Toll-Free
Phone Book USA

A Directory of Toll-Free Telephone Numbers for
Businesses and Organizations Nationwide

20
23rd

Containing Toll-Free Nu̲̲̲̲̲ lephone Numbers, and Mailing Addresses ̲̲̲̲̲ U.S. Businesses, Organizations, Agencies, ̲̲̲̲̲̲̲̲tutions, Including Companies, Associations, Educational Institutions, Media, Political Organizations, Societies, Travel Providers, and U.S. Government Agencies. Arranged Alphabetically by Name of Organization and in a Classified Section by Type of Business.

OMNIGRAPHICS

Omnigraphics

Pearline Jaikumar, *Editor*
Karthikeyan Ponnambalam, *Research Manager*

* * *

ISBN 978-0-7808-1667-1

ISSN 1092-0085

Printed in the United States of America

Omnigraphics
615 Griswold, Ste. 901, Detroit, MI 48226
Phone Orders: 800-234-1340 • Fax Orders: 800-875-1340
Mail Orders: P.O. Box 8002 • Aston, PA 19014-8002
www.omnigraphics.com

Table of Contents

How To Use This Directory

Toll-Free Phone Book USA provides toll-free numbers, along with other key contact information, for some of the largest and most important corporations, organizations, and institutions in the United States. This 23rd edition contains **more than 40,500** individual listings, presented alphabetically by company or organization name as well as in a classified subject arrangement according to business or organization type. The directory is intended as a convenient resource for toll-free calling nationwide, with supplemental contact data provided as an aid to follow-up correspondence or additional research.

What's Included in Toll-Free Phone Book USA?

Toll-free phone numbers, addresses, and local telephone numbers are provided for major businesses and industries located throughout the United States, as well as for organizations that serve as important information resources for businesses. Included also are listings for top Canadian companies and organizations.

Types of businesses listed in *Toll-Free Phone Book USA* include:
- manufacturing, retail, and wholesale companies;
- construction, mining, transportation, and utilities industries;
- agricultural interests;
- media and communications;
- and a full range of service industries.

Examples of other types of organizations listed include:
- associations;
- colleges and universities;
- libraries;
- research centers; and
- US Government agencies and offices.

How Do I Find What I'm Looking For?

Toll-Free Phone Book USA is organized in two main sections: an **Alphabetical Section,** in which listings are presented alphabetically according to company or organization name; and a **Classified Section**, where listings are organized under subject headings and subheadings according to business or organization type. All of the 40,500 plus entries are listed in each section.

- ### Alphabetizing in *Toll-Free Phone Book USA*
Alphabetizing throughout *Toll-Free Phone Book USA* is on a word-by-word, rather than letter-by-letter, basis. No distinction is made between upper and lower case letters, and articles, conjunctions, and most prepositions are ignored for sorting purposes. Names that begin with symbols or numerals rather than letters file first. Symbols that may accompany numerals (e.g., a pound sign [#] or dollar sign [$]) are ignored for alphabetical sorting.

The following example illustrates these alphabetizing rules:
> 1 on 1 Computing
> $1 Sunglasses Ltd
> 3M Co
> All Weather Vacuuming
> C & S Inc
> Calido Hotels
> Cambridge Fire Insurance
> Damon Corp
> DAS Co
> Data Generation Inc
> La Quinta Motor Inns
> Laacke Co

- ### Index to Classified Headings
All of the subject headings under which listings are organized in the Classified Section of *Toll-Free Phone*

4

Book USA are identified in the Index to Classified Headings located at the back of the directory. Page numbers given for each index citation refer to the page on which a particular subject category begins, rather than to a specific company or organization name. "See" and "See also" references are included to help guide users to appropriate subject categories.

Content of Individual Listings

Each listing in *Toll-Free Phone Book USA* provides the official name of the company, organization, or institution; street or other mailing address; city, state, and zip code; tollfree telephone number; and local telephone number (with area code). For publicly traded companies, stock exchange information is provided as well.

Classification Codes

In addition to these items of contact information, each listing in *Toll-Free Phone Book USA* contains a **classification code.** Classification codes are numbers that appear to the left of subject headings in the Classified Section and in a "Class" column to the right of listings in the Alphabetical Section, thus providing a common element that links the two sections. Users can determine a company's business activity by matching a number in a "Class" column to the corresponding subject heading number in the Classified Section.

Some listings in the Classified Section may be organized under a second level of subheadings within the broader category named in a heading. In situations where there are two levels of headings, two levels of classification codes are given as well. For instance, if a heading numbered as 200 is followed by a series of subheadings, the first subheading would be numbered 200-1, the second would be 200-2, and so on. Headings that have been created only to provide a reference to another heading category—i.e., "See" and "See also" references—are **not** numbered.

• Company Names

As a general rule, complete official names are given for companies and organizations listed in *Toll-Free Phone Book USA*. In the case of listings for companies that are clearly named after individuals, information usually is presented both by the person's first name and by the last name. For example, LL Bean Inc would also be listed as Bean LL Inc.

Companies that are well-known by an acronym or initialism — for example, IBM — usually are listed both by acronym and by full name (i.e., "IBM" and "International Business Machines Corp").

• Addresses

Most of the addresses provided in this directory are street addresses, unless mail cannot be accepted at a particular location, in which case a post office box or other mailing address is provided. All listings include the city, state, and zip code as well.

• Toll-Free Numbers

All ten digits, including the area code (800, 855, 866, 877, or 888), are given for each listing's toll-free number. If the toll-free number is intended for a specific use (e.g., customer service, human resources, or technical support) rather than for general calling, an asterisk is printed to the right of the toll-free number and an explanatory note (e.g., *Cust Svc) is printed on the line below the name/address data.

• Telephone Numbers

Local telephone numbers given in *Toll-Free Phone Book USA* are usually for the main switchboard of a company or organization, and area codes are included with all phone numbers listed.

• Stock Exchange Information

Trading symbols and corresponding stock exchanges for publicly traded companies are provided below the company's name and address.

Comments Welcome

Comments from readers concerning this publication, including suggestions for additions and improvements, are welcome. Please send to:

Editor — *Toll-Free Phone Book USA*
Omnigraphics
615 Griswold, Ste. 901
Detroit, MI 48226
editorial@omnigraphics.com

Area Codes in Numerical Order

201 ... New Jersey	331 ... Illinois	518 ... New York	707 ... California	850 ... Florida
202 ... District of Columbia	334 ... Alabama	519 ... Ontario	708 ... Illinois	855 ... Toll-free; all states
203 ... Connecticut	336 ... North Carolina	520 ... Arizona	709 ... Newfoundland	856 ... New Jersey
204 ... Manitoba	337 ... Louisiana	530 ... California	712 ... Iowa	857 ... Massachusetts
205 ... Alabama	339 ... Massachusetts	534 ... Wisconsin	713 ... Texas	858 ... California
206 ... Washington	340 ... US Virgin Islands	540 ... Virginia	714 ... California	859 ... Kentucky
207 ... Maine	345 ... Cayman Islands	541 ... Oregon	715 ... Wisconsin	860 ... Connecticut
208 ... Idaho	347 ... New York	551 ... New Jersey	716 ... New York	862 ... New Jersey
209 ... California	351 ... Massachusetts	559 ... California	717 ... Pennsylvania	863 ... Florida
210 ... Texas	352 ... Florida	561 ... Florida	718 ... New York	864 ... South Carolina
212 ... New York	360 ... Washington	562 ... California	719 ... Colorado	865 ... Tennessee
213 ... California	361 ... Texas	563 ... Iowa	720 ... Colorado	866 ... Toll-free; all states
214 ... Texas	385 ... Utah	567 ... Ohio	724 ... Pennsylvania	867 ... NorthWest Territories
215 ... Pennsylvania	386 ... Florida	570 ... Pennsylvania	727 ... Florida	868 ... Trinidad and Tobago
216 ... Ohio	401 ... Rhode Island	571 ... Virginia	731 ... Tennessee	869 ... Saint Kitts and Nevis
217 ... Illinois	402 ... Nebraska	573 ... Missouri	732 ... New Jersey	870 ... Arkansas
218 ... Minnesota	403 ... Alberta	574 ... Indiana	734 ... Michigan	876 ... Jamaica
219 ... Indiana	404 ... Georgia	575 ... New Mexico	740 ... Ohio	877 ... Toll-free; all states
224 ... Illinois	405 ... Oklahoma	580 ... Oklahoma	747 ... California	878 ... Pennsylvania
225 ... Louisiana	406 ... Montana	581 ... Quebec	754 ... Florida	880 ... Toll Calls: From Canada & The Caribbean
226 ... Ontario	407 ... Florida	585 ... New York	757 ... Virginia	
228 ... Mississippi	408 ... California	586 ... Michigan	758 ... Saint Lucia	881 ... Toll Calls: From Canada & The Caribbean
229 ... Georgia	409 ... Texas	587 ... Alberta	760 ... California	
231 ... Michigan	410 ... Maryland	601 ... Mississippi	762 ... Georgia	888 ... Toll-free; all states
234 ... Ohio	412 ... Pennsylvania	602 ... Arizona	763 ... Minnesota	901 ... Tennessee
239 ... Florida	413 ... Massachusetts	603 ... New Hampshire	765 ... Indiana	902 ... Nova Scotia
240 ... Maryland	414 ... Wisconsin	604 ... British Columbia	767 ... Dominica	903 ... Texas
242 ... Bahamas	415 ... California	605 ... South Dakota	769 ... Mississippi	904 ... Florida
246 ... Barbados	416 ... Ontario	606 ... Kentucky	770 ... Georgia	905 ... Ontario
248 ... Michigan	417 ... Missouri	607 ... New York	772 ... Florida	906 ... Michigan
250 ... British Columbia	418 ... Quebec	608 ... Wisconsin	773 ... Illinois	907 ... Alaska
251 ... Alabama	419 ... Ohio	609 ... New Jersey	774 ... Massachusetts	908 ... New Jersey
252 ... North Carolina	423 ... Tennessee	610 ... Pennsylvania	775 ... Nevada	909 ... California
253 ... Washington	424 ... California	612 ... Minnesota	778 ... British Columbia	910 ... North Carolina
254 ... Texas	425 ... Washington	613 ... Ontario	779 ... Illinois	912 ... Georgia
256 ... Alabama	430 ... Texas	614 ... Ohio	780 ... Alberta	913 ... Kansas
260 ... Indiana	432 ... Texas	615 ... Tennessee	781 ... Massachusetts	914 ... New York
262 ... Wisconsin	434 ... Virginia	616 ... Michigan	784 ... Saint Vincent & the Grenadines	915 ... Texas
264 ... Anguilla	435 ... Utah	617 ... Massachusetts		916 ... California
267 ... Pennsylvania	438 ... Quebec	618 ... Illinois	785 ... Kansas	917 ... New York
268 ... Antigua and Barbuda	440 ... Ohio	619 ... California	786 ... Florida	918 ... Oklahoma
269 ... Michigan	441 ... Bermuda	620 ... Kansas	787 ... Puerto Rico	919 ... North Carolina
270 ... Kentucky	442 ... California	623 ... Arizona	800 ... Toll-free; all states	920 ... Wisconsin
276 ... Virginia	443 ... Maryland	626 ... California	801 ... Utah	925 ... California
281 ... Texas	450 ... Quebec	630 ... Illinois	802 ... Vermont	928 ... Arizona
284 ... British Virgin Islands	458 ... Oregon	631 ... New York	803 ... South Carolina	931 ... Tennessee
289 ... Ontario	469 ... Texas	636 ... Missouri	804 ... Virginia	936 ... Texas
301 ... Maryland	470 ... Georgia	641 ... Iowa	805 ... California	937 ... Ohio
302 ... Delaware	473 ... Grenada	646 ... New York	806 ... Texas	939 ... Puerto Rico
303 ... Colorado	475 ... Connecticut	647 ... Ontario	807 ... Ontario	940 ... Texas
304 ... West Virginia	478 ... Georgia	649 ... Turks and Caicos	808 ... Hawaii	941 ... Florida
305 ... Florida	479 ... Arkansas	650 ... California	809 ... Dominican Republic	947 ... Michigan
306 ... Saskatchewan	480 ... Arizona	651 ... Minnesota	810 ... Michigan	949 ... California
307 ... Wyoming	484 ... Pennyslvania	657 ... California	812 ... Indiana	951 ... California
308 ... Nebraska	501 ... Arkansas	660 ... Missouri	813 ... Florida	952 ... Minnesota
309 ... Illinois	502 ... Kentucky	661 ... California	814 ... Pennsylvania	954 ... Florida
310 ... California	503 ... Oregon	662 ... Mississippi	815 ... Illinois	956 ... Texas
312 ... Illinois	504 ... Louisiana	664 ... Montserrat	816 ... Missouri	959 ... Connecticut
313 ... Michigan	505 ... New Mexico	671 ... Guam	817 ... Texas	970 ... Colorado
314 ... Missouri	506 ... New Brunswick	678 ... Georgia	818 ... California	971 ... Oregon
315 ... New York	507 ... Minnesota	681 ... West Virginia	819 ... Quebec	972 ... Texas
316 ... Kansas	508 ... Massachusetts	682 ... Texas	828 ... North Carolina	973 ... New Jersey
317 ... Indiana	509 ... Washington	684 ... American Samoa	829 ... Dominican Republic	978 ... Massachusetts
318 ... Louisiana	510 ... California	689 ... Florida	830 ... Texas	979 ... Texas
319 ... Iowa	512 ... Texas	701 ... North Dakota	831 ... California	980 ... North Carolina
320 ... Minnesota	513 ... Ohio	702 ... Nevada	832 ... Texas	985 ... Louisiana
321 ... Florida	514 ... Quebec	703 ... Virginia	843 ... South Carolina	989 ... Michigan
323 ... California	515 ... Iowa	704 ... North Carolina	845 ... New York	
325 ... Texas	516 ... New York	705 ... Ontario	847 ... Illinois	
330 ... Ohio	517 ... Michigan	706 ... Georgia	848 ... New Jersey	

Area Codes in State Order

Alabama
205	Birmingham & Tuscaloosa
251	Southwest
256	North & East Central
334	South

Alaska
907	All locations

American Samoa
684	All locations

Arizona
480	East of Phoenix including Tempe & Scottsdale
520	Southeast
602	Phoenix
623	West of Phoenix including Glendale
928	Most of State except South Central & Southeast areas

Arkansas
479	West Central & Northwest
501	Little Rock & surrounding areas
870	East & South

California
209	Central
213	Los Angeles
310	Long Beach/West
323	Los Angeles
408	West Central
415	San Francisco
424	Long Beach/West
442	Southeast except San Diego Area
510	Oakland
530	North
559	Central
562	Long Beach
619	San Diego & surrounding area (except North)
626	Pasadena/East
650	South of San Francisco
657	Northern Orange County
661	Bakersfield & Northern La County
707	Northwest
714	Northern Orange County
747	Burbank & Glendale Area
760	Southeast except San Diego Area
805	South
818	Burbank & Glendale Area
831	West Central
858	San Diego/North
909	San Bernardino & surrounding area
916	Sacramento & surrounding area
925	East of Oakland
949	Southern Orange County
951	Riverside & surrounding area (except North)

Canada
204	All locations in Manitoba
226	Southern Ontario
250	Outside Vancouver Area including Vancouver Island
289	North of Toronto
306	All locations in Saskatchewan
403	Southern Alberta
416	Toronto
418	Eastern Quebec
438	Montreal Metro Area
450	Outside Montreal Metro Area
506	All locations in New Brunswick
514	Montreal Metro Area
519	Southern Ontario
581	Eastern Quebec
587	All locations in Alberta
604	Vancouver Area
613	Northeast of Toronto
647	Toronto
705	Eastern Ontario
709	All locations in Newfoundland
778	Vancouver Area
780	Central & Northern Alberta
807	Western Ontario
819	Western Quebec
867	All locations in Yukon & Northwest Territories
902	All locations in Nova Scotia & Prince Edward Island
905	North of Toronto

Caribbean, Bahamas & Bermuda
242	Bahamas
246	Barbados
264	Anguilla
268	Antigua & Barbuda
284	British Virgin Islands
340	US Virgin Islands
345	Cayman Islands
441	Bermuda
473	Grenada
649	Turks & Caicos
664	Montserrat
758	Saint Lucia
767	Dominica
784	Saint Vincent & Grenadines
787	Puerto Rico
809	Dominican Republic
829	Dominican Republic
868	Trinidad & Tobago
869	Saint Kitts & Nevis
876	Jamaica
939	Puerto Rico

Colorado
303	Denver
719	South & East
720	Denver
970	West & North

Connecticut
203	Southwest
475	Southwest
860	Except Southwest
959	Except Southwest

Delaware
302	All locations

District of Columbia
202	All locations

Florida
239	Southwest (Lee, Collier & part of Monroe Counties)
305	Southeast
321	Central & East Central
352	Gainesville, Ocala & surrounding areas
386	Northeast except Jacksonville, St. Augustine & surrounding areas
407	Central
561	Palm Beach County
689	Central & East Central
727	Saint Petersburg/Clearwater
754	Fort Lauderdale & surrounding area
772	Martin, St. Lucie, Indian River & part of Brevard Counties
786	Southeast
813	Tampa
850	Northwest
863	South Central
904	Jacksonville, St. Augustine & surrounding areas
941	Southwest (Sarasota, Char Lotte & Manatee Counties)
954	Fort Lauderdale & surrounding area

Georgia
229	Southwest
404	Atlanta
470	Atlanta & surrounding area
478	Central
678	Atlanta Area
706	North except Atlanta Area
762	North except Atlanta Area
770	Atlanta suburbs
912	Southeast

Guam
671	All locations

Hawaii
808	All locations

Idaho
208	All locations

Illinois
217	Central
224	Suburban Chicago
309	West
312	Chicago
331	Northeast
618	South
630	Northeast
708	Northeast
773	Chicago (outside central commercial area)
779	North
815	North
847	Suburban Chicago

Indiana
219	North West
260	Northeast
317	Indianapolis Metro Area
574	North Central
765	Central except Indianapolis Metro Area
812	South

Iowa
319	East Central
515	Central including Des Moines & Ames
563	East
641	South central & East Central
712	West

Kansas
316	Wichita & surrounding area
620	South except Wichita & surrounding area
785	North except Kansas City
913	Kansas City

Kentucky
270	West & Central
502	North including Louisville
606	East
859	North Central

Louisiana
225	East Central
318	North & West
337	West Central & Southwest
504	New Orleans Area
985	Southeast except New Orleans Area

Maine
207	All locations

Maryland
240	West
301	West
410	East
443	East

Massachusetts
339	Outside Metro Boston
351	North
413	West
508	Southeast
617	Boston Metro Area
774	Southeast
781	Outside Metro Boston
857	Boston Metro Area
978	North

Michigan
231	Northwest
248	East (Oakland County)
269	Southwest
313	Detroit & inner suburbs
517	South Central
586	East (Macomb County)
616	West/Southwest
734	West of Detroit
810	East (except Oakland & Macomb Counties)
906	North
947	East (Oakland County)
989	Central

Minnesota
218	North
320	Central except Minneapolis/ Saint Paul Metro Area
507	South
612	Minneapolis
651	Saint Paul & East Central
763	Suburbs North & Northwest of Minneapolis
952	Suburbs South & Southwest of Minneapolis

Mississippi
228	Gulfport/Biloxi & surrounding area
601	South except Gulfport/ Biloxi & surrounding area
662	North
769	South except Gulfport/ Biloxi & surrounding area

Missouri
314	Saint Louis
417	Southwest
573	East except Saint Louis Metro Area
636	East (outside Saint Louis)
660	North except Kansas City & Saint Joseph
816	Kansas City & Saint Joseph

Montana
406	All locations

Nebraska
308	West
402	East

Nevada
702	Las Vegas Area
775	All locations except Las Vegas

New Hampshire
603	All locations

New Jersey
201	Northeast
551	Northeast
609	Southeast
732	East Central
848	East Central
856	Southwest
862	Northwest
908	West Central
973	Northwest

Area Codes in State Order (continued)

New Mexico
505	Northwest
575	Entire State except Northwest

New York
212	New York City
315	North Central
347	New York City
516	Nassau County
518	Northeast
585	West-Central
607	South Central
631	Suffolk County
646	New York City
716	West
718	New York City
845	North & West of Westchester County
914	Westchester County
917	New York City

North Carolina
252	East
336	Greensboro & Winston-Salem areas
704	Southwest
828	West
910	South Central
919	North Central
980	Southwest

North Dakota
701	All locations

Ohio
216	Cleveland Metro Area
234	Northeast except Cleveland
330	Northeast except Cleveland
419	Northwest
440	North Central except Cleveland Metro Area
513	Southwest
567	Northwest
614	Columbus Area
740	East & Central except

	Columbus Area
937	Southwest except Cincinnati Area

Oklahoma
405	Central
580	South & West
918	Northeast

Oregon
458	Outside Portland Area
503	Portland Area
541	Outside Portland Area
971	Portland Area

Pennsylvania
215	Philadelphia
267	Philadelphia
412	Pittsburgh Metro Area
484	Southeast
570	Northeast
610	Southeast
717	Southeast
724	Outside Pittsburgh Metro Area
814	West
878	Pittsburgh & surrounding area

Rhode Island
401	All locations

South Carolina
803	Central
843	East
864	Northwest

South Dakota
605	All locations

Tennessee
423	Northeast & Southeast
615	North Central
731	West except Shelby, Fayette & Tipton Counties
865	Knoxville & surrounding area
901	Southwest (Shelby, Fayette & Tipton Counties)

931	Nashville & North Central

Texas
210	San Antonio Metro Area
214	Dallas
254	North Central
281	Houston
325	Central
361	Corpus Christi & surrounding Area
409	East of Houston Area
430	Northeast
432	West Central
469	Dallas
512	Austin & surrounding area
682	Fort Worth Metro Area & Arlington
713	Houston
806	Northwest
817	Fort Worth Metro Area & Arlington
830	South Central
832	Houston
903	Northeast
915	West (including El Paso)
936	North of Houston Area
940	North
956	South
972	Dallas
979	West of Houston Area

Toll Calls: From Canada & The Caribbean
880	
881	

Toll-Free; All States
800	
855	
866	
877	
888	

Utah
385	Salt Lake City, Ogden & Provo Metro areas

435	All locations except Salt Lake City/Ogden/Provo Metro areas
801	Salt Lake City, Ogden & Provo Metro areas

Vermont
802	All locations

Virginia
276	Southwest
434	South & Central
540	North
571	Northeast
703	Northeast
757	Norfolk & surrounding area
804	East

Washington
206	Seattle Area
253	Tacoma Area
360	West except Seattle, Tacoma & Everett areas
425	East of Seattle between Everett & Kent
509	East

West Virginia
304	All locations
681	All locations

Wisconsin
262	Southeast except Milwaukee
414	Milwaukee
534	North
608	Southwest
715	North
920	Southeast except Milwaukee & surrounding area (South)

Wyoming
307	All locations

Toll-Free
Phone Book USA

Alphabetical Section

Listings here are presented in alphabetical order by company or organization name. Alphabetizing is on a word-by-word rather than letter-by-letter basis. For a detailed explanation of the scope and arrangement of listings in this directory, please refer to "How To Use This Directory" at the beginning of this book. An explanation of individual page elements is also provided under the "Sample Entry" on the back inside cover of the book.

SYMBOLS & NUMERALS

		Toll-Free	Phone	Class
1 Biotechnology				
PO Box 758 .... Oneco FL 34264		800-951-4246	941-355-8451	414
1 EDI Source Inc				
31875 Solon Rd .... Solon OH 44139		877-334-9650		
100 Fountain Spa at the Pillar & Post Inn				
48 John St				
PO Box 48 .... Niagara-on-the-Lake ON L0S1J0		888-669-5566	905-468-2123	703
1013 ESPN				
265 Hegeman Ave .... Colchester VT 05446		866-862-4267	802-655-0093	641
1015 Lite FM				
20450 NW Second Ave .... Miami FL 33169		877-790-1015		641-65
1025 KDON				
903 N Main St				
.... Monterey-Salinas-Santa Cruz CA 93906		888-558-5366	831-755-8181	641
1025 The Bull				
600 Beacon Pkwy W Ste 400 .... Birmingham AL 35209		877-811-3369	205-439-9600	641-14
1027Jack FM				
711 W 40th St .... Baltimore MD 21211		888-410-1027	410-366-7600	641-10
1037 KSON				
?9665 Granite Ridge Dr				
Ste 600 .... San Diego CA 92123		833-287-1037	619-291-9797	641-95
1041 KRBE				
9801 Westheimer Rd Ste 700 .... Houston TX 77042		888-955-2993	713-266-1000	641-46
1047 Kiss FM				
4686 E Van Buren St Ste 300 .... Phoenix AZ 85008		844-289-7234	602-374-6000	641-81
1059 SUNNY FM				
1800 Pembrook Dr Ste 400 .... Orlando FL 32810		877-919-1059	407-919-1000	641-75
1061 Kiss Fm Seattle				
645 Elliott Ave W Ste 400 .... Seattle WA 98119		888-343-1061	866-311-9806	641-98
1067 The Eagle				
13333 SW 68th Pkwy Ste 310 .... Tigard OR 97223		844-289-7234	503-323-6400	641-109
1075 KZL				
192 E Lewis St .... Greensboro NC 27406		800-682-1075	336-274-8042	641
1&1 Internet Inc				
701 Lee Rd Ste 300 .... Chesterbrook PA 19087		877-461-2631		686
1430 KLO				
257 East 200 South				
Ste 400 .... Salt Lake City UT 84111		866-627-1430	801-364-9836	641-93
1500 KSTP-AM LLC				
3415 University Ave .... Minneapolis MN 55414		877-615-1500	651-646-8255	641-64
1-800 Postcards Inc				
121 Varick St .... New York NY 10013		800-767-8227		623
1-800-Flowerscom Inc				
1 Old Country Rd Ste 110 .... Carle Place NY 11514		800-356-9377	516-739-3083	292
NASDAQ: FLWS				
1-800-Got-Junk				
887 Great Northern Way .... Vancouver BC V5T4T5		800-468-5865		310
1800PetSuppliescom				
395 Oakhill Rd Ste 210 .... Mountain Top PA 18707		800-738-7877		786
1-800-Water Damage				
1167 Mercer St .... Seattle WA 98109		800-928-3732	206-381-3041	310
1886 Crescent Hotel & Spa				
75 Prospect Ave .... Eureka Springs AR 72632		877-342-9766	855-725-5720	378
1888 Mills LLC				
375 Airport Rd .... Griffin GA 30224		800-346-3660		741
1928 Jewelry Co				
3000 West Empire Blvd .... Burbank CA 91504		800-227-1928	818-841-1928	407
1932 & 1980 Lake Placid Winter Olympic Museum				
2634 Main St .... Lake Placid NY 12946		800-462-6236	518-523-1655	519
1Cloud				
25 Lowell St Ste 407 .... Manchester NH 03101		855-256-8300		
1MAGE Software Inc				
7200 S Alton Way A206 .... Centennial CO 80112		800-844-1468		178-1
1st Colonial Bancorp Inc				
1040 Haddon Ave .... Collingswood NJ 08108		800-500-1044	856-858-1100	70
OTC: FCOB				
1st Discount Brokerage Inc				
8927 Hypoluxo Rd Ste A-5 .... Lake Worth FL 33467		888-642-2811	561-515-3200	686
1st Mechanical Services Inc				
303 Curie Dr .... Alpharetta GA 30005		888-346-0792	770-346-0792	606
1st Source Bank				
100 N Michigan St .... South Bend IN 46601		800-513-2360	574-235-2260	70
1STWEST Background Due Diligence LLC				
1536 Cole Blvd Ste 335 .... Lakewood CO 80401		866-670-3443		464
2 Checkoutcom Inc				
1785 O'Brien Rd .... Columbus OH 43228		877-294-0273	614-921-2450	457
2 Places At 1 Time Inc				
1000 NW 57th Crt Ste 590 .... Miami FL 33126		877-275-2237		461
2020 Exhibits Inc				
10550 S Sam Huston Pkwy W .... Houston TX 77071		800-856-6659	713-354-0900	196

		Toll-Free	Phone	Class
21st Century Christian Inc				
PO Box 40526 .... Nashville TN 37204		800-251-2477	615-383-3842	96
21st Mortgage Corp				
620 Market St Ste 100 .... Knoxville TN 37902		800-955-0021	865-523-2120	507
220 Group LLC, The				
3405 Kenyon St Ste 301 .... San Diego CA 92110		877-220-6584	619-758-9696	195
24 Asset Management Corp				
13155 SW 42nd Ste 200 .... Miami FL 33175		855-414-2424		392
247Sports				
12 Cadillac Dr Ste 230 .... Brentwood TN 37027		888-508-3055		
24hourtek LLC				
268 Bush St .... San Francisco CA 94104		855-378-0787	415-294-4449	175
320 Guest Ranch Inc				
205 Buffalo Horn Creek Rd				
.... Gallatin Gateway MT 59730		800-243-0320	406-995-4283	239
360 Business Consulting				
1576 N Batavia Ave .... Orange CA 92867		877-360-2492	949-916-9120	
360 Cloud Solutions LLC				
1475 N Scottsdale Rd .... Scottsdale AZ 85257		800-360-8150		
360 Imaging Inc				
2 Concourse Pkwy Ste 140 .... Atlanta GA 30328		866-360-6622	404-236-7700	92
360 Technologies Inc				
15401 Debba Dr .... Austin TX 78734		888-883-0360	512-266-7360	461
3balls LLC				
PO Box 90083 .... Raleigh NC 27675		888-289-0300	919-987-3222	707
3D Internet				
633 W Fifth St US Bank Twr				
28th Fl .... Los Angeles CA 90071		800-442-5299		5
3D Lacrosse LLC				
1301 S Jason St Unit K .... Denver CO 80223		800-941-9193		
3D Systems Inc				
333 Three D Systems Cir .... Rock Hill SC 29730		800-793-3669	803-326-3900	178-8
3Dlabs Inc Ltd				
1901 McCarthy Blvd .... Milpitas CA 95035		800-464-3348	408-530-4700	621
3M 28100 Cabot Dr Ste 200 .... Novi MI 48377		877-992-7749	248-374-9600	688
3M Canada Co				
300 Tartan Dr .... London ON N5V4M9		888-364-3577		727
3M Co 3M Ctr .... Saint Paul MN 55144		800-364-3577	651-733-1110	185
NYSE: MMM				
3M Dental Products Div				
3M Ctr .... Saint Paul MN 55144		888-364-3577		228
3M Electronic Handling & Protection Div				
6801 River Place Blvd .... Austin TX 78726		800-328-1368		253
3M Interconnect Solutions Div				
6801 River Place Blvd .... Austin TX 78726		800-225-5373	512-984-1800	253
3M Telecommunications Div				
6801 River Place Blvd .... Austin TX 78726		800-426-8688		248
3M Touch Systems				
501 Griffin Brook Dr .... Methuen MA 01844		866-407-6666	978-659-9000	173-1
3M Unitek				
2724 Peck Rd .... Monrovia CA 91016		800-634-5300		228
4 Wheel Parts				
20315 96 Ave .... Langley BC V1M0E4		855-554-2402	778-726-2787	750
411 Local Search Corp				
1500 Don Mills Rd				
Ste 600 N York .... Toronto ON M3B3K4		866-411-4411	647-723-9929	386
4Checkscom				
8245 N Union Blvd .... Colorado Springs CO 80920		800-995-9925		142
4D Inc				
3031 Tisch Way Ste 900 .... San Jose CA 95128		800-785-3303	408-557-4600	178-1
4Life Research				
9850 S 300 W .... Sandy UT 84070		888-454-3374*	801-256-3102	365
*Sales				
4Refuel Canada LP				
9440 - 202 ST Ste 215 .... Langley BC V1M4A6		888-473-3835		
4Sight Group LLC				
4023 Kennett Pk Ste 233 .... Wilmington DE 19807		800-490-2131		180
4-Star Trailers LLC				
10 000 NW Tenth St .... Oklahoma City OK 73127		800-848-3095	405-324-7827	774
4th Source Inc				
2502 N Rocky Point Dr Ste 960 .... Tampa FL 33607		855-875-4700		177
5 Alarm Fire & Safety Equipment LLC				
350 Austin Cir .... Delafield WI 53018		800-615-6789	262-646-5911	689
5 Star Equine Products Inc				
4589 Hwy 71 S .... Hatfield AR 71945		800-533-3377	870-389-6328	707
50 Forks				
3601 W Sunflower Ave .... Santa Ana CA 92704		855-784-1269		
511 Inc				
3201 N Airport Way .... Manteca CA 95356		866-451-1726		157-5
540 ESPN				
310 W Wisconsin Ave Ste 100 .... Milwaukee WI 53203		800-990-3776	414-273-3776	641-63
54th Street Grill				
18700 E 38th Terr .... Independence MO 64057		866-402-5454		
600 WREC				
2650 Thousand Oaks Blvd				
Ste 4100 .... Memphis TN 38118		800-474-9732	901-259-1300	641-62
63 Ranch				
PO Box 979 .... Livingston MT 59047		888-395-5151		239

	City	State	ZIP	Toll-Free	Phone	Class
6D Global Technologies Inc						
1500 Broadway Ste 505	New York	NY	10036	**800-787-3006**		
7 D Ranch						
7D Ranch PO Box 100	Cody	WY	82414	**888-587-9885**	307-587-9885	239
7-Eleven Inc						
1722 Routh Ste 100	Dallas	TX	75221	**800-255-0711**		204
7-sigma Inc						
2843 26th Ave S	Minneapolis	MN	55406	**888-722-8396**	612-722-5358	604
7strategy LLC						
117 N Cooper St	Olathe	KS	66061	**888-231-3062**		180
7Summits LLC						
1110 Old World Third St Ste 500	Milwaukee	WI	53203	**866-705-6372**	877-803-9286	195
84 Lumber Co						
1019 Rt 519	Eighty Four	PA	15330	**800-664-1984**	724-228-8820	191-3
891 WBOI						
3204 Clairmont Ct	Fort Wayne	IN	46808	**800-471-9264***	260-452-1189	641-39
*General						
8x8 Inc						
810 W Maude Ave	Sunnyvale	CA	94085	**888-898-8733**	408-727-1885	692
NASDAQ: EGHT						
923 FM KGON						
0700 SW Bancroft St	Portland	OR	97239	**800-222-9236**	503-223-1441	641-109
925 FM WVNN						
1717 Hwy 72 E	Athens	AL	35611	**866-494-9866**	256-830-8300	641
925 WESC-FM						
101 N Main St Ste 1000 10th Fl	Greenville	SC	29601	**800-248-0863**		641-43
927 KTOM						
903 N Main St	Salinas	CA	93906	**800-660-5866***	831-755-8181	641
*General						
92nd St Young Men's & Young Women's Hebrew Assn						
1395 Lexington Ave	New York	NY	10128	**800-385-1689**	212-415-5500	48-20
930 AM The Answer						
9601 McAllister Fwy Ste 1200	San Antonio	TX	78216	**866-308-8867**	210-344-8481	641-94
939 The Beat Honolulu						
650 Iwilei Rd Ste 400	Honolulu	HI	96817	**844-289-7234**	808-550-9200	641-45
94 HJY						
75 Oxford St Ste 301	Providence	RI	02905	**844-289-7234**	401-224-1994	641-84
957 Hallelujah FM						
2650 Thousand Oaks Blvd Ste 4100	Memphis	TN	38118	**844-885-9425**	901-259-1300	641-62
961 KISS FM						
4270 Byrd Dr	Loveland	CO	80538	**877-498-9600**	970-461-2560	641
965 FM KISS Country						
600 Old Marion Rd NE	Cedar Rapids	IA	52402	**800-258-0096**	319-395-0530	641-19
965 JACK-FM						
645 Elliott Ave W Ste 400	Seattle	WA	98119	**844-289-7234**		641-98
965 The Fox						
4303 Memorial Hwy	Mandan	ND	58554	**888-663-9650**	701-663-9600	641
973 Kiss FM						
245 Alfred St	Savannah	GA	31408	**800-543-3548**	912-964-7794	641-97
985 KFOX						
201 Third St Ste 1200	San Francisco	CA	94103	**877-410-5369**		
99 Cents Only Stores						
4000 Union Pacific Ave	Commerce	CA	90023	**888-582-5999**	323-980-8145	786
995 QYK						
9721 Executive Ctr Dr N Ste 200	Saint Petersburg	FL	33702	**800-992-1099**	727-579-1925	
995 WMAG						
2-B PAI Pk	Greensboro	NC	27409	**800-876-0995**	336-822-2000	641
997 Blitz, The						
1458 Dublin Rd	Columbus	OH	43215	**800-821-9970**	614-481-7800	641-28
@Comm Corp						
150 Dow St	Manchester	NH	03101	**800-641-5400**	603-624-4424	178-7

A

	City	State	ZIP	Toll-Free	Phone	Class
A & A Express Inc						
PO Box 707	Brandon	SD	57005	**800-658-3549**	605-582-2402	775
A & A Global Industries Inc						
17 Stenersen Ln	Cockeysville	MD	21030	**800-638-6000**	410-252-1020	481
A & A Maintenance Enterprise Inc						
965 Midland Ave	Yonkers	NY	10704	**800-280-0601**		192
A & B Aluminum & Brass Foundry						
11165 Denton Dr	Dallas	TX	75229	**800-743-4995**	972-247-3579	490
A & B Freight Line Inc						
4805 Sandy Hollow Rd	Rockford	IL	61109	**800-231-2235**	815-874-4700	314
A & d Technical Supply Company Inc						
4320 S 89th St	Omaha	NE	68127	**800-228-2753**	402-592-4950	113
A & K Railroad Materials Inc						
1505 S Redwood Rd	Salt Lake City	UT	84104	**800-453-8812***	801-974-5484	765
*Sales						
A & M Dental Laboratories Inc						
425 S Santa Fe St	Santa Ana	CA	92705	**800-487-8051**	714-547-8051	414
A & N Trailer Parts						
6028 S 118th E Ave	Tulsa	OK	74146	**800-272-1898**	918-461-8404	120
A & Z Hayward Co						
655 Waterman Ave	East Providence	RI	02914	**800-556-7462**	401-438-0550	407
A 1 Auto Recyclers						
7804 S Hwy 79	Rapid City	SD	57702	**800-456-0715**	605-348-8442	54
A 1 Termite & Pest Control Inc						
2686 Morganton Blvd SW	Lenoir	NC	28645	**800-532-7378**	828-758-4312	573
A A Blueprint Company Inc						
2757 Gilchrist Rd	Akron	OH	44305	**800-821-3700**	330-794-8803	776
A Bales Security Agency Inc						
625 E Twiggs St Ste 101	Tampa	FL	33602	**800-255-7328**		
A Better Chance Inc						
253 W 35th St 6th Fl	New York	NY	10001	**800-562-7865**	646-346-1310	48-11
A Betterway Rent-a-car Inc						
1092 Roswell Rd	Marietta	GA	30067	**800-527-0700**	770-240-3305	126

	City	State	ZIP	Toll-Free	Phone	Class
A C e International Company Inc						
85 Independence Dr	Taunton	MA	02780	**800-223-4685**		194
A C Nelson Rv World						
11818 L St	Omaha	NE	68137	**888-655-2332**	402-333-1122	57
A Colonial Moving & Storage Co						
17 Mercer St	Hackensack	NJ	07601	**877-549-7783**	201-343-5777	516
A Daigger & Company Inc						
620 Lakeview Pkwy	Vernon Hills	IL	60061	**800-621-7193**	847-816-5060	599
A Duchini Inc						
2550 McKinley Ave	Erie	PA	16503	**800-937-7317**	814-456-7027	183
A Duie Pyle Inc						
650 Westtown Rd PO Box 564	West Chester	PA	19381	**800-523-5020**	610-696-5800	447
A H Belo Corp						
1954 Commerce St PO Box 224866	Dallas	TX	75201	**800-230-1074**	214-977-8200	576
NYSE: AHC						
A J Sackett & Sons Co, The						
1701 S Highland Ave	Baltimore	MD	21224	**800-274-4466**	410-276-4466	478
A Lava & Son Co						
4800 S Kilbourn Ave	Chicago	IL	60632	**800-777-5282**	773-254-2800	320
A M Solutions						
100 Interstate Blvd	Edgerton	WI	53534	**800-410-6245**		
A Matter of Fax						
105 Harrison Ave	Harrison	NJ	07029	**800-433-3329**	973-482-3700	179
A P F Travel Inc						
1721 Garvey Ave 2nd Fl	Alhambra	CA	91803	**800-888-9168**		770
A Partner in Technology						
105 Dresden Ave	Gardiner	ME	04345	**877-582-0888**	207-582-0888	180
A Plus Benefits Inc						
395 W 600 N	Lindon	UT	84042	**800-748-5102**	801-443-1090	389
A Plus International Inc						
5138 Eucalyptus Ave	Chino	CA	91710	**800-762-1123**	909-591-5168	473
A Rifkin Co						
1400 Sans Souci Pkwy	Wilkes-Barre	PA	18706	**800-458-7300***	570-825-9551	67
*Cust Svc						
A Stucki Co						
2600 Neville Rd	Pittsburgh	PA	15225	**888-266-6630**	412-771-7300	646
A William Roberts Jr & Assoc Inc						
234 Seven Farms Dr Ste 210	Charleston	SC	29492	**800-743-3376**	843-722-8414	
A Yankee Line						
370 W First St	Boston	MA	02127	**800-942-8890**	617-268-8890	107
A'Gaci LLC						
12460 Network Blvd Ste 106	San Antonio	TX	78249	**866-265-3036**		157-6
A+ School Apparel						
401 Knoss Ave	Star City	AR	71667	**800-227-3215**		155-18
A/G (Assemblies of God)						
1445 N Boonville Ave	Springfield	MO	65802	**800-641-4310**	417-862-2781	48-20
A1 Staffing & Recruiting Agency Inc						
7407 NW 23rd St	Bethany	OK	73008	**800-233-1261**	405-787-7600	260
A2Z Field Services LLC						
7450 Industrial Pkwy Ste 105	Plain City	OH	43064	**800-713-2001**	614-873-0211	364
A3 Communications Inc						
1038 Kinley Rd Bldg B	Irmo	SC	29063	**888-809-1473**		
AA (Alcoholics Anonymous)						
475 Riverside Dr 11th Fl	New York	NY	10115	**800-437-3584**	212-870-3400	48-21
AA Importing Co Inc						
7700 Hall St	Saint Louis	MO	63147	**800-325-0602***	314-383-8800	360
*Cust Svc						
Aa Temps Inc						
7002 Little River Tpke	Annandale	VA	22003	**800-901-8367**	703-642-9050	5
AAA (American Academy of Audiology)						
11730 Plaza America Dr Ste 300	Reston	VA	20190	**800-222-2336**	703-226-1032	49-8
AAA (American Angus Assn)						
3201 Frederick Ave	Saint Joseph	MO	64506	**800-821-5478**	816-383-5100	48-2
AAA (American Ambulance Assn)						
8400 Westpark Dr 2nd Fl	McLean	VA	22102	**800-523-4447**	703-610-9018	49-21
AAA Chicago Motor Club						
975 Meridian Lake Dr	Aurora	IL	60504	**866-968-7222**		53
AAA Club Alliance Inc						
3201 Meijer Dr	Toledo	OH	43617	**800-763-9900**	419-843-1212	53
AAA Colorado						
4100 E Arkansas Ave	Denver	CO	80222	**866-625-3601**	303-753-8800	53
AAA East Penn						
1020 W Hamilton St	Allentown	PA	18101	**800-222-4357**		53
AAA Environmental Inc						
2036 Chesnee Hwy	Spartanburg	SC	29303	**888-296-3803**	864-582-1222	663
Aaa Flag & Banner Manufacturing Co						
8937 National Blvd	Los Angeles	CA	90034	**855-836-3200**	310-836-3200	287
AAA Hawaii						
1130 N Nimitz Hwy Ste A-170	Honolulu	HI	96817	**800-736-2886**	877-440-6943	53
AAA Michigan						
1 Auto Club Dr	Dearborn	MI	48126	**800-222-6424**		53
AAA Minnesota/Iowa						
600 W Travelers Trl	Burnsville	MN	55337	**800-222-1333**	952-707-4500	53
AAA MountainWest						
2100 11th Ave	Helena	MT	59601	**800-332-6119**	406-447-8100	53
Aaa Moving & Storage Inc						
747 E Ship Creek Ave	Anchorage	AK	99501	**888-995-3331**	888-927-3330	775
AAA Nebraska						
815 N 98th St	Omaha	NE	68114	**800-222-6327**	402-390-1000	53
AAA New York						
1415 Kellum Pl	Garden City	NY	11530	**855-374-1821**		
AAA North Penn						
1035 N Washington Ave	Scranton	PA	18509	**800-222-4357**	570-348-2511	53
AAA Northway						
112 Railroad St	Schenectady	NY	12305	**866-222-7283**	518-374-4696	53
AAA of Minnesota & Iowa						
600 W Travelers Trl	Burnsville	MN	55337	**800-222-1333**		
AAA Ohio Auto Club						
90 E Wilson Bridge Rd	Worthington	OH	43085	**888-222-6446**	614-431-7901	53
AAA Oklahoma						
2121 E 15th St	Tulsa	OK	74104	**800-222-2582**	918-748-1000	53
AAA Security						
180 Nature Pkwy	Winnipeg	MB	R3P0X7	**866-949-0078**	204-949-0078	689
AAA Southern Pennsylvania						
2840 Eastern Blvd	York	PA	17402	**800-222-1469**	717-600-8700	53
AAA Utica & Central New York						
409 Court St	Utica	NY	13502	**800-222-4357**		53

	Toll-Free	Phone	Class
AAA Western & Central New York 100 International Dr .... Williamsville NY 14221	800-836-2582	716-633-9860	53
AAAASF (American Assn for Accreditation of Ambulatory Surg) 5101 Washington St Ste 2F PO Box 9500 .... Gurnee IL 60031	888-545-5222	847-775-1985	48-1
AACCVB (Annapolis & Anne Arundel County Conference & Visit) 26 W St .... Annapolis MD 21401	888-302-2852	410-280-0445	206
AAAI (Association for the Advancement of Artificial Inte) 445 Burgess Dr Ste 100 .... Menlo Park CA 94025	800-548-4664	650-328-3123	48-9
AAAOM (American Assn of Acupunture & Oriental Medicine) PO Box 162340 .... Sacramento CA 95816	866-455-7999	916-443-4770	48-17
AAAP (American Academy of Addiction Psychiatry) 400 Massasoit Ave 2nd Fl Ste 307 .... East Providence RI 02914	800-263-6317	401-524-3076	49-15
AAB (American Association of Bioanalysts) 906 Olive St Ste 1200 .... Saint Louis MO 63101	800-457-3332	314-241-1445	49-8
Aabbitt Adhesives Inc 2403 N Oakley .... Chicago IL 60647	800-222-2488		3
AABBN (Alexandria & Arlington Bed & Breakfast Networks) 4938 Hampden Ln Ste 164 .... Bethesda MD 20814	888-549-3415	703-549-3415	375
AABC (Association for Biblical Higher Education) 5850 T G Lee Blvd Ste 130 .... Orlando FL 32822	800-525-1611	407-207-0808	48-1
AACA (Antique Automobile Club of America) 501 W Governor Rd PO Box 417 .... Hershey PA 17033	800-452-9910	717-534-1910	48-18
AACAP (American Academy of Child & Adolescent Psychiatry) 3615 Wisconsin Ave NW .... Washington DC 20016	800-333-7636	202-966-7300	49-15
AACC (Asset Acceptance Capital Corp) 28405 Van Dyke Ave .... Warren MI 48093 *NASDAQ: AACC*	800-545-9931	586-939-9600	160
AACC (American Assn for Clinical Chemistry Inc) 1850 K St NW Ste 625 .... Washington DC 20006 *Cust Svc	800-892-1400*	202-857-0717	49-19
AACD (American Academy of Cosmetic Dentistry) 402 W Wilson St .... Madison WI 53703	800-543-9220	608-222-8583	49-8
AACN (American Assn of Critical-Care Nurses) 101 Columbia .... Aliso Viejo CA 92656	800-809-2273	949-362-2000	49-8
AACOM (American Assn of Colleges of Osteopathic Medicine) 5550 Friendship Blvd Ste 310 .... Chevy Chase MD 20815	800-356-7836	301-968-4100	49-8
Aacom Inc 201 Stuyvesant Ave .... Lyndhurst NJ 07071	800-273-3719	201-438-2244	196
AACR (American Assn for Cancer Research) 615 Chestnut St 17th Fl .... Philadelphia PA 19106	866-423-3965	215-440-9300	49-8
AACRAO (American Association of Collegiate Registrars and) 1 Dupont Cir NW Ste 520 .... Washington DC 20036	800-222-4922	202-293-9161	49-5
AAD (American Academy of Dermatology) 9500 W Bryn Mawr Ave Ste 500 .... Rosemont IL 60018	888-462-3376		49-8
AADMM (American Assn of Daily Money Managers) 174 Crestview Dr .... Bellefonte PA 16823	877-326-5991		49-2
AADP (American Association of Drugless Practitioners) 2200 Market St Ste 803 .... Galveston TX 77550	888-764-2237	409-621-2600	48-17
AAE (American Assn of Endodontists) 211 E Chicago Ave Ste 1100 .... Chicago IL 60611	800-872-3636	312-266-7255	49-8
AAEP (American Assn of Equine Practitioners) 4075 Iron Works Pkwy .... Lexington KY 40511	800-443-0177	859-233-0147	48-3
AAES (American Assn of Engineering Societies) 1801 Alexander Bell Dr .... Reston VA 20191 *Orders	888-400-2237*	202-296-2237	49-19
AAF International Corp 10300 Ormsby Pk Pl Ste 600 .... Louisville KY 40223	888-223-2003	502-637-0011	18
AAFA (American Apparel & Footwear Assn) 740 sixth St NW 3rd & 4th Fl .... Washington DC 20001	800-520-2262	202-853-9080	49-4
AAFA (Asthma & Allergy Foundation of America) 8201 Corporate Dr Ste 1000 .... Landover MD 20785	800-727-8462	202-466-7643	48-17
AAFCS (American Assn of Family & Consumer Sciences) 400 N Columbus St Ste 202 .... Alexandria VA 22314	800-424-8080	703-706-4600	49-5
AAFD (American Assn of Franchisees & Dealers) PO Box 10158 .... Palm Desert CA 92255	800-733-9858	619-209-3775	49-18
AAFP (American Academy of Family Physicians) 11400 Tomahawk Creek Pkwy .... Leawood KS 66211	800-274-2237	913-906-6000	49-8
AAG (Association of American Geographers) 1710 16th St NW .... Washington DC 20009	800-696-7353	202-234-1450	49-19
AAGL (American Assn of Gynecological Laparoscopists) 6757 Katella Ave .... Cypress CA 90630	800-554-2245	714-503-6200	49-8
AAHA (American Animal Hospital Assn) 12575 W Bayaud Ave .... Lakewood CO 80228	800-252-2242	303-986-2800	48-3
AAI (American Athletic Inc) 200 American Ave .... Jefferson IA 50129	800-247-3978		345
AAI Corp 124 Industry Ln .... Hunt Valley MD 21030	800-655-2616	410-666-1400	525
AAIDD (American Assn on Intellectual & Developmental Disa) 444 N Capitol St NW Ste 846 .... Washington DC 20001	800-424-3688	202-387-1968	48-17
AAII (American Assn of Individual Investors) 625 N Michigan Ave Ste 1900 .... Chicago IL 60611	800-428-2244	312-280-0170	49-2
AAIS (American Assn of Insurance Services Inc) 701 Warrenville Rd Ste 100 .... Lisle IL 60532	800-564-2247	630-681-8347	49-9
AAJ (American Assn for Justice) 777 Sixth St NW Ste 200 .... Washington DC 20001	800-424-2725	202-965-3500	49-10
AAJ Technologies 6301 NW Fifth Way Ste 1700 .... Fort Lauderdale FL 33309	800-443-5210	954-689-3984	180
Aalborg Instruments & Controls Inc 20 Corporate Dr .... Orangeburg NY 10962	800-866-3837	845-770-3000	201
AALDEF (Asian American Legal Defense & Education Fund) 99 Hudson St 12th Fl .... New York NY 10013	800-966-5946	212-966-5932	48-8
AALU (Association for Advanced Life Underwriting) 11921 Freedom Dr Ste 1100 .... Reston VA 20190	888-275-0092	703-641-9400	49-9
AAM (American Assn of Museums) 1575 Eye St NW Ste 400 .... Washington DC 20005	866-226-2150	202-289-1818	48-4
AAMA (American Assn of Medical Assistants) 20 N Wacker Dr Ste 1575 .... Chicago IL 60606	800-228-2262	312-899-1500	49-8
A-American Self Storage Management Co Inc 11560 Tennessee Ave .... Los Angeles CA 90064	800-499-3524		798-3
AAMI (Association for the Advancement of Medical Instrum) 4301 N Fairfax Dr Ste 301 .... Arlington VA 22203	800-332-2264	703-525-4890	49-8
AAMRO (American Assn of Medical Review Officers) PO Box 12873 .... Research Triangle Park NC 27709	800-489-1839	919-489-5407	49-8
AAMVA (American Assn of Motor Vehicle Administrators) 4301 Wilson Blvd Ste 400 .... Arlington VA 22203	800-221-9253	703-522-4200	49-7
AAN (Association of Alternative Newsweeklies) 115615th St NW .... Washington DC 20005	866-415-0704	202-289-8484	49-14
AAN (American Academy of Neurology) 1080 Montreal Ave .... Saint Paul MN 55116	800-879-1960	651-695-1940	49-8
AANA (Arthroscopy Assn of North America) 9400 W Higgins Rd Ste 200 .... Rosemont IL 60018	877-924-0305	847-292-2262	49-8
AANA (American Assn of Nurse Anesthetists) 222 S Prospect Ave .... Park Ridge IL 60068	855-526-2262	847-692-7050	49-8
AANAPAC (American Association of Nurse Anesthetists PAC) 222 S Prospect Ave .... Park Ridge IL 60068	855-526-2262	847-692-7050	611
AANEM (American Assn of Neuromuscular & Electrodiagnostic) 2621 Superior Dr NW .... Rochester MN 55901	844-347-3277	507-288-0100	49-8
AANN (American Assn of Neuroscience Nurses) 4700 West Lake Ave .... Glenview IL 60025	888-557-2266	847-375-4733	49-8
AANP (American Academy of Nurse Practitioners) PO Box 12846 .... Austin TX 78711	800-981-2491	512-442-4262	49-8
AANP (American Assn of Naturopathic Physicians) 818 18th St Ste 250 .... Washington DC 20006	866-538-2267	202-237-8150	48-17
AANS (American Assn of Neurological Surgeons) 5550 Meadowbrook Dr .... Rolling Meadows IL 60008	888-566-2267	847-378-0500	49-8
AAO (American Assn of Orthodontists) 401 N Lindbergh Blvd .... Saint Louis MO 63141	800-424-2841	314-993-1700	49-8
AAO-HNS (American Academy of Otolaryngology-Head & Neck Sur) 1650 Diagonal Rd .... Alexandria VA 22314	877-722-6467	703-836-4444	49-8
AAOMS (American Assn of Oral & Maxillofacial Surgeons) 9700 W Bryn Mawr Ave .... Rosemont IL 60018	800-822-6637	847-678-6200	49-8
AAOS (American Academy of Orthopaedic Surgeons) 6300 N River Rd .... Rosemont IL 60018	800-346-2267	847-823-7186	49-8
AAP (American Academy of Pediatrics) 141 NW Pt Blvd .... Elk Grove Village IL 60007	800-433-9016	847-434-4000	49-8
AAP (American Academy of Periodontology) 737 N Michigan Ave Ste 800 .... Chicago IL 60611	800-282-4867	312-787-5518	49-8
AAPB (Association for Applied Psychophysiology & Biofeed) 10200 W 44th Ave Ste 304 .... Wheat Ridge CO 80033	800-477-8892	303-422-8436	49-8
AAPCC (American Assn of Poison Control Centers) 3201 New Mexico Ave Ste 310 .... Washington DC 20016	800-222-1222		49-8
AAPG (American Association of Petroleum Geologists) 1444 S Boulder Ave PO Box 979 .... Tulsa OK 74119	800-364-2274	918-584-2555	48-12
AAPG Explorer Magazine 1444 S Boulder Ave .... Tulsa OK 74119	800-364-2274	918-584-2555	455-21
AAPL (American Academy of Psychiatry & the Law) 1 Regency Dr PO Box 30 .... Bloomfield CT 06002	800-331-1389	860-242-5450	49-15
AAPS (American Assn of Pharmaceutical Scientists) 2107 Wilson Blvd Ste 700 .... Arlington VA 22201	877-998-2277	703-243-2800	49-19
AAPT (American Assn of Physics Teachers) 1 Physics Ellipse .... College Park MD 20740	800-446-8923	301-209-3311	49-5
AAR (Association of American Railroads) 425 Third St SW .... Washington DC 20024	800-533-6644	202-639-2100	49-21
AAR Corp 1100 N Wood Dale Rd .... Wood Dale IL 60191 *NYSE: AIR*	800-422-2213	630-227-2000	21
AAR Defense Systems & Logistics 1100 N Wood Dale Rd .... Wood Dale IL 60191	877-227-9200	630-227-2000	765
Aarch Caster & Equipment 314 Axminister Dr .... Fenton MO 63026	888-349-0220	866-206-8792	350
AARDA (American Autoimmune Related Disease Assn) 22100 Gratiot Ave .... Eastpointe MI 48021	800-598-4668	586-776-3900	48-17
Aaron & Company Inc PO Box 8310 .... Piscataway NJ 08855	800-734-4822	732-752-8200	608
Aaron Bros 8000 Bent Branch Dr .... Irving TX 75063	877-372-6370		
AaronEquipment Company Inc 735 E Green St .... Bensenville IL 60106	800-492-2766	630-350-2200	384
AARP Motoring Plan 601 E St NW .... Washington DC 20049	800-555-1121		53
AARP Public Policy Institute 601 E St NW .... Washington DC 20049	888-687-2277	202-434-2277	630
AARP Services Inc PO Box 1017 .... Montgomeryville PA 18936	800-523-5800		390-3
AARP the Magazine 601 E St NW .... Washington DC 20049	888-687-2277	202-434-3525	455-10
AASA (American Assn of School Administrators) 801 N Quincy St Ste 700 .... Arlington VA 22203	800-771-1162	703-528-0700	49-5
AASCU (American Assn of State Colleges & Universities) 1307 New York Ave NW 5th Fl .... Washington DC 20005	800-558-3417	202-293-7070	49-5
AASL (American Assn of School Librarians) 50 E Huron St .... Chicago IL 60611	800-545-2433	312-280-4386	49-11
Aasys Group 11301 N US Hwy 301 Ste 106 .... Thonotosassa FL 33592	800-852-7091	813-246-4757	180
AATBS (Association for Advanced Training in the Behaviora) 5126 Ralston St .... Ventura CA 93003	800-472-1931	805-676-3030	49-5
AATG (American Assn of Teachers of German) 112 Haddontowne Ct Ste 104 .... Cherry Hill NJ 08034	800-835-6770	856-795-5553	49-5
AATS (American Assn for Thoracic Surgery) 800 Cummings Ctr Ste 350-V .... Beverly MA 01915	800-424-5249	978-252-2200	49-8
AAU (Amateur Athletic Union of the US) 1910 Hotel Plaza Blvd .... Lake Buena Vista FL 32830	800-228-4872	407-934-7200	48-22
AAUP (American Assn of University Professors) 1133 Nineteenth St Ste 200 .... Washington DC 20036	800-424-2973	202-737-5900	49-5
AAUW (American Assn of University Women) 1111 16th St NW .... Washington DC 20036	800-326-2289	202-785-7700	49-5
AAUW Outlook Magazine 1111 16th St NW .... Washington DC 20036	800-326-2289	202-785-7700	455-10
Aava Whistler Hotel Ltd 4005 Whistler Way .... Whistler BC V0N1B4	800-663-5644	604-932-2522	377
Aaxon Laundry Systems 6100 N Powerline Rd .... Ft. Lauderdale FL 33309	800-826-1012	954-772-7100	111
AB (AllianceBernstein Holding LP) 1345 Ave of the Americas .... New York NY 10105 *NYSE: AB* ■ *Cust Svc	800-221-5672*	212-486-5800	400
A&B Process Systems Corp 201 S Wisconsin Ave .... Stratford WI 54484	888-258-2789	715-687-4332	490
AB Staffing Solutions LLC 3451 Mercy Rd .... Gilbert AZ 85297	888-515-3900	480-345-6668	627
A&B Wiper Supply Inc 11350 Norcom Rd .... Philadelphia PA 19154	800-333-7247	215-482-6100	506
ABA (American Bicycle Assn) 1645 W Sunrise Blvd .... Gilbert AZ 85233	866-650-4867	480-961-1903	48-22

Alphabetical Section

Name / Address	Toll-Free	Phone	Class
ABA (American Bankers Assn) 1120 Connecticut Ave NW — Washington DC 20036 *Cust Svc	800-226-5377*		49-2
ABA (American Baptist Assn) 4605 N State Line Ave — Texarkana TX 75503	800-264-2482	903-792-2783	48-20
ABA (American Bar Assn) 321 N Clark St — Chicago IL 60654	800-285-2221	312-988-5000	49-10
ABA (American Booksellers Assn) 333 Westchester Ave Ste S202 — White Plains NY 10604	800-637-0037		49-18
ABA Commission on Domestic Violence 321 N Clark St — Chicago IL 60654	800-285-2221	312-988-5000	49-10
ABA Marketing Network 1120 Connecticut Ave NW — Washington DC 20036	800-226-5377	202-663-5000	49-2
Abacus Corp 610 Gusryan St — Baltimore MD 21224	800-230-0043	410-633-1900	627
Abacus Technology Corp 5404 Wisconsin Ave Ste 1100 — Chevy Chase MD 20815	800-225-2135		180
ABAPAC (American Bankers Assn PAC) 1120 Connecticut Ave NW — Washington DC 20036	800-226-5377		611
Abatement Technologies 605 Satellite Blvd Ste 300 — Suwanee GA 30024	800-634-9091	678-889-4200	37
Abatix Corp 2400 Skyline Dr Ste 400 — Mesquite TX 75149	800-426-3983	214-381-0322	384
Abaxis Inc 3240 Whipple Rd — Union City CA 94587 NASDAQ: ABAX	800-822-2947	510-675-6500	418
Abba Technologies 5301 Beverly Hills Ave NE — Albuquerque NM 87113	888-222-2832	505-889-3337	194
Abbco Inc 304 Meyer Rd — Bensenville IL 60106	866-986-6546	630-595-7115	453
Abbey Delray 2000 Lowson Blvd — Delray Beach FL 33445	888-791-9363	561-454-2000	668
Abbey Resort & Fontana Spa 269 Fontana Blvd — Fontana WI 53125	800-709-1323	262-275-9000	665
Abbey Travel Ltd 522 N Washington St — Naperville IL 60563	800-338-0900	630-420-0400	
Abbi Home Care Inc 6453 SW Blvd — Benbrook TX 76132	877-383-2224	817-377-0889	362
Abbot & Abbot Box Corp 37-11 Tenth St — Long Island NY 11101	888-525-7186		200
Abbott 26531 Ynez Rd — Temecula CA 92591	800-227-9902		111
Abbott Diagnostics 675 N Field Dr — Lake Forest IL 60045	800-387-8378	224-667-6100	231
Abbott Greg (R) State Insurance Bldg 1100 San Jacinto PO Box 12428 — Austin TX 78701	800-843-5789	512-463-2000	
Abbott Interfast Corp 190 Abbott Dr — Wheeling IL 60090	800-877-0789	847-459-6200	617
Abbott Northwestern Hospital 800 E 28th St — Minneapolis MN 55407	800-582-5175	612-863-4000	373-3
AbbVie Pharmaceutical Contract Manufacturing 1401 Sheridan Rd — North Chicago IL 60064	888-299-7416	847-938-8524	580
Abbyland Foods Inc 502 E Linden St PO Box 69 — Abbotsford WI 54405	800-732-5483	715-223-6386	471
ABC (America's Blood Centers) 725 15th St NW Ste 700 — Washington DC 20005	888-872-5663	202-393-5725	49-8
ABC (ArcBest) 3801 Old Greenwood Rd — Fort Smith AR 72903 NASDAQ: ARCB	800-610-5544		775
ABC (Associated Builders & Contractors Inc) 4250 Fairfax Dr — Arlington VA 22203	877-889-5627	202-595-1505	49-3
Abc 33 40 800 Concourse Pkwy Ste 200 — Birmingham AL 35244	800-784-8669	205-403-3340	736-10
ABC American Bio-clinical 2730 N Main St — Los Angeles CA 90031	800-262-1688		417
ABC Appliance Inc 1 Silverdome Industrial Pk — Pontiac MI 48343	800-981-3866		35
ABC Compounding Company Inc & Acme Wholesale 6970 Jonesboro Rd — Morrow GA 30260	800-795-9222	770-968-9222	151
ABC Global Services 6001 Broken Sound Pkwy NW Ste 340 — Boca Raton FL 33487	800-722-5179		766
ABC Home Medical Supply Inc 397 Eagleview Blvd — Exton PA 19341	866-897-8588		473
ABC Industrie PO Box 77 — Warsaw IN 46581	800-426-0921	574-267-5166	369
ABC Metals Inc 500 W Clinton St — Logansport IN 46947	800-238-8470		490
A-B-C Packaging Machine Corp 811 Live Oak St — Tarpon Springs FL 34689	800-237-5975	727-937-5144	543
ABC Seamless 3001 Fiechtner Dr — Fargo ND 58103	800-732-6577	701-293-5952	191-4
ABC Supply Company Inc 1 ABC Pkwy — Beloit WI 53511	888-492-1047	608-362-7777	191-4
ABC-CLIO Inc 130 Cremona Dr — Goleta CA 93117	800-368-6868	805-968-1911	633-2
Abco Cleaning Products 6800 NW 36th Ave — Miami FL 33147	888-694-2226	305-694-2226	506
Abco Inc 1621 Wall St — Dallas TX 75215	800-969-2226	214-565-1191	86
Abco Laboratories Inc 2450 S Watney Way — Fairfield CA 94533	800-678-2226	707-432-2200	296-37
ABCO Printing 512 Trade Rd — Columbus OH 43204	800-821-9435		624
ABCT (Association for Behavioral & Cognitive Therapies) 305 Seventh Ave 16th Fl — New York NY 10001	800-685-2228	212-647-1890	49-15
Abell LLC 2201 Old Sterlington Rd PO Box 4150 — Monroe LA 71211	800-523-9871	866-765-9957	
ABELSoft Inc 3310 S Service Rd — Burlington ON L7M4K8	800-267-2235	905-333-3200	461
Abercrombie & Fitch Co 6301 Fitch Pass — New Albany OH 43054 NASDAQ: ANF	866-681-3115		157-4
Aberdeen & Rockfish Railroad Co 101 E Main St — Aberdeen NC 28315	800-849-8985	910-944-2341	644
Aberdeen American News 124 S Second St — Aberdeen SD 57402	800-925-4100	605-229-5555	528-2
Aberdeen Area Chamber of Commerce 516 S Main St — Aberdeen SD 57401	800-874-9038	605-225-2860	139
Aberdeen Convention & Visitors Bureau 10 Railroad Ave SW PO Box 78 — Aberdeen SD 57401	800-645-3851	605-225-2414	206
Aberdeen Group Inc 60 Hickory Dr 5th Fl — Waltham MA 02451	800-577-7891	617-854-5200	464
Aberdeen LLC 9130 Norwalk Blvd — Santa Fe Springs CA 90670	800-500-9526	562-699-6998	173-2
Aberhart Centre 11402 University Ave — Edmonton AB T6G2J3	866-407-1970	780-407-7510	541
ABG Communications 3810 Wabash Dr — Mira Loma CA 91752	888-685-7100	951-361-7100	623
ABI (Advanced Biotechnologies Inc) 1545 Progress Way — Eldersburg MD 21784	800-426-0764	410-792-9779	231
ABI (Atkinson-Baker Inc) 500 N Brand Blvd 3rd Fl — Glendale CA 91203	800-288-3376	818-551-7300	443
ABI (American Biltrite Inc Tape Products Div) 105 Whittendale Dr — Moorestown NJ 08057	888-224-6325	856-778-0700	727
Abilene Christian University Brown Library (ACU) 221 Brown Library — Abilene TX 79699	800-460-6228	325-674-2316	433-6
Abilene Convention & Visitors Bureau 1101 N First St — Abilene TX 79601	800-727-7704	325-676-2556	206
Abilene Convention & Visitors Bureau 201 NW Second St — Abilene KS 67410	800-569-5915	785-263-2231	206
Abilene Machine Inc PO Box 129 — Abilene KS 67410	800-255-0337	785-655-9455	274
Abilene Regional Medical Ctr 6250 S Hwy 83-84 — Abilene TX 79606	800-888-2504	325-428-1000	373-3
Abilene Reporter-News 101 Cypress St — Abilene TX 79601	866-604-2020	325-673-4271	528-2
Abilene Zoological Gardens 2070 Zoo Ln Nelson Pk — Abilene TX 79602	800-899-9841	325-676-6085	818
ABIM (American Board of Internal Medicine) 510 Walnut St Ste 1700 — Philadelphia PA 19106	800-441-2246	215-446-3590	48-1
Abingdon Convention & Visitors Bureau 335 Cummings St — Abingdon VA 24210	800-435-3440	276-676-2282	206
ABIOMED Inc 22 Cherry Hill Dr — Danvers MA 01923 NASDAQ: ABMD	800-422-8666	978-646-1400	250
Abipa Canada Inc 3700 Ave des Grandes Tourelles — Boisbraind QC J7H0A1	877-963-6888	450-963-6888	21
Abita Brewing Co 21084 Hwy 36 — Covington LA 70433	800-737-2311	985-893-3143	102
Abita Trace Animal Clinic 69142 Hwy 59 Ste E — Mandeville LA 70471	800-640-3274	985-892-5656	789
Abitec Corp Inc PO Box 569 — Columbus OH 43215 *Sales	800-555-1255*	614-429-6464	296-29
Able 2 Products Company Inc PO Box 543 — Cassville MO 65625	800-641-4098	417-847-4791	437
Able Services 868 Folsom St — San Francisco CA 94107	800-461-9577	415-546-6534	256
ABMA (American Boiler Manufacturers Assn) 8221 Old Courthouse Rd Ste 380 — Vienna VA 22182	800-227-1966	703-356-7172	49-13
ABMC (American Bio Medica Corp) 122 Smith Rd — Kinderhook NY 12106 OTC: ABMC ■ *General	800-227-1243*	518-758-8158	85
Abmech Inc 976 Forest Ave — West Homestead PA 15120	800-686-3626	412-462-7440	663
ABMP (Associated Bodywork & Massage Professionals) 25188 Genesee Trl Rd Ste 200 — Golden CO 80401	800-458-2267	303-674-8478	48-17
Above All Advertising Inc 9080 Activity Rd Ste A — San Diego CA 92126	866-552-2683	858-549-2226	8
ABRA (American Buckskin Registry Assn Inc) 1141 Hartnell Ave — Redding CA 96002	800-458-4283	530-223-1420	48-3
Abraham Baldwin Agricultural College 2802 Moore Hwy — Tifton GA 31793	800-733-3653	229-391-5001	162
Abraham Lincoln Presidential Library & Museum 112 N Sixth St — Springfield IL 62701	800-610-2094	217-557-6250	433-2
Abresist Corp PO Box 38 — Urbana IN 46990	800-348-0717	260-774-3327	183
Abrisa Technologies 200 S Hallock Dr — Santa Paula CA 93060	877-622-7472		331
A-Brite Plating Company Inc 3000 W 121st St — Cleveland OH 44111	800-252-2995		
Abscope Environmental Inc 7086 Commercial Dr — Canastota NY 13032	800-273-5318	315-697-8437	663
Absocold PO Box 1545 — Richmond IN 47374	800-843-3714		606
Absolut Aire Inc 5496 N Riverview Dr — Kalamazoo MI 49004	800-804-4000	269-382-1875	14
Absolute Analysis Inc 2393 Teller Rd Ste 109 — Newbury Park CA 91320	800-452-5174		
Absolute Machine Tools Inc 7420 Industrial Pkwy — Lorain OH 44053	800-852-7825	440-960-6911	357
Absolute Standards Inc 44 Rossotto Dr — Hamden CT 06514	800-368-1131	203-281-2917	738
Absopure Water Co 8845 General Dr — Plymouth MI 48170	800-422-7678		800
ABT Inc 259 Murdock Rd — Troutman NC 28166	800-438-6057		490
ABT Internet Inc 175 E Shore Rd — Great Neck NY 11023	800-367-3414	516-829-5484	397
ABTA (American Brain Tumor Assn) 2720 River Rd — Des Plaines IL 60018	800-886-2282	847-827-9910	48-17
Abundant Life Christian Academy 1494 Banks Rd — Margate FL 33063	800-948-6291	954-979-2665	148
ABWA (American Business Women's Assn) 11050 Roe Ave Ste 200 — Overland Park KS 66211	800-228-0007		49-12
Abx Engineering 880 Hinckley Rd — Burlingame CA 94010	800-366-4588	650-552-2322	256
AC & T Company Inc 11535 Hopewell Rd — Hagerstown MD 21740	800-458-3835	301-582-2700	316
AC Central Reservations Inc 201 Tilton Rd London Sq Mall Ste 17B — Northfield NJ 08225	888-227-6667	609-383-8880	375
AC Corp 301 Creek Ridge Rd — Greensboro NC 27406	800-422-7378	336-273-4472	189-10

Name / Address	Toll-Free	Phone	Class
AC Doctor LLC 2151 W Hillsboro Blvd Ste 400 .... Deerfield Beach FL 33442	866-264-1479		786
AC Horn & Co 1269 Majesty Dr .... Dallas TX 75247	800-657-6155	214-630-3311	693
AC Moore Arts & Crafts Inc 130 AC Moore Dr .... Berlin NJ 08009 *NASDAQ: ACMR*	888-226-6673		45
AC Nutrition 158 N Main St .... Winters TX 79567	800-588-3333	325-754-4546	445
AC. Coy Co 395 Valley Brook Rd ...... Canonsburg PA 15317	800-784-5773	724-820-1820	261
ACA (Auto Club of America Corp) 9411 N Georgia St .... Oklahoma City OK 73120	800-411-2007	405-751-4430	53
ACA (American Camp Assn) 5000 State Rd 67 N .... Martinsville IN 46151	800-428-2267	765-342-8456	48-23
ACA (American Canoe Assn) 503 Sophia St Ste 100 ... Fredericksburg VA 22401	888-229-3792	540-907-4460	48-22
ACA (American Chiropractic Assn) 1701 Clarendon Blvd Ste 200 .. Arlington VA 22209	800-986-4636	703-276-8800	49-8
ACA (American Correctional Assn) 206 N Washington St Ste 200 ... Alexandria VA 22314	800-222-5646	703-224-0000	49-7
ACA (American Counseling Assn) 5999 Stevenson Ave ...... Alexandria VA 22304	800-347-6647	703-823-9800	49-15
ACA (American AgCredit) PO Box 1120 .... Santa Rosa CA 95402	800-800-4865	707-545-1200	216
Academe Magazine 1133 Nineteenth St NW Ste 200 .... Washington DC 20036	800-424-2973	202-737-5900	455-8
Academic Apparel 20644 Superior St .... Chatsworth CA 91311	800-626-5000	818-886-8697	155-13
Academy Bus LLC 111 Paterson Ave .... Hoboken NJ 07030	800-442-7272	201-420-7000	755
Academy Fire Protection Inc 42 Broadway 2nd Fl .... Lynbrook NY 11563	800-773-4736		392
Academy Hotel Colorado Springs, The 8110 N Academy Blvd ... Colorado Springs CO 80920	800-766-8524	719-598-5770	378
Academy of Art University 79 New Montgomery St ... San Francisco CA 94105	800-544-2787	415-274-2200	166
Academy of General Dentistry (AGD) 211 E Chicago Ave Ste 900 .... Chicago IL 60611	888-243-3368	312-440-4300	49-8
Academy of Managed Care Pharmacy (AMCP) 100 N Pitt St Ste 400 ...... Alexandria VA 22314	800-827-2627	703-683-8416	49-8
Academy of Management (AOM) 235 Elm Rd PO Box 3020 .. Briarcliff Manor NY 10510	800-633-4931	914-923-2607	49-12
Academy of Model Aeronautics (AMA) 5161 E Memorial Dr .... Muncie IN 47302	800-435-9262		48-18
Academy of Osseointegration 85 W Algonquin Rd Ste 550 .... Arlington Heights IL 60005	800-656-7736	847-439-1919	49-8
Academy of Students of Pharmacy American Pharmacists Assn 1100 15th St NW Ste 400 ...... Washington DC 20005	800-237-2742	202-628-4410	49-8
Academy Sports & Outdoors 1800 N Mason Rd .... Katy TX 77449	888-922-2336	281-646-5200	707
AcademyOne Inc 101 Lindenwood Dr Ste 220 .. Malvern PA 19355	888-434-2150		
Acadia Divinity College 38 Highland Ave .... Wolfville NS B4P2R6	866-875-8975	902-585-2210	167-3
Acadia Inn 98 Eden St .... Bar Harbor ME 04609	800-638-3636	207-288-3500	378
ACADIA Pharmaceuticals Inc 3911 Sorrento Valley Blvd ... San Diego CA 92121 *NASDAQ: ACAD*	800-901-5231	858-558-2871	85
Acadia University 15 University Ave .... Wolfville NS B4P2R6	877-585-1121	902-542-2201	780
Acadian Ambulance Service Inc PO Box 98000 .... Lafayette LA 70509	800-259-3333		30
ACB (American Council of the Blind) 2200 Wilson Blvd Ste 650 ... Arlington VA 22201	800-424-8666	202-467-5081	48-11
ACB (America's Community Bankers) 1120 Connecticut Ave NW ... Washington DC 20036	800-226-5377		49-2
ACB Solutions 551 W Dimond Blvd .... Anchorage AK 99515	888-238-4225		180
ACBL (American Contract Bridge League) 6575 Windchase Blvd ..... Horn Lake MS 38637 *Sales*	800-264-2743*	662-253-3100	48-18
ACC (Alpena Community College) 665 Johnson St .... Alpena MI 49707	888-468-6222	989-356-9021	162
ACC (American College of Cardiology) 2400 N St NW .... Washington DC 20037 *Cust Svc*	800-253-4636*	202-375-6000	49-8
ACC (Association of Corporate Counsel) 1025 Connecticut Ave NW Ste 200 .... Washington DC 20036	877-647-3411	202-293-4103	49-10
ACC (Austin Community College) 5930 Middle Fiskville Rd ...... Austin TX 78752	877-442-3522	512-223-7000	162
Acc Technical Services Inc 106 Dwight Park Cir .... Syracuse NY 13209	855-484-4500	315-484-4500	461
ACCA (Air Conditioning Contractors of America) 2800 S Shirlington Rd Ste 300 .... Arlington VA 22206	888-290-2220	703-575-4477	49-3
ACCE (American Chamber of Commerce Executives) 4875 Eisenhower Ave Ste 250 ... Alexandria VA 22304	800-394-2223	703-998-0072	49-12
Accel Aviation Accessories LLC 11900 Lacy Ln .... Fort Myers FL 33966	888-686-4880	239-275-8202	358
Accelerated Genetics E 10890 Penny Ln .... Baraboo WI 53913	800-451-9275	608-356-8357	11-2
Acceles Inc 13771 N Fountain Hills Blvd Ste 114-115 .... Fountain Hills AZ 85268	877-260-6725		196
Accelian LLC 1222 Earnestine St .... Mc Lean VA 22101	888-543-0051	703-543-1616	804
Accelrys Inc 10188 Telesis Ct Ste 100 ... San Diego CA 92121	888-249-2284	858-799-5000	178-5
Accent 7171 Mercy Rd Ste 100 .... Omaha NE 68106	800-397-7243	402-397-9920	392
Accent Communication Services Inc 585 Sunbury Rd .... Delaware OH 43015	800-589-7379	740-548-7378	196
Accent Computer Solutions Inc 8438 Red Oak St ...... Rancho Cucamonga CA 91730	800-481-4369	909-204-4801	461
Accent Inns Ltd 3233 Maple St .... Victoria BC V8X4Y9	800-663-0298	250-475-7500	703
Accent Inns Vancouver Airport 10551 St Edwards Dr ...... Richmond BC V6X3L8	800-663-0298	604-273-3311	378
Accent Inns Vancouver-Burnaby 3777 Henning Dr .... Burnaby BC V5C6N5	800-663-0298	604-473-5000	378
Accent Packaging 10131 FM 2920 Rd .... Tomball TX 77375	800-383-8047	281-251-3700	
Access America 673 Emory Valley Rd ...... Oak Ridge TN 37830	800-860-2140	865-482-2140	731
Access America 2805 N Parham Rd .... Richmond VA 23294	800-284-8300		390-7
Access Business Group 7575 Fulton St E .... Ada MI 49355 *Cust Svc*	800-879-2732*		447
Access Energy Co-op 1800 W Washington St ... Mount Pleasant IA 52641	866-242-4232	319-385-1577	245
Access Innovations Inc 4725 Indian School Rd NE Ste 100 .... Albuquerque NM 87110	800-926-8328	505-265-3591	177
Access Intelligence Inc 4 Choke Cherry Rd 2nd Fl ... Rockville MD 20850	800-777-5006	301-354-2000	633-9
Access Magazine 444 N Michigan Ave Ste 3400 ... Chicago IL 60611	800-243-2342	312-440-8900	455-16
Access National Corp 1800 Robert Fulton Dr Ste 310 ... Reston VA 20191 *NASDAQ: ANCX*	800-931-0370	703-871-2100	359-2
Access Point Inc 1100 Crescent Green .... Cary NC 27518	877-419-4274	919-851-4838	731
Access Specialties International LLC 15230 Carrousel Way ...... Rosemount MN 55068	800-332-1013	651-453-1283	174
Access To Media 432 Front St .... Chicopee MA 01013	866-612-0034	413-206-0715	7
Access US 712 N Second St Ste 300 ... Saint Louis MO 63102	800-638-6373	314-655-7700	397
AccessPoint LLC 28800 Orchard Lake Rd ... Farmington Hills MI 48334	866-513-3861		729
Accident Fund Co 232 S Capitol Ave PO Box 40790 ... Lansing MI 48901 *Mktg*	888-276-0327*	517-342-4200	390-4
ACCO Engineered Systems 6265 San Fernando Rd .... Glendale CA 91201 *Cust Svc*	800-998-2226*	818-244-6571	189-10
Acco Material Handling Solutions 76 Acco Dr .... York PA 17402	800-967-7333		190
Accokeek Foundation 3400 Bryan Pt Rd .... Accokeek MD 20607	800-217-4273	301-283-2113	517
Accompass 1052 Yonge St .... Toronto ON M4W2L1	866-969-8588	416-969-8588	461
Accord Carton 6155 W 115th St .... Alsip IL 60803	800-648-6780		45
Accord Industries 4001 Forsyth Rd .... Winter Park FL 32792 *General*	800-876-6989*	407-671-6989	183
Accordant Company LLC 365 S St Ste 100 .... Morristown NJ 07960	800-363-1002	973-887-8900	179
Account Control Systems Inc 85 Chestnut Ridge Rd Ste 113 ... Montvale NJ 07645	800-482-8026		160
Accounts Payable Chexs Inc 1829 Ranchlands Blvd NW ... Calgary AB T3G2A7	888-437-0624	403-247-8913	2
ACCP (American College of Chest Physicians) 3300 Dundee Rd .... Northbrook IL 60062	800-343-2227	847-498-1400	49-8
Accram Inc 2901 W Clarendon Ave .... Phoenix AZ 85017	800-786-0288		175
Accrediting Commission of Career Schools & Colleges of Technology (ACCSCT) 2101 Wilson Blvd Ste 302 ... Arlington VA 22201	800-842-0229	703-247-4212	48-1
Accrediting Council for Independent Colleges & Schools (ACICS) 750 First St NE Ste 980 ... Washington DC 20002	800-258-3826	202-336-6780	48-1
Accredo Health Group Inc 1640 Century Ctr Pkwy ...... Memphis TN 38134	877-222-7336	901-385-3600	583
ACCSCT (Accrediting Commission of Career Schools & College) 2101 Wilson Blvd Ste 302 ... Arlington VA 22201	800-842-0229	703-247-4212	48-1
Accsense Inc 8437 Mayfield Rd .... Chesterland OH 44026	800-956-4437	440-729-2570	
ACCT (Association of Community College Trustees) 1101 17th St NW Ste 300 ... Washington DC 20036	866-895-2228	202-775-4667	49-5
Accu Reference Medical Lab 1901 E Linden Ave Unit 4 .... Linden NJ 07036	877-733-4522		414
ACCU Translations 3 Mays Crescent .... Waterdown ON L0R2H4	800-668-0831		
AccuCode Inc 6886 S Yosemite St Ste 100 ... Centennial CO 80112	866-705-9879	303-639-6111	177
AccuConference 5 Concourse Pkwy Ste 1600 ..... Atlanta GA 30328 *Cust Svc*	800-989-9239*	404-920-6600	317
Accufax PO Box 35563 .... Tulsa OK 74153	800-256-8898		631
Accu-Label Inc 2021 Research Dr ...... Fort Wayne IN 46808	888-482-5223	260-482-5223	623
Acculink 1055 Greenville Blvd SW .... Greenville NC 27834	800-948-4110	252-321-5805	623
Accumedic Computer Systems Inc 11 Grace Ave Ste 401 ...... Great Neck NY 11021	800-765-9300	516-466-6800	177
Accuplace 1800 NW 69th Ave .... Plantation FL 33313	866-820-0434	954-791-1500	
Accuplan Benefits Services 515 East 4500 South Ste G200 .... Salt Lake City UT 84107	800-454-2649	801-266-9900	49-2
Accuracy in Media Inc (AIM) 4350 EW Hwy Ste 555 ..... Bethesda MD 20814	800-787-4567	202-364-4401	49-14
Accurate Alloys Inc 5455 Irwindale Ave .... Irwindale CA 91706	800-842-2222	626-338-4012	490
Accurate Biometrics Inc 4849 N Milwaukee Ave Ste 101 ... Chicago IL 60630	866-361-9944	773-685-5699	399
Accurate Bushing Company Inc 443 N Ave .... Garwood NJ 07027 *Sales*	800-932-0076*	908-789-1121	75

Alphabetical Section

Listing	Toll-Free	Phone	Class
Accurate Chemical & Scientific Corp 300 Shames Dr .... Westbury NY 11590	800-645-6264	516-333-2221	231
Accurate Dial & Nameplate Inc 329 Mira Loma Ave .... Glendale CA 91204	800-400-4455	323-245-9181	412
Accurate Mailings Inc 215 O'Neill Ave .... Belmont CA 94002	800-732-3290	650-508-8885	5
Accurate Partitions Corp 160 Tower Dr PO Box 287 .... Burr Ridge IL 60527	800-933-4525	708-442-6800	605
Accurate Perforating Co 3636 S Kedzie Ave .... Chicago IL 60632	800-621-0273	773-254-3232	486
Accurate Surgical & Scientific Instruments Corp 300 Shames Dr .... Westbury NY 11590	800-645-3569	516-333-2570	474
Accuride Corp 7140 Office Cir .... Evansville IN 47715 NYSE: ACW ■ *Cust Svc	800-823-8332*	812-962-5000	60
Accuristix 2844 Bristol Cir .... Oakville ON L6H6G4	866-356-6830	905-829-9927	359-2
Accu-Sort Systems Inc 511 School House Rd .... Telford PA 18969	800-227-2633	215-723-0981	173-7
Accusource Inc 1240 E Ontario Ave Ste 102-140 .... Corona CA 92881	888-649-6272	951-734-8882	738
AccuTech LLC 2641 La Mirada Dr .... Vista CA 92081	800-749-9910	760-599-6555	474
Accutemp Products Inc 8415 N Clinton Pk .... Fort Wayne IN 46825	800-210-5907		
Accu-time Systems Inc 420 Somers Rd .... Ellington CT 06029	800-355-4648	860-870-5000	56
Accutron Inc 1733 Parkside Ln .... Phoenix AZ 85027	800-531-2221	623-780-2020	228
AccuWeather Inc 385 Science Pk Rd .... State College PA 16803 *Sales	800-566-6606*	814-235-8650	526
Accuzip 3216 El Camino Real .... Atascadero CA 93422	800-233-0555	805-461-7300	177
ACD Systems International Inc 129-1335 Bear Mtn Pkwy .... Victoria BC V9B6T9	888-767-9888	778-817-1168	
ACDI/VOCA 50 F St NW Ste 1000 .... Washington DC 20001	800-929-8622	202-638-4661	48-5
ACE (American Council on Exercise) 4851 Paramount Dr .... San Diego CA 92123	800-825-3636	858-576-6500	48-17
ACE (Altamont Commuter Express) 949 E Ch St .... Stockton CA 95202	800-411-7245		466
ACE (Auto Credit Express) 3271 Five Points Dr Ste 200 .... Auburn Hills MI 48326	888-535-2277		
ACE Bakery 1 Hafis Rd .... Toronto ON M6M2V6	800-443-7929	416-241-8433	
Ace Doran Hauling & Rigging Company Inc 1601 Blue Rock St .... Cincinnati OH 45223	800-829-0929	513-681-7900	775
Ace Forms of Kansas Inc 2900 N Rotary Terr .... Pittsburg KS 66762	800-223-9287		110
Ace Glass Inc 1430 NW Blvd PO Box 688 .... Vineland NJ 08360	800-223-4524	856-692-3333	332
Ace Hardware Corp 2200 Kensington Ct .... Oak Brook IL 60523	866-290-5334		363
Ace ImageWear 4120 Truman Rd .... Kansas City MO 64127	800-366-0564	816-231-5737	441
Ace Mart - Downtown San Antonio 1220 S St Mary's .... San Antonio TX 78210	888-898-8079	210-224-0082	114
Ace Medical Inc 94-910 Moloalo St .... Waipahu HI 96797	866-678-3601	808-678-3600	473
Ace Parking Management Inc 645 Ash St .... San Diego CA 92101 *General	855-223-7275*	619-233-6624	558
Ace Product Management Group Inc 12801 W Silver Spring Rd .... Butler WI 53007	800-294-9007	262-754-8490	461
ACE Rent A Car 8639 W Washington St .... Indianapolis IN 46241	877-822-3872	317-399-5247	126
Ace Sign Systems Inc 3621 W Royerton Rd .... Muncie IN 47304	800-607-6010	765-288-1000	697
Ace Tool Co 7337 Bryan Dairy Rd .... Largo FL 33777	800-777-5910	727-544-6652	61
Ace Wire & Cable Co Inc 7201 51st Ave .... Woodside NY 11377	800-225-2354	718-458-9200	808
Ace World Wide Moving 1900 E College Ave .... Cudahy WI 53110	800-558-3980	414-764-1000	516
ACEC (Allamakee-Clayton Electric Co-op) 229 Hwy 51 PO Box 715 .... Postville IA 52162	888-788-1551	563-864-7611	245
ACEC (American Council of Engineering Cos) 1015 15th St NW 8th Fl .... Washington DC 20005	800-338-1391	202-347-7474	49-19
Aceco 4419 Federal Way .... Boise ID 83716	800-359-7012	208-343-7712	349
ACEI (Association for Childhood Education International) 1101 16th St NW Ste 300 .... Washington DC 20036	800-423-3563	202-372-9986	49-5
ACEP (American College of Emergency Physicians) 1125 Executive Cir PO Box 619911 .... Dallas TX 75261	800-798-1822	972-550-0911	49-8
Acer America Corp 333 W San Carlos St Ste 1500 .... San Jose CA 95110	866-695-2237	408-533-7700	173-2
ACerS (American Ceramic Society) 600 N Cleveland Ave Ste 210 .... Westerville OH 43082	866-721-3322	614-890-4700	48-4
ACES (American College of Eye Surgeons/American Board of) 334 E Lake Rd Ste 135 .... Palm Harbor FL 34685	800-223-2233	727-366-1487	49-8
Ace-Tex Enterprises 7601 Central St .... Detroit MI 48210	800-444-3800	313-834-4000	441
ACF (American Culinary Federation Inc) 180 Ctr Pl Way .... Saint Augustine FL 32095	800-624-9458	904-824-4468	49-6
ACF Components & Fasteners Inc 31012 Huntwood Ave .... Hayward CA 94544 *Cust Svc	800-227-2901*	510-487-2100	246
ACFA (Alameda County Fair Assn) 4501 Pleasanton Ave .... Pleasanton CA 94566	800-874-9253	925-426-7600	638
ACFAS (American College of Foot & Ankle Surgeons) 8725 W Higgins Rd Ste 555 .... Chicago IL 60631	800-421-2237	773-693-9300	49-8
ACFC (American Coalition for Fathers & Children) 1718 M St NW Ste 1187 .... Washington DC 20036	800-978-3237		48-6
ACFC (Atlantic Coast Bank) 505 Haines Ave .... Waycross GA 31501 NASDAQ: ACFC	800-342-2824	912-283-4711	359-2
ACFE (Association of Certified Fraud Examiners) 716 W Ave .... Austin TX 78701	800-245-3321	512-478-9000	49-1
ACG (American Cotton Growers Textile Div) PO Box 2827 .... Lubbock TX 79408	800-333-8011	806-763-8011	740-1
ACG (Association for Corporate Growth) 125 S Wacker Dr Ste 3100 .... Chicago IL 60606	877-358-2220	312-957-4260	49-12
ACG Advisory Services Inc 1640 Huguenot Rd .... Midlothian VA 23113	800-231-6409	804-323-1886	524
ACH Foam Technologies LLC 5250 Sherman St .... Denver CO 80216	800-525-8697	303-297-3844	597
ACHE (Association for Continuing Higher Education) 1700 Asp Ave .... Norman OK 73072	800-807-2243		49-5
A-Check America Inc 1501 Research Park Dr .... Riverside CA 92507	877-345-2021	951-750-1501	260
AchieveGlobal Inc 8875 Hidden River Pkwy Ste 400 .... Tampa FL 33637	800-566-0630	813-631-5517	760
Achievement Incentives & Meetings 64 River Rd .... East Hanover NJ 07936	800-454-1424	973-386-9500	194
achoo! ALLERGY & AIR Products Inc 3411 Pierce Dr Ste 100 .... Atlanta GA 30341	800-339-7123		
ACI (Arkansas Correctional Industries) 6841 W 13th St .... Pine Bluff AR 71602	877-635-7213		626
ACI (Axis Communications Inc) 100 Apollo Dr .... Chelmsford MA 01824	800-444-2947	978-614-2000	176
ACI (ACI) 500 W 57th St .... New York NY 10019	800-724-4444	212-293-3000	722
ACI Worldwide Inc 3520 Kraft Rd Ste 300 .... Naples FL 34105	877-276-5554	402-390-7600	178-1
ACIC Pharmaceuticals Inc 81 St Claire Blvd .... Brantford ON N3S7X6	800-265-6727	519-751-3668	477
ACICS (Accrediting Council for Independent Colleges & Sch) 750 First St NE Ste 980 .... Washington DC 20002	800-258-3826	202-336-6780	48-1
Acier Picard Inc 3000 Rue De L' Etchemin .... Levis QC G6W7X6	888-834-0646	418-834-8300	490
ACIL (American Council of Independent Laboratories) 1875 I St NW Ste 500 .... Washington DC 20006	800-368-1131	202-887-5872	49-19
ACIPCO (American Cast Iron Pipe Co) 1501 31st Ave N .... Birmingham AL 35207	800-442-2347	205-325-7701	307
ACIST Medical Systems Inc 7905 Fuller Rd .... Eden Prairie MN 55344	888-667-6648	952-941-3507	474
Ackermann Public Relations & Marketing 1111 Northshore Dr Ste N-400 .... Knoxville TN 37919 *General	877-325-9453*	865-584-0550	632
Ackroo Inc 62 Steacie Dr Ste 201 .... Ottawa ON K2K2A9	888-405-0066	613-599-2396	317
ACLU (American Civil Liberties Union) 125 Broad St 18th Fl .... New York NY 10004	877-867-1025	212-549-2500	48-8
ACM (Association for Computing Machinery) 2 Penn Plz Ste 701 .... New York NY 10121	800-342-6626	212-626-0500	48-9
ACMA Computers Inc 1565 Reliance Way .... Fremont CA 94539 *Sales	800-786-6888*	510-683-9090	173-2
ACMC (Ashtabula County Medical Ctr) 2420 Lake Ave .... Ashtabula OH 44004	800-722-3330	440-997-2262	373-3
ACMC (Affiliated Community Medical Centers) 101 Willmar Ave SW .... Willmar MN 56201	888-225-6580	320-231-5000	373-3
ACME (Association for Couples in Marriage Enrichment) PO Box 21374 .... Winston-Salem NC 27120	800-634-8325		48-6
Acme Construction Company Inc 7695 Bond St .... Cleveland OH 44139	800-686-5077	440-232-7474	188-8
Acme Cryogenics Inc 2801 Mitchell Ave .... Allentown PA 18103	800-422-2790	610-966-4488	452
Acme Distribution Centers Inc 18101 E Colfax Ave .... Aurora CO 80011	800-444-3614	303-340-2100	798-1
Acme Dynamics Inc 3608 Sydney Rd PO Box 1780 .... Plant City FL 33566	800-622-9355	813-752-3137	637
Acme Electric N56 W13385 Silver Spring Dr .... Menomonee Falls WI 53051	800-334-5214		385
Acme Engineering & Manufacturing Corp PO Box 978 .... Muskogee OK 74402	800-382-2263	918-682-7791	18
Acme Food Sales Inc 5940 First Ave S .... Seattle WA 98108	800-777-2263	206-762-5150	297-8
Acme Industrial Co 441 Maple Ave .... Carpentersville IL 60110	800-323-5582	847-428-3911	491
Acme Markets Inc 75 Valley Stream Pkwy .... Malvern PA 19355	877-932-7948	610-889-4000	344
Acme Spirally Wound Paper Products Inc 4810 W 139th St PO Box 35320 .... Cleveland OH 44135	800-274-2797	216-267-2950	125
Acme Truck Line Inc 200 Westbank Expy PO Box 183 .... Gretna LA 70053	800-825-6246	504-368-2510	775
Acme United Corp 55 Walls Dr Ste 201 .... Fairfield CT 06824 NYSE: ACU	800-835-2263		474
Acme Wire Products Co 7 Broadway Ave .... Mystic CT 06355	800-723-7015	860-572-0511	447
ACNM (American College of Nurse-Midwives) 8403 Colesville Rd Ste 1550 .... Silver Spring MD 20910	800-468-3571	240-485-1800	49-8
Aco Polymer Products Inc 9470 Pinecore Dr .... Mentor OH 44060	800-543-4764	440-639-7230	604
ACOFP (American College of Osteopathic Family Physicians) 330 E Algonquin Rd Ste 1 .... Arlington Heights IL 60005	800-323-0794	847-952-5100	49-8
ACOM Solutions Inc 2850 E 29th St .... Long Beach CA 90806	800-347-3638	562-424-7899	178-1
Acoma Business Enterprise PO Box 310 .... Acoma NM 87034	888-759-2489		
Acor Orthopaedic Inc 18530 S Miles Pkwy .... Cleveland OH 44128	800-237-2267	216-662-4500	301
ACORD (Association for Co-op Operations Research & Develo) 1 Blue Hill Plz PO Box 1529 .... Pearl River NY 10965	800-444-3341	845-620-1700	49-9
Acorn Deck House Co 852 Main St .... Acton MA 01720	800-727-3325		106
Acorn Engineering Co 15125 Proctor Ave PO Box 3527 .... City of Industry CA 91744	800-488-8999	626-336-4561	605
Acorn Gencon Plastics Inc 15125 Proctor Ave .... City of Industry CA 91746	800-782-7706	626-968-6681	385
Acorn Manufacturing Company Inc 457 School St .... Mansfield MA 02048	800-835-0121	508-339-2977	349

Name / Address	City	State	ZIP	Toll-Free	Phone	Class
Acorn Wire & Iron Works Inc 2035 S Racine Ave	Chicago	IL	60608	**800-552-2676**	773-585-0600	279
Acousti Engineering Company of Florida Inc 4656 34th St SW	Orlando	FL	32811	**800-434-3467**	407-425-3467	189-9
Acoustic Neuroma Assn (ANA) 600 Peachtree Pkwy Ste 108	Cumming	GA	30041	**877-200-8211**	770-205-8211	48-17
Acoustic Sounds Inc 1500 S Ninth St	Salina	KS	67401	**888-926-2564**	785-825-8609	461
Acoustical Society of America (ASA) 1305 Walt Whitman Rd Ste 300	Melville	NY	11747	**800-828-8840**	516-576-2360	49-19
ACP (American College of Physicians) 190 N Independence Mall W	Philadelphia	PA	19106	**800-523-1546**	215-351-2400	49-8
ACPA (American Concrete Pavement Assn) 5420 Old OrchaRd Rd Ste A-100	Skokie	IL	60077	**800-281-7899**	847-966-2272	49-3
ACPA (American Chronic Pain Assn) PO Box 850	Rocklin	CA	95677	**800-533-3231**		48-17
ACPE (American College of Physician Executives) 400 N Ashley Dr Ste 400	Tampa	FL	33602	**800-562-8088**	813-287-2000	49-8
ACPHS (Albany College of Pharmacy) 106 New Scotland Ave *General	Albany	NY	12208	**888-203-8010***	518-694-7221	166
Acqua Hotel 555 Redwood Hwy	Mill Valley	CA	94941	**888-662-9555**	415-380-0400	378
Acqualina 17875 Collins Ave	Sunny Isles Beach	FL	33160	**877-312-9742**	305-918-8000	378
Acquizitionbiz Inc 1100 Rene-Levesque Blvd W 24th Fl	Montreal	QC	H3B4X9	**866-499-0334**	514-499-0334	386
ACR (American College of Radiology) 1891 Preston White Dr	Reston	VA	20191	**800-227-5463**	703-648-8900	49-8
ACR Electronics Inc 5757 Ravenswood Rd	Fort Lauderdale	FL	33312	**800-432-0227**	954-981-3333	674
ACR Supply Company Inc 4040 S Alston Ave	Durham	NC	27713	**800-442-4044**	919-765-8081	111
Acranet 521 W Maxwell Ave	Spokane	WA	99201	**800-304-1249**		180
ACRL (Association of College & Research Libraries) 50 E Huron St	Chicago	IL	60611	**800-545-2433**	312-280-2519	49-11
Acro Labels Inc 2530 Wyandotte Rd	Willow Grove	PA	19090	**800-355-2235**	215-657-5366	412
Acro Media Inc 2303 Leckie Rd Ste 103	Kelowna	BC	V1X6Y5	**877-763-8844**	250-763-8884	804
AcrobatAnt LLC 1336 E 15th St	Tulsa	OK	74120	**800-984-7239**	918-938-7901	195
Acromag Inc 30765 S Wixom Rd	Wixom	MI	48393	**877-295-7092**	800-882-2055	621
Acropolis Technology Group 300 Hunter Ave Ste 103	Clayton	MO	62095	**800-742-6316**	314-890-2208	175
Acroprint Time Recorder Co 5640 Departure Dr	Raleigh	NC	27616	**800-334-7190**	919-872-5800	530
ACRT Inc 1333 Home Ave	Akron	OH	44310	**800-622-2562**		193
Acrylic Design Assoc 6050 Nathan Ln N	Plymouth	MN	55442	**800-445-2167**	763-559-8395	233
Acrylic Plastic Products Company Inc 4815 Hwy 80 W	Jackson	MS	39209	**800-331-8819**	601-922-2651	604
Acryline USA Inc 2015 Becancour	Lyster	QC	G0S1V0	**800-567-0920**		349
ACS (American Cancer Society) 250 William St NW	Atlanta	GA	30303	**800-227-2345**	404-315-1123	48-17
ACS (American Chemical Society) 1155 16th St NW	Washington	DC	20036	**800-227-5558**	202-872-4600	49-19
ACS (American College of Surgeons) 633 N St Clair St	Chicago	IL	60611	**800-621-4111**	312-202-5000	49-8
ACS Group, The 2900 S 160th St	New Berlin	WI	53151	**800-423-3183**	262-641-8600	14
ACS Industries Inc 1 New England Way	Lincoln	RI	02865	**866-783-4838**	401-769-4700	684
ACSH (American Council on Science & Health) 110 E 42nd St Ste 1300	New York	NY	10017	**866-905-2694**	212-362-7044	49-19
ACSI (Association of Christian Schools International) 731 Chapel Hills Dr *Cust Svc	Colorado Springs	CO	80920	**800-367-0798***	719-528-6906	49-5
Act2 Retirement Consulting LLC 100 Painters Mill Rd	Owings Mills	MD	21117	**866-992-9256**	443-379-0375	461
ACTE (Association for Career & Technical Education) 1410 King St	Alexandria	VA	22314	**800-826-9972**	703-683-3111	49-5
ACTE (Association of Corporate Travel Executives) 526 King St Ste 215	Alexandria	VA	22314	**800-228-3669**	703-683-5322	
Actel Corp 2061 Stierlin Ct	Mountain View	CA	94043	**800-262-1060**	650-318-4200	692
ACTEON North America Inc 124 Gaither Dr Ste 140	Mount Laurel	NJ	08054	**800-289-6367**	856-222-9988	228
Actify LLC 7635 Interactive Way Ste 200	Indianapolis	IN	46278	**800-467-0830**		246
Action Against Hunger 247 W 37th St 10th Fl	New York	NY	10018	**877-777-1420**	212-967-7800	48-5
Action Aircraft 10570 Olympic Dr	Dallas	TX	75220	**800-909-7616**	214-351-1284	21
Action Capital Corp 230 Peachtree St Ste 1910	Atlanta	GA	30303	**800-525-7767**	404-524-3181	272
Action Co 1425 N Tennessee St *Sales	McKinney	TX	75069	**800-937-3700***	972-542-8700	430
Action Floor Systems LLC 4781 N US Hwy 51	Mercer	WI	54547	**800-746-3512**	715-476-3512	290
Action Lift Inc 1 Memco Dr	Pittston	PA	18640	**800-294-5438**	570-655-2100	357
Action Mailing Corp 3165 W Heartland Dr	Liberty	MO	64068	**866-990-9001**	816-415-9000	5
Action Pest Control Inc 2301 S Green River Rd	Evansville	IN	47715	**800-467-5530**	812-477-5546	573
Action Screen Print Inc 30w260 Butterfield Rd Unit 203	Warrenville	IL	60555	**800-661-5892**	630-393-1990	683
Action Sports Systems Inc 617 Carbon City Rd PO Box 1442	Morganton	NC	28655	**800-631-1091**	828-584-8000	155-18
ActionCOACH 5781 S Ft Apache Rd	Las Vegas	NV	89148	**888-483-2828**	702-795-3188	760
ActionTec Electronics Inc 760 N Mary Ave *Tech Supp	Sunnyvale	CA	94085	**888-436-0657***	408-752-7700	173-3
Activation Laboratories Ltd 1336 Sandhill Dr	Ancaster	ON	L9G4V5	**888-228-5227**	905-648-9611	738
Active Day/Senior Care Inc 6 Neshaminy Interplex Ste 401	Trevose	PA	19053	**877-435-3372**	888-338-6898	449
Active Network 10182 Telesis Ct Ste 100	San Diego	CA	92121	**888-543-7223**	858-964-3800	7
Active Parenting Publishers 1955 Vaughn Rd Ste 108	Kennesaw	GA	30144	**800-825-0060**	770-429-0565	510
Activeforevercom 10799 N 90th St	Scottsdale	AZ	85260	**800-377-8033**		321
activePDF Inc 27405 Puerta Real Ste 100	Mission Viejo	CA	92691	**866-468-6733**	949-582-9002	178-12
Activision Inc 3100 Ocean Pk Blvd	Santa Monica	CA	90405	**800-509-5586**	310-255-2000	178-6
Acton Institute 98 E Fulton St	Grand Rapids	MI	49503	**800-345-2286**	616-454-3080	630
Actors Theatre of Louisville 316 W Main St	Louisville	KY	40202	**800-428-5849**	502-584-1205	744
Actors' Equity Assn 1560 Broadway	New York	NY	10036	**866-270-4232**	212-869-8530	413
Actsoft Inc 10006 N Dale Mabry Hwy Ste 100	Tampa	FL	33618	**888-732-6638**	813-936-2331	177
Actuarial Systems Corp 15840 Monte St Ste 108	Sylmar	CA	91342	**800-950-2082**		389
ACU (Abilene Christian University Brown Library) 221 Brown Library	Abilene	TX	79699	**800-460-6228**	325-674-2316	433-6
ACU Serve Corp 2020 Front St Ste 205	Cuyahoga Fls	OH	44221	**800-887-8965**	330-923-5258	2
Acuity Insurance 2800 S Taylor Dr	Sheboygan	WI	53081	**800-242-7666**		390-4
Acumen Capital Finance Partners Ltd 404 Sixth Ave SW Ste 700	Calgary	AB	T2P0R9	**888-422-8636**	403-571-0300	400
Acumen Fiscal Agent 4542 E Inverness Ave Ste 210	Mesa	AZ	85206	**877-211-3738**		
Acumenex Com 2201 Brant St	Burlington	ON	L7P3N8	**877-788-5028**	905-319-2468	395
Acuren Group Inc 7450 - 18th St	Edmonton	AB	T6P1N8	**800-663-9729**	780-440-2131	782
Acushnet holdings Corp 333 Bridge St	Fairhaven	MA	02719	**800-225-8500**	508-979-2000	706
AcuSport Corp 1 Hunter Pl	Bellefontaine	OH	43311	**800-543-3150**	937-593-7010	706
Acxiom 301 E Dave Ward Dr *NASDAQ: ACXM*	Conway	AR	72032	**888-322-9466**	501-342-7799	5
Ad Art Co 3260 E 26th St	Los Angeles	CA	90058	**800-266-7522**	323-981-8941	697
A&D Environmental Services Inc PO Box 484	High Point	NC	27261	**800-434-7750**		63
ADA (American Dental Assn) 211 E Chicago Ave	Chicago	IL	60611	**800-621-8099**	312-440-2500	49-8
ADA (American Diabetes Assn) 1701 N Beauregard St	Alexandria	VA	22311	**800-232-3472**	703-549-1500	48-17
ADAA (Anxiety Disorders Assn of America) 8701 Georgia Ave Ste #412	Silver Spring	MD	20910	**800-922-8947**	240-485-1001	48-17
ADAA (American Dental Assistants Assn) 140 N Bloomingdale Rd	Bloomingdale	IL	60108	**877-874-3785**	312-541-1550	49-8
ADA-ES Inc 640 Plz Dr Ste 270 *NASDAQ: ADES*	Highlands Ranch	CO	80129	**888-822-8617**	720-598-3500	145
Adair Printing Technologies 7850 Second St	Dexter	MI	48130	**800-637-5025**	734-426-2822	622
Adam Broderick Salon & Spa 89 Danbury Rd	Ridgefield	CT	06877	**800-438-3834**	203-431-3994	77
Adamo Construction Inc 11980 Woodside Ave Ste 5	Lakeside	CA	92040	**800-554-6364**	619-390-6706	186
Adams Air & Hydraulics Inc 7209 E Adamo Dr	Tampa	FL	33619	**800-282-4165**	813-626-4128	357
Adams County 110 W Main St	West Union	OH	45693	**800-840-5711**	937-544-2011	337
Adams County Public Library 140 Baltimore St	Gettysburg	PA	17325	**800-548-3240**	717-334-5716	433-3
Adams County Travel & Visitors Bureau 509 E Main St	West Union	OH	45693	**877-232-6764**	937-544-5639	139
Adams County Winery 251 Peach Tree Rd	Orrtanna	PA	17353	**877-601-7936**	717-334-4631	50-7
Adams Direct & Media Services 39 Faranella Dr	East Hanover	NJ	07936	**800-631-6245**		195
Adams Electric Co-op PO Box 247	Camp Point	IL	62320	**800-232-4797**	217-593-7701	245
Adams Electric Co-op Inc 1338 Biglerville Rd PO Box 1055	Gettysburg	PA	17325	**888-232-6732**	717-334-2171	245
Adams Elevator Equipment Co 6310 W Howard St	Niles	IL	60714	**800-929-9247**	847-581-2900	674
Adams Funds 500 E Pratt St Ste 1300 *NYSE: ADX*	Baltimore	MD	21202	**800-638-2479**	410-752-5900	404
Adams Investment Co 2500 Industrial Pkwy	Dewey	OK	74029	**800-331-0920**		110
Adams Keegan Inc 6750 Poplar Ave Ste 400	Memphis	TN	38138	**800-621-1308**		627
Adams Museum 54 Sherman St	Deadwood	SD	57732	**800-335-0275**	605-578-1714	517
Adams Oceanfront Resort 4 Read St	Dewey Beach	DE	19971	**800-448-8080**	302-227-3030	378
Adams Products Co 5701 McCrimmon Pkwy	Morrisville	NC	27560	**800-672-3131**	919-467-2218	183
Adams Remco Inc 2612 Foundation Dr	South Bend	IN	46628	**800-627-2113**	574-288-2113	112
Adams Rural Electric Co-op Inc 4800 SR 125	West Union	OH	45693	**800-283-1846**	937-544-2305	245

Name / Address	City	State	ZIP	Toll-Free	Phone	Class
Adams State College						
208 Edgemont Blvd	Alamosa	CO	81102	**800-824-6494**	719-587-7712	166
Adams USA Inc						
610 S Jefferson Ave	Cookeville	TN	38501	**800-426-9784**		706
Adams-Burch Inc						
1901 Stanford Ct	Landover	MD	20785	**800-347-8093***	301-276-2000	300
*Cust Svc						
Adams-Columbia Electric Co-op						
401 E Lake St	Friendship	WI	53934	**800-831-8629**		245
Adamson Global Technology Corp						
13101 N Eron Church Rd	Chester	VA	23836	**800-525-7703**	804-748-6453	91
Adaptive Micro Systems Inc						
7840 N 86th St	Milwaukee	WI	53224	**800-558-4187**	414-357-2020	178-7
ADB (American Drill Bushings Co)						
5740 Hunt Rd	Valdosta	GA	31606	**800-423-4425**	229-253-8928	491
ADC (American-Arab Anti Discrimination Committee)						
1990 M St NW Ste 610	Washington	DC	20036	**800-253-3931**	202-244-2990	48-8
AdCare Hospital of Worcester						
107 Lincoln St	Worcester	MA	01605	**800-252-6465**	508-799-9000	722
Adco Inc						
1909 W Oakridge	Albany	GA	31707	**800-821-7556**		151
Adco Industries						
11333 Pagemill Rd	Dallas	TX	75243	**800-527-4609**	214-217-7800	43
Adco Manufacturing Inc						
2170 Academy Ave	Sanger	CA	93657	**888-608-5946**	559-875-5563	384
Adcolor Inc						
230 Charlois Blvd	Winston-Salem	NC	27103	**800-688-0629**		
ADDCO LLC						
240 Arlington Ave E	Saint Paul	MN	55117	**800-616-4408**	651-488-8600	696
Addison Biological Laboratory Inc						
507 N Cleveland Ave	Fayette	MO	65248	**800-331-2530**	660-248-2215	580
Addison House						
5201 NW 77th Ave Ste 400	Doral	FL	33166	**800-426-2988**	305-640-2400	321
Adducent Technology Inc						
PO Box 1057	Rohnert Park	CA	94927	**800-648-0656**		525
ADEA (American Dental Education Assn)						
1400 K St NW Ste 1100	Washington	DC	20005	**800-353-2237**	202-289-7201	49-5
A-dec Inc						
2601 Crestview Dr	Newberg	OR	97132	**800-547-1883***	503-538-7478	228
*Cust Svc						
Adec Industries						
2700 Industrial Pkwy	Elkhart	IN	46516	**866-730-3111**	574-295-3167	88
Adel Wiggins Group of Transdigm Inc						
5000 Triggs St	Los Angeles	CA	90022	**800-624-3576**	323-269-9181	
Adell Plastics Inc						
4530 Annapolis Rd	Baltimore	MD	21227	**800-638-5218**	410-789-7780	740-2
Adelman Travel Group						
6980 N Port Washington Rd	Milwaukee	WI	53217	**800-248-5562***	414-352-7600	766
*Cust Svc						
Adelphi Consulting Group Inc						
8209 SW Cirrus Dr	Beaverton	OR	97008	**800-698-1942**	503-641-3501	196
Adelphi University						
1 South Ave PO Box 701	Garden City	NY	11530	**800-233-5744**	516-877-3050	166
Adelphia Steel Equipment Co						
7372 State Rd	Philadelphia	PA	19136	**800-865-8211**	215-333-6300	319-1
Adena Regional Medical Ctr						
272 Hospital Rd	Chillicothe	OH	45601	**800-582-7277**	740-779-7500	373-3
Adept Corp						
4601 N Susquehanna Trial	York	PA	17406	**800-451-2254**	717-266-3606	357
Aderans Hair Goods Inc						
9135 Independence Ave	Chatsworth	CA	91311	**877-413-5225***		347
*Sales						
ADESA Inc						
13085 Hamilton Crossing Blvd	Carmel	IN	46032	**800-923-3725**	317-815-1100	51
ADEX Corp						
1035 Windward Ridge Pkwy						
Ste 500	Alpharetta	GA	30005	**800-451-9899**	678-393-7900	224
Adfirmative LLC						
11416 Hollister Dr	Austin	TX	78739	**866-966-9968**		195
ADG Promotional Products						
2300 Main St	Hugo	MN	55038	**800-852-5208**		9
ADHA (American Dental Hygienists' Assn)						
444 N Michigan Ave Ste 3400	Chicago	IL	60611	**800-243-2342**	312-440-8900	49-8
Adhesive Packaging Specialties Inc						
103 Foster St	Peabody	MA	01960	**800-222-1117**	978-531-3300	544
Adhesives Research Inc						
400 Seaks Run Rd PO Box 100	Glen Rock	PA	17327	**800-445-6240**	717-235-7979	3
AdHub LLC, The						
146 Alexander St	Rochester	NY	14607	**866-712-2986**	585-442-2585	392
Adi American Distributors Inc						
2 Emery Ave	Randolph	NJ	07869	**800-877-0510**	973-328-1181	246
Adirondack Community College						
640 Bay Rd	Queensbury	NY	12804	**888-786-9235**	518-743-2200	162
Adirondack Council						
103 Hand Ave Ste 3	Elizabethtown	NY	12932	**877-873-2240**	518-873-2240	48-13
Adirondack Mountain Club						
814 Goggins Rd	Lake George	NY	12845	**800-395-8080***	518-668-4447	48-23
*Orders						
Adirondack Regional Chambers of Commerce						
136 Glen St Ste 3	Glens Falls	NY	12801	**888-516-7247**	518-798-1761	139
ADL (Anti-Defamation League)						
605 Third Ave	New York	NY	10158	**866-386-3235**	212-885-7700	48-8
Adler Display						
7140 Windsor Blvd	Baltimore	MD	21244	**855-552-3537**		7
Adleta Co						
1645 Diplomat Dr	Carrollton	TX	75006	**800-423-5382**	972-620-5600	360
ADM (ADM Milling Co)						
8000 W 110th St	Overland Park	KS	66210	**800-422-1688**	913-491-9400	296-23
ADM Corp						
100 Lincoln Blvd	Middlesex	NJ	08846	**800-327-0718**	732-469-0900	263
ADM Milling Co (ADM)						
8000 W 110th St	Overland Park	KS	66210	**800-422-1688**	913-491-9400	296-23
ADM Natural Health & Nutrition						
Archer Daniels Midland Co						
4666 Faries Pkwy	Decatur	IL	62526	**800-637-5843**	217-451-7231	794
ADM Specialty Food Ingredients Div						
4666 E Faries Pkwy	Decatur	IL	62526	**800-637-5843**	217-424-5200	296-17
AdMail Express Inc						
31640 Hayman St	Hayward	CA	94544	**800-273-6245**		623
Admar Supply Co Inc						
1950 Brighton Henriett	Rochester	NY	14623	**800-836-2367**	585-272-9390	357
Administration on Aging (AoA)						
1 Massachusetts Ave NW	Washington	DC	20001	**800-677-1116**	202-357-3584	
Admiral Craft Equipment Corp						
940 S Oyster Bay Rd	Hicksville	NY	11801	**800-223-7750**	516-433-3535	486
Admiral Fell Inn						
888 S Broadway	Baltimore	MD	21231	**866-583-4162**	410-522-7377	378
Admiral Linen Service Inc						
2030 Kipling St	Houston	TX	77098	**800-321-1948**	713-529-2608	441
Admiral on Baltimore						
2 Baltimore Ave	Rehoboth Beach	DE	19971	**888-882-4188**	302-227-1300	378
Admiral Packaging Inc						
10 Admiral St	Providence	RI	02908	**800-556-6454**	401-274-7000	544
AdMobilize LLC						
1680 Michigan Ave Ste 918	Miami Beach	FL	33139	**888-628-7494**		386
Adobe Systems Inc						
345 Park Ave	San Jose	CA	95110	**800-833-6687**	408-536-6000	178-8
NASDAQ: ADBE						
Adobe Ventures LP						
345 Park Ave	San Jose	CA	95110	**877-722-7088**	408-536-6000	787
Department of Insurance						
100 N 15th Ave Ste 102	Phoenix	AZ	85007	**800-325-2548**	602-364-2499	
Adoption ARC Inc						
4247 Locust St Apt 16	Philadelphia	PA	19104	**888-558-6561**	215-748-1441	48-6
Adoptive Families Magazine						
108 W 39th St Ste 805	New York	NY	10018	**800-372-3300**	646-366-0830	455-10
Adorama Camera Inc						
42 W 18th St	New York	NY	10011	**800-223-2500**	212-741-0052	119
ADP (Association of Directory Publishers)						
PO Box 209	Traverse City	MI	49685	**800-267-9002**	231-486-2182	49-16
ADP (Automatic Data Processing Inc)						
1 ADP Blvd	Roseland	NJ	07068	**800-225-5237**		225
NASDAQ: ADP						
Adp Media Group LLC						
7700 Camp Bowie W Blvd Ste B	Fort Worth	TX	76116	**800-925-5700**	817-244-2740	623
ADP TotalSource Co						
10200 Sunset Dr	Miami	FL	33173	**800-447-3237**	800-225-5237	627
ADRA (Adventist Development & Relief Agency)						
12501 Old Columbia Pk	Silver Spring	MD	20904	**800-424-2372**		48-5
Adrenalin Inc						
54 W 11th Ave	Denver	CO	80204	**888-757-5646**	303-454-8888	343
Adrian College						
110 S Madison St	Adrian	MI	49221	**800-877-2246***	517-265-5161	166
*Admissions						
Adriance Memorial Library						
93 Market St	Poughkeepsie	NY	12601	**800-804-0092**	845-485-3445	434
Adrianna Papell						
500 Seventh Ave 10th Fl	New York	NY	10018	**800-325-9450**		155-20
Adroit Medical Systems Inc						
1146 CaRding Machine Rd	Loudon	TN	37774	**800-267-6077**	865-458-8600	475
ADS Environmental Services						
4940 Research Dr	Huntsville	AL	35805	**800-633-7246**	256-430-3366	201
ADS Security LP						
3001 Armory Dr Ste 100	Nashville	TN	37204	**800-448-5852**	615-269-4448	688
ADS/Transicoil						
9 Iron Bridge Dr	Collegeville	PA	19426	**800-323-7115**	484-902-1100	515
ADSA (American Dairy Science Assn)						
1111 N Dunlap Ave	Savoy	IL	61874	**888-670-2250**	217-356-5146	48-2
Adserts Inc						
14750 W Capitol Dr	Brookfield	WI	53005	**800-346-6919**		2
Adstrategies Inc						
101 Bay St Ste 201	Easton	MD	21601	**888-456-2450**		7
ADT Security Services Inc						
14200 E Exposition Ave	Aurora	CO	80012	**800-246-9147**	800-521-1734	688
Ad-tech Medical Instrument Corp						
400 W Oakview Pky	Oak Creek	WI	53154	**800-776-1555**	262-634-1555	474
ADTRAN Inc						
901 Explorer Blvd	Huntsville	AL	35806	**800-923-8726**	256-963-8000	730
NASDAQ: ADTN						
ADTRAV Travel Management						
4555 S Lake Pkwy	Birmingham	AL	35244	**800-476-2952**	205-444-4800	766
Advance Auto Parts Inc						
5008 Airport Rd	Roanoke	VA	24012	**877-238-2623**		54
NYSE: AAP						
Advance Bag & Packaging Technologies						
5720 Williams Lake Rd	Waterford	MI	48329	**800-475-2247**	248-674-3126	596
Advance Carbon Products Inc						
2036 National Ave	Hayward	CA	94545	**800-283-1249**	510-293-5930	127
Advance Communications & Consulting Inc						
8803 Swigert Ct Unit A	Bakersfield	CA	93311	**800-510-2148**	661-664-0177	196
Advance Corp Braille-Tac Div						
8200 97th St S	Cottage Grove	MN	55016	**800-328-9451**	651-771-9297	697
Advance Energy Technologies Inc						
1 Solar Dr	Clifton Park	NY	12065	**800-724-0198**	518-371-2140	660
Advance Engineering Co						
7505 Baron Dr	Canton	MI	48187	**800-497-6388**	313-537-3500	487
Advance Food Company Inc						
9987 Carver Rd Ste 500	Cincinnati	OH	45242	**800-969-2747**		299
Advance Group, The						
185 Price Pkwy	Farmingdale	NY	11735	**877-273-6481**		392
Advance Insurance Company of Kansas						
1133 SW Topeka Blvd	Topeka	KS	66629	**800-530-5989**	785-273-9804	390-2
Advance Lifts Inc						
701 Kirk Rd	Saint Charles	IL	60174	**800-843-3625**	630-584-9881	468
Advance Notice Inc						
24 Winter St	Peabody	MA	01960	**800-992-0313**		7
Advance Scale of MD LLC						
2400 Egg Harbor Rd	Lindenwold	NJ	08021	**888-447-2253**	856-627-0700	680
Advance Tabco						
200 Heartland Blvd	Edgewood	NY	11717	**800-645-3166**	631-242-8270	300
Advance Tank & Construction Co						
3700 E County Rd 64						
PO Box 219	Wellington	CO	80549	**800-422-3488**	970-568-3444	189-14
Advance Transportation Systems Inc						
10558 Taconic Ter	Cincinnati	OH	45215	**800-878-4849**	513-771-4848	311
Advanced Alarm Systems Inc						
101 Lindsey St	Fall River	MA	02720	**800-442-5276**	508-675-1937	689

	City	State	ZIP	Toll-Free	Phone	Class
Advanced Bionics LLC						
28515 Westinghouse Pl	Valencia	CA	91355	**877-829-0026**	661-362-1400	253
Advanced Biotechnologies Inc (ABI)						
1545 Progress Way	Eldersburg	MD	21784	**800-426-0764**	410-792-9779	231
Advanced Cable Ties Inc						
245 Suffolk Ln	Gardner	MA	01440	**800-861-7228**		707
Advanced California (NAAS)						
1510 Robert St Ste 103	Boise	ID	83705	**888-413-3669**		
Advanced Cell Diagnostics Inc						
3960 Point Eden Way	Hayward	CA	94545	**877-576-3636**	510-576-8800	664
Advanced Chemistry Development Inc						
110 Yonge St 14th Fl	Toronto	ON	M5C1T4	**800-304-3988**	416-368-3435	177
Advanced Circuits Inc						
21101 E 32nd Pkwy	Aurora	CO	80011	**800-979-4722**	303-576-6610	621
Advanced Computing Solutions Group Inc						
19125 Northcreek Pkwy	Bothell	WA	98011	**800-550-8007**	425-609-3165	177
Advanced Concrete Systems						
55 Advanced Ln	Middleburg	PA	17842	**800-521-3788**		
Advanced Digital Data Inc						
6 Laurel Dr	Flanders	NJ	07836	**800-922-0972**	973-584-4026	177
Advanced Drainage Systems Inc						
4640 Trueman Blvd	Hilliard	OH	43026	**800-821-6710**		592
Advanced Energy Corp						
909 Capability Dr Ste 2100	Raleigh	NC	27606	**800-869-8001**	919-857-9000	194
Advanced Energy Industries Inc						
1625 Sharp Pt Dr	Fort Collins	CO	80525	**800-446-9167**		691
NASDAQ: AEIS						
Advanced Hydraulics Inc						
13568 Vintage Pl	Chino	CA	91710	**888-581-8079**	909-590-7644	454
Advanced Image Direct						
1415 S Acacia Ave	Fullerton	CA	92831	**800-540-3848**	714-502-3900	457
Advanced Industrial Services Inc						
3250 Susquehanna Trial	York	PA	17406	**800-544-5080**	717-764-9811	186
Advanced Information Systems Group Inc						
11315 Corporate Blvd Ste 210	Orlando	FL	32817	**800-593-8359**	407-581-2929	180
Advanced Looseleaf Technologies Inc						
1424 Somerset Ave	Dighton	MA	02715	**800-339-6354**	508-669-6354	86
Advanced Machine & Engineering Co						
2500 Latham St	Rockford	IL	61103	**800-225-4263**	815-962-6076	491
Advanced Micro Devices Inc (AMD)						
1 AMD Pl PO Box 3453	Sunnyvale	CA	94088	**800-538-8450**	408-749-4000	692
NYSE: AMD						
Advanced MP Technology						
1010 Calle Sombra	San Clemente	CA	92673	**800-492-3113**	949-492-3113	246
Advanced Orthomolecular Research Inc						
3900 - 12 St NE	Calgary	AB	T2E8H9	**800-387-0177**	403-250-9997	344
Advanced Photographic Solutions						
1525 Hardeman Ln	Cleveland	TN	37312	**800-241-9234**	423-479-5481	584
Advanced Poly Packaging Inc						
1331 Emmitt Rd	Akron	OH	44306	**800-754-4403**	330-785-4000	553
Advanced Pressure Systems						
701 S Persimmon St Ste J	Tomball	TX	77375	**877-290-4277**	281-290-9950	
Advanced Probing Systems Inc						
2300 Central Ave	Boulder	CO	80301	**800-631-0005**	303-939-9384	590
Advanced Sterilization Products (ASP)						
33 Technology Dr	Irvine	CA	92618	**888-783-7723**		475
Advanced Support Products Inc						
20820 FM 2854 Rd	Montgomery	TX	77375	**800-941-5737**	936-597-4731	490
Advanced Technology Co						
2858 E Walnut St	Pasadena	CA	91107	**800-447-2442**	626-449-2696	22
Advanced Vacuum Company Inc						
1215 Business Pkwy N	Westminster	MD	21157	**800-272-2525**	410-876-8200	405
Advantage Credit Inc						
32065 Castle Ct Ste 300	Evergreen	CO	80439	**800-670-7993**		218
Advantage Electronic Product Development						
34 Garden Ctr	Broomfield	CO	80020	**866-841-5581**	303-410-0292	692
Advantage Funding Corp						
1000 Parkwood Cir SE	Atlanta	GA	30339	**800-241-2274**	770-955-2274	272
Advantage Home Health Care Inc						
4008 N Wheeling Ave	Muncie	IN	47304	**800-884-5088**	765-284-1211	362
Advantage Manufacturing Inc						
616 S Santa Fe St	Santa Ana	CA	92705	**800-636-8866**		
Advantage Metals Recycling LLC (AMR)						
510 Walnut St Ste 300	Kansas City	MO	64106	**866-527-4733**	816-861-2700	682
Advantage Mktg Inc						
14 W Main St	Ashland	OH	44805	**800-670-7479**	419-281-4762	96
Advantage Performance Group Inc						
700 Larkspur Landing Cir	Larkspur	CA	94939	**800-494-6646**	415-925-6832	194
Advantage Rent-A-Car						
1030 W Manchester Blvd	Inglewood	CA	94010	**800-777-5500**		126
Advantage RN LLC						
9021 Meridian Way	West Chester	OH	45069	**866-301-4045**		260
Advantage Truck Accessories Inc						
5400 S State Rd	Ann Arbor	MI	48108	**800-773-3110**		61
Advantec MFS Inc						
6723 Sierra Ct Ste A	Dublin	CA	94568	**800-334-7132**	925-479-0625	18
Advantech Corp						
380 Fairview Way	Milpitas	CA	95035	**888-576-9668**	408-519-3898	175
AdvanTech Inc						
2661 Riva Rd Ste 1050	Annapolis	MD	21401	**888-266-2841**	410-266-8000	
Advantech Manufacturing Inc						
2450 S Commerce Dr	New Berlin	WI	53151	**800-511-2096**	262-786-1600	461
AdVantis Hospitality Alliance LLC						
615 N Highland Ste 2A	Murfreesboro	TN	37130	**866-218-4782**	615-904-6133	703
Advantix Solutions Group						
1202 Richardson Dr Ste 200	Richardson	TX	75080	**866-238-2684**		386
Advantor Systems Corp						
12612 Challenger Pkwy Ste 300	Orlando	FL	32826	**800-238-2686**		688
Advent Capital Management LLC						
888 Seventh Ave 31st Fl	New York	NY	10019	**888-523-8368**	212-482-1600	400
Advent Software Inc						
600 Townsend St						
5th Fl Ste 500	San Francisco	CA	94103	**800-727-0605**	415-543-7696	178-1
NASDAQ: ADVS						
Adventist Community Services						
12501 Old Columbia Pk	Silver Spring	MD	20904	**877-227-2702**	301-680-6438	48-5
Adventist Development & Relief Agency (ADRA)						
12501 Old Columbia Pk	Silver Spring	MD	20904	**800-424-2372**		48-5

	City	State	ZIP	Toll-Free	Phone	Class
Adventist Health						
2100 Douglas Blvd	Roseville	CA	95661	**877-336-3566**	916-781-2000	352
Adventist Health Lodi Memorial						
975 S Fairmont Ave	Lodi	CA	95240	**800-323-3360**	209-334-3411	373-3
Adventure Alaska Tours Inc						
PO Box 64	Hope	AK	99605	**800-365-7057**	907-782-3730	755
Adventure Aquarium						
1 Riverside Dr	Camden	NJ	08103	**844-474-3474**		40
Adventure Connection						
PO Box 475	Coloma	CA	95613	**800-556-6060**	530-626-7385	755
Adventure Cycling Assn						
150 E Pine St PO Box 8308	Missoula	MT	59807	**800-755-2453**	406-721-1776	48-22
Adventure Life South America						
712 W Spruce St Ste 1	Missoula	MT	59802	**800-344-6118**	406-541-2677	755
Adventure Medical Kits						
7700 Edgewater Dr Ste 526						
PO Box 43309	Oakland	CA	94624	**800-324-3517**		
Ad-venture Promotions LLC						
2625 Regency Rd	Lexington	KY	40503	**800-218-5488**	859-263-4299	129
Adventuredome						
2880 Las Vegas Blvd S	Las Vegas	NV	89109	**866-456-8894**	702-691-5861	32
Adventureland Inn						
305 34th Ave NW	Altoona	IA	50009	**800-910-5382**	515-265-7321	378
Adventureland Park						
3200 Adventureland Dr	Altoona	IA	50009	**800-532-1286**	515-266-2121	32
Adventures Out West						
1680 S 21st St	Colorado Springs	CO	80904	**800-755-0935**		755
Advertising Council Inc						
815 Second Ave 9th Fl	New York	NY	10016	**888-200-4005**	212-922-1500	49-18
Advertising Specialties Institute						
4800 St Rd	Trevose	PA	19053	**800-546-1350**	215-942-8600	633-9
Advice Media LLC						
PO Box 982064	Park City	UT	84098	**800-260-9497**		627
Advisor Today						
2901 Telestar Ct	Falls Church	VA	22042	**877-866-2432**	703-770-8267	455-5
Advisors Excel LLC						
1300 SW Arrowhead Rd Ste 200	Topeka	KS	66604	**866-363-9595**		195
Advocacy Center for Persons With Disabilities						
2728 Centerview Dr Ste 102	Tallahassee	FL	32301	**800-342-0823**	850-488-9071	427
Advocal 1000 Q St	Sacramento	CA	95811	**800-446-9121**	916-446-6161	632
Advocate Christ Medical Ctr						
4440 W 95th St	Oak Lawn	IL	60453	**800-323-8622**	708-684-8000	373-3
Advocate Good Shepherd Hospital (AGSH)						
450 W Hwy 22	Barrington	IL	60010	**800-775-4784**	847-381-9600	373-3
Advocate Hospice						
1441 Branding Ave Ste 200	Downers Grove	IL	60515	**800-564-2025**	630-963-6800	370
Advocate Sherman Hospital						
1425 N Randall Rd	Elgin	IL	60123	**800-397-9000**	847-742-9800	373-3
Advocate, The						
7290 Blue Bonnet Blvd	Baton Rouge	LA	70810	**800-960-6397**	225-383-1111	528-2
Advocate, The						
22 N First St	Newark	OH	43055	**877-424-0208**	740-345-4053	528-2
Adzzup						
2600 N Central Ave Ste 1700	Phoenix	AZ	85004	**888-723-9987**		5
AE Petsche Company Inc						
1501 Nolan Ryan Expy	Arlington	TX	76011	**844-237-7600**		246
AEA Advocate Magazine						
345 E Palm Ln	Phoenix	AZ	85004	**800-352-5411**	602-264-1774	455-8
Aearo Technologies LLC						
5457 W 79th St	Indianapolis	IN	46268	**877-327-4332**		572
AEB (American Egg Board)						
8755 W Higgins Rd Ste 300	Chicago	IL	60631	**888-549-2140**	847-296-7043	48-2
AEB (American Exchange Bank)						
510 W Main St PO Box 818	Henryetta	OK	74437	**888-652-3321**	918-652-3321	70
AEC (Applied Energy Company Inc)						
1205 Venture Ct Ste 100	Carrollton	TX	75006	**800-580-1171**	214-355-4200	636
AEC (Allen Engineering Corp)						
819 S Fifth St PO Box 819	Paragould	AR	72450	**800-643-0095**	870-236-7751	190
AED (Associated Equipment Distributors)						
650 E Algonquin Rd Ste 305	Schaumburg	IL	60173	**800-388-0650**	630-574-0650	49-18
Aedes De Venustas						
16A Orchard St	New York	NY	10002	**888-233-3715**	212-206-8674	77
Aegis Assisted Living						
4585 W Lake Sammamish Pkwy NE	Redmond	WA	98052	**888-252-3447**	866-688-5829	449
Aegis Sciences Corp						
515 Great Cir Rd	Nashville	TN	37228	**800-533-7052**		256
Aegis Security Insurance Co						
4507 N Front St Ste 200	Harrisburg	PA	17110	**800-233-2160**		390-4
AEI (American Enterprise Institute for Public Policy Re)						
1789 Massachusetts Ave NW	Washington	DC	20036	**800-862-5801**	202-862-5800	630
AEI Speakers Bureau						
300 Western Ave Ste 2	Allston	MA	02134	**800-447-7325**	617-782-3111	704
AELE (Americans for Effective Law Enforcement)						
841 W Touhy Ave	Park Ridge	IL	60068	**800-763-2802**	847-685-0700	48-8
AEM (Association of Equipment Manufacturers)						
6737 W Washington St Ste 2400	Milwaukee	WI	53214	**866-236-0442**	414-272-0943	49-13
Aeon Nexus Corp						
174 Glen St	Glens Falls	NY	12801	**866-252-1251**	518-338-1551	177
AEP Industries Inc						
125 Phillips Ave	South Hackensack	NJ	07606	**800-999-2374**	201-641-6600	596
NASDAQ: AEPI						
AEPhi (Alpha Epsilon Phi Sorority)						
11 Lake Ave Ext Ste 1A	Danbury	CT	06811	**888-668-4293**	203-748-0029	48-16
Aer Mfg Inc						
PO Box 979	Carrollton	TX	75011	**800-753-5237**	972-417-2582	60
AERA (American Educational Research Assn)						
1430 K St NW Ste 1200	Washington	DC	20005	**800-893-7950**	202-238-3200	49-5
AERA (Automotive Engine Rebuilders Assn)						
500 Coventry Ln Ste 180	Crystal Lake	IL	60014	**888-326-2372**	847-541-6550	49-21
Aerco International Inc						
159 Paris Ave	Northvale	NJ	07647	**800-526-0288**	201-768-2400	356
Aereon Corp						
16310 Bratton Ln Bldg 3 Ste 350	Austin	TX	78728	**800-475-9473**	512-836-9473	
Aerial Innovations Inc						
3703 W Azeele St	Tampa	FL	33609	**800-223-1701**	813-254-7339	196
Aermotor Pumps Inc						
293 Wright St	Delavan	WI	53115	**800-230-1816**		637

Name / Address	City	State	ZIP	Toll-Free	Phone	Class
Aero Air LLC						
2050 NE 25th Ave	Hillsboro	OR	97124	**800-448-2376**	503-640-3711	13
Aero Industries Inc						
4243 W Bradbury Ave	Indianapolis	IN	46241	**800-535-9545***	317-244-2433	728
*Sales						
Aero Industries Inc						
5745 Huntsman Rd						
Richmond International Airport	Richmond	VA	23250	**800-845-1308**	804-226-7200	63
Aero Rubber Company Inc						
8100 W 185th St	Tinley Park	IL	60487	**800-662-1009**		369
Aero Tec Labs Inc						
45 Spear Rd Industrial Pk	Ramsey	NJ	07446	**800-526-5330**	201-825-1400	672
Aero Tech Designs Cycling Apparel						
1132 Fourth Ave	Coraopolis	PA	15108	**800-783-8326**	412-262-3255	707
Aerobics & Fitness Association of America (AFAA)						
1750 E Northrop Blvd Ste 200	Chandler	AZ	85286	**800-446-2322**		48-22
Aerofin Corp						
4621 Murray Pl PO Box 10819	Lynchburg	VA	24506	**800-237-6346**	434-845-7081	91
Aeroflot Russian International Airlines						
358 Fifth Ave Ste 1103	New York	NY	10001	**866-879-7647**		25
Aeroflow Inc						
3165 Sweeten Creek Rd	Asheville	NC	28803	**888-345-1780**		473
Aeroglide Corp						
100 Aeroglide Dr	Cary	NC	27511	**800-722-7483**	919-851-2000	385
Aerojet						
PO Box 13222	Sacramento	CA	95813	**800-637-7200**	916-355-4000	502
Aeromedixcom LLC						
Po Box 14730	Jackson	WY	83002	**888-362-7123**	307-732-2642	457
Aeromet Industries Inc						
739 S Arbogast St	Griffith	IN	46319	**800-899-7442**	219-924-7442	752
Aeronet Worldwide						
42 Corporate Pk	Irvine	CA	92606	**800-552-3869**	949-474-3000	12
Aerosoles Inc						
201 Meadow Rd	Edison	NJ	08817	**800-798-9478**	732-985-6900	301
Aerospace America Inc						
900 Harry Truman Pkwy	Bay City	MI	48706	**800-237-6414**		478
Aerospace America Magazine						
1801 Alexander Bell Dr Ste 500	Reston	VA	20191	**800-639-2422**	703-264-7500	455-21
Aerospace Products International (API)						
2871 Business Pk Dr	Memphis	TN	38118	**888-274-2497**	901-365-3470	22
Aero-Space Southwest Inc						
21450 N Third Ave	Phoenix	AZ	85027	**800-289-2779**	623-582-2779	350
Aerospec Inc						
505 E Alamo Dr	Chandler	AZ	85225	**888-854-2376**	480-892-7195	256
AeroVironment Inc						
181 W Huntington Dr Ste 202	Monrovia	CA	91016	**888-833-2148**	626-357-9983	20
NASDAQ: AVAV						
Aerus LLC						
300 E Valley Dr	Bristol	VA	24201	**800-243-9078**		37
Aervoe Industries Inc						
1100 Mark Cir	Gardnerville	NV	89410	**800-227-0196**	775-783-3100	546
AES (American Epilepsy Society)						
342 N Main St	West Hartford	CT	06117	**888-233-2334**	860-586-7505	48-17
AESC (Association of Energy Service Cos)						
14531 Fm 529 Ste 250	Houston	TX	77095	**800-692-0771**	713-781-0758	48-12
Aesco Electronics Inc						
2230 Picton Pkwy	Akron	OH	44312	**877-442-6987**	330-245-2630	246
AESCULAP Inc						
3773 Corporate Pkwy	Center Valley	PA	18034	**800-282-9000**		474
AESU Travel Inc						
3922 Hickory Ave	Baltimore	MD	21211	**800-638-7640**	410-366-5494	766
AETEA Information Technology Inc						
1445 Research Blvd Ste 210	Rockville	MD	20850	**888-772-3832**	301-721-4200	180
AETEK UV Systems						
1229 Lakeview Ct	Romeoville	IL	60446	**800-333-2304**	630-226-4200	436
Aethon Inc						
200 Business Ctr Dr	Pittsburgh	PA	15205	**888-201-9522**	412-322-2975	473
AETN (Arkansas Educational Television Network)						
350 S Donaghey Ave	Conway	AR	72034	**800-662-2386**	501-682-2386	628
Aetna Felt Corp						
2401 W Emaus Ave	Allentown	PA	18103	**800-526-4451**	610-791-0900	740-6
Aetna Inc						
151 Farmington Ave	Hartford	CT	06156	**800-872-3862**	860-273-0123	390-3
NYSE: AET						
Aetna Integrated Services						
646 Parsons Ave	Columbus	OH	43206	**866-238-6201**		392
Aetna Plastics Corp						
1702 St Clair Ave	Cleveland	OH	44114	**800-634-3074**	216-781-4421	599
Aexcel Corp						
7373 Production Dr	Mentor	OH	44060	**800-854-0782**	440-974-3800	546
AF & L Insurance Co						
580 Virginia Dr Ste 330	Ft. Washington	PA	19034	**800-659-9206**	215-918-0515	
AFA (American Fence Association)						
6404 Internationa Pkwy Ste 2250-A	Plano	TX	75093	**800-822-4342**		49-3
AFA (American Federation of Astrologers)						
6535 S Rural Rd	Tempe	AZ	85283	**888-301-7630**	480-838-1751	48-18
AFA (American Finance Assn)						
101 Station Landing350 Main St						
Ste 300	Medford	MA	02155	**800-835-6770**	781-388-8599	49-2
AFA (Air Force Assn)						
1501 Lee Hwy	Arlington	VA	22209	**800-727-3337**	703-247-5800	48-19
AFAA (Aerobics & Fitness Association of America)						
1750 E Northrop Blvd Ste 200	Chandler	AZ	85286	**800-446-2322**		48-22
AFAR (American Federation for Aging Research)						
55 W 39th St 16th Fl	New York	NY	10018	**888-582-2327**	212-703-9977	49-8
AFB (American Foundation for the Blind)						
1401 S Clark St Ste 730	Arlington	VA	22202	**800-232-5463**	212-502-7600	48-17
AFC (AMPAC Fine Chemicals)						
MS 1007 PO Box 1718	Rancho Cordova	CA	95741	**800-311-9668**	916-357-6880	145
AFC (Automotive Finance Corp)						
13085 Hamilton Crossing Blvd	Carmel	IN	46032	**888-335-6675**	865-384-8250	216
AFC Cable Systems Inc						
960 Flaherty Dr	New Bedford	MA	02745	**800-757-6996**	508-998-1131	808
AFC Industries Inc						
13-16 133rd Pl	College Point	NY	11356	**800-663-3412**	718-747-0237	194
AFCA (American Football Coaches Assn)						
100 Legends Ln	Waco	TX	76706	**877-557-5338**	254-754-9900	48-22
AFCEA (Armed Forces Communications & Electronics Assn)						
4400 Fair Lakes Ct	Fairfax	VA	22033	**800-336-4583**	703-631-6100	48-19
AFCI (Association of Film Commissioners International)						
9595 Wilshire Blvd						
Ste 900	Beverly Hills	CA	90212	**888-765-5777**	323-461-2324	48-4
AFCO (Alex C Fergusson LLC)						
5000 Letterkenny Rd	Chambersburg	PA	17201	**800-345-1329**		145
AFCO Credit Corp						
14 Wall St	New York	NY	10005	**800-288-6901**	212-401-4400	216
Afco Industries Inc						
3400 Roy St	Alexandria	LA	71302	**800-551-6576**		480
AFCU (Andrews Federal Credit Union)						
5711 Allentown Rd	Suitland	MD	20746	**800-487-5500**	301-702-5500	219
AFF (American Forest Foundation)						
2000 M St NW Ste 550	Washington	DC	20036	**800-325-2954**	202-765-3660	48-2
Affiliated Car Rental						
105 Hwy 36	Eatontown	NJ	07724	**800-367-5159**		126
Affiliated Chamber of Commerce of Greater Springfield						
1441 Main St	Springfield	MA	01103	**888-283-3757**	413-787-1555	139
Affiliated Community Medical Centers (ACMC)						
101 Willmar Ave SW	Willmar	MN	56201	**888-225-6580**	320-231-5000	373-3
Affiliated Control Equipment Inc						
640 Wheat Ln	Wood Dale	IL	60191	**800-942-8753**	630-595-4680	55
Affiliated Foods Inc						
1401 W Farmers Ave	Amarillo	TX	79118	**800-234-3661**	806-372-3851	297-8
Affiliated Medical Services Laboratory Inc						
2916 E Central Ave	Wichita	KS	67214	**800-876-0243**	316-265-4533	414
Affina Dumont						
150 E 34th St	New York	NY	10016	**866-233-4642**	212-481-7600	378
Affinia 50						
155 E 50th St	New York	NY	10022	**866-246-2203**	212-751-5710	378
Affinia Manhattan						
371 Seventh Ave	New York	NY	10001	**866-246-2203**	212-563-1800	378
Affinigent Inc						
4 Kent Rd Ste 200	York	PA	17402	**800-932-3380**	717-600-0033	225
Affinion Group Inc						
6 High Ridge Pk	Stamford	CT	06905	**800-252-2148**	203-956-1000	389
Affinitas Corp						
1015 N 98th St Ste 100	Omaha	NE	68114	**800-369-6495**	402-505-5000	194
Affinity Federal Credit Union						
73 Mountain View Blvd						
PO Box 621	Basking Ridge	NJ	07920	**800-325-0808**		219
Affinity Inc						
10850 W Park Pl Ste 470	Milwaukee	WI	53224	**877-399-2220**		
Affinity Wealth Management Inc						
1702 Lovering Ave	Wilmington	DE	19806	**800-825-8399**	302-652-6767	194
Affordabletourscom						
11150 Cash Rd	Stafford	TX	77477	**800-935-2620**		767
Affton Chamber of Commerce						
9815 Mackenzie Rd	Affton	MO	63123	**800-877-1234**	314-631-3100	139
Affymetrix Inc						
3420 Central Expy	Santa Clara	CA	95051	**888-362-2447**	866-356-0354	250
NASDAQ: AFFX						
AFI (American Film Institute)						
2021 N Western Ave	Los Angeles	CA	90027	**866-234-3378**	323-856-7600	48-4
AFI (Armed Forces Insurance Exchange)						
550 Eisenhower Rd	Leavenworth	KS	66048	**800-255-6792**		390-4
AFI Fest						
2021 N Western Ave	Los Angeles	CA	90027	**866-234-3378**	323-856-7600	282
AFIMAC Inc						
8160 Parkhill Dr	Milton	ON	L9T5V7	**800-554-4622**		194
AFLAC (American Family Life Assurance Company of Columbus)						
1932 Wynnton Rd	Columbus	GA	31999	**800-992-3522***	706-323-3431	390-2
*Cust Svc						
AFLAC Inc						
1932 Wynnton Rd	Columbus	GA	31999	**800-992-3522**	706-323-3431	359-4
NYSE: AFL						
AFLAC PAC (American Family Life Assurance Co PAC)						
1932 Wynnton Rd	Columbus	GA	31999	**800-992-3522***	706-323-3431	611
NYSE: AFL ■ *Cust Svc						
AFL-CIO Committee on Political Education						
815 16th St NW	Washington	DC	20006	**855-712-8441**		611
AFM (American Federation of Musicians of the US & Canad)						
1501 Broadway Ste 600	New York	NY	10036	**800-762-3444**	212-869-1330	413
Afni Inc						
404 Brock Dr	Bloomington	IL	61701	**866-377-8844**		160
AFP (Association of Fundraising Professionals)						
4300 Wilson Blvd Ste 300	Arlington	VA	22203	**800-666-3863**	703-684-0410	49-12
AFP International LLC						
1730 Berkeley St	Santa Monica	CA	90404	**888-895-0547**	310-559-9949	707
AFP Transformers Inc						
206 Talmedge Rd	Edison	NJ	08817	**800-843-1215**	732-248-0305	762
AF&PA (American Forest & Paper Assn)						
1111 19th St NW Ste 800	Washington	DC	20036	**800-878-8878**	202-463-2700	48-2
Africa Adventure Co, The						
2601 E Oakland Park Blvd						
Ste 600	Fort Lauderdale	FL	33308	**800-882-9453**	954-491-8877	755
African Safari Wildlife Park						
267 S Lightner Rd	Port Clinton	OH	43452	**800-521-2660**	419-732-3606	818
African Travel Inc						
330 N Brand Blvd Ste 225	Glendale	CA	91203	**800-421-8907**	818-507-7893	755
African Wildlife Foundation (AWF)						
1100 New Jersey Ave SE						
Ste 900	Washington	DC	20003	**888-494-5354**	202-939-3333	48-3
African-American Civil War Memorial & Museum						
1925 Vermont Ave NW	Washington	DC	20001	**800-753-9222**	202-667-2667	517
Africare Inc						
440 R St NW	Washington	DC	20001	**800-429-9493**	202-462-3614	48-5
Afro-American Newspapers Co						
2519 N Charles St	Baltimore	MD	21218	**800-237-6892**	410-554-8200	633-8
AFS (American Folklore Society)						
800 E Third St	Bloomington	IN	47405	**866-315-9403**	812-856-2379	48-14
AFS (American Foundry Society)						
1695 N Penny Ln	Schaumburg	IL	60173	**800-537-4237**	847-824-0181	49-13
AFSA (American Foreign Service Assn)						
2101 E St NW	Washington	DC	20037	**800-704-2372**	202-338-4045	49-7
AFSC (American Friends Service Committee)						
1501 Cherry St	Philadelphia	PA	19102	**800-621-4000**	215-241-7000	48-5

Name / Address	City	State	ZIP	Toll-Free	Phone	Class
AFSP (American Foundation for Suicide Prevention)						
120 Wall St 29th Fl	New York	NY	10005	**888-333-2377**	212-363-3500	48-17
AFT (American Farmland Trust)						
1200 18th St	Washington	DC	20036	**800-431-1499**	202-331-7300	48-2
AFT Healthcare						
555 New Jersey Ave NW	Washington	DC	20001	**800-238-1133**	202-879-4400	413
After Six						
118 W 20th St	New York	NY	10011	**800-444-8304**	646-638-9600	155-11
Aftermath Claim Science Inc						
4580 Weaver Pkwy Ste 200	Warrenville	IL	60555	**800-962-6831**	630-922-1900	392
AFTRA (American Federation of Television & Radio Artists)						
260 Madison Ave 7th Fl	New York	NY	10016	**800-638-6796**	212-532-0800	413
AFX Inc						
2345 Ernie Krueger Cir	Waukegan	IL	60087	**800-873-2326**	847-249-5970	438
AG Dealer Ltd						
44 Byward Market Sq	Ottawa	ON	K1N7A2	**800-665-1362**	613-596-8022	225
AG Partners Inc						
512 S Eigth St PO Box 467	Lake City	MN	55041	**800-772-2990**	651-345-3328	445
Ag Processing Inc						
12700 W Dodge Rd PO Box 2047	Omaha	NE	68103	**800-247-1345**	402-496-7809	296-29
Ag West Supply Inc						
9055 Rickreall Rd	Rickreall	OR	97371	**800-842-2224**	503-363-2332	274
AG. Ferrari Foods						
2000 N Loop Rd	Alameda	CA	94502	**877-878-2783**	510-351-5520	344
AGA (American Gastroenterological Assn)						
4930 Del Ray Ave	Bethesda	MD	20814	**800-227-7888**	301-654-2055	49-8
AGA (American Galvanizers Assn)						
6881 S Holly Cir Ste 108	Centennial	CO	80112	**800-468-7732**	720-554-0900	49-13
AGA (Association of Government Accountants)						
2208 Mt Vernon Ave	Alexandria	VA	22301	**800-242-7211**	703-684-6931	49-1
AGB (Association of Governing Boards of Universities &)						
1133 20th St NW Ste 300	Washington	DC	20036	**800-356-6317**	202-296-8400	49-5
AGC (Associated General Contractors of America)						
2300 Wilson Blvd Ste 300	Arlington	VA	22201	**800-242-1766**	703-548-3118	49-3
AGC Biologics						
22021 20th Ave SE	Bothell	WA	98021	**800-845-6973**	425-485-1900	85
Agcall Inc						
251 Midpark Blvd SE	Calgary	AB	T2X1S3	**877-273-4333**	403-256-1229	194
AGCO (AGCO Corp)						
4205 River Green Pkwy	Duluth	GA	30096	**877-525-4384**	770-813-9200	273
NYSE: AGCO						
AGCO Corp (AGCO)						
4205 River Green Pkwy	Duluth	GA	30096	**877-525-4384**	770-813-9200	273
NYSE: AGCO						
AGD (Academy of General Dentistry)						
211 E Chicago Ave Ste 900	Chicago	IL	60611	**888-243-3368**	312-440-4300	49-8
Agency for Healthcare Research & Quality						
540 Gaither Rd	Rockville	MD	20850	**800-358-9295**	301-427-1364	339-9
Agency for Toxic Substances & Disease Registry						
4770 Buford Hwy NE	Atlanta	GA	30341	**800-232-4636**		339-9
Agency Mabu						
1003 Gateway Ave	Bismarck	ND	58503	**800-568-9346**	701-250-0728	7
Agency Revolution 698 NW	Bend	OR	97701	**800-606-0477**		5
Agency Software Inc						
215 W Commerce Dr	Hayden Lake	ID	83835	**800-342-7327**	208-762-7188	389
agencyQ						
1825 K St NW Ste 500	Washington	DC	20006	**866-734-7932**	202-776-9090	
Aget Manufacturing Co						
1408 E Church St	Adrian	MI	49221	**800-832-2438**	517-263-5781	18
AGF Management Ltd						
66 Wellington St W 31st Fl	Toronto	ON	M5K1E9	**800-268-8583**	905-214-8203	400
Agfa Corp						
611 River Dr	Elmwood Park	NJ	07407	**888-274-8626**	201-440-2500	587
Agfinity 260 Factory Rd	Eaton	CO	80615	**800-433-4688**	970-454-4000	276
Aggreko						
15600 John F Kennedy Blvd						
Ste 600	Houston	TX	77032	**833-507-6491**		
AGI (Audio General Inc)						
1680 Republic Rd	Huntingdon Valley	PA	19006	**866-866-2600**	267-288-0300	511
AGI (Guttmacher Institute)						
125 Maiden Ln 7th Fl	New York	NY	10038	**800-355-0244**	212-248-1111	48-5
Agile Frameworks LLC						
1826 Buerkle Rd	Saint Paul	MN	55110	**800-779-1196**		
Agile Sourcing Partners Inc						
2385 Railroad St	Corona	CA	92880	**888-718-1988**		
AgileAssets Inc						
3001 Bee Caves Rd Ste 200	Austin	TX	78746	**800-877-8734**	512-327-4200	177
Agilith Capital Inc						
20 Queen St W Ste 3311						
PO Box 30	Toronto	ON	M5H3R3	**866-345-1231**	416-915-0284	524
AgilQuest Corp						
9407 Hull St Rd	Richmond	VA	23236	**888-745-7455**	804-745-0467	178-1
Agilysys NV LLC						
1000 Windward Concourse						
Ste 250	Alpharetta	GA	30005	**800-241-8768**	770-810-7800	177
Aging News Alert						
8204 Fenton St	Silver Spring	MD	20910	**800-666-6380**	301-588-6385	527-8
AGM Container Controls Inc						
3526 E Ft Lowell Rd	Tucson	AZ	85716	**800-995-5590**	520-881-2130	349
AGM Industries Inc						
16 Jonathan Dr	Brockton	MA	02301	**800-225-9990**	508-587-3900	806
AGMA (American Guild of Musical Artists)						
1430 Broadway 14th Fl	New York	NY	10018	**800-543-2462**	212-265-3687	48-4
AGN International-North America						
2851 S Parker Rd Ste 850	Aurora	CO	80014	**800-782-2272**	303-743-7880	49-1
Agnes Scott College						
141 E College Ave	Decatur	GA	30030	**800-868-8602**	404-471-6000	166
Agnico-Eagle Mines Ltd						
145 King St E Ste 500	Toronto	ON	M5C2Y7	**888-822-6714**	416-947-1212	500
NYSE: AEM						
AGO (American Guild of Organists)						
475 Riverside Dr Ste 1260	New York	NY	10115	**855-631-0759**	212-870-2310	48-4
AGPA (American Group Psychotherapy Assn)						
25 E 21st St 6th Fl	New York	NY	10010	**877-668-2472**	212-477-2677	49-15
AGR GROUP NEVADA LLC						
6275 S Pearl St Ste 100-300	Las Vegas	NV	89120	**877-860-5780**		392
AGRA Industries Inc						
1211 W Water St	Merrill	WI	54452	**800-842-8033**	715-536-9584	261

Name / Address	City	State	ZIP	Toll-Free	Phone	Class
Agralite Electric Co-op						
320 Hwy 12 SE	Benson	MN	56215	**800-950-8375**	320-843-4150	245
Agrex Inc						
10975 Grandview Dr St						
Ste 200	Overland Park	KS	66210	**800-523-8181**	913-851-6300	10-3
Agri Beef Co						
1555 Shoreline Dr Ste 320	Boise	ID	83702	**800-657-6305**	208-338-2500	10-1
agriCAREERS Inc						
613 Main St	Massena	IA	50853	**800-633-8387**	712-779-3300	260
Agricultural Retailers Assn (ARA)						
1156 15th St NW Ste 500	Washington	DC	20005	**800-535-6272**	202-457-0825	48-2
Agricultural Workers Mutual Auto Insurance Co						
PO Box 88	Fort Worth	TX	76101	**800-772-7424**	817-831-9900	390-4
Agri-Fab Inc						
809 S Hamilton St	Sullivan	IL	61951	**800-448-9282**		359-3
AgriGold Hybrids						
5381 Akin Rd	Saint Francisville	IL	62460	**800-262-7333**		690
Agri-King Inc						
18246 Waller Rd	Fulton	IL	61252	**800-435-9560**		445
Agri-Mark Inc						
PO Box 5800	Lawrence	MA	01842	**800-225-0532**	978-689-4442	296-27
Agri-Service						
300 Agri-Service Way	Kimberly	ID	83341	**800-388-3599**	208-734-7772	274
Agron Inc						
2440 S Sepulveda Blvd						
Ste 201	Los Angeles	CA	90064	**800-966-7697**		34
AGS (American Gem Society)						
8881 W Sahara Ave	Las Vegas	NV	89117	**866-805-6500**	702-255-6500	49-4
AGSH (Advocate Good Shepherd Hospital)						
450 W Hwy 22	Barrington	IL	60010	**800-775-4784**	847-381-9600	373-3
AGSI						
800 Battery Ave SE Ste 100	Atlanta	GA	30339	**800-768-2474**	404-816-7577	180
AGTA (American Gem Trade Assn)						
3030 LBJ Fwy Ste 840	Dallas	TX	75234	**800-972-1162**	214-742-4367	49-4
AGU (American Geophysical Union)						
2000 Florida Ave NW	Washington	DC	20009	**800-966-2481**	202-462-6900	49-19
AGVA (American Guild of Variety Artists)						
363 Seventh Ave 17th Fl	New York	NY	10001	**800-331-0890**	212-675-1003	48-4
AgVantage FS Inc						
1600 Eigth St SW	Waverly	IA	50677	**800-346-0058**	319-483-4900	276
A&h Lithoprint Inc						
2640 S 27th Ave	Broadview	IL	60155	**855-305-7628**	708-345-1196	623
AHA (American Heart Assn)						
7272 Greenville Ave	Dallas	TX	75231	**800-242-8721**	214-373-6300	48-17
AHA (American Hospital Assn)						
155 N Wacker Dr	Chicago	IL	60606	**800-424-4301**	312-422-3000	49-8
AHA (American Humane Assn)						
63 Inverness Dr E	Englewood	CO	80112	**800-227-4645**		48-6
AHA (American Homeowners Association)						
3001 Summer St	Stamford	CT	06905	**800-470-2242**	203-323-7715	
AHAM PAC (Association of Home Appliance Manufacturers PAC)						
1111 19th St NW Ste 402	Washington	DC	20036	**800-424-2970**	202-872-5955	611
AHAPAC (American Hospital Assn PAC)						
325 Seventh St NW	Washington	DC	20004	**800-424-4301**	202-638-1100	611
AHAVA North America						
330 Seventh Ave	New York	NY	10001	**800-366-7254**		214
AHC (American Horse Council)						
1616 H St NW 7th Fl	Washington	DC	20006	**800-443-0177**	202-296-4031	48-3
AHCA (American Health Care Assn)						
1201 L St NW	Washington	DC	20005	**800-321-0343**	202-842-4444	49-8
AHDI (Association for Healthcare Documentation Integrity)						
4230 Kiernan Ave Ste 130	Modesto	CA	95356	**800-982-2182**	209-527-9620	49-8
Ahead Hum Resources						
2209 Heather Ln	Louisville	KY	40218	**888-749-1000**	502-485-1000	177
Ahead LLC						
270 Samuel Barnet Blvd	New Bedford	MA	02745	**800-282-2246**	508-985-9898	155-8
AheadTek Inc						
6410 Via Del Oro	San Jose	CA	95119	**800-971-9191**	408-226-9991	643
Ahearn & Soper Inc						
100 Woodbine Downs Blvd	Rexdale	ON	M9W5S6	**800-263-4258**	416-675-3999	174
AHEPA (American Hellenic Educational Progressive Assn)						
1909 Q St NW Ste 500	Washington	DC	20009	**855-473-3512**	202-232-6300	48-14
Ahern Rentals Inc						
4241 Arville St	Las Vegas	NV	89103	**800-589-6797**	702-362-0623	264-3
AHF (American Homeowners Foundation)						
6776 Little Falls Rd	Arlington	VA	22213	**800-489-7776**		
AHI (AHI Facility Services Inc)						
1253 Round Table Dr	Dallas	TX	75247	**800-472-5749**	214-741-3714	
AHI Facility Services Inc (AHI)						
1253 Round Table Dr	Dallas	TX	75247	**800-472-5749**	214-741-3714	
AHI International Corp						
8550 W Bryn Mawr Ave Ste 600	Chicago	IL	60631	**800-323-7373**		755
AHI Supply Inc						
PO Box 884	Friendswood	TX	77549	**800-873-5794**	281-331-0088	191-1
AHIA (Association of Healthcare Internal Auditors)						
10200 W 44th Ave Ste 304	Wheat Ridge	CO	80033	**888-275-2442**	303-327-7546	49-1
AHIMA (American Health Information Management Assn)						
233 N Michigan Ave 21st Fl	Chicago	IL	60601	**800-335-5535**	312-233-1100	49-8
AHLA (Alberta Hotel & Lodging Assn)						
2707 Ellwood Dr	Edmonton	AB	T6X0P7	**888-436-6112**	780-436-6112	48-23
Ahmad, Zavitsanos, Anaipakos, Alavi & Mensing PC						
1 Houston Ctr 1221 McKinney St						
Ste 3460	Houston	TX	77010	**800-856-8153**	713-655-1101	427
AHNA (American Holistic Nurses Assn)						
2900 SW Plass Ct	Topeka	KS	66611	**800-278-2462**	785-234-1712	48-17
Ahola Corp, The						
6820 West Snowville Rd	Brecksville	OH	44141	**800-727-2849**		2
AHPA (American Herbal Products Assn)						
8630 Fenton St Ste 918	Silver Spring	MD	20910	**800-358-2104**	301-588-1171	49-8
AHRA (American Healthcare Radiology Administrators)						
490-B Boston Post Rd Ste 200	Sudbury	MA	01776	**800-334-2472**	978-443-7591	49-8
Ahrberg Milling Co						
200 S Depot PO Box 968	Cushing	OK	74023	**800-324-0267**	918-225-0267	445
AHS (American Hiking Society)						
8605 Second Ave	Silver Spring	MD	20910	**800-972-8608**	301-565-6704	48-23
AHS (American Horticultural Society)						
7931 E Blvd Dr	Alexandria	VA	22308	**800-777-7931**	703-768-5700	48-18

	Toll-Free	Phone	Class
AI Technology Inc (AIT)			
70 Washington Rd ....Princeton Junction NJ 08550	800-735-5040	609-799-9388	796
AIA (American Institute of Architects)			
1735 New York Ave NW ....Washington DC 20006	800-242-3837*	202-626-7300	48-4
*Orders			
AIA (Archaeological Institute of America)			
44 Beacon St ....Boston MA 02108	877-524-6300	617-353-9361	48-11
AIAA (American Institute of Aeronautics & Astronautics I)			
1801 Alexander Bell Dr Ste 500 ......Reston VA 20191	800-639-2422	703-264-7500	49-19
AIADA (American International Automobile Dealers Assn)			
500 Montgomery St Ste 800.........Alexandria VA 22314	800-462-4232		49-18
AIAG (Automotive Industry Action Group)			
26200 Lahser Rd Ste 200 ....Southfield MI 48033	877-275-2424	248-358-3570	49-21
AIB International Inc			
1213 Bakers Way PO Box 3999 ....Manhattan KS 66505	800-633-5137	785-537-4750	461
AICA (American-International Charolais Assn)			
11700 NW Plaza Cir ....Kansas City MO 64153	800-270-7711	816-464-5977	48-2
AIChE (American Institute of Chemical Engineers)			
120 Wall St 2nd Fl ....New York NY 10005	800-242-4363*	203-702-7660	49-19
*Cust Svc			
AICPA (American Institute of Certified Public Accountants)			
1211 Ave of the Americas ....New York NY 10036	888-777-7077	212-596-6200	49-1
AICPCU/IIA (American Institute for CPCU & Insurance Institute)			
720 Providence Rd Ste 100 ....Malvern PA 19355	800-644-2101	610-644-2100	49-9
AICR Newsletter			
1759 R St NW ....Washington DC 20009	800-843-8114	202-328-7744	527-8
Aid Maintenance Co			
300 Roosevelt Ave ....Pawtucket RI 02860	800-886-6627	401-722-6627	104
Aidells Sausage Co			
1625 Alvarado St ....San Leandro CA 94577	855-600-7697		296-26
AIDS Library			
1233 Locust St 2nd Fl ....Philadelphia PA 19107	877-613-4533	215-985-4851	433-4
AIDSinfo			
PO Box 6303 ....Rockville MD 20849	800-448-0440	301-315-2816	339-9
AIFP (American International Forest Products LLC)			
5560 SW 107th Ave ....Beaverton OR 97005	800-366-1611	503-641-1611	191-3
AIG SunAmerica Inc			
21650 Oxnard St ....Woodland Hills CA 91367	800-445-7862		359-4
AIGA (American Institute of Graphic Arts)			
164 Fifth Ave ....New York NY 10010	800-548-1634	212-807-1990	48-4
Aigner Index Inc			
23 Mac Arthur Ave ....New Windsor NY 12553	800-242-3919	845-562-4510	604
Aiken County			
420 Hampton Ave NE ....Aiken SC 29801	866-876-7074	803-642-2012	337
Aiken Electric Co-op Inc			
2790 Wagener Rd ....Aiken SC 29802	877-264-5368*	803-649-6245	245
*Tech Supp			
Aiken Regional Medical Centers			
302 University Pkwy ....Aiken SC 29801	800-245-3679	803-641-5000	373-3
Aiken State Natural Area			
1145 State Pk Rd ....Windsor SC 29856	866-345-7275	803-649-2857	561
Aiken Technical College			
2276 J Davis Hwy ....Graniteville SC 29829	800-246-6198	803-593-9231	162
AIL (American Income Life Insurance Co)			
1200 Wooded Acres ....Waco TX 76710	800-433-3405	254-761-6400	390-2
AILA (American Immigration Lawyers Assn)			
918 F St NW ....Washington DC 20004	800-982-2839	202-216-2400	49-10
AIM (Accuracy in Media Inc)			
4350 EW Hwy Ste 555 ....Bethesda MD 20814	800-787-4567	202-364-4401	49-14
Aim			
2 Berkeley St Ste 403 ....Toronto ON M5A4J5	866-645-2224	416-594-9393	179
AIM Supply Co			
7337 Bryan Dairy Rd ....Largo FL 33777	800-999-0125	727-544-6652	384
Aimco			
10000 SE Pine St ....Portland OR 97216	800-852-1368		384
AIME (American Institute of Mining Metallurgical & Petro)			
12999 E Adam Aircraft Cir ....Englewood CO 80112	888-702-0049	303-325-5185	48-12
Aimpoint Inc			
7309 Gateway Ct ....Manassas VA 20109	877-246-7646	703-263-9795	
Aims Community College			
5401 W 20th St ....Greeley CO 80634	800-301-5388	970-330-8008	162
AIMS Inc			
235 Desiard St ....Monroe LA 71201	800-729-2467	318-323-2467	178-10
Ainsworth Pet Nutrition			
984 Water St ....Meadville PA 16335	800-323-7738	814-724-7710	574
AIPB (American Institute of Professional Bookkeepers)			
6001 Montrose Rd Ste 500.........Rockville MD 20852	800-622-0121		49-1
AIPG (American Institute of Professional Geologists)			
1400 W 122nd Ave Ste 250 ......Westminster CO 80234	800-337-3140	303-412-6205	49-19
Air & Waste Management Assn (A&WMA)			
436 Seventh Ave Ste 2100 ....Pittsburgh PA 15219	800-270-3444	412-232-3444	48-12
Air Canada Centre			
40 Bay St ....Toronto ON M5J2X2	800-661-8747	416-815-5500	716
Air Center Inc			
1201 E Whitcomb Ave ....Madison Heights MI 48071	800-247-2959		357
Air Charter Team			
4151 N Mulberry Dr Ste 250.........Kansas City MO 64116	800-205-6610	816-283-3280	13
Air Chek Inc			
1936 Butler Bridge Rd ....Mills River NC 28759	800-247-2435		196
Air Cleaning Technologies Inc			
1300 W Detroit ....Broken Arrow OK 74012	800-351-1858	918-251-8000	35
Air Comfort Corp			
2550 Braga Dr ....Broadview IL 60155	800-466-3779	708-345-1900	189-10
Air Conditioning Contractors of America (ACCA)			
2800 S Shirlington Rd Ste 300..........Arlington VA 22206	888-290-2220	703-575-4477	49-3
Air Conditioning Heating & Refrigeration News			
2401 W Big Beaver Rd Ste 700............Troy MI 48084	800-837-8337	248-362-3700	455-21
Air Contact Transport Inc			
PO Box 570 ....Budd Lake NJ 07828	800-765-2769		187
Air Creebec Inc			
101 Fecteau St ....Val-d'or QC J9P0G4	800-567-6567	819-825-8375	12
Air Cycle Corp			
2200 Ogden Ave Ste 100 ....Lisle IL 60532	800-909-9709		295
Air Force Assn (AFA)			
1501 Lee Hwy ....Arlington VA 22209	800-727-3337	703-247-5800	48-19
Air Force Federal Credit Union			
1560 Cable Ranch Rd Ste 200 ....San Antonio TX 78245	800-227-5328	210-673-5610	219
Air Force Magazine			
1501 Lee Hwy ....Arlington VA 22209	800-727-3337	703-247-5800	455-12
Air India			
570 Lexington Ave 15th Fl ....New York NY 10022	800-223-7776		25
Air Ivanhoe Ltd			
George and Jeanne Theriault			
PO Box 99...................Foleyet ON P0M1T0	800-955-2951	705-899-2155	239
Air Land & Sea Travel Wedding Crdn			
126 N Orlando Ave ....Cocoa Beach FL 32931	800-799-1094	321-783-4900	770
Air Lift Co			
2727 Snow Rd ....Lansing MI 48917	800-248-0892	517-322-2144	54
Air Line Pilots Assn			
535 Herndon Pkwy ....Herndon VA 20170	877-331-1223	703-689-2270	413
AIR LIQUIDE USA LLC			
9811 Katy Fwy Ste 100.............Houston TX 77024	877-855-9533	713-624-8000	143
Air Logistics Inc			
4605 Industrial Dr ....New Iberia LA 70560	800-365-6771	337-365-6771	358
Air Monitor Corp			
1050 Hopper Ave ....Santa Rosa CA 95403	800-247-3569	707-544-2706	608
Air North Charter & Training Ltd			
150 Condor Rd ....Whitehorse YT Y1A0M7	800-661-0407	867-668-2228	12
Air Palm Springs			
145 N Gene Autry Trl			
Ste 14 ....Palm Springs CA 92262	800-760-7774		13
Air Products & Chemicals Inc			
7201 Hamilton Blvd ....Allentown PA 18195	800-345-3148*	610-481-4911	143
NYSE: APD ■ *Prod Info			
Air Quality Engineering Inc			
7140 Northland Dr N ....Brooklyn Park MN 55428	888-883-3273	763-531-9823	18
Air Sunshine			
PO Box 37698 ....San Juan PR 00937	800-435-8900	954-434-8900	25
Air Systems International Inc			
829 Juniper Crescent ....Chesapeake VA 23320	800-866-8100	757-424-3967	637
Air Technical Industries			
7501 Clover Ave ....Mentor OH 44060	800-321-9680	440-951-5191	468
Air Techniques Inc			
1295 Walt Whitman Rd ....Melville NY 11747	888-247-8481	516-433-7676	228
Air Trek Inc			
28000 A-5 Airport Rd ....Punta Gorda FL 33982	800-247-8735	941-639-7855	
Air Van			
2340 130th Ave NE Ste 201 ....Bellevue WA 98005	800-989-8905	425-629-4101	516
Air Vent Inc			
4117 Pinnacle Pnt Dr Ste 400............Dallas TX 75211	800-247-8368		693
Air Waves Inc			
7750 Green Meadows Dr N ....Lewis Center OH 43035	844-543-8339	740-548-1200	623
Air Zoo, The			
6151 Portage Rd ....Portage MI 49002	866-524-7966	269-382-6555	517
Airbiquity Inc			
1011 Western Ave Ste 600 ....Seattle WA 98104	888-334-7741	206-219-2700	643
Airbrush Action Inc			
PO Box 438 ....Allenwood NJ 08720	800-876-2472	732-223-7878	5
Airbus Helicopters Canada			
1100 Gilmore Rd PO Box 250..........Fort Erie ON L2A5M9	800-267-4999	905-871-7772	13
Airbus Helicopters Inc			
2701 Forum Dr ....Grand Prairie TX 75052	800-873-0001	972-641-0000	20
AirClean Systems Inc			
3248 Lake Woodard Dr ....Raleigh NC 27604	800-849-0472	919-255-3220	474
Aircraft Owners & Pilots Assn (AOPA)			
421 Aviation Way ....Frederick MD 21701	800-872-2672	301-695-2000	49-21
Aircraft Specialists Inc			
6005 Propeller Ln ....Sellersburg IN 47172	800-776-5387		
Aircraft Technical Publishers			
101 S Hill Dr ....Brisbane CA 94005	800-227-4610	415-330-9500	633-11
Airefco Inc			
18755 SW Teton Ave PO Box 1349.......Tualatin OR 97062	800-869-1349	503-692-3210	15
Aire-Master of America Inc			
1821 N State Hwy CC ....Nixa MO 65714	800-525-0957	417-725-2691	310
Airespring Inc			
6060 Sepulveda Blvd Ste 220.........Van Nuys CA 91411	888-389-2899	818-786-8990	386
Airfloat LLC			
2230 Brush College Rd ....Decatur IL 62526	800-888-0018	217-423-6001	207
Airflow Systems Inc			
11221 Pagemill Rd ....Dallas TX 75243	800-818-6185	214-503-8008	18
airG			
1133 Melville St Ste 710 ....Vancouver BC V6E4E5	866-874-8136	604-408-2228	386
Airgas Inc			
259 N Radnor-Chester Rd Ste 100 ....Radnor PA 19087	800-255-2165	610-687-5253	146
NYSE: ARG			
Airgas Specialty Products			
2530 Sever Rd Ste 300...........Lawrenceville GA 30043	800-295-2225		280
Airguard Industries Inc			
100 River Ridge Cir ....Jeffersonville IN 47130	866-247-4827		18
AirIQ Inc			
1845 Sandstone Manor Unit 10 ....Pickering ON L1W3X9	888-606-6444	905-831-6444	731
Airlie Conference Ctr			
6809 Airlie Rd ....Warrenton VA 20187	800-288-9573	540-347-1300	376
Airmaster Fan Co			
9229 S Meridian Rd ....Clarklake MI 49234	800-410-3267	517-764-2300	18
Airmate Co Inc			
16280 County Rd D ....Bryan OH 43506	800-544-3614	419-636-3184	9
AirNet Communications Corp			
295 North Dr Ste G.............Melbourne FL 32934	800-984-1990	321-984-1990	
Airosol Company Inc			
1206 Illinois St ....Neodesha KS 66757	800-633-9576	620-325-2666	145
Airparts Company Inc			
2310 NW 55th Ct ....Fort Lauderdale FL 33309	800-392-4999	954-739-3575	765
AIR-serv Group LLC			
1370 Mendota Heights Rd			
.................Mendota Heights MN 55120	800-247-8363		55
AirTek Indoor Air Solutions Inc			
1241 Johnson Ave			
Ste 209 ....San Luis Obispo CA 93401	877-858-6213		192
Airtel Plaza Hotel			
7277 Valjean Ave ....Van Nuys CA 91406	877-939-9268	818-997-7676	378
Airtex Consumer Products a Div of Federal Foam Technologies			
150 Industrial Pk Blvd ....Cokato MN 55321	800-851-8887		740-6
Airvoice Wireless LLC			
2425 Franklin Rd ....Bloomfield Hills MI 48302	888-944-2355		731

	Toll-Free	Phone	Class
Air-Way Manufacturing Co			
586 N Main St ....Olivet MI 49076	800-253-1036*	269-749-2161	785
*Cust Svc			
Airway Surgical Appliances Ltd			
189 Colonnade Rd ....Nepean ON K2E7J4	800-267-3476	613-723-4790	42
Airways Freight Corp			
3849 W Wedington Dr ....Fayetteville AR 72704	800-643-3525	479-442-6301	311
AIS RealTime			
4440 Bowen Blvd SE ....Grand Rapids MI 49508	877-314-1100		195
AISES (American Indian Science & Engineering Society)			
2305 Renard SE Ste 200........Albuquerque NM 87106	800-759-5219	505-765-1052	49-19
AIST (Association for Iron & Steel Technology)			
186 Thorn Hill Rd ....Warrendale PA 15086	800-759-4867	724-814-3000	49-13
AIT (AI Technology Inc)			
70 Washington Rd ....Princeton Junction NJ 08550	800-735-5040	609-799-9388	796
AITDomainscom			
421 Maiden Ln ....Fayetteville NC 28301	877-549-2881		395
AIUM (American Institute of Ultrasound in Medicine)			
14750 Sweitzer Ln Ste 100.........Laurel MD 20707	800-638-5352	301-498-4100	49-8
AIUSA (Amnesty International USA)			
5 Penn Plz 16th Fl ....New York NY 10001	866-273-4466	800-266-3789	48-5
AIV LP			
7140 W Sam Houston Pkwy N			
Ste 100 ....Houston TX 77040	800-447-4230	713-462-4181	384
Aixtek			
890 Cowan Rd Ste C...........Burlingame CA 94010	800-342-4525	415-282-1188	
AJ Desmond & Sons Funeral Directors			
2600 Crooks Rd ....Troy MI 48084	800-210-7135	248-362-2500	508
AJA (American Jail Assn)			
1135 Professional Ct ....Hagerstown MD 21740	800-211-2754	301-790-3930	49-7
Ajacs Die Sales Corp			
4625 Clay Ave SW ....Grand Rapids MI 49548	800-968-6868	616-452-1469	357
AJAX Electric Co			
60 Tomlinson Rd ....Huntingdon Valley PA 19006	800-516-9916	215-947-8500	318
Ajax Tocco Magnethermic Corp			
1745 Overland Ave NE ....Warren OH 44483	800-547-1527	330-372-8511	318
AJLI (Association of Junior Leagues International Inc)			
80 Maiden Ln Ste 305 ....New York NY 10038	800-955-3248	212-951-8300	48-15
AJWS (American Jewish World Service)			
45 West 36th St ....New York NY 10018	800-889-7146	212-792-2900	48-5
AK Draft Seal Ltd			
7470 Buller Ave ....Burnaby BC V5J4S5	888-520-9009	604-451-1080	234
AK Steel Corp			
9227 Centre Pt Dr ....West Chester OH 45069	800-331-5050	513-425-5000	719
NYSE: AKS			
AK Tube LLC			
30400 E Broadway ....Walbridge OH 43465	800-955-8031	419-661-4150	488
AKA Direct			
2415 N Ross Ave ....Portland OR 97227	800-647-8587		
AKA Direct Mail Services			
44 Joseph Mills Dr ....Fredericksburg VA 22408	800-232-1515		623
Akal Global Inc			
7 Infinity Loop ....Espanola NM 87532	888-325-2527	505-692-6600	688
Akamai Technologies Inc			
150 Broadway ....Cambridge MA 02142	877-425-2624	617-444-3000	178-7
NASDAQ: AKAM			
Akdo Intertrade Inc			
1435 State St ....Bridgeport CT 06605	800-811-2536	203-336-5199	720
Akers Packaging Service Inc			
2820 Lefferson Rd ....Middletown OH 45044	800-327-7308	513-422-6312	100
AKF (American Kidney Fund)			
6110 Executive Blvd Ste 1010 ....Rockville MD 20852	800-638-8299		48-17
Akkerman Inc			
58256 – 266th St ....Brownsdale MN 55918	800-533-0386		
Akorn Inc			
1925 W Field Ct ....Lake Forest IL 60045	800-932-5676	847-279-6100	231
NASDAQ: AKRX			
AKRF Inc			
440 Park Ave S ....New York NY 10016	800-899-2573	212-696-0670	261
Akrochem Corp			
255 Fountain St ....Akron OH 44304	800-321-2260	330-535-2100	601-3
Akro-Mils Inc			
1293 S Main St ....Akron OH 44301	800-253-2467		199
Akron Auto Auction Inc			
2471 Ley Dr ....Akron OH 44319	800-773-0033	330-773-8245	51
Akron General Medical Ctr			
400 Wabash Ave ....Akron OH 44307	800-221-4601	330-344-6000	373-3
Akron Paint & Varnish Inc			
1390 Firestone Pkwy ....Akron OH 44301	800-772-3452	330-773-8911	546
Akron Porcelain & Plastics Co			
2739 Cory Ave PO Box 15157 ....Akron OH 44314	800-737-9664	330-745-2159	600
Akron Steel Treating Co			
336 Morgan Ave ....Akron OH 44311	800-364-2782	330-773-8211	482
Akron/Summit County Convention & Visitors Bureau			
77 E Mill St ....Akron OH 44308	800-245-4254	330-374-8900	206
Akron-Canton Airport			
5400 Lauby Rd NW ....North Canton OH 44720	888-434-2359	330-499-4221	27
Aks Infotech			
2088 US 130 N Ste 203 .....Monmouth Junction NJ 08852	800-771-7000	609-301-4607	
AKSM (American Kidney Stone Management Ltd)			
797 Thomas Ln ....Columbus OH 43214	800-637-5188	614-447-0281	352
AKT Enterprises			
6424 Forest City Rd ....Orlando FL 32810	877-306-3651		5
Aktina Medical Physics Corp			
360 N Rt 9W ....Congers NY 10920	888-433-3380	845-268-0101	473
AKVMA (Alaska State Veterinary Medical Assn)			
1731 Bragaw St ....Anchorage AK 99508	800-272-1813	907-205-4272	790
Akzo Nobel Chemicals Inc			
10 Finderne Ave ....Bridgewater NJ 08807	888-331-6212		145
Al Betz & Associates Inc			
PO Box 665 Ste 30 ....Westminster MD 21158	877-402-3376		443
Al Copeland Investments Inc			
1001 Harimaw Ct S ....Metairie LA 70001	800-401-0401	504-830-1000	666
AL Gilbert Co			
304 N Yosemite Ave ....Oakdale CA 95361	800-400-6377	209-847-1721	445
Al Neyer Inc			
302 W Third St Ste 800 ....Cincinnati OH 45202	877-271-6400	513-271-6400	649

	Toll-Free	Phone	Class
ALA (Alliance for Lupus Research)			
28 W 44th St Ste 501 ....New York NY 10036	800-867-1743	212-218-2840	48-17
ALA (American Library Assn)			
50 E Huron St ....Chicago IL 60611	800-545-2433	312-944-6780	49-11
ALA (American Logistics Assn)			
1101 Vermont Ave NW Ste 1002......Washington DC 20005	800-791-7146	202-466-2520	48-19
ALA (American Lung Assn)			
14 Wall St ....New York NY 10005	800-586-4872	212-315-8700	48-17
ALA (American Lighting Assn)			
2050 Stemmons Fwy Ste 10046.........Dallas TX 75207	800-605-4448	214-698-9898	49-4
Ala Moana Hotel			
410 Atkinson Dr ....Honolulu HI 96814	800-367-6025	808-955-4811	378
Alabama			
Administrative Office of Alabama Courts			
300 Dexter Ave ....Montgomery AL 36104	866-954-9411	334-954-5000	338-1
Banking Dept			
401 Adams Ave Ste 680 ....Montgomery AL 36104	866-465-2279	334-242-3452	338-1
Crime Victims Compensation Commission			
5845 Carmichael Rd ....Montgomery AL 36117	800-541-9388	334-290-4420	338-1
Highway Patrol Div			
301 S Ripley St ....Montgomery AL 36104	800-272-7930	334-517-2950	
Housing Finance Authority			
7460 Halcyon Pointe Dr			
Ste 200....................Montgomery AL 36117	800-325-2432	334-244-9200	338-1
Mental Health & Mental Retardation Dept			
100 N Union St PO Box 301410....Montgomery AL 36130	800-367-0955	334-242-3454	338-1
National Guard			
1720 Congressman William L Dickinson Dr			
PO Box 3711 ....Montgomery AL 36109	800-464-8273	334-271-7200	338-1
Prepaid Affordable College Tuition (PACT)			
100 N Union St Ste 660 ....Montgomery AL 36104	800-252-7228		721
Public Health Dept			
201 Monroe St ....Montgomery AL 36104	800-252-1818	334-206-5300	338-1
Public Service Commission			
100 N Union St RSA Union			
PO Box 304260 ....Montgomery AL 36130	800-392-8050	334-242-5218	338-1
Rehabilitation Services Dept			
602 S Lawrence St ....Montgomery AL 36104	800-441-7607	334-293-7500	338-1
Securities Commission			
401 Adams Ave Ste 280 ....Montgomery AL 36104	800-222-1253	334-242-2984	338-1
Senior Services Dept			
201 Monroe Ste 350............Montgomery AL 36104	877-425-2243	334-242-5743	338-1
State Parks Div			
64 N Union St Rm 538 ....Montgomery AL 36130	800-252-7275		338-1
Tourism Department			
401 Adams Ave PO Box 4927.....Montgomery AL 36104	800-252-2262	334-242-4169	338-1
Alabama Agricultural & Mechanical University			
4900 Meridian St N PO Box 908.........Normal AL 35762	800-553-0816	256-372-5000	166
Alabama Art Supply Inc			
1006 23rd St S ....Birmingham AL 35205	800-749-4741*	205-322-4741	45
*Cust Svc			
Alabama Assn of Realtors			
522 Washington Ave			
PO Box 4070...............Montgomery AL 36104	800-446-3808	334-262-3808	652
Alabama Card Systems Inc			
500 Gene Reed Dr Ste 102......Birmingham AL 35215	800-985-7507	205-833-1116	756
Alabama Constitution Village			
109 Gates Ave ....Huntsville AL 35801	800-678-1819	256-564-8100	517
Alabama Crown Distributing			
421 Industrial Ln ....Birmingham AL 35211	800-548-1869	205-941-1155	81-3
Alabama Dental Assn			
836 Washington Ave ....Montgomery AL 36104	800-489-2532	334-265-1684	227
Alabama Educational Television Commission			
2112 11th Ave S Ste 400 ....Birmingham AL 35205	800-239-5233	205-328-8756	628
Alabama Eye Bank			
500 Robert Jemison Rd ....Birmingham AL 35209	800-423-7811		269
Alabama Farmers Co-op Inc			
PO Box 2227 ....Decatur AL 35609	800-589-3206	256-353-6843	280
Alabama Graphics & Engineering Supply Inc			
2801 Fifth Ave S ....Birmingham AL 35233	800-292-3806	205-252-8505	256
Alabama Lawyer Magazine			
415 Dexter Ave ....Montgomery AL 36104	800-354-6154	334-269-1515	455-15
Alabama Media Group			
200 Westside Sq Ste 100 ....Huntsville AL 35801	800-239-5271	256-532-4000	528-2
Alabama Medical Assn			
19 S Jackson St ....Montgomery AL 36104	800-239-6272		472
Alabama Metal Industries Corp (AMICO)			
3245 Fayette Ave ....Birmingham AL 35208	800-366-2642	205-787-2611	489
Alabama Motor Express Inc			
10720 E US Hwy 84 E ....Ashford AL 36312	800-633-7590		775
Alabama Newsnet			
3251 Harrison Rd ....Montgomery AL 36109	800-467-0401	334-270-9252	736-48
Alabama Pharmacy Assn			
1211 Carmichael Way ....Montgomery AL 36106	877-877-3962*	334-271-4222	581
*General			
Alabama Public Television (APT)			
2112 11th Ave S Ste 400 ....Birmingham AL 35205	800-239-5233	205-328-8756	628
Alabama School Journal			
422 Dexter Ave ....Montgomery AL 36104	800-392-5839	334-834-9790	455-8
Alabama Shakespeare Festival			
1 Festival Dr ....Montgomery AL 36117	800-841-4273		744
Alabama Southern Community College			
30755 Hwy 43 ....Thomasville AL 36784	800-381-3722	334-636-9642	162
Alabama Specialty Products Inc			
152 Metal Samples Rd PO Box 8 ....Munford AL 36268	888-388-1006	256-358-5200	318
Alabama State Bar			
415 Dexter Ave ....Montgomery AL 36104	800-392-5660	334-269-1515	72
Alabama State Nurses Assn (ASNA)			
360 N Hull St ....Montgomery AL 36104	800-270-2762	334-262-8321	529
Alabama State University			
915 S Jackson St ....Montgomery AL 36104	800-253-5037*	334-229-4100	166
*Admissions			
Alabama Theatre			
4750 Hwy 17 S ....North Myrtle Beach SC 29582	800-342-2262	843-272-1111	568
Alacare Home Health & Hospice			
2400 John Hawkins Pkwy ....Birmingham AL 35244	800-852-4724	205-981-8000	362
Alachua County Library District			
401 E University Ave ....Gainesville FL 32601	866-341-2730	352-334-3900	433-3

Alphabetical Section

	Toll-Free	Phone	Class

Alachua County Visitors & Convention Bureau
30 E University Ave . . . . .Gainesville FL 32601 — 866-778-5002 — 352-374-5260 — 206

ALACO Ladder Co
5167 G St . . . . .Chino CA 91710 — 888-310-7040 — 909-591-7561 — 420

Aladdin Steel Inc
PO Box 89 .Gillespie IL 62033 — 800-637-4455 — 217-839-2121 — 490

Alaglass Swimming Pools
165 Sweet Bay Rd . . . . Saint Matthews SC 29135 — 877-655-7179 — — 374

Alaka'i Mechanical Corp
2655 Waiwai Loop . . . . .Honolulu HI 96819 — 800-600-1085 — 808-834-1085 — 189-10

Alamance Community College
PO Box 8000 . . . . .Graham NC 27253 — 877-667-7533 — 336-578-2002 — 162

Alamar Resort Inn
311 16th St . . . . .Virginia Beach VA 23451 — 800-346-5681 — 757-428-7582 — 665

Alameda County
1221 Oak St Ste 555. . . . . .Oakland CA 94612 — 800-878-1313 — 510-272-6984 — 337

Alameda County Fair Assn (ACFA)
4501 Pleasanton Ave . . . . .Pleasanton CA 94566 — 800-874-9253 — 925-426-7600 — 638

Alameda County Library
2450 Stevenson Blvd . . . . .Fremont CA 94538 — 888-663-0660 — 510-745-1500 — 433-3

Alameda Times-Star
7677 Oakport St . . . . .Oakland CA 94621 — 866-225-5277 — 510-208-6300 — 633-8

Alameda-Contra Costa Transit District
1600 Franklin St 10th Fl . . . . .Oakland CA 94612 — 877-878-8883 — 510-891-4777 — 466

Alamo City Chverolet
9400 San Pedro Ave . . . . .San Antonio TX 78216 — 866-635-6971 — 210-987-2134 — 57

Alamo Group Inc
1627 E Walnut . . . . .Seguin TX 78155 — 800-788-6066* — 830-379-1480 — 273
NYSE: ALG ■ *Cust Svc*

Alamo Industrial Inc
1502 E Walnut St . . . . .Seguin TX 78155 — 800-356-6286 — — 295

Alamo Iron Works Inc
943 AT&T Ctr Pkwy . . . . .San Antonio TX 78219 — 800-292-7817 — 210-223-6161 — 384

Alamo Lumber Co
10800 Sentinel Dr . . . . .San Antonio TX 78217 — 855-828-9792 — 210-352-1300 — 191-3

Alamo Music Ctr
425 N Main Ave . . . . .San Antonio TX 78205 — 800-822-5010 — 844-251-1922 — 522

Alamo Tee's & Advertising
12814 Cogburn . . . . .San Antonio TX 78249 — 888-562-3800 — 210-699-3800 — 7

Alamo Tissue Service Ltd
5844 Rocky Point Dr . . . . .San Antonio TX 78249 — 800-226-9091 — 210-738-2663 — 541

Alamo Travel Group
8930 Wurzbach Rd . . . . .San Antonio TX 78240 — 800-692-5266 — 210-593-3997 — 766

Alamodome
100 Montana St . . . . .San Antonio TX 78203 — 800-884-3663 — 210-207-3663 — 716

Alamogordo Chamber of Commerce
1301 N White Sands Blvd . . . . .Alamogordo NM 88310 — 800-826-0294 — 575-437-6120 — 139

Alamos Gold Inc
181 Bay St Ste 3910. . . . . .Toronto ON M5J2T3 — 866-788-8801 — 416-368-9932
NYSE: AGI

Alan b Harris Attorney at Law
409 N Texas Ave . . . . .Odessa TX 79761 — 800-887-1676 — 432-580-3118 — 427

Alan Gordon Enterprises Inc
5625 Melrose Ave . . . . .Hollywood CA 90038 — 800-825-6684 — 323-466-3561 — 587

Alan Ritchey Inc
740 S I-35 E Frontage Rd . . . . .Valley View TX 76272 — 800-877-0273 — 940-726-3276 — 775

Al-Anon Family Group Inc
1600 Corporate Landing Pkwy
. . . . .Virginia Beach VA 23454 — 888-425-2666 — 757-563-1600 — 48-21

Alaris Group Inc
4108 N 79th Ave W . . . . .Duluth MN 55810 — 888-425-2747

Alaska
Arts Council
161 Klevin St Ste 102. . . . . .Anchorage AK 99508 — 888-278-7424 — 907-269-6610 — 338-2
Banking Securities & Corporations Div
333 Willoughby Ave 9th Fl
PO Box 110800 . . . . .Juneau AK 99801 — 888-925-2521 — 907-465-2521 — 338-2
Commission on Postsecondary Education
PO Box 110510 . . . . .Juneau AK 99811 — 800-770-8973 — 907-465-6671 — 721
Employment Security Div
PO Box 115509 . . . . .Juneau AK 99811 — 888-448-3527 — 907-465-2757 — 259
Enterprise Technology Services Div
State Office Bldg 333 Willoughby Ave
5th Fl . . . . .Juneau AK 99801 — 888-565-8680 — — 338-2
Housing Finance Corp
4300 Boniface Pkwy 99504 . . . . . . .Anchorage AK 99504 — 800-478-2432 — 907-338-6100 — 338-2
Postsecondary Education Commission
3030 Vintage Blvd PO Box 110510 . . . . .Juneau AK 99811 — 800-441-2962 — 907-465-2962 — 338-2
Vocational Rehabilitation Div
801 W Tenth St PO Box 115516. . . . . . . .Juneau AK 99801 — 800-478-2815 — 907-465-2814 — 338-2

Alaska Air Group Inc
19300 International Blvd . . . . .Seattle WA 98188 — 800-654-5669 — 206-433-3200 — 359-1
NYSE: ALK

Alaska Assn of Realtors
4205 Minnesota Dr . . . . .Anchorage AK 99503 — 800-478-3763 — 907-563-7133 — 652

Alaska Bible College
248 E Elmwood Ave . . . . .Palmer AK 99645 — 800-478-7884 — 907-745-3201 — 161

Alaska Business Monthly
501 W Northern Lights Blvd
Ste 100 .Anchorage AK 99503 — 800-770-4373 — 907-276-4373 — 455-5

Alaska Collection
509 W Fourth Ave . . . . .Anchorage AK 99501 — 800-808-8068 — 907-777-2800 — 755

Alaska Commercial Co
125 Main St . . . . .Aniak AK 99557 — 800-563-0002 — — 344

Alaska Communications Systems Group Inc
600 Telephone Ave . . . . .Anchorage AK 99503 — 800-808-8083 — 855-565-2556 — 731
NASDAQ: ALSK

Alaska Dental Society
9170 Jewel Lake Rd Ste 203. . . . . .Anchorage AK 99502 — 800-478-4675 — 907-563-3003 — 227

Alaska Industrial Hardware Inc
2192 Viking Dr . . . . .Anchorage AK 99501 — 800-478-7201 — 907-276-7201 — 363

Alaska Magazine
301 Arctic Slope Ave Ste 300 . . . . . .Anchorage AK 99518 — 800-288-5892 — 386-246-0444 — 455-22

Alaska Marine Highway System
6858 Glacier Hwy PO Box 112505 . . . . .Juneau AK 99811 — 800-642-0066 — 907-465-3941 — 466

Alaska Marine Lines Inc
5615 W Marginal Way SW . . . . .Seattle WA 98106 — 800-326-8346* — 206-763-4244 — 312
*Cust Svc

Alaska Municipal League Joint Insurance Assn
807 G St Ste 356 . . . . .Anchorage AK 99501 — 800-337-3682 — 907-258-2625 — 529

Alaska Native Heritage Ctr
8800 Heritage Ctr Dr . . . . .Anchorage AK 99504 — 800-315-6608 — 907-330-8000 — 517

Alaska Native Medical Ctr (ANMC)
4315 Diplomacy Dr . . . . .Anchorage AK 99508 — 800-478-6661* — 907-563-2662 — 373-3
*Admitting

Alaska Native Tribal Health Consortium Inc
4000 Ambassador Dr . . . . .Anchorage AK 99508 — 800-655-4837 — 907-729-1900 — 362

Alaska Pacific University
4101 University Dr . . . . .Anchorage AK 99508 — 800-252-7528 — 907-564-8248 — 166

Alaska Power & Telephone Co
193 Otto St PO Box 3222 . . . . . . .Port Townsend WA 98368 — 800-982-0136* — 360-385-1733 — 782
OTC: APTL ■ *Cust Svc

Alaska State Veterinary Medical Assn (AKVMA)
1731 Bragaw St . . . . .Anchorage AK 99508 — 800-272-1813 — 907-205-4272 — 790

Alaska Stock Images
2505 Fairbanks St . . . . .Anchorage AK 99503 — 800-487-4285 — 907-276-1343 — 589

Alaska Tour & Travel
3900 Arctic Blvd Ste 304
PO Box 221011. . . . . .Anchorage AK 99503 — 800-208-0200 — 907-245-0200 — 766

Alaska Travel Adventures Inc
9085 Glacier Hwy Ste 301 . . . . .Juneau AK 99801 — 800-323-5757 — 907-789-0052 — 766

Alaska USA Federal Credit Union
4000 Credit Union Dr
PO Box 196613. . . . . .Anchorage AK 99503 — 800-525-9094 — 907-563-4567 — 219

Alaskan Copper & Brass Co
3223 Sixth Ave S . . . . .Seattle WA 98134 — 800-552-7661 — 206-623-5800 — 490

Alban Tractor Co
8531 Pulaski Hwy . . . . .Baltimore MD 21237 — 800-492-6994 — 410-686-7777 — 357

Albany Area Chamber of Commerce
225 W Broad Ave . . . . .Albany GA 31701 — 800-475-8700 — 229-434-8700 — 139

Albany College of Pharmacy (ACPHS)
106 New Scotland Ave . . . . .Albany NY 12208 — 888-203-8010* — 518-694-7221 — 166
*General

Albany County Convention & Visitors Bureau
25 Quackenbush Sq . . . . .Albany NY 12207 — 800-258-3582 — 518-434-1217 — 206

Albany International Corp
216 Airport Dr . . . . .Rochester NH 03867 — 877-327-5378 — 518-445-2200 — 740-3
NYSE: AIN

Albany Law School of Union University (ALS)
80 New Scotland Ave . . . . .Albany NY 12208 — 800-448-3500 — 518-445-2311 — 167-1

Albany Medical Center
43 New Scotland Ave . . . . .Albany NY 12208 — 866-262-7476 — 518-262-3125 — 373-3

Albany Steel Inc
566 Broadway . . . . .Albany NY 12204 — 800-342-9317 — 518-436-4851 — 189-14

Albany Visitors Association
110 Third Ave SE PO Box 965 . . . . . . .Albany OR 97321 — 800-526-2256 — 541-928-0911 — 206

Albemarle Electric Membership Corp
PO Box 69 .Hertford NC 27944 — 800-215-9915 — 252-426-5735 — 245

Alberic Colon Auto Sales
551 Marginal JF Kennedy . . . . .San Juan PR 00920 — 888-510-0718 — 877-292-4610 — 57

Albert at Bay Suite Hotel
435 Albert St . . . . .Ottawa ON K1R7X4 — 800-267-6644 — 613-238-8858 — 378

Albert College
160 Dundas St W . . . . .Belleville ON K8P1A6 — 800-952-5237 — 613-968-5726 — 618

Albert E Sleeper State Park
6573 State Pk Rd . . . . .Caseville MI 48725 — 888-784-7328 — — 561

Albert Einstein Healthcare Network
5501 Old York Rd . . . . .Philadelphia PA 19141 — 800-346-7834 — 215-456-7890 — 352

Albert Einstein Medical Ctr
5501 Old York Rd . . . . .Philadelphia PA 19141 — 800-346-7834 — — 373-3

Albert Guarnieri Co
1133 E Market St . . . . .Warren OH 44483 — 800-686-2639 — 330-394-5636 — 297-8

Albert Kahn Assoc Inc
3011 W Grand Blvd Ste 1800 . . . . .Detroit MI 48202 — 800-833-0062 — 313-202-7000 — 261

Albert Lea Seed House
1414 W Main St . . . . .Albert Lea MN 56007 — 800-352-5247 — 507-373-3161 — 690

Albert Moving
4401 Barnett Rd . . . . .Wichita Falls TX 76310 — 800-460-9333 — 940-696-7020

Albert's Organics Inc
3268 E Vernon Ave . . . . .Vernon CA 90058 — 800-899-5944 — — 297-7

Alberta Bair Theater for the Performing Arts
2722 Third Ave N Ste 200
PO Box 1556. . . . . .Billings MT 59103 — 877-321-2074 — 406-256-8915 — 568

Alberta Blue Cross
10009 108th St NW . . . . .Edmonton AB T5J3C5 — 800-661-6995 — 780-498-8000 — 390-3

Alberta Chambers of Commerce
10025 - 102A Ave Ste 1808 . . . . . . .Edmonton AB T5J2Z2 — 800-272-8854 — 780-425-4180 — 137

Alberta College of Art & Design
1407 14th Ave NW . . . . .Calgary AB T2N4R3 — 800-251-8290 — 403-284-7600 — 780

Alberta Enterprise Corp
10088 102 Ave . . . . .Edmonton AB T5J2Z2 — 877-336-3474 — 587-402-6601 — 524

Alberta Hotel & Lodging Assn (AHLA)
2707 Ellwood Dr . . . . .Edmonton AB T6X0P7 — 888-436-6112 — 780-436-6112 — 48-23

Alberta Oil Tool
9530 60th Ave . . . . .Edmonton AB T6E0C1 — 877-432-3404 — 780-434-8566 — 533

Alberta Soccer
9023 111 Ave NW . . . . .Edmonton AB T5B0C3 — 866-250-2200 — 780-474-2200 — 138

Alberta Union of Prov Employees
10451 170 St NW . . . . .Edmonton AB T5P4S7 — 800-232-7284 — 780-930-3300 — 413

Alberta-Pacific Forest Industries Inc
PO Box 8000 . . . . .Boyle AB T0A0M0 — 800-661-5210 — 780-525-8000 — 634

Albertus Magnus College
700 Prospect St . . . . .New Haven CT 06511 — 800-578-9160* — 203-773-8550 — 166
*Admissions

Albion College
611 E Porter St . . . . .Albion MI 49224 — 800-858-6770 — 517-629-1000 — 166

Albion Hotel
1650 James Ave . . . . .Miami Beach FL 33139 — 877-782-3557* — 305-913-1000 — 378
*General

Albion Industries Inc
800 N Clark St . . . . .Albion MI 49224 — 800-835-8911 — 517-629-9441 — 349

Albion Laboratories Inc
67 S Main St Ste 100 . . . . .Layton UT 84041 — 800-453-2406 — 801-773-4631 — 445

Albright College
1621 N 13th St . . . . .Reading PA 19604 — 800-252-1856 — 610-921-2381 — 166

Albuquerque Convention & Visitors Bureau
20 First Plz Ste 601 . . . . .Albuquerque NM 87102 — 800-733-9918 — 505-842-9918 — 206

Name / Address	Toll-Free	Phone	Class
Albuquerque Public Schools (APS) 6400 Uptown Blvd NE, Albuquerque NM 87110	866-563-9297	505-880-3700	681
Alburg Dunes State Park 151 Coon Pt Rd, Alburg VT 05440	800-262-5226	802-796-4170	561
Alcazar Networks Inc 419 State Ave Ste 3, Emmaus PA 18049	800-349-6192	484-664-2800	461
Alchemy of England 3516 Roberts Cut Off Rd, Fort Worth TX 76114	800-578-1065	817-236-3141	360
ALCO Inc 6925 - 104 St, Edmonton AB T6H2L5	800-563-1498	780-435-3502	402
ALCO Sales & Service Co 6851 High Grove Blvd, Burr Ridge IL 60527	800-323-4282	630-655-1900	194
Alcoa Inc 201 Isabella St, Pittsburgh PA 15212 NYSE: AA	800-388-4825	412-553-4545	483
Alcoa Wheel Products International 1600 Harvard Ave, Cleveland OH 44105	800-242-9898	216-641-3600	481
Alcohol & Tobacco Tax & Trade Bureau 1310 G St NW PO Box 12, Washington DC 20005	877-882-3277	202-453-2180	339-17
Alcoholic Beverage Control PO Box 27491, Richmond VA 23261	800-552-3200	804-213-4565	527-7
Alcoholics Anonymous (AA) 475 Riverside Dr 11th Fl, New York NY 10115	800-437-3584	212-870-3400	48-21
Alcon Canada Inc 2665 Meadowpine Blvd, Mississauga ON L5N8C7	800-268-4574	905-826-6700	540
Alcon Laboratories Inc 6201 S Fwy, Fort Worth TX 76134	800-862-5266	817-293-0450	269
Alcop Adhesive Label Co 826 Perkins Ln, Beverly NJ 08010	888-313-3017	609-871-4400	412
Alcopro Inc 2547 Sutherland Ave, Knoxville TN 37919	800-227-9890	865-525-4900	414
Alcorn County Electric Power Association Inc 1909 S Tate St, Corinth MS 38834	844-741-7071	662-287-4402	245
ALCTS (Association for Library Collections & Technical Se) 50 E Huron St, Chicago IL 60611	800-545-2433	312-280-5037	49-11
Aldea Solutions Inc 8550 Cote de Liesse Blvd Ste 200, Saint-Laurent QC H4T1H2	866-344-5432	514-344-5432	
Alderbrook Resort & Spa 7101 E SR-106, Union WA 98592	800-622-9370	360-898-2200	665
Alderfer Inc 382 Main St PO Box 2, Harleysville PA 19438 *Sales	800-222-2319*		296-26
Alderson-Broaddus College 101 College Hill Rd, Philippi WV 26416 *Admissions	800-263-1549*	304-457-1700	166
Aldila Inc 14145 Danielson St Ste B, Poway CA 92064 OTC: ALDA	800-854-2786	858-513-1801	706
Aldine 150 Varick St 5th Fl, New York NY 10013	800-356-1818	212-226-2870	623
Aldo Shoes 2300 Emile Belanger, Montreal QC H4R3J4	888-818-2536	514-747-2536	301
Alebra Technologies Inc 3810 Pheasant Ridge Dr NE Ste 100, Minneapolis MN 55449	888-340-2727	651-366-6140	177
Alembic Inc 3005 Wiljan Ct, Santa Rosa CA 95407	800-322-5893	707-523-2611	523
Alemite LLC 1057-521 Corporate Ctr Dr Ste 100, Fort Mill SC 29715	800-267-8022	803-802-0001	385
Aleris International Inc 25825 Science Pk Dr Ste 400, Beachwood OH 44122	866-266-2586	216-910-3400	719
AlertOne Services Inc 1000 Commerce Park Dr Ste 300, Williamsport PA 17701 *Cust Svc	866-581-4540*		571
Alerus Retirement & Benefits 2 Pine Tree Dr Ste 400, Arden Hills MN 55112	800-433-1685	800-795-2697	524
Alesco Data Group LLC 5276 Summerlin Commons Way, Fort Myers FL 33907	800-701-6531	239-275-5006	4
Aleut Management Services LLC 5540 Tech Ctr Dr Ste 100, Colorado Springs CO 80919	800-377-7765	719-531-9090	194
Aleutians East Borough 3380 C St Ste 205, Anchorage AK 99503	888-383-2699	907-274-7555	337
Alex C Fergusson LLC (AFCO) 5000 Letterkenny Rd, Chambersburg PA 17201	800-345-1329		145
Alexander & Baldwin Inc 822 Bishop St, Honolulu HI 96813 NYSE: ALEX	866-442-6551	808-525-6611	185
Alexander Mfg Co 12978 Tesson Ferry Rd, Sappington MO 63128 *General	800-258-2743*	800-467-5343	9
Alexander Open Systems Inc 12851 Foster St, Overland Park KS 66213	800-473-1110	913-307-2300	174
Alexander Ramsey House (ARH) 265 S Exchange St, Saint Paul MN 55102	800-657-3773	651-296-8760	50-3
Alexander's Seafood Restaurant & Wine Bar 76 Queens Folly Rd, Hilton Head Island SC 29928	855-706-4319		667
Alexandra Hotel 77 Ryerson Ave, Toronto ON M5T2V4	800-567-1893	416-504-2121	376
Alexandria & Arlington Bed & Breakfast Networks (AABBN) 4938 Hampden Ln Ste 164, Bethesda MD 20814	888-549-3415	703-549-3415	375
Alexandria City Hall 301 King St, Alexandria VA 22314	800-543-8911	703-838-4000	336
Alexandria Convention & Visitors Assn 221 King St, Alexandria VA 22314	800-388-9119	703-746-3301	206
Alexandria Daily Town Talk PO Box 7558, Alexandria LA 71306	800-523-8391	318-487-6397	528-2
Alexandria Lakes Area Chamber of Commerce 206 Broadway, Alexandria MN 56308	800-235-9441	320-763-3161	139
Alexandria Moulding 20352 Powerdam Rd, Alexandria ON K0C1A0	866-377-2539	613-525-2784	309
Alexandria Veterans Affairs Medical Ctr 2495 Shreveport Hwy 71 N, Pineville LA 71360	800-375-8387	318-473-0010	373-8
Alexandria/Pineville Area Convention & Visitors Bureau (APACVB) 707 Main St PO Box 1070, Alexandria LA 71301	800-551-9546		206
Alexian Bros Health System 3040 Salt Creek Ln, Arlington Heights IL 60005	800-432-5005	847-385-7100	352
Alexian Bros Medical Ctr 800 Biesterfield Rd, Elk Grove Village IL 60007	800-432-5005	847-437-5500	373-3
Alexis Hotel 1007 First Ave, Seattle WA 98104	866-356-8894	206-624-4844	378
Alexis Park Resort 375 E Harmon Ave, Las Vegas NV 89169	800-582-2228	702-796-3300	665
ALF (American Liver Foundation) 39 Broadway, New York NY 10006	800-465-4837	212-668-1000	48-17
Alfa Aesar Co 26 Parkridge Rd, Ward Hill MA 01835	800-343-0660	978-521-6300	145
Alfa Corp 2108 E S Blvd, Montgomery AL 36116	800-964-2532		455-1
Alfa Wassermann Inc 4 Henderson Dr, West Caldwell NJ 07006	800-220-4488	973-882-8630	474
Alfalfa Electric Co-op Inc 121 E Main St, Cherokee OK 73728	888-736-3837	580-596-3333	245
Alfe Heat Treating Inc 6920 Pointe Inverness Way Ste 140, Fort Wayne IN 46804	888-747-2533		
Alfiniti Inc 1152 rue Manic, Chicoutimi QC G7K1A2	800-334-8731	418-696-2545	490
Alforex Seeds 38001 County Rd 27, Woodland CA 95695	877-560-5181	530-666-3331	276
Alfred A Loeb State Park 725 Summer St NE Ste C, Salem OR 97301	800-551-6949	503-986-0707	561
Alfred P Sloan Foundation 630 Fifth Ave 2550, New York NY 10111	800-401-8004	212-649-1649	305
Alfresco 1085 Bixby Dr, Hacienda Heights CA 91745	888-383-8800	323-722-7900	106
Alger Family of Funds PO Box 8480, Boston MA 02266	800-992-3863		524
Alger Precision Machining LLC 724 S Bon View Ave, Ontario CA 91761	800-854-9833		617
Algo Communication Products Ltd 4500 Beedie St, Burnaby BC V5J5L2	800-226-7722	604-438-3333	246
Algo Design Inc 6455 Doris Lussier Ste 300, Boisbriand QC J7H0E8	800-267-2584	450-681-2584	180
Algoma University 1520 Queen St E, Sault Sainte Marie ON P6A2G4	888-254-6628	705-949-2301	353
Algy Team Collection 440 NE First Ave, Hallandale FL 33009	800-458-2549	954-457-8100	155-18
Alhambra 8 Governor Wentworth Hwy, Wolfeboro NH 03894	800-329-9099	603-569-0600	178-7
ALI (American Law Institute) 4025 Chestnut St, Philadelphia PA 19104	800-253-6397	215-243-1600	49-10
ALI's Database Consultants 1151 Williams Dr, Aiken SC 29803	866-257-8970	803-648-5931	180
Alice Lloyd College 100 Purpose Rd, Pippa Passes KY 41844 *Admissions	888-280-4252*	606-368-6000	166
Alice Travel Luxury Cruises & Tour 277 Fairfield Rd Ste 218, Fairfield NJ 07004	800-229-2542	973-439-1700	767
Alidade Technology Inc 111 Knoll Dr, Collegeville PA 19426	877-265-1581		196
Align Technology Inc 2560 Orchard Pkwy, San Jose CA 95131 NASDAQ: ALGN	800-577-8767	408-470-1000	228
Aliments Asta Inc 767 Rte 289, St Alexandre-De-Kamouraska QC G0L2G0	800-463-1355	418-495-2728	296-26
ALine Inc 2206 E Gladwick St, Rancho Dominguez CA 90220	877-707-8575		738
Alisal Guest Ranch & Resort 1054 Alisal Rd, Solvang CA 93463	800-425-4725	805-693-4208	665
ALISE (Association for Library & Information Science Educ) 2150 N 107th St Ste 205, Seattle WA 98133	877-275-7547	206-209-5267	49-11
Alise Boston - A Staypineapple Hotel, The 54 Berkeley St, Boston MA 02116	800-842-3450	617-585-5625	378
Alive Hospice Inc 1718 Patterson St, Nashville TN 37203	800-327-1085	615-327-1085	370
Aljex Software Inc 50 Division St Ste 204, Somerville NJ 08876	833-262-2314		
Aljira Ctr for Contemporary Arts 591 Broad St, Newark NJ 07102	800-852-7699	973-622-1600	517
ALK 35-151 Brunel Rd, Mississauga ON L4Z2H6	800-663-0972	905-290-9952	231
Alken Inc 40 Hercules Dr, Colchester VT 05446	800-357-4777	802-655-3159	688
Alkermes Inc 852 Winter St, Waltham MA 02451 NASDAQ: ALKS	800-848-4876	781-609-6000	85
Alkinco PO Box 278, New York NY 10116	800-424-7118	212-719-3070	347
All - Fill Inc 418 Creamery Way, Exton PA 19341	866-255-3455		
All Aboard Benefits 6162 E Mockingird Ln Ste 104, Dallas TX 75214	800-462-2322	214-821-6677	390-7
All Aboard Cruises Inc 12383 SW 124 Ter, Miami FL 33186	800-883-8657	305-385-8657	766
All Aboard USA 2736 Kanasita Dr, Chattanooga TN 37343	800-499-9877	423-499-9977	755
All About Packaging Inc 2200 W Everett St, Appleton WI 54912	800-446-1552	920-830-2700	623
All American Grating Inc 3001 Grand Ave, Pittsburgh PA 15225	800-962-9692	412-771-6970	490
All American Ticket Service 2616 Philadelphia Pk Ste E, Claymont DE 19703	800-669-0571		745
All City Metal inc 54-35 46th St, Maspeth NY 11378	888-682-5757	718-472-5700	
All Classical Portland 211 SE Caruthers St Ste 200, Portland OR 97214	888-306-5277	503-943-5828	641-109
All Copy Products LLC 4141 Colorado Blvd, Denver CO 80216	800-332-2352	303-295-0741	45
All Cruise Travel 1723 Hamilton Ave, San Jose CA 95125	800-227-8473	408-295-1200	766
All Direct Travel Services Inc 19772 MacArthur Blvd Ste 150, Irvine CA 92612	800-862-1516	949-474-8100	767

Name / Address	City	State	ZIP	Toll-Free	Phone	Class
All Flex Flexible Circuits & Heaters						
1705 Cannon Ln	Northfield	MN	55057	**800-959-0865**		
All Foils Inc						
16100 Imperial Pkwy	Strongsville	OH	44149	**800-521-0054**	440-572-3645	490
All Graphic Supplies						
6691 Edwards Blvd	Mississauga	ON	L5T2H8	**800-501-4451**		786
All in One Poster Co						
8521 Whitaker St	Buena Park	CA	90621	**800-273-0307**	714-521-7720	45
All Languages Ltd						
306-421 Bloor St E	Toronto	ON	M4W3T1	**800-567-8100**	416-975-5000	317
All Makes Office Equipment Co						
2558 Farnam St	Omaha	NE	68131	**800-341-2413**	402-341-2413	321
All Market Inc						
250 Park Ave S 7th Fl	New York	NY	10003	**877-848-2262**	212-206-0763	
All Metals Industries Inc						
4 Higgins Dr	Belmont	NH	03220	**800-654-6043**	603-267-7023	490
All Native Systems LLC						
1 Mission Dr	Winnebago	NE	68071	**866-323-7636**		180
All New Stamping Co						
10801 Lower Azusa Rd	El Monte	CA	91731	**800-877-7775**		486
All Nippon Airways Company Ltd						
2050 W 190th St Ste 100	Torrance	CA	90504	**800-235-9262**		25
All Property Management						
PO Box 1013 Ste 325	Winthrop	WA	98862	**877-234-9723**		
All Source Security Container Mfg Corp						
40 Mills Rd	Barrie	ON	L4N6H4	**866-526-4579**	705-726-6460	798-1
All Star Glass Co Inc						
1845 Morena Blvd	San Diego	CA	92110	**800-225-4184**	619-275-3343	62-2
All State Fastener Corp						
15460 E 12 Mile Rd	Roseville	MI	48066	**800-755-8959**	586-773-5400	350
All States Inc						
602 N 12th St	Saint Charles	IL	60174	**800-621-5837***	773-728-0525	604
*Cust Svc						
All Systems Installation						
8300 Tenth Ave N Ste A	Golden Valley	MN	55427	**800-403-4832**	763-593-1330	180
All Tune & Lube International Inc						
ATL International Inc						
8334 Veterans Hwy	Millersville	MD	21108	**877-978-1758***		62-5
*Cust Svc						
All Weather Inc						
1165 National Dr	Sacramento	CA	95834	**800-824-5873**	916-928-1000	470
All Web Leads Inc						
7300 FM 2222 Bldg 2 Ste 100	Austin	TX	78730	**888-522-7355**		386
All West Coach Lines						
7701 Wilbur Way	Sacramento	CA	95828	**800-843-2121**	888-970-7233	107
All West Select Sires						
PO Box 507	Burlington	WA	98233	**800-426-2697**		444
All World Travel Inc						
314 Gilmer St	Sulphur Springs	TX	75482	**866-298-6067**	903-885-0896	770
Allagash Wilderness Waterway						
106 Hogan Rd Ste 7	Bangor	ME	04401	**800-332-1501**	207-941-4014	561
Allamakee County						
110 Allamakee St	Waukon	IA	52172	**800-728-0131**	563-864-7454	337
Allamakee-Clayton Electric Co-op (ACEC)						
229 Hwy 51 PO Box 715	Postville	IA	52162	**888-788-1551**	563-864-7611	245
All-American Co-op						
PO Box 125	Stewartville	MN	55976	**888-354-4058**	507-533-4222	273
Allamon Tool Company Inc						
18935 Freeport Dr	Montgomery	TX	77356	**877-449-5433**		535
Allan A Myers Inc						
1805 Berks Rd PO Box 1340	Worcester	PA	19490	**800-596-6118**	610-222-8800	188-4
Allan Hackel Organization						
1330 Ctr St	Newton Center	MA	02459	**800-970-2499**	617-965-4400	6
Allan Hancock College						
800 S College Dr	Santa Maria	CA	93454	**866-342-5242**	805-922-6966	162
Allana Buick & Bers Inc						
990 Commercial St	Palo Alto	CA	94303	**800-378-3405**	650-543-5600	256
Allant Group Inc, The						
2655 Warrenville Rd						
Ste 200	Downers Grove	IL	60515	**800-367-7311**		194
AllCare Health						
740 SE Seventh St	Grants Pass	OR	97526	**888-460-0185**	541-471-4106	362
All-Clad Metalcrafters LLC						
424 Morganza Rd	Canonsburg	PA	15317	**800-255-2523***	724-745-8300	484
*Cust Svc						
Allegacy Federal Credit Union						
1691 Westbrook Plaza Dr	Winston-Salem	NC	27103	**800-782-4670**	336-774-3400	219
Allegan County Tourist Council						
3255 122nd Ave	Allegan	MI	49010	**888-425-5342**	269-686-9088	206
Allegany College of Maryland						
12401 Willowbrook Rd SE	Cumberland	MD	21502	**800-974-0203**	301-784-5000	162
Alleghany Regional Hospital						
1 ARH Ln	Low Moor	VA	24457	**866-393-0026**	540-862-6011	373-3
Allegheny College						
520 N Main St	Meadville	PA	16335	**800-521-5293**	814-332-4351	166
Allegheny Petroleum Products Co						
999 Airbrake Ave	Wilmerding	PA	15148	**800-600-2900**	412-829-1990	576
Allegheny Technologies Inc						
1000 Six PPG Pl	Pittsburgh	PA	15222	**800-258-3586***	412-394-2800	719
NYSE: ATI ■ *Sales						
Allegheny Wesleyan College						
2161 Woodsdale Rd	Salem	OH	44460	**800-292-3153**	330-337-6403	161
Allegiance Health						
205 NE Ave	Jackson	MI	49201	**800-872-6480**	517-788-4800	373-3
Allegiant International LLC						
450 E 96th St Ste 500	Indianapolis	IN	46240	**866-841-3671**		260
Allegis Group Inc						
7301 Pkwy Dr	Hanover	MD	21076	**800-927-8090**		717
Allegro Coffee Co						
12799 Claude Ct	Thornton	CO	80241	**800-530-3995**	303-444-4844	296-7
Allegro Industries						
1360 Shiloh Church Rd	Piedmont	SC	29673	**800-622-3530**	864-846-8740	473
ALLEN						
525 Burbank St	Broomfield	CO	80020	**800-876-8600**	303-469-1857	188-4
Allen Blasting & Coating Inc						
1668 Old Hwy 61	Wever	IA	52658	**800-760-9186**	319-367-5500	186
Allen Bros Inc						
3737 S Halsted St	Chicago	IL	60609	**800-548-7777**	773-890-5100	471
Allen County						
1 N Washington St	Iola	KS	66749	**866-444-1407**	620-365-1407	337
Allen County Community College						
1801 N Cottonwood St	Iola	KS	66749	**800-444-0535**	620-365-5116	162
Allen Engineering Corp (AEC)						
819 S Fifth St PO Box 819	Paragould	AR	72450	**800-643-0095**	870-236-7751	190
Allen Industries Inc						
6434 Burnt Poplar Rd	Greensboro	NC	27409	**800-967-2553**	336-668-2791	697
Allen Lund Company Inc						
4529 Angeles Crest Hwy	La Canada	CA	91011	**800-811-0083**	800-777-6142	311
Allen Memorial Hospital						
1825 Logan Ave	Waterloo	IA	50703	**888-343-4165**	319-235-3941	373-3
Allen Organ Co						
150 Locust St	Macungie	PA	18062	**800-582-4466**	610-966-2202	523
Allen Parish						
8904 Hwy 165	Oberlin	LA	70655	**888-639-4868**	337-639-4868	337
Allen Press Inc						
810 E Tenth St PO Box 1897	Lawrence	KS	66044	**800-627-0932**	785-843-1234	47
Allen Systems Group Inc (ASG)						
1333 Third Ave S	Naples	FL	34102	**800-932-5536**	239-435-2200	178-12
Allen University						
1530 Harden St	Columbia	SC	29204	**877-625-5368**	803-376-5700	166
Allen-Edmonds Shoe Corp						
201 E Seven Hills Rd	Port Washington	WI	53074	**800-235-2348***	262-235-9261	301
*Cust Svc						
Allentown Equipment						
1733 90th St	Sturtevant	WI	53177	**800-553-3414**		385
Allen-Vanguard Corp						
2400 St Laurent Blvd	Ottawa	ON	K1G5B4	**800-644-9078**	613-739-9646	572
Allergan Inc						
2525 Dupont Dr	Irvine	CA	92612	**800-347-4500**	714-246-4500	578
NYSE: AGN						
Allergychoices Inc						
2800 National Dr Ste 100	Onalaska	WI	54650	**866-793-1680**	608-793-1580	237
ALLETE Inc						
30 W Superior St	Duluth	MN	55802	**800-228-4966**	218-279-5000	359-5
NYSE: ALE						
Allevity HR & Payroll						
870 Manzanita Ct Ste A	Chico	CA	95926	**800-447-8233**	530-345-2486	627
Alliance Abroad Group						
1645 E Sixth St Ste 100	Austin	TX	78702	**866-622-7623**	512-457-8062	41
Alliance Corp						
2395 Meadowpine Blvd	Mississauga	ON	L5N7W6	**888-821-4797**		490
Alliance for Children & Families Inc						
11700 West Lake Pk Dr	Milwaukee	WI	53224	**800-221-3726**		48-6
Alliance For Employee Growth & Development Inc, The						
80 Cottontail Ln Ste 320	Somerset	NJ	08873	**800-323-3436**		193
Alliance for Lupus Research (ALA)						
28 W 44th St Ste 501	New York	NY	10036	**800-867-1743**	212-218-2840	48-17
Alliance for Retired Americans						
815 16th St NW 4th Fl	Washington	DC	20006	**888-373-6497**	202-637-5399	48-6
Alliance for Telecommunications Industry Solutions (ATIS)						
1200 G St NW Ste 500	Washington	DC	20005	**800-649-1202**	202-628-6380	49-20
Alliance Grain Co						
1306 W Eigth St	Gibson City	IL	60936	**800-222-2451**	217-784-4284	275
Alliance Imaging Inc						
100 Bayview Cir Ste 400	Newport Beach	CA	92660	**800-544-3215**	949-242-5300	382
Alliance Limousine						
14553 Delano St Ste 210	Van Nuys	CA	91411	**800-954-5466**		440
Alliance Publishing Company Inc						
40 S Linden Ave	Alliance	OH	44601	**800-778-0098**	330-821-1200	528-3
Alliance Rubber Co						
210 Carpenter Dam Rd	Hot Springs	AR	71901	**800-626-5940**	501-262-2700	672
Alliance to Save Energy (ASE)						
1850 M St NW Ste 600	Washington	DC	20036	**800-862-2086**	202-857-0666	48-12
Alliance Worldwide Investigative Group Inc						
4 Executive Park Dr	Clifton Park	NY	12065	**800-579-2911**	518-514-2944	389
AllianceBernstein Holding LP (AB)						
1345 Ave of the Americas	New York	NY	10105	**800-221-5672***	212-486-5800	400
NYSE: AB ■ *Cust Svc						
Alliant Energy Corp						
4902 N Biltmore Ln Ste 1000	Madison	WI	53718	**800-255-4268**		782
NYSE: LNT						
Alliant International University						
10455 Pomerado Rd	San Diego	CA	92131	**866-825-5426**	858-635-4772	166
Alliant Powder						
2299 Snake River Ave	Lewiston	ID	83501	**800-276-9337**	800-379-1732	268
Allianz Global Investors of America LP						
600 West Broadway						
San Diego	Newport Beach	CA	92101	**800-656-6226**		400
Allianz Life Insurance Company of North America						
PO Box 1344	Minneapolis	MN	55416	**800-950-5872**		390-2
Allied Aerofoam Products LLC						
216 Kelsey Ln	Tampa	FL	33619	**800-338-9140**	813-626-0090	597
Allied Air Enterprises						
215 Metropolitan Dr	West Columbia	SC	29170	**800-448-5872**		15
Allied Automotive Group						
2302 ParkLake Dr						
Bldg 15 Ste 600	Atlanta	GA	30345	**800-476-2058**		
Allied Bindery LLC						
32501 Dequindre Rd	Madison Heights	MI	48071	**800-833-0151**	248-588-5990	776
Allied Bldg Products Corp						
15 E Union Ave	East Rutherford	NJ	07073	**800-541-2198**	201-507-8400	191-3
Allied Body Works Inc						
625 S 96th St	Seattle	WA	98108	**800-733-7450***	206-763-7811	513
*General						
Allied Construction Products LLC						
3900 Kelley Ave	Cleveland	OH	44114	**800-321-1046***	216-431-2600	190
*Cust Svc						
Allied Construction Services & Color Inc						
2122 Fleur Dr PO Box 937	Des Moines	IA	50304	**800-365-4855**	515-288-4855	189-9
Allied Container Systems Inc						
39 Ygnacio Valley Rd						
No 402	Walnut Creek	CA	94596	**800-943-6510**	925-944-7600	545
Allied Controls Inc						
150 E Aurora St	Waterbury	CT	06708	**800-788-0955**	203-757-4200	203
Allied Corrosion Industries Inc						
1550 Cobb Industrial Dr	Marietta	GA	30066	**800-241-0809**	770-425-1355	256

Company / Address	City	State	ZIP	Toll-Free	Phone	Class
Allied Electronics Inc 7151 Jack Newell Blvd S	Fort Worth	TX	76118	866-433-5722	817-595-3500	246
Allied Employer Group 4400 Buffalo Gap Rd Ste 4500	Abilene	TX	79606	800-495-3836	325-695-5822	627
Allied Fastener & Tool Inc 1130 Ng St	Lake Worth	FL	33460	877-353-3731	561-585-2113	349
Allied Fire & Security Inc 425 W Second Ave *Acctg	Spokane	WA	99201	888-333-2632*	509-321-8778	688
Allied Fire Protection LP PO Box 2842	Pearland	TX	77588	800-604-2600	281-485-6803	189-10
ALLIED Group Inc 1100 Locust St	Des Moines	IA	50391	800-532-1436		390-4
Allied Group Inc, The 25 Amflex Dr	Cranston	RI	02921	800-556-6310	401-946-6100	174
Allied Health Group LLC 6551 Park of Commerce Blvd	Boca Raton	FL	33487	800-873-9182		717
Allied Healthcare Products Inc 1720 Sublette Ave *NASDAQ: AHPI*	Saint Louis	MO	63110	800-444-3954	314-771-2400	475
Allied Insurance 1100 Locust St	Des Moines	IA	50391	800-532-1436		390-4
Allied International Credit Corp 16635 Young St Ste 26	Newmarket	ON	L3X1V6	877-451-2594		160
Allied International NA Inc 700 Oakmont Ln	Westmont	IL	60559	800-444-6787	630-570-3500	516
Allied Machine & Engineering Corp 120 Deeds Dr	Dover	OH	44622	800-321-5537	330-343-4283	491
Allied Mechanical Services Inc 145 N Plains Industrial Rd	Wallingford	CT	06492	888-237-3017	269-344-0191	189-10
Allied Moulded Products Inc 222 N Union St	Bryan	OH	43506	800-722-2679	419-636-4217	811
Allied Oil & Supply Inc 2209 S 24th St	Omaha	NE	68108	800-333-3717	402-267-1375	575
Allied Oilfield Machine & Pump LLC 202 Hulon Moreland Rd	Levelland	TX	79336	855-378-4787		534
Allied Pilots Association 14600 Trinity Blvd O'Connell Bldg Ste 500	Fort Worth	TX	76155	800-272-7456	817-302-2272	413
Allied Plastics Company Inc 2001 Walnut St *Cust Svc	Jacksonville	FL	32206	800-999-0386*		319-1
Allied Power Group LLC 10131 Mills Rd	Houston	TX	77070	888-830-3535	281-444-3535	261
Allied Services Rehabilitation Hospital 100 Abington Executive Pk	Clarks Summit	PA	18508	888-734-2272	570-348-1300	373-6
Allied Solutions LLC 350 Veterans Way	Carmel	IN	46032	800-826-9384		
Allied Steel Construction Co Inc 2211 NW First Terr	Oklahoma City	OK	73107	800-522-4658	405-232-7531	264-3
Allied Supply Company Inc 1100 E Monument Ave	Dayton	OH	45402	800-589-5690	937-224-9833	661
Allied Systems Co 21433 SW Oregon St	Sherwood	OR	97140	800-285-7000	503-625-2560	273
Allied Telesyn International Corp 19800 N Creek Pkwy Ste 100	Bothell	WA	98011	800-424-4284	425-481-3895	176
Allied Tool Products 9334 N 107th St	Milwaukee	WI	53224	800-558-5147	414-355-8280	453
Allied Toyotalift 1640 Island Home Ave	Knoxville	TN	37920	866-538-0667	865-573-0995	57
Allied Vaughn 7600 Parklawn Ste 300	Minneapolis	MN	55435	800-323-0281	952-832-3100	654
Allied-Horizontal Wireline Services 3200 Wilcrest Dr Ste 170	Houston	TX	77042	888-494-9580	713-343-7280	532
Allied-Locke Industries 1088 Corregidor Rd	Dixon	IL	61021	800-435-7752	815-288-1471	616
Alligato Inc 1450-1055 W Hastings St	Vancouver	BC	V6E2E9	866-355-0187		224
Alligator Records & Artist Management Inc PO Box 60234	Chicago	IL	60660	800-344-5609	773-973-7736	653
Allina Health System 710 E 24th St	Minneapolis	MN	55404	800-233-8504	612-813-3600	352
All-Inclusive Vacations Inc 1595 Iris St	Denver	CO	80215	866-980-6483	303-980-6483	766
Allison Payment Systems LLC 2200 Production Dr	Indianapolis	IN	46241	800-755-2440		110
Allmar Inc 287 Riverton Ave	Winnipeg	MB	R2L0N2	800-230-5516	204-668-1000	236
AllMed Healthcare Management Inc 111 SW Fifth Ave Ste 1400	Portland	OR	97204	800-400-9916		461
AllMeds Inc 151 Lafayette Dr Ste 401	Oak Ridge	TN	37830	888-343-6337	865-482-1999	39
Allmetal Inc 1 Pierce Pl Ste 295W	Itasca	IL	60143	800-638-2599	630-250-8090	
Allomatic Products Co 102 Jericho Tpke Ste 104 Floral Pk	Floral Park	NY	11001	800-568-0330	516-775-0330	61
Allor Manufacturing Inc 12534 Emerson Dr	Brighton	MI	48116	888-382-6300	248-486-4500	207
AlloSource 6278 S Troy Cir	Centennial	CO	80111	800-557-3587	720-873-0213	541
Allot Communications 300 Tradecenter Ste 4680	Woburn	MA	01801	877-255-6826	781-939-9300	178-10
Alloy Engineering & Casting Co 1700 W Washington St	Champaign	IL	61821	800-348-2880	217-398-3200	307
Alloy Stainless Products Co 611 Union Blvd	Totowa	NJ	07512	800-631-8372	973-256-1616	591
All-Pro Fasteners Inc 1916 Peyco Dr N	Arlington	TX	76001	800-361-6627	817-467-5700	350
Allpro Parking LLC 465 Main St Lafayette Court Bldg Ste 105	Buffalo	NY	14203	877-849-7275	716-849-7275	
All-Pro Printing 11548 Pyramid Dr	Odessa	FL	33556	866-472-3982		
Allscripts Healthcare Solutions 222 Merchandise Mart Plz Ste 2024 *NASDAQ: MDRX*	Chicago	IL	60654	800-654-0889		178-10
All-Search & Inspection Inc 1108 E South Union Ave	Midvale	UT	84047	800-227-3152		631
Allstar Fire Equipment Inc 12328 Lower Azusa Rd	Arcadia	CA	91006	800-425-5787	626-652-0900	675
Allstar Magnetics LLC 6205 NE 63rd St	Vancouver	WA	98661	800-356-5977	360-693-0213	246
All-Star Recruiting LLC 6119 Lyons Rd	Coconut Creek	FL	33073	800-928-0229		260
Allstate 2775 Sanders Rd	Northbrook	IL	60062	800-255-7828	847-402-5000	
Allstate Floral & Craft Inc 14038 Park Pl	Cerritos	CA	90703	800-433-4056	562-926-2302	293
Allstate Leasing Inc 1 Olympic Pl	Towson	MD	21204	800-223-4885	877-711-4211	289
Allstate Life Insurance Co 3100 Sanders Rd *Cust Svc	Northbrook	IL	60062	800-366-1411*	847-402-5000	390-2
Allsteel Inc 2210 Second Ave *Cust Svc	Muscatine	IA	52761	888-255-7833*	563-272-4800	319-1
Allstream Corp 200 Wellington St W *Cust Svc	Toronto	ON	M5V3G2	888-288-2273*	416-345-2000	731
Allsup Inc 300 Allsup Pl	Belleville	IL	62223	800-854-1418		194
Alltech Inc 3031 Catnip Hill Pk	Nicholasville	KY	40356	800-289-8324	859-885-9613	580
ALL-TEST Pro LLC 123 Spencer Plain Rd	Old Saybrook	CT	06475	800-952-8776	860-399-4222	201
Allway Tools Inc 1255 Seabury Ave	Bronx	NY	10462	800-422-5592	718-792-3636	753
All-Ways Adv Co 1442 Broad St	Bloomfield	NJ	07003	800-255-9291	973-338-0700	4
ALM (American Lawyer Media Inc) 120 Broadway 5th Fl	New York	NY	10271	877-256-2472	212-457-9400	633-9
Alma College 614 W Superior St	Alma	MI	48801	800-321-2562	989-463-7111	166
Alma Lasers Inc 485 Half Day Rd Ste 100	Buffalo Grove	IL	60089	866-414-2562		
Alma Products Co 2000 Michigan Ave	Alma	MI	48801	877-427-2624	989-463-1151	60
Almanac, The 3525 Alameda De Las Pulgas	Menlo Park	CA	94025	800-799-4811	650-854-2626	528-4
Almatis Inc 501 W Pk Rd	Leetsdale	PA	15056	800-643-8771	412-630-2903	143
Almo Corp 2709 Commerce Way	Philadelphia	PA	19154	800-345-2566	215-698-4000	38
Almost Family Inc 9510 Ormsby Stn Rd Ste 300 *NASDAQ: AFAM*	Louisville	KY	40223	800-828-9769	502-891-1000	362
Alnylam Pharmaceuticals Inc 300 Third St 3rd Fl *NASDAQ: ALNY*	Cambridge	MA	02142	866-330-0326	617-551-8200	85
ALOA (Associated Locksmiths of America) 3500 Easy St	Dallas	TX	75247	800-532-2562	214-819-9733	49-3
Aloft Broomfield Denver 8300 Arista Pl	Broomfield	CO	80021	866-716-8143	303-635-2000	703
Aloft Chicago O'hare 9700 Balmoral Ave	Rosemont	IL	60018	866-716-8143	847-671-4444	703
Aloha Medicinals Inc 2300 Arrowhead Dr	Carson City	NV	89706	877-835-6091	775-886-6300	231
Aloha Petroleum Ltd 1132 Bishop St Ste 1700	Honolulu	HI	96813	800-621-4654	808-522-9700	113
Alohilani Resort 2490 Kalakaua Ave	Honolulu	HI	96815	800-367-6060	808-922-1233	378
Alorica Inc 5 Park Plz Ste 1100	Irvine	CA	92614	866-256-7422		
Alostar Bank 3680 Grandview Pkwy Ste 200	Birmingham	AL	35243	877-738-6391	205-298-6391	70
Alpena Area Convention & Visitors Bureau 235 W Chisholm St	Alpena	MI	49707	800-425-7362	989-354-4181	206
Alpena Community College (ACC) 665 Johnson St	Alpena	MI	49707	888-468-6222	989-356-9021	162
Alpena County 720 W Chisholm St	Alpena	MI	49707	800-999-4487	989-354-9500	337
Alpena County George N Fletcher Public Library 211 N First Ave	Alpena	MI	49707	877-737-4106	989-356-6188	433-3
Alpena Oil Co Inc 235 Water St	Alpena	MI	49707	800-968-1098	989-356-1098	324
Alpenhof Lodge 3255 W Village Dr	Teton Village	WY	83025	800-732-3244	307-733-3242	378
Alpha & Omega Financial Management Consultants Inc 8580 La Mesa Blvd Ste 100	La Mesa	CA	91942	800-755-5060		194
Alpha 1 Induction Service Ctr Inc 1525 Old Alum Creek Dr	Columbus	OH	43209	800-991-2599	614-253-8900	318
Alpha Assoc Inc 145 Lehigh Ave	Lakewood	NJ	08701	800-631-5399	732-634-5700	740-2
Alpha Epsilon Phi Sorority (AEPhi) 11 Lake Ave Ext Ste 1A	Danbury	CT	06811	888-668-4293	203-748-0029	48-16
Alpha Group, The 3767 Alpha Way	Bellingham	WA	98226	800-322-5742	360-647-2360	253
Alpha Imaging Inc 4455 Glenbrook Rd	Willoughby	OH	44094	800-331-7327	440-953-3800	473
Alpha Industries Inc 14200 Park Meadow Dr Ste 110 S Tower *General	Chantilly	VA	20151	866-631-0719*		155-5
Alpha Lambda Delta 6800 Pittsford-Palmyra Rd Ste 340	Fairport	NY	14450	800-925-7421		48-16
Alpha Mechanical Service Inc 7200 Distribution Dr	Louisville	KY	40258	888-212-6324		606
Alpha Natural Resources Inc 636 Shelby St 3rd Fl *OTC: ANR*	Bristol	TN	37620	866-322-5742	423-574-5100	499
Alpha Omega International Dental Fraternity 50 W Edmonston Dr	Rockville	MD	20852	877-368-6326	301-738-6400	48-16
Alpha Omicron Pi International 5390 Virginia Way	Brentwood	TN	37027	855-230-1183	615-370-0920	48-16

Name / Address	City	State	Zip	Toll-Free	Phone	Class
Alpha Packaging						
1555 Page Industrial Blvd	Saint Louis	MO	63132	**800-421-4772**	314-427-4300	98
Alpha Pro Tech Ltd						
60 Centurian Dr	Markham	ON	L3R9R2	**800-749-1363**	905-479-0654	228
Alpha Rae Personnel Inc						
347 West Berry St 7th Fl	Fort Wayne	IN	46802	**800-837-8940**	260-426-8227	260
Alpha Source Inc						
6619 W Calumet Rd	Milwaukee	WI	53223	**800-654-9845**	414-760-2222	473
Alpha Tau Omega Fraternity (ATO)						
1 N Pennsylvania St 12th Fl	Indianapolis	IN	46204	**800-798-9286**	317-684-1865	48-16
Alpha Technologies Services LLC						
3030 Gilchrist Rd	Akron	OH	44305	**800-356-9886**	330-745-1641	201
Alpha Wire Co						
711 Lidgerwood Ave	Elizabeth	NJ	07207	**800-522-5742**	908-925-8000	809
AlphaGraphics Inc						
215 S State St Ste 320	Salt Lake City	UT	84111	**800-955-6246**	801-595-7270	623
AlphaKOR Group Inc						
7800 Twin Oaks Dr	Windsor	ON	N8N5B6	**877-944-6009**	519-944-6009	180
Alphanumeric Systems Inc						
3801 Wake Forest Rd	Raleigh	NC	27609	**800-638-6556**	919-781-7575	113
AlphaStaff Inc						
800 Corporate Dr Ste 600	Fort Lauderdale	FL	33334	**888-335-9545**	954-267-1760	627
Alphinat Inc						
2000 Peel Ste 680	Montreal	QC	H3A2W5	**877-773-9799**	514-398-9799	
Alpin Haus Ski Shop						
4850 State Hwy 30 N	Amsterdam	NY	12010	**888-454-3691**	518-843-4400	
Alpina Manufacturing LLC						
6460 W Cortland St	Chicago	IL	60707	**800-915-2828**	773-202-8887	45
Alpine Adventure Trails Tours Inc						
7495 Lower Thomaston Rd	Macon	GA	31220	**888-478-4004**	478-477-4702	755
Alpine Bank of Colorado						
2200 Grand Ave	Glenwood Springs	CO	81601	**888-425-7463**	970-945-2424	359-2
Alpine Electronics of America						
19145 Gramercy Pl	Torrance	CA	90501	**800-257-4631**	310-326-8000	52
Alpine Fresh Inc						
9300 NW 58th St Ste 201	Miami	FL	33178	**800-292-8777**	305-594-9117	297-7
Alpine Helen/White County Convention & Visitors Bureau						
726 Bruckenstrasse PO Box 730	Helen	GA	30545	**800-858-8027**	706-878-2181	206
Alpine Lodge						
434 Indian Creek Cir	Branson	MO	65616	**888-563-4388**	417-338-2514	703
Alpine Lumber Co						
10170 Church Ranch Way Ste 350	Westminster	CO	80021	**800-499-1634**	303-451-8001	191-3
Alpine Meats						
9850 Lowr Sacramento Rd	Stockton	CA	95210	**800-399-6328**	209-477-2691	471
Alpine Packaging Inc						
4000 Crooked Run Rd	North Versailles	PA	15137	**844-682-2361**	412-664-4000	623
Alpine Power Systems						
24355 Capitol	Redford	MI	48239	**877-993-8855**		754
Alpine Resort						
7715 Alpine Rd PO Box 200	Egg Harbor	WI	54209	**888-281-8128**	920-868-3000	665
Alpine Solutions Inc						
3222 Corte Malpaso Ste 203-206	Camarillo	CA	93012	**855-388-1883**	805-388-1699	381
Alpine Testing Inc						
51 W Ctr St Ste 514	Orem	UT	84057	**844-625-7463**		244
Alro Steel Corp						
3100 E High St	Jackson	MI	49204	**800-877-2576**	517-787-5500	490
ALS (Albany Law School of Union University)						
80 New Scotland Ave	Albany	NY	12208	**800-448-3500**	518-445-2311	167-1
ALSAC (American Lebanese Syrian Associated Charities)						
262 Danny Thomas Pl	Memphis	TN	38105	**800-822-6344**	901-578-2000	48-5
ALSC (Association for Library Service to Children)						
50 E Huron St	Chicago	IL	60611	**800-545-2433**	312-280-2163	49-11
Alsco Inc						
3370 W 1820 S	Salt Lake City	UT	84104	**800-408-0208**	801-973-7771	782
Alsea Bay Historic Interpretive Ctr						
725 Summer St NE Ste C	Salem	OR	97301	**800-551-6949**		561
Alt 1037						
4131 N Central Expy Ste 1000	Dallas	TX	75204	**877-787-1037**	214-525-7000	641-30
ALTA (American Land Title Assn)						
1800 M St NW Ste 300S	Washington	DC	20036	**800-787-2582**	202-296-3671	49-10
Alta Dena Dairy						
17851 E Railrd	City of Industry	CA	91748	**800-535-1369***		296-27
*Orders						
Alta Equipment Co						
28775 Beck Rd	Wixom	MI	48393	**800-261-9642**		357
Alta Lodge PO Box 8040	Alta	UT	84092	**800-707-2582***	801-742-3500	665
*Cust Svc						
Alta Resources						
120 N Commercial St	Neenah	WI	54956	**877-464-2582**		732
Alta Ski Lifts Co						
Alta Ski Area Hwy 210 Little Cottonwood Canyon	Alta	UT	84092	**800-453-8488**	801-359-1078	450
Alta Via Consulting LLC						
525 Tanasi Cir	Loudon	TN	37774	**877-258-2842**		177
Alta-Fab Structures Ltd						
1205-5th St	Nisku	AB	T9E7L6	**800-252-7990**	780-955-7733	774
Altair Engineering Inc						
1820 E Big Beaver Rd	Troy	MI	48083	**888-222-7822**	248-614-2400	194
Altamaha Electric Membership Corp						
611 W Liberty Ave PO Box 346	Lyons	GA	30436	**800-822-4563**	912-526-8181	245
Altamed Health Services Corp						
4650 W Sunset Blvd M/S 76	Los Angeles	CA	90027	**877-462-2582**	323-669-2113	362
Altametrics						
3191 Red Hill Ave Ste 100	Costa Mesa	CA	92626	**800-676-1281**		174
Altamont Commuter Express (ACE)						
949 E Ch St	Stockton	CA	95202	**800-411-7245**		466
Altapacific Technology Group Inc						
1525 E Shaw Ave Ste 201	Fresno	CA	93710	**800-659-3655**	559-439-5700	225
Altavista Wealth Management Inc						
4 Vanderbilt Park Dr Ste 310	Asheville	NC	28803	**866-684-2600**		
Altec Aluminum Technologies						
Bldg 242 America Pl	Jeffersonville	IN	47130	**800-922-9692**		483
Altech Services Inc						
695 US Rt 46W Ste 301B	Fairfield	NJ	07004	**888-725-8324**		177
Alten Construction						
1141 Marina Way S	Richmond	CA	94804	**800-360-6397**	510-234-4200	186
Altep Inc						
7450 Remcon Cir	El Paso	TX	79912	**800-263-0940**	915-533-8722	177
Alter Trading Corp						
700 Office Pkwy	Saint Louis	MO	63141	**888-337-2727**	314-872-2400	682
Altera Corp						
101 Innovation Dr	San Jose	CA	95134	**800-767-3753***	408-544-7000	692
NASDAQ: ALTR ■ *Cust Svc						
Altera Payroll Inc						
2400 Northside Crossing	Macon	GA	31210	**877-474-6060**	478-477-6060	2
Alternative Apparel Inc						
1650 Indian Brook Way Bldg 200	Norcross	GA	30093	**877-747-2915**	678-380-1890	
Althoff Industries Inc						
8001 S Rt 31	Crystal Lake	IL	60014	**800-225-2443**	815-455-7000	189-10
Altierus Career College						
14555 Potomac Mills Rd	Woodbridge	VA	22192	**833-692-4264**	571-408-2100	795
Brandon						
3924 Coconut Palm Dr	Tampa	FL	33619	**888-223-8556***	813-621-0041	795
*Cust Svc						
Orange Park						
805 Wells Rd	Orange Park	FL	32073	**888-223-8556**	904-264-9122	795
Thornton						
9065 Grant St	Thornton	CO	80229	**888-223-8556**	303-457-2757	795
Altieurs career college						
100 Forbes Ave Ste 1200	Pittsburgh	PA	15222	**800-603-2870**	412-261-4520	795
Tampa						
3319 W Hillsborough Ave	Tampa	FL	33614	**888-223-8556**	813-879-6000	795
AltiGen Communications Inc						
410 E Plumeria Dr	San Jose	CA	95134	**888-258-4436**	408-597-9000	730
OTC: ATGN						
Altimate Medical Inc						
262 West First St	Morton	MN	56270	**800-342-8968**	507-697-6393	474
Altium Inc						
4225 Executive Sq Level 7	La Jolla	CA	92037	**800-544-4186***	858-864-1500	178-5
*Sales						
Altius Broadband Inc						
3314 Papermill Rd Ste 100	Phoenix	MD	21131	**800-864-6546**	410-667-1638	224
Altman Weil Inc						
PO Box 625	Newtown Square	PA	19073	**866-886-3600**	610-359-9900	194
Altmeyer Home Stores Inc						
6515 Rt 22	Delmont	PA	15626	**800-394-6628**	724-468-3434	361
Alton National Cemetery						
600 Pearl St	Alton	IL	62003	**800-535-1117**	314-845-8320	136
Alton Regional Convention & Visitors Bureau (ARCVB)						
200 Piasa St	Alton	IL	62002	**800-258-6645**	618-465-6676	206
Altoona Mirror						
301 Cayuga Ave	Altoona	PA	16602	**800-222-1962**	814-946-7411	528-2
Altoona Regional Health System Altoona Hospital						
620 Howard Ave	Altoona	PA	16601	**877-855-8152**	814-889-2011	373-3
Altoona VA Medical Ctr						
2907 Pleasant Vly Blvd	Altoona	PA	16602	**877-626-2500**		373-8
Alto-Shaam Inc						
W 164 N 9221 Water St PO Box 450	Menomonee Falls	WI	53052	**800-329-8744**	262-251-3800	298
Altria Group Inc						
6601 W Broad St	Richmond	VA	23230	**800-627-5200**	804-274-2200	185
NYSE: MO						
Altru Hospital						
1200 S Columbia Rd	Grand Forks	ND	58201	**800-732-4277**	701-780-5000	373-3
Aluchem Inc						
1 Landy Ln	Cincinnati	OH	45215	**800-336-8519**	513-733-8519	485
Alumaweld Boats Inc						
1601 Ave F	White City	OR	97503	**800-401-2628**	541-826-7171	90
Alumicor Ltd						
290 Humberline Dr	Toronto	ON	M9W5S2	**877-258-6426**	416-745-4222	479
Aluminum & Stainless Inc						
PO Box 3484	Lafayette	LA	70502	**800-252-9074**	337-837-4381	490
Aluminum Distributing						
2930 SW Second Ave	Fort Lauderdale	FL	33315	**866-825-9271**	954-523-6474	490
Aluminum Ladder Co						
1430 W Darlington St	Florence	SC	29501	**800-752-2526**	843-662-2595	485
Aluminum Line Products Co						
24460 Sperry Cir	Westlake	OH	44145	**800-321-3154**	440-835-8880	693
Aluminum Precision Products Inc						
3333 W Warner St	Santa Ana	CA	92704	**800-411-8983**	714-546-8125	481
Alumni Center, The						
1241 University Dr N	Fargo	ND	58102	**800-279-8971**	701-231-6800	667
Alutiiq LLC						
3909 Arctic Blvd Ste 500	Anchorage	AK	99503	**800-829-8547**	907-222-9500	359-3
Alva-Amco Pharmacal Cos Inc						
7711 Merrimac Ave	Niles	IL	60714	**800-792-2582**	847-663-0700	578
Alvah Bushnell Co						
519 E Chelten Ave	Philadelphia	PA	19144	**800-255-7434**	800-814-7296	556
Alvarado Hospital Medical Ctr						
6655 Alvarado Rd	San Diego	CA	92120	**800-258-2723**	619-287-3270	373-3
Alvarado Mfg Company Inc						
12660 Colony St	Chino	CA	91710	**800-423-4143**	909-591-8431	489
Alvernia College						
540 Upland Ave	Reading	PA	19611	**888-258-3764**	610-796-8200	166
Alverno College						
PO Box 343922	Milwaukee	WI	53234	**800-933-3401**	414-382-6100	166
Alvin & Company Inc						
1335 Blue Hills Ave	Bloomfield	CT	06002	**800-444-2584**	860-243-8991	43
Alvin Hollis & Co						
1 Hollis St	South Weymouth	MA	02190	**800-649-5090**	781-335-2100	316
Alyeska Prince Hotel & Resort						
1000 Arlberg Ave PO Box 249	Girdwood	AK	99587	**800-880-3880**	907-754-1111	665
Alzheimer's Assn						
225 N Michigan Ave 1st Fl	Chicago	IL	60601	**800-272-3900**	312-335-8700	48-17
AM 880 KIXI						
3650 131st Ave SE Ste 550	Bellevue	WA	98006	**866-880-5494**	425-562-8964	641
AM Best Co Ambest Rd	Oldwick	NJ	08858	**800-424-2378**	908-439-2200	633-10
A-M Systems Inc						
131 Business Park Loop	Sequim	WA	98382	**800-426-1306**	360-683-8300	475
AM Technical Solutions Inc						
2213 RR 620 N Ste 105	Austin	TX	78734	**888-729-1548**		392
AMA (American Marketing Assn)						
311 S Wacker Dr Ste 5800	Chicago	IL	60606	**800-262-1150**	312-542-9000	49-18

Name / Address	Toll-Free	Phone	Class
AMA (American Medical Assn) 515 N State St ... Chicago IL 60610	800-621-8335	312-464-5000	49-8
AMA (American Motorcyclist Assn) 13515 Yarmouth Dr ... Pickerington OH 43147	800-262-5646	614-856-1900	48-22
AMA (Academy of Model Aeronautics) 5161 E Memorial Dr ... Muncie IN 47302	800-435-9262		48-18
AMACO (American Art Clay Co) 6060 Guion Rd ... Indianapolis IN 46254	800-374-1600	317-244-6871	43
Amada America Inc 7025 Firestone Blvd ... Buena Park CA 90621	800-626-6612	714-739-2111	454
Amadeus North America Inc 3470 NW 82nd Ave Ste 1000 ... Miami FL 33122	888-262-3387	305-499-6000	334
Amador County 810 Ct St ... Jackson CA 95642	800-775-9772	209-223-6470	337
AMAG Technology Inc 20701 Manhattan Pl ... Torrance CA 90501	800-889-9138	310-518-2380	688
Amalgamated Bank of New York 275 Seventh Ave ... New York NY 10001	800-662-0860		70
Amalgamated Life 333 Westchester Ave ... White Plains NY 10604	866-975-4089	914-367-5000	
Amalgamated Transit Union (ATU) 10000 New Hampshire Ave ... Silver Spring MD 20903	888-240-1196	202-537-1645	413
Amana Appliances Inc 2800 220th Trl ... Amana IA 52204 *Cust Svc	800-843-0304*	319-622-5511	15
Amana Colonies 622 46th Ave ... Amana IA 52203	800-579-2294	319-622-7622	10-3
Amangani Resort 1535 NE Butte Rd ... Jackson WY 83001	877-734-7333	307-734-7333	665
Amano Cincinnati Inc 140 Harrison Ave ... Roseland NJ 07068	800-526-2559	973-403-1900	111
Amarillo College 2201 S Washington St ... Amarillo TX 79109	800-227-8784	806-371-5000	162
Amarillo Convention & Visitor Council 1000 S Polk St ... Amarillo TX 79101	800-692-1338		206
Amarillo Economic Development Corp 801 S Fillmore Ste 205 ... Amarillo TX 79101	800-333-7892	806-379-6411	461
Amarillo Globe News PO Box 2091 ... Amarillo TX 79166	800-692-4052	806-376-4488	528-2
Amarillo National Bank 410 S Taylor St ... Amarillo TX 79101	800-253-1031	806-378-8000	70
Amarillo Wind Machine Co 20513 Ave 256 ... Exeter CA 93221	800-311-4498	559-592-4256	273
Amatech Inc 1160 Grimm Dr ... Erie PA 16501	800-403-6920		
Amateur Athletic Union of the US (AAU) 1910 Hotel Plaza Blvd ... Lake Buena Vista FL 32830	800-228-4872	407-934-7200	48-22
Amateur Trapshooting Assn (ATA) 601 W National Rd ... Vandalia OH 45377	800-671-8042	937-898-4638	48-22
Amatex Corp 1032 Stambridge St ... Norristown PA 19404	800-441-9680	610-277-6100	740-3
AmaWaterways 26010 Mureau Rd ... Calabasas CA 91302	800-626-0126		755
Amax Engineering Corp 1565 Reliance Way ... Fremont CA 94539 *Cust Svc	800-889-2629*	510-651-8886	173-2
Amazing Mail-print Ctr 2130 S Seventh Ave Ste 170 ... Phoenix AZ 85007	888-681-1214		5
Amazing Recycled Products Inc PO Box 312 ... Denver CO 80201	800-241-2174		657
Amazoncom Inc 1200 12th Ave S Ste 1200 ... Seattle WA 98144 NASDAQ: AMZN ■ *Cust Svc	800-201-7575*	206-266-1000	95
AMB Financial Corp 8230 Hohman Ave ... Munster IN 46321 OTC: AMFC	800-436-5113	219-836-5870	359-2
AMBAC Assurance Corp 1 State St Plz ... New York NY 10004	800-221-1854	212-658-7470	390-5
AMBAC Financial Group Inc 1 State St Plz ... New York NY 10004 NASDAQ: AMBC	800-221-1854	212-668-0340	359-4
AMBAC International Inc 910 Spears Creek Ct ... Elgin SC 29045	800-628-6894		60
Amber Lotus Publishing PO Box 11329 ... Portland OR 97211	800-326-2375	503-284-6400	130
AMBEST Inc 5115 Maryland Way ... Brentwood TN 37027	800-910-7220	615-371-5187	324
Ambit Energy LP 1801 N Lamar St Ste 200 ... Dallas TX 75202	877-282-6248		782
Ambius Plants 485 E Half Day Rd ... Buffalo Grove IL 60089	800-581-9946		
Amboy Bancorp 3590 US Hwy 9 S ... Old Bridge NJ 08857	800-942-6269	732-591-8700	359-2
Amboy National Bank 3590 US Hwy 9 S ... Old Bridge NJ 08857	800-942-6269	732-591-8700	70
Ambriola Company Inc 7 Patton Dr ... West Caldwell NJ 07006	800-962-8224		297-4
Ambrose Printing Co 210 Cumberland Bend ... Nashville TN 37228	800-334-6524	615-256-1151	623
Ambrosia House Tropical Lodging 622 Fleming St ... Key West FL 33040	800-535-9838	305-296-9838	378
AMBS 3003 Benham Ave ... Elkhart IN 46517	800-964-2627	574-295-3726	167-3
Ambush Boarding Co 1690 Roberts Blvd NW Ste 105 ... Kennesaw GA 30144	800-408-9945	770-420-9111	
AMC (Augusta Medical Ctr) 78 Medical Ctr Dr PO Box 1000 ... Fishersville VA 22939	800-932-0262	540-932-4000	373-3
AMC (Appalachian Mountain Club) 5 Joy St ... Boston MA 02108 *Orders	800-262-4455*	617-523-0655	48-13
AMC Theatres PO Box 725489 ... Atlanta GA 31139	888-440-4262		743
Amcest Nationwide Monitoring 1017 Walnut St ... Roselle NJ 07203	800-631-7370		196
AmChel Communications Inc 1703 Martinez Ln ... Wylie TX 75098	866-388-6959	972-442-1030	478
AMCI 5353 Grosvenor Blvd ... Los Angeles CA 90066	855-486-5527		7
Amcom Software Inc 10400 Yellow Cir Dr ... Eden Prairie MN 55343	800-852-8935	952-230-5200	178-7
AMCON Distributing Co 7405 Irvington Rd ... Omaha NE 68122 NYSE: DIT	888-201-5997	402-331-3727	751
AMCP (Academy of Managed Care Pharmacy) 100 N Pitt St Ste 400 ... Alexandria VA 22314	800-827-2627	703-683-8416	49-8
AMD (Advanced Micro Devices Inc) 1 AMD PI PO Box 3453 ... Sunnyvale CA 94088 NYSE: AMD	800-538-8450	408-749-4000	692
AMD Industries Inc 4620 W 19th St ... Cicero IL 60804	800-367-9999	708-863-8900	233
AMDA (American Medical Directors Assn) 10500 Little Patuxent Pkwy Ste 210 ... Columbia MD 21044	800-876-2632	410-740-9743	49-8
AME Inc 2467 Coltharp Rd PO Box 909 ... Fort Mill SC 29716	800-849-7766	803-548-7766	188-6
AME Label Corp 25155 W Ave Stanford ... Valencia CA 91355	866-278-9268	661-257-2200	412
Amedica Corp 1885 West 2100 South ... Salt Lake City UT 84119	855-839-3500		250
Amedisys 209 Tenth Ave S Ste 512 ... Nashville TN 37203	800-464-0020	423-587-9484	370
Amedisys Inc 5959 S Sherwood Forest Blvd ... Baton Rouge LA 70816 NASDAQ: AMED	800-464-0020	225-292-2031	351
Amegy Bank of Texas 4400 Post Oak Pkwy ... Houston TX 77027	800-287-0301	713-235-8800	70
Amelia Island Plantation 39 Beach Lagoon Rd ... Amelia Island FL 32034	800-834-4900	904-261-6161	665
Amelicor 1525 W 820 N ... Provo UT 84601	800-992-1344		178-11
Amendia Inc 1755 W Oak Pkwy ... Marietta GA 30062	877-755-3329		473
AmerCable Inc 350 Bailey Rd ... El Dorado AR 71730	800-643-1516	870-862-4919	808
Ameren Corp 1901 Chouteau Ave ... Saint Louis MO 63103 NYSE: AEE	800-552-7583	314-621-3222	359-5
Ameresco Canada Inc 90 Sheppard Ave E ... North York ON M2N3A1	888-483-7267	416-512-7700	464
Ameresco Inc 111 Speen St Ste 410 ... Framingham MA 01701	866-263-7372	508-661-2200	192
Amcrex Corp 7595 Gadsden Hwy ... Trussville AL 35173	800-654-5980	205-655-3271	
America First Credit Union 1344 W 4675 S ... Ogden UT 84405	800-999-3961	801-627-0900	219
America II Electronics Inc 2600 118th Ave N ... Saint Petersburg FL 33716	800-767-2637	727-573-0900	246
America Outdoors 5816 Kingston Pk ... Knoxville TN 37919	800-524-4814		48-23
America's Blood Centers (ABC) 725 15th St NW Ste 700 ... Washington DC 20005	888-872-5663	202-393-5725	49-8
America's Call Center Inc 7901 Baymeadows Way Ste 14 ... Jacksonville FL 32256	800-598-2580	904-224-2000	732
America's Car-Mart Inc 802 Southeast Plaza Ave Ste 200 ... Bentonville AR 72712 NASDAQ: CRMT	866-819-9944		
America's Community Bankers (ACB) 1120 Connecticut Ave NW ... Washington DC 20036	800-226-5377		49-2
America's Ctr Convention Ctr 701 Convention Plz Ste 300 ... Saint Louis MO 63101	800-325-7962	314-342-5036	205
America's Second Harvest 35 E Wacker Dr Ste 2000 ... Chicago IL 60601	800-771-2303		48-5
Americall 1502 Tacoma Ave S ... Tacoma WA 98402	800-964-3556	253-272-4111	41
American Academy McAllister Institute of Funeral Service 619 W 54th St 2nd Fl ... New York NY 10019	866-932-2264	212-757-1190	795
American Academy of Addiction Psychiatry (AAAP) 400 Massasoit Ave 2nd Fl Ste 307 ... East Providence RI 02914	800-263-6317	401-524-3076	49-15
American Academy of Art 332 S Michigan Ave ... Chicago IL 60604	888-461-0600	312-461-0600	164
American Academy of Audiology (AAA) 11730 Plaza America Dr Ste 300 ... Reston VA 20190	800-222-2336	703-226-1032	49-8
American Academy of Child & Adolescent Psychiatry (AACAP) 3615 Wisconsin Ave NW ... Washington DC 20016	800-333-7636	202-966-7300	49-15
American Academy of Cosmetic Dentistry (AACD) 402 W Wilson St ... Madison WI 53703	800-543-9220	608-222-8583	49-8
American Academy of Dermatology (AAD) 9500 W Bryn Mawr Ave Ste 500 ... Rosemont IL 60018	888-462-3376		49-8
American Academy of Dramatic Arts 120 Madison Ave ... New York NY 10016	800-463-8990		164
American Academy of Family Physicians (AAFP) 11400 Tomahawk Creek Pkwy ... Leawood KS 66211	800-274-2237	913-906-6000	49-8
American Academy of Neurology (AAN) 1080 Montreal Ave ... Saint Paul MN 55116	800-879-1960	651-695-1940	49-8
American Academy of Nurse Practitioners (AANP) PO Box 12846 ... Austin TX 78711	800-981-2491	512-442-4262	49-8
American Academy of Ophthalmology 655 Beach St ... San Francisco CA 94109	866-561-8558	415-561-8500	49-8
American Academy of Orthopaedic Surgeons (AAOS) 6300 N River Rd ... Rosemont IL 60018	800-346-2267	847-823-7186	49-8
American Academy of Otolaryngology-Head & Neck Surgery (AAO-HNS) 1650 Diagonal Rd ... Alexandria VA 22314	877-722-6467	703-836-4444	49-8
American Academy of Pediatrics (AAP) 141 NW Pt Blvd ... Elk Grove Village IL 60007	800-433-9016	847-434-4000	49-8
American Academy of Periodontology (AAP) 737 N Michigan Ave Ste 800 ... Chicago IL 60611	800-282-4867	312-787-5518	49-8
American Academy of Psychiatry & the Law (AAPL) 1 Regency Dr PO Box 30 ... Bloomfield CT 06002	800-331-1389	860-242-5450	49-15
American Accounts & Advisers PO Box 250 ... Cottage Grove MN 55016	866-714-0489	651-287-6100	160
American Achievement Corp 7211 Cir S Rd ... Austin TX 78745	800-531-5055	512-444-0571	408
American Advisors Group 3800 W Chapman Ave 3rd Fl ... Orange CA 92868	866-948-0003		215

	Toll-Free	Phone	Class
American Aerospace Controls Inc			
570 Smith St ....Farmingdale NY 11735	**888-873-8559**	631-694-5100	256
American AgCredit (ACA)			
PO Box 1120 ....Santa Rosa CA 95402	**800-800-4865**	707-545-1200	216
American Agriculturist			
5227-B Baltimore Pk ....Littlestown PA 17340	**800-441-1410**	717-359-0150	455-1
American Air Charter Inc			
577 Bell Ave ....Chesterfield MO 63005	**888-532-2710**	636-532-2707	13
American Airlines Employees Federal Credit Union			
4151 Amon Carter Blvd ....Fort Worth TX 76155	**800-533-0035**	817-952-4500	219
American Airlines Inc			
4333 Amon Carter Blvd ....Fort Worth TX 76155	**800-433-7300**	817-963-1234	25
American Ambulance Assn (AAA)			
8400 Westpark Dr 2nd Fl ....McLean VA 22102	**800-523-4447**	703-610-9018	49-21
American Amicable Life Insurance Co			
PO Box 2549 ....Waco TX 76702	**800-736-7311**	254-297-2777	390-2
American Angus Assn (AAA)			
3201 Frederick Ave ....Saint Joseph MO 64506	**800-821-5478**	816-383-5100	48-2
American Animal Hospital Assn (AAHA)			
12575 W Bayaud Ave ....Lakewood CO 80228	**800-252-2242**	303-986-2800	48-3
American Anti-Slavery Group, The			
198 Tremont St ....Boston MA 02116	**800-884-0719**	617-426-8161	48-5
American Apparel & Footwear Assn (AAFA)			
740 sixth St NW 3rd & 4th Fl ....Washington DC 20001	**800-520-2262**	202-853-9080	49-4
American Apparel LLC			
747 Warehouse St ....Los Angeles CA 90021	**888-747-0070**	213-488-0226	155-11
American Art Clay Co (AMACO)			
6060 Guion Rd ....Indianapolis IN 46254	**800-374-1600**	317-244-6871	43
American Artstone Co			
2025 N Broadway St ....New Ulm MN 56073	**800-967-2076**	507-233-3700	183
American Assn for Accreditation of Ambulatory Surgery Facilities Inc (AAAASF)			
5101 Washington St Ste 2F			
PO Box 9500. ....Gurnee IL 60031	**888-545-5222**	847-775-1985	48-1
American Assn for Cancer Research (AACR)			
615 Chestnut St 17th Fl ....Philadelphia PA 19106	**866-423-3965**	215-440-9300	49-8
American Assn for Clinical Chemistry Inc (AACC)			
1850 K St NW Ste 625 ....Washington DC 20006	**800-892-1400***	202-857-0717	49-19
*Cust Svc			
American Assn for Justice (AAJ)			
777 Sixth St NW Ste 200 ....Washington DC 20001	**800-424-2725**	202-965-3500	49-10
American Assn for Justice PAC			
777 Sixth St NW Ste 200 ....Washington DC 20001	**800-622-1791**	202-965-3500	611
American Assn for Thoracic Surgery (AATS)			
800 Cummings Ctr Ste 350-V ....Beverly MA 01915	**800-424-5249**	978-252-2200	49-8
American Assn of Acupuncture & Oriental Medicine (AAAOM)			
PO Box 162340 ....Sacramento CA 95816	**866-455-7999**	916-443-4770	48-17
American Assn of Colleges of Osteopathic Medicine (AACOM)			
5550 Friendship Blvd			
Ste 310 ....Chevy Chase MD 20815	**800-356-7836**	301-968-4100	49-8
American Assn of Critical-Care Nurses (AACN)			
101 Columbia ....Aliso Viejo CA 92656	**800-809-2273**	949-362-2000	49-8
American Assn of Daily Money Managers (AADMM)			
174 Crestview Dr ....Bellefonte PA 16823	**877-326-5991**		49-2
American Assn of Endodontists (AAE)			
211 E Chicago Ave Ste 1100 ....Chicago IL 60611	**800-872-3636**	312-266-7255	49-8
American Assn of Engineering Societies (AAES)			
1801 Alexander Bell Dr ....Reston VA 20191	**888-400-2237***	202-296-2237	49-19
*Orders			
American Assn of Equine Practitioners (AAEP)			
4075 Iron Works Pkwy ....Lexington KY 40511	**800-443-0177**	859-233-0147	48-3
American Assn of Family & Consumer Sciences (AAFCS)			
400 N Columbus St Ste 202 ....Alexandria VA 22314	**800-424-8080**	703-706-4600	49-5
American Assn of Franchisees & Dealers (AAFD)			
PO Box 10158 ....Palm Desert CA 92255	**800-733-9858**	619-209-3775	49-18
American Assn of Gynecological Laparoscopists (AAGL)			
6757 Katella Ave ....Cypress CA 90630	**800-554-2245**	714-503-6200	49-8
American Assn of Individual Investors (AAII)			
625 N Michigan Ave Ste 1900 ....Chicago IL 60611	**800-428-2244**	312-280-0170	49-2
American Assn of Insurance Services Inc (AAIS)			
701 Warrenville Rd Ste 100 ....Lisle IL 60532	**800-564-2247**	630-681-8347	49-9
American Assn of Medical Assistants (AAMA)			
20 N Wacker Dr Ste 1575 ....Chicago IL 60606	**800-228-2262**	312-899-1500	49-8
American Assn of Medical Review Officers (AAMRO)			
PO Box 12873 ....Research Triangle Park NC 27709	**800-489-1839**	919-489-5407	49-8
American Assn of Motor Vehicle Administrators (AAMVA)			
4301 Wilson Blvd Ste 400 ....Arlington VA 22203	**800-221-9253**	703-522-4200	49-7
American Assn of Museums (AAM)			
1575 Eye St NW Ste 400...........Washington DC 20005	**866-226-2150**	202-289-1818	48-4
American Assn of Naturopathic Physicians (AANP)			
818 18th St Ste 250 ....Washington DC 20006	**866-538-2267**	202-237-8150	48-17
American Assn of Neurological Surgeons (AANS)			
5550 Meadowbrook Dr ....Rolling Meadows IL 60008	**888-566-2267**	847-378-0500	49-8
American Assn of Neuromuscular & Electrodiagnostic Medicine (AANEM)			
2621 Superior Dr NW ....Rochester MN 55901	**844-347-3277**	507-288-0100	49-8
American Assn of Neuroscience Nurses (AANN)			
4700 West Lake Ave ....Glenview IL 60025	**888-557-2266**	847-375-4733	49-8
American Assn of Nurse Anesthetists (AANA)			
222 S Prospect Ave ....Park Ridge IL 60068	**855-526-2262**	847-692-7050	49-8
American Assn of Oral & Maxillofacial Surgeons (AAOMS)			
9700 W Bryn Mawr Ave ....Rosemont IL 60018	**800-822-6637**	847-678-6200	49-8
American Assn of Orthodontists (AAO)			
401 N Lindbergh Blvd ....Saint Louis MO 63141	**800-424-2841**	314-993-1700	49-8
American Assn of Orthodontists PAC			
401 N Lindbergh Blvd ....Saint Louis MO 63141	**800-424-2841**	314-993-1700	611
American Assn of Pharmaceutical Scientists (AAPS)			
2107 Wilson Blvd Ste 700 ....Arlington VA 22201	**877-998-2277**	703-243-2800	49-19
American Assn of Physics Teachers (AAPT)			
1 Physics Ellipse ....College Park MD 20740	**800-446-8923**	301-209-3311	49-5
American Assn of Poison Control Centers (AAPCC)			
3201 New Mexico Ave Ste 310.......Washington DC 20016	**800-222-1222**		49-8
American Assn of School Administrators (AASA)			
801 N Quincy St Ste 700 ....Arlington VA 22203	**800-771-1162**	703-528-0700	49-5
American Assn of School Librarians (AASL)			
50 E Huron St ....Chicago IL 60611	**800-545-2433**	312-280-4386	49-11
American Assn of State Colleges & Universities (AASCU)			
1307 New York Ave NW 5th Fl ....Washington DC 20005	**800-558-3417**	202-293-7070	49-5
American Assn of Teachers of German (AATG)			
112 Haddontowne Ct Ste 104.......Cherry Hill NJ 08034	**800-835-6770**	856-795-5553	49-5
American Assn of University Professors (AAUP)			
1133 Nineteenth St Ste 200 ....Washington DC 20036	**800-424-2973**	202-737-5900	49-5
American Assn of University Women (AAUW)			
1111 16th St NW ....Washington DC 20036	**800-326-2289**	202-785-7700	49-5
American Assn on Intellectual & Developmental Disabilities (AAIDD)			
444 N Capitol St NW Ste 846 ....Washington DC 20001	**800-424-3688**	202-387-1968	48-17
American Association for Homecare			
2011 Crystal Dr Ste 725 ....Arlington VA 22202	**800-988-4484**	703-836-6263	49-8
American Association of Bioanalysts (AAB)			
906 Olive St Ste 1200..........Saint Louis MO 63101	**800-457-3332**	314-241-1445	49-8
American Association of Collegiate Registrars & Admissions Officers (AACRAO)			
1 Dupont Cir NW Ste 520.........Washington DC 20036	**800-222-4922**	202-293-9161	49-5
American Association of Drugless Practitioners (AADP)			
2200 Market St Ste 803 ....Galveston TX 77550	**888-764-2237**	409-621-2600	48-17
American Association of Nurse Anesthetists PAC (AANAPAC)			
222 S Prospect Ave ....Park Ridge IL 60068	**855-526-2262**	847-692-7050	611
American Association of Petroleum Geologists (AAPG)			
1444 S Boulder Ave PO Box 979 ....Tulsa OK 74119	**800-364-2274**	918-584-2555	48-12
American Athletic Inc (AAI)			
200 American Ave ....Jefferson IA 50129	**800-247-3978**		345
American Augers Inc			
135 US Rt 42 ....West Salem OH 44287	**800-324-4930**	419-869-7107	57
American Autoimmune Related Disease Assn (AARDA)			
22100 Gratiot Ave ....Eastpointe MI 48021	**800-598-4668**	586-776-3900	48-17
American Backflow Specialties			
3940 Home Ave ....San Diego CA 92105	**800-662-5356**	619-527-2525	608
American Baler Co			
800 E Centre St ....Bellevue OH 44811	**800-843-7512**	419-483-5790	385
American Banker Magazine			
1 State St Plz 27th Fl ....New York NY 10004	**800-221-1809**	212-803-8200	455-5
American Bankers Assn (ABA)			
1120 Connecticut Ave NW ....Washington DC 20036	**800-226-5377***		49-2
*Cust Svc			
American Bankers Assn PAC (ABAPAC)			
1120 Connecticut Ave NW ....Washington DC 20036	**800-226-5377**		611
American Baptist Assn (ABA)			
4605 N State Line Ave ....Texarkana TX 75503	**800-264-2482**	903-792-2783	48-20
American Baptist Churches USA			
PO Box 851 ....Valley Forge PA 19482	**800-222-3872**	610-768-2000	48-20
American Baptist News Service			
PO Box 851 ....Valley Forge PA 19482	**800-222-3872**	610-768-2000	526
American Bar Assn (ABA)			
321 N Clark St ....Chicago IL 60654	**800-285-2221**	312-988-5000	49-10
American Battlefield Trust			
Civil War Trust, The			
1156 15th St NW Ste 900. ....Washington DC 20005	**888-606-1400**	202-367-1861	48-13
American Behavioral Benefits Managers			
2204 Lakeshore Dr Ste 135 ....Birmingham AL 35209	**800-925-5327**	205-871-7814	460
American Benefits Council			
1501 M St NW Ste 600...........Washington DC 20005	**877-829-5500**	202-289-6700	49-2
American Bicycle Assn (ABA)			
1645 W Sunrise Blvd ....Gilbert AZ 85233	**866-650-4867**	480-961-1903	48-22
American Biltrite Inc Tape Products Div (ABI)			
105 Whittendale Dr ....Moorestown NJ 08057	**888-224-6325**	856-778-0700	727
American Bio Medica Corp (ABMC)			
122 Smith Rd ....Kinderhook NY 12106	**800-227-1243***	518-758-8158	85
OTC: ABMC ■ *General			
American Biologics			
1180 Walnut Ave ....Chula Vista CA 91911	**800-227-4473**	619-429-8200	418
American Board of Internal Medicine (ABIM)			
510 Walnut St Ste 1700 ....Philadelphia PA 19106	**800-441-2246**	215-446-3590	48-1
American Boiler Manufacturers Assn (ABMA)			
8221 Old Courthouse Rd Ste 380.........Vienna VA 22182	**800-227-1966**	703-356-7172	49-13
American Bolt & Screw Manufacturing Corp			
14650 Miller Ave Ste 200...........Fontana CA 92336	**800-325-0844**	909-390-0522	349
American Booksellers Assn (ABA)			
333 Westchester Ave			
Ste S202................White Plains NY 10604	**800-637-0037**		49-18
American Borate Corp			
5700 Cleveland St			
Ste 350.................Virginia Beach VA 23462	**800-486-1072**	757-490-2242	501-1
American Botanical Council			
6200 Manor Rd ....Austin TX 78723	**800-373-7105**	512-926-4900	48-17
American Brain Tumor Assn (ABTA)			
2720 River Rd ....Des Plaines IL 60018	**800-886-2282**	847-827-9910	48-17
American Brass Manufacturing Co			
5000 Superior Ave ....Cleveland OH 44103	**800-431-6440**	216-431-6565	605
American Buckskin Registry Assn Inc (ABRA)			
1141 Hartnell Ave ....Redding CA 96002	**800-458-4283**	530-223-1420	48-3
American Buildings Co			
1150 State Docks Rd ....Eufaula AL 36027	**888-307-4338**	334-687-2032	105
American Bullion Inc			
12301 Wilshire Blvd Ste 650 .....Los Angeles CA 90025	**800-326-9598**	800-465-3472	787
American Bus Association			
111 K St NE 9th Fl ....Washington DC 20002	**800-283-2877**	202-842-1645	611
American Business Systems Inc			
315 Littleton Rd ....Chelmsford MA 01824	**800-356-4034**		178-1
American Business Women's Assn (ABWA)			
11050 Roe Ave Ste 200 ....Overland Park KS 66211	**800-228-0007**		49-12
American Camp Assn (ACA)			
5000 State Rd 67 N ....Martinsville IN 46151	**800-428-2267**	765-342-8456	48-23
American Cancer Society (ACS)			
250 William St NW ....Atlanta GA 30303	**800-227-2345**	404-315-1123	48-17
American Cancer Society Hope Lodge of Buffalo			
250 Williams St NW ....Atlanta GA 30303	**800-227-2345**		
American Cancer Society Hope Lodge of Charleston			
269 Calhoun St ....Charleston SC 29401	**800-227-2345**	843-958-0930	371
American Cancer Society Joe Lee Griffin Hope Lodge			
1104 Ireland Way ....Birmingham AL 35205	**800-227-2345**	205-558-7860	371
American Cancer Society Winn-Dixie Hope Lodge			
250 Williams St NW ....Atlanta GA 30303	**800-227-2345**	404-327-9200	371
American Canoe Assn (ACA)			
503 Sophia St Ste 100 ....Fredericksburg VA 22401	**888-229-3792**	540-907-4460	48-22
American Capital Group Inc			
23382 Mill Creek Dr			
Ste 115.................Laguna Hills CA 92653	**877-814-6871**	949-271-5800	787
American Capital Partners LLC			
205 Oser Ave ....Hauppauge NY 11788	**800-393-0493**	631-851-0918	400

	Toll-Free	Phone	Class
American Career College Inc 151 Innovation Dr . . . . . Irvine CA 92617	877-832-0790		166
American Cast Iron Pipe Co (ACIPCO) 1501 31st Ave N . . . . . Birmingham AL 35207	800-442-2347	205-325-7701	307
American Casting & Manufacturing Corp 51 Commercial St . . . . . Plainview NY 11803	800-342-0333	516-349-7010	326
American Century Investments Inc PO Box 419200 . . . . . Kansas City MO 64141	800-345-2021	816-531-5575	400
American Century Proprietary Holdings Inc PO Box 419200 . . . . . Kansas City MO 64141	800-345-2021	816-531-5575	524
American Ceramic Society (ACerS) 600 N Cleveland Ave Ste 210 . . . . . Westerville OH 43082	866-721-3322	614-890-4700	48-4
American Chamber of Commerce Executives (ACCE) 4875 Eisenhower Ave Ste 250 . . . . . Alexandria VA 22304	800-394-2223	703-998-0072	49-12
American Chemical Society (ACS) 1155 16th St NW . . . . . Washington DC 20036	800-227-5558	202-872-4600	49-19
American Chiropractic Assn (ACA) 1701 Clarendon Blvd Ste 200 . . . . . Arlington VA 22209	800-986-4636	703-276-8800	49-8
American Chiropractor, The 8619 NW 68th St . . . . . Miami FL 33166	888-369-1396		526
American Chrome Co 518 W Crossroads Pkwy . . . . . Bolingbrook IL 60440	800-562-4488	630-685-2200	490
American Chronic Pain Assn (ACPA) PO Box 850 . . . . . Rocklin CA 95677	800-533-3231		48-17
American Cinematographer Magazine 1782 N Orange Dr . . . . . Los Angeles CA 90028	800-448-0145	323-969-4333	455-9
American Civil Liberties Union (ACLU) 125 Broad St 18th Fl . . . . . New York NY 10004	877-867-1025	212-549-2500	48-8
American Clay Enterprises LLC 2418 Second St SW . . . . . Albuquerque NM 87102	866-404-1634	505-243-5300	501-6
American Cleaning Solutions 39-30 Review Ave PO Box 1943 . . . . . Long Island NY 11101	888-929-7587	718-392-8080	151
American Club, The 419 Highland Dr . . . . . Kohler WI 53044	800-344-2838	920-457-8000	665
American Coach Limousine 1100 Jorie Blvd Ste 314 . . . . . Oak Brook IL 60523	888-709-5466	630-629-0001	440
American Coalition for Fathers & Children (ACFC) 1718 M St NW Ste 1187 . . . . . Washington DC 20036	800-978-3237		48-6
American College 270 S Bryn Mawr Ave . . . . . Bryn Mawr PA 19010	888-263-7265	610-526-1000	795
American College of Cardiology (ACC) 2400 N St NW . . . . . Washington DC 20037 *Cust Svc	800-253-4636*	202-375-6000	49-8
American College of Chest Physicians (ACCP) 3300 Dundee Rd . . . . . Northbrook IL 60062	800-343-2227	847-498-1400	49-8
American College of Emergency Physicians (ACEP) 1125 Executive Cir PO Box 619911 . . . . . Dallas TX 75261	800-798-1822	972-550-0911	49-8
American College of Eye Surgeons/American Board of Eye Surgery (ACES) 334 E Lake Rd Ste 135 . . . . . Palm Harbor FL 34685	800-223-2233	727-366-1487	49-8
American College of Foot & Ankle Surgeons (ACFAS) 8725 W Higgins Rd Ste 555 . . . . . Chicago IL 60631	800-421-2237	773-693-9300	49-8
American College of Nurse-Midwives (ACNM) 8403 Colesville Rd Ste 1550 . . . . . Silver Spring MD 20910	800-468-3571	240-485-1800	49-8
American College of Osteopathic Family Physicians (ACOFP) 330 E Algonquin Rd Ste 1 . . . . . Arlington Heights IL 60005	800-323-0794	847-952-5100	49-8
American College of Physician Executives (ACPE) 400 N Ashley Dr Ste 400 . . . . . Tampa FL 33602	800-562-8088	813-287-2000	49-8
American College of Physicians (ACP) 190 N Independence Mall W . . . . . Philadelphia PA 19106	800-523-1546	215-351-2400	49-8
American College of Radiology (ACR) 1891 Preston White Dr . . . . . Reston VA 20191	800-227-5463	703-648-8900	49-8
American College of Surgeons (ACS) 633 N St Clair St . . . . . Chicago IL 60611	800-621-4111	312-202-5000	49-8
American Commerce Insurance Co 3590 Twin Creeks Dr . . . . . Columbus OH 43204	800-848-2945	614-308-3366	390-4
American Commercial Barge Lines Inc 1701 E Market St . . . . . Jeffersonville IN 47130	800-457-6377		314
American Concrete Pavement Assn (ACPA) 5420 Old OrchaRd Rd Ste A-100 . . . . . Skokie IL 60077	800-281-7899	847-966-2272	49-3
American Contract Bridge League (ACBL) 6575 Windchase Blvd . . . . . Horn Lake MS 38637 *Sales	800-264-2743*	662-253-3100	48-18
American Correctional Assn (ACA) 206 N Washington St Ste 200 . . . . . Alexandria VA 22314	800-222-5646	703-224-0000	49-7
American Cotton Growers Textile Div (ACG) PO Box 2827 . . . . . Lubbock TX 79408	800-333-8011	806-763-8011	740-1
American Council of Engineering Cos (ACEC) 1015 15th St NW 8th Fl . . . . . Washington DC 20005	800-338-1391	202-347-7474	49-19
American Council of Independent Laboratories (ACIL) 1875 I St NW Ste 500 . . . . . Washington DC 20006	800-368-1131	202-887-5872	49-19
American Council of the Blind (ACB) 2200 Wilson Blvd Ste 650 . . . . . Arlington VA 22201	800-424-8666	202-467-5081	48-11
American Council on Exercise (ACE) 4851 Paramount Dr . . . . . San Diego CA 92123	800-825-3636	858-576-6500	48-17
American Council on Science & Health (ACSH) 110 E 42nd St Ste 1300 . . . . . New York NY 10017	866-905-2694	212-362-7044	49-19
American Counseling Assn (ACA) 5999 Stevenson Ave . . . . . Alexandria VA 22304	800-347-6647	703-823-9800	49-15
American Craft Council 1224 Marshall St Ste 200 . . . . . Minneapolis MN 55413	800-836-3470	612-206-3100	48-4
American Crane & Equipment Corp 531 Old Swede Rd . . . . . Douglassville PA 19518	877-877-6778	610-385-6061	468
American Cruise Lines 741 Boston Post Rd Ste 200 . . . . . Guilford CT 06437	800-814-6880	203-453-8885	221
American Culinary Federation Inc (ACF) 180 Ctr Pl Way . . . . . Saint Augustine FL 32095	800-624-9458	904-824-4468	49-6
American Dairy Science Assn (ADSA) 1111 N Dunlap Ave . . . . . Savoy IL 61874	888-670-2250	217-356-5146	48-2
American Dehydrated Foods Inc 3801 E Sunshine . . . . . Springfield MO 65809	800-456-3447	417-881-7755	615
American Dental Assistants Assn (ADAA) 140 N Bloomingdale Rd . . . . . Bloomingdale IL 60108	877-874-3785	312-541-1550	49-8
American Dental Assn (ADA) 211 E Chicago Ave . . . . . Chicago IL 60611	800-621-8099	312-440-2500	49-8

	Toll-Free	Phone	Class
American Dental Assn 1111 14th St NW Ste 1100 . . . . . Washington DC 20005	800-353-2237	202-898-2424	611
American Dental Education Assn (ADEA) 1400 K St NW Ste 1100 . . . . . Washington DC 20005	800-353-2237	202-289-7201	49-5
American Dental Hygienists' Assn (ADHA) 444 N Michigan Ave Ste 3400 . . . . . Chicago IL 60611	800-243-2342	312-440-8900	49-8
American Dental Partners Inc 401 Edgewater Pl Ste 430 . . . . . Wakefield MA 01880	800-838-6563	781-213-6500	461
American Diabetes Assn (ADA) 1701 N Beauregard St . . . . . Alexandria VA 22311	800-232-3472	703-549-1500	48-17
American Diabetes Association Inc 2451 Crystal Dr Ste 900 . . . . . Arlington VA 22202	800-342-2383	800-806-7801	455-16
American Douglas Metals Inc 783 Thorpe Rd . . . . . Orlando FL 32824	800-428-0023	407-855-6590	490
American Drill Bushings Co (ADB) 5740 Hunt Rd . . . . . Valdosta GA 31606	800-423-4425	229-253-8928	491
American Eagle Federal Credit Union 417 Main St . . . . . East Hartford CT 06118	800-842-0145	860-568-2020	219
American Eagle Outfitters Inc 77 Hot Metal St . . . . . Pittsburgh PA 15203 *NYSE: AEO* ■ *Cust Svc	888-232-4535*	412-432-3300	157-4
American Ecotech LLC 100 Elm St Factory D . . . . . Warren RI 02885	877-247-0403		196
American Educational Products Inc 401 Hickory St PO Box 2121 . . . . . Fort Collins CO 80522	800-289-9299	970-484-7445	243
American Educational Research Assn (AERA) 1430 K St NW Ste 1200 . . . . . Washington DC 20005	800-893-7950	202-238-3200	49-5
American Educator Magazine 555 New Jersey Ave NW . . . . . Washington DC 20001	800-238-1133	202-879-4400	455-8
American Egg Board (AEB) 8755 W Higgins Rd Ste 300 . . . . . Chicago IL 60631	888-549-2140	847-296-7043	48-2
American Electric Power Company Inc 1 Riverside Plz . . . . . Columbus OH 43215 *NYSE: AEP* ■ *Cust Svc	800-277-2177*	614-716-1000	359-5
American Electronic Components 1101 Lafayette St . . . . . Elkhart IN 46516	888-847-6552	574-295-6330	247
American Engineering Testing Inc 550 Cleveland Ave N . . . . . Saint Paul MN 55114	800-972-6364	651-659-9001	261
American Enterprise Institute for Public Policy Research (AEI) 1789 Massachusetts Ave NW . . . . . Washington DC 20036	800-862-5801	202-862-5800	630
American Environmental Container Corp 2302 Lasso Ln . . . . . Lakeland FL 33801	800-535-7946	863-666-3020	100
American Epilepsy Society (AES) 342 N Main St . . . . . West Hartford CT 06117	888-233-2334	860-586-7505	48-17
American Equity Investment Life Insurance Co 6000 Westown Pkwy . . . . . West Des Moines IA 50266	888-221-1234	515-221-0002	390-2
American Excelsior Co 850 Ave H E . . . . . Arlington TX 76011	800-777-7645		597
American Exchange Bank (AEB) 510 W Main St PO Box 818 . . . . . Henryetta OK 74437	888-652-3321	918-652-3321	70
American Express Company Inc World Financial Ctr 200 Vesey St . . . . . New York NY 10285 *NYSE: AXP*	800-528-4800	212-640-2000	215
American Exteriors LLC 7100 E Belleview Ave Ste 210 . . . . . Littleton CO 80111	800-794-6369	208-424-7757	235
American Family Association 107 Parkgate Dr . . . . . Tupelo MS 38801	800-326-4543	662-844-5036	640
American Family Care 3700 Cahaba Beach Rd . . . . . Birmingham AL 35242	833-361-4643	800-258-7535	351
American Family Insurance 6000 American Pkwy . . . . . Madison WI 53783	800-692-6326		390-2
American Family Life Assurance Co PAC (AFLAC PAC) 1932 Wynnton Rd . . . . . Columbus GA 31999 *NYSE: AFL* ■ *Cust Svc	800-992-3522*	706-323-3431	611
American Family Life Assurance Company of Columbus (AFLAC) 1932 Wynnton Rd . . . . . Columbus GA 31999 *Cust Svc	800-992-3522*	706-323-3431	390-2
American Family Mutual Insurance Co 6000 American Pkwy . . . . . Madison WI 53783 *Cust Svc	800-374-0008*	800-692-6326	390-2
American Fan Company Inc 2933 Symmes Rd . . . . . Fairfield OH 45014	866-771-6266	513-874-2400	18
American Farm Bureau Federation 600 Maryland Ave SW Ste 1000-W . . . . . Washington DC 20024	800-327-6287	202-406-3600	48-2
American Farmland Trust (AFT) 1200 18th St . . . . . Washington DC 20036	800-431-1499	202-331-7300	48-2
American Faucet & Coating Corp 3280 Corporate Vw . . . . . Vista CA 92081	800-621-8383	760-598-5895	608
American Federation for Aging Research (AFAR) 55 W 39th St 16th Fl . . . . . New York NY 10018	888-582-2327	212-703-9977	49-8
American Federation of Astrologers (AFA) 6535 S Rural Rd . . . . . Tempe AZ 85283	888-301-7630	480-838-1751	48-18
American Federation of Government Employees 80 F St NW . . . . . Washington DC 20001	888-844-2343	202-737-8700	413
American Federation of Musicians of the US & Canada (AFM) 1501 Broadway Ste 600 . . . . . New York NY 10036	800-762-3444	212-869-1330	413
American Federation of Television & Radio Artists (AFTRA) 260 Madison Ave 7th Fl . . . . . New York NY 10016	800-638-6796	212-532-0800	413
American Fence Association (AFA) 6404 Internationa Pkwy Ste 2250-A . . . . . Plano TX 75093	800-822-4342		49-3
American Fence Inc 2502 N 27th Ave . . . . . Phoenix AZ 85009	888-691-4565	602-272-2333	191-2
American Fidelity Assurance Co PO Box 268886 . . . . . Oklahoma City OK 73126	800-662-1113		359-4
American Film Institute (AFI) 2021 N Western Ave . . . . . Los Angeles CA 90027	866-234-3378	323-856-7600	48-4
American Finance Assn (AFA) 101 Station Landing350 Main St Ste 300 . . . . . Medford MA 02155	800-835-6770	781-388-8599	49-2
American Fitness Magazine 1750 E Northrop Blvd Ste 200 . . . . . Chandler AZ 85286	800-446-2322		455-13
American Floor Products Company Inc 7977 Cessna Ave . . . . . Gaithersburg MD 20879	800-342-0424		291
American Folklore Society (AFS) 800 E Third St . . . . . Bloomington IN 47405	866-315-9403	812-856-2379	48-14
American Foods Group Inc 544 Acme St . . . . . Green Bay WI 54302	800-345-0293	920-437-6330	471

Name / Address	City	State	ZIP	Toll-Free	Phone	Class
American Football Coaches Assn (AFCA) 100 Legends Ln	Waco	TX	76706	877-557-5338	254-754-9900	48-22
American Foreign Service Assn (AFSA) 2101 E St NW	Washington	DC	20037	800-704-2372	202-338-4045	49-7
American Forest & Paper Assn (AF&PA) 1111 19th St NW Ste 800	Washington	DC	20036	800-878-8878	202-463-2700	48-2
American Forest Foundation (AFF) 2000 M St NW Ste 550	Washington	DC	20036	800-325-2954	202-765-3660	48-2
American Foundation for Suicide Prevention (AFSP) 120 Wall St 29th Fl	New York	NY	10005	888-333-2377	212-363-3500	48-17
American Foundation for the Blind (AFB) 1401 S Clark St Ste 730	Arlington	VA	22202	800-232-5463	212-502-7600	48-17
American Foundry Society (AFS) 1695 N Penny Ln	Schaumburg	IL	60173	800-537-4237	847-824-0181	49-13
American Freight Ohio Inc 2770 Lexington Ave	Mansfield	OH	44904	800-420-2337	419-884-2224	321
American Friends Service Committee (AFSC) 1501 Cherry St	Philadelphia	PA	19102	800-621-4000	215-241-7000	48-5
American Furniture Warehouse Co 8501 Grant St	Thornton	CO	80229	888-615-9415	303-289-3300	321
American Galvanizers Assn (AGA) 6881 S Holly Cir Ste 108	Centennial	CO	80112	800-468-7732	720-554-0900	49-13
American Gaming & Electronics 556 W Taylor Rd	Romeoville	IL	60446	800-727-6807	815-886-1447	322
American Gastroenterological Assn (AGA) 4930 Del Ray Ave	Bethesda	MD	20814	800-227-7888	301-654-2055	49-8
American Gem Society (AGS) 8881 W Sahara Ave	Las Vegas	NV	89117	866-805-6500	702-255-6500	49-4
American Gem Trade Assn (AGTA) 3030 LBJ Fwy Ste 840	Dallas	TX	75234	800-972-1162	214-742-4367	49-4
American Geophysical Union (AGU) 2000 Florida Ave NW	Washington	DC	20009	800-966-2481	202-462-6900	49-19
American Girl Inc 8400 Fairway Pl *Orders	Middleton	WI	53562	800-845-0005*		757
American Golf Corp 2951 28th St	Santa Monica	CA	90405	800-238-7267	310-664-4000	651
American Granby Inc 7652 Morgan Rd	Liverpool	NY	13090	800-776-2266	315-451-1100	608
American Greetings Corp 1 American Rd *NYSE: AM* ■ *Sales	Cleveland	OH	44144	800-777-4891*	216-252-7300	130
American Grinding & Machine Co 2000 N Mango Ave	Chicago	IL	60639	877-988-4343	773-889-4343	452
American Group Psychotherapy Assn (AGPA) 25 E 21st St 6th Fl	New York	NY	10010	877-668-2472	212-477-2677	49-15
American Guard Services Inc 1299 E Artesia Blvd	Carson	CA	90746	800-662-7372	310-645-6200	399
American Guild of Musical Artists (AGMA) 1430 Broadway 14th Fl	New York	NY	10018	800-543-2462	212-265-3687	48-4
American Guild of Organists (AGO) 475 Riverside Dr Ste 1260	New York	NY	10115	855-631-0759	212-870-2310	48-4
American Guild of Variety Artists (AGVA) 363 Seventh Ave 17th Fl	New York	NY	10001	800-331-0890	212-675-1003	48-4
American Gypsum 3811 Turtle Creek Blvd Ste 1200	Dallas	TX	75219	866-439-5800	214-530-5500	346
American Health Assoc 671 Ohio Pk Ste K	Cincinnati	OH	45245	800-522-7556		414
American Health Care Assn (AHCA) 1201 L St NW	Washington	DC	20005	800-321-0343	202-842-4444	49-8
American Health Information Management Assn (AHIMA) 233 N Michigan Ave 21st Fl	Chicago	IL	60601	800-335-5535	312-233-1100	49-8
American Healthcare Radiology Administrators (AHRA) 490-B Boston Post Rd Ste 200	Sudbury	MA	01776	800-334-2472	978-443-7591	49-8
American Heart Assn (AHA) 7272 Greenville Ave	Dallas	TX	75231	800-242-8721	214-373-6300	48-17
American Hellenic Educational Progressive Assn (AHEPA) 1909 Q St NW Ste 500	Washington	DC	20009	855-473-3512	202-232-6300	48-14
American Herbal Products Assn (AHPA) 8630 Fenton St Ste 918	Silver Spring	MD	20910	800-358-2104	301-588-1171	49-8
American Highway Users Alliance 1920 L St NW Ste 525	Washington	DC	20036	800-388-0650	202-857-1200	49-21
American Hiking Society (AHS) 8605 Second Ave	Silver Spring	MD	20910	800-972-8608	301-565-6704	48-23
American Holistic Nurses Assn (AHNA) 2900 SW Plass Ct	Topeka	KS	66611	800-278-2462	785-234-1712	48-17
American Home Base Inc PO Box 2430 *General	Pensacola	FL	32513	800-549-0595*	850-857-0860	732
American Home Furnishings 3535 Menaul Blvd NE	Albuquerque	NM	87107	800-854-6755	505-883-2211	321
American Home Shield 150 Peabody Pl	Memphis	TN	38102	888-682-1043	901-537-8000	366
American Homeowners Association (AHA) 3001 Summer St	Stamford	CT	06905	800-470-2242	203-323-7715	
American Homeowners Foundation (AHF) 6776 Little Falls Rd	Arlington	VA	22213	800-489-7776		
American HomePatient Inc 5200 Maryland Way Ste 400	Brentwood	TN	37027	800-890-7271	615-221-8884	362
American Honda Motor Company Inc 1919 Torrance Blvd	Torrance	CA	90501	800-999-1009	310-783-3170	59
American Horse Council (AHC) 1616 H St NW 7th Fl	Washington	DC	20006	800-443-0177	202-296-4031	48-3
American Horticultural Society (AHS) 7931 E Blvd Dr	Alexandria	VA	22308	800-777-7931	703-768-5700	48-18
American Hose & Rubber Co Inc 3645 E 44th St	Tucson	AZ	85713	800-272-7537	520-514-1666	369
American Hospital Assn (AHA) 155 N Wacker Dr	Chicago	IL	60606	800-424-4301	312-422-3000	49-8
American Hospital Assn PAC (AHAPAC) 325 Seventh St NW	Washington	DC	20004	800-424-4301	202-638-1100	611
American Hotel Register Co 100 S Milwaukee Ave	Vernon Hills	IL	60061	800-323-5686	847-743-3000	555
American Humane Assn (AHA) 63 Inverness Dr E	Englewood	CO	80112	800-227-4645		48-6
American Immigration Lawyers Assn (AILA) 918 F St NW	Washington	DC	20004	800-982-2839	202-216-2400	49-10
American Income Life Insurance Co (AIL) 1200 Wooded Acres	Waco	TX	76710	800-433-3405	254-761-6400	390-2
American Indian College Fund 8333 Greenwood Blvd	Denver	CO	80221	800-776-3863	303-426-8900	48-11
American Indian Science & Engineering Society (AISES) 2305 Renard SE Ste 200	Albuquerque	NM	87106	800-759-5219	505-765-1052	49-19
American Institute for Cancer Research 1759 R St NW	Washington	DC	20009	800-843-8114	202-328-7744	664
American Institute for CPCU & Insurance Institute of America (AICPCU/IIA) 720 Providence Rd Ste 100	Malvern	PA	19355	800-644-2101	610-644-2100	49-9
American Institute of Aeronautics & Astronautics Inc (AIAA) 1801 Alexander Bell Dr Ste 500	Reston	VA	20191	800-639-2422	703-264-7500	49-19
American Institute of Architects (AIA) 1735 New York Ave NW *Orders	Washington	DC	20006	800-242-3837*	202-626-7300	48-4
American Institute of Chemical Engineers (AIChE) 120 Wall St 2nd Fl *Cust Svc	New York	NY	10005	800-242-4363*	203-702-7660	49-19
American Institute of CPA's (AICPA) 1211 Ave of the Americas	New York	NY	10036	888-777-7077	212-596-6200	49-1
American Institute of Graphic Arts (AIGA) 164 Fifth Ave	New York	NY	10010	800-548-1634	212-807-1990	48-4
American Institute of Mining Metallurgical & Petroleum Engineers (AIME) 12999 E Adam Aircraft Cir	Englewood	CO	80112	888-702-0049	303-325-5185	48-12
American Institute of Physics 1 Physics Ellipse	College Park	MD	20740	800-892-8259	301-209-3100	49-19
American Institute of Professional Bookkeepers (AIPB) 6001 Montrose Rd Ste 500	Rockville	MD	20852	800-622-0121		49-1
American Institute of Professional Geologists (AIPG) 1400 W 122nd Ave Ste 250	Westminster	CO	80234	800-337-3140	303-412-6205	49-19
American Institute of Ultrasound in Medicine (AIUM) 14750 Sweitzer Ln Ste 100	Laurel	MD	20707	800-638-5352	301-498-4100	49-8
American Institutes for Research 1000 Thomas Jefferson St NW	Washington	DC	20007	877-334-3499	202-403-5000	664
American Intercontinental University 231 N Martingale Rd 6th Fl	Schaumburg	IL	60173	877-221-5800	877-701-3800	166
Atlanta 6600 Peachtree Dunwoody Rd 500 Embassy Row NE	Atlanta	GA	30328	800-491-0182	404-965-6500	166
Dunwoody 6600 Peachtree-Dunwoody Rd 500 Embassy Row	Atlanta	GA	30328	855-377-1888	404-965-6500	166
American InterContinental University Los Angeles 231 N Martingale Rd 6th Fl	Schaumburg	IL	60173	877-701-3800		166
American International Automobile Dealers Assn (AIADA) 500 Montgomery St Ste 800	Alexandria	VA	22314	800-462-4232		49-18
American International College 1000 State St *Admissions	Springfield	MA	01109	800-242-3142*	413-205-3201	166
American International Forest Products LLC (AIFP) 5560 SW 107th Ave	Beaverton	OR	97005	800-366-1611	503-641-1611	191-3
American International Inc 1040 Avendia Acaso	Camarillo	CA	93012	800-336-6500	805-388-6800	253
American Iron Magazine 1010 Summer St *Cust Svc	Stamford	CT	06905	877-693-3572*	203-425-8777	455-3
American Jail Assn (AJA) 1135 Professional Ct	Hagerstown	MD	21740	800-211-2754	301-790-3930	49-7
American Jewish World Service (AJWS) 45 West 36th St	New York	NY	10018	800-889-7146	212-792-2900	48-5
American Journal of Psychiatry 1000 Wilson Blvd Ste 1825	Arlington	VA	22209	800-368-5777	703-907-7300	455-16
American Kidney Fund (AKF) 6110 Executive Blvd Ste 1010	Rockville	MD	20852	800-638-8299		48-17
American Kidney Stone Management Ltd (AKSM) 797 Thomas Ln	Columbus	OH	43214	800-637-5188	614-447-0281	352
American Land Title Assn (ALTA) 1800 M St NW Ste 300S	Washington	DC	20036	800-787-2582	202-296-3671	49-10
American Law Institute (ALI) 4025 Chestnut St	Philadelphia	PA	19104	800-253-6397	215-243-1600	49-10
American Law Label Inc 1677 S Research Loop	Tucson	AZ	85710	888-529-5223		
American Lawyer Media Inc (ALM) 120 Broadway 5th Fl	New York	NY	10271	877-256-2472	212-457-9400	633-9
American Lebanese Syrian Associated Charities (ALSAC) 262 Danny Thomas Pl	Memphis	TN	38105	800-822-6344	901-578-2000	48-5
American Lecithin Company Inc 115 Hurley Rd Unit 2B	Oxford	CT	06478	800-364-4416	203-262-7100	296-29
American LegalNet Inc 16501 Ventura Blvd Ste 615	Encino	CA	91436	800-293-2771	818-817-9225	427
American Legion Auxiliary 8945 N Meridian St Ste 200	Indianapolis	IN	46260	800-504-4098	317-569-4500	48-19
American Legion, The 700 N Pennsylvania St *Cust Svc	Indianapolis	IN	46204	800-433-3318*	317-630-1200	48-19
American Library Assn (ALA) 50 E Huron St	Chicago	IL	60611	800-545-2433	312-944-6780	49-11
American Lighting Assn (ALA) 2050 Stemmons Fwy Ste 10046	Dallas	TX	75207	800-605-4448	214-698-9898	49-4
American Limousines Inc 4401 E Fairmount Ave	Baltimore	MD	21224	800-787-1690	410-522-0400	440
American Liver Foundation (ALF) 39 Broadway	New York	NY	10006	800-465-4837	212-668-1000	48-17
American Locker Security Systems Inc 608 Allen St *Sales	Jamestown	NY	14701	800-828-9118*		688
American Logistics Assn (ALA) 1101 Vermont Ave NW Ste 1002	Washington	DC	20005	800-791-7146	202-466-2520	48-19
American Louver Co 7700 N Austin Ave	Skokie	IL	60077	800-772-0355		438
American Lubrication Equipment Corp 11212A McCormick Rd PO Box 1350	Hunt Valley	MD	21030	888-252-9300	410-252-9300	537
American Lumber Distributors & Brokers Inc 2405 Republic Blvd	Birmingham	AL	35201	800-433-8578		
American Lung Assn (ALA) 14 Wall St	New York	NY	10005	800-586-4872	212-315-8700	48-17
American Marketing Assn (AMA) 311 S Wacker Dr Ste 5800	Chicago	IL	60606	800-262-1150	312-542-9000	49-18

				Toll-Free	Phone	Class
American Marking Systems Inc						
1015 Paulison Ave PO Box 1677	Clifton	NJ	07011	**800-782-6766**	973-478-5600	465
American Massage Therapy Assn (AMTA)						
500 Davis St Ste 900	Evanston	IL	60201	**877-905-2700**	847-864-0123	48-17
American Mathematical Society (AMS)						
201 Charles St	Providence	RI	02904	**800-321-4267***	401-455-4000	49-19
*Cust Svc						
American Medical Assn (AMA)						
515 N State St	Chicago	IL	60610	**800-621-8335**	312-464-5000	49-8
American Medical Assn PAC						
25 Massachusetts Ave NW # 600						
	Washington	DC	20001	**800-621-8335**	312-464-4430	611
American Medical Directors Assn (AMDA)						
10500 Little Patuxent Pkwy						
Ste 210	Columbia	MD	21044	**800-876-2632**	410-740-9743	49-8
American Medical ID						
949 Wakefield Ste 100	Houston	TX	77018	**800-363-5985**		473
American Medical Rehabilitation Providers Assn (AMRPA)						
1710 N St NW	Washington	DC	20036	**888-346-4624**	202-223-1920	49-8
American Medical Response (AMR)						
6200 S Syracuse Way						
Ste 200	Greenwood Village	CO	80111	**877-244-4890**	303-495-1200	30
American Medical Student Assn (AMSA)						
1902 Assn Dr	Reston	VA	20191	**800-767-2266**	703-620-6600	49-5
American Medical Technologists (AMT)						
10700 W Higgins Rd Ste 150	Rosemont	IL	60018	**800-275-1268**	847-823-5169	49-8
American Megatrends Inc (AMI)						
5555 Oakbrook Pkwy Bldg 200	Norcross	GA	30093	**800-828-9264**	770-246-8600	176
American Mensa Ltd						
1229 Corporate Dr W	Arlington	TX	76006	**800-666-3672**	817-607-0060	48-15
American Mental Health Counselors Assn (AMHCA)						
107 S W St Ste 779	Alexandria	VA	22314	**800-326-2642**	703-548-6002	49-15
American Metal Bearing Co						
7191 Acacia Ave	Garden Grove	CA	92841	**800-888-3048**	714-892-5527	616
American Metal Crafters LLC						
695 High St	Middletown	CT	06457	**800-840-9243**	860-343-1960	198
American Metalcraft Inc						
3708 N River Rd Ste 800	Franklin Park	IL	60131	**800-333-9133**	708-345-1177	486
American Meteorological Society (AMS)						
45 Beacon St	Boston	MA	02108	**800-824-0405**	617-227-2425	49-19
American Micro Products Inc						
4288 Armstrong Blvd	Batavia	OH	45103	**800-479-2193**		
American Modern Home Insurance Co						
PO Box 5323	Cincinnati	OH	45201	**800-543-2644**	513-943-7200	390-4
American Moistening Company Inc						
10402 Rodney St	Pineville	NC	28134	**800-948-5540**	704-889-7281	606
American Morgan Horse Assn (AMHA)						
4066 Shelburne Rd Ste 5	Shelburne	VT	05482	**888-436-3700**	802-985-4944	48-3
American Motel Management						
1872 Montreal Rd Ste A	Tucker	GA	30084	**800-580-8258**	770-939-1801	651
American Motorcyclist Assn (AMA)						
13515 Yarmouth Dr	Pickerington	OH	43147	**800-262-5646**	614-856-1900	48-22
American Moving & Storage Assn (AMSA)						
1611 Duke St	Alexandria	VA	22314	**888-849-2672**	703-683-7410	49-21
American Muscle						
7 Lee Blvd	Malvern	PA	19355	**888-332-7930**	610-251-2397	786
American Museum of Fly Fishing						
4104 Main Rd	Manchester	VT	05254	**800-333-1550**	802-362-3300	519
American Musical Supply						
PO Box 152	Spicer	MN	56288	**800-458-4076**	320-796-2088	522
American Musicological Society (AMS)						
6010 College Stn	Brunswick	ME	04011	**888-421-1442**	212-992-6340	48-4
American National Bank						
628 Main St	Danville	VA	24541	**800-240-8190**	434-792-5111	359-2
NASDAQ: AMNB						
American National Bank						
PO Box 2139	Omaha	NE	68103	**800-279-0007***	402-457-1077	70
*Cust Svc						
American National Property & Casualty Co						
1949 E Sunshine St	Springfield	MO	65899	**800-333-2860**	417-887-0220	390-4
American National Red Cross						
Portland Platelet Donation Ctr						
3131 N Vancouver Ave	Portland	OR	97227	**800-733-2767**		416
American National Rubber Co						
Main & High St	Ceredo	WV	25507	**800-624-3410***	304-453-1311	673
*Cust Svc						
American National Standards Institute (ANSI)						
25 W 43rd St 4th fl	New York	NY	10036	**800-374-3818**	212-642-4900	48-1
American Nephrology Nurses Assn (ANNA)						
200 E Holly Ave	Sewell	NJ	08080	**888-600-2662**	856-256-2320	49-8
American Nickeloid Co						
2900 Main St	Peru	IL	61354	**800-645-5643**	815-223-0373	479
American Nuclear Society (ANS)						
555 N Kensington Ave	La Grange Park	IL	60526	**800-323-3044**	708-352-6611	49-19
American Nurses Assn (ANA)						
8515 Georgia Ave Ste 400	Silver Spring	MD	20910	**800-274-4262**	301-628-5000	49-8
American Nurses Assn PAC (ANA PAC)						
8515 Georgia Ave Ste 400	Silver Spring	MD	20910	**800-274-4262**	301-628-5000	611
American Occupational Therapy Assn Inc (AOTA)						
4720 Montgomery Ln						
PO Box 31220	Bethesda	MD	20824	**800-877-1383**	301-652-2682	49-8
American Oil Chemists Society (AOCS)						
2710 S Boulder PO Box 17190	Urbana	IL	61802	**866-535-2730**	217-359-2344	48-12
American Orthodontics Corp						
1714 Cambridge Ave	Sheboygan	WI	53081	**800-558-7687**	920-457-5051	228
American Orthopaedic Society for Sports Medicine (AOSSM)						
9400 W Higgins Rd Ste 300	Rosemont	IL	60018	**877-321-3500**	847-292-4900	49-8
American Osteopathic Assn (AOA)						
142 E Ontario St	Chicago	IL	60611	**800-621-1773**	888-626-9262	49-8
American Outdoor Products Inc						
6350 Gunpark Dr	Boulder	CO	80301	**800-641-0500**		296-37
American Outfitters Ltd						
3700 Sunset Ave	Waukegan	IL	60087	**800-397-6081**	847-623-3959	707
American Packaging Corp						
777 Driving Park Ave	Rochester	NY	14613	**800-551-8801**	585-254-9500	544
American Packing & Gasket Co (APG)						
6039 Armour Dr PO Box 213	Houston	TX	77020	**800-888-5223**	713-675-5271	326
American Panel Corp						
5800 SE 78th St	Ocala	FL	34472	**800-327-3015**	352-245-7055	660
American Paper & Twine Co						
7400 Cockrill Bend Blvd	Nashville	TN	37209	**800-251-2437**	615-350-9000	555
American Park & Recreation Society (APRS)						
22377 Belmont Ridge Rd	Ashburn	VA	20148	**800-765-3110**	703-858-0784	48-23
American Parkinson Disease Assn (APDA)						
135 Parkinson Ave	Staten Island	NY	10305	**800-223-2732**	718-981-8001	48-17
American Pavilion						
1706 Warrington Ave	Danville	IL	61832	**800-424-9699**	217-443-0800	728
American Permanent Ware Inc						
729 Third Ave	Dallas	TX	75226	**800-527-2100**	214-421-7366	298
American Pet Products Manufacturers Assn (APPMA)						
255 Glenville Rd	Greenwich	CT	06831	**800-452-1225**	203-532-0000	49-4
American Pharmacists Assn PAC						
2215 Constitution Ave NW	Washington	DC	20037	**800-237-2742**	202-628-4410	611
American Pharmacists Association						
2215 Constitution Ave NW	Washington	DC	20037	**800-237-2742**	202-628-4410	49-8
American Physical Society (APS)						
1 Physics Ellipse	College Park	MD	20740	**866-918-1164**	301-209-3200	49-19
American Physical Therapy Assn (APTA)						
1111 North Fairfax St	Alexandria	VA	22314	**800-999-2782**	703-684-2782	49-8
American Pipe & Supply Company Inc						
4100 Eastlake Blvd	Birmingham	AL	35217	**800-476-9460**	205-252-9460	
American Plastic Toys Inc						
799 Ladd Rd	Walled Lake	MI	48390	**800-521-7080**	248-624-4881	757
American Playground Corp						
2328 Jefferson St	Anderson	IN	46016	**800-541-1602**	765-642-0288	345
American Pneumatic Tool Inc						
1000 S Grand Ave	Santa Ana	CA	92705	**800-532-7402**	562-204-1555	754
American Podiatric Medical Assn (APMA)						
9312 Old Georgetown Rd	Bethesda	MD	20814	**800-275-2762**	301-581-9200	49-8
American Polarizers Inc						
141 S Seventh St	Reading	PA	19602	**800-736-9031**	610-373-5177	540
American Polywater Corp						
11222 60th St N	Stillwater	MN	55082	**800-328-9384**	651-430-2270	145
American Power Conversion Corp (APC)						
132 Fairgrounds Rd	West Kingston	RI	02892	**800-788-2208***	401-789-5735	253
*Cust Svc						
American Power Pull Corp						
550 W Linfoot St PO Box 109	Wauseon	OH	43567	**800-808-5922**	419-335-7050	468
American Printing House for the Blind						
1839 Frankfort Ave						
PO Box 6085	Louisville	KY	40206	**800-223-1839**	502-895-2405	633-10
American Product Distributors Inc (APD)						
8350 Arrowridge Blvd	Charlotte	NC	28273	**800-049-5842**	704-522-9411	530
American Products LLC						
597 Evergreen Rd	Strafford	MO	65757	**855-736-2135**	417-736-2135	486
American Psychiatric Assn (APA)						
1000 Wilson Blvd Ste 1825	Arlington	VA	22209	**888-357-7924**	703-907-7300	49-15
American Psychiatric Nurses Assn (APNA)						
1555 Wilson Blvd Ste 530	Arlington	VA	22209	**866-243-2443**	703-243-2443	49-8
American Psychiatric Publishing Inc						
1000 Wilson Blvd Ste 1825	Arlington	VA	22209	**800-368-5777**	703-907-7322	633-9
American Psychological Assn (APA)						
750 First St NE	Washington	DC	20002	**800-374-2721**	202-336-5500	49-15
American Public Gas Assn (APGA)						
201 Massachusetts Ave NE						
Ste C-4	Washington	DC	20002	**800-927-4204**	202-464-2742	48-12
American Public Life Insurance Co						
2305 Lakeland Dr PO Box 925	Jackson	MS	39205	**800-256-8606**	601-936-6600	390-5
American Public Works Assn (APWA)						
2345 Grand Blvd Ste 700	Kansas City	MO	64108	**800-848-2792**	816-472-6100	49-7
American Quarter Horse Assn (AQHA)						
1600 Quarter Horse Dr	Amarillo	TX	79104	**800-291-7323**	806-376-4811	48-3
American Rabbit Breeders Assn (ARBA)						
PO Box 5667	Bloomington	IL	61702	**800-753-9448**	309-664-7500	48-3
American Radio Relay League (ARRL)						
225 Main St	Newington	CT	06111	**888-277-5289**	860-594-0200	49-14
American Radiolabeled Chemicals Inc (ARC)						
101 ARC Dr	Saint Louis	MO	63146	**800-331-6661**	314-991-4545	145
American Railcar Industries Inc						
100 Clark St	Saint Charles	MO	63301	**800-489-9888**	636-940-6000	646
NASDAQ: ARII						
American Ramp Sales Co						
601 S Mckinley Ave	Joplin	MO	64801	**800-949-2024**	417-206-6816	295
American Red Ball Transit Company Inc						
PO Box 1127	Indianapolis	IN	46206	**800-733-8139**		516
American Red Cross						
2025 E St NW	Washington	DC	20006	**800-257-7575**	202-303-4498	48-5
American Red Cross In Greater New York (Inc)						
520 W 49th St	New York	NY	10019	**877-733-2767**		351
American Reeling Devices Inc						
15 Airpark Vista Blvd	Dayton	NV	89403	**800-354-7335***		117
*Sales						
American Refugee Committee (ARC)						
430 Oak Grove St Ste 204	Minneapolis	MN	55403	**800-875-7060**	612-872-7060	48-5
American Registry of Diagnostic Medical Sonographers (ARDMS)						
1401 Rockville Pk Ste 600	Rockville	MD	20852	**800-541-9754**	301-738-8401	49-8
American Religious Town Hall Meeting Inc						
PO Box 180118	Dallas	TX	75218	**800-783-9828**	214-328-9828	449
American Renal Assoc Inc						
500 Cummings Ctr Ste 6550	Beverly	MA	01915	**877-997-3625**	978-922-3080	352
American Rental Assn (ARA)						
1900 19th St	Moline	IL	61265	**800-334-2177**	309-764-2475	49-4
American Residential Services LLC						
9010 Maier Rd Ste 105	Laurel	MD	20723	**866-399-2885**	901-271-9700	189-10
American Rifleman Magazine						
11250 Waples Mill Rd	Fairfax	VA	22030	**800-672-3888**		455-20
American River Bankshares						
3100 Zinfandel Dr						
Ste 450	Rancho Cordova	CA	95670	**800-544-0545**		359-2
NASDAQ: AMRB						
American River College						
4700 College Oak Dr	Sacramento	CA	95841	**800-700-4144**	916-484-8011	162
American Rivers						
1101 14th St NW Ste 1400	Washington	DC	20005	**877-347-7550**	202-347-7550	48-13
American Road & Transportation Builders Assn (ARTBA)						
1219 28th St NW	Washington	DC	20007	**800-636-2377**	202-289-4434	49-3
American Road Machinery Inc						
3026 Saratoga Ave	Canton	OH	44706	**844-294-5862**		

Alphabetical Section

Listing	Toll-Free	Phone	Class
American Roentgen Ray Society (ARRS) 44211 Slatestone Ct .... Leesburg VA 20176	800-438-2777	703-729-3353	49-8
American Rose Society (ARS) 8877 Jefferson Paige Rd .... Shreveport LA 71119	800-637-6534		48-18
American Running Assn 4405 E W Hwy Ste 405 .... Bethesda MD 20814	800-776-2732	301-913-9517	48-22
American Saddlebred Museum 4083 Iron Works Pkwy .... Lexington KY 40511	800-829-4438	859-259-2746	517
American Safety Technologies Inc 565 Eagle Rock Ave .... Roseland NJ 07068	800-631-7841		546
American Savings Bank FSB 1001 Bishop St .... Honolulu HI 96813	800-272-2566	808-627-6900	70
American School Counselor Assn (ASCA) 1101 King St Ste 625 .... Alexandria VA 22314	800-306-4722	703-683-2722	49-5
American Scientist Magazine 3106 E NC Hwy 54 PO Box 13975.......... Research Triangle Park NC 27709	800-243-6534	919-549-4691	455-19
American Seating Co 401 American Seating Ctr NW .... Grand Rapids MI 49504 *Cust Svc	800-748-0268*	616-732-6600	319-3
American Seed Trade Assn (ASTA) 1701 Duke St Ste 275............... Alexandria VA 22304	888-890-7333	703-837-8140	48-2
American Shared Hospital Services 4 Embarcadero Ctr Ste 3700...................... San Francisco CA 94111 *NYSE: AMS*	800-735-0641	415-788-5300	264-4
American Shore & Beach Preservation Assn (ASBPA) 5460 Beaujolais Ln .... Fort Myers FL 33919	800-331-1600	239-489-2616	48-13
American Slate Co 1900 Olympic Blvd .... Walnut Creek CA 94596	888-259-4249		
American Sleep Apnea Assn (ASAA) 6856 Eastern Ave NW Ste 203 .... Washington DC 20012	888-293-3650	202-293-3650	48-17
American Society for Adolescent Psychiatry (ASAP) PO Box 3948 .... Parker CO 80134	866-672-9060		
American Society for Aesthetic Plastic Surgery, The (ASAPS) 11262 Monarch St .... Garden Grove CA 92841	800-364-2147	562-799-2356	49-8
American Society for Clinical Pathology (ASCP) 33 W Monroe St Ste 1600 .... Chicago IL 60603 *Cust Svc	800-621-4142*	312-541-4999	49-8
American Society for Colposcopy & Cervical Pathology (ASCCP) 152 W Washington St .... Hagerstown MD 21740	800-787-7227	301-733-3640	49-8
American Society for Dermatologic Surgery (ASDS) 5550 Meadowbrook Dr Ste 120..................... Rolling Meadows IL 60008	800-714-1374	847-956-0900	49-8
American Society for Gastrointestinal Endoscopy (ASGE) 1520 Kensington Rd Ste 202 .... Oak Brook IL 60523	866-353-2743	630-573-0600	49-8
American Society for Horticultural Science (ASHS) 1018 Duke St...................... Alexandria VA 22314	800-331-1600	703-836-4606	48-2
American Society for Laser Medicine & Surgery Inc (ASLMS) 2100 Stewart Ave Ste 240............. Wausau WI 54401	877-258-6028	715-845-9283	49-8
American Society for Microbiology (ASM) 1752 N St NW .... Washington DC 20036	800-546-2416	202-737-3600	49-8
American Society for Nondestructive Testing Inc (ASNT) 1711 Arlingate Ln PO Box 28518...... Columbus OH 43228 *Orders	800-222-2768*	614-274-6003	49-19
American Society for Nutrition (ASNS) 9211 Corporate Blvd Ste 300.......... Rockville MD 20850	800-627-8723	240-428-3650	49-6
American Society for Parenteral & Enteral Nutrition (ASPEN) 8630 Fenton St Ste 412 .... Silver Spring MD 20910	800-727-4567	301-587-6315	49-8
American Society for Quality (ASQ) 600 N Plankinton Ave .... Milwaukee WI 53203	800-248-1946	414-272-8575	49-13
American Society for the Prevention of Cruelty to Animals (ASPCA) 424 E 92nd St .... New York NY 10128	800-582-5979	212-876-7700	48-3
American Society for Therapeutic Radiology & Oncology (ASTRO) 8280 Willow Oaks Corporate Dr Ste 500............................ Fairfax VA 22031	800-962-7876	703-839-7312	49-8
American Society of Agronomy (ASA) 5585 Guilford Rd .... Madison WI 53711	866-359-9161	608-273-8080	48-2
American Society of Appraisers (ASA) 555 Herndon Pkwy Ste 125 .... Herndon VA 20170	800-272-8258	703-478-2228	49-17
American Society of Assn Executives (ASAE) 1575 'I' St NW .... Washington DC 20005	888-950-2723	202-626-2723	49-12
American Society of Cataract & Refractive Surgery (ASCRS) 4000 Legato Rd Ste 700 .... Fairfax VA 22033	877-996-4464	703-591-2220	49-8
American Society of Cinematographers (ASC) 1782 N Orange Dr .... Hollywood CA 90028	800-448-0145	323-969-4333	48-4
American Society of Civil Engineers (ASCE) 1801 Alexander Bell Dr .... Reston VA 20191	800-548-2723	703-295-6300	455-21
American Society of Clinical Hypnosis (ASCH) 140 N Bloomingdale Rd .... Bloomingdale IL 60108	800-227-6963	630-980-4740	49-8
American Society of Clinical Oncology (ASCO) 2318 Mill Rd Ste 800 .... Alexandria VA 22314	888-282-2552	571-483-1300	49-8
American Society of Consultant Pharmacists (ASCP) 1321 Duke St .... Alexandria VA 22314	800-355-2727	703-739-1300	49-8
American Society of Health-System Pharmacists (ASHP) 7272 Wisconsin Ave .... Bethesda MD 20814	866-279-0681	301-664-8700	49-8
American Society of Heating Refrigerating & Air-Conditioning Engineers Inc (ASHRAE) 1791 Tullie Cir NE .... Atlanta GA 30329 *Cust Svc	800-527-4723*	404-636-8400	49-3
American Society of Home Inspectors (ASHI) 932 Lee St Ste 101 .... Des Plaines IL 60016	800-743-2744	847-759-2820	49-3
American Society of International Law, The (ASIL) 2223 Massachusetts Ave NW .... Washington DC 20008	800-828-7571	202-939-6000	49-10
American Society of Landscape Architects (ASLA) 636 'I' St NW .... Washington DC 20001	888-999-2752	202-898-2444	48-2
American Society of Limnology & Oceanography (ASLO) 5400 Bosque Blvd Ste 680................ Waco TX 76710	800-929-2756	254-399-9635	49-19
American Society of Military Comptrollers (ASMC) 415 N Alfred St .... Alexandria VA 22314	800-462-5637	703-549-0360	48-19
American Society of PeriAnesthesia Nurses (ASPAN) 90 Frontage Rd .... Cherry Hill NJ 08034	877-737-9696	856-616-9600	49-8
American Society of Professional Estimators (ASPE) 2525 Perimeter Pl Dr Ste 103.......... Nashville TN 37214	888-378-6283	615-316-9200	49-3
American Society of Radiologic Technologists (ASRT) 15000 Central Ave SE .... Albuquerque NM 87123	800-444-2778	505-298-4500	49-8
American Society of Regional Anesthesia & Pain Medicine (ASRA) 4 Penn Ctr W Ste 401............... Pittsburgh PA 15276	855-795-2772	412-471-2718	49-8
American Society of Travel Agents (ASTA) 675 N Washington St Ste 490......... Alexandria VA 22314	800-275-2782	703-739-2782	48-23
American Society of Travel Agents PAC 675 N Washington St Ste 490......... Alexandria VA 22314	800-275-2782	703-739-2782	611
American Society on Aging (ASA) 575 Market St Ste 2100 .... San Francisco CA 94105	800-537-9728	415-974-9600	48-6
American Sociological Assn (ASA) 1307 New York Ave .... Washington DC 20005	800-524-9400	202-383-9005	49-5
American Software Inc 470 E Paces Ferry Rd .... Atlanta GA 30305 *NASDAQ: AMSWA*	800-726-2946	404-261-4381	178-1
American Solutions for Business 31 E Minnesota Ave E .... Glenwood MN 56334	800-862-3690		530
American Southern Insurance Co 3715 Northside Pkwy NW Bldg 400 Ste 800 .... Atlanta GA 30327	800-241-1172	404-266-9599	390-4
American Soybean Assn (ASA) 12125 Woodcrest Executive Dr Ste 100........................... Saint Louis MO 63141	800-688-7692	314-576-1770	48-2
American Specialty Health Plans 10221 Wateridge Cir .... San Diego CA 92121	800-848-3555		390-3
American Spectator Magazine 933 N Kenmore St Ste 405 .... Arlington VA 22201	800-524-3469	703-807-2011	455-17
American Speech-Language-Hearing Assn (ASHA) 2200 Research Blvd .... Rockville MD 20850	800-498-2071	301-296-5700	49-8
American Spirit 1776 D St NW .... Washington DC 20006	800-449-1776	202-628-1776	455-10
American Spoon Foods Inc 1668 Clarion Ave .... Petoskey MI 49770	800-222-5886	888-735-6700	296-20
American Sports 74 Albe Dr Ste 1 .... Newark DE 19702	866-207-3179		706
American Stair Corp Inc 642 Forestwood Dr .... Romeoville IL 60446	800-872-7824		489
American Standard Cos Inc 1 Centennial Ave .... Piscataway NJ 08855	800-442-1902		359-3
American Standard Insurance Company of Wisconsin 6000 American Pkwy .... Madison WI 53783	800-692-6326	608-249-2111	390-2
American State Bank 1401 Ave Q .... Lubbock TX 79401	800-531-1401	806-767-7000	359-2
American States Water Co 630 E Foothill Blvd .... San Dimas CA 91773 *NYSE: AWR*	800-999-4033	909-394-3600	359-5
American Statistical Assn (ASA) 732 N Washington St............... Alexandria VA 22314	888-231-3473	703-684-1221	49-19
American Strip Steel Inc 901 Coopertown Rd .... Delanco NJ 08075	800-526-1216		490
American Systems Corp 14151 Pk Meadow Dr Ste 500 .... Chantilly VA 20151	800-733-2721	703-968-6300	180
American Tank & Fabricating Co (AT&F) 12314 Elmwood Ave .... Cleveland OH 44111	800-544-5316	216-252-1500	719
American Technology Network Corp 1341 San Mateo Ave .... South San Francisco CA 94080	800-910-2862	650-989-5100	540
American Textile Co 10 N Linden St .... Duquesne PA 15110 *Cust Svc	800-289-2826*	412-948-1020	741
American Theological Library Assn (ATLA) 300 S Wacker Dr Ste 2100 .... Chicago IL 60606	888-665-2852	312-454-5100	48-20
American Thermoplastic Co (ATC) 106 Gamma Dr .... Pittsburgh PA 15238	800-245-6600		86
American Tinnitus Assn (ATA) 522 SW Fifth Ave Ste 825............. Portland OR 97204	800-634-8978	503-248-9985	48-17
American Tire Depot 14407 Alondra Blvd .... La Mirada CA 90638	855-899-3764	562-677-3950	750
American Torch Tip Co 6212 29th St E .... Bradenton FL 34203	800-342-8477		
American Tower Corp 116 Huntington Ave 11th Fl .... Boston MA 02116 *NYSE: AMT*	877-282-7483	617-375-7500	170
American Traffic Safety Services Assn (ATSSA) 15 Riverside Pkwy Ste 100........................ Fredericksburg VA 22406	800-272-8772	540-368-1701	49-21
American Trails PO Box 491797 .... Redding CA 96049	866-363-7226	530-605-4395	48-23
American Trails West (ATW) 92 Middle Neck Rd .... Great Neck NY 11021	800-645-6260	516-487-2800	755
American Trucking Assn (ATA) 950 N Glebe Rd Ste 210............... Arlington VA 22203	800-282-5463	703-838-1700	49-21
American Trust Administrators Inc 7223 W 95th St Ste 301 .... Overland Park KS 66212	800-842-4121	913-378-9938	
American Type Culture Collection (ATCC) 10801 University Blvd PO Box 1549....................... Manassas VA 20108 *Cust Svc	800-638-6597*	703-365-2700	664
American Ultraviolet Co 40 Morristown Rd .... Bernardsville NJ 07924	800-288-9288	908-696-1130	806
American United Life Insurance Co 1 American Sq PO Box 368 .... Indianapolis IN 46206	800-537-6442	317-285-1877	390-2
American Urban Radio Networks 938 Penn Ave Ste 701 .... Pittsburgh PA 15222	800-456-4211	412-456-4099	642
American Urological Assn (AUA) 1000 Corporate Blvd .... Linthicum MD 21090	866-746-4282	410-689-3700	49-8
American Utility Management Inc 2211 S York Rd Ste 320............. Oak Brook IL 60523	866-520-1245		461
American Veterinary Medical Assn (AVMA) 1931 N Meacham Rd Ste 100....... Schaumburg IL 60173	800-248-2862	847-925-8070	49-8
American Veterinary Medical Assn PAC (AVMA) 1910 Sunderland Pl NW .... Washington DC 20036	800-321-1473	202-789-0007	611
American Watchmakers-Clockmakers Institute (AWI) 701 Enterprise Dr.................. Harrison OH 45030	866-367-2924	513-367-9800	49-4
American Water Ski Hall of Fame & Museum 1251 Holy Cow Rd .... Polk City FL 33868	800-533-2972	863-324-2472	519
American Water Works Assn (AWWA) 6666 W Quincy Ave .... Denver CO 80235	800-926-7337	303-794-7711	48-12
American Water Works Co Inc 1025 Laurel Oak Rd .... Voorhees NJ 08043 *NYSE: AWK*	888-282-6816	856-346-8200	359-5
American Welding Society (AWS) 550 NW 42nd Ave .... Miami FL 33126	800-443-9353	305-443-9353	49-3

	Toll-Free	Phone	Class
American Whitewater (AW) PO Box 1540 .... Cullowhee NC 28723	866-262-8429	828-586-1930	48-23
American Wilbert Vault Corp 4415 W Harrison PO Box 7245. .... Hillside IL 60162	800-328-5040	708-366-3210	134
American Window & Glass Inc 2715 Lynch Rd .... Evansville IN 47711	877-671-6943	812-464-9400	604
American Wire Rope & Sling 3122 Engle Rd .... Fort Wayne IN 46809	800-466-7520	866-578-4700	490
American Youth Soccer Organization (AYSO) 19750 S Vermont Ave Ste 200 .... Torrance CA 90502	800-872-2976		48-22
Americana Tickets NY 1535 Broadway .... New York NY 10036	800-833-3121	212-581-6660	745
American-Arab Anti Discrimination Committee (ADC) 1990 M St NW Ste 610. .... Washington DC 20036	800-253-3931	202-244-2990	48-8
AmericanChurch Inc 100 Noll Plz ....Huntington IN 46750	800-446-3035		263
American-International Charolais Assn (AICA) 11700 NW Plaza Cir .... Kansas City MO 64153	800-270-7711	816-464-5977	48-2
Americanna Co 101 Industrial .... Lakeville MA 02347 *Cust Svc	888-747-5550*	508-747-5550	9
Americans for Effective Law Enforcement (AELE) 841 W Touhy Ave ....Park Ridge IL 60068	800-763-2802	847-685-0700	48-8
Americans for Fair Taxation PO Box 4929 .... Clearwater FL 33758	800-324-7829		48-7
Americans for Peace Now (APN) 1101 14th St NW 6th Fl .... Washington DC 20005	877-429-0678	202-728-1893	48-7
Americans United for Separation of Church & State 518 C St NE .... Washington DC 20002	800-875-3707	202-466-3234	48-7
AmeriCares Foundation 88 Hamilton Ave .... Stamford CT 06902	800-486-4357	203-658-9500	48-5
Americas Styrenics LLC 24 Waterway Ave Ste 1200 .... Woodlands TX 77380	844-512-1212	832-616-7800	146
AmericasMart 240 Peachtree St NW Ste 2200. .... Atlanta GA 30303	800-285-6278		205
Americhem Inc 2000 Americhem Way .... Cuyahoga Falls OH 44221	800-228-3476	330-929-4213	143
AmericInn International LLC 250 Lake Dr E ....Chanhassen MN 55317 *Resv	800-634-3444*	952-294-5000	378
Americo Financial Life & Annuity Insurance Co PO Box 410288 ....Kansas City MO 64141	800-231-0801		390-2
Americo Financial Life & Annuity Insurance Co PO Box 410288 ....Kansas City MO 64141	800-231-0001		390-2
AmeriCom Inc PO Box 2146 .... Sandy UT 84091	800-820-6296	801-571-2446	731
Americu Credit Union 1916 Black River Blvd ....Rome NY 13440	866-210-3876		
Ameridial Inc 4535 Strausser St NW ....North Canton OH 44720	800-445-7128		732
Ameridrives 1802 Pittsburgh Ave .... Erie PA 16502	800-352-0141	814-480-5000	616
AmeriFactors 215 Celebration Pl Ste 340. .... Celebration FL 34747	800-884-3863		272
Ameri-Fax Corp 6520 W 20th Ave Unit 2 .... Hialeah FL 33016	800-262-8214	305-828-1701	550
Ameriflight Inc 1515 W 20th St PO Box 612763. ....DFW Airport TX 75261	800-800-4538		12
Ameri-Force Inc 9485 Regency Sq Blvd Ste 300. ....Jacksonville FL 32225	800-522-8998	904-633-9918	
AmeriGas Partners LP 460 N Gulph Rd .... King of Prussia PA 19406 NYSE: APU	800-427-4968	610-337-7000	316
AmeriGas Propane Inc PO Box 965 ....Valley Forge PA 19482	800-934-6802	610-337-7000	575
AMERIgreen Energy Inc 1650 Manheim Pk Ste 201 ....Lancaster PA 17601	888-423-8357	717-945-1392	532
AMERIGROUP Corp 4425 Corporation Ln ....Virginia Beach VA 23462 NYSE: AGP	800-600-4441	757-490-6900	390-3
Ameriguard Security Services Inc 5470 W Spruce Ave Ste 102. ....Fresno CA 93722	866-836-0117	559-271-5984	
AmeriHealth Mercy Health Plan 8040 Carlson Rd Ste 500 .... Harrisburg PA 17112	888-991-7200	717-651-3540	351
Ameril-Co Carriers Inc 1702 E Overland ....Scottsbluff NE 69361	800-445-5400	308-635-3157	775
Amerijet International Inc 2800 S Andrews Ave .... Fort Lauderdale FL 33316	800-927-6059	954-320-5300	12
Amerilist Inc 978 Rt 45 Ste L2. .... Pomona NY 10970	800-457-2899	845-362-6737	317
AmerillumBrands 3728 Maritime Way .... Oceanside CA 92056	800-439-0549	760-727-7675	438
Amerimade Technology Inc 449 Mtn Vista Pkwy .... Livermore CA 94551	800-938-3824	925-243-9090	604
Amerimax Home Products Inc 450 Richardson Dr .... Lancaster PA 17603	800-347-2586		478
Ameripack Inc 107 N Gold Dr ....Robbinsville NJ 08691	800-456-7963	609-259-7004	5
AmeriPride Services Inc 10801 Wayzata Blvd .... Minnetonka MN 55305 *Cust Svc	800-750-4628*	952-738-4200	441
Ameriprise Brokerage 70400 Ameriprise Financial Ctr ....Minneapolis MN 55474	800-535-2001		686
Ameriprise Financial Inc 834 Ameriprise Financial Ctr ....Minneapolis MN 55474 NYSE: AMP	866-673-3673	612-671-3131	400
Ameris Bank 24 Second Ave SE PO Box 3668. ....Moultrie GA 31768	866-616-6020		186
AMERISAFE 2301 Hwy 190 W .... DeRidder LA 70634 NASDAQ: AMSF	800-256-9052	337-463-9052	390-4
Ameriserv Financial 216 Franklin St PO Box 520 .... Johnstown PA 15907 NASDAQ: ASRV	800-837-2265		70
Amerisource Bergen 1300 Morris Dr Ste 100 .... Chesterbrook PA 19087 NYSE: ABC	800-829-3132	610-727-7000	238
Amerispa 100 boul From the Navy Ste 2A .... Varennes QC J3X2B1	866-263-7477		702
AmeriSpan 1500 Walnut St ....Philadelphia PA 19102	800-879-6640	215-751-1100	422
AmeriSpec Inc 3839 Forest Hill Irene Rd .... Memphis TN 38125	877-769-5217		364
Ameristar Casino Hotel Council Bluffs 2200 River Rd .... Council Bluffs IA 51501	866-667-3386	712-328-8888	133
Ameristar Casino Hotel Vicksburg 4116 Washington St .... Vicksburg MS 39180	800-700-7770	601-638-1000	133
Ameristar Fence Products Inc 1555 N Mingo Rd .... Tulsa OK 74116	888-333-3422	918-835-0898	489
Amerisure Insurance Co 26777 Halsted Rd .... Farmington Hills MI 48331	800-257-1900	248-615-9000	390-4
Amerit Fleet Solutions 1331 N California Blvd Ste 150 .... Walnut Creek CA 94596	877-512-6374		
Amerita Inc 7307 S Revere Pky Ste 200. .... Centennial CO 80112	800-360-4755	303-355-4745	362
Ameritas Direct 5900 'O' St .... Lincoln NE 68510	800-555-4655		390-2
Ameritas Life Insurance Corp 5900 'O' St .... Lincoln NE 68510	800-745-1112	402-467-1122	390-2
AmeriTrust Group Inc 26255 American Dr .... Southfield MI 48034 NYSE: MIG	800-482-2726	248-358-1100	359-4
AmeriWater Inc 1303 Stanley Ave .... Dayton OH 45404	800-535-5585	937-461-8833	45
Ameriwood Home 410 E S First St .... Wright City MO 63390 *General	800-489-3351*	636-745-3351	319-2
Amernet 315 Montgomery St .... San Francisco CA 94104	877-616-5100		
Amery Hospital & Clinic 265 Griffin St E .... Amery WI 54001	800-424-5273	715-268-8000	352
Ames 1327 Northbrook Pkwy Ste 400 .... Suwanee GA 30024	800-303-1827		753
Ames Chamber of Commerce 1601 Golden Aspen Dr Ste 110 .... Ames IA 50010	800-288-7470	515-232-2310	139
Ames True Temper Inc 465 Railroad Ave .... Camp Hill PA 17011	800-393-1846		753
Ametco Manufacturing Corp 4326 Hamann Industrial Pky .... Willoughby OH 44094	800-321-7042		486
Ametek HDR Power Systems Inc 3563 Interchange Rd .... Columbus OH 43204	888-797-2685	614-308-5500	253
AMETEK Inc Chemical Products Div 455 Corporate Blvd ....Newark DE 19702 *Orders	800-441-7777*	302-456-4431	740-3
AMETEK Inc Dixson Div 287 27 Rd .... Grand Junction CO 81503	888-302-0639	970-242-8863	493
AMETEK Inc Test & Calibration Instruments Div 8600 Somerset Dr .... Largo FL 33773	800-733-5427	727-538-6132	470
AMETEK National Controls Corp 1725 Western Dr .... West Chicago IL 60185	800-323-2593	630-231-5900	203
AMETEK Power Instruments 255 North Union St ....Rochester NY 14605	800-950-6686	610-647-2121	
AMETEK Sensor Technology Drexelbrook Div 205 Keith Valley Rd .... Horsham PA 19044 *Cust Svc	800-553-9092*	215-674-1234	493
AMETEK Solidstate Controls 875 Dearborn Dr .... Columbus OH 43085	800-635-7300	614-846-7500	253
AMETEKInc 1080 N Crooks .... Clawson MI 48017	800-635-0289	248-435-0700	201
Ameublements Tanguay Inc 7200 Armand-Viau St .... Quebec QC G2C2A7	800-826-4829	418-847-4411	
AMF Bakery Systems 2115 W Laburnum Ave .... Richmond VA 23227	800-225-3771	804-355-7961	207
AMF Bowling Worldwide Inc 7313 Bell Creek Rd ....Mechanicsville VA 23111	800-342-5263		99
Amfed Cos LLC 576 Highland Colony Pkwy .... Ridgeland MS 39157	800-264-8085	601-853-4949	389
AMFM Inc 240 Capitol St Ste 500 ....Charleston WV 25301	800-348-1623	304-344-1623	461
AMG Medical Inc 8505 Dalton .... Montreal QC H4T1V5	800-363-2381	514-737-5251	475
AMG Resources Corp 2 Robinson Plz # 350 .... Pittsburgh PA 15205	877-395-8338	412-777-7300	682
Am-Gard Security Inc 600 Main St .... Pittsburgh PA 15215	800-554-0412		689
Amgen Canada Inc 6775 Financial Dr Ste 100 ... Mississauga ON L5N0A4	800-665-4273	905-285-3000	85
Amgen Inc 1 Amgen Ctr Dr .... Thousand Oaks CA 91320	800-563-9798	805-447-1000	85
Amgraf Inc 1501 Oak St .... Kansas City MO 64108	800-304-4797	816-474-4797	180
AMHA (American Morgan Horse Assn) 4066 Shelburne Rd Ste 5 .... Shelburne VT 05482	888-436-3700	802-985-4944	48-3
AMHCA (American Mental Health Counselors Assn) 107 S W St Ste 770 ....Alexandria VA 22314	800-326-2642	703-548-6002	49-15
Amherst Area Chamber of Commerce 28 Amity St .... Amherst MA 01002	800-593-4052	413-253-0700	139
Amherst College 220 S Pleasant St .... Amherst MA 01002	866-542-4438	413-542-2000	166
AMI (American Megatrends Inc) 5555 Oakbrook Pkwy Bldg 200. .... Norcross GA 30093	800-828-9264	770-246-8600	176
AMI (Associated Materials Inc) 3773 State Rd .... Cuyahoga Falls OH 44223	800-922-6009		693
AMI Bearings Inc 570 N Wheeling Rd ....Mount Prospect IL 60056	800-882-8642	847-759-0620	
AMI Metals Inc 1738 General George Patton Dr .... Brentwood TN 37027	800-727-1903	615-377-0400	490
Amica Mutual Insurance Co 100 Amica Way .... Lincoln RI 02865	800-652-6422		390-4
Amicalola Electric Membership Corp 544 Hwy 515 S .... Jasper GA 30143	800-282-7411	706-253-5200	245

	Toll-Free	Phone	Class

Amick Farms Inc
2079 Batesburg Hwy .... Batesburg SC 29006 — 800-926-4257 — 803-532-1400 — 10-7

AMICO (Alabama Metal Industries Corp)
3245 Fayette Ave .... Birmingham AL 35208 — 800-366-2642 — 205-787-2611 — 489

Amico Corp
85 Fulton Way .... Richmond Hill ON L4B2N4 — 877-462-6426 — 905-764-0800 — 637

Amidon Graphics
1966 Benson Ave .... Saint Paul MN 55116 — 800-328-6502 — 651-690-2401 — 623

Amigos de las Americas
1800 W Loop S Ste 1325 .... Houston TX 77027 — 800-231-7796 — — 48-5

Amigos Library Services
14400 Midway Rd .... Dallas TX 75244 — 800-843-8482 — 972-851-8000 — 386

Aminian Business Services Inc
50 Tesla .... Irvine CA 92618 — 888-800-5207 — 949-724-1155 — 113

Amino Transport Inc
223 NE Loop 820 Ste 101 .... Hurst TX 76053 — 800-304-3360 — — 194

Amivest Capital Management
703 Market St 18th Fl .... San Francisco CA 94103 — 800-541-7774 — — 400

AMJ Campbell International
1445 Courtneypark Dr E .... Mississauga ON L5T2E3 — 800-363-6683 — 905-670-6683 — 314

Ammeraal Beltech USA
7501 N St Louis Ave .... Skokie IL 60076 — 800-323-4170* — 847-673-6720 — 369
*Cust Svc

AMN Healthcare Services Inc
12400 High Bluff Dr Ste 100 .... San Diego CA 92130 — 866-871-8519 — — 717
NYSE: AMN

Amnesty International USA (AIUSA)
5 Penn Plz 16th Fl .... New York NY 10001 — 866-273-4466 — 800-266-3789 — 48-5

AMOA (Amusement & Music Operators Assn)
380 Terra Cotta Rd Ste F .... Crystal Lake IL 60012 — 800-937-2662 — 815-893-6010 — 48-23

AMOA-National Dart Assn (NDA)
10070 W 190th Pl .... Mokena IL 60448 — 800-808-9884 — — 48-22

Amoco Federal Credit Union
PO Box 889 .... Texas City TX 77592 — 800-231-6053 — 409-948-8541 — 219

Amon Carter Museum
3501 Camp Bowie Blvd .... Fort Worth TX 76107 — 800-573-1933 — 817-738-1933 — 517

Amoray Dive Resort Inc
104250 Overseas Hwy .... Key Largo FL 33037 — 800-426-6729 — 305-451-3595 — 703

Amos Press Inc
911 S Vandemark Rd .... Sidney OH 45365 — 866-468-1622 — 937-498-2111 — 633-9

Amos-Hill Assoc Inc
112 Shelby Ave .... Edinburgh IN 46124 — 800-745-1778 — 812-526-2671 — 609

AMP (Applied Measurement Professionals Inc)
18000 W 105th St .... Olathe KS 66061 — 800-345-6559 — 913-895-4600 — 47

AMPAC Fine Chemicals (AFC)
MS 1007 PO Box 1718 .... Rancho Cordova CA 95741 — 800-311-9668 — 916-357-6880 — 145

Ampac Packaging LLC
12025 Tricon Rd .... Cincinnati OH 45246 — 800-543-7030 — 513-671-1777 — 66

Ampac Seed Co
32727 Hwy 99 E .... Tangent OR 97389 — 800-547-3230 — 541-928-1651 — 690

Ampacet Corp
660 White Plains Rd .... Tarrytown NY 10591 — 800-888-4267* — 914-631-6600 — 143
*Cust Svc

Ampco Manufacturers Inc
9 Burbidge St Ste 101 .... Coquitlam BC V3K7B2 — 800-663-5482 — 604-472-3800 — 623

Ampco Metal Inc
1117 E Algonquin Rd .... Arlington Heights IL 60005 — 800-844-6008 — 847-437-6000 — 483

Ampersand Art Supply
1235 S Loop 4 Ste 400 .... Buda TX 78610 — 800-822-1939 — 512-322-0278 — 43

Ampex Data Systems Corp
500 Broadway .... Redwood City CA 94063 — 800-752-7590 — 650-367-2011 — 173-8

Amphastar Pharmaceuticals Inc
11570 Sixth St .... Rancho Cucamonga CA 91730 — 800-423-4136 — 909-980-9484 — 578

Amphenol Aerospace
40-60 Delaware Ave .... Sidney NY 13838 — 800-678-0141 — 607-563-5011 — 253

Amphenol RF
4 Old Newtown Rd .... Danbury CT 06810 — 800-627-7100 — 203-743-9272 — 253

Amphenol Sine Systems
44724 Morley Dr .... Clinton Township MI 48036 — 800-394-7732

Amphenol Spectra-Strip
720 Sherman Ave .... Hamden CT 06514 — 800-846-6400 — 203-281-3200 — 253

AMPI 315 N Broadway .... New Ulm MN 56073 — 800-533-3580 — 507-354-8295 — 297-4

Amplicon Express Inc
2345 NE Hopkins Ct .... Pullman WA 99163 — 877-332-8080 — 509-332-8080 — 738

Amplify Education Inc
55 Washington St Ste 800 .... Brooklyn NY 11201 — 800-823-1969 — 212-213-8177

AmpliVox Sound Systems LLC
3995 Commercial Ave .... Northbrook IL 60062 — 800-267-5486 — 847-498-9000 — 52

Ampronix Inc
15 Whatney .... Irvine CA 92618 — 800-400-7972 — 949-273-8000 — 473

AMR (American Medical Response)
6200 S Syracuse Way Ste 200 .... Greenwood Village CO 80111 — 877-244-4890 — 303-495-1200 — 30

AMR (Advantage Metals Recycling LLC)
510 Walnut St Ste 300 .... Kansas City MO 64106 — 866-527-4733 — 816-861-2700 — 682

AMR Corp
4333 Amon Carter Blvd PO Box 619616 .... Fort Worth TX 76155 — 800-535-5225 — 817-963-1234 — 359-1
OTC: AAL

AmRad Engineering Inc
32 Hargrove Grade .... Palm Coast FL 32137 — 800-445-6033 — 386-445-6000 — 253

AmRent
250 E Broad St .... Columbus OH 43215 — 800-324-3681 — — 631

Amridge University
1200 Taylor Rd .... Montgomery AL 36117 — 888-790-8080 — 334-387-3877 — 166

Amro Music Stores
2918 Poplar Ave .... Memphis TN 38111 — 800-626-2676* — 901-323-8888 — 522
*General

AMRPA (American Medical Rehabilitation Providers Assn)
1710 N St NW .... Washington DC 20036 — 888-346-4624 — 202-223-1920 — 49-8

AMS (American Musicological Society)
6010 College Stn .... Brunswick ME 04011 — 888-421-1442 — 212-992-6340 — 48-4

AMS (American Mathematical Society)
201 Charles St .... Providence RI 02904 — 800-321-4267* — 401-455-4000 — 49-19
*Cust Svc

AMS (American Meteorological Society)
45 Beacon St .... Boston MA 02108 — 800-824-0405 — 617-227-2425 — 49-19

AMS Filling Systems
2500 Chestnut Tree Rd .... Honey Brook PA 19344 — 800-647-5390 — 610-942-4200 — 543

AMSA (American Medical Student Assn)
1902 Assn Dr .... Reston VA 20191 — 800-767-2266 — 703-620-6600 — 49-5

AMSA (American Moving & Storage Assn)
1611 Duke St .... Alexandria VA 22314 — 888-849-2672 — 703-683-7410 — 49-21

Amscan Inc
80 Grasslands Rd .... Elmsford NY 10523 — 800-444-8887 — 914-345-2020 — 562

AMSCO (Automotive Mfg & Supply Co)
90 Plant Ave .... Hauppauge NY 11788 — 800-645-5604 — 631-435-1400

Amsco Windows Inc
1880 S 1045 W .... Salt Lake City UT 84104 — 800-748-4661 — 801-972-6441 — 234

Amset Technical Consulting Inc
1864 S Elmhurst Rd .... Mount Prospect IL 60056 — 888-982-6783 — 847-229-1155 — 261

Amsher
4524 Southlake Pkwy Ste 15 .... Birmingham AL 35244 — 844-227-4627 — 205-322-4110 — 160

AMSNET Inc
502 Commerce Way .... Livermore CA 94551 — 800-893-3660 — — 177

Amsoil Inc
925 Tower Ave .... Superior WI 54880 — 800-777-7094* — 715-392-7101 — 537
*Sales

AMSplus Inc
400 Washington St .... Braintree MA 02184 — 888-239-9575 — — 225

Amstan Logistics Inc
101 Knightsbridge Dr .... Hamilton OH 45011 — 855-301-7599 — 513-817-0937 — 775

Amsterdam Printing & Litho Corp
166 Wallins Corners Rd .... Amsterdam NY 12010 — 800-833-6231* — — 9
*Cust Svc

Amster-Kirtz Co
2830 Cleveland Ave NW .... Canton OH 44709 — 800-257-9338 — 330-535-6021 — 297-8

AmSurg Corp
1A Burton Hills Blvd .... Nashville TN 37215 — 800-945-2301 — 615-665-1283 — 351
NASDAQ: AMSG

AMSUS (Association of Military Surgeons of the United Sta)
9320 Old Georgetown Rd .... Bethesda MD 20814 — 800-761-9320 — 301-897-8800 — 49-8

AMT (American Medical Technologists)
10700 W Higgins Rd Ste 150 .... Rosemont IL 60018 — 800-275-1268 — 847-823-5169 — 49-8

AMT (Association for Mfg Technology)
7901 Westpark Dr .... McLean VA 22102 — 800-524-0475 — 703-893-2900 — 49-12

AMT Datasouth Corp
803 Camarillo Springs Rd Ste D .... Camarillo CA 93012 — 800-215-9192 — 805-388-5799 — 173-6

AMT Pump Co
400 Spring St .... Royersford PA 19468 — 888-268-7867 — — 637

AMTA (American Massage Therapy Assn)
500 Davis St Ste 900 .... Evanston IL 60201 — 877-905-2700 — 847-864-0123 — 48-17

AMTEL
9707 Key West Ave Ste 202 .... Rockville MD 20850 — 800-989-5566 — 301-721-3010

Amtelco
4800 Curtin Dr .... McFarland WI 53558 — 800-356-9148 — 608-838-4194 — 730

Amtote International Inc
11200 Pepper Rd .... Hunt Valley MD 21031 — 800-345-1566 — 410-771-8700 — 322

AmTrust Bank
1801 E Ninth St .... Cleveland OH 44114 — 888-696-4444 — 216-736-3480 — 70

Amuneal Manufacturing Corp
4737 Darrah St .... Philadelphia PA 19124 — 800-755-9843 — 215-535-3000 — 693

Amusement & Music Operators Assn (AMOA)
380 Terra Cotta Rd Ste F .... Crystal Lake IL 60012 — 800-937-2662 — 815-893-6010 — 48-23

AMVETS
4647 Forbes Blvd .... Lanham MD 20706 — 877-726-8387 — 301-459-9600 — 48-19

Amvic Inc
501 McNicoll Ave .... Toronto ON M2H2E2 — 877-470-9991 — 416-410-5674 — 183

Amway Corp
7575 Fulton St E .... Ada MI 49355 — 800-253-6500 — 616-787-4000 — 365

Amway Grand Plaza Hotel
187 Monroe Ave NW .... Grand Rapids MI 49503 — 800-253-3590 — 616-774-2000 — 378

AN Deringer Inc
64 N Main St .... Saint Albans VT 05478 — 800-448-8108 — 802-524-8110 — 447

ANA (Acoustic Neuroma Assn)
600 Peachtree Pkwy Ste 108 .... Cumming GA 30041 — 877-200-8211 — 770-205-8211 — 48-17

ANA (American Nurses Assn)
8515 Georgia Ave Ste 400 .... Silver Spring MD 20910 — 800-274-4262 — 301-628-5000 — 49-8

ANA PAC (American Nurses Assn PAC)
8515 Georgia Ave Ste 400 .... Silver Spring MD 20910 — 800-274-4262 — 301-628-5000 — 611

ANAC (Association of Nurses in AIDS Care)
3538 Ridgewood Rd .... Akron OH 44333 — 800-260-6780 — 330-670-0101 — 49-8

Anacom General Corp
1240 S Claudina St .... Anaheim CA 92805 — 800-955-9540 — 714-774-8484 — 391

Anadarko Petroleum Corp
1201 Lake Robbins Dr .... The Woodlands TX 77380 — 800-800-1101 — 832-636-1000 — 532
NYSE: APC

Anaheim Automation
910 E Orangefair Ln .... Anaheim CA 92801 — 800-345-9401* — 714-992-6990 — 203
*Sales

Anaheim Custom Extruders
4640 E La Palma Ave .... Anaheim CA 92807 — 800-229-2760* — 714-693-8508 — 596
*Cust Svc

Anaheim Ducks
2695 E Katella Ave .... Anaheim CA 92806 — 877-945-3946 — — 712

Anaheim Extrusion Company Inc
1330 N Kraemer Blvd PO Box 6380 .... Anaheim CA 92806 — 800-660-3318 — 714-630-3111 — 483

Anaheim Hotel, The
1700 S Harbor Blvd .... Anaheim CA 92802 — 800-631-4144 — 714-772-5900 — 378

Anaheim Manufacturing Co
25300 Al Moen Dr .... North Olmsted OH 44070 — 800-767-6293* — — 36
*Cust Svc

Anaheim Marriott
700 W Convention Way .... Anaheim CA 92802 — 800-845-5279 — 714-750-8000 — 667

Anaheim University
1240 S State College Blvd Rm 110 .... Anaheim CA 92806 — 800-955-6040 — 714-772-3330 — 165

Analog Devices Inc
3 Technology Way .... Norwood MA 02062 — 800-262-5643 — 781-329-4700 — 692
NASDAQ: ADI

Analytic Investors LLC
555 W Fifth St 50th Fl .... Los Angeles CA 90013 — 800-618-1872 — 213-688-3015 — 400

Analytical Graphics Inc
220 Vly Creek Blvd .... Exton PA 19341 — 800-220-4785 — 610-981-8000 — 177

Analytics Corp
10329 Stony Run Ln .... Ashland VA 23005 — 800-888-8061 — 804-365-3000 — 738

Company / Address	City	State	ZIP	Toll-Free	Phone	Class
Ananke IT Solutions						
20 Main St	East Greenwich	RI	02818	**877-626-2653**	401-331-2780	
Anaren Microwave Inc						
6635 Kirkville Rd	East Syracuse	NY	13057	**800-544-2414**	315-432-8909	253
NASDAQ: ANEN						
AnaSpec Inc						
34801 Campus Dr	Fremont	CA	94555	**800-452-5530**	510-791-9560	231
Anatom-e Information Systems Ltd						
7505 Fannin St Ste 422	Houston	TX	77054	**800-561-0874**		
Ancestrycom						
360 W 4800 N	Provo	UT	84604	**800-262-3787***	801-705-7000	396
*Cust Svc						
Anchor Bar						
651 Delaware Ave	Buffalo	NY	14202	**866-248-9623**	716-883-1134	667
Anchor Benefit Consulting Inc						
2400 Maitland Ctr Pkwy Ste 111	Maitland	FL	32751	**800-845-7629**	407-667-8766	194
Anchor Computer Inc						
1900 New Hwy	Farmingdale	NY	11735	**800-728-6262**	631-293-6100	178-10
Anchor Fabrication						
1200 Lawson Rd	Fort Worth	TX	76131	**800-635-0386**		478
Anchor Hocking Co						
519 Pierce Ave	Lancaster	OH	43130	**800-562-7511**	740-681-6900	333
Anchor Industries Inc						
7701 Hwy 41 N	Evansville	IN	47725	**800-544-4445**	812-867-2421	728
Anchor Manufacturing Group inc						
12200 Brookpark Rd	Cleveland	OH	44130	**888-341-8910**	216-362-1850	752
Anchor Paper Company Inc						
480 Broadway St	Saint Paul	MN	55101	**800-652-9755**	651-298-1311	549
Anchor Tampa Inc						
3907 W Osborne Ave	Tampa	FL	33614	**800-879-8685**	813-879-8685	186
Anchorage Convention & Visitors Bureau						
524 W Fourth Ave	Anchorage	AK	99501	**800-478-6657**	907-276-4118	206
Anchorage Daily News						
1001 Northway Dr	Anchorage	AK	99508	**800-478-4200**	907-257-4200	528-2
Ancient Cedars Spa at the Wickaninnish Inn						
500 Osprey Ln PO Box 250	Tofino	BC	V0R2Z0	**800-333-4604**	250-725-3100	703
Ancira Winton Chevrolet						
6111 Bandera Rd	San Antonio	TX	78238	**800-299-5286***	210-681-4900	57
*General						
ANCO Insurance						
1111 Briarcrest Dr PO Box 3889	Bryan	TX	77802	**800-749-1733**	979-776-2626	389
Andersen Corp						
100 Fourth Ave N	Bayport	MN	55003	**888-888-7020**	651-264-5150	236
Andersen Manufacturing Inc						
3125 N Yellowstone Hwy	Idaho Falls	ID	83401	**800-635-6106**	208-523-6460	643
Anderson Brass Co						
1629 W Bobo Newsome Hwy	Hartsville	SC	29550	**800-476-9876**	843-332-4111	784
Anderson Chemical Co						
325 S Davis	Litchfield	MN	55355	**800-366-2477**	320-693-2477	145
Anderson Coach & Travel						
1 Anderson Plz	Greenville	PA	16125	**800-345-3435**	724-588-8310	755
Anderson Copper & Brass Co						
255 Industry Ave	Frankfort	IL	60423	**800-323-5284**	708-535-9030	605
Anderson County						
PO Box 8002	Anderson	SC	29622	**800-447-5375**	864-260-4000	337
Anderson Equipment Co						
1000 Washington Pk	Bridgeville	PA	15017	**800-414-4554**	412-343-2300	357
Anderson Erickson Dairy Co						
2420 E University Ave	Des Moines	IA	50317	**800-234-6455**	515-265-2521	296-27
Anderson Forest Products Inc						
1267 Old Edmonton Rd	Tompkinsville	KY	42167	**800-489-6778**	270-487-6778	547
Anderson Gallery						
325 N Harrison St	Richmond	VA	23284	**866-534-3201**	804-828-0100	
Anderson International Corp						
4545 Boyce Pkwy	Stow	OH	44224	**800-336-4730**	216-641-1112	298
Anderson Partners Advertising						
444 Regency Pkwy Dr Ste 311	Omaha	NE	68114	**800-551-9737**	402-341-4807	4
Anderson Ranch Arts Center						
5263 Owl Creek Rd						
PO Box 5598	Snowmass Village	CO	81615	**800-525-6363**	970-923-3181	50-2
Anderson Trucking Service Inc						
725 Opportunity St	Saint Cloud	MN	56301	**800-328-2316**	320-255-7400	775
Anderson Tube Company Inc						
1400 Fairgrounds Rd	Hatfield	PA	19440	**800-523-2258**	215-855-0118	608
Anderson University						
1100 E Fifth St	Anderson	IN	46012	**800-428-6414***		166
*Admissions						
Anderson/Madison County Visitors & Convention Bureau						
6335 S Scatterfield Rd	Anderson	IN	46013	**800-533-6569**	765-643-5633	206
Andersons Inc						
1947 Briarfield Blvd PO Box 119	Maumee	OH	43537	**800-537-3370**	419-893-5050	185
NASDAQ: ANDE						
Andex Industries Inc						
1911 Fourth Ave N	Escanaba	MI	49829	**800-338-9882**		88
Andis Co						
1800 Renaissance Blvd	Sturtevant	WI	53177	**800-558-9441**		37
Andover Healthcare Inc						
9 Fanaras Dr	Salisbury	MA	01952	**800-432-6686**	978-465-0044	474
Andover Newton Theological School						
210 Herrick Rd	Newton Center	MA	02459	**800-964-2687**	617-964-1100	167-3
Andreas Furniture Company Inc						
114 Dover Rd NE	Sugarcreek	OH	44681	**800-846-7448**	330-852-2494	321
Andreini & Co						
220 W 20th Ave	San Mateo	CA	94403	**800-969-2522**	650-573-1111	389
Andrew College						
501 College St	Cuthbert	GA	39840	**800-664-9250**		162
Andrew G Gordon Inc						
306 Washington St	Norwell	MA	02061	**866-243-2259**	781-659-2262	389
Andrew Garrett Inc						
52 Vanderbilt Ave Ste 510	New York	NY	10017	**800-899-1883**		
Andrew Technologies LLC						
1421 Edinger Ave Ste D	Tustin	CA	92780	**888-959-7674**		473
Andrews & Hamilton Company Inc						
3829 S Miami Blvd	Durham	NC	27703	**800-443-6866**	919-787-4100	357
Andrews Excavating Inc						
5 W Willow Rd PO Box 249	Willow Street	PA	17584	**800-730-6822**	717-464-3329	189-5
Andrews Federal Credit Union (AFCU)						
5711 Allentown Rd	Suitland	MD	20746	**800-487-5500**	301-702-5500	219
Andrews Hooper Pavlik Plc						
5300 Gratiot Rd	Saginaw	MI	48638	**888-754-8478**	989-497-5300	2
Andrews Hotel						
624 Post St	San Francisco	CA	94109	**800-926-3739**	415-563-6877	378
Andrews Logistics Inc						
2445 E Southlake Blvd	Southlake	TX	76092	**866-536-1234**	817-527-2770	194
Andrews University						
4355 International Ct	Berrien Springs	MI	49104	**800-253-2874**	269-471-7771	166
Andrews University James White Library						
4190 Admin Dr	Berrien Springs	MI	49104	**800-253-2874**	269-471-3264	433-6
Andrews University Seventh-day Adventist Theological Seminary						
4145 E Campus Cir Dr						
Andrews University	Berrien Springs	MI	49104	**800-253-2874**	269-471-3537	167-3
Andrie Inc						
561 E Western Ave	Muskegon	MI	49442	**800-722-2421**	231-728-2226	314
Andromed Inc						
5003 Levy St	Saint Laurent	QC	H4R2N9	**888-336-0043**	514-336-0043	
Andrus Transportation Services LLC						
3185 East Deseret Dr North						
	Saint George	UT	84790	**800-888-5838**	435-673-1566	359-2
Andy Frain Services Inc						
761 Shoreline Dr	Aurora	IL	60504	**877-707-4771**	630-820-3820	689
Anemostat						
1220 Watsoncenter Rd PO Box 4938	Carson	CA	90745	**877-423-7426**	310-835-7500	234
Anesthesia Service Inc						
1821 N Classen Blvd	Oklahoma City	OK	73106	**800-336-3356**	405-525-3588	473
ANG Federal Credit Union						
PO Box 170204	Birmingham	AL	35217	**800-237-6211**	205-841-4525	219
Angel Fire Resort						
PO Box 130	Angel Fire	NM	87710	**800-633-7463**	575-377-6401	665
Angela Hospice Home Care						
14100 Newburgh Rd	Livonia	MI	48154	**866-464-7810***	734-464-7810	370
*General						
Angell & Phelps Chocolate Factory						
154 S Beach St	Daytona Beach	FL	32114	**800-969-2634**	386-252-6531	667
Angelo State University						
2601 W Ave N ASU Stn 11014	San Angelo	TX	76909	**800-946-8627**	325-942-2041	166
Angelo State University Henderson Library						
2025 S Johnson St	San Angelo	TX	76909	**800-946-8627**	325-942-2051	433-6
Angels of the Valley Hospice Care						
2600 Foothill Blvd Ste 202	La Crescenta	CA	91214	**888-344-0880**	818-542-3070	788
Angie's Cantina						
11 E Buchanan St	Duluth	MN	55802	**800-706-7672**	210-727-6117	667
Angola Wire Products Inc						
803 Wohlert St	Angola	IN	46703	**800-800-7225**	260-665-9447	286
Angstrom Technologies Inc						
7880 Foundation Dr	Florence	KY	41042	**800-543-7358***	859-282-0020	145
*Cust Svc						
Anguil Environmental Systems Inc						
8855 N 55th St	Milwaukee	WI	53223	**800-488-0230**	414-365-6400	18
Anguilla Tourist Marketing Office						
246 Central Ave	White Plains	NY	10606	**800-553-4939**	914-287-2400	770
Angus Systems Group Ltd						
1125 Leslie St	Toronto	ON	M3C2J6	**877-442-6487**	416-385-8550	392
Anheuser-Busch Cos Inc						
1 Busch Pl	Saint Louis	MO	63118	**800-342-5283**		80-1
Anika Therapeutics Inc						
32 Wiggins Ave	Bedford	MA	01730	**800-299-7089**	781-457-9000	477
NASDAQ: ANIK						
Animal & Plant Health Inspection Service (APHIS)						
National Veterinary Services Laboratories						
4700 River Rd	Riverdale	MD	20737	**844-820-2234**		738
Animal Ark Wildlife Sanctuary & Nature Ctr						
1265 Deerlodge Rd	Reno	NV	89508	**866-366-5771**	775-970-3111	818
Animas Corp						
200 Lawrence Dr	West Chester	PA	19380	**877-937-7867**		475
Animation Mentor						
1400 65th St Ste 250	Emeryville	CA	94608	**877-326-4628**		759
Anixter Inc						
2301 Patriot Blvd	Glenview	IL	60026	**800-492-1212**	224-521-8000	189-4
ANL (Argonne National Laboratory)						
9700 S Cass Ave	Argonne	IL	60439	**800-632-8990**	630-252-2000	664
Anlin Industries						
1665 Tollhouse Rd	Clovis	CA	93611	**800-287-7996**	559-322-1531	497
ANMC (Alaska Native Medical Ctr)						
4315 Diplomacy Dr	Anchorage	AK	99508	**800-478-6661***	907-563-2662	373-3
*Admitting						
Ann Arbor Area Convention & Visitors Bureau						
120 W Huron St	Ann Arbor	MI	48104	**800-888-9487**	734-995-7281	206
Ann Arbor Transportation Authority						
2700 S Industrial Hwy	Ann Arbor	MI	48104	**800-835-4603**	734-973-6500	466
Ann Sacks Tile & Stone Inc						
8120 NE 33rd Dr	Portland	OR	97211	**800-278-8453**		746
ANNA (American Nephrology Nurses Assn)						
200 E Holly Ave	Sewell	NJ	08080	**888-600-2662**	856-256-2320	49-8
Anna Griffin Inc						
99 Armour Dr	Atlanta	GA	30324	**888-817-8170**	404-817-8170	548-2
Anna Maria College						
50 Sunset Ln	Paxton	MA	01612	**800-344-4586**		166
Annals of Internal Medicine Magazine						
190 N Independence Mall West						
	Philadelphia	PA	19106	**800-523-1546**	215-351-2400	455-16
Annan & Bird Lithographers Ltd						
1060 Tristar Dr	Mississauga	ON	L5T1H9	**800-565-5618**	905-670-0604	623
Annandale Chamber of Commerce						
7263 Maple Pl Ste 207	Annandale	VA	22003	**800-357-2110**	703-256-7232	139
Annapolis & Anne Arundel County Chamber of Commerce						
134 Holiday Ct Ste 316	Annapolis	MD	21401	**800-624-8887**	410-266-3960	139
Annapolis & Anne Arundel County Conference & Visitors Bureau (AAACCVB)						
26 W St	Annapolis	MD	21401	**888-302-2852**	410-280-0445	206
Annapolis Bancorp Inc						
1000 Bestgate Rd	Annapolis	MD	21401	**800-555-5455**	410-224-4455	359-2
NASDAQ: ANNB						
Annenberg Media						
1301 Pennsylvania Ave NW						
Ste 302	Washington	DC	20004	**800-532-7637**		628
Annex Brands Inc						
7580 Metropolitan Dr Ste 200	San Diego	CA	92108	**877-722-5236**	619-563-4800	113

Alphabetical Section

Name / Address	Toll-Free	Phone	Class
Annex Cloud 5301 Beethoven St Ste 260 .... Los Angeles CA 90066	866-802-8806		386
Annex Pro Inc 49 Dunlevy Ave Ste 220 .... Vancouver BC V6A3A3	800-682-6639	604-682-6639	522
Annie E Casey Foundation 701 St Paul St .... Baltimore MD 21202	800-222-1099	410-547-6600	305
Annie Penn Hospital 618 S Main St .... Reidsville NC 27320	866-391-2734	336-951-4000	373-3
Anniston Sportswear Corp 4305 McClellan Blvd PO Box 189 ...... Anniston AL 36206	866-814-9253	256-236-1551	155-11
Anniston Star 4305 McClellan Blvd PO Box 2285 .... Anniston AL 36206	866-814-9253	256-236-1551	528-2
AnnTaylor Inc 7 Times Sq .... New York NY 10036	800-342-5266	212-541-3300	157-6
Annual Reviews 4139 El Camino Way .... Palo Alto CA 94306	800-523-8635	650-493-4400	633-9
Annuvia Inc 1725 Clay St Ste 100 .... San Francisco CA 94109	866-364-7940		41
Anoka Technical College 1355 W Hwy 10 .... Anoka MN 55303	800-627-3529	763-433-1100	795
Anoka-Hennepin School District 2727 N Ferry St .... Anoka MN 55303	800-729-6164	763-506-1000	681
Anoka-Ramsey Community College 11200 Mississippi Blvd NW .... Coon Rapids MN 55433	800-627-3529	763-433-1230	162
Cambridge 300 Polk St S .... Cambridge MN 55008	800-627-3529	763-433-1100	162
Another Printer Inc 10 Bush River Ct .... Columbia SC 29210	888-689-6399	803-798-1380	623
ANR Pipeline Co 717 Texas St .... Houston TX 77002	800-827-5267	888-427-2875	325
Anresco Inc 1375 Van Dyke Ave ... San Francisco CA 94124	800-359-0920	415-822-1100	41
Anritsu Co 490 Jarvis Dr .... Morgan Hill CA 95037	800-267-4878	408-778-2000	248
ANRO Inc 931 S Matlack St .... West Chester PA 19382	800-355-2676	610-687-1200	623
Anron Air Systems Inc 440 Wyandanch Ave .... West Babylon NY 11704	800-421-0389	631-643-3433	189-10
ANS (American Nuclear Society) 555 N Kensington Ave .... La Grange Park IL 60526	800-323-3044	708-352-6611	49-19
Ansar Group Inc, The 242 S Eighth St Ste 1 st Fl .... Philadelphia PA 19107	888-883-7804	877-228-6863	473
Ansatel Communications Inc 940 Kingsway .... Vancouver BC V5V3C4	866-872-6500	604-872-6500	224
ANSI (American National Standards Institute) 25 W 43rd St 4th fl .... New York NY 10036	800-374-3818	212-642-4900	48-1
AnswerLive LLC 1101 Cherryville .... Shelby NC 28150	800-472-4495	704-333-8880	392
ANSYS Inc 275 Technology Dr .... Canonsburg PA 15317 *NASDAQ: ANSS*	800-937-3321	724-820-4367	178-5
Antares Technology Solutions 8282 Goodwood Blvd Ste W-2 ...... Baton Rouge LA 70806	800-366-8807	225-922-7748	
Antea Group 5910 Rice Creek Pkwy Ste 100 .... Saint Paul MN 55126	800-477-7411	651-639-9449	663
Antec Inc 47900 Fremont Blvd .... Fremont CA 94538	800-222-6832	510-770-1200	253
Antelope Valley Press 37404 Sierra Hwy .... Palmdale CA 93550	888-874-2527	661-273-2700	528-2
Anthelio Healthcare Solutions Inc 5400 LBJ Fwy Ste 200 .... Dallas TX 75240	855-268-4354	214-257-7000	362
Anthem Blue Cross & Blue Shield 2015 Staples Mill Rd .... Richmond VA 23230	800-451-1527	855-636-6136	390-3
Anthem Blue Cross & Blue Shield Maine 2 Gannett Dr .... South Portland ME 04106 *Cust Svc	800-482-0966*	855-636-6136	390-3
Anthem Blue Cross & Blue Shield of Connecticut 370 Bassett Rd .... North Haven CT 06473	855-636-6136		390-3
Anthem Blue Cross & Blue Shield of Nevada 9133 W Russell Rd .... Las Vegas NV 89148	855-636-6136		390-3
Anthem Blue Cross Blue Shield Colorado 700 Broadway .... Denver CO 80273	877-833-5742	303-831-2131	390-3
Anthem Inc 120 Monument Cir Ste 200 ... Indianapolis IN 46204	800-331-1476	317-488-6000	359-4
Anthem Life Insurance Co 6740 N High St Ste 200 .... Worthington OH 43085	800-551-7265	614-436-0688	390-2
Anthony & Sylvan Pools 3739 Easton Rd Rt 611 .... Doylestown PA 18901	877-729-7946	215-489-5605	724
Anthony Forest Products Co 309 N Washington Ave .... El Dorado AR 71730	800-221-2326	870-862-3414	679
Anthony International 12391 Montera Ave .... Sylmar CA 91342	800-772-0900	818-365-9451	329
Anthony-Thomas Candy Co 1777 Arlingate Ln .... Columbus OH 43228	877-226-3921	614-274-8405	296-8
Anthro Corp 10450 SW Manhasset Dr .... Tualatin OR 97062	800-325-3841	503-691-2556	319-1
Antibodies Inc PO Box 1560 .... Davis CA 95617	800-824-8540		85
AntiCancer Inc 7917 Ostrow St .... San Diego CA 92111	800-511-2555	858-654-2555	231
Anti-Defamation League (ADL) 605 Third Ave .... New York NY 10158	866-386-3235	212-885-7700	48-8
Antigua & Barbuda *Embassy* 3216 New Mexico Ave NW .... Washington DC 20016	866-978-7299	202-362-5122	257
Antigua & Barbuda Dept of Tourism & Trade 25 SE Second Ave Ste 300 .... Miami FL 33131	888-268-4227	305-381-6762	770
Antigua Group Inc, The 16651 N 84 Ave .... Peoria AZ 85382	800-528-3133	623-523-6000	155-11
Antillean Marine Shipping Corp 3038 NW N River Dr .... Miami FL 33142	888-633-6361	305-633-6361	313
Antimite Associates Inc 5867 Pine Ave .... Chino Hills CA 91709	800-974-2847	909-606-2300	573
Antiochian Orthodox Christian Archdiocese of North America 358 Mountain Rd .... Englewood NJ 07631	888-421-1442	201-871-1355	48-20
Antique Automobile Club of America (AACA) 501 W Governor Rd PO Box 417 .... Hershey PA 17033	800-452-9910	717-534-1910	48-18
Antique Collectors Club 116 Pleasant St .... EastHampton MA 01027	800-254-4100	413-529-0861	633-2
Antique Mall 1251 S Virginia St .... Reno NV 89502	888-316-6255	775-324-4141	458
Antique Trader 700 E State St .... Iola WI 54990	800-258-0929	503-319-0799	455-14
Antitrust & Trade Regulation Daily 1801 S Bell St .... Arlington VA 22202	800-372-1033		527-2
Antler Inn 43 W Pearl St PO Box 575 .... Jackson WY 83001	800-483-8667	307-733-2535	378
Anton/Bauer Inc 14 Progress Dr .... Shelton CT 06484	800-422-3473	203-929-1100	587
Antonelli Institute 300 Montgomery Ave .... Erdenheim PA 19038	800-722-7871	215-836-2222	164
Anvil Cases 15730 Salt Lake Ave .... City of Industry CA 91745	800-359-2684	626-968-4100	451
Anxiety Disorders Assn of America (ADAA) 8701 Georgia Ave Ste #412 .... Silver Spring MD 20910	800-922-8947	240-485-1001	48-17
AnyDoc Software Inc 5404 Cypress Ctr Dr Ste 140 .... Tampa FL 33609	888-495-2638		178-7
Anytime Fitness Inc 12181 Margo Ave S .... Hastings MN 55033	888-827-9262		
Anza ElectricCo-op Inc 58470 Hwy 371 PO Box 391909 .... Anza CA 92539	844-311-7201	951-763-4333	245
AO Smith Electrical Products Co 531 N Fourth St .... Tipp City OH 45371	800-543-9450	937-667-2431	515
AO Smith Water Products Co 500 Tennessee Waltz Pkwy .... Ashland City TN 37015	800-527-1953	866-362-9898	36
AOA (American Osteopathic Assn) 142 E Ontario St .... Chicago IL 60611	800-621-1773	888-626-9262	49-8
AoA (Administration on Aging) 1 Massachusetts Ave NW .... Washington DC 20001	800-677-1116	202-357-3584	
AOAC International 481 N Frederick Ave Ste 500 .... Gaithersburg MD 20877	800-379-2622	301-924-7077	49-19
AOAExcel Inc 243 N Lindbergh Blvd 1st Fl .... St. Louis MO 63141	800-365-2219		386
AOCA (Automotive Oil Change Assn) 330 N Wabash Ave Ste 2000 .... Chicago IL 60611	800-230-0702	312-321-5132	49-21
AOCS (American Oil Chemists Society) 2710 S Boulder PO Box 17190 .... Urbana IL 61802	866-535-2730	217-359-2344	48-12
AOM (Academy of Management) 235 Elm Rd PO Box 3020 .... Briarcliff Manor NY 10510	800-633-4931	914-923-2607	49-12
Aon Corp 200 E Randolph St .... Chicago IL 60601	877-384-4276	312-381-1000	359-4
Aon Risk Services Inc 200 E Randolph St .... Chicago IL 60601	877-384-4276	312-381-1000	389
AOPA (Aircraft Owners & Pilots Assn) 421 Aviation Way .... Frederick MD 21701	800-872-2672	301-695-2000	49-21
AOPA Pilot Magazine 421 Aviation Way .... Frederick MD 21701	800-872-2672	301-695-2000	455-14
AORN Inc 2170 S Parker Rd Ste 400 .... Denver CO 80231	800-755-2676	303-755-6300	49-8
Aos Thermal Compounds LLC 22 Meridian Rd Ste 6 .... Eatontown NJ 07724	888-662-7337	732-389-5514	575
AOSSM (American Orthopaedic Society for Sports Medicine) 9400 W Higgins Rd Ste 300 .... Rosemont IL 60018	877-321-3500	847-292-4900	49-8
AOTA (American Occupational Therapy Assn Inc) 4720 Montgomery Ln PO Box 31220 .... Bethesda MD 20824	800-877-1383	301-652-2682	49-8
AP Exhaust Technologies Inc 300 Dixie Trial .... Goldsboro NC 27530	800-277-2787	919-580-2000	60
APA (American Psychiatric Assn) 1000 Wilson Blvd Ste 1825 .... Arlington VA 22209	888-357-7924	703-907-7300	49-15
APA (American Psychological Assn) 750 First St NE .... Washington DC 20002	800-374-2721	202-336-5500	49-15
APA Services 4150 International Plaza Tower I Ste 510 .... Fort Worth TX 76109	877-425-5023		729
A-Pac Manufacturing Company Inc 2719 Courier NW .... Grand Rapids MI 49534	800-272-2634		344
Apache Corp 2000 Post Oak Blvd Ste 100 .... Houston TX 77056 *NYSE: APA*	800-272-2434	713-296-6000	532
Apache Greyhound Park 3801 E Washington .... Phoenix AZ 85034	800-772-0852	480-982-2371	133
Apache Hose & Belting Co Inc 4805 Bowling St SW .... Cedar Rapids IA 52404 *Sales	800-553-5455*	319-365-0471	369
Apache Stainless Equipment Corp 200 W Industrial Dr PO Box 538 .... Beaver Dam WI 53916	800-444-0398	920-356-9900	385
APACVB (Alexandria/Pineville Area Convention & Visitors Bu) 707 Main St PO Box 1070 .... Alexandria LA 71301	800-551-9546		206
Apartment Investment & Management Co 4582 S Ulster St Pkwy Ste 1100 .... Denver CO 80237 *NYSE: AIV* ■ *General	888-789-8600*	303-757-8101	651
APC (American Power Conversion Corp) 132 Fairgrounds Rd .... West Kingston RI 02892 *Cust Svc	800-788-2208*	401-789-5735	253
APC Integrated Services Inc 770 Spirit of St Louis Blvd .... Chesterfield MO 63005	888-294-7886		317
APCO Bulletin 351 N Williamson Blvd .... Daytona Beach FL 32114	888-272-6911	386-322-2500	527-8
APCO Employees Credit Union 750 17th St North .... Birmingham AL 35203	800-249-2726	205-257-3601	219
Apco Extruders Inc 180 National Rd .... Edison NJ 08817 *Orders	800-942-8725*	732-287-3000	544
APCO Graphics Inc 388 Grant St SE .... Atlanta GA 30312	877-988-2726	404-688-9000	697
APCON Inc 9255 SW Pioneer Ct .... Wilsonville OR 97070	800-624-6808	503-682-4050	174
APD (American Product Distributors Inc) 8350 Arrowridge Blvd .... Charlotte NC 28273	800-849-5842	704-522-9411	530

Name / Address	City	State	Zip	Toll-Free	Phone	Class
APDA (American Parkinson Disease Assn)						
135 Parkinson Ave	Staten Island	NY	10305	**800-223-2732**	718-981-8001	48-17
Apelles LLC						
3700 Corporate Dr Ste 240	Columbus	OH	43231	**800-825-4425**	614-899-7322	317
Apetito Canada Ltd						
12 Indell Ln	Brampton	ON	L6T3Y3	**800-268-8199**	905-799-1022	297-8
Apex Advertising Inc						
2959 Old Tree Dr	Lancaster	PA	17603	**800-666-5556**	717-396-7100	7
Apex Asset Management LLC						
2501 Oregon Pk Ste 201	Lancaster	PA	17601	**888-592-2149**	717-519-1770	195
Apex Color						
200 N Lee St	Jacksonville	FL	32204	**800-367-6790**		110
Apex Digital Imaging Inc						
16057 Tampa Palms Blvd W	Tampa	FL	33647	**866-973-3034**	813-973-3034	697
Apex Homes Inc						
7172 Rt 522	Middleburg	PA	17842	**800-326-9524**	570-837-2333	186
Apex Industries Inc						
100 Millennium Blvd	Moncton	NB	E1E2G8	**800-268-3331**	506-857-1620	478
Apex Mills Corp						
168 Doughty Blvd	Inwood	NY	11096	**800-989-2739**	516-239-4400	740-4
Apex Packing & Rubber Co Inc						
1855 New Hwy Ste D	Farmingdale	NY	11735	**800-645-9110**	631-420-8150	357
Apex Paper Box Co						
5601 Walworth Ave	Cleveland	OH	44102	**800-438-2269***	216-631-6900	101
*Cust Svc						
Apex Piping Systems Inc						
302 Falco Dr	Wilmington	DE	19804	**888-995-2739**		606
APG (Automation Products Group Inc)						
1025 W 1700 N	Logan	UT	84321	**888-525-7300**	435-753-7300	201
APG (American Packing & Gasket Co)						
6039 Armour Dr PO Box 213	Houston	TX	77020	**800-888-5223**	713-675-5271	326
APGA (American Public Gas Assn)						
201 Massachusetts Ave NE						
Ste C-4	Washington	DC	20002	**800-927-4204**	202-464-2742	48-12
ApHC (Appaloosa Horse Club)						
2720 W Pullman Rd	Moscow	ID	83843	**888-304-7768**	208-882-5578	48-3
APHIS (Animal & Plant Health Inspection Service)						
National Veterinary Services Laboratories						
4700 River Rd	Riverdale	MD	20737	**844-820-2234**		738
APHL (Association of Public Health Laboratories)						
8515 Georgia Ave Ste 700	Silver Spring	MD	20910	**800-899-2278**	240-485-2745	49-7
API (Aerospace Products International)						
2871 Business Pk Dr	Memphis	TN	38118	**888-274-2497**	901-365-3470	22
API Construction Co						
1100 Old Hwy 8 NW	New Brighton	MN	55112	**800-223-4922**	651-636-4320	189-9
APi Group Inc						
1100 Old Hwy 8 NW	New Brighton	MN	55112	**800-223-4922**		185
API Heat Transfer Inc						
2777 Walden Ave	Buffalo	NY	14225	**877-274-4328**	716-684-6700	91
APi Systems Group Inc						
10575 Vista Park Rd	Dallas	TX	75238	**800-566-0845***	214-349-2221	688
*General						
APIC (Association for Professionals in Infection Control)						
1275 K St NW Ste 1000	Washington	DC	20005	**800-650-9883**	202-789-1890	49-8
Apio Inc PO Box 727	Guadalupe	CA	93434	**800-454-1355***		296-21
*Sales						
APL Access & Security Inc						
115 S William Dillard Dr	Gilbert	AZ	85233	**866-873-2288**	480-497-9471	689
APL Logistics Inc						
17600 N Perimeter Dr Ste 150	Scottsdale	AZ	85255	**844-479-9620**	602-457-4297	447
Aplus						
3680 Victoria St N	Shoreview	MN	55126	**877-532-0132**	651-481-4598	397
APM Hexseal Corp						
44 Honeck St	Englewood	NJ	07631	**800-498-9034**	201-569-5700	326
APMA (American Podiatric Medical Assn)						
9312 Old Georgetown Rd	Bethesda	MD	20814	**800-275-2762**	301-581-9200	49-8
Apmetrix Inc						
2815 Forbs Ave						
Ste 107-40	Hoffman Estates	IL	60192	**800-490-3184**	312-416-0950	386
APN (Americans for Peace Now)						
1101 14th St NW 6th Fl	Washington	DC	20005	**877-429-0678**	202-728-1893	48-7
APN Media LLC						
PO Box 20113	New York	NY	10023	**800-470-7599**	212-581-3380	633-9
APNA (American Psychiatric Nurses Assn)						
1555 Wilson Blvd Ste 530	Arlington	VA	22209	**866-243-2443**	703-243-2443	49-8
Apogee Enterprises Inc						
4400 W 78th St Ste 520	Minneapolis	MN	55435	**877-752-3432**	952-835-1874	329
NASDAQ: APOG						
Apollo Chemical Company LLC						
2001 Willow Springs Ln	Burlington	NC	27253	**800-374-3827**	336-226-1161	145
Apollo Education Group Inc						
4025 S Riverpoint Pkwy	Phoenix	AZ	85040	**800-990-2765**		242
Apollo Oil LLC						
1175 Early Dr	Winchester	KY	40391	**800-473-5823**		316
Apollo Professional Svc						
29 Stiles Rd Ste 302	Salem	NH	03079	**866-277-3343**		261
Apollo Retail Specialists LLC						
4450 E Adamo Dr	Tampa	FL	33605	**866-872-0666**	813-712-2525	
ApolloMD						
5665 New Northside Dr Ste 200	Atlanta	GA	30328	**866-827-6556**	770-874-5400	
Apotex Corp						
2400 N Commerce Pkwy Ste 400	Weston	FL	33326	**877-427-6839**		579
Apothecary Products						
11750 12th Ave S Burnsville	Burnsville	MN	55337	**800-328-2742**		214
Appalachian Behavioral Healthcare						
100 Hospital Dr	Athens	OH	45701	**800-372-8862**	740-594-5000	373-5
Appalachian Mountain Club (AMC)						
5 Joy St	Boston	MA	02108	**800-262-4455***	617-523-0655	48-13
*Orders						
Appalachian Regional Healthcare Service (ARH)						
80 Hospital Dr PO Box 8086	Barbourville	KY	40906	**888-654-0015**	859-226-2440	352
Appalachian School of Law						
1169 Edgewater Dr	Grundy	VA	24614	**800-895-7411**	276-935-4349	167-1
Appalachian State University						
Belk Library						
218 College St PO Box 32026	Boone	NC	28608	**877-423-0086**	828-262-2300	433-6
Appalachian Trail Conservancy (ATC)						
799 Washington St						
PO Box 807	Harpers Ferry	WV	25425	**888-287-8673***	304-535-6331	48-23
*Sales						
Appaloosa Horse Club (ApHC)						
2720 W Pullman Rd	Moscow	ID	83843	**888-304-7768**	208-882-5578	48-3
Apparelmaster						
123 Harrison Ave	Harrison	OH	45030	**877-543-1678**	513-202-1600	441
AppDetex						
609 W Main St Ste 202	Boise	ID	83702	**855-693-3839**		196
APPI Energy						
224 Phillip Morris Dr Ste 402	Salisbury	MD	21804	**800-520-6685**		194
Appian Analytics Inc						
2000 Crow Canyon Pl Ste 300	San Ramon	CA	94583	**877-757-7646**		620
Apple & Assoc						
PO Box 996	Chapin	SC	29036	**800-326-8490**	803-932-2000	
Apple & Eve Inc						
2 Seaview Blvd	Port Washington	NY	11050	**800-969-8018**	516-621-1122	296-20
Apple Bank for Savings						
122 E 42nd St	New York	NY	10168	**800-824-0710**	914-902-2775	70
Apple Discount Drugs						
404 N Fruitland Blvd	Salisbury	MD	21801	**800-424-8401**	410-749-8401	23
Apple Farm Bakery						
2015 Monterey St	San Luis Obispo	CA	93401	**800-255-2040**	805-544-2040	377
Apple Inc						
1 Infinite Loop	Cupertino	CA	95014	**800-275-2273***	408-996-1010	173-2
NASDAQ: AAPL ■ *Cust Svc						
Apple Rubber Products Inc						
310 Erie St	Lancaster	NY	14086	**800-828-7745***	716-684-6560	326
*Cust Svc						
Apple Saddlery						
1875 Innes Rd	Ottawa	ON	K1B4C6	**800-867-8225**	613-744-4040	707
Apple Tree Inn						
9508 N Div St	Spokane	WA	99218	**800-323-5796**	509-466-3020	378
Apple Vacations Inc						
101 NW Pt Blvd	Elk Grove Village	IL	60007	**800-517-2000**		766
Apple Valley Chamber of Commerce						
14800 Galaxie Ave Ste 101	Apple Valley	MN	55124	**800-301-9435**	952-432-8422	139
Apple Valley Medical Clinic Ltd						
14655 Galaxie Ave	Apple Valley	MN	55124	**800-233-8504**	952-432-6161	237
Applegate Insulation Manufacturing Inc						
1000 Highview Dr	Webberville	MI	48892	**800-627-7536**	517-521-3545	388
Applegate Livestock Equipment Inc						
902 S State Rd 32	Union City	IN	47390	**800-354-9502**	765-964-4631	273
AppleOne						
327 West Broadway PO Box 29048	Glendale	CA	91209	**800-872-2677**		717
Appleton Coated LLC						
540 Prospect St	Combined Locks	WI	54113	**888-488-6742**		
Appleton Group LLC, The						
100 W Lawrence St Ste 306	Wisconsin	WI	54911	**866-993-7727**	920-993-7727	400
Appleton Medical Ctr						
1818 N Meade St	Appleton	WI	54911	**800-236-4101**	920-731-4101	373-3
Appleton Partners Inc						
1 Post Office Sq 6th Fl	Boston	MA	02109	**800-338-0745**	617-338-0700	400
Applewood Books Inc						
1 River Rd	Carlisle	MA	01741	**800-277-5312***		633-2
*General						
Applewood Manor Inn						
62 Cumberland Cir	Asheville	NC	28801	**800-442-2197**	828-254-2244	378
Appliance Recycling Centers of America Inc						
7400 Excelsior Blvd	Minneapolis	MN	55426	**800-452-8680**	952-930-9000	656
NASDAQ: ARCI						
Applicant Insight Ltd						
5652 Meadowlane St	New Port Richey	FL	34652	**800-771-7703**		631
Applied Business Software Inc						
2847 Gundry Ave	Long Beach	CA	90755	**800-833-3343**		177
Applied Card Systems						
50 Applied Card Way	Glen Mills	PA	19342	**866-227-5627**		215
Applied Diagnostics Inc						
1140 Business Center Dr Ste 370	Houston	TX	77043	**855-239-8378**	713-271-4133	414
Applied Energy Company Inc (AEC)						
1205 Venture Ct Ste 100	Carrollton	TX	75006	**800-580-1171**	214-355-4200	636
Applied Energy Solutions LLC						
1 Technology Pl	Caledonia	NY	14423	**800-836-2132**	585-538-4421	74
Applied Fiber Inc						
PO Box 1339	Leesburg	GA	31763	**800-226-5394**	229-759-8301	540
Applied Flow Technology Corp						
2955 Professional Pl						
Ste 301	Colorado Springs	CO	80904	**800-589-4943**	719-686-1000	261
Applied Fusion Inc						
1915 Republic Ave	San Leandro	CA	94577	**800-704-1078**	510-351-4511	806
Applied Imaging Inc						
5555 Glenwood Hills Pkwy SE						
	Grand Rapids	MI	49512	**800-521-0983**	616-554-5200	225
Applied Laser Technologies						
8404 Venture Cir	Schofield	WI	54476	**888-359-3002**	715-359-3002	490
Applied LNG						
5716 Corsa Ave Ste 200	Westlake Village	CA	91362	**800-609-1702**	818-450-3650	532
Applied Logic Inc						
11475 Olde Cabin Rd Ste 100	St Louis	MO	63141	**844-478-7225**	314-918-8877	804
Applied Marketing Research Inc						
420 W 98th St	Kansas City	MO	64114	**800-381-5599**		195
Applied Measurement Professionals Inc (AMP)						
18000 W 105th St	Olathe	KS	66061	**800-345-6559**	913-895-4600	47
Applied Medical Technology Inc						
8000 Katherine Blvd	Brecksville	OH	44141	**800-869-7382**	440-717-4000	473
Applied Membranes Inc						
2450 Business Park Dr	Vista	CA	92081	**800-321-9321**	760-727-3711	608
Applied Process Cooling Corp						
555 Price Ave	Redwood City	CA	94063	**877-231-6406**	650-595-0665	660
Applied Sciences Group Inc						
2495 Main St Ste 407	Buffalo	NY	14214	**877-274-9811**	716-626-5100	180
Applied Software Inc						
3915 National Dr Ste 200	Burtonsville	MD	20866	**888-624-8439**		177
Applied Systems Inc						
200 Applied Pkwy	University Park	IL	60484	**800-786-1362***	708-534-5575	178-11
*Sales						
Applied Technology & Management Inc						
411 Pablo Ave	Jacksonville Beach	FL	32250	**800-275-6488**	904-249-8009	261

	Toll-Free	Phone	Class
Applied Thermal Systems 8401 73rd Ave N Ste 74 .... Brooklyn Park MN 55428	800-479-4783	763-535-5545	608
APPMA (American Pet Products Manufacturers Assn) 255 Glenville Rd .... Greenwich CT 06831	800-452-1225	203-532-0000	49-4
AppNeta Inc 285 Summer St 4th Fl. ....Boston MA 02210	800-664-4401	800-508-5233	804
APPNETCOM 7883 NC Hwy 105 S Ste C .... Boone NC 28607	888-926-4584	828-963-7286	180
Appraisal Institute 550 W Van Buren St Ste 1000 ....Chicago IL 60607	888-756-4624	312-335-4100	49-17
Appraisal Journal 200 W Madison Ste 1500 ....Chicago IL 60606	888-756-4624		455-5
AppTech Corp 2011 Palomar Airport Rd Ste 102 ....Carlsbad CA 92011 *Support	877-720-0022*	760-707-5959	177
Apptopia Inc 132 Lincoln St 3rd Fl ....Boston MA 02111	855-277-8674		
APPX Software Inc 11363 San Jose Blvd Ste 301.............Jacksonville FL 32223	800-879-2779	904-880-5560	178-1
APQC 123 N Post Oak Ln Ste 300............Houston TX 77024	800-776-9676	713-681-4020	49-12
APRA (Automotive Parts Remanufacturers Assn) 4215 Lafayette Ctr Dr Ste 3.......... Chantilly VA 20151	877-734-4827	703-968-2772	49-21
Apria Healthcare Group Inc 26220 Enterprise Ct .... Lake Forest CA 92630	800-277-4288	949-639-2000	362
Apricorn Inc 12191 Kirkham Rd .... Poway CA 92064	800-458-5448	858-513-2000	173-8
Apriva Inc 8501 N Scottsdale Rd Ste 110 .... Scottsdale AZ 85253	877-277-0728	480-421-1210	177
APRO (Association of Progressive Rental Organizations) 1504 Robin Hood Trl ....Austin TX 78703	800-204-2776	512-794-0095	49-18
APRS (American Park & Recreation Society) 22377 Belmont Ridge Rd ....Ashburn VA 20148	800-765-3110	703-858-0784	48-23
APS (Albuquerque Public Schools) 6400 Uptown Blvd NE .... Albuquerque NM 87110	866-563-9297	505-880-3700	681
APS (American Physical Society) 1 Physics Ellipse .... College Park MD 20740	866-918-1164	301-209-3200	49-19
APS (Arizona Public Service Co) 400 N Fifth St PO Box 53999 ....Phoenix AZ 85004	800-253-9405	602-371-7171	782
Apscreen Inc PO Box 80639 ....Rancho Santa Margarita CA 92688	800-277-2733	949-646-4003	631
APSP (Association of Pool & Spa Professionals) 2111 Eisenhower Ave Ste 500 .... Alexandria VA 22314	800-323-3996	703-838-0083	49-4
APT (Alabama Public Television) 2112 11th Ave S Ste 400 .... Birmingham AL 35205	800-239-5233	205-328-8756	628
APTA (American Physical Therapy Assn) 1111 North Fairfax St .... Alexandria VA 22314	800-999-2782	703-684-2782	49-8
AptarGroup Inc 475 W Terra Cotta Ave Ste E.............Crystal Lake IL 60014 NYSE: ATR	800-401-1957	815-477-0424	154
APWA (American Public Works Assn) 2345 Grand Blvd Ste 700 .... Kansas City MO 64108	800-848-2792	816-472-6100	49-7
AQHA (American Quarter Horse Assn) 1600 Quarter Horse Dr ....Amarillo TX 79104	800-291-7323	806-376-4811	48-3
Aqtis 1001 De Maisonneuve East Blvd Ste 900 .... Montreal QC H2L4P9	888-647-0681	514-844-2113	
Aqua America Inc 762 W Lancaster Ave .... Bryn Mawr PA 19010 NYSE: WTR	877-987-2782		782
Aqua Bamboo Waikiki 2425 Kuhio Ave .... Honolulu HI 96815	855-747-0754	808-922-7777	378
Aqua Bath Company Inc 921 Cherokee Ave .... Nashville TN 37207	800-232-2284	615-227-0017	606
Aqua Cal Inc 2737 24th St N .... Saint Petersburg FL 33713	800-786-7751	727-823-5642	14
Aqua Data Inc 95 Fifth Ave ....Pincourt QC J7W5K8	800-567-9003	514-425-1010	242
Aqua Finance Inc 1 Corporate Dr Ste 300............ Wausau WI 54401	800-234-3663		
Aqua Rehab Inc 2145 rue Michelin .... Laval QC H7L5B8	800-661-3472	450-687-3472	242
Aqua Test Inc 28620 Maple Valley Black Diamond Rd SE .... Maple Valley WA 98038	800-221-3159		
Aqua-Aerobic Systems Inc 6306 N Alpine Rd ....Loves Park IL 61111	800-940-5008	815-654-2501	801
Aqua-Dyne Inc 701 S Persimmon St Ste 85 .... Tomball TX 77375	888-997-1483		637
Aqua-Leisure Industries Inc PO Box 239 .... Avon MA 02322	866-807-3998		706
Aqualung America Inc 2340 Cousteau Ct .... Vista CA 92083	800-446-2671	760-597-5000	706
Aquarion Co 835 Main St .... Bridgeport CT 06604	800-732-9678	203-336-7662	782
Aquarium du Quebec 1675 des Hotels Ave .... Quebec QC G1W4S3	866-659-5264	418-659-5264	40
Aquarius Casino Resort 1900 S Casino Dr .... Laughlin NV 89029	888-662-5825	702-298-5111	133
Aquatherm Industries Inc 1940 Rutgers University Blvd .... Lakewood NJ 08701	800-535-6307		356
Aquatic Informatics Inc 1111 West Georgia St Ste 2400 .... Vancouver BC V6E4M3	877-870-2782	604-873-2782	146
Aquatrol Inc 600 E North St PO Box 8012 .... Elburn IL 60119	800-323-0688	630-365-5400	
Aqueduct Medical Inc 665 Third St Ste 20. .... San Francisco CA 94107	877-365-4325		473
Aquent LLC 711 Boylston St .... Boston MA 02116	855-767-6333	617-535-5000	717
Aquila Group of Funds 380 Madison Ave Ste 2300............New York NY 10017	800-437-1020	212-697-6666	524
Aquinas College 4210 HaRding Rd .... Nashville TN 37205 *Admissions	800-649-9956*	615-297-7545	166
Aquinas Institute of Theology 23 S Spring Ave .... Saint Louis MO 63108	800-977-3869	314-256-8800	167-3
AR 160 Schoolhouse Rd .... Souderton PA 18964	800-933-8181	215-723-8181	643
A-r Editions Inc 1600 Aspen Cmns Ste 100........... Middleton WI 53562	800-736-0070	608-836-9000	520
AR Wilfley & Sons Inc 5870 E 56th Ave ....Commerce CO 80022	800-525-9930	303-779-1777	637
AR. Sandri Inc 400 Chapman St .... Greenfield MA 01301	800-628-1900		575
AR.M. Solutions Inc PO Box 2929 ....Camarillo CA 93011	888-772-6468		160
ARA (American Rental Assn) 1900 19th St ....Moline IL 61265	800-334-2177	309-764-2475	49-4
ARA (Agricultural Retailers Assn) 1156 15th St NW Ste 500...... Washington DC 20005	800-535-6272	202-457-0825	48-2
ARA (Awards and Personalization Assn) 8735 W Higgins Rd Ste 300 ....Chicago IL 60631	800-344-2148	847-375-4800	49-4
ARA (Automotive Recyclers Assn) 9113 Church St .... Manassas VA 20110	888-385-1005	571-208-0428	49-21
Arabel Inc 16301 NW 49th Ave .... Hialeah FL 33014 *Sales	800-759-5959*	305-623-8302	191-2
Arabian Horse World 1316 Tamson Dr Ste 101 .... Cambria CA 93428	800-955-9423	805-771-2300	455-14
Arachnid Inc 6212 Material Ave ....Loves Park IL 61111	800-435-8319	815-654-0212	322
Aram A Kaz Co, The 365 Silas Deane Hwy ....Wethersfield CT 06109	800-969-2251	860-529-6900	392
ARAMARK Corp 1101 Market St ....Philadelphia PA 19107	800-388-3300	215-238-3000	185
ARAMARK Uniform & Career Apparel LLC 2860 Rudder Rd .... Memphis TN 38118	800-272-6275		271
Aramsco Inc 1480 Grandview Ave .... Paulsboro NJ 08086	800-767-6933	856-686-7700	146
Arandell Inc N82 W13118 Leon Rd .... Menomonee Falls WI 53051	800-558-8724		623
Arapahoe Community College 5900 S Santa Fe Dr ....Littleton CO 80160	888-800-9198	303-797-0100	162
Arazoza Brothers Corp 15901 SW 242nd St ....Homestead FL 33031	800-238-1510	305-246-3223	293
ARBA (American Rabbit Breeders Assn) PO Box 5667 ....Bloomington IL 61702	800-753-9448	309-664-7500	48-3
Arbella Insuranc 1100 Crown Colony Dr PO Box 699103. ....Quincy MA 02269	800-972-5348	617-328-2800	390-4
Arbill PO Box 820542 ....Philadelphia PA 19154	800-523-5367		675
Arbitration Forums Inc 3350 Buschwood Pk Dr Ste 295 .... Tampa FL 33618 *Cust Svc	800-967-8889*	813-931-4004	41
Arbitron Inc 9705 Patuxent Woods Dr .... Columbia MD 21046 NYSE: ARB	800-543-7300	410-312-8000	464
Arbor Acres 1240 Arbor Rd .... Winston-Salem NC 27104	866-658-2724	336-724-7921	668
Arbor Centers for Eyecare 2640 W 183rd St .... Homewood IL 60430	866-798-6633	708-798-6633	237
Arbor Hospice & Home Care 2366 Oak Vly Dr .... Ann Arbor MI 48103	888-992-2273	734-662-5999	370
Arbor Realty Trust Inc 333 Earle Ovington Blvd Ste 900 .... Uniondale NY 11553 NYSE: ABR	800-272-6710		650
Arbor Research & Trading LLC 1000 Hart Rd Ste 260 .... Barrington IL 60010	800-606-1872		
Arboretum, The Arboretum Rd University of Guelph...................Guelph ON N1G2W1	877-674-1610	519-824-4120	97
ArborOakland Group 4303 Normandy Ct .... Royal Oak MI 48073	800-886-5661	248-549-0150	
Arborwell Inc 2337 American Ave ....Hayward CA 94545	888-969-8733		771
Arbutus Software Inc 6450 Roberts St ....Burnaby BC V5G4E1	877-333-6336	604-437-7873	179
ARC (American Radiolabeled Chemicals Inc) 101 ARC Dr .... Saint Louis MO 63146	800-331-6661	314-991-4545	145
ARC (American Refugee Committee) 430 Oak Grove St Ste 204.......Minneapolis MN 55403	800-875-7060	612-872-7060	48-5
ARC Industries Inc 2780 Airport Dr .... Columbus OH 43219	800-734-7007	614-479-2500	717
Arc of Stanly County, The 350 Pee Dee Ave Ste A .... Albemarle NC 28001	800-230-7525	704-986-1500	49-15
Arc of the US 1010 Wayne Ave Ste 650 .... Silver Spring MD 20910	800-433-5255	301-565-3842	48-17
ARC Resources Ltd 308 Fourth Ave SW Ste 1200 .... Calgary AB T2P0H7 TSX: ARX	888-272-4900	403-503-8600	671
Arc San Joaquin Inc 41 W Yokuts Ave .... Stockton CA 95207	800-847-3030	209-955-1625	260
ARC the Hotel Ottawa 140 Slater St .... Ottawa ON K1P5H6	800-699-2516	613-238-2888	378
Arcadia University 450 S Easton Rd .... Glenside PA 19038	877-272-2342	215-572-2900	166
Arcamed Inc 5101 Decatur Blvd Ste A........Indianapolis IN 46241	877-545-6622	317-822-7799	
ArcBest (ABC) 3801 Old Greenwood Rd ....Fort Smith AR 72903 NASDAQ: ARCB	800-610-5544		775
Arcet Equipment Company Inc 1700 Chamberlayne Ave .... Richmond VA 23222	800-388-0302		201
Arch Chemicals Inc 1200 Old Lower River Rd PO Box 800. ....Charleston TN 37310 NYSE: ARJ	800-638-8174	423-780-2724	145
Arch Crown Tags Inc 460 Hillside Ave .... Hillside NJ 07205	800-526-8353	973-731-6300	412
Arch Insurance Group Inc 1 Liberty Plz 53rd Fl ....New York NY 10006	866-993-9978	212-651-6500	390-2
Archadeck 2924 Emerywood Pkwy Ste 101 .... Richmond VA 23294	888-687-3325	804-353-6999	189-2

	Toll-Free	Phone	Class
Archaeological Institute of America (AIA)			
44 Beacon St ....Boston MA 02108	877-524-6300	617-353-9361	48-11
Archaeology Magazine			
36-36 33rd St ....Long Island NY 11106	877-275-9782	718-472-3050	455-19
Archdale-Trinity Chamber of Commerce			
213 Balfour Dr ....Archdale NC 27263	800-626-2672	336-434-2073	139
Archdiocese of Saint Paul & Minneapolis			
226 Summit Ave ....Saint Paul MN 55102	877-290-1605	651-291-4411	48-20
Archer Daniels Midland Co			
77 W Wacker Dr ....Chicago IL 60601	800-637-5843	217-424-5200	296-8
Archer Screw Products Inc			
11341 Melrose Ave ....Franklin Park IL 60131	800-952-7897		452
Archibald Gray & McKay Ltd			
3514 White Oak Rd ....London ON N6E2Z9	800-336-9708	519-685-5300	256
Archie Mcphee			
10915 47th Ave W ....Mukilteo WA 98275	800-886-2221	425-349-3838	328
Architectural & Transportation Barriers Compliance Board			
1331 F St NW Ste 1000 ......Washington DC 20004	800-872-2253	202-272-0080	339-19
Architectural Bronze Aluminum Corp			
655 Deerfield Rd Ste 100 ....Deerfield IL 60015	800-339-6581		772
Architectural Builders Hardware Manufacturing			
1222 Ardmore Ave Apt W ....Itasca IL 60143	800-932-9224	630-875-9900	349
Architectural Digest			
1 World Trade Ctr ....New York NY 10007	800-365-8032		455-2
Architex International			
3333 Commercial Ave ......Northbrook IL 60062	800-621-0827		360
Archive-cd LLC			
910 Beverly Way ....Jacksonville OR 97530	800-323-1868	541-899-5704	177
Archway Marketing Services Inc			
19850 S Diamond Lake Rd ....Rogers MN 55374	866-779-9855	763-428-3300	461
ARCO Coffee Co			
2206 Winter St ....Superior WI 54880	800-283-2726	715-392-4771	296-7
Arco Electric Products Corp			
2325 E Michigan Rd ....Shelbyville IN 46176	800-428-4370	317-398-9713	515
Arcos Industries			
1 Arcos Dr ....Mount Carmel PA 17851	800-233-8460	570-339-5200	806
Arctern Inc			
1133 Ave of the Americas			
15th Fl ....New York NY 10036	800-231-4973		
Arctic Industries Inc			
9731 NW 114th Way ....Miami FL 33178	800-325-0123		14
Arctic Slope Regional Corp			
1230 Agvik St PO Box 129 ....Barrow AK 99723	800-770-2772	907-852-8633	534
Arctic Star Refrigeration Mfg Company Inc			
3540 W Pioneer Pkwy ......Arlington TX 76013	800-229-6562	817-274-1396	660
Arctic Storm Management Group LLC			
2727 Alaskan Way Pier 69 ....Seattle WA 98121	800-929-0908	206-547-6557	285
Arctic Wolf Networks Inc			
111 West Evelyn Ste 115 ....Sunnyvale CA 94086	888-272-8429		196
ArcticDx Inc			
MaRs Ctr 661 University Ave			
Ste 455 ....Toronto ON M5G1M1	866-964-5182		415
Arcturus Advisors			
4320 Dunewood Pl ....Fernandina Beach FL 32034	866-593-2207		41
ARCVB (Alton Regional Convention & Visitors Bureau)			
200 Piasa St ....Alton IL 62002	800-258-6645	618-465-6676	206
Arcways Inc			
1076 Ehlers Rd ....Neenah WI 54956	800-558-5096		
Arcweb Technologies LLC			
234 Market St 5th Fl..........Philadelphia PA 19106	800-846-7980		461
Ardenwood Historic Farm			
34600 Ardenwood Blvd ....Fremont CA 94555	888-327-2757	510-544-2797	517
ARDEX Inc			
400 Ardex Park Dr ....Aliquippa PA 15001	888-512-7339	724-203-5000	
ARDMS (American Registry of Diagnostic Medical Sonographe)			
1401 Rockville Pk Ste 600 ....Rockville MD 20852	800-541-9754	301-738-8401	49-8
ARE (Association for Research & Enlightenment)			
215 67th St ....Virginia Beach VA 23451	800-333-4499	757-428-3588	48-17
Area Agency On Aging			
9549 Koger Blvd			
Gadsden Bldg Ste 100 .....St Petersburg FL 33702	800-963-5337	727-570-9696	448
Area Agency On Aging 10b Inc			
1550 Corporate Woods Pkwy ......Uniontown OH 44685	800-421-7277	330-896-9172	448
Area Development Magazine			
400 Post Ave ....Westbury NY 11590	800-735-2732	516-338-0900	455-5
Area Erectors Inc			
2323 Harrison Ave ....Rockford IL 61104	800-270-2732	815-398-6700	189-14
Areacall Inc			
7803 Stratford Rd ....Bethesda MD 20814	800-205-6268	301-657-2718	116
Arenac County			
PO Box 747 ....Standish MI 48658	800-232-5216	989-846-4626	337
Arends & Sons Inc			
715 S Sangamon Ave ....Gibson City IL 60936	800-637-6052	217-784-4241	274
Ares Sportswear Ltd			
3704 Lacon Rd ....Hilliard OH 43026	800-439-8614	614-767-1950	683
ARG Trucking Corp			
369 Bostwick Rd ....Phelps NY 14532	800-334-1314	315-789-8871	775
Argenia LLC			
11524 Fairview Rd ....Little Rock AR 72212	800-482-5968	501-227-9670	389
ARGI (ARGI Investment Services LLC)			
2110 High Wickham Pl........Louisville KY 40223	866-568-9719	502-753-0609	400
ARGI Investment Services LLC (ARGI)			
2110 High Wickham Pl........Louisville KY 40223	866-568-9719	502-753-0609	400
Argo International Corp			
71 Veronica Ave Unit 1 ....Somerset NJ 08873	866-289-2746	732-979-2996	246
Argo Sales inc			
717-7th Ave SW Ste 1300 ......Calgary AB T2P0Z3	866-930-6633	403-265-6633	
Argo Translation Inc			
1884 Johns Dr ....Glenview IL 60025	888-961-9291	847-901-4075	763
Argon Technologies Inc			
4612 Wesley St ....Greenville TX 75401	888-651-1010	903-455-5036	261
Argonaut Hotel			
495 Jefferson St ....San Francisco CA 94109	866-415-0704	415-563-0800	378
Argonne National Laboratory (ANL)			
9700 S Cass Ave ....Argonne IL 60439	800-632-8990	630-252-2000	664
Argosy Casino Alton			
1 Piasa St ....Alton IL 62002	800-711-4263		133
Argosy University			
1515 Central Pkwy ....Eagan MN 55121	888-844-2004	651-846-2882	166
Argosy University Hawaii			
400 ASB Tower 1001 Bishop St ....Honolulu HI 96813	888-323-2777	808-536-5555	795
Arguindegui Oil Companies			
4506 State 359 and Loop 20 ....Laredo TX 78042	800-722-5251	956-286-8330	316
Argus Interactive Agency Inc			
217 N Main St Ste 200 ....Santa Ana CA 92701	866-595-9597		526
Argus Machine Company Ltd			
5820 97th St NW ....Edmonton AB T6E3J1	888-434-9451	780-434-9451	535
Argus Supply Co			
46400 Continental Dr ....Chesterfield MI 48047	800-873-0456	800-332-0435	23
ARH (Alexander Ramsey House)			
265 S Exchange St ....Saint Paul MN 55102	800-657-3773	651-296-8760	50-3
ARH (Appalachian Regional Healthcare Service)			
80 Hospital Dr PO Box 8086. .....Barbourville KY 40906	888-654-0015	859-226-2440	352
ARHP (Association of Reproductive Health Professionals)			
1300 19th St NW Ste 200.......Washington DC 20036	877-311-8972	202-466-3825	49-8
ARI (Autism Research Institute)			
4182 Adams Ave ....San Diego CA 92116	866-366-3361	619-281-7165	48-17
ARi Industries Inc			
381 Ari Ct ....Addison IL 60101	800-237-6725	630-953-9100	201
ARI Network Services Inc			
10850 W Pk Pl Ste 1200.......Milwaukee WI 53224	877-805-0803	414-973-4300	178-10
Aria Athletic Club & Spa			
1300 Westhaven Dr ....Vail CO 81657	888-824-5772	970-479-5942	703
Aria Communications			
717 W Saint Germain St ....St. Cloud MN 56301	800-955-9924		732
Aria Health Bucks County Campus			
380 N Oxford Valley Rd ....Langhorne PA 19047	877-808-2742		
Aria Solutions Inc			
110 - 12th Ave SW Ste 600 ....Calgary AB T2R0G7	866-235-1181	403-235-0227	620
Ariba Inc			
807 11th Ave ....Sunnyvale CA 94089	866-772-7422		39
NYSE: SAP			
Aribex Inc 744 S 400 E ....Orem UT 84097	866-340-5522	801-226-5522	228
Ariel Technologies			
1980 E Lohman Ave ....Las Cruces NM 88001	877-524-6860		175
Ariens Co			
655 W Ryan St ....Brillion WI 54110	800-678-5443	920-756-2141	428
Aris Horticulture Inc			
115 Third St SE ....Barberton OH 44203	800-232-9557		368
Aristatek Inc			
710 E Garfield St Ste 220 ......Laramie WY 82070	877-912-2200	307-721-2126	177
Aristocrat Technologies			
7230 Amigo St ....Las Vegas NV 89119	800-748-4156	702-270-1000	322
Aristotle Capital Management LLC			
11100 Santa Monica Blvd			
Ste 1700 ....Los Angeles CA 90025	877-478-4722	310-478-4005	400
Aristotle Inc			
205 Pennsylvania Ave SE .....Washington DC 20003	800-296-2747*	202-543-8345	178-11
*Sales			
ARIZON COMPANIES			
11880 Dorsett Rd ....St. Louis MO 63043	800-325-1303	314-739-0037	
Arizona			
Agriculture Dept			
1688 W Adams St ....Phoenix AZ 85007	800-294-0308	602-542-4373	338-3
Department of Insurance			
100 N 15th Ave Ste 102 ....Phoenix AZ 85007	800-325-2548	602-364-2499	
Education Dept			
1535 W Jefferson St ....Phoenix AZ 85007	800-352-4558	602-542-5393	338-3
Financial Institutions			
2910 N 44th St Ste 310 ....Phoenix AZ 85018	800-544-0708	602-771-2800	338-3
Legislature			
Arizona State Capitol Complex 1700 W Washington St			
1700 W Washington St. ....Phoenix AZ 85007	800-352-8404	602-926-3559	338-3
Lottery			
4740 E University Dr ....Phoenix AZ 85034	800-639-8783	480-921-4400	450
Medical Board			
9545 Doubletree Ranch Rd .....Scottsdale AZ 85258	877-255-2212	480-551-2700	338-3
Rehabilitation Services Admin			
3321 N 16th St Ste 200 ....Phoenix AZ 85016	800-563-1221	602-266-9206	338-3
Secretary of State			
1700 W Washington St 7th Fl. ....Phoenix AZ 85007	800-458-5842	602-542-4285	338-3
Securities Div			
1300 W Washington St 3rd Fl .....Phoenix AZ 85007	866-837-4399	602-542-4242	338-3
Treasurer			
1700 W Washington St Ste 102 ....Phoenix AZ 85007	877-365-8310	602-542-7800	338-3
Vital Records Office			
1818 W Adams St ....Phoenix AZ 85007	888-816-5907	602-364-1300	338-3
Arizona Art Supply			
4025 N 16th St ....Phoenix AZ 85016	877-264-9514	602-264-9514	45
Arizona Assn of Realtors			
255 E Osborne Rd Ste 200 ....Phoenix AZ 85012	800-426-7274	602-248-7787	652
Arizona Attorney Magazine			
4201 N 24th St Ste 200 ....Phoenix AZ 85016	866-482-9227	602-252-4804	455-15
Arizona Automobile Dealers Association			
4701 N 24th St Ste B3 ....Phoenix AZ 85016	800-678-3875	602-468-0888	138
Arizona Biltmore Resort & Spa			
2400 E Missouri ....Phoenix AZ 85016	800-950-0086	602-955-6600	665
Arizona Cardinals			
8701 S Hardy Dr ....Tempe AZ 85284	800-999-1402	602-379-0101	711-2
Arizona Chamber of Commerce & Industry			
3200 N Central Ave Ste 1125 .....Phoenix AZ 85012	866-275-5816	602-248-9172	140
Arizona Charlie's Boulder Casino & Hotel			
4575 Boulder Hwy ....Las Vegas NV 89121	888-236-9066	702-951-5800	378
Arizona Community Foundation			
2201 E Camelback Rd Ste 405B ....Phoenix AZ 85016	800-222-8221	602-381-1400	303
Arizona Correctional Industries			
3701 W Cambridge Ave ....Phoenix AZ 85009	800-992-1738	602-272-7600	626
Arizona Culinary Institute			
10585 N 114th St Ste 401 ....Scottsdale AZ 85259	866-294-2433	480-603-1066	163
Arizona Daily Star			
4850 S Park Ave ....Tucson AZ 85714	800-695-4492	520-573-4343	528-2
Arizona Dental Assn			
3193 N Drinkwater Blvd ....Scottsdale AZ 85251	800-866-2732	480-344-5777	227
Arizona Federal Credit Union			
PO Box 60070 ....Phoenix AZ 85082	800-523-4603	602-683-1000	219

Alphabetical Section

Name / Address	City	State	ZIP	Toll-Free	Phone	Class
Arizona Golf Resort & Conference Ctr						
425 S Power Rd	Mesa	AZ	85206	**800-528-8282**	480-832-3202	665
Arizona Grand Resort						
8000 S Arizona Grand Pkwy	Phoenix	AZ	85044	**866-267-1321**	602-438-9000	665
Arizona Highways Magazine						
2039 W Lewis Ave	Phoenix	AZ	85009	**800-543-5432**		455-22
Arizona Leather Company Inc						
4235 Schaefer Ave	Chino	CA	91710	**888-669-5328**	909-993-5101	321
Arizona Limousines Inc						
8900 N Central Ave Ste 101	Phoenix	AZ	85020	**800-678-0033**	602-267-7097	440
Arizona Medical Assn, The (ArMA)						
810 W Bethany Home Rd	Phoenix	AZ	85013	**800-482-3480**	602-246-8901	472
Arizona Mills						
5000 Arizona Mills Cir	Tempe	AZ	85282	**877-746-6642**	317-636-1600	458
Arizona Osteopathic Medical Assn						
5150 N 16th St Ste A122	Phoenix	AZ	85016	**888-266-6699**	602-266-6699	529
Arizona Partsmaster						
7125 W Sherman St	Phoenix	AZ	85043	**888-924-7278**	602-233-3580	608
Arizona Precision Sheet Metal						
2140 W Pinnacle Peak Rd	Phoenix	AZ	85027	**800-443-7039**	623-516-3700	693
Arizona Public Service Co (APS)						
400 N Fifth St PO Box 53999	Phoenix	AZ	85004	**800-253-9405**	602-371-7171	782
Arizona Republic						
200 E Van Buren St	Phoenix	AZ	85004	**800-331-9303**	602-444-8000	528-2
Arizona State Capitol Museum						
1700 W Washington St	Phoenix	AZ	85007	**800-228-4710**	602-542-4675	517
Arizona State Hospital						
2500 E Van Buren St	Phoenix	AZ	85008	**877-588-5163**	602-244-1331	373-5
ARIZONA STATE PARKS						
Lyman Lake State Park						
PO Box 1428	Saint Johns	AZ	85936	**877-697-2757**	928-337-4441	
Arizona State Prison Complex-Eyman						
4374 E Butte Ave	Florence	AZ	85132	**866-333-2039**	520-868-0201	213
Arizona State Retirement System						
3300 N Central Ave	Phoenix	AZ	85012	**800-621-3778**	602-240-2000	524
Arizona State University						
Hayden Library						
300 E Orange Mall	Tempe	AZ	85281	**800-728-0209**	480-965-3417	433-6
Sandra Day O'Connor College of Law						
PO Box 877906	Tempe	AZ	85287	**855-278-5080**	480-727-8856	167-1
West PO Box 37100	Phoenix	AZ	85069	**855-278-5080**	602-543-5500	166
Arizona Western College						
2020 S Ave 8 E	Yuma	AZ	85366	**888-293-0392**	928-317-6000	162
ARJ Infusion Services Inc						
10049 Lakeview Ave	Lenexa	KS	66219	**866-451-8804**		237
Arjobex America Inc						
10901 Westlake Dr	Charlotte	NC	28273	**800-765-9278**		553
ARK Diagnostics Inc						
48089 Fremont Blvd	Fremont	CA	94538	**877-869-2320**		362
Ark TeleServices						
2 E Merrick Rd	Valley Stream	NY	11580	**800-898-5367**		392
Ark Valley Electric Co-op Assn						
10 E Tenth St	South Hutchinson	KS	67504	**888-297-9212**	620-662-6661	245
Arkadin Inc						
5 Concourse Pkwy Ste 1600	Atlanta	GA	30328	**866-551-1432**		386
Arkansas						
Administrative Office of the Courts						
625 Marshall St	Little Rock	AR	72201	**800-950-8221**	501-682-9400	338-4
Aging & Adult Services Div						
PO Box 1437 Slot S-530	Little Rock	AR	72203	**800-482-8049**	501-682-2441	338-4
Attorney General						
323 Ctr St Ste 200	Little Rock	AR	72201	**800-482-8982***	501-682-2007	338-4
*Consumer Info						
Consumer Protection Div						
323 Ctr St Ste 200	Little Rock	AR	72201	**800-482-8982**	501-682-2007	338-4
Crime Victims Reparations Board						
323 Ctr St Ste 200	Little Rock	AR	72201	**800-482-8982**	501-682-2007	338-4
Dept of Corrections Maximum Security Unit						
2501 State Farm Rd	Tucker	AR	72168	**866-801-3435**	501-842-3800	213
Environmental Quality Dept						
5301 Northshore Dr	Little Rock	AR	72118	**888-233-0326**	501-682-0744	338-4
Ethics Commission						
501 Woodlane St Ste 301n	Little Rock	AR	72203	**800-422-7773**	501-324-9600	265
Game & Fish Commission						
2 Natural Resource Dr	Little Rock	AR	72205	**800-364-4263**	501-223-6300	338-4
Highway & Transportation Dept						
10324 I-30	Little Rock	AR	72209	**800-245-1672**	501-569-2000	338-4
Insurance Dept						
1200 W Third St	Little Rock	AR	72201	**800-282-9134**	501-371-2600	338-4
Parks & Tourism Dept						
1 Capitol Mall Ste 4A-900	Little Rock	AR	72201	**800-628-8725**	501-682-7777	338-4
Rehabilitation Services						
525 W Capitol Ave	Little Rock	AR	72201	**800-330-0632**	501-296-1600	338-4
Securities Dept						
201 E Markham St Ste 300	Little Rock	AR	72201	**800-981-4429**	501-324-9260	338-4
State Medical Board						
1401 West Capitol Ave Ste 340	Little Rock	AR	72201	**888-228-1233**	501-296-1802	338-4
Arkansas Baptist Foundation						
10 Remington Dr	Little Rock	AR	72204	**800-838-2272**	501-376-4791	48-20
Arkansas Bar Assn						
2224 Cottondale Ln	Little Rock	AR	72202	**800-609-5668**	501-375-4606	72
Arkansas Blue Cross Blue Shield						
PO Box 2181	Little Rock	AR	72203	**800-238-8379**		390-3
Arkansas Business LP						
114 Scott St	Little Rock	AR	72201	**888-322-6397**	501-372-1443	455-5
Arkansas Capital Corp Group						
200 River Market Ave Ste 400	Little Rock	AR	72201	**800-216-7237**	501-374-9247	216
Arkansas City Area Chamber of Commerce						
PO Box 795	Arkansas City	KS	67005	**800-794-4780**	620-442-0230	139
Arkansas City Convention & Visitors Bureau						
106 S Summit St PO Box 795	Arkansas City	KS	67005	**800-794-4780**	620-442-0230	206
Arkansas Correctional Industries (ACI)						
6841 W 13th St	Pine Bluff	AR	71602	**877-635-7213**		626
Arkansas Democrat-Gazette						
121 E Capital St	Little Rock	AR	72203	**800-482-1121***	501-378-3400	528-2
*Cust Svc						
Arkansas Educational Television Network (AETN)						
350 S Donaghey Ave	Conway	AR	72034	**800-662-2386**	501-682-2386	628
Arkansas Educator Magazine						
1500 W Fourth St	Little Rock	AR	72201	**800-632-0624**	501-375-4611	455-8
Arkansas Graphics Inc						
800 S Gaines St	Little Rock	AR	72201	**877-918-4847**	501-376-8436	623
Arkansas Hospice						
14 Parkstone Cir	North Little Rock	AR	72116	**877-257-3400**	501-748-3333	370
Arkansas Lawyer Magazine						
2224 Cottondale Ln	Little Rock	AR	72202	**800-609-5668**	501-375-4606	455-15
Arkansas Museum of Natural Resources						
3853 Smackover Hwy	Smackover	AR	71762	**888-287-2757**	870-725-2877	561
Arkansas Poly Inc						
1248 S 28th St	Van Buren	AR	72956	**800-364-5036**	479-474-5036	344
Arkansas Power Steering & Hydraulics Inc						
900 Fiber Optic Dr	North Little Rock	AR	72117	**800-734-9411**	501-372-4828	112
Arkansas Realtors Assn						
11224 Executive Ctr Dr	Little Rock	AR	72211	**888-333-2206**	501-225-2020	652
Arkansas Repertory Theatre						
601 Main St PO Box 110	Little Rock	AR	72203	**866-684-3737**	501-378-0405	569-4
Arkansas State Dental Assn						
7480 Hwy 107	Sherwood	AR	72120	**800-501-2732**	501-834-7650	227
Arkansas State University						
PO Box 1630	State University	AR	72467	**800-382-3030**	870-972-3024	166
Arkansas State University Mountain Home						
1600 S College St	Mountain Home	AR	72653	**800-482-5964**	870-508-6100	162
Arkansas State University Museum						
PO Box 490	State University	AR	72467	**800-342-2923**	870-972-2074	517
Arkansas State University Newport						
7648 Victory Blvd	Newport	AR	72112	**800-976-1676**	870-512-7800	162
Arkansas Valley Electric Co-op Corp						
1811 W Commercial St PO Box 47	Ozark	AR	72949	**800-468-2176**	479-667-2176	245
Arkwin Industries Inc						
686 Main St	Westbury	NY	11590	**800-284-2551**	516-333-2640	785
Arley Wholesale						
700 N South Rd	Scranton	PA	18504	**800-233-4107**	570-344-9874	
Arlington Baptist College						
3001 W Div St	Arlington	TX	76012	**800-899-0012**	817-461-8741	166
Arlington Coal & Lumber Company Inc						
41 Park Ave	Arlington	MA	02476	**800-649-8101**	781-643-8100	363
Arlington Computer Products Inc						
851 Commerce Ct	Buffalo Grove	IL	60089	**800-548-5105***	847-541-6333	180
*Orders						
Arlington Convention & Visitors Bureau						
1905 E Randol Mill Rd	Arlington	TX	76011	**800-433-5374**		206
Arlington Industries Inc						
1616 Lakeside Dr	Waukegan	IL	60085	**800-323-4147**	847-689-2754	530
Arlington Industries Inc						
1 Stauffer Industrial Pk	Scranton	PA	18517	**800-233-4717**	570-562-0270	810
Arlington Resort Hotel & Spa						
239 Central Ave	Hot Springs	AR	71901	**800-643-1502**	501-623-7771	665
Arlington School District						
315 N French Ave	Arlington	WA	98223	**877-766-4753**	360-618-6200	681
Arlo G Lott Trucking Inc						
257 S 100 E	Jerome	ID	83338	**800-443-5688**	208-324-5053	775
Arlon Graphics						
2811 S Harbor Blvd	Santa Ana	CA	92704	**800-232-7161**	714-540-2811	3
ARM (Associated Risk Managers)						
2850 Golf Rd	Rolling Meadows	IL	60008	**800-735-5441**	630-285-4324	49-9
ArMA (Arizona Medical Assn, The)						
810 W Bethany Home Rd	Phoenix	AZ	85013	**800-482-3480**	602-246-8901	472
ARMA (Asphalt Roofing Manufacturers Assn)						
529 14th St NW Ste 750	Washington	DC	20045	**800-247-6637**	202-207-0917	49-3
ARMA International						
11880 College Blvd Ste 450	Overland Park	KS	66210	**800-422-2762**	913-341-3808	49-12
Armada Group, The						
325 Soquel Ave	Santa Cruz	CA	95062	**800-408-2120**		343
Armand Manufacturing Inc						
2399 Silver Wolf Dr	Henderson	NV	89011	**800-669-9811**	702-565-7500	66
Armanino Foods of Distinction Inc						
30588 San Antonio St	Hayward	CA	94544	**800-255-5855**	510-441-9300	296-36
OTC: AMNF						
Armanino LLP						
12657 Alcosta Blvd Ste 500	San Ramon	CA	94583	**844-582-8883**		
Armatron International Inc						
15 Highland Ave	Malden	MA	02148	**800-343-3280**	781-321-2300	428
Armed Forces Communications & Electronics Assn (AFCEA)						
4400 Fair Lakes Ct	Fairfax	VA	22033	**800-336-4583**	703-631-6100	48-19
Armed Forces Insurance Exchange (AFI)						
550 Eisenhower Rd	Leavenworth	KS	66048	**800-255-6792**		390-4
Armed Forces Retirement Home - Gulfport						
1800 Beach Dr	Gulfport	MS	39507	**800-422-9988**		668
Armed Forces Retirement Home - Washington						
3700 N Capitol St NW	Washington	DC	20011	**800-422-9988***		448
*Admissions						
Armed Services Mutual Benefit Assn (ASMBA)						
PO Box 160384	Nashville	TN	37216	**800-251-8434**	615-851-0800	48-19
Armellini Express Lines Inc						
3446 SW Armellini Ave	Palm City	FL	34990	**800-327-7887**	772-287-0575	775
Armentor Glenn Law Corp						
300 Stewart St	Lafayette	LA	70501	**800-960-5551**	337-233-1471	427
Armin Tool & Manufacturing Company Inc						
1500 N La Fox St	South Elgin	IL	60177	**800-427-3607**	847-742-1864	752
Armistead Mechanical Inc						
168 Hopper Ave	Waldwick	NJ	07463	**800-587-5267**	201-447-6740	189-10
Armor Group Inc, The						
4600 N Mason-Montgomery Rd	Mason	OH	45040	**800-255-0393**		318
Armor Protective Packaging						
951 Jones St	Howell	MI	48843	**800-365-1117**	517-546-1117	553
Armour Transportation Systems Inc						
689 Edinburgh Dr	Moncton	NB	E1E2L4	**800-561-7987**	506-857-0205	23
Arms Acres						
75 Seminary Hill Rd	Carmel	NY	10512	**800-989-2676**	845-225-3400	722
Armstrong Atlantic State University						
11935 Abercorn St	Savannah	GA	31419	**800-633-2349**		166
Armstrong County						
450 E Market St	Kittanning	PA	16201	**800-368-1066**	724-543-2500	337

Name / Address	City	State	Zip	Toll-Free	Phone	Class
Armstrong County Tourist Bureau 125 Market St	Kittanning	PA	16201	**888-265-9954**	724-543-4003	206
Armstrong International Inc 2081 SE Ocean Blvd 4th Fl	Stuart	FL	34996	**866-738-5125**	772-286-7175	784
Armstrong Lumber Co Inc 2709 Auburn Way N	Auburn	WA	98002	**800-868-9066**	253-833-6666	812
Armstrong Medical Industries Inc 575 Knightsbridge Pkwy *Cust Svc	Lincolnshire	IL	60069	**800-323-4220***	847-913-0101	475
Armstrong Mfg Co 2700 SE Tacoma St	Portland	OR	97202	**800-426-6226**	503-228-8381	492
Armstrong World Industries Inc 2500 Columbia Ave *NYSE: AWI* ■ *Cust Svc	Lancaster	PA	17603	**800-233-3823***	717-397-0611	291
Army & Navy Academy 2605 Carlsbad Blvd	Carlsbad	CA	92008	**888-762-2338**	760-729-2385	618
ARMY Magazine 2425 Wilson Blvd	Arlington	VA	22201	**800-336-4570**	703-841-4300	455-12
Army Residence Community 7400 Crestway	San Antonio	TX	78239	**800-725-0083**	210-646-5316	668
ARN (Association of Rehabilitation Nurses) 4700 West Lake Ave	Glenview	IL	60025	**800-229-7530**	847-375-4710	49-8
Arnaud's 813 Bienville St	New Orleans	LA	70112	**866-230-8895**	504-523-5433	667
Arneg Canada Inc 18 Rue Richelieu	Lacolle	QC	J0J1J0	**800-363-3439**	450-246-3837	606
Arnoff Moving & Storage Inc 1282 Dutchess Tpke	Poughkeepsie	NY	12603	**800-633-6683**	888-430-9542	516
Arnold & Assoc 14275 Midway Rd Ste 170	Addison	TX	75001	**800-535-6329**	972-991-1144	256
Arnold & Itkin LLP 6009 Memorial Dr	Houston	TX	77007	**888-493-1629**	713-222-3800	427
Arnold Lumber Co 251 Fairgrounds Rd	West Kingston	RI	02892	**800-339-0116**	401-783-2266	191-3
Arnot Ogden Medical Ctr 600 Roe Ave	Elmira	NY	14905	**800-952-2662**	607-737-4100	373-3
Aromaland Inc 1326 Rufina Cir	Santa Fe	NM	87507	**800-933-5267**	505-438-0402	77
Aroostook Home Health Services 658 Main St Ste 2	Caribou	ME	04736	**877-688-9977**	207-492-8290	362
AroundWireCom LLC 9455 De Soto Ave	Chatsworth	CA	91311	**888-382-3793**		386
ArQule Inc 19 Presidential Way *NASDAQ: ARQL*	Woburn	MA	01801	**800-373-7827**	781-994-0300	85
Arradiance Inc 142 N Rd Ste F-150	Sudbury	MA	01776	**800-659-2970**		
Array Marketing 45 Progress Ave	Toronto	ON	M1P2Y6	**800-295-4120**	416-299-4865	233
Arrington Jodey (Rep R - TX) 1029 Longworth House Office Bldg	Washington	DC	20515	**888-217-0281**	202-225-4005	
Arris Group Inc 3871 Lakefield Dr *NASDAQ: ARRS*	Suwanee	GA	30024	**866-362-7747**	678-473-2000	643
ARRL (American Radio Relay League) 225 Main St	Newington	CT	06111	**888-277-5289**	860-594-0200	49-14
ArroHealth 49 Wireless Blvd Ste 140	Hauppauge	NY	11788	**866-449-8844**	631-780-5000	392
Arrow 9201 E Dry Creek Rd	Centennial	CO	80112	**800-393-7627**	303-824-4000	656
Arrow Electric Company Inc 317 Wabasso Ave	Louisville	KY	40209	**888-999-5591**	502-367-0141	189-4
Arrow Engine Co 2301 E Independence St	Tulsa	OK	74110	**800-331-3662**	918-583-5711	262
Arrow Environmental Services Inc 6225 Tower Ln	Sarasota	FL	34240	**888-424-2324**	941-377-0888	573
Arrow Fastener Co Inc 271 Mayhill St	Saddle Brook	NJ	07663	**800-776-2228**	201-843-6900	753
Arrow Financial Corp 250 Glen St *NASDAQ: AROW*	Glens Falls	NY	12801	**888-444-0058**	518-415-4307	359-2
Arrow Florist & Park Avenue Greenhouses Inc 757 Park Ave	Cranston	RI	02910	**800-556-7097**	401-785-1900	292
Arrow Freight Management Inc 1001 Berryville st	El Paso	TX	79928	**888-598-9891**		311
Arrow Lock Co 100 Arrow Dr	New Haven	CT	06511	**800-839-3157**		349
Arrow Road Construction 3401 S Busse Rd	Mount Prospect	IL	60056	**800-523-4417**	847-437-0700	188-4
Arrow Stage Lines 720 E Norfolk Ave	Norfolk	NE	68701	**800-672-8302**	402-371-3850	107
Arrow Tank & Engineering Co 650 N Emerson St	Cambridge	MN	55008	**888-892-7769**	763-689-3360	91
Arrow Truck Sales Inc 3200 Manchester Trfy	Kansas City	MO	64129	**800-311-7144**	816-923-5000	57
Arrow Uniform Rental Inc 6400 Monroe Blvd	Taylor	MI	48180	**888-332-7769**	313-299-5000	441
Arrowhead Containers Inc 4330 Clary Blvd	Kansas City	MO	64130	**888-861-9225**	816-861-8050	100
Arrowhead Electric Co-op Inc 5401 West Hwy 61 PO Box 39	Lutsen	MN	55612	**800-864-3744**	218-663-7239	245
Arrowhead Regional Medical Ctr 400 N Pepper Ave	Colton	CA	92324	**855-422-8029**	909-580-1000	373-3
Arrow-Magnolia International 2646 Rodney Ln	Dallas	TX	75229	**800-527-2101**	972-247-7111	151
Arrowpoint Capital 3600 Arco Corporate Dr Ste 100	Charlotte	NC	28273	**866-236-7750**	704-522-2000	390-4
Arrowwood Resort & Conference Ctr 2100 Arrowwood Ln NW *Resv	Alexandria	MN	56308	**866-386-5263***	320-762-1124	665
ARRS (American Roentgen Ray Society) 44211 Slatestone Ct	Leesburg	VA	20176	**800-438-2777**	703-729-3353	49-8
ARS (American Rose Society) 8877 Jefferson Paige Rd	Shreveport	LA	71119	**800-637-6534**		48-18
ARS National Services Inc 201 W Grand Ave	Escondido	CA	92025	**800-456-5053**		392
Art Academy of Cincinnati 1212 Jackson St	Cincinnati	OH	45202	**800-323-5692**	513-562-6262	164
Art Brands LLC 225 Business Ctr Dr	Blacklick	OH	43004	**877-755-4278**	614-755-4278	683
Art Craft Display Inc 500 Business Centre Dr	Lansing	MI	48917	**800-878-0710**	517-485-2221	226
Art Gallery of Ontario 317 Dundas St W	Toronto	ON	M5T1G4	**877-225-4246**	416-979-6660	305
Art in America Magazine 110 Greene St 2nd Fl *Cust Svc	New York	NY	10012	**800-925-8059***	212-398-1690	455-2
Art Institute of Atlanta 6600 Peachtree Dunwoody Rd NE 100 Embassy Row	Atlanta	GA	30328	**800-275-4242**	770-394-8300	164
Art Institute of California						
Inland Empire 674 E Brier Dr	San Bernardino	CA	92408	**800-353-0812**	909-915-2100	164
Los Angeles 2900 31st St	Santa Monica	CA	90405	**888-646-4610**	855-784-1269	164
Orange County 3601 W Sunflower Ave	Santa Ana	CA	92704	**855-784-1269**		
San Diego 7650 Mission Valley Rd	San Diego	CA	92108	**866-275-2422**	858-598-1200	164
San Francisco 10 United Nations Plz	San Francisco	CA	94102	**888-493-3261**	415-865-0198	164
Art Institute of Charlotte 3 Lake Pointe Plz 2110 Water Ridge Pkwy	Charlotte	NC	28217	**800-872-4417**	704-357-8020	164
Art Institute of Colorado 1200 Lincoln St	Denver	CO	80203	**800-275-2420**	303-837-0825	164
Art Institute of Dallas 8080 Pk Ln Ste 100	Dallas	TX	75231	**800-275-4243**	214-692-8080	164
Art Institute of Fort Lauderdale 1799 SE 17th St	Fort Lauderdale	FL	33316	**800-275-7603**	954-463-3000	164
Art Institute of Houston 1900 Yorktown St	Houston	TX	77056	**800-275-4244**	855-784-1269	164
Art Institute of Indianapolis 3500 Depauw Blvd	Indianapolis	IN	46268	**866-441-9031**	855-784-1269	164
Art Institute of Las Vegas 2350 Corporate Cir	Henderson	NV	89074	**800-833-2678**	702-369-9944	164
Art Institute of New York City 218-232 W 40th St	New York	NY	10018	**855-784-1269**		
Art Institute of Ohio						
Cincinnati 8845 Covernor's Hill Dr Ste 100	Cincinnati	OH	45249	**866-613-5184**	855-784-1269	164
Art Institute of Philadelphia 1622 Chestnut St	Philadelphia	PA	19103	**800-275-2474**	855-784-1269	164
Art Institute of Pittsburgh 420 Blvd of the Allies	Pittsburgh	PA	15219	**800-275-2470**	855-784-1269	164
Art Institute of Portland 1122 NW Davis St	Portland	OR	97209	**888-228-6528**	855-784-1269	164
Art Institute of Seattle 2323 Elliott Ave	Seattle	WA	98121	**800-275-2471**	206-448-0900	164
Art Institute of Tampa 4401 N Himes Ave Ste 150	Tampa	FL	33614	**866-703-3277**	855-784-1269	164
Art Institute of Washington 1820 N Ft Myer Dr	Arlington	VA	22209	**877-303-3771**	703-358-9550	164
Art Institutes International Minnesota, The 15 S Ninth St	Minneapolis	MN	55402	**800-777-3643**	855-784-1269	164
Art Institutes, The 1400 Penn Ave	Pittsburgh	PA	15222	**800-275-2470**	855-784-1269	164
Art Iron Inc 860 Curtis St	Toledo	OH	43609	**800-472-1113**	419-241-1261	490
Art Material Services Inc 625 Joyce Kilmer Ave	New Brunswick	NJ	08901	**888-522-5526**	732-545-8888	361
Art Morrison Enterprises Inc 5301 Eighth St E	Fife	WA	98424	**888-640-0516**	253-922-7188	57
Art Resource Inc 65 Bleecker St 12th Fl	New York	NY	10012	**888-505-8666**	212-505-8700	620
Art Supply Warehouse 6672 Westminster Blvd	Westminster	CA	92683	**800-854-6467**	714-891-3626	45
Artafact LLC 43165 Sabercat	Fremont	CA	94539	**800-618-3228**	510-651-9178	464
ARTBA (American Road & Transportation Builders Assn) 1219 28th St NW	Washington	DC	20007	**800-636-2377**	202-289-4434	49-3
Artco-Bell Corp 1302 Industrial Blvd	Temple	TX	76504	**877-778-1811**	254-778-1811	319-3
Artcraft Company Inc, The 200 John L Dietsch Blvd	North Attleboro	MA	02763	**800-659-4042**	508-695-4042	428
Art-Craft Optical Company Inc 57 Goodway Dr S	Rochester	NY	14623	**800-828-8288**	585-546-6640	538
Artel 25 Bradley Dr	Westbrook	ME	04092	**888-406-3463**	207-854-0860	250
Artel Video Systems Corp 5B Lyberty Way	Westford	MA	01886	**800-225-0228**	978-263-5775	643
Artemus Group 317 Office Square Ln Ste 202B	Virginia Beach	VA	23462	**866-744-7101**		313
Artesian Resources Corp 664 Churchmans Rd *NASDAQ: ARTNA*	Newark	DE	19702	**800-332-5114**	302-453-6900	359-5
Artforum International Magazine 350 Seventh Ave	New York	NY	10001	**800-966-2783**	212-475-4000	455-2
Arthrex Inc 1370 Creekside Blvd	Naples	FL	34108	**800-934-4404**	239-643-5553	475
Arthritis Foundation 1330 W Peachtree St Ste 100	Atlanta	GA	30309	**800-283-7800**	404-872-7100	48-17
Arthroscopy Assn of North America (AANA) 9400 W Higgins Rd Ste 200	Rosemont	IL	60018	**877-924-0305**	847-292-2262	49-8
Arthur Consulting Group Inc 31355 Oak Crest Dr Ste 200	Westlake Village	CA	91361	**800-677-9792**	818-735-4800	729
Arthur G James Cancer Hospital & Richard J Solove Research Institute						
Bone Marrow Transplant Program 300 W Tenth Ave	Columbus	OH	43210	**800-293-5066**	614-293-5066	764
Arthur J Gallagher & Co 2 Pierce Pl *NYSE: AJG*	Itasca	IL	60143	**888-285-5106**	630-773-3800	389

	Toll-Free	Phone	Class

Arthur J Glatfelter Agency Inc
PO Box 2726 ....York PA 17405 — 800-233-1957 — 717-741-0911 — 389

Arthur, Chapman, Kettering, Smetak & Pikala PA
500 Young Quinlan Bldg 81 S Ninth St
..................................Minneapolis MN 55402 — 800-916-9262 — 612-339-3500 — 427

Artisan Colour Inc
8970 E Bahia Dr ....Scottsdale AZ 85260 — 800-274-2422 — 480-948-0009 — 776

Artisan Controls Corp
111 Canfield Ave Bldg B15-18 ....Randolph NJ 07869 — 800-457-4950 — 973-598-9400 — 203

Artisan Funds
PO Box 8412 ....Boston MA 02266 — 800-344-1770*
*Cust Svc — — 524

Artisan Laboratories Inc
2532 SE Hawthorne Blvd ....Portland OR 97214 — 800-222-6721 — 503-238-6006 — 474

Artisan's Bank
2961 Centerville Rd ....Wilmington DE 19808 — 800-282-8255 — 302-658-6881 — 70

Artisans Inc
PO Box 1059 ....Calhoun GA 30703 — 800-311-8756 — — 131

Artist Brand Canvas
2448 Loma Ave ....South El Monte CA 91733 — 888-579-2704* — 626-579-2740 — 43
*Orders

Artist's Magazine, The
4700 E Galbraith Rd ....Cincinnati OH 45236 — 800-422-2550 — 513-531-2222 — 455-2

Artistic Carton Co
1975 Big Timber Rd ....Elgin IL 60123 — 800-735-7225 — 847-741-0247 — 100

Artistic Checks
PO Box 40003 ....Colorado Springs CO 80935 — 800-824-3255 — — 142

Artists Club, The
13118 NE Fourth St ....Vancouver WA 98684 — 800-574-1323 — — 756

ARTnews Magazine
110 Greene St 2nd Fl ....New York NY 10012 — 800-284-4625 — 212-398-1690 — 455-2

Art-Phyl Creations
16250 NW 48th Ave ....Hialeah FL 33014 — 800-327-8318 — 305-624-2333 — 233

Arts Ctr of Coastal Carolina
14 Shelter Cove Ln ....Hilton Head Island SC 29928 — 888-860-2787 — 843-686-3945 — 568

Arts-Way Mfg Co Inc
5556 Hwy 9 PO Box 288. ....Armstrong IA 50514 — 800-535-4517 — 712-864-3131 — 273
NASDAQ: ARTW

Aruba Networks Inc
1344 Crossman Ave ....Sunnyvale CA 94089 — 800-943-4526 — 408-227-4500 — 177

Aruba Tourism Authority
1750 Powder Springs St Ste 190 ....Marietta GA 30064 — 800-862-7822 — 404-892-7822 — 770

Aruze Gaming America Inc
955 Grier Dr Ste A ....Las Vegas NV 89119 — 877-268-4119 — 702-361-3166

Arvco Container Corp
845 Gibson St ....Kalamazoo MI 49001 — 800-968-9127 — 269-381-0900 — 100

ArvinMeritor Inc
2135 W Maple Rd ....Troy MI 48084 — 800-535-5560 — 248-435-1000 — 60
NYSE: MTOR

Arvinyl Metal Laminates Corp
233 N Sherman Ave ....Corona CA 92882 — 800-278-4695 — — 483

ARVO (Association for Research in Vision & Ophthalmology)
12300 Twinbrook Pkwy Ste 250 ....Rockville MD 20852 — 888-503-1050 — 240-221-2900 — 49-8

Arzel Zoning Technology Inc
4801 Commerce Pkwy ....Cleveland OH 44128 — 800-611-8312 — — 201

ASA (Autism Society of America)
4340 EW Hwy Ste 350 ....Bethesda MD 20814 — 800-328-8476 — 301-657-0881 — 48-17

ASA (Acoustical Society of America)
1305 Walt Whitman Rd Ste 300 ....Melville NY 11747 — 800-828-8840 — 516-576-2360 — 49-19

ASA (American Society of Agronomy)
5585 Guilford Rd ....Madison WI 53711 — 866-359-9161 — 608-273-8080 — 48-2

ASA (American Society of Appraisers)
555 Herndon Pkwy Ste 125 ....Herndon VA 20170 — 800-272-8258 — 703-478-2228 — 49-17

ASA (American Society on Aging)
575 Market St Ste 2100 ....San Francisco CA 94105 — 800-537-9728 — 415-974-9600 — 48-6

ASA (American Sociological Assn)
1307 New York Ave ....Washington DC 20005 — 800-524-9400 — 202-383-9005 — 49-5

ASA (American Soybean Assn)
12125 Woodcrest Executive Dr
Ste 100 ....Saint Louis MO 63141 — 800-688-7692 — 314-576-1770 — 48-2

ASA (American Statistical Assn)
732 N Washington St ....Alexandria VA 22314 — 888-231-3473 — 703-684-1221 — 49-19

ASA (Automotive Service Assn)
1901 Airport Fwy ....Bedford TX 76021 — 800-272-7467*
*Cust Svc — — 49-21

ASA Alloys Inc
81 Steinway Blvd ....Etobicoke ON M9W6H6 — 800-387-9166 — 416-213-0000 — 490

ASA Computers Inc
645 National Ave ....Mountain View CA 94043 — 800-732-5727 — 650-230-8000 — 176

ASA Tire Master Software
651 S Stratford Rd ....Meridian ID 83642 — 800-241-8472 — 208-855-0781 — 174

ASAA (American Sleep Apnea Assn)
6856 Eastern Ave NW Ste 203 ....Washington DC 20012 — 888-293-3650 — 202-293-3650 — 48-17

ASAE (American Society of Assn Executives)
1575 'I' St NW ....Washington DC 20005 — 888-950-2723 — 202-626-2723 — 49-12

Asah 2125 Hwy 33 ....Trenton NJ 08690 — 800-955-2321 — 609-890-1400 — 472

Asahi Kasei Plastics North America Inc
900 E Van Riper Rd ....Fowlerville MI 48836 — 800-993-5382* — 517-223-5100 — 601-2
*Cust Svc

ASAP (American Society for Adolescent Psychiatry)
PO Box 3948 ....Parker CO 80134 — 866-672-9060

Asap Printing Corp
643 Billinis Rd ....Salt Lake City UT 84119 — 888-727-2863

ASAPS (American Society for Aesthetic Plastic Surgery, Th)
11262 Monarch St ....Garden Grove CA 92841 — 800-364-2147 — 562-799-2356 — 49-8

ASBO (Association of School Business Officials Internati)
11401 N Shore Dr ....Reston VA 20190 — 866-682-2729 — — 49-5

ASBPA (American Shore & Beach Preservation Assn)
5460 Beaujolais Ln ....Fort Myers FL 33919 — 800-331-1600 — 239-489-2616 — 48-13

Asbury Methodist Village
201 Russell Ave ....Gaithersburg MD 20877 — 800-327-2879 — 301-216-4001 — 668

Asbury Park Press
3601 Hwy 66 PO Box 1550. ....Neptune NJ 07754 — 800-822-9770 — 732-922-6000 — 528-2

Asbury University
1 Macklem Dr ....Wilmore KY 40390 — 800-888-1818* — 859-858-3511 — 166
*Admissions

ASC (American Society of Cinematographers)
1782 N Orange Dr ....Hollywood CA 90028 — 800-448-0145 — 323-969-4333 — 48-4

	Toll-Free	Phone	Class

ASC Profiles Inc
2110 Enterprise Blvd ....West Sacramento CA 95691 — 800-360-2477* — 916-372-0933 — 693
*Cust Svc

ASCA (American School Counselor Assn)
1101 King St Ste 625 ....Alexandria VA 22314 — 800-306-4722 — 703-683-2722 — 49-5

ASCCP (American Society for Colposcopy & Cervical Patholo)
152 W Washington St ....Hagerstown MD 21740 — 800-787-7227 — 301-733-3640 — 49-8

ASCD (Association for Supervision & Curriculum Developme)
1703 North Beauregard St ....Alexandria VA 22311 — 800-933-2723 — 703-578-9600 — 49-5

ASCDI (Association of Service & Computer Dealers Internat)
131 NW First Ave ....Delray Beach FL 33444 — 800-393-2505 — 561-266-9016 — 48-9

ASCE (American Society of Civil Engineers)
1801 Alexander Bell Dr ....Reston VA 20191 — 800-548-2723 — 703-295-6300 — 455-21

Ascend Federal Credit Union
520 Airpark Dr PO Box 1210 ....Tullahoma TN 37388 — 800-342-3086 — 931-455-5441 — 219

Ascend Therapeutics Inc
607 Herndon Pkwy Ste 110 ....Herndon VA 20170 — 888-412-5751 — 703-471-4744 — 231

Ascentium Capital LLC
23970 Hwy 59 N ....Kingwood TX 77339 — 866-722-8500 — — 507

Ascentra Credit Union
1710 Grant St ....Bettendorf IA 52722 — 800-426-5241 — 563-355-0152 — 219

ASCH (American Society of Clinical Hypnosis)
140 N Bloomingdale Rd ....Bloomingdale IL 60108 — 800-227-6963 — 630-980-4740 — 49-8

ASCLA (Association of Specialized & Co-op Library Agencie)
50 E Huron St ....Chicago IL 60611 — 800-545-2433 — 312-280-4395 — 49-11

ASCO (American Society of Clinical Oncology)
2318 Mill Rd Ste 800 ....Alexandria VA 22314 — 888-282-2552 — 571-483-1300 — 49-8

Ascom North America
300 Perimeter Park Dr ....Morrisville NC 27560 — 877-712-7266

ASCP (American Society of Consultant Pharmacists)
1321 Duke St ....Alexandria VA 22314 — 800-355-2727 — 703-739-1300 — 49-8

ASCP (American Society for Clinical Pathology)
33 W Monroe St Ste 1600 ....Chicago IL 60603 — 800-621-4142* — 312-541-4999 — 49-8
*Cust Svc

ASCRS (American Society of Cataract & Refractive Surgery)
4000 Legato Rd Ste 700 ....Fairfax VA 22033 — 877-996-4464 — 703-591-2220 — 49-8

ASD
600 Corporate Pointe
Ste 1000 10th Fl. ....Culver CA 90230 — 800-421-4511 — 323-817-2200 — 184

ASD Data Services LLC
PO Box 1184 ....Manchester TN 37349 — 877-742-7297 — 931-723-0204 — 633-6

ASDS (American Society for Dermatologic Surgery)
5550 Meadowbrook Dr
Ste 120. ....Rolling Meadows IL 60008 — 800-714-1374 — 847-956-0900 — 49-8

ASE (Alliance to Save Energy)
1850 M St NW Ste 600 ....Washington DC 20036 — 800-862-2086 — 202-857-0666 — 48-12

AseraCare Hospice
1000 Turave Way ....Fort Smith AR 72919 — 888-868-1957 — — 370

ASF (Atlantic Salmon Federation)
PO Box 5200 ....Saint Andrews NB E5B3S8 — 800-565-5666 — 506-529-1033 — 48-3

ASG (Allen Systems Group Inc)
1333 Third Ave S ....Naples FL 34102 — 800-932-5536 — 239-435-2200 — 178-12

ASG Renaissance
22226 Garrison St ....Dearborn MI 48124 — 800-238-0890 — 313-565-4700 — 261

ASGE (American Society for Gastrointestinal Endoscopy)
1520 Kensington Rd Ste 202 ....Oak Brook IL 60523 — 866-353-2743 — 630-573-0600 — 49-8

Ash Grove Cement Co
8900 Indian Creek Pkwy
Ste 200. ....Overland Park KS 66210 — 800-545-1882 — 913-451-8900 — 135
OTC: ASHG

ASHA (American Speech-Language-Hearing Assn)
2200 Research Blvd ....Rockville MD 20850 — 800-498-2071 — 301-296-5700 — 49-8

Ashaway Line & Twine Manufacturing Co
24 Laurel St ....Ashaway RI 02804 — 800-556-7260 — 401-377-2221 — 208

Ashbrook Ctr
401 College Ave
Ashland University ....Ashland OH 44805 — 877-289-5411 — 419-289-5411 — 630

Ashburn Consulting LLC
43848 Goshen Farm Ct ....Leesburg VA 20176 — 866-576-9382 — 703-652-9120

Ashe County Chamber of Commerce
1 N Jefferson Ave Ste C
PO Box 31. ....West Jefferson NC 28694 — 888-343-2743 — 336-846-9550 — 337

Asher's Chocolates
80 Wambold Rd ....Souderton PA 18964 — 800-223-4420 — 215-721-3000 — 296-8

Asheville Area Chamber of Commerce
36 Montford Ave ....Asheville NC 28802 — 888-314-1041 — 828-258-6101 — 139

Asheville Chevrolet Inc
205 Smokey Park Hwy ....Asheville NC 28806 — 866-921-1073 — 828-348-7326 — 57

Asheville Citizen Times
14 O'Henry Ave ....Asheville NC 28801 — 800-672-2472 — 828-252-5611 — 528-2

Asheville Regional Airport
61 Terminal Dr Ste 1. ....Fletcher NC 28732 — 866-719-3910 — 828-684-2226 — 27

Asheville Savings Bank S S B
PO Box 652 ....Asheville NC 28802 — 800-222-3230 — 828-254-7411 — 70

Ashfield Capital Partners LLC
801 Montgomery St Ste 200. ......San Francisco CA 94133 — 877-391-4747 — 415-391-4747 — 400

Ashford University
400 N Bluff Blvd ....Clinton IA 52732 — 800-242-4153 — 563-242-4023 — 166

ASHI (American Society of Home Inspectors)
932 Lee St Ste 101 ....Des Plaines IL 60016 — 800-743-2744 — 847-759-2820 — 49-3

Ashland Addison Florist Co
1640 W Fulton St ....Chicago IL 60612 — 800-348-1157 — 312-432-1800 — 292

Ashland Community & Technical College
1400 College Dr ....Ashland KY 41101 — 800-928-4256 — 606-326-2000 — 162

Ashland Inc
50 E River Ctr Blvd
PO Box 391. ....Covington KY 41012 — 877-546-2782 — 859-815-3333 — 185
NYSE: ASH

Ashland Industries Inc
1115 Rail Dr ....Ashland WI 54806 — 877-634-4622

Ashland University
401 College Ave ....Ashland OH 44805 — 800-882-1548 — 419-289-4142 — 166

Ashland University Library
401 College Ave ....Ashland OH 44805 — 866-434-5222 — 419-289-5400 — 433-6

Ashlar Inc
9600 Great Hills Trl
Ste 150W-1625. ....Austin TX 78759 — 800-877-2745 — 512-250-2186 — 178-5

Ashley Furniture Industries Inc
1 Ashley Way ....Arcadia WI 54612 — 800-477-2222 — 608-323-3377 — 319-2

Name / Address	City	State	Zip	Toll-Free	Phone	Class
Ashley Madison Agency, The 2300 Yonge St	Toronto	ON	M4P1E4	866-742-2218		226
Ashley-Chicot Electric Co-op Inc 307 E Jefferson St	Hamburg	AR	71646	800-281-5212	870-853-5212	245
ASHP (American Society of Health-System Pharmacists) 7272 Wisconsin Ave	Bethesda	MD	20814	866-279-0681	301-664-8700	49-8
ASHRAE (American Society of Heating Refrigerating & Air-Co) 1791 Tullie Cir NE *Cust Svc	Atlanta	GA	30329	800-527-4723*	404-636-8400	49-3
ASHS (American Society for Horticultural Science) 1018 Duke St	Alexandria	VA	22314	800-331-1600	703-836-4606	48-2
Ashta Chemicals Inc 3509 Middle Rd *Cust Svc	Ashtabula	OH	44004	800-492-5082*	440-997-5221	143
Ashtabula County Medical Ctr (ACMC) 2420 Lake Ave	Ashtabula	OH	44004	800-722-3330	440-997-2262	373-3
Ashtead Technology Inc 19407 Pk Row Ste 170	Houston	TX	77084	800-242-3910	281-398-9533	193
ASI Corp 48289 Fremont Blvd	Fremont	CA	94538	800-200-0274	510-226-8000	174
ASI DataMyte Inc 2800 Campus Dr Ste 60	Plymouth	MN	55441	800-455-4359	763-553-1040	178-10
Asi Networks Inc 19331 E Walnut Dr N	City Of Industry	CA	91748	800-251-1336		180
Asi System Integration Inc 48 W 37th St	New York	NY	10018	866-308-3920		113
Asi Technologies Inc 5848 N 95th Ct	Milwaukee	WI	53225	800-558-7068	414-464-6200	234
Asian American Legal Defense & Education Fund (AALDEF) 99 Hudson St 12th Fl	New York	NY	10013	800-966-5946	212-966-5932	48-8
Asian Pacific American Legal Center of Southern California 1145 Wilshire Blvd 2nd Fl	Los Angeles	CA	90017	800-520-2356	213-977-7500	427
Asics America Corp 29 Parker Ste 100	Irvine	CA	92618	800-333-8404	949-453-8888	301
ASIL (American Society of International Law, The) 2223 Massachusetts Ave NW	Washington	DC	20008	800-828-7571	202-939-6000	49-10
Ask Associates Inc 1201 Wakarusa Ste C-1	Lawrence	KS	66049	800-315-4333	785-841-8194	733
ASK Services Inc 42180 Ford Rd Ste 101	Canton	MI	48187	888-416-1313	734-983-9040	399
Aski Capital Inc 419 Notre Dame Ave	Winnipeg	MB	R3B1R3	866-987-7180	204-987-7180	138
ASKO Inc 501 W Seventh Ave	Homestead	PA	15120	800-321-1310	412-461-4110	491
ASL Distribution Services Ltd 2160 Buckingham Rd	Oakville	ON	L6H6M7	800-387-7995	905-829-5141	476
ASL Services 3700 Commerce Blvd Ste 216	Kissimmee	FL	34741	888-744-6275	407-518-7900	697
ASLA (American Society of Landscape Architects) 636 'I' St NW	Washington	DC	20001	888-999-2752	202-898-2444	48-2
ASLMS (American Society for Laser Medicine & Surgery Inc) 2100 Stewart Ave Ste 240	Wausau	WI	54401	877-258-6028	715-845-9283	49-8
ASLO (American Society of Limnology & Oceanography) 5400 Bosque Blvd Ste 680	Waco	TX	76710	800-929-2756	254-399-9635	49-19
ASLU LLC 12178 Fourth St Rancho	Cucamonga	CA	91730	800-588-3911	951-934-4200	
ASM (American Society for Microbiology) 1752 N St NW	Washington	DC	20036	800-546-2416	202-737-3600	49-8
ASM Industries Inc Pacer Pumps Div 41 Industrial Cir *Cust Svc	Lancaster	PA	17601	800-233-3861*	717-656-2161	637
ASM International 9639 Kinsman Rd	Materials Park	OH	44073	800-336-5152	440-338-5151	49-13
ASMBA (Armed Services Mutual Benefit Assn) PO Box 160384	Nashville	TN	37216	800-251-8434	615-851-0800	48-19
ASMC (American Society of Military Comptrollers) 415 N Alfred St	Alexandria	VA	22314	800-462-5637	703-549-0360	48-19
ASNA (Alabama State Nurses Assn) 360 N Hull St	Montgomery	AL	36104	800-270-2762	334-262-8321	529
ASNS (American Society for Nutrition) 9211 Corporate Blvd Ste 300	Rockville	MD	20850	800-627-8723	240-428-3650	49-6
ASNT (American Society for Nondestructive Testing Inc) 1711 Arlingate Ln PO Box 28518 *Orders	Columbus	OH	43228	800-222-2768*	614-274-6003	49-19
Asnuntuck Community College 170 Elm St	Enfield	CT	06082	800-501-3967	860-253-3000	162
Asolo Repertory Theatre 5555 N Tamiami Tr	Sarasota	FL	34243	800-361-8388	941-351-9010	744
ASP (Advanced Sterilization Products) 33 Technology Dr	Irvine	CA	92618	888-783-7723		475
ASP Inc 460 Brant St Ste 212	Burlington	ON	L7R4B6	877-552-5535	905-333-4242	689
ASPAN (American Society of PeriAnesthesia Nurses) 90 Frontage Rd	Cherry Hill	NJ	08034	877-737-9696	856-616-9600	49-8
ASPCA (American Society for the Prevention of Cruelty to) 424 E 92nd St	New York	NY	10128	800-582-5979	212-876-7700	48-3
ASPE (American Society of Professional Estimators) 2525 Perimeter Pl Dr Ste 103	Nashville	TN	37214	888-378-6283	615-316-9200	49-3
ASPE Inc 114 Edinburgh S Dr Ste 200	Cary	NC	27511	877-800-5221		759
ASPEN (American Society for Parenteral & Enteral Nutritio) 8630 Fenton St Ste 412	Silver Spring	MD	20910	800-727-4567	301-587-6315	49-8
Aspen Chamber Resort Assn 590 N Mill St	Aspen	CO	81611	800-670-0792	970-925-1940	139
Aspen Marketing Services 1240 N Ave	West Chicago	IL	60185	800-848-0212	630-293-9600	4
Aspen Meadows Resort 845 Meadows Rd	Aspen	CO	81611	800-452-4240	970-925-4240	665
Aspen Medical Products 6481 Oak Cyn	Irvine	CA	92618	800-295-2776		474
Aspen Santa Fe Ballet 0245 Sage Way	Aspen	CO	81611	866-449-0464	970-925-7175	569-1
Aspen Ski & Board Co 1170 E Powell Rd	Lewis Center	OH	43035	877-861-0777	614-848-6600	707
Aspen Surgical 6945 Southbelt Dr SE	Caledonia	MI	49316	888-364-7004	616-698-7100	475

Name / Address	City	State	Zip	Toll-Free	Phone	Class
Aspen Technology Inc 200 Wheeler Rd *NASDAQ: AZPN*	Burlington	MA	01803	888-996-7100	855-882-7736	178-5
Aspen Times, The 314 E Hyman Ave	Aspen	CO	81611	800-525-6200	970-925-3414	528-2
Asphalt Roofing Manufacturers Assn (ARMA) 529 14th St NW Ste 750	Washington	DC	20045	800-247-6637	202-207-0917	49-3
Aspirus Wausau Hospital 333 Pine Ridge Blvd	Wausau	WI	54401	800-283-2881	715-847-2121	373-3
Asplundh Tree Expert Co 708 Blair Mill Rd	Willow Grove	PA	19090	800-248-8733		771
Asponte Technology Inc 11523 Palmbrush Trl Ste 137	Lakewood Ranch	FL	34202	888-926-9434		180
ASPR (Association of Staff Physician Recruiters) 1000 Westgate Dr Ste 252	Saint Paul	MN	55114	800-830-2777		49-8
Aspyra LLC 7400 Baymeadows Way Ste 101 *OTC: APYI*	Jacksonville	FL	32256	800-437-9000		178-10
ASQ (American Society for Quality) 600 N Plankinton Ave	Milwaukee	WI	53203	800-248-1946	414-272-8575	49-13
ASRA (American Society of Regional Anesthesia & Pain Med) 4 Penn Ctr W Ste 401	Pittsburgh	PA	15276	855-795-2772	412-471-2718	49-8
ASRT (American Society of Radiologic Technologists) 15000 Central Ave SE	Albuquerque	NM	87123	800-444-2778	505-298-4500	49-8
ASSA ABLOY 110 Sargent Dr	New Haven	CT	06511	800-377-3948		234
Assa Abloy of Canada Ltd 160 Four Vly Dr	Vaughan	ON	L4K4T9	800-461-3007	905-738-2466	349
ASSA Inc 110 Sargent Dr	New Haven	CT	06511	800-235-7482	203-624-5225	349
Assante Financial Management Ltd 199 Bay St Ste 2700	Toronto	ON	M5L1E2	888-348-9994	416-348-9994	
Assateague State Park 7307 Stephen Decatur Hwy	Berlin	MD	21811	888-432-2267	410-641-2120	561
Assemblies of God (A/G) 1445 N Boonville Ave	Springfield	MO	65802	800-641-4310	417-862-2781	48-20
Assemblies of God Theological Seminary 1435 N Glenstone Ave	Springfield	MO	65802	800-467-2487	417-268-1000	167-3
Asset 15050 Ave of Science	San Diego	CA	92128	888-303-8755		366
Asset Acceptance Capital Corp (AACC) 28405 Van Dyke Ave *NASDAQ: AACC*	Warren	MI	48093	800-545-9931	586-939-9600	160
Asset Preservation Advisors Inc 3344 Peachtree Rd Ste 2050	Atlanta	GA	30326	800-833-8985	404-261-1333	524
Asset Strategy Consultants LLC 6 N Park Dr Ste 208	Hunt Valley	MD	21030	866-344-8282	410-528-8282	400
AssetMark Inc 1655 Grant St 10th Fl	Concord	CA	94520	800-664-5345		400
Assiniboine Park Zoo 55 Pavilion Crescent	Winnipeg	MB	R3P2N6	877-927-6006	204-927-8080	818
Assist Cornerstone Technologies Inc 150 W Civic Ctr Dr Ste 601	Sandy	UT	84070	800-732-0136		177
Assist-2-Sell Inc 1610 Meadow Wood Ln	Reno	NV	89502	800-528-7816	775-688-6060	648
Associated Bag Co 400 W Boden St	Milwaukee	WI	53207	800-926-6100	414-769-1000	66
Associated Banc-Corp 310 W Wisconsin Ave Ste 400	Milwaukee	WI	53202	800-236-8866	920-491-7000	70
Associated Banc-Corp 1305 Main St *NYSE: ASB* ■ *PR	Stevens Point	WI	54481	800-236-8866*	715-341-0400	359-2
Associated Bank 1305 Main St MS 7722	Stevens Point	WI	54481	800-236-8866		70
Associated Bank Green Bay NA 200 N Adams St	Green Bay	WI	54301	800-728-3501	920-433-3200	70
Associated Bank Illinois NA 612 N Main St	Rockford	IL	61103	800-236-8866	815-987-3500	70
Associated Behavioral Health 4700 42nd Ave SW Ste 470	Seattle	WA	98116	800-858-6702	206-935-1282	460
Associated Bodywork & Massage Professionals (ABMP) 25188 Genesee Trl Rd Ste 200	Golden	CO	80401	800-458-2267	303-674-8478	48-17
Associated Builders & Contractors Inc (ABC) 4250 Fairfax Dr	Arlington	VA	22203	877-889-5627	202-595-1505	49-3
Associated Building Maintenance Company Inc 2140 Priest Bridge Ct Ste 3	Crofton	MD	21114	800-721-9068	410-721-1818	
Associated Equipment Corp 5043 Farlan Ave	Saint Louis	MO	63115	800-949-1472	314-385-5178	248
Associated Equipment Distributors (AED) 650 E Algonquin Rd Ste 305	Schaumburg	IL	60173	800-388-0650	630-574-0650	49-18
Associated Fabrics Corp 15-01 Pollitt Dr Unit 7	Fair Lawn	NJ	07410	800-232-4077		590
Associated Floors 32 Morris Ave	Springfield	NJ	07081	800-800-4320		189-2
Associated Food Stores Inc 1850 West 2100 South *Cust Svc	Salt Lake City	UT	84119	888-574-7100*	801-973-4400	297-8
Associated General Contractors of America (AGC) 2300 Wilson Blvd Ste 300	Arlington	VA	22201	800-242-1766	703-548-3118	49-3
Associated General Contractors PAC 2300 Wilson Blvd Ste 400	Arlington	VA	22201	800-242-1767	703-548-3118	611
Associated Global Systems Inc 3333 New Hyde Pk Rd *Cust Svc	New Hyde Park	NY	11042	800-645-8300*	516-627-8910	447
Associated Grocers Inc 8600 Anselmo Ln	Baton Rouge	LA	70810	800-637-2021	225-444-1000	297-8
Associated Grocers of New England Inc 11 Co-op Way	Pembroke	NH	03275	800-242-2248	603-223-6710	297-8
Associated Grocers of the South 3600 Vanderbilt Rd	Birmingham	AL	35217	800-695-6051	205-841-6781	297-8
Associated Industries 1206 N Lincoln Ste 200	Spokane	WA	99201	800-720-4291	509-326-6885	194
Associated Industries Of Massachusetts Mutual Insurance Com PO Box 4070	Burlington	MA	01803	866-270-3354	781-221-1600	390-4
Associated Locksmiths of America (ALOA) 3500 Easy St	Dallas	TX	75247	800-532-2562	214-819-9733	49-3

	Toll-Free	Phone	Class
Associated Materials Inc (AMI) 3773 State Rd, Cuyahoga Falls OH 44223	800-922-6009		693
Associated Materials Inc Alside Div PO Box 2010, Akron OH 44309 *Cust Svc	800-922-6009*		235
Associated Petroleum Carriers Inc PO Box 2808, Spartanburg SC 29304 *Cust Svc	800-573-9301*	864-573-9301	775
Associated Risk Managers (ARM) 2850 Golf Rd, Rolling Meadows IL 60008	800-735-5441	630-285-4324	49-9
Associated Steel Corp 18200 Miles Rd, Cleveland OH 44128	800-321-9300		350
Associated Wholesalers Inc PO Box 67, Robesonia PA 19551	800-927-7771	610-693-3161	297-8
Association for Advanced Life Underwriting (AALU) 11921 Freedom Dr Ste 1100, Reston VA 20190	888-275-0092	703-641-9400	49-9
Association for Advanced Training in the Behavioral Sciences (AATBS) 5126 Ralston St, Ventura CA 93003	800-472-1931	805-676-3030	49-5
Association for Applied Psychophysiology & Biofeedback (AAPB) 10200 W 44th Ave Ste 304, Wheat Ridge CO 80033	800-477-8892	303-422-8436	49-8
Association for Assessment & Accreditation of Laboratory Animal Care International 5283 Corporate Dr Ste 203, Frederick MD 21703	800-926-0066	301-696-9626	48-1
Association for Behavioral & Cognitive Therapies (ABCT) 305 Seventh Ave 16th Fl, New York NY 10001	800-685-2228	212-647-1890	49-15
Association for Biblical Higher Education (AABC) 5850 T G Lee Blvd Ste 130, Orlando FL 32822	800-525-1611	407-207-0808	48-1
Association for Career & Technical Education (ACTE) 1410 King St, Alexandria VA 22314	800-826-9972	703-683-3111	49-5
Association for Childhood Education International (ACEI) 1101 16th St NW Ste 300, Washington DC 20036	800-423-3563	202-372-9986	49-5
Association for Computing Machinery (ACM) 2 Penn Plz Ste 701, New York NY 10121	800-342-6626	212-626-0500	48-9
Association for Continuing Higher Education (ACHE) 1700 Asp Ave, Norman OK 73072	800-807-2243		49-5
Association for Co-op Operations Research & Development (ACORD) 1 Blue Hill Plz PO Box 1529, Pearl River NY 10965	800-444-3341	845-620-1700	49-9
Association for Corporate Growth (ACG) 125 S Wacker Dr Ste 3100, Chicago IL 60606	877-358-2220	312-957-4260	49-12
Association for Couples in Marriage Enrichment (ACME) PO Box 21374, Winston-Salem NC 27120	800-634-8325		48-6
Association for Healthcare Documentation Integrity (AHDI) 4230 Kiernan Ave Ste 130, Modesto CA 95356	800-982-2182	209-527-9620	49-8
Association for Iron & Steel Technology (AIST) 186 Thorn Hill Rd, Warrendale PA 15086	800-759-4867	724-814-3000	49-13
Association for Library & Information Science Education (ALISE) 2150 N 107th St Ste 205, Seattle WA 98133	877-275-7547	206-209-5267	49-11
Association for Library Collections & Technical Services (ALCTS) 50 E Huron St, Chicago IL 60611	800-545-2433	312-280-5037	49-11
Association for Library Service to Children (ALSC) 50 E Huron St, Chicago IL 60611	800-545-2433	312-280-2163	49-11
Association for Linen Management 138 N Keeneland Dr Ste D, Richmond KY 40475	800-669-0863	859-624-0177	49-4
Association for Mfg Technology (AMT) 7901 Westpark Dr, McLean VA 22102	800-524-0475	703-893-2900	49-12
Association for Professionals in Infection Control & Epidemiology Inc (APIC) 1275 K St NW Ste 1000, Washington DC 20005	800-650-9883	202-789-1890	49-8
Association for Research & Enlightenment (ARE) 215 67th St, Virginia Beach VA 23451	800-333-4499	757-428-3588	48-17
Association for Research in Vision & Ophthalmology (ARVO) 12300 Twinbrook Pkwy Ste 250, Rockville MD 20852	888-503-1050	240-221-2900	49-8
Association for Supervision & Curriculum Development (ASCD) 1703 North Beauregard St, Alexandria VA 22311	800-933-2723	703-578-9600	49-5
Association for the Advancement of Artificial Intelligence (AAAI) 445 Burgess Dr Ste 100, Menlo Park CA 94025	800-548-4664	650-328-3123	48-9
Association for the Advancement of Medical Instrumentation (AAMI) 4301 N Fairfax Dr Ste 301, Arlington VA 22203	800-332-2264	703-525-4890	49-8
Association for Vascular Access (AVA) 5526 W 13400 S Ste 229, Herriman UT 84096	877-924-2821	801-792-9079	49-8
Association Headquarters Inc 1120 Rt 73 Ste 200, Mount Laurel NJ 08054	877-777-6753		
Association Management Magazine 1575 'I' St NW, Washington DC 20005	888-950-2723	202-371-0940	455-5
Association of Alternative Newsweeklies (AAN) 115615th St NW, Washington DC 20005	866-415-0704	202-289-8484	49-14
Association of American Chambers of Commerce in Latin America 1615 H St NW, Washington DC 20062	800-638-6582	202-463-5485	138
Association of American Geographers (AAG) 1710 16th St NW, Washington DC 20009	800-696-7353	202-234-1450	49-19
Association of American Railroads (AAR) 425 Third St SW, Washington DC 20024	800-533-6644	202-639-2100	49-21
Association of Certified Fraud Examiners (ACFE) 716 W Ave, Austin TX 78701	800-245-3321	512-478-9000	49-1
Association of Christian Schools International (ACSI) 731 Chapel Hills Dr, Colorado Springs CO 80920 *Cust Svc	800-367-0798*	719-528-6906	49-5
Association of College & Research Libraries (ACRL) 50 E Huron St, Chicago IL 60611	800-545-2433	312-280-2519	49-11
Association of Community College Trustees (ACCT) 1101 17th St NW Ste 300, Washington DC 20036	866-895-2228	202-775-4667	49-5
Association of Corporate Counsel (ACC) 1025 Connecticut Ave NW Ste 200, Washington DC 20036	877-647-3411	202-293-4103	49-10
Association of Corporate Travel Executives (ACTE) 526 King St Ste 215, Alexandria VA 22314	800-228-3669	703-683-5322	
Association of Directory Publishers (ADP) PO Box 209, Traverse City MI 49685	800-267-9002	231-486-2182	49-16
Association of Energy Service Cos (AESC) 14531 Fm 529 Ste 250, Houston TX 77095	800-692-0771	713-781-0758	48-12
Association of Equipment Manufacturers (AEM) 6737 W Washington St Ste 2400, Milwaukee WI 53214	866-236-0442	414-272-0943	49-13
Association of Film Commissioners International (AFCI) 9595 Wilshire Blvd Ste 900, Beverly Hills CA 90212	888-765-5777	323-461-2324	48-4
Association of Flight Attendants 501 Third St NW, Washington DC 20001	800-424-2401	202-434-1300	413
Association of Fundraising Professionals (AFP) 4300 Wilson Blvd Ste 300, Arlington VA 22203	800-666-3863	703-684-0410	49-12
Association of Governing Boards of Universities & Colleges (AGB) 1133 20th St NW Ste 300, Washington DC 20036	800-356-6317	202-296-8400	49-5
Association of Government Accountants (AGA) 2208 Mt Vernon Ave, Alexandria VA 22301	800-242-7211	703-684-6931	49-1
Association of Healthcare Internal Auditors (AHIA) 10200 W 44th Ave Ste 304, Wheat Ridge CO 80033	888-275-2442	303-327-7546	49-1
Association of Home Appliance Manufacturers PAC (AHAM PAC) 1111 19th St NW Ste 402, Washington DC 20036	800-424-2970	202-872-5955	611
Association of Junior Leagues International Inc (AJLI) 80 Maiden Ln Ste 305, New York NY 10038	800-955-3248	212-951-8300	48-15
Association of Magazine Media, The (MPA) 757 Third Ave 11th Fl, New York NY 10017	800-234-3368	212-872-3700	49-16
Association of Military Surgeons of the United States (AMSUS) 9320 Old Georgetown Rd, Bethesda MD 20814	800-761-9320	301-897-8800	49-8
Association of Nurses in AIDS Care (ANAC) 3538 Ridgewood Rd, Akron OH 44333	800-260-6780	330-670-0101	49-8
Association of Performing Arts Presenters 1211 Connecticut Ave NW Ste 200, Washington DC 20036	888-820-2787	202-833-2787	48-4
Association of Pool & Spa Professionals (APSP) 2111 Eisenhower Ave Ste 500, Alexandria VA 22314	800-323-3996	703-838-0083	49-4
Association of Progressive Rental Organizations (APRO) 1504 Robin Hood Trl, Austin TX 78703	800-204-2776	512-794-0095	49-18
Association of Public Health Laboratories (APHL) 8515 Georgia Ave Ste 700, Silver Spring MD 20910	800-899-2278	240-485-2745	49-7
Association of Public-Safety Communications Officials International Inc 351 N Williamson Blvd, Daytona Beach FL 32114	888-272-6911	386-322-2500	49-7
Association of Rehabilitation Nurses (ARN) 4700 West Lake Ave, Glenview IL 60025	800-229-7530	847-375-4710	49-8
Association of Reproductive Health Professionals (ARHP) 1300 19th St NW Ste 200, Washington DC 20036	877-311-8972	202-466-3825	49-8
Association of School Business Officials International (ASBO) 11401 N Shore Dr, Reston VA 20190	866-682-2729		49-5
Association of Service & Computer Dealers International (ASCDI) 131 NW First Ave, Delray Beach FL 33444	800-393-2505	561-266-9016	48-9
Association of Social Work Boards (ASWB) 400 S Ridge Pkwy Ste B, Culpeper VA 22701	800-225-6880	540-829-6880	49-7
Association of Specialized & Co-op Library Agencies (ASCLA) 50 E Huron St, Chicago IL 60611	800-545-2433	312-280-4395	49-11
Association of Staff Physician Recruiters (ASPR) 1000 Westgate Dr Ste 252, Saint Paul MN 55114	800-830-2777		49-8
Association of State Wetland Managers 32 Tandberg Trl Ste 2A, Windham ME 04062	800-451-6027	207-892-3399	49-7
Association of Surgical Technologists (AST) 6 W Dry Creek Cir Ste 200, Littleton CO 80120	800-637-7433	303-694-9130	49-8
Association of Test Publishers 601 Pennsylvania Ave NW Ste 900, Washington DC 20004	866-240-7909		49-5
Association of the US Army (AUSA) 2425 Wilson Blvd, Arlington VA 22201	800-336-4570	703-841-4300	48-19
Association of the Wall & Ceiling Industries International (AWCI) 513 W Broad St Ste 210, Falls Church VA 22046	800-233-8990	703-538-1600	49-3
Association of Universities for Research in Astronomy (AURA) 1200 New York Ave NW Ste 350, Washington DC 20005	888-624-8373	202-483-2101	49-5
Association of University Centers on Disabilities (AUCD) 1100 Wayne Ave Ste 1000, Silver Spring MD 20910	888-572-2249	301-588-8252	49-5
Association of University Presses 28 W 36th St Ste 602, New York NY 10018	800-678-2120	212-989-1010	49-16
Association of University Programs in Health Admin (AUPHA) 2000 N 14th St Ste 780, Arlington VA 22201	877-275-6462	703-894-0941	49-8
Association of Washington Business PO Box 658, Olympia WA 98507	800-521-9325	360-943-1600	140
Association of Women's Health Obstetric & Neonatal Nurses (AWHONN) 2000 L St NW Ste 740, Washington DC 20036	800-673-8499	202-261-2400	49-8
Assumption College 500 Salisbury St, Worcester MA 01609	888-882-7786	508-767-7000	166
AssuranceAmerica Corp 5500 I- N Pkwy Ste 600, Atlanta GA 30328	800-450-7857	770-952-0200	390-4
Assurant Employee Benefits 2323 Grand Blvd, Kansas City MO 64108	800-733-7879	816-474-2345	390-2
Assurant Group 11222 Quail Roost Dr, Miami FL 33157	800-852-2244	305-253-2244	359-4
Assurant Inc 1 Chase Manhattan Plz, New York NY 10005 *NYSE: AIZ*	800-852-2244		
AssuredPartners NL 2305 River Rd, Louisville KY 40206	888-499-8092	502-894-2100	194
Assurity Life Insurance Co 2000 Q St, Lincoln NE 68503	800-869-0355	402-476-6500	389
AST (Association of Surgical Technologists) 6 W Dry Creek Cir Ste 200, Littleton CO 80120	800-637-7433	303-694-9130	49-8
AST Bearings 115 Main Rd, Montville NJ 07045	800-526-1250	973-335-2230	75
AST Sports Science Inc 120 Capitol Dr, Golden CO 80401	800-627-2788	303-278-1420	794
ASTA (American Seed Trade Assn) 1701 Duke St Ste 275, Alexandria VA 22304	888-890-7333	703-837-8140	48-2
ASTA (American Society of Travel Agents) 675 N Washington St Ste 490, Alexandria VA 22314	800-275-2782	703-739-2782	48-23
Asta Funding Inc 210 Sylvan Ave, Englewood Cliffs NJ 07632 *NASDAQ: ASFI*	866-389-7627	201-567-5648	272
Astatech Inc 2525 Pearl Buck Rd, Bristol PA 19007	800-387-2269	215-785-3197	196
Astea International Inc 240 Gibraltar Rd, Horsham PA 19044 *NASDAQ: ATEA*	800-878-4657	215-682-2500	178-1
Astec Industries Inc 1725 Shepherd Rd, Chattanooga TN 37421 *NASDAQ: ASTE*	800-272-7100	423-899-5898	190
Astellas Pharma US Inc 1 Astellas Way, Northbrook IL 60062	800-695-4321		85
AstenJohnson 4399 Corporate Rd, Charleston SC 29405	800-529-7990	843-747-7800	740-3
Asthma & Allergy Foundation of America (AAFA) 8201 Corporate Dr Ste 1000, Landover MD 20785	800-727-8462	202-466-7643	48-17
Asticou Inn 15 Peabody Dr, Northeast Harbor ME 04662	800-258-3373	207-276-3344	378

	Toll-Free	Phone	Class

ASTM International
100 Barr Harbor Dr
PO Box C700 . . . . West Conshohocken PA 19428 | **800-814-1017** | 610-832-9500 | 49-19

Aston Hotels & Resorts
2155 Kalakaua Ave Ste 500 . . . . Honolulu HI 96815 | **800-775-4228** | 808-931-1400 | 378

Astor Crowne Plaza
739 Canal St . . . . New Orleans LA 70130 | **877-408-9661** | 504-962-0500 | 378

Astor Hotel, The
924 E Juneau Ave . . . . Milwaukee WI 53202 | **800-558-0200** | 414-271-4220 | 378

Astoria Ford
710 W Marine Dr . . . . Astoria OR 97103 | **888-760-9303** | 503-325-6411 | 57

Astoria-Pacific Inc
15130 SE 82nd Dr . . . . Clackamas OR 97015 | **800-536-3111** | 503-657-3010 | 292

AstraZeneca Canada Inc
1004 Middlegate Rd . . . . Mississauga ON L4Y1M4 | **800-565-5877** | 905-277-7111 | 578

AstraZeneca Pharmaceuticals LP
1800 Concord Pk PO Box 15437 . . . . . Wilmington DE 19850 | **800-236-9933** | | 578

ASTRO (American Society for Therapeutic Radiology & Oncol)
8280 Willow Oaks Corporate Dr
Ste 500 . . . . Fairfax VA 22031 | **800-962-7876** | 703-839-7312 | 49-8

Astro Industries Inc
4403 Dayton-Xenia Rd . . . . Dayton OH 45432 | **800-543-5810** | 937-429-5900 | 808

Astro Manufacturing & Design Corp
34459 Curtis Blvd . . . . Eastlake OH 44095 | **888-215-1746** |

Astro Pak Corp
270 E Baker St Ste 100 . . . . Costa Mesa CA 92626 | **888-278-7672** | | 738

Astrodyne Corp
375 Forbes Blvd . . . . Mansfield MA 02048 | **800-823-8082** | 508-964-6300 | 256

Astronomical Society of the Pacific
390 Ashton Ave . . . . San Francisco CA 94112 | **800-335-2624** | 415-337-1100 | 48-11

ASU Group, The
2120 University Park Dr . . . . Okemos MI 48805 | **800-968-0278** | 517-349-2212 | 194

Asure Software
110 Wild Basin Rd . . . . Austin TX 78746 | **888-323-8835** | 512-437-2700 | 178-7
NASDAQ: ASUR

ASW Global LLC
3375 Gilchrist Rd . . . . Mogadore OH 44260 | **888-826-5087** | 330-798-5172 | 798-1

ASWB (Association of Social Work Boards)
400 S Ridge Pkwy Ste B . . . . Culpeper VA 22701 | **800-225-6880** | 540-829-6880 | 49-7

AT & T Inc
175 E Houston St
PO Box 2933. . . . . San Antonio TX 78299 | **800-351-7221** | 210-821-4105 | 731
NYSE: AT&T

At Health LLC
2733 E Battlefield Ste 266. . . . . Springfield MO 65804 | **888-284-3258** | | 355

At Last Naturals Inc
401 Columbus Ave . . . . Valhalla NY 10595 | **800-527-8123** | 914-747-3599 | 214

AT. Still University of Health Sciences
800 W Jefferson St . . . . Kirksville MO 63501 | **866-626-2878** | 660-626-2121 | 162

ATA (American Tinnitus Assn)
522 SW Fifth Ave Ste 825. . . . . Portland OR 97204 | **800-634-8978** | 503-248-9985 | 48-17

ATA (Amateur Trapshooting Assn)
601 W National Rd . . . . Vandalia OH 45377 | **800-671-8042** | 937-898-4638 | 48-22

ATA (American Trucking Assn)
950 N Glebe Rd Ste 210 . . . . Arlington VA 22203 | **800-282-5463** | 703-838-1700 | 49-21

Ataco Steel Products Corp
PO Box 270 . . . . Cedarburg WI 53012 | **800-536-4822** | 262-377-3000 | 486

ATAP Inc
130 Industry way . . . . Eastaboga AL 36260 | **800-362-2827** | 256-362-2221 | 468

ATAS International Inc
6612 Snowdrift Rd . . . . Allentown PA 18106 | **800-468-1441** | 610-395-8445 | 489

Atascadero Chamber of Commerce
6904 El Camino Real . . . . Atascadero CA 93422 | **877-204-9830** | 805-466-2044 | 139

Atascadero State Hospital
10333 S Camino Real . . . . Atascadero CA 93422 | **844-210-6207** | 805-468-2000 | 373-5

ATC (American Thermoplastic Co)
106 Gamma Dr . . . . Pittsburgh PA 15238 | **800-245-6600** | | 86

ATC (Appalachian Trail Conservancy)
799 Washington St
PO Box 807. . . . . Harpers Ferry WV 25425 | **888-287-8673*** | 304-535-6331 | 48-23
*Sales

ATCC (American Type Culture Collection)
10801 University Blvd
PO Box 1549. . . . . Manassas VA 20108 | **800-638-6597*** | 703-365-2700 | 664
*Cust Svc

Atchison County
405 S Main St PO Box 243. . . . . Rock Port MO 64482 | **800-989-4115** | 660-744-6562 | 337

Atchison-Holt Electric Co-op
18585 Industrial Rd
PO Box 160. Rock Port MO 64482 | **888-744-5366** | 660-744-5344 | 245

ATCO Ltd
700 909 11th Ave SW . . . . Calgary AB T2R1N6 | **800-242-3447** | 403-292-7500 | 782
TSE: ACO/X

Atco Rubber Products Inc
7101 Atco Dr . . . . Fort Worth TX 76118 | **800-877-3828** | 817-595-2894 | 369

ATD-American Co
135 Greenwood Ave . . . . Wyncote PA 19095 | **866-283-9327** | 215-576-1380 | 320

ATEC Inc
12600 Executive Dr . . . . Stafford TX 77477 | **800-873-0001** | 281-276-2700 | 617

ATEL Capital Group
600 California St 9th Fl. . . . . San Francisco CA 94111 | **800-543-2835** | | 216

AT&F (American Tank & Fabricating Co)
12314 Elmwood Ave . . . . Cleveland OH 44111 | **800-544-5316** | 216-252-1500 | 719

Atfocus
394 Old Orchard Grove . . . . Toronto ON M5M2E9 | **866-349-2661** | 416-485-4220 | 193

Athabasca University
1 University Dr . . . . Athabasca AB T9S3A3 | **800-788-9041** | 780-675-6111 | 780

Athana International Inc
602 Faye . . . . Redondo Beach CA 90277 | **800-421-1591** | 310-539-7280 | 654

Athea Laboratories Inc
1900 W Cornell St . . . . Milwaukee WI 53209 | **800-743-6417** | | 145

Athena Controls Inc
5145 Campus Dr . . . . Plymouth Meeting PA 19462 | **800-782-6776** | 610-828-2490 | 201

Athena Diagnostics Inc
377 Plantation St 2nd Fl. . . . . Worcester MA 01605 | **800-394-4493** | 508-756-2886 | 231

athenahealth Inc
311 Arsenal St . . . . Watertown MA 02472 | **800-981-5084** | 617-402-1000 | 178-1
NASDAQ: ATHN

Atheneum Suite Hotel & Conference Ctr
1000 Brush Ave . . . . Detroit MI 48226 | **800-772-2323** | 313-962-2323 | 378

Athens Area Chamber of Commerce
449 E State St Ste 1 . . . . Athens OH 45701 | **877-360-3608** | 740-594-2251 | 139

Athens Banner-Herald
1 Press Pl . . . . Athens GA 30601 | **800-533-4252** | 706-549-0123 | 528-2

Athens Convention & Visitors Bureau
300 N Thomas St . . . . Athens GA 30601 | **800-653-0603** | 706-357-4430 | 206

Athens County Convention & Visitors Bureau
667 E State St . . . . Athens OH 45701 | **800-878-9767** | 740-592-1819 | 206

Athens Regional Medical Ctr
1114 W Madison Ave . . . . Athens TN 37303 | **800-855-2880** | 423-745-1411 | 373-3

Athens Services
14048 Valley Blvd . . . . La Puente CA 91746 | **888-336-6100** | 626-336-3636 | 799

Athens State Bank
6530 N State Rt 29 . . . . Springfield IL 62707 | **800-367-7576** | 217-487-7766 | 70

Athletic Training Equipment Company Inc
655 Spice Island Dr . . . . Sparks NV 89431 | **800-800-9931** |

ATIS (Alliance for Telecommunications Industry Solutions)
1200 G St NW Ste 500 . . . . Washington DC 20005 | **800-649-1202** | 202-628-6380 | 49-20

ATIS Elevator Inspections LLC
1976 Innerbelt Business Ctr . . . . St. Louis MO 63114 | **855-755-2847** | | 392

Atiwa Computer Leasing Exchange
6950 Portwest Dr Ste 100. . . . . Houston TX 77024 | **800-428-2532** | 713-467-9390 | 179

Atkins & Pearce Inc
1 Braid Way . . . . Covington KY 41017 | **800-837-7477** | 859-356-2001 | 208

Atkins Nutritionals Inc
1225 17th St Ste 1000 . . . . Denver CO 80202 | **800-628-5467** | | 794

Atkinson Conway & Gagnon Inc
420 L St Ste 500. . . . . Anchorage AK 99501 | **800-478-1900** | 907-276-1700 | 427

Atkinson County School System
98 Roberts Ave E . . . . Pearson GA 31642 | **800-639-0850** | 912-422-7373 | 681

Atkinson-Baker Inc (ABI)
500 N Brand Blvd 3rd Fl . . . . Glendale CA 91203 | **800-288-3376** | 818-551-7300 | 443

ATLA (American Theological Library Assn)
300 S Wacker Dr Ste 2100 . . . . Chicago IL 60606 | **888-665-2852** | 312-454-5100 | 48-20

Atlanta Attachment Company Inc
362 Industrial Pk Dr . . . . Lawrenceville GA 30045 | **877-206-5116** | 770-963-7369 | 36

Atlanta City Hall
55 Trinity Ave SW . . . . Atlanta GA 30303 | **800-897-1910** | 404-330-6004 | 336

Atlanta Civic Ctr
395 Piedmont Ave NE . . . . Atlanta GA 30308 | **877-430-7596** | 404-523-6275 | 568

Atlanta Cutlery Corp
2147 Gees Mill Rd . . . . Conyers GA 30013 | **800-883-0300** | 800-883-8838 | 222

Atlanta Fixture & Sales Co
3185 NE Expy . . . . Atlanta GA 30341 | **800-282-1977** | | 300

Atlanta Hardwood Corp
5596 Riverview Rd SE . . . . Mableton GA 30126 | **800-476-5393** | 404-792-2290 | 363

Atlanta Journal-Constitution
223 Perimeter Ctr Pkwy NE . . . . Atlanta GA 30346 | **800-933-9771** | 404-526-5151 | 528-2

Atlanta Magazine
260 Peachtree St Ste 300 . . . . Atlanta GA 30303 | **800-930-3019** | 404-527-5500 | 455-22

Atlanta Motor Speedway
PO Box 500 . . . . Hampton GA 30228 | **877-926-7849** | 770-946-4211 | 512

Atlanta Petroleum Equipment Co
4732 N Royal Atlanta Dr . . . . Tucker GA 30084 | **800-562-4060** | 770-491-6644 | 535

Atlanta Postal Credit Union
501 Pulliam St SW Ste 350 . . . . Atlanta GA 30312 | **800-849-8431** | 404-768-4126 | 219

Atlantech Online Inc
1010 Wayne Ave Ste 630 . . . . Silver Spring MD 20910 | **800-256-1612** | 301-589-3060 | 225

Atlantic British Ltd
Halfmoon Light Industrial Pk 6 Enterprise Ave
. . . . Clifton Park NY 12065 | **800-533-2210** | 518-664-6169 | 57

Atlantic Bulk Carrier Corp
PO Box 112 . . . . Providence Forge VA 23140 | **800-966-0030** | 804-966-5459 | 447

Atlantic Center For The Arts Inc
1414 Art Ctr Ave . . . . New Smyrna Beach FL 32168 | **800-393-6975** | 386-427-6975 | 327

Atlantic City Convention & Visitors Authority
2314 Pacific Ave . . . . Atlantic City NJ 08401 | **888-228-4748** | 609-348-7100 | 206

Atlantic Coast Bank (ACFC)
505 Haines Ave . . . . Waycross GA 31501 | **800-342-2824** | 912-283-4711 | 359-2
NASDAQ: ACFC

Atlantic Construction Fabrics Inc
2831 Cardwell Rd . . . . Richmond VA 23234 | **800-448-3636** | | 190

Atlantic County Library-Mays Landing
40 Farragut Ave . . . . Mays Landing NJ 08330 | **800-852-7899** | 609-345-6700 | 433-3

Atlantic Credit & Finance Inc
3353 Orange Ave . . . . Roanoke VA 24012 | **800-888-9419** | 540-772-7800 | 160

Atlantic Eyrie Lodge
6 Norman Rd . . . . Bar Harbor ME 04609 | **800-422-2883** | | 378

Atlantic Forest Products LLC
7000 Forest Dr . . . . Sparrows Point MD 21219 | **800-551-2374** | 410-752-8092 |

Atlantic Gasket Corp
3908 Frankford Ave . . . . Philadelphia PA 19124 | **800-229-8881** | 215-533-6400 | 326

Atlantic Health System
475 South St . . . . Morristown NJ 07960 | **800-247-9580** | 973-971-5000 | 373-3

Atlantic India Rubber Co
1437 Kentucky Rt 1428 . . . . Hagerhill KY 41222 | **800-476-6638** | | 673

Atlantic Information Services Inc
1100 17th St NW Ste 300 . . . . Washington DC 20036 | **800-521-4323** | 202-775-9008 | 633-9

Atlantic International University
900 Ft St Mall . . . . Honolulu HI 96813 | **800-993-0066** | 808-924-9567 | 166

Atlantic Lift Truck Inc
2945 Whittington Ave . . . . Baltimore MD 21230 | **800-638-4566** | 410-644-7777 | 384

Atlantic Monthly Magazine
600 New Hampshire Ave NW . . . . Washington DC 20037 | **800-234-2411*** | 202-266-6000 | 455-11
*Cust Svc

Atlantic Oceanside Hotel & Event Center
119 Eden St Rte 3. . . . . Bar Harbor ME 04609 | **800-336-2463** | 207-288-5801 | 665

Atlantic Packaging Co
806 N 23rd St . . . . Wilmington NC 28405 | **800-722-5841** | 910-343-0624 | 549

Atlantic Paper & Twine Co Inc
85 York Ave . . . . Pawtucket RI 02860 | **800-613-0950** | 401-725-0950 | 555

Atlantic Personnel Search Inc
9624 Pennsylvania Ave . . . . Upper Marlboro MD 20772 | **877-229-5254** | 301-599-2108 | 193

Atlantic Premium Shutters
29797 Beck Rd . . . . Wixom MI 48393 | **866-288-2726** | 248-668-6408 | 695

Alphabetical Section

	Toll-Free	Phone	Class
Atlantic Prsnnel Tnant Scrning Inc			
8895 N Military Trl Ste 301C.............. Palm Beach Gardens FL 33410	877-747-2104	561-776-1804	
Atlantic Publishing Co			
315 E Washington St .... Starke FL 32091	800-814-1132		633-2
Atlantic Relocation Systems Inc			
1314 Chattahoochee Ave NW .....Atlanta GA 30318 *Cust Svc	800-241-1140*	404-351-5311	516
Atlantic Salmon Federation (ASF)			
PO Box 5200 .... Saint Andrews NB E5B3S8	800-565-5666	506-529-1033	48-3
Atlantic Sands Hotel			
1 Baltimore Ave ....Rehoboth Beach DE 19971	800-422-0600	302-227-2511	378
Atlantic Spas & Billiards			
8721 Glenwood Ave .... Raleigh NC 27617	800-849-8827	919-783-7447	374
Atlantic Spring			
PO Box 650 .... Flemington NJ 08822	877-231-6474	908-788-5800	715
Atlantic Track & Turnout Co			
270 N Broad St ....Bloomfield NJ 07003	800-631-1274	973-748-5885	765
Atlantic Trust			
100 International Dr 23rd Fl ....Baltimore MD 21202	866-644-4144	202-783-4144	400
Atlantic Union College			
338 Main St ....South Lancaster MA 01561	800-282-2030	978-368-2000	166
Atlantica Oak Island Resort & Conference Ctr			
36 Treasure Dr PO Box 6 .... Western Shore NS B0J3M0	800-565-5075	902-627-2600	665
Atlantis Casino Resort			
3800 S Virginia St .... Reno NV 89502	800-723-6500	775-825-4700	665
Atlantis Seafood Steakhouse			
3800 S Virginia St Atlantis Casino Resort............... Reno NV 89502	800-723-6500		667
Atlas Advertising LLC			
1128 Grant St ....Denver CO 80203	800-543-4402	303-292-3300	7
Atlas Air Worldwide Holdings Inc			
2000 Westchester Ave .... Purchase NY 10577 NASDAQ: AAWW	866-434-1617	914-701-8000	12
Atlas Bolt & Screw Co			
1628 Troy Rd ....Ashland OH 44805	800-321-6977	419-289-6171	278
Atlas Bronze			
445 Bunting Ave .... Trenton NJ 08611	800-478-0887		490
Atlas Brown Investment Advisors Inc			
333 E Main St - 400 ....Louisville KY 40202	866-871-0334	502-271-2900	194
Atlas Carpet Mills Inc			
2200 Saybrook Ave ....Los Angeles CA 90040	800-272-8527	323-724-9000	131
Atlas Concrete Products			
65 Burritt St .... New Britain CT 06053	800-774-1112	860-224-2244	359-3
Atlas Construction Supply Inc			
4640 Brinnell St .... San Diego CA 92111	877-588-2100	858-277-2100	191-1
Atlas Container Corp			
8140 Telegraph Rd .... Severn MD 21144	800-394-4894	410-551-6300	100
Atlas Copco North America LLC			
7 Campus Dr Ste 200 ....Parsippany NJ 07054	800-732-6762	973-397-3400	359-3
Atlas Copco Tools & Assembly Systems LLC			
3301 Cross Creek Pkwy .... Auburn Hills MI 48326	800-859-3746	248-373-3000	754
Atlas Distributing Corp			
44 Southbridge St ....Auburn MA 01501	800-649-6221	508-791-6221	81-1
Atlas Match LLC			
1801 S Airport Cir .... Euless TX 76040	800-628-2426	817-354-7474	9
Atlas Metal Industries			
1135 NW 159th Dr .... Miami FL 33169 *Cust Svc	800-762-7565*	305-625-2451	298
Atlas Minerals & Chemicals Inc			
1227 Valley Rd ....Mertztown PA 19539 *Cust Svc	800-523-8269*	610-682-7171	3
Atlas Model Railroad Company Inc			
378 Florence Ave ....Hillside NJ 07205 *Orders	800-872-2521*	908-687-0880	757
Atlas Oil Co			
24501 Ecorse Rd ....Taylor MI 48180	800-878-2000	313-292-5500	575
Atlas Pacific Engineering Co			
1 Atlas Ave ....Pueblo CO 81001	800-588-5438	719-948-3040	298
Atlas Roofing Corp			
2322 Valley Rd .... Meridian MS 39307 *Cust Svc	800-478-0258*	601-483-7111	46
Atlas Roofing Falcon Foam Div			
8240 Byron Ctr Rd SW ....Byron Center MI 49315	800-917-9138		596
Atlas Sound			
1601 Jack McKay Blvd ....Ennis TX 75119	800-876-3333		52
Atlas Steel Products Co			
7990 Bavaria Rd .... Twinsburg OH 44087	800-444-1682	330-425-1600	490
Atlas Systems Inc			
5712 Cleveland St Ste 200 .... Virginia Beach VA 23462	800-567-7401	757-467-7872	177
Atlas Travel & Technology Group Inc			
200 Donald Lynch Blvd Ste 323 ....Milford MA 01752	800-362-8626	508-478-8626	770
Atlas Tube			
1855 E 122nd St ....Chicago IL 60633	800-733-5683	773-646-4500	488
Atlas Van Lines Inc			
1212 St George Rd ....Evansville IN 47711	800-638-9797	812-424-2222	516
Atlas World Group Inc			
1212 St George Rd ....Evansville IN 47711	800-252-8885	812-424-2222	359-3
Atm Merchant Systems			
1667 Helm Dr .... Las Vegas NV 89119	888-878-8166	702-837-8787	69
Atmos Energy Corp			
PO Box 650205 .... Dallas TX 75265 NYSE: ATO	888-286-6700	972-934-9227	359-5
AT-NET Services Inc			
3401 St Vardell Ln Ste D .... Charlotte NC 29217	866-708-0886	704-831-2500	
ATO (Alpha Tau Omega Fraternity)			
1 N Pennsylvania St 12th Fl ....Indianapolis IN 46204	800-798-9286	317-684-1865	48-16
Atomic USA			
2030 Lincoln Ave .... Ogden UT 84401	800-258-5020		706
Atom-Jet Industries Ltd			
2110 Park Ave ....Brandon MB R7B0R9	800-573-5048		273
AtoZdatabases com			
PO Box 27757 ....Omaha NE 68127	877-428-0101		392
ATRA (Automatic Transmission Rebuilders Assn)			
2400 Latigo Ave ....Oxnard CA 93030	866-464-2872	805-604-2000	49-21
Atrex Inc			
1633 Farm Way Ste 505 .... Middleburg FL 32068	800-874-4505	904-264-9086	643

	Toll-Free	Phone	Class
AtriCure Inc			
6217 Centre Pk Dr .... West Chester OH 45069 NASDAQ: ATRC	888-347-6403	513-755-4100	85
Atris Inc			
1151 S Trooper Rd Ste E.............Norristown PA 19403	800-724-3384		730
Atrium Hotel			
18700 MacArthur Blvd ....Irvine CA 92612	800-854-3012	949-833-2770	378
Atrium Medical Corp			
5 Wentworth Dr .... Hudson NH 03051	800-528-7486	603-880-1433	474
Atrium Medical Ctr			
1 Medical Ctr Dr .... Middletown OH 45005	800-338-4057	513-424-2111	373-3
Atrium Windows & Doors			
3890 W NW Hwy Ste 500 .... Dallas TX 75220	800-938-1000	214-630-5757	234
Ats All Tire Supply Co			
6600 Long Point Rd Ste 101.........Houston TX 77055	888-339-6665		54
ATS Systems Inc			
30222 Esperanza ....Rancho Santa Margarita CA 92688	800-321-1833	949-888-1744	693
ATS Tours			
300 Continental Blvd Ste 350........ El Segundo CA 90245	888-410-5770		755
ATSSA (American Traffic Safety Services Assn)			
15 Riverside Pkwy Ste 100...............Fredericksburg VA 22406	800-272-8772	540-368-1701	49-21
ATT Metrology Services Inc			
30210 SE 79th St Ste 100..........Issaquah WA 98027	888-320-7011	425-867-5356	23
Attendee Management Inc			
15572 Ranch Rd 12 Ste 1..........Wimberley TX 78676	877-947-5174	512-847-5174	620
Attica Hydraulic Exchange Inc			
48175 Gratiot Ave ....Chesterfield MI 48051	800-422-4279	586-949-4240	357
AtticSalt Greetings Inc			
PO Box 5773 ....Topeka KS 66605	888-345-6005		130
Attorney Aid Divorce & Bankruptcy Center Inc			
3605 Long Beach Blvd Ste 300....... Long Beach CA 90807	877-905-5297	562-988-0885	427
Attorney's Title Insurance Fund Inc			
6545 Corporate Ctr Blvd .... Orlando FL 32822	800-336-3863	407-240-3863	390-6
Attraction Inc			
672 Rue du Parc ....Lac-Drolet QC G0Y1C0	800-567-6095	819-549-2477	155-3
Attunity Inc			
70 BlanchaRd Rd ....Burlington MA 01803	866-288-8648	781-730-4070	178-1
Attwood Corp			
1016 N Monroe St ....Lowell MI 49331	844-808-5704	616-897-9241	349
ATU (Amalgamated Transit Union)			
10000 New Hampshire Ave ...... Silver Spring MD 20903	888-240-1196	202-537-1645	413
ATW (American Trails West)			
92 Middle Neck Rd ....Great Neck NY 11021	800-645-6260	516-487-2800	755
Atwater Chamber of Commerce			
1181 Third St ....Atwater CA 95301	844-269-9688	209-358-4251	139
Atwood Mobile Products			
1120 N Main St ....Elkhart IN 46514	800-546-8759	574-264-2131	60
Au Bon Pain			
19 Fid Kennedy Ave ....Boston MA 02210	800-825-5227	617-423-2100	68
Au Naturel Wellness & Medical Spa at the Brookstreet Hotel			
525 Legget Dr ....Ottawa ON K2K2W2	888-826-2220	613-271-1800	703
AUA (American Urological Assn)			
1000 Corporate Blvd .... Linthicum MD 21090	866-746-4282	410-689-3700	49-8
Auberge De La Fontaine b & b Inn			
1301 Rue Rachel E .... Montreal QC H2J2K1	800-597-0597	514-597-0166	703
Auberge du Soleil			
180 Rutherford Hill Rd .... Rutherford CA 94573	800-348-5406	707-963-1211	378
Auberge du Tresor			
20 Rue Sainte-Anne .... Quebec QC G1R3X2	800-566-1876	418-694-1876	667
Auberge du Vieux-Port			
97 Rue de la Commune E .... Montreal QC H2Y1J1	888-660-7678	514-876-0081	378
Auberge Saint-Antoine			
8 rue Saint-Antoine .... Quebec QC G1K4C9	888-692-2211	418-692-2211	378
Auburn Area Chamber of Commerce			
25 Second St NW ....Auburn WA 98001	800-395-0144	253-833-0700	139
Auburn Corp			
10490 W 164th Pl ....Orland Park IL 60467	800-393-1826		191-3
Auburn Leather Co			
125 N Caldwell St ....Auburn KY 42206	800-635-0617	270-542-4116	430
Auburn Manufacturing Co			
29 Stack St .... Middletown CT 06457	800-427-5387	860-346-6677	326
Auburn Public Library			
749 E Thach Ave ....Auburn AL 36830	800-888-2726	334-501-3190	433-3
Auburn Publishers Inc			
25 Dill St ....Auburn NY 13021	800-878-5311	315-253-5311	633-8
Auburn Regional Medical Ctr			
202 N Div St ....Auburn WA 98001	866-268-7223	253-833-7711	373-3
Auburn Systems LLC			
8 Electronics Ave .... Danvers MA 01923	800-255-5008	978-777-2460	201
Auburn University			
202 Mary Martin Hall .... Auburn University AL 36849 *Admissions	866-389-6770*	334-844-6425	166
Montgomery 7430 East Dr ....Montgomery AL 36117	800-227-2649	334-244-3000	166
Auburn-Opelika Tourism Bureau			
714 E Glenn Ave ....Auburn AL 36830	866-880-8747	334-887-8747	206
AUCD (Association of University Centers on Disabilities)			
1100 Wayne Ave Ste 1000 .... Silver Spring MD 20910	888-572-2249	301-588-8252	49-5
Aucoin-Hart			
1525 Metairie Rd ....Metairie LA 70005	800-992-8743	504-834-9999	409
Audi of America			
3800 Hamlin Rd ....Auburn Hills MI 48326	888-237-2834		59
Audible Inc			
1 Washington Pk ....Newark NJ 07102	888-283-5051	973-820-0400	394
Audio Advisor			
3427 Kraft Ave SE ....Grand Rapids MI 49512	800-942-0220		194
Audio America			
15132 Park Of Commerce Blvd ....Jupiter FL 33478	800-432-8532	561-863-7704	
Audio Authority Corp			
2048 Mercer Rd ....Lexington KY 40511	800-322-8346	859-233-4599	386
Audio Command Systems			
694 Main St .... Westbury NY 11590	800-382-2939	516-997-5800	52
Audio Direct			
2004 E Irvington Rd Ste 264.............Tucson AZ 85714 *Cust Svc	888-628-3467*		35
Audio Engineering Society			
60 E 42nd St Rm 2520 .... New York NY 10165	800-541-7299	212-661-8528	49-19

	Toll-Free	Phone	Class
Audio General Inc (AGI) 1680 Republic Rd ... Huntingdon Valley PA 19006	866-866-2600	267-288-0300	511
Audio-Digest Foundation 1577 E Chevy Chase Dr ... Glendale CA 91206	800-423-2308	818-240-7500	761
AudioQuest Inc 2621 White Rd ... Irvine CA 92614	800-747-2770	949-585-0111	253
Audiosears Corp 2 S St ... Stamford NY 12167	800-533-7863	607-652-7305	52
Audio-technica Us Inc 1221 Commerce Dr ... Stow OH 44224	800-667-3745	330-686-2600	246
Audiovisual & Integrated Experience Association (ICIA) 11242 Waples Mill Rd Ste 200 ... Fairfax VA 22030	800-659-7469	703-273-7200	49-20
Audiovox Corp 180 Marcus Blvd ... Hauppauge NY 11788 *NASDAQ: VOXX*	800-645-4994	631-231-7750	52
Audit & Adjustment Company Inc 20700 44th Ave W Ste 100 ... Lynnwood WA 98036	800-526-1074	425-776-9797	531
Auditorium Theatre 50 E Congress Pkwy ... Chicago IL 60605	800-982-2787	312-341-2310	568
Audubon Magazine 225 Varick St 7th Fl ... New York NY 10014 *Cust Svc	800-274-4201*	212-979-3000	455-19
Audubon Naturalist Society 8940 Jones Mill Rd ... Chevy Chase MD 20815	888-744-4723	301-652-9188	48-13
Audubon Nature Institute 6500 Magazine St ... New Orleans LA 70118	800-774-7394	504-581-4629	818
Auer Steel & Heating Supply Co 2935 W Silver Spring Dr ... Milwaukee WI 53209	800-242-0406	414-463-1234	14
Auglaize & Mercer Counties Convention & Visitors Bureau 900 Edgewater Dr ... Saint Marys OH 45885	800-860-4726	419-394-1294	206
Augsburg College 2211 Riverside Ave ... Minneapolis MN 55454	800-788-5678	612-330-1000	166
Augsburg Fortress PO Box 1209 ... Minneapolis MN 55440	800-328-4648	612-330-3300	633-3
August Inc 354 Congress Park Dr ... Centerville OH 45459	800-318-5242	937-434-2520	321
August Winter & Sons Inc 2323 N Roemer Rd ... Appleton WI 54911	800-236-8882	920-739-8881	189-13
Augusta Chronicle 725 Broad St ... Augusta GA 30901	866-249-8223	706-724-0851	528-2
Augusta Fiberglass Coatings Inc 86 Lake Cynthia Rd ... Blackville SC 29817	800-995-8265	803-671-4742	
Augusta Medical Ctr (AMC) 78 Medical Ctr Dr PO Box 1000 ... Fishersville VA 22939	800-932-0262	540-932-4000	373-3
Augusta Metro Chamber of Commerce 1 Tenth St Ste 120 ... Augusta GA 30901	888-639-8188	706-821-1300	139
Augusta Metropolitan Convention & Visitors Bureau 1450 Greene St ... Augusta GA 30901	800-726-0243	706-823-6600	206
Augustana College 639 38th St ... Rock Island IL 61201	800-798-8100	309-794-7000	166
Augustana College 2001 S Summit Ave ... Sioux Falls SD 57197	800-727-2844	605-274-0770	166
AUPHA (Association of University Programs in Health Admin) 2000 N 14th St Ste 780 ... Arlington VA 22201	877-275-6462	703-894-0941	49-8
AURA (Association of Universities for Research in Astron) 1200 New York Ave NW Ste 350 ... Washington DC 20005	888-624-8373	202-483-2101	49-5
Aura Systems Inc 1310 E Grand Ave ... El Segundo CA 90245 *OTC: AUSI*	800-909-2872		515
Aurora Area Convention & Visitors Bureau 43 W Galena Blvd ... Aurora IL 60506	800-477-4369	630-256-3190	206
Aurora Biomed Inc 1001 E Pender St ... Vancouver BC V6A1W2	800-883-2918	604-215-8700	
Aurora Chamber of Commerce 43 W Galena Blvd ... Aurora IL 60506	866-947-8081	630-256-3180	139
Aurora City Hall 15151 E Alameda Pkwy ... Aurora CO 80012	800-895-4999	303-739-7000	336
Aurora Contractors Inc 100 Raynor Ave ... Ronkonkoma NY 11779	866-423-2197	631-981-3785	606
Aurora Co-op Elevator Co 605 12th St PO Box 209 ... Aurora NE 68818	800-642-6795	402-694-2106	275
Aurora Corp of America 3500 Challenger St ... Torrance CA 90503	800-327-8508	310-793-5650	530
Aurora Las Encinas Hospital 2900 E Del Mar Blvd ... Pasadena CA 91107	800-792-2345	626-795-9901	373-5
Aurora National Life Assurance Co PO Box 4490 ... Hartford CT 06147	800-265-2652		390-2
Aurora Pictures Inc 5249 Chicago Ave ... Minneapolis MN 55417	800-346-9487	612-821-6490	511
Aurora Sinai Medical Ctr 945 N 12th St ... Milwaukee WI 53201	888-863-5502	414-219-2000	373-3
Aurora Specialty Textiles Group Inc 2705 N Bridge St ... Yorkville IL 60560	800-864-0303		740-7
Aurora Systems Consulting Inc 2510 W 237th St Ste 202 ... Torrance CA 90505	888-282-0696		461
Aurora University 347 S Gladstone Ave ... Aurora IL 60506	800-742-5281	630-844-5533	166
Aurum Ceramic Dental Laboratories Ltd 115 17 Ave SW ... Calgary AB T2S0A1	800-665-8815	403-228-5120	417
AUSA (Association of the US Army) 2425 Wilson Blvd ... Arlington VA 22201	800-336-4570	703-841-4300	48-19
Austad's Golf 2801 E Tenth St ... Sioux Falls SD 57103 *Cust Svc	800-444-1234*	605-331-4653	707
Aus-Tex Printing & Mailing 2431 Forbes Dr ... Austin TX 78754	800-472-7581	512-476-7581	623
Austin American-Statesman 305 S Congress Ave ... Austin TX 78704	800-445-9898	512-445-4040	528-2
Austin College 900 N Grand Ave ... Sherman TX 75090	800-526-4276	903-813-3000	166
Austin Community College (ACC) 5930 Middle Fiskville Rd ... Austin TX 78752	877-442-3522	512-223-7000	162
Eastview 3401 Webberville Rd ... Austin TX 78702	888-626-1697	512-223-5100	162
Northridge 11928 Stonehollow Dr ... Austin TX 78758	888-626-1697	512-223-4000	162
Pinnacle 7748 Hwy 290 W ... Austin TX 78736	888-626-1697	512-223-8001	162
Rio Grande 1212 Rio Grande ... Austin TX 78701	888-626-1697	512-223-3000	162
Riverside 1020 Grove Blvd ... Austin TX 78741	888-626-1697	512-223-6000	162
Austin Convention & Visitors Bureau 535 E Fifth St ... Austin TX 78701	800-926-2282	512-474-5171	206
Austin Film Festival 1801 Salina St ... Austin TX 78702	800-310-3378	512-478-4795	282
Austin Graduate School of Theology 7640 Guadalupe St ... Austin TX 78752	866-287-4723	512-476-2772	166
Austin Graphics Inc 1198 Second Ave E ... Owen Sound ON N4K2J1	800-265-6964	519-376-2116	343
Austin Peay State University 601 College St ... Clarksville TN 37044 *Admissions	800-844-2778*	931-221-7661	166
Austin Powder Co 25800 Science Pk Dr ... Cleveland OH 44122	800-321-0752	216-464-2400	268
Austin Pump & Supply Co PO Box 17037 ... Austin TX 78760	800-252-9692	512-442-2348	384
Austin State Hospital 4110 Guadalupe St ... Austin TX 78751	866-407-3773	512-452-0381	373-5
Austin Symphony Orchestra 1101 Red River St ... Austin TX 78701	888-462-3787	512-476-6064	569-3
Austin Williams 80 Arkay Dr Ste 220 ... Hauppauge NY 11788	877-386-6035	631-498-5756	
AustinMohawk & Company Inc 2175 Beechgrove Pl ... Utica NY 13501	800-765-3110	315-793-9390	91
Australian-American Chamber of Commerce - San Francisco PO Box 471285 ... San Francisco CA 94147	800-662-4455	415-485-6718	138
Austria *Consulate General* 11859 Wilshire Blvd Ste 501 ... Los Angeles CA 90025	800-255-2414	310-444-9310	257
Embassy 3524 International Ct NW ... Washington DC 20008	800-255-2414	202-895-6700	257
Autec Inc 2500 W Front St ... Statesville NC 28677	800-438-3028	704-871-9141	
Authentic Pine Floors Inc 4042 Hwy 42 ... Locust Grove GA 30248	800-283-6038		747
Authenticity Consulting Inc 4008 Lake Dr Ave N ... Minneapolis MN 55422	800-971-2250	763-971-8890	461
Author House 1663 Liberty Dr ... Bloomington IN 47403	888-519-5121	812-339-6000	633-2
Author Services Inc 7051 Hollywood Blvd ... Hollywood CA 90028	800-624-6504	323-466-3310	461
AuthorizeNet Corp PO Box 8999 ... San Francisco CA 94128	877-447-3938	801-492-6450	178-7
Autism Research Institute (ARI) 4182 Adams Ave ... San Diego CA 92116	866-366-3361	619-281-7165	48-17
Autism Society of America (ASA) 4340 EW Hwy Ste 350 ... Bethesda MD 20814	800-328-8476	301-657-0881	48-17
Autistic Treatment Center Inc 10503 Metric Dr ... Dallas TX 75243	877-666-2747	972-644-2076	148
Auto Builders 5715 Corporate Way ... West Palm Beach FL 33407	800-378-5946	561-622-3515	186
Auto Club of America Corp (ACA) 9411 N Georgia St ... Oklahoma City OK 73120	800-411-2007	405-751-4430	53
Auto Club Speedway 9300 Cherry Ave ... Fontana CA 92335	800-944-7223	909-429-5000	512
Auto Credit Express (ACE) 3271 Five Points Dr Ste 200 ... Auburn Hills MI 48326	888-535-2277		
Auto Data Direct Inc 1379 Cross Creek Cir ... Tallahassee FL 32301	866-923-3123	850-877-8804	224
Auto Europe 39 Commercial St ... Portland ME 04101	800-223-5555	207-842-2000	126
Auto FX Software 130 Inverness Plaz Ste 510 ... Birmingham AL 35242	800-839-2008	205-980-0056	178-8
Auto Lenders Liquidation Center 104 Rt 73 ... Voorhees NJ 08043	888-305-5968		57
Auto Meter Products Inc 413 W Elm St ... Sycamore IL 60178	866-248-6356	815-895-8141	493
Auto Profit Masters 250 E Dry Creek Rd ... Littleton CO 80122	866-826-7911	303-795-5838	461
Auto Truck Inc 1420 Brewster Creek Blvd ... Bartlett IL 60103	877-284-4440	630-860-5600	513
Autobahn Freight Lines Ltd 27 Automatic Rd ... Brampton ON L6S5N8	877-989-9994	416-741-5454	311
Autobell Car Wash Inc 1521 E Third St ... Charlotte NC 28204	800-582-8096	704-527-9274	62-1
Autobytel Inc 18872 MacArthur Blvd ... Irvine CA 92612 *NASDAQ: AUTO*	888-422-8999	949-225-4500	58
Autocam Corp 4070 E Paris Ave ... Kentwood MI 49512	800-747-6978	616-698-0707	60
Autodesk Inc 111 McInnis Pkwy ... San Rafael CA 94903 *NASDAQ: ADSK ■ *Tech Supp*	800-964-6432*	415-507-5000	178-5
Auto-Graphics Inc 430 N Vineyard Ave ... Ontario CA 91764	800-776-6939	909-595-7004	776
Autoland 170 Rt 22 E ... Springfield NJ 07081 *Sales	877-813-7239*	973-467-2900	57
AutoManager Inc 7301 Topanga Canyon Blvd Ste 200 ... Canoga Park CA 91303	800-300-2808	310-207-2202	804
Automated Bldg Components Inc 2359 Grant Rd ... North Baltimore OH 45872	800-837-2152	419-257-2152	812
Automated Medical Systems Inc 2310 N Patterson St Bldg H ... Valdosta GA 31602	800-256-3240	229-253-9526	179
Automated Packaging Systems Inc 10175 Phillip Pkwy ... Streetsboro OH 44241 *Sales	800-527-0733*	330-342-2000	543
Automated Precision Inc 15000 Johns Hopkins Dr ... Rockville MD 20850	800-537-2720		
Automated Quality Technologies Inc 563 Shoreview Park Rd ... St Paul MN 55126	800-250-9297	651-484-6544	693
Automatic Data Processing Inc (ADP) 1 ADP Blvd ... Roseland NJ 07068 *NASDAQ: ADP*	800-225-5237		225

	Toll-Free	Phone	Class
Automatic Funds Transfer Services			
151 S Landers St Ste C . . . . Seattle WA 98134	800-275-2033	206-254-0975	69
Automatic Systems Inc			
9230 E 47th St . . . . Kansas City MO 64133	800-366-3488	816-356-0660	207
Automatic Transmission Rebuilders Assn (ATRA)			
2400 Latigo Ave . . . . Oxnard CA 93030	866-464-2872	805-604-2000	49-21
Automation Products Group Inc (APG)			
1025 W 1700 N . . . . Logan UT 84321	888-525-7300	435-753-7300	201
Automation Service			
13871 Parks Steed Dr . . . . Earth City MO 63045	800-325-4808	314-785-6600	201
Autometrix Precision Cutting Systems Inc			
12098 Charles Dr . . . . Grass Valley CA 95945	800-635-3080	530-477-5065	111
Automobile Club of Southern California			
2601 S Figueroa St . . . . Los Angeles CA 90007	800-400-4222	213-741-3686	53
Automobile Consumer Services Inc			
6249 Stewart Rd . . . . Cincinnati OH 45227	800-223-4882	513-527-7700	58
Automotive Distribution Network			
3085 Fountainside Dr Ste 210 . . . . Germantown TN 38138	800-616-7587		49-18
Automotive Distributors Company Inc			
2981 Morse Rd . . . . Columbus OH 43231	800-421-5556		61
Automotive Engine Rebuilders Assn (AERA)			
500 Coventry Ln Ste 180 . . . . Crystal Lake IL 60014	888-326-2372	847-541-6550	49-21
Automotive Finance Corp (AFC)			
13085 Hamilton Crossing Blvd . . . . Carmel IN 46032	888-335-6675	865-384-8250	216
Automotive Industry Action Group (AIAG)			
26200 Lahser Rd Ste 200 . . . . Southfield MI 48033	877-275-2424	248-358-3570	49-21
Automotive Information Ctr			
18872 MacArthur Blvd . . . . Irvine CA 92612	888-422-8999		58
Automotive Mfg & Supply Co (AMSCO)			
90 Plant Ave . . . . Hauppauge NY 11788	800-645-5604	631-435-1400	
Automotive News Magazine			
1155 Gratiot Ave . . . . Detroit MI 48207	877-812-1584	313-446-0450	455-21
Automotive Oil Change Assn (AOCA)			
330 N Wabash Ave Ste 2000. . . . . Chicago IL 60611	800-230-0702	312-321-5132	49-21
Automotive Parts Headquarters			
2959 Clearwater Rd . . . . Saint Cloud MN 56301	800-247-0339	320-252-5411	61
Automotive Parts Remanufacturers Assn (APRA)			
4215 Lafayette Ctr Dr Ste 3 . . . . Chantilly VA 20151	877-734-4827	703-968-2772	49-21
Automotive Racing Products Inc			
1863 Eastman Ave . . . . Ventura CA 93003	800-826-3045	805-339-2200	349
Automotive Recyclers Assn (ARA)			
9113 Church St . . . . Manassas VA 20110	888-385-1005	571-208-0428	49-21
Automotive Resources Inc			
12775 Randolph Ridge Ln . . . . Manassas VA 20109	800-562-3250		295
Automotive Service Assn (ASA)			
1901 Airport Fwy . . . . Bedford TX 76021	800-272-7467*		49-21
*Cust Svc			
Automotive Training Center-Exton Campus			
114 Pickering Way . . . . Exton PA 19341	888-321-8992		166
Autonet Mobile Inc			
3636 N Laughlin Dr Ste 150 . . . . Santa Rosa CA 95403	800-977-2107	415-223-0316	641-9
Auto-Owners Insurance Co			
6101 Anacapri Blvd . . . . Lansing MI 48917	800-346-0346	517-323-1200	390-4
Autoquip Corp			
1058 W Industrial Rd . . . . Guthrie OK 73044	888-811-9876	405-282-5200	468
AutoRevo LTD			
3820 American Dr Ste 110 . . . . Plano TX 75075	888-311-7386*		57
*Support			
Autostar Solutions Inc			
1300 Summit Ave Ste 800 . . . . Fort Worth TX 76102	800-682-2215		174
Autotrol Corp			
365 E Prairie St . . . . Crystal Lake IL 60014	800-228-6207	815-459-3080	515
Autotruck Federal Credit Union			
3611 Newburg Rd . . . . Louisville KY 40218	800-459-2328	502-459-8981	219
AutoTruckToysco			
2814 W Wood St . . . . Paris TN 38242	800-544-6194	731-642-3535	786
AutoVIN Inc			
13085 Hamilton Crossing Blvd . . . . Carmel IN 46032	866-585-8080		58
AutoWeek Magazine			
1155 Gratiot Ave . . . . Detroit MI 48207	888-288-6954*	313-446-6000	455-3
*Circ			
AutoZone Inc			
123 S Front St . . . . Memphis TN 38103	800-288-6966	901-495-6500	54
NYSE: AZO			
Autry Greer & Sons Inc			
2850 W Main St . . . . Mobile AL 36612	800-999-7750	251-457-8655	344
AV Homes Inc			
8601 N Scottsdale Rd Ste 225 . . . . Scottsdale AZ 85253	800-284-6637	480-214-7400	649
NASDAQ: AVHI			
AVA (Association for Vascular Access)			
5526 W 13400 S Ste 229 . . . . Herriman UT 84096	877-924-2821	801-792-9079	49-8
AVAD Canada Ltd			
205 Courtneypark Dr W			
Ste 103 . . . . Mississauga ON L5W0A5	866-523-2823		174
Avalign Technologies Inc			
2275 Half Day R Ste 126. . . . . Bannockburn IL 60015	855-282-5446		
Avalign Technologies Inc			
272 E Deerpath Rd Ste 208. . . . . Lake Forest IL 60045	855-282-5446		473
Avalon Corporate Furnished Apartments			
1553 Empire Blvd . . . . Webster NY 14580	800-934-9763	585-671-4421	378
Avalon Fortress Security Corp			
2407 109th Ave NE Ste 110 . . . . Blaine MN 55449	844-788-9111	763-767-9111	689
Avanade Inc			
818 Stewart St . . . . Seattle WA 98101	844-282-6233	206-239-5600	39
Avancen MOD Corp			
1156 Bowman Rd Ste 200 . . . . Mount Pleasant SC 29464	800-607-1230		250
Avanquest Software USA			
1333 W 120th Ave . . . . Westminster CO 80234	800-011-2312		178-7
Avant Ministries			
10000 N Oak Trafficway . . . . Kansas City MO 64155	800-468-1892	816-734-8500	48-20
Avanti Destinations Inc			
111 SW Columbia St Ste 1200 . . . . Portland OR 97201	800-422-5053	503-295-1100	766
Avanti Foods			
109 Depot St . . . . Walnut IL 61376	800-243-3739	815-379-2155	296-36
Avanti Polar Lipids Inc			
700 Industrial Pk Dr . . . . Alabaster AL 35007	800-227-0651	205-663-2494	477
Avanti Press Inc			
155 W Congress St Ste 200 . . . . Detroit MI 48226	800-228-2684	313-961-0022	130

	Toll-Free	Phone	Class
Avantica Technologies			
2680 Bayshore Pkwy			
Ste 416 . . . . Mountain View CA 94043	877-372-1955	650-248-9678	196
Avantus			
15 W Strong St Ste 20A . . . . Pensacola FL 32501	800-600-2510	850-470-9336	178-10
Avanzado LLC			
25330 Interchange Ct . . . . . . Farmington Hills MI 48335	800-913-1058		457
Avatar Management Services Inc			
8157 Bavaria Dr E . . . . Macedonia OH 44056	800-728-2827	330-963-3900	461
Avatier Corp			
2603 Camino Ramon Ste 110. . . . . . . San Ramon CA 94583	800-609-8610	925-217-5170	178-12
Avaya Government Solutions Inc			
12730 Fair Lakes Cir . . . . Fairfax VA 22033	800-492-6769	703-653-8000	178-10
Avaya Inc			
211 Mt Airy Rd . . . . Basking Ridge NJ 07920	866-462-8292	908-953-6000	176
Ave Intervision LLC			
1840 W State St . . . . Alliance OH 44601	800-448-9126		681
Ave Maria University			
5050 Ave Maria Blvd . . . . Naples FL 34119	877-283-8648	239-280-2500	166
Aveda Corp			
4000 Pheasant Ridge Dr . . . . Blaine MN 55449	800-644-4831		214
Avedis Zildjian Co			
22 Longwater Dr . . . . Norwell MA 02061	800-229-8672	781-871-2200	523
Avemco Insurance Co			
8490 Progress Dr Ste 100 . . . . Frederick MD 21701	888-241-7891		390-4
Aventura Hospital			
20900 Biscayne Blvd . . . . Aventura FL 33180	800-523-5772	305-682-7000	373-3
Avenue Inn & Spa			
33 Wilmington Ave . . . . Rehoboth Beach DE 19971	800-433-5870		378
Avenue Plaza Resort			
2111 St Charles Ave . . . . New Orleans LA 70130	800-614-8685	504-566-1212	378
Avenue Stores Inc			
365 W Passaic St . . . . Rochelle Park NJ 07662	888-843-2836	201-845-0880	157-6
Avera Saint Luke's Hospital			
305 S State St . . . . Aberdeen SD 57401	800-658-3535	605-622-5000	373-3
Avere Systems			
910 River Ave . . . . Pittsburgh PA 15212	888-882-8373	412-894-2570	173-8
Averitt Express Inc			
1415 Neal St . . . . Cookeville TN 38501	800-283-7488		775
Avery Dennison Corp			
207 Goode Ave . . . . Glendale CA 91203	888-567-4387*	626-304-2000	727
NYSE: AVY ■ *Cust Svc			
Avery Dennison Fastener Div			
224 Industrial Rd . . . . Fitchburg MA 01420	800-225-5913		604
Avery Dennison Specialty Tapes			
250 Chester St . . . . Painesville OH 44077	866-462-8379		727
Avery Dennison Worldwide Office Products Div			
207 Goode Ave . . . . Glendale CA 91203	800-462-8379	626-304-2000	530
Avery Weigh-Tronix Inc			
1000 Armstrong Dr . . . . Fairmont MN 56031	800-458-7062	507-238-4461	680
Aves Audio Visual Systems Inc			
PO Box 500 . . . . Sugar Land TX 77487	800-365-2837	281-295-1300	38
AVG Automation			
4140 Utica St . . . . Bettendorf IA 52722	877-774-3279		253
Avi Systems Inc			
9675 W 76th St Ste 200 . . . . Eden Prairie MN 55344	800-488-4954	952-949-3700	643
Aviation Ground Equipment Corp			
53 Hanse Ave . . . . Freeport NY 11520	800-758-0044	516-546-0003	57
Aviation Supplies & Academics Inc			
7005 132nd PI SE . . . . Newcastle WA 98059	800-272-2359	425-235-1500	633-2
Aviation Week & Space Technology Magazine			
1200 G St NW . . . . Washington DC 20005	800-525-5003		455-19
AviationWeek			
1200 G St NW Ste 900 . . . . Washington DC 20005	800-525-5003		527-13
Avid Payment Solutions			
950 S Old Woodward Ste 220. . . . . . Birmingham MI 48009	888-855-8644		255
Avid Technology Inc			
65-75 Network Dri . . . . Burlington MA 01803	800-949-2843	978-640-6789	178-8
NASDAQ: AVID			
Avideon Corp			
PO Box 4830 . . . . Baltimore MD 21211	888-368-1237		195
Avidian Technologies Inc			
2053 152nd Ave NE . . . . Redmond WA 98052	800-860-5534	800-399-8980	177
Avila University			
11901 Wornall Rd . . . . Kansas City MO 64145	866-943-5787	816-501-2400	166
Avionic Instruments Inc			
1414 Randolph Ave . . . . Avenel NJ 07001	800-468-3571	732-388-3500	253
Avis Rent A Car System Inc			
6 Sylvan Way . . . . Parsippany NJ 07054	800-331-1212	973-496-3500	126
Avisen Securities Inc			
3620 American River Dr			
Ste 145 . . . . Sacramento CA 95864	800-230-7704	916-480-2747	686
Avista Corp			
1411 E Mission St . . . . Spokane WA 99252	800-227-9187		782
Avista Corp			
1411 E Mission St . . . . Spokane WA 99202	800-936-6629	509-489-0500	782
NYSE: AVA			
Avitus Group			
175 N 27th St . . . . Billings MT 59101	800-454-2446		729
Aviva Metals			
2929 W 12th St . . . . Houston TX 77008	800-231-0771		
Avjobs Inc			
9609 S University Blvd			
Unit 630830 . . . . Littleton CO 80163	888-624-8691	303-683-2322	260
AVMA (American Veterinary Medical Assn PAC)			
1910 Sunderland PI NW . . . . Washington DC 20036	800-321-1473	202-789-0007	611
AVMA (American Veterinary Medical Assn)			
1931 N Meacham Rd Ste 100 . . . . . . Schaumburg IL 60173	800-248-2862	847-925-8070	49-8
AvMed			
4300 NW 89th Blvd . . . . Gainesville FL 32606	800-346-0231	352-372-8400	390-3
AVMetrics LLC			
90 W Cochran St Ste C. . . . . Simi Valley CA 93065	800-240-1049	805-421-5056	
Avnet Inc			
2211 S 47th St . . . . Phoenix AZ 85034	888-822-8638	480-643-2000	246
NASDAQ: AVT			
Avnet Technology Solutions			
8700 S Price Rd . . . . Tempe AZ 85284	800-409-1483	480-794-6500	174
Avon Old Farms School			
500 Old Farms Rd . . . . Avon CT 06001	800-464-2866	860-404-4100	618

Name / Address	City	State	ZIP	Toll-Free	Phone	Class
AVS Companies 750 Morse Ave	Elk Grove Village	IL	60007	**800-441-0009**	847-439-9400	55
AVS Inc 60 Fitchburg Rd	Ayer	MA	01432	**800-772-0710**	978-772-0710	318
AVS Installations LLC 400 Raritan Ctr Pkwy Ste D	Edison	NJ	08837	**800-218-9177**	732-634-7903	180
Avstar Aviation Ltd 12 N Haven Ln	East Northport	NY	11731	**800-575-2359**	631-499-0048	13
Avtec Inc 6 Industrial Pk	Cahokia	IL	62206	**800-552-8832**	618-337-7800	437
Avtech Software Inc 16 Cutler St Cutler Mill	Warren	RI	02885	**888-220-6700**		177
Avtron Aerospace Inc 7900 E Pleasant Valley Rd	Cleveland	OH	44131	**800-783-7871**	216-750-5152	21
AW (American Whitewater) PO Box 1540	Cullowhee	NC	28723	**866-262-8429**	828-586-1930	48-23
Awards & Personalization Assn (ARA) 8735 W Higgins Rd Ste 300	Chicago	IL	60631	**800-344-2148**	847-375-4800	49-4
AWCI (Association of the Wall & Ceiling Industries Inter) 513 W Broad St Ste 210	Falls Church	VA	22046	**800-233-8990**	703-538-1600	49-3
AWF (African Wildlife Foundation) 1100 New Jersey Ave SE Ste 900	Washington	DC	20003	**888-494-5354**	202-939-3333	48-3
AWHONN (Association of Women's Health Obstetric & Neonatal) 2000 L St NW Ste 740	Washington	DC	20036	**800-673-8499**	202-261-2400	49-8
AWI (American Watchmakers-Clockmakers Institute) 701 Enterprise Dr	Harrison	OH	45030	**866-367-2924**	513-367-9800	49-4
A&WMA (Air & Waste Management Assn) 436 Seventh Ave Ste 2100	Pittsburgh	PA	15219	**800-270-3444**	412-232-3444	48-12
AWP Inc 826 Overholt Rd	Kent	OH	44240	**800-343-2650**		689
AWS (American Welding Society) 550 NW 42nd Ave	Miami	FL	33126	**800-443-9353**	305-443-9353	49-3
AWWA (American Water Works Assn) 6666 W Quincy Ave	Denver	CO	80235	**800-926-7337**	303-794-7711	48-12
Axcera Corp 103 Freedom Dr	Lawrence	PA	15055	**800-215-2614**	724-873-8100	643
Axcet HR Solutions *Axcet* 8325 Lenexa Dr Ste 410	Lenexa	KS	66214	**800-801-7557**	913-383-2999	627
Axcient Inc 1161 San Antonio Rd	Mountain View	CA	94043	**800-715-2339**		177
Axeon Specialty Products LLC 750 Washington Blvd Ste 600	Stamford	CT	06901	**855-378-4958**		575
AXIA Consulting LLC 1391 W Fifth Ave Ste 320	Columbus	OH	43212	**866-937-5550**	614-675-4050	196
Axial Networks Inc 443 Park Ave S 8th Fl	New York	NY	10016	**800-860-4519**		687
Axiobionics 6111 Jackson Rd Ste 200	Ann Arbor	MI	48103	**800-552-3539**	734-327-2946	250
Axiom Education LLC 4 Research Dr	Shelton	CT	06484	**888-801-8183**		386
Axiom Memory Solutions LLC 15 Chrysler	Irvine	CA	92618	**888-658-3326**	949-581-1450	174
Axiom Software Ltd 115 Stevens Ave Ste 320	Valhalla	NY	10595	**800-588-8805**	914-769-8800	177
AXIOS HR 528 Fourth St NW	Grand Rapids	MI	49504	**844-442-9467**		
Axis Communications Inc (ACI) 100 Apollo Dr	Chelmsford	MA	01824	**800-444-2947**	978-614-2000	176
Axley 2 E Mifflin St Ste 200	Madison	WI	53703	**800-368-5661**	608-257-5661	443
Axon Sports 505 S 24th Ave	Wausau	WI	54401	**877-399-2966**		
Axonify Inc 450 Phillip St Ste 300	Waterloo	ON	N2L5J2	**855-296-6439**	519-585-1200	242
Axsun Group 4900 Armand Frappier	Saint-Hubert	QC	J3Z1G5	**888-992-9786**	450-445-3003	311
Axsun Technologies Inc 1 Fortune Dr	Billerica	MA	01821	**866-462-9786**	978-262-0049	692
Axxiem Web Solutions 276 Fifth Ave Ste 704 *General	New York	NY	10001	**877-429-9436***	914-478-7600	
AXYS Technologies Inc 2045 Mills Rd	Sidney	BC	V8L5X2	**877-792-7878**	250-655-5850	604
Axyz Automation Inc 2844 E Kemper Rd	Cincinnati	OH	45241	**800-527-9670**	800-361-3408	180
AY McDonald Manufacturing Co 4800 Chavenelle Rd *Cust Svc	Dubuque	IA	52002	**800-292-2737***		591
Aya Kitchens & Baths Ltd 1551 Caterpillar Rd	Mississauga	ON	L4X2Z6	**866-292-4968**	905-848-1999	814
Ayres Hotel Anaheim 2550 E Katella Ave	Anaheim	CA	92806	**800-595-5692**	714-634-2106	378
AYSO (American Youth Soccer Organization) 19750 S Vermont Ave Ste 200	Torrance	CA	90502	**800-872-2976**		48-22
AZ Countertops Inc 1445 S Hudson Ave	Ontario	CA	91761	**800-266-3524**	909-983-5386	720
A-Z Sponge & Foam Products Ltd 811 Cundy Ave Annacis Is	Delta	BC	V3M5P6	**800-665-3990**	604-525-1665	597
Azar Computer Software Services Inc 1200 Regal Row	Austin	TX	78748	**800-525-7844**		
Azar Nut Co 1800 NW Dr	El Paso	TX	79912	**800-351-8178**	915-877-4079	296-28
Azon USA Inc 643 W Crosstown Pkwy	Kalamazoo	MI	49008	**800-788-5942**	269-385-5942	385
Azonix Corp 900 Middlesex Tpke Bldg 6	Billerica	MA	01821	**800-967-5558**	978-670-6300	201
Aztec International Inc 3010 Henson Rd	Knoxville	TN	37921	**800-369-5357**	865-588-5357	151
Aztec Supply 954 N Batavia St	Orange	CA	92867	**800-836-3210**	714-771-6580	599
AzTx Cattle Co 311 E Park Ave	Hereford	TX	79045	**800-999-5065**	806-364-8871	10-1
Azure Horizons Inc 7115 W North Ave Ste 185	Oak Park	IL	60302	**877-494-6070**	708-838-7031	180
Azusa Pacific University 901 E Alosta Ave PO Box 7000	Azusa	CA	91702	**800-825-5278**	626-969-3434	166

B

Name / Address	City	State	ZIP	Toll-Free	Phone	Class
B & B Agency of Boston 47 Commercial Wharf Apt 3	Boston	MA	02110	**800-248-9262**	617-720-3540	375
B & B Electronics Manufacturing Co PO Box 1040	Ottawa	IL	61350	**800-346-3119**	815-433-5100	692
B & B Trade Distribution Centre 1950 Oxford St E	London	ON	N5V2Z8	**800-265-0382**	519-679-1770	606
B & C Transportation Inc 427 Continental Dr	Maryville	TN	37804	**877-812-2287**	865-983-4653	107
B & D Litho of Arizona 3820 N 38th Ave	Phoenix	AZ	85019	**800-735-0375**	602-269-2526	623
B & G Foods Inc 4 Gatehall Dr Ste 110 *NYSE: BGS*	Parsippany	NJ	07054	**800-811-8975**		
B & G House of Printing 1825-A W 169th St	Gardena	CA	90247	**800-882-1844**	310-532-1533	623
B & G Mfg Company Inc 3067 Unionville Pk	Hatfield	PA	19440	**800-366-3067**	215-822-1921	278
B & H Manufacturing Co 3461 Roeding Rd	Ceres	CA	95307	**888-643-0444**	209-537-5785	543
B & H Manufacturing Inc 141 County Rd 34 E	Jackson	MN	56143	**800-240-3288**		273
B & H Photo-Video-Pro Audio Corp 420 Ninth Ave	New York	NY	10001	**800-947-9954**	212-444-6615	119
B & O Railroad Museum 901 W Pratt St	Baltimore	MD	21223	**866-468-7630**	410-752-2490	517
B & R Eckel's Transport Ltd 5514B - 50 Ave	Bonnyville	AB	T9N2K8	**800-661-3290**	780-826-3889	535
B Berger Co 1380 Highland Rd *Cust Svc	Macedonia	OH	44056	**800-288-8400***	330-425-3838	590
B Braun Medical Inc 824 12th Ave	Bethlehem	PA	18018	**800-523-9676**	610-691-5400	474
B E Meyers & Co Inc 9461 Willows Rd NE	Redmond	WA	98052	**800-327-5648**	425-881-6648	540
D E. Smith Inc 8801 Renner Ave	Lenexa	KS	66219	**855-296-6318**		193
B Green Innovations Inc 750 Hwy 34	Matawan	NJ	07747	**877-996-9333**		
B H G Inc PO Box 309	Garrison	ND	58540	**800-658-3485**	701-463-2201	623
B Jcc Inspections 1000 Banks Draw	Rexford	MT	59930	**877-248-6006**	406-882-4825	261
B M Ross & Assoc Ltd 62 N St	Goderich	ON	N7A2T4	**888-524-2641**	519-524-2641	256
B'nai B'rith International 2020 K St NW 7th Fl	Washington	DC	20006	**888-388-4224**	202-857-6600	48-20
B'Nai B'Rith Magazine 2020 K St NW 7th Fl	Washington	DC	20006	**888-388-4224**	202-857-6600	455-18
B2 Gold Corp 595 Burrard St Ste 3100 PO Box 49143	Vancouver	BC	V7X1J1	**800-316-8855**	604-681-8371	500
B2B2C Inc 2700 Rue Michelin	Laval	QC	H7L5Y1	**800-965-9065**	514-908-5420	
B3 Solutions LLC 901 North Pitt St Ste 300	Alexandria	VA	22314	**877-872-9839**	571-384-1400	461
BA Exhibits inc 2191 Mendenhall Dr Ste 101	North Las Vegas	NV	89081	**800-579-3888**		
BA Robinson Company Ltd 619 Berry St	Winnipeg	MB	R3H0S2	**866-903-6275**	204-784-0150	608
Baader-Johnson 2955 Fairfax Trafficway	Kansas City	KS	66115	**800-288-3434**	913-621-3366	298
BAB Inc 500 Lake Cook Rd Ste 475 *OTC: BABB*	Deerfield	IL	60015	**800-251-6101**		666
Babcock & Wilcox Co 13024 Ballantyne Corporate Pl Ste 700	Charlotte	NC	28277	**800-222-2625**	704-625-4900	91
Babcock Power Inc 6 Kimball Ln Ste 210	Lynnfield	MA	01940	**800-523-0480**	978-646-3300	91
Babcock-Davis 9300 73rd Ave N	Brooklyn Park	MN	55428	**888-412-3726**		234
Babe Ruth League Inc 1770 Brunswick Pk PO Box 5000	Trenton	NJ	08638	**800-880-3142**	609-695-1434	48-22
Babe Winkelman Productions PO Box 407	Brainerd	MN	56401	**800-333-0471**		737
Babson College 231 Forest St *Admissions	Babson Park	MA	02457	**800-488-3696***	781-235-1200	166
Baby Jogger Co 8575 Magellan Pkwy Ste 1000	Richmond	VA	23227	**800-241-1848**		64
Baby Trend Inc 1567 S Campus Ave *Cust Svc	Ontario	CA	91761	**800-328-7363***		64
BabyCenter LLC 163 Freelon St	San Francisco	CA	94107	**866-732-8243**	415-537-0900	355
BAC (Big Apple Circus) 321 W 44th St Ste 400	New York	NY	10036	**888-541-3750**	212-257-2330	149
BAC (International Union of Bricklayers & Allied Craftw) 1776 eye St NW	Washington	DC	20006	**888-880-8222**	202-783-3788	413
Baccarat New York LLC 20 W 53rd St	New York	NY	10019	**866-957-5139**	212-765-5300	703
Bacharach Inc 621 Hunt Vly Cir	New Kensington	PA	15068	**800-736-4666**	724-334-5000	201
Bachem Bioscience Inc 3132 Kashiwa St	Torrance	CA	90505	**888-422-2436**	310-539-4171	477
Bachem-Peninsula Laboratories Inc 3132 Kashiwa St	Torrence	CA	90505	**888-422-2436**	310-539-4171	231
Bachman's Inc 6010 Lyndale Ave S	Minneapolis	MN	55419	**888-222-4626**	612-861-7600	292

	City	State	ZIP	Toll-Free	Phone	Class
Bachmann Industries Inc						
1400 E Erie Ave	Philadelphia	PA	19124	**800-356-3910***	215-533-1600	757
*Cust Svc						
Back Country Horsemen of America (BCHA)						
59 Rainbow Rd	East Granby	CT	06029	**888-893-5161**	860-586-7540	48-23
Backchannelmedia Inc						
105 S St	Boston	MA	02111	**800-676-0823**		
Backcountry Gear LLC						
1855 W Second Ave	Eugene	OR	97402	**800-953-5499**	541-485-4007	707
Backcountrycom						
2607 S 3200 W Ste A	West Valley City	UT	84119	**800-409-4502***		457
*Orders						
Background Bureau Inc						
2019 Alexandria Pk	Highland Heights	KY	41076	**800-854-3990**	859-781-3400	631
Background Information Services Inc						
1800 30th St Ste 204	Boulder	CO	80301	**800-433-6010**	303-442-3960	631
Backroads						
801 Cedar St	Berkeley	CA	94710	**800-462-2848**	510-527-1555	755
Backtrack Inc						
8850 Tyler Blvd	Mentor	OH	44060	**800-991-9694**		260
Backupify 50 Milk St	Boston	MA	02109	**800-571-4984**		804
Bacon Don (Rep R - NE)						
1516 Longworth House Office Bldg						
	Washington	DC	20515	**888-221-7452**	202-225-4155	341-1
Bacon Veneer Co						
16W273 83rd St Ste A-1	Burr Ridge	IL	60527	**800-443-7995**	630-541-8312	609
Bacone College						
2299 Old Bacone Rd	Muskogee	OK	74403	**888-682-5514***	918-683-4581	166
*Admissions						
Bacon-Universal Company Inc						
918 Ahua St	Honolulu	HI	96819	**800-352-3508**	808-839-7202	357
BACVA (Baltimore Area Convention & Visitors Assn)						
100 Light St 12th Fl	Baltimore	MD	21202	**877-225-8466**	410-659-7300	206
Bad Dog Tools						
24 Broadcommon Rd	Bristol	RI	02809	**800-252-1330**	401-253-1330	349
Badge A Minit Ltd						
345 N Lewis Ave	Oglesby	IL	61348	**800-223-4103**		454
Badger Air Brush Co						
9128 Belmont Ave	Franklin Park	IL	60131	**800-247-2787**	847-678-3104	43
Badger Bus						
5501 Femrite Dr	Madison	WI	53718	**800-442-8259**	608-255-1511	107
Badger Coaches Inc						
5501 Femrite Dr	Madison	WI	53718	**800-442-8259**	608-255-1511	755
Badger Daylighting Corp						
919 11th Ave SW 4th Fl	Calgary	AB	T2R-1P3	**877-322-3437**	403-264-8500	535
Badger Express LLC						
181 Quality Ct	Fall River	WI	53932	**800-972-0084**	920-484-5808	192
Badger Liquor Company Inc						
850 S Morris St	Fond du Lac	WI	54936	**800-242-9708**	920-923-8160	81-3
Badger Meter Inc						
4545 W Brown Deer Rd	Milwaukee	WI	53224	**800-876-3837**	414-355-0400	493
NYSE: BMI						
Badger Mining Corp						
409 S Church St						
CA Chier Resource Ctr	Berlin	WI	54923	**800-932-7263**	920-361-2388	500
Badger Sportswear Inc						
111 Badger Ln	Statesville	NC	28625	**888-871-0990**	704-871-0990	155-3
Badger State Industries (BSI)						
3099 E Washington Ave						
PO Box 8990	Madison	WI	53708	**800-862-1086**	608-240-5200	626
Badger West Wine & Spirits LLC						
5400 Old Town Hall Rd	Eau Claire	WI	54701	**800-472-6674**	715-836-8600	81-3
Badgley Phelps & Bell Inc						
1420 Fifth Ave Ste 3200	Seattle	WA	98101	**800-869-7173**	206-623-6172	400
Badorf Shoe Co Inc						
1958 Auction Rd	Manheim	PA	17545	**800-325-1545**	717-653-0155	301
Baer Supply Co						
909 Forest Edge Dr	Vernon Hills	IL	60061	**800-944-2237**	800-289-2237	350
BAF Industries Inc						
1451 Edinger Ave	Tustin	CA	92780	**800-437-9893**	714-258-8055	151
Bag Makers Inc						
6606 S Union Rd	Union	IL	60180	**800-458-9031**		66
Bagby Elevator Company Inc						
3608 Messer Airport Hwy	Birmingham	AL	35222	**800-228-7544**		
BagcraftPapercon						
3900 W 43rd St	Chicago	IL	60632	**800-621-8468**	773-254-8000	550
Bagdad Roller Mills Inc						
5740 Elmburg Rd	Bagdad	KY	40003	**800-928-3333**	502-747-8968	445
Bahama Breeze						
8849 International Dr	Orlando	FL	32819	**877-500-9715**	407-248-2499	667
Bahama House						
2001 S Atlantic Ave						
	Daytona Beach Shores	FL	32118	**800-571-2001**		378
Bahamas Tourism Office						
1200 S Pine Island Rd						
Ste 450	Plantation	FL	33324	**800-327-7678**	954-236-9292	770
Bahia Mar Beach Resort & Yachting Ctr						
801 Seabreeze Blvd	Fort Lauderdale	FL	33316	**800-755-9558**	954-627-6309	665
Bahia Mar Resort & Conference Ctr						
3100 Padre Blvd	South Padre Island	TX	78597	**800-926-6926**		665
Bahia Resort Hotel						
998 W Mission Bay Dr	San Diego	CA	92109	**800-576-4229**	858-488-0551	665
Bahl & Gaynor Investment Counsel						
255 East Fifth St Ste 2700	Cincinnati	OH	45202	**800-341-1810**	513-287-6100	400
BAI (Bank Administration Institute)						
115 S LaSalle St Ste 3300	Chicago	IL	60603	**800-224-9889***	312-683-2464	49-2
*Cust Svc						
Baier Marine Company Inc						
2920 Airway Ave	Costa Mesa	CA	92626	**800-455-3917**		349
Bailard						
950 Tower Ln Ste 1900	Foster City	CA	94404	**800-224-5273**	650-571-5800	400
Bailey Company Inc, The						
501 Cowan St	Nashville	TN	37207	**800-342-1665**		357
Bailey Matthews Shell Museum						
3075 Sanibel-Captiva Rd						
PO Box 1580	Sanibel	FL	33957	**888-679-6450**	239-395-2233	517
Bailey Properties						
106 Aptos Beach Dr	Aptos	CA	95003	**800-347-6830**	831-688-7009	648
Bailey44						
4700 S Boyle Ave	Vernon	CA	90058	**844-894-8100**		
Baileys Furniture Outlet Inc						
350 W Intl Airport Rd Ste 100	Anchorage	AK	99518	**888-563-4083**		
Bailiwick Services LLC						
4260 Norex Dr	Chaska	MN	55318	**800-935-8840**		
Baille Lumber Co						
4002 Legion Dr PO Box 6	Hamburg	NY	14075	**800-950-2850**	716-649-2850	191-3
Baillio's Inc						
5301 Menaul Blvd NE	Albuquerque	NM	87110	**800-540-7511**	505-395-5611	39
Bain Pest Control Service Inc						
1320 Middlesex St	Lowell	MA	01851	**800-272-3661**	978-452-9621	573
Baird & Warner Inc						
120 S LaSalle St 20th Fl	Chicago	IL	60603	**888-661-1176**	312-368-1855	648
Baird Patrick & Company Inc						
305 Plz 10	Jersey City	NJ	07311	**800-221-7747**	201-680-7300	686
Baisch & Skinner Inc						
2721 Lasalle St	Saint Louis	MO	63104	**800-523-0013**	314-664-1212	292
Baja Expeditions Inc						
3096 Palm St	San Diego	CA	92104	**800-843-6967**	858-581-3311	220
Baja Fresh						
9311 E Via De Ventura	Scottsdale	AZ	85258	**866-452-4252**		667
Baka Communications Inc						
630 The East Mall	Etobicoke	ON	M9B4B1	**866-884-3329**	416-641-2800	196
Bake'n Joy Foods Inc						
351 Willow St S	North Andover	MA	01845	**800-666-4937**	978-683-1414	296-16
Baker & Taylor Inc						
2550 W Tyvola Rd Ste 300	Charlotte	NC	28217	**800-775-1800**		96
Baker Book House Company Inc						
6030 E Fulton St	Ada	MI	49301	**800-877-2665***	616-676-9185	633-3
*Orders						
Baker Book House Company Inc Revell Div						
6030 E Fulton St	Ada	MI	49301	**800-877-2665***	616-676-9185	633-3
*Orders						
Baker Charlie (R)						
State House 24 Beacon St						
Office of the Governor Rm 280	Boston	MA	02133	**888-870-7770**	617-725-4005	
Baker College						
Auburn Hills						
1500 University Dr	Auburn Hills	MI	48326	**888-429-0410**	248-340-0600	166
Cadillac						
9600 E 13th St	Cadillac	MI	49601	**888-313-3463**	231-876-3100	166
Flint 1050 W Bristol Rd	Flint	MI	48507	**800-964-4299**		166
Jackson						
2800 Springport Rd	Jackson	MI	49202	**888-343-3683**	517-788-7800	166
Owosso						
1020 S Washington St	Owosso	MI	48867	**800-879-3797**	989-729-3350	166
Port Huron						
3403 Lapeer Rd	Port Huron	MI	48060	**888-262-2442**	810-985-7000	166
Baker Communications Inc						
10101 SW Fwy #630	Houston	TX	77074	**877-253-8506**	713-627-7700	760
Baker Company Inc						
175 Gatehouse Rd	Sanford	ME	04073	**800-992-2537**	207-324-8773	419
Baker Concrete Construction Inc						
900 N Garver Rd	Monroe	OH	45050	**800-539-2224**	513-539-4000	189-3
Baker Distributing Co						
14610 Breakers Dr Ste 100	Jacksonville	FL	32258	**844-289-0033**	800-217-4698	608
Baker Donelson Bearman Caldwell & Berkowitz PC						
165 Madison Ave						
1st Tennessee Bldg Ste 2000	Memphis	TN	38103	**800-973-1177**	901-526-2000	427
Baker Foodservice Design Inc						
2220 E Paris Ave SE	Grand Rapids	MI	49546	**800-968-4011**	616-942-4011	461
Baker Group						
4224 Hubbell Ave	Des Moines	IA	50317	**855-262-4000**	515-262-4000	189-10
Baker Krizner Financial Planning						
2230 N Limestone St	Springfield	OH	45503	**888-390-8753**	937-390-8750	461
Baker Products						
55480 Hwy 21 N PO Box 128	Ellington	MO	63638	**800-548-6914**	573-663-7711	816
Baker Rock Resources						
21880 SW Farmington Rd	Beaverton	OR	97007	**800-340-7625**	503-642-2531	46
Baker Roofing Co						
517 Mercury St	Raleigh	NC	27603	**800-849-4096**	919-813-6681	189-12
Baker Tankhead Inc						
10405 N fwy	Fort Worth	TX	76177	**866-232-8030**	817-232-8030	478
Baker Triangle						
341 Hwy 80 E	Mesquite	TX	75150	**800-458-3480**	972-289-5534	189-9
Baker University						
618 E Eighth St	Baldwin City	KS	66006	**800-873-4282**	785-594-6451	165
Bal Seal Engineering Company Inc						
19650 Pauling	Foothill Ranch	CA	92610	**800-366-1006**	949-460-2100	326
Balance Rock Inn						
21 Albert Meadow	Bar Harbor	ME	04609	**800-753-0494**	207-288-2610	378
Balasa Dinverno Foltz LLC						
500 Park Blvd Ste 1400	Itasca	IL	60143	**800-840-4740**	630-875-4900	41
Balboa Travel Management Inc						
5414 Oberlin Dr Ste 300	San Diego	CA	92121	**800-359-8773**	858-678-3300	766
Balcan Plastics Ltd						
9340 Meaux St	Saint Leonard	QC	H1R3H2	**877-422-5226**	514-326-0200	597
Balchem Corp						
52 Sunrise Pk Rd PO Box 600	New Hampton	NY	10958	**877-407-8289**	845-326-5613	477
NASDAQ: BCPC						
Baldwin & Lyons Inc						
111 Congressional Blvd Ste 500	Carmel	IN	46032	**800-644-5501**	317-636-9800	390-4
NASDAQ: BWINB						
Baldwin County						
322 Courthouse Sq	Bay Minette	AL	36507	**800-403-4872**	251-937-9561	337
Baldwin EMC						
19600 State Hwy 59						
PO Box 220	Summerdale	AL	36580	**800-837-3374**	251-989-6247	245
Baldwin Filters						
4400 Hwy 30	Kearney	NE	68847	**800-822-5394**		60
Baldwin Hardware Corp						
841 E Wyomissing Blvd	Reading	PA	19611	**800-566-1986**	610-777-7811	349
Baldwin Richardson Foods Co						
1 Tower Ln Ste 2390	Oakbrook Terrace	IL	60181	**866-644-2732***	630-607-1780	296-25
*Cust Svc						
Baldwinsville Public Library						
33 E Genesee St	Baldwinsville	NY	13027	**800-388-2000**	315-635-5631	433-3

	City	State	Zip	Toll-Free	Phone	Class
Baldwin-Wallace College						
275 Eastland Rd	Berea	OH	44017	**877-292-7759**	440-826-2222	166
Balfour 7211 Cir S Rd	Austin	TX	78745	**800-225-3687**		408
Bali Steak & Seafood						
2005 Kalia Rd	Honolulu	HI	96815	**800-445-8667**	808-949-4321	667
Balihoo						
404 S Eighth St Ste 300	Boise	ID	83702	**866-446-9914**		179
Ball Beauty Supplies						
416 N Fairfax Ave	Los Angeles	CA	90036	**800-588-0244**		77
Ball Bounce & Sport Inc/Hedstrom Plastics						
1 Hedstrom Dr	Ashland	OH	44805	**800-765-9665**	419-289-9310	757
Ball Homes LLC						
3609 Walden Dr	Lexington	KY	40517	**888-268-1101**	865-556-0574	187
Ball Horticultural Co						
622 Town Rd	West Chicago	IL	60185	**800-879-2255**	630-231-3600	293
Ball State University						
2000 W University Ave	Muncie	IN	47306	**800-382-8540**	765-289-1241	166
Ballantine Corp						
55 Lane Rd	Fairfield	NJ	07004	**800-669-6801**	973-305-1500	5
Ballantyne Resort Hotel						
10000 Ballantyne Commons Pkwy	Charlotte	NC	28277	**866-248-4824**	704-248-4000	665
Ballantyne Strong Inc						
13710 FNB Pkwy	Omaha	NE	68154	**800-424-1215***		587
NYSE: BTN ■ *General						
Ballard's Farm Sausage Inc						
7275 Right Fork Wilson Creek	Wayne	WV	25570	**800-346-7675***	304-272-5147	296-26
*General						
Ballet British Columbia						
677 Davie St	Vancouver	BC	V6B2G6	**855-985-2787**	604-732-5003	569-1
Ballew's Aluminum Products Inc						
2 Shelter Dr	Greer	SC	29650	**800-231-6666**	864-272-4453	693
Balloons Everywhere Inc						
16474 Greeno Rd	Fairhope	AL	36532	**800-239-2000**		562
Ballymore Co						
501 Gunnard Carlson Dr	Coatesville	PA	19365	**800-762-8327**	610-593-5062	420
Balmoral Inn						
120 Balmoral Ave	Biloxi	MS	39531	**800-393-9131**	228-388-6776	378
Balnea Spa						
319 chemin du Lac Gale	Bromont	QC	J2L2S5	**866-734-2110**	450-534-0604	226
Baltimore Area Convention & Visitors Assn (BACVA)						
100 Light St 12th Fl	Baltimore	MD	21202	**877-225-8466**	410-659-7300	206
Baltimore Behavioral Health (BBH)						
1101 W Pratt St	Baltimore	MD	21223	**800-789-2647**	410-962-7180	722
Baltimore City Community College						
2901 Liberty Heights Ave	Baltimore	MD	21215	**888-203-1261**	410-462-8300	162
Baltimore City Public Schools						
200 E N Ave	Baltimore	MD	21202	**800-422-0009**	443-984-2000	681
Baltimore Convention Ctr						
1 W Pratt St	Baltimore	MD	21201	**800-327-4414**	410-649-7000	205
Baltimore County						
401 Bosley Ave	Towson	MD	21204	**800-332-6347**	410-887-2139	337
Baltimore County Revenue Authority						
115 Towsontown Blvd E	Baltimore	MD	21286	**888-246-5384**	410-887-8216	558
Baltimore Gas & Electric Co						
110 W Fayette St	Baltimore	MD	21201	**800-685-0123**		782
Baltimore International College						
17 Commerce St	Baltimore	MD	21202	**800-624-9926**	410-752-4710	163
Baltimore Life Cos						
10075 Red Run Blvd	Owings Mills	MD	21117	**800-628-5433**	410-581-6600	390-2
Baltimore Magazine						
1000 Lancaster St Ste 400	Baltimore	MD	21202	**800-935-0838***	443-873-3900	455-22
*Cust Svc						
Baltimore National Cemetery						
5501 Frederick Ave	Baltimore	MD	21228	**800-535-1117**	410-644-9696	136
Baltimore Rigging Company Inc, The						
6601 Tributary St	Baltimore	MD	21224	**800-626-2150**	443-696-4001	189-1
Baltimore Sun						
501 N Calvert St	Baltimore	MD	21278	**800-829-8000**	410-332-6000	528-2
Baltimore Symphony Orchestra						
1212 Cathedral St	Baltimore	MD	21201	**877-276-1444**	410-783-8100	569-3
Baltimore Teachers Union						
Seton Business Park 5800 Metro Dr 2nd Fl	Baltimore	MD	21215	**800-332-6347**	410-358-6600	260
Baltimore/Washington International Thurgood Marshall Airport (BWI)						
PO Box 8766	Baltimore	MD	21240	**800-435-9294**	410-859-7111	27
Balzer Pacific Equipment Co						
2136 SE Eigth Ave	Portland	OR	97214	**800-442-0966**	503-232-5141	357
BAM Advisor Services						
8182 Maryland Ave Ste 500	St Louis	MO	63105	**800-711-2027**		
Bamberger Polymers Inc						
2 Jericho Plz	Jericho	NY	11753	**800-888-8959**	516-622-3600	599
BAMC (Brooke Army Medical Center)						
3551 Roger Brooke Dr	Fort Sam Houston	TX	78234	**800-443-2262**		373-4
BAMC (Bay Area Medical Ctr)						
3100 Shore Dr	Marinette	WI	54143	**888-788-2070**	715-735-4200	373-3
Bamco Inc						
30 Baekeland Ave	Middlesex	NJ	08846	**800-245-0210**		
Bancker Construction Corp						
218 Blydenburgh Rd	Islandia	NY	11749	**800-767-7565**	631-582-8880	188-10
Bancorp Bank						
409 Silverside Rd Ste 105	Wilmington	DE	19809	**866-255-9831***	302-385-5000	70
NASDAQ: TBBK ■ *Cust Svc						
BancorpSouth Inc						
2910 W Jackson St	Tupelo	MS	38801	**888-797-7711**	662-680-2000	359-2
NYSE: BXS						
Bancroft Bag Inc						
425 Bancroft Blvd	West Monroe	LA	71292	**800-551-4950**	318-387-2550	65
Bandera County Convention & Visitors Bureau						
126 State Hwy 16 S PO Box 171	Bandera	TX	78003	**800-364-3833**	830-796-3045	206
Bandera Electric Co-op Inc						
3172 State Hwy 16 N	Bandera	TX	78003	**866-226-3372**		245
Bandit Industries Inc						
6750 W Millbrook Rd	Remus	MI	49340	**800-952-0178**	989-561-2270	190
Band-It-IDEX Inc						
4799 Dahlia St	Denver	CO	80216	**800-525-0758**		349
Banetti Inc						
55 NE 94th St	Miami	FL	33138	**855-855-7800**		180

	City	State	Zip	Toll-Free	Phone	Class
Banff Adventures Unlimited						
211 Bear St Bison Courtyard	Banff	AB	T1L1A8	**800-644-8888**	403-762-4554	755
Banff Centre for Arts & Creativity						
107 Tunnel Mtn Dr PO Box 1020	Banff	AB	T1L1H5	**800-884-7574**	403-762-6100	376
Banff National Park						
PO Box 900	Banff	AB	T1L1K2	**877-737-3783**	403-762-1550	559
Banfield the Pet Hospital						
18101 SE Sixth Way	Vancouver	WA	98683	**866-894-7927**		789
Bang Printing Inc						
3323 Oak St	Brainerd	MN	56401	**800-328-0450**	218-829-2877	622
Bangor Daily News						
491 Main St PO Box 1329	Bangor	ME	04402	**800-432-7964**	207-990-8000	528-2
Bangor Hydro Electric Co						
PO Box 932	Bangor	ME	04401	**800-499-6600**	207-945-5621	782
Bangor International Airport						
287 Godfrey Blvd	Bangor	ME	04401	**866-359-2264**	207-992-4600	27
Bangor Savings Bank						
99 Franklin St	Bangor	ME	04401	**877-226-4671**	207-942-5211	70
Bangor Symphony Orchestra						
PO Box 1441	Bangor	ME	04402	**800-639-3221***	207-942-5555	569-3
*General						
Bangor Theological Seminary						
159 State St	Portland	ME	04101	**800-287-6781**	207-942-6781	167-3
Bank Administration Institute (BAI)						
115 S LaSalle St Ste 3300	Chicago	IL	60603	**800-224-9889***	312-683-2464	49-2
*Cust Svc						
Bank Financial						
6415 W 95th St	Chicago Ridge	IL	60415	**800-894-6900**		70
Bank Independent						
710 S Montgomery Ave	Sheffield	AL	35660	**877-865-5050**	256-386-5000	359-2
Bank Leumi USA						
350 Madison Ave	New York	NY	10017	**800-892-5430**	917-542-2343	70
Bank Mutual Corp						
4949 W Brown Deer Rd	Milwaukee	WI	53223	**844-256-8684**	414-354-1500	359-2
NASDAQ: BKMU						
Bank of Albuquerque						
400 S Tijeras Ave North W Ste 150	Albuquerque	NM	87102	**800-583-0709**	505-855-0855	70
Bank of America Business Capital						
100 North Tryon St	Charlotte	NC	28255	**800-521-3984**		
Bank of Commerce Holdings						
1901 Churn Creek Rd	Redding	CA	96002	**800-421-2575**	530-224-3333	359-2
NASDAQ: BOCH						
Bank of Greene County, The						
PO Box 470	Catskill	NY	12414	**888-439-4272**	518-943-2600	359-2
NASDAQ: GCBC						
Bank of Hawaii Corp						
130 Merchant St 16th Fl	Honolulu	HI	96813	**888-643-3888**		359-2
NYSE: BOH						
Bank of Louisiana						
300 St Charles Ave	New Orleans	LA	70130	**866-392-9952**	504-592-0600	70
Bank of Marin						
504 Tamalpais Dr	Corte Madera	CA	94925	**800-654-5111**	415-927-2265	70
NASDAQ: BMRC						
Bank of Montreal (BMO)						
100 King St W 1 First Canadian Pl 19th Fl	Toronto	ON	M5X1A1	**800-340-5021**	416-867-6785	70
NYSE: BMO						
Bank of Montreal						
3 Times Sq	New York	NY	10036	**877-225-5266**		70
Bank of North Dakota						
1200 Memorial Hwy	Bismarck	ND	58504	**800-472-2166**	701-328-5600	70
Bank of Nova Scotia						
1 Liberty Plz 26th Fl	New York	NY	10006	**800-472-6842**	212-225-5000	70
TSE: BNS						
Bank of Oklahoma NA						
PO Box 2300	Tulsa	OK	74192	**800-234-6181**	918-588-6010	70
Bank of South Carolina Corp						
256 Meeting St	Charleston	SC	29401	**800-523-4175**	843-724-1500	359-2
NASDAQ: BKSC						
Bank of Springfield						
2600 Adlai Stevenson Dr	Springfield	IL	62703	**877-698-3278**	217-529-5555	70
Bank of Stockton						
PO Box 1110	Stockton	CA	95201	**800-941-1494**	209-929-1600	70
Bank of Sunset & Trust Co						
863 Napoleon Ave	Sunset	LA	70584	**800-264-5578**	337-662-5222	70
Bank of the Ozarks Inc						
PO Box 8811	Little Rock	AR	72231	**800-274-4482**	501-978-2265	359-2
NASDAQ: OZK						
Bank of the Sierra						
PO Box 1930	Porterville	CA	93258	**888-454-2265***	559-782-4900	70
*Cust Svc						
Bank Of Utica						
222 Genesee St	Utica	NY	13502	**800-442-1028**	315-797-2700	70
OTC: BKUT						
Bankcard Central Llc						
PO Box 12317	Kansas City	MO	64116	**800-331-8882**	816-221-1133	
BankCard Services						
21281 S Western Ave	Torrance	CA	90501	**888-339-0100**	213-365-1122	394
Bankers Data Services Inc						
521 W 11th St	Alma	GA	31510	**888-458-8652**	912-632-2060	395
Bankers Fidelity Life Insurance Co						
4370 Peachtree Rd NE	Atlanta	GA	30319	**866-458-7504**	800-241-1439	390-2
NASDAQ: AAME						
Bankers Financial Products Corp						
201 N Main St Ste 4	Fort Atkinson	WI	53538	**800-348-1831**		400
Bankers Petroleum Ltd						
3700 888 - Third St SW	Calgary	AB	T2P5C5	**888-797-7170**	403-513-2699	
Bankers' Bank						
7700 Mineral Point Rd	Madison	WI	53717	**800-388-5550**	608-833-5550	70
Bank-Fund Staff Federal Credit Union						
PO Box 27755	Washington	DC	20038	**800-923-7328**	202-458-4300	219
Bankruptcy Management Solutions Inc						
5 Peters Canyon Rd Ste 200	Irvine	CA	92606	**800-634-7734**		461
Banks Pest Control Inc						
215 Golden State Ave	Bakersfield	CA	93301	**800-662-6300**	661-323-7858	573
Bankshot Sports Organization						
330-U N Stonestreet Ave Ste 504	Rockville	MD	20852	**800-933-0140**	301-309-0260	706

Company / Address	City	State	ZIP	Toll-Free	Phone	Class
Bankwest 420 S Pierre St	Pierre	SD	57501	**800-253-0362**	605-224-7391	70
Banner Bank 10 S First Ave PO Box 907	Walla Walla	WA	99362	**800-272-9933**	509-527-3636	70
Banner Behavioral Health Hospital 7575 E Earll Dr	Scottsdale	AZ	85251	**800-254-4357**	480-941-7500	373-5
Banner Del E Webb Memorial Hospital 14502 W Meeker Blvd	Sun City West	AZ	85375	**800-254-4357**	623-214-4000	373-3
Banner Engineering Corp 9714 Tenth Ave N	Minneapolis	MN	55441	**888-373-6767**	763-544-3164	253
Banner Equipment Company Inc 1370 Bungalow Rd	Morris	IL	60450	**800-621-4625**		
Banner Life Insurance Co 1701 Research Blvd	Rockville	MD	20850	**800-638-8428**	301-279-4800	390-2
Banner Marketing 16201 E Indiana Ave Ste 3240	Spokane Valley	WA	99216	**800-843-9271**	509-922-7828	7
Banner Wholesale Grocers Inc 3000 S Ashland	Chicago	IL	60608	**844-421-2650**	312-421-2650	344
Bannister Family House 406 Dickinson St	San Diego	CA	92103	**800-926-8273**	619-543-7977	371
Banterra Corp 1404 US Rt 45 S	Eldorado	IL	62930	**877-541-2265**	618-273-9346	70
Banyan Air Service 5360 NW 20th Terr	Fort Lauderdale	FL	33309	**800-200-2031**	954-491-3170	63
Banyan International Corp 11629 49th Pl W	Mukilteo	WA	98275	**888-782-8548**		473
Banyan Resort 323 Whitehead St	Key West	FL	33040	**866-371-9222**	305-296-7786	665
Banyan Water Inc 11002-B Metric Blvd	Austin	TX	78758	**800-276-1507**		461
Bap-Geon Import Auto Parts 3403 Gulf Fwy	Houston	TX	77003	**888-868-2281**	713-227-1544	54
Baptist Bible College 628 E Kearney St	Springfield	MO	65803	**800-228-5754**		161
Baptist College of Florida 5400 College Dr	Graceville	FL	32440	**800-328-2660**	850-263-3261	166
Baptist General Convention of Texas 7557 Rambler Rd Ste 1200	Dallas	TX	75231	**888-244-9400**		48-20
Baptist Health 1 Trillium Way	Corbin	KY	40701	**800-395-4435**	606-528-1212	373-3
Baptist Medical Ctr 1225 N State St	Jackson	MS	39202	**800-948-6262**	601-968-1000	373-3
Baptist Medical Ctr 111 Dallas St	San Antonio	TX	78205	**866-309-2873**	210-297-7000	373-3
Baptist Medical Ctr South 2105 E S Blvd	Montgomery	AL	36116	**800-356-9596**	334-288-2100	373-3
Baptist Memorial Health Care Corp 350 N Humphreys Blvd	Memphis	TN	38120	**800-422-7847**	901-227-5920	352
Baptist Memorial Hospital Golden Triangle 2520 Fifth St N	Columbus	MS	39705	**800-422-7847**	662-244-1000	373-3
Baptist Memorial Hospital Union City 1201 Bishop St	Union City	TN	38261	**800-344-2470**	731-885-2410	373-3
Baptist Missionary Assn of America (BMA) 611 Locust Ave PO Box 878	Conway	AR	72034	**800-333-1442**	501-455-4977	48-20
Baptist Missionary Assn Theological Seminary 1530 E Pine St	Jacksonville	TX	75766	**800-259-5673**	903-586-2501	167-3
Baptist University of the Americas 7838 Barlite Blvd	San Antonio	TX	78224	**800-721-1396**	210-924-4338	161
Bar G Feed Yard 275 FM 1057 Rd	Summerfield	TX	79085	**800-569-3736**	806-357-2241	10-1
Bar Harbor Bankshares 82 Main St PO Box 400 *NYSE: BHB*	Bar Harbor	ME	04609	**888-853-7100**	207-288-3314	359-2
Bar Harbor Chamber of Commerce 2 Cottage St	Bar Harbor	ME	04609	**888-540-9990**	207-288-5103	139
Bar Harbor Hotel-Bluenose Inn 90 Eden St	Bar Harbor	ME	04609	**800-445-4077**	207-288-3348	378
Bar Harbor Inn Oceanfront Resort Newport Dr	Bar Harbor	ME	04609	**800-248-3351**	207-288-3351	665
Bar Harbor Town Hall 93 Cottage St	Bar Harbor	ME	04609	**800-232-4733**	207-288-4098	336
Bar Lazy J Guest Ranch 447 County Rd 3 PO Box N	Parshall	CO	80468	**800-396-6279**	970-725-3437	239
Bar None Auction Inc 4751 Power Inn Rd	Sacramento	CA	95826	**866-372-1700**		187
Bar Productscom Inc 1990 Lake Ave SE	Largo	FL	33771	**800-256-6396**	727-584-2093	321
Baraga Correctional Facility 13924 Wadaga Rd	Baraga	MI	49908	**800-326-4537**	906-353-7070	213
Barbara Ann Karmanos Cancer Institute 4100 John R St	Detroit	MI	48201	**800-527-6266**		664
Barbara B Mann Performing Arts Hall 13350 FSW Pkwy	Fort Myers	FL	33919	**800-440-7469**	239-481-4849	568
Barbershop Harmony Society 110 Seventh Ave N	Nashville	TN	37203	**800-876-7464**	615-823-3993	48-18
Barbizon International LLC 4950 W Kennedy Blvd Ste 200	Tampa	FL	33615	**800-330-8361**		505
Barbour Welting Company Div Barbour Corp 1001 N Montello St	Brockton	MA	02301	**800-955-9649**	508-583-8200	301
BARC Electric Co-op 84 High St PO Box 264	Millboro	VA	24460	**800-846-2272**		245
Barchartcom Inc 209 W Jackson 2nd Fl	Chicago	IL	60606	**800-238-5814**	312-554-8122	317
Barclay College 607 N Kingman St	Haviland	KS	67059	**800-862-0226**	620-862-5252	161
Barclay Products 4000 Porett Dr	Gurnee	IL	60031	**800-446-9700**	847-244-1234	605
Barclays 745 Seventh Ave	New York	NY	10019	**888-227-2275**	212-526-7000	686
Barco Electronic Systems Pvt Ltd 11101 Trade Ctr Dr	Rancho Cordova	CA	95670	**888-414-7226**	916-859-2500	173-4
BARCO Industries Inc 1020 MacArthur Rd *Cust Svc	Reading	PA	19605	**800-234-8665***		753
Barco Products 24 N Washington Ave	Batavia	IL	60510	**800-338-2697**		384
Barco Rent a Truck 717 South 5600 West	Salt Lake City	UT	84104	**800-453-4761**	801-532-7777	773
Barco Uniforms 350 W Rosecrans Ave	Gardena	CA	90248	**800-262-1559**	310-323-7315	155-18
Barcoding Inc 2220 Boston St	Baltimore	MD	21231	**888-412-7226**	888-860-7226	179
Barcontrol Systems & Services Inc 113 Edinburgh Ct	Greenville	SC	29607	**800-947-4362**	864-421-0050	177
Bard College PO Box 5000	Annandale-on-Hudson	NY	12504	**800-872-7423**	845-758-7472	166
Bard Inc Peripheral Vascular 1625 W Third St	Tempe	AZ	85281	**800-321-4254**	480-894-9515	474
Bard Mfg Co Inc 1914 Randolph Dr	Bryan	OH	43506	**800-563-5660**	419-636-1194	15
Barden & Robeson Corp 103 Kelly Ave	Middleport	NY	14105	**800-724-0141**	716-735-3732	106
Barden Corp 200 Park Ave	Danbury	CT	06810	**800-243-1060**	203-744-2211	616
Bardes Plastics Inc 5225 W Clinton Ave *Cust Svc	Milwaukee	WI	53223	**800-558-5161***		598
Barefoot Resort & Golf 4980 Barefoot Resort Bridge Rd	North Myrtle Beach	SC	29582	**866-638-4818**	843-390-3200	665
Barfield Inc 4101 NW 29th St	Miami	FL	33142	**800-321-1039**	305-894-5300	24
Bargain Supply Co 844 E Jefferson St	Louisville	KY	40206	**800-322-5226**	502-562-5000	350
Barger Packaging Inc 2901 Oakland Ave	Elkhart	IN	46517	**888-525-2845**		597
Bargreen Ellingson Inc 2925 70th Ave E	Fife	WA	98424	**866-722-2665**	253-722-2600	300
Bari-Jay Fashions Inc 1277 Bridge St Unit 1B	New Dundee	ON	N0B2E0	**800-735-5808**		155-20
Barker Air & Hydraulics Inc 1308 Miller Rd	Greenville	SC	29607	**800-922-3324**	864-288-3537	637
Barker Martin PS 719 Second Ave Ste 1200	Seattle	WA	98104	**888-381-9806**	360-756-9806	427
BarkerGilmore 1387 Fairport Rd Ste 845	Fairport	NY	14450	**877-571-5047**		717
Barkman Honey 120 Santa Fe St	Hillsboro	KS	67063	**800-364-6623**		296-24
Barksdale Inc 3211 Fruitland Ave	Los Angeles	CA	90058	**800-835-1060**	323-589-6181	201
Barletta Lou (Rep R - PA) 2049 Rayburn House Office Bldg	Washington	DC	20515	**855-241-5144**	202-225-6511	
Barlow Truck Lines inc 1305 SE Grand Dd Hwy	Faucett	MO	64448	**800-688-1202**	816-396-1430	775
Barnes & Thornburg LLP 11 S Meridian St	Indianapolis	IN	46204	**800-236-1352**	317-236-1313	427
Barnes Advertising Corp 1580 Fairview Rd	Zanesville	OH	43701	**800-458-1410**	740-453-6836	7
Barnes Bullets LLC 38 N Frontage Rd	Mona	UT	84645	**800-574-9200**	435-856-1000	
Barnes County 230 Fourth St NW Rm 202	Valley City	ND	58072	**800-352-0867**	701-845-8500	337
Barnes Distribution 1301 E Ninth St Ste 700	Cleveland	OH	44114	**800-726-9626**	216-416-7200	384
Barnes Farming Corp 7840 Old Bailey Hwy	Spring Hope	NC	27882	**800-367-2799**		10-9
Barnes International Inc 814 Chestnut St PO Box 1203	Rockford	IL	61105	**800-435-4877**	815-964-8661	453
Barnes Transportation Services Inc 2309 Whitley Rd	Wilson	NC	27895	**800-898-5897**		359-2
Barnes-Jewish Saint Peters Hospital 4901 Forest Park Ave	St. Louis	MO	63108	**800-536-2653**	314-747-9322	373-3
Barnet Associates LLC 2 Round Lake Rd	Ridgefield	CT	06877	**888-827-7070**		317
Barnet-Dulaney Eye Ctr 4800 N 22nd St	Phoenix	AZ	85016	**866-742-6581**	602-955-1000	793
Barnett & Ramel Optical Co 7154 N 16th St	Omaha	NE	68112	**800-228-9732**		539
Barnett Engineering Ltd 7710 5 St SE Ste 215	Calgary	AB	T2H2L9	**800-268-2646**	403-255-9544	261
Barney Trucking Inc 235 State Rt 24	Salina	UT	84654	**800-524-7930**		681
Barnhardt Mfg Co 1100 Hawthorne Ln	Charlotte	NC	28205	**800-277-0377**		228
Barnhill Bolt Company Inc 2500 Princeton Dr NE	Albuquerque	NM	87107	**800-472-3900**	505-884-1808	349
Barnsley Resort 597 Barnsley Gardens Rd	Adairsville	GA	30103	**877-773-2447**	770-773-7480	665
Barnstead Inn 349 Bonnet St	Manchester Center	VT	05255	**800-331-1619**	802-362-1619	378
Baron Funds 767 Fifth Ave 49th Fl	New York	NY	10153	**800-992-2766**	212-583-2000	524
Baron Metal Industries Inc 101 Ashbridge Cir	Woodbridge	ON	L4L3R5	**800-263-7515**	416-749-2111	478
Baron Mfg Company LLC 730 Baker St	Itasca	IL	60143	**800-368-8585**	630-628-9110	349
Baron Oilfield Supply Ltd 9515-108 St	Grande Prairie	AB	T8V5R7	**888-532-5661**	780-532-5661	357
Baron Sign Manufacturing 900 W 13th St	Riviera Beach	FL	33404	**800-531-9558**		
Barona Resort & Casino 1932 Wildcat Canyon Rd	Lakeside	CA	92040	**888-722-7662**	619-443-2300	133
Barr Engineering Co 4700 W 77th St	Minneapolis	MN	55435	**800-632-2277**	952-832-2600	261
Barrasso John (Sen R - WY) 307 Dirksen Senate Office Bldg	Washington	DC	20510	**866-235-9553**	202-224-6441	
Barrent Group, The 3056 104th St	Urbandale	IA	50322	**866-318-4448**		317
Barrett Business Services Inc 8100 NE Pkwy Dr Ste 200 *NASDAQ: BBSI*	Vancouver	WA	98662	**800-494-5669**	360-828-0700	627

Name / Address	City	State	ZIP	Toll-Free	Phone	Class
Barrett Carpet Mills Inc						
2216 Abutment Rd	Dalton	GA	30721	**800-241-4064**		131
Barrett Group LLC, The						
100 Jefferson Blvd Ste 310	Warwick	RI	02888	**800-304-4473**		
Barrick Gold Corp						
TD Canada Trust Tower 161 Bay St						
PO Box 212	Toronto	ON	M5J2S1	**800-720-7415**	416-861-9911	500
NYSE: ABX						
Barrick Gold Corp						
161 Bay St Ste 3700	Toronto	ON	M5J2S1	**800-720-7415**	416-861-9911	
Barrie						
Chamber of Commerce						
121 Commerce Park Dr Unit A	Barrie	ON	L4N8X1	**888-220-2221**	705-721-5000	
Barrie House Coffee Company Inc						
4 Warehouse ln	Elmsford	NY	10523	**800-876-2233**		297-2
Barrie Public Library						
60 Worsley St	Barrie	ON	L4M1L6	**800-222-8477**	705-728-1010	434
Barriere Construction Co LLC						
1 Galleria Blvd Ste 1650	Metairie	LA	70001	**800-234-5376**	504-581-7283	188-4
Barrington Hotel & Suites						
263 Shepherd of the Hills Expy	Branson	MO	65616	**800-760-8866**	417-334-8866	378
Barris, Sott, Denn & Driker PLLC						
333 W Fort St Ste 1200	Detroit	MI	48226	**877-529-8750**	313-965-9725	427
BarristerBooks Inc						
615 Florida St	Lawrence	KS	66044	**866-808-5635**		95
Barron Electric Co-op						
1434 State Hwy 25 N	Barron	WI	54812	**800-322-1008**	715-537-3171	245
Barron's Educational Series Inc						
250 Wireless Blvd	Hauppauge	NY	11788	**800-645-3476**	631-434-3311	633-2
Barrow Hanley Mewhinney & Strauss LLC						
2200 Ross Ave 31st Fl	Dallas	TX	75201	**800-543-0407**	214-665-1900	400
Barry Bunker Chevrolet Inc						
1307 N Wabash Ave	Marion	IN	46952	**866-603-8625***	866-726-5519	57
*Sales						
Barry Callebaut USA LLC						
400 Industrial Pk Rd	Saint Albans	VT	05478	**866-443-0460**	802-524-9711	296-8
Barry County						
220 W State St	Hastings	MI	49058	**888-876-0993**	269-945-1290	337
Barry Electric Co-op						
4015 Main St PO Box 307	Cassville	MO	65625	**866-847-2333**		245
Barry University						
11300 NE Second Ave	Miami Shores	FL	33161	**800-756-6000**	305-899-3000	166
Orlando						
1650 Sandlake Rd Ste 390	Orlando	FL	32809	**800-756-6000**	407-438-4150	166
Tallahassee Community College						
444 Appleyard Dr Bldg A	Tallahassee	FL	32304	**800-756-6000**	850-201-8650	166
Barry University Dwayne O Andreas School of Law						
6441 E Colonial Dr	Orlando	FL	32807	**800-756-6000**	321-206-5600	167-1
Barry-owen Co Inc						
5625 Smithway St	Los Angeles	CA	90040	**800-682-6682**	323-724-4800	292
Barry-Wehmiller Cos Inc Accraply Div						
3580 Holly Ln N	Plymouth	MN	55447	**800-328-3997**	763-557-1313	543
BARSKA Optics						
1721 Wright Ave	La Verne	CA	91750	**888-666-6769**		539
Bartech Group						
17199 N Laurel Park Dr Ste 224	Livonia	MI	48152	**800-828-4410**	734-953-5050	717
Bartell Hotels						
4875 N Harbor Dr	San Diego	CA	92106	**800-345-9995**	619-224-1556	703
Bartell Machinery Systems LLC						
6321 Elmer Hill Rd	Rome	NY	13440	**800-537-8473**	315-336-7600	492
Barth Electric Company Inc						
1934 N Illinois St	Indianapolis	IN	46202	**800-666-6226**	317-924-6226	189-4
Bartha Visual						
600 N Cassady Ave	Columbus	OH	43219	**800-513-1209**	800-363-2698	23
Bartholomew County Public Library						
536 Fifth St	Columbus	IN	47201	**800-685-0524**	812-379-1255	433-3
Bartholomew County Rural Electric Membership Corp						
1697 W Deaver Rd	Columbus	IN	47201	**800-927-5672**	812-372-2546	245
Bartizan Corp						
217 Riverdale Ave	Yonkers	NY	10705	**800-899-2278**	914-965-7977	530
Bartle & Gibson Company Ltd						
13475 Ft Rd NW	Edmonton	AB	T5A1C6	**800-661-5615**	780-472-2850	608
Bartlett & Co						
600 Vine St Ste 2100	Cincinnati	OH	45202	**800-800-4612**	513-621-4612	400
Bartlett & Co						
4900 Main St Ste 12	Kansas City	MO	64112	**800-888-6300**	816-753-6300	296-23
Bartlett & West Engineers Inc						
1200 SW Executive Dr	Topeka	KS	66615	**888-200-6464**	785-272-2252	261
Barton & Loguidice DPC						
443 Electronics Pkwy	Liverpool	NY	13088	**800-724-1070**	315-457-5200	
Barton Brescome Inc						
69 Defco Park Rd	North Haven	CT	06473	**800-922-4840**	203-239-4901	80-3
Barton College						
PO Box 5000	Wilson	NC	27893	**800-345-4973**	252-399-6300	166
Barton Cotton Inc						
3030 Waterview Ave	Baltimore	MD	21230	**800-638-4652**	800-348-1102	317
Barton County Community College						
245 NE 30th Rd	Great Bend	KS	67530	**800-722-6842**	620-792-2701	162
Barton County Electric Co-op						
91 US-160	Lamar	MO	64759	**800-286-5636**	417-682-5636	245
Barton Solvents Inc						
1920 NE Broadway Ave	Des Moines	IA	50313	**800-728-6488**	515-265-7998	146
Barton W Stone Christian Home						
873 Grove St	Jacksonville	IL	62650	**800-397-1313**	217-479-3400	448
Bartow County						
135 W Cherokee Ave	Cartersville	GA	30120	**800-715-4225**	770-387-5030	337
Bartow Ford Co						
2800 US Hwy 98 N	Bartow	FL	33830	**800-533-0425**		
Basalite Concrete Products LLC						
605 Industrial Way	Dixon	CA	95620	**800-776-6690**	707-678-1901	183
Basco Shower Enclosures						
7201 Snider Rd	Mason	OH	45040	**800-543-1938**	513-573-1900	329
Bascom Palmer Eye Institute						
900 NW 17th St	Miami	FL	33136	**800-329-7000**	305-326-6000	373-7
Bascom-Turner Instrument						
111 Downey St	Norwood	MA	02062	**800-225-3298**	781-769-9660	608

Name / Address	City	State	ZIP	Toll-Free	Phone	Class
Base Camp Franchising						
39 E Eagle Ridge Dr						
Ste 100	North Salt Lake	UT	84054	**855-637-3211**		
Baseball America Magazine						
4319 S Alston Ave Ste 103	Durham	NC	27713	**800-845-2726**		
Baseball Express Inc						
5750 NW Pkwy Ste 100	San Antonio	TX	78249	**800-937-4824**	210-348-7000	707
BASF Corp						
100 Campus Dr	Florham Park	NJ	07932	**800-526-1072**	973-245-6000	143
BASF Corp/Bldg Systems						
889 Valley Pk Dr	Shakopee	MN	55379	**800-433-9517***	952-496-6000	3
*Cust Svc						
Bashas Inc						
22402 S Bashas Rd	Chandler	AZ	85248	**800-755-7292**	480-895-5369	344
Basic American Foods						
2185 N California Blvd						
Ste 215	Walnut Creek	CA	94596	**800-227-4050**		
Basic Carbide Corp						
900 Main St	Lowber	PA	15660	**800-426-4291**	724-446-1630	1
Basic Components Inc						
1201 S Second Ave	Mansfield	TX	76063	**800-452-1780**	817-473-7224	191-2
Basic Metals Inc						
W180 Nn11819 River Ln	Germantown	WI	53022	**800-989-1996**	262-255-9034	490
Basic Software Systems						
905 N Kings Hwy	Texarkana	TX	75501	**800-252-4476**	903-792-4421	179
Basin Harbor Club						
4800 Basin Harbor Rd	Vergennes	VT	05491	**800-622-4000**	802-475-2311	665
Basin Tire & Auto Inc						
2700 E Main St	Farmington	NM	87402	**800-832-9832**	505-326-2231	62-5
Basis International Ltd						
5901 Jefferson St NE	Albuquerque	NM	87109	**800-423-1394***	505-345-5232	178-12
*Orders						
Basis Technology Corp						
1 Alewife Ctr	Cambridge	MA	02140	**800-697-2062**	617-386-2000	177
Baskin Auto Truck & Tractor Inc						
1844 Hwy 51 S	Covington	TN	38019	**877-476-2626**	901-476-2626	57
Baskin-Robbins Inc						
130 Royall St	Canton	MA	02021	**800-859-5339**	781-737-3000	380
Basler Flight Service						
Wittman Regional Airport						
PO Box 2464	Oshkosh	WI	54903	**800-564-6322**	920-236-7827	63
Bass Performance Hall						
4th & Calhoun Sts	Fort Worth	TX	76102	**877-212-4280**	817-212-4300	568
Bassett Furniture Industries Inc						
3525 Fairystone Pk Hwy						
PO Box 626	Bassett	VA	24055	**877-525-7070**	276-629-6000	319-2
NASDAQ: BSET						
Bassett Healthcare Network						
1 Atwell Rd	Cooperstown	NY	13326	**800-227-7388**	607-547-3456	373-3
Bassmaster						
3500 Blue Lake Dr Ste 330	Birmingham	FL	35243	**877-227-7872**		455-20
Bastian Solutions (BMH)						
10585 N Meridian St 3rd Fl	Indianapolis	IN	46290	**800-772-0464**	317-575-9992	55
Bastian Trucking Inc						
440 S Main	Aurora	UT	84620	**800-452-5126**	435-529-7453	775
Bat Conservation International (BCI)						
500 N Capital of Texas Hwy	Austin	TX	78746	**800-538-2287**	512-327-9721	48-3
Bates College						
2 Andrews Rd	Lewiston	ME	04240	**888-522-8371**	207-786-6255	166
Bates Communications Inc						
40 Grove St Ste 310	Wellesley	MA	02482	**800-908-8239**		
Bates Ford						
1673 W Main St	Lebanon	TN	37087	**888-834-4671**		57
Batesville Casket Co						
1 Batesville Blvd	Batesville	IN	47006	**800-622-8373***	812-934-7500	134
*Cust Svc						
Bath & Body Works						
7 Limited Pkwy E	Reynoldsburg	OH	43068	**800-395-1001**		214
Bath + Beyond, The						
77 Connecticut St	San Francisco	CA	94107	**800-696-6662**	415-689-6338	361
Bath County						
PO Box 309	Warm Springs	VA	24484	**888-823-1710**	540-839-7221	337
Bath Veterans Affairs Medical Ctr						
76 Veterans Ave	Bath	NY	14810	**877-845-3247**	607-664-4000	373-8
Bathcrest Inc						
3791 S 300 W	Salt Lake City	UT	84115	**855-662-7220**		189-11
Baton Rouge Community College (BRCC)						
201 Community College Dr	Baton Rouge	LA	70806	**866-217-9823**	225-216-8000	162
Baton Rouge Convention & Visitors Bureau						
359 Third St	Baton Rouge	LA	70801	**800-527-6843**	225-383-1825	206
Battalia Winston International						
555 Madison Ave	New York	NY	10022	**800-570-3118**	212-308-8080	266
Battelle Memorial Institute Inc						
505 King Ave	Columbus	OH	43201	**800-201-2011**	614-424-6424	664
Battered Women's Justice Project						
1801 Nicollet Ave S Ste 102	Minneapolis	MN	55403	**800-903-0111**	612-824-8768	49-10
Battery Ventures						
1 Marina Pk Dr Ste 1100	Boston	MA	02210	**800-449-0645**	617-948-3600	787
Battery Wharf Hotel, Boston Waterfront						
3 Battery Wharf	Boston	MA	02109	**866-898-3560**		703
Battle Creek Area Chamber of Commerce						
1 Riverwalk Ctr						
34 W Jackson St Ste 3A	Battle Creek	MI	49017	**800-397-2240**	269-962-4076	139
Battle Creek Enquirer						
77 E Michigan Ave Ste 101	Battle Creek	MI	49017	**800-333-4139**	269-964-7161	528-2
Battle Creek/Calhoun County Convention & Visitors Bureau						
1 Riverwalk Ctr						
34 W Jackson St	Battle Creek	MI	49017	**800-397-2240**		206
Battle River Regional Div						
5402 48a Ave	Camrose	AB	T4V0L3	**800-262-4869**	780-672-6131	681
Battlefield Farms Inc						
23190 Clarks Mtn Rd	Rapidan	VA	22733	**800-722-0744**		368
Baudville Inc						
5380 52nd St SE	Grand Rapids	MI	49512	**800-728-0888***	616-698-0889	178-1
*Orders						
Baue Funeral Homes						
620 Jefferson St	Saint Charles	MO	63301	**888-724-0073**	636-940-1000	508
Bauer Premium Fly Reels						
585 Clover Ln Ste 1	Ashland	OR	97520	**888-484-4165**	541-488-8246	706

Alphabetical Section

Company / Address	City	ST	ZIP	Toll-Free	Phone	Class
Bauerware LLC 3886 17th St	San Francisco	CA	94114	877-864-5662	415-864-3886	361
Baum Textile Mills Inc 812 Jersey Ave	Jersey City	NJ	07310	866-842-7631	201-659-0444	590
Bauman Associates Ltd PO Box 1225	Eau Claire	WI	54702	888-952-2866	715-834-2001	2
Baumfolder Corp 1660 Campbell Rd	Sidney	OH	45365	800-543-6107	937-492-1281	552
Baumgarten's 144 Ottley Dr	Atlanta	GA	30324	800-247-5547	404-874-7675	530
Bausch & Lomb Inc 1400 N Goodman St	Rochester	NY	14609	800-553-5340		538
Bausch & Lomb Pharmaceuticals Inc 8500 Hidden River Pkwy	Tampa	FL	33637	800-323-0000*	800-553-5340	578
*Cust Svc						
Bavarian Autosport Inc 275 Constitution Ave	Portsmouth	NH	03801	800-535-2002	603-427-2002	54
Baxter Corp 7125 Mississauga Rd	Mississauga	ON	L5N0C2	866-234-2345	905-369-6000	231
Baxter International Inc 1 Baxter Pkwy	Deerfield	IL	60015	800-422-9837	847-948-2000	475
NYSE: BAX						
BaxterBoo 148 Cypress Ridge Crt	Ridgeland	SC	29936	888-887-0063		686
Bay Area Hospital 1775 Thompson Rd	Coos Bay	OR	97420	800-798-0799	541-269-8111	373-3
Bay Area Medical Ctr (BAMC) 3100 Shore Dr	Marinette	WI	54143	888-788-2070	715-735-4200	373-3
Bay City Flower Company Inc 2265 Cabrillo Hwy S	Half Moon Bay	CA	94019	800-399-5858*	650-726-5535	368
*Sales						
Bay Club Hotel & Marina 2131 Shelter Island Dr	San Diego	CA	92106	800-672-0800	619-224-8888	378
Bay County 515 Center Ave	Bay City	MI	48708	877-229-9960	989-895-4280	337
Bay de Noc Community College 2001 N Lincoln Rd	Escanaba	MI	49829	800-221-2001	906-786-5802	162
Bay Dynamics 595 Market St Ste 1300	San Francisco	CA	94105	855-281-7362	415-912-3130	
Bay Hill Golf Club & Lodge 9000 Bay Hill Blvd	Orlando	FL	32819	888-422-9445	407-876-2429	665
Bay Houston Towing Co 2243 Milford St	Houston	TX	77253	800-324-3755	713-529-3755	463
Bay Landing Hotel 1550 Bayshore Hwy	Burlingame	CA	94010	866-783-9612	650-259-9000	377
Bay Mills Community College 12214 West Lakeshore Dr	Brimley	MI	49715	800-844-2622	906-248-3354	165
Bay Mills Resort & Casinos 11386 West Lakeshore Dr	Brimley	MI	49715	888-422-9645		450
Bay Park Hotel 1425 Munras Ave	Monterey	CA	93940	800-338-3564*	831-649-1020	378
*Resv						
Bay Path College 588 Longmeadow St	Longmeadow	MA	01106	800-782-7284		166
Bay Pointe Technology 2662 Brecksville Rd	Richfield	OH	44286	800-746-1420		
Bay Regional Juvenile Detention Ctr 450 E 11th St	Panama City	FL	32401	800-355-2280	850-872-4706	411
Bay Regional Medical Ctr (BRMC) 1900 Columbus Ave	Bay City	MI	48708	800-656-3950	989-894-3000	373-3
Bay State College 122 Commonwealth Ave	Boston	MA	02116	800-815-3276	617-217-9000	795
Bay State Milling Co 100 Congress St	Quincy	MA	02169	800-553-5687		296-23
Bay Technical Assoc Inc 5239 Ave A	Long Beach Industrial Park	MS	39560	800-523-2702	228-563-7334	174
Bay Valley Hotel & Resort 2470 Old Bridge Rd	Bay City	MI	48706	888-241-4653	989-686-3500	665
Bay View Plaza Furniture Inc 2181 E Pass Rd	Gulfport	MS	39507	800-748-9852	228-896-4400	321
BAYADA Home Health Care 1 W Main St	Moorestown	NJ	08057	877-591-1527	856-231-1000	362
Bayco Products Inc 640 Sanden Blvd	Wylie	TX	75098	800-233-2155	469-326-9400	436
Bayer CropScience 2 TW Alexander Dr	Research Triangle Park	NC	27709	800-331-2867	919-549-2000	85
Bayer Inc 77 Belfield Rd	Toronto	ON	M9W1G6	800-622-2937	416-248-0771	578
Bayerkohler & Graff Ltd 11132 Zealand Ave N	Champlin	MN	55316	866-315-2771	763-427-2542	729
Bayfield County PO Box 878	Washburn	WI	54891	800-447-4094	715-373-6100	337
Bayfield Electric Co-op Inc 68460 District St	Iron River	WI	54847	800-278-0166	715-372-4287	245
BAY-FM 945 (AC) 190 Pk Ctr Plz Ste 200	San Jose	CA	95113	800-948-5229	408-287-5775	
Bayforce 5100 W Kennedy Blvd Ste 425	Tampa	FL	33609	877-642-4727		
Bayhead Products Corp 173 Crosby Rd	Dover	NH	03820	800-229-4323	603-742-3000	468
Bayhealth Medical Ctr 21 W Clarke Ave	Milford	DE	19963	877-453-7107	302-422-3311	373-3
Baylis Medical Company Inc 5959 Trans-Canada Hwy	Montreal	QC	H4T1A1	800-850-9801	514-488-9801	475
Baylor County 301 N Washington	Seymour	TX	76380	800-633-0852	940-889-3148	337
Baylor Scott & White Health 1650 W College St	Grapevine	TX	76051	800-422-9567	817-481-1588	373-3
Baylor Trucking Inc 9269 E State Rd 48	Milan	IN	47031	800-322-9567	812-623-2020	775
Baylor University 1301 S University Parks Dr	Waco	TX	76798	800-229-5678		166
Title IX Office Clifton Robinson Tower Ste 285	Waco	TX	76798	800-229-5678	254-710-3821	167-1
Bayou Segnette State Park 7777 Westbank Expy	Westwego	LA	70094	888-677-2296	504-736-7140	561
Bays Corp PO Box 1455	Chicago	IL	60690	800-367-2297	312-346-5757	296-1
Bayshore Transportation System Inc 901 Dawson Dr	Newark	DE	19713	800-523-3319	302-366-0220	775
Bayside Resort Hotel 225 Massachusetts 28	West Yarmouth	MA	02673	800-243-1114	508-775-5669	665
Bayside Solutions Inc 3000 Executive Pkwy Ste 510	San Ramon	CA	94583	800-220-0074		260
Baystate Visiting Nurse Association & Hospice 50 Maple St	Springfield	MA	01199	800-249-8298	413-794-6411	370
Baytec Service LLC 4761 Hwy 146 200	Bacliff	TX	77518	800-560-2334		316
Baytex Energy Corp 2800 520 - Third Ave SW	Calgary	AB	T2P0R3	800-524-5521	587-952-3000	532
Bayview Limousine Service 15701 Nelson Pl S	Seattle	WA	98188	800-606-7880	206-824-6200	440
Bayview Press 30 Knox St PO Box 153	Thomaston	ME	04861	800-903-2346	207-354-9919	130
Bayway Lincoln-mercury Inc 12333 Gulf Fwy	Houston	TX	77034	888-356-1895	866-956-0972	57
Bazon Cox & Associates Inc 1244 Executive Blvd	Chesapeake	VA	23320	800-769-1763	757-410-2128	180
Bazz Houston Co 12700 Western Ave	Garden Grove	CA	92841	800-385-9608	714-898-2666	486
BB & T Corp 200 W Second St	Winston-Salem	NC	27101	800-226-5228		359-2
NYSE: BBT						
B&B Image Group 1712 Marshall St NE	Minneapolis	MN	55413	888-788-9461	612-788-9461	343
Bb Riverboats Inc 101 Riverboat Row	Newport	KY	41071	800-261-8586	859-261-8500	744
BBE 100 McMillan St	Yellowknife	NT	X1A3T2	866-746-4223	867-766-8666	314
BBH (Baltimore Behavioral Health) 1101 W Pratt St	Baltimore	MD	21223	800-789-2647	410-962-7180	722
BC One Call Ltd 4259 Canada Way Ste 130	Burnaby	BC	V5G1H3	800-474-6886	604-257-1900	194
BC Wire Rope & Rigging 2720 E Regal Park Dr	Anaheim	CA	92806	800-669-5919		490
BC. Government & Service Employees' Union 4911 Canada Way	Burnaby	BC	V5G3W3	800-663-1674	604-291-9611	413
BCA (Brent Coon & Associates) 215 Orleans St	Beaumont	TX	77701	866-335-2666	409-835-2666	427
BCC (Brevard Community College) Cocoa 1519 Clearlake Rd	Cocoa	FL	32922	888-747-2802	321-632-1111	162
BCC Research LLC 49 Walnut Pk Bldg 2	Wellesley	MA	02481	866-285-7215	781-489-7301	633-9
BCCR (Brown College of Court Reporting & Medical Transcr) 1900 Emery St NW Ste 200	Atlanta	GA	30318	800-849-0703	404-876-1227	795
BCF LLP 25th Fl 1100 Rene-Levesque Blvd W	Montreal	QC	H3B5C9	866-511-8501	514-397-8500	427
Bcg Attorney Search 175 S Lake Ave Unit 200	Pasadena	CA	91101	800-298-6440		260
BCG Connect 755 Middlesex Tpke	Billerica	MA	01821	800-767-0067		776
BCHA (Back Country Horsemen of America) 59 Rainbow Rd	East Granby	CT	06029	888-893-5161	860-586-7540	48-23
BCI (Benefit Communications Inc) 2977 Sidco Dr	Nashville	TN	37204	800-489-3786		389
BCI (Bat Conservation International) 500 N Capital of Texas Hwy	Austin	TX	78746	800-538-2333	512-327-9721	48-3
BCI Burke Company Inc 660 Van Dyne Rd	Fond du Lac	WI	54937	800-356-2070	920-921-9220	345
BCLC (British Columbia Lottery Corp) 74 W Seymour St	Kamloops	BC	V2C1E2	866-815-0222	250-828-5500	450
BCM Resources Corp 1040 W Georgia St	Vancouver	BC	V6E4H1	888-646-0144	604-646-0144	500
BCN (Bliss Clearing Niagara) 1004 E State St	Hastings	MI	49058	800-642-5477	269-948-3300	454
BCN Services Inc 3650 W Liberty Rd	Ann Arbor	MI	48103	800-891-9911	734-994-4100	461
BCS (Birmingham Board of Education) 2015 Park Place North	Birmingham	AL	35203	800-628-6673	205-231-4600	681
BCS Prosoft Inc 2700 Lockhill Selma	San Antonio	TX	78230	800-882-6705	210-308-5505	179
BCSCVB (Experience Bryan College Station) 715 University Dr E	College Station	TX	77840	800-777-8292	979-260-9898	206
BCVB (Bloomington Convention & Visitors Bureau) 7900 International Dr Ste 990	Bloomington	MN	55425	800-346-4289	952-858-8500	206
BCW Diversified 514 E 31st St	Anderson	IN	46016	800-433-4229	765-644-2033	623
BCWSA (Bucks County Water & Sewer Authority) 1275 Almshouse Rd	Warrington	PA	18976	800-222-2068	215-343-2538	801
BD Biosciences 2350 Qume Dr	San Jose	CA	95131	800-223-8226	877-232-8995	418
BD Biosciences PharMingen 10975 Torreyana Rd	San Diego	CA	92121	800-848-6227	858-812-8800	85
B&D Industries Inc 9720 Bell Ave SE	Albuquerque	NM	87123	866-315-8349	505-299-4464	246
BD Medical 9450 S State St	Sandy	UT	84070	888-237-2762	801-565-2300	474
Bde Computer Services LLC 399 Lakeview Ave	Clifton	NJ	07011	877-233-4877	973-772-8507	175
BDL Supply 15 Sprague Rd	South Charleston	OH	45368	888-728-9810		
B-D-R Transport Inc 7994 US Rt 5	Westminster	VT	05158	800-421-0126	802-463-0606	775
BDS Marketing LLC 10 Holland	Irvine	CA	92618	800-234-4237		195
Beach Camera 203 Rt 22 E	Green Brook	NJ	08812	800-572-3224	732-968-6400	119
Beach Manufacturing Co PO Box 129	Donnelsville	OH	45319	800-543-5942	937-882-6372	60
Beach Properties of Hilton Head 64 Arrow Rd	Hilton Head Island	SC	29928	800-671-5155	843-671-5155	652
Beach Realty & Construction 4826 N Croatan Hwy	Kitty Hawk	NC	27949	800-635-1559	252-261-3815	648

	City	State	ZIP	Toll-Free	Phone	Class
Beach Terrace Motor Inn						
3400 Atlantic Ave	Wildwood	NJ	08260	**800-841-8416**	609-522-8100	377
Beacher's Lodge						
6970 A1A S	Saint Augustine	FL	32080	**800-527-8849**	904-471-8849	378
Beacon Container Corp						
700 W First St	Birdsboro	PA	19508	**800-422-8383**	610-582-2222	100
Beacon Credit Union						
PO Box 627	Wabash	IN	46992	**800-762-3136**	260-563-7443	219
Beacon Financial Partners						
25800 Science Park Dr Ste 100	Beachwood	OH	44122	**866-568-3951**	216-910-1850	194
Beacon Health System						
615 N Michigan St	South Bend	IN	46601	**800-850-7913**	574-647-1000	373-3
Beacon Hotel						
720 Ocean Dr	Miami Beach	FL	33139	**877-674-8200**	305-674-8200	378
Beacon House						
1301 N Third St	Marquette	MI	49855	**800-562-9753**	906-225-7100	371
Beacon Industries Inc						
12300 Old Tesson Rd	Saint Louis	MO	63128	**800-454-7159**	314-487-7600	21
Beacon Medaes						
1059 Paragon Way	Rock Hill	SC	29730	**888-463-3427**	803-817-5600	250
Beacon Press Inc						
24 Farnsworth St	Boston	MA	02210	**800-253-9646**	617-742-2110	633-2
Beacon Products LLC						
2041 58th Ave Cir E	Bradenton	FL	34203	**800-345-4928**		361
Beacon Roofing Supply Inc						
1 Lakeland Pk Dr	Peabody	MA	01960	**877-645-7663**	978-535-7668	191-4
NASDAQ: BECN						
Beacon Trust Co						
163 Madison Ave Ste 600	Morristown	NJ	07960	**866-377-8090**	973-377-8090	400
Beacon Wireless						
815 Middlefield Rd Unit 1	Toronto	ON	M1V2P9	**866-867-7770**	416-696-7555	643
Bead Industries Inc						
11 Cascade Blvd	Milford	CT	06460	**800-297-4851**	203-301-0270	485
Beal College						
99 Farm Rd	Bangor	ME	04401	**800-660-7351**	207-947-4591	795
Beall Corp						
9200 N Ramsey Blvd	Portland	OR	97203	**855-219-5686**		774
Beals Martin						
2596 Bay Rd	Redwood City	CA	94063	**800-879-7730**	650-364-8141	187
Beam Mack Sales & Service Inc						
2674 W Henrietta Rd	Rochester	NY	14623	**877-650-8789**	585-424-4860	775
Beamers Hells Canyon Tours						
1451 Bridge St	Clarkston	WA	99403	**800-522-6966**	509-758-4800	755
Bear Creek Mountain Resort						
101 Doe Mtn Ln	Macungie	PA	18062	**866-754-2822**	610-641-7101	377
Bear Mountain Golf Course						
43101 Gold Mine Dr						
PO Box 77	Big Bear Lake	CA	92315	**844-462-2327**		665
BEAR, THE						
91 Radio Park Dr	Mount Clare	WV	26408	**877-232-7121**	304-623-6546	641
Bearcom Inc						
4009 Distribution Dr Ste 200	Garland	TX	75041	**800-527-1670***		246
*Sales						
Bearing Distributors Inc						
8000 Hub Pkwy	Cleveland	OH	44125	**888-423-4872**	216-642-9100	384
Bearing Inspection Inc						
4500 Mt Pleasant NW	North Canton	OH	44720	**800-416-8881***	234-262-3000	75
*Cust Svc						
Bearing Service Co of Pennsylvania						
630 Alpha Dr RIDC Park	Pittsburgh	PA	15238	**800-783-2327**	412-963-7710	75
Bearskin Airlines						
1475 W Walsh St	Thunder Bay	ON	P7E4X6	**800-465-2327**		25
Beartooth Electric Co-op Inc						
1306 N Broadway St						
PO Box 1110	Red Lodge	MT	59068	**800-472-9821**	406-446-2310	245
Beasley Allen Crow Methvin						
218 Commerce St	Montgomery	AL	36104	**800-898-2034**	334-269-2343	427
Beau Rivage Resort & Casino						
875 Beach Blvd	Biloxi	MS	39530	**888-750-7111**	228-386-7111	665
Beaufort Memorial Hospital						
955 Ribaut Rd	Beaufort	SC	29902	**877-532-6472**	843-522-5200	373-3
Beaufurn LLC						
5269 US Hwy 158	Advance	NC	27006	**888-766-7706**	336-941-3446	321
Beaulieu Vineyard						
1960 St Helena Hwy	Rutherford	CA	94573	**800-373-5896**	707-967-5200	80-3
Beaumont Civic Ctr Complex						
701 Main St	Beaumont	TX	77701	**800-782-3081**	409-838-3435	205
Beaumont Convention & Visitors Bureau						
505 Willow St	Beaumont	TX	77701	**800-392-4401**	409-880-3749	206
Beauregard Electric Co-op Inc						
1010 E First St	DeRidder	LA	70634	**800-367-0275**	337-463-6221	245
Beauregard Parish Library						
205 S Washington Ave	Deridder	LA	70634	**800-524-6239**	337-463-6217	433-3
Beauty Brands Inc						
4600 Madison St Ste 400	Kansas City	MO	64112	**877-640-2248**	816-531-2266	77
Beauty Craft Supply & Equipment Co						
11110 Bren Rd W	Minnetonka	MN	55343	**800-328-5010**	952-935-4420	77
Beaver Creek Lodge						
26 Avon Dale Ln	Beaver Creek	CO	81620	**800-525-7280**	970-845-9800	378
Beaver Creek Nature Area						
48351 264th St	Valley Springs	SD	57068	**800-710-2267**	605-594-3824	561
Beaver Dunes State Park						
Hwy 270 N	Beaver	OK	73932	**800-654-8240**	580-625-3373	561
Beaver Express Service LLC						
4310 Oklahoma Ave PO Box 1147	Woodward	OK	73802	**800-593-2328**	580-256-6460	775
Beaver Run Resort & Conference Ctr						
620 Village Rd	Breckenridge	CO	80424	**800-525-2253**	970-453-6000	665
Beaver Street Fisheries Inc						
1741 W Beaver St	Jacksonville	FL	32209	**800-874-6426**	904-354-8533	296-13
Beavers Bend Resort Park						
PO Box 10	Broken Bow	OK	74728	**800-435-5514**	580-494-6300	561
Beaverton Foods Inc						
7100 NW Century Blvd	Hillsboro	OR	97124	**800-223-8076**	503-646-8138	296-19
Beavertown Block Company Inc						
3612 Paxtonville Rd	Middleburg	PA	17842	**800-597-2565**	570-837-1744	183
bebe stores Inc						
400 Valley Dr	Brisbane	CA	94005	**877-232-3777**	415-715-3900	155-20
Becharas Brothers Coffee Co Inc						
14501 Hamilton Ave	Highland Park	MI	48203	**800-944-9675**	313-869-4700	297-2
Bechik Products Inc						
860 Blue Gentian Rd Ste 140	Eagan	MN	55121	**800-328-6569**		469
Beck/Arnley Worldparts Inc						
2375 Midway Ln	Smyrna	TN	37167	**888-464-2325**		
Becker Arena Products Inc						
6611 W Hwy 13	Savage	MN	55378	**800-234-5522**	952-890-2690	186
Becker College						
61 Sever St	Worcester	MA	01609	**877-523-2537**	508-791-9241	166
Becker Electric Supply Inc						
1341 E Fourth St	Dayton	OH	45402	**800-762-9515**	937-226-1341	246
Beckett Air Inc						
37850 Beckett Pkwy	North Ridgeville	OH	44039	**800-831-7839**	440-327-9999	18
Beckmanxmo						
376 Morrison Rd	Columbus	OH	43213	**800-864-2232**	614-864-2232	623
Be-Cool Inc						
903 Woodside Ave	Essexville	MI	48732	**800-691-2667**	989-895-9699	608
Becton Dickinson & Co						
1 Becton Dr	Franklin Lakes	NJ	07417	**888-237-2762***	201-847-6800	475
NYSE: BDX ■ *Cust Svc						
Bed Bath & Beyond Inc						
650 Liberty Ave	Union	NJ	07083	**800-462-3966**	908-688-0888	361
NASDAQ: BBBY						
BedandBreakfastcom						
700 Brazos St Ste B-700	Austin	TX	78701	**800-462-2632***	512-322-2700	768
*Sales						
Beden-Baugh Products Inc						
105 Lisbon Rd	Laurens	SC	29360	**866-598-5794**	864-682-3136	199
Bedford County Visitors Bureau						
131 S Juliana St	Bedford	PA	15522	**800-765-3331**	814-623-1771	206
Bedford Gazette						
424 W Penn St	Bedford	PA	15522	**800-242-4250**	814-623-1151	528-3
Bedford Industries Inc						
1659 Rowe Ave	Worthington	MN	56187	**877-233-3673***	507-376-4136	544
*Cust Svc						
Bedford Materials Co Inc						
7676 Allegheny Rd	Manns Choice	PA	15550	**800-773-4276**	814-623-9014	811
Bedford Road Pharmacy Inc						
11306 Bedford Rd NE	Cumberland	MD	21502	**800-788-6693**	301-777-1771	238
Bedford Rural Electric Co-op Inc						
8846 Lincoln Hwy	Bedford	PA	15522	**800-808-2732**	814-623-5101	245
Bedford Technology LLC						
2424 Armour Rd PO Box 609	Worthington	MN	56187	**800-721-9037**	507-372-5558	657
Bedford Village Inn						
2 Olde Bedford Way	Bedford	NH	03110	**800-852-1166**	603-472-2001	667
Bedrock Prime						
1309 N Wilson Rd Ste A	Radcliff	KY	40160	**866-334-5914**	270-351-8043	177
Bee-alive Inc						
151 N Rte 9 W	Congers	NY	10920	**800-543-2337**		231
Beech-Nut Nutrition Corp						
1 Nutritious Pl	Amsterdam	NY	12010	**800-233-2468**		296-36
Beechwood Hotel						
363 Plantation St	Worcester	MA	01605	**800-344-2589**	508-754-5789	378
Beef Magazine						
7900 International Dr						
Ste 300	Minneapolis	MN	55425	**800-722-5334***	952-851-9329	455-1
*Cust Svc						
Beef O'Bradys Inc						
5660 W Cypress St Ste A	Tampa	FL	33607	**800-728-8878**	813-226-2333	666
Beehive Botanicals Inc						
16297 W Nursery Rd	Hayward	WI	54843	**800-233-4483**	715-634-4274	794
Beekley Corp						
1 Prestige Ln	Bristol	CT	06010	**800-233-5539**	860-583-4700	474
Beelman Truck Co						
1 Racehorse Dr	East Saint Louis	IL	62205	**800-541-5918***	618-646-5300	775
*Sales						
Beemac Trucking						
2747 Legionville Rd	Ambridge	PA	15003	**800-282-8781**	724-266-8781	681
Beemer Precision Inc						
230 New York Dr						
PO Box 3080	Fort Washington	PA	19034	**800-836-2340**	215-646-8440	616
BeenVerified Inc (BV)						
48 W 38th St 8th Fl	New York	NY	10018	**888-579-5910**		317
Beer Institute						
440 First St NW Ste 350	Washington	DC	20001	**800-379-2739**	202-737-2337	49-6
Beginnings For Parents						
156 Wind Chime Ct Ste A	Raleigh	NC	27615	**800-541-4327**	919-715-4092	48-17
Begneaud Manufacturing Inc						
306 E Amedee Dr	Lafayette	LA	70583	**800-358-8970**	337-237-5069	295
Behan Communications Inc						
86 Glen St	New York	NY	12801	**877-792-3856**		632
Behlen Building Systems						
4025 E 23rd St	Columbus	NE	68601	**800-228-0340**		186
Behr Process Corp						
3400 W Segerstrom Ave	Santa Ana	CA	92704	**800-854-0133**	714-545-7101	546
BEI Technologies Inc Industrial Encoder Div						
7230 Hollister Ave	Goleta	CA	93117	**800-350-2727***	805-968-0782	253
*Sales						
Beistle Co						
1 Beistle Plz	Shippensburg	PA	17257	**800-445-2131**	717-532-2131	562
Beitler-Mckee Optical Co						
160 S 22nd St	Pittsburgh	PA	15203	**800-989-4700**	412-481-4700	538
Bekins Van Lines LLC						
8010 Castleton Rd	Indianapolis	IN	46250	**800-456-8092**		516
Bel Brands USA Inc						
30 S Wacker Dr Ste 3000	Chicago	IL	60606	**800-831-3724**	920-788-3524	
Bel Fuse Inc						
206 Van Vorst St	Jersey City	NJ	07302	**800-235-3873**	201-432-0463	725
NASDAQ: BELFA						
Bel Stewart Connector						
11118 Susquehanna Trl S	Glen Rock	PA	17327	**800-323-9612**	717-235-7512	253
Bel-Art Products Inc						
661 Rte 23 S	Wayne	NJ	07440	**800-423-5278**	973-694-0500	419
Belarus Tractor International Inc						
7842 N Faulkner Rd	Milwaukee	WI	53224	**800-356-2336**		274
Belcam Inc Delagar Div						
27 Montgomery St	Rouses Point	NY	12979	**800-328-3006**	518-297-3366	214

Alphabetical Section

	Toll-Free	Phone	Class
Belcan Corp			
10200 Anderson Way ....Cincinnati OH 45242	800-423-5226	513-891-0972	261
Belco Mfg Company Inc			
2303 Taylors Valley Rd ....Belton TX 76513	800-251-8265	254-933-9000	199
Belco Packaging Systems Inc			
910 S Mountain Ave ....Monrovia CA 91016	800-833-1833	626-357-9566	543
Belden Inc			
2200 US Hwy 27 S ....Richmond IN 47374	800-235-3362	765-983-5200	809
Belding Tank Technologies Inc			
200 N Gooding St PO Box 160 ....Belding MI 48809	800-253-4252	616-794-1130	606
Beldon			
100 S Canyonwood Dr ....Dripping Springs TX 78620	855-971-6936	512-337-1820	189-12
Belfast Area Chamber of Commerce			
14 Main St ....Belfast ME 04915	877-338-9015	207-338-5900	139
BELFOR (Canada) Inc			
3300 Bridgeway St ....Vancouver BC V5K1H9	888-432-1123	604-432-1123	663
Belhaven College			
1500 Peachtree St PO Box 153..........Jackson MS 39202	800-960-5940	601-968-5940	166
Beliefnet			
999 Waterside Dr Ste 1900.........Norfolk VA 23510	800-311-2458		171
Belknap White Group, The			
111 Plymouth St ....Mansfield MA 02048	866-298-0708	800-283-7500	
Bell + Howell			
3791 S Alston Ave ....Durham NC 27713	800-961-7282	847-675-7600	173-7
Bell Canada			
1050 Beaver Hall Hill ....Montreal QC H2Z1S4	800-667-0123		731
Bell County			
101 E Central Ave PO Box 768 ....Belton TX 76513	800-460-2355	254-939-3521	337
Bell Ford Inc			
2401 W Bell Rd ....Phoenix AZ 85023	800-688-1776	602-457-2144	57
Bell Harbor International Conference Ctr			
2211 Alaskan Way Pier 66 ....Seattle WA 98121	888-772-4422	206-441-6666	205
Bell Investment Advisors			
1111 Broadway Ste 1630 ....Oakland CA 94607	800-700-0089	510-433-1066	400
Bell Litho Inc			
370 Crossen Ave ....Elk Grove Village IL 60007	800-952-3306	847-952-3300	776
Bell Lumber & Pole Co			
778 First St NW			
PO Box 120786.................New Brighton MN 55112	877-633-4334	651-633-4334	813
Bell Techlogix			
4400 W 96th St ....Indianapolis IN 46268	866-782-2355	317-333-7777	180
Bell Tower Hotel			
300 S Thayer St ....Ann Arbor MI 48104	800-562-3559	734-769-3010	378
Bell Tower Inn			
1235 Second St SW ....Rochester MN 55902	800-448-7583	507-289-2233	378
Bellagio - Las Vegas			
3600 Las Vegas Blvd S ....Las Vegas NV 89109	866-259-7111	702-693-7111	667
Bellagio Hotel & Casino			
3600 Las Vegas Blvd S ....Las Vegas NV 89109	888-987-7111	888-987-6667	665
Bellarmine University			
2001 Newburg Rd ....Louisville KY 40205	800-274-4723	502-272-8000	166
Bellasera Hotel			
221 Ninth St S ....Naples FL 34102	844-898-4184	239-649-7333	378
Bellco First Federal Credit Union			
7600 E OrchaRd Rd			
Ste 400N..................Greenwood Village CO 80111	800-235-5261	303-689-7800	219
Bellco Glass Inc			
340 Edrudo Rd ....Vineland NJ 08360	800-257-7043	856-691-1075	332
Belle Bonfils Memorial Blood Ctr			
717 Yosemite St ....Denver CO 80230	800-365-0006	303-341-4000	89
Belle Meade Plantation			
5025 Harding Pk ....Nashville TN 37205	800-270-3991	615-356-0501	517
Belle of Baton Rouge Casino			
103 France St ....Baton Rouge LA 70802	800-676-4847		133
Belle Tire Inc			
1000 Enterprise Dr ....Allen Park MI 48101	888-462-3553	313-271-9400	62-5
Belle-Pak Packaging Inc			
7465 Birchmount Rd ....Markham ON L3R5X9	800-565-2137	905-475-5151	597
Belleville Area Chamber of Commerce			
248 Main St ....Belleville MI 48111	800-692-2274	734-697-7151	139
Belleville Chamber of Commerce			
5 Moira St E ....Belleville ON K8P2S3	888-852-9992	613-962-4597	137
Belleville General Hospital			
265 Dundas St E ....Belleville ON K8N5A9	800-483-2811	613-969-7400	373-2
Belleville News-Democrat			
120 S Illinois St ....Belleville IL 62220	800-642-3878	618-234-1000	528-2
Belleville Wire Cloth Inc			
18 Rutgers Ave ....Cedar Grove NJ 07009	800-631-0490	973-239-0074	684
Bellevue Arts Museum			
510 Bellevue Way NE ....Bellevue WA 98004	800-367-2648	425-519-0770	517
Bellevue Club Hotel			
11200 SE Sixth St ....Bellevue WA 98004	800-579-1110		378
Bellevue University			
1000 Galvin Rd S ....Bellevue NE 68005	800-756-7920	402-293-2000	166
Bellin College of Nursing			
3201 Eaton Rd ....Green Bay WI 54311	800-236-8707	920-433-6699	166
Bellingham Marine Industries Inc			
1001 C St ....Bellingham WA 98225	800-733-5679	360-676-2800	188-5
Bellingrath Gardens & Home			
12401 Bellingrath Garden Rd ....Theodore AL 36582	800-247-8420	251-973-2217	97
Bellmoor, The			
6 Christian St ....Rehoboth Beach DE 19971	800-425-2355	302-227-5800	378
Bellomy Research Inc			
175 Sunnynoll Ct ....Winston-Salem NC 27106	800-443-7344		195
Bel-Mar Wire Products Inc			
2343 N Damen Ave ....Chicago IL 60647	800-249-9450	773-342-3800	286
Belmont Abbey College			
100 Belmont-Mt Holly Rd ....Belmont NC 28012	888-222-0110	704-461-6700	166
Belmont Ctr for Comprehensive Treatment			
4200 Monument Rd ....Philadelphia PA 19131	800-220-4357		373-5
Belmont University			
1900 Belmont Blvd ....Nashville TN 37212	800-563-6765	615-460-6000	166
Beloit College			
700 College St ....Beloit WI 53511	800-331-4943*	608-363-2500	166
*Admissions			
Beloit Health System			
1969 W Hart Rd ....Beloit WI 53511	800-637-2641	608-363-5724	373-3

	Toll-Free	Phone	Class
Beloit Regional Hospice			
655 Third St Ste 200................Beloit WI 53511	877-363-7421	608-363-7421	370
Bel-Rea Institute of Animal Technology			
1681 S Dayton St ....Denver CO 80247	800-950-8001	303-751-8700	795
Belshaw Adamatic Bakery			
814 44th St NW Ste 103 ....Auburn WA 98001	800-578-2547	206-322-5474	298
Belshaw Bros Inc			
1750 22nd Ave S ....Seattle WA 98144	800-578-2547	206-322-5474	298
Belshire Environmental Services Inc			
25971 Towne Centre Dr ....Foothill Ranch CA 92610	800-995-8220	949-460-5200	63
Belson Outdoors Inc			
111 N River Rd ....North Aurora IL 60542	800-323-5664		319-4
Belstar Inc			
8408 Arlington Blvd Ste 200..........Fairfax VA 22031	800-548-5921	703-645-0280	
Belstra Milling Company Inc			
424 15th St ....Demotte IN 46310	800-276-2989		445
Belt Railway Co of Chicago			
6900 S Central Ave ....Bedford Park IL 60638	877-772-5772	708-496-4000	647
Belterra Casino Resort			
777 Belterra Dr ....Florence IN 47020	888-235-8377	812-427-7777	665
Belting Industries Group			
1090 Lousons Rd ....Union NJ 07083	800-843-2358	908-272-8591	369
Belton Industries Inc			
1205 Hanby Rd PO Box 127 ....Belton SC 29627	800-845-8753	864-338-5711	740-3
Beltone Electronics Corp			
2601 Patriot Blvd ....Glenview IL 60026	800-235-8663	847-832-3300	475
Beltrami Electric Co-op Inc			
4111 Technology Dr NW ....Bemidji MN 56601	800-955-6083	218-444-2540	245
Beltservice Corp			
4143 Rider Trl N ....Earth City MO 63045	800-727-2358	314-344-8555	207
Belvac Production Machinery Inc			
237 Graves Mill Rd ....Lynchburg VA 24502	800-423-5822	434-239-0358	492
Belvedere Terminals Inc			
111 NE Second Ave NE St ....Petersburg FL 33701	800-716-8515		534
Belvedere USA Corp			
1 Belvedere Blvd ....Belvidere IL 61008	800-435-5491		76
Belwith International Ltd			
3100 Broadway Ave ....Grandville MI 49418	800-235-9484		349
Bement School			
94 Main St PO Box 8 ....Deerfield MA 01342	877-405-3949	413-774-7061	618
Bemidji Area Chamber of Commerce			
300 Bemidji Ave ....Bemidji MN 56601	800-458-2223	218-444-3541	139
Bemidji State University			
1500 Birchmont Dr NE ....Bemidji MN 56601	800-475-2001*	218-755-2001	166
*Admissions			
Bemis Company Inc			
2301 Industrial Dr ....Neenah WI 54956	800-544-4672	920-527-5000	544
NYSE: BMS			
Bemis Manufacturing Co			
300 Mill St ....Sheboygan Falls WI 53085	800-558-7651	920-467-4621	319-4
Bemis Public Library			
6014 S Datura St ....Littleton CO 80120	800-895-1999	303-795-3961	433-3
Ben Bridge Jeweler Inc			
PO Box 1908 ....Seattle WA 98111	888-917-9171*	888-448-1912	409
*Cust Svc			
Ben Tire Distributors Ltd			
203 E Madison St PO Box 158 ....Toledo IL 62468	800-252-8961		750
Benchmark Electronics Inc			
4141 N Scottsdale Rd ....Scottsdale AZ 85251	800-322-2885	623-300-7000	621
NYSE: BHE			
Benchmark Group			
4053 Maple Rd ....Amherst NY 14226	800-876-0160	716-833-4986	650
Benchmark Technologies International Inc (BTI)			
411 Hackensack Ave ....Hackensack NJ 07601	800-265-8254	201-996-0077	194
Benco Electric Co-op			
20946 549 Ave PO Box 8 ....Mankato MN 56002	888-792-3626	507-387-7963	245
Bender Group			
345 Parr Cir ....Reno NV 89512	800-621-9402		447
Bender Plumbing Supplies Inc			
580 Grand Ave ....New Haven CT 06511	800-573-4288	203-787-4288	608
Bendix Commercial Vehicle Systems LLC			
901 Cleveland St ....Elyria OH 44035	800-247-2725	440-329-9000	61
Bendsen Signs & Graphics Inc			
1506 E McBride Ave ....Decatur IL 62526	866-275-6407	217-877-2345	343
BendTec Inc			
366 Garfield Ave ....Duluth MN 55802	800-236-3832	218-722-0205	591
Benecaid Health Benefit Solutions Inc			
185 The W Mall Ste 800 ....Toronto ON M9C5L5	877-797-7448	416-626-8786	390-3
Benedict College			
1600 Harden St ....Columbia SC 29204	800-868-6598	803-253-5000	166
Benedictine College			
1020 N Second St ....Atchison KS 66002	800-467-5340	913-367-5340	166
Benedictine Health System			
503 E Third St Ste 400 ....Duluth MN 55805	800-833-7208	218-786-2370	352
Benedictine University			
5700 College Rd ....Lisle IL 60532	888-829-6363	630-829-6300	166
Benefact Consulting Group			
6285 Northam Dr Ste 200..........Mississauga ON L4V1X5	855-829-2225		461
Beneficial Financial Group			
55 N 300 W ....Salt Lake City UT 84145	800-233-7979	801-933-1100	390-2
Beneficial Mutual Savings Bank			
530 Walnut St ....Philadelphia PA 19106	800-784-8490	888-742-5272	70
Benefit & Risk Management Services Inc (BRMS)			
80 Iron Point Cir Ste 200			
PO Box 2140....................Folsom CA 95763	888-326-2555		389
Benefit Advantage Inc			
3431 Commodity Ln ....Green Bay WI 54304	800-686-6829	920-339-0351	461
Benefit Communications Inc (BCI)			
2977 Sidco Dr ....Nashville TN 37204	800-489-3786		389
Benefit Express Services LLC			
1700 E Golf Rd Ste 1000 ....Schaumburg IL 60173	877-369-2153		177
Benefit Recovery Group			
6745 Lenox Center Ct Ste 100 ....Memphis TN 38115	866-384-4051		443
BenefitHelp Solutions Inc			
10505 SE 17th Ave ....Milwaukie OR 97222	888-398-8057	503-219-3679	531
BenefitMall Inc			
4851 LBJ Fwy Ste 1100 ....Dallas TX 75244	888-338-6293	469-791-3300	178-10

Name / Address	Toll-Free	Phone	Class
Benefitvision Inc 4522 RFD ...... Long Grove IL 60047	800-810-2200	877-737-5526	196
Benelogic LLC 9475 Deereco Rd Ste 310 ...... Timonium MD 21093	877-716-6615		
Benemax Inc 7 W Mill St ...... Medfield MA 02052	800-528-1530		194
Benetrends Inc 1180 Welsh Rd ...... North Wales PA 19454	866-423-6387	267-498-0059	461
Benewah County 701 College Ave ...... Saint Maries ID 83861	800-983-0937	208-245-3212	337
Benjamin Franklin Institute of Technology 41 Berkeley St ...... Boston MA 02116	877-400-2348	617-423-4630	795
Benjamin Franklin Plumbing 12 Greenway Plz Ste 250 ...... Houston TX 77046	800-471-0809	713-877-3500	310
Benjamin Manufacturing 3215 S Sweetwater Rd ...... Lithia Springs GA 30122	800-343-1756	770-941-1433	606
Benjamin Moore & Co 101 Paragon Dr ...... Montvale NJ 07645	800-344-0400	855-724-6802	546
Benjamin Office Supply & Services Inc 758 E Gude Dr ...... Rockville MD 20850	877-439-2677	301-340-1384	
Benjamin, The 125 E 50th St ...... New York NY 10022	866-222-2365	212-715-2500	378
Benner-Nawman Inc 3450 Sabin Brown Rd ...... Wickenburg AZ 85390	800-992-3833	928-684-2813	286
Bennett Brothers Inc 30 E Adams St ...... Chicago IL 60603	800-621-2626	312-263-4800	410
Bennett College 900 E Washington St ...... Greensboro NC 27401 *Admissions	800-413-5323*	336-370-8624	166
Bennett Jones LLP 855 Second St S W 4500 Bankers Hall E ...... Calgary AB T2P4K7	800-222-6479	403-298-3100	427
Bennett Pump Co 1218 Pontaluna Rd ...... Spring Lake MI 49456	800-235-7618	231-798-1310	635
Bennington College 1 College Dr ...... Bennington VT 05201	800-833-6845	802-440-4325	166
Bennington Museum 75 Main St ...... Bennington VT 05201	800-205-8033	802-442-2494	517
Benny Hinn Ministries PO Box 162000 ...... Irving TX 75016	888-377-7783		48-20
Benny Whitehead Inc 3576 S Eufaula Ave ...... Eufaula AL 36027	800-633-7617	334-687-8055	359-2
BenQ America Corp 15375 Barranca Ste A205 ...... Irvine CA 92618	866-600-2367	949-255-9500	173-7
Benson's Gourmet Seasonings PO Box 638 ...... Azusa CA 91702	800-325-5619	626-969-4443	296-37
Benson, The 309 SW Broadway ...... Portland OR 97205	800-663-1144	503-228-2000	378
Bent Gate Mountaineering 1313 Washington Ave ...... Golden CO 80401	877-236-8428	303-271-9382	707
Bentley Historical Library 1150 Beal Ave ...... Ann Arbor MI 48109	866-233-6661	734-764-3482	433-4
Bentley Motors Inc 2200 Ferdinand Porsche Dr ...... Herndon VA 20171	800-777-6923		
Bentley Prince Street 14641 E Don Julian Rd ...... City of Industry CA 91746	800-423-4709		131
Bentley Systems Inc 685 Stockton Dr ...... Exton PA 19341	800-236-8539	610-458-5000	178-5
Benton Rural Electric Assn (BREA) 402 Seventh St PO Box 1150 ...... Prosser WA 99350	800-221-6987	509-786-2913	245
Bentz Whaley Flessner 7251 Ohms Ln ...... Minneapolis MN 55439	800-921-0111	952-921-0111	317
Benz Communications LLC 209 Mississippi St ...... San Francisco CA 94107	888-550-5251		193
Benzel's Pretzel Bakery Inc 5200 Sixth Ave ...... Altoona PA 16602	800-344-4438	814-942-5062	296-9
Benzie County 448 Ct Pl ...... Beulah MI 49617	800-315-3593	231-882-9671	337
BeQuick Software Inc 601 Heritage Dr Ste 442 ...... Jupiter FL 33458	866-267-5105	561-721-9600	
Berco Inc 111 Winnebago ...... Saint Louis MO 63118	888-772-4788	314-772-4700	
Berding & Weil LLP 2175 N California Blvd Ste 500 ...... Walnut Creek CA 94596	800-838-2090	925-838-2090	427
Berdon LLP 360 Madison Ave 8th Fl ...... New York NY 10017	800-372-1033	212-832-0400	2
Berea College 101 Chestnut St ...... Berea KY 40403	800-326-5948	859-985-3500	166
Berendsen Fluid Power 401 S Boston Ave Ste 1200 ...... Tulsa OK 74103	800-360-2327	918-592-3781	384
Berenson Corp 2495 Main St ...... Buffalo NY 14214	800-333-0578	716-833-3100	349
Beretta USA Corp 17601 Beretta Dr ...... Accokeek MD 20607	800-237-3882	301-283-2191	284
Berg Equipment Co 2700 W Veterans Pkwy ...... Marshfield WI 54449	800-494-1738	715-384-2151	273
Berg's Ski & Snowboard Shop 367 W 13th Ave ...... Eugene OR 97401	800-800-1953	541-683-1300	707
Bergad Inc 747 Eljer Way ...... Ford City PA 16226	888-476-8664	724-763-2883	469
Bergamot Inc 820 E Wisconsin St ...... Delavan WI 53115 *Cust Svc	800-922-6733*	262-728-5572	9
Bergdorf Goodman Inc 754 Fifth Ave ...... New York NY 10019 *Cust Svc	888-774-2424*	212-753-7300	157-4
Bergen Community College 400 Paramus Rd ...... Paramus NJ 07652	877-612-5381	201-447-7200	162
Berger & Montague PC 1622 Locust St ...... Philadelphia PA 19103	800-424-6690	215-875-3000	427
Berger Bldg Products Inc 805 Pennsylvania Blvd ...... Feasterville PA 19053 *Cust Svc	800-523-8852*	215-355-1200	693
Berger Transfer & Storage Inc 2950 Long Lake Rd ...... Saint Paul MN 55113	877-268-2101		516
BERGEY'S AUTO DEALERSHIPS 462 Harleysville Pk ...... Souderton PA 18964	800-237-4397	215-723-6071	62-5
Bergmann Assoc Inc 280 E Broad St Ste 200 ...... Rochester NY 14614	800-724-1168		261
Bergquist Co 18930 W 78th St ...... Chanhassen MN 55317	800-347-4572	952-835-2322	253
Bergstrom of Kaukauna 2929 Lawe St ...... Kaukauna WI 54130	866-939-0130		57
Bering Air 1470 Sepalla Dr PO Box 1650 ...... Nome AK 99762	800-478-5422	907-443-5464	25
Berkeley Chamber of Commerce 1834 University Ave ...... Berkeley CA 94703	800-847-4823	510-549-7000	139
Berkeley College *Garrett Mountain* 44 Rifle Camp Rd ...... Woodland Park NJ 07424	800-446-5400	973-278-5400	795
New York City 3 E 43rd St ...... New York NY 10017	800-446-5400	212-986-4343	795
Paramus 64 E Midland Ave ...... Paramus NJ 07652	800-446-5400	201-967-9667	795
White Plains 99 Church St ...... White Plains NY 10601	800-446-5400	914-694-1122	795
Woodbridge 430 Rahway Ave ...... Woodbridge NJ 07095	800-446-5400	732-750-1800	795
Berkeley Communications Corp 1321 67th St ...... Emeryville CA 94608	877-237-5266	510-644-1599	194
Berkeley County Chamber of Commerce PO Box 968 ...... Moncks Corner SC 29461	800-882-0337	843-761-8238	139
Berkeley Hotel, The 1200 E Cary St ...... Richmond VA 23219	888-780-4422	804-780-1300	378
Berkeley Public Library 2090 Kittredge St ...... Berkeley CA 94704	800-870-3663	510-981-6100	433-3
Berkeley Pumps 293 Wright St ...... Delavan WI 53115	888-782-7483	262-728-5551	637
Berkeley Varitronics Systems Inc 255 Liberty St Liberty Corporate Pk ...... Metuchen NJ 08840	888-737-4287	732-548-3737	177
Berkeleys Northside Travel Inc 1824 Euclid Ave ...... Berkeley CA 94709	800-575-3411	510-843-1000	767
Berklee College of Music 1140 Boylston St ...... Boston MA 02215	800-421-0084	617-747-2221	166
Berkley Risk Administrators Company LLC 222 S Ninth St Ste 2700 ...... Minneapolis MN 55402	800-449-7707	612-766-3000	389
Berks Packing Company Inc 307-323 Bingaman St PO Box 5919 ...... Reading PA 19610	800-882-3757		296-26
Berks VNA 1170 Berkshire Blvd ...... Wyomissing PA 19610	855-843-8627		370
Berkshire Advisors Inc 2240 Ridgewood Rd ...... Wyomissing PA 19610	800-566-4325	610-376-6970	400
Berkshire Bancorp Inc 24 North St PO Box 1308 ...... Pittsfield MA 01202 *NYSE: BHLB*	800-773-5601		
Berkshire Bank PO Box 1308 ...... Pittsfield MA 01202	800-773-5601	413-443-5601	70
Berkshire Hathaway Homestates Cos (BHHC) PO Box 2048 ...... Omaha NE 68103	888-495-8949		390-4
Berkshire Hathaway Inc 3555 Farnam St Ste 1440 ...... Omaha NE 68131 *NYSE: BRK.A*	800-223-2064	402-346-1400	185
Berkshire Health & Rehabilitation Ctr 705 Clearview Dr ...... Vinton VA 24179	800-321-1245	540-982-6691	448
Berlin Metals LLC 3200 Sheffield Ave ...... Hammond IN 46327	800-754-8867	219-933-0111	490
Berlitz Languages Inc 7 Roszel Rd ...... Princeton NJ 08540	866-423-7548		
Bermuda Dept of Tourism 675 Third Ave 20th Fl ...... New York NY 10017	800-223-6106	212-818-9800	770
Bermuda Village 142 Bermuda Village Dr ...... Advance NC 27006 *Mktg	800-843-5433*		668
Bernard Food Industries Inc 1125 Hartrey Ave ...... Evanston IL 60204	800-323-3663	847-869-5222	296-18
Bernard L Madoff Investment Securities Co 45 Rockefeller Ctr 11th Fl ...... New York NY 10111	800-334-1343	212-230-2424	686
Bernards Inn 27 Mine Brook Rd ...... Bernardsville NJ 07924	888-766-0002	908-766-0002	378
Bernardus Lodge 415 Carmel Valley Rd ...... Carmel Valley CA 93924	800-223-2533	831-658-3400	378
Bernatello's PO Box 729 ...... Maple Lake MN 55358	800-666-9455	952-831-6622	296-21
Berne Apparel Co 2501 East 850 North PO Box 530 ...... Ossian IN 46777	800-843-7657	888-772-3763	155-18
Berner Foods Inc 2034 E Factory Rd ...... Dakota IL 61018	800-819-8199	815-563-4222	296-5
Berney Office Solutions LLC 10690 John Knight Close ...... Montgomery AL 36117	800-239-3025		623
Berney-Karp Inc 3350 E 26th St ...... Vernon CA 90058	800-237-6395	323-260-7122	333
Bernhardt Furniture Co 1839 Morganton Blvd ...... Lenoir NC 28645	800-638-2772		319-1
Bernicke Wealth Management 1565 Bluestem Blvd ...... Altoona WI 54720	866-832-1173	715-832-1173	
Berns Co 1250 W 17th St ...... Long Beach CA 90813	800-421-3773	562-437-0471	468
Bernzott Capital Advisors 888 W Ventura Blvd Ste B ...... Camarillo CA 93010	800-856-2646	805-389-9445	194
Berr Pet Supply Inc 929 N Market Blvd ...... Sacramento CA 95834	888-237-7738	916-921-0145	237
Berry Aviation Inc 1807 Airport Dr ...... San Marcos TX 78666	800-229-2379		13
Berry College 2277 Martha Berry Hwy NW ...... Mount Berry GA 30149	800-237-7942	706-232-5374	166
Berry Global Inc 101 Oakley St ...... Evansville IN 47710 *Sales	877-662-3779*	413-529-2183	
Berryman Products Inc 3800 E Randol Mill Rd ...... Arlington TX 76011	800-433-1704	817-640-2376	146
Bertek Systems Inc 133 Bryce Rd ...... Fairfax VT 05454	800-367-0210	802-752-3170	623
Bertelkamp Automation Inc 4716 Middle Creek Ln ...... Knoxville TN 37921	800-251-9134	865-588-7691	

	Toll-Free	Phone	Class
Berthel Fisher Companies			
4201 42nd St NE Ste 100 . . . . Cedar Rapids IA 52402	800-356-5234	319-447-5700	686
Berwick Hospital Ctr, The			
701 E 16th St . . . . Berwick PA 18603	800-654-5988	570-759-5000	373-3
Besl Transfer Co			
5700 Este Ave . . . . Cincinnati OH 45232	800-456-2375	513-242-3456	775
Besly Cutting Tools Inc			
520 Blackhawk Blvd Ste135 . . . . South Beloit IL 61080	800-435-2965	815-389-2231	491
Bessemer Area Chamber of Commerce			
321 N 18th St . . . . Bessemer AL 35020	888-423-7736	205-425-3253	139
Bessemer Trust Co			
630 Fifth Ave . . . . New York NY 10111	866-271-7403	212-708-9100	400
Besser Co			
801 Johnson St . . . . Alpena MI 49707	800-530-9980	800-968-0444	385
Bessire & Associates Inc			
7621 Little Ave Ste 106. . . . . Charlotte NC 28226	800-797-7355	704-341-1423	193
Best Access Systems			
6161 E 75th St . . . . Indianapolis IN 46250	855-365-2407	317-849-2250	349
Best Bath Systems			
723 Garber St . . . . Caldwell ID 83605	866-333-8657	208-342-6823	374
Best Buy Company Inc			
7601 Penn Ave S . . . . Richfield MN 55423	888-237-8289	612-291-1000	35
NYSE: BBY			
Best Impressions Catalog Co			
345 N Lewis Ave . . . . Oglesby IL 61348	800-635-2378	815-883-3532	786
Best Life & Health Insurance Co			
2505 McCabe Way . . . . Irvine CA 92614	800-433-0088	949-253-4080	390-2
Best Line Oil Co Inc			
219 N 20th St . . . . Tampa FL 33605	800-382-1811	813-248-1044	575
Best Maid Products Inc			
PO Box 1809 . . . . Fort Worth TX 76101	800-447-3581	817-335-5494	296-19
Best Plumbing Specialties			
3039 Ventrie Ct . . . . Myersville MD 21773	800-448-6710		608
Best Priced Products Inc			
PO Box 1174 . . . . White Plains NY 10602	800-824-2939	914-345-3800	406
Best Provision Company Inc			
144 Avon Ave . . . . Newark NJ 07108	800-631-4466	973-242-5000	296-26
Best Registration Services Inc			
1418 S Third St . . . . Louisville KY 40208	800-977-3475	502-637-4528	395
Best Telecom Inc			
278 E End Ave . . . . Beaver PA 15009	888-365-2273		386
Best Theratronics Ltd			
413 March Rd . . . . Ottawa ON K2K0E4	866-792-8598	613-591-2100	474
Best Vascular			
4350 International Blvd Ste A . . . . Norcross GA 30093	800-668-6783	770-717-0904	474
Best Way Logistics			
14004 Century Ln . . . . Grandview MO 64030	877-923-7892	816-767-8008	314
Best Western Chincoteague Island			
7105 Maddox Blvd . . . . Chincoteague Island VA 23336	800-780-7234	757-336-6557	378
Best Western Grandma's Feather Bed			
9300 Glacier Hwy . . . . Juneau AK 99801	888-781-5005	907-789-5005	667
Best Western InnTowner, The			
2424 University Ave . . . . Madison WI 53726	800-258-8321	608-233-8778	377
Best Western International Inc			
6201 N 24th Pkwy . . . . Phoenix AZ 85016	800-528-1234	602-957-4200	378
Best Western Plus Hood River Inn			
1108 E Marina Way . . . . Hood River OR 97031	800-828-7873	541-386-2200	703
Best Western Victorian Inn			
487 Foam St . . . . Monterey CA 93940	800-232-4141	831-373-8000	378
Best's Review			
Ambest Rd . . . . Oldwick NJ 08858	800-424-2378	908-439-2200	455-5
Best, Vanderlaan & Harrington			
25 E Washington St Ste 800 . . . . Chicago IL 60602	800-351-4316	312-819-1100	427
Bestar Inc			
4220 Villeneuve St . . . . Lac-Megantic QC G6B2C3	888-823-7827	819-583-1017	319-1
BestCo Inc			
288 Mazeppa Rd . . . . Mooresville NC 28115	888-211-5530	704-664-4300	296-8
BESTECH			
1040 Lorne St Unit 3 . . . . Sudbury ON P3C4R9	877-675-7720	705-675-7720	261
Bestforms Inc			
1135 Avenida Acaso . . . . Camarillo CA 93012	800-350-0618	805-383-6993	110
Bestolife Corp			
2777 Stemmons Fwy Ste 1800 . . . . Dallas TX 75207	855-243-9164	214-583-0271	3
BestPass Inc			
828 Washington Ave . . . . Albany NY 12203	888-410-9696	518-458-1579	392
Best-Rite Mfg			
2885 Lorraine Ave . . . . Temple TX 76501	800-749-2258		286
Best-Wade Petroleum Inc			
201 Dodge Dr . . . . Ripley TN 38063	888-888-6457	731-635-9661	
Bestway Inc			
12400 Coit Rd Ste 950 . . . . Dallas TX 75251	800-316-4567	214-630-6655	264-2
Bestway Tours & Safaris			
8678 Greenall Ave . . . . Burnaby BC V5J3M6	800-663-0844	604-264-7378	755
Beta Alpha Psi			
220 Leigh Farm Rd . . . . Durham NC 27707	800-362-5066	919-402-4044	48-16
Beta Gamma Sigma Inc (BGS)			
125 Weldon Pkwy . . . . Maryland Heights MO 63043	800-337-4677	314-432-5650	48-16
Beta LaserMike Inc			
8001 Technology Blvd . . . . Dayton OH 45424	800-886-9935	937-233-9935	470
Beta Screen Corp			
707 Commercial Ave . . . . Carlstadt NJ 07072	800-272-7336	201-939-2400	587
Bete Fog Nozzle Inc			
50 Greenfield St . . . . Greenfield MA 01301	800-235-0049	413-772-0846	349
Beth Israel Deaconess Hospital-Milton			
199 Reedsdale Rd . . . . Milton MA 02186	800-462-5540	617-696-4600	373-3
Beth Israel Deaconess Medical Ctr (BIDMC)			
330 Brookline Ave . . . . Boston MA 02215	800-667-5356	617-667-7000	373-3
Bethany Bible College			
26 Western St . . . . Sussex NB E4E1E6	888-432-4444	506-432-4400	780
Bethany College			
31 E Campus Dr . . . . Bethany WV 26032	800-922-7611	304-829-7000	166
Bethany College			
335 E Swensson St . . . . Lindsborg KS 67456	800-826-2281*	785-227-3380	166
*Admissions			
Bethany House Publishers			
11400 Hampshire Ave S . . . . Bloomington MN 55438	800-328-6109	616-676-9185	633-3
Bethany Lutheran College			
700 Luther Dr . . . . Mankato MN 56001	800-944-3066	507-344-7000	166

	Toll-Free	Phone	Class
Bethany Theological Seminary			
615 National Rd W . . . . Richmond IN 47374	800-287-8822	765-983-1800	167-3
Bethea Baptist Retirement Community			
157 Home Ave . . . . Darlington SC 29532	877-393-2867	843-393-2867	668
Bethel College			
1001 W McKinley Ave . . . . Mishawaka IN 46545	800-422-4101*	574-807-7000	166
*Admissions			
Bethel College			
300 E 27th St . . . . North Newton KS 67117	800-522-1887	316-283-2500	166
Beth-El College of Nursing & Health Sciences			
1420 Austin Bluffs Pkwy			
. . . . Colorado Springs CO 80918	800-990-8227	719-255-8227	166
Bethel Inn & Country Club			
21 Broad St . . . . Bethel ME 04217	800-654-0125		665
Bethel Seminary			
3949 Bethel Dr . . . . Saint Paul MN 55112	800-255-8706	651-638-6400	167-3
Bethel University			
3900 Bethel Dr . . . . Saint Paul MN 55112	800-255-8706	651-638-6400	166
Bethesda Hospital			
2951 Maple Ave . . . . Zanesville OH 43701	800-322-4762	740-454-4000	373-3
Bethpage Federal Credit Union			
899 S Oyster Bay Rd . . . . Bethpage NY 11714	800-628-7070		219
Bethpage State Park			
Bethpage Pkwy . . . . Farmingdale NY 11735	800-456-2267	516-249-0701	561
Bethune-Cookman College			
640 Dr Mary McLeod Bethune Blvd			
. . . . Daytona Beach FL 32114	800-448-0228*	386-481-2900	166
*Admissions			
Betson Enterprises Inc			
303 Patterson Plank Rd . . . . Carlstadt NJ 07072	800-524-2343	201-438-1300	55
Betsy Hotel			
1440 Ocean Dr . . . . Miami Beach FL 33139	866-792-3879	305-531-6100	378
Bettcher Industries Inc			
PO Box 336 . . . . Vermilion OH 44089	800-321-8763	440-965-4422	298
Bettendorf-Stanford			
1370 W Main St . . . . Salem IL 62881	800-548-2253	618-548-3555	360
Better Business Bureau Inc			
1000 Broadway Ste 625 . . . . Oakland CA 94607	866-411-2221	510-844-2000	79
Better Business Bureau of Acadiana			
4003 W Congress St . . . . Lafayette LA 70506	800-557-7392	337-981-3497	79
Better Business Bureau of Asheville/Western North Carolina			
112 Executive Pk . . . . Asheville NC 28801	800-452-2882	828-253-2392	79
Better Business Bureau of Canton Region/West Virginia			
1434 Cleveland Ave NW . . . . Canton OH 44703	800-362-0494	330-454-9401	79
Better Business Bureau of Central & Eastern Kentucky			
1460 Newtown Pk . . . . Lexington KY 40511	800-866-6668	859-259-1008	79
Better Business Bureau of Central Alabama & the Wiregrass Area			
2101 Highland Ave Ste 410 . . . . Birmingham AL 35205	800-824-5274	205-558-2222	79
Better Business Bureau of Central East Texas			
3600 Old BullaRd Rd Bldg 1 . . . . Tyler TX 75701	800-443-0131	903-581-5704	79
Better Business Bureau of Central Illinois			
8100 N University Peoria . . . . Peoria IL 61615	800-763-4222	309-688-3741	79
Better Business Bureau of Central Indiana			
151 N Delaware St . . . . Indianapolis IN 46204	866-463-9222	317-488-2222	79
Better Business Bureau of Central Northeast Northwest & Southwest Arizona			
4428 N 12th St . . . . Phoenix AZ 85014	877-291-6222	602-264-1721	79
Better Business Bureau of Central Ohio			
1169 Dublin Rd . . . . Columbus OH 43215	800-759-2400	614-486-6336	79
Better Business Bureau of Central Oklahoma			
17 S Dewey Ave . . . . Oklahoma City OK 73102	800-654-7757	405-239-6081	79
Better Business Bureau of Central Texas			
1805 Rutherford Ln Ste 100 . . . . Austin TX 78754	800-621-0508	512-445-2911	79
Better Business Bureau of Central Virginia			
720 Moorefield Pk Dr Ste 300 . . . . Richmond VA 23236	800-533-5501	804-648-0016	79
Better Business Bureau of Cincinnati			
1 E Fourth St Ste 600 . . . . Cincinnati OH 45202	800-388-2222	513-421-3015	79
Better Business Bureau of Dayton/Miami Valley			
15 W Fourth St Ste 300 . . . . Dayton OH 45402	800-776-5301	937-222-5825	79
Better Business Bureau of Eastern Massachusetts Maine Rhode Island & Vermont			
290 Donald Lynch Blvd			
Ste 102 . . . . Marlborough MA 01752	800-422-2811	508-652-4800	79
Better Business Bureau of Eastern Oklahoma			
1722 S Carson Ave Ste 3200 . . . . Tulsa OK 74119	800-955-5100	918-492-1266	79
Better Business Bureau of Eastern Ontario & the Outaouais Inc			
700 Industrial Ave Unit 505 . . . . Ottawa ON K1G0Y9	877-859-8566	613-237-4856	
Better Business Bureau of El Paso			
720 Arizona Ave . . . . El Paso TX 79902	800-621-0508	915-577-0191	79
Better Business Bureau of Greater Iowa Quad Cities & Sioux Land Region			
2625 Beaver Ave . . . . Des Moines IA 50310	800-239-1642	515-243-8137	79
Better Business Bureau of Greater Kansas City			
8080 Ward Pkwy Ste 401 . . . . Kansas City MO 64114	877-606-0695	816-421-7800	79
Better Business Bureau of Greater Maryland			
502 S Sharp St Ste 1200 . . . . Baltimore MD 21201	800-579-6239	410-347-3990	79
Better Business Bureau of Heartland			
11811 P St . . . . Omaha NE 68137	800-649-6814	402-391-7612	79
Better Business Bureau of Kansas Inc			
11811 P St . . . . Omaha NE 68137	800-856-2417	402-391-7612	79
Better Business Bureau of Louisville Southern Indiana			
844 S Fourth St . . . . Louisville KY 40203	800-388-2222	502-583-6546	79
Better Business Bureau of Metro Washington DC & Eastern Pennsylvania			
1411 K St NW Ste 1000 . . . . Washington DC 20005	800-864-1224	202-393-8000	79
Better Business Bureau of Metropolitan Dallas & Northeast Texas			
1601 Elm St Ste 3838 . . . . Dallas TX 75201	800-444-0686	214-220-2000	79
Better Business Bureau of Metropolitan Houston			
1333 W Loop S Ste 1200 . . . . Houston TX 77027	800-876-7060	713-868-9500	79
Better Business Bureau of Middle Tennessee Inc			
201 Fourth Ave N Ste 100 . . . . Nashville TN 37219	800-615-9720	615-242-4222	79
Better Business Bureau of Minnesota & North Dakota			
220 River Ridge Cir S . . . . Burnsville MN 55337	800-646-6222	651-699-1111	79
Better Business Bureau of Northeast California			
3075 Beacon Blvd . . . . West Sacramento CA 95691	866-334-6272	916-443-6843	79
Better Business Bureau of Northeast Ohio			
2800 Euclid Ave 4th Fl . . . . Cleveland OH 44115	800-233-0361	216-241-7678	79
Better Business Bureau of Northern Colorado & East Central Wyoming			
8020 S County Rd 5 Ste 100 . . . . Fort Collins CO 80528	800-564-0371	970-484-1348	79
Better Business Bureau of Northern Indiana			
4011 Parnell Ave . . . . Fort Wayne IN 46805	800-552-4631	260-423-4433	79

Listing	City	State	ZIP	Toll-Free	Phone	Class
Better Business Bureau of Northwest Florida						
912 E Gadsden St	Pensacola	FL	32501	**800-729-9226**	850-429-0002	79
Better Business Bureau of Northwest North Carolina						
500 W Fifth St Ste 202	Winston-Salem	NC	27101	**800-777-8348**	336-725-8348	79
Better Business Bureau of Northwest Ohio & Southeast Michigan						
7668 King's Pt Rd	Toledo	OH	43617	**800-743-4222**	419-531-3116	79
Better Business Bureau of Saskatchewan						
980 Albert St	Regina	SK	S4R2P7	**888-352-7601**	306-352-7601	78
Better Business Bureau of South Texas						
1333 W Loop S Ste 1200	Houston	TX	77027	**800-705-3994**	713-868-9500	79
Better Business Bureau of Southeast Florida & the Caribbean						
4411 Beacon Cir Ste 4	West Palm Beach	FL	33407	**866-966-7226**	561-842-1918	79
Better Business Bureau of Southeast Tennessee & Northwest Georgia						
508 N Market St	Chattanooga	TN	37405	**800-548-4456**	423-266-6144	79
Better Business Bureau of Southeast Texas						
550 Fannin St Ste 100	Beaumont	TX	77701	**800-685-7650**	409-835-5348	79
Better Business Bureau of Southern Arizona						
434 S Williams Blvd Ste 102	Tucson	AZ	85711	**800-697-4733**	520-888-5353	79
Better Business Bureau of Southern Nevada						
6040 S Jones Blvd	Las Vegas	NV	89118	**800-449-8693**	702-320-4500	79
Better Business Bureau of Southern Piedmont Carolinas						
9719 Northeast Pkwy	Matthews	NC	28105	**800-432-1000**	704-927-8611	79
Better Business Bureau of Southwest Louisiana Inc						
2309 E Prien Lake Rd	Lake Charles	LA	70601	**800-542-7085**	337-478-6253	79
Better Business Bureau of the Abilene Area						
3300 S 14th St Ste 307	Abilene	TX	79605	**800-705-3994**	325-691-1533	79
Better Business Bureau of the Bakersfield Area						
1601 H St Ste 101	Bakersfield	CA	93301	**800-675-8118**	661-322-2074	79
Better Business Bureau of the Denver-Boulder Metro Area						
1020 Cherokee St	Denver	CO	80204	**800-356-6333**	303-758-2100	79
Better Business Bureau of the Mid-South						
3693 Tyndale Dr	Memphis	TN	38125	**800-222-8754**	901-759-1300	79
Better Business Bureau of the Texas Panhandle						
600 S Tyler Ste 1300	Amarillo	TX	79101	**800-621-0508**	806-379-6222	79
Better Business Bureau of the Tri-Parish Area						
801 Barrow St Ste 400	Houma	LA	70360	**800-533-5501**	985-868-3456	79
Better Business Bureau of Upstate New York						
100 Bryant Woods S	Amherst	NY	14228	**800-828-5000**	716-881-5222	79
Better Business Bureau of Utah						
5673 S Redwood Rd	Salt Lake City	UT	84123	**800-456-3907**	801-892-6009	79
Better Business Bureau of Vancouver Island						
220-1175 Cook St Ste 220	Victoria	BC	V8V4A1	**877-826-4222**	250-386-6348	78
Better Business Bureau of West Florida						
2655 McCormick Dr	Clearwater	FL	33759	**800-525-1447**	727-535-5522	79
Better Business Bureau of Western Pennsylvania						
400 Holiday Dr Ste 220	Pittsburgh	PA	15220	**877-267-5222**		79
Better Business Bureau Online						
Council of Better Business Bureaus, The						
4200 Wilson Blvd Ste 800	Arlington	VA	22203	**800-459-8875**	703-276-0100	79
Better Business Bureau Serving Central & Western MA & Northeastern CT						
400 Grove St	Worcester	MA	01605	**866-566-9222**	508-755-3340	
Better Business Bureau Serving Central California						
4201 W Shaw Ave Ste 107	Fresno	CA	93722	**800-675-8118**	559-222-8111	79
Better Business Bureau Serving Mainland British Columbia						
788 Beatty St Ste 404	Vancouver	BC	V6B2M1	**888-803-1222**	604-682-2711	78
Better Business Bureau Serving Western Ontario						
190 Wortley Rd Ste 206	London	ON	N6C4Y7	**877-283-9222**	519-673-3222	78
Better Business Bureau Serving Winnipeg & Manitoba						
1030B Empress St	Winnipeg	MB	R3G3H4	**800-385-3074**	204-989-9010	78
Better Hearing Institute (BHI)						
1444 I St NW Ste 700	Washington	DC	20005	**800-639-3884**	202-449-1100	48-17
Better Homes & Gardens Wood Magazine						
1716 Locust St	Des Moines	IA	50309	**800-374-9663**		455-14
Better Investing						
PO Box 220	Royal Oak	MI	48068	**877-275-6242**	248-583-6242	49-2
Better Label & Products Inc						
3333 Empire Blvd SW	Atlanta	GA	30354	**800-448-1813**	404-763-8440	623
Better Made Snack Foods Inc						
10148 Gratiot Ave	Detroit	MI	48213	**800-332-2394**	313-925-4774	296-35
Better Packages Inc						
255 Canal St PO Box 711	Shelton	CT	06484	**800-237-9151**	203-926-3700	111
Betts Industries Inc						
1800 Pennsylvania Ave W	Warren	PA	16365	**800-482-2678**	814-723-1250	591
Betty Dain Creations Inc						
9701 NW 112 Ave Ste 10	Miami	FL	33178	**800-327-5256***	305-769-3451	76
*General						
Beulah Heights University						
892 Berne St SE	Atlanta	GA	30316	**888-777-2422**	404-627-2681	161
Bevco Precision Manufacturing Co						
21320 Doral Rd	Waukesha	WI	53186	**800-864-2991**	262-798-9200	319-1
Bevco Sales International Inc						
9354 194 St	Surrey	BC	V4N4E9	**800-663-0090**	604-888-1455	357
Beverage Distributors Co						
14200 E Moncrieff Pl	Aurora	CO	80011	**888-262-9787***	303-371-3421	81-3
*General						
Beverage Marketing Corp						
850 Third Ave Ste 13C	New York	NY	10022	**800-275-4630**	212-688-7640	195
Beverage-Air Corp						
3779 Champion Blvd	Winston-Salem	NC	27105	**800-845-9800**	336-245-6400	660
Beverly Beach State Park						
198 NE 123rd St	Newport	OR	97365	**800-551-6949**		561
Beverly Hills Hotel						
9641 Sunset Blvd	Beverly Hills	CA	90210	**800-650-1842**	310-276-2251	378
Beverly Hills Plaza Hotel						
10300 Wilshire Blvd	Los Angeles	CA	90024	**800-800-1234**	310-275-5575	377
Beverly Hills Public Library						
444 N Rexford Dr	Beverly Hills	CA	90210	**800-238-0172**	310-288-2220	433-3
Beverly Hills Transfer & Storage Co						
15500 S Main St	Gardena	CA	90248	**800-999-7114**	310-532-1121	516
Beverly Hilton						
9876 Wilshire Blvd	Beverly Hills	CA	90210	**800-605-8896**	310-274-7777	378
Beverly Hospital						
309 W Beverly Blvd	Montebello	CA	90640	**800-618-6664**	323-726-1222	373-3
Beverly Wilshire - A Four Seasons Hotel						
9500 Wilshire Blvd	Beverly Hills	CA	90212	**800-545-4000**	310-275-5200	378
Beverly Wilshire, A Four Seasons Hotel						
9500 Wilshire Blvd	Beverly Hills	CA	90212	**800-545-4000**	310-275-5200	703

Listing	City	State	ZIP	Toll-Free	Phone	Class
Bevill State Community College						
2631 Temple Ave N	Fayette	AL	35555	**800-648-3271**	205-932-3221	162
Jasper						
1411 Indiana Ave	Jasper	AL	35501	**800-648-3271**	205-387-0511	162
Bexley Hall Seminary						
1407 E 60th St	Chicago	IL	60637	**800-275-8235**	773-380-6780	167-3
Beyer Blinder Belle						
120 Broadway 20th Fl	New York	NY	10271	**800-777-7892**	212-777-7800	
Beyond Components						
5 Carl Thompson Rd	Westford	MA	01886	**800-971-4242**		246
Beyond Digital Imaging						
36 Apple Creek Blvd	Markham	ON	L3R4Y4	**888-689-1888**	905-415-1888	697
Beyond Pesticides						
701 E St SE Ste 200	Washington	DC	20003	**866-260-6653**	202-543-5450	48-13
BFC 1051 N Kirk Rd	Batavia	IL	60510	**800-774-6840**	630-879-9240	623
BFG Supply Co LLC						
14500 Kinsman Rd PO Box 479	Burton	OH	44021	**800-883-0234**	440-834-1883	276
BFGoodrich Tires Inc						
PO Box 19001	Greenville	SC	29602	**877-788-8899**		750
BFMA (Business Forms Management Assn)						
3800 Old Cheney Rd Ste 101-285	Lincoln	NE	68516	**888-367-3078**		49-12
B&G Equipment Company Inc						
135 Region S Dr	Jackson	GA	30233	**800-544-8811**	678-688-5601	295
B-G Mechanical Service Inc						
12 Second Ave	Chicopee	MA	01020	**800-992-7386**	413-888-1500	189-10
BG Products Inc						
740 S Wichita St	Wichita	KS	67213	**800-961-6228**		537
BGA (Lincoln Botanical Garden & Arboretum)						
c/o Landscape Services						
1309 N 17th St	Lincoln	NE	68588	**800-742-8800**	402-472-2679	97
BGD Cos Inc						
5323 Lakeland Ave N	Minneapolis	MN	55429	**800-699-3537**	612-338-6804	319-1
BGF Industries Inc						
3802 Robert Porcher Way	Greensboro	NC	27410	**800-476-4845**	336-545-0011	740-3
BGS (Beta Gamma Sigma Inc)						
125 Weldon Pkwy	Maryland Heights	MO	63043	**800-337-4677**	314-432-5650	48-16
B-H Transfer Co						
750 Sparta Rd PO Box 151	Sandersville	GA	31082	**800-342-6462**	478-552-5119	447
BHHC (Berkshire Hathaway Homestates Cos)						
PO Box 2048	Omaha	NE	68103	**888-495-8949**		390-4
BHI (Better Hearing Institute)						
1444 I St NW Ste 700	Washington	DC	20005	**800-639-3884**	202-449-1100	48-17
BHK Securities LLC						
2200 Lakeshore Dr Ste 250	Birmingham	AL	35209	**888-529-2610**	205-322-2025	686
BHP Billiton Petroleum (Americas) Inc						
1360 Post Oak Blvd Ste 150	Houston	TX	77056	**800-359-1692**	713-961-8500	532
BI Inc						
6400 Lookout Rd	Boulder	CO	80301	**800-241-2911**	303-218-1000	688
BIA (Brick Industry Assn)						
12007 Sunrise Valley Dr Ste 430	Reston	VA	20191	**866-644-1293**	703-620-0010	49-18
BIA (Bureau of Indian Affairs Regional Offices)						
Alaska Region						
3601 C St Ste 1100	Anchorage	AK	99503	**800-645-8397**	907-271-4085	339-12
Biamp Systems Inc						
9300 SW Gemini Dr	Beaverton	OR	97008	**800-826-1457**		52
Bianchi Honda						
8430 Peach St	Erie	PA	16509	**866-979-8132**	814-864-5809	513
Bibbero Systems Inc						
1300 N McDowell Blvd	Petaluma	CA	94954	**800-242-2376**		623
Bibby Financial Services						
600 TownPark Ln Ste 450	Kennesaw	GA	30144	**877-882-4229**		272
Bible Broadcasting Network Inc						
11530 Carmel Commons Blvd						
PO Box 7300	Charlotte	NC	28226	**800-888-7077**	704-523-5555	639
Bible League						
3801 Eagle Nest Dr	Crete	IL	60417	**866-825-4636**		48-20
Biblical Archaeology Review						
4710 41st St NW	Washington	DC	20016	**800-221-4644**	202-364-3300	455-18
Biblical Theological Seminary						
200 N Main St	Hatfield	PA	19440	**800-235-4021**	215-368-5000	167-3
Bickel's Snack Foods						
1120 Zinns Quarry Rd	York	PA	17404	**800-233-1933**	717-843-0738	296-35
Bickford's Family Restaurants Inc						
37 Oak St Ext	Brockton	MA	02301	**800-969-5653**		666
Bicon LLC 501 Arborway	Boston	MA	02130	**800-882-4266**	617-524-4443	228
Bicycle Garage of Indy Inc						
4340 E 82nd St	Indianapolis	IN	46250	**800-238-7389**	317-842-4140	707
Bicycling Magazine						
400 S Tenth St	Emmaus	PA	18098	**800-666-2806**		455-14
Biddeford Blankets						
300 Terr Dr	Mundelein	IL	60060	**800-789-6441**		741
Biddle Precision Components Inc						
701 S Main St	Sheridan	IN	46069	**800-428-4387**	317-758-4451	617
BIDMC (Beth Israel Deaconess Medical Ctr)						
330 Brookline Ave	Boston	MA	02215	**800-667-5356**	617-667-7000	373-3
Bid-Well Corp						
PO Box 97	Canton	SD	57013	**800-843-9824**		190
Bieber Transportation Group						
320 Fair St PO Box 180	Kutztown	PA	19530	**800-243-2374**	610-683-7333	107
Bienville House Hotel						
320 Decatur St	New Orleans	LA	70130	**800-535-7836**	504-529-2345	378
Bierlein Cos Inc						
2000 Bay City Rd	Midland	MI	48642	**800-336-6626**	989-496-0066	189-16
Bierschbach Equipment & Supply Co						
PO Box 1444	Sioux Falls	SD	57101	**800-843-3707**	605-332-4466	191-1
BIG 100						
1801 Rockville Pk	Rockville	MD	20852	**800-493-1003**	240-747-2700	641
Big 5 Sporting Goods Corp						
2525 E El Segundo Blvd	El Segundo	CA	90245	**800-898-2994**	310-536-0611	707
NASDAQ: BGFV						
Big Apple Bagels						
500 Lake Cook Rd Ste 475	Deerfield	IL	60015	**800-251-6101**	847-948-7520	68
Big Apple Car Inc						
169 Bay 17th St	Brooklyn	NY	11214	**800-251-5001**	718-630-0040	314
Big Apple Circus (BAC)						
321 W 44th St Ste 400	New York	NY	10036	**888-541-3750**	212-257-2330	149
Big Bang ERP Inc						
105 De Louvain W	Montreal	QC	H2N1A3	**844-361-4408**	514-360-4408	196

Name / Address	Toll-Free	Phone	Class
Big Bend Community College 7662 Chanute St, Moses Lake WA 98837	877-745-1212	509-793-2222	162
Big Bend Electric Co-op 1373 N Hwy 261, Ritzville WA 99169	866-844-2363	509-659-1700	245
Big Bend Telephone Company Inc 808 N Fifth St, Alpine TX 79830	800-520-0092	844-592-4781	116
Big C Lumber Inc 50860 Princess Way PO Box 176, Granger IN 46530	888-297-0010	574-277-4550	191-3
Big Ceramic Store LLC 543 Vista Blvd, Sparks NV 89434	888-513-5303		
Big Country Electric Co-op 1010 W S First St PO Box 518, Roby TX 79543	888-662-2232	325-776-2244	245
Big Dogs 519 Lincoln County Pkwy, Lincolnton NC 28092	800-244-3647	828-695-2800	155-3
Big Five Tours & Expeditions 1551 SE Palm Ct, Stuart FL 34994	800-244-3483		755
Big Flat Electric Co-op Inc 333 S Seventh St, Malta MT 59538	800-242-2040	406-654-2040	245
Big Frey Promotional Products 420 Lake Cook Rd Ste 117, Deerfield IL 60015	800-888-1636		7
Big G Cereals PO Box 9452, Minneapolis MN 55440	800-248-7310		296-4
Big G Express Inc 190 Hawkins Dr, Shelbyville TN 37160	800-955-9140	800-684-9140	775
Big Horn County 420 W C St, Basin WY 82410	800-500-2324	307-568-2357	337
Big Horn Rural Electric Co-op 208 S Fifth St PO Box 270, Basin WY 82410	800-564-2419	307-568-2419	245
Big Kaiser Precision Tooling Inc 641 Fargo Ave, Elk Grove Village IL 60007	888-866-5776	847-228-7660	491
Big Lots Inc (BLI) 300 Phillipi Rd, Columbus OH 43228 NYSE: BIG	877-998-1697	614-278-6800	786
Big Mountain Imaging 4725 Copper Sage St, Las Vegas NV 89115	877-229-4030		
Big O Tires LLC 4280 Professional Center Dr Ste 400, Palm Beach Gardens FL 33410	866-834-2652		
Big Ridge State Park 1015 Big Ridge Rd, Maynardville TN 37807	800-471-5305	865-992-5523	561
Big River Zinc Corp 2401 Mississippi Ave, Sauget IL 62201	800-274-4002	618-274-5000	483
Big Rock Sports LLC 173 Hankison Dr, Newport NC 28570	800-334-2661	252-808-3500	706
Big Sandy Community & Technical College 1 Bert T Combs Dr, Prestonsburg KY 41653	888-641-4132	606-886-3863	162
Big Sandy Rural Electric Cooperative Corp 504 11th St, Paintsville KY 41240	888-789-7322	606-789-4095	245
Big Shoals State Park 11330 SE County Rd 135, White Springs FL 32096	877-635-3655	386-397-2733	561
Big Sky Resort 50 Big Sky Resort Rd, Big Sky MT 59716	800-548-4486	406-995-5000	665
Big Spring 215 W Third St PO Box 3359, Big Spring TX 79720	866-222-7100	432-264-6032	206
Big Stone Lake State Park 35889 Meadowbrook State Pk Rd, Ortonville MN 56278	888-646-6367	320-839-3663	561
Big Timberworks Inc 1 Rabel Ln, Gallatin Gateway MT 59730	800-763-4639	406-763-4639	286
Big Y Foods Inc 2145 Roosevelt Ave, Springfield MA 01102 *Cust Svc	800-828-2688*	413-784-0600	344
Bigbend Hospice 1723 Mahan Ctr Blvd, Tallahassee FL 32308	800-772-5862	850-878-5310	370
BigByte Corp 47400 Seabridge Dr, Fremont CA 94538	800-536-6425	510-249-1100	175
Bigelow Tea 201 Black Rock Tpke, Fairfield CT 06825	888-244-3569		296-40
Bigge Crane & Rigging Co 10700 Bigge Ave, San Leandro CA 94577	888-337-2444	510-277-4747	189-1
Biggers Chevrolet 1385 E Chicago St, Elgin IL 60120	866-431-1555	847-742-9000	57
BIGMPG Design/Marketing 811 E Vienna Ave, Milwaukee WI 53212	866-332-3919		5
Bigrentz Inc 1063 Mcgaw Ave Ste 200, Irvine CA 92614	855-999-5438	888-325-5172	23
BII (Burgess Industries Inc) 7500 Boone Ave N Ste 111, Brooklyn Park MN 55428	800-233-2589	763-553-7800	625
Bike Friday Travel Systems 3364 W 11th Ave, Eugene OR 97402	800-777-0258	541-687-0487	770
Bike USA Inc 2811 Brodhead Rd, Bethlehem PA 18020	800-225-2453		
Bilbrey Insurance Services Inc 5701 Greendale Rd, Johnston IA 50131	800-383-0116		389
Bilenky Cycle Works Inc 5319 N Second St, Philadelphia PA 19120	844-889-8823	215-329-4744	707
Bil-Jax Inc 125 Taylor Pkwy, Archbold OH 43502	800-537-0540	419-445-8915	489
Bill & Hillary Clinton National Airport 1 Airport Dr, Little Rock AR 72202	800-897-1910	501-372-3439	27
Bill & Melinda Gates Foundation PO Box 23350, Seattle WA 98102	800-728-3843	206-709-3100	305
Bill & Ralphs Inc 118 B & R Dr, Sarepta LA 71071	800-406-3045		
Bill Smith Auto Parts 400 Ash St Ste 100, Danville IL 61832	800-252-3005	217-442-0156	
Billings Area Chamber of Commerce 815 S 27th St, Billings MT 59101	855-328-9116	406-245-4111	139
Billings Clinic 2800 Tenth Ave N, Billings MT 59101	800-332-7156	406-238-2501	373-3
Billings Convention & Visitors Bureau 815 S 27th St PO Box 31177, Billings MT 59107	800-735-2635	406-245-4111	206
Billings Gazette 401 N 28th St, Billings MT 59101	800-543-2505	406-657-1200	528-2
Billows Electric Supply 9100 State Rd, Philadelphia PA 19136	866-398-1162	215-332-9700	246
Billpro Management Systems Inc 30575 Euclid Ave, Wickliffe OH 44092	800-736-0587	440-516-3776	177
Billy Graham Evangelistic Assn 1 Billy Graham Pkwy, Charlotte NC 28201	877-247-2426	704-401-3200	48-20
Biltmore Greensboro Hotel 111 W Washington St, Greensboro NC 27401 *General	800-332-0303*	336-272-3474	378
Biltmore Hotel & Conference Ctr of the Americas 1200 Anastasia Ave, Coral Gables FL 33134 *Cust Svc	800-727-1926*	855-311-6903	665
Biltmore Suites 205 W Madison St, Baltimore MD 21201	800-868-5064	410-728-6550	378
Biltrite Corp 51 Sawyer Rd, Waltham MA 02454	800-877-8775	781-647-1700	672
Bimbo Bakeries USA PO Box 976, Horsham PA 19044	800-984-0989		296-1
Bimeda-MTC Animal Health Inc 420 Beaverdale Rd, Cambridge ON N3C2W4	888-524-6332	519-654-8000	580
Binary Group Inc 4250 N Fairfax Dr Ste 600, Arlington VA 22203	855-424-6279	571-480-4444	
Bindagraphics Inc 2701 Wilmarco Ave, Baltimore MD 21223	800-326-0300	410-362-7200	92
Binder Metal Products Inc 14909 S Broadway, Gardena CA 90248	800-233-0896	323-321-4835	295
Binders 284 S Sharon Amity Rd, Charlotte NC 28211	888-472-6866	704-442-2608	539
Binghamton Knitting Co Inc 11 Alice St, Binghamton NY 13904	877-746-3368		155-15
Binghamton University 4400 Vestal Pkwy E, Binghamton NY 13902	800-782-0289	607-777-2000	166
Binion's Gambling Hall & Hotel 128 E Fremont St, Las Vegas NV 89101	800-937-6537	702-382-1600	133
Binovia Corp 3021 N 204th St, Omaha NE 68022	877-331-0282	402-331-0202	
Binswanger Glass 965 Ridge Lake Blvd Ste 305, Memphis TN 38120	800-365-9922		329
Bio Compression Systems Inc 120 W Commercial Ave, Moonachie NJ 07074	800-888-0908	201-939-0716	474
Bio Medic Data Systems Inc 1 Silas Rd, Seaford DE 19973	800-526-2637		84
Bio Medical Innovations 814 Airport Way, Sandpoint ID 83864	800-201-3958		250
Bio/Data Corp PO Box 347, Horsham PA 19044	800-257-3282	215-441-4000	418
Bioanalytical Systems Inc 2701 Kent Ave, West Lafayette IN 47906 NASDAQ: BASI	800-845-4246	765-463-4527	418
Bio-Botanica Inc 75 Commerce Dr, Hauppauge NY 11788	800-645-5720	631-231-5522	477
BioCardia Inc 125 Shoreway Rd Ste B, San Carlos CA 94070	800-624-1179	650-226-0120	474
Biocare Medical LLC 60 Berry Dr, Pacheco CA 94553	800-799-9499	925-603-8000	578
Biocell Laboratories Inc 2001 University Dr, Rancho Dominguez CA 90220	800-222-8382	310-537-3300	231
BioCryst Pharmaceuticals Inc 2190 Pkwy Lake Dr, Birmingham AL 35244 NASDAQ: BCRX	800-361-0912	205-444-4600	85
Biodex Medical Systems Inc 20 Ramsay Rd, Shirley NY 11967	800-224-6339	631-924-9000	474
Biofit Engineered Products 15500 Biofit Way, Bowling Green OH 43402	800-597-0246	419-823-1089	319-1
BioFlex Laser Therapy 411 Horner Ave, Etobicoke ON M8W4W3	888-557-4004	416-251-1055	474
Bioforest Technologies Inc 59 Industrial Park Crescent Unit 1, Sault Sainte Marie ON P6B5P3	888-236-7378	705-942-5824	
BioGenex Laboratories Inc 4600 Norris Canyon Rd, San Ramon CA 94583	800-421-4149	925-275-0550	231
Biohelix Corp 500 Cummings Ste 5550, Beverly MA 01915	800-874-1517	978-927-5056	231
BioHorizons Inc 2300 Riverchase Ctr, Birmingham AL 35244	888-246-8338	205-967-7880	475
Biola University 13800 Biola Ave, La Mirada CA 90639 *Admissions	800-652-4652*	562-903-6000	166
BioLase Inc 4 Cromwell, Irvine CA 92618	888-424-6527		423
BioLegend Inc 11080 Roselle St, San Diego CA 92121	877-246-5343	858-455-9588	664
bioLytical Laboratories Inc 1108 - 13351 Commerce Pkwy, Richmond BC V6V2X7	866-674-6784	604-204-6784	664
Biomerica Inc 1533 Monrovia Ave, Newport Beach CA 92663 OTC: BMRA ■ *Cust Svc	800-854-3002*	949-645-2111	231
BioMerieux Inc 595 Anglum Rd, Hazelwood MO 63042	800-634-7656	314-731-8500	474
Biomet Inc 56 E Bell Dr PO Box 587, Warsaw IN 46582	800-348-9500	574-267-6639	475
Biomet Microfixation Inc 1520 Tradeport Dr, Jacksonville FL 32218	800-874-7711	904-741-4400	474
Biomune Co 8906 Rosehill Rd, Lenexa KS 66215	800-999-0297	913-894-0230	580
Bionetics Corp, The 101 Production Dr Ste 100, Yorktown VA 23693	800-868-0330	757-873-0900	261
Bionostics Inc 7 Jackson Rd, Devens MA 01434 *General	800-776-3856*	978-772-7070	231
BIOPAC Systems Inc 42 Aero Camino, Goleta CA 93117	877-524-6722	805-685-0066	738
BioPro Inc 2929 Lapeer Rd, Port Huron MI 48060	800-252-7707	810-982-7777	475
Bioqual Corp 4 Research Ct, Rockville MD 20850	800-208-3149	240-404-7654	85
Bioquant Image Analysis Corp 5611 Ohio Ave, Nashville TN 37209	800-221-0549	615-350-7866	511
Bio-Rad Laboratories 1000 Alfred Nobel Dr, Hercules CA 94547 NYSE: BIO	800-424-6723	510-724-7000	231
Bio-Recovery Corp 1863 Pond Rd Ste 4, Ronkonkoma NY 11779	800-556-0621	888-609-5735	83

Name / Address	City	State	Zip	Toll-Free	Phone	Class
Bio-Reference Laboratories Inc						
481 Edward H Ross Dr	Elmwood Park	NJ	07407	**800-229-5227**		415
BioReliance Corp						
14920 Broschart Rd	Rockville	MD	20850	**800-553-5372**	301-738-1000	85
Bio-Research Products Inc						
323 W Cherry St	North Liberty	IA	52317	**800-326-3511**	319-626-2423	738
Bios Corp						
309 E Dewey Ave	Sapulpa	OK	74066	**888-920-3600**		
Biosafe Engineering						
5750 W 80th St	Indianapolis	IN	46278	**888-858-8099**	317-858-8099	111
Biosan Laboratories Inc						
1950 Tobsal Ct	Warren	MI	48091	**800-253-6800**	586-755-8970	738
Bio-Scene Recovery						
13191 Meadow St NE	Alliance	OH	44601	**877-380-5500**	330-823-5500	83
BioScrip						
1600 Broadway Ste 700	Denver	CO	80202	**877-409-2301**	720-697-5200	582
NASDAQ: BIOS						
Bioseal						
167 W Orangethorpe Ave	Placentia	CA	92870	**800-441-7325**	714-528-4695	474
Biosense Webster Inc						
3333 S Diamond Canyon Rd	Diamond Bar	CA	91765	**800-729-9010**	909-839-8500	474
Bio-Serv						
3 Foster Ln Ste 201	Flemington	NJ	08822	**800-996-9908**	908-284-2155	580
BioSpace Inc						
10506 Justin Dr	Urbandale	IA	50322	**888-246-7722**	877-277-7585	396
Biotechnology Industry Organization						
1201 Maryland Ave SW Ste 900	Washington	DC	20024	**866-356-5155**	202-962-9200	49-19
Biotechnology Software						
140 Huguenot St 3rd Fl	New Rochelle	NY	10801	**800-654-3237**	914-740-2100	527-3
BioTek Instruments Inc						
100 Tigan St PO Box 998	Winooski	VT	05404	**888-451-5171**	802-655-4040	418
Biothera Pharmaceuticals						
3388 Mike Collins Dr Ste A	Eagan	MN	55121	**877-699-5100**	651-675-0300	738
bioTheranostics Inc						
9640 Towne Centre Dr Ste 200	San Diego	CA	92121	**877-886-6739**		738
Bio-Tissue						
7000 SW 97th Ave Ste 211	Miami	FL	33173	**888-296-8858**		541
Biovet Inc						
4375 Ave Beaudry	Saint-Hyacinthe	QC	J2S8W2	**888-824-6838**	450-771-7291	580
Biovet USA Inc						
1502 E 122nd St	Burnsville	MN	55337	**877-824-6838**	952-884-3113	580
BioZyme Inc						
6010 Stockyards Expy	Saint Joseph	MO	64504	**800-821-3070**	816-238-3326	445
Birch Communications						
2300 Main St Ste 340	Kansas City	MO	64108	**866-424-5100**	816-300-3000	731
Birch Hill Investment Advisors LLC						
24 Federal St 10th Fl	Boston	MA	02110	**800-441-3453**	617-502-8300	400
Birchwood automative group						
35D-3965 Portage Ave	Winnipeg	MB	R3K2H7	**866-990-6237**	204-831-4214	
Birchwood Laboratories Inc						
7900 Fuller Rd	Eden Prairie	MN	55344	**800-328-6156**	952-937-7900	145
Bird Electronic Corp						
30303 Aurora Rd	Solon	OH	44139	**866-695-4569**	440-248-1200	248
Bird Precision						
1 Spruce St PO Box 540569	Waltham	MA	02454	**800-454-7369***		616
*Cust Svc						
Bird Solutions International						
1338 N Melrose Dr Ste H	Vista	CA	92083	**800-210-9514**	760-758-9747	573
Bird Studies Canada						
115 Front St PO Box 160	Port Rowan	ON	N0E1M0	**888-448-2473**	519-586-3531	48-3
Bird Technologies Group Inc						
30303 Aurora Rd	Solon	OH	44139	**866-695-4569**	440-248-1200	248
Birdair Inc						
65 Lawrence Bell Dr Ste 100	Amherst	NY	14221	**800-622-2246**	716-633-9500	189-12
Birdie Golf Balls Golf Equipment						
208 Margate Ct	Margate	FL	33063	**800-333-7271**	954-973-2741	707
Birds & Blooms						
5400 S 60th St	Greendale	WI	53129	**888-860-8040**		455-14
BirdWatching Magazine						
25 Braintree Hill Office Pk Ste 404	Braintree	MA	02184	**877-252-8141**		455-14
Birks						
1240 du Sq-Phillips St	Montreal	QC	H3B3H4	**800-758-2511**		409
Birmingham Board of Education (BCS)						
2015 Park Place North	Birmingham	AL	35203	**800-628-6673**	205-231-4600	681
Birmingham Civil Rights Institute						
1720 University Blvd	Birmingham	AL	35203	**866-328-9696**	205-328-9696	517
Birmingham International Forest Products LLC						
300 Riverhills Business Pk	Birmingham	AL	35242	**800-767-2437**	205-972-1500	191-3
Birmingham News						
1731 First Ave N	Birmingham	AL	35203	**800-568-4123**	205-325-4444	528-2
Birmingham Race Course						
1000 John Rogers Dr	Birmingham	AL	35210	**800-998-8238**	205-838-7500	133
Birmingham Rail & Locomotive Company Inc						
PO Box 530157	Birmingham	AL	35253	**800-241-2260**	205-424-7245	765
Birmingham Vending Co						
540 Second Ave N	Birmingham	AL	35204	**800-288-7635**	205-324-7526	55
Birmingham-Southern College						
900 Arkadelphia Rd	Birmingham	AL	35254	**800-523-5793**	205-226-4600	166
Birnbaum Interpreting Services						
8730 Georgia Ave Ste 210	Silver Spring	MD	20910	**800-471-6441**	301-587-8885	763
Birner Dental Management Services Inc						
1777 S Harrison St Ste 1400	Denver	CO	80210	**877-898-1083**	303-691-0680	461
Birnie Bus Service Inc						
248 Otis St	Rome	NY	13441	**800-734-3950**	315-336-3950	109
Birthday Direct						
120 Commerce St	Muscle Shoals	AL	35661	**888-491-9185**	256-381-0310	292
Birthday In A Box Inc						
7951 Cessna Ave	Gaithersburg	MD	20879	**800-237-6545**		195
Biscayne Rod Manufacturing Inc						
425 E Ninth St	Hialeah	FL	33010	**866-969-0808**	305-884-0808	706
Bischoff Insurance Agency Inc						
1300 Oakridge Dr Ste 100	Fort Collins	CO	80525	**888-229-5558**	970-223-9400	389
Bisco Dental Products (Canada) Inc						
2571 Smith St	Richmond	BC	V6X2J1	**800-667-8811**	604-276-8662	473
Bisco Industries Inc						
1500 N Lakeview Ave	Anaheim	CA	92807	**800-323-1232**		246

Name / Address	City	State	Zip	Toll-Free	Phone	Class
Biscom Inc						
321 Billerica Rd	Chelmsford	MA	01824	**800-477-2472**	978-250-1800	173-3
Bishop Distributing Co						
5200 36th St SE	Grand Rapids	MI	49512	**800-748-0363***		360
*Cust Svc						
Bishop State Community College						
351 N Broad St	Mobile	AL	36603	**800-523-7000**	251-405-7000	162
Bishop's College School						
80 chemin Moulton Hill	Sherbrooke	QC	J1M1Z8	**877-570-7542**	819-566-0227	618
Bishop-Wisecarver Corp						
2104 Martin Way	Pittsburg	CA	94565	**888-580-8272**	925-439-8272	616
Bismarck Expressway Suites						
180 E Bismarck Expy	Bismarck	ND	58504	**888-774-5566**	701-222-3311	378
Bismarck State College						
1500 Edwards Ave	Bismarck	ND	58501	**800-445-5073**	701-224-5400	162
Bismarck Tribune						
707 E Front Ave	Bismarck	ND	58504	**866-476-5348**	701-223-2500	528-2
Bismarck-Mandan Convention & Visitors Bureau						
1600 Burnt Boat Dr	Bismarck	ND	58503	**800-767-3555**	701-222-4308	206
Bison Gear & Engineering Corp						
3850 Ohio Ave	Saint Charles	IL	60174	**800-282-4766**	630-377-4327	705
Bison Inc 603 L St	Lincoln	NE	68508	**800-247-7668**	402-474-3353	706
Bisque Imports						
1 Belmont Ave	Belmont	NC	28012	**888-568-5991**	704-829-9290	360
Bissell Inc						
2345 Walker NW	Grand Rapids	MI	49544	**800-237-7691**	616-453-4451	783
BITCO Insurance Cos						
3700 Market Square Cir	Davenport	IA	52807	**800-475-4477**		390-4
Bitterman Scales LLC						
413 Radcliff Rd	Willow Street	PA	17584	**877-464-3009**	717-464-3009	361
Bix Beiderbecke Memorial Society						
PO Box 3688	Davenport	IA	52808	**888-249-5487**	563-324-7170	48-4
Bix Produce Co						
1415 L'Orient St	Saint Paul	MN	55117	**800-642-9514**	651-487-8000	297-7
Bixby Knolls Towers						
3737 Atlantic Ave	Long Beach	CA	90807	**800-545-1833**	562-426-6123	668
Bixel & Co						
8721 Sunset Blvd Ste 101	Los Angeles	CA	90069	**855-854-9830**	310-854-3828	184
Bizco Technologies Inc						
7950 "O" St	Lincoln	NE	68510	**800-424-9677**		
BIZDOC Capital Group						
5024 Night Hawk Dr NE	Rio Rancho	NM	87144	**844-249-3621**		461
BizLand Inc						
70 BlanchaRd Rd	Burlington	MA	01803	**800-249-5263**		39
Bizlink Technology Inc						
3400 Gateway Blvd	Fremont	CA	94538	**800-326-4193**	510-252-0786	810
BizQuest						
101 California St 43rd Fl	San Francisco	CA	94111	**844-495-3091***	888-280-3815	392
*Advertising						
BL Co						
355 Research Pkwy	Meriden	CT	06450	**800-301-3077**	203-630-1406	261
B&L Pipeco Services						
20465 SH 249 Ste 200	Houston	TX	77070	**800-927-4732**	281-955-3500	
Blach Distributing Co						
131 W Main St	Elko	NV	89801	**800-310-5099**	775-738-7111	81-1
Blachly-Lane Inc						
PO Box 70	Junction City	OR	97448	**800-446-8418**	541-688-8711	245
Black Bart International LLC						
155 E Blue Heron Blvd Ste R2	Riviera Beach	FL	33404	**866-289-7050**	561-842-4550	707
Black Bear Casino Resort						
1785 Hwy 210 PO Box 777	Carlton	MN	55718	**888-771-0777**	218-878-2327	133
Black Box Corp						
1000 Pk Dr	Lawrence	PA	15055	**877-877-2269**		176
NASDAQ: BBOX						
Black Butte Ranch						
12930 Hawks BeaRd Rd PO Box 8000	Black Butte Ranch	OR	97759	**866-901-2961**	541-595-1252	665
Black Enterprise Magazine						
130 Fifth Ave	New York	NY	10011	**800-727-7777***	212-242-8000	455-5
*Cust Svc						
Black Equipment Co Inc						
1187 Burch Dr	Evansville	IN	47725	**866-414-7062**	812-477-6481	
Black Forest Decor LLC						
PO Box 297	Jenks	OK	74037	**800-605-0915**		786
Black Hat						
1932 First Ave Ste 204	Seattle	WA	98101	**866-203-8081**	206-443-5489	688
Black Hawk College						
East						
1501 State Hwy 78	Kewanee	IL	61443	**800-233-5671**	309-852-5671	162
Quad Cities						
6600 34th Ave	Moline	IL	61265	**800-334-1311**	309-796-5000	162
Black Hills Bentonite						
PO Box 9	Mills	WY	82644	**800-700-8666***	307-265-3740	501-2
*Orders						
Black Hills Caverns						
2600 Cavern Rd	Rapid City	SD	57702	**800-837-9358**	605-343-0542	50-5
Black Hills Corp						
625 Ninth St	Rapid City	SD	57701	**866-264-8003**	605-721-1700	359-5
NYSE: BKH						
Black Hills Electric Co-op						
25191 Co-op Way PO Box 792	Custer	SD	57730	**800-742-0085**	605-673-4461	245
Black Hills Health & Education Ctr						
13815 Battle Creek Rd PO Box 19	Hermosa	SD	57744	**866-757-0160***	605-255-4101	702
*Cust Svc						
Black Hills State University						
1200 University St Unit 9502	Spearfish	SD	57799	**800-255-2478**	605-642-6343	166
Black Mesa Casino						
25 Hagon Rd	Algodones	NM	87001	**877-529-2946**	505-867-6700	450
Black Mountain Ranch						
4000 Conger Mesa Rd	McCoy	CO	80463	**800-967-2401**	970-653-4226	239
Black Mountain-Swannanoa Chamber of Commerce						
201 E State St	Black Mountain	NC	28711	**800-669-2301**	828-669-2300	139
Black Radio Network						
375 Fifth Ave	New York	NY	10016	**866-342-6892**	212-686-6850	640
Black River Electric Co-op						
2600 Hwy 67 PO Box 31	Fredericktown	MO	63645	**800-392-4711**	573-783-3381	245

Name / Address	City	State	ZIP	Toll-Free	Phone	Class
Black River Electric Cooperative Inc						
1121 N Pike Rd W	Sumter	SC	29153	**866-731-2732**	803-469-8060	
Black River State Forest						
W10325 Hwy 12	Black River	WI	54615	**888-936-7463**		561
Black River Technical College						
1410 Hwy 304 E	Pocahontas	AR	72455	**866-890-6933**	870-248-4000	162
Blackbaud Inc						
2000 Daniel Island Dr	Charleston	SC	29492	**800-468-8996**	843-216-6200	178-1
NASDAQ: BLKB						
Blackboard Inc						
1899 L St NW 5th Fl	Washington	DC	20036	**800-424-9299**	202-463-4860	178-3
Blackbourn						
200 Fourth Ave N	Edgerton	MN	56128	**800-842-7550**		86
Blackburn College						
700 College Ave	Carlinville	IL	62626	**800-233-3550**		166
Blackburn Correctional Complex						
3111 Spurr Rd	Lexington	KY	40511	**800-808-1213**	859-246-2366	213
Blackburn's Physicians Pharmacy Inc						
301 Corbet St	Tarentum	PA	15084	**800-472-2440**	724-224-9100	474
Blackcomb Helicopters						
9960 Heliport Rd	Whistler	BC	V0N1B0	**800-330-4354**	604-938-1700	
Blackfoot Inn						
5940 Blackfoot Trl SE	Calgary	AB	T2H2B5	**800-661-1151**	403-252-2253	378
Blackhawk Bank						
400 Broad St PO Box 719	Beloit	WI	53511	**888-769-2600**	608-364-8911	69
Blackhawk Technical College						
6004 S County Rd G	Janesville	WI	53546	**800-498-1282**	608-758-6900	795
Blackledge Furniture						
233 SW Second St	Corvallis	OR	97333	**800-782-4851**	541-753-4851	321
Blacklion International Inc						
10635 Park Rd	Charlotte	NC	28210	**866-466-5466**		
Blackmer						
1809 Century Ave	Grand Rapids	MI	49503	**888-363-7886**	616-241-1611	637
Blackmore Company Inc						
10800 Blackmore Ave	Belleville	MI	48111	**800-874-8660**	734-483-8661	604
Blackstone Industries Inc						
16 Stoney Hill Rd	Bethel	CT	06801	**800-272-2885**	203-792-8622	754
Blackstone Valley Chamber of Commerce						
110 Church St	Whitinsville	MA	01588	**800-841-0919**	508-234-9090	139
Blackwell, The						
2110 Tuttle Pk Pl	Columbus	OH	43210	**866-247-4003**	614-247-4000	378
Blade						
541 N Superior St	Toledo	OH	43660	**800-245-3317**	419-724-6000	528-2
Blade Creative Branding Inc						
15 Gervais Dr Ste 103	Toronto	ON	M3C1Y8	**800-392-5233**	416-467-4770	7
Blade Energy Partners Ltd						
2600 Network Blvd Ste 550	Frisco	TX	75034	**800-849-1545**	972-712-8407	192
Blade-Tech Industries Inc						
5530 184th St E	Puyallup	WA	98375	**877-331-5793**	253-655-8059	707
Blain Supply Inc						
3507 E Racine St	Janesville	WI	53547	**800-210-2370**	608-754-2821	274
Blaine County						
145 Lincoln Ave	Brewster	NE	68821	**800-657-2113**	308-547-2222	337
Blaine County						
420 Ohio St	Chinook	MT	59523	**800-666-6124**	406-442-9830	337
Blaine Tech Services Inc						
1680 Rogers Ave	San Jose	CA	95112	**800-545-7558**	408-573-0555	194
Blaine's Art Supply						
1025 Photo Ave	Anchorage	AK	99503	**866-561-4278**	907-561-5344	45
Blair Cedar & Novelty Works Inc						
680 W US Hwy 54	Camdenton	MO	65020	**800-325-3943**	573-346-2235	328
Blair Rubber Co						
5020 Panther Pkwy	Seville	OH	44273	**800-321-5583**		131
Blake Medical Ctr						
2020 59th St W	Bradenton	FL	34209	**800-523-5827**	941-792-6611	373-3
Blakely Construction Company Inc						
2830 W I-20	Odessa	TX	79763	**800-604-9339**	432-381-3540	535
Blakely New York						
136 W 55th St	New York	NY	10019	**800-735-0710**	212-245-1800	378
Blanchard Compact Equipment						
1410 Ashville Hwy	Spartanburg	SC	29303	**888-799-3606**	864-582-1245	274
Blanco America Inc						
110 Mt Holly By-Pass	Lumberton	NJ	08048	**800-451-5782**		361
Bland County						
612 Main St Ste 104	Bland	VA	24315	**800-519-3468**	276-688-4622	337
Bland Farms Inc						
1126 Raymond Bland Rd	Glennville	GA	30427	**800-440-9543**		
Blank Quilting Corp						
Blank Quilting						
49 W 37th St 14th Fl	New York	NY	10018	**800-294-9495**		590
Blank Rome LLP						
1 Logan Sq 130 N 18th St	Philadelphia	PA	19103	**800-973-1177**	215-569-5500	427
Blanks/USA Inc						
7700 68th Ave N #7	Minneapolis	MN	55428	**800-328-7311**		556
Blantyre						
16 Blantyre Rd PO Box 995	Lenox	MA	01240	**844-881-0104**	413-637-3556	378
Blasingame, Burch, Garrard & Ashley PC						
440 College Ave Ste 320	Athens	GA	30601	**866-354-3544**	706-608-8212	427
Blast Advanced Media						
950 Reserve Dr Ste 150	Roseville	CA	95678	**888-252-7866**	916-724-6701	180
Blast Radius						
509 Richards St	Vancouver	BC	?V6B2Z6	**866-473-6800**	604-647-6500	7
Blauer Mfg Co Inc						
20 Aberdeen St	Boston	MA	02215	**800-225-6715**	617-536-6606	155-18
Blax Inc						
9861 Colbert	Montreal	QC	H1J1Z9	**888-523-2529**	514-523-4600	
Blaylock Oil Company Inc						
724 S Flagler Ave	Homestead	FL	33030	**877-944-4262**	305-247-7249	
Blazer Industries Inc						
PO Box 489	Aumsville	OR	97325	**877-211-3437**	503-749-1900	106
Blenko Glass Co						
PO Box 67	Milton	WV	25541	**877-425-3656**	304-743-9081	333
Blessing Health System						
Broadway at 11th St	Quincy	IL	62301	**866-460-3933**	217-223-8400	373-3
BlessingWhite						
200 Clocktower Dr	Hamilton	NJ	08690	**800-222-1349**	609-528-3535	
Bleyhl Farm Service Inc						
940 E Wine Country Rd	Grandview	WA	98930	**800-862-6806***	509-882-2248	276
*Cust Svc						
BLI (Bulk Lift International Inc)						
1013 Tamarac Dr	Carpentersville	IL	60110	**800-879-2247**	847-428-6059	67
BLI (Big Lots Inc)						
300 Phillipi Rd	Columbus	OH	43228	**877-998-1697**	614-278-6800	786
NYSE: BIG						
Blish-Mize Co						
223 S Fifth St	Atchison	KS	66002	**800-995-0525**	913-367-1250	350
Bliss Clearing Niagara (BCN)						
1004 E State St	Hastings	MI	49058	**800-642-5477**	269-948-3300	454
Bliss Direct Media						
641 15th Ave NE	Saint Joseph	MN	56374	**800-578-7947**	320-271-1600	386
Blissfield Manufacturing Co						
626 Depot St	Blissfield	MI	49228	**800-626-1772***	517-486-2121	14
*Cust Svc						
Blistex Inc						
1800 Swift Dr	Oak Brook	IL	60523	**800-837-1800***	630-571-2870	578
*Cust Svc						
Blitt & Gaines PC						
661 Glenn Ave	Wheeling	IL	60090	**888-920-0620**	847-403-4900	427
Blizzard Internet Marketing Inc						
1001 Grand Ave Ste 005	Glenwood Springs	CO	81601	**888-840-5893**	970-928-7875	225
Bloch Industries						
140 Commerce Dr	Rochester	NY	14623	**800-499-7871**	585-334-9600	115
Block & Co						
1111 S Wheeling Rd	Wheeling	IL	60090	**800-323-7556**		
Block Scientific Inc						
22 Sawgrass Dr	Bellport	NY	11713	**866-203-5777**	631-589-1118	
Blocker & Wallace Service LLC						
1472 Rogers Ave	Memphis	TN	38114	**800-843-0551**	901-274-0708	786
Blodgett Supply Co Inc						
100 Ave D PO Box 759	Williston	VT	05495	**888-888-3424**	802-864-9831	38
Blommer Chocolate Co						
600 W Kinzie St	Chicago	IL	60610	**800-621-1606**	312-226-7700	296-8
Blonder Tongue Laboratories Inc						
1 Jake Brown Rd	Old Bridge	NJ	08857	**877-407-8033**	732-679-4000	643
NYSE: BDR						
Blood Assurance Inc						
705 E Fourth St	Chattanooga	TN	37403	**800-962-0628**	423-756-0966	89
Blood Bank of Delmarva						
100 Hygeia Dr	Newark	DE	19713	**800-548-4009**	302-737-8405	89
Blood Bank of Hawaii						
2043 Dillingham Blvd	Honolulu	HI	96819	**800-372-9966**	808-845-9966	89
Blood Centers of the Pacific						
250 Bush St Ste 136	San Francisco	CA	94104	**888-393-4483**	415-567-6400	89
Blood Ctr, The						
2609 Canal St	New Orleans	LA	70119	**800-862-5663**	504-524-1322	89
Blood Donor Ctr at Presbyterian/St Luke's Medical Ctr						
1719 E 19th Ave	Denver	CO	80218	**800-231-2222**	303-839-6000	764
BloodCenter of Wisconsin						
638 N 18th St	Milwaukee	WI	53233	**877-232-4376**	414-933-5000	89
Blood-Horse Magazine						
PO Box 911088	Lexington	KY	40591	**800-866-2361**	859-278-2361	455-14
BloodSource						
1608 Q St	Sacramento	CA	95811	**800-995-4420**	916-456-1500	89
Bloodworks Northwest						
921 Terry Ave	Seattle	WA	98104	**800-366-2831**	206-292-6500	89
Bloomberg BNA						
1801 S Bell St	Arlington	VA	22022	**800-960-1220**	703-341-5777	527-7
Bloomfield College						
467 Franklin St	Bloomfield	NJ	07003	**800-848-4555**	973-748-9000	166
Bloomfield Township Public Library						
1099 Lone Pine Rd	Bloomfield Hills	MI	48302	**800-318-2596**	248-642-5800	433-3
Bloomington Convention & Visitors Bureau (BCVB)						
7900 International Dr						
Ste 990	Bloomington	MN	55425	**800-346-4289**	952-858-8500	206
Bloomington/Monroe County Convention & Visitors Bureau						
2855 N Walnut St	Bloomington	IN	47404	**800-800-0037**	812-334-8900	206
Bloomington-Normal Area Convention & Visitors Bureau						
3201 CIRA Dr Ste 201	Bloomington	IL	61704	**800-433-8226**	309-665-0033	206
BloomNation LLC						
8889 W Olympic Blvd	Beverly Hills	CA	90211	**877-702-5666**	210-405-5050	292
BloomNet Inc						
1 Old Country Rd Ste 500	Carle Place	NY	11514	**866-256-6663**		386
Bloomsburg Carpet Industries Inc						
4999 Columbia Blvd	Bloomsburg	PA	17815	**800-233-8773**	570-784-9188	131
Bloomsburg University						
400 E Second St	Bloomsburg	PA	17815	**888-651-6117**	570-389-3900	166
Blossman Gas Inc						
4601 Hanshaw Rd	Ocean Springs	MS	39564	**800-256-7762**	228-872-8747	316
Blough Tech Inc						
119 S Broad St	Cairo	GA	39828	**800-957-0554**	229-377-8825	180
Blount Memorial Hospital						
907 E Lamar Alexander Pkwy	Maryville	TN	37804	**800-448-0219**	865-983-7211	373-3
Blount Seafood Corp						
630 Currant Rd	Fall River	MA	02720	**800-274-2526***	774-888-1300	296-14
*Hotline						
Blount Small Ship Adventures						
461 Water St	Warren	RI	02885	**800-556-7450**	401-247-0955	220
Blower Application Company Inc						
N 114 W 19125 Clinton Dr	Germantown	WI	53022	**800-959-0880**	262-255-5580	385
Blowfish Direct LLC						
6160 Bristol Pkwy Ste 100	Culver City	CA	90230	**877-725-6934**	310-566-5700	686
Blowing Rock Chamber of Commerce						
PO Box 406	Blowing Rock	NC	28605	**877-750-4636**	828-295-7851	139
BLR (Business & Legal Reports Inc)						
141 Mill Rock Rd E	Old Saybrook	CT	06475	**800-727-5257**	860-510-0100	633-9
Blue Bird Inc						
10135 Mill Rd	Peshastin	WA	98847	**800-828-4106**	509-548-1700	315-3
Blue Care Network of Michigan						
20500 Civic Ctr Dr	Southfield	MI	48076	**800-662-6667**		390-3
Blue Chip Casino Inc						
777 Blue Chip Dr	Michigan City	IN	46360	**888-879-7711**	219-879-7711	133
Blue Chip Computer Systems						
2554 Lincoln Blvd Ste 232	Venice	CA	90291	**800-325-9868**	310-410-0126	
Blue Cross & Blue Shield Assn						
225 N Michigan Ave	Chicago	IL	60601	**888-630-2583**	312-297-6000	49-9

	Toll-Free	Phone	Class
Blue Cross & Blue Shield of Alabama			
450 Riverchase Pkwy E ....Birmingham AL 35244	800-292-8868	205-988-2200	390-3
Blue Cross & Blue Shield of Kansas City			
2301 Main St ....Kansas City MO 64108	800-892-6048	816-395-2222	390-3
Blue Cross & Blue Shield of Michigan			
600 Lafayette Blvd E ....Detroit MI 48226	855-237-3501	313-225-9000	390-3
Blue Cross & Blue Shield of Mississippi			
PO Box 1043 ....Jackson MS 39215	800-222-8046	601-932-3704	390-3
Blue Cross & Blue Shield of Montana			
560 N Park Ave PO Box 4309 ......Helena MT 59604	800-447-7828	406-437-5000	390-3
Blue Cross & Blue Shield of Nebraska			
1919 Aksarben Dr PO Box 3248.....Omaha NE 68180	800-422-2763	402-982-7000	390-3
Blue Cross & Blue Shield of New Mexico			
PO Box 27630 ....Albuquerque NM 87125	800-835-8699	505-291-3500	390-3
Blue Cross & Blue Shield of North Carolina			
1965 Ivory Creek Blvd			
PO Box 2291...............Durham NC 27707	800-446-8053*	919-489-7431	390-3
*Cust Svc			
Blue Cross & Blue Shield of Oklahoma			
1215 S Boulder Ave ....Tulsa OK 74119	800-942-5837*	918-560-3500	390-3
*Cust Svc			
Blue Cross & Blue Shield of Rhode Island			
500 Exchange St ....Providence RI 02903	800-637-3718	401-459-1000	390-3
Blue Cross & Blue Shield of Texas Inc			
1001 E Lookout Dr ....Richardson TX 75082	800-521-2227	972-766-6900	390-3
Blue Cross & Blue Shield of Vermont			
445 Industrial Ln ....Montpelier VT 05602	800-247-2583*	802-223-6131	390-3
*Cust Svc			
Blue Cross Blue Shield of Arizona			
2444 W Las Palmaritas Dr ....Phoenix AZ 85021	800-232-2345	602-864-4400	390-3
Blue Cross Blue Shield of Delaware			
PO Box 1991 ....Wilmington DE 19899	800-572-4400	800-876-7639	390-3
Blue Cross Blue Shield of Georgia			
3350 Peachtree Rd NE ....Atlanta GA 30326	800-441-2273*	404-842-8000	390-3
*Cust Svc			
Blue Cross Blue Shield of Illinois			
300 E Randolph St ....Chicago IL 60601	800-972-8382	312-653-6000	390-3
Blue Cross Blue Shield of Kansas			
1133 SW Topeka Blvd ....Topeka KS 66629	800-432-0216	785-291-7000	390-3
Blue Cross Blue Shield of Louisiana			
5525 Reitz Ave ....Baton Rouge LA 70898	800-599-2583	800-495-2583	390-3
Blue Cross Blue Shield of Massachusetts			
401 Pk Dr ....Boston MA 02215	800-262-2583	617-246-5000	390-3
Blue Cross Blue Shield of North Dakota			
4510 13th Ave S ....Fargo ND 58121	800-342-4718	701-282-1864	390-3
Blue Cross Blue Shield of Wyoming			
4000 House Ave ....Cheyenne WY 82001	800-851-9145	307-634-1393	390-3
Blue Cross of California			
2 Gannett Dr ....South Portland ME 04106	800-999-3643	855-636-6136	390-3
Blue Cross of Idaho			
3000 E Pine Ave ....Meridian ID 83642	800-274-4018	208-345-4550	390-3
Blue Fountain Media Inc			
102 Madison Ave 2nd Fl.......New York NY 10016	800-278-0816	212-260-1978	225
Blue Generation Div of M Rubin & Sons Inc			
34-01 38th Ave ....Long Island NY 11101	888-336-4687		155-18
Blue Giant Equipment Corp			
85 Heart Lake Rd S ....Brampton ON L6W3K2	800-668-7078	905-457-3900	357
Blue Granite Inc			
2750 Old Centre Rd Ste 150...........Portage MI 49024	877-817-0736		180
Blue Grass Airport			
4000 Terminal Dr ....Lexington KY 40510	800-800-4000	859-425-3100	27
Blue Grass Energy Co-op Corp			
1201 Lexington Rd ....Nicholasville KY 40356	888-546-4243	859-885-4191	245
Blue Grass Regional Library			
104 E Sixth St ....Columbia TN 38401	888-345-5575	931-388-9282	433-3
Blue Grass Regional Mental Health-Mental Retardation Board Inc			
1351 Newtown Pk Bldg 1 ....Lexington KY 40511	800-928-8000	859-253-1686	48-6
Blue Grass Stockyard			
1274 HWY 90 W PO Box 980...........Albany KY 42602	800-621-3972	606-387-4681	444
Blue Horizon Hotel			
1225 Robson St ....Vancouver BC V6E1C3	800-663-1333	604-688-1411	378
Blue Lakes Charters & Tours			
12154 N Saginaw Rd ....Clio MI 48420	800-282-4287	810-686-4287	107
Blue Lance Inc			
410 Pierce St ....Houston TX 77002	800-856-2583	713-255-4800	178-12
Blue Licks Battlefield State Resort Park			
10299 Maysville Rd ....Carlisle KY 40311	800-443-7008	859-289-5507	561
Blue Moon Hotel			
944 Collins Ave ....Miami Beach FL 33139	800-553-7739	305-673-2262	378
Blue Mounds State Park			
1410 161st St ....Luverne MN 56156	888-646-6367	507-283-6050	561
Blue Mountain Air Inc			
707 Aldridge Rd ....Vacaville CA 95688	800-889-2085		606
Blue Mountain Arts Inc			
PO Box 4549 ....Boulder CO 80306	800-545-8573*	303-449-0536	130
*Sales			
Blue Mountain College			
PO Box 160 ....Blue Mountain MS 38610	800-235-0136	662-685-4771	166
Blue Mountain Community College			
2411 NW Carden Ave PO Box 100 .....Pendleton OR 97801	888-441-7232	541-276-1260	162
Blue Mountain Quality Resources Inc			
475 Rolling Ridge Dr			
Ste 200.................State College PA 16801	800-982-2388	814-234-2417	177
Blue Nile Inc			
705 Fifth Ave S Ste 900 ....Seattle WA 98104	800-242-2728	206-336-6700	409
NASDAQ: NILE			
Blue Pillar Inc			
9025 N River Rd Ste 150 ....Indianapolis IN 46240	888-234-3212		192
Blue Quill Angler Inc			
1532 Bergen Pkwy ....Evergreen CO 80439	800-435-5353	303-674-4700	707
Blue Ribbon Home Warranty Inc			
95 S Wadsworth Blvd ....Lakewood CO 80226	800-571-0475	303-986-3900	366
Blue Ribbon Tag & Label Corp			
4035 N 29th Ave ....Hollywood FL 33020	800-433-4974	954-922-9292	412
Blue Ribbon Travel-american			
3601 W 76th St Ste 190 ....Minneapolis MN 55435	800-626-5309	952-835-2724	770
Blue Ridge Bank & Trust Co			
4240 Blue Ridge Blvd			
Ste 100................Kansas City MO 64133	800-569-4287	816-358-5000	70
Blue Ridge Community College			
1 College Ln PO Box 80 ....Weyers Cave VA 24486	888-750-2722	540-234-9261	162
Blue Ridge Electric Membership Corp			
1216 Blowing Rock Blvd ....Lenoir NC 28645	800-451-5474	828-758-2383	245
Blue Ridge Public Television			
1215 McNeil Dr ....Roanoke VA 24015	888-332-7788	540-344-0991	628
Blue Ridge X-Ray Company Inc			
120 Vista Blvd ....Arden NC 28704	800-727-7290		473
Blue Rock Technologies			
800 Kirts Blvd ....Troy MI 48084	866-390-8200	248-786-6100	225
Blue Seal Feeds Inc			
2905 US Hwy 61 N ....Muscatine IA 52761	866-647-1212*		445
*Cust Svc			
Blue Sky Cycling Inc			
2530 Randolph St ....Huntington Park CA 90255	800-585-4137	323-585-3934	707
Blue Sky Energy Inc			
2598 Fortune Way Ste K ....Vista CA 92081	800-493-7877	760-597-1642	606
Blue Sky Swimwear			
729 E International Speedway Blvd			
...............Daytona Beach FL 32118	800-799-6445*	386-255-2590	155-16
*Orders			
Blue Springs State Park			
2595 Alabama 10 ....Clio AL 36017	800-252-7275		
Blue Tangerine Solutions Llc			
1380 Sarno Rd Ste B ....Melbourne FL 32935	800-870-4293	321-309-6900	180
Blue Tent			
218 E Valley Rd ....Carbondale CO 81623	877-716-9648	970-704-3240	
Blue Water Area Chamber of Commerce			
512 McMorran Blvd ....Port Huron MI 48060	800-361-0526	810-985-7101	139
Blue Water Resort			
291 S Shore Dr ....South Yarmouth MA 02664	800-367-9393		665
Blue Water Sailing Magazine			
747 Aquidneck Ave Ste 201 ....Middletown RI 02842	888-800-7245	401-847-7612	455-4
Blue Williams LLP			
3421 N Causeway Blvd Ste 900 ......Metairie LA 70002	800-326-4991	504-831-4091	427
Blue Zebra Appointment Setting			
25 Pequot Ave Ste A..........Port Washington NY 11050	800-755-0094		7
BlueAlly			
8609 Westwood Center Dr Ste 100........Vienna VA 22182	888-768-2060		260
BlueCross BlueShield of Western New York			
257 W Genesee St ....Buffalo NY 14202	800-888-0757	716-887-6900	390-3
Bluecube Information Technology			
525 Milltown Rd			
Ste 301-B ....North Brunswick NJ 08902	888-380-6272	708-325-8328	
Bluefield College			
3000 College Ave ....Bluefield VA 24605	800-872-0175	276-326-3682	166
Bluefield State College			
219 Rock St ....Bluefield WV 24701	800-654-7798	304-327-4000	166
Blue-Grace Logistics LLC			
2846 S Falkenburg Rd ....Riverview FL 33578	800-697-4477		311
Bluegrass Care Navigators			
2312 Alexandria Dr ....Lexington KY 40504	855-492-0812		
Bluegrass Cellular Inc			
2902 Ring Rd ....Elizabethtown KY 42701	800-928-2355	270-769-0339	731
Bluegrass Community & Technical College			
Cooper Campus			
470 Cooper Dr ....Lexington KY 40506	866-774-4872	859-246-6200	162
Bluegreen Corp			
4960 Conference Way N			
Ste 100 ....Boca Raton FL 33431	800-456-2582	561-912-8000	748
NYSE: BXG			
Blueharbor Bank			
106 Corporate Park Dr ....Mooresville NC 28117	877-322-8228	704-662-7700	70
Bluelock LLC			
6325 Morenci Trl ....Indianapolis IN 46268	888-402-2583		180
Bluenose Inn & Suites			
636 Bedford Hwy ....Halifax NS B3M2L8	800-553-5339	800-565-2301	378
Blueox Energy Products & Services			
38 N Canal St ....Oxford NY 13830	877-233-8176		575
Bluepoint Leadership Development Ltd			
25 Whitney Dr ....Milford OH 45150	888-221-8685	513-683-4702	194
Blueport Commerce			
500 Harrison Ave Ste 3R..............Boston MA 02118	855-277-0614		
BlueRange Technology Inc			
9241 Globe Ctr Dr Ste 100 ......Morrisville NC 27560	877-928-4800		627
BlueSpire Strategic Marketing			
7650 Edinborough Way			
Ste 500.................Minneapolis MN 55435	800-727-6397		5
Bluestem Electric Co-op Inc			
614 E Hwy 24 PO Box 5 ......Wamego KS 66547	800-558-1580	785-456-2212	245
BlueTie Inc			
2480 Browncroft Blvd Ste 2b ....Rochester NY 14625	800-258-3843	585-586-2000	225
Bluewater Adventures Ltd			
252 E First St Ste 3............North Vancouver BC V7L1B3	888-877-1770	604-980-3800	220
Bluewater Thermal Solutions			
126 Millport Cir Ste 201 ....Greenville SC 29607	877-990-0050	864-990-0050	482
Bluffton Motor Works LLC			
410 E Spring St ....Bluffton IN 46714	800-579-8527	260-827-2200	515
Bluffton University			
1 University Dr ....Bluffton OH 45817	800-488-3257	419-358-3000	166
Blum Inc			
7733 Old Plank Rd ....Stanley NC 28164	800-438-6788	704-827-1345	349
Blumenthal Lansing Co			
30 Two Bridges Rd ....Fairfield NJ 07004	800-553-4158	201-935-6220	590
Blytheco LLC			
23161 Mill Creek Dr ....Laguna Hills CA 92653	800-425-9843	949-583-9500	180
BMA (Baptist Missionary Assn of America)			
611 Locust Ave PO Box 878..........Conway AR 72034	800-333-1442	501-455-4977	48-20
BMA Communications LLC			
15184 Hawk ....St Fontana CA 92336	800-850-4262		
BMC Software			
2202 NW Shore Blvd Ste 650 ....Tampa FL 33607	855-834-7487		178-12
BMC Software Inc			
2101 City W Blvd ....Houston TX 77042	800-841-2031	713-918-8800	178-1
BMDA (Building Material Dealers Assn)			
1006 SE Grand Ave Ste 301 ....Portland OR 97214	888-960-6329	503-208-3763	49-3
BMG Aviation Inc			
984 S Kirby Rd ....Bloomington IN 47403	888-457-3787	812-825-7979	63

	City	State	ZIP	Toll-Free	Phone	Class
BMG Metals Inc						
950 Masonic Ln	Richmond	VA	23231	**800-552-1510**	804-226-1024	490
BMH (Bastian Solutions)						
10585 N Meridian St 3rd Fl	Indianapolis	IN	46290	**800-772-0464**	317-575-9992	55
BMH Books						
1104 Kings Hwy PO Box 544	Winona Lake	IN	46590	**800-348-2756**		633-8
BMI (Brotherhood Mutual Insurance Co)						
6400 Brotherhood Way	Fort Wayne	IN	46825	**800-333-3735***		390-4
*Cust Svc						
BMI Educational Services						
PO Box 800	Dayton	NJ	08810	**800-222-8100**	732-329-6991	96
BMI Imaging Systems						
1115 E Arques Ave	Sunnyvale	CA	94085	**800-359-3456**	408-736-7444	494
BMM Testlabs						
815 Pilot Rd Ste G	Las Vegas	NV	89119	**800-791-6536**	702-407-2420	461
BMO (Bank of Montreal)						
100 King St W 1 First Canadian Pl 19th Fl	Toronto	ON	M5X1A1	**800-340-5021**	416-867-6785	70
NYSE: BMO						
Bmo Bankcorp Inc						
111 W Monroe St	Chicago	IL	60603	**888-340-2265**		359-2
BMO Financial Corp						
1 First Canadian Pl 21st Fl	Toronto	ON	M5X1A1	**800-553-0332**	416-359-4440	216
BMO Harris Bank						
111 W Monroe St	Chicago	IL	60603	**888-340-2265**	773-682-7481	70
BMS (Broadcast Microwave Services Inc)						
12305 Crosthwaite Cir	Poway	CA	92064	**800-669-9667**	858-391-3050	224
BMW of Darien						
140 Ledge Rd	Darien	CT	06820	**855-349-6240**	203-656-1804	57
BMW of Manhattan Inc						
555 W 57th St	New York	NY	10019	**877-855-4607**	212-586-2269	54
BMW of North America LLC						
300 Chestnut Ridge Rd	Woodcliff Lake	NJ	07677	**800-831-1117**	201-307-4000	59
BNC National Bank						
322 E Main Ave	Bismarck	ND	58501	**800-262-2265**	701-250-3000	70
BNN (Business News Network)						
299 Queen St W	Toronto	ON	M5V2Z5	**855-326-6266**	416-384-6600	735
BNSF (Burlington Northern & Santa Fe Railway)						
2650 Lou Menk Dr	Fort Worth	TX	76131	**800-795-2673**		644
BNZ Materials Inc						
6901 S Pierce St Ste 260	Littleton	CO	80128	**800-999-0890**	303-978-1199	658
Boa Technology Inc						
1760 Platte St	Denver	CO	80202	**844-203-1297**	303-455-5126	194
Boa-Franc						
1255-98th St	Saint-georges	QC	G5Y8J5	**800-463-1303**	418-227-1181	290
Boar's Head Inn						
200 Ednam Dr	Charlottesville	VA	22903	**800-476-1988**	434-296-2181	665
Boarder to Boarder Trucking Inc						
PO Box 328	Edinburg	TX	78541	**800-678-8789**	956-316-4444	681
Boardwalk Pipeline Partners LP						
3800 Frederica St	Owensboro	KY	42301	**866-913-2122**	270-686-3620	325
NYSE: BWP						
Boardwalk Plaza Hotel						
2 Olive Ave	Rehoboth Beach	DE	19971	**800-332-3224**	302-227-7169	378
Boart Longyear Co						
2640 W 1700 S	Salt Lake City	UT	84104	**800-453-8740**	801-972-6430	190
Boat Owners Assn of the US						
880 S Pickett St	Alexandria	VA	22304	**800-395-2628**	703-823-9550	48-22
Bob Barker Company Inc						
PO Box 429	Fuquay Varina	NC	27526	**800-334-9880**		590
Bob Davidson Ford Lincoln						
1845 E Joppa Rd	Baltimore	MD	21234	**877-885-7890**	410-661-6400	57
Bob Evans Farms Inc						
3776 S High St	Columbus	OH	43207	**800-939-2338**		666
NASDAQ: BOBE						
Bob Jones University						
1700 Wade Hampton Blvd	Greenville	SC	29614	**800-252-6363***	864-242-5100	166
*Admissions						
Bob Reeves Brass Mouthpieces						
25574 Rye Canyon Rd Ste D	Valencia	CA	91355	**800-837-0980**	661-775-8820	707
Bob Stall Chevrolet						
7601 Alvarado Rd	La Mesa	CA	91942	**800-295-2695**	619-458-3231	57
Bob Ward & Sons Inc						
3015 Paxson St	Missoula	MT	59801	**800-800-5083**	406-728-3220	707
Bob's Barricades Inc						
921 Shotgun Rd	Sunrise	FL	33326	**800-432-5031**	954-423-2627	295
Bob's Red Mill Natural Foods Inc						
13521 SE Pheasant Ct	Milwaukie	OR	97222	**800-553-2258**	503-654-3215	296-4
Bob's Stores Inc						
160 Corporate Ct	Meriden	CT	06450	**866-333-2627**	203-379-2260	157-2
Bobby Jones						
2625 N Berkeley Lake Rd NW Bldg 200 Ste 100	Duluth	GA	30096	**888-776-0076***		155-3
*Cust Svc						
Bobco Metals LLC						
2000 S Alameda St	Los Angeles	CA	90058	**800-262-2605**		490
BOC Partners Inc						
1030 South Ave W Ste 1	Westfield	NJ	07090	**877-310-8445**		7
Boca Raton Museum of Art						
501 Plaza Real Mizner Pk	Boca Raton	FL	33432	**866-481-1689**	561-392-2500	517
Boca Raton Resort & Club						
501 E Camino Real	Boca Raton	FL	33432	**888-543-1224**	561-447-3000	665
Bocada LLC						
5555 Lakeview Dr Ste 201	Kirkland	WA	98033	**866-262-2321**	425-898-2400	386
Boccardo Law Firm Inc, The						
111 W Saint John St Ste 400	San Jose	CA	95113	**800-662-9807**		443
Bock & Clark Corp						
3550 W Market St Ste 200	Akron	OH	44333	**800-787-8397**	330-665-4821	723
Bock Water Heaters Inc						
110 S Dickinson St	Madison	WI	53703	**800-794-2491**	608-257-2225	36
Bodega Bay Lodge						
103 Coast Hwy 1	Bodega Bay	CA	94923	**888-875-2250***	707-875-3525	378
*Resv						
Bodine Co						
PO Box 460	Collierville	TN	38027	**800-223-5728**	901-853-7211	762
Bodine Electric Co						
201 Northfield Rd	Northfield	IL	60093	**800-726-3463**	773-478-3515	515
Body-Solid Inc						
1900 Des Plaines Ave	Forest Park	IL	60130	**800-833-1227**		267
BoeFly LLC						
50 W 72nd St Ste C4	New York	NY	10023	**800-277-3158**		386
Boehringer Ingelheim Pharmaceuticals Inc						
900 Ridgebury Rd	Ridgefield	CT	06877	**800-243-0127**	203-798-9988	578
Boehringer Ingelheim Vetmedica Inc						
2621 N Belt Hwy	Saint Joseph	MO	64506	**800-821-7467**	816-233-2571	580
Boekel Scientific						
855 Pennsylvania Blvd	Feasterville	PA	19053	**800-336-6929**	215-396-8200	419
Boelter Cos Inc						
N22W23685 Ridgeview Pkwy W	West Waukesha	WI	53188	**800-263-5837**	262-523-6200	300
Boenning & Scattergood Inc						
200 Barr Harbor Dr Four Tower Bridge Ste 300	West Conshohocken	PA	19428	**800-883-1212**	610-832-1212	400
Bogen Communications International Inc						
50 Spring St	Ramsey	NJ	07446	**800-999-2809**	201-934-8500	52
OTC: BOGN						
Boh Bros Construction Co LLC						
730 S Tonti St	New Orleans	LA	70119	**800-284-3377**	504-821-2400	188-4
Bohannan Huston Inc						
7500 Jefferson St NE	Albuquerque	NM	87109	**800-877-5332**	505-823-1000	178-5
Boheme, The						
325 S Orange Ave	Orlando	FL	32801	**866-663-0024**	407-313-9000	667
Bohemian Hotel Celebration						
700 Bloom St	Celebration	FL	34747	**888-249-4007**	407-566-6000	378
Bohler-Uddeholm North America						
2505 Millenium Dr	Elgin	IL	60124	**800-638-2520**		490
Bohrens Moving & Storage Inc						
3 Applegate Dr	Robbinsville	NJ	08691	**800-326-4736**	609-208-1470	516
Boiling Springs Savings Bank (BSSB)						
25 Orient Way	Rutherford	NJ	07070	**888-388-7459**	201-939-5000	70
Boingo Wireless Inc						
10960 Wilshire Blvd Ste 800	Los Angeles	CA	90024	**800-880-4117**	310-586-5180	177
Boiron						
6 Campus Blvd	Newtown Square	PA	19073	**800-264-7661**	610-325-7464	
Bois Blanc Island Lighthouse National Historic Site						
30 Victoria St	Lachine	QC	J8X0B3	**888-773-8888**		
Boise Bible College						
8695 W Marigold St	Boise	ID	83714	**800-893-7755**	208-376-7731	161
Boise City Hall						
150 N Capitol Blvd	Boise	ID	83702	**800-377-3529**	208-384-4422	336
Boise Convention & Visitors Bureau						
250 S Fifth St Ste 300	Boise	ID	83702	**800-635-5240**	208-344-7777	206
Boise VA Medical Center						
500 W Fort St	Boise	ID	83702	**866-437-5093**	208-422-1000	373-8
Boise Valley Feeders LLC						
1555 Shoreline Dr Ste 320	Boise	ID	83702	**800-657-6305**	208-338-2605	10-1
Boiseries Raymond Inc						
11880 56e Ave	Montreal	QC	H1E2L6	**800-361-6577**	514-494-1141	497
Boise-Winnemucca Stages Inc						
1230 W Bannock St	Boise	ID	83702	**800-448-5692**	208-336-3300	107
Boite a Fleur De Laval Inc La						
3266 Boul Sainte-Rose	Laval	QC	H7P4K8	**800-784-3495**	450-622-0341	292
Bojangles' Restaurants Inc						
9432 Southern Pine Blvd	Charlotte	NC	28273	**800-366-9921**	704-335-1804	666
Boker's Inc						
3104 Snelling Ave	Minneapolis	MN	55406	**800-927-4377**	612-729-9365	617
Boland						
30 W Watkins Mill Rd	Gaithersburg	MD	20878	**800-552-6526**	240-306-3000	606
Bolden Lipkin PC						
3993 Huntingdon Pk	Huntingdon Valley	PA	19006	**888-947-3750**	215-947-3750	2
Bolger						
3301 Como Ave SE	Minneapolis	MN	55414	**866-264-3287**	651-645-6311	623
Bolin Marketing & Advertising						
2523 Wayzata Blvd Ste 300	Minneapolis	MN	55405	**800-876-6264**	612-374-1200	7
Bolt Products Inc						
16725 E Johnson Dr	City Of Industry	CA	91745	**800-423-6503**	626-961-4401	350
Bolthouse Farms						
7200 E Brundage Ln	Bakersfield	CA	93307	**800-467-4683**	661-366-7209	10-9
Bolton & Co						
3475 E Foothill Blvd Ste 100	Pasadena	CA	91107	**800-439-9337**	626-799-7000	389
Bolton & Hay Inc						
2701 Delaware Ave	Des Moines	IA	50317	**800-362-1861**	515-265-2554	300
Bolttech Mannings						
501 Mosside Blvd	North Versailles	PA	15137	**888-846-8827**	724-872-4873	384
BOMA (Building Owners & Managers Assn International)						
1101 15th St NW Ste 800	Washington	DC	20005	**800-426-6292**	202-408-2662	49-17
Bo-mac Contractors Ltd						
1020 Lindbergh Dr	Beaumont	TX	77707	**800-526-6221**	409-842-2125	188
Bombardier Aerospace						
400 Cote-Vertu Ouest	Dorval	QC	H4S1Y9	**866-855-5001***	514-855-5000	20
*General						
Bombardier Capital Inc						
1 Learjet Way Mailstop 1	Wichita	KS	05446	**800-949-5568**	802-764-5232	216
Bombardier Learjet						
1 Learjet Way	Wichita	KS	67209	**888-227-1428**	316-946-2287	20
Bombet Cashio & Assoc						
11220 N Harrells Ferry Rd	Baton Rouge	LA	70816	**800-256-5333**	225-275-0796	399
Bommarito Automotive Group						
15736 Manchester Rd	Ellisville	MO	63011	**800-367-2289**	636-391-7200	57
Bommer Industries Inc						
PO Box 187	Landrum	SC	29356	**800-334-1654**	864-457-3301	349
Bon Appetit Management Co						
100 Hamilton Ave Ste 400	Palo Alto	CA	94301	**800-765-9419**	650-798-8000	299
Bon Chef Inc						
205 SR- 94	Lafayette	NJ	07848	**800-331-0177**		
Bon Homme Yankton Electric Assn						
134 S Lidice St	Tabor	SD	57063	**800-925-2929**	605-463-2507	245
Bon Secours Saint Francis Hospital						
2095 Henry Tecklenburg Dr	Charleston	SC	29414	**800-863-2273**	843-402-1000	373-3
Bon Voyage Travel						
1640 E River Rd Ste 115	Tucson	AZ	85718	**800-439-7963**	520-797-1110	766
Bonadio Group, The						
171 Sully's Trl Ste 201	Pittsford	NY	14534	**877-917-3077**	585-381-1000	2
Bonair Daydreams						
PO Box 1522	Wrightsville Beach	NC	28480	**888-226-6247**	910-617-3887	130
Bonanza Creek Country Guest Ranch						
523 Bonanza Creek Rd	Martinsdale	MT	59053	**800-476-6045**	406-572-3366	239

	Toll-Free	Phone	Class
Bonanza Press Inc 19860 141st Pl NE .... Woodinville WA 98072	800-233-0008	425-486-3399	623
Bonanza Trade & Supply 6853 Lankershim Blvd ...... North Hollywood CA 91605	888-965-6577	818-765-6577	194
Bonaventure Tours 8 Boudreau Ln .... Haute-Aboujagane NB E4P5N1	800-561-1213	506-532-3674	755
Bond Place Hotel 65 Dundas St E .... Toronto ON M5B2G8	800-268-9390	416-362-6061	378
Bond Pro LLC 302 Knights Run Ave Ste 1160 .... Tampa FL 33602	888-789-4985	813-413-7576	390-5
Bondcote Corp PO Box 729 .... Pulaski VA 24301	800-368-2160	540-980-2640	740-2
Bonded Concrete Inc PO Box 189 .... Watervliet NY 12189	800-252-8589	518-273-5800	182
Bondhus Corp 1400 E Broadway St PO Box 660 .... Monticello MN 55362 *Cust Svc	800-328-8310*	763-295-2162	753
Bone Bank Allografts 4808 Research Dr .... San Antonio TX 78240 *Sales	800-397-0088*	210-696-7616	541
Bonfit America Inc 5741 Buckingham Pkwy Unit A ..... Culver City CA 90230	800-526-6348	310-204-7880	564
Bonhams & Butterfields 220 San Bruno Ave .... San Francisco CA 94103	800-223-2854	415-861-7500	51
Bonipak 1850 W Stowell Rd .... Santa Maria CA 93458	800-328-8816		10-9
Bonita Springs Area Chamber of Commerce 25071 Chamber of Commerce Dr .... Bonita Springs FL 34135	800-226-2943	239-992-2943	139
Bonland Industries Inc 50 Newark-Pompton Tpke .... Wayne NJ 07470	800-232-6600	973-694-3211	189-12
Bonnell Aluminum 25 Bonnell St PO Box 428 .... Newnan GA 30263	800-846-8885	770-253-2020	483
Bonneville Collections 6026 S Fashion Point Dr .... Ogden UT 84403	800-660-6138	801-621-7880	160
Bonnie Castle Resort 31 Holland St PO Box 127 .... Alexandria Bay NY 13607	800-955-4511	315-482-4511	665
Bonnie Lure State Recreation Area 11321 SW Terwilliger Blvd .... Portland OR 97219	800-551-6949		561
Bonstone Materials Corp 707 Swan Dr .... Mukwonago WI 53149	800-425-2214	262-363-9877	3
Bon-Ton Stores Inc 2801 E Market St .... York PA 17405 NASDAQ: BONTQ	800-945-4438	717-757-7660	229
Book Depot 67 Front St N .... Thorold ON L2V1X3	800-801-7193	905-680-7230	96
Book Passage 51 Tamal Vista Blvd ...... Corte Madera CA 94925	800-999-7909	415-927-0960	95
Bookazine Company Inc 75 Hook Rd .... Bayonne NJ 07002	800-221-8112	201-339-7777	96
Bookkeeping Express Enterprises LLC 671 N Glebe Rd Ste 1610 .... Arlington VA 22203	844-629-8797		
BookPal LLC 18101 Von Karman Ave Ste 120 ...... Irvine CA 92612	866-522-6657		95
BookPeople 603 N Lamar .... Austin TX 78703	800-853-9757	512-472-5050	95
Books of Discovery 2539 Spruce St .... Boulder CO 80302	800-775-9227		95
Books on the Square 471 Angell St .... Providence RI 02906	888-669-9660	401-331-9097	95
Books-A-Million Inc 402 Industrial Ln .... Birmingham AL 35211 NASDAQ: BAMM	800-201-3550	205-942-3737	95
Booksource Inc 1230 Macklind Ave .... Saint Louis MO 63110	800-444-0435	314-647-0600	96
Boomtown Casino Biloxi 676 Bayview Ave .... Biloxi MS 39530	800-627-0777	228-435-7000	133
Boomtown Inc 2100 Garson Rd .... Verdi NV 89439	800-648-3790	775-345-6000	132
Boomtown Internet Group Inc 111 Rosemary Ln .... Glenmoore PA 19343	888-454-3330		194
Boone County 222 S Fourth St .... Albion NE 68620	800-330-0755	402-395-2055	337
Boone County 801 E Walnut St Rm 333 .... Columbia MO 65201	800-552-7583	573-886-4270	337
Boone County Rural Electric Membership Corp 1207 Indianapolis Ave .... Lebanon IN 46052	800-897-7362	765-482-2390	245
Boone Electric Co-op 1413 Rangeline St .... Columbia MO 65201	800-225-8143	573-449-4181	245
Boone Tavern Hotel of Berea College 100 S Main St .... Berea KY 40404	800-366-9358	859-985-3700	378
Boos Dental Laboratory 1000 Boone Ave N Ste 660 ..... Golden Valley MN 55427	800-333-2667	763-544-1446	414
Boost Rewards 811 E Fourth St Ste B .... Dayton OH 45402	800-324-9756		195
Boostability Inc 2600 W Executive Pkwy Ste 200 .... Lehi UT 84043	800-261-1537		5
BootBarn Inc 620 Pan American Dr ...... Livingston TX 77351	888-440-2668		
Booth 4900 Nautilus Ct N Ste 220 ...... Boulder CO 80301	800-332-6684	303-581-1408	5
Booz Allen Hamilton Inc 8283 Greensboro Dr .... McLean VA 22102	866-390-3908	703-902-5000	194
Boral Material Technologies Inc 45 NE Loop 410 Ste 700 ..... San Antonio TX 78216	800-964-0951	210-349-4069	146
Borden Dairy Co 8750 N Central Expy Ste 400 ...... Dallas TX 75231	800-778-7879		
Border Gold Corp 15234 N Bluff Rd .... White Rock BC V4B3E6	888-312-2288		687
Border States Electric Supply 105 25th St N .... Fargo ND 58102	800-800-0199	701-293-5834	246
Boren, Oliver & Coffey LLP 59 N Jefferson St .... Martinsville IN 46151	800-403-9971	765-342-0147	427
Borla Performance Industries Inc 500 Borla Dr .... Johnson City TN 37604	877-462-6752	423-979-4000	60
Born Into It Inc 112 Burlington St .... Woburn MA 01801	800-560-2840	781-491-0707	
Borroughs Corp 3002 N Burdick St .... Kalamazoo MI 49004	800-748-0227	269-342-0161	286
Borsheim's Inc 120 Regency Pkwy .... Omaha NE 68114	800-642-4438	402-391-0400	409
Bosch Rexroth 14001 S Lakes Dr .... Charlotte NC 28273	800-739-7684	330-263-3300	785
Bosch Security Systems 130 Perinton Pkwy .... Fairport NY 14450	800-289-0096	585-223-4060	688
Bosch Thermotechnology 340 Mad River Pk .... Waitsfield VT 05673	800-283-3787		356
Bose Corp The Mountain .... Framingham MA 01701 *Cust Svc	800-379-2073*	508-766-1099	52
Boss Chair Inc 5353 Jillson St .... Commerce CA 90040	800-593-1888	323-262-1919	321
Bosshardt Realty Services LLC 5542 NW 43rd St .... Gainesville FL 32653	800-284-6110	352-371-6100	648
Boston Advisors Inc 1 Liberty Sq 10th Fl .... Boston MA 02109	800-523-5903	617-348-3100	400
Boston Architectural College 320 Newbury St .... Boston MA 02115	877-585-0100	617-585-0100	795
Boston Beer Co 1 Design Ctr Pl Ste 850 ..... Boston MA 02210 NYSE: SAM	888-661-2337	617-368-5000	102
Boston Centerless Inc 11 Presidential Way .... Woburn MA 01801	800-343-4111	781-994-5000	452
Boston College 140 Commonwealth Ave ..... Chestnut Hill MA 02467	800-360-2522	617-552-3100	166
Boston College Law School 885 Centre St .... Newton MA 02459	800-321-2211	617-552-8550	167-1
Boston Common Hotel 40 Trinity Pl .... Boston MA 02116	800-580-0194		377
Boston Consumers Checkbook 185 Franklin St .... Boston MA 02110	888-382-1222		95
Boston Duck Tours Ltd 4 Copley Pl Ste 4155 .... Boston MA 02116	800-226-7442	617-267-3825	755
Boston Family Office LLC, The 88 Broad St 2nd Fl .... Boston MA 02110	800-900-4401	617-624-0800	400
Boston Globe, The PO Box 55819 .... Boston MA 02205	888-694-5623		281
Boston Group 400 Riverside Ave .... Medford MA 02155	800-225-1633		286
Boston Harbor Hotel 70 Rowes Wharf .... Boston MA 02110	800-752-7077	617-439-7000	378
Boston Harbor Islands National Recreation Area 408 Atlantic Ave Ste 228 .... Boston MA 02110	877-874-2478	617-223-8666	560
Boston Language Institute Inc 648 Beacon St .... Boston MA 02215	877-998-3500	617-262-3500	763
Boston Market Corp 14103 Denver W Pkwy .... Golden CO 80401 *General	866-977-9090*	303-278-9500	666
Boston Medical Ctr 1 Boston Medical Ctr Pl .... Boston MA 02118	800-249-2007	617-638-8000	373-3
Boston Park Plaza Hotel & Towers 50 Park Plz .... Boston MA 02116	800-225-2008	617-426-2000	378
Boston Pizza Restaurants LP 14850 Quorum Dr Ste 201 .... Dallas TX 75234	866-277-8721	972-484-9022	666
Boston Pops 301 Massachusetts Ave Symphony Hall .... Boston MA 02115	888-266-1200	617-266-1492	569-3
Boston Sand & Gravel Company Inc 100 N Washington St .... Boston MA 02114 OTC: BSND	800-624-2724	617-227-9000	182
Boston Scientific Corp 300 Boston Scientific Way ..... Marlborough MA 01752 NYSE: BSX	800-876-9960	508-683-4000	474
Boston Symphony Hall 301 Massachusetts Ave .... Boston MA 02115	888-266-1200	617-266-1492	568
Boston Symphony Orchestra 301 Massachusetts Ave Symphony Hall .... Boston MA 02115	888-266-1200	617-266-1492	569-3
Boston University School of Law 765 Commonwealth Ave .... Boston MA 02215	800-321-2211	617-353-3100	167-1
Boston Whaler Inc 100 Whaler Way .... Edgewater FL 32141	877-294-5645		90
Boston's Best Chimney Sweep 76 Bacon St .... Waltham MA 02451 *Cust Svc	800-660-6708*	781-893-6611	152
Bostwick Laboratories 4355 Innslake Dr .... Glen Allen VA 23060	877-865-3262		
Bostwick-Braun Co 7349 Crossleigh Ct .... Toledo OH 43617	800-777-9640		350
Bothwell Regional Health Ctr 601 E 14th St .... Sedalia MO 65301	800-635-9194	660-826-8833	373-3
Bott Radio Network 10550 Barkley St Ste 100 .... Overland Park KS 66212	800-875-1903	913-642-7770	639
Bottega Veneta Inc 699 Fifth Ave .... New York NY 10022	800-845-6790		
Bottom Line Inc 3 Landmark Sq Ste 201 .... Stamford CT 06901	800-274-5611	203-973-5900	633-9
Bottomline Technologies 325 Corporate Dr .... Portsmouth NH 03801 NASDAQ: EPAY	800-243-2528	603-436-0700	178-1
Boulder Arts & Crafts 1421 Pearl St Mall .... Boulder CO 80302	866-656-2667	303-443-3683	458
Boulder Book Store 1107 Pearl St .... Boulder CO 80302	800-244-4651	303-447-2074	95
Boulder Convention & Visitors Bureau 2440 Pearl St .... Boulder CO 80302	800-444-0447	303-442-2911	206
Boulder Station Hotel & Casino 4111 Boulder Hwy .... Las Vegas NV 89121	800-683-7777	702-432-7777	133
Boulders Resort & Golden Door Spa 34631 N Tom Darlington Dr ..... Scottsdale AZ 85262	888-579-2631	480-488-9009	665
Bound to Stay Bound Books Inc (BTSB) 1880 W Morton Ave .... Jacksonville IL 62650	800-637-6586	217-245-5191	92
Bourbon & Boots Inc 314 Main St 2nd Fl .... North Little Rock AR 72114	877-435-8977		686
Bourbon Orleans - A Wyndham Historic Hotel 717 Orleans St .... New Orleans LA 70116	866-513-9744	504-523-2222	378

	City	State	ZIP	Toll-Free	Phone	Class
Bourns Inc						
1200 Columbia Ave	Riverside	CA	92507	**877-426-8767**	951-781-5690	621
Bovie Medical Corp						
5115 Ulmerton Rd	Clearwater	FL	33760	**800-537-2790**		250
NYSE: BVX						
Bow Plastics Ltd						
5700 Cote de Liesse	Montreal	QC	H4T1B1	**800-852-8527**	514-735-5671	603
Bowden Manufacturing Corp						
4590 Beidler Rd	Willoughby	OH	44094	**800-876-8970**	440-946-1770	752
Bowden Oil Company Inc						
PO Box 145	Sylacauga	AL	35150	**800-280-0393**	256-245-5611	316
Bowditch Ford Inc						
11291 Jefferson Ave	Newport News	VA	23601	**866-399-2616**	757-595-2211	54
Bowers Envelope Co						
5331 N Tacoma Ave	Indianapolis	IN	46220	**800-333-4321**	317-253-4321	263
Bowie Industries Inc						
1004 E Wise St	Bowie	TX	76230	**800-433-0934**	940-872-1106	273
Bowie State University						
14000 Jericho Pk Rd	Bowie	MD	20715	**877-772-6943**	301-860-4000	166
Bowie-Cass Electric Co-op Inc						
117 N St	Douglassville	TX	75560	**800-794-2919**	903-846-2311	245
Bowles Mattress Co Inc						
1220 Watt St	Jeffersonville	IN	47130	**800-223-7509**	812-288-8614	469
Bowlin Travel Centers Inc						
150 Louisiana Blvd NE	Albuquerque	NM	87108	**800-716-8413**		8
OTC: BWTL						
Bowling Green Area Chamber of Commerce						
710 College St	Bowling Green	KY	42101	**866-330-2422**	270-781-3200	139
Bowling Green State University						
1001 E Wooster St	Bowling Green	OH	43403	**866-246-6732**	419-372-2531	166
Bowling Proprietors' Assn of America (BPAA)						
621 Six Flags Dr PO Box 5802	Arlington	TX	76011	**800-343-1329**		48-23
Bowman Hollis Manufacturing Inc						
2925 Old Steele Creek Rd	Charlotte	NC	28208	**888-269-2358**	704-374-1500	739
Bowman Mfg Company Inc						
17301 51st Ave NE	Arlington	WA	98223	**800-962-4660**	360-435-5005	604
Box Elder County						
1 S Main St	Brigham City	UT	84302	**877-390-2326**	435-734-3300	337
Boxworks Technologies Inc						
2065 Pkwy Blve	Salt Lake City	UT	84119	**877-495-2250**	801-214-6100	180
Boy Scouts of America (BSA)						
1325 W Walnut Hill Ln						
PO Box 152079	Irving	TX	75015	**800-323-0732**	972-580-2000	48-15
Boyajian Inc						
144 Will Dr	Canton	MA	02021	**800-965-0665***	781-828-9966	296-41
*General						
Boyce Thompson Arboretum						
37615 US Hwy 60	Superior	AZ	85273	**877-763-5315**	520-689-2723	97
Boyd Bros Transportation Inc						
3275 Alabama 30	Clayton	AL	36016	**800-700-2693**	334-775-1400	775
Boyd Coffee Co						
19730 NE Sandy Blvd	Portland	OR	97230	**800-545-4077***	503-666-4545	296-7
*Cust Svc						
Boyd Group Inc, The						
3570 Portage Ave	Winnipeg	MB	R3K0Z8	**800-385-5451**	204-895-1244	62
Boyd Lighting Co						
944 Folsom St	San Francisco	CA	94107	**800-224-2693***	415-778-4300	438
*Cust Svc						
Boyett Petroleum						
601 McHenry Ave	Modesto	CA	95350	**800-545-9212**	209-577-6000	575
Boyne Country Sports						
1200 Bay View Rd	Petoskey	MI	49770	**800-462-6963**	231-439-4906	707
Boyne Highlands Resort						
600 Highlands Dr	Harbor Springs	MI	49740	**800-462-6963**	844-783-3175	665
Boyne Mountain Resort						
3951 Charlevoix Ave	Petoskey	MI	49770	**800-462-6963**	231-439-4750	665
Bozzuto's Inc						
275 School House Rd	Cheshire	CT	06410	**800-458-5114**	203-272-3511	297-8
OTC: BOZZ						
BP Lubricants USA Inc						
1500 Valley Rd	Wayne	NJ	07470	**800-333-3991**	973-633-2200	537
BP MotorClub						
PO Box 4441	Carol Stream	IL	60197	**800-334-3300**		53
BPA						
Bonneville Power Administration						
905 NE 11th Ave	Portland	OR	97232	**800-282-3713**	503-230-3000	339-8
BPAA (Bowling Proprietors' Assn of America)						
621 Six Flags Dr PO Box 5802	Arlington	TX	76011	**800-343-1329**		48-23
BPM Inc						
200 W Front St	Peshtigo	WI	54157	**800-826-0494**	715-582-4551	553
BPRR (Buffalo & Pittsburgh Railroad Inc)						
1200-C Scottsville Rd Ste 200	Rochester	NY	14624	**800-603-3385**	585-463-3307	644
BR Funsten & Co						
5200 Watt Ct Ste B	Fairfield	CA	94534	**888-261-2871**	209-825-5375	360
Brabazon Pumps & Compressor						
2484 Century Rd	Green Bay	WI	54303	**800-825-3222**	920-498-6020	172
Bracco Diagnostics Inc						
259 Prospect Plns Rd	Cranbury	NJ	08512	**800-631-5245**	609-514-2200	
Brackett Inc						
7115 SE Forbes Ave Bldg 451 J St	Topeka	KS	66619	**800-255-3506**	785-862-2205	625
Braco Window Cleaning Service Inc						
1 Braco International Blvd	Wilder	KY	41076	**800-969-4300**	859-442-6000	152
Bradbury Company Inc						
1200 E Cole	Moundridge	KS	67107	**800-397-6394**	620-345-6394	454
Bradco Inc						
107-11th Ave PO Box 997	Holbrook	AZ	86025	**800-442-4770**	928-524-3976	575
Braddock Hospital						
12500 Willowbrook Rd	Cumberland	MD	21502	**888-369-1122**	240-964-7000	373-3
Braden Mfg LLC						
5199 N Mingo Rd	Tulsa	OK	74117	**800-272-3360**		478
Braden Sutphin Ink Co						
3650 E 93rd St	Cleveland	OH	44105	**800-289-6872**	216-271-2300	387
Bradford & Galt Inc						
11457 Olde Cabin Rd Ste 200	Saint Louis	MO	63141	**800-997-4644**	314-997-4644	196
Bradford Health Services						
2101 Magnolia Ave S Ste 518	Birmingham	AL	35205	**800-217-2849**	205-251-7753	722
Bradford School						
2469 Stelzer Rd	Columbus	OH	43219	**800-678-7981**	614-416-6200	795
Bradford Scott Data Corp						
1001 Chestnut Hills Pkwy						
Ste 1	Fort Wayne	IN	46814	**800-430-5120**	260-625-5107	395
Bradford Technologies Inc						
302 Piercy Rd	San Jose	CA	95138	**866-445-8367**	408-360-8520	177
Bradford White Corp						
725 Talamore Dr	Ambler	PA	19002	**800-523-2931**	215-641-9400	36
Bradley Caldwell Inc						
200 Kiwanis Blvd	Hazleton	PA	18202	**800-257-9100***	570-455-7511	276
*Cust Svc						
Bradley Corp						
W 142 N 9101 Fountain Blvd						
	Menomonee Falls	WI	53051	**800-272-3539**	262-251-6000	605
Bradley County						
101 E Cedar St	Warren	AR	71671	**877-531-3282**		
Bradley Graphic Solutions Inc						
941 Mill Rd	Bensalem	PA	19020	**800-638-8223**	215-638-8771	623
Bradley University						
1501 W Bradley Ave	Peoria	IL	61625	**800-447-6460***	309-676-7611	166
*Admissions						
Bradmark Technologies Inc						
4265 San Felipe St Ste 700	Houston	TX	77027	**800-621-2808**	713-621-2808	178-1
Brady Corp						
6555 W Good Hope Rd	Milwaukee	WI	53223	**800-541-1686***	414-358-6600	412
NYSE: BRC ■ *Cust Svc						
Brady Identification Solutions						
6555 W Good Hope Rd	Milwaukee	WI	53223	**800-537-8791***	888-250-3082	178-1
*Cust Svc						
Brady Industries Inc						
7055 Lindell Rd	Las Vegas	NV	89118	**800-293-4698**	702-876-3990	405
Braff Group, The						
1665 Washington Rd Ste 3	Pittsburgh	PA	15228	**888-922-5169**	412-833-5733	474
Bragg Live Food Products Inc						
PO Box 7	Santa Barbara	CA	93102	**800-446-1990**		
Brahma Compression Ltd						
8825 Shepard Rd SE	Calgary	AB	T2C4N9	**800-230-6056**	403-287-6990	
Braille Institute of America Inc						
741 North Vermont Ave	Los Angeles	CA	90029	**800-272-4553**	323-663-1111	48-11
Brain Injury Assn of America						
1608 Spring Hill Rd Ste 110	Vienna	VA	22182	**800-444-6443**	703-761-0750	48-17
Brainerd Compressor						
3034 Sandbrook St	Memphis	TN	38116	**800-228-4138**		14
Brainerd International Raceway						
5523 Birchdale Rd	Brainerd	MN	56401	**866-444-4455**	218-824-7223	512
Brainerd Lakes Area Chamber of Commerce						
7393 State Hwy 371 PO Box 356	Brainerd	MN	56401	**800-450-2838**	218-829-2838	139
BrainLAB Inc						
5 Westbrook Corporate Ctr	Westchester	IL	60154	**800-784-7700**	708-409-1343	381
Brains II						
165 Konrad Crescent	Markham	ON	L3R9T9	**888-272-4672**		
Brainworks Software Inc						
100 S Main St	Sayville	NY	11782	**800-755-1111**	631-563-5000	178-1
BrainX Inc						
45 Rincon Dr	Camarillo	CA	93012	**844-927-2469**		
Brake Supply Company Inc						
5501 Foundation Blvd	Evansville	IN	47725	**800-457-5788**	812-467-1000	384
Brakebush Bros Inc						
N4993 Sixth Dr	Westfield	WI	53964	**800-933-2121**	608-296-2121	615
Brakeley Briscoe Inc						
322 W Bellevue Ave	San Mateo	CA	94402	**800-416-3086**	650-344-8883	317
Brakewell Steel Fabricator Inc						
55 Leone Ln	Chester	NY	10918	**888-914-9131**	845-469-9131	480
Brame Specialty Company Inc						
PO Box 271	Durham	NC	27702	**800-672-0011**	919-598-1500	555
Branch Banking & Trust Company of South Carolina						
301 College St	Greenville	SC	29601	**800-226-5228**		70
Branch Highways Inc						
442 Rutherford Ave	Roanoke	VA	24016	**800-353-3747**	540-982-1678	188-4
Brand Energy & Infrastructure Services Inc						
1325 Cobb International Dr						
Ste A-1	Kennesaw	GA	30152	**855-746-4477**	678-285-1400	489
Brand Iron 821 22nd St	Denver	CO	80205	**800-343-6405**	303-534-1901	195
Brand Protection Agency LLC						
8750 N Central Expwy Ste 720	Dallas	TX	75231	**866-339-5657**		195
Brandeis University						
415 S St	Waltham	MA	02454	**800-622-0622**	781-736-3500	166
BrandEquity International						
7 Great Meadow Rd	Newton	MA	02462	**800-969-3150**		343
Brandes Investment Partners LP						
11988 El Camino Real Ste 600	San Diego	CA	92191	**800-237-7119**	858-755-0239	400
Branding Brand						
2313 E Carson St	Pittsburgh	PA	15203	**888-979-5018**		386
Brandmovers Inc						
590 Means St Ste 250	Atlanta	GA	30318	**888-463-4933**	678-718-1850	627
Brandon Regional Hospital						
119 Oakfield Dr	Brandon	FL	33511	**800-733-0429**	813-681-5551	373-3
Brandpoint						
850 Fifth St S	Hopkins	MN	55343	**877-374-5270**		5
BrandsMart USA Corp						
3200 SW 42nd St	Hollywood	FL	33312	**800-432-8579**		35
Brandt Tractor Ltd						
Hwy 1 E PO Box 3856	Regina	SK	S4P3R8	**888-227-2638**	306-791-7777	111
Brandtjen & Kluge Inc						
539 Blanding Woods Rd						
	Saint Croix Falls	WI	54024	**800-826-7320**	715-483-3265	625
Brandywine Capital Associates Inc						
100 S Church St	West Chester	PA	19382	**888-344-2920**	610-344-2910	400
Brandywine Global Investment Management LLC						
2929 Arch St 8th Fl	Philadelphia	PA	19104	**800-348-2499**	215-609-3500	400
Brandywine Hospital						
201 Reeceville Rd	Coatesville	PA	19320	**800-430-3762**	610-383-8000	373-3
Brandywine Machine Company Inc						
300 Creek Rd	Downingtown	PA	19335	**800-523-7128**		452
Brandywine Realty Trust						
555 E Lancaster Ave Ste 100	Radnor	PA	19087	**866-426-5400**	610-325-5600	651
NYSE: BDN						
Brann & Isaacson						
184 Main St	Lewiston	ME	04243	**800-225-6964**	207-786-3566	427

	City	State	ZIP	Toll-Free	Phone	Class
Brannan Paving Coltd						
111 Elk Dr PO Box 3403	Victoria	TX	77903	**800-626-7064**	361-573-3130	186
Brannen Banks of Florida Inc						
PO Box 1929	Inverness	FL	34451	**866-546-8273**	352-726-1221	359-2
Branom Instrument Co						
5500 Fourth Ave So	Seattle	WA	98108	**800-767-6051**	206-762-6050	357
Branson 41 Eagle Rd	Danbury	CT	06813	**800-732-9262**		777
Branson's Best Reservations						
2875 Green Mtn Dr	Branson	MO	65616	**800-335-2555**	417-339-2204	375
Branson/Lakes Area Chamber of Commerce						
PO Box 1897	Branson	MO	65615	**800-214-3661**	417-334-4084	139
Brant Securities Ltd						
220 Bay St Ste 300	Toronto	ON	M5J2W4	**888-544-9318**	416-596-4545	686
Brasfield & Gorrie LLC						
3021 Seventh Ave S	Birmingham	AL	35233	**800-239-8017**	205-328-4000	186
Brasher Motor Company of Weimar Inc						
1700 I- 10	Weimar	TX	78962	**800-783-1746**	979-725-8515	57
Brasseler USA						
1 Brasseler Blvd	Savannah	GA	31419	**800-841-4522**		228
Brasstown Valley Resort						
6321 Hwy 76	Young Harris	GA	30582	**800-201-3205**		665
Braswell Food Co						
226 N Zetterower Ave	Statesboro	GA	30458	**800-673-9388**	912-764-6191	296-20
Brattleboro Area Chamber of Commerce						
180 Main St	Brattleboro	VT	05301	**877-254-4565**	802-254-4565	139
Brattleboro Memorial Hospital Inc						
17 Belmont Ave	Brattleboro	VT	05301	**866-972-5266**	802-257-0341	373-3
Brauer Material Handling Systems Inc						
226 Molly Walton Dr	Hendersonville	TN	37075	**800-645-6083**		384
Braun Industries Inc						
1170 Production Dr	Van Wert	OH	45891	**877-344-9990**		59
Braun Intertec Corp						
11001 Hampshire Ave S	Minneapolis	MN	55438	**800-279-6100**	952-995-2000	261
Bravo Sports Corp						
12801 Carmenita Rd	Santa Fe Springs	CA	90670	**800-234-9737***	562-484-5100	706
*Cust Svc						
Brawner Paper Company Inc						
5702 Armour Dr	Houston	TX	77020	**800-962-9384**	713-675-6584	549
Bray Real Estate						
637 N Ave	Grand Junction	CO	81501	**888-760-4251**	970-242-8450	648
Brazilian Court, The						
301 Australian Ave	Palm Beach	FL	33480	**800-552-0335**	561-655-7740	378
Brazilian Travel Service (BTS)						
16 W 46th St 2nd Fl	New York	NY	10036	**800-342-5746**	212-764-6161	16
Brazos Telecommunications Inc						
109 N Ave D	Olney	TX	76374	**800-687-3222**	940-564-5659	196
Brazos Urethane Inc						
1031 Sixth St North	Texas City	TX	77590	**866-527-2967**		189-12
Brazosport College						
500 College Dr	Lake Jackson	TX	77566	**877-717-7873**	979-230-3000	162
Brazosport Facts						
720 S Main St	Clute	TX	77531	**800-864-8340**	979-265-7411	528-2
BRB Publications Inc						
PO Box 27869	Tempe	AZ	85285	**800-929-3811**	480-829-7475	633-2
BRCC (Baton Rouge Community College)						
201 Community College Dr	Baton Rouge	LA	70806	**866-217-9823**	225-216-8000	162
BREA (Benton Rural Electric Assn)						
402 Seventh St PO Box 1150	Prosser	WA	99350	**800-221-6987**	509-786-2913	245
Bread for the World						
425 Third St SW Ste 1200	Washington	DC	20024	**800-822-7323***	202-639-9400	48-5
*Cust Svc						
Breakaway Tours						
337 Queen St W	Toronto	ON	M5V2A4	**800-465-4257**		755
Breakers at Waikiki, The						
250 Beach Walk	Honolulu	HI	96815	**800-426-0494**	808-923-3181	378
Breakers Hotel & Suites						
105 Second St	Rehoboth Beach	DE	19971	**800-441-8009**	302-227-6688	378
Breakers Palm Beach, The						
1 S County Rd	Palm Beach	FL	33480	**888-273-2537**	561-655-6611	703
Breakers Resort						
3002 N Ocean Blvd	Myrtle Beach	SC	29577	**800-952-4507**	843-448-8082	665
Breakers Resort Inn						
16th & Oceanfront	Virginia Beach	VA	23451	**800-237-7532**	757-428-1821	665
Breakers, The						
1 S County Rd	Palm Beach	FL	33480	**888-273-2537**	561-655-6611	665
BREC (Butler Rural Electric Co-op Inc)						
3888 Still-Beckett Rd	Oxford	OH	45056	**800-255-2732**	513-867-4400	245
Breck's PO Box 65	Guilford	IN	47022	**800-644-5505**	513-354-1511	323
Breeze-Eastern Corp						
35 Melanie Ln	Whippany	NJ	07981	**800-929-1919**	973-602-1001	468
Breezy Point Resort						
9252 Breezy Pt Dr	Breezy Point	MN	56472	**800-432-3777**		665
Breg Inc						
2885 Loker Ave E	Carlsbad	CA	92010	**800-897-2734**		48-2
Bremen Castings Inc						
500 N Baltimore St	Bremen	IN	46506	**800-837-2411**		307
Bremer Financial Corp						
372 St Peter St	Saint Paul	MN	55102	**800-908-2265**	651-288-3751	69
Bremner Biscuit Co						
4600 Joliet St	Denver	CO	80239	**800-668-3273***	855-972-0535	296-9
*Prod Info						
Brenau University						
500 Washington St	Gainesville	GA	30501	**800-252-5119**	770-534-6299	166
Brendan Vacations						
801 E Katella Ave	Anaheim	CA	92805	**800-687-1002**		755
Brenden Theatres						
531 Davis St	Vacaville	CA	95688	**866-857-5191**		
Brenham Wholesale Grocery Co						
602 W First St	Brenham	TX	77833	**800-392-4869**	979-836-7925	297-8
Brennan & Clark LLC						
721 E Madison Ste 200	Villa Park	IL	60181	**800-858-7600**	630-279-7600	160
Brenneman Printing Inc						
1909 Olde Homestead Ln	Lancaster	PA	17601	**800-222-2423**	717-299-2847	623
Brenner Printing Inc						
1234 Triplett St	San Antonio	TX	78216	**877-349-4024**	210-349-4024	623
Brenner Tank LLC						
450 Arlington Ave	Fond du Lac	WI	54935	**800-558-9750**		
Brenner-Fiedler & Associates Inc						
4059 Flat Rock Dr	Riverside	CA	92505	**800-843-5558**		357
Brenntag Canada Inc						
43 Jutland Rd	Toronto	ON	M8Z2G6	**866-516-9707**	416-243-9615	146
Brenntag North America Inc						
5083 Pottsville Pk	Reading	PA	19605	**877-363-5843**	610-926-6100	146
Brenntag Southwest Inc						
Industry Park W 17550	Citronelle	AL	36522	**800-732-0562**	903-759-7151	146
Brent Coon & Associates (BCA)						
215 Orleans St	Beaumont	TX	77701	**866-335-2666**	409-835-2666	427
Brent House Hotel						
1512 Jefferson Hwy	New Orleans	LA	70121	**800-535-3986**	504-842-4140	378
Brentech Inc						
9340 Carmel Mtn Rd Ste C	San Diego	CA	92129	**800-709-0440**	858-484-7314	175
Brenton LLC						
4750 County Rd 13 NE	Alexandria	MN	56308	**800-535-2730**	320-852-7705	543
Brentwood Corp						
453 Industrial Way PO Box 265	Molalla	OR	97038	**800-331-6013**	503-829-7366	
Brentwood Hospital						
1006 Highland Ave	Shreveport	LA	71101	**877-678-7500**	318-678-7500	373-5
Brescia University						
717 Frederica St	Owensboro	KY	42301	**877-273-7242***	270-685-3131	166
*Admissions						
Bresser's Cross Index Directory Co						
684 W Baltimore St	Detroit	MI	48202	**800-995-0570**	313-874-0570	633-6
Bretford Manufacturing Inc						
11000 Seymour Ave	Franklin Park	IL	60131	**800-521-9614**	847-678-2545	319-3
Brethren Press						
1451 Dundee Ave	Elgin	IL	60120	**800-441-3712**		633-3
Bretthauer Oil Co						
453 SW Washington St	Hillsboro	OR	97123	**800-359-3113**	503-648-2531	575
Brevard College						
1 Brevard College Dr	Brevard	NC	28712	**800-527-9090***	828-883-8292	166
*Admissions						
Brevard Community College (BCC)						
Cocoa 1519 Clearlake Rd	Cocoa	FL	32922	**888-747-2802**	321-632-1111	162
Melbourne						
3865 N Wickham Rd	Melbourne	FL	32935	**888-747-2802**	321-632-1111	162
Palm Bay						
250 Community College Pkwy	Palm Bay	FL	32909	**888-747-2802**	321-632-1111	162
Titusville						
1311 N US 1	Titusville	FL	32796	**888-747-2802**	321-632-1111	162
Brevard County Tourism Development						
2725 Judge Fran Jamieson Way	Viera	FL	32940	**800-955-8771**	321-633-2000	206
Brewer & Pritchard PC						
800 Bering Dr Ste 201A	Houston	TX	77057	**800-236-7468**		427
Brewer Co						
1354 US Hwy 50	Milford	OH	45150	**800-394-0017**	513-576-6300	46
Brewmatic Co						
20333 S Normandie Ave						
PO Box 2959	Torrance	CA	90509	**800-421-6860**	310-787-5444	298
Brewster Academy						
80 Academy Dr	Wolfeboro	NH	03894	**800-842-9961**	603-569-7200	618
Brewster Adventures						
PO Box 370	Banff	AB	T1L1A5	**800-691-5085**	403-762-5454	
Brewton-Parker College						
201 David-Eliza Fountain Cir Hwy 280						
PO Box 197	Mount Vernon	GA	30445	**800-342-1087**	912-583-2241	166
BRG (Business Resource Group)						
10440 N Central Expy Ste 1150	Dallas	TX	75231	**888-391-9166**	214-777-5100	194
Brian Gavin Diamonds						
7322 SW Frwy						
Ste 1810 - Arena One	Houston	TX	77074	**866-611-4465**		
Briar Cliff University						
3303 Rebecca St	Sioux City	IA	51104	**800-662-3303**	712-279-5321	166
Briarhurst Manor						
404 Manitou Ave	Manitou Springs	CO	80829	**877-685-1448**	719-685-1864	667
Briarwood College						
2279 Mt Vernon Rd	Southington	CT	06489	**800-952-2444**	860-628-4751	166
Brice's Crossroads National Battlefield Site						
2680 Natchez Trace Pkwy	Tupelo	MS	38804	**800-305-7417**	662-680-4025	560
Brick Bodies Fitness Services Inc						
212 W Padonia Rd	Timonium	MD	21093	**866-952-7425**	410-252-8058	353
Brick Industry Assn (BIA)						
12007 Sunrise Valley Dr Ste 430	Reston	VA	20191	**866-644-1293**	703-620-0010	49-18
Brickell Financial Services Motor Club Inc						
7300 Corporate Ctr Dr	Miami	FL	33126	**800-262-7262**	305-392-4300	53
BrickKicker						
849 N Ellsworth St	Naperville	IL	60563	**800-821-1820**		364
Bridal Guide Magazine						
228 E 45th St 11th Fl	New York	NY	10017	**800-472-7744**	212-838-7733	455-11
Bridal Veil Falls State Scenic Viewpoint						
I-84	Bridal Veil	OR	97010	**800-551-6949**		561
Bridgcom						
11388 W Olympic Blvd	Los Angeles	CA	90064	**855-455-5522**	323-510-3860	5
Bridge Bank						
55 Almaden Blvd Ste 200	San Jose	CA	95113	**866-273-4265***	408-423-8500	359-2
NASDAQ: BDGE ■ *General						
Bridge Home Health & Hospice						
15100 Birchaven Ln	Findlay	OH	45840	**800-982-3306**	419-423-5351	370
Bridgeline Digital						
80 BlanchaRd Rd	Burlington	MA	01803	**800-603-9936**	781-376-5555	180
Bridgepoint Education						
13500 Evening Creek Dr N						
Ste 600	San Diego	CA	92123	**866-475-0317**	858-668-2586	242
NYSE: BPI						
BridgePort Brewing Co						
1318 NW Northrup St	Portland	OR	97209	**888-834-7546**	503-241-7179	102
Bridgeport City Hall						
999 Broad St	Bridgeport	CT	06604	**800-978-2828**	203-576-7201	336
Bridgeport Hospital						
267 Grant St	Bridgeport	CT	06610	**800-688-4954**	203-384-3000	373-3
Bridgeport News						
1000 Bridgeport Ave	Shelton	CT	06484	**855-247-8573***	860-491-9988	528-4
*Advestisement						
Bridger Valley Extreme Access						
40014 Business Loop 1-80						
PO Box 399	Mountain View	WY	82939	**800-276-3481**	307-786-2800	245

Name / Address	Toll-Free	Phone	Class
Bridges Investment Counsel Inc 256 Durham Plz 8401 W Dodge Rd Ste 256 ....Omaha NE 68114	866-934-4700		
Bridgestone Americas Holding Inc 535 Marriott Dr ....Nashville TN 37214 *Cust Svc	877-201-2373*	615-937-1000	749
Bridgestone Arena 501 Broadway ....Nashville TN 37203	800-356-4840	615-770-2000	716
Bridgestone Golf Inc 15320 Industrial Pk Blvd NE ....Covington GA 30014	800-358-6319	770-787-7400	706
Bridgestone Multimedia Group Inc 300 N McKemy Ave ....Chandler AZ 85226	866-774-3774		
BridgeSTOR LLC 18060 Old Coach Dr ....Poway CA 92064	800-280-8204	858-375-7076	173-8
Bridgewater College 402 E College St ....Bridgewater VA 22812	800-759-8328	540-828-5375	166
Bridgewater Hotel 212 Wedgewood Dr ....Fairbanks AK 99701	800-528-4916		378
Bridge-world Language Center Inc, The 110 Second St S Ste 213 ....Waite Park MN 56387	800-835-6870	320-259-9239	763
Bridgford Foods Corp 1308 N Patt St ....Anaheim CA 92801 NASDAQ: BRID	800-854-3255	714-526-5533	296-26
Bridon Cordage LLC 909 E 16th St ....Albert Lea MN 56007	800-533-6002	507-377-1601	208
Briefingcom Inc 401 N Michigan Ste 2910............Chicago IL 60611 *General	800-752-3013*	312-670-4463	403
Brierley & Partners 5465 Legacy Dr Ste 300............Plano TX 75024	800-899-8700	214-760-8700	5
Briess Malting Co 625 S Irish Rd ....Chilton WI 53014	800-657-0806	920-849-7711	459
Briggs & Stratton Corp 12301 W Wirth St ....Milwaukee WI 53222 NYSE: BGG	800-444-7774	414-259-5333	262
Briggs Auto Group Inc 2312 Stagg Hill Rd ....Manhattan KS 66502	800-257-4004	785-537-8330	54
Briggs Equipment 10540 N Stemmons Fwy ....Dallas TX 75220	800-606-1833	214-630-0808	384
Briggs Industrial Equipment 10550 N Stemmons Fwy ....Dallas TX 75220	800-516-9206	214-630-0808	384
Briggs Plumbing 597 Old Mt Holly Rd ....Goose Creek SC 29445	800-888-4458		607
Brigham Young University Idaho 525 S Ctr ....Rexburg ID 83460	866-672-2984		166
Bright Chair Co 51 Railroad Ave ....Middletown NY 10940	888-524-5997	845-343-2196	319-1
Bright Co-op Inc 803 W Seale St ....Nacogdoches TX 75964	800-562-0730	936-564-8378	758
Bright Horizons Family Solutions LLC 200 Talcott Ave S ....Watertown MA 02472	800-324-4386	617-673-8000	148
Bright Image Corp 2830 S18th Ave ....Broadview IL 60155	888-449-5656		203
BrightMove Inc 320 High Tide Dr # 201 ....Saint Augustine FL 32080	877-482-8840		196
Brighton Ford Inc 8240 W Grand River ....Brighton MI 48114	888-644-9991	810-227-1171	57
Brighton Securities Corp 1703 Monroe Ave ....Rochester NY 14618	800-388-1703	585-473-3590	686
Brill Securities Inc 152 W 57th St 16th Fl............New York NY 10019	800-933-0800	212-957-5700	686
Brillacademic Publishers Inc 2 liberty Sq 11th Fl............Boston MA 02109	800-337-9255	617-263-2323	633-2
Brillio 5201 Great America Pkwy ....Santa Clara CA 95054	800-317-0575		461
Brimar Industries Inc 64 Outwater Ln ....Garfield NJ 07026	800-274-6271		623
Brinjac Engineering Inc 114 N Second St ....Harrisburg PA 17101	877-274-6526	717-233-4502	261
Brinker Brown Fastener & Supply Inc 12290 Crystal Commerce Loop ....Fort Myers FL 33966	800-527-5530	239-939-3535	384
Brinker International Inc 6820 LBJ Fwy ....Dallas TX 75240 NYSE: EAT	800-983-4637	972-980-9917	666
Brinkmann Corp 4215 McEwen Rd ....Dallas TX 75244	800-527-0717	972-387-4939	438
Brinly-Hardy Co 3230 Industrial Pkwy ....Jeffersonville IN 47130	877-728-8224	812-218-7200	428
BriskHeat Corp 1055 Gibbard Ave ....Columbus OH 43201	800-848-7673	614-294-3376	318
Bristol Aluminum 5514 Bristol Emilie Rd ....Levittown PA 19057	800-338-5532	215-946-3160	361
Bristol Herald-Courier 320 Bob Morrison Blvd ....Bristol VA 24201	888-228-2098	276-669-2181	528-2
Bristol Hotel 1055 First Ave ....San Diego CA 92101	800-662-4477	619-232-6141	378
Bristol Motor Speedway 151 Speedway Blvd ....Bristol TN 37620	866-415-4158	423-989-6933	512
Bristol Products Corp 700 Shelby St ....Bristol TN 37620 *Orders	800-336-8775*	423-968-4140	155-1
Bristol Public Library 5 High St ....Bristol CT 06010	877-603-7323	860-584-7787	433-3
Bristol West Insurance Group 900 S Pine Island Rd Ste 600........Plantation FL 33324	888-888-0080		390-2
Bristol, The 200 Boylston St ....Boston MA 02116	800-819-5053	617-338-4400	667
Bristol-Myers Squibb Canada Inc 2344 Alfred-Nobel Blvd Ste 300........Montreal QC H4S0A4 *Cust Svc	800-267-0005*	514-333-3200	578
Bristol-Myers Squibb Co 345 Park Ave ....New York NY 10154 NYSE: BMY	800-332-2056	212-546-4000	578
Brita Products Co 1221 Broadway ....Oakland CA 94612	800-242-7482	510-271-7000	801
Britax Child Safety Inc 4140 Pleasant Rd ....Fort Mill NC 29708	888-427-4829	704-409-1700	64
Brite-Line LLC 10660 E 51st Ave ....Denver CO 80239	888-201-6448		727
Britestar Business 1305-B Governor Ct ....Abingdon MD 21009	888-409-6227	410-679-0441	
BriteVision Media LLC 475 14th St Ste 200 ....Oakland CA 94612	877-479-7777		8
British Airways Executive Club PO Box 300743 ....Jamaica NY 11430	800-452-1201		26
British Columbia Lottery Corp (BCLC) 74 W Seymour St ....Kamloops BC V2C1E2	866-815-0222	250-828-5500	450
British Columbia's Women's Hospital & Health Centre 4500 Oak St ....Vancouver BC V6H3N1	888-300-3088	604-875-2424	373-2
British Standards Institution, The 12110 Sunset Hills Rd Ste 200............Reston VA 20190	800-862-4977	345-086-9001	455-5
Brittany Pointe Estates 1001 S Valley Forge Rd ....Lansdale PA 19446	800-504-2287	267-656-6008	668
Brivo Systems LLC 7700 Old Georgetown Rd Ste 300........Bethesda MD 20814 *Tech Supp	866-692-7486*	301-664-5242	688
Brixmor Property Group 450 Lexington Ave 13th Fl............New York NY 10017	800-468-7526	212-869-3000	651
BRK Brands Inc 3901 Liberty St Rd ....Aurora IL 60504	800-323-9005	630-851-7330	283
BRMC (Bay Regional Medical Ctr) 1900 Columbus Ave ....Bay City MI 48708	800-656-3950	989-894-3000	373-3
BRMS (Benefit & Risk Management Services Inc) 80 Iron Point Cir Ste 200 PO Box 2140............Folsom CA 95763	888-326-2555		389
Broad River Electric Co-op Inc 811 Hamrick St ....Gaffney SC 29342	866-687-2667	864-489-5737	245
Broadband Dynamics LLC 8757 E Via De Commercio ....Scottsdale AZ 85258	888-801-1034		386
Broadcast Microwave Services Inc (BMS) 12305 Crosthwaite Cir ....Poway CA 92064	800-669-9667	858-391-3050	224
Broadfield Distributing Inc 67A Glen Cove Ave ....Glen Cove NY 11542	800-634-5178	516-676-2378	246
Broadleaf Services Inc 6 Fortune Dr ....Billerica MA 01821	866-337-7733		180
Broadman & Holman Publishers 127 Ninth Ave N MSN 114 ....Nashville TN 37234	800-448-8032		633-3
Broadmoor, The 1 Lake Ave ....Colorado Springs CO 80906	866-837-9520	719-577-5775	665
Broadnet Teleservices LLC 1805 Shea Ctr Dr Ste 160............Highlands Ranch CO 80129	877-579-4929		116
Broadview Networks Holdings Inc 800 Westchester Ave Ste N-501 ....Rye Brook NY 10573	800-260-8766	914-922-7000	731
BroadVoice Inc 9221 Corbin Ave Ste 155 ....Northridge CA 91324 *Sales	866-247-3194*	888-325-5875	386
Broadway at the Beach 1325 Celebrity Cir ....Myrtle Beach SC 29577	800-386-4662	843-444-3200	50-6
Broadway Financial Corp 5055 Wilshire Blvd Ste 100 ....Los Angeles CA 90036 NASDAQ: BYFC	888-988-2265		359-2
Broadway In Chicago 24 W Randolph St ....Chicago IL 60601	800-359-2525	312-977-1700	568
Broadway League, The 729 Seventh Ave 5th Fl............New York NY 10019	866-442-9878	212-764-1122	48-4
Broadwaycom 729 Seventh Ave ....New York NY 10019	800-276-2392	212-541-8457	745
Broan-NuTone LLC 926 W State St ....Hartford WI 53027 *Cust Svc	800-558-1711*	262-673-4340	37
Brock & Company Inc 257 Great Vly Pkwy ....Malvern PA 19355	866-468-2783	610-647-5656	666
Brock & Scott PLLC 4550 country club Rd ....Winston-Salem NC 27104	844-856-6646	336-354-1797	
Brock Group 10343 Sam Houston Park Dr Ste 200............Houston TX 77064	800-600-9675	281-807-8200	189-8
Brock Solutions Inc 86 Ardelt Ave ....Kitchener ON N2C2C9	877-702-7625	519-571-1522	261
Brockville General Hospital 75 Charles St ....Brockville ON K6V1S8	800-567-7415	613-345-5645	373-2
Broco Inc 10868 Bell Ct ....Rancho Cucamonga CA 91730	800-845-7259	909-483-3222	483
Broco Products Inc 18624 Syracuse Ave ....Cleveland OH 44110	800-321-0837	216-531-0880	410
Brody School of Medicine at East Carolina University 600 Moye Blvd ....Greenville NC 27834	800-722-3281	252-744-1020	167-2
Broedell Plumbing Supply Inc 1601 Commerce Ln ....Jupiter FL 33458	800-683-6363	561-743-6663	608
Broich Enterprises Inc 6440 City W Pkwy ....Eden Prairie MN 55344	800-853-3508	952-941-2270	661
Brokers International Financial Services LLC 4135 NW Urbandale Dr ....Urbandale IA 50322	877-886-1939		689
Brokers Worldwide 701C Ashland Ave ....Folcroft PA 19032	800-624-5287	610-461-3661	457
Brolite Products Inc 1900 S Park Ave ....Streamwood IL 60107	888-276-5483	630-830-0340	296-42
Bronco Billy's Casino 233 E Bennett Ave ....Cripple Creek CO 80813	877-989-2142	719-689-2142	133
Bronco Wine Co 6342 Bystrum Rd ....Ceres CA 95307	855-874-2394	209-538-3131	80-3
Brondell Inc 1159 Howard St ....San Francisco CA 94103	888-542-3355		320
Bronner Bros Inc 2141 Powers Ferry Rd ....Marietta GA 30067	800-241-6151	770-988-0015	214
Bronx Community College 2155 University Ave ....Bronx NY 10453	866-888-8777	718-289-5100	162
Bronx Council on the Arts 1738 Hone Ave ....Bronx NY 10461	866-564-5226	718-931-9500	458
Bronx Library Ctr 310 E Kings Bridge Rd ....Bronx NY 10458	800-342-3688	718-579-4244	433-3
Bronx Psychiatric Ctr 1500 Waters Pl ....Bronx NY 10461	800-597-8481	718-931-0600	373-5
Bronx Zoo 2300 Southern Blvd ....Bronx NY 10460	800-433-4149	718-220-5100	818
BronxCare Family Wellness Center 1276 Fulton Ave ....Bronx NY 10456	877-451-9361	718-590-1800	373-3

Name / Address	City	State	ZIP	Toll-Free	Phone	Class
Bronze Craft Corp						
37 Will St	Nashua	NH	03060	**800-488-7747**		349
Brook Furniture Rental Inc						
100 N Field Dr Ste 220	Lake Forest	IL	60045	**877-285-7368**		264-2
Brook Mays Music Co						
8605 John Carpenter Fwy	Dallas	TX	75247	**800-637-8966***	214-631-0928	522
*Cust Svc						
Brookdale Community College						
765 Newman Springs Rd	Lincroft	NJ	07738	**866-767-9512**	732-842-1900	162
Brookdale Plastics						
6096 McKee Rd	Madison	WI	53719	**800-541-1535**	608-271-5634	
Brooke Army Medical Center (BAMC)						
3551 Roger Brooke Dr	Fort Sam Houston	TX	78234	**800-443-2262**		373-4
Brooke Chase Associates Inc						
1543 Second St	Sarasota	FL	34236	**877-374-0039**		717
Brookfield Engineering Lab Inc						
11 Commerce Blvd	Middleboro	MA	02346	**800-628-8139**	508-946-6200	201
Brookgreen Gardens						
1931 Brookgreen Dr	Murrells Inlet	SC	29576	**800-849-1931**	843-235-6000	97
Brookhaven-Lincoln County Chamber of Commerce						
230 S Whitworth Ave	Brookhaven	MS	39601	**800-613-4667**	601-833-1411	139
Brookline Bank						
131 Clarendon St						
PO Box 470469	Brookline	MA	02116	**877-668-2265***	617-425-4600	359-2
*Cust Svc						
Brookline College						
2445 W Dunlap Ave Ste 100	Phoenix	AZ	85021	**800-793-2428**	602-242-6265	681
Brookline Public Library						
361 Washington St	Brookline	MA	02445	**800-447-8844**	617-730-2370	433-3
Brooks Automation Inc						
15 Elizabeth Dr	Chelmsford	MA	01824	**800-698-6149**	978-262-2400	691
NASDAQ: BRKS						
Brooks Automation Inc Polycold Systems						
3800 Lakeville Hwy	Petaluma	CA	94954	**800-698-6149**	707-769-7000	14
Brooks Equipment Company Inc						
10926 David Taylor Dr Ste 300						
PO Box 481888	Charlotte	NC	28262	**800-433-9265**	800-826-3473	675
Brooks Instrument LLC						
407 West Vine St	Hatfield	PA	19440	**888-554-3569**		406
Brooks Lake Lodge & Guest Ranch						
458 Brooks Lake Rd	Dubois	WY	82513	**866-213-4022**		239
Brooks Sports Inc						
19910 N Creek Pkwy Ste 200	Bothell	WA	98011	**800-227-6657**		301
Brooks Tropicals Inc						
18400 SW 256th St	Homestead	FL	33090	**800-327-4833**	305-247-3544	315-4
Brooks Utility Products Group						
23847 Industrial Park Dr						
	Farmington Hills	MI	48335	**888-687-3008**	248-477-0250	635
Brookshire Suites						
120 E Lombard St	Baltimore	MD	21202	**855-345-5033**	410-625-1300	378
Brookside Resort						
463 E Pkwy	Gatlinburg	TN	37738	**800-251-9597**	865-436-5611	665
Brookstone Inc						
1 Innovation Way	Merrimack	NH	03054	**800-846-3000***		327
*Cust Svc						
Brookstown Inn						
200 Brookstown Ave	Winston-Salem	NC	27101	**800-845-4262**	336-725-1120	378
Brookwood Laminating						
275 Putnam Rd	Wauregan	CT	06387	**800-247-6658**	860-774-5001	740-2
Broome Community College						
901 Front St	Binghamton	NY	13905	**800-836-0689**	607-778-5000	162
Bro-Tex Inc						
800 Hampden Ave	Saint Paul	MN	55114	**800-328-2282**	651-645-5721	506
Brother International Corp						
100 Somerset Corporate Blvd						
	Bridgewater	NJ	08807	**877-552-6255***	908-704-1700	111
*Cust Svc						
Brotherhood Bank & Trust						
756 Minnesota Ave	Kansas City	MO	66101	**855-522-6722**	913-321-4242	70
Brotherhood Mutual Insurance Co (BMI)						
6400 Brotherhood Way	Fort Wayne	IN	46825	**800-333-3735***		390-4
*Cust Svc						
Brotherhood Winery						
100 Brotherhood Plaza Dr						
PO Box 190	Washingtonville	NY	10992	**800-724-3960**	845-496-3661	80-3
Broughton Foods						
1701 Green St	Marietta	OH	45750	**800-303-3400**	740-373-4121	296-27
Broward Community College						
Downtown Center						
111 E Las Olas Blvd	Fort Lauderdale	FL	33301	**888-654-6482**	954-201-7350	162
North						
1000 Coconut Creek Blvd	Coconut Creek	FL	33066	**888-654-6482**	954-201-2240	162
Broward County Historical Commission						
151 SW Second St	Fort Lauderdale	FL	33301	**866-682-2258**	954-765-4670	517
Broward Fire Equipment & Service Inc						
101 SW Sixth St	Fort Lauderdale	FL	33301	**800-866-3473**	954-467-6625	675
Brower Mechanical Inc						
4060 Alvis Ct	Rocklin	CA	95677	**877-816-6649**	916-624-0808	606
Brown & Bigelow Inc						
345 Plato Blvd E	Saint Paul	MN	55107	**800-628-1755***	651-293-7000	9
*Cust Svc						
Brown & Haley						
PO Box 1596	Tacoma	WA	98401	**800-426-8400**		296-8
Brown Automotive Group LP						
4300 S Georgia	Amarillo	TX	79110	**888-388-6728**	806-353-7211	57
Brown Bus Co						
2111 E Sherman Ave	Nampa	ID	83686	**800-574-1580**	208-466-4181	109
Brown Coach Inc						
50 Venner Rd	Amsterdam	NY	12010	**800-424-4700**	518-843-4700	107
Brown College of Court Reporting & Medical Transcription (BCCR)						
1900 Emery St NW Ste 200	Atlanta	GA	30318	**800-849-0703**	404-876-1227	795
Brown County						
305 E Walnut PO Box 23600	Green Bay	WI	54301	**800-362-9082**	920-448-4016	337
Brown County Convention & Visitors Bureau						
10 N Van Buren St PO Box 840	Nashville	IN	47448	**800-753-3255**	812-988-7303	206
Brown County Inn						
51 State Rd 46	Nashville	IN	47448	**800-772-5249**	812-988-2291	378
Brown County Rural Electric Assn						
24386 State Hwy 4 PO Box 529	Sleepy Eye	MN	56085	**800-658-2368**	507-794-3331	245

Name / Address	City	State	ZIP	Toll-Free	Phone	Class
Brown Hay & Stephens LLP						
205 S fifth St Ste 700	Springfield	IL	62701	**888-666-8491**		
Brown Investment Advisory & Trust Co						
901 S Bond St Ste 400	Baltimore	MD	21231	**800-645-3923**	410-537-5400	400
Brown Jordan Co						
9860 Gidley St	El Monte	CA	91731	**800-743-4252**	626-279-5537	319-4
Brown Machine LLC						
330 N Ross St	Beaverton	MI	48612	**877-702-4142**	989-435-7741	146
Brown Mackie College						
Merrillville						
1000 E 80th Pl Ste 205M	Merrillville	IN	46410	**800-258-3321**	219-769-3321	795
South Bend						
3454 Douglas Rd	South Bend	IN	46635	**800-743-2447**	574-237-0774	795
Brown Mackie College Lenexa						
9705 Lenexa Dr	Lenexa	KS	66215	**800-635-9101**	913-768-1900	795
Brown Mackie College Louisville						
3605 Fern Valley Rd	Louisville	KY	40219	**800-999-7387**	502-968-7191	795
Brown Mackie College Northern Kentucky						
309 Buttermilk Pk	Fort Mitchell	KY	41017	**800-888-1445**	859-341-5627	795
Brown Mackie College Salina						
2106 S Ninth St	Salina	KS	67401	**800-365-0433**	785-825-5422	795
Brown Mfg Corp						
6001 E Hwy 27	Ozark	AL	36360	**800-633-8909**		273
Brown Palace Hotel						
321 17th St	Denver	CO	80202	**800-321-2599**	303-297-3111	378
Brown Stove Works Inc						
1422 Carolina Ave PO Box 2490	Cleveland	TN	37320	**800-251-7485***	423-476-6544	36
*All						
Brown Wood Preserving Company Inc						
6201 Camp Ground Rd	Louisville	KY	40216	**800-537-1765**	502-448-2337	813
Brown Wood Products Co						
7040 N Lawndale Ave	Lincolnwood	IL	60712	**800-328-5858**		815
Brown's Wharf Inn						
121 Atlantic Ave	Boothbay Harbor	ME	04538	**800-334-8110**	207-633-5440	378
Browne & Co						
505 Apple Creek Blvd Unit 2	Markham	ON	L3R5B1	**866-306-3672**	905-475-6104	300
Browne Foodservice						
1122 US Rt 22 Ste 203	Mountainside	NJ	07092	**888-289-1005**	973-232-1065	300
Brownell World Travel						
216 Summit Blvd Ste 220	Birmingham	AL	35243	**800-999-3960**	205-802-6222	766
Brown-Forman						
850 Dixie Hwy	Louisville	KY	40210	**800-831-9146**	502-585-1100	185
NYSE: BFA						
Brownlie & Braden LLC						
2820 Ross Tower 500 N Akard	Dallas	TX	75201	**888-339-4650**	214-219-4650	194
Brownstone Real Estate Co						
1840 Fishburn Rd	Hershey	PA	17033	**877-533-6222**	717-533-6222	648
Brownstown Electric Supply Company Inc						
690 E State Rd 250	Brownstown	IN	47220	**800-742-8492**		782
Brown-Strauss Steel						
2495 Uravan St	Aurora	CO	80011	**800-677-2778***	303-371-2200	490
*Sales						
Brownsville Convention & Visitors Bureau						
650 Ruben M Torres Sr Blvd	Brownsville	TX	78521	**800-626-2639**	956-546-3721	206
Brownsville Herald, The						
1135 E Van Buren St	Brownsville	TX	78520	**800-488-4301**	956-542-4301	528-2
Browntrout Publishers Inc						
201 Continental Blvd	El Segundo	CA	90245	**800-777-7812**	310-607-9010	633-2
Brown-Wilbert Inc						
2280 Hamline Ave N	Saint Paul	MN	55113	**800-672-0709**		
Broyhill Co						
1 N Market Sq PO Box 475	Dakota City	NE	68731	**800-228-1003**	402-987-3412	273
Broyhill Furniture Industries Inc						
3483 Hickory Blvd	Hudson	NC	28638	**800-225-0265***		319-2
*Cust Svc						
Broyles Kight & Ricafort PC						
8250 Haverstick Rd Ste 100	Indianapolis	IN	46240	**888-834-2692**	317-571-3600	427
BRP Manufacturing Co						
637 N Jackson St	Lima	OH	45801	**800-858-0482**	419-228-4441	672
BRT Apartments Corp						
60 Cutter Mill Rd Ste 303	Great Neck	NY	11021	**800-450-5816**	516-466-3100	507
NYSE: BRT						
Bruce & Merrilees Electric Co						
930 Cass St	New Castle	PA	16101	**800-652-5560**	724-652-5566	189-4
Bruce Foods Corp						
221 Southpark Plz PO Box 1030	Lafayette	LA	70508	**800-299-9082**	337-365-8101	296-20
Bruce Telecom						
3145 Hwy 21 PO Box 80	Tiverton	ON	N0G2T0	**866-517-2000**	519-368-2000	731
Brueton Industries Inc						
146 Hanse Ave	Freeport	NY	11520	**800-221-6783***	516-379-3400	319-2
*Cust Svc						
Bruker Daltonics Inc						
40 Manning Rd	Billerica	MA	01821	**800-672-7676**	978-663-3660	418
Brulin Holding Co						
2920 Dr AJ Brown Ave	Indianapolis	IN	46205	**800-776-7149**	317-923-3211	145
Brumlow Mills Inc						
734 S River St PO Box 1779	Calhoun	GA	30701	**855-427-8656**		
Brunet-Garcia Advertising Inc						
1510 Hendricks Ave	Jacksonville	FL	32207	**866-346-1977**	904-346-1977	7
Brunswick & The Golden Isles of Georgia Visitors Bureau						
529 Beachview Dr	St Simons Island	GA	31522	**800-933-2627**	912-638-9014	206
Brunswick Community College						
50 College Rd	Bolivia	NC	28422	**800-754-1050**	910-755-7300	162
Brunswick Corp Mercury Marine Div						
W 6250 Pioneer Rd	Fond du Lac	WI	54935	**866-408-6372**	920-929-5040	262
Brunswick County						
30 Government Center Dr NE	Bolivia	NC	28422	**800-442-7033**	910-253-2657	337
Brunswick County Board of Education						
35 Referendum Dr	Bolivia	NC	28422	**800-662-7030**	910-253-2900	681
Brunswick County Chamber of Commerce						
114 Wall St	Shallotte	NC	28459	**800-426-6644**	910-754-6644	139
Brunswick Electric Membership Corp						
795 Ocean Hwy PO Box 826	Shallotte	NC	28459	**800-842-5871**	910-754-4391	245
Brunswick School Inc						
100 Maher Ave	Greenwich	CT	06830	**800-546-9425**	203-625-5800	41
Brush Research Mfg Company Inc						
4642 Floral Dr	Los Angeles	CA	90022	**800-572-6501**	323-261-2193	103
Brushfoil LLC						
1 Shoreline Dr Unit 6	Guilford	CT	06437	**800-493-2321**	203-453-7403	597

Name	Address	City	State	ZIP	Toll-Free	Phone	Class
Bruss Co	3548 N Kostner Ave	Chicago	IL	60641	**800-621-3882**		297-9
Bry-Air Inc	10793 SR 37 W	Sunbury	OH	43074	**877-427-9247**	740-965-2974	14
Bryan College	140 Landes Way	Dayton	TN	37321	**800-277-9522**	423-775-2041	166
Bryan Health	1600 S 48th St	Lincoln	NE	68506	**800-742-7844**	402-481-7333	373-3
Bryan Systems	14020 US 20A Hwy	Montpelier	OH	43543	**800-745-2796**		775
Bryan W Whitfield Memorial Hospital	105 Hwy 80 E PO Box 890	Demopolis	AL	36732	**800-453-2395**	334-289-4000	373-3
Bryan-College Station Eagle	1729 Briarcrest Dr	Bryan	TX	77802	**800-299-7355**	979-776-4444	528-2
Bryant & Stratton College *Cleveland*	3121 Euclid Ave	Cleveland	OH	44115	**866-948-0571**	216-771-1700	795
Bryant & Stratton College Albany	1259 Central Ave	Albany	NY	12205	**800-836-5627**	518-437-1802	795
Bryant & Stratton College Milwaukee	310 W Wisconsin Ave Ste 500-E	Milwaukee	WI	53203	**866-948-0571**	414-276-5200	795
Bryant & Stratton College Richmond	8141 Hull St Rd	Richmond	VA	23235	**866-948-0571**	804-745-2444	795
Bryant & Stratton College Syracuse North	8687 Carling Rd	Liverpool	NY	13090	**800-836-5627**	315-652-6500	795
Bryant Park Hotel	40 W 40th St	New York	NY	10018	**877-640-9300**	212-869-0100	378
Bryant University	1150 Douglas Pk	Smithfield	RI	02917	**800-622-7001***	401-232-6000	166
	*Admissions						
Bryce Corp	4505 Old Lamar Ave	Memphis	TN	38118	**800-238-7277**	901-369-4400	544
BryCoat Inc	207 Vollmer Ave	Oldsmar	FL	34677	**800-989-8788**	727-490-1000	546
BryLin Hospitals	1263 Delaware Ave	Buffalo	NY	14209	**800-727-9546**	716-886-8200	373-5
Bryn Mawr Rehab Hospital	414 Paoli Pk	Malvern	PA	19355	**866-225-5654**	484-596-5400	373-6
BSA (Boy Scouts of America)	1325 W Walnut Hill Ln PO Box 152079	Irving	TX	75015	**800-323-0732**	972-580-2000	48-15
BSC America Inc	803 Bel Air Rd	Bel Air	MD	21014	**800-764-7400**		461
BSCAI (Building Service Contractors Assn International)	401 N Michigan Ave Ste 2200	Chicago	IL	60611	**800-368-3414**	312-321-5167	49-13
BSI (Badger State Industries)	3099 E Washington Ave PO Box 8990	Madison	WI	53708	**800-862-1086**	608-240-5200	626
BSM Wireless Inc	75 International Blvd Ste 100	Toronto	ON	M9W6L9	**866-768-4771**	416-675-1201	688
BSN Medical Inc	5825 Carnegie Blvd	Charlotte	NC	28209	**800-552-1157**	704-554-9933	475
BSQUARE Corp	110 110th Ave NE Ste 300	Bellevue	WA	98004	**888-820-4500**	425-519-5900	178-2
	NASDAQ: BSQR						
BSSB (Boiling Springs Savings Bank)	25 Orient Way	Rutherford	NJ	07070	**888-388-7459**	201-939-5000	70
BT Conferencing Inc	30 Braintree Hill Office Pk Ste 301	Braintree	MA	02184	**866-766-8777**	617-801-6700	359-3
B&t Service Station Contractors	630 S Frontage Rd	Nipomo	CA	93444	**888-862-2552**	805-929-8944	324
BTA (Business Technology Assn)	12411 Wornall Rd Ste 200	Kansas City	MO	64145	**800-325-7219**	816-941-3100	49-18
BTD Manufacturing	1111 13th Ave SE	Detroit Lakes	MN	56501	**866-562-3986**		486
BTG International Inc	5 Tower Bridge 300 Barr Harbor Dr Ste 810	West Conshohocken	PA	19428	**888-327-1027**	610-278-1660	
BTI (Benchmark Technologies International Inc)	411 Hackensack Ave	Hackensack	NJ	07601	**800-265-8254**	201-996-0077	194
BTI Group	4 N Second St Ste 560	San Jose	CA	95113	**800-622-0192**	408-246-1102	196
BTM Solutions Inc	572 Yorkville Rd E	Columbus	MS	39702	**800-909-9381**	662-328-2400	177
BTS (IEEE Broadcast Technology Society)	445 Hoes Ln	Piscataway	NJ	08854	**800-678-4333**	732-562-5407	49-19
BTS (Brazilian Travel Service)	16 W 46th St 2nd Fl	New York	NY	10036	**800-342-5746**	212-764-6161	16
BTS Asset Management Inc	420 Bedford St Ste 340	Lexington	MA	02420	**800-343-3040**		400
BTS USA Inc	222 Kearny St Ste 1000	San Francisco	CA	94108	**800-445-7089**	415-362-4200	194
BTSB (Bound to Stay Bound Books Inc)	1880 W Morton Ave	Jacksonville	IL	62650	**800-637-6586**	217-245-5191	92
BTU International Inc	23 Esquire Rd	North Billerica	MA	01862	**800-998-0666**	978-667-4111	691
	NASDAQ: BTUI						
Bubba Gump Shrimp Co LLC	2501 Seawall Blvd	Galveston	TX	77550	**800-552-6379**	409-766-4952	666
Buchanan Automotive Group	707 S Washington Blvd	Sarasota	FL	34236	**888-349-4989**		
Buchanan Hauling & Rigging	4625 Industrial Rd	Fort Wayne	IN	46825	**888-544-4285**	260-471-1877	775
Bucher & Christian Consulting Inc	9777 N College	Indianapolis	IN	46280	**866-363-1132**		194
Buck & Knobby Equipment Co	6220 Sterns Rd	Ottawa Lake	MI	49267	**855-213-2825**	734-856-2811	264-3
Buck Chuck Co	2155 Traversefield Dr	Traverse City	MI	49686	**800-228-2825**		491
Buck Distributing Company Inc	15827 Commerce Ct	Upper Marlboro	MD	20774	**800-750-2825***	301-952-0400	81-1
	*Cust Svc						
Buck Knives Inc	660 S Lochsa St	Post Falls	ID	83854	**800-326-2825**	208-262-0500	222
Buck's Pizza Franchising Corp Inc	PO Box 405	Du Bois	PA	15801	**800-310-8848**		666
Buckeye Business Products Inc	3830 Kelley Ave	Cleveland	OH	44114	**800-837-4323**		624
Buckeye Career Ctr	545 University Dr NE	New Philadelphia	OH	44663	**800-227-1665**	330-339-2288	162
Buckeye International Inc	2700 Wagner Pl	Maryland Heights	MO	63043	**800-321-2583**	314-291-1900	151
Buckeye Nissan Inc	3820 Pkwy Ln	Hilliard	OH	43026	**800-686-4391**	614-771-2345	57
Buckeye Nutrition	330 E Schultz Ave	Dalton	OH	44618	**800-417-6460**		445
Buckeye Pacific LLC	4386 SW Macadam Ave Ste 200	Portland	OR	97207	**800-767-9191**	503-274-2284	191-3
Buckeye Power Sales Company Inc	6850 Commerce Ct Dr	Blacklick	OH	43004	**800-523-3587**	614-861-6000	616
Buckeye Rural Electric Co-op	4848 State Rt 325 PO Box 200	Patriot	OH	45658	**800-231-2732**	740-379-2025	245
Buckeye ShapeForm	555 Marion Rd	Columbus	OH	43207	**800-728-0776**	614-445-8433	254
Buckham Memorial Library	11 Div St E	Faribault	MN	55021	**800-658-2354**	507-334-2089	433-3
Buckhorn Inc	55 W Techne Ctr Dr	Milford	OH	45150	**800-543-4454**		199
Buckhorn Lake State Resort Park	4441 Ky Hwy 1833	Buckhorn	KY	41721	**800-325-0058**	606-398-7510	561
Buckingham County	13360 W James Anderson Hwy	Buckingham	VA	23921	**800-440-6116**	434-969-4242	337
Buckingham's Restaurant & Oasis	2820 W Hwy 76	Branson	MO	65616	**800-725-2236**	417-337-7777	667
Buckle Inc	2407 W 24th St	Kearney	NE	68845	**800-626-1255**	308-236-8491	157-4
	NYSE: BKE						
Buckles-Smith	801 Savaker Ave	San Jose	CA	95126	**800-833-7362**		246
Buckley Energy Group Ltd	154 Admiral St	Bridgeport	CT	06605	**800-937-2682**		316
Buckley Industries Inc	1850 E 53rd St N	Wichita	KS	67219	**800-835-2779**	316-744-7587	599
Buckley Oil Company Inc	1809 Rock Island St	Dallas	TX	75207	**800-721-4147**	214-421-4147	577
Buckley Powder Co	42 Inverness Dr E	Englewood	CO	80112	**800-333-2266**	303-790-7007	268
Bucklin Tractor & Implement Co	115 W Railroad PO Box 127	Bucklin	KS	67834	**800-334-4823**	620-826-3271	273
Buckman Buckman & Reid Inc	174 Patterson Ave	Shrewsbury	NJ	07702	**800-531-0303**	732-530-0303	400
Buckner International	700 N Pearl St Ste 1200	Dallas	TX	75201	**800-442-4800**	214-758-8000	48-6
Bucks County	55 E Ct St	Doylestown	PA	18901	**888-942-8257**	215-348-6000	337
Bucks County Water & Sewer Authority (BCWSA)	1275 Almshouse Rd	Warrington	PA	18976	**800-222-2068**	215-343-2538	801
Budco Inc	PO Box 3065	Tulsa	OK	74101	**800-747-7307**		457
Buddy Moore Trucking Inc	925 34th St N	Birmingham	AL	35222	**877-366-6566**		775
Buddy Rogers Music Inc	6891 Simpson Ave	Cincinnati	OH	45239	**800-536-2263**	513-729-1950	522
Buddy's Home Furnishings	4705 S Apopka Vineland Rd	Orlando	FL	32819	**855-298-9325***	866-779-5058	264-2
	*Cust Svc						
Budget Blinds Inc	1927 N Glassell St	Orange	CA	92865	**800-800-9250**	949-404-1100	87
Budget Finance Co	1849 Sawtelle Blvd	Los Angeles	CA	90025	**800-225-6267**	310-696-4050	217
Budget Host International	2307 Roosevelt Dr	Arlington	TX	76016	**800-283-4678**	817-861-6088	378
Budget Rent A Car System Inc	6 Sylvan Way	Parsippany	NJ	07054	**800-527-0700**	800-283-4382	126
Budreck Truck Lines Inc	2642 Joseph Ct	University Park	IL	60484	**800-621-0013**	708-496-0522	186
Buehler Companies	16456 E Airport Cir Ste 100	Aurora	CO	80011	**800-234-6683**	303-388-4000	516
Buehler Food Markets Inc	1401 Old Mansfield Rd	Wooster	OH	44691	**800-998-4438**	330-264-4355	344
Buehler Ltd	41 Waukegan Rd	Lake Bluff	IL	60044	**800-283-4537***	847-295-6500	418
	*Sales						
Buena Park Convention & Visitors Office	6601 Beach Blvd	Buena Park	CA	90621	**800-541-3953**		206
Buena Vista Motor Inn	1599 Lombard St	San Francisco	CA	94123	**800-835-4980**	415-923-9600	377
Buena Vista Regional Medical Ctr	PO Box 309	Storm Lake	IA	50588	**877-401-8030**	712-732-4030	373-3
Buena Vista University	610 W Fourth St	Storm Lake	IA	50588	**800-383-9600**	712-749-2253	166
Buff & Shine Manufacturing	2139 E Del Amo Blvd	Rancho Dominguez	CA	90220	**800-659-2833**	310-886-5111	295
Buffalo & Pittsburgh Railroad Inc (BPRR)	1200-C Scottsville Rd Ste 200	Rochester	NY	14624	**800-603-3385**	585-463-3307	644
Buffalo Bill's Resort & Casino	31900 Las Vegas Blvd S	Primm	NV	89019	**888-774-6668**	702-386-7867	133
Buffalo Bills	1 Bills Dr	Orchard Park	NY	14127	**877-228-4257**	716-648-1800	711-2
Buffalo City Hall	65 Niagara Sq	Buffalo	NY	14202	**800-541-2437**	716-851-4200	336
Buffalo Dental Manufacturing Company Inc	159 Lafayette Dr	Syosset	NY	11791	**800-828-0203**	516-496-7200	228
Buffalo Games Inc	220 James E Casey Dr	Buffalo	NY	14206	**855-895-4290**		757
Buffalo General Hospital	100 High St	Buffalo	NY	14203	**800-506-6480**	716-859-5600	373-3
Buffalo Industries Inc	99 S Spokane St	Seattle	WA	98134	**800-683-0052**	206-682-9900	740-8
Buffalo Museum of Science	1020 Humboldt Pkwy	Buffalo	NY	14211	**866-291-6660**	716-896-5200	517
Buffalo National River	402 N Walnut St Ste 136	Harrison	AR	72601	**800-447-7538**	870-439-2502	560
Buffalo News	1 News Plz PO Box 100	Buffalo	NY	14240	**800-777-8640**	716-849-4444	528-2
Buffalo Niagara Convention & Visitors Bureau	403 Main St Ste 630	Buffalo	NY	14203	**800-283-3256**	716-852-2356	206

Name	Address	City	State	ZIP	Toll-Free	Phone	Class
Buffalo Niagara Convention Ctr	153 Franklin St	Buffalo	NY	14202	**800-995-7570**	716-855-5555	205
Buffalo Niagara International Airport	4200 Genesee St	Cheektowaga	NY	14225	**877-359-2642**	716-630-6000	27
Buffalo Niagara Partnership	665 Main St	Buffalo	NY	14203	**844-308-9165**	716-566-5400	139
Buffalo Psychiatric Ctr	400 Forest Ave	Buffalo	NY	14213	**800-597-8481**	716-885-2261	373-5
Buffalo Specialties Inc	10706 Craighead Dr	Houston	TX	77025	**800-256-0838**	713-271-6107	683
Buffalo Spree Magazine	100 Corporate Pkwy Ste 220	Buffalo	NY	14226	**855-697-7733**	716-783-9119	455-22
Buffalo Supply Inc	1650A Coal Creek Dr	Lafayette	CO	80026	**800-366-1812**	303-666-6333	238
Buffalo Wire Works Co	1165 Clinton St	Buffalo	NY	14206	**800-828-7028**	716-826-4666	684
Buffelen Woodworking Co	1901 Taylor Way	Tacoma	WA	98421	**800-423-8810**	253-627-1191	497
Bugcrowd	921 Front St 1st Fl	San Francisco	CA	94111	**888-361-9734**		196
Buglisi Dance Theatre	229 W 42nd St Ste 502	New York	NY	10036	**800-754-0797**	212-719-3301	569-1
BUG-O Systems Inc	161 Hillpointe Dr	Canonsburg	PA	15317	**800-245-3186**	412-331-1776	806
Buhler Inc	13105 12th Ave N	Plymouth	MN	55441	**800-722-7483**	763-847-9900	201
Build-A-Bear Workshop Inc	1954 Innerbelt Business Ctr Dr; *NYSE: BBW*	Saint Louis	MO	63114	**877-789-2327**		756
BuildASigncom	11525B Stonehollow Dr Ste 100	Austin	TX	78758	**800-330-9622**	512-374-9850	177
Builder Magazine	1 Thomas Cir NW Ste 600	Washington	DC	20005	**800-325-6180**	202-452-0800	455-21
Builders General Supply Co	15 Sycamore Ave	Little Silver	NJ	07739	**800-570-7227**		191-3
Builders Hardware & Supply Company Inc	1516 15th Ave W	Seattle	WA	98119	**800-828-1437**	206-281-3700	350
Builders Redi-Mix Inc	30701 W 10 Mile Rd Ste 500 PO Box 2900	Farmington Hills	MI	48333	**888-988-4400**		182
Building & Earth Sciences Inc	5545 Derby Dr	Birmingham	AL	35210	**800-775-2468**		
Building Block Computer	3209 Terminal Dr Ste 100	Eagan	MN	55121	**800-272-2650**	651-687-9435	
Building Industry Credit Association	10601 Civic Center Dr	Rancho Cucamonga	CA	91730	**800-722-2422**	909-303-2300	218
Building Material Dealers Assn (BMDA)	1006 SE Grand Ave Ste 301	Portland	OR	97214	**888-960-6329**	503-208-3763	49-3
Building Owners & Managers Assn International (BOMA)	1101 15th St NW Ste 800	Washington	DC	20005	**800-426-6292**	202-408-2662	49-17
Building Performance Institute Inc	107 Hermes Rd Ste 210	Malta	NY	12020	**877-274-1274**	518-899-2727	194
Building Products Corp	950 Freeburg Ave	Belleville	IL	62220	**800-233-1996**	618-233-4427	182
Building Products Plus	12317 Almeda Rd	Houston	TX	77045	**800-460-8627**	713-434-8008	813
Building Service Contractors Assn International (BSCAI)	401 N Michigan Ave Ste 2200	Chicago	IL	60611	**800-368-3414**	312-321-5167	49-13
Bulk Lift International Inc (BLI)	1013 Tamarac Dr	Carpentersville	IL	60110	**800-879-2247**	847-428-6059	67
Bulk Transit Corp	7177 Industrial Pkwy	Plain City	OH	43064	**800-345-2855**	614-873-4632	775
Bulkmatic Transport Co	2001 N Cline Ave	Griffith	IN	46319	**800-535-8505**		775
Bull Moose Tube Co	1819 Clarkson Rd Ste 100	Chesterfield	MO	63017	**800-325-4467**	636-537-2600	488
Bull Shoals-White River State Park	153 Dam Overlook Ln	Bull Shoals	AR	72169	**877-879-2741**		
Bull Wealth Management Group Inc	4100 Yonge St Ste 612	Toronto	ON	M2P2B5	**866-623-2053**	416-223-2053	686
Bullard Abrasives Inc	6 Carol Dr	Lincoln	RI	02865	**800-227-4469**	401-333-3000	1
Bullard Co	1898 Safety Way	Cynthiana	KY	41031	**800-227-0423**	859-234-6611	572
Bulldog Bag Ltd	13631 Vulcan Way	Richmond	BC	V6V1K4	**800-665-1944**	604-273-8021	597
Bulldog Hiway Express	3390 Buffalo Ave	Charleston	SC	29418	**800-331-9515**	843-744-1651	447
Bulldog Solutions LLC	7600 N Capital of Texas Hwy Bldg C Ste 250	Austin	TX	78731	**877-402-9199**		5
Bullen Cos	1640 Delmar Dr PO Box 37	Folcroft	PA	19032	**800-444-8900**	610-534-8900	151
Bulletin, The	1777 Chandler Ave	Bend	OR	97702	**800-503-3933**	541-382-1811	528-2
Bullfrog Films Inc	372 Dautrich Rd	Reading	PA	19606	**800-543-3764**	610-779-8226	511
Bullhorn Inc	33-41 Farnsworth St 5th Fl	Boston	MA	02210	**800-206-7934**	617-478-9100	177
Bulloch & Bulloch Inc	309 Cash Memorial Blvd	Forest Park	GA	30297	**800-339-8177**	404-762-5063	25
Bullock Steve (D)	*State Capitol* PO Box 200801	Helena	MT	59620	**855-318-1330**	406-444-3111	
Bullseye Glass Co	3722 SE 21st Ave	Portland	OR	97202	**888-220-3002**	503-232-8887	329
Bulova Corp	Empire State Bldg 350 Fifth Ave	New York	NY	10118	**800-228-5682**	212-497-1875	153
Bumble Bee Seafoods Inc	PO Box 85362	San Diego	CA	92186	**800-800-8572**	858-715-4000	296-13
Bunker Hill Community College	*Charlestown* 250 New Rutherford Ave	Boston	MA	02129	**877-218-8829**	617-228-2000	162
Bunnell Inc	436 Lawndale Dr	Salt Lake City	UT	84115	**800-800-4358**	801-467-0800	474
Bunn-O-Matic Corp	1400 Stevenson Dr	Springfield	IL	62703	**800-637-8606**	217-529-6601	37
Bunting Bearings Corp	1001 Holland Pk Blvd	Holland	OH	43528	**888-286-8464**	419-866-7000	308
Bunting Magnetics Co	500 S Spencer Ave	Newton	KS	67114	**800-835-2526**	316-284-2020	483
Burbank Chamber of Commerce	200 W Magnolia Blvd	Burbank	CA	91502	**800-495-5005**	818-846-3111	139
Burberry Ltd (New York)	444 Madison Ave	New York	NY	10022	**877-217-4085**	212-407-7100	157-4
Burch Fabrics Group	4200 Brockton Dr SE	Grand Rapids	MI	49512	**800-841-8111**	616-698-2800	590
Burchell Nursery Inc, The	12000 Hwy 120	Oakdale	CA	95361	**800-828-8733**	209-845-8733	292
Burchfield Group Inc, The	1295 Northland Dr Ste 350	St Paul	MN	55120	**800-778-1359**	651-389-5640	194
Burd & Fletcher	5151 E Geospace Dr	Independence	MO	64056	**800-821-2776**		101
Burdette Beckmann Inc	5851 Johnson St	Hollywood	FL	33021	**888-575-7413**	954-983-4360	123
Bureau of Consular Affairs	2201 C St NW SA 17 9th Fl	Washington	DC	20522	**888-407-4747**	202-501-4444	339-15
	Office of Children's Issues 2201 C St NW SA-17 9th Fl	Washington	DC	20522	**888-407-4747**	202-501-4444	339-15
	Passport Services 600 19th St NW 1st Fl Sidewalk Level	Washington	DC	20006	**888-874-7793**	877-487-2778	339-15
Bureau of Diplomatic Security	DS Public Affairs Bureau of Diplomatic Security US. Department of St	Washington	DC	20522	**866-217-2089**	571-345-3146	
Bureau of Engraving & Printing	14th & C Sts SW	Washington	DC	20228	**877-874-4114**		339-17
Bureau of Indian Affairs Regional Offices (BIA)							
	Alaska Region 3601 C St Ste 1100	Anchorage	AK	99503	**800-645-8397**	907-271-4085	339-12
	Eastern Oklahoma Region 3100 W Peak Blvd PO Box 8002	Muskogee	OK	74402	**800-645-8397**	918-781-4600	339-12
	Northwest Region 911 NE 11th Ave	Portland	OR	97232	**800-645-8397**	503-231-6702	339-12
	Pacific Region 2800 Cottage Way	Sacramento	CA	95825	**800-645-8397**	916-978-6000	339-12
	Rocky Mountain Region 316 N 26th St	Billings	MT	59101	**800-645-8397**	406-247-7943	339-12
	Southern Plains Region PO Box 368	Anadarko	OK	73005	**800-645-8465**	405-247-6673	339-12
Bureau of Labor Statistics	*Southeast Information Office* 61 Forsyth St SW Rm 7T25	Atlanta	GA	30303	**800-347-3764**	404-893-4222	339-14
Bureau of Land Management	*Wild Horse & Burro Program* 1849 C St NW Rm 5665	Washington	DC	20240	**866-468-7826**	202-208-3801	339-12
Bureau of Land Management Regional Offices	*Eastern States Office* 7450 Boston Blvd	Springfield	VA	22153	**800-370-3936**	703-440-1600	339-12
Bureau of the Public Debt	PO Box 7015	Parkersburg	WV	26106	**800-722-2678**		339-17
	TreasuryDirect PO Box 7015	Parkersburg	WV	26106	**844-284-2676**		339-17
Burger & Brown Engineering Inc	4500 E 142nd St	Grandview	MO	64030	**800-764-3518**	816-878-6675	452
Burger King Corp	5505 Blue Lagoon Dr	Miami	FL	33126	**866-394-2493**	305-378-3000	666
Burger's Ozark Country Cured Hams Inc	32819 Hwy 87	California	MO	65018	**800-203-4424**	573-796-3134	296-26
Burgerville USA	109 W 17th St	Vancouver	WA	98660	**888-827-8369**		666
Burgess Group LLC, The	1701 Duke St Ste 300	Alexandria	VA	22314	**800-637-2004**	703-894-1800	
Burgess Industries Inc (BII)	7500 Boone Ave N Ste 111	Brooklyn Park	MN	55428	**800-233-2589**	763-553-7800	625
Burgess Pigment Company Inc	525 Beck Blvd PO Box 349	Sandersville	GA	31082	**800-841-8999**	478-552-2544	498
Burghardt Sporting Goods	14660 W Capitol Dr	Brookfield	WI	53005	**866-790-6606**	262-790-1170	707
Burgundy Asset Management Ltd	Bay Wellington Tower Brookfield Pl 181 Bay St Ste 4510	Toronto	ON	M5J2T3	**888-480-1790**	416-869-3222	686
Burke & Herbert Bank & Trust Co	100 S Fairfax St	Alexandria	VA	22314	**877-440-0800**	703-751-7701	70
Burke E Porter Machinery Co	730 Plymouth Ave NE	Grand Rapids	MI	49505	**800-562-9133**	616-234-1200	385
Burke Handling Systems	431 Hwy 49 S	Jackson	MS	39218	**800-222-5400**	601-939-6600	765
Burke Inc	1800 Merriam Ln; *Sales	Kansas City	KS	66106	**800-255-4147***		475
Burke International Tours Inc	PO Box 890	Newton	NC	28658	**800-476-3900**	828-465-3900	755
Burke Museum of Natural History & Culture	17th Ave NE & NE 45th St	Seattle	WA	98195	**800-411-9671**	206-543-5590	517
Burke Rehabilitation Hospital	785 Mamaroneck Ave	White Plains	NY	10605	**888-992-8753**	914-597-2500	373-6
Burkett Oil Company Inc	6788 Best Friend Rd	Norcross	GA	30071	**800-228-1786**	770-447-8030	575
Burkhalter Travel Agency	6501 Mineral Pt Rd	Madison	WI	53705	**800-556-9286**	608-833-5200	766
Burkhart Advertising Inc	1335 Mishawaka Ave	South Bend	IN	46615	**800-777-8122**	574-233-2101	7
Burkhart Dental Supply Co	2502 S 78th St; *Cust Svc	Tacoma	WA	98409	**800-562-8176***	253-474-7761	473
Burklund Distributors Inc	2500 N Main St Ste 3	East Peoria	IL	61611	**800-322-2876**	309-694-1900	297-3
Burks Tractor Co Inc	3140 Kimberly Rd	Twin Falls	ID	83301	**800-247-7419**	208-733-5543	274
Burleigh County	514 E Thayer Ave PO Box 1055	Bismarck	ND	58502	**877-222-6682**	701-222-6690	337
Burlington Coat Factory	1830 Rt 130 N	Burlington	NJ	08016	**855-355-2875**	609-387-7800	361

Alphabetical Section

Name	Address	City	State	ZIP	Toll-Free	Phone	Class
Burlington Drug Company Inc	91 Catamount Dr	Milton	VT	05468	**800-338-8703**	802-893-5105	231
Burlington Free Press	100 Bank St	Burlington	VT	05401	**800-427-3124**	802-660-1819	528-2
Burlington Hawk Eye Co	800 S Main St PO Box 10	Burlington	IA	52601	**800-397-1708**	319-754-8461	633-8
Burlington Mall	75 Middlesex Tpke	Burlington	MA	01803	**877-746-6642**	781-272-8667	458
Burlington Medical Supplies Inc	3 Elmhurst St	Newport News	VA	23603	**800-221-3466**		
Burlington Northern & Santa Fe Railway (BNSF)	2650 Lou Menk Dr	Fort Worth	TX	76131	**800-795-2673**		644
Burlington Public Library	22 Sears St	Burlington	MA	01803	**800-422-2462**	781-270-1690	433-3
Burlington/Alamance County Convention & Visitors Bureau	200 S Main St PO Box 519	Burlington	NC	27216	**800-637-3804**	336-570-1444	206
Burmax Co	28 Barretts Ave	Holtsville	NY	11742	**800-645-5118**		76
Burndy LLC	47 E Industrial Park Dr	Manchester	NH	03109	**800-346-4175**		810
Burnett County	7410 County Rd K	Siren	WI	54872	**800-788-3164**	715-349-2181	337
Burnett Dairy Co-op	11631 SR- 70	Grantsburg	WI	54840	**800-854-2716**	715-689-2468	296-5
Burney Co	1800 Alexander Bell Dr Ste 510	Reston	VA	20191	**866-928-7639**		
Burnham & Flower Group Inc	315 S Kalamazoo Mall	Kalamazoo	MI	49007	**888-748-7966**	269-381-1173	389
Burns & McBride Inc	18 Boulden Cir Ste 30	New Castle	DE	19720	**800-756-5110**	302-656-5110	316
Burns Bog Conservation Society	7953 120 St	Delta	BC	V4C6P6	**888-850-6264**	604-572-0373	138
Burns Burns Walsh & Walsh PA	704 Topeka Ave	Lyndon	KS	66451	**888-528-3186**	785-828-4418	427
Burns Controls Co	13735 Beta Rd	Dallas	TX	75244	**800-442-2010**	972-233-6712	357
Burns Engineering Inc	10201 Bren Rd E	Minnetonka	MN	55343	**800-328-3871**	952-935-4400	256
Burns Mailing & Printing Inc	6131 Industrial Heights Dr PO Box 52730	Knoxville	TN	37909	**866-288-5618**	865-584-2265	623
Burns Motor Freight Inc	500 Seneca Trl N	Marlinton	WV	24954	**800-598-5674**	304-799-6106	775
Burns Pest Elimination Inc	2620 Grovers Ave	Phoenix	AZ	85053	**877-971-4782**	602-971-4782	573
Burnsville Chamber of Commerce	350 W Burnsville Pkwy Ste 425	Burnsville	MN	55337	**800-521-6055**	952-435-6000	139
Burr Oak Tool Inc	405 W S St	Sturgis	MI	49091	**800-861-8864**	269-651-9393	453
Burrell Imaging	1311 Merrillville Rd	Crown Point	IN	46307	**800-348-8732**	219-663-3210	584
BurrellesLuce	30 B Vreeland Rd PO Box 674	Florham Park	NJ	07932	**800-631-1160**	973-992-6600	386
Burris Company Inc	331 E Eighth St	Greeley	CO	80631	**888-228-7747**	970-356-1670	540
Burris Logistics	501 SE Fifth St	Milford	DE	19963	**800-805-8135**	302-839-5157	798-2
Burrows Paper Corp	501 W Main St	Little Falls	NY	13365	**800-272-7122**	315-823-2300	553
Burrows Paper Corp Packaging Group	2000 Commerce Ctr Dr	Franklin	OH	45005	**800-732-1933**	937-746-1933	544
Burrtec Waste Industries Inc	9890 Cherry Ave	Fontana	CA	92335	**888-287-7832**	909-429-4200	799
Bursma Electronic Distributing Inc	2851 Buchanan Ave SW	Grand Rapids	MI	49548	**800-777-2604**	616-831-0080	38
Burstek	12801 Westlinks Dr Ste 101	Fort Myers	FL	33913	**800-709-2551**	239-495-5900	174
Burt County Public Power District	613 N 13th St	Tekamah	NE	68061	**888-835-1620**	402-374-2631	245
Burtco Inc	185 Rt 123	Westminster Station	VT	05159	**800-451-4401**	802-722-3358	183
Burton & Mayer Inc	W140 N9000 Lilly Rd	Menomonee Falls	WI	53051	**800-236-1770**	262-781-0770	623
Burton Neil & Assoc	1060 Andrew Dr Ste 160	West Chester	PA	19380	**866-696-2120**	610-696-2120	443
Bus Andrews Truck Equipment Inc	2828 N E Ave	Springfield	MO	65803	**800-273-0733**	417-869-1541	57
Busch Distributors Inc	7603 State Rt 270	Pullman	WA	99163	**800-752-2295**	509-339-6600	577
Busch Vacuum Technics Inc	1740 Lionel Bertrand	Boisbriand	QC	J7H1N7	**800-363-6360**	450-435-6899	637
Buscomm Inc	11696 Lilburn Park Rd	Saint Louis	MO	63146	**800-283-7755**	314-567-7755	177
Buse Timber & Sales Inc	3812 28th Pl NE	Everett	WA	98201	**800-305-2577**	425-258-2577	679
Bush Industries Inc	1 Mason Dr	Jamestown	NY	14701	**800-950-4782**	716-665-2000	319-2
Bushnell Corp	9200 Cody St	Overland Park	KS	66214	**800-423-3537**	913-752-3400	540
Bushnell Ctr for the Performing Arts	166 Capitol Ave	Hartford	CT	06106	**888-824-2874**	860-987-6000	568
Bushwacker Inc	6710 N Catlin Ave	Portland	OR	97203	**800-234-8920**	503-283-4335	60
Bushwick Metals LLC	560 N Washington Ave	Bridgeport	CT	06604	**888-399-4070**		719
Business & Legal Reports Inc (BLR)	141 Mill Rock Rd E	Old Saybrook	CT	06475	**800-727-5257**	860-510-0100	633-9
Business Council of Alabama	2 N Jackson St PO Box 76	Montgomery	AL	36101	**800-665-9647**	334-834-6000	140
Business Council of New York State Inc	152 Washington Ave	Albany	NY	12210	**800-358-1202**	518-465-7511	140
Business Facilities Magazine	44 Apple St Ste 3	Tinton Falls	NJ	07724	**800-524-0337**	732-842-7433	455-5
Business Forms Management Assn (BFMA)	3800 Old Cheney Rd Ste 101-285	Lincoln	NE	68516	**888-367-3078**		49-12
Business Furniture Corp	8421 Bearing Dr Ste 200	Indianapolis	IN	46278	**800-774-5544**	317-216-1600	320
Business Inn	180 MacLaren St	Ottawa	ON	K2P0L3	**800-363-1777**	613-232-1121	378
Business Insurance Magazine	711 Third Ave	New York	NY	10017	**877-812-1587**	212-210-0100	455-5
Business Interiors	1111 Valley View Ln	Irving	TX	75061	**800-568-9281**		321
Business Journal, The	25 E Boardman St	Youngstown	OH	44501	**800-837-6397**	330-744-5023	455-5
Business News Network (BNN)	299 Queen St W	Toronto	ON	M5V2Z5	**855-326-6266**	416-384-6600	735
Business News Publishing Co	2401 W Big Beaver Rd Ste 700	Troy	MI	48084	**800-837-7370**	248-362-3700	633-9
Business Professionals of America	5454 Cleveland Ave	Columbus	OH	43231	**800-334-2007**	614-895-7277	49-5
Business Protection Specialists Inc	1296 E Victor Rd	Victor	NY	14564	**800-560-2199**		689
Business Resource Group (BRG)	10440 N Central Expy Ste 1150	Dallas	TX	75231	**888-391-9166**	214-777-5100	194
Business Technology Assn (BTA)	12411 Wornall Rd Ste 200	Kansas City	MO	64145	**800-325-7219**	816-941-3100	49-18
Business Training Library Inc	14500 S Outer Forty Ste 500	Town and Country	MO	63017	**888-432-3077**		
Business Valuation Center LLC	1717 Pennsylvania Ave NW Ste 1025	Washington	DC	20006	**800-856-6780**	703-787-0012	461
Business Wire	101 California St 20th Fl	San Francisco	CA	94111	**800-227-0845**	415-986-4422	
BusinessBroker Network LLC	375 Northridge Rd Ste 475	Atlanta	GA	30350	**877-342-9786**		
BusinessPlans Inc	432 E Pearl St	Miamisburg	OH	45342	**800-865-4485**		461
Buskirk Lumber Co	319 Oak St	Freeport	MI	49325	**800-860-9663**		679
Busse/SJI Corp	124 N Columbus St	Randolph	WI	53956	**800-882-4995**		468
Butchart Gardens, The	800 Benvenuto Ave	Brentwood Bay	BC	V8M1J8	**866-652-4422**	250-652-4422	97
Butcher Distributors Inc	101 Boyce Rd	Broussard	LA	70518	**800-960-0008**	337-837-2088	608
Butler Brothers Supply Division Inc	2001 Lisbon St	Lewiston	ME	04240	**888-784-6875**	207-784-6875	186
Butler County	205 W Central Ave	El Dorado	KS	67042	**800-822-6104**	316-322-4300	337
Butler County	315 High St	Hamilton	OH	45011	**800-582-4267**	513-887-3278	337
Butler County Community College	107 College Dr	Butler	PA	16002	**888-826-2829**	724-287-8711	162
Butler County REC	521 N Main PO Box 98	Allison	IA	50602	**888-267-2726**	319-267-2726	245
Butler Eagle	114 W Diamond St	Butler	PA	16001	**800-842-8098**	724-282-8000	528-2
Butler Motor Transit	210 S Monroe St PO Box 1602	Butler	PA	16003	**800-222-8750**	724-282-1000	107
Butler Public Power District	1331 N Fourth St	David City	NE	68632	**800-230-0569**	402-367-3081	245
Butler Rural Electric Co-op Assn Inc	216 S Vine St PO Box 1242	El Dorado	KS	67042	**800-464-0060**	316-321-9600	245
Butler Rural Electric Co-op Inc (BREC)	3888 Still-Beckett Rd	Oxford	OH	45056	**800-255-2732**	513-867-4400	245
Butler Supply Inc	965 Horan Dr	St.Louis	MO	63026	**800-850-9949**	636-349-9000	246
Butler Technologies Inc	231 W Wayne St	Butler	PA	16001	**800-494-6656**	724-283-6656	174
Butler Transport Inc	347 N James St *Cust Svc	Kansas City	KS	66118	**800-345-8158***		775
Butler University	4600 Sunset Ave	Indianapolis	IN	46208	**800-368-6852**	317-940-8100	166
Butler-Dearden Paper Service Inc	PO Box 1069	Boylston	MA	01505	**800-634-7070**	508-869-9000	555
Butte College	3536 Butte Campus Dr *Hum Res	Oroville	CA	95965	**800-933-8322***	530-895-2511	162
Butte Electric Co-op	109 Dartmouth Ave	Newell	SD	57760	**800-928-8839**	605-456-2494	245
Butterfly House - Faust Park, The	15193 Olive Blvd	Chesterfield	MO	63017	**800-642-8842**	636-530-0076	50-5
Butters-Fetting Company Inc	1669 S First St	Milwaukee	WI	53204	**800-361-6154**	414-645-1535	189-10
Butte-Silver Bow Chamber of Commerce	1000 George St	Butte	MT	59701	**800-735-6814**	406-723-3177	139
Butts Foods Inc	2596 Bransford Ave	Nashville	TN	37204	**800-962-8570**	615-674-2030	297-10
Buurma Farms Inc	3909 Kok Rd	Willard	OH	44890	**888-428-8762**	419-935-6411	10-9
Buxton Co	245 Cadwell Dr	Springfield	MA	01104	**800-426-3638**	413-734-5900	429
Buxton Co	2651 S Polaris Dr	Fort Worth	TX	76137	**888-228-9866**		
Buyatab Online Inc	B1 - 788 Beatty St	Vancouver	BC	V6B2M1	**888-267-0447**		224
BV (BeenVerified Inc)	48 W 38th St 8th Fl	New York	NY	10018	**888-579-5910**		317
BW Container Systems	1305 Lakeview Dr	Romeoville	IL	60446	**800-527-0494**	630-759-6800	207
BW Papersystems	3333 Crocker Ave	Sheboygan	WI	53082	**888-310-1898**	920-458-2500	552
BWAY Corp	8607 Roberts Dr Ste 250	Atlanta	GA	30350	**800-527-2267**	770-645-4800	124
BWI (Baltimore/Washington International Thurgood Marsha)	PO Box 8766	Baltimore	MD	21240	**800-435-9294**	410-859-7111	27
Byard F Brogan Inc	PO Box 0369	Glenside	PA	19038	**800-232-7642**	215-885-3550	408
Bybee Stone Company Inc	6293 N Matthews Dr	Ellettsville	IN	47429	**800-457-4530**	812-876-2215	720

				Toll-Free	Phone	Class
Byerly Ford 4041 Dixie Hwy	Louisville	KY	40216	888-436-0819	502-448-1661	57
Byers-Evans House Museum 1310 Bannock St	Denver	CO	80204	800-824-0150	303-620-4933	517
Byram Healthcare Centers Inc 120 Bloomingdale Rd	White Plains	NY	10605	800-354-4054	877-902-9726	473
Byrd Cookie Company Inc 6700 Waters Ave	Savannah	GA	31406	800-291-2973	912-355-1716	344
Byron Originals Fuel Sales 119 E State Hwy 175 PO Box 279	Ida Grove	IA	51445	800-594-9421		575
Bytemobile Inc 4988 Great America Pkwy	Santa Clara	CA	95054	800-424-8749	408-790-8000	677
Bytespeed LLC 3131 24th Ave S	Moorhead	MN	56560	877-553-0777	218-227-0445	173-2

C

				Toll-Free	Phone	Class
C & A Industries Inc 13609 California St	Omaha	NE	68154	800-574-9829	402-891-0009	717
C & D Technologies Inc 1400 Union Meeting Rd PO Box 3053	Blue Bell	PA	19422	800-543-8630	215-619-2700	74
C & F Enterprises Inc 819 Bluecrab Rd	Newport News	VA	23606	888-889-9868	757-873-5688	360
C & F Financial Co 1313 E Main St Ste 400 *NASDAQ: CFFI*	Richmond	VA	23219	855-602-2001		359-2
C & H International 4751 Wilshire Blvd Ste 201	Los Angeles	CA	90010	800-833-8888	323-933-2288	16
C & H Sugar Co Inc 2300 Contra Costa Blvd Ste 600	Pleasant Hill	CA	94523	800-773-1803	925-688-1731	296-38
C & J Clark America Inc 156 Oak St *Cust Svc	Newton Upper Falls	MA	02464	800-211-5461*		301
C & L Supply Co PO Box 578	Vinita	OK	74301	800-256-6411		38
C & M Conveyor 4598 State Rd 37	Mitchell	IN	47446	800-551-3195	812-849-5647	207
C & R Mechanical 12825 Pennridge Dr	Bridgeton	MO	63044	800-524-3828	314-739-1800	189-10
C Cretors & Co 3243 N California Ave	Chicago	IL	60618	800-228-1885	773-588-1690	298
C J Horner Company Inc 105 W Grand Ave	Hot Springs	AR	71901	800-426-4261	501-321-9600	182
C L Smith 1311 S 39th St	Saint Louis	MO	63110	855-551-2625		604
C Lazy U Ranch 3640 Colorado Hwy 125 PO Box 379	Granby	CO	80446	800-228-9792	970-887-3344	239
C m Buck & Associates Inc 6850 Guion Rd	Indianapolis	IN	46268	800-382-3961	317-293-5704	392
C M S North America 4095 Korona Ct SE	Caledonia	MI	49316	800-931-6083	616-698-9970	357
C M School Supply Inc 940 N Central Ave	Upland	CA	91786	800-464-6681	909-982-9695	531
C Myers Corp 8222 S 48th St Ste 275	Phoenix	AZ	85044	800-238-7475		194
C P H & Assoc 711 S Dearborn St Unit 205	Chicago	IL	60605	800-875-1911	312-987-9823	389
C Spire 1018 Highland Colony Pkwy Ste 300	Ridgeland	MS	39157	855-277-4735		386
C W I Inc 650 Three Springs Raod	Bowling Green	KY	42104	888-626-7576		707
C'mon Inn Grand Forks 3051 32nd Ave S	Grand Forks	ND	58201	800-255-2323	701-775-3320	378
C2AE 106 W Allegan St Ste 500	Lansing	MI	48933	866-454-3923		261
C2F Inc 6600 SW 111th Ave	Beaverton	OR	97008	800-544-8825	503-643-9050	96
CA (Cocaine Anonymous World Services Inc) PO Box 492000	Los Angeles	CA	90049	800-347-8998	310-559-5833	48-21
CA Inc 1 CA Plz *NASDAQ: CA*	Islandia	NY	11749	800-225-5224		178-1
Ca Lindman Inc 10401 Guilford Rd	Jessup	MD	20794	877-737-8675	301-470-4700	186
CAA (Canadian Automobile Assn) 2151 Thurston Dr	Ottawa	ON	K1G6C9	800-267-8713	613-820-1890	48-23
CAA Club Group 60 Commerce Valley Dr E	Thornhill	ON	L3T7P9	866-988-8878	905-771-3000	53
CAA Maritimes Ltd 378 Westmorland Rd	Saint John	NB	E2J2G4	800-471-1611	506-634-1400	53
Caa Niagara 155 Main St E	Grimsby	ON	L3M1P2	800-263-7272		770
CAA North & East Ontario PO Box 8350	Ottawa	ON	K1G3T2	800-267-8713	613-820-1890	53
CAA Stoney Creek 75 Centennial Pkwy N	Hamilton	ON	L8E2P2	877-544-0445	905-664-8000	53
Cab Signs 38 Livonia Ave	Brooklyn	NY	11212	800-394-1690	718-385-1600	623
Cabarrus County Convention & Visitors Bureau 3003 Dale Earnhardt Blvd	Kannapolis	NC	28083	800-848-3740	704-782-4340	206
Cabela's Inc 1 Cabela Dr *NYSE: CAB*	Sidney	NE	69160	800-237-8888	800-850-8402	707
Cabell-Huntington Convention & Visitors Bureau PO Box 347	Huntington	WV	25708	800-635-6329	304-525-7333	206
Cabinet Tronix 280 Trousdale Dr Ste A	Chula Vista	CA	91910	866-876-6199		814
Cabinetry By Karman 6000 S Stratler St	Salt Lake City	UT	84107	800-255-3581	801-268-3581	115
CABLCF (Creditors Adjustment Bureau-LC Financial) 14226 Ventura Blvd	Sherman Oaks	CA	91423	800-800-4523	818-990-4800	160
Cable Connection, The 52 Heppner Dr	Carson City	NV	89706	800-851-2961	775-885-1443	116
Cable Markers Company Inc 13805-C Alton Pkwy	Irvine	CA	92618	800-746-7655		465
Cable One Inc 210 E Earll Dr	Phoenix	AZ	85012	877-692-2253	602-364-6000	116
Cable Public Affairs Channel (CPAC) PO Box 81099	Ottawa	ON	K1P1B1	877-287-2722		735
CableAmerica Corp 7822 E Gray Rd	Scottsdale	AZ	85260	866-871-4492	480-315-1820	116
Cable-Dahmer Chevrolet Inc 1834 S Noland Rd	Independence	MO	64055	866-650-1809		57
Cables to Go Inc 3599 Dayton Pk Dr	Dayton	OH	45414	800-826-7904	937-224-8646	809
Cabot Coach Builders Inc 99 Newark St	Haverhill	MA	01832	800-544-5587	978-374-4530	643
Cabot Corp 2 Seaport Ln Ste 1300 *NYSE: CBT*	Boston	MA	02210	800-322-1236	617-345-0100	145
Cabot Microelectronics Corp 870 N Commons Dr *NASDAQ: CCMP*	Aurora	IL	60504	800-811-2756	630-375-6631	145
Cabot Oil & Gas Corp 840 Gessner Rd Ste 1400 *NYSE: COG*	Houston	TX	77024	800-434-3985	281-848-2799	782
Cabot Specialty Fluids Inc Waterway Plz Two 10001 Woodlock Forest Dr Ste 275	The Woodlands	TX	77380	800-322-1236	281-298-9955	145
Cabot Supermetals 1095 Windward Ridge Pkwy Ste 200	Alpharetta	GA	30005	800-472-4889		
Cabot Wealth Management Inc 216 Essex St	Salem	MA	01970	800-888-6468	978-745-9233	524
Cabot Wealth Network 176 N St PO Box 2049 *Orders	Salem	MA	01970	800-326-8826*		527-9
Cabrillo College 6500 Soquel Dr	Aptos	CA	95003	888-442-4551	831-479-6100	162
Cabrillo National Monument 1800 Cabrillo Memorial Dr	San Diego	CA	92106	800-236-7916	619-557-5450	560
Cabrini College 610 King of Prussia Rd	Radnor	PA	19087	800-848-1003	610-902-8552	166
CABT (Coalition Against Bigger Trucks) 109 NFairfax St 2nd Fl	Alexandria	VA	22314	888-222-8123	703-535-3131	
CAC (Coating & Adhesive Corp) 1901 Popular St PO Box 1080	Leland	NC	28451	800-410-2999	910-371-3184	546
Cache Valley Electric Inc 875 N 1000 W	Logan	UT	84321	888-558-0600	435-752-6405	189-4
Cachet Financial Services 175 S Lake Ave Ste 200	Pasadena	CA	91101	855-591-9865		2
CACi 12855 Tesson Ferry Rd Ste 201	St. Louis	MO	63128	800-777-7971		160
CACI International Inc 1100 N Glebe Rd *NYSE: CACI*	Arlington	VA	22201	866-606-3471	703-841-7800	180
Cacique Inc 14923 Procter Ave	La Puente	CA	91746	800-521-6987	626-961-3399	296-5
Cactus Flower Florists 10822 N Scottsdale Rd	Scottsdale	AZ	85254	800-922-2887	480-483-9200	292
Cactus Mailing Co 16020 N 77th St	Scottsdale	AZ	85260	888-633-7939		5
Cactus Punch Inc 1224 Heil Quaker Blvd	LaVergne	TN	37086	800-446-2333		343
CACU (Community America Credit Union) 9777 Ridge Dr	Lenexa	KS	66219	800-892-7957	913-905-7000	219
Cad Control Systems 1017 Frenchman Dr	Broussard	LA	70518	800-543-1968	337-369-3737	534
Cad Technology Center Inc 8101 Fourth Ave S Ste 100	Bloomington	MN	55425	866-941-1181		180
CAD/CAM Consulting Services Inc (CCCS) 1525 Rancho Conejo Blvd Ste 103	Newbury Park	CA	91320	888-375-7676	805-375-7676	174
CADCA (CPA Auto Dealer Consultants Assn) 1801 W End Ave Ste 800	Nashville	TN	37203	800-231-2524	615-373-9880	49-1
CADE (Commission on Accreditation for Dietetics Educatio) 120 S Riverside Plz Ste 2000	Chicago	IL	60606	800-877-1600	312-899-0040	48-1
Cadence Design Systems Inc 2655 Seely Ave *NASDAQ: CDNS* ■ *Cust Svc	San Jose	CA	95134	800-746-6223*	408-943-1234	178-5
Cadence Group Inc 1095 Zonolite Rd Ste 105	Atlanta	GA	30306	888-346-8125		
Cadet Mfg Company Inc 2500 W Fourth Plain Blvd	Vancouver	WA	98660	800-442-2338	360-693-2505	37
Cadex Electronics Inc 22000 Fraserwood Way	Richmond	BC	V6W1J6	800-565-5228	604-231-7777	246
Cadillac Area Visitors Bureau 201 N Mitchell St	Cadillac	MI	49601	800-325-2525	231-775-0657	206
Cadillac Coffee Co 194 E Maple Rd	Troy	MI	48083	800-438-6900	248-545-2266	296-7
Cadnet Services 100 Carl Dr Ste 12	Manchester	NH	03103	866-522-3638		180
Cadnetics 400 Holiday Dri Ste 102	Pittsburgh	PA	15220	855-494-0043	412-642-2701	
Cadre Computer Resources Co 201 E Fifth St Ste 1800	Cincinnati	OH	45202	866-762-6700	513-762-7350	180
Cadwell Laboratories Inc 909 N Kellogg St	Kennewick	WA	99336	800-245-3001	509-735-6481	474
CAE Inc 8585 Cote de Liesse *NYSE: CAE*	Saint Laurent	QC	H4T1G6	866-999-6223	514-341-6780	699
CAEP (Canadian Assn of Emergency Physicians) 1785 Alta Vista Dr Ste 104	Ottawa	ON	K1G3Y6	800-463-1158	613-523-3343	49-8
Caesar's Palace 3570 Las Vegas Blvd S Caesar's Palace	Las Vegas	NV	89109	800-634-6001	866-227-5938	667
Caesars License Company LLC 3655 Las Vegas Blvd S	Las Vegas	NV	89109	877-796-2096	702-946-7000	378

				Toll-Free	Phone	Class
Caesars License Company LLC						
377 Riverside Dr E	Windsor	ON	N9A7H7	**800-991-7777**	519-258-7878	133
Cafe Centro						
200 Park Ave	New York	NY	10166	**866-972-8462**		
Cafe Fina						
47 Fisherman's Wharf Ste 1	Monterey	CA	93940	**800-843-3462**	831-372-5200	667
Cafe Marquesa						
600 Fleming St	Key West	FL	33040	**800-869-4631**	305-292-1244	667
Cafe Modern						
3200 Darnell St	Fort Worth	TX	76107	**866-824-5566**	817-738-9215	667
Cafe Pinot						
700 W Fifth St	Los Angeles	CA	90071	**866-972-8462**		
Cafe Rio						
215 N Admiral Byrd Rd Ste 100	Salt Lake City	UT	84116	**800-223-3746**	801-441-5000	
Cafepresscom Inc						
1850 Gateway Dr Ste 300	Foster City	CA	94404	**877-809-1659**	502-822-7501	204
Cagwin & Dorward Inc						
1565 S Novato Blvd Ste B	Novato	CA	94947	**800-891-7710**	415-892-7710	421
CAI (Community Assns Institute)						
6402 Arlington Blvd Ste 500	Falls Church	VA	22042	**888-224-4321**	703-970-9220	48-7
CAI (Chrysler Aviation Inc)						
7120 Hayvenhurst Ave Ste 309	Van Nuys	CA	91406	**800-995-0825**	818-989-7900	13
CAI-CLAC						
1809 S St Ste 101-245	Sacramento	CA	95811	**888-909-7403**	916-791-4750	529
Cailor Fleming & Associates Inc						
4610 Market St	Youngstown	OH	44512	**800-796-8495**	330-782-8068	389
Cajun Constructors Inc						
15635 Airline Hwy	Baton Rouge	LA	70817	**800-944-5857**	225-753-5857	188-7
Cal Farley's						
PO Box 1890	Amarillo	TX	79174	**800-687-3722**		48-6
Cal Net Technology Group						
9420 Topanga Canyon Blvd Ste 100	Chatsworth	CA	91311	**866-999-2638**		180
Cal Spas Inc						
1462 E Ninth St	Pomona	CA	91766	**800-225-7727**	909-623-8781	374
CALAMCO (California Ammonia Co)						
1776 W March Ln Ste 420	Stockton	CA	95207	**800-624-4200**	209-982-1000	280
Calamos Asset Management Inc						
2020 Calamos Ct	Naperville	IL	60563	**800-582-6959**	630-245-7200	400
NASDAQ: CLMS						
Cal-a-Vie Spa						
29402 Spa Havens Way	Vista	CA	92084	**866-772-4283**	760-945-2055	702
Calavo Growers Inc						
1141-A Cummings Rd	Santa Paula	CA	93060	**800-654-8758**	805-525-1245	315-4
NASDAQ: CVGW						
Calbag Metals Co						
2495 NW Nicolai St	Portland	OR	97210	**800-398-3441**	503-226-3441	682
Cal-Coast Dairy Systems Inc						
424 S Tegner Rd	Turlock	CA	95380	**800-732-6826***	209-634-9026	273
*Cust Svc						
Calculated Industries Inc						
4840 Hytech Dr	Carson City	NV	89706	**800-854-8075**	775-885-4900	118
Caldwell Chamber of Commerce						
704 Blaine St	Caldwell	ID	83605	**866-206-6944**	208-459-7493	139
Caldwell Securities Ltd						
150 King St W Ste 1710	Toronto	ON	M5H1J9	**800-387-0859**	416-862-7755	686
Caldwell Trust Co						
1400 Ctr Rd	Venice	FL	34292	**800-338-9476**	941-493-3600	400
Caldwell University						
120 Bloomfield Ave	Caldwell	NJ	07006	**888-864-9516***	973-618-3500	166
*Admissions						
CALEA (Commission on Accreditation for Law Enforcement Ag)						
13575 Heathcote Blvd Ste 320	Gainesville	VA	20155	**877-789-6904**	703-352-4225	49-7
Calea Ltd						
2785 Skymark Ave Unit 2	Mississauga	ON	L4W4Y3	**888-909-3299**	905-238-1234	362
Caledon Laboratories Ltd						
40 Armstrong Ave	Georgetown	ON	L7G4R9	**877-225-3366**	905-877-0101	226
Caledonia Haulers LLC						
420 West Lincoln St PO Box 31	Caledonia	MN	55921	**800-325-4728**	507-725-9000	466
Calendarscom LLC						
6411 Burleson Rd	Austin	TX	78744	**800-366-3645**		
Calex Express Inc						
58 Pittston Ave	Pittston	PA	18640	**800-292-2539**	570-603-0180	775
CALEX Manufacturing Co						
2401 Stanwell Dr	Concord	CA	94520	**800-542-3355**	925-687-4411	515
Calfrac Well Services Ltd						
411 8 Ave SW	Calgary	AB	T2P1E3	**866-770-3722**	403-266-6000	535
Calgary Economic Development						
731 First St SE	Calgary	AB	T2G2G9	**888-222-5855**	403-221-7831	341
Calgary Herald						
215-16th St SE	Calgary	AB	T2E7P5	**800-372-9219**	403-235-7100	528-1
Calgary International Airport						
2000 Airport Rd NE	Calgary	AB	T2E6W5	**877-254-7427**	403-735-1200	27
Calgary Laboratory Services						
3535 Research Rd NW	Calgary	AB	T2L2K8	**800-661-3450**	403-770-3500	414
Calgary Zoo Botanical Garden & Prehistoric Park						
1300 Zoo Rd NE	Calgary	AB	T2E7V6	**800-588-9993**	403-232-9300	818
Calgon Carbon Corp						
3000 GSK Dr	Moon Township	PA	15108	**800-422-7266***	412-787-6700	143
NYSE: CCC ■ *Cust Svc						
Calhoun Community College						
PO Box 2216	Decatur	AL	35609	**800-626-3628**	256-306-2500	162
Huntsville						
102B Wynn Dr	Huntsville	AL	35805	**800-626-3628**	256-890-4701	162
Redstone Arsenal						
6250 Hwy 31 N	Tanner	AL	35671	**800-626-3628**	256-306-2500	162
Calhoun County Electric Co-op Assn						
1015 Tonawanda St PO Box 312	Rockwell City	IA	50579	**800-821-4879**	712-297-7112	245
Calian Technology Ltd						
340 Legget Dr Ste 101	Ottawa	ON	K2K1Y6	**877-225-4264**	613-599-8600	717
TSX: CGY						
Calibre Systems Inc						
6354 Walker Ln Ste 300	Alexandria	VA	22310	**888-225-4273**	703-797-8500	180
Calico Building Services Inc						
15550-C Rockfield Blvd	Irvine	CA	92618	**800-576-7313**		104

				Toll-Free	Phone	Class
Califone International Inc						
9135 Alabama Ave Ste B	Chatsworth	CA	91311	**800-722-0500**	818-407-2400	253
California						
Arts Council						
1300 'I' St Ste 930	Sacramento	CA	95814	**800-201-6201**	916-322-6555	338-5
Bureau of Real Estate						
1651 Exposition Blvd	Sacramento	CA	95815	**877-373-4542**		338-5
Child Support Services Dept						
PO Box 419064	Sacramento	CA	95741	**866-901-3212**	916-464-5000	338-5
Consumer Affairs Dept						
1625 N Market Blvd Ste N 112	Sacramento	CA	95834	**800-952-5210**	916-445-1254	338-5
Corrections Dept						
PO Box 942883	Sacramento	CA	94283	**877-256-6877**	916-324-7308	338-5
Fair Political Practices Commission						
428 J St Ste 620	Sacramento	CA	95814	**866-275-3772**	916-322-5660	265
Health Care Services Dept						
PO Box 997413 MS 8502	Sacramento	CA	95899	**800-735-2929**		338-5
Housing Finance Agency						
500 Capitol Mall Ste 1400	Sacramento	CA	95814	**877-922-5432**		338-5
Judicial Council of California						
455 Golden Gate Ave	San Francisco	CA	94102	**800-900-5980**	415-865-4200	338-5
Medical Board						
2005 Evergreen St Ste 1200	Sacramento	CA	95815	**800-633-2322**	916-263-2382	338-5
Motor Vehicles Dept						
4700 Broadway	Sacramento	CA	95820	**800-777-0133**	916-657-6437	338-5
Public Utilities Commission						
505 Van Ness Ave	San Francisco	CA	94102	**800-848-5580**	415-703-2782	338-5
Rehabilitation Dept						
721 Capitol Mall	Sacramento	CA	95814	**800-952-5544**	916-324-1313	338-5
Veterans Affairs Dept						
1227 'O' St	Sacramento	CA	95814	**800-952-5626**	916-653-1402	338-5
Victim Compensation Board						
PO Box 3036	Sacramento	CA	95812	**800-777-9229**		338-5
California Ammonia Co (CALAMCO)						
1776 W March Ln Ste 420	Stockton	CA	95207	**800-624-4200**	209-982-1000	280
California Analytical Instruments Inc						
1312 W Grove Ave	Orange	CA	92865	**800-959-0949**	714-974-5560	418
California Bank & Trust						
11622 El Camino Real Ste 200	San Diego	CA	92130	**800-400-6080**	858-793-7400	70
California Baptist University						
8432 Magnolia Ave	Riverside	CA	92504	**877-228-8866**	951-689-5771	166
California Cartage Company Inc						
2931 Redondo Ave	Long Beach	CA	90806	**888-537-1432**		775
California Chamber of Commerce						
1215 K St Ste 1400 PO Box 1736	Sacramento	CA	95812	**800-649-4921**	916-444-6670	140
California Closet Co						
1716 Fourth St	Berkeley	CA	94710	**888-336-9707***	510-763-2033	189-11
*General						
California College of the Arts						
Oakland 5212 Broadway	Oakland	CA	94618	**800-447-1278**	510-594-3600	164
California Cryobank Inc						
11915 La Grange Ave	Los Angeles	CA	90025	**866-927-9622**	310-443-5244	541
California Cryobank Inc						
950 Massachusetts Ave	Cambridge	MA	02139	**888-810-2796**	617-497-8646	541
California Ctr for the Arts						
340 N Escondido Blvd	Escondido	CA	92025	**800-988-4253**	760-839-4138	568
California Dental Assn						
1201 K St 14th Fl	Sacramento	CA	95814	**800-736-7071**	916-443-0505	227
California Eastern Laboratories Inc (CEL)						
4590 Patrick Henry Dr	Santa Clara	CA	95054	**800-390-3232**	408-919-2500	246
California Flexrake Corp						
9620 Gidley St	Temple City	CA	91780	**800-266-4200**	626-443-4026	428
California Gasket & Rubber Corp						
533 W Collins Ave	Orange	CA	92867	**800-635-7084**	714-202-8500	326
California Hotel & Casino						
12 E Ogden Ave	Las Vegas	NV	89101	**800-634-6505**	702-385-1222	133
California Institute of the Arts						
24700 McBean Pkwy	Valencia	CA	91355	**800-545-2787**	661-255-1050	164
California ISO						
151 Blue Ravine Rd PO Box 639014	Folsom	CA	95630	**800-220-4907**	916-351-4400	782
California Lutheran University						
60 W Olsen Rd	Thousand Oaks	CA	91360	**877-258-3678**	805-493-3135	166
California Lutheran University Pearson Library						
60 W Olsen Rd	Thousand Oaks	CA	91360	**877-258-3678**	805-493-3250	433-6
California Maritime Academy						
200 Maritime Academy Dr	Vallejo	CA	94590	**800-561-1945**	707-654-1330	166
California Medical Assn						
1201 J St Ste 200	Sacramento	CA	95814	**800-300-1506**	916-444-5532	472
California Newspaper Service Bureau						
915 E First St	Los Angeles	CA	90012	**800-788-7840**	213-229-5500	526
California Office Furniture						
3480 Industrial Blvd Ste 100	West Sacramento	CA	95691	**877-442-6959**	916-442-6959	320
California Pacific Medical Ctr Research Institute						
475 Brannan St Ste 220	San Francisco	CA	94107	**855-354-2778**	415-600-1600	664
California Panel & Veneer Co						
14055 Artesia Blvd	Cerritos	CA	90703	**800-451-1745**	562-926-5834	609
California Parlor Car Tours						
500 Sutter St Ste 401	San Francisco	CA	94102	**800-227-4250**	415-474-7500	755
California Pharmacists Assn (CPhA)						
4030 Lennane Dr	Sacramento	CA	95834	**866-365-7472**	916-779-1400	581
California Portland Cement Co						
2025 E Financial Way	Glendora	CA	91741	**800-272-1891***	626-852-6200	135
*Cust Svc						
California Public Radio						
4100 Vachell Ln	San Luis Obispo	CA	93401	**800-549-8855**	805-549-8855	628
California Real Estate Magazine						
525 S Virgil Ave	Los Angeles	CA	90020	**888-811-5281**	213-739-8200	455-5
California Saw & Knife Works						
721 Brannan St	San Francisco	CA	94103	**888-729-6533**	415-861-0644	678
California State Archives						
1020 'O' St	Sacramento	CA	95814	**800-633-5155**	916-653-7715	517
California State Library						
900 N St	Sacramento	CA	95814	**800-952-5666**	916-654-0261	433-5
California State University						
401 Golden Shore	Long Beach	CA	90802	**800-325-4000**	562-951-4000	781
Chico 400 West First St	Chico	CA	95929	**800-542-4426***	530-898-6321	166
*Admissions						

Alphabetical Section

	Toll-Free	Phone	Class
Dominguez Hills 1000 E Victoria St ....Carson CA 90747	888-545-6512	310-243-3696	166
East Bay 25800 Carlos Bee Blvd ....Hayward CA 94542	800-884-1684	510-885-3000	166
Fresno 5241 N Maple Ave ....Fresno CA 93740	800-700-2320	559-278-4240	166
Fullerton 800 N State College Blvd ....Fullerton CA 92834	888-433-9406	657-278-2011	166
Long Beach 1250 Bellflower Blvd ....Long Beach CA 90840	800-663-1144	562-985-4111	166
Northridge 18111 Nordhoff St ....Northridge CA 91330	800-399-4529	818-677-1200	166
Sacramento 6000 J St ....Sacramento CA 95819	800-667-7531	916-278-3901	166
San Marcos 333 S Twin Oaks Valley Rd ....San Marcos CA 92096	888-225-5427	760-750-4000	166
Stanislaus 1 University Cir ....Turlock CA 95382	800-235-9292	209-667-3152	166
California Steel & Tube 16049 Stephens St ....City of Industry CA 91745	800-338-8823	626-968-5511	488
California University of Pennsylvania 250 University Ave ....California PA 15419	888-412-0479	724-938-4000	166
California Water Service Group 1720 N First St ....San Jose CA 95112 NYSE: CWT	866-734-0743	408-367-8200	782
California Western School of Law 225 Cedar St ....San Diego CA 92101	800-255-4252	619-239-0391	167-1
Caliper Life Sciences Inc 68 Elm St ....Hopkinton MA 01748	800-762-4000	781-663-6050	418
Calise & Sons Bakery Inc 2 Quality Dr ....Lincoln RI 02865	800-225-4737	401-334-3444	296-1
Calista Corp 301 Calista Ct Ste A ....Anchorage AK 99518	800-277-5516	907-279-5516	651
Calistoga Spa Hot Springs 1006 Washington St ....Calistoga CA 94515	866-822-5772	707-942-6269	702
Callahan Chemical Co Broad St & Filmore Ave ....Palmyra NJ 08065	800-257-7967		146
Callahan Financial Planning Co 3157 Farnam St Ste 7111 ....Omaha NE 68131	800-991-5195	402-341-2000	
Call-A-Head Corp 304 Cross Bay Blvd ....Broad Channel NY 11693	800-634-2085		
Callan & Woodworth Moving & Storage 900 Hwy 212 ....Michigan City IN 46360	800-584-0551	219-874-3274	516
Callan Associates Inc 600 Montgomery St Ste 800 ....San Francisco CA 94111	800-227-3288	516-150-2772	400
Callaway Cars Inc 3 High St ....Old Lyme CT 06371	866-927-9400	860-434-9002	57
Callaway Electric Co-op 1313 Co-op Dr PO Box 250 ....Fulton MO 65251	888-642-4840	573-642-3326	245
Callaway Gardens 17800 Hwy 27 ....Pine Mountain GA 31822	800-225-5292	706-663-2281	665
Callaway Golf Co 2180 Rutherford Rd ....Carlsbad CA 92008 NYSE: ELY	800-588-9836	760-931-1771	706
Callbright Corp 6700 Hollister ....Houston TX 77040	877-462-2552	855-225-5274	389
Caller-Times 820 N Lower Broadway ....Corpus Christi TX 78401	800-827-2011	361-884-2011	528-2
Calling Solutions By Phone Power Inc 2200 McCullough Ave ....San Antonio TX 78212 *Cust Svc	800-683-5500*	210-801-9630	732
Callisto Integration 635 Fourth Line Ste 16 ....Oakville ON L6L5B3	800-387-0467	905-339-0059	194
Callon Petroleum Co 200 N Canal St ....Natchez MS 39120 NYSE: CPE	800-451-1294	601-442-1601	536
Callware Technologies Inc 9100 S 500 W ....Sandy UT 84070	800-888-4226	801-988-6800	178-7
Calmont Leasing Ltd 14610 Yellowhead Trail NW ....Edmonton AB T5L3C5	855-474-2568		773
Calmoseptine Inc 16602 Burke Ln ....Huntington Beach CA 92647	800-800-3405	714-840-3405	231
Calnet Inc 12359 Sunrise Vly Dr Ste 270 ....Reston VA 20191 *General	877-322-5638*	703-547-6800	194
Calolympic Glove & Safety Company Inc 1720 Delilah St ....Corona CA 92879	800-421-6630	951-340-2229	675
Calphalon Corp PO Box 583 ....Toledo OH 43697	800-809-7267		484
Calpico Inc 1387 San Mateo Ave ....South San Francisco CA 94080	800-998-9115	650-588-2241	326
CalPortland 5975 E Marginal Way S ....Seattle WA 98134	800-750-0123	206-764-3000	182
Cal-Royal Products Inc 6605 Flotilla St ....City Of Commerce CA 90040	800-876-9258	323-888-6601	349
CalSurance 681 S Parker St Ste 300 ....Orange CA 92868	800-762-7800	714-939-0800	389
Calton & Assoc Inc 2701 N Rocky Point Dr Ste 1000 ....Tampa FL 33607	800-942-0262	813-264-0440	686
Calumet College of Saint Joseph 2400 New York Ave ....Whiting IN 46394	877-700-9100	219-473-4215	166
Calumet Diversified Meats Inc 10000 80th Ave ....Pleasant Prairie WI 53158	800-752-7427	262-947-7200	297-9
Calumet Specialty Products Partners LP 2780 Waterfront Pkwy E Dr Ste 200 ....Indianapolis IN 46214 NASDAQ: CLMT	800-437-3188	317-328-5660	576
Cal-Van Tools 7918 Industrial Village Rd ....Greensboro NC 27409	800-537-1077		753
Calvary Bible College & Theological Seminary 15800 Calvary Rd ....Kansas City MO 64147	800-326-3960	816-322-3960	161
Calvert County 175 Main St ....Prince Frederick MD 20678	800-492-7122	410-535-1600	337
Calvert County Chamber of Commerce PO Box 9 ....Prince Frederick MD 20678	800-972-4389	410-535-2577	139
Calvert Investments Inc 4550 Montgomery Ave Ste 1000N ....Bethesda MD 20814	800-368-2748	800-368-2745	524
Calvert Labs 1225 Crescent Green Ste 115 ....Cary NC 27518	800-300-8114	919-854-4453	417
Calvin College 3201 Burton St SE ....Grand Rapids MI 49546	800-688-0122	616-526-6000	166
Calvin Theological Seminary 3233 Burton St SE ....Grand Rapids MI 49546	800-388-6034	616-957-6036	167-3
Calyx Transportation Group Inc *National Fast Freight* 107 Alfred Kuehne Blvd ....Brampton ON L6T4K3	800-563-2223	905-494-4808	
Calzone Case Co 225 Black Rock Ave ....Bridgeport CT 06605 *Cust Svc	800-243-5152*	203-367-5766	451
CAM International LLC 503 Space Park S ....Nashville TN 37211	800-251-8544		61
Cam Services Inc 5664 Selmaraine Dr ....Culver City CA 90230	800-576-3050	310-390-3552	256
Camas-Washougal Chamber of Commerce 422 NE Fourth Ave ....Camas WA 98607	844-262-1100	360-834-2472	139
Cambelt International Corp 2820 West 1100 South ....Salt Lake City UT 84104	855-226-2358	801-972-5511	207
Camber Corp 670 Discovery Dr ....Huntsville AL 35806	800-998-7988	256-922-0200	180
Cambex Corp 337 Tpke Rd ....Southborough MA 01772 OTC: CBEX	800-325-5565	508-281-0209	176
Cambiar Investors Inc 2401 E Second Ave Ste 500 ....Denver CO 80206	888-673-9950		400
Cambrex Corp 1 Meadowlands Plz ....East Rutherford NJ 07073 NYSE: CBM	866-286-9133	201-804-3000	477
Cambria Capital LLC 488 E Winchester St Ste 200 ....Salt Lake City UT 84107	877-226-0477	801-320-9606	400
Cambria Pines Realty Inc 746-A Main St ....Cambria CA 93428	800-676-8616	805-927-8616	648
Cambridge Chamber of Commerce 750 Hespeler Rd ....Cambridge ON N3H5L8 *General	800-749-7560*	519-622-2221	137
Cambridge College Inc 360 Merrimack St 4th fl ....Lawrence MA 01843	800-829-4723	617-868-1000	795
Cambridge Engineering Inc PO Box 1010 ....Chesterfield MO 63006	800-899-1989	636-532-2233	318
Cambridge International 105 Goodwill Rd ....Cambridge MD 21613	800-638-9560	410-901-4979	207
Cambridge Isotope Laboratories Inc 3 Highwood Dr ....Tewksbury MA 01876	800-322-1174		145
Cambridge Medical Ctr (CMC) 701 S Dellwood St ....Cambridge MN 55008	800-252-4133	763-689-7700	373-3
Cambridge Packing Company Inc 41-43 Foodmart Rd ....Boston MA 02118	800-722-6726	617-269-6700	297-9
Cambridge Public Library 449 Broadway ....Cambridge MA 02138	800-327-5050	617-349-4040	433-3
Cambridge Savings Bank 1374 Massachusetts Ave ....Cambridge MA 02138	888-418-5626	617-441-4155	70
Cambridge Silversmith Ltd 116 Lehigh Dr ....Fairfield NJ 07004	800-890-3366	973-227-4400	360
Cambridge Street Metal Corp (CSM) 82 Stevens St ....East Taunton MA 02718	800-254-7580	508-822-2278	490
Cambridge Suites Hotel Halifax 1583 Brunswick St ....Halifax NS B3J3P5	800-565-1263	902-420-0555	378
Cambridge Suites Hotel Toronto 15 Richmond St E ....Toronto ON M5C1N2	800-463-1990	416-368-1990	378
Cambridge Whos Who Publishing Inc 498 RXR Plz ....Uniondale NY 11556	866-933-1555	516-535-1515	633-9
Cambridgeport Air Systems 8 Fanaras Dr ....Salisbury MA 01952	877-648-2872	978-465-8481	606
CambridgeSoft Corp 100 CambridgePark Dr ....Cambridge MA 02140	800-315-7300	617-588-9100	178-5
CambridgeWorld 34 Franklin Ave ....Brooklyn NY 11205	800-221-2253	718-858-5002	119
Cambro Manufacturing Co 5801 Skylab Rd ....Huntington Beach CA 92647	800-833-3003	714-848-1555	300
Camco Chemical Co 8145 Holton Dr ....Florence KY 41042 *Cust Svc	800-354-1001*	859-727-3200	151
Camco Manufacturing Inc 121 Landmark Dr ....Greensboro NC 27409	800-334-2004		247
Camden County 520 Market St Ste 306 ....Camden NJ 08102	866-226-3362	856-225-5300	337
Camden County Library 203 Laurel Rd ....Voorhees NJ 08043	877-222-3737	856-772-1636	433-3
Camden National Corp 2 Elm St ....Camden ME 04843 NASDAQ: CAC	800-860-8821	207-236-8821	359-2
Camden Property Trust 11 Greenway Plz Ste 2400 ....Houston TX 77046 NYSE: CPT	800-922-6336	713-354-2500	651
Camden Publications 331 E Bell St ....Camden MI 49232	800-222-6336	517-368-0365	528-4
Camel Rock Casino 17486A Hwy 84/285 ....Santa Fe NM 87506	800-483-1040	800-462-2635	133
Camelback Inn JW Marriott Resort Golf Club & Spa 5402 E Lincoln Dr ....Scottsdale AZ 85253	800-242-2635	480-948-1700	665
Camera Corner Inc PO Box 1899 ....Burlington NC 27216	800-868-2462	336-228-0251	119
Cameron Balloons US PO Box 3672 ....Ann Arbor MI 48106	866-423-6178	734-426-5525	28
Cameron Instruments Inc 173 Woolwich St ....Guelph ON N1H3V4	888-863-8010	519-824-7111	357
Cameron Parish Police Jury 148 Smith Cir PO Box 1280 ....Cameron LA 70631	844-503-7283	337-775-5718	
Cameron University 2800 W Gore Blvd ....Lawton OK 73505 *Admissions	888-454-7600*	580-581-2289	166
Cameron, Hodges, Coleman, LaPointe & Wright PA 111 N Magnolia Ave Ste 1350 ....Orlando FL 32801	888-841-5030	407-841-5030	427
Camesa Inc 1615 Spur 529 ....Rosenberg TX 77471	800-866-0001	281-342-4494	253
Camex Equipment Sales & Rental Inc 1806 Second St ....Nisku AB T9E0W8	877-955-2770	780-955-2770	535

Name / Address	City	State	Zip	Toll-Free	Phone	Class
Camp Butler National Cemetery 5063 Camp Butler Rd	Springfield	IL	62707	**877-907-8585**	217-492-4070	136
Camp Florence 4859 S Jetty Rd	Florence	OR	97439	**800-588-9003**	541-997-2076	411
Camp Lebanon 1205 Acorn Rd	Burtrum	MN	56318	**800-816-1502**	320-573-2125	239
Camp Olympia 723 Olympia Dr	Trinity	TX	75862	**800-735-6190**	936-594-2541	297-8
Camp Simcha 430 White Rd	Glen Spey	NY	12737	**888-756-1432**	845-856-1432	239
Campbell & Associates Inc 3485 Fortuna Dr Ste 100	Akron	OH	44312	**800-233-4117**	330-945-4117	723
Campbell & George Co 1100 Industrial Rd Ste 12	San Carlos	CA	94070	**800-682-4224**	650-654-5000	253
Campbell Christian Schools 1075 E Campbell Ave	Campbell	CA	95008	**800-264-7955**	408-370-4900	681
Campbell County 1635 Reata Dr	Gillette	WY	82718	**800-457-9312**	307-682-0552	337
Campbell Manufacturing Inc 127 E Spring St	Bechtelsville	PA	19505	**800-523-0224**	610-367-2107	591
Campbell Scientific Inc 815 W 1800 N	Logan	UT	84321	**844-454-2505**		
Campbell Soup Co 1 Campbell Pl *NYSE: CPB*	Camden	NJ	08103	**800-257-8443**	856-342-4800	296-36
Campbell University 450 Leslie Campbell Ave PO Box 546	Buies Creek	NC	27506	**800-334-4111**	910-893-1290	166
Campbell University Norman Adrian Wiggins School of Law 225 Hillsborough St	Raleigh	NC	27603	**800-334-4111**	919-865-4650	167-1
Campbell Wrapper Corp 1415 Fortune Ave	De Pere	WI	54115	**800-727-4210**	920-983-7100	543
Campbell's Resort 104 W Woodin Ave PO Box 278	Chelan	WA	98816	**800-553-8225**	509-682-2561	665
Campbellsville University 1 University Dr *Admissions	Campbellsville	KY	42718	**800-264-6014***	270-789-5000	166
Camperoo Inc 599 Third St Ste 309	San Francisco	CA	94109	**888-538-8809**		386
Camping Investigations 4427 N 27th Ave	Phoenix	AZ	85017	**800-862-8458**	602-864-7860	399
Camping World RV Sales 8155 Rivers Ave	Charleston	SC	29406	**888-586-5446**	888-471-3171	786
Campion College at the University of Regina 3737 Wascana Pkwy	Regina	SK	S4S0A2	**800-667-7282**	306-586-4242	780
Campmor Inc 400 Corporate Dr PO Box 680	Mahwah	NJ	07430	**800-226-7667**		
Campus Federal Credit Union PO Box 98036	Baton Rouge	LA	70898	**888-769-8841**	225-769-8841	219
Campus Text Inc 7 Bala Ave Ste 203	Bala Cynwyd	PA	19004	**888-606-8398**	610-664-6900	
Campus USA Credit Union PO Box 147029	Gainesville	FL	32614	**800-367-6440**	352-335-9090	219
Cam-Wal Electric Co-op Inc PO Box 135	Selby	SD	57472	**800-269-7676**	605-649-7676	245
Canaan Printing 4820 Jefferson Davis Hwy	Richmond	VA	23234	**800-332-3580**	804-271-4820	623
Canaan Valley Resort & Conference Ctr 230 Main Lodge Rd	Davis	WV	26260	**800-622-4121**	304-866-4121	665
CANAC Inc 6505 Trans-Canada Hwy Ste 405	St Laurent	QC	H4T1S3	**800-588-4387**	514-734-4700	646
Canad Inns - Club Regent Casino Hotel 1415 Regent Ave W	Winnipeg	MB	R2C3B2	**888-332-2623**	204-667-5560	378
Canad Inns Fort Garry 1824 Pembina Hwy	Winnipeg	MB	R3T2G2	**888-332-2623**	204-261-7450	378
Canad Inns Garden City 2100 McPhillips St	Winnipeg	MB	R2V3T9	**888-332-2623**	204-633-0024	378
Canad Inns Polo Park 1405 St Matthews Ave	Winnipeg	MB	R3G0K5	**888-332-2623**	204-775-8791	378
Canada 885 Second Ave 14th Fl	New York	NY	10017	**800-267-8376**	212-848-1100	779
Consulate General 500 N Akard St Ste 2900	Dallas	TX	75201	**800-267-8376**	214-922-9806	257
Consulate General 1251 Ave of the Americas Concourse Level	New York	NY	10020	**800-267-8376**	212-596-1628	257
Canada Agriculture & Food Museum 901 Prince of Wales Dr	Ottawa	ON	K2C3K1	**866-442-4416**	613-991-3044	517
Canada Colors & Chemicals Ltd 175 Bloor St E Ste 1300 N Twr	Toronto	ON	M4W3R8	**800-461-1638**	416-443-5500	146
Canada Deposit Insurance Corp 50 O'Connor St 17th Fl	Ottawa	ON	K1P6L2	**800-461-2342**	613-996-2081	507
Canada Flowers 4073 Longhurst Ave	Niagara Falls	ON	L2E6G5	**888-705-9999**	905-354-2713	292
Canada Forgings Inc 130 Hagar St	Welland	ON	L3B5P8	**800-263-0440**	905-735-1220	537
Canada Life Assurance Co, The 330 University Ave	Toronto	ON	M5G1R8	**888-252-1847**	416-597-1456	390-4
Canada Media Fund 50 Wellington St E Ste 202	Toronto	ON	M5E1C8	**877-975-0766**	416-214-4400	392
Canada School of Public Service 373 Sussex Dr	Ottawa	ON	K1N6Z2	**866-703-9598**	819-953-5400	619
Canada Science & Technology Museum 2421 Lancaster Rd	Ottawa	ON	K1G5A3	**866-442-4416**	613-991-3044	517
Canadian Academy of Sport Medicine (CASM) 55 Metcalfe St Ste 300	Ottawa	ON	K1P6L5	**877-585-2394**	613-748-5851	49-8
Canadian Assn of Emergency Physicians (CAEP) 1785 Alta Vista Dr Ste 104	Ottawa	ON	K1G3Y6	**800-463-1158**	613-523-3343	49-8
Canadian Assn of Occupational Therapists (CAOT) 1125 Colonel By Dr	Ottawa	ON	K1S5R1	**800-434-2268**	613-523-2268	48-1
Canadian Automobile Assn (CAA) 2151 Thurston Dr	Ottawa	ON	K1G6C9	**800-267-8713**	613-820-1890	48-23
Canadian Bar Assn 500-865 Carling Ave	Ottawa	ON	K1S5S8	**800-267-8860**	613-237-2925	138
Canadian Bearings Ltd 1600 Drew Rd	Mississauga	ON	L5S1S5	**800-229-2327**	905-670-6700	384
Canadian College of Naturopathic Medicine 1255 Sheppard Ave E	Toronto	ON	M2K1E2	**866-241-2266**	416-498-1255	780
Canadian Dental Association 1815 Alta Vista Dr	Ottawa	ON	K1G3Y6	**866-521-2322**	613-523-7114	48-1
Canadian Federation of Humane Societies (CFHS) 30 Concourse Gate Ste 102	Ottawa	ON	K2E7V7	**888-678-2347**	613-224-8072	48-3
Canadian Finance & Leasing Association 15 Toronto St	Toronto	ON	M5C2E3	**877-213-7373**	416-860-1133	138
Canadian Football League 50 Wellington St E 3rd Fl	Toronto	ON	M5E1C8	**855-264-4242**	416-322-9650	711-1
Canadian Golf Hall of Fame & Museum 1333 Dorval Dr Ste 1	Oakville	ON	L6M4X7	**800-263-0009**	905-849-9700	519
Canadian Home Income Plan Corp 1881 Yonge St Ste 300	Toronto	ON	M4S3C4	**866-758-2447**	416-925-4757	
Canadian Hospital Specialties ULC 2810 Coventry Rd	Oakville	ON	L6H6R1	**800-461-1423**	905-825-9300	473
Canadian Imperial Bank of Commerce (CIBC) 199 Bay St Commerce Ct W *NYSE: CM*	Toronto	ON	M5L1A2	**800-465-2422**		70
Canadian Information Processing Society (CIPS) 5090 Explorer Dr Ste 801	Mississauga	ON	L4W4T9	**877-275-2477**	905-602-1370	48-1
Canadian Kennel Club (CKC) 200 Ronson Dr Ste 400	Etobicoke	ON	M9W5Z9	**800-250-8040**	416-675-5511	48-3
Canadian Medical Assn (CMA) 1867 Alta Vista Dr	Ottawa	ON	K1G5W8	**800-663-7336**	613-731-9331	49-8
Canadian Memorial Chiropractic College 6100 Leslie St	Toronto	ON	M2H3J1	**800-463-2923**	416-482-2340	780
Canadian Mental Health Association 250 Dundas St W Ste 500	Toronto	ON	M5T2Z5	**800-616-8816**	416-646-5557	138
Canadian Museum of Civilization 100 Laurier St	Gatineau	QC	K1A0M8	**800-555-5621**	819-776-7000	517
Canadian Museum of Nature 240 McLeod St	Ottawa	ON	K2P2R1	**800-263-4433**	613-566-4700	517
Canadian National Railway Co 935 Rue de la Gauchetiere O *NYSE: CNI*	Montreal	QC	H3B2M9	**888-668-4626**	888-888-5909	644
Canadian Natural Resources Ltd (CNRL) 855 Second St SW Ste 2100 *NYSE: CNQ*	Calgary	AB	T2P4J8	**888-878-3700**	403-517-6700	532
Canadian Pacific 7550 Ogden Dale Rd SE	Calgary	AB	T2C4X9	**888-333-6370**		644
Canadian Parks & Wilderness Society (CPAWS) 250 City Ctr Ave Ste 506	Ottawa	ON	K1R6K7	**800-333-9453**	613-569-7226	48-13
Canadian Payroll Association 250 Bloor St E	Toronto	ON	M4W1E6	**800-387-4693**	416-487-3380	138
Canadian Peregrine Foundation 25 Crouse Rd Unit 20	Toronto	ON	M1R5P8	**888-709-3944**	416-481-1233	48-3
Canadian Professional Sales Association 310 Front St W Ste 800	Toronto	ON	M5V3B5	**888-267-2772**	416-408-2685	196
Canadian Society of Customs Brokers 55 Murray St Ste 320	Ottawa	ON	K1N5M3	**800-668-6870**	613-562-3543	138
Canadian Southern Baptist Seminary 200 Seminary View	Cochrane	AB	T4C2G1	**877-922-2727**	403-932-6622	167-3
Canadian Tire Corp Ltd 2180 Yonge St PO Box 770 Stn K *TSX: CTC.A*	Toronto	ON	M4P2V8	**800-387-8803**	416-480-3000	185
Canadian Tool & Die Ltd 1331 Chevrier Blvd	Winnipeg	MB	R3T1Y4	**800-204-4150**	204-453-6833	752
Canadian Valley Electric Co-op 11277 S 356 PO Box 751	Seminole	OK	74868	**877-382-3680**	405-382-3680	245
Canadian Veterinary Medical Assn (CVMA) 339 Booth St	Ottawa	ON	K1R7K1	**800-567-2862**	613-236-1162	49-8
Canadian Wildlife Federation (CWF) 350 Michael Cowpland Dr	Kanata	ON	K2M2W1	**800-563-9453**	613-599-9594	48-13
CanaDream Corp 292154 Crosspointe Dr Rocky View County	Calgary	AB	T4A0V2	**800-461-7368**	403-291-1000	121
Canal Park Lodge 250 Canal Pk Dr	Duluth	MN	55802	**800-777-8560**	218-279-6000	378
Canal Park Stadium 300 S Main St	Akron	OH	44308	**888-223-6000**	330-253-5151	716
Canal Wood LLC 2430 Main St	Conway	SC	29526	**866-587-1460**	843-488-9663	446
Canam Group Inc 11535 First Ave Bureau 500 *TSX: CAM*	Saint-Georges	QC	G5Y7H5	**877-499-6049**	418-228-8031	719
Can-am Plumbing Inc 151 Wyoming St	Pleasanton	CA	94566	**800-786-9797**	925-846-1833	606
Canamould Extrusions Inc 101a Roytec Rd	Woodbridge	ON	L4L8A9	**866-874-6762**	905-264-4436	497
Canandaigua Inn on the Lake 770 S Main St	Canandaigua	NY	14424	**800-228-2801**	585-394-7800	378
Canarie 45 O'Connor St Ste 500	Ottawa	ON	K1P1A4	**800-959-5525**	613-943-5454	48-9
Canary Hotel 31 W Carrillo	Santa Barbara	CA	93101	**866-999-5401**	805-884-0300	378
Canberra Corp 3610 Holland Sylvania Rd	Toledo	OH	43615	**800-832-8992**	419-841-6616	151
Canberra Industries Inc 800 Research Pkwy *Sales	Meriden	CT	06450	**800-243-3955***	203-238-2351	470
Cancap Pharmaceutical Ltd 13111 Vanier Pl Unit 180	Richmond	BC	V6V2J1	**877-998-2378**	604-278-2188	231
Cancer Care Inc 275 Seventh Ave 22nd Fl	New York	NY	10001	**800-813-4673**	212-712-8400	48-17
Cancer Genetics Inc Meadows Office Complex 201 Rt 17 N 2nd Fl	Rutherford	NJ	07070	**888-334-4988**	201-528-9200	231
Candela Corp 530 Boston Post Rd	Wayland	MA	01778	**800-733-8550**	508-358-7400	423
Candid Color Systems Inc 1300 Metropolitan Ave	Oklahoma City	OK	73108	**800-336-4550**	405-947-8747	584
Candlelighters Childhood Cancer Foundation 10920 Connecticut Ave Suuite A PO Box 498	Kensington	MD	20895	**800-366-2223**	301-962-3520	48-17
Candler Hospital 5353 Reynolds St	Savannah	GA	31405	**800-622-6877**	912-819-6000	373-3

Name / Address	Toll-Free	Phone	Class
Can-do Promotions Inc 6517 Wise Ave NW ....North Canton OH 44720	800-325-7981		184
Cando Railway Services Ltd 740 Rosser Ave ....Brandon MB R7A0K9	866-989-5310	204-725-2627	646
Candy Bouquet International Inc 510 Mclean St ....Little Rock AR 72202	877-226-3901	501-375-9990	123
Cane Creek Cycling Components 355 Cane Creek Rd ....Fletcher NC 28732	800-234-2725	828-684-3551	82
Cane Creek State Park 50 State Pk Rd ....Star City AR 71667	888-287-2757	870-628-4714	561
Caneel Bay Resort PO Box 720 ....St. John VI 00831	855-226-3358	212-845-0581	
Caney Fork Electric Co-op Inc 920 Smithville Hwy PO Box 272. ....McMinnville TN 37110	888-505-3030	931-473-3116	245
Caney Valley Electric Co-op Assn Inc, The 401 Lawrence St PO Box 308 ....Cedar Vale KS 67024	800-310-8911	620-758-2262	245
Canfield Connector Div 8510 Foxwood Ct ....Youngstown OH 44514	800-554-5071		201
Canfield Equipment Service 21533 Mound Rd ....Warren MI 48091	800-637-3956	586-757-2020	57
Cangro Industries Long Island Transmission Co 495 Smith St ....Farmingdale NY 11735	800-422-9210	631-454-9000	616
Canidium LLC 3801 Kirby Dr S456 ....Houston TX 77024	877-651-1837		196
Canine Companions for Independence Inc (CCI) 2965 Dutton Ave PO Box 446 ....Santa Rosa CA 95402	800-572-2275	707-577-1700	48-17
Canisius College 2001 Main St ....Buffalo NY 14208	800-843-1517	716-888-2200	166
Cankdeska Cikana Community College PO Box 269 ....Fort Totten ND 58335	888-783-1463	701-766-4415	165
CAN-med Healthcare 99 Susie Lake Crescent ....Halifax NS B3S1C3	800-565-7553	902-455-4649	473
Cannery Casino & Hotel, The *Cannery Casino Resorts LLC* 2121 E Craig Rd ....North Las Vegas NV 89030	866-999-4899	702-507-5700	378
Cannon & Dunphy Sc 595 N Barker Rd ....Brookfield WI 53045	855-570-2676		
Cannon Cochran Management Services Inc 2 E Main St Towne Centre Bldg Ste 208 ....Danville IL 61832	800-252-5059	217-446-1089	461
Cannon Muskegon Corp 2875 Lincoln St ....Muskegon MI 49441	800-253-0371	231-755-1681	483
Cannon Sports Inc 12701 Van Nuys Blvd Ste P ....Pacoima CA 91331	800-223-0064		707
Canoga Perkins Corp 20600 Prairie St ....Chatsworth CA 91311 *Tech Supp	800-360-6642*	818-718-6300	173-3
Canon Business Solutions-Central 425 N Martingale Rd Ste 100 ....Schaumburg IL 60173	844-443-4636	847-706-3400	112
Canon City Chamber of Commerce 403 Royal Gorge Blvd ....Canon City CO 81212	800-876-7922	719-275-2331	139
Canoochee Electric Membership Corp 342 E Brazell St ....Reidsville GA 30453	800-342-0134		245
Canplas Industries Ltd 500 Veterans Dr ....Barrie ON L4M4V3	800-461-1771	705-726-3361	601-2
Cansec Systems Ltd 3105 Unity Dr Unit 9 ....Mississauga ON L5L4L2	877-545-7755	905-820-2404	689
CanTalk (Canada) Inc 250-70 Arthur St ....Winnipeg MB R3B1G7	800-480-9686		763
Cantata Health LLC 8383 158th Ave NE Ste 100 ....Redmond WA 98052	800-426-2675		178-11
Canteen Service Co 712 Industrial Dr ....Owensboro KY 42301	800-467-2471	270-683-2471	299
Canteen Vending Services *Compass Group* 2400 Yorkmont Rd ....Charlotte NC 28217	800-357-0012	704-328-4000	299
Cantel Medical Corp 150 Clove Rd 9th Fl ....Little Falls NJ 07424 *NYSE: CMN*	800-714-4152	973-890-7220	474
Canter & Assoc LLC 12975 Coral Tree Pl ....Los Angeles CA 90066 *Cust Svc	800-669-9011*	310-578-4700	761
Canterbury Designs 5632 W Washington Blvd ....Los Angeles CA 90016	800-935-7111	323-936-7111	153
Canterbury Park Holding Corp 1100 Canterbury Rd ....Shakopee MN 55379 *NASDAQ: CPHC*	800-340-6361	952-445-7223	638
Canton Public Library 1200 S Canton Ctr Rd ....Canton MI 48188	888-988-6300	734-397-0999	433-3
Canton Regional Chamber of Commerce 222 Market Ave N ....Canton OH 44702	800-533-4302	330-456-7253	139
Cantrell 1400 S Bradford St ....Gainesville GA 30501	800-922-1232	770-536-3611	
Canvas Products Co 274 S Waterman St ....Detroit MI 48209	877-293-1669	313-496-1000	728
Canweb Internet Services 1086 Modeland Rd ....Sarnia ON N7S6L2	877-422-6932	519-332-6900	180
CanWest DHI 660 Speedvale Ave W ....Guelph ON N1K1E5	800-549-4373	519-824-2320	738
Canyon Chamber of Commerce 1518 Fifth Ave ....Canyon TX 79015	800-999-9481	806-655-7815	139
Canyon Creek Cabinet Co 16726 Tye St SE ....Monroe WA 98272	800-228-1830	360-348-4600	115
Canyon Creek Travel Inc 333 W Campbell Rd Ste 440 ....Richardson TX 75080	800-952-1998	972-238-1998	770
Canyon Explorations Inc 675 W Clay Ave ....Flagstaff AZ 86001	800-654-0723	928-774-4559	532
Canyon Ranch 165 Kemble St ....Lenox MA 01240 *Resv	800-742-9000*	413-637-4100	665
Canyon Ranch Tucson 8600 E Rockcliff Rd ....Tucson AZ 85750	800-742-9000	520-749-9000	665
Canyonlands National Park 2282 SW Resource Blvd ....Moab UT 84532	800-394-9978	435-719-2313	560
CAO Group Inc 4628 Skyhawk Dr ....West Jordan UT 84084	877-877-9778	801-256-9282	418
CAOT (Canadian Assn of Occupational Therapists) 1125 Colonel By Dr ....Ottawa ON K1S5R1	800-434-2268	613-523-2268	48-1
CAP (College of American Pathologists) 325 Waukegan Rd ....Northfield IL 60093	800-323-4040	847-832-7000	49-8
CAP (Children Awaiting Parents Inc) 595 Blossom Rd Ste 306 ....Rochester NY 14610	888-835-8802	585-232-5110	48-6
Capax Global LLC 410 N Michigan Ave ....Chicago IL 60611	866-780-0385		225
Cape Air 660 Barnstable Rd ....Hyannis MA 02601	800-227-3247	508-771-6944	25
Cape Arago State Park Cape Arago Hwy ....Coos Bay OR 97420	800-551-6949		561
Cape Breton University (CBU) 1250 Grand Lake Rd PO Box 5300 ....Sydney NS B1P6L2	888-959-9995	902-539-5300	780
Cape Cod Canal Regional Chamber of Commerce 70 Main St ....Buzzards Bay MA 02532	888-332-2732	508-759-6000	139
Cape Cod Chamber of Commerce 5 Shoot Flying Hill Rd ....Centerville MA 02632	888-332-2732	508-362-3225	139
Cape Cod Community College 2240 Iyanough Rd ....West Barnstable MA 02668	877-846-3672	508-362-2131	162
Cape Cod Five Cents Savings Bank 532 Rte 28 PO Box 20 ....Harwich Port MA 02646	800-678-1855	508-430-0400	70
Cape Cod Hospital 27 Park St ....Hyannis MA 02601	800-545-5014	508-771-1800	373-3
Cape Cod Life Magazine 13 Steeple St Ste 204 PO Box 1439 ....Mashpee MA 02649	800-698-1717	508-419-7381	455-22
Cape Cod Potato Chip Co 100 Breed's Hill Rd ....Hyannis MA 02601	888-881-2447		296-35
Cape Cod Regional Transit Authority (CCRTA) 215 Iyannough Rd PO Box 1988. ....Hyannis MA 02601	800-352-7155	508-775-8504	466
Cape Cod Times 319 Main St ....Hyannis MA 02601	800-451-7887	508-775-1200	528-2
Cape Codder Resort & Spa 1225 Iyanough Rd Rt 132 Bearse's Way ....Hyannis MA 02601	888-297-2200	508-771-3000	665
Cape Girardeau Convention & Visitors Bureau 400 Broadway Ste 100 ....Cape Girardeau MO 63701	800-777-0068	573-335-1631	206
Cape Hatteras Electric Co-op 47109 Light Plant Rd PO Box 9 ....Buxton NC 27920	800-454-5616	252-995-5616	245
Cape Lookout State Park 13000 Whiskey Creek Rd W ....Tillamook OR 97141	800-551-6949		
Cape May County 7 N Main St PO Box 5000 ....Cape May Court House NJ 08210	800-621-5388	609-465-1010	337
Capel Inc 831 N Main St ....Troy NC 27371	800-334-3711		131
Capella Education Co 225 S Sixth St 9th Fl ....Minneapolis MN 55402 *NASDAQ: CPLA ■ *Cust Svc	888-227-3552*	612-339-8650	242
Capezio 1 Campus Rd ....Totowa NJ 07512 *Acctg	888-227-3946*	973-595-9000	301
CapFinancial Partners LLC 4208 Six Forks Rd Ste 1700 ....Raleigh NC 27609	800-216-0645	919-870-6822	400
Capintec Inc 7 Vreeland Rd ....Florham Park NJ 07932	800-631-3826	201-825-9500	
Capital Advisors Limited LLC 20600 Chagrin Blvd ....Shaker Heights OH 44122	888-295-7908	216-295-7900	194
Capital Agricultural Property Services Inc 801 Warrenville Rd Ste 150 ....Lisle IL 60532	800-243-2060	630-434-9150	315-3
Capital Area District Libraries 401 S Capitol Ave ....Lansing MI 48933	866-561-2500	517-367-6300	433-3
Capital Brewery 7734 Terr Ave ....Middleton WI 53562	800-598-6352	608-836-7100	102
Capital City Bank 217 North Monroe St ....Tallahassee FL 32301	888-671-0400	850-402-7700	70
Capital City Bank Group Inc PO Box 900 ....Tallahassee FL 32302 *NASDAQ: CCBG*	888-671-0400	850-402-7500	359-2
Capital City Press Inc PO Box 588 ....Baton Rouge LA 70821	800-960-6397	225-383-1111	633-8
Capital Community College 950 Main St ....Hartford CT 06103	800-894-6126	860-906-5000	162
Capital Culinary Institute of Keiser College *Melbourne* 900 S Babcock St ....Melbourne FL 32901	877-636-3618	321-409-4800	163
Capital District Physicians' Health Plan 500 Patroon Creek Blvd ....Albany NY 12206	888-258-0477	518-641-3000	390-3
Capital Electric Co-op Inc 4111 State St ....Bismarck ND 58503	888-223-1513	701-223-1513	245
Capital Farm Credit Aca 7000 Woodway Dr ....Waco TX 76712	877-944-5500	254-776-7506	69
Capital Ford Inc 4900 Capital Blvd ....Raleigh NC 27616	877-659-2496	919-790-4600	57
Capital Grille 900 Boylston St ....Boston MA 02115	866-518-9113		667
Capital Growth Management LP 1 International Pl ....Boston MA 02110	800-345-4048	617-737-3225	400
Capital Health Plan PO Box 15349 ....Tallahassee FL 32317	800-390-1434	850-383-3333	390-3
Capital Hill Hotel & Suites 88 Albert St ....Ottawa ON K1P5E9	800-463-7705	613-235-1413	378
Capital Hospice Inc 2900 Telestar Ct ....Falls Church VA 22042	855-571-5700	703-538-2065	370
Capital Hotel 111 W Markham St ....Little Rock AR 72201	877-637-0037	501-374-7474	378
Capital Institutional Services Inc 1700 Pacific Ave Ste 1100 ....Dallas TX 75201	800-247-6729	214-720-0055	400
Capital Investment Advisors Inc 200 Sandy Springs Pl NE Ste 300 ....Atlanta GA 30328	888-531-0018	404-531-0018	194
Capital Journal 333 W Dakota Ave ....Pierre SD 57501	800-537-0025	605-224-7301	528-2
Capital Medical Ctr 3900 Capital Mall Dr SW ....Olympia WA 98502	888-677-9757	360-754-5858	373-3
Capital Merchant Solutions Inc 3005 Gill St ....Bloomington IL 61704	877-495-2419		251
Capital One Auto Finance Inc PO Box 60511 ....City of Industry CA 91716	800-946-0332		70
Capital One Financial Corp 1680 Capital One Dr ....McLean VA 22102 *NYSE: COF*	800-655-2265	800-926-1000	215

	Toll-Free	Phone	Class
Capital One FSB *Capital One Bank* 15000 Capital One Dr .... Richmond VA 23238	877-383-4802		70
Capital Premium Financing Inc 12235 South 800 East .... Draper UT 84020	877-730-1906	800-767-0705	
Capital Public Radio Inc 7055 Folsom Blvd .... Sacramento CA 95826	877-480-5900	916-278-8900	641-91
Capital Realty Advisors Inc 600 Sandtree Dr Ste 109 .... Palm Beach Gardens FL 33403	800-940-1088	561-624-5888	461
Capital Review Group (CRG) 2415 E Camelback Rd Ste 700 .... Phoenix AZ 85016	877-666-5539		
Capital Senior Living Corp 14160 Dallas Pkwy Ste 300 .... Dallas TX 75254 *NYSE: CSU*	800-635-1232	972-770-5600	668
Capital Times 1901 Fish Hatchery Rd .... Madison WI 53713	800-362-8333	608-252-6400	528-2
Capital University College & Main St .... Columbus OH 43209	866-544-6175	614-236-6101	166
Capitol Aggregates Ltd 2330 N Loop 1604 W .... San Antonio TX 78248	855-422-7244	210-871-6100	46
Capitol Aluminum & Glass Corp 1276 W Main St .... Bellevue OH 44811	800-331-8268		330
Capitol Archives & Record Storage Inc 133 Laurel St .... Hartford CT 06106	800-381-2277	860-951-8981	194
Capitol Broadcasting Co Inc 2619 Western Blvd .... Raleigh NC 27606	800-234-4857	919-890-6000	733
Capitol Chevrolet Montgomery 711 Eastern Blvd .... Montgomery AL 36117 *Sales	800-410-1137*	334-223-4458	57
Capitol City Container Corp 8240 Zionsville Rd .... Indianapolis IN 46268	800-233-5145	317-875-0290	100
Capitol City Produce 16550 Commercial Ave .... Baton Rouge LA 70816	800-349-1583	225-272-8153	296-21
Capitol City Speakers Bureau 1620 S Fifth St .... Springfield IL 62703	800-397-3183	217-544-8552	704
Capitol Connection 4400 University Dr MSN 1D2 .... Fairfax VA 22030	844-504-7161	703-993-3100	116
Capitol Federal Financial 700 Kansas Ave .... Topeka KS 66603 *NASDAQ: CFFN*	888-822-7333	785-235-1341	359-2
Capitol FSB 700 S Kansas Ave .... Topeka KS 66603	888-822-7333	785-235-1341	70
Capitol Hill Hotel 200 C St SE .... Washington DC 20003	800-491-2525	202-543-6000	378
Capitol Indemnity Corp 1600 Aspen Commons .... Middleton WI 53562	800-475-4450	608-829-4200	390-4
Capitol Lien Records & Research Inc 1010 N Dale St .... Saint Paul MN 55117	800-845-4077	651-488-0100	631
Capitol Plaza Hotel 415 W McCarty St .... Jefferson City MO 65101	800-338-8088	573-635-1234	667
Capitol Plaza Hotel & Conference Ctr 100 State St .... Montpelier VT 05602	800-274-5252	802-223-5252	378
Capitol Plaza Hotel Jefferson City 415 W McCarty St .... Jefferson City MO 65101	800-338-8088	573-635-1234	378
Capitol Reservations 1730 Rhode Island Ave NW .... Washington DC 20036	800-847-4832	202-452-1270	375
Capitol Services Inc 206 E Ninth St Ste 1300 .... Austin TX 78701	800-345-4647		631
Capitol Steps Productions Inc 210 N Washington St .... Alexandria VA 22314	800-733-7837	703-683-8330	628
Capitol Technology University 11301 Springfield Rd .... Laurel MD 20708	800-950-1992	301-369-2800	166
Capitol Uniform & Linen Service 195 Commerce Way .... Dover DE 19904	800-822-7352	302-674-1511	441
Caplugs LLC 2150 Elmwood Ave .... Buffalo NY 14207 *Cust Svc	888-227-5847*	716-876-9855	154
Capricorn Coffees Inc 353 Tenth St .... San Francisco CA 94103	800-541-0758	415-621-8500	297-2
Capsmith Inc 2240 Old Lake Mary Rd .... Sanford FL 32771	800-228-3889	407-328-7660	157-6
CapSouth Partners Inc 2216 W Main St .... Dothan AL 36301	800-929-1001	334-673-8600	461
CAPSPECIALTY 1600 Aspen Commons Ste 300 ... Middleton WI 53562	800-475-4450	608-829-4200	390-4
Capstead Mortgage Corp 8401 N Central Expy Ste 800 .... Dallas TX 75225 *NYSE: CMO*	800-358-2323	214-874-2323	650
Capstone Production Group 1638 S Saunders St .... Raleigh NC 27603	800-951-4005	919-838-8030	343
Capstone Therapeutics Corp 1275 W Washington St Ste 101 .... Tempe AZ 85281 *OTC: CAPS*	800-937-5520	602-286-5520	475
Capstone Turbine Corp 21211 Nordhoff St .... Chatsworth CA 91311 *NASDAQ: CPST*	866-422-7786	818-734-5300	262
Capt Harrys Fishing Supply Company Inc 8501 NW Seventh Ave .... Miami FL 33150	800-327-4088	305-374-4661	707
Captain D's LLC 624 Grassmere Park Dr Ste 30 .... Nashville TN 37211	800-314-4819	615-391-5461	666
CAPTE (Commission on Accreditation in Physical Therapy Ed) 1111 North Fairfax St .... Alexandria VA 22314	800-999-2782	703-706-3245	48-1
Captive Fastener Corp 19 Thornton Rd .... Oakland NJ 07436	800-526-4430	201-337-6800	278
Captive-aire Systems Inc 4641 Paragon Pk Rd .... Raleigh NC 27616	800-334-9256	919-882-2410	693
CAPTRUST 4208 Six Forks Rd Ste 1700 .... Raleigh NC 27609	800-216-0645		
Car City Motor Company Inc 3100 S US Hwy 169 .... Saint Joseph MO 64503	800-525-7008	816-233-9149	57
Car Clinic Productions 5675 N Davis Hwy .... Pensacola FL 32503	888-227-2546	850-478-3139	642
Car Toys Inc 400 Fairview Ave N Ste 900 .... Seattle WA 98109	888-227-8697		52
CARA Group Inc, The Drake Oak Brook Plz 2215 York Rd Ste 300 .... Oak Brook IL 60523	866-401-2272	630-574-2272	180
Cara Operations Ltd 199 Four Valley Dr .... Vaughan ON L4K0B8	800-860-4082	905-760-2244	299
Carahsoft Technology Corp 12369 Sunrise Vly Dr Ste D2 .... Reston VA 20191	888-662-2724	703-871-8500	225
Caraustar Industries Inc 5000 Austell-Powder Springs Rd Ste 300 .... Austell GA 30106	800-858-1438	770-948-3100	550
Caravan Facilities Management LLC 1400 Weiss St .... Saginaw MI 48602	855-211-7450		192
Caravelle Resort Hotel & Villas 6900 N Ocean Blvd .... Myrtle Beach SC 29572	800-297-3413	843-310-3420	665
Carbo Ceramics Inc 575 N Dairy Ashford Rd Ste 300 .... Houston TX 77079 *NYSE: CRR*	800-551-3247	281-921-6400	533
Carboline Co 350 Hanley Industrial Ct .... Saint Louis MO 63144	800-848-4645	314-644-1000	546
Carbon County 2 Hazard Sq PO Box 129 .... Jim Thorpe PA 18229	800-441-1315	570-325-3611	337
Carbon County PO Box 1017 .... Rawlins WY 82301	800-228-3547		337
Carbon Power & Light Inc 100 E Willow Ave PO Box 579 .... Saratoga WY 82331	800-359-0249	307-326-5206	245
Carbro Corp 15724 Condon Ave PO Box 278 .... Lawndale CA 90260	888-738-4400	310-643-8400	491
Carco Inc 10333 Shoemaker PO Box 13859 ......Detroit MI 48213	800-255-3924	313-925-9000	465
Carco International Inc 2721 Midland Blvd .... Fort Smith AR 72904	800-824-3215	479-441-3270	274
Carco National Lease Inc 2905 N 32nd St .... Fort Smith AR 72904	800-643-2596	479-441-3200	773
Cardell Cabinetry 3215 N Panam Expy .... San Antonio TX 78219	888-221-3872		
Cardiac Science Corp 3303 Monte Villa Pkwy .... Bothell WA 98021 *Cust Svc	800-426-0337*		250
CardiacAssist Inc 240 Alpha Dr .... Pittsburgh PA 15238	800-373-1607	412-963-7770	474
Cardiff Park Advisors 2257 Vista La Nisa .... Carlsbad CA 92009	888-332-2238	760-635-7526	196
Cardinal Aluminum Co 6910 Preston Hwy .... Louisville KY 40219 *Cust Svc	800-398-7833*	502-969-9302	483
Cardinal Gates 79 Amlajack Way .... Newnan GA 30265	800-318-3380	770-252-4200	64
Cardinal Health Distribution 7000 Cardinal Pl .... Dublin OH 43017	800-926-0834	614-757-5000	238
Cardinal Health Inc 7000 Cardinal Pl .... Dublin OH 43017 *NYSE: CAH*	800-926-0834	614-757-5000	359-3
Cardinal Health Nuclear Pharmacy Services 7000 Cardinal Pl .... Dublin OH 43017	800-326-6457	614-757-5000	238
Cardinal Industries Inc 21-01 51st Ave .... Long Island NY 11101	800-622-8339	718-784-3000	757
Cardinal Meat Specialists Ltd 155 Hedgedale Rd .... Brampton ON L6T5P3	800-363-1439	905-459-4436	297-9
Cardinal Office Products Inc 576 E Main St .... Frankfort KY 40601	800-589-5886	502-875-3300	530
Cardinal Scale Manufacturing Co 203 E Daugherty St PO Box 151 .... Webb City MO 64870	800-441-4237	417-673-4631	680
Cardinal Stritch University 6801 N Yates Rd .... Milwaukee WI 53217	800-347-8822	414-410-4000	166
Cardinal Transport Inc 7180 E Reed Rd .... Coal City IL 60416	800-435-9302	815-634-4443	775
CardioMed Supplies Inc 199 Saint David St .... Lindsay ON K9V5K7	800-387-9757	705-328-2518	473
Cardiovascular Systems Inc 1225 NO H 8 NW .... St Paul MN 55112	877-274-0360	651-259-1600	474
CardLogix 16 Hughes Ste 100 .... Irvine CA 92618	866-392-8326	949-380-1312	700
Cardlytics Inc 675 Ponce de Leon Ave NE Ste 6000 .... Atlanta GA 30308	888-798-5802	866-269-1020	5
Cardo Systems Inc 1204 Pkwy View Dr .... Pittsburgh PA 15205	800-488-0363	412-788-4533	452
Cardone Industries Inc 5501 Whitaker Ave .... Philadelphia PA 19124 *Cust Svc	800-777-4780*	800-777-4304	60
CardScan Inc 25 First St Ste 107 .... Cambridge MA 02141	800-942-6739	617-492-4200	173-7
CardSmart Retail Corp 11 Executive Ave .... Edison NJ 08817	888-782-7050	800-654-6960	310
CardTrak LLC 4055 Tamiami Trl .... Port Charlotte FL 33952	800-344-7714		392
Cardwell Distributing Inc 8137 S State St .... Midvale UT 84047	800-561-0051	801-561-4251	575
Cardwell Westinghouse Co 8400 S Stewart Ave .... Chicago IL 60620	800-821-2376	773-483-7575	646
CARE (Coalition for Auto Repair Equality) 105 Oronoco St Ste 115 .... Alexandria VA 22314	800-229-5380	703-519-7555	49-21
Care of Trees Inc 1500 N Mantua St .... Kent OH 44240	800-445-8733		771
Care Partners 68 Sweeten Creek Rd .... Asheville NC 28803	800-627-1533	828-252-2255	362
CARE USA 151 Ellis St NE .... Atlanta GA 30303	800-521-2273	404-681-2552	48-5
Care Zone Inc 1463 E Republican St Ste 198 .... Seattle WA 98112	888-407-7785		386
CareCentric Inc 20 Church St 12th Fl .... Hartford CT 06103	800-808-1902		178-10
Career Step LLC 4692 N 300 W Ste 150 .... Provo UT 84604	800-246-7837	801-489-9393	759
CareerBuilder Employment Screening LLC Atrium Corporate Ctr 3800 Golf Rd Ste 120 .... Rolling Meadows IL 60008	866-255-1852		399
CareerCurve LLC 5005 Rockside Rd Ste 600-076 .... Cleveland OH 44131	800-314-8230	216-406-5542	41
Careers The Next Generation Foundation 10470 176 St NW .... Edmonton AB T5S1L3	888-757-7172	780-426-3414	305

Name / Address	City	State	ZIP	Toll-Free	Phone	Class
CareerSource Flagler Volusia 359 Bill France Blvd	Daytona Beach	FL	32114	**800-476-7574**	386-323-7001	260
CareerStaff Unlimited Inc 6363 N State Hwy 161 Ste 100	Irving	TX	75038	**888-993-4599**	972-812-3200	717
Carefirst Seniors & Community Services Association 3601 Victoria Park Ave	Scarborough	ON	M1W3Y3	**800-268-7708**	416-502-2323	138
Carefree Resort & Conference Ctr 37220 Mule Train Rd	Carefree	AZ	85377	**888-692-4343**		703
Carefree Vacations Inc 11885 Carmel Mountain Rd Ste 906	San Diego	CA	92128	**800-266-3476**	800-795-0720	766
Caremark Rx Inc PO Box 832407	Richardson	TX	75083	**877-460-7766**		582
Carenet Healthcare Services 11845 Interstate 10 W Ste 400	San Antonio	TX	78230	**800-809-7000**		392
CareOne 57 Old Rd to Nine Acre Corner	Concord	MA	01742	**855-277-8550**		
CarePartners Mountain Area Hospice PO Box 5779	Asheville	NC	28813	**800-627-1533**	828-255-0231	370
Carepoint Inc 215 E Bay St Ste 304	Charleston	SC	29401	**800-296-1825**	843-853-6999	237
Carepro Health Services 1014 Fifth Ave SE	Cedar Rapids	IA	52403	**800-575-8810**		194
CareSource 230 N Main St	Dayton	OH	45402	**800-488-0134**	937-224-3300	351
Carestream Health 150 Verona St	Rochester	NY	14608	**888-777-2072**	585-627-1800	474
CAREstream Medical Ltd 20133 102 Ave Units 1	Langley	BC	V1M4B4	**888-310-2186**		
Care-Tech Laboratories Inc 3224 S KingsHwy Blvd	Saint Louis	MO	63139	**800-325-9681**	314-772-4610	578
CareWatch Inc 3483 Satellite Blvd Ste 211 S	Duluth	GA	30096	**800-901-2454**	770-409-0244	177
CareWorks Technologies Ltd 5555 Glendon Ct	Dublin	OH	43016	**800-669-9623**		196
Carey Color Inc 6835 Ridge Rd	Wadsworth	OH	44281	**800-555-3142**	330-239-1835	195
Carey Digital 1718 Central Pkwy	Cincinnati	OH	45214	**800-767-6071**	513-241-5210	776
Carey Executive Limousine 245 University Ave	Atlanta	GA	30315	**800-241-3943**	404-223-2000	440
Carey International Inc 4530 Wisconsin Ave NW	Washington	DC	20016	**800-336-4646**	301-698-3900	440
Carey Sales & Services Inc 3141-47 Frederick Ave	Baltimore	MD	21229	**800-848-7748**	410-945-7878	35
Carey Theological College 5920 Iona Dr	Vancouver	BC	V6T1J6	**844-862-2739**	604-224-4308	167-3
CARF (Commission on Accreditation of Rehabilitation Faci) 6951 E Southpoint Rd	Tucson	AZ	85756	**888-281-6531**	520-325-1044	48-1
Cargill Energy PO Box 9300	Minneapolis	MN	55440	**800-227-4455**		575
Cargill Foundation 15407 McGinty Rd W Ste 46	Wayzata	MN	55391	**800-227-4455**	877-765-8867	304
Cargill Inc 15407 McGinty Rd W	Wayzata	MN	55391	**800-227-4455**		275
Cargill Salt Inc PO Box 5621	Minneapolis	MN	55440	**888-385-7258**		676
Cargo Control USA Inc PO Box 2806	Sanford	NC	27331	**888-775-5059**	919-775-5059	365
Cargo Management Systems Llc 827 E Main St	Richmond	KY	40475	**855-484-9235**		195
Carhartt Inc 5750 Mercury Dr	Dearborn	MI	48126	**800-833-3118**	313-271-8460	155-18
Caribbean Products Ltd 3624 Falls Rd	Baltimore	MD	21211	**888-689-5068**		296-26
Caribbean Resort & Villas 3000 N Ocean Blvd	Myrtle Beach	SC	29577	**800-552-8509**		665
Caribe Royale 8101 World Ctr Dr *Resv	Orlando	FL	32821	**800-823-8000***	407-238-8000	378
Caribe Royale Orlando All-Suites Hotel & Convention Ctr 8101 World Ctr Dr *Resv	Orlando	FL	32821	**800-823-8300***	407-238-8000	378
Caribou Coffee Company Inc 3900 Lakebreeze Ave N *NASDAQ: CBOU*	Minneapolis	MN	55429	**888-227-4268**	763-592-2200	159
Caribou County 159 S Main	Soda Springs	ID	83276	**800-972-7660**	208-547-4324	337
Caribou Highlands Lodge 371 Ski Hill Rd	Lutsen	MN	55612	**800-642-6036**	218-663-7241	665
Caribou Road Services Ltd 5110 52nd Ave	Pouce Coupe	BC	V0C2C0	**800-667-2322**	250-786-5440	261
Carilion Roanoke Community Hospital (CRCH) 101 Elm Ave SE	Roanoke	VA	24013	**800-422-8482**	540-985-8000	373-3
Carilion Roanoke Memorial Hospital 1906 Belleview Ave	Roanoke	VA	24014	**800-422-8482**	540-981-7000	373-3
Carina Technology Inc 2366 Whitesburg Dr	Huntsville	AL	35801	**866-915-5464**	256-704-0422	177
Carithers Wallace Courtenay Co 4343 NE Expy	Atlanta	GA	30340	**800-292-8220**	770-493-8200	320
Carl Belt Inc 11521 Milnor Ave PO Box 1210	Cumberland	MD	21502	**888-729-1616**	301-729-8900	186
Carl Buddig & Co 950 175th St	Homewood	IL	60430	**888-633-5684**	708-798-0900	296-26
Carl Nelson Insurance Agency I 1519 N 11th Ave	Hanford	CA	93230	**800-582-4264**	559-584-4495	389
Carl Sandburg College 2400 Tom L Wilson Blvd	Galesburg	IL	61401	**877-236-1862**	309-344-2518	162
Carl Vinson Veterans Affairs Medical Ctr 1826 Veterans Blvd	Dublin	GA	31021	**800-595-5229**	478-272-1210	373-8
Carl Zeiss Inc 1 Zeiss Dr	Thornwood	NY	10594	**800-233-2343**	914-747-1800	540
Carl Zeiss Industrial Metrology 6250 Sycamore Ln N	Maple Grove	MN	55369	**800-327-9735**	763-744-2400	491
Carl's Golfland Inc 1976 S Telegraph Rd	Bloomfield Hills	MI	48302	**877-412-2757**	248-335-8095	707
Carle Hospice 611 W Park St	Urbana	IL	61801	**800-239-3620**	217-383-3311	370
Carleton College 100 S College St *Admissions	Northfield	MN	55057	**800-995-2275***	507-646-4000	166
Carleton University 1125 Colonel By Dr	Ottawa	ON	K1S5B6	**888-354-4414**	613-520-7400	780
Carley State Park 19041 Hwy 74	Altura	MN	55910	**888-646-6367**	507-932-3007	561
Carlisle & Finch Co, The 4562 W Mitchell Ave	Cincinnati	OH	45232	**800-828-3186**	513-681-6080	438
Carlisle FoodService Products Inc 4711 E Hefner Rd	Oklahoma City	OK	73131	**800-654-8210**	405-475-5600	300
Carlisle Industrial Brake 1031 E Hillside Dr	Bloomington	IN	47401	**800-873-6361**	812-336-3811	60
Carlisle Sanitary Maintenance Products 402 Black River St	Sparta	WI	54656	**800-654-8210**	608-269-2151	103
Carlisle SynTec 1285 Ritner Hwy PO Box 7000	Carlisle	PA	17013	**800-479-6832**		191-4
Carlisle Wide Plank Floors Inc 1676 Rt 9	Stoddard	NH	03464	**800-595-9663**	603-446-3937	363
Carlo Gavazzi Inc 750 Hastings Ln	Buffalo Grove	IL	60089	**800-222-2659**	847-465-6100	261
Carlow University 3333 Fifth Ave	Pittsburgh	PA	15213	**800-333-2275**	412-578-6000	166
Carlson Craft Inc 1750 Tower Blvd	North Mankato	MN	56003	**800-774-6848**		623
Carlson Tool & Manufacturing Corp W57 N14386 Doerr Way	Cedarburg	WI	53012	**800-532-2252**	262-377-2020	752
Carlson Wagonlit Travel Inc 701 Carlson Pkwy	Minnetonka	MN	55305	**800-213-7295**		767
Carlstar Group LLC, The 725 Cool Springs Blvd Ste 500	Franklin	TN	37067	**800-889-7367**	615-503-0220	369
Carlton Bates Co 3600 W 69th St	Little Rock	AR	72209	**866-600-6040**	501-562-9100	246
Carlton Foods Corp 880 Texas 46	New Braunfels	TX	78130	**800-628-9849**	830-625-7583	296-26
Carlton Group Inc 120 Landmark Dr	Greensboro	NC	27409	**800-722-7824**	336-668-7677	360
Carlyle Hotel, The 1731 New Hampshire Ave NW	Washington	DC	20009	**877-301-0019**	202-234-3200	378
Carlyle House Historic Park 121 N Fairfax St	Alexandria	VA	22314	**800-877-0954**	703-549-2997	517
Carlyle Johnson Machine Co (CJM) 291 Boston Tpke	Bolton	CT	06043	**888-629-4867**	860-643-1531	616
CarMax Inc 12800 Tuckahoe Creek Pkwy *NYSE: KMX*	Richmond	VA	23238	**800-519-1511**		57
Carmel Clay Public Library 55 Fourth Ave SE	Carmel	IN	46032	**800-908-4490**	317-844-3361	433-3
Carmel River Inn 26600 Oliver Rd	Carmel	CA	93923	**800-882-8142**	831-624-1575	378
Carmel Valley Manor 8545 Carmel Valley Rd	Carmel	CA	93923	**800-544-5546**	831-624-1281	668
Carmel Valley Ranch Resort 1 Old Ranch Rd	Carmel	CA	93923	**866-405-5037**	855-687-7262	665
Carmeuse North America 11 Stanwix St 11th Fl	Pittsburgh	PA	15222	**866-243-0965**	412-995-5500	439
Carmichael Chamber of Commerce 6825 Fair Oaks Blvd Ste 100	Carmichael	CA	95608	**800-991-6147**	916-481-1002	139
Carnations Home Fashions Inc 53 Jeanne Dr	Newburgh	NY	12550	**800-866-8949**	212-679-6017	360
Carnegie East House For Seniors 1844 Second Ave	New York	NY	10128	**888-410-0033**	212-410-0033	196
Carnegie Fabrics Llc 110 N Ctr Ave	Rockville Centre	NY	11570	**800-727-6770**	516-678-6770	
Carnegie Hotel 1216 W State of Franklin Rd	Johnson City	TN	37604	**866-757-8277**	423-979-6400	378
Carnegie Learning Inc 501 Grant St Ste 1075	Pittsburgh	PA	15219	**888-851-7094**		177
Carnegie Mellon University 5000 Forbes Ave	Pittsburgh	PA	15213	**844-625-4600**	412-268-2000	166
Carneros Resort & Spa 4048 Sonoma Hwy	Napa	CA	94559	**888-400-9000**	707-299-4900	703
Carney, Sandoe & Associates, LP 44 Bromfield St	Boston	MA	02108	**800-225-7986**	617-542-0260	242
Carnival Cruise Lines 3655 NW 87th Ave	Miami	FL	33178	**800-764-7419**	305-599-2600	220
Caro Foods Inc 2324 Bayou Blue Rd	Houma	LA	70364	**800-395-2276**	985-872-1483	297-7
Carol Woods Retirement Community 750 Weaver Dairy Rd	Chapel Hill	NC	27514	**800-518-9333**	919-968-4511	668
Carole Fabrics Inc PO Box 1436	Augusta	GA	30903	**800-241-0920**	706-863-4742	741
Carolina Advanced Digital Inc 133 Triangle Trade Dr	Cary	NC	27513	**800-435-2212**	919-460-1313	461
Carolina Apothecary Inc 726 S Scales St	Reidsville	NC	27320	**800-633-1447**	336-342-0071	473
Carolina Biological Supply Co 2700 York Rd	Burlington	NC	27215	**800-334-5551**	336-584-0381	243
Carolina Business Furniture LLC 535 Archdale Blvd	Archdale	NC	27263	**800-763-0212**	336-431-9400	319-1
Carolina Carports Inc 187 Cardinal Ridge Trl	Dobson	NC	27017	**800-670-4262**		485
Carolina Casualty Insurance Co 5011 Gate Pkwy Ste 200	Jacksonville	FL	32256	**800-874-8053**	904-363-0900	390-4
Carolina Container Co 909 Prospect St	High Point	NC	27260	**800-627-0825**	336-883-7146	100
Carolina Dragway 302 Dragstrip Rd	Aiken	SC	29803	**877-471-7223**	803-471-2285	512
Carolina Eye Assoc PA 2170 Midland Rd	Southern Pines	NC	28387	**800-733-5357**	910-295-2100	793
Carolina Filters Inc 109 E Newberry Ave	Sumter	SC	29150	**800-849-5646**		801
Carolina Foods Inc 1807 S Tryon St	Charlotte	NC	28203	**800-234-0441**	704-333-9812	296-1

Company / Address	City	State	ZIP	Toll-Free	Phone	Class
Carolina Glove Co 116 Mclin Creek Rd PO Box 999	Conover	NC	28613	**800-335-1918**	828-464-1132	155-7
Carolina Herrera 501 Seventh Ave 17th Fl	New York	NY	10018	**866-254-7660**		
Carolina Inn 211 Pittsboro St	Chapel Hill	NC	27516	**800-962-8519**	919-933-2001	378
Carolina International Trucks Inc 1619 Bluff Rd	Columbia	SC	29201	**800-868-4923**		57
Carolina Material Handling Services Inc PO Box 6	Columbia	SC	29202	**800-922-6709**	803-695-0149	384
Carolina Meadows 100 Carolina Meadows	Chapel Hill	NC	27517	**800-458-6756**	919-942-4014	668
Carolina Mfg 7025 Augusta Rd	Greenville	SC	29605	**800-845-2744**		155-12
Carolina Narrow Fabric Co 1100 N Patterson Ave	Winston-Salem	NC	27101	**877-631-3077**	336-631-3000	740-5
Carolina Opry 8901 Hwy 17 N	Myrtle Beach	SC	29572	**800-843-6779**		568
Carolina Packers Inc 2999 S Bright Leaf Blvd	Smithfield	NC	27577	**800-682-7675**	919-934-2181	471
Carolina Panthers Bank of America Stadium 800 S Mint St	Charlotte	NC	28202	**888-297-8673**	704-358-7000	711-2
Carolina Rim & Wheel Co 1308 Upper Asbury Ave	Charlotte	NC	28206	**800-247-4337**	704-334-7276	61
Carolina Trust Bank 901 E Main St *NASDAQ: CART*	Lincolnton	NC	28092	**877-983-5537**	704-735-1104	70
Carolinas Auto Supply House Inc 2135 Tipton Dr	Charlotte	NC	28206	**800-438-4070**	704-334-4646	61
Carolinas Investment Consulting LLC 5605 Carnegie Blvd Ste 400	Charlotte	NC	28209	**800-255-2904**	704-643-2455	400
Carolinas Medical Center-NorthEast 920 Church St N	Concord	NC	28025	**800-575-1275**	704-403-1275	373-3
Carolinas Medical Center-University 8800 N Tryon St	Charlotte	NC	28262	**800-821-1535**	704-863-6000	373-3
Carolinas Medical Ctr Mercy 2001 Vail Ave	Charlotte	NC	28207	**800-821-1535**		373-3
Caroline County Public Library 100 Market St	Denton	MD	21629	**800-832-3277**	410-479-1343	433-3
Carollo Engineers 2700 Ygnacio Valley Rd Ste 300	Walnut Creek	CA	94598	**800-523-5826**	925-932-1710	261
Caron Compactor Co 1204 Ullrey Ave	Escalon	CA	95320	**800-542-2766**	209-838-2062	190
Caroplast Inc PO Box 668405	Charlotte	NC	28266	**800-327-5797**	704-394-4191	608
Carousel Beachfront Hotel & Suites 11700 Coastal Hwy	Ocean City	MD	21842	**800-641-0011**	410-524-1000	378
Carousel Inn & Suites 1530 S Harbor Blvd	Anaheim	CA	92802	**800-854-6767**	714-758-0444	378
Carpedia International Ltd 75 Navy St	Oakville	ON	L6J2Z1	**877-445-8288**		461
Carpenter Co 5016 Monument Ave	Richmond	VA	23230	**800-288-3830**	804-359-0800	597
Carpenter Contractors of America Inc 3900 Ave D NW	Winter Haven	FL	33880	**800-959-8806**	863-294-6449	189-2
Carpenter Powder Products 600 Mayer St	Bridgeville	PA	15017	**866-790-9092**	412-257-5102	591
Carpenter Specialty Alloys Operations 101 W Bern St	Reading	PA	19601	**800-654-6543**	610-208-2000	719
Carpenter Technology Corp PO Box 14662 *NYSE: CRS*	Reading	PA	19612	**800-654-6543**	610-208-2000	719
Carpenter Technology Corp - Latrobe Operati 2626 Ligonier St	Latrobe	PA	15650	**800-241-8527**	724-537-7711	490
Carpet King Inc 1815 W River Rd N	Minneapolis	MN	55411	**800-375-3608**	612-588-7600	290
Carr Business Systems 130 Spagnoli Rd	Melville	NY	11747	**800-720-2277**	631-249-9880	112
Carr Concrete Corp 362 Waverly Rd	Williamstown	WV	26187	**800-837-8918**	304-464-4441	183
Carr Corp 1547 11th St	Santa Monica	CA	90401	**800-952-2398**	310-587-1113	587
Carr Lane Mfg 4200 Carr Ln Ct	Saint Louis	MO	63119	**800-622-4824**	314-647-6200	752
Carriage Services Inc 3040 Post Oak Blvd Ste 300 *NYSE: CSV*	Houston	TX	77056	**866-332-8400**	713-332-8400	508
Carrico Implement Company Inc 3160 US 24 Hwy	Beloit	KS	67420	**877-542-4099**	785-738-5744	274
Carrier Clinic 252 County Rd 601	Belle Mead	NJ	08502	**800-933-3579**		373-5
Carrier Vibrating Equipment Inc 3400 Fern Valley Rd	Louisville	KY	40213	**800-547-7278**	502-969-3171	207
Carrillo Business Technologies Inc 750 The City Dr S Ste 225	Orange	CA	92868	**888-241-7585**		179
Carrington Convention & Visitors Bureau 871 Main St	Carrington	ND	58421	**800-641-9668**	701-652-2524	206
Carroll & Co 425 N Canon Dr	Beverly Hills	CA	90210	**800-238-9400**	310-273-9060	157-3
Carroll Co 2900 W Kingsley Rd	Garland	TX	75041	**800-527-5722**		151
Carroll College 1601 N Benton Ave	Helena	MT	59625	**800-992-3648**	406-447-4300	166
Carroll Community College 1601 Washington Rd	Westminster	MD	21157	**888-221-9748**	410-386-8000	162
Carroll Cos Inc 1640 Old Hwy 421 S	Boone	NC	28607	**800-884-2521**	828-264-2521	430
Carroll County 114 E Main St Ste C PO Box 175	Delphi	IN	46923	**866-374-6813**	765-564-6757	337
Carroll County 8215 Black Oak Rd	Mount Carroll	IL	61053	**800-485-0145**	815-244-2035	337
Carroll County Chamber of Commerce & Economic Development 61 N Lisbon St PO Box 277	Carrollton	OH	44615	**877-727-0103**	330-627-4811	139
Carroll County Sheriff's Office 95 Water Village Rd PO Box 190	Ossipee	NH	03864	**800-552-8960**	603-539-2284	337

Company / Address	City	State	ZIP	Toll-Free	Phone	Class
Carroll Electric Co-op Corp 920 Hwy 62 Spur	Berryville	AR	72616	**800-432-9720**	870-423-2161	245
Carroll Electric Co-op Inc 350 Canton Rd NW	Carrollton	OH	44615	**800-232-7697**	330-627-2116	245
Carroll Electric Membership Corp (EMC) 155 N Hwy 113	Carrollton	GA	30117	**800-282-7411**	770-832-3552	245
Carroll Hospice 292 Stoner Ave	Westminster	MD	21157	**800-966-3877**	410-871-8000	370
Carroll Lutheran Village 300 St Luke Cir	Westminster	MD	21158	**877-848-0095**	410-848-0090	668
Carroll Seating Company Inc 10 Lincoln St	Kansas City	KS	66103	**800-972-3779**	816-471-2929	320
Carroll University 100 NE Ave	Waukesha	WI	53186	**800-227-7655**	262-547-1211	166
Carroll Valley Golf Resort 78 Country Club Trl	Carroll Valley	PA	17320	**855-784-0330**	717-642-8282	665
Carrollton Public Library 4220 N Josey Ln	Carrollton	TX	75010	**888-727-2978**	972-466-4800	433-3
Carrols Restaurant Group Inc 968 James St *NASDAQ: TAST*	Syracuse	NY	13203	**800-348-1074**	315-424-0513	666
Carron Net Company Inc 1623 17th St PO Box 177	Two Rivers	WI	54241	**800-558-7768**	920-793-2217	208
Carrot Medical LLC 22122 20th Ave SE Ste H-166	Bothell	WA	98021	**866-492-3533**	425-318-8089	738
Carscom 175 W Jackson Blvd Ste 800	Chicago	IL	60604	**888-246-6298**	312-601-5000	58
CarsDirectcom Inc 909 N Sepulveda Blvd 11th Fl *Cust Svc	El Segundo	CA	90245	**888-227-7347***		58
Carson 3125 NW 35th Ave	Portland	OR	97210	**800-998-7767**	503-224-8500	575
Carson Boxberger LLP 301 W Jefferson Blvd Ste 200	Fort Wayne	IN	46802	**800-900-4250**	260-423-9411	443
Carson City Nugget 507 N Carson St	Carson City	NV	89701	**800-426-5239**	775-882-1626	133
Carson Dunlop Home Inspection 120 Carlton St Ste 407	Toronto	ON	M5A4K2	**800-268-7070**	416-964-9415	
Carson Hot Springs 1500 Hot Springs Rd	Carson City	NV	89706	**888-917-3711**	775-885-8844	50-5
Carson Valley Chamber of Commerce 1477 Hwy 395 N Ste A	Gardnerville	NV	89410	**800-727-7677**	775-782-8144	139
Carson-Dellosa Publishing Company Inc 7027 Albert Pick Rd	Greensboro	NC	27409	**800-321-0943**	336-632-0084	243
Carsonite Composites LLC 19845 US Hwy 76	Newberry	SC	29108	**800-648-7916**	803-321-1185	674
Carson-Newman College 1646 Russell Ave	Jefferson City	TN	37760	**800-678-9061**	865-471-2000	166
CARSTAR Quality Collision Service 13750 W 108th St *Cust Svc	Lenexa	KS	66215	**800-227-7827***	913-696-0003	62-4
Carswell Distributing Co 3750 N Liberty St	Winston-Salem	NC	27105	**800-929-1948**	336-767-7700	428
Cartec International Inc 106 Powder Mill Rd	Canton	CT	06019	**800-821-4434**	860-693-9395	601-2
Carter Bros LLC 3015 RN Martin St	East Point	GA	30344	**888-818-0152**		688
Carter County 101 First Ave SW	Ardmore	OK	73401	**800-231-8668**	580-223-8162	337
Carter Ctr 1 Copenhill Ave 453 Freedom Pkwy	Atlanta	GA	30307	**800-550-3560**	404-420-5100	630
Carter Express Inc 4020 W 73rd St	Anderson	IN	46011	**800-738-7705**		194
Carter Healthcare 3105 S Meridian Ave	Oklahoma City	OK	73119	**888-951-1112**	405-947-7700	362
Carter Mario Injury Lawyers 176 Wethersfield Ave	Hartford	CT	06114	**844-634-5656**		427
Carteret County Chamber of Commerce 801 Arendell St Ste 1	Morehead City	NC	28557	**800-622-6278**	252-726-6350	139
Carteret-Craven Electric Co-op (CCEC) 1300 Hwy 24 W PO Box 1490	Newport	NC	28570	**800-682-2217**	252-247-3107	245
Carter-Lee ProBuild 1717 W Washington St	Indianapolis	IN	46222	**800-344-9242**	317-639-5431	497
Cartersville-Bartow County Chamber of Commerce 122 W Main St PO Box 307	Cartersville	GA	30120	**800-527-9395**	770-382-1466	139
Carthage College 2001 Alford Pk Dr *Admissions	Kenosha	WI	53140	**800-351-4058***	262-551-8500	166
Carthage Mills 4243 Hunt Rd *Sales	Cincinnati	OH	45242	**800-543-4430***		740-3
Cartier Place Suite Hotel 180 Cooper St	Ottawa	ON	K2P2L5	**800-236-8399**	613-236-5000	378
Carton Service Inc First Quality Dr PO Box 702 *General	Shelby	OH	44875	**800-533-7744***	419-342-5010	101
Cartus Corp 40 Apple Ridge Rd	Danbury	CT	06810	**888-767-9357**	203-205-3400	662
Cartwright Cos, The 11901 Cartwright Ave	Grandview	MO	64030	**800-821-2334**		516
Carus Corp 315 Fifth St	Peru	IL	61354	**800-435-6856**	815-223-1500	143
Caruso Inc 3465 Hauck Rd	Cincinnati	OH	45241	**800-759-7659**	513-860-9200	10-9
Carvel Express 200 Glenridge Pt Pkwy Ste 200	Atlanta	GA	30342	**800-322-4848**		380
Carvin Corp 12340 World Trade Dr	San Diego	CA	92128	**800-854-2235**	858-487-8700	523
Cary Academy 1500 N Harrison Ave	Cary	NC	27513	**800-948-2557**	919-677-3873	681
Cary Oil Company Inc 110 Mackenan Dr	Cary	NC	27511	**800-227-9645**	919-462-1100	577
CAS (Chemical Abstracts Service) 2540 Olentangy River Rd	Columbus	OH	43202	**800-848-6538**	614-447-3600	386
CAS (Coastal Administrative Services) PO Box 3070	Bellingham	WA	98227	**800-870-1831**		260
CAS (Casualty Actuarial Society) 4350 Fairfax Dr # 250	Arlington	VA	22203	**800-766-0070**	703-276-3100	49-9

				Toll-Free	Phone	Class
CAS Medical Systems Inc 44 E Industrial Rd *NASDAQ: CASM*	Branford	CT	06405	**800-227-4414**	203-488-6056	474
CASA (National CASA Assn) 100 W Harrison St North Tower Ste 500	Seattle	WA	98119	**800-628-3233**	206-270-0072	48-6
Casa Colina Hospital & Centers for Healthcare 255 E Bonita Ave	Pomona	CA	91767	**866-724-4127**		448
Casa Esperanza 1005 Yale NE	Albuquerque	NM	87106	**866-654-1338**	505-246-2700	371
Casa Grande Ruins National Monument 1100 W Ruins Dr	Coolidge	AZ	85128	**877-642-4743**	520-723-3172	560
Casa Herrerra Inc 2655 N Pine St	Pomona	CA	91767	**800-624-3916**	909-392-3930	298
Casa Linda Furniture Inc 4815 Whittier Blvd	Los Angeles	CA	90022	**888-783-0631**	323-263-3851	
Casa Madrona Hotel 801 Bridgeway *General	Sausalito	CA	94965	**800-288-0502***	415-332-0502	378
Casa Marina Resort & Beach Club 1500 Reynolds St	Key West	FL	33040	**888-303-5719**	305-296-3535	665
Casa Monica Hotel 95 Cordova St *Help Line	Saint Augustine	FL	32084	**800-648-1888***	904-827-1888	378
Casa Munras Hotel 700 Munras Ave	Monterey	CA	93940	**800-222-2446**	831-375-2411	378
Casa Palmero 1518 Cypress Dr	Pebble Beach	CA	93953	**800-654-9300**	831-622-6650	665
Casa Ybel Resort 2255 W Gulf Dr	Sanibel Island	FL	33957	**800-276-4753**	239-472-3145	665
Casablanca Resort 950 W Mesquite Blvd	Mesquite	NV	89027	**800-459-7529**	702-346-7529	665
Cascade Computer Maintenance Inc 750 Front St NE	Salem	OR	97302	**800-421-7934**	503-581-0081	
Cascade Corp 2201 NE 201st Ave *NYSE: CASC*	Fairview	OR	97024	**800-227-2233**	503-669-6300	468
Cascade Designs Inc 4000 First Ave S *Cust Svc	Seattle	WA	98134	**800-531-9531***	206-505-9500	706
Cascade Federal Credit Union 18020 80th Ave S	Kent	WA	98032	**800-562-2853**	425-251-8888	216
Cascade Financial Management Inc 950 17th St Ste 950	Denver	CO	80202	**800-353-0008**		194
Cascade Lodge 3719 W Hwy 61	Lutsen	MN	55612	**800-322-9543**	218-387-1112	665
Cascade Machinery & Electric Inc 4600 E Marginal Way S	Seattle	WA	98134	**800-289-0500**	206-762-0500	384
Cascade Natural Gas Corp (CNGC) 8113 W Grandridge Blvd	Kennewick	WA	99336	**888-522-1130**		782
Cascade Orthopedic Supply Inc 2638 Aztec Dr	Chico	CA	95928	**800-888-0865**		
Cascade Steel Rolling Mills Inc (CSRM) 3200 N Hwy 99 W PO Box 687	McMinnville	OR	97128	**800-283-2776**	503-472-4181	719
Cascade Wholesale Hardware Inc 5650 NW *General	Hillsboro	OR	97124	**800-877-9987***	503-614-2600	350
Cascade Wood Products Inc PO Box 2429	White City	OR	97503	**800-423-3311**	541-826-2911	497
Cascade365 1670 Corporate Cir Ste 202	Petaluma	CA	94954	**888-417-1531**	707-981-4002	392
Cascades Inc 404 Marie-Victorin Blvd *TSX: CAS*	Kingsey Falls	QC	J0A1B0	**800-361-4070**	819-363-5100	557
Cascadia Motivation 4646 Riverside Dr Ste 14	Red Deer	AB	T4N6Y5	**800-661-8360**	403-340-8687	
Cascio Interstate Music 13819 W National Ave	New Berlin	WI	53151	**800-462-2263**	262-789-7600	522
CASCO International Inc 4205 E Dixon Blvd	Shelby	NC	28152	**800-535-5690**		260
CASE (Council of Administrators of Special Education) Osigian Office Centre 101 Katelyn Cir Ste E	Warner Robins	GA	31088	**800-585-1753**	478-333-6892	49-5
CASE (Council for Advancement & Support of Education) 1307 New York Ave NW Ste 1000 *Orders	Washington	DC	20005	**800-554-8536***	202-328-5900	49-5
Case Design Corp 333 School Ln	Telford	PA	18969	**800-847-4176**	215-703-0130	199
Case Foundation Co 1325 West Lake St	Roselle	IL	60172	**800-999-4087**	630-529-2911	188-2
Case Logic Inc 6303 Dry Creek Pkwy	Longmont	CO	80503	**800-925-8111**	303-652-1000	530
Case Management Society of America (CMSA) 6301 Ranch Dr	Little Rock	AR	72223	**800-216-2672**	501-225-2229	49-8
Case Paper Company Inc 500 Mamaroneck Ave	Harrison	NY	10528	**800-222-2922**	888-227-3178	550
Case Western Reserve University 10900 Euclid Ave	Cleveland	OH	44106	**800-967-8898**	216-368-2000	166
Case Western Reserve University School of Law 11075 E Blvd	Cleveland	OH	44106	**800-756-0036**	216-368-3600	167-1
Casella Waste Systems Inc 25 Greens Hill Ln *NASDAQ: CWST*	Rutland	VT	05701	**800-227-3552**	802-775-0325	799
Cases By Source Inc 215 Island Rd	Mahwah	NJ	07430	**888-515-5255**		
Casey Research LLC 55 NE Fifth Ave	Delray Beach	FL	33483	**888-512-2739**	602-445-2736	400
Casey Robert P Jr. (Sen D - PA) 393 Russell Senate Office Bldg	Washington	DC	20510	**866-802-2833**	202-224-6324	
Casey State Bank 305-307 N Central Ave	Casey	IL	62420	**866-666-2754**	217-932-2136	70
Cash Acme Inc 2727 Paces Ferry Rd SE Ste 1800	Atlanta	GA	30339	**877-700-4242**		784
Cash Flow Solutions Inc 5166 College Corner Pk	Oxford	OH	45056	**800-736-5123**		196
Cashman Equipment Co 3300 St Rose Pkwy	Henderson	NV	89052	**800-937-2326**	702-649-8777	45
Cashtown Inn Restaurant 1325 Old Rt 30 PO Box 103	Cashtown	PA	17310	**800-367-1797**	717-334-9722	667
Cash-Wa Distributing Co 401 W Fourth St	Kearney	NE	68845	**800-652-0010**	308-237-3151	297-8
Casino Arizona at Salt River 524 N 92nd St *General	Scottsdale	AZ	85256	**866-877-9897***	480-850-7777	133
Casino Aztar 421 NW Riverside Dr	Evansville	IN	47708	**800-342-5386**	812-433-4000	133
Casino NB 21 Casino Dr	Moncton	NB	E1G0R7	**877-859-7775**		133
Casino Niagara 5705 Falls Ave	Niagara Falls	ON	L2E6T3	**888-325-5788**		133
Casino Queen 200 S Front St	East Saint Louis	IL	62201	**800-777-0777**	618-874-5000	133
Casino Royale Hotel 3411 Las Vegas Blvd S	Las Vegas	NV	89109	**800-854-7666**	702-737-3500	378
Cask 'n' Cleaver 8689 Ninth St	Rancho Cucamonga	CA	91730	**800-995-4452**	909-982-7108	666
Cask LLC 9350 Waxie Way Ste 210	San Diego	CA	92123	**866-535-8915**		196
CASM (Canadian Academy of Sport Medicine) 55 Metcalfe St Ste 300	Ottawa	ON	K1P6L5	**877-585-2394**	613-748-5851	49-8
Casper Area Convention & Visitors Bureau 139 W Second St Ste 1B	Casper	WY	82601	**800-852-1882**	307-234-5362	206
Casper College 125 College Dr	Casper	WY	82601	**800-442-2963**	307-268-2100	162
Casper Events Ctr 1 Events Dr	Casper	WY	82601	**800-442-2256**	307-235-8400	205
Cass Cable Tv Inc 100 Redbud Rd	Virginia	IL	62691	**800-252-1799**	217-452-7725	116
Cass County 346 Main St	Plattsmouth	NE	68048	**855-658-5736**	402-296-1028	337
Cass County Electric Co-op Inc 4100 32nd Ave SW	Fargo	ND	58104	**800-248-3292**	701-356-4400	245
Cass Information Systems Inc 13001 Hollenberg Dr *NASDAQ: CASS*	Bridgeton	MO	63044	**888-569-4707**	314-506-5500	225
Casselman River Bridge State Park 580 Taylor Ave	Annapolis	MD	21401	**877-620-8367**		561
Casswood Insurance Agency Ltd 5 Executive Pk Dr	Clifton Park	NY	12065	**800-972-2242**	518-373-8700	389
Castalloy Inc 1701 Industrial Ln PO Box 827	Waukesha	WI	53189	**800-211-0900**	262-547-0070	307
Cast-Crete Corp 6324 County Rd 579	Seffner	FL	33584	**800-999-4641**	813-621-4641	183
Caster Concepts Inc 16000 E Michigan Ave	Albion	MI	49224	**800-800-0036**	517-629-8838	357
Caster Technology Corp 11552 Markon Dr	Garden Grove	CA	92841	**866-547-8090**	714-893-6886	350
CastiaRx 701 Emerson Rd Ste 301	Creve Coeur	MO	63141	**800-652-9550**	314-652-3121	194
Castine Moving & Storage 1235 Chestnut St	Athol	MA	01331	**800-225-8068**	978-249-9105	516
Castle Branch Inc 1844 Sir Tyler Dr	Wilmington	NC	28405	**888-723-4263**		434
Castle Brands Inc 122 E 42nd St Ste 4700 *NYSE: ROX*	New York	NY	10168	**800-882-8140**	646-356-0200	81-3
Castle Hill Inn & Resort 590 Ocean Dr	Newport	RI	02840	**888-466-1355**	401-849-3800	665
Castle Impact Windows 7089 Hemstreet Pl	West Palm Beach	FL	33413	**800-643-6371**	561-683-4811	234
Castle in the Sand Hotel 3701 Atlantic Ave	Ocean City	MD	21842	**800-552-7263**	410-289-6846	378
Castle Pierce 2247 Ryf Rd	Oshkosh	WI	54904	**800-227-8537**		623
Castle Worldwide Inc 6001 Hospitality Ct Ste 100	Morrisville	NC	27560	**800-655-4845**	919-572-6880	244
Castlegarde Inc 4911 S W Shore Blvd	Tampa	FL	33611	**866-751-3203**	813-872-4844	689
Castleton State College 86 Seminary St	Castleton	VT	05735	**800-639-8521**	802-468-5611	166
Casto Technical Services Inc 540 Leon Sullivan Way	Charleston	WV	25301	**800-232-2221**	304-346-0549	606
Casto Travel Inc 2560 N First St Ste 150	San Jose	CA	95131	**800-832-3445**		766
Castrol Industrial North America Inc 150 W Warrenville Rd	Naperville	IL	60563	**877-641-1600**		537
Casual Designs Furniture Inc 36523 Lighthouse Rd	Selbyville	DE	19975	**888-629-1717**	302-436-8224	321
Casualty Actuarial Society (CAS) 4350 Fairfax Dr # 250	Arlington	VA	22203	**800-766-0070**	703-276-3100	49-9
Catal Restaurant & Uva Bar 1510 Disneyland Dr	Anaheim	CA	92802	**866-972-8462**		
Catalina Express Berth 95	San Pedro	CA	90731	**800-481-3470**	310-519-1212	466
Catalina Graphic Films Inc 27001 Agoura Rd Ste 100	Calabasas Hills	CA	91301	**800-333-3136**	818-880-8060	596
Catalogcom Inc 14000 Quail Springs Pkwy Ste 3600	Oklahoma City	OK	73134	**888-932-4376**	405-753-9300	803
Catalpha Advertising & Design Inc 6801 Loch Raven Blvd	Towson	MD	21286	**888-337-0066**	410-337-0066	7
Catapult Systems Inc 1221 S MoPac Expwy Ste 350	Austin	TX	78746	**800-528-6248**	512-328-8181	180
Catawba College 2300 W Innes St	Salisbury	NC	28144	**800-228-2922**	704-637-4772	166
Catawba Hospital 5525 Catawba Hospital Dr	Catawba	VA	24070	**800-451-5544**	540-375-4200	373-5
Catawba Print & Mail Inc 1215 15th St Dr NE	Hickory	NC	28601	**800-632-9513**		
Caterpillar 501 S W Jefferson Ave	Peoria	IL	61630	**888-614-4328**	309-675-2337	
Catfish Bend Casinos II LLC 3001 Winegard Dr	Burlington	IA	52601	**866-792-9948**		450

	Toll-Free	Phone	Class
Cathay General Bancorp Inc			
777 N Broadway ....Los Angeles CA 90012	**800-922-8429**	213-625-4700	359-2
NASDAQ: CATY			
Cathay Pacific Cargo			
6040 Avion Dr Ste 338 ....Los Angeles CA 90045	**800-628-6960**	310-417-0052	12
Cathedral Corp			
632 Ellsworth Rd Griffis Technology Pk			
..........................Rome NY 13441	**800-698-0299**	315-338-0021	623
Cathedral Press Inc			
600 NE Sixth St ....Long Prairie MN 56347	**800-874-8332***	320-732-6143	633-10
*Cust Svc			
Cathedral Village			
600 E Cathedral Rd ....Philadelphia PA 19128	**800-382-1385**	215-487-1300	392
Catholic Charities USA			
2050 Ballenger Ave Ste 400 ....Alexandria VA 22314	**800-919-9338**	703-549-1390	48-5
Catholic Digest			
PO Box 6015 ....New London CT 06320	**800-678-2836**		455-18
Catholic Extension			
150 S Wacker Dr Ste 2000 ....Chicago IL 60606	**800-842-7804**		48-20
Catholic Health Assn of the US (CHA)			
4455 Woodson Rd ....Saint Louis MO 63134	**800-230-7823**	314-427-2500	49-8
Catholic Healthcare West			
185 Berry St Ste 300..............San Francisco CA 94107	**844-274-8497**		
Catholic Medical Ctr (CMC)			
100 McGregor St ....Manchester NH 03102	**800-437-9666**	603-668-3545	373-3
Catholic Medical Mission Board (CMMB)			
100 Wall St 9th Fl................New York NY 10005	**800-678-5659**	212-242-7757	48-5
Catholic Mutual Group			
10843 Old Mill Rd ....Omaha NE 68154	**800-228-6108**	402-551-8765	390-5
Catholic News Publishing Co			
420 Railroad Way ....Mamaroneck NY 10543	**800-433-7771**		
Catholic Order of Foresters			
355 Shuman Blvd PO Box 3012 ....Naperville IL 60566	**800-552-0145**	630-983-4900	390-2
Catholic Relief Services (CRS)			
228 W Lexington St ....Baltimore MD 21201	**800-235-2772**	410-625-2220	48-5
Catholic Supply of st Louis Inc			
6759 Chippewa St ....Saint Louis MO 63109	**800-325-9026**	314-644-0643	48-20
Catholic Transcript Inc, The			
467 Bloomfield Ave ....Bloomfield CT 06002	**800-726-2381**	860-286-2828	48-20
Catholic University of America			
620 Michigan Ave NE ....Washington DC 20064	**800-673-2772**	202-319-5000	166
CatholicMatch LLC			
PO Box 154 ....Zelienople PA 16063	**888-605-3977**		386
Cato Corp, The			
8100 Denmark Rd ....Charlotte NC 28273	**800-758-2286**	704-554-8510	157-6
Cattaneo Bros Inc			
769 Caudill St ....San Luis Obispo CA 93401	**800-243-8537**		296-26
Cauthorne Paper Co			
12124 S Washington Hwy ....Ashland VA 23005	**800-552-3011**	804-798-6999	553
Cavalier Homes Alabama			
32 Wilson Blvd 100 PO Box 300 ....Addison AL 35540	**800-465-7923**		503
Cavaliers Operating Company LLC			
Quicken Loans Arena 1 Ctr Ct ....Cleveland OH 44115	**888-894-9424**	216-420-2000	710-1
Cavanagh Law Firm, The			
1850 N Central Ave ....Phoenix AZ 85004	**888-824-3476**	602-322-4000	427
Cavco Industries Inc			
1001 N Central Ave 8th Fl...........Phoenix AZ 85004	**800-790-9111**	602-256-6263	503
NASDAQ: CVCO			
Cave & Mine Adventures/Sierra Nevada Recreation Corporation			
5350 Moaning Cave Rd ....Vallecito CA 95251	**866-762-2837**	209-736-2708	50-5
Cayman Airways Cargo Services			
6103 NW 72nd Ave ....Miami FL 33166	**800-252-2746**	305-526-3190	12
Cayman Islands Dept of Tourism			
350 Fifth Ave ....New York NY 10118	**800-235-5888**	212-889-9009	770
Cayman Islands Dept of Tourism			
8300 NW 53rd St Ste 103.............Miami FL 33166	**800-553-4939**	305-599-9033	770
Cayman Technologies Inc			
12954 Stonecreek Dr Ste E.........Pickerington OH 43147	**877-370-9470**	614-759-9461	180
Cayuga Community College			
197 Franklin St ....Auburn NY 13021	**866-598-8883**	315-255-1743	162
Cayuga County			
160 Genesee St 1st Fl...............Auburn NY 13021	**800-771-7755**	315-253-1271	337
Cazenovia College			
8 Sullivan St ....Cazenovia NY 13035	**800-654-3210**	315-655-7208	166
CBA (Critical Business Analysis Inc)			
133 W Second St ....Perrysburg OH 43551	**800-874-8080**		
CBAN (Community Banking Advisory Network)			
1801 W End Ave Ste 800 ....Nashville TN 37203	**800-231-2524**	615-373-9880	49-2
CBB (Citizens Business Bank)			
701 N Haven Ave ....Ontario CA 91764	**888-222-5432***	909-980-4030	70
*Cust Svc			
CBC (Community Blood Center)			
4040 Main St ....Kansas City MO 64111	**888-647-4040**	816-753-4040	89
CBC Advertising			
56 Industrial Park Rd Ste 103 ....Saco ME 04072	**800-222-2682**	207-283-9191	
CBC Manitoba			
541 Portage Ave ....Winnipeg MB R3C2H1	**877-666-6292**	204-788-3222	641-117
CBCInnovis Inc			
250 E Town St ....Columbus OH 43215	**877-284-8322**		218
CBD (Cincinnati Bell Directory)			
312 Plum St Ste 600................Cincinnati OH 45202	**800-877-0475**		633-6
CBE Companies Inc			
1309 Technology Pkwy ....Cedar Falls IA 50613	**800-925-6686**		392
CBI			
600 Unicorn Park Dr ....Woburn MA 01801	**800-817-8601**	339-298-2100	194
CBI Laboratories			
4201 Diplomacy Rd ....Fort Worth TX 76155	**800-822-7546**	972-241-7546	214
CBM of America Inc			
1455 W Newport Ctr Dr ....Deerfield Beach FL 33442	**800-881-8202**	954-698-9104	180
CBMC (Christian Business Men's Connection)			
5746 Marlin Rd			
Ste 602 Osborne Ctr ....Chattanooga TN 37411	**800-566-2262**	423-698-4444	48-20
CBMR (Crested Butte Mountain Resort)			
12 Snowmass Rd			
PO Box 5700..................Crested Butte CO 81225	**877-547-5143**	970-349-2222	665
CBN (Christian Broadcasting Network)			
977 Centerville Tpke ....Virginia Beach VA 23463	**800-823-6053**		735
Cbord Group Inc, The			
950 Danby Rd Ste 100C ....Ithaca NY 14850	**844-462-2673**		180
CBOSS Inc			
827 Southwestern Run ....Poland OH 44514	**866-726-0429**	330-726-0429	
CBR-Technology Corp			
15581 Sunburst Ln ....Huntington Beach CA 92647	**800-227-0700**	714-901-5740	461
CBT Bank			
11 N Second St PO Box 171.......Clearfield PA 16830	**888-765-7551**	814-765-7551	70
CBU (Cape Breton University)			
1250 Grand Lake Rd PO Box 5300........Sydney NS B1P6L2	**888-959-9995**	902-539-5300	780
CBV Collection Services Ltd			
1490 Denison St Ste 100 ....Markham ON L3R9T7	**866-877-9323**	416-482-9323	160
CBVE-FM 1047 (CBC)			
PO Box 3220 Sta C ....Ottawa ON K1Y1E4	**866-306-4636**		
Cbw Automation			
3939 Automation Way ....Fort collins CO 80525	**800-229-9500**	970-229-9500	752
CBY Systems Inc			
33 S Duke St ....York PA 17401	**800-717-4229**		
C&C Fabrication Company Inc			
30 Fabrication Dr ....Lacey's Spring AL 35754	**888-485-5130**	256-881-7300	198
Cc Pollen Co			
3627 E Indian School Rd Ste 209 ....Phoenix AZ 85018	**800-875-0096**		794
CCA Global Partners			
4301 Earth City Expy ....Earth City MO 63045	**800-466-6984**	314-506-0000	360
CCA Industries Inc			
193 Conshohocken State Rd ....Penn Valley PA 19072	**800-595-6230***		214
NYSE: CAW ■ *Cust Svc			
Cca Medical Inc			
6 Southridge Ct ....Greenville SC 29607	**800-775-2556**	864-233-2700	180
CCC (Copyright Clearance Ctr Inc)			
222 Rosewood Dr ....Danvers MA 01923	**855-239-3415**	978-750-8400	49-16
CCC (Consolidated Container Co)			
3101 Towercreek Pkwy Ste 300 ....Atlanta GA 30339	**888-831-2184***	678-742-4600	544
*Sales			
CCC (Clovis Community College)			
417 Schepps Blvd ....Clovis NM 88101	**800-769-1409**	575-769-2811	162
CCC Information Services Inc			
222 Merchandise Mart Plz ....Chicago IL 60654	**800-621-8070**		225
CCCC (Conference on College Composition & Communication)			
1111 W Kenyon Rd ....Urbana IL 61801	**877-369-6283**	217-328-3870	49-5
CCCS (CAD/CAM Consulting Services Inc)			
1525 Rancho Conejo Blvd			
Ste 103 ....Newbury Park CA 91320	**888-375-7676**	805-375-7676	174
CCCVB (Clermont County Convention & Visitors Bureau)			
410 E Main St PO Box 100............Batavia OH 45103	**800-796-4282**	513-732-3600	206
CCEC (Carteret-Craven Electric Co-op)			
1300 Hwy 24 W PO Box 1490 ....Newport NC 28570	**800-682-2217**	252-247-3107	245
CCFA (Crohn's & Colitis Foundation of America)			
733 Third Ave Ste 510 ....New York NY 10017	**800-932-2423**		48-17
CCH Small Firm Services			
225 Chastain Meadows Ct NW			
Ste 200 ....Kennesaw GA 30144	**866-345-4171***		178-10
*Sales			
CCI (Canine Companions for Independence Inc)			
2965 Dutton Ave PO Box 446.......Santa Rosa CA 95402	**800-572-2275**	707-577-1700	48-17
CCI (Charlestown Retirement Community)			
715 Maiden Choice Ln ....Catonsville MD 21228	**800-917-8649**	410-242-2880	668
CCI (Columbia Collectors Inc)			
1104 Main St Ste 311 ....Vancouver WA 98660	**800-694-7585**	360-694-7585	160
CCI Network Services			
155 North 400 West			
Ste 100.................Salt Lake City UT 84103	**877-592-8049**	801-994-4100	
CCI Thermal Technologies Inc			
5918 Roper Rd ....Edmonton AB T6B3E1	**800-661-8529***	780-466-3178	318
*Cust Svc			
CCIM Institute			
430 N Michigan Ave Ste 800 ....Chicago IL 60611	**800-621-7027**	312-321-4460	49-17
CCM (Comprehensive Care Management Corp)			
1250 Waters Pl Tower 1 Ste 602.........Bronx NY 10461	**877-226-8500**		448
CCMG (Clark Capital Management Group Inc)			
1650 Market St			
1 Liberty Pl 53rd Fl............Philadelphia PA 19103	**800-766-2264**	215-569-2224	400
CCON (Columbia College of Nursing)			
4425 N Port Washington Rd ....Glendale WI 53212	**800-221-5573**	414-326-2330	166
CCP (Continental Commercial Products)			
11840 Westline Industrial Dr ....St. Louis MO 63146	**800-325-1051**		506
CCPS (Center for Chemical Process Safety)			
120 Wall St ....New York NY 10005	**800-242-4363**	646-495-1371	49-19
CCRKBA (Citizens Committee for the Right to Keep & Bear Ar)			
Liberty Park 12500 NE Tenth Pl ....Bellevue WA 98005	**800-486-6963**	425-454-4911	48-7
CCRTA (Cape Cod Regional Transit Authority)			
215 Iyannough Rd PO Box 1988.........Hyannis MA 02601	**800-352-7155**	508-775-8504	466
CCS (Custom Computer Specialists Inc)			
70 Suffolk Ct ....Hauppauge NY 11788	**800-598-8989**		180
CCS (Check Cashing Store)			
6340 NW Fifth Way ....Fort Lauderdale FL 33309	**800-361-1407**		141
CCS Medical Inc			
1505 LBJ Fwy Ste 600 ....Farmers Branch TX 75234	**800-726-9811**	800-260-8193	473
CCS Plas-Tech			
180 Shepard Ave ....Wheeling IL 60090	**800-747-1269**	847-459-8320	700
CCS Presentation Systems Inc			
17350 N Hartford Dr ....Scottsdale AZ 85255	**800-742-5036**	480-348-0100	196
CCSAA (Cross Country Ski Areas Assn)			
259 Bolton Rd ....Winchester NH 03470	**877-779-2754**	603-239-4341	48-22
CCSD (Charleston County School District)			
75 Calhoun St ....Charleston SC 29401	**800-241-8898**	843-937-6300	681
CCSD (Clark County School District)			
5100 West Sahara Ave ....Las Vegas NV 89146	**866-799-8997**	702-799-5000	681
CCSNH (Community College System of New Hampshire)			
26 College Dr ....Concord NH 03301	**866-945-2255**	603-230-3500	162
CCTF Corp			
5407 - 53 Ave NW ....Edmonton AB T6B3G2	**800-661-3633**	780-463-8700	111
CCUSD (Culver City Unified School District)			
4034 Irving Pl ....Culver City CA 90232	**855-446-2673**	310-842-4220	681
CD Ford & Sons Inc			
PO Box 300 ....Geneseo IL 61254	**800-383-4661**	309-944-4661	368
CD Publications			
8204 Fenton St ....Silver Spring MD 20910	**800-666-6380**	301-588-6380	527-2
CD Universe			
101 N Plains Industrial Rd ....Wallingford CT 06492	**800-231-7937**	203-294-1648	521

	Toll-Free	Phone	Class
C&D Valve Manufacturing Co			
201 NW 67th St ....Oklahoma City OK 73116	**800-654-9233**	405-843-5621	784
CDA (Chemically Dependent Anonymous)			
PO Box 423 ....Severna Park MD 21146	**888-232-4673**		48-21
CDC Distributors			
10511 Medallion Dr ....Cincinnati OH 45241	**800-678-2321**	513-771-3100	360
CDC Small Business Finance Corp			
2448 Historic Decatur Rd Ste 200 ....San Diego CA 92106	**800-611-5170**	619-291-3594	216
CDF (Children's Defense Fund)			
25 E St NW ....Washington DC 20001	**800-233-1200**	202-628-8787	48-6
CDF Corp			
77 Industrial Park Rd ....Plymouth MA 02360	**800-443-1920**		597
CDGRA (Colorado Dude & Guest Ranch Assn)			
PO Box D ....Shawnee CO 80475	**866-942-3472**		48-23
CDI (Consolidated Devices Inc)			
19220 San Jose Ave ....City of Industry CA 91748	**800-525-6319**	626-965-0668	753
CDI Corp			
1735 Market St Ste 200 ....Philadelphia PA 19103	**866-472-2203**	215-282-8300	261
CDI Credit Inc			
6160 Peachtree Dunwoody Rd NE Ste B-210 ....Atlanta GA 30328	**800-633-3961**	770-350-5070	631
CdLS (Cornelia de Lange Syndrome Foundation Inc)			
302 W Main St Ste 100.............Avon CT 06001	**800-753-2357**	860-676-8166	48-17
CDMA (Chain Drug Marketing Assn)			
43157 W Nine-Mile Rd PO Box 995.........Novi MI 48376	**800-935-2362**	248-449-9300	49-18
CDMS Inc			
550 Sherbrooke W West Tower Ste 250 ....Montreal QC H3A1B9	**866-337-2367**	514-286-2367	180
Cdo Technologies Inc			
5200 Sprngfeld St Ste 320 ....Dayton OH 45431	**866-307-6616**	937-258-0022	447
Cdr Assessment Group Inc			
1644 S Denver Ave ....Tulsa OK 74119	**888-406-0100**	918-488-0722	195
CDS Analytical Inc			
465 Limestone Rd ....Oxford PA 19363	**800-541-6593**	610-932-3636	418
CDS Logistics Management Inc			
1225 Bengies Rd Ste A ....Baltimore MD 21220	**866-649-9559**	410-314-8000	311
CDS-John Blue Co			
290 Pinehurst Dr ....Huntsville AL 35806	**800-253-2583**	256-721-9090	637
Cdspi 155 Lesmill Rd ....Toronto ON M3B2T8	**800-561-9401**	416-296-9401	390-3
CDT (Center for Democracy & Technology)			
1401 K St NW Ste 200 ....Washington DC 20005	**800-869-4499**	202-637-9800	40-7
CDW Corp			
200 N Milwaukee Ave ....Vernon Hills IL 60061	**800-800-4239**	847-465-6000	179
CE Niehoff & Co			
2021 Lee St ....Evanston IL 60202 *Tech Supp	**800-643-4633***	847-866-6030	247
CE Resource Inc			
PO Box 997581 ....Sacramento CA 95899	**800-707-5644**		461
CE Thurston & Sons Inc			
3335 Croft St ....Norfolk VA 23513	**800-444-7713**	757-855-7700	189-9
CEA (CEA Study Abroad)			
2999 N 44th St Ste 200 ....Phoenix AZ 85018	**866-987-8906**	800-266-4441	755
CEA Study Abroad (CEA)			
2999 N 44th St Ste 200 ....Phoenix AZ 85018	**866-987-8906**	800-266-4441	755
Cec Controls Co Inc			
14555 Barber Ave ....Warren MI 48088	**877-924-0303**	586-779-0222	201
CEC Entertainment Inc			
3903 W Airport Frwy ....Irving TX 75062 NYSE: CEC	**888-778-7193**	972-258-8507	666
CEC Industries Ltd			
599 Bond St ....Lincolnshire IL 60069	**800-572-4168**	847-821-1199	54
Cecil Community College			
1 Seahawk Dr ....North East MD 21901	**866-966-1001**	410-287-6060	162
CECO (Compressor Engineering Corp)			
5440 Alder Dr ....Houston TX 77081	**800-879-2326**	713-664-7333	172
Ceco Building Systems			
2400 Hwy 45 N ....Columbus MS 39705	**800-474-2326**	662-243-6400	105
CED (Committee for Economic Development)			
1530 Wilson Blvd Ste 400 ....Arlington VA 22209	**800-676-7353**	202-296-5860	630
Cedar City-Brian Head Tourism & Convention Bureau			
581 N Main St ....Cedar City UT 84721	**800-354-4849**	435-586-5124	206
Cedar County			
400 Cedar St ....Tipton IA 52772	**800-735-3942**	563-886-2101	337
Cedar Crest College			
100 College Dr ....Allentown PA 18104 *Admissions	**800-360-1222***	610-437-4471	166
Cedar Crest Specialties Inc			
7269 Hwy 60 PO Box 260.............Cedarburg WI 53012 *Hotline	**800-877-8341***	262-377-7252	296-25
Cedar Graphics Inc			
311 Parsons Dr ....Hiawatha IA 52233	**800-393-2399**	319-395-6900	392
Cedar Grove Composting Inc			
7343 E Marginal Way S ....Seattle WA 98108	**888-832-3008**	877-764-5748	186
Cedar Rapids Area Convention & Visitors Bureau			
87 16th Ave Ste 200 ....Cedar Rapids IA 52404	**800-735-5557**	319-398-5009	206
Cedar Springs Behavioral Health System			
2135 Southgate Rd ....Colorado Springs CO 80906	**800-888-1088**	719-633-4114	373-5
Cedar Springs Post			
36 E Maple PO Box 370 ....Cedar Springs MI 49319	**888-937-4514**	616-696-3655	528-4
Cedar Valley Hospice			
2101 Kimball Ave Ste 401 ....Waterloo IA 50702	**800-617-1972**	319-272-2002	370
Cedara Software Corp			
6303 Airport Rd Ste 500.............Mississauga ON L4V1R8	**800-724-5970**	905-364-8000	178-10
Cedarlane Laboratories Inc			
4410 Paletta Ct ....Burlington ON L7L5R2	**800-268-5058**	905-878-8891	231
Cedars Business Services LLC			
5230 Las Virgenes Ste 210.............Calabasas CA 91302	**800-804-3353**	818-224-3357	160
Cedars-Sinai Medical Ctr (CSMC)			
8700 Beverly Blvd ....Los Angeles CA 90048	**800-233-2771**	310-423-3277	373-3
Cedarville University			
251 N Main St ....Cedarville OH 45314	**800-233-2784**	937-766-7700	166
CEDIA (Custom Electronic Design & Installation Assn)			
7150 Winton Dr Ste 300.............Indianapolis IN 46268	**800-669-5329**	317-328-4336	49-19
CEF Industries Inc			
320 S Church St ....Addison IL 60101	**800-888-6419**	630-628-2299	22
Cegep De Matane			
616 Ave Holy Redeemer ....Matane QC G4W1L1	**800-463-4299**	418-562-1240	167
CEI			
801 NW St Mary Dr Ste 205 ....Blue Springs MO 64014	**800-473-1976**	816-228-2976	225
CEI Enterprises Inc			
245 WoodwaRd Rd SE ....Albuquerque NM 87102	**800-545-4034**		14
Ceilings & Interior Systems Construction Assn (CISCA)			
1010 Jorie Blvd Ste 30 ....Oak Brook IL 60523	**866-560-8537**	630-584-1919	49-3
Ceiva Logic Inc			
214 E Magnolia Blvd ....Burbank CA 91502 *Tech Supp	**877-693-7263***	818-562-1495	587
Cejka Search Inc			
4 Cityplace Dr Ste 300 ....Saint Louis MO 63141	**800-678-7858**	314-726-1603	717
CEL (California Eastern Laboratories Inc)			
4590 Patrick Henry Dr ....Santa Clara CA 95054	**800-390-3232**	408-919-2500	246
Celadon Trucking Services Inc			
9503 E 33rd St ....Indianapolis IN 46235	**800-235-2366**	317-972-7000	775
Celanese Corp			
1601 W LBJ Fwy ....Dallas TX 75234 NYSE: CE	**800-627-9581**	972-443-4000	144
Celerity Consulting Group Inc			
2 Gough St Ste 300 ....San Francisco CA 94103	**866-224-4333**	415-986-8850	196
Celestial Seasonings Inc			
4600 Sleepytime Dr ....Boulder CO 80301	**800-351-8175**		296-40
Celestica Inc			
844 Don Mills Rd ....Toronto ON M3C1V7 NYSE: CLS	**888-899-9998**	416-448-5800	253
Celgene Corp			
86 Morris Ave ....Summit NJ 07901 NASDAQ: CELG	**888-771-0141**	908-673-9000	85
Cell Signaling Technology Inc			
3 Trask Ln ....Danvers MA 01923	**877-678-8324**	978-867-2300	417
Cell-con Inc			
305 Commerce Dr Ste 300 ....Exton PA 19341	**800-771-7139**		74
Cellhire USA LLC			
3520 W Miller Rd Ste 100 ....Garland TX 75041	**877-244-7242**		731
Cellino & Barnes PC			
2500 Main Place Twr ....Buffalo NY 14202	**800-888-8888**		427
Cello Professional Products			
1354 Old Post Rd ....Havre de Grace MD 21078	**800-638-4850**	410-939-1234	151
Cellofoam North America Inc			
1917 Rockdale Industrial Blvd ....Conyers GA 30012	**800-241-3634**	770-929-3688	597
Cellotape Inc			
47623 Fremont Blvd ....Fremont CA 94538	**800-231-0608**	510-651-5551	412
Cell-Tel Government Systems Inc			
8226-B Phillips Hwy Ste 290.............Jacksonville FL 32256	**800-737-7545**	904-363-1111	246
Celtic Commercial Finance			
4 Park Plz Ste 300 ....Irvine CA 92614	**866-323-5842**		
Celtic Healthcare			
150 Scharberry Ln ....Mars PA 16046	**800-355-8894**		370
CEM Corp			
3100 Smith Farm Rd ....Matthews NC 28104	**800-726-3331**	704-821-7015	418
CEMCO			
263 N Covina Ln ....City Of Industry CA 91744	**800-775-2362**		105
Cement Industries Inc			
2925 Hanson St PO Box 823 ....Fort Myers FL 33902	**800-332-1440**	239-332-1440	183
Cemex USA			
929 Gessner Rd Ste 1900.............Houston TX 77024 NYSE: CX	**800-999-8529**	713-650-6200	135
Cemstone			
2025 Centre Pt Blvd Ste 300 ....Mendota Heights MN 55120	**800-642-3887**	651-688-9292	182
Cenergistic Inc			
5950 Sherry Ln ....Dallas TX 75225	**855-798-7779**		194
Cengage Learning			
PO Box 6904 ....Florence KY 41022	**800-354-9706**		633-2
Centaurus Financial			
2300 E Katella Ave Ste 200 ....Anaheim CA 92806	**800-880-4234**		
Centegra Memorial Medical Ctr			
3701 Doty Rd ....Woodstock IL 60098	**877-236-8347**	815-338-2500	373-3
Centenary College			
400 Jefferson St ....Hackettstown NJ 07840 *Admissions	**800-236-8679***	908-852-1400	166
Centenary College of Louisiana			
2911 Centenary Blvd ....Shreveport LA 71104 *Admissions	**800-234-4448***	318-869-5131	166
Centenary State Historic Site			
3522 College St ....Jackson LA 70748	**888-677-2364**	225-634-7925	561
Centene Corp			
7700 Forsyth Blvd ....Saint Louis MO 63105 NYSE: CNC ■ *General	**800-293-0056***	314-725-4477	390-3
Centennial Hall Convention Ctr			
101 Egan Dr ....Juneau AK 99801	**800-478-4176**	907-586-5283	205
Centennial Travelers			
7697 S Roslyn Ct ....Centennial CO 80112	**800-223-0675**	303-741-6685	755
Centennial Windows Ltd			
687 Sovereign Rd ....London ON N5V4K8	**800-265-1995**	519-451-0508	497
Center Enterprises Inc			
30 Shield St ....West Hartford CT 06110 *Orders	**800-542-2214***	860-953-4423	243
Center for Assn Resources Inc			
1901 N Roselle Rd Ste 920.............Schaumburg IL 60195	**888-705-1434**		47
Center for Association Growth, The (TCAG)			
1926 Waukegan Rd Ste 300 ....Glenview IL 60025	**800-492-6462**	847-657-6700	47
Center for Chemical Process Safety (CCPS)			
120 Wall St ....New York NY 10005	**800-242-4363**	646-495-1371	49-19
Center for Civic Education			
5145 Douglas Fir Rd ....Calabasas CA 91302	**800-350-4223**	818-591-9321	194
Center for Creative Photography			
1030 N Olive Rd ....Tucson AZ 85721	**888-472-4732**	520-621-7968	517
Center for Cultural Interchange			
746 N La Salle Dr ....Chicago IL 60654	**866-224-0061**	312-944-2544	194
Center for Democracy & Technology (CDT)			
1401 K St NW Ste 200 ....Washington DC 20005	**800-869-4499**	202-637-9800	48-7
Center for Diagnostic Imaging			
5775 Wayzata Blvd Ste 190 ....Saint Louis Park MN 55416	**800-537-0005**	952-541-1840	382
Center for Genetic Testing at Saint Francis			
6465 S Yale Ave ....Tulsa OK 74136	**877-789-6001**	918-502-1720	416

Name / Address	City	State	ZIP	Toll-Free	Phone	Class
Center for Grain & Animal Health Research						
1515 College Ave	Manhattan	KS	66502	**800-627-0388**		664
Center for Hospice Care Inc						
111 Sunnybrook Ct	South Bend	IN	46637	**800-413-9083**	574-243-3100	370
Center for Individual Rights (CIR)						
1100 Connecticut Ave NW						
Ste 625	Washington	DC	20036	**877-426-2665**	202-833-8400	48-8
Center for Law & Social Policy (CLASP)						
1015 15th St NW Ste 400	Washington	DC	20005	**800-821-4367**	202-906-8000	630
Center for Organ Recovery & Education (CORE)						
204 Sigma Dr RIDC Pk	Pittsburgh	PA	15238	**800-366-6777**	412-963-3550	269
Center for Policy Research						
Syracuse University						
426 Eggers Hall	Syracuse	NY	13244	**800-325-3535**	315-443-3114	630
Center for Practical Bioethics						
1111 Main St Ste 500	Kansas City	MO	64105	**800-344-3829**	816-221-1100	48-17
Center for Puppetry Arts						
1404 Spring St NW	Atlanta	GA	30309	**800-642-3629**	404-873-3089	50-2
Center for Space Plasma & Aeronomic Research						
University of Alabama Huntsville						
	Huntsville	AL	35899	**800-824-2255**	256-961-7403	664
Center for Western Studies						
2101 S Summit Ave						
Augustana College	Sioux Falls	SD	57197	**800-727-2844**	605-274-4007	517
Center of Vocational Alternative For Men						
3770 N High St	Columbus	OH	43214	**877-521-2682**	614-294-7117	242
Center on Human Development & Disability						
University of Washington						
PO Box 357920	Seattle	WA	98195	**800-636-1089**	206-543-7701	664
Center Stage Productions Inc						
20-10 Maple Ave	Fair Lawn	NJ	07410	**800-955-1663**	973-423-5000	392
Centerplate						
2187 Atlantic St	Stamford	CT	06902	**800-698-6992**	203-975-5900	299
CenterPoint Energy Inc						
1111 Louisiana St	Houston	TX	77002	**800-495-9880***	713-207-1111	359-5
NYSE: CNP ■ *Cust Svc						
National Center for Chronic Disease Prevention						
4770 Buford Hwy NE	Atlanta	GA	30341	**800-232-4636**		339-9
National Center for Emerging & Zoonotic Infectious						
1600 Clifton Rd	Atlanta	GA	30333	**800-232-4636**	404-639-3311	339-9
National Center for Environmental Health						
4770 Buford Hwy NE	Atlanta	GA	30341	**800-232-4636**		339-9
National Center for Health Marketing						
1600 Clifton Rd NE	Atlanta	GA	30333	**800-311-3435**	404-639-3311	339-9
National Center for HIV/AIDS Viral Hepatitis STD						
1600 Clifton Rd	Atlanta	GA	30333	**800-232-4636**		339-9
National Center for Immunization & Respiratory Disorders						
1600 Clifton Rd NE MS E-05	Atlanta	GA	30333	**800-232-4636**		339-9
National Center for Injury Prevention & Control						
4770 Buford Hwy NE	Atlanta	GA	30341	**800-232-4636**		339-9
National Center for Public Health Informatics						
1600 Clifton Rd NE	Atlanta	GA	30329	**888-232-6348**	800-232-4636	339-9
Centers for Disease Control & Prevention						
National Center on Birth Defects & Developmental Dept						
1600 Clifton Rd	Atlanta	GA	30329	**800-232-4636**	404-639-3311	339-9
National Institute for Occupational Safety & Health						
200 Independence Ave SW	Washington	DC	20201	**800-356-4674**	404-639-3286	339-9
National Office of Public Health Genomics						
1600 Clifton Rd MS K-89	Atlanta	GA	30329	**800-232-4636**		339-9
Travelers Health						
1600 Clifton Rd NE	Atlanta	GA	30333	**800-232-4636**		339-9
Centers for Medicare & Medicaid Services (CMS)						
7500 Security Blvd	Baltimore	MD	21244	**800-633-4227**		339-9
Medicare.gov						
7500 Security Blvd	Baltimore	MD	21244	**800-633-4227**		339-9
Centerstate Banks Inc						
42725 US Hwy 27	Davenport	FL	33837	**855-863-2265**		70
CenTex House Leveling						
1120 E 52nd St	Austin	TX	78723	**888-425-5438**	512-444-5438	186
Centimark Corp						
12 Grandview Cir	Canonsburg	PA	15317	**800-558-4100**		189-12
Centinela Elementary School						
1123 Marlborough Ave	Inglewood	CA	90302	**800-942-2761**	310-680-5440	681
Centra Health Inc						
1920 Atherholt Rd	Lynchburg	VA	24501	**800-947-5442**	434-200-3000	352
Central Address Systems Inc						
10303 Crown Point Ave	Omaha	NE	68134	**800-482-7705**	402-964-9998	7
Central Alabama Electric Co-op						
1802 Hwy 31 N	Prattville	AL	36067	**800-545-5735**	334-365-6762	245
Central Arizona College						
8470 N Overfield Rd	Coolidge	AZ	85228	**800-237-9814**	520-494-5444	162
Central Baptist College						
1501 College Ave	Conway	AR	72034	**800-205-6872**	501-329-6872	166
Central Boston Elder Services Inc						
2315 Washington St	Boston	MA	02119	**800-922-2275**	617-277-7416	448
Central Builders Supply Company Inc						
125 Bridge Ave PO Box 152	Sunbury	PA	17801	**800-326-9361**	570-286-6461	182
Central California Blood Ctr						
4343 W Herndon Ave	Fresno	CA	93722	**800-649-5399**	559-389-5433	89
Central Carolina Community College						
1105 Kelly Dr	Sanford	NC	27330	**800-682-8353**	919-775-5401	162
Central Carolina Hospital						
1135 Carthage St	Sanford	NC	27330	**800-292-2262**	919-774-2100	373-3
Central Carolina Technical College						
506 N Guignard Dr	Sumter	SC	29150	**800-221-8711**	803-778-1961	795
Central Christian College						
PO Box 1403	McPherson	KS	67460	**800-835-0078**	620-241-0723	166
Central Christian College of the Bible						
911 E Urbandale Dr	Moberly	MO	65270	**888-263-3900**	660-263-3900	161
Central College						
812 University St	Pella	IA	50219	**877-462-3687**	641-628-5285	166
Central Community College						
Grand Island						
3134 W Hwy 34 PO Box 4903	Grand Island	NE	68802	**877-222-0780**	308-398-4222	162
Central Concrete Supply Company Inc						
755 Stockton Ave	San Jose	CA	95126	**866-404-1000**	408-293-6272	182
Central Credit Services LLC						
9550 Regency Sq Blvd						
Ste 500A	Jacksonville	FL	32225	**888-904-1800**		

Name / Address	City	State	ZIP	Toll-Free	Phone	Class
Central Crude Inc						
4187 Hwy 3059 PO Box 1863	Lake Charles	LA	70602	**800-245-8408**	337-436-1000	577
Central Electric Membership Corp						
128 Wilson Rd	Sanford	NC	27331	**800-446-7752**	919-774-4900	245
Central Florida Electric Cooperative Inc						
11491 NW 50th Ave	Chiefland	FL	32626	**800-227-1302**	352-493-2511	245
Central Florida Visitors & Convention Bureau						
101 Adventure Ct	Davenport	FL	33837	**800-828-7655**	863-420-2586	206
Central Flying Service Inc						
1501 Bond St	Little Rock	AR	72202	**800-888-5387**	501-375-3245	63
Central Freight Lines Inc						
PO Box 2638	Waco	TX	76702	**800-782-5036**		775
Central Garden & Pet Co						
1340 Treat Blvd Ste 600	Walnut Creek	CA	94597	**800-356-2017**	925-948-4000	293
NASDAQ: CENT						
Central Georgia Electric Membership Corp						
923 S Mulberry St	Jackson	GA	30233	**800-222-4877**	770-775-7857	245
Central Georgia Technical College						
3300 Macon Tech Dr	Macon	GA	31206	**866-430-0135**	478-757-3400	795
Central Illinois Community Blood Ctr						
1999 Wabash Ave	Springfield	IL	62703	**866-448-3253***	217-753-1530	89
*Help Line						
Central Industries Inc						
11438 Cronridge Dr Ste W	Owings Mills	MD	21117	**800-304-8484**		535
Central Ink Corp						
1100 Harvester Rd	West Chicago	IL	60185	**800-345-2541**	630-231-6500	387
Central Insulation Systems Inc						
300 Murray Rd	Cincinnati	OH	45217	**800-544-7502**	513-242-0600	663
Central Insurance Cos						
800 S Washington St	Van Wert	OH	45891	**800-736-7000**	419-238-1010	390-4
Central Lakes College						
Brainerd						
501 W College Dr	Brainerd	MN	56401	**800-933-0346**	218-855-8199	162
Staples						
1830 Airport Rd	Staples	MN	56479	**800-247-6836**	218-894-5100	162
Central Louisiana State Hospital						
242 W Shamrock St	Pineville	LA	71360	**888-342-6207**	318-484-6200	373-5
Central Maine Community College						
1250 Turner St	Auburn	ME	04210	**800-891-2002***	207-755-5100	795
*Admissions						
Central Maine Power Co						
83 Edison Dr	Augusta	ME	04336	**800-565-0121**	207-623-3521	782
Central Maintenance & Welding Inc (CMW)						
2620 E Keysville Rd	Lithia	FL	33547	**877-704-7411**	813-737-1402	189-14
Central Mechanical Construction Company Inc						
631 Pecan Cir	Manhattan	KS	66502	**800-631-6999**	785-537-2437	189-10
Central Methodist University						
411 Central Methodist Sq	Fayette	MO	65248	**877-268-1854**	660-248-3391	166
Central Michigan University						
102 Warriner Hall	Mount Pleasant	MI	48859	**888-292-5366***	989-774-4000	166
*Admissions						
Central Mine Equipment Company Inc						
4215 Rider Trl N	Earth City	MO	63045	**800-325-8827**	314-291-7700	190
Central Minnesota Fabricating Inc						
2725 W Gorton Ave	Willmar	MN	56201	**800-839-8857**	320-235-4181	478
Central Missouri ElectricCo-op Inc						
22702 Hwy 65 PO Box 939	Sedalia	MO	65302	**855-875-7165**	660-826-2900	245
Central Nebraska Packing Inc						
2800 E Eigth St PO Box 550	North Platte	NE	69103	**800-445-2881***	308-532-1250	471
*Cust Svc						
Central New Mexico Community College						
10549 Universe Blvd NW	Albuquerque	NM	87114	**888-453-1304**	505-224-3000	795
Central New York Business Journal, The						
269 W Jefferson St	Syracuse	NY	13202	**800-836-3539**	315-579-3919	455-5
Central Ohio Technical College						
1179 University Dr	Newark	OH	43055	**800-963-9275**	740-366-9494	795
Central Ontario Healthcare Procurement Alliance						
95 Mural St	Richmond Hill	ON	L4B3G2	**866-897-8812**	905-886-5319	317
Central Oregon Visitors Assn						
57100 Beaver Dr Bldg 6 Ste 130	Sunriver	OR	97707	**800-800-8334**		206
Central Pacific Financial Corp						
PO Box 3590	Honolulu	HI	96811	**800-342-8422**	808-544-0500	359-2
NYSE: CPF						
Central Paper Products Co Inc						
350 Gay St						
John C Mongan Industrial Park	Manchester	NH	03103	**800-339-4065**	603-624-4065	555
Central Pennsylvania Blood Bank						
8167 Adams Dr	Hummelstown	PA	17036	**800-771-0059**	717-566-6161	89
Central Pennsylvania College						
600 Valley Rd PO Box 309	Summerdale	PA	17093	**800-759-2727**	717-732-0702	795
Central Petroleum Transport Inc (CPT)						
6115 Mitchell St	Sioux City	IA	51111	**800-798-6357**	712-258-6357	775
Central Piedmont Community College						
1201 Elizabeth Ave	Charlotte	NC	28204	**877-530-8815**	704-330-2722	162
Central Pipe Supply Inc						
101 Ware Rd PO Box 5470	Pearl	MS	39288	**800-844-7700**	601-939-3322	591
Central Power Systems & Services						
9200 W Liberty Dr	Liberty	MO	64068	**800-444-0442**	816-781-8070	384
Central Prairie Co-op						
225 S Broadway	Sterling	KS	67579	**800-861-3207**	620-278-2141	11-1
Central Products LLC						
7750 Georgetown Rd	Indianapolis	IN	46268	**800-215-9293**		
Central Puget Sound Regional Transit Authority						
401 S Jackson St	Seattle	WA	98104	**800-201-4900**	206-398-5000	466
Central Record						
PO Box 1027	Medford	NJ	08055	**800-825-7653**	609-654-5000	528-4
Central Rural Electric Co-op						
3304 S Boomer Rd PO Box 1809	Stillwater	OK	74076	**800-375-2884**	405-372-2884	245
Central Service Assn						
93 S Coley Rd	Tupelo	MS	38801	**877-842-5962**	662-842-5962	225
Central Signaling						
2033 Hamilton Rd	Columbus	GA	31904	**800-554-1101**		688
Central Specialties Ltd						
220 Exchange Dr	Crystal Lake	IL	60014	**800-873-4370**	815-459-6000	64
Central State University						
1400 Brush Row Rd						
PO Box 1004	Wilberforce	OH	45384	**800-388-2781**	937-376-6011	166
Central States Health & Life Company of Omaha						
1212 N 96th St	Omaha	NE	68114	**800-826-6587**		390-2

	Toll-Free	Phone	Class
Central Steel Fabricators Inc 1843 S 54th Ave .... Cicero IL 60804	855-652-7010	708-652-2037	478
Central Texas College PO Box 1800 .... Killeen TX 76540	800-792-3348	254-526-7161	162
Central Texas Electric Co-op Inc (CTEC) 386 Friendship Ln PO Box 553. .... Fredericksburg TX 78624 *General	800-900-2832*	830-997-2126	245
Central Texas Medical Ctr (CTMC) 1301 Wonder World Dr .... San Marcos TX 78666	800-927-9004	512-353-8979	373-3
Central Texas Veterans Health Care System 1901 Veterans Memorial Dr ..... Temple TX 76504	800-423-2111	254-778-4811	373-8
Central Transportation Systems 4105 Rio Bravo Ste 100 .... El Paso TX 79902	855-636-9780		447
Central Valley Community Bancorp 7100 N Financial Dr Ste 101. ..... Fresno CA 93720 NASDAQ: CVCY	866-294-9588	559-298-1775	359-2
Central Vermont Chamber of Commerce 33 Stewart Rd .... Berlin VT 05641	877-887-3678	802-229-5711	139
Central Vermont Home Health & Hospice 600 Granger Rd .... Barre VT 05641	800-286-1219	802-223-1878	362
Central Virginia Electric Co-op 800 Co-op Way PO Box 247. ... Lovingston VA 22949	800-367-2832	434-263-8336	245
Central Virginia Training Ctr 521 Colony Rd .... Madison Heights VA 24572	866-897-6095	434-947-6000	230
Central Washington Hospital 1201 S Miller St .... Wenatchee WA 98801	800-365-6428	509-662-1511	373-5
Central Washington University 400 E University Way ...... Ellensburg WA 98926 *Admissions	866-298-4968*	509-963-1111	166
Central Washington University Brooks Library 400 E University Way ...... Ellensburg WA 98926	800-290-3327	509-963-3682	433-6
Central Woodwork Inc 870 Keough Rd .... Collierville TN 38017	800-788-3775	901-363-4141	497
Central Wyoming College 2660 Peck Ave .... Riverton WY 82501	800-735-8418	307-855-2000	162
Centralia Correctional Ctr 9330 Shattuc Rd PO Box 1266 .... Centralia IL 62801	844-258-9071		
Centralia-Chehalis Chamber of Commerce 500 NW Chamber of Commerce Way .... Chehalis WA 98532	800-525-3323	360-748-8885	139
CentralVac International 23455 Hellman Ave PO Box 259. ...... Dollar Bay MI 49922	800-666-3133		783
Centrav Inc 511 E Travelers Trl .... Burnsville MN 55337	800-874-2033	952-886-7650	16
Centre College 600 W Walnut St .... Danville KY 40422	800-423-6236	859-238-5350	166
Centre County Convention & Visitors Bureau 800 E Park Ave .... State College PA 16803	800-358-5466	814-231-1400	206
Centre Daily Times 3400 E College Ave .... State College PA 16801	800-327-5500	814-238-5000	528-2
Centre for Skills Development & Training, The 3350 S Service Rd .... Burlington ON L7N3M6	888-315-5521	905-333-3499	148
Centre for Well-Being at the Phoenician 6000 E Camelback Rd .... Scottsdale AZ 85251	800-843-2392		703
Centre in the Square 101 Queen St N .... Kitchener ON N2H6P7	800-265-8977	519-578-1570	568
CENTRIA 1005 Beaver Grade Rd ...... Moon Township PA 15108	800-759-7474	412-299-8000	478
Centrix Pharmaceutical Inc 951 Clint Moore Rd Ste A. ... Boca Raton FL 33487	866-991-9870	205-991-9870	
Centron Data Services Inc 1175 Devin Dr .... Norton Shores MI 49441 *Cust Svc	800-732-8787*		5
CENTROSOLAR America Inc 14350 N 87th St Ste 105 ..... Scottsdale AZ 85260	877-348-2555		
Centrus Energy Corp 6903 Rockledge Dr .... Bethesda MD 20817 NYSE: LEU	800-273-7754	301-564-3200	143
Centurion Industries Inc 1107 N Taylor Rd .... Garrett IN 46738	888-832-4466	260-357-6665	190
Centurion Medical Products 100 Centurion Way .... Williamston MI 48895	800-248-4058	517-546-5400	475
CENTURY 21 Salvadori Realty 3500 N G St .... Merced CA 95340	800-557-6033	209-383-6475	648
Century Bancorp Inc 400 Mystic Ave .... Medford MA 02155 NASDAQ: CNBKA	866-823-6887	781-393-4160	359-2
Century Casinos Inc 2860 S Cir Dr Ste 350 ...... Colorado Springs CO 80906 NASDAQ: CNTY	888-966-2257	719-527-8300	132
Century College 3300 Century Ave N .... White Bear Lake MN 55110	800-228-1978	651-779-3300	162
Century Engineering Inc 10710 Gilroy Rd .... Hunt Valley MD 21031	800-318-6867	443-589-2400	261
Century Fasteners Corp 50-20 Ireland St .... Elmhurst NY 11373	800-221-0769	718-446-5000	246
Century Furniture LLC 401 11th St NW .... Hickory NC 28601	800-852-5552	828-328-1851	319-2
Century Graphics & Metals Inc 550 S N Lake Blvd Ste 1000 ...... Altamonte Springs FL 32701	800-373-5330		697
Century Group Inc, The 1106 W Napoleon St PO Box 228 ... Sulphur LA 70664	800-527-5232	337-527-5266	183
Century Health Solutions Inc 1500 SW Tenth Ave .... Topeka KS 66604	800-227-0089	785-270-4593	194
Century Insurance Group 550 Polaris Pkwy Ste 300. ...... Westerville OH 43082	877-855-8462	614-895-2000	390-5
Century Marketing Solutions LLC 3000 Cameron St .... Monroe LA 71201	800-256-6000		623
Century Martial Art Supply Inc 1000 Century Blvd .... Oklahoma City OK 73110 *Sales	800-626-2787*	405-732-2226	707
Century National Bank 14 S Fifth St .... Zanesville OH 43701 *Cust Svc	800-548-3557*	740-454-2521	70
Century Plaza Hotel & Spa 1015 Burrard St .... Vancouver BC V6Z1Y5	800-663-1818	604-687-0575	378
Century Ready-Mix Corp 3250 Armand St PO Box 4420 ...... Monroe LA 71211	800-732-3969	318-322-4444	182
Century Roof Tile 23135 Saklan Rd .... Hayward CA 94545	888-233-7548	510-780-9489	191-1
Century Spring Corp 222 E 16th St .... Los Angeles CA 90015	800-237-5225	213-749-1466	715
Century Steel Erectors Co 210 Washington Ave ...... Dravosburg PA 15034	888-601-8801	412-469-8800	189-14
Century Suites Hotel 300 SR-446 .... Bloomington IN 47401	800-766-5446	812-336-7777	378
Century Tile Supply Co 747 E Roosevelt Rd .... Lombard IL 60148	888-845-3968	630-495-2300	290
Century Tool & Mfg 90 McMillen Rd .... Antioch IL 60002	800-635-3831		706
Century Wealth Management LLC 1770 Kirby Pkwy Ste 117 ...... Memphis TN 38138	855-850-5532	901-850-5532	400
Century-National Insurance Co 16650 Sherman Way .... Van Nuys CA 91406 *Cust Svc	800-733-0880*		390-4
CEP Forensic inc 1345 Boul Louis-xiv Blvd ...... Quebec QC G2L1M4	855-622-4480	418-622-4480	
Cepheid 904 E Caribbean Dr .... Sunnyvale CA 94089	888-838-3222	408-541-4191	418
Cequent Towing Products 47774 Anchor Ct W .... Plymouth MI 48170	800-521-0510		758
Cequent Trailer Products 1050 Indianhead Dr .... Mosinee WI 54455	800-604-9466	715-693-1700	758
CERAGEM Co Inc 3699 Wilshire Blvd Ste 930 .... Los Angeles CA 90010	800-903-9333	213-480-7070	473
Ceramic Technology Inc 606 Wardell Industrial Pk ...... Cedar Bluff VA 24609	800-437-1142		563
Ceramo Company Inc 681 Kasten Dr .... Jackson MO 63755	800-325-8303	573-243-3138	333
CeramTec North America Corp Technology Pl .... Laurens SC 29360	800-752-7325	864-682-3215	249
CERC (Columbia Environmental Research Ctr) 4200 New Haven Rd .... Columbia MO 65201	888-283-7626	703-648-5953	664
Ceres Environmental Services Inc 3825 85th Ave N .... Minneapolis MN 55443	800-218-4424		
Ceres Solutions LLP 2112 Indianapolis Rd PO Box 132 ...... Crawfordsville IN 47933 *General	800-878-0952*	765-362-6700	275
Cerex Advanced Fabrics Inc 610 Chemstrand Rd .... Cantonment FL 32533	800-572-3739	850-937-3365	740-6
Ceridian Benefits Services Inc 3201 34th St S .... St. Petersburg FL 33711	800-689-7893		
Cermetek Microelectronics Inc 374 Turquoise St .... Milpitas CA 95035	800-882-6271	408-752-5000	173-3
Cernan Earth & Space Ctr 2000 Fifth Ave .... River Grove IL 60171	800-972-7000	708-583-3100	594
Ceros Financial Services Inc 1445 Research Blvd Ste 530. ...... Rockville MD 20850	866-842-3356		686
Cerritos Ctr for the Performing Arts 18000 Park Plaza Dr .... Cerritos CA 90703	800-300-4345	562-916-8501	568
Cerro Coso Community College Bishop 4090 W Line St .... Bishop CA 93514	888-537-6932	760-872-1565	162
Indian Wells Valley 3000 College Heights Blvd ...... Ridgecrest CA 93555	888-537-6932	760-384-6100	162
Kern River Valley 5520 Lake Isabella Blvd ...... Lake Isabella CA 93240	888-537-6932	760-379-5501	162
Mammoth 101 College Pkwy .... Mammoth Lakes CA 93546	888-537-6932	760-934-2875	162
South Kern 140 Methusa Ave .... Edwards AFB CA 93524	888-537-6932	661-258-8644	162
Cerro Flow Products Inc PO Box 66800 .... Saint Louis MO 63166	888-237-7611	618-337-6000	488
Cerro Wire & Cable Company Inc 1099 Thompson Rd SE .... Hartselle AL 35640	800-523-3869	256-773-2522	808
CERT (Computer Emergency Response Team) 4500 Fifth Ave .... Pittsburgh PA 15213	800-598-6831	412-268-7090	664
CertainTeed Corp 750 E Swedesford Rd ...... Valley Forge PA 19482 *Prod Info	800-782-8777*	610-341-7000	388
CertainTeed Gypsum 2424 Lakeshore Rd W ...... Mississauga ON L5J1K4	800-233-8990	905-823-9881	346
CertaPro Painters Ltd 150 Green Tree Rd Ste 1003 ...... Oaks PA 19456	800-689-7271		189-8
Certex USA Inc 1721 W Culver St .... Phoenix AZ 85007	800-225-2103	602-271-9048	490
Certicom Corp 4701 Tahoe Blvd Bldg A ...... Mississauga ON L4W0B5	800-561-6100	905-507-4220	178-12
Certif-a-gift Company the 1625 E Algonquin Rd ...... Arlington Heights IL 60005	800-545-5156		
Certified Financial Planner Board of Standards Inc 1425 K St NW Ste 500 ...... Washington DC 20005	800-487-1497	202-379-2200	49-2
Certified Horsemanship Assn (CHA) 1795 Alysheba Way Ste 7102 ..... Lexington KY 40509	800-399-0138	859-259-3399	48-3
Certified Languages International LLC 4800 SW Macadam Ave Ste 400. .... Portland OR 97239	800-362-3241		763
Certified Power Inc 970 Campus Dr .... Mundelein IL 60060	888-905-7411	847-573-3800	616
Certified Restoration DryCleaning Network LLC 2060 Coolidge Hwy .... Berkley MI 48072	800-963-2736		310
Certified Safety Manufacturing Inc 1400 Chestnut Ave .... Kansas City MO 64127	800-854-7474		474
Certipay 199 Ave B NW Ste 270 ...... Winter Haven FL 33881	800-422-3782	863-299-2400	2
Certis USA LLC 9145 Guilford Rd Ste 175. ...... Columbia MD 21046	800-250-5024		280
Certus International 9 Cedarwood Dr Ste 8. .... Bedford NH 03110	800-969-3218	603-627-1212	193
CES (Community Eldercare Services LLC) PO Box 3667 .... Tupelo MS 38803	877-461-1062		
Cesium Telecom Inc 5798 Ferrier .... Montreal QC H4P1M7	877-798-8686	514-798-8686	731
Cessco Fabrication & Engineering Ltd 7310-99 St .... Edmonton AB T6E3R8	800-272-9698	780-433-9531	478

Listing	Toll-Free	Phone	Class
CET			
1223 Central Pkwy .... Cincinnati OH 45214	**800-808-0445**	513-381-4033	736-18
Cetac Technologies Inc			
14306 Industrial Rd .... Omaha NE 68144	**800-369-2822**	402-733-2829	418
CETCO (Colloid Environmental Technologies Co)			
2870 Forbs Ave .... Hoffman Estates IL 60192	**800-527-9948**	847-851-1899	3
Cetera Financial Group Inc			
200 N Sepulveda Blvd			
Ste 1200 .... El Segundo CA 90245	**866-489-3100**		686
Cev Multimedia Ltd			
1020 SE Loop 289 .... Lubbock TX 79404	**877-610-5017**		511
CF Industries Inc			
4 Pkwy N Ste 400 .... Deerfield IL 60015	**800-462-8565**	847-405-2400	280
CF Martin & Company Inc			
510 Sycamore St PO Box 329 .... Nazareth PA 18064	**888-433-9177**	610-759-2837	523
CFA Institute			
915 E High St .... Charlottesville VA 22902	**800-247-8132**	434-951-5499	49-2
CFBank			
7000 N High St .... Worthington OH 43085	**866-668-4606**	614-334-7979	359-2
NASDAQ: CFBK			
CFC Farm & Home Ctr			
15172 Brandy Rd PO Box 2002 .... Culpeper VA 22701	**800-284-2667**	540-825-2200	280
CFC International Inc			
500 State St .... Chicago Heights IL 60411	**800-393-4505**	708-891-3456	3
CFCA (Christian Foundation for Children & Aging)			
1 Elmwood Ave .... Kansas City KS 66103	**800-875-6564**	913-384-6500	48-6
CFCC (Cuyahoga Falls Chamber of Commerce)			
151 Portage Trl Ste 1 .... Cuyahoga Falls OH 44221	**800-248-4040**	330-929-6756	139
CFCU Community Credit Union			
1030 Craft Rd .... Ithaca NY 14850	**800-428-8340**	607-257-8500	219
CFG (Creative Financial Group)			
16 Campus Blvd .... Newtown Square PA 19073	**800-893-4824**	610-325-6100	400
CFHS (Canadian Federation of Humane Societies)			
30 Concourse Gate Ste 102 .... Ottawa ON K2E7V7	**888-678-2347**	613-224-8072	48-3
CFMA (Construction Financial Management Assn)			
100 Village Blvd Ste 200 .... Princeton NJ 08540	**888-421-9996**	609-452-8000	49-1
CFP (CFP inc)			
4560 L B Mcleod Rd .... Orlando FL 32811	**800-683-0693**	407-843-5811	
CFP inc (CFP)			
4560 L B Mcleod Rd .... Orlando FL 32811	**800-683-0693**	407-843-5811	
CGH (Coral Gables Hospital Inc)			
3100 Douglas Rd .... Coral Gables FL 33134	**866-728-3677**	305-445-8461	373-3
CGH Medical Ctr (CGHMC)			
100 E LeFevre Rd .... Sterling IL 61081	**800-625-4790**	815-625-0400	373-3
CGHMC (CGH Medical Ctr)			
100 E LeFevre Rd .... Sterling IL 61081	**800-625-4790**	815-625-0400	373-3
CGI Group Inc			
1350 Ren,-L,vesque Blvd W			
15th Fl .... Montreal QC H3G1T4	**800-828-8377**	514-841-3200	180
TSX: GIB/A			
CGM Funds PO Box 8511 .... Boston MA 02266	**800-345-4048**	617-859-7714	524
CGNAD (Compass Group North American Div)			
2400 Yorkmont Rd .... Charlotte NC 28217	**800-357-0012**	704-328-4000	299
CGR Products Inc			
4655 US Hwy 29 N .... Greensboro NC 27405	**877-313-6785**	336-621-4568	326
CH (Clarion Hospital)			
1 Hospital Dr .... Clarion PA 16214	**800-522-0505**	814-226-9500	373-3
CH Ellis Co Inc			
2432 SE Ave .... Indianapolis IN 46201	**800-466-3351***	317-636-3351	451
*Sales			
CH Energy Group Inc			
284 S Ave .... Poughkeepsie NY 12601	**800-527-2714**	845-452-2000	359-5
NYSE: CHG			
CH Hanson Co			
2000 N Aurora Rd .... Naperville IL 60563	**800-827-3398**	630-848-2000	465
CH Robinson Worldwide Inc			
14701 Charlson Rd .... Eden Prairie MN 55347	**855-229-6128***	952-683-3950	447
NASDAQ: CHRW ■ *Cust Svc			
CHA (Certified Horsemanship Assn)			
1795 Alysheba Way Ste 7102 .... Lexington KY 40509	**800-399-0138**	859-259-3399	48-3
CHA (Catholic Health Assn of the US)			
4455 Woodson Rd .... Saint Louis MO 63134	**800-230-7823**	314-427-2500	49-8
CHA (Craft & Hobby Assn)			
319 E 54th St .... Elmwood Park NJ 07407	**800-822-0494**	201-835-1200	48-18
CHA (Community Hospital Anderson)			
1515 N Madison Ave .... Anderson IN 46011	**800-777-7775**	765-298-4242	373-3
CHA Hollywood Presbyterian Medical Center			
1300 N Vermont Ave .... Los Angeles CA 90027	**800-465-3203**	213-413-3000	373-3
CHADD (Children & Adults with Attention-Deficit/Hyperacti)			
4601 Presidents Dr Ste 300 .... Lanham MD 20706	**800-233-4050**		48-17
Chadderton Trucking Inc			
40 Stewart Way PO Box 687 .... Sharon PA 16146	**800-327-6868**	724-981-5050	775
Chadron State College			
1000 Main St .... Chadron NE 69337	**800-242-3766**	308-432-6000	166
Chadwick's of Boston			
75 Aircraft Rd .... Southington CT 06489	**877-330-3393**		457
Chaffey College			
5885 Haven Ave .... Rancho Cucamonga CA 91737	**800-535-2421**	909-652-6000	162
Chahinkapa Zoo Park & Carousel			
1004 RJ Hughes Dr .... Wahpeton ND 58075	**800-342-4671**	701-642-8709	818
Chain Drug Marketing Assn (CDMA)			
43157 W Nine-Mile Rd PO Box 995 .... Novi MI 48376	**800-935-2362**	248-449-9300	49-18
Chain Store Guide			
10117 Princess Palm Ave Ste 375 .... Tampa FL 33610	**800-927-9292**		633-6
Chalk & Vermilion Fine Arts Inc			
55 Old Post Rd Ste 2 .... Greenwich CT 06830	**800-877-2250**	203-869-9500	633-10
Challenge Dairy Products Inc			
PO Box 2369 .... Dublin CA 94568	**800-733-2479**		
Challenge Printing Co, The			
2 Bridewell Pl .... Clifton NJ 07014	**800-654-1234**	973-471-4700	623
Challenge Publications Inc			
21835 Nordhoff St .... Chatsworth CA 91311	**800-562-9182**	818-700-6868	633-9
Challenger Ctr for Space Science Education			
422 First St SE 3rd Fl .... Washington DC 20003	**800-969-5747***	202-827-1580	48-11
*General			
Challenger Gray & Christmas Inc			
150 S Wacker Dr Ste 2800 .... Chicago IL 60606	**855-242-3424**	312-332-5790	193

Listing	Toll-Free	Phone	Class
Challenger Learning Ctr (CLC)			
316 Washington Ave			
Wheeling Jesuit University .... Wheeling WV 26003	**800-624-6992**	304-243-2279	517
Chalmers & Kubeck Inc			
150 Commerce Dr .... Aston PA 19014	**800-242-5637**	610-494-4300	452
Chamber Music America (CMA)			
305 Seventh Ave 5th Fl .... New York NY 10001	**888-221-9836**	212-242-2022	48-4
Chamber of Business & Industry of Centre County			
200 Innovation Blvd			
Ste 150 .... State College PA 16803	**877-234-5050**	814-234-1829	139
Chamber of Southern Saratoga County			
58 Clifton Country Rd			
Ste 102 .... Clifton Park NY 12065	**800-766-9001**	518-371-7748	139
Chamberlain College of Nursing			
11830 Westline Industrial			
Ste 106 .... Saint Louis MO 63146	**888-556-8226**	314-991-6200	166
Chamberlain West Hollywood			
1000 Westmount Dr .... West Hollywood CA 90069	**877-686-2082**	310-657-7400	378
Chambers of Commerce / Tourism			
106 E Jefferson St .... Tallahassee FL 32301	**800-628-2866**	850-606-2305	206
Chambre de Commerce du Quebec			
555 boul Ren,-L,vesque W			
Ste 1100 .... Montreal QC H2Z1B1	**800-361-5019**	514-844-9571	
Chameleon Consulting Inc			
89 Falmouth Rd W .... Arlington MA 02474	**866-903-7912**	781-646-2272	180
Chameleon Group LLC			
951 Islington St .... Portsmouth NH 03801	**800-773-9182**	603-570-4300	196
Chaminade College Preparatory School			
425 S Lindbergh Blvd .... Saint Louis MO 63131	**877-378-6847**	314-993-4400	618
Chaminade Resort & Spa			
1 Chaminade Ln .... Santa Cruz CA 95065	**800-283-6569**	831-475-5600	376
Chaminade University			
3140 Waialae Ave .... Honolulu HI 96816	**800-735-3733**	808-735-4711	166
Champaign County Chamber of Commerce			
107 N Main St .... Urbana OH 43078	**877-873-5764**	937-653-5764	139
Champion Bus Inc			
331 Graham Rd .... Imlay City MI 48444	**800-776-4943**	810-724-6474	513
Champion Chemical Co			
8319 S Greenleaf Ave .... Whittier CA 90602	**800-424-9300**		151
Champion College Services Inc			
7776 S Pointe Pkwy W Ste 250 .... Tempe AZ 85044	**800-761-7376**	480-947-7375	194
Champion Industries Inc			
PO Box 2968 .... Huntington WV 25728	**800-624-3431**	304-528-2791	623
OTC: CHMP			
Champion Photochemistry			
7895 Tranmere Dr .... Mississauga ON L5S1V9	**800-387-3430**	905-670-7900	587
Champion Power Equipment			
12039 Smith Ave .... Santa Fe Springs CA 90670	**877-338-0999**		61
Champion Solutions Group			
791 Pk of Commerce Blvd			
Ste 200 .... Boca Raton FL 33487	**800-771-7000**	561-997-2900	174
Champion Technologies Inc			
845 Mckinley St .... Eugene OR 97402	**800-547-6180**		247
Champion Window Mfg Inc			
12121 Champion Way .... Cincinnati OH 45241	**877-424-2674**	513-346-4600	235
Champion-Arrowhead LLC			
5147 Alhambra Ave .... Los Angeles CA 90032	**800-332-4267**	323-221-9137	605
Champions Way			
4333 Still Creek Dr 2nd Fl .... Burnaby BC V5C6S6	**877-774-5425**		804
Champlain Cable Corp			
175 Hercules Dr .... Colchester VT 05446	**800-451-5162**		809
Champlain College			
163 S Willard St .... Burlington VT 05401	**800-570-5858**	802-860-2700	166
Champlain Oil Company Inc			
45 San Remo Dr .... South Burlington VT 05403	**800-649-3229**	802-864-5380	
Chancellor Hotel on Union Square			
433 Powell St .... San Francisco CA 94102	**800-428-4748**	415-362-2004	378
Chandler Asset Management Inc			
6225 Lusk Blvd .... San Diego CA 92121	**800-317-4747**		524
Chandler Chamber of Commerce			
25 S Arizona Pl Ste 201 .... Chandler AZ 85225	**800-963-4571**	480-963-4571	139
Chandler Hall Hospice			
99 Barclay St .... Newtown PA 18940	**888-603-1973**	215-860-4000	370
Chanel Inc			
15 E 57th St .... New York NY 10022	**800-550-0005**	212-355-5050	570
Chaney Enterprises			
12480 Mattawoman Dr PO Box 548 ...... Waldorf MD 20604	**888-244-0411**	301-932-5000	183
Chaney Instrument Co			
965 Wells St .... Lake Geneva WI 53147	**877-221-1252**	262-729-4852	201
Channel 45 WHFT TV			
3324 Pembroke Rd .... Miami FL 33021	**800-447-7235**	954-962-1700	736
Channel Solutions LLC			
3145 E Chanl Blvd Ste 110 .... Phoenix AZ 85048	**866-501-9690**		196
Channellock Inc			
1306 S Main St .... Meadville PA 16335	**800-724-3018***		753
*Cust Svc			
Channing Bete Co			
1 Community Pl .... South Deerfield MA 01373	**800-477-4776**	413-665-7611	633-10
Chanticleer Inn			
1458 E Dollar Lake Rd .... Eagle River WI 54521	**800-752-9193**	715-479-4486	665
CHAP (Community Health Accreditation Program Inc)			
1275 K St NW Ste 800 .... Washington DC 20005	**800-656-9656**	202-862-3413	48-1
Chapel Hill/Orange County Visitors Bureau			
501 W Franklin St .... Chapel Hill NC 27516	**888-968-2060**		206
Chapel Hill-Carrboro Chamber of Commerce			
104 S Estes Dr .... Chapel Hill NC 27515	**800-694-9784**	919-967-7075	139
Chapel Steel Co			
590 N Bethlehem Pk .... Lower Gwynedd PA 19002	**800-570-7674**	215-793-0899	452
Chapin & Bangs Co, The			
165 River St .... Bridgeport CT 06604	**800-972-9615**		
Chapin Davis Investments			
1411 Clarkview Rd .... Baltimore MD 21209	**800-222-3246**	410-435-3200	
Chapman University			
1 University Dr .... Orange CA 92866	**888-282-7759**	714-997-6815	166
Chapman/Leonard Studio Equipment Inc			
12950 Raymer St .... North Hollywood CA 91605	**888-883-6559**	818-764-6726	718
Char-Broil			
1442 Belfast Ave .... Columbus GA 31902	**800-241-7548**		36

	Toll-Free	Phone	Class

Chardon Laboratories Inc
7300 Tussing Rd . . . . Reynoldsburg OH 43068　**888-660-1724**　　738

Charisma Magazine
600 Rinehart Rd . . . . Lake Mary FL 32746　**800-749-6500**　407-333-0600　455-18

Chariton Valley Electric Co-op
2090 Hwy 5 PO Box 486 . . . . Albia IA 52531　**800-475-1702**　641-932-7126　245

CharityUSAcom LLC
600 University St
Ste 1000 One Union Square . . . . Seattle WA 98101　**888-811-5271**　206-268-5400　386

Charles & Colvard Ltd
170 Southport Dr . . . . Morrisville NC 27560　**800-210-4367**　919-468-0399　410
NASDAQ: CTHR

Charles A Lindbergh State Park
1615 Lindbergh Dr S . . . . Little Falls MN 56345　**888-646-6367**　320-616-2525　561

Charles Bond Co
11 Green St PO Box 105 . . . . Christiana PA 17509　**800-922-0125**　610-596-5171　705

Charles C Parks Co
388 N Belvedere Dr . . . . Gallatin TN 37066　**800-873-2406**　615-452-2406　297-11

Charles C Thomas Publisher
2600 S First St . . . . Springfield IL 62704　**800-258-8980***　217-789-8980　633-2
*Sales

Charles County Chamber of Commerce
101 Centennial St Ste A . . . . La Plata MD 20646　**800-992-3194**　301-932-6500　139

Charles E Gillman Co
907 E Frontage Rd . . . . Rio Rico AZ 85648　**800-783-2589**　520-281-1141　810

Charles Gabus Ford Inc
4545 Merle Hay Rd . . . . Des Moines IA 50310　**800-934-2287***　515-270-0707　57
*Sales

Charles GG Schmidt & Company Inc
301 W Grand Ave . . . . Montvale NJ 07645　**800-724-6438**　201-391-5300　753

Charles Hotel Harvard Square
1 Bennett St . . . . Cambridge MA 02138　**800-882-1818**　617-864-1200　378

Charles Industries Ltd
5600 Apollo Dr . . . . Rolling Meadows IL 60008　**800-458-4747**　847-806-6300　730

Charles Jones LLC
PO Box 8488 . . . . Trenton NJ 08650　**800-792-8888**　　631

Charles L Crane Agency Co
100 N Broadway Ste 900 . . . . Saint Louis MO 63102　**800-264-8722**　314-241-8700　389

Charles Leonard Inc
145 Kennedy Dr . . . . Hauppauge NY 11788　**800-999-7202**　631-273-6700　349

Charles Machine Works Inc, The
1959 W First Ave PO Box 1902 . . . . Perry OK 73077　**844-572-1902**

Charles Mix Electric Assn Inc
440 Lake St . . . . Lake Andes SD 57356　**800-208-8587**　605-487-7321　245

Charles River Laboratories Inc
251 Ballardvale St . . . . Wilmington MA 01887　**800-772-3271**　781-222-6000　664
NYSE: CRL

Charles Ross & Son Co
710 Old Willets Path . . . . Hauppauge NY 11788　**800-243-7677**　631-234-0500　385

Charles Ryan Assoc Inc
601 Morris St Ste 301 . . . . Charleston WV 25301　**877-342-0161**　　632

Charles Schwab & Co Inc
211 Main St . . . . San Francisco CA 94105　**800-648-5300***　415-667-1009　686
*Cust Svc

Charleston Area Convention & Visitors Bureau
423 King St . . . . Charleston SC 29403　**800-868-8118**　800-774-4444　206

Charleston County
4045 Bridge View Dr . . . . North Charleston SC 29405　**800-735-2905**　843-958-4030　337

Charleston County Public Library
68 Calhoun St . . . . Charleston SC 29401　**800-768-3676**　843-805-6930　433-3

Charleston County School District (CCSD)
75 Calhoun St . . . . Charleston SC 29401　**800-241-8898**　843-937-6300　681

Charleston Harbor Resort & Marina
20 Patriots Pt Rd . . . . Mount Pleasant SC 29464　**888-856-0028**　843-856-0028

Charleston Newspapers Ltd
1001 Virginia St E . . . . Charleston WV 25301　**800-982-6397**　304-348-4848　528-3

Charleston Place
205 Meeting St . . . . Charleston SC 29401　**888-635-2350**　843-722-4900　378

Charleston Regional Chamber of Commerce
1116 Smith St . . . . Charleston WV 25301　**800-792-4326**　304-340-4253　139

Charleston Southern University
9200 University Blvd . . . . Charleston SC 29423　**800-947-7474**　843-863-7050　166

Charlestown Retirement Community (CCI)
715 Maiden Choice Ln . . . . Catonsville MD 21228　**800-917-8649**　410-242-2880　668

Charlevoix County
203 Antrim St . . . . Charlevoix MI 49720　**800-548-9157**　231-547-7200　337

Charleys Philly Steaks
2500 Farmers Dr Ste 140 . . . . Columbus OH 43235　**800-437-8325**　614-923-4700　666

Charlotte Anodizing Products Inc
591 E Packard Hwy . . . . Charlotte MI 48813　**800-818-6945**　517-543-1911　479

Charlotte Appliances Inc
3200 Lake Ave . . . . Rochester NY 14612　**800-244-0405**　585-663-5050　321

Charlotte City Hall
Charlotte-Mecklenburg Government Ctr
600 E 4th St . . . . Charlotte NC 28202　**800-418-2065**　704-336-2241　336

Charlotte Convention & Visitors Bureau
500 S College St . . . . Charlotte NC 28202　**800-722-1994**　704-334-2282　206

Charlotte Hawkins Brown Museum
PO Box B . . . . Sedalia NC 27342　**800-767-1560**　336-449-4846　517

Charlotte Institute of Rehabilitation
1100 Blythe Blvd . . . . Charlotte NC 28203　**800-634-2256**　704-355-4300　373-6

Charlotte Motor Speedway
5555 Concord Pkwy S . . . . Concord NC 28027　**800-455-3267**　704-455-3200　638

Charlotte Observer, The
600 S Tryon St . . . . Charlotte NC 28202　**800-332-0686**　704-358-5000　528-2

Charlotte Pipe & Foundry Co
2109 Randolph Rd . . . . Charlotte NC 28207　**800-438-6091**　704-372-5030　488

Charlotte Russe Inc
5910 Pacific Center Blvd . . . . San Diego CA 92121　**888-211-7271**　　157-6

Charlton County
68 Kingsland Ste B . . . . Folkston GA 31537　**800-436-7442**

Charlton Memorial Hospital
363 Highland Ave . . . . Fall River MA 02720　**800-276-0103**　508-679-3131　373-3

Charm Sciences Inc
659 Andover St . . . . Lawrence MA 01843　**800-343-2170**　978-687-9200　477

Charms Co
7401 S Cicero Ave . . . . Chicago IL 60629　**800-267-0037**　773-838-3400　296-8

Charnstrom
5391 12th Ave E . . . . Shakopee MN 55379　**800-328-2962***　　468
*Cust Svc

Charter Communications Inc
12405 Powerscourt Dr . . . . Saint Louis MO 63131　**888-438-2427**　314-965-0555　116
NASDAQ: CHTR

Charter Films Inc
1901 Winter St PO Box 277 . . . . Superior WI 54880　**877-411-3456**　715-395-8258　544

Charter Flight Inc
1928 S Blvd . . . . Charlotte NC 28208　**800-521-3148**　　13

Charter Industries
3900 S Greenbrooke Dr SE . . . . Kentwood MI 49512　**800-538-9088**　　350

Charter Medical Ltd
3948-A Westpoint Blvd . . . . Winston-Salem NC 27103　**866-458-3116**

Charter Mfg Company Inc
1212 W Glen Oaks Ln . . . . Mequon WI 53092　**800-437-8789**　262-243-4700　719

Charter Oak State College
55 Paul J Manafort Dr . . . . New Britain CT 06053　**800-235-6559**　860-832-3800　166

Charter Wire
3700 W Milwaukee Rd . . . . Milwaukee WI 53208　**800-436-9074**　414-390-3000　808

CharterBank
1233 OG Skinner Dr . . . . West Point GA 31833　**800-763-4444**　706-645-1391　70

Chartered Business Valuators
277 Wellington St W Ste 808 . . . . Toronto ON M5V3H2　**866-770-7315**　416-977-1117　767

Chartis Group LLC
220 W Kinzie St 3rd Fl . . . . Chicago IL 60654　**877-667-4700**　　461

Chartist Newsletter
PO Box 758 . . . . Seal Beach CA 90740　**800-942-4278**　562-596-2385　527-9

Chartpak Inc 1 River Rd . . . . Leeds MA 01053　**800-628-1910**　413-584-5446　43

Chartway Federal Credit Union
5700 Cleveland St . . . . Virginia Beach VA 23462　**800-678-8765**　757-552-1000　219

Chase & Sons Inc
295 University Ave . . . . Westwood MA 02090　**800-323-4182**　781-332-0700　811

Chase Bank
28 Liberty St . . . . New York NY 10005　**800-935-9935**　　70

Chase Brass & Copper Co
14212 Selwyn Dr . . . . Montpelier OH 43543　**800-537-4291**　419-485-3193　483

Chase Brexton Health Services Inc
1111 N Charles St . . . . Baltimore MD 21201　**866-392-4483**　410-837-2050

Chase Corp
26 Summer St . . . . Bridgewater MA 02324　**800-323-4182**　781-332-0700　3
NYSE: CCF

Chase Enterprises Inc
6509 W Reno Ave . . . . Oklahoma City OK 73127　**800-525-4970**　405-495-1722　196

Chase Industries Inc
10021 Commerce Park Dr . . . . Cincinnati OH 45246　**800-543-4455**　513-860-5565　478

Chase Paymentech Solutions LLC
14221 Dallas Pkwy . . . . Dallas TX 75254　**800-708-3740***　　255
*Cust Svc

Chase Plastic Services Inc
6467 Waldon Ctr Dr . . . . Clarkston MI 48346　**800-232-4273**　248-620-2120　686

Chateau Elan Winery
100 Tour de France . . . . Braselton GA 30517　**800-233-9463**　678-425-0900　50-7

Chateau Grille
415 N State Hwy 265 . . . . Branson MO 65616　**888-333-5253**　417-334-1161　667

Chateau Lacombe Hotel
10111 Bellamy Hill . . . . Edmonton AB T5J1N7　**800-661-8801**　780-428-6611　378

Chateau Louis Hotel & Conference Ctr
11727 Kingsway . . . . Edmonton AB T5G3A1　**800-661-9843**　780-452-7770　378

Chateau Morrisette Winery
287 Winery Rd SW . . . . Floyd VA 24091　**866-695-2001**　540-593-2865　50-7

Chateau on the Lake
415 N State Hwy 265 . . . . Branson MO 65616　**888-333-5253**　417-334-1161　378

Chateau Resort & Conference Center, The
475 Camelback Rd . . . . Tannersville PA 18372　**800-245-5900**　570-629-5900　703

Chateau Rouge
1505 S Broadway Ave . . . . Red Lodge MT 59068　**800-926-1601**　406-446-1601　703

Chateau Ste Michelle Winery
14111 NE 145th St . . . . Woodinville WA 98072　**800-267-6793**　425-488-1133　50-7

Château Vaudreuil Hotel & Suites
21700 Rt Transcanada Hwy
. . . . Vaudreuil-Dorion QC J7V8P3　**800-363-7896**　450-455-0955　378

Chateau Versailles
1659 Sherbrooke St W . . . . Montreal QC H3H1E3　**888-933-8111**　514-933-3611　378

Chateau-Sur-Mer
474 Bellevue Ave . . . . Newport RI 02840　**800-326-6030**　401-847-1000　50-3

Chatham Bars Inn
297 Shore Rd . . . . Chatham MA 02633　**800-527-4884**　　665

Chatham Chamber of Commerce
531 E Third St . . . . Siler City NC 27344　**800-329-7466**　919-742-3333　139

Chatham Hall
800 Chatham Hall Cir . . . . Chatham VA 24531　**877-644-2941**　434-432-2941　618

Chatham Steel Corp
501 W Boundary St . . . . Savannah GA 31401　**800-800-1337**　912-233-5751　490

Chatham University
1 Woodland Rd . . . . Pittsburgh PA 15232　**800-837-1290**　412-365-1100　166

Chatr Mobile
333 Bloor St E 8th Fl . . . . Toronto ON M4W1G9　**800-485-9745**　　224

Chatsworth Chamber of Commerce
10038 Old Depot Plaza Rd . . . . Chatsworth CA 91311　**800-613-5903**　818-341-2428　139

Chatsworth Products Inc
31425 Agoura Rd . . . . Westlake Village CA 91361　**800-834-4969**　818-735-6100　176

Chatsworth-Murray County Chamber of Commerce
1001 Green Rd . . . . Chatsworth GA 30705　**800-969-9490**　706-695-6060　139

Chattahoochee River National Recreation Area
1978 Island Ford Pkwy . . . . Atlanta GA 30350　**877-874-2478**　678-538-1200　560

Chattanooga Area Chamber of Commerce
811 Broad St . . . . Chattanooga TN 37402　**877-756-1684**　423-756-2121　139

Chattanooga Area Convention & Visitors Bureau
215 Broad St . . . . Chattanooga TN 37402　**800-322-3344**　423-756-8687　206

Chattanooga City Hall
101 E 11th St Rm 100 . . . . Chattanooga TN 37402　**866-894-5026**　423-643-6311　336

Chattanooga Convention Ctr
1150 Carter St . . . . Chattanooga TN 37402　**800-962-5213**　423-756-0001　205

Chattanooga Group
4717 Adams Rd . . . . Hixson TN 37343　**800-592-7329**　423-870-2281　475

Chattanooga National Cemetery
1200 Bailey Ave . . . . Chattanooga TN 37404　**877-907-8585**　423-855-6590　136

Name / Address	City	State	ZIP	Toll-Free	Phone	Class
Chattanooga State Technical Community College 4501 Amnicola Hwy	Chattanooga	TN	37406	**866-547-3733**	423-697-4400	162
Chattanoogan, The 1201 Broad St	Chattanooga	TN	37402	**877-756-1684**	423-756-3400	376
Chattooga County PO Box 211	Summerville	GA	30747	**800-436-7442**		
Chautauqua County 3 N Erie St	Mayville	NY	14757	**800-252-8748**	716-753-4211	337
Chautauqua County Visitors Bureau Chautauqua Main Gate Rt 394 PO Box 1441	Chautauqua	NY	14722	**800-242-4569**	716-357-4569	206
Chauvin Arnoux Inc 15 Faraday Dr	Dover	NH	03820	**800-343-1391**	603-749-6434	406
Cheaha Resort State Park 19644 Hwy 281	Delta	AL	36258	**800-610-5801**	256-488-5111	561
Cheap Joe's Art Stuff Inc 374 Industrial Park Dr	Boone	NC	28607	**800-227-2788**	828-262-5459	519
Check Cashing Store (CCS) 6340 NW Fifth Way	Fort Lauderdale	FL	33309	**800-361-1407**		141
Check Cashing USA Inc 899 NW 37th Ave	Miami	FL	33125	**833-352-2274**	305-644-1840	141
Check Point Software Technologies Ltd 800 Bridge Pkwy *NASDAQ: CHKP*	Redwood City	CA	94065	**800-429-4391**	650-628-2000	178-12
Checkbox Survey Inc 44 Pleasant St	Watertown	MA	02472	**866-430-8274**	617-231-8890	
Checkered Flag Motor Car Corp 5225 Virginia Beach Blvd	Virginia Beach	VA	23462	**866-414-7820**	757-687-3486	57
Checkers Drive-In Restaurants Inc 4300 W Cypress St Ste 600	Tampa	FL	33607	**800-800-8072**	813-283-7000	666
Checkpoint Systems Inc 101 Wolf Dr *NYSE: CKP*	Thorofare	NJ	08086	**800-257-5540**	856-848-1800	688
Checks In The Mail Inc 2435 Goodwin Ln	New Braunfels	TX	78135	**800-733-4443**		142
Checks Unlimited PO Box 19000	Colorado Springs	CO	80935	**800-210-0468**		142
Cheeca Lodge & Spa 81801 Overseas Hwy Mile Marker 82	Islamorada	FL	33036	**800-327-2888**	305-664-4651	703
Chef's Requested Foods Inc 2600 Exchange Ave	Oklahoma City	OK	73108	**800-256-0259**		
Cheley Colorado Camps Inc 601 Steele St	Denver	CO	80206	**800-359-7200**	303-377-3616	239
Chella Professional Skin Care 507 Calle San Pablo	Camarillo	CA	93012	**877-424-3552**	805-383-7711	77
Chelsea Bldg Products 565 Cedar Way	Oakmont	PA	15139	**800-424-3573**		235
Chelsea Lumber Co 1 Old Barn Cir	Chelsea	MI	48118	**800-875-9126**	734-475-9126	191-3
Chelsea Milling Co 201 W N St PO Box 460	Chelsea	MI	48118	**800-727-2460**	734-475-1361	296-23
Chelsea Savoy Hotel 204 W 23rd St	New York	NY	10011	**866-929-9353**	212-929-9353	378
Chem Processing Inc 3910 Linden Oaks Dr	Rockford	IL	61109	**800-262-2119**		479
Chem USA Corp 38507 Cherry St	Newark	CA	94560	**800-866-2436**	510-608-8818	173-2
Chematics Inc PO Box 293	North Webster	IN	46555	**800-348-5174**	574-834-2406	231
Chembio Diagnostics Inc 3661 Horseblock Rd *NASDAQ: CEMI*	Medford	NY	11763	**844-243-6246**	631-924-1135	578
Chemed Corp 255 E Fifth St Ste 2600 *NYSE: CHE* ■ *General	Cincinnati	OH	45202	**800-224-3633***	513-762-6900	185
Chemetal 39 O'Neil St	EastHampton	MA	01027	**800-807-7341**		295
CHEMetrics Inc 4295 Catlett Rd	Midland	VA	22728	**800-356-3072**		
Chemical Abstracts Service (CAS) 2540 Olentangy River Rd	Columbus	OH	43202	**800-848-6538**	614-447-3600	386
Chemical Bank 333 E Main St *NASDAQ: CHFC*	Midland	MI	48640	**800-867-9757**	989-839-5350	359-2
Chemical Processing Magazine 1501 E Woodfield Rd Ste 400N	Schaumburg	IL	60173	**800-343-4048**	630-467-1300	455-21
Chemical Products Corp 102 Old Mill Rd *Cust Svc	Cartersville	GA	30120	**877-210-9814***	770-382-2144	143
Chemical Safety Corp 5901 Christie Ave	Emeryville	CA	94608	**888-594-1100**	510-594-1000	39
Chemical Waste Management Inc 1001 Fannin St Ste 4000	Houston	TX	77002	**800-633-7871**	713-512-6200	663
Chemical Week 140 E 45th St 2 Grand Central Tower40th Fl *Cust Svc	New York	NY	10017	**866-501-7540***	212-884-9528	455-21
Chemically Dependent Anonymous (CDA) PO Box 423	Severna Park	MD	21146	**888-232-4673**		48-21
Chemin-A-Haut State Park 14656 State Pk Rd	Bastrop	LA	71220	**888-677-2436**	318-283-0812	561
Chemineer Inc 5870 Poe Ave	Dayton	OH	45414	**800-643-0641**	937-454-3200	385
Chem-pak Inc 242 Corning Way	Martinsburg	WV	25405	**800-336-9828**		295
Chemprene Inc 483 Fishkill Ave	Beacon	NY	12508	**800-431-9981**	845-831-2800	369
Chemstar Products Co 3915 Hiawatha Ave	Minneapolis	MN	55406	**800-328-5037**	612-722-0079	144
Chem-Tainer Industries Inc 361 Neptune Ave	West Babylon	NY	11704	**800-275-2436**	631-661-8300	199
Chem-Trend LP 1445 McPherson Pk Dr	Howell	MI	48843	**800-727-7730**	517-546-4520	537
Chemtrol Div NIBCO Inc 1516 Middlebury St	Elkhart	IN	46516	**800-234-0227**	574-295-3000	592
Chemtron Corp 35850 Schneider Ct	Avon	OH	44011	**800-676-5091**	440-937-6348	656
Chemtronics Inc 8125 Cobb Centre Dr	Kennesaw	GA	30152	**800-645-5244**	770-424-4888	145
Chemung Supply Corp PO Box 527	Elmira	NY	14903	**800-733-5508**	607-733-5506	191-2
Chenoweth Ford Inc 1564 E Pike St *Sales	Clarksburg	WV	26301	**877-289-8348***	800-344-1108	57
CHEP USA 8517 S Pk Cir *Cust Svc	Orlando	FL	32819	**866-855-2437***	407-370-2437	644
Cher-Make Sausage Co 2915 Calumet Ave	Manitowoc	WI	54220	**800-242-7679**		296-26
Cherokee Brick & Tile Co Inc 3250 Waterville Rd	Macon	GA	31206	**800-277-2745**		150
Cherokee Electric Cooperative 1550 Clarence Chestnut Bypass PO Box O	Centre	AL	35960	**800-952-2667**	256-927-5524	245
Cherokee Heritage Ctr & National Museum 21192 S Keeler Dr	Park Hill	OK	74451	**888-999-6007**	918-456-6007	517
Cherokee State Park N 4475 Rd	Langley	OK	74350	**866-602-4653**	918-435-8066	561
Cherokee Steel Supply 196 Leroy Anderson Dr	Monroe	GA	30655	**800-729-0334**	770-207-4621	490
Cherry Brook Zoo Inc 901 Foster Thurston Dr	Saint John	NB	E2K5H9	**800-321-1433**	506-634-1440	818
Cherry Corp 11200 88th Ave	Pleasant Prairie	WI	53158	**800-510-1689**	262-942-6500	810
Cherry Creek State Park 4201 S Parker Rd	Aurora	CO	80014	**866-265-6447**	303-690-1166	561
Cherry Demolition 6131 Selinsky Rd	Houston	TX	77048	**800-444-1123**	713-987-0000	189-16
Cherry Hill Photo Enterprises Inc 4 E Stow Rd	Marlton	NJ	08003	**800-969-2440**	856-663-1616	586
Cherry Systems Inc 2270 Northwest Pkwy Ste 125	Marietta	GA	30067	**800-500-2840**	770-955-2395	620
Cherry's Industrial Equipment 600 Morse Ave	Elk Grove Village	IL	60007	**800-350-0011**	847-364-0200	357
Cherrydale Farms Fundraising 707 N Vly Forge Rd	Lansdale	PA	19446	**877-619-4822**		296-8
Cherryland Electric Co-op 5930 US 31 S PO Box 298	Grawn	MI	49637	**800-442-8616**	231-486-9200	245
Cherryroad Technologies Inc 301 Gibraltar Dr Ste 2C	Morris Plains	NJ	07950	**877-402-7804**	973-402-7802	177
Cherry-Todd Electric Co-op Inc 625 W Second St	Mission	SD	57555	**800-856-4417**	605-856-4416	245
Cheryl & Co 646 McCorkle Blvd	Westerville	OH	43082	**800-443-8124**		68
Chesapeake Bay Magazine 601 Sixth St Ste 180	Annapolis	MD	21403	**877-804-8624**	410-263-2662	455-22
Chesapeake Convention & Visitors Bureau 1224 Progressive Dr	Chesapeake	VA	23320	**888-889-5551**	757-382-6411	206
Chesapeake Lodging Trust (CLT) 1997 Annapolis Exchange Pkwy Ste 410 *NYSE: CHSP*	Annapolis	MD	21401	**800-698-2820**	571-349-9450	650
Chesapeake Regional Medical Ctr 736 Battlefield Blvd N	Chesapeake	VA	23320	**800-456-8121**	757-312-8121	373-3
Cheshire Center Pediatric Comm 2500 N Church St	Greensboro	NC	27405	**800-360-1099**	336-375-2240	7
Cheshire Public Library 104 Main St	Cheshire	CT	06410	**800-275-2273**	203-272-2245	433-3
Chester County 313 W Market St Ste 6202 PO Box 2748	West Chester	PA	19380	**800-692-1100**	610-344-6100	337
Chester County Bar Association, The 15 W Gay St 2nd Fl	West Chester	PA	19380	**800-701-5161**	610-692-1889	529
Chester Fritz Auditorium 3475 University Ave	Grand Forks	ND	58202	**800-375-4068**	701-777-3076	568
Chester Mental Health Ctr 1315 Lehman Dr	Chester	IL	62233	**800-843-6154**	618-826-4571	373-5
Chester Water Authority PO Box 467	Chester	PA	19016	**800-793-2323**	610-876-8185	800
Chester-Jensen Company Inc PO Box 908	Chester	PA	19016	**800-685-3750**	610-876-6276	298
Chestnut Hill College 9601 Germantown Ave	Philadelphia	PA	19118	**800-248-0052**	215-248-7001	166
Chestnut Hill Hotel 8229 Germantown Ave	Philadelphia	PA	19118	**800-628-9744**	215-242-5905	378
Chestnut Mountain Resort 8700 W Chestnut Mountain Rd	Galena	IL	61036	**800-397-1320**		377
Chevron Canada Ltd 1200 - 1050 W Pender St	Vancouver	BC	V6E3T4	**800-663-1650**	604-668-5300	576
Chevron Corp 6001 Bollinger Canyon Rd *NYSE: CVX* ■ *Cust Svc	San Ramon	CA	94583	**800-368-8357***	925-842-1000	532
Chevron Global Marine Products LLC 9401 Williamsburg Plz Ste 201	Louisville	KY	40222	**800-283-9582**	914-285-7390	576
Chevron Phillips Chemical Company LP 10001 Six Pines Dr	The Woodlands	TX	77380	**800-231-1212**	832-813-4100	144
Chevron Phillips Chemical Company Performance Pipe Division 5085 W Pk Blvd Ste 500	Plano	TX	75093	**800-527-0662**	972-599-6600	592
Chevron Pipe Line Co 4800 Fournace Pl	Bellaire	TX	77401	**877-596-2800**		593
Chevron Texaco Credit Card Ctr PO Box P	Concord	CA	94524	**800-243-8766**		215
Cheyenne Area Convention & Visitors Bureau 121 W 15th St Ste 202	Cheyenne	WY	82001	**800-426-5009**	307-778-3133	206
Cheyenne City Hall 2101 O'Neil Ave	Cheyenne	WY	82001	**855-491-1859**	307-637-6200	336
Cheyenne Mountain Conference Resort 3225 Broadmoor Valley Rd	Colorado Springs	CO	80906	**800-428-8886**	719-538-4000	376
Cheyney University of Pennsylvania 1837 University Cir PO Box 200	Cheyney	PA	19319	**800-243-9639**	610-399-2275	166
CHF Industries Inc 1 Park Ave 9th Fl *Cust Svc	New York	NY	10016	**800-243-7090***	212-951-7800	741

	Toll-Free	Phone	Class
Chi Corp 5265 Naiman Pkwy ....Cleveland OH 44139	800-828-0599	440-498-2300	180
CHI Health Good Samaritan 10 E 31st St ....Kearney NE 68847	800-277-4306	308-865-7100	373-3
CHI Solutions Inc 5414 Oberlin Dr Ste 202...........San Diego CA 92121	800-860-5454		
CHI St Alexius Health Bismarck 900 E Broadway Ave ....Bismarck ND 58501	877-530-5550	701-530-7000	373-3
Chicago Boiler Co 1300 Northwestern Ave ....Gurnee IL 60031 *Cust Svc	800-522-7343*	847-662-4000	91
Chicago City Hall 121 N La Salle St ....Chicago IL 60602	800-832-6352	312-744-4958	336
Chicago Display Marketing Corp 2021 W St ....River Grove IL 60171	800-681-4340	708-842-0001	233
Chicago Extruded Metals Co (CXM) 1601 S 54th Ave ....Cicero IL 60804 *Cust Svc	800-323-8102*		483
Chicago Faucets A Geberit Co 2100 S Clearwater Dr ....Des Plaines IL 60018	800-323-5060	847-803-5000	605
Chicago Fire 7000 S Harlem Ave ....Bridgeview IL 60455	888-657-3473	708-594-7200	713
Chicago Gasket Co 1285 W N Ave ....Chicago IL 60642	800-833-5666	773-486-3060	326
Chicago Heights Steel 211 E Main St ....Chicago Heights IL 60411	800-424-4487	708-756-5648	
Chicago Lakeshore Hospital 4840 N Marine Dr ....Chicago IL 60640 *Cust Svc	800-888-0560*	773-878-9700	373-5
Chicago Magazine 435 N Michigan Ave Ste 1100 ....Chicago IL 60611	800-999-0879	312-222-8999	455-22
Chicago Meat Authority Inc (CMA) 1120 W 47th Pl ....Chicago IL 60609	800-383-3811	773-254-3811	296-26
Chicago Metal Fabricators Inc 3724 S Rockwell St ....Chicago IL 60632	877-400-5995	773-523-5755	480
Chicago Metallic Corp 4849 S Austin Ave ....Chicago IL 60638	800-323-7164		
Chicago Nannies Inc 101 N Marion St Ste 300 ....Oak Park IL 60301	866-900-9605	708-524-2101	260
Chicago Nut & Bolt Inc 150 Covington Dr ....Bloomingdale IL 60108	888-529-8600	630-529-8600	349
Chicago Office of Tourism & Culture 78 E Washington St 4th Fl ....Chicago IL 60602	888-871-5311	312-744-2400	206
Chicago Parking Meters LLC 205 N Michigan Ave Ste 1910 ....Chicago IL 60601	877-242-7901		
Chicago Pneumatic Tool Co 1800 Overview Dr ....Rock Hill SC 29730	800-624-4735	803-817-7000	754
Chicago Sky 20 W Kinzie St Ste 1000...........Chicago IL 60610	877-329-9622	312-828-9550	710-2
Chicago Southland CVB 2304 173rd St ....Lansing IL 60438	888-895-8233	708-895-8200	206
Chicago Southshore & South Bend Railroad 505 N Carroll Ave ....Michigan City IN 46360	800-356-2079	219-874-9000	644
Chicago State University 9501 S King Dr ....Chicago IL 60628	800-937-3898	773-995-2513	166
Chicago Steel Container Corp 1846 S Kilbourn Ave ....Chicago IL 60623	800-633-4933		198
Chicago Symphony Orchestra 220 S Michigan Ave ....Chicago IL 60604	800-223-7114	312-294-3000	569-3
Chicago Title & Trust Co 171 N Clark St ....Chicago IL 60601	800-621-1919	312-223-2000	390-6
Chicago Tribune 160 N Stetson Ave ....Chicago IL 60601	800-874-2863	312-222-3232	528-4
Chicago Tube & Iron Co 1 Chicago Tube Dr...........Romeoville IL 60446 *Cust Svc	800-972-0217*	815-834-2500	490
Chicago Wilcox Mfg Co Inc 16928 State St ....South Holland IL 60473	800-323-5282	708-339-5000	326
Chicagoland Speedway 500 Speedway Blvd ....Joliet IL 60433	888-629-7223	815-722-5500	512
Chicago-Read Mental Health Ctr 4200 N Oak Park Ave ....Chicago IL 60634	800-322-7143	773-794-4000	373-5
Chick Master Incubator Co 945 Lafayette Rd ....Medina OH 44256	800-727-8726	330-722-5591	273
Chico News & Review 353 E Second St ....Chico CA 95928	866-703-3873	530-894-2300	528-5
Chico Produce Inc 70 Pepsi Way PO Box 1069 ....Durham CA 95938	888-232-0908	530-893-0596	297-7
Chico's FAS Inc 11215 Metro Pkwy ....Fort Myers FL 33966 *NYSE: CHS*	888-855-4986		157-6
Chicopee Provision Co Inc 19 Sitarz St ....Chicopee MA 01013	800-924-6328	413-594-4765	296-26
Chief Automotive Systems Inc 1924 E Fourth St ....Grand Island NE 68802	800-445-9262	308-384-9747	385
Chief Manufacturing 301 Mcintosh Pkwy ....Thomaston GA 30286	800-722-2061		349
Chignecto-central Regional 60 Lorne St ....Truro NS B2N3K3	800-770-0008		681
Child Development Associates Inc 180 Otay Lakes Rd Ste 310..........Bonita CA 91902	888-755-2445	619-427-4411	148
Child Evangelism Fellowship Inc 17482 Hwy M ....Warrenton MO 63383	800-748-7710	636-456-4321	48-20
Child Find Canada 212-2211 McPhillips St ....Winnipeg MB R2V3M5	800-387-7962	204-339-5584	48-6
Child Lures Prevention 5166 Shelburne Rd ....Shelburne VT 05482	800-552-2197	802-985-8458	48-6
Child Welfare Information Gateway Children's Bureau/ACYF 330 C St SW.................Washington DC 20201	800-394-3366	703-385-7565	339-9
Childcare Network 3009 University Ave ....Columbus GA 31909	866-521-5437	706-819-6297	148
Childhelp USA 4350 E Camelback Rd Bldg F250 ....Phoenix AZ 85018	800-422-4453	480-922-8212	48-6
Children & Adults with Attention-Deficit/Hyperactivity Disorder (CHADD) 4601 Presidents Dr Ste 300 ....Lanham MD 20706	800-233-4050		48-17
Children & Youth Funding Report 8204 Fenton St ....Silver Spring MD 20910	800-666-6380	301-588-6380	527-8
Children Awaiting Parents Inc (CAP) 595 Blossom Rd Ste 306 ....Rochester NY 14610	888-835-8802	585-232-5110	48-6
Children First Home Healthcare Service 4448 Edgewater Dr ....Orlando FL 32804	800-207-0802	407-513-3000	260
Children Inc 4205 Dover Rd ....Richmond VA 23221	800-538-5381	804-359-4562	48-6
Children International 2000 E Red Bridge Rd ....Kansas City MO 64131	800-888-3089	816-942-2000	48-5
Children of the Night 14530 Sylvan St ....Van Nuys CA 91411	800-551-1300	818-908-4474	48-6
Children's Bureau of Southern California 1910 Magnolia Ave ....Los Angeles CA 90004	800-730-3933	213-342-0100	351
Children's Defense Fund (CDF) 25 E St NW ....Washington DC 20001	800-233-1200	202-628-8787	48-6
Children's Healthcare of Atlanta at Egleston 1405 Clifton Rd NE ....Atlanta GA 30322	888-785-7778	404-785-6000	373-1
Children's Healthcare of Atlanta at Scottish Rite 1001 Johnson Ferry Rd NE ....Atlanta GA 30342	888-785-7778	404-785-5252	373-1
Children's Hospital 200 Henry Clay Ave ....New Orleans LA 70118	800-299-9511	504-899-9511	373-1
Children's Hospital Boston 300 Longwood Ave ....Boston MA 02115	800-355-7944	617-355-6000	373-1
Children's Hospital Medical Ctr of Akron 1 Perkins Sq ....Akron OH 44308	800-262-0333	330-543-1000	373-1
Children's Hospital of Alabama 1600 Seventh Ave S ....Birmingham AL 35233	800-504-9768	205-939-9100	373-1
Children's Hospital of Eastern Ontario 401 Smyth Rd ....Ottawa ON K1H8L1	866-797-0007	613-737-7600	373-2
Children's Hospital of Orange County Blood & Donor Services 505 S Main St ....Orange CA 92868	800-228-5234	714-509-8339	764
Children's Hospital of Philadelphia Stem Cell Transplant Program 3401 Civic Ctr Blvd ....Philadelphia PA 19104	800-879-2467		764
Children's Hospital of the King's Daughters 601 Children's Ln ....Norfolk VA 23507	800-395-2453	757-668-7000	373-1
Children's Hospital of Wisconsin 9000 W Wisconsin Ave ....Milwaukee WI 53226	800-266-0366	414-266-2000	373-1
Children's Hospitals & Clinics Minneapolis 2525 Chicago Ave ....Minneapolis MN 55404	866-225-3251	612-813-6000	373-1
Children's Institute of Pittsburgh 1405 Shady Ave ....Pittsburgh PA 15217	877-433-1109	412-420-2400	373-1
Children's Medical Ctr 1 Children's Plz ....Dayton OH 45404	800-228-4055	937-641-3000	373-1
Children's Mercy Hospital & Clinics 2401 Gillham Rd ....Kansas City MO 64108	866-512-2168	816-234-3000	373-1
Children's Museum of Indianapolis 3000 N Meridian St ....Indianapolis IN 46208	800-820-6214	317-334-3322	517
Children's Museum of Oak Ridge 461 W Outer Dr ....Oak Ridge TN 37830	877-524-1223	865-482-1074	518
Children's National Medical Ctr (CNMC) 111 Michigan Ave NW ....Washington DC 20010	800-884-5433	202-476-5000	373-1
Children's Organ Transplant Assn (COTA) 2501 W Cota Dr ....Bloomington IN 47403	800-366-2682	812-336-8872	48-17
Children's Place Retail Stores Inc 500 Plaza Dr ....Secaucus NJ 07094 *NASDAQ: PLCE*	877-752-2387	201-558-2400	157-1
Children's Press 557 Broadway ....New York NY 10012	800-724-6527		633-2
Children's Research Institute Children's National Medical Ctr 111 Michigan Ave NW ....Washington DC 20010	888-884-2327	202-476-5000	664
Children's Specialized Hospital 150 New Providence Rd ....Mountainside NJ 07092	888-244-5373		373-1
Children's Tumor Foundation 120 Wall St 16th Fl...........New York NY 10005	800-323-7938	212-344-6633	48-17
Children's Wish Foundation International 8615 Roswell Rd ....Atlanta GA 30350	800-323-9474	770-393-9474	48-17
Childrens Discovery Museum, The 177 Main St ....Acton MA 01720	800-544-6666	978-264-4200	517
Childrens Plus Inc 1387 Dutch American Way ....Beecher IL 60401	800-230-1279		95
Chillicothe Gazette 50 W Main St ....Chillicothe OH 45601	877-424-0215	740-773-2111	528-2
Chiltern Inn 11 Cromwell Harbor Rd ....Bar Harbor ME 04609	800-709-0114	207-288-3371	378
Chime Master Systems PO Box 936 ....Lancaster OH 43130	800-344-7464		523
Chimney Rock Park 431 Main St ....Chimney Rock NC 28720	800-277-9611		97
Chimney Rock Public Power District 128 Eighth St PO Box 608 ....Bayard NE 69334	877-773-6300	308-586-1824	245
China Ocean Shipping Co Americas Inc (COSCO) 100 Lighting Way ....Secaucus NJ 07094	800-242-7354	201-422-0500	220
China Travel Service Chicago Inc 2145b S China Pl ....Chicago IL 60616	800-793-8856	312-328-0688	770
Chinatrust Bank USA 801 S Figueroa St Ste 2300 ....Los Angeles CA 90017	888-308-0986	310-791-2828	70
Chinese Chamber of Commerce of Hawaii 8 S King St Ste 201 ....Honolulu HI 96813	877-533-2444	808-533-3181	138
Chinese Laundry Shoes 3485 S La Cienega Blvd ....Los Angeles CA 90016	888-935-8825	310-838-2103	301
Chino Hills Ford 4480 Chino Hills Pkwy ....Chino CA 91710	866-261-0153		57
Chino Valley Ranchers 331 W Citrus St ....Colton CA 92324	800-354-4503	626-652-0890	297-10
Chinois on Main 2709 Main St ....Santa Monica CA 90405	888-646-3387	310-432-1500	667
Chinook Winds Casino Resort 1777 NW 44th St ....Lincoln City OR 97367	888-244-6665		450
Chippewa Falls Area Chamber of Commerce 10 S Bridge St ....Chippewa Falls WI 54729	888-723-0024	715-723-0331	139
Chippewa Valley Electric Co-op 317 S Eigth St ....Cornell WI 54732	800-300-6800	715-239-6800	245
Chippewa Valley Technical College 620 W Clairemont Ave ....Eau Claire WI 54701	800-547-2882	715-833-6200	795
Chipton-ross Inc 343 Main St ....El Segundo CA 90245	800-927-9318	310-414-7800	627
Chiricahua National Monument 12856 E Rhyolite Creek Rd ....Willcox AZ 85643	877-444-6777	520-824-3560	560

Alphabetical Section

Name / Address	City	State	ZIP	Toll-Free	Phone	Class
Chiropractic Health Plan of California PO Box 190	Clayton	CA	94517	800-995-2442		390-3
Chisago County 313 N Main St	Center City	MN	55012	888-234-1246	651-257-1300	337
Chisesi Bros Meat Packing Co 5221 Jefferson Hwy	New Orleans	LA	70123	800-966-3550	504-822-3550	471
Chisholm Fleming & Assoc 317 Renfrew Dr Ste 301	Markham	ON	L3R9S8	888-241-4149	905-474-1458	256
Chocolates a la Carte 24836 Ave Rockefeller *Cust Svc	Valencia	CA	91355	800-818-2462*		296-8
Choctaw Casino Resorts 3735 Choctaw Rd	Durant	OK	74701	888-652-4628	580-920-0160	450
Choctaw Management Services Enterprise 2101 W Arkansas St	Durant	OK	74701	866-326-1000		260
Choctawhatchee Electric Co-op Inc 1350 W Baldwin Ave	DeFuniak Springs	FL	32435	800-342-0990	850-892-2111	245
Choi Bros Inc 3401 W Div St	Chicago	IL	60651	800-524-2464	773-489-2800	155-1
Choice Books LLC 2387 Grace Chapel Rd	Harrisonburg	VA	22801	800-827-1894	540-434-1827	96
Choice Hotels International Inc 1 Choice Hotels Cir Ste 400 *NYSE: CHH*	Rockville	MD	20850	800-424-6423	301-592-5000	378
CHOMP (Community Hospital of the Monterey Peninsula) 23625 Holman Hwy	Monterey	CA	93940	888-452-4667	831-624-5311	373-3
Chop House Ann Arbor, The 322 S Main St	Ann Arbor	MI	48104	888-456-3463		
Chopra Ctr at La Costa Resort & Spa 2013 Costa del Mar Rd	Carlsbad	CA	92009	888-424-6772	760-494-1600	669
Choptank Electric Co-op Inc 24820 Meeting House Rd PO Box 430	Denton	MD	21629	877-892-0001		245
Choristers Guild 2834 W Kingsley Rd	Garland	TX	75041	800-246-7478	469-398-3606	48-4
Chowan University 1 University Pl *Admissions	Murfreesboro	NC	27855	888-424-6926*	252-398-6439	166
CHP International Inc 1040 N Blvd Ste 220	Oak Park	IL	60301	800-449-2614	708-848-9650	196
Chris Alston Chassisworks Inc 8661 Younger Creek Dr	Sacramento	CA	95828	800-722-2269	916-388-0288	54
Chrisad Inc 11 Professional Ctr Pkwy	San Rafael	CA	94903	800-505-4150	415-924-8575	7
Christ School 500 Christ School Rd	Arden	NC	28704	800-422-3212	828-684-6232	618
Christel DeHaan Fine Arts Ctr 1400 E Hanna Ave University of Indianapolis	Indianapolis	IN	46227	800-232-8634	317-788-3566	568
Christendom College 134 Christendom Dr	Front Royal	VA	22630	800-877-5456	540-636-2900	166
Christian & Missionary Alliance 8595 Explorer Dr	Colorado Springs	CO	80920	800-700-2651	719-599-5999	48-20
Christian Appalachian Project 485 Ponderosa Dr PO Box 1768	Paintsville	KY	41240	800-755-5322		48-5
Christian Broadcasting Network (CBN) 977 Centerville Tpke	Virginia Beach	VA	23463	800-823-6053		735
Christian Bros University 650 E Pkwy S *Admissions	Memphis	TN	38104	800-288-7576*	901-321-3000	166
Christian Business Men's Connection (CBMC) 5746 Marlin Rd Ste 602 Osborne Ctr	Chattanooga	TN	37411	800-566-2262	423-698-4444	48-20
Christian Church (Disciples of Christ) 130 E Washington St	Indianapolis	IN	46204	800-668-8016	317-635-3100	48-20
Christian Foundation for Children & Aging (CFCA) 1 Elmwood Ave	Kansas City	KS	66103	800-875-6564	913-384-6500	48-6
Christian Horizons 200 N Postville Dr	Lincoln	IL	62656	800-535-8717	217-732-9651	362
Christian Leadership Alliance (CLA) 635 Camino De Los Mares Ste 216	San Clemente	CA	92673	800-263-6317	949-487-0900	49-12
Christian Legal Society (CLS) 8001 Braddock Rd Ste 300	Springfield	VA	22151	800-225-4008	703-642-1070	49-10
Christian Medical & Dental Assn (CMDA) 2604 Hwy 421 PO Box 7500	Bristol	TN	37620	888-231-2637	423-844-1000	49-8
Christian Reformed Church in North America (CRC) 2850 Kalamazoo Ave SE	Grand Rapids	MI	49560	800-272-5125	616-241-1691	48-20
Christian Reformed World Relief Committee (CRWRC) 2850 Kalamazoo Ave SE	Grand Rapids	MI	49560	800-552-7972	616-241-1691	48-5
Christian Schools International (CSI) 3350 E Paris Ave SE	Grand Rapids	MI	49512	800-635-8288	616-957-1070	49-5
Christian Science Publishing Society 210 Massachusetts Ave P02-15	Boston	MA	02115	800-456-2220	617-450-2300	633-8
Christian Television Network Inc (CTN) 6922 142nd Ave N	Largo	FL	33771	800-716-7729	727-535-5622	733
Christiana Care Health System 501 W 14th St	Wilmington	DE	19801	855-250-9594	302-366-1929	352
Christianity Today 465 Gundersen Dr *Cust Svc	Carol Stream	IL	60188	800-222-1840*	630-260-6200	455-11
Christianity Today International 465 Gundersen Dr	Carol Stream	IL	60188	800-222-1840	630-260-6200	633-9
Christianity Today Magazine 465 Gundersen Dr	Carol Stream	IL	60188	800-999-1704	630-260-6200	455-18
Christianson Systems Inc 20421 15th St SE PO Box 138	Blomkest	MN	56216	800-328-8896	320-995-6141	207
Christie Cookie Co 1205 Third Ave N	Nashville	TN	37208	800-458-2447	615-242-3817	296-9
Christie Lodge PO Box 1196	Avon	CO	81620	888-325-6343	970-845-4504	377
Christman Co, The 2400 Sutherland Ave	Knoxville	TN	37919	800-583-0148	865-546-2440	186
Christopher Enterprises 155 W 2050 N	Spanish Fork	UT	84660	800-453-1406		354
Christopher Guy 8900 Beverly Blvd	West Hollywood	CA	90048	800-476-9505	323-509-4034	

Name / Address	City	State	ZIP	Toll-Free	Phone	Class
Christopher Newport University 1 University Pl *Admissions	Newport News	VA	23606	800-333-4268*	757-594-7015	166
Christopher Ranch 305 Bloomfield Ave	Gilroy	CA	95020	800-779-1156	408-847-1100	10-9
Christopher Reeve Foundation 636 Morris Tpke Ste 3A	Short Hills	NJ	07078	800-225-0292	973-379-2690	48-17
Christophers, The 5 Hanover Sq	New York	NY	10004	888-298-4050	212-759-4050	48-20
CHRISTUS Shreveport-Bossier Health System 1453 E Bert Kouns	Shreveport	LA	71105	888-681-4138	318-681-4500	373-3
CHRISTUS Southeast Texas Health System 2830 Calder St	Beaumont	TX	77702	866-683-3627	409-892-7171	373-3
CHRISTUS Southeast Texas Health System 3600 Gates Blvd PO Box 3696	Port Arthur	TX	77642	866-683-3627	409-985-7431	373-3
Chrom Tech Inc PO Box 240248	Apple Valley	MN	55124	800-822-5242	952-431-6000	418
ChromaGen Vision LLC 326 W Cedar St Ste 1	Kennett Square	PA	19348	855-473-2323		540
Chromaline Corp 4832 Grand Ave	Duluth	MN	55807	800-328-4261	218-628-2217	624
Chromium Corp 14911 Quorum Dr Ste 600	Dallas	TX	75254	888-346-4747	216-271-4910	262
Chronicle Books 680 Second St	San Francisco	CA	94107	800-722-6657	415-537-4200	633-2
Chronicle Herald, The PO Box 610	Halifax	NS	B3J2T2	800-563-1187	902-426-2811	528-1
Chronicle of Higher Education, The 1255 23rd St NW Ste 700	Washington	DC	20037	800-728-2803	202-466-1000	455-8
Chrysalis Inn & Spa 804 Tenth St	Bellingham	WA	98225	888-808-0005	360-756-1005	378
Chrysler Aviation Inc (CAI) 7120 Hayvenhurst Ave Ste 309	Van Nuys	CA	91406	800-995-0825	818-989-7900	13
Chrysler Group LLC 1000 Chrysler Dr *Cust Svc	Auburn Hills	MI	48326	800-423-6343*		59
CHS Inc 5500 Cenex Dr *NASDAQ: CHSCP*	Inver Grove Heights	MN	55077	800-232-3639	651-355-6000	276
CHSI (Comprehensive Health Services Inc) 10701 Parkridge Blvd Ste 200	Reston	VA	20191	800-638-8083	703-760-0700	390-3
CHU Sainte-Justine 3175 Ch de la Cote-Sainte-Catherine	Montreal	QC	H3T1C5	888-235-3667	514-345-4931	373-2
Chubb & Son 15 Mountain View Rd	Warren	NJ	07059	800-252-4670	908-903-2000	390-4
Chubb Specialty Insurance 82 Hopmeadow St	Simsbury	CT	06070	800-252-4670	860-408-2000	390-5
Chugach Electric Assn Inc 5601 Electron Dr	Anchorage	AK	99518	800-478-7494	907-563-7494	245
Chugach State Park 18620 Seward Hwy	Anchorage	AK	99516	800-478-6196	907-345-5014	561
Chukchansi Gold Resort & Casino 711 Lucky Ln	Coarsegold	CA	93614	866-794-6946		377
Chula Vista Resort 2501 River Rd	Wisconsin Dells	WI	53965	800-388-4782	608-254-8366	665
Chumash Casino Resort 3400 E Hwy 246	Santa Ynez	CA	93460	800-248-6274	805-686-0855	450
Chumney & Associates 660 US-1 2nd Fl	North Palm Beach	FL	33408	877-816-7347	561-768-5818	
Church & Chapel Metal Arts Inc 2616 W Grand Ave	Chicago	IL	60612	800-992-1234		508
Church & Dwight Company Inc 469 N Harrison St *NYSE: CHD*	Princeton	NJ	08543	800-617-4220		214
Church Mutual Insurance Co 3000 Schuster Ln	Merrill	WI	54452	800-554-2642	715-536-5577	390-4
Church of God in Christ Inc 930 Mason St	Memphis	TN	38126	877-746-8578	901-947-9300	48-20
Church of God Ministries 1201 E Fifth St	Anderson	IN	46012	800-848-2464	765-642-0256	48-20
Church of God World Missions (COGWM) 2490 Keith St	Cleveland	TN	37311	800-345-7492		48-20
Church of Jesus Christ of Latter-Day Saints 50 E N Temple St	Salt Lake City	UT	84150	800-453-3860	801-240-1000	48-20
Church of the Brethren 1451 Dundee Ave	Elgin	IL	60120	800-323-8039	847-742-5100	48-20
Church Women United (CWU) 475 Riverside Dr Ste 243	New York	NY	10115	800-298-5551	212-870-2347	48-20
Church World Service 28606 Phillips St PO Box 968	Elkhart	IN	46515	800-297-1516	574-264-3102	48-5
Church World Service Emergency Response Program 475 Riverside Dr Ste 700	New York	NY	10115	888-297-2767	212-870-2061	48-5
Churchill Cabinet Co 4616 W 19th St *Sales	Cicero	IL	60804	800-379-9776*	708-780-0070	286
Churchill Corporate Services 56 Utter Ave	Hawthorne	NJ	07506	800-941-7458	973-636-9400	210
Churchill Downs Inc 600 N Hurstbourne Pkwy Ste 400 *NASDAQ: CHDN*	Louisville	KY	40222	800-283-3729	502-636-4400	638
Churchill Hotel 1914 Connecticut Ave NW	Washington	DC	20009	800-424-2464	202-797-2000	378
Churchill Nature Tours PO Box 429	Erickson	MB	R0J0P0	877-636-2968	204-636-2968	755
Churchwell Co 814 S Edgewood Ave	Jacksonville	FL	32205	877-537-6166	904-356-5721	9
CI (Conservation International) 2011 Crystal Dr Ste 500	Arlington	VA	22202	800-406-2306	703-341-2400	48-13
CI Financial Corp 20 Second Queen St E	Toronto	ON	M5C3G5	800-268-9374	416-585-5420	782
Ci Radar LLC 40 Technology Pkwy S Ste 150	Peachtree Corners	GA	30092	888-421-0617	678-680-2103	392
Cianbro Corp 101 Cianbro Sq	Pittsfield	ME	04967	866-242-6276	207-487-3311	188-4

	Toll-Free	Phone	Class
CIBC (Canadian Imperial Bank of Commerce)			
199 Bay St Commerce Ct W .... Toronto ON M5L1A2	800-465-2422		70
NYSE: CM			
CIBC Wood Gundy Capital			
425 Lexington Ave .... New York NY 10017	800-999-6726	212-856-4000	787
CIBER Inc			
6363 S Fiddler's Green Cir			
Ste 1400 .... Greenwood Village CO 80111	800-242-3799	303-220-0100	180
NYSE: CBR			
CICA-TV Ch 19 (Ind)			
2180 Yonge St Stn Q PO Box 200 .... Toronto ON M4T2T1	800-613-0513	416-484-2600	736-80
Cicero Inc			
8000 Regency Pkwy Ste 542 .... Cary NC 27518	866-538-3588	919-380-5000	178-1
CID Bio-Science Inc			
4845 NW Camas Meadows Dr .... Camas WA 98607	800-767-0119	360-833-8835	635
CID Performance Tooling Inc			
6 Willey Rd .... Saco ME 04072	800-964-2331		693
CiDRA Corp			
50 Barnes Pk N .... Wallingford CT 06492	877-243-7277	203-265-0035	730
CIEE (Council on International Educational Exchange)			
300 Fore St .... Portland ME 04101	888-268-6245*	207-553-4000	49-5
*Cust Svc			
CIENA Corp			
7035 Ridge Rd .... Hanover MD 21076	800-207-3714	410-694-5700	
Cigarcom Inc			
1911 Spillman Dr .... Bethlehem PA 18015	800-357-9800		751
CIGNA			
900 Cottage Grove Rd .... Hartford CT 06002	800-244-6224	860-226-6000	390-2
CIGNA Behavioral Health Inc			
11095 Viking Dr Ste 350 .... Eden Prairie MN 55344	800-753-0540	800-433-5768	460
CIGNA Foundation			
900 Cottage Grove Rd .... Bloomfield CT 06002	866-438-2446		304
NYSE: CI			
CIGNA Healthcare of North Carolina Inc			
701 Corporate Ctr Dr .... Raleigh NC 27607	800-942-1654	888-521-5869	390-3
Cimarron Electric Co-op			
PO Box 299 .... Kingfisher OK 73750	800-375-4121	405-375-4121	245
CIMCO Refrigeration			
65 Villiers St .... Toronto ON M5A3S1	800-267-1418	416-465-7581	660
Cimmaron Field Services Inc			
303 W Wall St Rank of America Tower			
Ste 600 .... Midland TX 79701	877 944-2705		532
CIMplify			
720 Cool Springs Blvd Ste 500 .... Franklin TN 37067	888-232-7026	615-261-6700	194
Cincinnati Art Museum			
953 Eden Pk Dr .... Cincinnati OH 45202	877-472-4226	513-721-2787	517
Cincinnati Bell Directory (CBD)			
312 Plum St Ste 600 .... Cincinnati OH 45202	800-877-0475		633-6
Cincinnati Bengals			
1 Paul Brown Stadium .... Cincinnati OH 45202	866-621-8383	513-621-3550	711-2
Cincinnati Children's Hospital Medical Ctr			
3333 Burnet Ave .... Cincinnati OH 45229	800-344-2462	513-636-4200	373-1
Cincinnati Christian University			
2700 Glenway Ave .... Cincinnati OH 45204	800-949-4228	513-244-8100	161
Cincinnati College of Mortuary Science			
645 W N Bend Rd .... Cincinnati OH 45224	888-377-8433	513-761-2020	795
Cincinnati Enquirer			
312 Elm St .... Cincinnati OH 45202	800-876-4500	513-721-2700	528-2
Cincinnati Financial Corp			
6200 S Gilmore Rd .... Fairfield OH 45014	800-364-3400	513-870-2000	359-4
NASDAQ: CINF			
Cincinnati Floor Company Inc			
5162 Broerman Ave .... Cincinnati OH 45217	800-886-4501	513-641-4500	189-2
Cincinnati History Museum			
1301 Western Ave			
Cincinnati Museum Ctr. .... Cincinnati OH 45203	800-733-2077	513-287-7000	517
Cincinnati Playhouse in the Park			
962 Mt Adams Cir .... Cincinnati OH 45202	800-582-3208	513-345-2242	568
Cincinnati Preserving Company Inc			
3015 E Kemper Rd .... Sharonville OH 45241	800-222-9966*		296-20
*Cust Svc			
Cincinnati Reds			
100 Joe Nuxhall Way .... Cincinnati OH 45202	877-647-7337	513-381-7337	709
Cincinnati State Technical & Community College			
3520 Central Pkwy .... Cincinnati OH 45223	877-569-0115	513-569-1500	162
Cincinnati Zoo & Botanical Garden			
3400 Vine St .... Cincinnati OH 45220	800-944-4776	513-281-4700	818
Cincinnatian Hotel			
601 Vine St .... Cincinnati OH 45202	800-942-9000	513-381-3000	378
Cincinnati-Northern Kentucky International Airport			
PO Box 752000 .... Cincinnati OH 45275	800-990-8841	859-767-3151	27
Cincom Systems Inc			
55 Merchant St .... Cincinnati OH 45246	800-224-6266	513-612-2300	178-1
Cindus Corp			
515 Stn Ave .... Cincinnati OH 45215	800-543-4691		550
Cine Magnetics Inc (CMI)			
9 W Broad St .... Stamford CT 06902	800-431-1102	203-989-9955	654
Cinemark USA Inc			
3900 Dallas Pkwy Ste 500 .... Plano TX 75093	800-246-3627	972-665-1000	743
Cineplex Entertainment LP			
1303 Yonge St .... Toronto ON M4T2Y9	800-333-0061	416-323-6600	743
Cinergy Children's Museum			
1301 Western Ave			
Cincinnati Museum Ctr. .... Cincinnati OH 45203	800-733-2077	513-287-7000	518
Cinmar LLC			
5566 W Chester Rd .... West Chester OH 45069	888-263-9850		457
Cintas Corp			
PO Box 625737 .... Cincinnati OH 45262	800-786-4367	513-573-4155	441
NASDAQ: CTAS			
Cintrex Audio Visual			
656 Axminister Dr .... Fenton MO 63026	800-325-9541	636-343-0178	511
Cipher Systems LLC			
185 Admiral Cochrane Dr			
Ste 210 .... Annapolis MD 21401	888-899-1523	410-412-3326	194
CIPS (Canadian Information Processing Society)			
5090 Explorer Dr Ste 801 ...... Mississauga ON L4W4T9	877-275-2477	905-602-1370	48-1
CIR (Center for Individual Rights)			
1100 Connecticut Ave NW			
Ste 625 .... Washington DC 20036	877-426-2665	202-833-8400	48-8

	Toll-Free	Phone	Class
CIR Law Offices International LLP			
2650 Camino Del Rio N Ste 308 ..... San Diego CA 92108	800-496-8909	858-496-8909	41
Circa Enterprises Inc			
535 - 10333 Southport Rd SW .... Calgary AB T2W3X6	877-257-4588	403-258-2011	
Circadian Technologies Inc			
2 Main St Ste 310. .... Stoneham MA 02180	800-284-5001	781-439-6300	194
Circle Bolt & Nut Company Inc			
158 Pringle St .... Kingston PA 18704	800-548-2658	570-718-6001	349
Circle City Bar & Grille			
350 W Maryland St .... Indianapolis IN 46225	877-640-7666	317-405-6100	667
Circle Graphics LLC			
120 Ninth Ave .... Longmont CO 80501	800-367-2472	303-532-2370	623
Circle J Trailers			
312 W Simplot Blvd .... Caldwell ID 83065	800-247-2535	208-459-0842	774
Circle Media Inc			
5817 Old Leeds Rd .... Irondale AL 35210	800-356-9916		528-3
Circle Seal Controls Inc			
2301 Wardlow Cir .... Corona CA 92880	800-991-2726	951-270-6200	784
Circle Z Ranch			
PO Box 194 .... Patagonia AZ 85624	888-854-2525	520-394-2525	239
Circleville City School District			
388 Clark Dr .... Circleville OH 43113	800-418-6423	740-474-4340	681
Circor Aerospace Inc			
2301 Wardlow Cir .... Corona CA 92880	800-344-8724	951-270-6200	349
Circuit Express Inc			
229 S Clark Dr .... Tempe AZ 85281	800-979-4722		621
Circus Circus Hotel & Casino Reno			
500 N Sierra St .... Reno NV 89503	800-648-5010	775-329-0711	133
Circus Circus Hotel Casino & Theme Park Las Vegas			
2880 Las Vegas Blvd S .... Las Vegas NV 89109	800-634-3450*	702-734-0410	133
*Resv			
Circus World Museum			
550 Water St .... Baraboo WI 53913	866-693-1500	608-356-8341	517
Cirque Corp			
2463 South 3850 West .... Salt Lake City UT 84120	800-454-3375	801-467-1100	173-1
Cirrascale Corp			
12140 Community Rd .... Poway CA 92064	888-942-3800	858-874-3800	173-8
Cirro Energy			
2745 Dallas Pkwy Ste 200 .... Plano TX 75093	800-692-4776		461
Cirrus Design Corp			
4515 Taylor Cir .... Duluth MN 55811	800-279-4322	218-727-2737	
Cirrus Logic Inc			
2901 Via Fortuna .... Austin TX 78746	800-888-5016	512-851-4000	692
NASDAQ: CRUS			
Cirrus9 Inc			
15 Market Sq .... Saint John NB E2L1E8	855-643-6691		224
CIS (Citadel Information Services Inc)			
33 Wood Ave S Ste 720 .... Iselin NJ 08830	888-862-4823	732-238-0072	
CIS Group			
55 Castonguay St Ste 301 .... St-jerome QC J7Y2H9	888-432-1550	450-432-1550	
CISCA (Ceilings & Interior Systems Construction Assn)			
1010 Jorie Blvd Ste 30 .... Oak Brook IL 60523	866-560-8537	630-584-1919	49-3
Cisco			
3333 Susan St .... Costa Mesa CA 92626	866-398-8749	714-662-5600	730
Cisco Air Systems Inc			
214 27th St .... Sacramento CA 95816	800-813-6763	916-444-2525	357
CISCO Inc			
1702 Townhurst .... Houston TX 77043	800-231-3686	713-461-9407	
Cisco Systems Inc			
170 W Tasman Dr .... San Jose CA 95134	800-553-6387	408-526-4000	176
NASDAQ: CSCO			
Cisco-Eagle			
2120 Valley View Ln .... Dallas TX 75234	888-877-3861	972-406-9330	384
Cision US Inc			
130 E Randolph St 7th Fl .... Chicago IL 60601	800-588-3827	312-922-2400	633-6
Cistera Networks Inc			
5045 Lorimar Dr Ste 180 .... Plano TX 75024	866-965-8646	972-381-4699	
Citadel Information Services Inc (CIS)			
33 Wood Ave S Ste 720 .... Iselin NJ 08830	888-862-4823	732-238-0072	
Citadel, The			
171 Moultrie St .... Charleston SC 29409	800-868-1842	843-953-5230	166
Citation Communications Inc			
1855 Indian Rd Ste 207 .... West Palm Beach FL 33409	800-286-5109	561-688-0330	386
Citibank NA			
399 Park Ave .... New York NY 10022	800-627-3999		70
Cities of Gold Casino			
10-B Cities of Gold Rd .... Santa Fe NM 87506	800-455-3313	505-455-4232	133
CitiMortgage Inc			
1000 Technology Dr .... O'Fallon MO 63368	800-283-7918*		507
*Cust Svc			
CitiusTech Inc			
2 Research Way .... Princeton NJ 08540	877-248-4871		225
Citizant Inc			
15000 Conference Center Dr			
Ste 500 .... Chantilly VA 20151	877-248-4926	703-667-9420	177
Citizen Auto Stage Co			
3594 E Lincoln St .... Tucson AZ 85714	800-276-1528	520-622-8811	107
Citizen National Bank Of Bluffton, The			
102 S Main St PO Box 88 .... Bluffton OH 45817	800-262-4663	419-358-8040	70
Citizen Systems America Corp			
363 Van Ness Way Ste 404 .... Torrance CA 90501	800-421-6516	310-781-1460	173-6
Citizen Tribune			
1609 W First N St PO Box 625 ...... Morristown TN 37815	800-624-0281	423-581-5630	528-2
Citizen Watch Co of America Inc			
1000 W 190th St .... Torrance CA 90502	800-321-1023	310-532-8463	153
Citizens Bank of Clovis			
420 Wheeler .... Texico NM 88135	844-657-3553	575-482-3381	70
Citizens Bank of Massachusetts			
28 State St .... Boston MA 02109	800-610-7300		70
Citizens Bank of Mukwonago			
301 N Rochester St PO Box 223 ..... Mukwonago WI 53149	877-546-5868	262-363-6500	70
Citizens Bank of Rhode Island			
1 Citizens Plz .... Providence RI 02903	800-922-9999*	401-456-7000	70
*Cust Svc			
Citizens Business Bank (CBB)			
701 N Haven Ave .... Ontario CA 91764	888-222-5432*	909-980-4030	70
*Cust Svc			
Citizens Committee for the Right to Keep & Bear Arms (CCRKBA)			
Liberty Park 12500 NE Tenth Pl ..... Bellevue WA 98005	800-486-6963	425-454-4911	48-7

					Toll-Free	Phone	Class
Citizens Equity First Credit Union	5401 W Dirksen Pkwy; *Cust Svc	Peoria	IL	61607	800-633-7077*	309-633-7000	219
Citizens Financial Corp	12910 Shelbyville Rd Ste 300; *OTC: CFIN*	Louisville	KY	40243	800-843-7752	502-244-2420	359-4
Citizens Financial Group Inc	1 Citizens Dr	Riverside	RI	02915	800-922-9999	401-456-7000	359-2
Citizens Financial Services	707 Ridge Rd	Munster	IN	46321	800-205-3464	219-836-5500	70
Citizens Gas & Coke Utility	2020 N Meridian St	Indianapolis	IN	46202	800-427-4217	317-924-3311	782
Citizens Gas Fuel Co	127 North Main St	Adrian	MI	49221	800-482-7171	517-265-2144	532
Citizens Insurance Company of America	400 E Anderson Ln	Austin	TX	78752	800-880-5044	512-837-7100	390-2
Citizens Security Life Insurance Co	12910 Shelbyville Rd Ste 300	Louisville	KY	40243	800-843-7752	502-244-2420	390-2
Citizens State Bank & Trust Co	203 N Douglas PO Box 518	Ellsworth	KS	67439	800-472-3145	785-472-3141	
Citizens Telephone Co-op	PO Box 137	Floyd	VA	24091	800-941-0426	540-745-2111	731
Citizens Trust Bank	1700 Third Ave N	Birmingham	AL	35203	888-214-3099	205-328-2041	70
Citizens' Electric Co	1775 Industrial Blvd PO Box 551	Lewisburg	PA	17837	877-487-9384	570-524-2231	245
Citrix Systems Inc	851 W Cypress Creek Rd; *NASDAQ: CTXS*	Fort Lauderdale	FL	33309	800-393-1888	954-267-3000	178-12
Citrus County Chamber of Commerce	28 NW US Hwy 19	Crystal River	FL	34428	800-665-6701	352-795-3149	139
Citrus Memorial Hospital	502 W Highland Blvd	Inverness	FL	34452	800-437-2672	352-726-1551	373-3
Citterio USA Corp	2008 SR- 940	Freeland	PA	18224	800-435-8888	570-636-3171	296-26
City	33 Dundas St E	Toronto	ON	M5B1B8	888-336-9978	416-764-3003	736-80
City Auto Glass Inc	116 S Concord Exchange	South Saint Paul	MN	55075	888-552-4272	651-552-1000	62-2
City College of San Francisco	50 Phelan Ave	San Francisco	CA	94112	800-433-3243	415-239-3000	162
City Colleges of Chicago	226 W Jackson	Chicago	IL	60606	866-908-7582	312-553-2500	162
City Escape Holidays	13470 Washington Blvd Ste 101	Marina del Rey	CA	90292	800-222-0022		766
City Furniture Inc	6701 N Hiatus Rd	Tamarac	FL	33321	866-930-4233	954-597-2200	321
City Holding Co	25 Gatewater Rd; *NASDAQ: CHCO*	Charleston	WV	25313	800-528-2273	304-769-1100	359-2
City National Bank	400 N Roxbury Dr; *Cust Svc	Beverly Hills	CA	90210	800-773-7100*	310-888-6000	70
City National Bank of Florida	450 E Las Olas Blvd	Fort Lauderdale	FL	33301	800-762-2489	954-467-6667	70
City National Bank of New Jersey (CNB)	900 Broad St	Newark	NJ	07102	877-350-3524	973-624-0865	70
City National Bank of West Virginia	3601 McCorckle Ave	Charleston	WV	25304	888-816-8064	304-926-3324	70
City of Chula Vista	276 Fourth Ave	Chula Vista	CA	91910	877-478-5478	619-691-5047	52
City of Clarksville	199 Tenth St	Clarksville	TN	37040	800-342-1003	931-645-7464	256
City of Com, The	1559 S Brownlee Blvd	Corpus Christi	TX	78404	888-785-0500		7
City of Henderson	*Henderson Convention Ctr* 200 S Water St	Henderson	NV	89015	877-775-5252	702-267-2171	205
City of Hope National Medical Ctr Hematology & Hematopoietic Cell Transplantation Div	1500 E Duarte Rd	Duarte	CA	91010	800-826-4673	626-256-4673	764
City of Palm Springs	300 S Sunrise Way	Palm Springs	CA	92262	800-611-1911	760-322-7323	433-3
City of Pendleton	500 SW Dorion Ave	Pendleton	OR	97801	800-238-5355	541-966-0201	205
City of Portland, Oregon	1221 SW Fourth Ave Rm 110	Portland	OR	97204	800-729-8807	503-823-4000	336
City Of Salem	101 S Broadway	Salem	IL	62881	800-755-5000	618-548-2222	206
City of Vacaville Inc, The	650 Merchant St	Vacaville	CA	95688	800-759-7159	707-449-5100	256
City of Wetaskiwin Recreation	4705-50 Ave	Wetaskiwin	AB	T9A2E9	800-419-2913	780-361-4446	702
City Pipe & Supply Corp	PO Box 2112	Odessa	TX	79760	844-307-4044	432-332-1541	490
City Plumbing & Electric Supply Co	730 EE Butler Pkwy	Gainesville	GA	30501	800-260-2024	770-532-4123	608
City Public Service Board	PO Box 1771	San Antonio	TX	78296	800-870-1006	210-353-2222	782
City Supply Corp	2326 Bell Ave	Des Moines	IA	50321	800-400-2377	515-288-3211	608
City University	521 Wall St Ste100; *Admissions	Seattle	WA	98121	800-426-5596*	888-422-4898	166
City University of New York (CUNY)	535 E 80th St	New York	NY	10075	800-286-9937	212-997-2869	781
Cityfeetcom Inc	101 California St 43rd Fl	San Francisco	CA	94111	866-527-0540	212-924-6450	
Cityfone	PO Box 19372	Burnaby	BC	V5H4J8	888-499-7566		
Civacon	4304 N Mattox Rd; *Sales	Kansas City	MO	64150	888-526-5657*	816-741-6600	785
CIVCO Medical Solutions	102 First St	Kalona	IA	52247	877-329-2482	319-248-6757	381
Civil & Environmental Consultants Inc	333 Baldwin Rd	Pittsburgh	PA	15205	800-365-2324	412-429-2324	261
Civil Engineering Magazine	1801 Alexander Bell Dr	Reston	VA	20191	800-548-2723	703-295-6300	455-21
Civil Service Employees Insurance Co	2121 N California Blvd Ste 900	Walnut Creek	CA	94596	800-282-6848		390-4
Civista Bank	100 E Water St	Sandusky	OH	44870	888-645-4121	419-625-4121	69
Civitan International	PO Box 130744	Birmingham	AL	35213	800-248-4826	205-591-8910	48-15
CJK	3962 Virginia Ave	Cincinnati	OH	45227	800-598-7808	513-271-6035	622
CJM (Carlyle Johnson Machine Co)	291 Boston Tpke	Bolton	CT	06043	888-629-4867	860-643-1531	616
CJT Koolcarb Inc	494 Mission St	Carol Stream	IL	60188	800-323-2299	630-690-5933	491
CJW Medical Ctr	7101 Jahnke Rd	Richmond	VA	23225	800-468-6620	804-320-3911	373-3
CK Worldwide Inc	3501 C St NE	Auburn	WA	98002	800-426-0877	253-854-5820	806
CKC (Canadian Kennel Club)	200 Ronson Dr Ste 400	Etobicoke	ON	M9W5Z9	800-250-8040	416-675-5511	48-3
CKHS (Crozer-Keystone Health System)	190 W Sproul Rd	Springfield	PA	19064	800-254-3258	610-328-8700	352
CLA (Christian Leadership Alliance)	635 Camino De Los Mares Ste 216	San Clemente	CA	92673	800-263-6317	949-487-0900	49-12
CLA (Coin Laundry Assn)	1s660 Midwest Rd Ste 205	Oakbrook Terrace	IL	60181	800-570-5629	630-953-7920	49-4
Claflin University	400 Magnolia St	Orangeburg	SC	29115	800-922-1276	803-535-5000	166
Claims Verification Inc	6700 N Andrews Ave Ste 200	Ft. Lauderdale	FL	33309	888-284-2000		399
Claimsnetcom Inc	14860 Montfort Dr Ste 250	Dallas	TX	75254	800-356-1511	972-458-1701	225
Claire Manufacturing Co	1005 S Westgate Ave; *Sales	Addison	IL	60101	800-252-4731*	630-543-7600	145
Claire's Accessories	3 SW 129th Ave	Pembroke Pines	FL	33027	800-252-4737	954-433-3000	157-6
Claitor's Law Books & Publishing Di	PO Box 261333	Baton Rouge	LA	70826	800-274-1403	225-344-0476	622
Clallam County	223 E Fourth St	Port Angeles	WA	98362	800-424-5555	360-417-2318	337
Clamp Swing Pricing Company Inc	8386 Capwell Dr	Oakland	CA	94621	800-227-7615	510-567-1600	412
Clamshell Structures Inc	1101 Maulhardt Ave	Oxnard	CA	93030	800-360-8853	805-988-1340	728
Clara Maass Medical Ctr	1 Clara Maass Dr	Belleville	NJ	07109	800-300-0628	973-450-2000	373-3
Clare Inc	78 Cherry Hill Dr	Beverly	MA	01915	800-272-5273	978-524-6700	692
Claremont Companies Inc	1 Lakeshore Ctr	Bridgewater	MA	02324	800-848-9077	508-279-4300	524
Claremont Resort & Spa	41 Tunnel Rd	Berkeley	CA	94705	800-551-7266	510-843-3000	665
Claremont Sales Corp	35 Winsome Dr PO Box 430	Durham	CT	06422	800-222-4448	860-349-4499	388
Clarendon College	1122 College Dr PO Box 968	Clarendon	TX	79226	800-687-9737	806-874-3571	162
Claret Canada Inc	1400 Rue Joliot-curie	Boucherville	QC	J4B7L9	800-567-7442	450-449-5774	752
Claridge Products & Equipment Inc	601 Hwy 62 65 PO Box 910	Harrison	AR	72602	800-434-4610	870-743-2200	243
Clarion Corp of America	6200 Gateway Dr	Cypress	CA	90630	800-347-8667	310-327-9100	52
Clarion Hospital (CH)	1 Hospital Dr	Clarion	PA	16214	800-522-0505	814-226-9500	373-3
Clarion University of Pennsylvania	840 Wood St	Clarion	PA	16214	800-672-7171	814-393-2306	166
	Venango 1801 W First St	Oil City	PA	16301	800-672-7171	814-676-6591	166
Clarion-Ledger, The	201 S Congress St	Jackson	MS	39201	877-850-5343	601-961-7000	528-2
Clarity Innovations Inc	1001 SE Water Ave Ste 400	Portland	OR	97214	877-683-3187	503-248-4300	256
Clark Atlanta University	223 James P Brawley Dr SW; *Admissions	Atlanta	GA	30314	800-688-3228*	404-880-8000	166
Clark Capital Management Group Inc (CCMG)	1650 Market St 1 Liberty Pl 53rd Fl	Philadelphia	PA	19103	800-766-2264	215-569-2224	400
Clark Construction Group LLC	7500 Old Georgetown Rd	Bethesda	MD	20814	800-655-1330	301-272-8100	186
Clark County REMC	7810 State Rd 60 PO Box 411	Sellersburg	IN	47172	800-462-6988	812-246-3316	245
Clark County School District (CCSD)	5100 West Sahara Ave	Las Vegas	NV	89146	866-799-8997	702-799-5000	681
Clark Electric Co-op	124 N Main St PO Box 190	Greenwood	WI	54437	800-272-6188	800-927-5707	245
Clark Foam Products Corp	655 Remington Blvd	Bolingbrook	IL	60440	888-284-2290	630-226-5900	597
Clark Grave Vault Co, The	375 E Fifth Ave	Columbus	OH	43201	800-848-3570		
Clark Material Handling Co	700 Enterprise Dr	Lexington	KY	40510	866-252-5275	859-422-6400	468
Clark Nuber PS	10900 NE Fourth St Ste 1400; *General	Bellevue	WA	98004	800-504-8747*	425-454-4919	2
Clark Planetarium	110 S 400 W	Salt Lake City	UT	84101	800-501-2885	385-468-7827	594
Clark Schaefer Hackett & Co	1 E Fourth St Ste 1200	Cincinnati	OH	45202	800-772-8144	513-241-3111	2
Clark Transfer Inc	800A Paxton St	Harrisburg	PA	17104	800-488-7585		186
Clark University	950 Main St	Worcester	MA	01610	800-462-5275	508-793-7711	166
Clark, Gagliardi & Miller PC	99 Court St	White Plains	NY	10601	800-734-5694		427

	Toll-Free	Phone	Class

Clark-Dunbar Flooring Superstore
3232 Empire Dr .... Alexandria LA 71301 — 800-256-1467 — 318-445-0262 — 290

Clarke College
1550 Clarke Dr .... Dubuque IA 52001 — 888-825-2753 — 563-588-6300 — 166

Clarke House Museum
1827 S Indiana Ave .... Chicago IL 60616 — 800-798-0988 — 312-744-4958 — 517

Clarke Power Services Inc
3133 E Kemper Rd .... Cincinnati OH 45241 — 800-513-9591 — 513-771-2200 — 357

Clark-Floyd Counties Convention & Tourism Bureau
315 Southern Indiana Ave
.... Jeffersonville IN 47130 — 800-552-3842 — 812-282-6654 — 206

Clark-Lindsey Village
101 W Windsor Rd .... Urbana IL 61802 — 800-998-2581 — 217-344-2144 — 668

Clark-Reliance Corp
16633 Foltz Pkwy .... Strongsville OH 44149 — 800-238-4027 — 440-572-1500 — 493

Clarksburg Exponent Telegram
324 Hewes Ave .... Clarksburg WV 26301 — 800-982-6034 — 304-626-1400 — 528-2

Clarksdale Municipal School District
135 Washington Ave
PO Box 1088 .... Clarksdale MS 38614 — 877-820-7831 — 662-627-8500 — 186

Clarksdale-Coahoma County Chamber of Commerce & Industrial Foundation
1540 DeSoto Ave PO Box 160 ...... Clarksdale MS 38614 — 800-626-3764 — 662-627-7337 — 139

Clarkson College
101 S 42nd St .... Omaha NE 68131 — 800-647-5500 — 402-552-3100 — 166

Clarkson University
10 Clarkson Ave .... Potsdam NY 13699 — 800-527-6577* — 315-268-6480 — 166
*Admissions

Clarkston Consulting
Research Triangle Park
2655 Meridian Pkwy .... Durham NC 27713 — 800-652-4274 — 919-484-4400 — 180

Clarksville Area Chamber of Commerce
25 Jefferson St Ste 300 .... Clarksville TN 37040 — 800-530-2487 — 931-647-2331 — 139

Clarksville Montgomery County Public Library
350 Pageant Ln .... Clarksville TN 37040 — 877-239-6635 — 931-648-8826 — 433-3

Clarksville/Montgomery County Tourist Commission
25 Jefferson St Ste 300 .... Clarksville TN 37040 — 800-530-2487 — 931-647-2331 — 206

Clarus Mktg Group LLC
500 Enterprise Dr 2nd Fl. .... Rocky Hill CT 06067 — 855-226-7047 — 860-358-9198 — 194

Clary Corp
150 E Huntington Dr .... Monrovia CA 91016 — 800-551-6111 — 626-359-4486 — 253

CLASP (Center for Law & Social Policy)
1015 15th St NW Ste 400 .... Washington DC 20005 — 800-821-4367 — 202-906-8000 — 630

Class Act Federal Credit Union
3620 Fern Valley Rd .... Louisville KY 40219 — 800-292-2960 — 502-964-7575 — 219

Class Action Litigation Report
1801 S Bell St .... Arlington VA 22202 — 800-372-1033 — — 527-7

Classic Brands LLC
8214 Wellmoor Ct .... Jessup MD 20794 — 877-707-7533 — 410-904-0006 — 469

Classic Brass Inc
2051 Stoneman Cir .... Lakewood NY 14750 — 800-869-3173 — 716-763-1400 — 349

Classic Custom Vacations
5893 Rue Ferrari .... San Jose CA 95138 — 800-635-1333 — — 766

Classic Hostess Inc
2 Skillman St Ste 313 .... Brooklyn NY 11205 — 888-280-6539 — 718-534-0690 — 392

Classic Medallics Inc
520 S Fulton Ave .... Mount Vernon NY 10550 — 800-221-1348 — 914-530-6259 — 772

Classic Student Tours
75 Rhoads Ctr Dr .... Dayton OH 45458 — 800-860-0246 — 937-439-0032 — 755

Classic Touch Limousine Inc
908 N Walnut St .... Bloomington IN 47404 — 800-319-0082 — 812-339-7269 — 440

Classic Trains Magazine
21027 Crossroads Cir
PO Box 1612 .... Waukesha WI 53187 — 800-533-6644 — 262-796-8776 — 455-14

Classic Travel Inc
4767 Okemos Rd .... Okemos MI 48864 — 800-643-3449 — 517-349-6200 — 767

Classic Tube
80 Rotech Dr .... Lancaster NY 14086 — 800-882-3711 — 716-759-1800 — 591

Classical Marketing LLC
2300 Cabot Dr Ste 390 .... Lisle IL 60532 — 800-613-3489 — 847-969-1696 — 195

Clatsop Community College
1653 Jerome Ave .... Astoria OR 97103 — 855-252-8767 — 503-325-0910 — 162

Clausing Industrial Inc
3963 Emerald Dr .... Kalamazoo MI 49001 — 800-323-0972

Claverack Rural Electric Co-op Inc
32750 W US 6 .... Wysox PA 18854 — 800-326-9799 — 570-265-2167 — 245

Clawson Tank Co
4701 White Lake Rd .... Clarkston MI 48346 — 800-272-1367 — 248-625-8700 — 91

Claxton Poultry Farms
8816 Hwy 301 N .... Claxton GA 30417 — 888-739-3181 — 912-739-3181 — 615

Clay County
PO Box 519 .... Fort Gaines GA 39851 — 800-436-7442

Clay County Electric Co-op Corp
3111 US-67 .... Corning AR 72422 — 800-521-2450 — 870-857-3521 — 245

Clay Electric Co-operative Inc
10 Citrus Dr
PO Box 308 .... Keystone Heights FL 32656 — 800-224-4917 — 352-473-4917 — 245

Clay Lacy Aviation
7435 Valjean Ave .... Van Nuys CA 91406 — 800-423-2904 — 818-989-2900 — 13

Clay Today
3513 US Hwy 17 .... Fleming Island FL 32003 — 888-434-9844 — 904-264-3200 — 528-4

Claybar Constracting Inc
424 Macnab St .... Dundas ON L9H2L3 — 866-801-9305 — 905-627-8000 — 606

Clayton Block Co
PO Box 3015 .... Lakewood NJ 08701 — 800-662-3044 — — 183

Clayton Corp
866 Horan Dr .... Fenton MO 63026 — 800-729-8220* — 636-349-5333 — 597
*Cust Svc

Clayton Holdings LLC
1500 Market St .... Philadelphia PA 19102 — 877-291-5301 — 215-231-1563 — 359-3

Clayton Industries
17477 Hurley St .... City of Industry CA 91744 — 800-423-4585 — 626-435-1200 — 470

Clayton Metals Inc
546 Clayton Ct .... Wood Dale IL 60191 — 800-323-7628 — — 490

Clay-Union Electric Corp
1410 E Cherry St PO Box 317 .... Vermillion SD 57069 — 800-696-2832 — 605-624-2673 — 245

CLC (Challenger Learning Ctr)
316 Washington Ave
Wheeling Jesuit University ...... Wheeling WV 26003 — 800-624-6992 — 304-243-2279 — 517

Clean Air Engineering Inc
500 W Wood St .... Palatine IL 60067 — 800-553-5511 — 847-991-3300 — 41

Clean Air Report
1919 S Eads St Ste 201 .... Arlington VA 22202 — 800-424-9068 — 703-416-8505 — 527-5

Clean Air Technology Inc
41105 Capital Dr .... Canton MI 48187 — 800-459-6320 — — 447

Clean Diesel Technologies Inc
4567 Telephone Rd Ste 206 ...... Ventura CA 93003 — 800-661-9963 — 805-639-9458 — 385
NASDAQ: CDTI

Clean Earth of North Jersey Inc
115 Jacobus Ave .... South Kearny NJ 07032 — 877-445-3478 — 973-344-4004 — 656

Clean Foods Inc
4561 Market St Ste B .... Ventura CA 93003 — 800-526-8328

Clean Harbors Inc
42 Longwater Dr PO Box 9149 ...... Norwell MA 02061 — 800-282-0058 — 781-792-5000 — 663
NYSE: CLH

Clean Ones Corp
317 SW Alder St Ste 350 .... Portland OR 97204 — 800-367-4587 — — 256

Clean Power LLC
124 N 121st St .... Milwaukee WI 53226 — 800-588-1608 — 414-302-3000 — 152

Clean Street Inc
1937 W 169th St .... Gardena CA 90247 — 800-225-7316 — — 663

Clean Water Action
4455 Connecticut Ave NW .... Washington DC 20008 — 800-657-3864 — 202-895-0420 — 48-13

Cleaning Authority
7230 Lee DeForest Dr .... Columbia MD 21046 — 888-658-0659 — 443-602-9154 — 310

CleanNet USA
9861 Brokenland Pkwy Ste 208 ...... Columbia MD 21046 — 800-735-8838 — 410-720-6444 — 152

Cleanroom Systems
7000 Performance Dr .... North Syracuse NY 13212 — 800-825-3268 — 315-452-7400 — 18

Cleantech Open, The
425 Broadway .... Redwood City CA 94063 — 888-989-6736 — — 461

Clear Brook Manor
1100 E Northampton St .... Laurel Run PA 18706 — 800-582-6241 — — 722

Clear Creek Baptist Bible College
300 Clear Creek Rd .... Pineville KY 40977 — 866-340-3196 — 606-337-3196 — 161

Clear Edge Technical Fabrics
7160 Northland Cir N .... Minneapolis MN 55428 — 800-328-3036 — 763-535-3220 — 740-3

Clear Lake Convention & Visitors Bureau
205 Main Ave PO Box 188 .... Clear Lake IA 50428 — 800-285-5338 — 641-357-2159 — 206

Clear Seas Research
2401 W Big Beaver Rd .... Troy MI 48084 — 800-811-6640 — 248-786-1683 — 464

Clear View Bag Co
5 Burdick Dr .... Albany NY 12205 — 800-458-7153 — 518-458-7153 — 68

Clearbridge Technology Group
6 Fortune Dr .... Billerica MA 01821 — 877-808-2284 — 781-916-2284 — 260

Clear-Com USA
850 Marina Village Pkwy .... Alameda CA 94501 — 800-462-4357 — 510-337-6600 — 391

Clearfield Hospital
809 Tpke Ave PO Box 992 .... Clearfield PA 16830 — 800-281-8000 — 814-765-5341 — 373-3

ClearOne Communications Inc
5225 Wiley Post Way .... Salt Lake City UT 84116 — 800-945-7730 — 801-975-7200 — 730

ClearSail Communications LLC
3950 Braxton .... Houston TX 77063 — 888-905-0888 — 713-230-2800 — 397

ClearStream Energy Services
311 - 6 Ave SW Ste 415 .... Calgary AB T2P3H2 — 855-410-9835 — 587-318-0997 — 532

Clearwater Power Co
4230 Hatwai Rd PO Box 997 .... Lewiston ID 83501 — 888-743-1501 — 208-743-1501 — 245

Cleary Building Corp
190 Paoli St .... Verona WI 53593 — 800-373-5550 — 608-845-9700 — 186

Cleary Millwork Company Inc
235 Dividend Rd .... Rocky Hill CT 06067 — 800-486-7600 — 800-899-4533 — 191-3

Cleary University
2793 Plymouth Rd .... Ann Arbor MI 48105 — 800-686-1883 — — 795
Livingston
3750 Cleary Dr .... Howell MI 48843 — 800-686-1883 — 517-548-3670 — 795

Cleaver Brooks
221 Law St .... Thomasville GA 31792 — 800-250-5883 — 229-226-3024 — 91

Cleburne Chamber of Commerce
1511 W Henderson St .... Cleburne TX 76033 — 800-621-8566 — 817-645-2455 — 139

Cleco Corp
2030 Donahue Ferry Rd
PO Box 5000 .... Pineville LA 71361 — 800-622-6537* — — 782
*Cust Svc

Cleft Palate Foundation (CPF)
1504 E Franklin St Ste 102 .... Chapel Hill NC 27514 — 800-242-5338 — 919-933-9044 — 48-17

Clement Communications Inc
3 Creek Pkwy .... Upper Chichester PA 19061 — 800-253-6368 — 610-459-4200 — 633-10

Clement Industries Inc
PO Box 914 .... Minden LA 71058 — 800-562-5948* — 318-377-2776 — 774
*Cust Svc

Clemson University
105 Sikes Hall .... Clemson SC 29634 — 800-640-2657 — 864-656-3311 — 166

Clermont County Convention & Visitors Bureau (CCCVB)
410 E Main St PO Box 100 .... Batavia OH 45103 — 800-796-4282 — 513-732-3600 — 206

Cleveland Bros Equipment Company Inc
5300 Paxton St .... Harrisburg PA 17111 — 866-551-4602 — 717-564-2121 — 357

Cleveland City Hall
601 Lakeside Ave .... Cleveland OH 44114 — 800-589-3101 — 216-664-2000 — 336

Cleveland Corp
42810 N Green Bay Rd .... Zion IL 60099 — 800-281-3464 — 847-872-7200 — 682

Cleveland Foundation
1422 Euclid Ave Ste 1300 .... Cleveland OH 44115 — 877-554-5054 — 216-861-3810 — 303

Cleveland Gear Co
3249 E 80th St .... Cleveland OH 44104 — 800-423-3169 — 216-641-9000 — 705

Cleveland Golf Co
5601 Skylab Rd .... Huntington Beach CA 92647 — 800-999-6263* — — 706
*Cust Svc

Cleveland HeartLab Inc
6701 Carnegie Ave Ste 500 .... Cleveland OH 44103 — 866-358-9828 — — 414

Cleveland Institute of Art
11141 E Blvd .... Cleveland OH 44106 — 800-223-4700 — — 164

Cleveland Institute of Electronics
1776 E 17th St .... Cleveland OH 44114 — 800-243-6446 — 216-781-9400 — 795

Cleveland Institute of Music
11021 E Blvd .... Cleveland OH 44106 — 800-686-1141 — 216-791-5000 — 166

Cleveland Magazine
1422 Euclid Ave Ste 730 .... Cleveland OH 44115 — 800-210-7293 — 216-771-2833 — 455-22

				Toll-Free	Phone	Class

Cleveland Motion Controls Inc
7550 Hub Pkwy ....Cleveland OH 44125 · 800-321-8072 · 216-524-8800 · 203

Cleveland Museum of Art, The
11150 E Blvd ....Cleveland OH 44106 · 877-262-4748* · 216-421-7350 · 517
*Sales

Cleveland Museum of Natural History
1 Wade Oval Dr ....Cleveland OH 44106 · 800-317-9155 · 216-231-4600 · 517

Cleveland Orchestra, The
11001 Euclid Ave
Severance Hall ....Cleveland OH 44106 · 800-686-1141 · 216-231-1111 · 569-3

Cleveland Plant & Flower Co
12920 Corporate Dr ....Cleveland OH 44130 · 888-231-7569 · 216-898-3500 · 293

Cleveland Plumbing Supply Company Inc
143 E Washington St ....Chagrin Falls OH 44022 · 800-331-1078 · 440-247-2555 · 608

Cleveland Public Library
325 Superior Ave ....Cleveland OH 44114 · 800-362-1262 · 216-623-2800 · 433-3

Cleveland Punch & Die Co
666 Pratt St PO Box 769 ....Ravenna OH 44266 · 888-451-4342 · · 752

Cleveland Range Co
1333 E 179th St ....Cleveland OH 44110 · 800-338-2204 · 216-481-4900 · 298

Cleveland State Community College
3535 Adkisson Dr ....Cleveland TN 37312 · 800-604-2722 · 423-472-7141 · 162

Cleveland State University
2121 Euclid Ave ....Cleveland OH 44115 · 888-278-6446 · 216-687-2000 · 166

Cleveland State University Cleveland-Marshall College of Law
1801 Euclid Ave LB 138 ....Cleveland OH 44115 · 866-687-2304 · 216-687-2344 · 167-1

Cleveland Tool & Machine
5240 Smith Rd ....Brook Park OH 44142 · 800-253-4502 · 216-267-6010 · 452

Cleveland Wire Cloth & Manufacturing Co
3573 E 78th St ....Cleveland OH 44105 · 800-321-3234 · 216-341-1832 · 684

Cleveland/Bradley Chamber of Commerce
225 Keith St ....Cleveland TN 37311 · 800-533-9930 · 423-472-6587 · 139

Clever Devices Ltd
300 Crossways Pk Dr ....Woodbury NY 11797 · 800-872-6129 · 516-433-6100 · 180

Clevest Solutions Inc
13911 Wireless Way Ste 100 ....Richmond BC V6V3B9 · 866-915-0088 · 604-214-9700 · 224

CLIA (Cruise Lines International Assn)
1201 F St NW Ste 250 ....Washington DC 20004 · 855-444-2542 · 202-759-9370 · 48-23

Click2mail
3103 Tenth St N Ste 201 ....Arlington VA 22201 · 866-665-2787 · 703-521-9029 · 623

ClickSafetycom Inc
2185 N California Blvd
Ste 425 ....Walnut Creek CA 94596 · 800-971-1080 · · 760

ClickSoftware Inc
35 Corporate Dr Ste 400 ....Burlington MA 01803 · 888-438-3308 · 781-272-5903 · 178-7

Clients First Business Solutions LLC
670 N Beers St Bldg 4 ....Holmdel NJ 07733 · 866-677-6290 · · 177

Cliff House at Pikes Peak
306 Canyon Ave ....Manitou Springs CO 80829 · 888-212-7000 · 719-785-1000 · 378

Cliff Spa at Snowbird
PO Box 929000 ....Snowbird UT 84092 · 800-453-3000 · 801-933-2225 · 703

Cliff Viessman Inc
215 First Ave PO Box 175 ....Gary SD 57237 · 800-328-2408 · 605-272-5241 · 466

Cliff Weil Inc
8043 Industrial Pk Rd ....Mechanicsville VA 23116 · 800-446-9345 · 804-746-1321 · 539

Clifford & Rano Associates Inc
57 Cedar St ....Worcester MA 01609 · 800-660-8284 · 508-752-8284 · 389

Clifton Savings Bancorp Inc
1433 Van Houten Ave ....Clifton NJ 07013 · 888-562-6727 · 973-473-2200 · 359-2
NASDAQ: CSBK

Clifton T Perkins Hospital Ctr (CTPHC)
1 Renaissance Blvd ....Oakbrook IL 60181 · 800-994-6610 · · 373-5

CliftonLarsonAllen - CLA
301 SW Adams St Ste 1000 ....Peoria IL 61602 · 888-529-2648 · 309-671-4500 · 2

Climate Design Air ConditioningIn
12530 47th Way N ....Clearwater FL 33762 · 888-572-7245 · · 189-10

Climate Registry, The
PO Box 811488 ....Los Angeles CA 90081 · 866-523-0764 · · 192

ClimateMaster Inc
7300 SW 44th St ....Oklahoma City OK 73179 · 800-299-9747 · 405-745-6000 · 14

Climbing Magazine
5720 Flatiron Pkwy ....Boulder CO 80301 · 800-829-5895 · 303-253-6412 · 455-20

Cline Falls State Scenic Viewpoint
7100 OR-126 ....Redmond OR 97756 · 800-551-6949 · · 561

C-Line Products Inc
1100 E Business Ctr Dr ....Mount Prospect IL 60056 · 800-323-6084 · 847-827-6661 · 530

Cline Tool & Service Co
PO Box 866 ....Newton IA 50208 · 866-561-3022 · · 491

ClingZ Inc
841 Market St ....Nekoosa WI 54457 · 800-826-4886 · ·

Clinic Service Corp
3464 S Willow St ....Denver CO 80231 · 800-929-5395 · 303-755-2900 · 2

Clinical Pathology Laboratories Inc
9200 Wall St ....Austin TX 78754 · 800-595-1275 · 512-339-1275 · 414

CliniComp International
9655 Towne Ctr Dr ....San Diego CA 92121 · 800-350-8202 · 858-546-8202 · 178-10

Clinique Laboratories Inc
767 Fifth Ave ....New York NY 10153 · 800-419-4041 · 212-572-3983 · 214

Clinton Community College
1000 Lincoln Blvd ....Clinton IA 52732 · 877-495-3320 · 563-244-7001 · 162

Clinton Community College
136 Clinton Pt Dr ....Plattsburgh NY 12901 · 800-552-1160 · 518-562-4200 · 162

Clinton County
1900 N Third St PO Box 2957 ....Clinton IA 52733 · 866-227-9040 · 563-243-6210 · 337

Clinton County Economic Partnership
212 N Jay St ....Lock Haven PA 17745 · 888-388-6991 · 570-748-5782 · 139

Clinton County Electric Co-op Inc
475 N Main St PO Box 40 ....Breese IL 62230 · 800-526-7282 · 618-526-7282 · 245

Clinton Electronics Corp
6701 Clinton Rd ....Loves Park IL 61111 · 800-549-6393 · 815-633-1444 · 253

Clinton Fences Company Inc
2630 Old Annapolis Rd ....Waldorf MD 20601 · 800-323-6869 · 301-645-8808 · 186

Clinton Inn Hotel
145 Dean Dr ....Tenafly NJ 07670 · 800-275-4411 · 201-871-3200 · 378

Clinton Memorial Hospital (CMH)
610 W Main St ....Wilmington OH 45177 · 800-803-9648 · 937-382-6611 · 373-3

Clippard Instrument Lab
7390 Colerain Ave ....Cincinnati OH 45239 · 877-245-6247 · 513-521-4261 · 223

Clipper Exxpress Inc
9014 Heritage Pkwy Ste 300 ....Woodridge IL 60517 · 800-678-2547 · 630-739-0700 · 447

Clipper Fund
2949 E Elvira Rd Ste 101 ....Tucson AZ 85756 · 800-432-2504 · · 524

Clipper Navigation Inc
2701 Alaskan Way Pier 69 ....Seattle WA 98121 · 800-888-2535 · 206-443-2560 · 766

CLLA (Commercial Law League of America)
3005 Tollview Dr ....Rolling Meadows IL 60008 · 800-978-2552 · 312-240-1400 · 49-10

Clm Equipment Company Inc
3135 Hwy 90 E ....Broussard LA 70518 · 800-256-0490 · 337-837-6693 · 190

Clock Mobility
6700 Clay Ave ....Grand Rapids MI 49548 · 800-732-5625 · 616-698-9400 · 62-7

Clofine Dairy Products Inc
1407 New Rd ....Linwood NJ 08221 · 800-441-1001 · 609-653-1000 · 297-4

Cloisters Museum
Fort Tryon Pk ....New York NY 10040 · 800-662-3397 · 212-923-3700 · 517

Clopay Bldg Products Inc
8585 Duke Blvd ....Mason OH 45040 · 800-225-6729 · · 234

Cloquet Area Chamber of Commerce
225 Sunnyside Dr ....Cloquet MN 55720 · 800-554-4350 · 218-879-1551 · 139

Clos du Bois
19410 Geyserville Ave ....Geyserville CA 95441 · 800-222-3189* · · 80-3
*Sales

Close To My Heart
1199 W 700 S ....Pleasant Grove UT 84062 · 888-655-6552 · · 157-6

Close Up Foundation
1330 Braddock Pl Ste 400 ....Alexandria VA 22314 · 800-256-7387 · 703-706-3300 · 48-7

Closet Factory
12800 S Broadway ....Los Angeles CA 90061 · 800-838-7995 · 310-516-7000 · 189-11

Clothworks
6301 W Marginal Way SW ....Seattle WA 98106 · 800-874-0541 · 206-762-7886 · 258

Cloud 9 Living
11101 W 120th Ave Ste 150 ....Broomfield CO 80021 · 866-525-6839 · · 196

Cloud County Community college
2221 Campus Dr ....Concordia KS 66901 · 800-729-5101 · · 337

Cloud County Community College
2221 Campus Dr ....Concordia KS 66901 · 800-729-5101 · 785-243-1435 · 162

Cloud Peak Energy Inc
505 S Gillette Ave PO Box 3009 ....Gillette WY 82717 · 866-470-4300 · 307-687-6000 · 499

CloudCheckr Inc
342 N Goodman St ....Rochester NY 14607 · 833-253-2425 · ·

Cloud-rider Designs Ltd
1260 Eighth Ave ....Regina SK S4R1C9 · 800-632-1255 · 306-761-2119 · 349

CloudSway LLC
711 Pacific Ave ....Tacoma WA 98402 · 855-212-5683 · · 386

Cloudwerx Data Solutions Inc
1440 28th St NE Ste 2 ....Calgary AB T2A7W6 · 855-550-5004 · 403-538-6659 ·

Clougherty Packing Co
3049 E Vernon Ave ....Los Angeles CA 90058 · 800-846-7635* · · 471
*Sales

Clover Farms Dairy
PO Box 14627 ....Reading PA 19612 · 800-323-0123 · 610-921-9111 · 296-27

Clover Wireless
2700 W Higgins Rd
Ste 100 ....Hoffman Estates IL 60169 · 866-734-6548 · ·

Cloverdale Equipment Co
13133 Cloverdale St ....Oak Park MI 48237 · 800-822-7999 · 248-399-6600 · 264-3

Cloverdale Foods Co
3015 34th St NW ....Mandan ND 58554 · 800-669-9511 · · 296-26

Cloverland Green Spring Dairy Inc
2701 Loch Raven Rd ....Baltimore MD 21218 · 800-492-0094* · 410-235-4477 · 296-27
*Orders

Clover-Stornetta Farms Inc
PO Box 750369 ....Petaluma CA 94975 · 800-237-3315 · · 297-4

Clovis Community College (CCC)
417 Schepps Blvd ....Clovis NM 88101 · 800-769-1409 · 575-769-2811 · 162

Clovis Unified School District
1450 Herndon Ave ....Clovis CA 93611 · 877-544-6664 · 559-327-9300 · 681

Clovis/Curry County Chamber of Commerce
105 E Third St ....Clovis NM 88101 · 800-261-7656 · 575-763-3435 · 139

Clow Valve Co
902 S Second St ....Oskaloosa IA 52577 · 800-829-2569 · 641-673-8611 · 784

Clowns of America International (COAI)
PO Box 122 ....Eustis FL 32727 · 877-816-6941 · 352-357-1676 · 48-4

CLS (Christian Legal Society)
8001 Braddock Rd Ste 300 ....Springfield VA 22151 · 800-225-4008 · 703-642-1070 · 49-10

CLS Investments LLC
17605 Wright St ....Omaha NE 68130 · 888-455-4244 · 402-493-3313 · 686

CLT (Chesapeake Lodging Trust)
1997 Annapolis Exchange Pkwy
Ste 410 ....Annapolis MD 21401 · 800-698-2820 · 571-349-9450 · 650
NYSE: CHSP

Club Cal Neva Hotel Casino, The
38 E Second St PO Box 2071 ....Reno NV 89501 · 877-777-7303 · 775-323-1046 · 665

Club Europa
802 W Oregon St ....Urbana IL 61801 · 800-331-1882 · 217-344-5863 · 755

Club Managers Assn of America (CMAA)
CMAA - 1733 King St ....Alexandria VA 22314 · 800-409-7755 · 703-739-9500 · 49-12

ClubCorp Inc
3030 Lyndon B Johnson Fwy
Ste 600 ....Dallas TX 75234 · 800-433-5079 · 972-243-6191 · 651

Clubfurniturecom
11535 Carmel Commons Blvd
Ste 202 ....Charlotte NC 28226 · 888-378-8383 · · 786

ClubLink Corp
15675 Dufferin St ....King City ON L7B1K5 · 800-661-1818 · · 651

Clyde Peeling's Reptiland
18628 US Rt 15 ....Allenwood PA 17810 · 800-737-8452 · 570-538-1869 · 818

Clyde's Transfer Inc
8015 Industrial Pk Rd ....Mechanicsville VA 23116 · 800-342-8758 · 804-746-1135 · 681

CM ALMY 28 Kaysal Ct ....Armonk NY 10504 · 800-225-2569 · 207-487-3232 · 155-13

CM Paula Co
6049 Hi-Tek Ct ....Mason OH 45040 · 800-543-4464 · · 327

CM Ranch
167 Fish Hatchery Rd PO Box 217 ....Dubois WY 82513 · 800-455-0721 · 307-455-2331 · 239

CM Services Inc
800 Roosevelt Rd
Bldg C Ste 312 ....Glen Ellyn IL 60137 · 800-613-6672 · 630-858-7337 · 47

Name / Address	City	State	ZIP	Toll-Free	Phone	Class
CM Trailers Inc 200 County Rd	Madill	OK	73446	**888-268-7577**		774
CMA (Chicago Meat Authority Inc) 1120 W 47th Pl	Chicago	IL	60609	**800-383-3811**	773-254-3811	296-26
CMA (Chamber Music America) 305 Seventh Ave 5th Fl	New York	NY	10001	**888-221-9836**	212-242-2022	48-4
CMA (Canadian Medical Assn) 1867 Alta Vista Dr	Ottawa	ON	K1G5W8	**800-663-7336**	613-731-9331	49-8
CMA (Crystal Meth Anonymous) 4470 W Sunset Blvd Ste 107 PO Box 555	Los Angeles	CA	90027	**877-262-6691**		48-21
CMA Consulting Services Inc 700 Troy Schenectady Rd	Latham	NY	12110	**800-276-6101**	518-783-9003	177
CMA Dishmachines 12700 Knott St	Garden Grove	CA	92841	**800-854-6417**	714-898-8781	385
CMAA (Crane Manufacturers Assn of America) 8720 Red Oak Blvd Ste 201	Charlotte	NC	28217	**800-345-1815**	704-676-1190	49-13
CMAA (Club Managers Assn of America) CMAA - 1733 King St	Alexandria	VA	22314	**800-409-7755**	703-739-9500	49-12
CMC (Catholic Medical Ctr) 100 McGregor St	Manchester	NH	03102	**800-437-9666**	603-668-3545	373-3
CMC (Communications Manufacturing Co) 2234 Colby Ave *Orders	Los Angeles	CA	90064	**800-462-5532***	310-828-3200	248
CMC (Geisinger Health System) 1800 Mulberry St	Scranton	PA	18510	**800-230-4565**	570-703-8000	373-3
CMC (Community Medical Ctr) 99 Hwy 37 W	Toms River	NJ	08755	**888-724-7123**	732-557-8000	373-3
CMC (Cambridge Medical Ctr) 701 S Dellwood St	Cambridge	MN	55008	**800-252-4133**	763-689-7700	373-3
CMC (Colleton Medical Ctr) 501 Robertson Blvd	Walterboro	SC	29488	**866-492-9083**	843-782-2000	373-3
CMC Capitol City Steel 14501 S IH 35	Buda	TX	78610	**888-682-7337**	512-282-8820	478
CMC Construction Services 9103 E Almeda Rd	Houston	TX	77054	**877-297-9111**	713-799-1150	384
CMC Rebar Georgia 251 Hosea Rd	Lawrenceville	GA	30046	**888-682-7337**	770-963-6251	478
CMD Products 1410 Flightline Dr Ste D	Lincoln	CA	95648	**800-210-9949**	916-434-0228	428
CMDA (Christian Medical & Dental Assn) 2604 Hwy 421 PO Box 7500	Bristol	TN	37620	**800-231-2637**	423-844-1000	49-8
CME Group Inc 20 S Wacker Dr *NASDAQ: CME*	Chicago	IL	60606	**866-716-7274**	312-930-1000	687
CMH (Clinton Memorial Hospital) 610 W Main St	Wilmington	OH	45177	**800-803-9648**	937-382-6611	373-3
CMI (Cine Magnetics Inc) 9 W Broad St	Stamford	CT	06902	**800-431-1102**	203-989-9955	654
Cmi 6704 Guada Coma Dr	Schertz	TX	78154	**800-840-1070**	210-967-6169	417
CMI Credit Mediators Inc 414 Sansom St	Upper Darby	PA	19082	**800-456-3328**	610-352-5151	160
CMI EFCO Inc 435 W Wilson St	Salem	OH	44460	**877-225-2674**	330-332-4661	318
CMI Inc 316 E Ninth St	Owensboro	KY	42303	**866-835-0690**		525
CMI Plastics Inc 222 Pepsi Way	Ayden	NC	28513	**877-395-1920**	252-746-2171	604
CMIC (Connecticut Medical Insurance Co) 80 Glastonbury Blvd 3rd Fl	Glastonbury	CT	06033	**800-228-0287**	860-633-7788	
CMMB (Catholic Medical Mission Board) 100 Wall St 9th Fl	New York	NY	10005	**800-678-5659**	212-242-7757	48-5
CMS (College Music Society) 312 E Pine St	Missoula	MT	59802	**800-729-0235**	406-721-9616	49-5
CMS (Centers for Medicare & Medicaid Services) 7500 Security Blvd	Baltimore	MD	21244	**800-633-4227**		339-9
Cms Communications Inc 722 Goddard Ave	Chesterfield	MO	63005	**800-755-9169**		246
CMS Electric Co-op Inc 509 E Carthage St	Meade	KS	67864	**800-794-2353**	620-873-2184	245
CMS Energy Corp 1 Energy Plz *NYSE: CMS*	Jackson	MI	49201	**800-477-5050**	517-788-0550	359-5
CMS Mid-Atlantic Inc 295 Totowa Rd	Totowa	NJ	07512	**800-267-1981**		392
CMS Peripherals Inc 12 Mauchly Unit E	Irvine	CA	92618	**800-327-5773**	714-424-5520	173-8
CMSA (Case Management Society of America) 6301 Ranch Dr	Little Rock	AR	72223	**800-216-2672**	501-225-2229	49-8
CMW (Central Maintenance & Welding Inc) 2620 E Keysville Rd	Lithia	FL	33547	**877-704-7411**	813-737-1402	189-14
CNA Financial Corp 333 S Wabash Ave *NYSE: CNA*	Chicago	IL	60604	**800-262-4357**	312-822-5000	359-4
CNA National Warranty Corp 4150 N Drinkwater Blvd Ste 400	Scottsdale	AZ	85251	**800-345-0191**		
CNB (City National Bank of New Jersey) 900 Broad St	Newark	NJ	07102	**877-350-3524**	973-624-0865	70
CNB Financial Corp 1 S Second St PO Box 42 *NASDAQ: CCNE*	Clearfield	PA	16830	**800-492-3221**	814-765-9621	359-2
CNC Industries Ltd 9331 39 Ave	Edmonton	AB	T6E5T3	**877-262-2343**	780-469-2346	452
CNC Software Inc 671 Old Post Rd	Tolland	CT	06084	**800-228-2877**	860-875-5006	225
CNGC (Cascade Natural Gas Corp) 8113 W Grandridge Blvd	Kennewick	WA	99336	**888-522-1130**		782
CNMC (Children's National Medical Ctr) 111 Michigan Ave NW	Washington	DC	20010	**800-884-5433**	202-476-5000	373-1
CNRL (Canadian Natural Resources Ltd) 855 Second St SW Ste 2100 *NYSE: CNQ*	Calgary	AB	T2P4J8	**888-878-3700**	403-517-6700	532
COA (Council on Accreditation) 45 Broadway 29th Fl	New York	NY	10006	**866-262-8088**	212-797-3000	48-1
Coach & Equipment Manufacturing Corp 130 Horizon Pk Dr PO Box 36	Penn Yan	NY	14527	**800-724-8464**	315-536-2321	513

Name / Address	City	State	ZIP	Toll-Free	Phone	Class
Coach House Inc 3480 Technology Dr	Nokomis	FL	34275	**800-235-0984**	941-485-0984	120
Coach Inc 342 Madison Ave *NYSE: COH*	New York	NY	10173	**800-444-3611**	212-599-4777	429
Coach Tours Ltd 475 Federal Rd	Brookfield	CT	06804	**800-822-6224**	203-740-1118	755
Coact Associates Ltd 2748 Centennial Rd	Toledo	OH	43617	**866-646-4400**		196
Co-Advantage Resources 3350 Buschwood Park Dr Ste 200	Tampa	FL	33618	**800-868-1016**	855-351-4731	627
COAI (Clowns of America International) PO Box 122	Eustis	FL	32727	**877-816-6941**	352-357-1676	48-4
Coair Industrial Air Compressor & Sandblasting 5405 Sarosto St	Levis	QC	G6V5B6	**888-835-0141**	418-835-0141	
Coalition Against Bigger Trucks (CABT) 109 NFairfax St 2nd Fl	Alexandria	VA	22314	**888-222-8123**	703-535-3131	
Coalition Against Insurance Fraud 1012 14th St NW Ste 200	Washington	DC	20005	**800-835-6422**	202-393-7330	49-9
Coalition for Auto Repair Equality (CARE) 105 Oronoco St Ste 115	Alexandria	VA	22314	**800-229-5380**	703-519-7555	49-21
Coalition of Health Services Inc 301 S Polk St Ste 740	Amarillo	TX	79101	**800-442-7893**	806-337-1700	461
Co-Alliance LLP 5250 E US Hwy 36 Bldg 1000	Avon	IN	46123	**800-525-0272**	317-745-4491	275
Coast Capital Savings 800-9900 King George Blvd	Surrey	BC	V3T0K7	**888-517-7000**	250-483-7000	70
Coast Central Credit Union Inc 2650 Harrison Ave	Eureka	CA	95501	**800-974-9727**	707-445-8801	219
Coast Edmonton House Suite Hotel 1090 W Georgia S Ste 900	Vancouver	BC	V6E3V7	**800-716-6199**	604-682-7982	378
Coast Electric Power Assn 18020 Hwy Ste 603 *Cust Svc	Kiln	MS	39556	**877-769-2372***	228-363-7000	245
Coast Guard Exchange System 510 Independence Pkwy Ste 500	Chesapeake	VA	23320	**800-572-0230**		786
Coast Property Management 2829 Rucker Ave	Everett	WA	98201	**800-339-3634**		648
Coast to Coast Corporate Housing 10773 Los Alamitos Blvd	Los Alamitos	CA	90720	**800-451-9466**		210
Coast to Coast Moving & Storage Co 136 41st St	Brooklyn	NY	11232	**800-872-6683**	718-443-5800	516
Coast2Coast Diagnostics Inc 600 N Tustin Ave Ste 110	Santa Ana	CA	92705	**800-730-9263**		414
Coastal Administrative Services (CAS) PO Box 3070	Bellingham	WA	98227	**800-870-1831**		260
Coastal Agrobusiness Inc 112 Staton Rd	Greenville	NC	27834	**800-758-1828**	252-756-1126	280
Coastal Alabama Community College 1900 Hwy 31 S	Bay Minette	AL	36507	**800-381-3722**		162
Coastal Bend Blood Ctr 209 N Padre Island Dr	Corpus Christi	TX	78406	**800-299-4943**	361-855-4943	89
Coastal Bend College *Beeville* 3800 Charco Rd	Beeville	TX	78102	**866-722-2838**	361-358-2838	162
Coastal Building Maintenance 8651 NW 70th St	Miami	FL	33166	**800-357-7790**	305-681-6100	104
Coastal Carolina Community College 444 Western Blvd	Jacksonville	NC	28546	**800-908-9946**	910-455-1221	162
Coastal Carolina University PO Box 261954	Conway	SC	29528	**800-277-7000**	843-349-2170	166
Coastal Casting Service Inc 2903 Gano St	Houston	TX	77009	**800-433-6223**	713-223-4439	752
Coastal Corrosion Control Surveys LLC 10172 Mammoth Ave	Baton Rouge	LA	70814	**800-894-2120**	225-275-6131	490
Coastal Electric Co-op 1265 S Coastal Hwy	Midway	GA	31320	**800-421-2343**	912-884-3311	245
Coastal Federal Credit Union 1000 St Albans Dr	Raleigh	NC	27609	**800-868-4262**	919-420-8000	219
Coastal Harbor Treatment Ctr 1150 Cornell Ave	Savannah	GA	31406	**844-657-2638**	912-354-3911	373-5
Coastal Helicopters Inc 8995 Yandukin Dr	Juneau	AK	99801	**800-789-5610**	907-789-5600	358
Coastal Hospice & Palliative Care 2604 Old Ocean City Rd PO Box 1733	Salisbury	MD	21804	**800-780-7886**	410-742-8732	370
Coastal Inn Concorde 379 Windmill Rd	Dartmouth	NS	B3A1J6	**800-565-1565**		378
Coastal Inns Inc 111 Warwick St PO Box 280	Digby	NS	B0V1A0	**800-401-1155**		378
Coastal Mechanical Services LLC 394 E Dr	Melbourne	FL	32904	**866-584-9528**	321-725-3061	189-10
Coastal Mountain Fuels 501 Industrial Park Pl	Gold River	BC	V0P2G0	**800-798-3835**		
Coastal Pacific Food Distributors Inc (CPFD) 1015 Performance Dr	Stockton	CA	95206	**800-500-2611**	209-983-2454	297-8
Coastal Palms Hotel 120th St Coastal Hwy	Ocean City	MD	21842	**800-641-0011**		378
Coastal Training Technologies Corp 500 Studio Dr	Virginia Beach	VA	23452	**866-333-6888**	757-498-9014	510
Coastal Transport Co Inc 1603 Ackerman Rd	San Antonio	TX	78219	**800-523-8612**	210-661-4287	775
Coastal Transportation Inc 4025 13th Ave W	Seattle	WA	98119	**800-544-2580**	206-282-9979	312
Coastline Community College 11460 Warner Ave	Fountain Valley	CA	92708	**866-422-2645**	714-546-7600	162
Coating & Adhesive Corp (CAC) 1901 Popular St PO Box 1080	Leland	NC	28451	**800-410-2999**	910-371-3184	546
Coats North America 3430 Toringdon Way Ste 301	Charlotte	NC	28277	**800-631-0965**	704-329-5800	740-9
Coaxial Dynamics 6800 Lake Abrams Dr	Middleburg Heights	OH	44130	**800-262-9425**	440-243-1100	643
Coaxis Inc 1515 SE Water Ave Ste 300	Portland	OR	97214	**800-333-3197**		177
COBA/Select Sires Inc 1224 Alton Darby Creek Rd	Columbus	OH	43228	**800-837-2621**	614-878-5333	11-2

Alphabetical Section

Name / Address	City	State	ZIP	Toll-Free	Phone	Class
Cobalt Boats LLC						
1715 N Eigth St	Neodesha	KS	66757	**800-468-5764**	620-325-2653	90
Cobalt Digital Inc						
2506 Galen Dr	Champaign	IL	61821	**800-669-1691**	217-344-1243	643
Cobb Travel & Tourism						
1 Galleria Pkwy	Atlanta	GA	30339	**800-451-3480**	678-303-2622	206
Cobblestone Capital Advisors LLC						
140 Allens Creek Rd	Rochester	NY	14618	**800-264-2769**	585-473-3333	686
Cobb-Vantress Inc						
PO Box 1030	Siloam Springs	AR	72761	**800-748-9719**	479-524-3166	11-2
Cober Evolving Solutions						
1351 Strasburg Rd	Kitchener	ON	N2R1H2	**800-263-7136**	519-745-7136	623
Cobon Plastics Corp						
90 S St	Newark	NJ	07114	**800-360-1324**	973-344-6330	369
Cobra Mfg Co Inc						
7909 E 148th St S	Bixby	OK	74008	**800-352-6272**		706
Coburn Co, The						
PO Box 147	Whitewater	WI	53190	**800-776-7042**	262-473-2822	596
Coburn Supply Company Inc						
390 Park St Ste 100	Beaumont	TX	77701	**800-832-8492**	409-838-6363	608
Coca-Cola Consolidated						
4100 Coca-Cola Plz						
PO Box 31487	Charlotte	NC	28211	**800-866-2653**	704-557-4000	81-2
NASDAQ: COKE						
Coca-Cola Foundation Inc						
PO Box 1734	Atlanta	GA	30301	**800-438-2653**		304
Coca-Cola Nonpartisan Committee for Good Government						
PO Box 1734	Atlanta	GA	30301	**800-438-2653**		611
Cocaine Anonymous World Services Inc (CA)						
PO Box 492000	Los Angeles	CA	90049	**800-347-8998**	310-559-5833	48-21
Cocca's Inn & Suites						
42 Wolf Rd	Albany	NY	12205	**888-426-2227**	518-459-5670	378
Cocciardi & Associates Inc						
4 Kacey Ct	Mechanicsburg	PA	17055	**800-377-3024**	717-766-4500	427
Cochise College						
4190 W Hwy 80	Douglas	AZ	85607	**800-966-7943**	520-364-7943	162
Sierra Vista						
901 N Colombo Ave	Sierra Vista	AZ	85635	**800-966-7943**	520-515-0500	162
Cochran Firm LLC						
111 E Main St	Dothan	AL	36301	**800-843-3476**	334-793-1555	427
Cochran, Kroll & Associates PC						
15510 Farmington Rd	Livonia	MI	48154	**800-322-5543**		
Cochrane Technologies Inc						
PO Box 81276	Lafayette	LA	70598	**800-346-3745**	337-837-3334	723
Cocoa Beach Area Chamber of Commerce						
400 Fortenberry Rd	Merritt Island	FL	32952	**800-248-5955**	321-459-2200	139
Coconino Community College						
Lonetree						
2800 S Lone Tree Rd	Flagstaff	AZ	86005	**800-350-7122**	928-527-1222	162
Coconino County						
219 E Cherry Ave	Flagstaff	AZ	86001	**800-559-9289**	928-774-5011	337
Coconut Mallory Resort & Marina						
1445 S Roosevelt Blvd	Key West	FL	33040	**866-316-1843**		376
CODA (Co-Dependents Anonymous Inc)						
PO Box 33577	Phoenix	AZ	85067	**888-444-2359**	602-277-7991	48-21
Codale Electric Supply Inc						
5225 West 2400 South						
PO Box 702070	Salt Lake City	UT	84120	**800-300-6634**	801-975-7300	246
Co-Dependents Anonymous Inc (CODA)						
PO Box 33577	Phoenix	AZ	85067	**888-444-2359**	602-277-7991	48-21
Codington-Clark Electric Co-op						
3520 Ninth Ave SW PO Box 880	Watertown	SD	57201	**800-463-8938**	605-886-5848	245
Coe College						
1220 First Ave NE	Cedar Rapids	IA	52402	**877-225-5263**	319-399-8500	166
COECO Office Systems Co						
2521 N Church St	Rocky Mount	NC	27804	**800-682-6844**	252-977-1121	320
Coeur d'Alene Area Chamber of Commerce						
105 N First St Ste 100	Coeur d'Alene	ID	83814	**877-782-9232**	208-664-3194	139
Coeur d'Alene Convention & Visitor Bureau Inc						
105 N 1st Ste 100	Coeur d'Alene	ID	83814	**877-782-9232**		
Coeur d'Alene Resort						
115 S Second St	Coeur D'Alene	ID	83814	**800-688-5253**	855-703-4648	665
Coface Services North America Inc						
50 Millstone Rd	East Windsor	NJ	08520	**877-626-3223**	609-469-0400	218
Coffee Bean International						
9120 NE Alderwood Rd	Portland	OR	97220	**800-877-0474**		297-2
Coffee Beanery Ltd, The						
3429 Pierson Pl	Flushing	MI	48433	**800-441-2255**	810-733-1020	159
Coffee County						
101 S Peterson Ave Ste A-15	Douglas	GA	31533	**800-436-7442**	912-384-4895	337
Coffee Holding Company Inc						
3475 Victory Blvd	Staten Island	NY	10314	**800-458-2233**	718-832-0800	296-7
NASDAQ: JVA						
Coffee Masters Inc						
7606 Industrial Ct	Spring Grove	IL	60081	**800-334-6485**	815-675-0088	297-2
Coffee Regional Medical Ctr (CRMC)						
1101 Ocilla Rd	Douglas	GA	31533	**800-555-4444**	912-384-1900	373-3
Coffeyville Regional Medical Ctr						
1400 W Fourth St	Coffeyville	KS	67337	**800-540-2762**	620-251-1200	373-3
Coffin Turbo Pump Inc						
326 S Dean St	Englewood	NJ	07631	**800-568-9798**	201-568-4700	637
Coffman Truck Sales						
1149 West Lake St	Aurora	IL	60507	**800-255-7641**	630-892-7093	57
Cogeco Peer 1						
413 Horner Ave	Etobicoke	ON	M8W4W3	**877-720-2228**	877-504-0091	225
Cogent Communications Group Inc						
1015 31st St NW	Washington	DC	20007	**877-875-4432**	202-295-4200	393
NASDAQ: CCOI						
Coghlan's Ltd						
121 Irene St	Winnipeg	MB	R3T4C7	**877-264-4526**	204-284-9550	707
Cognify						
PO Box 69337	Oro Valley	AZ	85737	**888-264-6439**		224
Cognizant Technology Solutions Corp						
500 Frank W Burr Blvd	Teaneck	NJ	07666	**888-937-3277**	201-801-0233	180
NASDAQ: CTSH						
Cogswell Polytechnical College						
1175 Bordeaux Dr	Sunnyvale	CA	94089	**800-264-7955**	408-541-0100	166
COGWM (Church of God World Missions)						
2490 Keith St	Cleveland	TN	37311	**800-345-7492**		48-20

Name / Address	City	State	ZIP	Toll-Free	Phone	Class
Cohber Press						
PO Box 93100	Rochester	NY	14692	**800-724-3032**	585-475-9100	776
Cohen & Steers Inc						
280 Park Ave 10th Fl	New York	NY	10017	**800-330-7348**		400
NYSE: CNS						
Cohen Highley LLP						
255 Queens Ave	London	ON	N6A5R8	**800-563-1020**	519-672-9330	427
Coherent Inc						
5100 Patrick Henry Dr	Santa Clara	CA	95054	**800-527-3786***	408-764-4000	424
NASDAQ: COHR ■ *Sales						
Coilcraft Inc						
1102 Silver Lake Rd	Cary	IL	60013	**800-322-2645**	847-639-2361	253
Coin Acceptors Inc						
300 Hunter Ave	Saint Louis	MO	63124	**800-325-2646**	314-725-0100	55
Coin Laundry Assn (CLA)						
1s660 Midwest Rd						
Ste 205	Oakbrook Terrace	IL	60181	**800-570-5629**	630-953-7920	49-4
COINage Magazine						
3585 Maple St Ste 232	Ventura	CA	93003	**800-764-6278**		455-14
CoinLab Inc						
71 Columbia St Ste 300	Seattle	WA	98104	**855-522-2646**		392
Coinstar Inc						
1800 114th Ave SE	Bellevue	WA	98004	**800-928-2274**	425-943-8000	55
Coker College						
300 E College Ave	Hartsville	SC	29550	**800-950-1908**	843-383-8000	166
Coker Consulting						
2400 Lakeview Pkwy Ste 400	Alpharetta	GA	30009	**800-345-5829**		461
Coker Tire Co						
1317 Chestnut St	Chattanooga	TN	37402	**866-516-3215**		
Cokesbury Village						
726 Loveville Rd	Hockessin	DE	19707	**800-530-2377**	302-235-6000	668
COLA						
9881 Broken Land Pkwy Ste 200	Columbia	MD	21046	**800-981-9883**	410-381-6581	49-8
Colad Group						
801 Exchange St	Buffalo	NY	14210	**800-950-1755**	716-961-1776	551
Colborne Foodbotics LLC						
28495 N Ballard Dr	Lake Forest	IL	60045	**800-626-9501**	847-371-0101	298
Colby Attorneys Service Company Inc						
111 Washington Ave Ste 703	Albany	NY	12210	**800-832-1220**		631
Colby College						
4800 Mayflower Hill	Waterville	ME	04901	**800-723-3032***	207-859-4800	166
*Admissions						
Colby Community College						
1255 S Range	Colby	KS	67701	**888-634-9350**	785-462-3984	162
Colby Convention & Visitors Bureau						
350 S Range Ste 10	Colby	KS	67701	**800-499-7928**	785-460-7643	206
Colby Equipment Company Inc						
3048 Ridgeview Dr	Indianapolis	IN	46226	**800-443-2981**	317-545-4221	357
Colby Hill Inn						
33 The Oaks PO Box 779	Henniker	NH	03242	**800-531-0330**	603-428-3281	378
Colby-Sawyer College						
541 Main St	New London	NH	03257	**800-272-1015***	603-526-3700	166
*Admissions						
Cold Shot Chillers						
14020 InterDr W	Houston	TX	77032	**800-473-9178**	281-227-8400	14
Cold Stone Creamery Inc						
9311 E Via De Ventura	Scottsdale	AZ	85258	**866-452-4252***	480-362-4800	380
*Cust Svc						
Coldiron Companies Inc						
200 N Sooner Rd	Edmond	OK	73034	**800-293-4369**	405-562-2910	311
Coldspring						
17482 Granite W Rd	Cold Spring	MN	56320	**800-328-5040**		720
ColdStar Solutions Inc						
1015 Henry Eng Pl	Victoria	BC	V9B6B2	**800-201-1277**	250-381-3399	311
Coldwell Banker Residential Brokerage						
600 Grant St Ste 900	Denver	CO	80203	**833-472-7283***	303-320-5733	648
*All						
Cole Industrial Inc						
5924 203rd St SW	Lynnwood	WA	98036	**800-627-2653**	425-774-6602	606
Cole Information Services						
17041 Lakeside Hills Plz Ste 2	Omaha	NE	68130	**800-283-2855***		633-6
*Consumer Info						
Cole Papers Inc						
1300 N 38th St	Fargo	ND	58102	**800-800-8090**	701-282-5311	549
Cole Sport Inc						
1615 Park Ave	Park City	UT	84060	**800-345-2938**	435-649-4800	707
Cole Tool & Die Co						
241 Ashland Rd	Mansfield	OH	44905	**800-837-2653**	419-522-1272	752
Cole-Haan						
8701 Keystone Crossing	Indianapolis	IN	46240	**800-695-8945**		301
Coleman A Young International Airport						
11499 Conner	Detroit	MI	48213	**800-874-9426**	313-628-2146	27
Coleman Company Inc						
3600 North Hydraulic	Wichita	KS	67219	**800-835-3278***		706
*Cust Svc						
Coleman County Electric Co-op Inc						
3300 N Hwy 84 PO Box 860	Coleman	TX	76834	**800-560-2128**	325-625-2128	245
Coleman Dairy Inc						
6901 I-30	Little Rock	AR	72209	**800-365-1551**	501-748-1700	296-27
Coleman E Adler & Sons Inc						
722 Canal St	New Orleans	LA	70130	**800-925-7912**	504-523-5292	409
Coleman Instrument Co						
11575 Goldcoast Dr	Cincinnati	OH	45249	**800-899-5745**	513-489-5745	357
Coleman Professional Services						
3920 Lovers Ln	Ravenna	OH	44266	**800-673-1347**	330-296-3555	722
Coleman Worldwide Moving						
PO Box 960	Midland City	AL	36350	**877-693-7060**		775
Cole-Parmer Instrument Co						
625 E Bunker Ct	Vernon Hills	IL	60061	**800-323-4340**	847-549-7600	419
Colgate Rochester Crozer Divinity School						
1100 S Goodman St	Rochester	NY	14620	**888-937-3732**	585-271-1320	167-3
Colite International Ltd						
5 Technology Cir	Columbia	SC	29203	**800-760-7926**	803-926-7926	606
CollabNet Inc						
8000 Marina Blvd Ste 600	Brisbane	CA	94005	**888-532-6823**	650-228-2500	177
Collectcents Inc						
1450 Meyerside Dr 2nd Fl	Mississauga	ON	L5T2N5	**800-256-8964**	905-670-7575	160
Collective[i]						
130 Madison Ave	New York	NY	10016	**888-890-0020**		464

	Toll-Free	Phone	Class
Collectors Universe Inc			
PO Box 6280 .... Newport Beach CA 92658	800-325-1121	949-567-1234	51
College & University Professional Assn for Hum Res (CUPA-HR)			
1811 Commons Pt Dr .... Knoxville TN 37932	877-287-2474	865-637-7673	49-5
College Board			
45 Columbus Ave .... New York NY 10023	800-927-4302	212-713-8000	244
College Health Services LLC			
112 Turnpike Rd Ste 304 .... Westborough MA 01581	866-636-8336		177
College Hospital			
10802 College Pl .... Cerritos CA 90703	800-352-3301	562-924-9581	373-5
College Hospital Costa Mesa			
301 Victoria St .... Costa Mesa CA 92627	800-773-8001	949-642-2734	373-5
College Merici			
755 Grande All,e Ouest .... Quebec QC G1S1C1	800-208-1463	418-683-1591	162
College Music Society (CMS)			
312 E Pine St .... Missoula MT 59802	800-729-0235	406-721-9616	49-5
College of American Pathologists (CAP)			
325 Waukegan Rd .... Northfield IL 60093	800-323-4040	847-832-7000	49-8
College of American Pathologists PAC			
1350 I St NW Ste 590 .... Washington DC 20005	800-392-9994	202-354-7100	611
College of Biblical Studies-Houston			
7000 Regency Sq Blvd Ste 110.... Houston TX 77036	844-227-9673	713-785-5995	161
College of Court Reporting Inc			
111 W Tenth St Ste 111 .... Hobart IN 46342	866-294-3974		795
College of Eastern Utah			
451 E 400 N .... Price UT 84501	800-336-2381	435-613-5000	162
San Juan 639 W 100 S .... Blanding UT 84511	800-395-2969	435-678-2201	162
College of Idaho			
2112 Cleveland Blvd .... Caldwell ID 83605	800-224-3246*	208-459-5011	166
*Admissions			
College of Marin			
Indian Valley			
1800 Ignacio Blvd .... Novato CA 94949	800-579-2878	415-883-2211	162
College of Menominee Nation			
PO Box 1179 .... Keshena WI 54135	800-567-2344	715-799-5600	165
College of Mount Saint Joseph			
5701 Delhi Rd .... Cincinnati OH 45233	800-654-9314	513-244-4200	166
College of Mount Saint Vincent			
6301 Riverdale Ave .... Riverdale NY 10471	800-722-4867	718-405-3304	166
College of New Rochelle			
29 Castle Pl .... New Rochelle NY 10805	800-933-5923	914-654-5000	166
College of Nurses of Ontario			
101 Davenport Rd .... Toronto ON M5R3P1	800-387-5526	416-928-0900	162
College of Registered Nurses of Manitoba			
890 Pembina Hwy .... Winnipeg MB R3M2M8	800-665-2027	204-774-3477	165
College of Saint Catherine			
2004 Randolph Ave .... Saint Paul MN 55105	800-945-4599	651-690-6000	166
Minneapolis			
601 25th Ave S .... Minneapolis MN 55454	800-945-4599	651-690-7700	166
College of Saint Elizabeth			
2 Convent Rd .... Morristown NJ 07960	800-210-7900*	973-290-4700	166
*Admissions			
College of Saint Joseph in Vermont			
71 Clement Rd .... Rutland VT 05701	877-270-9998*	802-773-5900	166
*Admissions			
College of Saint Mary			
7000 Mercy Rd .... Omaha NE 68106	800-926-5534	402-399-2400	166
College of Saint Rose			
979 Madison Ave .... Albany NY 12203	800-637-8556		166
College of Saint Scholastica			
1200 Kenwood Ave .... Duluth MN 55811	800-447-5444	218-723-6046	166
College of Santa Fe			
1600 St Michaels Dr .... Santa Fe NM 87505	800-862-7759	877-732-5977	166
College of Southern Idaho			
PO Box 1238 .... Twin Falls ID 83303	800-680-0274	208-733-9554	162
College of Southern Maryland			
Leonardtown			
22950 Hollywood Rd .... Leonardtown MD 20650	800-933-9177	240-725-5300	162
Prince Frederick			
115 J W Williams Rd .... Prince Frederick MD 20678	800-933-9177	443-550-6000	162
College of Staten Island			
2800 Victory Blvd .... Staten Island NY 10314	888-442-4551	718-982-2000	166
College of the Albemarle			
PO Box 2327 .... Elizabeth City NC 27906	800-335-9050	252-335-0821	162
College of the Atlantic			
105 Eden St .... Bar Harbor ME 04609	800-528-0025*	207-288-5015	166
*Admissions			
College of the Canyons			
26455 Rockwell Canyon Rd .... Santa Clarita CA 91355	800-695-4858	661-259-7800	162
College of the Holy Cross			
1 College St .... Worcester MA 01610	800-442-2421	508-793-2011	166
College of the Holy Cross Dinand Library			
1 College St .... Worcester MA 01610	877-433-1843	508-793-2642	433-6
College of the Mainland			
1200 N Amburn Rd .... Texas City TX 77591	888-258-8859	409-938-1211	162
College of the Ozarks			
1 Industrial Dr PO Box 17...... Point Lookout MO 65726	800-222-0525*	417-334-6411	166
*Admissions			
College of the Redwoods			
7351 Tompkins Hill Rd .... Eureka CA 95501	800-641-0400	707-476-4100	162
Del Norte			
883 W Washington Blvd .... Crescent City CA 95531	800-641-0400	707-465-2300	162
Mendocino Coast			
440 Alger St .... Fort Bragg CA 95437	800-641-0400	707-962-2600	162
College of the Siskiyous			
800 College Ave .... Weed CA 96094	888-397-4339	530-938-4461	162
College of the Southwest			
6610 N Lovington Hwy .... Hobbs NM 88240	800-530-4400	575-392-6561	166
College of Westchester (CW)			
325 Central Ave .... White Plains NY 10606	800-660-7093		795
College of Wooster			
1189 Beall Ave .... Wooster OH 44691	800-877-9905	330-263-2000	166
College Outlook & Career Opportunities Magazine			
20 E Gregory Blvd .... Kansas City MO 64114	800-274-8867	816-361-0616	455-11
College Parents of America (CPA)			
2200 Wilson Blvd Ste 102-396.... Arlington VA 22201	888-761-6702		48-11
College Park Marriott Hotel & Conference Center			
3501 University Blvd E .... Hyattsville MD 20783	800-721-7033	301-985-7300	376
College Savings Bank			
PO Box 3769 .... Princeton NJ 08543	800-888-2723		70
College Station Ford			
1351 Earl Rudder Freeway Fwy			
.... College Station TX 77845	888-508-0241	979-431-3382	57
Colleton Medical Ctr (CMC)			
501 Robertson Blvd .... Walterboro SC 29488	866-492-9083	843-782-2000	373-3
Collier County School Board			
5775 Osceola Trl .... Naples FL 34109	800-950-6264	239-377-0001	681
Collier Insurance			
606 S Mendenhall Rd Ste 200 .... Memphis TN 38117	866-600-2655*	901-529-2900	389
*General			
Colligo Networks Inc			
400-1152 Mainland St .... Vancouver BC V6B4X2	866-685-7962	604-685-7962	179
Collin County			
2300 Bloomdale Rd Ste 2106......... McKinney TX 75071	800-974-2437	972-548-4185	337
Collin Street Bakery Inc			
401 W Seventh Ave .... Corsicana TX 75110	800-267-4657*		68
*Sales			
Collington Episcopal Community			
10450 Lottsford Rd .... Mitchellville MD 20721	888-257-9468		668
Collins & Lacy PC			
1330 Lady St 6th Fl .... Columbia SC 29201	888-648-0526	803-256-2660	427
Collins Cos			
1618 SW First Ave Ste 500......... Portland OR 97201	800-329-1219		679
Collins Electric Co Inc			
53 Second Ave .... Chicopee MA 01020	877-553-2810	413-592-9221	189-4
Collins Law Firm PC, The			
1770 Park St Ste 200 .... Naperville IL 60563	866-480-8223	630-687-9838	443
Collins Manufacturing Co			
2000 Bowser Rd .... Cookeville TN 38506	800-292-6450	931-528-5151	76
Colloid Environmental Technologies Co (CETCO)			
2870 Forbs Ave .... Hoffman Estates IL 60192	800-527-9948	847-851-1899	3
Colmac Coil Manufacturing Inc			
370 N Lincoln St PO Box 571... Colville WA 99114	800-845-6778	509-684-2595	14
Colmac Industries Inc			
PO Box 72 .... Colville WA 99114	800-926-5622	509-684-4505	426
Colmery-O'Neil Veterans Affairs Medical Ctr			
2200 SW Gage Blvd .... Topeka KS 66622	800-574-8387	785-350-3111	373-8
Cologix Inc			
2300 15th St Ste 300 .... Denver CO 80202	800-638-6336	720-230-7000	224
Coloma Frozen Foods Inc			
4145 Coloma Rd .... Coloma MI 49038	800-642-2723	269-849-0500	296-21
Colonial Bag Corp			
205 E Fullerton Ave .... Carol Stream IL 60188	800-445-7496	630-690-3999	66
Colonial Bronze Co			
511 Winsted Rd .... Torrington CT 06790	800-355-7903*	860-489-9233	349
*All			
Colonial Diversified Polymer Products LLC			
2055 Forrest St Ext .... Dyersburg TN 38024	800-303-3606	731-287-3636	
Colonial Engineering Inc			
6400 Corporate Ave .... Portage MI 49002	800-374-0234	269-323-2495	591
Colonial Farm Credit Aca			
7104 Mechanicsville Tpke			
.... Mechanicsville VA 23111	800-777-8908	804-746-1252	216
Colonial Freight Systems Inc			
10924 McBride Ln .... Knoxville TN 37932	800-826-1402	865-966-9711	775
Colonial Group Inc			
101 N Lathrop Ave .... Savannah GA 31415	800-944-3835		
Colonial Life & Accident Insurance Co			
1200 Colonial Life Blvd .... Columbia SC 29210	800-325-4368	803-213-7250	390-2
Colonial Millwork Ltd			
PO Box 436 .... Beverly WV 26253	800-833-7612		497
Colonial National Historical Park			
PO Box 210 .... Yorktown VA 23690	866-945-7920	757-898-3400	560
Colonial Nursing & Rehabilitation Inc			
125 Broad St .... Weymouth MA 02188	800-245-8389	781-337-3121	448
Colonial Penn Life Insurance Co			
399 Market St .... Philadelphia PA 19181	800-523-9100	877-877-8052	390-2
Colonial Pipeline Co			
1185 Sanctuary Pkwy Ste 100 .... Alpharetta GA 30009	800-275-3004	678-762-2200	593
Colonial Quarter			
33 St George St .... Saint Augustine FL 32084	888-991-0933		517
Colonial Truck Co			
1833 Commerce Rd .... Richmond VA 23224	800-234-8782	804-232-3492	775
Colonial Williamsburg Foundation			
PO Box 1776 .... Williamsburg VA 23187	800-447-8679	757-229-1000	305
ColonialWebb Contractors Co			
2820 Ackley Ave .... Richmond VA 23228	877-208-3894	804-916-1400	189-10
Colonna's Shipyard Inc			
400 E Indian River Rd .... Norfolk VA 23523	800-265-6627	757-545-2414	694
Colonnade Hotel			
120 Huntington Ave .... Boston MA 02116	800-962-3030	617-424-7000	378
Colony Hotel			
140 Ocean Ave .... Kennebunkport ME 04046	800-552-2363	207-967-3331	665
Colony Hotel & Cabana Club			
525 E Atlantic Ave .... Delray Beach FL 33483	800-552-2363	561-276-4123	378
Colony Inc			
2500 Galvin Dr .... Elgin IL 60123	800-735-1300	847-426-5300	233
Colony Palms Hotel			
572 N Indian Canyon Dr .... Palm Springs CA 92262	800-557-2187	760-969-1800	132
Color Ad Inc			
18601 S Santa Fe Ave .... Rancho Dominguez CA 90221	888-264-6991		623
Color Communication Inc			
4000 W Fillmore St .... Chicago IL 60624	800-458-5743		776
Color House Graphics Inc			
3505 Eastern Ave SE .... Grand Rapids MI 49508	800-454-1916	616-241-1916	776
Color Imaging Inc			
4350 Peachtree Industrial Blvd			
Ste 100 .... Norcross GA 30071	800-783-1090	770-840-1090	624
Color Me Beautiful			
7000 Infantry Ridge Rd Ste 200 .... Manassas VA 20109	800-265-6763		365
Color Merchants			
6 E 45th St Rm 1704............. New York NY 10017	800-356-3851	212-682-4788	409
Color Pigments Manufacturers Association Inc			
1400 Crystal Dr Ste 630 .... Arlington VA 22202	888-233-9527	571-348-5130	49-13
Color Spot Nurseries Inc			
2575 Olive Hill Rd .... Fallbrook CA 92028	800-554-4065	760-695-1480	368

Alphabetical Section

	Toll-Free	Phone	Class
Colorado			
Children Youth & Families Office			
1575 Sherman St ....Denver CO 80203	**800-799-5876**		338-6
CollegeInvest			
1560 Broadway Ste 1700 ....Denver CO 80202	**800-448-2424**	303-376-8800	721
Division Of Criminal Justice			
700 Kipling St Ste 1000 ....Denver CO 80215	**888-282-1080**	303-239-4442	338-6
Emergency Management Office			
9195 E Mineral Ave ....Centennial CO 80112	**877-820-7831**	720-279-0026	338-6
Insurance Div			
1560 Broadway Ste 850 ....Denver CO 80202	**800-930-3745**	303-894-7499	338-6
Labor & Employment Dept			
633 17th St Ste 201 ....Denver CO 80202	**800-388-5515**	303-318-9000	259
Lottery 225 N Main St ....Pueblo CO 81003	**800-999-2959**	719-546-2400	450
Natural Resources Dept			
1313 Sherman St Rm 718 ....Denver CO 80203	**800-536-5308**	303-866-3311	338-6
Parks and Wildlife			
1313 Sherman St Rm 618 ....Denver CO 80203	**800-678-2267***	303-866-3437	338-6
*Campground Resv			
Public Utilities Commission			
1560 Broadway Ste 250 ....Denver CO 80202	**800-888-0170**	303-894-2000	338-6
Regulatory Agencies Dept			
1560 Broadway Ste 110 ....Denver CO 80202	**800-886-7675**	303-894-7855	338-6
State Court Administrator			
1300 Broadway Ste 210 ....Denver CO 80203	**800-888-0001**	720-625-5000	338-6
Supreme Court			
1300 Broadway Ste 500 ....Denver CO 80203	**877-888-1370**	303-457-5800	338-6
Colorado Assn of Realtors			
309 Inverness Way S ....Englewood CO 80112	**800-944-6550**	303-790-7099	652
Colorado Avalanche			
Pepsi Ctr 1000 Chopper Cir ....Denver CO 80204	**800-559-2333**	303-405-1100	712
Colorado Bar Assn			
1900 Grant St Ste 900 ....Denver CO 80203	**800-332-6736**	303-860-1115	72
Colorado Belle Hotel & Casino			
2100 S Casino Dr ....Laughlin NV 89029	**877-460-0777***	702-298-4000	133
*Resv			
Colorado Business Bank			
821 17th St ....Denver CO 80202	**800-574-4714**	303-293-2265	359-2
Colorado Charter Lines			
4960 Locust St ....Commerce CO 80022	**800-821-7491**	303-287-0239	107
Colorado Christian University			
8787 W Alameda Ave ....Lakewood CO 80226	**800-443-2484**	303-963-3000	166
Colorado College			
14 E Cache La Poudre St			
................Colorado Springs CO 80903	**800-542-7214**	719-389-6344	166
Colorado Container Corp			
4221 Monaco St ....Denver CO 80216	**800-456-4725**		
Colorado Correctional Industries			
4999 Oakland St ....Denver CO 80239	**800-685-7891***	719-226-4206	211
*Cust Svc			
Colorado Dude & Guest Ranch Assn (CDGRA)			
PO Box D ....Shawnee CO 80475	**866-942-3472**		48-23
Colorado Farm Bureau Mutual Insurance Co			
PO Box 5647 ....Denver CO 80217	**800-315-5998**	303-749-7500	390-4
Colorado Fsb			
8400 E Prentice Ave			
Ste 840 ....Greenwood Village CO 80111	**877-484-2372**	303-793-3555	70
Colorado Lawyer Magazine			
1900 Grant St 9th Fl ....Denver CO 80203	**800-332-6736**	303-860-1115	455-15
Colorado Medical Society			
7351 Lowry Blvd ....Denver CO 80230	**800-654-5653**	720-859-1001	472
Colorado Mountain College			
Alpine			
1330 Bob Adams Dr ......Steamboat Springs CO 80487	**800-621-8559**	970-870-4444	162
Aspen 0255 Sage Way ....Aspen CO 81611	**800-621-8559**	970-925-7740	162
Spring Valley			
3000 County Rd 114 ....Glenwood Springs CO 81601	**800-621-8559**	970-945-7481	162
Colorado National Monument			
1750 Rim Rock Dr ....Fruita CO 81521	**866-945-7920**	970-858-3617	560
Colorado Northwestern Community College			
500 Kennedy Dr ....Rangely CO 81648	**800-562-1105**	970-675-3335	162
Craig 50 College Dr ....Craig CO 81625	**800-562-1105**		162
Colorado Prime Foods			
500 Bi-County Blvd Ste 400........Farmingdale NY 11735	**800-365-2404**	631-694-1111	365
Colorado Railroad Museum			
17155 W 44th Ave ....Golden CO 80403	**800-365-6263**	303-279-4591	517
Colorado Rapids			
6000 Victory Way ....Commerce CO 80022	**800-979-3370**	303-727-3500	713
Colorado School of English			
331 14th St ....Denver CO 80202	**877-234-0654**	720-932-8900	422
Colorado School of Mines			
1600 Maple St ....Golden CO 80401	**800-446-9488**	303-273-3000	166
Colorado School of Mines Foundation			
1812 Illinois St ....Golden CO 80401	**800-446-9488**	303-273-3275	305
Colorado Serum Co			
4950 York St PO Box 16428........Denver CO 80216	**800-525-2065***	303-295-7527	85
*Orders			
Colorado Springs Convention & Visitors Bureau			
515 S Cascade Ave ......Colorado Springs CO 80903	**800-888-4748**	719-635-7506	206
Colorado Springs Utilities			
111 S Cascade Ave ......Colorado Springs CO 80903	**800-238-5434**	719-448-4800	782
Colorado State University			
200 West Lake St ....Fort Collins CO 80523	**800-491-4366**	970-491-1101	166
Colorado State Veterans Nursing Home-Rifle			
851 E Fifth St ....Rifle CO 81650	**800-828-4580**	970-625-0842	
Colorado Symphony Orchestra			
1245 Champa St ....Denver CO 80204	**877-292-7979**	303-292-5566	569-3
Colorado Technical University			
4435 N Chestnut St ....Colorado Springs CO 80907	**855-230-0555**	719-598-0200	166
Colorado Technical University Denver			
3151 S Vaughn Way ....Aurora CO 80014	**866-813-1836**	303-632-2300	795
Colorado Time Systems			
1551 E 11th St ....Loveland CO 80537	**800-279-0111**	970-667-1000	697
Colorado Trails Ranch			
12161 County Rd 240 ....Durango CO 81301	**800-323-3833**	866-942-3472	239
Colorado Trust			
1600 Sherman St ....Denver CO 80203	**888-847-9140**	303-837-1200	303
Colorado Valley Transit Inc			
108 Cardinal Ln PO Box 940 ....Columbus TX 78934	**800-548-1068**	979-732-6281	108
Coloradoan, The			
1300 Riverside Ave ....Fort Collins CO 80524	**877-424-0063**	970-493-6397	528-2
Colorfx Inc			
10776 Aurora Ave ....Des Moines IA 50322	**800-348-9044**		174
Colorid LLC			
20480 Chartwls Ctr Dr ....Cornelius NC 28031	**888-682-6567**	704-987-2238	357
Colors on Parade			
125 Daytona St PO Box 50940 ......Conway SC 29526	**866-756-4207***	843-347-8818	62-4
*Cust Svc			
Colosseum Online Inc			
800 Petrolia Rd ....Toronto ON M3J3K4	**877-739-7873**	416-739-7873	225
Colquitt Regional Medical Ctr (CRMC)			
3131 S Main St PO Box 40.........Moultrie GA 31768	**888-262-2762**	229-985-3420	373-3
Colt's Plastics Co			
969 N Main St ....Dayville CT 06241	**800-222-2658**	860-774-2301	98
Coltene/Whaledent Inc			
235 Ascot Pkwy ....Cuyahoga Falls OH 44223	**800-221-3046**	330-916-8800	228
Columbia Air Services			
175 Tower Ave			
Groton-New London Airport ....Groton CT 06340	**800-787-5001**	860-449-1400	63
Columbia Bank			
1301 A St Ste 800..............Tacoma WA 98402	**800-305-1905**	253-305-1900	359-2
NASDAQ: COLB			
Columbia Bank			
506 SW Coast Hwy ....Newport OR 97365	**800-304-0050***	877-272-3678	70
*Cust Svc			
Columbia Bank, The			
7168 Columbia Gateway Dr ....Columbia MD 21046	**888-822-2265**		70
Columbia Bible College			
2940 Clearbrook Rd ....Abbotsford BC V2T2Z8	**800-283-0881**	604-853-3358	780
Columbia Cascade Co			
1300 SW Sixth Ave Ste 310 ....Portland OR 97201	**800-547-1940**	503-223-1157	345
Columbia City Ballet			
1545 Main St ....Columbia SC 29201	**800-899-7408**	803-799-7605	569-1
Columbia Collectors Inc (CCI)			
1104 Main St Ste 311.........Vancouver WA 98660	**800-694-7585**	360-694-7585	160
Columbia College			
1001 Rogers St ....Columbia MO 65216	**800-231-2391**	573-875-8700	166
Columbia College			
1301 Columbia College Dr ....Columbia SC 29203	**800-277-1301**		166
Columbia College			
11600 Columbia College Dr ....Sonora CA 95370	**888-722-2873**	209-588-5100	162
Columbia College Chicago			
600 S Michigan Ave ....Chicago IL 60605	**866-705-0200**	312-663-1600	166
Columbia College Hollywood			
18618 Oxnard St ....Tarzana CA 91356	**800-785-0585**	818-345-8414	166
Columbia College Jefferson City			
3314 Emerald Ln ....Jefferson City MO 65109	**800-231-2391**	573-634-3250	166
Columbia College Lake of the Ozarks			
900 College Blvd ....Osage Beach MO 65065	**800-231-2391**	573-348-6463	166
Columbia College of Nursing (CCON)			
4425 N Port Washington Rd ....Glendale WI 53212	**800-221-5573**	414-326-2330	166
Columbia College Orlando			
2600 Technology Dr Ste 100 ....Orlando FL 32804	**800-231-2391**	407-293-9911	166
Columbia Community Mental Health			
58646 McNulty Way ....Saint Helens OR 97051	**800-294-5211**	503-397-5211	722
Columbia County			
135 NE Hernando Ave # 203 ....Lake City FL 32055	**800-342-8170**	386-755-4100	337
Columbia Crest Winery			
178810 State Rt 221 PO Box 231.......Paterson WA 99345	**888-309-9463**	509-875-4227	80-3
Columbia Daily Tribune			
101 N Fourth St ....Columbia MO 65201	**800-333-6799**	573-815-1700	528-2
Columbia Data Products Inc			
925 Sunshine Ln			
Ste 1080................Altamonte Springs FL 32714	**800-613-6288***	407-869-6700	178-12
*Sales			
Columbia Elevator Products Company Inc			
380 Horace St ....Bridgeport CT 06610	**888-858-1558**		189-1
Columbia Environmental Research Ctr (CERC)			
4200 New Haven Rd ....Columbia MO 65201	**888-283-7626**	703-648-5953	664
Columbia Forest Products Inc Columbia Plywood Div			
7900 McCloud Dr Suit 200........Greensboro NC 27409	**800-637-1609**		609
Columbia Gas of Ohio Inc			
200 Civic Ctr Dr ....Columbus OH 43215	**800-807-9781**	800-344-4077	782
Columbia Gas of Virginia Inc			
1809 Coyote Dr ....Chester VA 23836	**800-544-5606***	800-543-8911	782
*Cust Svc			
Columbia Gear Corp			
530 County Rd 50 ....Avon MN 56310	**800-323-9838**	320-356-7301	705
Columbia Industries Inc			
PO Box 746 ....Hopkinsville KY 42241	**800-531-5920**	270-881-1200	706
Columbia International University			
7435 Monticello Rd ....Columbia SC 29203	**800-777-2227**	803-754-4100	161
Columbia Legal Services			
600 Larson Bldg 6 S Second St ....Seattle WA 98901	**800-631-1323**	509-575-5593	443
Columbia Magazine			
1 Columbus Plz ....New Haven CT 06510	**800-380-9995**	203-752-4000	455-10
Columbia Memorial Hospital			
71 Prospect Ave ....Hudson NY 12534	**866-539-1370**	518-828-7601	373-3
Columbia Mfg Corp			
14400 S San Pedro St ....Gardena CA 90248	**800-729-3667**	310-327-9300	234
Columbia Missourian			
221 S Eigth St ....Columbia MO 65201	**855-270-6572**	573-882-5700	528-2
Columbia Montour chamber of Commerce, The			
238 Market St ....Bloomsburg PA 17815	**800-342-5775**	570-784-2522	139
Columbia Pipe & Supply Co			
1120 W Pershing Rd ....Chicago IL 60609	**888-429-4635**	773-927-6600	490
Columbia River Knife & Tool Inc			
18348 SW 126th Pl ....Tualatin OR 97062	**800-891-3100**	503-685-5015	349
Columbia Rural Electric Assn Inc			
115 E Main St ....Dayton WA 99328	**800-642-1231**	509-382-2578	245
Columbia Saint Mary's Hospital Ozaukee			
13111 N Port Washington Rd ....Mequon WI 53097	**800-457-6004**	262-243-7300	373-3
Columbia Savings Bank			
19-01 Rt 208 ....Fair Lawn NJ 07410	**800-747-4428***	800-522-4167	70
*Cust Svc			
Columbia Sportswear Co			
14375 NW Science Park Dr ....Portland OR 97229	**800-622-6953**	503-985-4000	155-1
NASDAQ: COLM			

	Toll-Free	Phone	Class
Columbia State Bank			
PO Box 2156 ... Tacoma WA 98401	**800-305-1905**	253-305-1900	70
Columbia State Community College			
1665 Hampshire Pk ... Columbia TN 38401	**800-848-0298**	931-540-2722	162
Clifton 795 Main St ... Clifton TN 38425	**888-346-6581**	931-676-6966	
Columbia Steel Casting Co Inc			
10425 N Bloss Ave ... Portland OR 97203	**800-547-9471**	503-286-0685	307
Columbia Theological Seminary			
701 S Columbia Dr ... Decatur GA 30030	**888-601-8916**	404-378-8821	167-3
Columbia Threadneedle Investments			
PO Box 8081 ... Boston MA 02266	**800-426-3750**		400
Columbia University Press			
615 W 131st St ... New York NY 10027	**800-944-8648**	212-459-0600	633-4
Columbia Utilities Heating Corp			
8751 18th Ave ... Brooklyn NY 11214	**877-726-5862**		316
Columbia Winery			
14030 NE 145th St ... Woodinville WA 98072	**800-488-2347**	425-482-7490	50-7
Columbia-Montour Visitors Bureau			
121 Papermill Rd ... Bloomsburg PA 17815	**800-847-4810**	570-784-8279	206
Columbian			
701 W Eigth St PO Box 180 ... Vancouver WA 98660	**800-743-3391**	360-694-3391	528-2
Columbian Chemicals Co			
1800 W Oak Commons Ct ... Marietta GA 30062	**800-235-4003**	770-792-9400	145
Columbus Area Visitors Ctr			
506 Fifth St ... Columbus IN 47201	**800-468-6564**	812-378-2622	206
Columbus Bank & Trust Co			
1148 Broadway ... Columbus GA 31901	**800-334-9007**	706-649-4900	70
Columbus Blue Jackets			
Nationwide Arena 200 W Nationwide Blvd			
Ste Level ... Columbus OH 43215	**800-645-2657**		
Columbus Business First			
303 W Nationwide Blvd ... Columbus OH 43215	**800-486-3289**	614-461-4040	455-5
Columbus College of Art & Design			
60 Cleveland Ave ... Columbus OH 43215	**877-997-2223**	614-224-9101	164
Columbus Convention & Visitors Bureau			
900 Front Ave ... Columbus GA 31901	**800-999-1613**	706-322-1613	206
Columbus County			
PO Box 1587 ... Whiteville NC 28472	**800-553-9759**	910-641-3000	337
Columbus Electric Co-op Inc			
900 N Gold St PO Box 631 ... Deming NM 88031	**800-950-2667**	575-546-8838	245
Columbus Ledger-Enquirer			
17 W 12th St ... Columbus GA 31901	**800-282-7859**	706-324-5526	528-2
Columbus Life Insurance Co			
400 E Fourth St ... Cincinnati OH 45202	**800-677-9595**		390-2
Columbus Marble Works Corp			
2415 Hwy 45 N ... Columbus MS 39705	**800-647-1055***	662-328-1477	720
*Cust Svc			
Columbus McKinnon Corp			
140 John James Audubon Pkwy ... Amherst NY 14228	**800-888-0985**	716-689-5400	468
NASDAQ: CMCO			
Columbus Public Library			
3000 Macon Rd ... Columbus GA 31906	**800-652-0782**	706-243-2669	433-3
Columbus Regional Hospital			
2400 E 17th St ... Columbus IN 47201	**800-841-4938**	812-379-4441	373-3
Columbus State Community College			
550 E Spring St ... Columbus OH 43215	**800-621-6407**	614-287-2400	162
Columbus State University			
4225 University Ave ... Columbus GA 31907	**866-264-2035**	706-507-8800	166
Columbus Symphony Orchestra			
55 E State St ... Columbus OH 43215	**800-653-8000**	614-228-9600	569-3
Columbus-Lowndes Convention & Visitors Bureau			
117 Third St S PO Box 789 ... Columbus MS 39703	**800-327-2686**	662-329-1191	206
Column Technologies Inc			
10 E 22nd St Ste 300 ... Lombard IL 60148	**866-265-8665**	630-515-6660	174
Columns, The			
3811 St Charles Ave ... New Orleans LA 70115	**800-445-9308**	504-899-9308	378
Colyer Jeff (R)			
State Capitol			
300 SW Tenth Ave Ste 241S ... Topeka KS 66612	**877-579-6757**	785-296-3232	
Comal County			
199 Main Plz ... New Braunfels TX 78130	**877-724-9475**	830-221-1100	337
Comanche Electric Co-op Assn			
201 W Wrights Ave ... Comanche TX 76442	**800-915-2533**	325-356-2533	245
Comar Inc 1 Comar Pl ... Buena NJ 08310	**800-962-6627**	856-692-6100	199
Comarco Products Inc			
501 Jackson St ... Camden NJ 08104	**800-524-2128**		
COMARK Communications			
104 Feeding Hills Rd ... Southwick MA 01077	**800-288-8364**	413-998-1100	643
Comark Corp 93 W St ... Medfield MA 02052	**800-280-8522**	508-359-8161	173-2
Comark Direct			
507 S Main St ... Ft. Worth TX 76104	**888-742-0405**		5
Comark Instruments Inc			
PO Box 500 ... Beaverton OR 97077	**800-555-6658**	503-643-5204	
Combe Inc			
1101 Westchester Ave ... White Plains NY 10604	**800-431-2610**		214
CombiMatrix Corp			
300 Goddard Ste 100 ... Irvine CA 92618	**800-710-0624**	949-753-0624	85
NASDAQ: CBMX			
Combined Express Inc			
3685 Marshall Ln ... Bensalem PA 19020	**800-777-0458**		311
Combined Specialities International Inc			
205 San Marin Dr Ste 5 ... Novato CA 94945	**866-893-9510**	415-209-0012	
Combined Transport Inc			
5656 Crater Lake Ave ... Central Point OR 97502	**800-547-2870**	541-734-7418	775
Comcar Industries Inc			
502 E Bridgers Ave ... Auburndale FL 33823	**800-524-1101***		775
*Cust Svc			
Comcast Cable Communications LLC			
1701 John F Kennedy Blvd ... Philadelphia PA 19103	**800-624-0331**	215-665-1700	116
Comcast Corp			
1701 JFK Blvd ... Philadelphia PA 19103	**800-266-2278**	215-665-1700	359-3
NASDAQ: CMCSA			
Comco Inc			
2151 N Lincoln St ... Burbank CA 91504	**800-796-6626**	818-841-5500	1
Comco Plastics Inc			
98-31 Jamaica Ave ... Woodhaven NY 11421	**800-221-9555**	718-849-9000	598
Comdata Corp			
5301 Maryland Way ... Brentwood TN 37027	**800-266-3282**	615-370-7000	69

	Toll-Free	Phone	Class
Comdel Inc			
11 Kondelin Rd ... Gloucester MA 01930	**800-468-3144**	978-282-0620	253
Comerica Bank			
411 W Lafayette ... Detroit MI 48226	**800-292-1300**	313-222-4000	70
Comerica Bank-California			
333 W Santa Clara St ... San Jose CA 95113	**800-522-2265**	408-556-5300	70
Comerica Bank-Texas			
1717 Main St ... Dallas TX 75201	**800-925-2160**		70
Cometic Gasket Inc			
8090 Auburn Rd ... Concord OH 44077	**800-752-9850**	440-354-0777	326
Com-Fab Inc			
4657 Price HilliaRds Rd ... Plain City OH 43064	**866-522-1794**	740-857-1107	758
ComForcare Senior Services Inc			
2520 Telegraph Rd			
Ste 100 ... Bloomfield Hills MI 48302	**800-886-4044**	248-745-9700	310
Comfort Inn & Suites			
2485 Hotel Circle Pl ... San Diego CA 92108	**888-221-6039**		
Comfort Inn & Suites Milwaukee			
916 E State St ... Milwaukee WI 53202	**888-221-6039**		378
Comfort Products Distributing LLC			
13202 I St ... Omaha NE 68137	**800-779-8299**	402-334-7777	608
Comfort Systems USA Inc			
675 Bering Ste 400 ... Houston TX 77057	**800-723-8431**	713-830-9600	189-10
NYSE: FIX			
Comfortex Inc			
1680 Wilkie Dr ... Winona MN 55987	**800-445-4007**	507-454-6579	469
Comfortex Window Fashions Inc			
21 Elm St ... Maplewood NY 12189	**800-843-4151***		87
*Cust Svc			
comFrank B Ross Co Inc			
970-H New Brunswick Ave ... Rahway NJ 07065	**800-541-6752**	732-669-0810	151
Comm Source Data			
200 Waler Way Bldg 1			
Unit 1 ... Saint Augustine FL 32086	**800-434-5750**		180
Command Ctr Inc			
3609 S Wadsworth Blvd Ste 250 ... Lakewood ID 80235	**866-464-5844**		717
NASDAQ: CCNI			
Command Plastic Corp			
124 W Ave ... Tallmadge OH 44278	**800-321-8001**	330-434-3497	544
Command Spanish Inc			
PO Box 1091 ... Petal MS 39465	**800-250-8637**	601-582-8378	96
Commander Hotel			
1401 Atlantic Ave ... Ocean City MD 21842	**888-289-6100**		378
CommCare Corp			
601 Poydras St 2755 Pan American Life Ctr			
... New Orleans LA 70130	**877-792-5434**	504-324-8950	370
Commemorative Brands Inc			
7211 Cir S Rd ... Austin TX 78745	**800-225-3687**		633-2
Commenco Inc			
4901 Bristol Ave ... Kansas City MO 64129	**800-292-9725**	816-753-2166	731
Commerce Corp			
7603 Energy Pkwy ... Baltimore MD 21226	**800-883-0234**	410-255-3500	428
Commercial & Architectural Products Inc			
PO Box 250 ... Dover OH 44622	**800-377-1221**	330-343-6621	497
Commercial Appeal			
495 Union Ave ... Memphis TN 38103	**800-444-6397**	901-529-2345	528-2
Commercial Bank			
301 N State St PO Box 638 ... Alma MI 48801	**800-547-8531**	989-463-2185	70
OTC: CEFC			
Commercial Cutting & Graphics LLC			
208 Central Ave ... Mansfield OH 44905	**800-995-2251**	419-526-4800	550
Commercial Driver Training			
600 Patton Ave ... West Babylon NY 11704	**800-649-7447**	631-249-1330	795
Commercial Law League of America (CLLA)			
3005 Tollview Dr ... Rolling Meadows IL 60008	**800-978-2552**	312-240-1400	49-10
Commercial Lighting Industries			
81161 Indio Blvd ... Indio CA 92201	**800-755-0155**		438
Commercial Lumber & Pallet Co			
135 Long Ln ... City Of Industry CA 91746	**800-252-4968**		200
Commercial Mailing Accessories Inc			
28220 Playmor Beach Rd ... Rocky Mount MO 65072	**800-325-7303**		4
Commercial National Financial Corp			
900 Ligonier St ... Latrobe PA 15650	**800-803-2265**	724-539-3501	359-2
OTC: CNAF			
Commercial Programming Systems Inc			
4400 Coldwater Canyon Ave ... Studio City CA 91604	**888-277-4562**	323-851-2681	177
Commercial Properties Realty Trust			
100 North St ... Baton Rouge LA 70802	**800-648-9064**	225-924-7206	650
Commercial Siding & Maintenance Co, The			
8059 Crile Rd ... Painesville OH 44077	**800-229-4276**	440-352-7800	189-12
Commercial-News			
17 W N St ... Danville IL 61832	**877-732-8258**	217-446-1000	528-2
Commission Junction Inc			
530 E Montecito St ... Santa Barbara CA 93103	**800-761-1072**	805-730-8000	7
Commission on Accreditation for Dietetics Education (CADE)			
120 S Riverside Plz Ste 2000 ... Chicago IL 60606	**800-877-1600**	312-899-0040	48-1
Commission on Accreditation for Law Enforcement Agencies (CALEA)			
13575 Heathcote Blvd			
Ste 320 ... Gainesville VA 20155	**877-789-6904**	703-352-4225	49-7
Commission on Accreditation in Physical Therapy Education (CAPTE)			
1111 North Fairfax St ... Alexandria VA 22314	**800-999-2782**	703-706-3245	48-1
Commission on Accreditation of Rehabilitation Facilities International (CARF)			
6951 E Southpoint Rd ... Tucson AZ 85756	**888-281-6531**	520-325-1044	48-1
Commission on Presidential Scholars			
US Presidential Scholars Program			
400 Maryland Ave SW			
US. Department of Education ... Washington DC 20202	**800-872-5327**	202-401-0961	
Committee for Economic Development (CED)			
1530 Wilson Blvd Ste 400 ... Arlington VA 22209	**800-676-7353**	202-296-5860	630
Commodity Futures Trading Commission			
1155 21 St NW ... Washington DC 20581	**866-366-2382**	202-418-5000	339-19
Commodity Futures Trading Commission Regional Offices			
Central Region			
525 W Monroe St ... Chicago IL 60661	**800-621-3570**	312-596-0700	339-19
Commodity Information Systems Inc			
3030 NW Expy Ste 725 ... Oklahoma City OK 73112	**800-231-0477**	405-604-8726	633-9
Commodity Research Bureau			
330 S Wells St Ste 612 ... Chicago IL 60606	**800-621-5271**	312-554-8456	527-9

	Toll-Free	Phone	Class
Commodity Systems Inc			
200 W Palmetto Park Rd Ste 200 ... Boca Raton FL 33432	**800-274-4727**	561-392-8663	224
Common Census Inc			
90 Bridge St Ste 105 ... Westbrook ME 04092	**800-552-7373**	207-854-5454	
Commons at Orlando Lutheran Towers, The			
300 E Church St ... Orlando FL 32801	**800-859-1033**	407-422-4103	48-20
Commonwealth Biotechnologies Inc			
601 Biotech Dr ... Richmond VA 23235	**800-735-9224**	804-648-3820	416
Commonwealth Canvas Inc			
5 Perkins Way ... Newburyport MA 01950	**877-922-6827**	978-499-3900	728
Commonwealth Club, The			
555 Post St ... San Francisco CA 94102	**800-847-7730**	415-597-6700	628
Commonwealth Credit Union			
PO Box 978 ... Frankfort KY 40602	**800-228-6420**	502-564-4775	219
Commonwealth Financial Network			
29 Sawyer Rd ... Waltham MA 02453	**800-237-0081**	781-736-0700	400
Commonwealth Health Corporation Inc			
800 Park St ... Bowling Green KY 42101	**800-786-1581**	270-745-1500	362
Commonwealth Laminating & Coating Inc			
345 Beaver Creek Dr ... Martinsville VA 24112	**888-321-5111***	276-632-4991	695
*General			
Commonwealth Land Title Insurance Co			
601 Riverside Ave ... Jacksonville FL 32204	**888-866-3684**		390-6
Commonwealth Park Suites Hotel			
901 Bank St ... Richmond VA 23219	**888-343-7301**	804-343-7300	378
Commonwealth Public Broadcasting			
23 Sesame St ... Richmond VA 23235	**800-476-2357**	804-320-1301	
Commonwealth Telephone Co			
1 Newbury St Ste 103 ... Peabody MA 01960	**800-439-7170**	978-536-9500	731
CommScope Inc			
1100 Commscope Pl SE PO Box 339 ... Hickory NC 28603	**800-982-1708**	828-324-2200	809
Communica 31 N Erie St ... Toledo OH 43604	**800-800-7890**		511
Communication Data Services			
1901 Bell Ave ... Des Moines IA 50315	**866-897-7987**	515-246-6837	225
Communication Technologies Inc			
14151 Newbrook Dr Ste 400 ... Chantilly VA 20151	**888-266-8358**	703-961-9080	730
Communications & Power Industries LLC			
607 Hansen Way ... Palo Alto CA 94303	**800-231-4818**	650-846-2900	253
Communications Daily			
2115 Ward Ct NW ... Washington DC 20037	**800-771-9202**	202-872-9200	527-11
Communications Manufacturing Co (CMC)			
2234 Colby Ave ... Los Angeles CA 90064	**800-462-5532***	310-828-3200	248
*Orders			
Communications News			
PO Box 866 ... Osprey FL 34229	**800-827-9715**	941-539-7579	455-5
Communications Resource Inc			
8280 Greensboro Dr Ste 500 ... Mc Lean VA 22102	**888-900-9757**	703-245-4120	177
Communications Supply Service Assn (CSSA)			
5700 Murray St ... Little Rock AR 72209	**800-252-2772**	501-562-7666	49-20
Communications Test Design Inc			
1339 Enterprise Dr ... West Chester PA 19380	**800-223-3910**	610-436-5203	730
CommuniGate Systems Inc			
655 Redwood Hwy Ste 275 ... Mill Valley CA 94941	**800-262-4722**	415-383-7164	178-12
Communispond Inc			
12 Barns Ln ... East Hampton NY 11937	**800-529-5925**	631-907-8010	194
Community America Credit Union (CACU)			
9777 Ridge Dr ... Lenexa KS 66219	**800-892-7957**	913-905-7000	219
Community Assns Institute (CAI)			
6402 Arlington Blvd Ste 500 ... Falls Church VA 22042	**888-224-4321**	703-970-9220	48-7
Community Banc Investments Inc			
26 E Main St ... New Concord OH 43762	**800-224-1013**		
Community Bank			
505 E Colorado Blvd ... Pasadena CA 91101	**800-788-9999**		69
Community Bank of Raymore			
PO Box 200 ... Raymore MO 64083	**800-523-4175**	816-322-2100	70
Community Bank System Inc			
5790 Widewaters Pkwy ... Syracuse NY 13214	**866-764-8638**	315-445-2282	359-2
NYSE: CBU			
Community Banking Advisory Network (CBAN)			
1801 W End Ave Ste 800 ... Nashville TN 37203	**800-231-2524**	615-373-9880	49-2
Community Blood Bank of Northwest Pennsylvania			
2646 Peach St ... Erie PA 16508	**877-842-0631**	814-456-4206	89
Community Blood Center (CBC)			
4040 Main St ... Kansas City MO 64111	**888-647-4040**	816-753-4040	89
Community Blood Ctr			
349 S Main St ... Dayton OH 45402	**800-388-4483**		89
Community Blood Ctr			
4040 Main St ... Kansas City MO 64111	**888-647-4040**	816-753-4040	89
Community Blood Ctr Inc			
4406 W Spencer St ... Appleton WI 54914	**800-280-4102**	920-738-3131	89
Community Blood Ctr of the Ozarks			
220 W Plainview Rd ... Springfield MO 65810	**800-280-5337**	417-227-5000	89
Community Blood Services			
102 Chestnut Ridge Rd ... Montvale NJ 07645	**866-228-1500**	201-444-3900	89
Community Care			
218 W Sixth St ... Tulsa OK 74119	**800-278-7563**	918-594-5200	390-3
Community Care Inc			
1555 S Layton Blvd ... Milwaukee WI 53215	**866-992-6600**	414-385-6600	194
Community Coffee Co			
3332 Partridge Ln Bldg A ... Baton Rouge LA 70809	**800-688-0990**	800-884-5282	296-7
Community College of Aurora			
16000 E Centretech Pkwy ... Aurora CO 80011	**844-493-8255**	303-360-4700	162
Community College of Baltimore County			
Essex			
7201 Rossville Blvd ... Baltimore MD 21237	**877-557-2575**	410-682-6000	162
Community College of Beaver County			
1 Campus Dr ... Monaca PA 15061	**800-335-0222**	724-775-8561	162
Community College of Rhode Island			
Flanagan			
1762 Louisquisset Pk ... Lincoln RI 02865	**800-494-8100**	401-333-7000	162
Liston 1 Hilton St ... Providence RI 02905	**800-494-8100**	401-455-6000	162
Community College of Vermont			
Bennington			
324 Main St ... Bennington VT 05201	**800-431-0025**	802-447-2361	162
Brattleboro			
70 Landmark Hill Ste 101 ... Brattleboro VT 05301	**800-431-0025**	802-254-6370	162
Middlebury			
10 Merchants Row Ste 223 ... Middlebury VT 05753	**800-431-0025**	802-388-3032	162
Montpelier			
PO Box 489 ... Montpelier VT 05602	**800-228-6686**	802-828-4060	162
Morrisville			
197 Harrell St Ste 2 ... Morrisville VT 05661	**800-431-0025**	802-888-4258	162
Newport			
100 Main St Ste 150 ... Newport VT 05855	**800-431-0025**	802-334-3387	162
Upper Valley			
145 Billings Farm Rd ... White River Junction VT 05001	**800-431-0025**	802-295-8822	162
Community College System of New Hampshire (CCSNH)			
26 College Dr ... Concord NH 03301	**866-945-2255**	603-230-3500	162
Community Development Digest			
8204 Fenton St ... Silver Spring MD 20910	**800-666-6380**	301-588-6380	527-7
Community Eldercare Services LLC (CES)			
PO Box 3667 ... Tupelo MS 38803	**877-461-1062**		
Community Electric Co-op			
52 W Windsor Blvd ... Windsor VA 23487	**855-700-2667**	757-242-6181	245
Community Foundation for Greater New Haven			
70 Audubon St ... New Haven CT 06510	**877-829-5500**	203-777-2386	303
Community Health Accreditation Program Inc (CHAP)			
1275 K St NW Ste 800 ... Washington DC 20005	**800-656-9656**	202-862-3413	48-1
Community Health Charities			
1199 N Fairfax St ... Alexandria VA 22314	**800-654-0845**	703-528-1007	48-5
Community Health Systems Inc			
4000 Meridian Blvd ... Franklin TN 37067	**888-373-9600**	615-465-7000	352
NYSE: CYH			
Community Hospice			
1480 Carter Ave ... Ashland KY 41101	**800-926-6184**	606-329-1890	370
Community Hospice Inc			
4368 Spyres Way ... Modesto CA 95356	**866-645-4567**	209-578-6300	370
Community Hospice of Northeast Florida			
4266 Sunbeam Rd ... Jacksonville FL 32257	**800-274-6614**	904-268-5200	370
Community Hospice of Texas			
6100 Western Pl Ste 105 ... Fort Worth TX 76107	**800-226-0373**		370
Community Hospital Anderson (CHA)			
1515 N Madison Ave ... Anderson IN 46011	**800-777-7775**	765-298-4242	373-3
Community Hospital of the Monterey Peninsula (CHOMP)			
23625 Holman Hwy ... Monterey CA 93940	**888-452-4667**	831-624-5311	373-3
Community Investors Bancorp Inc			
119 S Sandusky Ave ... Bucyrus OH 44820	**800-222-4955**	419-562-7055	359-2
OTC: CIBN			
Community Medical Ctr (CMC)			
99 Hwy 37 W ... Toms River NJ 08755	**888-724-7123**	732-557-8000	373-3
Community of Christ			
1001 W Walnut St ... Independence MO 64050	**800-825-2806**	816-833-1000	48-20
Community Oriented Policing Services (COPS)			
145 N St NE ... Washington DC 20530	**800-421-6770**		339-13
Community Pharmacies			
16 Commerce Dr Ste 1 PO Box 528 ... Augusta ME 04332	**800-730-4840**		237
Community Professional Loudspeakers			
333 E Fifth St ... Chester PA 19013	**800-523-4934**	610-876-3400	52
Community Regional Medical Ctr			
2823 Fresno St ... Fresno CA 93721	**800-994-6610**	559-459-6000	373-3
Community Resource Federal Credit Union			
20 Wade Rd ... Latham NY 12110	**888-783-2211**	518-783-2211	219
Community Services Group (CSG)			
320 Highland Dr PO Box 597 ... Mountville PA 17554	**877-907-7970**	717-285-7121	352
Community Shores Bank Corp			
1030 W Norton Ave ... Muskegon MI 49441	**888-853-6633**	231-780-1800	359-2
NASDAQ: CSHB			
Community Surgical Supply Inc			
1390 Rt 37 W ... Toms River NJ 08755	**800-349-2990**	732-349-2990	475
Community Tissue Services			
2900 College Dr ... Kettering OH 45420	**800-684-7783**		541
Community Transportation Assn of America (CTAA)			
1341 G St NW 10th Fl ... Washington DC 20005	**800-891-0590**		49-21
Community Trust Bank NA			
346 N Mayo Trl PO Box 2947 ... Pikeville KY 41501	**800-422-1090**	606-432-1414	70
Community VNA			
10 Emory St ... Attleboro MA 02703	**800-220-0110**	508-222-0118	370
Comm-Works Holdings LLC			
1405 Xenium Ln N Ste 120 ... Minneapolis MN 55441	**800-853-8090**	763-258-5800	252
Com-Net Services			
7786 S Commerce Ave ... Baton Rouge LA 70815	**800-676-2137**	225-928-1231	224
Comnexia Corp			
590 W Crssvlle Rd ... Roswell GA 30075	**877-600-6550**		
Co-Mo Electric Co-op Inc			
29868 Hwy 5 PO Box 220 ... Tipton MO 65081	**800-781-0157**	660-433-5521	245
Comox Valley Chamber of Commerce			
2040 Cliffe Ave ... Courtenay BC V9N2L3	**888-357-4471**	250-334-3234	137
Com-Pac International Inc			
800 W Industrial Park Rd ... Carbondale IL 62901	**800-824-0817**		
Compact Power Equipment Centers LLC			
PO Box 40 ... Fort Mill SC 29716	**888-266-7228**		
Compaction Technologies Inc			
8324 89th Ave N ... Brooklyn Park MN 55445	**877-860-6900**		192
Compak Asset Management			
1801 Dove St ... Newport Beach CA 92660	**800-388-9700**		400
COMPanion Corp			
1831 Ft Union Blvd ... Salt Lake City UT 84121	**800-347-6439**	801-943-7277	177
Companion Life Insurance Co			
7909 Parklane Rd Ste 200 ... Columbia SC 29223	**800-753-0404**	803-735-1251	390-2
Companion Pets Inc (CPI)			
2001 N Black Canyon Hwy ... Phoenix AZ 85009	**800-646-3611**	602-255-0166	574
Companions & Homemakers Inc			
613 New Britain Ave ... Farmington CT 06032	**800-348-4663**	860-677-4948	805
Company Car Chauffeured Transportation			
7138 Envoy Ct ... Dallas TX 75247	**888-559-0708**	214-824-0011	440
Compass Bancshares Inc			
15 S 20th St ... Birmingham AL 35233	**800-266-7277**	205-297-1986	359-2
Compass Cove Ocean Resort			
2311 S Ocean Blvd ... Myrtle Beach SC 29577	**800-331-0934**	843-448-8373	665
Compass Group North American Div (CGNAD)			
2400 Yorkmont Rd ... Charlotte NC 28217	**800-357-0012**	704-328-4000	299
Compass Minerals International			
9900 W 109th St Ste 100 ... Overland Park KS 66210	**866-755-1743***	913-344-9200	676
NYSE: CMP ■ *Cust Svc			

	Toll-Free	Phone	Class
Compassion & Choices PO Box 101810 .... Denver CO 80250	800-247-7421		48-17
Compassion Canada 985 Adelaide St S .... London ON N6E4A3	800-563-5437	519-668-0224	48-20
Compassion International 12290 Voyager Pkwy ... Colorado Springs CO 80921	800-336-7676	719-487-7000	48-5
Compassionate Care Hospice 3331 St Rd Ste 410 .... Bensalem PA 19020	800-584-8165	215-245-3525	370
Compassionate Friends PO Box 3696 .... Oak Brook IL 60522	877-969-0010	630-990-0010	48-21
CompassLearning Inc 203 Colorado St .... Austin TX 78701	800-232-9556	512-478-9600	178-3
Compatico Inc 5005 Kraft Ave SE Ste A ... Grand Rapids MI 49512	800-336-1772	616-940-1772	350
CompBenefits Corp 100 Mansell Ct E Ste 400 .... Roswell GA 30076	800-633-1262	770-552-7101	390-3
Compensation Resources Inc 310 Rt 17 North ...... Upper Saddle River NJ 07458	877-934-0505	201-934-0505	194
Competency & Credentialing Institute 2170 S Parker Rd Ste 295 .... Denver CO 80231	888-257-2667		148
Competition Cams Inc 3406 Democrat Rd .... Memphis TN 38118	800-999-0853	901-795-2400	60
Competitor Magazine 9477 Waples St Ste 150 .... San Diego CA 92121	800-311-1255		455-20
Compex Legal Services Inc 325 S Maple Ave .... Torrance CA 90503 *Cust Svc	800-426-6739*		443
Complemar Partners 500 Lee Rd .... Rochester NY 14606	800-388-7254	585-647-5800	551
Complete Innovations Inc WaterPark Pl 88 Queens Quay W Ste 200 .... Toronto ON M5J0B8	800-220-0779	905-944-0863	177
Complete Payroll Processing Inc 7488 SR- 39 Po Box 190 .... Perry NY 14530	888-237-5800	585-237-5800	2
Complex Steel & Wire Corp 36254 Annapolis St .... Wayne MI 48184	800-521-0666	734-326-1600	307
Complexe Les Ailes 705 rue Sainte-Catherine Ouest .... Montreal QC H3B4G5	800-998-6844	514-288-3708	
Compli /11 SW Alder Ste 200 .... Portland OR 97205 *Support	877-522-4276*	800-481-8309	177
Complia Health 1827 Walden Office Sq Ste 104 .... Schaumburg IL 60173	866-802-7704		521
Compmanagement Inc PO Box 884 .... Dublin OH 43017	800-825-6755	614-376-5300	461
Component Enterprises Co Inc 235 E Penn St PO Box 189 ..... Norristown PA 19401	877-232-7253		810
Component Hardware Group Inc 1890 Swarthmore Ave .... Lakewood NJ 08701	800-526-3694	732-363-4700	349
ComponentOne LLC 201 S Highland Ave 3rd Fl .... Pittsburgh PA 15206	800-858-2739	412-681-4343	178-12
Comporium Communications PO Box 470 .... Rock Hill SC 29731	888-403-2667	803-326-6064	731
Composite Panel Assn 19465 Deerfield Ave Ste 306 ...... Leesburg VA 20176	866-426-6767	703-724-1128	49-3
Compositech Inc 5315 Walt Pl .... Indianapolis IN 46254	800-447-8372	317-481-1120	514
Composition Materials Company Inc 249 Pepes Farm Rd .... Milford CT 06460	800-262-7763	203-874-6500	1
Comprehensive Care Management Corp (CCM) 1250 Waters Pl Tower 1 Ste 602 .... Bronx NY 10461	877-226-8500		448
Comprehensive Financial Planning LLC 530 Main Ave Ste A .... Durango CO 81301	877-901-5227	970-385-5227	194
Comprehensive Health Service 8600 Astronaut Blvd ...... Cape Canaveral FL 32920	800-638-8083	321-783-2720	
Comprehensive Health Services Inc (CHSI) 10701 Parkridge Blvd Ste 200 ...... Reston VA 20191	800-638-8083	703-760-0700	390-3
Comprehensive Pharmacy Services Inc (CPS) 6409 N Quail Hollow Rd .... Memphis TN 38120	800-968-6962	901-748-0470	194
Comprehensive Traffic Systems Inc 4300 Harlan St .... Wheat Ridge CO 80033	888-353-9002		
Compressed Air Systems Inc 9303 Stannum St .... Tampa FL 33619	800-626-8177	813-626-8177	172
Compressor Engineering Corp (CECO) 5440 Alder Dr .... Houston TX 77081	800-879-2326	713-664-7333	172
Compressor Products International 4410 Greenbriar Dr .... Stafford TX 77477	800-675-6646	281-207-4600	128
ComPsych Corp 455 N City Front Plaza Dr 13th Fl .... Chicago IL 60611	800-851-1714	312-595-4000	460
Comptroller of the Currency 250 E St SW .... Washington DC 20219 *Cust Svc	800-613-6743*	202-874-5000	339-17
CompuCom Systems Inc 7171 Forest Ln .... Dallas TX 75230 *Cust Svc	800-597-0555*	972-856-3600	176
Compugen Inc 100 Via Renzo Dr ...... Richmond Hill ON L4S0B8	800-387-5045	905-707-2000	394
Compulink Inc 1205 Gandy Blvd N ...... Saint Petersburg FL 33702	800-231-6685	727-579-1500	809
Compunetix Inc 2420 Mosside Blvd .... Monroeville PA 15146	800-879-4266		730
Compunnel Software Group Inc 103 Morgan Ln Ste 102 .... Plainsboro NJ 08536	800-696-8128		717
CompuOne Corp 9888 Carroll Centre Rd Ste 201 .... San Diego CA 92126	888-226-6781	858-404-7000	196
Compusearch Software Systems Inc 21251 Ridgetop Cir .... Dulles VA 20166	855-817-2720	571-449-4000	177
Computer Aided Technology Inc 165 N Arlington Heights Rd Ste 101 .... Buffalo Grove IL 60089	888-308-2284		174
Computer Arts Inc 320 SW Fifth Ave .... Meridian ID 83642	800-365-9335	208-385-9335	177
Computer Dynamics Inc 3030 Whitehall Pk Dr ...... Charlotte NC 28273	866-599-6512		174
Computer Emergency Response Team (CERT) 4500 Fifth Ave .... Pittsburgh PA 15213	800-598-6831	412-268-7090	664
Computer Explorers 12715 Telge Rd .... Cypress TX 77429	800-531-5053		148
Computer Magazine 10662 Los Vaqueros Cir ...... Los Alamitos CA 90720 *Orders	800-272-6657*	714-821-8380	455-7
Computer Power Solutions Inc 4644 Katella Ave .... Los Alamitos CA 90720	800-444-1938	562-493-4487	180
Computer Pundits Corp (CPC) 5001 American Blvd W Ste 310 .... Bloomington MN 55437	888-786-3487	952-854-2422	180
Computer Services Inc 3901 Technology Dr .... Paducah KY 42001 OTC: CSVI	800-545-4274	270-442-7361	225
Computer Solutions 814 Arion Pkwy Ste 101 .... San Antonio TX 78216	800-326-4304	210-369-0300	177
Computer Task Group Inc (CTG) 800 Delaware Ave .... Buffalo NY 14209 OTC: CTG	800-992-5350	716-882-8000	180
Computer Team Inc 1049 State St .... Bettendorf IA 52722	800-355-0450	563-355-0426	177
Computer Technology Law Report 1801 S Bell St .... Arlington VA 22202	800-372-1033		527-7
Computer Troubleshooters USA 7100 E Pleasant Valley Rd Ste 300 .... Independence OH 44131	877-704-1702	216-674-0645	310
Computer Workshop Inc, The 5131 Post Rd Ste 102 .... Dublin OH 43017	800-639-3535	614-798-9505	759
ComputerJobscom Inc 1995 N Pk Pl SE .... Atlanta GA 30339	800-850-0045	770-850-0045	260
ComputerLogic Inc 4951 Forsyth Rd .... Macon GA 31210	800-933-6564	478-474-5593	177
ComputerPlus Sales & Service Inc 5 Northway Ct .... Greer SC 29651	800-849-4426	864-801-9003	175
Computers in Libraries Magazine 143 Old Marlton Pk .... Medford NJ 08055	800-300-9868	609-654-6266	455-7
Computers Unlimited 2407 Montana Ave .... Billings MT 59101	800-763-0308	406-255-9500	178-10
Computerwise Inc 302 N Winchester Ln .... Olathe KS 66062	800-255-3739	913-829-0600	173-7
Computerworks of Chicago Inc 5153 N Clark St .... Chicago IL 60640	800-977-8212	773-275-4437	177
Computerworld Magazine 1 Speen St .... Framingham MA 01701	800-343-6474	508-879-0700	455-7
Computrition Inc 8521 Fallbrook Ave Ste 100 .... West Hills CA 91304	800-222-4488		177
Computype Inc 2285 W County Rd C .... St. Paul MN 55113	800-328-0852		623
COMRES Inc 424 SW 12th Ave ...... Deerfield Beach FL 33442	877-379-9600	954-462-9600	
comScore Inc 11950 Democracy Dr # 600 .... Reston VA 20190	866-276-6972	703-438-2000	464
ComSonics Inc 1350 Port Republic Rd PO Box 1106 .... Harrisonburg VA 22801	800-336-9681	540-434-5965	635
Comstar Enterprises Inc PO Box 6698 .... Springdale AR 72766	800-533-2343	479-361-2111	48-11
ComStar Networks LLC 1820 NE Jensen Beach Blvd Ste 1 .... Jensen Beach FL 34957	800-516-1595		195
Comstock Historic House 506 Eigth St S .... Moorhead MN 56560	800-657-3773	218-291-4211	50-3
Comstock Resources Inc 5300 Town & Country Blvd Ste 500 ...... Frisco TX 75034 NYSE: CRK	800-929-4884	972-668-8800	532
Comstor 520 White Plains Rd .... Tarrytown NY 10591	800-955-9590	914-829-7000	174
Comstor Productivity Ctr Inc 441 W Sharp Ave .... Spokane WA 99201	800-776-2451	509-534-5080	494
Comtech Network Systems Inc 1320 Lincoln Ave Ste 4 .... Holbrook NY 11741	877-267-0750		
Comtel Corp 39810 Grand River Ave Ste 180 .... Novi MI 48375	800-335-2505	248-888-4730	246
Comtran Cable 330A Turner St .... Attleboro MA 02703	800-842-7809	508-399-7004	
Comtrol 100 Fifth Ave NW ...... Maple Grove MN 55112	800-926-6876	763-957-6000	176
Comware Technical Services Inc 17922 Sky Park Cir Ste E .... Irvine CA 92614	800-460-1970	949-851-9600	175
Comwave Networks Inc 61 Wildcat Rd .... Toronto ON M3J2P5	877-474-6638	416-663-9700	386
Con Cast Pipe LP 299 Brock Rd S .... Puslinch ON N0B2J0	800-668-7473	519-763-8655	183
Con Forms 777 Maritime Dr ...... Port Washington WI 53074	800-223-3676	262-284-7800	183
Conagra Brands Inc 1 ConAgra Dr .... Omaha NE 68102 NYSE: CAG	877-266-2472	402-240-4000	359-3
ConAgra Foods Foodservice Co 5 ConAgra Dr .... Omaha NE 68102	800-357-6543	800-722-1344	297-6
Conair Corp 1 Cummings Point Rd .... Stamford CT 06902 OTC: CNGA	800-326-6247	203-351-9000	37
Conax Buffalo Technologies LLC 2300 Walden Ave .... Buffalo NY 14225	800-223-2389	716-684-4500	201
Concensus Consulting LLC 51 Dutilh Rd Ste 140 ... Cranberry Township PA 16066	888-349-1014		
Concentra Inc 5080 Spectrum Dr Ste 1200 W .... Addison TX 75001	866-944-6046		461
Concentrix Corp 44201 Nobel Dr .... Fremont CA 94538	800-747-0505		113
Concepts Av Integration 4610 S 133rd St Ste 106 .... Omaha NE 68137	877-422-3933	402-298-5011	606
ConceptShare Inc 130 Slater St .... Ottawa ON K1P6E2	844-227-7848	613-903-4431	386
Conceptual Financial Planning Inc 2561 E Calumet St .... Appleton WI 54915	866-809-6411	920-731-9500	686

Alphabetical Section

				Toll-Free	Phone	Class
Concern America						
2015 N Broadway	Santa Ana	CA	92706	**800-266-2376**	714-953-8575	48-5
Concerned United Birthparents Inc (CUB)						
PO Box 503475	San Diego	CA	92150	**800-822-2777**		48-21
Concerns of Police Survivors Inc (COPS)						
846 Old S 5 PO Box 3199	Camdenton	MO	65020	**800-784-2677**	573-346-4911	48-21
Concerto Marketing Group Inc						
128 Hastings St W	Vancouver	BC	V6B1G8	**877-873-2738**	604-642-5901	7
Conch House Heritage Inn						
625 Truman Ave	Key West	FL	33040	**800-207-5806**	305-293-0020	378
Conch House Marina Resort						
57 Comares Ave	Saint Augustine	FL	32080	**800-940-6256**	904-829-8646	378
Concord Confections Ltd						
345 Courtland Ave	Concord	ON	L4K5A6	**800-267-0037**	905-660-8989	296-6
Concord Document Services Inc						
1321 W 12th St	Los Angeles	CA	90015	**800-246-7881**	213-745-3175	225
Concord Group Insurance Cos						
4 Bouton St	Concord	NH	03301	**800-852-3380**		390-4
Concord Litho Group						
92 Old Tpke Rd	Concord	NH	03301	**800-258-3662**	603-225-3328	623
Concord Marketing Solutions Inc						
195 Exchange Blvd	Glendale Heights	IL	60139	**800-648-8588**	630-893-6453	461
Concord Regional Visiting Nurse Assoc Hospice Program						
30 Pillsbury St	Concord	NH	03301	**800-924-8620**	603-224-4093	370
Concord Servicing Corp						
4150 N Drinkwater Blvd	Scottsdale	AZ	85251	**866-493-6393**		317
Concord University						
PO Box 1000	Athens	WV	24712	**800-344-6679**	304-384-3115	166
Concorde Career Colleges Inc						
5800 Foxridge Dr Ste 500	Mission	KS	66202	**800-693-7010**	913-831-9977	795
Aurora 111 N Havana St	Aurora	CO	80010	**800-693-7010**	303-861-1151	
Miramar						
10933 Marks Way	Miramar	FL	33025	**800-693-7010**	954-731-8880	795
San Bernardino						
201 E Airport Dr	San Bernardino	CA	92408	**800-693-7010**	909-884-8891	795
San Diego						
4393 Imperial Ave Ste 100	San Diego	CA	92113	**800-693-7010**	619-688-0800	795
Concorde Inc						
1835 Market St Ste 1200	Philadelphia	PA	19103	**800-662-1676**		
Concordia College						
901 Eigth St S	Moorhead	MN	56562	**800-699-9897**	218-299-4000	166
Concordia College New York						
171 White Plains Rd	Bronxville	NY	10708	**800-937-2655***	914-337-9300	166
*Admissions						
Concordia Electric Co-op Inc						
1865 Hwy 84 W PO Box 98	Jonesville	LA	71343	**800-617-6282**	318-339-7969	245
Concordia Hospital						
1095 Concordia Ave	Winnipeg	MB	R2K3S8	**888-315-9257**	204-667-1560	373-2
Concordia Language Villages						
8659 Thorsonveien Rd	Bemidji	MN	56601	**800-450-2214**	800-222-4750	239
Concordia Publishing House Inc						
3558 S Jefferson Ave	Saint Louis	MO	63118	**800-325-3040***	314-268-1000	633-3
*Cust Svc						
Concordia Seminary						
801 Seminary Pl	Saint Louis	MO	63105	**800-822-9545**	314-505-7000	167-3
Concordia Theological Seminary						
6600 N Clinton St	Fort Wayne	IN	46825	**800-481-2155**	260-452-2100	167-3
Concordia University						
1455 de Maisonneuve Blvd W	Montreal	QC	H3G1M8	**866-333-2271**	514-848-2424	780
Concordia University Chicago						
7400 Augusta St	River Forest	IL	60305	**888-258-6773**	708-771-8300	166
Concordia University College of Alberta						
7128 Ada Blvd NW	Edmonton	AB	T5B4E4	**866-479-5200**	780-479-9220	780
Concordia University Irvine						
1530 Concordia W	Irvine	CA	92612	**800-229-1200**	949-854-8002	166
Concordia University Nebraska						
800 N Columbia Ave	Seward	NE	68434	**800-535-5494**	402-643-3651	166
Concordia University Portland						
2811 NE Holman St	Portland	OR	97211	**800-321-9371**	503-288-9371	166
Concordia University Texas						
11400 Concordia University Dr	Austin	TX	78726	**800-865-4282**	512-313-3000	166
Concordia University Wisconsin						
12800 N Lake Shore Dr	Mequon	WI	53097	**888-628-9472***	262-243-5700	166
*Admissions						
Concrete Systems Inc						
9 Commercial St	Hudson	NH	03051	**800-342-3374**	603-889-4163	
Conde Group Inc						
4141 Jutland Dr Ste 130	San Diego	CA	92117	**800-838-0819**		196
Conder Flag Co						
4705 Dwight Evans Rd	Charlotte	NC	28217	**855-344-1500**	704-529-1976	553
Condo Control Central						
2 Carlton St Ste 1000	Toronto	ON	M5B1J3	**888-762-6636**	416-961-7884	224
Condon Oil Co						
126 E Jackson St	Ripon	WI	54971	**800-452-1212**	920-748-3186	575
Condor Earth Technologies Inc						
21663 Brian Ln	Sonora	CA	95370	**800-800-0490**	209-532-0361	194
Condor Outdoor Products						
5268 Rivergrade Rd	Irwindale	CA	91706	**800-552-2554**		707
Condortech Services Inc						
6621-A Electronic Dr	Springfield	VA	22151	**800-842-9171**	703-916-9200	180
Conduant Corp						
1501 S Sunset St Ste D	Longmont	CO	80501	**888-497-7327**	303-485-2721	
Conductix 10102 F St	Omaha	NE	68127	**800-521-4888**	402-339-9300	117
Conduit Pipe Products Co						
1501 W Main St	West Jefferson	OH	43162	**800-848-6125**	614-879-9114	811
Condustrial Inc						
514 East N St	Greenville	SC	29601	**888-794-7798**	864-235-3619	260
Cone Drive Operations Inc - A Textron Co						
240 E 12th St	Traverse City	MI	49684	**888-994-2663***	231-946-8410	705
*Sales						
Coneco Engineers & Scientists Inc						
4 First St	Bridgewater	MA	02324	**800-548-3355**	508-697-3191	261
Conestoga Capital Advisors LLC						
CrossPoint at Valley Forge 550 E Swedesford Rd						
Ste 120	Radnor	PA	19087	**800-320-7790**	484-654-1380	400
Conestoga Tours Inc						
1619 Manheim Pk	Lancaster	PA	17601	**800-538-2222**	717-569-1111	107

				Toll-Free	Phone	Class
Conestoga Valley School District						
2110 Horseshoe Rd	Lancaster	PA	17601	**800-732-0025**	717-397-2421	681
Conestoga Wood Specialties Inc						
245 Reading Rd	East Earl	PA	17519	**800-964-3667**		115
CoNetrix LLC						
5214 68th St Ste 200	Lubbock	TX	79424	**800-356-6568**	806-687-8600	177
Confer Plastics Inc (CPI)						
97 Witmer Rd	North Tonawanda	NY	14120	**800-635-3213**	716-693-2056	600
Conference & Travel						
5655 Coventry Ln	Fort Wayne	IN	46804	**800-346-9807**	260-434-6600	184
Conference & Visitors Bureau of Montgomery County MD Inc						
1801 Rockville Pk Ste 320	Rockville	MD	20852	**877-789-6904**	240-641-6750	206
Conference Ctr at NorthPointe						
100 Green Meadows Dr S	Lewis Center	OH	43035	**844-475-5045**	614-880-4300	376
Conference Group, The						
254 Chapman Rd Topkis Bldg						
Ste 200	Newark	DE	19702	**877-716-8255**	302-224-8255	
Conference on College Composition & Communication (CCCC)						
1111 W Kenyon Rd	Urbana	IL	61801	**877-369-6283**	217-328-3870	49-5
Confluent Translations LLC						
340 Mansfield Ave	Pittsburgh	PA	15220	**888-539-9077**	412-539-1410	7
Conforma Laboratories Inc						
4705 Colley Ave	Norfolk	VA	23508	**800-426-1700**	757-321-0200	538
Congdon's Aids To Daily Living Ltd						
10550 - Mayfield Rd	Edmonton	AB	T5P4X4	**800-252-9368**	780-483-1762	
Conger & Elsea Inc						
9870 Hwy 92	Woodstock	GA	30188	**800-875-8709**	770-926-1131	461
Conglom Inc						
2600 Marie-Curie Ave	Saint-Laurent	QC	H4S2C3	**877-333-0098**	514-333-6666	597
Congoleum Corp						
3500 Quakerridge Rd						
PO Box 3127	Mercerville	NJ	08619	**800-274-3266**	609-584-3601	291
Congress Watch						
215 Pennsylvania Ave SE	Washington	DC	20003	**800-289-3787**	202-546-4996	48-7
Conifer Park						
79 Glenridge Rd	Schenectady	NY	12302	**800-989-6446**	518-399-6446	722
Conifex Timber Inc						
980-700 W Georgia St						
PO Box 10070	Vancouver	BC	V7Y1B6	**866-301-2949**	604-216-2949	279
Conine Clubhouse						
1005 Joe DiMaggio Dr	Hollywood	FL	33021	**866-532-4362**	954-265-5324	371
Conklin Company Inc						
551 Valley Pk Dr	Shakopee	MN	55379	**800-888-8838**	952-445-6010	365
Conklin Office Furniture						
56 N Canal St	Holyoke	MA	01040	**800-817-1187**	413-315-6777	
Conley Transport Ii Inc						
2104 Eastline Rd	Searcy	AR	72143	**800-338-8700**		447
Conlin Travel Inc						
3270 Washtenaw Ave	Ann Arbor	MI	48104	**800-426-6546**	734-677-0900	766
Conmed Corp						
525 French Rd	Utica	NY	13502	**800-448-6506**	315-797-8375	474
NASDAQ: CNMD						
CONMED Linvatec						
11311 Concept Blvd	Largo	FL	33773	**800-448-6506***	727-392-6464	474
*Cust Svc						
Conn's Inc						
3295 College St	Beaumont	TX	77701	**800-511-5750***	409-832-1696	35
NASDAQ: CONN ■ *Cust Svc						
Conneaut Savings Bank						
305 Main St PO Box 740	Conneaut	OH	44030	**888-453-2311**	440-599-8121	70
Connect PR						
1 Market St 36th Fl	San Francisco	CA	94105	**800-455-8855**	415-222-9691	632
Connect Tech Inc						
42 Arrow Rd	Guelph	ON	N1K1S6	**800-426-8979**	519-836-1291	180
Connect-Air International Inc						
4240 'B' St NW	Auburn	WA	98001	**800-247-1978**	253-813-5599	490
Connected Nation						
191 W Professional Park Ct b						
	Bowling Green	KY	42104	**877-846-7710**	270-781-4320	464
ConnectiCare Inc						
175 Scott Swamp Rd	Farmington	CT	06032	**800-251-7722***	860-674-5700	390-3
*Cust Svc						
Connecticut						
Aging Commission						
210 Capitol Ave	Hartford	CT	06106	**866-218-6631**	860-424-5274	338-7
Banking Dept						
260 Constitution Plz	Hartford	CT	06103	**800-831-7225**	860-240-8230	338-7
Chief Medical Examiner						
11 Shuttle Rd	Farmington	CT	06032	**800-842-8820**	860-679-3980	338-7
Child Support Assistance						
55 Farmington Ave	Hartford	CT	06106	**800-228-5437**		338-7
Consumer Protection Dept						
450 Columbus Blvd Ste 901	Hartford	CT	06106	**800-838-6554**	860-713-6100	338-7
Emergency Management and Homeland Security Div						
25 Sigourney St 6th Fl	Hartford	CT	06106	**800-397-8876**	860-256-0800	338-7
Higher Education Dept						
450 Columbus Blvd Ste 510	Hartford	CT	06103	**800-842-0229**	860-947-1800	338-7
Insurance Dept						
153 Market St	Hartford	CT	06103	**800-203-3447**	860-297-3800	338-7
Public Utility Control Dept						
10 Franklin Sq	New Britain	CT	06051	**800-382-4586**	860-827-1553	338-7
Real Estate & Professional Trades Div						
165 Capitol Ave	Hartford	CT	06106	**800-838-6554**	860-713-6100	338-7
Rehabilitation Services Bureau						
55 Farmington Ave 1st Fl	Hartford	CT	06105	**800-537-2549**	860-424-4844	338-7
Treasurer 55 Elm St	Hartford	CT	06106	**800-618-3404**	860-702-3000	338-7
Veterans Affairs Dept						
287 W St	Rocky Hill	CT	06067	**800-447-0961**	860-721-5891	338-7
Victim Services Office						
225 Spring St 4th Fl	Wethersfield	CT	06109	**800-822-8428**		338-7
Weights & Measures Div						
450 Columbus Blvd	Hartford	CT	06103	**800-838-6554**	860-713-6100	338-7
Workers' Compensation Commission						
21 Oak St 4th Fl	Hartford	CT	06106	**800-223-9675**	860-493-1500	338-7
Connecticut Assn of Realtors						
111 Founders Plz Ste 1101	East Hartford	CT	06108	**800-335-4862**	860-290-6601	652
Connecticut College						
270 Mohegan Ave	New London	CT	06320	**800-892-3363**	860-439-2000	166

Name / Address	Toll-Free	Phone	Class
Connecticut Laminating Company Inc 162 James St ....New Haven CT 06513	**800-753-9119**	203-787-2184	595
Connecticut Magazine 100 Gando Dr ....New Haven CT 06513	**877-396-8937**	203-789-5300	455-22
Connecticut Medical Insurance Co (CMIC) 80 Glastonbury Blvd 3rd Fl....Glastonbury CT 06033	**800-228-0287**	860-633-7788	
Connecticut Post 410 State St ....Bridgeport CT 06604 *Edit	**800-542-2517***	203-333-0161	528-2
Connecticut Public Broadcasting Inc (CPBI) 1049 Asylum Ave ....Hartford CT 06105	**877-444-4485**	860-278-5310	628
Connecticut Radio Holding Inc 1208 Cromwell Ave PO Box 487....Rocky Hill CT 06067	**800-527-8855**	860-563-4867	
Connecticut State Library 231 Capitol Ave ....Hartford CT 06106	**866-886-4478**	860-757-6510	433-5
Connecticut Water Service Inc 93 W Main St ....Clinton CT 06413 *NASDAQ: CTWS*	**800-286-5700**		359-5
Connection, The 11351 Rupp Dr ....Burnsville MN 55337 *Sales	**800-883-5777***	952-948-5488	732
ConnectOne Bank 301 Sylvan Ave ....Englewood Cliffs NJ 07632 *NASDAQ: CNOB*	**844-266-2548**		
Connectria Hosting 10845 Olive Blvd Ste 300....Saint Louis MO 63141	**800-781-7820**	314-587-7000	39
ConnectWise Inc 4110 George Rd Ste 200....Tampa FL 33634	**800-671-6898**	813-463-4700	179
Conner Prairie Living History Museum 13400 Allisonville Rd ....Fishers IN 46038	**800-966-1836**	317-776-6000	517
Connors Investor Services Inc 1210 Broadcasting Rd Ste 200....Wyomissing PA 19610	**877-376-7418**	610-376-7418	400
Conn-Selmer Inc 600 Industrial Pkwy ....Elkhart IN 46516	**800-348-7426**	574-522-1675	523
Conolog Corp 5 Columbia Rd ....Somerville NJ 08876 *NASDAQ: CNLG*	**800-526-3984**	908-722-8081	643
Conoptics International Sales Corp 19 Eagle Rd ....Danbury CT 06810	**800-748-3349**	203-743-3349	540
Conproco Corp 17 Production Dr ....Dover NH 03820	**800-258-3500**		182
Conrad Forest Products 68765 Wildwood Dr ....North Bend OR 97459	**800-356-7146**		813
Conrad Schmitt Studios Inc 2405 S 162nd St ....New Berlin WI 53151	**800-969-3033**	262-786-3030	186
Conrad-American Inc 609 Main St ....Houghton IA 52631 *General	**800-553-1791***	319-469-4141	273
Conroe Regional Medical Ctr 504 Medical Ctr Blvd ....Conroe TX 77304	**888-633-2687**	936-539-1111	373-3
Conseco Inc 11825 N Pennsylvania St ....Carmel IN 46032 *NYSE: CNO*	**866-595-2255**		359-4
Conseco Senior Health Insurance Co 11825 N Pennsylvania St ....Carmel IN 46032	**866-595-2255**		390-2
Conservation International (CI) 2011 Crystal Dr Ste 500....Arlington VA 22202	**800-406-2306**	703-341-2400	48-13
CONSOL Energy Inc 1000 Consol Energy Dr ....Canonsburg PA 15317 *NYSE: CNX*	**800-544-8024**	724-485-4000	359-3
Consolidated Brick 650 Bodwell St Ext ....Avon MA 02322	**800-321-0021**		
Consolidated Catfish Cos LLC 299 S St PO Box 271 ....Isola MS 38754	**800-228-3474**	662-962-3101	296-14
Consolidated Container Co (CCC) 3101 Towercreek Pkwy Ste 300 ....Atlanta GA 30339 *Sales	**888-831-2184***	678-742-4600	544
Consolidated Devices Inc (CDI) 19220 San Jose Ave ....City of Industry CA 91748	**800-525-6319**	626-965-0668	753
Consolidated Disposal Services Inc 12949 Telegraph Rd ....Santa Fe Springs CA 90670	**800-299-4898**		799
Consolidated Edison Inc 4 Irving Pl ....New York NY 10003 *NYSE: ED*	**800-752-6633**	212-460-4600	359-5
Consolidated Electric Co-op 3940 E Liberty St ....Mexico MO 65265	**800-621-0091**	573-581-3630	245
Consolidated Electronic Wire & Cable Co 11044 King St ....Franklin Park IL 60131	**800-621-4278**	847-455-8830	809
Consolidated Energy Co 910 Main St ....Jesup IA 50648	**800-338-3021**		575
Consolidated Fibers 8100 S Blvd ....Charlotte NC 28273	**800-243-8621**	704-554-8621	601-1
Consolidated Metco Inc 5701 SE Columbia Way ....Vancouver WA 98661 *Sales	**800-547-9473***		60
Consolidated Rail Corp 1717 Arch St 13th Fl....Philadelphia PA 19103	**800-272-0911**	215-209-2000	644
Consolidated Shoe Company Inc 22290 Timberlake Rd ....Lynchburg VA 24502	**800-368-7463**	434-239-0391	301
Consolidated Steel Services Inc 632 Glendale Vly Blvd ....Fallentimber PA 16639	**800-237-8783**	814-944-5890	490
Consolidated Supply Co 7337 SW Kable Ln ....Tigard OR 97224	**800-929-5810**	503-620-7050	608
Consortium for School Networking (CoSN) 1025 Vermont Ave NW Ste 1010....Washington DC 20005	**866-267-8747**	202-861-2676	48-9
ConSova Corp 1536 Cole Blvd Ste 350 ....Lakewood CO 80401	**866-529-9107**		196
Constantine's Wood Ctr 1040 E Oakland Pk Blvd ....Fort Lauderdale FL 33334	**800-443-9667**	954-561-1716	609
Constellation Brands Inc 207 High Pt Dr Bldg 100 ....Victor NY 14564 *NYSE: STZ*	**888-724-2169**		81-3
Constellation Technology Corp 7887 Bryan Dairy Rd Ste 100....Largo FL 33777	**800-335-7355**	727-547-0600	218
Constitutional Rights Foundation 601 S Kingsley Dr ....Los Angeles CA 90005	**800-488-4273**	213-487-5590	48-7
Construction Book Express Inc 990 Park Center Dr Ste E ....Vista CA 92081	**800-253-0541**		

Name / Address	Toll-Free	Phone	Class
Construction Claims Monthly 2222 Sedwick Rd ....Durham NC 27713	**800-223-8720**		527-13
Construction Financial Management Assn (CFMA) 100 Village Blvd Ste 200 ....Princeton NJ 08540	**888-421-9996**	609-452-8000	49-1
Construction Labor Report 1801 S Bell St ....Arlington VA 22202	**800-372-1033**		527-13
Construction Metals LLC 13169 B Slover Ave ....Fontana CA 92337	**800-576-9810**	909-390-9880	236
Construction Process Solutions Ltd 3950 Virginia Ave ....Cincinnati OH 45227	**877-295-9876**	513-271-9026	535
Construction Products Inc 1631 Ashport Rd ....Jackson TN 38305	**800-238-8226**	731-668-7305	183
Construction Specialties Inc 3 Werner Way ....Lebanon NJ 08833	**800-972-7214**	908-236-0800	489
Construction Systems Software Inc PO Box 203184 ....Austin TX 78720	**800-531-1035**		178-10
Constructors Association of Western Pennsylvania 800 Cranberry Woods Dr Ste 110....Cranberry Township PA 16066	**877-343-2297**	412-343-8000	138
Construx Software 11820 Northup Way Ste E-200....Bellevue WA 98005	**866-296-6300**	425-636-0100	177
Consulate General Of Italy *Consulate General* 150 S Independence Mall W 1026 Public Ledger Bldg ....Philadelphia PA 19106	**800-531-0840**	215-592-7329	257
Consult Dynamics Inc 1016 Delaware Ave ....Wilmington DE 19806	**800-784-4788**	302-654-1019	180
Consult Usa Inc 634 Alpha Dr ....Pittsburgh PA 15238	**866-963-8621**	412-963-8621	177
Consumer Attorneys of California 770 L St Ste 1200....Sacramento CA 95814	**800-424-2725**	916-442-6902	427
Consumer Product Safety Commission (CPSC) 4340 E W Hwy Ste 502....Bethesda MD 20814	**800-638-2772**	301-504-7923	339-19
Consumer Reports Magazine 101 Truman Ave ....Yonkers NY 10703 *Orders	**800-333-0663***	914-378-2000	455-11
Consumers Energy 2074 242nd St ....Marshalltown IA 50158	**800-696-6552**	641-752-1593	245
Consumers Energy Co 1 Energy Plz ....Jackson MI 49201 *Cust Svc	**800-477-5050***	517-788-0550	782
Consumers Pipe & Supply Co 13424 Arrow Blvd ....Fontana CA 92335	**800-338-7473**	909-728-4828	490
Consumers Power Inc (CPI) 6990 W Hills Rd ....Philomath OR 97370	**800-872-9036**	541-929-3124	245
Consumers Union of US Inc 101 Truman Ave ....Yonkers NY 10703	**800-927-4357**	914-378-2000	633-9
Consumers' Research Council of America (CRCA) 2020 Pennsylvania Ave NW Ste 300-A....Washington DC 20006	**877-774-6337**	202-835-9698	48-10
Contact Industries Inc 9200 SE Sunnybrook Blvd Ste 200....Clackamas OR 97015	**800-547-1038**	503-228-7361	497
Contact Lens Manufacturers Assn PO Box 29398 ....Lincoln NE 68529	**800-344-9060**	402-465-4122	49-4
Contactpointe of Pittsburgh 2593 Wexford Bayne Rd Ste 200 ....Sewickley PA 15143	**877-255-4916**	412-788-0680	378
Container Research Corp (CRC) 2 New Rd ....Aston PA 19014	**844-220-9574**		198
Container Store, The 500 Freeport Pkwy ....Coppell TX 75019	**800-733-3532**	972-538-6000	361
ContainerWorld Forwarding Services Inc 16133 Blundell Rd ....Richmond BC V6W0A3	**877-838-8880**	604-276-1300	311
Contech Construction Products Inc 9025 Centre Pt Dr Ste 400 ....West Chester OH 45069	**800-338-1122**	513-645-7000	693
Con-Tech Lighting 2783 Shermer Rd ....Northbrook IL 60062	**800-728-0312**	847-559-5500	438
Con-tek Machine Inc 3575 Hoffman Rd E ....Saint Paul MN 55110	**800-968-9801**	651-779-6058	111
Contemar Silo Systems Inc 30 Pennsylvania Ave Unit 8 ....Concord ON L4K4A5	**800-567-2741**	905-669-3604	296
Contemporary Arts Ctr 44 E Sixth St ....Cincinnati OH 45202	**800-644-6862**	513-345-8400	50-2
Contemporary Arts Museum Houston 5216 Montrose Blvd ....Houston TX 77006	**800-982-2787**	713-284-8250	517
Contemporary Tours 100 Crossways Park Dr W Ste 400....Westbury NY 11797	**800-627-8873**	516-484-5032	755
Content Management Corp 4287 Technology Dr ....Fremont CA 94538	**877-495-3720**	510-505-1100	623
Conterra Ultra Broadband LLC 2101 Rexford Rd Ste 200E....Charlotte NC 28211	**800-634-1374**	704-365-6701	648
Contiki Holidays 801 E Katella Ave ....Anaheim CA 92805	**800-944-5708**	866-266-8454	755
Continental Airlines Inc 900 Grand Plaza Dr ....Houston TX 77067	**800-621-7467**	713-952-1630	26
Continental Battery Corp 4919 Woodall St ....Dallas TX 75247	**800-442-0081**	214-631-5701	74
Continental Binder & Specialty Corp 407 W Compton Blvd ....Gardena CA 90248	**800-872-2897**	310-324-8227	86
Continental Book Company Inc 6425 Washington St ....Denver CO 80229	**800-364-0350**	303-289-1761	95
Continental Cast Stone Manufacturing Inc 22001 W 83rd St ....Shawnee KS 66227	**800-989-7866**		720
Continental Casualty Co 333 S Wabash Ave ....Chicago IL 60604	**800-262-2000**	312-822-5000	390-4
Continental Cement Company LLC 16401 Swingley Ridge Rd Ste 610....Chesterfield MO 63017	**800-625-1144**	636-532-7440	135
Continental Coin & Jewlery Co 5627 Sepulveda Blvd ....Van Nuys CA 91411	**800-552-6467**	818-781-4232	410
Continental Commercial Products (CCP) 11840 Westline Industrial Dr ....St. Louis MO 63146	**800-325-1051**		506
Continental Concession Supplies Inc 575 Jericho Tpke Ste 300....Jericho NY 11753	**800-516-0090**	516-739-8777	297-3
Continental Design & Engineering Inc 1524 Jackson St ....Anderson IN 46016	**800-875-4557**	765-778-9999	302
Continental Electric Motors Inc 23 Sebago St ....Clifton NJ 07013	**800-335-6718**		515

Alphabetical Section

	Toll-Free	Phone	Class

Continental Electronics Corp
4212 S Buckner Blvd .... Dallas TX 75227 | 800-733-5011 | 214-381-7161 | 643

Continental Fire Sprinkler Co
4518 S 133rd St .... Omaha NE 68137 | 800-543-5170 | 402-330-5170 | 606

Continental Flowers Inc
8101 NW 21 St .... Miami FL 33122 | 800-327-2715 | | 292

Continental Graphics Corp
4060 N Lakewood Blvd
Bldg 801 5th Fl .... Long Beach CA 90808 | 800-862-5691 | 714-503-4200 | 225

Continental Linen Services
4200 Manchester Rd .... Kalamazoo MI 49001 | 800-878-4357 | | 441

Continental Machines Inc
5505 W 123rd St .... Savage MN 55378 | 888-362-5572 | 952-890-3300 | 453

Continental Maritime of San Diego Inc
1995 Bay Front St .... San Diego CA 92113 | 877-631-0020 | 619-234-8851 | 694

Continental Motors Inc
2039 Broad St .... Mobile AL 36615 | 800-326-0089 | 251-436-8292 | 21

Continental Resources Inc
175 Middlesex Tpke .... Bedford MA 01730 | 800-937-4688 | 781-275-0850 | 176

Continental Safety Equipment
2935 Waters Rd Ste 140 .... Eagan MN 55121 | 800-844-7003 | 651-454-7233 | 675

Continental Service Group Inc
200 Cross Keys Office Pk ...... Fairport NY 14450 | 800-724-7500 | 585-421-1000 | 160

Continental Studwelding Ltd
35 Devon Rd .... Brampton ON L6T5B6 | 800-848-9442 | 905-792-3650 | 479

Continental Traffic Service Inc (CTSI)
5100 Poplar Ave 15th Fl .... Memphis TN 38137 | 888-836-5135 | 901-766-1500 | 311

Continental Western Group
11201 Douglas Ave .... Urbandale IA 50322 | 800-235-2942 | 515-473-3000 | 390-4

Contingent Workforce Solutions Inc
2430 Meadowpine Blvd
Ste 101 .... Mississauga ON L5N6S2 | 866-837-8630 | | 2

Continuing Education of The Bar Suite 410
300 Frank H Ogawa Plz Ste 410 .... Oakland CA 94612 | 800-232-3444 | 510-302-2000 | 166

Continuum
3150 Central Expy .... Santa Clara CA 95051 | 888-532-1064 | 408-727-3240 | 424

Contour Saws Inc
900 Graceland Ave .... Des Plaines IL 60016 | 800-259-6834 | | 678

Contra Costa County Library
75 Santa Barbara Rd .... Pleasant Hill CA 94523 | 800-984-4636 | | 433-3

Contra Costa Health Services
2500 Alhambra Ave .... Martinez CA 94553 | 877-661-6230 | 925-370-5000 | 373-3

Contract Converting LLC
W6580 Quality Ct .... Greenville WI 54942 | 800-734-0990 | |

Contract Design Magazine
100 Broadway 14th fl .... New York NY 10005 | 800-697-8859 | | 455-5

Contract Land Staff LLC
2245 Texas Dr Ste 200 .... Sugar Land TX 77479 | 800-874-4519 | 281-240-3370 | 194

Contractors Register Inc
800 E Main St ....Jefferson Valley NY 10535 | 800-431-2584 | 914-245-0200 | 633-6

Contractors Steel Co
36555 Amrhein Rd .... Livonia MI 48150 | 800-521-3946 | 734-464-4000 | 490

Contrex Inc
8900 Zachary Ln N .... Maple Grove MN 55369 | 800-342-4411 | 763-424-7800 | 203

Control Flow Inc
9201 Fairbanks N Houston Rd .... Houston TX 77064 | 800-231-9922 | 281-890-8300 | 785

Control Line Equipment Inc
14750 Industrial Pkwy ....Cleveland OH 44135 | 888-895-1440 | 216-433-7766 | 223

Control Printing Group Inc
4212 S Hocker Dr Ste 150 ... Independence MO 64055 | 800-333-2820 | 816-350-8100 | 623

Control Techniques Americas
7078 Shady Oak Rd .... Eden Prairie MN 55344 | 800-893-2321 | 952-995-8000 |

Controlled Access Inc
1515 W 130th St .... Hinckley OH 44233 | 800-942-0829 | 330-273-6185 | 635

Controlled Contamination Services LLC
6150 Lusk Blvd Ste B205 .... San Diego CA 92121 | 888-979-9608 | | 256

Controlled Power Co
1955 Stephenson Hwy .... Troy MI 48083 | 800-521-4792 | 248-528-3700 | 762

Controls Corporation of America
1501 Harpers Rd .... Virginia Beach VA 23454 | 800-225-0473 | 757-422-8330 | 45

CONVENTION & SPORTS FACILITIES
900 E Market St ....San Antonio TX 78205 | 877-504-8895 | 210-207-8500 | 568

Convention Consultants Historic Savannah Foundation
117 W Perry St ....Savannah GA 31401 | 800-559-6627 | 912-234-4088 | 184

Conventus Orthopaedics Inc
10200 73rd Ave N Ste 122 .... Maple Grove MN 55369 | 855-418-6466 | 763-515-5000 | 475

Convergys Corp
201 E Fourth St .... Cincinnati OH 45202 | 888-284-9900 | 513-723-7000 | 732
NYSE: CVG

Conversant LLC
30699 Russell Ranch Rd
Ste 250 .... Westlake Village CA 91362 | 877-361-3316 | 818-575-4500 | 7
NASDAQ: VCLK

Converse College
580 E Main St ....Spartanburg SC 29302 | 800-766-1125* | 864-596-9000 | 166
Admissions

Converse County
107 North Fifth St ....Douglas WY 82633 | 800-460-5657 | 307-358-2244 | 337

Conveyco Technologies Inc
PO Box 1000 .... Bristol CT 06011 | 800-229-8215 | 860-589-8215 | 384

Conveyer & Caster Corp
3501 Detroit Ave ....Cleveland OH 44113 | 800-777-0600 | 216-631-4448 | 350

Conveyor Components Co
130 Seltzer Rd .... Croswell MI 48422 | 800-233-3233* | 810-679-4211 | 207
Cust Svc

Conveyor Handling Company Inc
6715 Santa Barbara Ct .... Elkridge MD 21075 | 877-553-2296 | |

Conveyors Inc
620 S Fourth Ave ....Mansfield TX 76063 | 800-243-9327 | 817-473-4645 | 207

Convio Inc
11501 Domain Dr Ste 200 .... Austin TX 78758 | 888-528-9501 | 512-652-2600 | 180

Conway Area Chamber of Commerce
900 Oak St .... Conway AR 72032 | 800-750-8155 | 501-327-7788 | 139

Conway Cemetery State Park
1 Capitol Mall
1 Capitol Mall .... Little Rock AR 72201 | 888-287-2757 | | 561

Conway Import Co Inc
11051 W Addison St ....Franklin Park IL 60131 | 800-323-8801 | 847-455-5600 | 296-19

Conway Management Co
547 Amherst St Ste 106 .... Nashua NH 03063 | 800-359-0099 | 603-889-1130 | 461

Conway Marketing Communications
6400 Baum Dr .... Knoxville TN 37919 | 800-882-7875 | 865-588-5731 | 7

Cook Aviation Inc
970 S Kirby Rd .... Bloomington IN 47403 | 800-880-3499 | 812-825-2392 | 63

Cook Biotech Inc
1425 Innovation Pl ...... West Lafayette IN 47906 | 888-299-4224 | 765-497-3355 | 85

Cook Coggin Engineers Inc
703 Crossover Rd PO Box 1526 ....Tupelo MS 38802 | 877-807-4667 | 662-842-7381 |

Cook Hotel & Conference Ctr
3848 West Lakeshore Dr .... Baton Rouge LA 70808 | 866-610-2665 | 225-383-2665 | 376

Cook Inc
PO Box 4195 .... Bloomington IN 47402 | 800-457-4500 | 812-339-2235 | 474

Cook Medical Inc
PO Box 4195 .... Bloomington IN 47402 | 800-457-4500 | 812-339-2235 | 474

Cook Moving Systems Inc
1845 Dale Rd ....Buffalo NY 14225 | 800-828-7144 | | 516

Cook Security Group Inc
5841 SE International Way ...... Milwaukie OR 97222 | 844-305-2665 | |

Cook Travel
1025 Acuff Rd .... Bloomington IN 47404 | 800-542-1687 | 812-336-6811 | 766

Cook Truck Equipment & Tools
3701 Harlee Ave .... Charlotte NC 28208 | 800-241-4210 | 704-392-4138 | 57

Cook Urological Inc
PO Box 4195 .... Bloomington IN 47402 | 800-457-4500 | 812-339-2235 | 474

Cook's Ham Inc
200 S Second St .... Lincoln NE 68508 | 800-332-8400 | 402-475-6700 | 296-26

Cook's Illustrated Magazine
PO Box 470739 ....Brookline MA 02447 | 800-526-8442* | 617-232-1000 | 455-11
Circ

Cookbook Publishers
11633 W 83rd St .... Lenexa KS 66214 | 800-227-7282 | 913-492-5900 | 622

Cooke County Electric Co-op
11799 W US Hwy 82 PO Box 530 .... Muenster TX 76252 | 800-962-0296 | 940-759-2211 | 245

Cooke Trucking Co Inc
1759 S Andy Griffith Pkwy ....Mount Airy NC 27030 | 800-888-9502 | 336-786-5181 | 775

Cookeville Area-Putnam County Chamber of Commerce
1 W First St ....Cookeville TN 38501 | 800-264-5541 | 931-526-2211 | 139

Cookeville Regional Medical Ctr (CRMC)
1 Medical Ctr Blvd ....Cookeville TN 38501 | 800-897-1898 | 931-528-2541 | 373-3

Cookies By Design Inc
1865 Summit Ave Ste 605 .... Plano TX 75074 | 800-945-2665 | 972-398-9536 | 310

Cookies From Home Inc
1605 W University Dr Ste 106 .... Tempe AZ 85281 | 800-543-8133 | 480-894-1944 |

Cooking & Hospitality Institute of Chicago
361 W Chestnut St ....Chicago IL 60610 | 877-828-7772* | 312-944-0882 | 163
Admissions

Cooking Light Magazine
2100 Lakeshore Dr ....Birmingham AL 35209 | 800-366-4712 | 205-445-6000 | 455-13

Cookshack
2304 N Ash St .... Ponca City OK 74601 | 800-423-0698 | 580-765-3669 | 360

Cookson Co
2417 S 50th Ave .... Phoenix AZ 85043 | 800-294-4358 | 602-272-4244 | 234

Cookson Hills Electric Cooperative Inc
1002 N Main St .... Stigler OK 74462 | 800-328-2368 | | 245

CookTek LLC
156 N Jefferson St Ste 300 ....Chicago IL 60661 | 888-266-5835 | 312-563-9600 | 36

Cool Gear International LLC
10 Cordage Park Cir ....Plymouth MA 02360 | 855-393-2665 | | 360

Coolant Control Inc
5353 Spring Grove Ave .... Cincinnati OH 45217 | 800-535-3885 | 513-471-8770 | 146

Cooley Group
50 Esten Ave .... Pawtucket RI 02860 | 800-992-0072* | 401-724-9000 | 740-2
Cust Svc

Cooling Tower Technologies
52410 Clark Rd .... White Castle LA 70788 | 800-882-1361 | 225-545-3970 |

Coontail
5466 Park St .... Boulder Junction WI 54512 | 888-874-0885 | | 707

Co-op America
1612 K St NW Ste 600 .... Washington DC 20006 | 800-584-7336 | 202-872-5307 | 48-13

Co-op Elevator Co
7211 E Michigan Ave ....Pigeon MI 48755 | 800-968-0601 | 989-453-4500 | 275

Co-op Feed Dealers Inc
380 Broome Corporate Pkwy
PO Box 670 .... Conklin NY 13748 | 800-333-0895* | 607-651-9078 | 276
Cust Svc

Co-op Finance Assn Inc, The
10100 N Ambassador Dr Ste 315
PO Box 842702 .... Kansas City MO 64153 | 877-835-5232 | 816-214-4200 | 216

CO-OP Financial Services Inc
9692 Haven Ave ....Rancho Cucamonga CA 91730 | 800-782-9042 | | 392

Co-op Gas Inc
PO Box 27 .... Pauline SC 29374 | 888-578-5752 | 864-583-6546 |

Cooper Aerial Survey Co
1692 W Grant Rd ....Tucson AZ 85745 | 800-229-2279 | 520-884-7580 | 723

Cooper Atkins Corp
33 Reeds Gap Rd .... Middlefield CT 06455 | 800-835-5011* | 860-349-3473 | 201
Sales

Cooper B-Line Inc
509 W Monroe St ....Highland IL 62249 | 800-851-7415 | | 811

Cooper Bussmann Inc
114 Old State Rd ....Ellisville MO 63021 | 855-287-7626 | 636-394-2877 | 810

Cooper Cos Inc
6140 Stoneridge Mall Rd
Ste 590 ....Pleasanton CA 94588 | 888-822-2660 | 925-460-3600 | 538
NYSE: COO

Cooper Crouse-Hinds
1201 Wolf St ....Syracuse NY 13208 | 866-764-5454 | 315-477-5531 | 810

Cooper Industries
600 Travis St Ste 5400 ....Houston TX 77002 | 866-853-4293 | 713-209-8400 | 810
NYSE: ETN

Cooper Legal Services Dwayne E Cooper Attorney at Law
718 S Washinton St ....Marion IN 46953 | 800-959-1825 | 765-573-3133 | 427

Cooper Motors Inc
985 York St .... Hanover PA 17331 | 866-414-2809 | | 57

Cooper Power Systems Inc
2300 Badger Dr .... Waukesha WI 53188 | 800-223-5227 | 262-896-2400 | 762

Name / Address	City	State	ZIP	Toll-Free	Phone	Class
Cooper Smith Advertising 3500 Granite Cir	Toledo	OH	43617	**800-215-8812**	419-470-5900	4
Cooper Tire & Rubber Co 701 Lima Ave *NYSE: CTB*	Findlay	OH	45840	**800-854-6288**	419-423-1321	749
Cooper University Hospital 3 Cooper Plz	Camden	NJ	08103	**800-826-6737**	856-342-2000	373-3
Cooper Wellness Program 12230 Preston Rd	Dallas	TX	75230	**800-444-5192**	972-386-4777	702
Cooper Wiring Devices Inc 203 Cooper Cir *Cust Svc	Peachtree City	GA	30269	**866-853-4293***	770-631-2100	810
Cooper Young Business Assn 2120 Young Ave	Memphis	TN	38104	**800-342-3308**	901-276-7222	50-6
CooperSurgical Inc 95 Corporate Dr	Trumbull	CT	06611	**800-645-3760**	203-929-6321	474
CooperVision Inc 209 High Point Dr	Victor	NY	14564	**800-538-7850**	585-385-6810	538
Cooptel 5521 Valcourt Airport Rd *Consumer Assistance	Valcourt	QC	J0E2L0	**888-532-2667***	450-532-2667	
CoorsTek Inc 600 Ninth St	Golden	CO	80401	**800-821-6110**	303-278-4000	249
Coos Bay-North Bend Visitor & Convention Bureau 200 S Bayshore Dr	Coos Bay	OR	97420	**800-824-8486**	541-269-0215	206
Coos County 250 N Baxter St	Coquille	OR	97423	**800-452-6010**	541-396-3121	337
Coosa Pines Federal Credit Union 17591 Plant Rd	Childersburg	AL	35044	**800-237-9789**	256-378-5559	219
COPE Inc 1120 G St NW Ste 550	Washington	DC	20005	**800-247-3054**	202-628-5100	460
Cope Plastics Inc 4441 Industrial Dr	Godfrey	IL	62002	**800-851-5510**	618-466-0221	599
Copernicus Group Independent Review Board 5000 CentreGreen Way Ste 200	Cary	NC	27513	**888-303-2224**	919-465-4310	
Copesan Services Inc W175 N5711 Technology Dr	Menomonee Falls	WI	53051	**800-267-3726**		573
Copia International Ltd 1220 Iroquois Dr Ste 180 *Sales	Naperville	IL	60187	**800-689-8898***	630-778-8898	173-3
Copic Insurance Co 7351 Lowry Blvd	Denver	CO	80230	**800-421-1834**	720-858-6000	390-5
Copiers Northwest Inc 601 Dexter Ave N	Seattle	WA	98109	**866-692-0700**	206-282-1200	112
Copley Hospital System 528 Washington Hwy	Morrisville	VT	05661	**800-564-1612**	802-888-8888	373-3
Copley Place 100 Huntington Ave Ste 100	Boston	MA	02116	**877-746-6642**	617-262-6600	458
Copley Square Hotel 47 Huntington Ave	Boston	MA	02116	**800-225-7062**	617-536-9000	378
Coppel Corp 503 Scaroni Rd	Calexico	CA	92231	**800-220-7735**		
Copper Development Assn Inc 260 Madison Ave 16th Fl	New York	NY	10016	**800-232-3282**	212-251-7200	49-13
Copper Hills Youth Ctr 5899 Rivendell Dr	West Jordan	UT	84081	**800-776-7116**		373-1
Copper Mountain Resort 209 Ten Mile Cir	Copper Mountain	CO	80443	**888-219-2441**	866-841-2481	665
Copper Valley Electric Assn Inc (CVEA) Mile 187 Glenn Hwy PO Box 45	Glennallen	AK	99588	**866-835-2832**	907-822-3211	245
CopperWynd Resort & Club 13225 N Eagle Ridge Dr	Scottsdale	AZ	85268	**877-707-7760**	480-333-1900	665
Coppin State University 2500 W N Ave *Admissions	Baltimore	MD	21216	**800-635-3674***	410-951-3600	166
Copple, Rockey, Mckeever & Schlecht PC LLO 2425 Taylor Ave	Norfolk	NE	68701	**888-860-2425**	402-371-4300	427
COPS (Community Oriented Policing Services) 145 N St NE	Washington	DC	20530	**800-421-6770**		339-13
COPS (Concerns of Police Survivors Inc) 846 Old S 5 PO Box 3199	Camdenton	MO	65020	**800-784-2677**	573-346-4911	48-21
Copy Cat Printing 365 N Broadwell Ave	Grand Island	NE	68803	**800-400-8520**	308-384-8520	623
Copyright Clearance Ctr Inc (CCC) 222 Rosewood Dr	Danvers	MA	01923	**855-239-3415**	978-750-8400	49-16
Coquille Myrtle Grove State Natural Site Powers Hwy	Myrtle Point	OR	97458	**800-551-6949**		561
Coral Beach Resort & Suites 1105 S Ocean Blvd	Myrtle Beach	SC	29577	**800-843-2684**	800-314-8060	665
Coral Cay Resort 2300 Caravelle Cir	Kissimmee	FL	34746	**866-357-3682**	407-787-0718	703
Coral Chemical Co 1915 Industrial Ave	Zion	IL	60099	**800-228-4646**	847-246-6666	145
Coral Color Process Ltd 50 Mall Dr	Commack	NY	11725	**800-564-7303**	631-543-5200	623
Coral Gables Hospital Inc (CGH) 3100 Douglas Rd	Coral Gables	FL	33134	**866-728-3677**	305-445-8461	373-3
Coral Reef Restaurant 106 N Baltimore Ave	Ocean City	MD	21842	**866-627-8483**	410-289-2612	667
Coral Springs Auto Mall 9400 W Atlantic Blvd	Coral Springs	FL	33071	**800-353-8660**	954-369-1016	57
Coral Springs Chamber of Commerce 11805 Heron Bay Blvd	Coral Springs	FL	33076	**800-816-1256**	954-752-4242	139
Coram Healthcare Corp 555 17th St Ste 1500	Denver	CO	80202	**800-267-2642**		362
Corban Onesource 235 Third St S Ste 300	St Petersburg	FL	33701	**844-267-2261**		
Corbett Lighting Inc 14508 Nelson Ave	City of Industry	CA	91744	**800-533-8769**	626-336-4511	438
Corbin 2360 Technology Pkwy	Hollister	CA	95023	**800-538-7035**		514
Corby Industries Inc 1501 E Pennsylvania St *Sales	Allentown	PA	18109	**800-652-6729***	610-433-1412	688
Corcoran 660 Madison Ave 12th Fl	New York	NY	10065	**800-544-4055**	212-355-3550	648
Cord Sets Inc 1015 Fifth St N	Minneapolis	MN	55411	**800-752-0580**	612-337-9700	810
Cordis Corp 14201 NW 60th Ave	Miami Lakes	FL	33014	**800-327-7714**	786-313-2000	474
CORE (Center for Organ Recovery & Education) 204 Sigma Dr RIDC Pk	Pittsburgh	PA	15238	**800-366-6777**	412-963-3550	269
Core Bts Inc 5875 Castle Creek Pkwy N Dr Ste 320	Indianapolis	IN	46250	**855-267-3287**		113
Core Health & Fitness LLC 4400 NE 77th Ave Ste 300	Vancouver	WA	98662	**888-678-2476**	360-326-4090	
Core Management Resources Group Inc 515 Mulberry St	Macon	GA	31201	**888-741-2673**	478-741-3521	196
Core Vision IT Solutions 1266 NW Hwy	Palatine	IL	60067	**855-788-5835**		196
CoreCivic 10 Burton Hills Blvd *NYSE: CXW*	Nashville	TN	37215	**800-624-2931**	615-263-3000	211
Corel Corp 1600 Carling Ave *Orders	Ottawa	ON	K1Z8R7	**800-772-6735***	613-728-8200	178-8
CoreNet Global Inc 260 Peachtree St NW Ste 1500	Atlanta	GA	30303	**800-726-8111**	404-589-3200	49-17
CoreTech 550 American Ave Ste 301	King of Prussia	PA	19406	**800-220-3337**		194
Corey Steel Co 2800 S 61st Ct	Cicero	IL	60804	**800-323-2750**	708-735-8000	719
Coriell Institute for Medical Research 403 Haddon Ave	Camden	NJ	08103	**800-752-3805**	856-966-7377	664
Corinthian Partners LLC 850 Third Ave Ste 16C	New York	NY	10022	**800-899-8950**	212-287-1500	686
Corix Utilities (US) Inc 11020 West Plank Crt Ste 100	Milwaukee	WI	53226	**877-678-3842**	414-203-8700	
Corizon 105 Westpark Dr Ste 200	Brentwood	TN	37027	**800-729-0069**		461
Corken Inc 3805 NW 36th St	Oklahoma City	OK	73112	**800-631-4929**	405-946-5576	637
Corn Belt Energy Corp 1 Energy Way	Bloomington	IL	61705	**800-879-0339**	309-662-5330	245
Corn Palace 604 N Main St	Mitchell	SD	57301	**800-289-7469**	605-995-8430	50-3
Cornelia de Lange Syndrome Foundation Inc (CdLS) 302 W Main St Ste 100	Avon	CT	06001	**800-753-2357**	860-676-8166	48-17
Cornelius Seed Corn Co 14760 317th Ave	Bellevue	IA	52031	**800-218-1862**		296-20
Cornell Botanic Gardens 1 Plantations Rd	Ithaca	NY	14850	**800-269-8368**	607-255-2400	97
Cornell College 600 First St SW *Admissions	Mount Vernon	IA	52314	**800-747-1112***	319-895-4215	166
Cornell Iron Works Inc 24 Elmwood Rd	Mountain Top	PA	18707	**800-233-8366**		234
Cornell Storefront Systems Inc 140 Maffet St	Wilkes-Barre	PA	18705	**800-882-6772**	570-706-2775	234
Cornell University Press 512 E State St *Sales	Ithaca	NY	14850	**800-666-2211***	607-277-2338	633-4
CornerCap Investment Counsel Inc 1355 Peachtree St NE The Peachtree Ste 1700	Atlanta	GA	30309	**800-728-0670**	404-870-0700	524
Cornerstone Advisors Asset Management Inc 74 W Broad St Ste 340	Bethlehem	PA	18018	**800-923-0900**	610-694-0900	400
Cornerstone Hospice & Palliative Care 2445 Ln Pk Rd	Tavares	FL	32778	**866-742-6655**		370
Cornerstone Medical Arts Ctr Hospital 159-05 Union Tpke	Fresh Meadows	NY	11366	**800-233-9999**	718-906-6700	722
Cornerstone residential management Llc 2100 Hollywood Blvd	Hollywood	FL	33020	**800-809-4099**		649
Cornerstone Systems Inc 3250 Players Club Pkwy	Memphis	TN	38125	**800-278-7677**	901-842-0660	194
Cornerstone University 1001 E Beltline Ave NE *Admissions	Grand Rapids	MI	49525	**800-787-9778***	616-222-1426	166
Cornhusker Bank 1101 Cornhusker Hwy	Lincoln	NE	68521	**877-837-4481**	402-434-2265	70
Cornhusker Casualty Co PO Box 2048	Omaha	NE	68103	**888-495-8949**		390-4
Cornhusker Hotel, The 333 S 13th St	Lincoln	NE	68508	**866-706-7706**	402-474-7474	378
Cornhusker Public Power District 23169 235th Ave PO Box 9	Columbus	NE	68602	**800-955-2773**	402-564-2821	245
Cornhusker State Industries 800 Pioneers Blvd	Lincoln	NE	68502	**800-348-7537**	402-471-4597	626
Corning Area Chamber of Commerce 1 W Market St Ste 202	Corning	NY	14830	**866-463-6264**	607-936-4686	139
Corning Cable Systems 800 17th St NW	Hickory	NC	28603	**800-743-2671**	607-974-9000	809
Corning Data Services Inc 139 Wardell St	Corning	NY	14830	**800-455-5996**	607-936-4241	177
Corning Hospital 176 Denison Pkwy E	Corning	NY	14830	**877-750-2042**	607-937-7200	373-3
Corning Inc Life Sciences Div 836 N St Bldg 300 Ste 3401	Tewksbury	MA	01876	**800-492-1110**	607-974-9000	418
Corning Museum of Glass 1 Museum Way *Cust Svc	Corning	NY	14830	**800-732-6845***	607-937-5371	517
Cornish College of the Arts 1000 Lenora St	Seattle	WA	98121	**800-726-2787**	206-726-5141	164
Cornucopia Tool & Plastics Inc 448 Sherwood Rd PO Box 1915	Paso Robles	CA	93447	**800-235-4144**	805-369-0030	253
Cornwall Community Hospital 840 McConnell Ave	Cornwall	ON	K6H5S5	**866-263-1560**	613-938-4240	373-2
Cornwall Manor 1 Boyd St	Cornwall	PA	17016	**800-222-2476**	717-273-2647	668
Cornwell Quality Tools 667 Seville Rd	Wadsworth	OH	44281	**800-321-8356**	330-336-3506	753
Corona Brushes Inc 5065 Savarese Cir	Tampa	FL	33634	**800-458-3483**	813-885-2525	103
Corona Clipper Inc 22440 Tomasco Canyon Rd	Corona	CA	92883	**800-234-2547**	951-737-6515	428

	Toll-Free	Phone	Class
Corotec Corp 145 Hyde Rd .... Farmington CT 06032	800-423-0348	860-678-0038	385
Corp for National & Community Service *AmeriCorps USA* 1201 New York Ave NW .... Washington DC 20525	800-833-3722	202-606-5000	339-19
Learn & Serve America 1201 New York Ave NW .... Washington DC 20525	800-833-3722	202-606-5000	339-19
CorpCare Associates Inc 7000 Peachtree Dunwoody Rd Bldg 4 Ste 300 .... Atlanta GA 30328	800-728-9444	770-200-8085	460
Corporate Accountability International 10 Milk St Ste 610 .... Boston MA 02108	800-688-8797	617-695-2525	48-8
Corporate Air LLC 15 Allegheny County Airport .... West Mifflin PA 15122	888-429-5377	412-469-6800	63
Corporate Business Solutions 1523 Johnson Ferry Rd Ste 200 .. Marietta GA 30062	800-239-8182	404-521-6030	566
Corporate Claims Management Inc 782 Spirit 40 Pk .... Chesterfield MO 63005	800-449-2264		389
Corporate Disk Co 4610 Crime Pkwy .... McHenry IL 60050	800-634-3475		240
Corporate Executive Board Co 1919 N Lynn St .... Arlington VA 22209 *NYSE: IT*	866-913-2632	571-303-3000	194
Corporate Helicopters of San Diego 3753 John J Montgomery Dr Ste 2 .... San Diego CA 92123	800-345-6737	858-505-5650	358
Corporate It Solutions Inc 661 Pleasant St .... Norwood MA 02062	888-521-2487		196
Corporate Telephone Services 184 W Second St .... Boston MA 02127	800-274-1211	617-625-1200	246
Corporate Writer & Editor 111 E Wacker Dr Ste 500 ...... Chicago IL 60601	800-878-5331	312-960-4140	527-2
Corporation for National & Community Service *Senior Corps* 1201 New York Ave NW .... Washington DC 20525	800-833-3722	202-606-5000	339-19
Corporation for Public Broadcasting (CPB) 401 Ninth St NW .... Washington DC 20004	800-272-2190	202-879-9600	305
Corporation Service Co 2711 Centerville Rd Ste 400 .... Wilmington DE 19808	866-403-5272	302-636-5400	113
Corptax LLC 1751 Lake Cook Rd Ste 100 ..... Deerfield IL 60015	800-966-1639		177
Corpus Christi Convention & Visitors Bureau 101 N Shoreline Blvd Ste 430 .... Corpus Christi TX 78401	800-678-6232	361-881-1888	206
Corpus Christi Gasket & Fastener Inc PO Box 4074 .... Corpus Christi TX 78469	800-460-6366	361-884-6366	326
Corradino Group 200 s Fifth st .... Louisville KY 40202	800-880-8241	502-587-7221	256
Correct Craft Inc 14700 Aerospace Pkwy .... Orlando FL 32832	800-346-2092	407-855-4141	90
Correct Rx Pharmacy Services Inc 1352-C Charwood Rd .... Hanover MD 21076	800-636-0501		238
Correctional Enterprises of Connecticut 24 Wolcott Hill Rd .... Wethersfield CT 06109	800-842-1146	860-263-6839	626
Correlated Products Inc 5616 Progress Rd .... Indianapolis IN 46242	800-428-3266	317-243-3248	151
Correvio Pharma Corp 1441 Creekside Dr 6th Fl ...... Vancouver BC V6J4S7 *NASDAQ: CORV*	800-330-9928	604-677-6905	85
Corridor Group Inc, The 6405 Metcalf Ste 108 .... Overland Park KS 66202	866-263-3795		194
Corridor Resources Inc 5475 Spring Garden Rd .... Halifax NS B3J3T2	888-429-4511	902-429-4511	532
Corrigan Moving Systems 23923 Research Dr ...... Farmington Hills MI 48335	800-267-7442		516
Corrosion Monitoring Services Inc 902 Equity Dr .... Saint Charles IL 60174	800-637-6592		
Corrpro Cos Inc 1055 W Smith Rd .... Medina OH 44256	800-443-3516	330-723-5082	261
CORSAIR 46221 Landing Pkwy .... Fremont CA 94538	888-222-4346	510-657-8747	173-5
Corsicana Bedding Inc PO Box 1050 .... Corsicana TX 75151	800-323-4349	903-872-2591	469
Corsicana Public Library 100 N 12th St .... Corsicana TX 75110	877-648-2836	903-874-4731	433-3
Cortac Group 609 Deep Valley Dr Ste 200 .... Rolling Hills Estates CA 90274	877-216-1717		
Cortec Corp 4119 White Bear Pkwy .... Saint Paul MN 55110	800-426-7832	651-429-1100	145
Cortelco Inc 1703 Sawyer Rd .... Corinth MS 38834	800-288-3132	662-287-5281	246
Cortera 901 Yamato Rd Ste 210 E ...... Boca Raton FL 33431	877-569-7376		178-1
Cortex Consultants Inc 1027 Pandora Ave .... Victoria BC V8V3P6	866-931-1192	250-360-1492	461
Corum Group Ltd 19805 N Creek Pkwy Ste 300 .... Bothell WA 98011	800-228-8281	425-455-8281	461
Corvallis Area Chamber of Commerce 420 NW Second St .... Corvallis OR 97330	800-562-8526	541-757-1505	139
Corvallis Tourism 420 NW Second St .... Corvallis OR 97330	800-334-8118	541-757-1544	206
CorVel Corp 2010 Main St Ste 600 .... Irvine CA 92614 *NASDAQ: CRVL*	888-726-7835	949-851-1473	461
Corvirtus 4360 Montebello Dr Ste 400 .... Colorado Springs CO 80918	800-322-5329		461
Corwin Press Inc 2455 Teller Rd .... Thousand Oaks CA 91320 *Orders*	800-233-9936*		633-2
Cory Watson Crowder & DeGaris 2131 Magnolia Ave .... Birmingham AL 35205	800-852-6299	205-328-2200	427
Cosanti Originals Inc 6433 Doubletree Ranch Rd .... Paradise Valley AZ 85253	800-752-3187	480-948-6145	50-3
COSCO (China Ocean Shipping Co Americas Inc) 100 Lighting Way .... Secaucus NJ 07094	800-242-7354	201-422-0500	220
Cosco Fire Protection Inc 1075 W Lambert Rd Bldg D .... Brea CA 92821	800-485-3795	714-989-1800	189-13
Cosco Industries Inc 7220 W Wilson Ave ...... Harwood Heights IL 60706	800-296-8970		465
CoServ Electric 7701 S Stemmons Fwy .... Corinth TX 76210	800-274-4014	940-321-7800	245
COSI Columbus 333 W Broad St .... Columbus OH 43215	888-819-2674	614-228-2674	517
COSI Toledo 1 Discovery Way .... Toledo OH 43604	800-590-9755	419-244-2674	517
Cosmopolitan Hotel Toronto 8 Colborne St .... Toronto ON M5E1E1	800-958-3488	416-350-2000	378
Cosmopolitan International PO Box 7351 .... Lancaster PA 17604	800-648-4331	717-295-7142	48-15
Cosmos Communications Inc 11-05 44th Dr .... Long Island NY 11101	800-223-5751	718-482-1800	623
CoSN (Consortium for School Networking) 1025 Vermont Ave NW Ste 1010 .... Washington DC 20005	866-267-8747	202-861-2676	48-9
Cossatot River State Park-Natural Area 1980 Hwy 278 W .... Wickes AR 71973	877-665-6343	870-385-2201	561
Cost Control Associates Inc 310 Bay Rd .... Queensbury NY 12804	800-836-3787	518-798-4437	196
Cost Plus Inc 200 Fourth St .... Oakland CA 94607 *NASDAQ: CPWM*	877-967-5362	510-893-7300	361
Costa Cruise Lines 200 S Pk Rd Ste 200 .... Hollywood FL 33021	800-462-6782	954-266-5600	220
Costa Del Mar 2361 Mason Ave Ste 100 ...... Daytona Beach FL 32117	800-447-3700	386-274-4000	538
Costa Fruit & Produce 18 Bunker Hill Industrial Pk ..... Boston MA 02129	800-322-1374	617-241-8007	297-7
Costa Nursery Farms Inc 21800 SW 162nd Ave .... Miami FL 33170	800-327-7074		368
Costanoa Coastal Lodge & Camp 2001 Rossi Rd .... Pescadero CA 94060	877-262-7848	650-879-1400	665
CoStar Group Inc 1331 L St NW .... Washington DC 20005 *NASDAQ: CSGP*	888-226-7404	800-204-5960	178-10
Costco Wholesale Corp 999 Lake Dr .... Issaquah WA 98027 *NASDAQ: COST* ■ *Cust Svc*	800-774-2678*	425-313-8100	807
Costume Gallery 700 Creek Rd .... Delanco NJ 08075	800-222-8125	609-386-6601	155-6
Costume Specialists Inc 211 N Fifth St .... Columbus OH 43215	800-596-9357	614-464-2115	155-6
COTA (Children's Organ Transplant Assn) 2501 W Cota Dr .... Bloomington IN 47403	800-366-2682	812-336-8872	48-17
Cota & Cota Inc 56 Bridge St .... Bellows Falls VT 05101	888-268-2645		
Cothern Computer Systems Inc 1640 Lelia Dr Ste 200 .... Jackson MS 39216	800-844-1155		178-7
Cotiviti Corp 1 Glenlake Pkwy Ste 1400 .... Atlanta GA 30328	800-530-1013	770-379-2800	
Cotterman Co 130 Seltzer Rd .... Croswell MI 48422	800-552-3337	810-679-4400	420
Cottey College 1000 W Austin Blvd .... Nevada MO 64772	888-526-8839	417-667-8181	162
Cotton Belt Inc 401 E Sater St .... Pinetops NC 27864	800-849-4192	252-827-4192	469
Cotton Inc 6399 Weston Pkwy .... Cary NC 27513	800-334-5868	919-678-2220	48-2
CottonimagesCom Inc 10481 NW 28th St .... Miami FL 33172	888-642-7999	305-251-2560	343
Cottonwood County 900 Third Ave .... Windom MN 56101	800-967-1763	507-831-1905	337
Cottrell Inc 2125 Candler Rd .... Gainesville GA 30507 *Sales*	800-827-0132*	770-532-7251	774
Cottrell Paper Company Inc 1135 Rock City Rd PO Box 35 .... Rock City Falls NY 12863	800-948-3559	518-885-1702	811
Couch & Philippi Inc 10680 Fern Ave PO Box A ...... Stanton CA 90680 *Orders*	800-854-3360*	714-527-2261	697
Cougar Drilling Solutions Inc 7319 - 17 St .... Edmonton AB T6P1P1	877-439-3376		
Cougle Commission Co 345 N Aberdeen St .... Chicago IL 60607	800-568-2240	312-666-7861	471
Coulson Group of Companies 4890 Cherry Creek Rd .... Port Alberni BC V9Y8E9	800-663-3456	250-724-7600	782
Coulter Forge Technology Inc 1494 67th St .... Emeryville CA 94608	800-648-4884	510-420-3500	481
Coulter Lake Guest Ranch 80 County Rd 273 .... Rifle CO 81650	800-858-3046	970-625-1473	239
Council Bluffs Area Chamber of Commerce 149 W Broadway .... Council Bluffs IA 51503	800-228-6878	712-325-1000	139
Council for Advancement & Support of Education (CASE) 1307 New York Ave NW Ste 1000 .... Washington DC 20005 *Orders*	800-554-8536*	202-328-5900	49-5
Council for Professional Recognition 2460 16th St NW .... Washington DC 20009	800-424-4310	202-265-9090	49-5
Council of Administrators of Special Education (CASE) Osigian Office Centre 101 Katelyn Cir Ste E .... Warner Robins GA 31088	800-585-1753	478-333-6892	49-5
Council of Better Business Bureaus Inc *Dispute Resolution Services & Mediation Training* 4200 Wilson Blvd Ste 800 ..... Arlington VA 22203	855-748-4600	703-276-0100	41
Council of Better Business Bureaus Inc Wise Giving Alliance 4200 Wilson Blvd Ste 800 ..... Arlington VA 22203	800-248-4040	703-276-0100	48-10
Council of Canadians 170 Laurier Ave W Ste 700 .... Ottawa ON K1P5V5	800-387-7177	613-233-2773	48-7
Council of Residential Specialists 430 N Michigan Ave Ste 300 ..... Chicago IL 60611	800-462-8841	312-321-4400	49-17
Council of State Governments (CSG) 2760 Research Pk Dr .... Lexington KY 40511 *Sales*	800-800-1910*	859-244-8000	49-7
Council of the Section of Legal Education & Admissions to the Bar 321 N Clark St 21st Fl .... Chicago IL 60654	800-238-2667	312-988-6738	48-1

Name / Address	City	State	ZIP	Toll-Free	Phone	Class
Council on Academic Accreditation in Audiology & Speech-Language Pathology						
2200 Research Blvd	Rockville	MD	20850	**800-498-2071**	301-296-5700	48-1
Council on Accreditation (COA)						
45 Broadway 29th Fl	New York	NY	10006	**866-262-8088**	212-797-3000	48-1
Council on Chiropractic Education Commission on Accreditation						
8049 N 85th Way	Scottsdale	AZ	85258	**888-443-3506**	480-443-8877	48-1
Council on Foundations						
2121 Crystal Dr Ste 700	Arlington	VA	22202	**800-673-9036**	703-879-0600	48-5
Council on International Educational Exchange (CIEE)						
300 Fore St	Portland	ME	04101	**888-268-6245***	207-553-4000	49-5
*Cust Svc						
Council on Occupational Education						
7840 Roswell Rd						
Bldg 300 Ste 325	Atlanta	GA	30350	**800-917-2081**	770-396-3898	48-1
Count Me In						
5955 Edmond St	Las Vegas	NV	89118	**866-514-5888**		84
Counter Pro Inc						
210 Lincoln St	Manchester	NH	03103	**800-899-2444**	603-647-2444	191-3
Country Bank for Savings						
75 Main St	Ware	MA	01082	**800-322-8233**	413-967-6221	70
Country Cablevision Inc						
9449 State Hwy 197 S	Burnsville	NC	28714	**800-722-4074**	828-682-4074	116
Country Hearth Inn Inc						
50 Glenlake Pkwy NE Ste 350	Atlanta	GA	30328	**888-443-2784**	770-393-2662	377
Country House						
4830 Kennett Pk	Wilmington	DE	19807	**800-976-7610**	302-501-7155	668
Country Inn at the Mall						
936 Stillwater Ave	Bangor	ME	04401	**800-244-3961***	207-941-0200	378
*Resv						
COUNTRY Insurance & Financial Services						
1705 Towanda Ave	Bloomington	IL	61701	**888-211-2555**	866-268-6879	390-2
Country Lane Flower Shop						
729 S Michigan Ave	Howell	MI	48843	**800-764-7673**	517-546-1111	292
Country Mark Co-op						
1200 Refinery Rd	Mount Vernon	IN	47620	**800-832-5490**		593
Country Music Hall of Fame & Museum						
222 Fifth Ave S	Nashville	TN	37203	**800-852-6437**	615-416-2001	517
Country Mutual Insurance Co						
1701 Towanda Ave	Bloomington	IL	61701	**888-211-2555***	866-268-6879	390-4
*Cust Svc						
Country Pride Co-op (CPC)						
201 S Monroe PO Box 529	Winner	SD	57580	**888-325-7743**	605-842-2711	10-4
Country Springs Hotel & Conference Ctr						
2810 Golf Rd	Pewaukee	WI	53072	**800-247-6640**	262-547-0201	376
Country's Barbecue						
2016 12th Ave	Columbus	GA	31901	**800-285-4267***	706-327-7702	667
*General						
Countryside Co-op						
514 E Main St	Durand	WI	54736	**800-236-7585**	715-672-8947	276
CountryTyme Inc						
3451 Cincinnati-Zanesville Rd SW	Lancaster	OH	43130	**800-213-8365**	740-475-6001	649
County College of Morris						
214 Ctr Grove Rd	Randolph	NJ	07869	**888-726-3260**	973-328-5000	162
County of Greene						
93 E High St	Waynesburg	PA	15370	**888-852-5399**	724-852-5210	337
Courier Graphics Corp						
2621 S 37th St	Phoenix	AZ	85034	**800-454-6381**	602-437-9700	623
Courier Printing						
1 Courier Pl	Smyrna	TN	37167	**800-467-0444**	615-355-4000	623
Courier-Journal						
525 W Broadway PO Box 740031	Louisville	KY	40201	**800-765-4011**	502-582-4011	528-2
Courier-Post						
301 Cuthbert Blvd	Cherry Hill	NJ	08002	**800-677-6289**	856-663-6000	528-2
Courier-Tribune						
500 Sunset Ave	Asheboro	NC	27203	**800-488-0444**	336-625-2101	528-2
Court Thomas Wingert						
11800 Monarch St						
PO Box 6207	Garden Grove	CA	92841	**800-359-7337**	714-379-5519	801
CourtCall						
6383 Arizona Cir	Los Angeles	CA	90045	**888-882-6878**	310-342-0888	
Courtemanche & Assoc						
4475 Morris Park Dr Ste B	Charlotte	NC	28227	**800-356-2501**	704-573-4535	
Courtesy Assoc						
2025 M St NW Ste 800	Washington	DC	20036	**800-647-4689**		184
Courtesy Building Services Inc						
2154 W Northwest Hwy Ste 214	Dallas	TX	75220	**800-479-3853**	972-831-1444	104
Courtesy Chevrolet						
1233 E Camelback Rd	Phoenix	AZ	85014	**877-295-4648**	602-235-0255	57
Courtesy Chrysler Jeep Dodge						
9207 Adamo Dr E	Tampa	FL	33619	**866-343-9730**		57
Courtroom Sciences Inc						
4950 N O'Connor Rd	Irving	TX	75062	**800-514-5879**	972-717-1773	443
Courtyard Cafe						
18 St Thomas St	Toronto	ON	M5S3E7	**877-999-2767***	416-971-9666	667
*Cust Svc						
Courtyard Fort Lauderdale Beach						
440 Seabreeze Blvd	Fort Lauderdale	FL	33316	**888-236-2427**	954-524-8733	378
Coushatta Casino Resort						
777 Coushatta Dr PO Box 1510	Kinder	LA	70648	**800-584-7263**		133
Cousineau Inc						
3 Valley Rd PO Box 58	North Anson	ME	04958	**877-268-7463**	207-635-4445	446
Cousins Submarines Inc						
N83 W13400 Leon Rd	Menomonee Falls	WI	53051	**800-238-9736**	262-253-7700	666
Covalon Technologies Ltd						
405 Britannia Rd E Ste 106	Mississauga	ON	L4Z3E6	**877-711-6055**	905-568-8400	578
Covance Inc						
210 Carnegie Ctr	Princeton	NJ	08540	**888-268-2623**	609-452-4440	85
NYSE: CVD						
Covanta Energy Corp						
445 South St	Morristown	NJ	07960	**800-950-8749**	862-345-5000	782
NYSE: CVA						
Cove Haven Pocono Palace						
5222 Milford Rd	East Stroudsburg	PA	18302	**800-432-9932**		665
Cove Inn						
900 Broad Ave S	Naples	FL	34102	**800-255-4365**	239-262-7161	378
Cove Lake State Park						
110 Cove Lake Ln	Caryville	TN	37714	**800-250-8615**	423-566-9701	561
Cove Palisades State Park						
7300 Jordan Rd	Culver	OR	97734	**800-551-6949**		
Covenant Care Home						
5700 Old Orchard Rd	Skokie	IL	60077	**877-708-7689**		370
Covenant College						
14049 Scenic Hwy	Lookout Mountain	GA	30750	**888-451-2683**	706-820-1560	166
Covenant Hospice						
5041 N 12th Ave	Pensacola	FL	32504	**800-541-3072**	850-433-2155	370
Covenant Transport Inc						
400 Birmingham Hwy	Chattanooga	TN	37419	**800-334-9686**	423-821-1212	775
NASDAQ: CVTI						
Covenant Village of Cromwell & Pilgrim Manor						
52 Missionary Rd	Cromwell	CT	06416	**800-255-8989**	860-635-2690	668
Covenant Village of Golden Valley						
5800 St Croix Ave	Minneapolis	MN	55422	**877-825-9763**	763-546-6125	668
Coventry First LLC						
7111 Vly Green Rd	Fort Washington	PA	19034	**877-836-8300**		791
Coventry Health Care Inc						
6730-B Rockledge Dr Ste 700	Bethesda	MD	20817	**800-348-2922**	301-581-0600	390-3
Coventry Health Care of Delaware Inc						
750 Prides Crossing Ste 200	Newark	DE	19713	**800-833-7423**		390-3
Coventry Health Care of Georgia Inc						
1100 Cir 75 Pkwy Ste 1400	Atlanta	GA	30339	**800-470-2004**	678-202-2100	390-3
Coventry Health Care of Iowa Inc						
4320 114th St	Urbandale	IA	50322	**800-470-6352**	515-225-1234	390-3
Coventry Health Care of Kansas Inc						
8320 Ward Pkwy	Kansas City	MO	64114	**800-969-3343**		390-3
Coventry Lumber Inc						
2030 Nooseneck Hill Rd	Coventry	RI	02816	**800-390-0919**	401-821-2800	191-3
Coverall Cleaning Concepts						
5201 Congress Ave Ste 275	Boca Raton	FL	33487	**800-537-3371**	866-296-8944	152
Coverbind Corp						
3200 Corporate Dr	Wilmington	NC	28405	**800-366-6060**	910-799-4116	604
Covington Electric Co-op Inc						
18836 US Hwy 84	Andalusia	AL	36421	**800-239-4121**	334-222-4121	245
Covington Travel						
4800 Cox Rd Ste 200	Glen Allen	VA	23060	**800-922-9218**	804-747-7077	766
Cowan Graphics Inc						
4864 - 93 Ave NW	Edmonton	AB	T6B2R9	**800-661-6996**	780-577-5700	623
Cowboy Village Resort						
120 S Flat Creek Dr PO Box 38	Jackson	WY	83001	**800-962-4988**	307-733-3121	378
Coweta-Fayette Electric Membership Corp						
807 Collinsworth Rd	Palmetto	GA	30268	**877-746-4362**	770-502-0226	245
Cowley County						
311 E Ninth Ave	Winfield	KS	67156	**800-876-3469**	620-221-5400	337
Cowley County Community College & Area Vocational-Technical School						
PO Box 1147	Arkansas City	KS	67005	**800-593-2222**	620-442-0430	162
CoWorx Staffing Services LLC						
1375 Plainfield Ave	Watchung	NJ	07069	**800-754-7000**	908-757-5300	260
Cowtown Boots						
11401 Gateway Blvd W	El Paso	TX	79936	**800-580-2698**	915-593-2929	301
Cox Communications Inc						
1400 Lake Hearn Dr	Atlanta	GA	30319	**866-961-0027**	404-843-5000	116
Cox Elearning Consultants Llc						
3848 Macgregor Cmn	Livermore	CA	94551	**866-240-3540**	925-373-6558	717
Cox Hospital North						
1423 N Jefferson Ave	Springfield	MO	65802	**800-711-9455**	417-269-3000	373-3
Cox Industries Inc						
860 Cannon Bridge Rd						
PO Box 1124	Orangeburg	SC	29116	**800-476-4401**	803-534-7467	813
Cox Interior Inc						
1751 Old Columbia Rd	Campbellsville	KY	42718	**800-733-1751**		497
Cox Manufacturing Co						
5500 N Loop 1604 E	San Antonio	TX	78247	**800-900-7981**	210-657-7731	617
Cox Media Group Tampa						
11300 Fourth St N						
Ste 300	Saint Petersburg	FL	33716	**888-723-9388**	727-579-2000	641-108
Cox Medical Center South						
3801 S National Ave	Springfield	MO	65807	**800-711-9455**	417-269-6000	373-3
Cox Schepp Construction Inc						
2410 Dunavant St	Charlotte	NC	28203	**800-954-0823**	704-716-2100	186
Cox Transportation Services Inc						
10448 Dow Gil Rd	Ashland	VA	23005	**800-288-8118**	804-798-1477	775
Coyle Hospitality Group						
244 Madison Ave #369	New York	NY	10016	**800-891-9292**	212-629-2083	461
Coyle Reproductions Inc						
2850 Orbiter St	Brea	CA	92821	**866-269-5373**	714-690-8200	623
Coyne College Inc						
330 N Green St	Chicago	IL	60607	**800-707-1922**	773-577-8100	759
Coyote Logistics LLC						
2545 W Diversey Ave	Chicago	IL	60647	**877-626-9683**		447
Cozad Asset Management Inc						
2501 Galen Dr	Champaign	IL	61821	**800-437-1686**	217-356-8363	524
Cozen O'Connor						
1900 Market St	Philadelphia	PA	19103	**800-523-2900**	215-665-2000	427
CP Capital Securities Inc						
3390 Mary St Ste 116	Coconut Grove	FL	33133	**866-596-5500**	305-702-5500	
C-P Flexible Packaging						
15 Grumbacher Rd	York	PA	17406	**800-815-0667**	717-764-1193	550
CP Franchising LLC						
3300 University Dr	Coral Springs	FL	33065	**800-683-0206**	954-344-8060	767
CP Medical Inc						
1775 Corporate Dr Ste 150	Norcross	GA	30093	**800-950-2763**	678-710-2016	474
CPA (College Parents of America)						
2200 Wilson Blvd Ste 102-396	Arlington	VA	22201	**888-761-6702**		48-11
CPA Auto Dealer Consultants Assn (CADCA)						
1801 W End Ave Ste 800	Nashville	TN	37203	**800-231-2524**	615-373-9880	49-1
CPAC (Cable Public Affairs Channel)						
PO Box 81099	Ottawa	ON	K1P1B1	**877-287-2722**		735
CPAWS (Canadian Parks & Wilderness Society)						
250 City Ctr Ave Ste 506	Ottawa	ON	K1R6K7	**800-333-9453**	613-569-7226	48-13
CPB (Corporation for Public Broadcasting)						
401 Ninth St NW	Washington	DC	20004	**800-272-2190**	202-879-9600	305
CPBI (Connecticut Public Broadcasting Inc)						
1049 Asylum Ave	Hartford	CT	06105	**877-444-4485**	860-278-5310	628
CPC (Country Pride Co-op)						
201 S Monroe PO Box 529	Winner	SD	57580	**888-325-7743**	605-842-2711	10-4

110 CPC

Toll-Free Phone Book USA

Alphabetical Section

Name / Address	City	State	ZIP	Toll-Free	Phone	Class
CPC (Computer Pundits Corp) 5001 American Blvd W Ste 310	Bloomington	MN	55437	**888-786-3487**	952-854-2422	180
CPC Logistics Inc 14528 S Outer 40 Rd Ste 210	Chesterfield	MO	63017	**800-274-3746**	314-542-2266	717
CPCU Society 720 Providence Rd	Malvern	PA	19355	**800-932-2728**		49-9
CPF (Cleft Palate Foundation) 1504 E Franklin St Ste 102	Chapel Hill	NC	27514	**800-242-5338**	919-933-9044	48-17
CPFD (Coastal Pacific Food Distributors Inc) 1015 Performance Dr	Stockton	CA	95206	**800-500-2611**	209-983-2454	297-8
CPH Engineers 500 W Fulton St	Sanford	FL	32771	**866-609-0688**		261
CPhA (California Pharmacists Assn) 4030 Lennane Dr	Sacramento	CA	95834	**866-365-7472**	916-779-1400	581
CPI (Companion Pets Inc) 2001 N Black Canyon Hwy	Phoenix	AZ	85009	**800-646-3611**	602-255-0166	574
CPI (Consumers Power Inc) 6990 W Hills Rd	Philomath	OR	97370	**800-872-9036**	541-929-3124	245
CPI (Confer Plastics Inc) 97 Witmer Rd	North Tonawanda	NY	14120	**800-635-3213**	716-693-2056	600
CPI Group Inc, The 112 Fifth St N PO Box 828	Columbus	MS	39703	**888-566-8303**	662-328-1042	260
CPM Wolverine Proctor LLC 251 Gibraltar Rd	Horsham	PA	19044	**800-428-0846**	215-443-5200	298
CPP Inc 185 N Wolfe Rd	Sunnyvale	CA	94086	**800-624-1765**	650-969-8901	633-2
Cpr Savers & First Aid Supply 7904 E Chaparral Rd Ste A110-242	Scottsdale	AZ	85250	**800-480-1277**		505
CPS (Comprehensive Pharmacy Services Inc) 6409 N Quail Hollow Rd	Memphis	TN	38120	**800-968-6962**	901-748-0470	194
CPS Cards 7520 Morris Ct	Allentown	PA	18106	**888-817-8121**	610-231-1860	623
CPSC (Consumer Product Safety Commission) 4340 E W Hwy Ste 502	Bethesda	MD	20814	**800-638-2772**	301-504-7923	339-19
CPT (Central Petroleum Transport Inc) 6115 Mitchell St	Sioux City	IA	51111	**800-798-6357**	712-258-6357	775
CPT Group Inc 50 Corporate Park	Irvine	CA	92606	**800-542-0900**	877-705-5021	
Parks and Wildlife 1313 Sherman St Rm 618 *Campground Resv	Denver	CO	80203	**800-678-2267***	303-866-3437	338-6
CR Bard Inc Urological Div 8195 Industrial Blvd	Covington	GA	30014	**800-526-4455**	770-784-6100	474
CR England & Sons Inc 4701 West 2100 South	Salt Lake City	UT	84120	**800-453-8826**	801-972-2712	775
CR Laurence Company Inc 2503 E Vernon Ave PO Box 58923	Los Angeles	CA	90058	**800-421-6144**	323-588-1281	191-2
CRA (CRAssoc Inc) 8580 Cinderbed Rd Ste 2400	Newington	VA	22122	**877-272-8960**		461
Crabtree & Evelyn Ltd 102 Peake Brook Rd	Woodstock	CT	06281	**800-272-2873**	860-928-2761	214
Cracker Barrel Old Country Store Inc PO Box 787 *NASDAQ: CBRL*	Lebanon	TN	37088	**800-333-9566**	615-235-4054	666
Crafco Inc 420 N Roosevelt Ave	Chandler	AZ	85226	**800-528-8242**	602-276-0406	46
Craft & Hobby Assn (CHA) 319 E 54th St	Elmwood Park	NJ	07407	**800-822-0494**	201-835-1200	48-18
CRAFT Ideas 911 S Vandemark Rd	Sidney	OH	45365	**800-253-4555**	937-498-2111	455-14
Craft Inc 1929 County St PO Box 3049	South Attleboro	MA	02703	**800-827-2388**	508-761-7917	349
Craftmade 650 S Royal Ln *OTC: CRFT*	Coppell	TX	75019	**800-486-4892**		37
Crafts Technology 91 Joey Dr	Elk Grove Village	IL	60007	**800-323-6802**	847-758-3100	453
Craftsman Printing Inc 120 Citation Ct	Birmingham	AL	35209	**800-543-1051**	205-942-3939	623
Cragun's Conference & Golf Resort 11000 Cragun's Dr	Brainerd	MN	56401	**800-272-4867**		665
Craig Envelope Corp 12-01 44th Ave	Long Island City	NY	11101	**888-272-4436**		
Craig Hospital 3425 S Clarkson St	Englewood	CO	80113	**800-247-0257**	303-789-8000	373-6
Craig Manufacturing Ltd 96 Mclean Ave	Hartland	NB	E7P2K5	**800-565-5007**		478
Craig Transportation Co 819 Kingsbury St	Maumee	OH	43537	**800-521-9119**	419-872-3333	775
Craig-Botetourt Electric Cooperative 26198 Craigs Creek Rd PO Box 265	New Castle	VA	24127	**800-760-2232**	540-864-5121	
Craighead Electric Co-op Corp 4314 Stadium Blvd PO Box 7503	Jonesboro	AR	72403	**800-794-5012**	870-932-8301	245
Crain Communications Inc 1155 Gratiot Ave	Detroit	MI	48207	**888-288-6954**	313-446-6000	633-9
Crain's Chicago Business Magazine 150 N Michigan Ave 16th Fl	Chicago	IL	60601	**877-812-1590**	312-649-5200	455-5
Crain's Cleveland Business Magazine 700 W St Clair Ave Ste 310	Cleveland	OH	44113	**888-909-9111**	216-522-1383	455-5
Crain's Detroit Business Magazine 1155 Gratiot Ave	Detroit	MI	48207	**888-909-9111**	313-446-6000	455-5
Crain's New York Business Magazine 685 Third Ave	New York	NY	10017	**877-824-9379**	212-210-0100	455-5
Cramer Fish Sciences 7525 NE Ambassador Pl Ste C	Portland	OR	97220	**888-224-1221**	503-491-9577	
Cramer Inc 1523 Grand Blvd	Kansas City	MO	64108	**800-366-6700**		319-1
Cramer Products Inc 153 W Warren St	Gardner	KS	66030	**800-345-2231**		475
Crandall Engineering Ltd 1077 St George Blvd	Moncton	NB	E1E4C9	**866-857-2777**	506-857-2777	194
Crandall University 333 Gorge Rd	Moncton	NB	E1G3H9	**888-968-6228**	506-858-8970	780
Crane & Co Inc 30 S St *Cust Svc	Dalton	MA	01226	**800-268-2281***		548-2
Crane Company Stockham Div 2129 Third Ave SE	Cullman	AL	35055	**800-786-2542**	203-363-7300	784
Crane Composites Inc 23525 W Eames St	Channahon	IL	60410	**800-435-0080**	815-467-8600	602
Crane Manufacturers Assn of America (CMAA) 8720 Red Oak Blvd Ste 201	Charlotte	NC	28217	**800-345-1815**	704-676-1190	49-13
CRANE Merchandising Systems 3330 Crane Way PO Box 719	Williston	SC	29853	**800-628-8363**	800-621-7278	111
Crane Nuclear Inc 2825 Cobb International Blvd	Kennesaw	GA	30152	**800-795-8013**	770-429-4600	470
Crane Worldwide Logistics LLC 1500 Rankin Rd	Houston	TX	77073	**888-870-2726**	281-443-2777	447
Cranesmart Systems Inc 4908 97 St NW	Edmonton	AB	T6E5S1	**888-562-3222**	780-437-2986	406
Craneveyor Corp 1524 Potrero Ave	South El Monte	CA	91733	**888-501-0050**		468
Cranston Machinery Company Inc 2251 SE Oak Grove Blvd	Oak Grove	OR	97267	**800-547-1012**	503-654-7751	552
Cranston Print Works Co 1381 Cranston St	Cranston	RI	02920	**800-876-2756**	401-943-4800	740-7
Cranwell Resort Spa & Golf Club 55 Lee Rd	Lenox	MA	01240	**800-272-6935**	413-637-1364	665
CRAssoc Inc (CRA) 8580 Cinderbed Rd Ste 2400	Newington	VA	22122	**877-272-8960**		461
Craters & Freighters 331 Corporate Cir Ste J	Golden	CO	80401	**800-736-3335**		310
Craters of the Moon National Monument & Preserve PO Box 29	Arco	ID	83213	**800-562-3408**	208-527-1335	560
Craven County 406 Craven St	New Bern	NC	28560	**800-437-5767**	252-636-6600	337
Craven County Convention & Visitors Bureau 203 S Front St	New Bern	NC	28560	**800-437-5767**	252-637-9400	206
Crawford Consulting Services Inc 239 Highland Ave	East Pittsburgh	PA	15112	**800-365-9010**	412-823-0400	261
Crawford County 903 Diamond Sq	Meadville	PA	16335	**800-585-3737**	814-333-7465	337
Crawford County 225 N Beaumont Rd	Prairie du Chien	WI	53821	**877-794-2372**	608-326-0200	337
Crawford County 302 Main St PO Box AS	Steelville	MO	65565	**866-566-8267**	573-775-2376	337
Crawford Electric Co-op Inc 10301 N Service Rd PO Box 10	Bourbon	MO	65441	**800-677-2667**	573-732-4415	245
Crawford Industries 1414 Crawford Dr	Crawfordsville	IN	47933	**800-428-0840**		544
Crawford Technologies Inc 45 St Clair Ave W Ste 102	Toronto	ON	M4V1K9	**866-679-0864**	416-923-0080	179
Crazy Shirts Inc 99-969 Iwaena St	Aiea	HI	96701	**800-771-2720**	808-487-9919	155-3
Crazy Woman Creek Bancorp Inc PO Box 1020	Buffalo	WY	82834	**877-684-2766**	307-684-5591	359-2
CRB (Rebi) 430 N Michigan Ave	Chicago	IL	60611	**800-621-8738**		49-17
CRC (Christian Reformed Church in North America) 2850 Kalamazoo Ave SE	Grand Rapids	MI	49560	**800-272-5125**	616-241-1691	48-20
CRC (Container Research Corp) 2 New Rd	Aston	PA	19014	**844-220-9574**		198
CRC Evans Pipeline International Inc 10700 E Independence St	Tulsa	OK	74116	**800-664-9224**	918-438-2100	190
CRC Industries Inc 885 Louis Dr *Cust Svc	Warminster	PA	18974	**800-556-5074***	215-674-4300	537
CRC Press LLC 6000 Broken Sound Pkwy NW Ste 300 *Cust Svc	Boca Raton	FL	33487	**800-272-7737***	561-994-0555	633-9
CRCA (Consumers' Research Council of America) 2020 Pennsylvania Ave NW Ste 300-A	Washington	DC	20006	**877-774-6337**	202-835-9698	48-10
CRCH (Carilion Roanoke Community Hospital) 101 Elm Ave SE	Roanoke	VA	24013	**800-422-8482**	540-985-8000	373-3
Cream City Music 12505 W Bluemound Rd	Brookfield	WI	53005	**800-800-0087**	262-860-1800	522
Creamer Metal Products Inc 77 S Madison Rd	London	OH	43140	**800-362-1603**	740-852-1752	295
Cream-O-Land Dairy Inc 529 Cedar Ln	Florence	NJ	08518	**800-220-6455**	609-499-3601	297-4
Create-a-card Inc 16 Brasswood Rd	Saint James	NY	11780	**800-753-6867**	631-584-2273	531
Creatine Marketing 2121 Natomas Crossing Ste 200- 105	Sacramento	CA	95834	**800-357-6242**	916-302-4742	
Creating Keepsakes Magazine 14850 Pony Express Rd	Bluffdale	UT	84065	**888-247-5282**	801-816-8300	455-14
Creation Engine 425 North Whisman Rd Ste 300	Mountain View	CA	94043	**800-431-8713**	650-934-0176	180
Creative Colors International Inc 19015 S Jodi Rd Ste E	Mokena	IL	60448	**800-933-2656**	708-478-1437	310
Creative Communications For The Parish Inc 1564 Fencorp Dr	Fenton	MO	63026	**800-325-9414**	636-305-9777	633-2
Creative Educational Concepts Inc 501 Darby Creek Dr Unit 15	Lexington	KY	40509	**866-226-9650**	859-260-1717	
Creative Financial Group (CFG) 16 Campus Blvd	Newtown Square	PA	19073	**800-893-4824**	610-325-6100	400
Creative Foam Corp 300 N Alloy Dr	Fenton	MI	48430	**800-529-4149**	810-629-4149	597
Creative Glass Center of America 1501 Glasstown Rd	Millville	NJ	08332	**800-998-4552**	856-825-6800	517
Creative Impact Group Inc 801 Skokie Blvd Ste 108	Northbrook	IL	60062	**800-445-2171**		184
Creative Kid Stuff 3939 E 46th St	Minneapolis	MN	55406	**800-353-0710**	612-929-2431	756
Creative Kids Magazine PO Box 8813	Waco	TX	76714	**800-998-2208**	254-756-3337	455-6
Creative Mktg International Corp 11460 Tomahawk Creek Pkwy	Leawood	KS	66211	**800-992-2642**	913-814-0510	390-2

	Toll-Free	Phone	Class
Creative Outdoor Advertising			
2402 Stouffville Rd .... Stouffville ON L4A2J4	800-661-6088		7
Creative Pultrusions Inc			
214 Industrial Ln .... Alum Bank PA 15521	888-274-7855	814-839-4186	191-3
Creative Sign Designs			
12801 Commodity Pl .... Tampa FL 33626	800-804-4809		317
Creative Teaching Press Inc			
6262 Katella Ave .... Cypress CA 90630	800-444-4287	714-895-5047	243
Creative Training Techniques International Inc			
14530 Martin Dr .... Eden Prairie MN 55344	800-383-9210	952-829-1954	760
Creativity for Kids			
9450 Allen Dr .... Cleveland OH 44125	800-311-8684	216-643-4660	757
Credit Acceptance Corp			
25505 W 12 Mile Rd .... Southfield MI 48034	800-634-1506	248-353-2700	217
Credit Consulting Services Inc			
201 John St Ste E. .... Salinas CA 93901	800-679-6888	831-424-0606	160
Credit Human Federal Credit Union			
PO Box 1356 .... San Antonio TX 78295	800-234-7228	210-258-1234	219
Credit Management LP			
4200 International Pkwy .... Carrollton TX 75007	800-377-7713		160
Credit Plus Inc			
31550 WinterPl Pkwy .... Salisbury MD 21804	800-258-3287	410-742-9551	226
Credit Union Acceptance Company LLC			
9601 Jones Rd Ste 108. .... Houston TX 77065	866-970-2822	281-970-2822	219
Credit Union Executives Society (CUES)			
5510 Research Pk Dr .... Madison WI 53711	800-252-2664	608-271-2664	49-2
Credit Union National Association (CUNA)			
99 M St SE Ste 300 .... Washington DC 20003	800-356-9655		
Credit Union of Southern California			
PO Box 200 .... Whittier CA 90608	866-287-6225	562-698-8326	219
Credit Union of Texas			
PO Box 517028 .... Dallas TX 75251	800-314-3828	972-263-9497	219
Creditors Adjustment Bureau-LC Financial (CABLCF)			
14226 Ventura Blvd .... Sherman Oaks CA 91423	800-800-4523	818-990-4800	160
Creditors Bureau Assoc			
420 College St .... Macon GA 31201	866-949-4213	478-750-1111	218
Cree Inc			
4600 Silicon Dr .... Durham NC 27703	800-533-2583	919-313-5300	692
NASDAQ: CREE			
Creedmoor Psychiatric Ctr			
79-25 Winchester Blvd .... Queens Village NY 11427	800-597-8481	718-464-7500	373-5
Creekside Inn			
3400 El Camino Real .... Palo Alto CA 94306	800-492-7335	650-493-2411	378
Creform Corp PO Box 830 .... Greer SC 29652	800-839-8823	864-989-1700	719
Creighton University			
2500 California Plz .... Omaha NE 68178	800-282-5835	402-280-2700	166
Creighton University Medical Ctr			
601 N 30th St .... Omaha NE 68131	800-368-5097	402-280-2700	373-3
Creor Group			
952 School St Ste 310 .... Napa CA 94559	877-774-4312		195
Creps United Publications			
1163 Water St .... Indiana PA 15701	800-752-0555	724-463-8522	623
Crescendo Systems Corp			
1600 Montgolfier .... Laval QC H7T0A2	800-724-2930	450-973-8029	177
Crescent Cardboard Company LLC			
100 W Willow Rd .... Wheeling IL 60090	888-293-3956	847-537-3400	556
Crescent Manufacturing Co			
1310 Majestic Dr .... Fremont OH 43420	800-537-1330	419-332-6484	222
Cresco Lines Inc			
15220 S Halsted St .... Harvey IL 60426	800-323-4476	708-339-1186	775
Cres-Cor			
5925 Heisley Rd .... Mentor OH 44060	877-273-7267	440-350-1100	286
Crespi Carmelite High School Inc			
5031 Alonzo Ave .... Encino CA 91316	800-540-4000	818-345-1672	681
Crest Craft Co			
3860 Virginia Ave .... Cincinnati OH 45227	800-860-1662	513-271-4858	623
Crest Foods Company Inc			
905 Main St .... Ashton IL 61006	877-273-7893	800-435-6972	296-17
Crest Healthcare Supply			
195 Third St .... Dassel MN 55325	800-328-8908		391
Crest Ultrasonics Corp			
18 Graphics Dr .... Ewing Township NJ 08628	800-992-7378	609-883-4000	777
Crestcom International Ltd			
6900 E Belleview Ave .... Greenwood Village CO 80111	800-333-7680	303-267-8200	760
Crested Butte Mountain Resort (CBMR)			
12 Snowmass Rd			
PO Box 5700. .... Crested Butte CO 81225	877-547-5143	970-349-2222	665
Crestliner Inc			
9040 Quaday Ave NE .... Ostego MN 55330	866-301-8544		90
Crestmark Bank			
5480 Corporate Dr Ste 350. .... Troy MI 48098	888-999-8050		272
Crestwood Advisors LLC			
50 Federal St Ste 810 .... Boston MA 02110	877-273-7896	617-523-8880	400
Crestwood Manor			
50 Lacey Rd .... Whiting NJ 08759	877-467-1652*	732-849-4900	668
*General			
Crestwood Tubulars Inc			
PO Box 6950 .... St. Louis MO 63123	800-238-7473		
Crete Carrier Corp			
400 NW 56th St PO Box 81228 .... Lincoln NE 68528	800-998-4095*	402-475-9521	775
*Cust Svc			
Creutzfeldt-Jakob Disease Foundation Inc			
3610 W Market St Ste 110 .... Fairlawn OH 44333	800-659-1991		48-17
Crew Outfitters Inc			
1001 Virginia Ave .... Atlanta GA 30354	888-345-5353		156
Crexendo Inc			
1615 S 52nd St .... Tempe AZ 85281	866-621-6111	602-714-8500	39
OTC: CXDO			
CRG (Capital Review Group)			
2415 E Camelback Rd Ste 700 .... Phoenix AZ 85016	877-666-5539		
CRG Global Inc			
3 Signal Ave Ste A .... Ormond Beach FL 32174	800-831-1718	386-677-5644	664
CRH Americas Inc			
900 Ashwood Pkwy Ste 700 .... Atlanta GA 30338	800-241-7074	770-522-5600	
Cricket Media Inc			
1751 Pinnacle Dr Ste 600. .... McLean VA 22102	800-821-0115		455-6
Crime Alert			
690 Lenfest Rd .... San Jose CA 95133	800-367-1094		
Criminal Law Reporter			
1801 S Bell St .... Arlington VA 22202	800-372-1033		527-7
Crissey Field State Recreation Site			
1655 Hwy 101 N .... Brookings OR 97415	800-551-6949	541-469-2021	561
Cristi Cleaning Service			
77 Trinity Pl .... Hackensack NJ 07608	800-287-6173	201-883-1717	104
Criswell Automotive			
503 Quince Orchard Rd .... Gaithersburg MD 20878	888-672-7559		57
Criswell College			
4010 Gaston Ave .... Dallas TX 75246	800-899-0012	214-821-5433	166
Criterion Thread Company Inc			
21744 98th Ave .... Queens Village NY 11429	800-695-0080*	718-464-4200	590
*General			
Critical Business Analysis Inc (CBA)			
133 W Second St .... Perrysburg OH 43551	800-874-8080		
Critical Mention Inc			
521 Fifth Ave .... New York NY 10175	855-306-2626	212-398-1141	
Criticom Inc			
4211 Forbes Blvd .... Lanham MD 20706	800-449-3384	301-306-0600	731
Criticom International Corp			
715 W State Rd Ste 434 .... Longwood FL 32750	866-705-7705		689
CRM Dynamics			
5800 Ambler Dr Unit 106 .... Mississauga ON L5W4J4	866-740-2424		196
CRM Learning			
11400 SE Eighth St Ste 210 .... Bellevue WA 92004	800-421-0833	760-431-9800	510
CRMC (Coffee Regional Medical Ctr)			
1101 Ocilla Rd .... Douglas GA 31533	800-555-4444	912-384-1900	373-3
CRMC (Colquitt Regional Medical Ctr)			
3131 S Main St PO Box 40. .... Moultrie GA 31768	888-262-2762	229-985-3420	373-3
CRMC (Cookeville Regional Medical Ctr)			
1 Medical Ctr Blvd .... Cookeville TN 38501	800-897-1898	931-528-2541	373-3
Crocker & Winsor Seafoods Inc			
PO Box 51905 .... Boston MA 02205	800-225-1597	617-269-3100	296-14
Crocs Inc			
6328 Monarch Pk Pl .... Niwot CO 80503	866-306-3179	303-848-7000	301
NASDAQ: CROX			
Croft LLC			
107 Oliver Emmerich Dr .... McComb MS 39648	800-222-3195	601-684-6121	483
Crohn's & Colitis Foundation of America (CCFA)			
733 Third Ave Ste 510 .... New York NY 10017	800-932-2423		48-17
Cromers Pnuts LLC			
3030 North Main St .... Columbia SC 29201	800-322-7688		290-36
Cronland Lumber Co			
PO Box 574 .... Lincolnton NC 28093	800-237-2428	704-736-2691	679
Cronomagic Canada Inc			
3333 boul Graham Ste 700. .... Mont-Royal QC H3R3L5	800-427-6012	514-341-1579	180
Crook County			
300 NE Third St			
Crook County Courthouse Rm 23. .... Prineville OR 97754	800-735-2900	541-447-6553	337
Crop Science Society of America (CSSA)			
677 S Segoe Rd .... Madison WI 53711	800-755-2751	608-273-8080	48-2
CropKing Inc 134 W Dr .... Lodi OH 44254	800-321-5656	330-302-4203	276
CropLife America			
1156 15th St NW .... Washington DC 20005	800-266-9432	202-296-1585	48-2
CROPP Co-op			
1 Organic Way .... LaFarge WI 54639	888-444-6455		10-9
Crosbie & Company Inc			
150 King St W Sun Life Financial Tower			
15th Fl .... Toronto ON M5H1J9	866-873-7002	416-362-7726	317
Crosby Group, The			
2801 Dawson Rd .... Tulsa OK 74110	800-772-1500	918-834-4611	468
Crosman Corp			
7629 Rt 5 & 20 .... Bloomfield NY 14469	800-724-7486		284
Cross Bros Inc			
5255 Sheila St .... Los Angeles CA 90040	866-939-1057	323-266-2000	480
Cross Co			
4400 Piedmont Pkwy .... Greensboro NC 27410	800-858-1737	336-856-6000	384
Cross Country Healthcare Inc			
6551 Pk of Commerce Blvd .... Boca Raton FL 33487	800-347-2264	561-998-2232	717
NASDAQ: CCRN			
Cross Country Home Services			
1625 NW 136th Ave Ste 200. .... Sunrise FL 33323	800-778-8000*	954-845-2468	366
*Cust Svc			
Cross Country Ski Areas Assn (CCSAA)			
259 Bolton Rd .... Winchester NH 03470	877-779-2754	603-239-4341	48-22
Cross Creek Resort			
3815 Pennsylvania 8 .... Titusville PA 16354	800-461-3173	814-827-9611	378
Cross Financial Corp			
74 Gilman Rd PO Box 1388 .... Bangor ME 04401	800-999-7345	207-947-7345	389
Cross Keys Village			
2990 Carlisle Pk .... New Oxford PA 17350	888-624-8242*	717-624-2161	668
*Mktg			
Cross Oil Refining & Marketing Inc			
484 E Sixth St .... Smackover AR 71762	800-725-3066	870-881-8700	576
Cross Petroleum Inc			
6920 Lockheed Dr .... Redding CA 96002	800-655-4427	530-221-2588	577
Crosscountry Courier Inc			
PO Box 4030 .... Bismarck ND 58502	800-521-0287	701-222-8498	542
Crosset Company Inc			
10295 Toebben Dr .... Independence KY 41051	800-347-4902	859-283-5830	297-7
Crossett Inc			
201 S Carver St .... Warren PA 16365	800-876-2778*		775
*General			
Crosslake Communications			
35910 County Rd 66 PO Box 70. .... Crosslake MN 56442	800-992-8220	218-692-2777	386
Crossmark Inc			
5100 Legacy Dr .... Plano TX 75024	877-699-6275	469-814-1000	195
Crossmatch			
3950 RCA Blvd			
Ste 5001 .... Palm Beach Garden FL 33410	866-725-3926	561-622-1650	
Crossroads Bible College			
601 North Shortridge Rd .... Indianapolis IN 46219	800-822-3119	317-789-8255	161
Crossroads College			
920 Mayowood Rd SW .... Rochester MN 55902	800-456-7651	507-288-4563	161
Crossville Cumberland County Chamber of Commerce			
34 S Main St .... Crossville TN 38555	877-465-3861	931-484-8444	139
Crossville Porcelain Stone/USA			
PO Box 1168 .... Crossville TN 38557	800-221-9093	931-484-2110	746

Name / Address	Toll-Free	Phone	Class
Crossworld 306 Bala Ave .... Bala Cynwyd PA 19004	888-785-0087		48-20
Croswell Bus Lines Inc 975 W Main St .... Williamsburg OH 45176	800-782-8747	513-724-2206	107
Crotched Mountain Foundation 1 Verney Dr .... Greenfield NH 03047	800-433-2900	603-547-3311	373-6
Crouch Group Inc, The 300 N Carroll Blvd Ste 103 .... Denton TX 76201	888-211-0273	940-383-1990	7
Crow Executive Air Inc 28331 Lemoyne Rd Toledo Metcalf Airport .... Millbury OH 43447	800-972-2769	567-200-0057	63
Crow Wing Co-op Power & Light Co Hwy 371 N PO Box 507 ...... Brainerd MN 56401	800-648-9401	218-829-2827	245
Crow Wing County 326 Laurel St .... Brainerd MN 56401	888-829-6680	218-824-1067	337
Crow Wing State Park 3124 State Pk Rd ...... Brainerd MN 56401	888-646-6367	218-825-3075	561
Crowder College 601 Laclede Ave ...... Neosho MO 64850	866-238-7788	417-451-3223	162
Crowder Constructors Inc 6425 Brookshire Blvd ...... Charlotte NC 28230	800-849-2966	704-372-3541	188-4
CrowdSource Solutions Inc 33 Bronze Pointe ...... Swansea IL 62226	855-276-9376	877-642-7331	627
Crowell Weedon & Co 1 Wilshire Bldg 624 S Grand Ave 26th Fl ...... Los Angeles CA 90017	800-227-0319	213-620-1850	686
Crowley Maritime Corp 9487 Regency Square Blvd .... Jacksonville FL 32225	800-276-9539	904-727-2200	312
Crowley's Ridge College 100 College Dr ...... Paragould AR 72450	800-264-1096	870-236-6901	162
Crown American Hotels Co Pasquerilla Plz ...... Johnstown PA 15907	800-245-9295	814-533-4600	378
Crown Battery Manufacturing Co 1445 Majestic Dr ...... Fremont OH 43420	800-487-2879	419-334-7181	74
Crown Castle International Corp 1220 Augusta Dr Ste 500 ...... Houston TX 77057 NYSE: CCI	877-486-9377	713-570-3000	170
Crown College 8700 College View Dr ...... Saint Bonifacius MN 55375	800-346-9252	952-446-4100	161
Crown Column & Millwork Co LLC 3810 Pleasant Valley Rd ...... Attalla AL 35954	888-862-0880		497
Crown Crafts Inc 916 S Burnside ...... Gonzales LA 70737 NASDAQ: CRWS	800-433-9560	225-647-9100	741
Crown Energy Co 1117 NW 24th St ...... Oklahoma City OK 73106	877-228-0801	405-526-0111	
Crown Financial Ministries 601 Broad St SE ...... Gainesville GA 30501	800-722-1976	770-534-1000	400
Crown Holdings Inc 1 Crown Way ...... Philadelphia PA 19154 NYSE: CCK	800-523-3644	215-698-5100	124
Crown Motors Ltd 196 Regent Blvd ...... Holland MI 49423	800-466-7000	616-396-5268	57
Crown Packaging Corp 17854 Chesterfld Airport Rd ...... Chesterfield MO 63005	888-880-0852	314-731-4927	544
Crown Plastics Co 116 May Dr ...... Harrison OH 45030	800-368-0238	513-367-0238	596
Crown Point State Historic Site 21 Grandview Dr ...... Crown Point NY 12928	800-456-2267	518-597-4666	561
Crown Products Company Inc 6390 Phillips Hwy ...... Jacksonville FL 32216	800-683-7144	904-737-7144	693
Crown Reef Resort 2913 S Ocean Blvd ...... Myrtle Beach SC 29577	800-291-6598	843-626-8077	378
Crown Roll Leaf Inc 91 Illinois Ave ...... Paterson NJ 07503	800-631-3831	973-742-4000	295
Crown Travel & Cruises 240 Newton Rd Ste 106 ...... Raleigh NC 27615	800-869-7447	919-870-1986	766
Crowne Plaza Niagara Falls - Fallsview 5685 Falls Ave ...... Niagara Falls ON L2E6W7	800-263-7135	905-374-4447	377
Crowne Plaza Syracuse 701 E Genesee St ...... Syracuse NY 13210	866-305-4134	315-479-7000	378
CrownTonka Inc 15600 37th Ave N Ste 100 ...... Plymouth MN 55446	800-523-7337	763-541-1410	660
Crozer-Keystone Health System (CKHS) 190 W Sproul Rd ...... Springfield PA 19064	800-254-3258	610-328-8700	352
CRRG Inc PO Box 170904 ...... Arlington TX 76003	800-687-9030		
CRS (Catholic Relief Services) 228 W Lexington St ...... Baltimore MD 21201	800-235-2772	410-625-2220	48-5
CRS Inc 4851 White Bear Pkwy ...... Saint Paul MN 55110	800-333-4949	651-294-2700	112
CRS Jet Spares Inc 6701 NW 12th Ave ...... Fort Lauderdale FL 33309	800-338-5387	954-972-2807	22
CRS Onesource 2803 Tamarack Rd PO Box 1984 .... Owensboro KY 42302	800-264-0710	270-684-1469	297-11
CRT Custom Products Inc 7532 Hickory Hills Ct ...... Whites Creek TN 37189	800-453-2533	615-876-5490	756
CRU Acquisitions Group LLC 1000 SE Tech Ctr Dr Ste 160 ...... Vancouver WA 98683	800-260-9800	360-816-1800	173-8
Crucial Technology 3475 E Commercial Ct ...... Meridian ID 83642	800-336-8915	208-363-5790	621
Crucible Materials Corp 575 State Fair Blvd ...... Syracuse NY 13209	800-365-1180	315-487-4111	719
Cruise America 11 W Hampton Ave ...... Mesa AZ 85210	800-671-8042	480-464-7300	120
Cruise Brokers 2803 W Busch Blvd Ste 100 ...... Tampa FL 33618	800-409-1919	813-288-9597	766
Cruise Brothers, The 100 Boyd Ave ...... East Providence RI 02914	800-827-7779	401-941-3999	767
Cruise Concepts 1329 Enniswood Pkwy ...... Palm Harbor FL 34683	800-752-7963	727-784-7245	766
Cruise Connection LLC 7932 N Oak St Ste 210 ...... Kansas City MO 64118	800-572-0004	816-420-8688	766
Cruise Lines International Assn (CLIA) 1201 F St NW Ste 250 ...... Washington DC 20004	855-444-2542	202-759-9370	48-23
Cruise People Inc 10191 W Sample Rd Ste 215 ...... Coral Springs FL 33065	800-642-2469	954-340-2016	766
Cruise Shop, The 700 Pasquinelli Dr Ste C ...... Westmont IL 60559	800-622-6456	858-433-1506	766
Cruise Specialists Inc 221 First Ave W Ste 210 ...... Seattle WA 98119	888-993-1318		
Cruise Vacation Ctr 2042 Central Park Ave ...... Yonkers NY 10710	800-803-7245		766
Cruise Web Inc 3901 Calverton Blvd Ste 350 ...... Calverton MD 20705	800-377-9383	240-487-0155	766
Cruisecheapcom 220 Congress Park Dr Ste 330 ...... Delray Beach FL 33445	800-543-1915		767
CruiseOne Inc 1201 W Cypress Creek Rd Ste 100 ...... Fort Lauderdale FL 33309	800-278-4731		767
Cruises Inc 1201 W Cypress Creek Rd Ste 100 ...... Fort Lauderdale FL 33309 *Cust Svc	888-282-1249*		766
Cruisescom 100 Fordham Rd Bldg C ...... Wilmington MA 01887	800-288-6006		768
Cruising Gide Publications Inc 1130 Pinehurst Rd Ste B ...... Dunedin FL 34698	800-330-9542	727-733-5322	5
Crum & Forster Insurance Inc 305 Madison Ave PO Box 1973 ...... Morristown NJ 07962	800-690-5520	973-490-6600	390-4
Crum & Forster Pet Insurance Group 305 Madison Ave ...... Morristown NJ 07962	844-592-4879		390-1
Crum Electric Supply Co 1165 W English Ave ...... Casper WY 82601	800-726-2239	307-266-1278	246
Crusader Paper Company Inc 350 Holt Rd ...... North Andover MA 01845	800-421-0007		550
Crutchfield Corp 1 Crutchfield Pk ...... Charlottesville VA 22911 *Sales	888-955-6000*	434-817-1000	457
CRWRC (Christian Reformed World Relief Committee) 2850 Kalamazoo Ave SE ...... Grand Rapids MI 49560	800-552-7972	616-241-1691	48-5
Crye-Leike Inc 6525 N Quail Hollow Rd ...... Memphis TN 38120	866-310-3102		648
Cryobiology Inc 4830D Knightsbridge Blvd ...... Columbus OH 43214	800-359-4375	614-451-4375	541
Cryolife Inc 1655 Roberts Blvd NW ...... Kennesaw GA 30144 NYSE: CRY	800-438-8285	770-419-3355	85
Cryovac Food Packaging & Food Solutions 100 Rogers Bridge Rd ...... Duncan SC 29334	800-391-5645		544
Crystal Beach Suites & Health Club 6985 Collins Ave ...... Miami Beach FL 33141	888-643-4630	305-865-9555	378
Crystal Communications Ltd 1525 Lakeville Dr Ste 230 ...... Kingwood TX 77339	888-949-6603	281-361-5199	196
Crystal Group Inc 850 Kacena Rd ...... Hiawatha IA 52233	877-279-7863	319-378-1636	176
Crystal Inn 185 S State St Ste 1300 ...... Salt Lake City UT 84111 *General	800-662-2525*	801-320-7200	378
Crystal Inn Salt Lake City Downtown 230 W 500 S ...... Salt Lake City UT 84101	800-662-2525	801-328-4466	378
Crystal Lake State Park 96 Bellwater Ave ...... Barton VT 05822	888-409-7579	802-525-6205	561
Crystal Meth Anonymous (CMA) 4470 W Sunset Blvd Ste 107 PO Box 555 ...... Los Angeles CA 90027	877-262-6691		48-21
Crystal Mountain Resort 12500 Crystal Mtn Dr ...... Thompsonville MI 49683	800-968-7686	231-378-2000	665
Crystal Rock Holdings Inc 1050 Buckingham St ...... Watertown CT 06795 NYSE: CRVP	800-525-0070	860-945-0661	80-2
Crystal Valley Coop 721 W Humphry PO Box 210 ...... Lake Crystal MN 56055	800-622-2910	507-726-6455	276
Crystal Wealth Management System Ltd 3385 Harvester Rd Ste 200 ...... Burlington ON L7N3N2	877-299-2854	905-332-4414	791
Crystallex International Corp 8 King St E Ste 1201 ...... Toronto ON M5C1B5	800-738-1577	416-203-2448	500
Crystal-Like Plastics 21701 Plummer St ...... Chatsworth CA 91311	800-554-6091	818-846-1818	604
Crysteel Mfg Inc 52182 Ember Rd ...... Lake Crystal MN 56055 *Orders	800-533-0494*	507-726-2728	468
Crysteel Truck Equipment Inc 52248 Ember Rd ...... Lake Crystal MN 56055 *General	800-722-0588*		775
Crystek Crystals Corp 12730 Commonwealth Dr ...... Fort Myers FL 33913	800-237-3061	239-561-3311	253
CS & P Technologies LP 18119 Telge Rd ...... Cypress TX 77429	800-262-6103	713-467-0869	637
CS Mott Children's Hospital 1500 E Medical Ctr Dr ...... Ann Arbor MI 48109	800-211-8181	734-936-4000	373-1
CSA Group 178 Rexdale Blvd ...... Toronto ON M9W1R3	800-463-6727	416-747-4000	317
CSC (Curtis Steel Company) 6504 Hurst St ...... Houston TX 77008	800-749-4621	713-861-4621	483
CSC ServiceWorks 303 Sunnyside Blvd Ste 70 ...... Plainview NY 11803	877-264-6622	516-349-8555	425
CSDP (Customer Service Delivery Platform) 15615 Alton Pkwy Ste 310 ...... Irvine CA 92618	888-741-2737		177
CSE Corp 1001 Corporate Ln ...... Export PA 15632	800-245-2224	412-856-9200	674
CSG (Council of State Governments) 2760 Research Pk Dr ...... Lexington KY 40511 *Sales	800-800-1910*	859-244-8000	49-7
CSG (Community Services Group) 320 Highland Dr PO Box 597 ...... Mountville PA 17554	877-907-7970	717-285-7121	352
CSI (Christian Schools International) 3350 E Paris Ave SE ...... Grand Rapids MI 49512	800-635-8288	616-957-1070	49-5
Csi Industries Inc 6910 W Ridge Rd ...... Fairview PA 16415	800-937-9033	814-474-9353	198
CSI International Inc 8120 State Rt 138 ...... Williamsport OH 43164	800-795-4914	740-420-5400	178-12
CSI Worldwide Inc 40 Regency Plz ...... Glen Mills PA 19342	800-523-7118	610-558-4500	184

	Toll-Free	Phone	Class
CSM (Cambridge Street Metal Corp) 82 Stevens St .... East Taunton MA 02718	800-254-7580	508-822-2278	490
CSM Group Inc 600 E Michigan Ave Ste A .... Kalamazoo MI 49007	877-386-8214		
CSM Metal Fabricating & Engineering Inc 1800 S San Pedro St ....Los Angeles CA 90015	800-272-4806	213-748-7321	480
CSMC (Cedars-Sinai Medical Ctr) 8700 Beverly Blvd ....Los Angeles CA 90048	800-233-2771	310-423-3277	373-3
Cso Insights 36 Tamal Vista Blvd ....Corte Madera CA 94925	877-506-2975		
CSP Inc 43 Manning Rd ....Billerica MA 01821 NASDAQ: CSPI	800-325-3110	978-663-7598	173-2
CSRM (Cascade Steel Rolling Mills Inc) 3200 N Hwy 99 W PO Box 687....McMinnville OR 97128	800-283-2776	503-472-4181	719
CSRS (D+H CollateralGuard RC) 4126 Norland Ave Ste 200 ....Burnaby BC V5G3S8	866-873-9780	604-637-4000	631
CSS 10301 Democracy Ln Ste 300.......... Fairfax VA 22030	800-888-4612	703-691-4612	261
CSS International Inc 115 River Landing Dr Daniel Is ....Charleston SC 29492	800-814-7705		260
CSSA (Crop Science Society of America) 677 S Segoe Rd ....Madison WI 53711	800-755-2751	608-273-8080	48-2
CSSA (Communications Supply Service Assn) 5700 Murray St ....Little Rock AR 72209	800-252-2772	501-562-7666	49-20
Cst Data 10725 John Price Rd ....Charlotte NC 28273	866-383-3282	704-927-3282	225
CST/Berger Corp 255 W Fleming St ....Watseka IL 60970	800-435-1859	815-432-5237	540
CSTM (Mexico Tourism Board) 225 N Michigan Ave Ste 2060 ....Chicago IL 60601	800-446-3942		770
CSX Corp 500 Water St 15th Fl....Jacksonville FL 32202 NASDAQ: CSX	800-737-1663	904-359-3200	185
CSX Transportation Inc 500 Water St ....Jacksonville FL 32202	800-737-1663	904-359-3100	644
CT Consultants Inc 8150 Sterling Ct ....Mentor OH 44060	800-925-0988	440-951-9000	261
C&T Design & Equipment Company Inc 2750 Tobey Dr ....Indianapolis IN 46219	800-966-3374		405
Ct Gasket & Polymer Company Inc 12308 Cutten Rd ....Houston TX 77066	800-299-1685		326
CTAA (Community Transportation Assn of America) 1341 G St NW 10th Fl....Washington DC 20005	800-891-0590		49-21
CTB Inc 611 N Higbee St PO Box 2000 ....Milford IN 46542	800-261-8651	574-658-4191	273
CTC Packaging 5264 Lake St PO Box 456..........Sandy Lake PA 16145 *General	800-241-0900*	724-376-7315	547
CTEC (Central Texas Electric Co-op Inc) 386 Friendship Ln PO Box 553....Fredericksburg TX 78624 *General	800-900-2832*	830-997-2126	245
CTG (Computer Task Group Inc) 800 Delaware Ave ....Buffalo NY 14209 OTC: CTG	800-992-5350	716-882-8000	180
CTI Inc 11105 Norrth Casa Grande Hwy ....Rillito AZ 85654	800-362-4952	520-624-2348	775
CTLGroup 5400 Old OrchaRd Rd ....Skokie IL 60077	800-522-2285	847-965-7500	738
CTMC (Central Texas Medical Ctr) 1301 Wonder World Dr ....San Marcos TX 78666	800-927-9004	512-353-8979	373-3
CTN (Christian Television Network Inc) 6922 142nd Ave N ....Largo FL 33771	800-716-7729	727-535-5622	733
CTPHC (Clifton T Perkins Hospital Ctr) 1 Renaissance Blvd ....Oakbrook IL 60181	800-994-6610		373-5
CTSI (Continental Traffic Service Inc) 5100 Poplar Ave 15th Fl....Memphis TN 38137	888-836-5135	901-766-1500	311
CTV 299 Queen St W ....Toronto ON M5V2Z5	866-690-6179	416-384-5000	736
CTV-TV Ch 5 (CTV) 345 Graham Ave Ste 400 ....Winnipeg MB R3C5S6	800-461-1542	204-788-3300	736-85
CU America Financial Services Inc 200 W 22nd St Ste 280....Lombard IL 60148	800-351-0449	630-620-5200	194
CU*Answers 6000 28th St SE Ste 100....Grand Rapids MI 49546	800-327-3478	616-285-5711	225
CUB (Concerned United Birthparents Inc) PO Box 503475....San Diego CA 92150	800-822-2777		48-21
Cuba 315 Lexington Ave ....New York NY 10016 *General	800-553-3210*	212-689-7215	779
Cubeit Portable Storage 100 Canadian Rd ....Scarborough ON M1R4Z5	844-897-3811		111
Cubix Corp 2800 Lockheed Way ....Carson City NV 89706 *Sales	800-829-0550*	775-888-1000	176
Cubix Labs Inc 1875 K St NW ....Washington DC 20006	866-978-2220		627
Cudahy Patrick Inc 1 Sweet Apple-Wood Ln ....Cudahy WI 53110	800-486-6900	414-744-2000	471
CUE Inc 11 Leonberg Rd ....Cranberry Township PA 16066	800-283-4621	724-772-5225	596
CUES (Credit Union Executives Society) 5510 Research Pk Dr ....Madison WI 53711	800-252-2664	608-271-2664	49-2
CUES Inc 3600 Rio Vista Ave ....Orlando FL 32805	800-327-7791	407-849-0190	201
Cuesta College PO Box 8106 ....San Luis Obispo CA 93403	877-732-0436	805-546-3100	162
CUI Global Inc 20050 SW 112th Ave ....Tualatin OR 97062 NASDAQ: CUI	800-275-4899	503-612-2300	359-3
Cuisinart 1 Cummings Pt Rd ....Stamford CT 06902	800-726-0190	203-975-4609	37
Cuisine Magazine 2200 Grand Ave ....Des Moines IA 50312	800-311-3995		455-11
Cuisine Solutions Corporate USA 22445 Sous Vide Ln Unit 100....Sterling VA 20166 OTC: CUSI	888-285-4679	703-270-2900	296-36
Cuivre River Electric Co-op 1112 E Cherry St ....Troy MO 63379	800-392-3709	636-528-8261	245
Culinary Depot Inc 2 Melnick Dr ....Monsey NY 10952	888-845-8200		405
Culinary Institute Alain & Marie LeNotre 7070 Allensby ....Houston TX 77022	888-536-6873	713-692-0077	163
Culinary Institute of America 1946 Campus Dr ....Hyde Park NY 12538 *Admissions	800-285-4627*	845-452-9600	163
Culinary Institute of Charleston 7000 Rivers Ave ....Charleston SC 29406	877-349-7184	843-574-6111	163
Culinary Software Services Inc 1900 Folsom St Ste 210 ....Boulder CO 80302	800-447-1466	303-447-3334	177
Cullen/Frost Bankers Inc 100 W Houston St ....San Antonio TX 78205 NYSE: CFR	800-562-6732	210-220-4011	359-2
Culligan International Co 9399 W Higgins Rd Ste 1100 ....Rosemont IL 60018	800-285-5442	847-430-2800	801
Cullinan Associates Inc 295 N Hubbards Ln 2nd Fl....Louisville KY 40207	800-611-4841	502-893-0300	400
Cullman Area Chamber of Commerce 301 Second Ave SW ....Cullman AL 35055	800-313-5114	256-734-0454	139
Cullman City School 301 First St NE Ste 100 ....Cullman AL 35055	800-548-2547	256-734-2233	681
Cullman Electric Cooperative 1749 Eva Rd NE ....Cullman AL 35055	800-242-1806	256-737-3201	245
Culpeper Wood Preservers Inc 15487 Braggs Corner Rd PO Box 1148....Culpeper VA 22701	800-817-6215		813
Culver Academies 1300 Academy Rd ....Culver IN 46511	800-528-5837	574-842-7000	618
Culver City Unified School District (CCUSD) 4034 Irving Pl ....Culver City CA 90232	855-446-2673	310-842-4220	681
Culver Duck Farms Inc 12215 CR 10 ....Middlebury IN 46540	800-825-9225	574-825-9537	10-7
Cumberland County College 3322 College Dr ....Vineland NJ 08360	800-792-8670	856-691-8600	162
Cumberland Electric Membership Corp 1940 Madison St ....Clarksville TN 37043	800-987-2362		245
Cumberland Falls State Resort Park 7351 Hwy 90 ....Corbin KY 40701	800-325-0063		561
Cumberland Furniture 321 Terminal St SW ....Grand Rapids MI 49548	800-401-7877		321
Cumberland Insurance Group 633 Shiloh Pk ....Bridgeton NJ 08302	800-232-6992		390-4
Cumberland Island National Seashore 101 Wheeler St ....Saint Marys GA 31558	877-860-6787	912-882-4336	560
Cumberland Private Wealth Management Inc 99 Yorkville Ave Ste 300....Toronto ON M5R3K5	800-929-8296	416-929-1090	400
Cumberland Truck Parts 15 Sylmar Rd ....Nottingham PA 19362	800-364-6995	610-932-1152	54
Cumberland University 1 Cumberland Sq ....Lebanon TN 37087	800-467-0562	615-444-2562	166
Cumberland Valley Electric Inc 6219 N US Hwy 25 E ....Gray KY 40734	800-513-2677		245
Cumbre Insurance Services LLC 3333 Concours Ste 5100 ....Ontario CA 91764	800-998-7986	909-484-2456	389
Cuming County Public Power District 500 S Main St ....West Point NE 68788	877-572-2463	402-372-2463	245
Cummings Signs 15 Century Blvd Ste 200....Nashville TN 37214	800-489-7446		697
Cummins Construction Company Inc 1420 W Chestnut Ave ....Enid OK 73702	800-375-6001	580-233-6000	188-4
Cummins Facility Services 5202 Marion Waldo Rd ....Prospect OH 43342	800-451-5629	740-726-9800	104
Cummins Filtration 26 Century Blvd ....Nashville TN 37214	800-777-7064	615-367-0040	60
Cummins Inc 500 Jackson St PO Box 3005 ....Columbus IN 47201 NYSE: CMI	800-343-7357	812-377-5000	262
Cummins-Allison Corp 852 Feehanville Dr ....Mount Prospect IL 60056	800-786-5528	847-299-9550	111
CUNA (Credit Union National Association) 99 M St SE Ste 300 ....Washington DC 20003	800-356-9655		
CUNA Mutual Group 5910 Mineral Point Rd ....Madison WI 53705	800-356-2644	608-238-5851	359-4
Cunard Line Ltd 24303 Town Center Dr Ste 200....Valencia CA 91355	800-728-6273	661-753-1000	220
Cunningham Manufacturing Co 318 S Webster St ....Seattle WA 98108	800-767-0038	206-767-3713	223
Cunningham Memorial Library 510 N 6 1/2 St ....Terre Haute IN 47809	800-851-4279	812-237-2580	433-6
CUNO Inc 400 Research Pkwy ....Meriden CT 06450	800-243-6894	203-237-5541	385
CUNY (City University of New York) 535 E 80th St ....New York NY 10075	800-286-9937	212-997-2869	781
CUPA-HR (College & University Professional Assn for Hum Res) 1811 Commons Pt Dr ....Knoxville TN 37932	877-287-2474	865-637-7673	49-5
Cupertino Inn 10889 N De Anza Blvd ....Cupertino CA 95014	800-222-4828	408-996-7700	703
Cupid Foundations Inc 475 Park Ave S ....New York NY 10016	877-649-5283	212-686-6224	155-17
Curatel LLC 1605 W Olympic Blvd Ste 800 ....Los Angeles CA 90015	866-287-2366		386
CureSearch for Children's Cancer 4600 East-West Hwy Ste 600 ....Bethesda MD 20814	800-458-6223	301-718-0047	664
Curran Investment Management 30 S Pearl St Omni Plz 9th Fl....Albany NY 12207	866-432-1246	518-391-4200	400
Current Analysis Inc 21335 Signal Hill Plz Ste 200....Sterling VA 20164	877-787-8947	703-404-9200	178-1
Current Inc 30 Tyler St PO Box 120183....East Haven CT 06512	877-436-6542	203-469-1337	595
Current USA Inc 1005 E Woodmen Rd ....Colorado Springs CO 80920 *Cust Svc	800-848-2848*		457
Curriculum Assoc Inc 153 Rangeway Rd ....North Billerica MA 01862	800-225-0248		633-2

Company / Address	Toll-Free	Phone	Class
Curry College 1071 Blue Hill Ave .... Milton MA 02186	800-669-0686	617-333-2210	166
CURTAIN & BATH OUTLET 1 Ann & Hope Way .... Cumberland RI 02864	877-228-7824		229
Curtain Call Costumes 333 E Seventh Ave .... York PA 17404	888-808-0801	800-677-7053	155-6
Curtis 1000 Inc 1725 Breckinridge Pkwy Ste 500 .... Duluth GA 30096	877-287-8715	678-380-9095	263
Curtis Industries Inc 2400 S 43rd St PO Box 343925 .... Milwaukee WI 53219	800-657-0853	414-649-4200	810
Curtis Industries LLC 70 Hartwell St .... West Boylston MA 01583	800-343-7676	508-853-2200	513
Curtis Institute of Music 1726 Locust St .... Philadelphia PA 19103	800-640-4155	215-893-5252	166
Curtis Instruments Inc 200 Kisco Ave .... Mount Kisco NY 10549	800-777-3433	914-666-2971	248
Curtis M Phillips Ctr for the Performing Arts 3201 Hull Rd PO Box 112750 .... Gainesville FL 32611	800-905-2787	352-392-1900	568
Curtis Machine Company Inc 2500 E Trl St .... Dodge City KS 67801	800-835-9166	620-227-7164	705
Curtis Packing Co 2416 Randolph Ave .... Greensboro NC 27406	800-852-7890	336-275-7684	471
Curtis Steel Co (CSC) 6504 Hurst St .... Houston TX 77008	800-749-4621	713-861-4621	483
Curtis, The 1405 Curtis St .... Denver CO 80202	800-525-6651	303-571-0300	378
Curtiss-Wright Corp 10 Waterview Blvd 2nd Fl .... Parsippany NJ 07054 *NYSE: CW*	855-449-0995	973-541-3700	22
Curtis-Toledo Inc 1905 Kienlen Ave .... Saint Louis MO 63133	800-925-5431	314-383-1300	172
Cusack Wholesale Meat Inc 301 SW 12th St .... Oklahoma City OK 73109	800-241-6328	405-232-2114	297-9
Cushing-Malloy Inc 1350 N Main St .... Ann Arbor MI 48104	888-295-7244	734-663-8554	622
Custer Public Power District 625 E South St PO Box 10 .... Broken Bow NE 68822	888-749-2453	308-872-2451	245
Custom Air 5338 Pinkney Ave .... Sarasota FL 34233	888-856-4507		606
Custom Aircraft Interiors 3701 Industry Ave .... Lakewood CA 90712	800-423-2904	562-426-5098	685
Custom Aluminum Products Inc 414 Div St .... South Elgin IL 60177	800-745-6333		483
Custom Bldg Products 13001 Seal Beach Blvd .... Seal Beach CA 90740	800-272-8786	562-598-8808	3
Custom Brackets 32 Alpha Pk .... Cleveland OH 44143	800-530-2289	440-446-0819	452
Custom Cable Corp 242 Butler St .... Westbury NY 11590	800-832-3600	516-334-3600	116
Custom Cable Industries Inc 3221 Cherry Palm Dr .... Tampa FL 33619	800-552-2232	813-623-2232	189-4
Custom Chrome Inc 155 E Main Ave Ste 150 .... Morgan Hill CA 95037	800-729-3332	408-825-5000	61
Custom Communications Inc 1661 Greenview Dr SW .... Rochester MN 55902	855-288-5522	507-288-5522	
Custom Computer Specialists Inc (CCS) 70 Suffolk Ct .... Hauppauge NY 11788	800-598-8989		180
Custom Culinary 2505 S Finley Rd .... Lombard IL 60148	800-621-8827		
Custom Drapery Blinds & Shutters 3402 E T C Jester .... Houston TX 77018	800-929-9211	713-225-9211	741
Custom Electronic Design & Installation Assn (CEDIA) 7150 Winton Dr Ste 300 .... Indianapolis IN 46268	800-669-5329	317-328-4336	49-19
Custom Environmental Services Inc 8041 N I 70 Frontage Rd Unit 11 .... Arvada CO 80002	800-310-7445	303-423-9949	663
Custom Exhibits Corp 1830 N Indianwood Ave .... Broken Arrow OK 74012	800-664-0309	918-250-2121	392
Custom Fiberglass Mfg Corp *Snugtop* 1711 Harbor Ave PO Box 121 ...... Long Beach CA 90813	800-768-4867	562-432-5454	120
Custom Global Logistics LLC 317 West Lake St .... Northlake IL 60164	800-446-8336		314
Custom Metal Fabricators Inc 7601 Whitepine Rd .... Richmond VA 23237	800-220-4084		693
Custom Mold Engineering Inc 9780 S Franklin Dr .... Franklin WI 53132	800-448-2005	414-421-5444	752
Custom Pack Inc 662 Exton Cmns .... Exton PA 19341	800-722-7005	610-363-1900	597
Custom Paper Tubes 15900 Industrial Pkwy PO Box 35140 .... Cleveland OH 44135	800-343-8823	216-362-2964	125
Custom Products of Litchfield Inc 1715 S Sibley Ave .... Litchfield MN 55355	800-222-5463	320-693-3221	273
Custom Toll Free 10940 Wilshire Blvd 17th Fl ....Los Angeles CA 90024	800-287-8664		386
Custom Truck Accessories Inc 13408 Hwy 65 NE ....Ham Lake MN 55304	800-333-1282	763-757-5326	54
Customer Communicator, The (TCC) 712 Main St Ste 187B .... Boonton NJ 07005	800-232-4317	973-265-2300	527-2
Customer Group, The 641 W Lake St Ste 304 .... Chicago IL 60661	844-802-7867		461
Customer Paradigm Inc 5353 Manhattan Cir Ste 103 .... Boulder CO 80303	888-772-0777	303-499-9318	225
Customer Service Delivery Platform (CSDP) 15615 Alton Pkwy Ste 310 .... Irvine CA 92618	888-741-2737		177
Cutera Inc 3240 Bayshore Blvd .... Brisbane CA 94005 *NASDAQ: CUTR*	888-428-8372	415-657-5500	474
Cuthbert Greenhouses Inc 4900 Hendron Rd .... Groveport OH 43125	800-321-1939	614-836-3866	368
Cutlery & More LLC 135 Prairie Lake Rd .... East Dundee IL 60118	800-650-9866		361
Cutten Realty Inc 2120 Campton Rd Ste C .... Eureka CA 95503	800-776-4458	707-445-8811	648
Cutter & Buck Inc 701 N 34th St Ste 400 .... Seattle WA 98103	800-713-7810	888-338-9944	155-1
Cutter Aviation 2802 E Old Tower Rd .... Phoenix AZ 85034	800-234-5382	602-273-1237	24
Cutting Edge Networked Storage 435 W Bradley Ave Ste C ....El Cajon CA 92020	800-257-1666	619-258-7800	177
Cutting Edge Products LLC 350 Turk Hill Pk .... Fairport NY 14450	800-889-4184		474
Cuyahoga Community College *Eastern* 4250 Richmond Rd .... Highland Hills OH 44122	800-954-8742	216-987-2024	162
Western 11000 Pleasant Valley Rd .... Parma OH 44130	800-954-8742	216-987-2800	162
Cuyahoga County Public Library 2111 Snow Rd .... Parma OH 44134	800-749-5560	216-398-1800	433-3
Cuyahoga Falls Chamber of Commerce (CFCC) 151 Portage Trl Ste 1 .... Cuyahoga Falls OH 44221	800-248-4040	330-929-6756	139
Cuyahoga Hills Juvenile Correctional Facility 4321 Green Rd .... Highland Hills OH 44128	800-872-3132	216-464-8200	411
Cuyahoga Molded Plastics Corp 1265 Babbitt Rd .... Cleveland OH 44132	800-805-9549	216-261-2744	600
Cuyahoga Valley National Park 15610 Vaughn Rd .... Brecksville OH 44141	800-445-9667	216-524-1497	560
Cuyamaca College 900 Rancho San Diego Pkwy .... El Cajon CA 92019	800-234-1597	619-660-4275	162
CVAC Systems Inc 26820 Hobie Cir Ste B .... Murrieta CA 92562	866-753-2822	951-699-2086	250
CVB Financial Corp 701 N Haven Ave PO Box 51000 .... Ontario CA 91764 *NASDAQ: CVBF*	888-222-5432	909-980-4030	359-2
CVD Diamond Corp 2061 Piper Ln .... London ON N5V3S5	877-457-9903	519-457-9903	479
CVEA (Copper Valley Electric Assn Inc) Mile 187 Glenn Hwy PO Box 45 .... Glennallen AK 99588	866-835-2832	907-822-3211	245
Cvikota Company Inc 2031 32nd St S .... La Crosse WI 54601	800-657-5175	608-788-8103	
CVMA (Canadian Veterinary Medical Assn) 339 Booth St .... Ottawa ON K1R7K1	800-567-2862	613-236-1162	49-8
CVS Corp 1 CVS Dr ....Woonsocket RI 02895 *Cust Svc	888-607-4287*	401-765-1500	237
CW (College of Westchester) 325 Central Ave .... White Plains NY 10606	800-660-7093		795
CW Seattle 1000 Dexter Ave N Ste 205 .... Seattle WA 98109	866-313-5789	206-441-1111	736
C&W Technologies 2522 SE Federal Hwy ....Stuart FL 34994	844-241-6442	772-287-5215	175
CWB Maxium Financial 30 Vogell Rd Ste 1 .... Richmond Hill ON L4B3K6	800-379-5888	905-780-6150	565
CWC Textron 1085 W Sherman Blvd .... Muskegon MI 49441	800-999-0853	231-733-1331	60
CWCVB (Wausau Central Wisconsin Convention & Visitors Bur) 219 Jefferson St .... Wausau WI 54403	888-948-4748	715-355-8788	206
CWF (Canadian Wildlife Federation) 350 Michael Cowpland Dr .... Kanata ON K2M2W1	800-563-9453	613-599-9594	48-13
CWI Gifts & Crafts 77 Cypress St SW .... Reynoldsburg OH 43068	800-666-5858	740-964-6210	44
CWPS Inc 14120 A Sullyfield Cir .... Chantilly VA 20151	877-297-7472	703-263-9539	180
CWU (Church Women United) 475 Riverside Dr Ste 243 .... New York NY 10115	800-298-5551	212-870-2347	48-20
CXM (Chicago Extruded Metals Co) 1601 S 54th Ave .... Cicero IL 60804 *Cust Svc	800-323-8102*		483
CXtec 5404 S Bay Rd .... Syracuse NY 13221 *Orders	800-767-3282*	315-476-3000	809
Cyanotech Corp 73-4460 Queen Kaahumanu Hwy Ste 102 .... Kailua-Kona HI 96740 *NASDAQ: CYAN* ■ *Sales	800-453-1187*	808-326-1353	477
Cyber Power Systems Inc 4241 12th Ave E Ste 400 ....Shakopee MN 55379	877-297-6937	952-403-9500	253
Cyber-Ark Software Inc 60 Wells Ave .... Newton MA 02459	888-808-9005	617-965-1544	177
Cyberdata Corp 3 Justin Ct .... Monterey CA 93940	800-363-8010	831-373-2601	176
Cybereason Inc 200 Clarendon St 5th Fl ....Boston MA 02116	855-695-8200		
Cyberex 5900 Eastport Blvd .... Richmond VA 23231	800-238-5000	804-236-3300	253
Cyberonics Inc 100 Cyberonics Blvd .... Houston TX 77058 *NASDAQ: CYBX*	800-332-1375	281-228-7262	475
CyberOptics Corp 5900 Golden Hills Dr .... Minneapolis MN 55416 *NASDAQ: CYBE* ■ *Cust Svc	800-746-6315*	763-542-5000	248
Cyber-Rain Inc 5535 Balboa Blvd Ste 115 .... Encino CA 91316	877-888-1452		406
Cybex International Inc 10 Trotter Dr .... Medway MA 02053	888-462-9239	508-533-4300	267
Cycle Country Access Corp 205 N Depot St PO Box 107 .... Fox Lake WI 53933 *Sales	800-841-2222*		29
Cycle-safe Inc 5211 Cascade Rd SE Ste 210 .... Grand Rapids MI 49546	888-950-6531	616-954-9977	707
Cyclonaire Corp 2922 N Division Ave .... York NE 68467	800-445-0730	402-362-2000	207
Cycom Canada Corp 31 Prince Andrew Pl .... North York ON M3C2H2	800-268-3171	416-494-5040	196
Cy-Fair Houston Chamber of Commerce 8711 Hwy 6 N Ste 120 .... Houston TX 77095	800-403-6120	281-373-1390	139
Cygnus Systems Inc 24700 Northwestern Hwy Ste 600 .... Southfield MI 48075	800-388-2280	248-557-4600	196
Cykic Software Inc PO Box 3098 .... San Diego CA 92163	800-438-7325	619-459-8799	178-7
Cyl-tec Inc 971 W Industrial Dr .... Aurora IL 60506	888-429-5832	630-844-8800	738
Cyma Systems Inc 2330 W University Dr Ste 4 ...... Tempe AZ 85281	800-292-2962		178-1
Cyn Oil Corp 1771 Washington St .... Stoughton MA 02072	800-242-5818	781-341-1777	663

	Toll-Free	Phone	Class
Cynosure Inc			
5 Carlisle Rd .... Westford MA 01886	800-886-2966	978-256-4200	423
NASDAQ: CYNO			
Cynthia C & William E. Perry Pavilion			
9400 Turkey Lake Rd .... Orlando FL 32819	800-447-1435	321-842-8844	371
Cyphers Agency Inc, The			
1682 Village Green .... Crofton MD 21114	888-412-7469		7
CypherWorX Inc			
130 Andrews St .... Rochester NY 14604	888-685-4440		386
Cypremort Point State Park			
306 Beach Ln .... Cypremort Point LA 70538	888-867-4510	337-867-4510	561
Cypress Bayou Casino			
832 Martin Luther King Rd .... Charenton LA 70523	800-284-4386		450
Cypress Care Inc			
2736 Meadow Church Rd Ste 300 ...... Duluth GA 30097	800-419-7191		366
Cypress Hills National Cemetery			
625 Jamaica Ave .... Brooklyn NY 11208	800-535-1117	631-454-4949	136
Cypress Networks			
4125 Walker Ave .... Greensboro NC 27407	866-625-3502	336-841-3030	180
Cypress Security LLC			
478 Tehama St .... San Francisco CA 94103	866-345-1277		689
Cypress Semiconductor Corp			
198 Champion Ct .... San Jose CA 95134	800-541-4736	408-943-2600	692
NASDAQ: CY			
Cyquent Inc			
5410 Edson Ln Ste 210C .... Rockville MD 20852	866-509-0331	240-292-0230	180
Cystic Fibrosis Foundation			
6931 Arlington Rd Ste 200 ...... Bethesda MD 20814	800-344-4823	301-951-4422	48-17
Cytak			
6001 Shellmound St .... Emeryville CA 94608	877-759-7464		
CytoSport			
1340 Treat Blvd Ste 350 .... Walnut Creek CA 94597	888-298-6629		794
Czech Airlines			
147 West 35th St Ste 1505 .... New York NY 10119	855-359-2932		25
Czech Airlines OK Plus			
147 W 35th St Ste 1505 .... New York NY 10001	855-359-2932		26
CZ-USA Inc			
PO Box 171073 .... Kansas City KS 66117	800-955-4486	913-321-1811	707

D

	Toll-Free	Phone	Class
D & D Commodities Ltd			
PO Box 359 .... Stephen MN 56757	800-543-3308		445
D & D Foods Inc			
9425 N 48th St .... Omaha NE 68152	800-208-0364	402-571-4113	296-36
D & D Manufacturing Inc			
500 Territorial Dr .... Bolingbrook IL 60440	888-300-6869		752
D & H Distributing Company Inc			
2525 N Seventh St .... Harrisburg PA 17110	800-340-1001		174
D & W Inc 941 Oak St .... Elkhart IN 46514	800-255-0829	574-264-9674	329
D F Richard Inc			
124 Broadway .... Dover NH 03821	800-649-6457	603-742-2020	316
D Hilton Associates Inc			
9450 Grogans Mill Rd			
Ste 200 .... The Woodlands TX 77380	800-367-0433	281-292-5088	194
D K Global			
420 Missouri Ct .... Redlands CA 92373	866-375-2214	909-747-0201	225
D L Evans Bank			
397 N Overland PO Box 1188 ...... Burley ID 83318	888-873-9777	208-678-9076	70
D M Bowman Inc			
10228 Governor Ln Blvd			
Ste 3006 .... Williamsport MD 21795	800-326-3274		775
D Net Internet Service			
189 E Palmer St .... Franklin NC 28734	877-601-3638	828-349-3638	225
D P Brown of Saginaw Inc			
2845 Universal Dr .... Saginaw MI 48603	877-799-9400	989-799-9400	392
D P. Curtis Trucking Inc			
1450 S Hwy 118 .... Richfield UT 84701	800-257-9151		775
D River State Recreation Site			
725 Summer St NE Ste C .... Salem OR 97301	800-551-6949	541-994-7341	561
D'Angelo Sandwich Shops			
600 Providence Hwy .... Dedham MA 02026	800-727-2446		666
D'Arrigo Bros Company of California Inc			
PO Box 850 .... Salinas CA 93902	800-995-5939*	831-455-4500	10-9
*Cust Svc			
D'Artagnan Inc			
280 Wilson Ave Ste 1 .... Newark NJ 07105	800-327-8246	973-344-0565	296-26
D'vontz 7208 E 38th St .... Tulsa OK 74145	877-322-3600	918-622-3600	606
D'Youville College			
320 Porter Ave .... Buffalo NY 14201	800-777-3921	716-829-7600	166
D+H CollateralGuard RC (CSRS)			
4126 Norland Ave Ste 200 .... Burnaby BC V5G3S8	866-873-9780	604-637-4000	631
d50 Media			
1330 Boylston St Ste 200 .... Chestnut Hill MA 02461	800-582-9606		195
DA (Debtors Anonymous)			
PO Box 920888 .... Needham MA 02492	800-421-2383	781-453-2743	48-21
D-A Lubricant Co			
1340 W 29th St .... Indianapolis IN 46208	800-645-5823	317-923-5321	537
Dabney State Recreation Area			
725 Summer St NE Ste C .... Salem OR 97301	800-551-6949	503-695-2261	561
DAC International Inc			
6702 McNeil Dr .... Austin TX 78729	800-527-2531	512-331-5323	765
Dac Products Inc			
625 Montroyal Rd .... Rural Hall NC 27045	800-431-1982		497
DAC Technologies			
3630 W Miller Ste 350 .... Garland TX 75041	800-800-1550	972-677-2700	538
DACC (Doca Ana Community College)			
2800 N Sonoma Ranch Blvd ..... Las Cruces NM 88011	800-903-7503	575-528-7000	162
Dacotah Paper Co			
3940 15th Ave N .... Fargo ND 58102	800-270-6352	701-281-1730	555
Dadant & Sons Inc			
51 S Second St .... Hamilton IL 62341	888-922-1293	217-847-3324	122

	Toll-Free	Phone	Class
Daemen College			
4380 Main St .... Amherst NY 14226	800-462-7652	716-839-8225	166
DAG Media Inc			
125-10 Queens Blvd Ste 14 ...... Kew Gardens NY 11415	800-261-2799	718-263-8454	633-6
Daggett County			
95 N First W .... Manila UT 84046	800-764-0844	435-784-3154	337
Daggett Truck Line Inc			
32717 County Rd 10 .... Frazee MN 56544	800-262-9393	218-334-3711	775
Dahl Arts Ctr			
713 Seventh St .... Rapid City SD 57701	800-487-3223	605-394-4101	50-2
Dahle North America Inc			
49 Vose Farm Rd .... Peterborough NH 03458	800-243-8145	603-924-0003	530
Dahlsten Truck Line Inc			
101 W Edgar PO Box 95 .... Clay Center NE 68933	800-228-4313	402-762-3511	775
DAI (Denali Advance Integration)			
17735 NE 65th St Ste 130 .... Redmond WA 98052	877-467-8008	425-885-4000	180
Daikin America Inc			
20 Olympic Dr .... Orangeburg NY 10962	800-365-9570*	792-831-8666	601-2
*Cust Svc			
Daily Advertiser, The			
1100 Bertrand Dr .... Lafayette LA 70506	800-259-8852	337-289-6300	528-2
Daily American Republic			
208 Poplar St PO Box 7 .... Poplar Bluff MO 63901	888-276-2242	573-785-1414	528-2
Daily Courier			
409 SE Seventh St .... Grants Pass OR 97526	800-228-0457	541-474-3700	528-2
Daily Environment Report			
1801 S Bell St .... Arlington VA 22202	800-372-1033		527-5
Daily Express Inc			
1072 Harrisburg Pk .... Carlisle PA 17013	800-735-3136	717-243-5757	775
Daily Gazette Co, The			
2345 Maxon Rd Ext			
PO Box 1090 .... Schenectady NY 12301	800-262-2211	518-374-4141	528-2
Daily Globe, The			
118 E McLeod Ave PO Box 548 ...... Ironwood MI 49938	800-236-2887	906-932-2211	633-8
Daily Herald			
1555 N Freedom Blvd .... Provo UT 84604	800-880-8075	801-373-5050	528-2
Daily Herald			
155 E Algonquin Rd .... Arlington Heights IL 60005	888-903-4070	847-427-4300	528-2
Daily Item, The			
110 Munroe St .... Lynn MA 01901	800-876-7060	781-593-7700	528-2
Daily Item, The			
200 Market St .... Sunbury PA 17001	800-326-9600	570-286-5671	528-3
Daily Journal			
777 Walnut St .... Franklin IN 46131	888-736-7101	317-736-2777	528-2
Daily Journal			
1513 St Joe Dr PO Box A .... Park Hills MO 63601	800-660-8166	573-431-2010	528-2
Daily Journal			
8 Dearborn Sq .... Kankakee IL 60901	866-299-9256	815-937-3300	528-2
NASDAQ: DJCO			
Daily Journal			
891 E Oak Rd .... Vineland NJ 08360	800-222-0104	856-691-5000	528-2
Daily Journal of Commerce			
921 SW Washington St Ste 210 ...... Portland OR 97205	800-451-9998	503-226-1311	528-2
Daily Labor Report			
1801 S Bell St .... Arlington VA 22202	800-372-1033		527-7
Daily Local News			
250 N Bradford Ave .... West Chester PA 19382	800-568-7355	610-696-1775	528-2
Daily News			
770 11th Ave PO Box 189 .... Longview WA 98632	800-341-4745	360-577-2500	528-2
Daily Nonpareil			
535 W Broadway Ste 300 .... Council Bluffs IA 51503	800-283-1882	712-328-1811	528-2
Daily Progress			
685 W Rio Rd .... Charlottesville VA 22901	866-469-4866	434-978-7200	633-8
Daily Racing Form			
100 Broadway 7th Fl .... New York NY 10005	800-306-3676*	212-366-7600	455-14
*Cust Svc			
Daily Record			
212 E Liberty St PO Box 918 .... Wooster OH 44691	800-686-2958	330-264-1125	528-2
Daily Record			
16 W Main St .... Rochester NY 14614	800-451-9998	585-232-6920	528-2
Daily Report for Executives			
1801 S Bell St .... Arlington VA 22202	800-372-1033		527-2
Daily Sentinel			
701 Veterans Dr .... Scottsboro AL 35768	877-985-9212	256-259-1020	528-2
Daily Star			
102 Chestnut St .... Oneonta NY 13820	800-721-1000	607-432-1000	528-2
Daily Tax Report			
1801 S Bell St .... Arlington VA 22202	800-372-1033		527-2
Daily Times			
618 Beam St .... Salisbury MD 21801	877-335-6278	410-749-7171	528-2
Daily Times			
201 N Allen Ave .... Farmington NM 87401	877-599-3331	505-325-4545	528-2
DaimlerChrysler Corp Jeep Div			
PO Box 21-8004 .... Auburn Hills MI 48321	800-992-1997*		59
*Cust Svc			
Dairiconcepts LP			
3253 E Chestnut Expy .... Springfield MO 65802	877-596-4374	417-829-3400	296-5
Dairy Farmers of America Inc			
10220 N Ambassador Dr ...... Kansas City MO 64153	888-332-6455	816-801-6455	296-5
Dairy Management Inc (DMI)			
10255 W Higgins Rd Ste 900 .... Rosemont IL 60018	800-853-2479		48-2
Dairy One			
730 Warren Rd .... Ithaca NY 14850	800-344-2697	607-257-1272	11-2
Dairy Queen			
7505 Metro Blvd .... Minneapolis MN 55439	800-883-4279	952-830-0200	380
Dairyamerica Inc			
7815 N Palm Ave Ste 250 .... Fresno CA 93711	800-722-3110	559-251-0992	49-18
Dairyland Laboratories Inc			
217 E Main St .... Arcadia WI 54612	800-658-2481	608-323-2123	738
Daisy IT Supplies Sales & Service			
8575 Red Oak Ave .... Rancho Cucamonga CA 91730	800-266-5585	909-989-5585	112
Daisy Outdoor Products			
400 W Stribling Dr .... Rogers AR 72756	800-643-3458	479-636-1200	706
Daisy Rock Guitars			
16320 Roscoe Blvd Ste 100 ...... Van Nuys CA 91410	877-693-2479	855-417-8677	523
Daiwa Corp			
11137 Warland Dr .... Cypress CA 90630	800-736-4653	562-375-6800	706

Alphabetical Section

Name / Address	Toll-Free	Phone	Class
DAKE 724 Robbins Rd .... Grand Haven MI 49417	800-846-3253	800-937-3253	350
Dakota Brands International Inc 2121 13th St NE ...... Jamestown ND 58401	800-844-5073	701-252-5073	296-1
Dakota Central 630 Fifth St N .... Carrington ND 58421	800-771-0974	701-652-3184	731
Dakota County Technical College 1300 E 145th St ...... Rosemount MN 55068	877-937-3282	651-423-8301	795
Dakota Drug Inc 28 Main St N .... Minot ND 58703	800-437-2018	701-852-2141	238
Dakota Electric Assn 4300 220th St W ...... Farmington MN 55024	800-874-3409	651-463-6144	245
Dakota Energy Cooperative Inc PO Box 830 .... Huron SD 57350	800-353-8591	605-352-8591	245
Dakota Gasification Co PO Box 5540 .... Bismarck ND 58506	866-747-3546	701-221-4400	782
Dakota Granite Co 48391 150th St PO Box 1351 ...... Milbank SD 57252	800-843-3333		720
Dakota Growers Pasta Company Inc 1 Pasta Ave ...... Carrington ND 58421	866-569-4411	701-652-2855	296-31
Dakota Line Inc PO Box 476 ...... Vermillion SD 57069	800-532-5682	605-624-5228	775
Dakota Lions Sight & Health 4501 W 61st St N ...... Sioux Falls SD 57107	800-245-7846	605-373-1008	269
Dakota Mfg Company Inc 1909 S Rowley St ...... Mitchell SD 57301	800-232-5682	605-996-5571	774
Dakota Riggers & Tool Supply Inc 704 E Benson Rd ...... Sioux Falls SD 57104	800-888-1612	605-335-0041	
Dakota State University 820 N Washington Ave ...... Madison SD 57042	888-378-9988	605-256-5139	166
Dakota Supply Group (DSG) 2601 Third Ave N ...... Fargo ND 58102	800-437-4702	701-237-9440	246
Dakota Valley Electric Co-op 7296 Hwy 281 ...... Edgeley ND 58433	800-342-4671	701-493-2281	245
Dakota Wesleyan University 1200 W University Ave ...... Mitchell SD 57301	800-333-8506	605-995-2600	166
Dakotacare 2600 W 49th St PO Box 7406 ...... Sioux Falls SD 57117	800-325-5598	605-334-4000	390-3
Daktronics Inc 201 Daktronics Dr ...... Brookings SD 57006 NASDAQ: DAKT	800-325-8766	605-692-0200	173-4
Dale Barton Agency 1100 East 6600 South ...... Salt Lake City UT 84121	866-288-1666	801-288-1600	389
Dale Buchanan & Associates 1206 Pointe Ctr Dr Ste 110 ...... Chattanooga TN 37421	800-945-4950		427
Dale Carnegie & Assoc Inc 290 Motor Pkwy ...... Hauppauge NY 11788	800-231-5800		760
Dale Laboratories 2960 Simms St ...... Hollywood FL 33020	800-327-1776	954-925-0103	584
Dale Medical Products Inc PO Box 1556 ...... Plainville MA 02762	800-343-3980		474
Dallas Baptist University 3000 Mtn Creek Pkwy ...... Dallas TX 75211	800-460-1328	214-333-7100	166
Dallas Christian College 2700 Christian Pkwy ...... Dallas TX 75234	800-688-1029	972-241-3371	161
Dallas Convention & Visitors Bureau 325 N St Paul St Ste 700 ...... Dallas TX 75201	800-232-5527	214-571-1000	206
Dallas Convention Ctr 650 S Griffin St ...... Dallas TX 75202	877-850-2100	214-939-2750	205
Dallas Data Center Inc 110 S Main St Ste 600 ...... Wichita KS 67202	800-326-6059	316-462-4001	
Dallas Fan Fares Inc 5485 Beltline Rd Ste 270 ...... Dallas TX 75254	800-925-6979	972-239-9969	181
Dallas Independent School District 3700 Ross Ave ...... Dallas TX 75204	866-796-3682	972-925-3700	681
Dallas Johnson Greenhouse Inc 2802 Twin City Dr ...... Council Bluffs IA 51501	800-445-4794	712-366-0407	368
Dallas Morning News 508 Young St ...... Dallas TX 75202	800-925-1500	214-977-8222	528-2
Dallas Theological Seminary 3909 Swiss Ave ...... Dallas TX 75204	800-992-0998	800-387-9673	167-3
Dallas-Fort Worth International Airport (DFW) 2400 Aviation Dr PO Box 619428 ...... Dallas TX 75261	800-252-7522	972-973-3112	27
Dalrymple Gravel & Contracting Company Inc 2105 S Broadway ...... Pine City NY 14871	800-957-3130	607-737-6200	46
Dalton Enterprises Inc 131 Willow St ...... Cheshire CT 06410	800-851-5606	203-272-3221	46
Dalton Gear Co 212 Colfax Ave N ...... Minneapolis MN 55405	800-328-7485	612-374-2150	705
Dalton Greiner Hartman Maher & Company LLC 565 Fifth Ave Ste 2101 ...... New York NY 10017	800-653-2839	212-557-2445	400
Dalton State College 650 N College Dr ...... Dalton GA 30720	800-829-4436	706-272-4436	166
Daly City Public Library 40 Wembley Dr ...... Daly City CA 94015	888-227-7669	650-991-8025	433-3
Daly Computers Inc 22521 Gateway Ctr Dr ...... Clarksburg MD 20871	800-955-3259	301-670-0381	176
Daman Products Co Inc 1811 N Home St ...... Mishawaka IN 46545	800-959-7841	574-259-7841	785
Damascus Bakery Inc 56 Gold St ...... Brooklyn NY 11201	800-367-7482	718-855-1456	68
Damascus Steel Casting Co Blockhouse Rd Run Extn ...... New Brighton PA 15066	800-920-2210	724-846-2770	490
Dameron Alloy Foundries Inc 6330 Gateway Dr Ste B ...... Cypress CA 90630	800-421-1985	714-820-6699	
Damon Industries Inc 12435 Rockhill Ave NE ...... Alliance OH 44601	800-362-9850	330-821-5310	151
Dan Bailey Fly Shop 209 W Park St ...... Livingston MT 59047	800-356-4052	406-222-1673	707
Dan Schantz Farm & Greenhouses LLC 8025 Spinnerstown Rd ...... Zionsville PA 18092	800-451-3064	610-967-2181	368
Dan'l Webster Inn 149 Main St ...... Sandwich MA 02563	800-444-3566	508-888-3622	378
Dan's Comp 1 Competition Way ...... Mount Vernon IN 47620	888-888-3267		707
Dana Innovations 212 Avenida Fabricante ...... San Clemente CA 92672	800-582-7777	949-492-7777	52
Dana Transport Inc 210 Essex Ave E ...... Avenel NJ 07001	800-733-3262	732-750-9100	775
Dana-Farber Cancer Institute 44 Binney St ...... Boston MA 02115	866-408-3324	617-632-3000	373-7
Dana-Farber Cancer Institute 450 Brookline Ave ...... Boston MA 02115	866-408-3324	617-632-3591	764
Danamark Watercare Ltd 2-90 Walker Dr ...... Brampton ON L6T4H6	888-326-2627		606
Danbury Hospital (DH) 24 Hospital Ave ...... Danbury CT 06810	800-516-3658	203-739-7000	373-3
Dance Magazine 333 Seventh Ave 11th Fl ...... New York NY 10001	800-331-1750	212-979-4800	455-9
Dane Media 170 NE Second St Ste 394 ...... Boca Raton FL 33429	888-233-2863		195
Danfords Hotel & Marina 25 E Broadway ...... Port Jefferson NY 11777	800-332-6367		377
Daniel & Henry Co 1001 Highlands Plaza Dr W Ste 500 ...... Saint Louis MO 63110	800-256-3462	314-421-1525	389
Daniel & Stark Law Offices 100 W William Joel Bryan Pkwy ...... Bryan TX 77803	800-474-1233	979-846-8686	427
Daniel & Yeager (D&Y) 6767 Old Madison Pk Ste 690 ...... Huntsville AL 35806	800-955-1919		266
Daniel Boone Regional Library 100 W Broadway ...... Columbia MO 65203	800-324-4806	573-443-3161	433-3
Daniel Drake Center 151 W Galbraith Rd ...... Cincinnati OH 45216	800-948-0003	513-418-2500	373-6
Daniel F Young Inc 1235 Westlakes Dr Ste 255 ...... Berwyn PA 19312	866-407-0083	610-725-4000	447
Daniel Group Ltd, The 400 Clarice Ave Ste 200 ...... Charlotte NC 28204	877-967-4242		447
Daniele Inc PO Box 106 ...... Pascoag RI 02859	800-451-2535	401-568-6228	296-26
Daniels & Roberts Inc 209 N Seacrest Blvd ...... Boynton Beach FL 33435	800-488-0066	561-241-0066	7
Danis Building Construction Co 3233 Newmark Dr ...... Dayton OH 45342	800-326-4701	937-228-1225	
Danly IEM 6779 Engle Rd Ste A-F ...... Cleveland OH 44130	800-652-6462		752
Dannemiller Inc 5711 NW Pkwy ...... San Antonio TX 78249	800-328-2308		355
Danner Shoe Manufacturing Co 17634 NE Airport ...... Portland OR 97230 *Cust Svc	800-345-0430*	503-262-0103	301
Danny Herman Trucking Inc PO Box 55 ...... Mountain City TN 37683	800-251-7500		447
Danson Decor Inc 3425 Douglas B Floreani ...... St Laurent QC H4S1Y6	800-363-1865	514-335-2435	292
Danver 1 Grand St ...... Wallingford CT 06492	888-441-0537	203-269-2300	319-1
Danville Area Community College 2000 E Main St ...... Danville IL 61832	877-342-3042	217-443-3222	162
Danville Community College 1008 S Main St ...... Danville VA 24541	800-560-4291	434-797-2222	162
Danville Correctional Ctr 3820 E Main St ...... Danville IL 61834	844-258-9071		
Danville Pittsylvania County Chamber of Commerce 8653 US Hwy 29 PO Box 99 ...... Blairs VA 24527	800-826-2355	434-836-6990	139
Danville Regional Medical Ctr 142 S Main St ...... Danville VA 24541	800-688-3762	434-799-2100	373-3
Danville Signal Processing Inc 38570 100th Ave ...... Cannon Falls MN 55009	877-230-5682	507-263-5854	194
Danville-Boyle County Chamber of Commerce 105 E Walnut St ...... Danville KY 40422	800-548-4229	859-236-2805	139
DAP Products Inc 2400 Boston St Ste 200 ...... Baltimore MD 21224 *Cust Svc	800-543-3840*	888-327-8477	3
DAR (National Society Daughters of the American Revolut) 1776 D St NW ...... Washington DC 20006	800-449-1776	202-628-1776	48-19
DAR Constitution Hall 1776 D St NW ...... Washington DC 20006	800-449-1776	202-628-1776	568
Darby Dan Farm 3225 Old Frankfort Pk ...... Lexington KY 40510	888-321-0424	859-254-0424	367
Dardanelle & Russellville Railroad Co 4416 S Arkansas Ave ...... Russellville AR 72802	888-877-7267	479-968-6455	644
Dare 2 Share Ministries International PO Box 745323 ...... Arvada CO 80006	800-462-8355	303-425-1606	48-20
Dare Products Inc 860 Betterly Rd PO Box 157 ...... Battle Creek MI 49015	800-922-3273	269-965-2307	279
Darex 210 E Hersey St PO Box 730 ...... Ashland OR 97520	800-597-6170		453
Darice Inc 13000 Darice Pkwy ...... Strongsville OH 44149	866-432-7423		44
Darien Lake Theme Park Resort 9993 Allegheny Rd PO Box 91 ...... Darien Center NY 14040	866-640-0652	585-599-4641	32
Dark Horse Comics Inc 10956 SE Main St ...... Milwaukie OR 97222	800-862-0052	503-652-8815	633-5
Darke County Chamber of Commerce 209 E Fourth St ...... Greenville OH 45331	800-396-0787	937-548-2102	139
Darling International Inc 251 O'Connor Ridge Blvd Ste 300 ...... Irving TX 75038 NYSE: DAR	800-800-4841	972-717-0300	296-12
Darlington Raceway 1301 Harry Bird Hwy ...... Darlington SC 29532	866-459-7223		512
Darlington School 1014 Cave Spring Rd ...... Rome GA 30161	800-368-4437	706-235-6051	618
Darlington Veneer Company Inc 225 Fourth St ...... Darlington SC 29532	800-845-2388	843-393-3861	609
Darlingtonia State Natural Site 84505 Hwy 101 S ...... Florence OR 97439	800-551-6949	541-997-3851	561
Daron Worldwide Trading Inc 24 Stewart Pl Unit 4 ...... Fairfield NJ 07004	800-776-2324	973-882-0035	756
Dar-Ran Furniture Industries 2402 Shore Rd ...... High Point NC 27263	800-334-7891	336-861-2400	319-1
Darrow School 110 Darrow Rd ...... New Lebanon NY 12125	877-432-7769	518-794-6000	618
Dart Aerospace Ltd 1270 Aberdeen St ...... Hawkesbury ON K6A1K7	800-556-4166	613-632-3336	21

	City	State	ZIP	Toll-Free	Phone	Class
Dart Appraisalcom						
2600 W Big Beaver Rd Ste 540	Troy	MI	48084	**888-327-8123**		648
Dart Container Corp						
500 Hogsback Rd	Mason	MI	48854	**800-248-5960**		597
Dart Entities						
1430 S Eastman Ave	Los Angeles	CA	90023	**800-285-0560**	323-264-1011	798-1
Dart World Inc						
140 Linwood St	Lynn	MA	01905	**800-225-2558**	781-581-6035	707
Dar-tech Inc						
16485 Rockside Rd	Cleveland	OH	44137	**800-228-7347**	216-663-7600	146
Dartmouth College						
6016 McNutt Hall	Hanover	NH	03755	**800-490-7010**	603-646-1110	166
Dartmouth-Hitchcock Medical Ctr						
1 Medical Ctr Dr	Lebanon	NH	03756	**800-543-1624**	603-650-5000	373-3
Daryl Flood Inc						
450 Airline Dr Ste 100	Coppell	TX	75019	**800-325-9340**	972-471-1496	186
DAS Inc 724 Lawn Rd	Palmyra	PA	17078	**866-622-7979**	717-964-3642	38
DASAN Zhone Solutions Inc						
7195 Oakport St	Oakland	CA	94621	**877-946-6320**	510-777-7000	730
NASDAQ: DZSI						
Dasco Pro Inc						
340 Blackhawk Park Ave	Rockford	IL	61104	**800-327-2690**	815-962-3727	753
Dash Tours						
1024 Winnipeg St	Regina	SK	S4R8P8	**800-265-0000**	306-352-2222	755
Dashwood Industries Ltd						
69323 Richmond St	Centralia	ON	N0M1K0	**800-265-4284**	519-228-6624	497
Dassault Falcon Jet Corp						
PO Box 2000	South Hackensack	NJ	07606	**800-527-2463**	201-440-6700	20
Dastmalchi Enterprises Inc						
4490 Von Karman Ave						
Ste 150	Newport Beach	CA	92660	**888-358-0331**		4
Data Access Corp						
14000 SW 119th Ave	Miami	FL	33186	**800-451-3539**	305-238-0012	178-2
Data Banque Ltd						
4117 Liberty Ave	Pittsburgh	PA	15224	**877-860-2702**		
DATA Communications Management Corp (DCM)						
9195 Torbram Rd	Brampton	ON	L6S6H2	**800-268-0128**	905-791-3151	
Data Consulting Group Inc						
965 E Jefferson Ave	Detroit	MI	48207	**800-258-4343**	313-963-7771	180
Data Conversion Laboratory Inc						
61-18 190th St Ste 205	Fresh Meadows	NY	11365	**800-321-2816**	718-357-8700	224
Data Dash Inc						
3928 Delor St	Saint Louis	MO	63116	**800-211-5988**	314-832-5788	225
Data Device Corp						
105 Wilbur Pl	Bohemia	NY	11716	**800-332-5757***	631-567-5600	253
*Cust Svc						
Data Exchange Corp						
3600 Via Pescador	Camarillo	CA	93012	**800-237-7911**	805-388-1711	175
Data Financial Inc						
1100 Glen Oaks Ln	Mequon	WI	53092	**800-334-8334**	262-243-5511	177
Data I/O Corp						
6464 185th Ave NE Ste 101	Redmond	WA	98052	**800-426-1045**	425-881-6444	691
NASDAQ: DAIO						
Data Impressions						
17418 Studebaker Rd	Cerritos	CA	90703	**800-777-6488**	562-207-9050	174
Data Label Inc						
1000 Spruce St	Terre Haute	IN	47807	**800-457-0676**	812-232-0408	412
Data Management Inc						
537 New Britain Ave	Farmington	CT	06034	**800-243-1969***	860-677-8586	86
*Orders						
Data Papers Inc						
468 Industrial Pk Rd	Muncy	PA	17756	**800-233-3032**		110
Data Partners						
12857 Banyan Creek Dr	Fort Myers	FL	33908	**866-423-1818**		194
Data Path						
318 McHenry Ave	Modesto	CA	95354	**888-693-2827**	209-521-0055	196
Data Pro Acctg Software Inc						
111 Second Ave NE						
Ste 1200	Saint Petersburg	FL	33701	**800-237-6377**	727-803-1500	178-1
Data Records Management Services Llc						
1400 Husband Rd	Paducah	KY	42003	**800-443-1610**	270-443-1255	461
Data Sales Company Inc						
3450 W Burnsville Pkwy	Burnsville	MN	55337	**800-328-2730**	952-890-8838	174
Data Sciences International						
119 14th St NW Ste 100	St. Paul	MN	55112	**800-262-9687**	651-481-7400	664
Data Select Systems Inc						
2829 Townsgate Rd						
Ste 300	Westlake Village	CA	91361	**800-535-9978**	805-446-2090	177
Data Services Inc						
31516 Winterplace Pkwy	Salisbury	MD	21804	**800-432-4066**	410-546-2206	225
Data Source Inc						
1400 Universal Ave	Kansas City	MO	64120	**877-846-9120**	816-483-3282	110
Data Square LLC						
396 Danbury Rd	Wilton	CT	06897	**877-328-2738**	203-964-9733	
Data Storage Systems Ctr (DSSC)						
Carnegie Mellon University						
ECE Department	Pittsburgh	PA	15213	**800-864-8287**	412-268-6600	664
Data Systems Analysts Inc (DSA)						
Eigth Neshaminy Interplex						
Ste 209	Trevose	PA	19053	**877-422-4372**	215-245-4800	180
Data Technology Inc						
14225 Dayton Cir Ste 4	Omaha	NE	68137	**888-334-9300***	402-891-0711	543
*General						
Data Transmission Network Corp						
9110 W Dodge Rd Ste 200	Omaha	NE	68114	**800-485-4000**	402-390-2328	386
Data Ventures Inc						
6101 Carnegie Blvd Ste 520	Charlotte	NC	28209	**888-431-2676**	704-887-1012	177
Data Vista Inc						
5198 US-130 Ste A	Mansfield	NJ	08016	**800-797-3527**	609-702-9300	
DataCard Corp						
11111 Bren Rd W	Minnetonka	MN	55343	**800-328-8623**	952-933-1223	700
Dataclarity Corp						
7200 Falls of Neuse Rd Ste 202	Raleigh	NC	27615	**800-963-5508**	919-256-6700	177
DataComm Networks Inc						
6801 N 54th St	Tampa	FL	33610	**800-544-4627**		
Datacore Consulting LLC						
1300 E Granger Rd	Brooklyn Heights	OH	44131	**800-244-4241**	216-398-8499	627
DataDirect Networks						
9351 Deering Ave	Chatsworth	CA	91311	**800-837-2298**	818-700-7600	173-8
Datafirst Corp						
2700 Sumner Blvd	Raleigh	NC	27616	**800-634-8504**	919-876-6650	177
Dataforth Corp						
3331 E Hemisphere Loop	Tucson	AZ	85706	**800-444-7644**	520-741-1404	173-3
Data-Graphics Inc						
240 Hartford Ave	Newington	CT	06111	**800-639-4316**		
Dataline LLC						
6703 Albunda Dr PO Box 50816	Knoxville	TN	37950	**888-588-7740**	865-588-7740	261
Datalink Corp						
10050 Crosstown Cir Ste 500						
	Eden Prairie	MN	55344	**800-448-6314**	952-944-3462	173-8
DataLink Interactive Inc						
1120 Benfield Blvd Ste G	Millersville	MD	21108	**888-565-3279**	410-729-0440	180
Datalogic Scanning						
959 Terry St	Eugene	OR	97402	**800-695-5700**	541-683-5700	173-7
Datalux Corp						
155 Aviation Dr	Winchester	VA	22602	**800-328-2589**	540-662-1500	173-2
Datamann Inc						
1994 Hartford Ave	Wilder	VT	05088	**800-451-4263**	802-295-6600	178-11
Datamark Inc						
123 W Mills Ave Ste 400	El Paso	TX	79901	**800-477-1944**		225
Datamatics Management Services Inc						
330 New Brunswick Ave	Fords	NJ	08863	**800-673-0366**	732-738-9600	178-1
Data-Matique						
2110 Sherwin St	Garland	TX	75041	**866-706-0981**	972-272-3446	693
Datamine Internet Marketing Solutions Inc						
330 S Lake St	Gary	IN	46403	**877-328-2646**	219-939-9987	7
DataMotion Inc						
35 Airport Rd Ste 120	Morristown	NJ	07960	**800-672-7233**	973-455-1245	178-7
Datapro Solutions Inc						
6336 E Utah Ave	Spokane	WA	99212	**888-658-6881**	509-532-3530	180
Dataram Corp						
777 Alexander Rd Ste 100	Princeton	NJ	08540	**800-328-2726**	609-799-0071	621
NASDAQ: DRAM						
Datarealm Internet Services Inc						
PO Box 1616	Hudson	WI	54016	**877-227-3783**		803
Datascan LP						
2210 Hutton Dr Ste 100	Carrollton	TX	75006	**866-441-4848**		196
Dataserv Corp 8625 F St	Omaha	NE	68127	**888-901-8700**	402-339-8700	175
Datashield LLC						
455 E 200 S Ste 100	Salt Lake City	UT	84111	**866-428-4567**		196
Dataskill Inc						
2190 Carmel Valley Rd Ste D	DelMar	CA	92014	**800-481-3282**	858-755-3800	180
DataSphere Technologies Inc						
3350 161st Ave SE	Bellevue	WA	98008	**866-912-7090**		5
Datassential						
1762 Westwood Blvd Ste 250	Los Angeles	CA	90024	**888-556-3687**	312-655-0622	464
Datatech Labs						
8000 E Quincy Ave	Denver	CO	80237	**888-288-3282**	303-770-3282	620
Datatel Inc						
4375 Fair Lakes Ct	Fairfax	VA	22033	**800-223-7036**		178-10
Datatel Resources Corp						
1729 Pennsylvania Ave	Monaca	PA	15061	**800-245-2688**	724-775-5300	110
Datatel Solutions Inc						
875 Laurel Dr	Roseville	CA	95678	**888-224-8647**		196
DataTicket Inc						
4600 Campus Dr Ste 200	Newport Beach	CA	92660	**888-752-0512**	949-752-6937	160
DataTrail Corp						
7056B Farrell Rd SE	Calgary	AB	T2H0T2	**877-885-6254**	403-253-3651	
Datatrend Technologies Inc						
121 Cheshire Ln Ste 700	Minnetonka	MN	55305	**800-367-7472**	952-931-1203	180
DataViz Inc						
612 Wheelers Farms Rd	Milford	CT	06460	**800-733-0030**	203-874-0085	178-12
Datawatch Corp						
271 Mill Rd	Chelmsford	MA	01824	**800-445-3311**	978-441-2200	178-12
NASDAQ: DWCH						
DataWorks Plus LLC						
728 N Pleasantburg Dr	Greenville	SC	29607	**866-632-2780**	864-672-2780	177
Dates Weiser Furniture Corp						
1700 Broadway St	Buffalo	NY	14212	**800-466-7037**	716-891-1700	321
Datex Billing Services Inc						
5520 Explorer Dr Ste 202	Mississauga	ON	L4W5L1	**855-553-2839**		
DATTCO Inc						
583 S St	New Britain	CT	06051	**800-229-4879**	860-229-4878	107
Datum Filing Systems Inc						
89 Church Rd	Emigsville	PA	17318	**800-828-8018**	717-764-6350	286
Dauphin County						
2 S Second St 3rd Fl	Harrisburg	PA	17101	**800-328-0058**	717-780-6130	337
Dauphin North America						
300 Myrtle Ave	Boonton	NJ	07005	**800-631-1186***	973-263-1100	319-1
*Cust Svc						
Dauphine Orleans Hotel						
415 Dauphine St	New Orleans	LA	70112	**800-521-7111**	504-586-1800	378
DAV (Disabled American Veterans)						
3725 Alexandria Pk	Cold Spring	KY	41076	**877-426-2838**	859-441-7300	48-19
Davco Advertising Inc						
89 N Kinzer Rd PO Box 288	Kinzers	PA	17535	**800-283-2826**	717-442-4155	7
Davco Technology LLC						
1600 Woodland Dr PO Box 487	Saline	MI	48176	**800-328-2611**	734-429-5665	60
Dave & Buster's						
3000 Oakwood Blvd	Hollywood	FL	33020	**888-300-1515**	954-923-5505	667
Dave & Buster's Inc						
2481 Manana Dr	Dallas	TX	75220	**800-842-5369**	214-357-9588	655
Dave Thomas Foundation for Adoption						
716 Mt Airyshire Blvd Ste 100	Columbus	OH	43235	**800-275-3832**		305
Davenport & Co LLC						
901 E Cary St						
1 James Center Ste 1100	Richmond	VA	23219	**800-846-6666**	804-780-2000	686
Davenport Cos, The						
20 N Main St	South Yarmouth	MA	02664	**800-822-3422**	508-398-2293	186
Davenport Machine Inc						
167 Ames St	Rochester	NY	14611	**800-344-5748**	585-235-4545	453
Davenport University						
Dearborn						
4801 Oakman Blvd	Dearborn	MI	48126	**800-585-1479**	313-581-4400	166
Flint						
4318 Miller Rd Ste A	Flint	MI	48507	**800-727-1443**	810-732-9977	166

				Toll-Free	Phone	Class
Lansing						
220 E Kalamazoo St	Lansing	MI	48933	**800-686-1600**	517-484-2600	166
Lettinga Campus						
6191 Kraft Ave SE	Grand Rapids	MI	49512	**866-925-3884**	616-698-7111	166
Saginaw 5300 Bay Rd	Saginaw	MI	48604	**800-968-8133**	989-799-7800	166
Warren						
27650 Dequindre Rd	Warren	MI	48092	**800-724-7708**	586-558-8700	166
Davey Tree Expert Co						
1500 N Mantua St	Kent	OH	44240	**800-445-8733**	330-673-9511	771
David A Noyes & Co						
209 S LaSalle St	Chicago	IL	60604	**800-669-3732**	312-782-0400	41
David A Smith Printing Inc						
742 S 22nd St	Harrisburg	PA	17104	**800-564-3117**	717-564-3719	623
David A Straz Jr Ctr for the Performing Arts						
1010 N WC MacInnes Pl	Tampa	FL	33602	**800-955-1045**	813-222-1000	568
David Berman Developments						
340 Selby Ave	Ottawa	ON	K2A3X6	**800-665-1809**	613-728-6777	343
David Clark Co						
360 Franklin St	Worcester	MA	01604	**800-298-6235***	508-751-5800	572
*Cust Svc						
David Dobbs Enterprises Inc						
4600 US Hwy 1 N	Saint Augustine	FL	32095	**800-889-6368**	904-824-6171	92
David Evans & Assoc Inc (DEA)						
2100 SW River Pkwy	Portland	OR	97201	**800-721-1916**	503-223-6663	261
David H Fell & Company Inc						
6009 Bandini Blvd	Commerce	CA	90040	**800-822-1996**	323-722-9992	406
David Horowitz Freedom Ctr						
PO Box 55089	Sherman Oaks	CA	91499	**800-752-6562**		
David Weekley Homes Inc						
1111 N Post Oak Rd	Houston	TX	77055	**800-390-6774**	713-963-0500	649
David Yurman Designs Inc						
24 Vestry St	New York	NY	10013	**888-398-7626**		408
David's Bridal Inc						
1001 Washington St	Conshohocken	PA	19428	**844-400-3222**	610-943-5000	157-6
Davidsmeyer Bus Service Inc						
2513 E Higgins Rd	Elk Grove Village	IL	60007	**800-323-0312**	847-437-3767	109
Davidson College						
209 Ridge Rd PO Box 7156	Davidson	NC	28035	**800-768-0380**		166
Davidson County Community College						
PO Box 1287	Lexington	NC	27293	**800-233-4050**	336-249-8186	162
Davidson-Kennedy Co						
800 Industrial Park Dr	Marietta	GA	30062	**800-733-3434**	770-427-9467	120
Davies Molding LLC						
350 Kehoe Blvd	Carol Stream	IL	60188	**800-554-9208**	630-510-8188	617
Davies Pearson PC						
920 Fawcett Ave	Tacoma	WA	98401	**800-439-1112**	253-620-1500	427
Daviess County Metal Sales Inc						
9929 E US Hwy 50	Cannelburg	IN	47519	**800-279-4299**	812-486-4299	693
Daviess-Martin County REMC						
12628 E 75 N PO Box 430	Loogootee	IN	47553	**800-762-7362**	812-295-4200	245
Davis & Elkins College						
100 Campus Dr	Elkins	WV	26241	**800-624-3157**	304-637-1900	166
Davis College						
400 Riverside Dr	Johnson City	NY	13790	**800-331-4137**	607-729-1581	161
Davis College						
4747 Monroe St	Toledo	OH	43623	**800-477-7021**	419-473-2700	795
Davis Correctional Facility						
6888 E 133rd Rd	Holdenville	OK	74848	**877-834-1550**	405-379-6400	213
Davis Cos						
325 Donald J Lynch Blvd	Marlborough	MA	01752	**800-482-9494**	763-231-0700	717
Davis Demographics & Planning Inc						
11850 Pierce St Ste 200	Riverside	CA	92505	**888-337-4471**	951-270-5211	461
Davis Direct Inc						
1241 Newell Pkwy	Montgomery	AL	36110	**877-277-0878**	334-277-0878	623
Davis Express Inc						
PO Box 1276	Starke	FL	32091	**800-874-4270**		775
Davis Funds						
2949 E Elvira Rd Ste 101	Tucson	AZ	85756	**800-279-0279**		524
Davis Hospital & Medical Ctr (DHMC)						
1600 W Antelope Dr	Layton	UT	84041	**877-898-6080**	801-807-1000	373-3
Davis Instrument Corp						
3465 Diablo Ave	Hayward	CA	94545	**800-678-3669**	510-732-9229	470
Davis Law Firm						
10500 Heitage Blvd Ste 102	San Antonio	TX	78216	**800-770-0127**	210-444-4444	427
Davis Oil Co						
904 Jernigan St	Perry	GA	31069	**888-448-5657**		316
Davis Paint Company Inc						
1311 Iron St	North Kansas City	MO	64116	**800-821-2029**	816-471-4447	546
Davis Vision Inc						
711 Troy-Schenectady Rd	Latham	NY	12110	**800-999-5431**		390-3
Davisco International Inc						
719 N Main St	Le Sueur	MN	56058	**800-757-7611**	507-665-8811	296-10
Davis-Ulmer Sprinkler Company Inc						
1 Commerce Dr	Amherst	NY	14228	**877-691-3200**	716-691-3200	385
DaVita Inc						
1551 Wewatta St	Denver	CO	80202	**800-310-4872**	303-405-2100	351
NYSE: DVA						
Davol Inc						
100 Crossings Blvd	Warwick	RI	02886	**800-556-6756***		474
*Cust Svc						
Daw Construction Group LLC						
12552 South 125 West # 100	Draper	UT	84020	**800-748-4778**	801-553-9111	186
Dawahares Inc						
1845 Alexandria Dr	Lexington	KY	40504	**800-677-9108**	859-278-0422	157-2
Dawn Food Products Inc						
3333 Sargent Rd	Jackson	MI	49201	**800-292-1362***	517-789-4400	296-16
*Cust Svc						
Dawson Co						
1681 W Second St	Pomona	CA	91766	**800-832-9766**	626-797-9710	608
Dawson Community College						
300 College Dr	Glendive	MT	59330	**800-821-8320**	406-377-3396	162
Dawson Geophysical Co						
508 W Wall St Ste 800	Midland	TX	79701	**800-332-9766**	432-684-3000	534
NASDAQ: DWSN						
Dawson Insurance Agency Inc						
721 First Ave N	Fargo	ND	58107	**800-220-4514**	701-237-3311	
Dawson Public Power District						
75191 Rd 433	Lexington	NE	68850	**800-752-8305**	308-324-2386	245

				Toll-Free	Phone	Class
Day & Zimmermann Group Inc						
1500 Spring Garden St	Philadelphia	PA	19130	**877-319-0270**	215-299-8000	723
Day Publishing Co						
47 Eugene O'Neill Dr	New London	CT	06320	**800-542-3354**	860-442-2200	633-8
Daybreak Star Ctr						
3801 W Government Way						
PO Box 99100	Seattle	WA	98199	**800-321-4321**	206-285-4425	50-2
Daybreak Venture LLC						
401 N Elm St	Denton	TX	76201	**800-345-5603**	940-387-4388	370
Day-Lee Foods Inc						
13055 Molette St	Santa Fe Springs	CA	90670	**800-329-5331**	562-903-3020	297-9
Daylight Donut Flour Company LLC						
11707 E 11th St	Tulsa	OK	74128	**800-331-2245**	918-438-0800	68
Daylight Transport						
1501 Hughes Way Ste 200	Long Beach	CA	90810	**800-468-9999**		775
Daymark Recovery Services Inc Stanly Center						
1000 N First St Ste 1	Albemarle	NC	28001	**866-275-9552**	704-983-2117	722
Days Inn Hinton-Jasper Hotel						
358 Smith St	Hinton	AB	T7V2A1	**800-259-4827**	780-817-1960	377
Days Inns Worldwide Inc						
215 W 94th St Broadway	New York	NY	10025	**800-225-3297**	212-866-6400	378
DaySpa Magazine						
7628 Densmore Ave	Van Nuys	CA	91406	**800-442-5667**	818-782-7328	455-21
DaySpring Cards Inc						
21154 Hwy 16 E	Siloam Springs	AR	72761	**800-944-8000**	877-751-4347	130
Daystar Television Network						
3901 Hwy 121 PO Box 610546	Bedford	TX	76021	**800-329-0029**	817-571-1229	735
Dayton Art Institute						
456 Belmonte Pk N	Dayton	OH	45405	**800-272-8258**	937-223-5277	517
Dayton City Paper						
126 N Main St Ste 240	Dayton	OH	45402	**888-228-3630**	937-222-8855	528-5
Dayton Contemporary Dance Co						
840 Germantown St	Dayton	OH	45402	**888-228-3630**	937-228-3232	569-1
Dayton Daily News						
1611 S Main St	Dayton	OH	45409	**888-397-6397**	937-225-2000	528-2
Dayton Foundation						
40 N Main St Ste 500	Dayton	OH	45423	**877-222-0410**	937-222-0410	303
Dayton Mark (D)						
130 State Capitol						
75 Rev Dr Martin Luther King Jr Blvd	St. Paul	MN	55155	**800-657-3717**	651-201-3400	
Dayton Parts LLC						
3500 Industrial Rd						
PO Box 5795	Harrisburg	PA	17110	**800-225-2159***	717-255-8500	60
*Cust Svc						
Dayton Philharmonic Orchestra						
126 N Main St Ste 210	Dayton	OH	45402	**888-228-3630**	937-224-3521	569-3
Dayton Power & Light Co						
PO Box 1247	Dayton	OH	45401	**800-433-8500**	937-331-3900	782
Dayton Reliable Air Filter Inc						
2294 N Moraine Dr	Dayton	OH	45439	**800-699-0747***		17
*Orders						
Dayton Rogers Manufacturing Co						
8401 W 35 W Service Dr	Minneapolis	MN	55449	**800-677-8881**	763-784-7714	486
Dayton Superior Corp						
1125 Byers Rd	Miamisburg	OH	45342	**800-745-3700**	937-866-0711	349
Dayton Va Medical Ctr						
4100 W Third St	Dayton	OH	45428	**800-368-8262**	937-268-6511	373-8
Dayton/Montgomery County Convention & Visitors Bureau						
1 Chamber Plz Ste A	Dayton	OH	45402	**800-221-8235**	937-226-8211	206
Daytona Beach Community College						
1200 W International Speedway Blvd						
	Daytona Beach	FL	32114	**877-822-6669**	386-506-3000	162
Daytona Beach Resort & Conference Ctr						
2700 N Atlantic Ave	Daytona Beach	FL	32118	**800-654-6216**	386-672-3770	378
Daytona Inn Beach Resort						
219 S Atlantic Ave	Daytona Beach	FL	32118	**800-874-1822***	386-252-3626	378
*General						
Dayton-Phoenix Group Inc						
1619 Kuntz Rd	Dayton	OH	45404	**800-657-0707**	937-496-3900	646
Dazian LLC						
18 Central Blvd	South Hackensack	NJ	07606	**877-232-9426**	201-549-1000	740-2
Dazor Lighting Solutions						
430 Industrial Dr	Maryland Heights	MO	63043	**800-345-9103**	314-652-2400	438
DB (Deutsche Bank Canada)						
199 Bay St Commerce Ct W						
Ste 4700	Toronto	ON	M5L1E9	**800-735-7777**	416-682-8000	70
D&B 103 JFK Pkwy	Short Hills	NJ	07078	**800-234-3867**	973-921-5500	633-2
NYSE: DNB						
DB Becker Company Inc						
46 Leigh St	Clinton	NJ	08809	**800-394-3991**	908-730-6010	146
D&B Sales & Marketing Solutions						
103 JFK Pkwy	Short Hills	NJ	07078	**866-473-3932**	973-921-5500	178-1
DBA Engineering Ltd						
401 Hanlan Rd	Vaughan	ON	L4L3T1	**800-819-8833**	905-851-0090	256
DBI Inc						
912 E Michigan Ave	Lansing	MI	48912	**800-968-1324**	517-485-3200	531
DBK Concepts Inc						
12905 SW 129 Ave	Miami	FL	33186	**800-725-7226**	305-596-7226	175
DBS Bank Ltd						
725 S Figueroa St	Los Angeles	CA	90017	**800-209-4555**	213-627-0222	70
DBSA (Depression & Bipolar Support Alliance)						
730 N Franklin St Ste 501	Chicago	IL	60610	**800-826-3632**	312-642-0049	48-17
DBU (Duluth Business University)						
4724 Mike Colalilo Dr	Duluth	MN	55807	**800-777-8406**	218-722-4000	795
DC Group Inc						
1977 W River Rd N	Minneapolis	MN	55411	**800-838-7927**		762
DC Humphrys Inc						
5744 Woodland Ave	Philadelphia	PA	19143	**800-645-2059***	215-724-8181	728
*Sales						
DC Taylor Co						
312 29th St NE	Cedar Rapids	IA	52402	**800-876-6346**	319-363-2073	189-12
DC101						
1801 Rockville Pk	Rockville	MD	20852	**866-913-2101**	240-747-2700	641
DCA (Diamond Council of America)						
3212 W End Ave Ste 202	Nashville	TN	37203	**877-283-5669**	615-385-5301	49-4
DCAT (Drug Chemical & Associated Technologies Assn)						
1 Washington Blvd Ste 7	Robbinsville	NJ	08691	**800-640-3228**	609-448-1000	49-19
DCCI (Dow Chemical Canada Inc)						
450 First St SW Ste 2100	Calgary	AB	T2P5H1	**800-447-4369**	403-267-3500	144

	Toll-Free	Phone	Class

DCD (Diamond Comic Distributors Inc)
10150 York Rd Ste 300................Hunt Valley MD 21030   800-452-6642   443-318-8001   633-5

DCEC (Delaware County Electric Co-op)
39 Elm St PO Box 471.................Delhi NY 13753   866-436-1223   607-746-2341   245

DCH Health System
809 University Blvd E.............Tuscaloosa AL 35401   800-266-4324   205-759-7111   352

DCH Honda of Nanuet
10 NY-304.................Nanuet NY 10954   888-495-8660   845-367-7050   57

DCH Regional Medical Ctr
809 University Blvd E.............Tuscaloosa AL 35401   800-356-9596   205-759-7111   373-3

DCI (Drum Corps International)
110 W Washington St Ste C.........Indianapolis IN 46204   800-495-7469*   317-275-1212   48-4
*Orders

DCL (Downey City Library)
11121 Brookshire Ave..............Downey CA 90241   877-846-3452   562-904-7360   433-3

DCM (Distribution Center Management)
712 Main St Ste 187B..............Boonton NJ 07005   800-232-4317   973-265-2300   527-2

DCM (DATA Communications Management Corp)
9195 Torbram Rd...............Brampton ON L6S6H2   800-268-0128   905-791-3151

Dcs Netlink
1800 Macauley Ave..............Rice Lake WI 54868   877-327-6385   715-236-7424   180

DCT (Diversified Chemical Technologies Inc)
15477 Woodrow Wilson St............Detroit MI 48238   800-243-1424   313-867-5444   145

DD Bean & Sons Co
207 Peterborough St..............Jaffrey NH 03452   800-326-8311   603-532-8311   467

D&D Sexton Inc
PO Box 156.................Carthage MO 64836   800-743-0265   417-358-8727   775

DD Williamson & Company Inc
100 S Spring St.................Louisville KY 40206   800-227-2635   502-895-2438   296-15

DDC (DNA Diagnostics Ctr)
1 DDC Way................Fairfield OH 45014   800-613-5768   513-881-7800   416

DDL Inc
10200 Vly View Rd Ste 101.........Eden Prairie MN 55344   800-229-4235   952-941-9226   738

DDLC Energy
410 Bank St.................New London CT 06320   888-225-5540

De Graff Memorial Hospital
445 Tremont St...........North Tonawanda NY 14120   800-506-6480   716-694-4500   373-3

De Kadt Marketing & Research Inc
162 Danbury Rd.................Ridgefield CT 06877   800-243-2991   203-431-1212   195

De Marque inc
400 Boul Jean-Lesage Bureau 540....Quebec QC G1K8W1   888-458-9143   418-658-9143   174

De Ronde Tire Supply Inc
2010 Elmwood Ave.................Buffalo NY 14207   800-227-4647   716-897-6690   750

de Saisset Museum at Santa Clara University
500 El Camino Real.................Santa Clara CA 95053   866-554-6800   408-554-4528   517

De Wafelbakkers LLC
10000 Crystal Hill Rd
.................North Little Rock AR 72113   800-924-3391   501-791-3320   296-1

DEA (David Evans & Assoc Inc)
2100 SW River Pkwy.............Portland OR 97201   800-721-1916   503-223-6663   261

Deaconess Hospital
600 Mary St.................Evansville IN 47747   800-677-3422   812-450-5000   373-3

Deaf Inter-link
100 rue St Francois Ste 206......Florissant MO 63031   800-330-7062   314-837-7757   138

Deaf-Talk Inc
14 E Main St.................Carnegie PA 15106   877-304-0004   412-563-3177   763

Deal, The
14 Wall St 15th Fl.............New York NY 10005   888-667-3325*   633-9
*Cust Svc

Dealer Tire LLC
7012 Euclid Ave.................Cleveland OH 44103   800-933-2537   216-432-0088   750

Dealers Truck Equipment Co
2460 Midway St.................Shreveport LA 71108   800-259-7569   318-635-7567   513

DealersEdge
PO Box 606.................Barnegat Light NJ 08006   800-321-5312   609-879-4456   527-13

DealerTrack Holdings Inc
1111 Marcus Ave Ste M04.........Lake Success NY 11042   877-357-8725   516-734-3600   178-10
NASDAQ: TRAK

DealNet Capital Corp
325 Milner Ave Ste 300.............Toronto ON M1B5N1   855-912-3444   461

Dean College
99 Main St.................Franklin MA 02038   877-879-3326   508-541-1508   162

Dean Foods Co
2711 N Haskell Ave Ste 3400...........Dallas TX 75204   800-395-7004   214-303-3400   296-27
NYSE: DF

Dean Health Insurance Inc
1277 Deming Way.................Madison WI 53717   800-279-1301   390-3

Dean Team Automotive Group Inc
15121 Manchester Rd.............Ballwin MO 63011   888-699-0663   636-227-0100   57

Dean Transportation Inc
4812 Aurelius Rd.................Lansing MI 48910   800-282-3326   517-319-8300   109

Dean Word Company Ltd
1245 River Rd.................New Braunfels TX 78130   800-683-3926   830-625-2365   188-4

Deansteel Manufacturing Co
111 Merchant.................San Antonio TX 78204   800-825-8271   210-226-8271   234

Dearborn County Chamber of Commerce
320 Walnut St.................Lawrenceburg IN 47025   800-322-8198   812-537-0814   139

Dearborn Federal Credit Union
400 Town Ctr Dr.................Dearborn MI 48126   888-336-2700   313-336-2700   219

Dearborn Times-Herald
13730 Michigan Ave.................Dearborn MI 48126   866-468-7630   313-584-4000   528-4

Dearden's Furniture Co
700 S Main St.................Los Angeles CA 90014   800-545-5509   213-362-9600   321

Dearing Compressor & Pump Co
3974 Verona Rd PO Box 6044........Youngstown OH 44501   800-850-3440   330-599-5720   172

Dearth Chrysler Dodge Jeep Ram
520 Eigth St.................Monroe WI 53566   877-495-5321   866-949-3653   57

Death Valley Museum
Death Vly National Pk
PO Box 579.................Death Valley CA 92328   800-544-0551   760-786-3200   517

Deauville Beach Resort
6701 Collins Ave.................Miami Beach FL 33141   800-327-6656   305-865-8511   665

DEB Inc
2815 Coliseum Centre Dr
Ste 600.................Charlotte NC 28217   800-248-7190   704-263-4240   214

DeBourgh Manufacturing
27505 Otero Ave.................La Junta CO 81050   800-328-8829   286

DeBra-Kuempel
3976 Southern Ave.................Cincinnati OH 45227   800-395-5741   513-271-6500   189-10

DebtFolio Inc
35 Braintree Hill Office Pk
Ste 107.................Braintree MA 02184   866-876-3654   386

Debtors Anonymous (DA)
PO Box 920888.................Needham MA 02492   800-421-2383   781-453-2743   48-21

DeCarolis Truck Rental Inc
333 Colfax St.................Rochester NY 14606   800-666-1169   585-254-1169   773

Decatur Area Convention & Visitors Bureau
202 E N St.................Decatur IL 62523   800-331-4479   217-423-7000   206

Decatur Co-op Assn
305 S York Ave.................Oberlin KS 67749   800-886-2293   785-475-2234   48-2

Decatur County
22 W Main St PO Box 488.........Decaturville TN 38329   800-525-6834   731-852-2131   337

Decatur County
150 Courthouse Sq Ste 244........Greensburg IN 47240   800-622-4941   812-663-8223   337

Decatur County Rural Electric Membership Corp
1430 W Main St PO Box 46.........Greensburg IN 47240   800-844-7362   812-663-3391   245

Decatur Daily
201 First Ave SE.................Decatur AL 35601   888-353-4612   256-353-4612   528-2

Decatur Memorial Hospital
2300 N Edward St.................Decatur IL 62526   866-364-3600   217-876-8121   373-3

Deccofelt Corp
555 S Vermont Ave.................Glendora CA 91741   800-543-3226*   626-963-8511   740-2
*Cust Svc

Decision Academic Inc
1705 Tech Ave Ste 1.........Mississauga ON L4W0A2   888-661-1933

DecisionOne Corp
426 W Lancaster Ave.................Devon PA 19333   800-767-2876   610-296-6000   175

DecisionPoint Systems Inc
19655 Descartes.........Foothill Ranch CA 92610   800-336-3670   949-465-0065   177
OTC: DPSI

DecisionQuest
21535 Hawthorne Blvd Ste 310.........Torrance CA 90503   800-887-5696   310-618-9600   443

Decker Advertising
99 Citizens Dr.................Glastonbury CT 06033   800-777-3677   860-659-1311   7

Decker Tape Products Inc
2 Stewart Pl.................Fairfield NJ 07004   800-227-5252   973-227-5350   727

Decker Truck Line Inc
4000 Fifth Ave S.................Fort Dodge IA 50501   800-247-2537   515-576-4141   775

Declara Inc
977 Commercial St.................Palo Alto CA 94303   877-216-0604   386

DECO Inc
11156 Zealand Ave N.........Champlin MN 55316   800-968-9114   689

Deco Products Co
506 Sanford St.................Decorah IA 52101   800-327-9751   563-382-4264   308

DecoArt Inc
49 Cotton Ave.................Stanford KY 40484   800-367-3047   606-365-3193   43

Decorative Crafts Inc
50 Chestnut St.................Greenwich CT 06830   800-431-4455   203-531-1500   360

Decore-ative Specialties Inc
2772 S Peck Rd.................Monrovia CA 91016   800-729-7277   626-254-9191   115

DeCoty Coffee Company Inc
1920 Austin St.................San Angelo TX 76903   800-588-8001   296-7

Dec-Tam Corp
50 Concord St.................North Reading MA 01864   800-332-8261   978 470 2860   663

Dectro International Inc
1000 Blvd du Parc-Technologique....Quebec QC G1P4S3   800-463-5566   418-650-0303   473

Dedham Institution For Savings
55 Elm St PO Box 9107.............Dedham MA 02026   888-289-0342   781-329-6700   70

Dedicated Computing
N26 W23880 Commerce Cir..........Waukesha WI 53188   877-333-4848   262-951-7200   173-2

Dedicated Distribution Inc
640 Miami Ave.................Kansas City KS 66105   800-325-8367   473

Dee Cramer Inc
4221 E Baldwin Rd.................Holly MI 48442   888-342-6995   810-579-5000   189-12

Dee Electronics Inc
2500 16th Ave SW.........Cedar Rapids IA 52404   800-747-3331   319-365-7551   246

Dee Paper Box Company Inc
100 Broomall St.................Chester PA 19013   800-359-0041   610-876-9285   101

Deen Meats
PO Box 4155.................Fort Worth TX 76164   800-333-3953   817-335-2257   297-9

Deep East Texas Council of Governments
274 E Lamar St.................Jasper TX 75951   800-256-6848   409-384-5704   461

Deep East Texas Electric Co-op Inc
880 Texas Hwy 21 E
PO Box 736.................San Augustine TX 75972   800-392-5986   936-275-2314   245

Deepwater Chemicals Inc
1210 Airpark Rd.................Woodward OK 73801   800-854-4064   580-256-0500   801

Deer Creek State Park
20635 State Pk Rd 20
PO Box 125.................Mount Sterling OH 43143   866-644-6727*   740-869-3124
*Resv

Deer Valley Federal Credit Union
16215 N 28th Ave.................Phoenix AZ 85053   800-579-5051   602-375-7300   219

Deer Valley Resort Lodging
PO Box 889.................Park City UT 84060   800-558-3337   435-645-6626   665

Deere & Co
1 John Deere Pl.................Moline IL 61265   800-765-9588   309-765-8000   185
NYSE: DE

Deerfield Episcopal Retirement Community
1617 Hendersonville Rd.............Asheville NC 28803   800-284-1531   828-274-1531   668

Deerfield Public Library Inc
920 Waukegan Rd.................Deerfield IL 60015   800-829-4059   847-945-3311   434

Deerfield Spa
650 Resica Falls Rd......East Stroudsburg PA 18302   800-852-4494   570-223-0160   702

Deerfoot Inn & Casino
1000 11500 35th St SE.............Calgary AB T2Z3W4   877-236-5225   403-236-7529   378

Deerhurst Resort
1235 Deerhurst Dr.................Huntsville ON P1H2E8   800-461-6522*   800-461-4393   665
*Sales

Deering Banjo Co
3733 Kenora Dr.................Spring Valley CA 91977   800-845-7791   619-464-8252   523

DeFehr Furniture Ltd
125 Furniture Pk.................Winnipeg MB R2G1B9   877-333-3471   204-988-5630   319-2

Defence Construction Canada
Constitution Sq 350 Albert St
19th Fl.................Ottawa ON K1A0K3   800-514-3555   613-998-9548

Defender Inc
3750 Priority Way S Dr...........Indianapolis IN 46240   800-860-0303   317-810-4720

	Toll-Free	Phone	Class
Defender Industries Inc			
42 Great Neck Rd ....Waterford CT 06385	800-628-8225	860-701-3400	765
Defenders of Wildlife			
1130 17th St NW ....Washington DC 20036	800-385-9712	202-682-9400	48-3
DefendX Software			
119 Drum Hill Rd Ste 383.........Chelmsford MA 01824	800-390-6937	603-622-4400	178-12
Defense Commissary Agency			
1300 E Ave ....Fort Lee VA 23801	877-332-2471	804-734-8000	339-3
Defense Contract Audit Agency			
8725 John J Kingman Rd			
Ste 2135 ....Fort Belvoir VA 22060	855-414-5892	703-767-3265	339-3
Defense Contract Management Agency			
6350 Walker Ln Ste 300 ....Alexandria VA 22310	888-576-3262		339-3
Defense Finance & Acctg Service			
8899 E 56th St ....Indianapolis IN 46249	888-332-7411		729
Defense Logistics Agency (DLA)			
8725 John J Kingman Rd ......Fort Belvoir VA 22060	877-352-2255		339-3
Defense Nuclear Facilities Safety Board			
625 Indiana Ave NW Ste 700 ....Washington DC 20004	800-788-4016	202-694-7000	339-19
Defense Technical Information Center (DTIC)			
8725 John J Kingman Rd			
Ste 0944....................Fort Belvoir VA 22060	800-225-3842		339-3
Defense Technology			
Safariland Group			
1855 S Loop Ave ....Casper WY 82601	877-248-3835	307-235-2136	284
Defense Threat Reduction Agency			
8725 John T Kingman Rd			
MS 6201.......................Fort Belvoir VA 22060	800-701-5096	703-767-5870	339-3
Defiance College			
701 N Clinton St ....Defiance OH 43512	800-520-4632	419-784-4010	166
Defiance County			
500 Ct St ....Defiance OH 43512	800-675-3953	419-782-4761	337
Defibtech LLC			
741 Boston Post Rd Ste 201..........Guilford CT 06437	866-333-4248	203-453-4507	474
Deflect-O Corp			
7035 E 86th St ....Indianapolis IN 46250	800-428-4328		530
Degesch America Inc			
PO Box 116 ....Weyers Cave VA 24486	800-330-2525	540-234-9281	280
DeGraaf Nature Ctr			
600 Graafschap Rd ....Holland MI 49423	888-535-5792	616-355-1057	50-5
DeGray Lake Resort State Park			
2027 State Pk Entrance Rd ....Bismarck AR 71929	800-737-8355	501-865-5810	561
DeGrazia Gallery in the Sun			
6300 N Swan Rd ....Tucson AZ 85718	800-545-2185	520-299-9191	517
Degree Controls Inc			
18 Meadowbrook Dr ....Milford NH 03055	877-334-7332	603-672-8900	256
DeHumidification Technologies LP			
6609 Ave U ....Houston TX 77011	866-736-8348	713-939-1166	14
DEI Holdings Inc			
1 Viper Way ....Vista CA 92081	800-876-0800	760-598-6200	52
OTC: DEI			
Deighton Associates Ltd			
223 Brock St N Unit 7..................Whitby ON L1N4H6	888-219-6605	905-665-6605	261
Dejana Truck & Utility Equipment Company Inc			
490 Pulaski Rd ....Kings Park NY 11754	877-335-2621	631-544-9000	775
DeKalb Convention & Visitors Bureau			
1957 Lakeside Pkwy Ste 510 ....Tucker GA 30084	866-633-5252	770-492-5000	206
Dekko 2505 Dekko Dr ....Garrett IN 46738	800-829-3101	260-357-3621	810
Del Amo Fashion Ctr			
3525 Carson St ....Torrance CA 90503	877-746-6642	310-542-8525	458
Del Amo Hospital			
23700 Camino Del Sol ....Torrance CA 90505	800-533-5266	310-530-1151	373-5
Del Mar College			
East			
101 Baldwin Blvd ....Corpus Christi TX 78404	800-652-3357	361-698-1200	162
Del Mar Scientific Acquisition Ltd			
4951 Airport Pkwy Ste 803 ....Addison TX 75001	800-722-4270	972-661-5160	201
Del Mar Thoroughbred Club			
2260 Jimmy Durante Blvd ....Del Mar CA 92014	800-467-7385	858-755-1141	638
Del Monte Foods Co			
1 Maritime Plz ....San Francisco CA 94111	800-543-3090*	415-247-3000	296-20
Cust Svc			
Del Monte Fresh			
PO Box 149222 ....Coral Gables FL 33114	800-950-3683*	305-520-8400	297-7
Cust Svc			
Del Monte Lodge Renaissance Rochester Hotel & Spa, The			
41 N Main St ....Pittsford NY 14534	866-237-5979	800-983-4240	378
Del Rey Beach State Recreation Site			
100 Peter Iredale Rd ....Hammond OR 97121	800-551-6949		561
Del Sol Medical Ctr			
10301 Gateway W ....El Paso TX 79925	800-322-0712	915-595-9000	373-3
DelaGet LLC			
5320 W 23rd St Ste 140 ....St Louis Park MN 55416	888-335-2438		196
Delaney Capital Management Ltd			
TD Bank Twr			
4410-66 Wellington St W ....Toronto ON M5K1H1	800-268-2733	416-361-0688	
Delaney Computer Services Inc			
575 Corporate Dr Ste 400..........Mahwah NJ 07430	844-832-4437	201-669-4300	
Delaney Educational Enterprises Inc			
1455 W Morena Blvd ....San Diego CA 92110	800-788-5557		
Delaware			
Aging & Adults with Physical Disabilites Services			
1901 N DuPont Hwy ....New Castle DE 19720	800-223-9074		338-8
Agriculture Dept			
2320 S DuPont Hwy ....Dover DE 19901	800-282-8685	302-698-4500	338-8
Consumer Protection Unit			
820 N French St 5th Fl ....Wilmington DE 19801	800-220-5424	302-577-8600	338-8
Emergency Management Agency			
165 Brick Store Landing Rd ....Smyrna DE 19977	877-729-3362	302-659-3362	338-8
Housing Authority			
18 The Green ....Dover DE 19901	888-363-8808	302-739-4263	338-8
Parks & Recreation Div			
89 Kings Hwy ....Dover DE 19901	877-987-2757*	302-739-9220	338-8
Campground Resv			
Thoroughbred Racing Commission			
2320 S DuPont Hwy ....Dover DE 19901	800-282-8685	302-698-4500	708
Tourism Office			
99 Kings Hwy ....Dover DE 19901	866-284-7483	302-739-4271	338-8

	Toll-Free	Phone	Class
Veterans Affairs Commission			
802 Silverlake Blvd Ste 100 ....Dover DE 19904	800-344-9900	302-739-2792	338-8
Weights & Measures Office			
2320 S DuPont Hwy ....Dover DE 19901	800-282-8685	302-698-4575	338-8
Delaware Art Museum			
2301 Kentmere Pkwy ....Wilmington DE 19806	866-232-3714	302-571-9590	517
Delaware County			
101 N Sandusky St ....Delaware OH 43015	800-277-2177	740-833-2100	337
Delaware County			
301 E Main St ....Manchester IA 52057	800-839-5005		337
Delaware County Daily Times			
639 S Chester Rd ....Swarthmore PA 19081	888-799-6299	610-622-8800	528-2
Delaware County Electric Co-op (DCEC)			
39 Elm St PO Box 471 ....Delhi NY 13753	866-436-1223	607-746-2341	245
Delaware County Intermediate Unit			
200 Yale Ave ....Morton PA 19070	800-441-3215	610-938-9000	681
Delaware County Memorial Hospital			
501 N Lansdowne Ave ....Drexel Hill PA 19026	877-884-1564	610-284-8100	373-3
Delaware Democratic Party			
19 E Commons Blvd 2nd Fl .....New Castle DE 19720	800-685-5544	302-328-9036	612-1
Delaware Electric Co-op Inc			
14198 Sussex Hwy ....Greenwood DE 19950	800-282-8595	302-349-3147	245
Delaware Employment & Training Div			
4425 N Market St ....Wilmington DE 19802	800-794-3032	302-761-8085	259
Delaware Hospice Inc			
1786 Wilmington-W Chester Pk			
Ste 200 A ....Glen Mills DE 19342	800-838-9800	302-478-5707	362
Delaware Mfg Industries Corp			
3776 Commerce Ct ....Wheatfield NY 14120	800-248-3642	716-743-4360	262
Delaware National Scenic River			
Delaware Water Gap National Recreation Area			
1978 River Rd.....................Bushkill PA 18324	800-543-4295	570-426-2435	560
Delaware North Cos Inc			
40 Fountain Plz ....Buffalo NY 14202	800-828-7240	716-858-5000	185
Delaware Nurses Assn (DNA)			
4765 Ogletown-Stanton Rd Ste L10 ....Newark DE 19713	800-626-4081	302-733-5880	529
Delaware Psychiatric Ctr			
1901 N Dupont Hwy ....New Castle DE 19720	800-652-2929	302-255-2700	373-5
Delaware Racing Assn			
777 Delaware Park Blvd ....Wilmington DE 19804	888-850-8888		
Delaware State Chamber of Commerce			
1201 N Orange St Ste 200			
PO Box 671...................Wilmington DE 19899	800-292-9507	302-655-7221	140
Delaware State News			
110 Galaxy Dr ....Dover DE 19901	800-282-8586	302-674-3600	528-2
Delaware State Park			
5202 US Rt 23 N ....Delaware OH 43015	866-644-6727	740-363-4561	561
Delaware State University			
1200 N DuPont Hwy ....Dover DE 19901	800-845-2544*	302-857-6351	166
Admissions			
Delaware Transit Corp			
119 Lower Beach St ....Wilmington DE 19805	800-652-3278		466
Delaware Valley College			
700 E Butler Ave ....Doylestown PA 18901	800-233-5825	215-489-2211	166
Delbridge Solutions			
7560 Airport Rd Unit 12 ....Mississauga ON L4T4H4	888-815-2996		317
Delco Diesel Services Inc			
1100 S Agnew Ave ....Oklahoma City OK 73108	800-256-0395	405-232-3595	54
Delcom Group LP			
2525B E SH 121 Ste 400 ....Lewisville TX 75056	800-308-9228	214-389-5500	196
Delden Manufacturing Company Inc			
3530 N Kimball Dr ....Kansas City MO 64161	800-821-3708	816-413-1600	497
DeLeon's Bromeliads Co			
13745 SW 216th St ....Miami FL 33170	800-448-8649	305-238-6028	368
Delfield Co			
980 S Isabella Rd ....Mount Pleasant MI 48858	800-733-8821	989-773-7981	298
Delfin Design & Manufacturing Inc			
23301 Antonio Pkwy			
.................Rancho Santa Margarita CA 92688	800-354-7919	949-888-4644	
Deli Express			
16101 W 78th St ....Eden Prairie MN 55344	800-328-8184		296-36
Deliverycom LLC			
235 Park Ave S 5th Fl.............New York NY 10038	800-709-7191		
Delkor Systems Inc			
4300 Round Lake Rd W ....St. Paul MN 55112	800-328-5558		543
Dell Inc			
1 Dell Way ....Round Rock TX 78682	800-879-3355	512-338-4400	173-2
NASDAQ: DELL			
DELLEMC			
6801 Koll Ctr Pkwy ....Pleasanton CA 94566	866-438-3622		
Dellenbach Motors			
3111 S College Ave ....Fort Collins CO 80525	866-963-5689		57
Dellisart Lodging LLC			
10800 Alpharetta Hwy			
Ste 208-776 ....Roswell GA 30076	877-606-0591	847-306-0954	376
Delmarva Power			
PO Box 231 ....Wilmington DE 19899	800-898-8042*		782
Cust Svc			
Delmont Laboratories Inc			
715 Harvard Ave PO Box 269 ....Swarthmore PA 19081	800-562-5541	610-543-2747	580
Delo Screw Products			
700 London Rd ....Delaware OH 43015	800-935-9935	740-363-1971	617
Delphi Energy Corp			
333 - 7 Ave SW Ste 2300 ....Calgary AB T2P2Z1	800-430-7207	403-265-6171	532
Delphos Herald Inc			
405 N Main St ....Delphos OH 45833	800-589-6950	419-695-0015	633-8
Delsey Luggage			
6735 Business Pkwy Ste A ....Elkridge MD 21075	800-558-3344	410-796-5655	451
Delta Air Lines Inc			
1030 Delta Blvd ....Atlanta GA 30354	800-221-1212	404-715-2600	25
NYSE: DAL			
Delta Air Lines Inc			
PO Box 20559 ....Atlanta GA 30320	800-352-2737		12
Delta Apparel Inc			
2750 Premiere Pkwy Ste 100 ....Duluth GA 30097	800-285-4456	678-775-6900	155-3
NYSE: DLA			
Delta Centrifugal Corp			
PO Box 1043 ....Temple TX 76503	888-433-3100*	254-773-9055	307
Sales			

	Toll-Free	Phone	Class
Delta Children			
114 W 26th St ....New York NY 10001	800-377-3777		64
Delta College of Arts & Technology			
7380 Exchange Pl ....Baton Rouge LA 70806	800-858-0551	225-928-7770	162
Delta Consolidated Industries Inc			
4800 Krueger Dr ....Jonesboro AR 72401	800-643-0084	870-935-3711	486
Delta Cooling Towers Inc			
PO Box 315 ....Rockaway NJ 07866	800-289-3358	973-586-2201	470
Delta Corporate Services Inc			
129 Littleton Rd ....Parsippany NJ 07054	800-335-8220	973-334-6260	180
Delta Data			
1500 Sixth Ave Ste 1 ....Columbus GA 31901	800-723-8274	706-324-0855	177
Delta Delta Delta Fraternity			
2331 Brookhollow Plaza Dr .....Arlington TX 76006	877-746-7333	817-633-8001	48-16
Delta Dental Insurance Company of Alaska			
PO Box 1809 ....Alpharetta GA 30023	800-521-2651		390-3
Delta Dental of Arizona			
PO Box 43026 ....Phoenix AZ 85080	800-352-6132		390-3
Delta Dental of Arkansas			
1513 Country Club Rd ....Sherwood AR 72120	800-462-5410	501-835-3400	390-3
Delta Dental of Colorado			
4582 S Ulster St Ste 800 ....Denver CO 80237	800-233-0860	303-741-9300	390-3
Delta Dental of Idaho			
555 E Parkcenter Blvd PO Box 2870......Boise ID 83706	800-356-7586	208-489-3580	390-3
Delta Dental of Indiana			
PO Box 30416 ....Lansing MI 48909	800-524-0149		390-3
Delta Dental of Iowa			
9000 Northpark Dr ....Johnston IA 50131	800-544-0718*	515-331-4594	390-3
*Cust Svc			
Delta Dental of Kansas			
1619 N Waterfront Pkwy			
PO Box 789769...............Wichita KS 67278	800-234-3375	316-264-4511	390-3
Delta Dental of Kentucky			
10100 Linn Station Rd ....Louisville KY 40223	800-955-2030*		390-3
*Cust Svc			
Delta Dental of Louisiana			
PO Box 1803 ....Alpharetta GA 30023	800-422-4234		390-3
Delta Dental of Massachusetts			
465 Medford St ....Boston MA 02129	800-872-0500*		390-3
*Cust Svc			
Delta Dental of Michigan			
PO Box 30416 ....Lansing MI 48909	800-524-0149		390-3
Delta Dental of Minnesota			
PO Box 330 ....Minneapolis MN 55440	800-553-9536	651-406-5900	390-3
Delta Dental of Missouri			
PO Box 8690 ....Saint Louis MO 63126	800-335-8266	314-656-3000	390-3
Delta Dental of Montana			
PO Box 1803 ....Alpharetta GA 30023	800-422-4234		390-3
Delta Dental of New Jersey			
1639 State Rt 10 ....Parsippany NJ 07054	800-624-2633	973-285-4000	390-3
Delta Dental of New Mexico			
2500 Louisiana Blvd NE			
Ste 600 ....Albuquerque NM 87110	800-999-0963	505-883-4777	390-3
Delta Dental of New York Inc			
1 Delta Dr ....Mechanicsburg PA 17055	800-932-0783		390-3
Delta Dental of North Carolina			
4242 Six Forks Rd Ste 970...........Raleigh NC 27609	800-587-9514	919-424-1046	390-3
Delta Dental of Ohio			
PO Box 30416 ....Lansing MI 48909	800-524-0149		390-3
Delta Dental of Oklahoma			
16 NW 63rd St ....Oklahoma City OK 73116	800-522-0188	405-607-2100	390-3
Delta Dental of Pennsylvania			
1 Delta Dr ....Mechanicsburg PA 17055	800-932-0783		390-3
Delta Dental of Pennsylvania & Alpha Dental Programs Inc			
PO Box 2105 ....Mechanicsburg PA 17055	800-932-0783		390-3
Delta Dental of Rhode Island			
10 Charles St ....Providence RI 02904	800-598-6684	401-752-6000	390-3
Delta Dental of South Dakota			
720 N Euclid Ave PO Box 1157 ....Pierre SD 57501	800-627-3961	605-224-7345	390-3
Delta Dental of Tennessee			
240 Venture Cir ....Nashville TN 37228	800-223-3104*		390-3
*Cust Svc			
Delta Dental of Virginia			
4818 Starkey Rd ....Roanoke VA 24018	800-237-6060	540-989-8000	390-3
Delta Dental of West Virginia			
PO Box 2105 ....Mechanicsburg PA 17055	800-932-0783		390-3
Delta Dental of Wisconsin			
2801 Hoover Rd PO Box 828 ....Stevens Point WI 54481	800-236-3713	715-344-6087	390-3
Delta Dental of Wyoming			
6234 Yellowstone Rd PO Box 29 ....Cheyenne WY 82009	800-735-3379	307-632-3313	390-3
Delta Downs Racetrack			
2717 Delta Downs Dr ....Vinton LA 70668	800-589-7441		638
Delta Education LLC			
80 NW Blvd ....Nashua NH 03063	800-258-1302	603-889-8899	243
Delta Employees Credit Union			
1025 Virginia Ave ....Atlanta GA 30354	800-544-3328	404-715-4725	219
Delta Gamma			
3250 Riverside Dr Ste A-2 ....Columbus OH 43221	800-644-5414	614-481-8169	48-16
Delta Hotels			
2685 Rue King O ....Sherbrooke QC J1L1C1	800-268-1133	819-822-1989	376
Delta King Riverboat Hotel			
1000 Front St ....Sacramento CA 95814	800-825-5464	916-444-5464	378
Delta M Corp			
1003 Larsen Dr ....Oak Ridge TN 37830	800-922-0083	865-483-1569	406
Delta Medical Center (DMC)			
3000 Getwell Rd ....Memphis TN 38118	877-627-4395		373-3
Delta Medical Systems Inc			
3280 Gateway Rd Ste 200.........Brookfield WI 53045	800-798-7574		473
Delta Natural Gas Co Inc			
3617 Lexington Rd ....Winchester KY 40391	800-262-2012	859-744-6171	782
NASDAQ: DGAS			
Delta Polymers Midwest Inc			
6685 Sterling Dr N ....Sterling Heights MI 48312	800-860-6848	586-795-2900	599
Delta Risk LLC			
106 S St Mary's St Ste 601.........San Antonio TX 78205	888-763-3582	210-293-0707	
Delta Sigma Theta Sorority Inc			
1707 New Hampshire Ave NW ....Washington DC 20009	866-615-6464	202-986-2400	48-16
Delta Star Inc			
270 Industrial Rd ....San Carlos CA 94070	800-892-8673		762
Delta State University			
1003 W Sunflower Rd ....Cleveland MS 38733	800-468-6378	662-846-4020	166
Delta Steel Inc			
7355 Roundhouse Ln ....Houston TX 77078	800-324-0220	713-635-1200	490
Delta T Inc			
8323 Loch Lomond Dr ....Pico Rivera CA 90660	800-928-5828	310-355-0355	608
Delta t Systems Inc			
2171 HWY 175 ....Richfield WI 53076	800-733-4204	262-628-0331	357
Delta Theta Phi			
225 Hillsborough St Ste 432 ....Raleigh NC 27603	800-783-2600		48-16
Delta Unit Arkansas Department of Corrections			
880 E Gaines ....Dermott AR 71638	800-482-1127	870-538-2000	213
Delta Waterfowl			
PO Box 3128 ....Bismarck ND 58502	888-987-3695	701-222-8857	48-3
Delta Western Inc			
420 L St Ste 101 ....Anchorage AK 99501	800-478-2688	907-276-2688	316
Deltacom Inc			
7037 Old Madison Pk ....Huntsville AL 35806	800-239-3000		731
Delta-Montrose Electric Assn			
11925 6300 Rd ....Montrose CO 81401	877-687-3632		
DeltaTRAK Inc			
PO Box 398 ....Pleasanton CA 94566	800-962-6776	925-249-2250	202
Deltec Homes Inc			
69 Bingham Rd ....Asheville NC 28806	800-642-2508		186
Del-Tech Manufacturing Inc			
9703 Penn Rd ....Prince George BC V2N5T6	800-736-7733	250-564-3585	752
Deltrol Fluid Products			
3001 Grant Ave ....Bellwood IL 60104	800-477-9772	708-547-0500	785
Deltronic Corp			
3900 W Segerstrom Ave ....Santa Ana CA 92704	800-451-6922	714-545-5800	491
Deluxe Bldg Systems Inc			
499 W Third St ....Berwick PA 18603	800-843-7372	570-752-5914	106
Deluxe Corp			
3680 Victoria St N ....Shoreview MN 55126	800-328-0304*	651-483-7111	359-3
NYSE: DLX ■ *Cust Svc			
Deluxe Stitcher Company Inc			
3747 Acorn Ln ....Franklin Park IL 60131	800-634-0810	847-455-4400	752
Delyse Inc			
505 Reactor Way ....Reno NV 89502	800-441-6887	775-857-1811	296-9
DEMA (Diving Equipment & Marketing Assn)			
3750 Convoy St Ste 310.........San Diego CA 92111	800-862-3483	858-616-6408	49-4
Demand Metric			
463 King St ....London ON N6B1S8	866-947-7744	519-495-9619	464
Dematic			
507 Plymouth Ave NE ....Grand Rapids MI 49505	877-725-7500*		468
*Cust Svc			
DEMCO (Dixie Electric Membership Corp)			
PO Box 15659 ....Baton Rouge LA 70895	800-262-0221	225-261-1221	245
DEMCO (Dethmers Manufacturing Co)			
4010 320th St ....Boyden IA 51234	800-543-3626	712-725-2311	758
Demco Inc			
4810 Forest Run Rd ....Madison WI 53704	800-356-1200*	608-241-1201	556
*Orders			
DeMesy & Company Ltd			
4514 Cole Ave Ste 808 ....Dallas TX 75205	800-635-9006	214-855-8777	786
Democrat & Chronicle			
55 Exchange Blvd ....Rochester NY 14614	800-790-9565	585-232-7100	528-2
Democrat Printing & Lithographing Company Inc			
6401 Lindsey Rd ....Little Rock AR 72206	800-622-2216		
DEMOCRATIC PARTY OF VIRGINIA			
919 E Main St Ste 2050 ....Richmond VA 23219	800-552-9745	804-644-1966	612-1
DeMolay International			
10200 NW Ambassador Dr ....Kansas City MO 64153	800-336-6529*	816-891-8333	48-15
*Orders			
DeMontrond 888 I- 45 S ....Conroe TX 77304	888-843-6583*	281-443-2500	57
*Sales			
DeMoulin Bros & Company Inc			
1025 S Fourth St ....Greenville IL 62246	800-228-8134	618-664-2000	155-18
Den Hartog Industries Inc			
4010 Hospers Dr S PO Box 425.........Hospers IA 51238	800-342-3408	712-752-8432	604
Denali Advance Integration (DAI)			
17735 NE 65th St Ste 130.........Redmond WA 98052	877-467-8008	425-885-4000	180
Denali Commission			
510 L St Ste 410.........Anchorage AK 99501	888-480-4321	907-271-1414	339-19
Denali State Park			
7278 E Bogard Rd ....Wasilla AK 99654	800-478-6196	907-745-3975	561
Denbury Resources Inc			
5320 Legacy Dr ....Plano TX 75024	800-348-9030*	972-673-2000	532
NYSE: DNR ■ *General			
Dendreon Corp			
1700 Saturn Way ....Seal Beach CA 90740	877-256-4545		85
OTC: DNDNQ			
Denier Electric Co Inc			
10891 SR- 128 ....Harrison OH 45030	800-676-3282	513-738-2641	245
Denim Group Ltd			
1354 N Loop 1604 E Ste 110 ....San Antonio TX 78232	844-572-4400		177
DENIS CIMAF Inc			
211 rue Notre-Dame ....Roxton Falls QC J0H1E0	877-279-2300	450-548-7007	190
Denison University			
100 W College St ....Granville OH 43023	877-336-8648	740-587-6394	166
Den-Mat Corp			
2727 Skyway Dr ....Santa Maria CA 93455	800-433-6628	805-922-8491	228
Dennis K Burke Inc			
284 Eastern Ave ....Chelsea MA 02150	800-289-2875	617-884-7800	447
Dennis Supply Co			
PO Box 3376 ....Sioux City IA 51102	800-352-4618	712-255-7637	661
Dennis Uniform Mfg Company Inc			
135 SE Hawthorne Blvd ....Portland OR 97214	800-854-6951		155-18
Denny's Corp			
203 E Main St ....Spartanburg SC 29319	800-733-6697*	864-597-8000	666
NASDAQ: DENN ■ *Cust Svc			
Denso North America Inc			
9747 Whithorn Dr ....Houston TX 77095	888-821-2300	281-821-3355	146
Dent Wizard International			
4710 Earth City Expy ....Bridgeton MO 63044	800-336-8949		62-4
Dental Economics Magazine			
1421 S Sheridan Rd ....Tulsa OK 74112	800-331-4463		455-16
Dental Lifeline Network			
1800 15th St Ste 100 ....Denver CO 80202	888-471-6334	303-534-5360	48-17

				Toll-Free	Phone	Class
Dental Systems Inc						
PO Box 7331	Baytown	TX	77522	**800-683-2501**		180
Dental Technologies Inc (DTI)						
5601 Arnold Rd	Dublin	CA	94568	**800-229-0936**	925-829-3611	414
DEN-TAL-EZ Group Inc						
2 W Liberty Blvd Ste 160	Malvern	PA	19355	**866-383-4636**	610-725-8004	228
DentalEZ Inc						
2500 Hwy 31 S	Bay Minette	AL	36507	**866-383-4636**	251-937-6781	228
DenTek Oral Care Inc						
307 Excellence Way	Maryville	TN	37801	**800-433-6835**		228
Dentists Insurance Co, The						
1201 K St 17th Fl	Sacramento	CA	95814	**800-733-0633**		390-5
Denton County						
1450 E McKinney	Denton	TX	76209	**800-388-8477**	940-349-2012	337
Denton Record-Chronicle						
314 E Hickory St	Denton	TX	76201	**800-275-1722**	940-387-3811	528-2
Dentsply International Inc Tulsa Dental Div						
5100 E Skelly Dr Ste 300	Tulsa	OK	74135	**800-662-1202**	918-493-6598	228
Dentsply Sirona						
221 W Philadelphia St PO Box 872	York	PA	17405	**800-877-0020**	717-845-7511	228
NASDAQ: XRAY						
Denver Ctr for the Performing Arts						
1101 13th St	Denver	CO	80204	**800-641-1222**	303-893-4000	568
Denver Fire Dept Federal Credit Union (DFDFCU)						
12 Lakeside Ln	Denver	CO	80212	**866-880-7770**	303-228-5300	219
Denver International Airport						
8500 Pena Blvd	Denver	CO	80249	**800-247-2336**	303-342-2000	27
Denver Metro Convention & Visitors Bureau						
1555 California St Ste 300	Denver	CO	80202	**800-480-2010**	303-892-1112	206
Denver Newspaper Agency						
101 W Colfax Ave	Denver	CO	80202	**800-336-7678**	303-954-1010	633-8
Denver Seminary						
6399 S Santa Fe Dr	Littleton	CO	80120	**800-922-3040**	303-761-2482	167-3
Denver Veterans Affairs Medical Ctr						
1055 Clermont St	Denver	CO	80220	**888-336-8262**	303-399-8020	373-8
Denver Wholesale Florists Co						
4800 Dahlia St	Denver	CO	80216	**800-829-8280**	303-399-0970	293
Denver Wire Rope & Supply Inc						
4100 Dahlia St	Denver	CO	80216	**800-873-3697**	303-377-5166	350
Denver7						
123 E Speer Blvd	Denver	CO	80203	**800-824-3463**	303-832-7777	736-23
Department of Agriculture (USDA)						
1400 Independence Ave SW	Washington	DC	20250	**844-433-2774**	202-720-3631	339-1
Department of Education						
400 Maryland Ave SW	Washington	DC	20202	**800-872-5327**	202-401-2000	339-7
Inspector General's Fraud & Abuse Hotline						
400 Maryland Ave SW	Washington	DC	20202	**800-647-8733**		339-7
Department of Health & Human Services (HHS)						
330 Independence Ave SW	Washington	DC	20201	**877-696-6775**	202-619-0150	339-9
Department of Health & Human Services						
Office on Women's Health						
200 Independence Ave SW	Washington	DC	20201	**800-994-9662**	202-690-7650	339-9
Department of Health & Human Services Regional Offices						
Region 7						
601 E 12th St	Kansas City	MO	64106	**800-447-8477**	816-426-2821	339-9
Department of Homeland Security						
Ready Campaign						
500 C St SW	Washington	DC	20472	**800-462-7585**	800-621-3362	339-10
Department of Housing & Urban Development (HUD)						
451 Seventh St SW	Washington	DC	20410	**800-569-4287**	202-708-0685	339-11
Department of Housing & Urban Development Regional Offices						
Boston Regional Office						
Thomas P O'Neill Jr Federal Bldg						
10 Causeway St 3rd Fl	Boston	MA	02222	**800-225-5342**	617-994-8200	339-11
Chicago Regional Office						
Ralph Metcalfe Federal Bldg						
77 W Jackson Blvd	Chicago	IL	60604	**800-955-2232**	312-353-6236	
Mid-Atlantic Region						
100 Penn Sq E	Philadelphia	PA	19107	**800-225-5342**	215-656-0500	339-11
New York City Regional Office						
26 Federal Plz Ste 3541	New York	NY	10278	**800-496-4294**	212-264-8000	339-11
Rocky Mountain Region						
1670 Broadway 25th Fl	Denver	CO	80202	**800-955-2232**	303-672-5440	339-11
Department of Labor (DOL)						
200 Constitution AveNW	Washington	DC	20210	**866-487-2365**		339-14
Job Corps						
200 Constitution Ave NW						
Ste N4463	Washington	DC	20210	**800-733-5627**	202-693-3000	339-14
Department of Labor Regional Offices						
Region 1 - Boston						
JFK Federal Bldg Rm E-260	Boston	MA	02203	**800-347-8029**	866-487-2365	339-14
Region 8 - Denver						
1999 Broadway Ste 1620	Denver	CO	80202	**800-827-5335**	303-844-1286	339-14
Department of the Treasury						
1500 Pennsylvania Ave NW	Washington	DC	20220	**800-359-3898**	202-622-2000	339-17
Department of Veterans Affairs (VA)						
810 Vermont Ave NW	Washington	DC	20420	**800-827-1000***	202-461-7600	339-18
*Cust Svc						
Public & Intergovernmental Affairs Office						
810 Vermont Ave NW	Washington	DC	20420	**800-273-8255**		339-18
DePauw University						
204 E Seminary St	Greencastle	IN	46135	**800-447-2495**	765-658-4006	166
DePauw University West Library						
11 E Larabee St	Greencastle	IN	46135	**800-447-2495**	765-658-4420	433-6
DePelchin Children's Ctr						
4950 Memorial Dr	Houston	TX	77007	**888-730-2335**	713-730-2335	48-6
Dependable Highway Express Inc						
2440 S 48th Ave	Phoenix	AZ	85043	**800-472-2037**	602-278-4401	447
Depobook Reporting Services						
1600 G St Ste 101	Modesto	CA	95354	**800-830-8885**	209-544-6466	443
Deposition Sciences Inc						
3300 Coffey Ln	Santa Rosa	CA	95403	**866-433-7724**	707-573-6700	479
Depression & Bipolar Support Alliance (DBSA)						
730 N Franklin St Ste 501	Chicago	IL	60610	**800-826-3632**	312-642-0049	48-17
DEPTCOR						
163 N Olden Ave	Trenton	NJ	08625	**800-321-6524**		626
Derby Industries LLC						
4451 Robards Ln	Louisville	KY	40218	**800-569-4812**	502-451-7373	798-1

				Toll-Free	Phone	Class
Derma Sciences						
311 Enterprise Dr	Plainsboro	NJ	08536	**800-825-4325**	609-514-4744	473
Dermatology Assoc of Atlanta PC						
5555 Peachtree Dunwoody Rd NE						
Ste 190	Atlanta	GA	30342	**800-233-0706**	404-256-4457	373-7
Dero Bike Racks Inc						
504 Malcolm Ave SE Ste 100	Minneapolis	MN	55414	**888-337-6729**	612-359-0689	61
DeRoyal Industries Inc						
200 DeBusk Ln	Powell	TN	37849	**800-251-9864**	865-938-7828	475
DeRoyal Textiles						
141 E York St	Camden	SC	29020	**800-845-1062**	803-432-2403	740-1
Derr Flooring Company Inc						
525 Davisville Rd						
PO Box 912	Willow Grove	PA	19090	**800-523-3457**	215-657-6300	360
Derrick Publishing Co						
1510 W First St	Oil City	PA	16301	**800-352-1002**	814-676-7444	633-8
Der-Tex Corp 1 Lehner Rd	Saco	ME	04072	**800-669-0364**		740-2
Des Moines						
100 Fourth St	Des Moines	IA	50309	**800-673-4763**	515-288-3336	455-5
Des Moines Area Community College						
Ankeny						
2006 S Ankeny Blvd	Ankeny	IA	50021	**800-362-2127**	515-964-6200	162
Boone 1125 Hancock Dr	Boone	IA	50036	**800-362-2127**	515-432-7203	162
Carroll						
906 N Grant Rd	Carroll	IA	51401	**800-622-3334**	712-792-1755	162
Urban/Des Moines						
1100 Seventh St	Des Moines	IA	50314	**800-622-3334**	515-244-4226	162
Des Moines Independent School District						
901 Walnut St	Des Moines	IA	50309	**800-452-1111**	515-242-7911	681
Des Moines International Airport						
5800 Fleur Dr	Des Moines	IA	50321	**877-686-0029**	515-256-5050	27
Des Moines Register						
715 Locust St	Des Moines	IA	50309	**800-247-5346**	515-284-8000	528-2
Des Plaines Chamber of Commerce & Industry						
1401 E Oakton St	Des Plaines	IL	60018	**800-933-2412**	847-824-4200	139
Des Plaines Journal						
622 Graceland Ave	Des Plaines	IL	60016	**800-719-4881**	847-299-5511	528-4
DES Reprographics						
2450 Scott Blvd Ste 300	Santa Clara	CA	95050	**888-788-1898**	408-970-8551	756
Descartes Systems Group Inc						
120 Randall Dr	Waterloo	ON	N2V1C6	**800-419-8495**	519-746-8110	178-12
TSE: DSG						
Desco Dental Systems LLC						
5005 W Loomis Rd Ste 100	Greenfield	WI	53220	**800-392-7610**	414-281-9192	177
Desco Plumbing & Heating Supply Inc						
65 Worcester Rd	Etobicoke	ON	M9W5N7	**800-564-5146**	416-213-1555	608
Deseret Book Co						
45 W S Temple	Salt Lake City	UT	84101	**800-453-4532**	801-534-1515	633-3
Deseret News						
55 North 300 West						
Ste 500	Salt Lake City	UT	84101	**866-628-4677**	801-204-6100	528-2
Desert Canyon Golf Resort						
1030 Desert Canyon Blvd	Orondo	WA	98843	**800-258-4173**	509-784-1111	665
Desert Financial Credit Union						
148 N 48th St	Phoenix	AZ	85034	**800-456-9171**	602-433-7000	219
Desert Springs Marriott Resort & Spa						
74855 Country Club Dr	Palm Desert	CA	92260	**888-538-9459**	760-341-2211	665
Desert Sun						
750 N Gene Autry Trl	Palm Springs	CA	92263	**800-233-3741**	760-322-8889	528-2
Design Design Inc						
19 La Grave SE	Grand Rapids	MI	49503	**800-334-3348**	866-935-2648	130
Design Homes Inc						
600 N Marquette Rd	Prairie du Chien	WI	53821	**800-627-9443**	608-326-6041	106
Design Institute of San Diego						
8555 Commerce Ave	San Diego	CA	92121	**800-619-4337**	858-566-1200	166
Design It Yourself Gift Baskets LLC						
7999 Hansen Rd Ste 204	Houston	TX	77061	**800-589-7553**	713-944-3440	129
Design News						
225 Wyman St	Waltham	MA	02451	**800-869-6882**	763-746-2792	455-21
Design ProfessionalXL Group						
2959 Salinas Hwy	Monterey	CA	93940	**800-227-4284**	831-649-5522	400
Design Toscano Inc						
1400 Morse Ave	Elk Grove Village	IL	60007	**800-525-5141**		457
Design Within Reach Inc						
711 Canal St 3rd Fl	Stamford	CT	06902	**800-944-2233**	203-614-0600	361
NASDAQ: DWRI						
DESIGNASHIRTCOM						
905 N Scottsdale Rd	Tempe	AZ	85281	**800-594-1206**	480-966-3500	623
Designatronics Inc						
2101 Jericho Tpke	New Hyde Park	NY	11040	**800-345-1144***	800-819-8900	705
*Orders						
Designer Decal Inc						
1120 E First Ave	Spokane	WA	99202	**800-622-6333**	509-535-0267	683
Designing Health Inc						
28410 Witherspoon Pkwy	Valencia	CA	91355	**800-774-7387**	661-257-1705	477
Desire2Learn Corp						
151 Charles St W Ste 400	Kitchener	ON	N2G1H6	**888-772-0325**	519-772-0325	174
Desjardins Securities Inc						
1170 Peel St Ste 300	Montreal	QC	H3B0A9	**866-985-7585**	514-985-7585	400
Desktop Consulting Services						
43311 Joy Rd	Canton	MI	48187	**888-600-2731**		175
DeSoto County Library						
125 N Hillsboro Ave	Arcadia	FL	34266	**800-843-5678**		
DeSoto Parish Chamber of Commerce						
115 N Washington Ave	Mansfield	LA	71052	**800-844-4646**	318-872-1310	139
DeSoto Public Library						
211 E Pleasant Run Rd	Desoto	TX	75115	**800-886-9008**	972-230-9656	433-3
Desoto Sales Inc						
20945 Osborne St	Canoga Park	CA	91304	**800-826-9779**	818-998-0853	350
Despatch Industries Inc						
8860 207th St W	Lakeville	MN	55044	**800-726-0110**	952-469-5424	318
Dessert Innovations Inc						
25-B Enterprise Blvd	Atlanta	GA	30336	**800-359-7351**	404-691-5000	296-2
DESTACO						
15 Corporate Dr	Auburn Hills	MI	48326	**888-337-8226**	248-836-6700	349
Destination Gettysburg						
571 W Middle St	Gettysburg	PA	17325	**800-337-5015**		206
Destination Hotels & Resorts Inc						
10333 E Dry Creek Rd Ste 450	Englewood	CO	80112	**855-893-1011**	303-799-3830	378

	Toll-Free	Phone	Class

Destination Maternity Corp
232 Strawbridge Dr ....Moorestown NJ 08057 — 800-466-6223 — — 157-6
NASDAQ: DEST

Destination Services of Colorado Inc (DSC)
PO Box 3660 ....Avon CO 81620 — 855-866-5290 — 970-476-6565 — 184

Destination toledo
401 Jefferson Ave ....Toledo OH 43604 — 800-243-4667 — 419-321-6404 — 206

Destination XL Group Inc (DXL)
555 Tpke St ....Canton MA 02021 — 855-746-7395
NASDAQ: DXLG

Destiny Industries LLC
250 R W Bryant Rd ....Moultrie GA 31788 — 866-782-6600 — — 503

Destiny Solutions Inc
40 Holly St ....Toronto ON M4S3C3 — 866-403-0500 — 416-480-0500 — 225

Destron Fearing
2805 E 14th St ....Irving TX 75261 — 800-328-0118 — — 643

Detechtion Technologies
1100 Eighth Ave SW Ste 277 ....Calgary AB T2P3T8 — 800-780-9798 — 403-250-9220

Detecto Scale Co
203 E Daugherty St PO Box 151.......Webb City MO 64870 — 800-641-2008 — 417-673-4631 — 680

Detex Corp
302 Detex Dr ....New Braunfels TX 78130 — 800-729-3839 — 830-629-2900 — 688

Dethmers Manufacturing Co (DEMCO)
4010 320th St ....Boyden IA 51234 — 800-543-3626 — 712-725-2311 — 758

Detroit Edge Tool Co
6570 E Nevada St ....Detroit MI 48234 — 800-404-2038 — 313-366-4120 — 491

Detroit Free Press
615 W Lafayette Blvd ....Detroit MI 48226 — 800-395-3300 — 313-222-6400 — 528-2

Detroit Hoist Co
6650 Sterling Dr N ....Sterling Heights MI 48312 — 800-521-9126 — 586-268-2600 — 468

Detroit Lakes Regional Chamber of Commerce
700 Summit Ave ....Detroit Lakes MN 56501 — 800-542-3992 — 218-847-9202 — 139

Detroit Legal News Co
1409 Allen Rd Ste B ....Troy MI 48083 — 800-875-5275 — 248-577-6100 — 633-8

Detroit Metropolitan Convention & Visitors Bureau
211 W Fort St Ste 1000 ....Detroit MI 48226 — 877-424-5554 — 313-202-1800 — 206

Detroit News
615 W Lafayette Blvd ....Detroit MI 48226 — 800-395-3300* — 313-222-2300 — 528-2
*General

Detroit Pump & Mfg Co
450 Fair St Bldg D ....Ferndale MI 48220 — 800-686-1662 — 248-544-4242 — 384

Detroit Quality Brush Mfg
32165 Schoolcraft Rd ....Livonia MI 48150 — 800-722-3037 — 734-525-5660 — 103

Detroit Radiant Product Co
21400 Hoover Rd ....Warren MI 48089 — 800-222-1100 — 586-756-0950 — 318

Detroit Regional Chamber
1 Woodward Ave Ste 1900 ....Detroit MI 48226 — 800-427-5100 — 313-964-4000 — 139

Detroit Stoker Co
1510 E First St ....Monroe MI 48161 — 800-786-5374 — 734-241-9500 — 318

Detroit Symphony Orchestra
3711 Woodward Ave ....Detroit MI 48201 — 800-434-6340 — 313-576-5111 — 569-3

Detroit WMYD TV20
20777 W Ten Mile Rd ....Southfield MI 48034 — 800-825-0770 — 248-827-7777 — 736

Deuel County
408 Fourth St W ....Clear Lake SD 57226 — 800-872-6190 — 605-874-2312 — 337

Deutsche Bank Canada (DB)
199 Bay St Commerce Ct W
Ste 4700 ....Toronto ON M5L1E9 — 800-735-7777 — 416-682-8000 — 70

Devcon Inc
30 Endicott St ....Danvers MA 01923 — 800-626-7226 — 855-489-7262 — 3

Developers Diversified Realty Corp
3300 Enterprise Pkwy ....Beachwood OH 44122 — 877-225-5337 — 216-755-5500 — 651
NYSE: DDR

Development Dimensions International
1225 Washington Pk ....Bridgeville PA 15017 — 800-933-4463* — 412-257-0600 — 193
*Mktg

Development Director's Letter
8204 Fenton St ....Silver Spring MD 20910 — 800-666-6380 — 301-588-6380 — 527-7

Devereux
1291 Stanley Rd NW PO Box 1688.....Kennesaw GA 30156 — 800-342-3357 — 678-303-5233 — 373-1

Devereux Advanced Behavioral Health
8000 Devereux Dr ....Viera FL 32940 — 800-338-3738 — 321-242-9100 — 373-1

Devereux Cleo Wallace
8405 Church Ranch Blvd ....Westminster CO 80021 — 800-456-2536 — 303-466-7391 — 373-1

DevFacto Technologies Inc
2250 Scotia Place Tower 1 10060 Jasper Ave
.............................Edmonton AB T5J3R8 — 877-323-3832 — — 461

deView Electronics USA Inc
1420 Lakeside Pkwy Ste 110 ....Lewisville TX 75057 — 877-433-8439 — 214-222-3332 — 688

Devil's Den Preserve
33 Pent Rd ....Weston CT 06883 — 800-628-6860 — — 50-5

Devil's Head Resort & Convention Ctr
S 6330 Bluff Rd ....Merrimac WI 53561 — 800-472-6670 — 608-493-2251 — 665

Devon Energy Corp
333 West Sheridan Ave ....Oklahoma City OK 73102 — 800-361-3377 — 405-235-3611 — 532
NYSE: DVN

DeVry University
Colorado Springs
1175 Kelly Johnson Blvd
.......................Colorado Springs CO 80920 — 877-784-1997* — 719-632-3000 — 795
*Help Line
Denver
1870 W 122nd Ave ....Westminster CO 80234 — 866-338-7934 — 303-280-7400 — 795
Houston
11125 Equity Dr ....Houston TX 77041 — 866-338-7934 — 713-973-3026 — 795
Long Beach
3880 Kilroy Airport Way ....Long Beach CA 90806 — 866-338-7934 — 562-427-0861 — 795
Long Island City
3020 Thomson Ave ....Long Island city NY 11101 — 866-338-7934 — 718-361-0004 — 795
Phoenix
2149 W Dunlap Ave ....Phoenix AZ 85021 — 866-338-7934* — 602-749-4500 — 795
*Cust Svc
Sherman Oaks
15301 Ventura Blvd
Bldg D-100.................Sherman Oaks CA 91403 — 866-338-7934 — 818-713-8111 — 795

DeVry University North Brunswick
630 US Hwy 1 ....North Brunswick NJ 08902 — 866-338-7934 — 732-729-3960 — 795

Dew Distribution Services Inc
2201 Touhy Ave ....Elk Grove Village IL 60007 — 800-837-3391 — — 645

DeWAL Industries Inc
15 Ray Trainor Dr ....Narragansett RI 02882 — 800-366-8356 — 401-789-9736 — 727

Dewey Services Inc
939 E Union St ....Pasadena CA 91106 — 877-339-3973 — — 573

Dewied International Inc
5010 IH- 10 E ....San Antonio TX 78219 — 800-992-5600 — 210-661-6161 — 296-26

Dewitt Products Co
5860 Plumer Ave ....Detroit MI 48209 — 800-962-8599* — 313-554-0575 — 46
*Cust Svc

DeWitt Wallace Decorative Arts Museum
326 Francis St W ....Williamsburg VA 23185 — 800-447-8679 — — 517

DexCom Inc
6340 Sequence Dr ....San Diego CA 92121 — 888-738-3646 — 858-200-0200 — 85
NASDAQ: DXCM

Dexta Corp 962 Kaiser Rd ....Napa CA 94558 — 800-733-3982 — 707-255-2454 — 228

Dexter & Chaney Inc
9700 Lake City Way NE ....Seattle WA 98115 — 800-875-1400 — 206-364-1400 — 179

Dexter Solutions
3493 Lamar Ave ....Memphis TN 38118 — 800-641-3398 — — 7

Dexter-Russell Inc
44 River St ....Southbridge MA 01550 — 800-343-6042 — 508-765-0201 — 222

D&F Travel Inc
331 Alberta Dr Ste 103 ....Amherst NY 14226 — 800-335-1982 — 716-835-9227 — 767

DFC (Duke Diet & Fitness Ctr)
501 Douglas St ....Durham NC 27705 — 800-235-3853 — — 702

DFDFCU (Denver Fire Dept Federal Credit Union)
12 Lakeside Ln ....Denver CO 80212 — 866-880-7770 — 303-228-5300 — 219

DFI 2404 51 Ave NW ....Edmonton AB T6P0E4 — 877-334-7453 — — 532

DFS 500 Main St ....Groton MA 01471 — 800-225-9528* — — 110
*General

DFT Communications
38 Temple St ....Fredonia NY 14063 — 877-653-3100 — 716-673-3000 — 386

DFW (Dallas-Fort Worth International Airport)
2400 Aviation Dr PO Box 619428.........Dallas TX 75261 — 800-252-7522 — 972-973-3112 — 27

DGA-PAC
7920 W Sunset Blvd ....Los Angeles CA 90046 — 800-421-4173 — 310-289-2000 — 611

DGT Associates
1071 Worcester Rd ....Framingham MA 01701 — 800-696-2874 — 508-879-0030 — 261

DH (Dominican Hospital)
1555 Soquel Dr ....Santa Cruz CA 95065 — 866-466-1401 — 831-462-7700 — 373-3

DH (Danbury Hospital)
24 Hospital Ave ....Danbury CT 06810 — 800-516-3658 — 203-739-7000 — 373-3

Dh Web Inc
11377 Robinwood Dr Ste D ....Hagerstown MD 21742 — 877-567-6599 — 301-733-7672 — 177

Dharma Trading Co
1604 Fourth St ....San Rafael CA 94901 — 800-542-5227 — 415-456-1211 — 707

DHI Mortgage Co Ltd
10700 Pecan Park Blvd Ste 450 ....Austin TX 78750 — 800-315-8434 — 512-502-0545 — 217

DHL Global Forwarding
6200 Edwards Blvd ....Mississauga ON L5T2V7 — 855-345-7447 — 289-562-6500 — 311

DHMC (Davis Hospital & Medical Ctr)
1600 W Antelope Dr ....Layton UT 84041 — 877-898-6080 — 801-807-1000 — 373-3

Diabetes Forecast Magazine
1701 N Beauregard St ....Alexandria VA 22311 — 800-676-4065 — 703-549-1500 — 455-13

Diabetes Research Institute
1450 NW Tenth Ave ....Miami FL 33136 — 800-321-3437 — 954-964-4040 — 664

Diablo Valley College
321 Golf Club Rd ....Pleasant Hill CA 94523 — 800-227-1060 — 925-685-1230 — 162

Diagnostic Laboratory of Oklahoma LLC
225 N East 97th St ....Oklahoma City OK 73114 — 800-891-2917 — 405-608-6100 — 414

Diagraph
2538 Wisconsin Ave ....Downers Grove IL 60515 — 800-626-3464 — 630-968-0646 — 465

Dial800
10940 Wilshire Blvd 17th Fl........Los Angeles CA 90024 — 800-700-1987 — — 224

Dialink Corp
1660 S Amphlett Blvd Ste 340 ....San Mateo CA 94402 — 800-896-3425 — — 386

Dialog One Llc
2380 Wycliff St Ste 200 ....Saint Paul MN 55114 — 877-300-5326 — 651-379-8600

Dialogic Inc
1504 Mccarthy Blvd ....Milpitas CA 95035 — 800-755-4444 — 408-750-9400 — 180

Diamond Aircraft Industries Inc
1560 Crumlin Sideroad ....London ON N5V1S2 — 888-359-3220 — 519-457-4000 — 20

Diamond Attachments LLC
2801A S Mississippi ....Atoka OK 74525 — 800-445-1917 — 580-889-6202 — 786

Diamond Chain Co
402 Kentucky Ave ....Indianapolis IN 46225 — 800-872-4246* — 317-638-6431 — 616
*Cust Svc

Diamond Coach Corp
2300 W Fourth St ....Oswego KS 67356 — 800-442-4645 — 620-795-2191 — 513

Diamond Comic Distributors Inc (DCD)
10150 York Rd Ste 300............Hunt Valley MD 21030 — 800-452-6642 — 443-318-8001 — 633-5

Diamond Council of America (DCA)
3212 W End Ave Ste 202 ....Nashville TN 37203 — 877-283-5669 — 615-385-5301 — 49-4

Diamond Drugs Inc
645 Kolter Dr ....Indiana PA 15701 — 800-882-6337 — 724-349-1111 — 231

Diamond Equipment Inc
1060 E Diamond Ave ....Evansville IN 47711 — 800-258-4428 — 812-425-4428 — 357

Diamond H2O
N1022 Quality Dr ....Greenville WI 54942 — 800-236-8931 — 920-757-5440 — 104

Diamond Manufacturing Co
243 West Eighth St PO Box 4174 .....Wyoming PA 18644 — 800-233-9601 — — 486

Diamond Offshore Drilling Inc
15415 Katy Fwy ....Houston TX 77094 — 800-848-1980 — 281-492-5300 — 536
NYSE: DO

Diamond Oil Well Drilling Company Inc
15415 Katy Fwy Ste 100...............Houston TX 77094 — 800-848-1980 — 281-492-5300 — 535

Diamond Packaging Company Inc
111 Commerce Dr PO Box 23620........Rochester NY 14692 — 800-333-4079 — 585-334-8030 — 101

Diamond Perforated Metals Inc
7300 W Sunnyview Ave ....Visalia CA 93291 — 800-642-4334 — 559-651-1889 — 486

Diamond Plastics Corp
1212 Johnstown Rd
PO Box 1608..................Grand Island NE 68802 — 800-782-7473 — 308-384-4400 — 592

Diamond Products Inc
333 Prospect ....Elyria OH 44035 — 800-321-5336 — — 1

Diamond Saw Works Inc
12290 Olean Rd ....Chaffee NY 14030 — 800-828-1180 — 716-496-7417 — 678

	Toll-Free	Phone	Class
Diamond Services Corp			
503 S DeGravelle Rd ....Amelia LA 70340	**800-879-1162**	985-631-2187	535
Diamond Tool & Die Inc			
508 29th Ave ....Oakland CA 94601	**800-227-1084**	510-534-7050	752
Diamond Tour			
202 Lucas St Unit A ....Sycamore IL 60178	**800-826-5340**	815-787-2649	707
Diamond V			
2525 60th Ave SW			
PO Box 74570. ....Cedar Rapids IA 52404	**800-373-7234**	319-366-0745	445
Diamond Z			
11299 Bass Ln ....Caldwell ID 83605	**800-949-2383**	208-585-3031	295
DiamondJacks Casino Resort			
711 Diamond Jacks Blvd ....Bossier City LA 71111	**866-552-9629**	318-678-7777	133
Dian Fossey Gorilla Fund International			
800 Cherokee Ave SE ....Atlanta GA 30315	**800-851-0203**	404-624-5881	48-3
Diane Von Furstenberg			
440 W 14th St ....New York NY 10014	**888-472-2383**	212-741-6607	277
DIANON Systems Inc			
1 Forest Pkwy ....Shelton CT 06484	**800-328-2666**	203-926-7100	417
DiaSorin Inc			
1951 NW Ave ....Stillwater MN 55082	**855-677-0600**	651-439-9710	231
DiaSorin Molecular LLC			
11331 Vly View St ....Cypress CA 90630	**800-838-4548**	562-240-6500	417
DiAZiT Company Inc			
8105 Diazit Dr ....Wake Forest NC 27587	**800-334-6641***	919-556-5188	697
*Cust Svc			
Dicalite Management Group Inc			
1 Bala Ave Ste 310 ....Bala Cynwyd PA 19004	**866-728-3303**	610-660-8808	498
DiCarlo Distributors Inc			
1630 N Ocean Ave ....Holtsville NY 11742	**800-342-2756**	631-758-6000	297-8
Dice Inc			
4101 NW Urbandale Dr ....Urbandale IA 50322	**877-386-3323**	515-280-1144	260
Dicentra			
603-7 St Thomas St ....Toronto ON M5S2B7	**866-647-3279**	416-361-3400	193
Dick Blick Co			
PO Box 1267 ....Galesburg IL 61402	**800-447-8192***	309-343-6181	45
*Orders			
Dick Brantmeier Ford Inc			
3624 Kohler Memorial Dr ....Sheboygan WI 53082	**800-498-6111**	920-458-6111	57
Dick Gores Rv World			
14590 Duval Pl W ....Jacksonville FL 32218	**800-635-7008**	904-741-5100	513
Dick Lavy Trucking Inc			
8848 State Rt 121 ....Bradford OH 45308	**800-345-5289**	937-448-2104	775
Dick Masheter Ford Inc			
1090 S Hamilton Rd ....Columbus OH 43227	**888-839-9646**		57
Dick's Sporting Goods Inc			
345 Court St ....Coraopolis PA 15108	**877-846-9997**		
Dicke Safety Products			
1201 Warren Ave ....Downers Grove IL 60515	**877-891-0050**	630-969-0050	359-3
Dickey Transport			
401 E Fourth St ....Packwood IA 52580	**800-247-1081**		575
Dickinson Brands Inc			
31 E High St ....East Hampton CT 06424	**888-860-2279**	860-267-2279	578
Dickinson College			
PO Box 1773 ....Carlisle PA 17013	**800-644-1773**	717-243-5121	166
Dickinson College Waidner-Spahr Library			
PO Box 1773 ....Carlisle PA 17013	**800-543-3809**	717-245-1397	433-6
Dickinson Convention & Visitors Bureau			
72 E Museum Dr ....Dickinson ND 58601	**800-279-7391**	701-483-4988	206
Dickinson Homes Inc			
404 N Stephenson Ave Hwy US-2			
PO Box 2245. ....Iron Mountain MI 49801	**800-438-4687**	906-774-2186	106
Dickinson State University			
291 Campus Dr ....Dickinson ND 58601	**800-279-4295**	701-483-2507	166
Dickson Co			
930 S Westwood Ave ....Addison IL 60101	**800-757-3747**	630-543-3747	201
Didax Inc 395 Main St ....Rowley MA 01969	**800-458-0024**		243
Die Services International			
45000 Van Born Rd ....Belleville MI 48111	**800-555-1212**	734-699-3400	752
Diebold Nixdorf Inc			
5995 Mayfair Rd ....North Canton OH 44720	**800-999-3600**	330-490-4000	796
NYSE: DBD			
Dielectric Communications Inc			
22 Tower Rd ....Raymond ME 04071	**800-341-9678**		643
Dielectrics Industries Inc			
300 Burnett Rd ....Chicopee MA 01020	**800-472-7286**	413-594-8111	596
Diesel Injection Service Company Inc			
4710 Allmond Ave ....Louisville KY 40209	**877-361-2531**		
Dieterich-Post Co			
616 Monterey Pass Rd ....Monterey Park CA 91754	**800-955-3729**		112
Dietz & Watson Inc			
5701 Tacony St ....Philadelphia PA 19135	**800-333-1974**	215-831-9000	296-26
Diffenbaugh Inc			
6865 Airport Dr ....Riverside CA 92504	**800-394-5334**	951-351-6865	186
Dig Corp			
1210 Activity Dr ....Vista CA 92081	**800-322-9146**	760-727-0914	273
Digestive Care Inc			
1120 Win Dr ....Bethlehem PA 18017	**877-882-5950**		231
Digi International Inc			
11001 Bren Rd E ....Minnetonka MN 55343	**877-912-3444**	952-912-3444	176
NASDAQ: DGII			
Digi-Key Corp			
701 Brooks Ave S ....Thief River Falls MN 56701	**800-344-4539**	218-681-6674	246
Digimap Data Services Inc			
40 Kodiak Cres Unit 13. ....Toronto ON M3J3G5	**877-344-4627**		226
Digimarc Corp			
9405 SW Gemini Dr ....Beaverton OR 97008	**800-344-4627**	503-469-4800	178-12
NASDAQ: DMRC			
DIGIOP			
9340 Priority Way West Dr ....Indianapolis IN 46240	**800-968-3606**		689
Digipen Institute of Technology			
9931 Willows Rd NE ....Redmond WA 98052	**866-478-5236**	425-558-0299	166
Digirad Corp			
13100 Gregg St Ste A ....Poway CA 92064	**800-947-6134**	858-726-1600	381
NASDAQ: DRAD			
Digiscribe International LLC			
150 Clearbrook Rd Ste 125. ....Elmsford NY 10523	**800-686-7577**		226
Digistream Investigation			
417 Mace Blvd ....Davis CA 95618	**800-747-4329**		689

	Toll-Free	Phone	Class
Digital Air Strike Co			
6991 E Camelback Rd Ste B111.......Scottsdale AZ 85251	**888-713-8958**		365
Digital ChoreoGraphics			
PO Box 8268 ....Newport Beach CA 92658	**800-548-1969**	949-548-1969	177
Digital Design Inc			
67 Sand Pk Rd ....Cedar Grove NJ 07009	**800-967-7746**	973-857-9500	173-6
Digital Employees' Federal Credit Union			
220 Donald Lynch Blvd ....Marlborough MA 01752	**800-328-8797**	508-263-6700	219
Digital Health Canada			
1100 - 151 Yonge St ....Toronto ON M5C2W7	**844-220-3468**	647-775-8555	138
Digital Intelligence Systems Corp (DISYS)			
8270 Greensboro Dr Ste 1000 ....McLean VA 22102	**855-765-8553**	703-752-7900	
Digital I-Ollc			
1424 30th St ....San Diego CA 92154	**866-423-4433**	619-423-4433	177
Digital Machining Systems LLC			
929 Ridge Rd ....Duson LA 70529	**800-530-8945**	337-984-6013	452
Digital Measures			
301 N Broadway 4th Fl ....Milwaukee WI 53202	**866-348-5677**		180
Digital Monitoring Products Inc			
2500 N Partnership Blvd ....Springfield MO 65803	**800-641-4282**	417-831-9362	664
Digital Peripheral Solutions Inc			
8015 E Crystal Dr ....Anaheim CA 92807	**877-998-3440**		173-8
Digital Photographer Magazine			
12121 Wilshire Blvd 12th Fl........Los Angeles CA 90025	**800-537-4619**	310-820-1500	455-14
Digital Power Corp			
41324 Christy St ....Fremont CA 94538	**866-344-7697**	510-353-4023	253
Digital River Inc			
10380 Bren Rd W ....Minnetonka MN 55343	**800-598-7450**		39
NASDAQ: DRIV			
Digital Room Inc			
8000 Haskell Ave ....Van Nuys CA 91406	**866-266-5047**		623
Digital Security Controls (DSC)			
3301 Langstaff Rd ....Concord ON L4K4L2	**888-888-7838**	905-760-3000	688
Digital Storage Inc			
7611 Green Meadows Dr . Lewis Center OH 43035	**800-232-3475**	740-548-7179	174
Digital Street Inc			
69550 Hwy 111 Ste 201 . Rancho Mirage CA 92270	**866-464-5100**		461
Digital Traffic Systems Inc			
8401 Jefferson St NE Ste A.........Albuquerque NM 87113	**855-328-2487**	505-881-4470	
Digital Video Services			
401 Hall St SW Ste 489.........Grand Rapids MI 49503	**800-747-8273**	616-975-9911	240
Digital Watchdog Inc			
5436 W Crenshaw St ....Tampa FL 33634	**866-446-3595**	813-888-9555	689
DigitalWork Inc			
14300 N Northsight Blvd			
Ste 206 ....Scottsdale AZ 85260	**877-496-7571**		39
Digitek Software Inc			
650 Radio Dr 43035 ....Lewis Center OH 43035	**888-764-8845**		
Digi-Trax			
650 Heathrow Dr ....Lincolnshire IL 60069	**800-356-6126**	847-613-2100	350
DignityUSA Inc			
PO Box 376 ....Medford MA 02155	**800-877-8797**	202-861-0017	48-21
DII (Doucette Industries Inc)			
20 Leigh Dr ....York PA 17406	**800-445-7511**	717-845-8746	14
Dillard's Inc			
1600 Cantrell Rd ....Little Rock AR 72201	**800-643-8274**	501-376-5200	229
NYSE: DDS			
Dillon Aero Inc			
8009 E Dillons Way ....Scottsdale AZ 85260	**800-881-4231**	480-333-5450	
Dilmar Oil Company Inc			
1951 W Darlington St			
PO Box 5629. ....Florence SC 29501	**800-922-5823**		775
Dimco Steel Inc			
3901 S Lamar St ....Dallas TX 75215	**877-428-8336**	214-428-8336	682
Dime Bank, The			
820 Church St PO Box 509.........Honesdale PA 18431	**888-469-3463**	570-253-1902	70
Dime Community Bancshares Inc			
209 Havemeyer St ....Brooklyn NY 11211	**800-321-3463**	718-782-6200	359-2
NASDAQ: DCOM			
Dimension Consulting Inc			
501 W Broadway ....San Diego CA 92101	**855-222-6444**	703-636-0933	196
Dinah's Garden Hotel			
4261 El Camino Real ....Palo Alto CA 94306	**800-227-8220**	650-493-2844	378
Diners Club International			
8430 W Bryn Mawr Ave ....Chicago IL 60631	**800-234-6377**	773-380-5160	215
Dings Co			
4740 W Electric Ave ....Milwaukee WI 53219	**800-494-1918**	414-672-7830	385
Dinkel's Bakery			
3329 N Lincoln Ave ....Chicago IL 60657	**800-822-8817***	773-281-7300	296-1
*Orders			
Dinkes & Schwitzer			
820 Second Ave 1st Fl ....New York NY 10017	**800-933-1212**	212-683-3800	427
Dinklage Feedyards			
PO Box 274 ....Sidney NE 69162	**888-343-5940**	308-254-5940	10-1
Dino Software Corp			
PO Box 7105 ....Alexandria VA 22307	**800-480-3466**	703-768-2610	177
Dino's Trucking Inc			
9615 Continental Indus Dr ....Saint Louis MO 63123	**800-771-7805**	314-631-3001	775
Dinova LLC			
6455 E Johns Crossing			
Ste 220 ....Johns Creek GA 30097	**888-346-6828**		392
Diocese of Rochester			
1150 Buffalo Rd ....Roch NY 14624	**800-388-7177**	585-328-3210	48-20
Diocese of St Augustine Inc			
11625 Old St Augustine ....Jacksonville FL 32258	**800-775-4659**	904-262-3200	48-20
Diocese of Steubenville Catholic Charities			
PO Box 969 ....Steubenville OH 43952	**800-339-7890**	740-282-3631	633-8
Dipert Travel & Transportation Ltd			
PO Box 580 ....Arlington TX 76004	**800-433-5335**		755
Dircks Moving Services Inc			
4340 W Mohave St ....Phoenix AZ 85043	**800-523-5038**	602-267-9401	775
Direct Connection Printing & Mailing			
1968 Yeager Ave ....La Verne CA 91750	**800-420-9937**	909-392-2334	623
Direct Edge Media			
2900 E White Star Ave ....Anaheim CA 92806	**800-556-5576**	714-221-8686	343
Direct Holdings Americas Inc			
8280 Willow Oaks Corporate Dr ....Fairfax VA 22031	**800-950-7887**		96
Direct Marketing Assn Inc (DMA)			
1120 Ave of the Americas ....New York NY 10036	**855-422-0749**	212-768-7277	49-18

Alphabetical Section

Name / Address	Toll-Free	Phone	Class
Direct Online Marketing 4727 Jacob St ... Wheeling WV 26003	800-979-3177	304-214-4850	225
Direct Relief International 6100 Wallace Becknell Rd ... Santa Barbara CA 93117	800-676-1638	805-964-4767	48-5
Direct Response Insurance Administrative Services (DRIASI) 7930 Century Blvd ... Chanhassen MN 55317	800-688-0760		
Direct Source Inc 8176 Mallory Ct ... Chanhassen MN 55317	800-934-8055	952-934-8000	178-5
Direct Sports Inc 1720 Curve Rd ... Pearisburg VA 24134	800-456-0072		707
Direct Travel 95 New Jersey 17 ... Paramus NJ 07652	800-366-2496	201-847-9000	766
DirectBuy Inc 8450 Broadway ... Merrillville IN 46410	800-320-3462	219-736-1100	310
Directec Corp 908 Lily Creek Rd Ste 101 ... Louisville KY 40243	800-588-7800	502-357-5000	196
DirectMailcom 5351 Ketch Rd ... Prince Frederick MD 20678	866-284-5816	301-855-1700	5
Directors Guild of America 7920 W Sunset Blvd ... Los Angeles CA 90046	800-421-4173	310-289-2000	413
Directory One Inc 9135 Katy Fwy Ste 204 ... Houston TX 77024	800-477-1324	713-465-0051	225
DIRECTV Inc 2230 E Imperial Hwy ... El Segundo CA 90245 *Cust Svc	800-531-5000*		116
DirectWest 355 Longman Crescent ... Regina SK S4W1A1	800-667-8201	306-777-0333	225
Dirks Group, The 3802 Hummingbird Rd ... Wausau WI 54401	800-866-1486	715-848-9865	180
Dirksen Screw Products Co 14490 23 Mile Rd Shelby ... Township MI 48315	800-732-5569	586-247-5400	617
Dirxion LLC 1859 Bowles Ave Ste 100 ... Fenton MO 63026	888-391-0202	636-717-2300	174
DIS Corp 1315 Cornwall Ave ... Bellingham WA 98225 *Cust Svc	800-426-8870*	360-733-7610	178-10
Disability Rights Ctr Inc 18 Low Ave ... Concord NH 03301	800-834-1721	603-228-0432	48-17
Disabled & Alone/Life Services for the Handicapped 1440 Broadway 23rd Fl ... New York NY 10018	800-995-0066	212-532-6740	48-17
Disabled American Veterans (DAV) 3725 Alexandria Pk ... Cold Spring KY 41076	877-426-2838	859-441-7300	48-19
Disabled Sports USA (DS/USA) 451 Hungerford Dr Ste 100 ... Rockville MD 20850	800-543-2754	301-217-0960	48-22
DISC (Document Imaging Systems Corp) 1523 Fenpark Dr ... Fenton MO 63026	800-710-3472		
Disc Makers 7905 N Rt 130 ... Pennsauken NJ 08110	800-468-9353		173-8
Discount Car & Truck Rentals Ltd 720 Arrow Rd ... North York ON M9M2M1	866-742-5968	416-744-7942	126
Discount Drug Mart Inc 211 Commerce Dr ... Medina OH 44256	800-833-6278	330-725-2340	237
Discount Labels Inc 4115 Profit Ct ... New Albany IN 47150	800-995-9500		412
Discount RampsCom LLC 760 S Indiana Ave ... West Bend WI 53095	888-651-3431		478
Discount School Supplies 2 Lower Ragsdale Rd Ste 125 ... Monterey CA 93940	800-919-5238		756
DiscountMugscom 12610 NW 115th Ave ... Medley FL 33178	800-569-1980		686
Discover Bank PO Box 30416 ... Salt Lake City UT 84130	800-347-7000	302-323-7810	70
Discover Communications Inc 30 Victoria Crescent ... Brampton ON L6T1E4	888-456-8989	905-455-5600	224
Discover Group Inc 2741 W 23rd St ... Brooklyn NY 11224	866-456-6555	718-456-4500	531
Discover Jamestown North Dakota 404 Louis L'Amour Ln ... Jamestown ND 58401	800-222-4766	701-251-9145	206
Discover Klamath 205 Riverside Dr Ste B ... Klamath Falls OR 97601	800-445-6728	541-882-1501	206
Discover The Palm Beaches 1555 Palm Beach Lakes Blvd Ste 800 ... West Palm Beach FL 33401	800-554-7256	561-233-3000	206
Discovery Communications Inc 1 Discovery Pl ... Silver Spring MD 20910 *NASDAQ: DISCA*	877-324-5850	240-662-2000	735
Discovery Ctr (TDC) 1944 N Winery Ave ... Fresno CA 93703	800-946-3039	559-251-5533	518
Discovery Ctr of Springfield 438 E St Louis St ... Springfield MO 65806	888-636-4395	417-862-9910	518
Discovery Place 301 N Tryon St ... Charlotte NC 28202	800-935-0553	704-372-6261	518
Disguise 12120 Kear Pl ... Poway CA 92064	877-875-2557	858-391-3600	155-6
DISH Network LLC 9601 S Meridian Blvd ... Englewood CO 80112 *NASDAQ: DISH*	800-823-4929		116
Disney Consumer Products 500 S Buena Vista St ... Burbank CA 91521 *PR	855-553-4763*	818-560-1000	633-9
Disney Vacation Club 1390 Celebration Blvd ... Celebration FL 34747	800-500-3990	407-566-3100	748
Disney's California Adventure 1313 S Disneyland Dr ... Anaheim CA 92802	800-225-2024	714-781-7290	32
Disney/Little Blue State Park Hwy 28 E ... Disney OK 74340	800-622-6317	918-435-8066	561
Dispensing Dynamics International 1020 Bixby Dr ... City of Industry CA 91745	800-888-3698	626-961-3691	606
Display Smart LLC 801 W 27th Terr ... Lawrence KS 66046	888-843-1870	785-843-1869	233
Display Technologies LLC 1111 Marcus Ave Ste M68 ... Lake Success NY 11042	800-424-4220		233
Dissolve Inc 425 78 Ave SW ... Calgary AB T2V5K5	800-518-6748		224
Disston Precision Inc 6795 State Rd ... Philadelphia PA 19135 *Cust Svc	800-238-1007*	215-338-1200	678
Distillata Co 1608 E 24th St ... Cleveland OH 44114 *Cust Svc	800-999-2906*	216-771-2900	800
Distinctive Dental Studio Ltd Inc 1504 Wall St ... Naperville IL 60563	800-552-7890		414
Distinctive Designs International Inc 120 Sibley Dr ... Russellville AL 35654	800-243-4787		293
Distinguished Programs Group LLC, The 1180 Ave Of The Americas 16th Fl ... New York NY 10036	888-355-4626	212-297-3100	389
Distribution Center Management (DCM) 712 Main St Ste 187B ... Boonton NJ 07005	800-232-4317	973-265-2300	527-2
District of Columbia *Convention & Tourism Corp* 901 Seventh St NW 4th Fl ... Washington DC 20001	800-422-8644	202-789-7000	338-9
Tuition Assistance Grant Program 810 First St NE ... Washington DC 20001	877-485-6751	202-727-2824	721
District of Columbia Bar, The 1101 K St NW Ste 200 ... Washington DC 20005	877-333-2227	202-737-4700	72
DISYS (Digital Intelligence Systems Corp) 8270 Greensboro Dr Ste 1000 ... McLean VA 22102	855-765-8553	703-752-7900	
DIT-MCO International Corp 5612 Brighton Terr ... Kansas City MO 64130	800-821-3487	816-444-9700	248
Diva at the Met 645 Howe St ... Vancouver BC V6C2Y9	800-667-2300	604-602-7788	667
Divers Academy International 1500 Liberty Pl ... Erial NJ 08081	800-238-3483		795
Diverse Power Inc 1400 S Davis Rd ... LaGrange GA 30241	800-845-8362	706-845-2000	245
Diversified Chemical Technologies Inc (DCT) 15477 Woodrow Wilson St ... Detroit MI 48238	800-243-1424	313-867-5444	145
Diversified Electronics Co Inc PO Box 566 ... Forest Park GA 30298	800-646-7278	404-361-4840	246
Diversified Funding Services Inc 125 Habersham Dr 2nd Fl ... Fayetteville GA 30214	888-603-0055	770-603-0055	272
Diversified Labeling Solutions 1285 Hamilton Pkwy ... Itasca IL 60143	800-397-3013	630-625-1225	548-1
Diversified Lenders Inc 5607 S Ave Q ... Lubbock TX 79412	800-288-3024	806-795-7782	194
Diversified Search Cos 2005 Market St 33rd Fl ... Philadelphia PA 19103	800-423-3932	215-732-6666	266
Diversified Transfer & Storage Inc (DTS) 1640 Monad Rd ... Billings MT 59101	800-755-5855	406-245-4695	775
Diversitec LLC 14321 Sommerville Ct ... Midlothian VA 23113	800-229-6772	804-379-6772	317
DiversiTech Corp 6650 Sugarloaf Pkwy Ste 100 ... Duluth GA 30097	800-995-2222	678-542-3600	14
Divine Providence Hospital 1100 Grampian Blvd ... Williamsport PA 17701	800-433-0816	570-326-8000	373-3
Divine Word College 102 Jacoby Dr SW ... Epworth IA 52045	800-553-3321	563-876-3353	166
Diving Equipment & Marketing Assn (DEMA) 3750 Convoy St Ste 310 ... San Diego CA 92111	800-862-3483	858-616-6408	49-4
Divisions Maintenance Group 1 RiverFrnt Pl Ste 510 ... Newport KY 41071	877-448-9730		192
Dixie Construction Products Inc 970 Huff Rd NW ... Atlanta GA 30318	800-992-1180	404-351-1100	350
Dixie Electric Co-op 9100 Atlanta Hwy ... Montgomery AL 36117	888-349-4332	334-288-1163	245
Dixie Electric Membership Corp (DEMCO) PO Box 15659 ... Baton Rouge LA 70895	800-262-0221	225-261-1221	245
Dixie Electric Power Assn 1863 US-184 PO Box 88 ... Laurel MS 39443	888-465-9209	601-425-2535	245
Dixie Group Inc 475 Reed Rd PO Box 2007 ... Dalton GA 30722 *NASDAQ: DXYN*	800-289-4811	423-510-7000	131
Dixie Gun Works Inc 1412 W Reelfoot Ave ... Union City TN 38261 *Orders	800-238-6785*	731-885-0561	707
Dixie Industries 3510 N Orchard Knob Ave ... Chattanooga TN 37406	800-933-4943	423-698-3323	349
Dixie Pipe Sales Inc 2407 Broiller ... Houston TX 77054	800-733-3494	713-796-2021	488
Dixie Power 71 E Hwy 56 ... Beryl UT 84714	800-874-0904	435-439-5311	245
Dixie State University 225 S 700 E ... Saint George UT 84770	855-628-8140	435-652-7500	166
Dixie Store Fixtures & Sales Company Inc 2425 First Ave N ... Birmingham AL 35203	800-323-4943	205-322-2442	286
Dixon Ticonderoga Co 195 International Pkwy ... Heathrow FL 32746	800-824-9430		567
Dixon Valve & Coupling Company Inc 800 High St ... Chestertown MD 21620	877-963-4966	410-778-2000	785
Dize Company Inc, The 1512 S Main St ... Winston-Salem NC 27127	800-583-8243	336-722-5181	349
DJ & A PC 3203 S Russell St ... Missoula MT 59801	800-398-3522	406-721-4320	256
DJ Jacobetti Home for Veterans 425 Fisher St ... Marquette MI 49855	800-433-6760	906-226-3576	788
DJ Orthopedics Inc 1430 Decision St ... Vista CA 92081	800-321-9549	760-727-1280	475
Djg Investigative Services Inc 19501 W Catawba Ave Ste 220 ... Cornelius NC 28031	866-597-7457	704-536-8025	689
Dk Security 5160 falcon view ave SE ... Grand rapids MI 49512	800-535-0646	616-656-0123	
D&L Art Glass Supply 1440 W 52nd Ave ... Denver CO 80221	800-525-0940	303-449-8737	44
DL Geary Brewing Company Inc 38 Evergreen Dr ... Portland ME 04103	800-452-4633	207-878-2337	102
DLA (Defense Logistics Agency) 8725 John J Kingman Rd ... Fort Belvoir VA 22060	877-352-2255		339-3
D-Link Systems Inc 17595 Mt Herrmann St ... Fountain Valley CA 92708	800-326-1688		176
DLL 1111 Old Eagle School Rd ... Wayne PA 19087	800-873-2474	610-386-5000	216
Dlt Solutions 13861 Sunrise Valley Dr Ste 400 ... Herndon VA 20171	800-262-4358	703-709-7172	174
DM Camp & Sons 31798 Merced Ave ... Bakersfield CA 93308	800-826-0200	661-399-5511	10-3
DM Figley Company Inc 10 Kelly Ct ... Menlo Park CA 94025	800-292-9919	650-329-8700	146

Name / Address	City	State	Zip	Toll-Free	Phone	Class
DM Transportation Management Services Inc						
740 Reading Ave	Boyertown	PA	19512	**888-399-0162**	610-367-0162	194
DMA (Direct Marketing Assn Inc)						
1120 Ave of the Americas	New York	NY	10036	**855-422-0749**	212-768-7277	49-18
DMC (Delta Medical Center)						
3000 Getwell Rd	Memphis	TN	38118	**877-627-4395**		373-3
DMC Sinai-Grace Hospital						
6071 W Outer Dr	Detroit	MI	48235	**888-362-2500**	313-966-3300	373-3
D-M-E Co						
29111 Stephenson Hwy	Madison Heights	MI	48071	**800-626-6653**	248-398-6000	600
DME-Direct Inc						
28486 Westinghouse Pl Ste 120	Valencia	CA	91355	**877-721-7701**		194
DMI (Dairy Management Inc)						
10255 W Higgins Rd Ste 900	Rosemont	IL	60018	**800-853-2479**		48-2
DMS Facility Services						
1040 Arroyo Dr	South Pasadena	CA	91030	**800-443-8677**	626-305-8500	104
DMS Laboratories Inc						
2 Darts Mill Rd	Flemington	NJ	08822	**800-567-4367**	908-782-3353	580
DMS Pharmaceutical Group Inc						
810 Busse Hwy	Park Ridge	IL	60068	**877-788-1100**	847-518-1100	231
DNA (Delaware Nurses Assn)						
4765 Ogletown-Stanton Rd Ste L10	Newark	DE	19713	**800-626-4081**	302-733-5880	529
DNA Diagnostics Ctr (DDC)						
1 DDC Way	Fairfield	OH	45014	**800-613-5768**	513-881-7800	416
DNC Parks & Resorts at KSC Inc						
250 Delaware Ave	Buffalo	NY	14202	**855-433-4210**		376
Do My Own Pest Control						
4260 Communications Dr	Norcross	GA	30093	**866-581-7378**		
Doane College						
1014 Boswell Ave	Crete	NE	68333	**800-333-6263**	402-826-2161	166
Grand Island						
3180 W US Hwy 34	Grand Island	NE	68801	**800-333-6263**	308-398-0800	166
Lincoln 303 N 52nd St	Lincoln	NE	68504	**888-803-6263**	402-466-4774	166
DOAR Inc						
1370 Broadway 15th Fl	New York	NY	10018	**800-875-8705**	212-235-2700	443
DOBER						
11230 Katherine Crossing Ste 100	Woodridge	IL	60517	**800-323-4983**	630-410-7300	145
Doble Engineering Co Inc						
85 Walnut St	Watertown	MA	02472	**888-443-6253**	617-926-4900	248
Doc 2 E-file Inc						
4500 S Wayside Ste 102	Houston	TX	77087	**888-649-2006**	713-649-2006	225
Docken & Co						
900-800 6 Ave SW	Calgary	AB	T2P3G3	**877-269-3612**	403-269-3612	427
Doctors Foster & Smith Inc						
2253 Air Pk Rd PO Box 100	Rhinelander	WI	54501	**800-826-7206**	800-381-7179	574
Doctors Hospital						
5100 W Broad St	Columbus	OH	43228	**800-432-3309**	614-544-1000	373-3
Doctors Hospital of Laredo						
10700 McPherson Rd	Laredo	TX	78045	**844-244-4874**	956-523-2000	373-3
Doctors Without Borders USA Inc						
40 Rector St 16th Fl	New York	NY	10006	**888-392-0392**	212-679-6800	48-5
Doctors' Co, The						
185 Greenwood Rd	Napa	CA	94558	**800-421-2368**		390-5
Document Imaging Systems Corp (DISC)						
1523 Fenpark Dr	Fenton	MO	63026	**800-710-3472**		
Doc-U-Search Inc						
63 Pleasant St	Concord	NH	03301	**800-332-3034**	603-224-2871	631
Dodd Camera						
2077 E 30th St	Cleveland	OH	44115	**855-544-1705**	216-361-6800	119
Dodge & Cox						
555 California St 40th Fl	San Francisco	CA	94104	**800-621-3979**	415-981-1710	400
Dodge & Cox Funds						
30 Dan Rd	Canton	MA	02021	**800-621-3979**		524
Dodge City Community College						
2501 N 14th Ave	Dodge City	KS	67801	**800-367-3222**	620-225-1321	162
Dodge County 435 N Pk	Fremont	NE	68025	**800-331-5666**	402-727-2767	337
Dodger Industries						
2075 Stultz Rd PO Box 711	Martinsville	VA	24112	**800-436-3437***		155-1
*Cust Svc						
Doe Run Co, The						
1801 Pk 270 Dr Ste 300	Saint Louis	MO	63146	**800-356-3786**	314-453-7100	483
Doerfer Engineering Corp						
PO Box 816	Waverly	IA	50677	**877-483-4700**		261
doggyloot LLC						
213 N Racine Ave	Chicago	IL	60607	**800-398-6081***		
*Cust Svc						
DogLeggs LLC 1155 Elm St	York	PA	17403	**800-313-1218**		
Dogwood Productions Inc						
757 Government St	Mobile	AL	36602	**800-254-9903**	251-476-0858	7
Dohrn Transfer Co						
625 Third Ave	Rock Island	IL	61201	**888-364-7621**	309-794-0723	447
Doka USA Ltd						
214 Gates Rd	Little Ferry	NJ	07643	**877-365-2872**	201-329-7839	191-3
DOL (Department of Labor)						
200 Constitution AveNW	Washington	DC	20210	**866-487-2365**		339-14
DOL (United States Department of Labor)						
Office of Workers' Compensation Programs						
200 Constitution Ave Ste S3524	Washington	DC	20210	**866-487-2365**		339-14
Dolce Hayes Mansion						
200 Edenvale Ave	San Jose	CA	95136	**866-981-3300**	408-226-3200	376
Dolce Hotels & Resorts						
201 Aberdeen Pkwy	Peachtree City	GA	30269	**800-983-6523**	770-487-2666	376
Dole Food Company Hawaii						
802 Mapunapuna St	Honolulu	HI	96819	**800-697-9100**	808-861-8015	297-7
Dole Food Company Inc						
1 Dole Dr	Westlake Village	CA	91362	**800-232-8888**	818-879-6600	315-4
NYSE: DOLE						
Dole Packaged Foods Co						
1 Dole Dr	Westlake Village	CA	91362	**800-356-3111**		
Dole Refrigerating Co						
1420 Higgs Rd	Lewisburg	TN	37091	**800-251-8990**	931-359-6211	660
Dollar Bank FSB						
225 Forbes Ave	Pittsburgh	PA	15222	**800-828-5527**		70
Dollar Bill Copying						
611 Church St	Ann Arbor	MI	48104	**877-738-9200**	734-665-9200	
Dollar General Corp						
100 Mission Rdg	Goodlettsville	TN	37072	**800-678-9258**	615-855-4000	786
NYSE: DG						
Dollar Loan Ctr LLC						
6122 W Sahara Ave	Las Vegas	NV	89146	**866-550-4352**	702-693-5626	217
Dollar Rent A Car Inc						
5330 E 31st St	Tulsa	OK	74135	**800-800-4000**	918-669-3000	126
Dollar Tree Stores Inc						
500 Volvo Pkwy	Chesapeake	VA	23320	**877-530-8733**		786
NASDAQ: DLTR						
Dollywood						
2700 Dollywood Parks Blvd	Pigeon Forge	TN	37863	**800-365-5996**		32
Dolphin Beach Resort						
4900 Gulf Blvd	Saint Pete Beach	FL	33706	**800-237-8916**	727-360-7011	378
Dolphin Shirt Co						
757 Buckley Rd	San Luis Obispo	CA	93401	**800-377-3256**	805-541-2566	623
Dolphin Swim School Inc						
1530 El Camino Ave	Sacramento	CA	95815	**800-436-5744**	916-929-8188	707
Dolphins Plus Inc						
31 Corrine Pl	Key Largo	FL	33037	**866-860-7946**	305-451-0315	799
Domaine Chandon Inc						
1 California Dr	Yountville	CA	94599	**888-242-6366**		80-3
Domain-It!						
9891 Montgomery Rd	Cincinnati	OH	45242	**866-269-2355***	513-351-4222	395
*General						
DomainPeople Inc						
550 Burrard St Ste 200 Bentall 5	Vancouver	BC	V6C2B5	**877-734-3667**	604-639-1680	395
Dome Printing						
2031 Dome Ln	McClellan Park	CA	95652	**800-343-3139**		623
DOmedia LLC						
274 Marconi Blvd One Marconi Pl Ste 400	Columbus	OH	43215	**866-939-3663**		225
Domengeaux Wright Roy & Edwards LLC						
556 Jefferson St Ste 500	Lafayette	LA	70501	**800-375-6186**	337-233-3033	427
Dometic Corp						
2320 Industrial Pkwy	Elkhart	IN	46516	**800-544-4881**	574-294-2511	14
Domini Social Investments						
PO Box 9785	Providence	RI	02940	**800-582-6757**		524
Dominican College						
470 Western Hwy	Orangeburg	NY	10962	**866-432-4636**	845-359-7800	166
Dominican Hospital (DH)						
1555 Soquel Dr	Santa Cruz	CA	95065	**866-466-1401**	831-462-7700	373-3
Dominican School of Philosophy & Theology						
2301 Vine St	Berkeley	CA	94708	**888-450-3778**	510-849-2030	167-3
Dominican University						
7900 W Div St	River Forest	IL	60305	**800-828-8475**	708-366-2490	166
Dominican University of California						
50 Acacia Ave	San Rafael	CA	94901	**888-323-6763***	415-457-4440	166
*Admissions						
Dominion Aviation Services Inc						
7511 Airfield Dr	Richmond	VA	23237	**800-366-7793**	804-271-7793	575
Dominion Electric Supply Company Inc						
5053 Lee Hwy	Arlington	VA	22207	**800-525-5006**	703-536-4400	246
Dominion Energy						
PO Box 45360	Salt Lake City	UT	84145	**800-323-5517**	801-324-5111	782
Dominion Energy						
120 Tredegar St	Richmond	VA	23219	**888-216-3718**		782
Dominion Energy Generation Marketing Inc						
701 E Cary St	Richmond	VA	23219	**866-366-4357**	757-857-2112	782
Dominion Hope						
701 E Cary St	Richmond	VA	23219	**866-366-4357**	888-366-8280	782
Dominion Lending Centres Inc						
2215 Coquitlam Ave	Port Coquitlam	BC	V3B1J6	**866-928-6810**		507
Dominion Resources Inc						
120 Tredegar St	Richmond	VA	23219	**800-552-4034**	804-819-2000	359-5
NYSE: D						
Dominion Veterinary Laboratories Inc						
1199 Sanford St	Winnipeg	MB	R3E3A1	**800-465-7122**	204-589-7361	580
Domino's Pizza Inc						
30 Frank Lloyd Wright Dr	Ann Arbor	MI	48106	**800-253-8182**	734-930-3030	666
NYSE: DPZ						
Doms Outdoor Outfitters						
1870 First St	Livermore	CA	94550	**800-447-9629**	925-447-9629	707
Domtech Inc						
40 East Davis St	Trenton	ON	K8V6S4	**888-278-8258**	613-394-4884	490
Don Beyer Motors Inc						
1231 W Broad St	Falls Church	VA	22046	**855-892-6528**	855-844-0659	
Don CeSar Beach Resort - A Loews Hotel						
3400 Gulf Blvd	Saint Pete Beach	FL	33706	**888-430-4999**	727-360-1881	665
Don Garlits Museums						
13700 SW 16th Ave	Ocala	FL	34473	**877-271-3278**	352-245-8661	519
Don Hutson Organization						
516 Tennessee St Ste 219	Memphis	TN	38103	**800-647-9166**	901-767-0000	760
Don Johnson Motors						
2101 Central Blvd	Brownsville	TX	78520	**888-653-0794**	956-546-2288	
Don Laughlin's Riverside Resort & Casino						
1650 Casino Dr	Laughlin	NV	89029	**800-227-3849**	702-298-2535	133
Don McGill Toyota Inc						
11800 Katy Fwy	Houston	TX	77079	**866-938-0767**	281-496-2000	57
Don Pepino Sales Co						
123 Railroad Ave	Williamstown	NJ	08094	**888-281-6400**	856-629-7429	296-20
Don Small & Sons Oil Distributing Co Inc						
112 Third St NW PO Box 626	Auburn	WA	98071	**800-626-3213**	253-833-0430	577
Don Stevens Inc						
980 Discovery Rd	Eagan	MN	55121	**800-444-2299**	651-452-0872	661
Don Young Co						
8181 Ambassador Row	Dallas	TX	75247	**800-367-0390**	214-630-0934	478
Doña Ana Community College (DACC)						
2800 N Sonoma Ranch Blvd	Las Cruces	NM	88011	**800-903-7503**	575-528-7000	162
Dona Ana County						
845 N Motel Blvd	Las Cruces	NM	88007	**800-477-3632**	575-647-7200	337
Donahuefavret Contractors Inc						
3030 E Causeway Approach	Mandeville	LA	70448	**800-626-4431**	985-626-4431	186
Donaldson Company Inc						
1400 W 94th St	Bloomington	MN	55431	**800-365-1331**	952-887-3131	18
NYSE: DCI						
Donan Engineering LLC						
12450 Lk Sta Pl	Louisville	KY	40299	**800-482-5611**		399

Alphabetical Section

	Toll-Free	Phone	Class
Donatech Corp 2094 185th St Ste 110 . . . . .Fairfield IA 52556	**800-328-2133**	641-472-7474	177
Donatello, The 501 Post St . . . . .San Francisco CA 94102	**800-258-2366**	415-441-7100	378
Donatos Pizza 935 Taylor Stn Rd . . . . .Columbus OH 43230	**800-366-2867**		666
Donegal Group Inc 1195 River Rd . . . . .Marietta PA 17547 *NASDAQ: DGICA*	**800-877-0600**	717-426-1931	359-4
Donegal Mutual Insurance Co 1195 River Rd PO Box 302 . . . . .Marietta PA 17547	**800-877-0600**		390-4
Doniphan County PO Box 278 . . . . .Troy KS 66087	**800-232-0170**	785-985-3513	337
Doniphan Electric Co-op Assn Inc 530 W Jones St PO Box 699 . . . . .Troy KS 66087	**800-699-0810**	785-985-3523	
Donlen Corp 2315 Sanders Rd . . . . .Northbrook IL 60062	**800-323-1483**	847-714-1400	289
Donley County 300 S Sully St 2nd Fl-Courthouse PO Box 909. . . . . .Clarendon TX 79226	**800-388-8075**	806-874-3625	337
Don-Nan 3427 E Garden City Hwy 158 . . . . .Midland TX 79706	**800-348-7742**		112
Donnell Systems Inc 130 S Main St Ste 375 . . . . .South Bend IN 46601	**800-232-3776**	574-232-3784	196
Donnelly College 608 N 18th St . . . . .Kansas City KS 66102	**800-908-9946**	913-621-8700	162
Donohoe & Stapleton LLC 2781 Zelda Rd . . . . .Montgomery AL 36106	**800-365-6896**	334-269-3355	427
Donor Alliance Inc 720 S Colorado Blvd Ste 800-N . . . . .Denver CO 80246	**888-868-4747**	303-329-4747	541
Donor Network of Arizona 201 W Coolidge St . . . . .Phoenix AZ 85013	**800-447-9477**	602-222-2200	269
Donor Network West 12667 Alcosta Blvd Ste 500 . . . . .Oakland CA 94583	**888-570-9400**		541
Donovan Marine Inc 6316 Humphreys St . . . . .Harahan LA 70123	**800-347-4464**	504-488-5731	765
Donriver Inc 701 Brazos St . . . . .Austin TX 78701	**866-733-1684**		196
Dooley's Petroleum Inc 304 Main Ave . . . . .Murdock MN 56271	**800-520-2466**	320-875-2641	577
Doonan Trailer Corp 36 NE Hwy 156 . . . . .Great Bend KS 67530	**800-734-0608**	620-792-6222	774
Dooney & Bourke Inc 1 Regent St . . . . .East Norwalk CT 06855 *Cust Svc	**800-347-5000***	203-853-7515	429
Door Components Inc 7980 Redwood Ave . . . . .Fontana CA 92336	**866-989-3667**		234
Door Engineering & Mfg LLC 400 Cherry St .Kasota MN 56050	**800-959-1352**	507-931-6910	349
Door Systems Inc PO Box 511 . . . . .Framingham MA 01704	**800-545-3667**	508-875-3508	191-3
Doormark Inc 430 Goolsby Blvd . . . . .Deerfield Beach FL 33442	**888-969-0124**	954-418-4700	115
Doral Arrowwood Conference Resort 975 Anderson Hill Rd . . . . .Rye Brook NY 10573	**844-211-0512**	844-214-5500	376
Dorchester County Council 501 Court Ln . . . . .Cambridge MD 21613	**800-272-9829**	410-228-1700	337
Dorchester Minerals LP 3838 Oak Lawn Ave Ste 300 . . . . .Dallas TX 75219 *NASDAQ: DMLP*	**800-690-6903**	214-559-0300	532
Dordt College 498 Fourth Ave NE . . . . .Sioux Center IA 51250	**800-343-6738**	712-722-6080	166
Dorling Kindersley Ltd 375 Hudson St . . . . .New York NY 10014 *Cust Svc	**800-631-8571***	646-674-4047	633-2
DORMA Architectural Hardware DORMA Dr Drawer AC . . . . .Reamstown PA 17567	**800-523-8483**	717-336-3881	486
DORMA Group North America Dorma Dr . . . . .Reamstown PA 17567	**800-523-8483**	717-336-3881	349
Dorman Products Inc 3400 E Walnut St . . . . .Colmar PA 18915 *NASDAQ: DORM*	**800-523-2492**	215-997-1800	60
Dormont Manufacturing Co 6015 Enterprise Dr . . . . .Export PA 15632	**800-367-6668**		369
Dornbracht Americas Inc 1700 Executive Dr S Ste 600 . . . . .Duluth GA 30096	**800-774-1181**	770-564-3599	606
Dorothy Bramlage Public Library Junction City 230 W Seventh St . . . . .Junction City KS 66441	**800-727-2785**	785-238-4311	433-3
Dorris Lumber & Moulding Co, The 2601 Redding Ave . . . . .Sacramento CA 95820	**800-827-5823**	916-452-7531	497
Dorsett & Jackson Inc 3800 Noakes St . . . . .Los Angeles CA 90023	**800-871-8365**	323-268-1815	146
Dorsett Industries Inc 1304 May St PO Box 805 . . . . .Dalton GA 30721	**800-241-4035**	706-278-1961	131
Dortronics Systems Inc 1668 Sag Harbor Tpke . . . . .Sag Harbor NY 11963	**800-906-0137**		349
Doss Aviation Inc 3670 Rebecca Ln . . . . .Colorado Springs CO 80917	**888-803-4415**	719-570-9804	575
Dostal Alley Casino 1 Dostal Alley . . . . .Central City CO 80427	**888-949-2757**	303-582-1610	133
Dot Com Holdings of Buffalo Inc 1460 Military Rd . . . . .Buffalo NY 14217	**877-636-3673**		686
Dot Foods Inc 1 Dot Way PO Box 192 . . . . .Mount Sterling IL 62353	**800-366-3687**	217-773-4411	297-6
Dot Hill Systems Corp 1351 S Sunset St . . . . .Longmont CO 80501 *NASDAQ: HILL*	**800-872-2783**	303-845-3200	176
Dothan Area Chamber of Commerce 102 Jamestown Blvd . . . . .Dothan AL 36301	**800-221-1027**	334-792-5138	139
Dothan Chrysler-Dodge Inc 4074 Ross Clark Cir NW . . . . .Dothan AL 36303	**877-674-9574**	334-794-0606	57
Dothan Eagle PO Box 1968 . . . . .Dothan AL 36302	**800-811-1771**	334-792-3141	528-2
Dot-Line Transportation PO Box 8739 . . . . .Fountain Valley CA 92728	**800-423-3780**	323-780-9010	188-5
Dotronix Inc 160 First St SE . . . . .New Brighton MN 55112	**800-720-7218**	651-633-1742	173-4
Dotster 8100 NE Pkwy Dr Ste 300 PO Box 821066. . . . . .Vancouver WA 98682	**800-401-5250**	360-449-5800	395
Double Diamond Co 5495 Belt Line Rd Ste 200 . . . . .Dallas TX 75254	**800-324-7438**	214-706-9801	649
Double Eagle Hotel & Casino 442 E Bennett Ave . . . . .Cripple Creek CO 80813	**800-711-7234**	719-689-5000	133
Double H Plastics Inc 50 W St Rd . . . . .Warminster PA 18974	**800-523-3932**		600
DoubleCheck LLC 101 Gilbraltar Dr . . . . .Morris Plains NJ 07950	**888-299-3980**	973-984-2229	177
Doublehorn Communications 1601 Rio Grande St # 500 . . . . .Austin TX 78701	**855-618-6423**	512-637-5200	224
DoublePositive 1111 Light St Ste 350. . . . . .Baltimore MD 21230	**888-376-7484**	410-332-0464	
DoubleTree by Hilton Hotel Downtown Wilmington - Legal District 700 N King St . . . . .Wilmington DE 19801	**855-610-8733**	302-655-0400	378
Doucette Industries Inc (DII) 20 Leigh Dr . . . . .York PA 17406	**800-445-7511**	717-845-8746	14
Dougherty & Company LLC 90 S Seventh St Ste 4300. . . . . .Minneapolis MN 55402	**800-328-4000**	612-376-4000	686
Douglas Battery Manufacturing Co 500 Battery Dr . . . . .Winston-Salem NC 27107	**800-368-4527**		74
Douglas Bros 423 Riverside Industrial Pkwy . . . . .Portland ME 04103	**800-341-0926**	207-797-6771	591
Douglas Corp 9650 Valley View Rd . . . . .Eden Prairie MN 55344	**800-806-6113**		697
Douglas Cuddle Toys Company Inc 69 Krif Rd PO Box D. . . . . .Keene NH 03431	**800-992-9002**	603-352-3414	757
Douglas Industries Co 3441 S 11th Ave . . . . .Eldridge IA 52748	**800-553-8907**	563-285-4162	706
Douglas Laboratories Inc 600 Boyce Rd . . . . .Pittsburgh PA 15205	**800-245-4440**		794
Douglas Press Inc 2810 Madison St . . . . .Bellwood IL 60104	**800-323-0705**	708-547-8400	322
Douglas Stewart Co, The 2402 Advance Rd . . . . .Madison WI 53718	**800-279-2795**	608-221-1155	530
Douglas-Guardian Services Corp 14800 St Mary's Ln . . . . .Houston TX 77079	**800-255-0552**	281-531-0500	398
Douglass Colony Group Inc 5901 E 58th Ave . . . . .Commerce City CO 80022	**877-288-0650**	303-288-2635	189-12
Douglass Distributing Co 325 E Forest Ave . . . . .Sherman TX 75090	**800-736-4316**	903-893-1181	677
Douglass Truck Bodies Inc 231 21st St . . . . .Bakersfield CA 93301	**800-635-7641**	661-327-0258	513
Douthitt Corp 245 Adair St . . . . .Detroit MI 48207	**800-368-8448**	313-259-1565	587
Dove Cleaners Inc 1560 Yonge St . . . . .Toronto ON M4T2S9	**866-999-3683**	416-413-7900	425
Dover Chemical Corp 3676 Davis Rd NW . . . . .Dover OH 44622 *General	**800-321-8805***	330-343-7711	145
Dover Downs Hotel & Casino 1131 N DuPont Hwy . . . . .Dover DE 19901 *NYSE: DDE*	**800-711-5882**	302-674-4600	638
Dover International Speedway 1131 N Dupont Hwy PO Box 843 . . . . .Dover DE 19901	**800-441-7223**	302-883-6500	638
Dover Motorsports Inc 1131 N Dupont Hwy PO Box 843 . . . . .Dover DE 19901 *NYSE: DVD*	**800-441-7223**	302-883-6500	
Dover Post 1196 S Little Creek Rd . . . . .Dover DE 19901	**800-942-1616**	302-678-3616	528-4
Dover Saddlery Inc 525 Great Rd . . . . .Littleton MA 01460 *NASDAQ: DOVR*	**800-406-8204**	978-952-8062	706
Doverco Inc 2111 32e Ave . . . . .Lachine QC H8T3J1	**800-363-0697**	514-420-6060	
DOVICO Software Inc 236 St George St Ste 119 . . . . .Moncton NB E1C1W1	**800-618-8463**		179
Dow Chemical Canada Inc (DCCI) 450 First St SW Ste 2100 . . . . .Calgary AB T2P5H1	**800-447-4369**	403-267-3500	144
Dow Chemical Co 2030 Dow Ctr . . . . .Midland MI 48674	**800-331-6451**	989-636-1000	304
Dow Chemical Co 2030 Dow Ctr . . . . .Midland MI 48674 *NYSE: DWDP* ■ *Cust Svc	**800-422-8193***	989-636-1463	144
Dow Corning Corp 2200 W Salzburg Rd PO Box 994. . . . . . . .Auburn MI 48611 *Cust Svc	**800-248-2481***	989-496-4000	144
Dow Cover Co Inc 373 Lexington Ave . . . . .New Haven CT 06513	**800-735-8877**	203-469-5394	348
Dow Electronics Inc 8603 E Adamo Dr . . . . .Tampa FL 33619	**800-627-2900**	813-626-5195	246
Dow Liquid Separations PO Box 1206 . . . . .Midland MI 48642	**800-447-4369**	989-636-1000	801
Dow Theory Forecasts 7412 Calumet Ave . . . . .Hammond IN 46324	**800-233-5922**		527-9
Dow-Key Microwave Corp 4822 McGrath St . . . . .Ventura CA 93003	**800-266-3695**	805-650-0260	253
Dowling College 150 Idle Hour Blvd . . . . .Oakdale NY 11769	**800-369-5464**	631-244-3000	166
Down East 680 Commercial St . . . . .Rockport ME 04856	**800-766-1670**	207-594-9544	455-22
Down Under Bedding & Mattresses 5170 Dixie Rd Unit 3 . . . . .Mississauga ON L4W1E3	**888-624-6484**	905-624-5854	360
Downeast Graphics & Printing Inc 477 Washington Jct Rd . . . . .Ellsworth ME 04605	**800-427-5582**	207-667-5582	623
Downers Grove Public Library 1050 Curtiss St . . . . .Downers Grove IL 60515	**800-227-0625**	630-960-1200	433-3
Downey City Library (DCL) 11121 Brookshire Ave . . . . .Downey CA 90241	**877-846-3452**	562-904-7360	433-3
Downey Regional Medical Ctr 11500 Brookshire Ave . . . . .Downey CA 90241	**800-954-8000**	562-904-5000	373-3
Downing Displays Inc 550 Techne Ctr Dr . . . . .Milford OH 45150	**800-883-1800**	513-248-9800	232
Downs Crane & Hoist Company Inc 8827 Juniper Ave . . . . .Los Angeles CA 90002	**800-748-5994**	323-589-6061	468
Downs Food Group 418 Benzel Ave SW . . . . .Madelia MN 56062	**800-967-2474**	507-642-3203	344

Name / Address	City	State	ZIP	Toll-Free	Phone	Class
Downtown Athletic Store Inc 1180 Seminole Trl Ste 210	Charlottesville	VA	22901	**800-348-2649**	434-975-3696	707
Downtown Erie Hotel 18 W 18th St	Erie	PA	16501	**800-832-9101**	814-456-2961	378
DoxTek Inc 264 W Center St	Orem	UT	84057	**877-705-7226**	801-356-2230	225
Doyle Security Systems Inc 792 Calkins Rd	Rochester	NY	14623	**866-463-6953**	585-244-3400	688
Doyon Drilling Inc 11500 C St Ste 200	Anchorage	AK	99515	**800-478-9675**	907-563-5530	536
Doyon Ltd 1 Doyon Pl Ste 300	Fairbanks	AK	99701	**888-478-4755**	907-459-2000	532
Dp Murphy Company Inc 945 Grand Blvd	Deer Park	NY	11729	**800-424-8724**	631-673-9400	5
DP Technology Corp 1150 Avenida Acaso	Camarillo	CA	93012	**800-627-8479**	805-388-6000	178-5
DPE Systems Inc 120 Lakeside Ave Ste 230	Seattle	WA	98122	**800-541-6566**	206-223-3737	180
DPF Data Services 1345 Campus Pkw Unit A8	Wall Township	NJ	07753	**800-431-4416**		225
DPL Inc 1065 Woodman Dr *NYSE: AES*	Dayton	OH	45432	**800-433-8500**	800-736-3001	359-5
DPL Wireless 53 Clark Rd	Rothesay	NB	E2E2K9	**800-561-8880**	506-847-2347	386
DPSI Inc 1801 Stanley Rd Ste 301	Greensboro	NC	27407	**800-897-7233**	336-854-7700	178-11
DPT Laboratories Ltd 318 McCullough	San Antonio	TX	78215	**866-225-5378**		578
Dr Delphinium Designs & Events 5806 W Lovers Ln & Tollway	Dallas	TX	75225	**800-783-8790**	214-522-9911	292
Dr Fresh Inc 6645 Caballero Blvd	Buena Park	CA	90620	**866-373-7371**		473
DR Horton Inc 301 Commerce St Ste 500 *NYSE: DHI*	Fort Worth	TX	76102	**800-846-7866**	817-390-8200	649
Dr Pepper/Seven-Up Inc 5301 Legacy Dr	Plano	TX	75024	**800-696-5891**	972-673-7000	80-2
DR Sperry & Co 623 Rathbone Ave	Aurora	IL	60506	**888-997-9297**	630-892-4361	454
Dr Vinyl & Assoc Ltd 1350 SE Hamblen Rd *General	Lees Summit	MO	64081	**800-531-6600***	816-525-6060	62-1
Draeger Medical Inc 3135 Quarry Rd	Telford	PA	18969	**800-437-2437**		250
DRAIVER 9393 W 110th St Ste 500	Overland Park	KS	66210	**844-366-6837**		224
Drake Hotel, The 140 E Walton Pl	Chicago	IL	60611	**800-553-7253**	312-787-2200	378
Drake Software 235 E Palmer St	Franklin	NC	28734	**800-890-9500**		178-1
Drake University 2507 University Ave	Des Moines	IA	50311	**800-443-7253**	515-271-3181	166
Drake University Law School 2507 University Ave	Des Moines	IA	50311	**800-443-7253**	515-271-2824	167-1
Drake-Scruggs Equipment Inc 2000 S Dirksen Pkwy	Springfield	IL	62703	**877-799-0398**	217-753-3871	468
Dramm & Echter Inc 1150 Quail Gardens Dr	Encinitas	CA	92024	**800-854-7021**	760-436-0188	368
Dranetz-BMI 1000 New Durham Rd	Edison	NJ	08818	**800-372-6832**	732-287-3680	248
Draper Knitting Co 28 Draper Ln	Canton	MA	02021	**800-808-7707**	781-828-0029	740-4
Draper Shade & Screen Co 411 S Pearl St	Spiceland	IN	47385	**800-238-7999**	765-987-7999	587
Draper Valley Farms 1500 E College Way PMB449 Ste A	Mount Vernon	WA	98273	**800-682-1468**		
Drapers & Damons 9 Pasteur Ste 200	Irvine	CA	92618	**800-843-1174**		157-6
DRAXIMAGE Inc 16751 Transcanada Hwy	Kirkland	QC	H9H4J4	**888-633-5343**	514-630-7080	238
Drayton Group 2295 N Opdyke Rd Ste D	Auburn Hills	MI	48326	**888-655-4442**		104
Dreamland Bar-B-que 1427 14th Ave S	Birmingham	AL	35205	**800-752-0544**	205-933-2133	667
DreamMaker Bath & Kitchen by Worldwide 510 N Valley Mills Dr Ste 304	Waco	TX	76710	**800-583-2133**		189-11
DreamWorld Backdrops by Dazian 10671 Lorne St	Sun Valley	CA	91352	**877-232-9426**		718
Drees Co 211 Grandview Dr	Fort Mitchell	KY	41017	**866-265-2980**	859-578-4200	187
Dremel Inc 4915 21st St	Racine	WI	53406	**800-437-3635**	262-554-1390	754
Dresser & Associates Inc 243 US Rt 1	Scarborough	ME	04074	**866-885-7212**	207-885-0809	461
Dreumex USA 3445 BoaRd Rd	York	PA	17406	**800-233-9382**	717-767-6881	151
Drew & Rogers Inc 30 Plymouth St	Fairfield	NJ	07004	**800-610-6210**	973-575-6210	623
Drew Shoe Corp 252 Quarry Rd	Lancaster	OH	43130	**800-837-3739**	740-653-4271	301
Drexel University 3141 Chestnut St *Admissions	Philadelphia	PA	19104	**866-358-1010***	215-895-2000	166
Drexel University Hagerty Library 3300 Market St	Philadelphia	PA	19104	**888-278-8825**	215-895-2767	433-6
Dreyfus-Cortney & Lowery Bros Rigging 4400 N Galvez St	New Orleans	LA	70117	**800-228-7660**	504-944-3366	765
Dreyfuss Planetarium 49 Washington St	Newark	NJ	07102	**888-370-6765**	973-596-6529	594
Dri Mark Products Inc 999 S Oyster Bay Rd Ste 312	Bethpage	NY	11714	**800-645-9662**	516-484-6200	567
DRIASI (Direct Response Insurance Administrative Services) 7930 Century Blvd	Chanhassen	MN	55317	**800-688-0760**		
Driehaus Capital Management Inc 25 E Erie St	Chicago	IL	60611	**800-688-8819**	312-587-3800	400
Driftwood Beach State Recreation Site 5580 S Coast Hwy	Newport	OR	97366	**800-551-6949**		561
Driftwood Hotel 435 Willoughby Ave	Juneau	AK	99801	**800-544-2239**	907-586-2280	378
Driftwood Shores Resort 88416 First Ave	Florence	OR	97439	**800-422-5091**	541-997-8263	378
Drillers Service Inc 1792 Highland Ave NE	Hickory	NC	28601	**800-334-2308**	828-322-1100	533
Dril-Quip Inc 6401 N Eldridge Pkwy *NYSE: DRQ*	Houston	TX	77041	**877-316-2631**	713-939-7711	533
Drink More Water Store 7595-A Rickenbacker Dr	Gaithersburg	MD	20879	**800-697-2070**		14
DRIP Investor 7412 Calumet Ave	Hammond	IN	46324	**800-233-5922**	219-852-3220	527-9
Dripping Springs State Park 16830 Dripping Springs Rd	Okmulgee	OK	74447	**800-622-6317**	918-756-5971	561
Driscoll Children's Hospital 3533 S Alameda St	Corpus Christi	TX	78411	**800-324-5683**	361-694-5000	373-1
Driscoll Strawberry Assoc Inc PO Box 50045	Watsonville	CA	95077	**800-871-3333**		315-1
DRISTEEM Corp 14949 Technology Dr	Eden Prairie	MN	55344	**800-328-4447**	952-949-2415	14
Drive Thru Technology Inc 1755 N Main St	Los Angeles	CA	90031	**800-933-8388**	866-388-7877	173-2
Drive Train Industries Inc 5555 Joliet St	Denver	CO	80239	**800-525-6177**	303-292-5176	61
Drivekore Inc 101 Wesley Dr	Mechanicsburg	PA	17055	**800-382-1311**	717-766-7636	349
Driveline Holdings Inc 700 Freeport Pkwy Ste 100	Coppell	TX	75019	**888-824-7505**		195
Drivers License Guide Co 1492 Oddstad Dr	Redwood City	CA	94063	**800-227-8827**	650-369-4849	633-10
DriveTime Corp 4020 E Indian School Rd	Phoenix	AZ	85018	**888-418-1212**		57
Driving Records Facilities PO Box 1086	Glen Burnie	MD	21061	**800-772-5510**		631
DrivingSales LLC 8871 S Sandy Pkwy Ste 250	Sandy	UT	84070	**866-943-8371**		386
DRMP (Dyer Riddle Mills & Precourt Inc) 941 Lake Baldwin Ln	Orlando	FL	32814	**800-375-3767**	407-896-0594	261
Dropbox Inc 401 S Ninth St	Ironton	OH	45638	**888-388-7768**		478
DropThought Inc 2755 Great America Way Ste 425	Santa Clara	CA	95054	**855-437-6776**		5
Drowsy Water Ranch PO Box 147	Granby	CO	80446	**800-845-2292**	970-725-3456	239
Drug Chemical & Associated Technologies Assn (DCAT) 1 Washington Blvd Ste 7	Robbinsville	NJ	08691	**800-640-3228**	609-448-1000	49-19
Drug Enforcement Administration Regional Offices						
Dallas Div 10160 Technology Blvd E	Dallas	TX	75220	**800-882-9539**	214-366-6900	339-13
Washington DC Div 800 K St NW Ste 500	Washington	DC	20001	**800-488-3111**	202-305-8500	339-13
Drug Package Inc 901 Drug Package Ln	O'Fallon	MO	63366	**800-325-6137**		623
Drug Topics Magazine 25115 Country Club Blvd Millennium Pl E *Cust Svc	North Olmsted	OH	44070	**877-922-2022***	440-891-2792	455-5
DrugScan Inc 200 Precision Rd Ste 200 PO Box 347	Horsham	PA	19044	**800-235-4890**		415
Druide informatique Inc 1435 rue Saint-Alexandre Bureau 1040	Montreal	QC	H3A2G4	**800-537-8433**	514-484-4998	180
Drum Corps International (DCI) 110 W Washington St Ste C *Orders	Indianapolis	IN	46204	**800-495-7469***	317-275-1212	48-4
Drummac Inc 251 Levy Rd	Atlantic Beach	FL	32233	**800-780-0111**	904-241-4999	
Drummer Online & Wright County Journal Press 108 Central Ave PO Box 159	Buffalo	MN	55313	**800-880-5047**	763-682-1221	528-3
Drury Hotels Company LLC 721 Emerson Rd Ste 400	Saint Louis	MO	63141	**800-378-7946**	314-429-2255	378
Drury University 900 N Benton Ave	Springfield	MO	65802	**800-922-2274**	417-873-7879	166
Druva 150 Mathilda Pl Ste 450	Sunnyvale	CA	94086	**844-303-7882**	650-241-3501	386
Dry Tortugas National Park PO Box 6208	Key West	FL	33041	**800-788-0511**	305-242-7700	560
Drycleaning & Laundry Institute 14700 Sweitzer Ln	Laurel	MD	20707	**800-638-2627**	301-622-1900	49-4
Drysdales Inc 3220 S Memorial Dr	Tulsa	OK	74145	**800-444-6481**	918-664-6481	328
Dryvit Systems Inc 1 Energy Way	West Warwick	RI	02893	**800-556-7752**	401-822-4100	388
DS Brown Co 300 E Cherry St	North Baltimore	OH	45872	**800-848-1730**	419-257-3561	191-2
D&S Communications Inc 1355 N Mclean Blvd	Elgin	IL	60123	**800-227-8403**		461
D-S Pipe & Supply Company Inc 1301 Wicomico St Ste 3	Baltimore	MD	21230	**800-368-8880**	410-539-8000	608
DS Services of America Inc 5660 New Northside Dr Ste 500 *Cust Svc	Atlanta	GA	30328	**800-201-6218***		800
DS/USA (Disabled Sports USA) 451 Hungerford Dr Ste 100	Rockville	MD	20850	**800-543-2754**	301-217-0960	48-22
DSA (Data Systems Analysts Inc) Eigth Neshaminy Interplex Ste 209	Trevose	PA	19053	**877-422-4372**	215-245-4800	180
DSC (Destination Services of Colorado Inc) PO Box 3660	Avon	CO	81620	**855-866-5290**	970-476-6565	184
DSC (Digital Security Controls) 3301 Langstaff Rd	Concord	ON	L4K4L2	**888-888-7838**	905-760-3000	688
DSC Logistics 1750 S Wolf Rd	Des Plaines	IL	60018	**800-372-1960**		447

Name / Address	Toll-Free	Phone	Class
DSG (Dakota Supply Group) 2601 Third Ave N .... Fargo ND 58102	800-437-4702	701-237-9440	246
DSG Tag Systems Inc 5455 152nd St Ste 214 .... Surrey BC V3S5A5	877-589-8806		386
DSL extreme 9221 Corbin Ave Ste 260 .... Northridge CA 91324	866-243-8638		397
DSM Desotech Inc 1122 St Charles St .... Elgin IL 60120	800-222-7189	847-697-0400	145
DSM Engineering Plastics Inc 2267 W Mill Rd .... Evansville IN 47720	800-333-4237	812-435-7500	601-2
DSM Food Specialties Inc 45 Waterview Blvd .... Parsippany NJ 07054	800-526-0189		296-42
DSM Resins Inc 31 Columbia Nitrogen Rd PO Box 2452 .... Augusta GA 30903	800-277-9975	706-849-6706	144
DSN Group Inc 152 Lorraine Dr .... Lake Zurich IL 60047	888-445-2919		521
DS&O Electric Cooperative Inc 129 W Main St PO Box 286 .... Solomon KS 67480	800-376-3533	785-655-2011	245
DSSC (Data Storage Systems Ctr) Carnegie Mellon University ECE Department .... Pittsburgh PA 15213	800-864-8287	412-268-6600	664
DST Controls 651 Stone Rd .... Benicia CA 94510	800-251-0773		203
DSX Access Systems Inc 10731 Rockwall Rd .... Dallas TX 75238	888-419-8353	214-553-6140	689
D-Ta Systems Inc 2500 Lancaster Rd .... Ottawa ON K1B4S5	877-382-3222	613-745-8713	177
DTE Energy Co 1 Energy Plz .... Detroit MI 48226 *NYSE: DTE*	800-477-4747	313-235-4000	359-5
DTI (Dental Technologies Inc) 5601 Arnold Rd .... Dublin CA 94568	800-229-0936	925-829-3611	414
DTIC (Defense Technical Information Center) 8725 John J Kingman Rd Ste 0944 .... Fort Belvoir VA 22060	800-225-3842		339-3
DTNIQ Inc 9110 W Dodge Rd Ste 200 .... Omaha NE 68114	800-475-4755	402-390-2328	406
DTS (Diversified Transfer & Storage Inc) 1640 Monad Rd .... Billings MT 59101	800-755-5855	406-245-4695	775
Du Page Airport Authority 2700 International Dr Ste 200 .... West Chicago IL 60185	800-208-5690	630-584-2211	27
Du Quebec 1400 Blvd Guillaume-Couture .... Levis QC G6W8K7	800-749-3646	418-838-5602	
Dualite Sales & Service Inc 1 Dualite Ln .... Williamsburg OH 45176	800-543-7271	513-724-7100	697
Dual-Lite Inc 701 Millennium Blvd .... Greenville SC 29607	866-898-0131	864-678-1000	438
Duane's 3649 Mission Inn Ave .... Riverside CA 92501	800-843-7755	951-784-0300	667
Duarte Unified School District 1620 Huntington Dr .... Duarte CA 91010	888-225-7377	626-599-5000	681
Dublin Convention & Visitors Bureau 9 S High St .... Dublin OH 43017	800-245-8387	614-792-7666	206
Dubois & King Inc 28 N Main St .... Randolph VT 05060	866-783-7101	802-728-3376	261
Dubois Chemicals 3630 E Kemper Rd .... Cincinnati OH 45241	800-438-2647		151
DuBois Regional Medical Ctr 100 Hospital Ave .... Du Bois PA 15801	800-254-5164	814-371-2200	373-3
Dubuque Area Chamber of Commerce 300 Main St Ste 200 .... Dubuque IA 52001	800-798-4748	563-557-9200	139
Dubuque County 720 Central Ave .... Dubuque IA 52001	800-637-0128	563-589-4432	337
Dubuque Symphony Orchestra 2728 Asbury Rd Ste 900 .... Dubuque IA 52001	866-803-9280	563-557-1677	569-3
Duca Financial Services Credit Union Ltd 5290 Yonge St .... Toronto ON M2N5P9	866-900-3822	416-223-8502	219
Duck Co 5601 Gray St .... Arvada CO 80002	800-255-3565		
Duckback 101 Prospect Ave .... Cleveland OH 44115	800-825-5382		546
Ducks Unlimited Magazine 1 Waterfowl Way .... Memphis TN 38120	800-453-8257	901-758-3825	455-20
Ducommun Inc 23301 Wilmington Ave .... Carson CA 90745 *NYSE: DCO*	800-522-6645	310-513-7280	203
Duct-O-Wire Co 345 Adams Cir .... Corona CA 92882	800-752-6001	951-735-8220	203
Dude Ranchers Assn 1122 12th St PO Box 2307 .... Cody WY 82414	866-399-2339	307-587-2339	48-23
Due North Consulting Inc 3112 Blue Lake Dr Ste 110 .... Birmingham AL 35243	800-899-2676	205-989-9394	196
Duff & Phelps Investment Management Co 200 S Wacker Dr Ste 500 .... Chicago IL 60606	800-338-8214	312-263-2610	400
Duffield Aquatic 113 Metro Dr .... Anderson SC 29625	888-669-7551	864-226-5500	186
Duffield Assoc Inc 5400 Limestone Rd .... Wilmington DE 19808	877-732-9633	302-239-6634	186
Duffy Sean P (Rep R - WI) 2330 Rayburn House office Bldg .... Washington DC 20515	855-584-4251	202-225-3365	
Duininck Inc 408 Sixth St PO Box 208 .... Prinsburg MN 56281 *General	800-328-8949*		188-4
Dukal Corp 2 Fleetwood Ct .... Ronkonkoma NY 11779	800-243-0741	631-656-3800	
Duke Diet & Fitness Ctr (DFC) 501 Douglas St .... Durham NC 27705	800-235-3853		702
Duke Law 210 Science Dr PO Box 90362 .... Durham NC 27708	888-529-2586	919-613-7006	167-1
Duke Manufacturing Co 2305 N Broadway .... Saint Louis MO 63102	800-735-3853	314-231-1130	298
Duke Realty Corp 600 E 96th St Ste 100 .... Indianapolis IN 46240 *NYSE: DRE*	800-875-3366	317-808-6000	651
Duke University 2138 Campus Dr PO Box 90586 .... Durham NC 27708	800-443-3853	919-684-3214	166
Duke University Divinity School 407 Chapel Dr PO Box 90968 .... Durham NC 27708	800-367-3853	919-660-3400	167-3
Duke University Press 905 W Main St Ste 18-B .... Durham NC 27701 *Cust Svc	888-651-0122*	919-687-3600	633-4
Duke's 8th Avenue Hotel 630 W Eigth Ave .... Anchorage AK 99501	800-478-4837	907-274-6213	378
Dukes County PO Box 190 .... Edgartown MA 02539	800-244-4630	508-696-3840	337
Dultmeier Sales LLC 13808 Industrial Rd .... Omaha NE 68137	888-677-5054	402-333-1444	428
Duluth Business University (DBU) 4724 Mike Colalilo Dr .... Duluth MN 55807	800-777-8406	218-722-4000	795
Duluth Entertainment Convention Ctr 350 Harbor Dr .... Duluth MN 55802	800-628-8385	218-722-5573	205
Duluth International Airport 4701 Grinden Dr .... Duluth MN 55811	855-787-2227	218-727-2968	27
Duluth News-Tribune 424 W First St .... Duluth MN 55802 *Circ	800-456-8080*	218-723-5281	528-2
Duluth Pack 365 Canal Park Dr .... Duluth MN 55802	800-777-4439		707
Dumbell Man Fitness Equipment, The 655 Hawaii Ave .... Torrance CA 90503	800-432-6266	310-381-2900	353
DuMor Inc PO Box 142 .... Mifflintown PA 17059	800-598-4018	717-436-2106	319-4
Dumore Corp 1030 Veterans St .... Mauston WI 53948	888-467-8288	608-847-6420	515
Dunbar Mechanical Inc 2806 N Reynolds Rd .... Toledo OH 43615	800-719-2201	419-537-1900	189-10
Dunbarton Corp PO Box 8577 .... Dothan AL 36304	800-633-7553		234
Duncan & Son Lines Inc 23860 W US Hwy 85 .... Buckeye AZ 85326	800-528-4283	623-386-4511	775
Duncan Aviation Inc 3701 Aviation Rd .... Lincoln NE 68524	800-228-4277	402-475-2611	24
Duncan Enterprises 5673 E Shields Ave .... Fresno CA 93727	800-438-6226	559-291-4444	43
Duncan Oil Company Inc 849 Factory Rd .... Beavercreek OH 45434	800-527-2559		575
Duncan Solutions Inc 033 W Wisconsin Ave Ste 1600 .... Milwaukee WI 53203	888-993-8622		493
Duncan Supply Company Inc 910 N Illinois St .... Indianapolis IN 46204	800-382-5528	317-634-1335	608
Duncan Systems Inc 29391 Old US Hwy 33 .... Elkhart IN 46516	800-551-9149		54
Duncan Valley Electric Co-op Inc PO Box 440 .... Duncan AZ 85534	800-669-2503	928-359-2503	245
Duncan-Parnell Inc 900 S McDowell St .... Charlotte NC 28204	800-849-7708	704-372-7766	113
Dundee Internet Service Inc 168 Riley St .... Dundee MI 48131	888-222-8485	734-529-5331	225
Dunes Manor Hotel 2800 Baltimore Ave .... Ocean City MD 21842	800-523-2888	410-289-1100	378
Dunham's Sports 5000 Dixie Hwy .... Waterford MI 48329	844-636-4109		157-5
Dunhill Hotel 237 N Tryon St .... Charlotte NC 28202	800-354-4141	704-332-4141	378
Dunkin' Donuts 130 Royall St .... Canton MA 02021 *Cust Svc	800-859-5339*	781-737-3000	68
Dunkin's Diamonds Inc 897 Hebron Rd .... Heath OH 43056	877-343-4883	740-522-1468	409
Dunlap Industries Inc 297 Industrial Park Rd .... Dunlap TN 37327	800-251-7214		590
Dunlap Oil Company Inc 759 S Haskell Ave .... Willcox AZ 85643	800-854-1646	520-384-2248	324
Dunlop Tires 200 Innovation Way .... Akron OH 44316	800-522-7458		749
Dunmore Corp 145 Wharton Rd .... Bristol PA 19007	800-444-0242	215-781-8895	596
Dunn Energy Co-op PO Box 220 .... Menomonie WI 54751	800-924-0630	715-232-6240	245
Dunn School 2555 Hwy 154 PO Box 98 .... Los Olivos CA 93441	800-287-9197	805-688-6471	618
Dunn-Edwards Corp 4885 E 52nd Pl .... Los Angeles CA 90058	800-537-4098	323-771-3330	546
Dunwoody College of Technology 818 Dunwoody Blvd .... Minneapolis MN 55403	800-292-4625	612-374-5800	795
Duo-Fast Construction 155 Harlem Ave .... Glenview IL 60025 *Cust Svc	877-489-2726*		753
Duo-Safety Ladder Corp 513 W Ninth Ave .... Oshkosh WI 54902	877-386-5377	920-231-2740	420
Dupaco Community Credit Union 3999 Pennsylvania Ave .... Dubuque IA 52002	800-373-7600	563-557-7600	219
DuPage Convention & Visitors Bureau 915 Harger Rd Ste 240 .... Oak Brook IL 60523	800-232-0502	630-575-8070	206
Dupli Graphics Corp 6761 Thompson Rd N .... Syracuse NY 13211	800-724-2477		623
Duplin County 112 Duplin St .... Kenansville NC 28349	800-685-8916	910-296-2150	337
Dupli-Systems Inc 8260 Dow Cir .... Strongsville OH 44136	800-321-1610	440-234-9415	110
DuPont Advanced Fibers Systems 5401 Jefferson Davis Hwy .... Richmond VA 23234	800-441-7515	804-383-3845	601-1
DuPont Chemical Solutions 1007 Market St .... Wilmington DE 19898	800-441-7515	302-774-1000	145
DuPont Crop Protection CRP 705/L1S11 PO Box 80705 .... Wilmington DE 19880	800-922-2368	302-774-1000	280
DuPont Engineering Polymers Lancaster Pike Rt 141 Barley Mill Plz Bldg 22 .... Wilmington DE 19805	800-441-7515	302-999-4592	601-2
DuPont Packaging & Industrial Polymers Barley Mill Plz 26-2122 PO Box 80026 .... Wilmington DE 19880	800-438-7225	703-305-7666	544
DuPont Performance Coatings 1007 Market St .... Wilmington DE 19898	800-441-7515	302-774-1000	546

	Toll-Free	Phone	Class
DuPont Qualicon Henry Clay Rd Bldg 400 Rt 141 PO Box 80400 ... Wilmington DE 19880	800-863-6842	302-695-5300	231
DuPont Surfaces 4417 Lancaster Pk CRP 728/3105 ... Wilmington DE 19805	800-448-9835	302-774-1000	595
DuPont Titanium Technologies 1007 Market St ... Wilmington DE 19898	800-441-7515	302-774-1000	143
Duquesne Light Holdings Inc 411 Seventh Ave ... Pittsburgh PA 15219	888-393-7000	412-393-7000	359-5
Duquesne University 600 Forbes Ave ... Pittsburgh PA 15282	800-456-0590	412-396-6000	166
DuQuoin Tourism Commission Inc 20 N Chestnut St PO Box 1037 ... Du Quoin IL 62832	800-455-9570	618-542-8338	206
Dura Wax Co 4101 W Albany St ... Mchenry IL 60050	800-435-5705		151
Durable Products Inc PO Box 826 ... Crossville TN 38557	800-373-3502	931-484-3502	672
Duracell 14 Research Dr ... Bethel CT 06801	800-551-2355		74
Duraclean International Inc 220 Campus Dr ... Arlington Heights IL 60004	800-251-7070		152
Duracote Corp 350 N Diamond St ... Ravenna OH 44266	800-321-2252	330-296-3487	740-2
Duralee Fabrics Ltd Inc 1775 Fifth Ave ... Bay Shore NY 11706 *Cust Svc	800-275-3872*	631-273-8800	590
DuraLine Imaging Inc 578 Upward Rd Ste 11 ... Flat Rock NC 28731	800-982-3872	828-692-1301	624
Durango Area Tourism Office 828 Main Ave ... Durango CO 81301	800-525-8855	970-247-3500	206
Durango Herald 1275 Main Ave ... Durango CO 81301	800-530-8318	970-247-3504	528-2
Dura-Stress Inc 11325 County Rd 44 ... Leesburg FL 34788 *General	800-342-9239*	352-787-1422	183
DuraTech Industries International Inc PO Box 1940 ... Jamestown ND 58401	800-243-4601	701-252-4601	273
Dura-Vent Inc 877 Cotting Ct ... Vacaville CA 95688	800-835-4429	707-446-1786	693
Duravit USA Inc 2205 Northmont Pkwy Ste 200 ... Duluth GA 30096	888-387-2848	770-931-3575	608
Durham Academy Inc 3130 Pickett Rd ... Durham NC 27705	888-904-9149	919-489-9118	681
Durham Convention & Visitors Bureau 101 E Morgan St ... Durham NC 27701	800-446-8604	919-687-0288	206
Durham Manufacturing Co 201 Main St ... Durham CT 06422	800-243-3774	860-349-3427	286
Durkin Equipment Company Inc 2383 Chaffee Dr ... Saint Louis MO 63146	800-264-3875	314-432-2040	357
Duro Dyne Corp 81 Spence St ... Bay Shore NY 11706	800-899-3876	631-249-9000	14
Durocher Auto Sales Inc 4651 Rt 9 ... Plattsburgh NY 12901	877-215-8954	518-563-3587	57
DUSA Pharmaceuticals Inc 25 Upton Dr ... Wilmington MA 01887 NASDAQ: DUSA	877-533-3872	978-657-7500	85
Dustex Corp 100 Chastain Ctr Blvd Ste 195 ... Kennesaw GA 30144	800-647-6167	770-429-5575	18
Dutailier Group Inc 299 Rue Chaput ... Sainte-Pie QC J0H1W0	800-363-9817	450-772-2403	319-2
Dutch Gold Honey Inc 2220 Dutch Gold Dr ... Lancaster PA 17601	800-846-2753	717-393-1716	296-24
Dutch Quality Stone 18012 Dover Rd ... Mount Eaton OH 44659	877-359-7866	330-359-7866	
Dutch Valley Bulk Food Distributors Inc 7615 Lancaster Ave ... Myerstown PA 17067	800-733-4191	717-933-4191	297-8
Dutch Wonderland 2249 Lincoln Hwy E ... Lancaster PA 17602	866-386-2839	717-291-1888	32
Dutchmen Mfg Inc 2164 Caragana Ct PO Box 2164 ... Goshen IN 46527	866-425-4369	574-537-0600	120
Dutt & Wagner of Virginia Inc 1142 W Main St ... Abingdon VA 24210	800-688-2116	276-628-2116	297-10
Duvinage Corp 60 W Oak Ridge Dr ... Hagerstown MD 21740	800-541-2645	301-733-8255	489
DuVoice Corp 608 State St S ... Kirkland WA 98033	800-888-1057	425-889-9790	225
DVD Empire 2140 Woodland Rd ... Warrendale PA 15086	888-383-1880		792
DVFlora (DVWF) 520 Mantua Blvd N ... Sewell NJ 08080	800-676-1212	856-468-7000	293
DVWF (DVFlora) 520 Mantua Blvd N ... Sewell NJ 08080	800-676-1212	856-468-7000	293
DW Green Co 8100 S Priest Dr ... Tempe AZ 85284	800-253-7146	480-491-8483	4
Dwfritz Automation Inc 12100 SW Tualatin Rd ... Wilsonville OR 97070	800-763-4161	503-598-9393	535
Dwight D Eisenhower Presidential Library & Museum 200 SE Fourth St ... Abilene KS 67410	877-746-4453	785-263-6700	433-2
Dwight D Eisenhower V A Medical Ctr 4101 S Fourth St ... Leavenworth KS 66048	800-952-8387	913-682-2000	373-8
Dworshak State Park 9934 Freeman Creek ... Lenore ID 83541	888-922-6743	208-476-5994	561
Dwyer Instruments Inc 102 Indiana Hwy 212 PO Box 373 ... Michigan City IN 46360	800-872-9141		
DXL (Destination XL Group Inc) 555 Tpke St ... Canton MA 02021 NASDAQ: DXLG	855-746-7395		
DXP Enterprises Inc 7272 Pinemont Dr ... Houston TX 77040 NASDAQ: DXPE	800-830-3973	713-996-4700	384
DXStormcom Inc 824 Winston Churchill Blvd ... Oakville ON L6J7X2	877-397-8676	905-842-8262	224
D&Y (Daniel & Yeager) 6767 Old Madison Pk Ste 690 ... Huntsville AL 35806	800-955-1919		266
DyAnsys Inc 300 N Bayshore Blvd ... San Mateo CA 94401	888-950-4321		738

	Toll-Free	Phone	Class
Dyatech 381 Highland Colony Pky ... Ridgeland MS 39157	866-651-4222	601-914-0533	389
Dycor Technologies Ltd 1851 94 St ... Edmonton AB T6N1E6	800-663-9267	780-486-0091	664
Dyer Riddle Mills & Precourt Inc (DRMP) 941 Lake Baldwin Ln ... Orlando FL 32814	800-375-3767	407-896-0594	261
Dymax Corp 318 Industrial Ln ... Torrington CT 06790	877-396-2963	860-482-1010	3
Dymedix Diagnostics 5985 Rice Creek Pkwy ... Shoreview MN 55126	888-212-1100	763-789-8280	
Dyna Flex Ltd PO Box 99 ... Saint Ann MO 63074	800-489-4020	314-426-4020	738
Dynabrade Inc 8989 Sheridan Dr ... Clarence NY 14031 *Cust Svc	800-828-7333*	716-631-0100	754
Dynadot LLC PO Box 345 ... San Mateo CA 94401 *Cust Svc	866-652-2039*	650-585-1961	395
Dynaflair Corp 8147 Eagle Palm Dr ... Tampa FL 33605	800-624-3667		
Dynagraphics Corp 4080 Norex St ... Chaska MN 55318	800-959-0108		203
Dynalco 3690 NW 53rd St ... Fort Lauderdale FL 33309	800-368-6666	954-739-4300	201
DynaLifeDX Diagnostic Laboratory Services 10150 - 102 St Ste 200 ... Edmonton AB T5J5E2	800-661-9876	780-451-3702	414
Dynaloy LLC 6445 Olivia Ln ... Indianapolis IN 46226	800-669-5709	317-788-5694	145
Dynamation Research Inc 2301 Pontius Ave ... Los Angeles CA 90064	800-726-7997	310-477-1224	349
Dynamet Inc 195 Museum Rd ... Washington PA 15301	800-237-9655	724-228-1000	483
DynaMetric Inc 717 S Myrtle Ave ... Monrovia CA 91016	800-525-6925	626-358-2559	730
Dynamic Computer Corp 23400 Industrial Pk Ct ... Farmington Hills MI 48335	866-257-2111	248-473-2200	174
Dynamic Homes LLC 525 Roosevelt Ave ... Detroit Lakes MN 56501	800-492-4833	218-847-2611	106
Dynamic Network Factory Inc 21353 Cabot Blvd ... Hayward CA 94545	800-947-4742	510-265-1122	173-8
DynamiCard Inc 215 S Hickory St Ste 220 ... Escondido CA 92025	800-928-7670		5
Dynamics Edge Inc 2635 N First St Ste #148 ... San Jose CA 95134	800-453-5961		196
Dynapar 1675 Delany Rd ... Gurnee IL 60031 *General	800-873-8731*		796
Dynapower Corp 85 Meadowland Dr ... South Burlington VT 05403	800-332-1111	802-860-7200	762
Dynaquip Controls 10 Harris Industrial Pk ... Saint Clair MO 63077	800-545-3636	636-629-3700	785
Dynarex Corp 10 Glenshaw St ... Orangeburg NY 10962	888-335-7500	845-365-8201	475
Dynasplint Systems Inc 770 Ritchie Hwy Ste W21 ... Severna Park MD 21146	800-638-6771	410-544-9530	264-4
Dynasty Gallery 2765 16th St ... San Francisco CA 94103	800-227-3344	415-864-5084	782
Dynasty Suites 1235 W Colton Ave ... Redlands CA 92374 *General	800-874-8958*	909-793-6648	378
Dynatem Inc 23263 Madero Ste C ... Mission Viejo CA 92691	800-543-3830	949-855-3235	621
Dynatronics Corp 7030 Pk Centre Dr ... Salt Lake City UT 84121 NASDAQ: DYNT	800-874-6251		250
Dynavax Technologies Corp 2929 Seventh St Ste 100 ... Berkeley CA 94710 NASDAQ: DVAX	877-848-5100	510-848-5100	578
Dynetics 1002 Explorer Blvd ... Huntsville AL 35806	800-964-4291	256-964-4000	531
Dynetics Engineering Corp 515 Bond St ... Lincolnshire IL 60069	800-888-8110	847-541-7300	111
Dynisco LLC 38 Forge Pkwy ... Franklin MA 02038 *General	800-396-4726*	508-541-9400	470
Dyno Nobel Inc 2795 E Cottonwood Pkwy Ste 400 ... Salt Lake City UT 84121	800-473-2675	801-364-4800	268
Dyonyx LP 1235 N Loop W ... Houston TX 77008 *General	855-749-6758*	713-485-7000	180
Dystonia Medical Research Foundation 1 E Wacker Dr Ste 2810 ... Chicago IL 60601 *General	800-377-3978*	312-755-0198	48-17
Dywidag Systems International 320 Marmon Dr ... Bolingbrook IL 60440	800-457-7633	630-739-1100	189-3

E

	Toll-Free	Phone	Class
E & V Energy 5700 State Rt 34 ... Auburn NY 13021	800-455-6522	315-253-6522	577
E Boineau & Co 128 Beaufain St ... Charleston SC 29401	800-579-2628	843-723-1462	632
E Commerce Partners 59 Franklin St ... New York NY 10013	866-431-6669	212-334-3390	225
E Dillon & Co 2522 Swords Creek Rd PO Box 160 ... Swords Creek VA 24649	800-234-8970	276-873-6816	183
E Gluck Corp 60-15 Little Neck Pkwy ... Little Neck NY 11362	800-840-2933	718-784-0700	153
E H Lynn Industries Inc 524 Anderson Dr ... Romeoville IL 60446	800-633-2948	815-328-8800	785

	Toll-Free	Phone	Class
E Hofmann Plastics Inc			
51 Centennial Rd . . . . Orangeville ON L9W3R1	**877-707-7245**	519-943-5050	599
E J Harrison & Sons			
PO Box 4009 . . . . Ventura CA 93007	**800-418-7274**	805-647-1414	799
E S Robbins Corp			
2802 Avalon Ave . . . . Muscle Shoals AL 35661	**866-934-6018**	256-248-2400	596
E Sam Jones Distributor Inc			
4898 S Atlanta Rd . . . . Atlanta GA 30339	**800-624-9849**	404-351-3250	246
E T & F Fastening Systems			
29019 Solon Rd . . . . Solon OH 44139	**800-248-2376**	440-248-8655	278
E*Trade Bank			
671 N Glebe Rd . . . . Arlington VA 22203	**877-800-1208**		70
E*Trade Financial Corp			
1271 Ave of the Americas			
14th Fl . . . . New York NY 10020	**800-387-2331**		686
NASDAQ: ETFC			
E3 Consulting Inc			
3333 S Bannock St Ste 500 . . . . Englewood CO 80110	**877-788-6676**	303-762-7060	
EAA (Experimental Aircraft Assn)			
3000 Poberezny Rd . . . . Oshkosh WI 54902	**800-236-4800**	920-426-4800	48-18
EAA AirVenture Museum			
3000 Poberezny Rd . . . . Oshkosh WI 54902	**888-322-3229**	920-426-4800	517
eAcceleration Corp			
1050 NE Hostmark St Ste 100-B . . . . Poulsbo WA 98370	**800-803-4588***	360-779-6301	178-7
*Sales			
EADS Group			
1126 Eigth Ave . . . . Altoona PA 16602	**800-626-0904**	814-944-5035	261
Eagan Convention & Visitors Bureau			
1501 Central Pkwy . . . . Eagan MN 55121	**866-324-2620**	651-675-5546	206
Eagan Insurance Agency Inc			
2629 N Cswy Blvd . . . . Metairie LA 70002	**888-882-9600**	504-836-9600	389
Eagle Asset Management			
880 Carillon Pkwy . . . . Saint Petersburg FL 33716	**800-237-3101**		400
Eagle Aviation			
2861 Aviation Way			
Columbia Metropolitan Airport . . . . West Columbia SC 29170	**800-849-3245**	803-822-5555	63
Eagle Bancorp Inc			
7815 Woodmont Ave . . . . Bethesda MD 20814	**800-364-8313**	301-986-1800	359-2
NASDAQ: EGBN			
Eagle Cleaning Service Inc			
525 Belview St . . . . Bessemer AL 35020	**877-864-5696**	205-424-5252	104
Eagle Communications Inc			
2703 Hall St Ste 15. . . . . Hays KS 67601	**877-613-2453**	785-625-5910	639
Eagle Comtronics Inc			
7665 Henry Clay Blvd . . . . Liverpool NY 13088	**800-448-7474**	315-622-3402	643
Eagle Copters Ltd			
823 Mctavish Rd NE . . . . Calgary AB T2E7G9	**800-564-6469**	403-250-7370	358
Eagle County			
500 Broadway - PO Box 850 . . . . Eagle CO 81631	**800-225-6136**	970-328-8600	337
Eagle Direct			
1 Printer's Dr . . . . Hermon ME 04401	**800-675-7669**	207-848-7300	7
Eagle Energy Trust			
500 4 Ave SW Ste 2710 . . . . Calgary AB T2P2V6	**855-531-1575**	403-531-1575	532
Eagle Family Foods Group LLC			
1 Strawberry Ln . . . . Orrville OH 44667	**888-550-9555**		296-27
Eagle Grips Inc			
460 Randy Rd . . . . Carol Stream IL 60188	**800-323-6144**	630-260-0400	707
Eagle Group Inc			
100 Industrial Blvd . . . . Clayton DE 19938	**800-441-8440**		300
Eagle Marketing Inc Perfume Originals Products Div			
150 W First St . . . . Cortland NE 68331	**800-233-7424**		570
Eagle Materials Inc			
3811 Turtle Creek Blvd Ste 1100 . . . . Dallas TX 75219	**800-759-7625**	214-432-2000	135
NYSE: EXP			
Eagle Mountain Casino			
681 S Reservation Rd			
PO Box 1659. . . . . Porterville CA 93257	**800-903-3353**		133
Eagle Mountain House			
179 Carter Notch Rd PO Box 804 . . . . Jackson NH 03846	**800-966-5779**	603-383-9111	378
Eagle One Golf Products Inc			
1340 N Jefferson St . . . . Anaheim CA 92807	**800-448-4409**	714-983-0050	706
Eagle Parts & Products Inc			
1411 Marvin Griffin Rd . . . . Augusta GA 30906	**888-972-9911**	706-790-6687	61
Eagle Pass Chamber of Commerce			
400 E Garrison St . . . . Eagle Pass TX 78852	**888-355-3224**	830-773-3224	139
Eagle Point National Cemetery			
2763 Riley Rd . . . . Eagle Point OR 97524	**800-535-1117**	541-826-2511	136
Eagle Point Software Corp			
600 Star Brewery Dr Ste 200. . . . . Dubuque IA 52001	**800-678-6565**		178-10
Eagle Professional Resources Inc			
170 Laurier Ave W Ste 902 . . . . Ottawa ON K1P5V5	**800-281-2339**	613-234-1810	717
Eagle Radio Inc			
2703 Hall St Ste 15. . . . . Hays KS 67601	**877-613-2453**		639
Eagle Recognition			
2706 Mtn Industrial Blvd . . . . Tucker GA 30084	**888-287-4240**	770-985-0808	184
Eagle Ridge Hospital & Health Care Ctr			
475 Guildford Way . . . . Port Moody BC V3H3W9	**800-465-4911**	604-461-2022	373-2
Eagle Ridge Inn & Resort			
444 Eagle Ridge Dr . . . . Galena IL 61036	**800-892-2269**	815-777-2444	665
Eagle Roller Mill Co			
1101 Airport Rd . . . . Shelby NC 28150	**800-223-9108**	704-487-5061	445
Eagle Stainless Tube & Fabrication Inc			
10 Discovery Way . . . . Franklin MA 02038	**800-528-8650**	508-528-8650	
Eagle Technology Inc			
11019 N Towne Sq Rd . . . . Mequon WI 53092	**800-388-3268**	262-241-3845	177
Eagle Transport Corp			
300 S Wesleyan Blvd Ste 202. . . . . . . Rocky Mount NC 27804	**800-776-9937**	252-937-2464	775
Eagle's Flight, Creative Training Excellence Inc			
489 Clair Rd W . . . . Guelph ON N1L0H7	**800-567-8079**	519-767-1747	461
Eagle's Nest Foundation			
43 Hart Rd . . . . Pisgah Forest NC 28768	**800-951-7442**	828-877-4349	239
Eagle:XM LLC			
5105 E 41st Ave . . . . Denver CO 80216	**800-426-5376**	303-320-5411	623
Eagle-Picher Minerals Inc			
9785 Gateway Dr . . . . Reno NV 89521	**800-228-3865***	775-824-7600	498
*Cust Svc			
Eagle-Tribune			
100 Tpke St . . . . North Andover MA 01845	**800-927-9200**	978-946-2000	528-2
Eagleville Hospital			
100 Eagleville Rd . . . . Eagleville PA 19408	**800-255-2019***	610-539-6000	722
*General			
Eaglewood Resort & Spa			
1401 Nordic Rd . . . . Itasca IL 60143	**877-285-6150**	630-773-1400	665
Eakes Office Plus			
617 W Third St . . . . Grand Island NE 68801	**800-652-9396**	308-382-8026	531
EANGUS (Enlisted Assn of the National Guard of the US)			
3133 Mt Vernon Ave . . . . Alexandria VA 22305	**800-234-3264**	703-519-3846	48-19
EAP Systems			
500 W Cummings Pk . . . . Woburn MA 01801	**800-535-4841**	781-935-8850	460
EAPA (Employee Assistance Professionals Assn Inc)			
4350 N Fairfax Dr Ste 740 . . . . Arlington VA 22203	**800-937-8461**	703-387-1000	49-12
Earhart Petroleum Inc			
PO Box 39 . . . . Troy OH 45373	**800-686-2928**	937-335-2928	575
Earl Burns Miller Japanese Garden			
1250 Bellflower Blvd . . . . Long Beach CA 90840	**800-985-8880**	562-985-8885	97
Earl G Graves Ltd			
130 Fifth Ave 10th Fl . . . . New York NY 10011	**800-727-7777***	212-242-8000	633-9
*Cust Svc			
Earl L Henderson Trucking Inc			
8118 Bunkum Rd . . . . Caseyville IL 62232	**800-447-8084**	618-623-0057	775
Earl May Seed & Nursery			
208 N Elm St . . . . Shenandoah IA 51603	**800-843-9608**	712-246-1020	323
Earl's Apparel Inc			
908 S Fourth St . . . . Crockett TX 75835	**800-527-3148**	936-544-5521	155-18
Earle M Jorgensen Co			
10650 S Alameda St . . . . Lynwood CA 90262	**800-336-5365***	323-567-1122	488
*Sales			
Earlham College			
801 National Rd W . . . . Richmond IN 47374	**800-327-5426**	765-983-1600	166
Earlham School of Religion			
228 College Ave . . . . Richmond IN 47374	**800-432-1377**	765-983-1423	167-3
Early County			
PO Box 693 . . . . Blakely GA 39823	**800-436-7442**		
Early Learning Coalition of Miami Dade & Monroe			
2555 Ponce De Leon Blvd			
Ste 500 . . . . Coral Gables FL 33134	**800-962-2873**	305-646-7220	242
Earnest Partners LLC			
1180 Peachtree St Ste 2300 . . . . Atlanta GA 30309	**800-322-0068**	404-815-8772	400
Earnhardt Auto Centers			
7300 W Orchid Ln . . . . Chandler AZ 05220	**888-378-7711**	480-926-4000	57
Earth Island			
9201 Owensmouth Ave . . . . Chatsworth CA 91311	**888-394-3949**	818-725-2820	296-33
Earth Networks Inc			
12410 Milestone Ctr Dr			
Ste 300 . . . . Germantown MD 20876	**800-544-4429**	301-250-4000	192
Earth Share			
7735 Old Georgetown Rd Ste 900. . . . . . . Bethesda MD 20814	**800-875-3863**	240-333-0300	48-13
Earth Systems Services Inc			
720 Aerovista Pl			
Ste 102 . . . . San Luis Obispo CA 93401	**866-781-0112**	805-781-0112	192
Earthbound Farm			
1721 San Juan Hwy . . . . San Juan Bautista CA 95045	**800-690-3200**	831-623-7880	10-9
EarthLink Inc			
1170 Peachtree St Ste 900 . . . . Atlanta GA 30309	**866-383-3080**		397
NASDAQ: ELNK			
EarthLinked Technologies Inc			
4151 S Pipkin Rd . . . . Lakeland FL 33811	**866-211-6102**	863-701-0096	35
EarthRes Group Inc			
6912 Old Easton Rd			
PO Box 468. . . . . Pipersville PA 18947	**800-264-4553**	215-766-1211	261
Earthwatch Institute			
114 Western Ave . . . . Boston MA 02134	**800-776-0188**	978-461-0081	48-13
EarthWay Products Inc			
1009 Maple St . . . . Bristol IN 46507	**800-294-0671**	574-848-7491	428
Ease Technologies Inc			
10320 Little Patuxent Pkwy			
Ste 1104 . . . . Columbia MD 21044	**888-327-3911**	301-854-0010	225
EASI 7301 Pkwy Dr . . . . Hanover MI 21076	**888-963-7740**	410-567-8061	461
East Arkansas Community College			
1700 Newcastle Rd . . . . Forrest City AR 72335	**877-797-3222**	870-633-4480	162
East Balt Inc			
1801 W 31st Pl . . . . Chicago IL 60608	**800-621-8555**	773-376-4444	68
East Bay Tire Co			
2200 Huntington Dr Unit C. . . . . Fairfield CA 94533	**800-831-8473**	707-437-4700	750
East Boston Savings Bank			
10 Meridian St . . . . East Boston MA 02128	**800-657-3272**	617-567-1500	70
East Carolina University			
E Fifth St . . . . Greenville NC 27858	**800-328-0577**	252-328-6131	166
East Central College			
1964 Prairie Dell Rd . . . . Union MO 63084	**800-392-6848**	636-583-5193	162
East Central Community College			
15738 Hwy 15 S PO Box 129 . . . . Decatur MS 39327	**877-462-3222**	601-635-2111	162
East Central Energy			
PO Box 39 . . . . Braham MN 55006	**800-254-7944**		245
East Coast Metal Distributors Inc			
1313 S Briggs Ave . . . . Durham NC 27703	**844-227-9531**	919-596-2136	608
East Coast Metals			
171 Ruth Rd . . . . Harleysville PA 19438	**800-355-2060**	215-256-9550	490
East Fairfield Coal Co (EFCC)			
10900 S Ave PO Box 217 . . . . North Lima OH 44452	**800-241-7074**	330-549-2165	499
East Georgia College			
131 College Cir . . . . Swainsboro GA 30401	**800-715-4255**	478-289-2000	162
East Georgia Regional Medical Ctr (EGRMC)			
1499 Fair Rd . . . . Statesboro GA 30458	**844-455-8708**	912-486-1000	373-3
East Hampton Star Inc, The			
153 Main St PO Box 5002 . . . . East Hampton NY 11937	**844-324-0777**	631-324-0002	633-8
East Houston Regional Medical Ctr			
13111 E Fwy . . . . Houston TX 77015	**800-979-3627**	713-393-2000	373-3
East Jefferson General Hospital (EJGH)			
4200 Houma Blvd . . . . Metairie LA 70006	**866-280-7737**	504-454-4000	373-3
East Jordan Plastics Inc			
PO Box 575 . . . . East Jordan MI 49727	**800-353-1190**		598
East Lion Corp			
318 Brea Canyon Rd . . . . City of Industry CA 91789	**877-939-1818**	626-912-1818	301
East Mfg Corp			
1871 State Rt 44 PO Box 277 . . . . Randolph OH 44265	**888-405-3278**	330-325-9921	774

	Toll-Free	Phone	Class

East Orange Campus of the VA New Jersey Health Care System (NJHCS)
385 Tremont Ave .... East Orange NJ 07018 · **844-872-4681*** · · 373-8
*General

East River Energy Inc
401 Soundview Rd PO Box 388 .... Guilford CT 06437 · **800-336-3762** · 203-453-1200 · 575

East Side Moving & Storage
4836 SE Powell Blvd .... Portland OR 97206 · **800-547-4600** · 503-777-4181 · 516

East Side Plating Inc
8400 SE 26th Pl .... Portland OR 97202 · **800-394-8554** · 503-654-3774 · 479

East Stroudsburg University
200 Prospect St .... East Stroudsburg PA 18301 · **877-230-5547*** · 570-422-3542 · 166
*Admissions

East Stroudsburg University Kemp Library
200 Prospect St .... East Stroudsburg PA 18301 · **877-422-1378** · 570-422-3465 · 433-6

East Teak Trading Group Inc
1106 Drake Rd .... Donalds SC 29638 · **800-338-5636** · 864-379-2111 · 349

East Tennessee Historical Society
601 S Gay St PO Box 1629 .... Knoxville TN 37901 · **800-407-4324** · 865-215-8824 · 517

East Tennessee State University
PO Box 70731 .... Johnson City TN 37614 · **800-462-3878** · 423-439-4213 · 166

East Texas Baptist University
1209 N Grove St .... Marshall TX 75670 · **800-804-3828** · 903-935-7963 · 166

East Valley Tribune
120 W First Ave .... Mesa AZ 85210 · **877-728-5414** · 480-898-6500 · 528-2

East West Bank
135 N Los Robles Ave 7th Fl .... Pasadena CA 91101 · **888-895-5650** · 626-768-6000 · 359-2
NASDAQ: EWBC

East West Bookshop
324 Castro St .... Mountain View CA 94041 · **800-909-6161** · 650-988-9800 · 95

East West Label Co
1000 E Hector St .... Conshohocken PA 19428 · **800-441-7333** · 610-825-0410 · 412

East-Central Iowa Rural Electric Co-op
2400 Bing Miller Ln .... Urbana IA 52345 · **877-850-4343** · 319-443-4343 · 245

Easter Owens Electric Co
6692 Fig St .... Arvada CO 80004 · **866-204-3707** · 303-431-0111 · 203

Easter Seals
230 W Monroe St Ste 1800 .... Chicago IL 60606 · **800-221-6827** · 312-726-6200 · 48-17

Eastern Arizona College
615 N Stadium Ave .... Thatcher AZ 85552 · **800-678-3808** · 928-428-8472 · 162

Eastern Bank
1 Eastern Pl .... Lynn MA 01901 · **800-327-8376** · 800-333-7234 · 70

Eastern Bank Corp
265 Franklin St .... Boston MA 02110 · **800-327-8376*** · 800-333-7234 · 359-2
*Cust Svc

Eastern Business Forms Inc
PO Box 10 .... Mauldin SC 29662 · **800-387-2648** · · 110

Eastern Co, The
112 Bridge St PO Box 460 .... Naugatuck CT 06770 · **800-221-0982** · 203-729-2255 · 349
NASDAQ: EML

Eastern Concrete Materials Inc
475 Market St .... Elmwood Park NJ 07407 · **800-822-7242** · 817-835-4105 · 182

Eastern Connecticut State University
83 Windham St .... Willimantic CT 06226 · **877-353-3278*** · 860-465-5000 · 166
*Admissions

Eastern Connecticut State University Smith Library
83 Windham St .... Willimantic CT 06226 · **800-578-1449** · 860-465-4506 · 433-6

Eastern Floral & Gift Shop
818 Butterworth St SW .... Grand Rapids MI 49504 · **800-494-2202** · 616-949-2200 · 292

Eastern Foods Inc
1000 Naturally Fresh Blvd .... Atlanta GA 30349 · **800-765-1950** · 800-236-1119 · 296-19

Eastern Gateway Community College
4000 Sunset Blvd .... Steubenville OH 43952 · **800-682-6553** · 740-264-5591 · 795

Eastern Idaho Technical College
1600 S 25th E .... Idaho Falls ID 83404 · **800-662-0261** · 208-524-3000 · 795

Eastern Illini Electric Co-op
330 W Ottawa PO Box 96 .... Paxton IL 60957 · **800-824-5102** · 217-379-2131 · 245

Eastern Illinois University
600 Lincoln Ave .... Charleston IL 61920 · **800-252-5711*** · 217-581-2223 · 166
*Admissions

Eastern Iowa Light & Power Co-op
600 E Fifth St PO Box 3003 .... Wilton IA 52778 · **800-728-1242** · 563-732-2211 · 245

Eastern Kentucky University
521 Lancaster Ave .... Richmond KY 40475 · **800-465-9191** · 859-622-2106 · 166

Eastern Lift Truck Company Inc
549 E Linwood Ave .... Maple Shade NJ 08052 · **866-980-7175** · 856-779-8880 · 384

Eastern Maine Community College
354 Hogan Rd .... Bangor ME 04401 · **800-286-9357** · 207-974-4600 · 795

Eastern Maine Electric Co-op Inc
21 Union St .... Calais ME 04619 · **800-696-7444** · 207-454-7555 · 245

Eastern Maine Healthcare Systems (EMHS)
797 Wilson St Ste 4 .... Brewer ME 04412 · **877-366-3662** · 207-973-5578 · 352

Eastern Mennonite University
1200 Pk Rd .... Harrisonburg VA 22802 · **800-368-2665*** · 540-432-4118 · 166
*Admissions

Eastern Metal/USA-SIGN
1430 Sullivan St .... Elmira NY 14901 · **800-872-7446*** · 607-734-2295 · 697
*Sales

Eastern Michigan University
900 Oakwood St .... Ypsilanti MI 48197 · **800-468-6368** · 734-487-1849 · 166

Eastern Michigan University Halle Library
955 W Cir Dr .... Ypsilanti MI 48197 · **888-888-3465** · 734-487-0020 · 433-6

Eastern Mountain Sports
1 Vose Farm Rd .... Peterborough NH 03458 · **888-463-6367** · 203-379-2233 · 707

Eastern Nazarene College
23 E Elm Ave .... Quincy MA 02170 · **800-883-6288** · 617-745-3000 · 166

Eastern New Mexico University
1500 S Ave K .... Portales NM 88130 · **800-367-3668** · 575-562-1011 · 166

Eastern New Mexico University Roswell
52 University Blvd .... Roswell NM 88203 · **800-243-6687** · 575-624-7000 · 162

Eastern New Mexico University-ruidoso
709 Mechem Dr .... Ruidoso NM 88345 · **800-934-3668** · 575-257-2120 · 166

Eastern Oklahoma District Library System
801 W Okmulgee Ave .... Muskogee OK 74401 · **888-291-8152** · 918-682-6657 · 433-3

Eastern Oregon University
1 University Blvd .... La Grande OR 97850 · **800-452-8639** · 541-962-3393 · 166

Eastern Pennsylvania Supply Co
700 Scott St .... Wilkes-Barre PA 18705 · **800-432-8075** · 570-823-1181 · 608

Eastern Sheet Metal LLC
8959 Blue Ash Rd .... Blue Ash OH 45242 · **800-348-3440** · ·

Eastern Shore Natural Gas Co
1110 Forest Ave Ste 201 .... Dover DE 19904 · **877-650-1257** · 302-734-6720 · 782

Eastern Skateboard Supply Inc
6612 Amsterdam Way .... Wilmington NC 28405 · **800-358-7588** · 910-791-8240 · 707

Eastern University
1300 Eagle Rd .... Wayne PA 19087 · **800-452-0996*** · 610-341-5800 · 166
*Admissions

Eastern Washington University
102 Sutton Hall .... Cheney WA 99004 · **800-280-1256** · 509-359-6200 · 166

Eastern West Virginia Community & Technical College
316 Eastern Dr .... Moorefield WV 26836 · **877-982-2322** · 304-434-8000 · 162

Eastern Wholesale Fence Co Inc
274 Middle Island Rd .... Medford NY 11763 · **800-339-3362** · 631-698-0900 · 191-2

Eastern Wyoming College
3200 W 'C' St .... Torrington WY 82240 · **800-658-3195** · 307-532-8200 · 162

Eastex Telephone Co-op Inc
PO Box 150 .... Henderson TX 75653 · **800-232-7839** · 903-854-1000 · 731

EastGroup Properties Inc
188 E Capitol St .... Jackson MS 39201 · **800-695-1564** · 601-354-3555 · 651
NYSE: EGP

Eastland Shoe Mfg Corp
4 Meeting House Rd .... Freeport ME 04032 · **888-988-1998** · 207-865-6314 · 301

Eastman Chemical Co
200 S Wilcox Dr .... Kingsport TN 37660 · **800-327-8626*** · 423-229-2000 · 144
NYSE: EMN ■ *Cust Svc

Eastman Machine Co
779 Washington St .... Buffalo NY 14203 · **800-872-5571** · 716-856-2200 · 739

Easton Hospital
250 S 21st St .... Easton PA 18042 · **866-800-3880** · 610-250-4000 · 373-3

Eastover Estate & Eco-Village
430 East St PO Box 2282 .... Lenox MA 01240 · **866-264-5139** · ·

Eastridge Workforce Solutions
2355 Northside Dr .... San Diego CA 92108 · **800-778-0197** · 619-260-2100 · 729

Easy Ice LLC
925 W Washington St Ste 100 .... Marquette MI 49855 · **866-327-9423** · · 786

easyDNS Technologies Inc
219 Dufferin St Ste 300A .... Toronto ON M6K3J1 · **855-321-3279** · 416-535-8672 · 395

Easyriders Magazine
28210 Dorothy Dr .... Agoura Hills CA 91301 · **800-323-3484** · 818-889-8740 · 455-3

EasyStreet
9705 SW Sunshine Ct .... Beaverton OR 97005 · **800-207-0740*** · 503-646-8400 · 225
*Support

Easyturf
2750 La Mirada Dr .... Vista CA 92081 · **866-353-3518** · 866-327-9887 · 604

Eat With Us
PO Box 1368 .... Columbus MS 39703 · **888-222-9550** · 662-327-6982 · 667

Eat'n Park Hospitality Group
285 E Waterfront Dr .... Homestead PA 15120 · **800-947-4033** · 412-461-2000 · 666

EATELCORP Inc
913 S Burnside Ave .... Gonzales LA 70737 · **800-621-4211** · 225-621-4300 · 731

Eaton Metal Products Co
4803 York St .... Denver CO 80216 · **800-208-2657** · 303-296-4800 · 91

Eaton Office Supply Company Inc
180 John Glenn Dr .... Buffalo NY 14228 · **800-365-3237** · 716-691-6100 · 530

Eaton Oil Tools Inc
118 Rue DuPain .... Broussard LA 70518 · **800-232-5317** · 337-856-8820 · 535

Eaton Steel Corp
10221 Capital Ave .... Oak Park MI 48237 · **800-527-3851** · 248-398-3434 · 490

Eaton Vance Mutual Funds
2 International Pl .... Boston MA 02110 · **800-225-6265** · 800-836-2414 · 524

Eatons' Ranch
270 Eatons' Ranch Rd .... Wolf WY 82844 · **800-210-1049** · 307-655-9285 · 239

EatStreet Inc
316 Washington Ave Ste 725 .... Madison WI 53703 · **866-654-8777** · · 386

EB Bradley Co
5080 S Alameda St .... Los Angeles CA 90058 · **800-533-3030** · 323-585-9201 · 350

Ebara Technologies Inc
51 Main Ave .... Sacramento CA 95838 · **800-535-5376** · 916-920-5451 · 691

eBay Inc
2065 Hamilton Ave .... San Jose CA 95125 · **800-322-9266** · 408-376-7400 · 51
NASDAQ: EBAY

Eberhard Hardware Manufacturing Ltd
1523 Bellmill Rd .... Tillsonburg ON N4GOC9 · **800-567-3344** · 519-688-3443 · 349

Eberhard Mfg Co
21944 Drake Rd .... Strongsville OH 44149 · **800-334-6706** · 440-238-9720 · 349

EBI Consulting Inc
21 B St .... Burlington MA 01803 · **800-786-2346** · 781-273-2500 · 196

Ebix BPO 151 N Lyon Ave .... Hemet CA 92543 · **800-996-9964** · 951-658-4000 · 225

Ebix Inc
5 Concourse Pkwy Ste 3200 .... Atlanta GA 30328 · **800-755-2326** · 678-281-2020 · 178-11
NASDAQ: EBIX

Ebonite International Inc
PO Box 746 .... Hopkinsville KY 42241 · **800-326-6483** · 270-881-1200 · 706

ebQuickstart
3000 S IH 35 Ste 320 .... Austin TX 78704 · **800-566-3050** · 512-637-9696 · 195

EBSCO Creative Concepts
3500 Blue Lake Dr Ste 150 .... Birmingham AL 35243 · **800-756-7023** · 205-980-6789 · 9

EBSCO Information Services
PO Box 1943 .... Birmingham AL 35201 · **800-758-5995** · 205-991-6600 · 386

EBSCO Information Services
10 Estes St .... Ipswich MA 01938 · **800-653-2726** · 978-356-6500 · 96

EBSCO Publishing Inc
10 Estes St .... Ipswich MA 01938 · **800-633-4604** · 978-356-6500 · 633-10

E-Builder Inc
1800 NW 69 Ave Ste 201 .... Plantation FL 33313 · **800-580-9322** · 954-556-6701 · 39

Ebus Inc
9250 Washburn Rd .... Downey CA 90242 · **888-925-4263** · 562-904-3474 · 513

eBX LLC
101 Federal St Ste 1010 .... Boston MA 02110 · **800-958-4813** · 617-350-1600 · 686

Eby Co 4300 H St .... Philadelphia PA 19124 · **800-329-3430** · 215-537-4700 · 253

Eby-Brown Co
1415 W Diehl Rd Ste 300N .... Naperville IL 60563 · **800-553-8249** · 630-778-2800 · 751

EC Ernst Inc
132 Log Canoe Cir .... Stevensville MD 21666 · **800-683-7770** · 301-350-7770 · 189-4

ECA (Evangelical Church Alliance)
205 W Broadway St PO Box 9 .... Bradley IL 60915 · **888-855-6060** · 815-937-0720 · 48-20

ECA Edinburg Citrus Association
PO Box 428 .... Edinburg TX 78540 · **877-381-1322** · 956-383-2743 ·

Alphabetical Section

Name / Address	Toll-Free	Phone	Class
ECCB (Erie 2-Chautauqua Cattaraugus Boces) 8685 Erie Rd ....Angola NY 14006	800-228-1184	716-549-4454	681
ECCO 833 W Diamond St ....Boise ID 83705	800-635-5900		696
EcElectric 2121 NW Thurman St ....Portland OR 97210	800-659-3511	503-224-3511	189-4
Ecessa Corp 13755 First Ave N Ste 100 ....Plymouth MN 55441	800-669-6242	763-694-9949	730
ECFA (Evangelical Council for Financial Accountability) 440 W Jubal Early Dr Ste 130 ....Winchester VA 22601	800-323-9473	540-535-0103	48-5
ECG Management Consultants 1111 Third Ave Ste 2500 ....Seattle WA 98101	800-729-7635	206-689-2200	194
Echelon Corp 550 Meridian Ave ....San Jose CA 95126 NASDAQ: ELON	888-324-3566	408-938-5200	176
Echo Design Group 10 E 40th St 16th Fl ....New York NY 10016 *General	800-327-3896*	212-686-8771	155-12
Echo Global Logistics Inc 600 W Chicago Ave Ste 725 ....Chicago IL 60654	800-354-7993		194
Echo Group Inc, The 15 Washington St ....Conway NH 03818	800-635-8209	603-447-8600	177
Echo Inc 400 Oakwood Rd ....Lake Zurich IL 60047	800-673-1558	855-706-1522	428
Echo Lake Farm Produce Co PO Box 279 ....Burlington WI 53105	800-888-3447		10-7
EchoData Services Inc 121 N Shirk Rd ....New Holland PA 17557	800-511-3870		392
Echomountain Llc 1483 Patriot Blvd ....Glenview IL 60026	877-311-1980		180
Echota Fabrics Inc 1394 US 41 N ....Calhoun GA 30701	800-763-9750	706-629-9750	741
ECI (Engine Components Inc) 9503 Middlex ....San Antonio TX 78217	800-324-2359	210-820-8101	21
ECI Systems 68 Stiles Rd Unit C ....Salem NH 03079	800-639-2086	603-898-6823	689
ECII (Engineered Controls International Inc) 100 Rego Dr PO Box 247 ....Elon NC 27244	800-650-0061	336-449-7707	784
eCivis Inc 418 N Fair Oaks Ave Ste 301 ....Pasadena CA 91103	877-232-4847		69
Eckards Home Improvement 2402 N Delt I Iwy ....Saint Jocoph MO 64506	800-264-2794	816-279-4522	290
Eckel Mfg Company Inc 8035 N County Rd W ....Odessa TX 79764	800-654-4779	432-362-4336	223
Eckerd College 4200 54th Ave S ....Saint Petersburg FL 33711 *Admissions	800-456-9009*	727-867-1166	166
Eckhart & Company Inc 4011 W 54th St ....Indianapolis IN 46254	800-443-3791	317-347-2665	86
Eclectic Products Inc 1075 Arrowsmith St PO Box 2280 ....Eugene OR 97402	800-693-4667		3
Eclipse Colour & Imaging Corp 875 Laurentian Dr ....Burlington ON L7N3W7	800-668-6369	905-634-1900	623
Eclipse Inc 1665 Elmwood Rd ....Rockford IL 61103	888-826-3473	815-877-3031	318
Eclipse Marketing Services Inc 240 Cedar Knolls Rd Ste 100 ....Cedar Knolls NJ 07927	800-837-4648		195
ECO Canada 308 – 11th Ave SE Ste 200 ....Calgary AB T2G0Y2	800-251-7773	403-233-0748	759
Eco Lips Inc 329 Tenth Ave SE Ste 213 ....Cedar Rapids IA 52401	866-326-5477	319-364-2477	
Eco Water Systems Inc 1890 Woodlane Dr ....Woodbury MN 55125	800-808-9899		426
Ecodyne Ltd 4475 Corporate Dr ....Burlington ON L7L5T9	888-326-3963	905-332-1404	385
ECOF (Eye Centers of Florida) 4101 Evans Ave ....Fort Myers FL 33901	888-393-2455	239-939-3456	793
Ecojustice Canada 131 Water St Ste 214 ....Vancouver BC V6B4M3	800-926-7744	604-685-5618	48-13
eCollect PO Box 241548 ....Mayfield OH 44124	888-569-6001		392
Ecolo Odor Control Technologies Inc 59 Penn Dr ....Toronto ON M9L2A6	800-667-6355	416-740-3900	104
E-Commerce Times (ECT) 16133 Ventura Blvd Ste 700 ....Encino CA 91436	877-328-5500	818-461-9700	455-5
Econoco Corp 300 Karin Ln ....Hicksville NY 11801	800-645-7032	516-935-7700	286
Econ-o-copy Inc 4437 Trenton St Ste A ....Metairie LA 70006	877-256-0310	504-457-0032	531
Econolite Control Products Inc 3360 E La Palma Av ....Anaheim CA 92806	800-225-6480	714-630-3700	696
Economic Development Administration Regional Office *Atlanta* 401 W Peachtree St NW Ste 1820 ......Atlanta GA 30308	800-518-4726	404-730-3002	339-2
Seattle 915 Second Ave Rm 1890 ....Seattle WA 98174	800-518-4726	206-220-7660	339-2
Economical Insurance 111 Westmount Rd S PO Box 2000 .....Waterloo ON N2J4S4	800-265-2180	519-570-8200	390-4
eContent Magazine 143 Old Marlton Pk ....Medford NJ 08055	800-300-9868	609-654-6266	455-7
eCornell 950 Danby Rd Ste 150 ....Ithaca NY 14850	866-326-7635	607-330-3200	242
Ecosmart 3315 N West 167th St ....Miami Gardens FL 33056	877-474-6473		
EcoTarium 222 Harrington Way ....Worcester MA 01604	800-625-7738	508-929-2700	518
eCreative Group Inc 1827 First St W Ste B PO Box 66 ....Independence IA 50644	877-334-5115	319-334-5115	
ECRI Institute 5200 Butler Pk ....Plymouth Meeting PA 19462	866-247-3004	610-825-6000	48-17
ECS (Electronic Cash Systems Inc) 29883 Santa Margarita Pkwy ....Rancho Santa Margarita CA 92688	888-327-2860	949-888-8580	56
ECS & R 3237 US Hwy 19 ....Cochranton PA 16314	866-815-0016	814-425-7773	196
ECS Financial Services Inc 3400 Dundee Rd ....Northbrook IL 60062	800-826-7070	847-291-1333	2
ECT (E-Commerce Times) 16133 Ventura Blvd Ste 700 ....Encino CA 91436	877-328-5500	818-461-9700	455-5
Ectaco Inc 31-21 31st St ....Long Island NY 11106	800-710-7920	718-728-6110	173-2
ECU (Educators Credit Union) 1400 N Newman Rd PO Box 081040 ......Racine WI 53406	800-236-5898	262-886-5900	219
E-cubed Media Synthesis Ltd 3807 William St ....Burnaby BC V5C3J1	800-294-1556	604-294-1556	225
ECWA (Erie County Water Authority) 295 Main St Rm 350 ....Buffalo NY 14203	855-748-1076	716-849-8484	782
eCycle LLC 4105 Leap Rd Ste 250 ....Hilliard OH 43026	877-215-5255		
ED Etnyre & Co 1333 S Daysville Rd ....Oregon IL 61061	800-995-2116	815-732-2116	190
Ed Fagan Inc 769 Susquehanna Ave ....Franklin Lakes NJ 07417	800-335-6827	201-891-4003	490
Ed Martin Inc 3800 E 96th St ....Indianapolis IN 46240	800-211-5410	317-846-3800	57
Ed Staub & Sons Petroleum Inc 1301 Esplanade Ave ....Klamath Falls OR 97601	800-435-3835		316
Eda Staffing Inc 132 Central St Ste 206 ....Foxboro ME 02035	800-886-9332	508-543-0333	
EDC (Education Development Ctr Inc) 55 Chapel St ....Newton MA 02458	800-225-4276	617-969-7100	48-11
Edcomm Inc 1300 Virginia Dr Ste 220 ....Fort Washington PA 19034	888-433-2666	215-542-6900	244
Eddie Bauer LLC PO Box 7001 ....Groveport OH 43125 *Orders	800-426-8020*		157-4
Eddington Thread Manufacturing Co PO Box 446 ....Bensalem PA 19020	800-220-8901	215-639-8900	740-9
Eddy Packing Company Inc 404 Airport Dr ....Yoakum TX 77995	800-292-2361	361-293-2361	471
Eddyline Kayaks 11977 Westar Ln ....Burlington WA 98233	800-635-5205	360-757-2300	706
Edelbrock Corp 2700 California St ....Torrance CA 90503	800-739-3737	310-781-2222	60
Eden Foods Inc 701 Tecumseh Rd ....Clinton MI 49236 *Cust Svc	800-248-0320*	517-456-7424	296-36
Eden House 1015 Fleming St ....Key West FL 33040	800-533-5397	305-296-6868	378
Eden i & r inc 570 B St ....Hayward CA 94541	888-886-9660	510-537-2710	138
Eden Labs LLC 309 S Cloverdale St ....Seattle WA 98108	888-626-3271		332
Eden Prairie Chamber of Commerce 11455 Viking Dr Ste 270 ....Eden Prairie MN 55344	800-932-8677	952-944-2830	139
Eden Roc - A Renaissance Beach Resort & Spa 4525 Collins Ave ....Miami Beach FL 33140	855-433-3676	305-531-0000	665
Eden Stone Company Inc W4520 Lime Rd ....Eden WI 53019	800-472-2521	920-477-2521	501-6
Eden Theological Seminary 475 E Lockwood Ave ....Saint Louis MO 63119	877-627-5652	314-961-3627	167-3
Edgar Evins State Park 1630 Edgar Evins State Pk Rd ....Silver Point TN 38582	800-250-8619	931-858-2114	561
Edgar Lomax Co 6564 Loisdale Ct Ste 310 ....Springfield VA 22150	866-205-0524	703-719-0026	400
Edge Electronics Inc 75 Orville Dr ....Bohemia NY 11716	800-647-3343		173-8
Edge Information Management Inc 1682 W Hibiscus Blvd ....Melbourne FL 32901	800-725-3343		631
EDge Interactive Inc 67 Mowat Ave Ste 533 ....Toronto ON M6K3E3	800-211-5577	416-494-3343	224
Edge Products 1080 S Depot Dr ....Ogden UT 84404	888-360-3343	801-476-3343	247
Edge Systems LLC 3S721 W Ave Ste 200 ....Warrenville IL 60555 *Tech Supp	800-352-3343*	630-810-9669	177
EDGE Tech Corp 9101 Harlan St Unit 260 ....Westminster CO 80031	800-259-6565		621
Edge Technologies 12110 Sunset Hills Rd Ste 600 ....Reston VA 22030	888-771-3343	703-691-7900	178-1
Edgecombe-Martin County Electric Membership Corp PO Box 188 ....Tarboro NC 27886	800-445-6486		245
Edgenet 2948 Sidco Dr ....Nashville TN 37204	877-334-3638		177
Edgewater Beach Hotel 1901 Gulf Shore Blvd N ....Naples FL 34102	866-624-1695	239-403-2000	378
Edgewater Hotel 2411 Alaskan Way ....Seattle WA 98121	800-624-0670	206-728-7000	378
Edgewater Hotel & Casino 2020 S Casino Dr ....Laughlin NV 89029 *Resv	866-352-3553*	702-298-2453	133
Edgewater Pointe Estates 23315 Blue Water Cir ....Boca Raton FL 33433 *General	888-339-2287*	561-391-6305	668
Edgewater Resort 200 Edgewater Cir ....Hot Springs AR 71913	800-234-3687	501-767-3311	378
Edgewater Resort & Waterpark 2400 London Rd ....Duluth MN 55812	800-777-7925	218-728-3601	378
EdgeWave Inc 15333 Ave of Science ....San Diego CA 92128	800-782-3762	858-676-2277	177
Edgewood College 1000 Edgewood College Dr ....Madison WI 53711	800-444-4861	608-663-2294	166
EDI Specialists Inc 31 Bellows Rd ....Raynham MA 02767	800-821-4644		193
Edible Arrangements LLC 95 Barnes Rd ....Wallingford CT 06492 *Cust Svc	877-363-7848*	304-894-8901	310
Edinboro University of Pennsylvania 200 E Normal St ....Edinboro PA 16444	888-846-2676	814-732-2761	166
Edinboro University of Pennsylvania Baron-Forness Library (EUB) 200 Tartan Rd ....Edinboro PA 16444	888-845-2890	814-732-2273	433-6
eDirectory 7004 Little River Tpke Ste O ....Annandale VA 22003	800-630-4694		

Name / Address	City	State	ZIP	Toll-Free	Phone	Class
Edison Biotechnology Institute						
1 Ohio University	Athens	OH	45701	**800-444-2420**	740-593-4713	664
Edison Carrier Solutions						
2 Innovation Way 1st Fl	Pomona	CA	91768	**800-634-7999**		386
Edison Chouest Offshore						
16201 E Main St	Galliano	LA	70354	**866-925-5161**	985-601-4444	463
Edison College						
Charlotte						
26300 Airport Rd	Punta Gorda	FL	33950	**800-749-2322**	941-637-5629	162
Edison Community College						
1973 Edison Dr	Piqua	OH	45356	**888-442-4551**	937-778-8600	162
Edison Electric Institute (EEI)						
701 Pennsylvania Ave NW	Washington	DC	20004	**800-649-1202**	202-508-5000	48-12
Edison International						
2244 Walnut Grove Ave	Rosemead	CA	91770	**800-655-4555***	626-302-1212	359-5
NYSE: EIX ■ *Cust Svc						
Edison Properties LLC						
100 Washington St	Newark	NJ	07102	**888-727-5327**	973-643-0895	558
Edison Venture Fund						
281 Witherspoon St	Princeton	NJ	08540	**800-899-3975**	609-896-1900	787
eDist 97 McKee Dr	Mahwah	NJ	07430	**800-800-6624**	201-512-1400	688
Edisto Beach State Park						
8377 State Cabin Rd	Edisto Island	SC	29438	**866-345-7275**	843-869-2156	561
Edisto Electric Co-op Inc						
896 Calhoun St	Bamberg	SC	29003	**800-433-3292**	803-245-5141	245
Edith J Carrier Arboretum & Botanical Gardens at James Madison University						
780 University Blvd						
MSC 3705	Harrisonburg	VA	22807	**888-568-2586**	540-568-3194	97
Editor & Publisher Magazine						
17782 Cowan Ste C	Irvine	CA	92614	**855-896-7433**	949-660-6150	455-5
Edlund Company Inc						
159 Industrial Pkwy	Burlington	VT	05401	**800-772-2126**	802-862-9661	298
EDMC (Education Management Corp)						
210 Sixth Ave 33rd Fl	Pittsburgh	PA	15222	**800-275-2440**	412-562-0900	242
NASDAQ: EDMC						
Edmo Distributors Inc						
12830 E Mirabeau Pkwy	Spokane Valley	WA	99216	**800-235-3300**	509-535-8280	765
Edmond Area Chamber of Commerce						
825 E Second St Ste 100	Edmond	OK	73034	**800-717-2601**	405-341-2808	139
Edmonds Community College						
20000 68th Ave W	Lynnwood	WA	98036	**866-886-4854**	425-640-1500	162
Edmonson County						
PO Box 830	Brownsville	KY	42210	**800-368-8683**	270-597-2624	337
Edmonton International Airport						
1000 Airport Rd Edmonton International Airport						
Ste 1	Edmonton	AB	T9E0V3	**800-268-7134**	780-890-8900	
Edmonton Journal						
10006 - 101 St	Edmonton	AB	T5J0S1	**800-232-9486**	780-429-5100	528-1
Edmonton Oilers						
10214 104 Ave NW	Edmonton	AB	T5J0H6	**800-559-2333**	780-414-4625	712
Edmonton Sun						
10006 101 St	Edmonton	AB	T5J0S1	**888-786-7821**	780-468-0100	528-1
Edmonton Symphony Orchestra						
9720 102nd Ave	Edmonton	AB	T5J4B2	**800-563-5081**	780-428-1108	569-3
Edmund Optics Inc						
101 E Gloucester Pk	Barrington	NJ	08007	**800-363-1992**		540
Edmunds & Associates Inc						
301 Tilton Rd	Northfield	NJ	08225	**888-336-6999***	609-645-7333	5
*Sales						
Edmunds Gages						
45 Spring Ln	Farmington	CT	06032	**800-878-1622**	860-677-2813	491
Edo Japan International Inc						
4838 - 32nd St SE	Calgary	AB	T2B2S6	**888-336-9888**	403-215-8800	666
Edom Laboratories Inc						
100 E Jefryn Blvd Ste M	Deer Park	NY	11729	**800-723-3366**	631-586-2266	794
Edon Farmers Co-op Assn Inc						
205 S Michigan St PO Box 308	Edon	OH	43518	**800-878-4093**	419-272-2121	276
EDR (Environmental Data Resources Inc)						
6 Armstrong Rd 4th Fl	Shelton	CT	06484	**800-352-0050**	203-783-0300	386
Edstrom Industries Inc						
819 Bakke Ave	Waterford	WI	53185	**800-558-5913**	262-534-5181	419
EDTA (Educational Theatre Assn)						
2343 Auburn Ave	Cincinnati	OH	45219	**800-848-2263**	513-421-3900	48-4
Education Ctr Inc						
3515 W Market St Ste 200	Greensboro	NC	27403	**800-714-7991**	336-854-0309	243
Education Development Ctr Inc (EDC)						
55 Chapel St	Newton	MA	02458	**800-225-4276**	617-969-7100	48-11
Education Grants Alert						
360 Hiatt Dr	Palm Beach Gardens	FL	33418	**800-621-5463**	561-622-6520	527-4
Education Management Corp (EDMC)						
210 Sixth Ave 33rd Fl	Pittsburgh	PA	15222	**800-275-2440**	412-562-0900	242
NASDAQ: EDMC						
Education Management Solutions Inc						
436 Creamery Way Ste 300	Exton	PA	19341	**877-367-5050**	610-701-7002	178-7
Education Management Systems Inc						
4110 Shipyard Blvd	Wilmington	NC	28403	**800-541-8999**	910-799-0121	177
Education Resource Information Ctr (ERIC)						
655 15th St NW Ste 500	Washington	DC	20005	**800-538-3742**		197
Education Week Magazine						
6935 Arlington Rd	Bethesda	MD	20814	**800-346-1834**	301-280-3100	455-8
Educational Development Corp						
5402 S 122nd E Ave	Tulsa	OK	74146	**800-475-4522**	918-622-4522	96
NASDAQ: EDUC						
Educational Employees Credit Union						
PO Box 5242	Fresno	CA	93755	**800-538-3328**	559-437-7700	219
Educational Housing Services Inc						
55 Clark St	Brooklyn	NY	11201	**800-385-1689**	800-297-4694	49-5
Educational Insights Inc						
380 N Fairway Dr	Vernon Hills	IL	60061	**800-995-4436**	847-968-3722	243
Educational Leadership Magazine						
1703 N Beauregard St	Alexandria	VA	22311	**800-933-2723**	703-578-9600	455-8
Educational Media Foundation						
5700 W Oaks Blvd	Rocklin	CA	95765	**800-525-5683***	800-877-5600	639
*General						
Educational Research Newsletter						
PO Box 2347	South Portland	ME	04116	**800-321-7471**	207-632-1954	527-4
Educational Theatre Assn (EDTA)						
2343 Auburn Ave	Cincinnati	OH	45219	**800-848-2263**	513-421-3900	48-4
Educational Tours						
1123 Sterling Rd	Inverness	FL	34450	**800-343-9003**		755
Educational Travel Consultants (ETC)						
PO Box 1580	Hendersonville	NC	28793	**800-247-7969**	828-693-0412	755
Educators Credit Union (ECU)						
1400 N Newman Rd PO Box 081040	Racine	WI	53406	**800-236-5898**	262-886-5900	219
Educators Publishing Service Inc (EPS)						
PO Box 9031	Cambridge	MA	02139	**800-225-5750**		633-2
Educators Resource Inc						
2575 Schillingers Rd	Semmes	AL	36575	**800-868-2368***		243
*Cust Svc						
Eduficient Inc						
6 Forest Ave 2nd Fl	Paramus	NJ	07652	**888-648-1811**	201-881-0030	195
Edufii Inc						
130 Buena Vista Ave	Mill Valley	CA	94941	**888-414-7276**		386
Edvest College Savings Plan						
PO Box 55189	Boston	MA	02205	**888-338-3789**		721
Edward C Levy Co						
9300 Dix Ave	Dearborn	MI	48120	**877-938-0007**	313-843-7200	501-5
Edward Don & Co						
9801 Adam Don Pkw	Woodridge	IL	60517	**800-777-4366***		300
*Cust Svc						
Edward J Darby & Son Inc						
2200 N Eigth St						
PO Box 50049	Philadelphia	PA	19133	**800-875-6374**	215-236-2203	684
Edward Jones						
12555 Manchester Rd	Saint Louis	MO	63131	**800-441-2357**	314-515-2000	686
Edward Joy Electric						
905 Canal St	Syracuse	NY	13210	**800-724-0664**	315-474-3361	361
Edwards Company Inc						
41 Woodford Ave	Plainville	CT	06062	**800-336-4206**		689
Edwards County						
721 Marsh Ave PO Box 161	Kinsley	KS	67547	**877-464-3929**	620-659-2711	337
Edwards Graphic Arts Inc						
2700 Bell Ave	Des Moines	IA	50321	**800-280-9765**	515-280-9765	623
Edwards Instrument Co						
530 S Hwy H	Elkhorn	WI	53121	**800-562-6838**	262-723-4221	523
Edwards Jet Center						
1691 Aviation Pl	Billings	MT	59105	**866-353-8245**	406-252-0508	63
Edwards John Bel (D)						
PO Box 94004	Baton Rouge	LA	70804	**866-366-1121**	225-342-7015	342
Edwards Lifesciences Corp						
1 Edwards Way	Irvine	CA	92614	**800-424-3278**	949-250-2500	578
NYSE: EW						
Edwards Manufacturing Co						
1107 Sykes St	Albert Lea	MN	56007	**800-373-8206**	507-373-8206	454
Edwin Gaynor Corp						
200 Charles St	Stratford	CT	06615	**800-342-9667**	203-378-5545	810
Edwin L Heim Co						
1918 Greenwood St	Harrisburg	PA	17104	**800-692-7316**	717-233-8711	189-4
Edwin Shaw Rehab						
1621 Flickinger Rd	Akron	OH	44312	**800-221-4601**	330-784-1271	373-6
EE Schenck Co						
6000 N Cutter Cir	Portland	OR	97217	**800-433-0722**	503-284-4124	590
EECO Switch						
1240 Pioneer St Ste A	Brea	CA	92821	**800-854-3808**		810
EEI (Edison Electric Institute)						
701 Pennsylvania Ave NW	Washington	DC	20004	**800-649-1202**	202-508-5000	48-12
EEI (Engineering Economics Inc)						
780 Simms St Ste 210	Golden	CO	80401	**800-869-6902**		186
EEI (Environmental Enterprises Inc)						
10163 Cincinnati-Dayton Rd	Cincinnati	OH	45241	**800-722-2818**		663
EEL River Fuels Inc						
3371 N State St	Ukiah	CA	95482	**800-343-8354**	707-462-5554	575
EEOC (Equal Employment Opportunity Commission)						
1801 L St NW	Washington	DC	20507	**800-669-4000**	202-663-4191	339-19
EF Center						
2 Education Cir	Cambridge	MA	02141	**800-637-8222**	800-665-5364	755
EF Precision Design Inc						
2301 Computer Rd	Willow Grove	PA	19090	**800-536-3900**	215-784-0861	752
EFC (Evangelical Fellowship of Canada)						
9821 Leslie St Ste 103	Richmond Hill	ON	L4B3Y4	**866-302-3362**	905-479-5885	48-20
EFCC (East Fairfield Coal Co)						
10900 S Ave PO Box 217	North Lima	OH	44452	**800-241-7074**	330-549-2165	499
EFCO Corp						
1000 County Rd	Monett	MO	65708	**800-221-4169**	417-235-3193	234
Efco Products						
136 Smith St	Poughkeepsie	NY	12601	**800-284-3326**		
Effective Data Inc						
1515 E Wdfield Rd	Schaumburg	IL	60173	**877-825-5233**	847-969-9300	225
Effective Solar Products LLC						
601 Crescent Ave	Lockport	LA	70374	**888-824-0090**	985-532-0800	606
Effective Training Inc						
14143 Farmington Rd	Livonia	MI	48154	**800-886-0909**		
Efficas Inc						
7007 Winchester Cir Ste 120	Boulder	CO	80301	**866-446-0388**	303-381-2070	574
Effingham Convention & Visitors Bureau						
201 E Jefferson Ave	Effingham	IL	62401	**800-772-0750**	217-342-5305	206
Effingham County						
601 N Laurel St	Springfield	GA	31329	**800-338-6745**	912-754-2123	337
Effingham Equity Inc						
201 W Roadway Ave	Effingham	IL	62401	**800-223-1337**	217-342-4101	275
E-filliate Inc						
11321 White Rock Rd	Rancho Cordova	CA	95742	**800-592-7031**	916-858-1000	457
EFJohnson Technologies						
1440 Corporate Dr	Irving	TX	75038	**800-328-3911**	972-819-0700	643
EFP Corp						
223 Middleton Run Rd	Elkhart	IN	46516	**800-205-8537**	574-295-4690	600
EFR (Employee & Family Resources)						
505 Fifth Ave Ste 600	Des Moines	IA	50309	**800-327-4692**	515-288-9020	
EG Systems LLC						
6200 Village Pkwy	Dublin	CA	94568	**800-538-5124**	408-528-3000	691
Eg Tax Service						
2475 Niagara Falls Blvd	Amherst	NY	14228	**800-829-9998**	716-632-7886	
eGain Corp						
1252 Borregas Ave	Sunnyvale	CA	94089	**888-603-4246**	408-636-4500	39
NASDAQ: EGAN						

Name / Address	City	State	ZIP	Toll-Free	Phone	Class
Egan Bernard & Co 1900 Old Dixie Hwy	Fort Pierce	FL	34946	**800-327-6676**		315-2
Egenera Inc 80 Central St	Boxborough	MA	01719	**866-301-3117**	978-206-6300	176
Egge Machine Company Inc 11707 Slauson Ave	Santa Fe Springs	CA	90670	**800-866-3443**	562-945-3419	452
Eglin Federal Credit Union 838 Eglin Pkwy NE	Fort Walton Beach	FL	32547	**800-367-6159**	850-862-0111	219
eGov Strategies LLC 101 W Ohio St Ste 2250	Indianapolis	IN	46204	**877-634-3468**		225
EGRMC (East Georgia Regional Medical Ctr) 1499 Fair Rd	Statesboro	GA	30458	**844-455-8708**	912-486-1000	373-3
Egroup Inc 482 Wando Park Blvd	Mount Pleasant	SC	29464	**877-347-6871**		
eGumBall Inc 7525 Irvine Ctr Dr Ste 100	Irvine	CA	92618	**800-890-8940**		195
Egyptian Electric Co-op Assn PO Box 38	Steeleville	IL	62288	**800-606-1505**		245
Egyptian Workspace Partner 129 W Main St *Cust Svc	Belleville	IL	62220	**800-642-3949***	618-234-2323	531
EH Ashley & Company Inc 1 White Squadron Rd	Riverside	RI	02915	**800-735-7424**	401-431-0950	410
EH Wachs Co 600 Knightsbridge Pkwy	Lincolnshire	IL	60069	**800-323-8185**	847-537-8800	453
eHDL Inc 3106 Commerce Pkwy	Miramar	FL	33025	**800-338-1079**		
Ehlers & Assoc Inc 3060 Centre Pointe Dr	Roseville	MN	55113	**800-552-1171**	651-697-8500	194
Ehob Inc 250 N Belmont Ave	Indianapolis	IN	46222	**800-899-5553**	317-972-4600	475
Ehrhardt Engineered Solutions 25 Central Industrial Dr	Granite City	IL	62040	**877-386-7856**	314-436-6900	752
Ehs-International Inc 1011 SW Klickitat Way Ste 104	Seattle	WA	98134	**800-666-2959**	206-381-1128	
EI Electronics LLC 1800 Shames Dr	Westbury	NY	11590	**877-346-3837**	516-334-0870	37
EI Group Inc, The 2101 Gateway Centre Blvd Ste 200	Morrisville	NC	27560	**800-717-3472**	919-657-7500	186
EI Microcircuits Inc 1651 Pohl Rd	Mankato	MN	56001	**800-713-4015**	507-345-5786	621
EIA (Environmental Information Assn) 6935 Wisconsin Ave Ste 306	Chevy Chase	MD	20815	**888-343-4342**	301-961-4999	48-13
Eichelbergers Inc 107 Texaco Rd	Mechanicsburg	PA	17050	**800-371-3313**	717-766-4800	317
Eide Industries Inc 16215 Piuma Ave	Cerritos	CA	90703	**800-422-6827**	562-402-8335	728
Eielson Air Force Base 354 Broadway St Unit 2B	Eielson AFB	AK	99702	**800-538-6647**	907-377-1110	495-1
Eigen 13366 Grass Vly Ave	Grass Valley	CA	95945	**888-924-2020**	530-274-1240	250
Eisai Inc 100 Tice Blvd	Woodcliff Lake	NJ	07677	**866-613-4724**	201-692-1100	578
Eisenbach Consulting LLC 5759 Eagles Nest Blvd Ste 1	Tyler	TX	75703	**800-977-4020**		461
Eizo Nanao Technologies Inc 5710 Warland Dr	Cypress	CA	90630	**800-800-5202**	562-431-5011	173-4
EJ Group Inc 301 Spring St	East Jordan	MI	49727	**800-874-4100**	231-536-2261	307
EJGH (East Jefferson General Hospital) 4200 Houma Blvd	Metairie	LA	70006	**866-280-7737**	504-454-4000	373-3
Ejh Construction Inc 30896 W 8 Mile Rd	Farmington Hills	MI	48336	**800-854-4534**		186
Ekahau 1925 Isaac Newton Sq E Ste 200	Reston	VA	20190	**866-435-2428**		386
EKRiley Investments LLC 1420 Fifth Ave Ste 3300	Seattle	WA	98101	**800-809-9317**	206-832-1520	
El Al Israel Airlines Inc 15 E 26th St	New York	NY	10010	**800-223-6700**	212-852-0600	25
El Camino College 16007 Crenshaw Blvd	Torrance	CA	90506	**866-352-2646**	310-532-3670	162
El Camino Store, The 420 Athena Dr	Athens	GA	30601	**888-685-5987**		57
El Caribe Resort 2125 S Atlantic Ave	Daytona Beach	FL	32118	**800-445-9889**	386-252-1558	703
El Centro Public Library 539 State St	El Centro	CA	92243	**877-482-5656**	760-337-4565	433-3
El Chico 8409 I-30	Little Rock	AR	72209	**800-242-5353**		
El Conquistador Resort & Golden Door Spa 1000 El Conquistador Ave *Resv	Fajardo	PR	00738	**888-543-1282***	787-863-1000	665
El Cortez Hotel & Casino 600 E Fremont St	Las Vegas	NV	89101	**800-634-6703**	702-385-5200	133
El Dorado County Chamber of Commerce 542 Main St	Placerville	CA	95667	**800-457-6279**	530-621-5885	139
El Dorado Furniture Corp 4200 NW 167th St	Miami	FL	33054	**888-451-7800**	305-624-2400	321
El Dorado Nature Ctr 7550 E Spring St	Long Beach	CA	90815	**800-662-8887**	562-570-1745	50-5
El Dorado Savings Bank 4040 El Dorado Rd	Placerville	CA	95667	**800-874-9779**	530-622-1492	70
El Dorado Trading Group Inc 760 San Antonio Rd	Palo Alto	CA	94303	**800-227-8292**		112
El Encanto Inc 2001 Fourth St SW PO Box 293	Albuquerque	NM	87103	**800-888-7336**	505-243-2722	296-36
El Fenix Corp 1845 Woodall Rodgers Ste 1100	Dallas	TX	75201	**877-591-1918**	972-241-2171	666
EL Harvey & Sons Inc 68 Hopkinton Rd	Westborough	MA	01581	**800-321-3002**	508-836-3000	799
El Mexicano 5801 Rue Ferrari	San Jose	CA	95138	**800-858-1119**		528-2
El Nuevo Herald 3511 NW 91st Ave	Doral	FL	33172	**866-949-6722**	305-376-3535	528-2

Name / Address	City	State	ZIP	Toll-Free	Phone	Class
El Paso Community College *Valle Verde* 919 Hunter Dr	El Paso	TX	79915	**800-531-8292**	404-679-4500	162
El Paso Convention & Performing Arts Ctr 1 Civic Ctr Plz	El Paso	TX	79901	**800-351-6024**	915-534-0600	205
El Paso Electric Co 100 N Stanton Stanton Tower *NYSE: EE*	El Paso	TX	79901	**800-351-1621**	915-543-5711	782
El Paso Health 1145 Westmoreland Dr	El Paso	TX	79925	**877-532-3778**	915-532-3778	48-17
El Paso International Airport 6701 Convair Rd	El Paso	TX	79925	**800-288-1784**	915-780-4749	27
El Pollo Loco 3535 Harbor Blvd Ste 100	Costa Mesa	CA	92626	**877-375-4968**	714-599-5000	666
El Ran Furniture Ltd 2751 Transcanada Hwy	Pointe-Claire	QC	H9R1B4	**800-361-6546**	514-630-5656	319-2
El Tovar Hotel 1 El Tovar Rd	Grand Canyon	AZ	86023	**888-297-2757**	928-638-2631	378
Ela Area Public Library District 275 Mohawk Trl	Lake Zurich	IL	60047	**800-436-0709**	847-438-3433	433-3
Elaine P Nunez Community College 3710 Paris Rd	Chalmette	LA	70043	**800-256-3000**	504-278-7497	162
Elam Construction Inc 556 Struthers Ave	Grand Junction	CO	81501	**800-675-4598**	970-242-5370	188-4
Elan Financial Services Commerce Ct 4 Stn Sq Ste 620	Pittsburgh	PA	15219	**800-343-7064**		400
Elan Hotel 8435 Beverly Blvd	Los Angeles	CA	90048	**866-203-2212**	323-658-6663	378
Elanco Animal Health 2500 Innovation Way	Greenfield	IN	46140	**877-352-6261**	317-276-2000	580
Elant Inc 46 Harriman Dr	Goshen	NY	10924	**800-501-3936**		389
Elantas PDG Inc 5200 N Second St	Saint Louis	MO	63147	**800-325-7492**	314-621-5700	145
Elavon 2 Concourse Pkwy Ste 800	Atlanta	GA	30328	**800-725-1243**	678-731-5000	178-4
eLawMarketing 25 Robert Pitt Dr Ste 209G	Monsey	NY	10952	**866-833-6245**		317
Elbar Duplicator Corp 10526 Jamaica Ave	Richmond Hill	NY	11418	**800-540-1123**	718-441-1123	113
Elbeco Inc 4418 Pottsville Pk	Reading	PA	19605	**800-468-4661**	610-921-0651	155-18
ELCA (Evangelical Lutheran Church in America) 8765 W Higgins Rd	Chicago	IL	60631	**800-638-3522**	773-380-2700	48-20
Elco Corp 1000 Belt Line St	Cleveland	OH	44109	**800-321-0467**	216-749-2605	537
ELCO Mutual Life & Annuity 916 Sherwood Dr	Lake Bluff	IL	60044	**888-872-7954**	800-321-3526	390-2
Eldercare Locator 1730 Rhode Island Ave NW Ste 1200	Washington	DC	20036	**800-677-1116**		197
Elderhostel Inc 11 Ave de Lafayette	Boston	MA	02111	**800-454-5768**		48-23
Elderlee Inc 729 Cross Rd	Oak Corners	NY	14518	**800-344-5917**	315-789-6670	
Elderly Instruments 1100 N Washington Ave	Lansing	MI	48906	**888-473-5810**	517-372-7890	522
ElderWood Senior Care 5271 Main St	Williamsville	NY	14221	**888-826-9663**	716-565-9663	449
Eldorado Gold Corp 550 Burrard St *NYSE: ELD*	Vancouver	BC	V6C2B5	**888-353-8166**	604-687-4018	500
Eldorado Hotel 309 W San Francisco St	Santa Fe	NM	87501	**800-955-4455**	505-988-4455	378
Eldorado Hotel Casino 345 N Virginia St *Resv	Reno	NV	89501	**800-879-8879***	775-786-5700	378
Eldorado Resort Casino Shreveport 451 Clyde Fant Pkwy	Shreveport	LA	71101	**877-602-0711**	318-220-0711	133
Eldridge Hotel 701 Massachusetts St	Lawrence	KS	66044	**800-527-0909**	785-749-5011	378
Eldridge Products Inc 465 Reservation Rd	Marina	CA	93933	**800-321-3569**	831-648-7777	201
Eleanor Roosevelt National Historic Site 4097 Albany Post Rd	Hyde Park	NY	12538	**800-337-8474**	845-229-9115	560
Eleanor Slater Hospital 14 Harrington Rd	Cranston	RI	02920	**800-438-8477**	401-462-2339	373-7
eLease Funding Inc 550 First Ave N	St. Petersburg	FL	33701	**800-499-2577**	727-209-1200	23
Election Systems & Software Inc 11208 John Galt Blvd *General	Omaha	NE	68137	**877-377-8683***	402-593-0101	796
Electralloy Corp 175 Main St	Oil City	PA	16301	**800-458-7273**	814-678-4100	719
Electrex Inc 6 N Walnut St	Hutchinson	KS	67501	**800-319-3676**		253
Electric City Printing Co 730 Hampton Rd	Williamston	SC	29697	**800-277-1920**	864-224-6331	623
Electric Cooperatives of South Carolina Inc, The 808 Knox Abbott Dr	Cayce	SC	29033	**800-459-2141**	803-796-6060	138
Electric Heater Co 45 Seymour St	Stratford	CT	06615	**800-647-3165**	203-378-2659	36
Electric Materials Co 50 S Washington St	North East	PA	16428	**800-356-2211**	814-725-9621	308
Electric Motors & Specialties Inc 701 W King St PO Box 180	Garrett	IN	46738	**800-474-0520**	260-357-4141	515
Electric Power Door 522 W 27th St	Hibbing	MN	55746	**800-346-5760**	218-263-8366	234
Electric Regulator Corp 6189 El Camino Real	Carlsbad	CA	92009	**800-458-6566**	760-438-7873	203
Electric Research & Mfg Co-op Inc PO Box 1228	Dyersburg	TN	38025	**800-238-5587**	731-285-9121	762
Electric Supply & Equipment Co 1812 E Wendover Ave	Greensboro	NC	27405	**800-632-0268**	336-272-4123	246
Electric Supply Inc 4407 N Manhattan Ave	Tampa	FL	33614	**800-678-1894**	813-872-1894	246
Electrical Distributing Inc 4600 NW St Helens Rd	Portland	OR	97210	**800-877-4229**	503-226-4044	38

	Toll-Free	Phone	Class
Electri-Flex Co 222 Central Ave ....Roselle IL 60172	800-323-6174	630-529-2920	811
Electro Brand Inc 1127 S Mannheim Rd Ste 305 ....Westchester IL 60154	800-982-3954		246
Electro Rent Corp 6060 Sepulveda Blvd ....Van Nuys CA 91411 *NASDAQ: ELRC ■ *Sales*	800-688-1111*	818-787-2100	264-1
Electro Scientific Industries Inc 13900 NW Science Pk Dr ....Portland OR 97229 *NASDAQ: ESIO ■ *Cust Svc*	800-331-4708*	503-641-4141	424
Electro Standards Laboratories Inc 36 Western Industrial Dr ....Cranston RI 02921	877-943-1164	401-943-1164	730
Electro Static Technology 31 Winterbrook Rd ......Mechanic Falls ME 04256	866-738-1857	207-998-5140	635
Electro Steam Generator Corp 50 Indel Ave PO Box 438 ....Rancocas NJ 08073	866-617-0764	609-288-9071	262
Electrocon International Inc 405 Little Lake Dr ....Ann Arbor MI 48103	888-240-4044	734-761-8612	177
Electrocube Inc 3366 Pomona Blvd ....Pomona CA 91768	800-515-1112	909-595-4037	253
Electro-Flex Heat Inc 5 Northwood Rd ....Bloomfield CT 06002	800-585-4213	860-242-6287	356
Electrolux Appliances PO Box 212237 ....Augusta GA 30907	877-435-3287		36
Electrolux Home Care Products Inc PO Box 3900 ....Peoria IL 61612 *Cust Svc*	800-282-2886*		783
Electro-Matic Products Inc 23409 Industrial Pk Ct ......Farmington Hills MI 48335	888-879-1088	248-478-1182	246
Electromek Diagnostic Systems Inc 412 W US Hwy 40 ....Troy IL 62294	800-466-6761	618-667-6761	473
Electron Energy Corp 924 Links Ave ....Landisville PA 17538	800-824-2735	717-898-2294	456
Electronic Cash Systems Inc (ECS) 29883 Santa Margarita Pkwy ...Rancho Santa Margarita CA 92688	888-327-2860	949-888-8580	56
Electronic Commerce & Law Report 1801 S Bell St ....Arlington VA 22202	800-372-1033		527-1
Electronic Contracting Co 6501 N 70th St ....Lincoln NE 68507	800-366-5320	402-466-8274	189-4
Electronic Environments Corp 410 Forest St ....Marlborough MA 01752	800-342-5332	508-229-1400	174
Electronic Security Assn Inc (ESA) 6333 North State Hwy 161 Ste 350 ......Irving TX 75038	888-447-1689	972-807-6800	49-3
Electronic Tele-Communications Inc 1915 MacArthur Rd ....Waukesha WI 53188 *OTC: ETCIA*	888-746-4382	262-542-5600	730
Electronic Theatre Controls Inc 3031 Pleasantview Rd ....Middleton WI 53562	800-688-4116	608-831-4116	203
Electronic Transactions Association, The 1101 16th St NW Ste 402 ....Washington DC 20036	800-695-5509	202-828-2635	138
Electronics Technicians Assn International (ETA) 5 Depot St ....Greencastle IN 46135	800-288-3824	765-653-8262	49-19
Electro-Sensors Inc 6111 Blue Circle Dr ....Minnetonka MN 55343 *NASDAQ: ELSE*	800-328-6170	952-930-0100	493
Electrosonics 17150 15 Mile Rd ....Fraser MI 48026	800-858-8448	586-415-5555	175
Electroswitch 2010 Yonkers Rd ....Raleigh NC 27604	888-768-2797	919-833-0707	810
Electroswitch Corp 180 King Ave ....Weymouth MA 02188	800-572-0479	781-335-5200	725
ElectroTech Inc 7101 Madison Ave W ....Minneapolis MN 55427	800-544-4288		246
ElectSolve Technology Solutions & Services Inc 4300 Youree Dr Bldg 1 ....Shreveport LA 71105	877-221-2055	318-221-2055	
Elegant Voyages 1802 Keesling Ct ....San Jose CA 95125	800-555-3534	408-239-0300	766
Elektro Assemblies 5140 Moundview Dr ....Red Wing MN 55066	800-533-1558		738
Elementis Specialties Inc 469 Old Trenton Rd ....East Windsor NJ 08512	800-866-6800		143
Elenco Electronics Inc 150 Carpenter Ave ....Wheeling IL 60090	800-533-2441	847-541-3800	242
Eleni's 205 E 42nd St ....New York NY 10017	888-435-3647		68
Elevating Boats LLC 201 Dean Ct ....Houma LA 70363	800-843-2895	985-868-9655	694
Elevator Equipment Corp 4035 Goodwin Ave ....Los Angeles CA 90039	888-577-3326	323-245-0147	256
Eleven 315 SW 11th Ave ....Portland OR 97205	866-435-3836	503-222-4321	
Elgin Area Convention & Visitors Bureau 60 S Grove Ave ....Elgin IL 60120	800-217-5362	847-695-7540	206
Elgin Community College 1700 Spartan Dr ....Elgin IL 60123	855-850-2525	847-697-1000	162
Elgin Molded Plastics 909 Grace St ....Elgin IL 60120	800-548-5483	847-931-2455	600
ELI (Environmental Law Institute) 2000 L St NW Ste 620 ....Washington DC 20036	800-433-5120	202-939-3800	49-10
ELI Inc 2675 Paces Ferry Rd SE Ste 470 ....Atlanta GA 30339	800-497-7654	770-319-7999	196
Eli Lilly & Co Lilly Corporate Ctr ....Indianapolis IN 46285 *NYSE: LLY ■ *Prod Info*	800-545-5979*	317-276-2000	578
Eli Lilly Canada Inc 3650 Danforth Ave ....Toronto ON M1N2E8	888-545-5972	416-694-3221	578
Eli's Cheesecake Co 6701 W Forest Preserve Dr ....Chicago IL 60634	800-999-8300	773-736-3417	296-2
Eliason Corp 9229 Shaver Rd ....Portage MI 49024 *Cust Svc*	800-828-3655*	269-327-7003	660
Eliassen Group LLC 55 Walkers Brook Dr 6th Fl. ......Reading MA 01867	800-354-2773		260
Elim Park Place 140 Cook Hill Rd ....Cheshire CT 06410	800-994-1776	203-272-3547	668
eLine Technology 9500 W 49th Ave Ste D106. ......Wheat Ridge CO 80033	800-683-6835		
Eliot Hotel, The 370 Commonwealth Ave ....Boston MA 02215	800-443-5468	617-267-1607	378
Eliot Rose Asset Management LLC 1000 Chapel View Blvd Ste 240 ....Cranston RI 02920	866-585-5100	401-588-5100	400
Elisa Act Biotechnologies 109 Carpenter Dr Ste 100 ....Sterling VA 20164	800-553-5472	703-796-0400	414
Elisabet Ney Museum 304 E 44th St ....Austin TX 78751	800-680-7289	512-458-2255	517
Elite PO Box 9630 ....Rancho Santa Fe CA 92067	800-204-3548		760
Elite Coach 1685 W Main St ....Ephrata PA 17522	800-722-6206	717-733-7710	107
Elite Corp 2878 Camino Del Rio S Ste 260 ....San Diego CA 92108	855-809-2047	619-574-1589	
Elite Island Resorts Inc 1065 SW 30th Ave ....Deerfield Beach FL 33442	800-771-4711	954-481-8787	703
Elite Lighting Company Inc 412 S Cypress St ....Mullins SC 29574	800-343-0764		
Elite Limousine Service Inc 1059 12th Ave Ste E ....Honolulu HI 96816	800-776-2098	808-735-2431	440
Elite Sportswear LP 2136 N 13th St ....Reading PA 19604 *Cust Svc*	800-345-4087*	610-921-1469	155-1
Elitexpo Cargo Systems 845 Commerce Dr ....South Elgin IL 60177	800-543-5484		461
Elixir Industries Inc 24800 Chrisanta Dr Ste 210 ....Mission Viejo CA 92691	800-421-1942	949-860-5000	234
Elizabeth Arden Inc 880 SW 145th Ave Ste 200 .....Pembroke Pines FL 33027 *NASDAQ: RDEN*	800-326-7337	954-364-6900	570
Elizabeth City State University 1704 Weeksville Rd ....Elizabeth City NC 27909 *Admissions*	800-347-3278*	252-335-3400	166
Elizabeth Hospice 500 La Terraza Blvd Ste 130 ....Escondido CA 92025	800-797-2050	760-737-2050	370
Elizabethtown Community & Technical College 600 College St Rd ....Elizabethtown KY 42701	877-246-2322	270-769-2371	162
Elizabethtown Gas Co 1 Elizabethtown Plz 1085 Morris Ave.................Union NJ 07083	800-242-5830	908-289-5000	782
Eljer Inc 1 Centennial Ave ....Piscataway NJ 08855	800-442-1902		607
Elk Country Inn 480 W Pearl St PO Box 1255 ....Jackson WY 83001	800-483-8667	307-733-2364	378
Elk County PO Box 606 ....Howard KS 67349	877-504-2490	620-374-2490	337
Elk Environmental Services 1420 Clarion St ....Reading PA 19601	800-851-7156	610-372-4760	196
Elk Grove Village Public Library 1001 Wellington Ave ....Elk Grove Village IL 60007	800-252-8980	847-439-0447	433-3
Elk Lighting Inc 12 Willow Ln ....Nesquehoning PA 18240	800-613-3261		438
Elk Mountain Ranch PO Box 910 ....Buena Vista CO 81211	800-432-8812		239
ELK Products Inc 3266 US 70 W ....Connelly Springs NC 28612	800-797-9355	828-397-4200	688
Elk River Systems Inc 22 S Central Ave PO Box 6934 ....Harlowton MT 59036	888-771-0809		174
Elk Valley Rancheria 2332 Howland Hill Rd ....Crescent City CA 95531	866-464-4680	707-464-4680	704
Elkay Manufacturing Co 2222 Camden Ct ....Oak Brook IL 60523	800-476-4106	630-574-8484	605
Elkhart County Convention & Visitors Bureau 219 Caravan Dr ....Elkhart IN 46514	800-262-8161	574-262-8161	206
Elkhorn Rural Public Power District 206 N Fourth St ....Battle Creek NE 68715	800-675-2185	402-675-2185	245
Elko Convention & Visitors Authority 700 Moren Way ....Elko NV 89801	800-248-3556	775-738-4091	205
Elks Magazine 2750 N Lakeview Ave ....Chicago IL 60614	800-892-8384	773-755-4700	455-10
Ellie Mae Inc 4155 Hopyard Rd Ste 200.........Pleasanton CA 94588	800-848-4904	925-227-7000	177
Elliot Companies, The 673 Blue Sky Pkwy ....Lexington KY 40509	888-768-2530	859-263-5148	
Elliot Equipment Corp 1131 Country Club Rd ....Indianapolis IN 46234	800-823-7527	317-271-3065	111
Elliot Hospital 1 Elliot Way Ste 100 ....Manchester NH 03103	800-922-4999	603-627-1669	373-3
Elliott & Frantz Inc 450 E Church Rd ....King Of Prussia PA 19406	800-220-3025	610-279-5200	357
Elliott Aviation Inc 6601 74th Ave PO Box 100...........Milan IL 61264	800-447-6711	309-799-3183	24
Elliott Bay Book Co 1521 Tenth Ave ....Seattle WA 98122	800-962-5311	206-624-6600	95
Elliott Company of Indianapolis Inc 9200 Zionsville Rd ....Indianapolis IN 46268 *Orders*	800-545-1213*	317-291-1213	597
Elliott Electric Supply Co 2526 N Stallings Dr PO Box 630610.........Nacogdoches TX 75963	877-777-0242	936-569-1184	246
Elliott Group 901 N Fourth St ....Jeannette PA 15644	888-352-7278	724-527-2811	172
Elliott Machine Works Inc 1351 Freese Works Pl ....Galion OH 44833	800-299-0412	419-468-4709	513
Elliott Wave International (EWI) PO Box 1618 ....Gainesville GA 30503 *Cust Svc*	800-336-1618*	770-536-0309	633-9
Elliott Wave Theorist PO Box 1618 ....Gainesville GA 30503	800-336-1618	770-536-0309	527-9
Elliott, Ostrander & Preston PC Union Bank Tower 707 SW Washington St Ste 1500..............Portland OR 97205	866-716-3410	503-224-7112	427
ElliptiGO Inc 722 Genevieve St Ste O ....Solana Beach CA 92075	888-796-8227	858-876-8677	
Ellis 1333 Corporate Dr Ste 266.........Irving TX 75038	888-988-3767	972-256-3767	196
Ellis Coffee Co 2835 Bridge St ....Philadelphia PA 19137	800-822-3984		297-11

				Toll-Free	Phone	Class
Ellis Corp						
1400 W Bryn Mawr Ave	Itasca	IL	60143	**800-611-6806**	630-250-9222	426
Ellison Bakery						
4108 W Ferguson Rd	Fort Wayne	IN	46809	**800-711-8091**		
Ellison Educational Equipment Inc						
25862 Commercentre Dr	Lake Forest	CA	92630	**800-253-2240**	949-598-8822	357
Ellmaker State Wayside						
198 NE 123rd St	Newport	OR	97365	**800-551-6949**		561
Ellsworth Adhesives						
W129 N10825 Washington Dr	Germantown	WI	53022	**877-454-9224**	262-253-8600	146
Ellsworth Community College						
1100 College Ave	Iowa Falls	IA	50126	**800-322-9235**	641-648-4611	162
Ellucian						
4375 Fair Lakes Ct	Fairfax	VA	22033	**800-223-7036**	610-647-5930	178-10
Ellwood City Forge						
800 Commercial Ave	Ellwood City	PA	16117	**800-843-0166**	724-752-0055	481
ELM Resources						
12950 Race Track Rd Ste 201	Tampa	FL	33626	**866-524-8198**		386
Elmar Worldwide Inc						
200 Gould Ave PO Box 245	Depew	NY	14043	**800-433-3562***	716-681-5650	543
*Cust Svc						
Elmer Candy Corp						
401 N Fifth St	Ponchatoula	LA	70454	**800-843-9537**	985-386-6166	296-8
Elmer's Products Inc						
1 Easton Oval	Columbus	OH	43219	**888-435-6377**		3
Elmet Technologies Inc						
1560 Lisbon St	Lewiston	ME	04240	**800-343-8008**	207-333-6100	483
Elmhurst College						
190 Prospect Ave	Elmhurst	IL	60126	**800-697-1871**	630-617-3400	166
Elmhurst Mutual Power & Light Co						
120 132nd St S	Tacoma	WA	98444	**855-841-2178**	253-531-4646	245
Elmira College 1 Pk Pl	Elmira	NY	14901	**800-935-6472***	607-735-1724	166
*Admissions						
Elmira Psychiatric Ctr						
100 Washington St	Elmira	NY	14901	**800-597-8481**	607-737-4711	373-5
Elmira Savings Bank						
333 E Water St	Elmira	NY	14901	**888-372-9299**	607-734-3374	70
NASDAQ: ESBK						
ELMS College						
291 Springfield St	Chicopee	MA	01013	**800-255-3567***	413-592-3189	166
*Admissions						
Elmwood Park Zoo						
1661 Harding Blvd	Norristown	PA	19401	**800-652-4143**	610-277-3825	818
Elo TouchSystems Inc						
301 Constitution Dr	Menlo Park	CA	94025	**800-557-1458**	650-361-4700	173-1
eLocal Listing						
25240 Hancock Ave Ste 410	Murrieta	CA	92563	**800-285-0484**		5
Elon University						
100 Campus Dr	Elon	NC	27244	**800-334-8448**	336-278-2000	166
Elsevier Science Ltd						
360 Park Ave S	New York	NY	10010	**888-437-4636**	212-989-5800	633-9
Elster American Meter Co						
2221 Industrial Rd	Nebraska City	NE	68410	**877-595-6254**	402-873-8200	493
Elte 80 Ronald Ave	Toronto	ON	M6E5A2	**888-276-3583**	416-785-7885	290
Elvis Presley Enterprises Inc						
3734 Elvis Presley Blvd						
PO Box 16508	Memphis	TN	38116	**800-238-2000**	901-332-3322	359-3
Elward Construction Co						
680 Harlan St	Lakewood	CO	80214	**800-933-5339**	303-239-6303	189-1
Elwood Corp High Performance Motors Group						
2701 N Green Bay Rd	Racine	WI	53404	**800-558-9489**	262-637-6591	515
Elyria Mfg Corp						
145 Northrup St PO Box 479	Elyria	OH	44035	**866-365-4171**	440-365-4171	617
eMagine						
1082 Davol St	Fall River	MA	02720	**877-530-7993**		180
Email Co, The						
15 Kainona Ave	Toronto	ON	M3H3H4	**877-933-6245**		365
Embassy Hotel & Suites						
25 Cartier St	Ottawa	ON	K2P1J2	**800-661-5495**	613-237-2111	378
EmblemHealth Co						
55 Water St	New York	NY	10041	**800-447-8255**	646-447-5000	390-3
Embossed Graphics						
1175 S Frontenac Rd	Aurora	IL	60504	**800-362-6773**		
EmbroidMe Inc						
2121 Vista Pkwy	West Palm Beach	FL	33411	**877-877-0234**	561-640-7367	310
Embryotech Laboratories Inc						
140 Hale St	Haverhill	MA	01830	**800-673-7500**	978-373-7300	738
Embry-Riddle Aeronautical University						
Daytona Beach						
600 S Clyde Morris Blvd	Daytona Beach	FL	32114	**800-862-2416**	386-226-6000	166
Embry-Riddle Aeronautical University Prescott						
3700 Willow Creek Rd	Prescott	AZ	86301	**800-888-3728**	928-777-3728	166
EMC (Carroll Electric Membership Corp)						
155 N Hwy 113	Carrollton	GA	30117	**800-282-7411**	770-832-3552	245
EMC (Grady Electric Membership Corp)						
1499 US Hwy 84 W	Cairo	GA	39828	**877-757-6060**	229-377-4182	245
EMC (IEEE Electromagnetic Compatibility Society)						
445 and 501 Hoes Ln	Piscataway	NJ	08854	**800-678-4333**	732-981-0060	49-19
EMC (Equipment Manufacturing Corp)						
14930 Marquardt Ave	Santa Fe Springs	CA	90670	**888-833-9000**	562-623-9394	385
EMC Insurance Group Inc						
717 Mulberry St	Des Moines	IA	50309	**800-447-2295**	515-280-2511	359-4
NASDAQ: EMCI						
EMC School						
875 Montreal Way	Saint Paul	MN	55102	**800-328-1452**	651-290-2800	633-2
EMCOR Construction Services Inc						
1420 Spring Hill Rd Ste 500	McLean	VA	22102	**866-890-7794**		
EMCOR Group Inc						
301 Merritt 7 6th Fl	Norwalk	CT	06851	**866-890-7794**	203-849-7800	189-4
NYSE: EME						
EMCOR Services Betlem						
704 Clinton Ave S	Rochester	NY	14620	**800-423-8536**		261
EMD Serono Inc						
1 Technology Pl	Rockland	MA	02370	**800-283-8088**	781-982-9000	85
Emdeon Business Services LLC						
3055 Lebanon Pk	Nashville	TN	37214	**800-735-8254**	615-932-3000	39
Emeco 805 W Elm Ave	Hanover	PA	17331	**800-366-5951**	717-637-5951	319-1
eMedia Music Corp						
664 NE Northlake Way	Seattle	WA	98105	**888-363-3424**	206-329-5657	180
Emera Energy Inc						
1223 Lower Water St PO Box 910	Halifax	NS	B3J2W5	**866-474-7800**	902-474-7800	534
Emerald City Graphics						
23328 66th Ave S	Kent	WA	98032	**877-631-5178***		623
*General						
Emerald Downs						
2300 Emerald Downs Dr PO Box 617	Auburn	WA	98001	**888-931-8400**	253-288-7000	133
Emerald Kalama Chemical LLC						
1296 Third St NW	Kalama	WA	98625	**877-300-9545**	360-673-2550	296-15
Emerald Queen Casino (EQC)						
2024 E 29th St	Tacoma	WA	98404	**888-831-7655**	253-594-7777	133
Emerald Queen Hotel & Casino						
5700 Pacific Hwy E	Fife	WA	98424	**888-831-7655***	253-594-7777	378
*Resv						
Emergency Ambulance Service Inc						
3200 E Birch St Ste A	Brea	CA	92821	**800-400-0689**	714-990-1331	30
Emergency Nurses Assn (ENA)						
915 Lee St	Des Plaines	IL	60016	**800-900-9659**	847-460-4000	49-8
EMERgency24 Inc						
999 E Touhy	Des Plaines	IL	60018	**800-800-3624**	773-725-0222	
Emergycare Inc						
1926 Peach St	Erie	PA	16502	**800-814-1038**	814-870-1010	30
Emerson						
7070 Winchester Cir	Boulder	CO	80301	**800-522-6277**	303-530-8400	201
Emerson Climate Technologies - Retail Solutions						
1065 Big Shanty Rd NW Ste 100	Kennesaw	GA	30144	**800-829-2724**	770-425-2724	202
Emerson Industrial Automation						
8000 W Florissant Ave						
PO Box 4100	St Louis	MO	63136	**888-213-0970**	314-553-2000	705
Emerson Network Power Connectivity Solutions						
1050 Dearborn Dr	Columbus	OH	43085	**800-275-3500**	614-888-0246	253
Emerson Thomson & Bennett LLC						
1914 Akron Peninsula Rd	Akron	OH	44313	**800-822-8113**	330-434-9999	427
Emerson-Swan Inc						
300 Pond St	Randolph	MA	02368	**800-346-9219**	781-986-2000	608
Emery & Webb Inc						
989 Main St	Fishkill	NY	12524	**800-942-5818**	845-896-6727	389
Emery Air Charter Inc						
1 Airport Cir	Rockford	IL	61109	**800-435-8090**	815-968-8287	186
Emery Corp						
PO Box 1104	Morganton	NC	28680	**800-255-0537**	828-433-1536	454
Emery Winslow Scale Co						
73 Cogwheel Ln	Seymour	CT	06483	**800-891-3952**	203-881-9333	680
EMF Corp						
505 Pokagon Trl	Angola	IN	46703	**800-847-2818**	260-665-9541	253
Emf Inc 60 Foundry St	Keene	NH	03431	**800-992-3003**	603-352-8400	175
EMG Corp						
10461 Mill Run Cir						
Ste 1100	Owings Mills	MD	21117	**800-733-0660**		652
EMHS (Eastern Maine Healthcare Systems)						
797 Wilson St Ste 4	Brewer	ME	04412	**877-366-3662**	207-973-5578	352
Eminence Speaker LLC						
838 Mulberry Pk PO Box 360	Eminence	KY	40019	**800-897-8373**	502-845-5622	52
Emkay Inc						
805 W Thorndale Ave	Itasca	IL	60143	**800-621-2001**	630-250-7400	289
EMM (Episcopal Migration Ministries)						
815 Second Ave	New York	NY	10017	**800-334-7626**	212-716-6000	48-5
Emmanuel College						
181 Spring St	Franklin Springs	GA	30639	**800-860-8800**	706-245-7226	166
Emmaus Bible College						
2570 Asbury Rd	Dubuque	IA	52001	**800-397-2425**	563-588-8000	161
Emme E2MS LLC						
PO Box 2251	Bristol	CT	06011	**800-396-0523**		406
Emmet County						
200 Div St Ste 130	Petoskey	MI	49770	**866-731-1204**	231-348-1702	337
Emory & Henry College						
PO Box 10	Emory	VA	24327	**800-848-5493***	276-944-4121	166
*Admissions						
Emory Conference Ctr Hotel						
1615 Clifton Rd	Atlanta	GA	30329	**800-933-6679**	404-712-6000	376
Emory University						
201 Dowman Dr	Atlanta	GA	30322	**800-727-6036***	404-727-6036	166
*Admissions						
Empire Bakery Equipment						
171 Greenwich St	Hempstead	NY	11550	**800-878-4070**	516-538-1210	452
Empire Bldg Materials Inc						
PO Box 220	Bozeman	MT	59771	**800-548-8201**		191-2
Empire Building Services						
1570 E Edinger Ave	Santa Ana	CA	92705	**888-296-2078**	714-836-7700	138
Empire Company Ltd						
115 King St	Stellarton	NS	B0K1S0	**800-387-0825**	902-755-4440	185
TSE: EMP.A						
Empire Diamond Corp						
350 Fifth Ave Ste 4000	New York	NY	10118	**800-728-3425**	212-564-4777	410
Empire District Electric Co, The						
602 Joplin St PO Box 127	Joplin	MO	64802	**800-206-2300**	417-625-5100	782
NYSE: EDE						
Empire Electric Assn Inc						
801 N Broadway	Cortez	CO	81321	**800-709-3726**	970-565-4444	245
Empire Industries Inc						
180 Olcott St	Manchester	CT	06040	**800-243-4844**	860-647-1431	591
Empire Level Manufacturing Corp						
929 Empire Dr PO Box 800	Mukwonago	WI	53149	**800-558-0722**		753
Empire Livestock Marketing LLC						
5001 Brittonfield Pkwy	East Syracuse	NY	13057	**800-462-8802**	315-433-9129	444
Empire Safety & Supply Inc						
10624 Industrial Ave	Roseville	CA	95678	**800-995-1341**		675
Empire Southwest Co						
1725 S Country Club Dr	Mesa	AZ	85210	**800-367-4731**	480-633-4000	357
Empire State Bldg						
350 Fifth Ave Ste 100	New York	NY	10118	**877-692-8439**	212-736-3100	50-4
Empire Telephone Corp						
34 Main St PO Box 349	Prattsburgh	NY	14873	**800-338-3300**	607-522-3712	731
Empire West Inc						
9270 Graton Rd PO Box 511	Graton	CA	95444	**800-521-4261**	707-823-1190	598
EmpireWorks Inc						
1940 Olivera Rd	Concord	CA	94520	**888-278-8200**		260

	Toll-Free	Phone	Class
Employee & Family Resources (EFR)			
505 Fifth Ave Ste 600 ....Des Moines IA 50309	**800-327-4692**	515-288-9020	
Employee Assistance Professionals Assn Inc (EAPA)			
4350 N Fairfax Dr Ste 740 ....Arlington VA 22203	**800-937-8461**	703-387-1000	49-12
Employee Development Systems Inc			
7308 S Alton Way Ste 2J ....Centennial CO 80112	**800-282-3374**		179
Employee Management Services			
435 Elm St ....Cincinnati OH 45202	**888-651-1536**	513-651-3244	627
Employer Flexible			
7102 N Sam Houston Pkwy W			
Ste 200 ....Houston TX 77064	**866-501-4942**		729
Employer Plan Services Inc			
2180 N Loop W Ste 400 ....Houston TX 77018	**800-447-6588**	713-351-3500	193
Employers Group			
400 N Continental Blvd			
Ste 300 ....El Segundo CA 90245	**800-748-8484**		529
Employers Insurance Company of Nevada			
9790 Gateway Dr Ste 100 ....Reno NV 89521	**888-682-6671**		389
Employers Resource Management Co			
1301 S Vista Ave Ste 200 ....Boise ID 83705	**800-574-4668**	208-376-3000	566
Employment & Training Administration			
200 Constitution Ave NW ....Washington DC 20210	**866-487-2365**		339-14
Employment Discrimination Report			
1801 S Bell St ....Arlington VA 22202	**800-372-1033**		527-7
Employment Guide LLC, The			
4460 Corporation Ln			
Ste 317 ....Virginia Beach VA 23462	**877-876-4039**		260
Employment Screening Services Inc			
627 E Sprague St Ste 100 ....Spokane WA 99202	**800-473-7778**	509-624-3851	631
Employment Standards Administration			
200 Constitution Ave NW			
Rm N-1301 ....Washington DC 20210	**866-487-2365**		339-14
Office of Labor-Management Standards (OLMS)			
200 Constitution Ave NW ......Washington DC 20210	**866-487-2365**		339-14
Wage & Hour Div			
200 Constitution Ave NW ......Washington DC 20210	**866-487-9243**		
Emporia Area Chamber of Commerce			
719 Commercial St ....Emporia KS 66801	**800-279-3730**	620-342-1600	139
Emporia State University			
1200 Commercial St ....Emporia KS 66801	**877-468-6378**	620-341-1200	166
Empress Software Inc			
11785 Beltsville Dr ....Beltsville MD 20705	**866-626-8888**	301-572-1600	178-2
Emprise Corp			
3900 Kennesaw 75 Pkwy N W			
Ste 125 ....Kennesaw GA 30144	**800-278-2119**	770-425-1420	261
Emprise Financial Corp			
257 N Broadway St PO Box 2970 ....Wichita KS 67202	**800-201-7118***	316-383-4301	69
*Cust Svc			
EmpXtrack			
150 Motor Pkwy Ste 401 ....Hauppauge NY 11788	**888-840-2682**		41
Ems-tech Inc			
699 Dundas St W ....Belleville ON K8N4Z2	**844-450-8324**	613-966-6611	256
Emtek Products Inc			
15250 Stafford St ......City of Industry CA 91744	**800-356-2741**	626-961-0413	349
Emteq Inc			
5349 S Emmer Dr ....New Berlin WI 53151	**888-679-6170**	262-679-6170	24
Emtex Inc			
42 Cherry Hill Dr Ste B..............Danvers MA 01923	**800-840-7035**	978-907-4500	740-2
ENA (Emergency Nurses Assn)			
915 Lee St ....Des Plaines IL 60016	**800-900-9659**	847-460-4000	49-8
Enbridge Energy Partners LP			
1100 Louisiana Ste 3300 ....Houston TX 77002	**800-481-2804**	713-821-2000	593
NYSE: EEP			
EnCana Corp			
500 Ctr St SE Po Box 2850.............Calgary AB T2G1A6	**888-568-6322**	403-645-2000	532
TSE: ECA			
Enchantment Resort			
525 Boynton Canyon Rd ....Sedona AZ 86336	**800-826-4180**	844-244-9489	665
Encinitas Chamber of Commerce			
527 Encinitas Blvd ....Encinitas CA 92024	**800-953-6041**	760-753-6041	139
Encision Inc			
6797 Winchester Cir ....Boulder CO 80301	**800-998-0986**	303-444-2600	474
OTC: ECIA			
Enclave Suites of Orlando			
6165 Carrier Dr ....Orlando FL 32819	**800-457-0077**	407-351-1155	378
Enclos Corp			
2770 Blue Water Rd ....Eagan MN 55121	**888-234-2966**		189-6
Encoder Products Co			
464276 Hwy 95 S PO Box 249..........Sagle ID 83860	**800-366-5412**	208-263-8541	201
Encompass Group LLC			
615 Macon Rd ....McDonough GA 30253	**800-284-4540**	770-957-1211	155-18
Encompass Health			
3660 Grandview Pkwy Ste 200 ....Birmingham AL 35243	**800-765-4772**	205-967-7116	351
NYSE: EHC			
Encompass Health Corp			
3660 Grandview Pkwy Ste 200 ....Birmingham AL 35243	**800-310-4919**	205-967-7116	373-6
Encompass Health Corp			
107 Governors Dr ....Huntsville AL 35801	**800-467-3422**	256-535-2300	373-6
Encompass Health Corp			
1212 W Lancaster ....Fort Worth TX 76102	**800-870-2336**	817-870-2336	373-6
Encompass Health Corp			
6701 Oakmont Blvd ....Fort Worth TX 76132	**800-325-3591**	817-370-4700	373-6
Encompass Health Rehabilitation Hospital of Austin			
330 W Ben White Blvd ....Austin TX 78704	**800-765-4772**	512-730-4800	373-6
Encon Group Inc			
500-1400 Blair Pl ....Ottawa ON K1J9B8	**800-267-6684**	613-786-2000	389
Encon Safety Products Co			
6825 W Sam Houston Pkwy N			
PO Box 3826...................Houston TX 77041	**800-283-6266**	713-466-1449	674
Encore Bank			
3003 Tamiami Trail N Ste 100............Naples FL 34103	**800-472-3272**	239-919-5888	70
Encore Capital Group Inc			
3111 Camino Del Rio N			
Ste 1300......................San Diego CA 92108	**877-445-4581**	858-560-2600	160
NASDAQ: ECPG			
Encore Event Technologies			
1 N Arlington 1500 W Shure Dr			
Ste 175............Arlington Heights IL 60004	**800-836-8361**		52
Encore Image Group Inc			
1445 W Sepulveda Blvd ....Torrance CA 90509	**800-729-4853**		5
Encore Manufacturing Company Inc			
2415 Ashland Ave ....Beatrice NE 68310	**800-267-4255**		428
Encore Medical Corp			
9800 Metric Blvd ....Austin TX 78758	**800-456-8696**	512-832-9500	85
Encore Wire Corp			
1329 Millwood Rd ....McKinney TX 75069	**800-962-9473**	972-562-9473	808
NASDAQ: WIRE			
Encyclopaedia Britannica Inc			
331 N La Salle St ....Chicago IL 60654	**800-323-1229**	312-347-7159	633-2
Enderes Tool Co			
1521 E Hawthorne St ....Albert Lea MN 56007	**800-874-7776**	507-373-2396	753
Endevco Corp			
30700 Rancho Viejo Rd			
................San Juan Capistrano CA 92675	**800-982-6732**	949-493-8181	470
Endicott College			
376 Hale St ....Beverly MA 01915	**800-325-1114***	978-927-0585	166
*Admissions			
Endo Pharmaceuticals Inc			
1400 Atwater Dr ....Malvern PA 19355	**800-462-3636***	484-216-0000	578
*Cust Svc			
Endocrine Society			
8401 Connecticut Ave			
Ste 900 ....Chevy Chase MD 20815	**888-363-6274**	301-941-0200	49-8
Endologix Inc			
11 Studebaker ....Irvine CA 92618	**800-983-2284**	949-457-9546	474
NASDAQ: ELGX			
Endometriosis Assn			
8585 N 76th Pl ....Milwaukee WI 53223	**800-992-3636**	414-355-2200	48-17
EndoShape Inc			
5425 Airport Blvd Ste 101 ....Boulder CO 80301	**844-870-5070**	303-951-6898	473
Endot Industries Inc			
60 Green Pond Rd ....Rockaway NJ 07866	**800-443-6368**	973-625-8500	592
Endress+Hauser Inc			
2350 Endress Pl ....Greenwood IN 46143	**888-363-7377**	317-535-7138	201
Endries International Inc			
714 W Ryan St PO Box 69 ....Brillion WI 54110	**800-852-5821**	920-756-5381	384
Endura Products Inc			
8817 W Market St ....Colfax NC 27235	**800-334-2006**		236
Enduro Composites Inc			
16602 Central Green Blvd ....Houston TX 77032	**800-231-7271**	713-358-4000	597
Eneflux Armtek Magnetics Inc			
700 Hicksville Rd Ste 110............Bethpage NY 11714	**877-363-3589**	516-576-3434	456
Enerac Inc			
67 Bond St ....Westbury NY 11590	**800-695-3637**	516-997-2100	201
Enerbank USA Inc			
1245 E Brickyard Rd			
Ste 600..............Salt Lake City UT 84106	**888-390-1220**		217
Enercon Engineering Inc			
201 Altorfer Ln ....East Peoria IL 61611	**800-218-8831**	309-694-1418	203
Enerfab Inc			
4955 Spring Grove Ave ....Cincinnati OH 45232	**800-772-5066**	513-641-0500	91
Enerflex Systems Ltd			
1331 Macleod Trail SE Ste 904.........Calgary AB T2G0K3	**800-242-3178**	403-387-6377	385
TSX: EFX			
Ener-G Foods Inc			
5960 First Ave S PO Box 84487 ....Seattle WA 98124	**800-331-5222**	206-767-3928	296-36
Energen Corp			
605 Richard Arrington Blvd N			
........................Birmingham AL 35203	**800-654-3206**	205-326-2700	359-5
NYSE: EGN			
Energent Inc			
22 Frederick St Ste 1114 ....Kitchener ON N2H6M6	**866-441-1143**		177
EnergX LLC			
1000 B Clearview Ct ....Oak Ridge TN 37830	**866-932-1333**		193
Energy Alloys LLC			
3 Waterway Square Pl			
Ste 600.............The Woodlands TX 77380	**866-448-9831**	832-601-5800	488
Energy Concepts Inc			
404 Washington Blvd ....Mundelein IL 60060	**800-621-1247**	847-837-8191	699
Energy Efficiency & Renewable Energy Information Ctr			
1000 Independence Ave SW ......Washington DC 20585	**877-337-3463**	202-586-4849	197
Energy Focus Inc			
32000 Aurora Rd ....Solon OH 44139	**800-327-7877**	440-715-1300	438
OTC: EFOI			
Energy Laboratories Inc			
2393 Salt Creek Hwy ....Casper WY 82601	**888-235-0515**	307-235-0515	
Energy Panel Structures Inc			
603 N Van Gordon Ave ....Graettinger IA 51342	**800-967-2130**		
Energy Petroleum Co			
2130 Kienlen Ave ....St. Louis MO 63121	**800-536-6828**	314-383-3700	316
Energy Transformation Systems Inc			
43353 Osgood Rd ....Fremont CA 94539	**800-752-8208**	510-656-2012	762
EnergyExplorium			
13339 Hagers Ferry Rd ....Huntersville NC 28078	**800-777-9898**	980-875-5600	517
EnergyUnited Electric Membership Corp			
PO Box 1831 ....Statesville NC 28687	**800-522-3793**	704-873-5241	245
Enerpac PO Box 3241 ....Milwaukee WI 53201	**800-433-2766***	262-293-1600	754
*Cust Svc			
EnerSys			
2366 Bernville Rd ....Reading PA 19605	**800-538-3627**	610-208-1991	74
NYSE: ENS			
Enesco LLC			
225 Windsor Dr ....Itasca IL 60143	**800-436-3726**	630-875-5300	333
Enflo Corp			
315 Lake Ave ....Bristol CT 06010	**888-887-4093**	860-589-0014	596
Enforcer Products Inc			
PO Box 1060 ....Cartersville GA 30120	**888-805-4357**		280
Engage Technologies Corp			
7041 Boone Ave N ....Brooklyn Park MN 55428	**800-877-5658**		387
Engelberth Construction Inc			
463 Mtn View Dr			
Ste 200 Second Fl..............Colchester VT 05446	**800-639-9011**	802-655-0100	186
EngenderHealth			
505 Ninth St NW Ste 601 ....Washington DC 20004	**800-564-2872**	202-902-2000	48-17
Enghouse Systems Ltd			
80 Tiverton Ct Ste 800 ....Markham ON L3R0G4	**866-233-4606**	905-946-3200	178-10
TSX: ENGH			

	Toll-Free	Phone	Class
Engine Components Inc (ECI)			
9503 Middlex ....San Antonio TX 78217	800-324-2359	210-820-8101	21
Engine Power Source Inc			
348 Bryant Blvd ....Rock Hill SC 29732	800-374-7522	704-944-1999	515
Engineered Controls International Inc (ECII)			
100 Rego Dr PO Box 247 ....Elon NC 27244	800-650-0061	336-449-7707	784
Engineered Polymer Solutions Inc			
1400 N State St ....Marengo IL 60152	800-654-4242		601-2
Engineered Products Co (EPCO)			
601 Kelso St PO Box 108 ....Flint MI 48506	888-414-3726	810-767-2050	349
Engineered Products Inc			
500 Furman Hall Rd ....Greenville SC 29609	888-301-1421	864-234-4868	207
Engineered Protection Systems Inc			
750 Front Ave NW ....Grand Rapids MI 49504	800-966-9199	616-459-0281	189-4
Engineering & Environmental Consultants Inc			
4625 E Ft Lowell Rd ....Tucson AZ 85712	800-887-2103	520-321-4625	261
Engineering Data Design Corp			
105 Daventry Ln Ste 100 ....Louisville KY 40223	888-678-0683	502-412-4000	256
Engineering Economics Inc (EEI)			
780 Simms St Ste 210 ....Golden CO 80401	800-869-6902		186
Engineering News-Record (ENR)			
350 fifth Ave Ste 6000 ....New York NY 10118	877-876-8208	646-849-7100	455-21
Engineers Canada			
180 Elgin St Ste 1100..............Ottawa ON K2P2K3	877-408-9273	613-232-2474	48-1
Enginetech Inc			
1205 W Crosby Rd ....Carrollton TX 75006	800-869-8711	972-245-0110	61
Engis Corp			
105 W Hintz Rd ....Wheeling IL 60090	800-993-6447	847-808-9400	385
England Logistics Inc			
1325 South 4700 West ....Salt Lake City UT 84104	800-848-7810	801-656-4500	194
Englander International			
1308 Teasley Ln Ste 183........Denton TX 76205	800-489-9994	888-909-0551	469
Englefield Oil Co			
447 James Pkwy ....Heath OH 43056	800-837-4458*	740-928-8215	324
*Cust Svc			
English Inn, The			
677 S Michigan Rd ....Eaton Rapids MI 48827	800-858-0598	517-663-2500	667
Englund Marine & Industrial Supply Co			
95 Hamburg Ave PO Box 296......Astoria OR 97103	800-228-7051	503-325-4341	221
Engman-Taylor Company Inc (ETCO)			
W142 N9351 Fountain Blvd			
......................Menomonee Falls WI 53051	800-236-1975	262-255-9300	304
Enhanced Software Products Inc			
1811 N Hutchinson Rd ....Spokane WA 99212	800-456-5750	509-534-1514	225
Enid News & Eagle			
227 W Broadway PO Box 1192............Enid OK 73701	800-299-6397	580-548-8186	528-2
Enidine Inc			
7 Centre Dr ....Orchard Park NY 14127	800-852-8508	716-662-1900	470
Enlisted Assn of the National Guard of the US (EANGUS)			
3133 Mt Vernon Ave ....Alexandria VA 22305	800-234-3264	703-519-3846	48-19
Enloe Medical Ctr			
1531 Esplanade ....Chico CA 95926	800-822-8102	530-332-7300	373-3
ENMAX Corp			
141 50 Ave SE ....Calgary AB T2G4S7	877-571-7111	403-245-7222	782
Ennis Inc			
2441 Presidential Pkwy ....Midlothian TX 76065	800-972-1069	972-775-9801	623
Enoch Manufacturing Co			
14242 SE 82nd Dr ....Clackamas OR 97015	888-659-2660	503-659-2660	617
ENOCHS Examining Room Furniture			
14701 Cumberland Rd Ste 107.......Noblesville IN 46060	800-428-2305*		319-3
*Cust Svc			
Enphase Energy Inc			
1420 N Mcdowell Blvd ....Petaluma CA 94954	877-797-4743	707-763-4784	692
Enprecis Inc			
60 Courtneypark Dr W Unit 3 ....Mississauga ON L5W0B3	877-476-9274	905-565-5777	
Enpro Inc			
121 S LombaRd Rd ....Addison IL 60101	800-323-2416		384
EnPro Industries Inc Fairbanks Morse Engine			
701 White Ave ....Beloit WI 53511	800-356-6955		262
ENR (Engineering News-Record)			
350 fifth Ave Ste 6000 ....New York NY 10118	877-876-8208	646-849-7100	455-21
Ensave Energy Performance Inc			
65 Millet St Ste 105 ....Richmond VT 05477	800-732-1399		461
ENSCO Inc			
3110 Fairview Pk Dr			
Ste 300......................Falls Church VA 22042	800-367-2682	703-321-9000	261
Ensearch Management Consultants			
905 E Cotati Ave ....Cotati CA 94931	888-667-5627		717
Ensemble Travel			
256 W 38th St 11th Fl...........New York NY 10018	800-576-2378	212-545-7460	767
Ensign Corp			
201 Ensign Rd ....Bellevue IA 52031	888-797-8658	630-628-9999	762
Ensinger Putnam Precision Molding			
11 Danco Rd ....Putnam CT 06260	800-752-7865	860-928-7911	600
ENSTAR Natural Gas Co			
401 E International Airport Rd			
..........................Anchorage AK 99518	800-907-9767	907-277-5551	782
Ent Federal Credit Union			
7250 Campus Dr ....Colorado Springs CO 80920	800-525-9623	719-574-1100	219
Entact LLC			
3129 Bass Pro Dr ....Grapevine TX 76051	800-255-2771		
Entegee Inc			
70 BlanchaRd Rd Ste 102...........Burlington MA 01803	800-368-3433	781-221-5800	717
Entelechy Enterprises Inc			
889 E Shore Dr ....Silver Lake NH 03875	800-376-8368	603-424-1237	461
Entergy Arkansas Inc			
425 W Capitol Ave ....Little Rock AR 72201	800-368-3749		782
Entergy Louisiana Inc			
639 Loyola Ave ....New Orleans LA 70113	800-368-3749*	504-576-6116	782
*Cust Svc			
Entergy Mississippi Inc			
PO Box 1640 ....Jackson MS 39215	800-368-3749		
Entergy New Orleans Inc			
639 Loyola Ave ....New Orleans LA 70113	800-368-3749		782
Entergy Texas Inc			
350 Pine St ....Beaumont TX 77701	800-368-3749		782
Entero Corp			
1040 Seventh Ave SW Ste 500 ....Calgary AB T2P3G9	877-261-1820	403-261-1820	177

	Toll-Free	Phone	Class
Enterprise Bank of SC			
13497 Broxton Bridge Rd			
PO Box 8....................Ehrhardt SC 29081	800-554-8969	803-267-3191	70
Enterprise Community Partners Inc			
10227 Wincopin Cir ....Columbia MD 21044	800-624-4298	410-964-1230	48-5
Enterprise Financial Services Corp			
150 N Meramec Ave ....Clayton MO 63105	800-396-8141	314-725-5500	359-2
NASDAQ: EFSG			
Enterprise Products Partners LP			
1100 Louisiana St 10th Fl............Houston TX 77002	866-230-0745	713-381-6500	325
NYSE: EPD			
Enterprise Rent-A-Car			
600 Corporate Pk Dr ....Saint Louis MO 63105	800-307-6666	314-512-5000	126
Enterprise Wireless Alliance (EWA)			
8484 Westpark Dr Ste 630 ....McLean VA 22102	800-482-8282	703-528-5115	49-20
Entertainment Software Assn (ESA)			
601 Massachusetts Ave NW			
Ste 300 ....Washington DC 20001	800-949-3660	202-223-2400	48-9
Entertainment Weekly Magazine			
225 Liberty St ....New York NY 10281	800-828-6882		455-9
Entest Inc			
15020 Beltway Dr ....Addison TX 75001	800-955-0077	972-980-9876	
Enthermics Inc			
W164 N9221 Water St ....Menomonee Falls WI 53051	800-862-9276	262-251-8356	473
Entitle Direct Group Inc			
200 Marshall Dr ....Pittsburgh PA 15108	877-936-8485		390-6
Entomological Society of America			
10001 Derekwood Ln Ste 100...........Lanham MD 20706	800-523-8635	301-731-4535	49-19
Entrepreneur Media Inc			
18061 Fitch ....Irvine CA 92614	800-779-5295	949-261-2325	633-9
Entrust Datacard			
5420 LBJ Fwy Ste 300 ....Dallas TX 75240	888-690-2424*		178-12
*Sales			
Entwistle Co Dietzco Div			
6 Bigelow St ....Hudson MA 01749	800-445-8909	508-481-4000	552
Envirologic Technologies Inc			
2960 Interstate Pkwy ....Kalamazoo MI 49048	800-272-7802	269-342-1100	461
EnviroLogix Inc			
500 Riverside Industrial Pkwy ....Portland ME 04103	866-408-4597	207-797-0300	738
Environamics Inc			
13935 S Point Blvd ....Charlotte NC 28273	800-262-3613	704-376-3613	186
Environics Analytics Group Ltd			
33 Bloor St E Ste 400 ....Toronto ON M4W3H1	888-339-3304	416-969-2733	195
Environment Reporter			
1801 S Bell St ....Arlington VA 22202	800-372-1033		527-5
Environmental & Safety Designs Inc			
5724 Summer Trees Dr ....Memphis TN 38134	800-588-7962	901-372-7962	192
Environmental Data Resources Inc (EDR)			
6 Armstrong Rd 4th Fl ....Shelton CT 06484	800-352-0050	203-783-0300	386
Environmental Defense			
257 Park Ave S ....New York NY 10010	800-505-0703	212-505-2100	48-13
Environmental Earthscapes Inc			
5075 S Swan Rd ....Tucson AZ 85706	800-571-1575	520-571-1575	421
Environmental Enterprises Inc (EEI)			
10163 Cincinnati-Dayton Rd ....Cincinnati OH 45241	800-722-2818		663
Environmental Health & Engineering Inc			
117 Fourth Ave ....Needham MA 02494	800-825-5343	781-247-4300	256
Environmental Information Assn (EIA)			
6935 Wisconsin Ave Ste 306 ....Chevy Chase MD 20815	888-343-4342	301-961-4999	48-13
Environmental Law Institute (ELI)			
2000 L St NW Ste 620 ....Washington DC 20036	800-433-5120	202-939-3800	49-10
Environmental Protection Agency (EPA)			
1200 Pennsylvania Ave NW ....Washington DC 20460	888-372-8255	202-564-4700	339-19
US National Response Team			
1200 Pennsylvania Ave NW ....Washington DC 20593	800-424-9346	202-267-2675	339-19
Environmental Protection Agency Regional Offices			
Region 1			
1 Congress St Ste 1100 ....Boston MA 02114	888-372-7341	617-918-1111	339-19
Region 2			
290 Broadway ....New York NY 10007	800-621-8431	212-637-3000	339-19
Region 3			
1650 Arch St ....Philadelphia PA 19103	800-438-2474	215-814-5000	339-19
Region 4			
Sam Nunn Atlanta Federal Ctr			
61 Forsyth St SW ....Atlanta GA 30303	800-241-1754	404-562-9900	339-19
Region 5			
77 W Jackson Blvd ....Chicago IL 60604	800-621-8431	312-353-2000	339-19
Region 6			
1445 Ross Ave Ste 1200 ....Dallas TX 75202	800-887-6063	214-665-2200	339-19
Region 7			
901 N Fifth St ....Kansas City KS 66101	800-223-0425	913-551-7003	339-19
Region 8			
1595 Wynkoop St ....Denver CO 80202	800-227-8917	303-312-6312	339-19
Region 9			
75 Hawthorne St ....San Francisco CA 94105	866-372-9378	415-947-8000	339-19
Region 10			
1200 Sixth Ave Ste 900 ....Seattle WA 98101	800-424-4372	206-553-1200	339-19
Environmental Systems Products Inc			
7 Kripes Rd ....East Granby CT 06026	800-446-4708	860-392-2100	406
Environmental Systems Research Institute Inc			
380 New York St ....Redlands CA 92373	800-447-9778*	909-793-2853	178-10
*Sales			
Enviro-Tote Inc			
15 Industrial Dr ....Londonderry NH 03053	800-868-3224	603-647-7171	66
Envirovantage			
629 Calef Hwy Rt 125 ....Epping NH 03042	800-640-5323	603-679-9682	663
Envision Capital Management Inc			
2301 Rosecrans Ave Ste 4180 ....El Segundo CA 90245	800-400-0989	310-445-3252	400
Envision Inc			
610 N Main St ....Wichita KS 67203	888-425-7072	316-440-1500	48-6
Envision Payment Solutions Inc			
PO Box 157 ....Suwanee GA 30024	800-290-3957	770-709-3007	179
Envoy Plan Services Inc			
901 Calle Amanecer Ste 200.......San Clemente CA 92673	800-248-8858	949-366-5070	531
Enwood Structures Inc			
5724 McCrimmon Pkwy			
PO Box 2002..................Morrisville NC 27560	800-777-8648	919-518-0464	812

Name / Address	City	State	ZIP	Toll-Free	Phone	Class
Enzi Michael B (Sen R - WY)						
379A Russell Senate Office Bldg	Washington	DC	20510	**888-250-1879**	202-224-3424	
Enzo Biochem Inc						
527 Madison Ave	New York	NY	10022	**800-522-5052**	212-583-0100	231
NYSE: ENZ						
Enzo Life Sciences Inc						
10 Executive Blvd	Farmingdale	NY	11735	**800-942-0430**	631-694-7070	231
Enzymatic Therapy						
825 Challenger Dr	Green Bay	WI	54311	**800-783-2286**	920-469-1313	794
Eoff Electric Company Inc						
3241 NW Industrial St	Portland	OR	97210	**800-285-3633**	503-222-9411	253
EOG Resources Inc						
1111 Bagby Sky Lobby 2	Houston	TX	77002	**877-363-3647**	713-651-7000	534
NYSE: EOG						
EOI Service Company Inc						
1820 E First St Ste 400	Santa Ana	CA	92705	**800-229-4364**	714-935-0503	
Eola Hills Wine Cellars						
501 S Pacific Hwy 99 W	Rickreall	OR	97371	**800-291-6730**	503-623-2405	50-7
Eoriginal Inc						
351 W Camden St Ste 800	Baltimore	MD	21201	**866-935-1776**		
Eos Systems Inc						
10 Kearney Rd Ste 102	Needham	MA	02494	**855-453-2600**	781-453-2600	180
EP Henry Corp						
201 Park Ave	Woodbury	NJ	08096	**800-444-3679**		183
EP Wealth Advisors Inc						
21515 Hawthorne Blvd Ste 1200	Torrance	CA	90503	**800-272-2328**	310-543-4559	194
EPA (Environmental Protection Agency)						
1200 Pennsylvania Ave NW	Washington	DC	20460	**888-372-8255**	202-564-4700	339-19
Epac Software Technologies Inc						
42 Ladd St	East Greenwich	RI	02818	**888-336-3722**		177
E-pak Machinery Inc						
1535 S State Rd 39	La Porte	IN	46350	**800-328-0466**	219-393-5541	543
EPCO (Engineered Products Co)						
601 Kelso St PO Box 108	Flint	MI	48506	**888-414-3726**	810-767-2050	349
EPCOS Inc						
485-B Rt 1 S Ste 200	Iselin	NJ	08830	**800-689-3717**	732-906-4304	253
ePerformax Contact Centers & BPO						
100 Saddle Springs Blvd Ste 100	Thompsons Station	TN	37179	**888-384-7004**		
Epes Carriers Inc						
3400 Edgefield Ct	Greensboro	NC	27409	**800-869-3737**	336-668-3358	775
Ephor Group LLC						
24 E Greenway Plz Ste 440	Houston	TX	77046	**800-379-9330**		461
EPI Marketing Services						
5404 Wayne Rd	Battle Creek	MI	49037	**800-562-9733**		623
Epic Cos						
24955 Interstate 45 N	The Woodlands	TX	77380	**800-844-3742**		
Epic Labs						
95 Third St NE PO Box 7430	Waite Park	MN	56387	**877-374-2522**		539
Epic Life Insurance Co						
1717 W Broadway	Madison	WI	53713	**800-520-5750***		390-2
*Sales						
Epic Metals Corp						
11 Talbot Ave	Rankin	PA	15104	**877-696-3742**	412-351-3913	693
Epicurean Inc						
257 B Main St	Superior	MN	54880	**866-678-3500**	218-740-3500	
Epilepsy Foundation						
8301 Professional Pl Ste 200	Landover	MD	20785	**800-332-1000**	301-459-3700	48-17
Epilog Corp						
16371 Table Mtn Pkwy	Golden	CO	80403	**888-437-4564**	303-277-1188	540
Episcopal Church USA						
815 Second Ave	New York	NY	10017	**800-334-6946**	212-716-6000	48-20
Episcopal Diocese of West Texas						
111 Torcido Dr	San Antonio	TX	78209	**888-824-5387**	210-824-5387	48-20
Episcopal High School						
1200 N Quaker Ln	Alexandria	VA	22302	**877-933-4347**	703-933-4062	618
Episcopal Life Magazine						
815 Second Ave Episcopal Church Ctr	New York	NY	10017	**800-334-7626**	212-716-6000	455-18
Episcopal Migration Ministries (EMM)						
815 Second Ave	New York	NY	10017	**800-334-7626**	212-716-6000	48-5
Episcopal Relief & Development						
815 Second Ave	New York	NY	10017	**800-334-7626**	855-312-4325	48-5
Epitomics Inc						
863 Mitten Rd Ste 103	Burlingame	CA	94010	**888-772-2226**		664
EPL Bio Analytical Services						
9095 W Harristown Blvd	Niantic	IL	62551	**866-963-2143**	217-963-2143	738
ePlus Inc						
13595 Dulles Technology Dr	Herndon	VA	20171	**888-482-1122**	703-984-8400	39
NASDAQ: PLUS						
Epoch 5 Public Relations						
755 New York Ave	Huntington	NY	11743	**800-628-7070**	631-427-1713	632
Epoch Design						
17617 NE 65th St Ste 2	Redmond	WA	98052	**800-589-7990**		321
Epoch Online						
324 W Pershing Blvd Ste 11	North Little Rock	AR	72114	**877-312-7500**	501-907-7500	
Epoch Universal Inc						
9341 Irvine Blvd	Irvine	CA	92618	**877-907-1144**		
Eppendorf North America Inc						
102 Motor Pkwy	Hauppage	NY	11788	**800-645-3050**		418
Eppinger Manufacturing Co						
6340 Schaefer Rd	Dearborn	MI	48126	**888-771-8277**	313-582-3205	706
Epps Aviation Inc						
1 Aviation Way DeKalb Peachtree Airport	Atlanta	GA	30341	**800-241-6807**	770-458-9851	63
EPRI Journal						
3420 Hillview Ave	Palo Alto	CA	94304	**800-313-3774**	650-855-2121	455-21
Epro Tile Inc						
10890 E CR 6	Bloomville	OH	44818	**866-818-3776**		746
ePromos Promotional Products Inc						
113 Fifth Ave S Ste 1360	St Cloud	NY	10271	**800-564-6216**	212-286-8008	96
EPS (Educators Publishing Service Inc)						
PO Box 9031	Cambridge	MA	02139	**800-225-5750**		633-2
Epson America Inc						
3840 Kilroy Airport Way	Long Beach	CA	90806	**800-463-7766**		173-6
Epson Electronics America Inc						
214 Devcon Dr	San Jose	CA	95112	**800-228-3964**	408-474-0500	692

Name / Address	City	State	ZIP	Toll-Free	Phone	Class
EQ Inc						
1235 Bay St Ste 401	Toronto	ON	M5R3K4	**888-597-8889**		
EQC (Emerald Queen Casino)						
2024 E 29th St	Tacoma	WA	98404	**888-831-7655**	253-594-7777	133
EQT Corp						
625 Liberty Ave Ste 1700	Pittsburgh	PA	15222	**800-242-1776**	412-553-5700	782
NYSE: EQT						
Equal Employment Opportunity Commission (EEOC)						
1801 L St NW	Washington	DC	20507	**800-669-4000**	202-663-4191	339-19
Equal Employment Opportunity Commission Regional Office						
Atlanta District						
100 Alabama St SW Ste 4R30	Atlanta	GA	30303	**800-669-6820**		339-19
Birmingham District						
1130 22nd St S Ste 2000	Birmingham	AL	35205	**800-669-4000**	205-212-2100	339-19
Charlotte District						
129 W Trade St Ste 400	Charlotte	NC	28202	**800-669-4000**	704-344-6682	339-19
Chicago District						
500 W Madison St Ste 2000	Chicago	IL	60661	**800-669-4000**	312-869-8084	339-19
Dallas District						
207 S Houston St 3rd Fl	Dallas	TX	75202	**800-669-4000**	214-253-2700	339-19
Houston District						
1201 Louisiana St 6th Fl	Houston	TX	77002	**800-669-4000**		339-19
Los Angeles District						
255 E Temple St 4th Fl	Los Angeles	CA	90012	**800-669-4000**		339-19
New York District						
33 Whitehall St 5th Fl	New York	NY	10004	**866-408-8075**	212-336-3620	339-19
Philadelphia District						
801 Market St Ste 1300	Philadelphia	PA	19107	**800-669-4000**		339-19
Saint Louis District						
1222 Spruce St Rm 8100	Saint Louis	MO	63103	**800-669-4000**	314-539-7800	339-19
San Francisco District						
450 Golden Gate Ave 5 W PO Box 36025	San Francisco	CA	94102	**800-669-4000**		339-19
Equal Rights Advocates (ERA)						
1170 Market St Ste 700	San Francisco	CA	94102	**800-839-4372**	415-621-0672	48-24
EQUESTRIAN CANADA QUESTRE						
2685 Queensview Dr	Ottawa	ON	K2B8K2	**866-282-8395**	613-248-3484	648
Equias Alliance LLC						
8000 Ctrview Pkwy Ste 525	Cordova	TN	38018	**844-553-7872**		
Equifax Credit Marketing Services						
1550 Peachtree St NW	Atlanta	GA	30309	**800-660-5125***	404-885-8000	218
NYSE: EFX ■ *Sales						
Equifax Inc						
1550 Peachtree St NW	Atlanta	GA	30309	**888-202-4025***	404-885-8000	218
NYSE: EFX ■ *Sales						
Equinox, The						
3567 Main St	Manchester Village	VT	05254	**800-362-4747**	802-362-4700	665
Equipment Development Company Inc						
100 Thomas Johnson Dr	Frederick	MD	21702	**800-638-3326**		
Equipment Manufacturing Corp (EMC)						
14930 Marquardt Ave	Santa Fe Springs	CA	90670	**888-833-9000**	562-623-9394	385
Equipment Technology LLC						
341 NW 122nd St	Oklahoma City	OK	73114	**888-748-3841**		264-3
Equipoise Dental Laboratory Inc						
85 Portland Ave	Bergenfield	NJ	07621	**800-999-4950**	201-385-4750	417
EQUIPTO 225 Main St	Tatamy	PA	18085	**800-323-0801**	610-253-2775	286
Equipto Electronics Corp						
351 Woodlawn Ave	Aurora	IL	60506	**800-204-7225**	630-897-4691	254
Equis International						
90 South 400 West Ste 620	Salt Lake City	UT	84101	**800-882-3040***	801-265-9996	178-10
*Sales						
Equitable Bank (MHC)						
113 N Locust St	Grand Island	NE	68801	**877-821-5783**	308-382-3136	70
Equitable Life & Casualty Insurance Co						
3 Triad Ctr	Salt Lake City	UT	84180	**877-358-4060***		390-2
*Cust Svc						
Equity Co-op Livestock Sales Assn						
401 Commerce Ave	Baraboo	WI	53913	**800-362-3989**	608-356-8311	444
Equity Investment Corp						
3007 Piedmont Rd Ste 200	Atlanta	GA	30305	**877-342-0111**	404-239-0111	524
Equity Lifestyle Properties Inc						
2 N Riverside Plz Ste 800	Chicago	IL	60606	**800-274-7314**	312-279-1400	651
NYSE: ELS						
Equity Residential						
2 N Riverside Plz	Chicago	IL	60606	**800-733-5001**	312-474-1300	651
NYSE: EQR						
Equus Computer Systems Inc						
7725 Washington Ave S	Edina	MN	55439	**866-378-8727**	800-641-1475	173-2
Equus Magazine						
656 Quince OrchaRd Rd Ste 600	Gaithersburg	MD	20878	**800-829-5910**	301-977-3900	455-14
EQUUS Total Return Inc						
700 Louisiana St 48th Fl	Houston	TX	77002	**888-323-4533**		787
ER Wagner Mfg Company Inc						
W130 N8691 Old Orchard Rd	Menomonee Falls	WI	53051	**800-558-5596**		349
ERA (Equal Rights Advocates)						
1170 Market St Ste 700	San Francisco	CA	94102	**800-839-4372**	415-621-0672	48-24
Era Helicopters LLC						
600 Airport Service Rd PO Box 6550	Lake Charles	LA	70606	**888-503-8172**	337-478-6131	13
ERA Wilder Realty Inc						
120A Columbia Ave	Chapin	SC	29036	**866-593-7653**	803-345-6713	648
Erb Equipment Co Inc						
200 Erb Industrial Dr	Fenton	MO	63026	**800-634-9661**	636-349-0200	357
Erchonia Corp						
650 Atlantis Rd	Melbourne	FL	32904	**888-242-0571**	321-473-1251	
Erdman 1 Erdman Pl	Madison	WI	53717	**866-855-1001**		
Erect-A-Tube Inc						
PO Box 100	Harvard	IL	60033	**800-624-9219**	815-943-4091	105
Ergodyne Corp						
1021 Bandana Blvd E Ste 220	Saint Paul	MN	55108	**800-225-8238**	651-642-9889	475
ErgoGenesis Workplace Solutions LLC						
1 BodyBilt Pl	Navasota	TX	77868	**800-364-5299**	936-825-1700	319-3
Ergotron Inc						
1181 Trapp Rd	Saint Paul	MN	55121	**800-888-8458***	651-681-7600	319-1
*Sales						

	City	ST	Zip	Toll-Free	Phone	Class
Erhard BMW of Bloomfield						
1845 S Telegraph	Bloomfield Hills	MI	48302	**888-481-4058**	248-642-6565	57
ERIC (Education Resource Information Ctr)						
655 15th St NW Ste 500	Washington	DC	20005	**800-538-3742**		197
Eric A King						
301 Grant St Ste 4300	Pittsburgh	PA	15219	**888-742-2454**	281-667-4200	177
Eric Buchanan & Associates Pllc						
414 Mccallie Ave	Chattanooga	TN	37402	**877-634-2506**		443
Eric Javits						
21-35 44th Rd	Long Island City	NY	11101	**855-208-6200***	800-374-4287	34
*Consumer Info						
Erick Nielsen Enterprises Inc						
4453 County Rd Mm # O	Orland	CA	95963	**800-844-9409**	530-865-9409	196
Erickson's Flooring & Supply Company Inc						
1013 Orchard St	Ferndale	MI	48220	**866-541-9663**		360
ERICO Products Inc						
34600 Solon Rd	Solon	OH	44139	**800-248-2677**	440-248-0100	810
Erie 2-Chautauqua Cattaraugus Boces (ECCB)						
8685 Erie Rd	Angola	NY	14006	**800-228-1184**	716-549-4454	681
Erie County Library System						
160 E Front St	Erie	PA	16507	**800-352-0026**	814-451-6900	433-3
Erie County Water Authority (ECWA)						
295 Main St Rm 350	Buffalo	NY	14203	**855-748-1076**	716-849-8484	782
Erie Family Life Insurance Co						
100 Erie Insurance Pl	Erie	PA	16530	**800-458-0811**	814-870-2000	390-2
Erie Indemnity Co						
Erie Insurance Group						
100 Erie Insurance Pl	Erie	PA	16530	**800-458-0811**	814-870-2000	390-4
NASDAQ: ERIE						
Erie Insurance Exchange						
100 Erie Insurance Pl	Erie	PA	16530	**800-458-0811**	814-870-2000	390-4
Erie Insurance Property & Casualty Co						
100 Erie Insurance Pl	Erie	PA	16530	**800-458-0811**	814-870-2000	390-4
Erie Playhouse						
13 W Tenth St	Erie	PA	16501	**800-305-0669**	814-454-2852	569-4
Erie Strayer Co						
1851 Rudolph Ave PO Box 1031	Erie	PA	16502	**800-356-4848**	814-456-7001	190
Erie Times-News						
205 W 12th St	Erie	PA	16534	**800-352-0043**	814-870-1600	528-2
Erie VA Medical Ctr						
135 E 38th St	Erie	PA	16504	**800-274-8387**	814-868-8661	373-8
Erie Vehicle Co						
60 E 51st St	Chicago	IL	60615	**888-550-3743**	773-536-6300	513
ErieTec Inc						
1432 E 12th St	Erie	PA	16503	**800-777-6871**	814-453-6871	384
Eris Exchange LLC						
311 S Wacker Dr Ste 950	Chicago	IL	60606	**888-587-2699**		
Erlanger Health System						
975 E Third St	Chattanooga	TN	37403	**877-849-8338**	423-778-7000	373-3
Ernest F Mariani Company Inc						
573 West 2890 South	Salt Lake City	UT	84115	**800-453-2927**		661
Ernest Maier Inc						
4700 Annapolis Rd	Bladensburg	MD	20710	**888-927-8303**	301-927-8300	183
Ernest Paper Products						
5777 Smithway St	Commerce	CA	90040	**800-233-7788**		555
Ernie Ball						
151 Suburban Rd	San Luis Obispo	CA	93401	**866-823-2255**	800-543-2255	523
Ernst Enterprises Inc						
3361 Successful Way	Dayton	OH	45414	**800-353-1555**	937-233-5555	182
Ernst Publishing Co LLC						
1 Commerce Plz 99 Washington Ave						
Ste 309	Albany	NY	12210	**800-345-3822**		633-9
Erskine College						
2 Washington St	Due West	SC	29639	**888-359-4358***		166
*Admissions						
Erskine Theological Seminary						
2 Washington St PO Box 338	Due West	SC	29639	**888-359-4358**	864-379-6571	167-3
ERT						
1818 Market St Ste 1000	Philadelphia	PA	19103	**800-704-9698**	215-972-0420	178-10
NASDAQ: ERT						
Ervin Industries Inc						
3893 Research Pk Dr	Ann Arbor	MI	48108	**800-748-0055**	734-769-4600	1
ES Originals Inc						
440 Ninth Ave 7th Fl	New York	NY	10001	**800-677-6577***	212-736-8124	301
*General						
ES. Fox Ltd						
9127 Montrose Rd	Niagara Falls	ON	L2E7J9	**866-233-8933**	905-354-3700	261
ESA (Evangelicals for Social Action)						
PO Box 367	Wayne	PA	19087	**800-650-6600**	484-384-2988	48-7
ESA (Electronic Security Assn Inc)						
6333 North State Hwy 161 Ste 350	Irving	TX	75038	**888-447-1689**	972-807-6800	49-3
ESA (Entertainment Software Assn)						
601 Massachusetts Ave NW						
Ste 300	Washington	DC	20001	**800-949-3660**	202-223-2400	48-9
Esab Welding & Cutting Products						
256 Midway Dr	Union	SC	29379	**800-372-2123**	864-466-0921	806
Escalade Inc						
817 Maxwell Ave	Evansville	IN	47711	**800-426-1421***	812-467-1200	706
NASDAQ: ESCA ■ *Cust Svc						
Escalera Inc						
708 S Industrial Dr						
PO Box 1359	Yuba City	CA	95993	**800-622-1359**	530-673-6318	468
Escalon Premier Brands						
1905 McHenry Ave	Escalon	CA	95320	**800-255-5750**	209-838-7341	296-20
Escambia River Electric Co-op Inc						
3425 Florida 4	Jay	FL	32565	**800-235-3848**	850-675-4521	245
Escapees RV Club						
100 Rainbow Dr	Livingston	TX	77351	**888-757-2582**		48-23
Eschenbach Optik of America Inc						
22 Shelter Rock Ln	Danbury	CT	06810	**800-487-5389**		
Esco Corp						
2141 NW 25th Ave	Portland	OR	97210	**800-523-3795**	503-228-2141	190
eScreen Inc						
7500 W 110th St Ste 500	Overland Park	KS	66210	**800-881-0722**	913-327-5915	386
ESE Inc						
3600 DownWind Dr	Marshfield	WI	54449	**800-236-4778**		256
Eseeola Lodge, The						
175 Linville Ave PO Box 99	Linville	NC	28646	**800-742-6717**	828-733-4311	665
ESGR (National Committee for Employer Support of the Gua)						
1555 Wilson Blvd Ste 319	Arlington	VA	22209	**800-336-4590**		48-19
ESI Technologies						
1550 Metcalfe St Ste 1100	Montreal	QC	H3A1X6	**800-260-3311**		
eSignal						
3955 Pt Eden Way	Hayward	CA	94545	**800-815-8256**	510-266-6000	178-1
eSilicon Corp						
501 Macara Ave	Sunnyvale	CA	94085	**877-769-2447**	408-616-4600	253
Eskaton Inc						
5105 Manzanita Ave	Carmichael	CA	95608	**800-729-2999**	916-334-0810	668
Eskaton Village						
3939 Walnut Ave	Carmichael	CA	95608	**800-300-3929**	916-974-2000	668
Esker Inc						
1212 Deming Way Ste 350	Madison	WI	53717	**800-368-5283**	608-828-6000	178-12
Esmark Steel Group						
2500 Euclid Ave	Chicago Heights	IL	60411	**800-323-0340**	708-756-0400	359-3
Esmeralda County						
PO Box 547	Goldfield	NV	89013	**800-884-4072**	775-485-6309	337
ESOP Assn						
1726 M St NW Ste 501	Washington	DC	20036	**866-366-3832**	202-293-2971	49-12
ESPE Mfg Company Inc						
9220 Ivanhoe St	Schiller Park	IL	60176	**800-367-3773***	847-678-8950	349
*Cust Svc						
Esplanade Tours						
160 Commonwealth Ave Ste U-1A	Boston	MA	02116	**800-628-4893**	617-266-7465	755
ESPN Deportes						
2 Alhambra Plz	Coral Gables	FL	33134	**800-337-6783**	305-567-3797	735
ESPN Richmond 950						
2809 Emerywood Pkwy Ste 300	Richmond	VA	23294	**877-994-4950**	804-672-9299	641-89
Esprit Miami						
11475 NW 39th St	Miami	FL	33178	**800-327-2320**	305-591-2244	293
ESRI Canada Ltd						
12 Concorde Pl Ste 900	Toronto	ON	M3C3R8	**866-625-4577**	416-441-6035	174
Essence Communications Inc						
241 37th St 4th Fl	Brooklyn	NY	11232	**800-274-9398***		633-9
*Sales						
Essence Magazine						
241 37th St 4th Fl	Brooklyn	NY	11232	**800-274-9398**		455-11
Essentia Health						
502 E Second St	Duluth	MN	55805	**855-469-6532**	218-786-8376	373-3
Essential Technologies Inc						
1107 Hazeltine Blvd Ste 477	Chaska	MN	55318	**844-375-7219**	952-368-9001	175
Essentra PLC						
7400 W Industrial Dr	Forest Park	IL	60130	**800-847-0486**		154
Essex County						
305 Prince St	Tappahannock	VA	22560	**800-552-9745**	804-443-4611	337
Essex Financial Services Inc						
176 Westbrook Rd	Essex	CT	06426	**800-900-5972**	860-767-4300	524
Essex Food Ingredients						
9 Lee Blvd	Frazer	PA	19355	**800-441-1017**		297-11
Essex Manufacturing Inc						
PO Box 92864	Southlake	TX	76092	**888-643-7739**	817-847-4555	155-5
Essex Meadows						
30 Bokum Rd	Essex	CT	06426	**866-721-4838**	860-767-7201	668
Essex Savings Bank						
PO Box 950	Essex	CT	06426	**877-377-3922**	860-767-4414	70
Essick Air Products Inc						
5800 Murray St	Little Rock	AR	72209	**800-643-8341**	501-562-1094	91
Essilor of America Inc						
13515 N Stemmons Fwy	Dallas	TX	75234	**800-377-4567**		538
Esskay Inc						
111 Commerce St	Smithfield	VA	23430	**855-411-7675**		471
Essmueller Co						
334 Ave A PO Box 1966	Laurel	MS	39440	**800-325-7175**	601-649-2400	207
Estabrook Capital Management LLC						
900 Third Ave Ste 1004	New York	NY	10022	**888-447-7443**	212-605-5595	
Esterline Interface Technologies						
600 W Wilbur Ave	Coeur d'Alene	ID	83815	**800-444-5923**	208-765-8000	173-1
Esterline Mason						
13955 Balboa Blvd	Sylmar	CA	91342	**800-232-7700**	818-361-3366	502
Estes Equipment Company Inc						
2007 Polk St	Chattanooga	TN	37408	**800-933-7837**	423-756-0090	
Estes-Cox Corp						
1295 H St	Penrose	CO	81240	**800-525-7561**	719-372-6565	757
Estex Mfg Co Inc						
402 E Broad St PO Box 368	Fairburn	GA	30213	**800-749-1224**		728
Esther Price Candies Inc						
1709 Wayne Ave	Dayton	OH	45410	**800-782-0326**	937-253-2121	296-8
Estrada Hinojosa & Company Inc						
1717 Main St LB47	Dallas	TX	75201	**800-676-5352**	214-658-1670	400
ET Horn Co						
16050 Canary Ave	La Mirada	CA	90638	**800-442-4676**	714-523-8050	146
ETA (Evangelical Training Assn)						
1551 Regency Ct	Calumet City	IL	60409	**800-369-8291***		48-20
*General						
ETA (Electronics Technicians Assn International)						
5 Depot St	Greencastle	IN	46135	**800-288-3824**	765-653-8262	49-19
Eta Sigma Gamma						
2000 University Ave	Muncie	IN	47306	**800-715-2559**	765-285-2258	48-16
ETC (Educational Travel Consultants)						
PO Box 1580	Hendersonville	NC	28793	**800-247-7969**	828-693-0412	755
ETCO (Engman-Taylor Company Inc)						
W142 N9351 Fountain Blvd						
	Menomonee Falls	WI	53051	**800-236-1975**	262-255-9300	384
ETCO Inc						
25 Bellows St	Warwick	RI	02888	**800-689-3826**	401-467-2400	810
ETCO Inc Automotive Products Div						
3004 62nd Ave E	Bradenton	FL	34203	**800-689-3826**	941-756-8426	247
Etera Consulting						
1100 17th St NW Ste 605	Washington	DC	20036	**800-674-3141**	202-349-0177	196
Etera Solutions Llc						
354 TurnPark St Ste 203	Canton	MA	02021	**888-536-6515**		395
Eternabond						
75 E Div St	Mundelein	IL	60060	**888-336-2663**	847-837-9400	727
Eternity Healthcare Inc						
8755 Ash St	Vancouver	BC	V6P6T3	**855-324-1110**	604-324-1113	474
Etex Telephone Co-op Inc						
1013 Hwy 155 N	Gilmer	TX	75644	**877-482-3839**	903-797-4357	

		Toll-Free	Phone	Class

Ethan Allen Hotel
21 Lake Ave Ext ....Danbury CT 06811 · **800-742-1776** · 203-744-1776 · 378

Ethan Allen Interiors Inc
Ethan Allen Dr ....Danbury CT 06811 · **888-324-3571** · · 321
NYSE: ETH

Ethics & Public Policy Ctr
1730 M St NW Ste 910. ....Washington DC 20036 · **800-935-0699** · 202-682-1200 · 630

Ethos Risk Services Inc
300 First Ave S Ste 300 ....St. Petersburg FL 33701 · **866-783-0525**

ETNA Supply
4901 Clay Ave SW ....Grand Rapids MI 49548 · **855-839-8011** · 616-245-4373

Etobicoke Ironworks Ltd
141 Rivalda Rd ....Weston ON M9M2M6 · **866-274-6971** · 416-742-7111 · 478

EtQ Management Consultants Inc
399 Conklin St Ste 208. ....Farmingdale NY 11735 · **800-354-4476** · 516-293-0949 · 195

Ettore Products Co
2100 N Loop Rd ....Alameda CA 94502 · **800-438-8673** · 510-748-4130 · 506

ETV (South Carolina Educational Television Commission)
1101 George Rogers Blvd ....Columbia SC 29201 · **800-922-5437** · 803-737-3200 · 628

EUB (Edinboro University of Pennsylvania Baron-Forness)
200 Tartan Rd ....Edinboro PA 16444 · **888-845-2890** · 814-732-2273 · 433-6

Eubanks Engineering Co
3022 Inland Empire Blvd ....Ontario CA 91764 · **800-729-4208** · 909-483-2456 · 808

Eubel Brady & Suttman Asset Management Inc
10100 Innovation Dr Ste 410 ....Dayton OH 45342 · **800-391-1223** · 937-291-1223 · 194

Euclid Chemical Co
19218 Redwood Rd ....Cleveland OH 44110 · **800-321-7628** · 216-531-9222 · 3

Euclid Heat Treating Co
1340 E 222nd St ....Euclid OH 44117 · **800-962-2909** · 216-481-8444 · 482

Euclid Hospital
18901 Lake Shore Blvd ....Euclid OH 44119 · **800-223-2273**

Eufaula/Barbour County Chamber of Commerce
333 E Broad St ....Eufaula AL 36027 · **800-524-7529** · 334-687-6664 · 139

Eugene Airport
28801 Douglas Dr ....Eugene OR 97402 · **800-741-5097** · 541-682-5430 · 27

Eugene Burger Management Corp
6600 Hunter Dr ....Rohnert Park CA 94928 · **800-788-0233** · 707-584-5123 · 651

Eugene Cascades Coast
754 Olive St ....Eugene OR 97440 · **800-547-5445** · 541-484-5307 · 206

Eugene O'Neill National Historic Site
1000 Kuss Rd ....Danville CA 94526 · **866-945-7920** · 925-838-0249 · 560

Euler Hermes ACI
800 Red Brook Blvd ....Baltimore MD 21117 · **877-883-3224** · 410-753-0753 · 390-5

Eureka College
300 E College Ave ....Eureka IL 61530 · **888-438-7352*** · 309-467-6350 · 166
*Admissions

Eureka Homestead
1922 Veterans Memorial Blvd ....Metairie LA 70005 · **855-858-5179** · 504-834-0242 · 69

Eureka Welding Alloys Inc
2000 E Avis Dr ....Madison Heights MI 48071 · **800-962-8560** · 248-588-0001 · 806

Euro Pacific Capital Inc
88 Post Rd W 2nd Fl. ....Westport CT 06880 · **800-727-7922** · 203-662-9700 · 70

Eurofase Inc
33 W Beaver Creek Rd ....Richmond Hill ON L4B1L8 · **800-660-5391** · 905-695-2055 · 41

Eurofins Spectrum Analytical Inc
830 Silver St ....Agawam MA 01001 · **800-789-9115** · 413-789-9018 · 738

Euromoney Institutional Investor PLC
225 Park Ave S ....New York NY 10003 · **800-715-9197** · 212-224-3300 · 633-9

Euro-Pharm International Canada Inc
9400 Boul Langelier ....Montreal QC H1P3H8 · **888-929-0835** · 514-323-8757 · 231

EuroPharma Inc
955 Challenger Dr ....Green Bay WI 54311 · **866-598-5487** · 920-406-6500 · 344

Euro-Suites Hotel
University Centre 501 Chestnut Ridge Rd
...............Morgantown WV 26505 · **800-678-4837** · · 378

Eutectic Corp
N94 W14355 Garwin Mace Dr
...............Menomonee Falls WI 53051 · **800-558-8524** · 262-532-4677 · 806

EV Connect Inc
615 North Nash St Ste 203. ....El Segundo CA 90245 · **866-790-3155**

EVA Airways
200 N Sepulveda Blvd
Ste 1600. ....El Segundo CA 90245 · **800-695-1188** · 310-362-6600 · 25

Evan K Thalenberg Law Offices
216 E Lexington St ....Baltimore MD 21202 · **800-778-1181** · 410-625-9100 · 427

Evana Automation
5825 Old Boonville Hwy ....Evansville IN 47715 · **800-468-6774** · 812-479-8246 · 207

Evangel University
1111 N Glenstone Ave ....Springfield MO 65802 · **800-382-6435*** · 417-865-2815 · 166
*Admissions

Evangelical Church Alliance (ECA)
205 W Broadway St PO Box 9. ....Bradley IL 60915 · **888-855-6060** · 815-937-0720 · 48-20

Evangelical Council for Financial Accountability (ECFA)
440 W Jubal Early Dr Ste 130. ....Winchester VA 22601 · **800-323-9473** · 540-535-0103 · 48-5

Evangelical Fellowship of Canada (EFC)
9821 Leslie St Ste 103 ....Richmond Hill ON L4B3Y4 · **866-302-3362** · 905-479-5885 · 48-20

Evangelical Free Church of America, The
901 E 78th St ....Minneapolis MN 55420 · **800-745-2202** · 952-854-1300 · 48-20

Evangelical Lutheran Church in America (ELCA)
8765 W Higgins Rd ....Chicago IL 60631 · **800-638-3522** · 773-380-2700 · 48-20

Evangelical School of Theology
121 S College St ....Myerstown PA 17067 · **800-532-5775** · 717-866-5775 · 167-3

Evangelical Training Assn (ETA)
1551 Regency Ct ....Calumet City IL 60409 · **800-369-8291*** · · 48-20
*General

Evangelicals for Social Action (ESA)
PO Box 367 ....Wayne PA 19087 · **800-650-6600** · 484-384-2988 · 48-7

Evan-Moor Educational Publishers Inc
18 Lower Ragsdale Dr ....Monterey CA 93940 · **800-777-4362** · 831-649-5901 · 243

Evans & Assoc Construction Company Inc
3320 N 14th St ....Ponca City OK 74601 · **800-324-6693** · 580-765-6693 · 188-4

Evans & Sutherland Computer Corp
770 Komas Dr ....Salt Lake City UT 84108 · **800-327-5707*** · 801-588-1000 · 699
*OTC: ESCC ■ *Sales*

Evans Bancorp Inc
1 Grimsby Dr ....Hamburg NY 14075 · **866-310-0763** · 716-926-2000 · 359-2
NYSE: EVBN

Evans Data Corp
340 Soquel Ave ....Santa Cruz CA 95062 · **800-831-3080** · 831-425-8451 · 664

		Toll-Free	Phone	Class

Evans Delivery Company Inc
PO Box 268 ....Pottsville PA 17901 · **800-666-7885** · 570-385-9048 · 311

Evans Enterprises Inc
1536 S Western Ave ....Oklahoma City OK 73109 · **800-423-8267** · 405-631-1344 · 246

Evans Food Group Ltd
4118 S Halsted St ....Chicago IL 60609 · **888-643-8267** · 773-254-7400 · 296-35

Evans Tempcon Michigan LLC
701 Ann St NW ....Grand Rapids MI 49504 · **800-878-7147** · 616-361-2681 · 15

Evans Tire & Service Centers Inc
510 N Broadway ....Escondido CA 92025 · **877-338-2678** · · 62-5

Evanston Hospital
2650 Ridge Ave ....Evanston IL 60201 · **888-364-6400** · 847-570-2000 · 373-3

Evanston Public Library
1703 Orrington Ave ....Evanston IL 60201 · **888-253-7003** · 847-448-8600 · 433-3

Evansville Convention & Visitors Bureau
401 SE Riverside Dr ....Evansville IN 47713 · **800-433-3025** · 812-421-2200 · 206

Evansville Courier & Press
300 E Walnut St ....Evansville IN 47713 · **844-900-7104** · 812-464-7620 · 528-2

Evansville Teachers Federal Credit Union
PO Box 5129 ....Evansville IN 47716 · **800-800-9271** · 812-477-9271 · 219

Evco Plastics
100 W N St PO Box 497 ....DeForest WI 53532 · **800-507-6000** · · 600

Evenflo Company Inc
1801 Commerce Dr ....Piqua OH 45356 · **800-233-5921** · · 64

Evening Observer
8-10 E Second St PO Box 391 ....Dunkirk NY 14048 · **800-836-0931** · 716-366-3000 · 528-2

Evening Sun
135 Baltimore St ....Hanover PA 17331 · **888-256-0125** · 717-755-4452 · 528-2

Evensky & Katz LLC
4000 Ponce de Leon Blvd
Ste 850. ....Coral Gables FL 33146 · **800-448-5435** · 305-448-8882 · 194

Eventure Interactive Inc
3420 Bristol St 6th Fl ....Costa Mesa CA 92626 · **855-986-5669** · · 394

Ever-Bloom Inc
4701 Foothill Rd ....Carpinteria CA 93013 · **800-388-8112** · 805-684-5566 · 368

Everbrite Inc
4949 S 110th St PO Box 20020 ....Greenfield WI 53220 · **800-558-3888** · 414-529-3500 · 697

Everest College Alhambra
2215 W Mission Rd ....Alhambra CA 91803 · **888-223-8556** · 626-979-4940 · 795

Everest College San Jose
3095 Yerba Buena Rd ....San Jose CA 95135 · **888-223-8556** · 408-260-5166 · 795

Everest Institute
21107 Lahser Rd ....Southfield MI 48033 · **800-611-2101*** · 248-799-9933 · 795
*General

Everest Re Group Ltd
477 Martinsville Rd
PO Box 830. ....Liberty Corner NJ 07938 · **800-269-6660** · 908-604-3000 · 359-4

Everest Reinsurance Co
477 Martinsville Rd ....Liberty Corner NJ 07938 · **800-269-6660** · 908-604-3000 · 390-5

Everest University
Pompano Beach
225 N Federal Hwy ....Pompano Beach FL 33062 · **800-468-0168** · 954-783-7339 · 795

Everett Community College
2000 Tower St ....Everett WA 98201 · **866-575-9027** · 425-388-9100 · 162

Everett J Prescott Inc
32 Prescott St ....Gardiner ME 04345 · **800-357-2447** · 207-582-1851 · 608

Everfast Inc
203 Gale Ln ....Kennett Square PA 19348 · **800-213-6366*** · 610-444-9700 · 270
*Cust Svc

eVerge Group Inc
4965 Preston Pk Blvd Ste 700 ....Plano TX 75093 · **888-548-1973** · 972-608-1803 · 180

Everglades Boats
544 Air Pk Rd ....Edgewater FL 32132 · **800-368-5647** · 386-409-2202 · 90

Everglades National Park
40001 SR-9336 ....Homestead FL 33034 · **800-788-0511** · 305-242-7700 · 560

Evergreen Engineering Portland LLC
1740 Willow Creek Cir ....Eugene OR 97402 · **888-484-4771**

Evergreen Enterprises Inc
5915 Midlothian Tpke ....Richmond VA 23225 · **800-774-3837** · · 320

Evergreen FS Inc
402 N Hershey Rd ....Bloomington IL 61704 · **877-963-2392** · · 276

Evergreen Lodge
250 S Frontage Rd W ....Vail CO 81657 · **800-284-8245** · 970-476-7810 · 378

Evergreen Marriott Conference Resort
4021 Lakeview Dr ....Stone Mountain GA 30083 · **800-983-4240** · · 376

EVERGREEN MORTUARY & CEMETERY
3015 N Oracle Rd ....Tucson AZ 85705 · **800-852-0269** · 520-257-4831

Evergreen Resort
7880 Mackinaw Trl ....Cadillac MI 49601 · **800-634-7302** · · 665

Evergreen State College, The
2700 Evergreen Pkwy ....Olympia WA 98505 · **888-492-9480** · 360-867-6000 · 166

Evergreen Woods
88 Notch Hill Rd ....North Branford CT 06471 · **866-413-6378*** · 203-488-8000 · 668
*General

Evergreens, The
309 Bridgeboro Rd ....Moorestown NJ 08057 · **877-673-8234** · 856-242-7435 · 668

Everhard Products Inc
1016 Ninth St SW ....Canton OH 44707 · **800-225-0984** · 330-453-7786 · 753

EverHome Mortgage Co
301 W Bay St ....Jacksonville FL 32202 · **888-882-3837*** · · 507
*Cust Svc

Everi Holdings Inc (GCA)
7250 S Tenaya Way Ste 100 ....Las Vegas NV 89113 · **800-833-7110** · 702-855-3000 · 56
NYSE: EVRI

Everist Genomics Inc
709 W Ellsworth Rd ....Ann Arbor MI 48108 · **855-383-7478** · · 738

Everlaw
2036 Bancroft Way ....Berkeley CA 94704 · **844-383-7529** · · 386

Everlube Products
100 Cooper Cir ....Peachtree City GA 30269 · **800-428-7802** · 770-261-4800 · 479

Everson Cordage Works Inc
7180 Everson-Goshen Rd ....Everson WA 98247 · **800-966-0203**

Eversource
800 Boylston St ....Boston MA 02199 · **800-592-2000** · · 359-5
NYSE: NST

Eversource
56 Prospect St ....Hartford MA 06103 · **800-286-2000** · 860-665-3495 · 782

EverStaff LLC
6150 oak Tree Blvd Ste 175 ....Cleveland OH 44131 · **877-392-6151** · 216-369-2566 · 260

Company / Address	City	State	ZIP	Toll-Free	Phone	Class
EverTrue LLC						
330 Congress St 2nd Fl	Boston	MA	02210	**855-387-8783**		386
Everwise Corp						
1178 Broadway 4th Fl	New York	NY	10001	**888-734-0011**		386
EVINE Live Inc						
6740 Shady Oak Rd	Eden Prairie	MN	55344	**800-676-5523**		735
Evo Exhibits						
399 Wegner Dr	West Chicago	IL	60185	**888-404-4224**	630-520-0710	7
Evolution Computing						
7000 N 16th St Ste 120 514	Phoenix	AZ	85020	**800-874-4028**		178-5
Evolve IP LLC						
989 Old Eagle School Rd Ste 815	Wayne	PA	19087	**877-459-4347**		
EVS Ltd						
3702 W Sample St	South Bend	IN	46619	**800-364-3218**	574-233-5707	320
EW Wylie Corp						
1520 Second Ave NW	West Fargo	ND	58078	**800-437-4132***		775
*Cust Svc						
EWA (Enterprise Wireless Alliance)						
8484 Westpark Dr Ste 630	McLean	VA	22102	**800-482-8282**	703-528-5115	49-20
eWareness Inc						
1900 S Harbor City Blvd						
Ste 122	Melbourne	FL	32901	**800-517-4130**	321-953-2435	804
EWASTE+						
7318 Victor Mendon Rd	Victor	NY	14564	**888-563-1340**		179
EWI (Executive Women International)						
3860 South 2300 East						
Ste 211	Salt Lake City	UT	84109	**877-439-4669**	801-355-2800	49-12
EWI (Elliott Wave International)						
PO Box 1618	Gainesville	GA	30503	**800-336-1618***	770-536-0309	633-9
*Cust Svc						
Ewing-Foley Inc						
10061 Bubb Rd Ste 1000	Cupertino	CA	95014	**800-399-3319**	408-342-1200	246
Exact Metrology						
11575 Goldcoast Dr	Cincinnati	OH	45249	**866-722-2600**	513-831-6620	357
Exactax Inc						
2301 W Lincoln Ave Ste 100	Anaheim	CA	92801	**844-327-6740**	714-284-4802	729
Exactech Inc						
2320 NW 66th Ct	Gainesville	FL	32653	**800-392-2832**	352-377-1140	475
NASDAQ: EXAC						
Exar Corp						
48720 Kato Rd	Fremont	CA	94538	**855-755-1330**	510-668-7000	692
NYSE: EXAR						
Excalibre Engineering						
9201 Irvine Blvd	Irvine	CA	92618	**877-922-5427**	949-454-6603	738
Excalibur Extrusions Inc						
110 E Crowther Ave	Placentia	CA	92870	**800-648-6804**	714-528-8834	592
Excalibur Hotel & Casino						
3850 S Las Vegas Blvd	Las Vegas	NV	89109	**877-750-5464**	702-597-7777	133
Excel Bridge Manufacturing Co						
12001 Shoemaker Ave	Santa Fe Springs	CA	90670	**800-548-0054**	562-944-0701	478
Excel Homes Inc						
10642 S Susquehanna Trl	Liverpool	PA	17045	**844-875-9160**		
Excel Machinery Ltd						
12100 I-40 E	Amarillo	TX	79120	**800-858-4002**	806-335-1553	752
Excel Staffing						
2100 Osuna Rd NE Ste 100	Albuquerque	NM	87113	**888-607-1695**	505-262-1871	193
Excel Telecommunications						
433 Las Colinas Blvd Ste 400	Irving	TX	75039	**877-668-0808**	972-910-1900	731
Ex-Cell Metal Products Inc						
11240 Melrose St	Franklin Park	IL	60131	**800-392-3557**	847-451-0451	286
Excellent Coffee Co						
259 E Ave	Pawtucket	RI	02860	**800-345-2007**		
Excelleris Technologies Inc						
200-3500 Gilmore Way	Burnaby	BC	V5C2W7	**866-728-4777***	604-658-2111	45
*Support						
Excellon Automation Inc						
20001 S Rancho Way	Rancho Dominguez	CA	90220	**800-392-3556**	310-668-7700	468
Excellus BlueCross BlueShield						
PO Box 22999	Rochester	NY	14692	**800-278-1247**	585-454-1700	390-3
Excellus BlueCross BlueShield of Central New York						
333 Butternut Dr	Syracuse	NY	13214	**800-633-6066**	315-671-6400	390-3
Excelsior College						
7 Columbia Cir	Albany	NY	12203	**888-647-2388**	518-464-8500	166
Excelsior Defense Inc						
2232 Central Ave	Saint Petersburg	FL	33712	**877-955-4636**	727-527-9600	689
Excelsior Marking Products						
888 W Waterloo Rd	Akron	OH	44314	**800-433-3615**	330-745-2300	465
Exchange State Bank						
3992 Chandler St PO Box 68	Carsonville	MI	48419	**888-488-9300**	810-657-9333	70
Exchange, The						
3911 S Walton Walker Blvd	Dallas	TX	75236	**800-527-2345**		786
EXCO Resources Inc						
12377 Merit Dr Ste 1700	Dallas	TX	75251	**888-788-9449**	214-368-2084	534
OTC: XCO						
Exec Air Montana Inc						
2430 Airport Rd	Helena	MT	59601	**800-513-2190**	406-442-2190	13
ExecSuite						
702 3 Ave SW	Calgary	AB	T2P3B4	**800-667-4980**	403-294-5800	210
Execu/Tech Systems Inc						
537 Harrison Ave	Panama City	FL	32401	**800-232-1626***	850-747-0581	177
*Sales						
ExecUNet Inc						
295 Westport Ave	Norwalk	CT	06851	**800-637-3126**		260
Execusys Inc						
6767 N Wickham Rd	Melbourne	FL	32940	**800-454-3081**	321-253-0077	177
Executive Car Leasing Inc						
7807 Santa Monica Blvd	Los Angeles	CA	90046	**800-994-2277**	323-654-5000	289
Executive Hotel Vintage Court						
650 Bush St	San Francisco	CA	94108	**888-388-3932**	415-392-4666	378
Executive Inn Group Corp						
Executive Hotels & Resorts						
1080 Howe St 8th Fl	Vancouver	BC	V6Z2T1	**866-642-6888**	604-642-5250	378
Executive Jet						
4556 Airport Rd	Cincinnati	OH	45226	**877-356-5387**	513-979-6600	13
Executive Pacific Plaza Hotel						
400 Spring St	Seattle	WA	98104	**888-388-3932**	206-623-3900	378
Executive Protection Institute						
16 Penn Plz Ste 1570	New York	NY	10001	**800-947-5827**	212-268-4555	761

Company / Address	City	State	ZIP	Toll-Free	Phone	Class
Executive Speakers Bureau						
3012 Ctr Oak Way Ste 102	Germantown	TN	38138	**800-754-9404**	901-754-9404	704
Executive Women International (EWI)						
3860 South 2300 East						
Ste 211	Salt Lake City	UT	84109	**877-439-4669**	801-355-2800	49-12
Exerplay Inc						
12001 State Hwy 14 N	Cedar Crest	NM	87008	**800-457-5444**	505-281-0151	707
Exerve Inc						
2909 Langford Rd Ste 400B	Norcross	GA	30071	**800-364-0637**	770-447-1566	729
EXFO Inc 400 Godin Ave	Quebec	QC	G1M2K2	**800-663-3936**	418-683-0211	248
NASDAQ: EXFO						
Exhibit Concepts Inc						
700 Crossroads Ct	Vandalia	OH	45377	**800-324-5063**		184
Exhibit Source Inc, The						
145 Wells Ave	Newton Center	MA	02459	**866-949-6113**	781-449-1600	392
Exide Technologies						
13000 Deerfield Pkwy Bldg 200	Milton	GA	30004	**888-563-6300**	678-566-9000	74
NASDAQ: XIDE						
Exiss Aluminum Trailers Inc						
900 E Trailer Blvd	El Reno	OK	73036	**800-256-6668**	877-553-9477	120
ExitCertified						
8950 Cal Center Dr						
Bldg 1 Ste 110	Sacramento	CA	95826	**800-803-3948**	916-669-3970	179
Exocor Inc						
271 Ridley Rd	St. Catharines	ON	L2R6P7	**888-317-2209**	905-704-0603	111
Expanding Light						
14618 Tyler Foote Rd	Nevada City	CA	95959	**800-346-5350**	530-478-7518	669
Expanko Resilient Flooring						
180 Gordon Dr Ste 107	Exton	PA	19341	**800-345-6202**		291
Expansion Management Magazine						
1300 E Ninth St	Cleveland	OH	44114	**866-505-7173**	216-696-7000	455-5
Expedient Communications						
810 Parish St	Pittsburgh	PA	15220	**877-570-7827**		397
Expedition Tripscom						
5932 California Ave SW	Seattle	WA	98136	**877-412-8527**	206-547-0700	767
Expeditor Systems Inc						
4090 Nine McFarland Dr	Alpharetta	GA	30004	**800-843-9651**		473
Expense Reduction Analysts Inc						
16415 Addison Rd Ste 410	Addison	TX	75001	**877-299-7801**	469-310-2970	461
ExpenseVisor						
910 Kenyon Ct Ste 110	Charlotte	NC	28210	**877-219-5448**	704-644-0019	
Experience Bryan College Station (DOSOVD)						
715 University Dr E	College Station	TX	77840	**800-777-8292**	979-260-9898	206
Experience Columbia SC						
1101 Lincoln St	Columbia	SC	29201	**800-264-4884**	803-545-0000	206
Experience Works Inc						
4401 Wilson Blvd Ste 1100	Arlington	VA	22203	**866-397-9757**	703-522-7272	48-6
Experient Inc						
2500 E Enterprise Pkwy	Twinsburg	OH	44087	**800-935-8333**	330-294-4194	184
Experimental Aircraft Assn (EAA)						
3000 Poberezny Rd	Oshkosh	WI	54902	**800-236-4800**	920-426-4800	48-18
Experis Data Centers Inc						
7811 Montrose Rd Ste 360	Potomac	MD	20854	**877-689-3282**		
ExPert E&P Consultants LLC						
101 Ashland Way	Madisonville	LA	70447	**888-231-8639**	844-522-7900	535
Expert Evidence Report						
1801 S Bell St	Arlington	VA	22202	**800-372-1033**		527-7
Expert Laser Service						
62 Pleasant St PO Box 744	Southbridge	MA	01550	**800-622-3535**		175
Expert Recruiters						
883 Helmcken St	Vancouver	BC	V6Z1B1	**888-407-7799**	604-689-3600	260
Explore Information Services LLC						
2750 Blue Water Rd Ste 200	Eagan	MN	55121	**800-531-9125**		631
Explore Saint Louis						
Executive Conference Ctr						
701 Convention Plz	Saint Louis	MO	63101	**800-325-7962**	314-421-1023	205
Explorica Inc						
145 Tremont St	Boston	MA	02111	**888-310-7120**		755
Expo Group, The						
5931 W Campus Cir Dr	Irving	TX	75063	**800-736-7775**	972-580-9000	184
ExpoMarketing LLC						
2741 Dow Ave	Tustin	CA	92780	**800-867-3976**		184
Expon Exhibits						
909 Fee Dr	Sacramento	CA	95815	**800-783-9766**	916-924-1600	232
Exponent Inc						
149 Commonwealth Dr	Menlo Park	CA	94025	**888-656-3976**	650-326-9400	664
NASDAQ: EXPO						
Exponent Telegram						
324 Hewes Ave	Clarksburg	WV	26301	**800-982-6034**		528-2
Export-Import Bank of the US						
811 Vermont Ave NW	Washington	DC	20571	**800-565-3946**	202-565-3946	339-19
Express						
1 Limited Pkwy	Columbus	OH	43230	**888-397-1980**		157-6
NYSE: EXPR						
Express Cargo USA LLC						
1790 Yardley-Langhorne Rd						
Carriage House 202	Yardley	PA	19067	**888-505-7361**	201-603-9155	
Express Employment Professionals						
9701 Boardwalk Blvd	Oklahoma City	OK	73162	**800-222-4057**	405-840-5000	717
Express Image Inc						
2942 Rice St	Little Canada	MN	55113	**866-482-8602**		683
Express Oil Change & Tire Engineers						
1880 S Pk Dr	Hoover	AL	35244	**888-945-1771**	205-940-2226	62-5
Expresscopycom						
6623 NE 59th Pl	Portland	OR	97218	**800-260-5887**		623
Express-News Corp						
PO Box 2171	San Antonio	TX	78297	**800-555-1551**	210-250-3000	633-8
Expressway Hotels						
4303 17th Ave S	Fargo	ND	58103	**877-239-4303**	701-239-4303	378
Extended Care Hospital Westminster						
206 Hospital Cir	Westminster	CA	92683	**800-236-9747**	714-891-2769	448
Extended Presence						
3570 E 12th Ave Ste 200	Denver	CO	80206	**800-398-8957**	303-892-5881	317
Extended Stay America						
11525 N Community House Rd						
Ste 100	Charlotte	NC	28277	**800-804-3724**	980-345-1600	378
Crossland Economy Studios						
11525 N Community House Rd						
Ste 100	Charlotte	NC	28277	**877-398-3633**	980-345-1600	378

Name	Address	City	State	ZIP	Toll-Free	Phone	Class
Extended Stay Hotels	530 Woods Lake Rd	Greenville	SC	29607	**800-804-3724**		378
Extensis	1800 SW First Ave Ste 500	Portland	OR	97201	**800-796-9798**	503-274-2020	177
Externetworks	10 Corporate Pl S	Piscataway	NJ	08854	**800-238-6360**	732-465-0001	177
EXTOL International Inc	529 Terry Reiley Way	Pottsville	PA	17901	**800-542-7284**	570-628-5500	178-7
Exton Region Chamber of Commerce	185 Exton Square Mall	Exton	PA	19341	**800-666-0191**	610-363-7746	139
Extra Mile Mktg Inc	12600 SE 38th St Ste 205	Bellevue	WA	98006	**866-907-1753**	425-746-1572	194
Extraco Technology	PO Box 2299	Waco	TX	76703	**866-428-9070**		507
Extreme Networks Inc	3585 Monroe St *NASDAQ: EXTR*	Santa Clara	CA	95051	**888-257-3000**	408-579-2800	176
Extreme Plastics Plus	360 Epic Circle Dr	Fairmont	WV	26554	**866-408-2837**		532
Extreme Reach Crew Services	3601 W Olive Ave Ste 500	Burbank	CA	91505	**800-301-1992**	818-729-0080	627
Extreme Reach Inc	75 Second Ave Ste 720	Needham	MA	02494	**877-769-9382**	781-577-2016	509
Extron Electronics	1230 S Lewis St *Tech Supp	Anaheim	CA	92805	**800-633-9876***	714-491-1500	52
Extrude Hone LLC	235 Industry Blvd	Irwin	PA	15642	**800-835-3668**	724-863-5900	453
Extrudex Aluminum Ltd	411 Chrislea Rd	Woodbridge	ON	L4L8N4	**800-668-7210**	416-745-4444	490
Extrutech Plastics Inc D/B/A Epi	5902 W Custer St	Manitowoc	WI	54220	**888-818-0118**		
Exxon Mobil Corp	5959 Las Colinas Blvd *NYSE: XOM*	Irving	TX	75039	**800-252-1800**	972-444-1000	532
Eyak Corp, The	360 W Benson Blvd Ste 210	Anchorage	AK	99503	**800-478-7161**	907-334-6971	359-3
Eyde Co	300 S Washington Sq Ste 400	Lansing	MI	48933	**800-422-3933**	517-351-2480	187
Eye Bank for Sight Restoration Inc	120 Wall St 3rd Fl	New York	NY	10005	**866-287-3937**	212-742-9000	269
Eye Bank of British Columbia	855 W 12th Ave JPPN - B205	Vancouver	BC	V5Z1M9	**800-667-2060**	604-875-4567	269
Eye Center Surgeons & Associates Ll	401 Meridian St N Ste 200	Huntsville	AL	35801	**800-233-9083**	256-705-3937	237
Eye Centers of Florida (ECOF)	4101 Evans Ave	Fort Myers	FL	33901	**888-393-2455**	239-939-3456	793
Eye Communication Systems Inc	455 E Industrial Dr	Hartland	WI	53029	**800-558-2153**	262-367-1360	494
Eye Glass World Inc	2435 Commerce Ave Bldg 2200	Duluth	GA	30096	**800-637-3597**		539
Eye Lighting International NA	9150 Hendricks Rd *Cust Svc	Mentor	OH	44060	**888-665-2677***	440-354-2938	436
Eyefinity Inc	10875 International Dr Ste 200	Rancho Cordova	CA	95670	**877-448-0707**		177
Eye-Kraft Optical Inc	8 McLeland Rd	Saint Cloud	MN	56303	**888-455-2022**		538
Eye-Mart Express Inc	13800 Senlac Dr Ste 200	Farmers Branch	TX	75234	**888-372-2763**	972-488-2016	539
EyeMed Vision Care	4000 Luxottica Pl	Mason	OH	45040	**866-939-3633**	513-765-4321	390-3
Eyre Bus Service Inc	13600 Triadelphia Rd PO Box 239	Glenelg	MD	21737	**800-321-3973**	410-442-1330	107
EZ Loader Boat Trailers Inc	717 N Hamilton St	Spokane	WA	99202	**800-398-5623**	509-489-0181	758
EZ Trail Inc	1050 E Columbia St PO Box 168	Arthur	IL	61911	**800-677-2802**	217-543-3471	273
ezCater Inc	101 Arch St Ste 1510	Boston	MA	02110	**800-488-1803**		386
EZCORP Inc	1901 Capital Pkwy *NASDAQ: EZPW*	Austin	TX	78746	**800-873-7296**	855-241-1261	565
Eze Castle Integration Inc	260 Franklin St 12th Fl	Boston	MA	02110	**800-752-1382**	617-217-3000	195
Eze Lap Diamond Products	3572 Arrowhead Dr	Carson City	NV	89706	**800-843-4815**	775-888-9500	693
Ezenia! Inc	14 Celina Ave Ste 17	Nashua	NH	03063	**800-966-2301**	253-509-7850	176
EZG Manufacturing	1833 North Riverview Rd	Malta	OH	43758	**800-417-9272**		135
E-Z-GO	1451 Marvin Griffin Rd	Augusta	GA	30906	**800-241-5855**		513

F

Name	Address	City	State	ZIP	Toll-Free	Phone	Class
F & A Dairy Products Inc	Hwy 35	Dresser	WI	54009	**800-826-5558**	715-755-3485	
F & D Head Co	3040 E Peden Rd	Fort Worth	TX	76179	**800-451-2684**	817-236-8773	719
F & H Ribbon Co Inc	3010 S Pipeline Rd	Euless	TX	76040	**800-877-5775**		772
F & M Hat Co Inc	103 Walnut St PO Box 40	Denver	PA	17517	**800-953-4287**	717-336-5505	155-8
F C Kerbeck & Sons	100 Rt 73 N *General	Palmyra	NJ	08065	**855-846-1500***	855-581-5700	57
F Mcconnell & Sons Inc	11102 Lincoln Hwy E	New Haven	IN	46774	**800-552-0835**	260-493-6607	297-8
F p i s Inc	220 Story Rd	Ocoee	FL	34761	**800-346-5977**	407-656-8818	7
F+W, A Content + eCommerce Co	10151 Carver Rd Ste 300 *Sales	Cincinnati	OH	45242	**800-289-0963***	513-531-2690	633-9
F5 Networks Inc	401 Elliott Ave W *NASDAQ: FFIV*	Seattle	WA	98119	**888-882-4447**	206-272-5555	176
FA Bartlett Tree Expert Co	1290 E Main St	Stamford	CT	06902	**877-227-8538**	203-323-1131	771
FA Davis Co	1915 Arch St	Philadelphia	PA	19103	**800-323-3555**	215-568-2270	633-2
FAA (Federal Aviation Administration)	800 Independence Ave SW	Washington	DC	20591	**866-835-5322**		339-16
Faa Federal Credit Union	3920 Whitebrook Dr	Memphis	TN	38118	**800-346-0069**	901-366-0066	219
Faac Inc	1229 Oak Valley Dr	Ann Arbor	MI	48108	**877-322-2387**	734-761-5836	699
FAAN (Food Allergy & Anaphylaxis Network)	11781 Lee Jackson Hwy Ste 160	Fairfax	VA	22033	**800-929-4040**	703-691-3179	48-17
Fabcon Precast	6111 Hwy 13 W	Savage	MN	55378	**800-727-4444**	952-890-4444	183
Fabgroups Technologies Inc	1100 Saint Amour	Saint-laurent	QC	H4S1J2	**800-561-8910**	514-331-3712	111
Fabral Inc	3449 Hempland Rd	Lancaster	PA	17601	**800-477-2741**	717-397-2741	478
Fabreeka International Inc	1023 Tpke St *Cust Svc	Stoughton	MA	02072	**800-322-7352***	781-341-3655	673
Fabricated Components Inc	PO Box 431	Stroudsburg	PA	18360	**800-233-8163**	570-421-4110	480
Fabrication JR Tardif Inc	62 Blvd Cartier	Rivi Re-Du-Loup	QC	G5R6B2	**877-962-7273**	418-862-7273	273
Fabricators & Manufacturers Assn International (FMA)	833 Featherstone Rd	Rockford	IL	61107	**888-394-4362**	815-399-8700	49-13
Fabricut Inc	9303 E 46th St	Tulsa	OK	74145	**800-999-8200**	918-622-7700	360
Fabri-Kal Corp	600 Plastics Pl	Kalamazoo	MI	49001	**800-888-5054**	269-385-5050	598
Fabri-Quilt Inc	901 E 14th Ave	North Kansas City	MO	64116	**800-279-0622**	816-421-2000	258
Fabritech Inc	5740 Salmen St	New Orleans	LA	70123	**888-733-5009**	504-733-5009	740-8
Fabulous Fox, The	527 N Grand Blvd	Saint Louis	MO	63103	**800-293-5949**	314-534-1678	568
Face Stockholm Ltd	324 Joslen Blvd	Hudson	NY	12534	**888-334-3223**	518-828-6600	231
Facets Multimedia Inc	1517 W Fullerton Ave *Cust Svc	Chicago	IL	60614	**800-331-6197***	773-281-9075	509
Facility Solutions Group (FSG)	4401 Westgate Blvd Ste 310	Austin	TX	78745	**800-854-6465**	512-440-7985	246
Facing History & Ourselves	16 HuRd Rd	Brookline	MA	02445	**800-856-9039**	617-232-1595	48-11
FactSet Research Systems Inc	601 Merritt 7 *NYSE: FDS*	Norwalk	CT	06851	**877-322-8738**	203-810-1000	403
Factual Data	5200 Hahns Peak Dr	Loveland	CO	80538	**800-929-3400**		218
FACVB (Fayetteville Area Convention & Visitors Bureau)	245 Person St	Fayetteville	NC	28301	**800-255-8217**	910-483-5311	206
FAE (Foundation for Acctg Education)	14 Wall St 19th Fl *General	New York	NY	10005	**800-537-3635***	212-719-8300	49-1
Faegre & Benson LLP	90 S Seventh St 2200 Wells Fargo Bldg	Minneapolis	MN	55402	**800-328-4393**	612-766-7000	427
FAF (Form-A-Feed Inc)	740 Bowman St	Stewart	MN	55385	**800-422-3649**	320-562-2413	445
FAF	26 Lark Industrial Pkwy	Greenville	RI	02828	**800-949-3311**		410
Fafco Inc	435 Otterson Dr	Chico	CA	95928	**800-994-7652**	530-332-2100	91
Fafinski Mark & Johnson PA	775 Prairie Center Dr Ste 400	Eden Prairie	MN	55344	**855-806-1525**	952-995-9500	427
FAFP (Florida Academy of Family Physicians)	13241 Bartram Pk Blvd Ste 1321	Jacksonville	FL	32258	**800-223-3237**	904-726-0944	
Fager's Island Restaurant	201 60th St	Ocean City	MD	21842	**855-432-4377**	410-524-5500	667
FAHC (University of Vermont Medical Center, The)	111 Colchester Ave	Burlington	VT	05401	**800-358-1144**	802-847-0000	373-3
Fahlgren Mortine	4030 Easton Stn Ste 300	Columbus	OH	43219	**800-731-8927**	614-383-1500	4
FAIA (Pekin Insurance)	2505 Court St	Pekin	IL	61558	**800-322-0160**	309-346-1161	390-4
FAIR (Federation for American Immigration Reform)	25 Massachusetts Ave NW Ste 330	Washington	DC	20001	**877-627-3247**	202-328-7004	48-7
Fair Grounds Race Course	1751 Gentilly Blvd	New Orleans	LA	70119	**800-262-7983**	504-944-5515	638
Fair Haven Beach State Park	14985 State Park Rd *General	Fair Haven	NY	13156	**800-456-2267***	315-947-5205	561
Fair Hills Resort	24270 County Hwy 20 *Resv	Detroit Lakes	MN	56501	**800-323-2849***	218-847-7638	665
Fair Isaac Corp	2665 Long Lake Rd Bldg C *NYSE: FICO* ■ *Cust Svc	Roseville	MN	55113	**888-342-6336***	612-758-5200	225
Fair Lawn Chamber of Commerce	12-45 River Rd	Fair Lawn	NJ	07410	**800-474-1299**	201-796-7050	139
Fair Wind Air Charter	2525 SE Witham Field Hangar 7	Stuart	FL	34996	**800-989-9665**		13
Fairbanks Convention & Visitors Bureau	101 Dunkel St Ste 111	Fairbanks	AK	99701	**800-327-5774**	907-456-5774	206
Fairbanks Correctional Ctr	1931 Eagan Ave	Fairbanks	AK	99701	**844-934-2381**	907-458-6700	213
Fairbanks Hospital	8102 Clearvista Pkwy	Indianapolis	IN	46256	**800-225-4673**	317-849-8222	722

	Toll-Free	Phone	Class
Fairbanks North Star Borough			
809 Pioneer Rd ....Fairbanks AK 99701	800-331-6158	907-459-1000	337
Fairbanks Princess Riverside Lodge			
4477 Pikes Landing Rd ....Fairbanks AK 99709	800-426-0500	907-455-4477	378
Fairbanks Scales Inc			
821 Locust St ....Kansas City MO 64106	800-451-4107		680
Fairchild Auto-mated Parts Inc			
10 White St ....Winsted CT 06098	800-927-2545	860-379-2725	617
Fairchild Imaging Inc			
1801 McCarthy Blvd ....Milpitas CA 95035	800-325-6975	408-433-2500	692
Fairchild Industrial Products Co			
3920 Westpoint Blvd ....Winston-Salem NC 27103	800-334-8422	336-659-3400	201
Fairfax County Convention & Visitors Bureau (FXVA)			
3702 Pender Dr Ste 420 ....Fairfax VA 22030	800-732-4732	703-790-0643	206
Fairfield Chair Co			
PO Box 1710 ....Lenoir NC 28645	800-841-6279	828-758-5571	319-2
Fairfield County			
210 E Main St ....Lancaster OH 43130	800-450-8845	740-652-7075	337
Fairfield Industries Inc			
1111 Gillingham Ln ....Sugar Land TX 77478	800-231-9809	281-275-7500	470
Fairfield Medical Ctr (FMC)			
401 N Ewing St ....Lancaster OH 43130	800-548-2627	740-687-8000	373-3
Fairfield Processing Corp			
88 Rose Hill Ave ....Danbury CT 06810	800-980-8000	203-744-2090	601-1
Fairfield University			
1073 N Benson Rd ....Fairfield CT 06824	800-822-8428	203-254-4000	166
Fairhaven			
435 W Starin Rd...............................Whitewater WI 53190	877-624-2298	262-473-2140	668
FairHope Hospice & Palliative Care Inc			
282 Sells Rd ....Lancaster OH 43130	800-994-7077	740-654-7077	370
Fairlane Town Ctr			
18900 Michigan Ave ....Dearborn MI 48126	800-992-9500		458
Fairleigh Dickinson University			
285 Madison Ave ....Madison NJ 07940	800-338-8803	973-443-8500	166
Metropolitan			
1000 River Rd ....Teaneck NJ 07666	800-338-8803	201-692-2000	166
FairMarket Life Settlements Corp			
435 Ford Rd Ste 120...............St Louis Park MN 55426	866-326-3757		389
Fairmont Chateau Lake Louise			
111 Lake Louise Dr ....Lake Louise AB T0L1E0	800-441-1414	403-522-3511	665
Fairmont Chateau Whistler			
4599 Chateau Blvd ....Whistler BC V0N1B4	800-441-1414	604-938-8000	665
Fairmont Convention & Visitors Bureau			
323 E Blue Earth Ave ....Fairmont MN 56031	800-657-3280	507-235-8585	206
Fairmont Hot Springs Resort			
1500 Fairmont Rd ....Fairmont MT 59711	800-332-3272	406-797-3241	665
Fairmont Kea Lani			
4100 Wailea Alanui Dr ....Maui HI 96753	800-659-4100	808-875-4100	665
Fairmont Le Chateau Montebello			
392 Notre Dame St ....Montebello QC J0V1L0	800-441-1414	819-423-6341	665
Fairmont Orchid Hawaii			
1 N Kaniku Dr ....Kohala Coast HI 96743	800-845-9905	808-885-2000	665
Fairmont San Francisco Hotel, The			
950 Mason St ....San Francisco CA 94108	800-257-7544	415-772-5000	377
Fairmont Scottsdale Princess			
7575 E Princess Dr ....Scottsdale AZ 85255	800-257-7544	480-585-4848	665
Fairmont Sonoma Mission Inn & Spa, The			
PO Box 1447 ....Sonoma CA 95476	866-540-4499	707-938-9000	665
Fairmont State University			
1201 Locust Ave ....Fairmont WV 26554	800-641-5678*	304-367-4892	166
*Admissions			
Fairmont Supply Co			
437 Jefferson Ave ....Washington PA 15301	800-245-9900		384
Fairmount Behavioral Health System			
561 Fairthorne Ave ....Philadelphia PA 19128	800-235-0200	215-487-4000	373-5
Fairmount Hotel, The			
401 S Alamo St ....San Antonio TX 78205	877-229-8808	210-224-8800	378
FairPoint Communications Inc			
521 E Morehead St Ste 250 ....Charlotte NC 28202	866-984-2001	704-344-8150	731
NASDAQ: FRP			
Fair-Rite Products Corp			
1 Commerical Row PO Box J ....Wallkill NY 12589	888-324-7748	845-895-2055	249
Fairview Health Services			
2450 Riverside Ave ....Minneapolis MN 55454	800-824-1953	612-672-2020	352
Fairview Hospice			
2450 26th Ave S ....Minneapolis MN 55406	800-285-5647	612-728-2455	370
Fairview Hospital			
18101 Lorain Ave ....Cleveland OH 44111	800-801-2273	216-444-0261	373-3
Fairview University Medical Ctr Mesabi			
750 E 34th St ....Hibbing MN 55746	888-870-8626	218-262-4881	373-3
Fairview-Riverside State Park			
119 Fairview Dr ....Madisonville LA 70447	888-677-3247	985-845-3318	561
Fairway Lincoln			
10101 Abercorn St ....Savannah GA 31406	888-716-2924	888-762-8050	57
Fairwinds Federal Credit Union			
3087 N Alafaya Trl ....Orlando FL 32826	800-443-6887	407-277-5045	219
FaithTalk 570 & 910 WTBN			
5211 W Laurel St ....Tampa FL 33607	800-576-3771	813-639-1903	641-108
FaithTrust Institute			
2400 N 45th St Ste 101 ....Seattle WA 98103	877-860-2255	206-634-1903	48-17
Fakouri Electrical Engineering Inc			
30001 Comercio ....Rancho Santa Margarita CA 92688	800-669-8862		261
Falcon Crest Aviation Supply Inc			
8318 Braniff ....Houston TX 77061	800-833-8229	713-644-2290	256
Falcon Executive Aviation Inc			
4766 E Falcon Dr ....Mesa AZ 85215	800-237-2359	480-832-0704	357
Falcon Express Inc			
2250 E Church St ....Philadelphia PA 19124	800-544-6566	215-992-3140	775
Falcon Express Transportation Inc			
12200 Indian Creek Ct ....Beltsville MD 20705	800-296-9696	240-264-1215	314
Falcon Safety Products Inc			
25 Imclone Dr ....Branchburg NJ 08876	800-332-5266	908-707-4900	151
Fall Creek State Recreation Area			
84610 Peninsula Rd ....Fall Creek OR 97438	800-551-6949		561
Fall River Public Library			
104 N Main St ....Fall River MA 02720	800-331-3764	508-946-8600	433-3
Fall River Rural Electric Co-op Inc			
1150 N 3400 E ....Ashton ID 83420	800-632-5726	208-652-7431	245

	Toll-Free	Phone	Class
Fallon Chamber of Commerce			
85 N Taylor St ....Fallon NV 89406	800-242-0478	775-423-2544	139
Fallon Community Health Plan Inc			
10 Chestnut St ....Worcester MA 01608	800-333-2535	508-799-2100	390-3
Falmouth Chamber of Commerce			
20 Academy Ln ....Falmouth MA 02540	800-526-8532	508-548-8500	139
False Cape State Park			
4001 Sandpiper Rd ....Virginia Beach VA 23456	800-933-7275*	757-426-7128	561
*General			
Fam Funds			
384 N Grand St PO Box 310...........Cobleskill NY 12043	800-721-5391	518-234-4393	317
Finance Authority of Maine			
5 Community Dr PO Box 949 ....Augusta ME 04332	800-228-3734	207-623-3263	721
Familiprix Inc			
6000 Rue Armand-Viau ....Quebec QC G2C2C5	800-463-5160	418-847-3311	238
Family Business Institute Inc, The			
4050 Wake Forest Rd Ste 110 ....Raleigh NC 27609	877-326-2493		
Family Campers & RVers (FCRV)			
4804 Transit Rd Bldg 2 ....Depew NY 14043	800-245-9755		48-23
Family Caregiver Alliance (FCA)			
101 Montgomery St			
Ste 2150 ....San Francisco CA 94104	800-445-8106	415-434-3388	48-17
Family Cir Magazine			
375 Lexington Ave 9th Fl ....New York NY 10017	800-627-4444		455-11
Family Circle Tennis Ctr			
161 Seven Farms Dr ....Daniel Island SC 29492	800-677-2293	843-856-7900	461
Family Credit Management			
111 N Wabash Ste 1410 ....Chicago IL 60602	877-322-8319	800-994-3328	41
Family Dollar Stores Inc			
PO Box 1017 ....Charlotte NC 28201	866-377-6420	844-636-7687	786
NASDAQ: DLTR			
Family Handyman Magazine			
2915 Commers Dr Ste 700 ....Eagan MN 55121	800-285-4961		455-14
Family Hospice & Palliative Care			
50 Moffett St ....Pittsburgh PA 15243	800-513-2148	412-572-8800	370
Family Life Communications Inc			
PO Box 35300 ....Tucson AZ 85740	800-776-1070		640
Family Motor Coach Assn (FMCA)			
8291 Clough Pk ....Cincinnati OH 45244	800-543-3622	513-474-3622	48-23
Family Motor Coaching Magazine			
8291 Clough Pk ....Cincinnati OH 45244	800-543-3622	513-474-3622	455-22
Family of the Americas Foundation			
5929 Talbot Rd ....Lothian MD 20711	800-443-3395	301-627-3346	48-17
Family Practice Management			
11400 Tomahawk Creek Pkwy ....Leawood KS 66211	800-274-2237	913-906-6000	455-16
Family Radio			
290 Hegenberger Rd ....Oakland CA 94621	800-543-1495		639
Family Research Council (FRC)			
801 G St NW ....Washington DC 20001	800-225-4008	202-393-2100	48-6
Family Stations Inc			
290 Hegenberger Rd ....Oakland CA 94621	800-543-1495		641
Family Tree Magazine			
4700 E Galbraith Rd ....Cincinnati OH 45236	855-278-0408		
Family Video			
2500 Lehigh Ave ....Glenview IL 60026	888-332-6843	847-904-9000	792
Familymeds Inc			
312 Farmington Ave ....Farmington CT 06032	888-787-2800		238
FamilySearch			
35 N W Temple St ....Salt Lake City UT 84150	866-406-1830		386
Famous Dave's Barbeque			
181 Jennifer Rd ....Annapolis MD 21401	877-833-9335	410-224-2207	667
Famous Dave's of America Inc			
12701 Whitewater Dr Ste 200 ....Minnetonka MN 55343	800-929-4040	952-294-1300	666
NASDAQ: DAVE			
Famous Footwear			
247 Junction Rd ....Madison WI 53717	800-888-7198*	608-833-3340	301
*Cust Svc			
Fandango Inc			
12200 W Olympic Blvd			
Ste 400 ....Los Angeles CA 90064	855-646-2580		
Fandor Homes			
68 Romina Dr ....Vaughan ON L4K4Z7	800-844-9936	905-669-5820	187
Fannie Mae			
3900 Wisconsin Ave NW ....Washington DC 20016	800-732-6643	800-232-6643	507
OTC: FNMA			
Fannin County Board of Education			
2290 E First St ....Blue Ridge GA 30513	800-308-2145	706-632-3771	681
Fanshawe College			
1001 Fanshawe College Blvd ....London ON N5Y5R6	800-717-4412	519-452-4430	165
Fantagraphics Books			
7563 Lake City Way NE ....Seattle WA 98115	800-657-1100	206-524-1967	633-5
Fantastic Tours & Travel			
6143 Jericho Tpke ....Commack NY 11725	800-552-6262	631-462-6262	755
Fan-Tastic Vent Corp			
2083 S Almont Ave ....Imlay City MI 48444	800-521-0298	810-724-3818	37
Fantasy Diamond Corp			
1550 W Carrol Ave ....Chicago IL 60607	800-621-4445	312-583-3200	409
Fantasy Springs Resort Casino			
84-245 Indio Springs Pkwy ....Indio CA 92203	800-827-2946*	760-342-5000	133
*Cust Svc			
Fantini Baking Company Inc			
375 Washington St ....Haverhill MA 01832	800-223-9037		296-1
Fantus Paper Products PS. Greetings Inc			
5730 N Tripp Ave ....Chicago IL 60646	800-621-8823*	800-334-2141	130
*Sales			
FANUC America Corp			
3900 W Hamlin Rd ....Rochester Hills MI 48309	800-477-6268	248-377-7000	385
Fanzz			
3775 W California Ave			
Ste 100...............................Salt Lake City UT 84104	888-326-9946		707
Fapco Inc			
216 Post Rd ....Buchanan MI 49107	800-782-0167		545
Far East Broadcasting Co Inc			
15700 Imperial Hwy PO Box 1 ....La Mirada CA 90638	800-523-3480		639
Farewell Bend State Recreation Area			
23751 Old Hwy 30 ....Huntington OR 97907	800-551-6949		
Fargo C'mon Inn Hotel			
4338 20th Ave SW ....Fargo ND 58103	800-334-1570	701-277-9944	378

Name / Address	City	State	Zip	Toll-Free	Phone	Class
Fargo Jet Center Inc						
3802 20th St N	Fargo	ND	58102	**800-770-0538**	701-235-3600	63
FARGODOME						
1800 N University Dr	Fargo	ND	58102	**855-694-6367**	701-241-9100	716
Fargo-Moorhead Convention & Visitors Bureau						
2001 44th St S	Fargo	ND	58103	**800-235-7654**	701-282-3653	206
Faribo Insurance Agency Inc						
1404 Seventh St NW	Faribault	MN	55021	**888-923-0430**	507-334-3929	389
Farm Boy Meats						
2761 N Kentucky Ave	Evansville	IN	47711	**800-852-3976**	812-425-5231	471
Farm Bureau Bank						
2165 Green Vista Dr Ste 204	Sparks	NV	89431	**800-492-3276**	775-673-4566	70
Farm Bureau Life Insurance Co						
5400 University Ave	West Des Moines	IA	50266	**800-247-4170**	515-225-5400	390-2
Farm Business Consultants Inc						
150 3015 Fifth Ave NE	Calgary	AB	T2A6T8	**800-265-1002**	403-735-6105	729
Farm Credit Leasing (FCL)						
600 Hwy 169 S Ste 300	Minneapolis	MN	55426	**800-444-2929**	952-417-7800	216
Farm Credit Of Central Florida Aca						
115 S Missouri Ave Ste 400	Lakeland	FL	33815	**800-533-2773**	863-682-4117	216
Farm Credit Of Northwest Florida Aca						
5052 Hwy 90	Marianna	FL	32446	**800-527-0647**	850-526-4910	216
Farm Credit of The Virginias Aca						
106 Sangers Ln	Staunton	VA	24401	**800-559-1016**	540-886-3435	217
Farm Family Casualty Insurance Co						
PO Box 656	Albany	NY	12201	**800-843-3276**	518-431-5000	390-4
Farm Family Life Insurance Co						
PO Box 656	Albany	NY	12201	**800-948-3276**	518-431-5000	390-2
Farm First Dairy Co-op						
4001 Nakoosa Trl Ste 100	Madison	WI	53714	**800-525-7704**	608-244-3373	392
Farm Implement & Supply Company Inc						
1200 S Washington Hwy 183	Plainville	KS	67663	**888-589-6029**	785-434-4824	274
Farm Industry News						
7900 International Dr						
Ste 300	Minneapolis	MN	55425	**800-722-5334***	630-524-4749	455-1
*Cust Svc						
Farm Journal						
30 S 15th Ste 900	Philadelphia	PA	19102	**800-331-9310**	215-557-8757	455-1
Farm Service Co-op						
2308 Pine St	Harlan	IA	51537	**800-452-4372**	712-755-3185	276
Farm Show Magazine						
20088 Kenwood Trial	Lakeville	MN	55044	**800-834-9665**		455-1
Farmdale Creamery Inc						
1049 W Baseline St	San Bernardino	CA	92411	**800-346-7306**	909-889-3002	296-5
Farmer Boy Ag						
50 W Stoever Ave	Myerstown	PA	17067	**800-845-3374**		274
Farmer Bros Co						
20333 S Normandie Ave	Torrance	CA	90502	**800-735-2878**	310-787-5200	296-7
NASDAQ: FARM						
Farmer's Co-op Assn						
110 S Keokuk Wash Rd	Keota	IA	52248	**877-843-4893**	641-636-3748	48-2
Farmers Alliance Mutual Insurance Co						
1122 N Main PO Box 1401	McPherson	KS	67460	**800-362-1075**	620-241-2200	390-4
Farmers Electric Co-op Inc						
2000 E I-30	Greenville	TX	75402	**800-541-2662**	903-455-1715	245
Farmers Electric Co-op Inc						
3701 Thornton PO Box 550	Clovis	NM	88101	**800-445-8541**	575-762-4466	245
Farmers Fire Insurance Co						
2875 Eastern Blvd	York	PA	17402	**800-537-0928**	717-751-4435	389
Farmers Insurance Exchange						
6301 Owensmouth Ave	Woodland Hills	CA	91367	**855-808-6599**	800-493-4917	390-4
Farmers Insurance Group of Companies						
6301 Owensmouth Ave	Woodland Hills	CA	91367	**888-327-6335**		2
Farmers Mutual Hail Insurance Company of Iowa						
6785 Westown Pkwy	West Des Moines	IA	50266	**800-247-5248**		390-4
Farmers Mutual Insurance Company of Nebraska						
501 S 13th St PO Box 81529	Lincoln	NE	68501	**800-742-7433**	402-434-8300	390-4
Farmers New World Life Insurance						
3003 77th Ave SE	Mercer Island	WA	98040	**800-493-4917**		
Farmers Ranchers Coop						
224 S Main St	Ainsworth	NE	69210	**800-233-6627**	402-387-2811	575
Farmers Rice Co-op						
PO Box 15223	Sacramento	CA	95851	**800-326-2799**	916-923-5100	296-23
Farmers Rural Electric Co-op Corp						
504 S Broadway St	Glasgow	KY	42141	**800-253-2191**	270-651-2191	245
Farmers Supply Sales Inc						
1409 E Ave	Kalona	IA	52247	**800-493-4917**	319-656-2291	274
Farmers Telecommunications Co-op (FTC)						
144 McCurdy Ave N PO Box 217	Rainsville	AL	35986	**866-638-2144**	256-638-2144	731
Farmers Telephone Co-op Inc						
1101 E Main St	Kingstree	SC	29556	**888-218-5050**	843-382-2333	731
Farmers West						
5300 Foothill Rd	Carpinteria	CA	93013	**800-549-0085**	805-684-5531	368
Farmers Win Coop (FFC)						
110 N Jefferson	Fredericksburg	IA	50630	**800-562-8389**	563-237-5324	10-3
Farmers' Electric Co-op						
201 W Business 36						
PO Box 680	Chillicothe	MO	64601	**800-279-0496**	660-646-4281	245
Farmingdale State University of New York						
2350 Broadhollow Rd	Farmingdale	NY	11735	**800-557-7392**	631-420-2482	166
Farmington Convention & Visitors Bureau						
3041 E Main St	Farmington	NM	87402	**800-448-1240**	505-326-7602	206
Farmington Correctional Ctr						
1012 W Columbia St	Farmington	MO	63640	**800-844-6591**	573-218-7100	213
Farmington Press						
218 N Washington St	Farmington	MO	63640	**800-455-0206**	573-756-8927	528-4
Farmland Dairies LLC						
520 Main Ave	Wallington	NJ	07057	**866-648-5252**		
FarmLink Marketing Solutions Inc						
93 Lombard Ave Ste 110	Winnipeg	MB	R3B3B1	**877-376-5465**		195
FarmTek						
1395 John Fitch Blvd	South Windsor	CT	06074	**800-327-6835***	860-528-1119	10-3
*Sales						
Farner-Bocken Co						
1751 US Hwy 30 E PO Box 368	Carroll	IA	51401	**800-274-8692**	712-792-3503	297-8
Farouk Systems Inc						
250 Pennbright Dr	Houston	TX	77090	**800-237-9175**	281-876-2000	214
Farr Regional Library						
1939 61st Ave	Greeley	CO	80634	**888-861-7323**		433-3
Farr's Ice Cream - SLC						
2575 South 300 West						
	South Salt Lake City	UT	84115	**877-553-2777**	801-484-8724	296-25
Farr, Farr, Emerich, Hackett & Carr PA						
99 Nesbit St						
Earl D Farr Bldg	Punta Gorda	FL	33950	**855-327-7529**	941-639-1158	427
Farrar Corp						
142 W Burns St	Norwich	KS	67118	**800-536-2215**	620-478-2212	307
Farrar Pump & Machinery Company Inc						
1701 S Big Bend Blvd	Saint Louis	MO	63117	**800-752-1050**	314-644-1050	
Farrel Corp						
25 Main St	Ansonia	CT	06401	**800-800-7290**	203-736-5500	385
Farrell-Calhoun Inc						
221 E Carolina Ave	Memphis	TN	38126	**888-832-7735**	901-526-2211	546
Farrey's Wholesale Hardware Company Inc						
1850 NE 146th St	North Miami	FL	33181	**888-854-5483**	305-947-5451	360
Farris Evans Insurance Agency Inc						
1568 Union Ave	Memphis	TN	38104	**800-395-8207**	901-274-5424	389
Farris Vaughan Wills & Murphy						
700 W Georgia St Pacific Centre S 25th Fl						
PO Box 10026	Vancouver	BC	V7Y1B3	**877-684-9151**	604-684-9151	41
Farwest Corrosion Control Co						
1480 W Artesia Blvd	Gardena	CA	90248	**888-532-7937**	310-532-9524	261
FASB (Financial Acctg Standards Board)						
401 Merritt 7 PO Box 5116	Norwalk	CT	06856	**800-748-0659**	203-847-0700	49-1
FASEB (Federation of American Societies for Experimental)						
9650 Rockville Pk	Bethesda	MD	20814	**800-433-2732**	301-634-7000	49-19
Fashion Architectural Designs						
4005 Carnegie Ave	Cleveland	OH	44103	**800-362-9930***	216-904-1380	797
*Orders						
Fashion Institute of Design & Merchandising						
Los Angeles						
919 S Grand Ave	Los Angeles	CA	90015	**800-624-1200***	213-624-1200	164
*Admissions						
Orange County						
17590 Gillette Ave	Irvine	CA	92614	**888-974-3436**	949-851-6200	164
San Diego						
350 Tenth Ave	San Diego	CA	92101	**800-243-3436**	619-235-2049	164
San Francisco						
55 Stockton St	San Francisco	CA	94108	**800-422-3436**	415-675-5200	164
Fashion Island Shopping Ctr						
401 Newport Ctr Dr	Newport Beach	CA	92660	**855-658-8527**	949-721-2000	458
Fasig-Tipton Co Inc						
2400 Newtown Pk	Lexington	KY	40511	**877-945-2020**	859-255-1555	51
Fasken Martineau DuMoulin LLP						
333 Bay St Bay Adelaide Ctr Ste 2400						
PO Box 20	Toronto	ON	M5H2T6	**800-268-8424**	416-366-8381	41
Fassberg Construction Co						
17000 Ventura Blvd Ste 200	Encino	CA	91316	**800-795-1747**	818-386-1800	186
Fast Company Magazine						
7 World Trade Ctr	New York	NY	10007	**800-542-6029**	800-501-9571	455-5
Fast Fastfurnishings						
340 S Lemon Ave Ste 6043	Walnut	CA	91789	**866-720-0126**	443-371-3278	321
Fast Heat Inc						
776 Oaklawn Ave	Elmhurst	IL	60126	**877-747-8575**	630-359-6300	318
Fastbolt Corp						
200 Louis St	South Hackensack	NJ	07606	**800-631-1980**	201-440-9100	349
Fastec Industrial						
112 Sherlake Rd	Knoxville	TN	37922	**800-837-2505**		350
Fastenal Co						
2001 Theurer Blvd	Winona	MN	55987	**877-507-7555**	507-454-5374	350
NASDAQ: FAST						
Fast-Fix Jewelry & Watch Repairs						
451 Altamonte Ave	Altamonte Springs	FL	32701	**800-359-0407**	407-261-1595	310
Fastframe USA Inc						
212 Marine St Ste 100	Santa Monica	CA	90405	**800-631-4964**		45
FasTracKids International Ltd						
6900 E Belleview Ave						
Ste 100	Greenwood Village	CO	80111	**888-576-6888**	303-224-0200	310
FASTSIGNS International Inc						
2542 Highlander Way	Carrollton	TX	75006	**800-327-8744**	214-346-5600	697
Fat Brain Toys LLC						
20516 Nicholas Cir	Elkhorn	NE	68022	**800-590-5987**	402-779-3181	756
Father Hennepin State Park						
41294 Father Hennepin Pk Rd						
PO Box 397	Isle	MN	56342	**888-646-6367**	320-676-8763	561
FAU (Florida Atlantic University)						
777 Glades Rd	Boca Raton	FL	33431	**800-299-4328***	561-297-3000	166
*Admissions						
Faulk & Winkler LLC						
6811 Jefferson Hwy	Baton Rouge	LA	70806	**800-927-6811**	225-927-6811	194
Faulkner Information Services						
7905 Browning Rd	Pennsauken	NJ	08109	**800-843-0460**	856-662-2070	633-11
Faulkner University						
5345 Atlanta Hwy	Montgomery	AL	36109	**800-879-9816**	334-272-5820	166
Fauquier Bank, The (TFB)						
10 Courthouse Sq	Warrenton	VA	20186	**800-638-3798**	540-347-2700	70
Fauquier Bankshares Inc						
10 Courthouse Sq	Warrenton	VA	20186	**800-638-3798**	540-347-2700	359-2
NASDAQ: FBSS						
Fauske & Assoc LLC						
16w070 83rd St	Burr Ridge	IL	60527	**877-328-7531**	630-323-8750	192
Favorite Office Automation						
2011 W State St	New Castle	PA	16101	**800-466-8338**	724-658-8300	
Faxaway						
417 Second Ave W	Seattle	WA	98119	**800-906-4329**	206-479-7000	731
FaxBack Inc						
7007 SW Cardinal Ln Ste 105	Portland	OR	97224	**800-329-2225**	503-597-5350	731
Fay Block Materials Inc						
130 Builders Blvd	Fayetteville	NC	28302	**800-326-9198**		191-1
Fayette County Library						
216 W Market St	Somerville	TN	38068	**866-465-3591**	901-465-5248	433-3
Fayette County Public Library						
531 Summit St	Oak Hill	WV	25901	**855-275-5737**	304-465-0121	433-3
Fayette County Public Library						
828 N Grand Ave	Connersville	IN	47331	**844-829-3746**	765-827-0883	433-3

Listing	Toll-Free	Phone	Class
Fayette Electric Co-op Inc			
357 N Washington St ... La Grange TX 78945	**800-874-8290**	979-968-3181	245
Fayetteville Area Convention & Visitors Bureau (FACVB)			
245 Person St ... Fayetteville NC 28301	**800-255-8217**	910-483-5311	206
Fayetteville Observer			
458 Whitfield St ... Fayetteville NC 28306	**800-345-9895**	910-323-4848	528-2
Fayetteville Public Utilities			
408 W College St ... Fayetteville TN 37334	**800-379-2534**	931-433-1522	245
Fayetteville State University			
1200 Murchison Rd ... Fayetteville NC 28301	**800-222-2594***	910-672-1371	166
*Admissions			
Fayetteville-Lincoln County Chamber of Commerce			
208 S Elk Ave ... Fayetteville TN 37334	**888-433-1238**	931-433-6154	139
Faygo Beverages Inc			
3579 Gratiot Ave ... Detroit MI 48207	**800-347-6591**	313-925-1600	80-2
FBFC (First Bank Financial Centre)			
155 W Wisconsin Ave			
PO Box 1004 ... Oconomowoc WI 53066	**888-569-9909**	262-569-9900	70
FBG Service Corp			
407 S 27th Ave ... Omaha NE 68131	**800-777-8326**		104
FBI Buildings Inc			
3823 W 1800 S ... Remington IN 47977	**800-552-2981**		
FBLA-PBL (Future Business Leaders of America-Phi Beta Lambda)			
1912 Assn Dr ... Reston VA 20191	**800-325-2946**		48-11
FBN Metal Products			
5020 S Nathaniel Lyon St ... Battlefield MO 65619	**800-538-2830**	417-882-2830	295
FBS (Fullerton Bldg Systems Inc)			
34620 250th St PO Box 308 ... Worthington MN 56187	**800-450-9782**	507-376-3128	812
FC Haab Company Inc			
2314 Market St ... Philadelphia PA 19103	**800-486-5663**	215-563-0800	316
FCA (Family Caregiver Alliance)			
101 Montgomery St			
Ste 2150 ... San Francisco CA 94104	**800-445-8106**	415-434-3388	48-17
FCA (Fellowship of Christian Athletes)			
8701 Leeds Rd ... Kansas City MO 64129	**800-289-0909**	816-921-0909	48-22
FCA (First Co-op Assn)			
960 Riverview Dr PO Box 60 ... Cherokee IA 51012	**877-753-5400**	712-225-5400	445
FCC (Federal Communications Commission)			
445 12th St SW ... Washington DC 20554	**888-225-5322**		339-19
FCC (Fremont Contract Carriers Inc)			
865 S Bud Blvd ... Fremont NE 68025	**800-228-9842**		447
FCC Commercial Furniture Inc			
8452 Old Hwy 99 N ... Roseburg OR 97470	**800-322-7328**		321
FCCI Insurance Group			
6300 University Pkwy ... Sarasota FL 34240	**800-226-3224**	941-907-3224	390-4
FCCU (First Community Credit Union)			
17151 Chesterfield Airport Rd			
... Chesterfield MO 63005	**800-767-8880**	636-728-3333	219
FCF (Fremont Correctional Facility)			
E US Hwy 50 Evans Blvd			
PO Box 999 ... Canon City CO 81215	**800-886-7683**	719-269-5002	213
FCG (Florida City Gas)			
955 E 25th St ... Hialeah FL 33013	**800-993-7546**		782
FCI (Federal Correctional Institution)			
Bastrop			
1341 Hwy 95 N PO Box 730 ... Bastrop TX 78602	**800-995-6429**	512-321-3903	212
FCI Lender Services Inc			
8180 E Kaiser Blvd ... Anaheim Hills CA 92808	**800-931-2424**	714-282-2424	392
FCL (Farm Credit Leasing)			
600 Hwy 169 S Ste 300 ... Minneapolis MN 55426	**800-444-2929**	952-417-7800	216
FCL Graphics Inc			
4600 N Olcott Ave ... Harwood Heights IL 60706	**800-274-3380**	708-867-5500	623
FCNL (Friends Committee on National Legislation)			
245 Second St NE ... Washington DC 20002	**800-630-1330**	202-547-6000	611
FCRV (Family Campers & RVers)			
4804 Transit Rd Bldg 2 ... Depew NY 14043	**800-245-9755**		48-23
FCx Performance			
3000 E 14th Ave ... Columbus OH 43219	**800-253-6223**		384
FD Lawrence Electric Co			
3450 Beekman St ... Cincinnati OH 45223	**800-582-4490***	513-542-1100	246
*Cust Svc			
FDA (Food & Drug Administration)			
5600 Fishers Ln ... Rockville MD 20857	**888-463-6332**	301-827-2410	339-9
FDB (First DataBank Inc)			
701 Gateway Blvd			
Ste 600 ... South San Francisco CA 94080	**800-633-3453***		178-10
*General			
FDC Graphics Films Inc			
3820 William Richardson Dr ... South Bend IN 46628	**800-634-7523**	574-273-4400	511
FDF Energy Services			
240 Jasmine Rd ... Crowley LA 70526	**800-252-3104**	337-783-8685	146
FDI Group			
39500 High Pointe Blvd Ste 400 ... Novi MI 48375	**800-828-0759**		389
FDLI (Food & Drug Law Institute)			
1155 15th St NW Ste 910 ... Washington DC 20005	**800-956-6293**	202-371-1420	49-10
Fdr & Cp Services Llc			
2503 Tabor Rd ... Bryan TX 77803	**800-337-5325**		
F&E Sportswear Corp			
1230 Newell Pkwy ... Montgomery AL 36110	**800-523-7762**	334-244-6477	683
Fearrington House			
2000 Fearrington Village Ctr ... Pittsboro NC 27312	**800-277-0130**	919-542-2121	378
Feather River College			
570 Golden Eagle Ave ... Quincy CA 95971	**800-442-9799**	530-283-0202	162
Featherlite Bldg Products Corp			
508 McNeil St PO Box 425 ... Round Rock TX 78681	**800-792-1234**	512-255-2573	183
Featherlite Trailers			
Hwy 63 & 9 PO Box 320 ... Cresco IA 52136	**800-800-1230**	563-547-6000	774
Fechheimer Bros Company Inc			
4545 Malsbary Rd ... Cincinnati OH 45242	**800-543-1939**	513-793-5400	155-18
Federal Assistance Monitor			
8204 Fenton St ... Silver Spring MD 20910	**800-666-6380**	301-588-6380	527-7
Federal Aviation Administration (FAA)			
800 Independence Ave SW ... Washington DC 20591	**866-835-5322**		339-16
Aviation Research Div			
800 Independence Ave SW ... Washington DC 20591	**866-835-5322**	202-267-8442	664
Flight Standards Service			
800 Independence Ave SW ... Washington DC 20591	**866-835-5322**	202-267-8237	
Safety Hotline			
800 Independence Ave SW ... Washington DC 20591	**800-255-1111**		339-16
Federal Aviation Administration Northwest Mountain Region			
1601 Lind Ave SW ... Renton WA 98057	**800-220-5715**	425-227-2001	339-16
Federal Block Corp			
247 Walsh Ave ... New Windsor NY 12553	**800-724-1999**	845-561-4108	183
Federal Bureau of Prisons			
National Institute of Corrections			
320 First St NW ... Washington DC 20534	**800-995-6423**	202-307-3106	339-13
National Institute of Corrections Information Ctr			
11900 E Cornell Ave Unit C ... Aurora CO 80014	**800-877-1461**		339-13
Federal Cartridge Co			
900 Ehlen Dr ... Anoka MN 55303	**800-379-1732**		284
Federal Communications Commission (FCC)			
445 12th St SW ... Washington DC 20554	**888-225-5322**		339-19
Federal Computer Week Magazine			
3141 Fairview Pk Dr			
Ste 777 ... Falls Church VA 22042	**877-534-2208**	703-876-5100	455-7
Federal Contracts Report			
1801 S Bell St ... Arlington VA 22202	**800-372-1033**		527-7
Federal Correctional Institution (FCI)			
Bastrop			
1341 Hwy 95 N PO Box 730 ... Bastrop TX 78602	**800-995-6429**	512-321-3903	212
Butner			
Old NC Hwy 75 PO Box 1000 ... Butner NC 27509	**877-623-8426**	919-575-4541	212
Englewood			
9595 W Quincy Ave ... Littleton CO 80123	**877-623-8426**	303-763-4300	212
Fairton			
655 Fairton-Millville Rd			
PO Box 280 ... Fairton NJ 08320	**877-623-8426**	856-453-1177	212
Forrest City			
1400 Dale Bumpers Rd ... Forrest City AR 72335	**877-623-8426**	870-630-6000	212
Loretto			
772 St Joseph St ... Loretto PA 15940	**877-623-8426**	814-472-4140	212
Manchester			
805 Fox Hollow Rd ... Manchester KY 40962	**877-623-8426**	606-598-1900	212
MCKEAN FCI			
6975 Rt 59 ... Lewis Run PA 16738	**877-623-8426**	814-362-8900	212
Oxford PO Box 500 ... Oxford WI 53952	**800-995-6423**	608-584-5511	212
Yazoo City			
2225 Haley Barbour Pkwy			
PO Box 5050 ... Yazoo City MS 39194	**877-623-8426**	662-751-4800	212
Federal Deposit Insurance Corp			
550 17th St NW ... Washington DC 20429	**877-275-3342**		339-19
Federal Deposit Insurance Corp Regional Offices			
Atlanta Regional Office			
10 Tenth St NW Ste 800 ... Atlanta GA 30309	**800-765-3342**	678-916-2200	339-19
Boston Area Office			
15 Braintree Hill Office Pk			
Ste 300 ... Braintree MA 02184	**866-728-9953**	781-794-5500	339-19
Chicago Area Office			
300 S Riverside Plz Ste 1700 ... Chicago IL 60606	**800-944-5343**	312-382-6000	339-19
Dallas Area Office			
1601 Bryan St ... Dallas TX 75201	**800-568-9161**	214-754-0098	339-19
Kansas City Area Office			
2345 Grand Blvd Ste 1200 ... Kansas City MO 64108	**800-209-7459**	816-234-8000	339-19
Memphis Area Office			
5100 Poplar Ave Ste 1900 ... Memphis TN 38137	**800-210-6354**	901-685-1603	339-19
New York Area Office			
350 Fifth Ave Ste 1200 ... New York NY 10118	**800-334-9593**	917-320-2500	339-19
San Francisco Area Office			
25 Jessie St at Ecker Sq			
Ste 2300 ... San Francisco CA 94105	**800-756-3558**	415-546-0160	339-19
Federal Direct			
150 Clove Rd 5th Fl ... Little Falls NJ 07424	**800-927-5123**	973-667-9800	110
Federal Election Commission			
999 E St NW ... Washington DC 20463	**800-424-9530**	202-694-1100	265
Federal Emergency Management Agency (FEMA)			
500 C St SW ... Washington DC 20472	**800-621-3362**	202-646-2500	339-10
FEMA for Kids			
500 C St SW ... Washington DC 20472	**800-621-3362**		339-10
National Flood Insurance Program			
500 C St SW ... Washington DC 20472	**800-427-4661**		339-10
US Fire Administration			
16825 S Seton Ave ... Emmitsburg MD 21727	**888-382-3827**	301-447-1000	339-10
Region 3			
1 Independence Mall			
615 Chestnut St 6th Fl ... Philadelphia PA 19106	**800-621-3362**	215-931-5500	339-10
Federal Emergency Management Agency Regional Office (FEMA)			
Region 1 99 High St ... Boston MA 02110	**877-336-2627**	877-336-2734	339-10
Region 5			
536 S Clark St 6th Fl ... Chicago IL 60605	**877-336-2627**	312-408-5500	339-10
Federal Emergency Management Agency Regional Offices			
Region 6			
800 N Loop 288 ... Denton TX 76209	**800-426-5460**	940-898-5399	339-10
Region 9			
1111 Broadway Ste 1200 ... Oakland CA 94607	**877-336-2627**	510-627-7100	339-10
Federal Energy Regulatory Commission			
888 First St NE ... Washington DC 20426	**866-208-3372**	202-502-8200	339-8
Federal Energy Regulatory Commission Regional Offices			
New York			
19 W 34th St Ste 400 ... New York NY 10001	**844-434-0053**		
San Francisco			
100 First St Ste 2300 ... San Francisco CA 94105	**844-434-0053**		
Federal Equipment Co			
5298 River Rd ... Cincinnati OH 45233	**877-435-4723**	513-621-5260	172
Federal Express Europe Inc			
3610 Hacks Cross Rd ... Memphis TN 38125	**800-463-3339**	901-369-3600	542
Federal Flange			
4014 Pinemont St ... Houston TX 77018	**800-231-0150**	713-681-0606	481
Federal Foam Technologies Inc			
600 Wisconsin Dr ... New Richmond WI 54017	**800-898-9559**	715-246-9500	597
Federal Hearings & Appeals Services Inc			
117 W Main St ... Plymouth PA 18651	**800-664-7177**	570-779-5122	529
Federal Heating & Engineering Company Inc			
611 Main St Ste 202 ... Winchester MA 01890	**855-721-2468***		
*Cust Svc			
Federal Highway Administration			
National Highway Institute			
4600 Fairfax Dr Ste 800 ... Arlington VA 22203	**877-558-6873**	703-235-0500	339-16

	Toll-Free	Phone	Class
Federal Industries Div Standex Corp			
215 Federal Ave .... Belleville WI 53508	800-356-4206		660
Federal Labor Relations Authority			
1400 K St NW .... Washington DC 20424	800-331-3572	202-357-6029	339-19
Federal Law Enforcement Training Ctr			
1131 Chapel Crossing Rd .... Glynco GA 31524	800-743-5382	912-267-2100	339-10
Federal Life Insurance Co Mutual			
3750 W Deerfield Rd .... Riverwoods IL 60015	800-233-3750	847-520-1900	390-2
Federal Motor Carrier Safety Administration (FMCSA)			
1200 New Jersey Ave SE .... Washington DC 20590	800-832-5660		339-16
Federal Prison Industries Inc			
320 First St NW .... Washington DC 20534	800-827-3168		626
Federal Protection Inc			
2500 N Airport Commerce Ave			
.... Springfield MO 65803	800-299-5400		689
Federal Railroad Administration Regional Offices (FRA)			
Region 1			
55 Broadway Rm 1077 .... Cambridge MA 02142	800-724-5991	202-366-4000	339-16
Region 2			
Baldwin Tower			
1510 Chester Pike .... Crum Lynne PA 19022	800-724-5991	202-366-4000	339-16
Region 3			
61 Forsyth St SW Ste 16T20 .... Atlanta GA 30303	800-724-5993	202-366-4000	339-16
Region 4			
200 W Adams St .... Chicago IL 60606	800-724-5040	202-366-4000	339-16
Region 6			
901 Locust St Ste 464 ...... Kansas City MO 64106	800-724-5996	202-366-4000	339-16
Region 8			
703 Broadway St Ste 650 .... Vancouver WA 98660	800-724-5998	202-366-4000	339-16
Federal Realty Investment Trust			
1626 E Jefferson St .... Rockville MD 20852	800-658-8980	301-998-8100	651
NYSE: FRT			
Federal Reserve Bank of Atlanta			
1000 Peachtree St NE .... Atlanta GA 30309	888-500-7390	404-498-8500	71
New Orleans Branch			
525 St Charles Ave .... New Orleans LA 70130	877-638-7003	504-593-3200	71
Federal Reserve Bank of Cleveland			
1455 E Sixth St PO Box 6387 ....Cleveland OH 44101	877-372-2457	216-579-2000	71
Cincinnati Branch			
150 E Fourth St .... Cincinnati OH 45202	877-372-2457	513-721-4787	71
Federal Reserve Bank of Dallas			
2200 N Pearl St .... Dallas TX 75201	800-333-4460	214-922-6000	71
El Paso Branch			
301 E Main St ....El Paso TX 79901	800-333-4460	915-521-5200	71
San Antonio Branch			
402 Dwyer Ave ....San Antonio TX 78204	800-333-4460	210-978-1200	71
Federal Reserve Bank of Kansas City			
1 Memorial Dr PO Box 1200 .... Kansas City MO 64198	800-333-1010	816-881-2000	71
Denver Branch			
1 Memorial Dr .... Kansas City MO 64198	888-851-1920		71
Oklahoma City Branch			
211 North Robinson			
2 Leadership Sq Ste 300 .... Oklahoma City OK 73102	800-333-1030	405-270-8400	71
Federal Reserve Bank of Minneapolis			
90 Hennepin Ave ....Minneapolis MN 55401	800-553-9656	612-204-5000	71
Federal Reserve Bank of Philadelphia			
10 Independence Mall ....Philadelphia PA 19106	866-574-3727	215-574-6000	71
Federal Reserve Bank of Richmond			
Baltimore Branch			
502 S Sharp St .... Baltimore MD 21201	800-446-7045	410-576-3300	71
Federal Reserve Bank of Saint Louis			
1 Federal Reserve Bank Plz			
Broadway and Locust St .... Saint Louis MO 63102	800-333-0810	314-444-8444	71
Little Rock Branch			
111 Ctr St			
Ste 1000 Stephens Bldg.......... Little Rock AR 72201	877-372-2457	501-324-8300	71
Federal Reserve Bank of San Francisco (FRBSF)			
101 Market St .... San Francisco CA 94105	800-227-4133	415-974-2000	71
Portland Branch			
101 Market St .... San Francisco CA 94105	800-227-4133	503-276-3000	71
Salt Lake City Branch			
101 Market St .... San Francisco CA 94105	800-227-4133	415-974-2000	71
Federal Signal Corp Emergency Products Div			
2645 Federal Signal Dr .... University Park IL 60466	800-264-3578	708-534-3400	696
Federal Staffing Resources LLC			
2200 Somerville Rd Ste 300 .... Annapolis MD 21401	866-886-2300	410-990-0795	260
Federal Trade Commission (FTC)			
600 Pennsylvania Ave NW .... Washington DC 20580	877-382-4357	202-326-2222	339-19
National Do Not Call Registry			
600 Pennsylvania Ave NW .... Washington DC 20580	888-382-1222		339-19
Federal Trade Commission Regional Offices			
East Central Region			
1111 Superior Ave Ste 200........Cleveland OH 44114	877-382-4357	216-263-3455	339-19
Midwest Region			
55 W Monroe St Ste 1825 .... Chicago IL 60603	877-382-4357		339-19
Northeast Region			
1 Bowling Green .... New York NY 10004	877-382-4357	212-607-2829	339-19
Northwest Region			
915 Second Ave Rm 2896 .... Seattle WA 98174	877-382-4357		339-19
Southeast Region			
225 Peachtree St NE .... Atlanta GA 30303	877-382-4357		339-19
Southwest Region			
1999 Bryan St Ste 2150 ....Dallas TX 75201	877-382-4357	214-979-9350	339-19
Western Region			
901 Market St Ste 570 .... San Francisco CA 94103	877-382-4357		339-19
Federal Wage & Labor Institute			
7001 W 43rd St ....Houston TX 77092	800-767-9243	713-690-5676	747
Federal White Cement Ltd			
PO Box 1609 ....Woodstock ON N4S0A8	800-265-1806*	519-485-5410	135
*Sales			
Federal-Mogul Corp			
27300 W 11 Mile Rd .... Southfield MI 48034	800-325-8886*	248-354-7700	60
*Cust Svc			
Federated Co-operatives Ltd			
401 22nd St E PO Box 1050........ Saskatoon SK S7K0H2	800-848-6347	306-244-3311	275
Federated Co-ops Inc			
502 S Second St .... Princeton MN 55371	800-638-8228	763-389-2582	575
Federated Insurance Cos			
121 E Pk Sq PO Box 328 ......Owatonna MN 55060	800-533-0472	507-455-5200	359-4

	Toll-Free	Phone	Class
Federated Investors			
1001 Liberty Ave			
Federated Investors Twr .... Pittsburgh PA 15222	800-245-0242	412-288-1900	400
NYSE: FII			
Federated Life Insurance Co			
121 E Pk Sq PO Box 328 ....Owatonna MN 55060	800-533-0472	507-455-5200	390-2
Federated Media			
245 Edison Rd Ste 250 ....Mishawaka IN 46545	888-333-6133		
Federated Mutual Insurance Co			
121 E Pk Sq PO Box 328 ....Owatonna MN 55060	800-533-0472	507-455-5200	390-2
Federated Rural Electric Assn			
77100 US Hwy 71 PO Box 69....... Jackson MN 56143	800-321-3520	507-847-3520	245
Federation Co-op			
108 N Water St .... Black River Falls WI 54615	800-944-1784	715-284-5354	276
Federation for American Immigration Reform (FAIR)			
25 Massachusetts Ave NW			
Ste 330 .... Washington DC 20001	877-627-3247	202-328-7004	48-7
Federation of American Societies for Experimental Biology (FASEB)			
9650 Rockville Pk .... Bethesda MD 20814	800-433-2732	301-634-7000	49-19
Federation of State Medical Boards of the US Inc (FSMB)			
400 Fuller Wiser Rd Ste 300 .... Euless TX 76039	800-793-7939	817-868-4000	49-8
Federation of Tax Administrators (FTA)			
444 N Capitol St NW Ste 348 ...... Washington DC 20001	800-829-9188	202-624-5890	49-7
FedEx			
3875 Airways Module H3 Dept 4634			
.... Memphis TN 38116	800-463-3339		110
FedEx Corp			
3610 Hacks Cross Rd .... Memphis TN 38125	800-463-3339	901-369-3600	359-3
NYSE: FDX			
FedEx Custom Critical Inc			
1475 Boettler Rd .... Uniontown OH 44685	800-463-3339		542
FedEx Supply Chain Services Inc			
5455 Darrow Rd .... Hudson OH 44236	800-463-3339	901-369-3600	447
Fedmet Resources Corp			
PO Box 278 .... Montreal QC H3Z2T2	800-609-5711	514-931-5711	659
Fednav Ltd			
1000 Rue de la GauchetiFre O			
Bureau 3500 .... Montreal QC H3B4W5	800-678-4842*	514-878-6500	313
*General			
FEE (Foundation for Economic Education)			
1819 Peachtree Rd NE Ste 300.......... Atlanta GA 30309	800-960-4333	404-554-9980	630
Feeco International Inc			
3913 Algoma Rd .... Green Bay WI 54311	800-373-9347		207
Feed the Children (FTC)			
PO Box 36 .... Oklahoma City OK 73101	800-627-4556	405-942-0228	48-5
Feesers Inc			
5561 Grayson Rd .... Harrisburg PA 17111	800-326-2828	717-564-4636	297-8
FEI Behavioral Health			
648 N Plankinton Ave Ste 425 .... Milwaukee WI 53203	800-987-4368		460
FEI Co			
5350 NE Dawson Creek Dr .... Hillsboro OR 97124	866-693-3426*	503-726-7500	418
*NASDAQ: FEIC ■ *Cust Svc*			
Feingold Association of the US			
11849 Suncatcher Dr .... Fishers IN 46037	800-321-3287	631-369-9340	48-17
Feizy Import & Export Co Ltd			
1949 Stemmons Fwy .... Dallas TX 75207	800-779-0877	214-747-6000	290
Feld Entertainment Inc			
8607 Westwood Ctr Dr .... Vienna VA 22182	800-844-3545	703-448-4000	149
Feldmeier Equipment Inc			
6800 Townline Rd .... Syracuse NY 13211	800-258-0118	315-454-8608	298
Felician College			
262 S Main St ....Lodi NJ 07644	888-442-4551	201-559-6000	166
Rutherford			
223 Montross Ave .... Rutherford NJ 07070	888-442-4551	201-559-6000	166
Felix Neck Wildlife Sanctuary			
100 Felix Neck Dr .... Edgartown MA 02539	866-627-2267	508-627-4850	818
Felix Storch Inc			
770 Garrison Ave ....Bronx NY 10474	800-932-4267	718-893-3900	38
Felker Bros Corp			
22 N Chestnut Ave .... Marshfield WI 54449	800-826-2304	715-384-3121	488
Fellowes Inc			
1789 Norwood Ave ....Itasca IL 60143	800-945-4545	630-893-1600	111
Fellowship Hall Inc			
5140 Dunstan Rd .... Greensboro NC 27405	800-659-3381		722
Fellowship of Christian Athletes (FCA)			
8701 Leeds Rd .... Kansas City MO 64129	800-289-0909	816-921-0909	48-22
Fellowship Senior Living			
8000 Fellowship Rd .... Basking Ridge NJ 07920	877-824-4909	877-343-6059	
Felly's Flowers Inc			
205 E Broadway .... Madison WI 53716	800-993-7673	608-221-4200	292
Fels Institute for Cancer Research & Molecular Biology			
3307 N Broad St			
Pharmacy Allied Health Bldg Rm 154 ..Philadelphia PA 19140	800-331-2839	215-204-7000	664
Felton Brush Inc			
7 Burton Dr .... Londonderry NH 03053	800-258-9702	603-425-0200	103
Felts Field Aviation Inc			
6205 E Rutter Ave ....Spokane WA 99212	800-676-5538	509-535-9011	63
FEM Electric Assn Inc			
PO Box 468 .... Ipswich SD 57451	800-587-5880	605-426-6891	245
FEMA (Federal Emergency Management Agency)			
500 C St SW .... Washington DC 20472	800-621-3362	202-646-2500	339-10
FEMA (Federal Emergency Management Agency Regional Offic)			
Region 1 99 High St .... Boston MA 02110	877-336-2627	877-336-2734	339-10
Femco Machine Co			
754 S Main St Ext .... Punxsutawney PA 15767	800-458-3445	814-938-9763	452
Fender Musical Instruments Corp			
17600 N Perimeter Dr Ste 100 .... Scottsdale AZ 85255	800-488-1818*	480-596-9690	523
*Cust Svc			
Fenner Drives			
311 W Stiegel St .... Manheim PA 17545	800-243-3374*	717-665-2421	369
*Sales			
Fenton Art Glass Co			
700 Elizabeth St ....Williamstown WV 26187	800-933-6766*	304-375-6122	333
*Cust Svc			
Fentress Inc			
945 Sunset Vly Dr .... Sykesville MD 21784	888-329-0040		196
Fenway Park			
4 Yawkey Way .... Boston MA 02215	877-733-7699	617-226-6000	716

Name / Address	City	State	ZIP	Toll-Free	Phone	Class
Ferguson Enterprises Inc						
12500 Jefferson Ave	Newport News	VA	23602	**800-721-2590**	757-874-7795	608
Ferguson Perforating & Wire Co						
130 Ernest St	Providence	RI	02905	**800-341-9800**	401-941-8876	481
Ferguson Supply & Box Manufacturing Co						
10820 Quality Dr	Charlotte	NC	28278	**800-821-1023**	704-597-0310	100
Ferguson Wellman Capital Management Inc						
888 S W Fifth Ave	Portland	OR	97204	**800-327-5765**	503-226-1444	524
Fernco Inc						
300 S Dayton St	Davison	MI	48423	**800-521-1283**	810-653-9626	592
Ferndale Chamber of Commerce						
1938 Burdette St Ste 112	Ferndale	MI	48220	**800-495-5464**	248-542-2160	139
Ferno-Washington Inc						
70 Weil Way	Wilmington	OH	45177	**800-733-3766**	937-382-1451	475
Fernwood Resort						
5785 Milford Rd	East Stroudsburg	PA	18302	**888-337-6966**		665
Feroleto Steel Company Inc						
300 Scofield Ave	Bridgeport	CT	06605	**800-243-2839**	203-366-3263	719
Ferrandino & Son Inc						
71 Carolyn Blvd	Farmingdale	NY	11735	**866-571-4609**	516-735-0097	606
Ferrara Fiorenza Larrison Barrett & Reitz PC						
5010 Campuswood Dr	East Syracuse	NY	13057	**800-777-4742**	315-437-7600	427
Ferrara Fire Apparatus Inc						
PO Box 249	Holden	LA	70744	**800-443-9006**	225-567-7100	59
Ferrellgas Partners LP						
1 Liberty Plz	Liberty	MO	64068	**888-337-7355**	816-792-1600	316
NYSE: FGP						
Ferrero USA Inc						
600 Cottontail Ln	Somerset	NJ	08873	**800-688-3552**	732-764-9300	296-8
Ferrilli						
41 S Haddon Ave Ste 7	Haddonfield	NJ	08033	**888-864-3282**		461
Ferring Pharmaceuticals Inc						
100 Interpace Pkwy	Parsippany	NJ	07054	**888-337-7464**	973-796-1600	238
Ferris School						
959 Centre Rd	Wilmington	DE	19805	**800-292-9582**	302-993-3800	411
Ferris State University						
1201 S State St	Big Rapids	MI	49307	**800-433-7747**	231-591-2000	166
FLITE Library						
1010 Campus Dr	Big Rapids	MI	49307	**800-433-7747**	231-591-3602	433-6
Traverse City						
2200 Dendrinos Dr Ste 100	Traverse City	MI	49684	**866-857-1954**	231-995-1734	166
Ferrum College						
215 Ferrum Mtn Rd	Ferrum	VA	24088	**800-868-9797**	540-365-2121	166
FESCO Agencies NA Inc						
1000 Second Ave Ste 1310	Seattle	WA	98104	**800-275-3372**	206-583-0860	311
Festiva Resorts						
1 Vance Gap Rd	Asheville	NC	28805	**866-933-7848***	828-254-3378	748
*Resv						
Festival Concert Hall						
North Dakota State University						
12th Ave N	Fargo	ND	58105	**800-726-1724**	701-231-7932	568
Festival Flea Market Mall						
2900 W Sample Rd	Pompano Beach	FL	33073	**800-353-2627**	954-979-4555	458
Festival Inn, The						
1144 Ontario St	Stratford	ON	N5A6Z3	**800-463-3581**	519-273-1150	703
Festive Holidays Inc						
5501 New Jersey Ave	Wildwood Crest	NJ	08260	**800-257-8920**	609-522-6316	755
Festo Corp						
395 Moreland Dr	Hauppauge	NY	11788	**800-993-3786**		452
Fetch Logistics Inc						
25 Northpointe Pkwy Ste 200	Amherst	NY	14228	**800-964-4940**	716-689-4556	311
Fey Industries Inc						
200 Fourth Ave N	Edgerton	MN	56128	**800-533-5340**	507-442-4311	86
FFB (First Financial Bancorp)						
255 E Fifth St Ste 700	Cincinnati	OH	45202	**877-322-9530**		359-2
NASDAQ: FFBC						
FFC (Farmers Win Coop)						
110 N Jefferson	Fredericksburg	IA	50630	**800-562-8389**	563-237-5324	10-3
FFE Transportation Inc						
1145 Empire Central Pl	Dallas	TX	75247	**800-569-9200**	214-630-8090	775
FFF Enterprises Inc						
41093 County Ctr Dr	Temecula	CA	92591	**800-843-7477**	951-296-2500	5
FFP (Food for the Poor Inc)						
6401 Lyons Rd	Coconut Creek	FL	33073	**800-427-9104**	954-427-2222	48-5
FGI (FOIA Group Inc)						
1250 Connecticut Ave NW						
Ste 200	Washington	DC	20036	**888-461-7951**	716-608-0800	386
FGS (Freedom Graphic Systems Inc)						
1101 S Janesville St	Milton	WI	53563	**800-334-3540**		110
FH Bonn Co						
338 W Columbus Rd	South Charleston	OH	45368	**800-323-0143**	937-323-7024	740-3
FHN Memorial Hospital						
1045 W Stephenson St	Freeport	IL	61032	**800-747-4131**	815-599-6000	373-3
Fibar Group LLC, The						
80 Business Park Dr Suit 300	Armonk	NY	10504	**800-342-2721**	914-273-8770	707
Fiber Instruments Sales Inc						
161 Clear Rd	Oriskany	NY	13424	**800-500-0347***	315-736-2206	470
*Sales						
Fiber Optic Center New Trust						
23 Centre St	New Bedford	MA	02740	**800-473-4237**	508-992-6464	246
Fiber SenSys LLC						
2925 NW Aloclek Dr Ste 120	Hillsboro	OR	97124	**800-641-8150**	503-692-4430	688
Fibercomm Lc						
1605 Ninth St	Sioux City	IA	51101	**800-836-2472**	712-224-2020	116
Fiberesin Industries Inc						
37031 E Wisconsin Ave						
PO Box 88	Oconomowoc	WI	53066	**800-450-0051**	262-567-4427	595
Fiberglass Specialties Inc						
PO Box 1340	Henderson	TX	75653	**800-527-1459**	903-657-6522	604
Fibergrate Composite Structures Inc						
5151 Beltline Rd Ste 700	Dallas	TX	75254	**800-527-4043**	972-250-1633	602
FiberMark North America Inc						
161 Wellington Rd	Brattleboro	VT	05302	**800-784-8558***	802-257-0365	557
*Cust Svc						
Fibernetics Corp						
605 Boxwood Dr	Cambridge	ON	N3E1A5	**866-973-4237**	519-489-6700	224
Fiberoptics Technology Inc						
1 Quassett Rd	Pomfret	CT	06258	**800-433-5248***	860-928-0443	330
*Cust Svc						
FiberPlus Inc						
8240 Preston Ct Ste C	Jessup	MD	20794	**800-394-3301**	301-317-3300	180
Fiber-Tech Industries Inc						
2000 Kenskill Ave	Washington Court House	OH	43160	**800-879-4377**	740-335-9400	609
Fiberwave Inc						
140 58th St Bldg B Unit 6E	Brooklyn	NY	11220	**800-280-9011**	718-802-9011	808
Fibre Craft Materials Corp						
7603 New Gross Point Rd	Skokie	IL	60077	**800-323-4316**	847-929-5600	756
Fibre Noire Internet Inc						
550 Ave Beaumont Ste 320	Montreal	QC	H3N1V1	**877-907-3002**		224
Fibrebond Corp						
1300 Davenport Dr	Minden	LA	71055	**800-824-2614**	318-377-1030	183
Fibre-Metal						
2000 Plainfield Pk	Cranston	RI	02921	**800-430-4110**		572
Fidelco Guide Dog Foundation Inc						
103 Vision Way	Bloomfield	CT	06002	**800-225-7566**	860-243-5200	689
Fidelifacts						
42 Broadway Ste 1548	New York	NY	10004	**800-678-0007**	212-425-1520	631
Fidelitone Inc						
1260 Karl Ct	Wauconda	IL	60084	**800-475-0917**		246
Fidelity Advisor Funds						
PO Box 770002	Cincinnati	OH	45277	**800-522-7297**		524
Fidelity Bancshares Nc Inc						
PO Box 8	Fuquay Varina	NC	27526	**800-816-9608**	919-552-2242	70
Fidelity Bank						
100 E English St	Wichita	KS	67201	**800-658-1637**		70
Fidelity Bank & Trust						
208 Second St SE PO Box 277	Dyersville	IA	52040	**800-403-8333**	563-875-7157	70
Fidelity Engineering Corp						
25 Loveton Cir PO Box 2500	Sparks	MD	21152	**800-787-6000**	410-771-9400	14
Fidelity Federal Bancorp						
18 NW Fourth St	Evansville	IN	47708	**800-280-8280**	812-424-0921	359-2
OTC: FDLB						
Fidelity Investment Funds						
PO Box 770001	Cincinnati	OH	45277	**800-343-3548**		524
Fidelity Investments						
483 Bay St Ste 200	Toronto	ON	M5G2N7	**800-263-4077**	416-307-5200	524
Fidelity Investments Charitable Gift Fund						
PO Box 770001	Cincinnati	OH	45277	**800-262-6039**		404
Fidelity Investments Institutional Operations Co Inc						
PO Box 770002	Cincinnati	OH	45277	**877-208-0098**		524
Fidelity Investments Institutional Services Co Inc						
82 Devonshire St	Boston	MA	02109	**800-343-3548**	617-563-9840	400
Fidelity National Title Group Inc						
601 Riverside Ave	Jacksonville	FL	32204	**888-866-3684**	904-854-8100	390-6
Fidelity National Title Insurance Co						
601 Riverside Ave	Jacksonville	FL	32204	**888-866-3684**		390-6
Fiducial						
10100 Old Columbia Rd	Columbia	MD	21046	**800-323-9000**	410-290-8296	729
Fiduciary Management Inc of Milwaukee						
100 E Wisconsin Ave Ste 2200	Milwaukee	WI	53202	**800-264-7684**	414-226-4545	400
Fieger Law						
19390 W 10-Mile Rd	Southfield	MI	48075	**800-294-6637**	248-558-2315	
Field Fresh Foods Inc						
14805 S San Pedro St	Gardena	CA	90248	**800-411-0588**		
Field Law						
10175 101 ST NW Ste 2500	Edmonton	AB	T5JOH3	**800-222-6479**	780-423-3003	427
Field Museum						
1400 S Lake Shore Dr	Chicago	IL	60605	**800-438-9644**	312-922-9410	517
Field Nation LLC						
901 Marquette Ave Ste 2300	Minneapolis	MN	55402	**877-573-4353**		317
Field Paper Co						
3950 D St	Omaha	NE	68107	**800-969-3435**		549
Field Trip Factory						
2211 N Elston Ave Ste 304	Chicago	IL	60614	**800-987-6409**		297-8
Fieldale Farms Corp						
PO Box 558	Baldwin	GA	30511	**800-241-5400**		615
Fields Company LLC						
2240 Taylor Way	Tacoma	WA	98421	**800-627-4098**		46
FieldWorker Products Ltd						
88 Queens Quay W Ste 200	Toronto	ON	M5J0B8	**800-220-0779**	905-944-0863	
Fiesta Henderson						
777 West Lake Mead Pkwy	Henderson	NV	89015	**888-899-7770**	702-558-7000	378
Fiesta Rancho Casino Hotel						
2400 N Rancho Dr	Las Vegas	NV	89130	**800-731-7333***	702-631-7000	133
*Resv						
Fifield Land Co						
4307 Fifield Rd	Brawley	CA	92227	**800-536-6395**	760-344-6391	276
Fifth Third Bank Central Ohio						
21 E State St	Columbus	OH	43215	**866-671-5353**	800-972-3030	70
Figaro's Italian Pizza Inc						
1500 Liberty St SE Ste 160	Salem	OR	97302	**888-344-2767**	503-371-9318	666
Fiji Embassy						
1707 L St NW Ste 200	Washington	DC	20036	**800-932-3454**	202-466-8320	257
Fiji Visitors Bureau						
5777 W Century Blvd Ste 220	Los Angeles	CA	90045	**800-932-3454**	310-568-1616	770
Fiji Water						
11444 W Olympic Blvd 2nd Fl	Los Angeles	CA	90064	**888-426-3454**	310-312-2850	80-2
Fike Corp						
704 SW Tenth St	Blue Springs	MO	64015	**877-342-3453**	816-229-3405	283
FileCatalyst Inc						
1725 St Laurent Blvd Ste 205	Ottawa	ON	K1G3V4	**877-327-9387**	613-667-2439	177
FileMaker Inc						
5201 Patrick Henry Dr	Santa Clara	CA	95054	**800-325-2747***	408-987-7000	178-1
*Cust Svc						
FileTrail Inc						
1990 The Alameda	San Jose	CA	95126	**800-310-0299**	408-289-1300	
Fillauer Inc						
PO Box 5189	Chattanooga	TN	37406	**800-251-6398**	423-624-0946	475
Fillmore Glen State Park						
1686 St Rt 38	Moravia	NY	13118	**800-456-2267**	315-497-0130	561
Film Society of Lincoln Center						
70 Lincoln Center Plz	New York	NY	10023	**888-313-6085**	212-875-5610	455-9
Filson Historical Society						
1310 S Third St	Louisville	KY	40208	**800-928-7000**	502-635-5083	517
Filter LLC						
1425 Fourth Ave Ste 1000	Seattle	WA	98101	**800-336-0809**		260

	Toll-Free	Phone	Class

FilterBoxx Water & Environmental Corp
200 Rivercrest Dr SE Ste 160 .... Calgary AB T2C2X5 — **877-868-4747** — 403-203-4747 — 317

Filterspun
624 N Fairfield St .... Amarillo TX 79107 — **800-323-5431** — 806-383-3840 — 801

Filtertek Inc
11411 Price Rd .... Hebron IL 60034 — **800-248-2461** — 815-648-1001 — 600

Filtration Group Inc
912 E Washington St .... Joliet IL 60433 — **877-603-1003** — 815-726-4600 — 18

FIMAC Solutions LLC
Denver Technological Ctr 7000 E Belleview
Ste 310 .... Greenwood Village CO 80111 — **877-789-5905** — 303-320-1900 — 686

Fimc Commercial Realty
1619 Tyler .... Amarillo TX 79102 — **800-658-2616** — 806-358-7151 — 648

FinAid Page LLC
PO Box 2056 .... Cranberry Township PA 16066 — **800-433-3243** — 724-538-4500 — 721

Final Draft Inc
26707 W Agoura Rd Ste 205 .... Calabasas CA 91302 — **800-231-4055** — 818-995-8995 — 178-10

Finance & Commerce
730 Second Ave S
US Trust Bldg Ste 100. .... Minneapolis MN 55402 — **800-451-9998** — 617-249-2600 — 455-5

Finance Factors Ltd
1164 Bishop St .... Honolulu HI 96813 — **800-648-7136** — 808-548-4940 — 217

Financial & Realty Services LLC
1110 Bonifant St Ste 301 .... Silver Spring MD 20910 — **800-650-9714** — 301-650-9112 — 271

Financial Acctg Standards Board (FASB)
401 Merritt 7 PO Box 5116. .... Norwalk CT 06856 — **800-748-0659** — 203-847-0700 — 49-1

Financial Engines Inc
1804 Embarcadero Rd .... Palo Alto CA 94303 — **888-443-8577** — 408-498-6000 — 178-10
NASDAQ: FNGN

Financial Guaranty Insurance Co
463 Seventh Ave .... New York NY 10018 — **800-352-0001** — 212-312-3000 — 390-5

Financial Industry Regulatory Authority (FINRA)
9509 Key W Ave .... Rockville MD 20850 — **800-321-6273** — 301-590-6500 — 49-2

Financial Institutions Inc
220 Liberty St .... Warsaw NY 14569 — **866-296-3743** — 585-786-1100 — 359-2
NASDAQ: FISI

Financial Managers Society (FMS)
100 W Monroe St Ste 810 .... Chicago IL 60603 — **800-275-4367*** — 312-578-1300 — 49-2
*Cust Svc

FINANCIAL PACIFIC LEASING INC
3455 S 344th Way Ste 300 .... Federal Way WA 98001 — **800-447-7107** — 253-568-6000 — 216

Financial Partners Credit Union
PO Box 7005 .... Downey CA 90241 — **800-950-7328** — 562-923-0311 — 219

Financial Planning Assn (FPA)
7535 E Hampden Ave Ste 600 .... Denver CO 80231 — **800-322-4237** — 303-759-4900 — 49-2

Financial Publishing Co
PO Box 570 .... South Bend IN 46624 — **800-433-0090*** — 574-243-6040 — 633-2
*Cust Svc

Financial Resource Group LLC
12900 Preston Rd Ste 100 LB-104 ... Dallas TX 75230 — **866-473-7132** — 972-960-7790 — 400

FinancialCAD Corp
13450 102nd Ave Ste 1750 .... Surrey BC V3T5X3 — **800-304-0702** — 604-957-1200 — 39

FINCA (Foundation for International Community Assistance)
1201 15th St NW 8th fl .... Washington DC 20005 — **855-903-4622** — 202-682-1510 — 48-5

Fincantieri Marine Systems North America Inc
800-C Principal Ct .... Chesapeake VA 23320 — **877-436-7643** — 757-548-6000 — 686

Finch Paper LLC
1 Glen St .... Glens Falls NY 12801 — **800-833-9983** — 518-793-2541 — 553

Finck Cigar Co
414 Vera Cruz St .... San Antonio TX 78207 — **800-221-0638*** — 210-226-4191 — 751
*Orders

Find the Children
2656 29th St Ste 203 .... Santa Monica CA 90405 — **888-477-6721** — 310-314-3213 — 48-6

Findings Inc
160 Water St .... Keene NH 03431 — **800-225-2706** — 603-352-3717 — 406

FindLaw 610 Opperman Dr .... Eagan MN 55123 — **800-392-6206** — 651-687-6393 — 396

Findlay Inn & Conference Ctr
200 E Main Cross St .... Findlay OH 45840 — **800-825-1455*** — 419-422-5682 — 378
*Cust Svc

Fine Homebuilding Magazine
63 S Main St PO Box 5506 .... Newtown CT 06470 — **800-309-8955*** — 203-426-8171 — 455-21
*Edit

Fine Line Production
2221 Regal Pkwy .... Euless TX 76040 — **800-887-5625** — 817-267-6750 — 481

Fine Organics Corp
420 Kuller Rd PO Box 2277 .... Clifton NJ 07015 — **800-526-7480** — 973-478-1000 — 151

Fine Woodworking Magazine
63 S Main St PO Box 5506 .... Newtown CT 06470 — **800-283-7252** — 203-426-8171 — 455-14

Fineline Printing Group
8081 Zionsville Rd .... Indianapolis IN 46268 — **877-334-7687** — 317-872-4490 — 623

Fineline Technologies Inc
3145 Medlock Bridge Rd .... Norcross GA 30071 — **800-500-8687** — 678-969-0835

Finger Lakes Gaming & Race Track
5857 Rt 96 .... Farmington NY 14425 — **877-846-7369** — 585-924-3232 — 638

Finger Lakes Library System
1300 Dryden Rd .... Ithaca NY 14850 — **800-909-3557** — 607-273-4074 — 433-3

Finger Lakes Times
218 Genesse St .... Geneva NY 14456 — **800-388-6652** — 315-789-3333 — 633-8

Finger Lakes Visitors Connection
25 Gorham St .... Canandaigua NY 14424 — **877-386-4669** — 585-394-3915 — 206

Fingerhut
6250 Ridgewood Dr .... St. Cloud MN 56303 — **800-208-2500** — 457

Finial Co, The
4030 La Reunion Pkwy .... Dallas TX 75212 — **800-392-4341** — 214-678-0805 — 360

Finish Line Inc, The
3308 N Mitthoeffer Rd .... Indianapolis IN 46235 — **888-777-3949** — 317-899-1022 — 301
NASDAQ: FINL

FinishMaster Inc
115 W Washington St 700 S .... Indianapolis IN 46204 — **888-311-3678** — 317-237-3678 — 546

Finity Inc
1200 NW Natio Pkwy Ste 220. .... Portland OR 97209 — **800-509-1346** — 503-808-9240 — 195

Finken Plumbing Heating & Cooling
628 19th Ave NE .... Saint Joseph MN 56374 — **877-346-5367** — 320-258-2005 — 606

Finlandia Sauna Products Inc
14010 SW 72nd Ave Ste B .... Portland OR 97224 — **800-354-3342** — 503-684-8289 — 707

Finlandia University
601 Quincy St .... Hancock MI 49930 — **800-682-7604** — 906-482-5300 — 166

Finley Hospital
350 N Grandview Ave .... Dubuque IA 52001 — **800-582-1891** — 563-582-1881 — 373-3

Finn Corp
9281 Le St Dr .... Fairfield OH 45014 — **800-543-7166** — 513-874-2818 — 273

Finnleo Sauna
575 Cokato St E .... Cokato MN 55321 — **800-346-6536** — 319-2

FINRA (Financial Industry Regulatory Authority)
9509 Key W Ave .... Rockville MD 20850 — **800-321-6273** — 301-590-6500 — 49-2

FINRA 1735 K St NW .... Washington DC 20006 — **800-289-9999** — 202-728-8000 — 49-2

FintronX LED LLC
5995 Chapel Hill Rd Ste 119 ...... Raleigh NC 27607 — **800-541-9082** — 919-324-3960 — 77

Finzer Roller Co
129 Rawls Rd .... Des Plaines IL 60018 — **888-486-1900** — 847-390-6200 — 673

Fire & Life Safety America
3017 Vernon Rd .... Richmond VA 23228 — **800-252-5069** — 804-222-1381 — 283

Fire Fighters Equipment Co
3053 Rt 10 E .... Denville NJ 07834 — **800-523-7222** — 973-366-4466 — 675

Fire Lite Alarms
1 Fire-Lite Pl .... Northford CT 06472 — **800-627-3473** — 203-484-7161 — 283

Fire Mountain Gems Inc
1 Fire Mountain Way .... Grants Pass OR 97526 — **800-355-2137** — 410

Fire-End & Croker Corp
7 Westchester Plz .... Elmsford NY 10523 — **800-759-3473** — 914-592-3640 — 572

Firefighters Community Credit Union Inc
2300 St Clair Ave NE .... Cleveland OH 44114 — **800-621-4644** — 216-621-4644 — 219

Firefighters' Museum
226 W Washington Blvd .... Fort Wayne IN 46802 — **800-767-7752** — 260-426-0051 — 517

Firehouse Image Ctr
2000 N Illinois St .... Indianapolis IN 46202 — **800-382-9179** — 317-236-1747 — 623

FireKeepers
Nottawaseppi Huron Band of the Potawatomi
11177 E Michigan Ave .... Battle Creek MI 49014 — **800-270-7117** — 877-353-8777 — 292

FireKing Security Group
101 Security Pkwy .... New Albany IN 47150 — **800-457-2424** — 812-948-8400 — 688

Firelands Electric Co-op Inc
1 Energy Pl PO Box 32 .... New London OH 44851 — **800-533-8658** — 419-929-1571 — 245

Firelands Regional Medical Ctr
1111 Hayes Ave .... Sandusky OH 44870 — **800-342-1177** — 419-557-7400 — 373-3

Fireside Inn & Suites
25 Airport Rd .... West Lebanon NH 03784 — **877-258-5900** — 603-298-5900 — 378

Firestone Fibers & Textiles Co
100 Firestone Ln
PO Box 1369. .... Kings Mountain NC 28086 — **800-441-1336** — 704-734-2132 — 740-3

Firestone Industrial Products Co
250 W 96th St .... Indianapolis IN 46260 — **800-888-0650** — 800-247-4337 — 60

Fireworks
3307 Utah Ave S .... Seattle WA 98134 — **800-505-8882** — 206-682-8707 — 517

Firm Consulting Group
2107 W Cass St Ste B. .... Tampa FL 33606 — **877-636-9525** — 461

FIRMA Foreign Exchange Corp
10205 101 St NW Ste 400 .... Edmonton AB T5J4H5 — **866-426-2605** — 780-426-5971

FIRST
200 Bedford St .... Manchester NH 03101 — **800-871-8326** — 603-666-3906 — 48-11

First - Call Medical Inc
574 Boston Rd Unit 11 .... Billerica MA 01821 — **800-274-5399**

First Act Inc
745 Boylston St .... Boston MA 02116 — **888-551-1115** — 522

First Action Security Security Team Inc
525 Northern Ave PO Box 2070 ... Hagerstown MD 21742 — **800-372-7447*** — 301-797-2124 — 688
*Cust Svc

First Alarm Security & Patrol Inc
1111 Estates Dr .... Aptos CA 95003 — **800-684-1111** — 831-476-1111 — 689

First Alert Inc
3901 Liberty St Rd .... Aurora IL 60504 — **800-323-9005** — 283

First American Bank
1650 Louis Ave
PO Box 0794. .... Elk Grove Village IL 60009 — **866-449-1150** — 847-952-3700 — 359-2

First American Bank & Trust
2785 Hwy 20 W PO Box 550 ...... Vacherie LA 70090 — **800-738-2265** — 225-265-2265 — 70

First American Corp
1 First American Way .... Santa Ana CA 92707 — **800-854-3643** — 714-250-3000 — 390-6
NYSE: FAF

First American Funds
PO Box 701 .... Milwaukee WI 53201 — **800-677-3863** — 524

First American Home Buyers Protection
1 First American Way .... Santa Ana CA 92707 — **800-854-3643** — 714-250-3000

First BanCorp
PO Box 9146 .... San Juan PR 00908 — **866-695-2511** — 787-725-2511 — 359-2
NYSE: FBP

First Bancorp
341 N Main St .... Troy NC 27371 — **800-548-9377** — 910-576-6171 — 359-2
NASDAQ: FBNC

First Bank Financial Centre (FBFC)
155 W Wisconsin Ave
PO Box 1004. .... Oconomowoc WI 53066 — **888-569-9909** — 262-569-9900 — 70

First Bank Of Highland Park
1835 First St .... Highland Park IL 60035 — **877-651-7800** — 847-432-7800 — 681

First Bank of Muleshoe
202 S 1st PO Box 565 .... Muleshoe TX 79347 — **888-653-9558** — 806-272-4515 — 70

First Busey Corp
100 West University Ave .... Champaign IL 61820 — **800-672-8739** — 217-365-4516 — 359-2
NASDAQ: BUSE

First Calgary Savings
510 16th Ave NE .... Calgary AB T2E1K4 — **866-923-4778** — 70

First Candle
49 Locust Ave Ste 104 .... New Canaan CT 06840 — **800-221-7437** — 120-396-6130 — 48-17

First Chemical Corp
1001 Industrial Rd .... Pascagoula MS 39581 — **877-243-6178** — 228-762-0870 — 144

First Choice Health Plan
600 University St Ste 1400 .... Seattle WA 98101 — **800-467-5281** — 390-3

First Church of Christ Scientist
210 Massachusetts Ave .... Boston MA 02115 — **800-288-7155** — 617-450-2000 — 48-20

First Citizens Bank
350 S Beverly D Ste 150. .... Beverly Hills CA 90212 — **888-323-4732** — 310-552-1776 — 359-2

First Citizens National Bank Charitable Foundation
PO Box 1708 .... Mason City IA 50402 — **800-423-1602** — 641-423-1600 — 359-2

First Class Services Inc
9355 US Hwy 60 E .... Lewisport KY 42351 — **800-467-8684*** — 270-295-3746 — 775
*General

First Command Financial Services Inc
1 FirstComm Plz .... Fort Worth TX 76109 — **800-443-2104** — 817-731-8621 — 194

Company / Address	City	State	ZIP	Toll-Free	Phone	Class
First Commonwealth Financial Corp 601 Philadelphia St; *NYSE: FCF*	Indiana	PA	15701	**800-711-2265**	724-463-8555	359-2
First Community Credit Union (FCCU) 17151 Chesterfield Airport Rd	Chesterfield	MO	63005	**800-767-8880**	636-728-3333	219
First Community Village 1800 Riverside Dr	Columbus	OH	43212	**877-364-2570**	614-324-4455	668
First Co-op Assn (FCA) 960 Riverview Dr PO Box 60	Cherokee	IA	51012	**877-753-5400**	712-225-5400	445
First DataBank Inc (FDB) 701 Gateway Blvd Ste 600; *General	South San Francisco	CA	94080	**800-633-3453***		178-10
First Defiance Financial Corp 601 Clinton St; *NASDAQ: FDEF*	Defiance	OH	43512	**800-472-6292**	419-782-5015	359-2
First Dental Health 5771 Copley Dr Ste 101	San Diego	CA	92111	**800-334-7244**		414
First Electric Co-op Corp 1000 S JP Wright Loop Rd	Jacksonville	AR	72076	**800-489-7405**	501-982-4545	245
First Equity Mortgage Bankers 9300 S Dadeland Blvd Ste 500	Miami	FL	33156	**800-973-3654**	305-666-3333	507
First Farmers & Merchants National Bank 816 S Garden St PO Box 1148; *OTC: FFMH*	Columbia	TN	38401	**800-882-8378**	931-388-3145	681
First Federal Bank Fsb 6900 N Executive Dr	Kansas City	MO	64120	**888-651-4759**	816-241-7800	70
First Federal Lakewood 14806 Detroit Ave	Lakewood	OH	44107	**800-966-7300**	216-529-2700	70
First Federal Savings Bank of Frankfort 216 W Main St PO Box 535	Frankfort	KY	40602	**888-818-3372**	502-223-1638	359-2
First Fidelity Capital Markets Inc 10463 Stonebridge Blvd	Boca Raton	FL	33498	**800-485-3670**	561-558-0730	
First Financial Bancorp (FFB) 255 E Fifth St Ste 700; *NASDAQ: FFBC*	Cincinnati	OH	45202	**877-322-9530**		359-2
First Financial Bank PO Box 2122	Terre Haute	IN	47802	**800-511-0045**	812-238-6000	70
First Financial Bank 300 High St; *Cust Svc	Hamilton	OH	45011	**877-322-9530***	513-867-4744	70
First Financial Bank PO Box 2122	Terre Haute	IN	47802	**800-511-0045**	812-238-6000	
First Financial Bankshares Inc 400 Pine St PO Box 701; *NASDAQ: FFIN*	Abilene	TX	79601	**855-660-5862**	325-627-7155	359-2
First Financial Corp 1 First Financial Plz; *NASDAQ: THFF*	Terre Haute	IN	47807	**800-511-0045**	812-238-6000	359-2
First Flight Island Restaurant & Brewery 301 Whitehead St	Key West	FL	33040	**800-507-9955**	305-293-8484	667
First Foundation Bank 18101 Von Karman Ave Ste 750	Irvine	CA	92612	**800-224-7931**	949-202-4100	70
First Gold Hotel 270 Main St	Deadwood	SD	57732	**800-274-1876**	605-578-9777	378
First Hawaiian Bank 999 Bishop St	Honolulu	HI	96813	**888-844-4444**	808-525-6340	70
First Health Group Corp *Coventry* 3200 Highland Ave	Downers Grove	IL	60515	**800-247-2898**	630-737-7900	461
First Horizon National Corp 165 Madison; *NYSE: FHN*	Memphis	TN	38103	**800-489-4040**	901-523-4444	359-2
First Insight Corp 6723 NE Bennett St Ste 200	Hillsboro	OR	97124	**800-920-1940**		177
First Insurance Company of Hawaii Ltd 1100 Ward Ave PO Box 2866	Honolulu	HI	96803	**800-272-5202**	808-527-7777	390-4
First Insurance Funding Corp 450 Skokie Blvd Ste 1000	Northbrook	IL	60062	**800-837-3707**		217
First Interstate Bancsystem Inc 401 N 31st St; *NASDAQ: FIBK*	Billings	MT	59101	**888-752-3341**	406-255-5000	359-2
First Interstate Bank 401 N 31st St	Billings	MT	59101	**888-752-3341**	406-255-5000	70
First Jackson Bank 43243 US Hwy 72	Stevenson	AL	35772	**888-950-2265**	256-437-2107	70
First Lease Inc 1 Walnut Grove Dr Ste 300	Horsham	PA	19044	**866-493-4778**		264-4
First Mercantile Trust Co 57 Germantown Ct 4th Fl	Cordova	TN	38018	**800-753-3682**	901-753-9080	70
First Merchants Corp 200 E Jackson St; *NASDAQ: FRME*	Muncie	IN	47305	**800-205-3464**		359-2
First Midwest Bancorp Inc 1 Pierce Pl Ste 1500; *NASDAQ: FMBI*	Itasca	IL	60143	**800-322-3623**	630-875-7450	359-2
First National Bank PO Box 578	Fort Collins	CO	80521	**800-883-8773**	970-495-9450	70
First National Bank 4220 William Penn Hwy	Monroeville	PA	15146	**800-555-5455**		359-2
First National Bank Alaska 101 W 36 Ave PO Box 100720; *OTC: FBAK*	Anchorage	AK	99510	**800-856-4362**	907-777-4362	70
First National Bank Creston PO Box 445	Creston	IA	50801	**877-782-2195**	641-782-2195	70
First National Bank Jasper 301 E Houston St	Jasper	TX	75951	**800-340-7167**	409-384-3486	70
First National Bank of Omaha 1620 Dodge St	Omaha	NE	68197	**800-462-5266**	402-602-3022	70
First National Bank of Oneida, The 18418 Alberta St PO Box 4699	Oneida	TN	37841	**866-546-8273**	423-569-8586	70
First National Bank of Santa Fe PO Box 609	Santa Fe	NM	87504	**888-912-2265**	505-992-2000	70
First National Bankers Bankshares Inc (FNBB) 7813 Office Pk Blvd	Baton Rouge	LA	70809	**800-421-6182**	225-924-8015	70
First National of Nebraska Inc PO Box 2490	Omaha	NE	68103	**800-688-7070**	402-341-0500	359-2
First Nations Development Institute 2217 Princess Anne St Ste 111-1	Fredericksburg	VA	22401	**888-371-3686**	540-371-5615	48-14
First Nations University of Canada (FNUniv) *Saskatoon* 229 Fourth Ave S	Saskatoon	SK	S7K4K3	**800-267-6303**	306-931-1800	780
First Office 1204 E Sixth St	Huntingburg	IN	47542	**800-983-4415**		319-1
First Pacific Advisors Inc 11601 Wilshire Blvd Ste 1200	Los Angeles	CA	90025	**800-982-4372**	310-473-0225	400
First Palmetto Savings Bank Fsb PO Box 430	Camden	SC	29021	**800-922-7411**	803-432-2265	70
First Priority Inc 1590 Todd Farm Dr	Elgin	IL	60123	**800-650-4899**	847-289-1600	578
First Quantum Minerals Ltd 543 Granville St 14th Fl; *TSX: FM*	Vancouver	BC	V6C1X8	**888-688-6577**	604-688-6577	500
First Rate Staffing 1920 W Camelback Rd Ste 102	Phoenix	AZ	85015	**800-357-6242**	602-442-5277	
First Republic Bank 111 Pine St; *NYSE: FRC*	San Francisco	CA	94111	**800-392-1400**	415-392-1400	70
First Run Features 630 Ninth Ave Ste 1213	New York	NY	10036	**800-229-8575**	212-243-0600	509
First Savings Bank 2804 N Telshor Blvd	Las Cruces	NM	88011	**800-555-6895**	575-521-7931	70
First Security Bank of Missoula 1704 Dearborn PO Box 4506	Missoula	MT	59801	**888-782-3115**	406-728-3115	70
First Security Bank of Sleepy Eye 100 Main St E PO Box 469	Sleepy	MN	56085	**800-535-8440**	507-794-3911	70
First Shore Federal 106-108 S Div St PO Box 4248	Salisbury	MD	21803	**800-634-6309**	410-546-1101	71
First Southern Bank 301 S Ct St; *General	Florence	AL	35630	**800-625-7131***	256-718-4200	359-2
First State Bank 730 Harry Sauner Rd; *General	Hillsboro	OH	45133	**800-987-2566***	937-393-9170	359-2
First State Bank 708 Azalea Dr PO Box 506	Waynesboro	MS	39367	**866-408-3582**		70
First State Bank & Trust Co 1005 E 23rd St	Fremont	NE	68025	**888-674-4344**	402-721-2500	70
First State Bank of Kansas City 650 Kansas Ave	Kansas City	KS	66105	**800-883-1242**	913-371-1242	70
First Student Inc 600 Vine St	Cincinnati	OH	45202	**800-844-5588**	513-241-2200	109
First Sun EAP 2700 Middleburg Dr Ste 208	Columbia	SC	29204	**800-968-8143**	803-376-2668	
First Tennessee Bank 165 Madison Ave	Memphis	TN	38103	**800-382-5465**	901-523-4883	70
First Texas Bank 501 E Third St	Lampasas	TX	76550	**866-220-1598**	512-556-3691	70
First to The Finish Inc 1325 N Broad St	Carlinville	IL	62626	**800-747-9013**		707
First Trinity Financial Corp 7633 E 63rd Pl Ste 230	Tulsa	OK	74133	**888-883-1499**		
First Truck Centre Inc 11313 170 St	Edmonton	AB	T5M3P5	**888-882-8530**	780-413-8800	57
First United Bank 1400 W Main St	Durant	OK	74701	**800-924-4427**	580-924-2211	70
First United Bank & Trust 19 S Second St; *NASDAQ: FUNC*	Oakland	MD	21550	**888-692-2654**		359-2
First UNUM Life Insurance Co 2211 Congress St	Portland	ME	04122	**800-633-7491**	207-575-2211	390-2
First Western Advisors 6440 Millrock Dr	Salt Lake City	UT	84121	**800-937-3500**	801-930-6500	461
First Western Bank & Trust PO Box 1090	Minot	ND	58702	**800-688-2584**	701-852-3711	70
Firstbase Services Ltd 34609 Delair Rd	Abbotsford	BC	V2S2E1	**800-758-2922**	604-850-5334	343
FirstCare 1901 W Loop 289 Ste #9	Lubbock	TX	79407	**800-884-4901**	806-784-4300	390-2
FirstCash Inc 1600 W Seventh St; *NASDAQ: FCFS*	Fort Worth	TX	76102	**800-290-4598**	817-335-1100	565
FirstCom Music 1325 Capital Pkwy Ste 109; *Cust Svc	Carrollton	TX	75006	**800-858-8880***	972-389-2800	521
FirstEnergy Corp 76 S Main St; *NYSE: FE*	Akron	OH	44308	**800-633-4766**		359-5
Firstexpress Inc 1137 Freightliner Dr	Nashville	TN	37210	**800-848-9203**		775
FirstFed Bancorp Inc 1630 Fourth Ave N PO Box 340	Bessemer	AL	35020	**800-436-5112**	205-428-8472	359-2
FirstGiving Inc 100 Cambridge Park Dr	Cambridge	MA	02240	**800-687-8505**		386
First-Knox National Bank 1 S Main St PO Box 1270	Mount Vernon	OH	43050	**800-837-5266**	740-399-5500	70
Firstrust Savings Bank 15 E Ridge Pk 4th Fl	Conshohocken	PA	19428	**800-220-2265**	610-238-5000	70
firstSTREET for Boomers & Beyond Inc 1998 Ruffin Mill Rd	Colonial Heights	VA	23834	**800-958-8324**	804-524-9888	195
Firstwave Technologies Inc 99 MedTech Dr	Batavia	NY	14020	**877-784-0269**		178-11
Fisc Investment Services Corp 1849 Clairmont Rd	Decatur	GA	30033	**800-241-3203**	404-321-1212	686
Fischer Environmental Service Inc 1980 Surgi Dr	Mandeville	LA	70448	**800-391-2565**		573
Fischer International Systems Corp 9045 Strada Stell Ct Ste 201; *Tech Supp	Naples	FL	34109	**800-776-7258***	239-643-1500	178-1
Fiserv Inc 255 Fiserv Dr PO Box 979; *NASDAQ: FISV* ■ *Sales	Brookfield	WI	53008	**800-872-7882***	262-879-5000	69
Fisgard Capital Corp 3378 Douglas St	Victoria	BC	V8Z3L3	**866-382-9255**	250-382-9255	686

Alphabetical Section

Company / Address	City	State	ZIP	Toll-Free	Phone	Class
Fish Oven & Equipment Corp						
120 W Kent Ave PO Box 875	Wauconda	IL	60084	**877-526-8720**	847-526-8686	298
Fish Window Cleaning Services Inc						
200 Enchanted Pkwy	Manchester	MO	63021	**877-707-3474**	636-779-1500	310
Fisher & Arnold Inc						
9180 Crestwyn Hills Dr	Memphis	TN	38125	**888-583-9724**	901-748-1811	194
Fisher & Ludlow Nucor Grating Inc						
2000 Corporate Dr PO Box 1238	Wexford	PA	15090	**800-334-2047**	724-934-5320	489
Fisher & Paykel Appliances Inc						
5900 Skylab Rd	Huntington Beach	CA	92647	**888-936-7872**		36
Fisher & Paykel Healthcare Inc						
173 Technology Dr Ste 100	Irvine	CA	92618	**800-446-3908**	949-453-4000	250
Fisher Athletic Equipment Inc						
2060 Cauble Rd	Salisbury	NC	28144	**800-438-6028**		707
Fisher Auction Company Inc						
2112 E Atlantic Blvd	Pompano Beach	FL	33062	**800-331-6620**	954-942-0917	
Fisher Canvas Products Inc						
415 St Mary St	Burlington	NJ	08016	**800-892-6688**		728
Fisher College						
118 Beacon St	Boston	MA	02116	**866-266-6007**	617-236-8800	162
Fisher Container Corp						
1111 Busch Pkwy	Buffalo Grove	IL	60089	**800-837-2247**	847-541-0000	544
Fisher Group Inc						
4517 W 1730 S	Salt Lake City	UT	84104	**800-365-8920**	801-262-6451	392
Fisher Investments						
13100 Skyline Blvd	Woodside	CA	94062	**800-550-1071**		400
Fisher Island Club & Resort						
1 Fisher Island Dr	Miami	FL	33109	**800-537-3708***	305-535-6000	665
*Resv						
Fisher Manufacturing Co						
PO Box 60	Tulare	CA	93275	**800-421-6162**		605
Fisher Printing Inc						
8640 S Oketo Ave	Bridgeview	IL	60455	**800-366-0006**	708-598-1500	683
Fisher Research Laboratory Inc						
1120 Alza Dr	El Paso	TX	79907	**800-685-5050**	915-225-0333	470
Fisher Sand & Gravel Co						
3020 Energy Dr PO Box 1034	Dickinson	ND	58602	**800-932-8740**	701-456-9184	501-4
Fisher Science Education						
4500 Turnberry Dr	Hanover Park	IL	60133	**800-955-1177**	800-766-7000	243
Fisher Space Pen Co						
711 Yucca St	Boulder City	NV	89005	**800-102-7366**	702-293-3011	567
Fisher Textiles Inc						
139 Business Pk Dr	Indian Trail	NC	28079	**800-554-8886**	704-821-8870	740-6
Fisher Theatre						
3011 W Grand Blvd	Detroit	MI	48202	**800-982-2787**	313-872-1000	568
Fisheries Museum of the Atlantic						
68 Bluenose Dr PO Box 1363	Lunenburg	NS	B0J2C0	**866-579-4909**	902-634-4794	517
Fisheries Supply Co						
1900 N Northlake Way	Seattle	WA	98103	**800-426-6930**	206-632-4462	765
Fisher-Price Inc						
636 Girard Ave	East Aurora	NY	14052	**800-432-5437**	716-687-3000	757
Fisher-Titus Medical Ctr (FTMC)						
272 Benedict Ave	Norwalk	OH	44857	**800-589-3862**	419-668-8101	373-3
Fisk University						
1000 17th Ave N	Nashville	TN	37208	**888-702-0022**	615-329-8500	166
Fiskars Brands Inc						
7800 Discovery Dr	Middleton	WI	53562	**866-348-5661**		222
Fiske Bros Refining Co						
129 Lockwood St	Newark	NJ	07105	**800-733-4755**	973-589-9150	537
Fit & Fresh Inc						
295 Promenade St	Providence	RI	02908	**800-858-8840**		
Fitch Co						
2201 Russell St	Baltimore	MD	21230	**800-933-4824**	410-539-1953	405
Fitch Ratings Inc						
1 State St Plz	New York	NY	10004	**800-753-4824**	212-908-0500	218
Fitness Club Warehouse Inc						
2210 S Sepulveda Blvd	Los Angeles	CA	90064	**800-348-4537**	310-235-2040	707
Fitness Depot						
1808 Lower Roswell Rd	Marietta	GA	30068	**800-974-6828**		353
Fitness Zone						
3439 Colonnade Pkwy Se 800	Birmingham	AL	35243	**800-875-9145**		707
FITNESSRX FOR MEN						
60 Rt 25A Ste 1	Setauket	NY	11733	**800-653-1151**	631-751-9696	455-13
Fitzgerald Electro-mechanical Co						
6 S Linden Ave						
Ste 4	South San Francisco	CA	94080	**800-448-9832**	650-589-9935	
Fitzgeralds Casino & Hotel Tunica						
711 Lucky Ln	Robinsonville	MS	38664	**888-766-5825**	662-363-5825	133
Fitzpatrick Manhattan Hotel						
687 Lexington Ave	New York	NY	10022	**800-367-7701**	212-355-0100	378
Five Below Inc						
1818 Market St	Philadelphia	PA	19103	**844-452-3569**	215-546-7909	757
Five Star Electric of Houston Inc						
19424 Pk Row Dr Ste 100	Houston	TX	77084	**888-492-7090**	281-492-7090	515
Five Star Quality Care Inc						
400 Centre St	Newton	MA	02458	**866-230-1286**	617-796-8387	449
NYSE: FVE						
Five Star Trucking Inc						
4380 Glenbrook Rd	Willoughby	OH	44094	**800-321-3658**	440-953-9300	775
FIX Flyer LLC						
525 Seventh Ave Ste 812	New York	NY	10018	**888-349-3593**		251
Fixtureworks LLC						
33792 Doreka	Fraser	MI	48026	**888-794-8687**	586-294-1188	452
FJH Music Company Inc, The						
2525 Davie Rd Ste 360	Davie	FL	33317	**800-262-8744**	954-382-6061	95
Fkg Oil Co						
721 W Main	Belleville	IL	62220	**800-873-3546**	618-233-6754	204
FL Crane & Sons Inc						
508 S Spring St PO Box 428	Fulton	MS	38843	**800-748-9523**	662-862-2172	189-9
FL Emmert Co Inc						
2007 Dunlap St	Cincinnati	OH	45214	**800-441-3343**	513-721-5808	445
FL Smidth Inc						
2040 Ave C	Bethlehem	PA	18017	**800-523-9482**	610-264-6011	468
FLA (Forest Landowners Assn)						
950 Glenn Dr Ste 150	Folsom	CA	95630	**800-325-2954**	404-325-2954	48-13
Flagler College						
74 King St	Saint Augustine	FL	32084	**800-304-4208**	904-829-6481	641
Flagler College						
74 King St	Saint Augustine	FL	32084	**800-304-4208***	904-829-6481	166
*Admissions						
Flagship All Suites Resort						
60 N Maine Ave	Atlantic City	NJ	08401	**800-647-7890**	609-343-7447	378
Flagship Fire Inc						
1500 15th Ave dr e	Palmetto	FL	34221	**866-242-3307**	941-723-7230	138
Flagship Press Inc						
150 Flagship Dr	North Andover	MA	01845	**800-733-1520**	978-975-3100	623
Flagstaff Convention & Visitors Bureau						
323 W Aspen Ave	Flagstaff	AZ	86001	**800-217-2367**	928-779-7611	206
Flagstaff Pulliam Airport						
6200 S Pulliam Dr	Flagstaff	AZ	86001	**800-463-1389**	928-213-2930	27
Flagstaff Symphony Orchestra						
113 E Aspen Ave # A	Flagstaff	AZ	86001	**888-520-7214**	928-774-5107	569-3
Flagstar Bank FSB						
5151 Corporate Dr	Troy	MI	48098	**800-945-7700**	248-312-5400	70
FlagZone LLC						
105A Industrial Dr	Gilbertsville	PA	19525	**800-976-4201**		258
Flaherty & Collins Properties Inc						
1 Indiana Sq Ste 3000	Indianapolis	IN	46240	**888-684-0338**	317-816-9300	
Flambeau Inc						
15981 Valplast Rd	Middlefield	OH	44062	**800-457-5252**	440-632-1631	600
Flame Enterprises Inc						
21500 Gledhill St	Chatsworth	CA	91311	**800-854-2255**	818-700-2905	246
Flamer's Grill						
1515 International Pkwy						
Ste 2013	Heathrow	FL	32746	**866-749-4889**	407-574-8363	666
Flamingo Resort Hotel & Conference Ctr						
2777 Fourth St	Santa Rosa	CA	95405	**800-848-8300**	707-545-8530	665
Flanders Corp						
531 Flanders Filters Rd	Washington	NC	27889	**800-637-2803**	252-946-8081	18
OTC: FLDR						
FLANDERS Inc						
8101 Baumgart Rd	Evansville	IN	47725	**855-875-5888**	812-867-7421	515
Flanigan's						
5059 NE 18th Ave	Fort Lauderdale	FL	33334	**800-833-5239**	954-377-1961	666
NYSE: BDL						
Flashbanc LLC						
185 NW spanish river blvd	Boca Raton	FL	33431	**800-808-1622**	561-278-8888	138
Flat Rock Playhouse						
2661 Greenville Hwy	Flat Rock	NC	28731	**866-732-8008**	828-693-0731	568
Flathead Convention & Visitors Bureau						
PO Box 2164	Bigfork	MT	59911	**800-543-3105**	406-756-9091	206
Flathead Electric Co-op Inc						
2510 US Hwy 2 E	Kalispell	MT	59901	**800-735-8489**	406-751-4483	245
Flathead Valley Community College						
777 Grandview Dr	Kalispell	MT	59901	**800-313-3822**	406-756-3822	162
Libby 225 Commerce Way	Libby	MT	59923	**800-313-3822**	406-293-2721	162
Flatout Inc						
1422 Woodland Dr	Saline	MI	48176	**888-254-5480**		296
Flavor Dynamics Inc						
640 Montrose Ave	South Plainfield	NJ	07080	**888-271-8424**	908-822-8855	297-8
Flax Art & Design						
Fort Mason Ctr 2 Marina Blvd						
Bldg D	San Francisco	CA	94123	**844-352-9278**	415-530-3510	45
Fleet Engineers Inc						
1800 E Keating Ave	Muskegon	MI	49442	**800-333-7890***	231-777-2537	513
*Cust Svc						
Fleet Equipment Corp						
567 Commerce St	Franklin Lakes	NJ	07417	**800-631-0873**	201-337-3294	513
Fleet Landing Retirement Community						
1 Fleet Landing Blvd	Atlantic Beach	FL	32233	**877-591-6547***	904-246-9900	668
*General						
Fleet Reserve Assn (FRA)						
125 NW St	Alexandria	VA	22314	**800-372-1924**	703-683-1400	48-19
FleetBoss Global Positioning Solutions Inc						
241 O'Brien Rd	Fern Park	FL	32730	**877-265-9559**	407-265-9559	730
Fleetgistics Holdings Inc						
2251 Lynx Ln Ste 7	Orlando	FL	32804	**800-280-9097**	407-843-6505	
Fleetwash Inc						
26 Law Dr	Fairfield	NJ	07004	**800-847-3735**		62-1
Fleetwing Corp						
742 S Combee Rd	Lakeland	FL	33801	**800-282-5678**	863-665-7557	575
Fleetwood Group Inc						
11832 James St	Holland	MI	49424	**800-257-6390**		319-3
Fleetwood Homes						
7007 Jurupa Ave	Riverside	CA	92504	**888-568-2080**		106
Fleetwood Homes of Idaho Inc						
2611 E Comstock Ave	Nampa	ID	83687	**800-334-8958**	877-413-9849	503
Fleetwood Homes of Virginia Inc						
90 Weaver St	Rocky Mount	VA	24151	**866-890-6206**	540-483-5171	503
Fleetwood-Signode						
3624 West Lake Ave	Glenview	IL	60026	**800-862-7997**	847-657-5111	555
Fleming College						
200 Albert St S	Lindsay	ON	K9V5E6	**866-353-6464**	705-324-9144	162
Fleming Door Products Ltd						
101 Ashbridge Cir	Woodbridge	ON	L4L3R5	**800-263-7515**		234
Fleming Mason Energy Co-op						
1449 Elizaville Rd						
PO Box 328	Flemingsburg	KY	41041	**800-464-3144**	606-845-2661	
Flesh Co						
2118 59th St	Saint Louis	MO	63110	**800-869-3330**	314-781-4400	110
Fletch's Inc						
825 Charlevoix Ave PO Box 265	Petoskey	MI	49770	**888-764-0308**	231-347-9651	57
FletchAir Inc						
103 Turkey Run Ln	Comfort	TX	78013	**800-329-4647**	830-995-5900	22
Fletcher Music Centers Inc						
3966 Airway Cir	Clearwater	FL	33762	**800-258-1088**	727-571-1088	522
Fletcher's Medical Supplies Inc						
6851 S Distribution Ave	Jacksonville	FL	32256	**855-541-7809**	904-387-4481	362
Flex Foam						
617 N 21st Ave	Phoenix	AZ	85009	**800-266-3626**	602-252-5819	131
Flex Hr						
10700 Medlock Bridge Rd						
Ste 206	Johns Creek	GA	30097	**877-735-3947**	770-814-4225	353
Flexaust Co						
1510 Armstrong Rd	Warsaw	IN	46580	**800-343-0428**	574-267-7909	369

Name / Address	Toll-Free	Phone	Class
Flexbar Machine Corp 250 Gibbs Rd ... Islandia NY 11749	800-879-7575	631-582-8440	693
Flex-Cable Inc 5822 N Henkel Rd ... Howard City MI 49329	800-245-3539	231-937-8000	811
Flexfab LLC 1699 W M-43 Hwy ... Hastings MI 49058	800-331-0003		369
FlexHead Industries Inc 56 Lowland St ... Holliston MA 01746	800-829-6975	508-893-9596	52
Flexi Display Marketing Inc 24669 Halsted Rd ... Farmington Hills MI 48335	800-875-1725	248-987-6400	195
Flexible Lifeline Systems Inc 14325 W Hardy Rd ... Houston TX 77060	800-353-9425		
Flexible Materials Inc 1202 Port Rd ... Jeffersonville IN 47130	800-244-6492	812-280-7000	609
Flexible Plan Investments Ltd 3883 Telegraph Rd Ste 100 ... Bloomfield Hills MI 48302	800-347-3539	248-642-6640	400
Flexible Steel Lacing Co 2525 Wisconsin Ave ... Downers Grove IL 60515	800-323-3444	630-971-0150	207
Flexicon Corp 2400 Emrick Blvd ... Bethlehem PA 18020	888-353-9426	610-814-2400	543
FlexiInternational Software Inc 2 Enterprise Dr ... Shelton CT 06484 *OTC: FLXI*	800-353-9492	203-925-3040	178-1
Flexi-Van Leasing Inc 251 Monroe Ave ... Kenilworth NJ 07033	866-965-9288	908-276-8000	264-5
Flexmag Industries Inc 107 Industry Rd ... Marietta OH 45750	800-543-4426	740-374-8024	456
Flex-N-Gate Corp 1306 E University Ave ... Urbana IL 61802	800-398-1496		60
Flexo Impressions 8647 Eagle Creek Pkwy ... Savage MN 55378	800-752-2357	952-884-9442	623
Flexospan Steel Buildings Inc 253 Railroad St ... Sandy Lake PA 16145	800-245-0396		106
Flex-Pay Business Services Inc 723 Coliseum Dr Ste 200 ... Winston-Salem NC 27106	800-457-2143	336-773-0128	194
FlexPrint Inc 2845 N Omaha St ... Mesa AZ 85215	888-353-9774		585
FLEXSTAR Packaging Inc 13320 River Rd ... Richmond BC V6V1W7	800-663-1177	604-273-9277	597
Flexsys America LP 260 Springside Dr ... Akron OH 44333	800-455-5622	330-666-4111	672
Flextron Industries Inc 720 Mt Rd ... Aston PA 19014	800-633-2181	610-459-4600	544
Flex-Y-Plan Industries Inc 6960 W Ridge Rd ... Fairview PA 16415 *Cust Svc	800-458-0552*	814-474-1565	319-1
Flight Dimensions International Inc 4835 Cordell Ave Ste 150 ... Bethesda MD 20814	866-235-6870	301-634-8201	21
Flight Light Inc 2708 47th Ave ... Sacramento CA 95822	800-806-3548		63
Flight Systems Inc 505 Fishing Creek Rd ... Lewisberry PA 17339	800-403-3728	717-932-9900	247
FlightAware Eleven Greenway Plz Ste 2900 ... Houston TX 77046	800-713-8570	713-877-9010	19
Flightline Data Services Inc 138 Peachtree Ct ... Fayetteville GA 30215	800-659-9859	770-487-3482	225
Flightstar Corp 7 Airport Rd Willard Airport ... Savoy IL 61874	800-747-4777	217-351-7700	13
FLIK Conference Centers & Hotels 2 International Dr 2nd Fl ... Rye Brook NY 10573 *Resv	855-832-3545*	914-629-0542	
Flint & Walling Inc 95 N Oak St ... Kendallville IN 46755 *Sales	800-345-9422*		637
Flint Energies 3 S Macon St ... Reynolds GA 31076	800-342-3616	478-847-3415	245
Flint Institute of Arts 1120 E Kearsley St ... Flint MI 48503	800-222-7270	810-234-1695	517
Flint Machine Tools Inc 3710 Hewatt Ct ... Snellville GA 30039	800-984-2620	770-985-2626	357
Flint River Mills Inc 1100 Dothan Rd ... Bainbridge GA 39817	800-841-8502		445
Flint Surveying & Engineering Company Inc 5370 Miller Rd ... Swartz Creek MI 48473	800-624-6089	810-230-1333	261
Flintco LLC 1624 W 21st St ... Tulsa OK 74107	800-947-2828	918-587-8451	186
Flippen Group, The 1199 Haywood Dr ... College Station TX 77845	800-316-4311	979-693-7660	461
FLIR Systems Inc 27700-A SW Pkwy Ave ... Wilsonville OR 97070 *NASDAQ: FLIR*	877-773-3547	503-498-3547	525
Floe International Inc 48473 State Hwy 65 ... Mcgregor MN 55760	800-336-6337		
Flood & Peterson 2000 S Colorado Blvd Twr 1 4000 ... Denver CO 80222	800-356-2295	970-356-0123	
Floor Coverings International 5250 Triangle Pwy Ste 100 ... Norcross GA 30092 *Sales	800-955-4324*	770-874-7600	290
Flooring Sales Group 1251 First Ave S ... Seattle WA 98134	877-478-3577	206-624-7800	290
Florence Convention & Visitors Bureau 3290 W Radio Dr ... Florence SC 29501 *General	800-325-9005*	843-664-0330	206
Florence County 180 N Irby St ... Florence SC 29501	800-523-3577	843-665-3035	337
Florence Eiseman company LLC 1966 S Fourth St ... Milwaukee WI 53204	800-558-9013		155-4
Florence National Cemetery 803 E National Cemetery Rd ... Florence SC 29506	877-907-8585	843-669-8783	136
Florence-Darlington Technical College 2715 W Lucas St ... Florence SC 29502	800-228-5745	843-661-8324	795
Florentine Opera Co 700 N Water St Ste 950 ... Milwaukee WI 53202	800-326-7372	414-291-5700	569-2
Florestone Products Company Inc 2851 Falcon Dr ... Madera CA 93637	800-446-8827	559-661-4171	606
Florexpo LLC 1960 Kellogg Ave ... Carlsbad CA 92008	800-830-3567		704

Name / Address	Toll-Free	Phone	Class
Florida			
Attorney General State Capitol PL-01 ... Tallahassee FL 32399	866-966-7226	850-245-0140	338-10
Business & Professional Regulation Dept 2601 Blair Stone Rd ... Tallahassee FL 32399	866-532-1440	850-487-1395	338-10
Chief Financial Officer 200 E Gaines St ... Tallahassee FL 32399	877-693-5236	850-413-3089	338-10
Colleges & Universities Div 325 W Gaines St Ste 1414 ... Tallahassee FL 32399	888-224-6684	850-245-3200	338-10
Consumer Services Div 2005 Apalachee Pkwy ... Tallahassee FL 32399	800-435-7352		338-10
Education Dept 325 W Gaines St Ste 1514 ... Tallahassee FL 32399	800-445-6739	850-245-0505	338-10
Financial Services Dept 200 E Gaines St ... Tallahassee FL 32399	800-342-2762	850-413-3149	338-10
Insurance Regulation Office 200 E Gaines St ... Tallahassee FL 32399	800-342-2762	850-413-3140	338-10
Prepaid College Board PO Box 6567 ... Tallahassee FL 32314	800-552-4723		721
Public Service Commission 2540 Shumard Oak Blvd ... Tallahassee FL 32399	800-342-3552	850-413-6042	338-10
Recreation & Parks Div 3900 Commonwealth Blvd ... Tallahassee FL 32399 *Campground Resv	800-326-3521*	850-245-2157	338-10
Secretary of State RA Gray Bldg 500 S Bronough St ... Tallahassee FL 32399	800-955-8771	850-245-6500	338-10
Vocational Rehabilitation Services Div 4070 Esplanade Way ... Tallahassee FL 32399	800-451-4327	850-245-3399	338-10
Florida A & M University 1700 Lee Hall Dr ... Tallahassee FL 32307	866-642-1198	850-599-3000	166
Florida Academy of Family Physicians (FAFP) 13241 Bartram Pk Blvd Ste 1321 ... Jacksonville FL 32258	800-223-3237	904-726-0944	
Florida Aquarium 701 Channelside Dr ... Tampa FL 33602	800-353-4741	813-273-4000	40
Florida Assn of Realtors 7025 Augusta National Dr ... Orlando FL 32822	800-669-4327	407-438-1400	652
Florida Atlantic University (FAU) 777 Glades Rd ... Boca Raton FL 33431 *Admissions	800-299-4328*	561-297-3000	166
Davie 3200 College Ave ... Davie FL 33314	800-764-2222	954-236-1000	166
Treasure Coast 777 Glades Rd PO Box 3091 ... Boca Raton FL 33431	800-552-4723	772-873-3300	166
Florida Bar 651 E Jefferson St ... Tallahassee FL 32399	800-342-8060	850-561-5600	72
Florida Christian College 1011 Bill Beck Blvd ... Kissimmee FL 34744	888-468-6322	407-847-8966	161
Florida City Gas (FCG) 955 E 25th St ... Hialeah FL 33013	800-993-7546		782
Florida Coastal School of Law 8787 Bay Pine Rd ... Jacksonville FL 32256	877-210-2591	904-680-7700	167-1
Florida College 119 N Glen Arven Ave ... Temple Terrace FL 33617	800-326-7655	813-988-5131	166
Florida Community College at Jacksonville *Downtown* 101 State St W ... Jacksonville FL 32202	877-633-5950	904-633-8100	162
Florida Council Against Sexual Violence Inc 1820 E Park Ave Ste 100 ... Tallahassee FL 32301	888-956-7273	850-297-2000	41
Florida Dental Assn 1111 E Tennessee St ... Tallahassee FL 32308	800-877-9922	850-681-3629	227
Florida Family Insurance 27599 Riverview Ctr Blvd Ste 100 ... Bonita Springs FL 34134	888-850-4663	888-486-4663	390-4
Florida Farm Bureau Insurance Cos 5700 SW 34th St ... Gainesville FL 32608	866-275-7322	352-378-1321	390-4
Florida Grand Opera 8390 NW 25th St ... Miami FL 33122	800-741-1010	305-854-1643	569-2
Florida Handling Systems Inc 2651 State Rd 60 W ... Bartow FL 33830	800-664-3380	863-534-1212	357
Florida Hospital Heartland Medical Ctr 4200 Sun 'n Lake Blvd ... Sebring FL 33871	800-756-4447	863-314-4466	373-3
Florida Hospital North Pinellas 1395 S Pinellas Ave ... Tarpon Springs FL 34689	800-558-6365	727-942-5000	373-3
Florida Hospital Oceanside 264 S Atlantic Ave ... Ormond Beach FL 32176	800-558-6365	386-672-4161	373-3
Florida Hospital Zephyrhills 7050 Gall Blvd ... Zephyrhills FL 33541	800-558-6365	813-788-0411	373-3
Florida Institute of Technology 150 W University Blvd ... Melbourne FL 32901	800-888-4348	321-674-8000	166
Florida Keys Community College 5901 College Rd ... Key West FL 33040	866-567-2665	305-296-9081	162
Florida Keys Electric Co-op Assn 91630 Overseas Hwy ... Tavernier FL 33070	800-858-8845	305-852-2431	245
Florida Memorial University 15800 NW 42nd Ave ... Miami Gardens FL 33054	800-822-1362	305-626-3600	166
Florida Museum of Natural History 3215 Hull Rd ... Gainesville FL 32611	800-595-7760	352-392-1721	517
Florida National Cemetery 6502 SW 102nd Ave ... Bushnell FL 33513	877-907-8585	352-793-7740	136
Florida Newsclips LLC PO Box 2190 ... Palm Harbor FL 34682	800-442-0332		620
Florida Pneumatic Manufacturing Corp 851 Jupiter Pk Ln ... Jupiter FL 33458	800-327-9403	561-744-9500	754
Florida Power & Light Co (FPL) 700 Universe Blvd ... Juno Beach FL 33408	800-226-3545	561-691-7574	782
Florida Presbyterian Homes 16 Lake Hunter Dr ... Lakeland FL 33803	866-294-3352	863-688-5521	668
Florida Public Interest Research Group 3110 First Ave N Ste 2H ... St. Petersburg FL 33713	800-838-6554	727-431-9686	
Florida Public Utilities Co (FPUC) 401 S Dixie Hwy ... West Palm Beach FL 33401	800-427-7712		782
Florida Repertory Theatre Inc 2267 Bay St ... Fort Myers FL 33901	877-787-8053	239-332-4665	716
Florida Southern College 111 Lake Hollingsworth Dr ... Lakeland FL 33801 *Admissions	800-274-4131*	863-680-4131	166

	Toll-Free	Phone	Class
Florida State College at Jacksonville			
Kent 3939 Roosevelt Blvd ....Jacksonville FL 32205	800-700-2795	904-381-3400	162
South 11901 Beach Blvd ....Jacksonville FL 32246	800-700-2795	904-646-2111	162
Florida Surplus Lines Service Office 1441 Maclay Commerce Dr ....Tallahassee FL 32312	800-562-4496	850-224-7676	41
Florida Theatre 128 E Forsyth St Ste 300 ....Jacksonville FL 32202	800-734-4667	904-355-5661	568
Florida Tile Industries Inc 998 Governors Ln Ste 300 ....Lexington KY 40513 *Cust Svc	800-352-8453*	859-219-5200	746
Florida Times-Union 1 Riverside Ave ....Jacksonville FL 32202	800-472-6397	904-359-4111	528-2
Florida Venture Forum Inc, The 707 W Azeele St ....Tampa FL 33606	888-375-7136	813-335-8116	138
Floridagriculture Magazine PO Box 147030 ....Gainesville FL 32614	866-275-7322		
Florist Distributing Inc 2403 Bell Ave ....Des Moines IA 50321	800-373-3741	515-243-5228	293
Florsheim Inc 333 W Estabrook Blvd ....Glendale WI 53212	866-454-0449		301
Flournoy Development Co 900 Brookstone Ctr Pkwy ....Columbus GA 31904	888-801-3404	706-324-4000	649
Flow Dry Technology Inc 379 Albert Rd PO Box 190 ....Brookville OH 45309	800-533-0077	937-833-2161	326
Flow International Corp 23500 64th Ave S ....Kent WA 98032 *NASDAQ: FLOW*	800-446-3569	253-850-3500	453
Flower City Tissue Mills Inc 700 Driving Park Ave ....Rochester NY 14613	800-595-2030	585-458-9200	544
Flower Patch Inc 4370 S 300 W ....Murray UT 84107 *General	888-865-6858*	801-747-2824	292
Flower Pot Florists 2314 N Broadway St ....Knoxville TN 37917	800-824-7792	865-523-5121	292
Flowerbudcom PO Box 761 ....Lake Oswego OR 97034	877-524-5400		
Flowers Auto Parts Co 935 Hwy 70 SE ....Hickory NC 28602 *Cust Svc	800-538-6272*	828-322-5414	61
Flowers by Sleeman for All Seasons & Reasons Ltd 1201 Memorial Rd ....Houghton MI 49931	800-400-4023	906-482-4023	292
Flowerwood Garden Center Inc 7625 US Hwy 14 ....Crystal Lake IL 60012	800-643-5443	815-459-6200	323
Flow-Eze Co 3209 Auburn St ....Rockford IL 61101	800-435-4873	815-965-1062	683
Flowroute Inc 1218 Third Ave 600th Fl ....Seattle WA 98101	855-356-9768		
Flowserve Corp 5215 N O'Connor Blvd Ste 2300 ....Irving TX 75039 *NYSE: FLS*	800-543-3927	972-443-6500	637
Floyd Browne Group 3875 Embassy Pkwy ....Akron OH 44333 *General	800-362-2764*	330-375-0800	193
Floyd E Tut Fann State Veterans Home 2701 Meridian St ....Huntsville AL 35811	855-212-8028	256-851-2807	788
Floyd Medical Ctr 304 Turner McCall Blvd ....Rome GA 30165	866-874-2772	706-509-5000	373-3
Fluent 7319 104 St NW ....Edmonton AB T6E4B9	855-238-4826		689
Fluent Language Solutions Inc 8801 JM Keynes Dr Ste 400 ....Charlotte NC 28262	888-225-6056	704-532-7446	763
Fluid Components International 1755 La Costa Meadows Dr ....San Marcos CA 92078	800-863-8703	760-744-6950	201
Fluid Management Inc 1023 S Wheeling Rd ....Wheeling IL 60090	800-462-2466	847-537-0880	385
Fluid Metering Inc 5 Aerial Way Ste 500 ....Syosset NY 11791	800-223-3388	516-922-6050	636
Fluidmaster Inc 30800 Rancho Viejo Rd ....San Juan Capistrano CA 92675	800-631-2011	949-728-2000	605
Fluidware 12 York St 2nd Fl ....Ottawa ON K1N5S6	866-218-5127		386
Fluke Biomedical 6920 Seaway Blvd ....Everett WA 98203	800-443-5853	425-446-6945	248
Fluke Corp 6920 Seaway Blvd ....Everett WA 98203	877-355-3225	425-446-6100	248
Fluke Corp 6920 Seaway Blvd ....Everett WA 98203	800-903-5853	425-347-6100	
Fluke Networks Inc 6920 Seaway Blvd ....Everett WA 98203	800-283-5853	425-446-4519	248
Flushing Financial Corp 1979 Marcus Ave ....New Hyde Park NY 11042 *NASDAQ: FFIC*	800-581-2889	718-961-5400	359-2
Fluvanna County 132 Main St ....Palmyra VA 22963	800-814-5339	434-591-1910	337
FlyData Inc 1043 N Shoreline Blvd Ste 200 ....Mountain View CA 94043	855-427-9787		620
FlyerCom 201 Kelsey Ln ....Tampa FL 33619	800-995-4433		633-10
Flying E Ranch 2801 W Wickenburg Way ....Wickenburg AZ 85390	888-684-2650	928-684-2690	239
Flying Magazine 460 N Orlando Ave Ste 200 ....Winter Park FL 32789 *Cust Svc	800-678-0797*	407-628-4802	455-14
F&M Bank 50 Franklin St ....Clarksville TN 37040	800-645-4199	931-906-0005	70
FM Brown's Sons Inc 205 Woodrow Ave PO Box 2116 ....Sinking Spring PA 19608	800-334-8816		445
F&M Expressions Inc 211 Island Rd ....Mahwah NJ 07430	888-788-7133		
FM Global 270 Central Ave PO Box 7500 ....Johnston RI 02919	800-343-7722	401-275-3000	390-4
F&M Mafco Inc PO Box 11013 ....Cincinnati OH 45211	800-333-2151	513-367-2151	190
FMA (Fabricators & Manufacturers Assn International) 833 Featherstone Rd ....Rockford IL 61107	888-394-4362	815-399-8700	49-13
FMA Alliance Ltd 80 Garden Ctr Ste 3 ....Broomfield CO 80020	800-955-5598	281-931-5050	160
FMC (Foothills Medical Centre) 1403 29th St NW ....Calgary AB T2N2T9	888-342-2471	780-342-2000	373-2
FMC (Fairfield Medical Ctr) 401 N Ewing St ....Lancaster OH 43130	800-548-2627	740-687-8000	373-3
FMC Corp 2929 Walnut St ....Philadelphia PA 19104 *NYSE: FMC*	888-548-4486	215-299-6000	143
FMC Ice Sports 100 Schoosett St Bldg 3 ....Pembroke MA 02359	888-747-5283	781-826-3085	713
FMCA (Family Motor Coach Assn) 8291 Clough Pk ....Cincinnati OH 45244	800-543-3622	513-474-3622	48-23
FMCI (Grassley Group, The) 600 State St Ste A ....Cedar Falls IA 50613	866-619-5580		47
FMCSA (Federal Motor Carrier Safety Administration) 1200 New Jersey Ave SE ....Washington DC 20590	800-832-5660		339-16
FMG Enterprises Inc 1125 Memorex Dr ....Santa Clara CA 95050	800-327-6177	408-982-0110	637
FMI (Food Marketing Institute) 2345 Crystal Dr Ste 800 ....Arlington VA 22202	800-732-2639	202-452-8444	49-18
FMR Corp 82 Devonshire St ....Boston MA 02109	800-343-3548		400
FMS (Financial Managers Society) 100 W Monroe St Ste 810 ....Chicago IL 60603 *Cust Svc	800-275-4367*	312-578-1300	49-2
FMS Inc 8150 Leesburg Pk Ste 600 ....Vienna VA 22182	866-367-7801	703-356-4700	178-2
FNBB (First National Bankers Bankshares Inc) 7813 Office Pk Blvd ....Baton Rouge LA 70809	800-421-6182	225-924-8015	70
FNUniv (First Nations University of Canada) *Saskatoon* 229 Fourth Ave S ....Saskatoon SK S7K4K3	800-267-6303	306-931-1800	780
FOA (Friends of Animals Inc) 777 Post Rd Ste 205 ....Darien CT 06820	800-321-7387	203-656-1522	48-3
Foam Fabricators Inc 950 Progress Blvd ....New Albany IN 47150	800-626-1197	812-948-1696	597
Foam Molders & Specialty Corp 20004 State Rd ....Cerritos CA 90703	800-378-8987		597
Focus Camera Inc 905 McDonald Ave ....Brooklyn NY 11218	800-221-0828		119
Focus Direct LLC 9707 Broadway ....San Antonio TX 78217	800-555-1551	210-805-9185	5
Focus Logistics Inc 1311 Howard Dr ....West Chicago IL 60185	877-924-3600	630-231-8200	314
Focus on the Family 8605 Explorer Dr ....Colorado Springs CO 80920 *Sales	800-232-6459*	719-531-3400	48-6
FocusCFO 1010 Jackson Hole Dr Ste 202 ....Columbus OH 43004	855-236-0600		461
FocusVision Worldwide Inc 1266 E Main St ....Stamford CT 06902	800-433-8128	203-961-1715	386
Fogarty Creek State Recreation Area US-101 ....Depoe Bay OR 97341	800-452-5687	800-551-6949	561
FOI Services Inc 704 Quince OrchaRd Rd Ste 275 ....Gaithersburg MD 20878	800-654-1147	301-975-9400	386
FOIA Group Inc (FGI) 1250 Connecticut Ave NW Ste 200 ....Washington DC 20036	888-461-7951	716-608-0800	386
Foley Carrier Services LLC 140 Huyshope Ave ....Hartford CT 06106	800-253-5506		461
Foley Equipment 1550 SW St ....Wichita KS 67213	877-761-9027		357
Foley House Inn 14 West Hull St ....Savannah GA 31401	800-647-3708		378
Foley Inc 855 Centennial Ave ....Piscataway NJ 08854	888-417-6464	732-885-5555	62-7
Folk Art Ctr PO Box 9545 ....Asheville NC 28815	888-672-7717	828-298-7928	517
Follett Corp 1340 Ridgeview Dr ....McHenry IL 60050	877-899-8550	815-759-1700	96
Follett Corp 3 Westbrook Corporate Ctr Ste 200 ....Westchester IL 60154	800-365-5388	708-884-0000	96
Follett Corp 801 Church Ln ....Easton PA 18040 *Cust Svc	800-523-9361*	610-252-7301	660
Follett Higher Education Group 3 Westbrook Corporate Ctr ....Westchester IL 60154	800-323-4506		95
Foltz Concrete Pipe Co LLC 11875 N NC Hwy 150 ....Winston-Salem NC 27127	800-229-8525		183
Fond du Lac Area Assn of Commerce 235 N National Ave ....Fond du Lac WI 54935	800-279-8811	920-921-9500	139
Fond du Lac Band of Lake Superior Chippewa 1720 Big Lake Rd ....Cloquet MN 55720	888-888-6007	218-879-4593	132
Fond du Lac Convention & Visitors Bureau 171 S Pioneer Rd ....Fond du Lac WI 54935	800-937-9123	920-923-3010	206
Fond du Lac Tribal & Community College 2101 14th St ....Cloquet MN 55720	800-657-3712	218-879-0800	165
Fondaction Bureau 501 125 boul Charest Est ....Montreal QC H2K4S3	800-253-6665	514-525-5505	524
Fonds de solidarite FTQ 545 Cremazie Blvd E Ofc 200 ....Montreal QC H2M2W4	800-567-3663		
FONEX Data Systems Inc 5400 Ch St-Francois ....St-Laurent QC H4S1P6	800-363-6639	514-333-6639	
Fontaine Fifth Wheel 7574 Commerce Cir ....Trussville AL 35173	800-874-9780	205-847-3250	60
Fontaine Modification 9827 Mt Holly Rd ....Charlotte NC 28214	800-366-8246	704-391-1355	513
Fontaine Trailer Co 430 Letson Rd PO Box 619 ....Haleyville AL 35565	800-821-6535	205-486-5251	774
Fontaine Truck Equipment Co 7574 Commerce Cir ....Trussville AL 35173	800-874-9780	205-661-4900	513
Fontainebleau Miami Beach 4441 Collins Ave ....Miami Beach FL 33140	800-548-8886		665
Fontainebleau State Park 67825 US Hwy 190 ....Mandeville LA 70448	888-677-3668	985-624-4443	561

Company	Location	Toll-Free	Phone	Class
Fontana Village Resort 300 Woods Rd PO Box 68	Fontana Dam NC 28733	800-849-2258	828-498-2211	665
Food & Drug Administration (FDA) 5600 Fishers Ln	Rockville MD 20857	888-463-6332	301-827-2410	339-9
Center for Devices & Radiological Health (CDRH) 10903 New Hampshire Ave	Silver Spring MD 20993	800-638-2041	301-796-7100	339-9
CFSAN 5100 Paint Branch Pkwy	College Park MD 20740	888-723-3366		339-9
Food & Drug Law Institute (FDLI) 1155 15th St NW Ste 910	Washington DC 20005	800-956-6293	202-371-1420	49-10
Food & Water Watch 1616 P St NW Ste 300	Washington DC 20036	855-340-8083	202-683-2500	305
Food & Wine Magazine 1120 Sixth Ave Ste 9	New York NY 10036	800-333-6569	813-979-6625	455-11
Food Allergy & Anaphylaxis Network (FAAN) 11781 Lee Jackson Hwy Ste 160	Fairfax VA 22033	800-929-4040	703-691-3179	48-17
Food City 1005 N Arizona Ave	Chandler AZ 85224	800-755-7292	480-857-2198	344
Food Consulting Co, The 13724 Recuerdo Dr	Del Mar CA 92014	800-793-2844	858-793-4658	471
Food for the Poor Inc (FFP) 6401 Lyons Rd	Coconut Creek FL 33073	800-427-9104	954-427-2222	48-5
Food Marketing Institute (FMI) 2345 Crystal Dr Ste 800	Arlington VA 22202	800-732-2639	202-452-8444	49-18
Food Services of America Inc 16100 N 71st St Ste 400	Scottsdale AZ 85254	800-528-9346	480-927-4000	297-8
Food Warming Equipment Company Inc 1540 Carlemont Dr Ste A *Sales	Crystal Lake IL 60014	800-222-4393*	815-459-7500	298
Foodbank of Southeastern Virginia & the Eastern Shore 800 Tidewater Dr	Norfolk VA 23504	877-486-4379	757-627-6599	
FoodChek Systems Inc 1414 8 St SW Ste 450	Calgary AB T2R1J6	877-298-0208	403-269-9424	406
Foodscience Corp 20 New England Dr Ste 10	Essex Junction VT 05452	800-451-5190	802-878-5508	794
Foot Locker Inc 112 W 34th St *NYSE: FL	New York NY 10120	800-952-5210	212-720-3700	301
Foot of the Mountain Motel 200 W Arapahoe Ave	Boulder CO 80302	866-773-5489	303-442-5688	378
Foot Solutions 4101 Roswell Rd	Marietta GA 30062	866-338-2597		
Foothill College 12345 El Monte Rd	Los Altos Hills CA 94022	800-234-1597	650-949-7777	162
Foothills Asset Management Ltd 8767 E Via de Ventura Ste 175	Scottsdale AZ 85258	800-663-9870	480-777-9870	400
Foothills Inn 1625 N La Crosse St	Rapid City SD 57701	877-428-5666	605-348-5640	378
Foothills Medical Centre (FMC) 1403 29th St NW	Calgary AB T2N2T9	888-342-2471	780-342-2000	373-2
Footlockercom Inc 112 W 34th St	New York NY 10120	800-863-8932	715-261-9719	301
FOP (Fraternal Order of Police) 701 Marriott Dr	Nashville TN 37214	800-451-2711	615-399-0900	48-15
Forbes Hospice 4800 Friendship Ave	Pittsburgh PA 15224	800-381-8080	412-578-5000	370
Forbes Inc 60 Fifth Ave	New York NY 10011	800-295-0893	212-620-2200	633-9
Forbes Magazine 60 Fifth Ave	New York NY 10011	800-295-0893		455-5
Forbes Snyder Tristate Cash 54 Northampton St	Easthampton MA 01027	800-222-4064	413-529-2950	253
Forbo Flooring North America 8 Maplewood Dr Humboldt Industrial Pk	Hazleton PA 18202	800-842-7839		131
Forbo Flooring Systems 8 Maplewood Dr Humboldt Industrial Pk *Cust Svc	Hazleton PA 18202	800-842-7839*		291
Force 3 Inc 2151 Priest Bridge Dr	Crofton MD 21114	800-391-0204		180
FORCE America Inc 501 E Cliff Rd	Burnsville MN 55337	800-328-2732	952-707-1300	357
Force Control Industries Inc 3660 Dixie Hwy	Fairfield OH 45014	800-829-3244	513-868-0900	616
Force Flow Inc 2430 Stanwell Dr	Concord CA 94520	800-893-6723		361
Force10 Networks Inc 1415 N McDowell Blvd	Petaluma CA 94954	866-600-5100	707-665-4400	677
Ford Audio-Video Systems Inc 4800 W I- 40	Oklahoma City OK 73128	800-654-6744	405-946-9966	52
Ford Equity Research Inc 11722 Sorrento Valley Rd Ste I	San Diego CA 92121	800-842-0207	858-755-1327	400
Ford Fasteners Inc 110 S Newman St	Hackensack NJ 07601	800-272-3673	201-487-3151	278
Ford Hotel Supply Company Inc 2204 N Broadway	Saint Louis MO 63102	800-472-3673	314-231-8400	703
Ford Motor Co PO Box 6248 *NYSE: F	Dearborn MI 48126	800-392-3673	313-845-8540	59
Ford Motor Credit Co 1 American Rd	Dearborn MI 48126	800-727-7000	313-322-3000	217
Ford of Montebello Inc 2747 Via Campo	Montebello CA 90640	888-313-2305	323-358-2880	57
Ford of Ocala Inc 2816 NW Pine Ave	Ocala FL 34475	888-255-1788	352-732-4800	513
FordDirect 1740 US Hwy 60 PO Box 700	Republic MO 65738	888-578-8478	417-732-2626	57
Fordham Auto Sales Inc 236 N Fordham Rd	Bronx NY 10468	800-407-1153		57
Fordham Plastics 1204 Village Market Pl Ste 262	Morrisville NC 27560	866-467-0708	919-467-0708	319-3
Fordham University 441 E Fordham Rd	Bronx NY 10458	800-367-3426	718-817-3240	166
College at Lincoln Ctr 113 W 60th St	New York NY 10023	800-367-3426	212-636-6000	166
Westchester 400 Westchester Ave	West Harrison NY 10604	800-606-6090	914-367-3426	166
Fordia Inc 2745 de Miniac Ville Saint Laurent	Saint Laurent QC H4S1E5	800-768-7274	514-336-9211	357
Forecast International 22 Commerce Rd	Newtown CT 06470	800-451-4975	203-426-0800	633-10
Foreign Affairs 58 E 68th St *Cust Svc	New York NY 10065	800-829-5539*	212-434-9527	455-17
Foreign Policy Assn (FPA) 470 Park Ave S	New York NY 10016	800-628-5754	212-481-8100	48-7
Foremost Farms USA E10889A Penny Ln	Baraboo WI 53913	800-362-9196	608-355-8700	296-10
Foremost Insurance Co 5600 Beech Tree Ln	Caledonia MI 49316	800-532-4221		390-4
Foremostco Inc 8457 NW 66th St	Miami FL 33166	800-421-8986	305-592-8986	690
Forest at Duke 2701 Pickett Rd	Durham NC 27705	800-474-0258		668
Forest City Trading Group LLC 10250 SW Greenburg Rd Ste 300	Portland OR 97223	800-767-3284	503-246-8500	191-3
Forest Landowners Assn (FLA) 950 Glenn Dr Ste 150	Folsom CA 95630	800-325-2954	404-325-2954	48-13
Forest Lawn Memorial-Parks & Mortuaries 1712 S Glendale Ave	Glendale CA 91205	800-204-3131	323-254-3131	508
Forest Preserve Dist of Dupage County 1717 31st St	Oak Brook IL 60523	800-526-0857	630-616-8424	226
Forest Service (USFS) 1400 Independence Ave SW	Washington DC 20050	800-832-1355	202-205-8333	339-1
Forest Service Regional Offices *Region 8 (Southern Region)* 1720 Peachtree Rd NW	Atlanta GA 30309	877-372-7248	414-297-3600	339-1
Forest Travel 2440 NE Miami Gardens Dr Ste 107	Miami FL 33180	800-432-2132	305-932-5560	
Forestry Suppliers Inc 205 W Rankin St *Cust Svc	Jackson MS 39201	800-752-8460*	601-354-3565	457
Forestville/Mystery Cave State Park 21071 County 118	Preston MN 55965	888-646-6367	507-352-5111	561
Foretravel Motorcoach Inc 1221 NW Stallings Dr	Nacogdoches TX 75964	800-955-6226	936-564-8367	120
Forever 21 Inc 2001 S Alameda St *Cust Svc	Los Angeles CA 90058	800-966-1355*	213-741-5100	157-6
Forever Living Products International Inc 7501 E McCormick Pkwy	Scottsdale AZ 85258	888-440-2563	480-998-8888	214
Forever Spring 2629 E Craig Rd Ste E	Las Vegas NV 89030	800-523-4334	702-633-4283	238
Forex Newscom 55 Water St 50th Fl	New York NY 10041	888-503-6739		386
Forged Products Inc (FPI) 6505 N Houston Rosslyn Rd	Houston TX 77091	800-876-3416	713-462-3416	481
Forkardt 2155 Traverse Field Dr	Traverse City MI 49686	800-544-3823	231-995-8300	491
Forked Deer Electric Co-op PO Box 67	Halls TN 38040	844-333-2729	731-836-7508	245
Forklifts of Minnesota Inc 2201 W 94th St	Bloomington MN 55431	800-752-4300	952-887-5400	384
Form-A-Feed Inc (FAF) 740 Bowman St	Stewart MN 55385	800-422-3649	320-562-2413	445
Formaggio Kitchen on Line LLC 244 Huron Ave	Cambridge MA 02138	888-212-3224	617-354-4750	292
Formall Inc 3908 Fountain Vly Dr	Knoxville TN 37918	800-643-3676	865-259-6298	598
Formax Manufacturing Corp 168 Wealthy St SW	Grand Rapids MI 49503	800-242-2833	616-456-5458	1
Former Governors' Mansion State Historic Site 612 E Blvd Ave	Bismarck ND 58505	866-243-5352	701-328-2666	561
Formetco Inc 2963 Pleasant Hill Rd	Duluth GA 30096	800-367-6382	770-476-7000	697
Formflex Inc PO Box 218	Bloomingdale IN 47832	800-255-7659		86
Formica Corp 10155 Reading Rd	Cincinnati OH 45241	800-367-6422	513-786-3400	595
Formosa Plastics Corp USA 9 Peach Tree Hill Rd	Livingston NJ 07039	888-664-4040	973-992-2090	601-2
Forms Manufacturers Inc 312 E Forest Ave	Girard KS 66743	800-835-0614		110
Formsprag Clutch Inc 23601 Hoover Rd	Warren MI 48089	800-348-0881		
Formtek Metal Forming Inc 4899 Commerce Pkwy	Cleveland OH 44128	800-631-0520	216-292-4460	670
Forney Corp 16479 N Dallas Pkwy Ste 600 *Cust Svc	Addison TX 75001	800-356-7740*	972-458-6100	201
FORNEY LLC 2050 Jackson's Pointe Ct	Zelienople PA 16063	800-367-6397	724-346-7400	
Forrest General Hospital 6051 US Hwy 49	Hattiesburg MS 39402	800-503-5980	601-288-7000	373-3
Forrest Hills Mountain Resort & Conference Ctr 135 Forrest Hills Rd	Dahlonega GA 30533	800-654-6313	706-864-6456	665
ForSaleByOwnercom Llc 701 Griswold	Detroit MI 48226	888-367-7253		
Forsbergs Inc 1210 Pennington Ave PO Box 510 *Cust Svc	Thief River Falls MN 56701	800-654-1927*	218-681-1927	273
Forsyth County Public Library 201 North Chestnut St	Winston-Salem NC 27101	866-345-1884	336-703-2665	433-3
Fort Atkinson Memorial Hospital 611 Sherman Ave E	Fort Atkinson WI 53538	800-844-5575	920-568-5000	373-3
Fort Casey State Park 1280 S Engle Rd	Coupeville WA 98239	888-226-7688	360-678-4519	
Fort Caspar Museum 4001 Fort Caspar Rd	Casper WY 82604	800-877-7353	307-235-8400	517
Fort Cobb Lake State Park 27022 Copperhead Rd	Fort Cobb OK 73038	800-622-6317	405-643-2249	561

	Toll-Free	Phone	Class
Fort Collins Area Chamber of Commerce			
225 S Meldrum St .... Fort Collins CO 80521	877-652-8607	970-482-3746	139
Fort Collins Convention & Visitors Bureau			
19 Old Town Sq Ste 137 .... Fort Collins CO 80524	800-274-3678	970-232-3840	206
Fort Detrick			
810 Schreider St .... Frederick MD 21702	800-256-7621	301-619-7613	495-2
Fort Edward Express Company Inc			
1402 Rt 9 .... Fort Edward NY 12828	800-342-1233	518-792-6571	775
Fort Erie Race Track			
230 Catherine St PO Box 1130 .... Fort Erie ON L2A5N9	800-295-3770	905-871-3200	638
Fort Garry, The			
222 Broadway .... Winnipeg MB R3C0R3	800-665-8088	204-942-8251	378
Fort Hays State University			
600 Park St .... Hays KS 67601	800-628-3478*	785-628-4000	166
*Admissions			
Fort Henry National Historic Site			
PO Box 213 .... Kingston ON K7L4V8	800-437-2233*	613-542-7388	517
*Cust Svc			
Fort Hill The John C Calhoun House			
Clemson University .... Clemson SC 29634	800-777-1004	864-656-3311	50-3
Fort Jesup State Historic Site			
32 Geoghagan Rd .... Many LA 71449	888-677-5378	318-256-4117	561
Fort Kent State Historic Site			
106 Hogan Rd .... Bangor ME 04401	800-332-1501	207-941-4014	561
Fort Knox Federal Credit Union			
PO Box 900 .... Radcliff KY 40159	800-756-3678	502-942-0254	219
Fort Lauderdale Behavioral Health Center			
5757 N Dixie Hwy .... Oakland Park FL 33334	800-585-7527	954-734-2000	373-5
Fort Lauderdale Executive Airport			
5101 NW 21st Ave .... Fort Lauderdale FL 33309	800-955-8770	954-828-4955	27
Fort Lauderdale/Hollywood International Airport			
100 Aviation Blvd .... Fort Lauderdale FL 33315	866-682-2258	954-359-1200	27
Fort Lewis College			
1000 Rim Dr .... Durango CO 81301	877-352-2656	970-247-7010	166
Fort McAllister State Historic Park			
3894 Ft McAllister Rd .... Richmond Hill GA 31324	800-864-7275	912-727-2339	561
Fort McDowell Casino			
10424 N Ft McDowell Rd .... Fort Mcdowell AZ 85264	800-843-3678		133
Fort McHenry National Monument & Historic Shrine			
2400 E Fort Ave .... Baltimore MD 21230	866-945-7920	410-962-4290	517
Fort Meigs State Memorial			
29100 W River Rd .... Perrysburg OH 43551	800-283-8916	419-874-4121	50-3
Fort Morgan Area Chamber of Commerce			
300 Main St .... Fort Morgan CO 80701	800-354-8660	970-867-6702	139
Fort Mountain State Park			
181 Ft Mtn Pk Rd .... Chatsworth GA 30705	800-864-7275	706-422-1932	
Fort Ridgely State Park			
72158 County Rd 30 .... Fairfax MN 55332	888-646-6367	507-426-7840	561
Fort Rock State Natural Area			
725 Summer St NE Ste C .... Salem OR 97301	800-551-6949		561
Fort Saint Jean Baptiste State Historic Site			
155 Jefferson St .... Natchitoches LA 71457	888-677-7853	318-357-3101	561
Fort Scott Community College			
2108 S Horton St .... Fort Scott KS 66701	800-874-3722	620-223-2700	162
Fort Smith Convention & Visitors Bureau			
2 N 'B' .... Fort Smith AR 72901	800-637-1477	479-783-8888	206
Fort Smith National Cemetery			
522 Garland Ave .... Fort Smith AR 72901	800-535-1117	479-783-5345	136
Fort Smith Regional Airport			
6700 McKennon Blvd Ste 200 .... Fort Smith AR 72903	800-992-7433	479-452-7000	27
Fort Snelling State Park			
101 Snelling Lake Rd .... Saint Paul MN 55111	888-646-6367	612-279-3550	561
Fort Valley State University			
1005 State University Dr .... Fort Valley GA 31030	877-462-3878	478-825-6211	166
Fort Washington Investment Advisors Inc			
303 Broadway Ste 1200 .... Cincinnati OH 45202	888-244-8167	513-361-7600	400
Fort Wayne Newspapers Inc			
600 W Main St .... Fort Wayne IN 46802	800-444-3303	260-461-8444	633-8
Fort Wayne/Allen County Convention & Visitors Bureau			
927 S Harrison St .... Fort Wayne IN 46802	800-767-7752	260-424-3700	206
Fort William Henry Corp, The			
48 Canada St .... Lake George NY 12845	800-234-0267	518-668-3081	377
Fort Worth Chamber of Commerce			
777 Taylor St Ste 900 .... Fort Worth TX 76102	800-433-5747	817-336-2491	139
Fort Worth City Credit Union			
PO Box 100099 .... Fort Worth TX 76185	888-732-3085	817-732-2803	219
Fort Worth Community Credit Union			
1905 Forest Ridge Dr			
PO Box 210848. .... Bedford TX 76021	800-817-8234	817-835-5000	219
Fort Worth Convention & Visitors Bureau			
111 W Fourth St Ste 200 .... Fort Worth TX 76102	800-433-5747	817-336-8791	206
Fort Worth Convention Ctr			
200 Texas St .... Fort Worth TX 76102	866-630-2588	800-433-5747	205
Fort Worth Museum of Science & History			
1600 Gendy St .... Fort Worth TX 76107	888-255-9300	817-255-9300	517
Fort Worth Opera			
1300 Gendy St .... Fort Worth TX 76107	877-396-7372	817-731-0833	569-2
Fort Worth Public Library			
200 Texas St .... Fort Worth TX 76102	800-433-5747		
Forte Data Systems Inc			
3330 Paddock Pkwy .... Suwanee GA 30024	800-571-8702	678-208-0206	225
Forth Inc			
6080 Ctr Dr Ste 600 .... Los Angeles CA 90045	800-553-6784	310-999-6784	178-2
Fortifiber Building Systems Group			
300 Industrial Dr .... Fernley NV 89408	800-773-4777	775-333-6400	548-1
Fortin Consulting Inc			
215 Hamel Rd .... Hamel MN 55340	844-273-3117	763-478-3606	196
Fortrend Engineering			
2220 O'Toole Ave .... San Jose CA 95131	888-937-3637	408-734-9311	691
Fortress Technology Inc			
51 Grand Marshall Dr .... Toronto ON M1B5N6	888-220-8737	416-754-2898	688
Fortun Insurance Agency Inc			
365 Palermo Ave .... Coral Gables FL 33134	877-643-2055	305-445-3535	389
Fortune Bay Resort & Casino			
1430 Bois Forte Rd .... Tower MN 55790	800-992-7529	218-753-6400	450
Fortune Brands Inc			
520 Lake Cook Rd .... Deerfield IL 60015	800-225-2719	847-484-4400	185
NYSE: FBHS			
Fortune Contract Inc			
272 Kraft Dr .... Dalton GA 30721	800-359-4508		
Fortune Practice Management			
1265 El Camino Real Ste 205 .... Santa Clara CA 95050	800-628-1052		461
Forum Publishing Co			
383 E Main St .... Centerport NY 11721	800-635-7654	631-754-5000	633-9
Forum, The			
101 N Fifth St .... Fargo ND 58102	800-274-5445	701-235-7311	528-2
Forward Air Corp			
1915 Snapps Ferry Rd Bldg N .... Greeneville TN 37745	800-726-6654	423-636-3380	775
NASDAQ: FWRD			
Forward Corp			
219 N Front St .... Standish MI 48658	800-664-4501	989-846-4501	324
Forward Technology Inc			
260 Jenks Ave .... Cokato MN 55321	800-307-6040*	320-286-2578	385
*Cust Svc			
Foss Maritime Co			
1151 Fairview Ave N .... Seattle WA 98109	800-426-2885	206-281-3800	463
Foss National Leasing			
125 Commerce Valley Dr W			
Ste 801 .... Markham ON L3T7W4	800-461-3677	905-886-4244	126
Foster Blue Water Oil LLC			
36065 Water St .... Richmond MI 48062	800-426-3800	586-727-3996	
Foster Construction Products Inc			
1105 S Frontenac Rd .... Aurora IL 60504	800-231-9541		3
Foster Farms Inc			
PO Box 306 .... Livingston CA 95334	800-255-7227		10-7
Foster Fuels Inc			
16720 Brookneal Hwy .... Brookneal VA 24528	800-344-6457	434-376-2322	575
Foster Grandparent Program c/o Senior Corps			
1201 New York Ave NW .... Washington DC 20525	800-942-2677	202-606-5000	197
Foster Thomas Inc			
1788 Forest Dr .... Annapolis MD 21401	800-372-3626		390-3
Foster Townsend LLP			
150 Dufferin Ave .... London ON N6A5N6	888-354-0448	519-672-5272	427
Fotoprint			
975 Pandora Ave .... Victoria BC V8V3P4	888-382-8211	250-382-8218	623
Foulkeways at Gwynedd			
1120 Meetinghouse Rd .... Gwynedd PA 19436	800-211-2713	215-643-2200	668
Foundation Constructors Inc			
81 Big Break Rd .... Oakley CA 94561	800-841-8740	925-754-6633	189-5
Foundation Ctr			
32 Old Slip 24th Fl .... New York NY 10005	800-424-9836	212-620-4230	48-11
Foundation Fighting Blindness			
11435 Cron Hill Dr .... Owings Mills MD 21117	800-683-5555	410-568-0150	48-17
Foundation for Acctg Education (FAE)			
14 Wall St 19th Fl .... New York NY 10005	800-537-3635*	212-719-8300	49-1
*General			
Foundation for Economic Education (FEE)			
1819 Peachtree Rd NE Ste 300 .... Atlanta GA 30309	800-960-4333	404-554-9980	630
Foundation for International Community Assistance (FINCA)			
1201 15th St NW 8th fl............. Washington DC 20005	855-903-4622	202-682-1510	48-5
Foundation for the Carolinas			
217 S Tryon St .... Charlotte NC 28202	800-973-7244	704-973-4500	303
Foundation Laboratory			
1716 W Holt Ave .... Pomona CA 91768	800-843-7190	909-623-9301	414
Foundation Technologies Inc			
1400 Progress Industrial Blvd			
.... Lawrenceville GA 30043	800-773-2368	678-407-4640	191-1
Founders Financial Inc			
1020 Cromwell Bridge Rd .... Towson MD 21286	800-288-3035	410-308-9988	791
Founders Inn			
5641 Indian River Rd .... Virginia Beach VA 23464	800-926-4466	757-424-5511	376
Fountain County			
301 Fourth St .... Covington IN 47932	800-800-5556	765-793-2411	337
Fountain Grove Inn, The			
101 Fountaingrove Pkwy ....Santa Rosa CA 95403	800-222-6101	707-578-6101	377
Fountain Industries Co			
922 E 14th St .... Albert Lea MN 56007	800-328-3594	507-373-2351	111
Fountain Valley Regional Hospital & Medical Ctr			
17100 Euclid St .... Fountain Valley CA 92708	866-904-6871	714-966-7200	373-3
Fountainhead College of Technology			
3203 Tazewell Pk .... Knoxville TN 37918	888-218-7335	865-688-9422	795
Fountainhead Group Inc			
23 Garden St .... New York Mills NY 13417	800-311-9903	315-736-0037	172
Four County Electric Membership Corp			
1822 NC Hwy 53 W PO Box 667 .... Burgaw NC 28425	888-368-7289	910-259-2171	245
Four Flags Area Chamber of Commerce			
321 E Main St .... Niles MI 49120	800-719-2188	269-683-3720	139
Four Points by Sheraton Charlotte			
315 E Woodlawn Rd .... Charlotte NC 28217	800-368-7764	704-522-0852	378
Four Points by Sheraton French Quarter			
541 Bourbon St .... New Orleans LA 70130	866-716-8133	504-524-7611	378
Four Queens Hotel & Casino			
202 Fremont St .... Las Vegas NV 89101	800-634-6045	702-385-4011	378
Four Sails Resort Hotel			
3301 Atlantic Ave .... Virginia Beach VA 23451	800-227-4213	757-491-8100	378
Four Seasons Hospice & Palliative Care			
571 S Allen Rd .... Flat Rock NC 28731	866-466-9734	828-692-6178	370
Four Seasons Hotels & Resorts			
1165 Leslie St .... Toronto ON M3C2K8	800-332-3442	416-449-1750	748
Four Seasons Hotels Inc			
1165 Leslie St .... Toronto ON M3C2K8	800-332-3442	416-449-1750	378
Four Seasons Hotels Ltd			
2800 Pennsylvania Ave NW .... Washington DC 20007	800-819-5053	202-342-0444	703
Four Seasons Inc			
1801 Waters Ridge Dr ....Lewisville TX 75057	888-505-4567	972-316-8100	608
Four Seasons Resort & Club Dallas at Las Colinas			
4150 N MacArthur Blvd .... Irving TX 75038	800-332-3442	972-717-0700	665
Four Seasons Resort Hualalai			
100 Ka'upulehu Dr .... Kailua-Kona HI 96740	888-340-5662	808-325-8000	665
Four Seasons Resort Maui			
Four Seasons Spa			
3900 Wailea Alanui Dr .... Maui HI 96753	800-334-6284	808-874-8000	703
Four Seasons Resort Maui at Wailea			
3900 Wailea Alanui Dr .... Wailea HI 96753	800-334-6284	808-874-8000	665
Four Seasons Resort Palm Beach			
2800 S Ocean Blvd .... Palm Beach FL 33480	800-432-2335	561-582-2800	665

	Toll-Free	Phone	Class

Four Seasons Resort Santa Barbara
1260 Ch Dr .... Santa Barbara CA 93108 — 800-819-5053 — 805-969-2261 — 665

Four Seasons Resort Scottsdale at Troon North
10600 E Crescent Moon Dr .... Scottsdale AZ 85262 — 800-332-3442 — 480-513-5145 — 665

Four Seasons Solar Products LLC
5005 Veterans Memorial Hwy .... Holbrook NY 11741 — 800-368-7732 — 631-563-4000 — 105

Four Seasons Spa at the Four Seasons Hotel Las Vegas
3960 Las Vegas Blvd S .... Las Vegas NV 89119 — 800-332-3442 — 702-632-5302 — 703

Four Seasons Spa at the Four Seasons Hotel Los Angeles at Beverly Hills
300 S Doheny Dr ....Los Angeles CA 90048 — 800-819-5053 — 310-786-2229 — 703

Four Seasons Spa at the Four Seasons Resort Jackson Hole
7680 Granite Loop Rd
PO Box 544 .... Teton Village WY 83025 — 800-819-5053 — 307-732-5120 — 703

Four Seasons Spa at the Four Seasons Resort Santa Barbara
1260 Ch Dr .... Santa Barbara CA 93108 — 800-819-5053* — 805-565-8250 — 703
*General

Four Wheel Campers
1460 Churchill Downs Ave .... Woodland CA 95776 — 800-242-1442 — 530-666-1442 — 120

Four Winds Casino Resort
11111 Wilson Rd ......New Buffalo MI 49117 — 866-494-6371 — — 132

Four Winds Hospital
800 Cross River Rd ....Katonah NY 10536 — 800-528-6624 — 914-763-8151 — 373-5

Fournitures De Bureau Denis Inc
2990 boul Le Corbusier .... Laval QC H7L3M2 — 800-338-5567

Foursome Inc
3570 Vicksveurg Ln N Ste 100 .... Plymouth MN 55447 — 888-368-7766 — 763-473-4667 — 157-2

Fowler State Bank
300 E Fifth St PO Box 511 ...... Fowler IN 47944 — 800-439-3951 — 765-884-1200 — 70

Fowler's Chocolate Co
100 River Rock Dr Ste 102 ....Buffalo NY 14207 — 800-824-2263 — 716-877-9983 — 296-8

Fownes Bros & Company Inc
16 E 34th St ....New York NY 10016 — 800-345-6837* — — 155-7
*All

Fox Chase Cancer Ctr
333 Cottman Ave ....Philadelphia PA 19111 — 888-369-2427 — 215-728-6900 — 373-7

Fox Cities Convention & Visitors Bureau
3433 W College Ave .... Appleton WI 54914 — 800-236-6673 — 920-734-3358 — 206

Fox Cities Performing Arts Ctr
400 W College Ave .... Appleton WI 54911 — 800-982-2787 — 800-216-7469 — 519

Fox Creek Leather Inc
2029 Elk Crook Pkwy .... Independence VA 24348 — 800-766-4165 — — 707

FOX Engineering Associates Inc
414 S 17th St Ste 107.............Ames IA 50010 — 800-433-3469 — 515-233-0000 — 261

Fox Harb'r Resort & Spa
1337 Fox Harbour Rd .... Wallace NS B0K1Y0 — 866-257-1801 — 902-257-1801 — 703

Fox Industries Inc
3100 Falls Cliff Rd ....Baltimore MD 21211 — 888-760-0369 — 410-646-8405 — 3

Fox Pool Corp
3490 BoaRd Rd ....York PA 17406 — 800-723-1011 — — 724

Fox Rothschild LLP
2000 Market St 10th Fl.............Philadelphia PA 19103 — 800-580-9136 — 215-299-2000 — 427

Fox Run Vineyards
670 State Rt 14 ....Penn Yan NY 14527 — 800-636-9786 — 315-536-4616 — 442

FOX Sports Radio 1400
316 Greystone Blvd .... Columbia SC 29210 — 844-289-7234 — 803-343-1100

Fox Theatre
660 Peachtree St NE .... Atlanta GA 30308 — 855-285-8499 — 404-881-2100 — 568

Fox Valley Spring Company Inc
N915 Craftsmen Dr .... Greenville WI 54942 — 800-776-2645 — 920-757-7777 — 490

Fox Valley Technical College
1825 N Bluemound Dr
PO Box 2277.......................Appleton WI 54912 — 800-735-3882 — 920-735-5600 — 795

Foxdale Village
500 E Marylyn Ave ....State College PA 16801 — 800-253-4951 — 814-238-3322 — 668

Foxes Music Co
416 S Washington St .... Falls Church VA 22046 — 800-446-4414 — 703-533-7393 — 522

Foxworth-Galbraith Lumber Co
4965 Preston Pk Blvd Ste 400 ....Plano TX 75093 — 800-688-8082 — 972-665-2400 — 191-3

Foxx Equipment Co
421 SW Blvd .... Kansas City MO 64108 — 800-821-2254 — 816-421-3600 — 357

Foxy 1071
8001-101 Creedmoor Rd .... Raleigh NC 27613 — 800-467-3699 — 919-848-9736 — 641-85

FP Mailing Solutions
140 N Mitchell Ct .... Addison IL 60101 — 800-341-6052 — — 112

FPA (Foreign Policy Assn)
470 Park Ave S ....New York NY 10016 — 800-628-5754 — 212-481-8100 — 48-7

FPA (Financial Planning Assn)
7535 E Hampden Ave Ste 600 ....Denver CO 80231 — 800-322-4237 — 303-759-4900 — 49-2

FPC Flexible Packaging Corp
1891 Eglinton Ave E .... Toronto ON M1L2L7 — 888-288-7386 — 416-288-3060 — 544

FPI (Forged Products Inc)
6505 N Houston Rosslyn Rd ....Houston TX 77091 — 800-876-3416 — 713-462-3416 — 481

FPL (Florida Power & Light Co)
700 Universe Blvd .... Juno Beach FL 33408 — 800-226-3545 — 561-691-7574 — 782

FPL Group Inc
NextEra Energy Inc
700 Universe Blvd .... Juno Beach FL 33408 — 888-218-4392 — 561-694-4000 — 359-5
NYSE: NEE

FPM LLC
1501 S Lively Blvd ....Elk Grove Village IL 60007 — 877-437-6432 — 847-228-2525 — 482

FPMI Solutions Inc
1033 N Fairfax St Ste 200........... Alexandria VA 22314 — 888-644-3764 — — 193

FPUC (Florida Public Utilities Co)
401 S Dixie Hwy ....West Palm Beach FL 33401 — 800-427-7712 — — 782

FRA (Fleet Reserve Assn)
125 NW St .... Alexandria VA 22314 — 800-372-1924 — 703-683-1400 — 48-19

FRA (Federal Railroad Administration Regional Offices)
Region 1
55 Broadway Rm 1077...........Cambridge MA 02142 — 800-724-5991 — 202-366-4000 — 339-16

FRA Today
125 NW St .... Alexandria VA 22314 — 800-372-1924 — 703-683-1400 — 455-12

Framingham Heart Study
73 Mt Wayte Ave Ste 2 .... Framingham MA 01702 — 800-854-7582 — 508-935-3418 — 664

Framingham State College
100 State St PO Box 9101 .... Framingham MA 01701 — 866-361-8970 — 508-620-1220 — 166

France
Consulate General
3475 Piedmont Rd NE Ste 1840........ Atlanta GA 30305 — 888-937-2623 — 404-495-1660 — 257

Consulate General
1395 Brickell Ave Ste 1050 .... Miami FL 33131 — 877-624-8737 — 305-403-4185 — 257

Consulate General
205 N Michigan Ave Ste 3700 .... Chicago IL 60601 — 866-858-4430 — 312-327-5200 — 257

Consulate General
777 Post Oak Blvd Ste 600........... Houston TX 77056 — 888-902-5322 — 713-572-2799 — 257

Consulate General
540 Bush St .... San Francisco CA 94108 — 800-553-4133 — 415-397-4330 — 257

Embassy
4101 Reservoir Rd NW .... Washington DC 20007 — 800-622-6232 — 202-944-6000 — 257

Franchise Co, The (TFC)
14502 N Dale Mabry Ste 200 .... Tampa FL 33618 — 800-294-5591 — — 461

Franchise Handbook
5555 N Port Washington Rd
Ste 305.............Milwaukee WI 53217 — 800-272-0246 — 414-882-2878 — 455-11

Franchise Information Services Inc
4075 Wilson Blvd Ste 410 .... Arlington VA 22203 — 800-485-9570 — — 386

Franchoice Inc
7500 Flying Cloud Dr
Ste 600...............Eden Prairie MN 55344 — 888-307-1371 — 952-345-8400 — 194

Francis Investment Counsel LLC
19435 W Capitol Dr .... Brookfield WI 53045 — 866-232-6457 — — 791

Francis Marion Hotel, The
387 King St ....Charleston SC 29403 — 877-756-2121 — 843-722-0600 — 378

Francis Marion University
PO Box 100547 ....Florence SC 29501 — 800-368-7551 — 843-661-1231 — 166

Francis Marion University Rogers Library
PO Box 100547 ....Florence SC 29502 — 800-368-7551 — — 433-6

Francis Scott Key Family Resort
12806 Ocean Gateway ....Ocean City MD 21842 — 800-213-0088 — 410-213-0088 — 665

Franciscan Health Inc
1501 Hartford St .... Lafayette IN 47904 — 800-371-6011 — 765-423-6011 — 373-3

Franciscan Missionaries of Our Lady University
Our Lady of the Lake College
5414 Brittany Dr .... Baton Rouge LA 70808 — 877-242-3509* — 225-768-1700 — 166
*Admissions

Franciscan School of Theology
1712 Euclid Ave .... Berkeley CA 94709 — 855-355-1550 — 760-547-1800 — 167-3

Franciscan Sisters of Chicago Inc
11500 Theresa Dr .... Lemont IL 60439 — 800-524-6126 — — 48-20

Franciscan Skemp Health Care
700 W Ave S .... La Crosse WI 54601 — 800-362-5454 — 608-785-0940 — 373-3

Francisco Grande Hotel & Golf Resort
26000 Gila Bend Hwy .... Casa Grande AZ 85222 — 800-237-4238* — 520-836-6444 — 665
*General

Frank B Fuhrer Wholesale Co
3100 E Carson St .... Pittsburgh PA 15203 — 800-837-2212 — 412-488-8844 — 81-1

Frank C Alegre Trucking Inc
PO Box 1508 ....Lodi CA 95241 — 800-769-2440 — 209-334-2112 — 775

Frank Edmunds & Co
6111 S Sayre ....Chicago IL 60638 — 800-447-3516 — 773-586-2772 — 815

Frank Kent Cadillac Inc
3500 W Loop 820 S ....Fort Worth TX 76116 — 877-558-5468 — — 57

Frank Lloyd Wright's Martin House Complex
125 Jewett Pkwy ....Buffalo NY 14214 — 877-377-3858 — 716-856-3858 — 50-3

Frank Lynn & Associates Inc
500 Park Blvd Ste 785 ....Itasca IL 60143 — 800-245-5966 — 312-263-7888 — 196

Frank Mayer & Assoc Inc
1975 Wisconsin Ave ....Grafton WI 53024 — 855-294-2875 — — 233

Frank Miller Lumber Company Inc
1690 Frank Miller Rd ....Union City IN 47390 — 800-345-2643 — 765-964-3196 — 191-3

Frank Paxton Lumber Co
7455 Dawson Rd .... Cincinnati OH 45243 — 800-325-9800 — 888-826-5580 — 191-3

Frank Roberts & Sons Inc
1130 Robertsville Rd ...... Punxsutawney PA 15767 — 800-262-8955 — 814-938-5000 — 191-4

Frankenmuth Convention & Visitors Bureau
635 S Main St .... Frankenmuth MI 48734 — 800-386-8696 — 989-652-6106 — 206

Frankenmuth Insurance
1 Mutual Ave .... Frankenmuth MI 48787 — 800-234-4433 — 989-652-6121 — 390-4

Frankfort Regional Medical Ctr
299 King's Daughters Dr .... Frankfort KY 40601 — 888-696-4505 — 502-875-5240 — 373-3

Frankfort/Franklin County Tourist & Convention Commission
100 Capitol Ave .... Frankfort KY 40601 — 800-960-7200 — 502-875-8687 — 206

Franklin & Marshall College
PO Box 3003 ....Lancaster PA 17604 — 877-678-9111 — 717-291-3951 — 166

Franklin & Marshall College Shadek-Fackenthal Library
450 College Ave ....Lancaster PA 17604 — 866-366-7655 — 717-358-4216 — 433-6

Franklin College
101 Branigin Blvd ....Franklin IN 46131 — 800-852-0232 — — 166

Franklin Community Health Network
111 Franklin Health Commons .... Farmington ME 04938 — 800-398-6031 — 207-778-6031 — 373-3

Franklin County
355 W Main St .... Malone NY 12953 — 800-397-8686 — 518-481-1681 — 337

Franklin County
1016 N Fourth Ave ....Pasco WA 99301 — 800-647-7706 — 509-545-3535 — 337

Franklin Covey Co
2200 West PkwyBlvd ....Salt Lake City UT 84119 — 800-827-1776 — 801-817-1776 — 760
NYSE: FC

Franklin Credit Management Corp
101 Hudson St ....Jersey City NJ 07302 — 800-255-5897 — — 217

Franklin D Roosevelt Presidential Library & Museum
4079 Albany Post Rd .... Hyde Park NY 12538 — 800-337-8474 — 845-486-7770 — 433-2

Franklin Electric Co Inc
9255 Coverdale Rd .... Fort Wayne IN 46809 — 800-962-3787 — 260-824-2900 — 515
NASDAQ: FELE

Franklin Empire
8421 Darnley Rd .... Montreal QC H4T2B2 — 800-361-5044 — 514-341-3720 — 253

Franklin Fibre-Lamitex Corp
903 E 13th St .... Wilmington DE 19802 — 800-233-9739 — 302-652-3621 — 595

Franklin Homes Inc
10655 Hwy 43 ....Russellville AL 35653 — 800-332-4511 — — 503

Franklin Imaging LLC
500 Schrock Rd .... Columbus OH 43229 — 877-885-6894 — 614-885-6894 — 623

Franklin International
2020 Bruck St .... Columbus OH 43207 — 800-877-4583 — 614-443-0241 — 3

Franklin Local School District
4000 Milllers Ln .... Duncan Falls OH 43734 — 800-846-4976 — 740-674-5203 — 681

		Toll-Free	Phone	Class
Franklin Mills				
1455 Franklin Mills Cir ....Philadelphia PA 19154		**877-746-6642***	317-636-1600	458
*General				
Franklin Mutual Insurance Co				
5 Broad St ....Branchville NJ 07826		**800-842-0551**	973-948-3120	390-4
Franklin Pierce University				
Keene 17 Bradco St ....Keene NH 03431		**800-325-1090**	603-899-4000	166
Lebanon				
24 Airport Rd Ste 19...... West Lebanon NH 03784		**800-325-1090**	603-298-5549	166
Manchester				
670 N Commercial St ....Manchester NH 03101		**800-437-0048***	603-626-4972	166
*Admissions				
Portsmouth				
73 Corporate Dr ....Portsmouth NH 03801		**800-325-1090**	603-433-2000	166
Rindge				
40 University Dr ....Rindge NH 03461		**800-437-0048***	603-899-4000	166
*Admissions				
Franklin Resources Inc				
1 Franklin Pkwy				
Bdge 970 1st Fl................San Mateo CA 94403		**800-632-2301**	650-312-2000	400
NYSE: BEN				
Franklin Rural Electric Co-op				
1560 Hwy 65 PO Box 437...........Hampton IA 50441		**800-750-3557**	641-456-2557	245
Franklin Sports Inc				
17 Campanelli Pkwy ....Stoughton MA 02072		**800-225-8649**	781-344-1111	706
Franklin Square Hospital Ctr				
9000 Franklin Sq Dr ....Baltimore MD 21237		**888-404-3549**	443-777-7000	373-3
Franklin Street Properties Corp (FSP)				
401 Edgewater Pl ....Wakefield MA 01880		**877-686-9496**	800-950-6288	650
NYSE: FSP				
Franklin Templeton Investments				
3344 Quality Dr ....Rancho Cordova CA 95670		**800-632-2350**	650-312-2000	686
Franklin University				
201 S Grant Ave ....Columbus OH 43215		**877-341-6300**	614-797-4700	166
Franklin, The				
164 E 87th St ....New York NY 10128		**800-607-4009**	212-369-1000	378
Franks Supply Company Inc				
3311 Stanford Dr NE ....Albuquerque NM 87107		**800-432-5254**	505-884-0000	357
Frankston Packaging				
699 N Frankston Hwy ....Frankston TX 75763		**800-881-1495**	903-876-2550	553
FRAN-PAC				
1501 K St Ste 350................Washington DC 20005		**800-543-1038**	202-628-8000	611
Frantz Group Inc, The				
1245 Cheyenne Ave ....Grafton WI 53024		**800-707-0064**	262-204-6000	195
Frasco Investigative Services				
215 W Alameda Ave ....Burbank CA 91502		**877-372-7261**		
Fraser Stryker PC LLO				
500 Energy Plz 409 S 17th St ....Omaha NE 68102		**800-544-6041**	402-341-6000	427
Fraternal Order of Alaska State Troopers Museum				
245 W Fifth Ave ....Anchorage AK 99501		**800-770-5050**	907-279-5050	517
Fraternal Order of Police (FOP)				
701 Marriott Dr ....Nashville TN 37214		**800-451-2711**	615-399-0900	48-15
Fraze Pavilion				
695 Lincoln Pk Blvd ....Dayton OH 45429		**800-514-3849**	937-296-3300	568
Frazier Industrial Co				
91 Fairview Ave ....Long Valley NJ 07853		**800-859-1342**	908-876-3001	286
Frazier Rehabilitation Institute				
220 Abraham Flexner Way ....Louisville KY 40202		**800-333-2230**	502-582-7400	373-6
FRBSF (Federal Reserve Bank of San Francisco)				
101 Market St ....San Francisco CA 94105		**800-227-4133**	415-974-2000	71
FRC (Family Research Council)				
801 G St NW ....Washington DC 20001		**800-225-4008**	202-393-2100	48-6
FRCC (Front Range Community College)				
Boulder County				
2190 Miller Dr ....Longmont CO 80501		**888-800-9198**	303-678-3722	162
Fred Loya Insurance				
1800 Lee Trevino Ste 201..............El Paso TX 79936		**800-554-0595**	915-590-5692	389
Fred M Schildwachter & Sons Inc				
1400 Ferris Pl ....Bronx NY 10461		**800-642-3646**	718-828-2500	316
Fred Olivieri Construction Company Inc				
6315 Promway Ave NW ....North Canton OH 44720		**800-847-5085**	330-494-1007	186
Fred Pryor Seminars				
9757 Metcalf Ave ....Overland Park KS 66212		**800-780-8476**		760
Fred Usinger Inc				
1030 N Old World Third St ....Milwaukee WI 53203		**800-558-9998**	414-276-9100	296-26
Fred Weber Inc				
2320 Creve Coeur Mill Rd				
...............Maryland Heights MO 63043		**866-739-8855**	314-344-0070	188-4
Fred's Inc				
4300 New Getwell Rd ....Memphis TN 38118		**800-374-7417**	901-365-8880	229
NASDAQ: FRED				
Freddie Mac				
8200 Jones Branch Dr ....McLean VA 22102		**800-424-5401**	703-903-2000	507
North Central Region				
333 W Wacker Dr Ste 2500 ....Chicago IL 60606		**800-373-3343**	312-407-7400	507
Northeast Region				
8200 Jones Branch Dr ....McLean VA 22102		**800-373-3343**	703-903-2000	507
Southeast/Southwest Region				
2300 Windy Ridge Pkwy Ste 200N......Atlanta GA 30339		**800-373-3343**	770-857-8800	507
Frederick Goldman Inc				
154 W 14th St ....New York NY 10011		**800-221-3232**		410
Frederick Motor Co, The				
1 Waverley Dr ....Frederick MD 21702		**800-734-9118**		57
Frederick News Post				
351 Ballenger Ctr Dr ....Frederick MD 21703		**800-486-1177**	301-662-1177	528-2
Frederick Taylor University				
2050 W Chapman Ave Ste 108 ....Orange CA 92868		**888-370-7589**	714-949-2304	505
Frederick Wildman & Sons Ltd				
307 E 53rd St ....New York NY 10022		**800-733-9463***	212-355-0700	81-3
*General				
Fredericks Co, The				
2400 Philmont Ave ....Huntingdon Valley PA 19006		**800-367-2919**	215-947-2500	331
Fredericksburg Regional Chamber of Commerce				
2300 Fall Hill Ave				
Ste 240 ....Fredericksburg VA 22401		**888-338-0252**	540-373-9400	139
Frederik Meijer Gardens & Sculpture Park				
1000 E Beltline Ave NE ....Grand Rapids MI 49525		**877-975-3171**	616-957-1580	97
Fredonia State University of New York				
Fredonia				
280 Central Ave ....Fredonia NY 14063		**800-642-4272**	716-673-3111	166
Fredrickson, Mazeika & Grant LLP				
5720 Oberlin Dr ....San Diego CA 92121		**800-231-8440**	858-642-2002	427
Free Flow Packaging International Inc				
1090 Mills Way ....Redwood City CA 94063		**800-866-9946**	650-261-5300	597
Free Lance Star				
616 Amelia St ....Fredericksburg VA 22401		**800-877-0500**	540-374-5000	528-2
Free Methodist Foundation, The				
8050 Spring Arbor Rd ....Spring Arbor MI 49283		**800-325-8975**	517-750-2727	305
Free Press				
418 S Second St ....Mankato MN 56001		**800-657-4662**	507-625-4451	528-2
Free Service Tire Co Inc				
PO Box 6187 ....Johnson City TN 37602		**855-646-1423**	423-979-2250	750
Free Spirit Publishing Inc				
217 Fifth Ave N Ste 200 ....Minneapolis MN 55401		**800-735-7323**	612-338-2068	633-2
Freeborn-Mower Co-op Services				
2501 E Main St ....Albert Lea MN 56007		**800-734-6421**	507-373-6421	245
Freed-Hardeman University				
158 E Main St ....Henderson TN 38340		**800-348-3481**	731-989-6651	166
Freedman Seating Co				
4545 W Augusta Blvd ....Chicago IL 60651		**800-443-4540**	773-524-2440	685
Freedom Alliance				
22570 Markey Ct Ste 240 ....Sterling VA 20166		**800-475-6620**	703-444-7940	611·
Freedom from Hunger				
1460 Drew Ave Ste 300 ....Davis CA 95618		**800-708-2555**	530-758-6200	48-5
Freedom Graphic Systems Inc (FGS)				
1101 S Janesville St ....Milton WI 53563		**800-334-3540**		110
Freedom Investments Inc				
375 Raritan Ctr Pkwy ....Edison NJ 08837		**800-944-4033**		686
Freedom Medical Inc				
219 Welsh Pool Rd ....Exton PA 19341		**800-784-8849**	610-903-0200	264-4
Freedom Scientific Inc				
11800 31st Ct N ....St. Petersburg FL 33716		**800-444-4443**	727-803-8000	177
Freedom Village				
23442 El Toro Rd ....Lake Forest CA 92630		**800-584-8084**	949-472-4700	668
Freedom Village				
5275 Rt 14 ....Lakemont NY 14857		**800-842-8679**	607-243-8126	668
FreedomWorks				
400 North Capitol St NW				
Ste 765 ....Washington DC 20001		**888-564-6273**	202-783-3870	48-7
Freelancers Union				
408 Jay St 2nd Fl ....Brooklyn NY 11201		**888-447-9883**	718-532-1515	
Freelin-Wade Co				
1730 NE Miller St ....McMinnville OR 97128		**888-373-9233**	503-434-5561	369
Freeman				
1600 Viceroy Dr Ste 100. ....Dallas TX 75235		**800-453-9228**	214-445-1000	
Freeman Gas Inc				
113 Peake Rd ....Roebuck SC 29376		**800-277-5730**	864-582-5475	356
Freeman Health System				
1102 W 32nd St ....Joplin MO 64804		**800-297-3337**	417-347-1111	373-3
Freeman Manufacturing Co				
900 W Chicago Rd ....Sturgis MI 49091		**800-253-2091**	269-651-2371	475
Freeman Marcus Jewelers				
76 Merchants Row ....Rutland VT 05701		**800-451-4167**	802-773-2792	409
Freeman Mfg & Supply Co				
1101 Moore Rd ....Avon OH 44011		**800-321-8511**	440-934-1902	563
Freeman's Flowers & Event Consultants				
2934 Duniven Cir ....Amarillo TX 79109		**800-846-3104**	806-355-4451	292
Freeman, The				
30 S Broadway ....Irvington-on-Hudson NY 10533		**800-960-4333***	914-591-7230	455-17
*Sales				
Freeserverscom				
1253 N Research Way Ste Q-2500 ....Orem UT 84097		**800-396-1999**		803
Freestone Inn at Wilson Ranch				
31 Early Winters Dr ....Mazama WA 98833		**800-639-3809**	509-996-3906	665
Freestyle Photo Biz				
5124 Sunset Blvd ....Hollywood CA 90027		**800-292-6137**		586
FreeWave Technologies Inc				
5395 Pearl Pkwy ....Boulder CO 80301		**866-923-6168***	303-381-9200	173-3
*Cust Svc				
Freight Logistics Inc				
PO Box 1712 ....Medford OR 97501		**800-866-7882**	541-734-5617	311
Freight Transportation Research Associates Inc				
1720 N Kinser Pk ....Bloomington IN 47404		**888-988-1699**	812-988-1699	
FreightCar America Inc				
17 Johns St ....Johnstown PA 15901		**800-458-2235**		646
NASDAQ: RAIL				
Freightliner Northwest				
277 Stewart Rd SW ....Pacific WA 98047		**800-523-8014**		57
Freightliner of Hartford Inc				
222 Roberts St ....East Hartford CT 06108		**800-453-6967**		57
Freightliner Specialty Vehicles Inc				
2300 S 13th St ....Clinton OK 73601		**800-358-7624**	580-323-4100	59
FreightPros				
3307 Northland Dr Ste 360. ....Austin TX 78731		**888-297-6968**		476
Freightquote				
901 W Carondelet Dr ....Kansas City MO 64114		**800-323-5441**		312
Fremont City Hall				
PO Box 5006 ....Fremont CA 94537		**800-462-3271**	510-284-4000	336
Fremont Contract Carriers Inc (FCC)				
865 S Bud Blvd ....Fremont NE 68025		**800-228-9842**		447
Fremont Correctional Facility (FCF)				
E US Hwy 50 Evans Blvd				
PO Box 999. ....Canon City CO 81215		**800-886-7683**	719-269-5002	213
Fremont County				
450 N Second St ....Lander WY 82520		**800-967-2297**	307-332-2405	337
Fremont Hotel & Casino				
200 Fremont St ....Las Vegas NV 89101		**800-634-6460**	702-385-3232	133
Fremont Industries Inc				
4400 Vly Industrial Blvd N				
PO Box 67. ....Shakopee MN 55379		**800-436-1238**	952-445-4121	145
Fremont Main Library				
2400 Stevenson Blvd ....Fremont CA 94538		**800-434-0222**	510-745-1400	433-3
Fremont Unified School District				
4210 Technology Dr ....Fremont CA 94538		**800-544-5248**	510-657-2350	681
French Broad Electric Membership Corp				
3043 Nc 213 Hwy ....Marshall NC 28753		**800-222-6190**	828-649-2051	245

				Toll-Free	Phone	Class
French Country Waterways Ltd						
24 Bay Rd	Duxbury	MA	02332	800-222-1236	781-934-2454	221
French Culinary Institute						
462 Broadway	New York	NY	10013	888-324-2433		163
French Lick Resort						
8670 W State Rd 56	French Lick	IN	47432	888-936-9360	812-936-9300	665
French Quarter Suites Hotel						
1119 N Rampart St	New Orleans	LA	70116	800-457-2253	504-524-7725	378
French-American Chamber of Commerce in New York						
1350 Broadway Ste 2101	New York	NY	10018	800-821-2241	212-867-0123	138
Frenchman Valley Farmers Co-op Exchange						
202 Broadway	Imperial	NE	69033	800-538-2667	308-882-3200	276
Fresenius Medical Care						
920 Winter St	Waltham	MA	02451	800-662-1237	781-699-9000	473
Fresenius Medical Care North America						
920 Winter St	Waltham	MA	02451	800-662-1237	781-699-9000	351
Fresh Air Educators Inc						
203-1568 Carling Ave	Ottawa	ON	K1Z7M4	866-495-4868		244
Fresh Air Fund						
633 Third Ave 14th Fl	New York	NY	10017	800-367-0003		239
Fresh Express Inc						
PO Box 80599	Salinas	CA	93912	800-242-5472*		11-1
*Cust Svc						
FreshAddress Inc						
36 Crafts St	Newton	MA	02458	800-321-3009		196
FreshDirect Inc						
23-30 Borden Ave	Long Island	NY	11101	866-511-1240	718-928-1000	344
FreshPoint Inc						
1390 Enclave Pkwy	Houston	TX	77077	800-367-5690		
Freshwater Society						
2500 Shadywood Rd	Excelsior	MN	55331	888-471-9773	952-471-9773	48-13
Freskeeto Frozen Foods Inc						
8019 Rt 209	Ellenville	NY	12428	800-356-3663	845-647-5111	296-18
Fresno & Clovis Convention & Visitors Bureau						
1550 E Shaw Ave Ste 101	Fresno	CA	93710	800-788-0836	559-981-5500	206
Fresno Bee 1626 E St	Fresno	CA	93786	800-877-3400	559-441-6111	528-2
Fresno Distributing Company Inc						
2055 E McKinley Ave	Fresno	CA	93703	800-655-2542	559-442-8800	608
Fresno Valves & Castings Inc						
7736 E Springfield Ave PO Box 40	Selma	CA	93662	800-333-1658	559-834-2511	785
Fresno Yosemite International Airport						
5175 E Clinton Way	Fresno	CA	93727	866-275-7772	559-621-4500	27
Freud America Inc						
218 Feld Ave	High Point	NC	27263	800-334-4107	336-434-3171	349
Freundlich Supply Co Inc						
2200 Arthur Kill Rd	Staten Island	NY	10309	800-221-0260	718-356-1500	765
Freyberg Hinkle Ashland Powers & Stowell SC CPA						
15420 W Capitol Dr	Brookfield	WI	53005	800-413-8799	262-784-6210	2
Freyssinet Inc						
44880 Falcon Pl Ste 100	Sterling	VA	20166	800-423-6587	703-378-2500	261
Friary of Lakeview Ctr, The						
4400 Hickory Shores Blvd	Gulf Breeze	FL	32563	800-332-2271	850-932-9375	722
Frick Hospital						
508 S Church St	Mount Pleasant	PA	15666	877-771-1234	724-547-1500	373-3
Fridgedoorcom						
21 Dixwell Ave	Quincy	MA	02169	800-955-3741	617-770-7913	328
Friedman Bros Decorative Arts						
9015 NW 105th Way	Medley	FL	33178	800-327-1065	305-887-3170	333
Friedman Electric						
1321 Wyoming Ave	Exeter	PA	18643	800-545-5517	570-654-3371	246
Friedrich						
10001 Reunion Pl Ste 500	San Antonio	TX	78216	800-541-6645	210-546-0500	14
Friend Tire Co						
11 Industrial Dr	Monett	MO	65708	800-950-8473	417-235-7836	750
Friend's Professional Stationery Inc						
1535 Lewis Ave	Zion	IL	60099	800-323-4394		531
Friendfinder Network Inc						
6800 Broken Sound Pkwy						
Ste 200	Boca Raton	FL	33487	888-575-8383	561-912-7000	226
TSE: FFN						
Friendly Cruises						
3081 S Sycamore Village Dr						
	Superstition Mountain	AZ	85118	800-842-1786	480-358-1496	766
Friendly Excursions Inc						
PO Box 69	Sunland	CA	91041	800-775-5018	818-353-7726	755
Friendly Ice Cream Corp						
1855 Boston Rd	Wilbraham	MA	01095	800-966-9970		666
Friends Committee on National Legislation (FCNL)						
245 Second St NE	Washington	DC	20002	800-630-1330	202-547-6000	611
Friends Hospital						
4641 Roosevelt Blvd	Philadelphia	PA	19124	800-889-0548	215-831-4600	373-5
Friends of Animals Inc (FOA)						
777 Post Rd Ste 205	Darien	CT	06820	800-321-7387	203-656-1522	48-3
Friends of the Earth						
1717 Massachusetts Ave NW						
Ste 600	Washington	DC	20036	877-843-8687	202-783-7400	48-13
Friends of the Earth Magazine						
1100 15th St NW	Washington	DC	20005	877-843-8687	202-783-7400	455-19
Friends of the River						
1418 20th St Ste 100	Sacramento	CA	95811	888-464-2477	916-442-3155	48-13
Friends Research Institute Inc						
1040 Park Ave Ste 103	Baltimore	MD	21201	800-822-3677	410-823-5116	664
Social Research Ctr						
1040 Park Ave Ste 103	Baltimore	MD	21201	800-705-7757	410-837-3977	664
Friends University						
2100 W University Ave	Wichita	KS	67213	800-794-6945	316-295-5000	166
Friendship Village Kalamazoo						
1400 N Drake Rd	Kalamazoo	MI	49006	800-613-3984	269-381-0560	668
Friendsview Retirement Community						
1301 E Fulton St	Newberg	OR	97132	866-307-4371	503-538-3144	668
Fringe Benefits Management Co						
3101 Sessions Rd	Tallahassee	FL	32303	800-872-0345	850-425-6200	389
Friona Industries						
500 S Taylor St Ste 601	Amarillo	TX	79101	800-658-6014	806-374-1811	10-1
Frisch's Restaurants Inc						
2800 Gilbert Ave	Cincinnati	OH	45206	800-873-3633	513-961-2660	666
NYSE: FRS						

				Toll-Free	Phone	Class
Fristam Pumps USA LP						
2410 Parview Rd	Middleton	WI	53562	800-841-5001	608-831-5001	637
Frit Industries Inc						
1792 Jodie Parker Rd	Ozark	AL	36360	800-633-7685	334-774-2515	280
Frito-Lay North America						
7701 Legacy Dr	Plano	TX	75024	800-352-4477		296-35
Fritz Industries Inc						
180 Gordon Dr Ste 107	Exton	PA	19341	800-345-6202		183
Frize Corp						
16605 E Gale Ave	City of Industry	CA	91745	800-834-2127		186
FRL Furniture						
460 Grand Blvd	Westbury	NY	11590	800-529-4375	516-333-4400	660
Froedtert Hospital Bone Marrow Transplant Program						
9200 W Wisconsin Ave	Milwaukee	WI	53226	800-272-3666	414-805-3666	764
Frog Street Press Inc						
800 Industrial Blvd Ste 100	Grapevine	TX	76051	800-884-3764		243
Frog Switch & Mfg Co						
600 E High St	Carlisle	PA	17013	800-233-7194	717-243-2454	307
FROGGY 1077						
275 Radio Rd	Hanover	PA	17331	800-366-9489	717-637-3831	641
Fromm Electric Supply						
2101 Centre Ave PO Box 15147	Reading	PA	19605	800-360-4441	610-374-4441	246
Front End Audio						
130 Hunter Village Dr Ste D	Irmo	SC	29063	888-228-4530	803-748-0914	522
Front Porch Communities & Services						
800 N Brand Blvd 19th Fl	Glendale	CA	91203	800-233-3709		448
Front Range Community College (FRCC)						
Boulder County						
2190 Miller Dr	Longmont	CO	80501	888-800-9198	303-678-3722	162
Larimer						
4616 S Shields St	Fort Collins	CO	80526	888-800-9198	970-226-2500	162
Front Row USA Entertainment						
900 N Federal Hwy	Hallandale beach	FL	33009	800-277-8499		745
Front Runner Consulting LLC						
6850 O'Bannon Bluff	Loveland	OH	45140	877-328-3360	513-697-6850	194
Frontenac State Park						
29223 County 28 Blvd	Frontenac	MN	55026	888-646-6367	651-345-3401	561
Frontier Adjusters of America Inc						
4745 N Seventh St Ste 320	Phoenix	AZ	85014	800-426-7228		389
Frontier Airlines Inc						
7001 Tower Rd	Denver	CO	80249	800-265-5505	720-374-4200	359-1
Frontier Communications Corp						
3 High Ridge Pk	Stamford	CT	06905	800-877-4390	203-614-5600	731
NASDAQ: FTR						
Frontier Co-op						
211 S Lincoln PO Box 37	Brainard	NE	68626	800-869-0379	402-545-2811	275
Frontier Cooperative Herbs						
3021 78th St	Norway	IA	52318	800-669-3275		800
Frontier Electronic Systems Corp						
4500 W Sixth Ave	Stillwater	OK	74074	800-677-1769	405-624-1769	525
Frontier Ford						
3701 Stevens Creek Blvd	Santa Clara	CA	95051	844-480-0574		57
Frontier Health						
PO Box 9054	Gray	TN	37615	877-928-9062	423-467-3600	
Frontier Logistics LP						
1806 S 16th St	La Porte	TX	77571	800-610-6808		311
Frontier Metal Stamping						
3764 Puritan Way	Frederick	CO	80516	888-316-1266	877-549-5955	481
Frontier Natural Products Co-op						
3021 78th St PO Box 299	Norway	IA	52318	800-669-3275	319-227-7996	296-37
Frontier Networks Inc						
530 Kipling Ave	Toronto	ON	M8Z5E3	866-833-2323	416-847-5240	386
Frontier Power Co						
770 S Second St PO Box 280	Coshocton	OH	43812	800-624-8050	740-622-6755	245
Frontier-Kemper Constructors Inc						
1695 Allen Rd	Evansville	IN	47710	877-554-8600	812-426-2741	188-10
Frontiers International Travel						
600 Warrendale Rd	Gibsonia	PA	15044	800-245-1950	724-935-1577	755
Frontiers of Flight Museum						
6911 Lemon Ave	Dallas	TX	75209	800-568-8924	214-350-1651	517
Frontline Communications						
PO Box 98	Orangeburg	NY	10962	888-376-6854		397
Frontline Group of Texas LLC						
15021 Katy Fwy Ste 575	Houston	TX	77094	800-285-5512	281-453-6000	760
Frontline Logistics Inc						
10315 Grand River Ste 300	Brighton	MI	48116	800-245-6632	734-449-9474	314
Frontline Systems Inc						
PO Box 4288	Incline Village	NV	89450	888-831-0333	775-831-0300	804
FrontPage Local						
1660 Hotel Cir N Ste 600	San Diego	CA	92108	800-219-1755		627
Frosch International Travel Inc						
1 Greenway Plz Ste 800	Houston	TX	77046	800-866-1623		767
Frost & Sullivan						
7550 IH 10 W Ste 400	San Antonio	TX	78229	877-463-7678	210-348-1000	527-12
Fruit Co, The						
2900 Van Horn Dr	Hood River	OR	97031	800-387-3100	541-387-3100	292
Fruit Growers Laboratory Inc						
853 Corporation St	Santa Paula	CA	93060	800-440-7821	805-392-2000	738
Fruit of the Loom Inc						
1 Fruit of the Loom Dr						
PO Box 90015	Bowling Green	KY	42102	888-378-4829	270-781-6400	155-3
Fruitful Yield Inc						
229 W Roosevelt Rd	Lombard	IL	60148	800-469-5552		
Fruitridge Printing & Lithograph Inc						
3258 Stockton Blvd	Sacramento	CA	95820	800-835-4846	916-452-9213	623
Frullati Cafe & Bakery						
9311 E Via de Ventura	Scottsdale	AZ	85258	866-452-4252	480-362-4800	666
Frutarom Corp						
9500 Railroad Ave	North Bergen	NJ	07047	866-229-7198	201-861-9500	296-15
Fruth Pharmacy Inc						
4016 Ohio River Rd	Point Pleasant	WV	25550	800-438-5390	304-675-1612	237
Fry Communications Inc						
800 W Church Rd	Mechanicsburg	PA	17055	800-334-1429		623
Fry's Food Stores of Arizona Inc						
500 S 99th Ave	Tolleson	AZ	85353	866-221-4141		344
Fryer-Knowles Inc						
205 S Dawson St	Seattle	WA	98108	800-544-6052	206-767-7710	291

Alphabetical Section

	Toll-Free	Phone	Class
Frymaster LLC			
8700 Line Ave ....Shreveport LA 71106	**800-221-4583***	318-865-1711	298
*Cust Svc			
Fry-Wagner Moving & Storage Co			
3700 Rider Trl S ....Earth City MO 63045	**800-899-4035**	314-291-4100	775
FS Tool Corp			
71 Hobbs Gate ....Markham ON L3R9T9	**800-387-9723**	905-475-1999	693
FSC Securities Corp			
2300 Windy Ridge Pkwy Ste 1100 ...Atlanta GA 30339	**800-372-5646**	800-547-2382	686
FSG (Facility Solutions Group)			
4401 Westgate Blvd Ste 310..Austin TX 78745	**800-854-6465**	512-440-7985	246
FSG Lighting			
4401 Westgate Blvd Ste 310..Austin TX 78745	**800-854-6465**	512-440-7985	246
FSI Technologies Inc			
668 E Western Ave ....Lombard IL 60148	**800-468-6009**	630-932-9380	203
FSMB (Federation of State Medical Boards of the US Inc)			
400 Fuller Wiser Rd Ste 300..Euless TX 76039	**800-793-7939**	817-868-4000	49-8
FSP (Franklin Street Properties Corp)			
401 Edgewater Pl ....Wakefield MA 01880	**877-686-9496**	800-950-6288	650
NYSE: FSP			
FTA (Federation of Tax Administrators)			
444 N Capitol St NW Ste 348........Washington DC 20001	**800-829-9188**	202-624-5890	49-7
FTC (Federal Trade Commission)			
600 Pennsylvania Ave NW ....Washington DC 20580	**877-382-4357**	202-326-2222	339-19
FTC (Farmers Telecommunications Co-op)			
144 McCurdy Ave N PO Box 217 ...Rainsville AL 35986	**866-638-2144**	256-638-2144	731
FTC (Feed the Children)			
PO Box 36 ....Oklahoma City OK 73101	**800-627-4556**	405-942-0228	48-5
FTD Inc			
3113 Woodcreek Dr ....Downers Grove IL 60515	**800-736-3383***		292
*Cust Svc			
FTI Consulting			
909 Commerce Rd ....Annapolis MD 21401	**800-334-5701**		443
NYSE: FCN			
FTJ FundChoice LLC			
2300 Litton Ln Ste 102.................Hebron KY 41048	**800-379-2513**		386
FTMC (Fisher-Titus Medical Ctr)			
272 Benedict Ave ....Norwalk OH 44857	**800-589-3862**	419-668-8101	373-3
Fuchs North America			
3800 Hampstead Mexico Rd ....Hampstead MD 21074	**800-365-3229**	410-363-1700	296-37
Fuel Education LLC			
2300 Corporate Park Dr ....Herndon VA 20171	**866-912-8588**		178-3
Fuel Tech Inc			
27601 Bella Vista Pkwy ....Warrenville IL 60555	**800-666-9688***	630-845-4500	18
NASDAQ: FTEK ■ *General			
FuelFX LLC			
1811 Bering Dr ....Houston TX 77057	**855-472-7316**		195
Fugro-Roadware Inc			
2505 Meadowvale Blvd ....Mississauga ON L5N5S2	**800-828-2726**	905-567-2870	406
Fuji Chemical Industries USA			
3 Terri Ln Unit 12 ....Burlington NJ 08016	**877-385-4777**	609-386-3030	297-8
FUJIFILM Graphic System USA Inc			
45 Crosby Dr ....Bedford MA 01730	**800-755-3854**	781-271-4400	384
Fujitsu America Inc			
1250 E Arques Ave ....Sunnyvale CA 94085	**800-538-8460**	408-746-6200	730
Fujitsu Computer Products of America Inc			
1255 E Arques Ave ....Sunnyvale CA 94085	**800-626-4686**	408-746-7000	173-8
Fujitsu Computer Systems Corp			
1250 E Arques Ave ....Sunnyvale CA 94085	**800-538-8460**	408-746-6000	176
Fujitsu Consulting			
1250 E Arques Ave ....Sunnyvale CA 94085	**800-831-3183**		180
Fujitsu General America Inc			
353 Rt 46 W ....Fairfield NJ 07004	**888-888-3424**	973-575-0380	606
Fujitsu Ten Corp of America			
19600 S Vermont Ave ....Torrance CA 90502	**800-233-2216**	310-327-2151	52
Fulflex Inc			
32 Justin Holden Dr ....Brattleboro VT 05301	**800-283-2500**	802-257-5256	740-5
Full Access Brokerage			
1240 Charnelton St ....Eugene OR 97401	**866-890-5743**	541-284-5070	686
Full Sail University			
3300 University Blvd ....Winter Park FL 32792	**800-226-7625**	407-679-6333	795
Full Swing Golf Inc			
10890 Thornmint Rd ....San Diego CA 92127	**800-798-9094**	858-675-1100	253
Fullen Dock & Warehouse Inc			
382 Klinke Rd ....Memphis TN 38127	**800-467-7104**	901-358-9544	191-1
Fuller Brush Co, The			
1 Fuller Way PO Box 729 ....Great Bend KS 67530	**800-522-0499***	620-792-1711	103
*Cust Svc			
Fuller Craft Museum			
455 Oak St ....Brockton MA 02301	**800-639-4808**	508-588-6000	517
Fuller Industrial			
65 Nelson Rd ....Lively ON P3Y1P4	**888-524-3777**	705-682-2777	591
Fuller Theological Seminary			
135 N Oakland Ave ....Pasadena CA 91182	**800-235-2222**	626-584-5200	167-3
Fullerton Bldg Systems Inc (FBS)			
34620 250th St PO Box 308........Worthington MN 56187	**800-450-9782**	507-376-3128	812
Fullerton Tool Company Inc			
121 Perry St ....Saginaw MI 48602	**855-722-7243**	989-799-4550	491
Fulton 58			
Fulton Missouri			
2 Hornet Dr ....Fulton MO 65251	**800-456-2634**	573-590-8000	681
Fulton Corp			
303 Eighth Ave ....Fulton IL 61252	**800-252-0002**		349
Fulton County			
122 W Market St Ste 202 ....McConnellsburg PA 17233	**800-328-0058**	717-485-6862	337
Fulton Industries Inc			
135 E Linfoot St ....Wauseon OH 43567	**800-537-5012**	419-335-3015	438
Fulton-Denver Co			
3500 Wynkoop St ....Denver CO 80216	**800-521-1414**	303-294-9292	67
Fun 1013 FM			
1996 Auction Rd ....Manheim PA 17545	**800-655-4101**	717-653-0800	641
Function Point Productivity Software Inc			
2034 11th Ave W Ste 140 ....Vancouver BC V6J2C9	**877-731-2522**		
Fund for Animals, The			
200 West 57th St ....New York NY 10019	**866-482-3708**		
Funeral Consumers Alliance			
33 Patchen Rd ....South Burlington VT 05403	**800-765-0107**	802-865-8300	48-10
Funeral Service Insider			
3349 Hwy 138 Bldg D Ste B ....Wall NJ 07719	**800-500-4585**		527-13

G

	Toll-Free	Phone	Class
G & C Equipment Corp			
1875 W Redondo Beach Blvd			
Ste 102 ....Gardena CA 90247	**800-559-5529**	310-515-6715	264-3
G & G Fitness Equipment Inc			
7350 Transit Rd ....Williamsville NY 14221	**800-537-0516**	716-633-2527	353
G & H Decoys Inc			
PO Box 1208 ....Henryetta OK 74437	**800-443-3269***	918-652-3314	706
*Orders			
G & H Wire Company Inc			
2165 Earlywood Dr ....Franklin IN 46131	**800-526-1026**	317-346-6655	228
G & J Land & Marine Food Distributors			
506 Front St ....Morgan City LA 70380	**800-256-9187**	985-385-2620	344
G & O Thermal Supply Co			
5435 N Northwest Hwy ....Chicago IL 60630	**800-621-4997**	773-763-1300	111
G & T Industries Inc			
1001 76th St SW ....Byron Center MI 49315	**800-968-6035**	616-452-8611	597
G & W Laboratories Inc			
111 Coolidge St ....South Plainfield NJ 07080	**800-922-1038**		578
G D G Environment Group Ltd			
430 rue St-Laurent ....Trois-Rivières QC G8T6H3	**888-567-8567**		192
G G Schmitt & Sons Inc			
2821 Old Tree Dr ....Lancaster PA 17603	**866-724-6488**	717-394-3701	349
G r Manufacturing Inc			
4800 Commerce Dr ....Trussville AL 35173	**800-841-8001**	205-655-8001	297-8
G2 Web Services LLC			
1750 112th Ave NE Ste C101 ....Bellevue WA 98004	**888-788-5353**		180
G3 Communications			
777 Terrace Ave			
Ste 202 ....Hasbrouck Heights NJ 07604	**888-603-3626**		195
G3 Enterprises Inc			
502 E Whitmore Ave ....Modesto CA 95358	**800-321-8747**		124
G6 Hospitality LLC			
Motel 6			
4001 International Pkwy ....Carrollton TX 75007	**800-466-8356**	972-360-9000	378
GA Braun Inc			
79 General Irwin Blvd ....Syracuse NY 13212	**800-432-7286**	315-475-3123	426
GA Wintzer & Son Co			
204 W Auglaize St ....Wapakoneta OH 45895	**800-331-1801**	419-739-4900	296-12
GableSigns Inc			
7440 Ft Smallwood Rd ....Baltimore MD 21226	**800-854-0568**	410-255-6400	697
Gabriel Roeder Smith & Co (GRS)			
1 Towne Sq Ste 800 ....Southfield MI 48076	**800-521-0498**	248-799-9000	193
Gachman Metals & Recycling Company Inc			
2600 Shamrock Ave ....Fort Worth TX 76107	**800-749-0423**	817-334-0211	682
Gaco Western Inc			
200 W Mercer St Ste 202 ....Seattle WA 98119	**800-456-4226**	800-331-0196	597
Gadabout Inc			
3501 E Kindale ....Tucson AZ 85716	**800-600-3662**	520-325-0000	77
Gadsden & Etowah County Chamber			
1 Commerce Sq ....Gadsden AL 35901	**800-659-2955**	256-543-3472	139
Gadsden State Community College			
1001 George Wallace Dr			
PO Box 227 ....Gadsden AL 35902	**800-226-5563**	256-549-8200	162
Gaggle Net			
2205 E Empire St Ste B			
PO Box 1352 ....Bloomington IL 61704	**800-288-7750**	309-665-0572	
Gaiam Inc			
833 W S Boulder Rd Bldg G ....Louisville CO 80027	**877-989-6321**	303-222-3600	457
NASDAQ: GAIA			
Gainesville City Schools			
508 Oak St ....Gainesville GA 30501	**800-533-0682**	770-536-5275	681
Gainesville Times			
345 Green St NW ....Gainesville GA 30501	**800-395-5005**	770-532-1234	528-2
Gainey Suites Hotel			
7300 E Gainey ....Scottsdale AZ 85258	**800-970-4666**	480-922-6969	377
Gainshare Inc			
3110 N Central Ave Ste 160 ....Phoenix AZ 85012	**800-264-9029**	602-266-8500	759
GAI-Tronics Corp			
400 E Wyomissing Ave ....Mohnton PA 19540	**800-492-1212**	610-777-1374	730
Galapagos Holidays			
7800 Red Rd Ste 112 ....South Miami FL 33143	**800-327-9854**	305-665-0841	766
Galasso's Inc			
10820 San Sevaine Way ....Mira Loma CA 91752	**800-339-7494**	951-360-1211	68
Galaxie Coffee Services			
110 Sea Ln ....Farmingdale NY 11735	**800-564-9104**	631-694-2688	113
Galaxie Defense Marketing Services			
5330 Napa St ....San Diego CA 92110	**888-711-3427**	619-299-9950	186
Galaxy Hotel Systems LLC			
5 Peters Canyon Ste 375 ....Irvine CA 92606	**800-624-2953**	714-258-5800	178-11
Galaxy Nutritional Foods Inc			
66 Whitecap Dr ....North Kingstown RI 02852	**800-441-9419**	401-667-5000	296-5
Galaxy Software Solutions Inc			
5820 N Lilley Rd Ste 8 ....Canton MI 48187	**877-269-4774**		260
Galco Industrial Electronics Inc			
26010 Pinehurst Dr ....Madison Heights MI 48071	**888-783-4611**	248-542-9090	246
Galderma Laboratories Inc			
14501 N Fwy ....Fort Worth TX 76177	**866-735-4137**	817-961-5000	578
Gale Cengage Learning			
27500 Drake Rd ....Farmington Hills MI 48331	**800-877-4253***	248-699-4253	633-2
*Cust Svc			
Galena Gazette			
716 S Bench St ....Galena IL 61036	**800-373-6397**	815-777-0019	528-4
Galesburg Area Convention & Visitors Bureau			
2163 E Main St ....Galesburg IL 61401	**800-916-3330**	309-343-2485	206
Galesburg Printing & Publishing Co			
140 S Prairie St ....Galesburg IL 61401	**800-733-2767**	309-343-7181	633-8
Galison Publishing LLC			
28 W 44th St Ste 1411 ....New York NY 10036	**800-670-7441**	212-354-8840	130
Gallade Chemical Inc			
1230 E St Gertrude Pl ....Santa Ana CA 92707	**888-830-9092**	714-546-9901	146

Name / Address	City	State	Zip	Toll-Free	Phone	Class
Gallagher Asphalt Corp 18100 S Indiana Ave	Thornton	IL	60476	**800-536-7160**		188-4
Gallagher Corp 3908 Morrison Dr	Gurnee	IL	60031	**800-524-8597**	847-249-3440	601-2
Gallagher, Gams, Pryor, Tallan & Littrell LLP 471 E Broad St 19th Fl	Columbus	OH	43215	**866-378-1624**	614-228-5151	427
Gallant Greetings Corp 4300 United Pkwy	Schiller Park	IL	60176	**800-621-4279**	847-671-6500	130
Gallaudet University 800 Florida Ave NE	Washington	DC	20002	**800-995-0550**	202-651-5000	166
Gallaudet University Library 800 Florida Ave NE	Washington	DC	20002	**800-995-0550**	202-651-5217	433-6
Gallegos Corp PO Box 821	Vail	CO	81658	**800-425-5346**	970-926-3737	189-7
Galleon Resort & Marina 617 Front St	Key West	FL	33040	**800-544-3030**	305-296-7711	665
Gallerie 454 15105 Kercheval Ave	Grosse Pointe Park	MI	48230	**800-914-3538**	313-822-4454	517
Gallery 78 Inc 796 Queen St	Fredericton	NB	E3B1C6	**888-883-8322**	506-454-5192	42
Gallery of History Inc 3601 W Sahara Ave	Las Vegas	NV	89102	**800-425-5379**	702-364-1000	51
Galliard Capital Management Inc 800 La Salle Ave Ste 1100	Minneapolis	MN	55402	**800-717-1617**	612-667-3220	401
Galliker Dairy Company Inc 143 Donald Ln	Johnstown	PA	15907	**800-477-6455**	814-266-8702	296-27
Gallo Salame 2411 Baumann Ave	San Lorenzo	CA	94580	**800-988-6464**		296-26
Galloup 3838 Clay Ave SW	Wyoming	MI	49548	**888-755-3110**	269-965-4005	191-2
Galls Inc 2680 Palumbo Dr	Lexington	KY	40509	**800-477-7766**	859-266-7227	572
Gallun Snow 1920 Market St Ste 201	Denver	CO	80202	**866-846-7514**	303-433-9500	392
Gallup Inc 1001 Gallup Dr	Omaha	NE	68102	**888-500-8282**	402-951-2003	464
Galt House Hotel 140 N Fourth St	Louisville	KY	40202	**800-843-4258**	502-589-5200	378
Galvan Industries Inc 7320 Millbrook Rd *General	Harrisburg	NC	28075	**800-277-5678***	704-455-5102	479
Galvanic Applied Sciences USA Inc 41 Wellman St	Lowell	MA	01851	**866-252-8470**	970-040-2701	201
Galveston Central Appraisal District 9850 Emmett F Lowry Expy Ste A	Texas City	TX	77591	**866-277-4725**	409-935-1980	317
Galveston College 4015 Ave Q	Galveston	TX	77550	**866-483-4242**	409-944-4242	162
Galveston County Daily News 8522 Teichman Rd PO Box 628	Galveston	TX	77553	**800-561-3611**	409-683-5200	528-2
Galvestonian Condominium Association 1401 E Beach Dr	Galveston	TX	77550	**888-526-6161**	409-765-6161	703
GAMA (General Aviation Manufacturers Association) 1400 K St NW Ste 801	Washington	DC	20005	**866-427-3287**	202-393-1500	49-21
Gama Aviation LLC 2 Corporate Dr Ste 1050	Shelton	CT	06484	**800-468-1110**	203-337-4600	21
GAMA International 2901 Telestar Ct *Cust Svc	Falls Church	VA	22042	**800-345-2687***		49-9
Gamajet Cleaning Systems Inc 604 Jeffers Cir *Sales	Exton	PA	19341	**877-426-2538***	610-408-9940	385
Gambrill State Park 8602 Gambrill Pk Rd	Frederick	MD	21702	**800-830-3974**	816-842-8600	561
Gambrinus Co, The 14800 San Pedro 3rd Fl	San Antonio	TX	78232	**800-596-6486**	210-496-6525	81-1
Gambro BCT 10811 W Collins Ave	Lakewood	CO	80215	**877-339-4228**	303-231-4357	418
GAMCO Investors Inc 1 Corporate Ctr *NYSE: GBL*	Rye	NY	10580	**800-422-3554**	914-921-5100	524
GamePlan Financial Marketing LLC 300 ParkBrooke Pl Ste 200 *Cust Svc	Woodstock	GA	30189	**800-886-4757***	678-238-0601	401
GameStop Corp 625 Westport Pkwy *NYSE: GME*	Grapevine	TX	76051	**800-883-8895**	817-424-2000	179
Gamewell FCI 12 Clintonville Rd	Northford	CT	06472	**800-606-1983**	203-484-7161	283
Gaming Partners International Inc 3945 W Cheyenne Ave Ste 208 *NASDAQ: GPIC*	Las Vegas	NV	89032	**800-728-5766**	702-384-2425	322
Gamma Beta Phi Society 5204 Kingston Pk Ste 31-33	Knoxville	TN	37919	**800-628-9920**	865-483-6212	48-16
Gamma Dynacare Medical Laboratories Inc 115 Midair Ct	Brampton	ON	L6T5M3	**800-668-2714**		414
Gamma Sports 200 Waterfront Dr	Pittsburgh	PA	15222	**800-333-0337**	412-323-0335	706
Gandy Co 528 Gandrud Rd	Owatonna	MN	55060	**800-443-2476**	507-451-5430	273
Ganesh Machinery 20869 Plummer St	Chatsworth	CA	91311	**888-542-6374**	818-349-9166	384
Gannett Company Inc 7950 Jones Branch Dr *NYSE: GCI*	McLean	VA	22107	**800-778-3299**	703-854-6000	733
Gannett Fleming Inc 207 Senate Ave	Camp Hill	PA	17011	**800-233-1055**	717-763-7211	261
Gannett Welsh & Kotler LLC 222 Berkeley St	Boston	MA	02116	**800-225-4236**	617-236-8900	400
Gannon University 109 University Sq *Admissions	Erie	PA	16541	**800-426-6668***	814-871-7000	166
Gans Ink & Supply Company Inc 1441 Boyd St	Los Angeles	CA	90033	**800-421-6167**		387
Gant Travel Management 400 W Seventh St Ste 233 *Cust Svc	Bloomington	IN	47404	**800-742-4198***	630-227-3800	766
Gap Inc 2 Folsom St *NYSE: GPS*	San Francisco	CA	94105	**800-333-7899**		157-4
Gapco Inc 2151 Centennial Dr	Gainesville	GA	30504	**866-534-7928**	770-534-7928	
Garaga Inc 8500 25th Ave	St Georges	QC	G6A1K5	**800-464-2724**	418-227-2828	478
Garan Lucow Miller PC 1000 Woodbridge St	Detroit	MI	48207	**800-875-1530**	313-446-1530	427
GARBC (General Assn of Regular Baptist Churches) 1300 N Meacham Rd	Schaumburg	IL	60173	**888-588-1600**		48-20
Garco Bldg Systems 2714 S Garfield Rd	Airway Heights	WA	99001	**800-941-2291**	509-244-5611	105
Gard Communications 1140 SW 11th Ave Ste 300	Portland	OR	97205	**800-800-7132**	503-221-0100	
Garden City Community College 801 N Campus Dr	Garden City	KS	67846	**800-658-1696**	620-276-7611	162
Garden City Group LLC 105 Maxess Rd	Melville	NY	11747	**888-404-8013**	631-470-5000	427
Garden City Hotel 45 Seventh St	Garden City	NY	11530	**877-549-0400**	516-747-3000	378
Garden Court Hotel 520 Cowper St	Palo Alto	CA	94301	**800-824-9028**	650-322-9000	378
Garden Grove Chamber of Commerce 12866 Main St Ste 102	Garden Grove	CA	92840	**800-959-5560**	714-638-7950	139
Garden of Life Inc 4200 NorthCrop Pkwy Ste 200	Palm Beach Gardens	FL	33410	**866-465-0051**	561-748-2477	794
Garden Spa at MacArthur Place 29 E MacArthur St	Sonoma	CA	95476	**800-722-1866**	707-933-3193	703
Garden State Community Bank (GSCB) 36 Ferry St *NYSE: NYCB*	Newark	NJ	07105	**877-786-6560**	973-589-8616	70
Garden State Engine & Equipment 3509 Rt 22 E	Somerville	NJ	08876	**800-479-3857**	908-534-5444	357
Garden State Growers 99 Locust Grove Rd	Pittstown	NJ	08867	**800-288-8484**	908-730-8888	368
Gardens Hotel 526 Angela St	Key West	FL	33040	**800-526-2664**	305-294-2661	378
Gardens of the American Rose Ctr 8877 Jefferson-Paige Rd	Shreveport	LA	71119	**800-637-6534**	318-938-5402	97
Gardenside Ltd 808 Anthony St	Berkeley	CA	94710	**888-999-8325**	415-455-4500	319-4
Gardner Denver Water Jetting Systems Inc 785 Greens Pkwy Ste 225	Houston	TX	77067	**800-580-5300**		
Gardner Glass Products Inc 301 Elkin Hwy PO Box 1570	North Wilkesboro	NC	28659	**800-334-7267**		333
Gardner Inc 3641 Interchange Rd	Columbus	OH	43204	**800-848-8946**	614-456-4000	274
Gardner Manufacturing Inc 1201 West Lake St	Horicon	WI	53032	**800-558-8890**		
Gardner Publications Inc 6915 Valley Ave	Cincinnati	OH	45244	**800-950-8020**	513-527-8800	633-9
Gardner Village 1100 W 7800 S	West Jordan	UT	84088	**800-662-4335**	801-566-8903	458
Gardner-Gibson PO Box 5449	Tampa	FL	33675	**800-237-1155**	813-248-2101	46
Gardners Candies Inc 2600 Adams Ave PO Box E	Tyrone	PA	16686	**800-242-2639**	814-684-3925	123
Gardner-Webb University 110 S Main St PO Box 997	Boiling Springs	NC	28017	**800-253-6472**	704-406-4000	166
Gare Inc 165 Rosemont St	Haverhill	MA	01832	**888-289-4273**	978-373-9131	43
Gared Sports Inc 707 N Second St Ste 220	Saint Louis	MO	63102	**800-325-2682**	314-421-0044	706
Garfield Refining Co 810 E Cayuga St	Philadelphia	PA	19124	**800-523-0968**		409
Gargoyles Inc 500 George Washington Hwy	Smithfield	RI	02917	**866-807-0195**	401-231-3800	538
Garick Corp 13600 Broadway Ave	Cleveland	OH	44125	**800-242-7425**		
Garkane Energy Co-op 120 W 300 S PO Box 465	Loa	UT	84747	**800-747-5403**		245
Garland C Norris Co 1101 Terry Rd	Apex	NC	27502	**800-331-8920**	919-387-1059	555
Garland Commercial Industries 185 S St	Freeland	PA	18224	**800-424-2411**	570-636-1000	298
Garland Company Inc 3800 E 91st St	Cleveland	OH	44105	**800-321-9336**	216-641-7500	46
Garland County 501 Ouachita Ave	Hot Springs	AR	71901	**800-482-5964**	501-622-3610	337
Garland Independent School District (GISD) 501 S Jupiter PO Box 469026	Garland	TX	75042	**800-252-5555**	972-494-8201	681
Garland Resort 4700 N Red Oak Rd	Lewiston	MI	49756	**877-442-7526**		665
Garland Sales Inc PO Box 1870	Dalton	GA	30720	**800-524-0361**	706-278-7880	131
Garland, The 4222 Vineland Ave	North Hollywood	CA	91602	**800-238-3759**	818-980-8000	378
Garlich Printing Co 525 Rudder Rd	Fenton	MO	63026	**844-449-4752**		622
Garlock Printing & Converting Corp 164 Fredette St	Gardner	MA	01440	**800-473-1328**	978-630-1028	623
Garmin Ltd 1200 E 151st St *NASDAQ: GRMN*	Olathe	KS	66062	**888-442-7646**	913-397-8200	525
Garner Industries Inc 7201 N 98th St PO Box 29709	Lincoln	NE	68507	**800-228-0275**	402-434-9100	604
Garner Printing Co 1697 NE 53rd Ave	Des Moines	IA	50313	**800-747-2171**	515-266-2171	623
Garnet Hill Inc 231 Main St	Franconia	NH	03580	**800-870-3513**	603-823-5545	740-1
Garney Construction 1333 NW Vivion Rd	Kansas City	MO	64118	**800-832-1517**	816-741-4600	188-10
Garr Tool Co 7800 N Alger Rd	Alma	MI	48801	**800-248-9003**	989-463-6171	491
Garrett College 687 Mosser Rd	McHenry	MD	21541	**866-554-2773**	301-387-3000	162

	Toll-Free	Phone	Class
Garrett Metal Detectors 1881 W State St .... Garland TX 75042	800-234-6151	972-494-6151	470
Garrett's Desert Inn 311 Old Santa Fe Trl ...... Santa Fe NM 87501	800-888-2145	505-982-1851	378
Garry Packing Inc 11272 E Central Ave ...... Del Rey CA 93616	800-248-2126	559-888-2126	296-18
Garsite LLC 539 S Tenth St ...... Kansas City KS 66105	888-427-7483	913-342-5600	21
Gartner Inc 56 Top Gallant Rd ...... Stamford CT 06902 *NYSE: IT*	866-471-2526	203-964-0096	464
Gartner Studios 220 Myrtle St E ...... Stillwater MN 55082	888-235-0484		
Garvan Woodland Gardens 550 Arkridge Rd PO Box 22240 ...... Hot Springs AR 71903	800-366-4664	501-262-9300	97
Garvey Corp 208 S Rt 73 ...... Blue Anchor NJ 08037	800-257-8581	609-561-2450	207
Garvey Wholesale Beverage Inc 2542 San Gabriel Blvd ...... Rosemead CA 91770	800-287-2075	626-280-5244	80-3
Garvin County 201 W Grant St 2nd Fl ...... Pauls Valley OK 73075	800-231-8668	405-238-2772	337
Garvin-Allen Solutions Ltd 155 Chain Lake Dr Unit 12 ...... Halifax NS B3S1B3	877-325-9062	902-453-3554	180
Gary Plastic Packaging Corp 1340 Viele Ave ...... Bronx NY 10474	800-221-8150	718-893-2200	596
Gary Soren Smith Ctr for the Fine & Performing Arts *Ohlone College* 43600 Mission Blvd ...... Fremont CA 94539	800-309-2131	510-659-6031	568
GAS (Glass Art Society) 6512 23rd Ave NW Ste 329 ...... Seattle WA 98117	800-636-2377	206-382-1305	48-4
Gas Equipment Company Inc 11616 Harry Hines Blvd ...... Dallas TX 75229	800-821-1829	972-241-2333	384
Gas Technology Energy Concepts LLC 401 William L Gaiter Pkwy Ste 4 ...... Buffalo NY 14215	800-451-8294		172
Gas Transmission-Northwest 1400 SW Fifth Ave Ste 900 ...... Portland OR 97201	888-750-6275		325
GasAmerica Services Inc 2700 W Main St ...... Greenfield IN 46140	800-643-1948	866-920-5550	324
Gasboy International Inc 7300 W Friendly Ave ...... Greensboro NC 27420 *Sales	800-444-5579*	336-547-5000	635
Gascosage Electric Co-op 803 S Hwy 28 PO Box G ...... Dixon MO 65459	866-568-8243	573-759-7146	245
Gas-Fired Products Inc 305 Doggett St ...... Charlotte NC 28203	800-830-3983	704-372-3485	318
Gaska-Tape Inc 1810 W Lusher Ave ...... Elkhart IN 46517	800-423-1571	574-294-5431	727
Gasket Manufacturing Co 18001 Main St ...... Gardena CA 90248	800-442-7538	310-217-5600	326
Gaskets Inc 301 W Hwy 16 ...... Rio WI 53960	800-558-1833	920-992-3137	326
Gaspard Inc 200 N Janacek Rd ...... Brookfield WI 53045	800-784-6868	262-784-6800	155-13
Gassaway Mansion 106 Dupont Dr ...... Greenville SC 29607	888-912-7469	864-271-0188	50-3
Gassco Inc PO Box 9866 ...... Bakersfield CA 93389	800-390-7837	661-832-7406	575
Gastonian, The 220 E Gaston St ...... Savannah GA 31401	800-322-6603	912-232-2869	378
Gatan Inc 5794 W Las Positas Blvd ...... Pleasanton CA 94588	888-887-3377	925-463-0200	418
Gatco Inc 1550 Factor Ave ...... San Leandro CA 94577	800-227-5640	510-352-8770	782
Gate Petroleum Co 9540 San Jose Blvd PO Box 23627 ...... Jacksonville FL 32241	866-571-1982	904-737-7220	324
GateHouse Media Inc 350 Willowbrook Office Pk ...... Fairport NY 14450 *NYSE: GHSE*	800-544-9218	585-598-0030	633-8
Gatekeeper Systems Inc 8 Studebaker ...... Irvine CA 92618	888-808-9433	949-453-1940	199
Gates Bar-B-Q 4621 Paseo Blvd ...... Kansas City MO 64110	800-662-7427	816-923-0900	666
Gates Corp 1551 Wewatta St ...... Denver CO 80202	800-709-6001	303-744-1911	369
Gates County 200 Court St ...... Gatesville NC 27938	800-272-9829	252-357-2411	337
Gates Family Foundation 1390 Lawrence St ...... Denver CO 80204	866-590-4377	303-722-1881	305
Gates of the Arctic National Park & Preserve 4175 Geist Rd ...... Fairbanks AK 99709	866-869-6887	907-457-5752	560
Gateway Arch 50 S Leonor K Sullivan Blvd ...... Saint Louis MO 63102	877-982-1410		50-4
Gateway Community & Technical College (GCTC) 500 Technology Wy ...... Florence KY 41042	855-346-4282	859-441-4500	795
GateWay Community College 108 N 40th St ...... Phoenix AZ 85034	888-994-4433	602-286-8000	162
Gateway Community College 20 Church St ...... New Haven CT 06510	800-390-7723	203-285-2000	162
Gateway Ctr 1 Gateway Dr ...... Collinsville IL 62234	800-289-2388	618-345-8998	205
Gateway Energy Services Corp 400 Rella Blvd Ste 300 ...... Montebello NY 10901	800-805-8586		316
Gateway Foundation Inc 1080 E Park St ...... Carbondale IL 62901	877-505-4673	618-529-1151	722
Gateway Inc 7565 Irvine Ctr Dr ...... Irvine CA 92618	800-846-2000	949-471-7040	173-2
Gateway Limousines 1550 Gilbreth Rd ...... Burlingame CA 94010	800-486-7077	650-697-5548	440
Gateway Logistics Group Inc, The 18201 Viscount Rd ...... Houston TX 77032	800-338-8017	281-443-7447	311
Gateway Mortgage Group LLC 244 S Gateway Pl PO Box 974 ...... Jenks OK 74037	877-764-9319	877-406-8109	217
Gateway Newstands 240 Chrislea Rd ...... Woodbridge ON L4L8V1	800-942-5351	905-851-9652	526
Gateway Supply Company Inc 1312 Hamrick St ...... Columbia SC 29201	800-922-5312	803-771-7160	608
Gateway Technical College 3520 - 30th Ave ...... Kenosha WI 53144	800-247-7122	262-564-2200	795
Gateway Travel Service Inc 28470 W 13 Mile Rd Ste 200 ...... Farmington Hills MI 48334	800-423-4898	248-432-8600	767
Gateway Truck & Refrigeration 921 Fournie Ln ...... Collinsville IL 62234	800-449-2131	618-345-0123	57
Gator Park 24050 SW Eigth St ...... Miami FL 33194	800-559-2205	305-559-2255	818
Gatorade Sports Science Institute 617 W Main St ...... Barrington IL 60010	800-616-4774		664
Gatorland 14501 S Orange Blossom Trl ...... Orlando FL 32837	800-393-5297	407-855-5496	818
GATRA 2 Oak St ...... Taunton MA 02780	800-483-2500	508-823-8828	108
Gavel International Corp 935 Lakeview Pkwy Ste 190 ...... Vernon Hills IL 60061	800-544-2835		184
Gay Men's Health Crisis (GMHC) 119 W 24th St ...... New York NY 10011	800-243-7692	212-367-1000	48-17
Gayla Industries Inc PO Box 920800 ...... Houston TX 77292	800-231-7508		757
Gaylor Electric 5750 Castle Creek Pkwy N Dr Ste 400 ...... Indianapolis IN 46250	800-878-0577	317-843-0577	189-4
Gaylord Bros 7282 William Barry Blvd ...... Syracuse NY 13212	800-345-5330	800-448-6160	319-3
Gaylord Hospital Gaylord Farms Rd PO Box 400 ...... Wallingford CT 06492	866-429-5673	203-284-2800	373-6
Gaylord Industries Inc 10900 SW Avery St ...... Tualatin OR 97062	800-547-9696	503-691-2010	18
Gaylord Manufacturing Co 1088 Montclaire Dr ...... Ceres CA 95307	800-375-0091	209-538-3313	811
Gaylord Opryland Hotel & Convention Ctr 2800 Opryland Dr ...... Nashville TN 37214	888-236-2427	615-889-1000	378
Gaymar Industries Inc 10 Centre Dr ...... Orchard Park NY 14127	800-828-7341	800-327-0770	474
Gazette, The 885 W Liberty St ...... Medina OH 44256	800-633-4623	330-725-4299	528-2
Gazette, The 501 Second Ave SE ...... Cedar Rapids IA 52401	800-397-8333	319-398-8333	528-2
GazetteXtra *Janesville Gazette* 1 S Parker Dr PO Box 5001 ...... Janesville WI 53547	800-362-6712	608-755-8250	528-2
GB Tubulars Inc 950 Threadneedle St Ste 130 ...... Houston TX 77079	888-245-3848	713-465-3585	490
GBCVB (Greater Boston Convention & Visitors Bureau) 2 Copley Pl Ste 105 ...... Boston MA 02116	888-733-2678	617-536-4100	206
GBH Communications Inc 1309 S Myrtle Ave ...... Monrovia CA 91016	800-222-5424		246
GBPD (Guardian Building Products) 979 Batesville Rd ...... Greer SC 29651	800-569-4262	864-297-6101	191-3
GBS Corp 7233 Freedom Ave NW ...... North Canton OH 44720	800-552-2427	330-494-5330	530
GBS Filing Solutions 224 Morges Rd ...... Malvern OH 44644	800-873-4427	330-494-5330	556
GBTA (Global Business Travel Assn, The) 123 N Pitt St ...... Alexandria VA 22314	888-574-6447	703-684-0836	48-23
GC America Inc 3737 W 127th St ...... Alsip IL 60803 *Cust Svc	800-323-7063*	708-597-0900	228
GC Services LP 6330 Gulfton St ...... Houston TX 77081	800-756-6524	713-777-4441	160
GCA (Everi Holdings Inc) 7250 S Tenaya Way Ste 100 ...... Las Vegas NV 89113 *NYSE: EVRI*	800-833-7110	702-855-3000	56
GCA Services Group 1350 Euclid Ave Ste 1500 ...... Cleveland OH 44115	800-422-8760		152
GCEC (Grayson-Collin Electric Cooperative) 14568 FM 121 PO Box 548 ...... Van Alstyne TX 75495	800-967-5235	903-482-7100	245
GCI Outdoor Inc 66 Killingworth Rd ...... Higganum CT 06441	800-956-7328	860-345-9595	321
GCS (Georgia Cancer Specialists Pc) 1835 Savoy Dr ...... Atlanta GA 30341	800-491-5991	770-496-9400	373-7
GCSAA (Golf Course Superintendents Assn of America) 1421 Research Pk Dr ...... Lawrence KS 66049	800-472-7878	785-841-2240	48-2
GCTC (Gateway Community & Technical College) 500 Technology Wy ...... Florence KY 41042	855-346-4282	859-441-4500	795
GCube Insurance Services Inc 3101 Wcoast Hwy Ste 100 ...... Newport Beach CA 92663	877-903-4777	949-515-9981	389
G&D Integrated 50 Commerce Dr ...... Morton IL 61550	800-451-6680		186
GDEB (General Dynamics Electric Boat Corp) 75 Eastern Pt Rd ...... Groton CT 06340	800-742-9692	860-433-3000	694
GE Analytical Instruments Inc 6060 Spine Rd ...... Boulder CO 80301	800-255-6964	303-444-2009	688
GE Fanuc Intelligent Platforms Embedded Systems Inc 7401 Snaproll NE ...... Albuquerque NM 87109	800-433-2682	505-875-0600	621
GE Healthcare 8200 W Tower Ave ...... Milwaukee WI 53223	800-558-5102	414-355-5000	250
GE Healthcare Bio-Sciences Corp 800 Centennial Ave ...... Piscataway NJ 08855	800-810-9118	732-457-8000	738
GE Lighting Systems Inc 3010 Spartanburg Hwy ...... East Flat Rock NC 28726	888-694-3533	828-693-2000	438
GE Richards Graphic Supplies Company Inc 928 Links Ave ...... Landisville PA 17538	800-233-0410	717-892-4620	686
GE Walker Inc 4420 E Adamo Dr Ste 206 ...... Tampa FL 33605	800-749-2483		473
Gear Energy Ltd 240 - Fourth Ave SW Ste 2600 ...... Calgary AB T2P2V6	877-494-3430	403-538-8435	532
Gear for Sports Inc 9700 Commerce Pkwy ...... Lenexa KS 66219	800-255-1065	913-693-3200	155-1
Gearhart By the Sea 1157 N Marion Ave ...... Gearhart OR 97138	800-547-0115	503-738-8331	665
Geary Pacific Corp 1908 N Enterprise St ...... Orange CA 92865	800-444-3279	714-279-2950	686
GEARYS Beverly Hills 351 N Beverly Dr ...... Beverly Hills CA 90210	800-793-6670		361

		Toll-Free	Phone	Class

Geauga County Transit
12555 Merritt Rd ....Chardon OH 44024 — **888-287-7190*** — 440-279-2150 — 108
*Cust Svc

GeBBS Healthcare Solutions Inc
600 Corporate Pointe
Ste 1250 ....Culver City CA 90230 — **888-539-4282** — — 177

Gebco Insurance Assoc
8600 LaSalle Rd Ste 338 ....Towson MD 21286 — **800-464-3226** — 410-668-3100 — 389

GEFCO (GEFCO Inc)
2215 S Van Buren ....Enid OK 73703 — **800-759-7441** — 580-234-4141 — 533

GEFCO Inc (GEFCO)
2215 S Van Buren ....Enid OK 73703 — **800-759-7441** — 580-234-4141 — 533

Gefran ISI Inc
8 Lowell Ave ....Winchester MA 01890 — **888-888-4474** — 781-729-5249 — 201

Gehl Foods
N116 W15970 Main St
PO Box 1004............Germantown WI 53022 — **800-521-2873** — 262-251-8572 — 296-10

Gehr Industries
7400 E Slauson Ave ....Los Angeles CA 90040 — **800-688-6606** — 323-728-5558 —

Gehring LP & Gehring Diato LP
24800 Drake Rd ....Farmington Hills MI 48335 — **888-923-9760** — 248-427-3901 —

Geiger
70 Mt Hope Ave ....Lewiston ME 04240 — **888-953-9340** — — 9

Geiger International Inc
6095 Fulton Industrial Blvd SW ....Atlanta GA 30336 — **800-456-6452** — 404-344-1100 — 319-1

Geisinger Health Plan
100 N Academy Ave ....Danville PA 17822 — **800-447-4000** — 570-271-8760 — 390-3

Geisinger Health System (CMC)
1800 Mulberry St ....Scranton PA 18510 — **800-230-4565** — 570-703-8000 — 373-3

Geisinger South Wilkes-Barre (GSWB)
25 Church St ....Wilkes-Barre PA 18765 — **800-230-4565** — 570-808-3100 — 373-3

Geisinger Wyoming Valley Medical Ctr
1000 E Mountain Dr ....Danville PA 17822 — **800-230-4565** — 570-271-8600 — 373-3

Gelia, Wells & Mohr Inc
390 S Youngs Rd ....Williamsville NY 14221 — **888-711-4884** — 716-629-3202 — 632

Gelita USA Inc
2445 Port Neal Industrial Rd
............Sergeant Bluff IA 51054 — **800-223-9244** — 712-943-5516 — 296-22

GELPAK
31398 Huntwood Ave ....Hayward CA 94544 — **888-621-4147** — 510-576-2220 — 692

Gem Dandy Inc
200 W Academy St ....Madison NC 27025 — **800-334-5101** — 336-548-9624 — 155-2

GEM Edwards Inc
5640 Hudson Industrial Pkwy
PO Box 429............Hudson OH 44236 — **800-733-7976** — — 474

GEM Group
9 International Way ....Lawrence MA 01843 — **800-800-3200** — 978-691-2000 — 67

Gem State Paper & Supply Co
1801 Highland Ave E ....Twin Falls ID 83303 — **800-727-2737** — 208-733-6081 — 555

GEMCOR Corp
1750 Union Rd ....West Seneca NY 14224 — **800-325-1596** — 716-674-9300 — 454

Gemex Systems Inc
6040 W Executive Dr Ste A............Mequon WI 53092 — **866-694-3639** — 262-242-1111 — 410

Gemini Coatings Inc
421 SE 27th St ....El Reno OK 73036 — **800-262-5710** — 405-262-5710 — 546

Gemini Companies, The
80 Arkay Dr Ste 110 ....Hauppauge NY 11788 — **855-891-0092** — —

Gemini Inc
103 Mensing Way ....Cannon Falls MN 55009 — **800-538-8377** — 507-263-3957 — 697

Gemini Valve
2 Otter Ct ....Raymond NH 03077 — **800-370-0936** — 603-895-4761 — 784

Gemmel Pharmacy Group Inc
143 N Euclid Ave ....Ontario CA 91762 — **888-302-0229** — 909-988-0591 — 237

Gemological Institute of America (GIA)
5345 Armada Dr ....Carlsbad CA 92008 — **800-421-7250** — 760-603-4000 — 49-4

Gems Sensors Inc
1 Cowles Rd ....Plainville CT 06062 — **800-378-1600** — 855-877-9666 — 201

Gemtex Abrasives
234 Belfield Rd ....Toronto ON M9W1H3 — **800-387-5100** — 416-245-5605 — 1

Gemtor Inc
1 Johnson Ave ....Matawan NJ 07747 — **800-405-9048** — 732-583-6200 — 674

GenBio
15222 Ave of Science Ste A ....San Diego CA 92128 — **800-288-4368*** — 858-592-9300 — 231
*Tech Supp

Gencor Industries Inc
5201 N Orange Blossom Trl ....Orlando FL 32810 — **888-887-1266*** — 407-290-6000 — 190
NASDAQ: GENC ■ *General*

Gene Codes Corp
775 Technology Dr ....Ann Arbor MI 48108 — **800-497-4939** — 734-769-7249 — 177

Genealogycom
360 W 4800 N ....Provo UT 84604 — **800-262-3787** — — 396

Genemed Biotechnologies Inc
458 Carlton Ct S San Francisco
............San Francisco CA 94080 — **877-436-3633** — 650-952-0110 — 664

Geneos Wealth Management Inc
9055 E Mineral Cir Ste 200 ....Centennial CO 80112 — **888-812-5043** — 303-785-8470 — 686

GenePOC Inc
360 Rue Franquet Porte 3 Technology Pk
............Quebec QC G1P4N3 — **844-616-1544** — 418-650-3535 — 738

Generac Power Systems Inc
PO Box 8 ....Waukesha WI 53187 — **888-436-3722** — 262-544-4811 — 515

General Air Service & Supply Company Inc
1105 Zuni St ....Denver CO 80204 — **877-782-8434** — 303-892-7003 — 146

General Assn of Regular Baptist Churches (GARBC)
1300 N Meacham Rd ....Schaumburg IL 60173 — **888-588-1600** — — 48-20

General Atomics
3550 General Atomics Ct
PO Box 85608............San Diego CA 92121 — **800-669-6820** — 858-455-3000 — 664

General Aviation Manufacturers Association (GAMA)
1400 K St NW Ste 801 ....Washington DC 20005 — **866-427-3287** — 202-393-1500 — 49-21

General Bearing Corp
44 High St ....West Nyack NY 10994 — **800-431-1766*** — 845-358-6000 — 75
*Sales

General Broach Co
307 Salisbury St ....Morenci MI 49256 — **800-889-7555** — 517-458-7455 — 491

General Butler State Resort Park
1608 US Hwy 227 ....Carrollton KY 41008 — **866-462-8853** — 502-732-4384 — 665

General Cable Corp
4 Tesseneer Dr ....Highland Heights KY 41076 — **800-572-8000** — 859-572-8000 — 809
NYSE: BGC

General Carbide Corp
1151 Garden St ....Greensburg PA 15601 — **800-245-2465** — — 752

General Code
781 Elmgrove Rd ....Rochester NY 14624 — **800-836-8834** — 585-328-1810 — 427

General Collection Company inc
402 W Third St ....Grand Island NE 68802 — **888-603-1423** — 308-381-1423 — 160

General Data Co Inc
4354 Ferguson Dr ....Cincinnati OH 45245 — **800-733-5252** — 513-752-7978 — 174

General Devices Company Inc
1410 S Post Rd ....Indianapolis IN 46239 — **800-821-3520** — 317-897-7000 — 201

General Digital Corp
8 Nutmeg Rd N ....South Windsor CT 06074 — **800-952-2535** — 860-282-2900 — 173-4

General Dynamics Advanced Information Systems
12450 Fair Lakes Cir ....Fairfax VA 22033 — **877-449-0600** — — 525

General Dynamics Electric Boat Corp (GDEB)
75 Eastern Pt Rd ....Groton CT 06340 — **800-742-9692** — 860-433-3000 — 694

General Dynamics Information Technology
3211 Jermantown Rd ....Fairfax VA 22030 — **800-242-0230** — 703-995-8700 — 180

General Educational Development Testing Service
American Council on Education
1 Dupont Cir NW ....Washington DC 20036 — **866-205-6267** — 202-939-9300 — 244

General Electric
1100 Technology Pk Dr ....Billerica MA 01821 — **800-833-9438** — 978-437-1000 — 201

General Electrodynamics Corporation Inc
8000 Calendar Ave ....Arlington TX 76001 — **800-551-6038** — 817-572-0366 — 22

General Equipment & Supplies Inc
4300 Main Ave ....Fargo ND 58103 — **800-437-2924** — 701-282-2662 — 357

General Equipment Co
620 Alexander Dr SW PO Box 334 ......Owatonna MN 55060 — **800-533-0524*** — 507-451-5510 — 385
*Cust Svc

General Fasteners Co
37584 Amrhein Rd ....Livonia MI 48150 — **800-945-2658** — — 350

General Federation of Women's Clubs (GFWC)
1734 N St NW ....Washington DC 20036 — **800-443-4392** — 202-347-3168 — 48-24

General Films Inc
645 S High St ....Covington OH 45318 — **888-436-3456** — —

General Filters Inc
43800 Grand River Ave ....Novi MI 48375 — **866-476-5101** — — 18

General Financial Supply Inc
1235 N Ave ....Nevada IA 50201 — **800-759-4374** — 515-382-3549 — 623

General Formulations Inc
309 S Union St ....Sparta MI 49345 — **800-253-3664** — 616-887-7387 — 596

General Growth Properties Inc
110 N Wacker Dr ....Chicago IL 60606 — **888-395-8037** — 312-960-5000 — 651
NYSE: GGP

General Healthcare Resources Inc
2250 Hickory Rd
Ste 240............Plymouth Meeting PA 19462 — **800-879-4471** — 610-834-1122 — 362

General Hearing Corp
175 Brookhollow Esplanade ....Harahan LA 70123 — **800-824-3021** — 504-733-3767 — 237

General Insulation Company Inc
278 Mystic Ave Ste 209 ....Medford MA 02155 — **800-229-9148** — 781-391-2070 — 191-4

General Loose Leaf Bindery Co
3811 Hawthorn Ct ....Waukegan IL 60087 — **800-621-0493** — 847-244-9700 — 86

General Machine Products Company Inc
3111 Old Lincoln Hwy ....Trevose PA 19053 — **800-345-6009*** — 215-357-5500 — 753
*Tech Supp

General Magnaplate Corp
1331 Us Rt 1 ....Linden NJ 07036 — **800-441-6173** — 908-862-6200 — 485

General Mills Foundation
PO Box 9452............Minneapolis MN 55440 — **800-248-7310** — — 304

General Mills Inc
1 General Mills Blvd ....Minneapolis MN 55426 — **800-248-7310** — — 299
NYSE: GIS

General Motors Acceptance Corp (GMAC)
200 Renaissance Ctr ....Detroit MI 48265 — **877-320-2559** — — 217

General Motors Corp (GMC)
100 Renaissance Ctr ....Detroit MI 48265 — **800-462-8782** — 313-556-5000 — 59
NYSE: GM

General Motors Corp Buick Motor Div
300 Renaissance Ctr ....Detroit MI 48265 — **877-825-8964*** — 800-521-7300 — 59
*Cust Svc

General Motors Foundation Inc
PO Box 33170............Detroit MI 48232 — **800-222-1020** — — 304

General Pet Supply Inc
7711 N 81st St ....Milwaukee WI 53223 — **800-433-9786** — 414-365-3400 — 96

General Plastic Extrusions Inc
1238 Kasson Dr ....Prescott WI 54021 — **800-532-3888** — 715-262-3806 — 544

General Plastics Mfg Co
4910 Burlington Way ....Tacoma WA 98409 — **800-806-6051** — 253-473-5000 — 597

General Produce Co
1330 N 'B' St ....Sacramento CA 95811 — **800-366-4991** — 916-441-6431 — 297-7

General Revenue Corp
4660 Duke Dr Ste 300 ....Mason OH 45040 — **800-234-6258** — — 160

General Services Administration
Federal Citizen Information Center
PO Box 100............Pueblo CO 81009 — **888-878-3256** — — 339-19

General Services Administration Regional Offices
Region 1 - New England
10 Cswy St
Thomas P O'Neill Federal Bldg Rm 900 ..Boston MA 02222 — **866-734-1727** — — 339-19
Region 4 - Southeast Sunbelt
1800 F St NW ....Washington DC 20405 — **800-333-4636** — — 339-19
Region 8 - Rocky Mountain
Denver Federal Ctr Bldg 41 ....Denver CO 80225 — **888-999-4777** — 303-236-7329 — 339-19

General Shale Products LLC
3015 Bristol Hwy ....Johnson City TN 37601 — **800-414-4661** — 423-282-4661 — 150

General Star National Insurance Co
120 Long Ridge Rd PO Box 10354 ......Stamford CT 06902 — **800-624-5237** — 203-328-5000 — 390-4

General Steel Inc
PO Box 1503............Macon GA 31202 — **800-476-2794** — 478-746-2794 — 490

General Theological Seminary
440 W 21st St ....New York NY 10011 — **888-487-5649** — 212-243-5150 — 167-3

General Tool & Supply Co Inc
2705 NW Nicolai St ....Portland OR 97210 — **800-526-9328** — 503-226-3411 — 384

Company / Address	Toll-Free	Phone	Class
General Tool Co 101 Landy Ln .... Cincinnati OH 45215	800-314-9817		752
General Tools Mfg Company LLC 80 White St .... New York NY 10013	800-697-8665	212-431-6100	753
General Tours 53 Summer St .... Keene NH 03431	800-221-2216		755
General Truck Body 7110 Jensen Dr .... Houston TX 77093	800-395-8585	713-692-5177	513
General Truck Parts & Equipment Co 4040 W 40th St .... Chicago IL 60632	800-621-3914	773-247-6900	61
General Vision Services LLC 520 Eigth Ave 9th Fl .... New York NY 10018	855-653-0586		539
General Wax & Candle Co 6863 Beck Ave PO Box 9398 ...... North Hollywood CA 91605	800-929-7867	818-765-5800	122
General Wire Spring Co 1101 Thompson Ave .... McKees Rocks PA 15136	800-245-6200	412-771-6300	714
Generex Biotechnology Corp 4145 N Service Rd Ste 200 ... Burlington ON L7L6A3 *OTC: GNBT*	800-391-6755		85
Genesee & Wyoming Inc 66 Field Pt Rd .... Greenwich CT 06830 *NYSE: GWR*	800-230-1059	203-629-3722	644
Genesee Community College 1 College Rd .... Batavia NY 14020	866-225-5422	585-343-0055	162
Genesee County Parks & Recreation 5045 Stanley Rd .... Flint MI 48506	800-648-7275	810-736-7100	50-5
Genesee District Library *Flint Township-McCarty Library* 2071 Graham Rd .... Flint MI 48532	866-732-1120	810-732-9150	433-3
Genesee Valley Ctr 3341 S Linden Rd .... Flint MI 48507	866-236-1128	810-732-4000	458
Genesis 10 950 Third Ave 2nd Fl .... New York NY 10022	800-261-1776	212-688-5522	180
Genesis Biosystems Inc 1500 Eagle Ct # 75057 .... Lewisville TX 75057	888-577-7335	972-315-7888	77
Genesis Energy LP 919 Milam Ste 2100 ...... Houston TX 77002 *NYSE: GEL*	800-284-3365	713-860-2500	593
Genesis HealthCare Corp 101 E State St .... Kennett Square PA 19348	800-944-7776	610-444-6350	449
Genesis Home Care Inc 116 E Heritage Dr .... Tyler TX 75703	800-947-0273	903-509-3374	362
Genesis Industries Inc 601 Pro Ject Dr .... Elmwood WI 54740	800-826-3301	715-639-2435	
Genesis Medical Ctr Illini Campus 801 Illini Dr .... Silvis IL 61282	800-250-6020	309-281-4000	373-3
Genesys Telecommunications Laboratories Inc 2001 Junipero Serra Blvd .... Daly City CA 94014	888-436-3797		730
Genetec Inc 2280 Alfred-Nobel Blvd Ste 400 ..... Montreal QC H4S2A4	866-684-8006	514-332-4000	225
Genetic Alliance Inc 4301 Connecticut Ave NW Ste 404 .... Washington DC 20008	800-860-8747	202-966-5557	48-17
Genetic Assays Inc 4711 Trousdale Dr Ste 209 ..... Nashville TN 37220	800-390-5280		
Genetic Engineering News 140 Huguenot St 3rd Fl ..... New Rochelle NY 10801	888-211-4235	914-740-2100	527-12
Genetics Associates Inc 1916 Patterson St Ste 400 ..... Nashville TN 37203	800-331-4363	615-327-4532	414
Genetics Society of America (GSA) 9650 Rockville Pk .... Bethesda MD 20814	866-486-4363	301-634-7300	49-19
Genetrack Biolabs Inc 401-1508 Broadway W .... Vancouver BC V6J1W8	888-828-1899	604-325-7282	417
Geneva Capital LLC 522 Broadway St Ste 4 ..... Alexandria MN 56308	800-408-9352		194
Geneva College 3200 College Ave ..... Beaver Falls PA 15010	800-847-8255	724-847-6500	166
Geneva State Park 4499 Pandanarum Rd ...... Geneva OH 44041	866-644-6727	440-466-8400	561
Geneva Woods Pharmacy Inc 501 W International Airport Rd Ste 1A .... Anchorage AK 99518	800-478-0005	907-565-6100	237
Genex Co-op Inc/CRI PO Box 469 .... Shawano WI 54166	888-333-1783	715-526-2141	11-2
Genex Services Inc 440 E Swedesford Rd Ste 1000 ...... Wayne PA 19087	888-464-3639	610-964-5100	194
Genghis Grill 8200 Springwood Dr Ste 230 ..... Irving TX 75063	888-436-4447		667
Genie Co 1 Door Dr PO Box 67 ..... Mount Hope OH 44660	800-354-3643		349
Genie Industries Inc 18340 NE 76th St .... Redmond WA 98052	800-536-1800	425-881-1800	468
Genie Repros Inc 2211 Hamilton Ave ...... Cleveland OH 44114	877-496-6611	216-696-6677	623
Genieco Inc 200 N Laflin St .... Chicago IL 60607	800-223-8217	312-421-2383	145
Genoa Business Forms Inc 445 Park Ave .... Sycamore IL 60178	800-383-2801		110
GenomeDx 1038 Homer St .... Vancouver BC V6B2W9	888-975-4540		738
Genomic Health Inc 101 Galveston Dr ...... Redwood City CA 94063 *NASDAQ: GHDX*	866-662-6897	650-556-9300	85
Genova Diagnostics 63 Zillicoa St .... Asheville NC 28801	800-522-4762	828-253-0621	417
Genova Products Inc 7034 E Court St .... Davison MI 48423	800-521-7488	888-309-1808	604
Genpak Carthage 505 E Cotton St .... Carthage TX 75633	800-626-6695	903-693-7151	300
Genpak Corp 68 Warren St .... Glens Falls NY 12801	800-626-6695		544
GenPore 1136 Morgantown Rd PO Box 380 ... Reading PA 19607	800-654-4391	610-374-5171	604
Gen-Probe Inc 10210 Genetic Center Dr .. San Diego CA 92121	800-523-5001	858-410-8000	231
GenQuest DNA Analysis Laboratory 133 Coney Island Dr ...... Sparks NV 89431	877-362-5227	775-358-0652	416
Gensco Inc 4402 20th St E .... Tacoma WA 98424	877-620-8203	253-620-8203	608
Gentec Inc 2625 Dalton .... Quebec QC G1P3S9	800-463-4480	418-651-8000	203
Gentek Bldg Products Inc 11 Craigwood Rd .... Avenel NJ 07001	800-489-1144	732-381-0900	693
GENTEX Corp 324 Main St .... Simpson PA 18407	888-894-1755	570-282-3550	538
Gentry Locke Rakes & Moore LLP 10 Franklin Rd S E Ste 900 ... Roanoke VA 24011	866-983-0866	540-983-9300	427
Genzyme Corp 500 Kendall St .... Cambridge MA 02142	800-745-4447	617-252-7500	85
Genzyme Genetics 3400 Computer Dr ...... Westborough MA 01581	800-255-7357	508-898-9001	416
GEO Drilling Fluids Inc 1431 Union Ave .... Bakersfield CA 93305	800-438-7436	661-325-5919	536
Geo Group Corp, The 6 Odana Ct .... Madison WI 53719	800-993-2262	608-230-1000	763
Geocel Corp 2504 Marina Dr .... Elkhart IN 46514	800-348-7615		3
Geo-Comm Inc 601 W St Germain St ...... Saint Cloud MN 56301	888-436-2666		
Geocomp Corp 1145 Massachusetts Ave ... Boxborough MA 01719 *Cust Svc*	800-822-2669*	978-635-0012	178-5
Geoforce Inc 750 Canyon Dr Ste 140 ...... Coppell TX 75019	888-574-3878	972-546-3878	532
Geographics 108 Main St 3rd Fl .... Norwalk CT 06851	800-436-4919		548-2
Geo-instruments Inc 24 Celestial Dr ...... Narragansett RI 02882	800-477-2506		461
Geological Museum 1000 E University Ave ...... Laramie WY 82071	800-842-2776	307-766-2646	517
Geological Society of America, The (GSA) 3300 Penrose Pl PO Box 9140 .... Boulder CO 80301	800-472-1988	303-357-1000	49-19
GeoLogics Corp 5285 Shawnee Rd Ste 300 ... Alexandria VA 22312	800-684-3455	703-750-4000	180
Geophysical Research Letter 2000 Florida Ave NW ...... Washington DC 20009	800-966-2481	202-462-6900	527-12
Geophysics GPR International Inc 100 - 2545 Delorimier St ..... Longueuil QC J4K3P7	800-672-4774	450-679-2400	723
George E DeLallo Co Inc 6390 Rt 30 .... Jeannette PA 15644	877-335-2556	724-523-6577	297-8
George Fox Evangelical Seminary 12753 SW 68th Ave .... Portland OR 97223	800-493-4937	503-554-6150	167-3
George Fox University 414 N Meridian St .... Newberg OR 97132	800-765-4369	503-538-8383	166
George H Crosby Manitou State Park c/o Tettegouche State Pk 5702 Hwy 61. .... Silver Bay MN 55614	888-646-6367	218-353-8800	561
George Heinl & Co 201 Church St .... Toronto ON M5B1Y7	800-387-7858	416-363-0093	523
George K Baum & Co 4801 Main St Ste 500 ..... Kansas City MO 64112	800-821-7195	816-474-1100	686
George Koch Sons LLC 10 S 11th Ave .... Evansville IN 47712	888-873-5624	812-465-9600	385
George Mason Mortgage Corp 4100 Monu Crnr Dr Ste 100 ..... Fairfax VA 22030	800-867-6859	703-273-2600	507
George Mason University 4400 University Dr .... Fairfax VA 22030	888-627-6612	703-993-1000	166
George R Brown Convention Ctr 1001 Avenida de Las Americas ... Houston TX 77010	800-427-4697	713-853-8000	205
George R Peters Assoc Inc PO Box 850 .... Troy MI 48099	800-929-5972	248-524-2211	246
George Reed Inc 140 Empire Ave .... Modesto CA 95354	877-823-2305		261
George Risk Industries Inc 802 S Elm St .... Kimball NE 69145 *OTC: RSKIA* ■ *Sales*	800-523-1227*	308-235-4645	688
George S Coyne Chemical Co 3015 State Rd .... Croydon PA 19021	800-523-1230	215-785-3000	146
George S Mickelson Trail 11361 Nevada Gulch Rd .... Lead SD 57754	800-888-1798	605-584-3896	561
George STREET Photo & Video LLC 230 W Huron St Ste 3W ...... Chicago IL 60654	866-831-4103		586
George T Bagby State Park & Lodge 330 Bagby Pkwy .... Fort Gaines GA 39851	877-591-5575	229-768-2571	561
George Uhe Company Inc 219 River Dr .... Garfield NJ 07026	800-850-4075	201-843-4000	477
George Washington University 2121 'I' St NW .... Washington DC 20052	866-498-3382	202-994-1000	166
George Washington University Hospital 900 23rd St NW .... Washington DC 20037	888-449-3627	202-715-4000	373-3
George Washington University School of Medicine & Health Sciences 2300 Eye St NW Ross Hall ... Washington DC 20037	866-846-1107	202-994-3506	167-2
George, Miles & Buhr LLC 206 W Main St .... Salisbury MD 21801	800-789-4462	410-742-3115	261
Georges Inc 402 W Robinson Ave ...... Springdale AR 72764	800-800-2449	479-927-7000	615
Georgeson Securities Corp 480 Washington Blvd .... Jersey City NJ 07310	800-428-0717		686
Georgetown College 400 E College St .... Georgetown KY 40324 *Admissions*	800-788-9985*	502-863-8000	166
Georgetown Convention & Visitors Bureau 1101 N College St .... Georgetown TX 78626	800-436-8696	512-930-3545	206
Georgetown County 129 Screven St PO Box 421270 ... Georgetown SC 29442	800-868-2284	843-545-3063	337
Georgetown County Chamber of Commerce 531 Front St .... Georgetown SC 29440	800-777-7705	843-546-8436	139
Georgia *Aging Services Div* 2 Peachtree St NW 3rd Fl ... Atlanta GA 30303	866-552-4464	404-657-5258	
Arts Council 260 14th St NW .... Atlanta GA 30318	800-222-6006	404-685-2400	338-11
Banking & Finance Dept 2990 Brandywine Rd Ste 200 ... Atlanta GA 30341	888-986-1633	770-986-1633	338-11
Community Affairs Dept 60 Executive Pk S NE ...... Atlanta GA 30329	800-359-4663	404-679-4940	338-11

				Toll-Free	Phone	Class
Composite Medical Board						
2 Peachtree St NW 36th Fl	Atlanta	GA	30303	**800-436-7442**	404-656-3913	338-11
Corrections Dept						
300 Patrol Rd Forsyth	Atlanta	GA	31029	**888-343-5627**	404-656-4661	338-11
Department of Behavioral Health & Developmental Disabilities						
2 Peachtree St NW 24th Fl	Atlanta	GA	30303	**800-436-7442**	404-657-2252	338-11
Division of Child Support Services						
2 Peachtree St NW	Atlanta	GA	30303	**800-436-7442**		
Economic Development Dept						
75 Fifth St NW Ste 845	Atlanta	GA	30308	**800-255-0056**	404-962-4005	338-11
Emergency Management Agency (GEMA)						
935 E Confederate Ave SE						
PO Box 18055	Atlanta	GA	30316	**800-879-4362**	404-635-7000	338-11
Environmental Protection Div						
2 Martin Luther King Jr Dr						
Ste 1456 E tower	Atlanta	GA	30334	**888-373-5947**	404-657-5947	338-11
Governor's Office of Consumer Protection						
2 ML King Jr Dr Ste 356	Atlanta	GA	30334	**800-869-1123**		338-11
Insurance Commissioner						
2 Martin Luther King Jr Dr						
W Tower Ste 704	Atlanta	GA	30334	**800-656-2298**	404-656-2070	338-11
Natural Resources Dept						
2 ML King Jr Dr SE Ste 1252E	Atlanta	GA	30334	**800-366-2661**	404-656-3500	338-11
Ports Authority						
2 Main St	Savannah	GA	31402	**800-342-8012**	912-964-3811	614
Professional Licensing Boards Div						
237 Coliseum Dr	Macon	GA	31217	**844-753-7825**	478-207-2440	
Public Service Commission						
244 Washington St SW	Atlanta	GA	30334	**800-282-5813**	404-656-4501	338-11
Revenue Dept						
1800 Century Ctr Blvd NE	Atlanta	GA	30345	**877-423-6711**	404-417-6760	338-11
Secretary of State						
214 State Capitol	Atlanta	GA	30334	**800-436-7442**		
Securities & Business Regulation Div						
2 Martin Luther King Jr Dr SE						
W Tower Ste 820	Atlanta	GA	30334	**844-753-7825**		338-11
Student Finance Commission						
2082 E Exchange Pl	Tucker	GA	30084	**800-505-4732**	800-436-7442	721
Tourism Div						
75 Fifth St NW Ste 1200	Atlanta	GA	30308	**800-255-0056***	404-962-4000	338-11
*Resv						
Transparency & Campaign Finance Commission						
200 Piedmont Ave SE						
Ste 1416 W Tower	Atlanta	GA	30334	**866-589-7327**	404-463-1980	265
Veterans Service Dept						
Floyd Veterans Memorial Bldg						
Ste 970E	Atlanta	GA	30334	**800-436-7442**	404-656-2300	338-11
Vital Records Office						
2600 Skyland Dr NE	Atlanta	GA	30319	**800-436-7442**	404-679-4702	338-11
Georgia Assn of Realtors						
6065 Barfield Rd	Atlanta	GA	30328	**866-280-0576**	770-451-1831	652
Georgia Bar Journal						
104 Marietta St NW Ste 100	Atlanta	GA	30303	**866-773-2782**	404-527-8700	455-15
Georgia Boot Inc						
39 E Canal St	Nelsonville	OH	45764	**877-795-2410**	866-442-4908	301
Georgia Cancer Specialists PC (GCS)						
1835 Savoy Dr	Atlanta	GA	30341	**800-491-5991**	770-496-9400	373-7
Georgia Chamber of Commerce						
270 Peachtree St NW	Atlanta	GA	30303	**800-241-2286**	404-223-2264	140
Georgia College & State University						
231 W Hancock St	Milledgeville	GA	31061	**800-342-0471**	478-445-5004	166
Macon						
433 Cherry St Ste B	Macon	GA	31206	**800-342-0471**	478-752-4278	166
Georgia Correctional Industries						
2984 Clifton Springs Rd	Decatur	GA	30034	**800-282-7130**	404-244-5100	626
Georgia Crown Distributing Co						
100 Georgia Crown Dr	McDonough	GA	30253	**800-342-2350**	770-302-3000	81-3
Georgia Cu Affiliates						
6705 Sugarloaf Pkwy Ste 200	Duluth	GA	30097	**800-768-4282**	770-476-9625	219
Georgia Dental Assn						
7000 Peachtree Dnwdy Rd NE						
Ste 200 Bldg 17	Atlanta	GA	30328	**800-432-4357**	404-636-7553	227
Georgia department of natural resources						
Fort King George State Historic Site Darien						
302 McIntosh Rd SE	Darien	GA	31305	**800-864-7275**	912-437-4770	
Georgia Dome						
1 Georgia Dome Dr NW	Atlanta	GA	30313	**888-333-4406**	404-223-9200	716
Georgia Farm Bureau News						
1620 Bass Rd	Macon	GA	31210	**800-342-1192**	478-474-8411	455-1
Georgia Hardy Tours						
20 Eglinton Ave E	Toronto	ON	M4R1K8	**800-813-4509**	416-483-7533	767
Georgia Highlands College						
Cartersville						
5441 Hwy 20 NE	Cartersville	GA	30121	**800-332-2406**	678-872-8000	162
Floyd 3175 Cedartown Hwy	Rome	GA	30161	**800-332-2406**	706-802-5000	162
Georgia Institute of Technology Library						
266 Fourth St NW	Atlanta	GA	30332	**888-225-7804**	404-894-4500	433-6
Georgia Lottery Corp						
250 Williams St NW Ste 3000	Atlanta	GA	30303	**800-425-8259**	404-215-5000	450
Georgia Military College						
201 E Green St	Milledgeville	GA	31061	**800-342-0413**	478-387-4900	162
Georgia Municipal Association						
201 Pryor St SW	Atlanta	GA	30303	**888-488-4462**	404-688-0472	529
Georgia Northwestern Technical College Foundation Inc						
1 Maurice Culberson Dr SW	Rome	GA	30161	**866-983-4682**	706-295-6842	305
Georgia Nurses Assn (GNA)						
3032 Briarcliff Rd NE	Atlanta	GA	30329	**800-324-0462**	404-325-5536	529
Georgia Pharmacy Assn (GPhA)						
50 Lenox Pointe NE	Atlanta	GA	30324	**888-871-5590**	404-231-5074	581
Georgia Printco						
90 S Oak St	Lakeland	GA	31635	**866-572-0146**		623
Georgia Public Broadcasting (GPB)						
260 14th St NW	Atlanta	GA	30318	**800-222-6006**		628
Georgia Public Broadcasting						
260 14th St NW	Atlanta	GA	30318	**800-222-4788**	404-685-2400	641-9
Georgia Public Library						
1800 Century Pl NE Ste 150	Atlanta	GA	30345	**800-248-6701**	404-235-7200	31
Georgia Regional Hospital at Atlanta						
3073 Panthersville Rd	Atlanta	GA	30034	**800-436-7442**	404-243-2100	373-5
Georgia Regional Hospital at Savannah						
1915 Eisenhower Dr	Savannah	GA	31406	**800-436-7442**	912-356-2011	373-5
Georgia Society of CPA's						
6 Concourse Pkwy Ste 800	Atlanta	GA	30328	**800-330-8889**	404-231-8676	138
Georgia Southwestern State University						
800 Gsw State University Dr	Americus	GA	31709	**800-338-0082***	229-928-1273	166
*Admissions						
Georgia Veterinary Medical Assn						
2200 Century Pkwy Ste 725	Atlanta	GA	30345	**800-853-1625**	678-309-9800	790
Georgia's Own Credit Union						
1155 Peachtree St NE Ste 600	Atlanta	GA	30309	**800-533-2062**		219
Georgian Court Hotel						
773 Beatty St	Vancouver	BC	V6B2M4	**800-663-1155**	604-682-5555	378
Georgian Court University						
900 Lakewood Ave	Lakewood	NJ	08701	**800-458-8422**		166
Georgian Hotel, The						
1415 Ocean Ave	Santa Monica	CA	90401	**800-538-8147**		378
Georgian Resort						
384 Canada St	Lake George	NY	12845	**800-525-3436**	518-668-5401	378
Georgian Terrace Hotel						
659 Peachtree St NE	Atlanta	GA	30308	**800-651-2316**	404-897-1991	378
Georgian, The						
411 University St	Seattle	WA	98101	**888-363-5022**	206-621-7889	667
Georgie's Ceramic & Clay Company Inc						
756 NE Lombard St	Portland	OR	97211	**800-999-2529**	503-283-1353	43
Geoscape International Inc						
2100 W Flagler St	Miami	FL	33135	**888-211-9353**		180
Geo-Solutions						
1250 Fifth Ave	New Kensington	PA	15235	**800-544-6235**	412-856-7700	189-5
GEOSPAN Corp						
6901 E Fish Lake Rd Ste 156	Minneapolis	MN	55369	**800-436-7726**	763-493-9320	225
GeoSyntec Consultants Inc						
900 Broken Sound Pkwy NW						
Ste 200	Boca Raton	FL	33487	**866-676-1101**	561-995-0900	261
GEOSYS Inc						
3030 Harbor Ln	Plymouth	MN	55447	**866-782-4661**		194
Geotab Inc						
1081 S Service Rd W	Oakville	ON	L6L6K3	**877-436-8221**	416-434-4309	386
Geotech Environmental Equipment Inc						
2650 E 40th Ave	Denver	CO	80205	**800-833-7958**	303-320-4764	201
Geotek Engineering & Testing Services Inc						
909 E 50th St N	Sioux Falls	SD	57104	**800-354-5512**	605-335-5512	256
GeoTrust Inc						
350 Ellis St Bldg J	Mountain View	CA	94043	**866-511-4141**	650-426-5010	178-7
Gerald H Phipps						
5995 Greenwood Florida Plaza Blvd						
Ste 100	Greenwood Village	CO	80111	**877-574-4777**	303-571-5377	186
Gerald J Sullivan & Assoc Inc						
800 W Sixth St Ste 1800	Los Angeles	CA	90017	**800-421-8969**	213-626-1000	
Gerald R Ford Conservation Ctr						
1326 S 32nd St	Omaha	NE	68105	**800-634-6932**	402-595-1180	50-2
Gerald R Ford Museum						
303 Pearl St NW	Grand Rapids	MI	49504	**800-888-9487**	616-254-0400	517
Gerard Daniel Worldwide						
34 Barnhart Dr	Hanover	PA	17331	**800-232-3332**	717-637-5901	684
Gerber Childrenswear Inc						
7005 Pelham Rd Ste D	Greenville	SC	29615	**800-642-4452**	877-313-2114	155-4
Gerber Collision & Glass						
400 W Grand Ave	Elmhurst	IL	60126	**877-743-7237**	847-679-0510	62-4
Gerber Collision & Glass						
400 W Grand Ave	Elmhurst	IL	60126	**877-743-7237***	630-628-5848	62-4
*General						
Gerber Legendary Blades Inc						
14200 SW 72nd Ave	Portland	OR	97224	**800-950-6161**		
Gerber Life Insurance Co						
1311 Mamaroneck Ave	White Plains	NY	10605	**800-704-2180**	914-272-4000	390-2
Gerber Products Co						
445 State St	Fremont	MI	49413	**800-284-9488**		296-36
Gerber Technology Inc						
24 Industrial Pk Rd W	Tolland	CT	06084	**800-826-3243**	860-871-8082	739
Gerber Tours Inc						
100 Crossways Park Dr W						
Ste 400	Woodbury	NY	11797	**800-645-9145**	516-826-5000	755
Gerdau AmeriSteel Corp						
4221 W Boy Scout Blvd Ste 600	Tampa	FL	33607	**800-876-7833***	813-286-8383	719
*Sales						
Gerhart Systems & Controls Corp						
754 Roble Rd Ste 140	Allentown	PA	18109	**888-437-4278**	610-264-2800	635
Gerloff Company Inc						
14955 Bulverde Rd	San Antonio	TX	78247	**800-486-3621**	210-490-2777	186
Germain Motor Co						
Mercedes-Benz of Easton						
4300 Morse Crossing	Columbus	OH	43219	**855-217-5986**		57
German American Bancorp						
711 Main St	Jasper	IN	47546	**800-482-1314**	812-482-1314	359-2
NASDAQ: GABC						
GermanDelicom						
601 Westport Pkwy Ste 100	Grapevine	TX	76051	**877-437-6269**	817-410-9955	344
Germania Farm Mutual Insurance Assn						
507 Hwy 290 E	Brenham	TX	77833	**800-392-2202**	979-836-5224	390-4
Germiphene Corp						
1379 Colborne St E	Brantford	ON	N3T5M1	**800-265-9931**		578
Gerontological Society of America, The						
1220 L St NW Ste 901	Washington	DC	20005	**800-677-1116**	202-842-1275	49-8
Gerry Cosby & Company Inc						
11 Pennsylvania Plz	New York	NY	10001	**877-563-6464**		707
Gershman, Brickner & Bratton Inc						
8550 Arlington Blvd Ste 304	Fairfax	VA	22031	**800-573-5801**	703-573-5800	192
Gerson Co						
1450 S Lone Elm Rd	Olathe	KS	66061	**800-444-8172**	913-262-7400	410
Gertrude Hawk Chocolates Inc						
9 Keystone Pk	Dunmore	PA	18512	**866-932-4295**	800-822-2032	296-8
GERZENY'S RV NOKOMIS						
2110 N Tamiami Trl	Nokomis	FL	34275	**800-262-2182**	941-966-2182	57
GES 7000 Lindell Rd	Las Vegas	NV	89118	**800-443-9767**	702-515-5500	184
GES (Groundwater & Environmental Services Inc)						
1599 Rte 34 Ste 1	Wall Township	NJ	07727	**800-220-3068**		192
GES Global Energy Services Inc						
3220 Cypress Creek Pkwy	Houston	TX	77068	**888-523-6797**		190

Company / Address	City	State	ZIP	Toll-Free	Phone	Class
Gessner Products Company Inc 241 N Main St PO Box 389	Ambler	PA	19002	**800-874-7808**	215-646-7667	604
Gestion P R Maintenance Inc 639 King St W Ste 203	Kitchener	ON	N2G1C7	**800-719-2828**	905-304-8300	192
GET Engineering Corp 9350 Bond Ave	El Cajon	CA	92021	**877-494-1820**	619-443-8295	203
Get It LLC 128 N Pitt St Ste 2	Alexandria	VA	22314	**877-285-7861**		386
Getconnect 14114 Dallas Pkwy Ste 430	Dallas	TX	75254	**888-200-1831**		365
GetMeFriends 7801 Broadway St	San Antonio	TX	78209	**888-663-9143**		627
Gettysburg Borough Hall 59 E High St	Gettysburg	PA	17325	**800-433-7317**	717-334-1160	336
Gettysburg College 300 N Washington St	Gettysburg	PA	17325	**800-431-0803**	717-337-6000	166
Gettysburg Hotel 1 Lincoln Sq	Gettysburg	PA	17325	**866-378-1797**	717-337-2000	667
Getzen Company Inc 530 S Cty Hwy H PO Box 440	Elkhorn	WI	53121	**800-366-5584**	262-723-4221	523
Gevity Consulting Inc 375 Water St Ste 350	Vancouver	BC	V6B5C6	**800-785-3303**	604-608-1779	177
GF Health Products Inc 2935 NE Pkwy	Atlanta	GA	30360	**800-347-5678**	770-447-1609	475
GF Machining Solutions 560 Bond St	Lincolnshire	IL	60069	**800-282-1336**	847-913-5300	453
GfG Instrumentation Inc 1194 Oak Vly Dr Ste 20	Ann Arbor	MI	48108	**800-959-0329**	734-769-0573	201
GFWC (General Federation of Women's Clubs) 1734 N St NW	Washington	DC	20036	**800-443-4392**	202-347-3168	48-24
GFX International Inc 333 Barron Blvd	Grayslake	IL	60030	**800-274-3225**	847-543-4600	683
GGS Technical Publications Services 3265 Farmtrail Rd	York	PA	17406	**800-927-4474**	717-764-2222	776
Ghafari Assoc Inc 17101 Michigan Ave	Dearborn	MI	48126	**800-289-7822**	313-441-3000	261
Ghent Manufacturing Inc 2999 Henkle Dr	Lebanon	OH	45036	**800-543-0550**	513-932-3445	243
GHG Corp 960 Clear Lake City Blvd	Webster	TX	77598	**866-380-4146**	281-488-8806	178-10
Ghiotto & Associates Inc 2426 Phillips Hwy	Jacksonville	FL	32207	**844-304-7262**	904-886-0071	723
Ghirardelli Chocolate Co 1111 139th Ave	San Leandro	CA	94578	**800-877-9338**		296-8
GHS Corp 2813 Wilber Ave	Battle Creek	MI	49037	**800-388-4447**		523
GHS Interactive Security Inc 21031 Warner Center Ln Ste D	Woodland Hills	CA	91367	**855-447-4961**		689
GHX (Global Health Care Exchange LLC) 1315 W Century Dr	Louisville	CO	80027	**800-968-7449**	720-887-7000	225
GIA (Gemological Institute of America) 5345 Armada Dr	Carlsbad	CA	92008	**800-421-7250**	760-603-4000	49-4
Giact Systems Inc 700 Central Expy S	Allen	TX	75013	**866-918-2409**		225
Giant Communications Inc 418 W Fifth St Ste C	Holton	KS	66436	**800-346-9084**	785-362-9331	116
Giant Eagle Inc 101 Kappa Dr *Cust Svc	Pittsburgh	PA	15238	**800-553-2324***	412-963-6200	344
Giant Food Inc 8301 Professional Pl Ste 115	Landover	MD	20785	**888-469-4426**		344
Giant Food Stores LLC 1149 Harrisburg Pk	Carlisle	PA	17013	**888-814-4268**	717-249-4000	344
Giant Resource Recovery - Harleyville Inc (GRR) 654 Judge St PO Box 352	Harleyville	SC	29448	**800-786-0477**		192
Giantbankcom 6300 NE First Ave	Fort Lauderdale	FL	33334	**877-446-4200**		70
Gibbs Wire & Steel Company Inc Metals Dr PO Box 520	Southington	CT	06489	**800-800-4422**	860-621-0121	490
Gibraltar Industries Inc 3556 Lakeshore Rd *NASDAQ: ROCK*	Buffalo	NY	14219	**800-247-8368**	716-826-6500	719
Gibraltar Steel Furniture Inc 9976 Westwanda Dr	Beverly Hills	CA	90210	**800-416-3635**	310-276-8889	321
Gibson 309 Plus Pk Blvd	Nashville	TN	37217	**800-444-2766**	615-871-4500	523
Gibson & Barnes 1900 Weld Blvd Ste 140 *Sales	El Cajon	CA	92020	**800-748-6693***	619-440-6977	155-18
Gibson Arnold & Assoc 5433 Westheimer Rd Ste 1016	Houston	TX	77056	**800-879-2007**	713-572-3000	717
Gibson Dunn & Crutcher LLP 333 S Grand Ave	Los Angeles	CA	90071	**888-203-1112**	213-229-7000	427
Gibson Electric Membership Corp 1207 S College St PO Box 47	Trenton	TN	38382	**800-977-4076**	731-855-4740	245
Gibson Guitar Corp 309 Plus Park Blvd	Nashville	TN	37217	**800-444-2766**		523
Gibson Laboratories Inc 1040 Manchester St	Lexington	KY	40508	**800-477-4763**	859-254-9500	231
Gideon Putnam Resort & Spa 24 Gideon Putnam Rd	Saratoga Springs	NY	12866	**800-452-7275**	518-584-3000	378
Giffels-Webster Engineers Inc 28 W Adams Ste 1200	Detroit	MI	48226	**866-271-9663**		
Gift Card Partners Inc 47 Pine Plain Rd	Wellesley	MA	02482	**800-413-9101**		7
Gift Card Systems Inc 218 Cedar St	Abilene	TX	79601	**888-745-4112**		
Gift of Hope Organ & Tissue Donor Network 425 Spring Lake Dr	Itasca	IL	60143	**877-577-3747**	630-758-2600	541
Gift of Life Bone Marrow Foundation 800 Yamato Rd Ste 101	Boca Raton	FL	33431	**800-962-7769**	561-982-2900	48-17
Gift of Life Donor Program 401 N Third St	Philadelphia	PA	19123	**800-543-6391**	215-557-8090	541
Gift of Life Michigan 3861 Research Park Dr	Ann Arbor	MI	48108	**866-500-5801**		292
Gift of Life Transplant House 705 Second St SW	Rochester	MN	55902	**800-479-7824**	507-288-7470	371
Gift Wrap Co 338 Industrial Blvd *General	Midway	GA	31320	**800-443-4429***		544
GiftCertificatescom 11510 Blondo St	Omaha	NE	68164	**800-773-7368**	402-445-2300	327
Gifts for You LLC 2425 Curtiss St	Downers Grove	IL	60515	**866-443-8748**		292
Gigasonic 260 E Gish Rd	San Jose	CA	95112	**888-246-4442**	408-573-1400	522
Giga-Tronics Inc 4650 Norris Canyon Rd *OTC: GIGA*	San Ramon	CA	94583	**800-726-4442**	925-328-4650	248
GigMasterscom Inc 33 S Main St	Norwalk	CT	06854	**866-342-9794**		386
Gil Tours Travel Inc 1511 Walnut St 2nd Fl	Philadelphia	PA	19102	**800-223-3855**	215-568-6655	766
Gila County 1400 E Ash St	Globe	AZ	85501	**800-304-4452**	928-425-3231	337
Gilbane Bldg Co 7 Jackson Walkway	Providence	RI	02903	**800-445-2263**	401-456-5800	188-7
Gilbane Bldg Co New England Regional Office 7 Jackson Walkway	Providence	RI	02903	**800-445-2263**	401-456-5800	186
Gilbane Bldg Company Southwest Regional Office 1331 Lamar St Ste 1170	Houston	TX	77010	**800-445-2263**	713-209-1873	186
Gilbane Inc 7 Jackson Walkway	Providence	RI	02903	**800-445-2263**	401-456-5890	649
Gilbert Displays Inc 110 Spagnoli Rd	Melville	NY	11747	**855-577-1100**	631-577-1100	232
Gilbert Industries Inc 5611 Krueger Dr	Jonesboro	AR	72401	**800-643-0400**	870-932-6070	573
Gilbert Southern Corp 3555 Farnam St	Omaha	NE	68131	**800-901-1087**	402-342-2052	188-4
Gilbreth Packaging Systems 3001 State Rd	Croydon	PA	19021	**800-630-2413**		412
Gilchrist Center Baltimore 11311 McCormick Rd Ste 350	Hunt Valley	MD	21301	**888-823-8880**		
Gilcrease Museum 1400 N Gilcrease Museum Rd	Tulsa	OK	74127	**888-655-2278**	918-596-2700	517
Gilead Sciences Inc 333 Lakeside Dr *NASDAQ: GILD*	Foster City	CA	94404	**800-445-3235**	650-574-3000	85
Giles & Kendall Inc 3470 Maysville Rd NE PO Box 188	Huntsville	AL	35804	**800-225-6738**	256-776-2978	812
Giles Engineering Assoc Inc N8 W22350 Johnson Dr	Waukesha	WI	53186	**800-782-0610**	262-544-0118	256
Gilford Johnson Flooring 1874 Defoor Ave NW	Atlanta	GA	30325	**877-722-5545**		131
Gill Athletics Inc 2808 Gemini Ct *Cust Svc	Champaign	IL	61822	**800-637-3090***	217-367-8438	706
Gill Foundation Inc 1550 Wewatta St	Denver	CO	80202	**888-530-4455**	303-292-4455	
Gill Services Inc 650 Aldine Bender Rd	Houston	TX	77060	**800-375-7881**	281-820-5400	357
Gillespie County 101 W Main St	Fredericksburg	TX	78624	**800-272-9829**	830-997-6515	337
Gillespie Graphics 27676 SW Pkwy Ave	Wilsonville	OR	97070	**800-547-6841**	503-682-1122	683
Gillespie Museum of Minerals 421 N Woodland Blvd Unit 8403	DeLand	FL	32723	**800-688-0101**	386-822-7330	517
Gillespie, Prudhon & Associates Inc 16111 SE 106th Ave Ste 100	Clackamas	OR	97015	**800-595-2145**	503-657-0424	261
Gillette Children's Specialty Healthcare 200 E University Ave	Saint Paul	MN	55101	**800-719-4040**	651-291-2848	373-1
Gillette Generators Inc 1340 Wade Dr	Elkhart	IN	46514	**800-777-9639**	574-264-9639	515
Gillig Corp 25800 Clawiter Rd	Hayward	CA	94545	**800-735-1500**	510-785-1500	513
Gillmore Security Systems Inc 26165 Broadway Ave	Cleveland	OH	44146	**800-899-8995**	440-232-1000	689
Gilman & Pastor LLP 63 Atlantic Ave Ste 3	Boston	MA	02110	**877-428-7374**	888-252-0048	192
Gilman USA 1230 Cheyenne Ave PO Box 5	Grafton	WI	53024	**800-445-6267**	262-377-2434	491
Gilmore Entertainment Group 8901-A Business 17 N	Myrtle Beach	SC	29572	**800-843-6779**	843-913-4000	181
Gilmour 7800 Discovery Dr *Cust Svc	Middleton	WI	53562	**866-348-5661***		428
Gilmour Academy 34001 Cedar Rd	Gates Mills	OH	44040	**800-533-5140**	440-442-1104	618
Gilpin Casino, The 111 Main St PO Box 50	Black Hawk	CO	80422	**800-522-4700**		
Gilroy Chevrolet 6720 Auto Mall Dr	Gilroy	CA	95020	**800-237-6318**	408-427-3708	57
Gilsbar 2100 Covington Ctr	Covington	LA	70433	**800-445-7227**	985-892-3520	460
Gina B Designs Inc 12700 Industrial Pk Blvd Ste 40	Plymouth	MN	55441	**800-228-4856**	763-559-7595	130
Ginger Cove 4000 River Crescent Dr	Annapolis	MD	21401	**800-299-2683**	410-266-7300	668
Ginsberg's Foods Inc 29 Ginsberg Ln PO Box 17	Hudson	NY	12534	**800-999-6006**	518-828-4004	354
Ginsu Brands 118 E Douglas Rd	Walnut Ridge	AR	72476	**800-982-5233**		222
Giordano s Solid Waste Removal 110 N Mill Rd	Vineland	NJ	08360	**800-636-8625**	856-696-2068	656
Giorgio Foods Inc PO Box 96	Temple	PA	19560	**800-220-2139**	610-926-2139	296-20
Giovanni's Restaurant & Convention Ctr 610 N Bell School Rd	Rockford	IL	61107	**877-926-8300**	815-398-6411	667
Girl Scouts of the USA 420 Fifth Ave	New York	NY	10018	**800-478-7248**	212-852-8000	48-15
Girls Inc 120 Wall St 18th Fl	New York	NY	10005	**800-374-4475**	212-509-2000	48-24

Name / Address	Toll-Free	Phone	Class
Girls Nation *American Legion Auxiliary* 8945 N Meridian St .... Indianapolis IN 46260	800-504-4098	317-569-4500	48-7
Girls' Life Acqusition Co 3 S Frederick St Ste 806 .... Baltimore MD 21202	800-931-2237	410-426-9600	455-6
Girtz Industries Inc 5262 N E Shafer Dr .... Monticello IN 47960	844-464-4789		
GISD (Garland Independent School District) 501 S Jupiter PO Box 469026 .... Garland TX 75042	800-252-5555	972-494-8201	681
Giselle's Travel Inc 1300 Ethan Way Ste 100 .... Sacramento CA 95825	800-782-5545	916-922-5500	766
Gislason & Hunter LLP 2700 S Broadway .... New Ulm MN 56073	800-469-0234	507-354-3111	427
Gita Sporting Goods Ltd 12500 Steele Creek Rd .... Charlotte NC 28273 *Consumer Info	800-729-4482*	800-366-4482	
GitHub 88 Colin P Kelly Junior St .... San Francisco CA 94107	877-448-4820		
Gitman Bros 2309 Chestnut St .... Ashland PA 17921	800-526-3929		155-11
Gits Manufacturing Co 4601 121st St .... Urbandale IA 50323	800-323-3238		
GIW Industries Inc 5000 Wrightsboro Rd .... Grovetown GA 30813	888-832-4449	706-863-1011	637
GK Industries Ltd 50 Precidio Ct .... Brampton ON L6S6E3	800-463-8889	905-799-1972	61
GKG (Global Knowledge Group Inc) 302 N Bryan Ave .... Bryan TX 77803	866-776-7584		803
G-L Veneer Co Inc 2224 E Slauson Ave .... Huntington Park CA 90255	800-588-5003	323-582-5203	609
Glacial Lakes Energy LLC 301 20th Ave SE PO Box 933 .... Watertown SD 57201	866-934-2676	605-882-8480	575
Glacial Lakes State Park 25022 County Rd 41 .... Starbuck MN 56381	888-646-6367	320-239-2860	561
Glacial Ridge Hospital Foundation Inc 10 Fourth Ave SE .... Glenwood MN 56334	866-667-4747	320-634-4521	373-3
Glacial Waters Spa at Grand View Lodge 23521 Nokomis Ave .... Nisswa MN 56468	866-801-2951		703
Glacier Bancorp Inc PO Box 27 .... Kalispell MT 59903 *NASDAQ: GBCI*	800-735-4371	406-756-4200	359-2
Glacier Clear Enterprises Inc 3291 Thomas St .... Innisfil ON L9S3W3 *Cust Svc	800-668-5118*	705-436-6363	800
Glacier Electric Co-op Inc 410 E Main St .... Cut Bank MT 59427	844-834-4457	406-873-5566	245
Glacier National Park PO Box 350 .... Revelstoke BC V0E2S0	866-787-6221	250-837-7500	559
Glacier Park Inc PO Box 2025 .... Columbia Falls MT 59912	844-868-7474	406-892-2525	665
Glacier Water Services Inc 1385 Park Center Dr .... Vista CA 92081 *OTC: GWSV*	800-452-2437		55
Glade & Grove Supply 305 CR 17A W .... Avon Park FL 33825	800-433-4451	877-513-8182	274
Glade Springs Resort 255 Resort Dr .... Daniels WV 25832	866-562-8054	304-763-2000	665
Gladstone Dodge Chrysler Jeep RAM 5610 North Oak Trafficway .... Gladstone MO 64118	866-695-2043	816-455-3500	57
Glamos Wire Products Company Inc 5561 N 152nd St .... Hugo MN 55038	800-328-5062	651-429-5386	73
Glance Networks Inc 1167 Massachusetts Ave .... Arlington MA 02476	877-452-6236	781-646-8505	225
Glasgow Inc 104 Willow Grove Ave .... Glenside PA 19038	877-222-5514	215-884-8800	188-4
Glasgow-Barren County Chamber of Commerce 118 E Public Sq .... Glasgow KY 42141	800-264-3161	270-651-3161	139
Glass Art Society (GAS) 6512 23rd Ave NW Ste 329 .... Seattle WA 98117	800-636-2377	206-382-1305	48-4
Glass House Inn 3202 W 26th St .... Erie PA 16506	800-956-7222	814-833-7751	378
Glass Jacobson Financial Group 10711 Red Run Blvd Ste 101 .... Owings Mills MD 21117	800-356-7666	410-356-1000	2
GlassCraft Door Co 2002 Brittmoore Rd .... Houston TX 77043	800-766-2196	713-690-8282	234
Glassfab Tempering Services Inc 1448 Mariani Ct .... Tracy CA 95376	800-535-2133	209-229-1060	261
Glassmere Fuel Service Inc 1967 Saxonburg Blvd .... Tarentum PA 15084	800-235-9054		316
Glasteel-stabilit America Inc 285 Industrial Dr .... Moscow TN 38057	800-238-5546	901-877-3010	604
Glastender Inc 5400 N Michigan Rd .... Saginaw MI 48604	800-748-0423	989-752-4275	385
Glastonbury Southern Gage 46 Industrial Pk Rd .... Erin TN 37061	800-251-4243		491
Glastron 925 Frisbie St .... Cadillac MI 49601	800-354-3141		90
Glauber Equipment Corp 1600 Commerce Pkwy .... Lancaster NY 14086	888-452-8237	716-681-1234	357
Glaucoma Research Foundation 251 Post St Ste 600 .... San Francisco CA 94108	800-826-6693	415-986-3162	48-17
Glaval Bus 914 County Rd 1 .... Elkhart IN 46514	800-445-2825	574-262-2212	59
GlaxoSmithKline Inc 7333 Mississauga Rd N .... Mississauga ON L5N6L4	800-387-7374	905-819-3000	578
Glaz-Tech Industries Inc 2207 E Elvira Rd .... Tucson AZ 85756	800-755-8062	520-629-0268	329
GLC (God's Learning Ch) PO Box 61000 .... Midland TX 79711	800-707-0420	432-563-0420	735
GLE Associates Inc 5405 Cypress Center Dr Ste 110 .... Tampa FL 33609	888-453-4531	813-241-8350	192
Gleaner's Food Bank of Indianapolis 3737 Waldemere Ave .... Indianapolis IN 46241	800-944-9166	317-925-0191	305
Gleason Reel Corp 600 S Clark St .... Mayville WI 53050	888-504-5151	920-387-4120	117
Glen Cove Mansion Hotel & Conference Ctr 200 Dosoris Ln .... Glen Cove NY 11542	877-782-9426	516-671-6400	376
Glen Eden Corp 25999 Glen Eden Rd .... Corona CA 92883	800-843-6833	951-277-4650	121
Glen Grove Suites 2837 Yonge St .... Toronto ON M4N2J6	800-565-3024	416-489-8441	378
Glen Meadows 11630 Glen Arm Rd .... Glen Arm MD 21057	877-246-4744	667-213-1835	668
Glen Mills Schools PO Box 5001 .... Concordville PA 19331	800-441-2064	610-459-8100	619
Glen Oaks Community College 62249 Shimmel Rd .... Centreville MI 49032	888-994-7818	269-467-9945	162
Glen Research Corp 22825 Davis Dr .... Sterling VA 20164	800-327-4536	703-437-6191	664
Glenair Inc 1211 Air Way .... Glendale CA 91201	888-465-4094	818-247-6000	810
Glenbeigh 2863 SR 45 .... Rock Creek OH 44084	800-234-1001	440-563-3400	722
Glencoe/McGraw-Hill 8787 Orion Pl .... Columbus OH 43240	800-848-1567		633-2
Glencrest Farm 1576 Moores Mill Rd PO Box 4468 .... Midway KY 40347	800-903-0136	859-233-7032	367
Glendale (AZ) City Hall 5850 W Glendale Ave .... Glendale AZ 85301	800-367-8939	623-930-2000	336
Glendale Community College 1500 N Verdugo Rd .... Glendale CA 91208	866-251-1977	818-240-1000	162
Glendinning Marine Products 740 Century Cir .... Conway SC 29526	800-500-2380	843-399-6146	203
Glendo Corp PO Box 1153 .... Emporia KS 66801	800-835-3519	620-343-1084	295
Glendorn 1000 Glendorn Dr .... Bradford PA 16701	800-843-8568	814-362-6511	378
Gleneden Beach State Recreation Site 198 NE 123rd St .... Newport OR 97365	800-551-6949		561
Glenerin Inn, The 1695 The Collegeway .... Mississauga ON L5L3S7	877-991-9971	905-828-6103	378
Glenmede Funds 1650 Market St Ste 1200 .... Philadelphia PA 19103	800-966-3200	215-419-6000	524
Glenmore Inn 1000 Glenmore Court SE .... Calgary AB T2C2E6	800-661-3163	403-279-8611	378
Glenn O Hawbaker Inc 1952 Waddle Rd Ste 203 .... State College PA 16803	800-221-1355	814-237-1444	46
GlenOaks Hospital 701 Winthrop Ave .... Glendale Heights IL 60139	866-751-7127	630-545-8000	373-3
Glenro Inc 39 McBride Ave .... Paterson NJ 07501	888-453-6761	973-279-5900	318
Glenrock International Inc 985 E Linden Ave .... Linden NJ 07036	800-453-6762		720
Glensheen Mansion 3300 London Rd .... Duluth MN 55804	888-454-4536	218-726-8910	50-3
Glenview Chamber of Commerce 2320 Glenview Rd .... Glenview IL 60025	800-459-4250	847-724-0900	139
Glenville State College 200 High St .... Glenville WV 26351 *Admissions	800-924-2010*	304-462-7361	166
Glenwood LLC 111 Cedar Ln .... Englewood NJ 07631	800-542-0772	201-569-0050	579
Glenwood State Bank 5 E Minnesota Ave PO Box 197 .... Glenwood MN 56334	800-207-7333	320-634-5111	70
Glidden House 1901 Ford Dr .... Cleveland OH 44106	866-812-4537	216-231-8900	378
Glidewell Laboratories Inc 4141 MacArthur Blvd .... Newport Beach CA 92660	800-854-7256		738
Glimmerglass Networks Inc 26142 Eden Landing Rd .... Hayward CA 94545	877-723-1900	510-723-1900	178-10
Glines & Rhodes Inc 189 E St .... Attleboro MA 02703	800-343-1196	508-226-2000	483
GLM Industries LP 1508 - Eighth St .... Nisku AB T9E7S6	800-661-9828	780-955-2233	478
GlobaFone Inc 1950 Lafayette Rd Ste 207 .... Portsmouth NH 03801	800-826-6152	603-433-7232	386
Global Air Response 5919 Approach Rd .... Sarasota FL 34238	800-631-6565		30
Global Building Services Inc 25129 The Old Rd Ste 102 .... Stevenson Ranch CA 91381	800-675-6643		392
Global Business Travel Assn, The (GBTA) 123 N Pitt St .... Alexandria VA 22314	888-574-6447	703-684-0836	48-23
Global Cash Card 7 Corporate Pk Ste 130 .... Irvine CA 92606	888-220-4477	949-751-0360	400
Global Cloud 30 W Third St Unit 2 .... Cincinnati OH 45202	866-244-0450		
Global Consultants Inc 25 Airport Rd .... Morristown NJ 07960	877-264-6424	973-889-5200	180
Global Contact Services LLC 118 S Main St .... Salisbury NC 28144	844-324-5427	704-647-9621	392
Global Elite Group 825 E Gate Blvd Ste 301 .... Garden City NY 11530	877-425-0999		689
Global Filtration Inc 9207 Emmott St .... Houston TX 77040	888-717-0888	713-856-9800	57
Global Ground Support LLC 540 Old Hwy 56 .... Olathe KS 66061	888-780-0303	913-780-0300	22
Global Health Care Exchange LLC (GHX) 1315 W Century Dr .... Louisville CO 80027	800-968-7449	720-887-7000	225
Global Help Desk Services Inc 2080 Silas Deane Hwy .... Rocky Hill CT 06067	800-770-1075		180
Global HR Research LLC 24201 Walden Ctr Dr Ste 206 .... Bonita Springs FL 34134	800-790-1205	239-274-0048	260
Global Imaging Inc 2011 Cherry St Ste 116 .... Louisville CO 80027	800-787-9801	303-673-9773	41
Global Imaging Systems 3903 Northdale Blvd Ste 200W .... Tampa FL 33624	888-628-7834	813-960-5508	112
Global Industries Inc 17 W Stow Rd .... Marlton NJ 08053	800-220-1900	856-596-3390	319-1
Global Knowledge Group Inc (GKG) 302 N Bryan Ave .... Bryan TX 77803	866-776-7584		803
Global Knowledge Training LLC 9000 Regency Pkwy Ste 400 .... Cary NC 27518 *Cust Svc	877-200-8866*	919-461-8600	759

Company / Address	Toll-Free	Phone	Class
Global Linguist Solutions LLC 1155 Herndon Pkwy Ste 100 . . . . .Falls ChurchHerndon VA 20170	800-349-9142		
Global Maxfin Investments Inc 100 Mural St Ste 201 . . . . Richmond Hill ON L4B1J3	866-666-5266	416-741-1544	686
Global Medical Imaging LLC 222 Rampart St . . . . Charlotte NC 28203	800-958-9986		473
Global Nest LLC 281 State Rt 79 N Ste 208 . . . . .Morganville NJ 07751	866-850-5872	732-333-5848	177
Global Neuro-Diagnostics LP 2670 Firewheel Dr Ste B . . . . Flower Mound TX 75028	866-848-2522		417
Global Pacific Financial Services Ltd 10430 144 St . . . . Surrey BC V3T4V5	800-561-1177		317
Global Partners LP 800 South St Ste 500 PO Box 9161 . . . . Waltham MA 02454 *NYSE: GLP*	800-685-7222	781-894-8800	575
Global Payments Inc 3550 Lenox Rd Ste 3000 . . . . Atlanta GA 30326 *NYSE: GPN*	800-560-2960	770-829-8000	255
Global Quality Assurance Inc 6900 Tavistock Lakes Blvd Ste 400 . . . . Orlando FL 32827	888-322-3330		461
Global Reach Internet Productions LLC 2321 N Loop Dr Ste 101 . . . . Ames IA 50010	877-254-9828	515-996-0996	177
Global Relay Communications Inc 220 cambie St . . . . Vancouver BC V6B2M9	866-484-6630	604-484-6630	224
Global Search Network Inc 118 S Fremont Ave . . . . Tampa FL 33606	800-254-3398	813-832-8300	193
Global Shop Solutions Inc 975 Evergreen Cir . . . . The Woodlands TX 77380 *Sales	800-364-5958*	281-681-1959	178-1
Global Software Inc 3201 Beechleaf Ct Ste 170 . . . . Raleigh NC 27604	800-326-3444	919-872-7800	178-1
Global Tax Network US LLC 7950 Main St N Ste 200 . . . . .Minneapolis MN 55369	888-486-2695	763-746-4556	729
Global Technology Resources Inc 990 S Broadway Ste 300 . . . . Denver CO 80209	877-603-1984	303-455-8800	180
Global Travel 900 W Jefferson St . . . . Boise ID 83702	800-584-8888	208-387-1000	766
Global Travel International 1060 Maitland Center Commons Ste 305 . . . . Maitland FL 32751	800-715-4440	407-660-7800	767
Global Turnkey Systems Inc 2001 US 46 . . . . .Parsippany NJ 07054	800-221-1746	973-331-1010	178-10
Global University 1211 S Glenstone Ave . . . . .Springfield MO 65804	800-443-1083	417-862-9533	761
GlobalDie 1130 Minot Ave PO Box 1120 . . . . .Auburn ME 04211	800-910-3747	207-514-7252	752
Globalspec Inc 350 Jordan Rd . . . . Troy NY 12180	800-261-2052	518-880-0200	180
Globalstar 300 Holiday Square Blvd . . . . Covington LA 70433	877-728-7466	877-452-5782	677
Globe Consultants Inc 3112 Porter St Ste D . . . . Soquel CA 95073	800-208-0663		193
Globe Electronic Hardware Inc 34-24 56th St . . . . Woodside NY 11377	800-221-1505	718-457-0303	203
Globe Food Equipment Co 2153 Dryden Rd . . . . Dayton OH 45439	800-347-5423	937-299-5493	298
Globe Mfg Co 37 Loudon Rd . . . . Pittsfield NH 03263	800-232-8323	603-435-8323	572
Globecomm Systems Inc 45 Oser Ave . . . . Hauppauge NY 11788 *NASDAQ: GCOM*	866-499-0223	631-231-9800	643
Globe-Gazette 300 N Washington . . . . Mason City IA 50402	800-421-0546	641-421-0500	528-2
Globex Corp 3620 Stutz Dr . . . . Canfield OH 44406	800-533-8610	330-533-0030	256
Globus 5301 S Federal Cir . . . . .Littleton CO 80123	866-755-8581		755
Glo-Quartz Electric Heater Company Inc 7084 Maple St . . . . .Mentor OH 44060 *Sales	800-321-3574*	440-255-9701	318
Glorietta Bay Inn 1630 Glorietta Blvd . . . . .Coronado CA 92118	800-283-9383	619-435-3101	378
Glorybee Foods Inc 29548 B Airport Rd . . . . .Eugene OR 97402	800-456-7923	541-689-0913	296-24
Gloucester County Times 309 S Broad St . . . . .Woodbury NJ 08096	800-300-9321	856-845-3300	528-2
Gloves Inc 1950 Collins Blvd . . . . Austell GA 30106	800-476-4568	770-944-9186	155-7
GLS (Government Liaison Services Inc) 200 N Glebe Rd Ste 321 . . . . Arlington VA 22203	800-642-6564	703-524-8200	631
Gls Group Inc 27850 Detroit Rd . . . . Westlake OH 44145	800-955-9435	440-899-7770	184
Glyph Language Services Inc 157 S Howard St Ste 603 . . . . .Spokane WA 99201	866-274-3218		
GM Nameplate Inc 2040 15th Ave W . . . . Seattle WA 98119	800-366-7668	206-284-2200	479
GMAC (General Motors Acceptance Corp) 200 Renaissance Ctr . . . . Detroit MI 48265	877-320-2559		217
GMAC (Graduate Management Admission Council) 11921 Freedom Dr Ste 300 . . . . .Reston VA 20190	866-505-6559	703-668-9600	48-11
GMC (General Motors Corp) 100 Renaissance Ctr . . . . Detroit MI 48265 *NYSE: GM*	800-462-8782	313-556-5000	59
GMHC (Gay Men's Health Crisis) 119 W 24th St . . . . .New York NY 10011	800-243-7692	212-367-1000	48-17
GMI Building Services Inc 8001 Vickers St . . . . San Diego CA 92111	866-803-4464		256
GMP Metal Products Inc 3883 Delor St . . . . Saint Louis MO 63116	800-325-9808	314-481-0300	273
GN Diamond LLC 800 Chestnut St . . . . .Philadelphia PA 19107	800-724-8810	215-925-5111	409
GN Hearing 8001 E Bloomington Fwy . . . . Bloomington MN 55420	888-735-4327		250
GNA (Georgia Nurses Assn) 3032 Briarcliff Rd NE . . . . Atlanta GA 30329	800-324-0462	404-325-5536	529
GNC Inc 300 Sixth Ave . . . . Pittsburgh PA 15222 *NYSE: GNC*	877-462-4700	412-228-4600	354
Go 2 Group 138 N Hickory Ave . . . . Bel Air MD 21014	877-442-4669		177
Go Apply Inc 27081 Aliso Creek Rd Ste 200 . . . . Aliso Viejo CA 92656	888-435-3239		565
GO Carlson Inc 350 Marshallton Thorndale Rd . . . . .Downingtown PA 19335	800-338-5622	610-384-2800	719
Go Next 8000 W 78th St Ste 345 . . . . .Minneapolis MN 55439	800-842-9023	952-918-8950	755
GO Transit 20 Bay St Ste 600 . . . . Toronto ON M5J2W3	888-438-6646	416-869-3200	466
Go Travel Inc 2811 W SR 434 . . . . Longwood FL 32779	800-848-3005		770
Go..With Jo! Tours & Travel Inc 121 W Tyler .Harlingen TX 78550	800-999-1446	956-423-1446	755
Goal Sporting Goods Inc 37 Industrial Pk Rd PO Box 236 . . . . .Essex CT 06426	800-334-4625	860-767-9112	706
GoalLine Solutions 3115 Harvester Rd Ste 200 . . . . Burlington ON L7N3H8	866-788-4625		195
Goals & Poles 7575 Jefferson Hwy . . . . Baton Rouge LA 70806	800-275-0317	225-923-0622	706
Goalsetter Systems Inc 1041 Cordova Ave . . . . Lynnville IA 50153	800-362-4625		706
Gobin's Inc 615 N Santa Fe Ave . . . . Pueblo CO 81003	800-425-2324	719-544-2324	531
God's Learning Ch (GLC) PO Box 61000 . . . . .Midland TX 79711	800-707-0420	432-563-0420	735
Goddard College 123 Pitkin Rd .Plainfield VT 05667	800-468-4888	802-454-8311	166
Goddard Systems Inc 1016 West Ninth Ave . . . . King of Prussia PA 19406	800-463-3273	877-256-7046	310
Godfrey Trucking Inc 6173 W 2100 S . . . . .West Valley City UT 84128	800-444-7669	801-972-0660	775
Goehring, Rutter & Boehm 437 Grant St 14th fl . . . . Pittsburgh PA 15219	866-677-5970	412-281-0587	
Goetz Printing Co, The 7939 Angus Ct . . . . .Springfield VA 22153	866-245-0977	703-569-8232	623
Goetze Dental 3939 NE 33 Terr . . . . Kansas City MO 64117	800-692-0804	816-413-1200	473
Goetze's Candy Company Inc 3900 E Monument St . . . . .Baltimore MD 21205 *Orders	800-295-8058*	410-342-2010	296-8
GOG (Gynecologic Oncology Group) 1600 JFK Blvd Ste 1020 . . . . .Philadelphia PA 19103	800-225-3053	215-854-0770	49-8
Gogebic Community College E 4946 Jackson Rd . . . . .Ironwood MI 49938	800-682-5910	906-932-4231	162
GOGO WorldWide Vacations 5 Paragon Dr . . . . Montvale NJ 07645	800-254-3477		766
Gohmert Louie (Rep R - TX) 2243 Rayburn House Office Bldg . . . . Washington DC 20515	866-535-6302	202-225-3035	
GOJO Industries Inc 1 GOJO Plz Ste 500 . . . . Akron OH 44311	800-321-9647	330-255-6000	214
Gokeyless 3646 Cargo Rd . . . . .Vandalia OH 45377	877-439-5377	937-890-2333	41
Gold Canyon Golf Resort 6100 S Kings Ranch Rd . . . . Gold Canyon AZ 85118	800-827-5281	480-982-9090	665
Gold Coast Hotel & Casino 4000 W Flamingo Rd . . . . Las Vegas NV 89103	800-331-5334	702-367-7111	133
Gold Coast Ingredients Inc 2429 Yates Ave . . . . .Commerce CA 90040	800-352-8673	323-724-8935	297-8
Gold Coast Tours 105 Gemini Ave . . . . Brea CA 92821	800-638-6427	714-449-6888	107
Gold Dust West Carson City 2171 E William St . . . . Carson City NV 89701	877-519-5567	775-885-9000	133
Gold Eagle Co 4400 S Kildare Ave . . . . .Chicago IL 60632	800-367-3245		145
Gold Key Technology Solutions 4212 S Fifth St . . . . Temple TX 76501	866-321-1531	254-774-9035	180
Gold Mechanical Inc 4735 W Division St . . . . .Springfield MO 65802	877-873-9770	417-873-9770	189-10
Gold Medal PO Box 9452 . . . . .Minneapolis MN 55440	800-248-7310		296-23
Gold Medal Bakery Inc 1397 Bay St . . . . .Fall River MA 02724	800-642-7568	508-674-5766	68
Gold Newsletter PO Box 84900 . . . . .Phoenix AZ 85071	800-877-8847		527-9
Gold Pure Food Products Inc 1 Brooklyn Rd . . . . .Hempstead NY 11550	800-422-4681		
Gold Reserve Inc 926 W Sprague Ave Ste 200 . . . . Spokane WA 99201 *OTC: GDRZF*	800-625-9550	509-623-1500	500
Gold Room 127 N Franklin St . . . . Juneau AK 99801	800-544-0970	907-586-2660	667
Gold Standard Enterprises Inc 5100 W Dempster St . . . . .Skokie IL 60077	888-942-9463	847-674-4200	442
Gold Star Chili 650 Lunken Pk Dr . . . . Cincinnati OH 45226	800-643-0465	513-231-4541	666
Gold Star FS Inc PO Box 135 . . . . .Cambridge IL 61238	800-443-8497	309-937-3369	276
Gold Strike Casino Resort 1010 Casino Ctr Dr . . . . Tunica Resorts MS 38664 *Resv	888-245-7829*	662-357-1111	133
Gold Strike Hotel & Gambling Hall 1 Main St . . . . Jean NV 89019	800-634-1359	702-477-5000	133
Gold Tip LLC 584 E 1100 S Ste 5 . . . . American Fork UT 84003	800-551-0541		707
Goldbelt Hotel Juneau 3025 Clinton Dr . . . . Juneau AK 99801	800-770-5866	907-790-4990	378
Goldberg & Osborne 4423 E Thomas Rd Ste 3 . . . . Phoenix AZ 85018	800-843-3245	602-808-6200	443
Goldberg Weisman Cairo 1 E Upper Wacker Dr Ste 3800 . . . . . . .Chicago IL 60601	800-464-4772	312-273-6745	427
Goldbug Inc 511 16th St Ste 400 . . . . Denver CO 80202	800-942-9442	303-371-2535	157-1

Name / Address	City	State	ZIP	Toll-Free	Phone	Class
Goldcorp Inc 666 Burrard St Ste 3400	Vancouver	BC	V6C2X8	**800-567-6223**	604-696-3000	500
NYSE: GG						
Goldcrest Wallcoverings PO Box 245	Slingerlands	NY	12159	**800-535-9513**	518-478-7214	797
Gold-Eagle Co-op PO Box 280	Goldfield	IA	50542	**800-825-3331**		10-3
Goldec Hamm's Manufacturing Ltd 6760 65 Ave	Red Deer	AB	T4P1A5	**800-661-1665**	403-343-6607	392
Golden & Silver Falls State Natural Area Glenn Creek Rd	Coos Bay	OR	97420	**800-551-6949**		
Golden Aluminum Inc 1405 14th St	Fort Lupton	CO	80621	**800-838-1004**		490
Golden Anchor Travel 1909 Southwood St	Sarasota	FL	34231	**800-299-1125**	941-922-4070	770
Golden Artists Colors Inc 188 Bell Rd	New Berlin	NY	13411	**800-959-6543**	607-847-6154	43
Golden Door 777 Deer Springs Rd	San Marcos	CA	92069	**866-420-6414**	760-744-5777	702
Golden Eagle Insurance 9145 Miller Rd	Johnstown	OH	43031	**800-461-9224**		390-4
Golden Eagle Resort 511 Mountain Rd	Stowe	VT	05672	**866-970-0786**	802-253-4811	378
Golden Flake Snack Foods Inc 1 Golden Flake Dr	Birmingham	AL	35205	**800-239-2447**	205-323-6161	296-35
Golden Flowers 2600 NW 79th Ave	Doral	FL	33122	**800-333-9929**	305-599-0193	
Golden Gate Bridge Golden Gate Bridge Toll Plz Presidio Stn PO Box 9000	San Francisco	CA	94129	**877-229-8655**	415-921-5858	50-4
Golden Gate University						
Roseville 7 Sierra Gate Plz Ste 101	Roseville	CA	95678	**800-448-4968**	415-442-7800	795
San Francisco 536 Mission St	San Francisco	CA	94105	**800-448-4968**	415-442-7000	795
Golden Gate University School of Law 536 Mission St	San Francisco	CA	94105	**800-448-4968**	415-442-6600	167-1
Golden Grain Energy LLC 1822 43rd St SW	Mason City	IA	50401	**888-443-2676**	641-423-8500	10-4
Golden Hotel, The 800 Eleventh St	Golden	CO	80401	**800-233-7214**	303-279-0100	378
Golden LivingCenter - Western Reserve 2601 Network Blvd Ste 102	Frisco	TX	75034	**877-823-8375**	479-201-2000	
Golden Neo-Life Diamite International 3500 Gateway Blvd	Fremont	CA	94538	**800-432-5842**		365
Golden Nugget Hotel 129 E Fremont St	Las Vegas	NV	89101	**800-634-3454**	702-385-7111	665
Golden Nugget Hotels & Casinos 151 Beach Blvd	Biloxi	MS	39530	**800-777-7568**	228-435-5400	133
Golden Nugget Laughlin 2300 S Casino Dr	Laughlin	NV	89029	**800-950-7700**	702-298-7111	133
Golden Oaks Village 5801 N Oakwood Rd	Enid	OK	73703	**800-259-0914**	580-249-2600	668
Golden Sports Tours 301 W Parker Rd Ste 206	Plano	TX	75023	**800-966-8258**		766
Golden Star Inc 4770 N Belleview Ave Ste 209	Kansas City	MO	64116	**800-821-2792**	816-842-0233	506
Golden Technologies Inc 401 Bridge St	Old Forge	PA	18518	**800-624-6374**		473
Golden Valley Bank 190 Cohasset Rd Ste 170	Chico	CA	95926	**800-472-3272**	530-894-1000	70
Golden Valley Electrical Assn Inc 758 Illinois St	Fairbanks	AK	99701	**800-770-4832**	907-452-1151	245
Golden West Casino 1001 S Union Ave	Bakersfield	CA	93307	**800-426-2537**	661-324-6936	133
Golden West Telecommunications 415 Crown St PO Box 411	Wall	SD	57790	**866-279-2161**	605-279-2161	731
Goldener Hirsch Inn 7570 Royal St E	Park City	UT	84060	**800-252-3373***	435-649-7770	378
*Cust Svc						
Golden-Tech International Inc 13555 SE 36th St Ste 330	Bellevue	WA	98006	**800-311-8090**	425-869-1461	297-5
Goldey Beacom College 4701 Limestone Rd	Wilmington	DE	19808	**800-833-4877**	302-998-8814	166
Goldline International Inc 1601 Cloverfield Blvd 100 S Tower	Santa Monica	CA	90404	**877-376-2646**	310-587-1423	489
Goldman Sachs 200 W St	New York	NY	10282	**800-526-7384**	212-902-1000	524
NYSE: GS						
Goldman Sachs Asset Management (GSAM) 200 W St	New York	NY	10282	**800-526-7384**	212-902-1000	400
Goldsmith & Eggleton Inc 300 First St	Wadsworth	OH	44281	**800-321-0954**	330-336-6616	601-2
Golf Course Superintendents Assn of America (GCSAA) 1421 Research Pk Dr	Lawrence	KS	66049	**800-472-7878**	785-841-2240	48-2
GolfBC Holdings Inc 1800-1030 W Georgia St	Vancouver	BC	V6E2Y3	**800-446-5322**		782
Golflogix Inc 15685 N Greenway-Hayden Loop Ste 100A	Scottsdale	AZ	85260	**877-977-0162**		148
GolfWorks, The 4820 Jacksontown Rd PO Box 3008	Newark	OH	43058	**800-848-8358**	740-328-4193	706
Golub Corp 461 Nott St	Schenectady	NY	12308	**800-666-7667**		344
gomembers Inc 1155 Perimeter Ctr W	Atlanta	GA	30338	**855-411-2783**		178-10
GoMotion Inc 10 Kendrick Rd Unit 3	Wareham	MA	02571	**866-446-1069**	508-322-7695	
Gompers & Assoc PLLC 117 Edgington Ln	Wheeling	WV	26003	**844-805-9844**	304-242-9300	2
Gonnella Baking Co 1117 E Wiley Rd	Schaumburg	IL	60173	**800-322-8829**		68
Gonzaga University 502 E Boone Ave	Spokane	WA	99258	**800-986-9585**	509-313-6572	166
Gonzaga University Foley Library 502 E Boone Ave	Spokane	WA	99258	**800-498-5941**	509-323-5931	433-6
Gonzaga University School of Law 721 N Cincinnati St PO Box 3528	Spokane	WA	99220	**800-793-1710***	509-313-3700	167-1
*Admissions						
Good Company Players 928 E Olive Ave	Fresno	CA	93728	**800-371-4747**	559-266-0660	568
Good Earth Inc PO Box 290	Lancaster	NY	14086	**800-877-0848**	716-684-8111	280
Good Earth Teasinc 831 Almar Ave	Santa Cruz	CA	95060	**888-625-8227**		123
Good Eats Inc 12200 Stemmons Fwy Ste 100	Dallas	TX	75234	**800-275-1337**	972-241-5500	666
Good Hotel						
Good Hotel 112 Seventh St	San Francisco	CA	94103	**800-444-5819**	415-621-7001	378
Good Leads 224 Main St Unit 2B	Salem	NH	03079	**866-894-5323**	603-894-5323	392
Good Printers Inc 213 Dry River Rd	Bridgewater	VA	22812	**800-296-3731**	540-828-4663	174
Good Sam Club PO Box 6888	Englewood	CO	80155	**800-234-3450**		48-23
Good Samaritan Hospital 2425 Samaritan Dr	San Jose	CA	95124	**800-307-7631**	408-559-2011	373-3
Good Samaritan Hospital (GSH) 407 14th Ave SE	Puyallup	WA	98372	**800-776-4048**	253-697-4000	373-3
Good Samaritan Hospital of Maryland 5601 Loch Raven Blvd	Baltimore	MD	21239	**855-633-5655**	410-532-8000	373-3
Good Samaritan Medical Ctr 235 N Pearl St	Brockton	MA	02301	**800-488-5959**	508-427-3000	373-3
Good Samaritan Regional Medical Ctr 3600 NW Samaritan Dr	Corvallis	OR	97330	**800-640-5339**	541-768-5111	373-3
Good Time Tours 455 Corday St	Pensacola	FL	32503	**800-446-0886**	850-476-0046	755
Good Times Travel Inc 17132 Magnolia St	Fountain Valley	CA	92708	**888-488-2287**	714-848-1255	755
Good Will Publishers Inc PO Box 269	Gastonia	NC	28052	**800-219-4663**	704-865-1256	633-2
Good Zoo & Benedum Planetarium 465 Lodge Dr	Wheeling	WV	26003	**877-436-1797**	304-243-4030	818
Goodale & Barbieri Co 818 W Riverside Ave Ste 300	Spokane	WA	99201	**800-572-9181**	509-459-6109	
Goodall Manufacturing Co 7558 Washington Ave S	Eden Prairie	MN	55344	**800-328-7730**	952-941-6666	247
Goode Co Texas Barbecue 5109 Kirby Dr	Houston	TX	77098	**800-627-3502**	713-522-2530	667
Goodell Devries Leech & Dann LLP 1 South St 20th Fl	Baltimore	MD	21202	**888-229-4354**	410-783-4000	427
Goodfellow Inc 225 Goodfellow St	Delson	QC	J5B1V5	**800-361-6503**	450-635-6511	812
Goodheart-Willcox Publisher 18604 W Creek Dr	Tinley Park	IL	60477	**800-323-0440**	708-687-5000	633-2
Goodhue County Co-op Electric Assn 1410 Northstar Dr	Zumbrota	MN	55992	**800-927-6864**	507-732-5117	245
Goodin Co 2700 N Second St	Minneapolis	MN	55411	**800-328-8433**	612-588-7811	608
Goodman Correctional Institution 4556 Broad River Rd	Columbia	SC	29210	**866-230-7761**	803-896-8565	213
Goodman Factors 3010 LBJ Fwy Ste 140	Dallas	TX	75234	**877-446-6362**	972-241-3297	272
Good-Nite Inn Fremont 4135 Cushing Pkwy	Fremont	CA	94538	**800-648-3466**	510-656-9307	378
Goodwill Industries International Inc 15810 Indianola Dr	Rockville	MD	20855	**800-741-0197**	800-466-3945	48-5
Goodwill Industries of Akron Ohio Inc, The 570 E Waterloo Rd	Akron	OH	44319	**800-989-8428**	330-724-6995	193
Goodwin Biotechnology Inc 1850 NW 69th Ave	Plantation	FL	33313	**800-814-8600**	954-327-9656	
Goodyear Canada Inc 450 Kipling	Toronto	ON	M8Z5E1	**800-387-3288**	416-201-4300	750
Goodyear Tire & Rubber Co 200 Innovation Way	Akron	OH	44316	**800-321-2136***	330-796-2121	749
NASDAQ: GT ■ *Cust Svc						
Goose Creek State Park 2190 Camp Leach Rd	Washington	NC	27889	**877-722-6762**	919-707-9300	561
Gooseberry Falls State Park 3206 Hwy 61	Two Harbors	MN	55616	**888-646-6367**	218-595-7100	561
Gooseneck Trailer Mfg Co 4400 E Hwy 21 PO Box 832	Bryan	TX	77808	**800-688-5490***	979-778-0034	758
*Cust Svc						
Gopher Electronics Company Inc 222 Little Canada Rd	Saint Paul	MN	55117	**800-592-9519**	651-490-4900	179
Gopher Sign Co 1310 Randolph Ave	Saint Paul	MN	55105	**800-383-3156**	651-698-5095	697
Gorant Candies 8301 Market St	Youngstown	OH	44512	**800-572-4139**	330-726-8821	123
Gordman 12100 W Ctr Rd	Omaha	NE	68144	**800-743-8730**		229
Gordon Brush Mfg Company Inc 3737 Capitol Ave	City of Industry	CA	90601	**800-950-7950**	323-724-7777	103
Gordon College 255 Grapevine Rd	Wenham	MA	01984	**800-343-1379**	978-927-2300	166
Gordon Flesch Company Inc 2675 Research Pk Dr	Madison	WI	53711	**800-333-5905**	800-677-7877	264-2
Gordon Glass Co 5116 Warrensville Center Rd	Maple Heights	OH	44137	**888-663-9830**		330
Gordon Paper Company Inc PO Box 1806	Norfolk	VA	23501	**800-457-7366**	757-464-3581	548-2
Gordon-Conwell Theological Seminary 130 Essex St	South Hamilton	MA	01982	**800-428-7329**	978-468-7111	167-3
Gorges State Park 976 Grassy Ridge Rd	Sapphire	NC	28774	**800-277-9611**	828-966-9099	561
Gorton's Inc 128 Rogers St	Gloucester	MA	01930	**800-222-6846**	978-283-3000	296-14
Goshen Chamber of Commerce 232 S Main St	Goshen	IN	46526	**800-307-4204**	574-533-2102	139
Goshen College 1700 S Main St	Goshen	IN	46526	**800-348-7422**	574-535-7000	166
Goshen News 114 S Main St PO Box 569	Goshen	IN	46527	**800-487-2151**	574-533-2151	528-2

Alphabetical Section

	Toll-Free	Phone	Class
Gosiger Inc 108 McDonough St ....Dayton OH 45402	877-288-1538	937-228-5174	384
GoSolo Technologies Inc 5410 Mariner St Ste 175.............Tampa FL 33609	866-246-7656		613
Gospel Light Publications 1957 Eastman Ave ....Ventura CA 93003	800-446-7735	805-644-9721	633-3
Gospel Publishing House 1445 N Boonville Ave ....Springfield MO 65802 *Orders	800-641-4310*	417-862-2781	622
Goss Inc 1511 William Flynn Hwy ....Glenshaw PA 15116	800-367-4677	412-486-6100	806
Gossen /Corp 2030 W Bender Rd ....Milwaukee WI 53209	800-558-8984	414-228-9800	191-2
Gossner Foods Inc 1051 N 1000 W ....Logan UT 84321	800-944-0454	435-227-2500	296-5
Gotham Distributing Corp 60 Portland Rd ....Conshohocken PA 19428	800-446-8426	610-649-7650	520
GotPrint 7651 N San Fernando Rd ....Burbank CA 91505	877-922-7374	818-252-3000	776
Gottlieb Martin & Associates Inc 4932 Sunbeam Rd ....Jacksonville FL 32257	800-833-9986	904-346-3088	461
Gottlieb Memorial Hospital 701 W N Ave ....Melrose Park IL 60160	800-424-4840	708-681-3200	373-3
Goucher College 1021 Dulaney Valley Rd ....Towson MD 21204	800-468-2437	410-337-6000	166
Gougler Industries Inc 711 Lake St ....Kent OH 44240	800-527-2282	330-673-5826	385
Gould & Goodrich Leather Inc 709 E McNeil St ....Lillington NC 27546	800-277-0732	910-893-2071	430
Gould Technology LLC 1121 Benfield Blvd Stes J-P ....Millersville MD 21108	800-544-6853	410-987-5600	540
Goulds Pumps Inc Goulds Water Technologies Group 240 Fall St ....Seneca Falls NY 13148	800-327-7700	315-568-2811	784
Gourmet Settings 245 W Beaver Creek Rd Ste 10 ....Richmond Hill ON L4B1L1	800-551-2649		
Gouverneur Hotel Montreal (Place-Dupuis) 1000 Sherbrooke St W Ste 2300........Montreal QC H3A3R3	888-910-1111		378
Govconnection Inc 7503 Standish Pl ....Rockville MD 20855	800-998-0009		179
Governing Magazine 1100 Connecticut Ave NW Ste 1300 ....Washington DC 20036	800-940-6039	202-862-8802	455-12
Government Employee Relations Report 1801 S Bell St ....Arlington VA 22202	800-372-1033		527-2
Government Island State Recreation Area 7005 NE Marine Dr ....Portland OR 97218	800-551-6949	503-281-0944	561
Government Liaison Services Inc (GLS) 200 N Glebe Rd Ste 321 ....Arlington VA 22203	800-642-6564	703-524-8200	631
Government National Mortgage Assn 451 Seventh St SW Rm B-133 ......Washington DC 20410	800-234-4662	202-708-1535	507
Government Research Service 1516 SW Boswell Ave ....Topeka KS 66604	800-346-6898	785-232-7720	633-2
Governor Calvert House 58 State Cir ....Annapolis MD 21401	800-847-8882	410-263-2641	378
Governor Patterson Memorial State Recreation Site 1770 SW Pacific Coast Hwy ....Waldport OR 97394	800-551-6949		561
Governor's Inn 700 W Sioux Ave ....Pierre SD 57501 *General	877-523-0080*	605-224-4200	378
Governor's Inn 210 Richards Blvd ....Sacramento CA 95811	800-999-6689	916-448-7224	378
Governors State University 1 University Pkwy ....University Park IL 60484	800-478-8478	708-534-5000	166
Gowan Company LLC PO Box 5569 ....Yuma AZ 85366	800-883-1844	928-783-8844	276
Gowans-Knight Co Inc 49 Knight St ....Watertown CT 06795	800-352-4871	860-274-8801	513
Goway Travel Ltd 3284 Yonge St Ste 300 ....Toronto ON M4N3M7	800-665-4432	416-322-1034	767
Goyette & Associates Inc 2366 Gold Meadow Way Ste 200 .....Gold River CA 95670	888-993-1600	916-851-1900	427
GP Strategies Corp 11000 Broken Land Pkwy Ste 200 ....Columbia MD 21044	888-843-4784	443-367-9600	180
Gpa Specialty Printable Sbstrt 8740 W 50th St ....McCook IL 60525	800-395-9000	773-650-2020	549
GPB (Georgia Public Broadcasting) 260 14th St NW ....Atlanta GA 30318	800-222-6006		628
GPB Education 260 14th St NW ....Atlanta GA 30318	888-501-8960	404-685-2550	628
GPCCVB (Greenville-Pitt County Convention & Visitors Burea) 417 Cotanche St Ste 100 ....Greenville NC 27858	800-537-5564	252-329-4200	206
GPhA (Georgia Pharmacy Assn) 50 Lenox Pointe NE ....Atlanta GA 30324	888-871-5590	404-231-5074	581
GPK Products Inc 1601 43rd St NW ....Fargo ND 58102	800-437-4670	701-277-3225	604
GPO (US Government Printing Office Bookstore) 732 N Capitol St NW ....Washington DC 20401	866-512-1800	202-512-1800	341
GR Sponaugle & Sons Inc 4391 Chambers Hill Rd ....Harrisburg PA 17111	800-868-9353	717-564-1515	189-10
GRAA (Greater Rockford Auto Auction Inc) 5937 Sandy Hollow Rd ....Rockford IL 61109	800-830-4722	815-874-7800	51
Graber Olive House Inc 315 E Fourth St ....Ontario CA 91764	800-996-5483		335
Grabill Cabinet Company Inc 13844 Sawmill Dr ....Grabill IN 46741	877-472-2782	260-376-1500	115
Grace A Dow Memorial Library 1710 W St Andrews Rd ....Midland MI 48640	800-422-5245	989-837-3430	433-3
Grace Bible College 1011 Aldon St SW PO Box 910. ....Grand Rapids MI 49509	800-968-1887	616-538-2330	161
Grace College 200 Seminary Dr ....Winona Lake IN 46590	800-544-7223	574-372-5100	166
Grace College & Theological Seminary 200 Seminary Dr ....Winona Lake IN 46590	800-544-7223	574-372-5100	167-3
Grace Davison 7500 Grace Dr ....Columbia MD 21044	800-638-6014	410-531-4000	145
Grace Hospice 6400 S Lewis Ave Ste 1000 ....Tulsa OK 74136	800-659-0307	918-744-7223	370
Grace Hospital 2201 S Sterling St ....Morganton NC 28655	800-624-3004	828-580-5000	373-3
Grace Mayflower Inn & Spa 118 Woodbury Rd Rte 47 ....Washington CT 06793	800-550-8095	860-868-9466	378
Grace University 1311 S Ninth St ....Omaha NE 68108	800-383-1422	402-449-2800	161
Graceland (Elvis Presley Mansion) 3734 Elvis Presley Blvd ....Memphis TN 38116	800-238-2000	901-332-3322	517
Graceland Fruit Inc 1123 Main St ....Frankfort MI 49635	800-352-7181	231-352-7181	296-18
Graceland University 1 University Pl ....Lamoni IA 50140	800-859-1215	641-784-5000	166
Graceland University Independence 1401 W Truman Rd ....Independence MO 64050	800-833-0524	816-833-0524	166
Gracious Home 1220 Third Ave ....New York NY 10021	800-338-7809	212-517-6300	361
Graco Inc 88 11th Ave NE PO Box 1441.......Minneapolis MN 55413 NYSE: GGG ■ *Cust Svc	800-328-0211*	612-623-6000	637
Gradall Industries Inc 406 Mill Ave SW ....New Philadelphia OH 44663	800-445-4752	330-339-2211	190
Graduate Management Admission Council (GMAC) 11921 Freedom Dr Ste 300............Reston VA 20190	866-505-6559	703-668-9600	48-11
Graduate Theological Union 2400 Ridge Rd ....Berkeley CA 94709	800-826-4488	510-649-2400	167-3
Grady Electric Membership Corp (EMC) 1499 US Hwy 84 W ....Cairo GA 39828	877-757-6060	229-377-4182	245
Grady Memorial Hospital 2220 Iowa Ave ....Chickasha OK 73018	800-299-9665	405-224-2300	373-3
Graeter's Inc 2145 Reading Rd ....Cincinnati OH 45202	800-721-3323	513-721-3323	296-25
Graf & Sons 4050 S Clark St ....Mexico MO 65265	800-531-2666	573-581-2266	707
Graff Truck Centers Inc 1401 S Saginaw St ....Flint MI 48503	888-870-4203	810-239-8300	57
Grafik Marketing Communications Ltd 625 N Washington St Ste 302.......Alexandria VA 22314	800-750-9772	703-299-4500	7
Grafton National Cemetery 431 Walnut St ....Grafton WV 26354	800-535-1117	304-265-2044	136
Grafton on Sunset 8462 West Sunset Blvd ....West Hollywood CA 90069	800-821-3660		378
Graham Architectural Products Corp 1551 Mt Rose Ave ....York PA 17403	800-755-6274	717-849-8100	234
Graham Co, The 1 Penn Sq W 25th Fl. ....Philadelphia PA 19102	888-472-4262	215-567-6300	389
Graham Corp 20 Florence Ave ....Batavia NY 14020 NYSE: GHM ■ *Orders	800-828-8150*	585-343-2216	385
Graham County 34 Wall St Ste 407 ....Asheville NC 28801	866-962-6246	828-255-0182	337
Graham County Chamber of Commerce 1111 Thatcher Blvd ....Safford AZ 85546	888-837-1841	928-428-2511	139
Graham County Electric Inc 9 W Center St ....Pima AZ 85543	800-577-9266	928-485-2451	245
Graham Medical Products 2273 Larsen Rd ....Green Bay WI 54303 *Cust Svc	800-558-6765*		572
GRAHAM OLESON 525 Communication Cir ......Colorado Springs CO 80905	800-776-7336		
Graham Packaging Co 2401 Pleasant Valley Rd ....York PA 17402	800-777-0065	717-849-8500	98
Grain Belt Supply Company Inc PO Box 615 ....Salina KS 67402	800-447-0522	785-827-4491	478
Grain Dealers Mutual Insurance Co 6201 Corporate Dr ....Indianapolis IN 46278	800-428-7081	317-388-4500	390-4
Grambling State University 403 Main St ....Grambling LA 71245	800-569-4714	318-247-3811	166
Gramercy Park Hotel 2 Lexington Ave ....New York NY 10010	866-784-1300	212-920-3300	378
Grammer Industries Inc 6320 E State St ....Columbus IN 47201	800-333-7410	812-579-5655	775
Grammy Magazine 3030 Olympic Blvd ....Santa Monica CA 90404	800-423-2017	310-392-3777	455-9
Grand 1894 Opera House 2020 Postoffice St ....Galveston TX 77550	800-821-1894	409-765-1894	568
Grand Aire Express Inc 11777 W Airport Service Rd ....Swanton OH 43558	800-704-7263		63
Grand America Hotel 555 S Main St ....Salt Lake City UT 84111	800-304-8696	801-258-6000	378
Grand Avenue Worldwide 186 N First St ....Nashville TN 37213	866-455-2823	615-714-5466	440
Grand Blanc Cement Products 10709 Ctr Rd ....Grand Blanc MI 48439	800-875-7500	810-694-7500	183
Grand Canyon Trust 2601 N Fort Valley Rd ....Flagstaff AZ 86001	800-827-5722	928-774-7488	48-13
Grand Canyon University 3300 W Camelback Rd ....Phoenix AZ 85017	800-800-9776	602-639-7500	166
Grand Casino Hinckley 777 Lady Luck Dr ....Hinckley MN 55037	800-472-6321		133
Grand Casino Mille Lacs 777 Grand Ave PO Box 343 ....Onamia MN 56359	800-626-5825		133
Grand Country Inn Grand Country Sq 1945 W 76 Country Blvd ....Branson MO 65616	888-505-4096		378
Grand Del Mar 5300 Grand Del Mar Ct ....San Diego CA 92130	855-314-2030	858-314-2000	378
Grand Electric Co-op Inc 801 Coleman Ave PO Box 39 ....Bison SD 57620	800-592-1803	605-244-5211	245
Grand European Tours 6000 Meadows Rd Ste 520 ......Lake Oswego OR 97035	877-622-9109		755
Grand Gateway Hotel 1721 N LaCrosse St ....Rapid City SD 57701	866-742-1300		378
Grand Geneva Resort & Spa 7036 Grand Geneva Way ....Lake Geneva WI 53147	800-558-3417	262-248-8811	665
Grand Harbor Resort & Waterpark 350 Bell St ....Dubuque IA 52001	866-690-4006	563-690-4000	665

Name / Address	City	State	ZIP	Toll-Free	Phone	Class
Grand Hotel Marriott Resort Golf Club & Spa 1 Grand Blvd PO Box 639	Point Clear	AL	36564	**800-544-9933**	251-928-9201	703
Grand Hotel Minneapolis, The 615 Second Ave S	Minneapolis	MN	55402	**866-843-4726**	612-288-8888	378
Grand Hotel of Cape May Beach Ave	Cape May	NJ	08204	**800-257-8550**	609-884-5611	378
Grand Hotel, The 149 State Rt 64	Grand Canyon	AZ	86023	**888-634-7263**	928-638-3333	
Grand Image Inc 560 Main St	Hudson	MA	01749	**888-973-2622**	978-212-3037	8
Grand Island Independent 422 W First St	Grand Island	NE	68801	**800-658-3160**	308-382-1000	528-2
Grand Island Veterans' Home 2300 W Capital Ave	Grand Island	NE	68803	**800-358-8802**	308-385-6252	788
Grand Isle State Park Admiral Craik Dr	Grand Isle	LA	70358	**888-787-2559**	985-787-2559	561
Grand Junction Area Chamber of Commerce 360 Grand Ave	Grand Junction	CO	81501	**800-352-5286**	970-242-3214	139
Grand Junction Visitors & Convention Bureau 740 Horizon Dr	Grand Junction	CO	81506	**800-962-2547**	970-244-1480	206
Grand Lake Gardens 401 Santa Clara Ave	Oakland	CA	94610	**800-416-6091**		668
Grand Lake Mental Health Center Inc 114 W Delaware	Nowata	OK	74048	**800-722-3611**	918-273-1841	722
Grand Lodge Crested Butte 6 Emmons Rd	Crested Butte	CO	81225	**877-547-5143**	970-349-8000	665
Grand Oaks Hotel 2315 Green Mountain Dr	Branson	MO	65616	**800-553-6423**		378
Grand Ole Opry 2804 opryland Dr	Nashville	TN	37214	**800-733-6779**	615-871-6779	568
Grand Pacific Palisades Resort & Hotel 5805 Armada Dr	Carlsbad	CA	92008	**800-725-4723**	760-827-3200	665
Grand Palms Hotel & Golf Resort 110 Grand Palms Dr	Pembroke Pines	FL	33027	**800-327-9246**	954-431-8800	665
Grand Portage Lodge & Casino PO Box 233	Grand Portage	MN	55605	**800-543-1384**	218-475-2401	665
Grand Portage State Park 9393 E Hwy 61	Grand Portage	MN	55605	**888-646-6367**	218-475-2360	561
Grand Prix of Long Beach 3000 Pacific Ave	Long Beach	CA	90806	**888-827-7333**	562-981-2600	638
Grand Rapids Area Chamber of Commerce 1 NW Third St	Grand Rapids	MN	55744	**800-472-6366**	218-326-6619	139
Grand Rapids Art Museum 101 Monroe Center St NW	Grand Rapids	MI	49503	**800-272-8258**	616-831-1000	517
Grand Rapids City Hall 300 Monroe Ave NW	Grand Rapids	MI	49503	**800-860-8610**	616-456-3010	336
Grand Rapids Label Co 2351 Oak Industrial Dr NE	Grand Rapids	MI	49505	**800-552-5215**	616-459-8134	412
Grand Rapids Scale Company Inc 4215 Stafford Ave SW	Grand Rapids	MI	49548	**800-348-5701**		361
Grand Rapids Symphony 300 Ottawa Ave NW Ste 100	Grand Rapids	MI	49503	**800-982-2787**	616-454-9451	569-3
Grand Rapids/Kent County Convention & Visitors Bureau 171 Monroe Ave NW Ste 545	Grand Rapids	MI	49503	**800-678-9859**	616-258-7388	206
Grand River Agricultural Society 7445 Wellington County Rd 21 RR 2	Elora	ON	N0B1S0	**800-898-7792**	519-846-5455	638
Grand Sierra Resort & Casino 2500 E Second St	Reno	NV	89595	**800-501-2651**	775-789-2000	665
Grand Summit Hotel 570 Springfield Ave	Summit	NJ	07901	**800-346-0773**	908-273-3000	378
Grand Targhee Resort 3300 E Ski Hill Rd	Alta	WY	83414	**800-827-4433**	307-353-2300	665
Grand Teton Lodge Company & Jackson Lake Lodge 101 Jackson Lake Lodge Rd *Resv	Moran	WY	83013	**800-628-9988***	307-543-2811	665
GRAND TIMES HOTEL 6515 Wilfrid-Hamel Blvd	Quebec	QC	G2E5W3	**888-902-4444**	418-877-7788	378
Grand Traverse Resort & Spa 100 Grand Traverse Blvd PO Box 404	Acme	MI	49610	**800-236-1577**	231-534-6000	665
Grand Valley Advance 2141 Port Sheldon St	Jenison	MI	49428	**800-878-1400**		
Grand Valley Rural Power Lines Inc 845 22 Rd PO Box 190	Grand Junction	CO	81505	**877-760-7435**	970-242-0040	245
Grand Valley State University 1 Campus Dr	Allendale	MI	49401	**800-748-0246**	616-331-5000	166
Grand Valley State University Zumberge Library 1 Campus Dr	Allendale	MI	49401	**800-879-0581**	616-331-3252	433-6
Grand View College 1200 Grandview Ave	Des Moines	IA	50316	**800-444-6083**	515-263-2800	166
Grand View Lodge 23521 Nokomis Ave	Nisswa	MN	56468	**866-801-2951**	218-963-2234	665
Grand View Media Group Inc (GVMG) 200 Croft St Ste 1	Birmingham	AL	35242	**888-431-2877**	205-262-4600	633-9
Grand Wailea Resort & Spa 3850 Wailea Alanui Dr	Wailea	HI	96753	**800-888-6100**	808-875-1234	665
Grande Cheese Co 301 E Main St	Lomira	WI	53048	**800-772-3210**		296-5
Grande Colonial 910 Prospect St	La Jolla	CA	92037	**888-828-5498**		378
Grande Prairie Public Library 3479 W 183rd St	Hazel Crest	IL	60429	**800-321-9511**	708-798-5563	433-3
Grande Prairie Regional College 10726 106 Ave	Grande Prairie	AB	T8V4C4	**888-539-4772**	780-539-2911	165
Grandite Inc PO Box 47133	Quebec	QC	G1S4X1	**866-808-3932**	581-318-2018	178-1
GrandLife Hotels 310 W Broadway	New York	NY	10013	**800-965-3000**	212-965-3000	377
Grandma's Saloon & Grill 522 Lake Ave S	Duluth	MN	55802	**800-706-7672**	218-727-4192	667
Grandover Resort & Conference Ctr 1000 Club Rd	Greensboro	NC	27407	**800-472-6301**	336-294-1800	376
Grandview Pharmacy 474 Southpoint Cir	Brownsburg	IN	46112	**866-827-7575**		237
Grandview Products Co 1601 Superior Dr	Parsons	KS	67357	**800-247-9105**	620-421-6950	115
Grandville Printing Company Inc 4719 Ivanrest Ave SW	Grandville	MI	49418	**800-748-0248**		623

Name / Address	City	State	ZIP	Toll-Free	Phone	Class
Grandwell Industries Inc 6109 S NC Hwy 55 *Cust Svc	Fuquay Varina	NC	27526	**800-338-6554***	919-557-1221	697
Grange Insurance 671 S High St	Columbus	OH	43206	**800-422-0550**		390-2
Grange Mutual Casualty Co 671 S High St	Columbus	OH	43206	**800-422-0550**		390-4
Grangetto's Farm & Garden Supply Co 1105 W Mission Ave	Escondido	CA	92025	**800-536-4671**	760-745-4671	276
Granite City Electric Supply Co 19 Quincy Ave	Quincy	MA	02169	**800-850-9400**	617-472-6500	361
Granite Farms Estates 1343 W Baltimore Pk	Media	PA	19063	**888-499-2287**	484-443-0070	668
Granite Group Wholesalers LLC 6 Storrs St	Concord	NH	03301	**800-258-3690**	603-545-3345	608
Granite Knitwear Inc 805 S Salberry Ave Hwy 52S *Cust Svc	Granite Quarry	NC	28072	**800-476-9944***	704-279-5526	155-11
Granite Security Products Inc 4801 Esco Dr	Fort Worth	TX	76140	**877-948-6723**	469-735-4901	349
Granite State College 8 Old Suncook Rd	Concord	NH	03301	**888-228-3000**	603-228-3000	166
Berlin 25 Hall St	Concord	NH	03301	**855-472-4255**	800-735-2964	166
Granite State Independent Living Foundation 21 Chenell Dr	Concord	NH	03301	**800-826-3700**	603-228-9680	305
Granite State Manufacturing Co 124 Joliette St	Manchester	NH	03102	**800-464-7646**		452
Granite Telecommunications LLC 100 Newport Ave Ext	Quincy	MA	02171	**866-847-1500**	866-847-5500	731
Grant Assembly Technologies 90 Silliman Ave	Bridgeport	CT	06605	**800-227-2150**	203-366-4557	454
Grant Bennett Accountants 1375 Exposition Blvd Ste 230	Sacramento	CA	95815	**888-763-7323**	916-922-5109	2
Grant County 301 W Main St	John Day	OR	97845	**800-769-5664**	541-575-0547	337
Grant County 35 C St NW PO Box 37	Ephrata	WA	98823	**800-572-0119**	509-754-2011	337
Grant County 1800 Bronson Blvd	Fennimore	WI	53809	**866-472-6894**	608-822-3501	337
Grant County Herald 35 Central Ave N	Elbow Lake	MN	56531	**877-852-2796**	218-685-5326	528-3
Grant Plaza Hotel 465 Grant Ave	San Francisco	CA	94108	**800-472-6899**	415-434-3883	378
Grant Street Group Inc 339 Sixth Ave Ste 1400	Pittsburgh	PA	15222	**800-410-3445**	412-391-5555	225
Grant, Konvalinka & Harrison PC Republic Ctr 633 Chestnut St 9th Fl	Chattanooga	TN	37450	**888-463-8117**	423-933-2731	
Grantek Systems Integration Inc 4480 Harvester Rd	Burlington	ON	L7L4X2	**866-936-9509**		
Grants Pass Chamber of Commerce 1995 NW Vine St	Grants Pass	OR	97526	**800-547-5927**	541-476-7717	139
Grants Pass Visitors & Convention Bureau 1995 NW Vine St	Grants Pass	OR	97526	**800-547-5927**	541-476-7574	206
Grants/Cibola County Chamber of Commerce 100 N Iron Ave	Grants	NM	87020	**866-270-5110**	505-287-4802	139
Grantsgov *U.S. Department of Health & Human Services* 200 Independence Ave SW	Washington	DC	20201	**877-696-6775**	800-518-4726	197
Granutech-Saturn Systems Corp 201 E Shady Grove	Grand Prairie	TX	75050	**877-582-7800**		
Granville Island Hotel 1253 Johnston St *Resv	Vancouver	BC	V6H3R9	**800-663-1840***	604-683-7373	378
Grapevine Convention Ctr, The 1209 S Main St	Grapevine	TX	76051	**866-782-7897**	817-410-3459	205
Graphel Corp 6115 Centre Pk Dr	West Chester	OH	45069	**800-255-1104**	513-779-6166	498
Graphic Arts Association 1210 Northbrook Dr Ste 200	Trevose	PA	19053	**800-475-6708**	215-396-2300	138
Graphic Controls LLC 400 Exchange St	Buffalo	NY	14204	**800-669-1535**		624
Graphic Products Inc PO Box 4030	Beaverton	OR	97076	**888-326-9244**	503-644-5572	174
Graphic Specialties Inc 3110 Washington Ave N	Minneapolis	MN	55411	**800-486-4605**	612-522-5287	697
Graphics Type & Color Enterprises Inc 2300 NW Seventh Ave	Miami	FL	33127	**800-433-9298**	305-591-7600	623
Graphique De France 9 State St *Sales	Woburn	MA	01801	**800-444-1464***		130
Graphite Sales Inc 16710 W Pk Cir Dr	Chagrin Falls	OH	44023	**800-321-4147**	440-543-8221	498
Grask Peterbilt 9201 Sixth St SW	Cedar Rapids	IA	52404	**888-434-2511**		775
Grass America Inc 1202 NC Hwy 66 S	Kernersville	NC	27284	**800-334-3512**		349
Grassland Dairy Products Company Inc N 8790 Fairgrounds Ave	Greenwood	WI	54437	**800-428-8837**		296-3
Grassland Equipment & Irrigation Corp 892-898 Troy Schenectady Rd	Latham	NY	12110	**800-564-5587**	518-785-5841	428
Grassley Group, The (FMCI) 600 State St Ste A	Cedar Falls	IA	50613	**866-619-5580**		47
Grassroots Motorsports Magazine 915 Ridgewood Ave	Holly Hill	FL	32117	**800-520-8292**	386-239-0523	455-3
Gratz College 7605 Old York Rd	Melrose Park	PA	19027	**800-475-4635**	215-635-7300	166
Graver Technologies LLC 200 Lake Dr	Newark	DE	19702	**800-249-1990**	302-731-1700	801
Graves Lumber Co 1315 S Cleveland-Massillon Rd	Copley	OH	44321	**877-500-5515**	330-666-1115	497
Graves Piano & Organ Company Inc 5798 Karl Rd	Columbus	OH	43229	**800-686-4322**	614-847-4322	522
Gravitec Systems Inc 21291 Urdahl Rd NW	Poulsbo	WA	98370	**800-755-8455**	206-780-2898	261
Gravograph-New Hermes Inc 2200 Northmont Pkwy	Duluth	GA	30096	**800-843-7637**	770-623-0331	625

	City	State	ZIP	Toll-Free	Phone	Class
Gray Chevrolet Cadillac						
1245 N Ninth St	Stroudsburg	PA	18360	866-505-3058		
Gray Construction						
10 Quality St	Lexington	KY	40507	800-814-8468	859-281-5000	186
Gray Glass Co						
217-44 98th Ave	Queens Village	NY	11429	800-523-3320	718-217-2943	329
Gray Line Corporation Inc						
1900 16th St Ste 210	Denver	CO	80202	800-472-9546	303-539-8502	755
Gray Matter Group						
88 Vilcom Ctr Dr Ste 180	Chapel Hill	NC	27514	877-970-4747	919-932-6150	180
Gray Transportation Inc						
2459 GT Dr	Waterloo	IA	50703	800-234-3930	319-234-3930	681
Graybar Electric Co Inc						
34 N Meramec Ave	Saint Louis	MO	63105	800-472-9227	314-573-9200	246
Grayhill Inc						
561 W Hillgrove Ave	La Grange	IL	60525	800-683-0366	708-354-1040	725
Graylyn International Conference Center Inc						
1900 Reynolda Rd	Winston-Salem	NC	27106	800-472-9596	336-758-2600	184
Graymills Corp						
3705 N Lincoln Ave	Chicago	IL	60613	877-465-7867	773-477-4100	637
Graymont Ltd						
10991 Shellbridge Way Ste 200	Richmond	BC	V6X3C6	866-207-4292	604-276-9331	439
Grays Harbor Chamber of Commerce						
506 Duffy St	Aberdeen	WA	98520	800-321-1924	360-532-1924	139
Grays Harbor College						
1620 Edward P Smith Dr	Aberdeen	WA	98520	800-562-4830	360-532-9020	162
Grays Harbor Raceway						
32 Elma McCleary Rd PO Box 911	Elma	WA	98541	800-667-7711	360-482-4374	638
Grays Harbor Tourism						
PO Box 1229	Elma	WA	98541	800-621-9625	360-482-2651	206
Grayson Rural Electric Co-op Corp						
109 Bagby Pk	Grayson	KY	41143	800-562-3532	606-474-5136	245
Grayson-Collin Electric Cooperative (GCEC)						
14568 FM 121 PO Box 548	Van Alstyne	TX	75495	800-967-5235	903-482-7100	245
Graystone Group Advertising						
2710 N ave	Bridgeport	CT	06604	800-544-0005	203-549-0060	7
GrayWolf Sensing Solutions LLC						
6 Research Dr	Shelton	CT	06484	800-218-7997	203-402-0477	418
GRE America Inc						
425 Harbor Blvd	Belmont	CA	94002	800-233-5973	650-591-1400	173-3
Grease Monkey International						
5575 DTC Pkwy Ste 100	Greenwood Village	CO	80111	800-822-7706	303-308-1660	62-5
Great American Cookie Company Inc						
3300 Chambers Rd	Horseheads	NY	14845	877-639-2361		68
Great American Life Insurance Co						
Great American Financial Resources Inc						
301 E Fourth St	Cincinnati	OH	45202	800-545-4269	513-369-5000	390-2
Great American Supplemental Benefits						
PO Box 26580	Austin	TX	78755	866-459-4272		390-3
Great Arrow Graphics						
2495 Main St Ste 457	Buffalo	NY	14214	800-835-0490	716-836-0408	130
Great Basin College						
1500 College Pkwy	Elko	NV	89801	888-590-6726	775-738-8493	166
Great Books Foundation						
35 E Wacker Dr Ste 400	Chicago	IL	60601	800-222-5870	312-332-5870	48-11
Great Clips Inc						
4400 W 78th St Ste 700	Minneapolis	MN	55435	800-999-5959	952-893-9088	77
Great Day Improvements LLC						
700 E Highland Rd	Macedonia	OH	44056	800-230-8301	330-468-0700	236
Great Falls Marketing LLC						
121 Mill St	Auburn	ME	04210	800-221-8895		195
Great Falls Tribune						
205 River Dr S	Great Falls	MT	59405	800-438-6600	406-791-1444	528-2
Great Harvest Bread Co						
28 S Montana St	Dillon	MT	59725	800-442-0424	406-683-6842	68
Great Lakes Aviation Ltd						
1022 Airport Pkwy	Cheyenne	WY	82001	800-554-5111	307-432-7000	25
OTC: GLUX						
Great Lakes Christian College						
6211 W Willow Hwy	Lansing	MI	48917	800-937-4522*	517-321-0242	161
*Admissions						
Great Lakes Crossing Outlets						
4000 Baldwin Rd	Auburn Hills	MI	48326	877-746-7452	248-454-5000	50-6
Great Lakes Cruise Co						
3270 Washtenaw Ave	Ann Arbor	MI	48104	888-891-0203		220
Great Lakes Dart Manufacturing Inc						
S84 W19093 Enterprise Dr	Muskego	WI	53150	800-225-7593	262-679-8730	756
Great Lakes Energy Co-op						
1323 Boyne Ave	Boyne City	MI	49712	888-485-2537	231-582-6521	245
Great Lakes Filters						
301 Arch Ave	Hillsdale	MI	49242	800-521-8565		18
Great Lakes Institute of Technology Toni & Guy Hair						
5100 Peach St	Erie	PA	16509	800-394-4548	814-864-6666	166
Great Lakes Mall						
7850 Mentor Ave	Mentor	OH	44060	877-746-6642	317-636-1600	458
Great Lakes Orthodontic Laboratories Div						
200 Cooper Ave	Tonawanda	NY	14150	800-828-7626		228
Great Lakes Packaging Corp						
W 190 N 11393 Carnegie Dr	Germantown	WI	53022	800-261-4572	262-255-2100	100
Great Lakes Towing Co						
4500 Div Ave	Cleveland	OH	44102	800-321-3663	216-621-4854	463
Great Neck Saw Manufacturing Inc						
165 E Second St	Mineola	NY	11501	800-457-0600*		678
*Cust Svc						
Great Northern Corp						
395 Stroebe Rd	Appleton	WI	54914	800-236-3671	920-739-3671	100
Great Pacific Fixed Income Securities Inc						
151 Kalmus Dr Ste H-8	Costa Mesa	CA	92626	800-284-4804	714-619-3000	686
Great Plains Coca-Cola Bottling Company Inc						
600 N May Ave	Oklahoma City	OK	73107	800-753-2653	405-280-2000	80-2
Great Plains Health Alliance Inc						
625 Third St	Phillipsburg	KS	67661	800-432-2779	785-543-2111	352
Great Plains Industries Inc						
5252 E 36th St N	Wichita	KS	67220	800-835-0113*	316-686-7361	637
*Sales						
Great Plains Laboratory Inc						
11813 W 77th St	Lenexa	KS	66214	800-288-0383	913-341-8949	417

	City	State	ZIP	Toll-Free	Phone	Class
Great Plains State Park						
22487 E 1566 Rd	Mountain Park	OK	73559	800-622-6317	580-569-2032	561
Great Plains Tribal Chairmen's Health Board						
1770 Rand Rd	Rapid City	SD	57702	800-745-3466	605-721-1922	194
Great Planes Model Distributors						
PO Box 9021	Champaign	IL	61826	800-637-7660	217-398-3630	757
Great River Bluffs State Park						
43605 Kipp Dr	Winona	MN	55987	888-646-6367	507-643-6849	561
Great Salt Lake Book Festival						
Utah Humanities Council						
202 W 300 N	Salt Lake City	UT	84103	877-786-7598	801-359-9670	281
Great Source Education Group						
181 Ballardvale St	Wilmington	MA	01887	800-289-4490		243
Great Steak & Potato Co						
9311 E Via de Ventura	Scottsdale	AZ	85258	866-452-4252	480-362-4800	666
Great West Casualty Co						
1100 W 29th St						
PO Box 277	South Sioux City	NE	68776	800-228-8602	402-494-2411	390-4
Great Western Bank						
6001 NW Radial Hwy	Omaha	NE	68104	800-952-2043	402-552-1200	70
Great Western Mfg Co Inc						
2017 S Fourth St PO Box 149	Leavenworth	KS	66048	800-682-3121	913-682-2291	298
Great Western Supply Inc						
2626 Industrial Dr	Ogden	UT	84401	866-776-8289		
Great Wolf Lodge of Sandusky LLC						
4600 Milan Rd US 250	Sandusky	OH	44870	800-641-9653		377
Great Wolf Lodge Williamsburg						
549 E Rochambeau Dr	Williamsburg	VA	23188	800-551-9653		665
Great Works Internet (GWI)						
43 Landry St	Biddeford	ME	04005	866-494-2020	207-494-2000	604
Great Wraps						
17 Executive Park Dr NE Ste 150	Atlanta	GA	30329	888-489-7277	404-248-9900	
Greater Aiken Chamber of Commerce						
121 Richland Ave E PO Box 892	Aiken	SC	29802	800-251-7234	803-641-1111	139
Greater Atlanta Christian						
1575 Indian Trl Lilburn Rd	Norcross	GA	30093	800-450-1327	770-243-2000	48-20
Greater Atlantic City Chamber						
12 S Virginia Ave	Atlantic City	NJ	08401	800-123-4567	609-345-4524	139
Greater Augusta Regional Chamber of Commerce						
30 Ladd Rd PO Box 1107	Fishersville	VA	22939	866-922-2514	540-324-1133	139
Greater Austin Performing Arts Center Inc						
701 W Riverside Dr	Austin	TX	78704	800-735-2989	512-457-5100	716
Greater Bakersfield Convention & Visitors Bureau						
515 Truxtun Ave	Bakersfield	CA	93301	866-425-7353	661-852-7282	206
Greater Beloit Chamber of Commerce						
500 Public Ave	Beloit	WI	53511	866-981-5969	608-365-8835	139
Greater Birmingham Convention & Visitors Bureau						
1819 Morris Ave	Birmingham	AL	35203	800-458-8085	205-458-8000	206
Greater Boston Chamber of Commerce						
265 Franklin St	Boston	MA	02110	800-476-3094	617-227-4500	139
Greater Boston Convention & Visitors Bureau (GBCVB)						
2 Copley Pl Ste 105	Boston	MA	02116	888-733-2678	617-536-4100	206
Greater Bridgeport Conference & Vistors Ctr						
164 W Main St	Bridgeport	WV	26330	800-368-4324	304-842-7272	206
Greater Cayce West Columbia Chamber of Commerce						
1006 12th St	Cayce	SC	29033	866-720-5400	803-794-6504	
Greater Chambersburg Chamber of Commerce						
100 Lincoln Way E Ste A	Chambersburg	PA	17201	800-840-9081	717-264-7101	139
Greater Cincinnati Convention & Visitors Bureau						
525 Vine St Ste 1200	Cincinnati	OH	45202	800-543-2613	513-621-2142	206
Greater Cincinnati Foundation						
200 W Fourth St	Cincinnati	OH	45202	800-742-6253	513-241-2880	303
Greater Cleveland Partnership						
1240 Huron Rd E Ste 300	Cleveland	OH	44115	888-304-4769	216-621-3300	139
Greater Columbus Chamber of Commerce						
1200 Sixth Ave PO Box 1200	Columbus	GA	31902	800-360-8552	706-327-1566	139
Greater Columbus Convention & Visitors Bureau						
277 W Nationwide Blvd Ste 125	Columbus	OH	43215	866-397-2657	614-221-6623	206
Greater Columbus Convention Ctr						
400 N High St	Columbus	OH	43215	800-626-0241	614-827-2500	205
Greater Concord Chamber of Commerce						
2280 Diamond Blvd Ste 200	Concord	CA	94520	800-427-8686	925-685-1181	139
Greater Concord Chamber of Commerce						
49 S Main St Ste 104	Concord	NH	03301	800-360-4839	603-224-2508	139
Greater Danbury Chamber of Commerce						
39 West St	Danbury	CT	06810	800-722-2936	203-743-5565	139
Greater Deerfield Beach Chamber of Commerce						
1601 E Hillsboro Blvd	Deerfield Beach	FL	33441	866-551-9805	954-427-1050	139
Greater Des Moines Convention & Visitors Bureau						
400 Locust St Ste 265	Des Moines	IA	50309	800-451-2625	515-286-4960	206
Greater Fort Lauderdale Convention & Visitors Bureau						
101 NE Third Ave						
Ste 100	Fort Lauderdale	FL	33301	800-227-8669	954-765-4466	206
Greater Fort Lauderdale-Broward County Convention Ctr						
1950 Eisenhower Blvd	Fort Lauderdale	FL	33316	800-327-1390	954-765-5900	205
Greater Fort Myers Chamber of Commerce						
2310 Edwards Dr	Fort Myers	FL	33901	800-366-3622	239-332-3624	139
Greater Fort Walton Beach Chamber of Commerce						
34 Miracle Strip Pkwy SE						
	Fort Walton Beach	FL	32548	800-225-5797	850-244-8191	139
Greater Giving Inc						
1920 N W Amberglen Pkwy						
Ste 140	Beaverton	OR	97006	800-276-5992		317
Greater Grand Forks Convention & Visitors Bureau						
4251 Gateway Dr	Grand Forks	ND	58203	800-866-4566	701-746-0444	206
Greater Green Bay Convention & Visitors Bureau						
1901 S Oneida St	Green Bay	WI	54304	888-867-3342	920-494-9507	206
Greater Greenbrier Chamber of Commerce						
200 W Washington St Ste C	Lewisburg	WV	24901	855-453-4858		
Greater Greenville Chamber of Commerce						
24 Cleveland St	Greenville	SC	29601	866-485-5262	864-242-1050	139
Greater Greenville Convention & Visitors Bureau						
148 River St Ste 222	Greenville	SC	29601	800-351-7180	864-421-0000	206
Greater Greenwood Chamber of Commerce						
65 Airport Pkwy	Greenwood	IN	46143	800-462-7585	317-888-4856	139
Greater Houston Convention & Visitors Bureau						
701 Avenida de las Americas						
Ste 200	Houston	TX	77010	800-446-8786		206

Name / Address	Toll-Free	Phone	Class
Greater Hutchinson Convention & Visitors Bureau 117 N Walnut St PO Box 519 .... Hutchinson KS 67504	800-691-4262	620-662-3391	206
Greater Jackson County Chamber of Commerce, The 407 E Willow St .... Scottsboro AL 35768	800-259-5508	256-259-5500	139
Greater Johnstown/Cambria County Chamber of Commerce 245 Market St Ste 100 .... Johnstown PA 15901	800-790-4522	814-536-5107	139
Greater Johnstown/Cambria County Convention & Visitors Bureau 111 Roosevelt Blvd Ste A .... Johnstown PA 15906	800-237-8590	814-536-7993	206
Greater Killeen Chamber of Commerce 1 Santa Fe Plz .... Killeen TX 76540	866-790-4769	254-526-9551	139
Greater Kirkland Chamber of Commerce 440 Central Way .... Kirkland WA 98033	800-501-7772	425-822-7066	139
Greater Lansing Convention & Visitors Bureau 500 E Michigan Ave Ste 180 .... Lansing MI 48912	888-252-6746	517-487-0077	206
Greater Lawrence County Area Chamber of Commerce 216 Collins Ave .... South Point OH 45680	800-408-1334	740-377-4550	139
Greater Lehigh Valley Chamber of Commerce 840 Hamilton St Ste 205 .... Allentown PA 18101	800-845-7941	610-841-5800	139
Greater Lexington Chamber of Commerce Inc 330 E Main St Ste 100 .... Lexington KY 40507	800-848-1224	859-254-4447	139
Greater Limestone County Chamber of Commerce 101 S Beaty St .... Athens AL 35611	866-953-6565	256-232-2600	139
Greater Liverpool Chamber of Commerce 314 Second St .... Liverpool NY 13088	800-388-2000	315-457-3895	139
Greater Lowell Chamber of Commerce 131 Merrimack St .... Lowell MA 01852	800-338-0221	978-459-8154	139
Greater Madison Chamber of Commerce PO Box 71 .... Madison WI 53701	800-750-5437	608-256-8348	139
Greater Madison Convention & Visitors Bureau 22 E Mifflin Ave st Ste 200 .... Madison WI 53703	800-373-6376	608-255-2537	206
Greater Mankato Growth 1961 Premier Dr .... Mankato MN 56001	800-697-0652	507-385-6640	206
Greater Marathon Chamber of Commerce 12222 Overseas Hwy .... Marathon FL 33050	800-262-7284	305-743-5417	139
Greater Menomonie Area Chamber of Commerce 342 E Main St .... Menomonie WI 54751	800-283-1862	715-235-9087	139
Greater Meriden Chamber of Commerce 3 Colony St Ste 301 .... Meriden CT 06451	877-283-8158	203-235-7901	139
Greater Miami Convention & Visitors Bureau 701 Brickell Ave Ste 2700 .... Miami FL 33131	800-933-8448	305-539-3000	206
Greater Milwaukee Convention & Visitors Bureau 648 N Plankinton Ave Ste 220 .... Milwaukee WI 53203	800-554-1448	414-273-7222	206
Greater Monticello Chamber of Commerce 116 N Main St .... Monticello IN 47960	800-541-7906	574-583-7220	139
Greater Morgantown Convention & Visitors Bureau 341 Chaplin Rd First Fl .... Morgantown WV 26501	800-458-7373	304-292-5081	206
Greater Mount Airy Chamber of Commerce 200 N Main St .... Mount Airy NC 27030	800-948-0949	336-786-6116	139
Greater Muskogee Area Chamber of Commerce PO Box 797 .... Muskogee OK 74402	866-381-6543	918-682-2401	139
Greater Naples Marco Island Everglades Convention & Visitors Bureau 2800 Horseshoe Dr .... Naples FL 34104	800-688-3600	239-252-2384	206
Greater New Braunfels Chamber of Commerce Inc, The 390 S Seguin Ave PO Box 311417 .... New Braunfels TX 78130	800-572-2626		206
Greater New Haven Chamber of Commerce 900 Chapel St 10th Fl .... New Haven CT 06510	800-953-4467	203-787-6735	139
Greater New Milford Chamber of Commerce 11 Railroad St .... New Milford CT 06776	800-998-2984	860-354-6080	139
Greater New Orleans Hotel & Lodging Assn 2020 St Charles Ave 5th Fl .... New Orleans LA 70130	866-366-1121	504-525-2264	375
Greater New York Dental Meeting 200 W 41st St Ste 800 .... New York NY 10036	844-797-7469	212-398-6922	194
Greater New York Chamber of Commerce 20 W 44th St 4th Fl .... New York NY 10036	800-344-6088	212-686-7220	139
Greater Newport Chamber of Commerce 555 SW Coast Hwy .... Newport OR 97365	800-262-7844	541-265-8801	139
Greater North Miami Chamber of Commerce 13100 W Dixie Hwy .... North Miami FL 33161	800-939-3848	305-891-7811	139
Greater Ocean City Chamber of Commerce 12320 Ocean Gateway .... Ocean City MD 21842	888-626-3386	410-213-0552	139
Greater Oklahoma City Chamber of Commerce 123 Park Ave .... Oklahoma City OK 73102	800-225-5652	405-297-8900	139
Greater Omaha Chamber of Commerce 1301 Harney St .... Omaha NE 68102	800-852-2622	402-346-5000	139
Greater Omaha Convention & Visitors Bureau 1001 Farnam St .... Omaha NE 68102	866-937-6624	402-444-4660	206
Greater Omaha Packing Company Inc 3001 L St .... Omaha NE 68107	800-747-5400	402-731-1700	471
Greater Parkersburg Convention & Visitors Bureau 350 Seventh St .... Parkersburg WV 26101	800-752-4982	304-428-1130	206
Greater Paterson Chamber of Commerce 100 Hamilton Plz Ste 1201 .... Paterson NJ 07505	800-220-2892	973-881-7300	139
Greater Peterborough Chamber of Commerce 175 George St N .... Peterborough ON K9J3G6	877-640-4037	705-748-9771	137
Greater Phoenix Convention & Visitors Bureau 400 E Van Buren St Ste 600 .... Phoenix AZ 85004	877-225-5749	602-254-6500	206
Greater Pittsburgh Convention & Visitors Bureau 120 Fifth Ave 5th Ave Pl Ste 2800 .... Pittsburgh PA 15222	800-359-0758	412-281-7711	206
Greater Pocatello Chamber of Commerce 324 S Main St .... Pocatello ID 83204	800-632-0905	208-233-1525	139
Greater Pompano Beach Chamber of Commerce 2200 E Atlantic Blvd .... Pompano Beach FL 33062	888-939-5711	954-941-2940	139
Greater Pueblo Chamber of Commerce 302 N Santa Fe Ave .... Pueblo CO 81003	800-233-3446	719-542-1704	139
Greater Raleigh Chamber of Commerce PO Box 2978 .... Raleigh NC 27602	888-456-8535	919-664-7000	139
Greater Raleigh Convention & Visitors Bureau 421 Fayetteville St Ste 1505 .... Raleigh NC 27601	800-849-8499	919-834-5900	206
Greater Renton Chamber of Commerce 625 S Fourth St .... Renton WA 98057	877-467-3686	425-226-4560	139
Greater Rockford Airport 60 Airport Dr .... Rockford IL 61109	800-517-2000	815-969-4000	27
Greater Rockford Auto Auction Inc (GRAA) 5937 Sandy Hollow Rd .... Rockford IL 61109	800-830-4722	815-874-7800	51
Greater Rome Convention & Visitors Bureau 402 Civics Ctr Dr .... Rome GA 30161	800-444-1834	706-295-5576	206

Name / Address	Toll-Free	Phone	Class
Greater Saint Charles Convention & Visitors Bureau 230 S Main St .... Saint Charles MO 63301	800-366-2427	636-946-7776	206
Greater San Antonio Chamber of Commerce 602 E Commerce St .... San Antonio TX 78205	888-828-8680	210-229-2100	139
Greater Seattle Chamber of Commerce 1301 Fifth Ave Ste 1500 .... Seattle WA 98101	866-978-2997	206-389-7200	139
Greater Spokane Inc 801 W Riverside Ave Ste 100 .... Spokane WA 99201	800-776-5263	509-624-1393	139
Greater Springfield Convention & Visitors Bureau 1441 Main St .... Springfield MA 01103	800-723-1548	413-787-1548	206
Greater Springfield Convention & Visitors Bureau 20 S Limestone St Ste 100 .... Springfield OH 45502	800-803-1553	937-325-7621	206
Greater Starkville Development Partnership 200 E Main St .... Starkville MS 39759	800-649-8687	662-323-3322	139
Greater Susquehanna Valley Chamber of Commerce 2859 N Susquehanna Trl PO Box 10 .... Shamokin Dam PA 17876	800-410-2880	570-743-4100	139
Greater Valley Area Chamber of Commerce 2102 S Broad Ave PO Box 205 .... Lanett AL 36863	800-245-2244	334-642-1411	139
Greater Vancouver Convention & Visitors Bureau 200 Burrard St .... Vancouver BC V6C3L6	800-561-0123	604-682-2222	206
Greater West Chester Chamber of Commerce 119 N High St .... West Chester PA 19380	800-210-8008	610-696-4046	139
Greater Williamsburg Chamber & Tourism Alliance 421 N Boundary St .... Williamsburg VA 23185	800-368-6511	757-229-6511	139
Greater Wilmington Convention & Visitors Bureau 100 W Tenth St Ste 20 .... Wilmington DE 19801	800-489-6664		206
Greater Winter Haven Area Chamber of Commerce 401 Ave 'B' NW .... Winter Haven FL 33881	800-260-9220	863-293-2138	139
Greater Woodfield Convention & Visitors Bureau 1375 E Woodfield Rd Ste 120 .... Schaumburg IL 60173	800-847-4849	847-490-1010	206
Greater Yellowstone Coalition (GYC) 215 S Wallace Ave .... Bozeman MT 59715	800-775-1834	406-586-1593	48-13
Great-West Life & Annuity Insurance Co 8515 E OrchaRd Rd .... Greenwood Village CO 80111	800-537-2033	303-737-3000	390-2
Grecian Delight Foods 1201 Tonne Rd .... Elk Grove Village IL 60007	800-621-4387		296-1
Greek Catholic Union of the USA 5400 Tuscarawas Rd .... Beaver PA 15009	800-722-4428	724-495-3400	390-2
Greek Peak Mountain Resort 2000 NYS Rt 392 .... Cortland NY 13045	855-677-7927		194
Greeley & Hansen 100 S Wacker Dr Ste 1400 .... Chicago IL 60606	800-837-9779	312-558-9000	261
Greeley Chamber of Commerce 902 Seventh Ave .... Greeley CO 80631	800-449-3866	970-352-3566	206
Greeley Tribune 501 Eigth Ave .... Greeley CO 80631	800-275-0321	970-352-0211	528-2
Greeley-Weld Chamber of Commerce 902 Seventh Ave .... Greeley CO 80631	800-449-3866	970-352-3566	139
Green Bay Drop Forge 1341 State St .... Green Bay WI 54304	800-824-4896	920-432-6401	481
Green Bay Packaging Inc 1700 Webster Ct .... Green Bay WI 54302	800-236-8400	920-433-5111	544
Green Bay Packers 1265 Lombardi Ave PO Box 10628 .... Green Bay WI 54304	800-895-0071	920-569-7500	711-2
Green Brick Partners Inc 2805 Dallas Pkwy Ste 400 .... Plano TX 75093	800-374-0137	469-573-6755	782
Green Circle Growers Inc 51051 US Hwy 20 .... Oberlin OH 44074	800-368-4759	440-775-1411	368
Green County 1016 16th Ave .... Monroe WI 53566	800-947-3529	608-328-9430	337
Green Depot Inc 1 Ivy Hill Rd .... Brooklyn NY 11211	800-238-5008	718-782-2991	428
Green Dot Corp 3465 E Foothill Blvd .... Pasadena CA 91107	866-795-7597		215
Green Earth Cleaning 51 W 135th St .... Kansas City MO 64145	877-926-0895	816-926-0895	116
Green Field Paper Co 7196 Clairemont Mesa Blvd .... San Diego CA 92111	888-402-9979	858-565-2585	553
Green Hills Software Inc 30 W Sola St .... Santa Barbara CA 93101	800-765-4733	805-965-6044	178-2
Green Lake County 492 Hill St .... Green Lake WI 54941	800-664-3588	920-294-4005	337
Green Lawn Fertilizing Inc 1004 Saunders Ln .... West Chester PA 19380	888-581-5296		573
Green Line Hose & Fittings (BC.) Ltd 1477 Derwent Way .... Delta BC V3M6N3	800-665-5444	604-525-6700	357
Green Mechanical Construction Inc 322 W Main St .... Glasgow KY 42141	800-264-6048		
Green Mountain at Fox Run 262 Fox Ln .... Ludlow VT 05149	800-448-8106	802-228-8885	702
Green Mountain College 1 Brennan Cir .... Poultney VT 05764 *Admissions	800-776-6675*	802-287-8000	166
Green Mountain Power Corp 163 Acorn Ln .... Colchester VT 05446	888-835-4672		782
Green Oaks Hospital 7808 Clodus Fields Dr .... Dallas TX 75251	800-866-6554	972-991-9504	373-5
Green Room at the Hotel duPont 42 W 11th St .... Wilmington DE 19801	800-441-9019	302-594-3100	667
Green Tortoise Adventure Travel & Hostels 494 Broadway .... San Francisco CA 94133	800-867-8647	415-834-1000	755
Green Valley Pecan Co 1625 E Sahuarita Rd .... Sahuarita AZ 85629	800-533-5269	520-791-2852	10-8
Green Valley Ranch Resort Casino & Spa 2300 Paseo Verde Pkwy .... Henderson NV 89052 *Resv	866-782-9487*	702-617-7777	378
Greenbelt Electric Co-op Inc PO Box 948 .... Wellington TX 79095	800-527-3082	806-447-2536	245
Greenbriar Inn, The 8735 N Foothills Hwy .... Boulder CO 80302	800-253-1474	303-440-7979	667
Greenbrier Co 1 Centerpointe Dr Ste 200 .... Lake Oswego OR 97035 *NYSE: GBX*	800-343-7188	503-684-7000	646
Greenbrier County 200 W Washington St .... Lewisburg WV 24901	800-833-2068	304-647-6602	337

Alphabetical Section

	Toll-Free	Phone	Class

Greenbrier Farms Inc
225 Sign Pine Rd . . . . Chesapeake VA 23322 | 800-829-2141 | 757-421-2141 | 323

Greenbrier, The
300 W Main St . . . . White Sulphur Springs WV 24986 | 800-453-4858 | 304-536-1110 | 665

Greenbusch Group Inc
1900 W Nickerson St Ste 201 . . . . Seattle WA 98119 | 855-476-2874 | 206-378-0569 | 196

Greene County
411 Main St . . . . Catskill NY 12414 | 800-355-2287 | 518-719-3270 | 337

Greene County
1034 Silver Dr . . . . Greensboro GA 30642 | 800-248-7689 | 706-453-7716 | 337

Greene County Chamber of Commerce
327 Main St PO Box 248 . . . . Catskill NY 12414 | 800-888-3586 | 518-943-4222 | 139

Greene County Convention & Visitors Bureau
1221 Meadowbridge Dr . . . . Beavercreek OH 45434 | 800-733-9109 | 937-429-9100 | 206

Greene Resources
6601 Six Forks Rd . . . . Raleigh NC 27615 | 800-784-9619 | 919-862-8602 | 260

Greenerd Press & Machine Company Inc
41 Crown St PO Box 886 . . . . Nashua NH 03061 | 800-877-9110 | 603-889-4101 | 454

Greeneville Light & Power System
PO Box 1690 . . . . Greeneville TN 37744 | 866-466-1438 | 423-636-6200 | 245

Greenfield Savings Bank
400 Main St PO Box 1537 . . . . Greenfield MA 01302 | 888-324-3191 | 413-774-3191 | 70

Greenfield Village
20900 Oakwood Blvd . . . . Dearborn MI 48124 | 800-835-5237 | 313-271-1620 | 517

GreenGeeks LLC
5739 Kanan Rd Ste 300 . . . . Agoura Hills CA 91301 | 877-326-7483 | 310-496-8946 | 225

Greenheart Farms Inc
902 Zenon Way . . . . Arroyo Grande CA 93420 | 800-549-5531 | 805-481-2234 | 10-9

Greenheck Fan Corp
1100 Greenheck Dr PO Box 410 . . . . Schofield WI 54476 | 800-355-5354 | 715-359-6171 | 18

Greenhorn Creek Guest Ranch
2116 Greenhorn Ranch Rd . . . . Quincy CA 95971 | 800-334-6939 | 530-283-0930 | 239

Greenlancer
615 Griswold St Ste 300 . . . . Detroit MI 48226 | 866-436-1440 | |

Greenleaf Nursery Co
28406 Hwy 82 . . . . Park Hill OK 74451 | 800-331-2982 | 918-457-5172 | 368

Greenlee Textron
1390 Aspen Way . . . . Vista CA 92081 | 800-642-2155 | 760-598-8900 | 253

Greenlee Textron Inc
4455 Boeing Dr . . . . Rockford IL 61109 | 800-435-0786 | | 754

Greenline Equipment
14750 S Pony Express Rd . . . . Bluffdale UT 84065 | 888-201-5500 | 801-966-4231 | 274

GreenLine Paper Company Inc
631 S Pine St . . . . York PA 17403 | 800-641-1117 | 717-845-8697 | 549

GreenMan Technologies Inc
7 Kimball Ln Bldg A . . . . Lynnfield MA 01940 | 866-994-7697 | 781-224-2411 | 656

Greenpages Inc
33 Badgers Island W . . . . Kittery ME 03904 | 888-687-4876 | 207-439-7310 | 180

Greenpeace Canada
33 Cecil St . . . . Toronto ON M5T1N1 | 800-320-7183 | 416-597-8408 | 48-13

Greenpeace USA
702 H St NW Ste 300 . . . . Washington DC 20001 | 800-326-0959 | 202-462-1177 | 48-13

Greensboro Area Convention & Visitors Bureau
2200 Pinecroft Rd Ste 200 . . . . Greensboro NC 27407 | 800-344-2282 | 336-274-2282 | 206

Greensboro College
815 W Market St . . . . Greensboro NC 27401 | 800-346-8226 | 336-272-7102 | 166

Greenscape Pump Services Inc
1425 Whitlock Ln Ste 108 . . . . Carrollton TX 75006 | 877-401-4774 | 972-446-0037 | 608

Greenstone Farm Credit Services Aca
3515 West Rd . . . . East Lansing MI 48823 | 800-444-3276 | 800-968-0061 | 216

Greentec
95 Struck Ct . . . . Cambridge ON N1R8L2 | 888-858-1515 | 519-624-3300 | 656

Greenview Data Inc
8178 Jackson Rd . . . . Ann Arbor MI 48103 | 800-458-3348 | 734-426-7500 | 196

Greenview Regional Hospital
1801 Ashley Cir . . . . Bowling Green KY 42104 | 800-605-1466 | 270-793-1000 | 373-3

Greenville City Hall
206 S Main St . . . . Greenville SC 29601 | 800-829-4477 | 864-232-2273 | 336

Greenville College
315 E College Ave . . . . Greenville IL 62246 | 800-345-4440 | 618-664-7100 | 166

Greenville News
305 S Main St . . . . Greenville SC 29601 | 800-800-5116 | 864-298-4100 | 528-2

Greenville Technical College
Barton
506 S Pleasantburg Dr . . . . Greenville SC 29607 | 800-723-0673* | 864-250-8000 | 162
*All
Greer
2522 Locust Hill Rd . . . . Taylors SC 29687 | 800-723-0673* | 864-250-8000 | 162

Greenville-Pitt County Convention & Visitors Bureau (GPCCVB)
417 Cotanche St Ste 100 . . . . Greenville NC 27858 | 800-537-5564 | 252-329-4200 | 206

Greenville-Spartanburg Airport (GSP)
2000 GSP Dr Ste 1 . . . . Greer SC 29651 | 800-331-1212 | 864-877-7426 | 27

Greenwald Industries
212 Middlesex Ave . . . . Chester CT 06412 | 800-221-0982 | 860-526-0800 | 493

Greenwell Chisholm Printing Co
420 E Parrish Ave . . . . Owensboro KY 42303 | 800-844-1876 | 270-684-3267 | 623

Greenwich Assoc LLC
6 High Ridge Park . . . . Stamford CT 06905 | 800-704-1027 | 203-629-1200 | 194

Greenwich Hospital
5 Perryridge Rd . . . . Greenwich CT 06830 | 800-657-8355 | 203-863-3000 | 373-3

Greenwood Mop & Broom Inc
312 Palmer St . . . . Greenwood SC 29646 | 800-635-6849 | 864-227-8411 | 103

Greenwood Park Mall
1251 US Hwy 31 N . . . . Greenwood IN 46142 | 877-746-6642 | 317-881-6758 | 458

Greenwood Racing Inc
3001 St Rd . . . . Bensalem PA 19020 | 888-238-2946 | 215-639-9000 | 359-2

Greenwood School District 50
1855 Calhoun Rd . . . . Greenwood SC 29648 | 888-260-9430 | 864-941-5400 | 681

Greer Garson Theatre Ctr
1600 St Michael's Dr . . . . Santa Fe NM 87505 | 800-456-2673 | 505-473-6011 | 568

Greer Laboratories Inc
639 Nuway Cir NE PO Box 800 . . . . Lenoir NC 28645 | 800-378-3906* | | 477
*Cust Svc

Greer Steel Co 624 Blvd . . . . Dover OH 44622 | 800-388-2868* | | 719
*Sales

Greeters of Hawaii Ltd
300 Rodgers Blvd Ste 266 . . . . Honolulu HI 96819 | 800-366-8559 | 808-836-0161 | 292

	Toll-Free	Phone	Class

Gregg Investigations Inc
500 E Milwaukee St . . . . Janesville WI 53545 | 800-866-1976 | | 399

Gregory Poole Equipment Co
4807 Beryl Rd PO Box 469 . . . . Raleigh NC 27606 | 800-451-7278 | 919-828-0641 | 385

Gregory Welteroth Advertising Inc
356 Laurens Rd . . . . Montoursville PA 17754 | 866-294-5765 | 570-433-3366 | 5

Greif Inc
425 Winter Rd . . . . Delaware OH 43015 | 877-781-9797 | | 198
NYSE: GEF

Grenzebach Glier & Assoc Inc
401 N Michigan Ave Ste 2800 . . . . Chicago IL 60611 | 800-222-9233 | 312-372-4040 | 317

Gresham Petroleum Co
415 Pershing Ave PO Box 690 . . . . Indianola MS 38751 | 800-748-8934 | 662-884-5000 | 577

Gressco Ltd
328 Moravian Valley Rd . . . . Waunakee WI 53597 | 800-345-3480 | 608-849-6300 | 321

Grey House Publishing
4919 Rt 22 PO Box 56 . . . . Amenia NY 12501 | 800-562-2139 | 518-789-8700 | 633-2

GreyCastle Security LLC
500 Federal St Ste 540 . . . . Troy NY 12180 | 800-403-8350 | 518-274-7233 | 196

Greyfield Inn
4 N Second St Ste 300 . . . . Fernandina Beach FL 32034 | 866-401-8581 | 904-261-6408 | 378

GREYHAWK
2000 Midlantic Dr Ste 210 . . . . Mount Laurel NJ 08054 | 888-280-4295 | 516-921-1900 |

Greyhound Canada Transportation Corp
1111 International Blvd
Ste 700 . . . . Burlington ON L7L6W1 | 800-661-8747 | | 107

Greyhound Hall of Fame
407 S Buckeye Ave . . . . Abilene KS 67410 | 800-932-7881 | 785-263-3000 | 519

Greylock Federal Credit Union
150 W St . . . . Pittsfield MA 01201 | 800-207-5555 | 413-236-4000 | 219

Greyston Bakery Inc
104 Alexander St . . . . Yonkers NY 10701 | 800-289-2253 | 914-375-1510 | 296-1

Greystone Construction Co
500 S Marschall Rd Ste 300 . . . . Shakopee MN 55379 | 888-742-6837 | 952-496-2227 | 186

Greystone Managed Investments Inc
300 Park Centre 1230 Blackfoot Dr
. . . . Regina SK S4S7G4 | 800-213-4286 | 306-779-6400 | 400

Greystone of Lincoln Inc
7 Wellington Rd . . . . Lincoln RI 02865 | 800-446-1761 | 401-333-0444 | 617

GRFI Ltd
400 E Randolph St Ste 700 . . . . Chicago IL 60601 | 888-856-5161 | | 464

Grid One Solutions Inc
700 Turner Way Ste 205 . . . . Aston PA 19014 | 800-606-7981 | | 392

Gries Seed Farms Inc
2348 N Fifth St . . . . Fremont OH 43420 | 800-472-4797 | 419-332-5571 | 690

Griffin Gate Marriott Resort
1800 Newtown Pk . . . . Lexington KY 40511 | 800-228-9290 | 859-231-5100 | 665

Griffin Memorial Hospital
900 E Main St . . . . Norman OK 73071 | 800-955-3468* | 405-321-4880 | 373-5
*General

Griffin Thermal Products
100 Hurricane Creek Rd . . . . Piedmont SC 29673 | 800-722-3723 | | 60

Griffin Transport Services
5360 Capital Ct . . . . Reno NV 89502 | 800-361-5028 | 775-331-8010 | 447

Griffith Rubber Mills
2625 NW Industrial St . . . . Portland OR 97210 | 800-321-9677 | 503-226-6971 | 673

Griffon Corp
712 Fifth Ave 18th Fl . . . . New York NY 10019 | 800-378-1475 | 212-957-5000 | 185
NYSE: GFF

Grifols USA LLC
2410 Lillyvale Ave . . . . Los Angeles CA 90032 | 888-474-3657 | | 85

Grill 225
225 E Bay St . . . . Charleston SC 29401 | 877-440-2250 | 843-266-4222 | 667

Grill at Hacienda del Sol
5501 N Hacienda del Sol Rd . . . . Tucson AZ 85718 | 800-728-6514 | 520-529-3500 | 667

Grimes Legal
8264 Louisville Rd . . . . Bowling Green KY 42101 | 800-875-3820 | 270-782-3820 | 260

Grimmway Farms Inc
PO Box 81498 . . . . Bakersfield CA 93380 | 800-301-3101 | | 10-9

Grimstad
S84w18887 Enterprise Dr . . . . Muskego WI 53150 | 877-474-6782 | 414-422-2300 | 357

Grindmaster-Cecilware Inc
4003 Collins Ln . . . . Louisville KY 40245 | 800-695-4500 | 502-425-4776 | 298

Grinnell College
1115 Eighth Ave . . . . Grinnell IA 50112 | 800-247-0113 | 641-269-3600 | 166

Grinnell College Burling Library
6th Ave High St . . . . Grinnell IA 50112 | 800-247-0113 | 641-269-3371 | 433-6

Grinnell Mutual Reinsurance Co
4215 Hwy 146 PO Box 790 . . . . Grinnell IA 50112 | 800-362-2041 | 641-269-8000 | 390-4

Griswold Home Care
717 Bethlehem Pk Ste 300 . . . . Erdenheim PA 19038 | 800-474-7965 | | 310

Griswold Industries
1701 Placentia Ave . . . . Costa Mesa CA 92627 | 800-942-6326 | 949-722-4800 |

Griswold LLC
1 River St PO Box 638 . . . . Moosup CT 06354 | 800-472-8788 | | 672

Griswold Machine & Engineering Inc
8530 M 60 . . . . Union City MI 49094 | 800-248-2054 | 517-741-4300 | 473

Grit Commercial Printing Inc
80 Choate Cir . . . . Montoursville PA 17754 | 800-872-0409 | 570-368-8021 | 623

Grizzly & Wolf Discovery Ctr
201 S Canyon St . . . . West Yellowstone MT 59758 | 800-257-2570 | 406-646-7001 | 818

Grob Inc
1731 Tenth Ave . . . . Grafton WI 53024 | 800-225-6481 | 262-377-1400 | 453

Grobet File Company of America Inc
750 Washington Ave . . . . Carlstadt NJ 07072 | 800-847-4188 | 201-939-6700 | 753

Grocery People Ltd, The (TGP)
14505 Yellowhead Trl . . . . Edmonton AB T5L3C4 | 800-461-9401 | 780-447-5700 | 297-8

Grocery Supply Co
130 Hillcrest Dr . . . . Sulphur Springs TX 75482 | 800-231-1938 | 903-885-7621 | 297-8

Groendyke Transport Inc
2510 Rock Island Blvd . . . . Enid OK 73701 | 800-843-2103 | 580-234-4663 | 775

Grogans Health Care Supply Inc
1016 S Broadway Ave . . . . Lexington KY 40504 | 800-365-1020 | 859-254-6661 | 473

Grohe America Inc
241 Covington Dr . . . . Bloomingdale IL 60108 | 800-444-7643 | 630-582-7711 | 605

Groovfold Inc
1050 W State St . . . . Newcomerstown OH 43832 | 800-367-1133 | 740-498-8363 | 309

Name / Address	Toll-Free	Phone	Class
Grosh Scenic Rentals 4114 Sunset Blvd ...Los Angeles CA 90029	877-363-7998		718
Gross Mendelsohn & Associates PA 36 S Charles St 18th fl ...Baltimore MD 21201	800-899-4623	410-685-5512	2
Grossenburg Implement Inc 31341 US Hwy 18 ...Winner SD 57580	800-658-3440	605-842-2040	274
Grossman Iron & Steel 5 N Market St ...Saint Louis MO 63102	800-969-9423	314-231-9423	682
Grote Industries Inc 2600 Lanier Dr ...Madison IN 47250	800-628-0809	812-273-1296	60
Groth Corp 13650 N Promenade Blvd ...Stafford TX 77477	800-354-7684	281-295-6800	784
Groton Public Library 52 Newtown Rd ...Groton CT 06340	800-989-0900	860-441-6750	433-3
Grotto Ristorante 129 E Fremont St ...Las Vegas NV 89101	800-634-3454	702-385-7111	667
Grounds For Play Inc 1050 Columbia Dr ...Carrollton GA 30117	800-552-7529		345
Groundwater & Environmental Services Inc (GES) 1599 Rte 34 Ste 1 ...Wall Township NJ 07727	800-220-3068		192
Group Management Services Inc 3296 Columbia Rd Ste 101 ...Richfield OH 44286	888-823-2084	330-659-0100	461
Group O Inc 4905 77th Ave ...Milan IL 61264 *Cust Svc	800-752-0730*	309-736-8300	113
Groupe Canimex 285 Saint-Georges St ...Drummondville QC J2C4H3	855-777-1335	819-477-1335	357
Groupe Desgagnes Inc 21 March-Champlain St ...Quebec QC G1K8Z8	800-463-0680	418-692-1000	313
Groupe Lacasse LLC 99 St-Pierre St ...Sainte-Pie QC J0H1W0	888-522-2773	450-772-2495	319-1
Groupe Maskatel Lp 770 Casavant Ouest Bd ...Saint-Hyacinthe QC J2S7S3	877-627-5283	450-250-5050	224
Grove Park Inn Resort & Spa 290 Macon Ave ...Asheville NC 28804	800-438-5800		665
Grove Printing Corp 4225 Howard Ave ...Kensington MD 20895	877-290-5793	301-571-1024	623
Grover Corp 2759 S 28th St ...Milwaukee WI 53234	800-776-3602	414-716-5900	128
Groves Industrial Supply Inc 7301 Pinemont Dr ...Houston TX 77040	800-343-8923	713-675-4747	111
Grower Direct Fresh Cut Flowers 6303 Wagner Rd ...Edmonton AB T6E4N4	877-277-4787	780-436-7774	292
Growth Assn of Southwestern Illinois 5800 Godfrey Rd Alden Hall ...Godfrey IL 62035	855-852-9460	618-467-2280	139
Growth Coach, The 10700 Montgomery Rd ...Montgomery OH 45242	855-300-2622		310
Growth Products Ltd 80 Lafayette Ave ...White Plains NY 10603	800-648-7626	914-428-1316	276
GRR (Giant Resource Recovery - Harleyville Inc) 654 Judge St PO Box 352 ...Harleyville SC 29448	800-786-0477		192
GRS (Gabriel Roeder Smith & Co) 1 Towne Sq Ste 800 ...Southfield MI 48076	800-521-0498	248-799-9000	193
Gruber Systems Inc 25636 Ave Stanford ...Valencia CA 91355	800-257-4070	661-257-4060	600
Grunau Company Inc 1100 W Anderson Ct ...Oak Creek WI 53154	800-365-1920	414-216-6900	189-10
Grundy County Rural Electric Co-op 303 N Park Ave PO Box 39 ...Grundy Center IA 50638	800-390-7605	319-824-5251	245
Grundy Electric Co-op Inc 4100 Oklahoma Ave ...Trenton MO 64683	800-279-2249	660-359-3941	245
Gryphon International Engineering Services Inc 80 King St Ste 404 ...Saint Catharines ON L2R7G1	800-268-9242	905-984-8383	256
GS Blodgett Corp 44 Lakeside Ave ...Burlington VT 05401	800-331-5842	802-658-6600	298
G-S Supplies 1150 University Ave Ste 5 ...Rochester NY 14607	800-295-3050	585-241-2370	540
GSA (US General Services Administration) 1275 First St NW ...Washington DC 20405	800-424-5210	202-208-7642	339-19
GSA (Geological Society of America, The) 3300 Penrose Pl PO Box 9140 ...Boulder CO 80301	800-472-1988	303-357-1000	49-19
GSA (Genetics Society of America) 9650 Rockville Pk ...Bethesda MD 20814	866-486-4363	301-634-7300	49-19
GSAM (Goldman Sachs Asset Management) 200 W St ...New York NY 10282	800-526-7384	212-902-1000	400
GSB (Guilford Savings Bank) PO Box 369 ...Guilford CT 06437	866-878-1480	203-453-2015	70
GSCB (Garden State Community Bank) 36 Ferry St ...Newark NJ 07105 NYSE: NYCB	877-786-6560	973-589-8616	70
GSE Lining Technology Inc 19103 Gundle Rd ...Houston TX 77073	800-435-2008	281-443-8564	596
GSE Systems Inc 1332 Londontown Blvd Ste 200 ...Sykesville MD 21784 NASDAQ: GVP ■ *Cust Svc	800-638-7912*	410-970-7800	178-1
GSH (Good Samaritan Hospital) 407 14th Ave SE ...Puyallup WA 98372	800-776-4048	253-697-4000	373-3
GSP (Greenville-Spartanburg Airport) 2000 GSP Dr Ste 1 ...Greer SC 29651	800-331-1212	864-877-7426	27
GST Inc 12881 166th St ...Cerritos CA 90703	800-833-0128	562-345-8700	177
GSWB (Geisinger South Wilkes-Barre) 25 Church St ...Wilkes-Barre PA 18765	800-230-4565	570-808-3100	373-3
GT Water Products Inc 5239 N Commerce Ave ...Moorpark CA 93021	800-862-5647		603
Gtcbio 635 W Foothill Blvd ...Monrovia CA 91016	800-422-8386	626-256-6405	184
GTI Corporate Travel 111 Township Line Rd ...Jenkintown PA 19046	800-223-3863	215-379-6800	767
GTO 2000 Inc PO Box 2819 ...Gainesville GA 30503	800-966-0801	770-287-9233	
GTSI Corp 2553 Dulles View Dr Ste 100 ...Herndon VA 20171 NASDAQ: GTSI	800-999-4874	703-502-2000	174
GTT Global 600 Data Dr Ste 101 ...Plano TX 75075	800-485-6828	972-490-3394	16
Guadalupe Credit Union 3601 Mimbres Ln ...Santa Fe NM 87507	800-540-5382	505-982-8942	219
Guadalupe Valley Electric Co-op Inc 825 E Sarah Dewitt Dr ...Gonzales TX 78629	800-223-4832	830-857-1200	245
Guadalupe Valley Telephone Co-op (GVTC) 36101 FM 3159 ...New Braunfels TX 78132	800-367-4882	830-885-4411	731
Guarantee Trust Life Insurance Co 1275 Milwaukee Ave ...Glenview IL 60025	800-338-7452	847-699-0600	390-2
Guaranteed Rate Inc 3940 N Ravenswood ...Chicago IL 60613	866-934-7283	773-290-0505	217
Guaranteed Supply Co 1211 Rotherwood Rd ...Greensboro NC 27406	800-326-0810	336-273-3491	
Guaranty Bancshares Inc 100 W Arkansas St PO Box 1158 ...Mount Pleasant TX 75455	888-572-9881	903-572-9881	359-2
Guaranty Bank 4000 W Brown Deer Rd ...Brown Deer WI 53209	800-235-4636		70
Guaranty State Bank & Trust Co Beloit Kansas, The 201 S Mill St ...Beloit KS 67420	888-738-8000	785-738-3501	70
Guard Publishing Co PO Box 10188 ...Eugene OR 97440	800-377-7428	541-485-1234	633-8
Guard Systems Inc 1190 Monterey Pass Rd ...Monterey Park CA 91754	800-606-6711	323-881-6711	689
Guardair Corp 47 Veterans Dr ...Chicopee MA 01022	800-482-7324	413-594-4400	172
Guardian Alarm 20800 Southfield Rd ...Southfield MI 48075	800-782-9688	248-423-1000	688
Guardian Building Products (GBPD) 979 Batesville Rd ...Greer SC 29651	800-569-4262	864-297-6101	191-3
Guardian Electric Mfg Company Inc 1425 Lake Ave ...Woodstock IL 60098	800-762-0369	815-334-3600	203
Guardian Industries Corp 2300 Harmon Rd ...Auburn Hills MI 48326	800-822-5599	248-340-1800	329
Guardian Interlock Systems 228 Church St ...Marietta GA 30060	800-499-0994		
Guardian Life Insurance Company of America 7 Hanover Sq ...New York NY 10004	888-600-4667	888-482-7342	390-2
Guardian Mobility Corp 43 Auriga Dr ...Ottawa ON K2E7Y8	888-817-8159	613-225-8885	643
Guardian Protection Services Inc 174 Thorn Hill Rd ...Warrendale PA 15086 *Cust Svc	877-314-7092*	855-779-2001	689
Guard-Line Inc 215 S Louise St PO Box 1030 ...Atlanta TX 75551	800-527-8822	903-796-4111	155-7
Guerbet LLC 120 W Seventh St Ste 108 ...Bloomington IN 47404	877-729-6679	812-333-0059	231
Guernsey-Muskingum Electric Co-op 17 S Liberty St ...New Concord OH 43762	800-521-9879	740-826-7661	245
Guest Services Inc 3055 Prosperity Ave ...Fairfax VA 22031	800-345-7534	703-849-9300	299
Guest Supply Inc 300 Davidson Ave ...Somerset NJ 08873 *Cust Svc	800-772-7676*	732-868-2200	214
Guhring Inc 1445 Commerce Ave ...Brookfield WI 53045	800-776-6170	262-784-6730	491
Guida-Seibert Dairy Co 433 Park St ...New Britain CT 06051	800-832-8929		296-27
Guide Dog Foundation for the Blind Inc 371 E Jericho Tpke ...Smithtown NY 11787	800-548-4337	631-930-9000	48-17
Guide Dogs for the Blind 350 Los Ranchitos Rd ...San Rafael CA 94903	800-295-4050	415-499-4000	48-17
Guide Dogs of America 13445 Glenoaks Blvd ...Sylmar CA 91342	800-459-4843	818-362-5834	48-17
Guide, The 24904 Sussex Hwy PO Box 1210 ...Seaford DE 19973	800-984-8433	302-629-5060	623
Guidecraft USA 55508 Hwy 19 W ...Winthrop MN 55396	800-524-3555	507-647-5030	757
Guided Discoveries 27282 Calle Arroyo ...San Juan Capistrano CA 92675	800-645-1423		
GuideOne Mutual Insurance Co 1111 Ashworth Rd ...West Des Moines IA 50265	877-448-4331	844-948-4968	390-4
Guidesoft Inc 5875 Castle Creek Pkwy Ste 400 ...Indianapolis IN 46250	877-256-6948	317-578-1700	41
Guido Perla & Associates 701 Fifth Ave Ste 1200 ...Seattle WA 98104	800-252-5232	206-768-1515	261
Guild Investment Management Inc 12400 Wilshire Blvd Ste 1080 ...Los Angeles CA 90025	800-645-4100	310-826-8600	524
Guild Mortgage Co 5898 Copley Dr 4th & 5th Fl ...San Diego CA 92111	800-365-4441		507
Guilford College 5800 W Friendly Ave ...Greensboro NC 27410 *Admissions	800-992-7759*	336-316-2000	166
Guilford County Schools 712 N Eugene St ...Greensboro NC 27401	866-286-7337	336-370-8100	681
Guilford Savings Bank (GSB) PO Box 369 ...Guilford CT 06437	866-878-1480	203-453-2015	70
Guitar Player Magazine 28 E 28th St 12th Fl ...New York NY 10016 *Cust Svc	800-289-9839*	212-378-0400	455-9
Guittard Chocolate Co 10 GuittaRd Rd ...Burlingame CA 94010	800-468-2462	650-697-4427	296-8
Gulf Business Forms Inc 2460 IH 35 S ...San Marcos TX 78666	800-433-4853	512-353-8313	110
Gulf Coast Autoplex Inc 414 W Fred&Ruth Zingler Dr ...Jennings LA 70546	888-526-2391		57
Gulf Coast Bank 4310 Johnston St ...Lafayette LA 70503	800-722-5363	337-989-1133	70
Gulf Coast Bank & Trust Co 200 St Charles Ave ...New Orleans LA 70130	800-223-2060	504-561-6100	681
Gulf Coast Community College 5230 W Hwy 98 ...Panama City FL 32401	800-311-3685	850-769-1551	162
Gulf Coast Electric Co-op Inc 722 W Hwy 22 PO Box 220 ...Wewahitchka FL 32465	800-333-9392	850-639-2216	245
Gulf Coast Medical Ctr 449 W 23rd St ...Panama City FL 32405	800-296-2611	850-769-8341	373-3
Gulf Coast Mental Health Center 1600 Broad Ave ...Gulfport MS 39501	800-681-0798	228-863-1132	722
Gulf Coast Regional Blood Ctr 1400 La Concha Ln ...Houston TX 77054	888-482-5663	713-790-1200	89

Company	Toll-Free	Phone	Class
Gulf Coast Treatment Ctr 1015 Mar-Walt Dr ... Fort Walton Beach FL 32547	800-537-5433	850-863-4160	373-1
Gulf Engineering LLC 611 Hill St ... Jefferson LA 70121	800-347-4749	504-733-4868	188
Gulf Hills Hotel 13701 Paso Rd ... Ocean Springs MS 39564	866-875-4211	228-875-4211	665
Gulf Interstate Engineering 16010 Barkers Pt Ln Ste 600 ... Houston TX 77079	800-521-8879	713-850-3400	261
Gulf Manufacturing LLC 1221 Indiana St ... Humble TX 77396	800-333-4493	281-446-0093	
Gulf Offshore Logistics LLC 120 White Rose Dr ... Raceland LA 70394	866-532-1060		535
Gulf Stream Coach Inc 503 S Oakland Ave PO Box 1005 ... Nappanee IN 46550	800-289-8787		120
Gulf Winds International Inc 411 Brisbane St ... Houston TX 77061	866-238-4909	713-747-4909	798-1
GulfMark Energy Inc 17 S Briar Hollow Ln Ste 100 ... Houston TX 77027	800-340-1495		
Gulfport City Hall 2309 15th St ... Gulfport MS 39501	800-901-7072	228-868-5700	336
Gulfside Hospice Inc 6224 Lafayette St ... New Port Richey FL 34652	800-561-4883	727-845-5707	370
Gump's 135 Post St ... San Francisco CA 94108	800-766-7628	415-982-1616	361
Gun Parts Corp 226 Williams Ln ... Kingston NY 12401	866-686-7424	845-679-4867	284
Gund Inc 1 Runyons Ln ... Edison NJ 08817 *Cust Svc	800-448-4863*	732-248-1500	757
Gundersen Lutheran at Home HomeCare & Hospice 914 Green Bay St ... La Crosse WI 54601 *General	800-362-9567*	608-775-8435	370
Gundersen Lutheran Medical Ctr 1836 S Ave ... La Crosse WI 54601	800-362-9567	608-782-7300	373-3
Gunlocke Company LLC 1 Gunlocke Dr ... Wayland NY 14572 *Cust Svc	800-828-6300*	585-728-5111	319-1
Gunn Automotive Group 227 Broadway ... San Antonio TX 78205	888-452-2856	210-472-2501	57
Gunnebo-Johnson Corp 1240 N Harvard Ave ... Tulsa OK 74115 *Sales	800-331-5460*	918-832-8933	468
Gunnison County Electric Assn Inc 37250 W Hwy 50 PO Box 180 ... Gunnison CO 81230	800-726-3523	970-641-3520	245
Gunster Yoakley & Stewart Pa 777 S Flagler Dr Ste 500 E ... West Palm Beach FL 33401	800-749-1980	561-655-1980	427
Guntert & Zimmerman Construction Div Inc 222 E Fourth St ... Ripon CA 95366	800-733-2912	209-599-0066	190
Gunther Mele Ltd 30 Craig St ... Brantford ON N3R7J1	888-486-8437	519-756-4330	597
Gupton-Jones College of Funeral Service 5141 Snapfinger Woods Dr ... Decatur GA 30035	800-848-5352	770-593-2257	795
Gurney's Montauk Resort & Seawater Spa 290 Old Montauk Hwy ... Montauk NY 11954	800-848-7639	631-668-2345	665
Gurstel Chargo LLP 6681 Country Club Dr ... Golden Valley MN 55427	877-750-6335	877-344-4002	427
Guru Labs 1148 W Legacy Crossing Blvd Ste 200 ... Centerville UT 84014	800-833-3582	801-298-5227	94
Gurucom 5001 Baum Blvd Ste 760 ... Pittsburgh PA 15213	888-678-0136		260
Gurwitch Products LLC 135 E 57th St ... New York NY 10022	888-637-2437	212-376-6300	214
Gustave A Larson Co W233 N2869 Roundy Circle W ... Pewaukee WI 53072	800-829-9609	262-542-0200	661
Gustavus Adolphus College 800 W College Ave ... Saint Peter MN 56082	800-487-8288	507-933-8000	166
Guthrie Healthcare System 1011 North Elmer Ave ... Sayre PA 18840	888-448-8474	570-887-4401	352
Guthrie Theater 818 S Second St ... Minneapolis MN 55415 *Resv	877-447-8243*	612-377-2224	568
Gutsy Women Travel LLC 801 E Katella Ave ... Anaheim CA 92806	866-464-8879		755
Guttenplans Frozen Dough 100 Hwy 36 ... Middletown NJ 07748 *General	888-422-4357*	732-495-9480	296-2
Guttmacher Institute (AGI) 125 Maiden Ln 7th Fl ... New York NY 10038	800-355-0244	212-248-1111	48-5
Guy M Turner Inc 4514 S Holden Rd PO Box 7776 ... Greensboro NC 27406	800-432-4859	336-294-4660	775
Guy Shavender Trucking Inc PO Box 206 ... Pantego NC 27860	800-682-2447	252-943-3379	681
Guzzler Manufacturing Inc 1621 S Illinois St ... Streator IL 61364	800-627-3171	815-672-3171	385
GVMG (Grand View Media Group Inc) 200 Croft St Ste 1 ... Birmingham AL 35242	888-431-2877	205-262-4600	633-9
GVTC (Guadalupe Valley Telephone Co-op) 36101 FM 3159 ... New Braunfels TX 78132	800-367-4882	830-885-4411	731
GW Lisk Company Inc 2 S St ... Clifton Springs NY 14432	800-776-9528	315-462-2611	253
GWI (Great Works Internet) 43 Landry St ... Biddeford ME 04005	866-494-2020	207-494-2000	604
Gwin's Travel Planners Inc 212 N Kirkwood Rd ... Saint Louis MO 63122	888-254-7775	314-822-1958	766
Gwynedd-Mercy College 1325 Sunneytown Pk PO Box 901 ... Gwynedd Valley PA 19437 *Admissions	800-342-5462*	215-646-7300	166
Gwynn Group 600 E Las Colinas Blvd Ste 520 ... Irving TX 75039	877-941-7075	214-941-7075	
GXS Inc 9711 Washingtonian Blvd ... Gaithersburg MD 20878	800-560-4347	301-340-4000	178-4
GYC (Greater Yellowstone Coalition) 215 S Wallace Ave ... Bozeman MT 59715	800-775-1834	406-586-1593	48-13
Gymboree Corp 500 Howard St ... San Francisco CA 94105 NASDAQ: GYMB	877-449-6932		157-1

Company	Toll-Free	Phone	Class
Gynecologic Oncology Group (GOG) 1600 JFK Blvd Ste 1020 ... Philadelphia PA 19103	800-225-3053	215-854-0770	49-8
Gypsum Express Ltd 8280 Sixty Rd PO Box 268 ... Baldwinsville NY 13027	800-621-7901	315-638-2201	447
Gyration Inc 3601-B Calle Tecate ... Camarillo CA 93012	888-340-0033		173-1
Gyrodata Inc 23000 Northwest Lake Dr ... Houston TX 77095	800-348-6063	281-213-6300	190
Gyrodyne Company of America Inc 1 Flowerfield Ste 24 ... Saint James NY 11780 NASDAQ: GYRO	800-322-2885	631-584-5400	651
Gyrus ACMI 6655 Wedgwood Rd Ste 160 ... Maple Grove MN 55311	800-387-0437	763-416-3000	474
Gyrus Medical Inc ENT Div 136 Turnpike Rd ... Southborough MA 01772	800-757-2942	508-804-2600	475

H

Company	Toll-Free	Phone	Class
H & C Tool Supply Corp 235 Mt Read Blvd ... Rochester NY 14611	800-323-4624	585-235-5700	349
H & E Equipment Services Inc 7500 Pecue Ln ... Baton Rouge LA 70809 NASDAQ: HEES	866-467-3682	225-298-5200	264-3
H & H Chevrolet LLC 4645 S 84 St ... Omaha NE 68127	855-866-1733		
H & H Color Lab Inc 8906 E 67th St ... Raytown MO 64133	800-821-1305	816-358-6677	584
H & H Industrial Corp 7612 Rt 130 ... Pennsauken NJ 08110	800-982-0341	856-663-4444	693
H & H Publishing Company Inc 1231 Kapp Dr ... Clearwater FL 33765	800-366-4079	727-442-7760	244
H & H Swiss Screw Machine Products Company Inc 1478 Chestnut Ave ... Hillside NJ 07205	800-826-9985		617
H & L Advantage Inc 3500 Busch Dr SW ... Grandville MI 49418	800-581-2343	616-532-1012	349
H & L Tooth Company Inc 10055 E 56 St N ... Tulsa OK 74117	800-458-6684		481
H & M International Transportation Inc 485B Rt 1 S ... Iselin NJ 08830	800-446-4685	732-510-4640	775
H & P Leasing Inc 1849 Flowood Dr ... Flowood MS 39232	877-377-7052	601-939-2200	
H & R 1871 60 Industrial Rowe ... Gardner MA 01440	866-776-9292		284
H & R Block Tax Services Inc 4400 Main St ... Kansas City MO 64111	800-472-5625		729
H & S Bakery Inc 601 S Caroline St ... Baltimore MD 21231	800-959-7655	410-276-7254	296-1
H & W Computer Systems Inc 6154 N Meeker Pl Ste 100 ... Boise ID 83713	800-338-6692	208-377-0336	177
H & W Trucking Company Inc 1772 N Andy Griffith Pkwy PO Box 1545 ... Mount Airy NC 27030	800-334-9181	336-789-2188	775
H B Fuller Construction Products Inc 1105 S Frontenac Rd ... Aurora IL 60504	800-832-9002		3
H B. Van Duzer Forest State Scenic Corridor 8300 Salmon River Hwy ... Otis OR 97368	800-551-6949		561
H Barber & Sons Inc 15 Raytkwich Rd ... Naugatuck CT 06770	800-355-8318	203-729-9000	663
H E Anderson Company Inc 2025 Anderson Dr ... Muskogee OK 74403	800-331-9620	918-687-4426	707
H E Whitlock Inc PO Box 8030 ... Pueblo CO 81008	866-933-0709	719-544-9475	447
H E. Murdock Co Inc 88 Main St ... Waterville ME 04901	888-974-1805	800-439-3297	409
H Freeman & Son Inc 411 N Cranberry Rd ... Westminster MD 21157	800-876-7700	410-857-5774	155-11
H G Makelim Co 219 Shaw Rd ... South San Francisco CA 94080	800-471-0590	650-873-4757	384
H Gr Industrial Surplus 20001 Euclid Ave ... Euclid OH 44117	866-447-7117	216-486-4567	357
H Kramer & Co 1345 W 21st St ... Chicago IL 60608	800-621-2305	312-226-6600	483
H Lee Moffitt Cancer Ctr & Research Institute Blood & Marrow Transplantation Program 12902 Magnolia Dr ... Tampa FL 33612	888-663-3488		764
H O Wolding Inc 9642 Western Way ... Amherst WI 54406	800-950-0054	715-824-5513	775
H Pearce Real Estate Co 393 State St ... North Haven CT 06405	800-373-3411	203-281-3400	648
H Smith Packing Corp 99 Ft Fairfield Rd ... Presque Isle ME 04769	800-393-9898	207-764-4540	297-7
H Stern Jewelers Inc 645 Fifth Ave ... New York NY 10022	800-747-8376	212-688-0300	409
H. T. Berry Co Inc PO Box B ... Canton MA 02021	800-736-2206	781-828-6000	555
H2O Concepts International Inc 22405 N 19th Ave ... Phoenix AZ 85027	888-275-4261	623-582-5222	
H3 Solutions Inc 10432 Balls Ford Rd Ste 230 ... Manassas VA 20109	855-464-5914		196
HA Guden Company Inc 99 Raynor Ave ... Ronkonkoma NY 11779	800-344-6437	631-737-2900	349
HA Logistics Inc 5175 Johnson Dr ... Pleasanton CA 94588	800-449-5778	925-251-9300	311
Haag Engineering Co 4949 W Royal Ln ... Irving TX 75063	800-527-0168	214-614-6500	261
Haas & Wilkerson Inc 4300 Shawnee Mission Pkwy ... Fairway KS 66205	800-821-7703	913-432-4400	389
Haas Automation Inc 2800 Sturgis Rd ... Oxnard CA 93030	800-331-6746	805-278-1800	452
Haas Cabinet Company Inc 625 W Utica St ... Sellersburg IN 47172	800-457-6458	812-246-4431	115
Habana Inn 2200 NW 40th St ... Oklahoma City OK 73112	800-988-2221	405-528-2221	378

Company	Address	City	State	ZIP	Toll-Free	Phone	Class
Habanero Consulting Group Inc	510-1111 Melville St	Vancouver	BC	V6E3V6	**866-841-6201**	604-709-6201	225
Habasit ABT Inc	150 Industrial Pk Rd	Middletown	CT	06457	**800-522-2358**	860-632-2211	369
Habasit America	805 Satellite Blvd	Suwanee	GA	30024	**800-458-6431**		604
Habasit Belting Inc	1400 Clinton St	Buffalo	NY	14206	**800-325-1585**	716-824-8484	369
Habco	501 Gordon Baker Rd	Toronto	ON	M2H2S6	**800-448-0244**	416-491-6008	798-1
Habegger Corp, The	4995 Winton Rd	Cincinnati	OH	45232	**800-459-4822**	513-681-5600	608
Haber Vision LLC	15710 W Colfax Ave Ste 204	Golden	CO	80401	**800-621-4381**	303-459-2220	45
Habersham County Chamber of Commerce	668 Clarkesville St	Cornelia	GA	30531	**800-835-2559**	706-778-4654	139
Habersham Electric Membership Corp	6135 Georgia 115	Clarkesville	GA	30523	**800-640-6812**	706-754-2114	245
Habersham Funding LLC	3495 Piedmont Rd NE Ste 910	Atlanta	GA	30305	**888-874-2402**	404-233-8275	791
Habitat for Humanity International Inc	121 Habitat St	Americus	GA	31709	**800-422-4828**	229-924-6935	48-5
Habitat Housewares	800 E Dimond Blvd Ste 3-207	Anchorage	AK	99515	**800-770-1856**	907-561-1856	361
Habitat Suites	500 E Highland Mall Blvd	Austin	TX	78752	**800-535-4663**	512-467-6000	378
Habitec Security Inc	2926 S Republic Blvd	Toledo	OH	43615	**888-422-4832**	419-537-6768	689
HAC (Housing Assistance Council)	1025 Vermont Ave NW Ste 606	Washington	DC	20005	**866-234-2689**	202-842-8600	48-5
Hach Co	PO Box 389	Loveland	CO	80539	**800-227-4224**	970-669-3050	418
Hachette Book Group	237 Park Ave	New York	NY	10017	**800-759-0190**		633-2
Hacienda del Sol Guest Ranch Resort	5501 N Hacienda Del Sol Rd	Tucson	AZ	85718	**800-728-6514**	520-299-1501	665
Hacienda Mexican Restaurants	1501 N Ironwood Dr	South Bend	IN	46635	**800-541-3227**		666
Hacienda The at Hotel Santa Fe	1501 Paseo del Peralta	Santa Fe	NM	87501	**855-825-9876**	505-955-7805	378
Hackbarth Delivery Service Inc	3504 Brookdale Dr N	Mobile	AL	36618	**800-277-3322**	251-478-1401	314
Hacker Johnson & Smith PA	500 N Wshore Blvd Ste 1000	Tampa	FL	33609	**800-366-7126**	813-286-2424	2
Hackney	911 W Fifth St PO Box 880	Washington	NC	27889	**800-763-0700**	252-946-6521	513
Hackworth Reprographics	1700 Liberty St	Chesapeake	VA	23324	**800-676-2424**	757-545-7675	113
HACU (Hispanic Assn of Colleges & Universities)	8415 Datapoint Dr Ste 400	San Antonio	TX	78229	**800-780-4228**	210-692-3805	49-5
Hader/Seitz Inc	15600 W Lincoln Ave	New Berlin	WI	53151	**877-388-2101**		223
Hadley Exhibits Inc	1700 Elmwood Ave	Buffalo	NY	14207	**800-962-8088**	716-874-3666	232
Hadley House Co	PO Box 245	Madison Lake	MN	56063	**800-423-5390**	952-983-8208	633-10
Hadronics Inc	4570 Steel Pl	Cincinnati	OH	45209	**800-829-0826**	513-321-9350	479
Haemonetics Corp	400 Wood Rd *NYSE: HAE*	Braintree	MA	02184	**800-225-5242**	781-848-7100	474
Hafele America Company Inc	3901 Cheyenne Dr *Cust Svc	Archdale	NC	27263	**800-423-3531***	336-434-2322	489
Hagemeyer North America Inc	1460 Tobias Gadson Blvd	Charleston	SC	29407	**877-462-7070**	843-745-2400	384
Hager Co	139 Victor St	Saint Louis	MO	63104	**800-325-9995**	314-772-4400	349
Hagerstown/Washington County Convention & Visitors Bureau	16 Public Sq	Hagerstown	MD	21740	**888-257-2600**	301-791-3246	206
Hagerty Insurance Agency LLC	141 River's Edge Dr Ste 200 PO Box 1303	Traverse City	MI	49684	**877-922-9701**	800-922-4050	390-4
Hagerty Steel & Aluminum Co	601 N Main	East Peoria	IL	61611	**800-322-2600**	309-699-7251	693
Hagey Coach & Tours Nrt	210 Schoolhouse Rd	Souderton	PA	18964	**800-544-2439**	215-723-4381	755
Haggar Clothing Co	11818 Harry Hines Blvd Ste 202	Dallas	TX	75234	**877-841-2219**	972-481-1579	155-11
Haggard & Stocking Assoc	5318 Victory Dr	Indianapolis	IN	46203	**800-622-4824**	317-788-4661	384
Haggen Inc	2900 Woburn St	Bellingham	WA	98226	**800-995-1902**	360-676-5300	344
Haggerty Enterprises Inc	370 Kimberly Dr	Carol Stream	IL	60188	**800-336-5282**	630-315-3300	333
Hagie Manufacturing Co	721 Central Ave W	Clarion	IA	50525	**800-247-4885**	515-532-2861	273
Hagopian & Sons Inc	14000 W 8 Mile Rd	Oak Park	MI	48237	**800-424-6742**		290
Hagyard-Davidson-McGee Assoc PSC	4250 Iron Works Pk	Lexington	KY	40511	**888-323-7798**	859-255-8741	11-2
Hahn & Bowersock Corp	151 Kalmus Dr Ste L1	Costa Mesa	CA	92626	**800-660-3187**		443
Hahn Systems LLC	8416 Zionsville Rd	Indianapolis	IN	46268	**800-201-4246**	317-243-3796	384
HAI (Helicopter Assn International)	1920 Ballenger Ave 4th Fl	Alexandria	VA	22314	**800-435-4976**	703-683-4646	49-21
HAI (Hohman Assoc Inc)	6951 W Little York	Houston	TX	77040	**800-324-0978**	713-896-0978	48-2
Haida Corp	PO Box 89	Hydaburg	AK	99922	**800-478-3721**	907-285-3721	747
Hain Celestial Group Inc	4600 Sleepytime Dr *NASDAQ: HAIN*	Boulder	CO	80301	**877-612-4246**		297-11
Haines & Company Inc	8050 Freedom Ave	North Canton	OH	44720	**800-843-8452**		633-6
Haines Borough	103 Third Ave S PO Box 1209	Haines	AK	99827	**800-572-8006**	907-766-2231	337
Haines City Citrus Growers Assn (HCCGA)	8 Railroad Ave PO Box 337 *Sales	Haines City	FL	33844	**800-327-6676***	863-422-1174	11-1
Hair Club for Men LTD Inc	1515 S Federal Hwy Ste 401	Boca Raton	FL	33432	**800-251-2658**	561-361-7600	
Hal Leonard Corp	960 E Mark St	Winona	MN	55987	**800-321-3408**	507-454-2920	633-7
Halabi Inc	2100 Huntington Dr	Fairfield	CA	94533	**800-660-4167**	707-402-1600	115
Hale Farm & Village	2686 Oakhill Rd PO Box 296	Bath	OH	44210	**877-425-3327**	330-666-3711	517
Hale Products Inc	700 Spring Mill Ave	Conshohocken	PA	19428	**800-220-4253**	800-533-3569	637
Hale Trailer Brake & Wheel Inc	76 Cooper Rd PO Box 1400	Voorhees	NJ	08043	**800-232-6535**	856-768-1330	126
Halekulani Hotel	2199 Kalia Rd	Honolulu	HI	96815	**800-367-2343**	808-923-2311	378
Halex Co	23901 Aurora Rd	Bedford Heights	OH	44146	**800-749-3261**		308
Haley Bros Inc	6291 Orangethorpe Ave	Buena Park	CA	90620	**800-854-5951**	714-670-2112	236
Haley Marketing Group	6028 Sheridan Dr PO Box 410	Williamsville	NY	14221	**888-696-2900**		
Half Hitch Tackle Company Inc	2206 Thomas Dr	Panama City	FL	32408	**888-668-9810**	850-234-2621	707
Half Moon Bay Lodge & Conference Ctr	2400 S Cabrillo Hwy	Half Moon Bay	CA	94019	**800-710-0778**	650-726-9000	378
Halifax Community College	100 College Dr	Weldon	NC	27890	**800-228-8443**	252-536-2551	162
Halifax Electric Membership Corp	208 Whitfield St	Enfield	NC	27823	**800-690-0522**	252-445-5111	245
Halifax Historical Museum	252 S Beach St	Daytona Beach	FL	32114	**800-677-6884**	386-255-6976	517
Halifax Marriott Harborfront Hotel	1919 Upper Water St	Halifax	NS	B3J3J5	**800-450-4442**	902-421-1700	378
Hall Hodges & Associates Inc	700 N Brand Blvd Ste 650	Glendale	CA	91203	**800-490-1447**	818-244-8930	461
Hall Laughlin China Co	672 Fiesta Dr	Newell	WV	26050	**800-452-4462**	330-385-2900	726
Hall Signs Inc	4495 W Vernal Pk	Bloomington	IN	47404	**800-284-7446**		697
Halliburton House Inn	5184 Morris St	Halifax	NS	B3J1B3	**888-512-3344**	902-420-0658	378
Hallie Ford Museum of Art	700 State St	Salem	OR	97301	**844-232-7228**	503-370-6855	517
Hallmark Ch	12700 Ventura Blvd	Studio City	CA	91604	**888-390-7474**	818-755-2400	735
Hallmark Corp Foundation	2501 McGee St	Kansas City	MO	64108	**800-425-5627**		304
Hallmark Inns & Resorts	1400 S Hemlock St	Cannon Beach	OR	97110	**888-448-4449**	503-436-1566	378
Hallmark Nameplate Inc	1717 E Lincoln Ave	Mount Dora	FL	32757	**800-874-9063**		697
Halo Group LLC	39475 13 Mile Rd Ste 201	Novi	MI	48377	**877-456-4256**		
Halocarbon Products Corp	6525 The Corners Pkwy Ste 200	Peachtree Corners	GA	30092	**800-338-5803**	470-419-6364	578
Halron Lubricants Inc	1618 State St	Green Bay	WI	54304	**800-236-5845**	920-436-4000	575
Halstead International Inc	15 Oakwood Ave	Norwalk	CT	06850	**866-843-8453**		360
Halsted Corp	51 Commerce Dr Ste 3	Cranbury	NJ	08512	**800-843-5184**	609-235-4444	67
Halston LLC	1201 W Fifth St 11th fl	Los Angeles	CA	90017	**844-425-7866**		157-2
Halvorson Trane	2220 NW 108th St	Clive	IA	50325	**800-798-0004**	515-270-0004	606
Hamacher Resource Group Inc	W 229 N 2510 Duplainville Rd	Waukesha	WI	53186	**800-888-0889**		362
Hamburg Sud North America Inc	465 S St	Morristown	NJ	07960	**888-228-8241**	973-775-5300	313
Hamilton Beach/Proctor-Silex Inc	4421 Waterfront Dr *Cust Svc	Glen Allen	VA	23060	**800-851-8900***	804-273-9777	37
Hamilton Capital Management	5025 Arlington Centre Blvd	Columbus	OH	43220	**888-833-5951**	614-273-1000	400
Hamilton Co	4970 Energy Way	Reno	NV	89502	**800-648-5950**	775-858-3000	418
Hamilton College	198 College Hill Rd *Admissions	Clinton	NY	13323	**800-843-2655***	315-859-4421	166
Hamilton County	625 Georgia Ave	Chattanooga	TN	37402	**800-342-1003**	423-209-6500	337
Hamilton County Convention & Visitors Bureau Inc	37 E Main St	Carmel	IN	46032	**800-776-8687**	317-848-3181	206
Hamilton County Electric Co-op Assn	420 N Rice St PO Box 753	Hamilton	TX	76531	**800-595-3401**	254-386-3123	245
Hamilton County Speedway	1200 Bluff St	Webster City	IA	50595	**800-873-1507**	515-832-6000	512
Hamilton Ctr Inc	620 Eighth Ave	Terre Haute	IN	47804	**800-742-0787**		373-5
Hamilton Form Company Ltd	7009 Midway Rd	Fort Worth	TX	76118	**800-332-7090**	817-590-2111	693
Hamilton Group	100 Elwood Davis Rd	North Syracuse	NY	13212	**800-351-3066**	315-413-0086	272
Hamilton Health Sciences	1200 Main St W	Hamilton	ON	L8N3Z5	**800-680-9868**	905-522-3863	373-2
Hamilton Park Hotel & Conference Ctr	175 Park Ave	Florham Park	NJ	07932	**877-999-3223**	973-377-2424	376
Hamilton Port Authority	605 James St N 6th Fl	Hamilton	ON	L8L1K1	**800-263-2131**	905-525-4330	614
Hamilton Sorter Co Inc	3158 Production Dr	Fairfield	OH	45014	**800-503-9966**	513-870-4400	286
Hamilton Telecommunications	1001 12th St	Aurora	NE	68818	**800-821-1831**	402-694-5101	116

Company	Address	City	State	ZIP	Toll-Free	Phone	Class
Hamline University	1536 Hewitt Ave	Saint Paul	MN	55104	**800-753-9753**	651-523-2207	166
Hammacher Schlemmer & Co	9307 N Milwaukee Ave	Niles	IL	60714	**800-321-1484**		361
Hammel Green & Abrahamson Inc	701 Washington Ave N	Minneapolis	MN	55401	**888-442-8255**	612-758-4000	261
Hammelmann Corp	600 Progress Rd	Dayton	OH	45449	**800-783-4935**	937-859-8777	637
Hammer Nutrition Ltd	4952 Whitefish Stage Rd *Cust Svc	Whitefish	MT	59937	**800-336-1977***		794
Hammerman Bros Inc	50 W 57th St 12th Fl.	New York	NY	10019	**800-223-6436**	212-956-2800	408
Hammersmith Mfg & Sales Inc	401 Central Ave	Horton	KS	66439	**800-375-8245**	785-486-2121	91
Hammock Beach Resort	200 Ocean Crest Dr	Palm Coast	FL	32137	**866-841-0287**		665
Hammond Communications Group Inc	173 Trade St	Lexington	KY	40511	**888-424-1878**	859-254-1878	510
Hammond Electronics Inc	1230 W Central Blvd *Sales	Orlando	FL	32805	**800-929-3672***	407-849-6060	246
Hamon Research-Cottrell Inc	58 E Main St PO Box 10 E	Somerville	NJ	08876	**800-445-6578**	908-333-2000	385
Hampden-Sydney College	PO Box 667 *Admissions	Hampden Sydney	VA	23943	**800-755-0733***	434-223-6120	166
Hampel Oil Distributors Inc	3727 S W St	Wichita	KS	67217	**800-530-5848**		
Hampton Behavioral Health Center	650 Rancocas Rd	Westampton	NJ	08060	**800-603-6767**		722
Hampton Conventions & Visitors Bureau	1919 Commerce Dr Ste 290	Hampton	VA	23666	**800-487-8778**	757-722-1222	206
Hampton (Independent City)	22 Lincoln St	Hampton	VA	23669	**800-555-3930**	757-727-8311	337
Hampton Plantation State Historic Site	1950 Rutledge Rd	McClellanville	SC	29458	**866-345-7275**	843-546-9361	561
Hampton Products International Corp	50 Icon	Foothill Ranch	CA	92610	**800-562-5625**	949-472-4256	349
Hampton Public Library	4207 Victoria Blvd	Hampton	VA	23669	**800-552-7096**	757-727-1154	433-3
Hampton Securities Ltd	141 Adelaide St W Ste 1800	Toronto	ON	M5H3L5	**877-225-0229**	416-862-7800	686
Hampton University	100 E Queen St	Hampton	VA	23668	**800-624-3341**	757-727-5000	166
Hamrick Mills Inc	515 W Buford St PO Box 48	Gaffney	SC	29341	**800-600-4305**	864-489-4731	740-1
Hanalei Bay Resort & Suites	5380 Honoiki Rd	Princeville	HI	96722	**877-344-0688**	808-826-6522	665
Hanauma Bay Nature Preserve	100 Hanauma Bay Rd	Honolulu	HI	96825	**800-690-6200**	808-396-4229	50-5
Hancock County	300 S Main St	Findlay	OH	45840	**888-534-1432**	419-424-7037	337
Hancock County	PO Box 367	New Cumberland	WV	26047	**800-642-9066**	304-564-3311	337
Hancock County	418 Harrison St PO Box 575	Sneedville	TN	37869	**800-332-0900**	423-733-2519	337
Hancock County	12630 Broad St	Sparta	GA	31087	**800-255-0135**	706-444-5746	337
Hancock County Co-op Oil Assn	245 State St	Garner	IA	50438	**800-924-2667**	641-923-2635	344
Hancock-Wood Electric Co-op Inc (HWEC)	1399 Business Pk Dr S PO Box 190	North Baltimore	OH	45872	**800-445-4840**		245
Hancor Inc	PO Box 1047	Findlay	OH	45839	**888-892-2694**	419-422-6521	592
Handel Group Llc	247 Limestone Rd	Ridgefield	CT	06877	**800-617-7040**	917-670-8782	461
Handgards Inc	901 Hawkins Blvd	El Paso	TX	79915	**800-351-8161**		572
Handi-Ramp	510 N Ave	Libertyville	IL	60048	**800-876-7267**	847-680-7700	357
Handlery Hotel & Resort	950 Hotel Cir N	San Diego	CA	92108	**800-676-6567**	619-298-0511	665
Handley Industries Inc	2101 Brooklyn Rd	Jackson	MI	49203	**800-870-5088**	517-787-8821	199
Hands on Technology Transfer Inc	14 Fletcher St 1 Village Sq Ste 8	Chelmsford	MA	01824	**800-413-0939**	978-250-4299	
Handy Store Fixtures Inc	337 Sherman Ave	Newark	NJ	07114	**800-631-4280**		286
Handyman Connection Inc	11115 Kenwood Rd	Blue Ash	OH	45242	**800-466-5530**	513-771-3003	189-11
HandyTrac Systems LLC	510 Staghorn Ct	Alpharetta	GA	30004	**800-665-9994**	678-990-2305	688
Hanes Cos Inc	500 N McLin Creek Rd	Conover	NC	28613	**877-252-3052**	828-464-4673	590
Hanger Inc	10910 Domain Dr Ste 300	Austin	TX	78758	**877-442-6437**	512-777-3800	475
Hanger Orthopedic Group Inc	10910 Domain Dr Ste 300	Austin	TX	78758	**877-442-6437**	512-777-3800	351
Hangsterfer's Laboratories Inc	175 Ogden Rd	Mantua	NJ	08051	**800-433-5823**	856-468-0216	537
HANK AM 1550 & 977 FM	730 Ray O Vac Dr	Madison	WI	53711	**888-974-4265**	608-273-1000	641-60
Hankook Tire America Corp	1450 Valley Rd	Wayne	NJ	07470	**800-426-5665**	973-633-9000	749
Hanley-Wood LLC	1 Thomas Cir NW Ste 600	Washington	DC	20005	**800-227-8839**	202-452-0800	633-9
Hanmi Bank	3660 Wilshire Blvd PH-A	Los Angeles	CA	90010	**877-808-4266**	213-382-2200	359-2
Hanna Andersson Corp	1010 NW Flanders St *Cust Svc	Portland	OR	97209	**800-222-0544***		457
Hanna Steel Corp	3812 Commerce Ave PO Box 558	Fairfield	AL	35064	**800-633-8252**	205-780-1111	488
Hannaford Bros Co LLC	145 Pleasant Hill Rd	Scarborough	ME	04074	**800-213-9040**		297-8
Hannay Reels Inc	553 State Rt 143	Westerlo	NY	12193	**877-467-3357**	518-797-3791	117
Hannibal Carbide Tool Inc	5000 Paris Gravel Rd	Hannibal	MO	63401	**800-451-9436**	573-221-2775	491
Hannibal Regional Hospital	6500 Hospital Dr	Hannibal	MO	63401	**888-426-6425**	573-248-1300	373-3
Hannibal-LaGrange Univ	2800 Palmyra Rd *Admissions	Hannibal	MO	63401	**800-454-1119***	573-221-3675	166
Hannon Hydraulics LLC	625 N Loop 12	Irving	TX	75061	**800-333-4266**	972-438-2870	223
Hanover College	484 Ball Dr	Hanover	IN	47243	**800-213-2178**	812-866-7000	166
Hanover Foods Corp	1550 York St PO Box 334 *OTC: HNFSA*	Hanover	PA	17331	**800-888-4646**	717-632-6000	296-36
Hanover Hospital	300 Highland Ave	Hanover	PA	17331	**800-673-2426**	717-637-3711	373-3
Hanover Inn Dartmouth	2 E Wheelock St	Hanover	NH	03755	**800-443-7024**	603-643-4300	378
Hanover Insurance Co	440 Lincoln St	Worcester	MA	01653	**800-853-0456**	508-855-1000	390-4
Hanover Marriott	1401 Rt 10 E	Whippany	NJ	07981	**800-983-4240**		
Hans Johnsen Co	8901 Chancellor Row *Sales	Dallas	TX	75247	**800-879-1515***	214-879-1550	350
Hans Rudolph Inc	8325 Cole Pkwy	Shawnee	KS	66227	**800-456-6695**	913-422-7788	475
Hansa GCR LLC	308 SW First Ave	Portland	OR	97204	**800-755-7683**	503-241-8036	195
Hanscom Inc	331 Market St	Warren	RI	02885	**877-725-6788**	401-247-1999	604
Hansen Architectural Systems	5500 SE Alexander St	Hillsboro	OR	97123	**800-599-2965**		490
Hansen Corp	901 S First St	Princeton	IN	47670	**800-328-8996**	812-385-3415	515
Hansen Manufacturing Corp	5100 W 12th St	Sioux Falls	SD	57107	**800-328-1785**	605-332-3200	207
Hansen Software Corp	1855 Kirschner Rd Ste 380	Kelowna	BC	V1Y4N7	**877-795-2274**		521
Hansen Surfboards	1105 S Coast Hwy 101	Encinitas	CA	92024	**800-480-4754**		707
Hansen Technologies Corp	6827 High Grove Blvd	Burr Ridge	IL	60527	**800-426-7368**	630-325-1565	202
Hanser & Associates	1001 Office Park Rd Ste 210	West Des Moines	IA	50265	**800-229-4879**	515-224-1086	7
Hanser Music Group	9615 Inter-Ocean Dr	Cincinnati	OH	45246	**800-999-5558**	859-817-7100	523
Hansgrohe Inc	1490 Bluegrass Lakes Pkwy	Alpharetta	GA	30004	**800-334-0455**		605
Hanson Information System	2433 W White Oaks Dr	Springfield	IL	62704	**888-245-8468**	217-726-2400	177
Hanson Logistics	2900 S State St	Saint Joseph	MI	49085	**888-772-1197**	269-982-1390	447
Hanson Medical Systems Inc	1954 Howell Branch Rd	Winter Park	FL	32792	**877-671-3883**	407-671-3883	473
Hanson Sign Companies	82 Carter St	Falconer	NY	14733	**800-522-2009**	716-484-8564	
Hantronix Inc	10080 Bubb Rd	Cupertino	CA	95014	**800-525-0811**	408-252-1100	173-4
Hapag-Lloyd America Inc	401 E Jackson St	Tampa	FL	33602	**800-282-8977**	813-276-4600	313
Hapco Inc	26252 Hillman Hwy	Abingdon	VA	24210	**800-368-7171**	276-628-7171	489
Hapman	6002 E N Ave	Kalamazoo	MI	49048	**800-427-6260**	269-343-1675	207
Happy Time Tours & Travel	1475 Walsh St W	Thunder Bay	ON	P7E4X6	**800-473-5955**	807-473-5955	767
Hapuna Beach Resort	62-100 Kauna'oa Dr	Kamuela	HI	96743	**800-882-6060**	808-880-1111	665
Haralson County	70 Murphy Campus Blvd	Waco	GA	30182	**800-955-7766**	770-537-5594	337
Harbec Inc	358 Timothy Ln	Ontario	NY	14519	**888-521-4416**	585-265-0010	604
Harbor Freight Tools	3491 Mission Oaks Blvd	Camarillo	CA	93011	**800-444-3353**	805-445-4791	350
Harbor Health Systems LLC	PO Box 11779	Newport Beach	CA	92658	**888-626-1737**	949-273-7020	239
Harbor Hospital Ctr	3001 S Hanover St	Baltimore	MD	21225	**800-280-9006**	410-350-3200	373-3
Harbor Light Hospice	1 N 131 County Farm Rd	Winfield	IL	60190	**800-419-0542**	630-682-3871	370
Harbor Sales	1000 Harbor Ct	Sudlersville	MD	21668	**800-345-1712**		609
Harbor View Hotel	131 N Water St Martha's Vineyard PO Box 7	Edgartown	MA	02539	**800-225-6005**	508-627-7000	378
HarborOne Credit Union	770 Oak St PO Box 720	Brockton	MA	02301	**800-244-7592**	508-895-1000	219
Harbors Home Health & Hospice	201 Seventh St	Hoquiam	WA	98550	**800-772-1319**	360-532-5454	370
Harborside Inn	1 Christie's Landing	Newport	RI	02840	**800-427-9444**	401-846-6600	378
Harborside Suites At Little Harbor	536 Bahia Beach Blvd	Ruskin	FL	33570	**800-327-2773**		665
Harbour Industries Inc	4744 Shelburne Rd PO Box 188	Shelburne	VT	05482	**800-659-4733**	802-985-3311	809
Harbour Investments Inc	575 D'Onofrio Dr Ste 300	Madison	WI	53719	**888-855-6960**	608-662-6100	
Harbour's Edge	401 E Linton Blvd	Delray Beach	FL	33483	**888-417-9281**	561-272-7979	668
Harco Company Ltd	5610 McAdam Rd	Mississauga	ON	L4Z1P1	**800-387-9503**	905-890-1220	35
Harcourt Equipment	313 Hwy 169 & 175 E	Harcourt	IA	50544	**800-445-5646**	515-354-5332	274
Harcourt Outlines Inc	7765 S 175 W PO Box 128	Milroy	IN	46156	**800-428-6584**		55

	Toll-Free	Phone	Class
Harcros			
5200 Speaker Rd .... Kansas City KS 66106	800-424-9300	913-321-3131	146
Harcum College			
750 Montgomery Ave .... Bryn Mawr PA 19010	800-537-3000	610-525-4100	162
Hard Mfg Company Inc			
230 Grider St .... Buffalo NY 14215	800-873-4273		319-3
Hard Rock Cafe			
45 Monroe St .... Detroit MI 48226	888-519-6683	313-964-7625	667
Hard Rock Cafe International Inc			
5701 Stirling Rd .... Davie FL 33314	888-519-6683	954-585-5703	
Hard Rock Cafe International Inc			
6100 Old Pk Ln .... Orlando FL 32835	888-519-6683	407-445-7625	666
Hard Rock Hotel & Casino			
4455 Paradise Rd .... Las Vegas NV 89169	800-473-7625	702-693-5000	665
Hard Rock Hotel & Casino Biloxi			
777 Beach Blvd .... Biloxi MS 39530	877-877-6256	228-374-7625	133
Hard Rock Hotel at Universal Orlando Resort			
5800 Universal Blvd .... Orlando FL 32819	888-430-4999	407-503-2000	665
Hard Rock Hotel San Diego			
207 Fifth Ave .... San Diego CA 92101	866-751-7625	619-702-3000	378
Hardeman County			
100 N Main St .... Bolivar TN 38008	800-336-2036	731-658-3541	337
Harder Corp			
7029 Raywood Rd .... Monona WI 53713	800-261-3400	608-271-5127	555
HARDI Hydronic Heating & Cooling Council			
445 Hutchinson Ave Ste 550 .... Columbus OH 43235	888-253-2128	614-345-4328	49-18
Hardi Inc			
1500 W 76th St .... Davenport IA 52806	866-770-7063	563-386-1730	273
Hardin County			
495 Main St .... Savannah TN 38372	800-552-3866	731-925-3921	337
Hardin Memorial Hospital			
913 W Dixie Ave .... Elizabethtown KY 42701	800-955-9455	270-706-1212	373-3
Harding Instruments			
7741 Wagner Rd NW .... Edmonton AB T6E5B1	888-792-1171	780-462-7100	201
Harding University			
915 E Market Ave .... Searcy AR 72149	800-477-4407*	501-279-4000	167-3
*Admissions			
Harding University			
915 E Market Ave .... Searcy AR 72149	800-477-4407	501-279-4000	166
Hardinge Inc			
1 Hardinge Dr .... Elmira NY 14902	800-843-8801	607-734-2281	453
NASDAQ: HDNG			
Hardin-Simmons University			
2200 Hickory St .... Abilene TX 79698	877-464-7889	325-670-1206	166
Hardware Distribution Warehouses Inc (HDW)			
6900 Woolworth Rd .... Shreveport LA 71129	800-256-8527*	318-686-8527	350
*Cust Svc			
Hardware Suppliers of America Inc (HSI)			
1400 E Fire Tower Rd .... Greenville NC 27858	800-334-5625		350
Hardwick Clothes Inc			
3800 Old Tasso Rd .... Cleveland TN 37312	800-251-6392		155-11
Hardwoods of Michigan Inc			
430 Div St .... Clinton MI 49236	800-327-2812	517-456-7431	679
Hardy Corp			
350 Industrial Dr .... Birmingham AL 35211	800-289-4822	205-252-7191	189-10
Harford County Public Library			
1221-A Brass Mill Rd .... Belcamp MD 21017	800-944-7403	410-575-6761	433-3
Hargrave Military Academy (HMA)			
200 Military Dr .... Chatham VA 24531	800-432-2480	434-432-2481	618
Harkcon			
1390 Chain Bridge Rd 570 .... Mclean VA 22101	800-499-6456		461
Harkins Builders Inc			
10490 Little Patuxent Pkwy Ste 400 .... Columbia MD 21044	800-227-2345	410-750-2600	186
Harlan ARH Hospital			
81 Ballpark Rd .... Harlan KY 40831	800-274-9375	606-573-8100	373-3
Harlan County			
311 Main St .... Alma NE 68920	800-762-5498		337
Harlan County			
201 S Main St .... Harlan KY 40831	800-988-4660	606-573-4495	337
Harlan Global Manufacturing LLC			
27 Stanley Rd .... Kansas City KS 66115	800-255-4262	913-342-5650	468
Harlem Globetrotters International Inc			
400 E Van Buren St Ste 300 .... Phoenix AZ 85004	800-641-4667	208-568-6644	181
Harlequin			
233 Broadway Ste 1001 .... New York NY 10279	800-873-8635	212-553-4200	633-2
Harley-Davidson Financial Services Inc			
PO Box 21489 .... Carson City NV 89721	888-691-4337		217
Harley-Davidson Inc			
3700 W Juneau Ave .... Milwaukee WI 53208	800-424-9393	414-342-4680	514
NYSE: HOG			
Harleysville Bank			
271 Main St .... Harleysville PA 19438	888-256-8828	215-256-8828	359-2
NASDAQ: HARL			
Harlingen Area Chamber of Commerce			
311 E Tyler St .... Harlingen TX 78550	800-225-5345	956-423-5440	139
Harman International Industries Inc			
400 Atlantic St 15th Fl .... Stamford CT 06901	800-473-0602	203-328-3500	52
NYSE: HAR			
Harman, Claytor, Corrigan & Wellman PC			
PO Box 70280 .... Richmond VA 23255	877-747-4229	804-747-5200	427
Harmon Electric Assn Inc (HEA)			
114 N First St PO Box 393 .... Hollis OK 73550	800-643-7769	580-688-3342	245
Harmon Stores Inc			
650 Liberty Ave .... Union NJ 07083	866-427-6661	908-688-7023	237
Harmonic Drive LLC			
247 Lynnfield St .... Peabody MA 01960	800-921-3332	978-532-1800	61
Harmonic Inc			
4300 N First St .... San Jose CA 95134	800-322-2885	408-542-2500	643
NASDAQ: HLIT			
Harmonie State Park			
3451 Harmonie State Pk Rd .... New Harmony IN 47631	866-622-6746	812-682-4821	561
Harmony Dental Lab			
758 W Duval St .... Jacksonville FL 32202	888-354-3594		417
Harmony Foundation Inc			
1600 Fish Hatchery Rd .... Estes Park CO 80517	866-686-7867	970-586-4491	722
Harms Oil Co			
337 22nd Ave S .... Brookings SD 57006	800-376-8476	605-696-5000	576
Harnack Co			
6016 Nordic Dr .... Cedar Falls IA 50613	800-772-2022*	319-277-0660	428
*Cust Svc			
Harnett County Board of Education			
1008 S 11th St .... Lillington NC 27546	800-342-9647	910-893-8151	681
Harney Rock & Paving Co			
457 S Date Ave .... Burns OR 97720	888-298-2681	541-573-7855	501-5
Haro Bicycles			
1230 Avenida Chelsea .... Vista CA 92081	800-289-4276		
Harold G Butzer Inc			
730 Wicker Ln .... Jefferson City MO 65109	800-769-1065	573-636-4115	189-10
Harold Levinson Assoc (HLA)			
21 Banfi Plz .... Farmingdale NY 11735	800-325-2512	631-962-2400	297-3
Harper Brush Works Inc			
400 N Second St .... Fairfield IA 52556	800-223-7894	641-472-5186	103
HARPER CHEVROLET-BUICK-GMC			
200 Hwy 531 .... Minden LA 71055	800-259-0395	318-268-3320	198
Harper County			
201 N Jennings Ave .... Anthony KS 67003	877-537-2110	620-842-5555	337
Harper Engraving & Printing Co			
2626 Fisher Rd .... Columbus OH 43204	800-848-5196	614-276-0700	623
Harper Industries Inc			
960 N H C Mathis Dr .... Paducah KY 42001	800-669-0077	270-442-2753	188-4
Harper Trucks Inc			
PO Box 12330 .... Wichita KS 67277	800-835-4099	316-942-1381	468
Harper's Magazine			
666 Broadway 11th Fl. .... New York NY 10012	800-444-4653	212-420-5720	455-11
Harrah's Ak-Chin Casino Resort			
15406 Maricopa Rd .... Maricopa AZ 85139	800-427-7247*	480-802-5000	665
*General			
Harrah's Council Bluffs			
1 Harrahs Blvd .... Council Bluffs IA 51501	800-342-7724	712-329-6000	133
Harrah's Las Vegas			
3475 Las Vegas Blvd S .... Las Vegas NV 89109	800-214-9110		
Harrah's New Orleans			
228 Poydras St .... New Orleans LA 70130	800-427-7247		133
Harrah's Resort Atlantic City			
777 Harrah's Blvd .... Atlantic City NJ 08401	800-342-7724	609-441-5000	133
Harrang Long Gary Rudnick PC			
360 E Tenth Ave Ste 300 .... Eugene OR 97401	800-315-4172	541-485-0220	427
Harraseeket Inn			
162 Main St .... Freeport ME 04032	800-342-6423	207-865-9377	378
Harriman State Park			
3489 Green Canyon Rd .... Island Park ID 83429	866-634-3246	208-558-7368	561
Harrington Hoists Inc			
401 W End Ave .... Manheim PA 17545	800-233-3010	717-665-2000	385
Harrington Hospital (HMH)			
100 South St .... Southbridge MA 01550	800-416-6072	508-765-9771	373-3
Harrington Industrial Plastics LLC			
14480 Yorba Ave .... Chino CA 91710	800-213-4528	909-597-8641	384
Harrington Investments Inc			
1001 Second St Ste 325 .... Napa CA 94559	800-788-0154		400
Harrington Raceway			
15 W Rider Rd .... Harrington DE 19952	888-887-5687		638
Harris Corp			
1025 W NASA Blvd .... Melbourne FL 32919	800-442-7747	321-727-9100	643
NYSE: HRS			
Harris Corp RF Communications Div			
1680 University Ave .... Rochester NY 14610	866-264-8040	585-244-5830	643
Harris Cos Inc			
909 Montreal Cir .... Saint Paul MN 55102	800-466-3993	651-602-6500	189-3
Harris County			
159 S College St PO Box 426. .... Hamilton GA 31811	888-478-0010	706-628-0010	337
Harris County			
1019 Congress St 1st Fl .... Houston TX 77002	800-983-9933	713-755-5000	337
Harris Farms Inc			
27366 W Oakland Ave .... Coalinga CA 93210	800-311-6211	559-884-2859	10-9
Harris Financial Services Inc			
940 Spokane Ave .... Whitefish MT 59937	800-735-7895	406-862-4400	686
Harris Industries Inc			
5181 Argosy Ave .... Huntington Beach CA 92649	800-222-6866	714-898-8048	727
Harris Miniature Golf			
141 W Burk Ave .... Wildwood NJ 08260	888-294-6530	609-522-4200	188-3
Harris myCFO Inc			
2200 Geng Rd Ste 100 .... Palo Alto CA 94303	866-966-1130	650-210-5000	403
Harris Products Group			
4501 Quality Pl .... Mason OH 45040	800-733-4043	513-754-2000	806
Harris Ranch Beef Co			
16277 S McCall Ave PO Box 220 .... Selma CA 93662	800-742-1955		471
Harris Teeter Inc			
PO Box 10100 .... Mathews NC 28106	800-432-6111		185
Harris Wyatt & Amala Attorneys at Law			
5778 Commercial St SE .... Salem OR 97306	800-853-2144	503-378-7744	427
Harrisburg Area Community College			
1 HACC Dr .... Harrisburg PA 17110	800-222-4222	717-780-2300	162
Gettysburg			
731 Old Harrisburg Rd .... Gettysburg PA 17325	800-222-4222	717-337-3855	162
Lebanon			
735 Cumberland St .... Lebanon PA 17042	800-222-4222	717-270-4222	162
Harrisburg Dairies Inc			
2001 Herr St .... Harrisburg PA 17105	800-692-7429		296-27
Harrisburg Hospital			
111 S Front St .... Harrisburg PA 17101	888-782-5678	717-782-3131	373-3
Harrisburg Regional Chamber			
3211 N Front St Ste 201 .... Harrisburg PA 17110	877-883-8339	717-232-4099	139
HarrisData			
13555 Bishops Ct Ste 300 .... Brookfield WI 53005	800-225-0585	262-784-9099	178-1
Harrison County			
301 W Main St .... Clarksburg WV 26301	888-509-6568	304-624-8500	337
Harrison Hot Springs Resort & Spa			
100 Esplanade Ave .... Harrison Hot Springs BC V0M1K0	800-663-2266	604-796-2244	665
Harrison Paint Co			
1329 Harrison Ave SW .... Canton OH 44706	800-321-0680	330-455-5125	546
Harrison Steel Castings Co Inc			
900 S Mound St .... Attica IN 47918	800-659-4722	765-762-2481	307
Harrisonburg (Independent City)			
345 S Main St .... Harrisonburg VA 22801	800-272-9829	540-432-7701	337

Alphabetical Section

	Toll-Free	Phone	Class
Harry & David Holdings Inc 2500 S Pacific Hwy ....Medford OR 97501 *Cust Svc	877-322-1200*		335
Harry Cooper Supply Company Inc 605 N Sherman Pkwy ....Springfield MO 65802	800-426-6737	417-865-8392	608
Harry Davis & Co 1725 Blvd of Allies ....Pittsburgh PA 15219	800-775-2289	412-765-1170	51
Harry G Barr Co 6500 S Zero St ....Fort Smith AR 72903	800-829-2277	479-646-7891	235
Harry Grodsky & Co Inc 33 Shaws Ln PO Box 880 ....Springfield MA 01101	800-843-4424	413-785-1947	189-10
Harry Hynes Memorial Hospice 313 S Market St ....Wichita KS 67202	800-767-4965	316-265-9441	370
Harry Klitzner Inc 530 Wellington Ave Ste 11 ....Cranston RI 02910	800-621-0161		408
Harry London Candies Inc 5353 Lauby Rd ....North Canton OH 44720 *Cust Svc	800-333-3629*	330-494-0833	296-8
Harry Ritchie's Jewelers Inc 956 Willamette St ....Eugene OR 97401 *Cust Svc	800-935-2850*	541-686-1787	409
Harry S Truman College 1145 W Wilson Ave ....Chicago IL 60640	877-863-6339	773-907-4000	162
Harry S Truman Presidential Library & Museum 500 W Hwy 24 ....Independence MO 64050	800-833-1225	816-268-8200	433-2
Harry Winston Inc 718 Fifth Ave ....New York NY 10019	800-988-4110	212-399-1000	408
Harry's 17711 NE Riverside Pkwy ....Portland OR 97230	800-307-7687	503-257-7687	297-8
Harsco Corp 350 Poplar Church Rd ....Camp Hill PA 17011 NYSE: HSC	866-470-3900	717-763-7064	185
Harsco Industrial Air-X-Changers 5616 S 129th E Ave ....Tulsa OK 74134	800-404-3904	918-619-8000	91
Hart & Price Corp PO Box 36368 ....Dallas TX 75235	800-777-9129	214-521-9129	661
Hart Corp 900 Jaymor Rd ....SouthHampton PA 18966	800-368-4278	215-322-5100	648
Hart Electric Membership Corp 1071 Elberton Hwy ....Hartwell GA 30643	800-241-4109	706-376-4714	245
Hart Industries Inc 11412 Cronridge Dr ....Owings Mills MD 21117	800-638-2700	410-581-1900	623
Hart InterCivic 15500 Wells Port Dr ....Austin TX 78728	800-223-4278		796
Hart King 4 Hutton Centre Dr Ste 900.........Santa Ana CA 92707	866-718-7148	714-432-8700	
Hart Petroleum 323 Skidmores Rd ....Deer Park NY 11729	800-796-3342	631-667-3200	576
Hart Publications Inc 1616 S Voss Rd Ste 1000...........Houston TX 77057	800-874-2544	713-260-6400	633-9
Hart Ranch Camping Resort Club 23756 Arena Dr ....Rapid City SD 57702	800-605-4278	605-399-2582	121
Hart Specialties Inc 5000 New Horizons Blvd ....Amityville NY 11701	800-221-6966	631-226-5600	
Harte Nissan 165 W Service Rd ....Hartford CT 06120	866-687-8971	860-549-2800	57
Harte-Hanks Inc 9601 McAllister Fwy Ste 610 ......San Antonio TX 78216 NYSE: HHS	800-456-9748	210-829-9000	5
Harte-Hanks Response Management 2800 Wells Branch Pkwy ....Austin TX 78728	800-456-9748	512-434-1100	732
Hartford Casualty Insurance Co 690 Asylum Ave ....Hartford CT 06155	800-243-5860	860-547-5000	390-4
Hartford Courant 285 Broad St ....Hartford CT 06115	800-524-4242	860-241-6200	528-2
Hartford Electric Supply Co (HESCO) 30 Inwood Rd Ste 1 ....Rocky Hill CT 06067	800-969-5444	860-236-6363	246
Hartford Financial Services Group Inc 690 Asylum Ave ....Hartford CT 06115 NYSE: HIG	866-553-5663	860-547-5000	359-4
Hartford Funds 30 Dan Rd Ste 55022 ....Canton MA 02021	888-843-7824		524
Hartford Hospital 80 Seymour St ....Hartford CT 06102	800-545-7664	860-545-5000	373-3
Hartford Life & Accident Insurance Co 1 Hartford Plz ....Hartford CT 06155	877-896-9320	860-547-5000	390-2
Hartford Seminary 77 Sherman St ....Hartford CT 06105	877-860-2255	860-509-9500	166
Hartness International Inc 500 Hartness Dr PO Box 26509 ....Greenville SC 29615	800-845-8791	864-297-1200	543
Hartnett Law Firm, The 2920 N Pearl St ....Dallas TX 75201	800-900-9702	214-742-4655	427
Hartsfield-Jackson Atlanta International Airport 6000 N Terminal Pkwy Ste 4000.......Atlanta GA 30320	800-897-1910	404-530-6600	27
Hartson-kennedy Cabinet Top Company Inc 522 W 22nd St PO Box 3095.......Marion IN 46953	800-388-8144		595
Hartung Bros Inc 708 Heartland Trl Ste 2000...........Madison WI 53717	800-362-2522	608-829-6000	10-9
Hartung Glass Industries 17830 W Valley Hwy ....Tukwila WA 98188	800-552-2227		329
Hartung Glass Industries 10450 SW Ridder Rd ....Wilsonville OR 97070	800-552-2227	503-682-3846	329
Hartwell Medical Corp 6354 Corte del Abeto Ste F..........Carlsbad CA 92011	800-633-5900	760-438-5500	474
Hartwick College 1 Hartwick Dr ....Oneonta NY 13820	888-427-8942	607-431-4150	166
Harty Integrated Solutions 25 James St ....New Haven CT 06513	800-654-0562	203-562-5112	623
Hartz Mountain Corp, The 400 Plaza Dr ....Secaucus NJ 07094	800-275-1414		574
Hartzell Engine Technologies LLC 2900 Selma Hwy ....Montgomery AL 36108	877-359-5355	334-386-5400	21
Hartzell Fan Inc 910 S Downing St ....Piqua OH 45356	800-336-3267	937-773-7411	18
Hartzell Propeller Inc 1 Propeller Pl ....Piqua OH 45356	800-942-7767	937-778-4200	22
Harvard Bioscience Inc 84 October Hill Rd Ste 10........Holliston MA 01746 NASDAQ: HBIO	800-272-2775	508-893-8999	418
Harvard Business Review 60 Harvard Way ....Boston MA 02163	800-274-3214	617-783-7500	455-5
Harvard Business School Publishing 60 Harvard Way ....Boston MA 02163	800-795-5200		633-4
Harvard Law Review 1511 Massachusetts Ave Gannett House ....Cambridge MA 02138	800-828-7571	617-495-4650	455-15
Harvard Medical School 25 Shattuck St ....Boston MA 02115	866-606-0573	617-432-1550	167-2
Harvard Pilgrim Health Care Inc 93 Worcester St ....Wellesley MA 02481	888-888-4742	617-509-1000	390-3
Harvard Square Hotel 110 Mt Auburn St Harvard Sq........Cambridge MA 02138	800-458-5886	617-864-5200	378
Harvard University Press 79 Garden St ....Cambridge MA 02138	800-405-1619	617-495-2600	633-4
Harvard Women's Health Watch PO Box 9308 ....Big Sandy TX 75755	877-649-9457		527-8
Harvest Inn 1 Main St ....Saint Helena CA 94574	800-950-8466	707-963-9463	378
Harvest Operations Corp 700 Second St SW Ste 1500............Calgary AB T2P2W1	866-666-1178	403-265-1178	671
Harvest Partners 280 Park Ave 25th Fl ....New York NY 10017	866-771-1000	212-599-6300	787
Harvey Cadillac Co 2600 28th St SE ....Grand Rapids MI 49512 *Sales	877-845-1557*	616-949-1140	57
Harvey Industries Inc 1400 Main St ....Waltham MA 02451	800-598-5400		191-4
Harvey Mudd College 301 Platt Blvd ....Claremont CA 91711	877-827-5462	909-621-8000	166
Harvey Software Inc 7050 Winkler Rd Ste 104 ....Fort Myers FL 33919	800-231-0296		177
Harvey Watt & Co 475 N Central Ave ....Atlanta GA 30354	800-241-6103	404-767-7501	390-2
Hasbro Inc 1027 Newport Ave ....Pawtucket RI 02861 NASDAQ: HAS	800-242-7276	401-431-8697	757
Hasco Oil Company Inc 2800 Temple Ave ....Long Beach CA 90806	800-456-8491	562-595-8491	575
Haskel International Inc 100 E Graham Pl ....Burbank CA 91502	800-743-2720	818-843-4000	637
Haskel Thompson & Associates LLC 12734 Kenwood Ln Ste 74 ....Fort Myers FL 33907	800-470-4226	239-437-4600	260
Haskell Co 111 Riverside Ave ....Jacksonville FL 32202	800-622-4326	904-791-4500	188-7
Hassayampa Inn 122 E Gurley St ....Prescott AZ 86301 *Cust Svc	800-322-1927*	928-778-9434	378
Hastings & Sons Publishing 38 Exchange St ....Lynn MA 01901	800-243-4636	781-593-7700	633-8
Hastings City Bank 150 W Court St ....Hastings MI 49058	888-422-2280		
Hastings College 710 N Turner Ave ....Hastings NE 68901	800-532-7642	402-463-2402	166
Hastings Equity Mfg 1900 Summit Ave PO Box 1007 ....Hastings NE 68901	888-883-2189	402-462-2189	273
Hastings House Country House Hotel 160 Upper Ganges Rd ....Salt Spring Island BC V8K2S2	800-661-9255		378
Hastings HVAC Inc 3606 Yost Ave PO Box 669...........Hastings NE 68902 *Cust Svc	800-228-4243*	402-463-9821	14
Hastings Manufacturing Co 325 N Hanover St ....Hastings MI 49058	800-776-1088	269-945-2491	128
Hat World Corp 7555 Woodland Dr ....Indianapolis IN 46278	888-564-4287		157-5
Hatch & Kirk Inc 5111 Leary Ave NW ....Seattle WA 98107	800-426-2818	206-783-2766	262
HatchBeauty LLC 10951 W Pico Blvd Ste 300 ....Los Angeles CA 90064	855-895-6980		195
Hatfield Quality Meats Inc 2700 Clemens Rd ....Hatfield PA 19440	800-743-1191	215-368-2500	471
Hatteras Hammocks Inc 305 Industrial Blvd ....Greenville NC 27834	800-643-3522	252-758-0641	319-4
Hattiesburg American 825 N Main St ....Hattiesburg MS 39401	800-844-2637	601-582-4321	528-2
Hattiesburg Zoo 107 S 17th Ave ....Hattiesburg MS 39401	800-733-2767	601-545-4500	818
Hatton Brown Publishers Inc PO Box 2268 ....Montgomery AL 36102	800-669-5613	334-834-1170	633-9
Hause Machines 809 S Pleasant St ....Montpelier OH 43543	800-932-8665	419-485-3158	453
Hausmann Industries Inc 130 Union St ....Northvale NJ 07647	888-428-7626	201-767-0255	319-1
Havenwood-Heritage Heights Havenwood Campus 33 Christian Ave ....Concord NH 03301	800-457-6833	603-224-5363	668
Havenwyck Hospital 1525 University Dr ....Auburn Hills MI 48326	800-401-2727	248-373-9200	373-5
Haverford Trust Co, The 3 Radnor Corp Ctr 100 Matsonford Rd Ste 450.................Radnor PA 19087	888-995-1979	610-995-8700	404
Haverhill Gazette 100 Turnpike St ....N Andover MA 01845	888-411-3245	978-946-2000	528-2
Haverty Furniture Cos Inc 780 Johnson Ferry Rd NE Ste 800 ....Atlanta GA 30342 NYSE: HVT	888-428-3789		321
Haviland Enterprises Inc 421 Ann St NW ....Grand Rapids MI 49504	800-456-1134		146
Havre Daily News 119 Second St ....Havre MT 59501	800-993-2459	406-265-6795	528-3
HAWAI'I GAS 515 Kamake'e St ....Honolulu HI 96814	866-499-3941	808-535-5933	782
Hawaii *Child Support Enforcement Agency* Kakuhihewa Bldg 601 Kamokila Blvd Ste 251.................Kapolei HI 96707	888-317-9081	808-692-8265	338-12
Consumer Protection Office 235 S Beretania St 9th fl. ....Honolulu HI 96813	800-394-1902	808-586-2630	338-12
Taxation Dept 830 Punchbowl St Rm 221..........Honolulu HI 96813	800-222-3229	808-587-4242	338-12

	Toll-Free	Phone	Class
Vocational Rehabilitation Div 1901 Bachelot St .... Honolulu HI 96817	800-316-8005	808-586-9744	338-12
Hawaii Assn of Realtors 1259 A'ala St Ste 300 .... Honolulu HI 96817	866-693-6767	808-733-7060	652
Hawaii Bar Journal 1100 Alakea St Ste 1000 .... Honolulu HI 96813	888-586-1056	808-537-1868	455-15
Hawaii Coffee Co 1555 Kalani St .... Honolulu HI 96817	800-338-8353	808-847-3600	159
Hawaii Community Foundation 65-1279 Kawaihae Rd .... Kamuela HI 96743	888-731-3863	808-537-6333	303
Hawaii Convention Ctr 1801 Kalakaua Ave .... Honolulu HI 96815	800-295-6603	808-943-3500	205
Hawaii Democratic Party 627 S St Ste 105. .... Honolulu HI 96813	844-596-2980	808-596-2980	612-1
Hawaii Dental Assn 1345 S Beretania St Ste 301 .... Honolulu HI 96814	800-359-6725	808-593-7956	227
Hawaii Dental Service 700 Bishop St Ste 700 .... Honolulu HI 96813	800-232-2533	808-521-1431	390-3
Hawaii Dept of Education Honolulu District Office 4967 Kilauea Ave .... Honolulu HI 96816	800-437-8641	808-733-4950	681
Hawaii Information Consortium (HIC) 201 Merchant St Ste 1805 .... Honolulu HI 96813	800-295-0089	808-695-4620	561
Hawaii Island Chamber of Commerce 117 Keawe St .... Hilo HI 96720	877-482-4411	808-935-7178	139
Hawaii Medical Assn 1360 S Beretania St .... Honolulu HI 96816	888-536-2792	808-536-7702	472
Hawaii Medical Service Assn 818 Keeaumoku St .... Honolulu HI 96814	800-776-4672	808-948-6111	390-3
Hawaii National Bank 45 N King St .... Honolulu HI 96817	800-528-2273	808-528-7711	69
Hawaii Nurses Assn (HNA) 949 Kapiolani Blvd Ste 107 .... Honolulu HI 96814	800-617-2677	808-531-1628	529
Hawaii Opera Theatre 848 S Beretania St Ste 301 .... Honolulu HI 96813	800-836-7372	808-596-7372	569-2
Hawaii Pacific University 1164 Bishop St Ste 200 .... Honolulu HI 96813	866-225-5478	808-544-0200	166
Hawaii Planing Mill Ltd (HPM) 16-166 Melekahiwa St .... Keaau HI 96749	877-841-7633	808-966-5693	191-3
Hawaii Preparatory Academy 65-1692 Kohala Mountain Rd .... Kamuela HI 96743	800-644-4481	808-885-7321	618
Hawaii Public Television 2350 Dole St .... Honolulu HI 96822	800-238-4847	808-973-1000	628
Hawaii State Bar Assn (HSBA) 1100 Alakea St Ste 1000. .... Honolulu HI 96813	800-932-0311	808-537-1868	72
Hawaii Visitors & Convention Bureau 2270 Kalakaua Ave Ste 801 .... Honolulu HI 96815	800-464-2924		206
Hawaii's Best Bed & Breakfasts 571 Pauku St .... Kailua HI 96734	800-262-9912	808-263-3100	375
Hawaiian Airlines HawaiianMiles PO Box 30008 .... Honolulu HI 96820	877-426-4537		26
Hawaiian Airlines Inc 3375 Koapaka St Ste G350 .... Honolulu HI 96819	800-367-5320	808-835-3700	25
Hawaiian Electric Industries Inc 1001 Bishop St Ste 2900 .... Honolulu HI 96813	877-871-8461	808-543-5662	782
Hawaiian Inn 2301 S Atlantic Ave .... Daytona Beach Shores FL 32118	800-922-3023	386-255-5411	378
Hawaiian Isles Kona Coffee Co 2839 Mokumoa St .... Honolulu HI 96819 *Orders	800-657-7716*		296-7
Hawk Eye, The 800 S Main St PO Box 10 .... Burlington IA 52601	800-397-1708	319-754-8461	528-2
Hawk Inn & Mountain Resort 75 Billings Rd .... Plymouth VT 05056	800-685-4295	802-672-3811	665
Hawk Ridge Systems 4 Orinda Way Bldg B Ste 100 .... Orinda CA 94563	877-266-4469		177
Hawk's Cay Resort & Marina 61 Hawk's Cay Blvd .... Duck Key FL 33050	888-395-5539	866-347-2675	665
Hawker Powersource Inc 9404 Ooltewah Industrial Dr PO Box 808. .... Ooltewah TN 37363	800-238-8658	423-238-5700	74
Hawkeye Community College 1501 E Orange Rd .... Waterloo IA 50704	800-670-4769	319-296-2320	162
Hawkeye Stages Inc 703 Dudley St .... Decorah IA 52101	877-464-2954		107
Hawkins Inc 3100 E Hennepin Ave .... Minneapolis MN 55413 *NASDAQ: HWKN*	800-328-5460	612-331-6910	143
Hawley Mountain Guest Ranch 4188 Main Boulder Rd .... McLeod MT 59052	877-496-7848	406-932-5791	239
Hawn State Park 12096 Pk Dr .... Sainte Genevieve MO 63670	877-422-6766	573-883-3603	
Haworth Inc 1 Haworth Ctr .... Holland MI 49423	800-344-2600	616-393-3000	319-1
Haws Corp 1455 Kleppe Ln .... Sparks NV 89431	888-640-4297	775-359-4712	660
Hawthorne Inn & Conference Ctr 420 High St .... Winston-Salem NC 27101	877-777-3099	336-777-3000	378
Hawthorne Machinery Co 16945 Camino San Bernardo .... San Diego CA 92127	800-437-4228	858-674-7000	264-3
Hay Group Inc 1650 Arch St .... Philadelphia PA 19103	800-716-4429	215-861-2000	194
Hay House Inc PO Box 5100 .... Carlsbad CA 92018	800-654-5126	760-431-7695	633-3
Hay-Adams Hotel 800 16th St NE .... Washington DC 20006	800-853-6807	202-638-6600	378
Hayden Automotive 1801 Waters Ridge Dr .... Lewisville TX 75057	888-505-4567		60
Hayes & Stolz Industrial Manufacturing Co 3521 Hemphill St PO Box 11217. .... Fort Worth TX 76110	800-725-7272	817-926-3391	298
Hayes Handpiece Franchises Inc 5375 Avenida Encinas Ste C .... Carlsbad CA 92008	800-228-0521		310
Hayes School Publishing Co Inc 321 Pennwood Ave .... Pittsburgh PA 15221	800-926-0704	412-371-2373	243
Hayes Specialties Corp 1761 E Genesee .... Saginaw MI 48601	800-248-3603	989-755-6541	328
Haynes International Inc 1020 W Park Ave PO Box 9013 .... Kokomo IN 46904 *NASDAQ: HAYN*	800-354-0806	765-456-6000	483
Hays Convention & Visitors Bureau 2700 Vine St PO Box 490 .... Hays KS 67601	800-569-4505	785-628-8202	206
Hays Fluid Controls 114 Eason Rd .... Dallas NC 28034	800-354-4297	704-922-9565	785
Hays Medical Ctr (HMC) 2220 Canterbury Dr .... Hays KS 67601	800-248-0073	785-650-2759	373-3
Haystak Digital Marketing LLC 1514 Broadway Ste 201 .... Fort Myers FL 33901	866-292-0194		5
Hayward Baker Inc 7550 Teague Rd Ste 300 .... Hanover MD 21076	800-456-6548	410-551-8200	189-5
Haywood County 1 N Washington St .... Brownsville TN 38012	800-273-8712	731-772-1432	337
Haywood Electric Membership Corp 376 Grindstone Rd .... Waynesville NC 28785	800-951-6088	828-452-2281	245
Haywood Mall 700 Haywood Rd .... Greenville SC 29607	800-331-5479	864-288-0511	458
Haywood Securities Inc Waterfront Centre 200 Burrard St Ste 700 .... Vancouver BC V6C3L6	800-663-9499	604-697-7100	400
Hazard Community & Technical College 1 Community College Dr .... Hazard KY 41701	800-246-7521	606-436-5721	162
Hazard Campus 101 Vo Tech Dr .... Hazard KY 41701	800-246-7521	606-436-5721	162
Lees College Campus Library 601 Jefferson Ave .... Jackson KY 41339	800-246-7521	606-666-7521	162
Hazelden Foundation 15251 Pleasant Valley Rd .... Center City MN 55012	800-257-7810	651-213-4200	722
Hazelden New York 322 Eigth Ave 12th Fl .... New York NY 10001	800-257-7800	212-420-9520	722
Hazelden Springbrook 1901 Esther St .... Newberg OR 97132	866-866-4662	503-554-4300	722
Hazen & Sawyer PC 498 Seventh Ave 11th Fl .... New York NY 10018	888-514-2936	212-539-7000	261
Hazen Transport Inc 27050 Wick Rd .... Taylor MI 48180	800-251-2120	313-292-2120	775
Hazle Park Packing Co 260 Washington Ave Hazle Pk .... Hazletownship PA 18202	800-238-4331	570-455-7571	296-26
Hazleton Standard Speaker 21 N Wyoming St .... Hazleton PA 18201 *Cust Svc	800-843-6680*	570-455-3636	528-2
HB Fuller Co 1200 Willow Lake Blvd PO Box 64683. .... St. Paul MN 55164 *NYSE: FUL*	888-423-8553	651-236-5900	3
HB Management Group Inc 7100 Broadway Ste 6L .... Denver CO 80221	866-440-1100		104
HB Mellot Estate Inc 100 Mellott Dr .... Warfordsburg PA 17267	800-634-5634	301-678-2050	501-5
HB Rentals LC 5813 Hwy 90 E .... Broussard LA 70518	800-262-6790	337-839-1641	264-3
HBD Inc 3901 Riverdale Rd .... Greensboro NC 27406	800-403-2247	336-275-4800	67
HBD/Thermoid Inc 1301 W Sandusky Ave .... Bellefontaine OH 43311	800-543-8070	937-593-5010	369
HB&G Inc PO Box 589 .... Troy AL 36081	800-264-4424	334-566-5000	497
HBI (Hickory Brands Inc) 429 27th St NW .... Hickory NC 28601	800-438-5777	828-322-2600	740-5
HBP (Huttig Bldg Products Inc) 555 Maryville University Dr Ste 400 .... Saint Louis MO 63141 *NASDAQ: HBP*	800-325-4466	314-216-2600	497
HBP Inc 952 Frederick St .... Hagerstown MD 21740	800-638-3508	301-733-2000	623
HBPL (Huntington Beach Public Library) 7111 Talbert Ave .... Huntington Beach CA 92648	800-565-0148	714-842-4481	433-3
HBSC Strategic Services 100 North Hill Dr Bldg 26. .... Brisbane CA 94005	800-970-7995	415-715-8767	
HC&A (Hettrick Cyr & Associates) 59 Sycamore St .... Glastonbury CT 06033	888-805-0300	860-652-9997	399
HCA Midwest Health System 903 E 104th St Ste 500 .... Kansas City MO 64131	800-386-9355	816-508-4000	352
HCAA (National CPA Health Care Advisors Assn) 1801 W End Ave Ste 800 .... Nashville TN 37203	800-231-2524	615-373-9880	49-1
HCC (Highland Community College) 606 W Main .... Highland KS 66035	800-985-9781	785-442-6000	162
HCC Inc 1501 First Ave .... Mendota IL 61342	800-548-6633	815-539-9371	273
HCCGA (Haines City Citrus Growers Assn) 8 Railroad Ave PO Box 337. .... Haines City FL 33844 *Sales	800-327-6676*	863-422-1174	11-1
HCI (Health Communications Inc) 3201 SW 15th St .... Deerfield Beach FL 33442 *Cust Svc	800-441-5569*	954-360-0909	633-2
HCI Group, The 6440 Southpoint Pkwy Ste 300 .... Jacksonville FL 32216	866-793-2484	904-337-6300	196
Hcpro Inc 75 Sylvan St Ste A-10. .... Danvers MA 01923	800-650-6787		195
HCS (Health Care Software) 1599 Rt 34 S Ste 2 .... Wall Township NJ 07727	800-524-1038		177
H-D Electric Co-op Inc 423 Third Ave S .... Clear Lake SD 57226	800-781-7474	605-874-2171	245
HD Hudson Manufacturing Co 500 N Michigan Ave .... Chicago IL 60611	800-977-7293	312-644-2830	273
HD Vest Financial Services 6333 N State Hwy 161 4th Fl .... Irving TX 75038	866-218-8206	972-870-6000	400
HDR Engineering Inc 8404 Indian Hills Dr .... Omaha NE 68114	800-366-4411	402-399-1000	261
HDSA (Huntington's Disease Society of America) 505 Eigth Ave Ste 902 .... New York NY 10018	800-345-4372	212-242-1968	48-17
HDT Global 30500 Aurora Rd Ste 100 .... Solon OH 44139	800-969-8527	216-438-6111	15
HDW (Hardware Distribution Warehouses Inc) 6900 Woolworth Rd .... Shreveport LA 71129 *Cust Svc	800-256-8527*	318-686-8527	350

	Toll-Free	Phone	Class
HE Neumann Inc 100 Middle Creek Rd ....Triadelphia WV 26059	800-627-5312	304-232-3040	189-10
he Press & Sun-Bulletin 33 Lewis Rd Ste 9.........Binghamton NY 13905	800-253-5343	607-798-1234	
HE Williams Inc 831 West Fairview Ave ....Carthage MO 64836	866-358-4065	417-358-4065	438
HEA (Harmon Electric Assn Inc) 114 N First St PO Box 393 ....Hollis OK 73550	800-643-7769	580-688-3342	245
HEAD USA Inc 3125 Sterling Cir Ste 101 ....Boulder CO 80301	800-874-3235		706
Headquarter Toyota 5895 NW 167th St ....Miami FL 33015	800-549-0947	305-600-4663	57
Headrick Companies Inc, The 1 Freedom Sq ....Laurel MS 39440	800-933-1365	601-649-1977	5
Headsets Direct Inc 1454 W Gurley St Ste A ....Prescott AZ 86305	800-914-7996	928-777-9100	246
Headstart Hair For Men Inc 3395 Cypress Gardens Rd ....Winter Haven FL 33884	800-645-6525	863-324-5559	347
Health & Safety Institute Inc 1450 Westec Dr ....Eugene OR 97402	800-447-3177		759
Health Alliance Plan 2850 W Grand Blvd ....Detroit MI 48202	800-422-4641	313-872-8100	390-3
Health Care Daily Report 1801 S Bell St ....Arlington VA 22202	800-372-1033		527-8
Health Care Software (HCS) 1599 Rt 34 S Ste 2 ....Wall Township NJ 07727	800-524-1038		177
Health Coalition Inc 8320 NW 30th Terr ....Doral FL 33122	800-456-7283	305-662-2988	238
Health Communications Inc (HCI) 3201 SW 15th St ....Deerfield Beach FL 33442 *Cust Svc	800-441-5569*	954-360-0909	633-2
Health Decisions Inc 2510 Meridian Pkwy ....Durham NC 27713	888-779-3771	919-967-2399	461
Health Forum 155 N Wacker Dr Ste 400 ....Chicago IL 60606	800-821-2039	312-893-6800	633-11
Health Industry Business Communications Council (HIBCC) 2525 E Arizona Biltmore Cir Ste 127 ....Phoenix AZ 85016	800-755-5505	602-381-1091	49-8
Health Industry Distributors Association (HIDA) 310 Montgomery St ....Alexandria VA 22314	800-549-4432	703-549-4432	49-18
Health Integrated 10008 N Dale Mabry Hwy ....Tampa FL 33618	877-267-7577		
Health Law Reporter 1801 S Bell St ....Arlington VA 22202	800-372-1033		527-7
Health Management Systems Inc 401 Park Ave S ....New York NY 10016	877-357-3268	212-857-5000	225
Health Net Of Arizona Inc 1230 W Washington St ....Tempe AZ 85281	800-291-6911	602-794-1400	352
Health Network Laboratory 2024 Lehigh St ....Allentown PA 18103	877-402-4221	610-402-8170	417
Health Partners 8170 33rd Ave S ....Minneapolis MN 55425	800-247-7015	952-883-6877	370
Health Physics Society 1313 Dolley Madison Blvd Ste 402 ....Mclean VA 22101	888-624-8373	703-790-1745	48-17
Health Resources & Services Administration (HRSA) 5600 Fishers Ln ....Rockville MD 20857	888-275-4772	301-443-2216	339-9
Health Smart Rx 1301 E Ninth St ....Cleveland OH 44114	800-681-6912		582
Health Tradition Health Plan 1808 E Main St ....Onalaska WI 54650	800-545-8499	608-781-9692	390-3
Health Unit Brant County 194 Ter Hill St ....Brantford ON N3R1G7	800-565-8603	519-753-4937	138
HealthAlliance Leominster Hospital 60 Hospital Rd ....Leominster MA 01453	800-462-5540	978-466-2000	373-3
HealthAxis Inc 7301 N State Hwy 161 ....Irving TX 75039	888-974-2947	972-443-5000	461
Healthcare Financial Management Assn (HFMA) 2 Westbrook Corporate Ctr Ste 700 ....Westchester IL 60154	800-252-4362		49-8
HealthCareSource Inc 100 Sylvan Rd Ste 100 ....Woburn MA 01801	800-869-5200		260
Healthco Information Systems 7657 SW Mohawk St ....Tualatin OR 97062	888-740-7734		
Healthcom 1600 W Jackson St ....Sullivan IL 61951	800-525-6921		473
HealthDrive Corp 888 Worcester St ....Wellesley MA 02482	888-964-6681		351
HealthForce Ontario Marketing & Recruitment Agency 163 Queen St E ....Toronto ON M5A1S1	800-596-4046	416-862-2200	260
Healthforce Partners Inc 18323 Bothell Everett Hwy ....Bothell WA 98012	877-437-2497	425-806-5700	194
Healthlinx Transitional Leadership Inc 1404 Goodale Blvd Ste 400 ....Columbus OH 43212	800-980-4820		461
HealthMarkets Inc 9151 Blvd 26 ....North Richland Hills TX 76180	800-827-9990		359-4
HealthPartners Inc PO Box 1309 ....Minneapolis MN 55440	800-883-2177	952-883-5000	390-3
Healthplex Inc 333 Earl Ovington Blvd ....Uniondale NY 11553 *Cust Svc	800-468-0608*	516-542-2200	390-3
Healthpoint 3909 Hulen St ....Fort Worth TX 76107 *Cust Svc	800-441-8227*	817-900-4000	579
HealthSmart International 1931 Norman Dr ....Waukegan IL 60085	800-526-4753		473
HealthSource Saginaw 3340 Hospital Rd ....Saginaw MI 48603	800-662-6848	989-790-7700	722
HealthSouth MountainView Regional Rehabilitation Hospital 1160 Van Voorhis Rd ....Morgantown WV 26505	800-388-2451	304-598-1100	373-6
HealthSouth Nittany Valley Rehabilitation Hospital 550 W College Ave ....Pleasant Gap PA 16823	800-842-6026	814-359-3421	373-6
HealthSouth Rehabilitation Hospital of Altoona 2005 Vly View Blvd ....Altoona PA 16602	800-873-4220	814-944-3535	373-6
HealthSouth Rehabilitation Hospital of Fayetteville 153 E Monte Painter ....Fayetteville AR 72703	800-749-2257	479-444-2200	373-6
HealthSouth Rehabilitation Hospital of Kingsport 113 Cassel Dr ....Kingsport TN 37660	800-454-7422	423-246-7240	373-6
Healthspace USA Inc 4860 Cox Rd Ste 200 ....Glen Allen VA 23060	866-860-4224	804-935-8532	201
HealthStream Inc 209 Tenth Ave S Ste 450.........Nashville TN 37203 NASDAQ: HSTM	800-933-9293	615-301-3100	760
Healthtrax Fitness & Wellness 100 Simsbury Rd ....Avon CT 06001	800-505-5000	860-284-1190	353
HealthTronics Inc 9825 Spectrum Dr Bldg 3.........Austin TX 78717	888-252-6575	512-328-2892	250
Healthways Inc 701 Cool Springs Blvd ....Franklin TN 37067 NASDAQ: HWAY	800-327-3822		351
Healthy Back Store LLC 10300 Southard Dr ....Beltsville MD 20705	800-469-2225		321
Healthy Directions LLC 7811 Montrose Rd ....Potomac MD 20854	866-599-9491		633-9
Healthy n Fit International Inc 435 Yorktown Rd ....Croton On Hudson NY 10520	800-338-5200	914-271-6040	
Healthy Pet 6960 Salashan Pkwy ....Ferndale WA 98248	800-242-2287	360-734-7415	574
Healy Group Inc, The 17535 Generations Dr ....South Bend IN 46635	800-667-4613	574-271-6000	389
Heard & Smith LLP 3737 Broadway Ste 310 ....San Antonio TX 78209	800-584-3700	210-820-3737	427
Hearing Loss Assn of America 7910 Woodmont Ave Ste 1200 ....Bethesda MD 20814	800-221-6827	301-657-2248	48-17
Hearn Paper Co 556 N Meridian Rd ....Youngstown OH 44509	800-225-2989		549
Hearst Foundation, The 300 W 57th St 26th Fl. ....New York NY 10019	800-841-7048	212-649-3750	305
Hearst San Simeon State Historical Monument 750 Hearst Castle Rd ....San Simeon CA 93452	800-444-4445	805-927-2020	561
Heart & Soul Magazine 15480 Annapolis Rd Ste 202-225.........Bowie MD 20715	800-834-8813		455-13
Heart of Texas Electric Co-op 1111 Johnson Dr PO Box 357 ....McGregor TX 76657	800-840-2957	254-840-2871	245
Heart of the House Hospitality 2346 S Lynhurst Dr Ste A-201 ....Indianapolis IN 46241	888-365-1440		260
Hearth & Home Technologies Inc 7571 215th St W ....Lakeville MN 55044	888-427-3973	952-985-6000	356
Heartland Blood Centers 1200 N Highland Ave ....Aurora IL 60506	800-786-4483	630-892-7055	89
Heartland Co-op 2829 Westown Pkwy Ste 350 ....West Des Moines IA 50266	800-513-3938	515-225-1334	275
Heartland Equipment Inc 2100 N Falls Blvd ....Wynne AR 72396	800-530-7617		273
Heartland Express Inc 901 N Kansas Ave ....North Liberty IA 52317 NASDAQ: HTLD	800-654-1175		775
Heartland Funds 789 N Water St Ste 500 ....Milwaukee WI 53202	800-432-7856	414-347-7777	524
Heartland Hands-Hope Hospice 137 N Belt Hwy ....Saint Joseph MO 64506	800-443-1143	816-271-7190	370
Heartland Hospice Services 333 N Summit St ....Toledo OH 43604	800-366-1232	419-252-5500	370
Heartland Inns 87-2nd St ....Coralville IA 52241 *Resv	800-334-3277*	319-351-8132	378
Heartland Label Printers Inc 1700 Stephen St ....Little Chute WI 54140 *General	800-236-7914*		246
Heartland Library Co-op 319 W Center Ave ....Sebring FL 33870	800-843-5678		
Heartland Lions Eye Bank 10100 N Ambassador Dr Ste 200 ....Kansas City MO 64153	800-753-2265	816-454-5454	269
Heartland Meat Company Inc 3461 Main St ....Chula Vista CA 91911	888-407-3668	619-407-3668	297-9
Heartland Paper Co 808 W Cherokee St ....Sioux Falls SD 57104 *Cust Svc	800-843-7922*	605-336-1190	555
Heartland Park Topeka 7530 SW Topeka Blvd ....Topeka KS 66619	844-200-6472	785-862-4781	512
Heartland Petroleum LLC 4001 E Fifth Ave ....Columbus OH 43219	800-889-7831	614-441-4001	575
Heartland Power Co-op 216 Jackson St PO Box 65 ....Thompson IA 50478	888-584-9732	641-584-2251	245
Heartland Rural Electric Co-op 110 N Enterprise St ....Girard KS 66743	888-835-9585	800-835-9586	245
Heartline Fitness Products Inc 8041 Cessna Ave Ste 200 ....Gaithersburg MD 20879	800-262-3348	301-921-0661	267
Heat & Control Inc 21121 Cabot Blvd ....Hayward CA 94545	800-227-5980	510-259-0500	298
Heat Seal LLC 4580 E 71st St Ste 100.........Cleveland OH 44125	800-342-6329	216-341-2022	543
Heat Transfer Products Group LLC 201 Thomas French Dr ....Scottsboro AL 35769	800-288-9488	256-259-7400	606
Heat Transfer Sales of the Carolinas Inc 4101 Beechwood Dr ....Greensboro NC 27410	800-842-3328	336-294-3838	608
Heatcraft Refrigeration Products 2175 W Pk Pl Blvd ....Stone Mountain GA 30087	800-321-1881	770-465-5600	660
Heath Consultants Inc 9030 Monroe Rd ....Houston TX 77061	800-432-8487	713-844-1300	192
Heatrex Inc PO Box 515 ....Meadville PA 16335	800-394-6589	814-724-1800	318
Heaven's Best Carpet & Upholstery Cleaning PO Box 607 ....Rexburg ID 83440	800-359-2095	208-359-1106	152
Heavy Machines Inc 3926 E Rains Rd ....Memphis TN 38118	888-366-9028	901-260-2200	357
Hebeler Corp 2000 Military Rd ....Tonawanda NY 14150	800-486-4709	716-873-9300	616
Hebrew Union College Los Angeles 3077 University Ave ....Los Angeles CA 90007	800-899-0925	213-749-3424	166
Hebron Academy 339 Rd PO Box 309 ....Hebron ME 04238	888-432-7664	207-966-2100	618
Heceta Head Lighthouse State Scenic Viewpoint 93111 Hwy 101 N ....Florence OR 97439	800-551-6949		561

Alphabetical Section

	Toll-Free	Phone	Class
Hector International Airport			
2801 32nd Ave NW ....Fargo ND 58102	800-451-5333	701-241-8168	27
Hed Cycling Products			
1735 TERRACE Dr ....Roseville MN 55113	888-246-3639		514
Hedwin Corp			
1600 Roland Heights Ave ....Baltimore MD 21211	800-638-1012	410-467-8209	199
Heely-Brown Company Inc			
1280 Chattahoochee Ave ....Atlanta GA 30318	800-241-4628	404-352-0022	46
Heerema Co			
200 Sixth Ave ....Hawthorne NJ 07506	800-346-4729	973-423-0505	707
Heffel Gallery Ltd			
2247 Granville St ....Vancouver BC V6H3G1	800-528-9608	604-732-6505	42
Heidel House Resort			
643 Illinois Ave ....Green Lake WI 54941	800-444-2812	920-294-3344	665
Heidelberg University			
310 E Market St ....Tiffin OH 44883	800-434-3352	419-448-2000	166
Heidelberg USA Inc			
1000 Gutenberg Dr ....Kennesaw GA 30144	888-472-9655*	770-419-6500	625
*Cust Svc			
Heidler Roofing Services Inc			
2120 Alpha Dr ....York PA 17408	866-792-3549	717-792-3549	189-12
Heifer International			
1 World Ave ....Little Rock AR 72202	800-422-0474	501-907-2600	48-5
Heil Environmental Ltd			
2030 Hamilton Pl Blvd			
Ste 200 ....Chattanooga TN 37421	866-367-4345	423-899-9100	513
Heilind Electronics Inc			
58 Jonspin Rd ....Wilmington MA 01887	800-400-7041	978-657-4870	246
Heim LP			
6360 W 73rd St ....Chicago IL 60638	800-927-9393	708-496-7450	454
Heinemann			
361 Hanover St ....Portsmouth NH 03801	800-541-2086	603-431-7894	633-2
Heinen's Inc			
4540 Richmond Rd ....Cleveland OH 44128	855-475-2300		344
Heiners Bakery Inc			
1300 Adams Ave ....Huntington WV 25704	800-776-8411	304-523-8411	296-1
Heinrich Envelope Corp			
925 Zane Ave N ....Minneapolis MN 55422	800-346-7957	763-544-3571	263
Heintz & Weber Co Inc			
150 Reading Ave ....Buffalo NY 14220	800-438-6878	716-852-7171	296-41
Heinz Hall for the Performing Arts			
600 Penn Ave ....Pittsburgh PA 15222	800-743-8560	412-392-4900	568
Heisler Industries Inc			
224 Passaic Ave ....Fairfield NJ 07004	800-496-7621	973-227-6300	543
Hei-Tek Automation			
2102 West Quail Ave Ste 4 ....Phoenix AZ 85027	800-926-2099		
Helac Corp			
225 Battersby Ave ....Enumclaw WA 98022	800-327-2589	360-825-1601	223
Helen DeVos Children's Hospital			
100 Michigan NE ....Grand Rapids MI 49503	866-989-7999	616-391-9000	764
Helen of Troy Ltd			
1 Helen of Troy Plz ....El Paso TX 79912	800-487-7273		38
NASDAQ: HELE			
Helena Area Chamber of Commerce			
225 Cruse Ave ....Helena MT 59601	800-743-5362	406-442-4120	139
Helena Laboratories Inc			
1530 Lindbergh Dr ....Beaumont TX 77704	800-231-5663	409-842-3714	231
Helene Fuld College of Nursing			
24 E 120th St ....New York NY 10035	800-262-3257	212-616-7200	795
Helical Products Co Inc			
901 W McCoy Ln ....Santa Maria CA 93455	877-353-9873	805-928-3851	616
Helicopter Assn International (HAI)			
1920 Ballenger Ave 4th Fl............Alexandria VA 22314	800-435-4976	703-683-4646	49-21
Heli-Mart Inc			
3184 Airway Ave Unit E ....Costa Mesa CA 92626	800-826-6899	714-755-2999	765
Heliodyne Corp			
4910 Seaport Ave ....Richmond CA 94804	888-878-8750	510-237-9614	321
Helix Design Inc			
175 Lincoln St Ste 201 ....Manchester NH 03103	800-511-5593		
Helix Energy Solutions Inc			
400 N Sam Houston Pkwy E			
Ste 400 ....Houston TX 77060	888-345-2347	281-618-0400	535
NYSE: HLX			
Helixstorm Inc			
27238 Via Industria ....Temecula CA 92590	888-434-3549		386
Hello Direct Inc			
77 NE Blvd ....Nashua NH 03062	800-435-5634		457
HelloWorld			
3000 Town Ctr Ste 2100.........South Field MI 48075	877-837-7493		7
Helly Hansen US Inc			
3703 I St NW ....Auburn WA 98001	800-435-5901		
Helm Inc			
47911 Halyard Dr Ste 200 ....Plymouth MI 48170	800-782-4356		88
Helmel Engineering Products Inc			
6520 Lockport Rd ....Niagara Falls NY 14305	800-237-8266	716-297-8644	174
Helmerich & Payne Inc			
1437 S Boulder Ave ....Tulsa OK 74119	800-205-4913	918-742-5531	536
NYSE: HP			
Helmut Guenschel Inc			
10 Emala Ave ....Baltimore MD 21220	800-852-2525	410-686-5900	115
Help At Home Inc			
1 N State St Ste 800 ....Chicago IL 60602	800-404-3191	312-762-0900	362
Helpjuice Inc			
211 E Seventh St ....Austin TX 78701	888-230-3420		386
Helwig Carbon Products Inc			
8900 W Tower Ave ....Milwaukee WI 53224	800-365-3113	414-354-2411	127
Helzberg Diamonds			
1825 Swift Ave ....North Kansas City MO 64116	800-435-9237	816-842-7780	409
Hemacare Corp			
15350 Sherman Way Ste 350 ....Van Nuys CA 91406	877-310-0717	877-397-3087	89
Hemagen Diagnostics Inc			
9033 Red Branch Rd ....Columbia MD 21045	800-436-2436	443-367-5500	231
OTC: HMGN			
HemaSource Inc			
4158 Nike Dr ....West Jordan UT 84088	888-844-4362		
Hemenway's Seafood Grille			
121 S Main St ....Providence RI 02903	888-759-5557	401-351-8570	667
Hemmings Motor News			
222 Main St ....Bennington VT 05201	800-227-4373	802-442-3101	455-3

	Toll-Free	Phone	Class
Henderson Auctions			
13340 Florida Blvd			
PO Box 336. ....Livingston LA 70754	800-334-7443	225-686-2252	51
Henderson Community College			
2660 S Green St ....Henderson KY 42420	800-696-9958	270-827-1867	162
Henderson County Tourist Commission			
101 N Water St Ste B ....Henderson KY 42420	800-648-3128	270-826-3128	206
Henderson Glass Inc			
715 S Blvd E ....Rochester Hills MI 48307	800-694-0672		331
Henderson Hills Baptist Church			
1200 E I 35 Frontage Rd ....Edmond OK 73034	877-901-4639	405-341-4639	48-20
Henderson Manufacturing Inc			
1085 S Third St ....Manchester IA 52057	800-359-4970	563-927-2828	273
Henderson Sewing Machine Company Inc			
Waits Dr Industrial Pk ....Andalusia AL 36420	800-824-5113	334-222-2451	357
Henderson State University			
1100 Henderson St ....Arkadelphia AR 71999	800-228-7333	870-230-5000	166
Henderson Wheel & Warehouse Supply			
1825 South 300 West ....Salt Lake City UT 84115	800-748-5111	801-486-2073	61
Henderson-Johnson Co Inc			
918 Canal St ....Syracuse NY 13210	800-492-3434	315-479-5561	189-9
Hendrick Hospice Care			
1682 Hickory St ....Abilene TX 79601	800-622-8516	325-677-8516	370
Hendrick Manufacturing Co			
1 Seventh Ave ....Carbondale PA 18407	800-225-7373*		486
*Cust Svc			
Hendrick Motorsports Museum			
4400 Papa Joe Hendrick Blvd ....Charlotte NC 28262	877-467-4890		519
Hendricks County Flyer			
8109 Kingston St Ste 500...............Avon IN 46123	800-359-3747	317-272-5800	528-4
Hendricks Power Co-op			
86 N County Rd 500 E ....Avon IN 46123	800-876-5473	317-745-5473	245
Hendrickson International			
800 S Frontage Rd ....Woodridge IL 60517	855-743-3733	630-910-2800	60
Hendrix College			
1600 Washington Ave ....Conway AR 72032	800-277-9017	501-329-6811	166
Hengehold Capital Management LLC			
6116 Harrison Ave ....Cincinnati OH 45247	877-598-5120	513-598-5120	400
Henig Inc			
4135 Carmichael Rd ....Montgomery AL 36106	800-521-2037	334-277-7610	157-6
Henkel Corp			
1 Henkel Way ....Rocky Hill CT 06067	800-243-4874*	860-571-5100	3
*Cust Svc			
Henley Park Hotel			
926 Massachusetts Ave NW ....Washington DC 20001	800-222-8474	202-638-5200	378
Henley Park Hotel, The			
926 Massachusetts Ave NW ....Washington DC 20001	800-222-8474	202-638-5200	
Henlopen Hotel			
511 N Boardwalk ....Rehoboth Beach DE 19971	800-441-8450	302-227-2551	378
Hennepin Technical College			
9000 Brooklyn Blvd ......Brooklyn Park MN 55445	800-345-4655	952-995-1300	795
Hennessy Industries Inc			
1601 JP Hennesey Dr ....La Vergne TN 37086	800-688-6359	855-876-3864	60
Henny Penny Corp			
1219 US 35 W PO Box 60 ....Eaton OH 45320	800-417-8417	937-456-8400	298
Henri Bendel Inc			
712 Fifth Ave ....New York NY 10019	866-875-7975	212-247-1100	157-6
Henry A Bromelkamp & Co			
106 E 24th St ....Minneapolis MN 55404	877-767-6703	612-870-9087	180
Henry Brick Co Inc			
3409 Water Ave ....Selma AL 36703	800-218-3906	334-875-2600	150
Henry Co			
909 N Sepulveda Blvd Ste 650 ......El Segundo CA 90245	800-598-7663	310-955-9200	46
Henry County			
140 Henry Pkwy ....McDonough GA 30253	800-955-7766	770-954-2400	337
Henry Equestrian Insurance Brokers Ltd			
53 Prospect St ....Newmarket ON L3Y3T1	800-565-4321	905-727-1144	390-1
Henry Ford Community College			
5101 Evergreen Rd ....Dearborn MI 48128	800-585-4322	313-845-9600	162
Henry Ford Health System			
1 Ford Pl ....Detroit MI 48202	800-436-7936		352
Department of Food and Nutrition Services			
2799 W Grand Blvd ....Detroit MI 48202	800-436-7936	313-916-1071	370
Henry Ford Hospital			
2799 W Grand Blvd ....Detroit MI 48202	800-999-4340	313-916-2600	373-3
Henry Ford Museum			
20900 Oakwood Blvd ....Dearborn MI 48124	800-835-5237	313-271-1620	517
Henry Glass & Co			
49 W 37th St ....New York NY 10018	800-294-9495		740-1
Henry Margu Inc			
540 Commerce St ....Yeadon PA 19050	800-345-8284	610-622-0515	347
Henry Pratt Co			
401 S Highland Ave ....Aurora IL 60506	877-436-7977	630-844-4000	785
Henry Products Inc			
302 S 23rd Ave ....Phoenix AZ 85009	800-525-5533	602-253-3191	191-1
Henry Quentzel Plumbing Supply Co			
379 Throop Ave ....Brooklyn NY 11221	800-889-2294	718-455-6600	608
Henry Schein Inc			
135 Duryea Rd ....Melville NY 11747	800-582-2702	631-843-5500	473
NASDAQ: HSIC			
Henry Technologies			
701 S Main St ....Chatham IL 62629	800-964-3679	217-483-2406	14
Henry Troemner LLC			
201 Wolf Dr ....Thorofare NJ 08086	800-352-7705	856-686-1600	474
Henrys Lake State Park			
3917 E 5100 N ....Island Park ID 83429	888-922-6743	208-558-7532	
Hensley Industries Inc			
2108 Joe Field Rd ....Dallas TX 75229	888-406-6262	972-241-2321	190
Hentzen Coatings Inc			
6937 W Mill Rd ....Milwaukee WI 53218	800-236-6589	414-353-4200	546
Hepaco Inc			
2711 Burch Dr PO Box 26308 ....Charlotte NC 28269	800-888-7689	704-598-9782	689
Hepatitis Foundation International (HFI)			
504 Blick Dr ....Silver Spring MD 20904	800-891-0707	301-622-4200	48-17
Her Interactive Inc			
1150 114th Ave SE Ste 200 ....Bellevue WA 98004	800-461-8787*	425-460-8787	178-6
*Orders			

				Toll-Free	Phone	Class

Herald Bulletin
1133 Jackson St .... Anderson IN 46016 — 800-750-5049 — 765-622-1212 — 528-2

Herald Democrat
603 S Sam Rayburn Fwy .... Sherman TX 75090 — 800-827-7183 — 903-893-8181 — 528-2

Herald Journal
75 W 300 N .... Logan UT 84321 — 800-275-0423 — 435-752-2121 — 528-2

Herald Publishing Co
PO Box 153 .... Houston TX 77001 — 888-421-1866 — 713-630-0391 — 633-8

Herald Times Reporter
902 Franklin St .... Manitowoc WI 54220 — 800-783-7323 — 920-684-4433 — 528-2

Herald, The
52 S Dock St .... Sharon PA 16146 — 800-981-1692 — 724-981-6100 — 528-2

Herald-Dispatch
946 Fifth Ave .... Huntington WV 25701 — 800-444-2446 — 304-526-4000 — 528-2

Herald-Mail Co, The
100 Summit Ave PO Box 439 .... Hagerstown MD 21741 — 800-626-6397 — 301-733-5123 — 633-8

Herald-Palladium
3450 Hollywood Rd .... Saint Joseph MI 49085 — 800-356-4262 — 269-429-2400 — 528-2

Herald-Standard
8 E Church St .... Uniontown PA 15401 — 800-342-8254 — 724-439-7500 — 528-2

Herald-Star
401 Herald Sq .... Steubenville OH 43952 — 800-526-7987 — 740-283-4711 — 633-8

Herald-Times Inc
PO Box 909 .... Bloomington IN 47402 — 800-422-0070 — 812-332-4401 — 633-8

Herb Chambers Chevrolet
90 Andover St Rt 114 .... Danvers MA 01923 — 877-907-1965 — 978-774-2000 — 57

Herb Gordon Nissan
3131 Automobile Blvd ...... Silver Spring MD 20904 — 877-345-9869 — — 57

Herb Growing & Marketing Network (HGMN)
PO Box 245 .... Silver Spring PA 17575 — 800-753-9199 — 717-393-3295 — 48-2

Herb Research Foundation (HRF)
4140 15th St .... Boulder CO 80304 — 800-748-2617 — 303-449-2265 — 48-17

Herbal Magic Inc
1867 Yonge St Ste 700 .... Toronto ON M4S1Y5 — 866-514-0786

Herbalist, The
2106 NE 65th St .... Seattle WA 98115 — 800-694-3727 — 206-523-2600 — 794

Herber Aircraft Service Inc
1401 E Franklin Ave .... El Segundo CA 90245 — 800-544-0050 — 310-322-9575 — 478

Herbert Gary Richard (R)
Utah State Capitol Complex 350 N State St Ste 200
PO Box 142220............. Salt Lake City UT 84114 — 800-705-2464 — 801-538-1000

Herbert H Landy Insurance Agency Inc
75 Second Ave Ste 410............ Needham MA 02494 — 800-336-5422 — — 389

Hercules Chemical Company Inc
111 S St....................... Passaic NJ 07055 — 800-221-9330 — — 3

Hercules Industries Inc
1310 W Evans Ave .... Denver CO 80223 — 800-356-5350 — 303-937-1000 — 608

Hercules Manufacturing Co
800 Bob Posey St .... Henderson KY 42420 — 800-633-3031 — 270-826-9501 — 513

Hercules Tire & Rubber Co
16380 E US Rt 224 - 200 .... Findlay OH 45840 — 800-677-9535 — 419-425-6400 — 749

Herc-U-Lift Inc
5655 Hwy 12 W .... Maple Plain MN 55359 — 800-362-3500 — 763-479-2501 — 384

Herculite Products Inc
105 E Sinking Springs Ln ...... Emigsville PA 17318 — 800-772-0036* — 717-764-1192 — 740-2
*Cust Svc

Heritage Bags
1648 Diplomat Dr .... Carrollton TX 75006 — 800-527-2247 — — 66

Heritage Bank
101 N Main St .... Jonesboro GA 30236 — 866-971-0106 — 770-478-8881 — 359-2

Heritage Bank
201 Fifth Ave SW .... Olympia WA 98501 — 800-455-6126 — 360-943-1500 — 359-2

Heritage Bible College
1747 Bud Hawkins Rd PO Box 1628........ Dunn NC 28334 — 800-297-6351 — 910-892-3178 — 166

Heritage Christian University
3625 Helton Dr PO Box HCU .... Florence AL 35630 — 800-367-3565 — 256-766-6610 — 161

Heritage Co, The
2402 Wildwood Ave .... Sherwood AR 72120 — 800-643-8822 — 501-835-5000 — 5

Heritage College & Seminary
175 Holiday Inn Dr .... Cambridge ON N3C3T2 — 800-465-1961 — 519-651-2869 — 780

Heritage Corridor Convention & Visitors Bureau
339 W Jefferson St .... Joliet IL 60435 — 800-926-2262 — 815-727-2323 — 206

Heritage Ctr
1201 W Buena Vista Rd .... Evansville IN 47710 — 800-704-0700 — 812-429-0700 — 448

Heritage Equipment Co
9000 Heritage Rd .... Plain City OH 43064 — 800-282-7961 — 614-873-3941 — 357

Heritage Foundation
214 Massachusetts Ave NE ...... Washington DC 20002 — 800-546-2843 — 202-546-4400 — 630

Heritage Global Solutions Inc
230 N Maryland Ave .... Glendale CA 91206 — 800-915-4474 — 818-547-4474 — 196

Heritage Group Inc
1101 12th St .... Aurora NE 68818 — 888-463-6611 — 402-694-3136 — 70

Heritage Hill State Historical Park
2640 S Webster Ave .... Green Bay WI 54301 — 800-721-5150 — 920-448-5150 — 561

Heritage Hospice Inc
120 Enterprise Dr PO Box 1213 ...... Danville KY 40423 — 800-203-6633 — 859-236-2425 — 370

Heritage Hotels & Resorts Inc
201 Third St NW Ste 1150 ...... Albuquerque NM 87102 — 877-901-7666 — 505 836-6700

Heritage Mechanical Services Inc
305 Suburban Ave .... Deer Park NY 11729 — 800-734-0384 — 516-558-2000 — 189-10

Heritage Mint Ltd
PO Box 13750 .... Scottsdale AZ 85267 — 888-860-6245 — 480-860-1300 — 726

Heritage Office Furnishings
1588 Rand Ave .... Vancouver BC V6P3G2 — 888-775-4555 — 604-688-2381 — 320

Heritage Petroleum LLC
516 N Seventh Ave .... Evansville IN 47710 — 800-422-3645 — 812-422-3251

Heritage Place Inc
2829 S MacArthur .... Oklahoma City OK 73128 — 888-343-9831 — 405-682-4551 — 51

Heritage Plastics Inc
1002 Hunt St .... Picayune MS 39466 — 800-245-4623 — 601-798-8663 — 601-2

Heritage Square Museum
3800 Homer St .... Los Angeles CA 90031 — 800-375-1771 — 323-225-2700 — 517

Heritage Summit HealthCare of Florida Inc
PO Box 2928 .... Lakeland FL 33806 — 800-282-7644 — 863-665-6629 — 390-3

Heritage University
3240 Ft Rd .... Toppenish WA 98948 — 888-272-6190 — 509-865-8500 — 166

Heritage Valley Health System
1000 Dutch Ridge Rd .... Beaver PA 15009 — 877-771-4847 — 724-728-7000 — 373-3

Heritage-Crystal Clean Inc
2175 Pt Blvd Ste 375 .... Elgin IL 60123 — **877-938-7948** — 847-836-5670 — 151

Herkimer County Chamber of Commerce
28 W Main St .... Mohawk NY 13407 — **877-984-4636** — 315-866-7820 — 139

Herkimer County Community College
100 Reservoir Rd .... Herkimer NY 13350 — **844-464-4375** — 315-866-0300 — 162

Herman Goldner Co Inc
7777 Brewster Ave .... Philadelphia PA 19153 — **800-355-5997** — 215-365-5400 — 189-10

Herman H Sticht Company Inc
45 Main St Ste 701 .... Brooklyn NY 11201 — **800-221-3203** — 718-852-7602 — 470

Herman Herman Katz & Cotlar LLP
820 Okeefe Ave .... New Orleans LA 70113 — **844-943-7626** — 504-581-4892 — 427

Herman Miller Inc
855 E Main Ave .... Zeeland MI 49464 — **888-443-4357** — 616-654-3000 — 319-1
NASDAQ: MLHR

Herman Seekamp Inc
1120 W Fullerton Ave .... Addison IL 60101 — **888-874-6814** — — 296-1

Hermann Oak Leather Co
4050 N First St .... Saint Louis MO 63147 — **800-325-7950** — 314-421-1173 — 431

Hermann Sons Life
515 S Saint Marys St
PO Box 1941 .... San Antonio TX 78205 — **800-234-4124** — 210-226-9261 — 703

Hermell Products Inc
9 Britton Dr .... Bloomfield CT 06002 — **800-233-2342** — 860-242-6550 — 475

Hermes Abrasives Ltd
524 Viking Dr .... Virginia Beach VA 23452 — **800-464-8314** — 757-486-6623 — 1

Hermes Music
401 S Broadway .... Pharr TX 78501 — **800-994-9150** — — 522

Hermitage Hotel
231 Sixth Ave N .... Nashville TN 37219 — **888-888-9414** — 615-244-3121 — 378

Hermosa County
5532 N Palo Cristi Rd .... Paradise Valley AZ 85253 — **800-241-1210** — 602-955-8614 — 378

Hernando County
16110 Aviation Loop Dr .... Brooksville FL 34604 — **800-601-4580** — 352-754-4000 — 337

Herndon Plant Oakley Ltd
800 N Shoreline Blvd
Ste 2200 South .... Corpus Christi TX 78401 — **800-888-4894** — 361-888-7611 — 400

Heroix Corp
165 Bay State Dr .... Braintree MA 02184 — **800-229-6500** — 781-848-1701 — 178-12

Heron Point of Chestertown
501 E Campus Ave .... Chestertown MD 21620 — **800-327-9138** — 443-214-3605 — 668

HEROweb Marketing & Design Inc
1976 Garden Ave .... Eugene OR 97403 — **888-257-2567** — 541-746-6418 — 5

Herr Foods Inc
20 Herr Dr PO Box 300 .... Nottingham PA 19362 — **800-344-3777** — 610-932-9330 — 296-35

Herr Tavern & Public House
900 Chambersburg Rd .... Gettysburg PA 17325 — **800-362-9849** — 717-334-4332 — 667

Herrschners Inc
2800 Hoover Rd .... Stevens Point WI 54481 — **800-713-1239** — 800-441-0838 — 258

HERS (Hysterectomy Educational Resources & Services Foun)
422 Bryn Mawr Ave .... Bala Cynwyd PA 19004 — **888-750-4377** — 610-667-7757 — 48-17

Hersam Acorn Newspapers
16 Bailey Ave .... Ridgefield CT 06877 — **800-372-2790** — 203-438-6544 — 633-8

Herschel-Adams Inc
1301 N 14th St .... Indianola IA 50125 — **800-247-2167** — — 273

Hershey Co
100 Crystal A Dr .... Hershey PA 17033 — **800-468-1714*** — — 296-8
NYSE: HSY ■ *Cust Svc

Hershey Creamery Co
301 S Cameron St .... Harrisburg PA 17101 — **888-240-1905** — 717-238-8134 — 296-25

Hershey Harrisburg Region Visitors Bureau
3211 N Front St Ste 301-A .... Harrisburg PA 17110 — **877-727-8573** — 717-231-7788 — 206

Hershey Lodge
325 University Dr .... Hershey PA 17033 — **844-330-1802** — 717-533-3311 — 378

Hersheypark
100 Hershey Pk Dr .... Hershey PA 17033 — **844-330-1813** — 717-534-3900 — 32

Herson's Inc
15525 Frederick Rd .... Rockville MD 20855 — **888-203-8318** — 301-279-8600 — 57

Hertz Global Holdings Inc
225 Brae Blvd .... Park Ridge NJ 07656 — **800-654-3131** — 201-307-2000 — 126
NYSE: HTZ

Hertz Schram & Saretsky PC
1760 S Telegraph Rd
Ste 300 .... Bloomfield Hills MI 48302 — **866-775-5987** — 248-335-5000 — 427

Herweck's Art & Drafting Supplies
300 Broadway St .... San Antonio TX 78205 — **800-725-1349** — 210-227-1349 — 45

Herzing College
Atlanta
3393 Peachtree Rd Ste 1003 .... Atlanta GA 30326 — **800-573-4533** — 404-816-4533 — 795

Herzing College Birmingham
280 W Valley Ave .... Birmingham AL 35209 — **800-425-9432** — 205-791-5860 — 795

Herzing College Madison
5218 E Terr Dr .... Madison WI 53718 — **800-582-1227** — 608-249-6611 — 795

HESCO (Hartford Electric Supply Co)
30 Inwood Rd Ste 1 .... Rocky Hill CT 06067 — **800-969-5444** — 860-236-6363 — 246

Hesse Inc
6700 St John Ave .... Kansas City MO 64123 — **800-821-5562** — 816-483-7808 — 774

Hesston College
325 S College Dr PO Box 3000 .... Hesston KS 67062 — **800-995-2757** — 620-327-4221 — 162

Hettrick Cyr & Associates (HC&A)
59 Sycamore St .... Glastonbury CT 06033 — **888-805-0300** — 860-652-9997 — 399

Heubel Shaw
6311 NE Equitable Rd .... Kansas City MO 64120 — **800-283-4177** — — 765

Heuss Printing Inc
903 N Second St .... Ames IA 50010 — **800-232-6710** — 515-232-6710 — 623

Hewlett Packard Enterprise (Canada) Co (HP)
5150 Spectrum Way .... Mississauga ON L4W5G1 — **800-447-4636** — 905-206-4725 — 173-2

Hewlett-Packard Co
3000 Hanover St .... Palo Alto CA 94304 — **800-752-0900*** — 650-857-1501 — 173-2
NYSE: HPQ ■ *Sales

Hexavest Inc
1250 Ren, L,vesque Blvd W
Ste 4200 .... Montreal QC H3B4W8 — **800-225-6265** — 514-390-8484 — 461

Hexcel Corp
281 Tresser Blvd 16th Fl .... Stamford CT 06901 — **800-444-3923** — 800-688-7734 — 601-1
NYSE: HXL

Heyburn State Park
57 Chatcolet Rd .... Plummer ID 83851 — **866-634-3246** — 208-686-1308 — 561

Name / Address	City	State	ZIP	Toll-Free	Phone	Class
Heyco Products 1800 Industrial Way N	Toms River	NJ	08755	**800-526-4182**	732-286-1800	486
Heyman HospiceCare 420 E Second Ave	Rome	GA	30161	**800-324-1078**	706-509-3200	370
HF Group Inc 203 W Artesia Blvd	Compton	CA	90220	**800-421-5000**	310-605-0755	494
HF Group, The 8844 Mayfield Rd	Chesterland	OH	44026	**800-444-7534**	440-729-2445	92
HF scientific Inc 3170 Metro Pkwy	Fort Myers	FL	33916	**888-203-7248**		
HFA (Hospice Foundation of America) 1707 L St NW Ste 220	Washington	DC	20036	**800-854-3402**	202-457-5811	49-8
HFI (Hepatitis Foundation International) 504 Blick Dr	Silver Spring	MD	20904	**800-891-0707**	301-622-4200	48-17
HFIA (Home Furnishings Independents Assn) 500 Giuseppe Ct Ste 6	Roseville	CA	95678	**800-422-3778**		49-4
HFMA (Healthcare Financial Management Assn) 2 Westbrook Corporate Ctr Ste 700	Westchester	IL	60154	**800-252-4362**		49-8
HFTP (Hospitality Financial & Technology Professionals) 11709 Boulder Ln Ste 110	Austin	TX	78726	**800-646-4387**	512-249-5333	49-1
Hg Solutions 3701 S Lawrence St	Tacoma	WA	98409	**866-988-2626**	253-588-2626	461
HGI Skydyne 100 River Rd	Port Jervis	NY	12771	**800-428-2273**		199
HGMN (Herb Growing & Marketing Network) PO Box 245	Silver Spring	PA	17575	**800-753-9199**	717-393-3295	48-2
HH Angus & Assoc Ltd 1127 Leslie St	Toronto	ON	M3C2J6	**866-955-8201**	416-443-8200	256
HH Arnold Co Inc 529 Liberty St	Rockland	MA	02370	**866-868-9603**	781-878-0346	739
H&H Group, The 854 N Prince St	Lancaster	PA	17603	**866-338-7569**	717-393-3941	343
H&H X-Ray Services Inc 104 Enterprise St	West Monroe	LA	71292	**800-551-5093**		738
HHI (Hoag Hospital Irvine) 16200 Sand Canyon Ave	Irvine	CA	92618	**800-309-9729**	949-764-4624	373-3
HHS (Department of Health & Human Services) 330 Independence Ave SW	Washington	DC	20201	**877-696-6775**	202-619-0150	339-9
Hi Tech Seals Inc 9211-41 Ave	Edmonton	AB	T6E6R5	**800-661-6055**	780-438-6055	349
Hi TecMetal Group Inc 1101 E 55th St	Cleveland	OH	44103	**877-484-2867**	216-881-8100	482
Hiawatha Correctional Facility 4533 W Industrial Pk Dr	Kincheloe	MI	49786	**800-642-4838**	906-495-5661	213
Hiawatha Rubber 1700 67th Ave N	Minneapolis	MN	55430	**800-782-7776**	763-566-0900	673
HI-AYH (Hostelling International USA - American Youth Host) 8401 Colesville Rd Ste 600	Silver Spring	MD	20910	**888-449-8727**	240-650-2100	48-23
Hibbing Community College 1515 E 25th St	Hibbing	MN	55746	**800-224-4422**	218-262-7200	162
Hibbs Hallmark & Co 501 Shelley Dr	Tyler	TX	75701	**800-765-6767**		389
HIBCC (Health Industry Business Communications Council) 2525 E Arizona Biltmore Cir Ste 127	Phoenix	AZ	85016	**800-755-5505**	602-381-1091	49-8
Hibco Plastics Inc 1820 Us 601 Hwy	Yadkinville	NC	27055	**800-849-8683**	336-463-2391	597
HIC (Hawaii Information Consortium) 201 Merchant St Ste 1805	Honolulu	HI	96813	**800-295-0089**	808-695-4620	561
Hickey Freeman 1155 N Clinton Ave *Cust Svc	Rochester	NY	14621	**844-755-7344***	585-467-7021	155-11
Hickok Inc 10514 Dupont Ave *OTC: HICKA*	Cleveland	OH	44108	**800-342-5080**	216-541-8060	248
Hickory Brands Inc (HBI) 429 27th St NW	Hickory	NC	28601	**800-438-5777**	828-322-2600	740-5
Hickory Farms Inc 811 Madison Ave	Toledo	OH	43604	**800-753-8558**		335
Hickory Knob State Resort Park 1591 Resort Dr	McCormick	SC	29835	**800-491-1764**	864-391-2450	561
Hickory Metro Convention & Visitors Bureau 1960 13th Ave Dr SE	Hickory	NC	28602	**800-509-2444**	828-322-1335	206
Hickory Motor Speedway 3130 Hwy 70 SE	Newton	NC	28658	**800-843-8725**	828-324-4535	512
Hickory Point Bank & Trust FSB PO Box 2548 *Cust Svc	Decatur	IL	62525	**800-872-0081***	217-875-3131	70
Hickory Printing Group Inc 725 Reese Dr SW	Conover	NC	28613	**800-442-5679**	828-465-3431	623
Hickory Ridge Marriott Conference Hotel 10400 Fernwood Rd	Bethesda	MD	20817	**800-334-0344**	301-380-3000	376
Hickory Springs Mfg Co 235 Second Ave NW	Hickory	NC	28601	**800-438-5341**		715
Hickory Yarns Inc 1025 Tenth St NE PO Box 1975	Hickory	NC	28601	**800-713-1484**	828-322-1550	740-9
HID Global Corp 611 Center Ridge Dr	Austin	TX	78753	**800-237-7769**	512-776-9000	178-12
HIDA (Health Industry Distributors Association) 310 Montgomery St	Alexandria	VA	22314	**800-549-4432**	703-549-4432	49-18
Hidalgo County 100 N Closner	Edinburg	TX	78539	**888-318-2811**	956-318-2100	337
Hidden Valley Resort & Conference Ctr 1 Craighead Dr PO Box 4420	Hidden Valley	PA	15502	**800-452-2223**	814-443-8000	376
Hideout Lodge & Guest Ranch, The PO Box 206	Shell	WY	82441	**800-354-8637**	307-765-2080	239
Higdon Florist 201 E 32nd St	Joplin	MO	64804	**800-641-4726**	417-624-7171	292
High Arctic Energy Services Inc 700-2nd St SW Ste 500	Calgary	AB	T2P2T8	**800-668-7143**	403-508-7836	
High Concrete Structures Inc 125 Denver Rd	Denver	PA	17517	**800-773-2278**	717-336-9300	183
High Country News 119 Grand Ave	Paonia	CO	81428	**800-311-5852**	970-527-4898	528-3
High End Systems Inc 2105 Gracy Farms Ln	Austin	TX	78758	**800-890-8989**	512-836-2242	438
High Hampton Inn & Country Club 1525 Hwy 107 S	Cashiers	NC	28717	**800-334-2551**		665
High Peaks Resort 2384 Saranac Ave	Lake Placid	NY	12946	**800-755-5598**	518-523-4411	665
High Performance Computing Collaboratory 2 Research Blvd	Starkville	MS	39762	**800-521-4041**	662-325-6768	664
High Plains Power Inc 1775 E Monroe PO Box 713	Riverton	WY	82501	**800-445-0613**	307-856-9426	245
High Plains Publishers Inc 1500 W Wyatt Earp Blvd	Dodge City	KS	67801	**800-452-7171**	620-227-7171	633-8
High Point Convention & Visitors Bureau 1634 North Main St Ste 102	High Point	NC	27262	**800-720-5255**	336-884-5255	206
High Point Furniture Industries Inc 1104 Bedford St PO Box 2063	High Point	NC	27261	**800-447-3462**	336-434-5141	319-1
High Point Regional Health System (HPRHS) 601 N Elm St PO Box HP-5	High Point	NC	27262	**877-878-7644**	336-878-6000	373-3
High Point University 833 Montlieu Ave	High Point	NC	27262	**800-345-6993**	336-841-9216	166
High Power Technical Services Inc (HPTS) 2230 Ampere Dr	Louisville	KY	40299	**866-398-3474**	502-271-2469	116
High River Hospital 560 Ninth Ave W	High River	AB	T1V1B3	**800-332-1414**	403-652-2200	373-2
High Steel Service Center LLC 400 Steel Way	Lancaster	PA	17601	**800-732-0346**	717-299-8989	
High Vacuum Apparatus LLC (HVA) 12880 Moya Blvd	Reno	NV	89506	**800-551-4422**	775-359-4442	784
High West Energy Inc (HWE) 6270 County Rd 212	Pine Bluffs	WY	82082	**888-834-1657**	307-245-3261	245
Highcom Security 2451 McMullen Booth Rd Ste 242	Clearwater	FL	33759	**800-987-9098**		689
Higher Ed Growth LLC 1702 E McNair Dr	Tempe	AZ	85283	**866-433-8532**		447
Highfield Manufacturing Co 5144 S Intl Dr	Cudahy	WI	53110	**855-443-4353**	414-489-7700	591
HighJump Software 5600 W 83rd St Ste 600	Minneapolis	MN	55437	**800-328-3271**	952-947-4088	178-1
Highland Community College (HCC) 606 W Main	Highland	KS	66035	**800-985-9781**	785-442-6000	162
Highland Computer Forms Inc 1025 W Main St	Hillsboro	OH	45133	**800-669-5213**	937-393-4215	110
Highland County 119 Governor Foraker Pl	Hillsboro	OH	45133	**800-774-1202**	937-393-1911	337
Highland Hospital of Rochester 1000 S Ave	Rochester	NY	14620	**800-499-9298**	585-473-2200	373-3
Highlands Fuel Delivery LLC 190 Commerce Way	Portsmouth	NH	03801	**888-310-1924**		575
Highlands Regional Medical Ctr (HRMC) 5000 KY Rt 321	Prestonsburg	KY	41653	**800-533-4762**	606-886-8511	373-3
Highlights for Children Inc 1800 Watermark Dr *Cust Svc	Columbus	OH	43216	**800-255-9517***	614-486-0631	633-9
Highline Electric Assn 1300 S Interocean Ave	Holyoke	CO	80734	**800-816-2236**	970-854-2236	245
Highmark Inc 120 Fifth Ave Pl	Pittsburgh	PA	15222	**800-992-0246**	412-544-7000	390-3
HighPoint Technology Solutions Inc 2332 Galiano St 2nd Fl	Coral Gables	FL	33134	**800-767-0893**		260
Highway Machine Company Inc (HMC) 3010 S Old US Hwy 41	Princeton	IN	47670	**866-990-9462**	812-385-3639	452
Highway To Health Inc 1 Radnor Corporate Ctr Ste 100	Radnor	PA	19087	**888-243-2358**		390-7
Highwoods Properties Inc 3100 Smoketree Ct Ste 600 *NYSE: HIW*	Raleigh	NC	27604	**866-449-6637**	919-872-4924	651
Hikma 246 Industrial Way W *Cust Svc	Eatontown	NJ	07724	**800-631-2174***		579
Hiland Dairy Co PO Box 2270	Springfield	MO	65801	**800-641-4022**	417-862-9311	296-27
Hilbert College 5200 S Park Ave	Hamburg	NY	14075	**800-649-8003**	716-649-7900	166
Hilco Electric Co-op Inc 115 E Main PO Box 127	Itasca	TX	76055	**800-338-6425**	254-687-2331	245
Hilford Moving & Storage 1595 Arundell Ave	Ventura	CA	93003	**800-739-6683**	805-210-8252	516
Hilgard House Hotel & Suites 927 Hilgard Ave	Los Angeles	CA	90024	**800-826-3934**	310-208-3945	378
Hilgraeve Inc 1287 N Telegraph Rd *Sales	Monroe	MI	48162	**800-826-2760***	734-243-0576	178-7
Hill & Griffith Co 1085 Summer St	Cincinnati	OH	45204	**800-543-0425**	513-921-1075	498
Hill & Valley Premium Bakery 320 44th St	Rock Island	IL	61201	**800-480-0055**	309-793-0161	68
Hill Barth & King LLC 6603 Summit Dr	Canfield	OH	44406	**800-733-8613**	330-758-8613	2
Hill Bros Chemical Co 1675 N Main St	Orange	CA	92867	**800-994-8801**	714-998-8800	146
Hill City Oil Company Inc 1409 Dunn St	Houma	LA	70360	**800-492-8377**	985-851-4000	575
Hill Country Furniture Partners Ltd 1431 Fm 1101	New Braunfels	TX	78130	**877-314-8457**		
Hill County Electric Co-op Inc PO Box 2330	Havre	MT	59501	**877-394-7804**		245
Hill Crest Behavioral Health Services 6869 Fifth Ave S	Birmingham	AL	35212	**800-292-8553**	205-833-9000	373-5
Hill Group, The 11045 Gage Ave	Franklin Park	IL	60131	**800-233-8990**	847-451-5000	189-10
Hill Mfg Company Inc 1500 Jonesboro Rd SE	Atlanta	GA	30315	**800-445-5123**	404-522-8364	151
Hill PHOENIX Inc 1003 Sigman Rd	Conyers	GA	30013	**800-518-6630**	770-285-3264	660
Hill Physicians Medical Group Inc 2409 Camino Ramon PO Box 5080	San Ramon	CA	94583	**800-445-5747**	925-820-8300	461
Hill School 860 Beech St	Pottstown	PA	19464	**877-651-2800**	610-326-1000	618

Alphabetical Section

	Toll-Free	Phone	Class
Hill Wood Products Inc 9483 Ashawa Rd .... Cook MN 55723	800-788-9689		547
Hillcrest Garden 95 W Century Rd .... Paramus NJ 07652	800-437-7000	201-599-3030	292
Hillcrest Historic District Markham & Kavanaugh .... Little Rock AR 72216	877-637-0037	501-371-0075	50-6
Hillcrest Hospital 6780 Mayfield Rd .... Mayfield Heights OH 44124	800-707-8922	440-312-4500	373-3
Hiller Aviation Museum 601 Skyway Rd .... San Carlos CA 94070	888-500-1555	650-654-0200	517
Hilliard Energy Inc 3001 W Loop 250 N Ste E103 .... Midland TX 79705	800-287-0014	432-683-9100	535
Hillman Group Inc 10590 Hamilton Ave .... Cincinnati OH 45231	800-800-4900	513-851-4900	350
Hill-Rom Services Inc 1069 SR 46 E .... Batesville IN 47006	800-267-2337	812-934-7777	319-3
Hills Bank & Trust Co 131 Main St PO Box 70 .... Hills IA 52235	800-445-5725		70
Hillsboro Argus 1500 SW First Ave .... Portland OR 97201	800-544-0505	503-648-1131	528-4
Hillsboro Equipment Inc E18898 Hwy 33 .... Hillsboro WI 54634	800-521-5133	608-489-2275	274
Hillsborough Community College *Dale Mabry* 4001 Tampa Bay Blvd .... Tampa FL 33614	866-253-7077	813-253-7000	162
Hillsborough County Public Schools 901 E Kennedy Blvd .... Tampa FL 33602	800-962-2873	813-272-4000	681
Hillsborough Regional Juvenile Detention Ctr West 3948 ML King Jr Blvd .... Tampa FL 33614	800-355-2280	813-871-7650	411
Hillsdale College 33 E College St .... Hillsdale MI 49242	888-886-1174	517-437-7341	166
Hillsdale Free Will Baptist College PO Box 7208 .... Moore OK 73153	800-460-6328	405-912-9000	166
Hillside Candy Co 35 Hillside Ave .... Hillside NJ 07205	800-524-1304	973-926-2300	296-8
Hillside School 404 Robin Hill Rd .... Marlborough MA 01752	800-344-8328	508-485-2824	618
Hillstone Restaurant Group 147 S Beverly Dr .... Beverly Hills CA 90212	800-230-9787		666
Hilltop Inn of Vermont 3472 Airport Rd .... Montpelier VT 05602	877-609-0003	802-229-5766	378
Hillyard Chemical Company Inc 302 N Fourth St PO Box 909 ... St. Joseph MO 64501	800-365-1555	816-233-1321	151
Hilman Inc 12 Timber Ln .... Marlboro NJ 07746 *Cust Svc	888-276-5548*	732-462-6277	468
Hilmar Cheese Company Inc PO Box 910 .... Hilmar CA 95324	800-577-5772	209-667-6076	296-5
Hilti Inc 5400 S 122nd E Ave .... Tulsa OK 74146 *Cust Svc	800-879-8000*		754
Hilton Grand Vacations Company LLC 6355 Metro W Blvd Ste 180 ...... Orlando FL 32835	800-230-7068	407-613-3100	748
Hilton Hawaiian Village 2005 Kalia Rd .... Honolulu HI 96815	800-445-8667	808-949-4321	665
Hilton Head Health Institute 14 Valencia Rd .... Hilton Head Island SC 29928	800-292-2440	843-785-3919	702
Hilton Head Island Beach & Tennis Resort 40 Folly Field Rd .... Hilton Head Island SC 29928 *Resv	800-475-2631*	843-842-4402	665
Hilton Head Island Visitor & Convention Bureau, The 1 Chamber of Commerce Dr PO Box 5647 .... Hilton Head Island SC 29938	800-523-3373	843-785-3673	139
Hilton Head Island Visitors & Convention Bureau 1 Chamber of Commerce Dr PO Box 5647 .... Hilton Head Island SC 29938	800-523-3373	843-785-3673	206
Hilton Key Largo Resort 97000 S Overseas Hwy .... Key Largo FL 33037 *Resv	888-871-3437*	305-852-5553	665
Hilton Myrtle Beach Resort 10000 Beach Club Dr .... Myrtle Beach SC 29572	800-445-8667	843-449-5000	665
Hilton San Diego Resort 1775 E Mission Bay Dr .... San Diego CA 92109	800-445-8667	619-276-4010	665
Hilton Sandestin Beach Golf Resort & Spa 4000 Sandestin Blvd S ...... Miramar Beach FL 32550	800-559-1805	850-267-9500	665
Hilton Santa Barbara Beachfront Resort 633 E Cabrillo Blvd .... Santa Barbara CA 93103	800-879-2929	805-564-4333	665
Hilton Savannah Desoto 15 E Liberty St .... Savannah GA 31401	844-279-5094		377
Hilton Short Hills 41 JFK Pkwy .... Short Hills NJ 07078	800-445-8667	973-379-0100	703
Hilton Waikoloa Village 425 Waikoloa Beach Dr .... Waikoloa HI 96738	866-931-1679	808-886-1234	665
Hilton Whistler Resort & Spa 4050 Whistler Way .... Whistler BC V0N1B4	800-515-4050	604-932-1982	665
Hilton Worldwide 7930 Jones Branch Dr .... McLean VA 22102	800-445-8667	703-883-1000	378
Himalayan Institute Ctr for Health & Healing 952 Bethany Tpke .... Honesdale PA 18431	800-822-4547	570-253-5551	702
HimoInsa Power Systems Inc 16002 W 110th St .... Lenexa KS 66219	866-710-2988	913-495-5557	515
Hindley Mfg Company Inc 9 Havens St .... Cumberland RI 02864	800-323-9031	401-722-2550	349
Hinds Community College 501 E Main St PO Box 1100 .... Raymond MS 39154	800-446-3722	601-857-3212	162
Hingham Mutual Fire Insurance Co 230 Beal St .... Hingham MA 02043	800-341-8200	781-749-0841	390-4
Hiniker Co 58766 240th St .... Mankato MN 56002	800-433-5620	507-625-6621	273
Hinkle Insurance Agency Inc 600 Olde Hickory Rd Ste 200 .... Lancaster PA 17601	877-408-1418	717-560-9733	389
Hinkley Lighting 12600 Berea Rd .... Cleveland OH 44111	800-446-5539	216-671-3300	438
Hinsdale County 311 N Henson St .... Lake City CO 81235	877-944-7575	970-944-2225	337
Hippocrates Health Institute 1466 Hippocrates Way ...... West Palm Beach FL 33411	800-842-2125	561-471-8876	702
Hiram College PO Box 67 .... Hiram OH 44234 *Admissions	800-362-5280*	330-569-5169	166
Hire Image LLC 6 Alcazar Ave .... Johnston RI 02919	888-433-0090	401-490-2202	717
Hire Quest LLC 4560 Great Oak Dr .... North Charleston SC 29418	800-835-6755	843-723-7400	260
Hireology 303 E Wacker Dr Ste 400 .... Chicago IL 60601	844-383-2633	312-253-7870	
HireRight Inc 5151 California Ave .... Irvine CA 92617	800-400-2761		631
Hirschbach Motor Lines Inc 18355 US Hwy 20 .... East Dubuque IL 61025	800-554-2969		775
Hirsh Industries Inc 3636 Westown Pkwy Ste 100 .... West Des Moines IA 50266	800-383-7414	515-299-3200	319-1
Hirshfield's Inc 725 Second Ave N .... Minneapolis MN 55405	800-432-3701	612-377-3910	
Hirzel Canning Company & Farms 411 Lemoyne Rd .... Northwood OH 43619	800-837-1631	419-693-0531	296-20
His radio 893 2420 Wade Hampton Blvd .... Greenville SC 29615	800-447-7234	864-292-6040	641-43
Hispanic Assn of Colleges & Universities (HACU) 8415 Datapoint Dr Ste 400 .... San Antonio TX 78229	800-780-4228	210-692-3805	49-5
Historic Bullock Hotel 633 Main St .... Deadwood SD 57732	800-336-1876	605-578-1745	378
Historic Fort Snelling 200 Tower Ave Ft Snelling History Ctr .... Saint Paul MN 55111	800-657-3773	612-726-1171	50-3
Historic French Market Inn 509 Decatur St .... New Orleans LA 70130	800-366-2743	504-561-5621	378
Historic Inns of Annapolis 58 State Cir .... Annapolis MD 21401	800-847-8882	410-263-2641	378
Historic New England 141 Cambridge St .... Boston MA 02114	800-722-2256	617-227-3956	48-13
Historic New Orleans Collection 533 Royal St .... New Orleans LA 70130	800-535-9595	504-523-4662	517
Historic Roswell District 617 Atlanta St .... Roswell GA 30075	800-776-7935		50-3
Historic Tours of America Inc 201 Front St .... Key West FL 33040 *Consumer Info	800-844-7601*	855-629-8777	755
Historical Lawmen Museum 845 Motel Blvd .... Las Cruces NM 88007	877-827-7200	575-647-7200	517
Historical Research Ctr Inc 2107 Corporate Dr .... Boynton Beach FL 33426	800-985-9956		327
History Ch *A&E Television Networks LLC* 235 E 45th St .... New York NY 10017	888-371-5848	212-210-1400	735
Hit Promotional Products Inc 7150 Bryan Dairy Rd .... Largo FL 33777	800-237-6305	727-541-5561	9
Hitachi America Ltd 50 Prospect Ave .... Tarrytown NY 10591	800-448-2244	914-332-5800	185
Hitachi America Ltd Computer Div 2000 Sierra Pt Pkwy .... Brisbane CA 94005	800-448-2244		173-8
Hitachi Chemical Diagnostics 630 Clyde Ct .... Mountain View CA 94043	800-233-6278	650-961-5501	231
Hitachi Credit America Ltd 800 Connecticut Ave .... Norwalk CT 06854	866-718-4222	203-956-3000	
Hitachi Kokusai Electric America Ltd 150 Crossways Pk Dr .... Woodbury NY 11797	855-490-5124	516-921-7200	643
Hitachi Medical Systems America Inc 1959 Summit Commerce Pk .... Twinsburg OH 44087	800-800-3106	330-425-1313	381
Hitachi Metals America Ltd 2 Manhattanville Rd Ste 301 ...... Purchase NY 10577	800-777-5757	914-694-9200	307
Hitachi Systems Security Inc 955 Michele-Bohec Blvd Ste 244 .... Blainville QC J7C5J6	866-430-8166	450-430-8166	363
Hitch Enterprises Inc 309 Northridge Cir PO Box 1308 ... Guymon OK 73942	800-951-2533	580-338-8575	359-3
HITCO Carbon Composites Inc 1600 W 135th St .... Gardena CA 90249	800-421-5444	310-527-0700	502
Hite Co 3101 Beale Ave .... Altoona PA 16601	800-252-3598	814-944-6121	246
HITEC Group Ltd 1743 Quincy Ave Unit #155 ...... Naperville IL 60540	800-288-8303		246
Hitt Marking Devices Inc 3231 W MacArthur Blvd .... Santa Ana CA 92704	800-969-6699	714-979-1405	465
Hive Modern Design 820 NW glisan st .... Portland OR 97209	866-663-4483	503-242-1967	138
Hivelocity Ventures Corp 8010 Woodland Ctr Blvd Ste 700 .... Tampa FL 33614	888-869-4678	813-471-0355	225
Hiwassee College 225 Hiwassee College Dr .... Madisonville TN 37354	800-356-2187	423-442-2001	162
Hix Corp 1201 E 27th Terr .... Pittsburg KS 66762	800-835-0606	620-231-8568	739
Hixardt Technologies Inc 119 W Intendencia St .... Pensacola FL 32502	866-985-3282	850-439-3282	180
HJ Foundation Inc 8275 N W 80 St .... Miami FL 33166	866-751-4545	305-592-8181	261
HKA Enterprises Inc 337 Spartangreen Blvd .... Duncan SC 29334	800-825-5452	864-661-5100	192
Hkm Direct Market Communications Inc 5501 Cass Ave .... Cleveland OH 44102 *General	800-860-4456*	216-651-9500	5
HL Dalis Inc 35-35 24th St .... Long Island NY 11106	800-453-2547	718-361-1100	246
HL Turner Group Inc, The 27 Locke Rd .... Concord NH 03301	800-305-2289	603-228-1122	261
HLA (Harold Levinson Assoc) 21 Banfi Plz .... Farmingdale NY 11735	800-325-2512	631-962-2400	297-3
HLI (Human Life International) 4 Family Life Ln .... Front Royal VA 22630 *Orders	800-549-5433*	540-635-7884	48-6
Hli Properties Inc 1003 Central Ave .... Fort Dodge IA 50501	800-247-2000	515-955-1600	633-9
HM Royal Inc 689 Pennington Ave .... Trenton NJ 08601	800-257-9452	609-396-9176	146
HM Stauffer & Sons Inc 33 Glenola Dr PO Box 567 .... Leola PA 17540	800-662-2226	717-656-2811	812
HMA (Hargrave Military Academy) 200 Military Dr .... Chatham VA 24531	800-432-2480	434-432-2481	618

Company / Address	Toll-Free	Phone	Class
HMC (Highway Machine Company Inc) 3010 S Old US Hwy 41 ....Princeton IN 47670	866-990-9462	812-385-3639	452
HMC (Hays Medical Ctr) 2220 Canterbury Dr ....Hays KS 67601	800-248-0073	785-650-2759	373-3
HMC Archtiect 3546 Councours St ....Ontario CA 91764	800-350-9979	909-989-9979	261
HME Inc 1950 Byron Ctr Ave SW ....Wyoming MI 49519	800-269-7335	616-534-1463	513
HMH (Harrington Hospital) 100 South St ....Southbridge MA 01550	800-416-6072	508-765-9771	373-3
HMN Financial Inc 1016 Civic Ctr Dr NW ....Rochester MN 55901 NASDAQ: HMNF	888-257-2000	507-535-1309	359-2
Hn Burns Engineering Corp 3275 Progress Dr Ste A ....Orlando FL 32826	800-728-6506	407-273-3770	261
HN. Funkhouser & Company Inc 2150 S Loudoun St ....Winchester VA 22601	800-343-6556	540-662-9000	575
HNA (Hawaii Nurses Assn) 949 Kapiolani Blvd Ste 107 ....Honolulu HI 96814	800-617-2677	808-531-1628	529
HNA (Hockey North America) 45570 Shepard Dr ....Sterling VA 20164	800-446-2539	703-430-8100	48-22
HNC (Hospice of Northern Colorado) 2726 W 11th St Rd ....Greeley CO 80634	800-564-5563	970-352-8487	370
HO Bostrom Company Inc 818 Progress Ave ....Waukesha WI 53186	800-332-5415	262-542-0222	685
HO Trerice Co 12950 W Eight-Mile Rd ....Oak Park MI 48237	888-873-7423	248-399-8000	201
HO.T. Printing & Graphics Inc 2595 Tracy Ct ....Northwood OH 43619	800-848-8259	419-242-7000	623
Hoag Hospital Irvine (HHI) 16200 Sand Canyon Ave ....Irvine CA 92618	800-309-9729	949-764-4624	373-3
Hoard's Dairyman Magazine 28 Milwaukee Ave W PO Box 801. ....Fort Atkinson WI 53538	800-245-8222	920-563-5551	455-1
Hobart & William Smith Colleges 300 Pulteney St ....Geneva NY 14456 *Admissions	800-852-2256*	315-781-3000	166
Hobart Bros Co 101 Trade Sq E ....Troy OH 45373	800-424-1543	937-332-4000	806
Hobart Corp 701 S Ridge Ave ....Troy OH 45374 *Cust Svc	800-333-7447*	937-332-3000	298
Hobas Pipe USA LP 1413 E Richey Rd ....Houston TX 77073	800-856-7473	281-821-2200	592
Hobbs Bonded Fibers Inc 200 Commerce Dr ....Waco TX 76710	800-433-3357	254-741-0040	740-6
Hobby Lobby 7717 SW 44th St ....Oklahoma City OK 73179	800-888-0321	405-745-1275	44
Hobe Sound Bible College PO Box 1065 ....Hobe Sound FL 33475	800-881-5534	772-546-5534	161
Hobson & Motzer Inc 30 Air Line Dr ....Durham CT 06422	800-476-5111	860-349-1756	486
HOC Industries Inc 3511 N Ohio ....Wichita KS 67219	800-999-9645	316-838-4663	577
Ho-Chunk Inc 1 Mission Dr ....Winnebago NE 68071	800-439-7008	402-878-2809	317
Hockessin Library 1023 Valley Rd ....Hockessin DE 19707	888-352-7722	302-239-5160	433-3
Hockey North America (HNA) 45570 Shepard Dr ....Sterling VA 20164	800-446-2539	703-430-8100	48-22
Hocking College 3301 Hocking Pkwy ....Nelsonville OH 45764	877-462-5464	740-753-3591	795
Hocking Valley Bank 7 W Stimson Ave ....Athens OH 45701	888-482-5854	740-592-4441	70
Hodell-natco Industries Inc 7825 Hub Pkwy ....Cleveland OH 44125	800-321-4862	216-447-0165	350
Hodge Products Inc PO Box 1326 ....El Cajon CA 92022	800-778-2217		295
Hodges University 2655 Northbrooke Dr ....Naples FL 34119 Fort Myers	800-466-8017	239-513-1122	166
4501 Colonial Blvd ....Fort Myers FL 33966	800-466-0019	239-938-7701	166
Hoegemeyer Hybrids Inc 1755 Hoegemeyer Rd ....Hooper NE 68031	800-245-4631	402-654-3399	10-4
Hoffman California Fabrics Inc 25792 Obrero Dr ....Mission Viejo CA 92691	800-547-0100		590
Hoffman Car Wash & Hoffman Jiffy Lube 1757 Central Ave ....Albany NY 12205	877-446-3362	518-862-1658	
Hoffman Planning, Design, & Construction Inc 122 E College Ave Ste 1G ....Appleton WI 54911	800-236-2370	920-731-2322	186
Hoffman Products 9600 Vly View Rd ....Macedonia OH 44056	800-645-2014	216-525-4320	810
Hoffmaster 2920 N Main St ....Oshkosh WI 54901	800-327-9774	920-235-9330	554
Hofstra University 1000 Fulton Ave ....Hempstead NY 11549	800-463-7872	516-463-6600	166
Hog Slat Inc PO Box 300 ....Newton Grove NC 28366	800-949-4647	910-594-0219	10-5
Hog's Breath Saloon Key West 400 Front St ....Key West FL 33040	800-826-6969	305-296-4222	667
Hogan Larry (R) 100 State Cir ....Annapolis MD 21401	800-811-8336	410-974-3901	
Hogan-Knotts Financial Group, The 298 Broad St ....Red Bank NJ 07701	800-801-3190	732-842-7400	686
Hoggan Scientific LLC 3653 W 1987 S ....Salt Lake City UT 84104	800-678-7888	801-572-6500	267
Hogue Cellars 2800 Lee Rd ....Prosser WA 99350	800-565-9779		80-3
Hohman Assoc Inc (HAI) 6951 W Little York ....Houston TX 77040	800-324-0978	713-896-0978	48-2
Hohmann & Barnard Inc 30 Rasons Ct ....Hauppauge NY 11788	800-645-0616	631-234-0600	278
Hohner Inc 12020 Volunteer Blvd ....Mt. Juliet TN 37122	888-627-3987		523
Hoigaards Inc 5425 Excelsior Blvd ....Minneapolis MN 55416	800-266-8157	952-929-1351	707
Hoist Fitness Systems Inc 9990 Empire St Ste 130 ....San Diego CA 92126	800-548-5438	858-578-7676	267
Holabird Sports LLC 9220 Pulaski Hwy ....Middle River MD 21220	866-860-1416	410-687-6400	707
Holaday Circuits Inc 11126 Bren Rd W ....Minnetonka MN 55343	800-362-3303	952-933-3303	621
Holden Industries Inc 5624 S State Hwy 43 ....South West City MO 64863	800-488-4487	417-762-3218	774
Holderness School 33 Chapel Ln ....Holderness NH 03245	877-262-1492	603-536-1257	618
Hole in One International 6195 Ridgeview Ct Ste A ....Reno NV 89519	800-827-2249	775-828-4653	755
Holiday Acres Resort 4060 S Shore Dr PO Box 460 ....Rhinelander WI 54501	800-261-1500	715-369-1500	665
Holiday Builders Inc 2293 W Eau Gallie Blvd ....Melbourne FL 32935	866-431-2533		649
Holiday Cos 4567 American Blvd W PO Box 1224. ....Bloomington MN 55437	800-745-7411	952-830-8700	185
Holiday Diver Inc 180 Gulf Stream Way ....Dania Beach FL 33004	800-348-3872	954-925-7630	707
Holiday Express Corp 721 S 28th St ....Estherville IA 51334	800-831-5078	712-362-5812	681
Holiday Hair 7201 Metro Blvd ....Minneapolis MN 55439	800-345-7811		77
Holiday Inn 301 Government St ....Mobile AL 36602	888-465-4329	251-694-0100	378
Holiday Inn Baltimore Inner Harbor Hotel 301 W Lombard St ....Baltimore MD 21201	877-834-3613	410-685-3500	377
Holiday Inn By the Bay 88 Spring St ....Portland ME 04101	800-345-5050	207-775-2311	377
Holiday Inn Express & Suites Oceanfront 3301 S Atlantic Ave ....Daytona Beach Shores FL 32118	800-633-8464	386-767-1711	665
Holiday Inn Express DFW North 4550 W John Carpenter Fwy ....Irving TX 75063	800-465-4329	972-929-4499	378
Holiday Inn Resort Daytona Beach Oceanfront 1615 S Atlantic Ave ....Daytona Beach FL 32118	877-834-3613	386-255-0921	378
Holiday Inn SunSpree Resort Wrightsville Beach 1706 N Lumina Ave ....Wrightsville Beach NC 28480	888-211-9874	910-256-2231	665
Holiday Isle Beach Resort & Marina 84001 Overseas Hwy ....Islamorada FL 33036	855-314-2829	305-664-2321	665
Holiday Retirement 480 N Orlando Ave Ste 236 ....Winter Park FL 32789	800-322-0999		651
Holiday River Expeditions 544 East 3900 South ....Salt Lake City UT 84107	800-624-6323	801-266-2087	755
Holiday Stationstores 4567 American Blvd W ....Bloomington MN 55437	800-745-7411	952-830-8700	204
Holiday Tree Farms Inc 800 NW Cornell Rd ....Corvallis OR 97330	800-289-3684	541-753-3236	747
Holiday Valley Resort 6557 Holiday Valley Rd PO Box 370. ....Ellicottville NY 14731	800-323-0020	716-699-2345	665
Holiday World & Splashin' Safari 452 E Christmas Blvd ....Santa Claus IN 47579	877-463-2645	812-937-4401	32
Holland America Line 450 Third Ave W ....Seattle WA 98119	800-426-0327	206-281-3535	220
Holland Area Convention & Visitors Bureau 76 E Eighth St ....Holland MI 49423	800-506-1299	616-394-0000	206
Holland College 140 Weymouth St ....Charlottetown PE C1A4Z1	800-446-5265	902-566-9510	162
Holland Litho Printing Service Inc 10972 Chicago Dr ....Zeeland MI 49464	800-652-6565	616-392-4644	588
Holland LP 1000 Holland Dr ....Crete IL 60417	800-895-4389	708-672-2300	646
Holland Mfg Co Inc 15 Main St PO Box 404 ....Succasunna NJ 07876	800-345-0492	973-584-8141	727
Hollander Home Fashions Corp 6501 Congress Ave Ste 300 ....Boca Raton FL 33487	800-233-7666	561-997-6900	741
Hollar & Greene Produce Co Inc 230 Cabbage Rd PO Box 3500 ....Boone NC 28607	800-222-1077	828-264-2177	297-7
Holler Classic 1150 N Orlando Ave ....Sanford FL 32789	866-937-1398	407-645-4969	57
Hollins University 7916 Williamson Rd ....Roanoke VA 24020 *Admissions	800-456-9595*	540-362-6401	166
Hollis Marketing 2130 Brenner St ....Saginaw MI 48602	866-797-3301	989-797-3300	195
Hollister Inc 2000 Hollister Dr ....Libertyville IL 60048	800-323-4060	847-680-1000	475
Holloman Corp 333 N Sam Houston Pkwy E Ste 600 ....Houston TX 77060	800-521-2461	281-878-2600	186
Holloway Credit Solutions LLC 1286 Carmichael Way ....Montgomery AL 36106	800-264-2700	334-396-1200	
Holly Energy Partners LP 100 Crescent Ct Ste 1600 ....Dallas TX 75201	800-642-1687	214-871-3555	359-5
Holly Hill Hospital 3019 Falstaff Rd ....Raleigh NC 27610	800-447-1800	919-250-7000	373-5
Holly Shores Best Holiday 491 Rt 9 ....Cape May NJ 08204	877-494-6559		703
Hollyhock PO Box 127 ....Mansons Landing BC V0P1K0	800-933-6339	250-935-6576	669
Hollywood Casino at Charles Town Races 750 Hollywood Dr ....Charles Town WV 25414	800-795-7001	304-725-7001	638
Hollywood Casino Baton Rouge 1717 River Rd N ....Baton Rouge LA 70802	800-447-6843	225-709-7777	133
Hollywood Casino Bay Saint Louis 711 Hollywood Blvd ....Bay Saint Louis MS 39520	866-758-2591		133
Hollywood Casino Joliet 777 Hollywood Blvd ....Joliet IL 60436	800-426-2537		133
Hollywood Reporter 5055 Wilshire Blvd Ste 500 ....Los Angeles CA 90036	866-525-2150	323-525-2000	455-9
Hollywood Wax Museum 3030 W Hwy 76 ....Branson MO 65616	800-214-3661	417-337-8277	517
Hol-Mac Corp PO Box 349 ....Bay Springs MS 39422	800-844-3019	601-764-4121	223
Holman Cadillac Co 1200 Rt 73 S ....Mount Laurel NJ 08054	866-865-6973	877-209-6052	57

	Toll-Free	Phone	Class

Holman Group
9451 Corbin Ave ....Northridge CA 91324 — 800-321-2843 — 818-704-1444 — 460

Holman Transportation Services Inc
1010 Holman Ct ....Caldwell ID 83605 — 800-375-2416 — 208-454-0779 — 775

Holmes Community College
PO Box 399 ....Goodman MS 39079 — 800-465-6374 — 662-472-2312 — 162

Holmes Murphy & Assoc Inc
3001 Westown Pkwy ....West Des Moines IA 50266 — 800-247-7756 — 515-223-6800 — 389

Holmes Regional Medical Ctr
1350 Hickory St ....Melbourne FL 32901 — 800-716-7737 — 321-434-7000 — 373-3

Holmes-Wayne Electric Co-op Inc
6060 Ohio 83 ....Millersburg OH 44654 — 866-674-1055 — 330-674-1055 — 245

Holmstad, The
700 W Fabyan Pkwy ....Batavia IL 60510 — 877-420-5046 — 630-879-4000

Hologic Inc
35 Crosby Dr ....Bedford MA 01730 — 800-523-5001 — 781-999-7300 — 381
NASDAQ: HOLX

Holophane
3825 Columbus Rd
Granville Business Park Bldg A. .... Granville OH 43023 — 866-759-1577 — 438

Holstein Assn USA Inc
1 Holstein Pl PO Box 808 ....Brattleboro VT 05302 — 800-952-5200* — 802-254-4551 — 48-2
*Orders

Holt & Bugbee Co
1600 Shawsheen St ....Tewksbury MA 01876 — 800-325-6010 — 191-3

Holt Hosiery Mills Inc
PO Box 1757 ....Burlington NC 27216 — 800-545-4658

Holt Marketing Services Inc
3075 Boardwalk Ste 2.................Saginaw MI 48603 — 800-698-2449 — 989-791-2475 — 461

HOLT Texas Ltd
3302 S WW White Rd ....San Antonio TX 78222 — 800-275-4658 — 210-648-1111 — 274

Holts Cigar Co
1522 Walnut St ....Philadelphia PA 19102 — 800-523-1641 — 215-732-8500 — 751

Holum & Sons Company Inc
740 Burr Oak Dr ....Westmont IL 60559 — 800-447-4479 — 630-654-8222 — 86

Holy Cross Energy
PO Box 2150 ....Glenwood Springs CO 81602 — 877-833-2555 — 970-945-5491 — 245

Holy Cross Family Ministries
518 Washington St ....North Easton MA 02356 — 800-299-7729 — 508-238-4095 — 48-20

Holy Cross Hospital
4725 N Federal Hwy ....Fort Lauderdale FL 33308 — 888-419-3456 — 954-771-8000 — 373-3

Holy Family Memorial
2300 Western Ave PO Box 1450.......Manitowoc WI 54221 — 800-994-3662 — 920-320-2011 — 373-3

Holy Family University
9801 Frankford Ave ....Philadelphia PA 19114 — 800-422-0010 — 215-637-7700 — 166

Holy Names University
3500 Mountain Blvd ....Oakland CA 94619 — 800-430-1321 — 510-436-1000 — 166

Holy Redeemer Home Care & Hospice
12265 Townsend Rd Ste 400 ....Philadelphia PA 19154 — 888-678-8678 — 370

Holy Redeemer Hospital & Medical Ctr
1648 Huntingdon Pk ....Meadowbrook PA 19046 — 800-818-4747 — 215-947-3000 — 373-3

Holy Rosary Healthcare
2600 Wilson St ....Miles City MT 59301 — 800-843-3820 — 406-233-2600 — 373-3

Holyoke Community College
303 Homestead Ave ....Holyoke MA 01040 — 800-325-3252 — 413-538-7000 — 162

Holz Rubber Company Inc
1129 S Sacramento St ....Lodi CA 95240 — 800-285-1600 — 209-368-7171 — 673

Homark Company Inc
100 Third St PO Box 309 ....Red Lake Falls MN 56750 — 800-382-1154 — 218-253-2777 — 503

Homasote Co
932 Lower Ferry Rd
PO Box 7240. ....West Trenton NJ 08628 — 800-257-9491 — 609-883-3300 — 814
OTC: HMTC

Homax Products Inc
1835 Barkley Blvd Ste 101 ....Bellingham WA 98226 — 888-890-9029 — 360-733-9029

Home Automated Living Inc
14401 Sweitzer Ln Ste 600.................Laurel MD 20707 — 800-935-5313 — 301-498-7000 — 174

Home Bound Healthcare Inc
14216 McCarthy Rd ....Lemont IL 60439 — 800-444-7028 — 708-798-0800 — 362

Home Care Industries Inc ALFCO Div
1 Lisbon St ....Clifton NJ 07013 — 800-325-1908* — 973-365-1600 — 18
*Cust Svc

Home Care Network Inc
190A E Spring Valley Rd ....Centerville OH 45458 — 800-417-0291 — 937-435-1142 — 362

Home City Financial Corp
2454 N Limestone St ....Springfield OH 45503 — 866-421-2331 — 937-390-0470 — 359-2
OTC: HCFL

Home Depot Inc
2455 Paces Ferry Rd NW ....Atlanta GA 30339 — 800-553-3199* — 770-433-8211 — 363
NYSE: HD ■ *Cust Svc

Home Design Outlet Ctr
400 County Ave ....Secaucus NJ 07094 — 800-701-0388 — 360

Home Dynamix
100 Porete Ave ....North Arlington NJ 07031 — 800-726-9290 — 131

Home Entertainment Distribution Inc
120 Shawmut Rd ....Canton MA 02021 — 888-567-7557

Home Essentials & Beyond Inc
200 Theodore Conrad Dr ....Jersey City NJ 07305 — 800-417-6218 — 732-590-3600 — 360

Home Federal Bank
1602 Cumberland Ave ....Middlesboro KY 40965 — 800-354-0182 — 606-248-1095 — 359-2
OTC: HFBA

Home Furnishings Independents Assn (HFIA)
500 Giuseppe Ct Ste 6 ....Roseville CA 95678 — 800-422-3778 — 49-4

Home Health & Hospice Care
7 Executive Park Dr ....Merrimack NH 03054 — 800-887-5973 — 603-882-2941 — 370

Home Healthcare, Hospice & Community Services Inc
312 Marlboro St ....Keene NH 03431 — 800-541-4145 — 603-352-2253 — 362

Home Hospice of Grayson County
505 W Ctr St ....Sherman TX 75090 — 888-233-7455 — 903-868-9315 — 370

Home Instead Inc
13323 California St ....Omaha NE 68154 — 888-484-5759 — 402-498-4466 — 362

Home Market Foods Inc
140 Morgan Dr ....Norwood MA 02062 — 800-367-8325 — 781-948-1500 — 296-36

Home News Enterprises
333 Second St ....Columbus IN 47201 — 800-876-7811 — 633-8

Home Paramount Pest Control Cos Inc
PO Box 850 ....Forest Hill MD 21050 — 888-888-4663 — 410-510-0700 — 573

Home Products International Inc
4501 W 47th St ....Chicago IL 60632 — 800-457-9881 — 773-890-8923 — 603

Home Savings & Loan Company of Youngstown
275 W Federal St ....Youngstown OH 44503 — 888-822-4751 — 330-742-0500 — 70

Home Security of America Inc
310 N Midvale Blvd ....Madison WI 53705 — 800-367-1448 — 366

Home Staff Health Services
40 Millbrook St ....Worcester MA 01606 — 800-779-3312

Home Staff Inc
5509 N Cumberland Ave Ste 514 ....Chicago IL 60656 — 888-806-6924 — 773-467-6002 — 362

HomeAdvisor
14023 Denver W Pkwy Ste 200..........Golden CO 80401 — 800-474-1596 — 303-963-7200 — 396

HomeCare & Hospice
1225 W State St ....Olean NY 14760 — 800-339-7011 — 716-372-5735 — 370

HomeCare of East Alabama Medical Ctr
665 Opelika Rd ....Auburn AL 36830 — 866-542-4768 — 334-826-3131 — 370

Homecare of Mid Missouri Inc
102 W Reed St ....Moberly MO 65270 — 800-246-6400 — 660-263-1517 — 362

HomeGaincom Inc
6001 Shellmound St Ste 550 ....Emeryville CA 94608 — 888-542-0800 — 510-655-0800 — 648

Homeland Security Information Ctr
National Technical Information Service
5301 Shawnee Rd.................Alexandria VA 22312 — 800-553-6847 — 703-605-6000

HomEquity Bank
1881 Yonge St Ste 300.................Toronto ON M4S3C4 — 866-522-2447 — 416-925-4757 — 69

Homer Electric Assn Inc
3977 Lake St ....Homer AK 99603 — 800-478-8551 — 907-235-8551 — 245

Homer Laughlin China Co
672 Fiesta Dr ....Newell WV 26050 — 800-452-4462 — 304-387-1300 — 726

Homer Optical Company Inc
2401 Linden Ln ....Silver Spring MD 20910 — 800-627-2710 — 301-585-9060 — 538

Homer Public Library
500 Hazel Ave ....Homer AK 99603 — 800-478-4441 — 907-235-3180 — 433-3

Homes & Land Magazine Affiliates LLC
1830 E Park Ave ....Tallahassee FL 32301 — 800-277-7800 — 850-701-2300 — 633-9

Homes by Keystone Inc
13338 Midvale Rd PO Box 69. ....Waynesboro PA 17268 — 800-890-7926 — 106

HomeServices of America Inc
333 S Seventh St 27th Fl ....Minneapolis MN 55402 — 888-485-0018 — 648

Homestead Mills
221 N River St PO Box 1115. ....Cook MN 55723 — 800-652-5233 — 218-666-5233 — 296-4

Homestead Resort
700 N Homestead Dr ....Midway UT 84049 — 800-327-7220 — 435-654-1102 — 665

Homestead Technologies Inc
180 Jefferson Dr ....Menlo Park CA 94025 — 800-797-2958 — 650-944-3100 — 803

HomeSteps
500 Plano Pkwy ....Carrollton TX 75010 — 800-972-7555 — 507

HomeStreet Bank
601 Union St Ste 2000.................Seattle WA 98101 — 800-654-1075 — 206-623-3050 — 70

HomeTeam Inspection Service Inc
575 Chamber Dr ....Milford OH 45150 — 800-598-5297 — 364

Hometown Quotes LLC
304 Inverness Pkwy S Ste 395 ....Englewood CO 80112 — 800-820-2981

Hometrust Bank, The
PO Box 10 ....Asheville NC 28802 — 800-627-1632 — 828-259-3939 — 70

HomeVestors of America Inc
6500 Greenville Ave Ste 400. ....Dallas TX 75206 — 866-200-6475 — 972-761-0046 — 310

Homewatch CareGivers
7100 E Belleview Ave
Ste 101 ....Greenwood Village CO 80111 — 800-777-9770 — 362

Homewood at Williamsport
16505 Virginia Ave ....Williamsport MD 21795 — 877-849-9244 — 301-582-1750 — 668

HON Co
101 Oak St ....Muscatine IA 52761 — 800-553-8230 — 563-272-7100 — 319-1

Honda of Santa Monica
1720 Santa Monica Blvd ....Santa Monica CA 90404 — 800-269-2031 — 57

Honda World
10645 Studebaker Rd ....Downey CA 90241 — 888-458-9404 — 562-929-7000 — 57

Hondros College of Nursing
4140 Executive Pkwy ....Westerville OH 43081 — 855-906-8773 — 166

Honegger Ringger & Company Inc
1905 N Main St ....Bluffton IN 46714 — 888-853-5906 — 260-824-4107 — 2

Honey Acres
1557 Hwy 67 N ....Ashippun WI 53003 — 800-558-7745 — 296-24

Honey Baked Ham Company LLC, The
1081 E Long Lake Rd ....Troy MI 48098 — 800-367-7720 — 248-689-4890

Honey Bee Manufacturing Ltd
PO Box 120 ....Frontier SK S0N0W0 — 855-330-2019 — 306-296-2297

Honey Creek State Park
901 State Pk Rd ....Grove OK 74344 — 800-622-6317 — 918-786-9447 — 561

Honey Dew Assoc Inc
2 Taunton St ....Plainville MA 02762 — 800-946-6393 — 508-699-3900 — 68

Honeys Place Inc
640 Glenoaks Blvd ....San Fernando CA 91340 — 800-910-3246 — 231

Honeytree Inc
8570 M 50 ....Onsted MI 49265 — 800-968-1889 — 517-467-2482 — 296-24

Honeyville Grain Inc
11600 Dayton Dr ....Rancho Cucamonga CA 91730 — 888-810-3212 — 909-980-9500 — 296-4

Honeyville Metal Inc
4200 S 900 West ....Topeka IN 46571 — 800-593-8377 — 18

Honeywell Aerospace
1944 E Sky Harbor Cir ....Phoenix AZ 85034 — 800-601-3099 — 22

Honeywell Electronic Materials
1349 Moffett Pk Dr ....Sunnyvale CA 94089 — 877-841-2840 — 253

Honeywell International Inc
115 Tabor Rd ....Morris Plains NJ 07950 — 877-841-2840 — 480-353-3020

Honeywell International Inc
101 Columbia Rd PO Box 2245 ......Morristown NJ 07962 — 877-841-2840 — 480-353-3020 — 730
NYSE: HON

Honeywell Safety Products
2000 Plainfield Pk ....Cranston RI 02921 — 800-430-4110* — 401-943-4400 — 572
*Cust Svc

Honeywell Security Group
2 Corporate Ctr Dr Ste 100.................Melville NY 11747 — 800-467-5875 — 516-577-2000 — 688

Honeywell Sensing & Control
11 W Spring St ....Freeport IL 61032 — 800-537-6945* — 815-235-5500 — 203
*Cust Svc

Honeywood Winery
1350 Hines St SE ....Salem OR 97302 — 800-726-4101 — 503-362-4111 — 50-7

Honkamp Krueger & Company PC
2345 JFK Rd PO Box 699 ....Dubuque IA 52004 — 888-556-0123 — 563-556-0123 — 2

Name / Address	City	State	ZIP	Toll-Free	Phone	Class
Honolulu Advertiser 500 Ala Moana Blvd Ste 7-210	Honolulu	HI	96813	**800-801-5999**	808-529-4747	528-2
Honolulu Magazine 1000 Bishop St Ste 405	Honolulu	HI	96813	**800-788-4230**	808-534-7546	455-22
Honolulu Publishing Co Ltd 707 Richards St Ste PH3	Honolulu	HI	96813	**800-272-5245**	808-524-7400	633-9
Honor Foods 1801 N Fifth St	Philadelphia	PA	19122	**800-462-2890**	215-236-1700	297-8
HonorHealth John C Lincoln Medical Center 250 E Dunlap Ave	Phoenix	AZ	85020	**800-223-3131**	623-580-5800	373-3
Hoober Inc 3452 Old Philadelphia Pk PO Box 518	Intercourse	PA	17534	**800-446-6237**	717-768-8231	274
Hood College 401 Rosemont Ave	Frederick	MD	21701	**800-922-1599**	301-696-3400	166
Hood County Public Library 222 N Travis St	Granbury	TX	76048	**800-452-9292**	817-573-3569	433-3
Hood Packaging Corp 25 Woodgreen Pl	Madison	MS	39110	**800-321-8115**	601-853-7260	65
Hooker Furniture Corp 440 E Commonwealth Blvd *NASDAQ: HOFT* ■ *Cust Svc	Martinsville	VA	24112	**800-422-1511***	276-632-0459	319-2
Hooper Corp 2030 Pennsylvania Ave	Madison	WI	53704	**877-630-7554**	608-249-0451	189-10
Hooper Handling Inc 5590 Camp Rd	Hamburg	NY	14075	**800-649-5590**	716-649-5590	357
Hoosier Co 5421 W 86th St PO Box 681064	Indianapolis	IN	46268	**800-521-4184**	317-872-8125	286
Hoosier Park Racing & Casino 4500 Dan Patch Cir	Anderson	IN	46013	**800-526-7223**	765-642-7223	638
Hooters Casino Hotel 115 E Tropicana Ave	Las Vegas	NV	89109	**866-584-6687**	702-739-9000	133
Hoover & Strong Inc 10700 Trade Rd *Cust Svc	North Chesterfield	VA	23236	**800-759-9997***	804-794-3700	483
Hoover Construction Co 302 S Hoover Rd PO Box 1007	Virginia	MN	55792	**800-741-0970**	218-741-3280	188-4
Hoover Inc 1205 Bridgestone Pkwy	Lavergne	TN	37086	**800-944-9200**		
Hoover's Inc 5800 Airport Blvd	Austin	TX	78752	**800-486-8666**	512-374-4500	633-6
Hop-A-Jet 5525 NW 15th Ave Ste 150	Fort Lauderdale	FL	33309	**800-556-6633**	954-771-5779	13
Hope College 69 E Tenth St PO Box 9000 *Admissions	Holland	MI	49422	**800-968-7850***	616-395-7850	166
Hope College Van Wylen Library 53 Graves Pl	Holland	MI	49423	**800-968-7850**	616-395-7790	433-6
Hope Hospice 9470 HealthPark Cir	Fort Myers	FL	33908	**800-835-1673**	239-482-4673	370
Hope Hospice 611 N Walnut Ave	New Braunfels	TX	78130	**800-499-7501**	830-625-7500	370
Hope International University 2500 E Nutwood Ave	Fullerton	CA	92831	**866-722-4673**	714-879-3901	166
Hope Network 3075 Orchard Vista Dr SE	Grand Rapids	MI	49546	**800-695-7273**	616-301-8000	448
Hope Pharmaceuticals Inc 16416 N 92nd St Ste 125	Scottsdale	AZ	85260	**800-755-9595**	480-607-1970	578
HOPE Worldwide 4231 Balboa Ave Ste 330	San Diego	CA	92117	**866-551-7327**	610-254-8800	
Hopewell (Independent City) 300 N Main St	Hopewell	VA	23860	**800-552-7096**	804-541-2243	337
Hopkins Ctr for the Arts 6041 Wilson Hall	Hanover	NH	03755	**800-451-4067**	603-646-2422	568
Hopkins Manufacturing Corp 428 Peyton St	Emporia	KS	66801	**800-524-1458**	620-342-7320	60
Hopkins Printing Inc 2246 CityGate Dr	Columbus	OH	43219	**800-319-3352**	614-509-1080	623
Hopkins Sporting Goods Inc 5485 NW Beaver Dr	Johnston	IA	50131	**800-362-2937**	515-270-0132	707
Hopkins-Carter Company Inc 3300 NW 21st St	Miami	FL	33142	**800-595-9656**	305-635-7377	463
Hopkinsville Community College 720 N Dr	Hopkinsville	KY	42240	**866-534-2224**	270-886-3921	162
Hopkinsville-Christian County Chamber of Commerce 2800 Port Campbell Blvd	Hopkinsville	KY	42240	**800-842-9959**	270-885-9096	139
Horace Mann Educators Corp 1 Horace Mann Plz *NYSE: HMN*	Springfield	IL	62715	**800-999-1030**	217-789-2500	359-4
Horace Mann Life Insurance Co 1 Horace Mann Plz	Springfield	IL	62715	**800-999-1030**	217-789-2500	390-2
Horan Capital Management LLC 20 Wight Ave Ste 115	Hunt Valley	MD	21030	**800-592-7534**	410-494-4380	194
Horiba Instruments Inc 17671 Armstrong Ave	Irvine	CA	92614	**800-446-7422**	949-250-4811	418
Horizon Air Freight Inc 152-15 Rockaway Blvd	Jamaica	NY	11434	**800-221-6028**	718-528-3800	447
Horizon Books 243 E Front St	Traverse City	MI	49684	**800-587-2147**	231-946-7290	95
Horizon Convention Ctr 401 S High St PO Box 842	Muncie	IN	47305	**888-288-8860**		205
Horizon Credit Union 13224 E Mansfield Ste 300	Spokane Valley	WA	99216	**800-808-6402**		219
Horizon Freight System Inc 6600 Bessemer Ave	Cleveland	OH	44127	**800-480-6829**	216-341-7410	466
Horizon Services Co 250 Governor St	East Hartford	CT	06108	**800-949-5323**		104
Horizon Shipbuilding Inc 13980 Shell Belt Rd	Bayou La Batre	AL	36509	**800-777-2014**	251-824-1660	694
Horizon Software International LLC 2850 Premier Pkwy Ste 100	Duluth	GA	30097	**800-741-7100**	770-554-6353	
Horizon Termite & Pest Control Corp 45 Cross Ave	Midland Park	NJ	07432	**888-612-2847**	201-447-2530	573
Horizons Window Fashions Inc 1705 Waukegan Rd	Waukegan	IL	60085	**800-858-2352**		360

Name / Address	City	State	ZIP	Toll-Free	Phone	Class
Hormel Foods Corp 1 Hormel Pl *NYSE: HRL*	Austin	MN	55912	**800-523-4635**	507-437-5838	296-26
Hornady Manufacturing Co 3625 W Old Potash Hwy	Grand Island	NE	68803	**800-338-3220**	308-382-1390	284
Hornbeck Offshore Services Inc 103 Northpark Blvd Ste 300 *NYSE: HOS*	Covington	LA	70433	**800-642-9816**	985-727-2000	463
Horner Millwork Corp 1255 Grand Army Hwy	Somerset	MA	02726	**800-543-5403**	508-679-6479	497
Hornerxpress Inc 5755 Powerline Rd	Fort Lauderdale	FL	33309	**800-432-6966**	954-772-6966	724
Hornor Townsend & Kent Inc (HTK) 600 Dresher Rd Ste C1C	Horsham	PA	19044	**800-289-9999**		401
Hornung's Golf Products Inc 815 Morris St	Fond du Lac	WI	54935	**800-323-3569**	920-922-2640	328
Horowitt, Darryl J - Coleman & Horowitt LLP 499 W Shaw Ave Ste 116	Fresno	CA	93704	**800-891-8362**	559-248-4820	427
Horry County Solid Waste Authority Inc 1886 Hwy 90	Conway	SC	29526	**800-768-7348**	843-347-1651	656
Horry Electric Cooperative Inc 2774 Cultra Rd	Conway	SC	29526	**800-877-8339**	843-369-2211	245
Horry Telephone Co-op Inc (HTC) 3480 Hwy 701 N PO Box 1820	Conway	SC	29528	**800-824-6779**	843-365-2151	731
Horry-Georgetown Technical College 2050 E Hwy 501	Conway	SC	29526	**855-544-4482**	843-347-3186	795
Grand Strand Campus 743 Hemlock Ave	Myrtle Beach	SC	29577	**855-544-4482**	843-477-0808	795
Horse Illustrated 4101 Tates Creek Centre Dr Ste 150-324	Lexington	KY	40517	**844-330-6373**		455-14
Horsehead Corp 4955 Steubenville Pk Ste 405	Pittsburgh	PA	15205	**800-648-8897**	724-774-1020	143
HorseLoverZ com 254 N Cedar St	Hazleton	PA	18201	**877-804-7810**	570-399-3469	157-5
Horseshoe Council Bluffs 2701 23rd Ave	Council Bluffs	IA	51501	**800-895-0711**	712-323-2500	133
Horseshoe Valley Resort Ltd 1101 Horseshoe Valley Rd - Comp 10 RR 1	Barrie	ON	L4M4Y8	**800-461-5627**	705-835-2790	377
Horsham Clinic 722 E Butler Pk	Ambler	PA	19002	**800-237-4447**	215-643-7800	373-5
Horspool & Romine Manufacturing Inc 5850 Marshall St	Oakland	CA	94608	**800-446-2263**		617
Hortica Insurance 1 Horticultural Ln PO Box 428	Edwardsville	IL	62025	**800-851-7740**	618-656-4240	390-4
Horton Emergency Vehicles 3800 McDowell Rd	Grove City	OH	43123	**800-282-5113**	614-539-8181	59
Horton Grand Hotel 311 Island Ave	San Diego	CA	92101	**800-542-1886**	619-544-1886	378
Horton Group, The 10320 Orland Pkwy	Orland Park	IL	60467	**800-383-8283**	708-845-3000	389
Horton Inc 2565 Walnut St	Saint Paul	MN	55113	**800-621-1320**	651-361-6400	616
Horwith Trucks Inc PO Box 7	NorthHampton	PA	18067	**800-220-8807**	610-261-2220	57
Hosanna 2421 Aztec Rd NE	Albuquerque	NM	87107	**800-545-6552**	505-881-3321	95
Hosokawa Polymer Systems 63 Fuller Way	Berlin	CT	06037	**800-233-6112**	860-828-0541	385
Hospice & Palliative Care Center of Alamance-Caswell 914 Chapel Hill Rd	Burlington	NC	27215	**800-588-8879**	336-532-0100	370
Hospice & Palliative Care of Cape Cod Inc 765 Attucks Ln	Hyannis	MA	02601	**800-642-2423**	508-957-0200	370
Hospice & Palliative Care of Western Colorado 2754 Compass Dr Ste 377	Grand Junction	CO	81506	**866-310-8900**	970-241-2212	370
Hospice & Palliative CareCenter 101 Hospice Ln	Winston-Salem	NC	27103	**888-876-3663**	336-768-3972	370
Hospice Alliance 10220 Prairie Ridge Blvd	Pleasant Prairie	WI	53158	**800-830-8344**	262-652-4400	370
Hospice at Charlotte 1420 E Seventh St	Charlotte	NC	28204	**800-835-5306**	704-375-0100	370
Hospice at Home 4025 Health Pk Ln	Saint Joseph	MI	49085	**800-717-3811**	269-429-7100	370
Hospice Austin 4107 Spicewood Springs Rd Ste 100	Austin	TX	78759	**800-445-3261**	512-342-4700	370
Hospice Brazos Valley 502 W 26th St	Bryan	TX	77803	**800-824-2326**	979-821-2266	370
Hospice Care Inc 4277 Middle Settlement Rd	New Hartford	NY	13413	**800-317-5661**	315-735-6484	370
Hospice Care Network 99 Sunnyside Blvd	Woodbury	NY	11797	**800-405-6731**	516-832-7100	370
Hospice Community Care PO Box 993	Rock Hill	SC	29731	**800-895-2273**	803-329-1500	370
Hospice Family Care 550 E Main St	Batavia	NY	14020	**800-719-7129**	585-343-7596	370
Hospice Foundation of America (HFA) 1707 L St NW Ste 220	Washington	DC	20036	**800-854-3402**	202-457-5811	49-8
Hospice Ministries 450 Towne Center Blvd	Ridgeland	MS	39157	**800-273-7724**	601-898-1053	370
Hospice of Boulder County 2594 Trlridge Dr E	Lafayette	CO	80026	**877-986-4766**	303-449-7740	370
Hospice of Central Ohio 2269 Cherry Valley Rd	Newark	OH	43055	**800-804-2505**	740-788-1400	370
Hospice of Central Pennsylvania 1320 Linglestown Rd	Harrisburg	PA	17110	**866-779-7374**	717-732-1000	370
Hospice of Chattanooga 4411 Oakwood Dr	Chattanooga	TN	37416	**800-267-6828**	423-892-4289	370
Hospice of Cullman County 1912 Alabama Hwy 157	Cullman	AL	35058	**877-271-4176**	256-737-2502	370
Hospice of Dayton 324 Wilmington Ave	Dayton	OH	45420	**800-653-4490**	937-256-4490	370
Hospice of East Texas 4111 University Blvd	Tyler	TX	75701	**800-777-9860**	903-266-3400	370
Hospice of Holland Inc 270 Hoover Blvd	Holland	MI	49423	**800-255-3522**	616-396-2972	370

Alphabetical Section

	Toll-Free	Phone	Class
Hospice of Huntington			
1101 Sixth Ave . . . . .Huntington WV 25701	800-788-5480	304-529-4217	370
Hospice of Kankakee Valley Inc			
482 Main St NW .Bourbonnais IL 60914	855-871-4695	815-939-4141	370
Hospice of Lake Cumberland			
100 Pkwy Dr . . . . .Somerset KY 42503	800-937-9596	606-679-4389	370
Hospice of Lancaster County			
685 Good Dr PO Box 4125 . . . . .Lancaster PA 17604	888-236-9563	717-295-3900	370
Hospice of Lincolnland			
1000 Health Center Dr . . . . .Mattoon IL 61938	800-454-4055	217-258-2525	370
Hospice of Marion County			
3231 SW 34th Ave . . . . .Ocala FL 34474	888-482-5018	352-873-7400	370
Hospice of Marshall County			
408 Martling Rd . . . . .Albertville AL 35951	888-334-9336	256-891-7724	370
Hospice of Medina County			
5075 Windfall Rd . . . . .Medina OH 44256	800-700-4771	330-722-4771	370
Hospice of Michigan			
400 Mack Ave . . . . .Detroit MI 48201	888-247-5701	313-578-6259	370
Hospice of NE Georgia Medical Ctr			
2150 Limestone Pkwy Ste 222 . . . .Gainesville GA 30501	888-572-3900	770-533-8888	370
Hospice of North Central Ohio			
1050 Dauch Dr . . . . .Ashland OH 44805	800-952-2207	419-281-7107	370
Hospice of Northeast Florida			
4266 Sunbeam Rd . . . . .Jacksonville FL 32257	866-253-6681	904-268-5200	370
Hospice of Northern Colorado (HNC)			
2726 W 11th St Rd .Greeley CO 80634	800-564-5563	970-352-8487	370
Hospice of Northwest Ohio			
30000 E River Rd . . . . .Perrysburg OH 43551	866-661-4001	419-661-4001	370
Hospice of Orange & Sullivan Counties			
800 Stony Brook Ct . . . . .Newburgh NY 12550	800-924-0157	845-561-6111	370
Hospice of Redlands Community Hospital			
350 Terracina Blvd . . . . .Redlands CA 92373	888-397-4999	909-335-5643	370
Hospice of Saint Francis Inc			
1250 Grumman Pl Ste B. . . . . .Titusville FL 32780	866-269-4240	321-269-4240	370
Hospice of San Angelo			
36 E Twohig St PO Box 471 . . . . .San Angelo TX 76903	800-499-6524	325-658-6524	370
Hospice of Siouxland			
4300 Hamilton Blvd . . . . .Sioux City IA 51104	800-383-4545	712-233-4144	370
Hospice of South Texas			
605 E Locust Ave . . . . .Victoria TX 77901	800-874-6908	361-572-4300	370
Hospice of Southeastern Connecticut Inc			
227 Dunham St . . . . .Norwich CT 06360	877-654-4035	860-848-5699	370
Hospice of Southern Illinois			
305 S Illinois St . . . . .Belleville IL 62220	800-233-1708	618-235-1703	370
Hospice of Southwest Georgia			
114 A Mimosa Dr . . . . .Thomasville GA 31792	800-290-6567	229-584-5500	370
Hospice of Stanly County			
960 N First St . . . . .Albemarle NC 28001	800-230-4236	704-983-4216	370
Hospice of the Carolina Foothills			
374 Hudlow Rd PO Box 336 . . . . .Forest City NC 28043	800-218-2273	828-245-0095	370
Hospice of the Chesapeake			
John & Cathy Belcher Campus 90 Ritchie Hwy			
. . . . .Pasadena MD 21122	877-462-1101*	410-987-2003	370
*General			
Hospice of the Cleveland Clinic			
6801 Brecksville Rd . . . . .Independence OH 44131	866-223-8100	800-223-2273	370
Hospice of the North Shore			
75 Sylvan St Ste B-102. . . . . .Danvers MA 01923	888-283-1722	978-774-7566	370
Hospice of the Panhandle			
330 Hospice Ln . . . . .Kearneysville WV 25430	800-345-6538	304-264-0406	370
Hospice of the Piedmont			
675 Peter Jefferson Pkwy			
Ste 300. .Charlottesville VA 22911	800-975-5501	434-817-6900	370
Hospice of the Red River Valley			
1701 38th ST S Ste 101 . . . . .Fargo ND 58103	800-237-4629		370
Hospice of the Valley			
240 Johnston St SE PO Box 2745 . . . .Decatur AL 35602	877-260-3657	256-350-5585	370
Hospice of the Western Reserve			
300 E 185th St . . . . .Cleveland OH 44119	800-707-8922	216-383-2222	370
Hospice of Visiting Nurse Service			
3358 Ridgewood Rd . . . . .Akron OH 44333	800-335-1455	330-665-1455	370
Hospice of Wake County Inc			
250 Hospice Cir . . . . .Raleigh NC 27607	888-900-3959	919-828-0890	370
Hospice of West Alabama			
3851 Loop Rd . . . . .Tuscaloosa AL 35404	877-362-7522	205-523-0101	370
Hospice of Westchester			
1025 Westchester Ave			
Ste 200. .White Plains NY 10604	800-860-9808	914-682-1484	370
Hospice of Wichita Falls			
4909 Johnson Rd . . . . .Wichita Falls TX 76310	800-378-2822	940-691-0982	370
HospiceCare			
5395 E Cheryl Pkwy . . . . .Madison WI 53711	800-553-4289	608-276-4660	370
Hospital Employee Labor Pool			
765 The City Dr S Ste 405 . . . . .Orange CA 92868	888-435-7689		
Hospital Marketing Services Company Inc			
162 Great Hill Rd . . . . .Naugatuck CT 06770	800-786-5094	203-723-1466	474
Hospital of Saint Raphael			
1450 Chapel St .New Haven CT 06511	888-700-6543	203-789-3000	373-3
Hospitality Financial & Technology Professionals (HFTP)			
11709 Boulder Ln Ste 110 . . . . .Austin TX 78726	800-646-4387	512-249-5333	49-1
Hospitality International Inc			
1726 Montreal Cir . . . . .Tucker GA 30084	800-251-1962		378
Master Hosts Inns & Resorts			
1726 Montreal Cir Ste 110 . . . . .Tucker GA 30084	800-892-8405	770-270-1180	378
Passport Inn			
1726 Montreal Cir Ste 110. . . . . .Tucker GA 30084	800-892-8405	770-270-1180	378
Red Carpet Inn			
1726 Montreal Cir . . . . .Tucker GA 30084	800-247-4677		378
Scottish Inns			
1726 Montreal Cir . . . . .Tucker GA 30084	800-251-1962		378
Hospitality Suites Resort			
409 N Scottsdale Rd . . . . .Scottsdale AZ 85257	800-445-5115	480-949-5115	378
Host Department LLC			
45277 Fremont Blvd Ste 11 . . . . .Fremont CA 94538	866-887-4678		386
Host Depot Inc			
4613 N University Dr			
Ste 227. . . . . .Coral Springs FL 33067	888-340-3527	954-340-3527	803
Hostcentric Inc			
70 BlanchaRd Rd 3rd Fl . . . . .Burlington MA 01803	866-897-5418*	602-716-5396	803
*Tech Supp			
Hostedware Corp			
16 Technology Dr Ste 116 . . . . .Irvine CA 92618	800-211-6967	949-585-1500	803
Hostelling International USA - American Youth Hostels (HI-AYH)			
8401 Colesville Rd			
Ste 600 . . . . .Silver Spring MD 20910	888-449-8727	240-650-2100	48-23
Hostway Corp			
100 N Riverside Plz 8th Fl . . . . .Chicago IL 60606	866-467-8929	312-238-0125	803
Hot 96 FM			
1162 Mt Auburn Rd . . . . .Evansville IN 47720	888-685-1961	812-491-9468	641-37
Hot Dog on a Stick			
5942 Priestly Dr . . . . .Carlsbad CA 92008	877-639-2361	877-922-9215	666
Hot Rod Magazine			
6420 Wilshire Blvd . . . . .Los Angeles CA 90048	800-800-4681*	323-782-2000	455-3
*Orders			
Hot Rooms			
444 N Michigan Ave Ste 1200 . . . . .Chicago IL 60611	800-468-3500	773-468-7666	375
Hot Shot Delivery Inc			
335 Garden Oaks Blvd . . . . .Houston TX 77018	866-261-3184	713-869-5525	542
Hot Springs Convention & Visitors Bureau			
134 Convention Blvd . . . . .Hot Springs AR 71901	800-543-2284	501-321-2277	206
Hot Springs Convention Ctr (HSCVB)			
134 Convention Blvd			
PO Box 6000. . . . . .Hot Springs AR 71902	800-625-7576	501-321-2277	205
Hot Springs Lodge & Pool			
415 E Sixth St . . . . .Glenwood Springs CO 81601	800-537-7946	970-945-6571	665
Hot Springs Memorial Field			
525 Airport Rd . . . . .Hot Springs AR 71913	800-992-7433	501-321-6750	27
Hot Springs National Park			
101 Reserve St . . . . .Hot Springs AR 71901	800-582-2244	501-620-6715	560
Hot Stuff Pizza			
2930 W Maple St . . . . .Sioux Falls SD 57107	800-336-1320	605-336-6961	68
Hot Water Products			
7500 N 81st St . . . . .Milwaukee WI 53223	877-377-0011	414-434-1371	
Hotan Corp			
751 N Canyons Pkwy . . . . .Livermore CA 94551	800-656-1888	925-290-1000	246
Hotcards Com Inc			
2400 Superior Ave . . . . .Cleveland OH 44114	800-787-4831	216-241-4040	343
Hotel & Restaurant Supply Inc			
5020 Arundel Rd PO Box 6. . . . . .Meridian MS 39302	800-782-6651	601-482-7127	300
Hotel & Suites Normandin			
4700 Pierre-Bertrand Blvd . . . . .Quebec QC G2J1A4	800-463-6721	418-622-1611	378
Hotel 43 981 Grove St . . . . .Boise ID 83702	800-243-4622	208-342-4622	378
Hotel 71			
71 St Pierre St . . . . .Quebec QC G1K4A4	888-692-1171	418-692-1171	378
Hotel Allegro Chicago			
171 W Randolph St .Chicago IL 60601	800-643-1500	312-236-0123	378
Hotel Ambassadeur			
3401 Blvd Ste-Anne . . . . .Quebec QC G1E3L4	800-363-4619		378
Hotel Andra			
2000 Fourth Ave . . . . .Seattle WA 98121	877-448-8600	206-448-8600	378
Hotel at Auburn University & Dixon Conference Ctr, The			
241 S College St . . . . .Auburn AL 36830	800-228-2876	334-821-8200	376
Hotel at Old Town Wichita			
830 E First St . . . . .Wichita KS 67202	877-265-3869	316-267-4800	378
Hotel Beacon			
2130 Broadway .New York NY 10023	800-572-4969	212-787-1100	378
Hotel Blue			
717 Central Ave NW . . . . .Albuquerque NM 87102	877-878-4868	505-924-2400	377
Hotel Boulderado			
2115 13th St . . . . .Boulder CO 80302	800-433-4344	303-442-4344	378
Hotel Captain Cook			
939 W Fifth Ave .Anchorage AK 99501	800-843-1950	907-276-6000	378
Hotel Chateau Bellevue			
16 Rue de la Porte . . . . .Quebec QC G1R4M9	877-849-1877	418-692-2573	378
Hotel Chateau Laurier			
1220 Pl George-V Ouest . . . . .Quebec QC G1R5B8	877-522-8108	418-522-8108	378
Hotel Cheribourg			
2603 chemin du Parc . . . . .Orford QC J1X8C8	877-845-5344	819-843-3308	665
Hotel Classique			
2815 Laurier Blvd . . . . .Quebec QC G1V4H3	800-463-1885		378
Hotel Colorado			
526 Pine St . . . . .Glenwood Springs CO 81601	800-544-3998	970-945-6511	378
Hotel Congress			
311 E Congress St . . . . .Tucson AZ 85701	800-722-8848	520-622-8848	378
Hotel Contessa			
306 W Market St . . . . .San Antonio TX 78205	866-435-0900	210-229-9222	378
Hotel de Anza			
233 W Santa Clara St . . . . .San Jose CA 95113	800-843-3700	408-286-1000	378
Hotel Deca			
4507 Brooklyn Ave NE . . . . .Seattle WA 98105	800-899-0251	206-634-2000	378
Hotel Del Coronado			
1500 Orange Ave .Coronado CA 92118	800-468-3533	619-435-6611	665
Hotel Del Sol			
3100 Webster St . . . . .San Francisco CA 94123	877-433-5765	415-921-5520	378
Hotel Derek			
2525 W Loop S . . . . .Houston TX 77027	866-292-4100	713-961-3000	378
Hotel Dieu Hospital			
166 Brock St . . . . .Kingston ON K7L5G2	855-544-3400	613-544-3310	373-2
Hotel Drisco			
2901 Pacific Ave . . . . .San Francisco CA 94115	800-634-7277	415-346-2880	378
Hotel du Pont			
11th & Market Sts . . . . .Wilmington DE 19801	800-441-9019	302-594-3100	378
Hotel Edison			
228 W 47th St . . . . .New York NY 10036	800-637-7070	212-840-5000	378
Hotel Encanto de Las Cruces			
705 S Telshor Blvd . . . . .Las Cruces NM 88011	866-383-0443	575-522-4300	378
Hotel Fusion			
140 Ellis St . . . . .San Francisco CA 94102	866-753-4244	415-568-2525	132
Hotel Galvez - A Wyndham Historic Hotel			
2024 Seawall Blvd . . . . .Galveston TX 77550	800-996-3426	409-765-7721	378
Hotel George			
15 E St NW . . . . .Washington DC 20001	800-576-8331*	202-347-4200	378
*General			
Hotel Grand Pacific			
463 Belleville St .Victoria BC V8V1X3	800-663-7550	250-386-0450	378

Alphabetical Section

Name / Address	Toll-Free	Phone	Class
Hotel Granduca 1080 Uptown Pk Blvd ....Houston TX 77056	888-472-6382	713-418-1000	378
Hotel Griffon 155 Steuart St ....San Francisco CA 94105	800-321-2201	415-495-2100	378
Hotel Hershey, The 100 Hotel Rd ....Hershey PA 17033	844-330-1711	717-533-2171	665
Hotel Jerome 330 E Main St ....Aspen CO 81611	855-331-7213		378
Hotel La Rose 308 Wilson St ....Santa Rosa CA 95401	800-527-6738	707-579-3200	378
Hotel Le Bleu 370 Fourth Ave ....Brooklyn NY 11215	866-427-6073	718-625-1500	378
Hotel Le Cantlie Suites 1110 Sherbrooke St W ....Montreal QC H3A1G9	800-567-1110	514-842-2000	378
Hotel Le Capitole 972 Rue St-Jean ....Quebec QC G1R1R5	800-261-9903	418-694-4444	378
Hotel Le Clos Saint-Louis 69 St Louis St ....Quebec QC G1R3Z2	800-461-1311	418-694-1311	378
Hotel Le Marais 717 Conti St ....New Orleans LA 70130	800-935-8740	504-525-2300	378
Hotel le Priori 15 Sault-au-Matelot St ....Quebec QC G1K3Y7	800-351-3992	418-692-3992	378
Hotel Le Soleil 567 Hornby St ....Vancouver BC V6C2E8	877-632-3030	604-632-3000	378
Hotel Le St-James 355 St Jacques St ....Montreal QC H2Y1N9	866-841-3111	514-841-3111	378
Hotel Lombardy 2019 Pennsylvania Ave NW ....Washington DC 20006	800-424-5486	202-828-2600	378
Hotel Lord-Berri 1199 Berri St ....Montreal QC H2L4C6	800-363-0363	514-845-9236	378
Hotel Lucia 400 SW Broadway ....Portland OR 97205	877-225-1717	503-225-1717	378
Hotel Manoir Victoria 44 Cote du Palais ....Quebec QC G1R4H8	800-463-6283	418-692-1030	378
Hotel Marlowe Cambridge 25 Edwind H Land Blvd ....Cambridge MA 02141	800-825-7140	617-868-8000	378
Hotel Max 620 Stewart St ....Seattle WA 98101	866-833-6299	206-728-6299	378
Hotel Mead 451 E Grand Ave ....Wisconsin Rapids WI 54494	800-843-6323		378
Hotel Mela 120 W 44th St ....New York NY 10036	877-452-6352	212-710-7000	378
Hotel Metro 411 E Mason St ....Milwaukee WI 53202	877-638-7620	414-272-1937	378
Hotel Monaco Chicago 225 N Wabash Ave ....Chicago IL 60601	866-610-0081	312-960-8500	378
Hotel Monaco Denver 1717 Champa St ....Denver CO 80202	800-990-1303	303-296-1717	378
Hotel Monaco Portland 506 SW Washington at Fifth Ave ....Portland OR 97204	866-861-9514	503-222-0001	378
Hotel Monaco Salt Lake City 15 West 200 South ....Salt Lake City UT 84101 *Resv	800-805-1801*	801-595-0000	378
Hotel Monaco Seattle 1101 Fourth Ave ....Seattle WA 98101	800-715-6513	206-621-1770	378
Hotel Monte Vista 100 N San Francisco St ....Flagstaff AZ 86001	800-545-3068	928-779-6971	378
Hotel Monteleone 214 Royal St ....New Orleans LA 70130	866-338-4684	504-523-3341	378
Hotel Mortagne 1228 Rue Nobel ....Boucherville QC J4B5H1	877-655-9966	450-655-9966	703
Hotel Nikko San Francisco 222 Mason St ....San Francisco CA 94102	866-636-4556	415-394-1111	378
Hotel Northampton 36 King St ....NorthHampton MA 01060	800-547-3529	413-584-3100	378
Hotel Oceana Santa Barbara 202 W Cabrillo Blvd ....Santa Barbara CA 93101	800-965-9776	805-965-4577	378
Hotel Omni Mont-Royal 1050 Sherbrooke St W ....Montreal QC H3A2R6	800-843-6664	514-284-1110	378
Hotel Orrington 1710 Orrington Ave ....Evanston IL 60201	888-677-4648	847-866-8700	378
Hotel Phillips 106 W 12th St ....Kansas City MO 64105	877-704-5341	816-221-7000	378
Hotel Plaza Athenee 37 E 64th St ....New York NY 10065	800-447-8800	212-734-9100	378
Hotel Plaza Quebec 3031 Laurier Blvd ....Qu‚bec QC G1V2M2	800-567-5276	418-658-2727	378
Hotel Plaza Real 125 Washington Ave ....Santa Fe NM 87501	855-752-9273	505-988-4900	378
Hotel Provincial 1024 Rue Chartres ....New Orleans LA 70116	800-535-7922	504-581-4995	378
Hotel Rex San Francisco 562 Sutter St ....San Francisco CA 94102 *Resv	800-433-4434*	415-433-4434	378
Hotel Roanoke & Conference Ctr 110 Shenandoah Ave ....Roanoke VA 24016	866-594-4722	540-985-5900	376
Hotel Rodney 142 Second St ....Lewes DE 19958	800-824-8754	302-645-6466	378
Hotel Roger Williams 131 Madison Ave ....New York NY 10016 *Resv	888-448-7788*	212-448-7000	378
Hotel Rouge 1315 16th St NW ....Washington DC 20036	800-738-1202	202-232-8000	378
Hotel Ruby Foo's 7655 Decarie Blvd ....Montreal QC H4P2H2	800-361-5419	514-731-7701	378
Hotel Saint Francis 210 Don Gaspar Ave ....Santa Fe NM 87501	800-529-5700	505-983-5700	378
Hotel Saint Regis Detroit 3071 W Grand Blvd ....Detroit MI 48202 *Resv	855-408-7738*	313-873-3000	378
Hotel San Carlos 202 N Central Ave ....Phoenix AZ 85004	866-253-4121	602-253-4121	378
Hotel Santa Barbara 533 State St ....Santa Barbara CA 93101	800-549-9869	805-957-9300	378
Hotel Santa Fe 1501 Paseo de Peralta ....Santa Fe NM 87501	855-825-9876	505-982-1200	378
Hotel Sepia 3135 Ch St-Louis ....Sainte-Foy QC G1W1R9	888-301-6837	418-653-4941	378
Hotel Shelley 844 Collins Ave ....Miami Beach FL 33139	877-762-3477	305-531-3341	378
Hotel Spero 405 Taylor St ....San Francisco CA 94102	866-575-9941	415-885-2500	378
Hotel Strasburg, The 213 S Holliday St ....Strasburg VA 22657	800-348-8327	540-465-9191	378
Hotel Teatro 1100 Fourteenth St ....Denver CO 80202	888-727-1200	303-228-1100	378
Hotel Triton 342 Grant Ave ....San Francisco CA 94108	800-800-1299	415-394-0500	378
Hotel Universel 2300 Ch St-Foy ....Quebec QC G1V1S5	800-463-4495		378
Hotel Valencia Riverwalk 150 E Houston St ....San Antonio TX 78205	855-596-3387	210-227-9700	703
Hotel Valley Ho 6850 E Main St ....Scottsdale AZ 85251	866-882-4484	480-376-2600	378
Hotel Viking 1 Bellevue Ave ....Newport RI 02840	800-556-7126	401-847-3300	378
Hotel Villagio 6481 Washington St ....Yountville CA 94599	800-351-1133	707-944-8877	703
Hotel Vintage Park 1100 Fifth Ave ....Seattle WA 98101	800-853-3914	206-624-8000	378
Hotel Wales 1295 Madison Ave ....New York NY 10128	866-925-3746	212-876-6000	378
Hotel ZaZa Dallas 2332 Leonard St ....Dallas TX 75201	800-597-8399	214-468-8399	378
Hotel ZaZa Houston 5701 Main St ....Houston TX 77005 *Resv	888-880-3244*	713-526-1991	378
Hotelroomscom Inc 108-18 Queens Blvd ....Forest Hills NY 11375	800-486-7000	718-730-6000	396
Hotels Etc Inc 910 Athens Hwy Ste K-214. ....Loganville GA 30052	877-967-7283		376
Hot-Line Freight System Inc PO Box 205 ....West Salem WI 54669	800-468-4686	608-486-1600	775
Hotwire Communications LLC 2100 W Cypress Creek Rd ....Fort Lauderdale FL 33309	800-355-5668		224
Hotwire Inc PO Box 26205 ....San Francisco CA 94126 *Cust Svc	866-468-9473*	866-381-3981	768
Houchen Bindery Ltd 340 First St ....Utica NE 68456	800-869-0420	402-534-2261	622
Houff Transfer Inc 46 Houff Rd ....Weyers Cave VA 24486	800-476-4683	540-234-9233	775
Hougen Manufacturing Inc 3001 Hougen Dr ....Swartz Creek MI 48473 *Orders	800-426-7818*	810-635-7111	491
Hough Petroleum Corp 340 Fourth St ....Ewing NJ 08638	800-400-7154	609-771-1022	576
Houghton Chemical Corp 52 Cambridge St ....Allston MA 02134	800-777-2466	617-254-1010	145
Houghton College 1 Willard Ave PO Box 128 ....Houghton NY 14744	800-777-2556	585-567-9200	166
Houghton International Inc 945 Madison Ave PO Box 930 ....Valley Forge PA 19482	888-459-9844	610-666-4000	3
Houghton Mifflin Harcourt 222 Berkeley St ....Boston MA 02116	800-225-5425		
Houma Area Convention & Visitors Bureau 114 Tourist Dr ....Gray LA 70359	800-688-2732	985-868-2732	206
Houma-Terrebonne Chamber of Commerce 6133 Louisiana 311 ....Houma LA 70360	800-649-7346	985-876-5600	139
Hound Ears Club 328 Shulls Mill Rd ....Boone NC 28607	800-243-8652	828-963-4321	665
House Foods America Corp 7351 Orangewood Ave ....Garden Grove CA 92841	877-333-7077	714-901-4350	296-20
House of Brick Technologies LLC 9300 Underwood Ave Ste 300 ....Omaha NE 68114	877-780-7038	402-445-0764	180
House of Flavors Inc 110 N William St ....Ludington MI 49431	800-930-7740	231-845-7369	379
House-Autry Mills Inc 7000 US Hwy 301 S ....Four Oaks NC 27524	800-849-0802		296-23
House-Hasson Hardware Inc 3125 Water Plant Rd ....Knoxville TN 37914	800-333-0520		350
HouseLens Inc 150 Fourth Ave N 20th Fl ....Nashville TN 37219	888-552-3851		5
HouseMaster 92 E Main St Ste 301 ....Somerville NJ 08876	800-526-3939	732-469-6565	364
Housh-the Home Energy Experts 18 S Main St ....Monroe OH 45050	800-793-6374	513-793-6374	606
Housing Assistance Council (HAC) 1025 Vermont Ave NW Ste 606. ....Washington DC 20005	866-234-2689	202-842-8600	48-5
Housing Authority Risk Retention Group Inc PO Box 189 ....Cheshire CT 06410	800-873-0242		389
Houston Arboretum & Nature Ctr 4501 Woodway Dr ....Houston TX 77024	866-510-7219	713-681-8433	50-5
Houston Astros Minute Maid Pk 501 Crawford St ....Houston TX 77002	800-771-2303	713-259-8000	709
Houston Ballet 601 Preston St ....Houston TX 77002	800-828-2787	713-523-6300	569-1
Houston Baptist University 7502 Fondren Rd ....Houston TX 77074 *Admissions	800-969-3210*	281-649-3000	166
Houston Chronicle 801 Texas Ave ....Houston TX 77002	800-735-3800	713-362-7171	528-2
Houston County 401 E Houston Ave PO Box 370 ....Crockett TX 75835	800-275-8777	936-544-3255	337
Houston Food Bank, The 535 Portwall St ....Houston TX 77029	866-384-4277	713-223-3700	324
Houston Grand Opera 510 Preston St ....Houston TX 77002	800-626-7372	713-546-0200	569-2
Houston Harris Div Patrol Inc 6420 Richmond Ave ....Houston TX 77057	877-975-9922	713-975-9922	689
Houston Independent School District 228 McCarty St ....Houston TX 77029	800-446-2821	713-556-6000	681

	Toll-Free	Phone	Class
Houston LifeStyle Magazine			
10707 Corporate Dr Ste 170 ....Stafford TX 77477	866-505-4456	281-240-2445	455-22
Houston Mfg Specialty Company Inc			
9909 Wallisville Rd ....Houston TX 77013	800-231-6030	713-675-7400	326
Houston Press			
1621 Milam St Ste 100...............Houston TX 77002	877-926-8300	713-280-2400	528-5
Houston Service Industries Inc			
7901 Hansen Rd ....Houston TX 77061	800-725-2291	713-947-1623	18
Houston Wire & Cable Co (HWC)			
10201 N Loop E ....Houston TX 77029	800-468-9473	713-609-2100	246
Houstonian Hotel Club & Spa			
111 N Post Oak Ln ....Houston TX 77024 *Resv	800-231-2759*	713-680-2626	665
Houston-Pasadena Apache Oil Company LP			
5136 Spencer Hwy ....Pasadena TX 77505	800-248-6388		577
Hover Networks Inc			
40 Gardenville Pkwy w ....Buffalo NY 14224	855-552-8900		
Hoveround Corp			
2151 Whitfield Industrial Way ....Sarasota FL 34243	800-542-7236		475
HOW Design Magazine			
4700 E Galbraith Rd ....Cincinnati OH 45236 *Cust Svc	800-333-1115*	513-531-2690	455-2
Howard Bros Florists			
8700 S Pennsylvania Ave ......Oklahoma City OK 73159	800-648-0524	405-632-4747	292
Howard College			
1001 Birdwell Ln ....Big Spring TX 79720	877-898-3833	432-264-5000	162
Howard County			
104 N Buckeye Rm 104B ....Kokomo IN 46901	800-913-6050	765-456-2204	337
Howard County General Hospital			
5755 Cedar Ln ....Columbia MD 21044	866-323-4615	410-740-7890	373-3
Howard County Tourism Council			
3430 Court House Dr ....Ellicott City MD 21043	866-313-6300	410-313-1900	206
Howard E Nyhart Company Inc, The			
8415 Allison Pointe Blvd Ste 300..................Indianapolis IN 46250	800-428-7106	317-845-3500	260
Howard F Baer Inc			
1301 Foster Ave ....Nashville TN 37210	800-447-7430	615-255-7351	775
Howard Greeley Rural Power			
422 Howard Ave PO Box 105 ....Saint Paul NE 68873	800-280-4962	308-754-4457	245
Howard Industries Inc			
3225 Pendorff Rd ....Laurel MS 39440	800-663-5598	601-425-3151	762
Howard Leight Industries			
7828 Waterville Rd ....San Diego CA 92154	800-430-5490		475
Howard Payne University			
1000 Fisk St ....Brownwood TX 76801	800-950-8465	325-646-2502	166
Howard Precision Metals Inc			
PO Box 240127 ....Milwaukee WI 53224	800-444-0311	414-355-9611	490
Howard Sheppard Inc			
PO Box 797 ....Sandersville GA 31082	800-846-1726	478-552-5127	775
Howard Systems International			
2777 Summer St ....Stamford CT 06905	800-326-4860		180
Howard Uniform Co			
1915 Annapolis Rd ....Baltimore MD 21230	800-628-8299	410-727-3086	155-18
Howard University			
2400 Sixth St NW ....Washington DC 20059	800-822-6363	202-806-6100	166
Howard University School of Divinity			
2400 Sixth St NW ....Washington DC 20059	800-822-6363	202-806-6100	167-3
Howco Metals Management			
9611 Telge Rd ....Houston TX 77095	800-392-7720	281-649-8800	307
Howden Buffalo Inc			
7909 Parklane Rd Ste 300 ....Columbia SC 29223	866-757-0908	803-741-2700	18
Howe Military School			
PO Box 240 ....Howe IN 46746	888-462-4693	260-562-2131	618
Howell Tractor & Equipment LLC			
480 Blaine St ....Gary IN 46406	800-852-8816		786
Howell's Motor Freight Inc			
PO Box 12308 ....Roanoke VA 24024	800-444-0585	540-966-3200	775
Howell-Oregon Electric Co-op Inc			
6327 N US Hwy 63 PO Box 649 ......West Plains MO 65775	855-385-9903	417-256-2131	245
HowGood Inc			
93 Commercial St ....Brooklyn NY 11222	888-601-3015		461
Howse Implement Company Inc			
2013 Hwy 184 E ....Laurel MS 39443	888-358-3377		
Hoxworth Blood Ctr University of Cincinnati Medical Ctr			
3130 Highland Ave ML0055 ....Cincinnati OH 45267	800-265-1515	513-451-0910	89
Hoyt			
543 N Neil Armstrong Rd ....Salt Lake City UT 84116	800-474-8733	801-363-2990	706
HP (Hewlett Packard Enterprise (Canada) Co)			
5150 Spectrum Way ....Mississauga ON L4W5G1	888-447-4636	905-206-4725	173-2
H-P Products Inc			
512 W Gorgas St ....Louisville OH 44641	800-822-8356	330-875-5556	591
HPC Foods Ltd			
288 Libby St ....Honolulu HI 96819	877-370-0919	808-848-2431	296-21
HPH Corp			
1529 SE 47th Terr ....Cape Coral FL 33904	800-654-9884	239-540-0085	347
HPL Stampings Inc			
425 Enterprise Pkwy ....Lake Zurich IL 60047	800-927-0397	847-540-1400	486
HPM (Hawaii Planing Mill Ltd)			
16-166 Melekahiwa St ....Keaau HI 96749	877-841-7633	808-966-5693	191-3
HPRHS (High Point Regional Health System)			
601 N Elm St PO Box HP-5 ....High Point NC 27262	877-878-7644	336-878-6000	373-3
HPTS (High Power Technical Services Inc)			
2230 Ampere Dr ....Louisville KY 40299	866-398-3474	502-271-2469	116
HR Advisors Inc			
25411 Cabot Rd Ste 212............Laguna Hills CA 92653	877-344-8324		
H&R Construction Parts & Equipment Inc			
20 Milburn St ....Buffalo NY 14212	800-333-0650	716-891-4311	57
HR Focal Point LLC			
3948 Legacy Dr Ste 106 PO Box 369 ....Plano TX 75023	855-464-4737		196
HR People & Strategy (HRPS)			
1800 Duke St ....Alexandria VA 22314	888-602-3270	703-535-6056	49-12
HR Works Inc			
200 WillowBrook Ofc Pk ....Fairport NY 14450	877-219-9062	585-381-8340	260
HRA - Healthcare Research & Analytics LLC			
400 Lanidex Plz ....Parsippany NJ 07054	800-929-5400	973-240-1200	464
HRC (Humboldt Redwood Company)			
125 Main St PO Box 565 ....Scotia CA 95565	888-225-7339	707-764-4472	
HRDQ			
827 Lincoln Ave Ste B-10..........West Chester PA 19380	800-633-4533	610-279-2002	196
HRF (Herb Research Foundation)			
4140 15th St ....Boulder CO 80304	800-748-2617	303-449-2265	48-17
HRI Inc			
1750 W College Ave ....State College PA 16801	877-474-9999	814-238-5071	188-4
HRMagazine			
1800 Duke St ....Alexandria VA 22314	800-283-7476	703-548-3440	455-5
HRMC (Highlands Regional Medical Ctr)			
5000 KY Rt 321 ....Prestonsburg KY 41653	800-533-4762	606-886-8511	373-3
HRMC (Huron Regional Medical Ctr)			
172 Fourth St SE ....Huron SD 57350	800-529-0115	605-353-6200	373-3
HRO Partners LLC			
855 Willow Tree Cir Ste 100..........Cordova TN 38018	866-822-0123		
HR&P			
9621 W Sam Houston Pkwy N Ste 100............................Houston TX 77064	877-880-4477	281-880-6525	
HRP Associates Inc			
197 Scott Swamp Rd ....Farmington CT 06032	800-246-9021		261
HRPS (HR People & Strategy)			
1800 Duke St ....Alexandria VA 22314	888-602-3270	703-535-6056	49-12
HRSA (Health Resources & Services Administration)			
5600 Fishers Ln ....Rockville MD 20857	888-275-4772	301-443-2216	339-9
Hru Inc Technical Resources			
3451 Dunckel Rd ....Lansing MI 48911	888-205-3446	517-272-5888	461
H&S Constructors Inc			
1616 Valero Way ....Corpus Christi TX 78469	800-727-8602	361-289-5272	256
HSBA (Hawaii State Bar Assn)			
1100 Alakea St Ste 1000.............Honolulu HI 96813	800-932-0311	808-537-1868	72
HSBC Bank USA			
2929 Walden Ave ....Depew NY 14043	800-975-4722	866-379-5621	507
HSBC Bank USA			
452 Fifth Ave ....New York NY 10018	800-975-4722		400
HSC Pediatric Ctr			
1731 Bunker Hill Rd NE ....Washington DC 20017	800-226-4444	202-832-4400	373-1
HSCVB (Hot Springs Convention Ctr)			
134 Convention Blvd PO Box 6000................Hot Springs AR 71902	800-625-7576	501-321-2277	205
HSHS St Joseph's Hospital			
2661 County Hwy I ....Chippewa Falls WI 54729	877-723-1811	715-723-1811	373-3
HSHS St Vincent Hospital			
835 S Van Buren St ....Green Bay WI 54301	800-211-2209		373-3
HSI (Hardware Suppliers of America Inc)			
1400 E Fire Tower Rd ....Greenville NC 27858	800-334-5625		350
HSQ Technology			
26227 Research Rd ....Hayward CA 94545	800-486-6684	510-259-1334	201
HSUS (Humane Society of the US)			
1255 23rd St NW Ste 450..........Washington DC 20037	866-720-2676	202-452-1100	48-3
HT Hackney Co			
502 S Gay St PO Box 238.............Knoxville TN 37901	800-406-1291	865-546-1291	185
HTC (Horry Telephone Co-op Inc)			
3480 Hwy 701 N PO Box 1820.........Conway SC 29528	800-824-6779	843-365-2151	731
HTK (Hornor Townsend & Kent Inc)			
600 Dresher Rd Ste C1C.............Horsham PA 19044	800-289-9999		401
Hub City Inc			
2914 Industrial Ave ....Aberdeen SD 57401	800-482-2489	605-225-0360	705
Hub Folding Box Co Inc			
774 Norfolk St ....Mansfield MA 02048	800-334-1113	508-339-0005	101
Hub Group Inc			
2000 Clearwater Dr ....Oak Brook IL 60523 NASDAQ: HUBG	800-377-5833	630-271-3600	447
HUB International Insurance Services			
333 W El Camino Real Ste 330........Sunnyvale CA 94087	877-530-8897	650-964-8000	
Hub International Ltd			
1065 Ave of the Americas ....New York NY 10018	800-456-5293	212-338-2000	389
Hubbard & Drake General Mechanical Contractors Inc			
PO Box 1867 ....Decatur AL 35602	800-353-9245	256-353-9244	189-10
Hubbard Feeds Inc			
111 W Cherry St Ste 500 ....Mankato MN 56001	800-869-7219	507-388-9400	445
Hubbard Street Dance Chicago			
1147 W Jackson Blvd ....Chicago IL 60607	800-982-2787	312-850-9744	569-1
Hubbard`s Impala Parts Inc			
1676 Anthony Rd ....Burlington NC 27215	800-846-7252	336-227-1589	786
Hubbard-Hall Inc			
563 S Leonard St ....Waterbury CT 06708	800-331-6871	866-441-5831	146
Hubbell Lighting Inc			
701 Millennium Blvd ....Greenville SC 29607	800-345-4928	864-678-1000	438
Hubbell Power Systems Inc			
210 N Allen St ....Centralia MO 65240	800-346-3062	573-682-5521	253
Hubbell Premise Wiring Inc			
23 Clara Dr ....Mystic CT 06355	800-626-0005		810
Hubbell Wiring Device-Kellems			
40 Waterview Dr ....Shelton CT 06484 *Cust Svc	800-288-6000*	203-882-4800	810
Huber's Orchard & Winery			
19816 Huber Rd ....Borden IN 47106	800-345-9463	812-923-9463	50-7
HubTech			
44 Norfolk Ave Ste 4...........South Easton MA 02375	877-482-8324		180
Hubtrucker Inc			
315 Freeport St Ste B ....Houston TX 77015	866-913-6553	713-547-5482	311
HUD (Department of Housing & Urban Development)			
451 Seventh St SW ....Washington DC 20410	800-569-4287	202-708-0685	339-11
HUD Office of Public & Indian Housing			
Real Estate Assessment Ctr 550 12th St SW Ste 100.......Washington DC 20410	888-245-4860	202-708-1112	339-11
Hudson Color Concentrates Inc			
50 Francis St ....Leominster MA 01453	888-858-9065	978-537-3538	546
Hudson Lock Inc			
81 Apsley St ....Hudson MA 01749	800-434-8960		349
Hudson Printing & Graphic Design			
611 S Mobberly Ave ....Longview TX 75602	800-530-4888	903-758-1773	343
Hudson River Fruit Distributors			
65 Old Indian Rd ....Milton NY 12547	800-640-2774		315-3
Hudson River Healthcare Inc			
1037 Main St ....Peekskill NY 10566	844-474-2273		
Hudson River Islands State Park			
Schodack Island State Pk ....Schodack Landing NY 12156	800-456-2267	518-732-0187	561

Name / Address	City	State	ZIP	Toll-Free	Phone	Class
Hudson Valley Community College 80 Vandenburgh Ave	Troy	NY	12180	**877-325-4822**	518-629-4822	162
Hudson Valley Federal Credit Union 159 Barnegat Rd	Poughkeepsie	NY	12601	**800-468-3011**	845-463-3011	219
Hudson Valve Company Inc 5301 Office Pk Dr Ste 330	Bakersfield	CA	93309	**800-748-6218**	661-869-1126	784
Hudspeth County 109 Brown St	Sierra Blanca	TX	79851	**888-368-4689**	915-369-2331	337
Hueco Tanks State Historic Site 6900 Hueco Tanks Rd Ste 1	El Paso	TX	79938	**800-792-1112**	915-857-1135	561
Hueneme Elementary School Dist 205 N Ventura Rd	Port Hueneme	CA	93041	**866-431-2478**	805-488-3588	681
Hueston Woods Lodge & Conference Ctr 5201 Lodge Rd	College Corner	OH	45003	**800-282-7275**	513-664-3500	665
Hufcor Inc 2101 Kennedy Rd	Janesville	WI	53545	**800-356-6968**	608-756-1241	286
Huffman Corp 1050 Huffman Way	Clover	SC	29710	**888-483-3626**	803-222-4561	453
Huffman Laboratories Inc 4630 Indiana St	Golden	CO	80403	**877-886-6225**	303-278-4455	738
Huffmaster Crisis Management 1055 W Maple Rd	Clawson	MI	48017	**800-446-1515**		
Huffy Bicycle Co 6551 Centerville Business Pkwy	Centerville	OH	45459	**800-872-2453**	937-865-2800	82
Hu-Friedy Mfg Company Inc 3232 N Rockwell St	Chicago	IL	60618	**800-483-7433**	773-975-6100	228
Hughes Bros Inc 210 N 13th St	Seward	NE	68434	**800-869-0359**	402-643-2991	811
Hughes Corp Weschler Instruments Div 16900 Foltz Pkwy	Cleveland	OH	44149	**800-557-0064**	440-238-2550	248
Hughes Federal Credit Union Inc PO Box 11900	Tucson	AZ	85734	**866-760-3156**	520-794-8341	219
Hughes Supply Company of Thomasville Inc 175 Kanoy Rd PO Box 1003	Thomasville	NC	27360	**800-747-8141**	336-475-8146	452
HughesNet 11717 Exploration Ln	Germantown	MD	20876	**866-347-3292**	301-428-5500	397
Hughston Orthopedic Hospital 100 Frist Ct	Columbus	GA	31908	**855-795-3609**	706-494-2100	373-7
Hugo Boss Fashions Inc 601 West 26th St Ste #M281	New York	NY	10001	**800-484-6267**		
Hugoton Royalty Trust 2911 Turtle Creek Blvd Ste 850 PO Box 962020 *NYSE: HGT*	Dallas	TX	75219	**855-588-7839**		671
Huhtamaki Inc North America 9201 Packaging Dr	DeSoto	KS	66018	**800-255-4243**	913-583-3025	544
Hull Lift Truck Inc 28747 Old US 33 W	Elkhart	IN	46516	**888-284-0364**	574-293-8651	384
Human Capital 2055 Crooks Rd Level B	Rochester Hills	MI	48309	**888-736-9071**		627
Human Factors International Inc 410 W Lowe Ave	Fairfield	IA	52556	**800-242-4480**	641-472-4480	177
Human Growth Foundation 997 Glen Cove Ave Ste 5	Glen Head	NY	11545	**800-451-6434**	516-671-4041	48-17
Human Kinetics 1607 N Market St	Champaign	IL	61820	**800-747-4457**	217-351-5076	633-2
Human Life International (HLI) 4 Family Life Ln *Orders	Front Royal	VA	22630	**800-549-5433***	540-635-7884	48-6
Human Resource Development Press Inc 22 Amherst Rd	Amherst	MA	01002	**800-822-2801**		194
Human Rights Campaign 1640 Rhode Island Ave NW	Washington	DC	20036	**800-777-4723**	202-628-4160	48-8
Human Touch 3030 Walnut Ave	Long Beach	CA	90807	**800-742-5493**	562-426-8700	319-2
Humana Inc 500 W Main St *NYSE: HUM*	Louisville	KY	40202	**800-486-2620**	502-580-1000	390-3
Humana Military Healthcare Services 500 W Main St *General	Louisville	KY	40202	**800-444-5445***		390-3
Humane Society of the US (HSUS) 1255 23rd St NW Ste 450	Washington	DC	20037	**866-720-2676**	202-452-1100	48-3
Humboldt County Convention & Visitors Bureau 1034 Second St	Eureka	CA	95501	**800-346-3482**	707-443-5097	206
Humboldt Manufacturing Co 875 Tollgate Rd	Elgin	IL	60123	**800-544-7220**		406
Humboldt Redwood Co (HRC) 125 Main St PO Box 565	Scotia	CA	95565	**888-225-7339**	707-764-4472	
Humboldt State University 1 Harpst St	Arcata	CA	95521	**866-850-9556**	707-826-3011	166
Humco Holding Group Inc 201 W Fifth St	Austin	TX	78701	**800-662-3435**	855-925-4736	578
Hume Travel Corp 1130 W Pender St Ste 510	Vancouver	BC	V6E4A1	**800-663-9787**	604-682-7581	767
Hummert International Inc 4500 Earth City Expy	Earth City	MO	63045	**800-325-3055**		276
Humphrey Products Co 5070 E N Ave PO Box 2008	Kalamazoo	MI	49048	**800-477-8707**		784
Humphrey's Half Moon Inn & Suites 2303 Shelter Island Dr	San Diego	CA	92106	**800-542-7400**	619-224-3411	378
Hunger Project, The 5 Union Sq W	New York	NY	10003	**800-228-6691**	212-251-9100	48-5
Hunt & Sons Inc 5750 S Watt Ave	Sacramento	CA	95829	**800-734-2999**	916-383-4868	324
Hunt Forest Products 401 E Reynolds Dr PO Box 1263	Ruston	LA	71273	**800-390-8589**	318-255-2245	679
Hunt Guillot & Assoc LLC 603 Reynolds Dr	Ruston	LA	71270	**866-255-6825**	318-255-6825	256
Hunt Insurance Agency Inc 12000 S Harlem Ave	Palos Heights	IL	60463	**800-772-6484**	708-361-5300	389
Hunt Midwest Enterprises Inc 8300 NE Underground Dr	Kansas City	MO	64161	**800-551-6877**	816-455-2500	651
Hunt Midwest Mining Inc 8300 NE Underground Dr	Kansas City	MO	64161	**800-551-6877**	816-455-2500	501-5
Hunt Pan Am Aviation Inc 505 Amelia Earhart Dr	Brownsville	TX	78521	**800-888-7524**	956-542-9111	63

Name / Address	City	State	ZIP	Toll-Free	Phone	Class
Hunt Valve Company Inc 1913 E State St	Salem	OH	44460	**800-321-2757**	330-337-9535	785
Hunter Business Group LLC 4650 N Port Washington Rd	Milwaukee	WI	53212	**800-423-4010**		195
Hunter Co 3300 W 71st Ave	Westminster	CO	80030	**800-676-4868**	303-427-4626	706
Hunter Engineering Co 11250 Hunter Dr	Bridgeton	MO	63044	**800-448-6848**	314-731-3020	62-5
Hunter Fan Co 7130 Goodlett Farms Pkwy Ste 400	Memphis	TN	38016	**888-830-1326**	901-743-1360	37
Hunter Heavy Equipment Inc 2829 Texas Ave	Texas City	TX	77590	**800-562-7368**	409-945-2382	190
Hunter House 424 Bellevue Ave	Newport	RI	02840	**800-326-6030**	401-847-1000	50-3
Hunter Woodworks Inc 21038 S Wilmington Ave PO Box 4937	Carson	CA	90749	**800-966-4751**	323-775-2544	547
Hunterdon County Democrat 8 Minneakoning Rd	Flemington	NJ	08822	**888-782-7533**	908-782-4747	528-4
Huntingdon College 1500 E Fairview Ave *Admissions	Montgomery	AL	36106	**800-763-0313***	334-833-4497	166
Huntingdon County 223 Penn St	Huntingdon	PA	16652	**800-373-0209**	814-643-3091	337
Huntingdon County Visitors Bureau 6993 Seven Pt Rd Ste 2	Hesston	PA	16647	**888-729-7869**	814-658-0060	206
Huntington Bancshares Inc 7 Easton Oval *NASDAQ: HBAN*	Columbus	OH	43219	**800-480-2265**		359-2
Huntington Beach Marketing & Visitors Bureau 301 Main St Ste 212	Huntington Beach	CA	92648	**800-729-6232**	714-969-3492	206
Huntington Beach Public Library (HBPL) 7111 Talbert Ave	Huntington Beach	CA	92648	**800-565-0148**	714-842-4481	433-3
Huntington Beach State Park 16148 Ocean Hwy	Murrells Inlet	SC	29576	**800-491-1764**	843-237-4440	561
Huntington County Visitors & Convention Bureau 407 N Jefferson St	Huntington	IN	46750	**800-848-4282**	260-359-8687	206
Huntington Ingalls Industries Inc 1000 Access Rd	Pascagoula	MS	39568	**877-871-2058**	228-935-1122	694
Huntington Junior College 900 Fifth Ave	Huntington	WV	25701	**800-344-4522**	304-697-7550	795
Huntington Learning Centers Inc 496 Kinderkamack Rd	Oradell	NJ	07649	**800-653-8400**	201-261-8400	148
Huntington Mortgage Co 7575 Huntington Pk Dr	Columbus	OH	43235	**800-323-4695**	614-480-6505	507
Huntington National Bank 41 S High St Huntington Ctr	Columbus	OH	43287	**800-480-2265**	614-480-8300	70
Huntington Park Rubber Stamp Co 2761 E Slauson Ave PO Box 519	Huntington Park	CA	90255	**800-882-0129**	323-582-6461	465
Huntington State Park PO Box 1343	Huntington	UT	84528	**800-322-3770**	435-687-2491	561
Huntington University 2303 College Ave *Admissions	Huntington	IN	46750	**800-642-6493***	260-356-6000	166
Huntington Veterans Affairs Medical Ctr 1540 Spring Valley Dr	Huntington	WV	25704	**800-827-8244**	304-429-6741	373-8
Huntington's Disease Society of America (HDSA) 505 Eigth Ave Ste 902	New York	NY	10018	**800-345-4372**	212-242-1968	48-17
Huntleigh Securities Corp 7800 Forsyth Blvd 5th Fl	Saint Louis	MO	63105	**800-727-5405**	314-236-2400	686
Huntsman Corp 500 Huntsman Way *NYSE: HUN*	Salt Lake City	UT	84108	**888-490-8484**	801-584-5700	601-2
Huntsville Board of Education 200 White St	Huntsville	AL	35801	**877-517-0020**	256-428-6800	681
Huntsville Botanical Garden 4747 Bob Wallace Ave	Huntsville	AL	35805	**877-930-4447**	256-830-4447	97
Huntsville Museum of Art 300 Church St SW	Huntsville	AL	35801	**800-786-9095**	256-535-4350	517
Huntsville/Madison County Convention & Visitor's Bureau 500 Church St NW Ste 1	Huntsville	AL	35801	**800-843-0468**	256-551-2230	206
Huntsville-Walker County Chamber of Commerce 1327 11th St	Huntsville	TX	77340	**800-289-0389**	936-295-8113	139
Huntwood Industries 23800 E Apple Way	Liberty Lake	WA	99019	**800-873-7350**	509-924-5858	115
Huot Manufacturing Co 550 Wheeler St N	Saint Paul	MN	55104	**800-832-3838**	651-646-1869	319-1
Hurckman Mechanical Industries Inc 1450 Velp Ave	Green Bay	WI	54303	**844-499-8771**	920-499-8771	189-10
Hurco Cos Inc 1 Technology Way *NASDAQ: HURC* ■ *Sales	Indianapolis	IN	46268	**800-634-2416***	317-293-5309	453
Hurco Technologies Inc 409 Enterprise St	Harrisburg	SD	57032	**800-888-1436**		478
Hurley Medical Ctr 1 Hurley Plz	Flint	MI	48503	**800-336-8999**	810-262-9000	373-3
Huron Chamber & Visitors Bureau 1725 Dakota Ave S	Huron	SD	57350	**800-487-6673**	605-352-0000	206
Huron County 250 E Huron Ave Rm 305	Bad Axe	MI	48413	**800-358-4862**	989-269-6431	337
Huron Daily Tribune 211 N Heisterman St	Bad Axe	MI	48413	**800-322-1184**	989-269-6461	528-2
Huron Machine Products Inc 228 SW 21st Terr	Fort Lauderdale	FL	33312	**800-327-8186**	954-587-4541	491
Huron Regional Medical Ctr (HRMC) 172 Fourth St SE	Huron	SD	57350	**800-529-0115**	605-353-6200	373-3
Huron Valley Financial Inc 2395 Oak Vly Dr Ste 200	Ann Arbor	MI	48103	**800-650-7441**	734-669-8000	524
Hurst Boiler & Welding Company Inc 100 Boilermaker Ln	Coolidge	GA	31738	**877-994-8778**	229-346-3545	91
Hurst Chemical Co 2020 Cunningham Rd	Rockford	IL	61102	**800-723-2004**		624
Hurst Farm Supply Inc 105 Ave D	Abernathy	TX	79311	**800-535-8903**	806-298-2541	274
Hurst Group 500 Buck Pl	Lexington	KY	40511	**800-926-4423**	859-255-4422	531

Alphabetical Section

	City	State	ZIP	Toll-Free	Phone	Class
Hurst Public Library						
901 Precinct Line Rd	Hurst	TX	76053	**800-344-8377**	817-788-7300	433-3
Hurwitz-Mintz Furniture Co						
1751 Airline Dr	Metairie	LA	70001	**888-957-9555**	504-378-1000	321
Huse Publishing Co						
525 Norfolk Ave	Norfolk	NE	68701	**877-371-1020**	402-371-1020	633-8
Hush Puppies Co						
9341 Courtland Dr NE	Rockford	MI	49351	**866-699-7365**	616-866-5500	301
Husky Energy Inc						
707 Eigth Ave SW						
PO Box 6525 Stn D	Calgary	AB	T2P1H5	**877-262-2111**	403-298-6111	532
TSE: HSE						
Husky Injection Molding Systems Ltd						
500 Queen St S	Bolton	ON	L7E5S5	**800-465-4875**	905-951-5000	385
Husqvarna Construction Products						
17400 W 119th St	Olathe	KS	66061	**800-288-5040**	913-928-1000	491
Hussey Copper Ltd						
100 Washington St	Leetsdale	PA	15056	**800-733-8866**	724-251-4200	483
Hussey Seating Co						
38 Dyer St Ext	North Berwick	ME	03906	**800-341-0401**	207-676-2271	319-3
Hussmann Corp						
12999 St Charles Rock Rd	Bridgeton	MO	63044	**800-592-2060**	314-291-2000	660
Husson College						
1 College Cir	Bangor	ME	04401	**800-448-7766**	207-941-7000	166
Hussong Manufacturing Company Inc						
204 Industrial Park Rd	Lakefield	MN	56150	**800-253-4904**	507-662-6641	361
Hussung Mechanical Contractors						
6913 Enterprise Dr	Louisville	KY	40214	**800-446-2738**	502-375-3500	606
Huston-Patterson Corp						
123 W N St PO Box 260	Decatur	IL	62522	**800-866-5692**		112
Huston-Tillotson University						
900 Chicon St	Austin	TX	78702	**800-343-3822**	512-505-3000	166
Hutchens Construction Co						
1007 Main St	Cassville	MO	65625	**888-728-3482**	417-847-2489	188-4
Hutchens Industries Inc						
215 N Patterson Ave	Springfield	MO	65802	**800-654-8824**	417-862-5012	60
Hutchens Petroleum Corp						
22 Performance Dr	Stuart	VA	24171	**800-537-7433**	276-694-7000	576
Hutchinson Aerospace & Industry Inc						
82 S St	Hopkinton	MA	01748	**800-227-7962**	508-417-7000	672
Hutchinson Community College & Area Vocational School						
1300 N Plum St	Hutchinson	KS	67501	**800-289-3501**	620-665-3500	162
Hutchinson Co-Op						
PO Box 158	Hutchinson	MN	55350	**800-795-1299**	320-587-4647	276
Hutchinson Manufacturing Inc						
720 Hwy 7 W PO Box 487	Hutchinson	MN	55350	**800-795-1276**	320-587-4653	693
Hutchinson News						
300 W Second St	Hutchinson	KS	67504	**800-766-3311**	620-694-5700	528-2
Hutchinson Regional Healthcare System						
1701 E 23rd Ave	Hutchinson	KS	67502	**800-267-6891**	620-665-2000	373-3
Hutchinson/Mayrath/TerraTrack Industries						
514 W Crawford St	Clay Center	KS	67432	**800-523-6993**	785-632-2161	273
Hutchinson/Reno County Chamber of Commerce						
117 N Walnut St	Hutchinson	KS	67501	**800-691-4262**	620-662-3391	139
Hutson 306 Andrus Dr	Murray	KY	42071	**866-488-7662**	270-886-3994	428
Huttig Bldg Products Inc (HBP)						
555 Maryville University Dr						
Ste 400	Saint Louis	MO	63141	**800-325-4466**	314-216-2600	497
NASDAQ: HBP						
Hutton Communications Inc						
2520 Marsh Ln	Carrollton	TX	75006	**800-725-5264**	972-417-0100	246
Huxley Communications Co-op						
102 N Main Ave	Huxley	IA	50124	**800-231-4922**	515-597-2212	224
HV Food Products Co						
1221 Broadway	Oakland	CA	94612	**877-853-7262**		
HVA (High Vacuum Apparatus LLC)						
12880 Moya Blvd	Reno	NV	89506	**800-551-4422**	775-359-4442	784
HVH Transportation Inc						
181 E 56th Ave Ste 200	Denver	CO	80216	**866-723-0586**	303-292-3656	775
HWC (Houston Wire & Cable Co)						
10201 N Loop E	Houston	TX	77029	**800-468-9473**	713-609-2100	246
HWE (High West Energy Inc)						
6270 County Rd 212	Pine Bluffs	WY	82082	**888-834-1657**	307-245-3261	245
HWEC (Hancock-Wood Electric Co-op Inc)						
1399 Business Pk Dr S						
PO Box 190	North Baltimore	OH	45872	**800-445-4840**		245
HWH Corp						
2096 Moscow Rd	Moscow	IA	52760	**800-321-3494**	563-724-3396	60
Hy Cite Enterprises LLC						
333 Holtzman Rd	Madison	WI	53713	**877-494-2289**		
Hyannis Holiday Motel						
131 Ocean St	Hyannis	MA	02601	**800-423-1551**	508-775-1639	378
Hyannis Travel Inn						
18 N St	Hyannis	MA	02601	**800-352-7190**	508-775-8200	378
Hyatt Corp						
Hyatt Regency Hotels						
396 Alhambra Cir Ste 788	Coral Gables	FL	33134	**800-233-1234***	312-750-1234	378
*Resv						
Hyatt Hotels Corp						
71 S Wacker Dr	Chicago	IL	60606	**888-591-1234**	312-750-1234	378
NYSE: H						
Hyatt Place Hotels						
150 N Riverside Plz	Chicago	IL	60606	**888-492-8847**	312-750-1234	378
Hyatt Place Waikiki Beach						
175 Paoakalani Ave	Honolulu	HI	96815	**877-367-1912**	808-922-3861	378
Hyatt Regency						
Orange County						
11999 Harbor Blvd	Garden Grove	CA	92840	**800-233-1234**	714-750-1234	667
Hyatt Regency Waikiki Beach Resort & Spa						
2424 Kalakaua Ave	Honolulu	HI	96815	**800-233-1234**		703
Hyatt Vacation Ownership Inc						
140 Fountain Pkwy N						
Ste 570	Saint Petersburg	FL	33716	**800-926-4447**	727-803-9400	748
Hycor Biomedical Inc						
7272 Chapman Ave	Garden Grove	CA	92841	**800-382-2527***	714-933-3000	231
*Cust Svc						
Hyde Tools Co						
54 Eastford Rd	Southbridge	MA	01550	**800-872-4933**	508-764-4344	753

	City	State	ZIP	Toll-Free	Phone	Class
Hydraulic Controls Inc						
4700 San Pablo Ave	Emeryville	CA	94608	**800-847-6900**	510-658-8300	357
Hydrel						
12881 Bradley Ave	Sylmar	CA	91342	**866-533-9901**		438
Hydro Carbide						
4439 SR-982	Latrobe	PA	15650	**800-245-2476**	724-539-9701	752
Hydro One Networks Inc						
483 Bay St S Tower						
8th Fl Reception	Toronto	ON	M5G2P5	**877-955-1155**	888-664-9376	782
Hydro Tube Enterprises Inc						
137 Artino St	Oberlin	OH	44074	**800-226-3553**	440-774-1022	591
HydroCAD Software Solutions LLC						
PO Box 477	Chocorua	NH	03817	**800-927-7246**	603-323-8666	178-8
HYDRO-FIT Inc						
160 Madison St	Eugene	OR	97402	**800-346-7295***	541-484-4361	267
*Cust Svc						
Hydrolevel Co						
83 Water St	New Haven	CT	06511	**800-654-0768**	203-776-0473	203
Hydromatic Pump Co						
740 E Ninth St	Ashland	OH	44805	**888-957-8677**		637
Hydro-Photon Inc						
262 Ellsworth Rd	Blue Hill	ME	04614	**888-783-7473**	207-374-5800	738
HydroPoint Data Systems Inc						
1720 Corporate Cir	Petaluma	CA	94954	**800-362-8774**		406
HydroPressure Cleaning Inc						
413 Dawson Dr	Camarillo	CA	93012	**800-934-2399**		637
Hydrotex Inc						
12920 Senlac Dr	Farmers Branch	TX	75234	**800-527-9439**		537
Hydro-Thermal Corp						
400 Pilot Ct	Waukesha	WI	53188	**800-952-0121**	262-548-8900	385
Hygenic Corp						
1245 Home Ave	Akron	OH	44310	**800-321-2135**	330-633-8460	228
hygiena LLC						
941 Avenida Acaso	Camarillo	CA	93012	**877-494-4364**	805-388-8007	418
Hygieneering Inc						
7575 Plaza Ct	Willowbrook	IL	60527	**800-444-7154**	630-654-2550	461
Hygolet Inc						
349 SE Second Ave	Deerfield Beach	FL	33441	**800-494-6538**	954-481-8601	604
Hygrade Metal Moulding Manufacturing Corp						
1990 Highland Ave	Bethlehem	PA	18020	**800-645-9475**	610-866-2441	234
Hy-Grade Precast Concrete						
2411 First St	St Catharines	ON	L2R6P7	**800-229-8568**	905-684-8568	183
Hygrade Precision Technologies Inc						
329 Cooke St	Plainville	CT	06062	**800-457-1666**	860-747-5773	752
HyGreen Inc						
3630 SW 47th Ave Ste 100	Gainesville	FL	32608	**877-574-9473**		738
Hy-Ko Products Co						
60 Meadow Ln	Northfield	OH	44067	**800-292-0550**	330-467-7446	697
Hyland Software Inc						
28500 Clemens Rd	Westlake	OH	44145	**888-495-2638**	440-788-5000	178-7
Hylant Group						
811 Madison Ave	Toledo	OH	43604	**800-249-5268**	419-255-1020	389
Hynes Industries						
3760 Oakwood	Youngstown	OH	44515	**800-321-9257**		490
Hypertherm Inc						
21 Great Hollow Rd PO Box 5010	Hanover	NH	03755	**800-643-0030**	603-643-3441	453
Hypneumat Inc						
5900 W Franklin Dr	Franklin	WI	53132	**800-228-9949**	414-423-7400	453
Hyson Products						
10367 Brecksville Rd	Brecksville	OH	44141	**800-876-4976**	440-526-5900	785
Hysterectomy Educational Resources & Services Foundation (HERS)						
422 Bryn Mawr Ave	Bala Cynwyd	PA	19004	**888-750-4377**	610-667-7757	48-17
Hy-Tape International						
PO Box 540	Patterson	NY	12563	**800-248-0101**		475
Hy-Tek Material Handling Inc						
2222 Rickenbacker Pkwy W	Columbus	OH	43217	**800-837-1217**		
Hytrol Conveyor Company Inc						
2020 Hytrol St	Jonesboro	AR	72401	**800-852-3233**	870-935-3700	207
Hyundai Motor America						
10550 Talbert Ave	Fountain Valley	CA	92708	**800-633-5151***	714-965-3000	59
*Cust Svc						

I

	City	State	ZIP	Toll-Free	Phone	Class
I & I Sling Inc						
PO Box 2423	Aston	PA	19014	**800-874-3539**	610-485-8500	208
I Am Athlete LLC						
6701 Center Dr Ste 700	Los Angeles	CA	90045	**877-462-7979**		386
I D Booth Inc						
620 William St PO Box 579	Elmira	NY	14902	**888-432-6684**	607-733-9121	608
I E T Inc						
3539 Glendale Ave	Toledo	OH	43614	**800-278-1031**	419-385-1233	261
I Rice & Company Inc						
11500 Roosevelt Blvd						
Bldg D	Philadelphia	PA	19116	**800-232-6022**	215-673-7423	296-15
I Wireless						
4135 NW Urbandale Dr	Urbandale	IA	50322	**888-550-4497***		730
*Cust Svc						
i2M Inc						
755 Oak Hill Rd Crestwood Industrial Pk						
	Mountain Top	PA	18707	**800-242-3909**		596
IA (Irrigation Assn)						
6540 Arlington Blvd	Falls Church	VA	22042	**800-362-8774**	703-536-7080	48-2
IAAI (International Assn of Arson Investigators)						
2111 Baldwin Ave # 203	Crofton	MD	21114	**800-468-4224**	410-451-3473	49-7
IAAO (International Assn of Assessing Officers)						
314 W Tenth St	Kansas City	MO	64105	**800-616-4226**	816-701-8100	49-7
IABC (International Assn of Business Communicators)						
155 Montgomery St						
Ste 1210	San Francisco	CA	94104	**800-776-4222**	415-544-4700	49-12
IAC Industries						
895 Beacon St	Brea	CA	92821	**800-989-1422**	714-990-8997	319-1

Listing	Toll-Free	Phone	Class
IACP (International Assn of Culinary Professionals) 45 Rockefeller Plz Ste 2000 .... New York NY 10111	855-738-4227		49-6
IACP (International Academy of Compounding Pharmacists) 4638 Riverstone Blvd .... Missouri City TX 77459	800-927-4227	281-933-8400	49-8
IACP (International Assn of Chiefs of Police) 44 Canal Ctr Plz Ste 200 .... Alexandria VA 22314	800-843-4227	703-836-6767	49-7
IAEI (International Assn of Electrical Inspectors) 901 Waterfall Way Ste 602 .... Richardson TX 75080	800-786-4234	972-235-1455	49-3
IAFC (International Assn of Fire Chiefs) 4025 Fair Ridge Dr Ste 300 .... Fairfax VA 22033	866-385-9110	703-273-0911	49-7
IAFE (International Assn of Fairs & Expositions, The) 3043 E Cairo St .... Springfield MO 65802	800-516-0313	417-862-5771	48-23
IAFP (International Assn for Food Protection) 6200 Aurora Ave Ste 200W .... Des Moines IA 50322 *General	800-369-6337*	515-276-3344	49-6
IAHB (Institute for the Advancement of Human Behavior) PO Box 5527 .... Santa Rosa CA 95402	800-258-8411	650-851-8411	49-8
IAIA (Institute of American Indian Arts) 83 Avan Nu Po Rd .... Santa Fe NM 87508	800-804-6422	505-424-2300	165
IAMFC (International Assn of Marriage & Family Counselors) 5999 Stevenson Ave .... Alexandria VA 22304	800-347-6647		49-15
IAMGOLD Corp 401 Bay St Ste 3200 PO Box 153 .... Toronto ON M5H2Y4 *TSE: IMG*	888-464-9999	416-360-4710	500
IAMS Co 3700 Ohio 65 .... Leipsic OH 45856 *Cust Svc	800-675-3849*	419-943-4267	574
IANA (Intermodal Assn of North America) 11785 Beltsville Dr Ste 1100 .... Calverton MD 20705	877-438-8442	301-982-3400	49-21
IAPA (International Airline Passengers Assn) PO Box 700188 .... Dallas TX 75370	800-821-4272	972-404-9980	48-23
IAPMO (International Assn of Plumbing & Mechanical Offici) 4755 E Philadelphia St .... Ontario CA 91761	877-427-6601	909-472-4100	49-7
Iapp (International Association of Privacy Professionals) 75 Rochester Ave Ste 4 .... Portsmouth NH 03801	800-266-6501	603-427-9200	
IASP (International Assn for the Study of Pain) 111 Queen Anne Ave N Ste 501 .... Seattle WA 98109	866-574-2654	206-283-0311	48-17
IATSE (International Alliance of Theatrical Stage Employe) 1430 Broadway 20th Fl .... New York NY 10018	800-456-3863	212-730-1770	413
IATSE PAC 1430 Broadway 20th Fl .... New York NY 10018	844-422-9273	212-730-1770	611
IAVM (International Assn of Venue Managers Inc) 635 Fritz Dr Ste 100 .... Coppell TX 75019	800-935-4226	972-906-7441	49-12
IB.I.S. Inc 420 Technology Pkwy Ste 100 .... Peachtree Corners GA 30092	866-714-8422	770-368-4000	691
Ibaset 27442 Portola Pkwy .... Foothill Ranch CA 92610	877-422-7381	949-598-5200	180
Ibb Design Group 5798 Genesis Ct .... Frisco TX 75034	800-355-9195	214-618-6600	138
IBC Advanced Alloys Corp 401 Arvin Rd .... Franklin IN 46131	800-423-5612	317-738-2558	500
IBERIABANK Corp 200 W Congress St .... Lafayette LA 70501 *NASDAQ: IBKC*	800-968-0801		359-2
Iberville Parish Chamber of Commerce 23675 Church St .... Plaquemine LA 70764	800-266-2692	225-687-3560	139
IBHS (Institute for Business & Home Safety) 4775 E Fowler Ave .... Tampa FL 33617	866-657-4247	813-286-3400	49-9
IBISWorld Inc 11755 Wilshire blvd 11th fl .... Los Angeles CA 90025	800-330-3772		386
IBJ (Indianapolis Business Journal) 41 E Washington St Ste 200 .... Indianapolis IN 46204	800-428-7081	317-634-6200	455-5
IBM (International Business Machines Corp) 1 New OrchaRd Rd .... Armonk NY 10504 *NYSE: IBM*	800-426-4968	914-499-1900	173-2
IBML (Imaging Business Machines LLC) 2750 Crestwood Blvd .... Birmingham AL 35210	877-627-8325	205-956-4071	111
IBPA (Independent Book Publishers Assn, The) 1020 Manhattan Beach Blvd Ste 204 .... Manhattan Beach CA 90266	800-327-5113	310-546-1818	49-16
IBS (International Bible Society) *Biblica* 1820 Jet Stream Dr .... Colorado Springs CO 80921 *Cust Svc	800-524-1588*	719-488-9200	48-20
IBS Direct 431 Yerkes Rd .... King of Prussia PA 19406	800-220-1255	610-265-8210	110
IBS Electronics Inc Lake Center Dr .... Santa Ana CA 92704	800-527-2888	714-751-6633	246
IBT Enterprises LLC 1770 Indian Trail Rd Ste 300 .... Norcross GA 30093	877-242-8428	770-381-2023	194
IBT Inc 9400 W 55th St .... Merriam KS 66203	800-332-2114	913-677-3151	384
IBWA (International Bottled Water Association) 1700 Diagonal Rd Ste 650 .... Alexandria VA 22314	800-928-3711	703-683-5213	49-6
IC. System Inc PO Box 64378 .... St. Paul MN 55164	800-443-4123		
ICA (International Chiropractors Assn) 6400 Arlington Blvd Ste 800 .... Falls Church VA 22042	800-423-4690	703-528-5000	49-8
ICAC (Institute of Clean Air Cos) 1730 M St NW Ste 206 .... Washington DC 20036	800-631-9505	202-478-6188	48-12
iCAD Inc 98 Spit Brook Rd Ste 100 .... Nashua NH 03062 *NASDAQ: ICAD*	866-280-2239	603-882-5200	381
Icahn Enterprises LP 767 Fifth Ave 47th Fl .... New York NY 10153 *NASDAQ: IEP*	800-255-2737	212-702-4300	359-3
Icahn School of Medicine at Mount Sinai 1 Gustave L Levy Pl .... New York NY 10029	800-862-1674	212-241-6500	48-17
ICAM Technologies Corp 21500 Nassr St .... Sainte-anne-de-bellevue QC H9X4C1	800-827-4226	514-697-8033	179
Icare Industries Inc 4399 35th St N .... Saint Petersburg FL 33714	877-422-7352	727-526-0501	538
IcareLabs 4399 35th St N .... Saint Petersburg FL 33714	877-422-7352		538
ICBA (Independent Community Bankers of America) 1615 L St NW Ste 900 .... Washington DC 20036	800-422-8439	202-659-8111	49-2
ICC (International Code Council) 500 New Jersey Ave NW 6th Fl .... Washington DC 20001	888-422-7233	202-370-1800	49-3

Listing	Toll-Free	Phone	Class
ICC Chemical Corp 460 Park Ave .... New York NY 10022	800-422-1720	212-521-1700	146
ICC Industries Inc 460 Park Ave .... New York NY 10022	800-422-1720	212-521-1700	144
ICCFA (International Cemetery Cremation & Funeral Assn) 107 Carpenter Dr Ste 100 .... Sterling VA 20164	800-645-7700	703-391-8400	49-4
ICCP (Institute for Certification of Computing Professio) 2400 E Devon Ave Ste 281 .... Des Plaines IL 60018	800-843-8227	847-299-4227	48-9
ICD (Industrial Controls Distributors Inc) 1776 Bloomsbury Ave .... Wanamassa NJ 07712 *Sales	800-281-4788*	732-918-9000	384
ICE (US Immigration & Customs Enforcement) 425 'I' St NW .... Washington DC 20536	866-347-2423		339-10
Ice Technologies Inc 411 SE Ninth St .... Pella IA 50219	877-754-8420		180
Icelandair North America 1900 Crown Colony Dr .... Quincy MA 02169	800-223-5500		26
Ice-O-Matic 11100 E 45th Ave .... Denver CO 80239	800-423-3367	303-576-2940	660
ICF (International Contract Furnishings Inc) 19 Ohio Ave .... Norwich CT 06360	800-237-1625	860-886-1700	321
ICFG (International Church of the Foursquare Gospel) 1910 W Sunset Blvd PO Box 26902 .... Los Angeles CA 90026	888-635-4234	213-989-4234	48-20
ICFL (Idaho Commission for Libraries) 325 W State St .... Boise ID 83702	800-458-3271	208-334-2150	433-5
ICG Link Inc 7003 Chadwick Dr Ste 111 .... Brentwood TN 37027	877-397-7605	615-370-1530	352
ICG/Holliston 905 Holliston Mills Rd .... Church Hill TN 37642	800-251-0451	423-357-6141	740-2
Ichp Building Company LLC 4055 N Perryville Rd .... Loves Park IL 61111	800-363-8012	815-227-9292	529
ICI Mutual Insurance Co 1401 H St NW Ste 1000 .... Washington DC 20005	800-643-4246		
ICIA (Audiovisual and Integrated Experience Association) 11242 Waples Mill Rd Ste 200 .... Fairfax VA 22030	800-659-7469	703-273-7200	49-20
iCIMS Inc 90 Matawan Rd Pkwy 120 5th Fl .... Matawan NJ 07747	800-889-4422	732-847-1941	178-1
ICLA (International Collegiate Licensing Assn) 24651 Detroit Rd .... Westlake OH 44145	877-887-2261	440-892-4000	48-22
ICM Asset Management Inc 601 W Main Ave .... Spokane WA 99201	800-488-4075	509-455-3588	400
Icm Controls Corp 7313 William Barry Blvd .... North Syracuse NY 13212	800-365-5525	315-233-5266	203
ICMA (International City/County Management Assn) 777 N Capitol St NE Ste 500 .... Washington DC 20002	800-745-8780	202-289-4262	49-7
ICMARC 777 N Capitol St NE Ste 600 .... Washington DC 20002 *General	800-669-7471*	202-962-4600	524
ICO (Inter City Oil Company Inc) 1921 S St .... Duluth MN 55812	800-642-5542	218-728-3641	575
ICOI (International Congress of Oral Implantologists) 55 Ln Rd Ste 305 .... Fairfield NJ 07004	800-442-0525	973-783-6300	49-8
iCollectorcom 103-2071 Kingsway Ave .... Port Coquitlam BC V3C6N2	866-313-0123	604-941-2221	51
ICOM America Inc 2380 116th Ave NE .... Bellevue WA 98004	800-872-4266	425-454-8155	643
ICON Advisers Inc 5299 DTC Blvd Ste 1200 .... Greenwood Village CO 80111	800-828-4881	303-790-1600	400
ICON Health & Fitness Inc 1500 S 1000 W .... Logan UT 84321	800-999-3756	435-750-5000	267
Iconoculture Inc 111 Washington Ave S Ste 600 .... Minneapolis MN 55401	866-913-8101		
Icor Technology Inc 935 Ages Dr .... Ottawa ON K1G6L3	877-483-7978	613-745-3600	686
ICP Construction 150 Dascomb Rd .... Andover MA 01810	800-225-1141	978-965-2122	546
ICPI (Interlocking Concrete Pavement Institute) 14801 Murdock St Ste 230 .... Chantilly VA 20151	800-241-3652	703-657-6900	49-3
ICS (Information & Computing Services Inc) 1650 Prudential Dr Ste 300 .... Jacksonville FL 32207	800-676-4427	904-399-8500	178-1
ICS (Implementation & Consulting Services Inc) 500 Office Center Dr Ste 400 .... Washington PA 19034	844-432-8326		177
ICS Marketing Services Inc 4225 Legacy Pkwy .... Lansing MI 48911	888-394-1890	517-394-1890	195
ICTC (Inter-Community Telephone Co) PO Box 8 .... Nome ND 58062	800-350-9137	701-924-8815	731
ICTV Brands Inc 489 Devon Park Dr Ste 315 .... Wayne PA 19087	800-839-4906	484-598-2300	225
ICU Medical Inc 951 Calle Amanecer .... San Clemente CA 92673 *NASDAQ: ICUI*	800-824-7890	949-366-2183	475
ICW Group 11455 El Camino Real .... San Diego CA 92130	800-877-1111	858-350-2400	390-4
ICWM (Institute of Caster & Wheel Manufacturers) 8720 Red Oak Blvd Ste 201 .... Charlotte NC 28217	877-522-5431	704-676-1190	49-13
IcwUSACom Inc 1487 Kingsley Dr .... Medford OR 97504	800-558-4435	541-608-2824	321
ID Systems Inc 123 Tice Blvd Ste 101 .... Woodcliff Lake NJ 07677 *NASDAQ: IDSY*	866-410-0152	201-996-9000	643
IDA (In Defense of Animals) 3010 Kerner Blvd .... San Rafael CA 94901	800-705-0425	415-448-0048	48-3
IDACORP Inc 1221 W Idaho St .... Boise ID 83702 *NYSE: IDA*	800-242-0681	208-388-2200	359-5
Idaho			
Aging Commission (ICOA) 341 W Washington 3rd Fl .... Boise ID 83702	877-471-2777	208-334-3833	338-13
Arts Commission 2410 Old Penitentiary Rd .... Boise ID 83712	800-278-3863	208-334-2119	338-13
Crime Victims Compensation Program PO Box 83720 .... Boise ID 83720	800-950-2110	208-334-6000	338-13
Department of Commerce 700 W State St PO Box 83720 .... Boise ID 83720	800-842-5858	208-334-2470	338-13
Finance Dept 800 Pk Blvd Ste 200 PO Box 83720 ...... Boise ID 83712	888-346-3378	208-332-8000	338-13

	City	State	ZIP	Toll-Free	Phone	Class
Health & Welfare Dept						
450 W State St 10th Fl						
PO Box 83720	Boise	ID	83720	**877-456-1233**		338-13
Housing & Finance Assn						
565 W Myrtle Ave	Boise	ID	83702	**800-526-7145**	208-331-4700	338-13
Lottery						
1199 Shoreline Ln Ste 100	Boise	ID	83702	**800-432-5688**	208-334-2600	450
Parks & Recreation Dept						
5657 Warm Springs Ave	Boise	ID	83716	**855-514-2429**	208-334-4199	338-13
Public Utilities Commission						
472 W Washington Boise						
PO Box 83720	Boise	ID	83720	**800-432-0369**	208-334-0300	338-13
Tax Commission						
800 E Pk Blvd Plz 4	Boise	ID	83712	**800-972-7660**	208-334-7660	338-13
Tourism Development Div						
700 W State St PO Box 83720	Boise	ID	83720	**800-847-4843***	208-334-2470	338-13
*General						
Idaho Assn of Realtors						
10116 W Overland Rd	Boise	ID	83709	**800-621-7553**	208-342-3585	652
Idaho Botanical Garden						
2355 N Penitentiary Rd	Boise	ID	83712	**877-527-8233**	208-343-8649	97
Idaho Commission for Libraries (ICFL)						
325 W State St	Boise	ID	83702	**800-458-3271**	208-334-2150	433-5
Idaho Community Foundation Inc						
210 W State St	Boise	ID	83702	**800-657-5357**	208-342-3535	305
Idaho County Light & Power Co-op						
1065 Hwy 13	Grangeville	ID	83530	**877-212-0424**	208-983-1610	245
Idaho Democratic Party						
812 W Franklin St	Boise	ID	83701	**800-626-0471**	208-336-1815	612-1
Idaho Falls School District 91 Education Foundation Inc						
690 John Adams Pkwy	Idaho Falls	ID	83401	**888-993-7120**	208-525-7500	681
Idaho Labor Dept						
317 W Main St	Boise	ID	83735	**800-554-5627**	208-332-3570	259
Idaho Lions Eye Bank						
1090 N Cole Rd	Boise	ID	83704	**800-546-6889**	208-338-5466	269
Idaho National Laboratory (INL)						
2525 Fremont Ave	Idaho Falls	ID	83402	**866-495-7440**		664
Idaho Nurses Assn (INA)						
1850 E Southern Ave Ste 1	Tempe	AZ	85282	**888-721-8904**		529
Idaho Pacific Lumber Company Inc (IdaPac)						
1770 Spanish Sun Way	Meridian	ID	83642	**800-231-2310**		191-3
Idaho Power Co						
1221 W Idaho St	Boise	ID	83702	**800-488-6151**	208-388-2200	782
Idaho Public Television (IPTV)						
1455 N Orchard St	Boise	ID	83706	**800-543-6868**	208-373-7220	628
Idaho State Bar						
525 W Jefferson St	Boise	ID	83702	**800-221-3295**	208-334-4500	72
Idaho State Journal						
305 S Arthur Ave	Pocatello	ID	83204	**800-669-9777**	208-232-4161	528-2
Idaho State Veterans Home-Pocatello						
1957 Alvin Ricken Dr	Pocatello	ID	83201	**855-488-8440**	208-235-7800	788
Idaho Statesman						
PO Box 40	Boise	ID	83707	**800-635-8934**	208-377-6400	528-2
Idaho-Pacific Corp						
4723 E 100 N PO Box 478	Ririe	ID	83443	**800-238-5503***	208-538-6971	296-18
*Sales						
IdaPac (Idaho Pacific Lumber Company Inc)						
1770 Spanish Sun Way	Meridian	ID	83642	**800-231-2310**		191-3
IDC (IDC) 5 Speen St	Framingham	MA	01701	**800-343-4952**	508-872-8200	464
Idc Communications						
1385 Niakwa Rd E	Winnipeg	MB	R2J3T3	**800-474-7771**	204-254-8282	
IDD Process & Packaging						
5450 Tech Cir	Moorpark	CA	93021	**800-621-4144**	805-529-9890	261
IDDBA (International Dairy-Deli-Bakery Assn)						
636 Science Dr	Madison	WI	53711	**877-399-4925**	608-310-5000	49-6
Idea & Design Works LLC						
2765 Truxtun Rd	San Diego	CA	92106	**800-438-7325**	858-270-1315	392
IDEA Inc						
10455 Pacific Ctr Ct	San Diego	CA	92121	**800-999-4332**	858-535-8979	48-22
Idea Works Inc, The						
100 W Briarwood Ln	Columbia	MO	65203	**888-444-5772**	573-445-4554	177
Ideal Adv & Printing						
116 N Winnebago St	Rockford	IL	61101	**800-208-0294**	815-965-1713	4
Ideal Chemical & Supply Co						
4025 Air Park St	Memphis	TN	38118	**800-232-6776**	901-363-7720	146
Ideal Consulting Services Inco						
521 American Legion Hwy	Westport	MA	02790	**866-254-6136**	508-636-6615	196
Ideal Industries Inc						
1375 Park Ave	Sycamore	IL	60178	**800-435-0705**	815-895-5181	811
Ideal Jacobs Corp						
515 Valley St	Maplewood	NJ	07040	**877-873-4332**	973-275-5100	623
Ideal Manufacturing Inc						
2011 Harnish Blvd	Billings	MT	59101	**800-523-3888**	406-656-4360	490
Ideal Pet Products Inc						
24735 Ave Rockefeller	Valencia	CA	91355	**800-378-4385**	661-294-2266	604
Ideal Shield						
2525 Clark St	Detroit	MI	48209	**866-825-8659**	313-842-7290	295
Ideal Software Systems Inc						
4909 29th Ave	Meridian	MS	39305	**800-964-3325**	601-693-1673	177
Ideal Tape Co						
1400 Middlesex St	Lowell	MA	01851	**800-284-3325**		475
Ideal Window Manufacturing Inc						
100 West Seventh St	Bayonne	NJ	07002	**800-631-3400**		592
Idealease Inc						
430 N Rand Rd	North Barrington	IL	60010	**800-435-3273**	847-304-6000	773
IdeaTek						
111 Old Mill St	Buhler	KS	67522	**855-433-2835**		386
IDEC Corp						
1175 Elko Dr	Sunnyvale	CA	94089	**800-262-4332**	408-747-0550	203
Idegy Inc						
226 N Fifth St Ste 220	Columbus	OH	43215	**888-421-2288**	614-545-5000	184
Ident-A-Kid Services of America						
1780 102nd Ave N						
Ste 100	Saint Petersburg	FL	33716	**800-890-1000**	727-577-4646	310
Identatronics Inc						
165 N Lively Blvd	Elk Grove Village	IL	60007	**800-323-5403***	847-437-2654	587
*Cust Svc						
IDenticard Systems Inc						
25 Race Ave 1st Fl	Lancaster	PA	17603	**800-233-0298**	717-569-5797	688
Identification Plates Inc						
1555 High Point Dr	Mesquite	TX	75149	**800-395-2570**	972-216-1616	410
Identifix Inc						
2714 Patton Rd	Saint Paul	MN	55113	**800-745-9649**	651-633-8007	620
Identigene LLC						
2495 S West Temple	Salt Lake City	UT	84115	**888-404-4363**		417
Identity Automation LP						
8833 N Sam Houston Pkwy W	Houston	TX	77064	**877-221-8401**		357
Identity Genetics Inc						
1321 Sixth St	Brookings	SD	57006	**800-861-1054**	605-697-5300	416
Identity Theft Resource Center						
3625 Ruffin Rd Ste 204	San Diego	CA	92123	**888-400-5530**		627
Idesco Corp						
37 W 26th St	New York	NY	10010	**800-336-1383**	212-889-2530	357
IDEXX Laboratories Inc						
1 IDEXX Dr	Westbrook	ME	04092	**800-548-6733**	207-556-0300	231
NASDAQ: IDXX						
IDF (Immune Deficiency Foundation)						
40 W Chesapeake Ave Ste 308	Towson	MD	21204	**800-296-4433**		48-17
IDG (International Data Group Inc)						
492 Old Connecticut Path						
PO Box 9208	Framingham	MA	01701	**800-343-4952***	508-875-5000	633-9
*Orders						
IDI Distributors Inc						
8303 Audubon Rd	Chanhassen	MN	55317	**888-843-1318**	952-279-6400	686
iDirect Technologies Inc						
13865 Sunrise Valley Dr Ste 100	Herndon	VA	20171	**888-362-5475**	703-648-8118	730
IDP (Insurance Data Processing Inc)						
8101 Washington Ln	Wyncote	PA	19095	**800-523-6745**	215-885-2150	178-11
IDSA (IDSA)						
1300 Wilson Blvd Ste 300	Arlington	VA	22209	**888-463-6332**	703-299-0200	49-8
IDT (Integrated Document Technologies Inc)						
1009 W Hawthorn Dr	Itasca	IL	60143	**877-722-6438**	630-875-1100	196
IEA						
6325 Digital Way Ste 460	Indianapolis	IN	46278	**800-688-3775**		256
IEAP (Interface EAP Inc)						
10370 Richmond Ave Ste 1100						
PO Box 421879	Houston	TX	77042	**800-324-4327**	713-781-3364	460
IEC (International Environmental Corp)						
PO Box 2598	Oklahoma City	OK	73101	**800-264-5329**	405-605-5000	14
IEEE Broadcast Technology Society (BTS)						
445 Hoes Ln	Piscataway	NJ	08854	**800-678-4333**	732-562-5407	49-19
IEEE Computer Graphics & Applications Magazine						
10662 Los Vaqueros Cir						
PO Box 3014	Los Alamitos	CA	90720	**800-272-6657**	714-821-8380	455-7
IEEE Computer Society						
2001 L St NW Ste 700	Washington	DC	20036	**800-272-6657**	202-371-0101	49-19
IEEE Computer Society Press						
10662 Los Vaqueros Cir						
PO Box 3014	Los Alamitos	CA	90720	**800-272-6657**	714-821-8380	633-9
IEEE Electromagnetic Compatibility Society (EMC)						
445 and 501 Hoes Ln	Piscataway	NJ	08854	**800-678-4333**	732-981-0060	49-19
IEEE Geoscience & Remote Sensing Society						
3 Park Ave 17th Fl	New York	NY	10016	**800-678-4333**	212-419-7900	49-19
IEEE Magnetics Society						
445 Hoes Ln PO Box 459	Piscataway	NJ	08855	**800-678-4333**	908-981-0060	49-19
IEEE Micro Magazine						
10662 Los Vaqueros Cir						
PO Box 3014	Los Alamitos	CA	90720	**800-272-6657**	714-821-8380	455-7
IEEE Microwave Theory & Techniques Society (MTT-S)						
5829 Bellanca Dr	Elkridge	MD	21075	**800-678-4333**	410-796-5866	49-19
IEEE Nuclear & Plasma Sciences Society (NPSS)						
445 Hoes Ln	Piscataway	NJ	08854	**800-678-4333**	732-981-0060	49-19
IEEE Product Safety Engineering Society						
445 Hoes Ln	Piscataway	NJ	08854	**800-678-4333**	732-981-0060	49-19
IEEE Reliability Society (RS)						
IEEE Operations Ctr						
445 Hoes Ln	Piscataway	NJ	08854	**800-678-4333**	732-981-0060	49-19
IEEE Signal Processing Society						
445 Hoes Ln	Piscataway	NJ	08854	**800-678-4333**	732-981-0060	49-19
IEEE Society on Social Implications of Technology (SSIT)						
IEEE Operations Ctr						
445 and 501 Hoes Ln	Piscataway	NJ	08854	**800-678-4333**	732-981-0060	49-19
IEEE Technology & Engineering Management Society (IEEE TEMS)						
445 Hoes Ln	Piscataway	NJ	08854	**800-678-4333**	732-981-0060	49-19
IEEE TEMS (IEEE Technology & Engineering Management Society)						
445 Hoes Ln	Piscataway	NJ	08854	**800-678-4333**	732-981-0060	49-19
IEEE Ultrasonics Ferroelectrics & Frequency Control Society (UFFC-S)						
445 Hoes Ln	Piscataway	NJ	08854	**800-678-4333**	732-981-0060	49-19
Ieh Laboratories & Consulting Group						
15300 Bothell Way NE	Lake Forest Park	WA	98155	**800-491-7745**		789
IEHA (International Executive Housekeepers Assn)						
1001 Eastwind Dr Ste 301	Westerville	OH	43081	**800-200-6342**	614-895-7166	49-4
IEP Technologies LLC						
400 Main St	Ashland	MA	01721	**855-793-8407**		663
IeSmart Systems LLC						
15200 E Hardy Rd	Houston	TX	77032	**866-437-6278**	281-447-6278	196
IEWC (Industrial Electric Wire & Cable Inc)						
5001 S Towne Dr	New Berlin	WI	53151	**800-344-2323**	877-613-4392	246
IFA (International Franchise Assn)						
1501 K St NW Ste 350	Washington	DC	20005	**800-543-1038**	202-628-8000	49-18
IFAC (International Federation of Accountants)						
545 Fifth Ave 14th Fl	New York	NY	10017	**888-272-2001**	212-286-9344	49-1
IFAI (Industrial Fabrics Assn International)						
1801 County Rd 'B' W	Roseville	MN	55113	**800-225-4324**	651-222-2508	49-13
IFAW (International Fund for Animal Welfare)						
290 Summer St	Yarmouth Port	MA	02675	**800-932-4329**	508-744-2000	48-3
IFC Stone Crab						
81532 Overseas Hwy						
PO Box 283	Islamorada	FL	33036	**800-258-2559**		667
IFCA International						
3520 Fairlane Ave SW	Grandville	MI	49418	**800-347-1840**	616-531-1840	48-20
IFEBP (International Foundation of Employee Benefit Plans)						
18700 W Bluemound Rd	Brookfield	WI	53045	**888-334-3327**	262-786-6700	260
IFIC (International Fidelity Insurance Co)						
1 Newark Ctr 1111 Raymond Blvd						
20th Fl	Newark	NJ	07102	**800-333-4167**		390-5

Company / Address	Toll-Free	Phone	Class
IFIC (International Food Information Council Foundation) 1100 Connecticut Ave NW Ste 430 ....Washington DC 20036	888-723-3366	202-296-6540	49-6
iFly USA LLC 31310 Alvarado-Niles Rd ....Union City CA 94587	800-759-3861	510-489-4359	31
Ifocus Consulting Inc 100 39th St Ste 201 ....Astoria OR 97103	888-308-6192	503-338-7443	196
Ifrah Financial Services Inc 17300 Chenal Pkwy Ste 150 ....Little Rock AR 72223	800-954-3724	501-821-7733	251
IFS Financial Services Inc 250 Brownlow Ave Ste 1 ....Dartmouth NS B3B1W9	800-565-1153	902-481-6106	317
IFS North America Inc 300 Pk Blvd Ste 555 ....Chicago IL 60143	888-437-4968		178-1
IFT (Institute of Food Technologists) 525 W Van Buren St Ste 1000 ....Chicago IL 60607	800-438-3663	312-782-8424	49-6
IG Inc 720 S Sara Rd ....Mustang OK 73064	800-654-8433	405-376-9393	326
IGA Inc 8745 W Higgins Rd Ste 350 ....Chicago IL 60631	800-321-5442	773-693-4520	344
Igenex 795 San Antonio Rd ....Palo Alto CA 94303	800-832-3200	650-424-1191	417
IGI (Information Gatekeepers Inc) 1340 Soldiers Field Rd Ste 2 ....Brighton MA 02135	800-323-1088	617-782-5033	633-11
IGI (Insight Global Inc) 4170 Ashford Dunwoody Rd Ste 250 ....Atlanta GA 30319	888-336-7463	404-257-7900	193
Igloo Products Corp 777 Igloo Rd ....Katy TX 77494	866-509-3503	281-394-6800	603
Ignify Inc 200 Pine Ave 4th Fl ....Long Beach CA 90802	888-599-4332	562-219-2000	177
Ignition Systems & Controls LP 6300 W Hwy 80 ....Midland TX 79706	800-777-5559	432-697-6472	247
iGo Inc 17800 N Perimeter Dr Ste 200 ....Scottsdale AZ 85255 NASDAQ: IGOI	888-205-0093	480-596-0061	176
I-Go Van & Storage 9820 S 142nd St ....Omaha NE 68138	800-228-9276	402-891-1222	516
iGov Technologies Inc 9211 Palm River Rd Ste 110 ....Tampa FL 33619	800-777-9375	813-612-9470	226
IGS (Institute of General Semantics) 72-11 Austin St ....Forest Hills NY 11375	800-346-1359	212-729-7973	48-11
IGS (Industrial Gasket & Shim Company Inc) 200 Country Club Rd ....Meadow Lands PA 15347	800-229-1447	724-222-5800	326
IGSHPA (International Ground Source Heat Pump Assn) Oklahoma State University 374 Cordell S ....Stillwater OK 74078	800-626-4747	405-744-5175	49-13
IHA (International Housewares Assn) 6400 Shafer Ct Ste 650 ....Rosemont IL 60018	800-752-1052	847-292-4200	49-4
IHC (International Homes of Cedar Inc) PO Box 886 ....Woodinville WA 98072	800-767-7674	360-668-8511	106
iHealth Lab Inc 719 N Shoreline Blvd ....Mountain View CA 94043	855-816-7705		738
iHeartMedia Inc 200 E Basse Rd ....San Antonio TX 78209	800-829-6551	210-822-2828	185
IHG (InterContinental Hotels Group) 3 Ravinia Dr Ste 100 ....Atlanta GA 30346	866-803-2143	770-604-2000	378
IHI (Institute for Healthcare Improvement) 20 University Rd 7th Fl ....Cambridge MA 02138	866-787-0831	617-301-4800	49-8
IHL Group 1650 Murfreesboro Rd Ste 206 ....Franklin TN 37067	888-445-6777	615-591-2955	461
IHLIC (Investors Heritage Life Insurance Co) 200 Capital Ave PO Box 717 ....Frankfort KY 40602	800-422-2011		390-2
IHOP Corp 450 N Brand Blvd ....Glendale CA 91203	866-444-5144	818-240-6055	666
IHRIM (International Assn for Human Resource Information) PO Box 1086 ....Burlington MA 01803	800-804-3983		49-12
IHRSA (International Health Racquet & Sportsclub Assn) 70 Fargo St ....Boston MA 02210	800-228-4772	617-951-0055	48-22
IIABA (Independent Insurance Agents & Brokers of America) 127 S Peyton St ....Alexandria VA 22314	800-221-7917	703-683-4422	49-9
IICRC (Institute of Inspection Cleaning & Restoration Cer) 4043 S E Ave ....Las Vegas NV 89119	844-464-4272		
IID (Imperial Irrigation District) PO Box 937 ....Imperial CA 92251	800-303-7756	760-482-9600	203
IIDA (International Interior Design Assn) 222 Merchandise Mart Plz Ste 567 ....Chicago IL 60654	888-799-4432	312-467-1950	48-4
IIE (Institute of Industrial & Systems Engineers) 3577 PkwyLn Ste 200 ....Norcross GA 30092 *Cust Svc	800-494-0460*	770-449-0461	49-13
III (Insurance Information Institute Inc) 110 William St ....New York NY 10038	877-263-7995	212-346-5500	49-9
IIMC (International Institute of Municipal Clerks) 8331 Utica Ave Ste 200 ....Rancho Cucamonga CA 91730	800-251-1639	909-944-4162	49-7
IJO (Independent Jewelers Organization) 136 Old Post Rd ....Southport CT 06890	800-624-9252		49-4
Ika-Works Inc 2635 Northchase Pkwy SE ....Wilmington NC 28405	800-733-3037	910-452-7059	419
IKEA 420 Alan Wood Rd ....Conshohocken PA 19428	800-434-4532	809-567-4532	321
IKO International Inc 91 Walsh Dr Fox Hill Industrial Pk ....Parsippany NJ 07054	800-922-0337	973-402-0254	384
Il Fornaio America Corp 770 Tamalpais Dr Ste 400 ....Corte Madera CA 94925	888-454-6246	415-945-0500	666
ILA (Illinois Library Assn) 33 W Grand Ave Ste 401 ....Chicago IL 60654	877-565-1896	312-644-1896	434
ILC Dover Inc 1 Moonwalker Rd ....Frederica DE 19946	800-631-9567	302-335-3911	572
ILC Resources 3301 106th Cir ....Urbandale IA 50322	800-247-2133	515-243-8106	501-3
iLeadscom 567 San Nicolas Dr Ste 180 ....Newport Beach CA 92660	877-245-3237		224
iLearning Gateway Inc 2650 Vly View Ln Bldg 1 Ste 200 ....Dallas TX 75234	888-464-2672		
Ilene Industries Inc 301 Stanley Blvd ....Shelbyville TN 37160	800-251-1602	931-684-8731	326
Ilex Construction & Woodworking 3801 Northampton St NW Ste 3 ....Washington DC 20015	866-551-4539	410-820-4393	681
ILF (Indiana Library Federation) 941 E 86th St Ste 260 ....Indianapolis IN 46240	800-326-0013	317-257-2040	434
Iliff School of Theology 2201 S University Blvd ....Denver CO 80210	800-678-3360	303-744-1287	167-3
Ilikai Hotel & Suites 1777 Ala Moana Blvd ....Honolulu HI 96815	866-536-7973	808-949-3811	378
iLinc Communications Inc 2999 N 44th St Ste 650 ....Phoenix AZ 85018	800-767-9054	602-952-1200	176
Illinois			
Aging Dept 1 Natural Resources Way Ste 100 ....Springfield IL 62701	800-252-8966	217-785-3356	338-14
Agriculture Dept StateFairgrounds? PO Box 19281 ....Springfield IL 62794	866-287-2999	217-782-2172	
Banks & Real Estate Div 320 W Washington St ....Springfield IL 62786	888-473-4858		338-14
Commerce & Economic Opportunity Dept 620 E Adams St ....Springfield IL 62701	800-526-0844		
Commerce Commission 527 E Capitol Ave ....Springfield IL 62701	800-524-0795	217-782-2024	
Crime Victims Services Div 100 W Randolf Rd 13th Fl ....Chicago IL 60601	800-228-3368	312-814-2581	338-14
Emergency Management Agency 2200 S Dirksen Pkwy ....Springfield IL 62703	800-782-7860	217-782-2700	338-14
Environmental Protection Agency 1021 N Grand Ave E ....Springfield IL 62702	800-782-7860	217-782-3397	338-14
Human Services Dept 100 S Grand Ave E ....Springfield IL 62762	800-843-6154	217-557-1601	338-14
Lottery 101 W Jefferson St ....Springfield IL 62702	800-252-1775	217-524-6435	450
Mental Health Div 100 W Randolf St Ste 3-400 ....Chicago IL 60601	800-252-2923	800-526-0844	338-14
Revenue Dept 101 W Jefferson St ....Springfield IL 62702	800-732-8866	217-782-3336	338-14
Secretary of State 213 State Capitol ....Springfield IL 62756	800-252-8980	217-782-2201	338-14
State Board of Education 100 N First St ....Springfield IL 62777	866-262-6663	217-782-4321	338-14
Student Assistance Commission 1755 Lake Cook Rd ....Deerfield IL 60015	877-877-3724	800-899-4722	721
Tourism Bureau 100 W Randolph St Ste 3-400 ....Chicago IL 60601	800-226-6632	312-814-4732	338-14
Treasurer Capitol Bldg 219 Statehouse ....Springfield IL 62706	866-458-7327		338-14
Veterans Affairs Dept 69 W Washington George Dunn County Bldg Ste 1620 ....Chicago IL 60602	800-437-9824	312-814-2460	338-14
Workers' Compensation Commission 100 W Randolph St Ste 8-200 ....Chicago IL 60601	866-352-3033	312-814-6611	338-14
Illinois Blueprint Corp 800 SW Jefferson Ave ....Peoria IL 61605	800-747-7070	309-676-1300	240
Illinois College 1101 W College Ave ....Jacksonville IL 62650 *Admissions	866-464-5265*	217-245-3030	166
Illinois Fair Plan Assn 130 E Randolph PO Box 81469 ....Chicago IL 60601	800-972-4480	312-861-0385	686
Illinois Glove Co 650 Anthony Trl ....Northbrook IL 60062	800-342-5458	847-291-1700	155-7
Illinois Health Care Association 1029 S Fourth St ....Springfield IL 62703	800-252-8988	217-528-6455	529
Illinois Institute of Art *Chicago* 350 N Orleans St Ste 136-L ....Chicago IL 60654	800-351-3450	312-280-3500	164
Schaumburg 1000 N Plaza Dr ....Schaumburg IL 60173	800-314-3450	847-619-3450	164
Illinois Institute of Technology 10 W 33rd St ....Chicago IL 60616	800-448-2329	312-567-3025	166
Illinois Library Assn (ILA) 33 W Grand Ave Ste 401 ....Chicago IL 60654	877-565-1896	312-644-1896	434
Illinois Mutual Life Insurance Co 300 SW Adams St ....Peoria IL 61634	800-380-6688	309-674-8255	390-2
Illinois National Bank 322 E Capitol ....Springfield IL 62701	877-771-2316	217-747-5500	70
Illinois Nurses Assn (INA) 105 W Adams St Ste 2101 ....Chicago IL 60603	800-262-2500	312-419-2900	529
Illinois Rural Electric Co-op 2 S Main St ....Winchester IL 62694	800-468-4732	217-742-3128	245
Illinois South Tourism 4387 N Illinois St Ste 200 ....Swansea IL 62226	800-442-1488	618-257-1488	206
Illinois State Bar Assn 424 S Second St ....Springfield IL 62701	800-252-8908	217-525-1760	72
Illinois State Dental Society 1010 S Second St ....Springfield IL 62704	888-286-2447	217-525-1406	227
Illinois State Fairgrounds 801 E Sangamon Ave ....Springfield IL 62702	866-287-2999	217-782-4231	638
Illinois State Library 300 S Second St ....Springfield IL 62701	800-665-5576	217-782-2994	433-5
Illinois State Medical Inter-Insurance Exchange (ISMIE) 20 N Michigan Ave Ste 700 ....Chicago IL 60602	800-782-4767	312-782-2749	390-5
Illinois State Medical Society 20 N Michigan Ave Ste 700 ....Chicago IL 60602	800-782-4767	312-782-1654	472
Illinois State Military Museum 1301 N MacArthur Blvd ....Springfield IL 62702	800-732-8868	217-761-3910	517
Illinois State University 100 N University St ....Normal IL 61761 *Admissions	800-366-2478*	309-438-2111	166
Illinois State University Milner Library 201 N School St ....Normal IL 61790	800-366-2478	309-438-3451	433-6
Illinois Symphony Orchestra 524 E Capitol Ave ....Springfield IL 62701	800-401-7222	217-522-2838	569-3
Illinois Veterans Home-Anna 792 N Main St ....Anna IL 62906	800-437-9824	618-833-6302	788
Illinois Vietnam Veterans Memorial Oak Ridge Cemetery ....Springfield IL 62702	800-545-7300	217-782-2717	50-4
Illinois Wesleyan University 1312 Park St ....Bloomington IL 61701 *Admissions	800-332-2498*	309-556-3031	166

	Toll-Free	Phone	Class

Illinois Wholesale Cash Register Inc
2790 Pinnacle Dr .... Elgin IL 60124 | **800-544-5493** | 847-310-4200 | 112

Illumina Inc
9885 Towne Centre Dr .... San Diego CA 92121 | **800-809-4566** | 858-202-4500 | 418
NASDAQ: ILMN

iLookabout Corp
383 Richmond St Ste 408. .... London ON N6A3C4 | **866-963-2015** | 519-963-2015 | 177

ILS (International Launch Services)
1875 Explorer St Ste 700 .... Reston VA 20190 | **800-852-4980** | 571-633-7400 | 502

ILSCO
4730 Madison Rd .... Cincinnati OH 45227 | **800-776-9775*** | 513-533-6200 | 810
*Sales

ILX Lightwave Corp
31950 E Frontage Rd .... Bozeman MT 59715 | **800-459-9459** | | 248

IM. Systems Group Inc
3206 Tower Oaks Blvd Ste 300 ..... Rockville MD 20852 | **866-368-9880** | 240-833-1889 | 180

IMA (Institute of Management Accountants Inc)
10 Paragon Dr Ste 1 .... Montvale NJ 07645 | **800-638-4427** | 201-573-9000 | 49-1

IMA (Interchurch Medical Assistance Inc)
1730 M St NW Ste 1100....... Washington DC 20036 | **877-241-7952** | 202-888-6200 | 48-5

Image Labs International
PO Box 1545 .... Belgrade MT 59714 | **800-785-5995** | 406-585-7225 | 178-8

Image One Corp
13201 Capital St .... Oak Park MI 48237 | **800-799-5377** | 248-414-9955 | 624

Image Sport Inc
1115 SE Westbrooke Dr .... Waukee IA 50263 | **800-919-0520** | 515-987-7699 | 683

Image Studios Inc
1100 S Lynndale Dr .... Appleton WI 54914 | **877-738-4080** | |

Image Works
PO Box 443 ....Woodstock NY 12498 | **800-475-8801** | 845-679-8500 | 589

Imagemakers Inc
514 Lincoln Ave PO Box 368 .... Wamego KS 66547 | **888-865-8511** | |

ImageMark Business Services Inc
3145 Northwest Blvd .... Gastonia NC 28098 | **800-632-9513** | |

ImageWorks
250 Clearbrook Rd .... Elmsford NY 10523 | **800-592-6666** | 914-592-6100 | 381

Imagine Advertising & Publishing Inc
3100 Medlock Bridge Rd
Ste 370......... Peachtree Corners GA 30071 | **866-832-3214** | 770-734-0966 | 392

Imagine Air Jet Services LLC
460 Briscoe Blvd Ste 210 ..... Lawrenceville GA 30046 | **877-359-4242** | |

Imaginet Resources Corp
233 Portage Ave ....Winnipeg MB R3B2A7 | **800-989-6022** | 204-989-6022 | 177

Imaging Business Machines LLC (IBML)
2750 Crestwood Blvd .... Birmingham AL 35210 | **877-627-8325** | 205-956-4071 | 111

Imaging Healthcare Specialists Medical Group Inc
6256 Greenwich Dr Ste 150 ...... San Diego CA 92122 | **866-558-4320** | | 414

Imaging Office Systems Inc
4505 E Park 30 Dr .... Columbia City IN 46725 | **800-878-7731** | 260-248-9696 | 45

Imaging Supplies Company Inc
804 Woodland Ave .... Sanford NC 27330 | **800-518-1152** | 919-776-1152 | 585

iMakeNews Inc
7400 Wilshire Place Dr ....Houston TX 77040 | **866-964-6397** | 937-485-8030 | 180

Imanami Corp
2301 Armstrong St Ste 211 .... Livermore CA 94551 | **800-684-8515** | 925-371-3000 | 196

IMC (InterAmerican Motor Corp)
8901 Canoga Ave .... Canoga Park CA 91304 | **800-874-8925** | 818-678-1200 | 61

IMC (International Medical Corps)
1919 Santa Monica Blvd
Ste 400........Santa Monica CA 90404 | **800-481-4462** | 310-826-7800 | 48-5

IMC Networks Corp
19772 Pauling ....Foothill Ranch CA 92610 | **800-624-1070** | 949-465-3000 | 176

IMC USA (Institute of Management Consultants USA Inc)
2025 M St NW Ste 800........ Washington DC 20036 | **800-221-2557** | 800-793-4992 | 49-12

IMCA (Investments & Wealth Institute)
5619 DTC Pkwy Ste 500.....Greenwood Village CO 80111 | **800-250-9083** | 303-770-3377 | 49-2

IMCOR-Interstate Mechanical Corp
1841 E Washington St ....Phoenix AZ 85034 | **800-628-0211** | 602-257-1319 | 189-10

IMCU (Indiana Members Credit Union)
7110 W Tenth St ....Indianapolis IN 46214 | **800-556-9268** | 317-248-8556 | 219

iMemories
9181 E Bell Rd .... Scottsdale AZ 85260 | **800-845-7986** | | 584

Imerys Filtration Minerals Inc
130 Castilian Dr .... Goleta CA 93117 | **800-893-4445** | 805-562-0200 | 410

IMETCO (Innovative Metals Company Inc)
4648 S Old Peachtree Rd .... Norcross GA 30071 | **800-646-3826** | 770-908-1030 | 46

iMethods
8787 Perimeter Park Blvd ....Jacksonville FL 32216 | **888-306-2261** | | 196

Imex Veterinary Inc
1001 Mckesson Dr ....Longview TX 75604 | **800-828-4639** | 903-295-2196 | 789

IMF (International Monetary Fund)
700 19th St NW .... Washington DC 20431 | **800-548-5384** | 202-623-7000 | 778

IMG (International Motor Coach Group Inc)
12351 W 96th Ter ....Lenexa KS 66215 | **888-447-3466** | | 49-21

Imh Financial Corp
7001 N Scottsdale Rd
Ste 2050.............. Scottsdale AZ 85253 | **800-510-6445** | 480-840-8400 | 216

IMI (International Masonry Institute)
17101 Science Dr ....Bowie MD 20715 | **800-803-0295** | 301-291-2124 | 49-3

IMI Cornelius Inc
101 Broadway St W .... Osseo MN 55369 | **800-238-3600** | | 660

IMI Data Search Inc
4333 Park Terrace Dr
Ste 220........ Westlake Village CA 91361 | **866-984-1736** | 805-920-8617 | 631

I-Minerals Inc
880 - 580 Hornby St .... Vancouver BC V6C3B6 | **877-303-6573** | 604-303-6573 | 501-2

IMLA (International Municipal Lawyers Assn)
51 Monroe St Ste 404............ Rockville MD 20850 | **800-942-7732** | 202-466-5424 | 49-10

IMM Inc
758 Isenhauer Rd ....Grayling MI 49738 | **855-202-6384** | 989-344-7662 |

Immanuel Medical Ctr
6901 N 72nd St .... Omaha NE 68122 | **800-253-4368** | 402-572-2121 | 373-3

Immediatek
3301 Airport Fwy Ste 200......... Bedford TX 76021 | **888-661-6565** | | 224

Immigrant & Employee Rights Section-US. Department of Justice Civil Rights Division
950 Pennsylvania Ave NW
Ste 4706.......... Washington DC 20530 | **800-255-7688** | 202-616-5594 | 339-13

Immtech Pharmaceuticals
1 N End Ave .... New York NY 10282 | **877-898-8038** | 212-791-2911 | 578

ImmucorGamma Inc
3130 Gateway Dr PO Box 5625......... Norcross GA 30091 | **800-829-2553*** | 770-441-2051 | 231
NASDAQ: BLUD ■ *Cust Svc

Immune Deficiency Foundation (IDF)
40 W Chesapeake Ave Ste 308 ..... Towson MD 21204 | **800-296-4433** | | 48-17

Immuno Concepts NA Ltd
9825 Goethe Rd Ste 350....... Sacramento CA 95827 | **800-251-5115** | 916-363-2649 | 738

ImmunoDiagnostics Inc
1 Presidential Way Ste 104......... Woburn MA 01801 | **800-573-1700** | 781-938-6300 | 231

Immunovision Inc
1820 Ford Ave ....Springdale AR 72764 | **800-541-0960** | 479-751-7005 | 231

IMMVAC Inc
6080 Bass Ln ....Columbia MO 65201 | **800-944-7563** | 573-443-5363 | 580

IMMY (IMMY)
2701 Corporate Centre Dr .... Norman OK 73069 | **800-654-3639** | 405-360-4669 | 231

Imo Pump
1710 Airport Rd .... Monroe NC 28110 | **877-853-7867** | 704-289-6511 | 637

Impac International
11445 Pacific Ave .... Fontana CA 92337 | **800-227-9591** | 951-685-9660 | 8

Impac Mortgage Holdings Inc
19500 Jamboree Rd .... Irvine CA 92612 | **800-597-4101** | 949-475-3600 | 650
NYSE: IMH

Impact Drug & Alcohol Treatment Ctr
1680 N Fair Oaks Ave ....Pasadena CA 91103 | **866-734-4200** | 626-798-0884 | 722

Impact Group
12977 N Outer 40 Dr Ste 300 .... St. Louis MO 63141 | **800-420-2420** | 314-453-9002 | 260

Impact Guns
2710 S 1900 W .... Ogden UT 84401 | **800-917-7137** | | 679

Impact Label Corp
8875 Krum Ave ....Galesburg MI 49053 | **800-820-0362** | | 412

Impact Products LLC
2840 Centennial Rd .... Toledo OH 43617 | **800-333-1541*** | 419-841-2891 | 151
*Cust Svc

Impact Seven Inc
147 Lake Almena Dr .... Almena WI 54805 | **800-685-9353** | 715-357-3334 | 401

Impact Technologies Group Inc
615 S College St .... Charlotte NC 28202 | **800-438-6017** | 704-549-1100 |

Impatica Inc
2430 Don Reid Dr Ste 200 .... Ottawa ON K1H1E1 | **800-548-3475** | 613-736-9982 | 225

Impax Laboratories Inc
30831 Hun2od Ave ....Hayward CA 94544 | **877-994-6729** | 510-240-6450 | 579

IMPCO Technologies
5757 Farinon Dr ....San Antonio TX 78240 | **800-325-4534** | 210-495-9772 | 128

Imperial Bedding Co
720 11th St PO Box 5347..........Huntington WV 25703 | **800-529-3321** | 304-529-3321 | 469

Imperial Capital LLC
10100 Santa Monica Blvd
Ste 2400..........Los Angeles CA 90067 | **800-929-2299** | 310-246-3700 | 400

Imperial Graphics Inc
3100 Walkent Dr NW ......Grand Rapids MI 49544 | **800-777-2591** | | 110

Imperial Industries Inc
505 Industrial Park Ave ....Rothschild WI 54474 | **800-558-2945** | 715-359-0200 | 105

Imperial Irrigation District (IID)
PO Box 937 .... Imperial CA 92251 | **800-303-7756** | 760-482-9600 | 203

Imperial Manufacturing Group Inc
40 Industrial Park St .... Richibucto NB E4W4A4 | **800-561-3100** | 506-523-9117 | 606

Imperial of Waikiki
205 Lewers St .... Honolulu HI 96815 | **800-347-2582** | 808-923-1827 | 378

Imperial Oil Resources Ltd
237 Fourth Ave SW
PO Box 2480 Stn M .... Calgary AB T2P3M9 | **800-567-3776** | | 576

Imperial Pools Inc
33 Wade Rd ....Latham NY 12110 | **800-444-9977** | 518-786-1200 | 724

Imperial Toy LLC
16641 Roscoe Pl ....North Hills CA 91343 | **877-762-8253*** | 818-536-6500 | 757
*Cust Svc

Imperial Trading Co Inc
701 Edwards Ave .... Elmwood LA 70123 | **800-775-4504*** | 504-733-1400 | 297-8
*Cust Svc

Imperial Valley College
380 E Atten Rd PO Box 158 .... Imperial CA 92251 | **800-336-1642** | 760-352-8320 | 162

Imperial Woodworks Inc
PO Box 7835 ....Waco TX 76714 | **800-234-6624** | | 319-3

Implement Sales Company LLC
1574 Stone Ridge Dr .... Stone Mountain GA 30083 | **800-955-9592** | 770-908-9439 | 274

Implementation & Consulting Services Inc (ICS)
500 Office Center Dr Ste 400 ...... Washington PA 19034 | **844-432-8326** | | 177

Implementix Inc
4850 Ward Rd .... Wheat Ridge CO 80033 | **800-433-2257** | 888-831-2536 | 623

IMPO PO Box 639 ....Santa Maria CA 93456 | **800-367-4676** | | 301

Improv Asylum
216 Hanover St ....Boston MA 02113 | **888-396-6887** | 617-263-6887 | 519

Improve Group Inc, The
661 LaSalle St Ste 300 .... St Paul MN 55114 | **877-467-7847** | 651-315-8919 | 196

Improved Construction Methods
1040 N Redmond Rd ....Jacksonville AR 72076 | **877-494-5793** | | 357

Impulse Technologies Ltd
920 Gana Crt ....Mississauga ON L5S1Z4 | **800-667-5475** | 905-564-9266 | 686

IMS inc
245 Commerce Blvd ....Liverpool NY 13088 | **800-466-4189** | | 5

IMSA (International Municipal Signal Assn)
165 E Union St PO Box 539 ....Newark NY 14513 | **800-723-4672** | 315-331-2182 | 49-7

IMT (Iowa Mold Tooling Co Inc)
500 W US Hwy 18 .... Garner IA 50438 | **800-247-5958** | 641-923-3711 | 468

IMT (Lomont In-Mold Technologies)
1516 E Mapleleaf Dr .... Mount Pleasant IA 52641 | **800-776-0380** | 319-385-1528 | 597

IMT Group, The
PO Box 1336 ....Des Moines IA 50266 | **800-274-3531** | | 390-4

Imtech Graphics Inc
545 Dell Rd .... Carlstadt NJ 07072 | **800-468-3240** | | 776

IMVU Inc
PO Box 390012 ....Mountain View CA 94039 | **866-761-0975** | 650-321-8334 | 386

In Defense of Animals (IDA)
3010 Kerner Blvd .... San Rafael CA 94901 | **800-705-0425** | 415-448-0048 | 48-3

In The Line of Duty
10786 Indian Head Industrial Blvd
.... Saint Louis MO 63132 | **800-462-5232** | 314-890-8733 | 95

In The Swim Inc
320 Industrial Dr .... West Chicago IL 60185 | **800-288-7946** | | 707

	Toll-Free	Phone	Class
In Touch Business Consultants			
11370 66th St 132 ....Largo FL 33773	877-676-5492		461
INA (Idaho Nurses Assn)			
1850 E Southern Ave Ste 1 ....Tempe AZ 85282	888-721-8904		529
INA (Illinois Nurses Assn)			
105 W Adams St Ste 2101 ....Chicago IL 60603	800-262-2500	312-419-2900	529
Inc Magazine			
7 World Trade Ctr ....New York NY 10007	800-234-0999	212-389-5377	455-5
Incentive Publications Inc			
2400 Crestmoor Dr ....Nashville TN 37215	800-967-5325*	615-385-2934	243
*Mktg			
INCERTEC LLC			
160 83rd Ave NE ....Fridley MN 55432	800-638-2573	763-717-7016	256
Incline Village/Crystal Bay Visitors Bureau			
969 Tahoe Blvd ....Incline Village NV 89451	800-468-2463	775-832-1606	206
InComm Conferencing Inc			
208 Harristown Rd Ste 202.............Glen Rock NJ 07452	877-804-2062	201-612-9696	386
InCycle Software Inc			
1120 Avenue of The Americas			
4th Fl ....New York NY 10036	800-565-0510	212-626-2608	180
INDA: Assn of the Nonwoven Fabrics Industry			
1100 Crescent Green Ste 115			
PO Box 1288. ....Cary NC 27518	800-628-2112	919-459-3700	49-13
Indaco Metal			
3 American Way ....Shawnee OK 74804	877-750-5614	405-273-9200	106
Indco Inc			
4040 Earnings Way ....New Albany IN 47150	800-942-4383		190
Indeck Power Equipment Co			
1111 Willis Ave ....Wheeling IL 60090	800-446-3325	847-541-8300	384
Indelco Plastics Corp			
6530 Cambridge St ....Minneapolis MN 55426	800-486-6456	952-925-5075	601-2
Indepak Inc			
2136 NE 194th Ave ....Portland OR 97230	800-338-1857		
Independant Insurance Services In			
3956 N Pine St ....Davenport IA 52806	800-373-1562	563-383-5555	389
Independence Blue Cross			
1901 Market St ....Philadelphia PA 19103	800-275-2583		390-3
Independence Bowl Foundation			
PO Box 1723 ....Shreveport LA 71166	888-414-2695	318-221-0712	
Independence Chamber of Commerce			
210 W Truman Rd ....Independence MO 64050	800-222-6400	816-252-4745	139
Independence Community College			
1057 W College Ave			
PO Box 708. ....Independence KS 67301	800-842-6063	620-331-4100	162
Independence FSB			
1301 Ninth St NW ....Washington DC 20001	888-922-6537		
Independence National Historical Park			
143 S Third St ....Philadelphia PA 19106	800-537-7676	215-597-8787	560
Independence Tube Corp			
6226 W 74th St ....Chicago IL 60638	800-376-6000		
Independent Bank Corp			
230 W Main St ....Ionia MI 48846	888-300-3193	616-527-2400	359-2
NASDAQ: IBCP			
Independent Book Publishers Assn, The (IBPA)			
1020 Manhattan Beach Blvd			
Ste 204 ....Manhattan Beach CA 90266	800-327-5113	310-546-1818	49-16
Independent Chemical Corp			
79-51 Cooper Ave ....Glendale NY 11385	800-892-2578	718-894-0700	146
Independent Community Bankers of America (ICBA)			
1615 L St NW Ste 900 ....Washington DC 20036	800-422-8439	202-659-8111	49-2
Independent Health			
511 Farber Lakes Dr ....Buffalo NY 14221	800-247-1466	716-631-3001	390-3
Independent Ink Inc			
13700 Gramercy Pl ....Gardena CA 90249	800-446-5538	310-523-4657	387
Independent Institute			
100 Swan Way ....Oakland CA 94621	800-927-8733	510-632-1366	630
Independent Insurance Agents & Brokers of America Inc (IIABA)			
127 S Peyton St ....Alexandria VA 22314	800-221-7917	703-683-4422	49-9
Independent Jewelers Organization (IJO)			
136 Old Post Rd ....Southport CT 06890	800-624-9252		49-4
Independent Order of Foresters (IOF)			
789 Don Mills Rd ....Toronto ON M3C1T9	800-828-1540	416-429-3000	48-5
Independent Order of Odd Fellows			
422 N Trade St ....Winston-Salem NC 27101	800-235-8358	336-725-5955	48-15
Independent Petroleum Assn of America (IPAA)			
1201 15th St NW Ste 300 ....Washington DC 20005	800-433-2851	202-857-4722	48-12
Independent Protection Company Inc			
1607 S Main St ....Goshen IN 46526	800-860-8388	574-533-4116	810
Independent Publishers Group			
814 N Franklin St ....Chicago IL 60610	800-888-4741*	312-337-0747	96
*Orders			
Independent Record			
PO Box 4249 ....Helena MT 59604	800-523-2272	406-447-4000	528-2
Independent Television Service (ITVS)			
651 Brannan St Ste 410 ....San Francisco CA 94107	888-572-8918	415-356-8383	737
Independent, The			
2250 First St ....Livermore CA 94550	877-952-3588	925-447-8700	528-4
Independents Service Co			
2710 Market St ....Hannibal MO 63401	800-325-3694	573-221-4615	194
Indera Mills Co			
350 W Maple St PO Box 309 ....Yadkinville NC 27055	800-334-8605		155-17
Index Fresh Inc			
18184 Slover Ave ....Bloomington CA 92316	800-352-6931	909-877-0999	11-1
Index Funds Advisors Inc			
19200 Von Karman Ave Ste 150 ....Irvine CA 92612	888-643-3133	949-502-0050	686
Indexx Inc			
303 Haywood Rd ....Greenville SC 29607	800-252-8227	864-234-1024	623
Indian Arts & Crafts Board			
1849 C St NW MS 2528-MIB ....Washington DC 20240	888-278-3253	202-208-3773	339-19
Indian Bible College			
2237 E Cedar Ave ....Flagstaff AZ 86004	866-503-7789	928-774-3890	166
Indian Capital Technology Ctr			
2403 N 41st St E ....Muskogee OK 74403	800-757-0877	918-687-6383	795
Indian Creek Fabricators			
1350 Commerce Pk Dr ....Tipp City OH 45371	877-769-5880	937-667-5818	752
Indian Creek Recreation Area			
12905 288th Ave ....Mobridge SD 57604	800-710-2267*	605-845-7112	
*Resv			
Indian Electric Co-op Inc			
2506 E Hwy 64 ....Cleveland OK 74020	800-482-2750	918-295-9500	245
Indian Harvest Specialtifoods Inc			
1012 Paul Bunyan Dr SE ....Bemidji MN 56601	800-346-7032*		296-23
*Orders			
Indian Head Industries Inc			
8530 Cliff Cameron Dr ....Charlotte NC 28269	800-527-1534	704-547-7411	60
Indian Hills Community College			
525 Grandview Ave ....Ottumwa IA 52501	800-726-2585	641-683-5111	162
Indian Hot Springs			
302 Soda Creek Rd			
PO Box 1990. ....Idaho Springs CO 80452	800-884-3201	303-989-6666	665
Indian Pueblo Cultural Ctr			
2401 12th St NW ....Albuquerque NM 87104	866-855-7902	505-843-7270	517
Indian River Estates			
2250 Indian Creek Blvd W ....Vero Beach FL 32966	800-544-0277*	772-539-4762	668
*Mktg			
Indian River Lifesaving Station Museum			
25039 Costal Hwy ....Rehoboth Beach DE 19971	877-987-2757	302-227-6991	517
Indian River State College (IRSC)			
3209 Virginia Ave ....Fort Pierce FL 34981	866-792-4772	772-462-4772	162
Indian River Transport Co			
2580 Executive Rd ....Winter Haven FL 33884	800-877-2430	863-324-2430	775
Indian Springs Resort & Spa			
1712 Lincoln Ave ....Calistoga CA 94515	800-877-3623	707-709-8139	665
Indian Springs School			
190 Woodward Dr ....Pelham AL 35124	888-843-9477*	205-988-3350	618
*General			
Indian Summer Carpet Mills Inc			
601 Callahan Rd PO Box 3577 ....Dalton GA 30719	800-824-4010	706-277-6277	131
Indian Temple Mound Museum			
107 Miracle Strip Pkwy SW			
.............Fort Walton Beach FL 32548	866-847-1301	850-833-9500	517
Indian Valley Industries Inc			
PO Box 810 ....Johnson City NY 13790	800-659-5111	607-729-5111	67
Indian Wells Resort Hotel			
76-661 Hwy 111 ....Indian Wells CA 92210	800-248-3220	760-345-6466	665
Indiana			
Agriculture Dept			
101 W Washington St ....Indianapolis IN 46204	800-677-9800		
Arts Commission			
302 W Washington St ....Indianapolis IN 46204	800-677-9800		
Attorney General			
302 W Washington St			
Rm E114. ....Indianapolis IN 46204	800-677-9800		
Child Support Bureau			
302 W Washington St			
Rm E-205. ....Indianapolis IN 46204	800-840-8757	800-677-9800	338-15
Consumer Protection Div			
402 W Washington St			
Rm W-478 ....Indianapolis IN 46204	800-382-5516	317-232-3001	338-15
Correction Dept			
302 W Washington St ....Indianapolis IN 46204	800-677-9800		
Disability Aging & Rehabilitative Services Div			
402 W Washington St Ste W453			
PO Box 7083 ....Indianapolis IN 46207	800-545-7763	317-232-1147	338-15
Economic Development Corp			
1 N Capitol Ave Ste 700 ....Indianapolis IN 46204	800-463-8081	317-232-8800	338-15
Environmental Management Dept			
100 N Senate Ave ....Indianapolis IN 46204	800-451-6027	317-232-8603	338-15
Family & Social Services Admin			
402 W Washington St Rm W-392			
PO Box 7083 ....Indianapolis IN 46207	800-403-0864	800-677-9800	338-15
Fish & Wildlife Div			
402 W Washington St			
Rm W273 ....Indianapolis IN 46204	800-677-9800		
General Assembly			
State House			
200 W Washington St ....Indianapolis IN 46204	800-382-9842	317-232-9600	338-15
Health Dept			
2 N Meridian St ....Indianapolis IN 46204	800-382-9480	317-233-1325	338-15
Historical Bureau			
302 W Washington St			
Rm E018. ....Indianapolis IN 46204	800-677-9800		
Homeland Security Dept			
302 West Washington St ....Indianapolis IN 46204	800-457-8283	800-677-9800	338-15
Housing Finance Authority			
30 S Meridian St Ste 1000 ....Indianapolis IN 46204	800-872-0371	317-232-7777	338-15
Insurance Dept			
311 W Washington St			
Ste 300. ....Indianapolis IN 46204	800-622-4461*	317-232-2385	338-15
*Cust Svc			
Lieutenant Governor			
302 W Washington St			
Rm E018. ....Indianapolis IN 46204	800-677-9800		
Natural Resources Dept			
315 West Ohio St ....Indianapolis IN 46204	877-463-6367	800-677-9800	338-15
Parole Services Div			
302 West Washington St			
Rm E334. ....Indianapolis IN 46204	800-677-9800		
Port Commission			
150 W Market St Ste 100 ....Indianapolis IN 46204	800-232-7678	317-232-9200	614
Professional Licensing Agency			
302 West Washington St ....Indianapolis IN 46204	800-677-9800		
Revenue Dept			
100 N Senate Ave Rm N105 ....Indianapolis IN 46204	800-677-9800		
Securities Div			
302 W Washington St 5th Fl. ....Indianapolis IN 46204	800-382-5516	317-232-6201	338-15
State Ethics Commission			
315 W Ohio St Rm 104. ....Indianapolis IN 46202	866-805-8498	800-677-9800	265
State Government Information			
402 W Washington St			
Rm W160 ....Indianapolis IN 46204	800-457-8283	317-233-0800	338-15
State Parks & Reservoirs Div			
402 W Washington St			
Rm W298. ....Indianapolis IN 46204	800-622-4931	317-232-4124	338-15
State Police			
100 N Senate Ave ....Indianapolis IN 46204	800-677-9800		

Name / Address	City	State	ZIP	Toll-Free	Phone	Class
Students Assistance Commission						
150 W Market St Rm 414	Indianapolis	IN	46204	**888-528-4719**	317-232-2350	721
Technology Office						
100 N Senate Ave	Indianapolis	IN	46204	**800-382-1095**	317-233-2072	338-15
Tourism Development Office						
1 N Capitol Ave Ste 600	Indianapolis	IN	46204	**800-457-8283**	317-232-8860	338-15
Treasurer						
315 West Ohio St	Indianapolis	IN	46204	**800-677-9800**		
Utility Regulatory Commission						
302 W Washington St Rm E306	Indianapolis	IN	46204	**800-677-9800**		
Veterans' Affairs Dept						
302 W Washington St Rm E418	Indianapolis	IN	46204	**800-400-4520**	317-232-3910	
Victims Services Div						
101 W Washington St Ste 1170 East Tower	Indianapolis	IN	46204	**800-353-1484**	317-232-1233	338-15
Weights & Measures Div						
2525 Shadeland Ave C-3	Indianapolis	IN	46219	**800-677-9800**		
Worker's Compensation Board						
402 W Washington St Rm W196	Indianapolis	IN	46204	**800-677-9800**		
Workforce Development Dept						
402 W Washington St Rm W160	Indianapolis	IN	46204	**800-891-6499**	317-232-7670	259
Indiana County						
825 Philadelphia St 3rd Fl	Indiana	PA	15701	**888-559-6355**	724-465-3805	337
Indiana County Tourist Bureau						
2334 Oakland Ave Ste 68	Indiana	PA	15701	**877-746-3426**	724-463-7505	206
Indiana Credit Union League						
5975 Castle Creek Pkwy N Ste 300	Indianapolis	IN	46250	**800-285-5300**	317-594-5300	219
Indiana Democratic Party						
115 W Washington St Ste 1165	Indianapolis	IN	46204	**800-223-3387**	317-231-7100	612-1
Indiana Dental Assn						
1319 E Stop 10 Rd	Indianapolis	IN	46227	**800-562-5646**	317-634-2610	227
Indiana Dimension Inc						
1621 W Market St	Logansport	IN	46947	**888-875-4434**		679
Indiana Donor Network						
3760 Guion Rd	Indianapolis	IN	46222	**888-275-4676**		541
Indiana Dunes the Casual Coast						
1215 N State Rd 49	Porter	IN	46304	**800-283-8687**	219-926-2255	206
Indiana Farm Bureau Insurance Co						
225 SE St PO Box 1250	Indianapolis	IN	46206	**800-723-3276**	317-692-7200	390-2
Indiana Furniture						
1224 Mill St	Jasper	IN	47546	**800-422-5727**	812-482-5727	319-1
Indiana Landmarks						
1201 Central Ave	Indianapolis	IN	46202	**800-450-4534**	317-639-4534	50-3
Indiana Library Federation (ILF)						
941 E 86th St Ste 260	Indianapolis	IN	46240	**800-326-0013**	317-257-2040	434
Indiana Members Credit Union (IMCU)						
7110 W Tenth St	Indianapolis	IN	46214	**800-556-9268**	317-248-8556	219
Indiana Rail Road Co, The						
101 W Ohio St Ste 1600	Indianapolis	IN	46204	**888-596-2121**	317-262-5140	645
Indiana Ribbon Inc						
106 N Second St	Wolcott	IN	47995	**800-531-3100**	219-279-2112	544
Indiana State Bar Assn						
1 Indiana Sq Ste 530	Indianapolis	IN	46204	**800-266-2581**	317-639-5465	72
Indiana State Chamber of Commerce						
115 W Washington St Ste 850-S	Indianapolis	IN	46204	**800-824-6885**	317-264-3110	140
Indiana State Library (ISL)						
115 W Washington St Ste 960S	Indianapolis	IN	46204	**800-451-6028**	800-677-9800	433-5
Indiana State Medical Assn						
322 Canal Walk	Indianapolis	IN	46202	**800-257-4762**	317-261-2060	472
Indiana State Museum						
650 W Washington St	Indianapolis	IN	46204	**800-382-9842**	317-232-1637	517
Indiana State University						
200 N Seventh St	Terre Haute	IN	47809	**800-468-6478**		166
Indiana Tech						
1600 E Washington Blvd	Fort Wayne	IN	46803	**800-937-2448**	260-422-5561	166
Indiana Trust & Investment Management Co						
4045 Edison Lakes Pkwy Ste 100	Mishawaka	IN	46545	**800-362-7905**	574-271-3400	791
Indiana University						
East						
2325 Chester Blvd	Richmond	IN	47374	**800-959-3278**	765-973-8208	166
Kokomo						
2300 S Washington St PO Box 9003	Kokomo	IN	46904	**888-875-4485**	765-455-9217	166
Northwest 3400 Broadway	Gary	IN	46408	**888-968-7486**	219-980-6500	166
South Bend						
1700 Mishawaka Ave PO Box 7111	South Bend	IN	46634	**877-462-4872**	574-520-4870	166
Southeast						
4201 Grant Line Rd	New Albany	IN	47150	**800-852-8835**	812-941-2212	166
Indiana University Hospital						
550 N University Blvd	Indianapolis	IN	46202	**800-248-1199**	317-274-5000	373-3
Indiana University Melvin & Bren Simon Cancer Ctr						
535 Barnhill Dr	Indianapolis	IN	46202	**888-600-4822**	317-278-0070	764
Indiana University of Pennsylvania						
1011 South Dr	Indiana	PA	15705	**800-442-6830**	724-357-2100	166
Indiana University of Pennsylvania Stapleton Library						
1011 S Dr	Indiana	PA	15705	**888-342-2383**	724-357-2340	433-6
Indiana University Press						
601 N Morton St	Bloomington	IN	47404	**800-842-6796**	812-855-8817	633-4
Indiana University-Purdue University						
Fort Wayne						
2101 E Coliseum Blvd	Fort Wayne	IN	46805	**800-324-4739**	260-481-6100	166
Indiana University-Purdue University Indianapolis						
Library						
755 W Michigan St	Indianapolis	IN	46202	**888-422-0499**	317-274-0462	433-6
Indiana Veterans Home						
3851 N River Rd	West Lafayette	IN	47906	**800-400-4520**	765-463-1502	788
Indiana Veterinary Medical Assn						
1202 E 38th St Discovery Hall Ste 200	Indianapolis	IN	46205	**800-270-0747**	317-974-0888	790

Name / Address	City	State	ZIP	Toll-Free	Phone	Class
Indiana Wesleyan University						
4201 S Washington St	Marion	IN	46953	**800-332-6901**	765-677-2138	166
Indianapolis Business Journal (IBJ)						
41 E Washington St Ste 200	Indianapolis	IN	46204	**800-428-7081**	317-634-6200	455-5
Indianapolis Colts						
7001 W 56th St	Indianapolis	IN	46254	**800-805-2658**	317-297-2658	711-2
Indianapolis Convention & Visitors Assn						
200 S Capitol Ave Ste 300	Indianapolis	IN	46225	**800-862-6912**	317-262-3000	206
Indianapolis Fruit Company Inc						
4501 Massachusetts Ave	Indianapolis	IN	46218	**800-377-2425**	317-546-2425	297-7
Indianapolis Monthly Magazine						
40 Monument Cir Ste 100 *Circ	Indianapolis	IN	46204	**888-403-9005***	317-237-9288	455-22
Indianapolis Star						
307 N Pennsylvania St	Indianapolis	IN	46204	**800-669-7827**	317-444-4000	528-2
Indianapolis Symphony Orchestra						
45 Monument Cir	Indianapolis	IN	46204	**800-366-8457**	317-262-1100	569-3
Indianhead Federated Library System						
1538 Truax Blvd	Eau Claire	WI	54703	**800-321-5427**	715-839-5082	433-3
Indigo Books & Music Inc						
468 King St W Ste 500 *TSX: IDG* ■ *Cust Svc	Toronto	ON	M5V1L8	**800-832-7569***	416-364-4499	95
Indigo Dynamic Networks Llc						
2413 W Algonquin Rd	Algonquin	IL	60102	**888-464-6344**		180
Indigo Rose Corp						
123 Bannatyne Ave Ste 200	Winnipeg	MB	R3B0R3	**800-665-9668**	204-946-0263	179
Indital USA Ltd						
7947 Mesa Dr	Houston	TX	77028	**800-772-4706**		
Individual Software Inc						
4255 HopyaRd Rd Ste 2	Pleasanton	CA	94588	**800-822-3522**	925-734-6767	178-3
Indoff Inc						
11816 Lackland Rd	Saint Louis	MO	63146	**800-486-7867**	314-997-1122	384
Indoor Purification Systems Inc						
Surround Air Div						
334 N Marshall Way Ste C	Layton	UT	84041	**888-812-1516**	801-547-1162	17
Indros Group						
210 Richardson St	Brooklyn	NY	11222	**866-463-7671**		395
Indtai Inc						
2095 Chain Bridge Rd Ste 300	Vienna	VA	22182	**877-912-6672**		
Inductoheat Inc						
32251 N Avis Dr	Madison Heights	MI	48071	**800-624-6297**	248-585-9393	318
Inductotherm Group						
10 Indel Ave PO Box 157	Rancocas	NJ	08073	**800-257-9527**	609-267-9000	318
Indus International Inc						
340 S Oak St PO Box 890	West Salem	WI	54669	**800-843-9377**	608-786-0300	494
Indusco Group						
1200 West Hamburg St	Baltimore	MD	21230	**800-727-0665**		468
Industrial Alliance Insurance & Financial Services Inc						
1080 Grande Allee W PO Box 1907 Sta Therminus	Quebec	QC	G1K7M3	**888-266-2224**	418-684-5405	390-2
Industrial Battery & Charger Inc						
5831 Orr Rd	Charlotte	NC	28213	**800-833-8412**	704-597-7330	74
Industrial Brush Company Inc						
105 Clinton Rd	Fairfield	NJ	07004	**800-241-9860**	973-575-0455	103
Industrial Chemicals Inc						
2042 Montreat Dr *Cust Svc	Vestavia	AL	35216	**800-476-2042***	205-823-7330	146
Industrial Clutch						
2800 Fisher Rd	Waukesha	WI	53186	**800-964-3262**	262-547-3357	616
Industrial Commodities Inc						
PO Box 4380	Glen Allen	VA	23060	**800-523-7902**		297-11
Industrial Communications & Electronics Inc						
40 Lone St	Marshfield	MA	02050	**800-822-9999**	781-319-1100	643
Industrial Container & Supply Company Inc						
1845 South 5200 West	Salt Lake City	UT	84104	**800-748-4250**	801-972-1561	332
Industrial Container Services						
7152 First Ave S	Seattle	WA	98108	**800-273-3786**	206-763-2345	198
Industrial Contractors Inc						
701 Ch Dr	Bismarck	ND	58501	**800-467-3089**	701-258-9908	189-10
Industrial Controls Distributors Inc (ICD)						
1776 Bloomsbury Ave *Sales	Wanamassa	NJ	07712	**800-281-4788***	732-918-9000	384
Industrial Custom Products Inc						
2801 37th Ave NE	Minneapolis	MN	55421	**800-654-0886**	612-781-2255	326
Industrial Data Systems Inc						
3822 E La Palma Ave	Anaheim	CA	92807	**800-854-3311**	714-921-9212	680
Industrial Diesel Inc						
8705 Harmon Rd	Fort Worth	TX	76177	**800-323-3659**	817-232-1071	384
Industrial Door Company Inc						
360 Coon Rapids Blvd	Minneapolis	MN	55433	**888-798-0199**	763-786-4730	236
Industrial Electric Wire & Cable Inc (IEWC)						
5001 S Towne Dr	New Berlin	WI	53151	**800-344-2323**	877-613-4392	246
Industrial Fabrics Assn International (IFAI)						
1801 County Rd 'B' W	Roseville	MN	55113	**800-225-4324**	651-222-2508	49-13
Industrial Gasket & Shim Company Inc (IGS)						
200 Country Club Rd	Meadow Lands	PA	15347	**800-229-1447**	724-222-5800	326
Industrial Hardware & Specialties Inc						
17-B Kentucky Ave	Paterson	NJ	07503	**800-684-4010**	973-684-4010	350
Industrial Louvers Inc						
511 Seventh St S	Delano	MN	55328	**800-328-3421**	763-972-2981	693
Industrial Material Corp						
7701 Harborside Dr	Galveston	TX	77554	**800-701-4462**	409-744-4538	490
Industrial Paper Tube Inc						
1335 E Bay Ave	Bronx	NY	10474	**800-345-0960**		125
Industrial Pipe & Supply Company Inc						
1779 Martin Luther King Junior Blvd	Gainesville	GA	30501	**800-426-1458**	770-536-0517	608
Industrial Power & Lighting Corp						
60 Depost St	Buffalo	NY	14206	**800-639-3702**	716-854-1811	189-4
Industrial Revolution Inc						
5835 Segale Park Dr C	Tukwila	WA	98188	**888-297-6062**		693
Industrial Rubber Works						
1700 Nicholas Blvd	Elk Grove Village	IL	60007	**800-852-1855**	847-952-1800	369
Industrial Scientific Corp						
7848 Steubenville Pk	Oakdale	PA	15071	**800-338-3287**	412-788-4353	201
Industrial Soap Co						
722 S Vandeventer Ave	Saint Louis	MO	63110	**800-405-7627**	314-241-6363	405
Industrial Steel Treating Inc						
613 Carroll St	Jackson	MI	49202	**800-253-9534**		482

Name / Address	City	State	Zip	Toll-Free	Phone	Class
Industrial Supply Solutions Inc 520 Elizabeth St	Charleston	WV	25311	800-346-5341	304-346-5341	
Industrial Tectonics Inc 7222 Huron River Dr	Dexter	MI	48130	866-816-8904	734-426-4681	483
Industrial Timber & Lumber Corp (ITL) 23925 Commerce Park Rd	Beachwood	OH	44122	800-829-9663	216-831-3140	679
Industrial Tool Inc 9210 52nd Ave N *Sales	New Hope	MN	55428	800-776-4455*	763-533-7244	452
Industrial Tools Inc (ITI) 1111 S Rose Ave	Oxnard	CA	93033	800-266-5561	805-483-1111	491
Industrial Tube & Steel Corp 4658 Crystal Pkwy	Kent	OH	44240	800-662-9567	330-474-5530	686
Industries of the Blind Inc 920 W Lee St	Greensboro	NC	27403	800-909-7086	336-274-1591	103
Industronics Service Co 489 Sullivan Ave	South Windsor	CT	06074	800-878-1551	860-289-1551	318
Industry Specific Solutions LLC 24901 Northwestern Hwy Ste 400	Southfield	MI	48075	877-356-3450		260
Industry-Railway Suppliers Inc 577 W Lamont Rd	Elmhurst	IL	60126	800-728-0029	630-766-5708	765
Inertia Dynamics Inc 31 Industrial Park Rd	New Hartford	CT	06057	800-800-6445	860-379-1252	203
Inertia Engineering 6665 Hardaway Rd	Stockton	CA	95215	800-791-9997	209-931-1670	725
Inetsolution 2075 W Big Beaver Rd Ste 222	Troy	MI	48084	855-728-5839		180
Infaith Community Foundation 625 Fourth Ave S Ste 1500	Minneapolis	MN	55415	800-365-4172	612-844-4110	304
Infantino LLC 4920 Carroll Canyon Rd Ste 200	San Diego	CA	92121	800-840-4916		64
Infection Control Today Magazine 3300 N Central Ave Ste 300	Phoenix	AZ	85012	800-581-1811	480-990-1101	455-16
Infinera Corp 140 Caspian Ct *NASDAQ: INFN*	Sunnyvale	CA	94089	877-742-3427	408-572-5200	730
Infinite Campus Inc 4321 109th Ave NE	Blaine	MN	55449	800-850-2335	651-631-0000	177
Infinite Graphics Inc 4611 E Lake St *OTC: INFG*	Minneapolis	MN	55406	800-679-0676	612-721-6283	178-5
Infitec Inc 6500 Badgley Rd	East Syracuse	NY	13057	800-334-0837	315-433-1150	203
Info Cubic LLC 9250 E Costilla Ave Ste 525	Greenwood Village	CO	80112	877-360-4636	303-220-0170	317
InfoCision Management Corp 325 Springside Dr	Akron	OH	44333	800-210-6269	330-668-1400	732
InFocus Corp 13190 SW 68th Pkwy Ste 200	Portland	OR	97223	877-388-8385	503-207-4700	587
INFOCUS Marketing Inc 4245 Sigler Rd	Warrenton	VA	20187	800-708-5478		461
infoGroup Inc 1020 E First St	Papillion	NE	68046	866-414-7848	402-836-5290	5
Infolink Exp 2880 Zanker Rd Ste 203	San Jose	CA	95134	800-280-7703	915-577-9466	
InfoMart Inc 1582 Terrell Mill Rd	Marietta	GA	30067	800-800-3774	770-984-2727	193
InfoMine Inc 580 Hornby St Ste 900	Vancouver	BC	V6C3B6	888-683-2037	604-683-2037	225
Infopros 12325 Oracle Blvd Ste 100	Colorado Springs	CO	80921	888-235-3231		804
Infor Global Solutions 13560 Morris Rd Ste 4100	Alpharetta	GA	30004	866-244-5479	678-319-8000	178-10
Informant Technologies Inc 19 Jenkins Ave Ste 200	Lansdale	PA	19446	877-503-4636	215-412-9165	177
Information & Computing Services Inc (ICS) 1650 Prudential Dr Ste 300	Jacksonville	FL	32207	800-676-4427	904-399-8500	178-1
Information Builders Inc 2 Penn Plz	New York	NY	10121	800-969-4636	212-736-4433	178-7
Information Gatekeepers Inc (IGI) 1340 Soldiers Field Rd Ste 2	Brighton	MA	02135	800-323-1088	617-782-5033	633-11
Information Management Systems Inc 114 W Main St Ste 211 PO Box 2924	New Britain	CT	06050	888-403-8347	860-229-1119	631
Information Network Assoc Inc 5235 N Front St	Harrisburg	PA	17110	800-443-0824	717-599-5505	689
Information Resources Inc 150 N Clinton St	Chicago	IL	60661	866-262-5973	312-726-1221	464
INFORMS (Institute for Operations Research & the Management) 7240 Pkwy Dr Ste 300	Hanover	MD	21076	800-446-3676	443-757-3500	49-19
InfoSend Inc 4240 E La Palma Ave	Anaheim	CA	92807	800-955-9330	714-993-2690	392
Infosight Corp PO Box 5000	Chillicothe	OH	45601	800-401-0716	740-642-3600	465
Infosilem 99 Emilien-marcoux Ste 201	Blainville	QC	J7C0B4	866-420-5585	450-420-5585	177
Infosoft Group Inc 1123 N Water St Ste 400	Milwaukee	WI	53202	800-984-3775	414-278-0700	180
Infosource Inc 1300 City View Ctr	Oviedo	FL	32765	800-393-4636	407-796-5200	177
Infospan Inc 31878 Del Obispo St Ste 118	San Juan Capistrano	CA	92675	866-611-8611	949-260-9990	
Infotex Inc 416 Main St Ste 3	Lafayette	IN	47901	800-466-9939		
infoUSA Inc 5711 S 86th Cir	Omaha	NE	68127	800-321-0869	800-835-5856	386
InfoVista Corp 12950 Worldgate Dr Ste 250	Herndon	VA	20170	866-921-9219	703-435-2435	178-1
Infra Metals Co 4501 Curtis Ave	Baltimore	MD	21225	800-235-3979		
InfraReDx Inc 34 Third Ave	Burlington	MA	01803	888-680-7339	781-221-0053	
Infratech Corp 2036 Baker Ct	Kennesaw	GA	30144	800-574-6372		
Infusion Nurses Society (INS) 315 Norwood Pk S	Norwood	MA	02062	800-694-0298	781-440-9408	49-8
InfySource Ltd 8345 NW 66th St	Miami	FL	33166	800-275-7503		620
ING Funds 7337 E Doubletree Ranch Rd	Scottsdale	AZ	85258	800-992-0180		524
Ingenuity Ieq 3600 Centennial Dr	Midland	MI	48642	800-669-9726	989-496-2233	606
Ingenuity Systems Inc 1700 Seaport Blvd Ste 3	Redwood City	CA	94063	866-464-3684		
Ingham Regional Medical Ctr 401 W Greenlawn Ave	Lansing	MI	48910	800-261-8018	517-975-6000	373-3
Ingles Markets Inc 2913 US Hwy 70 W *NASDAQ: IMKTA*	Black Mountain	NC	28711	800-635-5066	828-669-2941	344
Ingleside Inn 200 W Ramon Rd	Palm Springs	CA	92264	800-772-6655	760-325-0045	378
Ingomar Packing Co 9950 S Ingomar Grade PO Box 1448	Los Banos	CA	93635	800-328-0026	209-826-9494	296-20
Ingot Metal Company Ltd 111 Fenmar Dr	Weston	ON	M9L1M3	800-567-7774	416-749-1372	479
Ingram Entertainment Inc 2 Ingram Blvd	La Vergne	TN	37089	800-621-1333	615-287-4000	509
Ingram Park Mall 6301 NW Loop 410	San Antonio	TX	78238	877-746-6642	210-684-9570	458
Injured Workers Insurance Fund 8722 Loch Raven Blvd	Towson	MD	21286	800-264-4943	410-494-2000	390-4
Ink Technology Corp 18320 Lanken Ave	Cleveland	OH	44119	800-633-2826	216-486-6720	624
INL (Idaho National Laboratory) 2525 Fremont Ave	Idaho Falls	ID	83402	866-495-7440		664
Inland Arts & Graphics Inc 14440 Edison Dr	New Lenox	IL	60451	800-437-6003		623
Inland Empire Paper Co 3320 N Argonne Rd	Millwood	WA	99212	866-437-7711	509-924-1911	553
Inland Mortgage Corp 2901 Butterfield Rd	Oak Brook	IL	60523	800-826-8228	630-218-8000	507
Inland Northwest Blood Ctr 210 W Cataldo Ave	Spokane	WA	99201	800-423-0151	509-624-0151	89
Inland Plywood Co 375 N Cass Ave	Pontiac	MI	48342	800-521-4355	248-334-4706	609
Inland Power & Light Company Inc 10110 W Hallett Rd	Spokane	WA	99224	800-747-7151	509-747-7151	245
Inland Seafood Corp 1651 Montreal Cir	Tucker	GA	30084	800-883-3474	404-350-5850	297-5
Inland Technologies Inc 14 Queen St PO Box 253	Truro	NS	B2N5C1	877-633-5263	902-895-6346	192
Inlet Tower Hotel & Suites 1020 W 12th Ave	Anchorage	AK	99501	800-544-0786	907-276-0110	378
Inline Fibreglass Ltd 30 Constellation Ct	Toronto	ON	M9W1K1	866-566-5656	416-679-1171	497
Inline Plastics Corp 42 Canal St	Shelton	CT	06484	800-826-5567	203-924-5933	598
Inman 75 N Woodward Ave Ste 80368	Tallahassee	FL	32313	800-775-4662	510-658-9252	526
INMED Partnerships for Children 21240 Ridgetop Cir Ste 115	Ashburn	VA	20147	800-552-7096	571-293-9849	48-5
Inmedius Inc 2247 Babcock Blvd	Pittsburgh	PA	15237	800-697-7110		177
Inn & Spa at Loretto 211 Old Santa Fe Trl	Santa Fe	NM	87501	800-727-5531	505-988-5531	378
Inn Above Tide, The 30 El Portal	Sausalito	CA	94965	800-893-8433	415-332-9535	378
Inn at Bay Harbor, The 3600 Village Harbor Dr	Bay Harbor	MI	49770	866-585-8123		665
Inn at Camachee Harbor 201 Yacht Club Dr	Saint Augustine	FL	32084	800-688-5379	904-825-0003	378
Inn at Gig Harbor 3211 56th St NW	Gig Harbor	WA	98335	800-795-9980	253-858-1111	378
Inn at Mamas Fish House 799 Poho Pl	Paia	HI	96779	800-860-4852	808-579-8488	377
Inn at Morro Bay 60 State Pk Rd	Morro Bay	CA	93442	800-321-9566	805-772-5651	378
Inn at Mystic 3 Williams Ave PO Box 526	Mystic	CT	06355	800-237-2415	860-536-9604	378
Inn at Otter Crest 301 Otter Crest Loop	Otter Rock	OR	97369	800-452-2101	541-765-2111	378
Inn at Pelican Bay 800 Vanderbilt Beach Rd	Naples	FL	34108	800-597-8770	239-597-8777	378
Inn at Perry Cabin 308 Watkins Ln	Saint Michaels	MD	21663	800-722-2949	410-745-2200	378
Inn at Rancho Santa Fe 5951 Linea Del Cielo PO Box 869	Rancho Santa Fe	CA	92067	800-843-4661	858-756-1131	665
Inn at Saint John 939 Congress St	Portland	ME	04102	800-636-9127	207-773-6481	378
Inn at Spanish Bay, The 2700 17-Mile Dr	Pebble Beach	CA	93953	800-654-9300	831-647-7500	665
Inn at Spanish Head 4009 SW Hwy 101	Lincoln City	OR	97367	800-452-8127	541-996-2161	378
Inn at the Market 86 Pine St	Seattle	WA	98101	800-446-4484	206-443-3600	378
Inn At The Quay 900 Quayside Dr	New Westminster	BC	V3M6G1	800-663-2001	604-520-1776	378
Inn at Union Square 440 Post St	San Francisco	CA	94102	800-288-4346	415-397-3510	378
Inn at Virginia Mason 1006 Spring St	Seattle	WA	98104	800-283-6453		371
Inn at Virginia Tech & Skelton Conference Ctr 901 Prices Fork Rd	Blacksburg	VA	24061	877-200-3360	540-231-8000	376
Inn at, The Tides, The 800 Coast Hwy 1	Bodega Bay	CA	94923	800-541-7788	707-875-2751	378
Inn of Long Beach 185 Atlantic Ave	Long Beach	CA	90802	800-230-7500	562-435-3791	378
Inn of the Anasazi 113 Washington Ave	Santa Fe	NM	87501	888-767-3966	505-988-3030	378

	Toll-Free	Phone	Class
Inn of the Governors			
101 W Alameda St ....Santa Fe NM 87501	800-234-4534	505-982-4333	378
Inn of the Hills River Resort			
1001 Junction Hwy ....Kerrville TX 78028	800-292-5690	830-895-5000	665
Inn of the Mountain Gods			
287 Carrizo Canyon Rd ....Mescalero NM 88340	800-545-9011		665
Inn on Biltmore Estate			
1 Antler Hill Rd ....Asheville NC 28803	800-411-3812	828-225-1600	378
Inn on Fifth			
699 Fifth Ave S ....Naples FL 34102	888-403-8778	239-403-8777	378
Inn on Gitche Gumee			
8517 Congdon Blvd ....Duluth MN 55804	800-317-4979	218-525-4979	378
Inn on Lake Superior			
350 Canal Pk Dr ....Duluth MN 55802	888-668-4352	218-726-1111	378
Inn on the Alameda			
303 E Alameda St ....Santa Fe NM 87501	888-984-2121		378
Inn on the Paseo			
630 Paseo de Peralta ....Santa Fe NM 87501	855-984-8200	505-984-8200	378
Inner Traditions International			
1 Park St ....Rochester VT 05767	800-246-8648	802-767-3174	633-2
Innis Maggiore Group Inc			
4715 Whipple Ave NW ....Canton OH 44718	800-460-4111	330-492-5500	4
Innisbrook Resort & Golf Club			
36750 US Hwy 19 N ....Palm Harbor FL 34684	800-492-6899	727-942-2000	665
In-N-Out Burger Inc			
4199 Campus Dr 9th Fl ....Irvine CA 92612	800-786-1000*	949-509-6200	666
*Cust Svc			
Innovated Packaging Company Inc			
38505 Cherry St Ste C ....Newark CA 94560	866-745-8180	510-745-8180	
Innovatia Inc			
1 Germain St ....Saint John NB E2L4V1	800-363-3358	506-640-4000	461
Innovative Data Management Systems LLC			
4006 W Azeele St ....Tampa FL 33609	866-706-4588	813-207-2025	177
Innovative Enterprises Inc			
25 Town & Country Dr ....Washington MO 63090	800-280-0300	636-390-0300	544
Innovative Fluid Handling Systems			
3300 E Rock Falls Rd ....Rock Falls IL 61071	800-435-7003		198
Innovative Industrial Solutions Inc			
2830 Skyline Dr ....Russellville AR 72802	888-684-8249	479-968-4266	689
Innovative Mattress Solutions LLC			
1721 Jaggie Fox Way ....Lexington KY 40511	800-766-4163		321
Innovative Metals Company Inc (IMETCO)			
4648 S Old Peachtree Rd ....Norcross GA 30071	800-646-3826	770-908-1030	46
Innovative Resources Consultant Group Inc			
1 Park Plz Ste 600 ....Irvine CA 92614	800-945-4724	949-252-0590	
Innovative Stamping Corp			
2068 E Gladwick St ....Compton CA 90220	800-400-0047	310-537-6996	486
Innovative Systems Group Inc			
799 Roosevelt Rd ....Glen Ellyn IL 60137	800-739-2400	630-858-8500	177
Innovative Systems Inc			
790 Holiday Dr ....Pittsburgh PA 15220	800-622-6390	412-937-9300	178-1
Innovative Technologies Corp (ITC)			
1020 Woodman Dr Ste 100 ....Dayton OH 45432	800-745-8050	937-252-2145	178-10
Innovative Telecom Solutions Inc			
9 Vela Way ....Edgewater NJ 07020	800-510-3000		386
Innovent Air Handling Equipment			
60 28th Ave N ....Minneapolis MN 55411	877-218-4129	612-877-4800	357
Innovize Inc			
500 Oak Grove Pkwy ....Saint Paul MN 55127	877-605-6580		598
InnSuites Hospitality Trust InnSuites Hotels & Suites			
475 N Granada Ave ....Tucson AZ 85701	800-842-4242	520-622-0923	378
InnSuites Hotel Tempe/Phoenix Airport			
1651 W Baseline Rd ....Tempe AZ 85283	800-842-4242	480-897-7900	378
Inolex Chemical Co			
2101 S Swanson St ....Philadelphia PA 19148	800-521-9891*	215-271-0800	144
*Cust Svc			
Inova Alexandria Hospital			
4320 Seminary Rd ....Alexandria VA 22304	800-526-7101	703-504-3000	373-3
Inova Diagnostics Inc			
9900 Old Grove Rd ....San Diego CA 92131	800-545-9495	858-586-9900	231
Inova Fairfax Hospital			
3300 Gallows Rd ....Falls Church VA 22042	800-838-8238	703-776-4001	373-3
Inova Health System			
8110 Gatehouse Rd ....Falls Church VA 22042	855-694-6682		352
Inova Payroll Inc			
176 Thompson Ln Ste 204 ....Nashville TN 37211	888-244-6106	615-921-0600	729
Inova Solutions Inc			
110 Avon St ....Charlottesville VA 22902	800-637-1077	434-817-8000	178-1
Inovar Inc			
1073 W 1700 N ....Logan UT 84321	866-898-4949	435-792-4949	392
Inovar Packaging Group LLC			
10470 Miller Rd ....Dallas TX 75238	800-285-2235		
In-O-Vate Technologies Inc			
810 Saturn St Ste 21 ....Jupiter FL 33477	888-443-7937	561-743-8696	191-1
Inovatia Laboratories LLC			
120 E Davis St ....Fayette MO 65248	800-280-1912	660-248-1911	738
Inovex Industries Inc			
45681 Oakbrook Ct Ste 102 ....Sterling VA 20166	888-374-3366	703-421-9778	3
Inovex Information Systems Inc			
7240 Pkwy Dr Ste 140 ....Hanover MD 21076	800-469-9705	443-782-1452	180
Inovio Pharmaceuticals Inc			
660 W Germantown Pk Ste 110 ....Plymouth PA 19462	877-446-6846	267-440-4200	250
NASDAQ: INO			
Inovise Medical Inc			
8770 SW Nimbus Ave Ste D ....Beaverton OR 97008	877-466-8473	503-431-3800	474
Inovo LLC			
213 S Ashley St Ste 300 ....Ann Arbor MI 48104	888-464-6686		461
InPath Devices			
3610 Dodge St Ste 200 ....Omaha NE 68131	800-988-1914	402-345-9200	173-7
Inpower LLC			
3555 Africa Rd ....Galena OH 43021	866-548-0965	740-548-0965	349
Input 1 LLC			
6200 Canoga Ave Ste 400 ....Woodland Hills CA 91367	888-882-2554	818-713-2303	178-10
Inquipco			
2730 N Nellis Blvd ....Las Vegas NV 89115	800-598-3465	702-644-1700	190
Inquiries Inc			
129 N W St ....Easton MD 21601	866-987-3767		399

	Toll-Free	Phone	Class
Inquiry Systems Inc			
1195 Goodale Blvd ....Columbus OH 43212	800-508-1116	614-464-3800	195
Inrad Inc			
4375 Donker Ct SE ....Kentwood MI 49512	800-558-4647	616-301-7800	474
INS (Infusion Nurses Society)			
315 Norwood Pk S ....Norwood MA 02062	800-694-0298	781-440-9408	49-8
Insco Distributing Inc			
12501 Network Blvd ....San Antonio TX 78249	855-282-4295	210-690-8400	661
In-Shape Health Clubs			
6 S El Dorado St Ste 600 ....Stockton CA 95210	877-446-7427	209-472-2450	353
Inside NRC			
2 Penn Plz 25th Fl ....New York NY 10121	800-752-8878		527-5
Inside Washington Publishers			
1919 S Eads St Ste 201 ....Arlington VA 22202	800-424-9068	703-416-8500	633-9
InsideUp Inc			
9245 Activity Rd Ste 210 ....San Diego CA 92126	800-889-6178	858-397-5733	392
Insight			
444 Scott Dr ....Bloomingdale IL 60108	800-467-4448		193
Insight 6820 S Harl Ave ....Tempe AZ 85283	800-467-4448		
Insight Computing LLC			
448 Ignacio Blvd Ste 490 ....Novato CA 94949	800-380-8985		175
Insight Enterprises Inc			
6820 S Harl Ave ....Tempe AZ 85283	800-467-4448	480-333-3000	179
NASDAQ: NSIT			
Insight Global Inc (IGI)			
4170 Ashford Dunwoody Rd Ste 250 ....Atlanta GA 30319	888-336-7463	404-257-7900	193
Insight Information			
214 King St W Ste 300 ....Toronto ON M5H3S6	888-777-1707		760
Insight Medical Holdings Ltd			
200 Meadowlark Health Ctr 156 St and 89 Ave ....Edmonton AB T5R5W9	866-771-9446	780-669-2222	414
Insight Service			
20338 Progress Dr ....Strongsville OH 44149	800-465-4329	216-251-2510	738
Insight Technology Inc			
9 Akira Way ....Londonderry NH 03053	866-509-2040	603-626-4800	21
Insignia Systems Inc			
8799 Brooklyn Blvd ....Minneapolis MN 55445	800-874-4648	763-392-6200	697
NASDAQ: ISIG			
Insinger Machine Co			
6245 State Rd ....Philadelphia PA 19135	800-344-4802	215-624-4800	298
In-Sink-Erator			
4700 21st St ....Racine WI 53406	800-558-5712	262-554-5432	36
Insituform Technologies Inc			
17988 Edison Ave ....St. Louis MO 63005	800-234-2992*	636-530-8000	188-10
*Cust Svc			
Insl-X			
101 Paragon Dr ....Montvale NJ 07645	855-724-6802		546
Insparisk LLC			
18-10 Whitestone Expy 3rd Fl ....Whitestone NY 11357	888-464-6772		364
Inspection Depot Inc			
3131 Saint Johns Bluff Rd ....Jacksonville FL 32246	888-589-2112		364
Insperity Inc			
19001 Crescent Springs Dr ....Kingwood TX 77339	800-237-3170	866-715-3552	461
Inspirage Inc			
600 108th Ave NE Ste 540 ....Bellevue WA 98004	855-517-4250		627
Inspiration Software Inc			
6443 SW Beaverton Hillsdale Hwy Ste 370 ....Portland OR 97221	800-877-4292	503-297-3004	178-1
Inspired eLearning Inc			
613 NW Loop 410 Ste 530 ....San Antonio TX 78216	800-631-2078	210-579-0224	225
InstaGift LLC			
1500 First Ave N Ste 65 ....Birmingham AL 35203	877-870-3463		392
InstaMed Communications LLC			
1880 John F Kennedy Blvd 12th Fl ....Philadelphia PA 19103	800-507-3800	215-789-3680	359-3
Instanet Solutions			
100 Wellington St Ste 201 ....London ON N6B2K6	800-668-8768		179
Instant Imprints			
6615 Flanders Dr Ste B ....San Diego CA 92121	800-542-3437	858-642-4848	310
Instantiations Inc			
Officers Row Ste 1325B ....Vancouver WA 98661	855-476-2558	503-649-3836	178-2
Instantwhip Foods Inc			
2200 Cardigan Ave ....Columbus OH 43215	800-544-9447*	614-488-2536	296-10
*Cust Svc			
Insteel Industries Inc			
1373 Boggs Dr ....Mount Airy NC 27030	800-334-9504	336-786-2141	808
NASDAQ: IIIN			
Institute for Business & Home Safety (IBHS)			
4775 E Fowler Ave ....Tampa FL 33617	866-657-4247	813-286-3400	49-9
Institute for Certification of Computing Professionals (ICCP)			
2400 E Devon Ave Ste 281 ....Des Plaines IL 60018	800-843-8227	847-299-4227	48-9
Institute for Health Freedom			
1825 K St NW Ste 1200 ....Washington DC 20006	800-433-5255	202-534-3700	
Institute for Healthcare Improvement (IHI)			
20 University Rd 7th Fl ....Cambridge MA 02138	866-787-0831	617-301-4800	49-8
Institute for Humane Studies			
3434 Washington Blvd MS 1C5 ....Arlington VA 22201	800-697-8799	703-993-4880	630
Institute for Natural Resources			
PO Box 5757 ....Concord CA 94524	877-246-6336	925-609-2820	21
Institute for Operations Research & the Management Sciences (INFORMS)			
7240 Pkwy Dr Ste 300 ....Hanover MD 21076	800-446-3676	443-757-3500	49-19
Institute for Supply Management (ISM)			
2055 Centennial Cir ....Tempe AZ 85284	800-888-6276*	480-752-6276	49-12
*Cust Svc			
Institute for the Advancement of Human Behavior (IAHB)			
PO Box 5527 ....Santa Rosa CA 95402	800-258-8411	650-851-8411	49-8
Institute of American Indian Arts (IAIA)			
83 Avan Nu Po Rd ....Santa Fe NM 87508	800-804-6422	505-424-2300	165
Institute of Caster & Wheel Manufacturers (ICWM)			
8720 Red Oak Blvd Ste 201 ....Charlotte NC 28217	877-522-5431	704-676-1190	49-13
Institute of Clean Air Cos (ICAC)			
1730 M St NW Ste 206 ....Washington DC 20036	800-631-9505	202-478-6188	48-12
Institute of Consumer Financial Education			
PO Box 34070 ....San Diego CA 92163	800-685-1111	619-239-1401	48-11
Institute of Corporate Directors			
2701 - 250 Yonge St ....Toronto ON M5B2L7	877-593-7741	416-593-7741	162
Institute of Culinary Education			
50 W 23rd St ....New York NY 10010	800-522-4610	212-847-0700	163

	Toll-Free	Phone	Class
Institute of Food Technologists (IFT)			
525 W Van Buren St Ste 1000 ....Chicago IL 60607	800-438-3663	312-782-8424	49-6
Institute of General Semantics (IGS)			
72-11 Austin St ....Forest Hills NY 11375	800-346-1359	212-729-7973	48-11
Institute of Gerontology			
University of Michigan ....Ann Arbor MI 48109	877-865-2167	734-764-1817	664
Institute of Industrial & Systems Engineers (IIE)			
3577 PkwyLn Ste 200 ....Norcross GA 30092	800-494-0460*	770-449-0461	49-13
*Cust Svc			
Institute of Inspection Cleaning & Restoration Certification (IICRC)			
4043 S E Ave ....Las Vegas NV 89119	844-464-4272		
Institute of Management Accountants Inc (IMA)			
10 Paragon Dr Ste 1 ....Montvale NJ 07645	800-638-4427	201-573-9000	49-1
Institute of Management Consultants USA Inc (IMC USA)			
2025 M St NW Ste 800..........Washington DC 20036	800-221-2557	800-793-4992	49-12
Institute of Packaging Professionals (IoPP)			
1833 Centre Point Cir			
Ste 123 ....Naperville IL 60563	800-432-4085	630-544-5050	49-13
Institute of Real Estate Management (IREM)			
430 N Michigan Ave ....Chicago IL 60611	800-837-0706	312-329-6000	49-17
Institute of Scrap Recycling Industries Magazine			
1250 H St NW Ste 400 ....Washington DC 20005	800-767-7236	202-662-8500	455-21
Institutional Wholesale Co			
535 Dry Valley Rd ....Cookeville TN 38506	800-239-9588	931-537-4000	299
Instrument Sales & Service Inc			
16427 NE Airport Way ....Portland OR 97230	800-333-7976	503-239-0754	61
Instrumentation Laboratory Inc			
180 Hartwell Rd ....Bedford MA 01730	800-955-9525*	781-861-0710	418
*Sales			
Insulectro			
20362 Windrow Dr ....Lake Forest CA 92630	800-279-7686	949-587-3200	246
Insulet Corp			
9 Oak Park Dr ....Bedford MA 01730	800-591-3455	781-457-5000	474
Insulfab Plastics Inc			
834 Hayne St ....Spartanburg SC 29301	800-845-7599	864-582-7506	595
Insultab Inc			
45 Industrial Pkwy ....Woburn MA 01801	800-468-4822*	781-935-0800	595
*Cust Svc			
Insurance Auto Auctions Inc			
2 Westbrook Corporate Ctr			
10th Fl ....Westchester IL 60154	800-872-1501	708-492-7000	51
Insurance Company of the West			
11455 El Camino Real ....San Diego CA 92130	800-877-1111	858-350-2400	390-4
Insurance Consultants International			
1840 Deer Creek Rd Ste 200.........Monument CO 80132	800-576-2674	719-573-9080	390-7
Insurance Data Processing Inc (IDP)			
8101 Washington Ln ....Wyncote PA 19095	800-523-6745	215-885-2150	178-11
Insurance Information Institute Inc (III)			
110 William St ....New York NY 10038	877-263-7995	212-346-5500	49-9
Insurance Marketing Agencies Inc			
306 Main St ....Worcester MA 01608	800-891-1226	508-753-7233	390-2
Insurance Services Office Inc (ISO)			
545 Washington Blvd ....Jersey City NJ 07310	800-888-4476	201-469-2000	389
InsurBanc			
10 Executive Dr ....Farmington CT 06032	866-467-2262	860-677-9701	70
INTA (International Trademark Assn)			
655 Third Ave 10th Fl...............New York NY 10017	800-995-3579	212-768-9887	49-12
Intaglio LLC			
3 Mile Rd NW Ste 3106 ....Grand Rapids MI 49534	800-632-9153	616-243-3300	510
Intec Video Systems Inc			
23301 Vista Grande Dr ....Laguna Hills CA 92653	800-468-3254	949-859-3800	689
Intedge Manufacturing			
1875 Chumley Rd Po Box 969 ....Woodruff SC 29388	866-969-9605	864-969-9605	300
Integra Capital Ltd			
2020 Winston Park Dr Ste 200 ....Oakville ON L6H6X7	800-363-2480	905-829-1131	400
Integra Group			
16 Triangle Park Dr Ste 1600 ....Cincinnati OH 45246	800-424-8384	513-326-5600	461
Integra LifeSciences Corp			
311 Enterprise Dr ....Plainsboro NJ 08536	800-654-2873	609-275-0500	473
Integra Services Technologies Inc			
5000 E 2nd Unit E....................Benicia CA 95410	800-779-2658	707-751-0685	
Integra Telecom Inc			
1201 NE Lloyd Blvd Ste 750...........Portland OR 97232	866-468-3472*		731
*General			
IntegraColor			
3210 Innovative Way ....Mesquite TX 75149	800-933-9511	972-289-0705	623
Integral Solutions Group			
5700 N Blockstock Rd ....Spartanburg SC 29303	800-428-7280		
Integranetics			
325 Park Plaza Dr 2b ....Owensboro KY 42301	800-291-9307	270-685-6016	175
Integrated Biometrics Inc			
121 Broadcast Dr ....Spartanburg SC 29303	888-840-8034	864-990-3711	688
Integrated BioPharma Inc			
225 Long Ave ....Hillside NJ 07205	888-319-6962	973-926-0816	794
OTC: INBP			
Integrated BioTherapeutics Inc			
4 Research Ct Ste 300 ....Rockville MD 20850	877-411-2041		738
Integrated Business Systems & Services Inc			
1601 Shop Rd Ste E ....Columbia SC 29201	800-553-1038	803-736-5595	178-1
Integrated Device Technology Inc			
6024 Silver Creek Valley Rd ....San Jose CA 95138	800-345-7015	408-284-8200	692
NASDAQ: IDTI			
Integrated Document Technologies Inc (IDT)			
1009 W Hawthorn Dr ....Itasca IL 60143	877-722-6438	630-875-1100	196
Integrated Flow Solutions LLC			
6461 Reynolds Rd ....Tyler TX 75708	800-859-7867	903-595-6511	637
Integrated Magnetics Inc			
11248 Playa Ct ....Culver City CA 90230	800-421-6692	310-391-7213	253
Integrated Regional Laboratories			
5361 NW 33rd Ave ....Ft. Lauderdale FL 33309	800-522-0232		414
Integrated Services Inc			
15115 SW Sequoia Pkwy Ste 110.........Portland OR 97224	800-922-3099		174
Integrated Support Command Miami Beach			
100 MacArthur Cswy ....Miami Beach FL 33139	866-772-8724	305-535-4300	158
Integration Technologies Group Inc			
2745 Hartland Rd Ste 200.........Falls Church VA 22043	800-835-7823	703-698-8282	175
INTEGRIS Baptist Regional Health Ctr			
200 Second Ave SW ....Miami OK 74355	888-951-2277	918-542-6611	373-3
INTEGRIS Bass Baptist Health Ctr			
600 S Monroe ....Enid OK 73701	888-951-2277	580-233-2300	373-3
INTEGRIS Health Inc			
3300 NW Expy ....Oklahoma City OK 73112	888-951-2277	405-951-2277	352
INTEGRIS Southwest Medical Ctr			
4401 S Western St ....Oklahoma City OK 73109	888-949-3816	405-636-7000	373-3
Integrity Marketing Solutions			
1311 Interquest Pkwy			
Ste 215 ....Colorado Springs CO 80921	877-352-2021		195
Integrity Music			
1646 Westgate Cir Ste 106 ....Brentwood TN 37027	888-888-4726		653
Integrity Systems & Solutions LLC			
1247 Highland Ave Ste 202 ....Cheshire CT 06410	866-446-8797		177
Intek Plastic Inc			
1000 Spiral Blvd ....Hastings MN 55033	888-468-3531		326
Intel Corp			
2200 Mission College Blvd ....Santa Clara CA 95052	800-628-8686*	408-765-8080	692
NASDAQ: INTC ■ *Cust Svc			
Intel Museum			
2200 Mission College Blvd ....Santa Clara CA 95052	800-628-8686	408-765-5050	517
Intelestream Inc			
27 North Wacker Dr Ste 370 ....Chicago IL 60606	800-391-4055		196
Intellect Resources Inc			
3824 N Elm St Ste 102 ....Greensboro NC 27455	877-554-8911		260
Intelletrace Inc			
936 B Seventh St ....Novato CA 94945	800-618-5877	415-493-2200	386
Intellicom Computer Consulting			
1702 Second Ave ....Kearney NE 68847	877-501-3375	308-237-0684	180
Intelligencer Printing Co			
330 Eden Rd ....Lancaster PA 17601	800-233-0107		623
Intelligent Computer Solutions Inc			
9350 Eton Ave ....Chatsworth CA 91311	888-994-4678	818-998-5805	174
Intelligent Decisions Inc			
21445 Beaumeade Cir ....Ashburn VA 20147	800-929-8331	703-554-1600	180
Intelligent Transportation Society of America (ITS)			
1100 New Jersey Ave SE			
Ste 850 ....Washington DC 20003	800-374-8472	202-484-4847	49-21
Intelligrated Products			
475 E High St PO Box 899 ....London OH 43140	866-936-7300	740-490-0300	207
IntelliSoft Group LLC			
61 Spit Brook Rd ....Nashua NH 03060	888-634-4464		180
Inter City Oil Company Inc (ICO)			
1921 S St ....Duluth MN 55812	800-642-5542	218-728-3641	575
Inter Mountain Cable Inc			
20 Laynesville Rd PO Box 159 ....Harold KY 41635	800-635-7052	606-478-9406	116
INTERA Inc			
1812 Centre Creek Dr Ste 300 ....Austin TX 78754	800-856-0217		
Interact Performance Systems Inc			
180 N Rverview Dr Ste 165...........Anaheim CA 92808	800-944-7553	714-283-8288	461
Interaction Assoc			
70 Fargo St Ste 908 ....Boston MA 02210	800-625-8049		194
Interactive Digital Solutions Inc			
14701 Cumberland Rd Ste 400.........Noblesville IN 46060	877-880-0022		52
Interamerican College of Physicians & Surgeons			
233 Broadway ....New York NY 10279	800-554-2245	212-777-3642	49-8
Inter-American Development Bank			
1300 New York Ave NW ....Washington DC 20577	877-782-7432	202-623-1000	778
InterAmerican Motor Corp (IMC)			
8901 Canoga Ave ....Canoga Park CA 91304	800-874-8925	818-678-1200	61
Interbond Corp of America			
3200 SW 42nd St ....Fort Lauderdale FL 33312	800-432-8579		35
InterCall			
8420 W Bryn Mawr Ste 1100 ....Chicago IL 60631	800-374-2441	773-399-1600	731
Intercept Energy Services Inc			
11464 - 149 St ....Edmonton AB T5M1W7	877-975-0558		534
Interchem Corp			
120 Rt 17 N ....Paramus NJ 07652	800-261-7332	201-261-7333	477
InterChez Logistics Systems Inc			
600 Alpha Pkwy ....Stow OH 44224	800-780-4707	330-923-5080	447
Interchurch Medical Assistance Inc (IMA)			
1730 M St NW Ste 1100.........Washington DC 20036	877-241-7952	202-888-6200	48-5
Intercollegiate Studies Institute (ISI)			
3901 Centerville Rd ....Wilmington DE 19807	800-526-7022	302-652-4600	48-11
Inter-Community Telephone Co (ICTC)			
PO Box 8 ....Nome ND 58062	800-350-9137	701-924-8815	731
Intercomp Co			
3839 County Rd 116 ....Medina MN 55340	800-328-3336	763-476-2531	680
InterContinental Hotels Group (IHG)			
3 Ravinia Dr Ste 100................Atlanta GA 30346	866-803-2143	770-604-2000	378
Crowne Plaza Atlanta Perimeter			
4355 Ashford Dunwoody Rd ....Atlanta GA 30346	800-621-0555	770-395-7700	378
Intercontinental San Francisco			
888 Howard St ....San Francisco CA 94103	888-811-4273		377
Inter-County Bakers Inc			
1095 Long Island Ave ....Deer Park NY 11729	800-696-1350	631-957-1350	70
Intercounty Electric Co-op			
102 Maple Ave ....Licking MO 65542	866-621-3679	573-674-2211	245
Inter-County Energy Co-op			
1009 Hustonville Rd ....Danville KY 40422	888-266-7322	859-236-4561	245
InterDev LLC			
2650 Holcomb Bridge Rd			
Ste 310 ....Alpharetta GA 30022	877-841-8069	770-643-4400	180
Interface EAP Inc (IEAP)			
10370 Richmond Ave Ste 1100			
PO Box 421879.......................Houston TX 77042	800-324-4327	713-781-3364	460
Interface Inc			
7401 E Butherus Dr ....Scottsdale AZ 85260	800-947-5598	480-948-5555	470
Interface Solutions Inc			
216 Wohlsen Way ....Lancaster PA 17603	800-942-7538		326
Intergraph Corp			
19 Interpro Rd ....Madison AL 35758	800-345-4856	256-730-2000	178-5
Interim HealthCare Inc			
1601 Sawgrass Corporate Pkwy ....Sunrise FL 33323	800-338-7786	954-858-6000	717
Interlaken Inn			
74 Interlaken Rd Rt 12 ....Lakeville CT 06039	800-222-2909	860-435-9878	665
Interlectric Corp			
1401 Lexington Ave ....Warren PA 16365	800-722-2184	814-723-6061	436

Listing	Toll-Free	Phone	Class
Interline Creative Group 553 North N Ct Ste 160 .... Palatine IL 60067	800-222-1208	847-358-4848	7
Interlink Network Systems Inc 495 Cranbury Rd .... East Brunswick NJ 08816	877-872-6947	732-846-2226	256
Interlocking Concrete Pavement Institute (ICPI) 14801 Murdock St Ste 230............ Chantilly VA 20151	800-241-3652	703-657-6900	49-3
Interlog USA Inc 9380 Central Ave NE Ste 350 ....Minneapolis MN 55434	800-603-6030		313
Intermark Group 101 25th St N ....Birmingham AL 35203	800-624-9239		4
InterMetro Industries Corp 651 N Washington St .... Wilkes-Barre PA 18705 *Cust Svc	800-992-1776*	570-825-2741	73
Intermodal Assn of North America (IANA) 11785 Beltsville Dr Ste 1100 ....Calverton MD 20705	877-438-8442	301-982-3400	49-21
Intermolecular Inc 3011 N First St .... San Jose CA 95134	877-251-1860	408-582-5700	692
Intermountain Farmers Assn 1147 West 2100 South ....Salt Lake City UT 84119	800-748-4432	801-972-2122	276
Intermountain Gas Co Inc 555 S Cole Rd ....Boise ID 83709 *Cust Svc	800-548-3679*	208-377-6840	782
Intermountain HealthCare 36 S State St ....Salt Lake City UT 84111 *Hum Res	800-843-7820*	801-442-2000	352
Intermountain Healthcare Logan Regional Hospital 500 E 1400 N .... Logan UT 84341	800-442-4845	435-716-1000	373-3
Intermountain Rural Electric Assn 5496 Hwy 85 ....Sedalia CO 80135	800-332-9540	303-688-3100	245
Internal Medicine News 5635 Fishers Ln Ste 6000............. Rockville MD 20852	877-524-9336	240-221-2400	455-16
Internal Revenue Service *Taxpayer Advocate Service* 77 K St NE Ste 1500............. Washington DC 20002	877-777-4778	202-803-9800	339-17
Internap Network Services Corp 250 Williams St Ste E-100 ....Atlanta GA 30303 *NASDAQ: INAP*	877-843-7627	404-302-9700	39
International Academy of Compounding Pharmacists (IACP) 4638 Riverstone Blvd ....Missouri City TX 77459	800-927-4227	281-933-8400	49-8
International Academy of Design & Technology *Las Vegas* 2495 Village View Dr ....Henderson NV 89074	866-400-4238	702-990-0150	164
International Aid Inc 17011 W Hickory St...............Spring Lake MI 49456	800-968-7490	616-846-7490	48-5
International Air Transport Assn 800 Pl Victoria PO Box 113 .... Montreal QC H4Z1M1	800-716-6326	514-874-0202	49-21
International Airline Passengers Assn (IAPA) PO Box 700188 .... Dallas TX 75370	800-821-4272	972-404-9980	48-23
International Alliance for Women (TIAW) 1101 Pennsylvania Ave NW 3rd Fl ....Washington DC 20004	888-712-5200		48-24
International Alliance of Theatrical Stage Employee (IATSE) 1430 Broadway 20th Fl..............New York NY 10018	800-456-3863	212-730-1770	413
International Assn for Food Protection (IAFP) 6200 Aurora Ave Ste 200W..........Des Moines IA 50322 *General	800-369-6337*	515-276-3344	49-6
International Assn for Human Resource Information Management Inc (IHRIM) PO Box 1086 .... Burlington MA 01803	800-804-3983		49-12
International Assn for the Study of Pain (IASP) 111 Queen Anne Ave N Ste 501 .... Seattle WA 98109	866-574-2654	206-283-0311	48-17
International Assn of Arson Investigators (IAAI) 2111 Baldwin Ave # 203 .... Crofton MD 21114	800-468-4224	410-451-3473	49-7
International Assn of Assessing Officers (IAAO) 314 W Tenth St ....Kansas City MO 64105	800-616-4226	816-701-8100	49-7
International Assn of Bridge Structural Ornamental & Reinforcing Iron Workers 1750 New York Ave NW Ste 400...... Washington DC 20006	800-368-0105	202-383-4800	413
International Assn of Business Communicators (IABC) 155 Montgomery St Ste 1210...................... San Francisco CA 94104	800-776-4222	415-544-4700	49-12
International Assn of Chiefs of Police (IACP) 44 Canal Ctr Plz Ste 200.............Alexandria VA 22314	800-843-4227	703-836-6767	49-7
International Assn of Culinary Professionals (IACP) 45 Rockefeller Plz Ste 2000 ....New York NY 10111	855-738-4227		49-6
International Assn of Electrical Inspectors (IAEI) 901 Waterfall Way Ste 602.......... Richardson TX 75080	800-786-4234	972-235-1455	49-3
International Assn of Fairs & Expositions, The (IAFE) 3043 E Cairo St ....Springfield MO 65802	800-516-0313	417-862-5771	48-23
International Assn of Fire Chiefs (IAFC) 4025 Fair Ridge Dr Ste 300 .... Fairfax VA 22033	866-385-9110	703-273-0911	49-7
International Assn of Lions Clubs 300 W 22nd St.................... Oak Brook IL 60523	800-710-7822	630-571-5466	48-15
International Assn of Marriage & Family Counselors (IAMFC) 5999 Stevenson Ave ....Alexandria VA 22304	800-347-6647		49-15
International Assn of Plumbing & Mechanical Officials (IAPMO) 4755 E Philadelphia St ....Ontario CA 91761	877-427-6601	909-472-4100	49-7
International Assn of Venue Managers Inc (IAVM) 635 Fritz Dr Ste 100 .... Coppell TX 75019	800-935-4226	972-906-7441	49-12
International Association of Privacy Professionals (Iapp) 75 Rochester Ave Ste 4............ Portsmouth NH 03801	800-266-6501	603-427-9200	
International Automotive Technicians' Network Inc PO Box 1599 ....Brea CA 92822	800-272-7467	714-257-1335	386
International Bible Society (IBS) *Biblica* 1820 Jet Stream Dr .... Colorado Springs CO 80921 *Cust Svc	800-524-1588*	719-488-9200	48-20
International Bottled Water Association (IBWA) 1700 Diagonal Rd Ste 650 ....Alexandria VA 22314	800-928-3711	703-683-5213	49-6
International Boundary & Water Commission - US & Mexico 2616 W Paisano Dr Ste C-100 .... El Paso TX 79922	800-262-8857	915-351-1030	339-15
International Bowling Museum & Hall of Fame 621 Six Flags Dr ....Arlington TX 76011	800-514-2695	817-385-8215	519
International Business College 5699 Coventry Ln .... Fort Wayne IN 46804	800-589-6363	260-459-4500	795
International Business Machines Corp (IBM) 1 New OrchaRd Rd.................. Armonk NY 10504 *NYSE: IBM*	800-426-4968	914-499-1900	173-2
International Carwash Assn 230 E Ohio St ....Chicago IL 60611	888-422-8422		49-21
International Cemetery Cremation & Funeral Assn (ICCFA) 107 Carpenter Dr Ste 100.............. Sterling VA 20164	800-645-7700	703-391-8400	49-4
International Ceramic Engineering 235 Brooks St .... Worcester MA 01606	800-779-3321	508-853-4700	249
International Chauffeured Service Worldwide 53 E 34th St ....New York NY 10016	800-266-5254	212-213-0302	440
International Chimney Corp 55 S Long St .... Williamsville NY 14221	800-828-1446		189-7
International Chiropractors Assn (ICA) 6400 Arlington Blvd Ste 800 .... Falls Church VA 22042	800-423-4690	703-528-5000	49-8
International Church of the Foursquare Gospel (ICFG) 1910 W Sunset Blvd PO Box 26902.....................Los Angeles CA 90026	888-635-4234	213-989-4234	48-20
International City/County Management Assn (ICMA) 777 N Capitol St NE Ste 500......... Washington DC 20002	800-745-8780	202-289-4262	49-7
International Civil Rights Ctr & Museum 134 S Elm St .... Greensboro NC 27401	800-748-7116	336-274-9199	517
International Coatings Co 13929 166th St .... Cerritos CA 90703	800-423-4103	562-926-1010	387
International Code Council (ICC) 500 New Jersey Ave NW 6th Fl....... Washington DC 20001	888-422-7233	202-370-1800	49-3
International Cold Storage Company Inc 215 E 13th St.........................Andover KS 67002	800-835-0001	316-733-1385	660
International Collegiate Licensing Assn (ICLA) 24651 Detroit Rd .... Westlake OH 44145	877-887-2261	440-892-4000	48-22
International Congress of Oral Implantologists (ICOI) 55 Ln Rd Ste 305 .... Fairfield NJ 07004	800-442-0525	973-783-6300	49-8
International Contract Furnishings Inc (ICF) 19 Ohio Ave ....Norwich CT 06360	800-237-1625	860-886-1700	321
International Cornea Project 9246 Lightwave Ave Ste 120.......... San Diego CA 92123	800-393-2265	858-694-0400	269
International Dairy Queen Corp 7505 Metro Blvd ....Minneapolis MN 55439	866-793-7582	952-830-0200	666
International Dairy-Deli-Bakery Assn (IDDBA) 636 Science Dr .... Madison WI 53711	877-399-4925	608-310-5000	49-6
International Data Group Inc (IDG) 492 Old Connecticut Path PO Box 9208.................... Framingham MA 01701 *Orders	800-343-4952*	508-875-5000	633-9
International Delivery Solutions 7340 S Howell Ave .... Oak Creek WI 53154	877-437-8722		5
International Engraved Graphics Assn 305 Plus Pk Blvd .... Nashville TN 37217	800-821-3138		49-4
International Environmental Corp (IEC) PO Box 2598 ....Oklahoma City OK 73101	800-264-5329	405-605-5000	14
International Executive Housekeepers Assn (IEHA) 1001 Eastwind Dr Ste 301 ....Westerville OH 43081	800-200-6342	614-895-7166	49-4
International Extrusions Inc 5800 Venoy Rd .... Garden City MI 48135	800-242-8876	734-427-8700	480
International Federation of Accountants (IFAC) 545 Fifth Ave 14th Fl ....New York NY 10017	888-272-2001	212-286-9344	49-1
International Fiber Corp 50 Bridge St................North Tonawanda NY 14120	888-698-1936	716-693-4040	601-1
International Fidelity Insurance Co (IFIC) 1 Newark Ctr 1111 Raymond Blvd 20th Fl ....Newark NJ 07102	800-333-4167		390-5
International Food Information Council Foundation (IFIC) 1100 Connecticut Ave NW Ste 430......................... Washington DC 20036	888-723-3366	202-296-6540	49-6
International Foundation of Employee Benefit Plans (IFEBP) 18700 W Bluemound Rd .... Brookfield WI 53045	888-334-3327	262-786-6700	260
International Franchise Assn (IFA) 1501 K St NW Ste 350 .... Washington DC 20005	800-543-1038	202-628-8000	49-18
International Fraternity of Phi Gamma Delta 1201 Red Mile Rd PO Box 4599..........Lexington KY 40544	888-668-4293	859-255-1848	48-16
International Fund for Animal Welfare (IFAW) 290 Summer St .... Yarmouth Port MA 02675	800-932-4329	508-744-2000	48-3
International Gourmet Foods Inc 7520 Fullerton Rd ....Springfield VA 22153	800-522-0377	703-569-4520	344
International Ground Source Heat Pump Assn (IGSHPA) Oklahoma State University 374 Cordell S .... Stillwater OK 74078	800-626-4747	405-744-5175	49-13
International Group Inc 85 Old Eagle School Rd .... Wayne PA 19087	800-852-6537	610-687-9030	576
International Health Racquet & Sportsclub Assn (IHRSA) 70 Fargo St ....Boston MA 02210	800-228-4772	617-951-0055	48-22
International Homes of Cedar Inc (IHC) PO Box 886 ....Woodinville WA 98072	800-767-7674	360-668-8511	106
International Hotel of Calgary 220 Fourth Ave SW .... Calgary AB T2P0H5	800-661-8627	403-265-9600	378
International Housewares Assn (IHA) 6400 Shafer Ct Ste 650............... Rosemont IL 60018	800-752-1052	847-292-4200	49-4
International Imaging Materials Inc 310 Commerce Dr .... Amherst NY 14228	888-464-4625	716-691-6333	530
International Immunology Corp 25549 Adams Ave .... Murrieta CA 92562	800-843-2853	951-677-5629	231
International Institute of Municipal Clerks (IIMC) 8331 Utica Ave Ste 200 ......Rancho Cucamonga CA 91730	800-251-1639	909-944-4162	49-7
International Interior Design Assn (IIDA) 222 Merchandise Mart Plz Ste 567...........................Chicago IL 60654	888-799-4432	312-467-1950	48-4
International Investigators Inc 3216 N Pennsylvania St............Indianapolis IN 46205	800-403-8111	317-925-1496	399
International Isotopes Inc 4137 Commerce Cir ....Idaho Falls ID 83401 *OTC: INIS*	800-699-3108	208-524-5300	231
International Jet Aviation Services 8511 Aviator Ln .... Centennial CO 80112	800-858-5891	303-790-0414	13
International Label & Printing Company Inc 2550 United Ln ....Elk Grove Village IL 60007	800-244-1442		412
International Launch Services (ILS) 1875 Explorer St Ste 700 .... Reston VA 20190	800-852-4980	571-633-7400	502
International Longshore & Warehouse Union 1188 Franklin St 4th Fl........... San Francisco CA 94109	866-266-0013	415-775-0533	413
International Masonry Institute (IMI) 17101 Science Dr ....Bowie MD 20715	800-803-0295	301-291-2124	49-3

	Toll-Free	Phone	Class
International Medical Corps (IMC) 1919 Santa Monica Blvd Ste 400 Santa Monica CA 90404	800-481-4462	310-826-7800	48-5
International Medical Device Regulatory Monitor 300 N Washington St Ste 200 Falls Church VA 22046	888-838-5578	703-538-7600	527-8
International Meeting Managers Inc 4550 Post Oak Pl Ste 342 Houston TX 77027	800-423-7175	713-965-0566	184
International Metal Hose Co 520 Goodrich Rd Bellevue OH 44811	800-458-6855	419-483-7690	488
International Mold Steel Inc 6796 Powerline Dr Florence KY 41042	800-625-6653	859-342-6000	490
International Monetary Fund (IMF) 700 19th St NW Washington DC 20431	800-548-5384	202-623-7000	778
International Montessori Council & The Montessori Foundation 19600 E State Rd 64 Bradenton FL 34212	800-655-5843	941-729-9565	48-11
International Motor Coach Group Inc (IMG) 12351 W 96th Ter Lenexa KS 66215	888-447-3466		49-21
International Municipal Lawyers Assn (IMLA) 51 Monroe St Ste 404 Rockville MD 20850	800-942-7732	202-466-5424	49-10
International Municipal Signal Assn (IMSA) 165 E Union St PO Box 539 Newark NY 14513	800-723-4672	315-331-2182	49-7
International Museum of the Horse 4089 Iron Works Pkwy Lexington KY 40511	800-678-8813	859-259-4232	517
International OCD Foundation (OCF) PO Box 961029 Boston MA 02196	800-331-3131	617-973-5801	48-17
International Order of the Golden Rule (OGR) 3520 Executive Ctr Dr Ste 300 Austin TX 78731	800-637-8030	512-334-5504	49-4
International Organization of Masters Mates & Pilots 700 Maritime Blvd Linthicum Heights MD 21090	877-667-5522	410-850-8700	413
International Orthodox Christian Charities (IOCC) 110 W Rd Ste 360 Towson MD 21204	877-803-4622	410-243-9820	48-5
International Paper Co 6400 Poplar Ave Memphis TN 38197 *NYSE: IP* ■ *Prod Info	800-223-1268*	901-419-9000	553
International Pentecostal Holiness Church (IPHC) PO Box 12609 Oklahoma City OK 73157	888-474-2966	405-787-7110	48-20
International Plastics Inc 185 Commerce Ctr Greenville SC 29615	800-820-4722	864-297-8000	344
International Playthings Inc 75D Lackawanna Ave Parsippany NJ 07054	800-631-1272	973-316-2500	757
International Poly Bag Inc 900 Park Center Dr Ste F & G Vista CA 92081	800-976-5922	760-598-2468	66
International Professional Rodeo Assn (IPRA) 1412 S Agnew Oklahoma City OK 73108	800-639-9002	405-235-6540	48-22
International Public Management Assn for Hum Res (IPMA-HR) 1617 Duke St Alexandria VA 22314	800-381-8378	703-549-7100	49-12
International Reprographic Assn (IRgA) 401 N Michigan Ave Ste 2200 Chicago IL 60611	800-833-4742	877-226-6839	49-16
International Revolving Door Co 2138 N Sixth Ave Evansville IN 47710	800-745-4726	812-425-3311	234
International Risk Management Institute Inc (IRMI) 12222 Merit Dr Ste 1600 Dallas TX 75251	800-827-4242	972-960-7693	
International Safe Transit Assn (ISTA) 1400 Abbott Rd Ste 160 East Lansing MI 48823	888-299-2208	517-333-3437	49-21
International Sanitary Supply Assn (ISSA) 3300 Dundee Rd Northbrook IL 60062	800-225-4772	847-982-0800	49-18
International Society for Animal Rights (ISAR) PO Box F Clarks Summit PA 18411	888-589-6397	570-586-2200	48-3
International Society for Performance Improvement (ISPI) PO Box 13035 Silver Spring MD 20910	800-825-7550	301-587-8570	49-12
International Society for Peritoneal Dialysis (ISPD) 66 Martin St Milton ON L9T2R2	888-834-1001	905-875-2456	49-8
International Society for Technology in Education (ISTE) 1530 Wilson Blvd Ste 730 Arlington VA 22209 *General	800-336-5191*		49-5
International Society for Traumatic Stress Studies (ISTSS) 111 Deer Lake Rd Ste 100 Deerfield IL 60015	877-469-7873	847-480-9028	49-15
International Society of Arboriculture (ISA) PO Box 3129 Champaign IL 61826	888-472-8733	217-355-9411	48-2
International Society of Certified Electronics Technicians (ISCET) 3608 Pershing Ave Fort Worth TX 76107	800-946-0201	817-921-9101	49-19
International Society of Certified Employee Benefits (ISCEBS) 18700 W Bluemond Rd PO Box 209 Brookfield WI 53008	888-334-3327	262-786-8771	49-12
International Society of Fire Service Instructors (ISFSI) 14001C St Germain Dr Centreville VA 20121	800-435-0005		49-7
International Society of Refractive Surgery (ISRS) 655 Beach St PO Box 7424 San Francisco CA 94109	866-561-8558	415-561-8581	49-8
International SOS 3600 Horizon Blvd Ste 300 Trevose PA 19053	800-523-6586	215-942-8000	390-7
International Trademark Assn (INTA) 655 Third Ave 10th Fl New York NY 10017	800-995-3579	212-768-9887	49-12
International Training Inc 1321 SE Decker Ave Stuart FL 34994	888-778-9073	207-729-4201	31
International Transplant Nurses Society (ITNS) 8735 W Higgins Rd Ste 300 Chicago IL 60631	800-776-8636	847-375-6340	49-8
International Travel Systems Inc 64 Madison Ave Wood-Ridge NJ 07075	800-258-0135	201-727-0470	16
International Union of Bricklayers & Allied Craftworkers (BAC) 1776 eye St NW Washington DC 20006	888-880-8222	202-783-3788	413
International Union of Painters & Allied Trades (IUPAT) 7234 Pkwy Dr Hanover MD 21076	800-554-2479	410-564-5900	413
International Union of Police Assn 1549 Ringling Blvd Ste 600 Sarasota FL 34236	800-247-4872	941-487-2560	413
International Union Security Police & Fire Professionals of America (SPFPA) 25510 Kelly Rd Roseville MI 48066	800-228-7492	586-772-7250	413
International Violin Co Ltd 1421 Clarkview Rd Baltimore MD 21209	800-542-3538	410-832-2525	522
International Visual Corp (IVC) 11500 Blvd Armand Bombardier Montreal QC H1E2W9	866-643-0570	514-643-0570	286
International Webmasters Assn (IWA) 119 E Union St Ste A Pasadena CA 91103	866-607-1773	626-449-3709	48-9
International Window Corp 5625 E Firestone Blvd South Gate CA 90280	800-477-4032	562-928-6411	234
International Women's Air & Space Museum 1501 N Marginal Rd Burke Lakefront Airport Cleveland OH 44114	877-287-4752	216-623-1111	517

	Toll-Free	Phone	Class
International Wood Products Assn (IWPA) 4214 King St Alexandria VA 22302	855-435-0005	703-820-6696	49-3
Interplastic Corp 1225 Wolters Blvd Saint Paul MN 55110	800-736-5497	651-481-6860	601-2
Interpreters Unlimited Inc 10650 Treena St Ste 308 San Diego CA 92131	800-726-9891		763
Interprint LLC 7111 Hayvenhurst Ave Van Nuys CA 91406	800-926-9873	818-989-3600	623
Interpublic Group 909 Third Ave New York NY 10036 *NYSE: IPG*	800-908-5395	212-704-1200	4
InterraTech Corp PO Box 4 Mount Ephraim NJ 08059	888-589-4889	856-854-5100	178-1
Interserve USA PO Box 418 Upper Darby PA 19082	800-809-4440	610-352-0581	48-20
Intersil Corp 1001 Murphy Ranch Rd Milpitas CA 95035 *NASDAQ: ISIL*	888-468-3774	408-432-8888	692
InterStar Communications 3900 North US 421 Hwy Clinton NC 28329	800-706-6538	910-564-4194	224
Inter-State Aviation 4800 Airport Complex N Pullman WA 99163	800-653-8420	509-332-6596	
Interstate Aviation Inc 62 Johnson Ave Plainville CT 06062	800-573-5519	860-747-5519	63
Interstate Chemical Co Inc 2797 Freedland Rd Hermitage PA 16148	800-422-2436	724-981-3771	143
Interstate Connecting Components Inc 120 Mt Holly By Pass Lumberton NJ 08048	800-422-3911		246
Interstate Electrical Supply Inc 2300 Second Ave Columbus GA 31901	800-903-4409	706-324-1000	246
Interstate Optical Co 680 Lindaire Ln Mansfield OH 44901	800-472-5790		
Interstate Transport Inc 324 First Ave N St Petersburg FL 33701	866-281-1281	727-822-9999	646
Interstock Premium Cabinets LLC 6300 Bristol Pk Levittown PA 19057	800-896-9842	267-442-0026	740-9
Interstyle Ceramics & Glass Ltd 3625 Brighton Ave Burnaby BC V5A3H5	800-667-1566	604-421-7229	746
InterSystems Corp 1 Memorial Dr Cambridge MA 02142	800-753-2571	617-621-0600	178-1
Intertech Corp 3240 N O'Henry Blvd Greensboro NC 27405	800-364-2255	336-621-1891	
InterTrust Technologies Corp 920 Stewart Dr Ste 100 Sunnyvale CA 94085	800-393-2272	408-616-1600	178-12
Interval International Inc 6262 Sunset Dr Miami FL 33143	800-828-8200	888-784-3447	748
InterVarsity Christian Fellowship/USA 6400 Schroeder Rd Madison WI 53711	866-734-4823	608-274-9001	48-20
Intervest Construction Inc 2379 Beville Rd Daytona Beach FL 32119	855-215-2974	844-349-6401	649
Interview Magazine 575 Broadway Ste 5 New York NY 10012	800-925-9574	212-941-2900	455-11
InterVision Systems Technologies Inc 2270 Martin Ave Santa Clara CA 95050	800-787-6707	408-980-8550	180
Interwest Capital Corp 4275 Executive Sq Ste 1020 La Jolla CA 92037	800-792-9639	858-622-4900	686
InterWest Insurance Services Inc 8950 Cal Ctr Dr Bldg 3 Ste 200 Sacramento CA 95826	800-444-4134	916-488-3100	389
InterWest Partners 2710 Sand Hill Rd Ste 200 Menlo Park CA 94025	866-803-9204	650-854-8585	787
InterWorks Inc 1425 S Sangre Rd Stillwater OK 74074	866-490-9643	405-624-3214	180
Intex Recreation Corp 1665 Hughes Way Long Beach CA 90810 *Cust Svc	800-234-6839*		706
Intland GmbH 968 Inverness Way Sunnyvale CA 94087	866-468-5210		392
Intoximeters Inc 2081 Craig Rd Saint Louis MO 63146	800-451-8639	314-429-4000	406
Intrada Technologies 31 Ashler Manor Dr Muncy PA 17756	800-858-5745		
Intradiem 3650 Mansell Rd Ste 500 Alpharetta GA 30022	888-566-9457	678-356-3500	178-10
IntraLinks Inc 150 E 42nd St New York NY 10017	888-546-5383	212-543-7700	39
Intraprisetechknowlogies LLC 3615 Harding Ave Ste 209 Honolulu HI 96816	866-737-9991		180
Intratek Computer Inc 5431 Industrial Dr Huntington Beach CA 92649	800-892-8282	714-892-0892	175
Intrepid Control Systems Inc 31601 Research Park Dr Madison Heights MI 48071	800-859-6265	586-731-7950	180
Intrepid Sea-Air-Space Museum W 46th St & 12th Ave Pier 86 New York NY 10036	877-957-7447	212-245-0072	517
Intrinium Inc 609 N Argonne Rd Spokane Valley WA 99212	866-461-5099		196
Intrinsix Corp 100 Campus Dr Marlborough MA 01752	800-783-0330	508-658-7600	261
Intronix Technologies Inc 26 McEwan Dr W Unit 15 Bolton ON L7E1E6	800-819-9996	905-951-3361	317
Intrusion Inc 1101 E Arapaho Rd Richardson TX 75081	888-637-7770	972-234-6400	178-12
Intsel Steel Distributors LP 11310 W Little York Houston TX 77041	800-762-3316	713-937-9500	719
Intuit Inc 2632 Marine Way Mountain View CA 94043 *NASDAQ: INTU* ■ *Cust Svc	800-446-8848*	650-944-6000	178-9
Intuitive Surgical Inc 1266 Kifer Rd Bldg 101 Sunnyvale CA 94086 *NASDAQ: ISRG*	888-868-4647	408-523-2100	474
Inuit Gallery of Vancouver Ltd 206 Cambie St Gastown Vancouver BC V6B2M9	888-615-8399	604-688-7323	42
Invacare Corp 1 Invacare Way Elyria OH 44036 *NYSE: IVC*	800-333-6900	440-329-6000	475
Invenio Marketing Solutions Inc 2201 Donley Dr Ste 200 Austin TX 78758	800-926-1754		195
Invent Now Inc 3701 Highland Park NW North Canton OH 44720	800-968-4332		517

	City	State	Zip	Toll-Free	Phone	Class
Inventory Sales Co						
9777 Reavis Rd	St Louis	MO	63123	**866-417-3801**		349
Inver Hills Community College						
2500 80th St E	Inver Grove Heights	MN	55076	**866-576-0689**	651-450-3000	162
Invesco						
11 Greenway Plz Ste 100	Houston	TX	77046	**800-959-4246**	713-626-1919	524
Invesco Canada Ltd						
5140 Yonge St Ste 800	Toronto	ON	M2N6X7	**800-874-6275**	416-590-9855	524
INVESCO Private Capital Inc						
1166 Ave of the Americas						
26th Fl	New York	NY	10036	**800-959-4246**	212-278-9000	787
Investing Daily						
7600A Leesburg Pk						
W Bldg Ste 300	Falls Church	VA	22043	**800-832-2330**	703-394-4931	527-9
Investment Planning Counsel						
5015 Spectrum Way Ste 200	Mississauga	ON	L4W0E4	**877-212-9799**	905-212-9799	687
Investment Professionals Inc (IPI)						
16414 San Pedro Ave Ste 300	San Antonio	TX	78232	**800-593-8800**	210-308-8800	
Investment Quality Trends (IQT)						
2888 Loker Ave E Ste 116	Carlsbad	CA	92010	**866-927-5250**		527-9
Investment Scorecard Inc						
601 Grassmere Park Dr Ste 1	Nashville	TN	37211	**800-555-6035**	615-301-1975	400
Investments & Wealth Institute (IMCA)						
5619 DTC Pkwy Ste 500	Greenwood Village	CO	80111	**800-250-9083**	303-770-3377	49-2
Investor's Business Daily						
12655 Beatrice St	Los Angeles	CA	90066	**800-831-2525**	310-448-6000	528-2
InvestorIdeascom						
1385 Gulf Rd Ste 102	Point Roberts	WA	98281	**800-665-0411**		464
InvestorPlace Media LLC						
9201 Corporate Blvd Ste 200	Rockville	MD	20850	**800-219-8592**		527-9
InvestorPlacecom						
2420A Gehman Ln	Lancaster	PA	17602	**800-219-8592**		403
Investors Bank						
101 Wood Ave S	Iselin	NJ	08830	**855-422-6548**	973-924-5100	70
NASDAQ: ISBC						
Investors Group Inc						
447 Portage Ave	Winnipeg	MB	R3B3H5	**888-746-6344**		400
TSE: IGM						
Investors Heritage Life Insurance Co (IHLIC)						
200 Capital Ave PO Box 717	Frankfort	KY	40602	**800-422-2011**		390-2
Investors Title Co						
121 N Columbia St	Chapel Hill	NC	27514	**800-326-4842**	919-968-2200	359-4
NASDAQ: ITIC						
Investrade Discount Securities						
950 N Milwaukee Ave Ste 102	Glenview	IL	60025	**800-498-7120***	847-375-6080	686
*Cust Svc						
Invincible Office Furniture Co						
842 S 26th St PO Box 1117	Manitowoc	WI	54220	**877-682-4601**	920-682-4601	319-1
Invisible Hand Networks Inc						
670 Broadway Ste 302	New York	NY	10012	**866-637-5286**	212-400-7416	392
INVISTA						
4123 E 37th St N	Wichita	KS	67220	**877-446-8478**	316-828-1000	601-1
InVite Health Inc						
1 Garden State Plz	Paramus	NJ	07652	**800-349-0929**	201-587-2222	344
Inviting Homecom						
4700 SW 51st St Unit 219	Davie	FL	33314	**866-751-6606**	781-444-8001	321
InVitro International						
330 E Orangethorpe Ave Ste D	Placentia	CA	92870	**800-246-8487**	949-851-8356	231
Invivoscribe Technologies Inc						
6330 Nancy Ridge Dr Ste 106	San Diego	CA	92121	**866-623-8105**	858-224-6600	231
InVue Security Products Inc						
10715 Sikes Pl Ste 200	Charlotte	NC	28277	**888-257-4272**	704-206-7849	253
IOA Re Inc						
190 W Germantown Pk						
Ste 200	East Norriton	PA	19401	**800-462-2300**	610-940-9000	390-3
IOActive Inc						
701 Fifth Ave Ste 6850	Seattle	WA	98104	**866-760-0222**	206-784-4313	180
IOCC (International Orthodox Christian Charities)						
110 W Rd Ste 360	Towson	MD	21204	**877-803-4622**	410-243-9820	48-5
IOF (Independent Order of Foresters)						
789 Don Mills Rd	Toronto	ON	M3C1T9	**800-828-1540**	416-429-3000	48-5
Ioline Corp						
14140 NE 200th St	Woodinville	WA	98072	**800-598-0029**	425-398-8282	739
Iomosaic Corp						
93 Stiles Rd	Salem	NH	03079	**844-466-6724**	603-893-7009	196
Ion						
948 W Seventh Ave W	Vancouver	BC	V5Z1C3	**888-336-2466**	604-682-6787	
ION Media Networks Inc						
875 Waimanu St Ste 630	Honolulu	HI	96813	**888-467-2988**	808-591-1275	736-33
ION Media Networks Inc						
601 Clearwater Pk Rd	West Palm Beach	FL	33401	**888-467-2988**	561-659-4122	
Ion Networks Inc						
120 Corporate Blvd						
Ste A	South Plainfield	NJ	07080	**800-722-8986**	908-546-3900	178-7
Iona College						
715 N Ave	New Rochelle	NY	10801	**800-264-6350**	914-633-2502	166
Ionia County						
100 W Main St	Ionia	MI	48846	**800-649-3777**	616-527-5322	337
IoPP (Institute of Packaging Professionals)						
1833 Centre Point Cir						
Ste 123	Naperville	IL	60563	**800-432-4085**	630-544-5050	49-13
Iowa						
Adult Children & Family Services Div						
1305 E Walnut St	Des Moines	IA	50319	**800-735-2942**	515-281-8977	338-16
Child Support Recovery Unit						
PO Box 9125	Des Moines	IA	50306	**888-229-9223**		338-16
Consumer Protection Div						
1305 E Walnut St 2nd Fl	Des Moines	IA	50319	**888-777-4590**	515-281-5926	338-16
Department on Aging						
510 E 12th St Ste 2	Des Moines	IA	50319	**800-532-3213**	515-725-3333	338-16
Human Services Dept						
1305 E Walnut St 5th Fl SE	Des Moines	IA	50319	**800-362-2178**	515-242-5880	338-16
Insurance Div						
601 Locust St 4th Fl	Des Moines	IA	50309	**877-955-1212**	515-281-5705	338-16
Medical Examiners Board						
400 SW Eigth St Ste C	Des Moines	IA	50309	**844-474-4321**	515-281-5171	338-16
Revenue & Finance Dept						
1305 E Walnut St						
Hoover State Office Bldg	Des Moines	IA	50319	**800-367-3388**	515-281-3114	338-16
Utilities Board						
1375 E Ct Ave Rm 69	Des Moines	IA	50319	**877-565-4450**	515-725-7300	338-16
Vital Records Bureau						
321 E 12th St						
Lucas State Office Bldg	Des Moines	IA	50319	**866-834-9671**	515-281-7689	338-16
Workforce Development						
1000 E Grand Ave	Des Moines	IA	50319	**866-239-0843**		259
Iowa Assn of Business & Industry						
400 E Ct Ave Ste 100	Des Moines	IA	50309	**800-383-4224**	515-280-8000	140
Iowa Assn of Realtors						
1370 NW 114th St Ste 100	Clive	IA	50325	**800-532-1515**	515-453-1064	652
Iowa Braille & Sight Saving School						
1002 G Ave	Vinton	IA	52349	**800-645-4579**	319-472-5221	166
Iowa Central Community College						
2031 Quail Ave	Fort Dodge	IA	50501	**800-362-2793**	515-576-7201	162
Iowa City/Coralville Area Convention & Visitors Bureau						
900 First Ave/Hayden Fry Way						
	Coralville	IA	52241	**800-283-6592**	319-337-6592	206
Iowa City/Coralville Area Convention & Visitors Bureau						
900 First Ave Hayden Fry Way						
	Coralville	IA	52241	**800-283-6592**	319-337-6592	206
Iowa College Student Aid Commission						
430 E Grand Ave 3rd Fl	Des Moines	IA	50309	**800-383-4222**	515-725-3400	721
Iowa Communications Network Inc						
Grimes State Office Bldg 400 E 14th St						
	Des Moines	IA	50319	**800-532-1290**	515-725-4692	386
Iowa Dental Assn						
8797 NW 54th Ave Ste 100	Johnston	IA	50131	**800-828-2181**	515-331-2298	227
Iowa Farm Bureau Spokesman Magazine						
5400 University Ave	West Des Moines	IA	50266	**866-598-3693**	515-225-5413	455-1
Iowa Gold Star Military Museum						
7105 NW 70th Ave	Johnston	IA	50131	**800-294-6607**	515-252-4531	517
Iowa Interstate Railroad						
5900 Sixth St SW	Cedar Rapids	IA	52404	**800-321-3891**	319-298-5400	644
Iowa Lakes Community College						
300 S 18th St	Estherville	IA	51334	**800-242-5106**	712-362-2604	162
Iowa Legal Aid						
1111 Ninth St Ste 230	Des Moines	IA	50314	**800-992-8161**	515-243-1193	427
Iowa Medical Society						
515 E Locust St Ste 400	Des Moines	IA	50309	**800-747-3070**	515-223-1401	472
Iowa Mold Tooling Co Inc (IMT)						
500 W US Hwy 18	Garner	IA	50438	**800-247-5958**	641-923-3711	468
Iowa Mortgage Association						
8800 NW 62nd Ave	Johnston	IA	50131	**800-800-2353**	515-286-4352	529
Iowa Northern Railway Co						
305 Second St SE Paramount Theatre Bldg						
Ste 400	Cedar Rapids	IA	52401	**800-392-3342**	319-297-6000	645
Iowa Prison Industries (IPI)						
1445 E Grand Ave	Des Moines	IA	50316	**800-670-4537**	515-242-5770	626
Iowa Public Television						
6450 Corporate Dr PO Box 6450	Johnston	IA	50131	**800-532-1290**	515-725-9700	736
Iowa Realty Company Inc						
3501 Westown Pkwy	West Des Moines	IA	50266	**800-247-2430**	515-453-6222	648
Iowa Soybean Association						
4554 114th St	Urbandale	IA	50322	**800-383-1423**	515-251-8640	138
Iowa Spring Manufacturing & Sales Co						
2112 Greene St	Adel	IA	50003	**800-622-2203**	515-993-4791	490
Iowa State Bar Assn						
625 E Ct Ave	Des Moines	IA	50309	**800-457-3729**	515-243-3179	72
Iowa State Library						
1007 E Grand Ave						
Capitol Bldg Second Fl	Des Moines	IA	50319	**800-248-4483**	515-281-4105	433-5
Iowa State Penitentiary						
Ave E & 1st St PO Box 409	Fort Madison	IA	52627	**800-382-0019**	319-372-1908	213
Iowa State Savings Bank						
401 W Adams St	Creston	IA	50801	**888-508-0142**	641-782-1000	70
Iowa State University						
100 Alumni Hall	Ames	IA	50011	**800-262-3810***	515-294-4111	166
*Admissions						
Iowa Veterans Home						
7105 NW 70th Ave						
Camp Dodge Bldg 3465	Johnston	IA	50131	**800-838-4692**	515-252-4698	788
Iowa Veterinary Medical Assn						
1605 North Ankeny Blvd Ste 110	Ankeny	IA	50023	**800-369-9564**	515-965-9237	790
Iowa Wesleyan College						
601 N Main St	Mount Pleasant	IA	52641	**800-582-2383**		166
Iowa Western Community College						
Clarinda						
923 E Washington St	Clarinda	IA	51632	**800-521-2073**	712-542-5117	162
IP Casino Resort & Spa						
850 Bayview Ave	Biloxi	MS	39530	**888-946-2847***	228-436-3000	133
*Resv						
Ip Convergence Inc						
PO Box 107	Argyle	TX	76226	**800-813-5106**		
IPAA (Independent Petroleum Assn of America)						
1201 15th St NW Ste 300	Washington	DC	20005	**800-433-2851**	202-857-4722	48-12
iPass Inc						
3800 Bridge Pkwy	Redwood Shores	CA	94065	**877-236-3807**	650-232-4100	393
NASDAQ: IPAS						
IPC Technologies Inc						
7200 Glen Forest Dr Ste 100	Richmond	VA	23226	**877-947-2835**		717
ipCapital Group Inc						
426 Industrial Ave Ste 150	Williston	VT	05495	**888-853-2212**	802-859-7800	
IPG Photonics Corp						
50 Old Webster Rd	Oxford	MA	01540	**877-980-1550**	508-373-1100	424
NASDAQ: IPGP						
IPHC (International Pentecostal Holiness Church)						
PO Box 12609	Oklahoma City	OK	73157	**888-474-2966**	405-787-7110	48-20
IPI (Iowa Prison Industries)						
1445 E Grand Ave	Des Moines	IA	50316	**800-670-4537**	515-242-5770	626
IPI (Investment Professionals Inc)						
16414 San Pedro Ave Ste 300	San Antonio	TX	78232	**800-593-8800**	210-308-8800	

	Toll-Free	Phone	Class
IPMA-HR (International Public Management Assn for Hum Res)			
1617 Duke St .... Alexandria VA 22314	**800-381-8378**	703-549-7100	49-12
IPRA (International Professional Rodeo Assn)			
1412 S Agnew .... Oklahoma City OK 73108	**800-639-9002**	405-235-6540	48-22
IPRO (Island Peer Review Organization Inc)			
1979 Marcus Ave .... Lake Success NY 11042	**888-880-9976**	516-326-7767	
Ipro Tech LLC			
1700 N Desert Dr Ste 101............... Tempe AZ 85281	**877-324-4776**		
IPS Corp			
455 W Victoria St .... Compton CA 90220	**800-888-8312**	310-898-3300	3
Ipsen Inc			
PO Box 6266 .... Rockford IL 61125	**800-727-7625**	815-332-4941	318
Ipss Inc			
150 Isabella St .... Ottawa ON K1S1V7	**866-532-2207**	613-232-2228	689
Ipswich Shellfish Group			
8 Hayward St .... Ipswich MA 01938	**800-477-9424**	978-356-4371	297-5
Ipswitch Inc			
83 Hartwell Ave .... Lexington MA 02421	**800-793-4825**	781-676-5700	178-12
IPTV (Idaho Public Television)			
1455 N Orchard St .... Boise ID 83706	**800-543-6868**	208-373-7220	628
IQ Technology Solutions			
5595 Equity Ave Ste 300................. Reno NV 89502	**866-842-4748**	775-352-2301	461
IQT (Investment Quality Trends)			
2888 Loker Ave E Ste 116............. Carlsbad CA 92010	**866-927-5250**		527-9
IQVIA			
16720 Trans-Canada Hwy .... Kirkland QC H9H5M3	**866-267-4479***	514-428-6000	578
*General			
IQware Inc			
5850 Coral Ridge Dr			
Ste 309........................ Coral Springs FL 33076	**877-698-5151**	954-698-5151	180
Ira Green Inc			
177 Georgia Ave .... Providence RI 02905	**800-663-7487***		408
*General			
Irc Building Sciences Group			
2121 Argentia Rd Ste 401.......... Mississauga ON L5N2X4	**888-607-5245**	905-607-7244	461
Iredale Mineral Cosmetics Ltd			
50 Church St .... Great Barrington MA 01230	**877-869-9420**		238
Consulate General			
100 Pine St Ste 3350.......... San Francisco CA 94111	**800-777-0133**	415-392-4214	257
Ireland			
Embassy			
2234 Massachusetts Ave NW ..... Washington DC 20008	**866-560-1050**	202-462-3939	257
IREM (Institute of Real Estate Management)			
430 N Michigan Ave .... Chicago IL 60611	**800-837-0706**	312-329-6000	49-17
IRET			
1400 31st Ave SW Ste 60................ Minot ND 58702	**888-478-4738**	701-837-4738	650
NYSE: IRET			
Irex Contracting Group			
120 N Lime St .... Lancaster PA 17608	**800-487-7255**		189-9
IRgA (International Reprographic Assn)			
401 N Michigan Ave Ste 2200 .... Chicago IL 60611	**800-833-4742**	877-226-6839	49-16
Iridex Corp			
1212 Terra Bella Ave .... Mountain View CA 94043	**800-388-4747***	650-940-4700	423
NASDAQ: IRIX ■ *Cust Svc			
Iris Group Inc, The			
1675 Faraday Ave .... Carlsbad CA 92008	**800-347-1103**	760-431-1103	4
Iris USA Inc			
11111 80th Ave .... Pleasant Prairie WI 53158	**800-320-4747**	262-612-1000	603
iRise			
2301 Rosecrans Ave Ste 4100 .... El Segundo CA 90245	**800-556-0399**		177
IRMI (International Risk Management Institute Inc)			
12222 Merit Dr Ste 1600 .... Dallas TX 75251	**800-827-4242**	972-960-7693	
Iron & Metals Inc			
5555 Franklin St .... Denver CO 80216	**800-776-7910**	303-292-5555	682
Iron City Distributing Co			
2670 Commercial Ave .... Mingo Junction OH 43938	**800-759-2671***	740-598-4171	81-1
*Cust Svc			
Iron City Workplace Services			
6640 Frankstown Ave .... Pittsburgh PA 15206	**800-532-2010**	412-661-2001	441
Iron Horse Energy Services Inc			
1901 Dirkson Dr NE................. Redcliff AB T0J2P0	**877-526-4666**	403-526-4600	536
Iron Mountain			
745 Atlantic Ave .... Boston MA 02111	**800-899-4766**		798-1
NYSE: IRM			
Iron Range Tourism Bureau			
111 Station 44 Rd .... Eveleth MN 55792	**800-777-8497**	218-749-8161	206
IronMaster LLC			
14562 167th Ave SE .... Monroe WA 98272	**800-533-3339**	360-217-7780	267
Ironplanet Inc			
3825 Hopyard Rd Ste 250............ Pleasanton CA 94588	**888-433-5426***	925-225-8600	51
*Cust Svc			
Ironrock Capital Inc			
1201 Millerton St SE .... Canton OH 44707	**800-325-3945**		746
Ironworkers			
1750 New York Ave NW Ste 400...... Washington DC 20006	**800-368-0105**	202-383-4800	611
Iroquois Gas Transmission System LP			
1 Corporate Dr Ste 600................ Shelton CT 06484	**800-888-3982**	203-925-7200	325
Iroquois New York			
49 W 44th St .... New York City NY 10036	**800-332-7220**	212-840-3080	378
Iroquois Products of Chicago			
2220 W 56th St .... Chicago IL 60636	**800-453-3355**		199
Irresistibles			
7 Hawkes St .... Marblehead MA 01945	**800-555-9865**	781-631-8903	157-6
Irrigation Assn (IA)			
6540 Arlington Blvd .... Falls Church VA 22042	**800-362-8774**	703-536-7080	48-2
IRS Practice Adviser			
1801 S Bell St .... Arlington VA 22202	**800-372-1033**		527-7
IRSC (Indian River State College)			
3209 Virginia Ave .... Fort Pierce FL 34981	**866-792-4772**	772-462-4772	162
Irvin Simon Photographers Inc			
146 Meacham Ave .... Elmont NY 11003	**800-540-4701**		588
Irvine Access Floors Inc			
9425 Washington Blvd .... Laurel MD 20723	**800-969-8870**	301-617-9333	489
Irvine Company Apartment Communities			
2500 Baypointe Dr .... Newport Beach CA 92660	**844-718-2918**		
Irvine Scientific			
2511 Daimler St .... Santa Ana CA 92705	**800-577-6097**	949-261-7800	85
Irvine Technology Corp			
17900 Von Karman Ste 100 .... Irvine CA 92614	**866-322-4482**		194
Irving Convention & Visitors Bureau			
500 W Las Colinas Blvd .... Irving TX 75039	**800-247-8464**	972-252-7476	206
Irwin Electric Membership Corp			
915 W Fourth St .... Ocilla GA 31774	**800-237-3745**	229-468-7415	245
Irwin Naturals			
5310 Beethoven St .... Los Angeles CA 90066	**800-297-3273**	310-306-3636	794
Irwin Seating Company Inc			
3251 Fruit Ridge NW .... Grand Rapids MI 49544	**866-464-7946**	616-574-7400	319-3
ISA (International Society of Arboriculture)			
PO Box 3129 .... Champaign IL 61826	**888-472-8733**	217-355-9411	48-2
Isabel Bloom LLC			
736 Federal St Ste 2100............. Davenport IA 52803	**800-273-5436**		183
ISABELLA FREEDMAN JEWISH RETREAT CENTER			
116 Johnson Rd .... Falls Village CT 06031	**800-398-2630**	860-824-5991	669
Isagenix International LLC			
2225 S Price Rd .... Chandler AZ 85286	**877-877-8111**	480-889-5747	296-11
Isanti County News			
234 S Main St .... Cambridge MN 55008	**800-927-9233**	763-689-1981	633-8
ISAR (International Society for Animal Rights)			
PO Box F .... Clarks Summit PA 18411	**888-589-6397**	570-586-2200	48-3
Isc Sales Inc			
4421 Tradition Trl .... Plano TX 75093	**800-836-7472**	972-964-2700	177
ISCEBS (International Society of Certified Employee Benefi)			
18700 W Bluemond Rd			
PO Box 209...................... Brookfield WI 53008	**888-334-3327**	262-786-8771	49-12
ISCET (International Society of Certified Electronics Tec)			
3608 Pershing Ave .... Fort Worth TX 76107	**800-946-0201**	817-921-9101	49-19
Isco Industries			
926 Baxter Ave PO Box 4545 .... Louisville KY 40204	**800-345-4726**	502-583-6591	592
ISCO International LLC			
444 E State Pkwy Ste 123.......... Schaumburg IL 60173	**888-948-4726**	630-283-3100	730
iSelect Internet Inc			
1420 W Kettleman Ln Ste E .... Lodi CA 95242	**877-837-1427**	209-334-0496	397
Iseli Co			
402 N Main St .... Walworth WI 53184	**800-403-8665**	262-275-2108	617
ISFSI (International Society of Fire Service Instructors)			
14001C St Germain Dr .... Centreville VA 20121	**800-435-0005**		49-7
Isgett Distributors Inc			
51 Highland Ctr Blvd .... Asheville NC 28806	**800-358-0080**	828-667-9846	575
ISGN (ISGN Corp)			
1333 Gateway Dr Ste 1000........... Melbourne FL 32901	**800-462-5545**	860-656-7550	178-1
ISGN Corp (ISGN)			
1333 Gateway Dr Ste 1000........... Melbourne FL 32901	**800-462-5545**	860-656-7550	178-1
ISI (Intercollegiate Studies Institute)			
3901 Centerville Rd .... Wilmington DE 19807	**800-526-7022**	302-652-4600	48-11
ISI Commercial Refrigeration LP			
640 W Sixth St .... Houston TX 77007	**800-777-5070**	214-631-7980	661
ISK Biosciences Corp			
7474 Auburn Rd Ste A .... Concord OH 44077	**877-706-4640**	440-357-4640	
ISL (Indiana State Library)			
115 W Washington St			
Ste 960S........................ Indianapolis IN 46204	**800-451-6028**	800-677-9800	433-5
Islamorada Chamber of Commerce			
PO Box 915 .... Islamorada FL 33036	**800-322-5397**	305-664-4503	139
Island Express Helicopter Service			
1175 Queens Hwy S .... Long Beach CA 90802	**800-228-2566***	310-510-2525	358
*Cust Svc			
Island Federal Credit Union			
120 Motor Pkwy .... Hauppauge NY 11788	**800-475-5263**	631-851-1100	219
Island Hotel, The			
690 Newport Ctr Dr .... Newport Beach CA 92660	**866-554-4620**	949-759-0808	378
Island Oasis Frozen Cocktail			
141 Norfolk St .... Walpole MA 02081	**800-777-4752**	508-660-1176	299
Island Pacific Inc			
17310 Red Hill Ave Ste 320 .... Irvine CA 92614	**800-994-3847**	250-250-1000	178-10
Island Packet, The			
10 Buck Island Rd .... Bluffton SC 29910	**877-706-8100**		528-2
Island Peer Review Organization Inc (IPRO)			
1979 Marcus Ave .... Lake Success NY 11042	**888-880-9976**	516-326-7767	
Island Surf			
1450 Miracle Strip Pkwy SE			
.... Fort Walton Beach FL 32548	**800-272-2065**		707
Island Timberlands LP			
65 Front St 4th Fl .... Nanaimo BC V9R5H9	**800-663-5555**	250-755-3500	452
Island View Casino Resort			
PO Box 1600 .... Gulfport MS 39502	**877-774-8439***	228-314-2100	133
*General			
Island Windjammers Inc			
165 Shaw Dr .... Acworth GA 30102	**877-772-4549**		31
Islander Resort			
82100 Overseas Hwy			
PO Box 766...................... Islamorada FL 33036	**800-753-6002**	305-664-2031	
Islands in the Sun Cruises & Tours Inc			
348 Thompson Creek Mall			
Ste 107......................... Stevensville MD 21666	**800-278-7786**	410-827-3812	766
ISLC Inc			
14 Savannah Hwy .... Beaufort SC 29906	**888-828-4752**	843-770-1000	386
Isle of Capri Casino Hotel Lake Charles			
100 West Lake Ave .... Westlake LA 70669	**800-843-4753**		
ISM (Institute for Supply Management)			
2055 Centennial Cir .... Tempe AZ 85284	**800-888-6276***	480-752-6276	49-12
*Cust Svc			
ISMIE (Illinois State Medical Inter-Insurance Exchange)			
20 N Michigan Ave Ste 700 .... Chicago IL 60602	**800-782-4767**	312-782-2749	390-5
ISN Global Enterprises Inc			
Po Box 1391 .... Claremont CA 91711	**877-376-4476**	909-670-0601	192
ISO (Insurance Services Office Inc)			
545 Washington Blvd .... Jersey City NJ 07310	**800-888-4476**	201-469-2000	389
Isolatek International Inc			
41 Furnace St .... Stanhope NJ 07874	**800-631-9600**	973-347-1200	388
Isolite Systems			
6868A Cortona Dr .... Santa Barbara CA 93117	**800-560-6066**		228
Iso-Tex Diagnostics Inc			
1511 County Rd 129 .... Pearland TX 77511	**800-477-4839**	281-481-1232	231
ISPD (International Society for Peritoneal Dialysis)			
66 Martin St .... Milton ON L9T2R2	**888-834-1001**	905-875-2456	49-8
ISPI (International Society for Performance Improvement)			
PO Box 13035 .... Silver Spring MD 20910	**800-825-7550**	301-587-8570	49-12

	Toll-Free	Phone	Class
ISPN Network Services 14303 W 95th St ....Lenexa KS 66215	866-584-4776		392
ISPOR (ISPOR) 505 Lawrence Sq Blvd S ....Lawrenceville NJ 08648	800-992-0643	609-586-4981	49-8
iSqFt Inc 3825 Edwards Rd Ste 800.........Cincinnati OH 45209	800-364-2059	513-645-8004	178-10
ISRS (International Society of Refractive Surgery) 655 Beach St PO Box 7424.......San Francisco CA 94109	866-561-8558	415-561-8581	49-8
ISSA (International Sanitary Supply Assn) 3300 Dundee Rd ....Northbrook IL 60062	800-225-4772	847-982-0800	49-18
Issuer Direct Corp 500 Perimeter Park Dr Ste D...Morrisville NC 27560	877-481-4014	919-481-4000	317
IS&T (Society for Imaging Science & Technology) 7003 Kilworth Ln ....Springfield VA 22151	800-654-2240	703-642-9090	49-16
ISTA (International Safe Transit Assn) 1400 Abbott Rd Ste 160 ....East Lansing MI 48823	888-299-2208	517-333-3437	49-21
ISTA Advocate Magazine 150 W Market St Ste 900........Indianapolis IN 46204	800-382-4037	317-263-3400	455-8
ISTE (International Society for Technology in Education) 1530 Wilson Blvd Ste 730 ....Arlington VA 22209 *General	800-336-5191*		49-5
Istech Inc 4691 Raycom Rd ....Dover PA 17315	800-555-4880	717-764-5565	180
iStreet Solutions LLC 1911 Douglas Blvd 85-200 ......Roseville CA 95661	866-976-3976		
ISTSS (International Society for Traumatic Stress Studies) 111 Deer Lake Rd Ste 100 ....Deerfield IL 60015	877-469-7873	847-480-9028	49-15
iT Services 2 2340 E Trinity Mills Rd Ste 300 ....Carrollton TX 75006	877-400-0293		196
IT Weapons 7965 Goreway Dr Unit 1 ....Brampton ON L6T5T5	866-202-5298	905-494-1040	180
IT. Blueprint Solutions Consulting Inc 170-422 Richards St ....Vancouver BC V6B2Z4	866-261-8981		196
Ita Inc 2162 Dana Ave ....Cincinnati OH 45207	800-899-8877		521
ITAGroup 4600 Westown Pkwy .....West Des Moines IA 50266	800-257-1985		383
Italgrani USA Inc 7900 Van Buren St ....Saint Louis MO 63111	800-274-1274	314-638-1447	275
iTalkBB CA 245 W Beaver Creek Rd Unit 9 ....Richmond Hill ON L4B1L1	877-482-5522		224
Itasca Community College 1851 E US Hwy 169 ....Grand Rapids MN 55744	800-996-6422	218-327-4460	162
Itasca County 123 NE Fourth St ....Grand Rapids MN 55744	800-422-0312	218-327-7363	337
Itasca-Mantrap Co-op Electrical Assn 16930 County Rd 6 ....Park Rapids MN 56470	888-713-3377	218-732-3377	245
ITC (Innovative Technologies Corp) 1020 Woodman Dr Ste 100 ....Dayton OH 45432	800-745-8050	937-252-2145	178-10
ITC Learning Corp 330 Himmarshee St Ste 108 ....Fort Lauderdale FL 33312	800-638-3757	703-286-0756	760
Itech Digital LLC 4287 W 96th St ....Indianapolis IN 46268	866-733-6673	317-704-0440	689
Iteck Solutions LLC 4909 Morning Glory Ct Ste 250 ....Rockville MD 20853	866-483-2544	301-929-1852	
ITEL Laboratories Inc 6676 Corporate Center Pkwy Ste 107 ....Jacksonville FL 32216	800-890-4835		
Iten Industries 4602 Benefit Ave ....Ashtabula OH 44004 *Orders	800-227-4836*	440-997-6134	595
Itergy 2075 University Ste 700 ....Montreal QC H3A2L1	866-522-5881	514-845-5881	180
Iteris Inc 1700 Carnegie Ave Ste 100 ....Santa Ana CA 92705 NASDAQ: ITI	888-254-5487	949-270-9400	643
ITG Inc 1 Liberty Plz 165 Broadway .....New York NY 10006	800-215-4484	212-588-4000	686
Ithaca College 953 Danby Rd ....Ithaca NY 14850 *Admissions	800-429-4274*	607-274-3124	166
Ithaca Journal 123 W State St ....Ithaca NY 14850	866-254-3068	607-272-2321	528-2
Ithaca/Tompkins County Convention & Visitors Bureau 904 E Shore Dr ....Ithaca NY 14850	800-284-8422	607-272-1313	206
ITI (Industrial Tools Inc) 1111 S Rose Ave ....Oxnard CA 93033	800-266-5561	805-483-1111	491
ITL (Industrial Timber & Lumber Corp) 23925 Commerce Park Rd ....Beachwood OH 44122	800-829-9663	216-831-3140	679
ITNS (International Transplant Nurses Society) 8735 W Higgins Rd Ste 300 ....Chicago IL 60631	800-776-8636	847-375-6340	49-8
ITR Group Inc 2520 Lexington Ave S Ste 500 ....Saint Paul MN 55120	866-290-3423		193
Itron Inc 2111 N Molter Rd ....Liberty Lake WA 99019 NASDAQ: ITRI	800-635-5461	509-924-9900	248
ITS (Intelligent Transportation Society of America) 1100 New Jersey Ave SE Ste 850 ....Washington DC 20003	800-374-8472	202-484-4847	49-21
Its Technologies Inc 7060 Spring Meadows Dr W Ste D.......Holland OH 43528	800-432-6607		260
ITSource Technology Inc 899 Northgate Dr Ste 304............San Rafael CA 94903	866-548-4911		180
ITT Goulds Pumps Industries/Goulds Industrial Pumps Group 240 Fall St ....Seneca Falls NY 13148	800-327-7700	315-568-2811	784
ITT Industries Inc 1133 Westchester Ave ....White Plains NY 10604 NYSE: ITT	800-254-2823	914-641-2000	253
ITT Industries Inc Engineered Valves Div 33 Centerville Rd ....Lancaster PA 17603	800-366-1111	717-509-2200	784
ITT Standard 175 Standard Pkwy ....Cheektowaga NY 14227	800-447-7700	800-281-4111	91
ITU AbsorbTech Inc 2700 S 160th St ....New Berlin WI 53151	888-729-4884		441
Ituran USA Inc 1700 NW 64th St Ste 100........Fort Lauderdale FL 33309	866-543-5433		224
ITVS (Independent Television Service) 651 Brannan St Ste 410 ....San Francisco CA 94107	888-572-8918	415-356-8383	737
ITW Brands 955 National Pkwy Ste 95500.......Schaumburg IL 60173	877-489-2726	847-944-2260	278
ITW Buildex 1349 W Bryn Mawr ....Itasca IL 60143	800-848-5611		278
ITW Dymon 805 E Old 56 Hwy ....Olathe KS 66061	800-443-9536	913-829-6296	151
ITW Fluids North America 475 N Gary Ave ....Carol Stream IL 60188	800-452-5823		537
ITW Insulation Systems 1370 E 40th St Ste 1 Bldg 7 ....Houston TX 77022	800-231-1024	713-691-7002	388
ITW Polymers Sealants North America 111 S Nursery R ....Irving TX 75060 *Hotline	800-878-7876*	972-438-9111	3
ITW Switches 195 E Algonquin Rd ....Des Plaines IL 60016	800-544-3354	847-876-9400	725
ITW Vortec 10125 Carver Rd ....Cincinnati OH 45242	800-441-7475	513-891-7485	14
Itx Corp 1169 Pittsford Victor Rd Ste 100.....................Pittsford NY 14534	800-600-7785	585-899-4888	224
IU School of Medicine - Office of Gift Development 1110 W Michigan St Lo 506 ......Indianapolis IN 46202	800-643-6975	317-274-3270	305
iUniverse 1663 Liberty Dr ....Bloomington IN 47403	800-288-4677	812-330-2909	633-2
IUPAT (International Union of Painters & Allied Trades) 7234 Pkwy Dr ....Hanover MD 21076	800-554-2479	410-564-5900	413
IV Most Consulting Inc 33 Park Dr ....Mt Kisco NY 10549	800-448-6678	914-864-2781	177
iv3 Solutions Corp 50 Minthorn Blvd Ste 301.........Markham ON L3T7X8	877-995-2651		364
Ivan Franko Museum 200 McGregor St ....Winnipeg MB R2W2K4	866-747-9323	204-589-4397	517
Ivanti 8660 E Hartford Dr Ste 300......Scottsdale AZ 85255	888-725-7828	480-970-1025	225
IVC (International Visual Corp) 11500 Blvd Armand Bombardier ....Montreal QC H1E2W9	866-643-0570	514-643-0570	286
IVCi LLC 601 Old Willets Path ....Hauppauge NY 11788	800-224-7083	631-273-5800	731
Ivenuecom 9925 Painter Ave Ste A........Whittier CA 90605	800-683-8314		177
Ivers-Lee Inc 31 Hansen S ....Brampton ON L6W3H7	800-265-1009	905-451-5535	85
Ivey Spencer Leadership Ctr 551 Windermere Rd ....London ON N5X2T1	800-407-9832	519-679-4546	376
Ivory Homes 970 E Woodoak Ln ....Salt Lake City UT 84117	888-455-5561		649
IVY Biomedical Systems Inc 11 Business Pk Dr ....Branford CT 06405	800-247-4614	203-481-4183	250
Ivy Tech Columbus College Columbus 4475 Central Ave ....Columbus IN 47203	800-922-4838	812-372-9925	795
Ivy Tech Community College Bloomington 200 Daniels Way ...Bloomington IN 47404	866-447-0700	812-330-6137	795
Central Indiana 50 W Fall Creek Pkwy N Dr ....Indianapolis IN 46208	888-489-5463	317-921-4800	795
Kokomo 1815 E Morgan St ....Kokomo IN 46901	800-459-0561	765-459-0561	795
Muncie 4301 S Cowan Rd ....Muncie IN 47302	800-589-8324	765-289-2291	795
North Central 220 Dean Johnson Blvd .... South Bend IN 46601	888-489-3478	888-489-5463	795
Northwest 1440 E 35th Ave ....Gary IN 46409	888-489-5463	219-981-1111	795
Richmond 2357 Chester Blvd ...Richmond IN 47374	800-659-4562	765-966-2656	795
Southeast 590 Ivy Tech Dr ....Madison IN 47250	800-403-2190	812-265-2580	795
Southern Indiana 8204 old Indiana 311 ....Sellersburg IN 47172	800-321-9021	812-246-3301	795
Southwest Indiana 3501 N First Ave .....Evansville IN 47710	888-489-5463		795
Wabash Valley 8000 S Education Dr ...Terre Haute IN 47802	888-489-5463	812-298-2293	795
IWA (International Webmasters Assn) 119 E Union St Ste A ....Pasadena CA 91103	866-607-1773	626-449-3709	48-9
iWay Software 2 Penn Plz ....New York NY 10121 *Sales	800-736-6130*	212-736-4433	194
iWeb Technologies Inc 20 Place du Commerce ......Montreal QC H3E1Z6	800-100-3276		
IWLA (Izaak Walton League of America) 707 Conservation Ln ....Gaithersburg MD 20878	800-453-5463	301-548-0150	48-13
IWM International LLC 500 E Middle St ....Hanover PA 17331	800-323-5585		
IWorld of Travel 25 Broadway 9th Fl............New York NY 10004	800-223-7460		755
IWPA (International Wood Products Assn) 4214 King St ....Alexandria VA 22302	855-435-0005	703-820-6696	49-3
IWS (Robert e Webber Institute for Worship Studies, The) 4001 Hendricks Ave ....Jacksonville FL 32207	800-282-2977	904-264-2172	681
Ixia 26601 W Agoura Rd ....Calabasas CA 91302 NASDAQ: XXIA	877-367-4942	818-871-1800	248
Izaak Walton League of America (IWLA) 707 Conservation Ln ....Gaithersburg MD 20878	800-453-5463	301-548-0150	48-13
Izzydesign 17237 Van Wagoner Rd ....Spring Lake MI 49456	800-543-5449	616-916-9369	319-1

J

Company / Address	City	State	ZIP	Toll-Free	Phone	Class
J & A Freight Systems Inc 4704 Irving Park Rd Ste 8	Chicago	IL	60641	**877-668-3378**	773-205-7720	311
J & A Printing Inc PO Box 457	Hiawatha	IA	52233	**800-793-1781**	319-393-1781	623
J & B Supply Inc 4915 S Zero PO Box 10450	Fort Smith	AR	72917	**800-262-2028**	479-649-4915	608
J & E Supply & Fastner Company Inc 1903 SE 59th St	Oklahoma City	OK	73129	**800-677-7922**	405-670-1234	350
J & J Industries Inc 818 J & J Dr PO Box 1287	Dalton	GA	30721	**800-241-4586**	706-529-2100	131
J & J Snack Foods Corp 6000 Central Hwy *NASDAQ: JJSF*	Pennsauken	NJ	08109	**800-486-9533**	856-665-9533	296-25
J & M Industries Inc 300 Ponchatoula Pkwy	Ponchatoula	LA	70454	**800-989-1002**	985-386-6000	67
J & M Plating Inc 4500 Kishwaukee St	Rockford	IL	61109	**877-344-3044**	815-964-4975	479
J Alexander's Corp 3401 W End Ave Ste 260 *NASDAQ: JAX*	Nashville	TN	37203	**888-528-1991**	615-269-1900	666
J C Foodservice Inc 415 S Atlantic Blvd	Monterey Park	CA	91754	**800-328-6688**	626-308-1988	111
J C Steele & Sons Inc 710 S Mulberry St	Statesville	NC	28677	**800-278-3353**	704-872-3681	452
J C Taylor Antique Automobile Agency Inc 320 S 69th St	Upper Darby	PA	19082	**800-345-8290**		389
J C. Macelroy Company Inc PO Box 850	Piscataway	NJ	08855	**800-622-3576**	732-572-7100	478
J Crew Group Inc 770 Broadway	New York	NY	10003	**800-562-0258**	212-209-2500	457
J D Beauty 5 Adams Ave	Hauppauge	NY	11788	**800-523-2889**	631-273-2800	77
J D'Addario & Company Inc 595 Smith St	Farmingdale	NY	11735	**800-323-2746**	631-439-3300	523
J Edgar Eubanks & Assoc 1 Windsor Cove Ste 305	Columbia	SC	29223	**800-445-8629**	803-252-5646	47
J Ennis Fabrics Ltd 12122 - 68 St	Edmonton	AB	T5B1R1	**800-663-6647**		405
J Fletcher Creamer & Son Inc 101 E Broadway	Hackensack	NJ	07601	**800-835-9801**	201-488-9800	189-5
J Freirich Foods Inc 815 W Kerr St PO Box 1529	Salisbury	NC	28144	**800-554-4788**	800-221-1315	471
J H. Bennett & Company Inc PO Box 8028 *General	Novi	MI	48376	**800-837-5426***	248-596-5100	384
J Knipper & Company Inc 1 Healthcare Way	Lakewood	NJ	08701	**888-564-7737**		195
J L Business Interiors Inc 515 Schoenhaar Dr PO Box 303	West Bend	WI	53090	**866-338-5524**	262-338-2221	320
J M Field Marketing Inc 3570 NW 53rd Ct	Fort Lauderdale	FL	33309	**844-523-1957**	954-523-1957	317
J P Noonan Transportation Inc 415 W St	West Bridgewater	MA	02379	**800-922-8026**	508-583-2880	775
J P. King Auction Company Inc 414 Broad St	Gadsden	AL	35901	**800-558-5464**		
J Polep Distribution Services Inc 705 Meadow St	Chicopee	MA	01013	**800-447-6537**	413-592-4141	751
J Robert Scott Inc 500 N Oak St	Inglewood	CA	90302	**877-207-5130**	310-680-4300	319-4
J S Logistics 4550 Gustine Ave	Saint Louis	MO	63116	**800-814-2634**	314-832-6008	314
J Sargeant Reynolds Community College PO Box 85622	Richmond	VA	23285	**800-922-3420**	804-371-3000	162
J Smith Lanier & Co 300 W Tenth St	West Point	GA	31833	**800-226-4522**	706-645-2211	389
J2 Global Communications Inc 6922 Hollywood Blvd *Sales	Hollywood	CA	90028	**888-718-2000***	323-860-9200	731
J4 Systems Inc 2521 Warren Dr Ste A	Rocklin	CA	95677	**866-547-9783**	916-303-7200	
JA (Jewelers of America) 52 Vanderbilt Ave 19th Fl	New York	NY	10017	**800-223-0673**	646-658-0246	49-4
JA Billipp Co 6925 Portwest Dr Ste 130	Houston	TX	77024	**800-216-9013**	713-426-5000	649
JA. Riggs Tractor Company Inc 9125 I-30	Little Rock	AR	72209	**800-759-3140**	501-570-3100	23
Jaapharm Canada Inc 510 Rowntree Dairy Rd Bldg B	Woodbridge	ON	L4L8H2	**800-465-9587**	905-851-7885	578
Jabil Circuit Inc 10560 ML King St N *NYSE: JBL*	Saint Petersburg	FL	33716	**877-217-6328**	727-577-9749	621
Jabo Supply Corp 5164 County Rd 64/66	Huntington	WV	25705	**800-334-5226**	304-736-8333	384
JACAN (Junior Achievement of Canada) 161 Bay St 27th Fl	Toronto	ON	M5J2S1	**800-265-0699**	416-622-4602	48-11
Jace Holdings Ltd 6649 Butler Crescent	Saanichton	BC	V8M1Z7	**800-667-8280**	250-544-1234	297-8
Jack B Parson Cos 2350 S 1900 W	Ogden	UT	84401	**888-672-7766**	801-731-1111	188-4
Jack Becker Distributors Inc 6800 Suemac Pl	Jacksonville	FL	32254	**800-488-8411**		577
Jack Conway 137 Washington St	Norwell	MA	02061	**800-283-1030**	781-871-0080	648
Jack Henry & Assoc Inc 663 W Hwy 60 PO Box 807 *NASDAQ: JKHY*	Monett	MO	65708	**800-299-4222**	417-235-6652	178-11
Jack in the Box Inc 9330 Balboa Ave *NASDAQ: JACK*	San Diego	CA	92123	**800-955-5225**	858-571-2121	666
Jack O'Dwyer's PR Newsletter 271 Madison Ave Ste 600	New York	NY	10016	**866-395-7710**	212-679-2471	527-11
Jack Richeson & Company Inc 557 Marcella Dr	Kimberly	WI	54136	**800-233-2404**	920-738-0744	43
Jack Williams Tire Co Inc PO Box 3655	Scranton	PA	18505	**800-833-5051**		62-5
Jack's Tire & Oil Inc 1795 N Main St	Logan	UT	84341	**866-804-8473**	435-752-7897	54
Jacknob Corp 290 Oser Ave	Hauppauge	NY	11788	**888-231-9333**	631-231-9400	349
Jacko Law Group PC 5920 Friars Rd Ste 208	San Diego	CA	92108	**866-497-2298**	619-298-2880	427
Jackpot Junction Casino Hotel 39375 County Hwy 24 PO Box 420	Morton	MN	56270	**800-946-2274**		133
Jackson & Hertogs LLP 201 Mission St Ste 700	San Francisco	CA	94105	**800-780-2008**	415-986-4559	427
Jackson & Perkins 2 Floral Ave *Cust Svc	Hodges	SC	29653	**800-292-4769***		457
Jackson Community College 2111 Emmons Rd	Jackson	MI	49201	**888-522-7344**	517-787-0800	162
Jackson County 401 Grindstaff Cove Rd	Sylva	NC	28779	**800-962-1911**	828-586-4055	337
Jackson County Chamber of Commerce 773 W Main St	Sylva	NC	28779	**800-962-1911**	828-586-2155	139
Jackson County Convention & Visitors Bureau 141 S Jackson St	Jackson	MI	49201	**800-245-5282**	517-764-4440	206
Jackson County Memorial Hospital 1200 E Pecan St	Altus	OK	73521	**800-595-0455**	580-379-5000	373-3
Jackson County Rural Electric Membership Corp 274 E Base Rd	Brownstown	IN	47220	**800-288-4458**	812-358-4458	245
Jackson County School System 1660 Winder Hwy	Jefferson	GA	30549	**800-760-3727**	706-367-5151	681
Jackson Electric Co-op N6868 County Rd F PO Box 546	Black River Falls	WI	54615	**800-370-4607**	715-284-5385	245
Jackson Electric Membership Corp 850 Commerce Rd	Jefferson	GA	30549	**800-462-3691**	706-367-5281	245
Jackson Energy Co-op 115 Jackson Energy Ln	McKee	KY	40447	**800-262-7480**	606-364-1000	245
Jackson George N Ltd 1139 Mcdermot Ave	Winnipeg	MB	R3E0V2	**800-665-8978**	204-786-3821	360
Jackson Hewitt Inc 3 Sylvan Way Ste 301 *OTC: JHTXQ*	Parsippany	NJ	07054	**800-234-1040**	973-630-1040	729
Jackson Hole Central Reservations (JHCR) 140 E Broadway Ste 24 PO Box 2618	Jackson	WY	83001	**888-838-6606**	307-733-4005	375
Jackson Hole Lodge 420 W Broadway PO Box 1805	Jackson	WY	83001	**800-604-9404**	307-733-2992	378
Jackson Hole Mountain Resort 3395 Cody Ln PO Box 290	Teton Village	WY	83025	**800-450-0477**	307-733-2292	665
Jackson HoleResort Lodging 3200 W McCollister Dr PO Box 510	Teton Village	WY	83025	**800-443-8613**	307-733-3990	665
Jackson ImmunoResearch Laboratories Inc 872 W Baltimore Pk PO Box 9	West Grove	PA	19390	**800-367-5296**		231
Jackson International Airport 100 International Dr Ste 300	Jackson	MS	39208	**800-227-7368**	601-939-5631	27
Jackson Laboratory, The 600 Main St	Bar Harbor	ME	04609	**800-422-6423**	207-288-6000	664
Jackson Lake Lodge PO Box 250	Moran	WY	83013	**800-628-9988**	307-543-2811	665
Jackson Marking Products Co 9105 N Rainbow Ln	Mount Vernon	IL	62864	**800-782-6722**	618-242-1334	465
Jackson Mattress Company Inc 3154 Camden Rd	Fayetteville	NC	28306	**800-763-7378**	910-425-0131	469
Jackson National Life Insurance Co 1 Corporate Way	Lansing	MI	48951	**800-644-4565**	517-381-5500	390-2
Jackson Oil & Solvents Inc 1970 Kentucky Ave	Indianapolis	IN	46221	**800-221-4603**	317-636-4421	537
Jackson Purchase Ag Credit Assn PO Box 309	Mayfield	KY	42066	**877-422-4203**	270-247-5613	216
Jackson Purchase Energy Corp 2900 Irvin Cobb Dr	Paducah	KY	42002	**800-633-4044**	270-442-7321	245
Jackson State University 1400 John R Lynch St	Jackson	MS	39217	**800-848-6817**	601-979-2121	166
Jackson Sun 245 W LaFayette St	Jackson	TN	38301	**800-372-3922**	731-427-3333	528-2
Jackson Tube Service Inc 8210 Industry Pk Dr	Piqua	OH	45356	**800-543-8910**	937-773-8550	488
Jacksonport State Park 205 Ave St	Newport	AR	72112	**877-879-2741**	870-523-2143	561
Jacksonville Area Chamber of Commerce 310 E State St	Jacksonville	IL	62650	**800-593-5678**	217-243-5678	139
Jacksonville Area Legal Aid (JALA) 126 W Adams St	Jacksonville	FL	32202	**866-356-8371**	904-356-8371	427
Jacksonville Chamber of Commerce 200 Dupree Dr	Jacksonville	AR	72076	**877-815-3111**	501-982-1511	139
Jacksonville Convention & Visitors Bureau 310 E State St	Jacksonville	IL	62650	**800-593-5678**	217-243-5678	206
Jacksonville Correctional Ctr 2268 E Morton Ave	Jacksonville	IL	62650	**800-526-0844**	217-245-1481	213
Jacksonville Independent School District 800 College Ave	Jacksonville	TX	75766	**800-583-6908**	903-586-6511	681
Jacksonville Magazine 1261 King St	Jacksonville	FL	32204	**800-962-0214**	904-389-3622	455-22
Jacksonville State University 700 Pelham Rd N	Jacksonville	AL	36265	**800-231-5291**	256-782-5781	166
Jacksonville University 2800 University Blvd N	Jacksonville	FL	32211	**800-225-2027**	904-256-8000	166
Jacksonville Zoo & Gardens 370 Zoo Pkwy	Jacksonville	FL	32218	**800-241-4113**	904-757-4463	818
Jaco Electronics Inc 415 Oser Ave *OTC: JACO*	Hauppauge	NY	11788	**877-373-5226**		246
Jacob Holtz Co 10 Industrial Hwy MS-6 Airport Business Complex B	Lester	PA	19029	**800-445-4337**	215-423-2800	349

	Toll-Free	Phone	Class
Jacob Leinenkugel Brewing Co			
124 E Elm St ....Chippewa Falls WI 54729	**888-534-6437***	715-723-5558	102
*General			
Jacobsen			
11108 Quality Dr ....Charlotte NC 28273	**800-848-1636**	704-504-6600	428
Jacobsen Homes			
600 Packard Ct ....Safety Harbor FL 34695	**800-843-1559**	727-726-1138	503
Jacquelyn Wigs			
15 W 37th St 4th Fl. ....New York NY 10018	**800-272-2424**	212-302-2266	347
Jacuzzi Brands LLC			
13925 City Ctr Dr Ste 200 ....Chino Hills CA 91709	**866-234-7727**		
Jade Engineered Plastic Inc			
121 Broadcommon Rd ....Bristol RI 02809	**800-557-9155**	401-253-4440	326
Jade Travel Group			
1650 Elgin Mills Rd E			
Unit 403 ....Richmond Hill ON L4S0B2	**800-387-0387**	905-787-9288	755
JAE Electronics Inc			
142 Technology Dr Ste 100 ....Irvine CA 92618	**800-523-7278**	949-753-2600	253
Jaeckle Wholesale Inc			
4101 Owl Creek Dr ....Madison WI 53718	**800-236-7225**	608-838-5400	191-1
JAG Advisors			
9841 Clayton Rd ....Saint Louis MO 63124	**800-966-4596**	314-997-1277	524
Jagemann Stamping Co			
5757 W Custer St ....Manitowoc WI 54220	**888-337-7853**	920-682-4633	486
Jaipur Living Inc			
1800 Cherokee pkwy ....Acworth GA 30102	**888-676-7330**	404-351-2360	131
JAK Enterprises Inc			
8309 N Knoxville Ave ....Peoria IL 61615	**800-752-3295**	309-692-8222	539
Jake A Parrott Insurance Agency Inc			
2508 N Herritage St ....Kinston NC 28501	**800-727-7688**	252-523-1041	389
Jake's Famous Crawfish			
401 SW 12th Ave SW Stark ....Portland OR 97205	**800-552-6379**	503-226-1419	667
Jaken Company Inc			
14420 My ford rf Ste 150 ....Irvine CA 92606	**800-401-7225**	714-522-1700	286
JAKKS Pacific Inc			
21749 Baker Pkwy ....Walnut CA 91789	**877-875-2557**	909-594-7771	757
JALA (Jacksonville Area Legal Aid)			
126 W Adams St ....Jacksonville FL 32202	**866-356-8371**	904-356-8371	427
JAMA (Journal of the American Medical Assn)			
PO Box 10946 ....Chicago IL 60654	**800-262-2350**	312-670-7827	455-16
Jamac Frozen Foods			
570 Grand St ....Jersey City NJ 07302	**800-631-0440**	201-333-6200	344
Jamaica Tourist Board			
5201 Blue Lagoon Dr Ste 670. ....Miami FL 33126	**800-526-2422**	305-665-0557	770
Jamak Fabrication Inc			
1401 N Bowie Dr ....Weatherford TX 76086	**800-543-4747**	817-594-8771	673
Jamar Co			
4701 Mike Colalillo Dr ....Duluth MN 55807	**800-644-3624**	218-628-1027	189-10
James Austin Co			
115 Downieville Rd PO Box 827..........Mars PA 16046	**800-245-1942**	724-625-1535	151
James Avery Craftsman Inc			
145 Avery Rd N ....Kerrville TX 78029	**800-283-1770**	830-895-6800	408
James Candy Co			
1519 Boardwalk ....Atlantic City NJ 08401	**800-441-1404***	609-344-1519	296-8
*Orders			
James Chicago, The			
55 E Ontario ....Chicago IL 60611	**888-526-3778**	312-337-1000	378
James D Morrissey Inc			
9119 Frankford Ave ....Philadelphia PA 19114	**877-536-6857**	215-708-8420	188-4
James Gettys Hotel			
27 Chambersburg St ....Gettysburg PA 17325	**888-900-5275**	717-337-1334	378
James Graham Brown Cancer Ctr			
529 S Jackson St ....Louisville KY 40202	**866-530-5516**	502-562-4369	764
James Greene & Assoc Inc			
275 W Kiehl Ave ....Sherwood AR 72120	**800-422-3384**	501-834-4001	389
James H Quillen Veterans Affairs Medical Ctr			
Corner of Lamont & Veterans Way			
..................Mountain Home TN 37684	**877-573-3529**	423-926-1171	373-8
James Hardie Bldg Products			
26300 La Alameda Ave			
Ste 400 ....Mission Viejo CA 92691	**888-542-7343**		191-4
James Hoyer PA			
2801 W Busch Blvd Ste 200. ....Tampa FL 33618	**800-651-2502**	813-375-3700	
James Investment Research Inc			
1349 Fairgrounds Rd ....Xenia OH 45385	**800-995-2637**	937-426-7640	400
James J Hill House			
240 Summit Ave ....Saint Paul MN 55102	**888-727-8386**	651-297-2555	50-3
James L Allen Ctr			
2211 Campus Dr ....Evanston IL 60208	**877-755-2227**	847-467-7000	376
James L Taylor Manufacturing Co			
108 Parker Ave ....Poughkeepsie NY 12601	**800-952-1320**	845-452-3780	816
James Lane Air Conditioning Company Inc			
5024 Old Jacksboro Hwy ....Wichita Falls TX 76302	**800-460-2204**	940-766-0244	606
James Machine Works LLC			
1521 Adams St ....Monroe LA 71201	**800-259-6104**	318-322-6104	189-1
James Mulligan Printing Corp			
1808 Washington Ave ....St. Louis MO 63103	**800-737-0874**	314-621-0875	623
James New York - NoMad, The			
88 Madison Ave ....New York NY 10016	**800-601-8500***	212-532-4100	378
*Resv			
James River Coal Co			
901 E Byrd St Ste 1600...........Richmond VA 23219	**877-283-6545**	804-780-3000	499
NASDAQ: JRVR			
James Wood Motors			
2111 US Hwy 287 S ....Decatur TX 76234	**866-232-6058**	940-539-9143	57
James, Stevens & Daniels Inc			
1283 College Park Dr ....Dover DE 19904	**800-305-0773**	302-735-4628	160
James, The			
460 W Tenth Ave ....Columbus OH 43210	**800-293-5066**		
Jamestown Area Chamber of Commerce			
120 Second St SE PO Box 1530 ....Jamestown ND 58402	**800-882-2500**	701-252-4830	139
Jamestown College			
6000 College Ln ....Jamestown ND 58405	**800-336-2554**	701-252-3467	166
Jamestown Community College			
525 Falconer St ....Jamestown NY 14702	**800-388-8557**	716-338-1000	162
Jamesway Incubator Co Inc			
30 High Ridge Ct ....Cambridge ON N1R7L3	**800-438-8077**	519-624-4646	273
Jamison Bedding Inc			
PO Box 681948 ....Franklin TN 37068	**800-255-1883***	615-794-1883	469
*Cust Svc			
Jamison Door Co			
55 JV Jamison Dr ....Hagerstown MD 21740	**800-532-3667**	301-733-3100	234
Jampro Antennas Inc			
6340 Sky Creek Dr ....Sacramento CA 95828	**800-732-7665**	916-383-1177	643
JAMS/Endispute			
500 N State College Blvd 14th Fl ....Orange CA 92868	**800-352-5267**	714-939-1300	41
Jamsan Hotel Management Inc			
440 Bedford St ....Lexington MA 02420	**800-523-5549**	781-863-8500	461
Jan Marini Skin Research Inc			
6951 Via Del Oro ....San Jose CA 95119	**800-347-2223**	408-362-0130	214
Jan's Mountain Outfitters			
1600 Park Ave PO Box 280. ....Park City UT 84060	**800-745-1020**	435-649-4949	707
Janalent			
2341 Renaissance Dr ....Las Vegas NV 89119	**888-290-4870**		196
Janazzo Services Corp			
140 Norton St Rt 10 PO Box 469 ....Milldale CT 06467	**800-297-3931**	860-621-7381	189-10
Jancyn Inc			
1100 Lincoln Ave Ste 367. ....San Jose CA 95125	**800-339-2861**		504
Jane Addams Hull-House Museum			
800 S Halsted St ....Chicago IL 60607	**800-625-2013**	312-413-5353	50-3
Jane Goodall Institute for Wildlife Research Education (JGI)			
1595 Spring Hill Rd Ste 550. ....Vienna VA 22182	**800-592-5263**	703-682-9220	48-3
Jane Rose Reporting			
80 Fifth Ave ....New York NY 10011	**800-825-3341**	212-727-7773	443
Janell Inc			
6130 Cornell Rd ....Cincinnati OH 45242	**888-489-9111**	513-489-9111	357
Janesville Sand & Gravel Co (JSG)			
1110 Harding St PO Box 427 ....Janesville WI 53547	**800-955-7702**	608-754-7701	501-4
Janet Mcafee Real Estate			
9889 Clayton Rd ....Saint Louis MO 63124	**888-991-4800**	314-997-4800	648
Janlynn Corp			
2070 Westover Rd ....Chicopee MA 01022	**800-445-5565**	413-206-0002	590
Janney Montgomery Scott LLC			
1801 Market St ....Philadelphia PA 19103	**800-526-6397**	215-665-6000	686
Jan-Pro International Inc (JPI)			
2520 Northwinds Pkwy Ste 375 ....Alpharetta GA 30009	**866-355-1064**	678-336-1780	152
Janson Industries			
1200 Garfield Ave SW ....Canton OH 44706	**800-548-8982**	330-455-7029	718
Janssen Pharmaceutica Inc			
1125 Trenton-Harbourton Rd ....Titusville NJ 08560	**800-526-7736**	908-218-6095	578
Jantek Industries			
230 Rt 70 ....Medford NJ 08055	**888-782-7937**	609-654-1030	234
Japan Travel Bureau USA Inc (JTB USA Inc)			
2 W 45th St Ste 305 ....New York NY 10036	**800-223-6104**	212-698-4900	766
Japanese American National Museum			
369 E First St ....Los Angeles CA 90012	**800-461-5266**	213-625-0414	517
Japanese Garden			
611 SW Kingston Ave ....Portland OR 97205	**800-955-8352**	503-223-1321	97
Jarden Consumer Solutions			
2381 Executive Ctr Dr ....Boca Raton FL 33431	**800-777-5452**	561-912-4100	37
Jaro Transportation Services Inc			
975 Post Rd ....Warren OH 44483	**800-451-3447**	330-393-5659	775
JARP Industries Inc			
1051 Pine St PO Box 923 ....Schofield WI 54476	**800-558-5950**	715-359-4241	223
Jarrard Phillips Cate & Hancock Inc			
219 Ward Cir ....Brentwood TN 37027	**888-844-6274**	312-419-0575	7
Jarrow Formulas Inc			
1824 S Robertson Blvd ....Los Angeles CA 90035	**800-726-0886**	310-204-6936	794
Jarvis Caster Co			
203 Kerth St ....St Joseph MI 49085	**800-253-0868**		349
JAS (Jo-Ann Stores Inc)			
5555 DARROW Rd ....Hudson OH 44236	**888-739-4120**		270
Jas Net Consulting Inc			
2053 Grant Rd Ste 321 ....Los Altos CA 94024	**888-527-6388**	408-257-3279	180
JASCO Inc			
28600 Mary's Ct ....Easton MD 21601	**800-333-5272**	410-822-1220	406
Jasco Products Co			
10 E Memorial Rd, Bldg B ......Oklahoma City OK 73114	**800-654-8483**	405-752-0710	246
Jason International Inc			
8328 MacArthur Dr ......North Little Rock AR 72118	**800-255-5766**	501-771-4477	374
Jasper County Rural Electric Membership Corp			
280 E 400 S ....Rensselaer IN 47978	**888-866-7362**	219-866-4601	245
Jasper Desk Co			
415 E Sixth St ....Jasper IN 47546	**800-365-7994***	812-482-4132	319-1
*Cust Svc			
JASPER Engines & Transmissions			
815 Wernsing Rd PO Box 650 ....Jasper IN 47547	**800-827-7455**	812-482-1041	60
Jasper Rubber Products Inc			
1010 First Ave ....Jasper IN 47546	**800-457-7457**	812-482-3242	673
Jasper Seating Company Inc			
Jasper Group			
225 Clay St ....Jasper IN 47546	**800-622-5661**	812-482-3204	319-1
Jasper Wyman & Son			
PO Box 100 ....Milbridge ME 04658	**800-341-1758***		315-1
*Sales			
Jasper's			
1201 W 103rd St ....Kansas City MO 64114	**800-810-3708**	816-941-6600	667
Java Dave's Executive Coffee Service			
6239 E 15th St ....Tulsa OK 74112	**800-725-7315**	918-836-5570	113
Javitch Block LLP			
700 Walnut St Ste 302 ....Cincinnati OH 45202	**800-837-0109**	513-744-9600	427
Jay Cee Sales & Rivet Inc			
32861 Chesley Dr ....Farmington MI 48336	**800-521-6777**	248-478-2150	350
Jay County Rural Electric Membership Corp			
484 S 200 W PO Box 904. ....Portland IN 47371	**800-835-7362**	260-726-7121	245
Jay Peak Resort			
830 Jay Peak Rd ....Jay VT 05859	**800-451-4449**	802-988-2611	665
Jay Roberts Jewelers			
515 Rt 73 S ....Marlton NJ 08053	**888-828-8463**	856-596-8600	409
Jayco Inc			
903 S Main St ....Middlebury IN 46540	**800-283-8267***	574-825-5861	120
*Cust Svc			
Jayhawk Bowling Supply & Equipment Inc			
355 N Iowa St PO Box 685 ....Lawrence KS 66044	**800-255-6436**	785-842-3237	706

Name / Address	Toll-Free	Phone	Class
Jaymie Scotto & Associates PO Box 20 ... Middlebrook VA 24459	866-695-3629		632
Jaypro Sports Inc 976 Hartford Tpke ... Waterford CT 06385 *Cust Svc	800-243-0533*		345
Jayson Home & Garden 1885 N Clybourn Ave ... Chicago IL 60614	800-472-1885	773-248-8180	321
Jazz Pharmaceuticals Inc 3180 Porter Dr ... Palo Alto CA 94304	866-997-3688	650-496-3777	578
Jazzercise Inc 2460 Impala Dr ... Carlsbad CA 92010 *Cust Svc	800-348-4748*	760-476-1750	805
JB Hunt Transport Services Inc 615 JB Hunt Corporate Dr ... Lowell AR 72745 *NASDAQ: JBHT*	800-643-3622	479-820-0000	447
JB Martin Co 645 Fifth Ave Ste 400 ... New York NY 10022	800-223-0525	212-421-2020	740-1
J&B Medical Supply Co Inc 50496 W Pontiac Trl ... Wixom MI 48393	800-980-0047	800-737-0045	238
JBFCS (Jewish Board of Family & Children Services) 135 W 50th St ... New York NY 10020	888-523-2769	212-582-9100	48-6
JBL Professional 8500 Balboa Blvd ... Northridge CA 91329	800-852-5776	800-397-1881	52
JBMH (Joseph Brant Memorial Hospital) 1230 N Shore Blvd ... Burlington ON L7S1W7	800-810-0000	905-632-3737	373-2
JC Penney Optical Co 821 N Central Expy ... Plano TX 75075	866-435-7111		539
JC Raulston Arboretum 4415 Beryl Rd Campus Box 7522 ... Raleigh NC 27695	888-842-2442	919-515-3132	97
JC Whitney 761 Progress Pkwy ... La Salle IL 61301	866-529-5530	312-431-6098	457
JCAHO (Joint Commission on Accreditation of Healthcare Or) 1 Renaissance Blvd ... Oakbrook Terrace IL 60181	800-994-6610	630-792-5000	48-1
JCI (Junior Chamber International) 15645 Olive Blvd ... Chesterfield MO 63017	800-905-5499	636-449-3100	48-7
JCVB (Johnston County Visitors Bureau) 234 Venture Dr ... Smithfield NC 27577	800-441-7829	919-989-8687	206
JD Calato Mfg Company Inc 4501 Hyde Pk Blvd ... Niagara Falls NY 14305 *Cust Svc	800-358-4590*	716-285-3546	523
JD Equipment Inc 1660 US 42 NE ... London OH 43140	800-659-5646	614-879-6620	274
JD Gould Co Inc 4707 Massachusetts Ave ... Indianapolis IN 46218	800-634-6853		785
JD McCarty Ctr for Children with Developmental Disabilities 2002 E Robinson St ... Norman OK 73071	800-777-1272	405-307-2800	373-1
JD Power & Assoc 2625 Townsgate Rd Ste 100 ... Westlake Village CA 91361	800-274-5372	805-418-8000	464
Jdk Consulting 4924 Balboa Blvd Ste 487 ... Encino CA 91316	855-535-7877	818-705-8050	196
JDR Microdevices Inc 229 Polaris Ave Ste 17 ... Mountain View CA 94043	800-538-5000	650-625-1400	457
JDRF (JDRF) 26 Broadway ... New York NY 10004	800-533-2873	212-785-9500	48-17
JE Adams Industries Ltd 1025 63rd Ave SW ... Cedar Rapids IA 52404	800-553-8861	319-363-0237	54
JE Herndon Company Inc 1020 J E Herndon Access Rd ... Kings Mountain NC 28086	800-277-0500	704-739-4711	740-8
JE Sawyer & Company Inc 64 Glen St ... Glens Falls NY 12801	800-724-3983		608
Jean Mayer USDA Human Nutrition Research Ctr on Aging 711 Washington St ... Boston MA 02111	800-738-7555	617-556-3000	664
Jean Paree Weegs Inc 4041 South 700 East Ste 2 ... Salt Lake City UT 84107 *Orders	800-422-9447*		347
Jeansonne & Remondet LLC 200 W Congress St Ste 1100 PO Box 91530 ... Lafayette LA 70509	800-446-2745	337-237-4370	427
Jedson Engineering 705 Central Ave ... Cincinnati OH 45202	866-729-3945	513-965-5999	256
Jeff Davis Bancshares Inc 507 N Main St PO Box 730 ... Jennings LA 70546 *OTC: JDVB*	800-789-5159	337-824-3424	70
Jefferds Corp 2070 Winfield Rd ... Saint Albans WV 25177	888-848-6216	304-755-8111	384
Jefferies Socks 2203 Tucker St ... Burlington NC 27215	800-334-6831	336-226-7315	155-9
Jeffers Inc 310 W Saunders Rd PO Box 100 ... Dothan AL 36301	800-533-3377	334-793-6257	574
Jefferson City Area Chamber of Commerce 213 Adams St ... Jefferson City MO 65101	866-223-6535	573-634-3616	139
Jefferson City Convention & Visitors Bureau 700 E Capitol Ave ... Jefferson City MO 65101	800-769-4183	573-632-2820	206
Jefferson City National Cemetery 1024 E McCarty St ... Jefferson City MO 65101	877-907-8585	314-845-8320	136
Jefferson Community & Technical College 109 E Broadway ... Louisville KY 40202	855-246-5282	502-213-5333	162
Jefferson Community College 1220 Coffeen St ... Watertown NY 13601	888-435-6522	315-786-2200	162
Jefferson County 155 Main St 2nd Fl ... Brookville PA 15825	800-852-8036	814-849-3696	337
Jefferson County 532 Patriot Dr PO Box 890 ... Dandridge TN 37725	877-237-3847	865-397-9642	337
Jefferson County 729 Maple St ... Hillsboro MO 63050	800-243-6060	636-797-5466	337
Jefferson County 302 E Broad St PO Box 630 ... Louisville GA 30434	866-527-2642	478-625-8134	337
Jefferson County 300 Jefferson St PO Box 458 ... Oskaloosa KS 66066	800-332-6633	785-403-0000	337
Jefferson County Chamber of Commerce 201 E Washington St ... Charles Town WV 25414	800-624-0577	304-725-2055	139
Jefferson County Convention & Visitors Bureau 37 Washington Ct ... Harpers Ferry WV 25425	866-435-5698		206
Jefferson County Journal 1405 N Truman Blvd ... Festus MO 63028	800-365-0820	636-937-9811	528-4
Jefferson Ctr 541 Luck Ave Ste 221 ... Roanoke VA 24016	866-345-2550	540-343-2624	568
Jefferson Davis Electric Co-op 906 N Lake Arthur Ave PO Box 1229 ... Jennings LA 70546	800-256-5332	337-824-4330	245
Jefferson Energy Co-op 3077 Hwy 17 N PO Box 457 ... North Wrens GA 30833	877-533-3377	706-547-2167	245
Jefferson Hotel 101 W Franklin St ... Richmond VA 23220	800-424-8014	804-649-4750	378
Jefferson Hotel Washington Dc, The 1200 16th St NW ... Washington DC 20036	877-313-9749	202-448-2300	703
Jefferson Lake State Park 2045 Morse Rd Bdg G ... Richmond OH 43229	800-945-3543		
Jefferson Medical College of Thomas Jefferson University 1015 Walnut St ... Philadelphia PA 19107	800-533-3669	215-955-6983	167-2
Jefferson National Expansion Memorial 11 N Fourth St ... Saint Louis MO 63102	855-733-4522	314-655-1700	560
Jefferson Partners LP 2100 E 26th St ... Minneapolis MN 55404 *Cust Svc	800-767-5333*	612-359-3400	108
Jefferson Regional Medical Ctr 1400 Hwy 61 S ... Festus MO 63028	800-318-2596	636-933-1000	373-3
Jefferson State Community College 2601 Carson Rd ... Birmingham AL 35215	800-239-5900	205-853-1200	162
Jefferson-Madison Regional Library 201 E Market St ... Charlottesville VA 22902	866-979-1555	434-979-7151	433-3
Jeffersonville Bancorp 4866 State Rt 52 PO Box 398 ... Jeffersonville NY 12748 *OTC: JFBC*	800-472-3272	845-482-4000	359-2
Jeffrey Byrne & Assoc 4042 Central St ... Kansas City MO 64111	800-222-9233	816-237-1999	41
Jeffrey Hale Saint Brigid's 1250 ch Sainte-Foy ... Quebec QC G1S2M6	888-984-5333	418-684-5333	373-2
Jeffrey Matthews Financial Group LLC, The 30B Vreeland Rd Ste 210 ... Florham Park NJ 07932	888-467-3636	973-805-6222	400
Jeffrey P Scott & Associates LLC 2356 University Ave W Ste 400 ... St. Paul MN 55114	866-442-3092	651-968-1457	
JEGS Performance Auto Parts 101 Jeg'S Pl ... Delaware OH 43015	800-345-4545	614-294-5050	61
Jekyll Island Club Hotel 371 Riverview Dr ... Jekyll Island GA 31527	800-535-9547	912-635-2600	665
Jel Sert Co 501 Conde St ... West Chicago IL 60185	800-323-2592	630-876-4838	296-15
Jeld-Wen Inc PO Box 1329 ... Klamath Falls OR 97601	800-535-3936		497
Jelliff Corp 354 Pequot Ave ... Southport CT 06890	800-243-0052	203-259-1615	684
Jelly Belly Candy Co 1 Jelly Belly Ln ... Fairfield CA 94533	800-323-9380	707-428-2838	296-8
Jem Engineering LLC 8683 Cherry Ln ... Laurel MD 20707	877-317-1070	301-317-1070	643
JEM Strapping Systems 116 Shaver St ... Brantford ON N3T5M1	877-536-6584	519-754-5432	652
Jemez Mountains Electric Co-op PO Box 128 ... Espanola NM 87532	888-755-2105	505-753-2105	245
Jenkins County 548 Cotton Ave ... Millen GA 30442	800-262-0128	478-982-5595	337
Jenkins Electric Inc 5933 Brookshire Blvd ... Charlotte NC 28216	800-438-3003		253
Jenkins Fenstermaker PLLC 325 Eighth St ... Huntington WV 25701	866-617-4736	304-523-2100	427
Jenkins Mfg Company Inc 1608 Frank Akers Rd ... Anniston AL 36207	800-633-2323	256-831-7000	236
Jennie Edmundson Hospital 933 E Pierce St ... Council Bluffs IA 51503	800-958-6498	712-396-6000	373-3
Jennie Stuart Medical Ctr 320 W 18th St PO Box 2400 ... Hopkinsville KY 42241	800-887-5762	270-887-0100	373-3
Jennie-O Turkey Store 2505 Willmar Ave SW PO Box 778 ... Willmar MN 56201	800-621-3505	320-235-2622	615
Jennings County Chamber of Commerce 203 N State St PO Box 340 ... North Vernon IN 47265	866-382-4968	812-346-2339	139
Jennings Technology Co 970 McLaughlin Ave ... San Jose CA 95122	800-292-4025	408-292-4025	203
Jensen Bridge & Supply Co 400 Stoney Creek Dr PO Box 151 ... Sandusky MI 48471	800-270-2852	810-648-3000	693
Jensen Distribution Services PO Box 3708 ... Spokane WA 99220 *General	800-234-1321*		350
Jensen Precast 521 Dunn Cir ... Sparks NV 89431	800-648-1134	855-468-5600	183
Jensen-Alvarado Historic Ranch & Museum 4307 Briggs St ... Riverside CA 92509	800-234-7275	951-369-6055	517
Jenzabar Inc 101 Huntington Ave Ste 2200 ... Boston MA 02199	800-593-0028	617-492-9099	178-10
Jeppesen Sanderson Inc 55 Inverness Dr E ... Englewood CO 80112	800-353-2107	303-799-9090	633-2
Jerdon Style 1820 N Glenville Dr Ste 124 ... Richardson TX 75081	800-223-3571		
Jergens Inc 15700 S Waterloo Rd ... Cleveland OH 44110	800-537-4367	877-486-1454	491
Jerith Mfg Company Inc 14400 McNulty Rd ... Philadelphia PA 19154	800-344-2242	215-676-4068	489
Jerome Cheese Co 547 W Nez Perce ... Jerome ID 83338	800-757-7611	208-324-8806	296-5
Jerome's Furniture Warehouse 16960 Mesamint St ... San Diego CA 92127	866-633-4094		321
Jerry Lipps Inc 3888 Nash Rd ... Cape Girardeau MO 63702	800-325-3331	573-335-0196	775
Jerry Pate Turf & Irrigation Inc 301 Schubert Dr ... Pensacola FL 32504	800-700-7004	850-479-4653	274
Jerry's Marine Service 100 SW 16th St ... Fort Lauderdale FL 33315	800-432-2231		765
Jerry's Sport Ctr Inc 100 Capital Rd ... Jenkins Township PA 18640	800-234-2612		706
Jerry's Systems Inc 702 Russell Ave Ste 306 ... Gaithersburg MD 20877	800-990-9176		666
Jersey Cape Realty Inc 739 Washington St ... Cape May NJ 08204	800-643-0043	609-884-5800	648

	Toll-Free	Phone	Class
Jersey City Free Public Library			
472 Jersey Ave .... Jersey City NJ 07302	800-443-0315	201-547-4501	433-3
Jersey Shore State Bank			
300 Market St .... Williamsport PA 17701	888-412-5772	570-322-1111	70
Jersey Shore Steel Co			
70 Maryland Ave			
PO Box 5055............ Jersey Shore PA 17740	800-833-0277	570-753-3000	719
Jersey Shore University Medical Ctr			
1945 Rt 33 .... Neptune NJ 07753	800-560-9990	732-775-5500	373-3
Jersey Strong			
762 SR- 18 .... East Brunswick NJ 08816	888-564-6969	732-390-7390	353
Jesco-Wipco Industries Inc			
950 Anderson Rd PO Box 388 .... Litchfield MI 49252	800-455-0019	517-542-2903	286
Jesse Engineering Co			
1840 Marine View Dr .... Tacoma WA 98422	800-468-3595	253-922-7433	478
Jessup Correctional Institution			
PO Box 534 .... Jessup MD 20794	877-304-9755	410-799-0100	
Jesuit School of Theology at Berkeley			
1735 LeRoy Ave .... Berkeley CA 94709	800-824-0122	510-549-5000	167-3
Jet Aviation			
112 Charles A Lindbergh Dr .... Teterboro NJ 07608	800-538-0832	201-288-8400	24
Jet Aviation			
114 Charles A Lindbergh Dr Teterboro Airport			
.... Teterboro NJ 07608	800-441-6016		260
Jet Industries Inc			
1935 Silverton Rd NE PO Box 7362 .... Salem OR 97303	800-659-0620	503-363-2334	606
Jet Logistics Inc			
5400 Airport Dr .... Charlotte NC 28208	866-824-9394		
Jet Star Inc			
10825 Andrade Dr .... Zionsville IN 46077	800-969-4222	317-873-4222	775
JetBlue Airways Corp			
118-29 Queens Blvd .... Forest Hills NY 11375	800-538-2583	718-286-7900	359-1
NASDAQ: JBLU			
Jet-Lube Inc			
4849 Homestead Rd Ste 232 .... Houston TX 77226	800-538-5823	713-670-5700	537
Jetstream of Houston LLP			
4930 Cranswick .... Houston TX 77041	800-231-8192	713-462-7000	785
JetSuite			
18952 MacArthur Blvd .... Irvine CA 92612	866-779-7770		13
Jewel Case Corp			
110 Dupont Dr .... Providence RI 02907	800-441-4447	401-943-1400	199
Jewel-Craft Inc			
4122 Olympic Blvd .... Erlanger KY 41018	800-525-5482	859-282-2400	410
Jewelers of America (JA)			
52 Vanderbilt Ave 19th Fl .... New York NY 10017	800-223-0673	646-658-0246	49-4
Jewelers Shipping Assn (JSA)			
125 Carlsbad St .... Cranston RI 02920	800-688-4572	401-943-6020	49-21
Jewell Group			
130 Research Pkwy .... Davenport IA 52806	800-831-8665	563-355-5010	452
Jewell Instruments LLC			
850 Perimeter Rd .... Manchester NH 03103	800-227-5955	603-669-6400	525
JewelryWebcom Inc			
98 Cuttermill Rd Ste 464 .... Great Neck NY 11021	800-955-9245	516-482-3982	409
Jewett-Cameron Trading Company Ltd			
32275 NW Hillcrest			
PO Box 1010............ North Plains OR 97133	800-547-5877	503-647-0110	191-3
NASDAQ: JCTCF			
Jewish Board of Family & Children Services (JBFCS)			
135 W 50th St .... New York NY 10020	888-523-2769	212-582-9100	48-6
Jewish Home Lifecare			
120 W 106th St .... New York NY 10025	800-544-0304	212-870-5000	448
Jewish Museum of Maryland			
15 Lloyd St .... Baltimore MD 21202	800-235-4045*	410-732-6400	517
*All			
Jewish National Fund (JNF)			
42 E 69th St .... New York NY 10021	800-542-8733	212-879-9300	48-20
Jewish Press Inc			
4915 16th Ave .... Brooklyn NY 11204	800-992-1600	718-330-1100	528-3
Jewish Publication Society			
2100 Arch St .... Philadelphia PA 19103	800-234-3151	215-832-0600	633-3
Jewish Reconstructionist Federation (JRF)			
101 Greenwood Ave .... Jenkintown PA 19046	877-226-7573	215-885-5601	48-20
Jewish United Fund/Jewish Federation of Metropolitan Chicago (JUF)			
30 S Wells St .... Chicago IL 60606	855-275-5237	312-346-6700	48-20
Jews for Jesus			
60 Haight St .... San Francisco CA 94102	800-366-5521	415-864-2600	48-20
JF Ahern Co			
855 Morris St .... Fond du Lac WI 54935	800-532-0155	920-921-9020	189-10
JF Drake State Technical College			
3421 Meridian St N .... Huntsville AL 35811	888-413-7253	256-539-8161	795
JF Shea Co Inc			
655 Brea Canyon Rd .... Walnut CA 91789	800-685-6494	909-594-9500	501-5
JF Shea Construction Inc			
655 Brea Canyon Rd .... Walnut CA 91789	888-779-7333	909-594-9500	188-4
JF White Contracting Co			
10 Burr St .... Framingham MA 01701	866-539-4400	508-879-4700	188-4
Jfm Enterprises Inc			
1770 Corporate Dr Ste 530........... Norcross GA 30093	800-462-3449	770-447-9740	
JG Tax Group			
1430 S Federal Hwy .... Deerfield Beach FL 33441	866-477-5291		729
JGI (Jane Goodall Institute for Wildlife Research Educa)			
1595 Spring Hill Rd Ste 550........... Vienna VA 22182	800-592-5263	703-682-9220	48-3
JH Baxter & Co			
PO Box 5902 .... San Mateo CA 94402	800-556-1098	650-349-0201	813
JH Fletcher & Co Inc			
402 High St .... Huntington WV 25705	800-327-6203	304-525-7811	190
JH Industries Inc			
1981 E Aurora Rd .... Twinsburg OH 44087	800-321-4968	330-963-4105	478
JH Routh Packing Company Inc			
4413 W Bogart Rd .... Sandusky OH 44870	800-446-6759	419-626-2251	471
JH Walker Trucking Company Inc			
152 N Hollywood Rd .... Houma LA 70364	800-581-2600	985-868-8330	775
JHCR (Jackson Hole Central Reservations)			
140 E Broadway Ste 24			
PO Box 2618............ Jackson WY 83001	888-838-6606	307-733-4005	375
JHL Digital Direct			
3100 Borham Ave .... Stevens Point WI 54481	800-236-0581	715-341-0581	195
JHL Industries			
10012 Nevada Ave .... Chatsworth CA 91311	800-255-6636	818-882-2233	727
Jiffy Lube			
PO Box 4427 .... Houston TX 77210	800-344-6933		62-5
Jif-Pak Manufacturing Inc			
1451 Engineer St .... Vista CA 92081	800-777-6613	760-597-2665	597
Jim Bishop Cabinets Inc			
5640 Bell Rd .... Montgomery AL 36116	800-410-2444		115
Jim Palmer Trucking			
9730 Derby Dr .... Missoula MT 59808	888-698-3422		775
Jiminy Peak Mountain Resort LLC			
37 Corey Rd .... Hancock MA 01237	800-835-2364	413-738-5500	703
Jimmie Davis State Park			
1209 State Pk Rd .... Chatham LA 71226	888-677-2263	318-249-2595	561
Jimmy John's Franchise Inc			
2212 Fox Dr .... Champaign IL 61820	800-546-6904	217-356-9900	666
Jimmy Swaggart Ministries (JSM)			
8919 World Ministry Blvd			
PO Box 262550............ Baton Rouge LA 70810	800-288-8350*	225-768-8300	48-20
*Orders			
Jive Communications Inc			
1275 W 1600 N Ste 100 .... Orem UT 84057	866-768-5429		179
JJ Haines & Company Inc			
6950 Aviation Blvd .... Glen Burnie MD 21061	800-922-9248		360
JJ Kane			
1000 Lenola Rd Bldg 1			
Ste 203 .... Maple Shade NJ 08052	855-462-5263		
JJ Keller & Assoc Inc			
3003 Breezewood Ln PO Box 368........ Neenah WI 54957	800-558-5011	877-564-2333	633-11
JJ MacKay Canada Ltd			
1342 Abercrombie Rd			
PO Box 338............ New Glasgow NS B2H5C6	888-462-2529	902-752-5124	765
JJ Powell Inc			
109 W Presqueisle St .... Philipsburg PA 16866	800-432-0866	814-342-3190	575
JJB Hilliard WL Lyons Inc			
500 W Jefferson St .... Louisville KY 40202	800-444-1854	502-588-8400	686
JL Clark Mfg Co			
923 23rd Ave .... Rockford IL 61104	877-482-5275	815-962-8861	124
JL Clark Mfg Co Lancaster Div			
303 N Plum St .... Lancaster PA 17602	877-482-5275	717-392-4125	124
JL Industries Inc			
4450 W 78th St Cir .... Bloomington MN 55435	800-554-6077	952-835-6850	286
J&L Marketing			
2100 Nelson Miller Pkwy .... Louisville KY 40223	800-651-5508		7
JL. Souser & Associates Inc			
3495 Industrial Dr .... York PA 17402	800-757-0181	717-505-3800	357
JLS Mailing Services			
672 Crescent St .... Brockton MA 02302	866-557-6245		5
JM Manufacturing Company Inc			
5200 W Century Blvd .... Los Angeles CA 90045	800-621-4404		592
JM Swank LLC			
395 Herky St .... North Liberty IA 52317	800-593-6375	319-626-3683	297-8
JM Test Systems Inc			
7323 Tom Dr .... Baton Rouge LA 70806	800-353-3411	225-925-2029	738
JM Turner Engineering Inc			
1325 College Ave .... Santa Rosa CA 95404	800-514-4220	707-528-4503	256
JM. Bozeman Enterprises Inc			
166 Seltzer Ln .... Malvern AR 72104	800-472-1836*		681
*General			
JM. Smucker Co, The			
1 Strawberry Ln .... Orrville OH 44667	888-550-9555		
J-Mar Enterprises Inc			
PO Box 4143 .... Bismarck ND 58502	800-446-8283	701-222-4518	775
JMF Co			
2735 62nd St Ct .... Bettendorf IA 52722	800-397-3739	563-332-9200	608
JMFA (John M Floyd & Associates Inc)			
125 N Burnett Dr .... Baytown TX 77520	800-809-2307	281-424-3800	194
JMMC (John Muir Medical Ctr)			
1601 Ygnacio Valley Rd .... Walnut Creek CA 94598	844-398-5376	925-939-3000	373-3
JMS Southeast Inc			
105 Temperature Ln .... Statesville NC 28677	800-873-1835		201
JMT (Johnson Mirmiran & Thompson)			
72 Loveton Cir .... Sparks MD 21152	800-472-2310	410-329-3100	261
JMT Consulting Group Inc			
2200-2202 Rt 22 .... Patterson NY 12563	888-368-2463	845-278-9262	524
JNF (Jewish National Fund)			
42 E 69th St .... New York NY 10021	800-542-8733	212-879-9300	48-20
JNJ Express Inc			
3935 Old Getwell Rd .... Memphis TN 38118	888-383-7157	901-362-3444	775
Jo-Ad Industries Inc			
31465 Stephenson Hwy .... Madison Heights MI 48071	800-331-8923	248-588-4810	752
Joan C Edwards School of Medicine at Marshall University			
1600 Medical Ctr Dr .... Huntington WV 25701	877-691-1600	304-691-1700	167-2
Jo-Ann Fabrics & Crafts			
5555 DARROW Rd .... Hudson OH 44236	888-739-4120		270
Jo-Ann Stores Inc (JAS)			
5555 DARROW Rd .... Hudson OH 44236	888-739-4120		270
JobDiva			
116 John St Ste 1406 .... New York NY 10038	866-562-3482		392
Jobe & Company Inc			
9004 Yellow Brick Rd Ste F............ Rosedale MD 21237	855-805-2599	410-288-0560	357
Jobe Hastings & Assoc CPA's			
745 S Church St Ste 105 .... Murfreesboro TN 37133	866-207-2384	615-893-7777	2
Jobelephantcom Inc			
5443 Fremontia Ln .... San Diego CA 92115	800-311-0563	619-795-0837	7
JobMonkey Inc			
1409 Post Alley .... Seattle WA 98101	800-230-1095		260
Jobscope Corp			
355 Woodruff Rd .... Greenville SC 29607	800-443-5794		178-11
JobsOhio			
41 S High St Ste 1500 .... Columbus OH 43215	855-874-2530	614-224-6446	461
JOC (Johnson Oil Company)			
1918 Church St .... Gonzales TX 78629	800-284-2432		575
Jo-Carroll Energy			
793 US Hwy 20 W .... Elizabeth IL 61028	800-858-5522		245
Jockey International Inc			
2300 60th St PO Box 1417 .... Kenosha WI 53140	800-562-5391		155-17
Jockeys' Guild Inc			
448 Lewis Hargett Cir Ste 220 ...Lexington KY 40503	866-465-6257	859-523-5625	48-22

Name / Address	City	State	ZIP	Toll-Free	Phone	Class
Joe Wheeler Resort Lodge & Convention Ctr						
4401 McLean Dr	Rogersville	AL	35652	**800-544-5639**	256-247-5461	665
Joe's Stone Crab						
11 Washington Ave	Miami Beach	FL	33139	**800-780-2722**	305-673-0365	667
Joey's Seafood Restaurants						
3048 - 9 St SE	Calgary	AB	T2G3B9	**800-661-2123**	403-243-4584	666
Joffrey's Coffee & Tea Co						
3803 Corporex Pk Dr	Tampa	FL	33619	**800-458-5282**	813-250-0404	297-11
Johanson Mfg Corp						
301 Rockaway Valley Rd	Boonton	NJ	07005	**800-477-1272**	973-334-2676	253
Johanson Transportation Service Inc						
5583 E Olive Ave	Fresno	CA	93727	**800-742-2053**	559-458-2200	311
John A Martin & Association Inc						
950 S Grand Ave 4th Fl.	Los Angeles	CA	90015	**800-776-2368**	213-483-6490	261
John A Van Den Bosch Co						
4511 Holland Ave	Holland	MI	49424	**800-968-6477**		445
John B Malouf Inc						
8201 Quaker Ave Ste 106	Lubbock	TX	79424	**800-658-9500**	806-794-9500	157-4
John Bean Co						
309 Exchange Ave	Conway	AR	72032	**800-225-5786**	501-450-1500	60
John Boos & Co						
3601 S Banker St PO Box 609	Effingham	IL	62401	**888-431-2667**	217-347-7701	286
John Boyd Thacher State Park						
1 Hailes Cave Rd	Voorheesville	NY	12186	**800-456-2267**	518-872-1237	561
John Brown University						
2000 W University St	Siloam Springs	AR	72761	**877-528-4636***	479-524-9500	166
*Admissions						
John C Heath, Attorney at Law PLLC						
360 N Cutler Dr						
PO Box 510290.	North Salt Lake	UT	84054	**877-575-2317**		427
John Carroll University						
20700 N Pk Blvd	Cleveland	OH	44118	**888-335-6800**	216-397-1886	166
John Cooper School						
1 John Cooper Dr	The Woodlands	TX	77381	**800-295-1162**	281-367-0900	681
John D Archbold Memorial Hospital						
915 Gordon Ave	Thomasville	GA	31792	**800-341-1009**	229-228-2000	373-3
John Daugherty Realtors						
520 Post Oak Blvd 6th Fl	Houston	TX	77027	**800-231-2821**	713-626-3930	648
John Day Co						
6263 Abbott Dr	Omaha	NE	68110	**800-767-2273**	402-455-8000	274
John Deere Coffeyville Works Inc						
1 John Deere Pl	Moline	IL	61265	**800-844-1337**	309-765-8000	616
John Deere Credit Co						
6400 NW 86th St	Johnston	IA	50131	**800-275-5322**	515-267-3000	216
John Deere Power Systems						
3801 W Ridgeway Ave	Waterloo	IA	50704	**800-533-6446**		262
John E Conner Museum						
905 W Santa Gertrudis Ave						
700 University Blvd.	Kingsville	TX	78363	**800-726-8192**	361-593-2810	517
John E Green						
220 Victor Ave	Highland Park	MI	48203	**888-918-7002**	313-868-2400	189-10
John E Jones Oil Co Inc						
1016 S Cedar PO Box 546	Stockton	KS	67669	**800-323-9821**	785-425-6746	186
John E Koerner & Company Inc						
4820 Jefferson Hwy	New Orleans	LA	70121	**800-333-1913**		297-11
John F Kennedy						
Space Ctr	Kennedy Space Center	FL	32899	**866-737-5235**	321-867-5000	664
John F Kennedy Presidential Library & Museum						
Columbia Point	Boston	MA	02125	**866-535-1960**	617-514-1600	433-2
John F Kennedy University						
100 Ellinwood Way	Pleasant Hill	CA	94523	**800-696-5358**	925-969-3300	166
John Fabick Tractor Co						
1 Fabick Dr	Fenton	MO	63026	**800-845-9188***	636-343-5900	357
*Cust Svc						
John G Ullman & Associates Inc						
51 E Market St	Corning	NY	14830	**800-936-3785**	607-936-3785	400
John Hancock Funds						
601 Congress St	Boston	MA	02210	**800-338-8080**	617-375-1500	524
John Hancock Life Insurance Co						
601 Congress St	Boston	MA	02210	**800-248-6110**	866-888-7803	390-2
John Hancock New York						
100 Summit Lake Dr 2nd Fl	Valhalla	NY	10595	**800-732-5543**	866-888-7803	390-2
John Harris-Simon Cameron Mansion, The						
219 S Front St	Harrisburg	PA	17104	**800-732-0099**	717-233-3462	50-3
John Henry Co						
5800 W Grand River Ave	Lansing	MI	48906	**800-748-0517**	517-323-9000	622
John J Pershing Veterans Affairs Medical Ctr						
1500 N Westwood Blvd	Poplar Bluff	MO	63901	**888-557-8262**	573-686-4151	373-8
John Jay Homestead State Historic Site						
PO Box 832	Katonah	NY	10536	**800-456-2267**	914-232-5651	561
John Johnson Co						
274 S Waterman St	Detroit	MI	48209	**800-991-1394**	313-496-0600	728
John Knox Village						
651 SW Sixth St	Pompano Beach	FL	33060	**800-998-5669**		668
John M Campbell & Co						
1215 Crossroads Blvd	Norman	OK	73072	**800-821-5933**	405-321-1383	261
John M Floyd & Associates Inc (JMFA)						
125 N Burnett Dr	Baytown	TX	77520	**800-809-2307**	281-424-3800	194
John Morrell & Co						
805 E Kemper Rd	Cincinnati	OH	45246	**800-722-1127**	513-346-3540	471
John Muir Medical Ctr (JMMC)						
1601 Ygnacio Valley Rd	Walnut Creek	CA	94598	**844-398-5376**	925-939-3000	373-3
John Paul Jones State Historic Site						
106 Hogan Rd Ste 7	Bangor	ME	04401	**800-452-1942**	207-941-4014	561
John Paul Mitchell Systems						
1888 Century Park E						
Ste 1600	Los Angeles	CA	90067	**800-793-8790***	800-027-4066	214
*Cust Svc						
John R Hess & Company Inc						
400 Stn St PO Box 3615	Cranston	RI	02910	**800-828-4377**	401-785-9300	146
John R White Company Inc						
PO Box 10043	Birmingham	AL	35202	**800-245-1183**	205-595-8381	146
John Roberts Co						
9687 E River Rd NW	Minneapolis	MN	55433	**800-551-1534**	763-755-5500	623
John S Knight Ctr						
77 E Mill St	Akron	OH	44308	**800-245-4254**	330-374-8900	205
John Simon Guggenheim Memorial Foundation						
90 Park Ave	New York	NY	10016	**800-232-0960**	212-687-4470	305
John T Cyr & Sons Inc						
153 Gilman Falls Ave	Old Town	ME	04468	**800-244-2335**	207-827-2335	109
John Tyler Community College						
13101 Jefferson Davis Hwy	Chester	VA	23831	**800-552-3490**	804-796-4000	162
John W Danforth Co						
300 Colvin Woods Pkwy	Tonawanda	NY	14150	**800-888-6119**	716-832-1940	189-10
John Watson Chevrolet						
3535 Wall Ave	Ogden	UT	84401	**866-647-9930**	801-394-2611	57
John Wayne Birthplace & Museum						
205 S John Wayne Dr	Winterset	IA	50273	**877-462-1044**	515-462-1044	517
John Wieland Homes & Neighborhoods						
4125 Atlanta Rd SE	Smyrna	GA	30080	**800-376-4663**	770-996-2400	649
John Wiley & Sons Inc						
111 River St	Hoboken	NJ	07030	**800-225-5945***	201-748-6000	633-2
NYSE: JW.A ■ *Sales						
John Wolf Florist						
6228 Waters Ave	Savannah	GA	31406	**800-944-6435**	912-352-9843	292
John Zink Hamworthy Combustion						
11920 E Apache St	Tulsa	OK	74116	**800-421-9242**	918-234-1800	356
John's Pass Village & Boardwalk						
150 John's Pass Boardwalk Pl	Madeira Beach	FL	33708	**800-853-1536**	727-398-6577	50-6
JohnDow Industries Inc						
151 Snyder Ave	Barberton	OH	44203	**800-433-0708**	330-753-6895	54
John-Kenyon Eye Ctr						
1305 Wall St	Jeffersonville	IN	47130	**800-342-5393**		793
Johnny's Fine Foods Inc						
319 E 25th St	Tacoma	WA	98421	**800-962-1462***	253-383-4597	296-37
*General						
Johnny's Selected Seeds						
955 Benton Ave	Winslow	ME	04901	**877-564-6697**		690
Johns Dental Laboratory Inc						
423 S 13th St	Terre Haute	IN	47807	**800-457-0504**	812-232-6026	382
Johns Eastern Co Inc						
PO Box 110259	Lakewood Ranch	FL	34211	**877-326-5326***	941-907-3100	389
*General						
Johns Hopkins University Applied Physics Laboratory						
11100 Johns Hopkins Rd	Laurel	MD	20723	**800-435-9294**	240-228-5000	664
Johns Hopkins University Press						
2715 N Charles St	Baltimore	MD	21218	**800-537-5487***	410-516-6900	633-4
*Orders						
Johns Manville Corp						
717 17th St PO Box 5108	Denver	CO	80217	**800-654-3103***	303-978-2000	388
*Prod Info						
Johnson & Johnson Consumer Products Co						
199 Grandview Rd	Skillman	NJ	08558	**866-565-2229**	908-874-1000	214
Johnson & Johnson Inc						
890 Woodlawn Rd W`	Guelph	ON	N1K1A5	**877-223-9807**		214
Johnson & Johnson Vision Care Inc						
7500 Centurion Pkwy	Jacksonville	FL	32256	**800-843-2020**	800-874-5278	538
Johnson & Rountree Premium Inc						
6160 Lusk Blvd Ste C-203	San Diego	CA	92121	**800-578-3300**	858-259-5846	
Johnson & Wales University						
Providence						
8 Abbott Pl	Providence	RI	02903	**800-342-5598**	401-598-1000	166
Johnson & Wales University Charlotte						
801 W Trade St	Charlotte	NC	28202	**866-598-2427**	980-598-1100	166
Johnson & Wales University Denver						
7150 E Montview Blvd	Denver	CO	80220	**877-598-3368**	303-256-9300	166
Johnson & Wales University North Miami						
1701 NE 127th St	North Miami	FL	33181	**866-598-3567**	800-342-5598	166
Johnson Bros Bakery Supply Inc						
10731 I H 35 N	San Antonio	TX	78233	**800-590-2575**		297-8
Johnson C Smith University						
100 Beatties Ford Rd	Charlotte	NC	28216	**800-782-7303***	704-378-1000	166
*Admissions						
Johnson City Press						
204 W Main St	Johnson City	TN	37604	**800-949-3111**	423-929-3111	528-2
Johnson College						
3427 N Main Ave	Scranton	PA	18508	**800-293-9675**	570-342-6404	795
Johnson Controls Systems						
9410 Bunsen Pkwy Ste 100-B	Louisville	KY	40220	**800-765-7773**	502-671-7300	202
Johnson County						
111 S Cherry St	Olathe	KS	66061	**800-766-3777**	913-715-5000	337
Johnson County Community College						
12345 College Blvd	Overland Park	KS	66210	**866-896-5893**	913-469-8500	162
Johnson County Rural Electric Membership Corp						
750 International Dr	Franklin	IN	46131	**800-382-5544**	317-736-6174	245
Johnson Electric Coil Co						
821 Watson St	Antigo	WI	54409	**800-826-9741**	715-627-4367	762
Johnson Financial Group Inc						
555 Main St Ste 400	Racine	WI	53403	**888-769-3796**		
Johnson Gas Appliance Co						
520 E Ave NW	Cedar Rapids	IA	52405	**800-553-5422**	319-365-5267	318
Johnson Investment Counsel Inc						
3777 W Fork Rd	Cincinnati	OH	45247	**800-541-0170**	513-661-3100	400
Johnson Matthey Medical Products						
1401 King Rd	West Chester	PA	19380	**800-442-1405**	610-648-8000	474
Johnson Mirmiran & Thompson (JMT)						
72 Loveton Cir	Sparks	MD	21152	**800-472-2310**	410-329-3100	261
Johnson Nursery Corp						
985 Johnson Nursery Rd	Willard	NC	28478	**800-624-8174**	910-285-7861	293
Johnson Oil Co (JOC)						
1918 Church St	Gonzales	TX	78629	**800-284-2432**		575
Johnson Oil Co						
507 S Otsego Ave PO Box 629	Gaylord	MI	49735	**800-292-3941**	989-732-2451	577
Johnson Refrigerated Truck Bodies						
215 E Allen St	Rice Lake	WI	54868	**800-922-8360***	715-234-7071	513
*Sales						
Johnson Scale Company Inc						
36 Stiles Ln	Pine Brook	NJ	07058	**800-572-2531**	973-226-2100	680
Johnson Screens Inc						
1950 Old Hwy 8 NW	New Brighton	MN	55112	**800-833-9473**	651-636-3900	295
Johnson State College						
337 College Hill	Johnson	VT	05656	**800-635-2356**	802-635-2356	166
Johnson Storage & Moving Co						
221 Broadway	Denver	CO	80202	**800-289-6683**		516
Johnson Supply Inc						
10151 Stella Link Rd	Houston	TX	77025	**800-833-5455**	713-830-2499	608

Alphabetical Section

Name / Address	City	State	ZIP	Toll-Free	Phone	Class
Johnson University 7900 Johnson Dr	Knoxville	TN	37998	**800-827-2122**	865-573-4517	161
Johnson Window Films Inc 20655 Annalee Ave	Carson	CA	90746	**800-448-8468**	310-631-6672	360
Johnson Youth Ctr 3252 Hospital Dr	Juneau	AK	99801	**800-780-9972**	907-586-9433	411
Johnson's Garden Centers 2707 W 13th St	Wichita	KS	67203	**888-542-8463**	316-942-1443	323
Johnsonite Inc 16910 Munn Rd	Chagrin Falls	OH	44023	**800-899-8916**	440-543-8916	131
Johnsonville Sausage LLC PO Box 906	Sheboygan Falls	WI	53085	**888-556-2728**		296-26
Johnston & Murphy Inc 1415 Murfreesboro Rd	Nashville	TN	37217	**800-424-2854**	615-367-7168	301
Johnston | Food Service & Cleaning Solutions 2 Eagle Dr	Auburn	NY	13021	**800-800-7123**	315-253-8435	555
Johnston Community College 245 College Rd	Smithfield	NC	27577	**800-510-9132**	919-934-3051	162
Johnston County Visitors Bureau (JCVB) 234 Venture Dr	Smithfield	NC	27577	**800-441-7829**	919-989-8687	206
Johnston the Florist Inc 14179 Lincoln Way	North Huntingdon	PA	15642	**800-356-9371**	412-751-2821	292
Johnstone Adams Bailey Gordon & Harris L L C 1 St Louis St Ste 4000	Mobile	AL	36602	**844-682-7682**	251-432-7682	
Joie de Vivre Hospitality Inc 650 California St 7th Fl	San Francisco	CA	94108	**800-738-7477**		
Joint Commission on Accreditation of Healthcare Organizations (JCAHO) 1 Renaissance Blvd	Oakbrook Terrace	IL	60181	**800-994-6610**	630-792-5000	48-1
Jolera Inc 365 Bloor St E 2nd Fl	Toronto	ON	M4W3L4	**800-292-4078**	416-410-1011	177
Joliet Area Community Hospice 250 Water Stone Cir	Joliet	IL	60431	**800-360-1817**	815-740-4104	370
Joliet Avionics Inc 43w730 US Hwy 30	Sugar Grove	IL	60554	**800-323-5966**	630-584-3200	246
Joliet Equipment Corp 1 Doris Ave	Joliet	IL	60433	**800-435-9350**	815-727-6606	515
Jolly Hotel Madison Towers 22 E 38th St *Resv	New York	NY	10016	**888-726-0528***	212-802-0600	378
Jolly Roger Inn 640 W Katella Ave	Anaheim	CA	92802	**888-296-5986**	714-782-7500	378
Jolt Consulting Group 112 Spring St Ste 301	Saratoga Springs	NY	12866	**877-249-6262**		461
Jomax Recovery Services 9242 W Union Hills Dr Ste 102	Peoria	AZ	85382	**888-866-0721**		392
Jon Renau Collection 2510 Island View Way	Vista	CA	92081	**800-462-9447**	760-598-0067	347
Jon's Nursery Inc 24546 Nursery Way	Eustis	FL	32736	**800-322-4289**	352-357-4289	292
Jonah Group Ltd, The 461 King St W 3rd Fl	Toronto	ON	M5V1K4	**888-594-6260**	416-304-0860	179
Jonas Fitness Inc 16969 N Texas Ave	Webster	TX	77598	**800-324-9800**		353
Jonathan Lord Corp 87 Carlough Rd	Bohemia	NY	11716	**800-814-7517**	631-517-1271	297-8
Jones & Frank Corp 1330 St Mary's St Ste 210	Raleigh	NC	27605	**800-286-4133**	919-838-7555	535
Jones Apparel Group Inc Jones New York Collection Div 1411 Broadway	New York	NY	10018	**888-880-8730**	212-642-3860	155-20
Jones County 500 W Main St	Anamosa	IA	52205	**800-622-3849**	319-462-2282	337
Jones Dairy Farm 800 Jones Ave	Fort Atkinson	WI	53538	**800-635-6637**		296-26
Jones Eye Clinic 4405 Hamilton Blvd	Sioux City	IA	51104	**800-334-2015**	712-239-3937	793
Jones Hamilton Co 30354 Tracy Rd	Walbridge	OH	43465	**888-858-4425**	419-666-9838	143
Jones Lake State Park 4117 NC 242 Hwy	Elizabethtown	NC	28337	**800-277-9611**	910-588-4550	561
Jones Metal Products Co 200 N Ctr St	West Lafayette	OH	43845	**888-868-6535**	740-545-6381	752
Jones Metal Products Inc 3201 Third Ave	Mankato	MN	56001	**800-967-1750**	507-625-4436	693
Jones Motor Group 654 Enterprise Dr	Limerick	PA	19468	**800-825-6637**	610-948-7900	775
Jones Stephens 3249 Moody Pkwy	Moody	AL	35004	**800-355-6637**		606
Jones Travel 511 S Lincoln St	Elkhorn	WI	53121	**800-236-3160**	262-723-4309	
Jonesboro Sun 518 Carson St	Jonesboro	AR	72401	**800-237-5341**	870-935-5525	528-2
Jones-Onslow Electric Membership Corp 259 Western Blvd	Jacksonville	NC	28546	**800-682-1515**	910-353-1940	245
JonesTrading Institutional Services LLC 32133 Lindero Canyon Rd Ste 208	Westlake Village	CA	91361	**800-423-5933**	818-991-5500	686
Joplin Convention & Visitors Bureau 602 S Main St	Joplin	MO	64801	**800-657-2534**	417-625-4789	
Joplin Globe 117 E Fourth St	Joplin	MO	64801	**800-444-8514**	417-623-3480	528-2
Jordan Essentials 1520 N Commercial Rd	Nixa	MO	65714	**877-662-8669**		353
Jordan Hospital 275 Sandwich St	Plymouth	MA	02360	**800-256-7326**	508-746-2000	373-3
Jordan Lake State Recreation Area 280 State Pk Rd	Apex	NC	27523	**877-722-6762**	919-362-0586	561
Jordan Tourism Board (JTB) 1307 Dolley Madison Blvd Ste 2A	McLean	VA	22101	**877-733-5673**	703-243-7404	770
Jordano's Inc 550 S Patterson Ave	Santa Barbara	CA	93111	**800-325-2278**	805-964-0611	297-8
Jorgensen Conveyors Inc 10303 N Baehr Rd	Mequon	WI	53092	**800-325-7705**	262-242-3089	207
Jorgensen Forge Corp 8531 E Marginal Way S	Tukwila	WA	98108	**800-231-5382**	206-762-1100	481
Jorgensen Laboratories Inc 1450 Van Buren Ave	Loveland	CO	80538	**800-525-5614**	970-669-2500	473
Jos A Bank Clothiers Inc 6380 Rogerdale Rd PO Box 1000 *Cust Svc	Houston	TX	77072	**800-285-2265***		155-11
Josam Co 525 W US Hwy 20	Michigan City	IN	46360	**800-365-6726**		605
Joseph Blank Inc 62 W 47th St Ste 808	New York	NY	10036	**800-223-7666**	212-575-9050	410
Joseph Brant Memorial Hospital (JBMH) 1230 N Shore Blvd	Burlington	ON	L7S1W7	**800-810-0000**	905-632-3737	373-2
Joseph C Sansone Co 18040 Edison Ave	Chesterfield	MO	63005	**800-394-0140**	636-537-2700	317
Joseph Cory Holdings LLC 150 Meadowlands Pkwy 4th Fl	Secaucus	NJ	07094	**877-267-9001**		359-3
Joseph H Stewart State Recreation Area 35251 Hwy 62	Trail	OR	97541	**800-452-5687**	541-560-3334	561
Joseph Meyerhoff Symphony Hall 1212 Cathedral St	Baltimore	MD	21201	**877-276-1444**	410-783-8100	568
Joseph, Greenwald & Laake PA 6404 Ivy Ln Ste 400	Rockville	MD	20770	**877-412-7429**	301-220-2200	427
Joslyn Art Museum 2200 Dodge St	Omaha	NE	68102	**800-965-2030**	402-342-3300	517
Jostens Inc 3601 Minnesota Ave Ste 400	Minneapolis	MN	55435	**800-235-4774**	952-830-3300	408
Jottan Inc PO Box 166	Florence	NJ	08518	**800-364-4234**	609-447-6200	189-12
Joule Inc 1235 Rt 1 S	Edison	NJ	08837	**800-341-0341**	732-548-5444	717
Journal & Courier 217 N Sixth St *News Rm	Lafayette	IN	47901	**800-456-3223***	765-423-5511	528-2
Journal & Topics Newspapers 622 Graceland Ave	Des Plaines	IL	60016	**800-719-4881**	847-299-5511	633-8
Journal Gazette 600 W Main St	Fort Wayne	IN	46802	**888-966-4532**	260-461-8773	528-2
Journal Inquirer 306 Progress Dr PO Box 510	Manchester	CT	06045	**800-237-3606**	860-646-0500	528-2
Journal of Accountancy 220 Leigh Farm Rd	Durham	NC	27707	**888-777-7077**		455-5
Journal of Financial Planning Assn 7535 E Hampden Ave Ste 600	Denver	CO	80231	**800-322-4237**	303-759-4900	455-5
Journal of Petroleum Technology 222 Palisades Creek Dr	Richardson	TX	75080	**800-456-6863**	972-952-9393	455-21
Journal of Property Management 430 N Michigan Ave	Chicago	IL	60611	**800-837-0706**		455-5
Journal of Protective Coatings & Linings 2100 Wharton St Ste 310	Pittsburgh	PA	15203	**800-837-8303**	412-431-8300	455-21
Journal of the American Dietetic Assn 1600 John F Kennedy Blvd	Philadelphia	PA	19103	**800-654-2452**		455-16
Journal of the American Medical Assn (JAMA) PO Box 10946	Chicago	IL	60654	**800-262-2350**	312-670-7827	455-16
Journal of the Kansas Bar Assn 1200 SW Harrison St	Topeka	KS	66612	**800-928-3111**	785-234-5696	455-15
Journal of the Louisiana State Medical Society 6767 Perkins Rd Ste 100	Baton Rouge	LA	70808	**800-375-9508**	225-763-8500	455-16
Journal of the Medical Assn of Georgia 1849 The Exchange Ste 200	Atlanta	GA	30339	**800-282-0224**	678-303-9290	455-16
Journal Publishing Co 1242 S Green St	Tupelo	MS	38804	**800-264-6397**	662-842-2611	633-8
Journal Record Oklahoma City 101 N Robinson St Ste 101	Oklahoma City	OK	73102	**800-451-9998**	405-235-3100	528-2
Journal Times 212 Fourth St	Racine	WI	53403	**888-460-8725**		528-2
Journal, The 207 W King St	Martinsburg	WV	25402	**800-448-1895**	304-263-8931	528-2
Journal-Standard 27 S State Ave	Freeport	IL	61032	**800-325-6397**	815-232-1171	528-2
JourneyEdcom Inc 80 E McDermott Dr	Allen	TX	75002	**800-876-3507**	972-481-2000	174
Journyx Inc 7600 Burnet Rd Ste 300	Austin	TX	78757	**800-755-9878**	512-834-8888	39
Joy Cone Co 3435 Lamor Rd	Hermitage	PA	16148	**800-242-2663**	724-962-5747	296-9
Joy Dog Food PO Box 305	Pinckneyville	IL	62274	**800-245-4125**		574
Joyce Honda 3166 State Rte 10	Denville	NJ	07834	**844-332-5955**		57
Joyce Koons Buick Gmc 10660 Automotive Dr	Manassas	VA	20109	**866-755-0072**	703-368-9100	513
Joyce Windows 1125 Berea Industrial Pkwy	Berea	OH	44017	**800-824-7988**	440-239-9100	234
JP Maguire Assoc Inc 266 Brookside Rd	Waterbury	CT	06708	**877-576-2484**	203-755-2297	83
Jp Mchale Pest Management Inc 241 Bleakley Ave	Buchanan	NY	10511	**800-479-2284**		573
JPI (Jan-Pro International Inc) 2520 Northwinds Pkwy Ste 375	Alpharetta	GA	30009	**866-355-1064**	678-336-1780	152
JPMorgan Fleming Asset Management PO Box 8528	Boston	MA	02266	**800-480-4111**		400
JR Filanc Construction Company Inc 740 North Andreasen Dr	Escondido	CA	92029	**877-225-5428**	760-941-7130	188-10
JR O'Dwyer Co 271 Madison Ave Ste 600	New York	NY	10016	**866-395-7710**	212-683-2750	633-9
JR Realty 101 E Horizon Dr	Henderson	NV	89015	**800-541-6780**	702-564-5142	648
JR Simplot Co PO Box 27	Boise	ID	83707	**800-832-8893**	208-336-2110	296-21
Jra Financial Advisors 7373 Kirkwood Ct Ste 300	Maple Grove	MN	55369	**800-278-5988**	763-315-8000	400
JRF (Jewish Reconstructionist Federation) 101 Greenwood Ave	Jenkintown	PA	19046	**877-226-7573**	215-885-5601	48-20
JRM Industries Inc 1 Mattimore St	Passaic	NJ	07055	**800-533-2697**	973-779-9340	740-5
JS Paluch Company Inc 3708 River Rd Ste 400	Franklin Park	IL	60131	**800-621-5197**	847-678-9300	41
JSA (Junior State of America) 111 Anza Blvd Ste 109	Burlingame	CA	94010	**800-334-5353**	650-347-1600	48-11
JSA (Jewelers Shipping Assn) 125 Carlsbad St	Cranston	RI	02920	**800-688-4572**	401-943-6020	49-21
Jsa Technologies 201 Main St Ste 1320	Fort Worth	TX	76102	**877-572-8324**		395

	Toll-Free	Phone	Class
JSG (Janesville Sand & Gravel Co)			
1110 Harding St PO Box 427 ....Janesville WI 53547	800-955-7702	608-754-7701	501-4
JSM (Jimmy Swaggart Ministries)			
8919 World Ministry Blvd			
PO Box 262550......... Baton Rouge LA 70810	800-288-8350*	225-768-8300	48-20
*Orders			
JTB (Jordan Tourism Board)			
1307 Dolley Madison Blvd Ste 2A .... McLean VA 22101	877-733-5673	703-243-7404	770
JTB USA Inc (Japan Travel Bureau USA Inc)			
2 W 45th St Ste 305 ....New York NY 10036	800-223-6104	212-698-4900	766
JTech Communications Inc			
6413 Congress Ave Ste 150 .... Boca Raton FL 33487	800-321-6221		730
JTEKT Corp			
29570 Clemens Rd .... Westlake OH 44145	800-263-5163*	440-835-1000	75
*Cust Svc			
JTM Provisions Company Inc			
200 Sales Dr ....Harrison OH 45030	800-626-2308		
JTS Direct LLC			
1180 Walnut Ridge Dr .... Hartland WI 53029	877-387-9500		
Juanita K Hammons Hall for the Performing Arts			
901 S National Ave .... Springfield MO 65897	888-476-7849	417-836-7678	568
Juanita's Foods Inc			
PO Box 847 .... Wilmington CA 90748	800-303-2965		296-36
Jubitz Corp			
33 NE Middlefield Rd .... Portland OR 97211	800-523-0600	503-283-1111	324
Judaica Press Inc			
123 Ditmas Ave .... Brooklyn NY 11218	800-972-6201	718-972-6200	633-2
Judd Wire Inc			
124 Tpke Rd .... Turners Falls MA 01376	800-545-5833*	413-863-4357	809
*Cust Svc			
Judge Group Inc			
300 Conshohocken State Rd			
Ste 300 .... West Conshohocken PA 19428	888-228-7162	610-667-7700	717
Judicare Wisconsin Inc Attys			
401 Fifth St Ste 200 .... Wausau WI 54403	800-472-1638	715-842-1681	427
Judicate West			
1851 E First St Ste 1600............ Santa Ana CA 92705	800-488-8805	714-834-1340	41
Judicial Watch Inc			
425 Third St SW Ste 800 .... Washington DC 20024	888-593-8442		48-7
Judson College			
302 Bibb St ....Marion AL 36756	800-447-9472*	334-683-5110	166
*Admissions			
Judson Park			
23600 Marine View Dr S ..... Des Moines WA 98198	800-401-4113	206-824-4000	668
Judson University			
1151 N State St .... Elgin IL 60123	800-879-5376*	847-628-2500	166
*Admissions			
JUF (Jewish United Fund/Jewish Federation of Metropolit)			
30 S Wells St ....Chicago IL 60606	855-275-5237	312-346-6700	48-20
Jugs Sports			
11885 SW Herman Rd .... Tualatin OR 97062	800-547-6843		706
Julian Charter School Inc			
1704 Cape Horn ....Julian CA 92036	866-853-0003	760-765-3847	681
Julian Tours			
1721 Crestwood Dr .... Alexandria VA 22302	800-541-7936	703-379-2300	755
Julie Inc			
3275 Executive Dr ....Joliet IL 60431	800-892-0123	815-741-5000	732
Julius Koch USA Inc			
387 Church St .... New Bedford MA 02745	800-522-3652*	508-995-9565	740-5
*Sales			
July Business Services			
215 Mary Ave Ste 302 .... Waco TX 76701	888-333-5859		41
Jump River Electric Co-op			
PO Box 99 .... Ladysmith WI 54848	866-273-5111	715-532-5524	245
JumpSport Inc			
2055 S Seventh St Ste A.............. San Jose CA 95112	888-567-5867	408-213-2551	41
Junction Networks Inc			
55 Broad St 20th Fl............. New York NY 10004	800-801-3381		386
Jundt Art Museum			
502 E Boone Ave ....Spokane WA 99258	800-986-9585	509-313-6611	517
Juneau Chamber of Commerce			
9301 Glacier Hwy Ste 110 .... Juneau AK 99801	888-581-2201	907-463-3488	139
Juneau Convention & Visitors Bureau			
800 Glacier Ave Ste 201 .... Juneau AK 99801	888-581-2201	907-586-1737	206
Juneau Harbor			
155 S Seward St ....Juneau AK 99801	800-642-0066	907-586-5255	614
Juneau Public Libraries			
292 Marine Way ....Juneau AK 99801	800-478-4176	907-586-5324	433-3
Jungle Adventures			
26205 E Colonial Dr .... Christmas FL 32709	877-424-2867	407-568-2885	818
Juniata College			
1700 Moore St .... Huntingdon PA 16652	877-586-4282	814-641-3000	166
Junior Achievement of Canada (JACAN)			
161 Bay St 27th Fl .... Toronto ON M5J2S1	800-265-0699	416-622-4602	48-11
Junior Chamber International (JCI)			
15645 Olive Blvd .... Chesterfield MO 63017	800-905-5499	636-449-3100	48-7
Junior State of America (JSA)			
111 Anza Blvd Ste 109 .... Burlingame CA 94010	800-334-5353	650-347-1600	48-11
Juniper Networks Inc			
1194 N Mathilda Ave .... Sunnyvale CA 94089	888-586-4737	408-745-2000	176
NYSE: JNPR			
Juniper Payments			
200 N Broadway Ste 700 .... Wichita KS 67202	800-453-9400	316-267-3200	174
Juniper Pharmaceuticals Inc			
33 Arch St ....Boston MA 02110	866-566-5636	617-639-1500	578
NASDAQ: JNP			
Jupiter Aluminum Corp			
2800 S River Rd .... Des Plaines IL 60018	800-392-7265	219-932-3322	656
Jupiter Beach Resort			
5 N A1A ....Jupiter FL 33477	877-389-0571	561-746-2511	665
Juran Institute Inc			
160 Main St ....Southington CT 06489	800-338-7726		113
Jury Research Institute			
2617 Danville Blvd PO Box 100 .... Alamo CA 94507	800-233-5879	925-932-5663	443
Just Born Inc			
1300 Stefko Blvd .... Bethlehem PA 18017	800-445-5787	610-867-7568	296-8
justClick media Inc			
16782-B Red Hill Ave .... Irvine CA 92606	866-623-8777		
Justia Inc			
1380 Pear Ave Unit 2b ....Mountain View CA 94043	800-300-0001	888-587-8421	177
Justice Jim (R)			
State Capitol			
1900 Kanawha Blvd E............... Charleston WV 25305	888-438-2731	304-558-2000	
Justice Solutions of America Inc			
2750 Taylor Ave Ste A-56 .... Orlando FL 32806	888-577-4766		
Justifacts Credential Verification Inc			
5250 Logan Ferry Rd .... Murrysville PA 15668	800-356-6885		704
Justin Boot Inc			
610 W Daggett Ave .... Fort Worth TX 76104	800-548-1021*	817-332-4385	301
*Cust Svc			
Justiss Oil Company Inc			
1120 E Oak St ....Jena LA 71342	800-256-2501	318-992-4111	536
Justrite Manufacturing Co			
2454 E Dempster St Ste 300......... Des Plaines IL 60016	800-798-9250	847-298-9250	198
JVC Professional Products Co			
1700 Valley Rd .... Wayne NJ 07470	800-252-5722	973-317-5000	52
JW Aluminum			
435 Old Mt Holly Rd ....Mount Holly SC 29445	877-586-5314*		483
*Sales			
JW Jung Seed Co			
335 S High St ....Randolph WI 53956	800-297-3123	920-326-3121	690
JW Marriott			
221 N Rampart Blvd .... Las Vegas NV 89144	877-869-8777	702-869-7807	703
JW Marriott Desert Springs Resort & Spa			
74855 Country Club Dr .... Palm Desert CA 92260	888-538-9459	760-341-2211	703
JW Marriott Orlando Grande Lakes Resort			
4040 Central Florida Pkwy .... Orlando FL 32837	800-576-5750	407-206-2300	665
JW Marriott Resort Las Vegas			
221 N Rampart Blvd .... Las Vegas NV 89145	877-869-8777	702-869-7777	665
JW Pepper & Son Inc			
2480 Industrial Blvd .... Paoli PA 19301	800-345-6296	610-648-0500	522
JW Peters Inc			
500 W Market St .... Burlington WI 53105	866-265-7888	262-763-2401	183
JW Speaker Corp			
N 120 W 19434 Freistadt Rd			
PO Box 1011................... Germantown WI 53022	800-558-7288	262-251-6660	437
JW Winco Inc			
2815 S Calhoun Rd .... New Berlin WI 53151	800-877-8351	262-786-8227	295

K

	Toll-Free	Phone	Class
K D M Enterprise LLC			
820 Commerce Pkwy ....Carpentersville IL 60110	877-591-9768	847-783-0333	553
K Line America Inc			
4860 Cox Rd Ste 300 .... Glen Allen VA 23060	800-609-3221	804-560-3600	313
K12 Inc			
2300 Corporate Pk Dr ....Herndon VA 20171	866-512-2273	703-483-7000	681
NYSE: LRN			
K2 Industrial Services			
3838 N Sam Houston Pkwy E			
Ste 285.....................Houston TX 77032	800-347-4813		189-8
K2 Sports			
4201 Sixth Ave S .... Seattle WA 98108	800-426-1617	206-805-4800	706
Kaba Ilco Corp			
400 Jeffreys Rd .... Rocky Mount NC 27804	800-334-1381	252-446-3321	349
Kabana Inc			
616 Indian School Rd NW .... Albuquerque NM 87102	800-521-5986		
KA-BAR Knives Inc			
200 Homer St .... Olean NY 14760	800-282-0130	716-372-5952	222
KABC-AM 790 (N/T)			
8965 Lindblade St ....Culver City CA 90232	800-222-5222	310-840-4900	641-57
Kabel Business Services			
1454 30th St Ste 105 .....West Des Moines IA 50266	800-300-9691	515-224-9400	113
KABX-FM 975 (Oldies)			
1020 W Main St .... Merced CA 95340	800-350-3777	209-723-2191	641
KABZ-FM 1037 (N/T)			
2400 Cottondale Ln .... Little Rock AR 72202	800-477-1037	501-661-1037	641-56
KACV-FM 90 (Alt)			
PO Box 447 .... Amarillo TX 79178	800-766-0176		641-5
Kadlec Regional Medical Ctr			
888 Swift Blvd .... Richland WA 99352	800-780-6067	509-946-4611	373-3
Kaepa USA Inc			
9050 Autobahn Dr Ste 500 .... Dallas TX 75237	800-880-9200		301
Kaeser & Blair Inc			
4236 Grissom Dr .... Batavia OH 45103	800-642-0790		365
KAFL Inc			
85 Allen St Ste 300................. Rochester NY 14608	800-272-6488	585-271-6400	389
KAFT-TV Ch 13 (PBS)			
350 S Donaghey Ave .... Conway AR 72034	800-662-2386	501-682-2386	736
KAG (Kenan Advantage Group Inc)			
4366 Mt Pleasant St NW .... North Canton OH 44720	800-969-5419		775
KAG West			
4076 Seaport Blvd ....West Sacramento CA 95691	800-547-1587	800-969-5419	775
Kagan			
981 Calle Amanecer .... San Clemente CA 92673	800-933-2667	949-369-6310	526
Kahala Hotel & Resort, The			
5000 Kahala Ave .... Honolulu HI 96816	800-367-2525	808-739-8938	703
Kahala Mandarin Oriental Hotel Hawaii Resort			
5000 Kahala Ave .... Honolulu HI 96816	800-367-2525	808-739-8888	378
Kahala Travel			
3838 Camino Del Rio N Ste 300....... San Diego CA 92108	800-852-8338	619-282-8300	767
Kahiki Foods Inc			
1100 Morrison Rd .... Gahanna OH 43230	855-524-4540		296-36
Kahler Grand Hotel, The			
1517 16th St SW .... Rochester MN 55902	800-533-1655		667
Kahn Litwin Renza & Company Ltd			
951 N Main St .... Providence RI 02904	888-557-8557	401-274-2001	2
Kahului Airport			
1 Kahului Airport Rd .... Kahului HI 96732	800-321-3712	808-872-3830	27

	Toll-Free	Phone	Class

Kahuna Inc
811 Hamilton St .... Redwood City CA 94063　844-465-2486　386

KAI (Kingsway America Inc)
150 NW Pt Blvd .... Elk Grove Village IL 60007　800-232-0631　847-700-9100　359-4

Kai 20 Jay St Ste 530 .... Brooklyn NY 11201　888-832-7832　718-250-4000　667

Kailua Chamber of Commerce
600 Kailua Rd Ste 107 .... Kailua HI 96734　888-261-7997　808-261-7997　139

Kaiser Aluminum Corp
27422 Portola Pkwy
Ste 200 .... Foothill Ranch CA 92610　800-873-2011*　949-614-1740　483
*Sales

Kaiser Foundation Health Plan Inc
1 Kaiser Plz .... Oakland CA 94612　800-464-4000　408-972-3000　390-3

Kaiser Permanente
3495 Piedmont Rd NE
9 Piedmont Center .... Atlanta GA 30305　800-611-1811　404-364-7000　390-3

Kaiser Permanente
6041 Cadillac Ave .... Los Angeles CA 90034　800-954-8000　373-3

Kaiser Permanente
3600 Broadway .... Oakland CA 94611　800-464-4000　510-752-1000　390-3

Kaiser Permanente Bellflower Medical Offices
9400 E Rosecrans Ave .... Bellflower CA 90706　800-823-4040　373-3

Kaiser Permanente Harbor City Medical Ctr
25825 S Vermont Ave .... Harbor City CA 90710　800-464-4000　310-325-5111　373-3

Kaiser Permanente Hawaii
1292 Waianuenue Ave .... Hilo HI 96720　800-966-5955　808-334-4400　390-3

Kaiser Permanente Hospital
441 N Lakeview Ave .... Anaheim CA 92807　800-464-4000　714-279-4000　373-3

Kaiser Permanente Medical Center-South Sacramento
6600 Bruceville Rd .... Sacramento CA 95823　800-464-4000　916-688-2000　373-3

Kaiser Permanente Medical Ctr
710 Lawrence Expy .... Santa Clara CA 95051　800-464-4000　408-851-1000　373-3

Kaiser Permanente Medical Ctr
1200 El Camino Real
.... South San Francisco CA 94080　800-464-4000　650-742-2000　373-3

Kaiser Permanente Medical Ctr San Francisco
2425 Geary Blvd .... San Francisco CA 94115　800-464-4000　415-833-2000　373-3

Kaiser Permanente Northwest
500 NE Multnomah St Ste 100 ....Portland OR 97232　800-813-2000　503-813-2000　390-3

Kaiser Permanente Riverside Medical Ctr
10800 Magnolia Ave .... Riverside CA 92505　800-464-4000*　951-353-2000　373-3
*Cust Svc

Kaiser Permanente Walnut Creek Medical Ctr
1425 S Main St .... Walnut Creek CA 94596　800-464-4000　925-295-4000　373-3

KaiserAir Inc
8735 Earhart Rd .... Oakland CA 94621　800-538-2625　510-569-9622　13

Kajun Kettle Foods
405 Alpha Dr .... Destrehan LA 70047　800-331-9612　504-733-8800

KAKM-TV Ch 7 (PBS)
3877 University Dr .... Anchorage AK 99508　800-478-8255　907-550-8400　736-2

Kal Plastics
2050 E 48th St .... Los Angeles CA 90058　800-321-3925　323-581-6194　598

Kalamazoo College
1200 Academy St .... Kalamazoo MI 49006　800-253-3602*　269-337-7166　166
*Admissions

Kalamazoo County Convention & Visitors Bureau
141 E Michigan Ave Ste 100 .... Kalamazoo MI 49007　800-888-0509　269-488-9000　206

Kalamazoo Psychiatric Hospital
1312 Oakland Dr .... Kalamazoo MI 49008　888-509-7007　269-337-3000　373-5

Kalamazoo Valley Community College
Texas Township
6767 W 'O' Ave PO Box 4070 ..... Kalamazoo MI 49003　800-221-2001　269-488-4400　162

Kalamazoo Valley Plant Growers Cooperative Inc
8937 Krum Ave .... Galesburg MI 49053　800-253-4898　186

Kalani Oceanside Retreat
12-6860 Kapoho Kalapana Rd .... Pahoa HI 96778　800-800-6886　808-965-7828　669

Kal-blue Reprographics Inc
914 E Vine St .... Kalamazoo MI 49001　800-522-0541　113

Kalibrate Technologies PLC
25B Hanover Rd .... Florham Park NJ 07932　800-727-6774*　973-549-1850　178-11
*Cust Svc

Kalispell Regional Medical Ctr
310 Sunnyview Ln .... Kalispell MT 59901　800-228-1574　406-752-5111　373-3

Kalitta Charters LLC
843 Willow Run Airport .... Ypsilanti MI 48198　800-525-4882　734-544-3400　21

Kalitta Flying Service
818 Willow Run Airport .... Ypsilanti MI 48198　800-521-1590　734-484-0088　12

Kalkomey Enterprises Inc
14086 Proton Rd .... Dallas TX 75244　800-830-2268　214-351-0461　95

Kallista Inc
1227 N Eigth St Ste 2 .... Sheboygan WI 53081　888-452-5547*　920-457-4441　374
*Cust Svc

Kallman Worldwide Inc
4 N St Ste 800 .... Waldwick NJ 07463　877-492-7028　201-251-2600　206

Kalman Floor Company Inc
1202 Bergen Pkwy Ste 110........... Evergreen CO 80439　800-525-7840　303-674-2290　189-2

Kalsec Inc
3713 W Main St .... Kalamazoo MI 49006　800-323-9320　269-349-9711　296-15

Kalwall Corp
1111 Candia Rd PO Box 237 ... Manchester NH 03105　800-258-9777　603-627-3861　604

Kaman Corp
1332 Blue Hills Ave PO Box 1 .... Bloomfield CT 06002　866-450-3663　860-243-7100　185
NYSE: KAMN

Kamet Manufacturing Solutions
171 Commercial St .... Sunnyvale CA 94086　800-888-2089　408-522-8000　452

Kamiya Biomedical Co
12779 Gateway Dr .... Seattle WA 98168　800-526-4925　206-575-8068　231

KAMMCO (KAMMCO)
623 SW Tenth Ave .... Topeka KS 66612　800-232-2259　785-232-2224　390-5

Kampgrounds of America Inc (KOA)
PO Box 30558 .... Billings MT 59114　888-562-0000　121

Kanata Energy Group Ltd
1900 112 - Fourth Ave SW
Sun Life Plz III - East Twr ...... Calgary AB T2P0H3　844-526-2822　587-774-7000　261

Kanatek Technologies Inc
359 Terry Fox Dr Ste 230 .... Kanata ON K2K2E7　800-526-2821　613-591-1482　180

Kanawha Hospice Care
1606 Kanawha Blvd W .... Charleston WV 25387　800-560-8523　304-768-8523　370

	Toll-Free	Phone	Class

Kanawha Scales & Systems Inc
Rock Branch Industrial Pk 303 Jacobson Dr
.... Poca WV 25159　800-955-8321　304-755-8321　360

Kane County 78 S 100 E ....Kanab UT 84741　800-733-5263　435-644-5033　337

Kane Graphical Corp
2255 W Logan Blvd .... Chicago IL 60647　800-992-2921　343

Kane Manufacturing Corp
515 N Fraley St .... Kane PA 16735　800-952-6399　814-837-6464　234

Kane Transport Inc
40925 403rd Ave .... Sauk Centre MN 56378　800-892-8557　320-352-2762　763

Kanebridge Corp
153 Bauer Dr .... Oakland NJ 07436　888-222-9221　201-337-2300　349

Kanguru Solutions
1360 Main St .... Millis MA 02054　888-526-4878*　508-376-4245　173-8
*Sales

Kanomax Usa Inc
219 US Hwy 206 .... Andover NJ 07821　800-247-8887　973-786-6386

Kansas
Attorney General
120 SW Tenth Ave 2nd Fl ...... Topeka KS 66612　888-428-8436　785-296-2215　338-17
Consumer Protection Div
534 S Kansas Ave Ste 1210 .... Topeka KS 66603　800-452-6727　785-296-5059　338-17
Healing Arts Board
800 SW Jackson Lower Level Ste A ..... Topeka KS 66612　888-886-7205　785-296-7413　338-17
Insurance Dept
420 SW Ninth St .... Topeka KS 66612　800-432-2484　785-296-3071　338-17
Lieutenant Governor
300 SW Tenth Ave .... Topeka KS 66612　800-766-3777　785-296-3232　338-17
Rehabilitation Services Div
915 SW Harrison
Docking State Office Bldg 9th Fl N ...... Topeka KS 66612　866-213-9079　785-368-7471　338-17
Workers' Compensation Div
401 SW Topeka Blvd Ste 2 .... Topeka KS 66603　800-332-0353　785-296-4000　338-17

Kansas Assn of Realtors
3644 SW Burlingame Rd .... Topeka KS 66611　800-366-0069　785-267-3610　652

Kansas Bankers Assn
610 SW Corporate View .... Topeka KS 66615　800-285-7878　785-272-7836

Kansas Bar Assn
1200 SW Harrison St .... Topeka KS 66612　800-928-3111　785-234-5696　72

Kansas Children's Service League (KCSL)
3545 SW Fifth St .... Topeka KS 66606　877-530-5275　785-274-3100　48-6

Kansas City Art Institute
4415 Warwick Blvd .... Kansas City MO 64111　800-522-5224　816-474-5224　164

Kansas City Chiefs
1 Arrowhead Dr .... Kansas City MO 64129　844-323-1227　816-920-9300　711-2

Kansas City Convention & Entertainment Centers
301 W 13th St .... Kansas City MO 64105　800-767-7700　816-513-5000　205

Kansas City Convention & Visitors Assn
1321 Baltimore Ave .... Kansas City MO 64105　800-767-7700　816-691-3800　206

Kansas City Kansas Community College
7250 State Ave .... Kansas City KS 66112　800-640-0352　913-334-1100　162

Kansas City Kansas Convention & Visitors Bureau Inc
PO Box 171517 .... Kansas City KS 66117　800-264-1563　913-321-5800　206

Kansas City (KS) City Hall
701 N Seventh St .... Kansas City KS 66101　800-432-2484　913-573-5000　336

Kansas City Life Insurance Co
3520 Broadway .... Kansas City MO 64111　800-821-6164　816-753-7000　359-4
OTC: KCLI

Kansas City Peterbilt Inc
8915 Woodend Rd .... Kansas City KS 66111　800-489-1122　913-441-2888　62-5

Kansas City Power & Light Co
1200 Main .... Kansas City MO 64141　888-471-5275　816-556-2200　782

Kansas City Royals
Kauffman Stadium 1 Royal Way
.... Kansas City MO 64129　800-676-9257*　816-921-8000　709
*Sales

Kansas City Southern Railway Co
427 W 12th St .... Kansas City MO 64105　800-468-6527　816-983-1303　644

Kansas City Star
1729 Grand Ave .... Kansas City MO 64108　877-962-7827　528-2

Kansas Cosmosphere
1100 N Plum St .... Hutchinson KS 67501　800-397-0330　620-662-2305　518

Kansas Department of Health & Environment
300 West Douglas Ste 700 .... Wichita KS 67202　800-842-0078　316-337-6020　799

Kansas Gas Service
7421 W 129th St .... Overland Park KS 66213　888-482-4950　782

Kansas Health Foundation
309 E Douglas .... Wichita KS 67202　800-373-7681　316-262-7676　305

Kansas Living Magazine
2627 KFB Plz .... Manhattan KS 66503　800-406-3053　785-587-6000　455-1

Kansas Medical Society
623 SW Tenth Ave .... Topeka KS 66612　800-332-0156　785-235-2383　472

Kansas Museum of History
6425 SW Sixth St .... Topeka KS 66615　800-279-3730　785-272-8681　517

Kansas Press Assn Inc
5423 SW Seventh St .... Topeka KS 66606　855-572-1863　785-271-5304　526

Kansas State University
119 Anderson Hall .... Manhattan KS 66506　800-432-8270*　785-532-6250　166
*Admissions

Kansas Wesleyan University
100 E Claflin Ave .... Salina KS 67401　800-874-1154　785-827-5541　166

Kanson Electronics Inc
245 Forrest Ave .... Hohenwald TN 38462　800-233-9354　931-796-3050　45

Kanto Corp
13424 N Woodrush Way ....Portland OR 97203　866-609-5571　503-283-0405　143

Kantola Productions LLC
55 Sunnyside Ave .... Mill Valley CA 94941　800-280-1180　415-381-9363　511

KANU-FM 915 (NPR)
1120 W 11th St
Kansas Public Radio .... Lawrence KS 66044　888-577-5268　785-864-4530　641

Kanzaki Specialty Papers
20 Cummings St .... Ware MA 01082　888-526-9254　413-967-6204　550

Kao Specialties Americas LLC
243 Woodbine St PO Box 2316 ...High Point NC 27261　800-727-2214　336-884-2214　145

Kaplan Early Learning Co
1310 Lewisville-Clemmons Rd ....Lewisville NC 27023　800-334-2014　336-766-7374　243

Kaplan Industries Inc
6255 Kilby Rd ....Harrison OH 45030　800-257-8299　856-779-8181

	Toll-Free	Phone	Class
Kaplan Trucking Co			
6600 Bessemer Ave ....Cleveland OH 44127	800-352-2848	216-341-3322	775
Kaplel (KTC)			
220 N Cushing Ave ....Kaplan LA 70548	866-643-7171	337-643-7171	731
Kappa Alpha Theta Fraternity			
8740 Founders Rd ....Indianapolis IN 46268	800-526-1870	888-526-1870	48-16
Kappa Delta Pi			
3707 Woodview Trace ....Indianapolis IN 46268	800-284-3167	317-871-4900	48-16
Kappa Delta Sorority			
3205 Players Ln ....Memphis TN 38125	800-536-1897	901-748-1897	48-16
Kappa Kappa Gamma			
PO Box 38 ....Columbus OH 43216	866-554-1870	614-228-6515	48-16
Kappler Inc			
55 Grimes Dr PO Box 490 ....Guntersville AL 35976	800-600-4019	256-505-4005	572
Kar's Nuts			
1200 E 14 Mile Rd ....Madison Heights MI 48071	800-527-6887		296-28
Karas & Karas Glass Company Inc			
455 Dorchester Ave ....Boston MA 02127	800-888-1235	617-268-8800	189-6
Kardex Systems Inc			
114 Westview Ave ....Marietta OH 45750	800-639-5805	740-374-9300	286
Karen Ann Quinlan Hospice			
99 Sparta Ave ....Newton NJ 07860	800-882-1117	973-383-0115	370
Karl Storz Endoscopy-america Inc			
600 Corporate Pt ....Culver City CA 90230	800-321-1304	310-338-8100	473
Karl Storz Imaging Inc			
175 Cremona Dr ....Goleta CA 93117	800-796-8909	805-968-3568	540
Karl W Richter Ltd			
350 Middlefield Rd ....Scarborough ON M1S5B1	877-597-8665	416-757-8951	350
Karmanos Cancer Institute Bone Marrow/Stem Cell Transplant Program			
4100 John R St ....Detroit MI 48201	800-527-6266		764
Karnak Corp, The			
330 Central Ave ....Clark NJ 07066	800-526-4236	732-388-0300	46
Karnes Electric Co-op Inc			
1007 N Hwy 123 ....Karnes City TX 78118	888-807-3952	830-780-3952	245
Karol Fulfillment			
Hanover Industrial Estates			
375 Stewart Rd ....Wilkes-Barre PA 18706	800-526-4773	570-822-8899	
Karthauser & Sons Inc			
W 147 N 11100 Fond du Lac Ave			
..................Germantown WI 53022	800-338-8620	262-255-7815	293
KAS Inc			
62 Veronica Ave ....Somerset NJ 08873	800-967-4254		131
Kasa Industrial Controls Inc			
418 E Ave B ....Salina KS 67401	800-755-5272	785-825-7181	725
Kaseya Corp			
400 Totten Pond Rd Ste 200 ......Waltham MA 02451	877-926-0001		196
Kasgro Rail Corp			
121 Rundle Rd ....New Castle PA 16102	888-203-5580	724-658-9061	646
Kashmir Fabrics + Furnishings			
3191 Commonwealth Dr ....Dallas TX 75247	800-527-4630	214-631-8040	
Kaskaskia College			
27210 College Rd ....Centralia IL 62801	800-642-0859	618-545-3090	162
Kaslen Textiles			
6099 Triangle Dr ....Commerce CA 90040	800-777-5789	323-588-7700	741
Kason Industries Inc			
57 Amlajack Blvd ....Newnan GA 30265	800-935-3550	770-304-3000	349
Katalyst Data Management LLC			
10311 Westpark Dr ....Houston TX 77042	855-529-6444	281-529-3200	535
Katalyst Surgical LLC			
754 Goddard Ave ....Chesterfield MO 63005	888-452-8259		686
Kate B Reynolds Charitable Trust			
128 Reynolda Vlg ....Winston-Salem NC 27106	800-485-9080	336-397-5500	305
Kate Spade			
135 Fifth Ave ....New York NY 10010	866-999-5283		348
Katharine Beecher			
1250 Slate Hill Rd ....Camp Hill PA 17011	800-233-7082		296-8
Katharine Ordway Preserve			
4245 N Fairfax Dr Ste 100 ....Arlington VA 22203	800-628-6860		50-5
Kathy Sisk Enterprises Inc			
PO Box 1754 ....Clovis CA 93613	800-477-1278	559-323-1472	732
Katz & Korin PC			
334 N Senate Ave			
The Emelie Bldg ....Indianapolis IN 46204	800-464-2427	317-464-1100	427
Katz Law Office Ltd			
2408 W Cermak Rd ....Chicago IL 60608	866-352-3033	773-847-8982	427
Kaufman Company Inc			
19 Walkhill Rd ....Norwood MA 02062	800-338-8023	781-255-1000	41
Kaufman Mfg Co			
547 S 29th St PO Box 1056 ....Manitowoc WI 54221	800-420-6641	920-684-6641	453
Kavaliro Staffing Services			
12001 Research Pkwy Ste 344 ....Orlando FL 32826	800-562-1470	407-243-6006	260
Kawada Hotel			
200 S Hill St ....Los Angeles CA 90012	800-752-9232	213-621-4455	378
Kay Chemical Co			
8300 Capital Dr ....Greensboro NC 27409	877-315-1115	844-880-8355	151
Kay County			
201 S Main St ....Newkirk OK 74647	800-255-9456	580-362-2565	337
Kay Dee Designs Inc			
177 Skunk Hill Rd ....Hope Valley RI 02832	800-537-3433		741
Kay Dee Feed Company Inc			
1919 Grand Ave ....Sioux City IA 51106	800-831-4815*	712-277-2011	445
*Cust Svc			
Kay El Bar Guest Ranch			
PO Box 2480 ....Wickenburg AZ 85358	800-684-7583	928-684-7593	239
Kay Electric Co-op (KEC)			
300 W Doolin Ave ....Blackwell OK 74631	800-535-1079	580-363-1260	245
Kay Jewelers			
375 Ghent Rd ....Akron OH 44333	800-527-8029		409
Kay Park Recreation Corp			
1301 Pine St ....Janesville IA 50647	800-553-2476*	877-529-7275	319-4
*Cust Svc			
Kay Toledo Tag			
6050 Benore Rd PO Box 5038 ....Toledo OH 43612	800-822-8247	419-729-5479	623
Kayem Foods Inc			
75 Arlington St ....Chelsea MA 02150	800-426-6100	617-889-1600	296-26
Kaye-Smith			
4101 Oakesdale Ave SW ....Renton WA 98057	800-822-9987	425-228-8600	110
Kaylor Dental Laboratory Inc			
619 N Florence St ....Wichita KS 67212	800-657-2549	316-943-3226	414
Kayne Anderson Capital Advisors LP			
1800 Ave of the Stars			
3rd Fl ....Los Angeles CA 90067	800-638-1496	310-282-7900	400
Kaytee Products Inc			
521 Clay St ....Chilton WI 53014	800-529-8331	920-849-2321	574
KAZ Inc			
250 Tpke Rd ....Southborough MA 01772	800-477-0457		37
KB Electronics Inc			
12095 NW 39th St ....Coral Springs FL 33065	800-221-6570	954-346-4900	203
KB Home			
10990 Wilshire Blvd 7th Fl ......Los Angeles CA 90024	800-304-0657	310-231-4000	649
NYSE: KBH			
KBFB-FM 979 (Urban)			
13760 Noel Rd Ste 1100...............Dallas TX 75240	844-787-1979	972-331-5400	641-30
KBH Corp, The			
395 Anderson Blvd ....Clarksdale MS 38614	800-843-5241	662-624-5471	273
KBHE-FM 893 (NPR)			
555 N Dakota St PO Box 5000 ....Vermillion SD 57069	800-456-0766	605-677-5861	641
KBHE-TV Ch 9 (PBS)			
555 N Dakota St PO Box 5000 ....Vermillion SD 57069	800-333-0789		736
KBIA-FM 913 (NPR)			
78 McReynolds Hall ....Columbia MO 65211	800-292-9136	573-882-3431	641
KBNP-AM 1410 (N/T)			
278 SW Arthur St ....Portland OR 97201	888-214-9237	503-223-6769	641-109
KBTC-TV Ch 28 (PBS)			
2320 S 19th St ....Tacoma WA 98405	888-596-5282	253-680-7700	736-70
KBXL-FM 941 (Rel)			
1440 S Weideman Ave ....Boise ID 83709	877-207-2276	208-377-3790	641-15
KC Electric Assn			
422 Third Ave ....Hugo CO 80821	800-700-3123	719-743-2431	245
KCAQ-FM 1047 (CHR)			
2284 S Victoria Ave Ste 2G..........Ventura CA 93003	877-440-1047	805-289-1400	641
KCEC-TV Ch 50 (Uni)			
777 Grant St 5th Fl ....Denver CO 80203	800-420-2757	303-832-0050	736-23
KCFR-FM 901 (NPR)			
7409 S Alton Ct ....Centennial CO 80112	800-722-4449	303-871-9191	641
KCG Inc			
15720 W 108th St Ste 100 ....Lenexa KS 66219	855-858-3344		
KCI Medical Canada Inc			
75 Courtneypark Dr W Unit 2 ......Mississauga ON L5W0E3	800-668-5403	905-565-7187	473
KCI Technologies Inc			
936 Ridgebrook Rd ....Sparks MD 21152	800-572-7496	410-316-7800	261
KCLB-FM 937 (Rock)			
1321 N Gene Autry Trl ....Palm Springs CA 92262	800-827-2946	760-322-7890	641-77
KCLR			
3215 Lemone Industrial Blvd ....Columbia MO 65201	800-455-5257	573-449-5257	641
KCM Investment Advisors LLC			
750 Lindaro St Ste 350..........San Rafael CA 94901	888-287-5555	415-461-7788	400
KCMQ			
3215 Lemone Industrial Blvd			
Ste 200 ....Columbia MO 65201	800-455-1967	573-875-1099	641
KCOS 13			
9050 Viscount Blvd Ste A440..........El Paso TX 79925	800-683-1899	915-590-1313	736-26
KCPT-TV Ch 19 (PBS)			
125 E 31st St ....Kansas City MO 64108	800-343-4727	816-756-3580	736-38
KCRG-TV Ch 9 (ABC)			
501 Second Ave SE ....Cedar Rapids IA 52401	800-332-5443	319-399-5999	736-14
KCSD-FM 909 (NPR)			
555 N Dakota St PO Box 5000 ....Vermillion SD 57069	800-456-0766	605-677-5861	641
KCSL (Kansas Children's Service League)			
3545 SW Fifth St ....Topeka KS 66606	877-530-5275	785-274-3100	48-6
KCSP-AM 610 (Sports)			
7000 Squibb Rd ....Mission KS 66202	800-234-6860	913-744-3650	641
KCTV-TV Ch 5 (CBS)			
4500 Shawnee Mission Pkwy ....Fairway KS 66205	800-767-7700	913-677-5555	736
KCUR-FM 893 (NPR)			
4825 Troost Ave Ste 202..........Kansas City MO 64110	855-778-5437	816-235-1551	641-53
KCVB (Kingsport Convention & Visitors Bureau)			
400 Clinchfield St Ste 100 ....Kingsport TN 37660	800-743-5282	423-392-8820	206
KCWC-TV Ch 4 (PBS)			
2660 Peck Ave ....Riverton WY 82501	800-495-9788	307-856-6944	736
K&D Pratt			
126 Glencoe Dr ....Mount Pearl NL A1N4S9	800-563-9595	709-722-5690	786
KDAQ-FM 899 (NPR)			
8675 Youree Dr ....Shreveport LA 71115	800-552-8502	318-798-0102	641-99
KDDI America Inc			
825 Third Ave 3rd Fl ....New York NY 10022	866-348-3370		
KDFW FOX 4			
400 N Griffin St ....Dallas TX 75202	800-677-5339	214-720-4444	736-21
KDIndustries			
1525 E Lake Rd ....Erie PA 16511	800-840-9577	814-453-6761	660
KDLT-TV Ch 46 (NBC)			
3600 S Westport Ave ....Sioux Falls SD 57106	800-727-5358	605-361-5555	736-72
KDM Signs Inc			
10450 N Medallion Dr ....Cincinnati OH 45241	855-232-7799		623
KDNL-TV Ch 30 (ABC)			
1215 Cole St ....St. Louis MO 63106	800-365-0820	314-436-3030	736-65
KDR (National Fraternity of Kappa Delta Rho)			
331 S Main St ....Greensburg PA 15601	800-536-5371	724-838-7100	48-16
Kea Lani Spa at the Fairmont Kea Lani Maui			
4100 Wailea Alanui Dr ....Maui HI 96753	800-659-4100	808-875-2229	703
KEA News			
401 Capital Ave ....Frankfort KY 40601	800-231-4532	502-875-2889	455-8
Kean University			
1000 Morris Ave Kean Hall ....Union NJ 07083	800-882-1037	908-737-7100	166
KEAN-FM 1051 (Ctry)			
3911 S First St ....Abilene TX 79605	800-588-5326	325-676-5326	641-1
Kearney Area Chamber of Commerce			
1007 Second Ave PO Box 607 ....Kearney NE 68848	800-227-8340	308-237-3101	139
Kearney Hub			
13 E 22nd PO Box 1988 ....Kearney NE 68847	800-950-6113	308-237-2152	526
Kearny FSB			
120 Passaic Ave ....Fairfield NJ 07004	800-273-3406		70
Keating Technologies Inc			
25 Royal Crest Ct Ste 120..........Markham ON L3R9X4	877-532-8464	905-479-0230	461

Name / Address	Toll-Free	Phone	Class
Keats, Connelly & Associates LLC 3336 N 32nd St Ste 100 ... Phoenix AZ 85018	800-678-5007	602-955-5007	400
KEC (Kay Electric Co-op) 300 W Doolin Ave ... Blackwell OK 74631	800-535-1079	580-363-1260	245
KEC (Kiamichi Electric Co-op Inc) 966 SW Hwy 2 PO Box 340 ... Wilburton OK 74578	800-888-2731	918-465-2338	245
Keds Corp 1400 Industries Rd ... Richmond IN 47374	800-680-0966		301
KEDT 3205 S Staples ... Corpus Christi TX 78411	800-307-5338	361-855-2213	641-29
Keefe Real Estate 1155 E Geneva St ... Delavan WI 53115	800-690-2292	262-728-8757	648
Keeler Motor Car Co 1111 Troy Schenectady Rd ... Latham NY 12110	800-474-4197	518-785-4197	57
Keeley Investment Corp 401 S La Salle St Ste 1201 ... Chicago IL 60605	800-533-5344	312-786-5000	169
Keeling Co PO Box 15310 ... North Little Rock AR 72231	800-343-9464	501-945-4511	608
Keen Technical Solutions LLC 158 E Front St PO Box 2109 ... Traverse City MI 49685	888-675-7772		192
Keenan & Assoc PO Box 4328 ... Torrance CA 90510	800-654-8102	310-212-3344	389
Keene Publishing Corp PO Box 546 ... Keene NH 03431	800-765-9994	603-352-1234	633-8
Keene State College 229 Main St ... Keene NH 03435	800-572-1909	603-352-1909	166
Keeneland Association Inc 4201 Versailles Rd ... Lexington KY 40510	800-456-3412	859-254-3412	444
Keeney Manufacturing Co 1170 Main St ... Newington CT 06111 *Cust Svc	800-243-0526*	860-666-3342	605
Keesal Young & Logan 400 Oceangate ... Long Beach CA 90802	800-877-7049	562-436-2000	
Keesler Federal Credit Union PO Box 7001 ... Biloxi MS 39534	888-533-7537	228-385-5500	219
KEGA-FM 1015 (Ctry) 50 West Broadway Ste 200 ... Salt Lake City UT 84101	866-551-1015	801-524-2600	641-93
Kegel's Produce Inc 2851 Old Tree Dr ... Lancaster PA 17603	800-535-3435	717-392-6612	297-7
Kegerreis Outdoor Advertising LLC 1310 Lincoln Way East ... Chambersburg PA 17202	800-745-4166	717-263-6700	8
Kehoe Component Sales Inc 34 Foley Dr ... Sodus NY 14551	800-228-7223		246
Keilson-Dayton Co 107 Commerce Park Dr ... Dayton OH 45404	800-759-3174	937-236-1070	751
Keim Lumber Company Inc 4465 State Rt 557 PO Box 40 ... Charm OH 44617	800-362-6682	330-893-2251	747
Keim T S Inc 1249 N Ninth St PO Box 226 ... Sabetha KS 66534	800-255-2450		775
Keir Surgical Ltd 126-408 E Kent Ave S ... Vancouver BC V5X2X7	800-663-4525	604-261-9596	473
Keiser University *Fort Lauderdale* 1500 W Commercial Blvd ... Fort Lauderdale FL 33309	800-749-4456	954-776-4456	795
Melbourne 900 S Babcock St ... Melbourne FL 32901	888-534-7379	321-409-4800	795
Sarasota 6151 Lake Osprey Dr ... Sarasota FL 34240	866-534-7372	941-907-3900	795
Keith Titus Corp PO Box 920 ... Weedsport NY 13166	800-233-2126	315-834-6681	775
Keith Watson Productions Inc 350 NW 39th Ave ... Gainesville FL 32609	800-584-1709	352-264-8814	33
Keithly-Williams Seeds Inc 420 Palm Ave ... Holtville CA 92250	800-533-3465	760-356-5533	690
Kejr Inc 1835 Wall St ... Salina KS 67401	800-436-7762	785-825-1842	406
Keller Army Community Hospital 900 Washington Rd ... West Point NY 10996	800-552-2907	845-938-7992	373-4
Keller Fay Group 65 Church St ... New Brunswick NJ 08901	800-273-8439	732-846-6800	461
Keller Inc N216 State Rd 55 ... Kaukauna WI 54130	800-236-2534	920-766-5795	186
Keller Laboratories Inc 160 Larkin Williams Industrial Ct ... Fenton MO 63026	800-325-3056	636-600-4200	417
Keller Supply Company Inc 3209 17th Ave W ... Seattle WA 98119	800-285-3302	206-285-3300	608
Kelley & Ferraro LLP Ernst & Young Tower 950 Main Ave Ste 1300 ... Cleveland OH 44113	800-398-1795	216-202-3450	427
Kelley Blue Book Company Inc 195 Technology Dr ... Irvine CA 92618	800-258-3266	949-770-7704	58
Kelley Manufacturing Co 80 Vernon Dr PO Box 1467 ... Tifton GA 31793	800-444-5449	229-382-9393	273
Kellogg Co 1 Kellogg Sq PO Box 3599 ... Battle Creek MI 49016 NYSE: K ■ *Cust Svc	800-962-1413*	269-961-2000	296-4
Kellogg Garden Products 350 W Sepulveda Blvd ... Carson CA 90745	800-232-2322		280
Kellogg Hotel & Conference Ctr Michigan State University 219 S Harrison Rd ... East Lansing MI 48824	800-875-5090	517-432-4000	378
Kellogg Marine Supply Inc 5 Enterprise Dr ... Old Lyme CT 06371	800-243-9303	860-434-6002	765
Kell-Strom Tool Co 214 Church St ... Wethersfield CT 06109	800-851-6851	860-529-6851	752
Kelly Aerospace 1404 E S Blvd ... Montgomery AL 36116	888-461-6077	334-286-8551	247
Kelly Home Care Services Inc 999 W Big Beaver Rd ... Troy MI 48084	800-755-8636	248-362-4444	362
Kelly Paper Co 288 Brea Canyon Rd ... Walnut CA 91789	800-675-3559		549
Kelly Pipe Company LLC 11680 Bloomfield Ave ... Santa Fe Springs CA 90670	800-305-3559	562-868-0456	591
Kelly Press Inc 1701 Cabin Branch Dr ... Cheverly MD 20785	888-535-5940	301-386-2800	623
Kelly Ryan Equipment Co 900 Kelly Ryan Dr ... Blair NE 68008	800-640-6967	402-426-2151	273
Kelly Systems Inc 422 N Western Ave ... Chicago IL 60612	800-258-8237	312-733-3224	468
Kelly's Janitorial Service Inc 228 Hazel Ave ... Trenton NJ 08638	800-227-0366	609-771-0365	256
Kelly-Moore Paint Company Inc 987 Commercial St ... San Carlos CA 94070	800-874-4436	650-592-8337	546
KELOLAND TV 501 S Phillips Ave ... Sioux Falls SD 57104	800-888-5356	605-336-1100	736
KELO-TV Ch 11 (CBS) 501 S Phillips Ave ... Sioux Falls SD 57104	800-888-5356	605-336-1100	736-72
Kelowna General Hospital (KGH) 2268 Pandosy St ... Kelowna BC V1Y1T2	888-877-4442	250-862-4000	373-2
KELP Christian Radio 6900 Commerce Ave ... El Paso TX 79915	800-658-6299	915-779-0016	641-34
Kelser Corp 43 Western Blvd ... Glastonbury CT 06033	800-647-5316	860-610-2200	225
Kelsey Museum of Archaeology 434 S State St University of Michigan ... Ann Arbor MI 48109	800-562-3559	734-763-3559	517
Keltic Transportation Inc 90 MacNaughton Ave Caledonia Industrial Pk ... Moncton NB E1H3L9	888-854-1233	506-854-1233	314
Kelty 6235 Lookout Rd ... Boulder CO 80301	800-423-2320	800-535-3589	64
Kelyniam Global Inc 97 River Rd ... Canton CT 06019	800-280-8192		250
KEM Electric Co-op Inc 107 S Broadway ... Linton ND 58552	800-472-2673	701-254-4666	245
Kemco Systems Inc 11500 47th St N ... Clearwater FL 33762	800-633-7055	727-573-2323	426
Kemin Industries Inc 2100 Maury St ... Des Moines IA 50317	800-777-8307	515-559-5100	445
Kemps LLC 1270 Energy Ln ... Saint Paul MN 55108	800-322-9566		296-27
Kemron Environmental Services Inc 8521 Leesburg Pk Ste 175 ... Vienna VA 22182	800-429-3516	703-893-4106	192
Kemwel 39 Commercial St ... Portland ME 04102	800-678-0678	207-842-2285	126
Ken Fowler Motors 1265 Airport Pk Blvd ... Ukiah CA 95482	800-287-0107	707-468-0101	57
Ken Garner Manufacturing - Rho Inc 1201 E 28th St # B ... Chattanooga TN 37404	888-454-7207	423-698-6200	261
Ken Jones Tire Inc 73 Chandler St ... Worcester MA 01609	800-225-9513	508-755-5255	750
Ken's Flower Shop 140 W S Boundary St ... Perrysburg OH 43551	800-253-0100	419-874-1333	292
Ken's Foods Inc 1 D'Angelo Dr ... Marlborough MA 01752	800-633-5800		
Kenall Mfg 1020 Lakeside Dr ... Gurnee IL 60031	800-453-6255	262-891-9700	438
Kenan Advantage Group Inc (KAG) 4366 Mt Pleasant St NW ... North Canton OH 44720	800-969-5419		775
Kenco Group Inc 2001 Riverside Dr ... Chattanooga TN 37406	800-758-3289		447
Kencoil Inc 2805 Engineers Rd ... Belle Chasse LA 70037	800-221-8577	504-394-4010	515
Kenda USA 7095 Americana Pkwy ... Reynoldsburg OH 43068	866-536-3287	614-866-9803	750
Kendal at Ithaca 2230 N Triphammer Rd ... Ithaca NY 14850	800-253-6325	607-266-5300	668
Kendal at Oberlin 600 Kendal Dr ... Oberlin OH 44074 *Mktg	800-548-9469*		668
Kendal Crosslands Communities 1109 E Baltimore Pk ... Kennett Square PA 19348	800-216-1920	610-388-1441	668
Kendall & Davis Company Inc 3668 S Geyer Rd Ste 100 ... St. Louis MO 63127	866-675-3755		260
Kendall College 900 N Branch St ... Chicago IL 60642	888-905-3632	312-752-2024	163
Kendall College of Art & Design of Ferris State University 17 Fountain St NW ... Grand Rapids MI 49503	800-676-2787		166
Kendall Electric Inc 131 Grand Trunk Ave ... Battle Creek MI 49037	800-632-5422	269-965-6897	246
Kendall Packaging Corp 10335 N Port Washington Rd ... Mequon WI 53092	800-237-0951	262-404-1200	596
Kendall/Hunt Publishing Co 4050 Westmark Dr PO Box 1840 ... Dubuque IA 52002 *Cust Svc	800-228-0810*	563-589-1000	633-2
Kendall-Jackson Wine Estates & Gardens 5007 Fulton Rd ... Fulton CA 95439	800-769-3649	866-287-9818	80-3
Kendra Scott LLC 1400 S Congress Ave Ste A-170 ... Austin TX 78704	866-677-7023		410
Kenergy Corp 6402 Old Corydon Rd ... Henderson KY 42419	800-844-4832	270-826-3991	245
Kenlake State Resort Park 542 Kenlake Rd ... Hardin KY 42048	800-325-0143	270-474-2211	561
Kenlee Precision Corp 1701 Inverness Ave ... Baltimore MD 21230	800-969-5278	410-525-3800	617
Ken-Mac Metals Inc 17901 Englewood Dr ... Cleveland OH 44130	800-831-9503	440-234-7500	490
Kenmore Air Harbor Inc 6321 NE 175th St ... Kenmore WA 98028	866-435-9524	425-486-1257	25
Kenmore Camera Inc 6708 NE 181st St PO Box 82467 ... Kenmore WA 98028	888-485-7447	425-485-7447	119
Kennametal 1662 MacMillan Park Dr ... Fort Mill SC 29707 NYSE: KMT ■ *Cust Svc	800-446-7738*		491
Kennametal Inc 2879 Aero Pk Dr ... Traverse City MI 49686 NYSE: KMT	800-662-2131	231-946-2100	1
Kennebec Savings Bank 150 State St PO Box 50 ... Augusta ME 04332	888-303-7788	207-622-5801	70
Kennebec Telephone Company Inc 220 S Main St PO Box 158 ... Kennebec SD 57544	888-868-3390	605-869-2220	731
Kennebec Valley Community College 92 Western Ave ... Fairfield ME 04937	800-528-5882	207-453-5000	162
Kennedy Ctr Opera House Orchestra John F Kennedy Ctr for the Performing Arts 2700 F St NW ... Washington DC 20566	800-444-1324		569-3

	Toll-Free	Phone	Class
Kennedy Health System-Cherry Hill			
2201 Chapel Ave W ....Cherry Hill NJ 08002	866-224-0264	856-488-6500	373-3
Kennedy Krieger Institute			
707 N Broadway ....Baltimore MD 21205	800-873-3377	443-923-9200	373-1
Kennedy Manufacturing Co			
1260 Industrial Dr ....Van Wert OH 45891	800-413-8665		486
Kennedy Office Supply			
4211-A Atlantic Ave ....Raleigh NC 27604	800-733-9401	919-878-5400	531
Kennedy Valve			
1021 E Water St ....Elmira NY 14902	800-782-5831	607-734-2211	784
Kennedy-King College			
6301 S Halsted St ....Chicago IL 60621	800-798-8100	773-602-5000	162
Kennerley-Spratling Inc			
2116 Farallon Dr ....San Leandro CA 94577	800-523-5474	510-351-8230	600
Kenneth Clark Company Inc			
10264 Baltimore National Pk			
...........................Ellicott City MD 21042	866-999-5116	410-465-5116	195
Kenneth Cole Productions Inc			
603 W 50th St ....New York NY 10019	800-536-2653		301
NYSE: KCP			
Kenney Mfg Co			
1000 Jefferson Blvd ....Warwick RI 02886	800-753-6639*	401-739-2200	87
*Cust Svc			
Kennickell Printing Co			
1700 E President St ....Savannah GA 31404	800-673-6455		623
KENNICOTT BROTHERS CO			
452 N Ashland Ave ....Chicago IL 60622	866-346-2826	312-492-8200	293
Kenny Construction Co			
2215 Sanders Rd Ste 400............Northbrook IL 60062	800-211-4226	831-724-1011	186
Kenosha Area Convention & Visitors Bureau			
812 56th St ....Kenosha WI 53140	800-654-7309	262-654-7307	206
Kenosha News			
5800 Seventh Ave ....Kenosha WI 53140	800-292-2700	262-657-1000	528-2
Kenosha Public Museum			
5500 First Ave ....Kenosha WI 53140	888-258-9966	262-653-4140	517
Kensington Computer Products Group			
333 Twin Dolphin Dr			
6th Fl ....Redwood Shores CA 94065	800-535-4242	855-692-0054	173-1
Kensington Hotel, The			
3500 S State St ....Ann Arbor MI 48108	800-344-7829*	734-761-7800	378
*Orders			
Kensington Park Hotel			
450 Post St ....San Francisco CA 94102	800-553-1900		378
Kensington Publishing Corp			
119 W 40th St ....New York NY 10018	800-221-2647	212-832-3753	633-2
Kensington Riverside Inn			
1126 Memorial Dr NW ....Calgary AB T2N3E3	877-313-3733	403-228-4442	378
Kent Chamber of Commerce			
524 W Meeker St Ste 1 ....Kent WA 98032	800-321-2808	253-854-1770	139
Kent District Library			
814 W River Ctr Dr NE ....Comstock Park MI 49321	877-243-2466	616-784-2007	433-3
Kent Elastomer Products Inc			
1500 St Claire Ave ....Kent OH 44240	800-331-4762*	330-673-1011	672
*Cust Svc			
Kent General Hospital			
640 S State St ....Dover DE 19901	888-761-8300	302-674-4700	373-3
Kent Hospital			
455 Toll Gate Rd ....Warwick RI 02886	800-892-9291	401-737-7000	373-3
Kent Quality Foods Inc			
703 Leonard St NW ....Grand Rapids MI 49504	800-748-0141		296-26
Kent School PO Box 2006 ....Kent CT 06757	800-538-5368	860-927-6111	618
Kent Security Services Inc			
14600 Biscayne Blvd ....North Miami Beach FL 33181	800-273-5368	305-919-9400	689
Kent State University			
800 E Summit St PO Box 5190.............Kent OH 44242	800-988-5368	330-672-3000	166
Ashtabula			
3300 Lake Rd W ....Ashtabula OH 44004	800-988-5368	440-964-3322	162
Stark			
6000 Frank Ave NW ....North Canton OH 44720	800-988-5368	330-499-9600	166
Trumbull Campus			
4314 Mahoning Ave NW ....Warren OH 44483	800-988-5368	330-847-0571	166
Tuscarawas			
330 University Dr NE ....New Philadelphia OH 44663	800-988-5368	330-339-3391	166
Kentec Medical Inc			
17871 Fitch ....Irvine CA 92614	800-825-5996	949-863-0810	473
Ken-Tool Co 768 E N St ....Akron OH 44305	800-872-4929	330-535-7177	753
Ken-Tron Manufacturing Inc			
PO Box 21250 ....Owensboro KY 42304	800-872-9336	270-684-0431	486
Kentucky			
Child Support Div			
730 Schenkel Ln ....Frankfort KY 40601	800-248-1163		338-18
Consumer Protection Div			
1024 Capital Ctr Dr Ste 200........Frankfort KY 40601	888-432-9257	502-696-5389	338-18
Correctional Institution for Women			
3000 Ash Ave ....Pewee Valley KY 40056	877-687-6818	502-241-8454	213
Crime Victims Compensation Board			
130 Brighton Pk Blvd ....Frankfort KY 40601	800-469-2120	502-573-2290	338-18
Emergency Management Div			
100 Minuteman Pkwy ....Frankfort KY 40601	800-255-2587		338-18
Fish & Wildlife Resources Dept			
#1 Sportsman's Ln ....Frankfort KY 40601	800-858-1549	502-564-3400	338-18
General Assembly			
700 Capitol Ave ....Frankfort KY 40601	800-372-7181	502-564-3449	338-18
Health & Family Services Cabinet			
275 E Main St ....Frankfort KY 40621	800-372-2973	502-564-7042	338-18
Higher Education Assistance Authority			
PO Box 798 ....Frankfort KY 40602	800-928-8926		721
Historical Society			
100 W Broadway ....Frankfort KY 40601	877-444-7867	502-564-1792	338-18
Housing Corp			
1231 Louisville Rd ....Frankfort KY 40601	800-633-8896	502-564-7630	338-18
Insurance Dept			
215 W Main St ....Frankfort KY 40601	800-595-6053	502-564-3630	338-18
Lottery Corp			
1011 W Main St ....Louisville KY 40202	800-937-8946	502-560-1500	450
Real Estate Commission (KREC)			
10200 Linn Stn Rd Ste 201 ....Louisville KY 40223	888-373-3300*	502-429-7250	338-18
*General			
Travel and Tourism Dept			
100 Airport Rd 2nd fl ....Frankfort KY 40601	800-225-8747	502-564-4930	338-18
Veterans Affairs Dept (KDVA)			
1111B Louisville Rd ....Frankfort KY 40601	800-572-6245	502-564-9203	338-18
Vocational Rehabilitation Dept			
275 E Main St ....Frankfort KY 40601	800-372-7172	502-564-4440	338-18
Kentucky Assn of Realtors			
2801 Palumbo Dr Ste 202 ....Lexington KY 40509	800-264-2185	859-263-7377	652
Kentucky Bank			
PO Box 157 ....Paris KY 40362	800-467-1939	859-987-1795	70
Kentucky Bankers Assn			
600 W Main St Ste 400..............Louisville KY 40202	800-392-4045	502-582-2453	529
Kentucky Christian University			
100 Academic Pkwy ....Grayson KY 41143	800-522-3181*		166
*Admissions			
Kentucky Correctional Industries			
1041 Leestown Rd ....Frankfort KY 40601	800-828-9524	502-573-1040	626
Kentucky Ctr for, The Performing Arts, The			
501 W Main St ....Louisville KY 40202	800-775-7777	502-562-0100	568
Kentucky Democratic Party			
190 Democrat Dr ....Frankfort KY 40601	800-995-3386	502-695-4828	612-1
Kentucky Dept for Libraries & Archives			
300 Coffee Tree Rd ....Frankfort KY 40602	800-372-2968	502-564-8300	433-5
Kentucky Derby Museum			
704 Central Ave ....Louisville KY 40208	800-593-3729	502-637-1111	517
Kentucky Educational Television (KET)			
600 Cooper Dr ....Lexington KY 40502	800-432-0951	859-258-7000	736
Kentucky Horse Park			
4089 Iron Works Pkwy ....Lexington KY 40511	800-678-8813	859-233-4303	818
Kentucky Hospital Assn			
2501 Nelson Miller Pkwy ....Louisville KY 40223	888-393-7353	502-426-6220	529
Kentucky International Convention Ctr			
221 S Fourth St ....Louisville KY 40202	800-701-5831	502-595-4381	205
Kentucky Mountain Bible College			
855 Hwy 541 ....Jackson KY 41339	800-879-5622	606-693-5000	161
Kentucky New Era			
1618 E Ninth St ....Hopkinsville KY 42240	877-463-9372	270-886-4444	
Kentucky Organ Donor Affiliates (KODA)			
10160 Linn Station Rd ....Louisville KY 40223	800-525-3456	502-581-9511	541
Kentucky Press Assn			
101 Consumer Ln ....Frankfort KY 40601	800-264-5721*	502-223-8821	620
*Cust Svc			
Kentucky Speedway			
1 Speedway Blvd ....Sparta KY 41086	888-652-7223*	859-578-2300	512
*Resv			
Kentucky State Parks			
Jenny Wiley State Resort Park			
75 Theatre Ct ....Prestonsburg KY 41653	800-325-0142	606-889-1790	561
Kentucky State University			
400 E Main St ....Frankfort KY 40601	800-325-1716*	502-597-6000	166
*Admissions			
Kentucky Veterinary Medical Assn			
108 Consumer Ln ....Frankfort KY 40601	800-552-5862	502-226-5862	790
Kentucky Wesleyan College			
3000 Frederica St ....Owensboro KY 42301	800-999-0592*	270-852-3120	166
*Admissions			
kentuky Blood center			
3121 Beaumont Centre Cir ....Lexington KY 40513	800-775-2522	859-276-2534	89
Kentwood Office Furniture Inc			
3063 Breton Rd SE ....Grand Rapids MI 49512	877-698-6250	616-957-2320	320
Kenway Distributors Inc			
6320 Strawberry Ln ....Louisville KY 40214	800-292-9478	502-367-2201	405
Kenwood USA			
PO Box 22745 ....Long Beach CA 90810	800-536-9663	310-639-9000	643
Kenworth Northwest Inc			
20220 International Blvd S ....SeaTac WA 98198	800-562-0060	206-433-5911	57
Kenworth of Indianapolis Inc			
2929 S Holt Rd ....Indianapolis IN 46241	800-827-8421	317-247-8421	57
Kenworth Sales Co			
2125 Constitution Blvd			
.....................West Valley City UT 84119	800-222-7831*	801-487-4161	775
*General			
Kenya Tourism Board			
6033 W Century Blvd Ste 900........Los Angeles CA 90045	800-223-6486	310-649-7718	770
Kenyon College			
103 College Dr ....Gambier OH 43022	800-848-2468	740-427-5000	166
Kenyon Industries Inc			
36 Sherman Ave ....Kenyon RI 02836	800-247-6658	401-364-3400	740-7
KEO Cutters Inc			
25040 Easy St ....Warren MI 48089	888-390-2050	586-771-2050	491
Kepco Inc			
131-38 Sanford Ave ....Flushing NY 11355	800-526-2324	718-461-7000	253
Kepner-Tregoe Inc			
PO Box 704 ....Princeton NJ 08542	800-537-6378	609-921-2806	194
Ker & Downey Inc			
6703 Hwy Blvd ....Katy TX 77494	800-423-4236	281-371-2500	755
KERA-FM 901 (NPR)			
3000 Harry Hines Blvd ....Dallas TX 75201	800-456-5372	214-871-1390	641-30
KERAMIDA Inc			
401 N College Ave ....Indianapolis IN 46202	800-508-8034	317-685-6600	192
Kerkau Manufacturing Co			
1321 S Valley Ctr Dr ....Bay City MI 48706	800-248-5060	989-686-0350	481
Kerley & Sears Inc			
4331 Cement Valley Rd ....Midlothian TX 76065	800-346-4381	972-775-3902	786
Kern County Board of Trade			
2101 Oak St ....Bakersfield CA 93301	800-500-5376*	661-868-5376	139
*General			
Kern Health Systems			
9700 Stockdale Hwy ....Bakersfield CA 93311	888-466-2219	661-664-5000	231
Kern River Gas Transmission Co			
2755 E Cottonwood Pkwy			
Ste 300 ....Salt Lake City UT 84121	800-420-7500	801-937-6000	325
Kern Schools Federal Credit Union			
PO Box 9506 ....Bakersfield CA 93389	800-221-3311	661-833-7900	219
Kerr Lakeside Inc			
26841 Tungsten Rd ....Euclid OH 44132	800-487-5377	216-261-2100	617
Kerr Pump & Supply			
12880 Cloverdale St ....Oak Park MI 48237	800-482-8259	248-543-3880	637

Name	Address	City	State	ZIP	Toll-Free	Phone	Class
Kerrington Group Inc	24 S Fifth St	Fernandina Beach	FL	32034	**800-582-0828**	904-491-1411	180
Kerrville Bus Co	1430 E Houston St	San Antonio	TX	78202	**800-256-2757**	210-226-7371	107
Kerrville Convention & Visitors Bureau	2108 Sidney Baker St	Kerrville	TX	78028	**800-221-7958**	830-792-3535	206
Kerrville State Hospital	721 Thompson Dr	Kerrville	TX	78028	**888-963-7111**	830-896-2211	373-5
Kerry's Nursery Inc	21840 SW 258th St	Homestead	FL	33031	**800-331-9127**		368
Kershaw County Chamber of Commerce	607 S Broad St	Camden	SC	29020	**800-968-4037**	803-432-2525	139
Kerusso Inc	402 Hwy 62 Spur	Berryville	AR	72616	**800-424-0943**	870-423-6242	683
Keryx Biopharmaceuticals Inc	1 Marina Park Dr 20th Fl *NASDAQ: KERX*	Boston	MA	02210	**800-903-0247**	617-466-3500	578
Kessler International	45 Rockefeller Plz Ste 2000	New York	NY	10111	**800-932-2221**	212-286-9100	399
Kessler Sign Co	5804 Poe Ave	Dayton	OH	45414	**800-686-1870**	937-898-0633	697
Kester Inc	800 W Thorndale Ave	Itasca	IL	60143	**800-253-7837**	630-616-4048	145
KET (Kentucky Educational Television)	600 Cooper Dr	Lexington	KY	40502	**800-432-0951**	859-258-7000	736
Ketchikan Visitors Bureau	131 Front St	Ketchikan	AK	99901	**800-770-3300**	907-225-6166	206
KETC-TV Ch 9 (PBS)	3655 Olive St	Saint Louis	MO	63108	**855-482-5382**	314-512-9000	736-65
KETG 9 Arkadelphia	350 S Donaghey Ave	Conway	AR	72034	**800-662-2386**	501-682-2386	736
KETS-TV Ch 2 (PBS)	350 S Donaghey Ave	Conway	AR	72034	**800-662-2386**	501-682-2386	736
Kettering University	1700 University Ave	Flint	MI	48504	**800-955-4464**	810-762-9500	166
Kettering-Moraine-Oakwood Area Chamber of Commerce	2977 Far Hills Ave	Kettering	OH	45419	**800-621-8931**	937-299-3852	139
KETV-TV Ch 7 (ABC)	2665 Douglas St	Omaha	NE	68131	**800-279-5388**	402-345-7777	736-53
Keurig Dr Pepper Inc	53 S Ave	Burlington	MA	01803	**866-901-2739**		102
Kewaunee Scientific Corp	2700 W Front St PO Box 1842 *NASDAQ: KEQU*	Statesville	NC	28687	**800-824-6626**	704-873-7202	419
Keweenaw Financial Corp	235 Quincy St	Hancock	MI	49930	**866-482-0404**	906-482-0404	359-2
KEX-AM 1190 (N/T)	13333 SW 68th Pkwy Ste 310	Poland	OR	97223	**844-289-7234**	503-323-6400	
Key Bank	65 Dutch Hill Rd *Cust Svc	Orangeburg	NY	10962	**800-539-2968***	845-398-2280	70
Key Bellevilles Inc	100 Key Ln	Leechburg	PA	15656	**800-245-3600**	724-295-5111	490
Key Club International	3636 Woodview Trace	Indianapolis	IN	46268	**800-549-2647**	317-875-8755	48-15
Key Container Corp	21 Campbell St	Pawtucket	RI	02861	**800-343-8811**	401-723-2000	100
Key Curriculum Press	1150 65th St	Emeryville	CA	94608	**800-338-3987**	510-595-7000	633-2
Key Equipment Finance	1000 S McCaslin Blvd	Superior	CO	80027	**888-301-6238**		216
Key Fire Hose Corp (KFH)	PO Box 7107	Dothan	AL	36302	**800-447-5666**	334-671-5532	369
Key Industries Inc	400 Marble Rd	Fort Scott	KS	66701	**800-835-0365**		155-18
Key Information Systems Inc	30077 Agoura Ct 1st Fl	Agoura Hills	CA	91301	**877-442-3249**	818-992-8950	178-11
Key Largo Marriott Bay Resort	103800 Overseas Hwy *Resv	Key Largo	FL	33037	**888-731-9056***	305-453-0000	665
Key Lime Inn	725 Truman Ave	Key West	FL	33040	**800-549-4430**	305-294-5229	378
Key Radio	307 S 1600 W	Provo	UT	84601	**855-539-4583**	801-374-5210	
Key Speakers Bureau Inc	3500 E Coast Hwy Ste 6	Corona del Mar	CA	92625	**800-675-1175**	949-675-7856	704
Key West Aloe	13095 N Telecom Pkwy	Tampa	FL	33637	**800-445-2563**		214
Key West Aquarium	1 Whitehead St	Key West	FL	33040	**888-544-5927**		40
Key West City Hall	3132 Flagler Ave	Key West	FL	33040	**800-955-8770**	305-809-3700	336
Key West International Airport	3491 S Roosevelt Blvd	Key West	FL	33040	**800-327-1390**	305-809-5200	27
Key West Key	726 Passover Ln	Key West	FL	33040	**800-881-7321**		375
Key West Visitors Ctr	510 Greene St 1st Fl *General	Key West	FL	33040	**800-533-5397***	305-294-2587	206
Keyano College	8115 Franklin Ave	Fort Mcmurray	AB	T9H2H7	**800-251-1408**	780-791-4800	95
Keyboard Magazine	28 E 28th St 12th Fl *Cust Svc	New York	NY	10016	**800-483-2433***	212-378-0400	455-9
Keybridge Medical Revenue Management	2348 Baton Rouge Ave	Lima	OH	45805	**877-222-4114**		
Keycentrix LLC	2420 N Woodlawn Bldg 500	Wichita	KS	67220	**800-444-8486**		
KeyCorp	127 Public Sq *NYSE: KEY*	Cleveland	OH	44114	**800-539-9055**	216-689-8481	359-2
Keyes Toyota	5855 Van Nuys Blvd	Van Nuys	CA	91401	**844-781-4304**		57
KeyImpact Sales & Systems Inc	1701 Crossroads Dr	Odenton	MD	21113	**800-955-0600**		687
KeyPoint Credit Union	2805 Bowers Ave	Santa Clara	CA	95051	**888-255-3637**	408-731-4100	219
Keyston Bros	2801 Academy Way	Sacramento	CA	95815	**800-453-1112**	916-927-5851	590
Keystone Aniline Corp	2501 W Fulton St	Chicago	IL	60612	**800-522-4393**	312-666-2015	143
Keystone Automotive Operations Inc	44 Tunkhannock Ave	Exeter	PA	18643	**800-521-9999**	570-655-4514	61
Keystone College	1 College Green	La Plume	PA	18440	**800-824-2764**	570-945-5141	166
Keystone Consolidated Industries Inc	7000 SW Adams St *Sales	Peoria	IL	61641	**800-447-6444***		808
Keystone Ctr	2001 Providence Ave	Chester	PA	19013	**800-558-9600**	610-876-9000	722
Keystone Dental Inc	144 Middlesex Tpke	Burlington	MA	01803	**866-902-9272**	781-328-3490	228
Keystone Electronics Corp	31-07 20th Rd	Astoria	NY	11105	**800-221-5510**	718-956-8900	349
Keystone Industries	480 S Democrat Rd	Gibbstown	NJ	08027	**800-333-3131**	856-663-4700	473
Keystone Information Systems	1000 S Lenola Rd	Maple Shade	NJ	08052	**800-735-4862**	856-722-0700	225
Keystone Learning Systems LLC	6030 Daybreak Cir Ste A150 116	Clarksville	MD	21029	**800-949-5590**	410-800-4000	510
Keystone Lodge & Spa	PO Box 38	Keystone	CO	80435	**877-625-1556**	970-496-4000	378
Keystone Payroll	355-C Colonnade Blvd	State College	PA	16803	**877-717-2272**	814-234-2272	2
Keystone Pretzels	124 W Airport Rd	Lititz	PA	17543	**888-572-4500**		296-9
Keystone Profiles Ltd	220 Seventh Ave	Beaver Falls	PA	15010	**800-777-1533**	724-506-1500	490
Keystone Property Group	125 E Elm St Ste 400	Conshohocken	PA	19004	**866-980-1818**	610-980-7000	648
Keystone Resort	21996 Hwy 6 PO Box 38	Keystone	CO	80435	**877-625-1556**	970-754-0001	665
Keystone Retaining Wall Systems Inc	4444 W 78th St	Minneapolis	MN	55435	**800-747-8971**	952-897-1040	720
Keystone Sporting Arms LLC	155 Sodom Rd	Milton	PA	17847	**800-742-0455**	570-742-2777	802
Keystone State Park	1926 S Hwy 151	Sand Springs	OK	74063	**800-654-8240**	918-865-4991	561
KEYW Corp	7740 Milestone Pkwy Ste 400	Hanover	MD	21076	**800-340-1001**	443-733-1600	177
KFH (Key Fire Hose Corp)	PO Box 7107	Dothan	AL	36302	**800-447-5666**	334-671-5532	369
KForce Government Soultions	2750 Prosperity Ave Ste 300	Fairfax	VA	22031	**800-200-7465**	703-245-7350	180
Kforce Inc	1001 E Palm Ave *NASDAQ: KFRC*	Tampa	FL	33605	**877-453-6723**	813-552-5000	717
KFRG-FM 951	900 E Washington St Ste 315	Colton	CA	92324	**888-431-3764**		641
Kfs Inc	1840 W Airfield Dr	Dallas	TX	75261	**800-364-4115**	817-488-4115	24
KFSN-TV Ch 30 (ABC)	1777 G St	Fresno	CA	93706	**800-423-3030**	559-442-1170	736-30
KFTV-TV Ch 21 (Uni)	601 W Univision Plz	Fresno	CA	93704	**866-783-2645**	559-222-2121	736-30
KFXA Fox 28	600 Old Marion Rd NE	Cedar Rapids	IA	52402	**800-222-5426**	800-642-6140	736-14
KGAN-TV Ch 2 (CBS)	600 Old Marion Rd NE	Cedar Rapids	IA	52402	**800-642-6140**	319-395-9060	736-14
KGGI-FM 991 (CHR)	2030 Iowa Ave Ste 100	Riverside	CA	92507	**866-991-5444**	951-684-1991	641-86
KGH (Kelowna General Hospital)	2268 Pandosy St	Kelowna	BC	V1Y1T2	**888-877-4442**	250-862-4000	373-2
KGNU-FM 885 (Var)	4700 Walnut St	Boulder	CO	80301	**800-737-3030**	303-449-4885	641
KGOU-FM 1063 (NPR)	860 Van Vleet Oval Rm 300	Norman	OK	73019	**866-533-2470**	405-325-3388	641
KGS Steel Inc	3725 Pine Ln	Bessemer	AL	35022	**800-533-3846**	205-425-0800	490
KGTV-TV Ch 10 (ABC)	4600 Airway	San Diego	CA	92102	**800-799-8881**	619-237-1010	736-68
Higher Education Assistance Authority	PO Box 798	Frankfort	KY	40602	**800-928-8926**		721
Khong Guan Corp	30068 Eigenbrodt Way	Union City	CA	94587	**877-889-8968**	510-487-7800	195
KHON-TV Ch 2 (Fox)	88 Piikoi St	Honolulu	HI	96814	**877-926-8300**	808-591-4278	736-33
Khoury Inc	1129 Webster Ave PO Box 1746	Waco	TX	76703	**800-725-6765**	254-754-5481	319-1
KHTK-AM 1140 (Sports)	5244 Madison Ave	Sacramento	CA	95841	**800-920-1140**	916-338-9200	641-91
KHVH-AM 830 (N/T)	650 Iwilei Rd Ste 400	Honolulu	HI	96817	**844-289-7234**	808-550-9200	641-45
KI	1330 Bellevue St	Green Bay	WI	54302	**800-424-2432**	920-468-8100	319-1
Kiamichi Electric Co-op Inc (KEC)	966 SW Hwy 2 PO Box 340	Wilburton	OK	74578	**800-888-2731**	918-465-2338	245
Kiawah Island Golf Resort	1 Sancturay Beach Dr *Resv	Kiawah Island	SC	29455	**800-654-2924***	843-768-2121	665
Kibble Equipment	1150 S Victory Dr	Mankato	MN	56001	**800-624-8983**	507-387-8201	357
Kibow Biotech Inc	4781 W Chester Pike Newtown Business Ctr	Newtown Square	PA	19073	**888-271-2560**	610-353-5130	231
Kice Industries Inc	5500 N Mill Heights Dr	Wichita	KS	67219	**877-289-5423**	316-744-7151	207
Kickhaefer Mfg Co (KMC)	1221 S Park St PO Box 348	Port Washington	WI	53074	**800-822-6080**	262-377-5030	486
Kidango Inc	44000 Old Warm Springs Blvd	Fremont	CA	94538	**800-262-4252**	408-258-3710	305
KidCo Inc	1013 Technology Way	Libertyville	IL	60048	**800-553-5529**	847-549-8600	64
Kidd Kraddick in The Morning	220 Las Colinas Blvd E Ste C-210	Irving	TX	75039	**800-543-3548**	972-432-9094	641-9

	Toll-Free	Phone	Class
Kidde-Fenwal Inc			
400 Main St ....Ashland MA 01721	**800-872-6527***	508-881-2000	202
*Hum Res			
Kiddesigns LLC			
1299 Main St ....Rahway NJ 07065	**800-777-5206**	732-382-1760	
Kids Help Phone			
300-439 University Ave ....Toronto ON M5G1Y8	**800-268-3062**	416-586-5437	138
KidsPeace Orchard Hills Campus			
5300 Kids Peace Dr ....Orefield PA 18069	**800-257-3223**		373-1
Kiefer Specialty Flooring Inc			
2910 Falling Waters Blvd ....Lindenhurst IL 60046	**800-322-5448**	847-245-8450	360
Kiewit Corp			
3555 Farnam St ....Omaha NE 68131	**800-901-1087**	402-342-2052	188-4
KIK Custom Products			
2730 Middlebury St ....Elkhart IN 46516	**800-479-6603**	574-295-0000	145
KIK Pool Additives Inc			
5160 E Airport Dr ....Ontario CA 91761	**800-745-4536**	909-390-9912	145
KIKO 2722 Fulton Dr NW ....Canton OH 44718	**800-533-5456**	330-453-9187	464
Kikusui America Inc			
1633 Bayshore Hwy Ste 331........ Burlingame CA 94010	**877-876-2807**	650-259-5900	246
Killington			
4763 Killington Rd ....Killington VT 05751	**800-734-9435**	802-422-3333	665
Killington Grand Resort Hotel & Conference Ctr			
4763 Killington Rd ....Killington VT 05751	**800-621-6867**	802-422-3333	378
Killion Industries Inc			
1380 Poinsettia Ave ....Vista CA 92081	**800-421-5352**	760 727 5102	286
KILO Radio			
1805 E Cheyenne Rd .... Colorado Springs CO 80905	**800-727-5456***	719-633-5456	641-26
*General			
Kilwins Quality Confections Inc (KQC)			
1050 Bay View Rd ....Petoskey MI 49770	**888-454-5946**		123
Kim Hotstart Manufacturing Co			
5723 E Alki Ave ....Spokane WA 99212	**800-224-5550**	509-536-8660	15
Kimball County			
114 E Third St ....Kimball NE 69145	**800-369-2850**	308-235-2241	337
Kimball Genetics Inc			
8490 Upland Dr Ste 100.............Englewood CO 80112	**800-444-9111**		414
Kimball Hospitality			
1180 E 16th St ....Jasper IN 47549	**800-634-9510**	276-666-8933	319-3
Kimball International Inc			
1600 Royal St ....Jasper IN 47549	**800-482-1616**		105
NASDAQ: KBAL			
Kimball Midwest			
4800 Robert Rd ....Columbus OH 43228	**800-233-1294**	800-214-9440	384
Kimball Office Furniture Co			
1600 Royal St ....Jasper IN 47549	**800-482-1818**		319-1
Kimball Terrace Inn			
10 Huntington Rd ....Northeast Harbor ME 04662	**800-454-6225**	207-276-3383	378
Kimball, Tirey & St John LLP			
7676 Hazard Center Dr .... San Diego CA 92108	**800-564-6611**		427
Kimberly Hotel			
145 E 50th St ....New York NY 10022	**800-683-0400**	212-755-0400	378
Kimberly-Clark Corp			
351 Phelps Dr ....Irving TX 75038	**888-525-8388**	972-281-1200	554
NYSE: KMB			
Kimble Companies Inc			
3596 State Rt 39 NW ....Dover OH 44622	**800-201-0005**		782
Kimco Realty Corp			
3333 New Hyde Pk Rd .... New Hyde Park NY 11042	**800-645-6292**	516-869-9000	651
NYSE: KIM			
Kimco Staffing Services Inc			
17872 Cowan Ave ....Irvine CA 92614	**800-649-5627**	949-752-6996	717
Kimmons Investigative Services Inc			
5177 Richmond Ave Ste 1190 ....Houston TX 77056	**800-681-5046**	713-532-5881	689
Kimpton Hotel & Restaurant Group			
422 SW Broadway ....Portland OR 97205	**800-263-2305**	503-228-1212	378
Kimpton Hotel & Restaurant Group LLC			
90 Tremont St ....Boston MA 02108	**866-906-9090**	617-772-5800	667
Kimpton Hotel & Restaurant Group LLC			
1733 N St NW ....Washington DC 20036	**800-775-1202**	202-393-3000	378
Kimpton Hotel & Restaurant Group LLC			
222 Kearny St Ste 200 .... San Francisco CA 94108	**800-546-7866**	415-397-5572	378
KIMT-TV Ch 3 (CBS)			
112 N Pennsylvania Ave .... Mason City IA 50401	**800-323-4883**	641-423-2540	736
Kimwood Corp			
77684 Oregon 99 .... Cottage Grove OR 97424	**800-942-4401**	541-942-4401	816
Kin Communications Inc			
736 Granville St Ste 100.......... Vancouver BC V6Z1G3	**866-684-6730**	604-684-6730	224
Kinamed Inc			
820 Flynn Rd ....Camarillo CA 93012	**800-827-5775**	805-384-2748	474
Kinark Child			
500 Hood Rd Ste 200 ....Markham ON L3R9Z3	**800-230-8533**	905-474-9595	392
Kinaxis			
700 Silver Seven Rd ....Ottawa ON K2V1C3	**877-546-2947***	613-592-5780	178-10
*General			
Kincaid Coach Lines Inc			
9207 Woodend Rd .... Kansas City KS 66111	**800-998-1901**	913-441-6200	755
Kincardine Cable TV Ltd			
223 Bruce Ave ....Kincardine ON N2Z2P2	**800-265-3064**	519-396-8880	116
Kinco International			
4286 NE 185th Dr ....Portland OR 97230	**800-547-8410***		155-7
*General			
Kinder Morgan			
1001 Louisiana St Ste 1000 ....Houston TX 77002	**800-247-4122**	713-369-9000	325
NYSE: KMI			
Kinder Morgan Bulk Terminals Inc			
7116 Hwy 22 ....Sorrento LA 70778	**800-232-1627**	225-675-5387	463
Kinder Morgan Inc KN Energy Retail Div			
370 Van Gordon St ....Lakewood CO 80228	**800-232-1627**	303-989-1740	782
KinderCare Learning Centers LLC			
650 NE Holladay St Ste 1400 ....Portland OR 97232	**800-633-1488**		148
Kinderdance International Inc			
5238 Valleypointe Pkwy ....Roanoke VA 24019	**800-554-2334**	540-904-2595	310
Kindred Healthcare Inc			
7710 Rialto Blvd Ste 150 .... Austin TX 78735	**866-546-3733**	512-288-0859	373-7
Kindred Healthcare Inc			
680 S Fourth Ave ....Louisville KY 40202	**800-545-0749**	502-596-7300	352
NYSE: KND			
Kindred Hospice			
190 Bilmar Dr Ste 200 .... Pittsburgh PA 15205	**866-546-3733**	412-494-5500	448
Kindred Hospital Fort Worth Southwest			
7800 Oakmont Blvd ....Fort Worth TX 76132	**800-359-7412**	817-346-0094	373-7
Kindred Hospital Greensboro			
2401 Southside Blvd ....Greensboro NC 27406	**877-836-2671**	336-271-2800	448
Kindred Hospital Louisville			
1313 St Anthony Pl ....Louisville KY 40204	**800-648-6057**	502-587-7001	373-3
Kindred Hospital Northland			
500 NW 68th St .... Kansas City MO 64118	**800-545-0749**	816-420-6300	373-7
Kinecta Federal Credit Union			
1440 Rosecrans Ave			
PO Box 10003. ....Manhattan Beach CA 90266	**800-854-9846**	310-643-5400	219
Kinesis Corp			
22030 20th Ave SE Ste 102 ....Bothell WA 98021	**800-454-6374**	425-402-8100	173-1
Kinetic Instrument Inc			
17 Berkshire Blvd ....Bethel CT 06801	**800-233-2346**	203-743-0080	228
Kinetico Inc			
10845 Kinsman Rd ....Newbury OH 44065	**800-944-9283**	440-564-9111	801
King & Prince Beach & Golf Resort			
201 Arnold Rd ....Saint Simons Island GA 31522	**800-342-0212**	912-638-3631	665
King & Prince Seafood Corp			
1 King & Prince Blvd ....Brunswick GA 31520	**888-391-5223**		296-14
King & Schickli PLLC			
800 Corporate Dr Ste 200.............Lexington KY 40503	**888-364-5712**	859-274-4287	427
King Architectural Metals Inc			
PO Box 271169 ....Dallas TX 75227	**800-542-2379**		489
King Bio			
3 Westside Dr ....Asheville NC 28806	**800-237-4100**	855-739-7127	578
King College			
1350 King College Rd ....Bristol TN 37620	**800-362-0014***	423-652-4861	166
*Admissions			
King County			
401 Fifth Ave 3rd Fl ....Seattle WA 98104	**800-325-6165**	206-296-1586	337
King Electrical Manufacturing Co			
9131 Tenth Ave S ....Seattle WA 98108	**800-603-5464**	206-762-0400	37
King Engineering Corp			
3201 S State St ....Ann Arbor MI 48106	**800-242-8871***	734-662-5691	18
*Cust Svc			
King Estate Winery			
80854 Territorial Rd ....Eugene OR 97405	**800-884-4441**	541-942-9874	50-7
King Features Syndicate Inc			
300 W 57th St ....New York NY 10019	**800-708-7311**	212-969-7550	526
King Industries Inc			
1 Science Rd ....Norwalk CT 06852	**800-431-7900**	203-866-5551	145
King Kamehameha's Kona Beach Hotel			
75-5660 Palani Rd ....Kailua-Kona HI 96740	**800-367-2111**	808-329-2911	378
King Koil Licensing Company Inc			
7501 S Quincy St ....Willowbrook IL 60527	**800-525-8331**		469
King Nut Co			
31900 Solon Rd ....Solon OH 44139	**800-860-5464**	440-248-8484	296-28
King of Prussia Mall			
160 N Gulph Rd .... King of Prussia PA 19406	**877-746-6642**	610-265-5727	458
King Pacific Lodge			
4850 Cowley Crescen ....Richmond BC V7E0B5	**855-825-9378**	604-503-5474	378
King Plastic Corp			
1100 N Toledo Blade Blvd ....North Port FL 34288	**800-780-5502**	941-493-5502	604
King Plastics Inc			
840 N Elm St ....Orange CA 92867	**800-363-9822**	714-997-7540	603
King Relocation Services			
13535 Larwin Cir ....Santa Fe Springs CA 90670	**800-854-3679**		516
King Wire Partitions Inc			
6044 N Figueroa St			
PO Box 42220.................Los Angeles CA 90042	**800-789-9608**	323-256-4848	684
King's College			
133 N River St ....Wilkes-Barre PA 18711	**800-955-5777**	570-208-5858	166
King's College Library			
322 Lamar Ave ....Charlotte NC 28204	**800-768-2255**	704-372-0266	166
King's Daughters Medical Ctr			
2201 Lexington Ave ....Ashland KY 41101	**888-377-5362**	606-408-8999	373-3
King's Jewelry & Loan			
800 S Vermont Ave ....Los Angeles CA 90005	**800-378-1111**	213-383-5555	409
King's Material Inc			
650 12th Ave SW ....Cedar Rapids IA 52404	**800-332-5298**	319-363-0233	183
King's University College			
9125 50th St ....Edmonton AB T6B2H3	**800-661-8582**	780-465-3500	780
Kingbridge Centre, The			
12750 Jane St ....King City ON L7B1A3	**800-827-7221**	905-833-3086	376
Kingdom of Morocco, The			
Consulate General			
10 E 40th St ....New York NY 10016	**800-787-8806**	212-758-2625	257
KING-FM 981 (Clas)			
10 Harrison St Ste 100.................Seattle WA 98109	**888-598-9810**	206-691-2981	641-98
Kingman Regional Medical Ctr (KRMC)			
3269 Stockton Hill Rd ....Kingman AZ 86409	**877-757-2101**	928-757-2101	373-3
Kings Credit Services			
510 N Douty St ....Hanford CA 93230	**800-366-0950**	559-587-4200	160
Kings Super Markets Inc			
700 Lanidex Plz ....Parsippany NJ 07054	**800-325-4647**		297-8
Kingsboro Psychiatric Ctr			
681 Clarkson Ave ....Brooklyn NY 11203	**800-597-8481**		373-5
Kingsbury Inc			
10385 Drummond Rd ....Philadelphia PA 19154	**866-581-5464***	215-824-4000	616
*Sales			
Kingsdale Capital Markets Inc			
130 King St W Ste 2950			
PO Box 156. .... Toronto ON M5X1C7	**877-373-6007**	416-867-4550	
Kingsdown Inc			
126 W Holt St ....Mebane NC 27302	**800-354-5464***	919-563-3531	469
*Cust Svc			
Kingsley Plantation			
11676 Palmetto Ave ....Jacksonville FL 32226	**877-874-2478**	904-251-3537	517
Kingsmill Resort & Spa			
1010 Kingsmill Rd ....Williamsburg VA 23185	**800-832-5665**	757-253-1703	665
Kingsport Convention & Visitors Bureau (KCVB)			
400 Clinchfield St Ste 100 ....Kingsport TN 37660	**800-743-5282**	423-392-8820	206
Kingsport Times-News			
701 Lynn Garden Dr ....Kingsport TN 37660	**800-251-0328**	423-246-8121	528-2

Name / Address	City	State	ZIP	Toll-Free	Phone	Class
Kingston National Bank 2 N Main St PO Box 613	Kingston	OH	45644	**800-337-4562**	740-642-2191	70
Kingston Technology Co 17600 Newhope St	Fountain Valley	CA	92708	**800-835-6575**	714-435-2600	288
Kingsway America Inc (KAI) 150 NW Pt Blvd	Elk Grove Village	IL	60007	**800-232-0631**	847-700-9100	359-4
Kingsway Charities 1119 Commonwealth Ave	Bristol	VA	24201	**800-321-9234**	276-466-3014	48-20
Kingwood College 20000 Kingwood Dr	Kingwood	TX	77339	**800-883-7939**	281-312-1600	162
Kinney Brick Co 100 Prosperity Rd PO Box 1804	Albuquerque	NM	87103	**800-464-4605**	505-877-4550	150
Kinray Inc 152-35 Tenth Ave	Whitestone	NY	11357	**800-854-6729**	718-767-1234	238
Kinross Correctional Facility 16770 S Watertower Dr	Kincheloe	MI	49788	**800-326-4537**	906-495-2282	213
Kinross Gold Corp 25 York St 17th Fl	Toronto	ON	M5J2V5	**866-561-3636**	416-365-5123	500
Kinsbursky Brothers Inc 125 E Commercial	Anaheim	CA	92801	**800-548-8797**	714-738-8516	196
Kinsley & Sons Inc 24 S Church St Ste A *General	Union	MO	63084	**800-468-4428***		408
Kintetsu World Express USA Inc 1 Jericho Plz Ste 100	Jericho	NY	11753	**800-275-4045**	516-933-7100	447
Kinyo Company Inc 14235 Lomitas Ave	La Puente	CA	91746	**800-735-4696**	626-333-3711	173-5
KIOA-FM 933 (Oldies) 1416 Locust St	Des Moines	IA	50309	**877-984-8786**	515-280-1350	641-32
Kiolbassa Provision Co 1325 S Brazos St	San Antonio	TX	78207	**800-456-5465**		
Kiosk Information Systems Inc (KIS) 346 S Arthur Ave *General	Louisville	CO	80027	**800-509-5471***	888-661-1697	610
Kiplinger Agriculture Letter 1729 H St NW	Washington	DC	20006	**800-544-0155**	202-887-6400	527-13
Kirby Agri Inc 500 Running Pump Rd PO Box 6277	Lancaster	PA	17607	**800-745-7524**	717-299-2541	280
Kirby Bldg Systems Inc 124 Kirby Dr	Portland	TN	37148	**800-348-7799**	615-325-4165	105
Kirby Co 1920 W 114th St	Cleveland	OH	44102	**800-437-7170**	216-228-2400	783
Kirby Electric Inc 415 Northgate D	Warrendale	PA	15086	**800-767-3263**	724-772-1800	189-4
Kirby Risk Corp 1815 Sagamore Pkwy N PO Box 5089	Lafayette	IN	47904	**877-641-0929**	765-448-4567	246
Kirkham's Outdoor Products 3125 S State St	Salt Lake City	UT	84115	**800-453-7756**	801-486-4161	707
Kirkland & Ellis LLP 200 E Randolph Dr	Chicago	IL	60601	**800-647-7600**	312-861-2000	427
Kirkland's Inc 5310 Maryland Way *NASDAQ: KIRK*	Brentwood	TN	37027	**877-541-4855**		361
Kirkridge Retreat & Study Ctr 2495 Fox Gap Rd	Bangor	PA	18013	**800-231-2222**	610-588-1793	669
Kirkwood Bank & Trust Co 2911 N 14th St	Bismarck	ND	58503	**800-492-4955**	701-258-6550	70
Kirkwood Community College 6301 Kirkwood Blvd SW	Cedar Rapids	IA	52404	**800-332-2055**	319-398-5411	162
Kirkwood Library 6000 Kirkwood Hwy	Wilmington	DE	19808	**888-352-7722**	302-995-7663	433-3
KIRO-FM 973 1820 Eastlake Ave E	Seattle	WA	98102	**800-756-5476**	206-726-7000	641-98
Kirr Marbach & Co Investment Management 621 Washington St	Columbus	IN	47201	**800-808-9444**	812-376-9444	400
Kirtland Air Force Base 2000 Wyoming Blvd SE Ste A-1	Kirtland AFB	NM	87117	**877-246-1453**	505-846-5991	495-1
Kirtland Community College 10775 N St Helen Rd	Roscommon	MI	48653	**866-632-9992**	989-275-5000	162
Kirtley Technology Corp 8328 Lemont Rd	Darien	IL	60561	**888-757-0778**	630-512-0213	225
Kirwan Surgical Products Inc 180 Enterprise Dr	Marshfield	MA	02050	**888-547-9267**	781-834-9500	474
KIS (Kiosk Information Systems Inc) 346 S Arthur Ave *General	Louisville	CO	80027	**800-509-5471***	888-661-1697	610
KIS (Knowledge Information Solutions Inc) 2877 Guardian Ln Ste 201	Virginia Beach	VA	23452	**877-547-7248**	757-463-3232	179
Kish Bancorp Inc 4255 E Main St PO Box 917 *OTC: KISB*	Belleville	PA	17004	**888-554-4748**	717-935-2191	70
Kishwaukee College 21193 Malta Rd	Malta	IL	60150	**888-656-7329**	815-825-2086	162
Kiski School 1888 Brett Ln	Saltsburg	PA	15681	**877-547-5448**	724-639-3586	618
Kiss 999 194 NW 187th St	Miami	FL	33169	**866-954-0999**	305-654-1700	641-65
KISS-FM 995 (Rock) 8122 Datapoint Dr Ste 600	San Antonio	TX	78229	**855-787-2227**	210-615-5400	641-94
Kissimmee Utility Authority Inc (KUA) 1701 W Carroll St	Kissimmee	FL	34741	**877-582-7700**	407-933-7777	782
Kissimmee/Osceola County Chamber of Commerce 1425 E Vine St	Kissimmee	FL	34744	**800-447-8206**	407-847-3174	139
Kistler-Morse Corp 150 Venture Blvd	Spartanburg	SC	29306	**800-426-9010**	864-574-2763	201
Kistner Concrete Products Inc 8713 Read Rd	East Pembroke	NY	14056	**800-809-2801**	585-762-8216	183
KISU-TV Ch 10 (PBS) 921 S Eighth Ave Stop 8111	Pocatello	ID	83209	**800-543-6868**	208-282-2857	736-58
KIT HomeBuilders West LLC 1124 Garber St	Caldwell	ID	83605	**800-859-0347**	208-454-5000	106
Kitano New York 66 Park Ave E 38th St	New York	NY	10016	**800-548-2666**	212-885-7000	378
Kitchen Academy 6370 W Sunset Blvd	Hollywood	CA	90028	**866-548-2223**		163

Name / Address	City	State	ZIP	Toll-Free	Phone	Class
Kitchen Collection Inc 71 E Water St *General	Chillicothe	OH	45601	**888-548-2651***	740-773-9150	361
Kitchen Craft Cookware 4129 United Ave	Mount Dora	FL	32757	**800-800-2850**	352-483-7600	
Kitchen Tune-Up 813 Cir Dr	Aberdeen	SD	57401	**800-333-6385**	605-225-4049	189-11
KitchenAid Div 553 Benson Rd	Benton Harbor	MI	49022	**800-422-1230**		37
KITCO Fiber Optics Inc 5269 Cleveland St	Virginia Beach	VA	23462	**866-643-5220**	757-518-8100	606
Kite Realty Group Trust 30 S Meridian St Ste 1100 *NYSE: KRG*	Indianapolis	IN	46204	**888-577-5600**	317-577-5600	650
Kitsap Regional Library 1301 Sylvan Way	Bremerton	WA	98310	**877-883-9900**	360-405-9100	433-3
Kittery Trading Post 301 US 1	Kittery	ME	03904	**888-587-6246**	603-334-1157	157-2
Kittredge Equipment Co Inc 100 Bowles Rd	Agawam	MA	01001	**800-423-7082**	413-304-4100	300
Kitty Askins Hospice Ctr 107 Handley Pk Ct	Goldsboro	NC	27534	**800-692-4442**	919-735-2145	370
Kivort Steel 380 Hudson River Rd	Waterford	NY	12188	**800-462-2616**	518-590-7233	490
Kiwanis International Foundation 3636 Woodview Trace	Indianapolis	IN	46268	**800-549-2647**	317-875-8755	305
Kiwash Electric Co-op Inc 120 W First St PO Box 100	Cordell	OK	73632	**888-832-3362**	580-832-3361	245
Kiwi Ii Construction Inc 28177 Keller Rd	Murrieta	CA	92563	**877-465-4942**	951-301-8975	186
KIZN-FM 923 (Ctry) 1419 West Bannock	Boise	ID	83702	**800-529-5264**	208-336-3670	641-15
KJB Security Products Inc 841-B Fessiers Pkwy	Nashville	TN	37210	**800-590-4272**	615-620-1370	246
KJLA-TV Ch 57 (Ind) 2323 Corinth Ave	Los Angeles	CA	90064	**800-588-5788**	310-943-5288	736-42
KJR-AM 950 (Sports) 645 Elliott Ave W Ste 400	Seattle	WA	98119	**800-829-0950**	206-494-2000	641-98
KJRH-TV Ch 2 (NBC) 3701 S Peoria Ave	Tulsa	OK	74105	**800-727-5574**	918-743-2222	736-81
KJUD-TV Ch 8 (ABC) 2700 E Tudor Rd	Anchorage	AK	99507	**877-304-1313**	907-561-1313	
KKBQ-FM 929 (Ctry) 1990 Post Oak Blvd Ste 2300	Houston	TX	77056	**877-745-6591**	713-963-1200	641-46
KKFI-FM 901 (Var) 3901 Main St Ste 203	Kansas City	MO	64111	**888-931-0901**	816-931-3122	641-53
KKPT-FM 941 2400 Cottondale Ln	Little Rock	AR	72202	**800-844-0094**	501-664-9410	641-56
K&L Freight Management Inc 745 S Rohlwing Rd	Addison	IL	60101	**800-770-9007**	630-607-1500	311
K&L Gates LLP 210 Sixth Ave	Pittsburgh	PA	15222	**800-452-8260**	412-355-6500	427
KL Industries Inc 1790 Sun Dolphin Dr	Muskegon	MI	49444	**800-733-2727**	231-733-2725	706
Klaff's 28 Washington St	South Norwalk	CT	06854	**800-552-3371**	203-866-1603	
Klafter's Inc 216 N Beaver St	New Castle	PA	16101	**800-922-1233**		751
Klamath County 305 Main St	Klamath Falls	OR	97601	**800-377-6094**	541-883-5134	337
KLAQ-FM 955 (Rock) 4180 N Mesa St	El Paso	TX	79902	**844-305-6210**	915-880-4955	641-34
Klass Ingredients Inc 3885 N Buffalo St	Orchard Park	NY	14127	**800-662-6577**	716-662-6665	344
KLAT-AM 1010 (Span N/T) 5100 SW Fwy	Houston	TX	77056	**800-646-6779**	713-961-1029	641-46
KLA-Tencor Corp 1 Technology Dr *NASDAQ: KLAC*	Milpitas	CA	95035	**800-600-2829**	408-875-3000	248
KLCA 961 Matley Ln Ste 120	Reno	NV	89502	**855-354-9111**	775-829-1964	641-87
KLCC-FM 897 (NPR) 136 W Eighth Ave	Eugene	OR	97401	**800-922-3682**	541-463-6000	641-36
Klean Industries Inc 700 W Georgia St	Vancouver	BC	V7Y1K8	**866-302-5928**	604-637-9609	
Kleen Test Products Corp 1611 Sunset Rd	Port Washington	WI	53074	**800-634-7328**	262-284-6600	554
Klein & Company Corporate Housing Services Inc 914 Washington Ave	Golden	CO	80401	**800-208-9826**	303-796-2100	210
Klein Electronics Inc 349 N Vinewood St	Escondido	CA	92029	**800-959-2899**	760-781-3220	643
Klein Independent School District 7200 Spring Cypress Rd	Klein	TX	77379	**888-703-0083**	832-249-4000	681
Klein Steel Service 105 Vanguarden Pkwy *Cust Svc	Rochester	NY	14606	**800-477-6789***	585-328-4000	490
Klein Tools Inc 450 Bond St *Cust Svc	Lincolnshire	IL	60069	**800-553-4676***		753
Kleinschmidt Inc 450 Lake Cook Rd	Deerfield	IL	60015	**800-824-2330**	847-945-1000	39
Klemmer & Associates Leaders 1340 Commerce St	Petaluma	CA	94954	**800-577-5447**	707-559-7722	461
KLFC-FM 881 205 W Atlantic St	Branson	MO	65616	**877-410-8592**	417-334-5532	641-17
KLH Audio Speakers 984 Logan St Ste 301	Noblesville	IN	46060	**833-554-8326**		
Kliklok-Woodman 5224 Snapfinger Woods Dr	Decatur	GA	30035	**800-621-4170**	770-981-5200	543
Kline & Company Inc 35 Waterview Blvd Ste 305	Parsippany	NJ	07054	**800-290-5214**	973-435-6262	194
Kline & Specter PC 1525 Locust St	Philadelphia	PA	19102	**800-243-1100**	215-772-1000	427
Klingelhofer Corp 165 Mill Ln	Mountainside	NJ	07092	**800-879-5546**	908-232-7200	453
Klipsch LLC 137 Hempstead 278	Hope	AR	71801	**888-250-8561**		52

Company	Address	City	State	Zip	Toll-Free	Phone	Class
KLJ Computer Solutions Inc	PO Box 2040	Fall River	NS	B2T1K6	**888-455-5669**	902-425-7010	179
KLJC-FM 885	8717 W 110th St Ste 480	Overland Park	KS	66210	**855-474-8850**	913-451-8850	
KLLM Inc	135 Riverview Dr	Richland	MS	39218	**800-925-5556**	800-925-1000	775
Klochko Equipment Rental Company Inc	2782 Corbin Ave	Melvindale	MI	48122	**800-783-7368**	313-386-7220	264-3
Kloppenberg & Co	2627 W Oxford Ave	Englewood	CO	80110	**800-346-3246**	303-761-1615	660
KLOS-FM 955 (CR)	3321 S La Cienega Blvd	Los Angeles	CA	90016	**800-955-5567**	310-840-4828	641-57
Klosterman Baking Company Inc	4760 Paddock Rd	Cincinnati	OH	45229	**877-301-1004**	513-242-1004	296-1
KLPB-TV Ch 24 (PBS)	7733 Perkins Rd	Baton Rouge	LA	70810	**800-272-8161**	225-767-5660	736-8
KLRN-TV Ch 9 (PBS)	501 Broadway St	San Antonio	TX	78215	**800-627-8193**	210-270-9000	736-67
KLRU-TV Ch 18 (PBS)	2504-B Whitis Ave PO Box 7158	Austin	TX	78712	**800-239-5233**	512-471-4811	736-6
Kluane National Park & Reserve of Canada	PO Box 5495	Haines Junction	YT	Y0B1L0	**877-852-3100**	867-634-7250	559
Kl ber Lubrication NA LP	32 Industrial Dr	Londonderry	NH	03053	**800-447-2238**	603-647-4104	537
KM Fabrics Inc	2 Waco St	Greenville	SC	29611	**800-845-1896**	864-295-2550	740-1
K&M Tire Inc	965 Spencerville Rd PO Box 279	Delphos	OH	45833	**877-879-5407**	419-695-1061	749
KMA One	6815 Meadowridge Ct	Alpharetta	GA	30005	**888-500-2536**	770-886-4000	365
K-Mac Enterprises Inc	PO Box 6538	Fort Smith	AR	72906	**800-947-9277**	479-646-2053	666
KMAJ-AM 1440	825 S Kansas Ave Ste 100	Topeka	KS	66612	**877-297-1077**	785-272-2122	641-111
KMAJ-FM 1077 (AC)	825 S Kansas Ave Ste 100	Topeka	KS	66612	**877-297-1077**	785-272-2122	641-111
KMAX-TV Ch 31 (CBS)	2713 Kovr Dr	West Sacramento	CA	95605	**800-374-8813**	916-374-1313	736
KMC (Kickhaefer Mfg Co)	1221 S Park St, PO Box 348	Port Washington	WI	53074	**800-822-6080**	262-377-5030	486
KMC Controls Inc	19476 Industrial Dr	New Paris	IN	46553	**877-444-5622**	574-831-5250	202
KMI Diagnostics Inc	8201 Central Ave NE Ste P	Minneapolis	MN	55432	**888-564-3424**	763-231-3313	231
KMIZ-TV Ch 17 (ABC)	501 Business Loop 70 E	Columbia	MO	65201	**800-345-4109**	573-449-0917	736
KMJ-AM 580 (N/T)	1071 W Shaw Ave	Fresno	CA	93711	**800-776-5858**	559-490-5800	641-40
KMJ-FM 1059	1071 W Shaw Ave	Fresno	CA	93711	**800-491-1899**	559-490-5800	641-40
KMLO-FM 1007 (Ctry)	214 W Pleasant Dr PO Box 1197	Pierre	SD	57501	**800-658-5439**	605-224-8686	641-82
KMOD-FM 975 (Rock)	7136 S Yale Ave Ste 500	Tulsa	OK	74136	**844-289-7234**	918-388-5100	
KMOS-TV Ch 6 (PBS)	University of Central Missouri	Warrensburg	MO	64093	**800-753-3436**		736
KMPH-TV Ch 26 (Fox)	5111 E McKinley Ave	Fresno	CA	93727	**800-101-2045**	559-453-8850	736-30
KMW Ltd	PO Box 327	Sterling	KS	67579	**800-445-7388**	620-278-3641	273
Knaack Manufacturing Co	420 E Terra Cotta Ave	Crystal Lake	IL	60014	**800-456-7865**		486
Knape & Vogt Manufacturing Co	2700 Oak Industrial Dr NE	Grand Rapids	MI	49505	**800-253-1561**		349
Knappen Milling Co	110 S Water St	Augusta	MI	49012	**800-562-7736**	269-731-4141	296-23
Knauf Insulation	1 Knauf Dr	Shelbyville	IN	46176	**800-825-4434**	317-398-4434	388
KNAU-FM 887 (NPR)	PO Box 5764	Flagstaff	AZ	86011	**800-523-5628**	928-523-5628	641-38
KNBA-FM 903 (NPR)	3600 San Geronimo Dr Ste 480	Anchorage	AK	99508	**800-996-2848**	907-793-3500	641-6
KNDR-FM 1047 (Rel)	1400 NE Third St PO Box 516	Mandan	ND	58554	**800-767-5095**	701-663-2345	641
Knichel Logistics LP	5347 William Flynn Hwy 2nd Fl	Gibsonia	PA	15044	**888-386-7450**	724-449-3300	311
Knife River Corp	3303 Rock Island Pl	Bismarck	ND	58504	**800-982-5339**	701-530-1380	135
Knight Dental Group	3659 Tampa Rd	Oldsmar	FL	34677	**800-359-2043**	813-854-3333	414
Knight Electronics Inc	10557 Metric Dr	Dallas	TX	75243	**800-323-2439**	214-340-0265	194
Knight Publishing Co	600 S Tryon St	Charlotte	NC	28202	**800-332-0686**	704-358-5000	633-8
Knight Rifles	213 Dennis st Athens	Athens	TN	37303	**866-518-4181**		284
Knight Security Systems LLC	10105 Technology Blvd W Ste 100	Dallas	TX	75220	**800-642-1632**	214-350-1632	689
Knight Transportation Inc	5601 W Buckeye Rd (*NYSE: KNX*)	Phoenix	AZ	85043	**800-489-2000**	602-269-2000	775
Knights of Columbus	1 Columbus Plz	New Haven	CT	06510	**800-380-9995*** (*Cust Svc)	203-752-4000	48-15
Knippelmier Chevrolet Inc	1811 E Hwy 62 E	Blanchard	OK	73010	**877-644-7255**		57
KNIS-FM 913 (Rel)	PO Box 21888	Carson City	NV	89721	**800-541-5647**	775-883-5647	641-87
Knit Rite Inc	120 Osage Ave	Kansas City	KS	66105	**800-821-3094**	913-281-4600	474
KNME-TV Ch 5 (PBS)	1130 University Blvd NE, University of New Mexico	Albuquerque	NM	87102	**800-328-5663**	505-277-2121	736-1
KNML-AM 610 (Sports)	500 Fourth St NW 5th Fl	Albuquerque	NM	87102	**888-922-0610**	505-767-6700	641-4
Knob Hill Inn	960 N Main St PO Box 1327	Ketchum	ID	83340	**800-526-8010**	208-726-8010	378
Knockout Pest Control Inc	1009 Front St	Uniondale	NY	11553	**800-244-7378**		573
Knoebels Amusement Resort	391 Knoebels Blvd	Elysburg	PA	17824	**800-487-4386**	570-672-2572	32
Knoll Inc	1235 Water St (*NYSE: KNL* ■ *Cust Svc)	East Greenville	PA	18041	**800-343-5665***		319-1
Knollwood	6200 Oregon Ave NW	Washington	DC	20015	**800-541-4255**	202-541-0400	668
Knopp Inc	1307 66th St	Emeryville	CA	94608	**800-227-1848**	510-653-1661	248
Knorr Beeswax Products Inc	14906 Via De La Valle	Del Mar	CA	92014	**800-807-2337**	760-431-2007	122
Knott's Berry Farm	8039 Beach Blvd	Buena Park	CA	90620	**800-742-6427**	714-220-5200	32
Knott's Berry Farm Resort	7675 Crescent Ave	Buena Park	CA	90620	**866-752-2444**	714-995-1111	665
Know Before You Go Reservations	8000 International Dr	Orlando	FL	32819	**800-749-1993**		375
Knowledge Anywhere Inc	3015 112th Ave NE #210	Bellevue	WA	98004	**800-850-2025**		
Knowledge Information Solutions Inc (KIS)	2877 Guardian Ln Ste 201	Virginia Beach	VA	23452	**877-547-7248**	757-463-3232	179
Knox County	200 S Cherry St	Galesburg	IL	61401	**800-916-3330**	309-343-3121	337
Knox County Convention & Visitors Bureau	107 S Main St	Mount Vernon	OH	43050	**800-837-5282**	740-392-6102	206
Knox McLaughlin Gornall & Sennett PC	120 W Tenth St	Erie	PA	16501	**800-939-9886**	814-459-2800	427
Knox Nursery Inc	940 Avalon Rd	Winter Garden	FL	34787	**800-441-5669**		368
Knox Services	2250 Fourth Ave	San Diego	CA	92101	**800-995-6694**		623
Knoxville Civic Auditorium/Coliseum	500 Howard Baker Jr Ave	Knoxville	TN	37915	**877-995-9961**	865-215-8900	568
Knoxville News-Sentinel	2332 News Sentinel Dr	Knoxville	TN	37921	**800-237-5821**	865-521-8181	528-2
Knoxville Symphony Orchestra	100 S Gay St Ste 302	Knoxville	TN	37902	**800-845-5665**	865-291-3310	569-3
Knoxville Tourism & Sports Corp	301 S Gay St	Knoxville	TN	37902	**800-727-8045**	865-523-7263	206
KNPR-FM 895 (NPR)	1289 S Torrey Pines Dr	Las Vegas	NV	89146	**888-258-9895**	702-258-9895	641-55
KNRK-FM 947 (Alt)	0700 SW Bancroft St	Portland	OR	97239	**800-777-0947**	503-733-5470	641-109
KOA (Kampgrounds of America Inc)	PO Box 30558	Billings	MT	59114	**888-562-0000**		121
KOAT-TV Ch 7 (ABC)	3801 Carlisle Blvd NE	Albuquerque	NM	87107	**877-871-0165**	505-884-7777	736-1
Kobelco Stewart Bolling Inc (KSBI)	1600 Terex Rd	Hudson	OH	44236	**800-464-0064**	330-655-3111	385
Koberg Beach State Recreation Site	725 Summer St NE Ste C	Salem	OR	97301	**800-551-6949**	503-986-0707	561
Kobussen Buses Ltd	W914 County Rd CE	Kaukauna	WI	54130	**800-447-0116**	920-766-0606	109
Koch Brothers	325 Grand Ave	Des Moines	IA	50306	**800-944-5624**	515-283-2451	531
Koch Filter Corp	625 W Hill St	Louisville	KY	40208	**800-757-5624**	502-634-4796	18
Koch Foods Inc	1300 Higgins Rd Ste 100	Park Ridge	IL	60068	**800-837-2778**	847-384-5940	615
Koch Membrane Systems Inc	850 Main St	Wilmington	MA	01887	**888-677-5624**	978-657-4250	385
Koch Specialty Plant Services	12221 E Sam Houston Pkwy N	Houston	TX	77044	**800-765-9177**	713-427-7700	535
KOCO-TV Ch 5 (ABC)	1300 E Britton Rd	Oklahoma City	OK	73131	**800-464-7928**	405-478-3000	736-52
KODA (Kentucky Organ Donor Affiliates)	10160 Linn Station Rd	Louisville	KY	40223	**800-525-3456**	502-581-9511	541
KODS-FM 1037 (Oldies)	961 Matley Ln Ste 120	Reno	NV	89502	**855-354-9111**	775-829-1964	641-87
Koegel Meats Inc	3400 W Bristol Rd	Flint	MI	48507	**800-678-1962**	810-238-3685	296-26
Koehler Lighting Products	380 Stewart Rd	Hanover Township	PA	18706	**800-788-1696*** (*Cust Svc)	570-825-1900	438
Koerner Distributors Inc	1601 Pike Ave	Effingham	IL	62401	**800-475-5162**		
Koeze Co	PO Box 9470	Grand Rapids	MI	49509	**800-555-9688**		296-8
Koger/Air Corp	PO Box 2098	Martinsville	VA	24113	**800-368-2096**	276-638-8821	151
Kohl & Frisch Ltd	7622 Keele St	Concord	ON	L4K2R5	**800-265-2520**		231
Kohl's Corp	N 56 W 17000 Ridgewood Dr (*NYSE: KSS*)	Menomonee Falls	WI	53051	**855-564-5705**	262-703-7000	229
Kohler Canada Company Hytec Plumbing Products Div	4150 Spallumcheen Dr	Armstrong	BC	V0E1B6	**800-871-8311**	250-546-3067	606
Kohler Co Inc	444 Highland Dr	Kohler	WI	53044	**800-456-4537**	920-457-4441	185
Kohler Engines	444 Highland Dr	Kohler	WI	53044	**800-544-2444**	920-457-4441	262
Kohler Waters Spa	444 Highland Dr	Kohler	WI	53044	**800-344-2838**		703
KOI Auto Parts	2701 Spring Grove Ave	Cincinnati	OH	45225	**800-354-0408**	513-357-2400	54
Koike Aronson Inc	635 W Main St PO Box 307	Arcade	NY	14009	**800-252-5232**	585-492-2400	453
Kois Bros Equipment Company Inc	5200 Colorado Blvd	Commerce	CO	80022	**800-672-6010**	303-298-7370	385
Kokomo Opalescent Glass Co	1310 S Market St	Kokomo	IN	46902	**877-475-6329**	765-457-8136	329
Kokomo Tribune (KT)	300 N Union St PO Box 9014	Kokomo	IN	46901	**800-382-0696**	765-459-3121	528-2
Kokomo-Howard County Public Library	220 N Union St	Kokomo	IN	46901	**800-837-0971**	765-457-3242	433-3

	Toll-Free	Phone	Class
Kokosing Construction Company Inc			
17531 Waterford Rd			
PO Box 226 . . . . Fredericktown OH 43019	800-800-6315	740-694-6315	188-4
Kokusai Semiconductor Equipment Corp			
2460 N First St Ste 290 . . . . San Jose CA 95131	800-800-5321	408-456-2750	691
Kolcraft Enterprises Inc			
10832 NC Hwy 211 E . . . . Aberdeen NC 28315	800-453-7673*	910-944-9345	469
*Cust Svc			
Kolene Corp			
12890 Westwood Ave . . . . Detroit MI 48223	800-521-4182	313-273-9220	145
Kolkhorst Petroleum Co			
1685 E Washington . . . . Navasota TX 77868	800-548-6671	936-825-6868	316
KOLN-TV Ch 10 (CBS)			
840 N 40th . . . . Lincoln NE 68503	800-475-1011	402-467-4321	736-41
Kolosso Toyota			
3000 W Wisconsin Ave . . . . Appleton WI 54914	877-756-2297	920-738-3666	57
Kolpak			
2915 Tennessee Ave N . . . . Parsons TN 38363	800-826-7036	731-847-5328	660
Kolpin Powersports			
9955 59th Ave N . . . . Plymouth MN 55442	877-956-5746	920-928-3118	706
Kombi			
5711 Ferrier St . . . . Montreal QC H4P1N3	800-203-0695	514-341-4321	
Komet Of America Inc			
2050 Mitchell Blvd . . . . Schaumburg IL 60193	800-865-6638	800-656-6381	617
Komline-Sanderson Engineering Corp			
12 Holland Ave . . . . Peapack NJ 07977	800-225-5457	908-234-1000	385
Komo Machine Inc			
1 Komo Dr . . . . Lakewood NJ 08701	800-255-5670	732-719-6222	679
KOMU-TV Ch 8 (NBC)			
5550 Hwy 63 S . . . . Columbia MO 65201	800-286-3932	573-884-6397	736
Kona International Airport			
73-200 Kupipi St . . . . Kailua-Kona HI 96740	800-321-3712	808-327-9520	27
Kona Kai Resort			
1551 Shelter Island Dr . . . . San Diego CA 92106	800-566-2524	619-221-8000	378
Konecranes America			
7300 Chippewa Blvd . . . . Houston TX 77086	800-231-0241	281-445-2225	468
Koneta Inc			
1400 Lunar Dr . . . . Wapakoneta OH 45895	800-331-0775	419-739-4200	672
KONI North America			
1961-A International Way . . . . Hebron KY 41048	800-965-5664	859-586-4100	60
Konop Cos			
1725 Industrial Dr . . . . Green Bay WI 54302	800-770-0477	920-468-8517	296-34
Konsyl Pharmaceuticals Inc			
8050 Industrial Park Rd . . . . Easton MD 21601	800-356-6795	410-822-5192	578
Kontiki Beach Resort			
2290 N Fulton Beach Rd . . . . Rockport TX 78382	800-388-0649	361-729-2318	377
Kontron S&T AG			
7631 Anagram Dr . . . . Eden Prairie MN 55344	888-343-5396	952-974-7000	173-2
KOOL 1055			
3071 Continental Dr . . . . West Palm Beach FL 33407	888-415-1055	561-616-6600	641-115
Koonce Securities Inc			
6550 Rock Spring Dr Ste 600 . . . . Bethesda MD 20817	800-368-2806	301-897-9700	400
Koontz-Wagner Electric Company Inc			
3801 Voorde Dr . . . . South Bend IN 46628	800-345-2051	574-232-2051	189-4
Koopman Lumber Company Inc			
665 Church St . . . . Whitinsville MA 01588	800-836-4545	508-234-4545	747
Kootenai County			
451 N Government Way . . . . Coeur d'Alene ID 83814	800-325-7940	208-446-1000	337
Kootenai Electric Co-op Inc			
2451 West Dakota Ave . . . . Hayden ID 83835	800-240-0459	208-765-1200	245
Kootenay Savings Credit Union			
1199 Cedar Ave . . . . Trail BC V1R4B8	800-665-5728		
Kop-Coat Inc			
3040 William Pitt Way . . . . Pittsburgh PA 15238	800-221-4466	412-227-2700	546
Kopf Builders Inc			
420 Avon Belden Rd . . . . Avon Lake OH 44012	888-933-5673	440-933-6908	187
KOPN-FM 895 (Var)			
915 E Broadway . . . . Columbia MO 65201	800-895-5676	573-874-1139	641
Koppers Inc			
436 Seventh Ave . . . . Pittsburgh PA 15219	800-385-4406	412-227-2001	813
NYSE: KOP			
KOR Water Inc			
95 Enterprise Ste 310 . . . . Aliso Viejo CA 92656	877-708-7567	714-708-7567	124
Koral Industries Inc			
1504 S Kaufman St . . . . Ennis TX 75119	800-627-2441	972-875-6555	374
Kordes Retreat Ctr			
802 E Tenth St . . . . Ferdinand IN 47532	800-880-2777	812-367-2777	669
Korean Air			
6101 W Imperial Hwy . . . . Los Angeles CA 90045	800-438-5000	310-417-5200	25
Korey Kay & Partners			
130 Fifth Ave . . . . New York NY 10011	800-264-8590	212-620-4300	4
Kor-it Inc			
1964 Auburn Blvd . . . . Sacramento CA 95815	888-727-4560		190
Korn/Ferry International			
1900 Ave of the Stars			
Ste 2600 . . . . Los Angeles CA 90067	877-345-3610	310-552-1834	266
NYSE: KFY			
Korney Board Aids Sporting			
312 Harrison Ave . . . . Roxton TX 75477	800-842-7772	903-346-3269	707
Kornylak Corp			
400 Heaton St . . . . Hamilton OH 45011	800-837-5676	513-863-1277	468
Kosciusko County			
100 W Center St . . . . Warsaw IN 46580	800-840-8757	574-372-2331	337
Kosciusko Rural Electric Membership Corp (REMC)			
370 S 250 E . . . . Warsaw IN 46582	800-790-7362	574-267-6331	245
Kosco 2926 Rt 32 N . . . . Saugerties NY 12477	800-755-6726	845-247-2200	316
Koshin America Corp			
1218 Remington Rd . . . . Schaumburg IL 60173	800-634-4092	847-884-1570	637
Koss Corp			
4129 N Port Washington Ave . . . . Milwaukee WI 53212	800-872-5677		52
NASDAQ: KOSS			
Koss Industrial Inc			
1943 Commercial Way . . . . Green Bay WI 54311	800-844-6261	920-469-5300	296
Kotler Marketing Group			
3509 Connecticut Ave			
Ste 1175 . . . . Washington DC 20008	800-331-9110	202-331-0555	
Kotter International			
5 Bennett St . . . . Cambridge MA 02138	855-400-4712	617-600-6787	461
Kovack Securities Inc			
6451 N Federal Hwy # 1201			
Ste 1201 . . . . Fort Lauderdale FL 33308	800-711-4078	954-782-4771	686
Kovasys Inc			
2550 Argentia Rd Ste 220 . . . . Mississauga ON L5N5R1	888-568-2747	416-800-4286	260
Koza Inc			
2910 S Main St . . . . Pearland TX 77581	800-594-5555	281-485-1462	623
KOZK-TV Ch 21 (PBS)			
901 S National Ave . . . . Springfield MO 65897	866-684-5695	417-836-3500	736-75
Kozy Heat Fireplace			
204 Industrial Park Dr . . . . Lakefield MN 56150	844-395-0405		
KP Tissue Inc			
1900 Minnesota Ct Ste 200 . . . . Mississauga ON L5N5R5	866-600-5869	905-812-6900	
KPAZ-TV Ch 21 (TBN)			
3551 E McDowell Rd . . . . Phoenix AZ 85008	800-447-7235	602-273-1477	736-56
KPBS Public Broadcasting			
5200 Campanile Dr . . . . San Diego CA 92182	888-399-5727	619-265-6438	641-95
KPBS-TV Ch 15 (PBS)			
5200 Campanile Dr . . . . San Diego CA 92182	888-399-5727	619-594-1515	736-68
KPDQ-FM 939 (Rel)			
6400 SE Lake Rd Ste 350 . . . . Portland OR 97222	800-845-2162	503-786-0600	641-109
KPDX-TV Ch 49 (MNT)			
14975 NW Greenbrier Pkwy . . . . Beaverton OR 97006	866-906-1249	503-906-1249	736
KPIG-FM 1075 (AAA)			
1110 Main St Ste 16 . . . . Watsonville CA 95076	877-744-5273	831-722-9000	
KPLO-FM 945 (Ctry)			
214 W Pleasant Dr . . . . Pierre SD 57501	800-658-5439*	605-224-8686	641-82
*General			
KPLZ-FM 1015 (AC)			
140 Fourth Ave N Ste 340 . . . . Seattle WA 98109	888-821-1015	206-404-4000	641-98
KPTS-TV Ch 8 (PBS)			
320 W 21 St . . . . Wichita KS 67203	800-794-8498	316-838-3090	736-84
KPTV-TV Ch 12 (Fox)			
14975 NW Greenbrier Pkwy . . . . Beaverton OR 97006	866-906-1249	503-906-1249	736
KPXE-TV Ch 50 (I)			
4220 Shawnee Mission Pkwy			
Ste 110 B . . . . Fairway KS 66205	888-467-2988	212-757-3100	736
KPXR-TV Ch 47			
1957 Blairs Ferry Rd NE . . . . . . Cedar Rapids IA 52402	888-467-2988		
KQC (Kilwins Quality Confections Inc)			
1050 Bay View Rd . . . . Petoskey MI 49770	888-454-5946		123
KQED-FM 885 (NPR)			
2601 Mariposa St . . . . San Francisco CA 94110	800-723-3566	415-864-2000	641-96
KQED-TV Ch 9 (PBS)			
2601 Mariposa St . . . . San Francisco CA 94110	866-573-3123	415-864-2000	736-69
Kraft Chemical Co			
1975 N Hawthorne Ave . . . . Melrose Park IL 60160	800-345-5200	708-345-5200	146
Kraft Fluid Systems Inc			
14300 Foltz Pkwy . . . . Strongsville OH 44149	800-257-1155	440-238-5545	637
Kraft Heinz Co			
200 E Randolph St . . . . Chicago IL 60601	800-543-5335		296-5
NASDAQ: KHC			
Kraft Power Corp			
199 Wildwood Ave . . . . Woburn MA 01801	800-969-6121	781-938-9100	515
Kraftmaid Cabinetry Inc			
15535 S State Ave			
PO Box 1055 . . . . Middlefield OH 44062	888-562-7744		115
Kraftware Corp			
270 Cox St . . . . Roselle NJ 07203	800-221-1728*		603
*Cust Svc			
Krannert Ctr for the Performing Arts			
500 S Goodwin Ave . . . . Urbana IL 61801	800-527-2849	217-333-6700	568
KRCC-FM 915 (NPR)			
912 N Weber St . . . . Colorado Springs CO 80903	800-748-2727	719-473-4801	641-26
KRCG-TV Ch 13 (CBS)			
10188 Old Hwy 54 N . . . . New Bloomfield MO 65063	800-773-6180	573-896-5144	736
KRCR News Channel			
755 Auditorium Dr . . . . Redding CA 96001	800-222-5727	530-243-7777	737
Kreamer Feed Inc			
PO Box 38 . . . . Kreamer PA 17833	800-767-4537	570-374-8148	276
Kreative Carriers Transportation & Logistic Services			
61 Bluewater Rd . . . . Bedford NS B4B1G8	888-274-2444		314
Kreher Steel Company LLC			
1550 N 25th Ave . . . . Melrose Park IL 60160	800-323-0745		490
Krehling Industries Inc			
1399 Hagy Way . . . . Harrisburg PA 17110	800-839-1654	717-232-7936	182
Kreider Farms			
1461 Lancaster Rd . . . . Manheim PA 17545	888-665-4415	717-665-4415	10-2
Kreinik Manufacturing Company Inc			
1708 Gihon Rd . . . . Parkersburg WV 26101	800-537-2166	304-422-8900	707
KREM-TV			
4103 S Regal St . . . . Spokane WA 99223	888-404-3922	509-448-2000	736-74
KREM-TV Ch 2 (CBS)			
4103 S Regal St . . . . Spokane WA 99223	888-404-3922	509-448-2000	736-74
Kress Employment Screening			
320 Westcott St Ste 108 . . . . Houston TX 77007	888-636-3693	713-880-3693	631
Krieger Specialty Products Co			
4880 Gregg Rd . . . . Pico Rivera CA 90660	866-203-5060	562-695-0645	234
Kripalu Ctr for Yoga & Health			
57 Interlaken Rd . . . . Stockbridge MA 01262	800-741-7353	413-448-3400	702
Krispy Kreme Doughnuts Corp			
PO Box 83 . . . . Winston-Salem NC 27102	800-457-4779	336-725-2981	68
NYSE: KKD			
Krist Oil Co			
303 Selden Rd . . . . Iron River MI 49935	800-722-6691	906-265-6144	344
Krm Information Services Inc			
200 Spring St . . . . Eau Claire WI 54703	800-775-7654		242
KRMA-TV Ch 6 (PBS)			
1089 Bannock St . . . . Denver CO 80204	800-274-6666	303-892-6666	736-23
KRMC (Kingman Regional Medical Ctr)			
3269 Stockton Hill Rd . . . . Kingman AZ 86409	877-757-2101	928-757-2101	373-3
KRMG-AM 740 (N/T)			
7136 S Yale Ave Ste 500 . . . . Tulsa OK 74136	855-297-9696	918-493-7400	641-112
Kroger Co			
1014 Vine St . . . . Cincinnati OH 45202	800-576-4377	513-762-4000	344
NYSE: KR			
Krohn Industries Inc			
PO Box 98 . . . . Carlstadt NJ 07072	800-526-6299	201-933-9696	406

Name / Address	City	State	Zip	Toll-Free	Phone	Class
Kroll Background America Inc 100 Centerview Dr Ste 300	Nashville	TN	37214	**800-697-7189**	615-320-9800	631
Kroll Inc 600 Third Ave	New York	NY	10016	**800-675-3772**	212-593-1000	194
Kroll Ontrack Inc 9023 Columbine Rd	Eden Prairie	MN	55347	**800-872-2599**	952-937-5161	178-12
Krones Inc 9600 S 58th St PO Box 321801	Franklin	WI	53132	**800-752-3787**	414-409-4000	543
Kronos Inc 297 Billerica Rd	Chelmsford	MA	01824	**888-293-5549**	978-250-9800	178-11
Kronos Products Inc 1 Kronos Dr	Glendale Heights	IL	60139	**800-621-0099**	224-353-5353	296-26
Kropp Equipment Inc 1020 Kennedy Ave	Schererville	IN	46375	**866-402-2222**		23
KROQ-FM 1067 (Alt) 5901 Venice Blvd	Los Angeles	CA	90034	**800-520-1067**	323-930-1067	641-57
Kroy LLC 3830 Kelley Ave *Cust Svc	Cleveland	OH	44114	**888-888-5769***	216-426-5600	173-6
KRTH-FM 1011 (Oldies) 5670 Wilshire Blvd Ste 200	Los Angeles	CA	90036	**800-232-5784**	323-936-5784	641-57
KRTR-FM 963 (AC) 900 Ft St Ste 700	Honolulu	HI	96813	**800-669-1010**	808-275-1000	641-45
Kruepke Trucking Inc 2881 Hwy P *Cust Svc	Jackson	WI	53037	**800-798-5000***	262-677-3155	775
Kruger Street Toy & Train Museum 144 Kruger St	Wheeling	WV	26003	**877-242-8133**	304-242-8133	517
Kruse Adhesive Tape Inc 1610 E McFadden Ave	Santa Ana	CA	92705	**800-992-7702**	714-640-2130	727
Kryptonite Kollectibles 1441 Plainfield Ave	Janesville	WI	53545	**877-646-1728**	608-758-2100	786
KSA Engineers Inc 140 E Tyler St Ste 600	Longview	TX	75601	**877-572-3647**	903-236-7700	261
KSAB-FM 501 Tupper Ln	Corpus Christi	TX	78417	**844-289-7234**	360-289-0111	
KSAN-FM 1077 (Alt) 750 Battery St Ste300	San Francisco	CA	94111	**888-303-2663**	415-995-6800	641-96
KSAZ-TV Ch 10 (Fox) 511 W Adams St	Phoenix	AZ	85003	**888-369-4762**	602-257-1234	736-56
KSBI (Kobelco Stewart Bolling Inc) 1600 Terex Rd	Hudson	OH	44236	**800-464-0064**	330-655-3111	385
KSFY Television 325 S First Ave Ste 100	Sioux Falls	SD	57104	**800-955-5739**	605-336-1300	
KSGN-FM 897 (Rel) 2048 Orange Tree Ln Ste 200	Redlands	CA	92374	**888-897-5746**	909-583-2150	641-86
KSKA-FM 911 3877 University Dr	Anchorage	AK	99508	**800-478-8255**	907-550-8400	641-6
KSKS-FM 937 (Ctry) 1071 W Shaw Ave	Fresno	CA	93711	**800-767-5477**	559-490-5800	641-40
KSLA-TV Ch 12 (CBS) 1812 Fairfield Ave	Shreveport	LA	71101	**800-444-5752**	318-222-1212	736-71
KSMQ-TV Ch 15 (PBS) 2000 Eigth Ave NW	Austin	MN	55912	**800-658-2539**	507-481-2095	736
KSMS-FM 905 (NPR) Missouri State University 901 S National	Springfield	MO	65897	**800-767-5768**	417-836-5878	641-103
KSMU-FM 911 (NPR) 901 S National	Springfield	MO	65897	**800-767-5768**	417-836-5878	641-103
KSNW-TV 833 N Main St	Wichita	KS	67203	**800-432-3924**	316-265-3333	736-84
KSPS Public TV 3911 S Regal St	Spokane	WA	99223	**800-735-2377**	509-443-7800	736-74
KSTP-TV Ch 5 (ABC) 3415 University Ave W	Saint Paul	MN	55114	**800-895-1999**	651-646-5555	736-46
KSTX-FM 891 (NPR) 8401 Datapoint Dr Ste 800	San Antonio	TX	78229	**800-622-8977**	210-614-8977	641-94
K-Systems Inc 2104 Aspen Dr	Mechanicsburg	PA	17055	**800-221-0204**	717-795-7711	178-1
KT (Kokomo Tribune) 300 N Union St PO Box 9014	Kokomo	IN	46901	**800-382-0696**	765-459-3121	528-2
Kta-Tator Inc 115 Technology Dr	Pittsburgh	PA	15275	**800-582-4243**	412-788-1300	261
KTBY-TV Ch 4 (Fox) 2700 E Tudor Rd	Anchorage	AK	99507	**877-304-1313**	907-561-1313	736-2
KTC (Kaplel) 220 N Cushing Ave	Kaplan	LA	70548	**866-643-7171**	337-643-7171	731
KTIK-AM 1350 (Sports) 1419 W Bannock St	Boise	ID	83702	**866-296-1350**	208-336-3670	641-15
KTKZ - AM 1380 The Answer 1425 River Pk Dr Ste 520	Sacramento	CA	95815	**888-923-1380**	916-924-9435	641-91
KTRS-AM 550 (N/T) 638 Westport Plz	Saint Louis	MO	63146	**888-550-5877**	314-453-5500	641-92
KTSD-FM 911 (NPR) 555 N Dakota St PO Box 5000	Vermillion	SD	57069	**800-456-0766**	605-677-5861	641
KTSD-TV Ch 10 (PBS) 555 N Dakota St PO Box 5000	Vermillion	SD	57069	**800-333-0789**		736
KTTC-TV Ch 10 (NBC) 6301 Bandel Rd NW	Rochester	MN	55901	**800-288-1656**	507-288-4444	736-62
K-Tube Technologies 13400 Kirkham Way	Poway	CA	92064	**800-394-0058**	858-513-9229	475
KTVB-TV Ch 7 (NBC) 5407 Fairview	Boise	ID	83706	**800-537-8939**	208-375-7277	736-11
KTVQ-TV Ch 2 (CBS) 3203 Third Ave N	Billings	MT	59101	**800-908-4490**	406-252-5611	736-9
KTWU-TV Ch 11 (PBS) 1700 College	Topeka	KS	66621	**800-866-5898**	785-670-1111	736-79
KUA (Kissimmee Utility Authority Inc) 1701 W Carroll St	Kissimmee	FL	34741	**877-582-7700**	407-933-7777	782
KUAD-FM 991 (Ctry) 600 Main St	Windsor	CO	80550	**800-500-2599**		641
KUAF 913 Public Radio 9 S School Ave	Fayetteville	AR	72701	**800-522-5823**	479-575-2556	641
Kubin-Nicholson *KN* 8440 N 87th St	Milwaukee	WI	53224	**800-858-9557**	414-586-4300	8
Kubota Tractor Corp 3401 Del Amo Blvd	Torrance	CA	90503	**888-458-2682**	310-370-3370	273
Kubotek USA 2 Mt Royal Ave Ste 500	Marlborough	MA	01752	**800-372-3872**	508-229-2020	178-5
KUBRA Data Transfer Ltd 5050 Tomken Rd	Mississauga	ON	L4W5B1	**800-766-6616**	905-624-2220	177
KUED-TV Ch 7 (PBS) 101 Wasatch Dr Rm 215	Salt Lake City	UT	84112	**800-477-5833**	801-581-7777	736-66
Kugler Co 209 W Third St PO Box 1748	McCook	NE	69001	**800-445-9116**	308-345-2280	276
KUHF-FM 887 (Clas) 4343 Elgin St	Houston	TX	77204	**877-252-0436**	713-748-8888	641-46
Kuhlman Corp 1845 Indian Woods Cir	Maumee	OH	43537	**800-669-3309**	419-897-6000	182
Kuhn Flowers Inc 3802 Beach Blvd	Jacksonville	FL	32207	**800-458-5846**	904-398-8601	292
Kula Hospital 100 Keokea Pl	Kula	HI	96790	**800-845-6733**	808-878-1221	448
Kultur International Films Ltd PO Box 755	Forked River	NJ	08731	**888-329-2580**		510
Kulzer LLC 4315 S Lafayette Blvd	South Bend	IN	46614	**800-431-1785**		
KUMD 1201 Ordean Ct 130 Humanities	Duluth	MN	55812	**800-566-5863**	218-726-7181	
Kumho Tire USA Inc 10299 Sixth St	Rancho Cucamonga	CA	91730	**800-445-8646**	909-428-3999	750
Kumon North America Inc 300 Frank W Burr Blvd Glenpointe Ctr E Ste 6	Teaneck	NJ	07666	**800-222-6284**	201-928-0444	148
KUNM-FM 899 (NPR) 1University of New Mexico MSC 06 3520	Albuquerque	NM	87131	**877-277-4806**	505-277-4806	641-4
Kuno Creative Group LLC 36901 American Wy Ste 2A	Avon	OH	44011	**800-303-0806**		4
KUOW-FM 949 (NPR) 4518 University Way NE Ste 310	Seattle	WA	98105	**800-289-5869**	206-543-2710	641-98
Kuraray America Inc 2625 Bay Area Blvd Ste 600	Houston	TX	77058	**800-423-9762**		740-1
Kuriyama of America Inc 360 E State Pkwy	Schaumburg	IL	60173	**800-800-0320**	847-755-0360	191-2
Kurt J Lesker Co 1925 Rt 51	Jefferson Hills	PA	15025	**800-245-1656**		
Kurt Manufacturing Co 5280 Main St NE	Minneapolis	MN	55421	**800-458-7855**	763-572-1500	452
Kurtz Bros Company Inc 400 Reed St PO Box 392	Clearfield	PA	16830	**800-252-3011**	814-765-6561	86
Kurtzon Lighting Inc 1420 S Talman Ave	Chicago	IL	60608	**800-837-8937**	773-277-2121	438
Kurz industrial Solutions 1325 McMahon Dr	Neenah	WI	54956	**800-776-3629**	920-886-8200	705
KUSC 1149 S Hill St Ste H100 PO Box 7913	Los Angeles	CA	90015	**800-421-5872**	213-225-7400	641-57
KUSD-TV Ch 2 (PBS) 555 N Dakota St PO Box 5000	Vermillion	SD	57069	**800-333-0789**		736
KUSM-TV Ch 9 (PBS) Visual Communications Bldg Rm 183	Bozeman	MT	59717	**800-426-8243**	406-994-3437	736
KUSP-FM 889 (NPR) 203 Eigth Ave	Santa Cruz	CA	95062	**800-655-5877**	831-476-2800	641
Kussmaul Electronics Company Inc 170 Cherry Ave	West Sayville	NY	11796	**800-346-0857**	631-567-0314	256
Kustom US 265 Hunt Park Cv	Longwood	FL	32750	**866-679-0699**		186
Kutztown University 15200 Kutztown Rd	Kutztown	PA	19530	**877-628-1915**	610-683-4000	166
Kuukpik Corp PO Box 89187	Nuiqsut	AK	99789	**866-480-6220**	907-480-6220	344
KUVO-FM 893 (Jazz) 2900 Welton St Ste 200	Denver	CO	80205	**800-574-5886**	303-480-9272	641-31
Kuwait Airways Oasis Club 400 Kelby St	Fort Lee	NJ	07024	**800-458-9248**	201-582-9222	26
KUWC-FM 913 (NPR) 1000 E University Ave	Laramie	WY	82071	**800-342-5996**	307-766-1121	641
Kuyper College 3333 E Beltline Ave NE	Grand Rapids	MI	49525	**800-511-3749**	616-222-3000	161
KVAL Inc 825 Petaluma Blvd So	Petaluma	CA	94952	**800-553-5825**	707-762-4363	816
K-VA-T Food Stores Inc PO Box 1158	Abingdon	VA	24212	**800-826-8451**	276-623-5100	344
KVI-AM 570 (N/T) 140 Fourth Ave N Ste 340	Seattle	WA	98109	**888-312-5757**	206-404-4000	641-98
KVIE-TV Ch 6 (PBS) 2030 W El Camino Ave	Sacramento	CA	95833	**800-347-5843**	916-929-5843	736-64
KVLC-FM 1011 (Oldies) 101 Perkins Dr	Las Cruces	NM	88005	**877-527-1011**	575-527-1111	641
KVLY-TV Ch 11 (NBC) 1350 21st Ave S	Fargo	ND	58103	**800-450-5844**	701-237-5211	736-29
KW Automotive North America Inc 300 W Pontiac Way	Clovis	CA	93612	**800-445-3767**		349
K&W Tire Company Inc 735 N Prince St	Lancaster	PA	17603	**877-598-4731**	800-732-3563	750
KWHE-TV 14 1188 Bishop St Ste 502	Honolulu	HI	96813	**800-218-1414**	808-538-1414	736-33
KWIC-FM 993 (Oldies) 825 S Kansas Ave Ste 100	Topeka	KS	66612	**844-366-8993**	913-795-2665	641-111
Kwik Goal Ltd 140 Pacific Dr	Quakertown	PA	18951	**800-531-4252**	215-536-2200	706
Kwik Kafe Company Inc 204 Furnace St	Bluefield	VA	24605	**800-533-4066**	276-322-4691	365
Kwik Lok Corp PO Box 9548	Yakima	WA	98909	**800-688-5945**	509-248-4770	298
Kwik Trip Inc 1626 Oak St PO Box 2107	La Crosse	WI	54602	**800-305-6666**	608-781-8988	204
Kwik-Covers LLC 811 Ridge Rd	Webster	NY	14580	**866-586-9620**	585-787-9620	361
Kwik-Wall Co 1010 E Edwards St	Springfield	IL	62703	**800-280-5945**	217-522-5553	286
KWJ Engineering Inc 8430 Central Ave Ste C	Newark	CA	94560	**800-472-6626**	510-794-4296	688
KWJJ-FM 995 (Ctry) 0700 SW Bancroft St	Portland	OR	97239	**866-239-9653**	503-733-9653	641-109

Alphabetical Section

Left column

Name / Address	Toll-Free	Phone	Class
KWMU-FM 907 (NPR) 3651 Olive St . . . . St. Louis MO 63108	866-240-5968	314-516-5968	641-92
KWPX-TV Ch 33 (I) 8112-C 304th Ave SE PO Box 426 . . . . Preston WA 98050	888-467-2988	212-757-3100	736
KWS Mfg Company Ltd 3041 Conveyor Dr . . . . Burleson TX 76028	800-543-6558	817-295-2247	207
KWTV-TV Ch 9 (CBS) 7401 N Kelley Ave . . . . . . Oklahoma City OK 73111	888-550-5988	212-931-1200	736-52
KWWL-TV Ch 7 (NBC) 500 E Fourth St . . . . Waterloo IA 50703	800-947-7746	319-291-1200	736
KWYR PO Box 491 . . . . Winner SD 57580	800-388-5997	605-842-3333	641
KXAN News 908 W Martin Luther King Jr Bl . . . . Austin TX 78701	800-843-5678	512-476-3636	736-6
KXAS-TV Ch 5 (NBC) 4805 Amon Carter Blvd . . . . . . Fort Worth TX 76155	800-232-5927	214-303-5119	736-21
KXFG-FM 929 900 E Washington St Ste 315 . . . . . Colton CA 92324	888-431-3764	909-433-3000	641
KXJB-TV Ch 4 (CBS) 1350 21st Ave S . . . . Fargo ND 58103	877-571-0774	701-237-5211	736-29
KXLN-TV Ch 45 (Uni) 5100 SW Fwy . . . . Houston TX 77056	800-500-4252	713-662-4545	736-34
KXPR-FM 889 (Clas) 7055 Folsom Blvd . . . . . . Sacramento CA 95826	877-480-5900	916-278-8900	641-91
KXSC-FM 1049 (Alt) 3607 Trousdale Pkwy . . . . Los Angeles CA 90089	888-966-5332	415-546-8710	
KY3 999 W Sunshine St . . . . . . Springfield MO 65807	888-476-6988	417-268-3000	736-75
KYCC-FM 901 9019 W Ln . . . . Stockton CA 95210	800-654-5254	209-477-3690	641-105
Kymera International 901 Lehigh Ave . . . . Union NJ 07083	800-232-3198	908-851-4500	490
Kyocera Communications Inc 9520 Towne Centre Dr . . . . San Diego CA 92121	800-349-4188	858-882-1400	643
Kyocera Industrial Ceramics Corp 5713 E Fourth Plain Rd . . . . Vancouver WA 98661	888-955-0800	360-696-8950	249
Kyocera International Inc 8611 Balboa Ave . . . . . . San Diego CA 92123	877-248-4237	858-576-2600	359-3
Kyocera Solar Inc 7812 E Acoma Dr . . . . . . Scottsdale AZ 85260	800-544-6466	480-948-8003	692
Kyocera Tycom Corp 3565 Cadillac . . . . . . Costa Mesa CA 92626	800-823-7284	714-428-3600	453
Kysor Panel Systems 4201 N Beach St . . . . . . Fort Worth TX 76137	800-633-3426	817-281-5121	660
Kysor Warren Corp 5201 Transport Blvd . . . . . . Columbus GA 31907	800-866-5596	706-568-1514	606
KYUR-TV Ch 13 (ABC) 2700 E Tudor Rd . . . . . . Anchorage AK 99507	877-304-1313	907-561-1313	736-2
KYW-NEWSRADIO 1060 (N/T) 1555 Hamilton St . . . . . . Philadelphia PA 19130	800-223-8477	215-977-5333	
KZNS-AM 1280 (Sports) 301 W South Temple . . . . Salt Lake City UT 84101	855-340-9663	801-325-2043	641-93

L

Name / Address	Toll-Free	Phone	Class
L & L Nursery Supply Co Inc 2552 Shenandoah Way . . . . San Bernardino CA 92407	800-624-2517	909-591-0461	293
L & m Mail Service Inc 2452 Truax Blvd . . . . . . Eau Claire WI 54703	800-507-7070	715-836-0138	5
L & M Radiator Inc 1414 E 37th St . . . . Hibbing MN 55746	800-346-3500	218-263-8993	61
L & N Federal Credit Union 9265 Smyrna Pkwy . . . . Louisville KY 40229	800-443-2479	502-368-5858	219
L B L Group 3631 S Harbor Blvd Ste 200 . . . . Santa Ana CA 92704	800-451-8037		686
L B Plastics Inc 482 E Plaza Dr . . . . . . Mooresville NC 28115	800-752-7739	704-663-1543	606
L H. P. Transportation Services Inc 2032 E Kearney Ste 213 . . . . Springfield MO 65803	800-642-1035	417-865-7577	311
L Keeley Construction 500 S Ewing Ave Ste G . . . . Saint Louis MO 63103	866-553-3539		
L M Scofield Co 6533 Bandini Blvd . . . . Los Angeles CA 90040	800-800-9900	323-720-3000	183
L Suzio Concrete Company Inc 975 Westfield Rd . . . . . . Meriden CT 06450	888-789-4626	203-237-8421	182
L' Appartement Hotel 455 Sherbrooke W . . . . . . Montreal QC H3A1B7	800-363-3010	514-284-3634	378
L'Acadie-Nouvelle 476 St-Pierre W PO Box 5536 . . . . Caraquet NB E1W1B7	800-561-2255	506-727-4444	528-1
L'Auberge de Sedona 301 L'Auberge Ln . . . . . . Sedona AZ 86336	855-905-5745	800-905-5745	667
L'Auberge Del Mar 1540 Camino del Mar PO Box 2889 . . . . Del Mar CA 92014	800-245-9757	858-259-1515	665
L'Ermitage Beverly Hills Hotel 9291 Burton Way . . . . Beverly Hills CA 90210	877-235-7582	310-278-3344	378
L'Hotel du Vieux-Quebec 1190 St Jean St . . . . . . Quebec QC G1R1S6	800-361-7787	418-692-1850	378
L'Hotel Quebec 3115 des Hotels Ave . . . . . . Quebec QC G1W3Z6	800-567-5276	418-658-5120	378
L'Oreal USA 575 Fifth Ave . . . . . . New York NY 10017	800-322-2036	212-818-1500	214
l'Usine Tactic Inc 127th St Ste 2050 . . . . Saint George QC G5Y2W8	800-933-5232		
L-3 Avionics Systems 5353 52nd St SE . . . . . . Grand Rapids MI 49512	800-253-9525	616-949-6600	525
L-3 Communications Corp Randtron Antenna Systems Div 130 Constitution Dr . . . . Menlo Park CA 94025 *Sales	866-900-7270*	650-326-9500	525
L-3 Communications Integrated Systems 600 Third Ave . . . . . . New York NY 10016	877-282-1168	903-455-3450	22
L-3 Communications Telemetry East Div 1515 Grundy's Ln . . . . . . Bristol PA 19007	800-351-8483	267-545-7000	643

Right column

Name / Address	Toll-Free	Phone	Class
L-3 Communications Telemetry West Div 9020 Balboa Ave . . . . . . San Diego CA 92123	800-351-8483	858-694-7500	643
L3 Technologies Inc 1 Federal St . . . . . . Camden NJ 08103	800-339-6197	856-338-3000	525
La Beau Bros Inc 295 N Harrison Ave . . . . . . Kankakee IL 60901	800-747-9519	815-933-5519	57
La Belle Dodge Chrysler Jeep Inc 501 S Main St . . . . . . Labelle FL 33935	800-226-1193	863-675-2701	57
La Capitol Federal Credit Union PO Box 3398 . . . . . . Baton Rouge LA 70821	800-522-2748	225-342-5055	219
LA Care Health Plan 555 W Fifth St 29th Fl. . . . . Los Angeles CA 90013	888-839-9909	213-694-1250	390-3
La Cie Canada Tire Inc 21500 Transcanadienne . . . . . . Baie-D'Urfe QC H9X4B7	888-267-5097	514-457-0155	749
La Cite 801 Aviation Dr . . . . . . Ottawa ON K1K4R3	800-267-2483	613-742-2483	
La Crete Sawmills Ltd Hwy 697 S PO Box 1090 . . . . La Crete AB T0H2H0	888-928-2298	780-928-2292	
La Crosse Area Convention & Visitors Bureau 410 Veterans Memorial Dr . . . . La Crosse WI 54601	800-658-9424	608-782-2366	206
La Crosse Graphics Inc 3025 E Ave S . . . . . . La Crosse WI 54601	800-832-2503	608-788-2500	623
La Crosse Tribune 401 N Third St . . . . . . La Crosse WI 54601	800-262-0420	608-782-9710	528-2
LA Darling Co 1401 Hwy 49B . . . . . . Paragould AR 72450	800-682-5730	870-239-9564	286
La Follette Utilities Board 302 N Tennessee Ave PO Box 1411 . . . . La Follette TN 37766	800-352-1340	423-562-3316	245
La Fonda 100 E San Francisco St . . . . Santa Fe NM 87501	800-523-5002	505-982-5511	378
La Grande-Union County Chamber of Commerce 102 Elm St . . . . . . La Grande OR 97850	800-848-9969	541-963-8588	139
La Habra Products Inc 4125 E La Palma Ave Ste 250 . . . . Anaheim CA 92807	866-516-0061	714-778-2266	498
La Hacienda Treatment Ctr 145 La Hacienda Way . . . . . . Hunt TX 78024	800-749-6160	830-238-4222	722
La Jolla Beach & Tennis Club 2000 Spindrift Dr . . . . . . La Jolla CA 92037	888-828-0948	858-454-7126	665
La Jolla Light Newspaper 565 Pearl St Ste 300 . . . . La Jolla CA 92037	800-691-0952	858-459-4201	528-3
La Jolla Nursing & Rehabilitation Ctr 2552 Torrey Pines Rd . . . . La Jolla CA 92037	800-861-0086	858-453-5810	448
La Leche League International Inc (LLLI) 957 N Plum Grove Rd . . . . Schaumburg IL 60173	800-525-3243	847-519-7730	48-17
La Marche Mfg Co 106 Bradrock Dr . . . . . . Des Plaines IL 60018	888-232-9562	847-299-1188	253
La Mesa Rv Ctr Inc 7430 Copley Pk Pl . . . . San Diego CA 92111 *Sales	800-496-8778*	858-874-8000	57
La Pastaia 233 W Santa Clara St . . . . . . San Jose CA 95113	800-843-3700	408-286-1000	667
La Pensione Hotel 606 W Date St . . . . . . San Diego CA 92101	800-232-4683	619-236-8000	378
La Petite Bretonne Inc 1210 Boul Mich Le-Bohec . . . . Blainville QC J7C5S4	800-361-3381	450-435-3381	297-8
La Plata Electric Assn Inc 45 Stewart St . . . . . . Durango CO 81303	888-839-5732	970-247-5786	245
La Playa Beach & Golf Resort 9891 Gulf Shore Dr . . . . . . Naples FL 34108	800-237-6883	239-597-3123	665
La Porte County 813 Lincolnway . . . . . . La Porte IN 46350	800-654-3441	219-326-6808	337
La Posada de Santa Fe Resort & Spa 330 E Palace Ave . . . . Santa Fe NM 87501	866-280-3810	505-986-0000	665
La Posada Hotel & Suites 1000 Zaragoza St . . . . . . Laredo TX 78040 *Resv	800-444-2099*	956-722-1701	378
La Quinta Inn & Suites Boise Towne Square 7965 W Emerald St . . . . . . Boise ID 83704	800-600-6001	208-378-7000	378
La Quinta Inn & Suites Pocatello 1440 Bench Rd . . . . . . Pocatello ID 83201	800-600-6001	208-234-7500	378
La Quinta Inn & Suites Secaucus Meadowlands 350 Lighting Way . . . . . . Secaucus NJ 07094 *General	800-753-3757*	201-863-8700	378
La Reina Inc 316 N Ford Blvd . . . . Los Angeles CA 90022	800-367-7522	323-268-2791	296-36
La Roche College 9000 Babcock Blvd . . . . . . Pittsburgh PA 15237 *Admissions	800-838-4572*	412-367-9300	166
La Salle University 1900 W Olney Ave . . . . Philadelphia PA 19141	800-328-1910	215-951-1500	166
La Salsa Fresh Mexican Grill 9311 E Via De Ventura . . . . Scottsdale AZ 85258	866-452-4252		666
La Sierra University 4500 Riverwalk Pkwy . . . . . . Riverside CA 92515	800-874-5587	951-785-2000	166
La Touraine Inc 110 W A St Ste 900 . . . . San Diego CA 92101	800-893-8871	619-237-5014	225
La Vida Llena 10501 Lagrima de Oro NE . . . . Albuquerque NM 87111	800-922-1344	505-293-4001	668
LA Weekly 6715 Sunset Blvd . . . . Los Angeles CA 90028	866-789-6188		528-5
Lab Products Inc 742 Sussex Ave . . . . . . Seaford DE 19973	800-526-0469	302-628-4300	73
LaBarge Coating LLC 211 N Broadway Ste 3050 . . . . Saint Louis MO 63102	866-992-4191	314-646-3400	535
Labatt Breweries of Canada 207 Queen's Quay W Ste 299 . . . . Toronto ON M5J1A7 *Cust Svc	800-268-2337*	416-361-5050	102
Labcon North America Inc 3700 Lkeville Hwy . . . . . . Petaluma CA 94954	800-227-1466	707-766-2100	418
Labconco Corp 8811 Prospect Ave . . . . Kansas City MO 64132 *Cust Svc	800-821-5525*	816-333-8811	419
Label Printers Lp, The 1710 N Landmark Rd . . . . . . Aurora IL 60506	800-229-9549	630-897-6970	623
Label Technology Inc 2050 Wardrobe Ave . . . . . . Merced CA 95341	800-388-1990	209-384-1000	623
Label Works 2025 Lookout Dr . . . . North Mankato MN 56003	800-522-3558		623

Name / Address	City	State	ZIP	Toll-Free	Phone	Class
Labelmaster Co						
5724 N Pulaski Rd	Chicago	IL	60646	**800-621-5808**	773-478-0900	412
Labeltape Inc						
5100 Beltway Dr SE	Caledonia	MI	49316	**800-928-4537**	616-698-1830	412
Labette Bank						
4th & Huston PO Box 497	Altamont	KS	67330	**800-711-5311**	620-784-5311	70
Labette Community College						
200 S 14th St	Parsons	KS	67357	**888-522-3883**	620-421-6700	162
LabOne Inc						
10101 Renner Blvd	Lenexa	KS	66219	**800-646-7788**	913-888-1770	417
Labor Finders						
11426 N Jog Rd	Palm Beach Gardens	FL	33418	**800-864-7749**	561-627-6507	717
Labor Racketeering & Fraud Investigations Office						
200 Constitution Ave NW						
Rm S-5506	Washington	DC	20210	**800-347-3756**	202-693-6999	
Laboratory Corp of America Holdings						
358 S Main St	Burlington	NC	27215	**800-334-5161**	336-584-5171	417
NYSE: LH						
Laboratory Institute of Merchandising						
12 E 53rd St	New York	NY	10022	**800-677-1323**	212-752-1530	166
Laborchex Co, The						
2506 Lakeland Dr Ste 200	Jackson	MS	39232	**800-880-0366**	601-664-6760	631
Laborers' International Union of North America						
905 16th St NW	Washington	DC	20006	**800-548-6242**	202-737-8320	413
Laboure College						
303 Adams St	Milton	MA	02186	**800-877-1600**	617-322-3575	795
Labrada Nutrition						
403 Century Plaza Dr Ste 440	Houston	TX	77073	**800-832-9948**		794
Labrie Enviroquip Group						
175-B Rte Marie-Victorin	Levis	QC	G7A2T3	**800-463-6638**	418-831-8250	513
LABS Inc						
6933 S Revere Pkwy	Centennial	CO	80112	**866-393-2244**	720-528-4750	416
Lac Courte Oreilles Ojibwa Community College						
13466 W Trepania Rd	Hayward	WI	54843	**888-526-6221**	715-634-4790	165
Lace For Less Inc						
1500 Main Ave	Clifton	NJ	07011	**800-533-5223**	973-478-2955	740-4
Lacks Valley Stores Ltd						
1300 San Patricia St	Pharr	TX	78577	**800-870-6999**	956-702-3361	321
Laclede Electric Co-op						
1400 E Rt 66	Lebanon	MO	65536	**800-299-3164**	417-532-3164	245
La-Co/Markal Co						
1201 Pratt Blvd	Elk Grove Village	IL	60007	**800-621-4025**	847-956-7600	465
Lacombe Hospital & Care Ctr						
5430 47th Ave	Lacombe	AB	T4L1G8	**800-291-2782**	403-782-3336	373-2
LaCrosse Footwear Inc						
17634 NE Airport	Portland	OR	97230	**800-323-2668***		301
*Cust Svc						
Lacrosse Unlimited Inc						
59 Gilpin Ave	Hauppauge	NY	11788	**877-800-5850**		
Lad Lake Inc						
W350s1401 Waterville Rd						
PO Box 158	Dousman	WI	53118	**877-965-2131**	262-965-2131	148
Lado International College						
401 Ninth St NW Ste C100	Washington	DC	20004	**800-281-7710**	202-223-0023	422
Lady Bird Johnson Wildflower Ctr						
4801 La Crosse Ave	Austin	TX	78739	**877-945-3357**	512-232-0100	97
Lady Grace Stores Inc						
238 W Cummings Pk	Woburn	MA	01801	**877-381-4629**		157-6
Laerdal Medical Corp						
167 Myers Corners Rd						
PO Box 1840	Wappingers Falls	NY	12590	**800-227-1143**	845-297-7770	473
Lafarge North America Inc						
8700 W Bryn Mawr Ave Ste 300	Chicago	IL	60631	**800-451-8346**	773-372-1000	135
Lafayette Convention & Visitors Commission						
1400 NW Evangeline Thwy	Lafayette	LA	70501	**800-346-1958**	337-232-3737	206
Lafayette Federal Credit Union (Inc)						
3535 University Blvd W	Kensington	MD	20895	**800-888-6560**	301-929-7990	219
Lafayette Hotel						
101 Front St	Marietta	OH	45750	**800-331-9336**	740-373-5522	378
Lafayette Life Insurance Co						
400 Broadway	Cincinnati	OH	45202	**800-443-8793**		390-2
Lafayette Museum						
1400 NW Evangeline Trwy	Lafayette	LA	70501	**800-346-1958**	337-234-2208	517
Lafayette Park Hotel						
3287 Mt Diablo Blvd	Lafayette	CA	94549	**855-382-8632**	800-394-3112	378
Lafayette Venetian Blind Inc						
3000 Klondike Rd						
PO Box 2838	West Lafayette	IN	47996	**800-342-5523**		87
Lafayette Wood-Works Inc						
3004 Cameron St	Lafayette	LA	70506	**800-960-3311**	337-233-5250	497
Lafayette-West Lafayette Convention & Visitors Bureau						
301 Frontage Rd	Lafayette	IN	47905	**800-872-6648**	765-447-9999	206
Laflamme Doors & Windows						
39 Industrielle St	St Apollinaire	QC	G0S2E0	**800-463-1922**		497
Lafontaine Honda						
2245 S Telegraph Rd	Dearborn	MI	48124	**866-567-5088**		57
LaForce Inc						
1060 W Mason St	Green Bay	WI	54303	**800-236-8858**		234
Lafourche Parish						
402 Green St PO Box 5548	Thibodaux	LA	70302	**800-834-8832**	985-446-8427	337
LaFrance Equipment Corp						
516 Erie St	Elmira	NY	14904	**800-873-8808**	607-733-5511	675
Lafromboise Communications Inc						
321 N Pearl St	Centralia	WA	98531	**800-356-4404**	360-736-3311	528-3
Lago Mar Resort & Club						
1700 S Ocean Ln	Fort Lauderdale	FL	33316	**855-209-5677**	954-523-6511	665
Lagoon & Pioneer Village						
375 N Lagoon Dr	Farmington	UT	84025	**800-748-5246**	801-451-8000	32
LaGrange College						
601 Broad St	LaGrange	GA	30240	**800-593-2885***	706-880-8000	166
*Admissions						
LaGrange County Rural Electric Membership Corp						
1995 E US Hwy 20	LaGrange	IN	46761	**877-463-7165**	260-463-7165	245
Lagrange Products Inc						
607 S Wayne St	Fremont	IN	46737	**800-369-6978**	260-495-3025	765
Laguna Beach Visitors & Conference Bureau						
381 Forest Ave	Laguna Beach	CA	92651	**800-877-1115**	949-497-9229	206
Laguna College of Art & Design						
2222 Laguna Canyon Rd	Laguna Beach	CA	92651	**800-255-0762**	949-376-6000	166

Name / Address	City	State	ZIP	Toll-Free	Phone	Class
Lahaina Shores Beach Resort						
475 Front St	Lahaina	HI	96761	**866-934-9176**		377
Lahey Clinic Foundation Inc						
41 Mall Rd	Burlington	MA	01805	**800-524-3955**	781-744-8000	373-3
Laibe Corp						
1414 Bates St	Indianapolis	IN	46201	**800-942-3388**	317-231-2250	490
Laird Noller Ford Inc						
2245 SW Topeka Blvd	Topeka	KS	66611	**877-803-1859**	785-235-9211	513
Laird Norton Tyee						
801 Second Ave Ste 1600	Seattle	WA	98104	**800-426-5105**		400
Laird Plastics Inc						
6800 Broken Sound Pkwy						
Ste 150	Boca Raton	FL	33487	**800-243-9696**	630-451-4688	599
Laitram LLC						
200 Laitram Ln	Harahan	LA	70123	**800-535-7631**	504-733-6000	525
Lake Agassiz Regional Library (LARL)						
118 Fifth St S PO Box 900	Moorhead	MN	56560	**800-247-0449**	218-233-3757	433-3
Lake Air						
7709 Winpark Dr	Minneapolis	MN	55427	**888-785-2422**	763-546-0994	487
Lake Area Technical Institute						
1201 Arrow Ave PO Box 730	Watertown	SD	57201	**800-657-4344**	605-882-5284	162
Lake Austin Spa Resort						
1705 S Quinlan Pk Rd	Austin	TX	78732	**800-847-5637**	512-372-7380	703
Lake Barkley State Resort Park						
3500 State Pk Rd	Cadiz	KY	42211	**800-325-1708**		561
Lake Bistineau State Park						
103 State Park Rd	Doyline	LA	71023	**888-677-2478**	318-745-3503	561
Lake Breeze Motel Resort						
9000 Congdon Blvd	Duluth	MN	55804	**800-738-5884**	218-525-6808	665
Lake Bruin State Park						
201 State Pk Rd	Saint Joseph	LA	71366	**888-677-2784**	318-766-3530	561
Lake Carmi State Park						
460 Marsh Farm Rd	Enosburg Falls	VT	05450	**888-409-7579***	802-933-8383	561
*Resv						
Lake Cascade State Park						
970 Dam Rd	Cascade	ID	83611	**866-634-3246**	208-382-6544	561
Lake Catherine Footwear						
3770 Malvern Rd PO Box 6048	Hot Springs	AR	71901	**800-819-1901**		301
Lake Champlain Regional Chamber of Commerce						
60 Main St Ste 100	Burlington	VT	05401	**877-686-5253**	802-863-3489	139
Lake Charles Civic Ctr						
900 Lakeshore Dr	Lake Charles	LA	70601	**888-620-1749**	337-491-1256	568
Lake Charles Memorial Health System (LCMH)						
1701 Oak Pk Blvd	Lake Charles	LA	70601	**800-494-5264**	337-494-3000	373-3
Lake Chicot State Park						
2542 Hwy 257	Lake Village	AR	71653	**800-264-2430**	870-265-5480	561
Lake Claiborne State Park						
225 State Pk Rd	Homer	LA	71040	**888-677-2524**	318-927-2976	561
Lake Clark National Park & Preserve						
240 W Fifth Ave Ste 236	Anchorage	AK	99501	**800-365-2267**	907-644-3626	560
Lake Country Power						
2810 Elida Dr	Grand Rapids	MN	55744	**800-421-9959**		245
Lake County						
105 Main St	Painesville	OH	44077	**800-899-5253**		337
Lake County Convention & Visitors Bureau						
5465 W Grand Ave Ste 100	Gurnee	IL	60031	**800-525-3669**	847-662-2700	206
Lake D'Arbonne State Park						
3628 Evergreen Rd	Farmerville	LA	71241	**888-677-5200**	318-368-2086	561
Lake Erie College						
391 West Washington St	Painesville	OH	44077	**800-533-4996**	440-375-7050	166
Lake Erie Electric						
25730 First St	Westlake	OH	44145	**855-877-9393**	440-835-5565	189-4
Lake Erie Frozen Foods Co						
1830 Orange Rd	Ashland	OH	44805	**800-766-8501**	419-289-9204	344
Lake Erie Graphics Inc						
5372 W 130th St	Brook Park	OH	44142	**888-293-7397**	216-265-7575	623
Lake Forest College						
555 N Sheridan Rd	Lake Forest	IL	60045	**800-828-4751**	847-234-3100	166
Lake Greenwood State Recreation Area						
302 State Pk Rd	Ninety Six	SC	29666	**866-345-7275**	864-543-3535	561
Lake Havasu Area Chamber of Commerce						
314 London Bridge Rd	Lake Havasu City	AZ	86403	**800-307-3610**	928-855-4115	139
Lake Immunogenics Inc						
348 Berg Rd	Ontario	NY	14519	**800-648-9990**		580
Lake Junaluska Assembly						
Lake Junaluska Conference						
Retreat Ctr 689 N Lakeshore Dr	Lake Junaluska	NC	28745	**800-482-1442**	828-452-2881	48-20
Lake Kegonsa State Park						
2405 Door Creek Rd	Stoughton	WI	53589	**888-947-2757***	608-873-9695	561
*General						
Lake Lawn Resort						
2400 E Geneva St	Delavan	WI	53115	**800-338-5253**	262-728-7950	665
Lake Louise Inn						
210 Village Rd PO Box 209	Lake Louise	AB	T0L1E0	**800-661-9237**	403-522-3791	378
Lake Lure Inn & Spa, The						
2771 Memorial Hwy	Lake Lure	NC	28746	**888-434-4970**		378
Lake Michigan College						
2755 E Napier Ave	Benton Harbor	MI	49022	**800-252-1562**	269-927-1000	162
Bertrand Crossing						
1905 Foundation Dr	Niles	MI	49120	**800-252-1562**	269-695-1391	162
Lake Morey Resort						
1 Clubhouse Rd	Fairlee	VT	05045	**800-423-1211**	802-333-4311	665
Lake Murray Resort Park						
3323 Lodge Rd	Ardmore	OK	73401	**800-622-6317**	580-223-6600	665
Lake Murray State Park						
900 N Stiles Ave	Oklahoma City	OK	73152	**800-652-6552**		561
Lake Norman State Park						
759 State Pk Rd	Troutman	NC	28166	**877-722-6762**	919-707-9300	
Lake of the Ozarks Convention & Visitors Bureau						
985 KK Dr	Osage Beach	MO	65065	**800-386-5253**	573-348-1599	206
Lake Oswego Chamber of Commerce						
459 Third St Lk	Oswego	OR	97034	**800-518-0760**	503-636-3634	139
Lake Owyhee State Park						
725 Summer St NE Ste C	Salem	OR	97301	**800-551-6949**	503-986-0707	561
Lake Park Retirement Residences						
1850 Alice St	Oakland	CA	94612	**866-384-3130**	510-835-5511	668
Lake Placid Lodge						
144 Lodge Way	Lake Placid	NY	12946	**877-523-2700**	518-523-2700	378

	Toll-Free	Phone	Class

Lake Powell Resorts & Marinas
100 Lakeshore Dr .... Page AZ 86040 — 800-622-6317 — 888-896-3829 — 665

Lake Quinault Lodge
345 S Shore Rd ....Quinault WA 98575 — 800-562-6672 — 360-288-2900 — 665

Lake Region Co-op Electrical Assn
1401 S Broadway
PO Box 643...........Pelican Rapids MN 56572 — 800-552-7658 — 218-863-1171 — 245

Lake Region Electric Assn Inc
1212 Main St ....Webster SD 57274 — 800-657-5869 — 605-345-3379 — 245

Lake Region Electric Co-op Inc
516 S Lake Region Rd ....Hulbert OK 74441 — 800-364-5732 — 918-772-2526 — 245

Lake Region Hospital
712 S Cascade St ....Fergus Falls MN 56537 — 800-439-6424 — 218-736-8000 — 373-3

Lake Region State College
1801 College Dr N ....Devils Lake ND 58301 — 800-443-1313 — 701-662-1600 — 162

Lake Sammamish State Park
2000 NW Sammamish Rd ......Issaquah WA 98027 — 888-226-7688 — 425-649-4275 — 561

Lake Shore Cryotronics
575 McCorkle Blvd ....Westerville OH 43082 — 877-969-0010 — 614-891-2243 — 201

Lake Shore Industries Inc (LSI)
1817 Poplar St PO Box 3427 ....Erie PA 16508 — 800-458-0463 — — 697

Lake Superior College
2101 Trinity Rd ....Duluth MN 55811 — 800-432-2884 — 218-733-7600 — 162

Lake Tahoe Community College
1 College Dr ....South Lake Tahoe CA 96150 — 800-877-1466 — 530-541-4660 — 162

Lake Tahoe Visitors Authority
3066 Lake Tahoe Blvd .....South Lake Tahoe CA 96150 — 800-288-2463 — 530-544-5050 — 206

Lake Thompson Recreation Area
21176 Flood Club Rd ....Lake Preston SD 57249 — 800-710-2267 — 605-847-4893 — 561

Lake Wales Area Chamber of Commerce
340 W Central Ave ....Lake Wales FL 33859 — 800-365-6380 — 863-676-3445 — 139

Lake Wapello State Park
15248 Campground Rd ......Drakesville IA 52552 — 866-495-4868 — 641-722-3371 — 561

Lake Wister State Park
25567 US Hwy 270 ....Wister OK 74966 — 800-622-6317 — 918-655-7212 — 561

Lakefront Lines Inc
13315 Brookpark Rd ....Brook Park OH 44142 — 800-543-9912 — 216-267-8810 — 755

Lakeland Bancorp Inc
250 Oak Ridge Rd ....Oak Ridge NJ 07438 — 866-224-1379 — 973-697-2000 — 359-2
NASDAQ: LBAI

Lakeland College
PO Box 359 ....Sheboygan WI 53082 — 800-569-2166 — 920-565-2111 — 166

Lakeland Community College
7700 Clocktower Dr ....Kirtland OH 44094 — 800-589-8520 — 440-525-7000 — 162

Lakeland Correctional Facility
141 First St ....Coldwater MI 49036 — 800-326-4537 — 517-278-6942 — 213

Lakeland Financial Corp
202 E Ctr St ....Warsaw IN 46580 — 800-827-4522 — 574-267-6144 — 359-2
NASDAQ: LKFN

Lakeland Industries Inc
701-7 Koehler Ave ....Ronkonkoma NY 11779 — 800-645-9291 — 631-981-9700 — 572
NASDAQ: LAKE

Lakeland Medical Center-Niles
31 N St Joseph Ave ....Niles MI 49120 — 800-968-0115 — 269-683-5510 — 373-3

Lakeland Plastics Inc (LP)
1550 McCormick Blvd ....Mundelein IL 60060 — 800-454-4006 — 847-680-1550 — 595

Lakeland Village Beach & Mountain Resort
3535 Lake Tahoe Blvd .....South Lake Tahoe CA 96150 — 888-484-7094 — 530-541-7711 — 665

Lakepoint Resort State Park
104 Lakepoint Dr ....Eufaula AL 36027 — 800-544-5253 — 334-687-8011 — 561

Lakeport Regional Chamber of Commerce
875 Lakeport Blvd ....Lakeport CA 95453 — 866-525-3767 — 707-263-5092 — 139

Lakeridge Health Oshawa
1 Hospital Ct ....Oshawa ON L1G2B9 — 866-338-1778 — 905-576-8711 — 373-2

Lakes Area Co-op
459 Third Ave SE PO Box 247 ....Perham MN 56573 — 866-346-5601 — 218-346-6240 — 276

Lakes Region Community College (LRCC)
379 Belmont Rd ....Laconia NH 03246 — 800-357-2992 — 603-524-3207 — 162

Lakeshore Learning Materials
2695 E Dominguez St ....Carson CA 90895 — 800-778-4456 — 310-537-8600 — 530

Lakeshore Technical College
1290 N Ave ....Cleveland WI 53015 — 888-468-6582 — 920-693-1000 — 795

Lakeside Behavioral Health System
2911 Brunswick Rd ....Memphis TN 38133 — 800-232-5253 — 901-377-4700 — 373-5

Lakeside Foods Inc
808 Hamilton St ....Manitowoc WI 54220 — 800-466-3834 — 920-684-3356 — 296-20

Lakeside Inn
100 N Alexander St ....Mount Dora FL 32757 — 800-556-5016 — 352-383-4101 — 378

Lakeside Manufacturing Inc
4900 W Electric Ave ....West Milwaukee WI 53219 — 800-558-8565 — 414-902-6400 — 319-1

Lakeview Golf Resort & Spa
1 Lakeview Dr ....Morgantown WV 26508 — 800-624-8300 — 304-594-1111 — 665

Lakeview Hotels & Resorts
Lakeview Inns & Suites - Hinton
185 Carlton St Ste 600............Winnipeg MB R3C3J1 — 877-355-3500 — 780-865-2575 — 377

Lakeview Professional Services Inc
104 S Maple St ....Corona CA 92880 — 800-287-1371 — 951-371-3390 — 196

Lakeview Regional Medical Ctr
95 Judge Tanner Blvd ....Covington LA 70433 — 866-452-5384 — 985-867-3800 — 373-3

Lakewold Gardens
12317 Gravelly Lake Dr SW ......Lakewood WA 98499 — 888-858-4106 — 253-584-4106 — 97

Lakewood Health System
49725 County 83 ....Staples MN 56479 — 800-525-1033 — 218-894-1515 — 362

Lakewood Hospital
14519 Detroit Ave ....Lakewood OH 44107 — 866-588-2264 — 216-521-4200 — 373-3

Lakewood Shores Resort
7751 Cedar Lake Rd ....Oscoda MI 48750 — 800-882-2493 — — 665

Lakin Tire West Inc
15305 Spring Ave ....Santa Fe Springs CA 90670 — 800-488-2752 — 562-802-2752 — 750

LallyPak Inc
1209 Central Ave ....Hillside NJ 07205 — 800-523-8484 — 908-351-4141 — 544

Lam Research Corp
4650 Cushing Pkwy ....Fremont CA 94538 — 800-526-7678 — 510-572-0200 — 691
NASDAQ: LRCX

Lamar Adv Co
5321 Corporate Blvd ....Baton Rouge LA 70808 — 800-235-2627 — 225-926-1000 — 8
NASDAQ: LAMR

Lamar Community College
2401 S Main St ....Lamar CO 81052 — 800-968-6920 — 719-336-2248 — 162

Lamar County Chamber of Commerce
1125 Bonham St ....Paris TX 75460 — 800-727-4789 — 903-784-2501 — 139

Lamar State College
Orange 410 Front St ....Orange TX 77630 — 877-673-6839 — 409-883-7750 — 162
Port Arthur
PO Box 310 ....Port Arthur TX 77641 — 800-477-5872 — 409-983-4921 — 162

Lamartek Inc
175 NW Washington St ....Lake City FL 32055 — 800-495-1046* — 386-752-1087 — 706
*Orders

Lamaze International
2025 M St NW Ste 800.........Washington DC 20036 — 800-368-4404 — 202-367-1128 — 49-8

Lambda Legal Defense & Education Fund
120 Wall St 19th Fl.............New York NY 10005 — 866-542-8336 — 212-809-8585 — 48-8

Lambeau Field Atrium
1265 Lombardi Ave ....Green Bay WI 54304 — 866-752-1265 — 920-569-7500 — 716

Lambert Saint Louis International Airport
10701 Lambert International Blvd
PO Box 10212...............Saint Louis MO 63145 — 855-787-2227 — 314-426-8000 — 27

Lamers Bus Lines Inc
2407 S Pt Rd ....Green Bay WI 54313 — 800-236-1240 — 920-496-3600 — 107

Lamey-Wellehan Inc
940 Turner St ....Auburn ME 04210 — 800-370-6900 — 207-784-6595 — 301

Laminar Consulting Services
424 S Olive St ....Orange CA 92866 — 888-531-9995 — — 196

Laminated Wood Systems Inc (LWS)
1327 285th Rd PO Box 386 ....Seward NE 68434 — 800-949-3526 — — 812

Lamination Depot Inc
1601 Alton Pkwy Ste E ....Irvine CA 92606 — 800-925-0054 — 714-954-0632 — 531

Laminations
3010 E Venture Dr ....Appleton WI 54911 — 800-925-2626 — 920-831-0596 — 544

Laminators Inc
3255 Penn St ....Hatfield PA 19440 — 877-663-4277 — 215-723-8107 — 812

Laminex Inc
4209 Pleasant Rd ....Fort Mill SC 29708 — 800-438-8850 — 704-679-4170 —

Lammes Candies Since 1885 Inc
PO Box 1885 ....Austin TX 78767 — 800-252-1885 — 512-310-2223 — 296-8

Lamons Gasket Co
7300 Airport Blvd ....Houston TX 77061 — 800-231-6906 — 713-222-0284 — 326

Lamont Engineers
548 Main St ....Cobleskill NY 12043 — 800-882-9721 — 518-234-4028 — 194

Lamont Ltd
1530 Bluff Rd ....Burlington IA 52601 — 800-553-5621 — 319-753-5131 — 319-2

Lamont, Hanley & Associates Inc
1138 Elm St ....Manchester NH 03105 — 800-639-2204 — 603-625-5547 — 160

Lamothe House Hotel
621 Esplanade Ave ....New Orleans LA 70116 — 800-535-7815 — — 378

LaMotte Co
802 Washington Ave ....Chestertown MD 21620 — 800-344-3100 — 410-778-3100 — 418

Lamps Plus Inc
20250 Plummer St ....Chatsworth CA 91311 — 800-782-1967 — — 361

Lamson & Goodnow Mfg Co
45 Conway St ....Shelburne Falls MA 01370 — 800-872-6564 — 413-625-0201 — 222

Lamvin Inc
4675 North Ave ....Oceanside CA 92056 — 800-446-6329 — 760-806-6400 — 604

Lancaster Archery Supply Inc
2195-A Old Philadelphia Pk ....Lancaster PA 17602 — 800-829-7408 — — 707

Lancaster Bible College
901 Eden Rd ....Lancaster PA 17601 — 800-544-7335 — 717-569-7071 — 161

Lancaster Commercial Products Inc
2353 Westbrooke Dr ....Columbus OH 43228 — 844-324-1444 — 614-263-2850 — 300

Lancaster County Chamber of Commerce
PO Box 430 ....Lancaster SC 29721 — 800-532-0335 — 803-283-4105 — 139

Lancaster Eagle-Gazette
138 W Chestnut St ....Lancaster OH 43130 — 877-513-7355 — 740-654-1321 — 528-2

Lancaster Group Inc, The
3411 Richmond Ave Ste 460 ....Houston TX 77046 — 888-365-7829 — 713-224-6000 —

Lancaster Host Resort
2300 Lincoln Hwy E ....Lancaster PA 17602 — 800-233-0121* — 717-299-5500 — 665
*Resv

Lancaster Hotel
701 Texas St ....Houston TX 77002 — 800-231-0336 — 713-228-9500 — 378

Lancaster Knives Inc
165 Ct St ....Lancaster NY 14086 — 800-869-9666 — 716-683-5050 — 491

Lancaster Pump Co
1340 Manheim Pk ....Lancaster PA 17601 — 800-442-0786 — 717-397-3521 — 801

Lancaster Theological Seminary
555 W James St ....Lancaster PA 17603 — 800-393-0654 — 717-393-0654 — 167-3

Lancaster Toyota Inc
5270 Manheim Pk ....East Petersburg PA 17520 — 888-424-1295 — — 57

Lancer Corp
6655 Lancer Blvd ....San Antonio TX 78219 — 800-729-1500 — 210-310-7000 — 660

Lancer Label
301 S 74th St ....Omaha NE 68114 — 800-228-7074* — 402-390-9119 — 412
*Cust Svc

Lancer Orthodontics Inc
1493 Poinsettia Ave Ste 143............Vista CA 92081 — 800-854-2896* — 760-744-5585 — 228
NYSE: LANZ ■ *Cust Svc

Land Line Magazine
1 NW Oodia Dr PO Box 1000........Grain Valley MO 64029 — 800-444-5791 — 816-229-5791 — 455-21

Land O'Lakes Inc Dairyman's Div
400 S 'M' St ....Tulare CA 93274 — 800-328-4155 — 559-687-8287 — 296-27

Land O'Lakes Inc Western Feed Div
4001 Lexington Ave N ....Arden Hills MN 55126 — 800-328-9680 — — 445

Land Rover North America Inc
555 MacArthur Blvd ....Mahwah NJ 07430 — 800-637-6837 — — 59

Land Rover of Calgary
175 Glendeer Cir SE ....Calgary AB T2H2V4 — 866-274-4080 — —

Landaal Packaging Systems Inc
3256 B Iron St ....Burton MI 48529 — 800-616-6619 — — 100

Landaas & Co
411 E Wisconsin Ave 20th Fl ....Milwaukee WI 53202 — 800-236-1096 — 414-223-1099 — 400

Landair Corp
1110 Myers St ....Greeneville TN 37743 — 888-526-3247 — — 775

LandaJob
222 W Gregory Blvd Ste 304 ....Kansas City MO 64114 — 800-931-8806 — 816-523-1881 — 195

Landau Uniforms
8410 W Sandidge Rd ....Olive Branch MS 38654 — 800-238-7513* — 662-895-7200 — 155-18
*General

Name / Address	City	State	ZIP	Toll-Free	Phone	Class
Landec Ag LLC						
201 N Michigan St	Oxford	IN	47971	**800-241-7252**	765-385-1000	280
Landel Telecom						
142 Martinvale Ln	San Jose	CA	95119	**855-624-5284**		386
Lander University						
320 Stanley Ave	Greenwood	SC	29649	**800-922-1117***	864-388-8307	166
*Admissions						
Landice Inc						
111 Canfield Ave	Randolph	NJ	07869	**800-526-3423**	973-927-9010	474
Landings Club Inc						
71 Green Island Rd	Savannah	GA	31411	**800-841-7011**	912-598-8050	353
Landis Construction LLC						
8300 Earhart Blvd Ste 300						
PO Box 4278	New Orleans	LA	70118	**800-880-3290**	504-833-6070	186
Landis Gyr Inc						
2800 Duncan Rd	Lafayette	IN	47904	**888-390-5733**	765-742-1001	248
Landiscor						
3401 E Broadway Rd	Phoenix	AZ	85040	**866-221-8578**	602-248-8989	723
Landmark Community Newspapers Inc						
601 Taylorsville Rd	Shelbyville	KY	40065	**800-939-9322**	502-633-4334	633-8
Landmark Credit Union						
5445 S Westridge Dr						
PO Box 510910	New Berlin	WI	53151	**800-801-1449**	262-796-4500	219
Landmark Financial Group LLC						
181 Old Post Rd	Southport	CT	06890	**800-437-4214**	203-254-8422	251
Landmark Inn						
230 N Front St	Marquette	MI	49855	**888-752-6362***	906-228-2580	378
*General						
Landmark International Trucks Inc						
4550 Rutledge Pk	Knoxville	TN	37914	**800-968-9999**	865-637-4881	775
Landmark Lincoln-Mercury Inc						
5000 S Broadway	Englewood	CO	80113	**888-318-9692**	303-761-1560	57
Landmark Plastic Corp						
1331 Kelly Ave	Akron	OH	44306	**800-242-1183**	330-785-2200	604
Landmark Resort						
7643 Hillside Rd	Egg Harbor	WI	54209	**800-273-7877**	920-868-3205	665
Landmark Resort						
1501 S Ocean Blvd	Myrtle Beach	SC	29577	**800-845-0658**	843-448-9441	665
Landmark School						
429 Hale St PO Box 227	Prides Crossing	MA	01965	**866-333-0859**	978-236-3010	618
Landmark Structures LP						
1665 Harmon Rd	Fort Worth	TX	76177	**800-888-6816**	817-439-8888	188-10
Landmark Theaters						
2222 S Barrington Ave	Los Angeles	CA	90064	**888-724-6362***	310-473-6701	743
*Cust Svc						
Landmark Tours Inc						
4001 Stinson Blvd Ste 430	Minneapolis	MN	55421	**888-231-8735**	651-490-5408	755
Landoll Corp						
1900 North St	Marysville	KS	66508	**800-446-5175***	785-562-5381	468
*Cust Svc						
Landpoint LLC						
5486 Airline Dr	Bossier City	LA	71111	**800-348-5254**	318-226-0100	723
Landrum & Shouse LLP						
106 W Vine St Ste 800	Lexington	KY	40507	**888-322-2505**	859-554-4038	
Landry's Restaurants Inc						
1510 W Loop S	Houston	TX	77027	**800-552-6379**	713-850-1010	666
Lands' End Inc						
1 Lands' End Ln	Dodgeville	WI	53595	**800-963-4816***		457
*Orders						
Landsberg Orora						
1640 S Greenwood Ave	Montebello	CA	90640	**888-526-3723***	323-832-2000	555
*Cust Svc						
Landscape Concepts Management						
31745 Alleghany Rd	Grayslake	IL	60030	**866-655-3800**	847-223-3800	421
Landscape Structures Inc						
601 Seventh St S	Delano	MN	55328	**800-328-0035**	763-972-3391	345
Landstar Express America Inc						
13410 Sutton Pk Dr S	Jacksonville	FL	32224	**800-872-9400**	904-398-9400	775
Landstar Inway Inc						
13410 Sutton Pk Dr S	Jacksonville	FL	32224	**800-872-9400**		775
Landstar Logistics Inc						
13410 Sutton Pk Dr S	Jacksonville	FL	32224	**800-872-9400**	904-398-9400	447
Lane Aviation Corp						
4389 International Gateway	Columbus	OH	43219	**800-848-6263**	614-237-3747	63
Lane Bryant Inc						
3344 Morse Crossing Rd	Columbus	OH	43219	**866-886-4731***	954-970-2205	157-6
*Cust Svc						
Lane College						
545 Ln Ave	Jackson	TN	38301	**800-960-7533***	731-426-7500	166
*Admissions						
Lane Community College						
4000 E 30th Ave	Eugene	OR	97405	**800-321-2211**	541-463-3000	162
Florence 3149 Oak St	Florence	OR	97439	**800-222-3290**	541-997-8444	162
Lane County						
125 E Eigth Ave	Eugene	OR	97401	**800-281-2800**	541-682-4203	337
Lane Press Inc						
87 Meadowland Dr	Burlington	VT	05403	**877-300-5933**		623
Lang Dental Manufacturing Co						
175 Messner Dr	Wheeling	IL	60090	**800-222-5264**		228
Langdon Hall Country House Hotel & Spa						
1 Langdon Dr	Cambridge	ON	N3H4R8	**800-268-1898**	519-740-2100	378
Langer Inc						
2905 Veterans' Memorial Hwy	Ronkonkoma	NY	11779	**800-645-5520**		475
Langham Boston, The						
250 Franklin St	Boston	MA	02110	**800-791-7781**	617-451-1900	378
Langhorne Carpet Co Inc						
201 W Lincoln Hwy PO Box 7175	Penndel	PA	19047	**800-372-6274**	215-757-5155	131
Langley Federal Credit Union						
1055 W Mercury Blvd	Hampton	VA	23666	**800-826-7490**	757-827-7200	219
Langston Cos Inc						
1760 S Third St	Memphis	TN	38109	**800-238-5798**		67
Langston University						
2017 Langston University						
PO Box 1500	Langston	OK	73050	**877-466-2231**		166
Langstons Co						
2034 NW Seventh St	Oklahoma City	OK	73106	**800-658-2831**	405-235-9536	229
Langtech Systems Consulting Inc						
733 Frnt St Ste 110	San Francisco	CA	94111	**800-480-8488**	415-364-9600	804

Name / Address	City	State	ZIP	Toll-Free	Phone	Class
Language Engineering Co						
135 Beaver St Ste 204	Waltham	MA	02452	**888-366-4532**	781-642-8900	178-3
Language Line Solutions						
1 Lower Ragsdale Dr Bldg 2	Monterey	CA	93940	**800-752-6096**		763
Language Scientific						
101 Station Landing Ste 500	Medford	MA	02155	**800-240-0246**	617-621-0940	
Language Services Associates Inc						
455 Business Ctr Dr - Ste 100	Horsham	PA	19044	**800-305-9673**		763
Languages Canada						
27282 - 12B AVE	Aldergrove	BC	V4W2P6	**888-277-0522**	604-574-1532	49-5
Lankota Inc						
270 Westpark Ave	Huron	SD	57350	**866-526-5682**	605-352-4550	57
LANL (Los Alamos National Laboratory)						
PO Box 1663	Los Alamos	NM	87545	**877-723-4101**	505-667-7000	664
Lanman Oil Co Inc						
PO Box 108	Charleston	IL	61920	**800-677-2819**		575
Lannett Company Inc (LCI)						
13200 Townsend Rd	Philadelphia	PA	19154	**800-325-9994**	215-333-9000	477
NYSE: LCI						
LANSA Inc						
2001 Butterfield Rd						
Ste 102	Downers Grove	IL	60515	**800-457-4083**	630-874-7000	178-2
Lansco Colors						
1 Blue Hill Plz 11th Fl						
PO Box 1685	Pearl River	NY	10965	**800-526-2783**	845-507-5942	546
Lansdale School of Business						
290 Wissahickon Ave	North Wales	PA	19454	**800-219-0486**	215-699-5700	795
Lansdowne Resort						
44050 Woodridge Pkwy	Leesburg	VA	20176	**877-513-8400**	703-729-8400	376
Lansing Community College						
411 N Grand Ave	Lansing	MI	48933	**800-644-4522**	517-483-1957	162
Lansing Ice & Fuel Co						
911 Ctr St	Lansing	MI	48906	**800-678-7230**	517-372-3850	316
Lansing State Journal						
120 E Lenawee St	Lansing	MI	48919	**800-234-1719**	517-377-1000	528-2
Lantal Textiles Inc						
1300 Langenthal Dr						
PO Box 965	Rural Hall	NC	27045	**800-334-3309**	336-969-9551	740-1
Lantana Communications Corp						
1700 Tech Centre Pkwy Ste 100	Arlington	TX	76014	**800-345-4211**		45
Lantech Inc						
11000 Bluegrass Pkwy	Louisville	KY	40299	**800-866-0322**	502-815-9109	543
Lantern Lodge Motor Inn						
411 N College St	Myerstown	PA	17067	**800-262-5564**	717-866-6536	378
Lantronix Inc						
167 Technology Dr	Irvine	CA	92618	**800-526-8766***	949-453-3990	730
NASDAQ: LTRX ■ *Orders						
Lanxess Corp						
111 RIDC Pk W Dr	Pittsburgh	PA	15275	**800-526-9377**	412-809-1000	601-3
LanXpert Corp						
605 Market St Ste 410	San Francisco	CA	94105	**888-499-1703**	415-543-1033	177
Lanz Cabinet Shop Inc						
3025 W Seventh Pl	Eugene	OR	97402	**800-788-6332**	541-485-4050	360
Lapco Inc						
12995 Rue Du Parc	Mirabel	QC	J7J0W5	**800-433-1988**	450-971-0432	
Lapels Dry Cleaning						
962 Washington St	Hanover	MA	02339	**866-695-2735**	781-829-9935	425
Lapham-Hickey Steel Corp						
5500 W 73rd St	Chicago	IL	60638	**800-323-8443**	708-496-6111	490
LapLink Software Inc						
600 108th Ave NE Ste 610	Bellevue	WA	98004	**800-527-5465**	425-952-6000	178-12
Lapmaster International LLC						
501 W Algonquin Rd	Mount Prospect	IL	60056	**877-352-8637**		489
Lapolla Industries Inc						
15402 Vantage Pkwy E Ste 322	Houston	TX	77032	**888-452-7655**	281-219-4700	
OTC: LPAD						
LaPorte County Convention & Visitors Bureau						
4073 S Franklin St	Michigan City	IN	46360	**800-634-2650**	219-872-5055	206
Laramie Area Chamber of Commerce						
800 S Third St	Laramie	WY	82070	**866-876-1012**	307-745-7339	139
Laramie County Community College						
1400 E College Dr	Cheyenne	WY	82007	**800-522-2993**	307-778-5222	162
Albany County						
1125 Boulder Dr	Laramie	WY	82070	**800-522-2993**	307-721-5138	162
Laramie River Dude Ranch						
25777 County Rd 103	Jelm	WY	82063	**800-551-5731**	970-435-5716	239
Larchmont Engineering & Irrigation Co						
11 Larchmont Ln PO Box 66	Lexington	MA	02420	**877-862-2550**	781-862-2550	274
Larco						
210 NE Tenth Ave	Brainerd	MN	56401	**800-523-6996***	218-829-9797	253
*Cust Svc						
Laredo Chamber of Commerce, The						
2310 San Bernardo	Laredo	TX	78040	**800-292-2122**	956-722-9895	139
Laredo Morning Times						
111 Esperanza Dr	Laredo	TX	78041	**800-232-7907**	956-728-2500	528-2
Larkin Enterprises Inc						
317 W Broadway PO Box 405	Lincoln	ME	04457	**800-990-5418**	207-794-8700	188
LARL (Lake Agassiz Regional Library)						
118 Fifth St S PO Box 900	Moorhead	MN	56560	**800-247-0449**	218-233-3757	433-3
LARON Inc						
4255 Santa Fe Dr	Kingman	AZ	86401	**800-248-3430**	928-757-8424	256
Larrabee Ventures Inc						
15165 Ventura Blvd Ste 450	Sherman Oaks	CA	91403	**800-232-3584**		194
Larsen Farms						
2650 N 2375 E	Hamer	ID	83425	**800-767-6104***	208-662-5501	296-18
*Sales						
Larson Boats LLC						
700 Paul Larson Memorial Dr						
	Little Falls	MN	56345	**800-220-6262***	320-632-5481	90
*General						
Larson Contracting Inc						
508 W Main St	Lake Mills	IA	50450	**800-765-1426**	641-592-5800	189-3
Larson Design Group Inc						
1000 Commerce Park Dr						
2nd Fl Ste 201	Williamsport	PA	17701	**877-323-6603**		261
Larson King LLP						
30 E Seventh St Ste 2800	Saint Paul	MN	55101	**877-373-5501**	651-312-6500	427

Name	Address	City	State	ZIP	Toll-Free	Phone	Class
Larson Manufacturing Co	2333 Eastbrook Dr *Cust Svc	Brookings	SD	57006	**888-483-3768***	605-692-6115	235
Larson-Juhl	3900 Steve Reynolds Blvd	Norcross	GA	30093	**800-221-4123**	770-279-5200	309
Larue Coffee	2631 S 156th Cir	Omaha	NE	68130	**800-658-4498**	402-333-9099	297-8
Las Cruces Sun-News	256 W Las Cruces Ave	Las Cruces	NM	88005	**877-827-7200**	575-541-5400	528-2
LAS Enterprises Inc	2413 L & A Rd	Metairie	LA	70001	**800-264-1527**	504-887-1515	187
Las Vegas Chamber of Commerce	575 Symphony Park Ave Ste 100	Las Vegas	NV	89106	**800-468-7272**	702-641-5822	139
Las Vegas Convention & Visitors Authority	3150 Paradise Rd	Las Vegas	NV	89109	**877-847-4858**	702-892-0711	206
Las Vegas Motor Speedway	7000 Las Vegas Blvd N	Las Vegas	NV	89115	**800-644-4444**	702-644-4444	512
LaSalle County	707 E Etna Rd	Ottawa	IL	61350	**800-247-5243**	815-433-3366	337
LASCCO (Los Angeles Smoking & Curing Co)	1100 W Ewing St	Seattle	WA	98119	**800-365-8950**	206-285-6800	296-13
Lasco Fittings Inc	414 Morgan St PO Box 116	Brownsville	TN	38012	**800-776-2756**	731-772-3180	592
Lasell College	1844 Commonwealth Ave *Admissions	Newton	MA	02466	**888-222-5229***	617-243-2225	166
Laser Excel	N6323 Berlin Rd	Green Lake	WI	54941	**800-285-6544**		452
Laser Institute of America (LIA)	13501 Ingenuity Dr Ste 128	Orlando	FL	32826	**800-345-2737**	407-380-1553	49-19
Laser Pros International	1 International Ln	Rhinelander	WI	54501	**888-558-5277**	715-369-5995	174
Laser Technology Inc	7070 S Tucson Way	Englewood	CO	80112	**800-280-6113**	303-649-1000	493
LaserCard Corp	1875 N Shoreline Blvd	Mountain View	CA	94043	**800-237-7769**	650-969-4428	654
Lasercycle USA Inc	528 S Taylor Ave	Louisville	CO	80027	**866-666-7776**	303-666-7776	585
LaserMax Corp	3495 Winton Pl	Rochester	NY	14623	**800-527-3703**	585-272-5420	540
Laserscope	3070 Orchard Dr	San Jose	CA	95134	**800-878-3399**	408-943-0636	423
LaserVue Eye Ctr	3540 Mendocino Ave #200	Santa Rosa	CA	95403	**888-527-3745**	707-522-6200	793
Lashbrook Designs	131 E 13065 S	Draper	UT	84020	**888-252-7388**		410
Lasko Metal Products Inc	820 Lincoln Ave	West Chester	PA	19380	**800-233-0268**	610-692-7400	37
LasscoWizer Inc	485 Hague St	Rochester	NY	14606	**800-854-6595**	585-436-1934	625
Lassen Community College	478-200 Hwy 139 PO Box 3000	Susanville	CA	96130	**800-461-9389**	530-257-6181	162
Lassen Volcanic National Park	38050 Hwy 36 E PO Box 100	Mineral	CA	96063	**800-427-7623**	530-595-4480	560
LassoSoft LLC	PO Box 33	Manchester	WA	98353	**888-286-7753**	954-302-3526	178-7
Lasting Impressions Inc	7406 43rd Ave NE	Marysville	WA	98270	**866-859-7625**	360-659-1255	623
LastMinuteTravelcom Inc	220 E Central Pkwy Ste 4000	Altamonte Springs	FL	32701	**800-442-0568**	407-667-8700	768
Lasvegasticketscom	5030 Paradise Rd Ste B108	Las Vegas	NV	89119	**800-597-7469**	702-597-1588	375
Latham & Phillips Ophthalmic Products Inc	224 James St	Bensenville	IL	60106	**800-729-1959**		
Latham Seed Co	131 180th St	Alexander	IA	50420	**877-465-2842**	641-692-3258	690
Lathem Time Corp	200 Selig Dr SW	Atlanta	GA	30336	**800-241-4990**	404-691-0400	111
Laticrete International Inc	91 Amity Rd	Bethany	CT	06524	**800-243-4788**	203-393-0010	3
Latitude Consulting Group Inc	100 E Michigan Ave Ste 200	Saline	MI	48176	**888-577-2797**		461
Latta Robert E (Rep R - OH)	2448 Rayburn House Office Bldg	Washington	DC	20515	**800-541-6446**	202-225-6405	
Latter Day Saints Business College	95 North 300 West	Salt Lake City	UT	84101	**800-999-5767**	801-524-8159	795
Lattice Semiconductor Corp	5555 NE Moore Ct *NASDAQ: LSCC*	Hillsboro	OR	97124	**800-528-8423**	503-268-8000	692
Laughing Elephant	3645 Interlake Ave N	Seattle	WA	98103	**800-354-0400**	800-509-4166	130
Laughlin Air Force Base	561 Liberty Dr Ste 3	Laughlin AFB	TX	78843	**866-966-1020**	830-298-3511	495-1
Laughlin Memorial Hospital	1420 Tuscolum Blvd	Greeneville	TN	37745	**800-852-7157**	423-787-5000	373-3
Launch Agency LP	4100 Midway Rd Ste 2110	Carrollton	TX	75007	**866-427-5013**	972-818-4100	4
Launch Pad	18130 Jorene Rd	Odessa	FL	33556	**888-920-3450**		179
Laura Ingalls Wilder Museum & Home	3068 Hwy A	Mansfield	MO	65704	**877-924-7126**		517
Laureate Education Inc	650 S Exeter St	Baltimore	MD	21202	**866-452-8732**	410-843-6100	242
Laurel Grocery Co Inc	129 Barbourville Rd	London	KY	40744	**800-467-6601**		297-8
Laurel Highlands Visitors Bureau	120 E Main St	Ligonier	PA	15658	**800-333-5661**	724-238-5661	206
Laurel Inn, The	444 Presidio Ave	San Francisco	CA	94115	**800-552-8735**	415-567-8467	378
Laurel Lake Retirement Community	200 Laurel Lake Dr	Hudson	OH	44236	**866-650-2100**		668
Laurel Park	Rt 198 & Racetrack Rd PO Box 130	Laurel	MD	20724	**800-638-1859**	301-725-0400	638
Lauren Mfg	2228 Reiser Ave SE	New Philadelphia	OH	44663	**800-683-0676**	330-339-3373	673
Laurentian Bank of Canada	1981 McGill College Ave *TSE: LB*	Montreal	QC	H3A3K3	**800-252-1846**	514-284-4500	70
Laurentian Bank Securities Inc	1981 McGill College Ave Ste 100	Montreal	QC	H3A3K3	**888-350-8577**	514-350-2800	400
Laurentian University	935 Ramsey Lake Rd	Sudbury	ON	P3E2C6	**800-461-4030**	705-675-1151	780
Laurie Raphael	117 Dalhousie St	Quebec	QC	G1K9C8	**877-876-4555**	418-692-4555	667
LAURUS Systems Inc	3460 Ellicott Ctr Dr Ste 101	Ellicott City	MD	21043	**800-274-4212**	410-465-5558	196
Lauterbach Group Inc	W222 N5710 Miller Way *Sales	Sussex	WI	53089	**800-841-7301***	262-820-8130	550
Lava Hot Springs State Foundation	430 E Main St PO Box 669	Lava Hot Springs	ID	83246	**800-423-8597**	208-776-5221	50-5
Laval University	2325 Rue University	Quebec	QC	G1V0A6	**877-785-2825**	418-656-2131	780
Lavanture Products Co	22825 Gallatin Way	Elkhart	IN	46515	**800-348-7625**	574-264-0658	596
Lavelle Industries Inc	665 McHenry St	Burlington	WI	53105	**800-528-3553**	262-763-2434	673
LaVezzi Precision Inc	250 Madsen Dr	Bloomingdale	IL	60108	**800-323-1772**		452
Lavigne Oil Company LLC	11203 Proverbs Ave	Baton Rouge	LA	70816	**800-349-0170**		534
Law Elder Law	2275 Church Rd	Aurora	IL	60502	**800-310-3100**	630-585-5200	683
Law Enforcement Assoc Corp (LEA-AID)	120 Penmarc Dr Ste 113 *OTC: LAWEQ*	Raleigh	NC	27603	**800-354-9669**	919-872-6210	52
Law Enforcement Technology Magazine	1233 Janesville Ave	Fort Atkinson	WI	53538	**800-547-7377**		455-5
Law Engine	7660-H Fay Ave Ste 342	La Jolla	CA	92037	**800-894-2889**	858-456-1234	396
Law Officer's Bulletin	610 Opperman Dr	Eagan	MN	55123	**800-344-5008**	651-687-7000	527-2
Lawgical Inc	11693 San Vicente Blvd Ste 910	Los Angeles	CA	90049	**800-811-4458**		195
Lawley Service Insurance	361 Delaware Ave *Cust Svc	Buffalo	NY	14202	**800-860-5741***	716-849-8618	389
Lawn Doctor Inc	142 SR 34	Holmdel	NJ	07733	**800-845-0580**		573
Lawn Equipment Parts Co	1475 River Rd PO Box 466	Marietta	PA	17547	**800-365-3726**	717-426-5200	428
Lawrence & Memorial Hospital	365 Montauk Ave	New London	CT	06320	**800-579-3341**	860-442-0711	373-3
Lawrence Behr Assoc Inc	3400 Tupper Dr	Greenville	NC	27834	**800-522-4464**	252-757-0279	196
Lawrence Companies (LTS)	872 Lee Hwy	Roanoke	VA	24019	**800-336-9626**		775
Lawrence County	216 Collins Ave	South Point	OH	45680	**800-408-1334**	740-377-4550	
Lawrence County	County Courthouse 430 Court St	New Castle	PA	16101	**855-564-6116**	724-658-2541	337
Lawrence County	315 W Main	Walnut Ridge	AR	72476	**800-621-4000**	870-886-2525	337
Lawrence County Tourist Promotion Agency	229 S Jefferson St	New Castle	PA	16101	**888-284-7599**	724-654-8408	206
Lawrence Equipment Inc	2034 Peck Rd	El Monte	CA	91733	**800-423-4500**	626-442-2894	298
Lawrence Journal-World	645 New Hampshire PO Box 888	Lawrence	KS	66044	**800-578-8748**	785-843-1000	633-8
Lawrence Memorial Hospital (LMH)	325 Maine St	Lawrence	KS	66044	**800-749-4144**	785-505-5000	373-3
Lawrence Memorial Hospital of Medford	170 Governors Ave	Medford	MA	02155	**800-540-9191**	781-306-6000	373-3
Lawrence Merchandising	1405 Xenium Ln N Ste 250	Plymouth	MN	55441	**800-328-3967**	763-383-5700	461
Lawrence Paper Co	2801 Lakeview Rd	Lawrence	KS	66049	**800-535-4553**		100
Lawrence Printing Co	400 Stribling Ave PO Box 886	Greenwood	MS	38935	**800-844-0338**	662-453-6301	
Lawrence Ragan Communications Inc	316 N Michigan Ave Ste 400	Chicago	IL	60601	**800-878-5331**	312-960-4100	527-3
Lawrence Technological University	21000 W 10-Mile Rd	Southfield	MI	48075	**800-225-5588**	248-204-3160	166
Lawrence University	115 S Drew St	Appleton	WI	54911	**800-432-5427**	920-832-7000	166
Lawrence University Mudd Library	711 E Boldt Way	Appleton	WI	54911	**800-432-5427**	920-832-6750	433-6
Lawrenceville School	2500 Main St PO Box 6008	Lawrenceville	NJ	08648	**800-735-2030**	609-896-0400	618
Lawry's Restaurants Inc	225 S Lake Ave Ste 1500	Pasadena	CA	91101	**888-552-9797**		666
Lawry's the Prime Rib	100 N La Cienega Blvd	Beverly Hills	CA	90211	**877-529-7984**	310-652-2827	667
Lawson Products Inc	1666 E Touhy Ave	Des Plaines	IL	60018	**800-323-5922**	847-827-9666	384
Lawson State Community College	*Bessemer* 1100 Ninth Ave SW	Bessemer	AL	35022	**800-373-4879**	205-925-2515	795
Lawton & Cates SC	10 E Doty St Ste 400	Madison	WI	53703	**800-900-4539**	608-282-6200	427
Lawton Industries Inc	4353 Pacific St	Rocklin	CA	95677	**800-692-2600**	916-624-7894	385
Lawton Public Library	110 SW Fourth St	Lawton	OK	73501	**855-895-8064**	580-581-3450	433-3
Lawton's Drug Stores Ltd	236 Brownlow Ave Ste 270	Dartmouth	NS	B3B1V5	**866-990-1599**	902-468-1000	231
Lawyers Diary & Manual	890 Mtn Ave Ste 300	New Providence	NJ	07974	**800-444-4041**	973-642-1440	633-2

	Toll-Free	Phone	Class
Lawyers Group Advertising Inc 28 Thorndal Cir .... Darien CT 06820	800-948-1080		
Lawyers Weekly Inc 10 Milk St Ste 1000 ....Boston MA 02108	800-444-5297	617-451-7300	528-3
Lawyers' Committee for Civil Rights Under Law 1401 New York Ave NW Ste 400...... Washington DC 20005	888-299-5227	202-662-8600	49-10
Lawyers' Travel Service 71 Fifth Ave ....New York NY 10003 *General	800-431-1112*		766
Lawyerscom 121 Chanlon Rd Ste 110........New Providence NJ 07974	800-526-4902	908-464-6800	171
Layer 3 Communications LLC 109 Park of Commerce Dr Ste 1 ....Savannah GA 31405	844-352-9373	770-225-5279	252
Layne 4520 N State Rd 37 ....Orleans IN 47452 *All	855-529-6301*	812-865-3232	188-10
Layton Manufacturing Corp 825 Remsen Ave ....Brooklyn NY 11236	800-545-8002	718-498-6000	14
Lazard 30 Rockefeller Plz ....New York NY 10112 NYSE: LAZ	866-867-4070	212-632-6000	686
La-Z-Boy Inc 1284 N Telegraph Rd ....Monroe MI 48162 NYSE: LZB	800-375-6890	734-242-1444	319-2
Lazer Grant Inc 309 Mcdermot Ave ....Winnipeg MB R3A1T3	800-220-0005	204-942-0300	2
Lazy L & B Ranch 1072 E Fork Rd ....Dubois WY 82513 *Cust Svc	800-453-9488*	307-455-2839	239
Lazzari Fuel Company LLC 11 Industrial Way ....Brisbane CA 94005	800-242-7265	415-467-2970	316
LB Foster Co 415 Holiday Dr ....Pittsburgh PA 15220 NASDAQ: FSTR	800-255-4500		646
LB Furniture Industries LLC 99 S Third St ....Hudson NY 12534	800-221-8752	518-828-1501	319-3
L&B Transport LLC 708 US190 PO Box 74870 ....Port Allen LA 70767	800-545-9401	225-387-0894	447
LB White Company Inc W 6636 LB White Rd ....Onalaska WI 54650	800-345-7200	608-783-5691	356
LBA Group Inc 3400 Tupper Dr ....Greenville NC 27834	800-522-4464	252-757-0279	261
LBJ Library & Museum 2313 Red River St ....Austin TX 78705	800-874-6451	512-721-0216	433-2
LBP Manufacturing Inc 1325 S Cicero Ave ....Cicero IL 60804	800-545-6200	708-652-5600	553
LBS (Library Binding Service) 1801 Thompson Ave ....Des Moines IA 50316	800-247-5323	515-262-3191	92
LBT Inc 11502 "I" St ....Omaha NE 68137	888-528-7278	402-333-4900	774
LC (LeChase Construction Services LLC) 205 Indigo Creek Dr ....Rochester NY 14626	888-953-2427	585-254-3510	
LC King Mfg Company Inc 24 Seventh St ....Bristol TN 37620	800-826-2510	423-764-5188	155-18
LC Whitford Company Inc 164 N Main St ....Wellsville NY 14895	800-321-3602	585-593-3601	188-4
LCC (Legal Cost Control Inc) 8 Kings Hwy W Ste C ....Haddonfield NJ 08033	800-493-7345	856-216-0800	443
LCD Lighting Inc 37 Robinson Blvd ....Orange CT 06477	800-826-9465	203-795-1520	436
LCEC 4980 Bayline Dr ....North Fort Myers FL 33917	800-282-1643	239-995-2121	245
LCH Paper Tube & Core Co 11930 Larc Industrial Blvd ....Burnsville MN 55337	800-472-3477	952-358-3587	125
LCI (Lannett Company Inc) 13200 Townsend Rd ....Philadelphia PA 19154 NYSE: LCI	800-325-9994	215-333-9000	477
LCMH (Lake Charles Memorial Health System) 1701 Oak Pk Blvd ....Lake Charles LA 70601	800-494-5264	337-494-3000	373-3
LCMS (Lutheran Church Missouri Synod) 1333 S Kirkwood Rd ....Saint Louis MO 63122	888-843-5267	314-965-9000	48-20
LCNB National Bank 3209 W Galbraith Rd ....Cincinnati OH 45239	800-344-2265	513-932-1414	70
LCS Technologies Inc 11230 Gold Express Dr Ste 310-140 ....Gold River CA 95670	855-277-5527		620
LD Systems LP 407 Garden Oaks ....Houston TX 77018	800-416-9327	713-695-9400	179
LDA (Learning Disabilities Assn of America) 4156 Library Rd ....Pittsburgh PA 15234	888-300-6710	412-341-1515	48-17
LDP Inc 75 Kiwanis Blvd PO Box O ....West Hazleton PA 18201	800-522-8413		178-3
LDR Industries Inc 600 N Kilbourn Ave ....Chicago IL 60624	800-545-5230	773-265-3000	605
LDS Hospital 8th Ave & C St ....Salt Lake City UT 84143	888-301-3880	801-408-1100	373-3
Le Baluchon Eco-resort 3550 chemin des Trembles ....Saint-Paulin QC J0K3G0	800-789-5968	819-268-2555	703
Le Bleu Corp 3134 Cornatzer Rd ....Advance NC 27006	800-854-4471	336-998-2894	800
Le Chamois 4557 Blackcomb Way ....Whistler BC V0N1B4	888-621-1177	604-932-8700	378
Le Devoir 1265 Berri 8th Fl..............Montreal QC H2L4X4	800-463-7559	514-985-3333	528-1
LE Johnson Products Inc 2100 Sterling Ave ....Elkhart IN 46516	800-837-5664	574-293-5664	349
Le Mars Insurance Co PO Box 1608 ....Le Mars IA 51031	800-545-6480		389
Le Meridian 20 Sidney St ....Cambridge MA 02139	800-543-4300	617-577-0200	378
Le Meridien Chambers Minneapolis 901 Hennepin Ave ....Minneapolis MN 55403 *General	877-782-0116*	612-767-6900	378
Le M,ridien Delfina Santa Monica 530 W Pico Blvd ....Santa Monica CA 90405	888-627-8532	310-399-9344	378
Le Montrose Suite Hotel 900 Hammond St ....West Hollywood CA 90069	800-776-0666	310-855-1115	378
Le Moyne College 1419 Salt Springs Rd ....Syracuse NY 13214 *Admissions	800-333-4733*	315-445-4100	166
Le Nouvel Montreal Hotel & Spa 1740 Rene-Levesque Blvd W ....Montreal QC H3H1R3	800-363-6063	514-931-8841	378
Le Port-Royal Hotel & Suites 144 St Pierre St ....Quebec QC G1K8N8	866-417-2777	418-692-2777	378
Le Quotidien & Progres Dimanche 1051 boul Talbot ....Chicoutimi QC G7H5C1	800-866-3658	418-545-4664	
Le Richelieu Hotel 1234 Chartres St ....New Orleans LA 70116	800-535-9653	504-529-2492	378
Le Saint Sulpice 414 Rue St Sulpice ....Montreal QC H2Y2V5 *General	877-785-7423*	514-288-1000	378
Lea County 100 N Main St Ste 11 ....Lovington NM 88260	800-658-9955	575-396-8619	337
Lea Regional Medical Ctr 5419 N Lovington Hwy ....Hobbs NM 88240	877-492-8001	575-492-5000	373-3
LEA-AID (Law Enforcement Assoc Corp) 120 Penmarc Dr Ste 113.............Raleigh NC 27603 OTC: LAWEQ	800-354-9669	919-872-6210	52
Leach International Corp 6900 Orangethorpe Ave ....Buena Park CA 90622	800-232-7700	714-736-7598	203
Lead Technologies Inc 1927 S Tryon St Ste 200.............Charlotte NC 28203	800-637-4699	704-332-5532	177
Leaders LLC 14 Maine St Ste 216G PO Box 18............. Brunswick ME 04011	888-583-7770	207-318-1893	686
Leadership Connect 1407 Broadway Ste 318 ....New York NY 10011	800-627-0311	212-627-4140	633-2
Leadership Journal 465 Gundersen Dr ....Carol Stream IL 60188	800-777-3136	630-260-6200	455-5
Leadership Management International Inc 4567 Lake Shore Dr ....Waco TX 76710	800-876-2389	254-776-2060	760
Leadership Performance Sustainability Laboratories 4647 Hugh Howell Rd ....Tucker GA 30084	800-241-8334		537
Leader-Telegram 701 S Farwell St ....Eau Claire WI 54701	800-236-8808	715-833-9200	528-2
Leading Age 2519 Connecticut Ave NW ....Washington DC 20008	866-898-2624	202-783-2242	48-6
Leading Authorities Inc 1725 Eye St NW Ste 200..........Washington DC 20006	855-827-0943		704
Leading Hotels of the World 485 Lexington Ave Ste 401.......New York NY 10017	800-745-8883	212-515-5600	375
Leading Lady 24050 Commerce Pk ....Beachwood OH 44122 *Cust Svc	800-321-4804*		155-17
LeadingResponse LLC 4805 Independence Pkwy ....Tampa FL 33634	800-660-2550		
Leadman Electronic USA Inc 382 Laurelwood Dr ....Santa Clara CA 95054	877-532-3626	408-738-1751	174
LeadRival 1207 S White Chapel Blvd Ste 250............Southlake TX 76092	800-332-8017		5
LEAF Commercial Capital Inc 1 Commerce Sq 2005 Market St 14th Fl ....Philadelphia PA 19103	800-819-5556		23
League of Kansas Municipalities, The 300 SW Eighth Ave Ste 100 ....Topeka KS 66603	800-445-5588	785-354-9565	529
Leahi Hospital 3675 Kilauea Ave ....Honolulu HI 96816	800-845-6733	808-733-8000	373-7
Leaktite Corp 40 Francis St ....Leominster MA 01453	800-392-0039	978-537-8000	604
Leam Drilling Systems Inc 2027a Airport Rd ....Conroe TX 77301	800-426-5349		535
Leanin' Tree Inc 6055 Longbow Dr ....Boulder CO 80301	800-525-0656		130
Leanin' Tree Museum of Western Art 6055 Longbow Dr ....Boulder CO 80301	800-525-0656		517
Leap/Carpenter/Kemps Insurance Agency 3187 Collins Dr ....Merced CA 95348	800-221-0864	209-384-0727	389
LeapFrog Enterprises Inc 6401 Hollis St Ste 100 ....Emeryville CA 94608 NYSE: LF	800-701-5327	510-420-5000	757
Lear Capital Inc 1990 S Bundy Dr Ste 600..........Los Angeles CA 90025	800-576-9355		251
Learning Disabilities Assn of America (LDA) 4156 Library Rd ....Pittsburgh PA 15234	888-300-6710	412-341-1515	48-17
Learning Express Inc 29 Buena Vista St ....Devens MA 01434	888-725-8697	978-889-1000	756
Learning Resources 380 N Fairway Dr ....Vernon Hills IL 60061	800-222-3909	847-573-8400	243
Learning Tree International Inc 1831 Michael Faraday Dr ....Reston VA 20190 OTC: LTRE ■ *Cust Svc	800-843-8733*	703-709-9119	759
Learning Unlimited 4137 S Harvard Ave Ste A............Tulsa OK 74135	888-622-4203	918-622-3292	461
Learning Wrap-Ups Inc 1660 W Gordon Ave Ste 4 ....Layton UT 84041	800-992-4966	801-497-0050	243
LearnSpectrum 9912 Georgetown Pke Ste D203.............Great Falls VA 22066	888-682-9485	703-757-8200	317
LeaseQ Inc 1 Burlington Woods Dr Ste 200 ....Burlington MA 01803	888-688-4519		392
Leasing Assoc Inc 12600 N Featherwood Dr Ste 400........Houston TX 77034	800-449-4807	832-300-1300	289
Leather Industries of America (LIA) 3050 K St NW Ste 400 ....Washington DC 20007	800-635-0617	202-342-8497	49-4
Leathercraft PO Box 639 ....Conover NC 28613	800-627-1561		319-2
Leatherman Tool Group Inc 12106 NE Ainsworth Cir ....Portland OR 97220	800-847-8665	503-253-7826	753
Leatherock International Inc 5285 Lovelock St ....San Diego CA 92110	800-466-6667	619-299-7625	431
Leave No Trace Ctr for Outdoor Ethics Inc 1830 17th St ....Boulder CO 80302	800-332-4100	303-442-8222	48-23
Leavenworth County 300 Walnut St ....Leavenworth KS 66048	855-893-9533	913-684-0421	337
Leavenworth Public Library 417 Spruce St ....Leavenworth KS 66048	800-829-3676	913-682-5666	433-3

	Toll-Free	Phone	Class
Leavenworth-Jefferson Electric Co-op Inc			
507 N Union St ....McLouth KS 66054	**888-796-6111**		245
leavitt group Enterprises			
216 S 200 W ....Cedar City UT 84720	**800-264-8085**	435-586-6553	389
Leavitt Machinery & Rentals Inc			
24389 Fraser Hwy ....Langley BC V2Z2L3	**877-850-6499**	604-607-4450	357
Leavitt Tube			
1717 W 115th St ....Chicago IL 60643	**800-532-8488**	773-239-7700	488
Lebanon Area Chamber of Commerce			
186 N Adams St ....Lebanon MO 65536	**888-588-5710**	417-588-3256	139
Lebanon Daily News			
718 Poplar St ....Lebanon PA 17042	**800-457-5929**	717-272-5611	528-2
Lebanon Seaboard Corp			
1600 E Cumberland St ....Lebanon PA 17042	**800-233-0628**	717-273-1685	280
Lebanon Valley College			
101 N College Ave ....Annville PA 17003	**866-582-4236**	717-867-6181	166
LEC (Lincoln Electric Co-op Inc)			
500 Osloski Rd PO Box 628 ....Eureka MT 59917	**800-442-2994**	406-889-3301	245
LeChase Construction Services LLC (LC)			
205 Indigo Creek Dr ....Rochester NY 14626	**888-953-2427**	585-254-3510	
Lechler Inc			
445 Kautz Rd ....Saint Charles IL 60174	**800-777-2926***	630-377-6611	485
*Cust Svc			
Leco Corp			
3000 Lakeview Ave ....Saint Joseph MI 49085	**800-292-6141**	269-985-5496	418
Leconte Wealth Management LLC			
703 William Blount Dr ....Maryville TN 37801	**888-236-6630**	865-379-8200	400
LeCroy Corp			
700 Chestnut Ridge Rd ....Chestnut Ridge NY 10977	**800-553-2769**	845-425-2000	248
NASDAQ: LCRY			
Lectrosonics Inc			
PO Box 15900 ....Rio Rancho NM 87174	**800-821-1121**	505-892-4501	52
LED Supply Co			
12340 W Cedar Dr ....Lakewood CO 80228	**877-595-4769**		196
Ledalite Architectural Products			
19750-92A Ave ....Langley BC V1M3B2	**800-665-5332**	604-888-6811	438
Ledding Library			
10660 SE 21st Ave ....Milwaukie OR 97222	**800-701-8560**	503-786-7580	433-3
Ledger, The			
300 W Lime St ....Lakeland FL 33815	**888-431-7323**	863-802-7000	528-2
Ledtronics Inc			
23105 Kashiwa Ct ....Torrance CA 90505	**800-579-4875**	310-534-1505	436
Ledwell & Son Enterprises			
3300 Waco St ....Texarkana TX 75501	**800-533-9355**	903-838-6531	774
Lee & Cates Glass Inc			
5355 Shawland Rd ....Jacksonville FL 32254	**888-844-1989**	904-358-8555	189-6
Lee Brass Co			
1800 Golden Springs Rd ....Anniston AL 36207	**800-876-1811***		308
*General			
Lee Brick & Tile Co			
3704 Hawkins Ave PO Box 1027 ....Sanford NC 27330	**800-672-7559**	919-774-4800	150
Lee Co			
2 Pellitaug Rd PO Box 424 ....Westbrook CT 06498	**800-533-7584**	860-399-6281	784
Lee College			
200 Lee Dr PO Box 818 ....Baytown TX 77520	**800-621-8724**	281-427-5611	162
Lee County Library			
2050 Central Ave ....Fort Myers FL 33901	**800-854-8195**	239-479-4636	433-3
Lee County Visitors & Convention Bureau			
2201 Second St Ste 600 ....Fort Myers FL 33901	**800-237-6444**	239-338-3500	206
Lee Dan Communications Inc			
155 Adams Ave ....Hauppauge NY 11788	**800-231-1414**	631-231-1414	391
Lee Jeans			
9001 W 67th St ....Merriam KS 66202	**800-453-3348***		155-10
*Cust Svc			
Lee Kum Kee Inc			
14841 Don Julian Rd ....City of Industry CA 91746	**800-654-5082***	626-709-1888	296-19
*Orders			
Lee Myles Auto Group			
914 Fern Ave ....Reading PA 19607	**800-533-6953**		62-6
Lee Products Co			
800 E 80th St ....Bloomington MN 55420	**800-989-3544**	952-854-3544	530
Lee Publications Inc			
6113 State Hwy 5 ....Palatine Bridge NY 13428	**800-836-2888**	518-673-3237	633-8
Lee Spring Company Inc			
140 58th St Unit 3C ....Brooklyn NY 11220	**800-110-2500**	718-236-2222	715
Lee Steel Holdings LLC			
27555 Executive Dr			
Ste 177 ....Farmington Hills MI 48331	**855-533-7833**	313-925-2100	
Lee Supply Corp			
6610 Guion Rd ....Indianapolis IN 46268	**800-873-1103**	317-290-2500	608
Lee University			
1120 N Ocoee St ....Cleveland TN 37311	**800-533-9930**	423-614-8000	166
Lee's Morvillo Group			
160 Niantic Ave ....Providence RI 02907	**800-821-1700**	401-353-1740	406
Lee's Summit Chamber of Commerce			
220 SE Main St ....Lees Summit MO 64063	**888-816-5757**	816-524-2424	139
Leebaw Mfg Company Inc			
PO Box 553 ....Canfield OH 44406	**800-841-8083**		468
Leech Lake Area Chamber of Commerce			
205 Minnesota Ave E ....Walker MN 56484	**800-833-1118**	218-547-1313	139
Leeches USA Ltd			
300 Shames Dr ....Westbury NY 11590	**800-645-3569**	516-333-2570	473
Leeco Steel LLC			
1011 Warrenville Rd Ste 500 ....Lisle IL 60532	**800-621-4366**	630-427-2100	786
Leed Selling Tools Corp			
9700 Hwy 57 ....Evansville IN 47725	**855-687-5333**	812-867-4340	86
Leelanau County			
8527 E Government Ctr Dr ....Suttons Bay MI 49682	**866-256-9711**	231-256-9824	337
Leelanau Fruit Co			
2900 SW Bay Shore Dr ....Suttons Bay MI 49682	**800-431-0718**	231-271-3514	296-21
Leer LP			
206 Leer St ....New Lisbon WI 53950	**800-766-5337***	608-562-7100	660
*Cust Svc			
Leerink Swann & Co			
1 Federal St 37th Fl ....Boston MA 02110	**800-808-7525**		400
Lees-McRae College			
191 Main St W ....Banner Elk NC 28604	**800-280-4562**	828-898-5241	166
Leeward Community College			
96-045 Ala Ike ....Pearl City HI 96782	**888-442-4551**	808-455-0011	162

	Toll-Free	Phone	Class
Leff Electric			
4700 Spring Rd ....Cleveland OH 44131	**800-686-5333**	216-432-3000	246
Leffler Energy Inc			
15 Mt Joy St ....Mount Joy PA 17552	**800-984-1411**		575
LeFiell Manufacturing Co			
13700 Firestone Blvd ....Santa Fe Springs CA 90670	**800-451-5971**		488
LeFleur's Bluff State Park			
2140 Riverside Dr ....Jackson MS 39202	**800-237-6278**	601-987-3923	561
Legacy Bank			
1580 E Cheyenne Mtn Blvd			
.................Colorado Springs CO 80906	**866-627-0800**	719-579-9150	70
Legacy Electronics Inc			
1220 N Dakota St PO Box 348 ....Canton SD 57013	**888-466-3853**	949-498-9600	174
Legacy Emanuel Hospital & Health Ctr			
2801 N Gantenbein Ave ....Portland OR 97227	**888-598-4232**	503-413-2200	373-3
Legacy Golf Resort			
6808 S 32nd St ....Phoenix AZ 85042	**866-729-7182**	602-305-5500	665
Legacy Good Samaritan Hospital			
1015 NW 22nd Ave ....Portland OR 97210	**800-733-9959**	503-335-3500	373-3
Legacy Meridian Park Hospital			
19300 SW 65th Ave ....Tualatin OR 97062	**800-944-4773**	503-692-1212	373-3
Legacy Salmon Creek Hospital			
2211 NE 139th St ....Vancouver WA 98686	**877-270-5566**	360-487-1000	373-3
Legal & General America Inc			
1701 Research Blvd ....Rockville MD 20850	**800-638-8428**	301-279-4800	359-4
Legal Aid of West Virginia Inc			
922 Quarrier St 4th Fl ....Charleston WV 25301	**866-255-4370**	304-343-4481	
Legal Aid Society of Palm Beach County Inc			
423 Fern St Ste 200 ....West Palm Beach FL 33401	**800-403-9353**	561-655-8944	427
Legal Club of America Corp			
7771 W Oakland Park Blvd			
Ste 217 ....Sunrise FL 33351	**800-316-5387**	954-377-0222	461
Legal Cost Control Inc (LCC)			
8 Kings Hwy W Ste C ....Haddonfield NJ 08033	**800-493-7345**	856-216-0800	443
Legal Resources Inc			
2877 Guardian Ln Ste 101 ....Virginia Beach VA 23452	**800-728-5768**	757-498-1220	260
LegalEase Inc			
205 E 42nd St 20th Fl ....New York NY 10017	**800-393-1277**	212-393-9070	631
Legend Data Systems Inc			
18024 72nd Ave S ....Kent WA 98032	**866-371-1670**	425-251-1670	45
Legend Power Systems Inc			
1480 Frances St ....Vancouver BC V5L1Y9	**866-772-8797**	604-420-1500	762
Legend Seeds Inc			
PO Box 241 ....De Smet SD 57231	**800-678-3346**	605-854-3346	276
Legendary Marketing			
3729 S Lecanto Hwy ....Lecanto FL 34461	**800-827-1663**	352-527-3553	195
Legendary Whitetails			
820 Enterprise Dr ....Slinger WI 53086	**800-875-9453**		360
Legends Theater			
1600 W Hwy 76 ....Branson MO 65616	**800-374-7469**	702-253-1333	568
Legg Company Inc			
325 E Tenth St ....Halstead KS 67056	**800-835-1003***		369
*Sales			
Legg Mason Inc (LMI)			
100 International Dr ....Baltimore MD 21202	**800-822-5544**	800-221-3627	686
NYSE: LM			
Leggett & Platt Inc			
1 Leggett Rd PO Box 757 ....Carthage MO 64836	**800-888-4569**	417-358-8131	715
NYSE: LEG			
Legion Lighting Company Inc			
221 Glenmore Ave ....Brooklyn NY 11207	**800-453-4466**	718-498-1770	438
LEGO Systems Inc			
555 Taylor Rd ....Enfield CT 06082	**877-518-5346**	860-749-2291	757
LEGOLAND California			
1 Legoland Dr ....Carlsbad CA 92008	**877-534-6526**	888-690-5346	32
Lehigh Asphalt Paving & Construction Co Inc			
1314 E Broad St ....Tamaqua PA 18252	**877-222-5514**	570-668-4303	188-4
Lehigh Carbon Community College			
4525 Education Pk Dr ....Schnecksville PA 18078	**800-414-3975***	610-799-2121	162
*General			
Lehigh Fluid Power Inc			
1413 Rt 179 ....Lambertville NJ 08530	**800-257-9515**		637
Lehigh Hanson Materials Ltd			
12640 Inland Way ....Edmonton AB T5V1K2	**800-252-9304***	780-420-2500	135
*Orders			
Lehigh Valley Hospice (LVHN)			
3080 Hamilton Blvd Ste 250 ....Allentown PA 18103	**888-402-5846**		370
Lehigh Valley International Airport			
3311 Airport Rd ....Allentown PA 18109	**800-359-5842**	610-266-6000	27
Lehigh Valley Plastics Inc			
187 North Commerce Way ....Bethlehem PA 18017	**800-354-5344**	484-893-5500	600
Lehman College			
250 Bedford Pk Blvd W ....Bronx NY 10468	**800-311-5656**	718-960-8000	166
Lehman Hardware & Appliances Inc			
4779 Kidron Rd ....Dalton OH 44618	**888-438-5346**	800-438-5346	392
Lehman Trikes Inc			
125 Industrial Dr ....Spearfish SD 57783	**888-394-3357**	605-642-2111	514
Leica Camera AG			
1 Pearl Ct ....Allendale NJ 07401	**800-222-0118**		540
Leica Microsystems Inc			
1700 Leider Ln ....Buffalo Grove IL 60089	**800-248-0123**		
Leidenheimer Baking Co			
1501 Simon Bolivar Ave ....New Orleans LA 70113	**800-259-9099**	504-525-1575	296-1
Leigh Baldwin & Company LLC			
112 Albany St ....Cazenovia NY 13035	**800-659-8044**	315-734-1410	686
Leisure Pro			
42 W 18th St ....New York NY 10011	**800-637-6880**	212-645-1234	707
Leisure Systems Inc			
502 TechneCenter Dr Ste D ....Milford OH 45150	**866-928-9644**	513-831-2100	121
LEK Consulting			
28 State St 16th Fl ....Boston MA 02109	**800-929-4535**	617-951-9500	194
LEKTRO Inc			
1190 SE Flightline Dr ....Warrenton OR 97146	**800-535-8767**	503-861-2288	57
Lemco Tool Corp			
1850 Metzger Ave ....Cogan Station PA 17728	**800-233-8713**	570-494-0620	452
Lemieux Bedard Communications Inc			
2665 King W Ste 315 ....Sherbrooke QC J1L2G5	**800-823-0850**	819-823-0850	224
Lemon Peak			
500 W Putnam Ave Ste 400 ....Greenwich CT 06830	**888-253-7348**		5

Company	Address	City	State	Zip	Toll-Free	Phone	Class
LemonStand eCommerce Inc	2416 Main St Ste 126	Vancouver	BC	V5T3E2	**855-332-0555**	604-398-4188	224
Len-Co Lumber Corp	1445 Seneca St	Buffalo	NY	14210	**800-258-4585**	716-822-0243	363
Lenning & Company Inc	13924 Seal Beach Blvd Ste C	Seal Beach	CA	90740	**800-200-4829**	562-594-9729	2
Lennox Industries Inc	2100 Lake Pk Blvd *Cust Svc	Richardson	TX	75080	**800-953-6669***		15
Lennox International Inc	2140 Lake Pk Blvd *NYSE: LII*	Richardson	TX	75080	**800-953-6669**	972-497-5000	15
Lenoir Community College	231 Hwy 58 S PO Box 188	Kinston	NC	28502	**866-866-2362**	252-527-6223	162
Lenoir Mirror Company Inc	401 Kincaid St	Lenoir	NC	28645	**800-438-8204**	828-728-3271	331
Lenoir-Rhyne University	625 Seventh Ave NE	Hickory	NC	28601	**800-277-5721**	828-328-7300	166
Lenox Corp	PO Box 2006	Bristol	PA	19007	**800-223-4311**		726
Lenox Hotel	61 Exeter St	Boston	MA	02116	**800-225-7676**	617-536-5300	378
Lenox Square Mall	3393 Peachtree Rd NE	Atlanta	GA	30326	**800-266-2278**	404-233-6767	458
LENSAR Inc	2800 Discovery Dr	Orlando	FL	32826	**888-536-7271**		473
LensCrafters Inc	4000 Luxottica Pl	Mason	OH	45040	**877-753-6727**	513-765-4321	539
Lentz Milling Co	2045 N 11th St	Reading	PA	19604	**800-523-8132**		800
Lenze	630 Douglas St	Uxbridge	MA	01569	**800-217-9100**	508-278-9100	705
Leo Wolleman Inc	31 S St Ste 4-N-3	Mt Vernon	NY	10550	**800-223-5667**	212-840-1881	410
Leola Village Inn & Suites	38 Deborah Dr	Leola	PA	17540	**877-669-5094**	717-656-7002	378
Leominster Credit Union	20 Adams St	Leominster	MA	01453	**800-649-4646**	978-537-8021	219
Leon Max Inc	3100 New York Dr	Pasadena	CA	91107	**888-334-4629**	626-797-9991	155-20
Leon S McGoogan Library of Medicine	University of Nebraska Medical Ctr 42nd and Emile	Omaha	NE	68198	**866-800-5209**	402-559-4000	433-1
Leon's Texas Cuisine Co	2100 Redbud Blvd	McKinney	TX	75069	**800-527-1243**	972-529-5050	296-36
Leonard Paper Co	725 N Haven St *Cust Svc	Baltimore	MD	21205	**800-327-5547***		555
Leonard Valve Co	1360 Elmwood Ave	Cranston	RI	02910	**800-222-1208**	401-461-1200	784
Lepel Corp	W227 N937 Westmound Dr	Waukesha	WI	53186	**800-548-8520**	631-586-3300	
Lerch Bates Inc	8089 S Lincoln St Ste 300	Littleton	CO	80122	**800-409-5471**	303-795-7956	261
Lereta LLC	1123 Parkview Dr	Covina	CA	91724	**800-537-3821**		648
Lerner Publishing Group	1251 Washington Ave N	Minneapolis	MN	55401	**800-328-4929**		633-2
LES (Loyd's Electric Supply Inc)	838 Stonetree Dr	Branson	MO	65616	**800-492-4030**	417-334-2171	246
Les Entreprises Energie Cardio	1040 Blvd Michele-Bohec Ste 120	Blainville	QC	J7C5E2	**877-363-7443**	450-979-3613	
Les Stanford Chevrolet Inc	21730 Michigan Ave	Dearborn	MI	48124	**800-836-0972**	313-769-3140	57
Les Suites Hotel Ottawa	130 Besserer St	Ottawa	ON	K1N9M9	**866-682-0879**	613-232-2000	378
Les Wilkins & Assoc Inc	6850 35th Ave NE	Seattle	WA	98115	**800-426-6634**	206-522-0908	473
Lesaffre Yeast Corp	7475 W Main St *Cust Svc	Milwaukee	WI	53214	**800-770-2714***	414-615-3300	296-42
LeSaint Logistics	868 W Crossroads Pkwy	Romeoville	IL	60446	**877-566-9375**	630-243-5950	447
LeSea Broadcasting Corp	61300 S Ironwood Rd	South Bend	IN	46614	**800-365-3732**	574-291-8200	733
Lesley University	29 Everett St	Cambridge	MA	02138	**800-999-1959**	617-868-9600	166
Leslie Controls Inc	12501 Telecom Dr	Tampa	FL	33637	**800-323-8366**	813-978-1000	784
Lesman Instrument Co	135 Bernice Dr	Bensenville	IL	60106	**800-953-7626**	630-595-8400	385
Leson Chevrolet Co Inc	1501 Westbank Express	Harvey	LA	70058	**877-496-2420**	504-366-4381	513
Lesperance & Martineau	1440 Ste-Catherine W Bureau 700	Montreal	QC	H3G1R8	**888-273-8387**	514-861-4831	427
Lester Bldg Systems LLC	1111 Second Ave S	Lester Prairie	MN	55354	**800-826-4439**	320-395-2531	106
Lester Inc	19 Business Pk Dr	Branford	CT	06405	**800-999-5265**	203-488-5265	732
Lester Sales Co Inc	4312 W Minnesota St	Indianapolis	IN	46241	**888-963-6270**	317-244-7811	246
Letco Medical Inc	1316 Commerce Dr NW	Decatur	AL	35601	**800-239-5288**	256-350-1297	579
LeTip International Inc	4838 E Baseline Rd Ste 123	Mesa	AZ	85206	**800-255-3847**	480-264-4600	392
LeTourneau University	2100 S Mobberly Ave	Longview	TX	75602	**800-759-8811**	903-233-3000	166
Leupold & Stevens Inc	14400 NW Greenbrier Pkwy	Beaverton	OR	97006	**800-538-7653**		540
Leuthold Weeden Capital Management LLC	33 S Sixth St Ste 4600	Minneapolis	MN	55402	**800-273-6886**	612-332-9141	194
Level Agency	235 Fort Pitt Blvd	Pittsburgh	PA	15222	**877-733-8625**		5
Level II Inc	555 Andover Park W Ste 110	Tukwila	WA	98188	**888-232-9609**	206-575-7682	
Levenger	420 S Congress Ave *Cust Svc	Delray Beach	FL	33445	**800-544-0880***	561-276-2436	457
Leventhal Ltd	PO Box 564 *General	Fayetteville	NC	28302	**800-847-4095***		155-18
Leviathan Corp	55 Washington St Ste 457	Brooklyn	NY	11201	**855-687-8721**		
Levin Sander (Rep D - MI)	1236 Longworth House Office Bldg	Washington	DC	20515	**888-810-3880**		341-1
Levinson Institute Inc	28 Main St Ste 100	Jaffrey	NH	03452	**800-290-5735**	603-532-4700	760
Levolor Kirsch Window Fashions	4110 Premier Dr	High Point	NC	27265	**800-752-9677**	336-812-8181	87
Levy Home Entertainment LLC	1420 Kensington Rd Ste 300	Oak Brook	IL	60523	**800-549-5389**	708-547-4400	526
Lew Jan Textile Corp	366 Veterans Memorial Hwy	Commack	NY	11725	**800-899-0531**		590
Lewcott Corp	86 Providence Rd *Sales	Millbury	MA	01527	**800-225-7725***	508-865-1791	601-2
Lewer Agency Inc	4534 Wornall Rd	Kansas City	MO	64111	**800-821-7715**		389
Lewin Group	3130 Fairview Pk Dr Ste 800	Falls Church	VA	22042	**877-227-5042**	703-269-5500	194
Lewis & Clark College	0615 SW Palatine Hill Rd *Admissions	Portland	OR	97219	**800-444-4111***	503-768-7040	166
Lewis & Clark Library	120 S Last Chance Gulch	Helena	MT	59601	**800-733-2767**	406-447-1690	433-3
Lewis & Clark State Recreation Site	725 Summer St NE Ste C	Salem	OR	97301	**800-551-6949**	503-986-0707	561
Lewis & Clark Trail Heritage Foundation	4201 Giant Springs Rd	Great Falls	MT	59405	**888-701-3434**	406-454-1234	48-23
Lewis & Knopf CPA's PC	5206 Gateway Centre Ste 100	Flint	MI	48507	**877-244-1787**	810-238-4617	2
Lewis County	112 Second St PO Box 129	Vanceburg	KY	41179	**800-230-5740**	606-796-2722	337
Lewis County Chamber of Commerce	7576 S State St	Lowville	NY	13367	**800-724-0242**	315-376-2213	139
Lewis County Rural Electric Co-op	18256 Hwy 16 PO Box 68	Lewistown	MO	63452	**888-454-4485**	573-215-4000	245
Lewis Direct Marketing	325 E Oliver St	Baltimore	MD	21202	**800-533-5394**	410-539-5100	5
Lewis Electric Supply Company Inc	1306 Second St PO Box 2237	Muscle Shoals	AL	35662	**800-239-0681**	256-383-0681	246
Lewis Label Products	2300 Race St	Ft Worth	TX	76111	**800-772-7728**		544
Lewis Tree Service Inc	300 Lucius Gordon Dr	West Henrietta	NY	14586	**800-333-1593**	585-436-3208	771
Lewis University	1 University Pkwy	Romeoville	IL	60446	**800-897-9000**	815-838-0500	166
Lewis Wagner LLP	501 Indiana Ave Ste 200	Indianapolis	IN	46202	**800-237-0505**	317-237-0500	427
Lewisburg Printing Co	170 Woodside Ave PO Box 2608	Lewisburg	TN	37091	**800-559-1526**		623
Lewis-Clark State College	500 Eighth Ave	Lewiston	ID	83501	**800-933-5272**	208-792-5272	166
Lewis-Gale Medical Ctr	1900 Electric Rd	Salem	VA	24153	**800-541-9992**	540-776-4000	373-3
Lewiston Sales Inc	21241 Dutchmans Crossing Rd	Lewiston	MN	55952	**800-732-6334**	507-523-2112	444
Lewistown News-Argus, The	521 W Main St PO Box 900	Lewistown	MT	59457	**800-879-5627**	406-535-3401	528-3
Lexar Media Inc	47300 Bayside Pkwy	Fremont	CA	94538	**877-747-4031**	408-933-1088	288
LexiCode	100 Executive Center Dr Ste 101	Columbia	SC	29210	**800-448-2633**		392
Lexicon International Corp	1400A Adams Rd	Bensalem	PA	19020	**800-448-8201**	215-639-8220	386
Lexicon Pharmaceuticals Inc	8800 Technology Forest Pl *NASDAQ: LXRX*	The Woodlands	TX	77381	**855-828-4651**	281-863-3000	85
Lexinet Corp, The	701 N Union St	Council Grove	KS	66846	**800-767-1577**	620-767-7000	5
Lexington Corporate Properties Trust	1 Penn Plz Ste 4015	New York	NY	10119	**800-850-3948**	212-692-7200	651
Lexington Home Brands	1300 National Hwy	Thomasville	NC	27360	**800-333-4300**	336-474-5300	319-2
Lexington Investment Company Inc	2365 Harrodsburg Rd Ste B375	Lexington	KY	40504	**800-264-7073**	859-224-7073	686
Lexington Philharmonic	161 N Mill St	Lexington	KY	40507	**888-494-4226**	859-233-4226	569-3
Lexington Theological Seminary	230 Lexington Green Cir Ste 300	Lexington	KY	40503	**866-296-6087**	859-252-0361	167-3
Lexington Visitors Ctr	401 W Main St	Lexington	KY	40507	**800-845-3959**	859-233-7299	206
LexisNexis	5000 Sawgrass Village Cir	Ponte Vedra Beach	FL	32082	**800-368-6955**	904-273-5000	178-11
LexisNexis Matthew Bender	744 Broad St	Newark	NJ	07102	**800-252-9257**	973-820-2000	633-2
LexJet Corp	1680 Fruitville Rd 3rd Fl	Sarasota	FL	34236	**800-453-9538**	941-330-1210	624
Lexmark International Inc	740 W New Cir Rd *NYSE: LXK* ■ *Cust Svc	Lexington	KY	40550	**800-539-6275***	859-232-2000	173-6
Leyman Manufacturing Corp	10335 Wayne Ave	Cincinnati	OH	45215	**866-539-6261**	513-891-6210	
LFA (Lupus Foundation of America Inc)	2000 L St NW Ste 410	Washington	DC	20036	**800-558-0121**	202-349-1155	48-17
LFCU (Lockheed Federal Credit Union)	2340 Hollywood Way	Burbank	CA	91505	**800-328-5328**	818-565-2020	219
LG Barcus & Sons Inc	1430 State Ave	Kansas City	KS	66102	**800-255-0180**	913-621-1100	188-2

	Toll-Free	Phone	Class
LG Electronics USA Inc			
1000 Sylvan Ave .... Englewood Cliffs NJ 07632	800-243-0000*	201-816-2000	173-4
*Tech Supp			
LG Everist Inc			
300 S Phillips Ave Ste 200 .... Sioux Falls SD 57117	800-843-7992	605-334-5000	501-4
LG2 Environmental Solutions Inc			
10475 Fortune Pkwy Ste 201 .... Jacksonville FL 32256	800-435-0072	904-288-8631	648
LGH (Lowell General Hospital)			
295 Varnum Ave .... Lowell MA 01854	800-544-2424	978-937-6000	373-3
LGInternational			
6700 SW Bradbury Ct .... Portland OR 97224	800-345-0534	503-620-0520	412
LGWM (Lloyd Gray Whitehead Monroe)			
880 Montclair Rd Ste 100 .... Birmingham AL 35213	800-967-7299	205-967-8822	427
LHC Group Inc			
901 Hugh Wallis Rd S .... Lafayette LA 70508	866-542-4768	337-289-8188	362
NASDAQ: LHCG			
LHotel Montreal			
262 St Jacques St W .... Old Montreal QC H2Y1N1	877-553-0019	514-985-0019	378
Li Cor Inc			
PO Box 4425 .... Lincoln NE 68504	800-447-3576	402-467-3576	418
LIA (Laser Institute of America)			
13501 Ingenuity Dr Ste 128 .... Orlando FL 32826	800-345-2737	407-380-1553	49-19
LIA (Leather Industries of America)			
3050 K St NW Ste 400 .... Washington DC 20007	800-635-0617	202-342-8497	49-4
Lia Auto Group, The			
1258 Central Ave .... Albany NY 12205	855-212-7985		57
Liacouras Ctr			
1776 N Broad St .... Philadelphia PA 19121	800-298-4200	215-204-2400	568
Libbey Inc			
300 Madison Ave PO Box 10060 .... Toledo OH 43699	888-794-8469	419-325-2100	333
NYSE: LBY			
Liberal Party of Canada			
81 Metcalfe St .... Ottawa ON K1P6M8	888-542-3725		611
Libertarian Party			
2600 Virginia Ave NW Ste 200 .... Washington DC 20037	800-735-1776	202-333-0008	612
Liberty Bank			
315 Main St .... Middletown CT 06457	800-622-6732	888-570-0773	70
Liberty Bank & Trust Co			
PO Box 60131 .... New Orleans LA 70160	800-883-3943	504-240-5100	70
Liberty Bell Equipment Corp			
3201 S 76th St .... Philadelphia PA 19153	800-541-5827	215-492-6700	200
Liberty Brass Turning Company Inc			
1200 Shames Dr .... Westbury NY 11590	800-345-5939	718-784-2911	617
Liberty Ch			
1971 University Blvd .... Lynchburg VA 24515	800-332-1883	434-582-2718	735
Liberty Diversified International Inc			
5600 Hwy 169 N .... New Hope MN 55428	800-421-1270	763-536-6600	359-3
Liberty Drug & Surgical Inc			
195 Main St .... Chatham NJ 07928	877-816-0111	973-635-6200	237
Liberty Forge Inc			
1507 Fort Worth St PO Box 1210 .... Liberty TX 77575	800-231-2377	936-336-5785	481
Liberty Fund Inc			
8335 Allison Pt Trial			
Ste 300 .... Indianapolis IN 46250	800-955-8335	317-842-0880	305
Liberty Group LLC			
411 30th St 2nd Fl .... Oakland CA 94609	888-588-5818	510-658-1880	686
Liberty Hardware Manufacturing Corp			
140 Business Pk Dr .... Winston-Salem NC 27107	800-652-7277	336-769-4077	349
Liberty Hardware Mfg Corp			
140 Business Pk Dr .... Winston-Salem NC 27107	800-542-3789	336-769-4077	349
Liberty Hospital			
2525 Glenn Hendren Dr .... Liberty MO 64068	800-344-3829	816-781-7200	373-3
Liberty Pumps Inc			
7000 Apple Tree Ave .... Bergen NY 14416	800-543-2550	585-494-1817	637
Liberty Safe & Security Products Inc			
1199 W Utah Ave .... Payson UT 84651	800-247-5625	801-925-1000	485
Liberty Savings Bank FSB			
3435 Airborne Rd Ste B .... Wilmington OH 45177	800-436-6300		70
Liberty Tax Service Inc			
1716 Corporate Landing Pkwy			
.... Virginia Beach VA 23454	800-790-3863*	757-493-8855	729
*Cust Svc			
Liberty Toyota Scion			
4397 Rt 130 S .... Burlington NJ 08016	888-809-7798	609-386-6300	513
Liberty Travel Inc			
69 Spring St .... Ramsey NJ 07446	888-271-1584		766
Liberty Tree Mall			
100 Independence Way .... Danvers MA 01923	877-746-6642	978-777-0794	458
Liberty University			
1971 University Blvd .... Lynchburg VA 24502	800-543-5317	434-582-2000	166
LibertyTree			
100 Swan Way .... Oakland CA 94621	800-927-8733	510-632-1366	95
Libertyville Chevrolet Inc			
1001 S Milwaukee Ave .... Libertyville IL 60048	877-520-1807*	847-362-1400	513
*Sales			
Libman Co			
220 N Sheldon St .... Arcola IL 61910	877-818-3380		103
Library & Information Technology Assn (LITA)			
50 E Huron St .... Chicago IL 60611	800-545-2433	312-280-4270	49-11
Library Binding Service (LBS)			
1801 Thompson Ave .... Des Moines IA 50316	800-247-5323	515-262-3191	92
Library Journal			
160 Varick St 11th Fl .... New York NY 10013	800-588-1030	646-380-0700	455-8
Library Leadership & Management Assn (LLAMA)			
50 E Huron St .... Chicago IL 60611	800-545-2433		49-11
Library of Congress			
National Library Service for the Blind			
1291 Taylor St NW .... Washington DC 20542	888-657-7323	202-707-5100	341
US Copyright Office			
101 Independence Ave SE .... Washington DC 20559	877-476-0778	202-707-3000	341
Library of Michigan, The			
702 W Kalamazoo St PO Box 30007 .... Lansing MI 48909	800-726-7323	517-373-1300	433-5
Library Reproduction Service			
19146 Van Ness Ave .... Torrance CA 90501	800-255-5002		622
Libyan Arab Jamahiriya			
309-315 E 48th St .... New York NY 10017	800-253-9646	212-752-5775	779
LICH (Long Island College Hospital)			
339 Hicks St .... Brooklyn NY 11201	800-227-8922	718-780-1000	373-3
Lick Observatory			
7281 Mt Hamilton Rd .... Mt Hamilton CA 95140	800-866-1131	408-274-5061	594
Licking Valley Oil Inc			
PO Box 246 .... Butler KY 41006	800-899-9449	859-472-7111	575
Licking Valley Rural Electric Co-op Corp			
271 Main St .... West Liberty KY 41472	800-596-6530	606-743-3179	245
Lido Beach Resort			
700 Ben Franklin Dr .... Sarasota FL 34236	800-441-2113	941-388-2161	703
Lied Ctr for Performing Arts			
301 N 12th St .... Lincoln NE 68588	800-432-3231	402-472-4700	568
Lied Lodge & Conference Center			
2700 Sylvan Rd .... Nebraska City NE 68410	800-546-5433	402-873-8733	205
Life Alert's Encino			
16027 Ventura blvd Ste 400 .... Encino CA 91436	800-920-3410		571
Life Flight Network LLC			
22285 Yellow Gate Ln NE .... Aurora OR 97002	800-232-0911	503-678-4364	13
Life Insurance Co of Alabama			
302 Broad St .... Gadsden AL 35901	800-226-2371	256-543-2022	390-2
Life of the South Insurance Co			
10151 Deerwood Pk Blvd			
Bldg 100 .... Jacksonville FL 32256	800-888-2738	904-350-9660	390-5
Life Pacific College			
1100 W Covina Blvd .... San Dimas CA 91773	877-886-5433	909-599-5433	161
Life Settlement Solutions Inc			
9201 Spectrum Ctr Blvd			
Ste 105 .... San Diego CA 92123	800-762-3387	858-576-8067	791
Life University			
1269 Barclay Cir .... Marietta GA 30060	800-543-3203	770-426-2884	166
Life-Assist Inc			
11475 Sunrise Park Dr .... Rancho Cordova CA 95742	800-824-6016		473
LifeBanc			
4775 Richmond Rd .... Cleveland OH 44128	888-558-5433	216-752-5433	541
Lifeblood Mid-South Regional Blood Center			
1040 Madison Ave .... Memphis TN 38104	888-543-3256	901-399-8120	89
LifeCore Biomedical LLC			
3515 Lyman Blvd .... Chaska MN 55318	800-348-4368*	952-368-4300	85
*Cust Svc			
LifeCourse Associates Inc			
9080 Eaton Park Rd .... Great Falls VA 22066	866-537-4999		193
LifeFone			
16 Yellowstone Ave .... White Plains NY 10607	888-687-0451		571
LIFEFORCE USA			
495 Raleigh Ave .... El Cajon CA 92020	800-531-4877	858-218-3200	344
LifeLearn Inc			
367 Woodlawn Rd W Unit 9 .... Guelph ON N1H7K9	888-770-2218	519-767-5043	242
Lifeline Medical Assoc LLC			
99 Cherry Hill Rd Ste 220 .... Parsippany NJ 07054	800-845-2785		373-3
Lifeline of Ohio			
770 Kinnear Rd Ste 200 .... Columbus OH 43212	800-525-5667	614-291-5667	541
Lifelink Foundation Inc			
9661 Delaney Creek Blvd .... Tampa FL 33619	800-262-5775	813-253-2640	362
LifeLink Tissue Bank			
9661 Delaney Creek Blvd .... Tampa FL 33619	800-683-2400	813-886-8111	541
Lifeloc Technologies Inc			
12441 W 49th Ave .... Wheat Ridge CO 80033	800-722-4817	303-431-9500	406
LifeNet			
1864 Concert Dr .... Virginia Beach VA 23453	800-847-7831		541
LifeNet Health Northwest			
501 SW 39th St .... Renton WA 98057	800-847-7831	425-981-8900	541
Lifenet Inc			
6225 St Michaels Dr .... Texarkana TX 75503	800-832-6395	903-832-8531	30
Lifepath Hospice			
3010 W Azeele St .... Tampa FL 33609	800-209-2200	813-877-2200	370
LifeRing Secular Recovery			
1440 Broadway Ste 312 .... Oakland CA 94612	800-811-4142	970-227-6650	48-21
LifeSafe Services LLC			
5971 Powers Ave Ste 108 .... Jacksonville FL 32217	888-767-0050		194
Lifescan Canada Ltd			
210-4321 Still Creek Dr .... Burnaby BC V5C6S7	800-663-5521	604-293-2266	474
LifeScan Inc			
1000 Gibraltar Dr .... Milpitas CA 95035	800-227-8862	408-263-9789	231
LifeServe Blood Ctr			
431 E Locust St .... Des Moines IA 50309	800-287-4903		89
LifeShare Blood Centers			
8910 Linwood Ave .... Shreveport LA 71106	800-256-4483	318-222-7770	89
LifeShare Community Blood Services			
105 Cleveland St .... Elyria OH 44035	800-317-5412	440-322-5700	89
LifeShare Transplant Donor Services of Oklahoma			
4705 NW Expy .... Oklahoma City OK 73132	888-580-5680	405-840-5551	541
Lifesharing			
7436 Mission Valley Rd .... San Diego CA 92108	888-423-6667	619-543-7225	541
LifeSize Communications Inc			
1601 S Mopac Expwy Ste 100 .... Austin TX 78746	877-543-3749	512-347-9300	52
LifeSouth Community Blood Centers			
4039 Newberry Rd .... Gainesville FL 32607	888-795-2707		89
Lifespring Inc			
460 Spring St .... Jeffersonville IN 47130	800-456-2117	812-280-2080	352
Lifetime Brands Inc			
1000 Steward Ave .... Garden City NY 11530	800-252-3390	516-683-6000	484
NASDAQ: LCUT			
Lifetime Products Inc			
Freeport Ctr Bldg D-11			
PO Box 160010 .... Clearfield UT 84016	800-242-3865	801-776-1532	706
Lifewings			
9198 Crestwyn Hills Dr .... Memphis TN 38125	800-290-9314		461
LifeWIRE Corp			
129 Blantyre Ave Ste 200 .... Toronto ON M1N2R6	888-738-4260		177
Lift Technologies Inc			
7040 S Hwy 11 .... Westminster SC 29693	888-946-3330		357
Lift-All Company Inc			
1909 McFarland Dr .... Landisville PA 17538	800-909-1964	717-898-6615	468
Liftone			
440 E Westinghouse Blvd .... Charlotte NC 28273	855-543-8663		468
Liftow			
3150 American Dr .... Toronto ON L4V1B4	866-465-4386		357
Lifts West Condominium Resort Hotel			
PO Box 330 .... Red River NM 87558	800-221-1859	505-754-2778	665

	Toll-Free	Phone	Class
Ligature, The 4909 Alcoa Ave ....Los Angeles CA 90058	800-944-5440	323-585-6000	776
Light 1039 FM, The 8001-101 Creedmoor Rd ....Raleigh NC 27613	877-310-9665	919-848-9736	641-85
Light Impressions 100 Carlson Rd ....Rochester NY 14610	800-975-6429		624
Light Metals Corp 2740 Prairie St SW ....Wyoming MI 49519	888-363-8257	616-538-3030	483
Light Sources Inc 37 Robinson Blvd ....Orange CT 06477	800-826-9465	203-799-7877	436
Lighthouse Club Hotel 201 60th St ....Ocean City MD 21842	888-371-5400	410-524-5400	378
Lighthouse Computer Services Inc 6 Blackstone Valley Pl Ste 205 ....Lincoln RI 02865	888-542-8030	401-334-0799	180
Lighthouse Hospice 1040 Kings Hwy N Ste 100..........Cherry Hill NJ 08034 *General	888-467-7423*	856-414-1155	370
Lighthouse Lodge & Cottages 1150 Lighthouse Ave ....Pacific Grove CA 93950	800-858-1249	831-655-2111	378
Lightner Electronics Inc 1771 Beaver Dam Rd ....Claysburg PA 16625	866-239-3888	814-239-8323	186
Lightning Transportation Inc 16820 Blake Rd ....Hagerstown MD 21740	800-233-0624	301-582-5700	775
Lightriver Technologies 2150 John Glenn Dr Ste 200.........Concord CA 94520	888-544-4825	925-363-9000	677
Lightspeed Aviation Inc 6135 Jean Rd ....Lake Oswego OR 97035	800-332-2421	503-968-3113	643
Lignite Energy Council 1016 E Owens Ave ....Bismarck ND 58502	800-932-7117	701-258-7117	138
Lil' Drug Store Products Inc 1201 Continental Pl NE ....Cedar Rapids IA 52402	800-553-5022		238
Lilleys' Landing Resort 367 River Ln ....Branson MO 65616	866-545-5397	417-334-6380	665
Lillie's Asian Cuisine 129 E Fremont St ....Las Vegas NV 89101	800-634-3454	702-385-7111	667
Lily Transportation Corp 145 Rosemary St ....Needham MA 02494	800-248-5459		773
Lima Estates 411 N Middletown Rd ....Media PA 19063	888-398-2287	484-443-0090	668
Lima Memorial Hospital 1001 Bellefontaine Ave ....Lima OH 45804	877-362-5672	419-228-3335	373-3
Lima News 3515 Elida Rd ....Lima OH 45807	800-686-9924	419-223-1010	528-2
Lima/Allen County Chamber of Commerce 144 S Main St Ste 100 ....Lima OH 45801	800-233-5462	419-222-6045	139
Lima/Allen County Convention & Visitors Bureau 144 S Main St Ste 101 ....Lima OH 45801	888-222-6075	419-222-6075	206
Lime Rock Park 60 White Hollow Rd ....Lakeville CT 06039	800-722-3577	860-435-5000	512
Limestone College 1115 College Dr ....Gaffney SC 29340	800-795-7151	864-489-7151	166
Limpert Bros Inc 202 NW Blvd ....Vineland NJ 08362	800-691-1353	856-691-1353	296-15
LIMRA International Inc 300 Day Hill Rd ....Windsor CT 06095	800-235-4672	860-688-3358	49-9
Lincare Holdings Inc 19387 US 19 N ....Clearwater FL 33764 NASDAQ: LNCR	800-284-2006		
Lincluden Investment Management 1275 N Service Rd W Ste 607.........Oakville ON L6M3G4	800-532-7071	905-825-9000	524
Lincoln Botanical Garden & Arboretum (BGA) c/o Landscape Services 1309 N 17th St ....Lincoln NE 68588	800-742-8800	402-472-2679	97
Lincoln Boyhood National Memorial 2916 E S St PO Box 1816...........Lincoln City IN 47552	800-445-9667	812-937-4541	560
Lincoln Christian College Seminary 100 Campus View Dr ....Lincoln IL 62656	888-522-5228	217-732-3168	167-3
Lincoln City Visitor & Convention Bureau 801 SW Hwy 101 Ste 401.........Lincoln City OR 97367	800-452-2151	541-996-1274	206
Lincoln College 300 Keokuk St ....Lincoln IL 62656	800-569-0556	217-732-3155	162
Lincoln College of Technology 11194 E 45th Ave ....Denver CO 80239	800-254-0547	303-722-5724	795
Lincoln College of Technology 2410 Metro Centre Blvd ....West Palm Beach FL 33407	800-254-0547	561-842-8324	795
Lincoln College of Technology 7225 Winton Dr Bldg 128...........Indianapolis IN 46268	800-228-6232	317-632-5553	795
Lincoln Convention & Visitors Bureau 3 Landmark Ctr 1128 Lincoln Mall Ste 100 ....Lincoln NE 68508	800-423-8212	402-434-5335	206
Lincoln County PO Box 978 ....Brookhaven MS 39602	800-613-4667	601-833-1411	337
Lincoln County WY 925 Sage Ave ....Kemmerer WY 83101	800-442-9001	307-877-9056	337
Lincoln County 111 W 'B' St Ste C ....Shoshone ID 83352	800-221-3295	208-886-7641	337
Lincoln County Courthouse PO Box 373 ....Hamlin WV 25523	800-859-7375	304-824-7990	337
Lincoln Ctr Theater 150 W 65th St ....New York NY 10023	800-432-7250		744
Lincoln Educational Services 200 Executive Dr ....West Orange NJ 07052 NASDAQ: LINC Suffield 8 Progress Dr ....Shelton CT 06484	800-254-0547 844-215-1513	973-736-9340 203-929-0592	242 163
Lincoln Electric Co 22801 St Clair Ave ....Cleveland OH 44117	888-935-3878	216-481-8100	806
Lincoln Electric Co-op Inc (LEC) 500 Osloski Rd PO Box 628 ....Eureka MT 59917	800-442-2994	406-889-3301	245
Lincoln FSB 1101 North St ....Lincoln NE 68508	800-333-2158	402-474-1400	71
Lincoln General Insurance Co 3501 Concord Rd ....York PA 17402	800-876-3350	717-757-0000	389
Lincoln Heritage Life Insurance Co 4343 E Camelback Rd Ste 400 ....Phoenix AZ 85018	800-438-7180	800-433-8181	390-2
Lincoln Industrial Corp 5148 N Hanley Rd ....Saint Louis MO 63134	800-424-5359	314-679-4200	385
Lincoln Journal-Star 926 P St ....Lincoln NE 68508	800-742-7315	402-475-4200	528-2
Lincoln Land Community College 5250 Shepherd Rd PO Box 19256...............Springfield IL 62794	800-727-4161	217-786-2200	162
Lincoln Land Oil Co PO Box 4307 ....Springfield IL 62708	800-238-4912	217-523-5050	316
Lincoln Memorial University 6965 Cumberland Gap Pkwy ....Harrogate TN 37752	800-325-0900	423-869-3611	166
Lincoln Motor Co PO Box 6248 ....Dearborn MI 48126	800-521-4140		59
Lincoln National Corp (LNC) 150 N Radnor-Chester Rd ....Radnor PA 19087 NYSE: LNC	877-275-5462	866-533-3410	359-4
Lincoln National Life Insurance Co 1300 S Clinton St ....Fort Wayne IN 46802	800-454-6265		390-2
Lincoln State Park Hwy 162 PO Box 216 ....Lincoln City IN 47552	877-478-3657	812-937-4710	561
Lincoln Trail College 11220 State Hwy 1 ....Robinson IL 62454	866-582-4322	618-544-8657	162
Lincoln University 820 Chestnut St ....Jefferson City MO 65101 *Admissions	800-521-5052*	573-681-5000	166
Lincoln University 1570 Old Baltimore Pk PO Box 179...........Lincoln University PA 19352 *Admissions	800-790-0191*	484-365-8000	166
Lincoln University 401 15th St ....Oakland CA 94612	888-810-9998	510-628-8010	166
Lincoln Wood Products Inc 1400 W Taylor St PO Box 375 ....Merrill WI 54452	800-967-2461	715-536-2461	236
Lincolnton-Lincoln County Chamber of Commerce 101 E Main St ....Lincolnton NC 28092	800-222-1167	704-735-3096	139
Linda Hall Library 5109 Cherry St ....Kansas City MO 64110	800-662-1545	816-363-4600	433-3
Lindal Cedar Homes Inc 4300 S 104th Pl ....Seattle WA 98178 *Prod Info	800-426-0536*	206-725-0900	106
Lindamar Industries Inc 1603 Commerce Way ....Paso Robles CA 93446	800-235-1811	805-237-1910	361
Lindblad Expeditions 96 Morton St 9th Fl ....New York NY 10014	800-397-3348		755
Lindeblad Piano Restoration 101 US 46 ....Pine Brook NJ 07058	888-687-4266		523
Linden Hall School for Girls 212 E Main St ....Lititz PA 17543	800-258-5778	717-626-8512	618
Linden Lab 945 Battery St ....San Francisco CA 94111	800-294-1067	415-243-9000	632
Linden Publishing 2006 S Mary St ....Fresno CA 93721 *Sales	800-345-4447*	559-233-6633	633-2
Linden Row Inn 100 E Franklin St ....Richmond VA 23219	800-348-7424	804-783-7000	378
Linden Warehouse & Distribution Co Inc 1300 Lower Rd ....Linden NJ 07036	800-333-2855	908-862-1400	775
Lindenmeyr Munroe 14 Research Pkwy ....Wallingford CT 06492	800-842-8480		549
Lindenmeyr Munroe Central Central National-Gottesman Inc 3 Manhattanville Rd ....Purchase NY 10577	800-221-3042		549
Lindenwood University 209 N Kings Hwy ....Saint Charles MO 63301	877-615-8212	636-949-2000	166
Lindey's Prime Steak House 3600 N Snelling Ave ....Arden Hills MN 55112	866-491-0538	651-633-9813	667
LINDO Systems Inc 1415 N Dayton St ....Chicago IL 60622 *Sales	800-441-2378*	312-988-7422	178-5
Lindquist Steels Inc 1050 Woodend Rd ....Stratford CT 06615	800-243-9637		490
Lindsay Corp 2222 N 111th St ....Omaha NE 68164 NYSE: LNN	800-829-5300	402-829-6800	273
Lindsay Manufacturing Inc PO Box 1708 ....Ponca City OK 74602	800-546-3729	580-762-2457	783
Lindsey & Company Inc 2302 Llama Dr ....Searcy AR 72143	800-890-7058	501-268-5324	174
Lindsey Wilson College 210 Lindsey Wilson St ....Columbia KY 42728	800-264-0138	270-384-2126	166
Lindt & Sprungli USA 1 Fine Chocolate Pl ....Stratham NH 03885	877-695-4638		296-8
Lineage Power Corp 601 Shiloh Rd ....Plano TX 75074	877-546-3243	972-244-9288	782
Linear Laboratories 42025 Osgood Rd ....Fremont CA 94539	800-536-0262	510-226-0488	201
Linemaster Switch Corp 29 Plaine Hill Rd ....Woodstock CT 06281	800-974-3668	860-974-1000	483
Linen Chest Inc 4455 AutoRt Des Laurentides ....Laval QC H7L5X8	800-363-3832	514-341-7077	363
LineStar Services Inc 5391 Bay Oaks Dr ....Pasadena TX 77505	800-790-3758	281-422-4989	
Linetec 725 S 75th Ave ....Wausau WI 54401	888-717-1472	715-843-4100	478
Linfield College 900 SE Baker St ....McMinnville OR 97128 *Admissions	800-640-2287*	503-883-2213	166
Lingo Inc 7901 Jones Branch Dr Ste 900..........Mclean VA 22102	888-546-4699		386
Lingo Manufacturing Co 7400 Industrial Rd ....Florence KY 41042 *Cust Svc	800-354-9771*	859-371-2662	233
Lingua Language Center 111 East Las Olas Blvd ....Fort Lauderdale FL 33301	888-654-6482	954-577-9955	422
Linguistic Society of America (LSA) 1325 18th St NW Ste 211 ....Washington DC 20036	800-726-0479	202-835-1714	48-11
Linguistics Systems Inc 201 Broadway ....Cambridge MA 02139	877-654-5006	617-528-7410	763
Link America Inc 3002 Century Dr ....Rowlett TX 75088	800-318-4955		224
Link Electronics Inc 2137 Rust Ave ....Cape Girardeau MO 63703	800-776-4411	573-334-4433	116
Link Energy Inc 211 1500 14 St SW ....Calgary AB T3C1C9	855-444-5465		577

Company / Address	City	State	ZIP	Toll-Free	Phone	Class
Link Medical Computing Inc 1208 B VFW Pkwy Ste 203	Boston	MA	02132	**888-893-0900**	617-676-6165	
Link-Burns Mfg Company Inc 253 American Way	Voorhees	NJ	08043	**800-457-4358**	856-429-6844	693
Linkus Enterprises Inc 5595 W San Madele Ave	Fresno	CA	93722	**888-854-6587**	559-256-6600	677
Linn Gear Co 100 N Eigth St PO Box 397	Lebanon	OR	97355	**800-547-2471**	541-259-1211	616
LINQ Services 1200 Steuart St Unit C3	Baltimore	MD	21230	**800-421-5467**		386
Linscomb & Williams Inc 1400 Post Oak Blvd Ste 1000	Houston	TX	77056	**800-960-1200**	713-840-1000	400
Linsly School 60 Knox Ln	Wheeling	WV	26003	**866-648-1893**	304-233-3260	618
Lintern Corp 8685 Stn St	Mentor	OH	44060	**800-321-3638**	440-255-9333	14
Linville Caverns Inc 19929 US 221 N	Marion	NC	28752	**800-419-0540**		50-5
Linx Industries Inc 2600 Airline Blvd	Portsmouth	VA	23701	**800-797-7476**		
Lion Apparel Inc 7200 Poe Ave Ste 400	Dayton	OH	45414	**800-548-6614**	937-898-1949	155-18
Lion Brand Yarn Co 135 Kero Rd	Carlstadt	NJ	07072	**800-795-5466**	212-243-8995	740-9
Lion Bros Company Inc 300 Red Brook Blvd *Cust Svc	Owings Mills	MD	21117	**800-365-6543***	410-363-1000	258
Lion Inc 320 E Main St	Lake Zurich	IL	60047	**800-867-6320**	872-228-5466	507
Lion Magazine 300 W 22nd St *Circ	Oak Brook	IL	60523	**800-710-7822***	630-571-5466	455-10
Lion Ribbon 2015 W Front St	Berwick	PA	18603	**800-551-5466**		
Lion World Travel 33 Kern Rd	Toronto	ON	M3B1S9	**800-387-2706**		769
Lionel com LLC 26750 23 Mile Rd	Chesterfield	MI	48051	**800-454-6635**	586-949-4100	757
Lionetti Associates LLC 450 S Front St	Elizabeth	NJ	07202	**800-734-0910**		682
Lionheart Publishing Inc 506 Roswell St	Marietta	GA	30060	**888-303-5639**		633-9
Lions Eye Bank of Nebraska Inc *University of Nebraska Medical Ctr* 985541 Nebraska Medical Ctr	Omaha	NE	68198	**800-225-7244**	402-559-4039	269
Lions Eye Bank of Wisconsin 2401 American Ln	Madison	WI	53704	**877-233-2354**	608-233-2354	269
Lions Foundation of Manitoba & Northwestern Ontario Inc 320 Sherbrook St	Winnipeg	MB	R3B2W6	**800-552-6820**	204-772-1899	269
Lions Gift of Sight 1000 Westgate Dr Ste 260 *Cust Svc	Saint paul	MN	55114	**866-887-4448***	612-625-5159	269
Lions Medical Eye Bank & Research Ctr of Eastern Virginia 600 Gresham Dr	Norfolk	VA	23507	**800-453-6059**		269
Lionshare Marketing Inc 7830 Barton St	Overland Park	KS	66214	**800-928-0712**	913-631-8400	195
LiphaTech Inc 3600 W Elm St	Milwaukee	WI	53209	**888-331-7900**	414-351-1476	85
Lipinski Landscape & Irrigation Contractors Inc 100 Sharp Rd	Marlton	NJ	08053	**800-644-6035**		421
Lipper International Inc 235 Washington St	Wallingford	CT	06492	**800-243-3129**	203-269-8588	726
Lippincott Marine 3420 Main St	Grasonville	MD	21638	**877-437-4193**	410-827-9300	693
Lippmann-Milwaukee Inc 3271 E Van Norman Ave	Cudahy	WI	53110	**800-648-0486**		190
Lipscomb University 3901 Granny White Pk	Nashville	TN	37204	**800-333-4358**	615-966-1000	166
Lipten Company LLC 28054 Ctr Oaks Ct	Wixom	MI	48393	**800-860-0790**	248-374-8910	384
Lipton Energy 458 S St	Pittsfield	MA	01201	**877-443-9191**	413-443-9191	
Liquid Networx Inc PO Box 780099	San Antonio	TX	78278	**866-547-8439**		196
Liquid Transport Corp 8470 Allison Pt Blvd Ste 400	Indianapolis	IN	46250	**800-942-3175**	317-841-4200	775
Liquidity Services Inc 1920 L St NW 6th Fl *NASDAQ: LQDT*	Washington	DC	20036	**800-310-4604**	202-467-6868	51
Liquidmetal Technologies Inc (LQMT) 30452 Esperanza *OTC: LQMT*	Rancho Santa Margarita	CA	92688	**888-203-1112**	949-635-2100	480
Liquor Mart Inc 1750 15th St	Boulder	CO	80302	**800-597-4440**	303-449-3374	442
LISI Inc 1600 W Hillsdale Blvd	San Mateo	CA	94402	**800-930-5190**	650-348-4131	389
Lisle Convention & Visitors Bureau 925 Burlington Ave	Lisle	IL	60532	**800-733-9811**	630-769-1000	206
Lisle Park District 1825 Short St	Lisle	IL	60532	**800-526-0854**	630-964-3410	31
List Industries Inc 401 Jim Moran Blvd	Deerfield Beach	FL	33442	**800-776-1342**	954-429-9155	319-3
Lista International Corp 106 Lowland St *Cust Svc	Holliston	MA	01746	**800-722-3020***	508-429-1350	286
Listel Hotel, The 1300 Robson St	Vancouver	BC	V6E1C5	**800-663-5491**	604-684-8461	378
Listo Pencil Corp 1925 Union St	Alameda	CA	94501	**800-547-8648**	510-522-2910	567
LITA (Library & Information Technology Assn) 50 E Huron St	Chicago	IL	60611	**800-545-2433**	312-280-4270	49-11
Litchfield Beach & Golf Resort 14276 Ocean Hwy	Pawleys Island	SC	29585	**888-734-8228**	843-237-3000	665
Litco International Inc 1 Litco Dr PO Box 150	Vienna	OH	44473	**800-236-1903**	330-539-5433	547
LiteCure LLC 250 Corporate Blvd Ste B	Newark	DE	19702	**877-627-3858**		
Litehaus Systems Inc 7445 132nd St Ste 2010	Surrey	BC	V3W1J8	**866-771-0044**		804
Litehouse Inc 1109 N Ella Ave	Sandpoint	ID	83864	**800-669-3169**		296-19
Litelab Corp 251 Elm St	Buffalo	NY	14203	**800-238-4120**	716-856-4491	361
Litetronics International Inc 4101 W 123rd St	Alsip	IL	60803	**800-860-3392**	708-389-8000	436
Lithia Motors Inc 360 E Jackson St *NYSE: LAD*	Medford	OR	97501	**866-318-9660**		57
Litho-Krome Co 5700 Old Brim Dr	Midland	GA	31820	**800-572-8028**	706-562-7900	623
Lithonia Lighting 1 Lithonia Way	Conyers	GA	30012	**800-858-7763**	770-922-9000	438
Lith-O-Roll Corp 9521 Telstar Ave	El Monte	CA	91731	**800-423-4176**	626-579-0340	452
Lithotone Inc 1313 W Hively Ave	Elkhart	IN	46517	**800-654-5671**		
Litigation Solution Inc (LSI) 5995 Greenwood Plz Blvd Ste 160	Greenwood Village	CO	80111	**888-767-7088**	303-820-2000	623
Lititz Mutual Insurance Co 2 N Broad St PO Box 900	Lititz	PA	17543	**800-626-4751**	717-626-4751	390-4
Litman Gregory Research Inc 100 Larkspur Landing Cir Ste 204	Larkspur	CA	94939	**800-960-0188**	925-254-8999	400
Littau Harvester Inc 855 Rogue Ave	Stayton	OR	97383	**866-262-2495**	503-769-5953	274
Littelfuse Inc 8755 W Higgins Rd Ste 500 *NASDAQ: LFUS* ■ *Sales	Chicago	IL	60631	**800-227-0029***	773-628-1000	725
Little America Hotel & Resort Cheyenne 2800 W Lincolnway	Cheyenne	WY	82009	**800-445-6945**	307-775-8400	378
Little America Hotel & Towers Salt Lake City 555 S Main St	Salt Lake City	UT	84101	**800-453-9450**	801-258-6568	378
Little America Hotel Flagstaff 2515 E Butler Ave	Flagstaff	AZ	86004	**800-352-4386**	928-779-7900	378
Little America Hotels & Resorts 500 S Main St	Salt Lake City	UT	84101	**800-281-7899**	801-596-5700	378
Little Brown & Co 237 Park Ave *Cust Svc	New York	NY	10017	**800-759-0190***	212-364-1100	633-2
Little Caesars Inc 2211 Woodward Ave	Detroit	MI	48201	**800-722-3727**	313-983-6000	666
Little Creek Casino Resort 91 W State Rt 108	Shelton	WA	98584	**800-667-7711**	360-427-7711	665
Little Falls Granite Works 10802 Hwy 10	Little Falls	MN	56345	**800-862-2417**		720
Little Gym International Inc 7500 N Dobson Rd Ste 220 *General	Paradise Valley	AZ	85256	**888-228-2878***		353
Little Kids Inc 225 Chapman St Ste 202	Providence	RI	02905	**800-545-5437**	401-454-7600	604
Little League Baseball Inc 539 US Rt 15 Hwy PO Box 3485	Williamsport	PA	17701	**800-811-7443**	570-326-1921	48-22
Little Nell, The 675 E Durant Ave	Aspen	CO	81611	**888-843-6355**	970-920-4600	378
Little Ocmulgee Electric Membership Corp 26 W Railroad Ave	Alamo	GA	30411	**800-342-1290**	912-568-7171	245
Little Palm Island Resort & Spa 28500 Overseas Hwy	Little Torch Key	FL	33042	**800-343-8567**	305-872-2524	665
Little Pee Dee State Park 1298 State Pk Rd	Dillon	SC	29536	**800-491-1764**	843-774-8872	561
Little River Electric Cooperative Inc (LRECI) 300 Cambridge St	Abbeville	SC	29620	**800-459-2141**	864-366-2141	245
Little Rock Air Force Base 1250 Thomas Ave	Little Rock AFB	AR	72099	**800-557-6815**	501-987-1110	495-1
Little Talbot Island State Park 12157 Heckscher Dr	Jacksonville	FL	32226	**800-326-3521**	904-251-2320	561
Little Tikes Co, The 2180 Barlow Rd *Cust Svc	Hudson	OH	44236	**800-321-0183***		757
Little White House State Historic Site 401 Little White House Rd	Warm Springs	GA	31830	**800-864-7275**		561
Littler Mendelson PC 650 California St 20th Fl	San Francisco	CA	94108	**888-548-8537**	415-433-1940	427
Littlestown Foundry Inc 150 Charles St PO Box 69	Littlestown	PA	17340	**800-471-0844**	717-359-4141	308
Littleton Adventist Hospital 7700 S Broadway	Littleton	CO	80122	**800-390-4166**	303-730-8900	373-3
Littleton Coin Company LLC 1309 Mt Eustis Rd	Littleton	NH	03561	**800-645-3122**		50-4
Litton Engineering Laboratories 200 Litton Dr Ste 200	Grass Valley	CA	95945	**800-821-8866**	530-273-6176	452
Liturgical Publications Inc 2875 S James Dr	New Berlin	WI	53151	**800-950-9952**	262-785-1188	633-9
Live Wire Net 4577 Pecos St	Denver	CO	80211	**866-913-5221**	303-458-5667	116
Livecareer 1 Hallidie Plz Ste 600	San Francisco	CA	94102	**800-652-8430**		395
Livengrin Foundation 4833 Hulmeville Rd	Bensalem	PA	19020	**800-245-4746**	215-638-5200	722
Livestock Marketing Assn (LMA) 10510 N Ambassador Dr	Kansas City	MO	64153	**800-821-2048**	816-891-0502	48-2
LiveWorld Inc 4340 Stevens Creek Blvd Ste 101	San Jose	CA	95129	**800-301-9507**		7
Living Assistance Services Inc 937 Haverford Rd Ste 200	Bryn Mawr	PA	19010	**800-365-4189**		310
Living Bank PO Box 6725	Houston	TX	77027	**800-528-2971**	713-961-9431	48-17
Living Color Enterprises Inc 6850 NW 12th Ave	Fort Lauderdale	FL	33309	**800-878-9511**	954-970-9511	41
Living Earth Crafts 3210 Executive Ridge Dr	Vista	CA	92081	**800-358-8292**	760-597-2155	76

Alphabetical Section

Name / Address	City	State	ZIP	Toll-Free	Phone	Class
Living Spa at El Monte Sagrado 317 Kit Carson Rd	Taos	NM	87571	**855-846-8267**	575-758-3502	703
Living Spaces Furniture LLC 14501 Artesia Blvd	La Mirada	CA	90638	**877-266-7300**		321
Livingston County Chamber of Commerce 4635 Millennium Dr	Geneseo	NY	14454	**800-538-7365**	585-243-2222	139
Livingston County Daily Press & Argus 323 E Grand River Ave	Howell	MI	48843	**888-999-1288**	517-548-2000	633-8
Livingston Memorial Visiting Nurse Assn Hospice 1996 Eastman Ave Ste 101	Ventura	CA	93003	**800-830-8881**	805-642-1608	370
Livingston Pipe & Tube Inc 1612 Rt 4 N	Staunton	IL	62088	**800-548-7473**	618-635-8700	490
Livingstone College 701 W Monroe St	Salisbury	NC	28144	**800-835-3435**	704-216-6000	166
LJB Inc 2500 Newmark Dr	Miamisburg	OH	45342	**866-552-3536**	937-259-5000	261
LKQ Corp 500 West Madison St Ste 2800 *NASDAQ: LKQX*	Chicago	IL	60661	**877-557-2677**		61
LL Bean Inc 15 Casco St	Freeport	ME	04033	**800-341-4341**	207-552-3080	457
Ll Roberts Group 7475 Skillman St Ste 102c	Dallas	TX	75231	**877-878-6463**	214-221-6463	260
LLAMA (Library Leadership & Management Assn) 50 E Huron St	Chicago	IL	60611	**800-545-2433**		49-11
Llano Estacado Winery 3426 E FM 1585	Lubbock	TX	79404	**800-634-3854**	806-745-2258	50-7
Llewellyn Worldwide Inc 2143 Wooddale Dr	Woodbury	MN	55125	**800-843-6666**	651-291-1970	633-2
LLLI (La Leche League International Inc) 957 N Plum Grove Rd	Schaumburg	IL	60173	**800-525-3243**	847-519-7730	48-17
Llorens Pharmaceuticals International Div 7080 NW 37th Ct	Miami	FL	33147	**866-595-5598**	305-716-0595	413
Lloyd & McDaniel PLC 11405 Park Rd Ste 200	Louisville	KY	40223	**866-548-2486**		427
Lloyd Gray Whitehead Monroe (LGWM) 880 Montclair Rd Ste 100	Birmingham	AL	35213	**800-967-7299**	205-967-8822	427
Lloyd Inc 604 W Thomas Ave PO Box 130	Shenandoah	IA	51601	**800-831-0004**	712-246-4000	580
Lloyd Pest Control Co Inc, The 1331 Morena Blvd Ste 300	San Diego	CA	92110	**800-223-2847**		573
Lloyd's Florist 9216 Preston Hwy	Louisville	KY	40229	**800-264-1825**	502-968-5428	292
LMA (Livestock Marketing Assn) 10510 N Ambassador Dr	Kansas City	MO	64153	**800-821-2048**	816-891-0502	48-2
LMC PO Box 428	Donalsonville	GA	39845	**800-332-8232**	229-524-2197	298
LMCG Investments LLC 200 Clarendon St 28th Fl	Boston	MA	02116	**877-241-5191**	617-380-5600	787
LMG Inc 2350 Investors Row	Orlando	FL	32837	**888-226-3100**	407-850-0505	264-2
LMH (Lawrence Memorial Hospital) 325 Maine St	Lawrence	KS	66044	**800-749-4144**	785-505-5000	373-3
LMI (Legg Mason Inc) 100 International Dr *NYSE: LM*	Baltimore	MD	21202	**800-822-5544**	800-221-3627	686
LN Curtis & Sons 1800 Peralta St	Oakland	CA	94607	**800-443-3556**	510-839-5111	675
LNC (Lincoln National Corp) 150 N Radnor-Chester Rd *NYSE: LNC*	Radnor	PA	19087	**877-275-5462**	866-533-3410	359-4
LNI Custom Manufacturing Inc 12536 Chadron Ave	Hawthorne	CA	90250	**800-338-3387**	310-978-2000	697
Loadcraft Industries Inc 3811 N Bridge St	Brady	TX	76825	**800-803-0183**	325-597-2911	774
Loaf N' Jug Mini Mart 442 Keeler Pkwy	Pueblo	CO	81001	**888-200-6211**		
Loan Science PO Box 81671	Austin	TX	78708	**866-311-9450**		215
loanDepot 26642 Towne Centre Dr	Foothill Ranch	CA	92610	**888-337-6888**		507
Loblaw Cos Ltd 1 President's Choice Cir	Brampton	ON	L6Y5S5	**888-495-5111**	905-459-2500	344
Lobster Sports Inc 7340 Fulton Ave	North Hollywood	CA	91605	**800-210-5992**	818-764-6000	706
LoBue & Majdalany Management Group 572B Ruger St PO Box 29920	San Francisco	CA	94129	**800-820-4690**	415-561-6110	47
LOC Enterprises LLC 7575 E Kemper Rd	Cincinnati	OH	45249	**888-963-6320**		195
Local Government Federal Credit Union 323 W Jones St Ste 600	Raleigh	NC	27603	**888-732-8562**	919-857-2150	219
Lochinvar Corp 300 Maddox Simpson Pkwy	Lebanon	TN	37090	**800-722-2101**	615-889-8900	36
Lochsa Engineering Inc 6345 S Jones Blvd Ste 100	Las Vegas	NV	89118	**866-606-9784**	702-365-9312	261
Lock Joint Tube Inc 515 W Ireland Rd	South Bend	IN	46614	**800-257-6859**	574-299-5326	488
Lockheed Federal Credit Union (LFCU) 2340 Hollywood Way	Burbank	CA	91505	**800-328-5328**	818-565-2020	219
Lockheed Martin Corp 6801 Rockledge Dr *NYSE: LMT*	Bethesda	MD	20817	**866-562-2363**	301-897-6000	20
Lockheed Martin Space Systems Co Michoud Operations 13800 Old Gentilly Rd	New Orleans	LA	70129	**866-562-2363**	504-257-3311	502
Lockheed Window Corp 925 S Main St PO Box 166	Pascoag	RI	02859	**800-537-3061**	401-568-3061	234
Lockmasters Security Institute 2101 John C Watts Dr	Nicholasville	KY	40356	**800-654-0637**	859-885-6041	349
Lockwood Advisors Inc 760 Moore Rd	King Of Prussia	PA	19406	**800-200-3033**		69
Lockwood Products Inc 5615 Willow Ln	Lake Oswego	OR	97035	**800-423-1625**		369
Lodal Inc 620 N Hooper St PO Box 2315	Kingsford	MI	49802	**800-435-3500**	906-779-1700	513
LoDan Electronics Inc 3311 N Kennicott Ave	Arlington Heights	IL	60004	**800-401-4995**	847-398-5311	811
Lodge & Club at Ponte Vedra Beach 607 Ponte Vedra Blvd	Ponte Vedra Beach	FL	32082	**800-243-4304**	888-839-9145	665
Lodge At Breckenridge, The 112 Overlook Dr	Breckenridge	CO	80424	**800-736-1607**	970-453-9300	378
Lodge at Pebble Beach 1700 17-Mile Dr	Pebble Beach	CA	93953	**800-654-9300**	831-624-3811	665
Lodge at Sonoma - A Renaissance Resort & Spa 1325 Broadway	Sonoma	CA	95476	**866-263-0758**	707-935-6600	665
Lodge at the Mountain Village 1850 Sidewinder Dr Ste 320	Park City	UT	84060	**800-453-1360**		378
Lodge at Tiburon, The 1651 Tiburon Blvd	Tiburon	CA	94920	**800-762-7770**	415-435-3133	377
Lodge at Ventana Canyon - A Wyndham Luxury Resort 6200 N Clubhouse Ln	Tucson	AZ	85750	**800-828-5701**	520-577-1400	665
Lodge Casino 240 Main St PO Box 50	Black Hawk	CO	80422	**800-522-4700**		
Lodge of Four Seasons 315 Four Seasons Dr *Resv	Lake Ozark	MO	65049	**888-265-5500***	573-365-3000	665
Lodi Conference & Visitors Bureau 115 S School St	Lodi	CA	95240	**800-798-1810**	209-365-1195	206
Lodi Pumb & Irrigation 1301 E Armstrong Rd	Lodi	CA	95242	**800-634-7272**		428
Loeb Equipment & Appraisal Co 4131 S State St	Chicago	IL	60609	**800-560-5632**	773-548-4131	41
Loeber Motors Inc 4255 W Touhy Ave	Lincolnwood	IL	60712	**888-211-4485**	847-675-1000	57
Loesel Schaaf Insurance Agency Inc 3537 W 12th St	Erie	PA	16505	**877-718-9935**	814-833-5433	389
Loews Hotel 1000 1000 First Ave	Seattle	WA	98104	**877-315-1088**	206-957-1000	378
Loews Hotels 4000 Coronado Bay Rd	Coronado	CA	92118	**888-674-1397**	619-628-8770	703
Loews Hotels & Co 667 Madison Ave	New York	NY	10065	**800-235-6397**		378
Loews Ventana Canyon 7000 N Resort Dr	Tucson	AZ	85750	**844-806-9740**	520-299-2020	665
Loftin Equipment Company Inc 12 N 45th Ave	Phoenix	AZ	85043	**800-437-4376**	602-272-9466	532
Loftness Specialized Farm Equipment Inc 650 S Main St PO Box 337	Hector	MN	55342	**800-828-7624**	320-848-6266	273
Lofton Label Inc 6290 Claude Way	Inver Grove Heights	MN	55076	**877-447-8118**	651-552-6257	548-1
Logan Capital Management Inc 6 Coulter Ave Ste 2000	Ardmore	PA	19003	**800-215-1100**		400
Logan Clay Products Co 201 S Walnut St	Logan	OH	43138	**800-848-2141**		150
Logan Corp 555 Seventh Ave	Huntington	WV	25701	**888-853-4751**	304-526-4700	384
Logan County 116 S Main St	Russellville	KY	42276	**800-693-3299**	270-726-2206	337
Logan County Chamber of Commerce 100 S Main St	Bellefontaine	OH	43311	**877-360-3608**	937-599-5121	139
Logan Regional Medical Ctr 20 Hospital Dr	Logan	WV	25601	**888-982-9144**	304-831-1101	373-3
Logan Trucking Inc 3224 Navarre Rd SW	Canton	OH	44706	**800-683-0142**	330-478-1404	186
LoganBritton Inc 1700 Park St Ste 111	Naperville	IL	60563	**800-362-4352**		225
Logansport Juvenile Correctional Facility 1118 S St Rd 25	Logansport	IN	46947	**800-800-5556**	800-677-9800	411
Logees Greenhouses Ltd 141 N St	Danielson	CT	06239	**888-330-8038**	860-774-8038	192
Logical Images Inc 3445 Winton Pl Ste 240	Rochester	NY	14623	**800-357-7611**	585-427-2790	177
Logical Net Corp 1462 Erie Blvd	Schenectady	NY	12305	**800-600-0638**	518-292-4500	386
Logicalis 1 Penn Plz 51st Fl Ste 5130	New York	NY	10119	**866-456-4422**		
Logicease Solutions Inc 1 Bay Plz Ste 520	Burlingame	CA	94010	**866-212-3273**	650-373-1111	180
Logility Inc 470 E Paces Ferry Rd	Atlanta	GA	30305	**800-762-5207**	404-261-9777	178-1
Logistic Dynamics Inc 155 Pineview Dr	Amherst	NY	14228	**800-554-3734**	716-250-3477	314
Logistics Plus Inc 1406 Peach St	Erie	PA	16501	**866-564-7587**	814-461-7600	311
Logitech Inc 6505 Kaiser Dr *Sales	Fremont	CA	94555	**800-231-7717***	510-795-8500	173-1
Logitek Electronic Systems Inc 5622 Edgemoor Dr	Houston	TX	77081	**877-231-5870**	713-664-4470	643
Logo Inc 117 SE Pkwy	Franklin	TN	37064	**844-564-6432**		
LogoNation Inc PO Box 3847 Ste 102	Mooresville	NC	28117	**800-955-7375**		623
Logos Christian College 6620 Southpoint Dr S Ste 115	Jacksonville	FL	32216	**800-776-0127**	904-329-1723	166
Loki Systems Inc 1258-13351 Commerce Pkwy	Richmond	BC	V6V2X7	**800-378-5654**		179
LOKRING Technology LLC 38376 Apollo Pkwy	Willoughby	OH	44094	**800-876-2323**	440-942-0880	719
LOMA 2300 Windy Ridge Pkwy Ste 600	Atlanta	GA	30339	**800-275-5662**	770-951-1770	49-9
Loma Linda University 11234 Anderson St	Loma Linda	CA	92354	**800-872-1212**	909-558-1000	166
Loma Linda University Medical Ctr 11234 Anderson St	Loma Linda	CA	92354	**877-558-6248**	909-558-4000	373-3
Loma Linda University School of Medicine 11175 Campus St	Loma Linda	CA	92350	**800-422-4558**	909-558-4467	167-2
Lomanco Inc 2101 W Main St	Jacksonville	AR	72076	**800-643-5596**	501-982-6511	14
Lomont In-Mold Technologies (IMT) 1516 E Mapleleaf Dr	Mount Pleasant	IA	52641	**800-776-0380**	319-385-1528	597
Lompoc Valley Chamber of Commerce & Visitors Bureau PO Box 626	Lompoc	CA	93438	**800-240-0999**	805-736-4567	139
London Computer Services 9140 Waterstone Blvd	Cincinnati	OH	45249	**800-669-0871**	513-583-1482	179
London Drugs Ltd 12251 Horseshoe Way	Richmond	BC	V7A4X5	**888-991-2299**		238

Alphabetical Section

Name / Address	Toll-Free	Phone	Class
London Fog 1615 Kellogg Dr ....Douglas GA 31535	877-588-8189	732-346-9009	155-5
London Free Press 369 York St PO Box 2280 ......London ON N6A4G1	866-541-6757	519-679-1111	528-1
London Life Insurance Co 255 Dufferin Ave ....London ON N6A4K1	800-990-6654	519-432-5281	390-2
London Luxury Bedding Inc 295 Fifth Ave Ste 817 .....New Rochelle NY 10016	877-636-2100	914-636-2100	
London Machinery Inc 15790 Robin's Hill Rd ....London ON N5V0A4	800-265-1098	519-963-2500	61
London West Hollywood Hotel 1020 N San Vicente Blvd .....West Hollywood CA 90069	866-282-4560		377
London/Laurel County Tourist Commission 140 Faith Assembly Church Rd .....London KY 40741	800-348-0095	606-878-6900	206
Lone Oak Lodge 2221 N Fremont St ....Monterey CA 93940 *General	800-283-5663*	831-372-4924	378
Lone Peak Labeling Systems 1785 South 4490 West ......Salt Lake City UT 84106	800-658-8599	801-975-1818	
Lone Star Container Corp 700 N Wildwood Dr ....Irving TX 75061	800-552-6937		100
Lone Star Flight Museum 11551 Aerospace Ave ......Houston TX 77034	888-359-5736	346-708-2517	517
Lone Star Legal Aid 500 Jefferson St 17th Fl ....Houston TX 77002	800-733-8394	713-652-0077	427
Lone Star Lions Eye Bank 102 E Wheeler PO Box 347 ....Manor TX 78653	800-977-3937	512-457-0638	269
Lone Star Park at Grand Prairie 1000 Lone Star Pkwy .....Grand Prairie TX 75050	800-795-7223	972-263-7223	638
Lone Star Percussion 10611 Control Pl ....Dallas TX 75238	866-792-0143	214-340-0835	522
Lone Star Railroad Contractors Inc 4201 S I-45 ....Ennis TX 75119	800-838-7225	972-878-9500	188
Lonely Planet Publications 50 Linden St ....Oakland CA 94607	800-275-8555	510-893-8555	633-2
Lonestar 987 6214 W 34th St ....Amarillo TX 79109	866-930-5225	806-355-9777	641-5
Long & Foster Realtors 14501 George Carter Way ....Chantilly VA 20151	800-237-8800	703-653-8500	648
Long & Foster Vacation Rentals 41 Maryland Ave ....Annapolis MD 21401	800-981-8234	410-263-3262	375
Long Beach Airport LGB 4100 Donald Douglas Dr ......Long Beach CA 90808	800-331-1212	562-570-2600	27
Long Beach City College 4901 E Carson St ....Long Beach CA 90808	888-442-4551	562-938-4111	162
Long Beach Convention & Visitors Bureau 301 E Ocean Blvd ....Long Beach CA 90802	800-452-7829	562-436-3645	206
Long Hollow Ranch 71105 Holmes Rd ....Sisters OR 97759	877-923-1901	541-923-1901	239
Long House Alaskan Hotel 4335 Wisconsin St ....Anchorage AK 99517	888-243-2133	907-243-2133	378
Long Island College Hospital (LICH) 339 Hicks St ....Brooklyn NY 11201	800-227-8922	718-780-1000	373-3
Long Island Convention & Visitors Bureau & Sports Commission 330 Motor Pkwy Ste 203 ....Hauppauge NY 11788	877-386-6654	631-951-3900	206
Long Island MacArthur Airport 100 Arrival Ave Ste 100 ....Ronkonkoma NY 11779	888-542-4776	631-467-3300	27
Long Island Power Authority 333 Earle Ovington Blvd Ste 403 ....Uniondale NY 11553 *Cust Svc	877-275-5472*	516-222-7700	782
Long Island Press 575 Underhill Blvd Ste 210.......Syosset NY 11791	800-545-6683	516-284-3300	528-5
Long Island University Brooklyn 1 University Plz ....Brooklyn NY 11201	800-548-7526	718-488-1011	166
Long Lines LLC 501 Fourth St PO Box 67 ....Sergeant Bluff IA 51054	866-901-5664	712-271-4000	225
Long Painting Co 21414 68th Ave S ....Kent WA 98032	800-687-5664	253-234-8050	189-8
Long Pond Ironworks State Park c/o Ringwood State Pk 1304 Sloatsburg Rd ....Ringwood NJ 07456	800-852-7899	973-962-7031	561
Long View Systems Corp 250-2 St SW Ste 2100 ....Calgary AB T2P0C1	866-515-6900	403-515-6900	174
Long Wharf Theatre 222 Sargent Dr ....New Haven CT 06511	800-782-8497	203-787-4282	568
Longboat Key Club 220 Sands Point Rd ....Longboat Key FL 34228	800-237-8821	941-383-8821	665
Longfellow-Evangeline State Historic Site 1200 N Main St ....Saint Martinville LA 70582	888-677-2900	337-394-3754	561
Longhorn Cavern State Park PO Box 732 ....Burnet TX 78611	877-441-2883	830-598-2283	
Longhorn Imports Inc 2202 E Union Bower ....Irving TX 75061	800-641-8348	972-721-9102	311
LongHorn Steakhouse 1000 Darden Ctr Dr ....Orlando FL 32837	888-221-0642		666
Longistics Transportation Inc 10900 World Trade Blvd ....Raleigh NC 27617	800-289-0082	919-872-7626	798-1
Longos a fresh tradition 8800 Huntington Rd ....Vaughan ON L4H3M6	800-956-6467		
Longue Vue House & Gardens 7 Bamboo Rd ....New Orleans LA 70124	800-476-9137	504-488-5488	517
Longust Distributing Inc 2432 W Birchwood Ave ....Mesa AZ 85202	800-352-0521	480-820-6244	360
Longview News-Journal 320 E Methvin St ....Longview TX 75601	800-825-9799	903-757-3311	528-2
Longview Solutions 65 Allstate Pkwy Ste 200 ....Markham ON L3R9X1	888-454-2549	905-940-1510	178-1
Longwood Elastomers Inc 706 Green Valley Rd Ste 212 ....Greensboro NC 27408	800-829-7231	336-272-3710	673
Longwood University 201 High St ....Farmville VA 23909	800-281-4677	434-395-2060	166
Lonsdale Quay Hotel 123 Carrie Cates Ct ....North Vancouver BC V7M3K7	800-836-6111	604-986-6111	378
Lonseal Inc 928 E 238th St ....Carson CA 90745	800-832-7111	310-830-7111	360

Name / Address	Toll-Free	Phone	Class
Loomis Armored US Inc 2500 Citywest Blvd Ste 900 ....Houston TX 77042	866-383-5069	713-435-6700	689
Loomis Communities 246 N Main St ....South Hadley MA 01075	800-865-7655	413-532-5325	668
Loomis Fargo & Co 2500 Citywest Blvd Ste 900 ....Houston TX 77042	866-383-5069	713-435-6700	688
Loomis Sayles & Company Inc LP 1 Financial Ctr ....Boston MA 02111	800-343-2029	800-633-3330	400
Loomis Sayles Funds 1 Financial Ctr ....Boston MA 02111	800-633-3330	617-482-2450	524
Loop Capital Markets LLC 111 W Jackson Blvd Ste 1901 ....Chicago IL 60604	888-294-8898	312-913-4900	686
Loop-Loc Ltd 390 Motor Pkwy ....Hauppauge NY 11788	800-562-5667	631-582-2626	728
LOPA (Louisiana Organ Procurement Agency) 3545 N I-10 Service Rd Ste 300 ....Metairie LA 70002	800-521-4483		541
Lopez Mchugh LLP 1123 Admiral Peary Way ....Philadelphia PA 19112	877-703-7070	215-952-6910	427
Lorain Correctional Institution 2075 Avon Belden Rd ....Grafton OH 44044	888-842-8464	440-748-1049	213
Lorain County 225 Ct St ....Elyria OH 44035	800-750-0750	440-329-5536	337
Lorain County Chamber of Commerce 226 Middle Ave ....Elyria OH 44035	800-633-4766	440-328-2550	139
Lorain County Community College 1005 N Abbe Rd ....Elyria OH 44035	800-995-5222	440-365-5222	162
Lorain County Visitors Bureau 8025 Leavitt Rd ....Amherst OH 44001	800-334-1673	440-984-5282	206
Lorain-Medina Rural Electric Co-op Inc 22898 W Rd ....Wellington OH 44090	800-222-5673	440-647-2133	245
Lorann Oils 4518 Aurelius Rd ....Lansing MI 48910	800-862-8620	517-882-0215	344
Loras College 1450 Alta Vista St ....Dubuque IA 52001	800-245-6727	563-588-7100	166
Lord & Taylor 424 Fifth Ave ....New York NY 10018	800-223-7440	212-391-3344	229
Lord Abbett & Co 90 Hudson St ....Jersey City NJ 07302	888-522-2388		400
Lord Corp 111 Lord Dr ....Cary NC 27511	877-275-5673	919-468-5979	3
Lord Elgin Hotel 100 Elgin St ....Ottawa ON K1P5K8	800-267-4298	613-235-3333	378
Lord Fairfax Community College Middletown 173 Skirmisher Ln ....Middletown VA 22645	800-906-5322	540-868-7000	162
Lord Nelson Hotel & Suites 1515 S Park St ....Halifax NS B3J2L2	800-565-2020	902-423-6331	378
Lord Stanley Suites on the Park 1889 Alberni St ....Vancouver BC V6G3G7	888-767-7829	604-688-9299	378
Lordco Parts Ltd 22866 Dewdney Trunk Rd ....Maple Ridge BC V2X3K6	877-591-1581	604-467-1581	57
Lorenz Corp 501 E Third St ....Dayton OH 45402	800-444-1144		633-7
LOREX Corp 3700 Koppers St Ste 504 ....Baltimore MD 21227	888-425-6739		689
Lori Bonn Jewelery 114 Linden St ....Oakland CA 94607	877-507-4206	510-286-8181	409
Lorin Industries 1960 S Roberts St ....Muskegon MI 49443	800-654-1159	231-722-1631	479
Loroco Industries Inc 5000 Creek Rd ....Cincinnati OH 45242	800-215-9474	513-891-9544	551
Lorraine Travel Bureau Inc 377 Alhambra Cir ....Coral Gables FL 33134	800-666-8911	305-446-4433	766
Los Abrigados Resort 160 Portal Ln ....Sedona AZ 86336	877-374-2582	928-282-1777	665
Los Adaes State Historic Site 6354 Hwy 485 ....Robeline LA 71469	888-677-5378	318-472-9449	561
Los Alamos National Laboratory (LANL) PO Box 1663 ....Los Alamos NM 87545	877-723-4101	505-667-7000	664
Los Alamos Technical Assoc Inc 6501 Americas Pkwy NE Ste 200 ....Albuquerque NM 87110	800-952-5282	505-884-3800	192
Los Angeles Air Force Base 483 N Aviation Blvd Los Angeles AFB ....El Segundo CA 90245	800-275-8777	310-653-1110	495-1
Los Angeles Athletic Club 431 W Seventh St ....Los Angeles CA 90014	800-421-8777	213-625-2211	378
Los Angeles Clippers 1212 S Flower St 5th Fl ....Los Angeles CA 90015	855-895-0872	213-742-7100	710-1
Los Angeles County Metropolitan Transportation Authority 1 Gateway Plz ....Los Angeles CA 90012	866-827-8646	213-922-6000	466
Los Angeles Downtown News 1264 W First St ....Los Angeles CA 90026	877-338-1010	213-481-1448	528-4
Los Angeles Federal Credit Union PO Box 53032 ....Los Angeles CA 90053	877-695-2328	818-242-8640	219
Los Angeles Galaxy 18400 Avalon Blvd ....Carson CA 90746	877-342-5299	310-630-2200	713
Los Angeles Kings Staples Ctr 1111 S Figueroa St ....Los Angeles CA 90015	888-546-4752	213-742-7100	712
Los Angeles Magazine 5900 Wilshire Blvd 10th Fl.......Los Angeles CA 90036 *Cust Svc	800-876-5222*	323-801-0100	455-22
Los Angeles Mission College 13356 Eldridge Ave ....Sylmar CA 91342	800-854-7771	818-364-7600	162
Los Angeles Police Federal Credit Union PO Box 10188 ....Van Nuys CA 91410	877-695-2732	818-787-6520	219
Los Angeles Smoking & Curing Co (LASCCO) 1100 W Ewing St ....Seattle WA 98119	800-365-8950	206-285-6800	296-13
Los Angeles Sparks 865 S Figueroa St Ste 104 ....Los Angeles CA 90017	888-694-3278	213-929-1300	710-2
Los Angeles Times 202 W First St ....Los Angeles CA 90012	800-528-4637	213-237-5000	528-2
Los Angeles Times Festival of Books Los Angeles Times 202 W First St ....Los Angeles CA 90012	800-528-4637	213-237-5000	281
Los Angeles Times-Washington Post News Service Inc 1150 15th St NW ....Washington DC 20071	800-627-1150	202-334-6000	526

Name / Address	City	State	ZIP	Toll-Free	Phone	Class
Los Medanos College						
2700 E Leland Rd	Pittsburg	CA	94565	**800-677-6337**	925-439-2181	162
Office of Student Financial Assistance						
602 N Fifth St	Baton Rouge	LA	70802	**800-259-5626**	225-219-1012	721
Losi 4710 E Guasti Rd	Ontario	CA	91761	**888-899-5674**	909-390-9595	757
Lost City Museum of Archeology						
721 S Moapa Valley Blvd	Overton	NV	89040	**800-326-6868**	775-687-4810	517
Lost Recovery Network Lrni						
406 Dixon St	Vidalia	GA	30474	**877-693-1456**	912-537-3901	461
Lost River Caverns						
726 Durham St PO Box M	Hellertown	PA	18055	**888-529-1907**	610-838-8767	50-5
Loudoun House						
209 Castlewood Dr	Lexington	KY	40505	**866-945-7920**	859-254-7024	50-3
Louhelen Baha'i School						
3208 S State Rd	Davison	MI	48423	**800-894-9716**	810-653-5033	669
Louis A Johnson Veterans Affairs Medical Ctr						
1 Medical Ctr Dr	Clarksburg	WV	26301	**800-733-0512**	304-623-3461	373-8
Louis A Weiss Memorial Hospital						
4646 N Marine Dr	Chicago	IL	60640	**800-503-1234**	773-878-8700	373-3
Louis Ferre Inc						
302 Fifth Ave	New York	NY	10001	**800-695-1061**		347
Louis M Gerson Company Inc						
16 Commerce Blvd	Middleboro	MA	02346	**800-225-8623**	508-947-4000	572
Louis M Martini Winery						
254 S St Helena Hwy	Saint Helena	CA	94574	**800-321-9463**	707-968-3362	80-3
Louis Padnos Iron & Metal Co						
PO Box 1979	Holland	MI	49422	**800-442-3509**	616-396-6521	682
Louis Riel School Div						
900 St Mary's Rd	Winnipeg	MB	R2M3R3	**800-940-3447**	204-257-7827	681
Louis Stokes Cleveland Veterans Affairs Medical Ctr						
10701 E Blvd	Cleveland	OH	44106	**888-838-6446**	216-791-3800	373-8
Louis Vuitton NA Inc						
1 E 57th St	New York	NY	10022	**866-884-8866***	212-758-8877	157-6
*Cust Svc						
Louisbourg Investments						
1000-770 Main St	Moncton	NB	E1C1E7	**888-608-7070**	506-853-5410	
Louisburg College						
501 N Main St	Louisburg	NC	27549	**800-775-0208**	919-496-2521	162
Louisiana						
Agriculture & Forestry Dept						
5825 Florida Blvd	Baton Rouge	LA	70806	**866-927-2476**	225-922-1234	338-19
Community Services Office						
627 N Fourth St	Baton Rouge	LA	70802	**888-524-3578**		338-19
Consumer Protection Office						
1885 N Third St	Baton Rouge	LA	70804	**800-351-4889**	225-326-6465	338-19
Contractors Licensing Board						
2525 Quail Dr	Baton Rouge	LA	70808	**800-256-1392**	225-765-2301	338-19
Crime Victims Reparations Board						
PO Box 3133	Baton Rouge	LA	70821	**888-684-2846**	225-342-1749	338-19
Education Dept						
PO Box 94064	Baton Rouge	LA	70804	**877-453-2721**		338-19
Environmental Quality Dept						
602 N Fifth St	Baton Rouge	LA	70802	**866-896-5337**	225-219-5337	338-19
Ethics Board						
617 N Third St						
LaSalle Bldg Ste 10-36	Baton Rouge	LA	70802	**800-842-6630**	225-219-5600	338-19
Financial Institutions Office						
PO Box 94095	Baton Rouge	LA	70804	**888-525-9414**	225-925-4660	338-19
Housing Finance Agency						
2415 Quail Dr	Baton Rouge	LA	70808	**888-454-2001**	225-763-8700	338-19
Insurance Dept						
1702 N Third Str	Baton Rouge	LA	70802	**800-259-5300**	225-342-5900	338-19
Legislature						
PO Box 94062	Baton Rouge	LA	70804	**800-256-3793**	225-342-2456	338-19
Lottery Corp						
555 Laurel St	Baton Rouge	LA	70801	**877-770-7867**	225-297-2000	450
Office of Student Financial Assistance						
602 N Fifth St	Baton Rouge	LA	70802	**800-259-5626**	225-219-1012	721
Office of the Governor						
PO Box 94004	Baton Rouge	LA	70804	**866-366-1121**	225-342-7015	338-19
Public Service Commission						
PO Box 91154	Baton Rouge	LA	70821	**800-256-2397**	225-342-4999	338-19
Rehabilitation Services						
627 N Fourth St	Baton Rouge	LA	70802	**888-524-3578**		
Revenue Dept						
617 N Third St PO Box 201	Baton Rouge	LA	70802	**855-307-3893**		338-19
State Parks Office						
PO Box 44426	Baton Rouge	LA	70804	**877-226-7652**	225-342-8111	338-19
Veterans Affairs Dept						
PO Box 94095	Baton Rouge	LA	70804	**877-432-8982**	225-219-5000	338-19
Weights & Measures Div						
5825 Florida Blvd	Baton Rouge	LA	70806	**866-927-2476**	225-922-1234	
Wildlife & Fisheries Dept						
2000 Quail Dr	Baton Rouge	LA	70898	**800-256-2749**	225-765-2800	338-19
Louisiana Assn For, The Blind, The						
1750 Claiborne Ave	Shreveport	LA	71103	**877-913-6471**	318-635-6471	548-2
Louisiana Assn of Business & Industry						
3113 Vly Creek Dr						
PO Box 80258	Baton Rouge	LA	70898	**888-816-5224**	225-928-5388	140
Louisiana Association of Educators						
8322 One Kalais Ave	Baton Rouge	LA	70809	**800-256-4523**	225-343-9243	455-8
Louisiana Banker						
PO Box 2871	Baton Rouge	LA	70821	**888-249-3050**	225-387-3282	527-1
Louisiana College						
1140 College Dr	Pineville	LA	71359	**800-487-1906**	318-487-7011	166
Louisiana Culinary Institute						
10550 Airline Hwy	Baton Rouge	LA	70816	**877-533-3198**		163
Louisiana Delta Community College						
7500 Millhaven Rd	Monroe	LA	71203	**866-500-5322**	318-345-9000	162
Louisiana Dental Assn						
7833 Office Pk Blvd	Baton Rouge	LA	70809	**800-388-6642**	225-926-1986	227
Louisiana Medical Mutual Insurance Co						
1 Galleria Blvd Ste 700	Metairie	LA	70001	**800-452-2120**		390-5
Louisiana Organ Procurement Agency (LOPA)						
3545 N I-10 Service Rd Ste 300	Metairie	LA	70002	**800-521-4483**		541
Louisiana Public Broadcasting						
7733 Perkins Rd	Baton Rouge	LA	70810	**800-973-7246**	225-767-5660	628

Name / Address	City	State	ZIP	Toll-Free	Phone	Class
Louisiana State Arboretum						
1300 Sudie Lawton Ln	Ville Platte	LA	70586	**888-677-6100**	337-363-6289	561
Louisiana State Bar Assn (LSBA)						
601 St Charles Ave	New Orleans	LA	70130	**800-421-5722**	504-566-1600	72
Louisiana State Medical Society						
6767 Perkins Rd Ste 100	Baton Rouge	LA	70808	**800-375-9508**	225-763-8500	472
Louisiana State Museum						
751 Chartres St	New Orleans	LA	70116	**800-568-6968**	504-568-6968	517
Louisiana State Nurses Assn (LSNA)						
543 Spanish Town Rd	Baton Rouge	LA	70802	**800-457-6378**	225-201-0993	529
Louisiana State University						
Alexandria						
8100 US Hwy 71 S	Alexandria	LA	71302	**888-473-6417***	318-445-3672	166
*Admissions						
Baton Rouge						
110 Thomas Boyd Hall	Baton Rouge	LA	70803	**888-846-6810**	225-578-3202	166
Eunice PO Box 1129	Eunice	LA	70535	**888-367-5783**	337-457-7311	162
Louisiana Veterinary Medical Assn						
8550 United Plaza Blvd						
Ste 1001	Baton Rouge	LA	70809	**800-524-2996**	225-928-5862	790
Louisiana-Pacific Corp						
414 Union St Ste 2000	Nashville	TN	37219	**888-820-0325**	615-986-5600	679
NYSE: LPX						
Louisville & Jefferson County Convention & Visitors Bureau						
401 W Main St Ste 2300	Louisville	KY	40202	**800-626-5646**	502-584-2121	206
Louisville Magazine						
137 W Muhammad Ali Blvd						
Ste 101	Louisville	KY	40202	**866-832-0011**	502-625-0100	455-22
Louisville Presbyterian Theological Seminary						
1044 Alta Vista Rd	Louisville	KY	40205	**800-264-1839**	502-895-3411	167-3
Louisville Science Ctr						
727 W Main St	Louisville	KY	40202	**800-591-2203**	502-561-6100	517
Louisville Slugger Museum						
800 W Main St	Louisville	KY	40202	**877-775-8443**		519
Louisville Technical Institute						
Sullivan College of Technology & Design						
3901 Atkinson Sq Dr	Louisville	KY	40218	**800-844-6528**	502-456-6509	795
Loup Public Power District (LPPD)						
2404 15th St PO Box 988	Columbus	NE	68602	**866-869-2087**	402-564-3171	245
Lourdes College						
6832 Convent Blvd	Sylvania	OH	43560	**800-878-3210**	419-885-5291	166
Lou-Rich Machine Tool Inc						
505 W Front St	Albert Lea	MN	56007	**800-893-3235**	507-377-8910	752
Love & Quiches Desserts						
178 Hanse Ave	Freeport	NY	11520	**800-525-5251**	516-623-8800	297-11
Love Envelopes Inc						
10733 E Ute St	Tulsa	OK	74116	**800-532-9747**	918-836-3535	263
Love's Travel Stops						
10601 N Pennsylvania Ave	Oklahoma City	OK	73120	**800-655-6837**		204
Lovegreen Industrial Services Inc						
2280 Sibley Ct	Eagan	MN	55122	**800-262-8284**	651-890-1166	468
Lovejoy Tool Company Inc						
133 Main St	Springfield	VT	05156	**800-843-8376**	802-885-2194	491
Lovelace Medical Ctr						
5400 Gibson Blvd SE	Albuquerque	NM	87108	**888-281-6531**	505-727-8000	373-3
Lovelace Respiratory Research Institute (LRRI)						
2425 Ridgecrest Dr SE	Albuquerque	NM	87108	**800-700-1016**	505-348-9400	664
Lovers Key State Park						
8700 Estero Blvd	Fort Myers Beach	FL	33931	**800-326-3521**	239-463-4588	561
Loveshaw Corp						
2206 Easton Tpke	South Canaan	PA	18459	**800-747-1586***	570-937-4921	543
*Cust Svc						
Lovitt & Touche Inc						
7202 E Rosewood St Ste 200						
PO Box 32702	Tucson	AZ	85710	**800-426-2756**	520-722-3000	389
Lowe Boats						
2900 Industrial Dr	Lebanon	MO	65536	**800-641-4372**	417-532-9101	90
Lowe Electric Supply Co						
1525 Forsyth St PO Box 4767	Macon	GA	31208	**800-868-8661**		246
Lowe Enterprises						
11777 San Vicente Blvd						
Ste 900	Los Angeles	CA	90049	**800-842-2252**	310-820-6661	651
Lowe's Cos Inc						
1000 Lowe's Blvd	Mooresville	NC	28117	**800-445-6937**	704-758-1000	363
NYSE: LOW						
Lowe's Home Centers Inc						
PO Box 1111	North Wilkesboro	NC	28656	**800-445-6937**		363
Lowell General Hospital (LGH)						
295 Varnum Ave	Lowell	MA	01854	**800-544-2424**	978-937-6000	373-3
Lowell Manufacturing Co						
100 Integram Dr	Pacific	MO	63069	**800-325-9660**	636-257-3400	52
Lowell Sun Publishing Co						
491 Dutton St	Lowell	MA	01854	**800-359-1300***	978-458-7100	633-8
*Cust Svc						
Lowe-Martin Company Inc						
400 Hunt Club Rd	Ottawa	ON	K1V1C1	**866-521-9871**	613-741-0962	225
Lowen Corp						
PO Box 1528	Hutchinson	KS	67504	**800-835-2365**	620-663-2161	623
Lower Bucks County Chamber of Commerce						
409 Hood Blvd	Fairless Hills	PA	19030	**800-786-2234**	215-943-7400	139
Lower Cape Fear Hospice & Life Care						
1414 Physicians Dr	Wilmington	NC	28401	**800-733-1476**	910-796-7900	370
Lower Columbia College						
1600 Maple St PO Box 3010	Longview	WA	98632	**866-900-2311**	360-442-2301	162
Lower Keys Chamber of Commerce						
31020 Overseas Hwy	Big Pine Key	FL	33043	**800-872-3722**	305-872-2411	139
Lower Keys Medical Ctr						
5900 College Rd	Key West	FL	33040	**800-355-2470**	305-294-5531	373-3
Lower Valley Energy						
236 N Washington PO Box 188	Afton	WY	83110	**800-882-5875**	307-885-3175	245
Lower Wekiva River Preserve State Park						
1800 Wekiwa Cir	Apopka	FL	32712	**800-326-3521**	407-884-2008	561
Lower Yellowstone Rural Electric Assn Inc						
3200 W Holly St PO Box 1047	Sidney	MT	59270	**844-441-5627**	406-488-1602	245
Lowes Food Stores Inc						
1381 Old Mill Cir Ste 200	Winston-Salem	NC	27103	**800-669-5693**	336-659-0180	344
Lowrance Electronics Inc						
12000 E Skelly Dr	Tulsa	OK	74128	**800-628-4487**	918-437-6881	525

				Toll-Free	Phone	Class
Lowrey Organ Co						
989 AEC Dr	Wood Dale	IL	60191	**800-451-5939**		523
Lowrider Magazine						
1821 E Dyer Rd PO Box 420235	Santa Ana	CA	92705	**800-283-2013**		
Loxcreen Co Inc, The						
1630 Old Dunbar Rd						
PO Box 4004	West Columbia	SC	29172	**800-330-5699**	803-822-8200	483
Loyalist College						
Wallbridge-Loyalist Rd	Belleville	ON	K8N5B9	**800-992-5866**	613-969-1913	162
Loyalty Methods Inc						
80 Yesler Way Ste 310	Seattle	WA	98104	**800-693-2040**	206-257-2111	461
Loyd's Aviation						
1601 Skyway Dr Ste 100						
PO Box 80958	Bakersfield	CA	93308	**800-284-1334**	661-393-1334	63
Loyd's Electric Supply Inc (LES)						
838 Stonetree Dr	Branson	MO	65616	**800-492-4030**	417-334-2171	246
Loyola College						
4501 N Charles St	Baltimore	MD	21210	**800-221-9107**	410-617-5012	166
Loyola Marymount University						
1 LMU Dr	Los Angeles	CA	90045	**800-568-4636**	310-338-2700	166
Loyola Press						
3441 North Ashland Ave	Chicago	IL	60657	**800-621-1008**	773-281-1818	95
Loyola University						
New Orleans						
6363 St Charles Ave	New Orleans	LA	70118	**800-456-9652***	504-865-3240	166
*Admissions						
Loyola University Chicago						
Lake Shore						
6525 N Sheridan Rd	Chicago	IL	60626	**800-262-2373**	773-508-3075	166
Water Tower						
820 N Michigan Ave	Chicago	IL	60611	**800-262-2373***	312-915-6500	166
*Admissions						
Loyola University Medical Ctr						
2160 S First Ave	Maywood	IL	60153	**888-584-7888**		373-3
Lozier Corp						
6336 John J Pershing Dr	Omaha	NE	68110	**800-228-9882**	402-457-8000	286
Lozier's Box R Ranch						
552 Willow Creek Rd PO Box 100	Cora	WY	82925	**800-822-8466**	307-367-4868	239
LP (Lakeland Plastics Inc)						
1550 McCormick Blvd	Mundelein	IL	60060	**800-454-4006**	847-680-1550	595
LPCH (Lucile Packard Children's Hospital)						
725 Welch Rd	Palo Alto	CA	94304	**800-995-5724**	650-497-8000	373-1
LPL Financial						
75 State St 22nd Fl	Boston	MA	02109	**800-877-7210**		686
LPPD (Loup Public Power District)						
2404 15th St PO Box 988	Columbus	NE	68602	**866-869-2087**	402-564-3171	245
LPS Industries Inc						
10 Caesar Pl	Moonachie	NJ	07074	**800-275-6577***	201-438-3515	544
*Sales						
LQ Management LLC						
909 Hidden Rdg Ste 600	Irving	TX	75038	**800-753-3757**	214-492-6600	378
La Quinta Inn & Suites						
909 Hidden Rdg Ste 600	Irving	TX	75038	**800-753-3757**	214-492-6600	378
LQMT (Liquidmetal Technologies Inc)						
30452 Esperanza	Rancho Santa Margarita	CA	92688	**888-203-1112**	949-635-2100	480
OTC: LQMT						
LR Services						
602 Hayden Cir	Allentown	PA	18109	**888-675-9650**	610-266-2500	13
LRCC (Lakes Region Community College)						
379 Belmont Rd	Laconia	NH	03246	**800-357-2992**	603-524-3207	162
LRECI (Little River Electric Cooperative Inc)						
300 Cambridge St	Abbeville	SC	29620	**800-459-2141**	864-366-2141	245
LRF (Lymphoma Research Foundation)						
115 Broadway Ste 1301	New York	NY	10006	**800-500-9976**	212-349-2910	48-17
LRP Publications						
360 Hiatt Dr	Palm Beach Gardens	FL	33418	**800-621-5463**	561-622-6520	633-2
LRRI (Lovelace Respiratory Research Institute)						
2425 Ridgecrest Dr SE	Albuquerque	NM	87108	**800-700-1016**	505-348-9400	664
LS Starrett Co						
121 Crescent St	Athol	MA	01331	**800-482-8710**	978-249-3551	678
NYSE: SCX						
LSA (Linguistic Society of America)						
1325 18th St NW Ste 211	Washington	DC	20036	**800-726-0479**	202-835-1714	48-11
LSB Industries Inc						
16 S Pennsylvania Ave	Oklahoma City	OK	73107	**800-657-4428**	405-235-4546	143
NYSE: LXU						
LSBA (Louisiana State Bar Assn)						
601 St Charles Ave	New Orleans	LA	70130	**800-421-5722**	504-566-1600	72
LSE Crane & Transportation						
313 Westgate Rd	Lafayette	LA	70506	**877-234-9435**	337-234-9435	189-14
LSI (Lake Shore Industries Inc)						
1817 Poplar St PO Box 3427	Erie	PA	16508	**800-458-0463**		697
LSI (Litigation Solution Inc)						
5995 Greenwood Plz Blvd						
Ste 160	Greenwood Village	CO	80111	**888-767-7088**	303-820-2000	623
LSI Industries Inc						
10000 Alliance Rd	Cincinnati	OH	45242	**800-436-7800**	513-793-3200	438
NASDAQ: LYTS						
LSL CPA's & Advisors						
1611 e Fourth st	Santa Ana	CA	92701	**800-821-5184**	714-569-1000	2
LSNA (Louisiana State Nurses Assn)						
543 Spanish Town Rd	Baton Rouge	LA	70802	**800-457-6378**	225-201-0993	529
LSP Products Group Inc						
3689 Arrowhead Dr	Carson City	NV	89706	**800-854-3215**		604
LSQ Funding Group LC						
2600 Lucien Way Ste 100	Maitland	FL	32751	**800-474-7606**		272
Lti Printing Inc						
518 N Centerville Rd	Sturgis	MI	49091	**800-592-6990**	269-651-7574	623
LTI Trucking Services Inc						
411 N Tenth St Ste 500	St. Louis	MO	63101	**800-642-7222**		314
LTS (Lawrence Companies)						
872 Lee Hwy	Roanoke	VA	24019	**800-336-9626**		775
Lts Lohmann Therapy Systems Corp						
21 Henderson Dr	West Caldwell	NJ	07006	**800-587-1872**	973-396-5345	
LTS Wireless Inc						
311 S LHS Dr	Lumberton	TX	77657	**800-255-5471**	409-755-4038	170
LUA (Lumbermen's Underwriting Alliance)						
1905 NW Corporate Blvd						
Ste 110	Boca Raton	FL	33431	**800-327-0630**	561-994-1900	390-4

				Toll-Free	Phone	Class
Lubbock Avalanche-Journal						
710 Ave J	Lubbock	TX	79401	**800-692-4021**	806-762-8844	528-2
Lubbock Christian University						
5601 19th St	Lubbock	TX	79407	**800-933-7601**	806-720-7151	166
Lubbock Convention & Visitors Bureau						
1500 Broadway St 6th Fl	Lubbock	TX	79401	**800-692-4035**	806-747-5232	206
Lubbock Regional Mental Health Mental Retardation Center						
1602 Tenth St PO Box 2828	Lubbock	TX	79408	**800-687-7581**	806-766-0310	370
Luber Bros Inc						
5224 Bear Creek Ct	Irving	TX	75061	**800-375-8237**	972-313-2020	274
Luberski Inc						
310 N Harbor Blvd Ste 205	Fullerton	CA	92832	**800-326-3220**	714-680-3447	297-4
Lubrication Engineers Inc						
300 Bailey Ave	Fort Worth	TX	76107	**800-537-7683**	817-834-6321	537
Lubrication Technologies Inc						
900 Mendelssohn Ave N	Golden Valley	MN	55427	**800-328-5573**	763-545-0707	537
Lubrizol Corp						
29400 Lakeland Blvd	Wickliffe	OH	44092	**800-380-5397**	440-943-4200	145
NYSE: LZ						
Luby's Inc						
13111 NW Fwy Ste 600	Houston	TX	77040	**800-886-4600**	713-329-6800	666
NYSE: LUB						
Lucas Assoc Inc						
950 E Paces Ferry Rd Ne						
Ste 2300	Atlanta	GA	30326	**800-515-0819**	404-239-5620	717
Lucas Precision LP						
13020 St Clair Ave	Cleveland	OH	44108	**800-336-1262**	216-451-5588	453
Lucas-Milhaupt Inc						
5656 S Pennsylvania Ave	Cudahy	WI	53110	**800-558-3856**	414-769-6000	483
Lucchese Boot Co						
20 ZANE GREY	El Paso	TX	79906	**800-637-6888**	888-582-1883	301
Luce, Schwab & Kase Inc						
9 Gloria Ln	Fairfield	NJ	07007	**800-458-7329**	973-227-4840	661
Lucidview LLC						
80 Rolling Links Blvd	Oak Ridge	TN	37830	**888-582-4384**	865-220-8440	196
Lucile Packard Children's Hospital (LPCH)						
725 Welch Rd	Palo Alto	CA	94304	**800-995-5724**	650-497-8000	373-1
Lucks Co, The						
3003 S Pine St	Tacoma	WA	98409	**800-426-9778**	253-383-4815	296-8
Lucky Eagle Casino						
12888 188th Ave SW	Rochester	WA	98579	**800-720-1788**	360-273-2000	133
Ludlow Composites Corp						
2100 Commerce Dr	Fremont	OH	43420	**800-628-5463**		672
Ludlum Measurements Inc						
501 Oak St	Sweetwater	TX	79556	**800-622-0828**	325-235-5494	470
Ludowici Roof Tile Inc						
4757 Tile Plant Rd						
PO Box 69	New Lexington	OH	43764	**800-945-8453***	740-342-1995	150
*Cust Svc						
Luitpold Pharmaceuticals Inc						
1 Luitpold Dr PO Box 9001	Shirley	NY	11967	**800-645-1706**	631-924-4000	580
Luke Air Force Base						
14185 W Falcon St	Luke AFB	AZ	85309	**855-655-1004**	623-856-5853	495-1
Lumbee River Electric Membership Corp						
PO Box 830	Red Springs	NC	28377	**800-683-5571**	910-843-4131	245
Lumber Liquidators Inc						
1455 VFW Pkwy	West Roxbury	MA	02132	**800-227-0332**	617-327-1222	290
Lumber River State Park						
2819 Princess Ann Rd	Orrum	NC	28369	**800-277-9611**	910-628-4564	561
Lumberjack Building Centers						
3470 Pointe Tremble Rd	Algonac	MI	48001	**800-466-5164**	810-794-4921	707
Lumbermen's Underwriting Alliance (LUA)						
1905 NW Corporate Blvd						
Ste 110	Boca Raton	FL	33431	**800-327-0630**	561-994-1900	390-4
Lumberton Area Visitors Bureau						
3431 Lackey St	Lumberton	NC	28360	**800-359-6971**	910-739-9999	206
Lumberton Honda Mitsubishi Inc						
301 Wintergreen Dr	Lumberton	NC	28358	**855-712-9438**	910-739-9871	513
Lumed Science Inc						
PO Box 102965	Denver	CO	80250	**866-526-7120**		
Lumedx Corp						
555 12th St Ste 2060	Oakland	CA	94607	**800-966-0699**	510-419-1000	178-10
Lumen Legal						
1025 N Campbell Rd	Royal Oak	MI	48067	**877-933-1330**	248-597-0400	717
Lumen, The						
6101 Hillcrest Ave	Dallas	TX	75205	**800-908-1140**	214-219-2400	378
Lumenis Ltd						
2033 Gateway Pl Ste 200	San Jose	CA	95110	**877-586-3647**	408-764-3000	423
Lumens Light & Living						
2028 K St	Sacramento	CA	95811	**877-445-4486**	916-444-5585	810
Lumina Foundation for Education						
30 S Meridian St Ste 700	Indianapolis	IN	46204	**800-834-5756**	317-951-5300	305
Luminator 900 Klein Rd	Plano	TX	75074	**800-388-8205**	972-424-6511	437
Luminex Corp						
12212 Technology Blvd	Austin	TX	78727	**888-219-8020**	512-219-8020	418
NASDAQ: LMNX						
Luminex Software Inc						
871 Marlborough Ave	Riverside	CA	92507	**888-586-4639***	951-781-4100	178-12
*Sales						
Luminite Products Corp						
148 Commerce Dr	Bradford	PA	16701	**888-545-2270**	814-817-1420	776
Lumitex Inc						
8443 Dow Cir	Strongsville	OH	44136	**800-969-5483**	440-600-3745	725
Lummus Corp						
225 Bourne Blvd PO Box 929	Savannah	GA	31408	**800-458-6687**	912-447-9000	739
Lumos & Assoc Inc						
800 E College Pkwy	Carson City	NV	89706	**800-621-7155**	775-883-7077	261
Luna Community College						
366 Luna Dr	Las Vegas	NM	87701	**800-588-7232**	505-454-2500	162
Lund International Holdings Inc						
4325 Hamilton Mill Rd Ste 400	Buford	GA	30518	**800-241-7219**		60
Lundbeck Canada Inc						
2600 Alfred-Nobel Blvd						
Ste 400	Saint Laurent	QC	H4S0A9	**800-586-2325**	514-844-8515	85
Lupus Foundation of America Inc (LFA)						
2000 L St NW Ste 410	Washington	DC	20036	**800-558-0121**	202-349-1155	48-17
Luster Products Inc						
1104 W 43rd St	Chicago	IL	60609	**800-621-4255**	773-579-1800	214

	Toll-Free	Phone	Class
Luth Research Inc			
1365 Fourth Ave .... San Diego CA 92101	800-465-5884	619-234-5884	464
Luther Burbank Savings			
804 Fourth St .... Santa Rosa CA 95404	888-205-6005	707-578-9216	70
Luther College			
700 College Dr .... Decorah IA 52101	800-458-8437	563-387-2000	166
Luther Consulting LLC			
10435 Commerce Dr Ste 140 .... Carmel IN 46032	866-517-6570	317-636-0282	196
Luther Luckett Correctional Complex			
Dawkins Rd PO Box 6 .... LaGrange KY 40031	800-511-1670	502-222-0363	213
Luther Rice College & Seminary			
3038 Evans Mill Rd .... Lithonia GA 30038	800-442-1577		
Luther Seminary			
2481 Como Ave .... Saint Paul MN 55108	800-588-4373	651-641-3456	167-3
Lutheran Church Missouri Synod (LCMS)			
1333 S Kirkwood Rd .... Saint Louis MO 63122	888-843-5267	314-965-9000	48-20
Lutheran Community at Telford			
12 Lutheran Home Dr .... Telford PA 18969	877-343-7518	215-723-9819	668
Lutheran Disaster Response			
8765 W Higgins Rd .... Chicago IL 60631	800-638-3522		48-5
Lutheran Home at Hollidaysburg, The			
916 Hickory St .... Hollidaysburg PA 16648	800-400-2285	814-696-4527	48-20
Lutheran Hospital of Indiana			
7950 W Jefferson Blvd .... Fort Wayne IN 46804	800-444-2001	260-435-7001	373-3
Lutheran Magazine			
8765 W Higgins Rd .... Chicago IL 60631	800-638-3522		455-18
Lutheran Metropolitan Ministry			
The Richard Sering Ctr 4515 Superior Ave			
.... Cleveland OH 44103	800-917-2081	216-696-2715	
Lutheran School of Theology at Chicago			
1100 E 55th St .... Chicago IL 60615	800-635-1116	773-256-0700	167-3
Lutheran Social Services of Illinois			
1001 E Touhy Ave Ste 50 .... Des Plaines IL 60018	888-671-0300	847-635-4600	48-15
Lutron Electronics Company Inc			
7200 Suter Rd .... Coopersburg PA 18036	800-523-9466*	610-282-6280	203
*Tech Supp			
Lutsen Resort			
5700 W Hwy 61 PO Box 9 .... Lutsen MN 55612	800-258-8736	218-663-7212	665
Lutz Frey Corp			
1195 Ivy Dr .... Lancaster PA 17601	800-280-6794	717-898-6808	189-10
Luv N' Care Ltd			
3030 Aurora Ave .... Monroe LA 71201	800-588-6227		258
Luvata Appleton LLC			
553 Carter Ct .... Kimberly WI 54136	800-749-5510	920-749-3820	483
Luvata Ohio Inc			
1376 Pittsburgh Dr .... Delaware OH 43015	800-749-5510	740-363-1981	483
Lux Bond & Green Inc			
46 Lasalle Rd .... West Hartford CT 06107	800-524-7336		409
Lux Scientiae Inc			
PO Box 326 .... Westwood MA 02090	800-441-6612		804
Luxe Hotel Sunset Blvd			
11461 Sunset Blvd .... Los Angeles CA 90049	800-468-3541	310-476-6571	378
Luxe Travel Management Inc			
16450 Bake Pkwy .... Irvine CA 92618	855-665-5900	949-336-1000	
Luxo Corp			
5 Westchester Plz .... Elmsford NY 10523	800-222-5896	914-345-0067	438
Luxor Hotel & Casino			
3900 Las Vegas Blvd S .... Las Vegas NV 89119	800-288-1000*	702-262-4000	133
*Resv			
Luxour			
2245 Delany Rd .... Waukegan IL 60087	800-323-4656	847-244-1800	319-1
Luxury Bath Technologies			
1800 Industrial Dr .... Libertyville IL 60048	800-263-9882		
Luxury Link LLC			
5200 W Century Blvd Ste 410 .... Los Angeles CA 90045	888-297-3299	310-215-8060	767
Luxury Retreats			
5530 St Patrick St Ste 2210 .... Montreal QC H4E1A8	877-993-0100		503
Luzerne County Community College			
1333 S Prospect St .... Nanticoke PA 18634	800-377-5222		162
LV Lomas Ltd			
99 Summerlea Rd .... Brampton ON L6T4V2	800-575-3382	905-458-1555	146
LVHN (Lehigh Valley Hospice)			
3080 Hamilton Blvd Ste 250 .... Allentown PA 18103	888-402-5846		370
LWS (Laminated Wood Systems Inc)			
1327 285th Rd PO Box 386 .... Seward NE 68434	800-949-3526		812
LXE Inc			
125 Technology Pkwy .... Norcross GA 30092	800-664-4593	770-447-4224	173-2
Lycoming College			
700 College Pl .... Williamsport PA 17701	800-345-3920	570-321-4000	166
Lycoming Engines			
652 Oliver St .... Williamsport PA 17701	800-258-3279	570-323-6181	525
Lycon Inc			
1110 Harding St PO Box 427 .... Janesville WI 53545	800-955-8758	608-754-7701	182
LycoRed 377 Crane St .... Orange NJ 07050	877-592-6733		477
Lyden Oil Company Inc			
30692 Tracy Rd .... Walbridge OH 43465	800-362-9410	419-666-1948	575
Lyman Products Corp			
475 Smith St .... Middletown CT 06457	800-225-9626	860-632-2020	284
Lymphoma Research Foundation (LRF)			
115 Broadway Ste 1301 .... New York NY 10006	800-500-9976	212-349-2910	48-17
Lyna Manufacturing Inc			
1125 15th St W .... North Vancouver BC V7P1M7	800-993-4007	604-990-0988	749
Lynch Livestock Co			
331 Third St NW .... Waucoma IA 52171	800-468-3178	563-776-3311	444
Lynch Metals Inc			
1075 Lousons Rd .... Union NJ 07083	888-272-9464	908-686-8401	786
Lynch, Traub, Keefe & Errante A Professional Corp			
52 Trumbull St .... New Haven CT 06510	888-692-7403	203-787-0275	427
Lynchburg College			
1501 Lakeside Dr .... Lynchburg VA 24501	800-426-8101	434-544-8100	166
Lynches River Electric Co-op Inc			
1104 W McGregor St .... Pageland SC 29728	800-922-3486	843-672-6111	245
Lyndacom Inc			
6410 Via Real .... Carpinteria CA 93013	888-335-9632	805-477-3900	194
Lynden Air Cargo LLC			
6441 S Airpark Pl .... Anchorage AK 99502	888-243-7248	907-243-7248	12

	Toll-Free	Phone	Class
Lynden Inc			
18000 International Blvd			
Ste 800 .... Seattle WA 98188	888-596-3361	206-241-8778	311
Lynden Transport Inc			
3027 Rampart Dr .... Anchorage AK 99501	800-327-9390		775
Lynde-Ordway Company Inc			
3308 W Warner Ave .... Santa Ana CA 92704	800-762-7057	714-957-1311	111
Lyndon State College			
1001 College Rd PO Box 919 .... Lyndonville VT 05851	800-225-1998	802-626-6413	166
Lynn Electronics Corp			
154 Railroad Dr .... Ivyland PA 18974	800-624-2220	215-355-8200	253
Lynn Ladder & Scaffolding Company Inc			
20 Boston St .... Lynn MA 01904	800-225-2510	781-598-6010	420
Lynn University			
3601 N Military Trl .... Boca Raton FL 33431	800-888-5966*	561-237-7900	166
*Admissions			
Lynnco Supply Chain Solutions Inc			
2448 E 81st St Ste 2600 .... Tulsa OK 74137	866-872-3264	918-664-5540	314
Lyntegar Electric Co-op Inc			
PO Box 970 .... Tahoka TX 79373	877-218-2308	806-561-4588	245
Lynx Brand Fence Products			
4330 76 Ave SE .... Calgary AB T2C2J2	800-665-5969	403-273-4821	191-1
Lynx Computer Technologies Inc			
7 Bristol Ct .... Wyomissing PA 19610	800-331-5969	610-678-8131	180
Lynx Grills Inc			
5895 Rickenbacker Rd .... Commerce CA 90040	888-289-5969	323-838-1770	361
Lynx Media Inc			
12501 Chandler Blvd			
Ste 202 .... Valley Village CA 91607	800-451-5969	818-761-5859	177
Lynx Software Technologies Inc			
855 Embedded Way .... San Jose CA 95138	800-255-5969	408-979-3900	178-10
Lyon & Healy Harps Inc			
168 N Ogden Ave .... Chicago IL 60607	800-621-3881	312-786-1881	523
Lyon College			
2300 Highland Rd .... Batesville AR 72501	800-423-2542	870-793-9813	166
Lyon Rural Electric Co-op			
116 S Marshall St .... Rock Rapids IA 51246	800-658-3976	712-472-2506	245
Lyon Work Space Products			
420 N Main St .... Montgomery IL 60538	800-433-8488	630-892-8941	286
Lyons Magnus Inc			
3158 E Hamilton Ave .... Fresno CA 93702	800-344-7130		296-20
Lyric Optical Company Whdslse			
3533 Cardiff Ave .... Cincinnati OH 45209	800-543-7376	513-321-2456	540
Lyster Army Health Clinic			
Andrews Ave .... Fort Rucker AL 36362	800-261-7193		373-4
LZ Truck Equipment Inc			
1881 Rice St .... Saint Paul MN 55113	800-247-1082	651-488-2571	513

M

	Toll-Free	Phone	Class
M & A Technology Inc			
2045 Chenault Dr .... Carrollton TX 75006	800-225-1452	972-490-5803	174
M & C Specialties Co			
90 James Way .... SouthHampton PA 18966	800-441-6996*	215-322-1600	727
*Cust Svc			
M & J Transportation			
3536 Nicholson Ave .... Kansas City MO 64120	866-298-3858	816-231-6733	447
M & K CPA's PLLC			
363 N Sam Houston Pkwy E			
Ste 650 .... Houston TX 77060	866-770-5931	832-242-9950	2
M & L Industries Inc			
1210 St Charles St .... Houma LA 70360	800-969-0068*	985-876-2280	384
*General			
M & M Designs Inc			
1981 Quality Blvd .... Huntsville TX 77320	800-627-0656		683
M & M Innovations			
7424 Blythe Island Hwy .... Brunswick GA 31523	800-688-3384	912-265-7110	228
M & W Transportation Company Inc			
1110 Pumping Sta Rd .... Nashville TN 37210	800-251-4209	615-256-5755	392
M B Klein Inc			
243-A Cockeysville Rd .... Cockeysville MD 21030	888-872-4675		
M Block & Sons Inc			
5020 W 73rd St .... Bedford Park IL 60638	800-621-8845	708-728-8400	360
M Conley Co			
1312 Fourth St SE .... Canton OH 44707	800-362-6001	330-456-8243	555
M Holland			
400 Skokie Blvd Ste 600 .... Northbrook IL 60062	800-872-7370		599
M K Products Inc			
16882 Armstrong Ave .... Irvine CA 92606	800-787-9707	949-863-1234	806
M K Specialty Metal Fabricators			
725 W Wintergreen Rd .... Hutchins TX 75141	866-814-4617	972-225-6562	693
M Lee Smith Publishers LLC			
PO Box 5094 .... Brentwood TN 37024	800-274-6774	615-373-7517	623
M R L Equipment Company Inc			
PO Box 31154 .... Billings MT 59107	877-788-2907	406-869-9900	357
M Steinert & Sons Co			
1 Columbus Ave .... Boston MA 02116	877-343-0662	617-426-1900	522
M/A/R/C Research			
1660 Westridge Cir .... Irving TX 75038	800-884-6272	972-983-0400	464
M/A-COM Technology Solutions Inc			
100 Chelmsford St .... Lowell MA 01851	800-366-2266	978-656-2500	692
M2 Logistics Inc			
2701 Executive Dr .... Green Bay WI 54304	800-391-5121	920-569-8800	461
M2 Technology Inc			
21702 Hardy Oak Ste 100 .... San Antonio TX 78258	800-267-1760	210-566-3773	178-1
m2M Strategies LLC			
33 Buford Village Way Ste 329 .... Buford GA 30518	800-345-1070	678-835-9080	464
MA Gedney Co			
2100 Stoughton Ave .... Chaska MN 55318	888-244-0653	952-448-2612	296-19
MAA (MAAC)			
6584 Poplar Ave .... Memphis TN 38138	866-620-1130		651
NYSE: MAA			

	Toll-Free	Phone	Class
MAA (Mathematical Assn of America)			
1529 18th St NW .... Washington DC 20036	800-331-1622	202-387-5200	49-19
MAA FOCUS			
1529 18th St NW .... Washington DC 20036	800-741-9415	202-387-5200	455-8
MAAC (MAA)			
6584 Poplar Ave .... Memphis TN 38138	866-620-1130		651
NYSE: MAA			
Maaco LLC			
440 S Church St Ste 700 .... Charlotte NC 28202	800-523-1180		62-4
Maas-Rowe Carillons Inc			
2255 Meyers Ave .... Escondido CA 92029	800-854-2023		523
Maax Corp			
160 St Joseph Blvd .... Lachine QC H8S2L3	888-957-7816	877-438-6229	606
Mac Haik Auto Group			
11711 Katy Fwy .... Houston TX 77079	866-721-8619		57
Mac Papers			
3300 Phillips Hwy			
PO Box 5369. .... Jacksonville FL 32207	800-622-2968	904-348-3300	549
Mac Tools Inc			
505 N Cleveland Ave .... Westerville OH 43082	800-622-8665	614-755-7000	753
Mac Trailer Mfg Inc			
14599 Commerce St NE .... Alliance OH 44601	800-795-8454	330-823-9900	774
Mac Valves Inc			
30569 Beck Rd .... Wixom MI 48393	800-622-8587	248-624-7700	784
Mac's Convenience Stores Inc			
305 Milner Ave Ste 400 4th Fl ...... Toronto ON M1B3V4	800-268-5574	416-291-4441	204
Macadamian Technologies Inc			
165 Rue Wellington .... Gatineau QC J8X2J3	877-779-6336	819-772-0300	461
Macalester College			
1600 Grand Ave .... Saint Paul MN 55105	800-231-7974*	651-696-6357	166
*Admissions			
MacAllister Machinery Company Inc			
7515 E 30th St .... Indianapolis IN 46219	800-382-1896	317-545-2151	357
MacArthur Co			
2400 Wycliff St .... Saint Paul MN 55114	800-777-7507	651-646-2773	191-4
MacArthur Place			
29 E MacArthur St .... Sonoma CA 95476	800-722-1866	707-938-2929	378
Macatawa Bank Corp			
10753 Macatawa Dr PO Box 3119 .... Holland MI 49424	877-820-2265	616-820-1444	359-2
NASDAQ: MCBC			
Macaulay-Brown Inc			
4021 Executive Dr .... Dayton OH 45430	800-432-3421	937-426-3421	261
MacCormac College			
29 E Madison St .... Chicago IL 60602	800-621-7740	312-922-1884	795
Macdonald Realty			
203 5188 Wminster Hwy .... Richmond BC V7C5S7	877-278-3888	604-279-9822	648
MacDonald-Miller Facility Solutions Inc			
7717 Detroit Ave SE .... Seattle WA 98106	800-962-5979	206-763-9400	189-10
Macera & Jarzyna LLP			
1200-427 Laurier Ave W .... Ottawa ON K1R7Y2	800-379-6668	613-238-8173	427
MacEwan College			
10700 104 Ave NW .... Edmonton AB T5J4S2	888-497-4622		162
MacEwen Petroleum Inc			
18 Adelaide St PO Box 100........... Maxville ON K0C1T0	800-267-7175		575
Mac-Gray Corp			
404 Wyman St Ste 400 .... Waltham MA 02451	888-622-4729	781-487-7600	384
NYSE: TUC			
Machaon Diagnostics Inc			
3023 Summit St .... Oakland CA 94609	800-566-3462	510-839-5600	417
Machias Savings Bank			
4 Ctr St PO Box 318............. Machias ME 04654	800-982-7179	207-255-3347	70
Machine Maintenance Inc			
2300 Cassens Dr .... Fenton MO 63026	800-325-3322	636-343-9970	190
Machine Specialty & Manufacturing Inc			
215 Rousseau Rd .... Youngsville LA 70592	800-256-1292	337-837-0020	481
Machinery & Equipment Company Inc			
3401 Bayshore Blvd .... Brisbane CA 94005	800-227-4544	415-467-3400	357
Machinery Dealers National Assn (MDNA)			
315 S Patrick St .... Alexandria VA 22314	800-872-7807	703-836-9300	49-18
Machinery Sales Co			
17253 Chestnut St .... City of Industry CA 91748	800-588-8111	626-581-9211	384
Machinery Sales Company Inc			
120 Webster Ave .... Memphis TN 38126	800-932-8376		816
Mackay Communications Inc			
3691 Trust Dr .... Raleigh NC 27616	888-798-7979	281-478-6245	525
Mackay Envelope Co			
2100 Elm St SE .... Minneapolis MN 55414	800-622-5299		263
Mack-Cali Realty Corp			
343 Thornall St .... Edison NJ 08837	800-317-4445	732-590-1000	651
NYSE: CLI			
Mackenzie Financial Corp			
180 Queen St W .... Toronto ON M5V3K1	888-653-7070	416-922-5322	400
Mackenzie House Museum			
82 Bond St .... Toronto ON M5B1X2	800-668-2437	416-392-6915	517
MacKenzie-Childs LLC			
3260 SR-90 .... Aurora NY 13026	888-665-1999	315-364-7123	321
Mackie Group			
933 Bloor St W .... Oshawa ON L1J5Y7	800-565-4646	905-728-2400	314
Mackinaw Area Visitors Bureau			
10800 US 23 .... Mackinaw City MI 49701	800-666-0160	231-436-5664	206
MacKissic Inc			
PO Box 111 .... Parker Ford PA 19457	800-348-1117	610-495-7181	428
Maclean Assoc LLC			
1700 Boston Post Rd .... Guilford CT 06437	877-819-6922*	866-924-4854	57
*Sales			
Maclean's			
1 Mount Pleasant Rd 11th Fl ...... Toronto ON M4Y2Y5	800-268-9119	416-764-1300	455-17
MacLean-Fogg Co			
1000 Allanson Rd .... Mundelein IL 60060	800-323-4536	847-566-0010	60
MacMurray College			
447 E College Ave .... Jacksonville IL 62650	800-252-7485	217-479-7056	166
MacNeal Hospital			
3249 S Oak Park Ave .... Berwyn IL 60402	888-622-6325	708-783-9100	373-3
MacNeill Engineering Company Inc			
140 Locke Dr .... Marlborough MA 01752	800-652-4267	508-481-8830	706
Macnica Americas Inc			
380 Stevens Ave Ste 206 .... Solana Beach CA 92075	888-399-4937	858-771-0846	246
Macomb Community College			
Center			
44575 Garfield Rd .... Clinton Township MI 48038	866-622-6621	586-445-7999	162
South			
14500 E 12-Mile Rd .... Warren MI 48088	866-622-6621	586-445-7000	162
Macomb County Chamber			
28 First St Ste B .... Mount Clemens MI 48043	800-564-3136	586-493-7600	139
Macon County			
410 N Missouri St Ste D........... Macon MO 63552	800-981-9409	660-676-0578	337
Macon Electric Co-op			
31571 Bus Hwy 36 E PO Box 157........ Macon MO 63552	800-553-6901	660-385-3157	245
Macon State College			
100 University Pkwy .... Macon GA 31206	800-272-7619	478-471-2700	166
MacPractice Inc			
233 N Eighth St Ste 300 .... Lincoln NE 68508	877-220-8418	402-420-2430	174
Macworld Magazine			
501 Second St Ste 600 ...... San Francisco CA 94107	800-288-6848*	415-243-0505	455-7
*Cust Svc			
Macy's Inc			
7 W Seventh St .... Cincinnati OH 45202	800-261-5385	513-579-7000	229
NYSE: M			
Mad Dogg Athletics Inc			
2111 Narcissus Ct .... Venice CA 90291	800-847-7746	310-823-7008	707
Mad Science Group			
8360 Bougainville St Ste 201 .... Montreal QC H4P2G1	800-586-5231	514-344-4181	310
Mada Medical Products Inc			
625 Washington Ave .... Carlstadt NJ 07072	800-526-6370	201-460-0454	473
Madame Tussauds New York Inc			
234 W 42nd St Times Sq .... New York NY 10036	800-434-7894	212-512-9600	517
Madan Plastics Inc			
108 North Union Ave Ste 3 .... Cranford NJ 07016	888-676-5926	908-276-8484	
MADD (Mothers Against Drunk Driving)			
511 E John Carpenter Fwy Ste 700.......... Irving TX 75062	877-275-6233		48-6
Madden Manufacturing Inc			
PO Box 387 .... Elkhart IN 46515	800-369-6233	574-295-4292	637
Madden's on Gull Lake			
11266 Pine Beach Peninsula .... Brainerd MN 56401	800-642-5363	800-233-2934	665
Madelaine Chocolate Novelties Inc			
9603 Beach Ch Dr .... Rockaway Beach NY 11693	800-322-1505	718-945-1500	296-8
Madera Chamber of Commerce			
120 NE St .... Madera CA 93638	800-872-7245	559-673-3563	
Madera County			
200 W Fourth St .... Madera CA 93637	800-427-6897	559-675-7703	337
MadgeTech Inc			
6 Warner Rd .... Warner NH 03278	877-671-2885	603-456-2011	256
Madico Inc			
64 Industrial Pkwy .... Woburn MA 01801	800-456-4331	781-935-7850	595
Madison			
1901 Fish Hatchery Rd			
PO Box 8056. .... Madison WI 53713	800-362-8333*	608-252-6200	633-8
*Sales			
Madison Area Chamber of Commerce			
301 E Main St .... Madison IN 47250	800-559-2956	812-265-3135	139
Madison Area Technical College			
1701 Wright St .... Madison WI 53704	800-322-6282	608-246-6100	795
Madison Cable Corp			
125 Goddard Memorial Dr .... Worcester MA 01603	877-623-4766	508-752-2884	809
Madison Concourse Hotel & Governors Club			
1 W Dayton St .... Madison WI 53703	800-356-8293	608-257-6000	378
Madison County			
146 W Ctr St .... Canton MS 39046	800-428-0584	601-859-1177	337
Madison County			
182 NW College Loop PO Box 817...... Madison FL 32341	877-272-3642	850-973-2788	337
Madison County			
73 Jefferson St .... Winterset IA 50273	800-298-6119	515-462-1185	337
Madison Gas & Electric Co			
133 S Blair St .... Madison WI 53703	800-245-1125	608-252-7000	782
Madison Hotel, The			
1 Convent Rd .... Morristown NJ 07960	800-526-0729	973-285-1800	378
Madison Investment Advisors Inc			
550 Science Dr .... Madison WI 53711	800-767-0300	608-274-0300	400
Madison National Life Insurance Company Inc			
PO Box 5008 .... Madison WI 53705	800-356-9601	608-830-2000	390-2
Madison Wood Preservers Inc			
216 Oak Park Rd .... Madison VA 22727	844-623-9663		813
Madison-Kipp Corp			
201 Waubesa St .... Madison WI 53704	800-356-6148		308
Madisonville Community College			
2000 College Dr .... Madisonville KY 42431	866-227-4812	270-821-2250	162
Madonna Rehabilitation Hospital			
5401 S St .... Lincoln NE 68506	800-676-5448	402-489-7102	373-6
Madonna University			
36600 Schoolcraft Rd .... Livonia MI 48150	800-852-4951	734-432-5339	166
Madwire			
3420 E Harmony Rd Bldg 5			
3rd Fl .... Fort Collins CO 80528	888-872-3734*	855-773-8171	7
*Sales			
MAF (Mission Aviation Fellowship)			
112 N Pilatus Ln .... Nampa ID 83687	800-359-7623	208-498-0800	48-20
Mafcote Industries Inc			
108 Main St .... Norwalk CT 06851	800-526-4280*	203-847-8500	550
*Cust Svc			
MAG (Medical Assn of Georgia)			
1849 The Exchange Ste 200 .... Atlanta GA 30339	800-282-0224	678-303-9290	472
Mag Instrument Inc			
2001 S Hillman Ave .... Ontario CA 91761	800-289-6241	909-947-1006	438
Magellan Health Services Inc			
55 Nod Rd .... Avon CT 06001	800-424-4399	860-237-4161	460
NASDAQ: MGLN			
Magellan Midstream Partners LP			
1 Williams Ctr .... Tulsa OK 74172	800-574-6671	918-574-7000	593
NYSE: MMP			
Maggie Valley Resort & Country Club			
1819 Country Club Dr ...... Maggie Valley NC 28751	800-438-3861		665
Magic Plastics Inc			
25215 Ave Stanford .... Valencia CA 91355	800-369-0303	661-257-4485	604
Magic Valley Electric Co-op Inc			
1 3/4 Mile W Hwy 83 .... Mercedes TX 78570	866-225-5683		245

Name / Address	City	State	ZIP	Toll-Free	Phone	Class
Magic Valley Newspapers						
132 Fairfield St W	Twin Falls	ID	83301	**800-658-3883**	208-733-0931	633-8
Magid Glove & Safety Manufacturing Co						
2060 N Kolmar Ave	Chicago	IL	60639	**800-444-8010**	773-384-2070	155-7
Magline Inc						
1205 W Cedar St	Standish	MI	48658	**800-624-5463**		468
Magna Chek Inc						
32701 Edward Ave	Madison Heights	MI	48071	**800-582-8947**	248-597-0089	738
Magna Design Inc						
12020 NE 26th PL	Bellevue	WA	98005	**800-426-1202**	206-852-5282	319-1
Magna IV						
2401 Commercial Ln	Little Rock	AR	72206	**800-946-2462**	501-376-2397	623
Magna Visual Inc						
9400 Watson Rd	Sappington	MO	63126	**800-843-3399**		530
Magnaserv Enterprises Inc						
2862 SE Monroe St	Stuart	FL	34997	**866-283-4288**		
Magnatech International Inc						
17 E Meadow Ave	Robesonia	PA	19551	**800-523-8193**	610-693-8866	111
Magnatex Pumps Inc						
3575 W 12th St	Houston	TX	77008	**866-624-7867**	713-972-8666	
Magnetech Industrial Services Inc						
800 Nave Rd SE	Massillon	OH	44646	**800-837-1614***	330-830-3500	483
*General						
MagneTek Inc						
N49 W13650 Campbell Dr	Menomonee Falls	WI	53051	**800-288-8178**		253
NASDAQ: MAG						
Magnetic Analysis Corp						
103 Fairview Park Dr	Elmsford	NY	10523	**800-463-8622**	914-530-2000	470
Magnetic Component Engineering Inc						
2830 Lomita Blvd	Torrance	CA	90505	**800-989-5656**	310-784-3100	456
Magnetic Metals Corp						
1900 Hayes Ave	Camden	NJ	08105	**800-257-8174**	856-964-7842	479
Magnetic Products Inc						
683 Town Center Dr	Highland	MI	48357	**800-544-5930**		563
Magnetic Springs Water Co						
1917 Joyce Ave	Columbus	OH	43219	**800-572-2990**	614-421-1780	297-8
Magnetrol International Inc						
5300 Belmont Rd	Downers Grove	IL	60515	**800-624-8765**	630-969-4000	201
Magnets Usa						
817 Connecticut Ave NE	Roanoke	VA	24012	**800-869-7562**		195
Magnetsoom						
51 Pacific Ave Ste 4	Jersey City	NJ	07304	**866-229-8237**		365
Mag-Nif Inc 8820 E Ave	Mentor	OH	44060	**800-869-5463**		757
Magnifying Ctr						
10086 W McNab Rd	Tamarac	FL	33321	**800-364-1612**	954-722-1580	539
Magnolia Brush Mfg Ltd						
1000 N Cedar st PO Box 932	Clarksville	TX	75426	**800-248-2261**	903-427-2261	103
Magnolia Financial Inc						
187 W Broad St	Spartanburg	SC	29306	**866-573-0611**	864-699-8178	272
Magnolia Forest Products Inc						
13252 I- 55 S PO Box 99	Terry	MS	39170	**800-366-6374**		191-3
Magnolia Hotel & Spa, The						
623 Courtney St	Victoria	BC	V8W1B8	**877-624-6654**	250-381-0999	378
Magnolia Hotel Dallas						
1401 Commerce St	Dallas	TX	75201	**888-915-1110**	214-915-6500	378
Magnolia Hotel Denver						
818 17th St	Denver	CO	80202	**888-915-1110**	303-607-9000	378
Magnolia Hotel Houston						
1100 Texas Ave	Houston	TX	77002	**888-915-1110**	713-221-0011	378
Magnolia Metal Corp						
10675 Bedford Ave Ste 200	Omaha	NE	68134	**800-228-4043**	402-455-8760	308
Magnolia Plantation & Gardens						
3550 Ashley River Rd	Charleston	SC	29414	**800-367-3517**	843-571-1266	97
Magnotta Winery Corp						
271 Chrislea Rd	Vaughan	ON	L4L8N6	**800-461-9463**	905-738-9463	80-3
Magnum Integrated Technologies Inc						
200 First Gulf Blvd	Brampton	ON	L6W4T5	**800-830-0642**	905-595-1998	670
Magnum Magnetics Corp						
801 Masonic Pk Rd	Marietta	OH	45750	**800-258-0991**	740-373-7770	456
Magnum Research Inc						
12602 33rd Ave SW	Pillager	MN	56473	**800-772-6168**	218-746-4597	707
Magnus Equipment						
4500 Beidler Rd	Willoughby	OH	44094	**800-456-6423**	440-942-8488	357
Magnus Mobility Systems Inc						
2805 Barranca Pkwy	Irvine	CA	92606	**800-858-7801**	714-771-2630	349
Magnuson Hotels						
525 E Mission Ave	Spokane	WA	99202	**866-904-1309**		
Magnussen Home Furnishings Ltd						
66 Hincks St	New Hamburg	ON	N3A2A3	**877-552-5670**		
Magtech Industries Corp						
5625 Arville St Ste A	Las Vegas	NV	89118	**888-954-4481**	702-364-9998	253
Magtrol Inc						
70 Gardenville Pkwy	Buffalo	NY	14224	**800-828-7844**	716-668-5555	616
MaguireZay						
17194 Preston Rd Ste 102-143	Dallas	TX	75248	**888-400-6929**	214-692-5002	
Mahaffey's Quality Printing Inc						
355 W Pearl St	Jackson	MS	39203	**800-843-1135**	601-353-9663	
Mahar Tool Supply Co Inc						
112 Williams St PO Box 1747	Saginaw	MI	48602	**800-456-2427**	989-799-5530	384
Maharishi University of Management						
1000 N Fourth St	Fairfield	IA	52557	**800-369-6480**	641-472-1110	166
Maher, Guiley & Maher PA						
271 West Canton Ave Ste 1						
PO Box 2209	Winter Park	FL	32789	**855-338-0720**		
MAHLE Industries Inc						
2020 Sanford St	Muskegon	MI	49444	**888-255-1942**	231-722-1300	128
Mahoning County						
120 Market St	Youngstown	OH	44503	**800-548-7175**	330-740-2104	337
Mahoning County Convention & Visitors Bureau						
21 W Boardman St	Youngstown	OH	44503	**800-447-8201**	330-740-2130	206
Mahuta Tool Corp						
N118W19137 Bunsen Dr	Germantown	WI	53022	**888-686-4940**	262-502-4100	752
MAI (Medical Action Industries Inc)						
500 Expy Dr S	Brentwood	NY	11717	**800-645-7042**	631-231-4600	475
Maibec Inc						
202 1984 Fifth St	Levis	QC	G6W5M6	**800-363-1930**	418-659-3323	679
Maid Brigade USA/Minimaid Canada						
4 Concourse Pkwy Ste 200	Atlanta	GA	30328	**866-800-7470**	800-722-6243	152

Name / Address	City	State	ZIP	Toll-Free	Phone	Class
Maid-Rite Steak Company Inc						
105 Keystone Industrial Pk	Dunmore	PA	18512	**800-233-4259**	570-343-4748	296-26
Maids International						
9394 W Dodge Rd Ste 140	Omaha	NE	68114	**800-843-6243**	402-558-8600	152
Mail Shark						
4125 New Holland Rd	Mohnton	PA	19540	**888-457-4275**	610-621-2994	365
Mailender Inc						
9500 Glades Dr	Hamilton	OH	45011	**800-998-5453**	513-942-5453	686
Mailing Services of Pittsburgh Inc						
155 Commerce Dr	Freedom	PA	15042	**800-876-3211**	724-774-3244	5
Mailing Systems Inc (MSI)						
2431 Mercantile Dr Ste A	Rancho Cordova	CA	95742	**877-577-2647**	916-631-7400	5
Mailings Unlimited						
116 Riverside Industrial Pkwy	Portland	ME	04103	**800-773-7417**	207-347-5000	5
Mailman Research Ctr						
McLean Hospital						
115 Mill St	Belmont	MA	02478	**800-333-0338**	617-855-2000	664
Main Source Bank						
201 N Broadway	Greensburg	IN	47240	**800-713-6083**		70
Main Street America Group, The						
4601 Touchton Rd E						
Ste 3400	Jacksonville	FL	32246	**800-258-5310**	877-425-2467	390-4
Main Street Capital Corp						
1300 Post Oak Blvd	Houston	TX	77056	**800-966-1559**	713-350-6000	404
NYSE: MAIN						
Main Street Gourmet Inc						
170 Muffin Ln	Cuyahoga Falls	OH	44223	**800-678-6246**	330-929-0000	296-2
Main Street Radiology						
136-25 37th Ave	Flushing	NY	11354	**888-930-4674**	718-428-1500	414
Main Street Station Hotel & Casino						
200 N Main St	Las Vegas	NV	89101	**800-713-8933**	702-387-1896	378
Main-Care Energy						
1 Booth Ln PO Box 11029	Albany	NY	12211	**800-542-5552**		575
Maine						
Bureau of Financial Institutions						
36 State House Sta	Augusta	ME	04333	**800-965-5235**	207-624-8570	338-20
Consumer Protection Unit						
85 Leighton Rd	Augusta	ME	04333	**800-436-2131**	207-287-2923	338-20
Elder Services Office						
41 Anthony Ave	Augusta	ME	04333	**888-568-1112**	207-287-9200	338-20
Employment Services Bureau						
55 State House Stn	Augusta	ME	04330	**888-457-8883**	207-623-7981	259
Environmental Protection Dept						
17 State House Stn	Augusta	ME	04333	**800-452-1942**	207-287-7688	338-20
Finance Authority of Maine						
5 Community Dr PO Box 949	Augusta	ME	04332	**800-228-3734**	207-623-3263	721
Governor						
1 State House Stn	Augusta	ME	04333	**855-721-5203**	207-287-3531	338-20
Housing Authority						
353 Water St	Augusta	ME	04330	**800-452-4668**	207-626-4600	338-20
Insurance Bureau						
34 State House Stn	Augusta	ME	04333	**800-300-5000**	207-624-8475	338-20
Public Utilities Commission						
18 State House Stn	Augusta	ME	04333	**800-437-1220**	207-287-3831	
Rehabilitation Services Bureau						
150 State House Sta	Augusta	ME	04333	**800-698-4440**		338-20
Securities Div						
76 Northern Ave	Gardiner	ME	04345	**877-624-8551**	207-624-8551	338-20
State Government Information						
26 Edison Dr	Augusta	ME	04330	**888-577-6690**	207-624-9494	338-20
Tourism Office						
59 State House Sta	Augusta	ME	04333	**888-624-6345**	207-624-7483	338-20
Vital Records Office						
220 Capitol St	Augusta	ME	04333	**888-664-9491**	207-287-3181	338-20
Workers' Compensation Board						
442 Civic Ctr Dr 27 State House Stn						
Ste 100	Augusta	ME	04333	**888-801-9087**	207-287-3751	338-20
Maine Biotechnology Services Inc						
1037 R Forest Ave	Portland	ME	04103	**800-925-9476**	207-797-5454	231
Maine Bucket Co						
21 Fireslate Pl	Lewiston	ME	04240	**800-231-7072**	207-784-6700	200
Maine College of Art						
522 Congress St	Portland	ME	04101	**800-639-4808**	207-775-3052	164
Maine Educator Magazine						
35 Community Dr	Augusta	ME	04330	**800-332-8529**	207-622-5866	455-8
Maine Folklife Ctr						
5773 S Stevens Rm 112B	Orono	ME	04469	**800-753-9044**	207-581-1840	50-2
Maine Instrument Flight Inc						
215 Winthrop St	Augusta	ME	04330	**888-643-3597**	207-622-1211	63
Maine Lobster Direct						
48 Union Wharf	Portland	ME	04101	**800-556-2783**		297-5
Maine Maritime Academy						
66 Pleasant St	Castine	ME	04420	**800-464-6565***	207-326-4311	166
*Admissions						
Maine Medical Ctr (MMC)						
22 Bramhall St	Portland	ME	04102	**877-339-3107**	207-662-0111	373-3
Maine Oxy						
22 Albiston Way	Auburn	ME	04210	**800-639-1108**	207-784-5788	806
Maine Plastics Inc						
1817 Kenosha Rd	Zion	IL	60099	**800-338-7728**	847-379-9100	599
Maine Potato Growers Inc						
261 Main St	Presque Isle	ME	04769	**800-649-3358**	207-764-3131	274
Maine State Bar Assn						
124 State St	Augusta	ME	04330	**800-475-7523**	207-622-7523	72
Maine State Chamber of Commerce						
125 Community Dr Ste 101	Augusta	ME	04330	**800-546-7866**	207-623-4568	140
Maine State Library						
64 State House Stn	Augusta	ME	04333	**800-427-8336**	207-287-5600	433-5
Maine Veterans' Homes						
310 Cony Rd	Augusta	ME	04330	**800-278-9494**	207-622-2454	788
Maine Veterans' Homes						
460 Civic Center Dr	Augusta	ME	04330	**800-278-9494**		
Maine Veterinary Medical Assn (MVMA)						
97A Exchange St Ste 305	Portland	ME	04101	**800-448-2772**		790
Maine Windjammer Cruises						
PO Box 617	Camden	ME	04843	**800-736-7981**	207-236-2938	220
Maine Wood Concepts Inc						
1687 New Vineyard Rd	New Vineyard	ME	04956	**800-374-6961**	877-728-4442	815

	Toll-Free	Phone	Class
MaineGeneral Medical Center (MGMC) *Augusta* 361 Old Belgrade Rd .... Augusta ME 04330	855-464-4463	207-621-6100	373-3
Mainegov *Fort O'Brien State Historic Site* c/o Cobscook Bay State Park 40 S Edmunds Rd .... Edmunds Township ME 04628	800-332-1501	207-726-4412	561
Maines Paper & Food Service Co 101 Broome Corporate Pkwy .... Conklin NY 13748	800-366-3669	607-779-1200	297-8
Mains'l Services Inc 7000 78th Ave N .... Brooklyn Park MN 55445	800-441-6525		362
Maintenx 2202 N Howard Ave .... Tampa FL 33607	855-751-0075		606
MAINTSTAR 28 Hammond Unit D.................... Irvine CA 92618	800-255-5675	949-458-7560	261
Mairs & Power Inc 332 Minnesota St W Ste 1520 First National Bank Bldg ..... Saint Paul MN 55101	800-304-7404	651-222-8478	524
Maison Dupuy Hotel 1001 Rue Toulouse .... New Orleans LA 70112	800-535-9177	504-586-8000	
Maison Dupuy Hotel 1001 Toulouse St................ New Orleans LA 70112	800-535-9177	504-586-8000	378
Majestic Drug Company Inc 4996 Main St Rt 42 ....South Fallsburg NY 12779	800-238-0220	845-436-0011	237
Majestic Hotel, The 528 W Brompton ....Chicago IL 60657	800-727-5108	773-404-3499	
Majestic Star Casino & Hotel 1 Buffington Harbor Dr ....Gary IN 46406	888-225-8259		133
Majestic Steel USA 5300 Majestic Pkwy ....Cleveland OH 44146	800-321-5590	440-786-2666	490
Majic 1057 6200 Oak Tree Blvd 4th Fl.............Cleveland OH 44131	800-669-1057	216-520-2600	641
Major Custom Cable Inc 281 Lotus Dr ....Jackson MO 63755	800-455-6224		808
Major Industries Inc 7120 Stewart Ave .... Wausau WI 54401	888-759-2678		693
Major League Baseball Ballpark 333 Camden St ....Baltimore MD 21201	888-848-2473	410-547-6100	716
Major Pharmaceutical Co 31778 Enterprise Dr...................Livonia MI 48150	800-875-0123	800-616-2471	578
Maka Beauty Systems 4042 W Kitty Hawk .... Chandler AZ 85226	800-293-6252	480-968-7980	77
Make-A-Wish Foundation of America 4742 N 24th St Ste 400 ....Phoenix AZ 85016	800-722-9474	602-279-9474	48-5
MakeMusic! Inc 7615 Golden Triangle Dr Ste M ....Eden Prairie MN 55344 *NASDAQ: MMUS*	800-843-2066	952-937-9611	178-6
Makino 7680 Innovation Way .... Mason OH 45040	888-625-4661	513-573-7200	453
Makita USA Inc 14930 Northam St .... La Mirada CA 90638	800-462-5482	714-522-8088	754
Makowski's Real Sausage 2710 S Poplar Ave ....Chicago IL 60608	800-746-9554	312-842-5330	296-26
Malaco Music Group Inc 3023 W Northside Dr ....Jackson MS 39213 *Cust Svc	800-272-7936*	601-982-4522	653
Malaga Inn 359 Church St ....Mobile AL 36602	800-235-1586	251-438-4701	378
Malarkey Roofing Products PO Box 17217 ....Portland OR 97217	800-545-1191	503-283-1191	46
Malaysia Airlines 100 N Sepulveda Blvd Ste 1710......................... El Segundo CA 90245 *Resv	800-552-9264*	310-535-9288	25
Malco Products Inc 14080 State Hwy 55 NW PO Box 400....................... Annandale MN 55302	800-328-3530	320-274-8246	753
Malco Products Inc 361 Fairview Ave PO Box 892...........Barberton OH 44203	800-253-2526	330-753-0361	151
Malcolm Wiener Ctr for Social Policy John F Kennedy School of Government Harvard Univer 79 John F Kennedy St...............Cambridge MA 02138	866-845-6596	617-384-9887	630
Malcolm X College 1900 W Jackson ....Chicago IL 60612	877-542-0285	312-850-7000	162
Malcom Randall VAMC NF/SGVHS 1601 SW Archer Rd ....Gainesville FL 32608	800-324-8387	352-376-1611	373-8
Male Survivor 4768 BRdway Ste 527................New York NY 10034	800-738-4181		48-17
Malema Engineering Corp 1060 S Rogers Cir .... Boca Raton FL 33487	800-637-6418	561-995-0595	201
Malibu Beach Inn 22878 Pacific Coast Hwy ....Malibu CA 90265	800-462-5428		
Malibu Chamber of Commerce 23805 Stuart Ranch Rd Ste 210 ....Malibu CA 90265	800-442-4988	310-456-9025	139
Mallet & Company Inc 51 Arch St Ext .... Carnegie PA 15106	800-245-2757	412-276-9000	296-23
Malleys Chocolates 13400 Brookpark Rd ....Cleveland OH 44135	800-275-6255	216-362-8700	296-8
Mallick Plumbing & Heating 8010 Cessna Ave .... Gaithersburg MD 20879	888-805-3354		606
Mallilo & Grossman 16309 Northern Blvd .... Flushing NY 11358	866-593-6274	718-461-6633	427
Mallin Casual Furniture 1 Minson Way .... Montebello CA 90640	800-251-6537		319-4
Malnati Organization Inc 3685 Woodhead Dr .... Northbrook IL 60062	800-568-8646	847-562-1814	666
Malnove Inc 13434 F St ....Omaha NE 68137	800-228-9877	402-330-1100	101
Malone College 2600 Cleveland Ave NW ....Canton OH 44709	800-521-1146		166
Maloney Technical Products 1300 E Berry St ....Fort Worth TX 76119	800-231-7236	817-923-3344	592
Malt Products Corp 88 Market St ....Saddle Brook NJ 07663	800-526-0180	201-845-4420	102
Maltby Electric Supply Company Inc 336 Seventh St .... San Francisco CA 94103	800-339-0668	415-863-5000	246
Maltz Jupiter Theatre 1001 E Indiantown Rd ....Jupiter FL 33477	800-445-1666	561-743-2666	744
Maltz Sales Company Inc 67 Green St ....Foxboro MA 02035	800-370-0439	508-203-2400	357
Malvern Systems Inc 81 Lancaster Ave Ste 219.............Malvern PA 19355	800-296-9642		178-1
MAMAC Systems Inc 8189 Century Blvd ....Minneapolis MN 55317	800-843-5116	952-556-4900	201
Mammoth Mountain Resort 10001 Minaret Rd PO Box 24.................... Mammoth Lakes CA 93546	800-626-6684	760-934-2571	665
Mammoth Times, The PO Box 3929 .... Mammoth Lakes CA 93546	800-427-7623	760-934-3929	528-4
Managed Care of America Inc 1910 Cochran Rd Ste 605............ Pittsburgh PA 15220	800-922-4966	412-922-2803	389
Managed Health Network Inc 1600 Los Gamos Dr Ste 300.......... San Rafael CA 94903	800-327-2133		460
Managed HealthCare Northwest Inc 422 E Burnside St Ste 215 PO Box 4629........................Portland OR 97208	800-648-6356	503-413-5800	389
Management Information Control Systems Inc (MICS) 2025 Ninth St ....Los Osos CA 93402	800-838-6427		178-10
Management International Inc 1828 SE First Ave .... Fort Lauderdale FL 33316	800-425-1995	954-763-8003	184
Management Network Group Inc (TMNG) 7300 College Blvd Ste 302......... Overland Park KS 66210 *NASDAQ: CRTN*	800-690-6903	913-345-9315	196
Management Recruiters International Inc 1735 Market St Ste 200 ....Philadelphia PA 19103	800-875-4000		266
Manager's Intelligence Report (MIR) 316 N Michigan Ave Ste 400 ....Chicago IL 60601	800-878-5331		527-2
Managing Editor Inc 610 York Rd # 250 .... Jenkintown PA 19046	800-638-1214	215-886-5662	178-10
Manarin Investment Counsel Ltd 505 N 210th St ....Omaha NE 68022	800-397-1167	402-676-8717	400
Manatron Inc 510 E Milham Ave .... Portage MI 49002 *Cust Svc	866-471-2900*	269-567-2900	178-11
Manatt's Inc 1775 Old 6 Rd .... Brooklyn IA 52211	800-532-1121	641-522-9206	188-4
Manchester College 604 E College Ave .... North Manchester IN 46962 *Admissions	800-852-3648*	260-982-5000	166
Manchester Community College PO Box 1046 .... Manchester CT 06045	888-999-5545	860-512-2800	162
Manchester Community College 1066 Front St .... Manchester NH 03102	800-924-3445	603-206-8000	162
Mancini Foods PO Box 157 ....Zolfo Springs FL 33890	800-741-1778		296-36
Manda Fine Meats 2445 Sorrel Ave .... Baton Rouge LA 70802	800-343-2642	225-344-7636	297-9
Mandalay Bay Resort & Casino 3950 Las Vegas Blvd S .... Las Vegas NV 89119	877-632-7800	702-632-7777	665
Mandarin Oriental Hotel Group (USA) 345 California St Ste 1250...................... San Francisco CA 94104	800-526-6566	415-772-8800	378
Mandarin Oriental Miami 500 Brickell Key Dr .... Miami FL 33131	800-526-6566	305-913-8288	378
Mandarin Oriental New York 80 Columbus Cir ....New York NY 10023	866-801-8880	212-805-8800	378
Mandarin Oriental Washington DC 1330 Maryland Ave SW ....Washington DC 20024	888-888-1778	202-554-8588	378
Mandel Co 727 W Glendale Ave Ste 100 ....Milwaukee WI 53209	800-888-6970	414-271-6970	623
Mandel Metals Inc 11400 W Addison Ave ....Franklin Park IL 60131	800-962-9851	847-455-6606	490
Mandel Scientific 2 Admiral Pl ....Guelph ON N1G4N4	888-883-3636	519-763-9292	418
Manex Resource Group Inc 1100 - 1199 W Hastings St .... Vancouver BC V6E3T5	888-456-1112	604-684-9384	194
Manhasset Specialty Co 3505 Fruitvale Blvd ....Yakima WA 98902	800-795-0965	509-248-3810	523
Manhattan Area Chamber of Commerce 501 Poyntz Ave .... Manhattan KS 66502	800-759-0134	785-776-8829	139
Manhattan Area Technical College 3136 Dickens .... Manhattan KS 66503	800-352-7575	785-587-2800	162
Manhattan Assoc Inc 2300 Windy Ridge Pkwy 10th Fl.......... Atlanta GA 30339 *NASDAQ: MANH*	877-756-7435	770-955-7070	178-10
Manhattan Beach State Recreation Site Hwy 101 N .... Rockaway Beach OR 97136	800-551-6949		561
Manhattan Christian College 1415 Anderson Ave .... Manhattan KS 66502	877-246-4622	785-539-3571	161
Manhattan College 4513 Manhattan College Pkwy ....Bronx NY 10471	855-841-2843	718-862-8000	166
Manhattan Convention & Visitors Bureau 501 Poyntz Ave .... Manhattan KS 66502	800-759-0134	785-776-8829	206
Manhattan Toy 300 First Ave North Ste 200 ....Minneapolis MN 55401	800-541-1345		64
Manhattanville College 2900 Purchase St .... Purchase NY 10577	800-328-4553	914-323-5464	166
Manildra Group USA 4210 Shawnee Mission Pkwy Ste 312A................... Shawnee Mission KS 66205	800-323-8435	913-362-0777	296-23
Manitex Inc 3000 S Austin Ave ....Georgetown TX 78626	877-314-3390	512-942-3000	468
Manitoba Chambers of Commerce, The 227 Portage Ave ....Winnipeg MB R3B2A6	877-444-5222	204-948-0100	137
Manitok Energy Inc 444 Seventh Ave SW Ste 700........... Calgary AB T2P0X8	877-503-5957	403-984-1750	
Manitou Cliff Dwellings Museum 10 Cliff Rd .... Manitou Springs CO 80829	800-354-9971	719-685-5242	517
Manitowoc Ice 2110 S 26th St ....Manitowoc WI 54220	800-545-5720		660
Manitowoc-Two Rivers Area Chamber of Commerce 1515 Memorial Dr ....Manitowoc WI 54220	866-727-5575	920-684-5575	139
Manke Lumber Company Inc 1717 Marine View Dr .... Tacoma WA 98422	800-426-8488	253-572-6252	679
Mann & Parker Lumber Company Inc, The 335 N Constitution Ave ....New Freedom PA 17349	800-632-9098	717-235-4834	497

	Toll-Free	Phone	Class
Mann Packing Co			
PO Box 690 . . . . Salinas CA 93902	800-285-1002		11-1
Mann's Jewelers Inc			
2945 Monroe Ave . . . . Rochester NY 14618	800-828-6234	585-271-4000	409
Manna Pro Corp			
707 Spirit 40 Pk Dr			
Ste 150 . . . . Chesterfield MO 63005	800-690-9908		445
Mannik & Smith Group Inc			
1800 Indian Wood Cir . . . . Maumee OH 43537	888-891-6321	419-891-2222	261
Mannington Mills Inc			
75 Mannington Mills Rd . . . . Salem NJ 08079	800-356-6787*	800-241-2262	291
*Cust Svc			
Manns Bait Co			
1111 State Docks Rd . . . . Eufaula AL 36027	800-841-8435	334-687-5716	706
Manoir du Lac Delage			
40 Ave du Lac . . . . Lac Delage QC G3C5C4	888-202-3242	418-848-2551	665
Manor House Inn			
106 West St . . . . Bar Harbor ME 04609	800-437-0088		378
Manor Park Inc			
2208 N Loop 250 W . . . . Midland TX 79707	800-523-9898	432-689-9898	668
Manor Vail Lodge			
595 E Vail Vly Dr . . . . Vail CO 81657	800-950-8245	970-476-5000	665
ManorCare Health Services - Mountainside			
1180 Rt 22 W . . . . Mountainside NJ 07092	800-366-1232	908-654-0020	448
Manpower Demonstration Research Corp			
16 E 34th St 19th Fl . . . . New York NY 10016	800-221-3165	212-532-3200	630
Mansfield Hotel, The			
12 W 44th St . . . . New York NY 10036	844-591-5565*	212-277-8700	378
*Admissions			
Mansfield Oil Co			
1025 Airport Pkwy SW . . . . Gainesville GA 30501	800-695-6626		535
Mansfield Plumbing Products Inc			
150 E First St . . . . Perrysville OH 44864	877-850-3060	419-938-5211	607
Mansfield State Historic Site			
15149 Hwy 175 . . . . Mansfield LA 71052	888-677-6267	318-872-1474	561
Mansfield University			
Alumni Hall . . . . Mansfield PA 16933	800-577-6826*	570-662-4000	166
*Admissions			
Mansfield-Richland County Public Library			
43 W Third St . . . . Mansfield OH 44902	877-795-2111	419-521-3100	433-3
Mansion on Forsyth Park			
700 Drayton St . . . . Savannah GA 31401	888-213-3671	912-238-5158	378
Mansion View Inn & Suites			
529 S Fourth St . . . . Springfield IL 62701	800-252-1083	217-544-7411	378
ManTech Advanced Systems International Inc			
12015 Lee Jackson Hwy . . . . Fairfax VA 22033	800-800-4857	703-218-6000	256
MantelsDirect			
217 N Seminary St . . . . Florence AL 35630	888-493-8898	256-765-2171	183
Manton Industrial Cork Products Inc			
415 Oser Ave Unit U . . . . Hauppauge NY 11788	800-663-1921		209
Mantros-Haeuser & Company Inc			
1175 Post Rd E . . . . Westport CT 06880	800-344-4229*	203-454-1800	546
*General			
Mantua Mfg Co			
7900 Northfield Rd . . . . Walton Hills OH 44146	800-333-8333*		319-2
*Orders			
Manual Woodworkers & Weavers Inc			
3737 HowaRd Gap Rd . . . . Hendersonville NC 28792	800-542-3139	828-692-7333	741
Manufactured Housing Enterprises Inc			
09302 St Rt 6 Rt 6 . . . . Bryan OH 43506	800-821-0220	419-636-4511	503
Manufacturing Jewelers & Suppliers of America Inc (MJSA)			
57 John L Dietsch Sq . . . . Attleboro MA 02763	800-444-6572	401-274-3840	49-4
Manus Group, The			
5000-18 Hwy 17 S Ste 134 . . . . Fleming Island FL 32003	888-735-8311		
Manzi Metals Inc			
15293 Flight Path Dr . . . . Brooksville FL 34604	800-799-8211	352-799-8211	490
MAP (Mississippi Action For Progress Inc)			
1751 Morson Rd . . . . Jackson MS 39209	800-924-4615	601-923-4100	147
MAP International			
4700 Glynco Pkwy . . . . Brunswick GA 31525	800-225-8550	912-265-6010	48-5
MAPEI Corp			
1144 E Newport Ctr Dr . . . . Deerfield Beach FL 33442	800-426-2734	954-246-8888	3
Mapes Panels LLC			
2929 Cornhusker Hwy			
PO Box 80069 . . . . Lincoln NE 68504	800-228-2391		693
MAPFRE Insurance			
211 Main St . . . . Webster MA 01570	800-221-1605	508-943-9000	390-4
MAPFRE Insurance			
211 Main St . . . . Webster MA 01570	800-922-8276		390-4
Maple City Ice Co Inc			
371 Cleveland Rd . . . . Norwalk OH 44857	800-736-6091*	419-668-2531	81-1
*Cust Svc			
Maple City Rubber Co			
55 Newton St . . . . Norwalk OH 44857	800-841-9434	419-668-8261	757
Maple Donuts Inc			
3455 E Market St . . . . York PA 17402	800-627-5348	717-757-7826	68
Maple Grove Farms of Vermont			
1052 Portland St . . . . Saint Johnsbury VT 05819	800-525-2540	802-748-5141	296-39
Maple Hill Farm Bed & Breakfast Inn			
11 Inn Rd . . . . Hallowell ME 04347	800-622-2708	207-622-2708	378
Maple Island Inc			
2497 Seventh Ave E Ste 105 . . . . St Paul MN 55109	800-369-1022	651-773-1000	296-10
Maple Leaf Farms Inc			
PO Box 167 . . . . Leesburg IN 46538	800-348-2812		10-7
Maple Leaf Foods Inc			
PO Box 61016 . . . . Winnipeg MB R3M3X8	800-268-3708		296-26
TSE: MFI			
Maplehurst Inc			
50 Maplehurst Dr . . . . Brownsburg IN 46112	800-428-3200	317-858-9000	296-2
Mapping Analytics LLC			
120 Allens Creek Rd Ste 10 . . . . Rochester NY 14618	877-893-6490		
MAQUET Cardiovascular LLC			
45 Barbour Pond Dr . . . . Wayne NJ 07470	888-627-8383		475
Maquoketa Valley Rural Electric Co-op			
109 N Huber St . . . . Anamosa IA 52205	800-927-6068	319-462-3542	245
MARAD (Maritime Administration)			
1200 New Jersey Ave SE . . . . Washington DC 20590	800-996-2723*	202-366-5807	339-16
*Hotline			
Maradyne Corp			
4540 W 160th St . . . . Cleveland OH 44135	800-537-7444	216-362-0755	14
Maranatha Baptist Bible College			
745 W Main St . . . . Watertown WI 53094	800-622-2947	920-206-2330	166
Marathon Coach			
91333 Coburg Industrial Way . . . . Coburg OR 97408	800-234-9991	541-343-9991	62-7
Marathon County			
500 Forest St . . . . Wausau WI 54403	800-247-5645	715-261-1500	337
Marathon Digital Services			
901 N Eighth st . . . . Kansas City KS 64108	877-568-1121	816-221-7881	177
Marathon Electric Inc			
100 E Randolf St PO Box 8003 . . . . Wausau WI 54402	800-616-7077	715-675-3311	515
Marathon Enterprises Inc			
9 Smith St . . . . Englewood NJ 07631	800-722-7388	201-935-3330	296-26
Marathon Equipment Co			
PO Box 1798 . . . . Vernon AL 35592	800-633-8974	205-695-9105	385
Marathon Press			
1500 Sq Turn Blvd PO Box 407 . . . . Norfolk NE 68702	800-228-0629		623
MarathonFoto			
3490 Martin Hurst Rd . . . . Tallahassee FL 32312	800-424-3686		586
Maravia Corp of Idaho			
602 E 45th St . . . . Boise ID 83714	800-223-7238	208-322-4949	706
Marborg Industries			
728 E Yanonali St . . . . Santa Barbara CA 93103	800-798-1852	805-963-1852	656
Marburger Farm Dairy Inc			
1506 Mars Evans City Rd . . . . Evans City PA 16033	800-331-1295	724-538-4800	10-2
Marc Jacobs International			
72 Spring St . . . . New York NY 10012	877-707-6272	212-965-4000	277
Marc Publishing Co			
600 Germantown Pk . . . . Lafayette Hill PA 19444	800-432-5478	610-834-8585	633-6
Marcive Inc			
PO Box 47508 Ste 160 . . . . San Antonio TX 78265	800-531-7678		433-3
Marck Industries Inc			
401 Main St Ste E PO Box 912 . . . . Cassville MO 65625	877-228-2565		
Marco Beach Ocean Resort			
480 S Collier Blvd . . . . Marco Island FL 34145	800-715-8517	239-393-1400	665
Marco Corp, The			
470 Hardy Rd . . . . Brantford ON N3V6T1	888-636-6161		7
Marco Crane & Rigging Co			
221 S 35th Ave . . . . Phoenix AZ 85009	800-668-2671	602-272-2671	264-3
Marco Island Chamber of Commerce			
1102 N Collier Blvd . . . . Marco Island FL 34145	888-330-1422	239-394-7549	139
Marco Promotional Products			
2640 Commerce Dr . . . . Harrisburg PA 17110	877-545-9322		9
Marco Rubber			
35 Woodworkers Way . . . . Seabrook NH 03874	800-775-6525	603-468-3600	326
MARCOA Publishing Inc			
9955 Black Mtn Rd . . . . San Diego CA 92126	800-854-2935	858-695-9600	633-1
Marcus Bros Textiles Inc			
980 Ave of the Americas . . . . New York NY 10018	800-548-8295	212-354-8700	590
Marcus Ctr for the Performing Arts			
929 N Water St . . . . Milwaukee WI 53202	888-612-3500	414-273-7206	568
Marcus Theatres Corp			
100 E Wisconsin Ave Ste 2000 . . . . Milwaukee WI 53202	800-274-0099*	414-905-1000	743
*Cust Svc			
Mardel Inc			
7727 SW 44th St . . . . Oklahoma City OK 73179	888-262-7335		
Maren Engineering			
111 W Taft Dr . . . . South Holland IL 60473	800-875-1038	708-333-6250	261
Mares America Corp			
1 Selleck St . . . . Norwalk CT 06855	800-874-3236	203-855-0631	706
Margaret Chase Smith Policy Ctr			
5784 York Complex Ste 4 . . . . Orono ME 04469	877-486-2364	207-581-1648	630
Margaret Mary Community Hospital Inc			
321 Mitchell Ave PO Box 226 . . . . Batesville IN 47006	800-562-5698	812-934-6624	373-3
Marian University			
3200 Cold Spring Rd . . . . Indianapolis IN 46222	800-772-7264*	317-955-6038	166
*Admissions			
Marian University			
45 S National Ave . . . . Fond du Lac WI 54935	800-262-7426		166
Mariani Packing Company Inc			
500 Crocker Dr . . . . Vacaville CA 95688	800-231-1287	707-452-2800	11-1
Marianjoy Rehabilitation Hospital			
26 W 171 Roosevelt Rd . . . . Wheaton IL 60187	800-462-2366	630-462-4000	373-6
Marianna Industries Inc			
11222 "I" St . . . . Omaha NE 68137	800-228-9060	402-593-0211	231
Maricopa Medical Ctr			
2601 E Roosevelt St . . . . Phoenix AZ 85008	866-749-2876	602-344-5011	373-3
Marie Callender Restaurant & Bakery			
27101 Puerta Real Ste 260 . . . . Mission Viejo CA 92691	800-776-7437		666
Marie Claire Magazine			
300 W 57th St 34th Fl . . . . New York NY 10019	800-777-3287	515-282-1607	455-11
Marietta College			
215 Fifth St . . . . Marietta OH 45750	800-331-7896*	740-376-4000	166
*Admissions			
Marietta Conference Ctr & Resort			
500 Powder Springs St . . . . Marietta GA 30064	888-685-2500	770-427-2500	376
Marietta Drapery & Window Coverings Company Inc			
22 Trammel St PO Box 569 . . . . Marietta GA 30064	800-241-7974		741
Marietta Hospitality			
37 Huntington St . . . . Cortland NY 13045	800-950-7772	607-753-6746	9
Marietta Memorial Hospital			
401 Matthew St . . . . Marietta OH 45750	800-523-3977	740-374-1400	373-3
Marietta National Cemetery			
500 Washington Ave . . . . Marietta GA 30060	866-236-8159		136
Marijuana Anonymous World Services (MAWS)			
PO Box 7807 . . . . Torrance CA 90504	800-766-6779		48-21
Marimba One Inc			
901 O St Ste D . . . . Arcata CA 95521	888-990-6663	707-822-9570	523
Marin Convention & Visitors Bureau			
1 Mitchell Blvd Ste B . . . . San Rafael CA 94903	866-925-2060	415-925-2060	206
Marin General Hospital			
250 Bon Air Rd . . . . Greenbrae CA 94904	888-996-9644	415-925-7000	373-3
Marin Independent Journal			
150 Alameda Del Prado . . . . Novato CA 94949	877-229-8655	415-883-8600	528-2
Marin Suites Hotel LLC			
45 Tamal Vista Blvd . . . . Corte Madera CA 94925	800-362-3372	415-924-3608	377

Alphabetical Section

	Toll-Free	Phone	Class
Marina Del Rey Hospital 4650 Lincoln Blvd ....Marina del Rey CA 90292	888-600-5600	310-823-8911	373-3
Marina Graphic Ctr 12901 Cerise Ave ....Hawthorne CA 90250	800-974-5777	310-970-1777	623
Marina Inn at Grande Dunes 8121 Amalfi Pl ....Myrtle Beach SC 29572 *Resv	877-913-1333*	843-913-1333	378
Marinco 2655 Napa Valley Corp Dr ....Napa CA 94558	800-307-6702	707-226-9600	810
Marine PO Box 5185 ....Des Plaines IL 60019	800-627-4637		339-6
Marine Corps Assn (MCA) PO Box 1775 ....Quantico VA 22134	800-336-0291	703-640-6161	48-19
Marine Corps Base Quantico 3250 Catlin Ave ....Quantico VA 22134	800-268-3710	703-432-0303	495-3
Marine Depot 14271 Corporate Dr ....Garden Grove CA 92843	800-566-3474		765
Marine Exhaust Systems of Alabama Inc 757 Nichols Ave ....Fairhope AL 36532	800-237-3160	251-928-1234	452
Marine Petroleum Trust 2911 Turtle Creek Blvd Ste 850 ....Dallas TX 75219 NASDAQ: MARPS	800-758-4672		671
Marine Room, The 2000 Spindrift Dr ....La Jolla CA 92037	866-644-2351	858-459-7222	667
Marineland of Florida 9600 Ocean Shore Blvd ....Saint Augustine FL 32080	877-933-3402	904-471-1111	40
Marinelife Ctr of Juno Beach 14200 US Hwy 1 Loggerhead Pk .....Juno Beach FL 33408	800-843-5451	561-627-8280	40
Mariner Wealth Advisors 1 Giralda Farms Ste 130 ....Madison NJ 07940	800-364-2468		194
Mariners' Museum 100 Museum Dr ....Newport News VA 23606	800-581-7245	757-596-2222	517
Mario Pastega Guest House 3505 NW Samaritan Dr ....Corvallis OR 97330	800-863-5241	541-768-4650	371
Marion Area Chamber of Commerce 267 W Ctr St Ste 100 ....Marion OH 43302	800-371-6688	740-387-2267	139
Marion Ceramics Inc PO Box 1134 ....Marion SC 29571	800-845-4010	843-423-1311	150
Marion Correctional Institution PO Box 57 ....Marion OH 43302	800-237-3454	740-382-5781	213
Marion County 200 E Washington St Ste W122 ....Indianapolis IN 46204	800-913-6050	317-327-4740	337
Marion County 200 S Third St Ste 104 ....Marion KS 66861	800-305-8851	620-382-2185	337
Marion County 118 Cross Creek Blvd ....Salem IL 62881	800-438-4318	618-548-3878	337
Marion Military Institute 1101 Washington St ....Marion AL 36756	800-664-1842	334-683-2322	162
Marion Star, The 163 E Center St ....Marion OH 43302	877-987-2782	740-387-0400	528-2
Marion-Grant County Convention & Visitors Bureau 1500 S Western Ave ....Marion IN 46953	800-662-9474	765-668-5435	206
Mariposa County 5100 Bullion St PO Box 784 ....Mariposa CA 95338	800-549-6741	209-966-3222	337
Marist College 3399 N Rd ....Poughkeepsie NY 12601	800-436-5483	845-575-3000	166
Maritime Administration (MARAD) 1200 New Jersey Ave SE ....Washington DC 20590 *Hotline	800-996-2723*	202-366-5807	339-16
Maritime Company For Navigation, The 249 Shipyard Blvd ....Wilmington NC 28412	800-626-4777	910-343-8900	311
Maritime Energy Inc 234 Park St PO Box 485 ....Rockland ME 04841	800-333-4489		575
Maritime Paper Products Ltd 25 Borden Ave PO Box 668 ....Dartmouth NS B2Y3Y9	800-565-5353	902-468-5353	550
Maritime Travel Inc 202-2000 Barrington St Cogswell Tower ....Halifax NS B3J3K1	800-593-3334	902-420-1554	770
MaritzCX Research LLC 1355 N Hwy Dr ....Fenton MO 63099	877-462-7489	385-695-2940	464
MarJam Supply Co Inc 20 Rewe St ....Brooklyn NY 11211 *All	800-848-8407*	718-388-6465	363
Marjorie Barrick Museum 4505 S Maryland Pkwy ....Las Vegas NV 89154	877-895-0334	702-895-3381	517
Mark Andy Inc 18081 Chesterfield Airport Rd ....Chesterfield MO 63005	800-700-6275	636-532-4433	625
Mark Hershey Farms Inc 479 Horseshoe Pk ....Lebanon PA 17042	888-801-3301	717-867-4624	445
Mark Morris Dance Group 3 Lafayette Ave ....Brooklyn NY 11217	800-957-1046	718-624-8400	569-1
Mark Sand & Gravel Co 525 Kennedy Pk Rd PO Box 458 ....Fergus Falls MN 56537	800-427-8316	218-736-7523	501-4
Mark Spencer Hotel 409 SW 11th Ave ....Portland OR 97205	800-548-3934	503-224-3293	378
Mark Twain Hotel 225 NE Adams St ....Peoria IL 61602	866-325-6351	309-676-3600	378
Mark's Plumbing Parts 3312 Ramona Dr ....Fort Worth TX 76116	800-772-2347	817-731-6211	608
Mark's Work Warehouse 1035 64th Ave SE Ste 30 ....Calgary AB T2H2J7	800-663-6275	403-255-9220	157-5
Mar-Kee Group, The 26248 Equity Dr ....Daphne AL 36526	888-300-4629		
Markel Corp 4521 Highwoods Pkwy ....Glen Allen VA 23060 NYSE: MKL	800-446-6671		359-4
Markel Corp 4521 Highwoods Pkwy ....Glen Allen VA 23060	800-446-6671		390-4
Markel Specialty Commercial 4600 Cox Rd ....Glen Allen VA 23060	800-416-4364	800-446-6671	390-4
Markem-Imaje Inc 100 Chastain Center Blvd Ste 165 ....Mississauga ON L4W2T7	800-267-5108		357
Market America Inc 1302 Pleasant Ridge Rd ....Greensboro NC 27409	866-420-1709	336-605-0040	114
Market Contractors 10250 NE Marx St ....Portland OR 97220	800-876-9133	503-255-0977	186
Market Data Retrieval 6 Armstrong Rd ....Shelton CT 06484	800-333-8802	203-926-4800	5
Market Decisions Research 75 Washington Ave Ste 2C ....Portland ME 04101	800-293-1538	207-767-6440	464
Market Force Information Llc 6025 The Corners Pkwy Ste 200 ....Peachtree Corners GA 30092	800-669-9939	770-441-5366	
Market Forge Industries Inc 35 Garvey St ....Everett MA 02149	866-698-3188	617-387-4100	298
Market Pavilion Hotel 225 E Bay St ....Charleston SC 29401	877-440-2250	843-723-0500	378
Market Scan Information Systems Inc 811 Camarillo Springs Ste B ....Camarillo CA 93012	800-658-7226		178-10
Market Strategies Inc 17430 College Pkwy ....Livonia MI 48152	800-420-9366	734-542-7600	464
Market Wire Inc 100 N Sepulveda Blvd Ste 325 ....El Segundo CA 90245 *General	800-774-9473*	310-765-3200	526
Marketing Innovators International Inc 9701 W Higgins Rd ....Rosemont IL 60018	800-543-7373		383
Marketing Library Services 143 Old Marlton Pk ....Medford NJ 08055	800-300-9868	609-654-6266	527-10
Marketing News 311 S Wacker Dr Ste 5800 ....Chicago IL 60606	800-262-1150	312-542-9000	455-5
Marketing Resource Group Inc (MRG) 225 S Washington Sq ....Lansing MI 48933	800-928-2086	517-372-4400	5
MarketingProfs LLC 419 N Larchmont Blvd #295 ....Los Angeles CA 90004	866-557-9625		195
Marketlab Inc 6850 Southbelt Dr ....Caledonia MI 49316	866-237-3722	616-656-2484	473
MarketLauncher Inc PO Box 916582 ....Longwood FL 32791	800-901-3803		7
MarketLeverage LLC 6314 Brookside Plz Ste 301 ....Kansas City MO 64113	888-653-8372		5
Marketocracy Inc 1208 W Magnolia Ste 236 ....Fort Worth TX 76104	877-462-4180		400
Marketri LLC 1700 Market St Ste 1005 ....Philadelphia PA 19103	800-695-1356		
Marketstar Corp 2475 Washington Blvd ....Ogden UT 84401	800-877-8259		
MarketVision Research Inc 5151 Pfeiffer Rd Ste 300 ....Cincinnati OH 45242	800-232-4250	513-791-3100	464
Marketware Inc 7070 Union Park Ctr Ste 300 ....Midvale UT 84047	800-777-6368		225
Markey Machinery Company Inc 7266 Eigth Ave S ....Seattle WA 98108	800-637-3430	206-622-4697	765
Marks Group P C 45 E city ave Ste 342 ....Bala Cynwyd PA 19004	888-224-0649		196
Marksville State Historic Site 837 ML King Dr ....Marksville LA 71351	888-253-8954	318-253-8954	561
MarkWest Energy Partners LP 1515 Arapahoe St Tower 1 Ste 1600 ....Denver CO 80202 NYSE: MWE	800-730-8388	303-925-9200	593
Markwort Sporting Goods Co 1101 Research Blvd ....St. Louis MO 63132	800-280-5555	314-942-1199	707
Marland Clutch 23601 Hoover Rd ....Warren MI 48089	800-216-3515		616
Marlboro College 2582 S Rd PO Box A ....Marlboro VT 05344	800-343-0049	802-257-4333	166
Marlboro College Graduate Ctr PO Box A ....Marlboro VT 05344	800-343-0049	802-258-9200	166
Marlborough Public Library 35 W Main St ....Marlborough MA 01752	800-592-2000	508-624-6900	433-3
Marlborough Regional Chamber of Commerce 11 Florence St ....Marlborough MA 01752	800-508-2265	508-485-7746	139
Marlen International Inc 4780 NW 41st St Ste 100 ....Riverside MO 64150	800-862-7536		298
Marley Engineered Products 470 Beauty Spot Rd E ....Bennettsville SC 29512	800-452-4179	843-479-4006	37
Marlin Business Services Inc 300 Fellowship Rd ....Mount Laurel NJ 08054 NASDAQ: MRLN	888-479-9111		264-2
Marlin Firearms Co PO Box 1871 ....Madison NC 27025 *Cust Svc	800-544-8892*		284
Marlow Industries Inc 10451 Vista Pk Rd ....Dallas TX 75238	877-627-5691		253
Marmon/Keystone Corp PO Box 992 ....Butler PA 16003	800-544-1748	724-283-3000	490
Marmon-Herrington Co 13001 Magisterial Dr ....Louisville KY 40223	800-227-0727		60
Marotta Controls Inc 78 Boonton Ave PO Box 427 ....Montville NJ 07045	888-627-6882	973-334-7800	784
Marposs Corp 3300 Cross Creek Pkwy ....Auburn Hills MI 48326	888-627-7677	248-370-0404	470
Marq Packaging Systems Inc 3801 W Washington Ave ....Yakima WA 98903	800-998-4301	509-966-4300	553
Marquesa Hotel 600 Fleming St ....Key West FL 33040	800-869-4631	305-292-1919	378
Marquette Asset Management 33 S Sixth St Ste 4540 ....Minneapolis MN 55402	866-661-3770	612-661-3770	400
Marquette Bank 10000 W 151st St ....Orland Park IL 60462	888-254-9500	708-226-8026	70
Marquette Country Convention & Visitors Bureau 117 West Washington St ....Marquette MI 49855	800-544-4321	906-228-7749	206
Marquette Savings Bank 920 Peach St ....Erie PA 16501	866-672-3743	814-455-4481	70
Marquette Transportation Company LLC 150 Ballard Cir ....Paducah KY 42001	800-456-9404	270-443-9404	314
Marquette University 1217 W Wisconsin Ave ....Milwaukee WI 53233 *Admissions	800-222-6544*	414-288-7302	166
Marquette University Raynor Memorial Library 1355 W Wisconsin Ave ....Milwaukee WI 53233	800-876-1715	414-288-7556	433-6
Marquez Bros International Inc 5801 Rue Ferrari ....San Jose CA 95138	800-858-1119	408-960-2700	297-8

Name / Address	City	State	ZIP	Toll-Free	Phone	Class
Marquis Spas Corp						
596 Hoffman Rd	Independence	OR	97351	**800-275-0888**	503-838-0888	374
Marquis Who's Who						
100 Connell Dr						
Ste 2300	Berkeley Heights	NJ	07922	**800-473-7020**	908-673-1000	633-2
Marrakech Express Inc						
720 Wesley Ave Ste 10	Tarpon Springs	FL	34689	**800-940-6566**	727-942-2218	623
Marriott Charleston Hotel						
170 Lockwood Blvd	Charleston	SC	29403	**888-236-2427**	843-723-3000	378
Marriott Columbus						
800 Front Ave	Columbus	GA	31901	**800-455-9261**	706-324-1800	378
Marriott International Inc						
10400 Fernwood Rd	Bethesda	MD	20817	**800-450-4442**	301-380-3000	378
NASDAQ: MAR						
Marriott Kaua'i Resort & Beach Club						
3610 Rice St Kalapaki Beach	Lihue	HI	96766	**800-220-2925**	808-245-5050	665
Marriott Montgomery Prattville at Capitol Hill						
2500 Legends Cir	Prattville	AL	36066	**800-593-6429***	334-290-1235	376
*Resv						
Marriott Vacation Club International						
6649 Westwood Blvd Ste 500	Orlando	FL	32821	**800-307-7312**	407-206-6000	748
Mars Stout Inc						
4500 Majestic Dr	Missoula	MT	59808	**800-451-6277**	406-721-6280	732
Marsh & Mclennan Agency						
250 Pehle Ave	Saddle Brook	NJ	07663	**800-669-6330**	800-642-0106	389
Marsh & McLennan Cos Inc						
1166 Ave of the Americas	New York	NY	10036	**866-374-2662**	212-345-5000	359-3
NYSE: MMC						
Marsh Bellofram Corp						
8019 Ohio River Blvd	Newell	WV	26050	**800-727-5646**	304-387-1200	201
Marsh Berry & Company Inc						
4420 Sherwin Rd	Willoughby	OH	44094	**800-426-2774**	440-354-3230	194
Marsh Electronics Inc						
1563 S 101st St	Milwaukee	WI	53214	**800-926-2774***	414-475-6000	246
*Cust Svc						
Marshal Mize Ford Inc						
5348 Hwy 153	Chattanooga	TN	37343	**888-633-5038**		57
Marshall & Sterling Inc						
110 Main St	Poughkeepsie	NY	12601	**800-333-3766**	845-454-0800	389
Marshall & Stevens Inc						
601 S Figueroa St Ste 2301	Los Angeles	CA	90017	**800-950-9588**	213-612-8000	194
Marshall & Sullivan Inc						
1109 First Ave Ste 200	Seattle	WA	98101	**800-735-7290**	206-621-9014	400
Marshall Area Convention & Visitors Bureau						
317 W Main St	Marshall	MN	56258	**800-581-0081**	507-537-2271	206
Marshall Dennehey Warner Coleman & Goggin						
1845 Walnut St	Philadelphia	PA	19103	**800-220-3308**	215-575-2600	427
Marshall Durbin Co						
2830 Commerce Blvd	Birmingham	AL	35210	**800-245-8204***	205-380-3251	615
*Sales						
Marshall Music Co						
4555 Wilson Ave SW Ste 1	Grandville	MI	49418	**800-242-4705**	616-530-7700	522
Marshall Screw Products Co						
3820 Chandler Dr NE	Minneapolis	MN	55421	**800-321-6727**		452
Marshall University						
1 John Marshall Dr	Huntington	WV	25755	**800-642-3463**	304-696-3170	166
Marshalls Inc						
770 Cochituate Rd	Framingham	MA	01701	**888-627-7425**		157-2
Marshalltown Co						
104 S Eigth Ave	Marshalltown	IA	50158	**800-888-0127**	641-753-5999	753
Marshalltown Community College						
3700 S Ctr St	Marshalltown	IA	50158	**866-622-4748**	641-844-5708	162
Marshfield Convention & Visitors Bureau						
700 S Central Ave PO Box 868	Marshfield	WI	54449	**800-422-4541**	715-384-3454	206
Marston House Museum & Gardens						
3525 Seventh Ave	San Diego	CA	92103	**800-577-6679**	619-297-9327	50-3
Martec						
105 W Adams St Ste 2900	Chicago	IL	60603	**888-811-5755**	312-606-9690	664
Marten Transport Ltd						
129 Marten St	Mondovi	WI	54755	**800-395-3000**	715-926-4216	775
NASDAQ: MRTN						
Martha Stewart Living Magazine						
601 W 26th St 9th Fl	New York	NY	10001	**800-999-6518**		455-11
Martin & Bayley Inc						
1311 A W Main	Carmi	IL	62821	**800-876-2511**	618-382-2334	344
Martin Community College						
1161 Kehukee Pk Rd	Williamston	NC	27892	**800-488-4101**	252-792-1521	162
Martin County Travel & Tourism Authority						
100 E Church St PO Box 382	Williamston	NC	27892	**800-776-8566**	252-792-6605	206
Martin Door Manufacturing Inc						
2828 South 900 West	Salt Lake City	UT	84119	**800-388-9310**	801-973-9310	363
Martin Eagle Oil Company Inc						
2700 James St	Denton	TX	76205	**800-316-6148**	940-383-2351	575
Martin Engineering						
1 Martin Pl	Neponset	IL	61345	**800-544-2947**	309-594-2384	207
Martin Furniture						
2345 Britannia Blvd	San Diego	CA	92154	**800-268-5669***		319-1
*Cust Svc						
Martin Glass Co						
25 Ctr Plz	Belleville	IL	62220	**800-325-1946**	618-277-1946	62-2
Martin Health System (MMHS)						
200 SE Hospital Ave PO Box 9010	Stuart	FL	34994	**844-630-4968**	772-287-5200	373-3
Martin Law Firm						
2059 N Green Acres Rd	Fayetteville	AR	72702	**800-633-2160**	479-442-2244	443
Martin Marietta Magnesia Specialties Inc						
8140 Corporate Dr Ste 220	Baltimore	MD	21236	**800-648-7400**	410-780-5500	143
Martin Methodist College						
433 W Madison St	Pulaski	TN	38478	**800-467-1273**	931-363-9804	166
Martin Midstream Partners LP						
4200 Stone Rd	Kilgore	TX	75662	**800-256-6644**	903-983-6200	575
NASDAQ: MMLP						
Martin Resource Management Corp (MRMC)						
PO Box 191	Kilgore	TX	75663	**888-334-7473**	903-983-6200	316
Martin Rosol Inc						
45 Grove St	New Britain	CT	06053	**800-937-2682**	860-223-2707	296-26
Martin Wells Industries						
5886 Compton Ave						
PO Box 01406	Los Angeles	CA	90001	**800-421-6000**	323-581-6266	128

Name / Address	City	State	ZIP	Toll-Free	Phone	Class
Martin Wheel Company Inc, The						
342 W Ave PO Box 157	Tallmadge	OH	44278	**800-462-7846**	330-633-3278	749
Martin Yale Industries Inc						
251 Wedcor Ave	Wabash	IN	46992	**800-225-5644**	260-563-0641	111
Martin's Famous Pastry Shoppe Inc						
1000 Potato Roll Ln	Chambersburg	PA	17202	**800-548-1200***	717-263-9580	296-1
*Cust Svc						
Martin's Potato Chips Inc						
5847 Lincoln Hwy W						
PO Box 28	Thomasville	PA	17364	**800-272-4477**	717-792-3565	296-35
Martin, Harding & Mazzotti LLP						
1222 Troy-Schenectady Rd	Niskayuna	NY	12309	**800-529-1010**	518-862-1200	427
Martin/F Weber Co						
2727 Southampton Rd	Philadelphia	PA	19154	**800-876-8076**	215-677-5600	43
MartinAire Aviation LLC						
4553 Glenn Curtiss Dr	Addison	TX	75001	**866-557-1861**	972-349-5700	12
Martindale Electric Co						
1375 Hird Ave	Cleveland	OH	44107	**800-344-9191**	216-521-8567	515
Martindale-Hubbell						
121 Chanlon Rd Ste 110	New Providence	NJ	07974	**800-526-4902**		386
Martinsville Bulletin						
PO Box 3711	Martinsville	VA	24115	**800-234-6575**	276-638-8801	528-2
Martinsville Speedway						
PO Box 3311	Martinsville	VA	24115	**877-722-3849**	276-666-7200	512
Martrex Inc						
1107 Hazeltine Blvd Ste 535	Minnetonka	MN	55318	**800-328-3627**	952-933-5000	276
Martronic Engineering Inc (MEI)						
874 Patriot Dr Unit D	Moorpark	CA	93021	**800-960-0808**	805-583-0808	261
Marts & Lundy Inc						
1200 Wall St W	Lyndhurst	NJ	07071	**800-526-9005**	201-460-1660	782
Marty Franich Ford Lincoln						
550 Auto Ctr Dr	Watsonville	CA	95076	**888-442-9037**		57
Martz First Class Coach Company Inc						
4783 37th St N	Saint Petersburg	FL	33714	**800-282-8020**		107
Martz Supply Co						
5330 Pecos St	Denver	CO	80221	**800-456-4672**		608
Maruka USA Inc						
1210 NE Douglas St	Lee's Summit	MO	64086	**800-262-7852**		385
Marvel Abrasive Products Inc						
6230 S Oak Park Ave	Chicago	IL	60638	**800-621-0673**		1
Marvel Consultants Inc						
28601 Chagrin Blvd Ste 210	Cleveland	OH	44122	**800-338-1257**	216-292-2855	627
Marvel Group Inc						
3843 W 43rd St	Chicago	IL	60632	**800-621-8846***	773-523-4804	319-1
*Cust Svc						
Marvel Mfg Company Inc						
3501 Marvel Dr	Oshkosh	WI	54902	**800-472-9464**	920-236-7200	678
Marvin Huffaker Consulting Inc						
PO Box 72643	Chandler	AZ	85050	**888-690-0013**	480-988-7215	196
Marvin W Foote Youth Services Ctr						
13500 E Fremont Pl	Englewood	CO	80112	**800-970-3468**	303-768-7501	411
Marvin Windows & Doors						
PO Box 100	Warroad	MN	56763	**888-537-7828**	218-386-1430	236
Mary Ann Liebert Publishers Inc						
140 Huguenot St 3rd Fl	New Rochelle	NY	10801	**800-654-3237**	914-740-2100	633-9
Mary Baldwin College						
318 Prospect St	Staunton	VA	24401	**800-468-2262***	540-887-7019	166
*Admissions						
Mary Bridge Children's Hospital & Health Ctr						
317 Martin Luther King Jr Way	Tacoma	WA	98405	**800-552-1419**	253-403-1400	373-1
Mary Free Bed Rehabilitation Hospital						
235 Wealthy St SE	Grand Rapids	MI	49503	**800-528-8989**	616-840-8000	373-6
Mary H Weirton Public Library						
3442 Main St	Weirton	WV	26062	**800-774-2429**	304-797-8510	433-3
Mary Jane Thurston State Park						
1466 State Rt 65	McClure	OH	43534	**866-644-6727**	419-832-7662	561
Mary Kay Inc						
PO Box 799045	Dallas	TX	75379	**800-627-9529***	972-687-6300	214
*Cust Svc						
Mary Lanning Memorial Hospital						
715 N St Joseph Ave	Hastings	NE	68901	**800-269-0473**	402-463-4521	373-3
Mary Maxim Inc						
2001 Holland Ave PO Box 5019	Port Huron	MI	48061	**800-962-9504**	810-987-2000	457
Mary Maxim Ltd						
75 Scott Ave	Paris	ON	N3L3G5	**888-442-2266**		756
Mary Washington Hospice						
5012 Southpoint Pkwy	Fredericksburg	VA	22407	**800-257-1667**	540-741-1667	370
Mary Washington Hospital						
1001 Sam Perry Blvd	Fredericksburg	VA	22401	**800-395-2455**	540-741-1100	373-3
Maryland						
Aging Dept						
301 W Preston St Ste 1007	Baltimore	MD	21201	**800-243-3425**	410-767-1100	338-21
Assessments & Taxation Dept						
301 W Preston St	Baltimore	MD	21201	**888-246-5941**	410-767-1184	338-21
Court of Appeals						
361 Rowe Blvd	Annapolis	MD	21401	**800-926-2583**	410-260-1500	338-21
Department of Budget & Management						
45 Calvert St	Annapolis	MD	21401	**800-705-3493**		338-21
Dept of Legislative Services						
90 State Cir	Annapolis	MD	21401	**800-492-7122**	410-946-5400	432
Education Dept						
200 W Baltimore St	Baltimore	MD	21201	**888-246-0016**	410-767-0100	338-21
Emergency Management Agency						
5401 Rue St Lo Dr	Reisterstown	MD	21136	**877-636-2872**	410-517-3600	338-21
Environment Dept						
1800 Washington Blvd	Baltimore	MD	21230	**800-633-6101**	410-537-3000	338-21
Ethics Commission						
45 Calvert St	Annapolis	MD	21401	**877-669-6085**	410-260-7770	265
Financial Regulation Div						
500 N Calvert St Ste 402	Baltimore	MD	21202	**888-784-0136**	410-230-6100	338-21
Fisheries Service						
580 Taylor Ave	Annapolis	MD	21401	**877-634-6361**		338-21
Governor						
State House 100 State Cir	Annapolis	MD	21401	**800-811-8336**	410-974-3901	338-21
Higher Education Commision						
839 Bestgate Rd Ste 400	Baltimore	MD	21201	**800-974-0203**	410-260-4500	338-21
Housing & Community Development Dept						
7800 Harkins Rd	Lanham	MD	21032	**800-756-0119**	301-429-7400	338-21

	Toll-Free	Phone	Class
Insurance Administration			
200 St Paul Pl Ste 2700 ... Baltimore MD 21202	**800-492-6116**	410-468-2000	338-21
Labor & Industry Div			
1100 N Eutaw St Rm 600 ... Baltimore MD 21201	**888-257-6674**	410-767-2241	338-21
Motor Vehicle Administration			
6601 Ritchie Hwy NE ... Glen Burnie MD 21062	**800-950-1682**	410-768-7000	338-21
Natural Resources Dept			
580 Taylor Ave ... Annapolis MD 21401	**877-620-8367**		338-21
Physician Quality Assurance Board			
4201 Patterson Ave ... Baltimore MD 21215	**800-492-6836**	410-764-4777	338-21
Public Service Commission			
6 St Paul St 16th Fl ... Baltimore MD 21202	**800-492-0474**	410-767-8000	338-21
Securities Div			
200 St Paul Pl ... Baltimore MD 21202	**888-743-0023**	410-576-6360	338-21
State Forest & Park Service			
580 Taylor Ave ... Annapolis MD 21401	**877-620-8367**		338-21
State Lottery			
1800 Washington Blvd Ste 330 ... Baltimore MD 21230	**800-201-0108**	410-230-8800	450
State Police			
1201 Reisterstown Rd ... Pikesville MD 21208	**800-525-5555**	410-653-4200	338-21
Teacher Certification & Accreditation Div			
200 W Baltimore St ... Baltimore MD 21201	**888-246-0016**	410-767-0412	338-21
Tourism Development Office			
401 E Pratt Str 14th Fl ... Baltimore MD 21202	**877-333-4455**	410-767-3400	338-21
Treasurer			
80 Calvert St Rm 109 ... Annapolis MD 21401	**800-974-0468**	410-260-7533	338-21
Vital Records Div			
6764-B Reisterstown Rd ... Baltimore MD 21215	**800-832-3277**	410-764-3038	338-21
Workers' Compensation Commission			
10 E Baltimore St ... Baltimore MD 21202	**800-492-0479**	410-864-5100	338-21
Maryland & Virginia Milk Producers Co-op Assn Inc			
1985 Isaac Newton Sq W ... Reston VA 20190	**800-552-1976**	703-742-6800	297-4
Maryland Assn of Realtors			
2594 Riva Rd ... Annapolis MD 21401	**800-638-6425**		652
Maryland Bar Journal			
520 W Fayette St ... Baltimore MD 21201	**800-492-1964**	410-685-7878	455-15
Maryland Cork Co Inc			
505 Blue Ball Rd Ste 190 ... Elkton MD 21921	**800-662-2675**	410-398-2955	209
Maryland Correctional Enterprises (MCE)			
7275 Waterloo Rd ... Jessup MD 20794	**800-735-2258**	410-540-5454	626
Maryland Correctional Training Center			
18800Roxbury Rd ... Hagerstown MD 21746	**877-692-8136**	240-420-1601	
Maryland Hall for the Creative Arts			
801 Chase St ... Annapolis MD 21401	**866-438-3808**	410-263-5544	568
Maryland Inn			
58 State Cir ... Annapolis MD 21401	**800-847-8882**	410-263-2641	378
Maryland Match Corp			
605 Alluvion St ... Baltimore MD 21230	**800-423-0013**	410-752-8164	467
Maryland Municipal League			
1212 W St ... Annapolis MD 21401	**800-492-7121**	410-295-9100	529
Maryland Plastics Inc			
251 E Central Ave ... Federalsburg MD 21632	**800-544-5582***	410-754-5566	603
*Cust Svc			
Maryland Public Television (MPT)			
11767 Owings Mills Blvd ... Owings Mills MD 21117	**800-223-3678**	410-581-4201	628
Maryland Renaissance Festival			
PO Box 315 ... Crownsville MD 21032	**800-296-7304**	410-266-7304	149
Maryland State Bar Assn Inc			
520 W Fayette St ... Baltimore MD 21201	**800-492-1964**	410-685-7878	72
Maryland State Dental Assn			
8901 Herrmann Dr ... Columbia MD 21045	**800-621-8099**	410-964-2880	227
Maryland State Medical Society			
1211 Cathedral St ... Baltimore MD 21201	**800-492-1056**	410-539-0872	472
Marylhurst University			
17600 Pacific Hwy 43			
PO Box 261 ... Marylhurst OR 97036	**800-634-9982**	503-636-8141	166
Marymount Hospital			
12300 McCracken Rd ... Garfield Heights OH 44125	**800-801-2273**	216-581-0500	373-3
Marymount University			
2807 N Glebe Rd ... Arlington VA 22207	**800-548-7638**	703-522-5600	166
Maryville College			
502 E Lamar Alexander Pkwy ... Maryville TN 37804	**800-597-2687**	865-981-8000	166
MAS Capital Inc			
2715 Coney Island Ave ... Brooklyn NY 11235	**866-553-7493**		687
Masco Cabinetry LLC			
5353 W US 223 ... Adrian MI 49221	**866-850-8557**	517-263-0771	115
Masergy			
2740 N Dallas Pkwy ... Plano TX 75093	**866-588-5885**		224
Masimo Corp 40 Parker ... Irvine CA 92618	**800-326-4890**	949-297-7000	250
Masland Carpets Inc			
716 Bill Myles Dr ... Saraland AL 36571	**800-633-0468**		131
Mason City Convention & Visitors Bureau			
2021 Fourth St SW Hwy 122 W ... Mason City IA 50401	**800-423-5724**	641-422-1663	206
Mason City Public Library			
225 Second St SE ... Mason City IA 50401	**800-532-1531**	641-421-3668	433-3
Mason Contractors Assn of America (MCCA) (MCAA)			
1481 Merchant Dr ... Algonquin IL 60102	**800-536-2225**	224-678-9709	49-3
Mason Corp			
123 W Oxmoor Rd ... Birmingham AL 35209	**800-868-4100**	205-942-4100	478
Mason County Garbage & Recycling			
81 E Wilburs Way PO Box 787 ... Shelton WA 98584	**877-722-0223**	360-426-8729	
Mason Structural Steel Inc			
7500 Northfield Rd ... Walton Hills OH 44146	**800-686-1223**	440-439-1040	361
Masonic Service Assn of North America (MSANA)			
8120 Fenton St Ste 203 ... Silver Spring MD 20910	**855-476-4010**	301-588-4010	48-15
Masonite International Corp			
201 N Franklin St Ste 300 ... Tampa FL 33602	**800-895-2723**	813-877-2726	236
Maspeth Federal Savings			
56-18 69th St ... Maspeth NY 11378	**888-558-1300**	718-335-1300	70
Mass Bay Transportation Authority (MBTA)			
10 Park Plz Ste 5610 ... Boston MA 02116	**800-392-6100**	617-222-3200	
Massa Products Corp			
280 Lincoln St ... Hingham MA 02043	**800-962-7543**	781-749-4800	664
Massachusetts			
Banks Div			
1000 Washington St 1st Fl ... Boston MA 02118	**800-495-2265**	617-956-1500	338-22
Child Support Enforcement Div			
51 Sleeper St 4th Fl ... Boston MA 02205	**800-332-2733**	617-660-1234	338-22

	Toll-Free	Phone	Class
Cultural Council			
10 St James Ave 3rd Fl ... Boston MA 02116	**800-232-0960**	617-858-2700	338-22
Governor			
24 Beacon St State House Rm 280 ... Boston MA 02133	**888-870-7770**	617-725-4005	338-22
Housing Finance Agency			
1 Beacon St ... Boston MA 02108	**800-882-1154**	617-854-1000	338-22
Insurance Div			
1000 Washington St Ste 810 ... Boston MA 02118	**877-563-4467**	617-521-7794	338-22
Medical Examiner			
720 Albany St ... Boston MA 02118	**800-962-7877**	617-267-6767	338-22
Mental Health Dept			
25 Staniford St ... Boston MA 02114	**800-221-0053**	617-626-8000	338-22
Parole Board			
12 Mercer Rd ... Natick MA 01760	**888-298-6272**	508-650-4500	338-22
Revenue Dept			
PO Box 7010 ... Boston MA 02204	**800-392-6089**	617-887-6367	338-22
Securities Div			
1 Ashburton Pl 17th Fl ... Boston MA 02108	**800-269-5428**	617-727-3548	338-22
Travel & Tourism Office			
136 Blackstone St 5th Fl ... Boston MA 02109	**800-227-6277**	617-973-8500	338-22
Massachusetts Assn of Realtors			
256 Second Ave ... Waltham MA 02451	**800-725-6272**	781-890-3700	652
Massachusetts Bay Community College			
Wellesley Hills			
50 Oakland St ... Wellesley Hills MA 02481	**800-233-3182**	781-239-3000	162
Massachusetts Board of Library Commissioners			
98 N Washington St ... Boston MA 02114	**800-952-7403**	617-725-1860	433-5
Massachusetts College of Art			
621 Huntington Ave ... Boston MA 02115	**800-834-3242**	617-879-7222	166
Massachusetts College of Pharmacy & Health Sciences			
179 Longwood Ave ... Boston MA 02115	**800-225-5506**	617-732-2850	166
Massachusetts Correctional Industries			
1 Industries Dr Bldg A			
PO Box 188 ... Norfolk MA 02056	**800-222-2211**	508-850-1070	626
Massachusetts Dental Society			
2 Willow St ... Southborough MA 01745	**800-342-8747**		227
Massachusetts Eye & Ear			
243 Charles St ... Boston MA 02114	**800-841-2900**	617-523-7900	373-7
Massachusetts Maritime Academy			
101 Academy Dr ... Buzzards Bay MA 02532	**800-544-3411***	508-830-5000	166
*Admissions			
Massachusetts Medical Society (MMS)			
860 Winter St ... Waltham MA 02451	**800-322-2303**	781-893-4610	472
Massachusetts Mutual Life Insurance Co			
100 Bright Meadow Blvd ... Enfield CT 06082	**800-272-2216**		
Massachusetts Nurses Assn (MNA)			
340 Tpke St ... Canton MA 02021	**800-882-2056**	781-821-4625	529
Massachusetts Society of Certified Public Accountants			
105 Chauncy St 10th Fl ... Boston MA 02111	**800-392-6145**	617-556-4000	2
Massanutten Military Academy			
614 S Main St ... Woodstock VA 22664	**877-466-6222**	540-459-2167	618
Massasoit Community College			
1 Massasoit Blvd ... Brockton MA 02302	**800-434-6000**	508-588-9100	162
massAV			
3 Radcliff Rd ... Tewksbury MA 01876	**800-423-7830**		232
Massey Cancer Ctr			
Virginia Commonwealth University			
401 College St PO Box 980037 ... Richmond VA 23298	**877-462-7739**	804-828-0450	664
Massey Services Inc			
315 Groveland St E ... Orlando FL 32804	**888-262-7739**	407-645-2500	573
Mast General Store Inc			
Hwy 194 ... Valle Crucis NC 28691	**866-367-6278**	828-963-6511	206
MasTec Inc			
800 Douglas Rd 12th Fl ... Coral Gables FL 33134	**800-531-5000**	305-599-1800	188-1
NYSE: MTZ			
Master Appliance Corp			
2420 18th St ... Racine WI 53403	**800-558-9413**	262-633-7791	754
Master Cutlery Inc			
700 Penhorn Ave ... Secaucus NJ 07094	**888-271-7229**		222
Master Finish Co			
2020 Nelson SE ... Grand Rapids MI 49510	**877-590-5819**	616-245-1228	479
Master Halco Inc			
3010 Lyndon B Johnson Fwy			
Ste 800 ... Dallas TX 75234	**800-883-8384**	972-714-7300	279
Master Industries Inc			
1001 S Linwood Ave ... Santa Ana CA 92705	**800-854-3794**	714-361-9767	
Master Lock Company LLC			
6744 S Howell Ave PO Box 927 ... Oak Creek WI 53154	**800-464-2088**		349
Master Package Corp, The			
200 Madson St ... Owen WI 54460	**800-396-8425**	715-229-2156	125
Master Spas Inc			
6927 Lincoln Pkwy ... Fort Wayne IN 46804	**800-860-7727**	260-436-9100	374
MASTER Teacher Inc, The			
2600 Leadership Ln ... Manhattan KS 66505	**800-669-9633**		524
Master's College			
21726 Placerita Canyon Rd			
... Santa Clarita CA 91321	**800-568-6248**	661-259-3540	166
Master-Bilt Products			
908 Hwy 15 N ... New Albany MS 38652	**800-647-1284**	662-534-9061	14
MasterCard Inc			
2000 Purchase St ... Purchase NY 10577	**800-100-1087**	914-249-2000	215
NYSE: MA			
Masterchem Industries LLC			
3135 Old Hwy M ... Imperial MO 63052	**866-774-6371**		546
MasterCraft Boat Co			
100 Cherokee Cove Dr ... Vonore TN 37885	**800-443-8774**	845-676-7876	90
Mastercraft Industries Inc			
777 South St ... Newburgh NY 12550	**800-835-7812**	845-565-8850	115
Masterfile Corp			
3 Concorde Gate 4th Fl ... Toronto ON M3C3N7	**800-387-9010**	416-929-3000	585
MasterGraphics Inc			
2979 Triverton Pike Dr ... Madison WI 53711	**800-873-7238**	608-256-4884	174
Masterman's LLP			
11 C St ... Auburn MA 01501	**800-525-3313**		45
Mastermind LP			
2134 Queen St E ... Toronto ON M4E1E3	**888-388-0000**	416-699-3797	95
Masters Advisors Inc			
480 New Holland Ave Ste 7201 ... Lancaster PA 17602	**800-571-1323**	717-581-1323	461

Name	Toll-Free	Phone	Class
Masters Gallery Foods Inc 328 County Hwy PP PO Box 170 ....Plymouth WI 53073 *General	800-236-8431*	920-893-8431	297-4
Masters Gallery Ltd 2115 Fourth St SW ....Calgary AB T2S1W8	866-245-0616	403-245-2064	42
Masters' Supply Inc 4505 Bishop Ln ....Louisville KY 40218	800-388-6353		608
Matanuska Telephone Assn Inc 1740 S Chugach St ....Palmer AK 99645	800-478-3211	907-745-3211	731
Match Eyewear LLC 1600 Shames Dr ....Westbury NY 11590	877-886-2824		
MatchCraft Inc 2701 Ocean Park Blvd Ste 220 ....Santa Monica CA 90405	888-502-7238	310-314-3320	7
Matco Tools 4403 Allen Rd ....Stow OH 44224	866-289-8665	330-926-5332	753
Matco-Norca Inc 1944 Rt 22 PO Box 27 ....Brewster NY 10509	800-431-2082	845-278-7570	606
Mate Precision Tooling Inc 1295 Lund Blvd ....Anoka MN 55303	800-328-4492	763-421-0230	752
Material Handling Industry of America (MHIA) 8720 Red Oak Blvd Ste 201 ....Charlotte NC 28217	800-345-1815	704-676-1190	49-13
Materials Transportation Co (MTC) 1408 S Commerce PO Box 1358 ....Temple TX 76503	800-433-3110	254-298-2900	385
Materion Corp 6070 Parkland Blvd ....Mayfield Heights OH 44124 NYSE: MTRN	800-321-2076	216-486-4200	500
Math Teachers Press Inc 4850 Park Glen Rd ....St Louis Park MN 55416	800-852-2435		
Mathematical Assn of America (MAA) 1529 18th St NW ....Washington DC 20036	800-331-1622	202-387-5200	49-19
Matheson Trucking Inc 9785 Goethe Rd ....Sacramento CA 95827	800-455-7678		775
Matheus Lumber 15800 Woodinville-Redmond Rd NE ....Woodinville WA 98072	800-284-7501	425-489-3000	191-3
Mathews Assoc Inc 220 Power Ct ....Sanford FL 32771	800-871-5262	407-323-3390	74
Mathews Bros Co 22 Perkins Rd ....Belfast ME 04915	800-615-2004	207-338-6490	236
Mathews Co 500 Industrial Ave ....Crystal Lake IL 60012	800-323-7045	815-459-2210	273
Mathias Ham House Historic Site 350 E Third St ....Dubuque IA 52001	800-226-3369	563-557-9545	50-3
Mathis Bros Furniture Inc 6611 S 101st East Ave ....Tulsa OK 74133 *Cust Svc	800-329-3434*	855-294-3434	321
Mathnasium LLC 5120 W Goldleaf Cir Ste 300 ....Los Angeles CA 90056	877-601-6284	323-421-8000	310
Matich Corp 1596 Harry Sheppard Blvd ....San Bernardino CA 92408	800-404-4975	909-382-7400	188-4
Matik Inc 33 Brook St ....West Hartford CT 06110	800-245-1628	860-232-2323	531
Matot Inc 2501 Van Buren St ....Bellwood IL 60104	800-369-1070	708-547-1888	256
Matrix Companies, The 7162 Reading Rd Ste 250 ....Cincinnati OH 45237	877-550-7973	513-351-1222	392
Matrix Energy Services Inc 3221 Ramos Cir ....Sacramento CA 95827	800-556-2123	916-363-9283	256
Matrix Hotel 10640-100 Ave ....Edmonton AB T5J3N8	866-465-8150	780-429-2861	378
Matrix Service Co 5100 E Skelly Dr 74135 ....Tulsa OK 74135 NASDAQ: MTRX	866-367-6879		535
Matrix Systems Inc 1041 Byers Rd ....Miamisburg OH 45342	800-562-8749	937-438-9033	688
Matrox Electronic Systems Ltd 1055 St Regis Blvd ....Dorval QC H9P2T4	800-361-1408	514-822-6000	173-5
Matson & Cuprill 100 E-Business Way Ste 160 ....Cincinnati OH 45249	800-944-8596	513-563-7526	
Matson Logistics Inc 555 12th St ....Oakland CA 94607	800-762-8766	510-628-4000	447
Matson Navigation Co 555 12th St ....Oakland CA 94607 *Cust Svc	800-462-8766*	510-628-4000	312
Matsui International Company Inc 1501 W 178th St ....Gardena CA 90248	800-359-5679	310-767-7812	387
Matsui Nursery Inc 1645 Old Stage Rd ....Salinas CA 93908	800-793-6433	831-422-6433	368
Matt Blatt Inc 501 Delsea Dr N ....Glassboro NJ 08028	877-462-5288	856-881-0005	57
Matt Castrucci Auto Mall of Dayton 3013 Mall Pk Dr ....Dayton OH 45459	855-204-5293		513
Mattel Inc 333 Continental Blvd ....El Segundo CA 90245 NASDAQ: MAT	800-524-8697	310-252-2000	757
Mattersight Corp 200 W Madison St Ste 3100 ....Chicago IL 60606	877-235-6925		461
Matthaei Botanical Gardens 1800 N Dixboro Rd ....Ann Arbor MI 48105	800-666-8693	734-647-7600	97
Matthews Book Co 11559 Rock Island Ct ....Maryland Heights MO 63043	800-633-2665	314-432-1400	95
Matthews Currie Ford Company Inc 130 N Tamiami Trl ....Nokomis FL 34275	855-491-3131	800-248-2378	57
Matthews International Corp Marking Products Div 6515 Penn Ave ....Pittsburgh PA 15206	800-775-7775	412-665-2500	465
Matthews Pierce & Lloyd Inc 830 Walker Rd Ste 12 ....Dover DE 19904	800-267-4026	302-678-5500	160
Matthews Studio Equipment Group 2405 W Empire Ave ....Burbank CA 91504	800-237-8263	818-843-6715	587
Matthijssen Inc 14 Rt 10 ....East Hanover NJ 07936	800-845-2200		175
Mattracks Inc 202 Cleveland Ave E ....Karlstad MN 56732	877-436-7800	218-436-7000	369
Mattress Firm Inc 5815 Gulf Fwy ....Houston TX 77023	800-821-6621	713-923-1090	361
Mattson Spray Equipment 230 W Coleman St ....Rice Lake WI 54868	800-877-4857	715-234-1617	172
Maui County 200 S High St ....Wailuku HI 96793	800-272-0117	808-270-7748	337
Maui Divers of Hawaii 1520 Liona St ....Honolulu HI 96814	800-462-4454	808-946-7979	408
Maui Jim Inc 721 Wainee St ....Lahaina HI 96761	888-352-2001	808-661-8841	538
Mauldin & Jenkins CPA's LLC 200 Galleria Pkwy SE ....Atlanta GA 30339	800-277-0080	770-955-8600	2
Maumee Bay Lodge & Conference Ctr 1750 Pk Rd Ste 2 ....Oregon OH 43616	800-282-7275	419-836-1466	378
Mauna Kea Beach Hotel 62-100 Maunakea Beach Dr ....Kohala Coast HI 96743	866-977-4589	808-882-7222	665
Mauna Lani Bay Hotel & Bungalows 68-1400 Mauna Lani Dr ....Kohala Coast HI 96743	800-367-2323	808-885-6622	665
Mauna Loa Macadamia Nut Corp 16-701 Macadamia Rd ....Keaau HI 96749 *Cust Svc	888-628-6256*	808-966-8618	10-8
Maupintour Inc 2690 Weston Rd Ste 200 ....Weston FL 33331	800-255-4266	954-653-3820	755
Maurey Manufacturing Corp 410 Industrial Pk Rd ....Holly Springs MS 38635	800-284-2161		616
Maurice Electrical Supply Co 6500A Seriff Rd ....Landover MD 20785	866-913-0922	301-333-5990	
Maurice's Gourmet Barbeque PO Box 6847 ....West Columbia SC 29171	800-628-7423	803-791-5887	296-19
Maurices Inc 105 W Superior St ....Duluth MN 55802	866-977-1542	218-727-8431	157-4
Mauritzon Inc 3939 W Belden Ave ....Chicago IL 60647	800-621-4352	773-235-6000	728
Maven Group LLC, The 320 N Salem St Ste 204 ....Apex NC 27502	800-343-6612	919-386-1010	260
MavenWire LLC 630 Freedom Business Ctr 3rd Fl ....King Of Prussia PA 19406	866-343-4870		461
Maverick Technologies 265 Admiral Trost Dr ....Columbia IL 62236	888-917-9109	618-281-9100	178-1
Maverick USA Inc 13301 Valentine Rd ....North Little Rock AR 72117	800-289-6600		775
Maverik Inc 880 W Center St ....North Salt Lake UT 84054 *Cust Svc	800-789-4455*	801-936-5573	204
Mawer Investment Management Ltd 517 - Tenth Ave S W Ste 600 ....Calgary AB T2R0A8	800-889-6248		524
MAWS (Marijuana Anonymous World Services) PO Box 7807 ....Torrance CA 90504	800-766-6779		48-21
Max Credit Union 400 Eastdale Cir ....Montgomery AL 36117	800-776-6776	334-260-2600	70
Max Environmental Technologies Inc 1815 Washington Rd ....Pittsburgh PA 15241	800-851-7845	412-343-4900	196
Max International Converters Inc 2360 Dairy Rd ....Lancaster PA 17601	800-233-0222		550
Max Levy Autograph Inc 2710 Commerce Way ....Philadelphia PA 19154	800-798-3675		479
Max Technical Training 4900 Pkwy Dr Ste 160 ....Mason OH 45040	866-595-6863	513-322-8888	196
MAX Technologies Inc 2051 Victoria Ave ....Saint-Lambert QC J4S1H1	800-361-1629	450-443-3332	664
Max Tool Inc 119b Citation Ct ....Birmingham AL 35209	800-783-6298	205-942-2466	350
Maxell Corp of America 3 Garret Mountain Plz 3rd Fl Ste 300 ....Woodland Park NJ 07424	800-533-2836	973-653-2400	
Maxim Crane Works 1225 Washington Pk ....Bridgeville PA 15017	877-629-5438	412-504-0200	264-3
Maxim Group LLC 405 Lexington Ave ....New York NY 10174	800-724-0761	212-895-3500	400
Maxim Integrated Products Inc 120 San Gabriel Dr ....Sunnyvale CA 94086 NASDAQ: MXIM	888-629-4642	408-737-7600	692
Maxim Technologies Inc 1607 Derwent Way ....Delta BC V3M6K8	800-663-9925		151
Maxima Technologies Stewart Warner 1811 Rohrerstown Rd ....Lancaster PA 17601	800-676-1837	717-581-1000	493
Maximizer Software Inc 1090 W Pender St 10th Fl ....Vancouver BC V6E2N7	800-804-6299	604-601-8000	180
MaxLinear Inc 2051 Palomar Airport Rd Ste 100 ....Carlsbad CA 92011 NYSE: MXL	888-505-4369	760-692-0711	691
Maxon Furniture Inc 200 Oak St ....Muscatine IA 52761	800-876-4274		319-1
Maxon Industries Inc 11921 Slauson Ave ....Santa Fe Springs CA 90670	800-227-4116	562-464-0099	468
Maxor National Pharmacy Services Corp 320 S Polk St Ste 100 ....Amarillo TX 79101	800-658-6146	806-324-5400	582
Maxsys 173 Dalhousie St ....Ottawa ON K1N7C7	800-429-5177	613-562-9943	260
Maxtec 2305 South 1070 West ....Salt Lake City UT 84119	800-748-5355	801-266-5300	474
Maxtex Inc 3620 Francis Cir ....Alpharetta GA 30004	800-241-1836	770-772-6757	360
MaxTool 5798 Ontario Mills Pkwy ....Ontario CA 91764	800-629-3325	909-568-2800	350
MaxVision Corp 495 Production Ave ....Madison AL 35758	800-533-5805	256-772-3058	173-2
Maxwell Air Force Base 55 Le May Plaza S ....Maxwell AFB AL 36112	877-353-6807	334-953-2014	495-1
Maxwell Noll 600 S Lake Ave ....Pasadena CA 91106	800-660-2466		
Maxwell Technologies Inc 5271 Viewridge Ct Ste 100 ....San Diego CA 92123 NASDAQ: MXWL	877-511-4324	858-503-3300	253
Maxxam 335 LaiRd Rd Unit 2 ....Guelph ON N1G4P7	877-706-7678		416
MaxYield Co-op 313 Third Ave NE PO Box 49 ....West Bend IA 50597	800-383-0003	515-887-7211	275
May Institute Inc 41 Pacella Pk Dr ....Randolph MA 02368	800-778-7601	781-440-0400	48-6

	Toll-Free	Phone	Class

May Supply Company Inc
1775 Erickson Ave ....Harrisonburg VA 22801　800-296-9997　540-433-2611　608

May Trucking Co
4185 Brooklake Rd ....Salem OR 97303　800-547-9169　503-393-7030　775

May, Adam, Gerdes & Thompson LLP
503 S Pierre St ....Pierre SD 57501　800-636-8803　605-224-8803　427

Maybelline New York
575 Fifth Ave PO Box 1010............New York NY 10017　800-944-0730　　214

Mayberry Fine Art Inc
212 Mcdermot Ave ....Winnipeg MB R3B0S3　877-871-9261　204-255-5690　42

Mayco Industries LLC
18 W Oxmoor Rd ....Birmingham AL 35209　800-749-6061　205-942-4242　693

Mayer Bros Apple Products Inc
3300 Transit Rd ....West Seneca NY 14224　800-696-2928　716-668-1787　296-20

Mayer Electric Supply Co
3405 Fourth Ave S ....Birmingham AL 35222　866-637-1255　205-583-3500　246

Mayesh Wholesale Florist Inc
5401 W 104th St ....Los Angeles CA 90045　888-462-9374　310-348-4921　292

Mayfair Hotel & Spa
3000 Florida Ave ....Coconut Grove FL 33133　800-433-4555　305-441-0000　378

Mayfield Paper Co
1115 S Hill St ....San Angelo TX 76903　800-725-1441　325-653-1444　555

Mayfield Transfer Company Inc
3200 West Lake St ....Melrose Park IL 60160　800-222-2959　708-681-4440　775

Mayflower Park Hotel
405 Olive Way ....Seattle WA 98101　800-426-5100　206-623-8700　378

Mayflower Retirement Community
1620 Mayflower Ct ....Winter Park FL 32792　800-228-6518　407-672-1620　668

Mayflower Tours Inc
1225 Warren Ave
PO Box 490. ....Downers Grove IL 60515　800-323-7604　630-435-8500　755

Mayflower Transit LLC
1 Mayflower Dr ....Fenton MO 63026　800-325-9970　636-305-4000　516

Mayhew Steel Products Inc
199 Industrial Blvd ....Turners Falls MA 01376　800-872-0037　413-863-4860　753

Mayland Community College
200 Mayland Dr PO Box 547 ....Spruce Pine NC 28777　800-462-9526　828-765-7351　162

Mayline Group
619 N Commerce St PO Box 728 ......Sheboygan WI 53082　800-822-8037　920-457-5537　319-1

Mayo Aviation Inc
7735 S Peoria St ....Englewood CO 80112　800-525-0194　303-792-4020　13

Mayo Civic Ctr
30 Civic Ctr Dr SE ....Rochester MN 55904　800-422-2199　507-328-2220　205

Mayo Clinic
4500 San Pablo Rd ....Jacksonville FL 32224　888-255-4458　904-992-9992　378

Mayo Clinic Health Letter
200 First St NW ....Rochester MN 55905　800-291-1128　　527-8

Mayo Clinic Health System Austin
1000 First Dr NW ....Austin MN 55912　888-609-4065　507-433-7351　373-3

Mayo Clinic Health System Southwest Minnesota
1025 Marsh St ....Mankato MN 56001　800-327-3721　507-625-4031　373-3

Mayo Clinic Hospital
5777 E Mayo Blvd ....Phoenix AZ 85054　888-266-0440　480-342-2000　373-3

Mayo Clinic Proceedings Magazine
Siebens Bldg 770 ....Rochester MN 55905　800-654-2452*　507-284-2094　455-16
*Cust Svc

Mayo Collaborative Services Inc
3050 Superior Dr NW ....Rochester MN 55901　800-533-1710　507-266-5700　414

Maytag Appliances
403 W Fourth St N ....Newton IA 50208　800-344-1274*　　36
*Cust Svc

Mayville State University
330 Third St NE ....Mayville ND 58257　800-437-4104　　166

Mazda North American Operations
7755 Irvine Center Dr
PO Box 19734. ....Irvine CA 92623　800-222-5500*　949-727-1990　59
*Cust Svc

Mazel & Company Inc
4300 W Ferdinand St ....Chicago IL 60624　800-525-4023　773-533-1600　490

Mazon Assoc Inc
800 W Airport Fwy Ste 900..........Irving TX 75062　800-442-2740　972-554-6967　272

Mazza Vineyards
11815 E Lake Rd ....North East PA 16428　800-796-9463　　50-7

Mazzella Lifting Technologies
21000 Aerospace Pkwy ....Cleveland OH 44142　800-362-4601　440-239-7000　468

Mb Bark LLC
100 Bark Mulch Dr ....Auburn ME 04210　800-866-4991

MB Financial Inc
6111 N River Rd ....Rosemont IL 60018　888-422-6562　　359-2
NASDAQ: MBFI

MB Trading Futures Inc
1926 E Maple Ave ....El Segundo CA 90245　866-628-3001　310-647-4281

MBA (Military Benefit Assn)
14605 Avion Pkwy
PO Box 221110. ....Chantilly VA 20153　800-336-0100　703-968-6200　48-19

MBA (Mortgage Bankers Assn)
1919 M St NW 5th Fl ....Washington DC 20036　800-793-6222　202-557-2700　49-2

MBAF
1450 Brickell Ave 18th Fl ....Miami FL 33131　800-239-3843　305-373-5500　2

MBC (Memorial Blood Centers)
737 Pelham Blvd ....Saint Paul MN 55114　888-448-3253*　　89
*Cust Svc

MBC (Medical Billing Concepts Inc)
16001 Ventura Blvd Ste 135.............Encino CA 91436　866-351-2852

MBDA (Minority Business Development Agency)
1401 Constitution Ave NW ....Washington DC 20230　888-324-1551　　339-2
San Francisco Region
1401 Constitution Ave ....Washington DC 20230　888-889-0538　202-482-2000　339-2

MBI Direct Mail
710 W New Hampshire Ave ....Deland FL 32720　800-359-4780　386-736-9998　7

MBL International Corp
4 H Constitution Way ....Woburn MA 01801　800-200-5459　　194

MBM (MBM Corp)
3134 Industry Dr ....North Charleston SC 29418　800-223-2508*　843-552-2700　111
*Cust Svc

MBM Corp (MBM)
3134 Industry Dr ....North Charleston SC 29418　800-223-2508*　843-552-2700　111
*Cust Svc

MBNA (Monument Builders of North America)
136 S Keowee St ....Dayton OH 45402　800-233-4472　　49-3

MBP (McDonough Bolyard Peck Inc)
3040 Williams Dr Williams Plz 1
Ste 300. ....Fairfax VA 22031　800-898-9088　703-641-9088　261

MBS Assoc Inc
7800 E Kemper Rd Ste 160...........Cincinnati OH 45249　888-469-9301　513-645-1600　261

MBS Textbook Exchange Inc
2711 W Ash St ....Columbia MO 65203　800-325-0530*　573-445-2243　96
*Cust Svc

MBT Financial Corp
102 E Front St ....Monroe MI 48161　800-321-0032　734-241-3431　359-2
NASDAQ: MBTF

MBTA (Mass Bay Transportation Authority)
10 Park Plz Ste 5610 ....Boston MA 02116　800-392-6100　617-222-3200

MBTC (Mifflinburg Bank & Trust Co)
250 E Chestnut St
PO Box 186. ....Mifflinburg PA 17844　888-966-3131　570-966-1041　70

MC & A Inc
615 Piikoi St Ste 1000 ....Honolulu HI 96814　877-589-5589*　808-589-5500　766
*General

Mc Glaughlin Oil Co, The
3750 E Livingston Ave ....Columbus OH 43227　800-839-6589　614-231-2518　575

MC Sign Company Inc
8959 Tyler Blvd ....Mentor OH 44060　800-627-4460　440-209-6200　697

MCA (Marine Corps Assn)
PO Box 1775 ....Quantico VA 22134　800-336-0291　703-640-6161　48-19

MCAA (Mason Contractors Assn of America (MCCA))
1481 Merchant Dr ....Algonquin IL 60102　800-536-2225　224-678-9709　49-3

MCAA (Mechanical Contractors Assn of America)
1385 Piccard Dr ....Rockville MD 20850　800-556-3653　301-869-5800　49-3

mcaConnect LLC
8055 E Tufts Ave Ste 1300 ....Denver CO 80237　866-662-0669　　196

McAfee & Taft A Professional Corp
211 N Robinson ....Oklahoma City OK 73102　800-235-9621　405-235-9621　427

McAfee Inc
2821 Mission College Blvd ....Santa Clara CA 95054　888-847-8766*　408-988-3832　178-12
*Cust Svc

McAllen Chamber of Commerce
1200 Ash Ave ....McAllen TX 78501　800-786-9199　956-682-2871　139

McAllister Towing & Transportation Co Inc
17 Battery Pl Ste 1200 ....New York NY 10004　888-764-5980　212-269-3200　463

MCAP Financial Corp
1140 W Pender St ....Vancouver BC V6E4G1　800-977-5877　604-681-8805　217

MCAP Service Corp
400-200 King St W ....Toronto ON M5H3T4　800-387-4405　416-598-2665　648

McBee Assoc Inc
997 Old Eagle School Rd ....Wayne PA 19087　800-767-6203　610-964-9680　194

MCC (Mennonite Central Committee)
21 S 12th St PO Box 500 ....Akron PA 17501　888-563-4676　717-859-1151　48-5

McCabe Software Inc
3300 N Ridge Rd ....Ellicott City MD 21043　800-638-6316　410-381-3710　178-12

McCain Foods Ltd
181 Bay St Ste 3600 ....Toronto ON M5J2T3　800-938-7799　416-955-1700　296-21

McCain Foods USA Inc
2275 Cabot Dr ....Lisle IL 60532　800-938-7799　630-955-0400　296-21

McCall Aviation
300 Deinhard Ln ....McCall ID 83638　800-992-6559　208-634-7137　63

McCall Handling Co
8801 Wise Ave ....Dundalk MD 21222　888-870-0685　410-388-2600　384

McCall Oil & Chemical Corp
5480 NW Front Ave ....Portland OR 97210　800-622-2558　503-221-6400　575

McCall Patterns Magazine
120 Broadway ....New York NY 10271　800-782-0323　　455-14

McCall Service Inc
2861 College St ....Jacksonville FL 32205　800-342-6948　904-389-5561　573

McCall's Quilting
741 Corporate Cir Ste A ....Golden CO 80401　800-944-0736　303-215-5600　455-14

McCallie School
500 Dodds Ave ....Chattanooga TN 37404　800-234-2163　423-624-8300　618

McCallum Theatre
73000 Fred Waring Dr ....Palm Desert CA 92260　866-889-2787　760-340-2787　568

Mccallum, Hoaglund, Cook & Irby LLP
905 Montgomery Hwy Ste 201 ....Vestavia AL 35216　866-974-8145　205-824-7767　427

McCamly Plaza Hotel
50 Capital Ave SW ....Battle Creek MI 49017　800-337-0300　269-963-7050　378

McClancy Seasoning Co
1 Spice Rd ....Fort Mill SC 29707　800-843-1968　803-548-2366　344

McClard's Bar-B-Q
505 Albert Pike Rd ....Hot Springs AR 71901　866-622-5273　501-623-9665　667

McClarin Plastics Inc
15 Industrial Dr ....Hanover PA 17331　800-233-3189　717-637-2241　602

McClatchy Newspapers
2100 Q St ....Sacramento CA 95816　866-807-2200　916-321-1000　633-8

McClelland Oilfield Rentals Ltd
8720-110 St ....Grande Prairie AB T8V8K1　866-539-3656　780-539-3656　536

McClure Co
4101 N Sixth St ....Harrisburg PA 17110　800-382-1319　717-232-9743　189-10

McCollister's Transportation Group Inc
1800 Rt 130 N ....Burlington NJ 08016　800-257-9595　609-386-0600　516

McCone Electric Co-op Inc
110 Main St ....Circle MT 59215　800-684-3605　406-485-3430　245

McConkey
1615 Puyallup St PO Box 1690 ....Sumner WA 98390　800-426-8124　253-863-8111　199

McCook Community College
1205 E Third St ....McCook NE 69001　800-658-4348　308-345-8100　162

McCook County
130 W Essex PO Box 504 ....Salem SD 57058　800-231-8346　605-425-2781　337

McCook Public Power District
1510 N Hwy 83 ....McCook NE 69001　800-658-4285　308-345-2500　245

McCormick & Company Inc McCormick Flavor Div
226 Schilling Cir ....Hunt Valley MD 21031　800-322-7742　　296-37

McCormick & Company Inc US Consumer Products Div
211 Schilling Cir ....Hunt Valley MD 21031　800-632-5847　　296-37

McCormick & Schmick's
200 S Tryon St ....Charlotte NC 28202　800-552-6379　704-377-0201　667

McCormick Ingredients
18 Loveton Cir ....Sparks MD 21152　800-632-5847　410-771-7301　296-37

Company / Address	City	State	ZIP	Toll-Free	Phone	Class
McCormick Theological Seminary 5460 S University Ave	Chicago	IL	60615	**800-228-4687**	773-947-6300	167-3
McCormick's Group LLC 216 W Campus Dr	Arlington Heights	IL	60004	**800-323-5201**	847-398-8680	
McCorvey Sheet Metal Works LP 8610 Wallisvile Rd	Houston	TX	77029	**800-580-7545**	713-672-7545	693
McCourt Label Co 20 Egbert Ln	Lewis Run	PA	16738	**800-458-2390**	814-362-3851	412
Mc-Coy-Mills 700 W Commonwealth *Sales	Fullerton	CA	92832	**888-434-3145***		513
McCracken County Public Library 555 Washington St	Paducah	KY	42003	**866-829-7532**	270-442-2510	433-3
McCranie, Sistrunk, Anzelmo, Hardy, McDaniel & Welch LLC 909 Poydras St Ste 1000	New Orleans	LA	70112	**800-977-8810**	504-831-0946	427
McCrea Equipment Company Inc 4463 Beech Rd	Temple Hills	MD	20748	**800-597-0091**		189-10
McCrometer Inc 3255 W Stetson Ave	Hemet	CA	92545	**800-220-2279**	951-652-6811	201
McCullough & Assoc 1746 NE Expy PO Box 29803	Atlanta	GA	30329	**800-969-1606**	404-325-1606	146
MCD Innovations 3303 N MCDonald St	Mckinney	TX	75071	**800-804-1757**	972-548-1850	497
McDaniel College 2 College Hill *Admissions	Westminster	MD	21157	**800-638-5005***	410-857-2230	166
McDaniel Motor Co 1111 Mt Vernon Ave	Marion	OH	43302	**877-362-0288**	740-389-2355	513
Mcdaniels Marketing Communications 11 Olt Ave	Pekin	IL	61554	**866-431-4230**	309-346-4230	195
McDantim Inc 750 Shepard Way	Helena	MT	59601	**888-735-5607**	406-442-5153	784
McDevitt Trucks Inc 1 Mack Ave	Manchester	NH	03108	**800-370-6225**		57
MCDI (Medical Care Development International) 8401 Colesville Rd Ste 425	Silver Spring	MD	20910	**800-427-7566**	301-562-1920	48-5
McDonald Carano LLP 2300 W Sahara Ave Ste 1200	Las Vegas	NV	89102	**800-872-3862**	702-873-4100	41
McDonald Partners LLC 1301 E Ninth St Ste 3700	Cleveland	OH	44114	**866-899-2997**	216-912-0567	
McDonald Publishing 567 Hanley Industrial Ct	Saint Louis	MO	63144	**800-722-8080**		243
McDonald Wholesale Co 2350 W Broadway St	Eugene	OR	97402	**877-722-5503**	541-345-8421	297-3
McDonald's Corp 1 McDonald's Plz *NYSE: MCD*	Oak Brook	IL	60523	**800-244-6227**	630-623-3000	666
McDonald's Restaurants of Canada Ltd PO Box 61023	Winnipeg	MB	R3M3X8	**888-424-4622**	416-443-1000	666
McDonough Bolyard Peck Inc (MBP) 3040 Williams Dr Williams Plz 1 Ste 300	Fairfax	VA	22031	**800-898-9088**	703-641-9088	261
McDowell County Tourism Development Authority 91 S Catawba Ave	Old Fort	NC	28762	**888-233-6111**	828-668-4282	206
MCE (Maryland Correctional Enterprises) 7275 Waterloo Rd	Jessup	MD	20794	**800-735-2258**	410-540-5454	626
MCE Technologies LLC 30 Hughes Ste 203	Irvine	CA	92618	**800-500-0622**	949-458-0800	95
McElroy Metal Inc 1500 Hamilton Rd	Bossier City	LA	71111	**800-562-3576**	318-747-8097	478
MCF Systems Atlanta Inc 4319 Tanners Church Rd	Ellenwood	GA	30294	**866-315-8116**		
McFarland & Company Inc 960 NC Hwy 88 W PO Box 611	Jefferson	NC	28640	**800-253-2187**	336-246-4460	633-2
McFarland Cascade 1640 E Marc St PO Box 1496 *Cust Svc	Tacoma	WA	98421	**800-426-8430***	253-572-3033	813
McFarlane Mfg Company Inc PO Box 100	Sauk City	WI	53583	**800-627-8569**	608-643-3321	276
McFarling Foods Inc 333 West 14th St	Indianapolis	IN	46202	**800-622-9003**		344
McGard LLC 3875 California Rd	Orchard Park	NY	14127	**800-444-5847**	716-662-8980	61
McGean-Rohco Inc 2910 Harvard Ave *Orders	Cleveland	OH	44105	**800-932-7006***	216-441-4900	145
McGee Company Inc 1140 S Jason St	Denver	CO	80223	**800-525-8888**		
MCGG (Morrow County Grain Growers Inc) 350 N Main St	Lexington	OR	97839	**800-452-7396**	541-989-8221	10-4
McGill Hose & Coupling Inc 41 Benton Dr PO Box 408	East Longmeadow	MA	01028	**800-669-1467**	413-525-3977	384
McGrath Auto 1548 Collins Rd NE	Cedar Rapids	IA	52402	**855-495-3118**		57
McGrath Ford Hyundai BMW 4001 First Ave SE	Cedar Rapids	IA	52402	**855-795-7289**	319-366-4000	57
McGraw-Hill Education 8787 Orion Pl	Columbus	OH	43240	**800-334-7344**		243
McGraw-Hill Higher Education Group 1333 Burr Ridge Pkwy	Burr Ridge	IL	60527	**800-634-3963**	630-789-4000	633-2
McGraw-Hill Professional Publishing Group 2 Penn Plz 9th Fl	New York	NY	10121	**877-833-5524**		633-2
McGriff Seibels & Williams Inc 2211 Seventh Ave S	Birmingham	AL	35233	**800-476-2211**	205-252-9871	389
McGuire W194 N11481 McCormick Dr PO Box 309	Germantown	WI	53022	**800-624-8473**	518-828-7652	468
McGuire Cadillac Inc 910 Rt 1 N	Woodbridge	NJ	07095	**866-552-4208**		513
McGuire Furniture Co 1201 Bryant St	San Francisco	CA	94103	**800-662-4847**	415-626-1414	319-2
McGuireWoods LLP Gateway Plz 800 E Canal St	Richmond	VA	23219	**877-712-8778**	804-775-1000	427
MCH Inc 601 E Marshall St	Sweet Springs	MO	65351	**800-776-6373**		
McHenry Area Chamber of Commerce 1257 N Green St	McHenry	IL	60050	**800-374-8373**	815-385-4300	139
McHenry County College 8900 US Hwy 14	Crystal Lake	IL	60012	**888-977-4847**	815-455-3700	162
McHenry Creative Services Inc 345 Main St	Harleysville	PA	19438	**877-627-0345**		
MCI Optonix LLC 2020 Contractors Rd Ste 8	Sedona	AZ	86336	**800-678-6649**		473
McIlhenny Co Hwy 329 *Orders	Avery Island	LA	70513	**800-634-9599***		296-19
McIntire Co 745 Clark Ave	Bristol	CT	06010	**800-437-9247**	860-585-0050	18
McIntosh County PO Box 584	Darien	GA	31305	**800-436-7442**		
McIntosh Laboratory Inc 2 Chambers St	Binghamton	NY	13903	**800-538-6576**	607-723-3512	52
McKay Nursery Company Inc 750 S Monroe St PO Box 185	Waterloo	WI	53594	**800-236-4242**	920-478-2121	323
McKean County 500 W Main St	Smethport	PA	16749	**800-482-1280**	814-887-5571	337
McKee Foods Corp PO Box 750 *Cust Svc	Collegedale	TN	37315	**800-522-4499***	423-238-7111	296-1
McKee Surfaces PO Box 230 *Cust Svc	Muscatine	IA	52761	**800-553-9662***	563-263-2421	590
McKee Wallwork Cleveland LLC 1030 18th St NW	Albuquerque	NM	87104	**888-821-2999**		
Mckeil Marine Ltd 208 Hillyard St	Hamilton	ON	L8L6B6	**800-454-4780**	905-528-4780	313
McKendree College 701 College Rd	Lebanon	IL	62254	**800-232-7228**	618-537-4481	166
Mckenna Distribution & Warehousing 1260 Lkshore Rd E	Mississauga	ON	L5E3B8	**800-561-4997**	905-274-1234	205
McKenna Pro Imaging 2815 Falls Ave *General	Waterloo	IA	50701	**800-238-3456***	319-235-6265	584
McKenney's Inc 1056 Moreland Industrial Blvd SE	Atlanta	GA	30316	**877-440-4204**	404-622-5000	189-10
McKenzie Electric Co-op Inc PO Box 649	Watford City	ND	58854	**800-584-9239**	701-444-9288	245
Mckenzie Lake Lawyers LLP 140 Fullarton St Ste 1800	London	ON	N6A5P2	**800-261-4844**	519-672-5666	427
McKenzie Tank Lines Inc 1966 Commonwealth Ln	Tallahassee	FL	32303	**800-828-6495**	850-576-1221	775
McKeon Door Co 44 Sawgrass Dr	Bellport	NY	11713	**800-266-9392**	631-803-3000	234
McKesson Medical Group Extended Care 8121 Tenth Ave N	Golden Valley	MN	55427	**800-328-8111**		473
McKesson Medical-Surgical 8741 Landmark Rd	Richmond	VA	23228	**800-446-3008**	415-983-8300	473
McKesson Pharmaceutical 1 Post St	San Francisco	CA	94104	**800-571-2889**	415-983-8300	583
McKey Perforating Company Inc 3033 S 166th St	New Berlin	WI	53151	**800-345-7373**	262-786-2700	198
McKinley Air Transport Inc 5430 Lauby Rd Bldg 4 *General	Canton	OH	44720	**800-225-6446***	330-499-3316	24
McKinley Equipment Corp 17611 Armstrong Ave	Irvine	CA	92614	**800-770-6094**	949-261-9222	384
Mckinney Petroleum Equipment Inc 3926 Halls Mill Rd	Mobile	AL	36693	**800-476-7867**	251-661-8800	357
McKinstry Co 5005 Third Ave S	Seattle	WA	98134	**800-669-6223**	206-762-3311	189-10
McKissock LP 218 Liberty St	Warren	PA	16365	**800-328-2008**	814-723-6979	177
McKnight's Long-Term Care News 900 Skokie Blvd Ste 114	Northbrook	IL	60062	**800-558-1703**	847-559-2884	633-9
MCL Inc 501 S Woodcreek Rd *Support	Bolingbrook	IL	60440	**800-743-4625***	630-759-9500	643
McLane Company Inc 4747 McLane Pkwy	Temple	TX	76504	**800-299-1401**	254-771-7500	297-8
McLane Foodservice Inc 2085 Midway Rd	Carrollton	TX	75006	**800-299-1401**	972-364-2000	297-8
McLaughlin Research Corp 132 Johnnycake Hill Rd	Middletown	RI	02842	**800-556-7154**	401-849-4010	261
McLaughlin Youth Ctr 2600 Providence Dr	Anchorage	AK	99508	**800-478-2221**	907-261-4399	411
McLean Contracting Co 6700 McLean Way	Glen Burnie	MD	21060	**800-677-1997**	410-553-6700	188-10
McLean Electric Co-op Inc 4031 Hwy 37 Bypass NW	Garrison	ND	58540	**800-263-4922**	701-463-2291	245
McLean Hospital 115 Mill St	Belmont	MA	02478	**800-333-0338**		373-5
McLean Inc 3409 E Miraloma Ave *Cust Svc	Anaheim	CA	92806	**800-451-2424***	714-996-5451	453
McLellan Botanicals 2352 San Juan Rd	Aromas	CA	95004	**800-467-2443**		368
McLellan Equipment Inc 251 Shaw Rd	South San Francisco	CA	94080	**800-848-8449**		190
McLennan Ross LLP 600 W Chambers 12220 Stony Plain Rd	Edmonton	AB	T5N3Y4	**800-567-9200**	780-482-9200	427
McLeod Co-op Power Assn 1231 Ford Ave N	Glencoe	MN	55336	**800-494-6272**	320-864-3148	245
McLeod Express LLC 5002 Cundiff Ct *General	Decatur	IL	62526	**800-709-3936***		681
McLeod Hospice 1203 E Cheves St	Florence	SC	29506	**800-768-4556**	843-777-2564	370
McLoone 75 Sumner St	La Crosse	WI	54603	**800-624-6641**	608-784-1260	697
MCM Elegante Suites 4250 Ridgemont Dr	Abilene	TX	79606	**888-897-9644**	325-698-1234	378
MCM Services Group 1300 Corporate Ctr Curve	Eagan	MN	55121	**888-507-6262**		196

Alphabetical Section

	Toll-Free	Phone	Class
McManis Faulkner			
Fairmont Plz 50 W San Fernando St			
10th Fl .... San Jose CA 95113	800-767-3263	408-279-8700	427
McMaster University			
1280 Main St W .... Hamilton ON L8S4L8	800-238-1623	905-525-9140	780
MCMC LLC			
300 Crown Colony Dr Ste 203 .... Quincy MA 02169	866-401-6262		317
McMenamins			
430 N Killingsworth ....Portland OR 97217	800-669-8610	503-223-0109	102
McMenamins on the Columbia			
1801 S Access Rd .... Vancouver WA 98661	800-669-8610	360-699-1521	667
McMurry University			
1400 Sayles Blvd .... Abilene TX 79697	800-460-2392	325-793-3800	166
McNally Industries LLC			
340 W Benson Ave ....Grantsburg WI 54840	800-366-1410	715-463-8300	637
McNally Robinson Booksellers Inc			
1120 Grant Ave .... Winnipeg MB R3M2A6	800-561-1833	204-475-0483	95
MCNB Bank & Trust Co			
PO Box 549 .... Welch WV 24801	800-532-9553	304-436-4112	70
McNeal Enterprises Inc			
2031 Ringwood Ave .... San Jose CA 95131	800-562-6325	408-922-7290	598
McNear Brick & Block			
1 McNear BrickyaRd Rd			
PO Box 151380. .... San Rafael CA 94901	888-442-6811	415-453-7702	150
McNeely Pigott & Fox (MP&F)			
611 Commerce St Ste 3000 ....Nashville TN 37203	800-818-6953	615-259-4000	632
McNeese State University			
4205 Ryan St .... Lake Charles LA 70609	800-622-3352		166
McNeil & NRM Inc			
96 E Crosier St .... Akron OH 44311	800-669-2525	330-253-2525	385
McNeilus Truck & Manufacturing Inc			
524 E Hwy St PO Box 70 ....Dodge Center MN 55927	888-686-7278	507-374-6321	513
McNichols Co			
9401 Corporate Lake Dr .... Tampa FL 33634	877-884-4653		490
McNulty's Tea & Coffee Company Inc			
109 Christopher St ....New York NY 10014	800-356-5200	212-242-5351	159
M-CON Products Inc			
2150 Richardson Side Rd ....Carp ON K0A1L0	800-267-5515	613-831-1736	183
McPherson College			
1600 E Euclid ....McPherson KS 67460	800-365-7402	620-242-0400	166
McQ Inc			
1551 Forbes St ....Fredericksburg VA 22405	866-373-2374	540-373-2374	256
MCR Safety			
5321 E Shelby Dr .... Memphis TN 38118	800-955-6887	901-795-5810	155-7
MCS Referral & Resources Inc			
6101 Gentry Ln ....Baltimore MD 21210	800-526-7234	410-889-6666	48-17
McShan Lumber Company Inc			
PO Box 27 .... McShan AL 35471	800-882-3712	205-375-6277	747
Mcswain & Co PS			
612 Woodland Sq Loop SE Ste 300 ....Lacey WA 98503	800-282-1301	360-357-9304	2
MCT Industries Inc			
500 Tierra Montana Loop ....Albuquerque NM 87004	800-876-8651	505-345-8651	774
MCT Transportation LLC			
1600 E Benson Rd ....Sioux Falls SD 57104	800-843-9904*	605-339-8400	775
*Cust Svc			
McTeague Higbee Case Cohen Whitney & Toker PA			
4 Union Pk PO Box 5000 ....Topsham ME 04086	800-482-0958	207-725-5581	427
MCVB (Merced Conference & Visitors Bureau)			
710 W 16th St .... Merced CA 95340	800-446-5353	209-384-2791	206
McVean Trading & Investments LLC			
850 Ridge Lake Blvd Ste One ....Memphis TN 38120	800-374-1937	901-761-8400	786
McVeigh Associates Ltd			
275 Dixon Ave ....Amityville NY 11701	800-726-5655	631-789-8833	196
McWane Inc			
2900 Hwy 280 Ste 300 ....Birmingham AL 35223	800-634-4746	205-414-3100	591
MD Anderson Cancer Ctr			
1515 Holcombe Blvd ....Houston TX 77030	800-889-2094	713-792-2121	373-7
M-D Bldg Products Inc			
4041 N Santa Fe Ave ....Oklahoma City OK 73118	800-654-8454*		234
*Cust Svc			
MD Financial Management			
1870 Alta Vista Dr ....Ottawa ON K1G6R7	800-267-4022	613-731-4552	524
M&D Printing			
515 University Ave ....Henry IL 61537	888-242-7552	309-364-3957	623
MD.M. Commercial Enterprises Inc			
1102 A1a N Ste 205 ....Ponte Vedra FL 32082	800-359-6741		38
MDA (Muscular Dystrophy Assn)			
3300 E Sunrise Dr ....Tucson AZ 85718	800-572-1717	520-529-2000	48-17
MDC Holdings Inc			
4350 S Monaco St Ste 500 ....Denver CO 80237	888-500-7060	303-773-1100	359-3
NYSE: MDC			
MDC Inc			
2547 Progress Rd .... Madison WI 53716	800-395-9405	608-221-3422	551
M-DCPS (Miami-Dade County Public Schools)			
1450 NE Second Ave .... Miami FL 33132	800-955-5504	305-995-1000	681
MDI (Molecular Devices Inc)			
1311 Orleans Dr .... Sunnyvale CA 94089	800-635-5577	408-747-1700	418
MDI Achieve			
10900 Hampshire Ave S			
Ste 100. .... Bloomington MN 55438	800-869-1322	952-995-9800	178-10
MDI Worldwide			
38271 W 12-Mile Rd ....Farmington Hills MI 48331	800-228-8925*	248-553-1900	233
*Sales			
Mdl Enterprise Inc			
9888 SW Fwy ....Houston TX 77074	800-879-0840	713-771-6350	180
MDNA (Machinery Dealers National Assn)			
315 S Patrick St ....Alexandria VA 22314	800-872-7807	703-836-9300	49-18
Mdr Fitness Corp			
14101 NW Fourth St ....Sunrise FL 33325	800-637-8227	954-845-9500	353
MDS (Mennonite Disaster Service)			
583 Airport Rd ....Lititz PA 17543	800-241-8111	717-735-3536	48-5
MDS Builders Inc			
301 NW Crawford Blvd Ste 201 ......Boca Raton FL 33432	844-637-2845		
MDT Advisors Inc			
125 High St Oliver St Twr			
21st Fl. .... Boston MA 02110	800-685-4277	617-235-7100	787
MDT Labor LLC			
2325 Paxton Church Rd Ste B ....Harrisburg PA 17110	888-454-9202		260
MDU (Montana-Dakota Utilities Co)			
400 N Fourth St ....Bismarck ND 58501	800-638-3278	701-222-7900	782
MDU Resources Group Inc			
1200 W Century Ave PO Box 5650......Bismarck ND 58506	866-760-4852	701-530-1000	185
NYSE: MDU			
MDX Medical Inc			
160 Chubb Ave Ste 301 ....Lyndhurst NJ 07071	866-325-8972	201-842-0760	
ME Heuck Co			
1600 Beech St .... Terre Haute IN 47804	866-634-3825*	812-238-5000	484
*Cust Svc			
ME Tile			
447 Atlas Dr .... Nashville TN 37211	888-348-8453		746
MEA Energy Association			
7825 Telegraph Rd .... Bloomington MN 55438	800-542-6096	651-289-9600	
MEA Voice Magazine			
1216 Kendale Blvd			
PO Box 2573. .... East Lansing MI 48826	800-292-1934		455-8
Mead Clark Lumber Co			
2667 Dowd Dr PO Box 529. ....Santa Rosa CA 95407	800-585-9663	707-576-3333	191-3
Mead Fluid Dynamics Inc			
4114 N Knox Ave ....Chicago IL 60641	877-632-3872*	773-685-6800	785
*Cust Svc			
Mead Johnson Nutritionals			
2701 Patriot Blvd 4th Fl ....Glenview IL 60026	800-231-5469	847-832-2420	296-10
Mead Metals Inc			
555 Cardigan Rd .... St. Paul MN 55126	800-992-1484	651-484-1400	490
Mead O'brien Inc			
1429 Atlantic Ave ....North Kansas City MO 64116	800-892-2769	816-471-3993	112
Mead Public Library			
710 N Eigth St ....Sheboygan WI 53081	800-441-4563	920-459-3400	433-3
Meade Instruments Corp			
27 Hubble .... Irvine CA 92618	800-626-3233	949-451-1450	540
Meador Staffing Services Inc			
722A Fairmont Pkwy ....Pasadena TX 77504	800-332-3310	713-941-0616	260
Meadow Lake Resort			
100 St Andrews Dr ....Columbia Falls MT 59912	800-321-4653	406-892-8700	665
Meadowmere Resort			
74 Main St .... Ogunquit ME 03907	800-633-8718	207-646-9661	377
Meadowood Napa Valley			
900 Meadowood Ln .... Saint Helena CA 94574	800-458-8080	877-963-3646	665
Meadows Foundation Inc			
3003 Swiss Ave .... Dallas TX 75204	800-826-9431	214-826-9431	305
Meadows Museum of Art at Centenary College			
2911 Centenary Blvd ....Shreveport LA 71104	800-234-4448	318-869-5169	517
Meadows Office Interiors			
885 Third Ave 29th Fl. .... New York NY 10022	800-337-6671	212-741-0333	
Meadows Psychiatric Ctr			
132 The Meadows Dr ....Centre Hall PA 16828	800-641-7529	814-364-2161	373-5
Meadows Regional Medical Ctr (MRMC)			
1 Meadows Pkwy ....Vidalia GA 30474	800-382-4023	912-535-5555	373-3
Meadville Lombard Theological School (MLTS)			
610 S Michigan Ave ....Chicago IL 60605	800-848-0979	773-256-3000	167-3
Meadville Medical Ctr (MMC)			
751 Liberty St .... Meadville PA 16335	800-254-5164	814-333-5000	373-3
Meadville Tribune			
947 Federal Ct .... Meadville PA 16335	800-879-0006	814-724-6370	528-2
Meagher County			
15 W Main St .... White Sulphur Springs MT 59645	800-332-2272	406-547-3612	337
Mears Transportation Group			
324 W Gore St .... Orlando FL 32806	800-759-5219	407-422-4561	440
Mearthane Products Corp			
16 W Industrial Dr .... Cranston RI 02921	888-883-8391	401-946-4400	
MECA Sportswear			
1120 Townline Rd .... Tomah WI 54660	800-729-6322	608-374-6450	155-5
Mecanica Solutions Inc			
10000 Blvd Henri-Bourassa Ouest			
.... Montreal QC H4S1R5	800-567-4223	514-340-1818	261
Mechanical Contractors Assn of America (MCAA)			
1385 Piccard Dr ....Rockville MD 20850	800-556-3653	301-869-5800	49-3
Mechanical Servants Inc			
2755 Thomas St ....Melrose Park IL 60160	800-351-2000		238
Mechanics Savings Bank			
100 Minot Ave PO Box 400 ....Auburn ME 04210	877-886-1020	207-786-5700	70
Mechanicsville Local			
6400 Mechanicsville Tpke			
.... Mechanicsville VA 23111	800-468-3382	804-746-1235	528-4
Mecklenburg Electric Co-op			
11633 Hwy Ninety Two .... Chase City VA 23924	800-989-4161	434-372-6100	245
Meckley Services Inc			
9704 Gunston Cove Rd Ste E .... Lorton VA 22079	877-632-5539	703-333-2040	606
Meclabs LLC			
1300 Marsh Landing Pkwy			
Ste 106 .... Jacksonville Beach FL 32250	800-517-5531		138
Med Fusion			
2501 S State Hwy 121 Business			
Ste 1100. .... Lewisville TX 75067	855-500-8535	972-966-7000	414
Med Shield Inc			
2424 E 55th St .... Indianapolis IN 46220	800-272-5454	317-613-3700	160
Med Team Home Health Care			
131 S Beckham Ave ....Tyler TX 75702	800-825-2873	903-592-9747	362
Medaille College			
18 Agassiz Cir .... Buffalo NY 14214	800-292-1582	716-880-2200	166
Medallion Cabinetry			
2222 Camden Ct ....Oak Brook IL 60523	800-543-4074	800-476-4181	115
Medallion Financial Corp			
437 Madison Ave 38th Fl. .... New York NY 10022	877-633-2554	212-328-2100	216
NASDAQ: MFIN			
Medallion Laboratories			
9000 Plymouth Ave N ....Minneapolis MN 55427	800-245-5615	763-764-4453	192
MedAltus			
944 College Park Rd Ste B ....Summerville SC 29486	800-393-3848		394
Medcare Products Inc			
151 E Cliff Rd .... Burnsville MN 55337	800-695-4479	952-894-7076	473
Medco Services Inc			
7037 Madison Pk Ste 450 .... Huntsville AL 35806	866-661-5739		
Medcom Inc			
6060 Phyllis Dr .... Cypress CA 90630	800-541-0253	800-877-1443	33

Listing	City	State	ZIP	Toll-Free	Phone	Class
Medcom Trainex 6060 Phyllis Dr *Cust Svc	Cypress	CA	90630	800-877-1443*		510
MedCost Benefit Services LLC 165 Kimel Park Dr	Winston-Salem	NC	27114	800-433-9178	800-795-1023	
MEDCURE 1811 NE Sandy Blvd	Portland	OR	97230	866-560-2525	503-257-9100	362
Medeco Security Locks Inc 3625 Alleghany Dr	Salem	VA	24153	800-839-3157	540-380-5000	349
Medegen Medical Products LLC 360 Motor Pkwy Ste 800	Hauppauge	NY	11788	800-511-6298		
Medela Inc 1101 Corporate Dr	Mchenry	IL	60050	800-435-8316	815-363-1166	680
Medexcel USA Inc 484 Temple Hill Rd	New Windsor	NY	12553	800-563-6384	845-565-3700	461
MedExpert International Inc 1300 Hancock St	Redwood City	CA	94063	800-999-1999	650-326-6000	194
Medflow Inc 14045 Ballantyne Corporate Pl Ste 300	Charlotte	NC	28277	844-366-5129	704-750-5927	179
Medford Leas 1 Medford Leas Way	Medford	NJ	08055	800-331-4302	609-654-3000	668
Medford Public Library 111 High St	Medford	MA	02155	800-447-8844	781-395-7950	433-3
MedGyn Products Inc 100 W Industrial Rd	Addison	IL	60101	800-451-9667	630-627-4105	604
Media Brokers International Inc 555 N Point Ctr E Ste 700	Alpharetta	GA	30022	866-514-1620		6
Media Cybernetics Inc 4340 E W Hwy Ste 400 *Sales	Bethesda	MD	20814	800-263-2088*	301-495-3305	178-10
Media Law Reporter 1801 S Bell St	Arlington	VA	22202	800-372-1033		527-11
Media Relations Report 316 N Michigan Ave Ste 400	Chicago	IL	60601	800-878-5331	312-960-4100	527-11
Media Services 500 S Sepulveda Blvd 4th Fl	Los Angeles	CA	90049	800-738-0409	310-440-9600	566
Media Space Solutions 5600 Rowland Rd Ste 170	Minnetonka	MN	55343	888-672-2100		6
Media Temple 6060 Center Dr 5th Fl	Los Angeles	CA	90045	877-578-4000		394
Media Watch PO Box 618	Santa Cruz	CA	95061	800-631-6355	831-423-6355	48-8
Media/Professional Insurance Inc 1201 Walnut Ste 1800	Kansas City	MO	64106	866-282-0565	816-471-6118	390-5
Media3 Technologies LLC 33 Riverside Dr N River Commerce Pk	Pembroke	MA	02359	800-903-9327	781-826-1213	803
Mediabidscom Inc 448 Main St *Cust Svc	Winsted	CT	06098	800-545-1135*		7
MediaBrains Inc 9015 Strada Stell Ct Ste 203	Naples	FL	34109	866-627-2467	239-594-3200	
MediaChoice LLC 3701 Bee Caves Rd	Austin	TX	78746	888-567-2424	512-693-9905	
Mediacom Communications Corp 100 Crystal Run Rd *General	Middletown	NY	10941	800-479-2082*	845-695-2600	116
Mediacom Communications Corp 1 Mediacom Way	Mediacom Park	NY	10918	855-633-4226		
Mediagrif Interactive Technologies Inc 1111 St-Charles St W E Tower Ste 255 *TSE: MDF*	Longueuil	QC	J4K5G4	877-677-9088	450-449-0102	178-1
MediaPro Inc 20021 120th Ave NE Ste 102	Bothell	WA	98011	800-726-6951	425-483-4700	180
MEDICA 401 Carlson Pkwy *Cust Svc	Minnetonka	MN	55305	800-952-3455*	866-317-1169	390-3
Medica Corp 5 Oak Park Dr	Bedford	MA	01730	800-777-5983	781-275-4892	474
Medical Action Industries Inc (MAI) 500 Expy Dr S	Brentwood	NY	11717	800-645-7042	631-231-4600	475
Medical Assn of Georgia (MAG) 1849 The Exchange Ste 200	Atlanta	GA	30339	800-282-0224	678-303-9290	472
Medical Associates Healthcare 911 Carter St NW	Elkader	IA	52043	800-648-6868	563-245-1717	539
Medical Assurance Inc 100 Brookwood Pl Ste 300 *Cust Svc	Birmingham	AL	35209	800-282-6242*	205-877-4400	390-5
Medical Benefits Mutual Life Insurance Co 1975 Tamarack Rd	Newark	OH	43058	800-423-3151	740-522-8425	390-3
Medical Billing Concepts Inc (MBC) 16001 Ventura Blvd Ste 135	Encino	CA	91436	866-351-2852		
Medical Care Development International (MCDI) 8401 Colesville Rd Ste 425	Silver Spring	MD	20910	800-427-7566	301-562-1920	48-5
Medical Center Pharmacy 2401 N Ocoee St	Cleveland	TN	37311	877-753-9555	423-476-5548	237
Medical Cost Management Corp 105 W Adams St Ste 2200	Chicago	IL	60603	800-367-9938	312-236-2694	362
Medical Ctr of South Arkansas 700 W Grove St	El Dorado	AR	71730	800-285-1131	870-863-2000	373-3
Medical Diagnostic Laboratories LLC 2439 Kuser Rd	Hamilton	NJ	08690	877-269-0090	609-570-1000	417
Medical Doctor Assoc 4775 Peachtree Industrial Blvd Ste 300	Norcross	GA	30092	800-780-3500		194
Medical Education Technologies Inc (METI) 6300 Edgelake Dr	Sarasota	FL	34240	866-462-7920	941-377-5562	250
Medical Eye Services Inc 345 Baker St E	Costa Mesa	CA	92626	800-877-6372	714-619-4660	389
Medical Genetics Consultants 819 DeSoto St	Ocean Springs	MS	39564	800-362-4363		416
Medical Graphics Corp 350 Oak Grove Pkwy *NASDAQ: ANGN*	Saint Paul	MN	55127	800-950-5597	651-484-4874	250
Medical Group Management Assn (MGMA) 104 Inverness Terr E	Englewood	CO	80112	877-275-6462	303-799-1111	49-8
Medical Instrument Development Laboratories Inc 557 McCormick St	San Leandro	CA	94577	800-929-5227	510-357-3952	414
Medical Library Assn (MLA) 65 E Wacker Pl Ste 1900	Chicago	IL	60601	800-523-1850	312-419-9094	49-11
Medical Management Specialists 4100 Embassy Dr SE Ste 200	Grand Rapids	MI	49546	888-707-2684	616-975-1845	2
Medical Mutual Group 700 Spring Forest Rd	Raleigh	NC	27609	800-662-7917	919-872-7117	390-5
Medical Mutual Insurance Company of Maine 1 City Ctr PO Box 15275	Portland	ME	04112	800-942-2791	207-775-2791	390-5
Medical Mutual Liability Insurance Society of Maryland 225 International Cir PO Box 8016	Hunt Valley	MD	21030	800-492-0193	410-785-0050	390-5
Medical Mutual of Ohio 2060 E Ninth St	Cleveland	OH	44115	800-700-2583	216-687-7000	390-3
Medical Products Laboratories Inc 9990 Global Rd	Philadelphia	PA	19115	800-523-0191	215-677-2700	578
Medical Protective Co 5814 Reed Rd	Fort Wayne	IN	46835	800-463-3776	260-485-9622	390-5
Medical Research Law & Policy Report 1801 S Bell St	Arlington	VA	22202	800-372-1033		527-7
Medical Risk Managers Inc 1170 Ellington Rd	South Windsor	CT	06074	800-732-3248		
Medical Security Card Company LLC 4911 E Broadway Blvd	Tucson	AZ	85711	800-347-5985	520-888-8070	582
Medical Services of America Inc (MSA) 171 Monroe Ln	Lexington	SC	29072	800-845-5850	803-957-0500	362
Medical Society of Virginia 2924 Emerywood Pkwy Ste 300	Richmond	VA	23294	800-746-6768		472
Medical Staffing Associates Inc 6731 Whittier Ave 3rd Fl	McLean	VA	22101	800-235-5105		717
Medical Staffing Network 6551 Park of Commerce Blvd	Boca Raton	FL	33487	800-676-8326		717
Medical Teams International (MTI) PO Box 10	Portland	OR	97207	800-959-4325	503-624-1000	48-5
MedicAlert Foundation International 5226 Pirrone Ct *Cust Svc	Salida	CA	95368	800-432-5378*		48-17
Medicalodges Inc 201 W Eighth St	Coffeyville	KS	67337	800-782-0120		788
Medicare Rights Ctr (MRC) 520 Eigth Ave N Wing 3rd Fl *Hotline	New York	NY	10018	800-333-4114*	212-869-3850	48-17
Medicat LLC 303 Perimeter Ctr N Ste 320	Atlanta	GA	30346	866-633-4053	404-252-2295	
Medicatech USA Inc 50 Maxwell Ave	Irvine	CA	92618	800-817-5030	949-679-2881	474
Medicines Co 8 Sylvan Way *NASDAQ: MDCO*	Parsippany	NJ	07054	800-388-1183	973-290-6000	85
Medicis Pharmaceutical Corp 7720 N Dobson Rd *Cust Svc	Scottsdale	AZ	85256	866-246-8245*	800-321-4576	578
Medico 1010 North 102nd St Ste 201	Omaha	NE	68114	800-547-2401		390-2
Medico Group 1515 S 75th St	Omaha	NE	68124	800-228-6080	402-391-6900	390-2
Medico Industries Inc 1500 Hwy 315	Wilkes-Barre	PA	18702	800-633-0027	570-825-7711	264-3
Medicomp Inc 600 Atlantis Rd	Melbourne	FL	32904	800-234-3278		635
MediConnect Global Inc 10897 S Riverfront Pkwy Ste 500	South Jordan	UT	84095	800-489-8710	801-545-3700	225
Medicount Management Inc 10361 Spartan Dr	Cincinnati	OH	45215	800-962-1484	513-772-4465	41
Medicus Healthcare Solutions LLC 22 Roulston Rd Ste 5	Windham	NH	03079	855-301-0563		193
Medifast Inc 11445 Cronhill Dr *NYSE: MED*	Owings Mills	MD	21117	800-209-0878		296-11
MedImpact Healthcare Systems Inc 10680 Treena St Ste 500	San Diego	CA	92131	800-788-2949	858-566-2727	582
Medin Corp 11 Jackson Rd	Totowa	NJ	07512	800-922-0476	973-779-2400	474
Medina Electric Co-op Inc PO Box 370	Hondo	TX	78861	866-632-3532		245
Medi-Nuclear Corp Inc 4610 Littlejohn St	Baldwin Park	CA	91706	800-321-5981	626-960-9822	474
MediRevv Inc 2600 University Pkwy	Coralville	IA	52241	888-665-6310		196
Medium Blue Search Engine Marketing 3365 Piedmont Rd NE St 1400 2nd Fl	Atlanta	GA	30305	866-436-2583	678-536-8336	461
MediUSA 6481 Franz Warner Pkwy	Whitsett	NC	27377	800-633-6334		156
Mediware Information Systems Inc 11711 W 79th St	Lenexa	KS	66214	800-255-0026	913-307-1000	178-11
Medix 222 S Riverside Plz Ste 2120	Chicago	IL	60606	866-446-3349		
MedjetAssist 3500 Colonnade Pkwy Ste 500 PO Box 43099	Birmingham	AL	35243	800-527-7478	205-595-6626	30
Medler Eelectric Company Inc 2155 Redman Dr	Alma	MI	48801	800-229-5740		249
Medline Industries Inc 1 Medline Pl *Cust Svc	Mundelein	IL	60060	800-633-5463*	847-949-5500	572
MedlinePlus US National Library of Medicine 8600 Rockville Pk	Bethesda	MD	20894	888-346-3656		355
Medlink Corp 10393 San Diego Mission Rd Ste 120	San Diego	CA	92108	800-452-2400	619-640-4660	194
Medmart Inc 10780 Reading Rd	Cincinnati	OH	45241	888-260-4430	513-733-8100	196
MedPlus Inc 4690 Pkwy Dr	Mason	OH	45040	800-444-6235	513-229-5500	178-10

	Toll-Free	Phone	Class
Med-Plus Medical Supplies			
PO Box 1242 .... Monsey NY 10942	888-433-2300	718-222-4416	418
MedPricer			
2346 Boston Post Rd Unit 2 .... Guilford CT 06437	888-453-4554	203-453-4554	225
MedRx Inc			
1200 Starkey Rd Ste 105 .... Largo FL 33771	888-392-1234	727-584-9600	474
MedShape Inc			
1575 Northside Dr NW Ste 440 .... Atlanta GA 30318	877-343-7016		
MedStar Health			
10980 Grantchester Way .... Columbia MD 21044	877-772-6505	410-772-6500	352
MedSupply			
5850 E Shields Ave Ste 105 .... Fresno CA 93727	800-889-9081	559-292-1540	473
Med-Tech Resource Inc			
29485 Airport Rd .... Eugene OR 97402	888-627-7779		521
MEDTOX Diagnostics Inc			
1238 Anthony Rd .... Burlington NC 27215	800-334-1116	336-226-6311	231
Medtronic			
710 Medtronic Pky .... Minneapolis MN 55432	800-633-8766	763-514-4000	250
Medtronic Inc			
710 Medtronic Pkwy NE .... Minneapolis MN 55432	800-328-2518*	763-514-4000	250
*NYSE: MDT ■ *Cust Svc*			
Medtronic MiniMed Inc			
18000 Devonshire St .... Northridge CA 91325	800-646-4633		475
Medtronic Neurosurgery			
125 Cremona Dr .... Goleta CA 93117	800-468-9710*	800-633-8766	474
*Cust Svc			
Medtronic of Canada Ltd			
99 Hereford St .... Brampton ON L6Y0R3	800-268-5346	905-826-6020	250
Medtronic Powered Surgical Solutions			
4620 N Beach St .... Fort Worth TX 76137	800-643-2773	817-788-6400	475
Medtronic Surgical Technologies			
6743 Southpoint Dr N .... Jacksonville FL 32216	800-874-5797	904-296-9600	475
Medusind Solutions Inc			
31103 Rancho Viejo Rd			
Ste 2150 .... San Juan Capistrano CA 92675	877-741-4573		461
Medvantx Inc			
5626 Oberlin Dr Ste 110 .... San Diego CA 92121	866-744-0621	866-526-1206	717
Mee Industries Inc			
16021 Adelante St .... Irwindale CA 91702	800-732-5364	626-359-4550	14
Meeder Equipment Co			
12323 Sixth St .... Rancho Cucamonga CA 91739	800-423-3711	909-463-0600	356
Meeting Connection Inc, The			
6373 Meadow Glen Dr N .... Westerville OH 43082	800-398-2568	614-898-9361	184
Meeting Professionals International (MPI)			
2711 Lyndon B Johnson Fwy			
Ste 600 .... Dallas TX 75234	866-318-2743	972-702-3053	49-12
Meeting Street Inn			
173 Meeting St .... Charleston SC 29401	800-842-8022	843-723-1882	378
Mega Care			
1883 Whitney Mesa Dr .... Henderson NV 89014	888-883-6342	626-382-9492	788
Mega Group Inc			
720-1st Ave N .... Saskatoon SK S7K6R9	800-265-9030	306-242-7366	41
MegaFab PO Box 457 .... Hutchinson KS 67504	800-338-5471	620-663-1127	454
Mega-Pro International Inc			
251 W Hilton Dr .... Saint George UT 84770	800-541-9469	435-673-1001	794
Megger 4271 Bronze Way .... Dallas TX 75237	800-723-2861	214-333-3201	248
Meggitt Training Systems Inc			
296 Brogdon Rd .... Suwanee GA 30024	800-813-9046	678-288-1090	699
Meguiar's Inc			
17991 Mitchell S .... Irvine CA 92614	800-347-5700*		151
*Cust Svc			
Meherrin Agricultural & Chemical Co Inc			
413 Main St .... Severn NC 27877	800-775-0333	252-585-1744	276
Mehron Inc			
100 Red Schoolhouse Rd			
Ste C2 .... Chestnut Ridge NY 10977	800-332-9955	845-426-1700	237
MEI (Martronic Engineering Inc)			
874 Patriot Dr Unit D .... Moorpark CA 93021	800-960-0808	805-583-0808	261
Meier Enterprises Inc			
12 W Kennewick Ave .... Kennewick WA 99336	800-239-7589	509-735-1589	261
Meier Supply Company Inc			
530 Bloomingburg Rd .... Middletown NY 10940	800-418-3216	845-733-5666	606
Meier's Wine Cellars			
6955 Plainfield Rd .... Cincinnati OH 45236	800-229-9813	513-891-2900	80-3
Meijer Inc			
2929 Walker Ave NW .... Grand Rapids MI 49544	800-543-3704	616-453-6711	344
Meisel			
2019 McKenzie Dr .... Carrollton TX 75006	800-527-5186	214-688-4950	584
Meister Media Worldwide			
37733 Euclid Ave .... Willoughby OH 44094	800-572-7740*	440-942-2000	633-9
*Orders			
Mej Personal Business Services Inc			
245 E 116th St .... New York NY 10029	866-418-3836	212-426-6017	113
Mel Bay Publications Inc			
1734 Gilsinn Ln .... Fenton MO 63026	800-863-5229	636-257-3970	633-2
Mel Rapton Inc			
3630 Fulton Ave .... Sacramento CA 95821	800-529-3053	916-482-5400	513
Melaleuca Inc			
3910 S Yellowstone Hwy .... Idaho Falls ID 83402	800-282-3000*	208-522-0700	365
*Sales			
Mele & Co			
2007 Beechgrove Pl .... Utica NY 13501	800-635-6353	315-733-4600	200
Melin Tool Co			
5565 Venture Dr Unit C .... Cleveland OH 44130	800-521-1078	216-362-4200	491
Melissa's/World Variety Produce Inc			
5325 S Soto St .... Vernon CA 90058	800-588-0151		297-7
Melitta Canada Inc			
50 Ronson Dr Unit 150 .... Toronto ON M9W1B3	800-565-4882		296-7
Melnor Inc			
109 Tyson Dr .... Winchester VA 22603	877-283-0697	540-722-5600	428
Melrose Hotel Washington DC, The			
2430 Pennsylvania Ave NW .... Washington DC 20037	800-635-7673	202-955-6400	377
Melting Pot of Charlotte, The			
901 S Kings Dr Ste 140B .... Charlotte NC 28204	800-783-0867	704-334-4400	667
Melting Pot of Columbia, The			
1410 Colonial Life Blvd .... Columbia SC 29210	800-783-0867	803-731-8500	667
Melting Pot of Indianapolis, The			
5650 E 86th St Ste A .... Indianapolis IN 46250	800-783-0867	317-841-3601	667

	Toll-Free	Phone	Class
Melting Pot of San Antonio, The			
14855 Blanco Rd Ste 110 .... San Antonio TX 78216	800-783-0867	210-479-6358	667
Melting Pot Restaurants Inc			
8810 Twin Lakes Blvd .... Tampa FL 33614	800-783-0867	813-881-0055	666
Melting Pot, The			
1601 Concord Pk			
Ste 43-47 Independence Mall .... Wilmington DE 19803	800-783-0867	302-652-6358	667
MemberPlanet			
23224 Crenshaw Blvd .... Torrance CA 90505	800-952-5210	916-445-1254	
Memorial Blood Centers (MBC)			
737 Pelham Blvd .... Saint Paul MN 55114	888-448-3253*		89
*Cust Svc			
Memorial Healthcare Ctr			
826 W King St .... Owosso MI 48867	800-206-8706		373-3
Memorial Hermann Healthcare System			
7600 Beechnut St .... Houston TX 77074	800-777-6330	713-456-4280	352
Memorial Hermann Memorial City Hospital			
921 Gessner Rd .... Houston TX 77024	800-526-2121	713-242-3000	373-3
Memorial Hermann Prevention & Recovery Ctr (MHPARC)			
3043 Gessner .... Houston TX 77080	877-464-7272	713-939-7272	373-5
Memorial Hospital & Health Care Ctr			
800 W Ninth St .... Jasper IN 47546	800-852-7279	812-996-2345	373-3
Memorial Hospital of Carbondale			
405 W Jackson St .... Carbondale IL 62902	800-457-1393	618-549-0721	373-3
Memorial Hospital of Rhode Island (MHRI)			
111 Brewster St .... Pawtucket RI 02860	800-647-4362	401-729-2000	373-3
Memorial Hospital of Salem County			
310 Woodstown Rd .... Salem NJ 08079	800-753-3779	856-935-1000	373-3
Memorial Hospital of Sweetwater County			
1200 College Dr .... Rock Springs WY 82901	866-571-0944*	307-362-3711	373-3
*General			
Memorial Medical Ctr			
1086 Franklin St .... Johnstown PA 15905	800-441-2555	814-534-9000	373-3
Memorial Medical Ctr (MMC)			
1700 Coffee Rd .... Modesto CA 95355	800-477-2258	209-526-4500	373-3
Memorial Medical Ctr			
1615 Maple Ln .... Ashland WI 54806	888-868-9292	715-685-5500	373-3
Memorial Sloan-Kettering Cancer Ctr			
1275 York Ave .... New York NY 10065	800-525-2225	212-639-2000	373-7
MemorialCare Medical Group			
17762 Beach Blvd .... Huntington Beach CA 92647	866-276-3627	714-848-0080	
Memphis College of Art			
1930 Poplar Ave .... Memphis TN 38104	800-727-1088	901-272-5100	164
Memphis Convention & Visitors Bureau			
47 Union Ave .... Memphis TN 38103	888-633-9099	901-543-5300	206
Memphis Flyer			
460 Tennessee St .... Memphis TN 38103	877-292-3804	901-521-9000	528-5
Memry Corp			
3 Berkshire Blvd .... Bethel CT 06801	866-466-3679	203-739-1100	483
Men's Health Magazine			
400 S Tenth St .... Emmaus PA 18098	800-666-2303		455-13
Men's Wearhouse Inc			
6380 Rogerdale Rd .... Houston TX 77072	877-986-9669	281-776-7000	157-3
NYSE: TLRD			
Mena Regional Health System			
311 Morrow St N .... Mena AR 71953	800-394-6185	479-394-6100	362
Mena Tours & Travel			
5209 N Clark St .... Chicago IL 60640	800-937-6362	773-275-2125	
Menard Electric Co-op			
14300 State Hwy 97			
PO Box 200 .... Petersburg IL 62675	800-872-1203	217-632-7746	245
Menardi 1 Maxwell Dr .... Trenton SC 29847	800-321-3218		67
Menasha Corp			
1645 Bergstrom Rd .... Neenah WI 54956	800-558-5073	920-751-1000	100
Menasha Packaging Co			
1645 Bergstrom Rd .... Neenah WI 54956	800-558-5073	920-751-1000	100
MENC: NA for Music Education			
1806 Robert Fulton Dr .... Reston VA 20191	800-336-3768	703-860-4000	49-5
Mended Hearts Inc, The			
8150 N Central Expy M2248 .... Dallas TX 75206	888-432-7899	214-296-9252	48-17
Mendocino Wine Co			
501 PaRducci Rd .... Ukiah CA 95482	800-362-9463	707-463-5350	80-3
Mendon Truck Leasing & Rental			
8215 Foster Ave .... Brooklyn NY 11236	877-636-3661	718-209-9886	773
Mendota Mental Health Institute			
301 Troy Dr .... Madison WI 53704	800-323-8942	608-301-1000	373-5
Menger Hotel			
204 Alamo Plz .... San Antonio TX 78205	800-345-9285	210-223-4361	378
Mengis Capital Management Inc			
1 SW Columbia St Ste 780 .... Portland OR 97258	877-916-0780	503-916-0776	
Menke Marking Devices			
13253 Alondra Blvd .... Santa Fe Springs CA 90670	800-231-6023	562-921-1380	465
Menlo College			
1000 El Camino Real .... Atherton CA 94027	800-556-3656	650-543-3753	166
Mennel Milling Co			
128 W Crocker St .... Fostoria OH 44830	800-688-8151		296-23
Menninger Clinic			
12301 Main St .... Houston TX 77035	800-351-9058	713-275-5000	373-5
Mennonite Brethren Biblical Seminary			
4824 E Butler Ave .... Fresno CA 93727	800-251-6227	559-453-2000	167-3
Mennonite Central Committee (MCC)			
21 S 12th St PO Box 500 .... Akron PA 17501	888-563-4676	717-859-1151	48-5
Mennonite Disaster Service (MDS)			
583 Airport Rd .... Lititz PA 17543	800-241-8111	717-735-3536	48-5
Mennonite Village			
5353 Columbus St SE .... Albany OR 97322	800-211-2713	541-928-7232	668
Menominee Hotel			
N277 Hwy 47/55 PO Box 760 .... Keshena WI 54135	800-343-7778		377
Menorah Medical Ctr			
5721 W 119th St .... Overland Park KS 66209	800-766-3777	913-498-6000	373-3
Mental Health America (MHA)			
2000 N Beauregard St 6th Fl .... Alexandria VA 22311	800-969-6642*	703-684-7722	48-17
*Help Line			
Mentholatum Company Inc			
707 Sterling Dr .... Orchard Park NY 14127	800-688-7660	716-677-2500	578
MENTIS			
3 Columbus Cir 15th Fl .... New York NY 10019	800-267-0858	212-203-4365	

	Toll-Free	Phone	Class
Mentor Corp			
201 Mentor Dr .... Santa Barbara CA 93111	800-525-0245	805-879-6000	475
NASDAQ: MENT			
Mentor Graphics Corp			
8005 SW Boeckman Rd ...... Wilsonville OR 97070	800-592-2210	503-685-7000	178-5
NASDAQ: MENT			
MENTOR Network, The			
313 Congress St 5th Fl. .... Boston MA 02210	800-388-5150	617-790-4800	460
MENTOR/National Mentoring Partnership			
201 South St Ste 615 .... Boston MA 02111	877-333-2464	703-224-2200	48-6
Menzner Lumber & Supply Co			
PO Box 217 .... Marathon WI 54448	800-257-1284		497
Mercantil Commercebank Holding Corp			
PO Box 226555 .... Miami FL 33222	888-629-0810	305-629-1212	
Mercantile Bank			
200 N 33rd St PO Box 3455 ...... Quincy IL 62305	800-405-6372	217-223-7300	359-2
NASDAQ: MBWM			
Merced College			
3600 M St .... Merced CA 95348	800-784-2433	209-384-6000	162
Merced Conference & Visitors Bureau (MCVB)			
710 W 16th St .... Merced CA 95340	800-446-5353	209-384-2791	206
Merced County Library			
2100 O St .... Merced CA 95340	866-249-0773	209-385-7643	433-3
Mercedes-Benz Financial Services USA LLC			
PO Box 685 .... Roanoke TX 76262	800-654-6222		217
Mercedes-Benz of San Francisco			
500 Eigth St .... San Francisco CA 94103	877-554-6016	415-673-2000	57
Mercedes-Benz of Seattle			
2025 Airport Way S .... Seattle WA 98134	855-263-5688	206-467-9999	57
Mercedes-Benz US. International Inc			
1 Mercedes Dr .... Vance AL 35490	888-286-8762	205-507-2252	59
Mercedes-Benz USA LLC			
1 Mercedes Dr .... Montvale NJ 07645	800-367-6372*		59
*Cust Svc			
Mercer County			
220 W Livingston St Ste 1 .... Celina OH 45822	800-686-1093	419-586-3289	337
Mercer County			
621 Commerce St PO Box 4088 ...... Bluefield WV 24701	800-221-3206	304-325-8438	337
Mercer County			
PO Box 39 .... Stanton ND 58571	800-441-2649		337
Mercer County Convention & Visitors Bureau			
621 Commerce St .... Bluefield WV 24701	800-221-3206	304-325-8438	206
Mercer County Joint Township Community Hospital			
800 W Main St .... Coldwater OH 45828	888-844-2341	419-678-2341	373-3
Mercer Engineering & Research			
135 Osigian Blvd .... Warner Robins GA 31088	877-650-6372	478-953-6800	138
Mercer Hotel			
147 Mercer St .... New York NY 10012	888-918-6060	212-966-6060	378
Mercer Transportation Co			
1128 W Main St .... Louisville KY 40203	800-626-5375	502-584-2301	775
Mercer University			
1400 Coleman Ave .... Macon GA 31207	800-637-2378	478-301-2650	166
Cecil B Day			
3001 Mercer University Dr ...... Atlanta GA 30341	800-840-8577	678-547-6089	166
Mercersburg Academy			
300 E Seminary St .... Mercersburg PA 17236	800-588-2550	717-328-6173	618
Mercersburg Printing			
9964 Buchanan Trl W .... Mercersburg PA 17236	800-955-3902	717-328-3902	623
Merchant & Evans Inc			
308 Connecticut Dr .... Burlington NJ 08016	800-257-6215	609-387-3033	478
Merchant Factors Corp			
1441 Broadway 22nd Fl .... New York NY 10018	800-970-9997*	212-840-7575	272
*All			
Merchant Law Group LLP			
2401 Saskatchewan Dr Saskatchewan Dr Plz			
.... Regina SK S4P4H8	888-567-7777	306-359-7777	41
Merchant One Inc			
524 Arthur Godfrey Rd			
3rd Fl .... Miami Beach FL 33140	800-910-8375	800-610-4189	95
Merchants & Medical Credit Corporation Inc			
6324 Taylor Dr .... Flint MI 48507	800-562-0273	810-239-3030	160
Merchants Building Maintenance			
606 Monterey Pass Rd .... Monterey Park CA 91754	800-560-6700		177
Merchants Co			
1100 Edwards St PO Box 1351 ...... Hattiesburg MS 39401	800-844-3663	601-583-4351	297-8
Merchants Credit Bureau			
955 Green St .... Augusta GA 30901	800-426-5265	706-823-6200	218
Merchants Grocery Co			
800 Maddox Dr PO Box 1268 ...... Culpeper VA 22701	877-897-9893	540-825-0786	344
Merchants Insurance Group			
250 Main St .... Buffalo NY 14202	800-462-1077		390-4
Merchants National Bank of Bangor Inc			
25 Broadway PO Box 227 .... Bangor PA 18013	877-678-6622	610-588-0981	70
Merchants Paper Co			
4625 SE 24th Ave .... Portland OR 97202	800-605-6301	503-235-2171	553
Merck & Company Inc			
2000 Galloping Hill Rd .... Kenilworth NJ 07033	800-444-2080*	908-740-4000	578
NYSE: MRK ■ *Cust Svc			
Merco-Savory Inc			
1111 N Hadley Rd .... Fort Wayne IN 46804	800-547-2513*	260-459-8200	298
*Cust Svc			
Mercury Insurance Group			
4484 Wilshire Blvd .... Los Angeles CA 90010	800-956-3728	323-937-1060	390-4
NYSE: MCY			
Mercury Lighting Products Company Inc			
20 Audrey Pl .... Fairfield NJ 07004	800-637-2584	973-244-9444	438
Mercury Medical			
11300 49th St N .... Clearwater FL 33762	800-237-6418	727-573-0088	474
Mercury Press Inc			
1910 S Nicklas St .... Oklahoma City OK 73128	800-423-5984	405-682-3468	623
Mercury Public Affairs			
200 Varick St Ste 600 .... New York NY 10014	800-325-4151	212-681-1380	632
Mercury Systems Inc			
50 Minuteman Rd .... Andover MA 01810	866-627-6951	978-256-1300	
NASDAQ: MRCY			
Mercy			
1235 E Cherokee .... Springfield MO 65804	800-909-8326	417-820-2000	373-3
Mercy			
615 S New Ballas Rd .... Saint Louis MO 63141	800-318-2596	314-251-6000	373-3
Mercy College			
555 Broadway .... Dobbs Ferry NY 10522	800-637-2969	914-674-7600	166
White Plains			
277 Martine Ave Ste 201 ...... White Plains NY 10601	888-464-6737	914-948-3666	166
Yorktown Heights			
2651 Strang Blvd .... Yorktown Heights NY 10598	877-637-2946	914-245-6100	166
Mercy Flights Inc			
2020 Milligan Way .... Medford OR 97504	800-903-9000	541-858-2600	30
Mercy Health			
Muskegon Campus			
1500 E Sherman Blvd .... Muskegon MI 49444	800-368-4125	231-672-2000	373-3
Mercy Health Ctr Fort Scott			
401 Woodland Hills Blvd .... Fort Scott KS 66701	800-464-7942	620-223-2200	373-3
Mercy Hospital			
144 State St .... Portland ME 04101	800-293-6583	207-879-3000	373-3
Mercy Hospital & Trauma Ctr			
1000 Mineral Point Ave .... Janesville WI 53548	800-756-4147	608-756-6000	373-3
Mercy Housing Inc			
1999 Broadway Ste 1000 .... Denver CO 80202	866-338-0557	303-830-3300	187
Mercy Iowa City			
500 E Market St .... Iowa City IA 52245	800-637-2942	319-339-0300	373-3
Mercy Medical Center North Iowa			
1000 Fourth St SW .... Mason City IA 50401	800-297-4719	641-428-7000	370
Mercy Medical Ctr (MMC)			
801 Fifth St .... Sioux City IA 51102	800-352-3559	712-279-2010	373-3
Mercy Medical Ctr			
1111 Sixth Ave .... Des Moines IA 50314	800-637-2993	515-247-3121	373-3
Mercy Medical Ctr (MMC)			
345 St Paul Pl .... Baltimore MD 21202	800-636-3729	410-332-9000	373-3
Mercy Medical Ctr			
1320 Mercy Dr NW .... Canton OH 44708	800-223-8662	330-489-1000	373-3
Mercy Medical Ctr (MMC)			
500 S Oakwood Rd .... Oshkosh WI 54904	800-894-9327	920-223-2000	373-3
Mercy Medical Ctr North Iowa			
1000 Fourth St SW .... Mason City IA 50401	800-433-3883	641-428-7000	373-3
Mercy Regional Medical Center			
1010 Third Springs Blvd .... Durango CO 81301	800-345-2516	970-247-4311	373-3
Mercy San Juan Medical Ctr			
6501 Coyle Ave .... Carmichael CA 95608	855-409-5280	916-537-5000	373-3
Mercyhurst College			
501 E 38th St .... Erie PA 16546	800-825-1926	814-824-2202	166
Mercy-USA for Aid & Development Inc (M-USA)			
44450 Pinetree Dr Ste 201 ...... Plymouth MI 48170	800-556-3729	734-454-0011	48-5
Meredith & Jeannie Ray Cancer Ctr			
255 N 30th St .... Laramie WY 82072	800-854-1115	307-742-7586	373-3
Meredith College			
3800 Hillsborough St .... Raleigh NC 27607	800-637-3348*	919-760-8600	166
*All			
Meredith Village Savings Bank (MVSB)			
24 State Rt 25 PO Box 177 ...... Meredith NH 03253	800-922-6872	603-279-7986	70
Mereen-Johnson Machine Co			
4401 Lyndale Ave N .... Minneapolis MN 55412	888-465-7297	612-529-7791	816
Merfish Pipe & Supply Co			
PO Box 15879 .... Houston TX 77220	800-869-5731	713-869-5731	490
Merge Helathcare			
350 N Orleans St 1st Fl. .... Chicago IL 60654	877-446-3743	312-565-6868	381
Mergenet Solutions Inc			
1701 W Hillsboro Blvd			
Ste 303 .... Deerfield Beach FL 33442	888-956-2526	561-208-3770	
Mergent FIS Inc			
580 Kingsley Pk Dr .... Fort Mill SC 29715	800-342-5647		633-10
Mergent Inc			
477 Madison Ave Ste 410. .... New York NY 10022	800-937-1398	212-413-7700	633-9
Mergenthaler Transfer & Storage			
1414 N Montana Ave .... Helena MT 59601	800-826-5463*	406-442-9470	775
*General			
Mergers & Acquisitions Law Report			
1801 S Bell St .... Arlington VA 22202	800-372-1033		527-7
Merial Ltd			
3239 Satellite Blvd Bldg 500 ...... Duluth GA 30096	888-637-4251	678-638-3000	580
Mericon Industries Inc			
8819 N Pioneer Rd .... Peoria IL 61615	800-242-6464	309-693-2150	579
Meridian Auto Parts			
10211 Pacific Mesa Blvd			
Ste 404 .... San Diego CA 92121	800-874-1974		54
Meridian Bioscience Inc			
3471 River Hills Dr .... Cincinnati OH 45244	800-543-1980*	513-271-3700	231
NASDAQ: VIVO ■ *Cust Svc			
Meridian Community College			
910 Hwy 19 N .... Meridian MS 39307	800-622-8431	601-483-8241	162
Meridian Display & Merchandising Inc			
162 York Ave E .... St Paul MN 55117	800-786-2501		5
Meridian Health System Inc			
1967 Hwy 34 Bldg C Ste 104 ...... Wall NJ 07719	800-560-9990		362
Meridian Medical Technologies Inc			
6350 Stevens Forest Rd Ste 301 ...... Columbia MD 21046	800-638-8093	443-259-7800	474
Meridian One Corp			
5775 General Washington Dr ...... Alexandria VA 22312	800-636-2377		
Meridian Plaza Resort			
2310 N Ocean Blvd .... Myrtle Beach SC 29577	888-590-0801	843-626-4734	378
Meridian Products			
124 Earland Dr Bldg 2 .... New Holland PA 17557	888-423-2804	717-355-7700	
Meridian Star Inc			
814 22nd Ave .... Meridian MS 39301	800-232-2525*	601-693-1551	633-8
*Cust Svc			
Meridian Technology Group Inc			
12909 SW 68th Pkwy Ste 100 ...... Portland OR 97223	800-755-1038	503-697-1600	177
Meridian Title Corp			
202 S Michigan St .... South Bend IN 46601	800-777-1574		390-6
Meridian/Lauderdale County Tourism Bureau			
212 Constitution Ave .... Meridian MS 39301	888-868-7720	601-482-8001	206
Merion Mercy Academy			
511 Montgomery Ave .... Merion Station PA 19066	800-352-7550	610-664-6655	681
Merion Publications Inc			
2900 Horizon Dr .... King of Prussia PA 19406	800-355-1088	484-804-4888	633-9
Merit Medical Systems Inc			
1600 W Merit Pkwy .... South Jordan UT 84095	800-356-3748	801-253-1600	474
NASDAQ: MMSI			

Alphabetical Section

	Toll-Free	Phone	Class

Merit Systems Protection Board (MSPB)
1615 M St NW . . . . Washington DC 20419 — **800-209-8960** — 202-653-7200 — 339-19
Merit Systems Protection Board Regional Offices (MSPB)
Atlanta Region
401 W Peachtree St NW 10th Fl . . . . Atlanta GA 30308 — **800-209-8960** — 404-730-2751 — 339-19
Central Region
230 S Dearborn St 31st Fl . . . . Chicago IL 60604 — **800-424-9121** — 312-353-2923 — 339-19
Merit Travel Group Inc
111 Peter St . . . . Toronto ON M5V2H1 — **866-341-1777** — 416-364-3775 — 766
Merit USA
620 Clark Ave . . . . Pittsburg CA 94565 — **800-445-6374** — — 490
Merits Health Products Inc
730 NE 19th Pl . . . . Cape Coral FL 33909 — **800-963-7487** — 239-772-0579 — 475
Meriwest Credit Union
PO Box 530953 . . . . San Jose CA 95153 — **877-637-4937** — — 219
Merix Financial
56 Temperance St Ste 400 . . . . Toronto ON M5H3V5 — **877-637-4911** — — 507
Merkle Wildlife Sanctuary
580 Taylor Ave . . . . Annapolis MD 21401 — **877-620-8367** — — 561
Merle Boes Inc
11372 E Lakewood Blvd . . . . Holland MI 49424 — **800-545-0706** — 616-392-7036 — 575
Merle Norman Cosmetics Inc
9130 Bellanca Ave . . . . Los Angeles CA 90045 — **800-421-6648** — 310-641-3000 — 214
Merlin
3815 E Main St Ste D . . . . Saint Charles IL 60174 — **800-652-9900** — 630-513-8200 — 310
Merrell Footwear
9341 Courtland Dr NE . . . . Rockford MI 49351 — **800-288-3124*** — 616-866-5500 — 301
*Cust Svc
Merrick & Co
2450 S Peoria St . . . . Aurora CO 80014 — **800-544-1714** — 303-751-0741 — 261
Merrick Industries Inc
10 Arthur Dr . . . . Lynn Haven FL 32444 — **800-345-8440** — 850-265-3611 — 680
Merrick's Inc
2415 Parview Rd PO Box 620307 . . . . . . Middleton WI 53562 — **800-637-7425** — 608-831-3440 — 445
Merrill Corp
1 Merrill Cir . . . . Saint Paul MN 55108 — **800-688-4400** — 651-646-4501 — 623
Merrill's Packaging Inc
1529 Rollins Rd . . . . Burlingame CA 94010 — **800-284-5910** — —
Merrimack Valley Hospice
360 Merrimack St Bldg 9 . . . . Lawrence MA 01843 — **800-933-5593** — — 370
Merrithew Corp
2200 Yonge St Ste 500 . . . . Toronto ON M4S2C6 — **800-910-0001** — 416-482-4050 — 782
Merritt Equipment Co
9339 Brighton Rd . . . . Henderson CO 80640 — **800-634-3036** — 303-289-2286 — 774
Merritt Interpreting Services
3626 N Hall St Ste 504 . . . . Dallas TX 75219 — **866-761-2585** — 214-969-5585 — 763
Merriweather Post Pavilion (MPP)
10475 Little Patuxent Pkwy . . . . Columbia MD 21044 — **877-435-9849** — 410-715-5550 — 568
Merry Maids
3839 Forrest Hill-Irene Rd . . . . Memphis TN 38125 — **800-798-8000** — — 152
Merry X-Ray Corp
4909 Murphy Canyon Rd Ste 120 . . . . . . San Diego CA 92123 — **800-635-9729** — —
Mersen Inc
374 Merrimac St . . . . Newburyport MA 01950 — **800-388-5428** — 978-462-6662 — 725
Mersen USA BN Corp
400 Myrtle Ave . . . . Boonton NJ 07005 — **800-526-0877*** — — 127
*General
Mervis Diamond Importers
1900 Mervis Way . . . . Tysons VA 22182 — **800-437-5683** — 703-448-9000 — 409
MERX Networks Inc
6 Antares Dr Phase II Unit 103 . . . . Ottawa ON K2E8A9 — **800-964-6379** — 613-727-4900 — 386
Merz Group, The
1570 Mcdaniel Dr . . . . West Chester PA 19380 — **800-600-9900** — 610-429-3160 — 7
Mesa Arizona Temple
101 S LeSueur . . . . Mesa AZ 85204 — **855-537-4357** — 480-833-1211 — 50-1
Mesa City Hall
PO Box 1466 . . . . Mesa AZ 85211 — **866-406-9659** — 480-644-2221 — 336
Mesa Community College
1833 W Southern Ave . . . . Mesa AZ 85202 — **866-532-4983** — 480-461-7000 — 162
Red Mountain
7110 E McKellips Rd . . . . Mesa AZ 85207 — **866-532-4983** — 480-654-7200 — 162
Mesa Laboratories Inc
12100 W Sixth Ave . . . . Lakewood CO 80228 — **800-992-6372*** — 303-987-8000 — 473
*NASDAQ: MLAB ■ *Sales*
Mesa State College
1100 N Ave . . . . Grand Junction CO 81501 — **800-982-6372** — 970-248-1020 — 166
Mesa Systems Inc
2275 South 900 West . . . . Salt Lake City UT 84119 — **800-523-4656** — — 359-2
Mesabi Range Community & Technical College
1100 Industrial Pk Dr
PO Box 648 . . . . Eveleth MN 55734 — **800-657-3860** — 218-741-3095 — 162
Mesco Bldg Solutions
5244 Bear Creek Ct . . . . Irving TX 75061 — **800-556-3726** — 214-687-9999 — 105
Mesirow Financial Inc
350 N Clark St . . . . Chicago IL 60654 — **800-453-0600** — 312-595-6000 — 686
Mesirow Financial Insurance Services Div
353 N Clark St . . . . Chicago IL 60654 — **800-453-0600** — 312-595-6200 — 389
Mesirow Financial Private Equity
353 N Clark St . . . . Chicago IL 60654 — **800-453-0600** — 312-595-6000 — 787
Mesko Glass & Mirror Company Inc
801 Wyoming Ave . . . . Scranton PA 18509 — **800-982-4055** — 570-346-0777 — 330
Meskwaki Bingo Hotel Casino
1504 305th St . . . . Tama IA 52339 — **800-728-4263** — — 133
MessageBank LLC
250 W 57th St Ste 1100 . . . . New York NY 10107 — **800-989-8001** — 212-333-9300 — 386
Messaging Architects
180 Peel St Ste 333 . . . . Montreal QC H3C2G7 — **866-497-0101** — 514-392-9220 — 179
Messenger, The
713 Central Ave . . . . Fort Dodge IA 50501 — **800-622-6613** — 515-573-2141 — 528-2
Messenger-Inquirer
1401 Fredrica St . . . . Owensboro KY 42301 — **800-633-2008** — 270-926-0123 — 528-2
Messiah College
PO Box 3005 . . . . Grantham PA 17027 — **800-233-4220** — 717-691-6000 — 166
Mesta Electronics Inc
11020 Parker Dr . . . . North Huntingdon PA 15642 — **800-535-6798** — 412-754-3000 — 762
Education Trust
PO Box 30198 . . . . Lansing MI 48909 — **800-638-4543*** — 517-335-4767 — 721
*General

Meta5 Inc
122 W Main St . . . . Babylon NY 11702 — **866-638-2555** — 631-587-6800 —
Metabolic Maintenance
601 N Larch St PO Box 940 . . . . Sisters OR 97759 — **800-772-7873** — —
Metafile Information Systems Inc
3428 Lakeridge Pl NW . . . . Rochester MN 55901 — **800-638-2445*** — 507-286-9232 — 178-11
*Sales
Metal Cladding Inc
230 S Niagara St . . . . Lockport NY 14094 — **800-432-5513** — — 479
Metal Cutting Corp
89 Commerce Rd . . . . Cedar Grove NJ 07009 — **800-783-6382** — 973-239-1100 — 453
Metal Marketplace International (MMI)
718 Sansom St . . . . Philadelphia PA 19106 — **800-523-9191** — 215-592-8777 — 410
Metal Masters Inc
3825 Crater Lake Hwy . . . . Medford OR 97504 — **800-866-9437** — 541-779-1049 — 186
Metal Supermarkets IP Inc
520 Abilene Dr 2nd Fl. . . . . Mississauga ON L5T2H7 — **866-867-9344** — 905-362-8226 — 490
Metal-Era Inc
1600 Airport Rd . . . . Waukesha WI 53188 — **800-558-2162** — — 693
Metalex Corp
700 Liberty Dr . . . . Libertyville IL 60048 — **877-667-8634** — 847-362-5400 — 719
Metal-Fab Inc
3025 May St . . . . Wichita KS 67213 — **800-835-2830** — 316-943-2351 — 693
Metalico Annaco Inc
943 Hazel St . . . . Akron OH 44305 — **800-966-1499** — 330-376-1400 — 682
Metalink Technologies Inc
417 Wayne Ave PO Box 1124 . . . . Defiance OH 43512 — **888-999-8002** — 419-782-3472 — 224
Metals Service Ctr Institute (MSCI)
4201 Euclid Ave . . . . Rolling Meadows IL 60008 — **800-634-2358** — 847-485-3000 — 49-18
Metals Week
2 Penn Plz . . . . New York NY 10121 — **800-752-8878** — — 527-13
Metaltech Service Center Inc
9915 Monroe . . . . Houston TX 77075 — **800-644-1204** — 713-991-5100 — 490
Metalworking Group Inc
9070 Pippin Rd . . . . Cincinnati OH 45251 — **800-476-9409** — 513-521-4114 — 485
Metalworking Lubricants Co
25 W Silverdome Industrial Park
. . . . Pontiac MI 48342 — **800-394-5494** — 248-332-3500 — 537
Metasense Inc
403 Commerce Ln #5 . . . . West Berlin NJ 08091 — **866-875-6382** — 856-873-9950 —
Metasystems Inc
13700 State Rd Ste 1 . . . . North Royalton OH 44133 — **800-788-5253** — 440-526-1454 — 461
Metcam Inc
305 Tidwell Cir . . . . Alpharetta GA 30004 — **888-394-9633** — 770-475-9633 — 693
Metcut Research Inc
3980 Rosslyn Dr . . . . Cincinnati OH 45209 — **877-847-1985** — 513-271-5100 — 738
Meteor Crater & Museum of Astrogeology
Exit 233 off I-40 . . . . Winslow AZ 86047 — **800-289-5898** — — 517
Metex Inc
789 Don Mills Rd Ste 218 . . . . North York ON M3C1T5 — **866-817-8137** — 416-203-8388 — 759
Metglas Inc
440 Allied Dr . . . . Conway SC 29526 — **800-581-7654** — 843-349-7319 — 483
Methanex Corp
1800 Waterfront Centre 200 Burrard St
. . . . Vancouver BC V6C3M1 — **800-661-8851** — 604-661-2600 — 144
TSX: MX
Methapharm Inc
11772 W Sample Rd . . . . Coral Springs FL 33065 — **800-287-7686** — 954-341-0795 — 238
Methode Electronics Inc
7401 W Wilson Ave . . . . Chicago IL 60706 — **877-316-7700** — 708-867-6777 — 253
NYSE: MEI
Methodist Alliance Hospice
6400 Shelby View Dr Ste 101 . . . . Memphis TN 38134 — **800-541-8277** — 901-516-1999 — 370
Methodist ElderCare Services
5155 N High St . . . . Columbus OH 43214 — **855-636-2225** — 614-396-4990 — 668
Methodist Health Care System
6565 Fannin St . . . . Houston TX 77030 — **877-726-9362** — 713-790-3311 — 352
Methodist Healthcare Ministries of South Texas Inc
4507 Medical Dr . . . . San Antonio TX 78229 — **800-959-6673** — 210-692-0234 — 352
Methodist Hospital
1305 N Elm St . . . . Henderson KY 42420 — **800-241-8322** — 270-827-7700 — 373-3
Methodist Hospital
1701 N Senate Blvd
PO Box 1367 . . . . Indianapolis IN 46202 — **800-899-8448** — 317-962-2000 — 373-3
Methodist Hospital
8109 Fredericksburg Rd . . . . San Antonio TX 78229 — **800-333-7333** — 210-575-0355 — 373-3
Methodist Hospital of Sacramento
7500 Hospital Dr . . . . Sacramento CA 95823 — **855-361-4103** — 916-423-3000 — 373-3
Methodist Hospital of Southern California
300 W Huntington Dr . . . . Arcadia CA 91007 — **888-388-2838** — 626-898-8000 — 373-3
Methodist Hospitals of Dallas
1441 N Beckley Ave . . . . Dallas TX 75203 — **800-725-9664** — 214-947-8181 — 352
Methodist Rehabilitation Ctr
1350 E Woodrow Wilson Dr . . . . Jackson MS 39216 — **800-223-6672** — 601-981-2611 — 373-6
Methodist Theological School in Ohio
3081 Columbus Pk . . . . Delaware OH 43015 — **800-333-6876** — 740-363-1146 — 167-3
Methodist University
5400 Ramsey St . . . . Fayetteville NC 28311 — **800-488-7110** — 910-630-7000 — 166
Methods Machine Tools Inc
65 Union Ave . . . . Sudbury MA 01776 — **877-668-4262** — 978-443-5388 — 357
METI (Medical Education Technologies Inc)
6300 Edgelake Dr . . . . Sarasota FL 34240 — **866-462-7920** — 941-377-5562 — 250
MetLife Foundation
27-01 Queens Plz N . . . . Long Island NY 11101 — **800-638-5433** — — 304
MetLife Inc
200 Park Ave . . . . New York NY 10166 — **800-638-5433** — 212-578-2211 — 390-2
NYSE: MET
Metl-Span LLC
1720 Lakepointe Dr Ste 101 . . . . Lewisville TX 75057 — **877-585-9969** — 972-221-6656 — 105
Met-Pro Corp Fybroc Div
700 Emlen Way . . . . Telford PA 18969 — **800-392-7621** — 215-723-8155 — 637
Met-Pro Corp Sethco Div
800 Emlen Way . . . . Telford PA 18969 — **800-645-0500** — 215-799-2577 — 637
Metra Electronics Corp
460 Walker St . . . . Holly Hill FL 32117 — **800-221-0932*** — 386-257-1186 — 52
*Sales
MetraPark
308 Sixth Ave N . . . . Billings MT 59101 — **800-366-8538** — 406-256-2400 — 205

				Toll-Free	Phone	Class
Metrex Research Corp						
1717 West Collins Ave	Orange	CA	92867	**800-841-1428**		228
Metrix Instrument Co						
8824 Fallbrook Dr	Houston	TX	77064	**800-638-7494**	281-940-1802	470
Metro - Sales Inc						
1640 E 78th St	Minneapolis	MN	55423	**800-862-7414**	612-861-4000	112
Metro Creative Graphics Inc						
519 Eigth Ave	New York	NY	10018	**800-223-1600**	212-947-5100	343
Metro Energy Group						
1011 Hudson Ave	Ridgefield	NJ	07657	**800-951-2941**	201-941-3470	316
Metro Express Transportation Services Inc						
875 Fee Fee Rd	St. Louis	MO	63043	**800-805-0073**	314-993-1511	311
Metro Health Hospital						
5900 Byron Ctr Ave	Wyoming	MI	49519	**800-968-0051**	616-252-7200	373-3
Metro Jackson Convention & Visitors Bureau						
111 E Capitol St Ste 102	Jackson	MS	39201	**800-354-7695**	601-960-1891	206
Metro Metals Northwest						
5611 NE Columbia Blvd	Portland	OR	97218	**800-610-5680**	503-287-8861	682
Metro Pavia Health System						
MaraMar Plaza Bldg Avenida San Patricio Ste 960	Guaynabo	PR	00968	**888-882-0882**	787-620-9770	362
Metro South Chamber of Commerce						
60 School St	Brockton	MA	02301	**877-777-4414**	508-586-0500	139
Metro Toronto Convention Centre						
255 Front St W	Toronto	ON	M5V2W6	**800-422-7969**	416-585-8000	205
Metro Wire & Cable Co						
6636 Metropolitan Pkwy	Sterling Heights	MI	48312	**800-633-1432**	586-264-3050	246
MetroActive Publishing Inc						
550 S First St	San Jose	CA	95113	**800-831-2345**	408-298-8000	633-8
Metrolina Greenhouses Inc						
16400 Huntersville-Concord Rd	Huntersville	NC	28078	**800-543-3915**	704-875-1371	368
Metromont Corp						
PO Box 2486	Greenville	SC	29602	**844-882-4015**		183
Metroplex Hospital						
2201 S Clear Creek Rd	Killeen	TX	76549	**800-926-7664**	254-526-7523	373-3
Metropolitan Ceramics						
1201 Millerton St SE	Canton	OH	44707	**800-325-3945**		746
Metropolitan Community College						
PO Box 3777	Omaha	NE	68103	**800-228-9553**	402-457-2400	162
Metropolitan Community College Penn Valley						
3200 Broadway	Kansas City	MO	64111	**866-676-6224**	816-604-1000	162
Metropolitan Grill						
2931 E Battlefield	Springfield	MO	65804	**800-225-6343**	417-889-4951	667
Metropolitan Hotel Vancouver						
645 Howe St	Vancouver	BC	V6C2Y9	**800-667-2300**	604-687-1122	378
Metropolitan Methodist Hospital						
1310 McCullough Ave	San Antonio	TX	78212	**800-553-6321**	210-757-2200	373-3
Metropolitan Milwaukee Assn of Commerce						
756 N Milwaukee St	Milwaukee	WI	53202	**855-729-1300**	414-287-4100	139
Metropolitan Museum of Art						
1000 Fifth Ave	New York	NY	10028	**800-468-7386**	212-535-7710	517
Metropolitan Nashville Airport Authority						
1 Terminal Dr Ste 501	Nashville	TN	37214	**800-628-6800**	615-275-1675	27
Metropolitan Nashville Public Schools (MNPS)						
2601 Bransford Ave	Nashville	TN	37204	**800-848-0298**	615-259-8531	681
Metropolitan Plant & Flower Exchange						
2125 Fletcher Ave	Fort Lee	NJ	07024	**800-638-7613**	201-944-1050	292
Metropolitan Poultry & Seafood Co						
1920 Stanford Ct	Landover	MD	20785	**800-522-0060**	301-772-0060	297-10
Metropolitan State University						
700 E Seventh St	Saint Paul	MN	55106	**888-234-2690**	651-793-1300	166
Metropolitan Vacuum Cleaner Co Inc						
5 Raritan Rd	Oakland	NJ	07436	**800-822-1602**	845-357-1600	783
Metropower						
798 21st Ave	Albany	GA	31701	**800-332-7345**	229-432-7345	
MetroStage						
1201 N Royal St	Alexandria	VA	22314	**800-494-8497**	703-548-9044	568
Metrovision Production Group LLC						
508 W 24th St	New York	NY	10011	**800-242-2424**	212-989-1515	733
MetroWest Daily News						
33 New York Ave	Framingham	MA	01701	**800-624-7355**	508-626-4412	528-2
MetroWest Medical Ctr						
115 Lincoln St	Framingham	MA	01702	**800-872-5473**	508-383-1000	373-3
Leonard Morse Campus 67 Union St	Natick	MA	01760	**800-872-5473**	508-650-7000	373-3
Metterra Hotel on Whyte						
10454 82nd Ave	Edmonton	AB	T6E4Z7	**866-465-8150**	780-465-8150	378
Metzgar Conveyor Co Inc						
901 Metzgar Dr NW	Comstock Park	MI	49321	**888-266-8390**	616-784-0930	207
Mexico						
2 United Nations Plz Rm DC2-2386	New York	NY	10017	**800-553-3210**	212-752-0220	779
Consulate General 4506 Carolinas St	Houston	TX	77004	**877-639-4835**	713-271-6800	257
Mexico Tourism Board (CSTM)						
225 N Michigan Ave Ste 2060	Chicago	IL	60601	**800-446-3942**		770
Meyenberg PO Box 934	Turlock	CA	95381	**800-891-4628**		296-10
Meyer & Najem Inc						
11787 Lantern Rd Ste 100	Fishers	IN	46038	**888-578-5131**	317-577-0007	186
Meyer Corp 1 Meyer Pl	Vallejo	CA	94590	**800-888-3883***	707-551-2800	484
*Cust Svc						
Meyer Gallery						
225 Canyon Rd Ste 14	Santa Fe	NM	87501	**800-779-7387**	505-983-1434	42
Meyer Plastics Inc						
5167 E 65th St	Indianapolis	IN	46220	**800-968-4131**	317-259-4131	598
Meziere Enterprises Inc						
220 S Hale Ave	Escondido	CA	92029	**800-208-1755**	760-746-3273	479
MFA Oil Co						
1 Ray Young Dr PO Box 519	Columbia	MO	65201	**800-366-0200**	573-442-0171	577
MFJ Enterprises Inc						
300 Industrial Pk Rd	Starkville	MS	39759	**800-647-1800**	662-323-5869	643
MFS Investment Management						
111 Huntington Ave	Boston	MA	02199	**800-637-8255**	617-954-5000	400
MG Oil Inc						
1180 Creek Dr	Rapid City	SD	57703	**800-333-5173**	605-342-0527	
Mg Scientific Inc						
8500 107th St	Pleasant Prairie	WI	53158	**800-343-8338**	262-947-7000	531
MG. Newell Corp						
301 Citation Ct	Greensboro	NC	27409	**800-334-0231**	336-393-0100	357
MGA Entertainment Inc						
16300 Roscoe Blvd Ste 150	Van Nuys	CA	91406	**800-222-4685**	818-894-2525	756
MGBW (Mitchell Gold & Bob Williams Co)						
135 One Comfortable Pl	Taylorsville	NC	28681	**800-789-5401**	828-632-9200	319-2
Jackson County 2300 Hwy 90	Gautier	MS	39553	**866-735-1122**	228-497-9602	162
MGE (Mohegan Gaming & Entertainment)						
1 Mohegan Sun Blvd	Uncasville	CT	06382	**888-777-7922***	888-226-7711	77
*Resv						
MGM Grand Detroit						
1777 Third St	Detroit	MI	48226	**877-888-2121**	313-465-1400	133
MGM Grand Hotel & Casino						
3799 Las Vegas Blvd S	Las Vegas	NV	89109	**877-880-0880**	702-891-1111	665
MGM Industries Inc						
287 Freehill Rd	Hendersonville	TN	37075	**800-476-5584**	615-824-6572	389
MGM Transformer Co						
5701 Smithway St	Commerce	CA	90040	**800-423-4366**	323-726-0888	762
MGMA (Medical Group Management Assn)						
104 Inverness Terr E	Englewood	CO	80112	**877-275-6462**	303-799-1111	49-8
MGMC (MaineGeneral Medical Center)						
Augusta 361 Old Belgrade Rd	Augusta	ME	04330	**855-464-4463**	207-621-6100	373-3
MGP Ingredients Inc						
100 Commercial St PO Box 130	Atchison	KS	66002	**800-255-0302**	913-367-1480	296-23
NASDAQ: MGPI						
Mgs Inc						
178 Muddy Creek Church Rd	Denver	PA	17517	**800-952-4228**		91
MGS Services LLC						
18775 N Frederick Ave Ste 205	Gaithersburg	MD	20879	**877-647-4255**	301-330-9793	535
MH EBY						
1194 Main St PO Box 127	Blue Ball	PA	17506	**800-292-4752**	717-354-4971	513
MH. Equipment Co						
2001 E Hartman Rd	Chillicothe	IL	61523	**877-884-8465**	309-579-8020	357
MHA (Mental Health America)						
2000 N Beauregard St 6th Fl	Alexandria	VA	22311	**800-969-6642***	703-684-7722	48-17
*Help Line						
Mha an Association of Montana Health Care Providers						
2625 Winne Ave	Helena	MT	59601	**800-351-3551**	406-442-1911	529
MHC (Equitable Bank)						
113 N Locust St	Grand Island	NE	68801	**877-821-5783**	308-382-3136	70
MHC Kenworth						
1524 N Corrington Ave	Kansas City	MO	64120	**888-259-4826**	816-483-7035	773
MHIA (Material Handling Industry of America)						
8720 Red Oak Blvd Ste 201	Charlotte	NC	28217	**800-345-1815**	704-676-1190	49-13
MHM Services Inc						
1593 Spring Hill Rd Ste 600	Vienna	VA	22182	**800-416-3649**	703-749-4600	461
MHNet Behavioral Health						
9606 N MoPac Exwy Ste 600	Austin	TX	78759	**888-646-6889**		460
MHPARC (Memorial Hermann Prevention & Recovery Ctr)						
3043 Gessner	Houston	TX	77080	**877-464-7272**	713-939-7272	373-5
MHPS (Mitsubishi Hitachi Power Systems Americas Inc)						
400 Colonial Ctr Pkwy	Lake Mary	FL	32746	**800-445-9723**	407-688-6100	194
MHRI (Memorial Hospital of Rhode Island)						
111 Brewster St	Pawtucket	RI	02860	**800-647-4362**	401-729-2000	373-3
Miami Beach Chamber of Commerce						
1920 Meridian Ave	Miami Beach	FL	33139	**800-501-0401**	305-674-1300	139
Miami Beach Resort & Spa						
4833 Collins Ave	Miami Beach	FL	33140	**866-765-9090**	305-532-3600	665
Miami Children's Hospital						
3100 SW 62nd Ave	Miami	FL	33155	**800-432-6837**	305-666-6511	373-1
Miami City Ballet						
2200 Liberty Ave	Miami Beach	FL	33139	**877-929-7010**	305-929-7000	569-1
Miami Corp, The						
720 Anderson Ferry Rd	Cincinnati	OH	45238	**800-543-0448**	513-451-6700	590
Miami Correctional Facility						
3038 W 850 S	Bunker Hill	IN	46914	**800-451-6028**	765-689-8920	213
Miami County Chamber of Commerce						
13 E Main St	Peru	IN	46970	**800-521-9945**	765-472-1923	139
Miami International Airport						
4200 NW 36th St 4th Fl	Miami	FL	33166	**800-825-5642**	305-876-7000	27
Miami International Airport Hotel						
NW 20th St & Le Jeune Rd	Miami	FL	33122	**800-327-1276**	305-871-4100	378
Miami International University of Art & Design						
1501 Biscayne Blvd	Miami	FL	33132	**800-225-9023**	305-428-5700	164
Miami University						
501 E High St	Oxford	OH	45056	**866-426-4643**	513-529-1809	166
Miami Valley Hospital						
1 Wyoming St	Dayton	OH	45409	**800-544-0630***	937-208-8000	373-3
*All						
Miami-Cass County Rural Electric Membership Corp						
3086 W 100 N PO Box 168	Peru	IN	46970	**800-844-6668***	765-473-6668	245
*General						
Miami-Dade County Public Schools (M-DCPS)						
1450 NE Second Ave	Miami	FL	33132	**800-955-5504**	305-995-1000	681
Miami-Luken Inc						
265 S Pioneer Blvd	Springboro	OH	45066	**800-856-0217**		
MIBRO Group						
111 Sinnott Rd	Toronto	ON	M1L4S6	**866-941-9006**	416-285-9000	753
MIC (Micro Instrument Corp)						
1199 Emerson St PO Box 60619	Rochester	NY	14606	**800-200-3150**	585-458-3150	452
Micato Safaris						
15 W 26th St 11th Fl	New York	NY	10010	**800-642-2861**	212-545-7111	755
Michael Angelo's Gourmet Foods Inc						
200 Michael Angelo Way	Austin	TX	78728	**877-482-5426**	512-218-3500	296-36
Michael Brandman Associates						
220 Commerce Ste 200	Irvine	CA	92602	**888-826-5814**	714-508-4100	196
Michael Foods Inc						
301 Carlson Pkwy Ste 400	Minnetonka	MN	55305	**800-328-5474**	952-258-4000	615
Michael J Fox Foundation for Parkinson's Research						
Grand Central Stn PO Box 4777	New York	NY	10163	**800-708-7644**		305
Michael J Liccar & Co						
231 S La Salle St	Chicago	IL	60604	**800-922-6604**	312-922-6600	2
Michael J O'Connor & Associates LLC						
608 W Oak St	Frackville	PA	17931	**800-518-4529**	570-874-3300	443

Name / Address	City	State	ZIP	Toll-Free	Phone	Class
Michael R Rubenstein & Assoc						
12527 New Brittany Blvd	Fort Myers	FL	33907	**888-616-1222**	239-489-4443	2
Michael Ramey & Assoc Inc						
PO Box 744	Danville	CA	94526	**800-321-0505**		399
Michael Weining Inc						
124 Crosslake Pk Dr						
PO Box 3158	Mooresville	NC	28117	**877-548-0929**	704-799-0100	816
Michael's						
9777 Las Vegas Blvd S	Las Vegas	NV	89183	**866-796-7111**	702-796-7111	667
Michael's Finer Meats & Seafoods						
3775 Zane Trace Dr	Columbus	OH	43228	**800-282-0518**	614-527-4900	297-9
Michael's Transportation Service Inc						
140 Yolano Dr	Vallejo	CA	94589	**800-295-2448***	707-643-2099	109
*Cust Svc						
Michael's Volkswagen of Bellevue						
15000 SE Eastgate Way	Bellevue	WA	98007	**888-480-5424**	425-641-2002	
Michaels Stores Inc						
8000 Bent Branch Dr	Irving	TX	75063	**800-642-4235***		45
*Cust Svc						
Michbi Doors Inc						
75 Emjay Blvd	Brentwood	NY	11717	**800-854-4541**	631-231-9050	497
Michelin Canada Inc						
2500 Blvd Daniel-Johnson Ste 500	Laval	QC	H7L23K8	**888-871-4444**		
Michelin North America Inc						
1 PkwyS PO Box 19001	Greenville	SC	29615	**866-866-6605***	864-458-5000	749
*Cust Svc						
Michell Consulting Group						
8240 NW 52nd Terr Ste 410	Doral	FL	33166	**800-442-5011**	305-592-5433	196
Michelman Inc						
9080 Shell Rd	Cincinnati	OH	45236	**800-333-1723**	513-793-7766	546
Michels Corp						
817 W Main St	Brownsville	WI	53006	**877-297-8663**	920-583-3132	188-10
Michel-Schlumberger Partners LP						
4155 Wine Creek Rd	Healdsburg	CA	95448	**800-447-3060**	707-433-7427	80-3
Michener Institute for Applied						
222 Saint Patrick St	Toronto	ON	M5T1V4	**800-387-9066**	416-596-3101	681
Michiana Health Information Network Llc						
220 W Colfax Ave Ste 300	South Bend	IN	46601	**800-814-6446**	574-968-1001	620
Michigan						
Attorney General						
525 W Ottawa St	Lansing	MI	48909	**877-765-8388**	517-373-1110	338-23
Career Education & Workforce Programs						
201 N Washington Sq						
Victor Office Center	Lansing	MI	48913	**888-253-6855**	517-335-5858	338-23
Child Support Office						
235 S Grand Ave PO Box 30037	Lansing	MI	48933	**866-661-0005**		338-23
Civil Service Dept						
400 S Pine St Capitol Commons Ctr						
PO Box 30002	Lansing	MI	48909	**800-788-1766**	517-373-3030	338-23
Consumer Protection Div						
PO Box 30213	Lansing	MI	48909	**877-765-8388**	517-373-1140	338-23
Crime Victims Services Commission						
320 S Walnut St Garden Level						
Lewis Cass Bldg	Lansing	MI	48933	**877-251-7373**	517-373-7373	338-23
Economic Development Corp (MEDC)						
300 N Washington Sq	Lansing	MI	48913	**888-522-0103**		338-23
Education Trust						
PO Box 30198	Lansing	MI	48909	**800-638-4543***	517-335-4767	721
*General						
eLibrary Information						
702 W Kalamazoo St PO Box 30007	Lansing	MI	48909	**877-479-0021**	517-373-4331	338-23
Financial & Insurance Regulation						
530 W Allegan St	Lansing	MI	48909	**877-999-6442**	517-373-0220	338-23
State Housing Development Authority						
PO Box 30044	Lansing	MI	48909	**866-466-7328**		
State Lottery						
101 E Hillsdale St PO Box 30023	Lansing	MI	48909	**844-887-6836**	517-335-5756	450
Student Financial Services Bureau						
Austin Bldg 430 W Allegan	Lansing	MI	48922	**888-447-2687**		721
Travel Michigan						
300 N Washington Sq	Lansing	MI	48913	**888-784-7328**	517-335-4590	338-23
Workers Compensation Agency						
2501 Woodlake Cir	Okemos	MI	48864	**888-396-5041**	517-284-8902	338-23
Michigan Assn of Realtors						
720 N Washington Ave	Lansing	MI	48906	**800-454-7842**	517-372-8890	652
Michigan Bankers Assn						
507 S Grand Ave	Lansing	MI	48933	**800-368-7764**	517-485-3600	138
Michigan Bar Journal						
306 Townsend St	Lansing	MI	48933	**888-726-3678**	517-346-6300	455-15
Michigan Chamber of Commerce						
600 S Walnut St	Lansing	MI	48933	**800-748-0266**	517-371-2100	140
Michigan Dental Assn						
3657 Okemos Rd Ste 200	Okemos	MI	48864	**800-589-2632**	517-372-9070	227
Michigan Fluid Power Inc						
4556 Spartan Industrial Dr SW						
	Grandville	MI	49418	**800-635-0289**	616-538-5700	385
Michigan Insurance Co						
1700 E Beltline NE Ste 100						
PO Box 152120	Grand Rapids	MI	49515	**888-606-6426**		389
Michigan International Speedway						
12626 US 12	Brooklyn	MI	49230	**800-354-1010**	517-592-6666	512
Michigan Masonic Home						
1200 Wright Ave	Alma	MI	48801	**800-321-9357**	989-463-3141	668
Michigan Mfg Technology Ctr						
47911 Halyard Dr	Plymouth	MI	48170	**888-414-6682**		664
Michigan Millers Mutual Insurance Co						
2425 E Grand River Ave						
PO Box 30060	Lansing	MI	48912	**800-888-1914**		390-4
Michigan Municipal League						
1675 Green Rd PO Box 1487	Ann Arbor	MI	48105	**800-653-2483**	734-662-3246	48-5
Michigan Stadium						
1201 S Main St						
University of Michigan	Ann Arbor	MI	48104	**866-296-6849**	734-647-2583	716
Michigan State Medical Society						
120 W Saginaw St	East Lansing	MI	48823	**800-482-4881**	517-337-1351	472
Michigan State University						
250 Hannah Admin Bldg	East Lansing	MI	48824	**800-500-1554**	517-355-1855	166
Michigan State University Library						
366 W Circle Dr	East Lansing	MI	48824	**800-500-1554**	517-353-8700	433-6

Name / Address	City	State	ZIP	Toll-Free	Phone	Class
Michigan Technological University						
1400 Townsend Dr	Houghton	MI	49931	**888-688-1885**	906-487-2335	166
Michigan Theological Seminary						
41550 E Ann Arbor Trl	Plymouth	MI	48170	**800-356-6639**	734-207-9581	167-3
Michigan United Conservation Clubs						
2101 Wood St	Lansing	MI	48912	**800-777-6720**	517-371-1041	455-22
Michigan Wheel Corp						
1501 Buchanan Ave SW	Grand Rapids	MI	49507	**800-369-4335**	616-452-6941	385
Mickey Thompson Tires						
4600 Prosper Dr	Stow	OH	44224	**800-222-9092**	330-928-9092	749
Mickey Truck Bodies Inc						
1305 Trinity Ave	High Point	NC	27261	**800-334-9061**	336-882-6806	774
Mickey's Linen						
4601 W Addison St	Chicago	IL	60641	**800-545-7511**		
Mico Inc						
1911 Lee Blvd	North Mankato	MN	56003	**800-477-6426**	507-625-6426	385
Mi-Corporation						
4601 Creekstone Dr Ste 180	Durham	NC	27703	**888-621-6230**	919-485-4819	
Micro 100 Tool Corp						
1410 E Pine Ave	Meridian	ID	83642	**800-421-8065**	208-888-7310	491
Micro Care Corp						
595 John Downey Dr	New Britain	CT	06051	**800-638-0125**	860-827-0626	151
Micro Control Co						
7956 Main St NE	Minneapolis	MN	55432	**800-328-9923**	763-786-8750	248
Micro Express Inc						
8 Hammond Dr Ste 105	Irvine	CA	92618	**800-989-9900**		173-2
Micro Instrument Corp (MIC)						
1199 Emerson St PO Box 60619	Rochester	NY	14606	**800-200-3150**	585-458-3150	452
Micro Matic USA Inc						
10726 N Second St	Machesney Park	IL	61115	**866-291-5756**	815-968-7557	660
Micro Plastics Inc						
11 Industry Ln Hwy 178 N						
PO Box 149	Flippin	AR	72634	**800-466-1467**	870-453-2261	604
Micro Strategies Inc						
1140 Parsippany Blvd	Parsippany	NJ	07054	**888-467-6588**		177
Micro Surface Engr Inc						
1550 E Slauson Ave	Los Angeles	CA	90011	**800-322-5832**	323-582-7348	483
Micro Surface Finishing Products Inc						
1217 W Third St	Wilton	IA	52778	**800-225-3006**	563-732-3240	1
MicroAire Surgical Instruments Inc						
3590 Grand Forks Blvd	Charlottesville	VA	22911	**800-722-0822**		474
MicroBiz Corp						
655 Oak Grove Ave Ste 493	Menlo Park	CA	94026	**800-937-2289**	702-749-5353	178-1
Microboards Technology LLC						
8150 Mallory Ct	Chanhassen	MN	55317	**800-646-8881**	952-556-1600	173-8
Micro-Clean Inc						
177 N Commerce Way	Bethlehem	PA	18017	**800-523-9852**	610-954-7803	738
Microcomputer Applications Inc						
777 S Wadsworth Blvd						
Bldg 4-220	Lakewood	CO	80226	**800-453-9565**	303-801-0338	
Microflex Corp						
2301 Robb Dr	Reno	NV	89523	**800-876-6866**	775-746-6600	
Microfluidics International Corp						
90 Glacier Dr Ste 1000	Westwood	MA	02090	**800-370-5452**	617-969-5452	298
MicroGroup Inc						
7 Industrial Pk Rd	Medway	MA	02053	**800-255-8823**	508-533-4925	591
Microlife USA Inc						
1617 Gulf to Bay Blvd Second Fl						
Ste B	Clearwater	FL	33755	**888-314-2599**	727-451-0484	474
Microlink Enterprise Inc						
20955 Pathfinder Rd Ste 100	Diamond Bar	CA	91765	**800-829-3688**	562-205-1888	178-1
MicroLumen Inc						
1 Microlumen Way	Oldsmar	FL	34677	**800-968-9014**	813-886-1200	474
Microlynx Systems Ltd						
1925 18 Ave NE Ste 107	Calgary	AB	T2E7T8	**866-835-4332**	403-275-7346	261
Micromatic LLC						
525 Berne St	Berne	IN	46711	**800-333-5752**	260-589-2136	223
Micromeritics Instrument Corp						
1 Micromeritics Dr	Norcross	GA	30093	**800-229-5052**	770-662-3620	418
Micrometals Inc						
5615 E La Palma Ave	Anaheim	CA	92807	**800-356-5977**	714-970-9400	762
MicroMetl Corp						
3035 N Shadeland Ave						
Ste 300	Indianapolis	IN	46226	**800-662-4822**		660
MicroMod Automation Inc						
75 Town Centre Dr	Rochester	NY	14623	**800-480-1975**	585-321-9200	201
Micron Technology Inc						
8000 S Federal Way	Boise	ID	83707	**888-363-2589**	208-368-4000	621
NASDAQ: MU						
Micronesia						
300 E 42nd St Ste 1600	New York	NY	10017	**800-469-4828**	212-697-8370	779
Consulate						
1725 N St NW	Washington	DC	20036	**877-730-9753**	202-223-4383	257
MicroPact						
12901 Worldgate Dr Ste 800	Herndon	VA	20170	**866-346-9492**	703-709-6110	177
Microphor Inc						
452 E Hill Rd	Willits	CA	95490	**800-358-8280***	707-459-5563	607
*Orders						
Micro-Poise Measurment Systems LLC						
555 Mondial Pkwy	Streetsboro	OH	44241	**800-428-3812**	330-541-9100	385
Microprocessor Report						
355 Chesley Ave	Mountain View	CA	94040	**800-413-2881**	408-270-3772	527-3
Micropump Inc						
1402 NE 136th Ave	Vancouver	WA	98684	**800-222-9565***	360-253-2008	637
*Sales						
MicroRam Electronics Inc						
222 Dunbar Ct	Oldsmar	FL	34677	**800-642-7671**	813-854-5500	246
Microsemi Corp						
2381 Morse Ave	Irvine	CA	92614	**800-713-4113**	949-221-7100	692
NASDAQ: MSCC						
Microsoft Corp						
1 Microsoft Way	Redmond	WA	98052	**800-642-7676**	425-882-8080	178-1
NASDAQ: MSFT						
MicroStrategy						
1850 Towers Crescent Plz	Tysons Corner	VA	22182	**888-266-0321**	703-848-8600	178-11
NASDAQ: MSTR						
Microthermics Inc						
3216-B Wellington Ct	Raleigh	NC	27615	**800-466-2369**	919-878-8045	296

				Toll-Free	Phone	Class
MicroVention Inc						
1311 Valencia Ave	Tustin	CA	92780	**800-990-8368**	714-247-8000	475
MicroVision Development Inc						
5541 Fermi Ct Ste 120	Carlsbad	CA	92008	**800-998-4555**	760-438-7781	178-8
MicroVote General Corp						
6366 Guilford Ave	Indianapolis	IN	46220	**800-257-4901**	317-257-4900	796
Microwave Filter Company Inc						
6743 Kinne St	East Syracuse	NY	13057	**800-448-1666**	315-438-4700	253
Microwest Software Systems Inc						
10981 San Diego Mson Rd Ste 210	San Diego	CA	92108	**800-969-9699**	619-280-0440	180
MICS (Management Information Control Systems Inc)						
2025 Ninth St	Los Osos	CA	93402	**800-838-6427**		178-10
Mid America Computer Corp						
PO Box 700	Blair	NE	68008	**800-622-2502**	402-426-6222	225
Mid America Motorworks						
17082 N US Hwy 45 PO Box 1368	Effingham	IL	62401	**866-350-4543**	217-540-4200	61
Mid Atlantic Center for The Arts						
1048 Washington St	Cape May	NJ	08204	**800-275-4278**	609-884-5404	517
Mid Atlantic Printers Ltd						
503 Third St	Altavista	VA	24517	**888-231-3175**	434-369-6633	528-3
Mid Ohio Energy Co-op Inc						
555 W Franklin St	Kenton	OH	43326	**888-382-6732**	419-673-7289	245
Mid Pines Inn & Golf Club						
1010 Midland Rd	Southern Pines	NC	28387	**800-747-7272**	910-692-2114	665
Mid South Lumber Inc						
6595 Marshall Blvd PO Box 1185	Lithonia	GA	30058	**800-759-3076**	770-482-4800	
MID-AM Bldg Supply Inc						
1615 Omar Bradley Dr PO Box 645	Moberly	MO	65270	**800-892-5850**		191-3
Midamar Corp						
PO Box 218	Cedar Rapids	IA	52406	**800-362-3711**	319-362-3711	297-9
Mid-America Charter Lines						
2513 E Higgins Rd	Elk Grove Village	IL	60007	**800-323-0312**	847-437-3779	107
Mid-America Christian University						
3500 SW 119th St	Oklahoma City	OK	73170	**888-888-2341**	405-691-3800	166
Midamerica Hotels Corp						
105 S Mt Auburn Rd	Cape Girardeau	MO	63703	**888-866-4326**	573-334-0546	377
Mid-America Merchandising Inc						
204 W Third St	Kansas City	MO	64105	**800-333-6737**	816-471-5600	9
Midamerica National Bancshares						
100 W Elm St	Canton	IL	61520	**877-647-5050**	309-647-5000	70
MidAmerica Nazarene University						
2030 E College Way	Olathe	KS	66062	**800-800-8887**	913-782-3750	166
Mid-America Publishing Corp						
9 Second St NW	Hampton	IA	50441	**800-558-1244**	641-456-2585	633-8
Mid-America Reformed Seminary						
229 Seminary Dr	Dyer	IN	46311	**888-440-6277**	219-864-2400	167-3
Mid-America Transplant Services (MTS)						
1110 Highlands Plaza Dr E Ste 100	Saint Louis	MO	63110	**888-376-4854**	314-735-8200	541
Mid-American Coaches Inc						
4530 Hwy 47	Washington	MO	63090	**866-944-8687**		755
MidAmerican Energy Holdings Co						
500 E Court Ave PO Box 657	Des Moines	IA	50303	**888-427-5632**		359-5
Midas International Corp						
823 Donald Ross Rd	Juno Beach	FL	33408	**800-621-8545**	630-438-3000	62-3
Mid-Atlantic Christian University						
715 N Poindexter St	Elizabeth City	NC	27909	**866-996-6228**	252-334-2000	161
Mid-Atlantic PenFed Realty Berkshire Hathaway HomeServices (PCR)						
3050 Chain Bridge Rd	Fairfax	VA	22030	**866-225-5778**	703-691-7653	651
Mid-Carolina Electric Co-op Inc						
PO Box 669	Lexington	SC	29071	**888-813-8000***	803-749-6555	245
*Cust Svc						
Midcontinent Airport						
2173 Air Cargo Rd	Wichita	KS	67209	**800-628-6800**	316-946-4700	27
Midcontinent Communications						
PO Box 5010	Sioux Falls	SD	57117	**800-888-1300**	605-274-9810	116
Mid-Continent Group						
1437 S Boulder Ave W PO Box 1409	Tulsa	OK	74119	**800-722-4994**	918-587-7221	390-4
Mid-Continent University						
99 Powell Rd E	Mayfield	KY	42066	**888-628-4723**	270-247-8521	166
Mid-Continental Restoration Company Inc						
401 E Hudson Rd PO Box 429	Fort Scott	KS	66701	**800-835-3700**	620-223-3700	189-7
Mid-Delta Health Systems Inc						
405 N Hayden St	Belzoni	MS	39038	**800-543-9055**	662-247-2418	370
Middle Georgia College						
1100 Second St SE	Cochran	GA	31014	**800-548-4221**	478-934-6221	162
Middle Georgia Electric Membership Corp						
600 Tippettville Rd	Vienna	GA	31092	**800-342-0144**	229-268-2671	245
Middle River Aircraft Systems (MRAS)						
103 Chesapeake Park Plz	Baltimore	MD	21220	**877-432-3272**	410-682-1500	22
Middle Tennessee Electric Membership Corp						
555 New Salem Hwy	Murfreesboro	TN	37129	**877-777-9020**		
Middle Tennessee Natural Gas Utility District (MTNG)						
1036 W Broad St PO Box 670	Smithville	TN	37166	**800-880-6373**	615-597-4300	782
Middle Tennessee State University						
1301 E Main St	Murfreesboro	TN	37132	**800-533-6878***	615-898-2300	166
*Admissions						
Middlebury College						
131 S Main St	Middlebury	VT	05753	**877-214-3330**	802-443-3000	166
Middleby Corp						
1400 Toastmaster Dr	Elgin	IL	60120	**800-331-5842**	847-741-3300	298
NASDAQ: MIDD						
Middlesboro Coca-Cola Bottling Works Inc						
1324 Cumberland Ave	Middlesboro	KY	40965	**800-442-0102**	877-692-4679	80-2
Middlesex Community College						
590 Springs Rd	Bedford	MA	01730	**800-818-3434**	978-656-3370	162
Middlesex Community College						
100 Training Hill Rd	Middletown	CT	06457	**800-818-5501**	860-343-5800	162
Middlesex Gases & Technologies Inc						
292 Second St PO Box 490249	Everett	MA	02149	**800-649-6704**	617-387-5050	786
Middlesex Hospital						
28 Crescent St	Middletown	CT	06457	**800-548-2394**	860-358-6000	373-3
Middlesex Mutual Assurance Co						
213 Ct St PO Box 891	Middletown	CT	06457	**800-622-3780**		390-4
Middlesex Research Mfg Company Inc						
27 Apsley St	Hudson	MA	01749	**800-424-5188**	978-562-3697	740-2

				Toll-Free	Phone	Class
Middlesex Savings Bank						
120 Flanders Rd	Westborough	MA	01581	**877-463-6287**	508-653-0300	70
Middlesex Water Co						
1500 Ronson Rd PO Box 1500	Iselin	NJ	08830	**800-549-3802**	732-634-1500	782
NASDAQ: MSEX						
Middleton & Company Inc						
600 Atlantic Ave 18th Fl	Boston	MA	02210	**800-357-5101**	617-357-5101	41
Middleton Place						
4300 Ashley River Rd	Charleston	SC	29414	**800-782-3608**	843-556-6020	667
MidFirst Bank						
PO Box 76149	Oklahoma City	OK	73147	**888-643-3477**	405-767-7000	70
Midian Electronic Comm Systems						
2302 E 22nd St	Tucson	AZ	85713	**800-643-4267**	520-884-7981	643
Mid-Kansas Co-op (MKC)						
PO Box D	Moundridge	KS	67107	**800-864-4428**		48-2
Mid-Lakes Distributing Inc						
1029 W Adams St	Chicago	IL	60607	**888-733-2700**	312-733-1033	608
Midland Area						
Chamber of Commerce						
300 Rodd St Ste 101	Midland	MI	48640	**800-999-3199**	989-839-9901	139
Midland by AMC, The						
1228 Main St	Kansas City	MO	64105	**800-653-8000**	816-283-9900	568
Midland College						
3600 N Garfield St	Midland	TX	79705	**800-474-7164**	432-685-4500	162
Midland County Convention & Visitors Bureau						
300 Rodd St Ste 101	Midland	MI	48640	**800-444-9979**	989-839-0340	206
Midland Ctr for the Arts Inc						
1801 W St Andrews Rd	Midland	MI	48640	**800-523-7649**	989-631-5930	517
Midland Daily News						
124 McDonald St	Midland	MI	48640	**877-411-2762**	989-835-7171	528-2
Midland Hospice Care						
200 SW Frazier Cir	Topeka	KS	66606	**800-491-3691**	785-232-2044	370
Midland Industries Inc						
1424 N Halsted St	Chicago	IL	60642	**800-662-8228**	312-664-7300	483
Midland Information Resources Co						
5440 Corporate Pk Dr	Davenport	IA	52807	**800-232-3696**	563-359-3696	623
Midland International Air & Space Port						
9506 Laforce Blvd PO Box 60305	Midland	TX	79706	**800-973-2867**	432-560-2200	27
Midland Memorial Hospital						
400 Rosalind Redfern Grover Pkwy	Midland	TX	79701	**800-833-2916**	432-685-1111	373-3
Midland Mortgage Co						
999 NW Grand Blvd Ste 100	Oklahoma City	OK	73118	**800-654-4566**		507
Midland National Bank						
527 Main St	Newton	KS	67114	**800-810-9457**	316-283-1700	70
Midland National Life Insurance Co						
1 Sammons Plz	Sioux Falls	SD	57193	**800-923-3223**	605-335-5700	390-2
Midland Paper						
101 E Palatine Rd	Wheeling	IL	60090	**800-323-8522**	847-777-2700	549
Midland Power Co-op						
1005 E Lincolnway PO Box 420	Jefferson	IA	50129	**800-833-8876**	515-386-4111	245
Midland Reporter-Telegram						
PO Box 1650	Midland	TX	79702	**800-542-3952**	432-682-5311	528-2
Midlands Technical College						
PO Box 2408	Columbia	SC	29202	**800-922-8038**	803-738-1400	162
Midmark Corp						
60 Vista Dr	Versailles	OH	45380	**800-643-6275**	937-526-7975	474
MidMichigan Home Care						
3007 N Saginaw Rd	Midland	MI	48640	**800-852-9350**	989-633-1400	370
Midnight Rose Hotel & Casino						
256 E Bennett Ave	Cripple Creek	CO	80813	**800-635-5825**		133
Midnight Sun Adventure Travel						
1027 Pandora Ave	Victoria	BC	V8V3P6	**800-255-5057**	250-480-9409	755
Midrange Solutions Inc						
20 Hillside Ave	Springfield	NJ	07081	**800-882-4008**	973-912-7050	196
MidSouth Bancorp Inc						
102 Versailles Blvd	Lafayette	LA	70501	**800-213-2265**	337-237-8343	359-2
NYSE: MSL						
Mid-South Community College						
2000 W Broadway	West Memphis	AR	72301	**866-733-6722**	870-733-6722	162
Mid-South Wire Company Inc						
1070 Visco Dr	Nashville	TN	37210	**800-714-7800**	615-743-2850	808
Midstate College						
411 W Northmoor Rd	Peoria	IL	61614	**800-251-4299**	309-692-4092	795
Midstate Electric Co-op Inc						
16755 Finley Butte Rd	La Pine	OR	97739	**800-722-7219**	541-536-2126	245
Mid-State Equipment Inc						
W 1115 Bristol Rd	Columbus	WI	53925	**877-677-4020**	920-623-4020	274
Mid-State Machine & Fabricating Corp						
2730 Mine and Mill Rd	Lakeland	FL	33801	**844-785-4180**		
Mid-States Bolt & Screw Co						
4126 Somers Dr	Burton	MI	48529	**800-482-0867**		278
Mid-States Screw Corp						
1817 18th Ave	Rockford	IL	61104	**888-354-6772**	815-397-2440	278
Mid-States Supply Co						
1716 Guinotte Ave	Kansas City	MO	64120	**800-825-1410**	816-842-4290	608
Midtown Hotel						
220 Huntington Ave	Boston	MA	02115	**800-343-1177**	617-262-1000	378
Midway College						
512 E Stephens St	Midway	KY	40347	**800-952-4122**		166
Midwesco Filter Resources Inc						
309 N Braddock St	Winchester	VA	22601	**800-336-7300**	540-773-4780	18
Midwest America Federal Credit Union						
1104 Medical Pk Dr	Fort Wayne	IN	46825	**800-348-4738**	260-482-3334	219
Midwest Bank						
105 E Soo St PO Box 40	Parkers Prairie	MN	56361	**877-365-5155**	218-338-6054	70
Midwest Bio-systems Inc						
28933 35 E St	Tampico	IL	61283	**877-649-2114**	815-438-7200	428
Midwest Corporate Aviation						
3512 N Webb Rd	Wichita	KS	67226	**800-435-9622**	316-636-9700	63
Midwest Dental Equipment Services & Supplies						
2700 Commerce St	Wichita Falls	TX	76301	**800-766-2025**		228
Midwest Designer Supply Inc						
N30 W22377 Green Rd Ste C	Waukesha	WI	53186	**888-523-2611**		360
Midwest Elastomers Inc						
700 Industrial Dr PO Box 412	Wapakoneta	OH	45895	**877-786-3539**	419-738-8844	601-3
Midwest Electric Co-op Corp						
104 Washington Ave	Grant	NE	69140	**800-451-3691**	308-352-4356	245

	Toll-Free	Phone	Class
Midwest Employers Casualty Co			
14755 N Outer 40 Dr			
Ste 300 ....Chesterfield MO 63017	**877-975-2667**	636-449-7000	390-4
Midwest Energy & Communications			
60590 Decatur Rd ....Cassopolis MI 49031	**800-492-5989**		245
Midwest Energy Inc			
1330 Canterbury Dr ....Hays KS 67601	**800-222-3121**		245
Midwest Folding Products Inc			
1414 S Western Ave ....Chicago IL 60608	**800-621-4716**	312-666-3366	319-3
Midwest Helicopter Airways Inc			
525 Executive Dr ....Willowbrook IL 60527	**800-323-7609**	630-325-7860	358
MIDWEST Homes for Pets			
3142 S Cowan Rd PO Box 1031 ....Muncie IN 47302	**800-428-8560**	765-289-3355	574
Midwest Industries Inc			
122 E State Hwy 175 ....Ida Grove IA 51445	**800-859-3028**	712-364-3365	758
Midwest Library Service Inc			
11443 St Charles Rock Rd ....Bridgeton MO 63044	**800-325-8833**	314-739-3100	96
Midwest Manufacturing Inc			
5311 Kane Rd ....Eau Claire WI 54703	**800-826-7126**	715-876-5555	810
Midwest Mechanical Group			
801 Parkview Blvd ....Lombard IL 60148	**800-214-3680**	630-850-2300	189-10
Midwest Metal Products Co			
2100 W Mt Pleasant Rd ....Muncie IN 47302	**888-741-1044**		478
Midwest Motor Express Inc			
5015 E Main Ave ....Bismarck ND 58502	**800-741-4097**	701-223-1880	775
Midwest Plan Service			
122 Davidson Hall ISU ....Ames IA 50011	**800-562-3618**	515-294-4337	633-2
Midwest Plastic Components			
7309 W 27th St ....Minneapolis MN 55426	**800-243-3221**	952-929-3312	600
Midwest Pro Painting Inc			
12845 Farmington Rd ....Livonia MI 48150	**800-860-6757**	734-427-1040	189-8
Midwest Products Company Inc			
400 S Indiana St ....Hobart IN 46342	**800-348-3497***	219-942-1134	757
*Orders			
Midwest Quality Gloves Inc			
835 Industrial Rd ....Chillicothe MO 64601	**800-821-3028**	660-646-2165	155-7
Midwest Sales & Service Inc			
917 S Chapin St ....South Bend IN 46601	**800-772-7262**	574-287-3365	38
Midwest Specialized Transportation Inc			
4515 Hwy 63 N PO Box 6418 ....Rochester MN 55906	**800-927-8007**	507-424-4838	447
Midwest Sports Supply Inc			
11613 Reading Rd ....Cincinnati OH 45241	**800-334-4580**	513-956-4900	707
Mid-West Spring & Stamping Co			
1404 Joliet Rd Unit C ....Romeoville IL 60446	**800-619-0909**	630-739-3800	715
Mid-West Steel Bldg Co			
7301 Fairview ....Houston TX 77041	**800-777-9378**	713-466-7788	105
Midwest Systems			
5911 Hall St ....Saint Louis MO 63147	**800-383-6281**	314-389-6280	774
Midwest Tile & Concrete Products Inc			
4309 Webster Rd ....Woodburn IN 46797	**800-359-4701**	260-749-5173	183
Midwest Tool & Cutlery Co Inc			
1210 Progress St PO Box 160 ....Sturgis MI 49091	**800-782-4659**	269-651-7964	222
Midwest Truck & Auto Parts Inc			
1001 W Exchange ....Chicago IL 60609	**800-934-2727**	773-247-3400	61
Midwest Walnut			
1914 Tostevin ....Council Bluffs IA 51503	**800-592-5688**	712-325-9191	446
Midwest Wire Products Inc			
PO Box 770 ....Sturgeon Bay WI 54235	**800-445-0225**	920-743-6591	486
Midwestern Baptist Theological Seminary			
5001 N Oak Trafficway ....Kansas City MO 64118	**800-944-6287**	816-414-3700	167-3
Midwestern Industries Inc			
915 Oberlin Rd SW ....Massillon OH 44647	**877-474-9464***	330-837-4203	190
*Cust Svc			
Midwestern Intermediate Unit Iv			
453 Maple St ....Grove City PA 16127	**800-942-8035**	724-458-6700	681
Midwestern Regional Medical Ctr (MRMC)			
2520 Elisha Ave ....Zion IL 60099	**800-615-3055**	847-872-4561	373-7
Midwestern State University			
3410 Taft Blvd ....Wichita Falls TX 76308	**800-842-1922***	940-397-4000	166
*Admissions			
Miele Inc			
9 Independence Way ....Princeton NJ 08540	**800-843-7231**	609-419-9898	36
Mifflinburg Bank & Trust Co (MBTC)			
250 E Chestnut St			
PO Box 186.................Mifflinburg PA 17844	**888-966-3131**	570-966-1041	70
Mighty Distributing System of America Inc			
650 Engineering Dr ....Norcross GA 30092	**800-829-3900**	770-448-3900	61
Migratory Bird Conservation Commission			
5275 Leesburg Pk ....Falls Church VA 22041	**800-344-9453**		
Mii Amo at Enchantment Resort			
525 Boynton Canyon Rd ....Sedona AZ 86336	**888-749-2137**	928-203-8500	703
Mijac Alarm			
9339 Charles Smith Ave			
Ste 100.................Rancho Cucamonga CA 91730	**800-982-7612**	909-982-7612	689
Mikasa Sports Usa			
556 Vanguard Way Unit D.................Brea CA 92821	**800-854-6927**		
Mike Collins & Associates Inc			
6048 Century Oaks Dr ....Chattanooga TN 37416	**800-347-6950**	423-892-8899	175
Mike Davis & Associates Inc			
15505 Long Vista Dr # 200 ....Austin TX 78728	**888-836-8442**	512-836-8442	343
Mike Ferry Organization, The			
7220 S Cimarron Rd Ste 300 ....Las Vegas NV 89113	**800-448-0647**	702-982-6260	260
Mike Kelly Law Group LLC			
500 Taylor St Ste 400 ....Columbia SC 29201	**866-692-0123**	803-726-0123	427
Mike Murach & Assoc Inc			
4340 N Knoll ....Fresno CA 93722	**800-221-5528**	559-440-9071	633-2
Mike Reed Chevrolet			
1559 E Oglethorpe ....Hinesville GA 31313	**877-228-3943**		57
Mike Rose's Auto Body Inc			
2260 Via de Marcardos ....Concord CA 94520	**855-340-1739**	925-689-1739	62-4
Mike-Sell's Potato Chip Co			
333 Leo St PO Box 115 ....Dayton OH 45404	**800-257-4742**	937-228-9400	296-35
Mikimoto (America) Company Ltd			
730 Fifth Ave ....New York NY 10019	**844-341-0579**		410
Mikros Engineering Inc			
8755 Wyoming Ave N ....Brooklyn Park MN 55445	**800-394-5499**	763-424-4642	261
Mila Displays Inc			
1315B Broadway Ste 108 ....Hewlett NY 11557	**800-295-6452**	516-791-2643	5
Milaeger's Inc			
4838 Douglas Ave ....Racine WI 53402	**800-669-1229**	262-639-2040	323
Milam County			
107 W Main St ....Cameron TX 76520	**800-299-2437**	254-697-7049	337
Milan Express Company Inc			
1091 Kefauver Dr ....Milan TN 38358	**800-231-7303**		775
Milbar Hydro-Test Inc			
651 Aero Dr ....Shreveport LA 71107	**800-259-8210**	318-227-8210	535
Mile High Shooting Accessories LLC			
3731 Monarch St ....Erie CO 80516	**877-871-9990**	303-255-9999	225
Mile Marker International Inc			
2121 BLOUNT Rd ....Pompano Beach FL 33069	**800-886-8647**		61
Miles & More			
PO Box 946 ....Santa Clarita CA 91380	**800-581-6400**		26
Miles College			
5500 Myron Massey Blvd ....Fairfield AL 35064	**800-445-0708***	205-929-1000	166
*Admissions			
Miles Community College			
2715 Dickinson St ....Miles City MT 59301	**800-541-9281**	406-874-6100	162
Miles Kimball Co			
250 City Ctr Bldg ....Oshkosh WI 54906	**855-202-7394***		457
*Cust Svc			
Miles Media Group LLLP			
6751 Professional Pkwy W			
Ste 200 ....Sarasota FL 34240	**800-683-0010**	941-342-2300	633-9
Miles Technologies Inc			
300 W Rt 38 ....Moorestown NJ 08057	**800-496-8001**	856-439-0999	180
MilesTek Corp			
1506 I-35 W ....Denton TX 76207	**800-958-5173**	940-484-9400	194
Milestone Contractors LP			
3410 S 650 E ....Elizabethtown IN 47232	**800-377-7727**	812-579-5248	188-4
Milestone Scientific Inc			
220 S Orange Ave ....Livingston NJ 07039	**800-862-1125**	973-535-2717	475
OTC: MLSS			
Milestone Technologies Inc			
3101 Skyway Ct ....Fremont CA 94539	**877-651-2454**		392
Milford Bank			
33 Broad St ....Milford CT 06460	**800-340-4862**	203-783-5700	70
Milford Federal Savings & Loan Assn			
246 Main St ....Milford MA 01757	**800-478-6990**	508-634-2500	71
Milford Markets Inc			
PO Box 7812 ....Edison NJ 08818	**800-746-7748**		344
Milford-Miami Township Chamber of Commerce			
745 Center St #302 ....Milford OH 45150	**800-837-3200**	513-831-2411	139
Milgram & Company Ltd			
400 – 645 Wellington ....Montreal QC H3C0L1	**800-879-6144**	514-288-2161	314
Military Benefit Assn (MBA)			
14605 Avion Pkwy			
PO Box 221110.................Chantilly VA 20153	**800-336-0100**	703-968-6200	48-19
Military Engineer Magazine			
607 Prince St ....Alexandria VA 22314	**800-336-3097***	703-549-3800	455-12
*Cust Svc			
Military Officers Assn of America (MOAA)			
201 N Washington St ....Alexandria VA 22314	**800-234-6622**		48-19
Milk Products LLC			
PO Box 150 ....Chilton WI 53014	**800-657-0793**	920-849-2348	296-10
Milk Specialties Co			
7500 Flying Cloud Dr			
Ste 500 ....Eden Prairie MN 55344	**800-323-4274**	952-942-7310	445
Milkco Inc			
220 Deaverview Rd ....Asheville NC 28806	**800-842-8021**	828-254-9560	296-27
Mill City Museum			
704 S Second St ....Minneapolis MN 55401	**800-657-3773**	612-341-7555	517
Mill Creek Mall			
654 Millcreek Mall ....Erie PA 16565	**800-615-3535**	814-868-9000	458
Mill Falls			
312 Daniel Webster Hwy ....Meredith NH 03253	**844-745-2931**		378
Mill Run Tours			
424 Madison Ave 12th Fl ....New York NY 10017	**855-645-5868**		
Mill Steel Co			
5116 36th St SE ....Grand Rapids MI 49512	**800-247-6455**		719
Mill Street Inn			
75 Mill St ....Newport RI 02840	**800-392-1316**	401-849-9500	378
Mill Supply Div			
266 Morse St ....Hamden CT 06517	**888-585-9354***	203-777-7668	87
*General			
Mill Valley Inn			
165 Throckmorton Ave ....Mill Valley CA 94941	**855-334-7946**	415-389-6608	378
Millard Lumber Inc			
12900 I St ....Omaha NE 68145	**800-228-9260**	402-896-2800	191-3
Millburn Veterinary Hospital			
147 Millburn Ave ....Millburn NJ 07041	**800-365-8295**	973-467-1700	789
Millcraft Paper Co			
6800 Grant Ave ....Cleveland OH 44105	**800-860-2482**	216-441-5500	549
Mille Lacs Band of Ojibwe			
43408 Oodena Dr ....Onamia MN 56359	**800-709-6445**	320-532-4181	132
Mille Lacs Electric Co-op			
PO Box 230 ....Aitkin MN 56431	**800-450-2191**	218-927-2191	245
Mille Lacs Health System			
200 Elm St N ....Onamia MN 56359	**877-535-3154**	320-532-3154	373-3
Millenia Products Group			
1345 Norwood Ave ....Itasca IL 60143	**800-822-0092**	630-741-7900	36
Millenium Aviation			
2365 Bernville Rd ....Reading PA 19605	**800-366-9419**	610-372-4728	63
Millennium Broadway Hotel New York			
145 W 44th St ....New York NY 10036	**800-622-5569**	212-768-4400	376
Millennium Industrial Tires LLC			
433 Lane Dr ....Florence AL 35630	**800-421-1180**	256-764-2900	
Millennium Marking Company Inc			
2600 Greenleaf Ave ....Elk Grove Village IL 60007	**800-453-5362**		
Millennium Resort Scottsdale McCormick Ranch			
7401 N Scottsdale Rd ....Scottsdale AZ 85253	**800-243-1332**	480-948-5050	665
Miller & Co LLC			
9700 W Higgins Rd Ste 1000 ....Rosemont IL 60018	**800-727-9847**	847-696-2400	498
Miller & Luring Company LPa			
314 W Main St ....Troy OH 45373	**800-381-9680**	937-339-2627	427
Miller Chemical & Fertilizer Corp			
120 Radio Rd PO Box 333 ....Hanover PA 17331	**800-233-2040**	717-632-8921	280

Alphabetical Section

Name / Address	City	State	Zip	Toll-Free	Phone	Class
Miller Consolidated Industries Inc						
2221 Arbor Blvd	Dayton	OH	45439	**800-589-4133**	937-294-2681	482
Miller County						
400 Laurel St Ste 105	Texarkana	AR	71854	**800-482-8998**	870-774-1501	337
Miller Electric Co						
2251 Rosselle St	Jacksonville	FL	32204	**800-554-4761***	904-388-8000	189-4
*Sales						
Miller Electric Mfg Co						
1635 W Spencer St	Appleton	WI	54914	**888-843-7693**	920-734-9821	806
Miller Energy Inc						
3200 S Clinton Ave	South Plainfield	NJ	07080	**800-631-5454**	908-755-6700	177
Miller Engineers & Scientists						
5308 S 12th St	Sheboygan	WI	53081	**800-969-7013**	920-458-6164	261
Miller Environmental Services Inc						
401 Navigation Blvd	Corpus Christi	TX	78408	**800-929-7227**	361-289-9800	63
Miller Industries Inc						
8503 Hilltop Dr	Ooltewah	TN	37363	**800-292-0330**	423-238-4171	513
NYSE: MLR						
Miller Packing Co						
PO Box 1390	Lodi	CA	95241	**800-624-2328**	209-339-2310	296-26
Miller Pipeline Corp						
8850 Crawfordsville Rd	Indianapolis	IN	46234	**800-428-3742**	317-293-0278	188-10
Miller Saint Nazianz Inc						
511 E Main St	Saint Nazianz	WI	54232	**800-247-5557**	920-773-2121	273
Miller Studio						
734 Fair Ave NW	New Philadelphia	OH	44663	**800-332-0050**	330-339-1100	498
Miller Supply Inc						
29902 Avenida de las Banderas						
	Rancho Santa Margarita	CA	92688	**888-240-9237**		549
Miller Thomson LLP						
Scotia Plz 40 King St W						
Ste 5800	Toronto	ON	M5H3S1	**888-762-5559**	416-595-8500	41
Miller Transporters Inc						
5500 Hwy 80 W	Jackson	MS	39209	**800-645-5378***	601-922-8331	775
*Cust Svc						
Miller Travel Services Inc						
4380 W 12th St	Erie	PA	16505	**800-989-8747**	814-833-8888	766
Miller Valentine Group						
137 North Main St Ste 600	Dayton	OH	45402	**877-684-7687**	937-293-0900	651
Miller-Leaman						
800 Orange Ave	Daytona Beach	FL	32114	**800-881-0320**	386-248-0500	693
Miller-Stephenson Chemical Co						
55 Backus Ave	Danbury	CT	06810	**800-992-2424***	203-743-4447	145
*Tech Supp						
Millersville University of Pennsylvania						
PO Box 1002	Millersville	PA	17551	**800-682-3648**	717-872-3011	166
Milligan College						
130 Richardson Rd	Milligan College	TN	37682	**800-262-8337**	423-461-8730	166
Milliken & Co's Live Oak Plant						
300 Industrial Dr	La Grange	GA	30240	**800-241-8666**		131
Millikin University						
1184 W Main St	Decatur	IL	62522	**800-373-7733**	217-424-6211	166
Milliman USA						
1301 Fifth Ave Ste 3800	Seattle	WA	98101	**866-767-1212**	206-624-7940	
Million Air						
4300 Westgrove Dr	Addison	TX	75001	**800-248-1602**	972-248-1600	63
Million Air Interlink Inc						
8501 Telephone Rd	Houston	TX	77061	**888-589-9059**	713-640-4000	24
Milliron Auto Parts						
2375 Springmill Rd	Mansfield	OH	44903	**800-747-4566**	419-747-4566	
Mill-Max Mfg Corp						
190 Pine Hollow Rd	Oyster Bay	NY	11771	**800-333-4237**	516-922-6000	810
Mill-Rose Co						
7995 Tyler Blvd	Mentor	OH	44060	**800-321-3533**	440-255-9171	103
Mills College						
5000 MacArthur Blvd	Oakland	CA	94613	**877-746-4557***	510-430-2135	166
*Admissions						
Mills Iron Works Inc						
14834 Maple Ave	Gardena	CA	90248	**800-421-2281**	323-321-6520	591
Millsap Fuel Distributors Ltd						
905 Ave P S	Saskatoon	SK	S7M2X3	**800-667-9767**	306-244-7916	576
Millsaps College						
1701 N State St	Jackson	MS	39210	**800-352-1050***	601-974-1000	166
*Admissions						
Millsite State Park						
Ferron Canyon Rd PO Box 1343	Huntington	UT	84528	**800-322-3770**	435-384-2552	561
Milpitas Post						
59 Marylinn Dr	Milpitas	CA	95035	**800-870-6397**	408-262-2454	528-4
Miltex Inc 589 Davies Dr	York	PA	17402	**866-854-8400**	717-840-9335	228
Milton CAT						
30 Industrial Dr	Londonderry	NH	03053	**800-473-5298**	603-665-4500	357
Milton Hershey School						
PO Box 830	Hershey	PA	17033	**800-322-3248**	717-520-2100	618
Milton Industries Inc						
4500 W Cortland	Chicago	IL	60639	**855-464-6458**		
Miltons Inc						
250 Granite St	Braintree	MA	02184	**888-645-8667**	781-848-1880	157-3
Milwaukee Area Technical College						
700 W State St	Milwaukee	WI	53233	**866-211-3380**	414-297-6600	795
Milwaukee Art Museum						
700 N Art Museum Dr	Milwaukee	WI	53202	**877-638-7620**	414-224-3200	517
Milwaukee Coast Guard Base						
2420 S Lincoln Memorial Dr	Milwaukee	WI	53207	**866-772-8724**	414-747-7100	158
Milwaukee County						
901 N Ninth St	Milwaukee	WI	53233	**877-652-6377**	414-278-4143	337
Milwaukee Electric Tool Corp						
13135 W Lisbon Rd	Brookfield	WI	53005	**800-729-3878**	262-783-8586	754
Milwaukee Institute of Art & Design						
273 E Erie St	Milwaukee	WI	53202	**888-749-6423**	414-276-7889	166
Milwaukee Magazine						
126 N Jefferson St	Milwaukee	WI	53202	**800-662-4818**	414-273-1101	455-22
Milwaukee Public Library						
814 W Wisconsin Ave	Milwaukee	WI	53233	**866-947-7363**	414-286-3000	433-3
Milwaukee School of Engineering						
1025 N Broadway	Milwaukee	WI	53202	**800-332-6763**	414-277-7300	166
Milwaukee Symphony Orchestra						
1101 N Market St Ste 100	Milwaukee	WI	53202	**888-367-8101**	414-291-7605	569-3
Milwaukee Valve Company Inc						
16550 W Stratton Dr	New Berlin	WI	53151	**800-348-6544**	262-432-2800	784
Milwhite Inc						
5487 S Padre Island Hwy	Brownsville	TX	78521	**800-442-0082**	956-547-1970	501-2
Mimaki USA Inc						
150 Satellite Blvd NE Ste A	Suwanee	GA	30024	**888-530-3988**		
MiMedx Group Inc						
1775 W Oak Commons Ct NE	Marietta	GA	30062	**888-543-1917**		474
Mimic Technologies Inc						
811 First Ave Ste 408	Seattle	WA	98104	**800-918-1670**	206-923-3337	177
Mind Your Business Inc (myb)						
305 Eighth Ave E	Hendersonville	NC	28792	**888-869-2462**		260
MINDBODY Inc						
4051 Broad St Ste 220	Sn Luis Obisp	CA	93401	**877-755-4279**		395
Mindgrub Technologies LLC						
1215 E Ft Ave Ste 200	Baltimore	MD	21230	**855-646-3472**	410-988-2444	4
Mindjet Corp						
1160 Battery St E 4th Fl	San Francisco	CA	94111	**877-646-3538**	415-229-4200	178-12
Mindlance						
80 River St 4th Fl	Hoboken	NJ	07030	**877-965-2623**		
MindPlay Educational Software						
4400 E Broadway Blvd Ste 400	Tucson	AZ	85711	**800-221-7911**	520-888-1800	178-3
MindSpark International Inc						
1205 Peachtree Pkwy Ste 1204	Cumming	GA	30041	**888-820-3616**		196
Mine & Mill Industrial Supply Company Inc						
2500 S Combee Rd	Lakeland	FL	33801	**800-282-8489**	863-665-5601	186
Mine Safety & Health Administration (MSHA)						
1100 Wilson Blvd	Arlington	VA	22209	**800-746-1553**	202-693-9400	339-14
Miner County						
Park Ave & Main St 401 N Main St 2nd Fl						
PO Box 86	Howard	SD	57349	**800-383-8000**	605-772-4671	337
Miner Enterprises Inc						
1200 E State St	Geneva	IL	60134	**888-822-5334**	630-232-3000	646
Mineral Resources International						
2720 Wadman Dr	Ogden	UT	84401	**800-731-7866**	801-731-7040	297-8
Mineral Wells Area Chamber of Commerce						
511 E Hubbard St	Mineral Wells	TX	76067	**800-252-6989**	940-325-2557	139
Minerals Metals & Materials Society, The (TMS)						
5700 Corporate Dr Ste 750	Pittsburgh	PA	15237	**800-759-4867**	724-776-9000	49-13
Minerva Networks Inc						
2150 Gold St	Santa Clara	CA	95002	**800-806-9594**	408-567-9400	643
Mines Press Inc, The						
231 Croton Ave	Cortlandt Manor	NY	10567	**800-447-6788**		623
Mingan Archipelago National Park Reserve of Canada						
1340 de la Digue St	Havre-Saint-Pierre	QC	G0G1P0	**877-737-3783**	418-538-3331	559
Minhas Craft Brewery						
1208 14th Ave	Monroe	WI	53566	**800-233-7205**		
Mini-Circuits Laboratories Inc						
13 Neptune Ave	Brooklyn	NY	11235	**800-654-7949**	718-934-4500	692
Ministry of Tourism of Dominican Republic						
848 Brickell Ave	Miami	FL	33131	**888-358-9594**	305-358-2899	770
Minitab Inc						
Quality Plz 1829 Pine Hall Rd						
	State College	PA	16801	**800-448-3555**	814-238-3280	178-10
Minka Group						
1151 W Bradford Ct	Corona	CA	92882	**800-221-7977**	951-735-9220	438
Minn-Dak Yeast Company Inc						
18175 Red River Rd W	Wahpeton	ND	58075	**800-348-0991**	701-642-3300	296-42
Minneapolis City Hall						
350 S Fifth St	Minneapolis	MN	55415	**800-766-3777**	612-673-2244	336
Minneapolis College of Art & Design						
2501 Stevens Ave	Minneapolis	MN	55404	**800-874-6223**	612-874-3760	164
Minneapolis Community & Technical College						
1501 Hennepin Ave	Minneapolis	MN	55403	**800-247-0911**	612-659-6200	162
Minneapolis Convention Ctr						
1301 Second Ave S	Minneapolis	MN	55403	**800-438-5547**	612-335-6000	205
Minneapolis Foundation						
80 S Eigth St 800 IDS Ctr	Minneapolis	MN	55402	**866-305-0543**	612-672-3878	303
Minneapolis Grain Exchange						
400 S Fourth St						
130 Grain Exchange Bldg	Minneapolis	MN	55415	**800-827-4746**	612-321-7101	687
Minneapolis Institute of Arts						
2400 Third Ave S	Minneapolis	MN	55404	**888-642-2787**	612-870-3000	517
Minneapolis Public Schools						
3345 Chicago Ave	Minneapolis	MN	55407	**800-543-7709**	612-668-0000	681
Minneapolis/St Paul City Pages						
401 N Third St Ste 550	Minneapolis	MN	55401	**844-387-6962**	612-375-1015	528-5
Minneapolis-Saint Paul Magazine						
220 S Sixth St Ste 500	Minneapolis	MN	55402	**800-999-5589**	612-339-7571	455-22
Minnesota						
Aging Board						
540 Cedar St	Saint Paul	MN	55155	**800-882-6262**	651-431-2500	338-24
Arts Board						
400 Sibley St Ste 200	Saint Paul	MN	55101	**800-866-2787**	651-215-1600	338-24
Attorney General						
445 Minnesota St Ste 1400	Saint Paul	MN	55101	**800-657-3787**	651-296-3353	338-24
Campaign Finance & Public Disclosure Board						
190 Centennial Office Bldg 658 Cedar St						
	Saint Paul	MN	55155	**800-657-3889**	651-539-1180	265
Child Support Enforcement Div						
444 Lafayette Rd N	Saint Paul	MN	55164	**800-747-5484**	651-431-2000	338-24
Commerce Dept						
85 Seventh Pl E Ste 500	Saint Paul	MN	55101	**800-657-3602**	651-539-1500	338-24
Department of Public Safety						
444 Minnesota St	Saint Paul	MN	55101	**800-657-3787**	651-201-7000	338-24
Employment & Economic Development Dept (DEED)						
332 Minnesota St Ste E200	Saint Paul	MN	55101	**800-657-3858**	651-259-7114	338-24
Governor						
130 State Capitol						
75 Rev Dr Martin Luther King Jr Blvd	Saint Paul	MN	55155	**800-657-3717**	651-201-3400	338-24
Health Dept						
625 Robert St N	Saint Paul	MN	55164	**888-345-0823**	651-201-4545	338-24
Housing Finance Authority						
400 Sibley St Ste 300	Saint Paul	MN	55101	**800-657-3769**	651-296-7608	338-24
Labor & Industry Dept						
443 Lafayette Rd N	Saint Paul	MN	55155	**800-342-5354**	651-284-5005	338-24
Legislature						
211 State Capitol	Saint Paul	MN	55155	**888-234-1112**	651-296-2314	338-24
Medical Practice Board						
2829 University Ave SE						
Ste 500	Minneapolis	MN	55414	**800-657-3709**	612-617-2130	338-24

Alphabetical Section

				Toll-Free	Phone	Class
Natural Resources Dept						
500 Lafayette Rd	Saint Paul	MN	55155	**888-646-6367**	651-259-5300	338-24
Office of Higher Education						
1450 Energy Pk Dr Ste 350	Saint Paul	MN	55108	**800-657-3866**	651-642-0567	721
Parks & Recreation Div						
500 Lafayette Rd	Saint Paul	MN	55155	**888-646-6367**	651-259-5300	338-24
Public Utilities Commission						
121 Seventh Pl E Ste 350	Saint Paul	MN	55101	**800-657-3782**	651-296-7124	338-24
Revenue Dept						
600 N Roberts St	Saint Paul	MN	55101	**800-657-3666**	651-556-3000	338-24
Transportation Dept						
395 John Ireland Blvd	Saint Paul	MN	55155	**800-657-3774**	651-296-3000	338-24
Workers" Compensation Div						
443 Lafayette Rd	Saint Paul	MN	55155	**800-342-5354**	651-284-5005	338-24
Minnesota Assn of Realtors						
5750 Lincoln Dr	Minneapolis	MN	55436	**800-862-6097**	952-935-8313	652
Minnesota Ballet						
301 W First St Ste 800	Duluth	MN	55802	**800-627-3529**	218-529-3742	569-1
Minnesota Chamber of Commerce						
400 Robert St N Ste 1500	Saint Paul	MN	55101	**800-821-2230**	651-292-4650	140
Minnesota Chemical Co						
2285 Hampden Ave	St. Paul	MN	55114	**800-328-5689**	651-646-7521	426
Minnesota Corrugated Box Inc						
2200 YH Hanson Ave	Albert Lea	MN	56007	**888-216-9454**		
Minnesota Dental Assn						
1335 Industrial Blvd						
Ste 200	Minneapolis	MN	55413	**800-950-3368**	612-767-8400	227
Minnesota Discovery Ctr						
1005 Discovery Dr	Chisholm	MN	55719	**800-372-6437**	218-254-7959	517
Minnesota Educator Magazine						
41 Sherburne Ave	Saint Paul	MN	55103	**800-652-9073**	651-227-9541	455-8
Minnesota Eye Consultants PA						
710 E 24th St Ste 100	Minneapolis	MN	55404	**800-526-7632**	612-813-3600	793
Minnesota Historical Society History Ctr Museum						
345 Kellogg Blvd W	Saint Paul	MN	55102	**800-657-3773**	651-259-3001	517
Minnesota Lawyers Mutual Insurance Co						
333 S Seventh St Ste 2200	Minneapolis	MN	55402	**800-422-1370**	877-880-1335	389
Minnesota Nurses Assn (MNA)						
345 Randolph Ave Ste 200	Saint Paul	MN	55102	**800-536-4662**	651-414-2800	529
Minnesota Orchestra						
1111 Nicollet Mall						
Orchestra Hall	Minneapolis	MN	55403	**800-292-4141**	612-371-5600	569-3
Minnesota Pharmacists Assn (MPhA)						
1000 Westgate Dr Ste 252	St. Paul	MN	55114	**800-451-8349**	651-697-1771	581
Minnesota Power						
30 W Superior St	Duluth	MN	55802	**800-228-4966**	218-722-2625	782
Minnesota Public Radio (MPR)						
480 Cedar St	Saint Paul	MN	55101	**800-228-7123**	651-290-1212	628
Minnesota Rubber & Plastics						
1100 Xenium Ln N	Minneapolis	MN	55441	**800-927-1422**	952-927-1400	600
Minnesota State Bar Assn						
600 Nicollet Mall Ste 380	Minneapolis	MN	55402	**800-882-6722**	612-333-1183	72
Minnesota State Community & Technical College						
Detroit Lakes						
900 Hwy 34 E	Detroit Lakes	MN	56501	**877-450-3322**	218-846-3700	162
Fergus Falls						
712 Cascade St S	Fergus Falls	MN	56537	**877-450-3322**		162
Moorhead						
1900 28th Ave S	Moorhead	MN	56560	**800-426-5603**	218-299-6500	162
Minnesota State University						
Mankato						
122 Taylor Ctr	Mankato	MN	56001	**800-722-0544***	507-389-1822	166
*Admissions						
Moorhead						
1104 Seventh Ave S	Moorhead	MN	56563	**800-593-7246**	218-477-2161	166
Minnesota State University Mankato						
Memorial Library						
601 Maywood Ave PO Box 8419	Mankato	MN	56002	**800-722-0544**	507-389-5952	433-6
Minnesota State University Moorhead Regional Science Ctr						
1104 Seventh Ave S	Moorhead	MN	56563	**800-593-7246**	218-477-2920	517
Minnesota Supply Company Inc						
6470 Flying Cloud Dr	Eden Prairie	MN	55344	**800-869-1028**	952-828-7300	384
Minnesota Timberwolves						
Target Ctr 600 First Ave N	Minneapolis	MN	55403	**855-895-0872**	612-673-1600	710-1
Minnesota Twins						
1 Twins Way	Minneapolis	MN	55403	**800-338-9467**	612-375-1366	709
Minnesota Valley Co-op Light & Power Assn						
501 S First St	Montevideo	MN	56265	**800-247-5051**	320-269-2163	245
Minnesota Valley Electric Co-op						
125 Minnesota Vly Electric Dr						
PO Box 77024	Jordan	MN	55352	**800-282-6832**	952-492-2313	245
Minnesota Veterans Home-Fergus Falls						
1821 N Park St	Fergus Falls	MN	56537	**877-838-4633**	218-736-0400	788
Minnesota Veterans Home-Minneapolis						
5101 Minnehaha Ave S	Minneapolis	MN	55417	**877-838-6757**	612-548-5700	788
Minnesota Veterans Home-Silver Bay						
56 Outer Dr	Silver Bay	MN	55614	**877-729-8387**	218-353-8700	788
Minnesota West Community & Technical College						
1450 Collegeway	Worthington	MN	56187	**800-657-3966**	507-372-3400	162
Minnesota Wire & Cable Co						
1835 Energy Park Dr	Saint Paul	MN	55108	**800-258-6922**	651-642-1800	810
Minnesota Zoo						
13000 Zoo Blvd	Apple Valley	MN	55124	**800-366-7811**	952-431-9200	818
Minnpar LLC						
5273 Program Ave	Mounds View	MN	55112	**800-889-3382**	612-379-0606	61
Minntech Corp						
14605 28th Ave N	Minneapolis	MN	55447	**800-328-3345**	763-553-3300	474
Minor Rubber Company Inc						
49 Ackerman St	Bloomfield	NJ	07003	**800-433-6886**	973-338-6800	673
Minor Tire & Wheel Company Inc						
3512 Sixth Ave SE	Decatur	AL	35603	**800-633-3936**	256-353-4957	54
Minority Business Development Agency (MBDA)						
1401 Constitution Ave NW	Washington	DC	20230	**888-324-1551**		339-2
San Francisco Region						
1401 Constitution Ave	Washington	DC	20230	**888-889-0538**	202-482-2000	339-2
Minority Business Development Agency Regional Offices						
Chicago Region						
105 W Adams St Ste 2300	Chicago	IL	60603	**888-324-1551**	312-353-0182	339-2
Minot Convention & Visitors Bureau						
1020 S Broadway	Minot	ND	58701	**800-264-2626**	701-857-8206	206
Minot Daily News						
301 Fourth St SE	Minot	ND	58702	**800-735-3119**	701-857-1900	
Minot Public Library						
516 Second Ave SW	Minot	ND	58701	**800-843-9948**	701-852-1045	433-3
Minot State University						
500 University Ave W	Minot	ND	58707	**800-777-0750**	701-858-3000	166
Minot State University Bottineau						
105 Simrall Blvd	Bottineau	ND	58318	**800-542-6866**	701-228-5451	162
Minova USA Inc						
150 Carley Ct	Georgetown	KY	40324	**800-626-2948**	502-863-6800	601-2
Minskoff Theatre						
200 W 45th St	New York	NY	10036	**800-714-8452**	212-869-0550	742
Minson Corp						
1 Minson Way	Montebello	CA	90640	**800-251-6537**	323-513-1041	319-4
Mint Magazine Inc						
6960 Bonneval Rd Ste 102	Jacksonville	FL	32216	**888-620-3877**		
Mintie Corp						
1114 San Fernando Rd	Los Angeles	CA	90065	**800-964-6843**	323-225-4111	35
Minto Rentals In Ottawa						
185 Lyons St N	Ottawa	ON	K1R7Y4	**800-267-3377**	613-232-2200	378
Minus Forty Technologies Corp						
30 Armstrong Ave	Georgetown	ON	L7G4R9	**800-800-5706**	905-702-1441	661
Minute Maid Park						
501 Crawford St	Houston	TX	77002	**877-927-8767**	713-259-8000	716
Minute Men Staffing Services						
3740 Carnegie Ave	Cleveland	OH	44115	**877-873-8856**	216-426-9675	717
Minuteman Group Inc						
35 Bedford St Ste 2	Lexington	MA	02420	**800-861-7493**	781-861-7493	
Minuteman International Inc						
14N845 US Rte 20	Pingree Grove	IL	60140	**800-323-9420**	847-264-5400	385
Minuteman Press International Inc						
61 Executive Blvd	Farmingdale	NY	11735	**800-645-3006**	631-249-1370	310
Minuteman Trucks Inc						
2181 Providence Hwy	Walpole	MA	02081	**800-231-8458**	508-668-3112	775
Minvalco Inc						
3340 Gorham Ave	Minneapolis	MN	55426	**800-642-9090**	952-920-0131	608
Minwax Co						
10 Mountainview Rd	Upper Saddle River	NJ	07458	**800-523-9299**		546
MinXray Inc						
3611 Commercial Ave	Northbrook	IL	60062	**800-221-2245**	847-564-0323	473
MIQ Logistics LLC						
11501 Outlook St Ste 500	Overland Park	KS	66211	**877-246-4909**	913-696-7100	447
MIR (Manager's Intelligence Report)						
316 N Michigan Ave Ste 400	Chicago	IL	60601	**800-878-5331**		527-2
Mira Monte Inn & Suites						
69 Mt Desert St	Bar Harbor	ME	04609	**800-553-5109**		378
Mira Vista Diagnostics						
4705 Decatur Blvd	Indianapolis	IN	46241	**866-647-2847**	317-856-2681	
Mirabito Fuel Group Inc						
49 Ct St PO Box 5306	Binghamton	NY	13902	**800-934-9480**	607-352-2800	316
Miracle Healthcare						
4322 N Hamilton Rd	Gahanna	OH	43230	**844-560-7775**	614-237-7702	362
Miracle Method US Corp						
4310 Arrowswest Dr	Colorado Springs	CO	80907	**800-444-8827**	719-594-9196	189-11
Miracle Recreation Equipment Co						
878 Hwy 60	Monett	MO	65708	**800-523-4202**	417-235-6917	345
Miracle-Ear Inc						
5000 Cheshire Pkwy N	Minneapolis	MN	55446	**800-464-8002**		475
MiraCosta College						
Oceanside						
1 Barnard Dr	Oceanside	CA	92056	**888-201-8480**	760-757-2121	162
San Elijo						
3333 Manchester Ave	Cardiff	CA	92007	**888-201-8480**	760-944-4449	162
Mirage, The						
3400 Las Vegas Blvd S	Las Vegas	NV	89109	**800-627-6667**	702-791-7111	665
Miramont Castle Museum						
9 Capitol Hill Ave	Manitou Springs	CO	80829	**888-685-1011**	719-685-1011	517
Miramonte Resort & Spa						
45000 Indian Wells Ln	Indian Wells	CA	92210	**800-237-2926**	760-341-2200	665
Miratel Solutions Inc						
2501 Steeles Ave W	North York	ON	M3J2P1	**866-647-2835**	416-650-7850	732
Miraval AZ Resort & Spa						
5000 E Via Estancia Miraval	Tucson	AZ	85739	**800-232-3969**		702
Mirbeau Inn & Spa						
851 W Genesee St	Skaneateles	NY	13152	**877-647-2328**	315-685-5006	378
Mircom						
25 Interchange Way	Vaughan	ON	L4K5W3	**888-660-4655**	905-660-4655	689
Mirrotek International LLC						
90 Dayton Ave	Passaic	NJ	07055	**888-659-3030**	973-472-1400	540
Mirus International Inc						
31 Sun Pac Blvd	Brampton	ON	L6S5P6	**888-866-4787**	905-494-1120	762
Misericordia University						
301 Lake St	Dallas	PA	18612	**866-262-6363**	570-674-6400	166
Mishawaka-Penn-Harris Public Library Indiana						
209 Lincoln Way E	Mishawaka	IN	46544	**800-622-4970**	574-259-5277	434
Miskelly Furniture						
101 Airport Rd	Jackson	MS	39208	**888-939-6288**	601-939-6288	321
Misonix Inc						
1938 NEW Hwy	Farmingdale	NY	11735	**800-694-9612**	631-694-9555	250
Miss Elaine Inc						
8430 Valcour Ave	Saint Louis	MO	63123	**800-458-1422**	314-631-1900	155-14
Mission Ambulance						
1055 E Third St	Corona	CA	92879	**800-899-9100**		30
Mission Aviation Fellowship (MAF)						
112 N Pilatus Ln	Nampa	ID	83687	**800-359-7623**	208-498-0800	48-20
Mission Chamber of Commerce						
202 W Tom Landry St	Mission	TX	78572	**800-827-8298**	956-585-2727	139
Mission Essential Personnel LLC						
4343 Easton Commons Ste 100	Columbus	OH	43219	**888-542-3447**	614-416-2345	761
Mission Federal Credit Union						
PO Box 919023	San Diego	CA	92191	**800-500-6328**	858-524-2850	219
Mission Foods						
1159 Cottonwood Ln Ste 200	Irving	TX	75038	**800-443-7994**	214-208-7010	296-35
Mission Golf Cars						
18865 Redland Rd	San Antonio	TX	78259	**800-324-7868**	210-545-7868	57

Name / Address	City	State	ZIP	Toll-Free	Phone	Class
Mission Inn						
3649 Mission Inn Ave	Riverside	CA	92501	**800-843-7755**	951-784-0300	378
Mission Inn Resort & Club						
10400 County Rd 48	Howey in the Hills	FL	34737	**800-874-9053**	352-324-3101	665
Mission Landscape Services Inc						
536 E Dyer Rd	Santa Ana	CA	92707	**800-545-9963**		421
Mission Petroleum Carriers Inc						
8450 Mosley	Houston	TX	77075	**800-737-9911**	713-943-8250	466
Mission Pharmacal						
PO Box 786099	San Antonio	TX	78278	**800-531-3333**	210-696-8400	578
Mission Point Mackinac Island						
1 Lakeshore Dr	Mackinac Island	MI	49757	**800-833-7711**	231-331-3419	665
Mission Search						
2203 N Lois Ave Ste 1225	Tampa	FL	33607	**877-479-1545**		
Mission Valley Ford Truck Sales Inc						
780 E Brokaw Rd	San Jose	CA	95112	**888-284-7471**	408-933-2300	57
Mission Wealth						
1123 Chapala St 3rd Fl	Santa Barbara	CA	93101	**888-642-7221**	805-882-2360	400
Mississippi						
Banking & Consumer Finance Dept						
PO Box 12129	Jackson	MS	39236	**800-844-2499**	601-321-6901	338-25
Contractors Board						
2679 Crane Ridge Dr Ste C	Jackson	MS	39216	**800-880-6161**	601-354-6161	338-25
Dept of Human Service						
200 S Lamar St	Jackson	MS	39201	**800-345-6347**	601-359-4500	338-25
Development Authority						
501 NW St	Jackson	MS	39201	**800-360-3323**	601-359-3449	338-25
Emergency Management Agency						
1 Mema Dr PO Box 5644	Pearl	MS	39288	**800-222-6362**	601-933-6362	338-25
Employment Security Commission						
1235 Echelon Pkwy PO Box 1699	Jackson	MS	39215	**888-844-3577**	601-321-6000	259
Enviromental Quality Dept						
515 E Amite St	Jackson	MS	39201	**888-786-0661**	601-961-5611	338-25
Insurance Dept						
1001 Woolfolk State Office Bldg 501 NW St 501 N West St	Jackson	MS	39201	**800-562-2957**	601-359-3569	338-25
Rehabilitation Services Dept						
1281 Hwy 51 PO Box 1698	Madison	MS	39110	**800-443-1000**		338-25
State Government Information						
200 S Lamar Ste 800	Jackson	MS	39201	**877-290-9487**	601-351-5023	338-25
Weights & Measures Div						
121 N Jefferson St	Jackson	MS	39201	**800-551-1830**	601-359-1100	338-25
Worker's Compensation Commission						
1428 Lakeland Dr	Jackson	MS	39216	**866-473-6922**	601-987-4200	338-25
Mississippi Action For Progress Inc (MAP)						
1751 Morson Rd	Jackson	MS	39209	**800-924-4615**	601-923-4100	147
Mississippi Agriculture & Forestry Museum/National Agricultural Aviation Museum						
1150 Lakeland Dr	Jackson	MS	39216	**800-844-8687**	601-359-1100	517
Mississippi Assn of Realtors						
4274 Lakeland Dr PO Box 321000	Jackson	MS	39232	**800-747-1103**	601-932-9325	652
Mississippi Bar						
643 N State St	Jackson	MS	39202	**800-682-6423**	601-948-4471	72
Mississippi Blood Services						
115 Tree St	Flowood	MS	39232	**888-902-5663**	601-981-3232	89
Mississippi Coast Coliseum & Convention Ctr						
2350 Beach Blvd	Biloxi	MS	39531	**800-726-2781**	228-594-3700	205
Mississippi College						
200 S Capitol St	Clinton	MS	39056	**800-738-1236**	601-925-3000	166
Mississippi County						
200 W Walnut St	Blytheville	AR	72315	**800-455-5600**	870-763-3212	337
Mississippi County Electric Co-op						
510 N Broadway St	Blytheville	AR	72315	**800-439-4563**	870-763-4563	245
Mississippi Dental Assn						
439 B katherine Dr	Flowood	MS	39232	**800-562-2957**	601-664-9691	227
Mississippi Economic Council						
PO Box 23276	Jackson	MS	39225	**800-748-7626**	601-969-0022	140
Mississippi Gulf Coast Community College						
51 Main St PO Box 548	Perkinston	MS	39573	**866-735-1122**	601-928-5211	162
Jackson County						
2300 Hwy 90	Gautier	MS	39553	**866-735-1122**	228-497-9602	162
Jefferson Davis						
2226 Switzer Rd	Gulfport	MS	39507	**866-735-1122**	228-896-3355	162
Mississippi Gulf Coast Convention & Visitors Bureau						
2350 Beach Blvd Ste A	Biloxi	MS	39531	**888-467-4853**	228-896-6699	206
Mississippi Lawyer Magazine						
643 N State St	Jackson	MS	39202	**800-682-6423**	601-948-4471	455-15
Mississippi Museum of Art						
380 S Lamar St	Jackson	MS	39201	**866-843-9278**	601-960-1515	517
Mississippi Museum of Natural Science						
2148 Riverside Dr	Jackson	MS	39202	**800-467-2757**	601-576-6000	517
Mississippi Music Inc						
222 N Main St	Hattiesburg	MS	39401	**800-844-5821**		521
Mississippi Public Broadcasting						
3825 Ridgewood Rd	Jackson	MS	39211	**800-850-4406**	601-432-6565	641-50
Mississippi River Museum						
125 N Front St	Memphis	TN	38103	**800-507-6507**	901-576-7241	517
Mississippi Sports Hall of Fame & Museum						
1152 Lakeland Dr	Jackson	MS	39216	**800-280-3263**	601-982-8264	519
Mississippi State Port Authority at Gulfport						
2510 14th St Ste 1450	Gulfport	MS	39501	**877-881-4367**	228-865-4300	614
Mississippi State Veterans' Home Collins						
3261 Hwy 49 S	Collins	MS	39428	**877-203-5632**	601-765-0403	788
Mississippi University for Women						
1100 College St MUW-1613	Columbus	MS	39701	**877-462-8439**	662-329-4750	166
Mississippi Valley Equipment Company Inc						
1198 Pershall Rd	Saint Louis	MO	63137	**800-325-8001**	314-869-8600	357
Mississippi Valley Regional Blood Ctr						
5500 Lakeview Pkwy	Davenport	IA	52807	**800-747-5401**		89
Mississippi Valley State University						
14000 Hwy 82	Itta Bena	MS	38941	**800-844-6885**	662-254-9041	166
Mississippi Valley Title Services Co						
1022 Highland Colony Pkwy Ste 200	Ridgeland	MS	39157	**800-647-2124**	601-969-0222	390-6
Missoula Electric Co-op Inc						
1700 West Broadway	Missoula	MT	59808	**800-352-5200**	406-541-4433	245
Missoulian						
PO Box 8029	Missoula	MT	59807	**800-366-7102**	406-523-5200	528-2

Name / Address	City	State	ZIP	Toll-Free	Phone	Class
Missouri						
Attorney General						
207 W High St PO Box 899	Jefferson City	MO	65102	**800-392-8222**	573-751-3321	338-26
Child Support Enforcement Div						
205 Jefferson St 1st Fl	Jefferson City	MO	65103	**800-859-7999**	573-522-8024	338-26
Consumer Protection Div						
207 W High St PO Box 899	Jefferson City	MO	65102	**800-392-8222**	573-751-3321	338-26
Finance Div						
Truman State Office Bldg Rm 630	Jefferson City	MO	65102	**888-246-7225**	573-751-3242	338-26
Higher Education Dept						
205 Jefferson St	Jefferson City	MO	65109	**800-473-6757**	573-751-2361	338-26
Historical Preservation Office						
1101 Riverside Dr	Jefferson City	MO	65101	**800-361-4827**	573-751-3443	338-26
Insurance Dept						
301 W High St Rm 530	Jefferson City	MO	65101	**800-726-7390**	573-751-4126	338-26
Lottery						
1823 Southridge Dr PO Box 1603	Jefferson City	MO	65109	**888-238-7633**	573-751-4050	450
Natural Resources Dept						
1101 Riverside Dr *Cust Svc	Jefferson City	MO	65102	**800-361-4827***	573-751-3443	338-26
Professional Registration Div						
3605 Missouri Blvd PO Box 1335	Jefferson City	MO	65102	**800-735-2466**	573-751-0293	338-26
Public Service Commission						
200 Madison St PO Box 360	Jefferson City	MO	65102	**800-819-3180**	573-751-3234	338-26
Real Estate Commission						
3605 Missouri Blvd PO Box 1339	Jefferson City	MO	65102	**800-735-2466**	573-751-2628	338-26
Securities Div						
600 W Main St Rm 229 PO Box 1276	Jefferson City	MO	65102	**800-721-7996**	573-751-4136	338-26
State Parks Div						
PO Box 176	Jefferson City	MO	65102	**800-334-6946**	573-751-2479	338-26
Supreme Court						
207 W High St	Jefferson City	MO	65101	**888-541-4894**	573-751-4144	338-26
Tourism Div						
PO Box 1055	Jefferson City	MO	65102	**800-519-2100**	573-751-4133	338-26
Transportation Dept						
105 W Capitol Ave PO Box 270	Jefferson City	MO	65102	**888-275-6636**	573-751-2551	338-26
Veterans Commission						
205 Jefferson St 12th Fl Jefferson Bldg PO Drawer 147	Jefferson City	MO	65102	**866-838-4636**	573-751-3779	338-26
Vocational & Adult Education Div						
3024 Dupont Cir PO Box 480	Jefferson City	MO	65109	**877-222-8963**	573-751-3251	338-26
Workers Compensation Div						
PO Box 58	Jefferson City	MO	65102	**800-775-2667**	573-751-4231	338-26
Missouri Assn of Realtors						
2601 Bernadette Pl	Columbia	MO	65203	**800-403-0101**	573-445-8400	652
Missouri Baptist Hospital of Sullivan						
751 Sappington Bridge Rd	Sullivan	MO	63080	**800-939-2273**	573-468-4186	373-3
Missouri Baptist Medical Ctr						
3015 N Ballas Rd	Saint Louis	MO	63131	**800-392-0936**	314-996-5000	373-3
Missouri Baptist University						
1 College Pk Dr	Saint Louis	MO	63141	**877-434-1115**	314-434-1115	166
Troy/Wentzville Extension						
1 College Park Dr	Saint Louis	MO	63141	**877-434-1115**	314-434-1115	
Missouri Bar, The						
326 Monroe St PO Box 119	Jefferson City	MO	65102	**888-253-6013**	573-635-4128	72
Missouri Botanical Garden						
4344 Shaw Blvd	Saint Louis	MO	63110	**800-642-8842**	314-577-5100	97
Missouri Dental Assn						
3340 American Ave	Jefferson City	MO	65109	**800-688-1907**	573-634-3436	227
Missouri Department Of Public Safety Veterans Commission						
1600 S Hickory	Mount Vernon	MO	65712	**866-838-4636**	417-466-7103	788
Missouri Enterprise						
900 Innovation Dr Ste 300	Rolla	MO	65401	**800-956-2682**		195
Missouri Gas Energy						
3420 Broadway	Kansas City	MO	64111	**800-582-1234**	816-360-5500	782
Missouri History Museum						
5700 Lindell Blvd PO Box 11940	Saint Louis	MO	63112	**800-610-2094**	314-746-4599	517
Missouri Medicine Magazine						
PO Box 1028	Jefferson City	MO	65102	**800-869-6762**	573-636-5151	455-16
Missouri Pharmacy Assn						
211 E Capitol Ave	Jefferson City	MO	65101	**800-468-4672**	573-636-7522	581
Missouri Protection & Advocacy Services						
925 S Country Club Dr	Jefferson City	MO	65109	**800-392-8667**	573-659-0678	
Missouri School Boards Assn						
2100 I-70 Dr SW	Columbia	MO	65203	**800-221-6722**	573-445-9920	681
Missouri Southern State University						
3950 Newman Rd	Joplin	MO	64801	**866-818-6778**	417-625-9300	166
Missouri Sports Hall of Fame						
3861 E Stan Musial Dr	Springfield	MO	65809	**800-498-5678**	417-889-3100	519
Missouri State Employees' Retirement System						
907 Wildwood Dr	Jefferson City	MO	65109	**800-827-1063**	573-632-6100	524
Missouri State Medical Assn						
113 Madison St	Jefferson City	MO	65101	**800-869-6762**	573-636-5151	472
Missouri State Teachers Assn						
407 S Sixth St *General	Columbia	MO	65201	**800-392-0532***	573-442-3127	455-8
Missouri State University (MSU)						
901 S National Ave	Springfield	MO	65897	**800-492-7900**	417-836-5000	166
Missouri University of Science & Technology						
Rolla 1870 Miner Cir	Rolla	MO	65409	**800-522-0938**	573-341-4111	166
Missouri Valley College						
500 E College St	Marshall	MO	65340	**800-999-8219**	660-831-4000	166
Missouri Veterans Home-Cape Girardeau						
2400 Veterans Memorial Dr	Cape Girardeau	MO	63701	**800-392-0210**	573-290-5870	788
Missouri Western State University						
4525 Downs Dr	Saint Joseph	MO	64507	**800-662-7041**	816-271-4266	166
Missourian Publishing Co						
14 W Main St	Washington	MO	63090	**888-239-7701**	636-239-7701	633-8

Alphabetical Section

	Toll-Free	Phone	Class
Mister Car Wash			
3101 E Speedway Blvd ....Tucson AZ 85716	**866-254-3229***	520-327-5656	62-1
*Cust Svc			
Mister Safety Shoes Inc			
2300 Finch Ave W Unit 6 ....North York ON M9M2Y3	**800-707-0051**	416-746-3001	357
Mister Transmission			
9555 Yonge St Ste 204 ....Richmond Hill ON L4C9M5	**800-373-8432**	905-884-1511	62-6
Misty Harbor & Barefoot Beach Resort			
118 Weirs Rd ....Gilford NH 03249	**800-336-4789**	603-293-4500	378
MIT Museum			
265 Massachusetts Ave ....Cambridge MA 02139	**800-228-9000**	617-253-4444	517
MIT Press, The			
1 Rogers St ....Cambridge MA 02142	**800-405-1619**	617-253-5646	633-4
Mitchell College			
437 Pequot Ave ....New London CT 06320	**800-443-2811***	860-701-5000	166
*Admitting			
Mitchell County			
26 N Ct St PO Box 187 ....Camilla GA 31730	**800-427-2457**	229-336-2000	337
Mitchell Electric Membership Corp			
475 Cairo Rd ....Camilla GA 31730	**800-479-6034**	229-336-5221	245
Mitchell Furniture Systems Inc			
1700 W St Paul Ave ....Milwaukee WI 53233	**800-290-5960**		319-3
Mitchell Gold & Bob Williams Co (MGBW)			
135 One Comfortable Pl ....Taylorsville NC 28681	**800-789-5401**	828-632-9200	319-2
Mitchell Golf Equipment Co			
954 Senate Dr ....Dayton OH 45459	**800-437-1314**	937-436-1314	707
Mitchell Industrial Tire Co			
2915 Eigth Ave ....Chattanooga TN 37407	**800-251-7226**	423-698-4442	749
Mitchell Institute, The			
75 Washington Ave Ste 2E ....Portland ME 04101	**888-220-7209**	207-773-7700	305
Mitchell Metal Products Inc			
19250 Hwy 12 E PO Box 789 ......Kosciusko MS 39090	**800-258-6137**	662-289-7110	693
Mitchell Rubber Products Inc			
10220 San Sevaine Way ....Mira Loma CA 91752	**800-453-7526**		672
Mitchell Selling Dynamics			
1360 Puritan Ave ....Birmingham MI 48009	**800-328-9696**	248-644-8092	461
Mitchell Supreme Fuel Co			
532 Freeman St ....Orange NJ 07050	**800-832-7090**	973-678-1800	316
Mitchell Technical Institute			
821 N Capital St ....Mitchell SD 57301	**800-684-1969**		162
MiTek Canada Inc			
100 Industrial Rd ....Bradford ON L3Z3G7	**800-268-3434**		
MiTek Industries Inc			
16023 Swingley Ridge Rd ....Chesterfield MO 63017	**800-325-8075**	314-434-1200	91
Mitel Networks Corp			
350 Legget Dr ....Kanata ON K2K2W7	**800-722-1301**	613-592-2122	730
Mitem Corp			
640 Menlo Ave ....Menlo Park CA 94025	**800-648-3660***	650-323-1500	178-12
*Sales			
Mitsubishi Digital Electronics America Inc			
9351 Jeronimo Rd ....Irvine CA 92618	**800-332-2119**	949-465-6000	52
Mitsubishi Electric Power Products Inc			
Thorn Hill Industrial Park 530 Keystone Dr			
..............Warrendale PA 15086	**800-887-7830**	724-772-2555	725
Mitsubishi Hitachi Power Systems Americas Inc (MHPS)			
400 Colonial Ctr Pkwy ....Lake Mary FL 32746	**800-445-9723**	407-688-6100	194
Mitsubishi Polyester Film LLC			
2001 Hood Rd ....Greer SC 29650	**800-334-1934**	864-879-5000	596
Mittler Corp			
10 Cooperative Way ....Wright City MO 63390	**800-467-2464**	636-745-7757	452
Mity-Lite Inc			
1301 W 400 N ....Orem UT 84057	**800-909-8034**	801-224-0589	319-3
Mix Software Inc			
1203 Berkeley Dr ....Richardson TX 75081	**800-333-0330**	972-231-0949	178-2
Mixer Systems Inc			
190 Simmons Ave ....Pewaukee WI 53072	**800-756-4937**	262-691-3100	190
Miyako Hotel Los Angeles			
328 E First St ....Los Angeles CA 90012	**800-228-6596**	213-617-2000	378
Mizkan Americas Inc			
1661 Feehanville Dr			
Ste 300 ....Mount Prospect IL 60056	**800-323-4358**	847-590-0059	296-41
Mizuho OSI Inc			
30031 Ahern Ave ....Union City CA 94587	**800-777-4674**	510-429-1500	473
Mizuno USA			
4925 Avalon Ridge Pkwy ....Norcross GA 30071	**800-966-1211**	770-441-5553	706
MJ Altman Cos Inc			
205 S Magnolia Ave ....Ocala FL 34471	**800-927-2655**	352-732-1112	160
MJ Soffe Co			
1 Soffe Dr ....Fayetteville NC 28312	**888-257-8673**		155-1
MJH (Sentara Martha Jefferson Hospital)			
500 Martha Jefferson Dr			
..........Charlottesville VA 22911	**888-652-6663**	434-654-7000	373-3
MJM Electric Co-op Inc (MJMEC)			
264 NE St PO Box 80 ....Carlinville IL 62626	**800-648-4729**	217-707-6156	245
MJMEC (MJM Electric Co-op Inc)			
264 NE St PO Box 80 ....Carlinville IL 62626	**800-648-4729**	217-707-6156	245
MJSA (Manufacturing Jewelers & Suppliers of America Inc)			
57 John L Dietsch Sq ....Attleboro MA 02763	**800-444-6572**	401-274-3840	49-4
MK Diamond Products Inc			
1315 Storm Pkwy ....Torrance CA 90501	**800-421-5830**	310-539-5221	678
MK Morse Co			
1101 11th St SE ....Canton OH 44707	**800-733-3377**	330-453-8187	678
MKC (Mid-Kansas Co-op)			
PO Box D ....Moundridge KS 67107	**800-864-4428**		48-2
MKS Instruments Inc			
2 Tech Dr Ste 201 ....Andover MA 01810	**800-428-9401**	978-645-5500	201
ML McDonald LLC			
50 Oakland St PO Box 315 ....Watertown MA 02471	**800-733-6243**	617-923-0900	189-8
MLA (Medical Library Assn)			
65 E Wacker Pl Ste 1900 ....Chicago IL 60601	**800-523-1850**	312-419-9094	49-11
MLA (Modern Language Assn)			
26 Broadway 3rd Fl. ....New York NY 10004	**800-323-4900**	646-576-5000	49-5
MLP Seating Corp			
950 Pratt Blvd ....Elk Grove Village IL 60007	**800-723-3030**	847-956-1700	319-3
MLQ Attorney Services			
2000 River Edge Pkwy Ste 885..........Atlanta GA 30328	**800-446-8794**	770-984-7007	631
MLS Property Information Network Inc			
904 Hartford Tpke ....Shrewsbury MA 01545	**800-695-3000**	508-845-1011	652
MLT Inc			
700 S Central Ave ....Atlanta GA 30354	**800-727-1111**	800-800-1504	755
MLTS (Meadville Lombard Theological School)			
610 S Michigan Ave ....Chicago IL 60605	**800-848-0979**	773-256-3000	167-3
M&M Meat Shops Ltd			
2240 Argentia Rd Ste 100..........Mississauga ON L5N2K7	**800-461-0171**	905-465-6325	
MM Systems Corp			
50 MM Way ....Pendergrass GA 30567	**800-241-3460**	706-824-7500	234
MMA Capital Management LLC (MuniMae)			
3600 O'Donnell St Ste 600 ....Baltimore MD 21224	**855-650-6932**	443-263-2900	507
OTC: MMAC			
MMA Creative Inc			
480 Neal St Ste 201 ....Cookeville TN 38501	**800-499-2332**	931-528-8852	7
Mmar Medical Group Inc			
9619 Yupondale Dr ....Houston TX 77080	**800-662-7633**	713-465-2003	473
MMC (Maine Medical Ctr)			
22 Bramhall St ....Portland ME 04102	**877-339-3107**	207-662-0111	373-3
MMC (Mercy Medical Ctr)			
801 Fifth St ....Sioux City IA 51102	**800-352-3559**	712-279-2010	373-3
MMC (Mercy Medical Ctr)			
345 St Paul Pl ....Baltimore MD 21202	**800-636-3729**	410-332-9000	373-3
MMC (Memorial Medical Ctr)			
1700 Coffee Rd ....Modesto CA 95355	**800-477-2258**	209-526-4500	373-3
MMC (Meadville Medical Ctr)			
751 Liberty St ....Meadville PA 16335	**800-254-5164**	814-333-5000	373-3
MMC (Mercy Medical Ctr)			
500 S Oakwood Rd ....Oshkosh WI 54904	**800-894-9327**	920-223-2000	373-3
MMC Group LP			
105 Decker Ct Ste 1100 ....Irving TX 75062	**800-779-2505**	972-893-0100	
MMF Industries			
1111 S Wheeling Rd ....Wheeling IL 60090	**800-323-8181**		688
MMG Insurance Co			
44 Maysville St PO Box 729........Presque Isle ME 04769	**800-343-0533**		
MMHS (Martin Health System)			
200 SE Hospital Ave PO Box 9010........Stuart FL 34994	**844-630-4968**	772-287-5200	373-3
MMI (Metal Marketplace International)			
718 Sansom St ....Philadelphia PA 19106	**800-523-9191**	215-592-8777	410
MMIC Group			
7701 France Ave S Ste 500..........Minneapolis MN 55435	**800-328-5532**		177
MMR Group Inc			
15961 Airline Hwy ....Baton Rouge LA 70817	**800-880-5090**	225-756-5090	189-4
MMS (Massachusetts Medical Society)			
860 Winter St ....Waltham MA 02451	**800-322-2303**	781-893-4610	472
MMS Education			
1 Summit Sq 1717 Langhorne-Newtown Rd			
Ste 301 ....Newtown PA 19047	**866-395-3193**		
MNA (Massachusetts Nurses Assn)			
340 Tpke St ....Canton MA 02021	**800-882-2056**	781-821-4625	529
MNA (Minnesota Nurses Assn)			
345 Randolph Ave Ste 200 ....Saint Paul MN 55102	**800-536-4662**	651-414-2800	529
MNAP Medical Solutions Inc			
9908 E Roosevelt Blvd ....Philadelphia PA 19115	**888-674-4381**	215-464-3300	382
MNPS (Metropolitan Nashville Public Schools)			
2601 Bransford Ave ....Nashville TN 37204	**800-848-0298**	615-259-8531	681
Mo Bio Laboratories			
2746 Loker Ave W Ste A ....Carlsbad CA 92010	**800-362-7737**		
MOAA (Military Officers Assn of America)			
201 N Washington St ....Alexandria VA 22314	**800-234-6622**		48-19
Moai Technologies Inc			
100 First Ave 9th Fl ....Pittsburgh PA 15222	**800-814-1548**	412-454-5550	178-7
Moberly Area Community College			
101 College Ave ....Moberly MO 65270	**800-622-2070**	660-263-4110	162
MOBI Wireless Management LLC			
6100 W 96th St Ste 150 ....Indianapolis IN 46278	**855-259-6624**		196
Mobile Area Chamber of Commerce			
451 Government St ....Mobile AL 36602	**800-422-6951**	251-433-6951	139
Mobile City Hall			
205 Government St ....Mobile AL 36602	**800-957-3676**	251-208-7411	336
Mobile Communication of Gwinnett Inc			
2241 Tucker Industrial Rd ....Tucker GA 30084	**800-749-7170**	770-963-3748	246
Mobile Fixture & Equipment Company Inc			
1155 Montlimar Dr ....Mobile AL 36609	**800-345-6458**	251-342-0455	405
Mobile Life Support Services Inc			
3188 Us Rt 9w ....New Windsor NY 12553	**800-209-8815**	845-562-4368	30
Mobile Medical International Corp			
2176 Portland St			
PO Box 672..........St. Johnsbury VT 05819	**800-692-5205**	802-748-2322	473
Mobile Nations LLC			
3151 E Thomas St ....Inverness FL 34453	**877-799-0143**		157-5
Mobile Paint			
4775 Hamilton Blvd ....Theodore AL 36582	**800-621-6952**	251-443-6110	546
Mobile Parts Inc			
2472 Evans Rd PO Box 327 ....Val Caron ON P3N1P5	**800-461-4055**	705-897-4955	357
Mobile Public Library			
701 Government St ....Mobile AL 36602	**877-322-8228**	251-208-7073	433-3
Mobile Regional Airport			
8400 Airport Blvd ....Mobile AL 36608	**800-357-5373**	251-633-4510	27
Mobile Smith			
5400 Trinity Rd Ste 208 ....Raleigh NC 27607	**855-516-2413**		39
Mobile Technologies Inc (MTI)			
1050 NW 229th Ave ....Hillsboro OR 97124	**888-684-0040**	503-648-6500	610
MobileIQ Inc			
4800 Baseline Rd Ste E104-247 ....Boulder CO 80303	**866-261-8600**		386
Mobility Center Inc			
6693 Dixie Hwy ....Bridgeport MI 48722	**866-361-7559**	989-777-0910	478
Mobivity Inc			
58 W Buffalo Ste 200 ....Chandler AZ 85225	**877-282-7660**		5
Mobridge Tribune			
1413 E Grand Xing ....Mobridge SD 57601	**800-594-9418**	605-845-3646	528-3
MOCAP Inc			
409 Pkwy Dr ....Park Hills MO 63601	**800-633-6775**	314-543-4000	604
Moccasin Bend Mental Health Institute			
100 Moccasin Bend Rd ....Chattanooga TN 37405	**800-560-5767**	423-265-2271	373-5
MODA Hotel			
900 Seymour St ....Vancouver BC V6B3L9	**877-683-5522**	604-683-4251	378
Modal Shop Inc, The			
1776 Mentor Ave ....Cincinnati OH 45212	**800-860-4867**	513-351-9919	418

Name / Address	City	State	ZIP	Toll-Free	Phone	Class
Model Coverall Service Inc 100 28th St SE	Grand Rapids	MI	49548	**800-968-6491**	616-241-6491	441
Model Electronics Inc 615 E Crescent Ave	Ramsey	NJ	07446	**800-433-9657**		45
Modell's Sporting Goods 498 Seventh Ave 20th Fl	New York	NY	10018	**800-275-6633**		157-5
Modern Art Museum of Fort Worth 3200 Darnell St	Fort Worth	TX	76107	**866-824-5566**	817-738-9215	517
Modern Automation Inc 134 Tennsco Dr	Dickson	TN	37055	**800-921-9705**	615-446-1990	357
Modern Business Associates Inc 9455 Koger Blvd Ste 200	St Petersburg	FL	33702	**888-622-6460**		
Modern Chevrolet of Winston-Salem 5955 University Pkwy *General	Winston-Salem	NC	27105	**888-306-0825***	336-793-5943	57
Modern Corp 4746 Model City Rd	Model City	NY	14107	**800-662-0012**	716-754-8226	799
Modern Dental Laboratory USA 500 Stephenson Hwy Ste 100	Troy	MI	48083	**877-711-8778**		414
Modern Distributors Inc 817 W Columbia St	Somerset	KY	42501	**800-880-5543**	606-679-1178	751
Modern Earth 449 Provencher Blvd	Winnipeg	MB	R2J0B8	**866-766-7640**	204-885-2469	225
Modern Group Ltd 2501 Durham Rd	Bristol	PA	19007	**800-223-3827**	215-943-9100	384
Modern Group Ltd 1655 Louisiana St *Cust Svc	Beaumont	TX	77701	**800-231-8198***	409-833-2665	273
MODERN Honolulu, The 1775 Ala Moana Blvd	Honolulu	HI	96815	**855-599-9604**	808-943-5800	
Modern Ice Equipment & Supply Co 5709 Harrison Ave	Cincinnati	OH	45248	**800-543-1581**		661
Modern Language Assn (MLA) 26 Broadway 3rd Fl	New York	NY	10004	**800-323-4900**	646-576-5000	49-5
Modern Machine & Engineering Corp 9380 Winnetka Ave N	Brooklyn Park	MN	55445	**800-443-5117**	612-781-3347	617
Modern Machine & Tool Company Inc 11844 Jefferson Ave	Newport News	VA	23606	**800-482-1835**	757-873-1212	406
Modern Machine Shop Magazine 6915 Valley Ave	Cincinnati	OH	45244	**800-950-8020**	513-527-8800	455-21
Modern Management Inc 253 Commerce Dr Ste 105	Grayslake	IL	60030	**800-323-1331**	847-945-7400	193
Modern Plastics Inc 88 Long Hill Cross Rd	Shelton	CT	06484	**800-243-9696**	203-333-3128	597
Modern Way Printing & Fulfillment 8817 Production Ln	Ooltewah	TN	37363	**800-603-5135**	423-238-4500	623
Modern Welding Company Inc 2880 New Hartford Rd	Owensboro	KY	42303	**800-922-1932**	270-685-4400	91
Modern Woodmen of America 1701 First Ave	Rock Island	IL	61201	**800-447-9811**		390-2
Moderne Glass Company Inc 1000 Industrial Blvd	Aliquippa	PA	15001	**800-645-5131**	724-857-5700	330
Modernfold Inc 215 W New Rd	Greenfield	IN	46140	**800-869-9685**		286
Modesto Bee 1325 H St	Modesto	CA	95354	**800-776-4233**	209-578-2000	528-2
Modesto City Schools 426 Locust St	Modesto	CA	95351	**800-942-3767**	209-574-1500	681
Modesto Convention & Visitors Bureau 1150 Ninth St Ste C	Modesto	CA	95354	**888-640-8467**	209-526-5588	206
Modesto Symphony Orchestra 911 13th St	Modesto	CA	95354	**877-488-3380**	209-523-4156	569-3
Modine Manufacturing Co 1500 De Koven Ave *NYSE: MOD*	Racine	WI	53403	**800-828-4328**	262-636-1200	15
Modis Inc 10 Bay St 7th Fl	Toronto	ON	M5J2R8	**800-842-5907**	904-360-2300	461
Modjeski & Masters Inc 100 Sterling Pkwy Ste 302	Mechanicsburg	PA	17050	**888-663-5375**	717-790-9565	261
Modo 20325 NW von Neumann Dr	Beaverton	OR	97006	**800-685-8784**		
MOD-PAC Corp 1801 Elmwood Ave *NASDAQ: MPAC* ■ *Cust Svc	Buffalo	NY	14207	**866-216-6193***	716-873-0640	101
Modulant Inc 15305 Dallas Pkwy Ste 300	Dallas	TX	75001	**800-470-3575**	972-378-6677	
Modular Connections LLC 1090 Industrial Blvd	Bessemer	AL	35022	**877-903-6335**	205-980-4565	186
Modular Genius Inc 1201 S Mountain Rd	Joppa	MD	21085	**888-420-1113**	410-676-3424	186
Moeller Mfg Company Inc Aircraft Div 30100 Beck Rd	Wixom	MI	48393	**800-321-8010**	248-960-3999	21
Moeller Mfg Company Inc Punch & Die Div 43938 Plymouth Oaks Blvd	Plymouth	MI	48170	**800-521-7613**	734-416-0000	752
Moen Inc 25300 Al Moen Dr *Cust Svc	North Olmsted	OH	44070	**800-289-6636***	440-962-2000	605
Moews Seed Co Route 89 S of Jct 89 & 71 PO Box 214	Granville	IL	61326	**800-663-9795**	815-339-2201	10-4
Moffatt & Nichol Engineers 3780 Kilroy Airport Way # 750	Long Beach	CA	90806	**888-399-6609**	562-590-6500	261
Moffitt Cancer Center University of S Florida 12902 Magnolia Dr	Tampa	FL	33612	**800-456-3434**	888-663-3488	373-7
Moffitt Corp Inc 1351 13th Ave S Ste 130	Jacksonville Beach	FL	32250	**800-474-3267**	904-241-9944	256
MOGL Loyalty Services Inc 9645 Scranton Rd Ste 110	San Diego	CA	92121	**888-664-5669**		386
Mohair Council of America 233 W Twohig Rd	San Angelo	TX	76903	**800-583-3161**	325-655-3161	48-2
Mohave Community College *Bullhead City* 3400 Hwy 95	Bullhead City	AZ	86442	**866-664-2832**	928-758-3926	162
Lake Havasu 1977 W Acoma Blvd	Lake Havasu City	AZ	86403	**866-664-2832**	928-855-7812	162
North Mohave PO Box 980	Colorado City	AZ	86021	**800-678-3992**	928-875-2799	162
Mohave Educational Services Cooperative Inc 625 E Beale St	Kingman	AZ	86401	**800-742-2437**	928-753-6945	433-3
Mohawk Fine Papers Inc 465 Saratoga St	Cohoes	NY	12047	**800-843-6455**	518-237-1740	548-2
Mohawk Industries Inc 160 S Industrial Blvd *NYSE: MHK*	Calhoun	GA	30703	**800-241-4494**	706-629-7721	131
Mohawk Industries Inc Lees Carpets Div 160 S Industrial Blvd	Calhoun	GA	30701	**800-241-4494**	706-629-7721	131
Mohawk Shared Services 5295 John Lucas Dr Unit 5	Burlington	ON	L7L6A8	**888-521-8300**	289-337-5000	460
Mohawk Valley Community College 1101 Sherman Dr	Utica	NY	13501	**800-733-6822**	315-792-5400	162
Mohawk Valley Psychiatric Ctr 1400 Noyes St	Utica	NY	13502	**800-597-8481**	315-738-3800	373-5
Mohegan Gaming & Entertainment (MGE) 1 Mohegan Sun Blvd *Resv	Uncasville	CT	06382	**888-777-7922***	888-226-7711	77
Mohegan Sun Resort & Casino 1 Mohegan Sun Blvd	Uncasville	CT	06382	**888-226-7711**	860-862-8150	133
Mohonk Mountain House 1000 Mtn Rest Rd	New Paltz	NY	12561	**855-883-3798**	845-255-1000	665
Mohr Corp PO Box 1600	Brighton	MI	48114	**800-223-6647**	810-225-9494	456
Mohr Power Solar Inc 1452 Pomona Rd	Corona	CA	92882	**800-637-6527**	951-736-2000	606
Mojave A Desert Resort 73721 Shadow Mtn Dr *Resv	Palm Desert	CA	92260	**800-391-1104***	760-346-6121	378
Mojio Inc 1080 Howe St 9th Fl	Vancouver	BC	V6Z2T1	**855-556-6546**		224
Mokara Hotel & Spa 212 W Crockett St	San Antonio	TX	78205	**866-605-1212**	210-396-5800	703
Molalla Communications Co-op 211 Robbins St PO Box 360	Molalla	OR	97038	**800-332-2344**	503-829-1100	731
Mold Base Industries Inc 7501 Derry St	Harrisburg	PA	17111	**800-241-6656**	717-564-7960	752
Mold-A-Matic Corp 147 River St	Oneonta	NY	13820	**866-886-2626**	607-433-2121	752
Molded Fiber Glass Cos 2026 MFG Pl PO Box 675	Ashtabula	OH	44005	**800-860-0196**	440-997-5851	600
Molded Fiber Glass Tray Co 6175 US Hwy 6 *Sales	Linesville	PA	16424	**800-458-6050***	814-683-4500	199
Moldex Metric Inc 10111 W Jefferson Blvd	Culver City	CA	90232	**800-421-0668**	310-837-6500	572
Molding Corp of America 10349 Norris Ave	Pacoima	CA	91331	**800-423-2747**	818-890-7877	600
Mold-Rite Plastics LLC 1 Plant St	Plattsburgh	NY	12901	**800-432-5277**	518-561-1812	604
Mole Hollow Candles Ltd 208 Charlton Rd Rt 20 PO Box 223 *Cust Svc	Sturbridge	MA	01566	**800-445-6653***		327
Mole Lake Casino Lodge & Conference Ctr 3084 State Hwy 55	Crandon	WI	54520	**800-236-9466**	715-478-3200	450
Molecular Devices Inc (MDI) 1311 Orleans Dr	Sunnyvale	CA	94089	**800-635-5577**	408-747-1700	418
Molecular Imaging Services Inc 10 Whitaker Ct	Bear	DE	19701	**866-937-8855**		414
Molecular Pathology Laboratory Network Inc 250 E Broadway	Maryville	TN	37804	**800-932-2943**	865-380-9746	416
Molex Inc 2222 Wellington Ct *Cust Svc	Lisle	IL	60532	**800-786-6539***	630-353-1314	253
Molin Concrete Products Co 415 Lilac St	Lino Lakes	MN	55014	**800-336-6546**	651-786-7722	183
Molina Healthcare Inc 200 Oceangate Ste 100 *NYSE: MOH*	Long Beach	CA	90802	**888-562-5442**	562-435-3666	390-3
Moline Dispatch Publishing Co 1720 Fifth Ave	Moline	IL	61265	**800-660-2472**	309-764-4344	633-8
Moline Machinery LLC 114 S Central Ave	Duluth	MN	55807	**800-767-5734**		361
Molle Toyota Inc 601 West 103rd St	Kansas City	MO	64114	**888-510-7705**	816-942-5200	57
Molloy College 1000 Hempstead Ave *Admissions	Rockville Centre	NY	11571	**888-466-5569***	516-678-5000	166
Molok North America Ltd 179 Norpark Ave	Mount Forest	ON	N0G2L0	**877-558-5576**	519-323-9909	38
Molon Motor & Coil Corp 300 N Ridge Ave	Arlington Heights	IL	60005	**800-526-6867**	847-253-6000	515
Moloney Securities 13537 Barrett Pkwy Dr Ste 300	Manchester	MO	63021	**800-628-6002**	314-909-0600	
Molpus Co, The 502 Vly View Dr PO Box 59	Philadelphia	MS	39350	**800-535-5434**	601-656-3373	812
Molson Coors Brewing Co 1225 17th St Ste 3200 *NYSE: TAP*	Denver	CO	80202	**800-645-5376**	303-927-2337	102
Momar Inc 1830 Ellsworth Industrial Dr	Atlanta	GA	30318	**800-556-3967**	404-355-4580	145
Moment Magazine 4115 Wisconsin Ave NW Ste 10	Washington	DC	20016	**800-777-1005**	202-363-6422	455-18
Momentum Bmw Ltd 10002 SW Fwy	Houston	TX	77074	**800-731-8114**	855-645-6452	513
Momo Automotive Accessories Inc 1161 N Knollwood Cir	Anaheim	CA	92801	**800-749-6666**	949-380-7556	54
Monaco Coach Corp 1031 US 224 E	Decatur	IN	46733	**877-466-6226**		120
Monaco Government Tourist Office 565 Fifth Ave 23rd Fl	New York	NY	10017	**800-753-9696**	212-286-3330	770
Monadnock Paper Mills Inc 117 Antrim Rd *Orders	Bennington	NH	03442	**800-221-2159***	603-588-3311	553
Monaghan Medical Corp 5 Latour Ave Ste 1600	Plattsburgh	NY	12901	**800-833-9653**		475

Alphabetical Section

Name / Address	Toll-Free	Phone	Class
Monarch Hotel & Conference Ctr 12566 SE 93rd Ave ....Clackamas OR 97015	800-492-8700	503-652-1515	378
Monarch Lathes 615 N Oaks Ave PO Box 4609 ....Sidney OH 45365	800-543-7666	937-492-4111	453
Monarch Recovery Management Inc 3260 Tillman Dr Ste 75....Bensalem PA 19020	800-220-0605	215-281-7500	
Monarch Textile Rental Services Inc 2810 Foundation Dr ....South Bend IN 46628	800-589-9434	574-233-9433	258
Moncton Flight College 1719 Champlain St ....Dieppe NB E1A7P5	800-760-4632	506-857-3080	23
Moncton Museum 20 Mountain Rd ....Moncton NB E1C2J8	800-363-4558	506-856-4383	519
Mondrian Hotel 8440 Sunset Blvd ....West Hollywood CA 90069	800-525-8029	323-650-8999	378
Monetta Financial Services Inc 1776A S Naperville Rd Ste 100....Wheaton IL 60189	800-241-9772	630-462-9800	524
Money & Politics Report 1801 S Bell St ....Arlington VA 22202	800-372-1033		527-7
Money Mailer LLC 12131 Western Ave ....Garden Grove CA 92841	800-468-5865	714-889-3800	5
Money Movers Inc PO Box 241 ....Sebastopol CA 95473	800-861-5029	707-829-5577	251
Money Tree Software Ltd 2430 NW Professional Dr ....Corvallis OR 97330	877-421-9815	541-754-3701	177
MoneyGram International Inc 2828 N Harwood 1st Fl ....Dallas TX 75201 *NASDAQ: MGI*	800-666-3947		69
Moneytree Inc 6720 Ft Dent Way Ste 230 ....Seattle WA 98188	877-613-6669	206-246-3500	69
Monin Inc 2100 Range Rd ....Clearwater FL 33765	855-352-8671		
Monitor Dynamics Inc 12500 Network Dr Ste 303 ....San Antonio TX 78249	866-435-7634	210-477-5400	688
Monitor, The 1400 E Nolana Loop ....Mcallen TX 78504	800-366-4343	956-683-4000	528-2
Monmouth College 700 E Broadway ....Monmouth IL 61462	888-827-8268	309-457-2311	166
Monmouth Historic Inn & Gardens 1358 John A Quitman Blvd ....Natchez MS 39120	800-828-4531	601-442-5852	378
Monmouth Medical Ctr 300 Second Ave ....Long Branch NJ 07740	888-724-7123	732-222-5200	373-3
Monmouth University 400 Cedar Ave ....West Long Branch NJ 07764	800-543-9671	732-571-3456	166
Monogram Biosciences Inc 345 Oyster Pt Blvd ....South San Francisco CA 94080	800-777-0177	650-635-1100	418
Monona Terrace Community & Convention Ctr 1 John Nolen Dr ....Madison WI 53703	800-947-3529	608-261-4000	205
MonoSol LLC 707 E 80th Pl Ste 301....Merrillville IN 46410	800-237-9552		
Monro Muffler Brake Inc 200 Holleder Pkwy ....Rochester NY 14615 *NASDAQ: MNRO*	800-876-6676	585-647-6400	62-3
Monroe Bank & Trust 102 E Front St ....Monroe MI 48161	800-321-0032	734-241-3431	70
Monroe Chamber of Commerce 212 Walnut St Ste 100 ....Monroe LA 71201	888-677-5200	318-323-3461	139
Monroe Clinic Hospital 515 22nd Ave ....Monroe WI 53566	800-338-0568	608-324-2000	373-3
Monroe College 2501 Jerome Ave ....Bronx NY 10468	800-556-6676	718-933-6700	795
Monroe Community College 1000 E Henrietta Rd ....Rochester NY 14623	800-875-6269	585-292-2000	162
Monroe County 124 W Commerce St ....Aberdeen MS 39730	800-457-5351	662-369-6488	337
Monroe County 38 W Main St PO Box 189 ....Forsyth GA 31029	800-282-5852	478-994-7000	337
Monroe County 106 E First St ....Monroe MI 48161	800-401-6402	734-240-7020	337
Monroe County Chamber of Commerce 1645 N Dixie Hwy Ste 20 ....Monroe MI 48162	855-386-1280	734-384-3366	139
Monroe County Chamber of Commerce 124 W Commerce St ....Aberdeen MS 39730	800-457-5351	662-369-6488	139
Monroe County Community College 1555 S Raisinville Rd ....Monroe MI 48161	877-937-6222	734-242-7300	162
Monroe County Electric Power Assn 601 N Main St ....Amory MS 38821	866-656-2962	662-256-2962	245
Monroe County Library System 3700 S Custer Rd ....Monroe MI 48161	800-462-2050	734-241-5277	433-3
Monroe County Tourist Development Council 1201 White St Ste 102 ....Key West FL 33040	800-242-5229	305-296-1552	206
Monroe County Water Authority 475 Norris Dr PO Box 10999 ....Rochester NY 14610	866-426-6292	585-442-2000	782
Monroe Electronics Inc 100 Housel Ave ....Lyndonville NY 14098	800-821-6001	585-765-2254	248
Monroe Environmental Corp 810 W Front St ....Monroe MI 48161	800-992-7707	734-242-7654	385
Monroe Financial Partners Inc 100 N Riverside Plz Ste 1620 ....Chicago IL 60606	800-766-5560	312-327-2530	194
Monroe Fluid Technology Inc 36 Draffin Rd ....Hilton NY 14468	800-828-6351	585-392-3434	145
Monroe Hardware Co 101 N Sutherland Ave ....Monroe NC 28110	800-222-1974	704-289-3121	350
Monroe Oil Co 519 E Franklin St ....Monroe NC 28112 *General	800-452-2717*	704-289-5438	324
Monroe Table Co 316 N Walnut St ....Salamanca NY 14779	844-822-5370	716-945-7700	
Monroe Title Insurance Corp 47 W Main St ....Rochester NY 14614	800-966-6763	585-232-4950	390-6
Monroe Tractor & Implement Company Inc 1001 Lehigh Stn Rd ....Henrietta NY 14467	866-683-5338	585-334-3867	357
Monroe Truck Equipment Inc 1051 W Seventh St ....Monroe WI 53566	800-356-8134	608-328-8127	513
Monroe Wheelchair 388 Old Niskayuna Rd ....Latham NY 12110	888-546-8595	518-783-1653	474
Monroeville Area Chamber of Commerce 4268 Northern Pk ....Monroeville PA 15146	800-527-8941	412-856-0622	139
Monroe-West Monroe Convention & Visitors Bureau 601 Constitution Dr PO Box 1436....West Monroe LA 71292	800-843-1872	318-387-5691	206
Monrovia Chamber of Commerce 620 S Myrtle Ave ....Monrovia CA 91016	800-755-1515	626-358-1159	139
Monster Cable Products Inc 455 Valley Dr ....Brisbane CA 94005	877-800-8989	415-840-2000	52
Montage Resort & Spa 30801 S Coast Hwy ....Laguna Beach CA 92651	866-271-6953	949-715-6000	665
Montana *Arts Council* PO Box 202201 ....Helena MT 59620	800-282-3092	406-444-6430	338-27
Banking & Financial Institutions Div 301 S Park Ste 316 PO Box 200546....Helena MT 59620	800-914-8423	406-841-2920	338-27
Child & Family Services Div PO Box 8005 ....Helena MT 59604	866-820-5437	406-841-2400	338-27
Consumer Protection Office 555 Fuller Ave ....Helena MT 59620	800-481-6896	406-444-4500	338-27
Higher Education Board of Regents 2500 Broadway St PO Box 203201....Helena MT 59620	877-501-1722	406-444-6570	721
Information Technology Services Div 125 N Roberts St PO Box 200113 ....Helena MT 59620	800-628-4917	406-444-2511	338-27
Office of Governor PO Box 200801 ....Helena MT 59620	855-318-1330	406-444-3111	338-27
Revenue Dept 125 N Roberts PO Box 5805....Helena MT 59604	866-859-2254	406-444-6900	338-27
Securities Dept 840 Helena Ave ....Helena MT 59601	800-332-6148	406-444-2040	338-27
Veterans Home 400 Veterans Dr ....Columbia Falls MT 59912	888-279-7532	406-892-3256	788
Victim Services Office 555 Fuller Ave PO Box 201410 ....Helena MT 59601	800-498-6455	406-444-1907	338-27
Montana Assn of Realtors 1 S Montana Ave Ste M1 ....Helena MT 59601	800-477-1864	406-443-4032	652
Montana Chamber of Commerce 900 GIBBON St PO Box 1730....Helena MT 59624	888-442-6668	406-442-2405	140
Montana Coffee Traders Inc 5810 Hwy 93 S ....Whitefish MT 59937	800-345-5282	406-862-7633	159
Montana Dental Assn 17 1/2 S Last Chance Gulch PO Box 1154....Helena MT 59624	800-257-4988	406-443-2061	227
Montana Historical Society Museum 225 N Roberts St ....Helena MT 59620	800-243-9900	406-444-2694	517
Montana Lawyer Magazine 7 W Sixth Ave Ste 2B ....Helena MT 59601	877-880-1335		455-15
Montana Manufacturing Extension Center 2310 University Way Bldg 2 ....Bozeman MT 59715	800-637-4634	406-994-3812	461
Montana Medical Assn 2021 11th Ave Ste 1 ....Helena MT 59601	877-443-4000	406-443-4000	472
Montana PBS 183 Visual Communications Bldg ....Bozeman MT 59717	800-426-8243	866-832-0829	628
Montana Public Radio 32 Campus Dr University of Montana....Missoula MT 59812	800-325-1565	406-243-4931	628
Montana Rail Link Inc 101 International Way ....Missoula MT 59808	800-338-4750	406-523-1500	644
Montana Refining Co 1900 Tenth St NE ....Great Falls MT 59404	800-437-3188	317-328-5660	576
Montana Standard 25 W Granite St ....Butte MT 59701	800-877-1074	406-496-5500	528-2
Montana State Prison 400 Conley Lake Rd ....Deer Lodge MT 59722	888-739-9122	406-846-1320	213
Montana State University *Billings* 1500 University Dr ....Billings MT 59101	800-565-6782	406-657-2011	166
Bozeman 1401 West Lincoln St ....Bozeman MT 59717 *Admissions	888-678-2287*	406-994-2452	166
Northern PO Box 7751 ....Havre MT 59501	800-662-6132	406-994-2452	166
Montana Tech of the University of Montana 1300 West Park St ....Butte MT 59701 *Admissions	800-445-8324*	406-496-4101	166
Montana-Dakota Utilities Co (MDU) 400 N Fourth St ....Bismarck ND 58501	800-638-3278	701-222-7900	782
Montauk Yacht Club Resort & Marina 32 Star Island Rd ....Montauk NY 11954	888-692-8668	631-668-3100	665
Montclair State University 1 Normal Ave ....Montclair NJ 07043 *Admissions	800-331-9205*	973-655-4000	166
Monte Carlo Inn-Airport Suites 7035 Edwards Blvd ....Mississauga ON L5T2H8	800-363-6400	905-564-8500	378
Monte Package Company Inc 3752 Riverside Rd ....Riverside MI 49084	800-653-2807	269-849-1722	200
Montello Inc 6106 E 32nd Pl Ste 100 ....Tulsa OK 74135	800-331-4628		145
Monterey Bay Inn 242 Cannery Row ....Monterey CA 93940	800-424-6242	831-373-6242	378
Monterey Conference Center 1 Portola Plz ....Monterey CA 93940 *Sales	800-742-8091*	831-646-3388	205
Monterey County 168 W Alisal St ....Salinas CA 93901	800-994-9662	831-755-5115	337
Monterey County Convention & Visitors Bureau PO Box 1770 ....Monterey CA 93942	888-221-1010		206
Monterey County Herald 2200 Garden Rd ....Monterey CA 93940	800-688-1808	831-372-3311	528-2
Monterey Financial Services Inc 4095 Avenida De La Plata ....Oceanside CA 92056	800-456-2225	760-639-3500	392
Monterey Mills Inc 1725 E Delavan Dr ....Janesville WI 53546	800-255-9665	608-754-2866	740-4
Monterey Mushrooms Inc 260 Westgate Dr ....Watsonville CA 95076	800-333-6874	831-763-5300	10-6
Monterey Pasta Co 2315 Moore Ave ....Fullerton CA 92833	800-588-7782		296-31
Monterey Peninsula College 980 Fremont St ....Monterey CA 93940	877-663-5433	831-646-4000	162
Monterey Plaza Hotel & Spa 400 Cannery Row ....Monterey CA 93940	877-862-7552		378

Name / Address	Toll-Free	Phone	Class
Monterey Public Library 580 Pacific St .... Monterey CA 93940	800-338-0505	831-646-3933	433-3
Monterey-Salinas Transit (MST) 19 Upper Ragsdale Dr Ste 200 .... Monterey CA 93940	888-678-2871		466
Montfort Bros Inc 44 Elm St .... Fishkill NY 12524	800-724-1777	845-896-6225	183
Montfort Group, The 44 Elm St .... Fishkill NY 12524	800-724-1777	845-896-6225	183
Montfort Hospital 713 Montreal Rd .... Ottawa ON K1K0T2	866-670-4621	613-746-4621	373-2
Montgomery Advertiser 425 Molton St .... Montgomery AL 36104	877-424-0007	334-262-1611	528-2
Montgomery Area Chamber of Commerce Convention & Visitor Bureau 300 Water St .... Montgomery AL 36104	800-240-9452	334-261-1100	206
Montgomery Bank 1 Montgomery Bank Plz PO Box 948 .... Sikeston MO 63801	800-455-2275	573-471-2275	70
Montgomery Bell State Resort Park 1020 Jackson Hill Rd .... Burns TN 37029	800-250-8613	615-797-9052	561
Montgomery County PO Box 311 .... Norristown PA 19404	800-932-4600	610-278-3346	337
Montgomery County Visitors & Convention Bureau 218 E Pike St .... Crawfordsville IN 47933	800-866-3973	765-362-5200	206
Montgomery Truss & Panel Inc 803 W Main St .... Grove City PA 16127	800-942-8010	724-458-7500	812
Monticello 556 Dettor Rd Ste 107 .... Charlottesville VA 22903	800-243-0743	434-984-9822	50-3
Monticello Corp, The PO Box 190645 .... Atlanta GA 31119	866-701-1561	404-478-6413	
Montisa 323 Acorn St .... Plainwell MI 49080 *Cust Svc	800-875-6836*	269-924-0730	319-1
Montmorency County PO Box 789 .... Atlanta MI 49709	877-742-7576	989-785-8022	337
Montour County 29 Mill St .... Danville PA 17821	800-632-9063	570-271-3010	337
Montpelier Glove Co Inc 129 N Main St .... Montpelier IN 47359	800-645-3931	765-728-2481	155-7
Montreal Beach Resort 1025 Beach Ave .... Cape May NJ 08204	800-525-7011	609-884-7011	665
Montreal Canadiens Bell Centre 1275 St-Antoine Ouest .... Montreal QC H3B5E8	800-363-8162	514-989-2836	712
Montreal Exchange 1800 - 1190 Ave des Canadiens-de-Montr,al PO Box 37 .... Montreal QC H3B0G7	800-361-5353	514-871-2424	687
Montreal Heart Institute 5000 Belanger St E .... Montreal QC H1T1C8	855-922-6387	514-376-3330	373-2
Montreat College 310 Gaither Cir PO Box 1267 .... Montreat NC 28757	800-622-6968	828-669-8012	166
Montrose Travel 2349 Honolulu Ave .... Montrose CA 91020	800-666-8767	818-553-3200	766
Montrose Visitor Center 107 S Cascade Ave .... Montrose CO 81401	855-497-8558	970-249-5000	206
Montserrat College of Art 23 Essex St .... Beverly MA 01915	800-836-0487	978-921-4242	166
Monument Builders of North America (MBNA) 136 S Keowee St .... Dayton OH 45402	800-233-4472		49-3
Monument Security Inc 5 Sierra Gate Plz Ste 305 .... Roseville CA 95678	877-506-1755	916-564-4234	689
Monumental Sales Inc 537 22nd Ave N PO Box 667 .... Saint Cloud MN 56302	800-442-1660	320-251-6585	720
Moody Bible Institute 820 N La Salle St .... Chicago IL 60610	800-967-4624	312-329-4400	161
Moody Dunbar Inc PO Box 6048 .... Johnson City TN 37602	800-251-8202	423-952-0100	296-20
Moody Foundation 2302 Post Office St Ste 704 .... Galveston TX 77550	866-742-1133	409-797-1500	305
Moody Gardens Convention Ctr 7 Hope Blvd .... Galveston TX 77554	888-388-8484	409-741-8484	205
Moody Medical Library 914 Market St .... Galveston TX 77555	866-235-5223	409-772-2372	433-1
Moody-Price LLC 18320 Petroleum Dr .... Baton Rouge LA 70809	800-272-9832		385
Moog Inc Jamison Rd .... East Aurora NY 14052 NYSE: MOG.A	800-336-2112	716-652-2000	203
Mooney Aircraft Corp 165 Al Mooney Rd .... Kerrville TX 78028	800-456-3033		20
Mooney General Paper Co 1451 Chestnut Ave PO Box 3800 .... Hillside NJ 07205	800-882-8846	973-926-3800	543
Moonworks 1137 Park E Dr .... Woonsocket RI 02895	800-975-6666		747
Moore & Neidenthal Inc 3034 N Wooster Ave .... Dover OH 44622	866-364-7774	330-364-7774	2
Moore College of Art & Design 20th St & the Pkwy .... Philadelphia PA 19103	800-523-2025	215-965-4000	164
Moore County Chamber of Commerce 10677 Hwy 15-501 .... Southern Pines NC 28387	800-346-5362	910-692-3926	139
Moore Industries International Inc 16650 Schoenborn St .... North Hills CA 91343	800-999-2900	818-894-7111	201
Moore Medical Corp 389 John Downey Dr .... New Britain CT 06050 *Sales	800-234-1464*	860-826-3600	473
Moore Regional Hospital 155 Memorial Dr PO Box 3000 .... Pinehurst NC 28374	866-415-2778	910-715-1000	373-3
Moore State Park Mill St .... Paxton MA 01612	800-437-5922	508-792-3969	561
Moore Stephens Lovelace PA 255 S Orange Ave Ste 600 .... Orlando FL 32801	800-683-5401	407-740-5400	2
Moores Electrical & Mechanical PO Box 119 .... Altavista VA 24517	888-722-2712	434-369-4374	186
Mooresville-South Iredell Chamber of Commerce 149 E Iredell Ave .... Mooresville NC 28115	800-764-7113	704-664-3898	139
Moorings Park 120 Moorings Pk Dr .... Naples FL 34105	866-802-4302	239-643-9111	668
Moors & Cabot Inc 111 Devonshire St .... Boston MA 02109	800-426-0501		404
Moose International Inc 155 S International Dr .... Mooseheart IL 60539	800-668-5901	630-859-2000	48-15
Moose Magazine 155 S International Dr .... Mooseheart IL 60539	800-544-4407	630-859-2000	455-10
Moose Travel Network 192 Spadina Ave Unit 408 .... Toronto ON M5T2C2	888-244-6673	604-297-0255	755
MOPS International 2370 S Trenton Way .... Denver CO 80231 *General	888-910-6677*	303-733-5353	48-6
Morabito Baking Company Inc 757 Kohn St .... Norristown PA 19401	800-525-7747	610-275-5419	296-1
Moraine Park Technical College 235 N National Ave .... Fond du Lac WI 54935	800-472-4554	920-922-8611	795
Moran Printing Inc 5425 Florida Blvd .... Baton Rouge LA 70806	800-211-8335	225-923-2550	622
Moran Technology Consulting Llc 1215 Hamilton Ln Ste 200 .... Naperville IL 60540	888-699-4440		196
Mora-San Miguel Electric Co-op Hwy 518 Main St .... Mora NM 87732	800-421-6773	575-387-2205	245
Moravian College 1200 Main St .... Bethlehem PA 18018	800-441-3191	610-861-1300	166
Moravian Theological Seminary 1200 Main St .... Bethlehem PA 18018	800-843-6541	610-861-1516	167-3
Morbark Inc 8507 S Winn Rd .... Winn MI 48896	800-831-0042	989-866-2381	446
More Hawaii for Less 11 Ash Tree Ln .... Irvine CA 92612	800-967-6687	949-724-5050	766
More Space Place Inc 5040 140th Ave N .... Clearwater FL 33760	888-731-3051		360
MoreDirect Inc 1001 Yamato Rd Ste 200 .... Boca Raton FL 33431	800-800-5555	561-237-3300	196
Morehead Memorial Hospital 117 E King's Hwy .... Eden NC 27288	800-291-4020	336-623-9711	373-3
Morehead State University 100 Admissions Ctr .... Morehead KY 40351	800-585-6781	606-783-2000	166
Morey's Seafood International LLC 1218 Hwy 10 S .... Motley MN 56466	800-808-3474	218-352-6345	296-14
Morga-Gallacher Inc 8707 Millergrove Dr .... Santa Fe Springs CA 90670	877-647-6279		
Morgan & Co 1131 Glendon Ave .... Los Angeles CA 90024	800-458-4367	310-208-3377	409
Morgan Adhesives Cu 4560 Darrow Rd .... Stow OH 44224	866-262-2822	330-688-1111	3
Morgan Community College 920 Barlow Rd .... Fort Morgan CO 80701	800-622-0216	970-542-3100	162
Morgan Corp 111 Morgan Way PO Box 588 .... Morgantown PA 19543	800-666-7426		513
Morgan County 180 S Main St .... Martinsville IN 46151	800-382-9467	765-342-1007	337
Morgan County Rural Electric Assn 20169 US Hwy 34 .... Fort Morgan CO 80701	877-495-6487	970-867-5688	245
Morgan Foods Inc 90 W Morgan St .... Austin IN 47102	888-430-1780	812-794-1170	296-20
Morgan Hunter Companies 7600 W 110th St .... Overland Park KS 66210	800-917-6447	913-491-3434	260
Morgan Lewis & Bockius LLP 1701 Market St .... Philadelphia PA 19103	866-963-7137	215-963-5000	427
Morgan Olson 1801 S Nottawa Rd .... Sturgis MI 49091	800-624-9005		513
Morgan Run Natural Environment Area Benrose Ln .... Westminster MD 21157	800-830-3974	410-461-5005	561
Morgan Run Resort & Club 5690 Cancha de Golf .... Rancho Santa Fe CA 92091 *Resv	800-378-4653*	800-433-5079	665
Morgan Schaffer Systems Inc 8300 rue Saint-Patrick Bureau 150 LaSalle .... Montreal QC H8N2H1	855-861-1967	514-739-1967	738
Morgan Scientific Inc 151 Essex St .... Haverhill MA 01832	800-525-5002	978-521-4440	474
Morgan Services Inc 323 N Michigan Ave .... Chicago IL 60601	888-966-7426	312-346-3181	441
Morgan Stanley 1585 Broadway .... New York NY 10036 NYSE: MS ■ *General	800-223-2440*	212-761-4000	686
Morgan Stanley Investment Management 1221 Ave of the Americas 5th Fl .... New York NY 10020 *General	800-223-2440*	212-296-6600	686
Morgan Stanley Venture Partners 1585 Broadway .... New York NY 10036	866-722-7310	212-761-4000	787
Morgan State University 1700 E Cold Spring Ln .... Baltimore MD 21251	800-319-4678	443-885-3333	166
Morgans Hotel Group 1685 Collins Ave .... South Beach FL 33139 NASDAQ: MHGC	800-606-6090	305-672-2000	378
Morgantown Area Chamber of Commerce 1029 University Ave Ste 101 .... Morgantown WV 26505 *General	800-618-2525*	304-292-3311	139
Mor-Gran-Sou Electric Co-op Inc 202 Sixth Ave W .... Flasher ND 58535	800-750-8212	701-597-3301	245
Moritz Embroidery Works Inc, The Pocono Mountain Business Park 405 Industrial Park PO Box 187 .... Mount Pocono PA 18344	800-533-4183	570-839-9600	258
Morley 100 High Grove Blvd .... Glendale Heights IL 60139	800-284-5172	847-639-4646	523
Morley Candy Makers Inc 23770 Hall Rd .... Clinton Township MI 48036	800-651-7263		296-8
Morley Companies Inc 1 Morley Plz .... Saginaw MI 48603	800-336-5554	989-791-2550	
Morley Financial Services Inc 1300 SW Fifth Ave Ste 3300 .... Portland OR 97201	800-548-4806	503-484-9300	400
Morley-Murphy Co 200 S Washington St Ste 305 .... Green Bay WI 54301	877-499-3171	920-499-3171	608
Morning Call PO Box 1260 .... Allentown PA 18105	800-666-5492	610-820-6500	528-2
Morning Journal 1657 Broadway Ave .... Lorain OH 44052	888-757-0727	440-245-6901	528-2
Morningside College 1501 Morningside Ave .... Sioux City IA 51106	800-831-0806	712-274-5000	166

	Toll-Free	Phone	Class
Morningside of Fullerton			
800 Morningside Dr ....Fullerton CA 92835	800-803-7597	714-256-8000	668
Morningstar Inc			
22 W Washington St ....Chicago IL 60602	800-735-0700*	312-696-6000	400
*NASDAQ: MORN ■ *Orders*			
Mornington Communications Co-operative Ltd			
16 Mill St E ....Milverton ON N0K1M0	800-250-8750	519-595-8331	224
Morongo Casino Resort & Spa			
49500 Seminole Dr ....Cabazon CA 92230	800-252-4499	951-849-3080	665
Morphix Business Consulting			
PO Box 5217 Stn A ....Calgary AB T2H1X3	866-680-2503	403-520-7710	196
MorphoTrak Inc			
5515 E La Palma Ave Ste 100.........Anaheim CA 92807	800-346-2674	714-238-2000	84
Morrill Motors Inc			
229 S Main Ave ....Erwin TN 37650	888-743-7001		515
Morrilton Packing Company Inc			
51 Blue Diamond Dr ....Morrilton AR 72110	800-264-2475	501-354-2474	471
Morris & Dickson Co Ltd			
410 Kay Ln ....Shreveport LA 71115	800-388-3833	318-797-7900	238
Morris Cerullo World Evangelism			
3545 Aero Ct Frnt ....San Diego CA 92123	866-756-4200		
Morris College			
100 W College St ....Sumter SC 29150	866-853-1345*	803-934-3200	166
Admissions			
Morris Communications Company LLC			
725 Broad St ....Augusta GA 30901	800-622-6358	706-724-0851	633-8
Morris Coupling Co			
2240 W 15th St ....Erie PA 16505	800-426-1579	814-459-1741	488
Morris Herald-News			
1804 N Division St ....Morris IL 60450	800-397-9397	815-942-3221	528-3
Morris Industries Inc			
777 Rt 23 ....Pompton Plains NJ 07444	800-835-0777	973-835-6600	533
Morris Material Handling Inc			
315 W Forest Hill Ave ....Oak Creek WI 53154	800-933-3001	414-764-6200	468
Morris Performing Arts Ctr			
211 N Michigan St ....South Bend IN 46601	800-537-6415	574-235-9190	568
Morris Products Inc			
53 Carey Rd ....Queensbury NY 12804	888-777-6678	518-743-0523	782
Morrison & Foerster LLP			
425 Market St ....San Francisco CA 94105	800-952-5210	415-268-7000	427
Morrison Bros Co			
570 E Seventh St ....Dubuque IA 52001	800-553-4840	563-583-5701	533
Morrison County			
213 SE First Ave ....Little Falls MN 56345	866-401-1111	320-632-2941	337
Morrison County Record			
216 SE First St ....Little Falls MN 56345	888-637-2345	320-632-2345	528-4
Morrison Hershfield Group Inc			
125 Commerce Valley Dr W			
Ste 300 ....Markham ON L3T7W4	888-649-4730	416-499-3110	261
Morrison Milling Co			
319 E Prairie St ....Denton TX 76201	800-531-7912	940-387-6111	296-23
Morrison Scott Alan Law Offices of pa			
141 W Patrick St Ste 300 ....Frederick MD 21701	866-220-5185	301-694-6262	427
Morrison Supply Company Inc			
311 E Vickery Blvd ....Fort Worth TX 76104	877-709-2227		608
Morristown Medical Ctr			
100 Madison Ave ....Morristown NJ 07960	877-310-7226	973-971-5000	373-3
Morrisville State College			
80 Eaton St PO Box 901 ....Morrisville NY 13408	800-258-0111*	315-684-6000	166
Admissions			
Morro Strand State Beach			
1416 Ninth St ....Sacramento CA 95814	800-777-0369		
Morrow Control & Supply Co			
810 Marion Motley Ave NE..............Canton OH 44705	800-362-9830	330-452-9791	608
Morrow County Grain Growers Inc (MCGG)			
350 N Main St ....Lexington OR 97839	800-452-7396	541-989-8221	10-4
Morse Industries Inc			
25811 74th Ave S ....Kent WA 98032	800-325-7513		693
Morse Operations Inc			
3790 W Blue Heron Blvd ....Riviera Beach FL 33404	800-755-2593	866-590-0873	513
Mortara Instrument Inc			
7865 N 86th St ....Milwaukee WI 53224	800-231-7437	414-354-1600	250
Mortech Manufacturing Inc			
411 N Aerojet Ave ....Azusa CA 91702	800-410-0100	626-334-1471	405
Mortgage Bankers Assn (MBA)			
1919 M St NW 5th Fl ....Washington DC 20036	800-793-6222	202-557-2700	49-2
Mortgage Banking Solutions			
Frost Bank Tower 401 Congress Ave			
Ste 1540 ....Austin TX 78701	800-476-0853	512-977-9900	461
Mortgage Builder			
24370 NW Hwy ....Southfield MI 48075	800-850-8060		178-10
Mortgage Guaranty Insurance Corp			
270 E Kilbourn Ave ....Milwaukee WI 53202	800-558-9900	414-347-6480	390-5
Mortgage Investors Group			
8320 E Walker Springs Ln ....Knoxville TN 37923	800-489-8910	865-691-8910	507
Mortgageflex Systems Inc			
25 N Market St ....Jacksonville FL 32202	800-326-3539*	904-356-2490	177
General			
Morton Buildings Inc			
252 W Adams St PO Box 399..........Morton IL 61550	800-447-7436		105
Morton Grove Pharmaceuticals Inc			
6451 Main St ....Morton Grove IL 60053	800-346-6854	847-967-5600	579
Morton Plant Hospital			
300 Pinellas St ....Clearwater FL 33756	800-229-2273	727-462-7000	373-3
Morton Salt Inc			
123 N Wacker Dr ....Chicago IL 60606	800-725-8847	312-807-2000	676
Morton's The Steakhouse			
618 Church St ....Nashville TN 37219	800-297-3276	615-259-4558	667
Moscot			
108 Orchard St ....New York NY 10002	866-667-2687	212-477-3796	
Moscow Chamber of Commerce			
411 S Main St ....Moscow ID 83843	866-770-2020	208-882-1800	139
Moseo Corp			
2722 Elake Ave E ....Seattle WA 98102	800-741-0926		386
Moser Corp			
601 N 13th St ....Rogers AR 72756	800-632-4564	479-636-3481	321
Moses H Cone Memorial Hospital			
1200 N Elm St ....Greensboro NC 27401	866-391-2734	336-832-7000	373-3

	Toll-Free	Phone	Class
Moses Lake Area Chamber of Commerce			
324 S Pioneer Way ....Moses Lake WA 98837	800-992-6234	509-765-7888	139
Mosquito Lake State Park			
1439 State Rt 305 ....Cortland OH 44410	866-644-6727	330-637-2856	
Moss Inc PO Box 189 ....Pasadena MD 21123	800-932-6677	410-768-3442	231
Moss Supply Company Inc			
5001 N Graham St ....Charlotte NC 28269	800-438-0770	704-596-8717	234
Mossberg & Company Inc			
301 E Sample St ....South Bend IN 46601	800-428-3340	574-289-9253	622
Mosser Hotel			
54 Fourth St ....San Francisco CA 94103	800-227-3804	415-986-4400	378
Motel 6 Wichita			
8302 E Kellogg Dr ....Wichita KS 67207	800-466-8356	800-899-9841	378
Mother Jones Magazine			
222 Sutter St Ste 600 ....San Francisco CA 94108	800-438-6656	415-321-1700	455-17
Mother Murphy's Labs Inc			
2826 S Elm St PO Box 16846..............Greensboro NC 27416	800-849-1277	336-273-1737	296-15
Mother's Market & Kitchen			
1890 Newport Blvd ....Costa Mesa CA 92627	800-595-6667	949-631-4741	344
Mothers Against Drunk Driving (MADD)			
511 E John Carpenter Fwy Ste 700........Irving TX 75062	877-275-6233		48-6
Motif Seattle			
1415 Fifth Ave ....Seattle WA 98101	855-515-1144	206-971-8000	703
Motion Control Engineering Inc			
11380 White Rock Rd ....Rancho Cordova CA 95742	800-444-7442	916-463-9200	256
Motion Industries Inc			
1605 Alton Rd ....Birmingham AL 35210	800-526-9328	205-956-1122	384
Motion Picture & Television Fund			
23388 Mulholland Dr ....Woodland Hills CA 91364	855-760-6783		48-4
Mo-Tires Ltd			
2830 5 Ave N ....Lethbridge AB T1H0P1	800-774-3888	403-329-4533	392
Motivation Through Incentives Inc			
10400 W 103 St Ste 10..............Overland Park KS 66214	800-826-3464	913-438-2600	383
Motley Fool Inc			
2000 Duke St 4th Fl ....Alexandria VA 22314	800-292-7677	703-838-3665	403
Motlow State Community College			
PO Box 8500 ....Lynchburg TN 37352	800-654-4877	931-393-1544	162
Motor Appliance Corp			
601 International Ave ....Washington DC 20004	800-622-3406	636-231-6100	515
Motor Products Owosso Corp			
201 S Delaney Rd ....Owosso MI 48867	800-248-3841		515
Motor Service Inc			
130 Byassee Dr ....Hazelwood MO 63042	800-966-5080	314-731-4111	186
Motor Trend Magazine			
6420 Wilshire Blvd 7th Fl..........Los Angeles CA 90048	800-800-6848	323-782-2000	455-3
Motorcar Parts & Accessories			
2929 California St ....Torrance CA 90503	800-890-9988	310-212-7910	247
Motorcars International			
3015 E Cairo St ....Springfield MO 65802	866-970-6800	417-831-9999	57
MotorCity Casino Hotel			
2901 Grand River Ave ....Detroit MI 48201	866-752-9622	866-782-9622	133
Motorcycle Consumer News Magazine			
3 Burroughs ....Irvine CA 92618	888-333-0354		455-3
Motorcycle Hall of Fame Museum			
13515 Yarmouth Dr ....Pickerington OH 43147	800-262-5646	614-856-2222	519
MotorHome Magazine			
2750 Park View Ct Ste 240..............Oxnard CA 93036	800-678-1201*	805-667-4100	455-22
Cust Svc			
Motorists Insurance Group			
471 E Broad St ....Columbus OH 43215	800-876-6642	614-225-8211	
Motorlease Corp			
1506 New Britain Ave ....Farmington CT 06032	800-243-0182	860-677-9711	289
Motor-Services Hugo Stamp Inc			
3190 SW Fourth Ave ....Fort Lauderdale FL 33315	800-622-6747	954-763-3660	752
Motson Graphics Inc			
1717 Bethlehem Pk ....Flourtown PA 19031	800-972-1986	215-233-0500	683
Mott Corp			
84 Spring Ln ....Farmington CT 06032	800-289-6688	860-747-6333	474
Mott's LLP			
PO Box 869077 ....Plano TX 75086	800-426-4891*		296-20
Consumer Info			
Moulton Logistics Management			
7850 Ruffner Ave ....Van Nuys CA 91406	800-808-3304		194
Moultrie Feeders			
150 Industrial Rd ....Alabaster AL 35007	800-653-3334	205-664-6700	706
Moultrie-Colquitt County Chamber of Commerce			
116 First Ave SE ....Moultrie GA 31768	888-408-4748	229-985-2131	139
Mount Aloysius College			
7373 Admiral Perry Hwy ....Cresson PA 16630	888-823-2220	814-886-6383	166
Mount Angel Seminary			
1 Abbey Dr ....Saint Benedict OR 97373	800-845-8272	503-845-3951	167-3
Mount Bachelor Village Resort & Conference Ctr			
19717 Mt Bachelor Dr ....Bend OR 97702	800-547-5204	888-691-3069	665
Mount Carmel West Hospital			
793 W State St ....Columbus OH 43222	800-346-1009	614-234-5000	373-3
Mount Gilead State Park			
4119 State Rte 95 ....Mount Gilead OH 43338	866-644-6727		
Mount Holyoke College			
50 College St ....South Hadley MA 01075	800-642-4483	413-538-2000	166
Mount Joy Wire Corp			
1000 E Main St ....Mount Joy PA 17552	800-321-2305	717-653-1461	808
Mount Laurel Library			
100 Walt Whitman Ave ....Mount Laurel NJ 08054	888-576-5529	856-234-7319	433-3
Mount Marty College			
1105 W Eigth St ....Yankton SD 57078	800-658-4552*	605-668-1545	166
Admissions			
Mount Mary College			
2900 N Menomonee River Pkwy .....Milwaukee WI 53222	800-321-6265*	414-256-1219	166
Admissions			
Mount Mercy College			
1330 Elmhurst Dr NE ....Cedar Rapids IA 52402	800-248-4504	319-368-6460	166
Mount Miguel Covenant Village			
325 Kempton St ....Spring Valley CA 91977	877-321-4895	619-479-4790	668
Mount Nittany Medical Ctr			
1800 E Park Ave ....State College PA 16803	866-686-6171	814-231-7000	373-3
Mount Olive College			
634 Henderson St ....Mount Olive NC 28365	800-653-0854	919-658-2502	166

Listing	Toll-Free	Phone	Class
Mount Regis Center 125 Knotbreak Rd, Salem VA 24153	866-302-6609	877-217-3447	722
Mount Revelstoke National Park of Canada PO Box 350, Revelstoke BC V0E2S0	866-787-6221	250-837-7500	559
Mount Saint Mary College 330 Powell Ave, Newburgh NY 12550	888-937-6762	845-569-3248	166
Mount Saint Mary's University 16300 Old Emmitsburg Rd, Emmitsburg MD 21727 *Admissions	800-448-4347*	301-447-5214	166
Mount Saint Vincent University 166 Bedford Hwy, Halifax NS B3M2J6	877-733-6788	902-457-6117	780
Mount San Jacinto College 1499 N State St, San Jacinto CA 92583	800-624-5561	951-487-6752	162
Mount Shasta Resort 1000 Siskiyou Lake Blvd, Mount Shasta CA 96067	800-958-3363	530-926-3030	665
Mount Sinai Hospital Bone Marrow Transplant Program 19 E 98th St, New York NY 10029	866-682-9380	212-241-6021	764
Mount Sinai Hospital Medical Ctr of Chicago California Ave 15th St, Chicago IL 60608	877-448-7848	773-542-2000	373-3
Mount Sinai Medical Ctr, The 1 Gustave L Levy Pl, New York NY 10029	800-637-4624	212-241-6500	373-3
Mount Sinai Memorial Park 5950 Forest Lawn Dr, Los Angeles CA 90068	800-600-0076	323-469-6000	508
Mount Sinai Queens 25-10 30th Ave, Astoria NY 11102	800-968-7637	718-932-1000	373-3
Mount Union College 1972 Clark Ave, Alliance OH 44601 *Admissions	800-334-6682*	330-823-2590	166
Mount Vernon Chamber of Commerce 66 Mount Vernon Ave, Mount Vernon NY 10550	888-868-2269	914-775-8127	
Mount Vernon Nazarene University 800 Martinsburg Rd, Mount Vernon OH 43050 *Admissions	800-766-8206*	740-392-6868	166
Mount View Hotel & Spa 1457 Lincoln Ave, Calistoga CA 94515	800-816-6877	707-942-6877	378
Mount Washington Hotel & Resort 310 Mount Washington Hotel Rd, Bretton Woods NH 03575	800-314-1752	603-278-1000	665
Mountain America Credit Union PO Box 9001, West Jordan UT 84084	800-748-4302	801-325-6228	219
Mountain Electric Co-op Inc PO Box 180, Mountain City TN 37683 *Cust Svc	800-638-3788*	423-727-1000	245
Mountain Empire Community College 3441 Mtn Empire Rd, Big Stone Gap VA 24219	800-981-0600	276-523-2400	162
Mountain Equipment Co-operative 149 W Fourth Ave, Vancouver BC V5Y4A6	800-722-1960	604-707-3300	707
Mountain Haus 292 E Meadow Dr, Vail CO 81657	800-237-0922	970-476-2434	378
Mountain High Resort 24510 State Hwy 2, Wrightwood CA 92397	888-754-7878		132
Mountain Home Air Force Base 366 Gunfighter Ave Ste 498, Mountain Home AFB ID 83648	855-366-0140	208-828-6800	495-1
Mountain Home Area Chamber of Commerce 1023 Hwy 62, Mountain Home AR 72653	800-822-3536	870-425-5111	139
Mountain Laurel 81 Treetops Dr, White Haven PA 18661	888-243-9300	570-443-8411	665
Mountain Laurel Spa at Stonewall Resort 940 Resort Dr, Roanoke WV 26447	888-278-8150	304-269-7400	703
Mountain Lion Foundation PO Box 1896, Sacramento CA 95812	800-319-7621	916-442-2666	48-3
Mountain Lodge at Telluride 457 Mtn Village Blvd, Telluride CO 81435	866-368-6867	970-369-5000	665
Mountain Ltd 19 Yarmouth Dr Ste 301, New Gloucester ME 04260	800-322-8627	207-688-6200	627
Mountain Parks Electric Inc 321 W Agate Ave, Granby CO 80446	877-887-3378	970-887-3378	245
Mountain Research LLC 825 25th St, Altoona PA 16601	800-837-4674	814-949-2034	738
Mountain Sky Guest Ranch PO Box 1219, Emigrant MT 59027	800-548-3392	406-333-4911	239
Mountain States Pipe & Supply Co 111 W Las Vegas St, Colorado Springs CO 80903	800-777-7173	719-634-5555	608
Mountain Supply Co 2101 Mullan Rd, Missoula MT 59808	800-821-1646	406-543-8255	608
Mountain Telephone Co 405 Main St, West Liberty KY 41472	800-939-3121	606-743-3121	386
Mountain Tools 225 Crossroads Blvd PO Box 222295, Carmel CA 93923	800-510-2514	831-620-0911	
Mountain Travel Sobek 1266 66th St Ste 4, Emeryville CA 94608	888-831-7526		755
Mountain Valley Bank 317 DAVIS Ave, Elkins WV 26241	800-555-3503	304-637-2265	70
Mountain View Electric Assn Inc 1655 Fifth St PO Box 1600, Limon CO 80828	800-388-9881	719-775-2861	245
Mountain View Hospital 1000 East 100 North, Payson UT 84651	877-865-9738	801-465-7000	373-3
Mountain Villas 9525 W Skyline Pkwy, Duluth MN 55810	866-688-4552		378
Mountaineers Books 1001 SW Klickitat Way Ste 201, Seattle WA 98134	800-553-4453	206-223-6303	95
Mountaineers, The 7700 Sand Pt Way NE, Seattle WA 98115	800-573-8484	206-521-6000	48-23
Mountainside Fitness 9745 W Happy Valley Rd, Peoria AZ 85383	866-686-3488		
Mountaire Corp PO Box 1320, Millsboro DE 19966	877-887-1490	302-934-1100	445
Mountaire Farms 17269 NC Hwy 71 N, Lumber Bridge NC 28357	877-887-1490	910-843-5942	615
Mountrail-Williams Electric Co-op 218 58th St W PO Box 1346, Williston ND 58802	800-279-2667	701-577-3765	245
Mouser Custom Cabinetry 2112 N Hwy 31 W, Elizabethtown KY 42701	800-345-7537	270-737-7477	115
Mouser Electronics Corp 1000 N Main St, Mansfield TX 76063	800-346-6873	817-804-3888	246
Mower Boston's One-Stop B2B Marketing Agency 134 Rumford Ave Ste 307, Newton MA 02466	800-553-6477	781-818-4201	7

Listing	Toll-Free	Phone	Class
Moyer & Son Inc 113 E Reliance Rd, Souderton PA 18964	866-669-3747	215-799-2000	445
Moyno Inc 1895 W Jefferson St, Springfield OH 45506	877-486-6966	937-327-3111	637
MP Biomedicals LLC 3 Hutton Ctr Dr Ste 100, Santa Ana CA 92707	800-633-1352	949-833-2500	475
MP Global Products 2500 Old Hadar Rd PO Box 2283, Norfolk NE 68702	888-379-9695		258
MP Husky Corp 204 Old Piedmont Hwy PO Box 16749, Greenville SC 29605	800-277-4810	864-234-4800	811
MP Metal Products Inc W1250 Elmwood Ave, Ixonia WI 53036	800-824-6744	920-261-9650	480
MP Pumps Inc 34800 Bennett Dr, Fraser MI 48026	800-563-8006	586-293-8240	637
MPA (Association of Magazine Media, The) 757 Third Ave 11th Fl, New York NY 10017	800-234-3368	212-872-3700	49-16
Mpa Media 5406 Bolsa Ave, Huntington Beach CA 92649	800-324-7758		461
MPC Promotions 4300 Produce Rd PO Box 34336, Louisville KY 40232	800-331-0989	502-451-4900	155-8
MPD Inc 316 E Ninth St, Owensboro KY 42303	866-225-5673	270-685-6200	418
Mpell Solutions LLC 3142 Tiger Run Ct Ste 108, Carlsbad CA 92010	800-450-1575	760-727-9600	
MP&F (McNeely Pigott & Fox) 611 Commerce St Ste 3000, Nashville TN 37203	800-818-6953	615-259-4000	632
MPhA (Minnesota Pharmacists Assn) 1000 Westgate Dr Ste 252, St. Paul MN 55114	800-451-8349	651-697-1771	581
MPI (Meeting Professionals International) 2711 Lyndon B Johnson Fwy Ste 600, Dallas TX 75234	866-318-2743	972-702-3053	49-12
MPI Label Systems Inc 450 Courtney Rd, Sebring OH 44672	800-423-0442	330-938-2134	412
MPI Media Group 16101 108th Ave, Orland Park IL 60467	800-323-0442		
MPI Technologies 37 E St, Winchester MA 01890	888-674-8088	781-729-8300	596
MPM Medical Inc 2301 Crown Ct, Irving TX 75038	800-232-5512	972-893-4090	474
MPP (Merriweather Post Pavilion) 10475 Little Patuxent Pkwy, Columbia MD 21044	077-435-9849	410 715 5550	568
MPR (Minnesota Public Radio) 480 Cedar St, Saint Paul MN 55101	800-228-7123	651-290-1212	628
MPT (Maryland Public Television) 11767 Owings Mills Blvd, Owings Mills MD 21117	800-223-3678	410-581-4201	628
MPW Industrial Services Group Inc 9711 Lancaster Ro SE, Hebron OH 43025	800-827-8790	740-929-1614	152
Mr Appliance Corp 304 E Church Ave, Killeen TX 76541	888-998-2011		310
Mr Button Products Inc 7840 Rockville Rd, Indianapolis IN 46214	800-777-0111		623
M&R Companies 440 Medinah Rd, Roselle IL 60172	800-736-6431	630-858-6101	623
Mr Crane Inc 647 N Hariton St, Orange CA 92868	800-598-3465	714-633-2100	190
Mr Goodcents Franchise Systems Inc 8997 Commerce Dr, DeSoto KS 66018	800-648-2368		666
Mr Handyman International LLC 3948 Ranchero Dr, Ann Arbor MI 48108 *Cust Svc	855-632-2126*		310
Mr Hero Restaurants 7010 Engle Rd Ste 100, Middleburg Heights OH 44130	888-860-5082	440-625-3080	666
Mr Jim's Pizza Inc *Franchise Service Ctr* 2521 Pepperwood St, Farmers Branch TX 75234	800-583-5960	972-267-5467	666
Mr Rooter Corp 1010 N University Parks Dr, Waco TX 76707	855-982-2028	254-340-1321	189-10
M-R Sign Company Inc 1706 First Ave N, Fergus Falls MN 56537	800-231-5564	218-736-5681	697
Mr Tire Auto Service Centers Inc 200 Holleder Pkwy, Rochester NY 14615	800-876-6676		62-5
MRAS (Middle River Aircraft Systems) 103 Chesapeake Park Plz, Baltimore MD 21220	877-432-3272	410-682-1500	22
MRC (Medicare Rights Ctr) 520 Eigth Ave N Wing 3rd Fl, New York NY 10018 *Hotline	800-333-4114*	212-869-3850	48-17
MRC Global Inc 2 Houston Ctr, Houston TX 77010	877-294-7574		782
MRG (Marketing Resource Group Inc) 225 S Washington Sq, Lansing MI 48933	800-928-2086	517-372-4400	5
MRI Group 2100 Harrisburg Pk, Lancaster PA 17601	888-674-1377	717-291-1016	414
MRMC (Midwestern Regional Medical Ctr) 2520 Elisha Ave, Zion IL 60099	800-615-3055	847-872-4561	373-7
MRMC (Martin Resource Management Corp) PO Box 191, Kilgore TX 75663	888-334-7473	903-983-6200	316
MRMC (Muhlenberg Regional Medical Ctr) Park Ave & Randolph Rd, Plainfield NJ 07060	877-271-4176	908-668-2000	373-3
MRMC (Meadows Regional Medical Ctr) 1 Meadows Pkwy, Vidalia GA 30474	800-382-4023	912-535-5555	373-3
Mrs Clark's Foods 740 SE Dalbey Dr, Ankeny IA 50021	800-736-5674	515-299-6400	296-21
Mrs Nelsons Library Service 1650 W Orange Grove Ave, Pomona CA 91768	800-875-9911	909-865-8550	95
MRS Systems Inc 19000 33rd Ave W Ste 130, Seattle WA 98036	800-253-4827		177
Ms Magazine 1600 Wilson Blvd Ste 801, Arlington VA 22209	866-672-6363	703-522-4201	455-11
MSA (Medical Services of America Inc) 171 Monroe Ln, Lexington SC 29072	800-845-5850	803-957-0500	362
MSA Aircraft Products Inc 10000 Iota Dr, San Antonio TX 78217	800-695-1212	210-590-6100	22
MSA Professional Services Inc 1230 South Blvd, Baraboo WI 53913	800-362-4505	608-356-2771	261
MSANA (Masonic Service Assn of North America) 8120 Fenton St Ste 203, Silver Spring MD 20910	855-476-4010	301-588-4010	48-15

	Toll-Free	Phone	Class
MSC Filtration Technologies			
198 Freshwater Blvd ....Enfield CT 06082	800-237-7359*	860-745-7475	801
*Cust Svc			
MSC Industrial Direct Co			
75 Maxess Rd ....Melville NY 11747	800-645-7270	516-812-2000	384
NYSE: MSM			
MSCI (Metals Service Ctr Institute)			
4201 Euclid Ave ....Rolling Meadows IL 60008	800-634-2358	847-485-3000	49-18
MSDSonline			
222 Merchandise Mart Plz Ste 1750 ....Chicago IL 60654	888-362-2007	312-881-2000	
MSF (Multiple Sclerosis Foundation)			
6520 N Andrews Ave ....Fort Lauderdale FL 33309	800-225-6495	954-776-6805	48-17
MSHA (Mine Safety & Health Administration)			
1100 Wilson Blvd ....Arlington VA 22209	800-746-1553	202-693-9400	339-14
MSI (Mailing Systems Inc)			
2431 Mercantile Dr Ste A ....Rancho Cordova CA 95742	877-577-2647	916-631-7400	5
MSI Benefits Group Inc			
245 Townpark Dr Ste 100 ....Kennesaw GA 30144	800-580-1629	770-425-1231	389
MSI International Inc			
650 Park Ave ....King of Prussia PA 19406	800-927-0919	610-265-2000	266
MSI Inventory Service Corp			
PO Box 320129 ....Flowood MS 39232	800-820-1460	601-939-0130	398
Msights Inc			
9935 Rea Rd Ste D-301 ....Charlotte NC 28277	877-267-4448		804
MSK Precision Products Inc			
10101 NW 67th St ....Tamarac FL 33321	800-992-5018	954-776-0770	617
MSM Industries Inc			
802 Swan Dr ....Smyrna TN 37167	800-648-6648	615-355-4355	672
MSPB (Merit Systems Protection Board)			
1615 M St NW ....Washington DC 20419	800-209-8960	202-653-7200	339-19
MSPB (Merit Systems Protection Board Regional Offices)			
Atlanta Region			
401 W Peachtree St NW 10th Fl ....Atlanta GA 30308	800-209-8960	404-730-2751	339-19
MSR Communications			
832 Sansome St 2nd Fl ....San Francisco CA 94111	866-247-6172	415-989-9000	632
MSS Technologies Inc			
1555 E Orangewood Ave ....Phoenix AZ 85020	800-694-1302	602-387-2100	180
MST (Monterey-Salinas Transit)			
19 Upper Ragsdale Dr Ste 200 ....Monterey CA 93940	888-678-2871		466
MSU (Missouri State University)			
901 S National Ave ....Springfield MO 65897	800-492-7900	417-836-5000	166
M&T Bank 345 Main St ....Buffalo NY 14203	800-724-2440	716-842-4470	70
NYSE: MTB			
Mt Shasta Spring Water Company Inc			
1878 Twin View Blvd ....Redding CA 96003	800-922-6227	530-246-8800	365
MTA Today Magazine			
20 Ashburton Pl ....Boston MA 02108	800-392-6175	617-878-8000	455-8
MTC (Materials Transportation Co)			
1408 S Commerce PO Box 1358 ....Temple TX 76503	800-433-3110	254-298-2900	385
MTD Products Inc			
5965 Grafton Rd ....Valley City OH 44280	800-800-7310	330-225-2600	428
MTE Corp			
PO Box 9013 ....Menomonee Falls WI 53051	800-455-4683		762
MTI (Mobile Technologies Inc)			
1050 NW 229th Ave ....Hillsboro OR 97124	888-684-0040	503-648-6500	610
MTI (Medical Teams International)			
PO Box 10 ....Portland OR 97207	800-959-4325	503-624-1000	48-5
MTI America			
1350 S Powerline Rd Ste 200 ....Pompano Beach FL 33069	800-553-2155		392
MTI Instruments Inc			
325 Washington Ave Ext ....Albany NY 12205	800-342-2203	518-218-2550	406
MTI Systems Inc			
59 Interstate D ....West Springfield MA 01089	800-644-4318	413-733-1972	178-12
MTM Assn for Standards & Research			
1111 E Touhy Ave Ste 280 ....Des Plaines IL 60018	844-300-5355		49-19
Mtm Recognition Corp			
3201 SE 29th St ....Oklahoma City OK 73115	877-686-7464	405-670-4545	408
MTNA (Music Teachers NA)			
441 Vine St Ste 3100 ....Cincinnati OH 45202	888-512-5278	513-421-1420	49-5
MTNG (Middle Tennessee Natural Gas Utility District)			
1036 W Broad St PO Box 670 ....Smithville TN 37166	800-880-6373	615-597-4300	782
MtronPTI			
1703 E Hwy 50 ....Yankton SD 57078	800-762-8800	605-665-9321	253
MTS (Mid-America Transplant Services)			
1110 Highlands Plaza Dr E Ste 100 ....Saint Louis MO 63110	888-376-4854	314-735-8200	541
MTS (MTS Safety Products Inc)			
PO Box 204 ....Golden MS 38847	800-647-8168*		572
*General			
MTS Ambulance			
2431 Greenup Ave ....Ashland KY 41101	800-598-3458	606-324-3286	30
MTS Safety Products Inc (MTS)			
PO Box 204 ....Golden MS 38847	800-647-8168*		572
*General			
MTS Seating Inc			
7100 Industrial Dr ....Temperance MI 48182	800-329-0687	734-847-3875	319-1
MTS Systems Corp			
14000 Technology Dr ....Eden Prairie MN 55344	800-328-2255*	952-937-4000	470
NASDAQ: MTSC ■ *Cust Svc			
MTT-S (IEEE Microwave Theory & Techniques Society)			
5829 Bellanca Dr ....Elkridge MD 21075	800-678-4333	410-796-5866	49-19
MTU Onsite Energy Corp			
100 Power Dr ....Mankato MN 56001	800-325-5450	507-625-7973	515
Mu Phi Epsilon			
1611 County Rd B West Ste 320 ....Saint paul MN 55113	888-259-1471		48-16
Mud Hole Custom Tackle Inc			
400 Kane Ct ....Oviedo FL 32765	866-790-7637	407-447-7637	707
Mudiam Inc			
7100 regency Sq blvd ....Houston TX 77036	888-306-2062	713-484-7266	225
Mueller Brass Co			
2199 Lapeer Ave ....Port Huron MI 48060	800-553-3336	810-987-7770	483
Mueller Co			
500 W Eldorado St ....Decatur IL 62522	800-423-1323	217-423-4471	784
Mueller Inc			
1913 Hutchins Ave ....Ballinger TX 76821	877-268-3553	325-365-3555	105
Mueller Industries Inc			
8285 Tournament Dr Ste 150 ....Memphis TN 38125	800-348-8464	901-753-3200	483
NYSE: MLI			
Mueller Metals LLC			
2152 Schwartz Rd ....San Angelo TX 76904	866-651-6702		
Mueller Plastics Corp			
3070 E Cedar ....Ontario CA 91761	800-348-8464	909-930-2060	592
Mueller Recreational Products Inc			
4825 S 16th St ....Lincoln NE 68512	800-925-7665	402-423-8888	707
Mueller Steam Specialty			
1491 NC Hwy 20 W ....Saint Pauls NC 28384	800-334-6259	910-865-8241	385
Muhlenberg Regional Medical Ctr (MRMC)			
Park Ave & Randolph Rd ....Plainfield NJ 07060	877-271-4176	908-668-2000	373-3
Mui Scientific			
145 Traders Blvd E ....Mississauga ON L4Z3L3	800-303-6611	905-890-5525	474
Muir Enterprises Inc			
3575 West 900 South PO Box 26775 ....Salt Lake City UT 84104	877-268-2002	801-363-7695	297-7
Muir Glen Organic			
PO Box 9452 ....Minneapolis MN 55440	800-832-6345		296-20
Mule Lighting Inc			
46 Baker St ....Providence RI 02905	800-556-7690	401-941-4446	438
Mulhern Belting Inc			
148 Bauer Dr ....Oakland NJ 07436	800-253-6300	201-337-5700	369
Muller Martini			
456 Wheeler Rd ....Hauppauge NY 11788	888-268-5537	631-582-4343	
Muller Systems Corp			
926 Juliana Dr ....Woodstock ON N4V1B9	800-668-6954	519-421-1800	180
MultAlloy Inc			
8511 Monroe St ....Houston TX 77061	800-568-9551		490
Multi Products Company Inc			
5301 21st St ....Racine WI 53406	877-444-1011	262-554-3700	
Multichannel News			
28 E 28th St 12th Fl ....New York NY 10016	888-343-5563*		455-9
*Cust Svc			
Multicoat Corp			
23331 Antonio Pkwy ....Rancho Santa Margarita CA 92688	877-685-8426		498
Multicom Inc			
1076 Florida Central Pkwy ....Longwood FL 32750	800-423-2594	407-331-7779	116
Multigon Industries			
525 Executive Blvd ....Elmsford NY 10523	800-289-6858	914-376-5200	186
MultiLingual Solutions Inc			
22 W Jefferson St Ste 404 ....Rockville MD 20850	800-815-1964	301-424-7444	
Multimatic Products Inc			
390 Oser Ave ....Hauppauge NY 11788	800-767-7633	631-231-1515	617
MultiMedia Schools Magazine			
143 Old Marlton Pk ....Medford NJ 08055	800-300-9868	609-654-6266	455-7
Multipet International Inc			
265 W Commercial Ave ....Moonachie NJ 07074	800-900-6738	201-438-6600	574
Multiple Media Inc			
465 McGill St Office 1000 ....Montreal QC H2Y2H1	866-790-6626	514-276-7660	180
Multiple Sclerosis Foundation (MSF)			
6520 N Andrews Ave ....Fort Lauderdale FL 33309	800-225-6495	954-776-6805	48-17
Multiquip Inc			
18910 Wilmington Ave ....Carson CA 90746	800-421-1244	310-537-3700	384
Multi-shifter Inc			
11110 Park Charlotte Blvd ....Charlotte NC 28278	800-457-4472	704-588-9611	357
Multisoft Corp			
1723 SE 47th Terr ....Cape Coral FL 33904	888-415-0554	239-945-6433	177
Multi-Tech Systems			
2205 Woodale Dr ....Mounds View MN 55112	800-328-9717*	763-785-3500	173-3
*Cust Svc			
Multivans Inc			
13289 Coleraine Dr ....Bolton ON L7E3B6	800-698-9249	905-857-3171	476
Multnomah University			
8435 NE Glisan St ....Portland OR 97220	800-275-4672	503-255-0332	167-3
Muncie Power Products Inc			
201 E Jackson St ....Muncie IN 47305	800-367-7867	765-284-7721	765
Muncie Star-Press			
345 S High St ....Muncie IN 47305	800-783-7827	765-213-5700	528-2
Muncie Visitors Bureau			
3700 S Madison St ....Muncie IN 47302	800-568-6862	765-284-2700	206
Muncie-Delaware County Chamber of Commerce			
401 S High St ....Muncie IN 47305	800-336-1373	765-288-6681	139
Municipal Credit Union			
PO Box 3205 ....New York NY 10007	866-512-6109	212-693-4900	219
MuniMae (MMA Capital Management LLC)			
3600 O'Donnell St Ste 600 ....Baltimore MD 21224	855-650-6932	443-263-2900	507
OTC: MMAC			
Munro & Co Inc			
3770 Malvern Rd 71901 PO Box 6048 ....Hot Springs AR 71902	800-819-1901	501-262-6000	301
Munson Healthcare			
1105 Sixth St ....Traverse City MI 49684	800-468-6766	231-935-5000	370
Munson's Candy Kitchen Inc			
174 Hop River Rd ....Bolton CT 06043	888-686-7667	860-649-4332	296-8
Munters Corp			
210 Sixth St PO Box 6428 ....Fort Myers FL 33907	800-843-5360	239-936-1555	14
Munters Corp DHI			
79 Monroe St ....Amesbury MA 01913	800-843-5360*	978-241-1100	14
*Sales			
Murata Electronics North America Inc			
2200 Lake Pk Dr ....Smyrna GA 30080	800-704-6079	770-436-1300	253
Murata Machinery USA Inc			
2120 Queen City Dr ....Charlotte NC 28208	800-428-8469		454
Murdock Industrial Supply			
1111 E 1st ....Wichita KS 67214	800-876-6867	316-262-4476	246
Murnane Paper Corp			
345 W Fischer Farm Rd ....Elmhurst IL 60126	855-632-8191	630-530-8222	549
Murphy Oil Corp			
200 Peach St ....El Dorado AR 71730	888-289-9314	870-862-6411	576
Murphy Plywood Co			
2350 Prairie Rd ....Eugene OR 97402	888-461-4545	541-461-4545	609
Murray Bank, The			
405 S 12th St ....Murray KY 42071	877-965-1122	270-753-5626	70
Murray Co			
1215 Fern Ridge Pkwy Ste 213 ....Saint Louis MO 63141	888-323-5560	314-576-2818	681

Name / Address	City	State	ZIP	Toll-Free	Phone	Class
Murray Guard Inc 58 Murray Guard Dr	Jackson	TN	38305	**800-238-3830**	731-668-3400	689
Murray Patty (Sen D - WA) 154 Russell Senate Office Bldg	Washington	DC	20510	**866-481-9186**	202-224-2621	
Murray Sheet Metal Co Inc 3112 Seventh St	Parkersburg	WV	26104	**800-464-8801**	304-422-5431	693
Murray State College 1 Murray Campus	Tishomingo	OK	73460	**800-342-0698**	580-371-2371	162
Murray State University 102 Curris Ctr	Murray	KY	42071	**800-272-4678**	270-809-3741	166
Hopkinsville 5305 Ft Campbell Blvd	Hopkinsville	KY	42240	**800-669-7654**	270-707-1525	166
Murrays Ford Inc 3007 Blinker Pkwy	Du Bois	PA	15801	**800-371-6601**		513
Murrey International Inc 14150 S Figueroa St	Los Angeles	CA	90061	**800-421-1022**	310-532-6091	706
Murrows Transfer Inc PO Box 4095 *Cust Svc	High Point	NC	27263	**800-669-2928***	336-475-6101	775
M-USA (Mercy-USA for Aid & Development Inc) 44450 Pinetree Dr Ste 201	Plymouth	MI	48170	**800-556-3729**	734-454-0011	48-5
Muscatine Community College 152 Colorado St	Muscatine	IA	52761	**888-336-3907**	563-288-6001	162
Muscle & Fitness Hers Magazine 21100 Erwin St	Woodland Hills	CA	91367	**800-340-8954**		455-13
Musco Sports Lighting LLC 100 First Ave W PO Box 808	Oskaloosa	IA	52577	**800-825-6020**	641-673-0411	438
Muscular Dystrophy Assn (MDA) 3300 E Sunrise Dr	Tucson	AZ	85718	**800-572-1717**	520-529-2000	48-17
Musculoskeletal Transplant Foundation 125 May St Ste 300	Edison	NJ	08837	**800-946-9008**	732-661-0202	541
Muse, The 130 W 46th St	New York	NY	10036	**877-692-6873**	212-485-2400	378
Museum Facsimiles 117 Fourth St	Pittsfield	MA	01201	**877-499-0020**	413-499-0020	130
Museum of Anthropology Wake Forest University	Winston-Salem	NC	27109	**888-925-3622**	336-758-5000	517
Museum of Art & Archaeology 1 Pickard Hall	Columbia	MO	65211	**866-447-9821**	573-882-3591	517
Museum of Arts & Sciences 352 S Nova Rd	Daytona Beach	FL	32114	**866-439-4769**	386-255-0285	517
Museum of Flight, The 9404 E Marginal Way S	Seattle	WA	98108	**800-833-6384**	206-764-5700	517
Museum of Geology *South Dakota School of Mines & Technology* 501 E St Joseph St	Rapid City	SD	57701	**800-544-8162**	605-394-2467	517
Museum of History & Art 1100 Orange Ave	Coronado	CA	92118	**866-599-7242**	619-435-7242	517
Museum of Natural History & Science 1301 Western Ave Cincinnati Museum Ctr	Cincinnati	OH	45203	**800-733-2077**	513-287-7000	517
Museum of Nebraska History 15th & P St PO Box 82554	Lincoln	NE	68508	**800-833-6747**	402-471-4754	517
Museum of North Idaho 115 NW Blvd PO Box 812	Coeur d'Alene	ID	83816	**800-344-4867**	208-664-3448	517
Museum of Science & History of Jacksonville 1025 Museum Cir	Jacksonville	FL	32207	**800-581-7245**	904-396-6674	517
Museum of Science & Industry 5700 S Lake Shore Dr	Chicago	IL	60637	**800-468-6674**	773-684-1414	517
Museum of Science & Industry 4801 E Fowler Ave	Tampa	FL	33617	**800-995-6674**	813-987-6000	517
Museum of the Mountain Man 700 E Hennick St	Pinedale	WY	82941	**877-686-6266**	307-367-4101	517
Museum of Tolerance 1399 S Roxbury Dr	Los Angeles	CA	90035	**800-900-9036**	310-553-8403	517
Museum of World Treasures 835 E First St	Wichita	KS	67202	**888-700-1311**	316-263-1311	517
Museums of Oglebay Institute 1330 National Rd	Wheeling	WV	26003	**800-624-6988**	304-242-7272	517
Musgrave Pencil Company Inc 701 W Ln St	Shelbyville	TN	37160	**800-736-2450**	931-684-3611	567
Music & Arts Centers Inc 4626 Wedgewood Blvd	Frederick	MD	21703	**888-731-5396**	301-620-4040	522
Music Celebrations International 1440 S Priest Dr Ste 102	Tempe	AZ	85281	**800-395-2036**		767
Music for All 39 W Jackson Pl Ste 150	Indianapolis	IN	46225	**800-848-2263**	317-636-2263	48-11
Music of the Baroque 111 N Wabash Ave Ste 810	Chicago	IL	60602	**800-595-4849**	312-551-1414	569-3
Music People Inc 154 Woodlawn Rd Ste C	Berlin	CT	06037	**800-289-8889**		246
Music Road Resort Inc 303 Henderson Chapel Rd	Pigeon Forge	TN	37863	**844-993-9644**		703
Music Teachers NA (MTNA) 441 Vine St Ste 3100	Cincinnati	OH	45202	**888-512-5278**	513-421-1420	49-5
Musiciansbuycom Inc 7830 Byron Dr Ste 1	West Palm Beach	FL	33404	**877-778-7845**	561-842-4246	522
Musictoday LLC 5391 Three Notch*f*?Td Rd	Crozet	VA	22932	**800-927-7821**	434-244-7200	225
Muska Electric Co 1985 Oakcrest Ave	Roseville	MN	55113	**800-694-0884**	651-636-5820	189-4
Muskegon Area Chamber of Commerce 380 W Western Ste 202	Muskegon	MI	49440	**800-659-2955**	231-722-3751	139
Muskegon Area District Library 4845 Airline Rd	Muskegon	MI	49444	**877-569-4801**	231-737-6248	433-3
Muskegon Community College 221 S Quarterline Rd	Muskegon	MI	49442	**866-711-4622**	231-773-9131	162
Muskegon County Convention & Visitors Bureau 610 W Western Ave	Muskegon	MI	49440	**800-250-9283**	231-724-3100	206
Muskingum College 163 Stormont St *Admissions	New Concord	OH	43762	**800-752-6082***	740-826-8211	166
Muskogee County 229 W Okmulgee Ave	Muskogee	OK	74401	**800-444-1187**	918-682-6602	337
Musson Rubber Company Inc 1320 E Archwood Ave *Cust Svc	Akron	OH	44306	**800-321-2381***	330-773-7651	672
Musson Theatrical Inc 890 Walsh Ave	Santa Clara	CA	95050	**800-843-2837**	408-986-0210	718
Mustang Dynamometer 2300 Pinnacle Pkwy	Twinsburg	OH	44087	**888-468-7826**	330-963-5400	470
Mustang Fuel Corp 9800 N Oklahoma Ave	Oklahoma City	OK	73114	**800-332-9400**	405-748-9400	534
Mustang Tractor & Equipment Co 12800 NW Fwy	Houston	TX	77040	**800-256-1001**	832-500-3674	357
Muth Electric Inc 1717 N Sanborn PO Box 1400	Mitchell	SD	57301	**800-888-1597**	605-996-3983	189-4
Mutiny Hotel 2951 S Bayshore Dr	Miami	FL	33133	**888-868-8469**	305-441-2100	378
Mutoh America Inc 2602 S 47th St Ste 102	Phoenix	AZ	85034	**800-996-8864**	480-968-7772	173-6
Mutual Benefit Group 409 Penn St PO Box 577	Huntingdon	PA	16652	**800-283-3531**	814-643-3000	524
Mutual Industries Inc 707 W Grange St	Philadelphia	PA	19120	**800-523-0888**	215-927-6000	740-3
Mutual Insurance Company of Arizona PO Box 33180	Phoenix	AZ	85067	**800-352-0402**	602-956-5276	390-2
Mutual Mobile Inc 206 E Ninth St Ste 1400	Austin	TX	78701	**800-208-3563**		177
Mutual of America Life Insurance Co 320 Park Ave	New York	NY	10022	**800-468-3785**	212-224-1600	390-2
Mutual of Enumclaw Insurance Co 1460 Wells St	Enumclaw	WA	98022	**800-366-5551**	360-825-2591	390-4
Mutual of Omaha Bank 3333 Farnam St	Omaha	NE	68131	**866-351-5646**	877-471-7896	70
Mutual of Omaha Co 3300 Mutual of Omaha Plz	Omaha	NE	68175	**800-775-6000**	866-688-7957	359-4
Mutual Trust Life Insurance Co 1200 Jorie Blvd	Oak Brook	IL	60522	**800-323-7320**		390-2
Mutual Wheel Co Inc 2345 Fourth Ave	Moline	IL	61265	**800-798-6926**	309-757-1200	61
MutualFirst Financial Inc 110 E Charles St *NASDAQ: MFSF*	Muncie	IN	47305	**800-382-8031**	765-747-2800	359-2
Muzi Motors Inc 557 Highland Ave	Needham Heights	MA	02494	**800-296-9440**		57
MVMA (Maine Veterinary Medical Assn) 97A Exchange St Ste 305	Portland	ME	04101	**800-448-2772**		790
MVP Health Care 625 State St	Schenectady	NY	12305	**800-777-4793**	518-370-4793	390-3
MVP Laboratories Inc 4805 G St	Omaha	NE	68117	**800-856-4648**	402-331-5106	580
MVS Group 1086 Goffle Rd	Hawthorne	NJ	07506	**800-619-9989**	201-447-1505	386
MVSB (Meredith Village Savings Bank) 24 State Rt 25 PO Box 177	Meredith	NH	03253	**800-922-6872**	603-279-7986	70
Mwh Global Inc 380 Interlocken Crescent Ste 200	Broomfield	CO	80021	**866-257-5984**	303-533-1900	192
MWI Corp 33 NW Second St	Deerfield Beach	FL	33441	**800-296-7004**	954-426-1500	637
MWM Dexter Inc 107 Washington Ave	Aurora	MO	65605	**888-833-1193**		
Mx Group, The 7020 High Grove Blvd	Burr Ridge	IL	60527	**800-827-0170**		194
MXL Industries Inc 1764 Rohrerstown Rd	Lancaster	PA	17601	**800-233-0159**	717-569-8711	600
My Alarm Center LLC 3803 W Chester Pk Ste 100	Newtown Square	PA	19073	**866-484-4800**		689
My Receptionist 800 Wisconsin St Ste 410	Eau Claire	WI	54703	**800-686-0162**		732
My Service Depot 8774 Cotter St	Lewis Center	OH	43035	**888-518-0818**		759
Myakka River State Park 13208 SR 72	Sarasota	FL	34241	**800-326-3521**	941-361-6511	561
MyClean Inc 247 W 35th St Ste 9R	New York	NY	10001	**855-692-5326**		
MyCorporation Business Services Inc 26025 Mureau Rd Ste 120	Calabasas	CA	91302	**877-692-6772**		386
Myers Brothers of Kansas City Inc 1210 W 28th St	Kansas City	MO	64108	**800-264-2404**	816-931-5501	54
Myers Container Corp 8435 NE Killingsworth	Portland	OR	97220	**800-406-9377**	503-501-5830	198
Myers Engineering Inc 8376 Salt Lake Ave	Bell	CA	90201	**877-652-4767**	323-560-4723	
myFreightWorld LLC 7133 W 95th St Ste 205	Overland Park	KS	66212	**877-549-9438**		392
Mylan 1000 Mylan Blvd	Canonsburg	PA	15317	**800-527-4278**	724-514-1800	578
Mylan Pharmaceuticals Inc 781 Chestnut Ridge Rd	Morgantown	WV	26505	**800-796-9526**	304-599-2595	578
Mylan Pharmaceuticals ULC 85 Advance Rd	Etobicoke	ON	M8Z2S6	**800-575-1379**	416-236-2631	579
MyLLCcom Inc 1910 Thomes Ave	Cheyenne	WY	82001	**888-886-9552**		461
MyOpenJobs LLC 203 Main St Ste 100	Lake Dallas	TX	75065	**800-396-4822**		260
Myotronics-noromed Inc 5870 S 194th St	Kent	WA	98032	**800-426-0316**	206-243-4214	228
MYR Group inc 1701 W Golf Rd Ste 1012	Rolling Meadows	IL	60008	**800-360-1321**	847-290-1891	189-4
Myre-Big Island State Park 19499 780th Ave	Albert Lea	MN	56007	**888-646-6367**	507-668-7060	561
Myriad Genetics Inc 320 Wakara Way *NASDAQ: MYGN*	Salt Lake City	UT	84108	**800-469-7423**	801-584-3600	85
Myriad RBM 3300 Duval Rd	Austin	TX	78759	**866-726-6277**	512-835-8026	578
Myrmidon Corp 10555 W Little York Rd	Houston	TX	77041	**800-880-0771**	713-880-0044	693
Myron Corp 205 Maywood Ave	Maywood	NJ	07607	**877-803-3358**		9
Myrtle Beach Area Chamber of Commerce 1200 N Oak St	Myrtle Beach	SC	29577	**800-356-3016**	843-626-7444	139

Alphabetical Section

Listing	Toll-Free	Phone	Class
Myrtle Beach International Airport			
1100 Jetport Rd, Myrtle Beach SC 29577	**800-778-4838**	843-448-1589	27
Myrtle Beach Resort Vacations			
5905 S Kings Hwy			
PO Box 3936, Myrtle Beach SC 29578	**888-627-3767**	843-238-1559	665
Mystic Lake Casino Hotel			
2400 Mystic Lake Blvd, Prior Lake MN 55372	**800-262-7799**	866-832-6402	133
Mystic Sea Resort			
2105 S Ocean Blvd, Myrtle Beach SC 29577	**800-443-7050**	843-448-8446	665
Mystic Seaport -- The Museum of America & the Sea			
75 Greenmanville Ave PO Box 6000, Mystic CT 06355	**888-973-2767**	860-572-0711	517
Mystic Stamp Co			
9700 Mill St, Camden NY 13316	**866-660-7147**	315-245-2690	457
Mythics Inc			
4525 Main St Ste 1500, Virginia Beach VA 23462	**866-698-4427**	757-412-4362	
MyUSACorporationcom Inc			
1 Radisson Plz Ste 800, New Rochelle NY 10801	**877-330-2677**		317
Mzinga 10 Mall Rd, Burlington MA 01803	**888-694-6428**		194

N

Listing	Toll-Free	Phone	Class
N E Florida Educational Consortium			
3841 Reid St, Palatka FL 32177	**800-227-6036**	386-329-3800	681
N R S I			
179 Lafayette Dr, Syosset NY 11791	**800-331-3117**	516-921-5500	242
N Tepperman Ltd			
2595 Ouellette Ave, Windsor ON N8X4V8	**800-265-5062**	519-969-9700	321
N Wasserstrom & Sons Inc			
2300 Lockbourne Rd, Columbus OH 43207	**800-444-4697**	614-228-5550	300
N'Ware Technologies Inc			
2885 81e Rue, Saint-georges QC G6A0C5	**800-270-9420**	418-227-4292	
NA for the Advancement of Colored People (NAACP)			
4805 Mt Hope Dr, Baltimore MD 21215	**877-622-2798**	410-580-5777	48-8
NA for Uniformed Services (NAUS)			
5535 Hempstead Way, Springfield VA 22151	**800-842-3451**	703-750-1342	48-19
NA of Colleges & Employers (NACE)			
62 Highland Ave, Bethlehem PA 18017	**800-544-5272**	610-868-1421	49-5
NA of Collegiate Directors of Athletics (NACDA)			
24651 Detroit Rd, Westlake OH 44145	**877-887-2261**	440-892-4000	48-22
NA of Convenience Stores (NACS)			
1600 Duke St 7th Fl, Alexandria VA 22314	**800-966-6227***	703-684-3600	49-18
*Cust Svc			
NA of Insurance & Financial Advisors (NAIFA)			
2901 Telestar Ct, Falls Church VA 22042	**877-866-2432***	703-770-8100	49-9
*Sales			
NA of Women in Construction (NAWIC)			
327 S Adams St, Fort Worth TX 76104	**800-552-3506**	817-877-5551	49-3
NAA (National Apartment Assn)			
4300 Wilson Blvd Ste 400, Arlington VA 22203	**800-632-3007**	703-518-6141	49-17
NAA (National Archery Association of the United States)			
4065 Sinton Rd Ste 110, Colorado Springs CO 80907	**800-775-8762**	719-866-4576	48-22
NAA (National Auctioneers Assn)			
8880 Ballentine St, Overland Park KS 66214	**877-657-1990**	913-541-8084	49-18
NAAA (National Auto Auction Assn)			
5320 Spectrum Dr Ste D, Frederick MD 21703	**800-232-5411**	301-696-0400	49-18
NAACP (NA for the Advancement of Colored People)			
4805 Mt Hope Dr, Baltimore MD 21215	**877-622-2798**	410-580-5777	48-8
NAADAC PAC			
44 Canal Center Plz Ste 301, Alexandria VA 22314	**800-377-1136**	703-741-7686	611
NAAS (Advanced California)			
1510 Robert St Ste 103, Boise ID 83705	**888-413-3669**		
Nabco Entrances Inc			
S82W18717 Gemini Dr, Muskego WI 53150	**888-679-3319**	877-622-2694	478
Nabet 700-M Unifor			
100 Lombard St Ste 203, Toronto ON M5C1M3	**800-889-9487**	416-536-4827	396
Nabors Industries Ltd			
515 W Greens Rd Ste 1200, Houston TX 77067	**800-422-2066**	281-874-0035	536
NAC (National Automobile Club)			
373 Vintage Park Dr Ste E, Foster City CA 94404	**800-622-2136**		
NAC Group Inc			
1790 Commerce Ave N, St Petersburg FL 33716	**866-651-2901**	727-828-0187	246
NACAC (North American Council on Adoptable Children)			
970 Raymond Ave Ste 106, Saint Paul MN 55114	**877-823-2237**	651-644-3036	48-6
Nacarato Volvo Truck			
519 New Paul Rd, La Vergne TN 37086	**888-392-8486**		513
NACB Group Corp			
10 Starwood Dr, Hampstead NH 03841	**800-370-2737**	603-329-4551	246
NACCAS (National Accrediting Commission of Cosmetology Art)			
4401 Ford Ave Ste 1300, Alexandria VA 22302	**877-212-5752**	703-600-7600	48-1
NACCC (National Association of Congregational Christian C)			
8473 S Howell Ave, Oak Creek WI 53154	**800-262-1620**	414-764-1620	48-20
NACCO Industries Inc			
5875 Landerbrook Dr Ste 220, Cleveland OH 44124	**877-756-5118**	440-229-5151	185
NYSE: NC			
NACDA (NA of Collegiate Directors of Athletics)			
24651 Detroit Rd, Westlake OH 44145	**877-887-2261**	440-892-4000	48-22
NACDS (National Association of Chain Drug Stores)			
413 N Lee St, Alexandria VA 22314	**800-678-6223**	703-549-3001	49-18
NACE (NA of Colleges & Employers)			
62 Highland Ave, Bethlehem PA 18017	**800-544-5272**	610-868-1421	49-5
NACE International: Corrosion Society			
1440 S Creek Dr, Houston TX 77084	**800-797-6223**	281-228-6200	49-13
NACHA - Electronic Payments Association			
2550 Wasser Terr Ste 400, Herndon VA 20171	**800-487-9180**	703-561-1100	49-2
Nachi America Inc			
715 Pushville Rd, Greenwood IN 46143	**888-340-2747**	317-530-1001	75
Na-Churs/Alpine Solutions			
421 Leader St, Marion OH 43302	**800-622-4877**	740-382-5701	280
NACM Gulf States			
10887 S Wilcrest Dr, Houston TX 77099	**866-252-6226**	281-228-6100	218
Nacogdoches Medical Ctr			
4920 NE Stallings Dr, Nacogdoches TX 75965	**866-898-8446**	936-569-9481	373-3

Listing	Toll-Free	Phone	Class
NACS (National Association of College Stores)			
500 E Lorain St, Oberlin OH 44074	**800-622-7498**	440-775-7777	49-18
NACS (NA of Convenience Stores)			
1600 Duke St 7th Fl, Alexandria VA 22314	**800-966-6227***	703-684-3600	49-18
*Cust Svc			
NACWA (National Association of Clean Water Agencies)			
1816 Jefferson Pl NW, Washington DC 20036	**888-267-9505**	202-833-2672	49-7
NADA (National Automobile Dealers Assn)			
8400 Westpark Dr, McLean VA 22102	**800-252-6232**	703-821-7000	49-18
NADAguidescom			
3186 K Airway Ave, Costa Mesa CA 92626	**800-966-6232**		
NAEA (National Art Education Assn)			
1806 Robert Fulton Dr, Reston VA 20191	**800-299-8321**	703-860-8000	49-5
NAED (National Association of Electrical Distributors)			
1181 Corporate Lake Dr, Saint Louis MO 63132	**888-791-2512**	314-991-9000	49-18
NAEIR (NAEIR)			
560 McClure St, Galesburg IL 61401	**800-562-0955**	309-343-0704	48-5
NAESP (National Association of Elementary School Principa)			
1615 Duke St, Alexandria VA 22314	**800-386-2377**	703-684-3345	49-5
NAF (National Abortion Federation)			
1755 Massachusetts Ave NW, Washington DC 20036	**800-772-9100**	202-667-5881	49-8
NAFC (National Acctg & Finance Council)			
American Trucking Assn			
950 N Glebe Rd, Arlington VA 22203	**800-517-7370**	703-838-1700	49-1
NAFCU (National Association of Federally-Insured Credit U)			
3138 Tenth St N, Arlington VA 22201	**800-336-4644**	703-522-4770	49-2
NAFEM (North American Assn of Food Equipment Manufacturer)			
161 N Clark St Ste 2020, Chicago IL 60601	**888-493-5961**	312-821-0201	49-13
NAFWB (National Association of Free Will Baptists Inc)			
5233 Mt View Rd, Antioch TN 37013	**877-767-7659**	615-731-6812	48-20
Nagel Chase Inc			
2323 Delaney Rd, Gurnee IL 60031	**800-323-4552**		349
Nagle & Associates			
380 Knollwood St Ste 320, Salem NC 27103	**800-411-1583**	336-723-4500	427
NAHB Research Ctr			
400 Prince Georges Blvd, Upper Marlboro MD 20774	**800-638-8556**	301-249-4000	664
Nahon, Saharovich & Trotz PLC			
488 S Menhenhall Rd, Memphis TN 38117	**800-529-4004**	901-683-7000	427
NAI solutions			
200 104th Ave Ste 324, Treasure Island FL 33706	**877-624-8311**		180
NAICS (North American Industry Classification System)			
US Census Bureau			
4600 Silver Hill Rd, Washington DC 20233	**800-923-8282**	301-763-4636	339-2
NAIFA (NA of Insurance & Financial Advisors)			
2901 Telestar Ct, Falls Church VA 22042	**877-866-2432***	703-770-8100	49-9
*Sales			
NAIHC (National American Indian Housing Council)			
122 C S NW Ste 350, Washington DC 20001	**800-284-9165**	202-789-1754	49-7
Nailpro Magazine			
7628 Densmore Ave, Van Nuys CA 91406	**800-442-5667**	818-782-7328	455-21
Najarian Furniture Company Inc			
265 North Euclid Ave, Pasadena CA 91101	**888-781-3088**	626-839-8700	320
Nakanishi Dental Laboratory Inc			
2959 Northup Way, Bellevue WA 98004	**800-735-7231**	425-822-2245	414
Nakase Bros Wholesale Nursery			
9441 Krepp Dr, Huntington Beach CA 92646	**800-747-4388**	714-962-6604	292
NAL			
10416 Investment Cir, Rancho Cordova CA 95670	**800-774-9555**	916-361-0555	192
NALC (National Association of Letter Carriers)			
100 Indiana Ave NW, Washington DC 20001	**800-424-5186**	202-393-4695	413
Nalco Co			
1601 W Diehl Rd, Naperville IL 60563	**800-288-0879**	630-305-1000	145
NALF (North American Limousin Foundation)			
6 Inverness Ct E Ste 260, Englewood CO 80112	**888-320-8747**	303-220-1693	48-2
Nalley Lexus Smyrna			
2750 Cobb Pkwy SE, Smyrna GA 30080	**877-454-4206**		57
NAM (National Arbitration & Mediation)			
990 Stewart Ave 1st Fl, Garden City NY 11530	**800-358-2550**		41
NAMA (North American Millers Assn)			
600 Maryland Ave SW			
Ste 825-W, Washington DC 20024	**800-633-5137**	202-484-2200	49-6
Name Maker Inc			
4450 Commerce Cir PO Box 43821, Atlanta GA 30336	**800-241-2890**	404-691-2237	740-5
Nameplate & Panel Technology			
387 Gundersen Dr, Carol Stream IL 60188	**800-833-8397**	630-690-9360	623
Namgis First Nation			
49 Atli St, Alert Bay BC V0N1A0	**888-962-6447**	250-974-5556	138
NAMI (National Alliance on Mental Illness)			
3803 N Fairfax Dr Ste 100, Arlington VA 22203	**800-950-6264**	703-524-7600	48-17
NAMM (NAMM)			
5790 Armada Dr, Carlsbad CA 92008	**800-767-6266**	760-438-8001	49-18
NANA Regional Corporation Inc			
1001 E Benson Blvd, Kotzebue AK 99752	**800-478-3301**	907-442-3301	535
Nana Wall Systems Inc			
707 Redwood Hwy, Mill Valley CA 94941	**800-873-5673**	415-383-3148	497
Nance International Inc			
2915 Milam St, Beaumont TX 77701	**877-626-2322**	409-838-6127	660
NANN (National Association of Neonatal Nurses)			
8735 W Higgins Rd Ste 300, Chicago IL 60631	**800-451-3795**	847-375-3660	49-8
NanoHorizons Inc			
270 Rolling Ridge Dr Ste 100, Bellefonte PA 16823	**866-584-6235**	814-355-4700	162
Nantucket Accommodations			
1 Macys Ln, Nantucket MA 02554	**866-743-3330**	508-228-9559	375
Nantucket Bank			
104 Pleasant St, Nantucket MA 02554	**800-533-9313**	508-228-0580	70
Nanz & Kraft Florists Inc			
141 Breckenridge Ln, Louisville KY 40207	**800-897-6551**	502-897-6551	292
NAO Inc			
1284 E Sedgley Ave, Philadelphia PA 19134	**800-523-3495***	215-743-5300	18
*Cust Svc			
NAP (National Association of Parliamentarians)			
213 S Main St, Independence MO 64050	**888-627-2929**	816-833-3892	49-12
NAP Windows & Doors Ltd			
2150 Enterprise Way, Kelowna BC V1Y6H7	**888-762-5311**	250-762-5343	597
NAPA (National Automotive Parts Assn)			
2999 Circle 75 Pkwy, Atlanta GA 30339	**800-538-6272**	770-953-1700	61
Napa County Library			
580 Coombs St, Napa CA 94559	**877-279-2987**	707-253-4241	433-3

Listing	City	State	ZIP	Toll-Free	Phone	Class
Napa River Inn 500 Main St	Napa	CA	94559	**877-251-8500**	707-251-8500	378
Napa State Hospital 2100 Napa-Vallejo Hwy	Napa	CA	94558	**866-327-4762**	707-253-5000	373-5
Napa Valley College 2277 Napa-Vallejo Hwy	Napa	CA	94558	**800-826-1077**	707-256-7000	162
Napa Valley Conference & Visitors Bureau 600 Main St	Napa	CA	94559	**855-847-6272**	707-251-5895	206
NAPCO (North American Publishing Co) 1500 Springarden St 12th Fl	Philadelphia	PA	19130	**800-627-2689**	215-238-5300	633-9
NAPCO Inc 120 Trojan Ave	Sparta	NC	28675	**800-854-8621**		86
NAPCO Security Systems Inc 333 Bayview Ave *NASDAQ: NSSC*	Amityville	NY	11701	**800-645-9445**	631-842-9400	688
Napco Steel Inc 1800 Arthur Dr	West Chicago	IL	60185	**800-292-8010**	630-293-1900	490
Napili Kai Beach Club 5900 Honoapiilani Rd	Lahaina	HI	96761	**800-367-5030**	808-669-6271	665
Naples Bay Resort 1500 Fifth Ave S	Naples	FL	34102	**866-605-1199**	239-530-1199	665
Naples Beach Hotel & Golf Club 851 Gulf Shore Blvd N	Naples	FL	34102	**800-237-7600**	239-261-2222	665
Naples Daily News 1100 Immokalee Rd	Naples	FL	34110	**800-404-7343**	239-213-6000	528-2
Naples Museum of Art 5833 Pelican Bay Blvd	Naples	FL	34108	**800-597-1900**	239-597-1111	517
Naples Ristorante e Pizzeria 1510 Disneyland Dr	Anaheim	CA	92802	**866-972-8462**		
Napoleon Spring Works 111 Weires Dr	Archbold	OH	43502	**800-338-5399**	419-445-1010	234
Napoleon/Henry County Chamber of Commerce 611 N Perry St	Napoleon	OH	43545	**800-322-6849**	419-592-1786	139
NAPWA (National Association of People With AIDS) 8401 Colesville Rd Ste 505	Silver Spring	MD	20910	**866-846-9366**	240-247-0880	48-17
NARA (National Archives & Records Administration) 8601 Adelphi Rd	College Park	MD	20740	**866-272-6272**		339-19
NARBHA (Northern Arizona Regional Behavioral Health Author) 1300 S Yale St	Flagstaff	AZ	86001	**877-923-1400**	928-774-7128	49-15
Narcolepsy Network Inc PO Box 2178 Ste A212	Lynnwood	WA	98036	**888-292-6522**	401-667-2523	48-17
Nardini Fire Equipment Company Inc 405 County Rd E W	Saint Paul	MN	55126	**888-627-3464**	651-483-6631	675
Nardone Bros Baking Company Inc 420 New Commerce Blvd	Wilkes-Barre	PA	18706	**800-822-5320**	570-823-0141	296-36
Nareit 1875 'I' St NW Ste 600	Washington	DC	20006	**800-362-7348**	202-739-9400	611
NARF (Native American Rights Fund) 1506 Broadway	Boulder	CO	80302	**888-280-0726**	303-447-8760	49-10
NARIC (National Rehabilitation Information Ctr) 8400 Corporate Dr Ste 500	Landover	MD	20785	**800-346-2742**	301-459-5900	48-17
Naropa University 2130 Arapahoe Ave	Boulder	CO	80302	**800-772-6951**	303-444-0202	166
Narrow Fabric Industries Corp 701 Reading Ave	Reading	PA	19611	**877-523-6373**	610-376-2891	740-5
NAS (National Audubon Society) 225 Varick St	New York	NY	10014	**800-274-4201**	212-979-3000	48-13
NAS Recruitment Communications 9700 Rockside Rd Ste 170	Cleveland	OH	44125	**866-627-7327**	216-503-9001	4
NASB (North American Savings Bank) 12520 S 71 Hwy	Grandview	MO	64030	**800-677-6272**	816-765-2200	70
NASB Financial Inc 12520 S 71 Hwy *NASDAQ: NASB*	Grandview	MO	64030	**800-677-6272**	816-765-2200	359-2
NASBE (National Association of State Boards of Education) 333 John Carlyle St Ste 530	Alexandria	VA	22314	**800-899-6693**	703-684-4000	49-5
NASCO International Inc 901 Janesville Ave *Orders	Fort Atkinson	WI	53538	**800-558-9595***	920-563-2446	457
Nash Produce Co 6160 S N Carolina 58	Nashville	NC	27856	**800-334-3032**		10-9
Nashua Corp 11 Trafalgar Sq 2nd Fl	Nashua	NH	03063	**800-430-7488**	603-880-2323	548-1
Nashua Homes of Idaho Inc PO Box 170008	Boise	ID	83717	**855-766-0222**	208-345-0222	503
Nashville Convention & Visitors Bureau (NCVB) 150 Fourth Ave N Ste G250	Nashville	TN	37219	**800-657-6910**	615-259-4730	206
Nashville Display 306 Hartmann Dr	Lebanon	TN	37087	**800-251-1150**	615-743-2900	233
Nashville General Hospital 1818 Albion St	Nashville	TN	37208	**800-318-2596**	615-341-4000	373-3
Nashville Office Interiors 1621 Church St	Nashville	TN	37203	**877-342-0294**	615-329-1811	321
Nashville State Community College (NSCC) 120 White Bridge Rd	Nashville	TN	37209	**800-272-7363**	615-353-3333	795
Nashville Wire Products Manufacturing Co 199 Polk Ave	Nashville	TN	37210	**800-448-2125**	615-743-2500	73
Nashville Zoo 3777 Nolensville Rd	Nashville	TN	37211	**800-456-6847**	615-833-1534	818
Nasiff Associates 841-1 County Rt 37	Central Square	NY	13036	**866-627-4332**	315-676-2346	474
NASS (National Agricultural Statistics Service) 1400 Independence Ave SW	Washington	DC	20250	**800-727-9540**	202-720-2707	339-1
NASS (North American Spine Society) 7075 Veterans Blvd	Burr Ridge	IL	60527	**877-774-6337**	630-230-3600	49-8
Nassau County PO Box 870	Fernandina Beach	FL	32035	**888-615-4398**	904-491-7300	337
Nassau County 240 Old Country Rd	Mineola	NY	11501	**800-460-5657**	516-571-2664	337
Nassau Financial Federal Credit Union 1325 Franklin Ave Ste 500	Garden City	NY	11530	**800-216-2328**	516-742-4900	219
Nassau Valley Vineyards 32165 Winery Way	Lewes	DE	19958	**800-425-2355**	302-645-9463	50-7
Nasseo Inc 13660 N 94th Dr D-7	Peoria	AZ	85381	**866-207-8919**		228
NASW News 750 First St NE Ste 700	Washington	DC	20002	**800-227-3590**	202-408-8600	455-16
NATA (National Air Transportation Assn) 4226 King St	Alexandria	VA	22302	**800-808-6282**	703-845-9000	49-21
NATA (National Athletic Trainers Assn) 2952 N Stemmons Fwy Ste 200	Dallas	TX	75247	**800-879-6282**	214-637-6282	48-22
NATCA (National Air Traffic Controllers Assn) 1325 Massachusetts Ave NW	Washington	DC	20005	**800-266-0895**	202-628-5451	413
Natchez Convention & Visitors Bureau 640 S Canal St	Natchez	MS	39120	**800-647-6724**	601-446-6345	206
Natchez Convention Ctr 211 Main St	Natchez	MS	39120	**888-475-9144**	601-442-5880	205
Natchez Trace National Scenic Trail 2680 Natchez Trace Pkwy	Tupelo	MS	38804	**800-305-7417**	662-680-4025	560
Natchez-Adams County *Chamber of Commerce* 211 Main St	Natchez	MS	39120	**800-647-6724**	601-445-4611	139
Natchitoches Area Chamber of Commerce 780 Front St Ste 101	Natchitoches	LA	71457	**877-646-6689**	318-352-6894	139
Natchitoches Regional Medical Center 501 Keyser Ave	Natchitoches	LA	71457	**888-728-8383**	318-214-4200	373-3
NATE (National Association of Tower Erectors) 8 Second St SE	Watertown	SD	57201	**888-882-5865**	605-882-5865	49-3
Natel Engineering Co Inc 9340 Owensmouth Ave	Chatsworth	CA	91311	**800-590-5774**	818-734-6580	621
Nation Magazine 33 Irving Pl *Cust Svc	New York	NY	10003	**800-333-8536***	212-209-5400	455-17
National Abortion Federation (NAF) 1755 Massachusetts Ave NW	Washington	DC	20036	**800-772-9100**	202-667-5881	49-8
National Academies 500 Fifth St NW	Washington	DC	20001	**800-624-6242**	202-334-2138	49-19
National Academy of Recording Arts & Sciences 3030 Olympic Blvd	Santa Monica	CA	90404	**800-423-2017**	310-392-3777	48-4
National Academy Press 500 Fifth St NW	Washington	DC	20001	**800-624-6242**	202-334-3313	633-2
National Accrediting Commission of Cosmetology Arts & Sciences (NACCAS) 4401 Ford Ave Ste 1300	Alexandria	VA	22302	**877-212-5752**	703-600-7600	48-1
National Acctg & Finance Council (NAFC) American Trucking Assn 950 N Glebe Rd	Arlington	VA	22203	**800-517-7370**	703-838-1700	49-1
National Active & Retired Federal Employees Assn 606 N Washington St	Alexandria	VA	22314	**800-627-3394**	703-838-7760	611
National Aeronautic Association Hanger 7 Ste 202	Washington	DC	20001	**800-644-9777**	703-416-4888	48-22
National Afro-American Museum & Cultural Ctr 1350 Brush Row Rd PO Box 578	Wilberforce	OH	45384	**800-752-2603**	937-376-4944	517
National Agricultural Library 10301 Baltimore Ave	Beltsville	MD	20705	**800-633-7701**	301-504-5755	339-1
National Agricultural Statistics Service (NASS) 1400 Independence Ave SW	Washington	DC	20250	**800-727-9540**	202-720-2707	339-1
National Air Traffic Controllers Assn (NATCA) 1325 Massachusetts Ave NW	Washington	DC	20005	**800-266-0895**	202-628-5451	413
National Air Transportation Assn (NATA) 4226 King St	Alexandria	VA	22302	**800-808-6282**	703-845-9000	49-21
National Alliance for Hispanic Health 1501 16th St NW	Washington	DC	20036	**866-783-2645**		
National Alliance for Youth Sports 2050 Vista Pkwy	West Palm Beach	FL	33411	**800-729-2057**	561-684-1141	48-22
National Alliance of Postal & Federal Employees 1628 11th St NW	Washington	DC	20001	**800-222-8733**	202-939-6325	413
National Alliance on Mental Illness (NAMI) 3803 N Fairfax Dr Ste 100	Arlington	VA	22203	**800-950-6264**	703-524-7600	48-17
National American Indian Housing Council (NAIHC) 122 C S NW Ste 350	Washington	DC	20001	**800-284-9165**	202-789-1754	49-7
National American University 5301 Mt Rushmore Rd	Rapid City	SD	57701	**800-843-8892**	605-394-4800	166
Sioux Falls 5801 S corporate Pl	Sioux Falls	SD	57108	**800-388-5430**	605-336-4600	166
National American University Colorado Springs 1915 Jamboree Dr Ste 185	Colorado Springs	CO	80920	**855-448-2318**	316-448-5400	166
National American University Denver 1325 S Colorado Blvd Ste 100	Denver	CO	80222	**855-448-2318**	303-758-6700	166
National American University Independence 3620 Arrowhead Ave	Independence	MO	64057	**866-628-1288**	816-412-7700	166
National Anti-Vivisection Society (NAVS) 53 W Jackson Blvd Ste 1552	Chicago	IL	60604	**800-888-6287**	312-427-6065	48-3
National Apartment Assn (NAA) 4300 Wilson Blvd Ste 400	Arlington	VA	22203	**800-632-3007**	703-518-6141	49-17
National Aquarium in Baltimore 501 E Pratt St	Baltimore	MD	21202	**800-628-9944**	410-576-3800	40
National Arbitration & Mediation (NAM) 990 Stewart Ave 1st Fl	Garden City	NY	11530	**800-358-2550**		41
National Arbor Day Foundation 100 Arbor Ave	Nebraska City	NE	68410	**888-448-7337**	402-474-5655	48-13
National Archery Association of the United States (NAA) 4065 Sinton Rd Ste 110	Colorado Springs	CO	80907	**800-775-8762**	719-866-4576	48-22
National Archives & Records Administration (NARA) 8601 Adelphi Rd	College Park	MD	20740	**866-272-6272**		339-19
Archival Research Catalog 8601 Adelphi Rd	College Park	MD	20740	**866-272-6272**		339-19
Office of the Federal Register 7 G St NW Ste A-734	Washington	DC	20401	**877-684-6448**	202-741-6000	339-19
National Archives & Records Administration Regional Offices						
Great Lakes Region 7358 S Pulaski Rd	Chicago	IL	60629	**800-447-1830**	773-948-9001	339-19
Northeast Region 380 Trapelo Rd	Waltham	MA	02452	**866-406-2379**	202-357-5946	339-19
Pacific Alaska Region 6125 Sand Pt Way NE	Seattle	WA	98115	**866-325-7208**	206-336-5115	339-19
Pacific Region 1000 Commodore Dr	San Bruno	CA	94066	**800-234-8861**	202-357-5946	339-19
Southeast Region 5780 Jonesboro Rd	Morrow	GA	30260	**800-447-1830**	202-357-5946	339-19
National Art Education Assn (NAEA) 1806 Robert Fulton Dr	Reston	VA	20191	**800-299-8321**	703-860-8000	49-5

	Toll-Free	Phone	Class
National Art Materials Trade Assn			
20200 Zion Ave ....Cornelius NC 28031	800-349-1039	704-892-6244	49-18
National Artcraft Supply Co			
300 Campus Dr ....Aurora OH 44202	**888-937-2723**	330-562-3500	43
National Assn of Credit Management			
8840 Columbia 100 Pkwy ....Columbia MD 21045	**800-955-8815**	410-740-5560	455-5
National Association of Chain Drug Stores (NACDS)			
413 N Lee St ....Alexandria VA 22314	**800-678-6223**	703-549-3001	49-18
National Association of Clean Water Agencies (NACWA)			
1816 Jefferson Pl NW ....Washington DC 20036	**888-267-9505**	202-833-2672	49-7
National Association of College Stores (NACS)			
500 E Lorain St ....Oberlin OH 44074	**800-622-7498**	440-775-7777	49-18
National Association of Congregational Christian Churches (NACCC)			
8473 S Howell Ave ....Oak Creek WI 53154	**800-262-1620**	414-764-1620	48-20
National Association of Electrical Distributors (NAED)			
1181 Corporate Lake Dr ....Saint Louis MO 63132	**888-791-2512**	314-991-9000	49-18
National Association of Elementary School Principals (NAESP)			
1615 Duke St ....Alexandria VA 22314	**800-386-2377**	703-684-3345	49-5
National Association of Federal Retirees			
865 Shefford Rd ....Ottawa ON K1J1H9	**855-304-4700**	613-745-2559	138
National Association of Federally-Insured Credit Unions (NAFCU)			
3138 Tenth St N ....Arlington VA 22201	**800-336-4644**	703-522-4770	49-2
National Association of Free Will Baptists Inc (NAFWB)			
5233 Mt View Rd ....Antioch TN 37013	**877-767-7659**	615-731-6812	48-20
National Association of Home Builders PAC			
1201 15th St NW ....Washington DC 20005	**800-368-5242**		611
National Association of Housing & Redevelopment Officials			
630 'I' St NW ....Washington DC 20001	**877-866-2476**	202-289-3500	455-5
National Association of Letter Carriers (NALC)			
100 Indiana Ave NW ....Washington DC 20001	**800-424-5186**	202-393-4695	413
National Association of Neonatal Nurses (NANN)			
8735 W Higgins Rd Ste 300 ....Chicago IL 60631	**800-451-3795**	847-375-3660	49-8
National Association of Nonprofit Accountants & Consultants (NSA)			
1801 W End Ave Ste 800 ....Nashville TN 37203	**800-231-2524**	615-373-9880	49-1
National Association of Parliamentarians (NAP)			
213 S Main St ....Independence MO 64050	**888-627-2929**	816-833-3892	49-12
National Association of People With AIDS (NAPWA)			
8401 Colesville Rd			
Ste 505 ....Silver Spring MD 20910	**866-846-9366**	240-247-0880	48-17
National Association of State Boards of Education (NASBE)			
333 John Carlyle St Ste 530 ....Alexandria VA 22314	**800-899-6693**	703-684-4000	49-5
National Association of Tower Erectors (NATE)			
8 Second St SE ....Watertown SD 57201	**888-882-5865**	605-882-5865	49-3
National Association of Town Watch (NATW)			
308 E Lancaster Ave Ste 115 ....Wynnewood PA 19096	**800-648-3688**		48-7
National Athletic Trainers Assn (NATA)			
2952 N Stemmons Fwy Ste 200 ....Dallas TX 75247	**800-879-6282**	214-637-6282	48-22
National Auctioneers Assn (NAA)			
8880 Ballentine St ....Overland Park KS 66214	**877-657-1990**	913-541-8084	49-18
National Audubon Society (NAS)			
225 Varick St ....New York NY 10014	**800-274-4201**	212-979-3000	48-13
National Australia Bank Americas			
245 Park Ave 28th Fl ....New York NY 10167	**866-706-0509**	212-916-9500	70
National Auto Auction Assn (NAAA)			
5320 Spectrum Dr Ste D..........Frederick MD 21703	**800-232-5411**	301-696-0400	49-18
National Automatic Sprinkler Industries			
8000 Corporate Dr ....Landover MD 20785	**800-638-2603**	301-577-1700	189-13
National Automobile Club (NAC)			
373 Vintage Park Dr Ste E.....Foster City CA 94404	**800-622-2136**		
National Automobile Dealers Assn (NADA)			
8400 Westpark Dr ....McLean VA 22102	**800-252-6232**	703-821-7000	49-18
National Automotive Parts Assn (NAPA)			
2999 Circle 75 Pkwy ....Atlanta GA 30339	**800-538-6272**	770-953-1700	61
National Aviation Academy			
150 Hanscom Dr ....Bedford MA 01730	**800-659-2080**	727-535-8727	795
National Bank of Arizona			
6001 N 24th St ....Phoenix AZ 85016	**800-655-7622**	602-235-6000	70
National Bank of Blacksburg			
PO Box 90002 ....Blacksburg VA 24062	**800-552-4123**	540-552-2011	70
National Bank, The			
852 Middle Rd ....Bettendorf IA 52722	**877-321-4347**	563-344-3935	70
National Bankshares Inc			
101 Hubbard St ....Blacksburg VA 24060	**800-552-4123**	540-951-6300	359-2
NASDAQ: NKSH			
National Baptist Convention of America International Inc			
1000 S Fourth St ....Louisville KY 40203	**844-610-6222**		
National Baptist Convention USA Inc			
1700 Baptist World Ctr Dr ....Nashville TN 37207	**866-531-3054**	615-228-6292	48-20
National Baseball Hall of Fame & Museum			
25 Main St ....Cooperstown NY 13326	**888-425-5633**	607-547-7200	519
National Basketball Players Assn (NBPA)			
1133 Avenue of Americas .....New York NY 10036	**800-955-6272**	212-655-0880	48-22
National Beef Packing Co LLC			
12200 Ambassador Dr Ste 500			
PO Box 20046..............Kansas City MO 64163	**800-449-2333**		471
National Beer Wholesalers Assn (NBWA)			
1101 King St Ste 600 ....Alexandria VA 22314	**800-300-6417**	703-683-4300	49-6
National Benevolent Assn (NBA)			
733 Union Blvd Ste 300 ....St. Louis MO 63108	**866-262-2669**	314-993-9000	48-5
National Billiard Manufacturing Co			
3315 Eugenia Ave ....Covington KY 41015	**800-543-0880**	859-431-4129	706
National Biodynamics Laboratory (NBDL)			
University of New Orleans College of Engineering			
2000 Lakeshore Dr ....New Orleans LA 70148	**888-514-4275**		664
National Board of Boiler & Pressure Vessel Inspectors			
1055 Crupper Ave ....Columbus OH 43229	**877-682-8772**	614-888-8320	49-7
National Book Festival			
Library of Congress			
101 Independence Ave SE..........Washington DC 20540	**888-714-4696**	202-707-5000	281
National Book Network Inc			
4501 Forbes Blvd Ste 200 ....Lanham MD 20706	**800-243-0495**	301-459-3366	95
National Border Patrol Museum			
4315 Woodrow Bean TransMtn Rd ....El Paso TX 79924	**877-276-8738**	915-759-6060	517
National Braille Press Inc			
88 St Stephen St ....Boston MA 02115	**888-965-8965**	617-266-6160	633-2
National Breast Cancer Coalition (NBCC)			
1101 17th St NW Ste 1300 ....Washington DC 20036	**800-622-2838**	202-296-7477	48-17
National Bureau of Economic Research			
1050 Massachusetts Ave ....Cambridge MA 02138	**800-621-8476**	617-868-3900	664
National Business Assn (NBA)			
5151 Beltline Rd Ste 1150 ....Dallas TX 75254	**800-456-0440**	972-458-0900	49-12
National Business Aviation Assn (NBAA)			
1200 18th St NW Ste 400..........Washington DC 20036	**800-394-6222**	202-783-9000	49-21
National Business Furniture Inc			
735 N Water St Ste 440 ....Milwaukee WI 53202	**800-558-1010***		320
*Sales			
National Businesswomen's Leadership Assn			
PO Box 419107 ....Kansas City MO 64141	**800-258-7246**		760
National Captioning Institute (NCI)			
3725 Concorde Pkwy Ste 100........Chantilly VA 20151	**800-825-6758**	703-917-7600	628
National Carriers Inc			
1501 E Eigth St ....Liberal KS 67901	**800-835-9180**		775
National CASA Assn (CASA)			
100 W Harrison St			
North Tower Ste 500 ....Seattle WA 98119	**800-628-3233**	206-270-0072	48-6
National Catholic Educational Assn (NCEA)			
1005 N Glebe Rd Ste 525 ....Arlington VA 22201	**800-711-6232**	571-257-0010	49-5
National Catholic Reporter Publishing Co			
115 E Armour Blvd ....Kansas City MO 64111	**800-333-7373**	816-531-0538	633-9
National Cattlemen's Beef Assn (NCBA)			
9110 E Nichols Ave Ste 300 ....Centennial CO 80112	**866-233-3872**	303-694-0305	48-2
National Center for Employee Development (NCED)			
2701 E Imhoff Rd ....Norman OK 73071	**866-438-6233**	405-366-4420	376
National Certification Commission for Acupuncture & Oriental Medicine (NCCAOM)			
2025 M St NW Ste 800..........Washington DC 20036	**888-381-1140**	202-381-1140	
National Chemical Laboratories Inc			
401 N Tenth St ....Philadelphia PA 19123	**800-628-2436**	215-922-1200	151
National Chemicals Inc			
105 Liberty St PO Box 32....... Winona MN 55987	**800-533-0027***	507-454-5640	151
*Cust Svc			
National Child Care Assn (NCCA)			
1325 G St NW Ste 500 ....Washington DC 20005	**866-536-1945**		48-6
National Christmas Tree Assn (NCTA)			
16020 Swingley Ridge Rd			
Ste 300 ....Chesterfield MO 63017	**800-975-5920**		
National Church Residences Inc			
2335 N Bank Dr ....Columbus OH 43220	**800-388-2151**		648
National Church Supply Co, The			
PO Box 269 ....Chester WV 26034	**800-627-9900**	304-387-5200	263
National Citizens' Coalition for Nursing Home Reform (NCCNHR)			
National Consumer Voice for Quality Long-Term Care			
1828 L St NW Ste 801 ....Washington DC 20036	**866-992-3668**	202-332-2275	48-17
National Cleaners Assn			
252 W 29th St ....New York NY 10001	**800-888-1622***	212-967-3002	49-4
*General			
National Clearinghouse for Alcohol & Drug Information			
5600 Fishers Ln ....Rockville MD 20857	**800-729-6686**		339-9
National Club Assn (NCA)			
1201 15th St NW Ste 450..........Washington DC 20005	**800-625-6221**	202-822-9822	48-23
National Coalition for Cancer Survivorship (NCCS)			
8455 Colesville Rd			
Ste 930 ....Silver Spring MD 20910	**877-622-7937**		48-17
National College			
Lexington			
2376 Sir Barton Way ....Lexington KY 40509	**877-540-3494**	859-253-0621	795
National College of Business & Technology			
8095 Connector Dr ....Florence KY 41042	**888-956-2732**	859-525-6510	795
Roanoke Valley			
1813 E Main St ....Salem VA 24153	**800-664-1886**	540-986-1800	795
National Commission Assn			
2501 Exchange Ave Ste 102.......Oklahoma City OK 73108	**800-999-8998**	405-232-3128	444
National Committee for Employer Support of the Guard & Reserve (ESGR)			
1555 Wilson Blvd Ste 319 ....Arlington VA 22209	**800-336-4590**		48-19
National Committee for Quality Assurance (NCQA)			
1100 13th St ....Washington DC 20005	**888-275-7585**	202-955-3500	48-10
National Committee to Preserve Social Security & Medicare (NCPSSM)			
10 G St NE Ste 600..........Washington DC 20002	**800-966-1935**	202-216-0420	48-7
National Community Pharmacists Assn (NCPA)			
100 Daingerfield Rd ....Alexandria VA 22314	**800-544-7447**	703-683-8200	49-8
National Concrete Masonry Assn			
13750 Sunrise Vly Dr ....Herndon VA 20171	**877-343-6268**	703-713-1900	49-3
National Conference of State Legislatures			
7700 E First Pl ....Denver CO 80230	**800-659-2656**	303-364-7700	49-7
National Congress of American Indians (NCAI)			
1516 P St NW ....Washington DC 20005	**800-388-2227**	202-466-7767	48-14
National Construction Rentals Inc			
15319 Chatsworth St ....Mission Hills CA 91345	**800-352-5675**		264-3
National Consumers League (NCL)			
1701 K St NW Ste 1200 ....Washington DC 20006	**800-388-2227**	202-835-3323	48-10
National Contract Management Assn (NCMA)			
21740 Beaumeade Cir Ste 125 ....Ashburn VA 20147	**800-344-8096**	571-382-0082	49-12
National Co-op Business Assn (NCBA)			
1401 New York Ave NW			
Ste 1100 ....Washington DC 20005	**800-356-9655**	202-638-6222	49-12
National Corvette Museum			
350 Corvette Dr ....Bowling Green KY 42101	**800-538-3883**	270-781-7973	517
National Council for Air & Stream Improvement Inc (NCASI)			
PO Box 13318 ....Research Triangle Park NC 27709	**888-448-2473**	919-941-6400	48-13
National Council for the Social Studies (NCSS)			
8555 16th St Ste 500 ....Silver Spring MD 20910	**800-683-0812***	301-588-1800	49-5
*Orders			
National Council of Examiners for Engineering & Surveying (NCEES)			
280 Seneca Creek Rd ....Seneca SC 29678	**800-250-3196**	864-654-6824	49-3
National Council of Farmer Co-ops (NCFC)			
50 F St NW Ste 900 ....Washington DC 20001	**800-344-2626**	202-626-8700	48-2
National Council of Juvenile & Family Court Judges (NCJFCJ)			
Univ of Nevada PO Box 8970 ....Reno NV 89507	**800-527-3223**	775-784-6012	49-10
National Council of State Boards of Nursing (NCSBN)			
111 E Wacker Dr Ste 2900 ....Chicago IL 60601	**866-293-9600**	312-525-3600	49-8
National Council of State Housing Agencies (NCSHA)			
444 N Capitol St NW Ste 438 ....Washington DC 20001	**800-475-2098**	202-624-7710	49-7
National Council of Teachers of English (NCTE)			
1111 W Kenyon Rd ....Urbana IL 61801	**877-369-6283**	217-328-3870	49-5
National Council of Teachers of Mathematics (NCTM)			
1906 Assn Dr ....Reston VA 20191	**800-235-7566***	703-620-9840	49-5
*Orders			

	Toll-Free	Phone	Class
National Council of Textile Organizations (NCTO) 1701 K St NW Ste 625 . . . . Washington DC 20006	**800-238-7192**	202-822-8028	49-13
National Council on Alcoholism & Drug Dependence Inc (NCADD) 217 Broadway Ste 712 . . . . New York NY 10007	**800-622-2255**	212-269-7797	48-17
National Council on Crime & Delinquency (NCCD) 1970 Broadway Ste 500 . . . . Oakland CA 94612	**800-306-6223**	510-208-0500	48-8
National Council on Economic Education (NCEE) 122 E 42nd St Ste 2600 . . . . New York NY 10168	**800-338-1192**	212-730-7007	49-5
National Council on Family Relations (NCFR) 1201 W River Pkwy Ste 200 . . . . Minneapolis MN 55454	**888-781-9331**		48-6
National Council on Problem Gambling Inc 730 11th St NW Ste 601 . . . . Washington DC 20001	**800-522-4700**	202-547-9204	49-8
National Council on Radiation Protection & Measurements (NCRP) 7910 Woodmont Ave Ste 400 . . . . Bethesda MD 20814	**800-462-3683**	301-657-2652	49-19
National Council on the Aging (NCOA) 1901 L St NW 4th Fl . . . . Washington DC 20036	**800-677-1116**	571-527-3900	48-6
National Court Reporters Assn (NCRA) 8224 Old Courthouse Rd . . . . Vienna VA 22182	**800-272-6272**	703-556-6272	49-10
National CPA Health Care Advisors Assn (HCAA) 1801 W End Ave Ste 800 . . . . Nashville TN 37203	**800-231-2524**	615-373-9880	49-1
National Credit Adjusters LLC 327 W Fourth Ave PO Box 3023 . . . . . . Hutchinson KS 67504	**888-768-0674**		360
National Credit Union Administration 1775 Duke St . . . . Alexandria VA 22314 *Fraud Hotline	**800-827-9650***	703-518-6300	339-19
National Credit Union Administration Regional Offices			
Region 1 9 Washington Sq Washington Ave Ext . . . . Albany NY 12205	**800-755-1030**	518-862-7400	339-19
Region 3 7000 Central Pkwy Ste 1600 . . . . Atlanta GA 30328	**800-827-9650**	678-443-3000	339-19
Region 5 1230 W Washington St Ste 301 . . . . Tempe AZ 85281	**800-995-9064**	602-302-6000	339-19
National Crime Prevention Council (NCPC) 2345 Crystal Dr Ste 500 . . . . Arlington VA 22202	**800-627-2911**	443-292-4565	48-8
National Criminal Justice Reference Service PO Box 6000 . . . . Rockville MD 20849	**800-851-3420**	202-836-6998	339-13
National Crop Insurance Services (NCIS) 8900 Indian Creek Pkwy Ste 600 . . . . Overland Park KS 66210	**800-951-6247**	913-685-2767	48-2
National Ctr for Genome Resources 2935 Rodeo Pk Dr E . . . . Santa Fe NM 87505	**800-450-4854**	505-982-7840	664
National Ctr for Juvenile Justice (NCJJ) 3700 S Water St Ste 200 . . . . Pittsburgh PA 15203	**800-851-3420**	412-227-6950	48-8
National Ctr for Mfg Sciences (NCMS) 3025 Boardwalk . . . . Ann Arbor MI 48108	**800-222-6267**	734-995-3457	664
National Ctr for Missing & Exploited Children (NCMEC) 699 Prince St . . . . Alexandria VA 22314	**800-843-5678**	703-274-3900	48-6
National Ctr for Retirement Benefits Inc 666 Dundee Rd Ste 1200 . . . . Northbrook IL 60062	**800-666-1000**		193
National Ctr for State Courts (NCSC) 300 Newport Ave . . . . Williamsburg VA 23185	**800-616-6164**	757-259-1525	49-7
National Ctr for Victims of Crime, The 2000 M St NW Ste 480 . . . . Washington DC 20036	**800-394-2255**	202-467-8700	48-8
National Cycle Inc 2200 S Maywood Dr PO Box 158 . . . . Maywood IL 60153	**877-972-7336**	708-343-0400	514
National Diagnostics Inc 305 Patton Dr . . . . Atlanta GA 30336	**800-526-3867**	404-699-2121	231
National Disaster Search Dog Foundation 6800 Wheeler Canyon Rd . . . . Ojai CA 93023	**888-459-4376**	805-646-1015	48-3
National Discount Cruise Co 1401 N Cedar Crest Blvd Ste 110 . . . . Allentown PA 18104	**800-788-8108**		766
National Disease Research Interchange (NDRI) 1628 John F Kennedy Blvd 8 Penn Ctr 8th Fl . . . . Philadelphia PA 19103	**800-222-6374**	215-557-7361	269
National Domestic Violence Hotline (NDVH) PO Box 161810 . . . . Austin TX 78716	**800-799-7233**	512-794-1133	48-6
National Down Syndrome Congress (NDSC) 30 Mansell Ct Ste 108 . . . . Roswell GA 30076	**800-232-6372**	770-604-9500	48-17
National Down Syndrome Society (NDSS) 666 Broadway 8th Fl . . . . New York NY 10012	**800-221-4602**		48-17
National Eating Disorders Assn 200 W 41st St Ste 1203 . . . . New York NY 10036	**800-931-2237**	212-575-6200	48-17
National Education Assn (NEA) 1201 16th St NW . . . . Washington DC 20036	**888-552-0624**	202-833-4000	49-5
National Electrical Carbon 251 Forrester Dr . . . . Greenville SC 29607	**800-471-7842**	864-284-9728	127
National Electrical Contractors Assn (NECA) 3 Bethesda Metro Ctr Ste 1100 . . . . Bethesda MD 20814	**800-214-0585**	301-657-3110	49-3
National Electrical Manufacturers Assn (NEMA) 1300 N 17th St Ste 1752 . . . . Rosslyn VA 22209	**800-699-9277**	703-841-3200	49-13
National Electrical Manufacturers Representatives Assn (NEMRA) 28 Deer St Ste 302 . . . . Portsmouth NH 03801	**800-446-3672**	914-524-8650	49-18
National Electronic Attachment Inc (NEA) 100 Ashford Ctr N Ste 300 . . . . Dunwoody GA 30338	**800-782-5150**		389
National Electronics Service Dealers Assn (NESDA) 3608 Pershing Ave . . . . Fort Worth TX 76107	**800-946-0201**	817-921-9061	49-18
National Emblem Inc 3925 E Vernon St PO Box 15680 . . . . Long Beach CA 90815	**800-877-6185**	310-515-5055	258
National Employee Assistance Services Inc N 17 W 24100 Riverwood Dr Ste 300 . . . . Waukesha WI 53188	**800-634-6433**	262-574-2500	460
National Endowment for the Humanities (NEH) 400 Seventh St SW . . . . Washington DC 20506	**800-634-1121**	202-606-8400	339-19
National Energy Research Scientific Computing Ctr (NERSC) Lawrence Berkeley National Laboratory . . . . Berkeley CA 94720	**800-666-3772**	510-486-5849	664
National Energy Technology Laboratory (NETL) 3610 Collins Ferry Rd . . . . Morgantown WV 26505	**800-432-8330**	304-285-4764	664
National Environmental Health Assn (NEHA) 720 S Colorado Blvd Ste 1000-N . . . . Denver CO 80246	**866-956-2258**	303-756-9090	49-7
National Environmental Satellite Data & Information Service *National Coastal Data Development Ctr* Bldg 1100 Ste 101 . . . . Stennis Space Center MS 39529	**866-732-2382**	228-688-2936	339-2
National Enzyme Co Inc 15366 US Hwy 160 . . . . Forsyth MO 65653	**800-825-8545**	417-546-4796	144
National Excelsior Co 1999 N Ruby St . . . . Melrose Park IL 60160	**855-373-9235**	708-343-4225	591
National Exchange Club 3050 W Central Ave . . . . Toledo OH 43606	**800-924-2643**	419-535-3232	48-15
National Eye Institute 2318 Mill Rd Ste 1300 . . . . Alexandria VA 22314	**800-372-3937**	703-548-4560	48-17
National Family Caregivers Assn (NFCA) 10400 Connecticut Ave Ste 500 . . . . Kensington MD 20895	**800-896-3650**	301-942-6430	48-6
National Farm Life Insurance Co 6001 Bridge St . . . . Fort Worth TX 76112	**800-772-7557**	817-451-9550	389
National Farmers Organization (NFO) 528 Billy Sunday Rd Ste 100 PO Box 2508 . . . . Ames IA 50010	**800-247-2110**	515-292-2000	48-2
National Farmers Union News (NFU) 20 F St NW Ste 300 . . . . Washington DC 20001	**800-442-8277**	202-554-1600	527-13
National Federation of Community Development Credit Unions (NFCDCU) 39 Broadway Ste 2140 . . . . New York NY 10006	**800-437-8711**	212-809-1850	49-2
National Federation of Republican Women (NFRW) 124 N Alfred St . . . . Alexandria VA 22314	**800-373-9688**	703-548-9688	48-7
National Federation of State High School Assn (NFHS) PO Box 690 . . . . Indianapolis IN 46206 *Cust Svc	**800-776-3462***	317-972-6900	48-22
National Federation of the Blind (NFB) 1800 Johnson St . . . . Baltimore MD 21230	**800-392-5671**	410-659-9314	48-17
National Fence Systems Inc 1033 Rt One . . . . Avenel NJ 07001	**800-211-2444**		186
National FFA Organization 6060 FFA Dr . . . . Indianapolis IN 46268	**800-772-0939**	317-802-6060	48-2
National Fiber Technology LLC 15 Union St . . . . Lawrence MA 01840 *Cust Svc	**800-842-2751***	978-686-2964	347
National Film Board of Canada Stn Centre-Ville PO Box 6100 . . . . Montreal QC H3C3H5	**800-267-7710**	514-283-9000	510
National Filter Media Corp 691 North 400 West . . . . Salt Lake City UT 84103	**800-777-4248**	801-363-6736	18
National Fingerprint Inc 6999 Dolan Rd . . . . Glouster OH 45732	**888-823-7873**	740-767-3853	688
National Fire & Marine Insurance Co 3024 Harney St . . . . Omaha NE 68131	**866-720-7861**	402-916-3000	390-4
National Fire Protection Assn (NFPA) 1 Batterymarch Pk . . . . Quincy MA 02169	**800-344-3555**	617-770-3000	48-17
National Fisherman Magazine 121 Free St . . . . Portland ME 04101	**800-959-5073**	207-842-5608	455-21
National Fitness Trade Journal PO Box 2490 . . . . White City OR 97503	**877-867-7835**	541-830-0400	455-21
National Flavors Inc 3680 Stadium Park Way . . . . Kalamazoo MI 49009	**800-525-2431**		297-8
National Floral Supply Inc 3825 LeonaRdtown Rd Ste 4 . . . . Waldorf MD 20601	**800-932-2772**	301-932-7600	292
National Football League Players (NFLPA) 1133 20th St NW . . . . Washington DC 20036	**800-372-2000**		48-22
National Foundation for Cancer Research (NFCR) 4600 E W Hwy Ste 525 . . . . Bethesda MD 20814	**800-321-2873**		305
National Foundation for Infectious Diseases (NFID) 4733 Bethesda Ave Ste 750 . . . . Bethesda MD 20814	**800-708-5478**	301-656-0003	49-8
National Frame Builders Assn (NFBA) 8735 W Higgins Rd Ste 300 . . . . Chicago IL 60631	**800-557-6957**		49-3
National Fraternity of Kappa Delta Rho (KDR) 331 S Main St . . . . Greensburg PA 15601	**800-536-5371**	724-838-7100	48-16
National Freedom of Information Coalition 344 Hearnes Ctr . . . . Columbia MO 65211	**866-682-6663**	573-882-4856	48-8
National Fruit Product Co Inc 701 Fairmont Ave . . . . Winchester VA 22601	**800-655-4022**	540-662-3401	315-3
National Fuel Gas Co 6363 Main St . . . . Williamsville NY 14221 *NYSE: NFG* ■ *Cust Svc	**800-365-3234***	716-857-7000	359-5
National Fuel Resources Inc 165 Lawrence Bell Dr Ste 120 . . . . Williamsville NY 14221	**800-839-9993**	716-630-6778	782
National Fulfillment Services 105 Commerce Dr . . . . Aston PA 19014	**800-637-1306**		225
National Funeral Directors & Morticians Assn (NFDMA) 6290 Shannon Pkwy . . . . Union City GA 30291	**800-434-0958**	770-969-0064	49-4
National Funeral Directors Assn (NFDA) 13625 Bishop's Dr . . . . Brookfield WI 53005	**800-228-6332**	262-789-1880	49-4
National Futures Assn (NFA) 300 S Riverside Plz Ste 1800 . . . . Chicago IL 60606	**800-621-3570**	312-781-1300	49-2
National Gallery of Art 6th St & Constitution Ave NW . . . . Washington DC 20565	**800-697-9350**	202-737-4215	517
National Garden Clubs Inc (NGC) 4401 Magnolia Ave . . . . Saint Louis MO 63110	**800-550-6007**	314-776-7574	48-18
National Gardening Assn (NGA) 1100 Dorset St . . . . South Burlington VT 05403	**800-538-7476**	802-863-5251	48-18
National Gaucher Foundation (NGF) 5410 Edson Ln Ste 220 . . . . Rockville MD 20852	**800-504-3189**		48-17
National Genealogical Society (NGS) 3108 Columbia Pk Ste 300 . . . . Arlington VA 22204	**800-473-0060**	703-525-0050	48-18
National Genetics Institute 2440 S Blvd Ste 235 . . . . Los Angeles CA 90064	**800-352-7788**	310-996-0036	417
National Geographic Society 1145 17th St NW . . . . Washington DC 20036	**800-647-5463**	202-857-7000	49-19
National Geographic Society Explorers Hall 1145 17th St NW . . . . Washington DC 20036	**800-647-5463**		517
National Geographic Traveler Magazine 1145 17th St NW . . . . Washington DC 20036	**800-647-5463**	202-857-7000	455-22
National Glass Assn (NGA) 8200 Greensboro Dr Ste 302 . . . . McLean VA 22102	**866-342-5642**	703-442-4890	49-13
National Golf Course Owners Assn (NGCOA) 291 Seven Farms Dr 2nd Fl . . . . Charleston SC 29492	**800-933-4262**	843-881-9956	48-23
National Golf Foundation (NGF) 1150 S US Hwy 1 Ste 401 . . . . Jupiter FL 33477	**800-733-6006**	561-744-6006	48-22
National Graduate School of Quality Management Inc, The 186 Jones Rd . . . . Falmouth MA 02540	**800-838-2580**		166
National Grange 1616 H St NW . . . . Washington DC 20006	**888-447-2643**	202-628-3507	48-2
National Grange Mutual Insurance Co 55 W St . . . . Keene NH 03431	**800-258-5310**	603-352-4000	390-4

	City	State	Zip	Toll-Free	Phone	Class
National Greyhound Assn (NGA)						
729 Old US 40	Abilene	KS	67410	**800-366-1471**	785-263-4660	48-22
National Grid USA Service Company Inc						
25 Research Dr	Westborough	MA	01582	**800-548-8000**	508-389-2000	359-5
National Grocers Assn (NGA)						
1005 N Glebe Rd Ste 250	Arlington	VA	22201	**800-627-6667**	703-516-0700	49-6
National Ground Water Assn (NGWA)						
601 Dempsey Rd	Westerville	OH	43081	**800-551-7379**	614-898-7791	48-12
National Guard Educational Foundation (NGAUS)						
1 Massachusetts Ave NW	Washington	DC	20001	**888-226-4287**	202-789-0031	48-19
National Guard Products Inc						
4985 E Raines Rd	Memphis	TN	38118	**800-647-7874**		234
National Guardian Life Insurance Co (NGL)						
2 E Gilman St	Madison	WI	53703	**800-548-2962**		390-2
National Guild for Community Arts Education						
520 Eighth Ave Ste 302	New York	NY	10018	**800-441-1414**	212-268-3337	49-5
National Gypsum Co						
2001 Rexford Rd	Charlotte	NC	28211	**800-628-4662**	704-365-7300	346
National Hansen's Disease Program (NHDP)						
1770 Physicians Pk Dr	Baton Rouge	LA	70816	**800-221-9393**		664
National Hardwood Lumber Assn (NHLA)						
6830 Raleigh-LaGrange Rd	Memphis	TN	38134	**800-933-0318**	901-377-1818	49-3
National Head Start Assn (NHSA)						
1651 Prince St	Alexandria	VA	22314	**866-677-8724**	703-739-0875	48-11
National HealthCare Corp						
100 E Vine St PO Box 1398	Murfreesboro	TN	37133	**800-877-1600**	615-890-2020	449
NYSE: NHC						
National Hemophilia Foundation (NHF)						
7 Penn Plz Ste 1204	New York	NY	10001	**800-424-2634**	212-328-3700	48-17
National Heritage Academies						
3850 Broadmoor Ave SE Ste 201	Grand Rapids	MI	49512	**877-223-6402***		242
*General						
National Highway Traffic Safety Administration (NHTSA)						
1200 New Jersey Ave SE	Washington	DC	20590	**888-327-4236**	202-366-9550	339-16
National Center for Statistics & Analysis						
1200 New Jersey Ave SE	Washington	DC	20590	**800-934-8517**	202-366-1503	339-16
Vehicle Research & Test Ctr						
10820 SR 347 PO Box B37	East Liberty	OH	43319	**800-262-8309**	937-666-4511	339-16
National Highway Traffic Safety Administration Regional Offices						
NHTSA Region 3						
1200 New Jersey Ave SE West Bldg	Washington	DC	20590	**888-327-4236**		339-16
National Hispanic University						
14271 Story Rd	San Jose	CA	95127	**877-762-9801**	408-254-6900	166
National Home Furnishings Assn (NHFA)						
500 Giuseppe Ct Ste 6	Roseville	CA	95678	**800-422-3778**		49-4
National Honor Society (NHS)						
1904 Assn Dr	Reston	VA	20191	**800-253-7746**	703-860-0200	48-11
National Hospice & Palliative Care Organization (NHPCO)						
1700 Diagonal Rd Ste 625	Alexandria	VA	22314	**800-658-8898***	703-837-1500	49-8
*Help Line						
National Hotel						
1677 Collins Ave	Miami Beach	FL	33139	**800-327-8370**	305-532-2311	378
National Indemnity Co						
1314 Douglas St Ste 1400	Omaha	NE	68102	**866-720-7861**	402-916-3000	
National Independent Automobile Dealers Assn (NIADA)						
2521 Brown Blvd	Arlington	TX	76006	**800-682-3837**	817-640-3838	49-18
National Independent Flag Dealers Assn (NIFDA)						
7984 S Chicago Ave	Chicago	IL	60617	**800-356-4085**	773-768-8076	49-18
National Industrial Lumber Co						
1 Chicago Ave	Elizabeth	PA	15037	**800-289-9352**		191-3
National Industries for the Blind (NIB)						
1310 Braddock Pl	Alexandria	VA	22314	**800-325-3535***	703-310-0500	48-17
*Cust Svc						
National Information Standards Organization (NISO)						
3600 Clipper Mill Rd Ste 302	Baltimore	MD	21211	**877-375-2160**	301-654-2512	49-16
National Inhalant Prevention Coalition (NIPC)						
PO Box 4117	Chattanooga	TN	37405	**855-704-4400**	423-265-4662	48-17
National Institute for Literacy (NIFL)						
1775 'I' St NW Ste 730	Washington	DC	20006	**800-228-8813**	202-233-2025	339-7
National Institute of Child Health & Human Development (NICHD)						
31 Center Dr Bldg 31 Rm 2A32	Bethesda	MD	20892	**800-370-2943**		664
National Institute of Governmental Purchasing Inc (NIGP)						
151 Spring St	Herndon	VA	20170	**800-367-6447**	703-736-8900	49-7
National Institutes of Health (NIH)						
9000 Rockville Pk	Bethesda	MD	20892	**800-411-1222**	301-496-4000	339-9
Center for Scientific Review						
6701 Rockledge Dr MSC 7950	Bethesda	MD	20892	**800-438-4380**	301-435-1115	339-9
National Cancer Institute						
9609 Medical Center Dr BG 9609 MSC 9760	Bethesda	MD	20892	**800-422-6237**	301-435-3848	664
National Institute of Arthritis & Musculoskeletal						
1 AMS Cir	Bethesda	MD	20892	**877-226-4267**	301-495-4484	339-9
National Institute of Mental Health						
6001 Executive Blvd Rm 6200 MSC 9663	Bethesda	MD	20892	**866-615-6464**	301-443-4513	339-9
National Institute of Neurological Disorders						
PO Box 5801	Bethesda	MD	20824	**800-352-9424**	301-496-5751	339-9
National Library of Medicine						
8600 Rockville Pk	Bethesda	MD	20894	**888-346-3656**	301-594-5983	339-9
Office of Rare Diseases						
6701 Democracy Blvd Ste 1001	Bethesda	MD	20892	**800-942-6825**	301-402-4336	339-9
The National Institute on Deafness and Other Communication Disorders						
31 Ctr Dr MSC 2320	Bethesda	MD	20892	**800-241-1044**	301-496-7243	664
National Instrument LLC						
4119 Fordleigh Rd	Baltimore	MD	21215	**866-258-1914**	410-764-0900	543
National Instruments Corp						
11500 N Mopac Expy	Austin	TX	78759	**800-433-3488***	512-683-0100	178-5
NASDAQ: NATI ■ *Cust Svc						
National Insulation Assn (NIA)						
99 Canal Ctr Plz Ste 222	Alexandria	VA	22314	**877-968-7642**	703-683-6422	49-3
National Insurance Crime Bureau (NICB)						
1111 E Touhy Ave Ste 400	Des Plaines	IL	60018	**800-447-6282**	847-544-7002	49-9
National Interagency Fire Ctr						
3833 S Development Ave	Boise	ID	83705	**877-471-2262**	208-387-5512	339-12
National Interstate Corp						
3250 I- Dr	Richfield	OH	44286	**800-929-1500**	330-659-8900	390-4
NASDAQ: NATL						

	City	State	Zip	Toll-Free	Phone	Class
National Inventors Hall of Fame						
3701 Highland Park NW	North Canton	OH	44720	**800-968-4332**		517
National Investment Co Service Assn (NICSA)						
8400 Westpark Dr 2nd Fl	Mclean	VA	22102	**800-426-1122**	508-485-1500	49-2
National Jets						
3495 SW Ninth Ave	Fort Lauderdale	FL	33315	**800-327-3710**	954-359-9900	63
National Jewish Medical & Research Ctr						
1400 Jackson St	Denver	CO	80206	**877-225-5654**	303-388-4461	373-7
National Journal						
600 New Hampshire Ave NW	Washington	DC	20037	**800-613-6701**	202-739-8400	455-17
National Kappa Kappa Iota Inc						
1875 E 15th St	Tulsa	OK	74104	**800-678-0389**	918-744-0389	48-16
National Kidney Foundation (NKF)						
30 E 33rd St	New York	NY	10016	**800-622-9010**	212-889-2210	48-17
National Kitchen & Bath Assn (NKBA)						
687 Willow Grove St	Hackettstown	NJ	07840	**800-843-6522**		49-3
National Labor College						
10000 New Hampshire Ave	Silver Spring	MD	20903	**888-427-8100**	301-431-6400	795
National Labor Relations Board (NLRB)						
1099 14th St NW	Washington	DC	20570	**866-667-6572**	202-273-1991	339-19
Region 1						
10 Causeway St 6th Fl	Boston	MA	02222	**866-667-6572**	617-565-6700	339-19
Region 2						
26 Federal Plz Rm 3614	New York	NY	10278	**866-667-6572**	212-264-0300	
Region 3						
Niagara Ctr Bldg 130 S Elmwood Ave Ste 630	Buffalo	NY	14202	**866-667-6572**	716-551-4931	339-19
Region 5						
103 S Gay St 8th Fl	Baltimore	MD	21202	**866-667-6572**	410-962-2822	
Region 6						
1000 Liberty Ave Rm 904	Pittsburgh	PA	15222	**866-667-6572**	412-395-4400	
Region 7						
477 Michigan Ave Rm 300	Detroit	MI	48226	**866-667-6572**	313-226-3200	
Region 8						
1240 E Ninth St Rm 1695	Cleveland	OH	44199	**866-667-6572**	216-522-3715	339-19
Region 9						
550 Main St Rm 3003	Cincinnati	OH	45202	**866-667-6572**	513-684-3686	339-19
National Labor Relations Board Regional Offices						
Region 10						
233 Peachtree St NE Ste 1000	Atlanta	GA	30303	**866-667-6572**	404-331-2896	
Region 11						
4035 University Pkwy Ste 200	Winston-Salem	NC	27106	**866-667-6572**	336-631-5201	339-19
Region 12						
201 E Kennedy Blvd Ste 530	Tampa	FL	33602	**866-667-6572**	813-228-2641	
Region 13						
200 W Adams St	Chicago	IL	60606	**866-667-6572**	312-353-7570	
Region 14						
1222 Spruce St Rm 8302	Saint Louis	MO	63103	**866-667-6572**	314-539-7770	339-19
Region 15						
1515 Poydras St Rm 610	New Orleans	LA	70112	**866-667-6572**	504-589-6361	
Region 16						
819 Taylor St Rm 8A24	Fort Worth	TX	76102	**866-667-6572**	817-978-2921	339-19
Region 17						
8600 Farley St Ste 100	Overland Park	KS	66212	**866-667-6572**	913-967-3000	
Region 18						
330 Second Ave S Ste 790	Minneapolis	MN	55401	**866-667-6572**	612-348-1757	339-19
Region 19						
915 Second Ave Rm 2948	Seattle	WA	98174	**844-762-6572**	206-220-6300	339-19
Region 20						
901 Market St Ste 400	San Francisco	CA	94103	**866-667-6572**	415-356-5130	339-19
Region 21						
888 S Figueroa St 9th Fl	Los Angeles	CA	90017	**866-667-6572**	213-894-5200	
Region 22						
20 Washington Pl 5th Fl	Newark	NJ	07102	**866-667-6572**	973-645-2100	
Region 24						
525 FD Roosevelt Ave Ste 1002	San Juan	PR	00918	**866-667-6572**	787-766-5347	
Region 25						
575 N Pennsylvania St Minton-Capehart Federal Bldg Ste 238	Indianapolis	IN	46204	**866-667-6572**	317-226-7381	339-19
Region 26						
80 Monroe Ave Ste 350	Memphis	TN	38103	**866-667-6572**	901-544-0018	339-19
Region 27						
1961 Stout St Ste 13-103	Denver	CO	80294	**844-762-6572**	303-844-3551	339-19
Region 28						
2600 N Central Ave Ste 1800	Phoenix	AZ	85004	**866-667-6572**	602-640-2160	
Region 29						
1 Metrotech Ctr 15th Fl	Brooklyn	NY	11201	**866-667-6572**	718-330-7713	
Region 30						
1015 Half St SE	Washington	DC	20570	**844-762-6572**	202-273-1000	339-19
Region 31						
11150 W Olympic Blvd Ste 700	Los Angeles	CA	90064	**866-667-6572**	310-235-7352	339-19
Region 32						
1301 Clay St Rm 300N	Oakland	CA	94612	**866-667-6572**	510-637-3300	
Region 34						
450 Main St	Hartford	CT	06103	**866-667-6572**	860-240-3522	
National League for Nursing (NLN)						
61 Broadway 33rd Fl	New York	NY	10006	**800-669-1656**	212-363-5555	49-8
National League of Cities (NLC)						
660 North Capitol St NW	Washington	DC	20001	**877-827-2385**		49-7
National Legal Aid & Defender Assn (NLADA)						
1140 Connecticut Ave NW Ste 900	Washington	DC	20036	**800-725-4513**	202-452-0620	49-10
National Lift Truck Inc						
3333 Mt Prospect Rd	Franklin Park	IL	60131	**800-469-6420**		111
National Little Britches Rodeo Assn (NLBRA)						
5050 Edison Ave Ste 105	Colorado Springs	CO	80915	**800-763-3694**	719-389-0333	48-22
National Luggage Dealers Association (NLDA)						
1817 Elmdale Ave	Glenview	IL	60026	**800-411-0705**	847-998-6869	49-18
National Mail Order Assn LLC (NMOA)						
2807 Polk St NE	Minneapolis	MN	55418	**800-992-1377**	612-788-1673	49-18
National Marfan Foundation (NMF)						
22 Manhasset Ave	Port Washington	NY	11050	**800-862-7326**	516-883-8712	48-17
National Marine Electronics Assn (NMEA)						
692 Ritchie Hwy Ste 104	Severna Park	MD	21146	**800-808-6632**	410-975-9425	49-13

	City	State	ZIP	Toll-Free	Phone	Class
National Marine Representatives Assn (NMRA)						
PO Box 360	Gurnee	IL	60031	**800-890-3819**	847-662-3167	49-18
National Marrow Donor Program (NMDP)						
500 N Fifth St	Minneapolis	MN	55401	**800-627-7692**		48-17
National Medical Assn (NMA)						
8403 Colesville Rd						
Ste 920	Silver Spring	MD	20910	**800-662-0554**	202-347-1895	49-8
National Mental Health Information Ctr						
PO Box 42557	Washington	DC	20015	**800-487-4889**		339-9
National Metal Fabricators						
2395 Greenleaf Ave	Elk Grove Village	IL	60007	**800-323-8849**		693
National Meter & Automation						
7220 S Fraser St	Centennial	CO	80112	**877-212-8340**	303-339-9100	606
National Middle School Assn (NMSA)						
4151 Executive Pkwy Ste 300	Westerville	OH	43081	**800-528-6672**	614-895-4730	49-5
National Minority Supplier Development Council (NMSDC)						
1359 Broadway 10th Fl	New York	NY	10018	**800-843-4898**	212-944-2430	49-18
National Mississippi River Museum & Aquarium						
350 E Third St	Dubuque	IA	52001	**800-226-3369**	563-557-9545	517
National Model Railroad Assn (NMRA)						
4121 Cromwell Rd	Chattanooga	TN	37421	**800-654-2256**	423-892-2846	48-18
National Monitoring Center						
26800 Aliso Viejo Pkwy						
Ste 250	Aliso Viejo	CA	92656	**800-662-1711**		689
National Motor Club of America Inc (NMC)						
130 E John Carpenter Fwy	Irving	TX	75062	**800-523-4582**		53
National Motor Freight Traffic Assn (NMFTA)						
1001 N Fairfax St Ste 600	Alexandria	VA	22314	**866-411-6632**	703-838-1810	49-21
National Motorists Assn (NMA)						
402 W Second St	Waunakee	WI	53597	**800-882-2785**	608-849-6000	49-21
National Multiple Sclerosis Society						
733 Third Ave 3rd Fl	New York	NY	10017	**800-344-4867**	212-986-3240	48-17
National Museum of Natural History (Smithsonian Institution)						
10th St & Constitution Ave NW						
	Washington	DC	20560	**866-868-7774**	202-633-1000	517
National Museum of Naval Aviation						
1750 Radford Blvd Ste C	Pensacola	FL	32508	**800-247-6289***	850-452-3604	517
*General						
National Museum of Racing & Hall of Fame						
191 Union Ave	Saratoga Springs	NY	12866	**800-562-5394**	518-584-0400	519
National Museum of the American Indian (Smithsonian Institution)						
1 Bowling Green	New York	NY	10004	**800-242-6624**	212-514-3700	517
National Museum of Wildlife Art						
2820 Rungius Rd PO Box 6825	Jackson	WY	83002	**800-313-9553**	307-733-5771	517
National Museum of Women in the Arts						
1250 New York Ave NW	Washington	DC	20005	**866-875-4627**	202-783-5000	517
National Mutual Benefit						
6522 Grand Teton Plz	Madison	WI	53719	**800-779-1936**	608-833-1936	390-2
National NeedleArts Assn, The (TNNA)						
1100-H Brandywine Blvd	Zanesville	OH	43701	**800-889-8662**	740-455-6773	48-18
National Newspaper Assn (NNA)						
PO Box 7540	Columbia	MO	65205	**800-829-4662**	217-241-1400	49-14
National Niemann-Pick Disease Foundation Inc (NNPDF)						
401 Madison Ave Ste B						
PO Box 49	Fort Atkinson	WI	53538	**877-287-3672**	920-563-0930	48-17
National Nonwovens						
PO Box 150	EastHampton	MA	01027	**800-333-3469**	413-527-3445	740-6
National Notary Assn (NNA)						
9350 DeSoto Ave	Chatsworth	CA	91313	**800-876-6827**		49-12
National Nursing Staff Development Organization (NNSDO)						
330 N Wabash Ave Ste 2000	Chicago	IL	60611	**800-489-1995**	312-321-5135	49-8
National Ocean Industries Assn (NOIA)						
1120 G St NW Ste 900	Washington	DC	20005	**800-558-9994**	202-347-6900	48-12
National Office Furniture						
1205 Kimball Blvd	Jasper	IN	47549	**800-482-1717**		319-1
National Office Systems Inc						
6804 Virginia Manor Rd						
Ste 400	Beltsville	MD	20705	**800-840-6264**	301-840-6264	
National Oil & Gas Inc						
409 N Main St	Bluffton	IN	46714	**800-322-8454**	260-824-2220	575
National Oilwell Varco (NOV)						
7909 Parkwood Cir Dr	Houston	TX	77036	**888-262-8645**	713-375-3700	183
NYSE: NOV						
National Optical Astronomy Observatory						
950 N Cherry Ave	Tucson	AZ	85719	**888-809-4012**	520-318-8000	664
National Oral Health Information Clearinghouse (NIDCR)						
1 NOHIC Way	Bethesda	MD	20892	**866-232-4528**	301-496-4261	48-17
National Organization for Albinism & Hypopigmentation (NOAH)						
PO Box 959	East Hampstead	NH	03826	**800-648-2310**	603-887-2310	48-17
National Organization for Rare Disorders (NORD)						
55 Kenosia Ave	Danbury	CT	06810	**800-999-6673**	203-744-0100	48-17
National Organization for the Reform of Marijuana Laws (NORML)						
1600 K St NW Ste 501	Washington	DC	20006	**888-420-8932**	202-483-5500	48-8
National Organization for Victim Assistance (NOVA)						
510 King St Ste 424	Alexandria	VA	22314	**800-879-6682**	703-535-6682	48-8
National Organization for Women (NOW)						
1100 H St NW 3rd Fl	Washington	DC	20005	**855-212-0212**	202-628-8669	48-24
National Organization of Circumcision Information Resource Centers (NOCIRC)						
PO Box 2512	San Anselmo	CA	94979	**800-727-8622**	415-488-9883	48-17
National Osteoporosis Foundation (NOF)						
251 18th St S Ste 630	Arlington	VA	22202	**800-231-4222**	202-223-2226	48-17
National Outdoor Leadership School (NOLS)						
284 Lincoln St	Lander	WY	82520	**800-710-6657**	307-332-5300	681
National Ovarian Cancer Coalition (NOCC)						
2501 Oak Lawn Ave Ste 435	Dallas	TX	75219	**888-682-7426**		48-17
National Paper & Sanitary Supply						
2511 S 156th Cir	Omaha	NE	68130	**800-647-2737**	402-330-5507	555
National Parking Assn (NPA)						
1112 16th St NW Ste 840	Washington	DC	20036	**800-647-7275**	202-296-4336	49-3
National Parks Conservation Assn (NPCA)						
1300 19th St NW Ste 300	Washington	DC	20036	**800-628-7275**	202-223-6722	48-13
National Parks Magazine						
777 Sixth St NW Ste 700	Washington	DC	20001	**800-628-7275***	202-223-6722	455-19
*General						
National Partitions						
10300 Goldenfern Ln	Knoxville	TN	37931	**800-996-7266**	865-670-2100	286
National Peace Corps Assn (NPCA)						
1900 L St NW Ste 610	Washington	DC	20036	**800-336-1616**	202-293-7728	48-5

	City	State	ZIP	Toll-Free	Phone	Class
National Pen Corp (NPC)						
12121 Scripps Summit Dr	San Diego	CA	92131	**888-672-7370**		9
National Pest Management Assn Inc (NPMA)						
10460 N St	Fairfax	VA	22030	**800-678-6722**	703-352-6762	49-4
National Pesticide Information Ctr (NPIC)						
333 Weniger Hall	Corvallis	OR	97331	**800-858-7378**		48-17
National Pipe & Plastics Inc						
3421 Old Vestal Rd	Vestal	NY	13850	**800-836-4350**		592
National Pork Producers Council (NPPC)						
122 C St NW Ste 875	Washington	DC	20001	**800-952-4629**	202-347-3600	49-6
National Precast Concrete Assn (NPCA)						
10333 N Meridian St						
Ste 272	Indianapolis	IN	46290	**800-366-7731**	317-571-9500	49-3
National Presto Industries Inc						
3925 N Hastings Way	Eau Claire	WI	54703	**800-877-0441**	715-839-2121	37
NYSE: NPK						
National Printing Converters Inc						
18 S Murphy Ave	Brazil	IN	47834	**800-877-6724**		412
National Propane Gas Assn (NPGA)						
1899 L St NW Ste 350	Washington	DC	20036	**800-328-1111**	202-466-7200	48-12
National Property Inspections Inc (NPI)						
9375 Burt St Ste 201	Omaha	NE	68114	**800-333-9807**	402-333-9807	364
National Psoriasis Foundation (NPF)						
6600 SW 92nd Ave Ste 300	Portland	OR	97223	**800-723-9166**	503-244-7404	48-17
National Psychological Assn for Psychoanalysis (NPAP)						
40 W 13th St	New York	NY	10011	**800-365-7006**	212-924-7440	49-15
National PTA						
1250 N Pitt St	Alexandria	VA	22314	**800-307-4782**	703-518-1200	305
National Public Radio (NPR)						
635 Massachusetts Ave NW	Washington	DC	20001	**800-989-8255**	202-513-3232	628
National Railroad Passenger Corp						
60 Massachusetts Ave NE	Washington	DC	20002	**800-872-7245**	202-906-3741	645
National Railway Equipment Co (NREC)						
14400 Robey St	Dixmoor	IL	60426	**800-253-2905**	708-388-6002	646
National Ready Mixed Concrete Assn (NRMCA)						
900 Spring St	Silver Spring	MD	20910	**888-846-7622**	301-587-1400	49-3
National Recreation & Park Assn (NSPR)						
22377 Belmont Ridge Rd	Ashburn	VA	20148	**800-626-6772**		48-23
National Rehabilitation Assn (NRA)						
633 S Washington St	Alexandria	VA	22314	**888-258-4295**	703-836-0850	48-17
National Rehabilitation Information Ctr (NARIC)						
8400 Corporate Dr Ste 500	Landover	MD	20785	**800-346-2742**	301-459-5900	48-17
National Renderers Association Inc (NRA)						
500 Montgomery St Ste 310	Alexandria	VA	22314	**800-366-2563**	703-683-0155	48-2
National Research Corp						
1245 Q St	Lincoln	NE	68508	**800-388-4264**	402-475-2525	464
NASDAQ: NRCI						
National Research Ctr for Coal & Energy (NRCCE)						
West Virginia University						
385 Evansdale Dr PO Box 6064	Morgantown	WV	26506	**800-624-8301**	304-293-2867	664
National Resource Center on Native American Aging (NRCNAA)						
1301 N Columbia Rd Ste E231						
PO Box 9037	Grand Forks	ND	58202	**800-896-7628**	701-777-3720	48-6
National Resource Ctr on Domestic Violence (NRCDV)						
6400 Flank Dr Ste 1300	Harrisburg	PA	17112	**800-799-7233**		48-6
National Restaurant Assn (NRA)						
2055 L St NW Ste 700	Washington	DC	20036	**800-424-5156**	202-331-5900	49-6
National Retail Federation (NRF)						
1101 New York Ave NW	Washington	DC	20005	**800-673-4692**	202-783-7971	49-18
National Retail Hardware Assn (NRHA)						
5822 W 74th St	Indianapolis	IN	46278	**800-772-4424***	317-290-0338	49-18
*Cust Svc						
National Reye's Syndrome Foundation (NRSF)						
426 N Lewis St	Bryan	OH	43506	**800-233-7393**	419-924-9000	48-17
National Right to Work Committee (NRTWC)						
8001 Braddock Rd Ste 500	Springfield	VA	22160	**800-325-7892**		49-12
National Rivet & Manufacturing Co						
21 E Jefferson St	Waupun	WI	53963	**888-324-5511**	920-324-5511	278
National Roofing Contractors Assn (NRCA)						
10255 W Higgins Rd Ste 600	Rosemont	IL	60018	**800-323-9545***	847-299-9070	49-3
*Cust Svc						
National Rosacea Society (NRS)						
196 James St	Barrington	IL	60010	**888-662-5874**		48-17
National Rubber Technologies Corp						
35 Cawthra Ave	Toronto	ON	M6N5B3	**800-387-8501**	416-657-1111	672
National Runaway Switchboard (NRS)						
3141 N Lincoln Ave	Chicago	IL	60657	**800-786-2929**	773-880-9860	48-6
National Rural Utilities Co-op Finance Corp						
2201 Co-op Way	Herndon	VA	20171	**800-424-2954**	703-709-6700	507
National Safety Apparel Inc (NSA)						
15825 Industrial Pkwy	Cleveland	OH	44135	**800-553-0672**		572
National Safety Council (NSC)						
1121 Spring Lake Dr	Itasca	IL	60143	**800-621-7615**	630-285-1121	48-17
National Salon Resources Inc						
3109 Louisiana Ave N	Minneapolis	MN	55427	**800-622-0003**		76
National School Products						
1523 Old Niles Ferry Rd	Maryville	TN	37803	**800-627-9393**	865-984-3960	243
National School Supply & Equipment Assn (NSSEA)						
8380 Colesville Rd						
Ste 250	Silver Spring	MD	20910	**800-395-5550**	301-495-0240	49-18
National Science Teachers Assn (NSTA)						
1840 Wilson Blvd	Arlington	VA	22201	**800-722-6782***	703-243-7100	49-5
*Sales						
National Securities Corp						
410 Park Ave 14th Fl	New York	NY	10022	**800-742-7730**	212-417-8000	686
National Seminars Training						
6900 Squibb Rd	Shawnee Mission	KS	66202	**800-258-7246**	913-432-7755	760
National Senior Golf Assn (NSGA)						
200 Perrine Rd Ste 201	Old Bridge	NJ	08857	**800-282-6772**		48-22
National Services Group Inc						
1682 Langley Ave	Irvine	CA	92614	**800-394-6000**	714-564-7900	189-8
National Sheriffs' Assn (NSA)						
1450 Duke St	Alexandria	VA	22314	**800-424-7827**	703-836-7827	49-7
National Shoe Retailers Assn (NSRA)						
7386 N La Cholla Blvd	Tucson	AZ	85741	**800-673-8446**	520-209-1710	49-18
National Shrine of Our Lady of the Snows						
442 S De Mazenod Dr	Belleville	IL	62223	**800-682-2879**	618-397-6700	50-1
National Slovak Society of the USA (NSS)						
351 Vly Brook Rd	McMurray	PA	15317	**800-488-1890**	724-731-0094	48-14

	Toll-Free	Phone	Class
National Small Business Assn (NSBA) 1156 15th St NW Ste 1100 Washington DC 20005	800-345-6728		49-12
National Soccer Coaches Assn of America (NSCAA) 800 Ann Ave Kansas City KS 66101	800-458-0678	913-362-1747	48-22
National Society Daughters of the American Revolution (DAR) 1776 D St NW Washington DC 20006	800-449-1776	202-628-1776	48-19
National Society of Accountants (NSA) 1010 N Fairfax St Alexandria VA 22314	800-966-6679	703-549-6400	49-1
National Society of Professional Engineers (NSPE) 1420 King St Alexandria VA 22314	888-285-6773		49-19
National Softball Hall of Fame & Museum 2801 NE 50th St Oklahoma City OK 73111	800-654-8337	405-424-5266	519
National Speakers Bureau 1177 W Broadway Ste 300 Vancouver BC V6H1G3	800-661-4110	604-734-3663	704
National Speakers Bureau Inc 14047 W Petronalla Dr Ste 102 Libertyville IL 60048	800-323-9442	847-295-1122	704
National Specialty Alloys LLC 18250 Keith Harrow Blvd Houston TX 77084 *General	800-847-5653*	281-345-2115	490
National Spinal Cord Injury Assn (NSCIA) 75-20 Astoria Blvd Ste 120 East Elmhurst NY 11370	800-962-9629	718-512-0010	48-17
National Sporting Goods Assn (NSGA) 1601 Feehanville Dr Ste 300 Mount Prospect IL 60056	800-815-5422	847-296-6742	49-4
National Sprint Car Hall of Fame & Museum 1 Sprint Capital Pl Knoxville IA 50138	800-874-4488	641-842-6176	519
National Staff Development Council (NSDC) 504 S Locust St Oxford OH 45056	800-727-7288	513-523-6029	49-5
National Standard Parts Assoc Inc 4400 Mobile Hwy Pensacola FL 32506	800-874-6813	850-456-5771	57
National Stock Exchange (NSX) 101 Hudson St Ste 1200 Jersey City NJ 07302	800-843-3924	201-499-3700	687
National Stock Sign Co 1040 El Dorado Ave Santa Cruz CA 95062	800-462-7726		697
National Stone Sand & Gravel Assn (NSSGA) 1605 King St Alexandria VA 22314	800-342-1415	703-525-8788	49-3
National Strength & Conditioning Assn (NSCA) 1885 Bob Johnson Dr Colorado Springs CO 80906	800-815-6826	719-632-6722	48-22
National Stroke Assn (NSA) 9707 E Easter Ln Centennial CO 80112 *Cust Svc	800-787-6537*		48-17
National Stuttering Assn (NSA) 119 W 40th St 14th Fl New York NY 10018	800-937-8888	212-944-4050	48-17
National Sunflower Assn PAC 2401 46th Ave SE Ste 206 Mandan ND 58554	888-718-7033	701-328-5100	611
National Super Service Company Inc 3115 Frenchman Rd Toledo OH 43607 *Cust Svc	800-677-1663*	419-531-2121	385
National System of Garage Ventilation Inc 714 N Church St PO Box 1186 Decatur IL 62525	800-728-8368	217-423-7314	15
National Tank Truck Carriers Inc 950 N Glebe Rd Ste 520 Arlington VA 22203 *Resv	800-228-9290*	703-838-1960	49-21
National Tay-Sachs & Allied Diseases Assn (NTSAD) 2001 Beacon St Ste 204 Brighton MA 02135	800-906-8723	617-277-4463	48-17
National Technical Information Service (NTIS) 5301 Shawnee Rd Alexandria VA 22312	800-363-2068	703-605-6060	197
National Technical Information Service (NTIS) 5285 Port Royal Rd Springfield VA 22161 *Orders	800-553-6847*	703-605-6000	664
National Technical Systems Inc (NTS) 2125 E Katella Ave Ste 250 Anaheim CA 92806 *NASDAQ: NTSC*	800-879-9225	818-591-0776	738
National Thoroughbred Racing Assn (NTRA) 2525 Harrodsburg Rd Ste 510 Lexington KY 40504	800-792-6872		48-22
National Tire & Wheel 5 Garden Ct Wheeling WV 26003	800-847-3287		57
National Tobacco Company LP 5201 Interchange Way Louisville KY 40229 *Cust Svc	800-579-0975*	502-778-4421	751
National Tooling & Machining Assn (NTMA) 6363 Oak Tree Blvd Independence OH 44131	800-248-6862		49-13
National Tour Assn (NTA) 546 E Main St Lexington KY 40508	800-682-8886	859-226-4444	48-23
National Trade Productions Inc 313 S Patrick St Alexandria VA 22314	800-687-7469	703-683-8500	184
National Truck Equipment Assn (NTEA) 37400 Hills Tech Dr Farmington Hills MI 48331	800-441-6832	248-489-7090	49-21
National Truck Leasing System 2651 Warrenville Rd Ste 560 Downers Grove IL 60515	800-729-6857		773
National Trust for Canada, The 190 Bronson Ave Ottawa ON K1R6H4	866-964-1066	613-237-1066	48-13
National Trust for Historic Preservation 1785 Massachusetts Ave NW Washington DC 20036	800-944-6847	202-588-6000	48-13
National Tube Supply Co 925 Central Ave University Park IL 60466	800-229-6872		490
National Turkey Federation (NTF) 1225 New York Ave NW Ste 400 Washington DC 20005	866-536-7593	202-898-0100	48-2
National Underwriter Co 4157 Olympic Blvd Ste 225 Erlanger KY 41018	800-543-0874		633-2
National United PO Box 779 Gatesville TX 76528	877-628-2265	254-865-2211	70
National University 11255 N Torrey Pines Rd La Jolla CA 92037	800-628-8648	858-642-8000	166
National University of Health Sciences 200 E Roosevelt Rd Lombard IL 60148	800-826-6285	630-629-2000	166
National Urban Technology Ctr 25 Broadway 9th Fl New York NY 10004	800-998-3212	212-528-7350	48-6
National Van Lines Inc 2800 W Roosevelt Rd Broadview IL 60155	877-590-2810	708-450-2900	516
National Veterinary Associates Inc 29229 Canwood St Ste 100 Agoura Hills CA 91301	888-767-7755	805-777-7722	789
National Vision Inc 2435 Commerce Ave Bldg 2200 Duluth GA 30096 *Cust Svc	800-637-3597*	770-822-3600	539

	Toll-Free	Phone	Class
National Waterways Conference Inc (NWC) 4650 Washington Blvd Ste 608 Arlington VA 22201	866-371-1390	703-243-4090	49-21
National Western Life Insurance Co 850 E Anderson Ln Austin TX 78752 *NASDAQ: NWLI*	800-531-5442	512-836-1010	390-2
National Wholesale Company Inc 400 National Blvd Lexington NC 27294	800-480-4673		457
National WIC Assn (NWA) 2001 S St NW Ste 580 Washington DC 20009	866-782-6246	202-232-5492	48-6
National Wild Turkey Federation (NWTF) 770 Augusta Rd PO Box 530 Edgefield SC 29824 *Cust Svc	800-843-6983*	803-637-3106	48-3
National Wildlife Federation (NWF) 11100 Wildlife Ctr Dr Reston VA 20190	800-822-9919	703-438-6000	48-3
National Wood Flooring Assn (NWFA) 111 Chesterfield Industrial Blvd Chesterfield MO 63005	800-422-4556	636-519-9663	49-3
National Woodland Owners Assn (NWOA) 374 Maple Ave E Ste 310 Vienna VA 22180	800-476-8733	703-255-2300	48-2
National Youth Sports Coaches Assn (NYSCA) 2050 Vista Pkwy West Palm Beach FL 33411	800-729-2057	561-684-1141	48-22
National/AZON 1148 Rochester Rd Troy MI 48083	800-325-5939	248-307-9308	548-1
National-Louis University 1000 Capitol Dr Wheeling IL 60090	800-443-5522	847-947-5718	166
Chicago 122 S Michigan Ave Chicago IL 60603	800-443-5522	888-658-8632	166
NationJob Inc 920 Morgan St Ste T Des Moines IA 50309	800-292-7731		260
Nations Financial Group Inc 4000 River Ridge Dr NE PO Box 908 Cedar Rapids IA 52406	800-351-2471	319-393-9541	687
Nationwide Adv Specialty Co 854 Angliana Ave Lexington KY 40508	800-683-5697	817-382-1616	
Nationwide Credit Inc (NCI) PO Box 14581 Des Moines IA 50306	800-456-4729		160
Nationwide Custom Homes 1100 Rives Rd Martinsville VA 24115	800-216-7001		106
Nationwide Life & Annuity Insurance Co 1 Nationwide Pl Columbus OH 43215	800-882-2822	855-473-6410	390-2
Nationwide Lift Trucks Inc 3900 N 28th Terr Hollywood FL 33020	800-327-4431	954-922-4645	57
Nationwide Medical Equipment Inc 1510 Stuart Rd NE Ste 109 Cleveland TN 37312	888-826-6245	423-478-7433	
Nationwide Mutual Fire Insurance Co 1 Nationwide Plz Columbus OH 43215	877-669-6877	800-882-2822	390-4
Nationwide Mutual Insurance Co 1 Nationwide Plz Columbus OH 43215	877-669-6877		390-2
Nationwide Truck Brokers Inc (NTB) 4203 Roger B Chaffee Memorial Blvd SE Ste 2 Grand Rapids MI 49548	800-446-0682	616-878-5554	775
Nationwide Van Lines Inc 1421 NW 65th Ave Plantation FL 33313	800-310-0056	954-585-3945	516
Native American Rights Fund (NARF) 1506 Broadway Boulder CO 80302	888-280-0726	303-447-8760	49-10
Native Eyewear Inc 1114 Neon Forest Cir Unit 5 Longmont CO 80504	888-776-2848		539
NATIVE INSTRUMENTS NORTH AMERICA INC 6725 Sunset Blvd 5th Fl Los Angeles CA 90028	866-556-6487	323-467-5260	
Native Pride 11359 Rt 20 Irving NY 14081	800-619-8618	716-934-5130	324
Nativo Lodge Hotel 6000 Pan American Fwy NE Albuquerque NM 87109	888-628-4861	505-798-4300	378
Natl Elevator Industrial Educational Program 11 Larsen Way Attleboro MA 02763	800-228-8220	508-699-2200	196
Natrol Inc 21411 Prairie St Chatsworth CA 91311	800-262-8765		794
NATSO Inc 1737 King St Ste 200 Alexandria VA 22314	800-956-9160	703-549-2100	49-21
Naturade 2030 Main St Ste 630 Irvine CA 92614	800-421-1830		794
Natural Alternatives International Inc 1185 Linda Vista Dr San Marcos CA 92078 *NASDAQ: NAII*	800-848-2646	760-744-7340	794
Natural Bridge Battlefield Historic State Park 7502 Natural Bridge Rd Tallahassee FL 32305	800-326-3521	850-922-6007	561
Natural Bridge State Resort Park 2135 Natural Bridge Rd Slade KY 40376	800-325-1710		561
Natural Factors Nutritional Products Ltd 1550 United Blvd Coquitlam BC V3K6Y2	800-663-8900	604-777-1757	794
Natural Habitat Adventures PO Box 3065 Boulder CO 80307	800-543-8917	303-449-3711	755
Natural Healthy Concepts 310 N Westhill Blvd Appleton WI 54914	866-505-7501	920-968-2350	344
Natural Organics Inc 548 Broadhollow Rd Melville NY 11747	800-645-9500		794
Natural Resource Partners LP 1201 Louisiana St Ste 3400 Houston TX 77002 *NYSE: NRP*	888-334-7102	713-751-7507	499
Natural Resources Research Institute (NRRI) *University of Minnesota Duluth* 5013 Miller Trunk Hwy Duluth MN 55811	800-234-0054	218-788-2694	664
NaturaLawn of America Inc 1 E Church St Frederick MD 21701	800-989-5444		573
Naturally Vitamins 4404 E Elwood St Phoenix AZ 85040	800-899-4499		794
Nature 529 14th St NW 968 National Press Bldg Washington DC 20045	800-524-0384	202-737-2355	455-19
Nature Conservancy 4245 N Fairfax Dr Ste 100 Arlington VA 22203 *Cust Svc	800-628-6860*	703-841-5300	48-13
Nature Conservancy of Canada 36 Eglinton Ave W Ste 400 Toronto ON M4R1A1	800-465-8005	416-932-3202	48-13
Nature's Trees Inc 550 Bedford Rd Bedford Hills NY 10507	800-341-8733	914-241-4999	771
Nature's Way Products Inc 825 Challenger Dr Ste 125 Green Bay WI 54311	800-962-8873		794

Name / Address	City	State	ZIP	Toll-Free	Phone	Class
Natures Best 6 Pt Dr Ste 300	Brea	CA	92821	800-800-7799	714-255-4600	344
Natus Medical Inc 1501 Industrial Rd *NASDAQ: BABY*	San Carlos	CA	94070	800-255-3901	650-802-0400	250
NATW (National Association of Town Watch) 308 E Lancaster Ave Ste 115	Wynnewood	PA	19096	800-648-3688		48-7
NAUS (NA for Uniformed Services) 5535 Hempstead Way	Springfield	VA	22151	800-842-3451	703-750-1342	48-19
Nautel Ltd 10089 Peggy'S Cove Rd	Hackett'S Cove	NS	B3Z3J4	877-662-8835	902-823-3900	643
Nautica Retail USA Inc 40 W 57th St	New York	NY	10019	866-376-4184		
NAUTICUS the National Maritime Ctr 1 Waterside Dr	Norfolk	VA	23510	800-664-1080	757-664-1000	517
Nautilus Inc 17750 SE Sixth Way *NYSE: NLS*	Vancouver	WA	98683	800-628-8458		267
Nautilus Insurance Group LLC 7233 E Butherus Dr	Scottsdale	AZ	85260	800-842-8972	480-951-0905	390-4
Nautilus Plus Inc 3550 1e Rue	SiŠge Social	QC	J3Y8Y5	800-363-6763	514-666-5814	702
NAV CANADA 77 Metcalfe St PO Box 3411 Stn D	Ottawa	ON	K1P5L6	800-876-4693	613-563-5588	19
NAV Canada Training & Conference Ctr 1950 Montreal Rd	Cornwall	ON	K6H6L2	877-832-6416	613-936-5800	376
Navajo Express Inc 1400 W 64 Ave	Denver	CO	80221	800-525-1969	303-287-3800	775
Naval Air Station Jacksonville 6801 Roosevelt Blvd	Jacksonville	FL	32212	800-849-6024	904-542-2338	495-4
Naval Air Station Joint Reserve Base New Orleans 301 Russell Ave	New Orleans	LA	70143	800-729-7327	504-678-3260	495-4
Naval Air Station Patuxent River 22268 Cedar Point Road Bldg 409	Patuxent River	MD	20670	877-995-5247	301-342-3000	495-4
Naval Enlisted Reserve Assn (NERA) 6703 Farragut Ave	Falls Church	VA	22042	800-776-9020		48-19
Naval Hospital Bremerton 1 Bo1 Rd	Bremerton	WA	98312	800-422-1383	360-475-4000	373-4
Naval Institute Press 291 Wood Rd	Annapolis	MD	21402	800-233-8764	410-268-6110	633-4
Naval Reserve Assn (NRA) 1619 King St	Alexandria	VA	22314	877-628-9411	703-548-5800	48-19
Naval Sea Systems Command 1333 Isaac Hull Ave SE Washington Navy Yard	Washington	DC	20376	800-356-8464	202-781-4123	339-5
Naval Station Great Lakes 2601E Paul Jones St	Great Lakes	IL	60088	800-393-0865	847-688-3500	495-4
Naval Surface Warfare Ctr *Dahlgren Div* 6149 Welsh Rd Ste 203	Dahlgren	VA	22448	877-845-5656		664
Naval Undersea Warfare Center (NUWC) 1176 Howell St	Newport	RI	02841	800-356-8464	401-832-7742	664
Navarro College 3200 W Seventh Ave	Corsicana	TX	75110	800-628-2776	903-874-6501	162
Navarro County Electric Co-op Inc 3800 Texas 22 PO Box 616	Corsicana	TX	75110	800-771-9095	903-874-7411	245
Navarro Discount Pharmacy 9400 NW 104 St	Medley	FL	33178	866-628-2776	786-245-8524	237
Navarro Research & Engineering Inc 1020 Commerce Park Dr	Oak Ridge	TN	37830	866-681-5265	865-220-9650	192
Navasota Valley Electric Co-op Inc 2281 E US Hwy 79 PO Box 848	Franklin	TX	77856	800-443-9462	979-828-3232	245
Navellier Securities Corp 1 E Liberty St Ste 504	Reno	NV	89501	800-887-8671	775-785-2300	400
Navhouse Corp 10 Loring Dr	Bolton	ON	L7E1J9	877-628-6667	905-857-8102	21
Naviant Inc 201 Prairie Heights Dr	Verona	WI	53593	888-686-4624		
Navigate Power 2211 N Elston Ste 208	Chicago	IL	60614	888-601-1789		461
Navigator Energy Services 2626 Cole Ave Ste 900	Dallas	TX	75204	888-991-1162	214-880-6000	
Navigators Group Inc 1 Penn Plz 32nd Fl *NASDAQ: NAVG*	New York	NY	10119	866-408-1922	212-244-2333	359-4
Navigators of Canada 11 St John'S Dr	Arva	ON	N0M1C0	866-202-6287	519-660-8300	48-20
Navigators, The 3820 N 30th St PO Box 6000	Colorado Springs	CO	80934	866-568-7827	719-598-1212	48-20
Navin, Haffty & Associates LLC 1900 West Park Dr Ste 180	Westborough	MA	01581	888-837-1300	781-871-6770	
Navis Pack & Ship Centers 12742 E Caley Ave Ste 2 A	Centennial	CO	80111	800-344-3528		113
Navitaire LLC 333 S Seventh St Ste 1700	Minneapolis	MN	55402	877-216-6787	612-317-7000	194
Navitar Inc 200 Commerce Dr *Cust Svc	Rochester	NY	14623	800-828-6778*	585-359-4000	587
Navopache Electric Co-op Inc 1878 W White Mtn Blvd	Lakeside	AZ	85929	800-543-6324	928-368-5118	245
NAVS (National Anti-Vivisection Society) 53 W Jackson Blvd Ste 1552	Chicago	IL	60604	800-888-6287	312-427-6065	48-3
Navtech Seminars & Gps Supply 5501 Backlick Rd Ste 230	Springfield	VA	22151	800-628-0885	703-256-8900	461
Navy Exchange Service Command (NEXCOM) 3280 Virginia Beach Blvd	Virginia Beach	VA	23452	800-628-3924	757-463-6200	786
Navy League of the US 2300 Wilson Blvd	Arlington	VA	22201	800-356-5760	703-528-1775	48-19
Navy Lodge Pensacola Naval Air Station Bldg 3875	Pensacola	FL	32508	800-628-9466	850-456-8676	495-4
Navy Personnel Command (NPC) 5720 Integrity Dr	Millington	TN	38055	866-827-5672		339-5
Navy-Marine Corps Relief Society (NMCRS) 875 N Randolph St Ste 225	Arlington	VA	22203	800-654-8364	703-696-4904	48-19
NAWIC (NA of Women in Construction) 327 S Adams St	Fort Worth	TX	76104	800-552-3506	817-877-5551	49-3
Naxos of America Inc 1810 Columbia Ave	Franklin	TN	37064	877-629-6723	615-771-9393	653
Naylor LLC 5950 NW First Pl	Gainesville	FL	32607	800-369-6220		7
Nazarene Theological Seminary 1700 E Meyer Blvd	Kansas City	MO	64131	800-831-3011	816-268-5400	167-3
Nazareth College of Rochester 4245 E Ave	Rochester	NY	14618	800-860-6942	585-389-2525	166
Nazcare Inc 599 White Spar Rd	Prescott	AZ	86303	877-756-4090	928-442-9205	138
Nazdar 8501 Hedge Ln Terr	Shawnee	KS	66227	800-767-9942	913-422-1888	387
NB.C. Truck Equipment Inc 28130 Groesbeck Hwy	Roseville	MI	48066	800-778-8207	586-774-4900	61
NBA (National Business Assn) 5151 Beltline Rd Ste 1150	Dallas	TX	75254	800-456-0440	972-458-0900	49-12
NBA (National Benevolent Assn) 733 Union Blvd Ste 300	St. Louis	MO	63108	866-262-2669	314-993-9000	48-5
NBAA (National Business Aviation Assn) 1200 18th St NW Ste 400	Washington	DC	20036	800-394-6222	202-783-9000	49-21
NBC 26 1391 N Rd	Green Bay	WI	54313	800-800-6619	920-494-2626	736-32
NBCC (National Breast Cancer Coalition) 1101 17th St NW Ste 1300	Washington	DC	20036	800-622-2838	202-296-7477	48-17
Nbcot 1 Bank St Ste 300	Gaithersburg	MD	20878	800-967-1139	301-990-7979	138
NBDL (National Biodynamics Laboratory) *University of New Orleans College of Engineering* 2000 Lakeshore Dr	New Orleans	LA	70148	888-514-4275		664
NBMDA (North American Bldg Material Distribution Assn) 330 N Wabash Ave Ste 2000	Chicago	IL	60611	888-747-7862	312-321-6845	49-18
Nbn Infusions 2 Pin Oak Ln Ste 250	Cherry Hill	NJ	08003	800-253-9111	856-669-0217	473
NBPA (National Basketball Players Assn) 1133 Avenue of Americas	New York	NY	10036	800-955-6272	212-655-0880	48-22
NBT Bancorp Inc 52 S Broad St *NASDAQ: NBTB*	Norwich	NY	13815	800-628-2265	607-337-2265	359-2
NBT Bank NA PO Box 351	Norwich	NY	13815	800-628-2265	607-337-2265	70
NBWA (National Beer Wholesalers Assn) 1101 King St Ste 600	Alexandria	VA	22314	800-300-0417	703-683-4300	49-6
NC Machinery Co 17025 W Valley Hwy	Tukwila	WA	98188	800-562-4735		384
NCA (National Club Assn) 1201 15th St NW Ste 450	Washington	DC	20005	800-625-6221	202-822-9822	48-23
NCA CASI (North Central Assn Commission on Accreditation & S) 9115 Westside Pkwy	Alpharetta	GA	30009	888-413-3669		48-1
NCADD (National Council on Alcoholism & Drug Dependence I) 217 Broadway Ste 712	New York	NY	10007	800-622-2255	212-269-7797	48-17
NCAE News Bulletin PO Box 27347	Raleigh	NC	27611	800-662-7924	919-832-3000	455-8
NCAI (National Congress of American Indians) 1516 P St NW	Washington	DC	20005	800-388-2227	202-466-7767	48-14
NCASI (National Council for Air & Stream Improvement Inc) PO Box 13318	Research Triangle Park	NC	27709	888-448-2473	919-941-6400	48-13
NCBA (National Cattlemen's Beef Assn) 9110 E Nichols Ave Ste 300	Centennial	CO	80112	866-233-3872	303-694-0305	48-2
NCBA (National Co-op Business Assn) 1401 New York Ave NW Ste 1100	Washington	DC	20005	800-356-9655	202-638-6222	49-12
NCCA (National Child Care Assn) 1325 G St NW Ste 500	Washington	DC	20005	866-536-1945		48-6
NCCAOM (National Certification Commission for Acupuncture) 2025 M St NW Ste 800	Washington	DC	20036	888-381-1140	202-381-1140	
NCCD (National Council on Crime & Delinquency) 1970 Broadway Ste 500	Oakland	CA	94612	800-306-6223	510-208-0500	48-8
NCCI Holdings Inc 901 Peninsula Corporate Cir *Cust Svc	Boca Raton	FL	33487	800-622-4123*	561-893-1000	389
NCCNHR (National Citizens' Coalition for Nursing Home Refo) *National Consumer Voice for Quality Long-Term Care* 1828 L St NW Ste 801	Washington	DC	20036	866-992-3668	202-332-2275	48-17
NCCS (National Coalition for Cancer Survivorship) 8455 Colesville Rd Ste 930	Silver Spring	MD	20910	877-622-7937		48-17
NCEA (National Catholic Educational Assn) 1005 N Glebe Rd Ste 525	Arlington	VA	22201	800-711-6232	571-257-0010	49-5
NCED (National Center for Employee Development) 2701 E Imhoff Rd	Norman	OK	73071	866-438-6233	405-366-4420	376
NCEE (National Council on Economic Education) 122 E 42nd St Ste 2600	New York	NY	10168	800-338-1192	212-730-7007	49-5
NCEES (National Council of Examiners for Engineering & Su) 280 Seneca Creek Rd	Seneca	SC	29678	800-250-3196	864-654-6824	49-3
NCFBMIC (North Carolina Farm Bureau Mutual Insurance Co) PO Box 27427	Raleigh	NC	27611	800-584-1143	919-782-1705	390-4
NCFC (National Council of Farmer Co-ops) 50 F St NW Ste 900	Washington	DC	20001	800-344-2626	202-626-8700	48-2
NCFI Polyurethanes 1515 Carter St	Mount Airy	NC	27030	800-346-8229	336-789-9161	191-4
NCFR (National Council on Family Relations) 1201 W River Pkwy Ste 200	Minneapolis	MN	55454	888-781-9331		48-6
NCH Corp 2727 Chemsearch Blvd	Irving	TX	75062	800-527-9919	972-438-0211	151
NCI (Nissan Canada Inc) 5290 Orbitor Dr	Mississauga	ON	L4W4Z5	800-387-0122		59
NCI (Nationwide Credit Inc) PO Box 14581	Des Moines	IA	50306	800-456-4729		160
NCI (National Captioning Institute) 3725 Concorde Pkwy Ste 100	Chantilly	VA	20151	800-825-6758	703-917-7600	628
NCI Bldg Systems Inc 10943 N Sam Houston PkwyWest *NYSE: NCS*	Houston	TX	77064	888-624-8677	281-897-7788	105
NCI Inc 11730 Plaza America Dr *NASDAQ: NCIT*	Reston	VA	20190	800-274-9694	703-707-6900	180
NCIS (National Crop Insurance Services) 8900 Indian Creek Pkwy Ste 600	Overland Park	KS	66210	800-951-6247	913-685-2767	48-2

	Toll-Free	Phone	Class
NCJFCJ (National Council of Juvenile & Family Court Judges)			
Univ of Nevada PO Box 8970 .... Reno NV 89507	**800-527-3223**	775-784-6012	49-10
NCJJ (National Ctr for Juvenile Justice)			
3700 S Water St Ste 200 .... Pittsburgh PA 15203	**800-851-3420**	412-227-6950	48-8
NCL (National Consumers League)			
1701 K St NW Ste 1200 .... Washington DC 20006	**800-388-2227**	202-835-3323	48-10
NCLA (North Carolina Library Assn)			
1811 Capital Blvd .... Raleigh NC 27604	**888-977-3143**	919-839-6252	434
NCMA (National Contract Management Assn)			
21740 Beaumeade Cir Ste 125 .... Ashburn VA 20147	**800-344-8096**	571-382-0082	49-12
NCMEC (National Ctr for Missing & Exploited Children)			
699 Prince St .... Alexandria VA 22314	**800-843-5678**	703-274-3900	48-6
NCMIC Insurance Co			
14001 University Ave .... Clive IA 50325	**800-769-2000**	800-247-8043	390-5
NCMS (National Ctr for Mfg Sciences)			
3025 Boardwalk .... Ann Arbor MI 48108	**800-222-6267**	734-995-3457	664
NCNA (North Carolina Nurses Assn)			
103 Enterprise St PO Box 12025 .... Raleigh NC 27605	**800-626-2153**	919-821-4250	529
NCOA (National Council on the Aging)			
1901 L St NW 4th Fl .... Washington DC 20036	**800-677-1116**	571-527-3900	48-6
NCOA (Non Commissioned Officers Assn)			
9330 Corporate Dr Ste 708 .... Selma TX 78154	**800-662-2620**	210-653-6161	48-19
NCPA (National Community Pharmacists Assn)			
100 Daingerfield Rd .... Alexandria VA 22314	**800-544-7447**	703-683-8200	49-8
NCPC (National Crime Prevention Council)			
2345 Crystal Dr Ste 500 .... Arlington VA 22202	**800-627-2911**	443-292-4565	48-8
NCPSSM (National Committee to Preserve Social Security & M)			
10 G St NE Ste 600 .... Washington DC 20002	**800-966-1935**	202-216-0420	48-7
NCQA (National Committee for Quality Assurance)			
1100 13th St .... Washington DC 20005	**888-275-7585**	202-955-3500	48-10
NCRA (National Court Reporters Assn)			
8224 Old Courthouse Rd .... Vienna VA 22182	**800-272-6272**	703-556-6272	49-10
NCRP (National Council on Radiation Protection & Measure)			
7910 Woodmont Ave Ste 400 .... Bethesda MD 20814	**800-462-3683**	301-657-2652	49-19
Ncs Global			
32 Innovation Dr .... Rochester NH 03867	**800-711-6010**	603-926-4300	174
NCSBN (National Council of State Boards of Nursing)			
111 E Wacker Dr Ste 2900 .... Chicago IL 60601	**866-293-9600**	312-525-3600	49-8
NCSC (National Ctr for State Courts)			
300 Newport Ave .... Williamsburg VA 23185	**800-616-6164**	757-259-1525	49-7
NCSD (Nye County School District Inc)			
PO Box 113 .... Tonopah NV 89049	**800-796-6273**	775-482-6258	681
NCSD (Niskayuna Central School District)			
1239 Van Antwerp Rd .... Schenectady NY 12309	**866-893-6337**	518-377-4666	681
NCSEAA (North Carolina State Education Assistance Authorit)			
PO Box 14103 .... Research Triangle Park NC 27709	**800-700-1775**	919-549-8614	721
NCSHA (National Council of State Housing Agencies)			
444 N Capitol St NW Ste 438 .... Washington DC 20001	**800-475-2098**	202-624-7710	49-7
NCSS (National Council for the Social Studies)			
8555 16th St Ste 500 .... Silver Spring MD 20910	**800-683-0812***	301-588-1800	49-5
*Orders			
NCTA (National Christmas Tree Assn)			
16020 Swingley Ridge Rd			
Ste 300 .... Chesterfield MO 63017	**800-975-5920**		
NCTE (National Council of Teachers of English)			
1111 W Kenyon Rd .... Urbana IL 61801	**877-369-6283**	217-328-3870	49-5
NCTM (National Council of Teachers of Mathematics)			
1906 Assn Dr .... Reston VA 20191	**800-235-7566***	703-620-9840	49-5
*Orders			
NCTM News Bulletin			
1906 Assn Dr .... Reston VA 20191	**800-235-7566**	703-620-9840	455-8
NCTO (National Council of Textile Organizations)			
1701 K St NW Ste 625 .... Washington DC 20006	**800-238-7192**	202-822-8028	49-13
NCVB (Nashville Convention & Visitors Bureau)			
150 Fourth Ave N Ste G250 .... Nashville TN 37219	**800-657-6910**	615-259-4730	206
NCVMA (North Carolina Veterinary Medical Assn)			
1611 Jones Franklin Rd Ste 108 .... Raleigh NC 27606	**800-446-2862**	919-851-5850	790
ND Graphic Product Ltd			
55 Interchange Way Unit 1 .... Concord ON L4K5W3	**800-811-0194**	416-663-6416	623
Nd Industries Inc			
1000 N Crooks Rd .... Clawson MI 48017	**800-471-5000**	248-288-0000	479
NDA (AMOA-National Dart Assn)			
10070 W 190th Pl .... Mokena IL 60448	**800-808-9884**		48-22
NDC Infrared Engineering			
5314 N Irwindale Ave .... Irwindale CA 91706	**800-866-4733**	626-960-3300	201
N-Dimension Solutions Inc			
9030 Leslie St Ste 300 .... Richmond Hill ON L4B1G2	**866-837-8884**		225
NDP (Neathawk Dubuque & Packett)			
2912 W Leigh St .... Richmond VA 23230	**800-847-2674**	804-783-8140	
NDRI (National Disease Research Interchange)			
1628 John F Kennedy Blvd			
8 Penn Ctr 8th Fl .... Philadelphia PA 19103	**800-222-6374**	215-557-7361	269
NDSC (National Down Syndrome Congress)			
30 Mansell Ct Ste 108 .... Roswell GA 30076	**800-232-6372**	770-604-9500	48-17
NDSE (Network Data Security Experts Inc)			
521 Branchway Rd .... North Chesterfield VA 23236	**877-440-6373**		
NDSL (North Dakota State Library)			
604 E Blvd Ave .... Bismarck ND 58505	**800-472-2104**	701-328-4622	433-5
NDSS (National Down Syndrome Society)			
666 Broadway 8th Fl .... New York NY 10012	**800-221-4602**		48-17
NDVH (National Domestic Violence Hotline)			
PO Box 161810 .... Austin TX 78716	**800-799-7233**	512-794-1133	48-6
NDX Stern Empire			
1805 W 34th St .... Houston TX 77018	**800-229-0214**	713-688-1301	228
NE.T. Inc			
5651 Palmer Way Ste C .... Carlsbad CA 92010	**800-888-4638**	760-929-5980	85
NEA (National Education Assn)			
1201 16th St NW .... Washington DC 20036	**888-552-0624**	202-833-4000	49-5
NEA (National Electronic Attachment Inc)			
100 Ashford Ctr N Ste 300 .... Dunwoody GA 30338	**800-782-5150**		389
Neapco Inc			
6735 Haggerty Rd .... Belleville MI 48111	**800-821-2374**	734-447-1380	60
Near North Business Machines			
86 W Rd .... Huntsville ON P1H1M1	**800-522-3836**	705-787-0517	
Near-Cal Corp			
512 Chaney St .... Lake Elsinore CA 92530	**800-969-3578**	951-245-5400	186
Nearly Me Technologies			
Po Box 21475 .... Waco TX 76702	**800-887-3370**	254-662-1752	475

	Toll-Free	Phone	Class
Nearman Maynard Vallez			
205 Brandywine Blvd			
Ste 200 .... Fayetteville GA 30214	**800-288-0293**		2
Neathawk Dubuque & Packett (NDP)			
2912 W Leigh St .... Richmond VA 23230	**800-847-2674**	804-783-8140	
Nebraska			
Arts Council			
1004 Farnam St .... Omaha NE 68131	**800-341-4067**	402-595-2122	338-28
Attorney General			
2115 State Capitol .... Lincoln NE 68509	**800-727-6432**	402-471-2683	338-28
Child Support Enforcement Div			
PO Box 94728 .... Lincoln NE 68509	**877-631-9973**	402-471-3121	338-28
Economic Development Dept			
301 Centennial Mall S .... Lincoln NE 68509	**800-426-6505**	402-471-3111	338-28
Emergency Management Agency			
2433 NW 24th St .... Lincoln NE 68524	**877-297-2368**	402-471-7421	338-28
Environmental Quality Dept			
1200 N St Ste 400 .... Lincoln NE 68508	**877-253-2603**	402-471-2186	338-28
Health & Human Services Dept			
301 Centennial Mall S .... Lincoln NE 68508	**800-430-3244**	402-471-3121	338-28
Historical Society			
1500 R St .... Lincoln NE 68508	**800-833-6747**	402-471-3270	338-28
Insurance Dept			
941 O St Ste 400 .... Lincoln NE 68508	**877-564-7323**	402-471-2201	338-28
Investment Finance Authority			
1230 'O' St Ste 200 .... Lincoln NE 68508	**800-204-6432**	402-434-3900	338-28
Lieutenant Governor			
PO Box 94848 .... Lincoln NE 68508	**800-747-8177**		
Public Accountancy Board			
1526 K St Ste 410 .... Lincoln NE 68508	**800-564-6111**	402-471-3595	338-28
Public Service Commission			
1200 N St Ste 300 .... Lincoln NE 68508	**800-526-0017**	402-471-3101	338-28
Revenue Dept			
301 Centennial Mall S			
PO Box 94818 .... Lincoln NE 68509	**800-742-7474**	402-471-5729	338-28
Travel & Tourism Div			
301 Centennial Mall S .... Lincoln NE 68509	**877-632-7275**	402-471-3796	338-28
Nebraska Bankers Association Inc			
233 S 13th St Ste 700 .... Lincoln NE 68508	**800-593-3881**	402-474-1555	138
Nebraska Beef Council			
1319 Central Ave .... Kearney NE 68848	**800-421-5326**	308-236-7551	138
Nebraska Book Co			
4700 S 19th St .... Lincoln NE 68512	**800-869-0366**	402-421-7300	96
Nebraska College of Technical Agriculture			
404 E 7th .... Curtis NE 69025	**800-328-7847**	308-367-4124	795
Nebraska Community Blood Bank			
100 N 84th St .... Lincoln NE 68505	**877-486-9414**	402-486-9414	89
Nebraska Educational Telecommunications (NET)			
1800 N 33rd St .... Lincoln NE 68503	**800-868-1868**		628
Nebraska Farm Bureau Federation			
5225 S 16th St .... Lincoln NE 68512	**800-742-4016**	402-421-4400	138
Nebraska Furniture Mart Inc			
700 S 72nd St .... Omaha NE 68114	**800-336-9136**	402-397-6100	321
Nebraska House			
983285 Nebraska Medical Ctr .... Omaha NE 68198	**800-401-4444**	402-559-5000	371
Nebraska Indian Community College			
PO Box 428 .... Macy NE 68039	**844-440-6422**	402-837-5078	165
Nebraska Library Commission			
1200 N St Ste 120 .... Lincoln NE 68508	**800-307-2665**	402-471-2045	433-5
Nebraska Lottery			
1800 "O" St PO Box 98901 .... Lincoln NE 68509	**800-587-5200**	402-471-6100	450
Nebraska Machinery Co Inc			
3501 S Jeffers St .... North Platte NE 69101	**800-494-9560**	308-532-3100	384
Nebraska Medical Ctr, The			
4350 Dewey Ave .... Omaha NE 68105	**800-922-0000**	402-552-2000	373-3
Nebraska Medicine			
987400 Nebraska Medical Ctr .... Omaha NE 68198	**800-922-0000**	402-559-2000	764
Nebraska Nurses Assn (NNA)			
PO Box 3107 .... Kearney NE 68848	**888-885-7025**		529
Nebraska Plastics Inc			
PO Box 45 .... Cozad NE 69130	**800-445-2887**	308-784-2500	592
Nebraska Public Power District			
1414 15th St PO Box 499 .... Columbus NE 68602	**877-275-6773**	402-564-8561	245
Nebraska Realtors Assn			
800 S 13th St Ste 200 .... Lincoln NE 68508	**800-777-5231**	402-323-6500	652
Nebraska Repertory Theatre			
PO Box 880201 .... Lincoln NE 68588	**800-432-3231**	402-472-7211	569-4
Nebraska State Bar Assn			
635 S 14th St Ste 200 .... Lincoln NE 68501	**800-927-0117**	402-475-7091	72
Nebraska Wesleyan University			
5000 St Paul Ave .... Lincoln NE 68504	**800-541-3818**		166
NEC (Nueces Electric Co-op)			
14353 Cooperative Ave .... Corpus Christi TX 78380	**800-632-9288**	361-387-2581	245
NEC America Inc			
6555 N State Hwy 161 .... Irving TX 75039	**866-632-3226***	214-262-2000	730
*Cust Svc			
NEC Display Solutions of America Inc			
500 Pk Blvd Ste 1100 .... Itasca IL 60143	**800-632-4662***	630-467-3000	173-4
*Cust Svc			
NECA (National Electrical Contractors Assn)			
3 Bethesda Metro Ctr Ste 1100 .... Bethesda MD 20814	**800-214-0585**	301-657-3110	49-3
Necco			
178 Private Dr .... South Point OH 45680	**866-996-3226**	513-771-9600	761
Neci 334 Hecla St .... Lake Linden MI 49945	**888-648-7283**	906-296-1000	231
NED Corp			
31 Town Forest Rd .... Oxford MA 01540	**800-343-6086**		491
Nedco Electronics			
594 American Way .... Payson UT 84651	**800-605-2323**	801-465-1790	246
Needham & Co Inc			
445 Park Ave .... New York NY 10022	**800-903-3268**	212-371-8300	686
Neenah Foundry Co			
2121 Brooks Ave .... Neenah WI 54956	**800-558-5075**	920-725-7000	307
NEH (National Endowment for the Humanities)			
400 Seventh St SW .... Washington DC 20506	**800-634-1121**	202-606-8400	339-19
NEHA (National Environmental Health Assn)			
720 S Colorado Blvd Ste 1000-N .... Denver CO 80246	**866-956-2258**	303-756-9090	49-7
Nehring Electric Works Inc			
1005 E Locust St .... DeKalb IL 60115	**800-435-4481**	815-756-2741	809

	Toll-Free	Phone	Class
NEI Global Relocation Inc 2707 N 118th St ....Omaha NE 68164	800-533-7353	402-397-8486	392
Neighbors Federal Credit Union PO Box 2831 ....Baton Rouge LA 70821	866-819-2178	225-819-2178	219
NeighborWorks America 999 N Capitol St NE Ste 900........Washington DC 20002	800-438-5547	202-760-4000	48-10
Neil Enterprises Inc 450 E Bunker Ct ....Vernon Hills IL 60061	800-621-5584	847-549-7627	604
Neil Medical Group Inc 2545 Jetport Rd ....Kinston NC 28504	800-735-9111		238
Neiman Funds Management LLC 6631 Main St ....Williamsville NY 14221	877-385-2720		400
NELCO Inc 3 Gill St Unit D ....Woburn MA 01801	800-635-2613	781-933-1940	475
Nellie Mae Education Foundation 1250 Hancock St Ste 205N...........Quincy MA 02169	877-635-5436	781-348-4200	305
Nello Corp 1201 S Sheridan St PO Box 1960.....................South Bend IN 46619	800-806-3556	574-288-3632	478
Nelnet Inc PO Box 8256 ....Lincoln NE 68501 *NYSE: NNI*	888-486-4722		217
Nelrod Co 3109 Lubbock Ave ....Fort Worth TX 76109	866-448-0961	817-922-9000	196
Nelson & Kennard 2180 Harvard St Stc 160...........Sacramento CA 95815	866-920-2295	916-920-2295	427
Nelson County 210 B Ave W Ste 203 ....Lakota ND 58344	800-472-2286	701-247-2462	337
Nelson County 84 Courthouse Sq PO Box 336....Lovingston VA 22949	888-662-9400	434-263-7000	337
Nelson Electric Supply Co Inc 926 State St ....Racine WI 53404	800-806-3576	262-635-5050	246
Nelson Ink 330 Second St N ....Middle River MN 56737	800-644-9311	218-222-3831	195
Nelson Jit Packaging Supplies Inc 4022 W Turney Ave Ste 3 ....Phoenix AZ 85019	800-939-3647	623-939-3365	553
Nelson Mullins Riley & Scarborough LLP 1320 Main St 17th Fl ....Columbia SC 29201	800-237-2000	803-799-2000	427
Nelson Packaging Company Inc 1801 Reservoir Rd ....Lima OH 45804	888-229-3471	419-229-3471	88
Nelson Publishing 2500 Tamiami Trl N ....Nokomis FL 34275	800-226-6113	941-966-9521	633-9
Nelson Tree Service llc 3300 Ofc Park Dr ....Dayton OH 45439	800-522-4311	937-294-1313	771
Nelson Westerberg Inc 1500 Arthur Ave ....Elk Grove Village IL 60007	800-245-2080	847-437-2080	516
Nelson-Jameson Inc 2400 E Fifth St PO Box 647 ....Marshfield WI 54449	800-826-8302	715-387-1151	384
Neltner Billing & Consulting Services 6463 Taylor Mill Rd ....Independence KY 41051	888-635-8637		196
NEMA (National Electrical Manufacturers Assn) 1300 N 17th St Ste 1752 ....Rosslyn VA 22209	800-699-9277	703-841-3200	49-13
Nemacolin Woodlands Resort & Spa 1001 Lafayette Dr ....Farmington PA 15437	800-422-2736	724-329-7500	665
Nemaha County 607 Nemaha ....Seneca KS 66538	800-259-2829	785-336-2106	337
Nemco Food Equipment Ltd 301 Meuse Argonne ....Hicksville OH 43526	800-782-6761	419-542-7751	296
Nemetschek North America 7150 Riverwood Dr ....Columbia MD 21046	888-646-4223	410-290-5114	178-8
NEMRA (National Electrical Manufacturers Representatives) 28 Deer St Ste 302 ....Portsmouth NH 03801	800-446-3672	914-524-8650	49-18
Nemschoff Inc 909 N Eigth St ....Sheboygan WI 53081 *Cust Svc	800-203-8916*		319-3
Neo Corp 289 Silkwood Dr ....Canton NC 28716	800-822-1247		192
Neogard Div Jones-blair Co 2728 Empire Central St ....Dallas TX 75235	800-492-9400	214-353-1600	546
Neogen Corp 620 Lesher Pl ....Lansing MI 48912 *NASDAQ: NEOG*	800-234-5333	517-372-9200	231
Neopost Inc Canada 150 Steelcase Rd W ....Markham ON L3R3J9	800-636-7678		111
Neos Therapeutics 2940 N Hwy 360 Ste 400 ....Grand Prairie TX 75050	844-375-8324	972-408-1300	578
Neosho County Community College Ottawa 900 E Logan St ....Ottawa KS 66067	888-466-2588	785-242-2067	162
NEP Electronics Inc 805 Mittel Dr ....Wood Dale IL 60191	800-284-7470	630-595-8500	246
Nephron Pharmaceuticals Corp 4500 12th St Ext ....West Columbia SC 29172	800-443-4313	803-569-2800	579
Neptco Inc 30 Hamlet St ....Pawtucket RI 02861	800-354-5445	401-722-5500	727
Neptune Chemical Pump Co 22069 Van Buren St ....Grand Terrace CA 92313	800-255-4017	215-699-8700	637
Neptune-Benson Inc 6 Jefferson Dr ....Coventry RI 02816	800-832-8002	401-821-2200	637
NERA (Naval Enlisted Reserve Assn) 6703 Farragut Ave ....Falls Church VA 22042	800-776-9020		48-19
Nerd Force Inc 26500 W Agoura Rd ....Calabasas CA 91302	800-979-6373		
NERSC (National Energy Research Scientific Computing Ctr) Lawrence Berkeley National Laboratory ....Berkeley CA 94720	800-666-3772	510-486-5849	664
NES Health 39 Main St ....Tiburon CA 94920	800-394-6376		
NESC Staffing Corp 150 Mirona Rd ....Portsmouth NH 03801	800-562-3463		717
Nesco/American Harvest 1700 Monroe St PO Box 237 ....Two Rivers WI 54241 *Cust Svc	800-288-4545*	920-793-1368	37
NESDA (National Electronics Service Dealers Assn) 3608 Pershing Ave ....Fort Worth TX 76107	800-946-0201	817-921-9061	49-18
NestFamily 1461 S Beltline Rd Ste 500...........Coppell TX 75019	800-634-4298	972-402-7100	33
Nestle Purina PetCare Co 801 Chouteau Ave ....Saint Louis MO 63102	800-778-7462	314-982-1000	574
NET (Nebraska Educational Telecommunications) 1800 N 33rd St ....Lincoln NE 68503	800-868-1868		628
Net Access Corp 2300 15th St Ste 300 ....Denver CO 80202	800-638-6336	973-590-5000	731
NET Radio 1800 N 33rd St ....Lincoln NE 68503	800-868-1868		736-41
Net2Phone Inc 520 Broad St ....Newark NJ 07102	800-386-6438	866-978-8260	731
Neta Scientific Inc 4206 Sylon Blvd ....Hainesport NJ 08036	800-343-6015	609-265-8210	473
Netcellent System Inc 4030 Valley Blvd ....Walnut CA 91789	888-595-3818	909-598-9019	177
Netcracker Technology Corp 95 Sawyer Rd University Ofc Pk III ....Waltham MA 02453	800-477-5785	781-419-3300	461
Netessentials Inc 705 Eighth St Ste 1000........Wichita Falls TX 76301	877-899-6387	940-767-6387	
Netfast Communications Inc 989 Ave of the Americas 4th Fl........New York NY 10018	888-678-6383	212-792-5200	224
NetFlix Inc 100 Winchester Cir ....Los Gatos CA 95032 *NASDAQ: NFLX*	866-579-7293	408-540-3700	792
Netfronts Web Hosting 459 N 300 W Ste 16 ....Kaysville UT 84037	800-675-4622	801-497-0878	395
Netgain Information Systems Co 128 W Columbus Ave ....Bellefontaine OH 43311	855-651-7001	937-593-7177	180
Netgain Networks Inc 8378 Attica Dr ....Riverside CA 92508	855-667-2364	951-656-0194	179
NetGain Technology LLC 720 W St Germain St ....Saint Cloud MN 56301	877-797-4700		
Netherland Rubber Co 2931 Exon Ave ....Cincinnati OH 45241	800-582-1877		326
Netherlands *Embassy* 4200 Linnean Ave NW ....Washington DC 20008	877-388-2443		257
NetIQ Corp 1233 W Loop S ....Houston TX 77027 *Sales	888-323-6768*	713-548-1700	178-12
NETL (National Energy Technology Laboratory) 3610 Collins Ferry Rd ....Morgantown WV 26505	800-432-8330	304-285-4764	664
Netlink Software Group America Inc 999 Tech Row ....Madison Heights MI 48071	800-485-4482		190
Netmarkcom 3135 E 17th St Ste B...............Ammon ID 83406	800-935-5133	208-522-1016	195
NetMotion Inc 701 N 34th St Ste 250 ....Seattle WA 98103	877-818-7626	206-691-5500	178-1
NetNation Communications Inc 550 Burrard St Ste 200.........Vancouver BC V6C2B5	888-277-0000	604-688-8946	803
Netorian LLC 210 Research Blvd Ste 160..........Aberdeen MD 21001	844-638-6742		
Netplanner Systems Inc 3145 Northwoods Pkwy Ste 800........Norcross GA 30071	800-795-1975	770-662-5482	176
Netrition Inc 25 Corporate Cir Ste 118 ....Albany NY 12203	888-817-2411	518-464-0765	354
NetScout Systems Inc 310 Littleton Rd ....Westford MA 01886 *NASDAQ: NTCT*	800-357-7666	978-614-4000	178-7
Netsertive Inc 2400 Perimeter Park Dr Ste 100......Research Triangle Region NC 27560	800-940-4351		195
Netsmart Technologies Inc 3500 Sunrise Hwy Ste D-122.........Great River NY 11739	800-421-7503	631-968-2000	178-11
Netspeed Learning Solutions 6245 36th Ave NE ....Seattle WA 98115	877-517-5271	206-517-5271	194
Netsville Inc 72 Cascade Dr ....Rochester NY 14614	888-638-7845	585-232-5670	189-4
Net-Temps Inc 55 Middlesex St Ste 220............North Chelmsford MA 01863	800-307-0062	978-251-7272	260
Netwolves Corp 4710 Eisenhower Blvd Ste E-8 ....Tampa FL 33634	855-638-9658		
Network Appliance Inc 495 E Java Dr ....Sunnyvale CA 94089 *NASDAQ: NTAP* ◼ *Sales	800-443-4537*	408-822-6000	176
Network Data Security Experts Inc (NDSE) 521 Branchway Rd ......North Chesterfield VA 23236	877-440-6373		
Network Dynamics Inc 700 Brooker Creek Blvd Ste 1000........Oldsmar FL 34677	877-818-8597	813-818-8597	176
Network Earth Inc 2501 Alida St ....Oakland CA 94602	888-201-5160		224
Network Global Logistics (NGL) 320 Interlocken Pkwy Ste 100.......Broomfield CO 80021	866-938-1870		542
Network Innovations Inc 4424 Manilla Rd SE ....Calgary AB T2G4B7	888-466-2772	403-287-5000	194
Network Medical Management Inc 1668 S Garfield Ave 2nd Fl..........Alhambra CA 91801	877-282-8272	626-282-0288	
Network Performance Inc 85 Green Mtn Dr ....South Burlington VT 05403	800-639-6091	802-859-0808	180
Network Solutions LLC 13861 Sunrise Valley Dr Ste 300 ....Herndon VA 20171	800-361-5712	703-668-4600	395
NetworkOmni 4353 Park Ter Dr ....Westlake Village CA 91361	800-543-4244	818-706-7890	
Networks of Florida 25 W Avery St ....Pensacola FL 32501	800-368-2315	850-434-8600	180
Networld Inc 300 Lanidex Plz Ste 1 ....Parsippany NJ 07054	800-992-3411	973-884-7474	755
Networld Media Group LLC 13100 Eastpoint Park Blvd Ste 100.......................Louisville KY 40223	877-441-7545	502-241-7545	392
NetXperts Inc 1777 Botelho Dr Ste 102 ....Walnut Creek CA 94596	888-271-9367	925-806-0800	180
NetZero Inc 21301 Burbank Blvd ....Woodland Hills CA 91367	800-638-9376	818-287-3000	397
Neuberger Berman Funds PO Box 8403 ....Boston MA 02266	800-877-9700	212-476-8800	524
Neuberger Berman LLC 605 Third Ave ....New York NY 10158	800-223-6448		400
Neudesic LLC 8105 Irvine Ctr Dr ....Irvine CA 92618	800-805-1805	949-754-4500	177

Name / Address	City	State	Zip	Toll-Free	Phone	Class
Neumann College						
1 Neumann Dr	Aston	PA	19014	**800-963-8626**	610-459-0905	166
Neumayer Equipment Company Inc						
5060 Arsenal St	Saint Louis	MO	63139	**800-843-4563**	314-772-4501	385
NeuroMetrix						
62 Fourth Ave	Waltham	MA	02451	**888-786-7287**	781-890-9989	250
NASDAQ: NURO						
Neuromonics Inc						
PO Box 351886	Westminster	CO	80035	**866-606-3876**		250
NeuroPace Inc						
455 N Bernardo Ave	Mountain View	CA	94043	**866-726-3876**		
Neuroscience Curriculum						
115 Mason Farm Rd						
Campus Box 7250	Chapel Hill	NC	27599	**800-862-4938**	919-843-8536	664
NeuroScience Inc						
373 280th St	Osceola	WI	54020	**888-342-7272**	715-294-2144	417
Neuro-Tec Inc						
975 Cobb Pl Blvd Ste 301	Kennesaw	GA	30144	**800-554-3407**		473
NeuStar Inc						
21575 Ridgetop Cir	Sterling	VA	20166	**855-638-2677**	571-434-5400	47
Neutral Posture Inc						
3904 N Texas Ave	Bryan	TX	77803	**800-446-3746**	979-778-0502	319-1
Neutrogena Corp						
5760 W 96th St	Los Angeles	CA	90045	**800-582-4048**	310-642-1150	214
Nevada						
Bill Status						
401 S Carson St	Carson City	NV	89701	**800-978-2878**	775-684-6827	432
Child Support Enforcement Office						
300 E Second St Ste 1200	Reno	NV	89501	**800-992-0900**	775-448-5150	338-29
Economic Development Commission						
808 W Nye Ln	Carson City	NV	89703	**800-336-1600**	775-687-9900	338-29
Motor Vehicles Dept						
555 Wright Way	Carson City	NV	89711	**877-368-7828**	775-684-4368	338-29
Tourism Commission						
401 N Carson St	Carson City	NV	89701	**800-638-2328**		338-29
Nevada Assn of Realtors						
760 Margrave Dr Ste 200	Reno	NV	89502	**800-748-5526**	775-829-5911	652
Nevada Dental Assn						
8863 W Flamingo Rd Ste 102	Las Vegas	NV	89147	**800-962-6710**	702-255-4211	227
Nevada Disability Advocacy & Law Center						
2820 W Charleston Blvd Ste 11	Las Vegas	NV	89102	**888-349-3843**	702-257-8150	
Nevada Donor Network Inc						
2055 E Sahara Ave	Las Vegas	NV	89104	**855-683-6667**	702-796-9600	541
Nevada Magazine						
401 N Carson St	Carson City	NV	89701	**855-729-7117**	775-687-5416	455-22
Nevada Power Co						
6226 W Sahara Ave	Las Vegas	NV	89146	**800-331-3103***	702-402-5555	782
NYSE: NVE ■ *Cust Svc						
Nevada State Bank						
PO Box 990	Las Vegas	NV	89125	**800-727-4743**	702-383-0009	70
Nevada State Library & Archives (NSLA)						
100 N Stewart St	Carson City	NV	89701	**800-922-2880**	775-684-3360	433-5
Nevers Industries Inc						
14125 21st Ave N	Minneapolis	MN	55447	**800-258-5591**	763-210-4206	320
Neville Chemical Co						
2800 Neville Rd	Pittsburgh	PA	15225	**877-704-4200***	412-331-4200	601-2
*Cust Svc						
Neville Public Museum of Brown County						
210 Museum Pl	Green Bay	WI	54303	**800-895-0071**	920-448-4460	517
New Balance Athletic Shoe Inc						
20 Guest St Brighton Landing	Brighton	MA	02135	**800-595-9138**	617-783-4000	301
New Bedford Whaling Museum						
18 Johnny Cake Hill	New Bedford	MA	02740	**800-453-5040**	508-997-0046	517
New Benefits Ltd						
14240 Proton Rd	Dallas	TX	75244	**800-800-8304**	972-404-8192	194
New Braunfels Public Library						
700 E Common St	New Braunfels	TX	78130	**800-434-8013**	830-221-4300	433-3
New Brunswick Museum						
1 Market Sq	Saint John	NB	E2L4Z6	**888-268-9595**	506-643-2300	517
New Castle County Detention Ctr						
963 Centre Rd	Wilmington	DE	19805	**800-969-4357**	302-633-3100	411
New Castle County Library						
750 Library Ave	Newark	DE	19711	**877-225-7351**	302-731-7550	433-3
New Castle Public Library						
424 Delaware St	New Castle	DE	19720	**877-225-7351**	302-328-1995	433-3
New Century Press Inc						
310 First Ave	Rock Rapids	IA	51246	**800-621-0801**	712-472-2525	528-3
New Choices Inc						
2501 18th St Ste 201	Bettendorf	IA	52722	**888-355-5502**	563-355-5502	362
NEW Co-op Inc						
2626 First Ave S	Fort Dodge	IA	50501	**800-362-2233**	515-955-2040	275
New Dimensions Research Corp						
260 Spagnoli Rd	Melville	NY	11747	**800-637-8870**	631-694-1356	233
New Directions Behavioral Health LLC						
PO Box 6729	Leawood	KS	66206	**800-624-5544**		460
New Edge Networks						
3000 Columbia House Blvd						
Ste 106	Vancouver	WA	98661	**877-725-3343**	360-693-9009	397
New England Airlines Inc						
56 Airport Rd	Westerly	RI	02891	**800-243-2460**	401-596-2460	25
New England Baptist Hospital						
125 Parker Hill Ave	Boston	MA	02120	**855-370-6324**	617-754-5000	373-3
New England Coffee Co						
100 Charles St	Malden	MA	02148	**800-225-3537**		296-7
New England College						
98 Bridge St	Henniker	NH	03242	**800-521-7642***	603-428-2223	166
*Admissions						
New England Computer Services Inc						
322 E Main St 3rd Fl	Branford	CT	06405	**800-766-6327***	475-221-8200	178-10
*Sales						
New England Conservatory						
290 Huntington Ave	Boston	MA	02115	**800-841-8371**	617-585-1100	166
New England Culinary Institute						
56 College St	Montpelier	VT	05602	**877-223-6324**	802-223-6324	163
New England Donor Services						
60 First Ave	Waltham	MA	02451	**800-446-6362**		541
New England Federal Credit Union						
PO Box 527	Williston	VT	05495	**800-400-8790**	802-879-8790	219

Name / Address	City	State	Zip	Toll-Free	Phone	Class
New England Garage Door						
15 Campanelli Cir	Canton	MA	02021	**800-676-7734**	781-821-2737	497
New England Homes						
270 Ocean Rd	Greenland	NH	03840	**800-800-8831**	603-436-8830	106
New England Institute of Technology						
2500 Post Rd	Warwick	RI	02886	**800-736-7744**	401-467-7744	795
New England Journal of Medicine						
10 Shattuck St	Boston	MA	02115	**800-843-6356**	617-734-9800	455-16
New England Life Flight Inc						
Robins St Hangar 1727 Hanscom Air Force Base						
	Bedford	MA	01730	**800-233-8998**	781-863-2213	13
New England Natural Bakers						
74 Fairview St E	Greenfield	MA	01301	**800-910-2884**	413-772-2239	296-4
New England Revolution						
Gillette Stadium 1 Patriot Pl	Foxboro	MA	02035	**877-438-7387**		713
New England School of Photography						
537 Commonwealth Ave	Boston	MA	02215	**800-676-3767**	617-437-1868	586
New England Wood Pellet LLC						
141 Old Sharon Rd	Jaffrey	NH	03452	**877-981-9663**		814
New Enterprise Rural Electric Co-op Inc						
3596 Brumbaugh Rd	New Enterprise	PA	16664	**800-270-3177**	814-766-3221	245
New Fairfield Free Public Library						
2 Brush Hill Rd	New Fairfield	CT	06812	**877-227-7487**	203-312-5679	433-3
New Generation Research Inc						
225 Friend St Ste 801	Boston	MA	02114	**800-468-3810**	617-573-9550	633-2
New Germany State Park						
349 Headquarters Ln	Grantsville	MD	21536	**800-830-3974**	301-895-5453	561
New Hampshire						
Banking Dept						
95 Pleasant St	Concord	NH	03301	**800-437-5991**	603-271-3561	338-30
Child Support Services						
129 Pleasant St	Concord	NH	03301	**800-852-3345**	603-271-4427	338-30
Employment Security						
32 S Main St	Concord	NH	03301	**800-852-3400**	603-224-3311	259
Environmental Services Dept						
29 Hazen Dr PO Box 95	Concord	NH	03301	**866-429-9278**	603-271-3503	338-30
Governor						
State House 107 N Main St	Concord	NH	03301	**800-852-3456**	603-271-2121	338-30
Housing Finance Authority						
32 Constitution Dr	Bedford	NH	03110	**800-439-7247**	603-472-8623	338-30
Lottery Commission						
14 Integra Dr	Concord	NH	03301	**800-852-3324**	603-271-3391	450
Public Utilities Commission						
21 S Fruit St Ste 10	Concord	NH	03301	**800-852-3793***	603-271-2431	338-30
*Consumer Assistance						
Teacher Credentialing Bureau						
101 Pleasant St	Concord	NH	03301	**866-444-4211**	603-271-3494	338-30
Treasury Dept						
25 Capitol St Rm 121	Concord	NH	03301	**800-791-0920**	603-271-2621	338-30
Victims' Assistance Commission						
33 Capitol St	Concord	NH	03301	**800-300-4500**	603-271-1284	338-30
Vocational Rehabilitation Office						
21 S Fruit St Ste 20	Concord	NH	03301	**800-299-1647**	603-271-3471	338-30
New Hampshire Catholic Charities Inc						
215 Myrtle St	Manchester	NH	03104	**800-562-5249**	603-669-3030	48-20
New Hampshire Dental Society						
23 S State St	Concord	NH	03301	**800-244-5961**	603-225-5961	227
New Hampshire Distributors Inc						
65 Regional Dr	Concord	NH	03301	**800-519-9770**	603-224-9991	81-1
New Hampshire Div of Travel & Tourism Development						
172 Pembroke Rd PO Box 1856	Concord	NH	03302	**800-262-6660**	603-271-2665	206
New Hampshire Educator Magazine						
9 S Spring St	Concord	NH	03301	**866-556-3264**	603-224-7751	455-8
New Hampshire Electric Co-op						
579 Tenney Mtn Hwy	Plymouth	NH	03264	**800-698-2007**	603-536-1800	245
New Hampshire Hospital						
36 Clinton St	Concord	NH	03301	**800-735-2964**	603-271-5200	373-5
New Hampshire Institute of Art						
148 Concord St	Manchester	NH	03104	**866-241-4918**	603-623-0313	517
New Hampshire Medical Society						
7 N State St	Concord	NH	03301	**800-564-1909**		472
New Hampshire Music Festival Orchestra						
42 Main St	Plymouth	NH	03264	**800-662-2739**	603-238-9007	569-3
New Hampshire Plastics Inc						
1 Bouchard St	Manchester	NH	03103	**800-258-3036**	603-669-8523	596
New Hampshire Public Television (NHPTV)						
268 Mast Rd	Durham	NH	03824	**800-639-8408**	603-868-1100	628
New Hampshire State Library						
20 Park St	Concord	NH	03301	**800-639-5290**	603-271-2144	433-5
New Hanover Regional Medical Ctr						
2131 S 17th St	Wilmington	NC	28401	**877-228-8135**	910-343-7000	373-3
New Haven Hotel						
229 George St	New Haven	CT	06510	**800-644-6835**	203-498-3100	378
New Haven Register						
40 Sargent Dr	New Haven	CT	06511	**888-969-0949**	203-789-5200	528-2
New Holland Church Furniture						
313 Prospect St PO Box 217	New Holland	PA	17557	**800-648-9663**		319-3
New Holland Engineering						
43 E Front St	New Holland	OH	43145	**800-734-8155**	740-495-5200	261
New Horizon Kids Quest Inc						
3405 Annapolis Ln N Ste 100	Plymouth	MN	55447	**800-941-1007**		148
New Horizons Computer Learning Centers Inc						
1900 S State College Blvd						
Ste 450	Anaheim	CA	92806	**888-236-3625**	714-940-8000	759
New Horizons RV Corp						
2401 Lacy Dr	Junction City	KS	66441	**800-235-3140**	785-238-7575	120
New Horizons Worldwide Inc						
1900 S State College Blvd						
Ste 450	Anaheim	CA	92806	**888-236-3625**		759
New ICM						
220 Sam Bishkin	El Campo	TX	77437	**800-987-9008**	979-578-0543	155-4
New Jersey						
Banking & Insurance Dept						
20 W State St PO Box 325	Trenton	NJ	08625	**800-446-7467**	609-292-7272	338-31
Bill Status						
State House Annex PO Box 068	Trenton	NJ	08625	**800-792-8630**	609-292-4840	432
Board of Public Utilities						
44 S Clinton Ave	Newark	NJ	07102	**800-624-0241**		338-31

				Toll-Free	Phone	Class
Child Support Office						
175 S Broad St PO Box 8068	Trenton	NJ	08650	**877-655-4371**		338-31
Consumer Affairs Div						
124 Halsey St	Newark	NJ	07102	**800-242-5846**	973-504-6200	338-31
Education Dept						
PO Box 500	Trenton	NJ	08625	**877-900-6960**	609-376-3500	338-31
Ethical Standards Commission						
28 W State St 8th Fl PO Box 082	Trenton	NJ	08625	**888-223-1355**	609-292-1892	265
Higher Education Student Assistance Authority						
4 Quakerbridge Plz PO Box 540	Trenton	NJ	08625	**800-792-8670**	609-584-4480	721
Mental Health Services Div						
PO Box 272	Trenton	NJ	08625	**800-382-6717**	609-777-0700	338-31
Military & Veterans' Affairs Dept						
101 Eggert Crossing Rd	Lawrenceville	NJ	08648	**800-624-0508**	609-530-4600	338-31
Parks & Forestry Div						
PO Box 404	Trenton	NJ	08625	**800-843-6420**	609-984-0370	338-31
Securities Bureau						
153 Halsey St 6th Fl	Newark	NJ	07102	**866-446-8378**	973-504-3600	338-31
Travel & Tourism Div						
225 W State St PO Box 460	Trenton	NJ	08625	**800-847-4865**	609-599-6540	338-31
Victims of Crime Compensation Board						
50 Pk Pl	Newark	NJ	07102	**877-658-2221**	973-648-2107	338-31
New Jersey Business Forms Manufacturing Co						
55 W Sheffield Ave	Englewood	NJ	07631	**800-466-6523**	201-569-4500	110
New Jersey City University						
2039 JFK Blvd	Jersey City	NJ	07305	**888-441-6528**	201-200-2000	166
New Jersey Herald						
2 Spring St	Newton	NJ	07860	**800-424-3725**	973-383-1500	528-2
New Jersey Legal Copy Inc						
501 King Ave	Cherry Hill	NJ	08002	**800-426-7965**	856-910-0202	113
New Jersey Machine Inc						
56 Etna Rd	Lebanon	NH	03766	**800-432-2990***	603-448-0300	543
*Sales						
New Jersey Medical Society						
2 Princess Rd	Lawrenceville	NJ	08648	**800-706-7893**	609-896-1766	472
New Jersey Monthly Magazine						
55 Pk Pl PO Box 920	Morristown	NJ	07963	**888-419-0419**	973-539-8230	455-22
New Jersey Nets						
390 Murray Hill Pkwy	East Rutherford	NJ	07073	**800-346-6387**	201-935-8888	710-1
New Jersey Performing Arts Ctr						
1 Ctr St	Newark	NJ	07102	**888-466-5722**	973-642-8989	568
New Jersey State Nurses Assn (NJSNA)						
1479 Pennington Rd	Trenton	NJ	08618	**800-662-0108**	609-883-5335	529
New Leaf Publishing Group						
PO Box 726	Green Forest	AR	72638	**800-999-3777**	870-438-5288	633-3
New Life Industries Inc						
140 Chappells Dairy Rd	Somerset	KY	42503	**800-443-9523**	606-679-3616	683
New Method Steel Stamps Inc						
31313 Kendall Ave	Fraser	MI	48026	**800-582-0199**	586-293-0200	465
New Mexico						
Aging Agency						
2550 Cerrillos Rd PO Box 27118	Santa Fe	NM	87505	**800-432-2080**	505-476-4799	338-32
Arts Div						
407 Galisteo St Ste 270	Santa Fe	NM	87501	**800-879-4278**	505-827-6490	338-32
Child Support Enforcement Div						
PO Box 25110	Santa Fe	NM	87504	**800-288-7207**	505-476-7207	338-32
Children Youth & Families Dept						
PO Box 5160	Santa Fe	NM	87502	**800-610-7610**	800-432-2075	338-32
Consumer Protection Div						
408 Galisteo St Villagra Bldg						
PO Box 1508	Santa Fe	NM	87501	**844-255-9210**	505-827-6000	338-32
Crime Victims Reparation Commission						
6200 Uptown Blvd Ste 210	Albuquerque	NM	87110	**800-306-6262**	505-841-9432	338-32
Economic Development Dept						
PO Box 20003	Santa Fe	NM	87504	**800-374-3061**	505-827-0300	338-32
Environment Dept						
1190 St Francis Dr Ste N4050	Santa Fe	NM	87505	**800-219-6157**	505-827-2855	338-32
Ethics Administration						
325 Don Gaspar St Ste 300	Santa Fe	NM	87501	**800-477-3632**	505-827-3600	265
Higher Education Dept						
2048 Galisteo St	Santa Fe	NM	87505	**800-279-9777**	505-476-8400	338-32
Highway & Transportation Dept (NMDOT)						
1120 Cerrillos Rd PO Box 1149	Santa Fe	NM	87504	**800-432-4269***	505-827-5100	338-32
*General						
Human Services Dept (NMHSD)						
PO Box 2348	Santa Fe	NM	87504	**888-997-2583**	505-827-3100	338-32
Lottery						
4511 Osuna Rd NE	Albuquerque	NM	87109	**800-572-1142**	505-342-7600	450
Mortgage Finance Authority						
344 Fourth St SW	Albuquerque	NM	87102	**800-444-6880**	505-843-6880	338-32
Secretary of State						
325 Don Gaspar Ste 300	Santa Fe	NM	87503	**800-477-3632**	505-827-3600	338-32
State Parks Division						
1220 S St Francis Dr	Santa Fe	NM	87505	**888-667-2757**	505-476-3355	338-32
Vital Records & Health Statistics Bureau						
1105 S St Francis Dr	Santa Fe	NM	87502	**866-534-0051**	505-827-0121	338-32
Vocational Rehabilitation Div						
435 St Michaels Dr Bldg D	Santa Fe	NM	87505	**800-224-7005**	505-954-8500	338-32
Workers' Compensation Admin						
2410 Ctr Ave SE						
PO Box 27198	Albuquerque	NM	87125	**800-255-7965**	505-841-6000	338-32
New Mexico Behavioral Health Institute						
3695 Hot Springs Blvd	Las Vegas	NM	87701	**800-446-5970**	505-454-2100	373-5
New Mexico Dental Assn						
9201 Montgomery Blvd NE						
Ste 601	Albuquerque	NM	87111	**888-787-1722**	505-294-1368	227
New Mexico Educational Retirement Board						
701 Camino de Los Marquez						
PO Box 26129	Santa Fe	NM	87502	**866-691-2345**	505-827-8030	524
New Mexico Highlands University						
PO Box 9000	Las Vegas	NM	87701	**877-850-9064**	505-425-7511	166
New Mexico Institute of Mining & Technology (NMT)						
801 Leroy Pl	Socorro	NM	87801	**800-428-8324***	505-835-5434	166
*Admissions						
New Mexico Junior College						
1 Thunderbird Cir	Hobbs	NM	88240	**800-657-6260**	505-392-4510	162
New Mexico Legal Aid Inc						
301 Gold Ave SW	Albuquerque	NM	87102	**866-416-1922**	505-243-7871	
New Mexico Lions Eye Bank						
2501 Yale Blvd SE Ste 100	Albuquerque	NM	87106	**888-616-3937**	505-266-3937	269
New Mexico Magazine						
PO Box 12002	Santa Fe	NM	87504	**800-898-6639**		455-22
New Mexico Medical Society (NMMS)						
316 Osuna Rd NE Ste 501	Albuquerque	NM	87107	**800-748-1596**	505-828-0237	472
New Mexico Museum of Art						
107 W Palace Ave	Santa Fe	NM	87501	**877-567-7380**	505-476-5072	517
New Mexico Museum of Space History						
Top of Hwy 2001	Alamogordo	NM	88311	**877-333-6589**	575-437-2840	517
New Mexico Mutual						
PO Box 27825	Albuquerque	NM	87125	**800-788-8851**	505-345-7260	390-4
New Mexico State University (NMSU)						
MSC-3A PO Box 30001	Las Cruces	NM	88003	**800-662-6678***	575-646-3121	166
*Admissions						
Carlsbad						
1500 University Dr	Carlsbad	NM	88220	**888-888-2199**	575-234-9200	162
New Mexico State Veterans Ctr						
992 S Broadway St						
	Truth or Consequences	NM	87901	**800-964-3976**	575-894-4200	788
New Milford Block & Supply						
574 Danbury Rd	New Milford	CT	06776	**800-724-1888**	860-355-1101	183
New Moon Magazine						
PO Box 161287	Duluth	MN	55816	**800-381-4743**	218-878-9673	455-6
New Objective Inc						
2 Constitution Way	Woburn	MA	01801	**888-220-2998**	781-933-9560	418
New Orleans Baptist Theological Seminary						
3939 Gentilly Blvd	New Orleans	LA	70126	**800-662-8701**	504-282-4455	167-3
New Orleans City Hall						
1300 Perdido St	New Orleans	LA	70112	**800-256-2748**	504-658-4000	336
New Orleans Firemens Federal Credit Union						
PO Box 689	Metairie	LA	70004	**800-647-1689**	504-889-9090	219
New Orleans Jazz National Historical Park						
419 Decatur St	New Orleans	LA	70130	**877-520-0677**	504-589-4806	560
New Orleans Magazine						
110 Veterans Blvd Ste 123	Metairie	LA	70005	**877-221-3512***	504-828-1380	455-22
*Edit						
New Orleans Metropolitan Convention & Visitors Bureau						
2020 St Charles Ave	New Orleans	LA	70130	**800-672-6124**		206
New Otani Kaimana Beach Hotel						
2863 Kalakaua Ave	Honolulu	HI	96815	**800-356-8264**	808-923-1555	378
New Penn Motor Express Inc						
625 S Fifth Ave	Lebanon	PA	17042	**800-285-5000***	717-274-2521	775
*Cust Svc						
New Pig Corp						
1 Pork Ave	Tipton	PA	16684	**800-468-4647**	814-684-0101	151
NEW Plastics Corp						
112 Fourth St	Luxemburg	WI	54217	**800-666-5207**	920-845-2326	98
New Process Steel Corp						
1322 N Post Oak	Houston	TX	77055	**800-392-4989**	713-686-9631	490
New Pros Data Inc						
155 Hidden Ravines Dr	Powell	OH	43065	**800-837-5478**	740-201-0410	386
New Readers Press						
101 Wyoming St	Syracuse	NY	13204	**800-448-8878**		633-2
New Republic, The						
1620 L St NW Ste 300C	Washington	DC	20036	**800-827-1289**	202-508-4444	455-17
New River Community College						
5251 College Dr	Dublin	VA	24084	**866-462-6722**	540-674-3600	162
New Riverside Ochre Co						
75 Old River Rd SE	Cartersville	GA	30120	**800-248-0176***	770-382-4568	501-1
*Orders						
New Seabury Resort						
20 Red Brook Rd	Mashpee	MA	02649	**877-687-3228**	508-539-8200	665
New Tech Network						
1250 Main St Ste 100	Napa	CA	94559	**800-856-7038**	707-253-6951	138
New Ulm Telecom Inc						
27 N Minnesota St	New Ulm	MN	56073	**888-873-6853**	507-354-4111	731
OTC: NULM						
New Vitality						
260 Smith St	Farmingdale	NY	11735	**888-997-2941**	888-271-7599	786
New Washington State Bank						
402 E Main St PO Box 10	New Washington	IN	47162	**800-883-0131**	812-293-3321	70
New Wave Enviro Products Inc						
6595 S Dayton St	Greenwood Village	CO	80111	**800-592-8371**		
New Wave Travel						
1075 Bay St	Toronto	ON	M5S2B1	**800-463-1512**	416-928-3113	767
New World Library						
14 Pamaron Way	Novato	CA	94949	**800-972-6657**	415-884-2100	633-3
New World Symphony						
500 17th St	Miami Beach	FL	33139	**800-597-3331**	305-673-3330	569-3
New York						
Aging Office						
2 Empire State Plz	Albany	NY	12223	**800-342-9871**		338-33
Athletic Commission						
123 William St 20th Fl	New York	NY	10038	**866-269-3769**	212-417-5700	708
Banking Dept						
1 State St	New York	NY	10004	**877-226-5697**	800-342-3736	338-33
Bill Status						
202 Legislative Office Bldg	Albany	NY	12248	**800-342-9860**	518-455-4218	432
Court of Appeals						
20 Eagle St	Albany	NY	12207	**800-268-7869**		
Department of Environmental Conservation						
625 Broadway	Albany	NY	12233	**800-678-6399**	518-408-5850	338-33
Division of Consumer Protection						
5 Empire State Plz Ste 2101	Albany	NY	12223	**800-697-1220**	518-474-8583	338-33
Empire State Development						
30 S Pearl St 7th Fl	Albany	NY	12245	**800-782-8369**	518-292-5100	338-33
Health Dept						
Empire State Plz Corning Tower	Albany	NY	12237	**866-881-2809**		338-33
Higher Education Services Corp						
99 Washington Ave	Albany	NY	12255	**888-697-4372**	518-473-1574	721
Housing Finance Agency						
641 Lexington Ave	New York	NY	10022	**866-275-3427**	212-688-4000	338-33
Labor Dept						
WA Harriman Campus Bldg 12	Albany	NY	12240	**888-469-7365**	518-457-9000	259
Mental Health Office						
44 Holland Ave	Albany	NY	12229	**800-597-8481**		338-33
Office of Court Admin						
4 ESP Ste 2001 Empire State Plz	Albany	NY	12223	**800-430-8457**	212-428-2100	338-33

Listing	City	State	Zip	Toll-Free	Phone	Class
Office of the Professions						
89 Washington Ave	Albany	NY	12234	**800-442-8106**	518-474-3817	338-33
Recreation and Historic Preservation						
625 Broadway	Albany	NY	12207	**800-456-2267**	518-474-0456	338-33
Temporary & Disability Assistance Office						
40 N Pearl St 16th Fl	Albany	NY	12243	**800-342-3009**	518-473-1090	338-33
Vital Records Office						
800 N Pearl St	Menands	NY	12204	**800-541-2831**		338-33
Workers' Compensation Board						
PO Box 5205	Binghamton	NY	13902	**877-632-4996**	518-402-6070	338-33
New York & Co						
330 W 34th St	New York	NY	10001	**800-961-9906**		157-6
New York Academy of Sciences						
250 Greenwich St 40th Fl	New York	NY	10007	**800-843-6927**	212-298-8600	49-19
New York Air Brake Co						
748 Starbuck Ave	Watertown	NY	13601	**888-836-6922**	315-786-5200	646
New York Banker						
99 Park Ave 4th Fl	New York	NY	10016	**800-346-3860**	212-297-1600	527-1
New York Barbells						
160 Home St	Elmira	NY	14904	**800-446-1833**		267
New York Blood Ctr						
310 E 67th St	New York	NY	10065	**800-688-0900**	646-456-4281	89
New York Blower Co						
7660 Quincy St	Willowbrook	IL	60527	**800-208-7918**	630-794-5700	18
New York Business Development Corp (NYBDC)						
50 Beaver St Ste 500	Albany	NY	12207	**800-923-2504**	518-463-2268	216
New York Central Mutual Fire Insurance Co (NYCM)						
1899 Central Plz E	Edmeston	NY	13335	**800-234-6926**		390-4
New York City Children's Ctr-Queens Campus (NYCCC)						
74-03 Commonwealth Blvd	Bellerose	NY	11426	**800-597-8481**	718-264-4500	373-1
New York City College of Technology						
300 Jay St	Brooklyn	NY	11201	**855-492-3633**	718-260-5000	166
New York Correctional Industries						
550 Broadway	Albany	NY	12204	**800-436-6321**	518-436-6321	626
New York County Lawyers Association						
14 Vesey St	New York	NY	10007	**800-255-0569**	212-267-6646	529
New York Daily News						
450 W 33rd St	New York	NY	10001	**800-692-6397**	646-473-0100	528-2
New York Eye & Ear Infirmary						
310 E 14th St	New York	NY	10003	**800-522-4582**	212-979-4000	373-7
New York Graphic Society Ltd						
129 Glover Ave	Norwalk	CT	06850	**800-221-1032**	203-661-2400	633-10
New York Institute of Technology						
New York Institute of Technology Northern Blvd						
PO Box 8000	Old Westbury	NY	11568	**800-345-6948**	516-686-1000	166
Manhattan						
1855 Broadway	New York	NY	10023	**800-345-6948**	212-261-1500	166
New York Islanders						
1535 Old Country Rd	Plainview	NY	11803	**800-843-5678**	516-501-6700	712
New York Law Journal						
120 Broadway 5th Fl	New York	NY	10271	**877-256-2472**		455-15
New York Library Assn (NYLA)						
6021 State Farm Rd	Guilderland	NY	12084	**800-252-6952***	518-432-6952	434
*General						
New York Life Insurance & Annuity Corp						
51 Madison Ave	New York	NY	10010	**800-598-2019**	212-576-7000	390-2
New York Magazine						
75 Varick St	New York	NY	10013	**800-678-0900**	212-508-0700	455-22
New York New York Hotel & Casino						
3790 Las Vegas Blvd S	Las Vegas	NV	89109	**800-689-1797**	702-740-6969	133
New York Palace Hotel						
455 Madison Ave 50th St	New York	NY	10022	**800-697-2522**	212-888-7000	378
New York Post						
1211 Ave of the Americas	New York	NY	10036	**800-552-7678**	212-930-8000	528-2
New York Presbyterian Hospital						
525 E 68th St	New York	NY	10021	**888-694-5700**	212-746-5454	373-3
New York Red Bulls						
600 Cape May St	Harrison	NJ	07029	**877-727-6223**		713
New York Replacement Parts Corp						
1462 Lexington Ave	Yonkers	NY	10128	**800-228-4718**		608
New York Review of Books						
435 Hudson St 3rd Fl	New York	NY	10014	**800-354-0050**	212-757-8070	455-11
New York School of Interior Design						
170 E 70th St	New York	NY	10021	**800-336-9743**	212-472-1500	166
New York State Assn of Realtors						
130 Washington Ave	Albany	NY	12210	**800-462-7585**	518-463-0300	652
New York State Bar Assn						
1 Elk St	Albany	NY	12207	**800-342-3661**	518-463-3200	72
New York State Bar News						
1 Elk St	Albany	NY	12207	**800-442-3863**	518-463-3200	455-15
New York State Canal Corp						
200 Southern Blvd PO Box 189	Albany	NY	12201	**800-422-6254**	518-449-6000	463
New York State Dental Assn						
20 Corporate Woods Blvd #602	Albany	NY	12211	**800-255-2100**	518-465-0044	227
New York State Electric & Gas Corp						
18 Link Dr PO Box 5240	Binghamton	NY	13904	**800-572-1111**		782
New York State Medical Society						
865 Merrick Ave PO Box 5404	Westbury	NY	11590	**800-523-4405**	516-488-6100	472
New York State Veterinary Medical Society						
300 Great Oaks Blvd Ste 314	Albany	NY	12203	**800-876-9867**	518-869-7867	790
New York Susquehanna & Western Railway Corp (NYSW)						
1 Railroad Ave	Cooperstown	NY	13326	**800-366-6979***	607-547-2555	644
*General						
New York Teacher Magazine						
800 Troy-Schenectady Rd	Latham	NY	12110	**800-342-9810**	518-213-6000	455-8
New York Times News Service Div						
620 Eigth Ave	New York	NY	10018	**800-698-4637**	866-870-2095	526
New York University						
22 Washington Sq N	New York	NY	10011	**888-243-2358**	212-998-4500	166
New York's Hotel Pennsylvania						
401 Seventh Ave	New York	NY	10001	**800-223-8585**	212-736-5000	378
New Zealand						
Embassy						
37 Observatory Cir NW	Washington	DC	20008	**866-639-9325**	202-328-4800	257
NewAge Industries Inc						
145 James Way	SouthHampton	PA	18966	**800-506-3924**	215-526-2300	369
NewAgeSys Inc						
231 Clarksville Rd						
Ste 200	Princeton Junction	NJ	08550	**888-863-9243**	609-919-9800	180
Newark Beth Israel Medical Ctr						
201 Lyons Ave	Newark	NJ	07112	**800-780-1140**	973-926-7000	373-3
Newark Chamber of Commerce						
37101 Newark Blvd	Newark	CA	94560	**844-245-8925**	510-578-4500	139
Newark Liberty International Airport						
3 Brewster Rd	Newark	NJ	07114	**888-397-4636**	973-961-6000	27
Newark Museum						
49 Washington St	Newark	NJ	07102	**888-370-6765**	973-596-6550	517
Neway Packaging Corp						
1973 E Via Arado	Rancho Dominguez	CA	90220	**800-456-3929**	310-898-3400	96
Newberry Area Tourism Assn, The						
PO Box 308	Newberry	MI	49868	**800-832-5216**	906-293-5562	206
Newberry College						
2100 College St	Newberry	SC	29108	**800-845-4955**	803-276-5010	166
Newberry County Chamber of Commerce						
1209 Caldwell St PO Box 396	Newberry	SC	29108	**800-288-2020**	803-276-4274	139
Newberry Electric Co-op Inc						
882 Wilson Rd	Newberry	SC	29108	**800-479-8838**	803-276-1121	245
Newbold Corp						
450 Weaver St	Rocky Mount	VA	24151	**800-552-3282**	540-489-4400	111
Newbridge Securities Corp						
1451 W Cypress Creek Rd						
	Fort Lauderdale	FL	33309	**877-447-9625**	954-334-3450	686
Newby Pridgen Sartip & Masel Llc						
4593 Oleander Dr	Myrtle Beach	SC	29577	**800-858-5592**	843-449-9417	
NewCloud Networks						
160 Inverness Dr W	Englewood	CO	80112	**855-255-5001**		386
Newcomb Spring Corp						
235 Spring St	Southington	CT	06489	**888-579-3051**	860-621-0111	715
NewComLink Inc						
3900 N Capital Of Texas Hwy						
Ste 150	Austin	TX	78746	**888-988-0603**		253
Newdea Inc						
6400 So Fiddlers Green Cir						
Ste 1970	Greenwood Village	CO	80111	**877-412-4829**	720-249-3030	
Newegg Inc						
16839 E Gale Ave	City of Industry	CA	91745	**800-390-1119**	626-271-9700	179
Newell Coach Corp						
3900 N Main St	Miami	OK	74354	**888-363-9355**	918-542-3344	120
Newell Paper Co						
1212 Grand Ave	Meridian	MS	39301	**800-844-8894**		549
Newell Rubbermaid Inc Irwin Tools Div						
8935 Northpointe Executive Dr						
	Huntersville	NC	28078	**800-866-5740**	704-987-4555	753
Newfield Exploration Co						
24 Waterway Ave Ste 900	The Woodlands	TX	77380	**866-902-0562**	281-847-6000	532
NYSE: NFX						
Newgistics Inc						
7171 Southwest Pkwy Bldg 300						
Ste 400	Austin	TX	78735	**877-860-5997**	512-225-6000	
Newhall Klein Inc						
6109 W Kl Ave	Kalamazoo	MI	49009	**866-639-4255**	269-544-0844	343
Newjac Inc						
415 S Grant St	Lebanon	IN	46052	**800-827-3259**	765-483-2190	693
Newlands Systems Inc						
602-30731 Simpson Rd	Abbotsford	BC	V2T6Y7	**877-855-4890**	604-855-4890	80-3
NewlineNoosh Inc						
625 Ellis St Ste 300	Mountain View	CA	94043	**888-286-6674**	650-637-6000	178-1
Newly Weds Foods Inc						
4140 W Fullerton Ave	Chicago	IL	60639	**800-621-7521**	773-489-7000	296-37
Newman & Company Inc						
6101 Tacony St	Philadelphia	PA	19135	**800-523-3256**	215-333-8700	557
Newman Theological College (NTC)						
10012-84 St	Edmonton	AB	T6A0B2	**844-392-2450**	780-392-2450	167-3
Newman University						
3100 McCormick Ave	Wichita	KS	67213	**877-639-6268**	316-942-4291	166
Newmar Corp						
355 Delaware St	Nappanee	IN	46550	**800-731-8300**	574-773-7791	120
Newmar Window Manufacturing Inc						
7630 Airport Rd	Mississauga	ON	L4T4G6	**800-263-5634**	905-672-1233	597
NewMarket Corp						
330 S Fourth St	Richmond	VA	23219	**800-625-5191**	804-788-5000	359-3
NYSE: NEU						
Newpark Mats & Integrated Services LLC						
2700 Research Forest Dr						
Ste 100	The Woodlands	TX	77381	**877-628-7623**	281-362-6800	535
Newport Aquarium						
1 Aquarium Way	Newport	KY	41071	**800-406-3474**		40
Newport Beach Conference & Visitors Bureau						
1200 Newport Ctr Dr						
Ste 120	Newport Beach	CA	92660	**800-216-1598**	949-719-6100	206
Newport Beach Hotel & Suites						
1 Wave Ave	Middletown	RI	02842	**800-655-1778**	401-846-0310	378
Newport Corp						
1791 Deere Ave	Irvine	CA	92606	**800-222-6440***	949-863-3144	540
NASDAQ: NEWP ■ *Sales						
Newport County Convention & Visitors Bureau						
23 America's Cup Ave	Newport	RI	02840	**800-326-6030**	401-849-8048	206
Newport Electronics Inc						
2229 S Yale St	Santa Ana	CA	92704	**800-639-7678***	203-968-7315	248
*Cust Svc						
Newport Harbor Hotel & Marina						
49 America's Cup Ave	Newport	RI	02840	**800-955-2558**	401-847-9000	378
Newport Leasing Inc						
4750 Von Karman Ave	Newport Beach	CA	92660	**800-274-0042***	949-476-8476	264-1
*Cust Svc						
Newport Medical Instruments Inc						
1620 Sunflower Ave	Costa Mesa	CA	92626	**800-255-6774**	714-427-5811	250
Newport News Tourism Development Office						
702 Town Center Dr	Newport News	VA	23606	**888-493-7386**	757-926-1400	206
Newport Partners LLC						
3760 Tanglewood Ln	Davidsonville	MD	21035	**866-302-0017**	301-889-0017	738
Newport State Park						
475 County Rd NP	Ellison Bay	WI	54210	**800-847-8882**	920-854-2500	561
NewRetirement LLC						
100 Pine St Ste 590	San Francisco	CA	94111	**866-441-0246**	415-738-2435	526
News & Advance						
PO Box 10129	Lynchburg	VA	24506	**800-275-8830**	434-385-5555	528-2

	Toll-Free	Phone	Class
News & Observer			
215 S McDowell St .... Raleigh NC 27602	800-522-4205	919-829-4500	528-2
News & Record			
200 E Market St .... Greensboro NC 27401	800-553-6880	336-373-7000	528-2
News America Marketing			
1185 Ave of the Americas 27 .... New York NY 10036	800-462-0852	212-782-8000	5
News Examiner, The			
847 Washington St .... Montpelier ID 83254	800-847-0465	208-847-0552	528-3
News Journal			
70 W Fourth St .... Mansfield OH 44903	877-424-0216	419-522-3311	528-2
News Journal			
950 W Basin Rd .... New Castle DE 19720	800-235-9100	302-324-2500	528-2
News Leader			
11 N Central Ave .... Staunton VA 24401	800-793-2459	540-885-7281	528-2
News Radio 1000 KTOK			
1900 NW Expy Ste 1000 ...... Oklahoma City OK 73118	844-289-7234	405-841-0200	641-73
News Radio 610			
70 Foundry St Ste 300 ...... Manchester NH 03102	866-999-7200	603-625-6915	641-61
News Radio 920 AM & 1047 FM			
75 Oxford St Ste 301 .... Providence RI 02905	866-920-9455		
News/Talk 951 & 790 KFYO			
4413 82nd St Ste 300 .... Lubbock TX 79424	800-687-0790	806-798-7078	641-59
Newsbank Inc			
5801 Pelican Bay Blvd Ste 600 ...... Naples FL 34108	800-243-7694	800-762-8182	386
News-banner Publications Inc			
125 N Johnson St .... Bluffton IN 46714	800-579-7476	260-824-0224	528-3
Newsday Inc			
598 Broadhollow Rd .... Melville NY 11747	888-280-4719	631-843-4050	528-2
News-Gazette Inc, The			
15 Main St .... Champaign IL 61820	800-660-7323	217-351-5252	528-2
News-Herald			
7085 Mentor Ave .... Willoughby OH 44094	800-947-2737	440-951-0000	528-2
News-Herald, The			
1 Heritage Dr Ste 100 .... Southgate MI 48195	888-361-6769	734-246-0800	
News-Sentinel			
600 W Main St .... Fort Wayne IN 46802	800-324-0505	260-461-8519	
NewStar Fresh Foods LLC			
850 Work St Ste 101 .... Salinas CA 93901	888-782-7220	805-487-3406	296-19
News-Times			
333 Main St .... Danbury CT 06810	877-542-6057	203-744-5100	528-2
News-Tribune			
426 Second St .... La Salle IL 61301	800-892-6452	815-223-3200	528-2
Newsweek Magazine			
7 Hanover Sq .... New York NY 10004	800-631-1040*		455-17
*Cust Svc			
NewTek Inc			
5131 Beckwith Blvd .... San Antonio TX 78249	800-862-7837*	210-370-8000	178-8
*Cust Svc			
Newtex Industries Inc			
8050 Victor Mendon Rd .... Victor NY 14564	800-836-1001	585-924-9135	740-3
Newton Convention & Visitor Bureau			
300 E 17th St S Ste 400 .... Newton IA 50208	800-798-0299	641-792-0299	206
Newton County			
201 N Third St .... Kentland IN 47951	888-663-9866	219-474-6081	337
Newton Distributing Company Inc			
245 W Central St .... Natick MA 01760	877-837-7745	617-969-4002	608
Newton Manufacturing Co			
854 Angliana Ave .... Lexington KY 40508	855-754-8123	641-316-0500	9
Newtown Savings Bank Foundation Inc			
39 Main St .... Newtown CT 06470	800-461-0672	203-426-2563	70
NexAge Technologies USA Inc			
75 Lincoln Hwy Ste 101 .... Iselin NJ 08830	866-866-5800	732-494-4944	195
NexBank Securities Inc			
2515 McKinney Ave Ste 1100 .... Dallas TX 75201	800-827-4818	972-308-6700	
Nexcessnet LLC			
21700 Melrose Ave .... Southfield MI 48075	866-639-2377		225
NEXCOM (Navy Exchange Service Command)			
3280 Virginia Beach Blvd			
.... Virginia Beach VA 23452	800-628-3924	757-463-6200	786
Nexen Group Inc			
560 Oak Grove Pkwy .... Vadnais Heights MN 55127	800-843-7445	651-484-5900	385
Nexio Group Inc			
2050 de Bleury St Ste 500 .... Montreal QC H3A2J5	888-798-3707	514-798-3707	627
Nexion			
6225 N State Hwy 161 Ste 450 .... Irving TX 75038	800-949-6410	408-280-6410	767
Nexogy			
2121 Ponce de leon Blvd			
Ste 200 .... Coral Gables FL 33134	866-639-6492		
Nexonia Inc			
2 St Clair Ave E Ste 750 .... Toronto ON M4T2T5	800-291-4829*	416-480-0688	
*Sales			
Next Day Flyers			
8000 Haskell Ave .... Van Nuys CA 91406	855-898-9870		5
NEXT Financial Holdings Inc			
2500 Wilcrest Dr Ste 620 .... Houston TX 77042	877-876-6398		686
Next Generation Films Inc			
230 Industrial Dr .... Lexington OH 44904	800-884-8150	419-884-8150	
Next Net Media LLC			
4801 Gulf Blvd Ste 334 .... St Pete Beach FL 33706	800-737-5820		386
Nexternal Solutions Inc			
785 Grand Ave Ste 216 .... Carlsbad CA 92008	800-914-6161	760-730-9015	395
NextG Networks Inc			
890 Tasman Dr .... Milpitas CA 95035	877-486-9377		610
Nextiva			
8800 E Chaparral Rd Ste 300 .... Scottsdale AZ 85250	800-799-0600	800-983-4289	386
Nextran Corp			
1986 W Beaver St .... Jacksonville FL 32209	800-347-6225	904-354-3721	57
NextServices Inc			
500 E Eisenhower Pkwy Ste 130 .... Ann Arbor MI 48108	866-362-6398	734-677-7700	
Nexus Corp			
10983 Leroy Dr .... Northglenn CO 80233	800-228-9639	303-457-9199	106
nexVortex Inc			
510 Spring St Ste 250 .... Herndon VA 20170	855-639-8888		
Nexxtworks Inc			
30798 US Hwy 19 N .... Palm Harbor FL 34684	888-533-8353		386
Ney Oil Company Inc			
145 S Water St .... Ney OH 43549	800-962-9839	419-658-2324	324
Neyra Industries			
10700 Evendale Dr .... Cincinnati OH 45241	800-543-7077	513-733-1000	46
Nez Perce National Historical Park			
39063 US Hwy 95 .... Spalding ID 83540	800-537-7962	208-843-2261	560
NFA (National Futures Assn)			
300 S Riverside Plz Ste 1800 .... Chicago IL 60606	800-621-3570	312-781-1300	49-2
NFB (National Federation of the Blind)			
1800 Johnson St .... Baltimore MD 21230	800-392-5671	410-659-9314	48-17
NFBA (National Frame Builders Assn)			
8735 W Higgins Rd Ste 300 .... Chicago IL 60631	800-557-6957		49-3
NFCA (National Family Caregivers Assn)			
10400 Connecticut Ave			
Ste 500 .... Kensington MD 20895	800-896-3650	301-942-6430	48-6
NFCDCU (National Federation of Community Development Credi)			
39 Broadway Ste 2140 .... New York NY 10006	800-437-8711	212-809-1850	49-2
NFCR (National Foundation for Cancer Research)			
4600 E W Hwy Ste 525 .... Bethesda MD 20814	800-321-2873		305
NFDA (National Funeral Directors Assn)			
13625 Bishop's Dr .... Brookfield WI 53005	800-228-6332	262-789-1880	49-4
NFDMA (National Funeral Directors & Morticians Assn)			
6290 Shannon Pkwy .... Union City GA 30291	800-434-0958	770-969-0064	49-4
NFHS (National Federation of State High School Assn)			
PO Box 690 .... Indianapolis IN 46206	800-776-3462*	317-972-6900	48-22
*Cust Svc			
NFI (NFI Industries)			
1515 Burnt Mill Rd .... Cherry Hill NJ 08003	877-634-3777		447
NFI Inc Dba Harrisonburg Honda Mitsubishi Hyundai			
2885 S Main St .... Harrisonburg VA 22801	800-433-1987	540-433-1467	
NFI Industries (NFI)			
1515 Burnt Mill Rd .... Cherry Hill NJ 08003	877-634-3777		447
NFID (National Foundation for Infectious Diseases)			
4733 Bethesda Ave Ste 750 .... Bethesda MD 20814	800-708-5478	301-656-0003	49-8
NFLPA (National Football League Players)			
1133 20th St NW .... Washington DC 20036	800-372-2000		48-22
NFO (National Farmers Organization)			
528 Billy Sunday Rd Ste 100			
PO Box 2508 .... Ames IA 50010	800-247-2110	515-292-2000	48-2
Nfocus Consulting Inc			
1594 Hubbard Dr .... Lancaster OH 43130	800-675-5809	740-654-5809	196
NFPA (National Fire Protection Assn)			
1 Batterymarch Pk .... Quincy MA 02169	800-344-3555	617-770-3000	48-17
NFR (North Fork Ranch)			
55395 Hwy 285 PO Box B .... Shawnee CO 80475	800-843-7895	303-838-9873	239
NFRW (National Federation of Republican Women)			
124 N Alfred St .... Alexandria VA 22314	800-373-9688	703-548-9688	48-7
NFU (National Farmers Union News)			
20 F St NW Ste 300 .... Washington DC 20001	800-442-8277	202-554-1600	527-13
NGA (National Gardening Assn)			
1100 Dorset St .... South Burlington VT 05403	800-538-7476	802-863-5251	48-18
NGA (National Glass Assn)			
8200 Greensboro Dr Ste 302 .... McLean VA 22102	866-342-5642	703-442-4890	49-13
NGA (National Greyhound Assn)			
729 Old US 40 .... Abilene KS 67410	800-366-1471	785-263-4660	48-22
NGA (National Grocers Assn)			
1005 N Glebe Rd Ste 250 .... Arlington VA 22201	800-627-6667	703-516-0700	49-6
NGAUS (National Guard Educational Foundation)			
1 Massachusetts Ave NW .... Washington DC 20001	888-226-4287	202-789-0031	48-19
NGC (National Garden Clubs Inc)			
4401 Magnolia Ave .... Saint Louis MO 63110	800-550-6007	314-776-7574	48-18
NGCOA (National Golf Course Owners Assn)			
291 Seven Farms Dr 2nd Fl .... Charleston SC 29492	800-933-4262	843-881-9956	48-23
NGF (National Gaucher Foundation)			
5410 Edson Ln Ste 220 .... Rockville MD 20852	800-504-3189		48-17
NGF (National Golf Foundation)			
1150 S US Hwy 1 Ste 401 .... Jupiter FL 33477	800-733-6006	561-744-6006	48-22
NGK Metals Corp			
917 Hwy 11 S .... Sweetwater TN 37874	800-523-8268	423-337-5500	308
NGK Spark Plugs Inc			
46929 Magellan .... Wixom MI 48393	877-473-6767	248-926-6900	247
NGL (National Guardian Life Insurance Co)			
2 E Gilman St .... Madison WI 53703	800-548-2962		390-2
NGL (Network Global Logistics)			
320 Interlocken Pkwy Ste 100 .... Broomfield CO 80021	866-938-1870		542
NGS (National Genealogical Society)			
3108 Columbia Pk Ste 300 .... Arlington VA 22204	800-473-0060	703-525-0050	48-18
NGWA (National Ground Water Assn)			
601 Dempsey Rd .... Westerville OH 43081	800-551-7379	614-898-7791	48-12
NH Yates & Company Inc			
117 Church Ln # C .... Cockeysville MD 21030	800-878-8181		637
NHDP (National Hansen's Disease Program)			
1770 Physicians Pk Dr .... Baton Rouge LA 70816	800-221-9393		664
Employment Security			
32 S Main St .... Concord NH 03301	800-852-3400	603-224-3311	259
NHF (National Hemophilia Foundation)			
7 Penn Plz Ste 1204 .... New York NY 10001	800-424-2634	212-328-3700	48-17
NHFA (National Home Furnishings Assn)			
500 Giuseppe Ct Ste 6 .... Roseville CA 95678	800-422-3778		49-4
NHK Laboratories Inc			
12230 E Florience Ave .... Santa Fe Springs CA 90670	866-645-5227	562-944-5400	477
NHLA (National Hardwood Lumber Assn)			
6830 Raleigh-LaGrange Rd .... Memphis TN 38134	800-933-0318	901-377-1818	49-3
NHPCO (National Hospice & Palliative Care Organization)			
1700 Diagonal Rd Ste 625 .... Alexandria VA 22314	800-658-8898*	703-837-1500	49-8
*Help Line			
NHPTV (New Hampshire Public Television)			
268 Mast Rd .... Durham NH 03824	800-639-8408	603-868-1100	628
NHS (National Honor Society)			
1904 Assn Dr .... Reston VA 20191	800-253-7746	703-860-0200	48-11
NHSA (National Head Start Assn)			
1651 Prince St .... Alexandria VA 22314	866-677-8724	703-739-0875	48-11
NHTI Concord's Community College			
31 College Dr .... Concord NH 03301	800-247-0179	603-271-6484	162
NHTSA (National Highway Traffic Safety Administration)			
1200 New Jersey Ave SE .... Washington DC 20590	888-327-4236	202-366-9550	339-16
NIA (National Insulation Assn)			
99 Canal Ctr Plz Ste 222 .... Alexandria VA 22314	877-968-7642	703-683-6422	49-3
Niacet Corp			
400 47th St .... Niagara Falls NY 14304	800-828-1207	716-285-1474	144

	Toll-Free	Phone	Class
NIADA (National Independent Automobile Dealers Assn)			
2521 Brown Blvd .... Arlington TX 76006	800-682-3837	817-640-3838	49-18
Niagara Blower Co Inc			
91 Sawyer Ave ....Tonawanda NY 14150	800-426-5169	716-875-2000	14
Niagara Conservation Corp			
45 Horsehill Rd .... Cedar Knolls NJ 07927	800-831-8383		608
Niagara Corp			
667 Madison Ave ....New York NY 10021	877-289-2277	212-317-1000	719
Niagara County			
PO Box 461 .... Lockport NY 14095	800-460-5657	716-439-7022	337
Niagara County Community College			
3111 Saunders Settlement Rd ....Sanborn NY 14132	800-875-6269	716-614-6222	162
Niagara Cutter Inc			
2805 Bellingham Dr ....Troy MI 48083	800-832-8326	248-528-5220	491
Niagara Duty Free Shop			
5726 Falls Ave .... Niagara Falls ON L2G7T5	877-642-4337	905-374-3700	241
Niagara Helicopters Ltd			
3731 Victoria Ave .... Niagara Falls ON L2E6V5	800-281-8034	905-357-5672	292
Niagara Parks Botanical Gardens			
7400 Portage Rd			
PO Box 150.................... Niagara Falls ON L2E6T2	877-642-7275		97
Niagara Tourism & Convention Corp			
10 Rainbow Blvd .... Niagara Falls NY 14303	877-325-5787	716-282-8992	206
Niagara Transformer Corp			
1747 Dale Rd........................Buffalo NY 14225	800-817-5652	716-896-6500	762
Niagara University			
5795 Lewiston Rd			
PO Box 2011............. Niagara University NY 14109	800-778-3450	716-285-1212	166
NIB (National Industries for the Blind)			
1310 Braddock Pl .... Alexandria VA 22314	800-325-3535*	703-310-0500	48-17
*Cust Svc			
NIBCO Inc			
1516 Middlebury St .... Elkhart IN 46515	800-234-0227	574-295-3000	591
NIC Inc			
25501 W Valley Pkwy Ste 300 .... Olathe KS 66061	877-234-3468		178-10
NASDAQ: EGOV			
Nicaragua			
Embassy			
1627 New Hampshire Ave NW ..... Washington DC 20009	800-333-4636	202-939-6570	257
NICB (National Insurance Crime Bureau)			
1111 E Touhy Ave Ste 400 .... Des Plaines IL 60018	800-447-6282	847-544-7002	49-9
Niceville-Valparaiso Chamber of Commerce			
1055 E John Sims Pkwy ....Niceville FL 32578	800-729-9226	850-678-2323	139
NICHD (National Institute of Child Health and Human Devel)			
31 Center Dr Bldg 31 Rm 2A32 .... Bethesda MD 20892	800-370-2943		664
Niche Directories LLC			
909 N Sepulveda Blvd 11th Fl .... El Segundo CA 90026	877-242-9330		386
Nicholas County			
Commission			
700 Main St Ste 1.............Summersville WV 26651	800-327-5405	304-872-7830	337
Nicholas Financial Inc			
2454 McMullen Booth Rd ....Clearwater FL 33759	800-237-2721	727-726-0763	217
NASDAQ: NICK			
Nichols PO Box 291 .... Muskegon MI 49443	800-442-0213	231-799-2120	555
Nichols College			
129 Center Rd ....Dudley MA 01571	800-470-3379		166
Nick & Stef's Steakhouse			
330 S Hope St ....Los Angeles CA 90071	866-972-8462		
Nick Strimbu Inc			
3500 PkwyRd ....Brookfield OH 44403	800-446-8785	330-448-4046	775
Nickell Moulding Company Inc			
3015 Mobile Dr ....Elkhart IN 46515	800-838-2151	574-264-3129	497
Nickers International Ltd			
PO Box 50066 .... Staten Island NY 10305	800-642-5377	718-448-6283	794
Nickerson Business Supplies			
876A Lebanon St ....Monroe OH 45050	888-385-9922	513-539-6600	321
Nicros Inc			
845 Phalen Blvd .... Saint Paul MN 55106	800-699-1975	651-778-1975	707
NICSA (National Investment Co Service Assn)			
8400 Westpark Dr 2nd Fl ....Mclean VA 22102	800-426-1122	508-485-1500	49-2
Nida Corp			
300 S John Rodes Blvd ....Melbourne FL 32904	800-327-6432	321-727-2265	699
The National Institute on Deafness and Other Communication Disorders			
31 Ctr Dr MSC 2320 .... Bethesda MD 20892	800-241-1044	301-496-7243	664
NIDCR (National Oral Health Information Clearinghouse)			
1 NOHIC Way .... Bethesda MD 20892	866-232-4528	301-496-4261	48-17
Nidec Motor Corp			
8050 W Florissant Ave .... Saint Louis MO 63136	888-637-7333		515
Nidek Inc			
47651 Westinghouse Dr .... Fremont CA 94539	800-223-9044	510-226-5700	473
Niedner, Bodeux, Carmichael, Huff, Lenox & Pashos LLP			
131 Jefferson St .... Saint Charles MO 63301	888-572-2192	636-949-9300	427
NIFDA (National Independent Flag Dealers Assn)			
7984 S Chicago Ave ....Chicago IL 60617	800-356-4085	773-768-8076	49-18
NIFL (National Institute for Literacy)			
1775 'I' St NW Ste 730 ....Washington DC 20006	800-228-8813	202-233-2025	339-7
Night Optics USA Inc			
15182 Triton Ln			
Ste 101 .... Huntington Beach CA 92649	800-306-4448		538
Nightingale-Conant Corp			
6245 W Howard St ....Niles IL 60714	800-557-1660*		510
*Cust Svc			
NIGP (National Institute of Governmental Purchasing Inc)			
151 Spring St ....Herndon VA 20170	800-367-6447	703-736-8900	49-7
NIH (National Institutes of Health)			
9000 Rockville Pk .... Bethesda MD 20892	800-411-1222	301-496-4000	339-9
NIH Osteoporosis & Related Bone Diseases-National Resource Ctr			
2 AMS Cir .... Bethesda MD 20892	800-624-2663	202-223-0344	339-9
Nihon Kohden America Inc			
90 Icon .... Foothill Ranch CA 92610	800-325-0283	949-580-1555	473
Nike Inc			
1 Bowerman Dr ....Beaverton OR 97005	800-344-6453*	503-671-6453	301
*NYSE: NKE ■ *Cust Svc*			
Nik-O-Lok Co			
3130 N Mitthoeffer Rd ....Indianapolis IN 46235	800-428-4348	317-899-6955	349
Nikon Inc			
1300 Walt Whitman Rd .... Melville NY 11747	800-645-6687*	631-547-4200	587
*Cust Svc			

	Toll-Free	Phone	Class
Niles Audio Corp			
1969 Kellog Ave .... Carlsbad CA 92008	800-289-4434	760-710-0992	253
Nill Bros Sports			
2814 S 44th St .... Kansas City KS 66106	800-748-7221	913-384-4242	707
Nimbix LLC			
800 E Campbell Ste 241 .... Richardson TX 75081	866-307-0819		
Nims & Assoc			
1445 Technology Ln Ste A8 .... Petaluma CA 94954	877-454-3200	707-781-6300	177
Nine Health Services Inc			
1139 Delaware St ....Denver CO 80204	800-332-3078	303-698-4455	632
Nine Star Enterprises Inc			
730 I St .... Anchorage AK 99501	800-478-7587	907-279-7827	260
Nine Zero Hotel			
90 Tremont St ....Boston MA 02108	866-906-9090	617-772-5800	378
Nines Hotel, The			
525 SW Morrison ....Portland OR 97204	877-229-9995		41
Ninety-Nines Inc			
4300 Amelia Earhart Rd ....Oklahoma City OK 73159	800-994-1929	405-685-7969	48-24
Ning Interactive Inc			
1906 El Camino Real .... Menlo Park CA 94027	855-233-6436		
Nintendo of America Inc			
4820 150th Ave NE ....Redmond WA 98052	800-255-3700*	425-882-2040	757
*Cust Svc			
NIPC (National Inhalant Prevention Coalition)			
PO Box 4117 .... Chattanooga TN 37405	855-704-4400	423-265-4662	48-17
Nipissing University			
100 College Dr PO Box 5002 ....North Bay ON P1B8L7	800-655-5154	705-474-3450	780
Nippon Kodo Inc			
2771 Plaza Del Amo Ste 805 .... Torrance CA 90503	888-775-5487	310-320-8881	782
NIR Roof Care Inc			
12191 Regency Pkwy .... Huntley IL 60142	800-221-7663	847-669-3444	189-12
NISH			
8401 Old Courthouse Rd ....Vienna VA 22182	888-411-8424		
Nishnabotna Valley Rural Electric Co-op			
1317 Chatburn Ave ....Harlan IA 51537	800-234-5122	712-755-2166	245
Niskayuna Central School District (NCSD)			
1239 Van Antwerp Rd .... Schenectady NY 12309	866-893-6337	518-377-4666	681
NISO (National Information Standards Organization)			
3600 Clipper Mill Rd Ste 302..........Baltimore MD 21211	877-375-2160	301-654-2512	49-16
Nissan Canada Inc (NCI)			
5290 Orbitor Dr .... Mississauga ON L4W4Z5	800-387-0122		59
Nissan Motor Corp USA Infiniti Div			
1 Nissan Way ....Franklin TN 37067	800-662-6200		59
Nissan North America Inc			
25 Vantage way ....Nashville TN 37228	800-647-7261		59
Nissei America Inc			
1480 N Hancock St .... Anaheim CA 92807	800-693-3231	714-693-3000	111
Nitel Inc			
1101 West Lake St 6th Fl ....Chicago IL 60607	888-450-2100		224
Nitelines USA Inc			
2180 Satellite Blvd Ste 400. ....Duluth GA 30097	844-661-9120		392
Nitrex Metal Inc			
3474 Poirier Blvd ....Saint-Laurent QC H4R2J5	877-335-7191	514-335-7191	482
Nitrous Express Inc			
5411 Seymour Hwy .... Wichita Falls TX 76310	888-463-2781	940-767-7694	57
Nitta Casings Inc			
141 Southside Ave .... Bridgewater NJ 08807	800-526-3970*	908-218-4400	298
*Cust Svc			
Nittany Lion Inn			
200 W Park Ave .... State College PA 16803	800-233-7505	814-865-8500	378
Nizhoni Health Systems LLC			
5 Middlesex Ave ....Somerville MA 02145	800-915-3211		362
NJHCS (East Orange Campus of the VA New Jersey Health Car)			
385 Tremont Ave .... East Orange NJ 07018	844-872-4681*		373-8
*General			
NJSNA (New Jersey State Nurses Assn)			
1479 Pennington Rd ....Trenton NJ 08618	800-662-0108	609-883-5335	529
NJTV 825 Eighth Ave ....New York NY 10019	800-882-6622	609-777-0031	
NKBA (National Kitchen & Bath Assn)			
687 Willow Grove St .... Hackettstown NJ 07840	800-843-6522		49-3
NKF (National Kidney Foundation)			
30 E 33rd St ....New York NY 10016	800-622-9010	212-889-2210	48-17
NKP Medical Marketing Inc			
8939 S Sepulveda Blvd			
Ste 320 .... Los Angeles CA 90045	866-539-2201		195
NKS Distributors Inc			
399 Churchmans Rd ....New Castle DE 19720	800-310-5099	302-322-1811	81-3
NKTelco Inc			
301 W S St PO Box 219 ..... New Knoxville OH 45871	888-658-3526	419-753-5000	224
NKYCVB (Northern Kentucky Convention & Visitors Bureau)			
50 E RiverCenter Blvd Ste 200 .... Covington KY 41011	877-659-8474	859-261-4677	206
NL Industries			
16801 Greenspoint Pk Dr ....Houston TX 77060	800-866-5600	281-423-3300	143
NYSE: NL			
NLADA (National Legal Aid & Defender Assn)			
1140 Connecticut Ave NW			
Ste 900 ....Washington DC 20036	800-725-4513	202-452-0620	49-10
NLBRA (National Little Britches Rodeo Assn)			
5050 Edison Ave			
Ste 105 .... Colorado Springs CO 80915	800-763-3694	719-389-0333	48-22
NLC (National League of Cities)			
660 North Capitol St NW .... Washington DC 20001	877-827-2385		49-7
NLC Products Inc			
PO Box 8300 .... Little Rock AR 72222	800-648-5483		
NLDA (National Luggage Dealers Association)			
1817 Elmdale Ave .... Glenview IL 60026	800-411-0705	847-998-6869	49-18
NLN (National League for Nursing)			
61 Broadway 33rd Fl. ....New York NY 10006	800-669-1656	212-363-5555	49-8
NLRB (National Labor Relations Board)			
1099 14th St NW ....Washington DC 20570	866-667-6572	202-273-1991	339-19
Region 16			
819 Taylor St Rm 8A24. .... Fort Worth TX 76102	866-667-6572	817-978-2921	339-19
NMA (National Motorists Assn)			
402 W Second St .... Waunakee WI 53597	800-882-2785	608-849-6000	49-21
NMA (National Medical Assn)			
8403 Colesville Rd			
Ste 920 .... Silver Spring MD 20910	800-662-0554	202-347-1895	49-8
NMC (National Motor Club of America Inc)			
130 E John Carpenter Fwy ....Irving TX 75062	800-523-4582		53

Name / Address	Toll-Free	Phone	Class
NMCC (Northern Maine Community College) 33 Edgemont Dr, Presque Isle ME 04769	800-535-6682	207-768-2700	795
NMCRS (Navy-Marine Corps Relief Society) 875 N Randolph St Ste 225, Arlington VA 22203	800-654-8364	703-696-4904	48-19
NMC-Wollard Inc 2021 Truax Blvd, Eau Claire WI 54703	800-656-6867	715-835-3151	468
NMDP (National Marrow Donor Program) 500 N Fifth St, Minneapolis MN 55401	800-627-7692		48-17
NMEA (National Marine Electronics Assn) 692 Ritchie Hwy Ste 104, Severna Park MD 21146	800-808-6632	410-975-9425	49-13
NMF (National Marfan Foundation) 22 Manhasset Ave, Port Washington NY 11050	800-862-7326	516-883-8712	48-17
NMFTA (National Motor Freight Traffic Assn) 1001 N Fairfax St Ste 600, Alexandria VA 22314	866-411-6632	703-838-1810	49-21
NMMS (New Mexico Medical Society) 316 Osuna Rd NE Ste 501, Albuquerque NM 87107	800-748-1596	505-828-0237	472
NMOA (National Mail Order Assn LLC) 2807 Polk St NE, Minneapolis MN 55418	800-992-1377	612-788-1673	49-18
NMRA (National Marine Representatives Assn) PO Box 360, Gurnee IL 60031	800-890-3819	847-662-3167	49-18
NMRA (National Model Railroad Assn) 4121 Cromwell Rd, Chattanooga TN 37421	800-654-2256	423-892-2846	48-18
NMS Capital Advisors LLC 433 N Camden Dr 4th Fl, Beverly Hills CA 90210	800-716-2080		687
NMS Labs 3701 Welsh Rd, Willow Grove PA 19090	800-522-6671	215-657-4900	417
NMSA (National Middle School Assn) 4151 Executive Pkwy Ste 300, Westerville OH 43081	800-528-6672	614-895-4730	49-5
NMSDC (National Minority Supplier Development Council) 1359 Broadway 10th Fl, New York NY 10018	800-843-4898	212-944-2430	49-18
NMSU (New Mexico State University) MSC-3A PO Box 30001, Las Cruces NM 88003 *Admissions	800-662-6678*	575-646-3121	166
NMT (New Mexico Institute of Mining & Technology) 801 Leroy Pl, Socorro NM 87801 *Admissions	800-428-8324*	505-835-5434	166
NN Inc 2000 Waters Edge Dr, Johnson City TN 37604 NASDAQ: NNBR	877-888-0002	423-434-8300	483
NNA (Nebraska Nurses Assn) PO Box 3107, Kearney NE 68848	888-885-7025		529
NNA (National Newspaper Assn) PO Box 7540, Columbia MO 65205	800-829-4662	217-241-1400	49-14
NNA (National Notary Assn) 9350 DeSoto Ave, Chatsworth CA 91313	800-876-6827		49-12
NNM Peterson Manufacturing Co 24133 W 143rd St, Plainfield IL 60544	800-826-9086	815-436-9201	286
NNPDF (National Niemann-Pick Disease Foundation Inc) 401 Madison Ave Ste B PO Box 49, Fort Atkinson WI 53538	877-287-3672	920-563-0930	48-17
NNSDO (National Nursing Staff Development Organization) 330 N Wabash Ave Ste 2000, Chicago IL 60611	800-489-1995	312-321-5135	49-8
NNT Corp 1320 Norwood Ave, Itasca IL 60143	800-556-9999	630-875-9600	453
No Fault Sports Products 2101 Briarglen Dr, Houston TX 77027	800-462-7766	713-683-7101	707
No Starch Press Inc 38 Ringold St, San Francisco CA 94103	800-420-7240	415-863-9900	633-2
NOAH (National Organization for Albinism & Hypopigmentat) PO Box 959, East Hampstead NH 03826	800-648-2310	603-887-2310	48-17
Noamex Inc 625 Wortman Ave, Brooklyn NY 11208	800-640-5917	718-342-2278	156
Nobel Biocare USA Inc 22715 Savi Ranch Pkwy, Yorba Linda CA 92887	800-993-8100	714-282-4800	228
NobelBiz Inc 1545 Faraday Ave, Carlsbad CA 92008	800-975-2844	760-405-0105	
Nobility Homes Inc 3741 SW Seventh St, Ocala FL 34474 OTC: NOBH	800-476-6624	352-732-5157	503
Noble Corp 13135 S Dairy Ashford Rd Ste 800, Sugar Land TX 77478 NYSE: NE	877-285-4162	281-276-6100	536
Noble County 101 N Orange St, Albion IN 46701	800-840-8757	260-636-2736	337
Noble Energy Inc 100 Glenborough Dr Ste 100, Houston TX 77067 NYSE: NBL	800-220-5824	281-872-3100	532
Noble Horizons 17 Cobble Rd, Salisbury CT 06068	800-733-2767	860-435-9851	448
Noble REMC 300 Weber Rd PO Box 137, Albion IN 46701	800-933-7362		245
Noble Roman's Pizza Inc 1 Virginia Ave Ste 300, Indianapolis IN 46204	800-585-0669		
Noble Royalties Inc (NRI) 15303 N Dallas Pkwy Ste 1350, Addison TX 75001	888-346-6253	972-720-1888	
Noble Trade Inc 7171 Jane St, Concord ON L4K1A7	800-529-9805	905-760-6800	111
Nobles Co-op Electric 22636 US Hwy 59 PO Box 788, Worthington MN 56187	800-776-0517	507-372-7331	245
Noblesville Chamber of Commerce 601 Conner St, Noblesville IN 46060	800-227-1376	317-773-0086	139
NobleWorks Inc 500 Paterson Plank Rd, Union City NJ 07087	800-346-6253	201-420-0095	130
NOCC (National Ovarian Cancer Coalition) 2501 Oak Lawn Ave Ste 435, Dallas TX 75219	888-682-7426		48-17
NOCIRC (National Organization of Circumcision Information) PO Box 2512, San Anselmo CA 94979	800-727-8622	415-488-9883	48-17
NOCO Energy Corp 2440 Sheridan Dr, Tonawanda NY 14150	800-500-6626	716-833-6626	575
Nodak Electric Co-op Inc 4000 32nd Ave S, Grand Forks ND 58201	800-732-4373	701-746-4461	245
Noevir USA Inc 1095 Main St, Irvine CA 92614	800-872-8817	949-660-1111	365
NOF (National Osteoporosis Foundation) 251 18th St S Ste 630, Arlington VA 22202	800-231-4222	202-223-2226	48-17
Nofa-ny Certified Organic LLC 840 Upper Front St, Binghamton NY 13905	800-853-2676	607-724-9851	138
Nogales-Santa Cruz County Chamber of Commerce 123 W Kino Pk, Nogales AZ 85621	800-508-7624	520-287-3685	139
NOIA (National Ocean Industries Assn) 1120 G St NW Ste 900, Washington DC 20005	800-558-9994	202-347-6900	48-12
Nolan Co 1016 Ninth St SW, Canton OH 44707	800-297-1383	330-453-7922	646
Noldus Information Technology Inc 1503 Edwards Ferry Rd NE Ste 201, Leesburg VA 20176	800-355-9541	703-771-0440	177
Nolin Rural Electric Co-op Corp 411 Ring Rd, Elizabethtown KY 42701	888-637-4247	270-765-6153	245
Nolocom 950 Parker St, Berkeley CA 94710	800-728-3555		178-9
NOLS (National Outdoor Leadership School) 284 Lincoln St, Lander WY 82520	800-710-6657	307-332-5300	681
Nomadic Display Capitol Inc 5617 Industrial Dr, Springfield VA 22151	800-336-5019		317
Nomanco Inc 501 Nmc Dr, Zebulon NC 27597	800-345-7279	919-269-6500	319-1
Nome Youth Facility 804 E Fourth St, Nome AK 99762	800-770-5650	907-443-5434	411
Non Commissioned Officers Assn (NCOA) 9330 Corporate Dr Ste 708, Selma TX 78154	800-662-2620	210-653-6161	48-19
Noninvasive Medical Technologies Inc 6412 S Arville St, Las Vegas NV 89118	888-466-8552	702-614-3360	461
Nook Industries 4950 E 49th St, Cleveland OH 44125	800-321-7800	216-271-7900	616
Nora Lighting Inc 6505 Gayhart St, Commerce CA 90040	800-686-6672	323-767-2600	246
Noran Instruments Inc 5225 Verona Rd, Madison WI 53711	800-532-4752	608-276-6100	418
Norandex Bldg Materials Distribution Inc 1 ABC Pkwy, Beloit WI 53511	800-528-0942		
Noraxon U.S.A. Inc 15770 N Greenway-Hayden Loop Ste 100, Scottsdale AZ 85260	800-364-8985	480-443-3413	473
Norbest Inc PO Box 890, Moroni UT 84646	800-453-5327		297-10
Nor-Cal Beverage Company Inc 2286 Stone Blvd, West Sacramento CA 95691	800-331-2059	916-372-0600	81-2
Nor-Cal Controls Inc 1952 Concourse Dr, San Jose CA 95131	800-233-2013	408-435-0400	418
NorCal Mutual Insurance Company Inc 575 Market St Ste 1000, San Francisco CA 94105	800-652-1051	855-882-3412	390-5
Nor-Cal Products Inc 1967 S Oregon St, Yreka CA 96097	800-824-4166	530-842-4457	591
Norco Products Furniture Mfrs 4985 Blue Mtn Rd, Missoula MT 59804	800-662-2300	406-251-3800	321
Nor-Cote International Inc 506 Lafayette Ave, Crawfordsville IN 47933	800-488-9180	765-362-9180	387
Norcraft cabinetry 950 Blue Gentian Rd Ste 200, Eagan MN 55121	866-802-7892		
NORD (National Organization for Rare Disorders) 55 Kenosia Ave, Danbury CT 06810	800-999-6673	203-744-0100	48-17
NORD Drivesystems 800 Nord Dr, Waunakee WI 53597	888-314-6673		54
Nordaas American Homes Company Inc 10091 State Hwy 22, Minnesota Lake MN 56068	800-658-7076	507-462-3331	187
Nordia Inc 3020 Jacques-Bureau 2nd Fl, Laval QC H7P6G2	866-858-4367	514-415-7088	732
Nordic Ware 5005 Hwy 7, Minneapolis MN 55416	877-466-7342	952-920-2888	484
Nordion 447 March Rd, Ottawa ON K2K1X8 NYSE: NDZ	800-465-3666	613-592-2790	85
Nordisk Systems Inc 13475 SE Johnson Rd, Milwaukie OR 97222	800-676-2777	503-353-7555	196
Nordon Inc 1 Cabot Blvd E, Langhorne PA 19047	800-544-0400	215-504-4700	111
Nordson Corp 28601 Clemens Rd, Westlake OH 44145 NASDAQ: NDSN	800-321-2881	440-892-1580	385
Nordson MEDICAL 3325 S Timberline Rd, Fort Collins CO 80525	888-404-5837		604
Nordson XALOY 1399 Countyline Rd, New Castle PA 16101	800-897-2830	724-656-5600	617
Nordyne Inc 8000 Phoenix Pkwy, O'Fallon MO 63368	800-422-4328	636-561-7300	14
Noregon Systems Inc 7009 Albert Pick Rd, Greensboro NC 27409	855-889-5776		804
Nor-Ell Inc 851 Hubbard Ave, Saint Paul MN 55104	877-276-4075	651-487-1441	479
Norfolk & Dedham Group 222 Ames St, Dedham MA 02027	800-688-1825		389
Norfolk Convention & Visitors Bureau 232 E Main St, Norfolk VA 23510	800-368-3097	757-664-6620	206
Norfolk Daily News PO Box 977, Norfolk NE 68702	877-371-1020	402-371-1020	528-2
Norfolk (Independent City) 999 Waterside Dr Ste 2430, Norfolk VA 23510	800-664-1080	757-664-4242	337
Norfolk Public Schools 800 E City Hall Ave, Norfolk VA 23510	800-846-4464	757-628-3843	681
Norfolk Southern Corp 3 Commercial Pl, Norfolk VA 23510 NYSE: NSC ■ *Cust Svc	800-635-5768*	855-667-3655	466
Norfolk Southern Railway Co 3 Commercial Pl, Norfolk VA 23510	800-635-5768	800-453-2530	644
Norfolk State University 700 Park Ave, Norfolk VA 23504	800-274-1821	757-823-8600	166
Norforge & Machining Inc 195 N Dean St, Bushnell IL 61422	800-839-3706	309-772-3124	481
Norgen Biotek Corp 3430 Schmon Pkwy, Thorold ON L2V4Y6	866-667-4362		417
Norgren 5400 S Delaware St, Littleton CO 80120	800-514-0129	303-794-5000	785
Noridian Healthcare Solutions LLC 900 42th St S PO Box 6055, Fargo ND 58103	800-633-4227		
Noritsu Technical Services 6900 Noritsu Ave, Buena Park CA 90620	888-435-7448	714-521-9040	392

	Toll-Free	Phone	Class
Nor-Lake Inc			
727 Second St PO Box 248 ... Hudson WI 54016	**800-388-5253**	715-386-2323	660
Norlift of Oregon Inc			
7373 SE Milwaukie Expy ... Portland OR 97222	**800-452-0050**	503-659-5438	765
Norm Thompson Outfitters Inc			
3188 NW Aloclek Dr ... Hillsboro OR 97124	**800-547-1160**	877-718-7899	457
Norm's Refrigeration & Ice Equipment Inc			
1175 N Knollwood Cir ... Anaheim CA 92801	**800-933-4423**	714-236-3600	661
Norman Convention & Visitors Bureau			
309 E Main St ... Norman OK 73069	**800-767-7260**	405-366-8095	206
Norman Frede Chevrolet Co			
16801 Feather Craft Ln ... Houston TX 77058	**888-307-1703**	281-486-2200	57
Norman Shatz Co USA			
3570 St Rd ... Bensalem PA 19020	**800-292-0292**		707
Normandale Community College			
9700 France Ave S ... Bloomington MN 55431	**866-880-8740**	952-487-8200	162
NormaTec			
480 Pleasant St ... Watertown MA 02472	**800-335-0960**		
NorMed PO Box 3644 ... Seattle WA 98124	**800-288-8200**		475
NORML (National Organization for the Reform of Marijuana)			
1600 K St NW Ste 501 ... Washington DC 20006	**888-420-8932**	202-483-5500	48-8
NORPAC Foods Inc			
930 W Washington St ... Stayton OR 97383	**800-733-9311**	503-769-6361	296-21
Norred & Associates Inc			
1003 Virginia Ave Ste 200 ... Atlanta GA 30354	**800-962-6363**	404-761-5058	
Norris Cylinder Co			
4818 W Loop 281 ... Longview TX 75603	**800-527-8418**	903-757-7633	223
Norris Ford			
901 Merritt Blvd ... Baltimore MD 21222	**888-205-0310***	410-285-0200	57
*Sales			
Norris Injury Lawyers			
10 Old Montgomery Hwy ... Birmingham AL 35209	**800-477-7510**		
Norris Public Power District			
606 Irving St PO Box 399 ... Beatrice NE 68310	**800-858-4707**	402-223-4038	245
Norsask Farm Equipment Ltd			
Hwy 16 E ... North Battleford SK S9A2X6	**888-446-8128**	306-445-8128	111
Norsat International Inc			
110-4020 Viking Way ... Richmond BC V6V2L4	**800-644-4562**	604-821-2800	730
TSX: NII			
Norscot Group Inc			
1000 W Donges Bay Rd ... Mequon WI 53092	**800-653-3313**	262-241-3313	9
Norshield Corp			
3232 Mobile Hwy ... Montgomery AL 36108	**855-859-3716**	334-551-0650	349
Nortech Systems Inc			
7550 Meridian Cir N Ste 150 ... Maple Grove MN 55369	**800-237-9576**	952-345-2244	253
NASDAQ: NSYS			
Nortek Inc			
50 Kennedy Plz ... Providence RI 02903	**800-422-4328**		
NASDAQ: NTK			
Nortek Security & Control LLC			
1950 Camino Vida Roble Ste 150 ... Carlsbad CA 92008	**800-421-1587***	760-438-7000	688
*Cust Svc			
North Alabama Electric Co-op			
41103 US Hwy 72 ... Stevenson AL 35772	**800-572-2900**	256-437-2281	245
North American Arms Inc			
2150 S 950 E ... Provo UT 84606	**800-821-5783**	801-374-9990	802
North American Assn of Food Equipment Manufacturers (NAFEM)			
161 N Clark St Ste 2020 ... Chicago IL 60601	**888-493-5961**	312-821-0201	49-13
North American Bldg Material Distribution Assn (NBMDA)			
330 N Wabash Ave Ste 2000 ... Chicago IL 60611	**888-747-7862**	312-321-6845	49-18
North American Container Corp			
1811 W Oak Pkwy Ste D ... Marietta GA 30062	**800-929-0610**	770-431-4858	100
North American Council on Adoptable Children (NACAC)			
970 Raymond Ave Ste 106 ... Saint Paul MN 55114	**877-823-2237**	651-644-3036	48-6
North American Industries Inc			
80 Holton St ... Woburn MA 01801	**800-847-8470**	781-897-4100	468
North American Industry Classification System (NAICS)			
US Census Bureau			
4600 Silver Hill Rd ... Washington DC 20233	**800-923-8282**	301-763-4636	339-2
North American Limousin Foundation (NALF)			
6 Inverness Ct E Ste 260 ... Englewood CO 80112	**888-320-8747**	303-220-1693	48-2
North American Millers Assn (NAMA)			
600 Maryland Ave SW			
Ste 825-W ... Washington DC 20024	**800-633-5137**	202-484-2200	49-6
North American Mission Board SBC			
4200 N Pt Pkwy ... Alpharetta GA 30022	**800-634-2462**	770-410-6000	48-5
North American Palladium Ltd			
1 University Ave Ste 402 ... Toronto ON M5J2P1	**888-360-7590**	416-360-7590	500
TSX: PDL			
North American Pipe Corp			
2801 Post Oak Blvd Ste 600 ... Houston TX 77056	**855-624-7473**	713-840-7473	592
North American Plywood Corp			
12343 Hawkins St ... Santa Fe Springs CA 90670	**800-421-1372***	562-941-7575	609
*Sales			
North American Products Corp			
1180 Wernsing Rd ... Jasper IN 47546	**800-457-7468***	812-482-2000	453
*Cust Svc			
North American Publishing Co (NAPCO)			
1500 Springarden St			
12th Fl ... Philadelphia PA 19130	**800-627-2689**	215-238-5300	633-9
North American Rescue LLC			
35 Tedwall Ct ... Greer SC 29650	**888-689-6277**		
North American Roofing Services Inc			
41 Dogwood Rd ... Asheville NC 28806	**800-551-5602**	828-687-7767	189-12
North American Savings Bank (NASB)			
12520 S 71 Hwy ... Grandview MO 64030	**800-677-6272**	816-765-2200	70
North American Science Assoc Inc			
6750 Wales Rd ... Northwood OH 43619	**866-666-9455**	419-666-9455	664
North American Specialty Glass			
2175 Kumry Rd PO Box 70 ... Trumbauersville PA 18970	**888-785-5962**	215-536-0333	331
North American Specialty Insurance Co			
650 Elm St 6th Fl ... Manchester NH 03101	**800-542-9200**	603-644-6600	390-4
North American Spine Society (NASS)			
7075 Veterans Blvd ... Burr Ridge IL 60527	**877-774-6337**	630-230-3600	49-8
North American Steel Co			
18300 Miles Ave ... Cleveland OH 44128	**800-321-9310**	216-475-7300	490
North American Tool Corp			
215 Elmwood Ave ... South Beloit IL 61080	**800-872-8277**	815-389-2300	491

	Toll-Free	Phone	Class
North American Van Lines Inc			
5001 US Hwy 30 W ... Fort Wayne IN 46818	**800-348-2111**	260-429-2511	219
North Arkansas College			
1515 Pioneer Dr ... Harrison AR 72601	**800-679-6622**	870-743-3000	162
North Atlantic			
29 Pippy Pl ... St. John's NL A1B3X2	**877-635-3645**	709-463-8811	532
North Atlantic Corp			
1255 Grand Army Hwy ... Somerset MA 02726	**800-543-5403**		
North Baldwin Chamber of Commerce			
301 McMeans Ave ... Bay Minette AL 36507	**800-634-8104**	251-937-5665	139
North Bay & District Chamber of Commerce			
205 Main St E ... North Bay ON P1B1B2	**888-249-8998**	705-472-8480	137
North Bay Nissan Inc			
1250 Auto Ctr Dr ... Petaluma CA 94952	**855-540-5697**		
North Bay Produce Inc			
PO Box 549 ... Traverse City MI 49685	**800-678-1941**		297-7
North Canton Area Chamber of Commerce			
121 S Main St ... North Canton OH 44720	**800-833-3722**	330-499-5100	139
North Carolina			
Agriculture Dept			
2 W Edenton St 1001 MSC ... Raleigh NC 27601	**800-735-2962**	919-733-7125	338-34
Department of Military and Veterans Affairs			
413 North Salisbury S ... Raleigh NC 27603	**844-624-8387**		
Housing Finance Agency			
3508 Bush St ... Raleigh NC 27609	**800-393-0988**	919-877-5700	338-34
Labor Dept			
1101 Mail Service Ctr ... Raleigh NC 27699	**800-625-2267**	919-807-2796	338-34
Marine Fisheries Div			
3441 Arendell St ... Morehead City NC 28557	**800-682-2632**	252-726-7021	338-34
Parks & Recreation Div			
121 W Jones St NRC Bldg 2nd Fl ... Raleigh NC 27603	**877-722-6762**	919-707-9300	338-34
Securities Div			
PO Box 29622 ... Raleigh NC 27626	**800-688-4507**	919-814-5400	338-34
Transportation Dept			
1 S Wilmington St ... Raleigh NC 27611	**877-368-4968**		338-34
Utilities Commission			
4325 Mail Service Ctr			
Dobbs Bldg ... Raleigh NC 27699	**866-380-9816**	919-733-7328	338-34
Victims Compensation Services Div			
4232 Mail Service Ctr ... Raleigh NC 27699	**800-826-6200**	919-733-7974	338-34
Vocational Rehabilitation Services Div			
2801 MSC ... Raleigh NC 27699	**800-689-9090**	919-855-3500	338-34
North Carolina A & T State University			
1601 E Market St ... Greensboro NC 27411	**800-443-8964***	336-334-7946	166
*Admissions			
North Carolina Assn of Realtors Inc			
4511 Weybridge Ln ... Greensboro NC 27407	**800-443-9956**	336-294-1415	652
North Carolina Central University			
1801 Fayetteville St ... Durham NC 27707	**877-667-7533***	919-530-6100	166
*Admissions			
North Carolina Dental Society			
1600 Evans Rd ... Cary NC 27513	**800-662-8754**	919-677-1396	227
North Carolina Eye Bank Inc			
3900 Westpoint Blvd Ste F ... Winston-Salem NC 27103	**800-552-9956**		269
North Carolina Farm Bureau Mutual Insurance Co (NCFBMIC)			
PO Box 27427 ... Raleigh NC 27611	**800-584-1143**	919-782-1705	390-4
North Carolina Granite Corp			
151 Granite Quarry Trl			
PO Box 151 ... Mount Airy NC 27030	**800-227-6242**	336-786-5141	720
North Carolina High Country Host			
1700 Blowing Rock Rd ... Boone NC 28607	**800-438-7500**	828-264-1299	206
North Carolina Library Assn (NCLA)			
1811 Capital Blvd ... Raleigh NC 27604	**888-977-3143**	919-839-6252	434
North Carolina Medical Society			
222 N Person St ... Raleigh NC 27601	**800-722-1350**	919-833-3836	472
North Carolina Mutual Life Insurance Co			
411 W Chapel Hill St ... Durham NC 27701	**800-626-1899**		390-2
North Carolina Mutual Wholesale Drug Co			
816 Ellis Rd ... Durham NC 27703	**800-800-8551**	919-596-2151	238
North Carolina Nurses Assn (NCNA)			
103 Enterprise St PO Box 12025 ... Raleigh NC 27605	**800-626-2153**	919-821-4250	529
North Carolina Sports Hall of Fame			
5 E Edenton St			
NC Museum of History ... Raleigh NC 27601	**877-627-6724**	919-807-7900	519
North Carolina State Bar			
217 E Edenton St PO Box 25996 ... Raleigh NC 27601	**800-662-7407**	919-828-4620	72
North Carolina State Education Assistance Authority (NCSEAA)			
PO Box 14103 ... Research Triangle Park NC 27709	**800-700-1775**	919-549-8614	721
North Carolina State University			
2200 Hillsborough St ... Raleigh NC 27695	**800-662-7301**	919-515-2011	166
North Carolina State University Libraries			
CB 7111 ... Raleigh NC 27695	**877-601-0590**	919-515-2843	433-6
North Carolina Veterinary Medical Assn (NCVMA)			
1611 Jones Franklin Rd Ste 108 ... Raleigh NC 27606	**800-446-2862**	919-851-5850	790
North Carolina Wesleyan College			
3400 N Wesleyan Blvd ... Rocky Mount NC 27804	**800-488-6292***	252-985-5100	166
*Admissions			
North Central Assn Commission on Accreditation & School Improvement (NCA CASI)			
9115 Westside Pkwy ... Alpharetta GA 30009	**888-413-3669**		48-1
North Central Assn Higher Learning Commission			
230 S LaSalle St ... Chicago IL 60604	**800-621-7440**	312-263-0456	49-5
North Central Bronx Hospital			
3424 Kossuth Ave ... Bronx NY 10467	**877-207-2134**	718-519-5000	373-3
North Central College			
30 N Brainard St ... Naperville IL 60540	**800-411-1861**	630-637-5800	166
North Central Electric Co-op Inc			
538 11th St W ... Bottineau ND 58318	**800-247-1197**	701-228-2202	245
North Central Electric Co-op Inc			
13978 E County Rd 56 ... Attica OH 44807	**800-426-3072**	419-426-3072	245
North Central Michigan College			
1515 Howard St ... Petoskey MI 49770	**888-298-6605**	231-348-6605	162
North Central Pennsylvania Regional Planning & Development Commission			
651 Montmorenci Rd ... Ridgway PA 15853	**800-942-9467**	814-773-3162	194
North Central Public Power District			
1409 Main St PO Box 90 ... Creighton NE 68729	**800-578-1060**	402-358-5112	245
North Central State College			
2441 Kenwood Cir ... Mansfield OH 44906	**888-755-4899**	419-755-4800	795

Name / Address	City	State	ZIP	Toll-Free	Phone	Class
North Central University						
910 Elliot Ave S	Minneapolis	MN	55404	**800-289-6222***	612-343-4460	166
*Admissions						
North Channel Capital Management Group						
5550 S 59th St Ste 26	Lincoln	NE	68516	**877-421-6501**	402-421-6500	
North Country Business Products Inc						
1112 S Railroad St SE	Bemidji	MN	56601	**800-937-4140**		320
North Country Community College						
23 Santanoni Ave	Saranac Lake	NY	12983	**888-879-6222**	518-891-2915	162
North Country Federal Credit Union Inc						
69 Swift St Ste 100	South Burlington	VT	05403	**800-660-3258**	802-657-6847	219
North Country Trail Assn						
229 E Main St	Lowell	MI	49331	**866-445-3628**	616-897-5987	48-23
North Dakota						
Accountancy Board						
2701 S Columbia Rd Ste D	Grand Forks	ND	58201	**800-532-5904**	701-775-7100	338-35
Aging Services Div						
1237 W Divide Ave Ste 6	Bismarck	ND	58501	**855-462-5465**	701-328-4649	338-35
Agriculture Dept						
600 E Blvd Ave Dept 602	Bismarck	ND	58505	**800-242-7535**	701-328-2231	338-35
Attorney General						
600 E Blvd Ave Dept 125	Bismarck	ND	58505	**800-472-2600**	701-328-2210	338-35
Child Support Enforcement Div						
1600 E Century Ave Ste 2 PO Box 2057	Bismarck	ND	58502	**800-231-4255**	701-328-3582	338-35
Consumer Protection Div						
1050 E Interstate Ave Ste 200	Bismarck	ND	58503	**800-472-2600**	701-328-3404	
Drivers License & Traffic Safety Div						
608 E Blvd Ave	Bismarck	ND	58505	**855-637-6237**	701-328-2500	338-35
Financial Institutions Dept						
2000 Schafer St Ste G	Bismarck	ND	58501	**800-366-6888**	701-328-9933	338-35
Governor						
600 E Blvd Ave	Bismarck	ND	58505	**888-328-2112**	701-328-2200	
Housing Finance Agency						
2624 Vermont Ave PO Box 1535	Bismarck	ND	58502	**800-292-8621**	701-328-8080	338-35
Insurance Dept						
600 E Blvd Ave	Bismarck	ND	58505	**800-247-0560**	701-328-2440	338-35
Labor and Human Rights Dept						
600 E Blvd Ave Dept 406	Bismarck	ND	58505	**800-582-8032**	701-328-2660	338-35
Parks & Recreation Dept						
1600 E Century Ave Ste 3 PO Box 5594	Bismarck	ND	58506	**800-366-6888**	701-328-5357	338-35
Secretary of State						
600 E Blvd Ave Dept 108	Bismarck	ND	58505	**800-352-0867**	701-328-2900	338-35
Securities Dept						
600 E Blvd Ave State Capitol 5th Fl	Bismarck	ND	58505	**800-297-5124**	701-328-2910	338-35
Tax Dept						
600 E Blvd Ave	Bismarck	ND	58505	**800-638-2901**	701-328-3470	338-35
Testing & Safety Div						
600 E Blvd Dept 408	Bismarck	ND	58505	**877-245-6685**	701-328-2400	338-35
Tourism Div						
1600 E Century Ave Ste 2	Bismarck	ND	58502	**800-435-5663**	701-328-2525	338-35
Transportation Dept						
608 E Blvd Ave	Bismarck	ND	58505	**855-637-6237**	701-328-2500	338-35
Veterans Affairs Dept						
4201 38th St SW Ste 104 PO Box 9003	Fargo	ND	58104	**866-634-8387**	701-239-7165	338-35
Vocational Rehabilitation Div						
1237 W Divide Ave Ste 2	Bismarck	ND	58501	**888-862-7342**	701-328-8800	338-35
Workers Compensation						
1600 E Century Ave Ste 1	Bismarck	ND	58503	**800-777-5033**	701-328-3800	338-35
North Dakota Assn of Realtors						
318 W Apollo Ave	Bismarck	ND	58503	**800-279-2361**	701-355-1010	652
North Dakota Dental Assn						
1720 Burnt Boat Dr Ste 201	Bismarck	ND	58503	**800-444-1330**	701-223-8870	227
North Dakota Mill & Elevator						
1823 Mill Rd	Grand Forks	ND	58203	**800-538-7721**	701-795-7000	296-23
North Dakota State College of Science						
800 Sixth St N	Wahpeton	ND	58076	**800-342-4325**	701-671-2401	162
North Dakota State Hospital						
2605 Cir Dr	Jamestown	ND	58401	**888-862-7342**	701-253-3650	373-5
North Dakota State Library (NDSL)						
604 E Blvd Ave	Bismarck	ND	58505	**800-472-2104**	701-328-4622	433-5
North Dakota State University						
1301 12th Ave N	Fargo	ND	58105	**800-488-6378**	701-231-8011	166
North Delta Planning & Development District						
220 Power Dr	Batesville	MS	38606	**800-844-2433**	662-561-4100	
North East Mall						
1101 Melbourne St Ste 1000	Hurst	TX	76053	**877-746-6642**	817-284-3427	458
North Face, The						
14450 Doolittle Dr	San Leandro	CA	94577	**855-500-8639**	877-992-0111	706
North Florida Community College						
325 NW Turner Davis Dr	Madison	FL	32340	**866-937-6322**	850-973-2288	162
North Florida Lincoln Mercury						
4620 Southside Blvd	Jacksonville	FL	32216	**888-457-1949**	877-941-1435	513
North Fork Ranch (NFR)						
55395 Hwy 285 PO Box B	Shawnee	CO	80475	**800-843-7895**	303-838-9873	239
North Greenville University						
7801 N Tigerville Rd PO Box 1892	Tigerville	SC	29688	**800-468-6642**	864-977-7000	162
North Hennepin Community College						
7411 85th Ave N	Brooklyn Park	MN	55445	**800-818-0395**	763-488-0391	162
North Idaho College						
1000 W Garden Ave	Coeur d'Alene	ID	83814	**877-404-4536**	208-769-3300	162
North Iowa Area Community College						
500 College Dr	Mason City	IA	50401	**888-466-4222**	641-423-1264	162
North Island College						
2300 Ryan Rd	Courtenay	BC	V9N8N6	**800-715-0914**	250-334-5000	166
North Island Credit Union						
5898 Copley Dr	San Diego	CA	92111	**800-334-8788**		219
North Itasca Electric Co-op Inc						
301 Main Ave PO Box 227	Bigfork	MN	56628	**800-762-4048**	218-743-3131	245
North Lake Tahoe Resort Assn						
100 N Lake Blvd	Tahoe City	CA	96145	**800-468-2463**	530-583-3494	206
North Lake Tahoe Visitors & Convention Bureau						
PO Box 1757	Tahoe City	CA	96145	**800-462-5196**	530-581-6900	206
North Light Color						
5008 Hillsboro Ave N	New Hope	MN	55428	**866-922-4700**	763-531-8222	
North Los Angel County Regional Ctr						
9200 Oakdale Ave Ste 100	Chatsworth	CA	91311	**800-430-4263**	818-778-1900	362
North Ontario Library Service						
334 Regent St	Sudbury	ON	P3C4E2	**800-461-6348**	705-675-6467	435
North Park Theological Seminary						
3225 W Foster Ave	Chicago	IL	60625	**800-964-0101**	773-244-6229	167-3
North Park University						
3225 W Foster Ave	Chicago	IL	60625	**800-888-6728**	773-244-5500	166
North Plains Electric Co-op Inc						
14585 Hwy 83 N PO Box 1008	Perryton	TX	79070	**800-272-5482**	806-435-5482	245
North Platte & Lincoln County Visitors Bureau						
101 Halligan Dr	North Platte	NE	69101	**800-955-4528**	308-532-4729	206
North Platte Community College						
North						
1101 Halligan Dr	North Platte	NE	69101	**800-658-4308**	308-535-3601	162
South						
601 W State Farm Rd	North Platte	NE	69101	**800-658-4348**		162
North Ridgeville City School District						
5490 Mills Creek Ln	North Ridgeville	OH	44039	**877-644-6457**	440-327-4444	681
North Ridgeville Visitors Bureau						
34845 Lorain Rd	North Ridgeville	OH	44039	**800-334-5910**	440-327-3737	206
North River Boats Inc						
1750 Green Siding Rd	Roseburg	OR	97471	**800-413-6351**	541-673-2438	694
North San Antonio Chamber of Commerce						
12930 Country Pkwy	San Antonio	TX	78216	**877-495-5888**	210-344-4848	139
North Santiam State Recreation Area						
PO Box 549	Detroit	OR	97342	**800-551-6949**		561
North Seattle Community College						
9600 College Way North	Seattle	WA	98103	**866-427-4747**	206-527-3600	162
North Shore Bank FSB						
15700 W Bluemound Rd	Brookfield	WI	53005	**800-236-4672**	877-672-2265	70
North Shore Community College						
1 Ferncroft Rd	Danvers	MA	01923	**800-841-2900**	978-762-4000	162
North Shore Gas Co						
3001 Grand Ave	Waukegan	IL	60085	**866-556-6004**		782
North Shore Medical Ctr						
1100 NW 95th St	Miami	FL	33150	**800-984-3434**	305-835-6000	373-3
North Shore University Hospital						
300 Community Dr	Manhasset	NY	11030	**888-214-4065**	516-562-0100	373-3
North Slope Borough						
PO Box 69	Barrow	AK	99723	**800-478-0267**	907-852-2611	337
North South Supply Inc						
686 Third Pl	Vero Beach	FL	32962	**800-940-3810**	772-569-3810	
North Star Electric Co-op						
441 State Hwy 172 NW PO Box 719	Baudette	MN	56623	**888-634-2202**	218-634-2202	245
North Star Glove Co						
2916 S Steele St	Tacoma	WA	98409	**800-423-1616**	253-627-7107	155-7
North Star Lighting Inc						
2150 Parkes Dr	Broadview	IL	60155	**800-229-4330**	708-681-4330	438
North Star Mall						
7400 San Pedro Ave	San Antonio	TX	78216	**800-866-6511**	210-340-6627	458
North Star Resource Group Inc						
2701 University Ave SE N Star Professional Ctr	Minneapolis	MN	55414	**800-820-4205**	612-617-6000	389
North State Bank Inc						
6204 Falls of Neuse Rd	Raleigh	NC	27609	**877-357-2265**	919-787-9696	359-2
North States Industries Inc						
1507 92nd Ln NE	Blaine	MN	55449	**800-848-8421**	763-486-1756	574
North Suburban Medical Ctr (NSMC)						
9191 Grant St	Thornton	CO	80229	**877-647-7440**	303-451-7800	373-3
North Toledo Bend State Park						
2907 N Toledo Pk Rd	Zwolle	LA	71486	**888-677-6400**	318-645-4715	561
North Western Electric Co-op Inc						
04125 State Rt 576 PO Box 391	Bryan	OH	43506	**800-647-6932**	419-636-5051	245
North Winds Investigations Inc						
119 S Second St PO Box 1654	Rogers	AR	72756	**800-530-4514**	479-925-1612	399
Northampton Community College						
3835 Green Pond Rd	Bethlehem	PA	18020	**877-543-0998**	610-861-5300	162
Northbridge Financial Corp						
105 Adelaide St W Ste 700	Toronto	ON	M5H1P9	**855-620-6262**	416-350-4400	359-2
Northcentral Technical College						
1000 W Campus Dr	Wausau	WI	54401	**888-682-7144**	715-675-3331	795
NorthCoast Asset Management LLC						
1 Greenwich Office Pk	Greenwich	CT	06831	**800-274-5448**	203-532-7000	400
Northeast Airmotive Inc						
1011 Westbrook St	Portland	ME	04102	**877-354-7881**	207-774-6318	63
Northeast Alabama Community College						
PO Box 159	Rainsville	AL	35986	**800-548-2546**	256-228-6001	162
Northeast Bancorp						
500 Canal St	Lewiston	ME	04240	**800-284-5989**	207-786-3245	359-2
NASDAQ: NBN						
Northeast Baptist Hospital						
8811 Village Dr	San Antonio	TX	78217	**800-201-9353**	210-297-2000	373-3
Northeast Battery & Alternator Inc						
240 Washington St	Auburn	MA	01501	**800-441-8824**	508-832-2700	61
Northeast Community College						
801 E Benjamin Ave PO Box 469	Norfolk	NE	68702	**800-348-9033**	402-371-2020	162
Northeast Florida Telephone Company Inc						
130 N Fourth St	Macclenny	FL	32063	**800-416-6707**	904-259-2261	386
Northeast Iowa Community College						
Calmar						
1625 Hwy 150 S PO Box 400	Calmar	IA	52132	**800-728-2256**	563-562-3263	162
Peosta 8342 NICC Dr	Peosta	IA	52068	**800-728-7367**	563-556-5110	162
Northeast Methodist Hospital						
12412 Judson Rd	San Antonio	TX	78233	**800-333-7333**	210-757-7000	373-3
Northeast Mississippi Community College						
101 Cunningham Blvd	Booneville	MS	38829	**800-555-2154**	662-728-7751	162
Northeast Mississippi Daily Journal						
1242 S Green St	Tupelo	MS	38804	**800-264-6397**	662-842-2611	528-2
Northeast Ohio Medical University						
4209 St Rt 44 PO Box 95	Rootstown	OH	44272	**800-686-2511**		167-2
Northeast Oklahoma Electric Co-op Inc						
443857 E Hwy 60 PO Box 948	Vinita	OK	74301	**800-256-6405**	918-256-6405	245
Northeast Remsco Construction Inc						
1433 Hwy 34 S Bldg B1	Farmingdale	NJ	07727	**800-879-8204**	732-557-6100	188-7
Northeast State Technical Community College						
PO Box 246	Blountville	TN	37617	**800-836-7822**	423-323-3191	795

Alphabetical Section

	Toll-Free	Phone	Class
Northeast Texas Community College 1735 Chapel Hill Rd .... Mount Pleasant TX 75455	800-870-0142	903-572-1911	162
Northeast Valley Health Corp 1172 N Maclay Ave .... San Fernando CA 91340	800-313-4942	818-898-1388	
Northeast Wisconsin Technical College PO Box 19042 .... Green Bay WI 54307	800-422-6982	920-498-5400	795
Northeastern Junior College 100 College Ave .... Sterling CO 80751	800-626-4637	970-521-6600	162
Northeastern Log Homes Inc 10 Ames Rd .... Kenduskeag ME 04450	800-624-2797	207-884-7000	106
Northeastern State University *Muskogee* 2400 W Shawnee .... Muskogee OK 74401	800-722-9614	918-683-0040	166
Tahlequah 600 N Grand Ave .... Tahlequah OK 74464	800-722-9614	918-456-5511	166
Northeastern Supply Inc 8323 Pulaski Hwy ....Baltimore MD 21237	877-637-8775	410-574-0010	608
Northeastern Technical College 1201 Chesterfield Hwy .... Cheraw SC 29520	800-921-7399	843-921-6900	162
Northeastern University 360 Huntington Ave .... Boston MA 02115	855-476-3391	617-373-2000	166
Northern 3625 Cincinnati Ave .... Rocklin CA 95765	855-388-7422	916-543-4000	246
Northern Arizona Regional Behavioral Health Authority Inc (NARBHA) 1300 S Yale St ....Flagstaff AZ 86001	877-923-1400	928-774-7128	49-15
Northern Arizona University PO Box 4084 ....Flagstaff AZ 86011 *Admissions	888-628-2968*	928-523-5511	166
Northern Arizona VA Health Care System 500 Hwy 89 N .... Prescott AZ 86313	800-949-1005	928-445-4860	373-8
Northern Business Products Inc PO Box 16127 .... Duluth MN 55816	800-647-8775	218-726-0167	
Northern California World Trade Ctr 1 Capitol Mall Ste 700 ...... Sacramento CA 95814	855-667-2259	916-447-9827	817
Northern Contours Inc 1355 Mendota Heights Rd Ste 100 ....Mendota Heights MN 55120	866-344-8132	651-695-1698	115
Northern Digital Inc 103 Randall Dr .... Waterloo ON N2V1C5	877-634-6340	519-884-5142	406
Northern Electric Inc 12789 Emerson St .... Thornton CO 80241	877-265-0794	303-428-6969	782
Northern Exposure Greeting Cards 2194 Northpoint Pkwy ....Santa Rosa CA 95407	800-237-3524		130
Northern Factory Sales Inc PO Box 660 .... Willmar MN 56201	800-328-8900	320-235-2288	61
Northern Illinois University 1425 W Lincoln Hwy ....DeKalb IL 60115	800-892-3050	815-753-1000	166
Northern Illinois University University Libraries 1425 W Lincoln Hwy ....DeKalb IL 60115	800-892-3050	815-753-1000	433-6
Northern Indiana Commuter Transportation District 33 E US Hwy 12 ....Chesterton IN 46304	800-743-3333	219-926-5744	466
Northern Industrial Sales Ltd 3526 Opie Cres .... Prince George BC V2N2P9	800-668-3317	250-562-4435	686
Northern Institutional Funds 801 S Canal St C5S .... Chicago IL 60607	800-637-1380		524
Northern Jet Management 5500 44th St SE ....Grand Rapids MI 49512	800-462-7709	616-336-4800	23
Northern Kentucky Convention & Visitors Bureau (NKYCVB) 50 E RiverCenter Blvd Ste 200 .... Covington KY 41011	877-659-8474	859-261-4677	206
Northern Kentucky University Nunn Dr ....Highland Heights KY 41099 *Admissions	800-637-9948*	859-572-5220	166
Northern Kentucky Water District 2835 Crescent Springs Rd ....Erlanger KY 41018	800-772-4636	859-578-9898	782
Northern Lights Inc 4420 14th Ave NW .... Seattle WA 98107	800-762-0165	206-789-3880	262
Northern Lights Inc 421 Cherry St PO Box 269 .... Sagle ID 83860	800-326-9594	208-263-5141	245
Northern Maine Community College (NMCC) 33 Edgemont Dr ....Presque Isle ME 04769	800-535-6682	207-768-2700	795
Northern Michigan University 1401 Presque Isle Ave .... Marquette MI 49855	800-682-9797	906-227-2650	166
Northern Natural Gas Co 1111 S 103rd St ....Omaha NE 68124	877-654-0646	402-398-7000	325
Northern Neck Electric Co-op Inc 85 St Johns St PO Box 288 .... Warsaw VA 22572	800-243-2860	804-333-3621	245
Northern New Mexico College 921 Paseo de Onate .... Espanola NM 87532	800-477-3632	505-747-2100	162
Northern New York Library Network 6721 US Hwy 11 .... Potsdam NY 13676	877-833-1674	315-265-1119	433-3
Northern Ohio Printing Inc 4721 Hinckley Indus Pkwy ....Cleveland OH 44109	800-407-7284	216-398-0000	623
Northern Oklahoma College 1220 E Grand St PO Box 310 ....Tonkawa OK 74653	800-522-0188	580-628-6200	162
Northern Plains Electric Co-op 1515 W Main St .... Carrington ND 58421	800-882-2500		245
Northern Power Systems Inc 29 Pitman Rd .... Barre VT 05641	877-906-6784	802-461-2955	664
Northern Quest Resort & Casino 100 N Hayford Rd ....Airway Heights WA 99001	877-871-6772		133
Northern Regional Correctional Facility 112 Northern Regional Correctional Dr ....Moundsville WV 26041	866-984-8463	304-843-4067	213
Northern Rockies Lodge Mile 462 Alaska Hwy ....Muncho Lake BC V0C1Z0	800-663-5269	250-776-3481	703
Northern Security Insurance Co PO Box 188 ....Montpelier VT 05601	800-451-5000	802-223-2341	390-4
Northern State Correctional Facility 2559 Glen Rd .... Newport VT 05855	800-347-0488	802-334-3364	213
Northern State University 1200 S Jay St .... Aberdeen SD 57401	800-678-5330		166
Northern States Financial Corp 1601 N Lewis Ave .... Waukegan IL 60085 OTC: NSFC	800-339-4432	847-244-6000	359-2
Northern States Metals Co 3207 Innovation Pl ....Youngstown OH 44509	800-689-0666		
Northern Technologies International Corp (NTIC) 4201 Woodland Rd PO Box 69 ....Circle Pines MN 55014 NASDAQ: NTIC	800-328-2433	763-225-6600	145
Northern Tool & Equipment Co 2800 Southcross Dr W .... Burnsville MN 55306 *Cust Svc	800-222-5381*	952-894-9510	363
Northern Trust Co 50 S LaSalle St .... Chicago IL 60603 NASDAQ: NTRS	888-289-6542	312-630-6000	70
Northern Trust Company of Connecticut 300 Atlantic St Ste 400 .... Stamford CT 06901	866-876-9944	312-630-0779	400
Northern Virginia Community College *Alexandria* 5000 Dawes Ave .... Alexandria VA 22311	855-259-1019	703-845-6200	162
Annandale 8333 Little River Tpke .... Annandale VA 22003	877-408-2028	703-323-3000	162
Manassas 6901 Sudley Rd .... Manassas VA 20109	855-259-1019	703-257-6620	162
Northern Virginia Electric Co-op PO Box 2710 .... Manassas VA 20108	888-335-0500	703-335-0500	245
Northern Waters Library Service 3200 E Lakeshore Dr .... Ashland WI 54806	800-228-5684	715-682-2365	433-3
Northern Westchester Hospital 400 E Main St .... Mount Kisco NY 10549	877-469-4362	914-666-1200	373-3
Northfield Lines Inc 1034 Gemini Rd ....Eagan MN 55121	888-670-8068	651-203-8888	107
Northfield Mount Hermon School 1 Lamplighter Way ....Gill MA 01354	866-664-4483	413-498-3227	618
Northfield Savings Bank (NSB) PO Box 7180 .... Barre VT 05641	800-672-2274		70
Northland Auto & Truck Accessories 1106 S 29th St W .... Billings MT 59102	800-736-5302	406-245-0595	54
Northland College 1411 Ellis Ave .... Ashland WI 54806	800-753-1840	715-682-1224	166
Northland Community & Technical College 1101 US Hwy 1 E ....Thief River Falls MN 56701	800-959-6282	218-681-0701	162
East Grand Forks 2022 Central Ave NE .....East Grand Forks MN 56721	800-451-3441	218-773-3441	162
Northland Furniture Co 681 SE Glenwood .... Bend OR 97702	800-497-7591		
Northland Insurance Co 385 Washington St .... Saint Paul MN 55102	800-237-9334		390-4
Northland Pioneer College PO Box 610 .... Holbrook AZ 86025	800-266-7845	928-532-6111	162
Northland Plastics Inc 1420 S 16th St PO Box 290 ....Sheboygan WI 53081	800-776-7163		596
Northland Securities Inc 150 S Fifth St Ste 3300 ....Minneapolis MN 55402	800-851-2920	612-851-5900	
Northland Services Inc 6700 W Marginal Way SW .... Seattle WA 98106	800-426-3113	206-763-3000	312
Northland Trucking Inc 1515 S 22nd Ave .... Phoenix AZ 85009	800-214-5564	602-254-0007	775
Northleaf Capital Partners 79 Wellington St W 6th Fl PO Box 120 .... Toronto ON M5K1N9	866-964-4141		787
Northport Medical Ctr 2700 Hospital Dr ....Northport AL 35476	866-840-0750	205-333-4500	373-3
Northrim BanCorp Inc 3111 C St .... Anchorage AK 99503 NASDAQ: NRIM	800-478-3311	907-562-0062	70
Northrop Grumman Newport News 13560 Jefferson Ave .... Newport News VA 23603	888-493-7386	757-886-7777	694
Northshire Information Inc 4869 Main St ....Manchester Center VT 05255	800-437-3700	802-362-2200	95
Northspan Group Inc, The 221 W First St .... Duluth MN 55802	800-232-0707	218-722-5545	196
Northstar Cruises PO Box 248 ....Essex Fells NJ 07021	800-249-9360		766
Northstar Investment Advisors LLC 700 17th St Ste 2350 ....Denver CO 80202	800-204-6199	303-832-2300	524
NorthStar Moving Corp 9120 Mason Ave .... Chatsworth CA 91311	800-275-7767	818-727-0128	516
Northstar-at-Tahoe PO Box 129 .... Truckee CA 96160	800-466-6784		665
Northtown Products Inc 5202 Argosy Ave ..... Huntington Beach CA 92649	800-972-7274	714-897-0700	537
Northumberland County 201 Market St 2nd Fl .... Sunbury PA 17801	800-692-4332	570-988-4167	337
Northville Downs 301 S Ctr St ....Northville MI 48167	888-349-7100	248-349-1000	638
Northway Toyota 727 New Loudon Rd ....Latham NY 12110	877-800-5098	518-213-5686	57
Northwell Health *North Shore University Hospital* 300 Community Dr 9 Tower Large Conference Rm ...... Manhasset NY 11030	888-321-3627	888-214-4065	764
Northwest 100 Liberty St PO Box 128 ....Warren PA 16365	877-672-5678	814-726-2140	70
Northwest Administrators Inc 2323 Eastlake Ave E .... Seattle WA 98102	877-304-6702	206-329-4900	389
Northwest Arctic Borough PO Box 1110 .... Kotzebue AK 99752	800-478-1110	907-442-2500	337
NorthWest Arkansas Community College 1 College Dr ....Bentonville AR 72712	800-995-6922	479-636-9222	162
Northwest Bank PO Box 128 ....Warren PA 16365	800-859-1000	814-728-7263	359-2
Northwest Chevrolet 35108 92nd Ave S .... McKenna WA 98558 *Sales	855-216-5183*	855-234-9884	
Northwest Christian College 828 E 11th Ave ....Eugene OR 97401	877-463-6622	541-343-1641	166
Northwest College 231 W Sixth St .... Powell WY 82435	800-560-4692	307-754-6000	162
Northwest Communications Coop 111 Railroad Ave PO Box 38 .... Ray ND 58849	800-245-5884	701-568-3331	386
Northwest Community Bank 86 Main St .... Winsted CT 06098	800-455-6668	860-379-7561	70
Northwest Data Solutions LLC 2627 C St .... Anchorage AK 99503	800-544-0786	907-227-1676	177
Northwest Designs Ink Inc 13456 SE 27th Pl Ste 200 ....Bellevue WA 98005	800-925-9327		157-5

				Toll-Free	Phone	Class
Northwest Georgia Trade & Convention Center						
2211 Dug Gap Battle Rd	Dalton	GA	30720	**800-824-7469**	706-272-7676	205
Northwest Grain Growers Inc						
850 N Fourth Ave	Walla Walla	WA	99362	**800-994-4290**	509-525-6510	275
Northwest Herald Inc						
PO Box 250	Crystal Lake	IL	60039	**800-589-8910**	815-459-4040	633-8
Northwest Hospital & Medical Ctr						
1550 N 115th St	Seattle	WA	98133	**877-694-4677**	206-364-0500	373-3
Northwest Hospital Ctr						
5401 Old Ct Rd	Randallstown	MD	21133	**800-876-1175**	410-521-2200	373-3
Northwest Indian College						
2522 Kwina Rd	Bellingham	WA	98226	**866-676-2772**	360-676-2772	165
Northwest Iowa Community College						
603 W Park St	Sheldon	IA	51201	**800-352-4907**	712-324-5061	162
Northwest Medical Ctr						
609 W Maple Ave	Springdale	AR	72764	**800-734-2024**	479-751-5711	373-3
Northwest Mississippi Regional Medical Ctr						
1970 Hospital Dr	Clarksdale	MS	38614	**800-582-2233**	662-627-3211	373-3
Northwest Missouri State University						
800 University Dr	Maryville	MO	64468	**800-633-1175**	660-562-1148	166
Northwest Natural Gas Co						
220 NW Second Ave	Portland	OR	97209	**800-422-4012**	503-226-4211	782
NYSE: NWN						
Northwest Nazarene University						
623 Holly St	Nampa	ID	83686	**877-668-4968***	208-467-8000	166
*Admissions						
Northwest Outlet						
1814 Belknap St	Superior	WI	54880	**800-569-8142**	715-392-9838	707
Northwest Pennsylvania's Great Outdoors Visitors Bureau						
2801 Maplevale Rd	Brookville	PA	15825	**800-348-9393**	814-849-5197	206
Northwest Pipe Co						
12005 N Burgard	Portland	OR	97203	**800-989-9631**	503-285-1400	488
NASDAQ: NWPX						
Northwest Pipe Fittings Inc						
33 S Eigth St W	Billings	MT	59102	**800-937-4737**	406-252-0142	608
Northwest Print Strategies Inc						
8175 SW Nimbus Ave	Beaverton	OR	97008	**800-648-5156**		585
Northwest Rural Public Power District						
5613 State Hwy 87						
PO Box 249	Hay Springs	NE	69347	**800-847-0492**	308-638-4445	245
Northwest Texas Hospital						
1501 S Coulter	Amarillo	TX	79106	**800-887-1114**	806-354-1000	373-3
Northwest University						
5520 108th Ave NE	Kirkland	WA	98033	**800-669-3781***	425-822-8266	166
*Admissions						
Northwest Wholesale Inc						
1567 N Wenatchee Ave	Wenatchee	WA	98801	**800-874-6607**	509-662-2141	276
Northwestern College						
101 Seventh St SW	Orange City	IA	51041	**800-747-4757**	712-707-7000	166
Northwestern College						
3003 Snelling Ave N	Saint Paul	MN	55113	**800-692-4020**	651-631-5100	166
Northwestern College Chicago Campus						
4829 N Lipps Ave	Chicago	IL	60630	**888-205-2283**	773-777-4220	795
Northwestern Counseling & Support Services Inc						
107 Fisher Pond Rd	Saint Albans	VT	05478	**800-834-7793**	802-524-6554	352
Northwestern Electric Cooperative						
2925 William Ave PO Box 2707	Woodward	OK	73801	**800-375-7423**	580-256-7425	245
Northwestern Industries Inc						
2500 W Jameson St	Seattle	WA	98199	**800-426-2771**	206-285-3140	329
Northwestern Medicine Kishwaukee Hospital						
1 Kish Hospital Dr	DeKalb	IL	60115	**800-397-1521**	815-756-1521	373-3
Northwestern Michigan College						
1701 E Front St	Traverse City	MI	49686	**800-748-0566**	231-995-1000	162
Northwestern Mutual Investment Services LLC						
611 E Wisconsin Ave Ste 300	Milwaukee	WI	53202	**866-664-7737**		400
Northwestern Pacific Indemnity Co						
15 Mtn View Rd	Warren	NJ	07059	**800-252-4670***	908-903-2000	390-4
*Claims						
Northwestern Polytechnic University						
47671 Westinghouse Dr	Fremont	CA	94539	**877-878-8883**	510-592-9688	166
Northwestern Publishing House						
1250 N 113th St	Milwaukee	WI	53226	**800-662-6022***		633-3
*Orders						
Northwestern State University						
175 Sam Sibley Dr	Natchitoches	LA	71497	**800-767-8115**	318-357-4078	166
Northwestern State University Watson Memorial Library						
913 University Pkwy	Natchitoches	LA	71497	**888-540-9657**	318-357-4477	433-6
Northwestern Tools Inc						
3130 Valleywood Dr	Dayton	OH	45429	**800-236-3956**	937-298-9994	752
Northwestern University						
1801 Hinman Ave	Evanston	IL	60208	**800-227-7368**	847-491-7271	166
Northwest-Shoals Community College						
Muscle Shoals						
800 George Wallace Blvd	Muscle Shoals	AL	35661	**800-645-8967**	256-331-5200	162
Phil Campbell						
2080 College Rd	Phil Campbell	AL	35581	**800-645-8967**	256-331-6200	162
Northwood University						
Texas						
1114 W FM 1382	Cedar Hill	TX	75104	**800-927-9663**	800-622-9000	166
Northwood University Florida						
2600 N Military Trl	West Palm Beach	FL	33409	**800-458-8325***	561-478-5500	166
*Admissions						
Northwood University Michigan						
4000 Whiting Dr	Midland	MI	48640	**800-622-9000**	989-837-4200	166
Norton Sandblasting Equipment						
1006 Executive Blvd	Chesapeake	VA	23320	**800-366-4341**	757-548-4842	1
Norton's Flowers & Gifts						
2900 Washtenaw Ave	Ypsilanti	MI	48197	**800-682-8667**	734-434-2700	292
Norvin Green State Forest						
c/o Ringwood State Pk						
1304 Sloatsburg Rd	Ringwood	NJ	07456	**800-852-7899**	973-962-7031	561
Norwalk Compressor Co						
1650 Stratford Ave	Stratford	CT	06615	**800-556-5001**		172
Norwalk Concrete Industries Inc						
80 Commerce Dr	Norwalk	OH	44857	**800-733-3624**	419-668-8167	183
Norwalk Public Library						
1 Belden Ave	Norwalk	CT	06850	**800-382-9463**	203-899-2780	433-3
Norwalk-Wilbert Vault Co						
425 Harral Ave	Bridgeport	CT	06604	**800-826-9406**	203-366-5678	134

				Toll-Free	Phone	Class
Norwegian-American Hospital						
1044 N Francisco St	Chicago	IL	60622	**877-624-9333**	773-292-8200	373-3
Norwell Manufacturing Inc						
82 Stevens St	East Taunton	MA	02718	**800-822-2831**	508-823-1751	438
Norwich University						
158 Harmon Dr	Northfield	VT	05663	**800-468-6679**	802-485-2001	166
Norwin Chamber of Commerce						
321 Main St	Irwin	PA	15642	**800-377-3539**	724-863-0888	139
Norwood Hotel						
112 Marion St	Winnipeg	MB	R2H0T1	**888-888-1878**	204-233-4475	378
Nossi College of Art						
590 Cheron Rd	Madison	TN	37115	**888-986-2787**	615-514-2787	166
Notions Marketing Corp						
1500 Buchanan Ave SW	Grand Rapids	MI	49507	**800-748-0250**	616-243-8424	195
Notre Dame College						
4545 College Rd	South Euclid	OH	44121	**877-632-6446**		166
Notre Dame de Namur University						
1500 Ralston Ave	Belmont	CA	94002	**800-263-0545**	650-508-3600	166
Nottoway Plantation						
31025 Louisiana Hwy 1	White Castle	LA	70788	**866-527-6884**	225-545-2730	517
Notus Career Management						
5 Centerpointe Dr Ste 400	Lake Oswego	OR	97035	**800-431-1990**	503-443-1113	41
NOV (National Oilwell Varco)						
7909 Parkwood Cir Dr	Houston	TX	77036	**888-262-8645**	713-375-3700	183
NYSE: NOV						
NOVA (National Organization for Victim Assistance)						
510 King St Ste 424	Alexandria	VA	22314	**800-879-6682**	703-535-6682	48-8
Nova Biologicals Inc						
1775 North Loop 336 E Ste 4	Conroe	TX	77301	**800-282-5416**		738
Nova Biomedical Corp						
200 Prospect St	Waltham	MA	02454	**800-458-5813***	781-894-0800	418
*Sales						
NOVA Chemicals Corp						
1000 Seventh Ave SW PO Box 2518	Calgary	AB	T2P5C6	**800-561-6682**	403-750-3600	601-2
Nova Express Millennium Inc						
105 - 14271 Knox Way	Richmond	BC	V6V2Z4	**877-566-6839**	604-278-8044	317
Nova Fisheries						
2532 Yale Ave E	Seattle	WA	98102	**888-458-6682**	206-781-2000	285
Nova Fitness Equipment						
4511 S 119th Cir	Omaha	NE	68137	**800-949-6682**	402-343-0552	707
Nova Libra Inc						
8609 W Bryn Mawr Ave Ste 208	Chicago	IL	60631	**866-724-1807**	773-714-1441	177
NOVA Medical Products						
1470 Beachey Pl	Carson	CA	90746	**800-557-6682**		473
NOVA of California						
6323 Maywood Ave	Los Angeles	CA	90255	**800-835-6682**	323-277-6266	361
Nova Pole International Inc						
2579 188 St	Surrey	BC	V3Z2A1	**866-874-8889**	604-881-0090	261
Nova Power Solutions						
23020 Eaglewood Ct Ste 100	Sterling	VA	20166	**800-999-6682**		762
Nova Scotia Dept of Tourism & Culture						
8 Water Str PO Box 667	Windsor	NS	B0N2T0	**800-565-0000**	902-798-6700	769
Nova Scotia Health Authority						
5788 University Ave	Halifax	NS	B3H1V7	**888-429-8167**	902-429-8167	541
Nova Scotia Power Inc						
PO Box 910	Halifax	NS	B3J2W5	**800-428-6230**	902-428-6230	782
Nova Solutions Inc						
421 Industrial Ave	Effingham	IL	62401	**800-730-6682**	217-342-7070	319-1
Nova Southeastern University						
3301 College Ave	Fort Lauderdale	FL	33314	**800-541-6682**	954-262-8000	166
Nova Southeastern University Shepard Broad Law Ctr						
3305 College Ave	Fort Lauderdale	FL	33314	**800-986-6529**	954-262-6100	167-1
Nova Tours & Travel Inc						
4255 Virgo Course	Liverpool	NY	13090	**800-543-6682**		770
Novacel 21 Third St	Palmer	MA	01069	**877-668-2235**	413-283-3468	544
Novacoast Inc						
1505 Chapala St	Santa Barbara	CA	93101	**800-949-9933**		180
Novagard Solutions Inc						
5109 Hamilton Ave	Cleveland	OH	44114	**800-380-0138**	216-881-8111	326
NovaGold Resources Inc						
789 W Pender St Ste 720	Vancouver	BC	V6C1H2	**866-669-6277**	604-669-6227	500
NYSE: NG						
Novalab						
2350 Power St	Drummondville	QC	J2C7Z4	**800-474-6682**	819-474-2580	228
Novar Controls Corp						
6060 Rockside Woods Blvd						
Ste 400	Cleveland	OH	44131	**800-348-1235**		202
Novare Capital Management						
521 E Morehead St The Morehead Bldg						
Ste 510	Charlotte	NC	28202	**877-334-3698**	704-334-3698	524
Novartis Pharmaceuticals Canada Inc						
385 boul Bouchard	Dorval	QC	H9S1A9	**800-465-2244**	514-631-6775	578
Novartis Pharmaceuticals Co						
25 Old Mill Rd	Suffern	NY	10901	**888-669-6682**	845-368-6000	578
Novasel & Schwarte Investments Inc						
3170 US Rte 50 Ste 10	South Lake Tahoe	CA	96150	**800-442-5052**	530-577-5050	
Novatec Inc						
222 Thomas Ave	Baltimore	MD	21225	**800-237-8379**	410-789-4811	318
Novatech						
4106 Charlotte Ave	Nashville	TN	37209	**800-264-0637**	615-577-7677	531
Novatech Group Inc						
1401 Nobel St	Sainte-julie	QC	J3E1Z4	**844-986-8001**		330
Novato Chamber of Commerce						
807 DeLong Ave	Novato	CA	94945	**800-897-1164**	415-897-1164	139
Novell Design Studio						
2100 Felver Ct	Rahway	NJ	07065	**888-668-3551**	732-428-8300	408
Noveo Technologies Inc						
9655 A Ignace St	Brossard	QC	J4Y2P3	**877-314-2044**	450-444-2044	606
Novex Software Developments Inc						
8743 Commercial St	New Minas	NS	B4N3C4	**888-542-1813**		177
Novi Chamber of Commerce, The						
41875 W 11 Mile Rd Ste 201	Novi	MI	48375	**888-440-7325**	248-349-3743	139
NOVIPRO Inc						
2055 Peel St Ste 701	Montreal	QC	H3A1V4	**866-726-5353**	514-744-5353	180
Novo Nordisk of North America Inc						
100 College Rd W	Princeton	NJ	08540	**800-727-6500**	609-987-5800	578

	Toll-Free	Phone	Class
Novo Nordisk Pharmaceuticals Inc			
800 Scudders Mill Rd ....Plainsboro NJ 08536	800-727-6500*	609-987-5800	578
*Cust Svc			
Novo Solutions Inc			
516 S Independence Blvd ....Virginia Beach VA 23452	888-316-4559	757-687-6590	180
Novosci			
2021 Airport Rd ....Conroe TX 77301	800-854-0567	281-363-4949	474
Novus Inc			
655 Calle Cubitas ....Guaynabo PR 00969	888-530-4546	787-272-4546	301
NOW (National Organization for Women)			
1100 H St NW 3rd Fl ....Washington DC 20005	855-212-0212	202-628-8669	48-24
Now Courier Inc			
PO Box 6066 ....Indianapolis IN 46206	800-543-6066		457
NowDocs International Inc			
1985 Lookout Dr ....North Mankato MN 56003	888-669-3627		177
Nox-Crete Inc			
1444 S 20th St ....Omaha NE 68108	800-669-2738	402-341-2080	145
Noxent Inc			
6400 Boul Taschereau Bureau 220			
..............................Brossard QC J4W3J2	800-268-4364	450-926-0662	196
Noxubee County			
198 Washington St PO Box 308 ....Macon MS 39341	800-487-0165	662-726-4456	337
NP Dodge Real Estate			
8701 W Dodge Rd Ste 300 ....Omaha NE 68114	800-642-5008	402-255-5099	648
NPA (National Parking Assn)			
1112 16th St NW Ste 840 ....Washington DC 20036	800-647-7275	202-296-4336	49-3
NPAP (National Psychological Assn for Psychoanalysis)			
40 W 13th St ....New York NY 10011	800-365-7006	212-924-7440	49-15
NPC (Navy Personnel Command)			
5720 Integrity Dr ....Millington TN 38055	866-827-5672		339-5
NPC (National Pen Corp)			
12121 Scripps Summit Dr ....San Diego CA 92131	888-672-7370		9
NPC Inc			
13710 Dunnings Hwy ....Claysburg PA 16625	800-847-5757	814-239-8787	623
NPC International Inc			
7300 W 129th St ....Overland Park KS 66213	866-299-1148	913-327-5555	666
NPCA (National Precast Concrete Assn)			
10333 N Meridian St			
Ste 272 ....Indianapolis IN 46290	800-366-7731	317-571-9500	49-3
NPCA (National Parks Conservation Assn)			
1300 19th St NW Ste 300 ....Washington DC 20036	800-628-7275	202-223-6722	48-13
NPCA (National Peace Corps Assn)			
1900 L St NW Ste 610 ....Washington DC 20036	800-336-1616	202-293-7728	48-5
NPD Group Inc			
900 W Shore Rd ....Port Washington NY 11050	866-444-1411	516-625-0700	464
NPES: Assn for Suppliers of Printing Publishing & Converting Technologies			
1899 Preston White Dr ....Reston VA 20191	866-381-9839	703-264-7200	49-16
NPF (National Psoriasis Foundation)			
6600 SW 92nd Ave Ste 300 ....Portland OR 97223	800-723-9166	503-244-7404	48-17
NPGA (National Propane Gas Assn)			
1899 L St NW Ste 350 ....Washington DC 20036	800-328-1111	202-466-7200	48-12
NPI (National Property Inspections Inc)			
9375 Burt St Ste 201 ....Omaha NE 68114	800-333-9807	402-333-9807	364
NPIC (National Pesticide Information Ctr)			
333 Weniger Hall ....Corvallis OR 97331	800-858-7378		48-17
NPMA (National Pest Management Assn Inc)			
10460 N St ....Fairfax VA 22030	800-678-6722	703-352-6762	49-4
NPPC (National Pork Producers Council)			
122 C St NW Ste 875 ....Washington DC 20001	800-952-4629	202-347-3600	49-6
NPR (National Public Radio)			
635 Massachusetts Ave NW ......Washington DC 20001	800-989-8255	202-513-3232	628
NPR Illinois 919 UIS			
University of Illinois at Springfield			
1 University Plz WUIS-130 ....Springfield IL 62703	866-206-9847	217-206-9847	641-102
NPSS (IEEE Nuclear & Plasma Sciences Society)			
445 Hoes Ln ....Piscataway NJ 08854	800-678-4333	732-981-0060	49-19
NPTA Alliance			
330 N Wabash Ave Ste 2000..........Chicago IL 60611	800-355-6782	312-321-4092	49-18
nQueue Inc			
7890 S Hardy Dr Ste 105 ....Tempe AZ 85284	800-299-5933		180
NRA (National Rehabilitation Assn)			
633 S Washington St ....Alexandria VA 22314	888-258-4295	703-836-0850	48-17
NRA (National Renderers Association Inc)			
500 Montgomery St Ste 310..........Alexandria VA 22314	800-366-2563	703-683-0155	48-2
NRA (National Restaurant Assn)			
2055 L St NW Ste 700 ....Washington DC 20036	800-424-5156	202-331-5900	49-6
NRA (Naval Reserve Assn)			
1619 King St ....Alexandria VA 22314	877-628-9411	703-548-5800	48-19
NRA Group LLC			
2491 Paxton St ....Harrisburg PA 17111	800-360-9953	800-773-4503	160
NRC Sports Inc			
206 Worcester Rd Ste 36-38.........Princeton MA 01541	800-243-5033	978-464-2433	457
NRCA (National Roofing Contractors Assn)			
10255 W Higgins Rd Ste 600 ....Rosemont IL 60018	800-323-9545*	847-299-9070	49-3
*Cust Svc			
NRCCE (National Research Ctr for Coal & Energy)			
West Virginia University			
385 Evansdale Dr PO Box 6064 ....Morgantown WV 26506	800-624-8301	304-293-2867	664
Nrccua			
3651 NE Ralph Powell Rd ....Lees Summit MO 64064	800-876-1117	816-525-2201	205
NRCDV (National Resource Ctr on Domestic Violence)			
6400 Flank Dr Ste 1300 ....Harrisburg PA 17112	800-799-7233		48-6
NRCNAA (National Resource Center on Native American Aging)			
1301 N Columbia Rd Ste E231			
PO Box 9037.....................Grand Forks ND 58202	800-896-7628	701-777-3720	48-6
NRD LLC			
2937 Alt Blvd PO Box 310 ....Grand Island NY 14072	800-525-8076	716-773-7634	201
NREC (National Railway Equipment Co)			
14400 Robey St ....Dixmoor IL 60426	800-253-2905	708-388-6002	646
NREC Power Systems			
5222 Hwy 311 ....Houma LA 70360	800-851-6732	985-872-5480	262
NRF (National Retail Federation)			
1101 New York Ave NW ....Washington DC 20005	800-673-4692	202-783-7971	49-18
NRHA (National Retail Hardware Assn)			
5822 W 74th St ....Indianapolis IN 46278	800-772-4424*	317-290-0338	49-18
*Cust Svc			
NRI (Noble Royalties Inc)			
15303 N Dallas Pkwy Ste 1350.........Addison TX 75001	888-346-6253	972-720-1888	
NRMCA (National Ready Mixed Concrete Assn)			
900 Spring St ....Silver Spring MD 20910	888-846-7622	301-587-1400	49-3
NRRI (Natural Resources Research Institute)			
University of Minnesota Duluth			
5013 Miller Trunk Hwy ....Duluth MN 55811	800-234-0054	218-788-2694	664
National Recreation Reservation Service			
PO Box 140 ....Ballston Spa NY 12020	877-444-6777	518-885-3639	768
NRS (National Runaway Switchboard)			
3141 N Lincoln Ave ....Chicago IL 60657	800-786-2929	773-880-9860	48-6
NRS (National Rosacea Society)			
196 James St ....Barrington IL 60010	888-662-5874		48-17
NRSF (National Reye's Syndrome Foundation)			
426 N Lewis St ....Bryan OH 43506	800-233-7393	419-924-9000	48-17
NRTA/AARP Bulletin			
601 E St NW ....Washington DC 20049	888-867-2277	202-434-3525	527-6
NRTWC (National Right to Work Committee)			
8001 Braddock Rd Ste 500.........Springfield VA 22160	800-325-7892		49-12
NRV Inc			
N8155 American St ....Ixonia WI 53036	800-558-0002	920-261-7000	445
NSA (National Stroke Assn)			
9707 E Easter Ln ....Centennial CO 80112	800-787-6537*		48-17
*Cust Svc			
NSA (National Association of Nonprofit Accountants & Co)			
1801 W End Ave Ste 800 ....Nashville TN 37203	800-231-2524	615-373-9880	49-1
NSA (National Safety Apparel Inc)			
15825 Industrial Pkwy ....Cleveland OH 44135	800-553-0672		572
NSA (National Stuttering Assn)			
119 W 40th St 14th Fl. ....New York NY 10018	800-937-8888	212-944-4050	48-17
NSA (National Sheriffs' Assn)			
1450 Duke St ....Alexandria VA 22314	800-424-7827	703-836-7827	49-7
NSA (National Society of Accountants)			
1010 N Fairfax St ....Alexandria VA 22314	800-966-6679	703-549-6400	49-1
NSB (Northfield Savings Bank)			
PO Box 7180 ....Barre VT 05641	800-672-2274		70
NSBA (National Small Business Assn)			
1156 15th St NW Ste 1100 ....Washington DC 20005	800-345-6728		49-12
NSC (National Safety Council)			
1121 Spring Lake Dr ....Itasca IL 60143	800-621-7615	630-285-1121	48-17
NSC Communications			
6820 Power Line Dr ....Florence KY 41042	800-543-1584	859-727-6640	643
NSCA (National Strength & Conditioning Assn)			
1885 Bob Johnson Dr ....Colorado Springs CO 80906	800-815-6826	719-632-6722	48-22
NSCAA (National Soccer Coaches Assn of America)			
800 Ann Ave ....Kansas City KS 66101	800-458-0678	913-362-1747	48-22
NSCC (Nashville State Community College)			
120 White Bridge Rd ....Nashville TN 37209	800-272-7363	615-353-3333	795
NSCIA (National Spinal Cord Injury Assn)			
75-20 Astoria Blvd			
Ste 120 ....East Elmhurst NY 11370	800-962-9629	718-512-0010	48-17
NSDC (National Staff Development Council)			
504 S Locust St ....Oxford OH 45056	800-727-7288	513-523-6029	49-5
NSEA Voice Magazine			
605 S 14th St Ste 200. ....Lincoln NE 68508	800-742-0047	402-475-7611	455-8
NSF International			
789 N Dixboro Rd			
PO Box 130140....................Ann Arbor MI 48105	800-673-6275	734-769-8010	2
NSGA (National Senior Golf Assn)			
200 Perrine Rd Ste 201. ....Old Bridge NJ 08857	800-282-6772		48-22
NSGA (National Sporting Goods Assn)			
1601 Feehanville Dr			
Ste 300 ....Mount Prospect IL 60056	800-815-5422	847-296-6742	49-4
NSK America Corp			
1800 Global Pkwy ....Hoffman Estates IL 60192	800-585-4675	847-843-7664	489
NSK Corp			
4200 Goss Rd ....Ann Arbor MI 48105	800-675-9930	734-913-7500	616
Nsl Analytical			
4450 Cranwood Pkwy ....Cleveland OH 44128	877-560-3943	877-560-3992	738
NSLA (Nevada State Library & Archives)			
100 N Stewart St ....Carson City NV 89701	800-922-2880	775-684-3360	433-5
NSMC (North Suburban Medical Ctr)			
9191 Grant St ....Thornton CO 80229	877-647-7440	303-451-7800	373-3
NSPE (National Society of Professional Engineers)			
1420 King St ....Alexandria VA 22314	888-285-6773		49-19
Nspire Health Inc			
1830 Lefthand Cir ....Longmont CO 80501	800-574-7374	303-666-5555	474
NSPR (National Recreation and Park Assn)			
22377 Belmont Ridge Rd ....Ashburn VA 20148	800-626-6772		48-23
NSRA (National Shoe Retailers Assn)			
7386 N La Cholla Blvd ....Tucson AZ 85741	800-673-8446	520-209-1710	49-18
NSS (National Slovak Society of the USA)			
351 Vly Brook Rd ....McMurray PA 15317	800-488-1890	724-731-0094	48-14
NSSEA (National School Supply & Equipment Assn)			
8380 Colesville Rd			
Ste 250 ....Silver Spring MD 20910	800-395-5550	301-495-0240	49-18
NSSGA (National Stone Sand & Gravel Assn)			
1605 King St ....Alexandria VA 22314	800-342-1415	703-525-8788	49-3
NSTA (National Science Teachers Assn)			
1840 Wilson Blvd ....Arlington VA 22201	800-722-6782*	703-243-7100	49-5
*Sales			
NSTAR Global Services Inc			
120 Partlo St ....Garner NC 27529	877-678-2766		260
NSX (National Stock Exchange)			
101 Hudson St Ste 1200. ....Jersey City NJ 07302	800-843-3924	201-499-3700	687
NTA (National Tour Assn)			
546 E Main St ....Lexington KY 40508	800-682-8886	859-226-4444	48-23
Nta Graphics South Inc			
501 Republic Cir ....Birmingham AL 35214	888-798-2123	205-798-2123	623
NTB (Nationwide Truck Brokers Inc)			
4203 Roger B Chaffee Memorial Blvd SE			
Ste 2. ....Grand Rapids MI 49548	800-446-0682	616-878-5554	775
NTC (Newman Theological College)			
10012-84 St ....Edmonton AB T6A0B2	844-392-2450	780-392-2450	167-3
NTEA (National Truck Equipment Assn)			
37400 Hills Tech Dr ....Farmington Hills MI 48331	800-441-6832	248-489-7090	49-21
NTF (National Turkey Federation)			
1225 New York Ave NW Ste 400 ....Washington DC 20005	866-536-7593	202-898-0100	48-2
NTG Clarity Networks Inc			
2820 Fourteenth Ave Ste 202 ....Markham ON L3R0S9	800-838-7894	905-305-1325	224

				Toll-Free	Phone	Class
NthGen Software Inc						
90 Sheppard Ave Ste 6	Toronto	ON	M2N3A1	**888-260-4604**	647-933-1169	
NTIC (Northern Technologies International Corp)						
4201 Woodland Rd PO Box 69	Circle Pines	MN	55014	**800-328-2433**	763-225-6600	145
NASDAQ: NTIC						
NTIS (National Technical Information Service)						
5301 Shawnee Rd	Alexandria	VA	22312	**800-363-2068**	703-605-6060	197
NTIS (National Technical Information Service)						
5285 Port Royal Rd	Springfield	VA	22161	**800-553-6847***	703-605-6000	664
*Orders						
NTMA (National Tooling & Machining Assn)						
6363 Oak Tree Blvd	Independence	OH	44131	**800-248-6862**		49-13
NTN Bearing Corp of America						
1600 E Bishop Ct	Mount Prospect	IL	60056	**800-323-2358**	847-298-7500	616
NTP Distribution Inc						
27150 SW Kinsman Rd	Wilsonville	OR	97070	**800-242-6987**	503-570-0171	61
NTRA (National Thoroughbred Racing Assn)						
2525 Harrodsburg Rd Ste 510	Lexington	KY	40504	**800-792-6872**		48-22
NTS (National Technical Systems Inc)						
2125 E Katella Ave Ste 250	Anaheim	CA	92806	**800-879-9225**	818-591-0776	738
NASDAQ: NTSC						
NTSAD (National Tay-Sachs & Allied Diseases Assn)						
2001 Beacon St Ste 204	Brighton	MA	02135	**800-906-8723**	617-277-4463	48-17
NTT DATA Inc						
100 City Sq	Boston	MA	02129	**800-745-3263**		180
NTT DoCoMo USA Inc						
757 Third Ave 16th Fl	New York	NY	10017	**888-362-6661**		731
Nu Horizons Electronics Corp						
70 Maxess Rd	Melville	NY	11747	**855-326-4757**	631-396-5000	246
Nu Way Co-op Inc						
PO Box Q	Trimont	MN	56176	**800-445-4118**		276
Nuance Communications Inc						
1 Wayside Rd	Burlington	MA	01803	**800-654-1187**	781-565-5000	178-7
NASDAQ: NUAN						
Nubenco Medical						
1 Kalisa Way	Paramus	NJ	07652	**800-633-1322**	201-967-9000	474
Nucara Pharmacy						
209 E San Marnan Dr	Waterloo	IA	50702	**800-359-2357**	319-236-8891	237
NuCare Pharmaceuticals Inc						
622 W Katella Ave	Orange	CA	92867	**888-482-9545**		579
US NRC Region II						
61 Forsyth St SW Ste 23T85	Atlanta	GA	30303	**800-577-8510**	404-562-4400	339-19
Nuclear Regulatory Commission Regional Offices						
Region 1						
2100 Renaissance Blvd	King of Prussia	PA	19406	**800-432-1156**	610-337-5000	339-19
Region 3						
2443 Warrenville Rd Ste 210	Lisle	IL	60532	**800-522-3025**	630-829-9500	339-19
Region 4						
1600 E Lamar Blvd	Arlington	TX	76011	**800-952-9677**	817-860-8100	339-19
Nuclear Security Services Corp						
701 Willowbrook Centre Pkwy	Willowbrook	IL	60527	**800-275-8319**	630-920-1488	689
NuCo2 Inc						
2800 SE Marketplace	Stuart	FL	34997	**800-472-2855**	772-221-1754	146
Nucor Corp						
1915 Rexford Rd	Charlotte	NC	28211	**800-294-1322**	704-366-7000	478
NYSE: NUE						
Nucor Corp Cold Finish Div						
2800 N Governor Williams Hwy	Darlington	SC	29540	**800-333-0590**	704-366-7000	719
Nucor Corp Vulcraft Div						
1501 W Darlington St	Florence	SC	29501	**888-000-0000**		
Nucor Steel Marion Inc						
912 Cheney Ave	Marion	OH	43302	**800-333-4011**	740-383-4011	490
Nucor-Yamato Steel Co						
5929 E State Hwy 18	Blytheville	AR	72315	**800-289-6977**	870-762-5500	719
Nucraft Furniture Co						
5151 W River Dr	Comstock Park	MI	49321	**877-682-7238**	616-784-6016	321
Nudo Products Inc						
1500 Taylor Ave	Springfield	IL	62703	**800-826-4132**	217-528-5636	746
Nueces Electric Co-op (NEC)						
14353 Cooperative Ave	Corpus Christi	TX	78380	**800-632-9288**	361-387-2581	245
NuGrowth Solutions						
4181 ArlingGate Plz	Columbus	OH	43228	**800-966-3051**		195
Nuherbs co						
14722 Wicks Blvd	San Leandro	CA	94577	**800-233-4307**	510-534-4372	297-8
Nu-Hope Laboratories Inc						
12640 Branford St	Pacoima	CA	91331	**800-899-5017**	818-899-7711	475
Nujak Development Inc						
714 N Massachusetts Ave	Lakeland	FL	33801	**888-685-2526**	863-686-1565	186
Nulaid Foods Inc						
200 W Fifth St	Ripon	CA	95366	**800-788-8871**	209-599-2121	297-10
Nu-Life Environmental Inc						
PO Box 1527	Easley	SC	29641	**800-654-1752**	864-855-5155	384
Nu-Lite Electrical Wholesalers						
850 Edwards Ave	Harahan	LA	70123	**800-256-1603**	504-733-3300	246
Numark Brands LLC						
105 Fieldcrest Ave Ste 502A	Edison	NJ	08837	**800-338-8079**	800-214-2379	578
Numerex Corp						
400 Interstate N Pkwy Ste 1350	Atlanta	GA	30339	**800-665-5686**	770-693-5950	730
Numeridex Inc						
632 S Wheeling Rd	Wheeling	IL	60090	**800-323-7737**	847-541-8840	112
Numero Uno Web Solutions Inc						
3300 Hwy 7 Ste 908	Concord	ON	L4K4M3	**855-736-9778**	905-669-1708	
Numonics Corp						
101 Commerce Dr PO Box 1005	Montgomeryville	PA	18936	**800-523-6716**	215-362-2766	173-1
Numotion						
126 Airport Rd	Scott City	MO	63780	**877-856-9154**	573-334-0600	473
Nunhems USA Inc						
1200 Anderson Corner Rd	Parma	ID	83660	**800-733-9505***	208-674-4000	690
*Cust Svc						
Nunn-Bush Shoe Co Inc						
333 W Estabrook Blvd	Glendale	WI	53212	**866-484-3718**		
Nuo Therapeutics Inc						
207A Perry Pkwy Ste 1	Gaithersburg	MD	20877	**866-298-6633**		85
OTC: NUOT						
Nupla Corp						
11912 Sheldon St	Sun Valley	CA	91352	**800-872-7661**	818-768-6800	606
Nurse Assist Inc						
3400 Northern Cross Blvd	Fort Worth	TX	76137	**800-649-6800**	817-231-1300	473
Nurse On Call Inc						
111 Westwood Pl Ste 400	Brentwood	TN	37027	**855-350-3800**		362
Nursecom						
1721 Moon Lake Blvd Ste 540	Hoffman Estates	IL	60169	**800-866-0919**		455-16
Nursefinders Inc						
12400 High Bluff Dr	San Diego	CA	92130	**800-445-0459**	877-214-4105	717
Nurserymen's Exchange						
2651 N Cabrillo Hwy	Half Moon Bay	CA	94019	**800-227-5229***	650-726-6361	368
*General						
Nurses Unlimited						
511 N Lincoln PO Box 4534	Odessa	TX	79761	**888-245-1061***	432-580-2085	
*Compliance						
Nursing Ctr						
323 Norristown Rd Ste 200	Ambler	PA	19002	**800-346-7844**	800-787-8985	396
Nushagak Electric & Telephone Co-op Inc						
557 Kenny Wren Rd	Dillingham	AK	99576	**800-478-5296**	907-842-5295	245
Nussbaum Trucking Inc						
19336 N 1425 East Rd	Normal	IL	61748	**800-322-7305**	309-452-4426	775
NuStar GP Holdings LLC						
19003 I-10 W	San Antonio	TX	78257	**800-866-9060**	210-918-2000	359-3
NYSE: NSH						
Nutech Medical Inc						
2641 Rocky Ridge Ln	Birmingham	AL	35216	**800-824-9194**	205-290-2158	474
Nutis Press Inc						
3540 E Fulton St	Columbus	OH	43227	**800-848-6266**	614-237-8626	623
Nutra-Blend Inc						
3200 Second St	Neosho	MO	64850	**800-657-5657**		580
Nutraceutical International Corp						
1400 Kearns Blvd	Park City	UT	84060	**800-669-8877**	435-655-6000	794
NutriCorp International						
4025 Rhodes Dr	Windsor	ON	N8W5B5	**888-446-8874**	519-974-8178	738
Nutrifaster Inc						
209 S Bennett St	Seattle	WA	98108	**800-800-2641**	206-767-5054	98
NutriSystem Inc						
600 Office Center Dr	Fort Washington	PA	19034	**800-585-5483**	215-706-5300	805
NASDAQ: NTRI						
Nuts & Volts Magazine						
430 Princeland Ct	Corona	CA	92879	**800-783-4624***	951-371-8497	455-14
*Orders						
Nuttall Gear LLC						
2221 Niagra Falls Blvd	Niagara Falls	NY	14304	**800-724-6710**	716-298-4100	705
Nutting						
450 Pheasant Ridge Dr	Watertown	SD	57201	**800-533-0337**	800-967-7333	468
NuVasive Inc						
7475 Lusk Blvd	San Diego	CA	92121	**800-475-9131**	858-909-1800	474
NASDAQ: NUVA						
Nuveen Investments Inc						
333 W Wacker Dr	Chicago	IL	60606	**800-257-8787**	312-917-7700	686
NuView Life Sciences Inc						
1389 Center Dr Ste 250	Park City	UT	84098	**888-902-7779**		738
NuVision Engineering Inc						
River Park Commons 2403 Sidney St Ste 700	Pittsburgh	PA	15203	**888-748-8232**	412-586-1810	256
Nuvite Chemical Compounds Corp						
85 Jetson Ln	Central Islip	NY	11722	**800-394-8351**	718-383-8351	151
Nuvue Business Solutions						
3061 Berks Way Ste 102	Raleigh	NC	27614	**800-688-8310**	919-562-5599	196
Nu-Wa Industries Inc						
3701 Johnson Rd	Chanute	KS	66720	**800-835-0676**	620-431-2088	120
Nu-Way Industries Inc						
555 Howard Ave	Des Plaines	IL	60018	**888-488-5631**	847-298-7710	693
NUWC (Naval Undersea Warfare Center)						
1176 Howell St	Newport	RI	02841	**800-356-8464**	401-832-7742	664
Nu-Wool Company Inc						
2472 Port Sheldon Rd	Jenison	MI	49428	**800-748-0128**	616-669-0100	388
Nu-Yale Cleaners						
6300 Hwy 62	Jeffersonville	IN	47130	**888-644-7400**	812-285-7400	425
NV5						
2525 Natomas Pk Dr Ste 300	Sacramento	CA	95833	**877-311-4180**	916-641-9100	261
NVC Logistics Group Inc						
1 Pond Rd	Rockleigh	NJ	07647	**800-526-0207**		
NVE Corp						
11409 Vly View Rd	Eden Prairie	MN	55344	**800-467-7141**	952-829-9217	692
NASDAQ: NVEC						
NVT Phybridge						
3495 Laird Rd Ste 12	Mississauga	ON	L5L5S5	**888-901-3633**	905-901-3633	606
NWA (National WIC Assn)						
2001 S St NW Ste 580	Washington	DC	20009	**866-782-6246**	202-232-5492	48-6
NWC (National Waterways Conference Inc)						
4650 Washington Blvd Ste 608	Arlington	VA	22201	**866-371-1390**	703-243-4090	49-21
NWF (National Wildlife Federation)						
11100 Wildlife Ctr Dr	Reston	VA	20190	**800-822-9919**	703-438-6000	48-3
NWFA (National Wood Flooring Assn)						
111 Chesterfield Industrial Blvd	Chesterfield	MO	63005	**800-422-4556**	636-519-9663	49-3
NWL Transformers Inc						
312 Rising Sun Rd	Bordentown	NJ	08505	**800-742-5695**	609-298-7300	253
NWOA (National Woodland Owners Assn)						
374 Maple Ave E Ste 310	Vienna	VA	22180	**800-476-8733**	703-255-2300	48-2
NWT Tourism						
PO Box 610	Yellowknife	NT	X1A2N5	**800-661-0788**	867-873-7200	769
NWTF (National Wild Turkey Federation)						
770 Augusta Rd PO Box 530	Edgefield	SC	29824	**800-843-6983***	803-637-3106	48-3
*Cust Svc						
NXC Imaging						
2118 Fourth Ave S	Minneapolis	MN	55404	**800-328-5016**		473
NxStage Medical Inc						
350 Merrimack St	Lawrence	MA	01843	**866-697-8243**	978-687-4700	474
NASDAQ: NXTM						
NYACK						
350 N Highland Ave	Nyack	NY	10960	**800-541-6891**	845-353-2020	167-3
Nyack College 1 S Blvd	Nyack	NY	10960	**800-336-9225***	845-358-1710	166
*Admissions						
NYBDC (New York Business Development Corp)						
50 Beaver St Ste 500	Albany	NY	12207	**800-923-2504**	518-463-2268	216

	Toll-Free	Phone	Class
NYCCC (New York City Children's Ctr-Queens Campus)			
74-03 Commonwealth Blvd ....Bellerose NY 11426	800-597-8481	718-264-4500	373-1
NYCE Corp			
400 Plaza Dr ....Secaucus NJ 07094	888-323-0310	904-438-6000	69
NYCM (New York Central Mutual Fire Insurance Co)			
1899 Central Plz E ....Edmeston NY 13335	800-234-6926		390-4
NYDJ Apparel LLC			
5401 S Soto St ....Vernon CA 90058	800-407-6001	323-581-9040	157-6
Nye County School District Inc (NCSD)			
PO Box 113 ....Tonopah NV 89049	800-796-6273	775-482-6258	681
NYLA (New York Library Assn)			
6021 State Farm Rd ....Guilderland NY 12084	800-252-6952*	518-432-6952	434
*General			
NYLIFE Securities Inc			
51 Madison Ave Rm 251 ....New York NY 10010	800-695-4785	800-695-9873	686
Nylok Corp			
15260 Hallmark Dr ....Macomb MI 48042	800-826-5161	586-786-0100	3
Nylon Corp of America			
333 Sundial Ave ....Manchester NH 03103	800-851-2001	603-627-5150	601-1
NYP Corp			
805 E Grand St ....Elizabeth NJ 07201	800-524-1052	908-351-6550	67
NYPIRG (NYPIRG)			
9 Murray St ....New York NY 10007	800-566-5020	212-349-6460	629
NYSCA (National Youth Sports Coaches Assn)			
2050 Vista Pkwy ....West Palm Beach FL 33411	800-729-2057	561-684-1141	48-22
NYSE Arce			
115 Samsone St ....San Francisco CA 94104	877-729-7291		687
NYSE Euronext			
11 Wall St ....New York NY 10005	866-873-7422	212-656-3000	687
NYSE: NYX			
Nystrom Inc			
9300 73rd Ave N ....Minneapolis MN 55428	800-547-2635	763-488-9200	234
NYSW (New York Susquehanna & Western Railway Corp)			
1 Railroad Ave ....Cooperstown NY 13326	800-366-6979*	607-547-2555	644
*General			
NYU School of Medicine			
560 First Ave ....New York NY 10016	855-698-2220	212-263-7300	167-2

O

	Toll-Free	Phone	Class
O & P Edge, The			
11154 Huron St Ste 104 ....Northglenn CO 80234	866-613-0257	303-255-0843	
O Berk Co 3 Milltown Ct ....Union NJ 07083	800-631-7392		384
O E C Graphics Inc			
555 W Waukau Ave PO Box 2443 ....Oshkosh WI 54902	800-388-7770	920-235-7770	479
O Henry Hotel			
624 Green Valley Rd ....Greensboro NC 27408	800-965-8259	336-854-2000	378
O Neill's Chevrolet & Buick Inc			
5 W Main St ....Avon CT 06001	844-315-0960	860-269-3637	57
O s u Center for Health Sciences			
1111 W 17th St ....Tulsa OK 74107	800-677-1972	918-582-1972	165
O'Brien Dental Lab Inc			
4311 SW Research Way ....Corvallis OR 97333	800-445-5941	541-754-1238	414
O'Brien International			
14615 NE 91st St ....Redmond WA 98052	800-662-7436	425-881-5900	706
O'Connell Electric Co			
830 Phillips Rd ....Victor NY 14564	800-343-2176	585-924-2176	189-4
O'Connell Oil Assoc Inc			
545 Merrill Rd ....Pittsfield MA 01201	800-464-4894	413-499-4800	324
O'connor Company Inc			
16910 W 116th St ....Lenexa KS 66219	888-800-3540	913-894-8788	41
O'Connor Woods			
3400 Wagner Heights Rd ....Stockton CA 95209	800-957-3308	209-956-3400	668
O'Day Equipment Inc			
1301 40th St NW ....Fargo ND 58102	800-654-6329	701-282-9260	635
O'Fallon Chamber of Commerce			
2145 Bryan Vly Commercial Dr ......O'Fallon MO 63366	888-349-1897	636-240-1818	139
O'Gara Coach Company LLC			
8833 W Olympic Blvd ....Beverly Hills CA 90211	888-291-5533	877-588-8862	57
O'halloran International Inc			
3311 Adventureland Dr ....Altoona IA 50009	800-800-6503	515-967-3300	765
O'Hare International Airport			
Dept of Aviation			
PO Box 66142 ....Chicago IL 60666	800-832-6352	773-686-3700	27
O'Keefe Drilling Co			
2000 4 Mile Rd ....Butte MT 59701	800-745-5554	406-494-3310	652
O'keefe Elevator Company Inc			
1402 Jones St ....Omaha NE 68102	800-369-6317	402-345-4056	357
O'Keeffe's Inc			
325 Newhall St ....San Francisco CA 94124	888-653-3333	415-822-4222	234
O'Leary Paint			
300 E Oakland Ave ....Lansing MI 48906	800-477-2066	517-487-2066	546
O'neal Flat Rolled Metals			
1229 S Fulton Ave ....Brighton CO 80601	800-336-3365	303-654-0300	490
O'Neal Steel Inc			
744 41st St N ....Birmingham AL 35222	800-861-8272	205-599-8000	490
O'Neill & Assoc LLC			
617 646 1000 Thirty-One New Chardon St			
.........................Boston MA 02114	866-989-4321	617-646-1000	194
O'Neill Wetsuits USA			
1071 41st Ave ....Santa Cruz CA 95063	800-213-6444	831-475-7500	706
O'Reilly & Assoc Inc			
1005 Gravenstein Hwy N ....Sebastopol CA 95472	800-998-9938	707-829-0515	633-11
O'Reilly Auto Parts			
233 S Patterson ....Springfield MO 65802	888-327-7153	417-862-6708	54
NASDAQ: ORLY			
O'Rourke Wrecking Co			
660 Lunken Pk Dr ....Cincinnati OH 45226	800-354-9850	513-871-1400	189-16
O'Ryan Group Inc			
4010 Pilot Ste 108 ....Memphis TN 38118	800-253-0750	901-794-4610	697
O'Sullivan Films Inc			
1944 Valley Ave ....Winchester VA 22601	800-336-9882	540-667-6666	596

	Toll-Free	Phone	Class
01 Communications Inc			
4359 Town Ctr Blvd			
Ste 217 ....El Dorado hills CA 95762	888-444-1111		731
OA (Overeaters Anonymous Inc)			
PO Box 44020 ....Rio Rancho NM 87174	866-505-4966	505-891-2664	48-21
OABA (Outdoor Amusement Business Assn Inc)			
1035 S Semoran Blvd			
Ste 1045A........................Winter Park FL 32792	800-517-6222	407-848-4958	611
OAG Worldwide			
3025 Highland Pkwy			
Ste 200 ....Downers Grove IL 60515	800-342-5624		633-10
Oahe Electric Co-op Inc			
102 S Cranford St PO Box 216...........Blunt SD 57522	800-640-6243	605-962-6243	245
Oak Associates Funds			
c/o Ultimus Fund Solutions 225 Pictoria Dr			
PO Box 46707....................Cincinnati OH 45246	888-462-5386		524
Oak Hall Inc			
6150 Poplar Ave Ste 146 ....Memphis TN 38119	844-625-4255	901-761-3580	157-4
Oak Hall Industries			
840 Union St ....Salem VA 24153	800-223-0429	540-387-0000	155-13
Oak Hills Christian College			
1600 Oak Hills Rd SW ....Bemidji MN 56601	888-751-8670	218-751-8670	161
Oak Park Area Convention & Visitors Bureau			
1118 Westgate ....Oak Park IL 60301	888-625-7275	708-524-7800	206
Oak Plantation Resort & Suites Condominium Assn			
4090 Enchanted Oaks Cir ....Kissimmee FL 34741	888-411-4141		377
Oak Ridge Financial			
701 Xenia Ave S Ste 100 ....Minneapolis MN 55416	800-231-8364	763-923-2200	69
Oakdale Electric Co-op			
PO Box 128 ....Oakdale WI 54649	800-241-2468	608-372-4131	245
Oakhill Hospital			
11375 Cortez Blvd ....Brooksville FL 34613	877-442-2362	352-596-6632	373-3
Oakhurst Dairy			
364 Forest Ave ....Portland ME 04101	800-482-0718	207-772-7468	296-27
Oakland City Hall			
1 Frank H Ogawa Plz ....Oakland CA 94612	800-834-3773	510-615-5566	336
Oakland City University			
138 North Lucretia St ....Oakland City IN 47660	800-737-5125	812-749-4781	166
Oakland Convention & Visitors Bureau			
481 Water St ....Oakland CA 94607	800-862-2543	510-839-9000	206
Oakland Museum of California			
1000 Oak St ....Oakland CA 94607	888-625-6873*	510-238-2200	517
*General			
Oakland Packaging & Supply			
3200 Regatta Blvd Unit F ....Richmond CA 94804	800-237-3103	510-307-4242	
Oakland Press			
2125 Butterfield Dr Ste 102N ....Troy MI 48084	888-977-3677	248-332-8181	633-8
Oakland Raiders, The			
1220 Harbor Bay Pkwy ....Alameda CA 94502	800-724-3377	510-864-5000	711-2
Oakland Unified School District			
1000 Broadway Ste 680 ....Oakland CA 94607	888-604-4636	510-879-8200	681
Oakland University			
2200 Squirrel Rd ....Rochester MI 48309	800-625-8648*	248-370-2100	166
*Admissions			
Oaklawn Park			
2705 Central Ave ....Hot Springs AR 71901	800-625-5296*	501-623-4411	638
*General			
Oaklawn Psychiatric Center Inc			
330 Lakeview Dr ....Goshen IN 46527	800-282-0809	574-533-1234	722
Oakley Inc			
1 Icon ....Foothill Ranch CA 92610	800-403-7449*	949-672-6925	538
*Cust Svc			
Oakley Transport Inc			
101 ABC Rd ....Lake Wales FL 33859	800-969-8265	863-638-1435	447
Oakley-Lindsay Ctr			
300 Civic Ctr Plz ....Quincy IL 62301	800-978-4748	217-223-1000	205
Oakmark Family of Funds			
330 W nineth St ....Kansas City MO 64105	800-625-6275	617-483-8327	524
Oaks at Denville, The			
19 Pocono Rd ....Denville NJ 07834	877-693-7650	973-586-6000	668
Oaks at Ojai			
122 E Ojai Ave ....Ojai CA 93023	800-753-6257	805-646-5573	702
Oakwood Capital Management LLC			
12121 Wilshire Blvd			
Ste 1250.....................Los Angeles CA 90025	800-586-0600	310-772-2600	194
Oakwood Crystal City			
400 15th St S ....Arlington VA 22202	877-902-0832	877-891-6844	210
Oakwood Heritage Hospital			
10000 Telegraph Rd ....Taylor MI 48180	800-543-9355	313-295-5000	373-3
Oakwood Products Inc			
1741 Old Dunbar Rd ....West Columbia SC 29172	800-467-3386	803-739-8800	144
Oakwood Southshore Medical Ctr			
5450 Fort St ....Trenton MI 48183	800-543-9355	734-671-3800	373-3
Oakwood Worldwide			
2222 Corinth Ave ....Los Angeles CA 90064	800-888-0808	310-478-1021	210
Oakworks Inc			
923 E Wellspring Rd ....New Freedom PA 17349	800-558-8850	717-235-6807	473
OANDA Corp			
140 Broadway 46th Fl.................New York NY 10005	800-826-8164	416-593-9436	69
Oar Net			
1224 Kinnear Rd ....Columbus OH 43212	800-627-6420	614-292-9191	180
Oasis Outsourcing Inc			
2054 Vista Pkwy Ste 300 ....West Palm Beach FL 33411	888-627-4735*		627
*General			
Oates Energy Inc			
14286 Beach Blvd Ste 12 ....Jacksonville FL 32250	800-717-9811		
Oatey Co			
4700 W 160th St ....Cleveland OH 44135	800-321-9532*	216-267-7100	605
*Cust Svc			
O-AT-KA Milk Products Co-op Inc			
700 Ellicott St ....Batavia NY 14020	800-828-8152	585-343-0536	296-3
OATS Inc			
2501 Maguire Blvd Ste 101 ....Columbia MO 65201	800-831-9219	573-443-4516	314
OB Macaroni Co			
3066 S E Loop 820 ....Fort Worth TX 76140	800-553-4336*	817-335-4629	296-31
*Orders			
Obagi Medical Products Inc			
3760 Kilroy Airport Way			
Ste 500 ....Long Beach CA 90806	800-636-7546	562-628-1007	214

				Toll-Free	Phone	Class
OBCI (Ocean Bio-Chem Inc)						
4041 SW 47th Ave	Fort Lauderdale	FL	33314	**800-327-8583**	954-587-6280	151
NASDAQ: OBCI						
ObdEdge LLC						
7117 Florida Blvd	Baton Rouge	LA	70806	**888-896-9753**		
Ober Gatlinburg Inc						
1001 Pkwy Ste 2	Gatlinburg	TN	37738	**800-251-9202**	865-436-5423	31
Oberbeck Grain Co						
700 Walnut St	Highland	IL	62249	**800-632-2012**	618-654-2387	445
Oberfields LLC						
1165 Alum Creek Dr	Columbus	OH	43209	**800-845-7644**	614-252-0955	191-4
Oberlin College & Conservatory						
38 E College St	Oberlin	OH	44074	**800-622-6243**	440-775-8411	
Oberto Sausage Co						
7060 S 238th St	Kent	WA	98032	**877-453-7591**		296-26
Oberweis Securities Inc						
3333 Warrenville Rd Ste 500	Lisle	IL	60532	**800-323-6166**	630-577-2300	
OBI (Oklahoma Blood Institute)						
1001 N Lincoln Blvd	Oklahoma City	OK	73104	**866-708-4995**	405-278-3100	89
Objectiva Software Solutions Inc						
12770 El Camino Real Ste 300	San Diego	CA	92130	**800-878-6975**	408-809-5950	196
Objectivity Inc						
3099 N First St Ste 200	San Jose	CA	95134	**800-767-6259**	408-992-7100	178-1
Obs Inc						
1324 WTuscarawas St PO Box 6210	Canton	OH	44706	**800-362-9592**	330-453-3725	513
Observer, The						
140 S Front St	Sarnia	ON	N7T7M8	**866-541-6757**	519-344-3641	528-1
Obsidian Energy Ltd						
Penn W Plz 207 - Ninth Ave SW						
Ste 200	Calgary	AB	T2P1K3	**866-693-2707**	403-777-2500	671
OC Tanner Co						
1930 S State St	Salt Lake City	UT	84115	**800-453-7490**		408
OC Weekly						
2975 Red Hill Ave Ste 150	Costa Mesa	CA	92626	**800-300-4345**	714-550-5900	528-5
Ocala-Marion County Chamber of Commerce						
310 SE Third St	Ocala	FL	34471	**800-466-5055**	352-629-8051	139
OCC (Optical Cable Corp)						
5290 Concourse Dr	Roanoke	VA	24019	**800-622-7711**	540-265-0690	809
NASDAQ: OCC						
Occasions Group, The						
1750 Tower Blvd	North Mankato	MN	56003	**800-296-9029**		
OCCC (Orange County Convention Ctr)						
9800 International Dr	Orlando	FL	32819	**800-345-9845**	407-685-9800	205
Occidental College						
1600 Campus Rd	Los Angeles	CA	90041	**800-825-5262***	323-259-2700	166
*Admissions						
Occupational Safety & Health Administration (OSHA)						
200 Constitution Ave NW	Washington	DC	20210	**800-321-6742**	202-693-1999	339-14
Occupational Safety & Health Administration Regional Offices						
Region 1						
JFK Federal Bldg Rm E-340	Boston	MA	02203	**800-321-6742**	617-565-9860	339-14
Region 2						
201 Varick St Rm 670	New York	NY	10014	**800-321-6742**	212-337-2378	339-14
Region 3						
Curtis Ctr 170 S Independence Mall W						
Ste 740W	Philadelphia	PA	19106	**800-321-6742**	215-861-4900	339-14
Region 4						
61 Forsyth St SW Rm 6T50	Atlanta	GA	30303	**800-321-6742**	678-237-0400	339-14
Region 10						
300 Fifth Ave Ste 1280	Seattle	WA	98104	**800-321-6742***	206-757-6700	339-14
*Help Line						
Occupational Safety & Health Review Commission Regional Offices						
Atlanta Region						
100 Alabama St SW Rm 2R90	Atlanta	GA	30303	**800-321-6742**	404-562-1640	339-19
OC&E Woods Line State Trail						
46000 Hwy 97 N	Chiloquin	OR	97624	**800-551-6949**	541-883-5558	561
Ocean Bank						
780 NW 42nd Ave	Miami	FL	33126	**877-688-2265**	305-442-2660	70
Ocean Beauty Seafoods Inc						
1100 W Ewing St	Seattle	WA	98119	**800-365-8950**	206-285-6800	296-14
Ocean Bio-Chem Inc (OBCI)						
4041 SW 47th Ave	Fort Lauderdale	FL	33314	**800-327-8583**	954-587-6280	151
NASDAQ: OBCI						
Ocean City City Hall						
301 Baltimore Ave	Ocean City	MD	21842	**800-626-2326**	410-289-8931	336
Ocean City Hotel-Motel-Restaurant Assn						
PO Box 340	Ocean City	MD	21843	**800-626-2326**	410-289-6733	375
Ocean City Maryland Hotels						
106 N Baltimore Ave	Ocean City	MD	21842	**800-837-3588**	410-524-5252	667
Ocean Conservancy						
1300 19th St NW 8th Fl	Washington	DC	20036	**800-519-1541**	202-429-5609	48-13
Ocean County						
118 Washington St	Toms River	NJ	08753	**800-722-0291**	732-929-2018	337
Ocean Ctr						
101 N Atlantic Ave	Daytona Beach	FL	32118	**800-858-6444**	386-254-4500	205
Ocean Edge Resort & Golf Club						
2907 Main St	Brewster	MA	02631	**800-343-6074**	508-896-9000	665
Ocean Forest Plaza						
201 74th Ave N	Myrtle Beach	SC	29572	**800-726-3783***		378
*General						
Ocean Kayak						
125 Gilman Falls Ave Bldg B	Old Town	ME	04468	**800-852-9257**		706
Ocean Key Resort						
424 Atlantic Ave	Virginia Beach	VA	23451	**800-955-9700**	757-425-2200	378
Ocean Key Resort & Spa						
0 Duval St	Key West	FL	33040	**800-328-9815**	305-296-7701	665
Ocean Management Systems Inc						
2021 Goshen Tpke	Wallkill	NY	12589	**800-325-8439**	619-236-1203	706
Ocean Manor Resort						
4040 Galt Ocean Dr	Fort Lauderdale	FL	33308	**800-955-0444**	954-566-7500	665
Ocean Medical Ctr (OMC)						
425 Jack Martin Blvd	Brick	NJ	08724	**800-560-9990**	732-840-2200	373-3
Ocean Mist Beach Hotel & Suites						
97 S Shore Dr	South Yarmouth	MA	02664	**800-655-1972**	508-398-2633	665
Ocean Place Resort & Spa						
1Ocean Blvd	Long Branch	NJ	07740	**800-411-6493**		665
Ocean Pointe Suites at Key Largo						
500 Burton Dr	Tavernier	FL	33070	**800-882-9464**	305-853-3000	378

				Toll-Free	Phone	Class
Ocean Reef Resort						
7100 N Ocean Blvd	Myrtle Beach	SC	29572	**888-322-6411**	843-449-4441	665
Ocean Sky Hotel & Resort						
4060 Galt Ocean Dr	Fort Lauderdale	FL	33308	**800-678-9022**	954-565-6611	378
Ocean Spray Cranberries Inc						
1 Ocean Spray Dr	Lakeville-Middleboro	MA	02349	**800-662-3263**	508-946-1000	296-20
Ocean Waters Spa						
600 N Atlantic Ave	Daytona Beach	FL	32118	**844-284-2685**	386-267-1660	702
Oceana Resorts LLC						
1000 Second Ave S						
Ste 110	North Myrtle Beach	SC	29582	**866-469-7853**		
Oceaneering International Inc						
11911 FM 529	Houston	TX	77041	**844-381-9324**	713-329-4500	535
NYSE: OII						
Oceanex						
630 boul Rene-Levesque W						
Ste 2550	Montreal	QC	H3B1S6	**888-875-9595**	514-875-9595	311
OceanFirst Bank						
975 Hooper Ave	Toms River	NJ	08753	**888-623-2633**	732-240-4500	70
Oceania Cruises Inc						
8300 NW 33rd St Ste 308	Miami	FL	33122	**800-531-5619**	305-514-2300	220
Oceanic USA						
2002 Davis St	San Leandro	CA	94577	**800-435-3483**	888-270-8595	706
Oceano Hotel & Spa Half Moon Bay Harbor						
280 Capistrano Rd	Half Moon Bay	CA	94019	**888-623-2661**	650-726-5400	377
Oceanside Beach State Recreation Site						
13000 Whiskey Creek Rd W	Tillamook	OR	97141	**800-551-6949**		561
Oceanside Photo & Telescope (OPT)						
918 Mission Ave	Oceanside	CA	92054	**800-483-6287**	760-400-0164	179
Oceanus Partners						
16540 Pointe Village Dr Ste 208	Lutz	FL	33558	**888-496-1117**		196
Oce-USA Inc						
5450 N Cumberland Ave	Chicago	IL	60656	**800-877-6232**	773-714-8500	585
OCF (International OCD Foundation)						
PO Box 961029	Boston	MA	02196	**800-331-3131**	617-973-5801	48-17
OCF (Omaha Community Foundation)						
302 S 36th St Ste 100	Omaha	NE	68131	**800-794-3458**	402-342-3458	303
Ochsner						
1514 Jefferson Hwy	New Orleans	LA	70121	**800-343-0269**	504-842-3000	373-3
Ochsner Medical Ctr Baton Rouge						
17000 Medical Ctr Dr	Baton Rouge	LA	70816	**800-231-5257**	225-752-2470	373-3
Ochsner Medical Ctr West Bank						
2500 Belle Chasse Hwy	Gretna	LA	70056	**800-231-5257**	504-391-5454	373-3
OCL (Orangeburg County Library)						
510 Louis St	Orangeburg	SC	29115	**800-922-2594**	803-531-4636	433-3
OCLC (Online Computer Library Ctr Inc)						
6565 Kilgour Pl	Dublin	OH	43017	**800-848-5878**		49-11
OCM (One Call Medical Inc)						
20 Waterview Blvd PO Box 614	Parsippany	NJ	07054	**800-872-2875**	973-257-1000	381
OCMC (Ouachita County Medical Ctr)						
PO Box 797	Camden	AR	71711	**877-836-2472**	870-836-1000	373-3
OCMMC (Orange Coast Memorial Medical Ctr)						
9920 Talbert Ave	Fountain Valley	CA	92708	**877-597-4777**	714-378-7000	373-3
Ocmulgee Electric Membership Corp						
5722 Eastman St	Eastman	GA	31023	**800-342-5509**	478-374-7001	245
Oconee Electric Membership Corp						
3445 US Hwy 80 W	Dudley	GA	31022	**800-522-2930**	478-676-3191	245
Oconomowoc Memorial Hospital						
791 Summit Ave	Oconomowoc	WI	53066	**800-242-0313**	262-569-9400	373-3
Oconto Electric Co-op						
PO Box 168	Oconto Falls	WI	54154	**800-472-8410**	920-846-2816	245
OCP (Oregon Catholic Press)						
5536 NE Hassalo St	Portland	OR	97213	**877-596-1653**	503-281-1191	633-3
Ocsea-Afscme Local						
390 Worthington Rd Ste A	Westerville	OH	43082	**800-969-4702**	614-865-4700	413
October Company Inc						
51 Ferry St	EastHampton	MA	01027	**800-628-9346**	413-527-9380	295
Ocwen Federal Bank FSB						
1661 Worthington Rd						
Ste 100	West Palm Beach	FL	33409	**800-746-2936**	561-681-8000	70
Ocwen Financial Corp						
1661 Worthington Rd						
Ste 100	West Palm Beach	FL	33409	**800-746-2936**	561-682-8000	359-2
NYSE: OCN						
Odan Laboratories						
325 Stillview Ave	Pointe-Claire	QC	H9R2Y6	**888-252-6467**	514-428-1628	231
Odawa Casino Resort, The						
1760 Lears Rd	Petoskey	MI	49770	**877-442-6464**		450
ODEF (Old Dominion Eye Bank)						
9200 Arboretum Pkwy Ste 104	Richmond	VA	23236	**800-832-0728**	804-560-7540	269
Oden & Associates Inc						
119 S Main St Ste 300	Memphis	TN	38103	**800-371-6233**	901-578-8055	343
Odessa American						
PO Box 2952	Odessa	TX	79760	**800-592-4433**	432-337-4661	528-2
Odessa Chamber of Commerce						
700 N Grant St Ste 200	Odessa	TX	79761	**800-780-4678**	432-332-9111	139
Odessa Regional Medical Ctr						
520 E Sixth St	Odessa	TX	79761	**877-898-6080**	432-582-8000	373-7
ODG (Ontario Drive & Gear Ltd)						
220 Bergey Ct	New Hamburg	ON	N3A2J5	**877-274-6288**	519-662-2840	29
ODL Inc						
215 E Roosevelt Ave	Zeeland	MI	49464	**800-253-3900**	616-772-9111	329
Odlum Brown Ltd						
250 Howe St Ste 1100	Vancouver	BC	V6C3S9	**866-636-8222**	604-669-1600	400
Odon Wagner Gallery						
196 Davenport Rd	Toronto	ON	M5R1J2	**800-551-2465**	416-962-0438	42
ODS Cos						
601 SW Second Ave	Portland	OR	97204	**888-221-0802**	503-228-6554	390-3
Odwalla Inc						
1 COCA-COLA Plz	Atlanta	GA	30313	**800-639-2552**		296-20
Odyssey Healthcare of Kansas City						
4911 S Arrowhead Dr	Independence	MO	64055	**800-944-4357**	816-795-1333	370
Odyssey Re Holdings Corp						
300 First Stamford Pl	Stamford	CT	06902	**866-745-4440**	203-977-8000	390-4
OEA (Ohio Education Assn)						
225 E Broad St	Columbus	OH	43215	**800-282-1500**	614-228-4526	455-8
OEA (Oregon Education Magazine)						
6900 SW Atlanta St Bldg 1	Portland	OR	97223	**800-858-5505**	503-684-3300	455-8

	Toll-Free	Phone	Class
OEC (Otsego Electric Co-op Inc)			
PO Box 128 .... Hartwick NY 13348	**844-843-6842**	607-293-6622	
OEC Medical Systems Inc			
384 Wright Brothers Dr .... Salt Lake City UT 84116	**800-874-7378**		
Oeconnection LLC			
4205 Highlander Pkwy .... Richfield OH 44286	**888-776-5792**	330-523-1830	177
OEM Systems LLC			
210 W Oklahoma Ave .... Okarche OK 73762	**800-810-7252**	405-263-7488	61
OF Mossberg & Sons Inc			
7 Grasso Ave .... North Haven CT 06473	**800-363-3555**	203-230-5300	284
OFA (Orphan Foundation of America)			
23811 Chagrin Blvd Ste 210. .... Cleveland OH 44122	**800-950-4673**	571-203-0270	48-6
Off the Beaten Path			
7 E Beall St .... Bozeman MT 59715	**800-445-2995**	406-586-1311	755
Offen Petroleum Inc			
5100 E 78th Ave .... Commerce CO 80022	**866-657-3835**	303-297-3835	575
Office Chairs Inc			
14815 Radburn Ave .... Santa Fe Springs CA 90670	**866-624-4968**	562-802-0464	319-1
Office Depot Inc			
2200 Old Germantown Rd .... Delray Beach FL 33445	**800-937-3600**	561-438-4800	531
NASDAQ: ODP			
Office Environments Inc			
11407 Granite St .... Charlotte NC 28273	**888-861-2525**	704-714-7200	320
Office Liquidators Inc			
11111 W Sixth Ave .... Denver CO 80215	**800-279-3375**	303-759-3375	317
Office of Disability Employment Policy			
200 Constitution Ave NW .... Washington DC 20210	**866-633-7365**	202-693-7880	339-14
Office of General Services			
Corning Tower Empire State Plz			
41st Fl Empire State Plz .... Albany NY 12242	**877-426-6006**	518-474-3899	205
Office of Justice Programs			
Bureau of Justice Assistance			
810 Seventh St NW .... Washington DC 20531	**888-744-6513**	202-616-6500	339-13
Office for Victims of Crime			
810 Seventh St NW .... Washington DC 20531	**800-363-0441**	202-307-5983	339-13
Office of Public Health & Science			
200 Independence Ave SW			
Rm 716G. .... Washington DC 20201	**877-696-6775**	202-690-7694	339-9
Office of Public Health & Science Regional Offices			
Region VII			
200 Independence Ave SW			
Rm 509F HHH Bldg .... Washington DC 20201	**877-696-6775**		339-9
Office of Special Counsel			
1730 M St NW Ste 218. .... Washington DC 20036	**800-872-9855**	202-254-3600	339-19
OSC Headquarters			
1730 M St NW Ste 218. .... Washington DC 20036	**800-872-9855**	202-254-3600	339-19
Office of the Pardon Attorney			
145 N St NE Rm 5E. .... Washington DC 20530	**800-514-0301**	202-616-6070	339-13
Office Solutions Inc			
217 Mt Horeb Rd .... Warren NJ 07059	**800-677-1778**		179
Office Star Products			
1901 S Archibald PO Box 3520 .... Ontario CA 91761	**800-950-7262**	909-930-2000	320
Official Payments Corp			
3550 Engineering Dr .... Norcross GA 30092	**877-754-4413**	770-325-3100	180
Offshore Energy Services Inc			
5900 US Hwy 90 E .... Broussard LA 70518	**800-489-6202**	337-837-1024	535
Offshore International Inc			
8350 E Old Vail Rd .... Tucson AZ 85747	**800-897-3158**		
Offwhite 521 Ft St .... Marietta OH 45750	**800-606-1610**	740-373-9010	343
OG & E Electric Services			
PO Box 24990 .... Oklahoma City OK 73124	**800-272-9741**	405-553-3000	782
Ogden Eccles Conference Ctr			
2415 Washington Blvd .... Ogden UT 84401	**866-472-4627**	801-689-8600	205
Ogden Regional Medical Ctr			
5475 Adams Ave Pkwy .... Ogden UT 84405	**877-870-3745**	801-479-2111	373-3
Ogden/Weber Convention & Visitors Bureau			
2438 Washington Blvd .... Ogden UT 84401	**800-255-8824**	801-778-6250	206
OGE Energy Corp			
321 N Harvey St .... Oklahoma City OK 73102	**800-272-9741**	405-553-3000	359-5
NYSE: OGE			
Ogle County			
105 S Fifth St .... Oregon IL 61061	**800-242-7642**	815-732-3201	337
Oglebay Institute's Stifel Fine Arts Ctr			
1330 National Rd .... Wheeling WV 26003	**800-624-6988**	304-242-7700	50-2
Oglebay Resort & Conference Ctr			
465 Lodge Dr Oglebay Pk. .... Wheeling WV 26003	**800-624-6988**	304-243-4000	665
Oglethorpe University			
4484 Peachtree RdNE .... Atlanta GA 30319	**800-428-4484**	404-364-8307	166
Ogontz Corp			
2835 Terwood Rd .... Willow Grove PA 19090	**800-523-2478**	215-657-4770	784
OGR (International Order of the Golden Rule)			
3520 Executive Ctr Dr Ste 300 .... Austin TX 78731	**800-637-8030**	512-334-5504	49-4
Ogren Insurance			
6929 Hohman Ave .... Hammond IN 46324	**800-936-4736**		389
OGS Industries			
976 Evans Ave .... Akron OH 44305	**800-321-2438**		
OHANA Waikiki Beachcomber Hotel			
2300 Kalakaua Ave .... Honolulu HI 96815	**866-956-4262**		378
Ohaus Corp			
7 Campus Dr Ste 310 .... Parsippany NJ 07054	**800-672-7722**		
Ohel Children's Home & Family Services Inc			
4510 16th Ave .... Brooklyn NY 11204	**800-603-6435**	718-851-6300	362
Ohio			
Aging Dept			
246 N High St 1st Fl. .... Columbus OH 43215	**800-266-4346**	614-466-5500	338-36
Agriculture Dept			
8995 E Main St .... Reynoldsburg OH 43068	**800-282-1955**	614-728-6201	338-36
Consumer Protection Section			
30 E Broad St 14th Fl. .... Columbus OH 43215	**800-282-0515**	614-466-4986	338-36
Education Dept			
25 S Front St .... Columbus OH 43215	**877-644-6338**		338-36
Financial Institutions Div			
77 S High St 21st Fl. .... Columbus OH 43266	**866-278-0003**	614-728-8400	338-36
Historical Society			
800 E 17th Ave .... Columbus OH 43211	**800-686-6124**	614-297-2300	338-36
Housing Finance Agency			
57 E Main St .... Columbus OH 43215	**888-362-6432**	614-466-7970	338-36
Insurance Dept			
50 W Town St Ste 300 3rd Fl .... Columbus OH 43215	**800-686-1526**	614-644-2658	338-36
Mental Health Dept			
30 E Broad St 8th Fl. .... Columbus OH 43215	**877-275-6364**	614-466-2596	338-36
Parks & Recreation Div			
2045 Morse Rd Bldg C-3. .... Columbus OH 43229	**866-644-6727**	614-265-6561	338-36
Parole Board			
770 W Broad St .... Columbus OH 43222	**888-344-1441**	614-752-1200	338-36
Public Utilities Commission			
180 E Broad St .... Columbus OH 43215	**800-686-7826**	614-466-3016	338-36
Taxation Dept			
PO Box 530 .... Columbus OH 43216	**888-405-4089**	614-466-2166	338-36
Travel & Tourism Div			
PO Box 1001 .... Columbus OH 43216	**800-282-5393**	614-466-8844	338-36
Treasurer			
30 E Broad St 9th Fl. .... Columbus OH 43215	**800-228-1102**	614-466-2160	338-36
Tuition Trust Authority			
35 E Chestnut St 8th Fl. .... Columbus OH 43215	**800-233-6734***	614-752-9400	721
*Cust Svc			
Wildlife Div			
2045 Morse Rd Bldg G. .... Columbus OH 43229	**800-945-3543**	614-265-6300	338-36
Workers' Compensation Bureau			
30 W Spring St .... Columbus OH 43215	**800-644-6292**	614-644-6292	338-36
Workforce Developement Office			
4020 E Fifth Ave PO Box 1618. ..... Columbus OH 43219	**888-296-7541**		338-36
Youth Services Dept			
30 W Spring St .... Columbus OH 43215	**855-577-7714**	614-466-4314	338-36
Ohio Art Co, The			
1 Toy St .... Bryan OH 43506	**800-800-3141**	419-636-3141	757
OTC: OART			
Ohio Associated Enterprises LLC			
97 Corwin Dr .... Painesville OH 44077	**888-637-4832**	440-354-2100	810
Ohio Casualty			
9450 SewaRd Rd .... Fairfield OH 45014	**800-843-6446**		390-4
Ohio Contractors Association			
1313 Dublin Rd .... Columbus OH 43215	**800-229-1388**	614-488-0724	138
Ohio Dominican University			
1216 Sunbury Rd .... Columbus OH 43219	**800-955-6446**	614-251-4500	166
Ohio Drilling Co			
2405 Bostic Blvd SW .... Massillon OH 44647	**800-272-1711**	330-832-1521	189-15
Ohio Edison Co			
76 S Main St .... Akron OH 44308	**800-736-3402**	330-436-4122	782
Ohio Education Assn (OEA)			
225 E Broad St .... Columbus OH 43215	**800-282-1500**	614-228-4526	455-8
Ohio Gas Co PO Box 528 .... Bryan OH 43506	**800-331-7396**	419-636-1117	532
Ohio Gasket & Shim Company Inc			
976 Evans Ave .... Akron OH 44305	**800-321-2438**		326
Ohio Historical Society			
1982 Velma Ave .... Columbus OH 43211	**800-686-6124**	614-297-2300	517
Ohio House Motel			
600 N La Salle Dr .... Chicago IL 60654	**866-601-6446**	312-943-6000	703
Ohio Indemnity Co			
250 E Broad St 7th Fl .... Columbus OH 43215	**800-628-8581**		390-4
Ohio Legal Assistance Foundation			
10 W Broad St Ste 950 .... Columbus OH 43215	**800-877-9772**	614-715-8560	427
Ohio Lottery Commission			
615 W Superior Ave .... Cleveland OH 44113	**800-686-4208**	216-787-3200	450
Ohio Machinery Co			
3993 E Royalton Rd .... Broadview Heights OH 44147	**800-837-6200**	440-526-6200	357
Ohio Magazine			
1422 Euclid Ave Ste 730. .... Cleveland OH 44115	**800-210-7293**	216-771-2833	455-22
Ohio Magnetics Inc			
5400 Dunham Rd .... Maple Heights OH 44137	**800-486-6446**	216-662-8484	468
Ohio Manufacturers' Association			
33 N High St .... Columbus OH 43215	**800-662-4463**	614-224-5111	138
Ohio Medical Transportation Inc			
2827 W Dblin Granville Rd .... Columbus OH 43235	**877-633-3598**	614-734-8001	13
Ohio Motorcycle Dealers Association			
655 Metro Pl S Ste 270 .... Dublin OH 43017	**800-686-9100**	614-766-9100	138
Ohio Northern University			
525 S Main St .... Ada OH 45810	**888-408-4668***	419-772-2000	166
*Admissions			
Ohio Northern University Claude W Pettit College of Law			
525 S Main St .... Ada OH 45810	**877-452-9668**	419-772-2211	167-1
Ohio Northern University Heterick Memorial Library			
525 S Main St .... Ada OH 45810	**866-943-5787**	419-772-2181	433-6
Ohio Nurses Assn (ONA)			
4000 E Main St .... Columbus OH 43213	**800-735-0056**	614-237-5414	529
Ohio Nut & Bolt Co			
5250 W 164th St .... Brook Park OH 44142	**800-437-1689**		278
Ohio Republican Party			
211 S Fifth St .... Columbus OH 43215	**800-282-0515**	614-228-2481	612-2
Ohio Restaurant Assn			
1525 Bethel Rd Ste 201 .... Columbus OH 43220	**800-282-9049**	614-442-3535	242
Ohio State Bar Assn (OSBA)			
1700 Lake Shore Dr .... Columbus OH 43204	**800-282-6556**	614-487-2050	72
Ohio State Medical Assn			
3401 Mill Run Dr .... Hilliard OH 43026	**800-766-6762**		472
Ohio State Medical Association, The			
5115 Parkcenter Ave Ste 200 .... Dublin OH 43017	**800-766-6762**		455-16
Ohio State University			
154 W 12th Ave .... Columbus OH 43210	**800-426-5046**	614-292-3980	166
Newark			
1179 University Dr .... Newark OH 43055	**800-963-9275**	740-366-3321	166
Ohio State University, The			
University Libraries			
1858 Neil Ave Mall .... Columbus OH 43210	**800-555-1212**	614-292-6785	433-6
Ohio Steel Sheet & Plate Inc			
7845 Chestnut Ridge Rd .... Hubbard OH 44425	**800-827-2401**		
Ohio Travel Association			
1801 Watermark Dr Ste 375 .... Columbus OH 43215	**800-896-4682**	614-572-1931	767
Ohio University			
120 Chubb Hall .... Athens OH 45710	**800-858-6843**	740-593-1000	166
Chillicothe			
101 University Dr .... Chillicothe OH 45601	**877-462-6824**	740-774-7200	166
Eastern			
45425 National Rd .... Saint Clairsville OH 43950	**800-648-3331**	740-695-1720	166
Lancaster			
1570 Granville Pk .... Lancaster OH 43130	**800-444-2910**	740-654-6711	166

Name / Address	City	State	ZIP	Toll-Free	Phone	Class
Southern						
1804 Liberty Ave	Ironton	OH	45638	**800-626-0513**	740-533-4600	166
Ohio Valley Aluminum Company LLC						
1100 Brooks Industrial Rd	Shelbyville	KY	40065	**800-692-4145**	502-633-2783	490
Ohio Valley Banc Corp						
420 Third Ave	Gallipolis	OH	45631	**800-468-6682**	740-446-2631	359-2
NASDAQ: OVBC						
Ohio Valley Supply Co						
3512 Spring Grove Ave	Cincinnati	OH	45223	**800-696-5608**	513-681-8300	191-3
Ohio Veterans Home						
3416 Columbus Ave	Sandusky	OH	44870	**800-572-7934***	419-625-2454	788
*Admissions						
Ohio Veterinary Medical Assn (OVMA)						
3168 Riverside Dr	Columbus	OH	43221	**800-662-6862**	614-486-7253	790
Ohio Wesleyan University						
61 S Sandusky St Slocum Hall	Delaware	OH	43015	**800-922-8953**	740-368-2000	166
Ohly Americas						
1115 Tiffany St	Boyceville	WI	54725	**800-321-2689**	320-587-2481	296-42
OHM (Orchard Hiltz & McCliment Inc)						
34000 Plymouth Rd	Livonia	MI	48150	**888-522-6711**	734-522-6711	261
Ohm Systems Inc						
10250 Chester Rd	Cincinnati	OH	45215	**800-878-0646**	513-771-0008	461
Ohmart/VEGA Corp						
4241 Allendorf Dr	Cincinnati	OH	45209	**800-367-5383**	513-272-0131	470
Ohmite Manufacturing Co						
1600 Golf Rd Ste 850	Rolling Meadows	IL	60008	**866-964-6483**		253
Ohmstede						
895 N Main St	Beaumont	TX	77704	**800-568-2328**	409-833-6375	91
OHSU (Oregon Health & Science University)						
Bone Marrow Transplant Clinic						
3181 SW Sam Jackson Pk Rd						
CB569	Portland	OR	97239	**800-452-1369**	503-494-8500	764
OI Corp						
151 Graham Rd						
PO Box 9010	College Station	TX	77842	**800-653-1711**	979-690-1711	418
OIA Global Logistics Inc						
2100 SW River Pkwy	Portland	OR	97201	**800-938-3109**	503-736-5900	311
State Ethics Commission						
315 W Ohio St Rm 104	Indianapolis	IN	46202	**866-805-8498**	800-677-9800	265
Oil & Gas Equipment Corp						
8 Rd 350	Flora Vista	NM	87415	**800-868-9624**	505-333-2300	305
Oil & Gas Journal						
1455 W Loop S	Houston	TX	77027	**800-633-1656**	918-831-9423	455-21
Oil Can Henry's						
19150 SW 90th Ave	Tualatin	OR	97062	**800-765-6244**	503-783-3888	195
Oil Creek Plastics Inc						
45619 State Hwy 27						
PO Box 385	Titusville	PA	16354	**800-537-3661**	814-827-3661	592
Oil Ctr Research LLC						
106 Montrose Ave	Lafayette	LA	70503	**800-256-8977**	337-993-3559	537
Oil Price Information Service						
3349 Hwy 138 Bldg D Ste D	Wall	NJ	07719	**888-301-2645***	732-901-8800	527-5
*Cust Svc						
Oil-Dri Corp of America						
410 N Michigan Ave Ste 400	Chicago	IL	60611	**800-645-3747**	312-321-1515	498
NYSE: ODC						
Oil-Law Records Corp						
8 N W 65th St	Oklahoma City	OK	73116	**888-464-5529**	405-840-1631	224
Ojai Valley Inn & Spa						
905 Country Club Rd	Ojai	CA	93023	**800-422-6524**	805-640-2068	665
Ojo Caliente Mineral Springs Resort						
50 Los Banos Dr PO Box 68	Ojo Caliente	NM	87549	**800-222-9162**	505-583-2233	702
OK Foods Inc						
PO Box 1787	Fort Smith	AR	72902	**800-635-9441**		615
Okanagan College						
1000 KLO Rd	Kelowna	BC	V1Y4X8	**800-621-3038**	250-762-5445	162
Okeechobee Correctional Institution						
3420 NE 168th St	Okeechobee	FL	34972	**800-574-5729**	863-462-5400	213
Okefenoke Rural Electric Membership Corp (REMC)						
14384 Cleveland St PO Box 602	Nahunta	GA	31553	**800-262-5131**	912-462-5131	245
Oki Data Americas Inc						
2000 Bishops Gate Blvd	Mount Laurel	NJ	08054	**800-654-3282***	856-235-2600	173-6
*Cust Svc						
OKI Developments Inc						
1416 112th Ave NE	Bellevue	WA	98004	**877-465-3654**	425-454-2800	359-3
Oklahoma						
Commerce Dept						
900 N Stiles Ave	Oklahoma City	OK	73104	**800-879-6552**	405-815-6552	338-37
Environmental Quality Dept						
707 N Robinson	Oklahoma City	OK	73102	**800-869-1400**	405-702-0100	338-37
Housing Finance Agency						
100 NW 63rd St Ste 200	Oklahoma City	OK	73116	**800-256-1489**	405-848-1144	338-37
Insurance Dept (OID)						
3625 NW 56th Ste 100	Oklahoma City	OK	73112	**800-522-0071**	405-521-2828	338-37
Real Estate Commission						
1915 N Stiles Ave Ste 200	Oklahoma City	OK	73105	**866-521-3389**	405-521-3387	338-37
Rehabilitative Services Dept						
3535 NW 58th St Ste 500	Oklahoma City	OK	73112	**800-845-8476**	405-951-3400	338-37
Travel Promotion Div						
900 N Stiles Ave	Oklahoma City	OK	73104	**800-652-6552**		338-37
Vital Records Div						
1000 NE Tenth St	Oklahoma City	OK	73117	**800-522-0203**	405-271-5600	338-37
Oklahoma Assn of Realtors						
9807 N Broadway	Oklahoma City	OK	73114	**800-375-9944**	405-848-9944	652
Oklahoma Baptist University						
500 W University St	Shawnee	OK	74804	**800-654-3285**	405-275-2850	166
Oklahoma Bar Assn						
1901 N Lincoln Blvd						
PO Box 53036	Oklahoma City	OK	73105	**800-522-8065**	405-416-7000	72
Oklahoma Blood Institute (OBI)						
1001 N Lincoln Blvd	Oklahoma City	OK	73104	**866-708-4995**	405-278-3100	89
Oklahoma Christian University						
PO Box 11000	Oklahoma City	OK	73136	**800-877-5010**		166
Oklahoma City Convention & Visitors Bureau						
123 Park Ave	Oklahoma City	OK	73102	**800-225-5652**	405-297-8912	206
Oklahoma City Museum of Art						
415 Couch Dr	Oklahoma City	OK	73102	**800-579-9278**	405-236-3100	517
Oklahoma City University						
2501 N Blackwelder Ave	Oklahoma City	OK	73106	**800-633-7242***	405-208-5050	166
*Admissions						
Oklahoma Correctional Industries						
3402 N Martin Luther King Ave						
	Oklahoma City	OK	73111	**800-522-3565**	405-425-7500	626
Oklahoma Democratic Party						
4100 N Lincoln Blvd	Oklahoma City	OK	73105	**800-547-5600**	405-427-3366	612-1
Oklahoma Dental Assn						
317 NE 13th St	Oklahoma City	OK	73104	**800-876-8890**	405-848-8873	227
Oklahoma Dept of Libraries						
200 NE 18th St	Oklahoma City	OK	73105	**800-522-8116**	405-521-2502	433-5
Oklahoma Education Association						
323 E Madison						
PO Box 18485	Oklahoma City	OK	73154	**800-522-8091**	405-528-7785	455-8
Oklahoma Electric Co-op						
242 24th Ave NW	Norman	OK	73069	**800-522-6543**	405-321-2024	245
Oklahoma Federal Credit Union						
517 NE 36th St	Oklahoma City	OK	73105	**800-522-8510**	405-524-6467	219
Oklahoma Forensic Ctr						
24800 S 4420 Rd	Vinita	OK	74301	**800-752-9475**	918-256-7841	373-5
Oklahoma Medical Research Foundation (OMRF)						
825 NE 13th St	Oklahoma City	OK	73104	**800-522-0211**	405-271-6673	664
Oklahoma Natural Gas Co						
401 N Harvey PO Box 401	Oklahoma City	OK	73101	**800-664-5463**		782
Oklahoma Panhandle State University						
323 Eagle Blvd	Goodwell	OK	73939	**800-664-6778**	580-349-2611	166
Oklahoma Press Service Inc						
3601 N Lincoln Blvd	Oklahoma City	OK	73105	**888-815-2672**	405-499-0020	620
Oklahoma State University						
219 Student Union Bldg	Stillwater	OK	74078	**800-852-1255**	405-744-5000	166
Oklahoma City						
900 N Portland Ave	Oklahoma City	OK	73107	**800-560-4099**	405-947-4421	162
Okmulgee						
1801 E Fourth St	Okmulgee	OK	74447	**800-722-4471**	918-293-4678	795
Oklahoma Telephone & Telegraph Inc						
26 N Otis Ave	Dustin	OK	74839	**800-869-1989**		386
Oklahoma Veterans Ctr Ardmore						
1015 S Commerce	Ardmore	OK	73401	**800-941-2160**	580-223-2266	788
Oklahoma Veterans Ctr Norman						
1776 E Robinson St	Norman	OK	73071	**800-782-5218**	405-360-5600	448
Oklahoma Veterans Ctr Talihina						
10014 SE 1138th Ave						
PO Box 1168	Talihina	OK	74571	**800-941-2160**	918-567-2251	788
Oklahoman, The						
100 W Main St	Oklahoma City	OK	73102	**877-987-2737**	405-475-3311	528-2
Old Alabama Town						
301 Columbus St	Montgomery	AL	36104	**888-240-1850**	334-240-4500	50-3
Old American Insurance Co						
3520 Broadway	Kansas City	MO	64111	**800-733-6242**	816-753-7000	390-2
Old Bridge Chemicals Inc						
554 Waterworks Rd	Old Bridge	NJ	08857	**800-275-3924**	732-727-2225	143
Old Colony Hospice						
1 Credit Union Way	Randolph	MA	02368	**800-370-1322**	781-341-4145	370
Old Dominion Brush Co						
5118 Glen Alden Dr	Richmond	VA	23231	**800-446-9823**		582
Old Dominion Capital Management Inc						
815 E Jefferson St	Charlottesville	VA	22902	**800-446-2029**	434-977-1550	524
Old Dominion Eye Bank (ODEF)						
9200 Arboretum Pkwy Ste 104	Richmond	VA	23236	**800-832-0728**	804-560-7540	269
Old Dominion Freight Line Inc						
500 Old Dominion Way	Thomasville	NC	27360	**800-432-6335**	336-889-5000	775
NASDAQ: ODFL						
Old Dominion University						
Rollins Hall	Norfolk	VA	23529	**800-348-7926**	757-683-3685	166
Old Edwards Inn & Spa						
445 Main St	Highlands	NC	28741	**866-526-8008**		377
Old Exchange & Provost Dungeon						
122 E Bay St	Charleston	SC	29401	**888-763-0448**	843-727-2165	50-3
Old Florida Museum						
259 San Marco Ave	Saint Augustine	FL	32084	**800-813-3208**	904-824-8874	517
Old Mansion Foods						
3811 Corporate Rd						
PO Box 1838	Petersburg	VA	23805	**800-476-1877**	804-862-9889	296-7
Old Mill Toronto						
21 Old Mill Rd	Toronto	ON	M8X1G5	**866-653-6455**	416-236-2641	378
Old Mill Winery						
403 S Broadway	Geneva	OH	44041	**800-227-6972**		80-3
Old National Bank						
1 Main St PO Box 718	Evansville	IN	47705	**800-731-2265**		70
Old Newbury Crafters						
36 Main St	Amesbury	MA	01913	**800-343-1388**	978-388-4026	698
Old Point Financial Corp						
1 W Mellen St PO Box 3392	Hampton	VA	23663	**800-952-0051**	757-728-1200	359-2
NASDAQ: OPOF						
Old Republic Insured Automotive Services Inc						
8282 S Memorial Dr	Tulsa	OK	74133	**800-331-3780**		390-5
Old Republic National Title Insurance Co (ORTIG)						
400 Second Ave S	Minneapolis	MN	55401	**800-328-4441**	612-371-1111	390-6
Old Republic Surety						
445 S Moorlands Rd Ste 200	Brookfield	WI	53005	**800-217-1792**	262-797-2640	390-5
Old Salem						
600 S Main St	Winston-Salem	NC	27101	**800-441-5305**	336-721-7300	517
Old Second Bancorp Inc						
37 S River St	Aurora	IL	60506	**877-866-0202**	630-892-0202	359-2
NASDAQ: OSBC						
Old Town Canoe Co						
125 Gilman Falls Ave Bldg B	Old Town	ME	04468	**800-343-1555**	207-827-1530	706
Old Wisconsin Sausage Co						
4036 Weeden Creek Rd	Sheboygan	WI	53083	**877-451-7988**	920-458-4304	296-26
Oldcastle BuildingEnvelope						
5005 Lyndon B Johnson Fwy						
Ste 1050	Dallas	TX	75244	**866-653-2278**		329
Oldcastle Precast Bldg Systems Div						
1401 Trimble Rd	Edgewood	MD	21040	**800-523-9144**	410-612-1213	189-3
Oldcastle Precast Inc						
7921 Southpark Plz Ste 200	Littleton	CO	80120	**800-642-3755**	303-209-8000	183
Olde Pink House						
29 Abercorn St	Savannah	GA	31401	**800-554-1187**		667

Name / Address	Toll-Free	Phone	Class
Oldham County Chamber of Commerce 412 E Main St ..... LaGrange KY 40031	800-264-0521	502-222-1635	139
Olds College 4500-50 St ..... Olds AB T4H1R6	800-661-6537	403-556-8281	162
Olds Products Co 10700 88th Ave ..... Pleasant Prairie WI 53158	800-233-8064	262-947-3500	296-19
Olean Times-Herald 639 Norton Dr ..... Olean NY 14760	800-722-8812	716-372-3121	528-2
Olean Wholesale Grocery Co-op Inc 1587 Haskell Rd PO Box 1070 ..... Olean NY 14760	888-835-3026	716-372-2020	297-8
Oleco Inc 18683 Trimble Ct ..... Spring Lake MI 49456	800-575-3282	616-842-6790	809
Olesky Associates Inc 865 Washington St Ste 3 ..... Newton MA 02460	800-486-4330	781-235-4330	260
Oleta River State Park 3400 NE 163rd St ..... North Miami Beach FL 33160	800-326-3521	305-919-1846	561
Oley Foundation 214 Hun Memorial MC-28 Albany Medical Ctr ..... Albany NY 12208	800-776-6539	518-262-5079	48-17
Olis Inc 130 Conway Dr Ste A B & C ..... Bogart GA 30622	800-852-3504	706-353-6547	418
Olive Branch Chamber of Commerce 9123 Pigeon Roost PO Box 608 ..... Olive Branch MS 38654	800-948-3090	662-895-2600	139
Oliver M Dean Inc 125 Brooks St ..... Worcester MA 01606	800-648-3326	508-856-9100	428
Oliver Machinery Co 6902 S 194th St ..... Kent WA 98032	800-559-5065	253-867-0334	816
Oliver of Adrian Inc 1111 E Beecher St PO Box 189 ..... Adrian MI 49221	877-668-0885	517-263-2132	453
Oliver Products Co 445 Sixth St NW ..... Grand Rapids MI 49504	800-253-3893	616-456-7711	298
Oliver Winery 8024 N SR-37 ..... Bloomington IN 47404	800-258-2783	812-876-5800	50-7
Olivet College 320 S Main St ..... Olivet MI 49076	800-456-7189	269-749-7000	166
Olivet Nazarene University 1 University Ave ..... Bourbonnais IL 60914	800-648-1463	815-939-5011	166
Olivia 434 Brannan St ..... San Francisco CA 94107	800-631-6277	415-962-5700	755
Ollie's Bargain Outlet Inc 6295 Allentown Blvd Ste 1 ..... Harrisburg PA 17112	800-219-7052	717-657-2300	786
Olney Central College 305 NW St ..... Olney IL 62450	866-529-4322	618-395-7777	162
Ologie LLC 447 E Main St ..... Columbus OH 43215	800-962-1107	614-221-1107	461
Olon Ricerca Bioscience 7528 Auburn Rd ..... Concord OH 44077	888-742-3722	440-357-3300	664
Olson Research Assoc Inc 10290 Old Columbia Rd ..... Columbia MD 21046	888-657-6680	410-290-6999	178-10
Olsun Electrics Corp 10901 Commercial St ..... Richmond IL 60071	800-336-5786		762
Olum's of Binghamton Inc 3701 Vestal Pkwy E ..... Vestal NY 13850 *Cust Svc	855-264-8674*	607-729-5775	321
Oly Penn Inc 245 E Washington St ..... Sequim WA 98382	800-303-8696	360-683-1456	225
Olymel LP 2200 Pratte Ave Pratte ..... Saint-Hyacinthe QC J2S4B6	800-361-7990	450-771-0400	615
Olympia City Hall PO Box 1967 ..... Olympia WA 98507	800-451-7985	360-753-8447	336
Olympia Financial Group Inc 125 Ninth Ave SE Ste 2300 ..... Calgary AB T2G0P6	888-668-8384	403-668-8384	782
Olympia Lacey Tumwater Visitor & Convention Bureau 103 Sid Snyder Ave SW ..... Olympia WA 98501	877-704-7500	360-704-7544	206
Olympia Promotions & Distribution 226 E Jericho Tpke ..... Mineola NY 11501	800-846-7874	516-775-4500	327
Olympia Resort & Spa 1350 Royale Mile Rd ..... Oconomowoc WI 53066	800-558-9573	262-369-4999	665
Olympia Sports 5 Bradley Dr ..... Westbrook ME 04092	844-511-1721	207-854-2794	707
Olympia Tile International Inc 1000 Lawrence Ave W ..... Toronto ON M6A1C6	800-268-1613	416-785-6666	191-4
Olympian, The PO Box 407 ..... Olympia WA 98507	800-905-0296	360-754-5400	528-2
Olympic College 1600 Chester Ave ..... Bremerton WA 98337	800-259-6718	360-792-6050	162
Shelton 937 W Alpine Way ..... Shelton WA 98584	800-259-6718	360-427-2119	162
Olympic Medical Ctr 939 Caroline St ..... Port Angeles WA 98362	888-362-6260	360-417-7000	373-3
Olympic Resource Management 19950 Seventh Ave NE Ste 200 ..... Poulsbo WA 98370 NASDAQ: POPE	800-522-6645	360-697-6626	747
Olympique Expert Building Care 26232 Enterprise Ct ..... Lake Forest CA 92630	866-659-6747	949-455-0796	461
Olympus Flag & Banner 9000 W Heather Ave ..... Milwaukee WI 53224	800-558-9620	414-355-2010	287
OMA (Oregon Medical Assn) 11740 SW 68th Pkwy Ste 100 ..... Portland OR 97223	877-605-3229	503-619-8000	472
Omaha Community Foundation (OCF) 302 S 36th St Ste 100 ..... Omaha NE 68131	800-794-3458	402-342-3458	303
Omaha Community Playhouse 6915 Cass St ..... Omaha NE 68132	888-782-4338	402-553-0800	569-4
Omaha Paper Co 6936 L St ..... Omaha NE 68117	800-288-7026	402-331-3243	634
Omaha Public Power District (OPPD) 444 S 16th St Mall ..... Omaha NE 68102	800-331-5666	402-536-4131	
Omaha World-Herald 1314 Douglas St ..... Omaha NE 68102	800-284-6397	402-444-1000	528-2
Oman Systems Inc 3334 Powell Ave ..... Nashville TN 37204	800-541-0803	615-385-2500	188
OMAX Corp 21409 72nd Ave S ..... Kent WA 98032	800-838-0343	253-872-2300	693
OMB Watch 1742 Connecticut Ave NW ..... Washington DC 20009	866-544-7573	202-234-8494	48-7
OMC (Ocean Medical Ctr) 425 Jack Martin Blvd ..... Brick NJ 08724	800-560-9990	732-840-2200	373-3
OMD Corp 3705 Missouri Blvd ..... Jefferson City MO 65109	866-440-8664	573-893-8930	178-1
Omedix Inc 7114 E Stetson Dr Ste 360 ..... Scottsdale AZ 85251	877-866-3349		395
Omega Engineering Inc 1 Omega Dr PO Box 4047 ..... Stamford CT 06907	800-826-6342	203-359-1660	201
Omega Flex Inc 451 Creamery Way ..... Exton PA 19341 NASDAQ: OFLX	800-355-1039	610-524-7272	785
Omega Healthcare Investors Inc 300 International Cir Ste 200 ..... Hunt Valley MD 21030 NYSE: OHI	877-511-2891	410-427-1700	651
Omega Institute for Holistic Studies 150 Lake Dr ..... Rhinebeck NY 12572	800-944-1001	845-266-4444	669
Omega Medical Health Systems Inc 1200 E High St Ste 106 ..... Pottstown PA 19464	866-716-6342		473
Omega Moulding Company Ltd 1 Saw Grass Dr ..... Bellport NY 11713	800-289-6634		360
Omega Products International 1681 California Ave ..... Corona CA 92881	800-600-6634	951-737-7447	191-3
Omega Protein Corp 2105 City W Blvd Ste 500 ..... Houston TX 77042	866-421-0831	713-623-0060	296-12
Omega Psi Phi Fraternity Inc 3951 Snapfinger Pkwy ..... Decatur GA 30035	800-829-4933	404-284-5533	48-16
Omega Rail Management 4721 Trousdale Dr Ste 206 ..... Nashville TN 37220	800-990-1961		645
Omega Shielding Products Inc 1384 Pompton Ave ..... Cedar Grove NJ 07009	800-828-5784	973-366-0080	326
Omega World Travel Inc 3102 Omega Office Pk Dr ..... Fairfax VA 22031	800-756-6342	703-359-0200	766
Omegachem 480 rue Perreault ..... St-romuald QC G6W7V6	800-661-6342	418-837-4444	238
OMHS (Owensboro Health) 811 E Parish Ave PO Box 20007 ..... Owensboro KY 42303	877-888-6647	270-691-8040	373-3
OMI (OMI Industries) 1 Corporate Dr Ste 100 ..... Long Grove IL 60047	800-662-6367		578
OMI Industries (OMI) 1 Corporate Dr Ste 100 ..... Long Grove IL 60047	800-662-6367		578
Omicron Architecture Engineering Construction Ltd 595 Burrard St Three Bentall Centre Fifth Fl PO Box 49369 ..... Vancouver BC V7X1L4	877-632-3350	604-632-3350	256
Omnetics Connector Corp 7260 Commerce Cir E ..... Minneapolis MN 55432 *Cust Svc	800-343-0025*	763-572-0656	810
Omni Barton Creek Resort & Spa 8212 Barton Club Dr ..... Austin TX 78735	800-336-6158	512-329-4000	665
Omni Cable Corp 2 Hagerty Blvd ..... West Chester PA 19382	888-292-6664	610-701-0100	246
Omni Cubed Inc 6125 Enterprise Dr Ste B155 ..... Diamond Springs CA 95619	877-311-1976		226
Omni Grove Park Inn, The 290 Macon Ave ..... Asheville NC 28804	800-438-5800		
Omni Hotels 4001 Maple Ave ..... Dallas TX 75219	800-843-6664	402-952-6664	378
Omni Hotels Select Guest Loyalty Program 11819 Miami St 3rd Fl ..... Omaha NE 68164 *Cust Svc	800-843-6664*		377
Omni Information Systems Inc PO Box 1429 ..... Dacula GA 30019	888-653-6664	678-377-5560	180
Omni Interlocken Resort 500 Interlocken Blvd ..... Broomfield CO 80021	800-843-6664	303-438-6600	665
Omni International Inc 435 12th St SW ..... Vernon AL 35592	800-844-6664	205-695-9173	
Omni Life Assocates Inc 375 N Broadway Ste 203 ..... Jericho NY 11753	800-966-6583	516-938-2465	
Omni Orlando Resort at Championsgate 1500 Masters Blvd ..... Champions Gate FL 33896	800-843-6664	407-390-6664	665
OMNI Products Inc 3911 Dayton St ..... Mchenry IL 60050	800-275-9848	815-344-3100	673
Omnia Group Inc, The 1501 W Cleveland St Ste 300 ..... Tampa FL 33606	800-525-7117	813-254-9449	
Omnicare Inc 201 E Fourth St ..... Cincinnati OH 45202 NYSE: OCR	800-342-5627	800-990-6664	583
Omnicell Inc 1201 Charleston Rd ..... Mountain View CA 94043 NASDAQ: OMCL	800-850-6664	650-251-6100	419
Omnigraphics Inc PO Box 31-1640 ..... Detroit MI 48231	800-234-1340		633-2
Omnilingua Worldwide LLC 306 Sixth Ave SE ..... Cedar Rapids IA 52401	800-395-6664		
Omni-Lite Industries Canada Inc 17210 Edwards Rd ..... Cerritos CA 90703	800-577-6664	562-404-8510	617
Omni-Medcom 160 Pope St ..... Cookshire QC J0B1M0	888-780-6081		179
OmniMetrix LLC 5225 Belle Wood Ct ..... Buford GA 30518	800-854-7342	770-209-0012	406
Omnipure Filter Company Inc 1904 Industrial Way ..... Caldwell ID 83605	800-398-0833	208-454-2597	45
Omnis Network LLC 3655 Torrance Blvd Ste 180 ..... Torrance CA 90503	877-393-4678	310-316-9600	
OmniSource Corp 7575 W Jefferson Blvd ..... Fort Wayne IN 46804	800-666-4789	260-422-5541	682
Omnitracs 717 North Harwood St Ste 1300 ..... Dallas TX 75201	800-348-7227		731
Omnitrans Inc 500 Merrick Rd ..... Lynbrook NY 11563	877-806-2541	516-561-9300	
OmniTRAX Inc 252 Clayton St 4th Fl ..... Denver CO 80206	800-533-9416	303-398-4500	647
Omnitronics LLC 6573 Cochran Rd ..... Solon OH 44139	800-762-9266	440-349-4900	52
Omnivex Corp 3300 Hwy 7 Ste 501 ..... Concord ON L4K4M3	800-745-8223	905-761-6640	179
OmniVue Business Solutions LLC 1355 Windward Concourse Ste 200 ..... Alpharetta GA 30005	866-900-6348	770-587-0095	196

	Toll-Free	Phone	Class
Omnni Associates Inc			
1 Systems Dr .... Appleton WI 54914	800-571-6677	920-735-6900	261
OMNOVA Solutions Inc Performance Chemicals Div			
165 S Cleveland Ave .... Mogadore OH 44260	888-253-5454	330-628-6536	145
OMRF (Oklahoma Medical Research Foundation)			
825 NE 13th St .... Oklahoma City OK 73104	800-522-0211	405-271-6673	664
OMRON Corp			
1 Commerce Dr .... Schaumburg IL 60173	800-556-6766	847-843-7900	203
Omron Healthcare Inc			
1925 W Field Ct .... Lake Forest IL 60045	877-216-1333	847-680-6200	473
OMRON Scientific Technologies Inc			
6550 Dumbarton Cir .... Fremont CA 94555	800-556-6766	510-608-3400	203
OMYA Inc 62 Main St .... Proctor VT 05765	800-451-4468	802-459-3311	143
ON Semiconductor Corp			
5005 E McDowell Rd .... Phoenix AZ 85008	800-282-9855	602-244-6600	692
NASDAQ: ON			
ON Services			
6779 Crescent Dr .... Norcross GA 30071	800-967-2419	770-457-0966	733
On The Border mexican grill & cantina			
1710 S Power Rd .... Mesa AZ 85206	888-682-6882		
On Time Staffing			
535 Rte 38 E Ste 412 .... Cherry Hill NJ 08002	855-866-2910	866-333-3007	260
On Time Transport Inc			
135 E Highland Pkwy .... Roselle NJ 07203	800-858-8463	908-298-9500	
ONA (Ohio Nurses Assn)			
4000 E Main St .... Columbus OH 43213	800-735-0056	614-237-5414	529
ONA (Oregon Nurses Assn)			
18765 SW Boones Ferry Rd ..... Tualatin OR 97062	800-634-3552	503-293-0011	529
Ona Beach State Park			
5580 S Coast Hwy .... Newport OR 97366	800-551-6949		561
OnCard Marketing Inc			
132 West 31st St Ste 702 ..... New York NY 10001	866-996-8729		464
Oncenter Complex			
800 S State St .... Syracuse NY 13202	800-776-7548	315-435-8000	205
Oncology Nursing Society (ONS)			
125 Enterprise Dr .... Pittsburgh PA 15275	866-257-4667	412-859-6100	49-8
Oncology Plus Inc			
1070 E Brandon Blvd .... Brandon FL 33511	877-410-0779		237
Oncor			
1616 Woodall Rodgers Fwy			
Ste 2M-012 .... Dallas TX 75202	800-313-6062*	888 313-4747	782
*General			
OnCorp Direct Inc			
1033 Bay St Ste 313 .... Toronto ON M5S3A5	800-461-7772	416-964-2677	317
Onduline North America Inc			
4900 Ondura Dr .... Fredericksburg VA 22407	800-777-7663	540-898-7000	191-4
One Call Medical Inc			
20 Waterview Blvd PO Box 614 ... Parsippany NJ 07054	800-872-2875	973-257-1000	381
One Inc Systems			
400 Imperial Blvd			
PO Box 9002 .... Cape Canaveral FL 32920	800-749-3160		730
One Lambda			
21001 Kittridge St .... Canoga Park CA 91303	800-822-8824	818-449-3230	477
One Link Wireless			
7321 Broadway Ext .... Oklahoma City OK 73116	800-259-2929	405-840-2345	246
One Source Industries LLC			
185 Technology Dr .... Irvine CA 92618	800-899-4990		542
One Southern Indiana			
4100 Charlestown Rd .... New Albany IN 47150	800-521-2232	812-945-0266	139
One Technologies LLC			
8144 Walnut Hill Ln Ste 600 ... Dallas TX 75231	888-550-8471	214-379-8216	225
OneAmerica Financial Partners Inc (PML)			
PO Box 368 .... Indianapolis IN 46206	800-249-6269	317-285-1877	390-2
OneBeacon Insurance Group			
605 Hwy 169 N Ste 800 .... Plymouth MN 55441	800-662-0156	781-332-7000	390-4
OneCoast Network LLC			
230 Spring St Ste 1800 .... Atlanta GA 30303	866-592-5514		360
Oneida County Convention & Visitors Bureau			
PO Box 551 .... Utica NY 13503	800-426-3132	315-724-7221	206
OneLegacy Transplant Donor Network			
221 S Figueroa St Ste 500 ..... Los Angeles CA 90012	800-786-4077	213-229-5600	541
OneMorePallet			
9891 Montgomery Rd Ste 122 ..... Cincinnati OH 45242	855-438-1667		386
OneSCM			
6805 Capital of Texas Hwy			
Ste 370 .... Austin TX 78731	800-324-5143	512-231-8191	178-1
Onesmartworld Inc			
79 Simcoe St .... Collingwood ON L9Y1H7	800-387-6278	705-444-1234	193
ONESPRING LLC			
980 Birmingham Rd			
Ste 501-165 .... Alpharetta GA 30004	888-472-1840		180
OneTouch Direct LLC			
4902 W Sligh Ave .... Tampa FL 33634	866-948-4005		41
OneUnited Bank			
3683 Crenshaw Blvd .... Los Angeles CA 90016	877-663-8648	323-290-4848	70
Onity Inc			
4001 Fairview Industrial Dr SE ... Salem OR 97302	800-424-1433		350
Online Computer Library Ctr Inc (OCLC)			
6565 Kilgour Pl .... Dublin OH 43017	800-848-5878		49-11
Online Copy Corp			
48815 Kato Rd .... Fremont CA 94539	800-833-4460		240
On-line Taxes Inc			
724 Jules St .... Saint Joseph MO 64501	800-829-1040		461
Online Transport System Inc			
6311 W Stoner Dr .... Greenfield IN 46140	866-543-1235	317-894-2159	775
OnlineMetals.com			
1848 Westlake Ave N Ste A ..... Seattle WA 98109	800-704-2157		490
Onondaga Cave State Park			
7556 Hwy H .... Leasburg MO 65535	877-422-6766	573-245-6576	561
Onondaga Coach Corp			
PO Box 277 .... Auburn NY 13021	800-451-1570	315-255-2216	107
OnPath Business Solutions Inc			
1165 Kenaston St .... Ottawa ON K1B3N9	855-420-3244		180
ONRAD Inc			
1770 Iowa Ave Ste 280 .... Riverside CA 92507	800-848-5876		
ONS (Oncology Nursing Society)			
125 Enterprise Dr .... Pittsburgh PA 15275	866-257-4667	412-859-6100	49-8

	Toll-Free	Phone	Class
Onset Computer Corp			
PO Box 3450 .... Pocasset MA 02559	800-564-4377		201
Onsite Health Diagnostics			
1199 S Beltline Rd Ste 120 ..... Coppell TX 75019	877-366-7483		415
Onslow County			
4024 Richland Hwy .... Jacksonville NC 28540	800-932-2144	910-347-4717	337
Onslow County Tourism			
1099 Gum Branch Rd .... Jacksonville NC 28540	800-932-2144		206
Onsrud Cutter LP			
800 Liberty Dr .... Libertyville IL 60048	800-234-1560	847-362-1560	491
Ontario Area Chamber of Commerce			
251 SW Ninth St .... Ontario OR 97914	866-989-8012	541-889-8012	206
Ontario Association of Architects			
111 Moatfield Dr .... North York ON M3B3L6	800-565-2724	416-449-6898	138
Ontario Centres of Excellence Inc			
156 Front St W Ste 200 .... Toronto ON M5J2L6	866-759-6014	416-861-1092	217
Ontario Clean Water Agency			
1 Yonge St Ste 1700 .... Toronto ON M5E1E5	800-667-6292	416-775-0500	192
Ontario College of Art & Design			
100 McCaul St .... Toronto ON M5T1W1	800-382-6516	416-977-6000	780
Ontario Convention & Visitors Bureau			
2000 E Convention Center Way ... Ontario CA 91764	800-455-5755	909-937-3000	206
Ontario Convention Ctr			
2000 E Convention Ctr Way ..... Ontario CA 91764	800-455-5755	909-937-3000	205
Ontario County			
20 Ontario St .... Canandaigua NY 14424	800-247-7273	585-396-4200	337
Ontario Dental Nurses & Assistants Association			
869 Dundas St .... London ON N5W2Z8	800-461-4348	519-679-2566	138
Ontario Drive & Gear Ltd (ODG)			
220 Bergey Ct .... New Hamburg ON N3A2J5	877-274-6288	519-662-2840	29
Ontario Knife Co			
26 Empire St .... Franklinville NY 14737	800-222-5233	716-676-5527	222
Ontario Lottery & Gaming Corp			
70 Foster Dr Ste 800 .... Sault Sainte Marie ON P6A6V2	800-563-5357	705-946-6464	638
Ontario Northland Transportation Commission			
555 Oak St E .... North Bay ON P1B8L3	800-363-7512	705-472-4500	311
Ontario Nurses Association			
85 Grenville St Ste 400 ...... Toronto ON M5S3A2	800-387-5580	416-964-8833	413
Ontario Pc Party			
59 Adelaide St E Ste 400 ..... Toronto ON M5C1K6	800-903-6453	416-861-0020	611
Ontario Real Estate Assn			
99 Duncan Mill Rd .... Don Mills ON M3B1Z2	800-444-5557	416 445 0010	648
Ontario Science Ctr			
770 Don Mills Rd .... Toronto ON M3C1T3	888-696-1110	416-696-1000	517
Ontario Society of Professional Engineers			
4950 Yonge St Ste 502 .... North York ON M2N6K1	866-763-1654	416-223-9961	
Ontario State Recreation Site			
23751 Old Hwy 30 .... Huntington OR 97907	800-551-6949		561
Ontellus			
1010 Lamar 18th Fl .... Houston TX 77002	800-467-9181		41
Ontor Ltd			
12 Leswyn Rd .... Toronto ON M6A1K3	800-567-1631	416-781-5286	660
Onyx Hotel			
155 Portland St .... Boston MA 02114	866-660-6699	617-557-9955	378
Onyx Medical Corp			
1800 N Shelby Oaks Dr .... Memphis TN 38134	800-238-6981		473
Oohology			
908 S Eighth St .... Louisville KY 40203	855-664-6564	502-416-0143	
OOIDA (Owner-Operator Independent Drivers Assn Inc)			
1 NW OOIDA Dr .... Grain Valley MO 64029	800-444-5791	816-229-5791	49-21
Opal Soft			
1288 Kifer Rd # 201 .... Sunnyvale CA 94086	800-632-2022	408-267-2211	225
OPB (Oregon Public Broadcasting Inc)			
7140 SW Macadam Ave .... Portland OR 97219	800-241-8123	503-244-9900	628
OPCMIA (Operative Plasterers' & Cement Masons' International)			
9700 Patuxent Woods Dr Ste 200 ... Columbia MD 21046	888-379-1558	301-623-1000	49-3
Open Air Cinema			
806 North 2800 West .... Lindon UT 84042	866-319-3280	801-796-6800	743
Open Arms Hospice			
1836 W Georgia Rd .... Simpsonville SC 29680	866-473-6276	864-688-1700	370
Open Automation Software			
5077 Bear Mtn Dr .... Evergreen CO 80439	800-533-4994	303-679-0898	179
Open Court Publishing Co			
70 E Lake St Ste 800 .... Chicago IL 60601	800-815-2280		633-2
Open Dental Software			
3995 Fairview Industrial Dr SE			
Ste 110 .... Salem OR 97302	866-239-0469	503-363-5432	177
Open Group			
44 Montgomery St Ste 960 ..... San Francisco CA 94104	800-433-6611	415-374-8280	48-9
Open Minds			
163 York St .... Gettysburg PA 17325	877-350-6463	717-334-1329	464
Open Spatial Inc			
5701 Lonetree Blvd Ste 211 ..... Rocklin CA 95765	800-696-1238		196
Open Storage Solutions Inc			
2 Castleview Dr .... Toronto ON L6T5S9	800-387-3419	905-790-0660	174
Open Systems Inc			
4301 Dean Lakes Blvd .... Shakopee MN 55379	800-328-2276*		178-1
*Sales			
Open Systems of Cleveland Inc			
22999 Forbes Rd Ste A .... Cleveland OH 44146	888-881-6660	440-439-2332	174
Open Text Corp			
275 Frank Tompa Dr .... Waterloo ON N2L0A1	800-499-6544*	519-888-7111	178-7
NASDAQ: OTEX ■ *General			
Open Text Corp (USA)			
100 Tri-State International Pkwy			
3rd Fl .... Lincolnshire IL 60069	800-499-6544*	847-267-9330	178-7
NASDAQ: OTEX ■ *Sales			
Openface Inc			
3445 Park Ave .... Montreal QC H2X2H6	800-865-8585	514-281-8585	225
OPENonline			
1650 Lake Shore Dr Ste 350 ..... Columbus OH 43204	888-381-5656	614-481-6999	631
OpenWorks			
4742 N 24th St Ste 450 .... Phoenix AZ 85016	800-777-6736	602-224-0440	310
Opera Colorado			
695 S Colorado Blvd Ste 20 ..... Denver CO 80246	800-414-2251	303-778-1500	569-2
Opera San Jose			
2149 Paragon Dr .... San Jose CA 95131	877-707-7827	408-437-4450	569-2

	Toll-Free	Phone	Class
Operation USA			
7421 Beverly Blvd PH ....Los Angeles CA 90036	800-678-7255	323-413-2353	48-5
Operative Plasterers' & Cement Masons' International Assn (OPCMIA)			
9700 Patuxent Woods Dr Ste 200.......Columbia MD 21046	888-379-1558	301-623-1000	49-3
Opex Corp			
305 Commerce Dr ....Moorestown NJ 08057	800-673-9288	856-727-1100	178-10
OPGI (Original Parts Group Inc)			
1770 Saturn Way ....Seal Beach CA 90740	800-243-8355	562-594-1000	54
Ophthalmic Consultants of Boston Inc			
50 Staniford St Ste 600.............Boston MA 02114	800-635-0489	617-367-4800	539
OPIC (Overseas Private Investment Corp)			
1100 New York Ave NW ....Washington DC 20527	800-225-5722	202-336-8400	339-19
Opinion Research Corp (ORC)			
902 Carnegie Ctr Ste 220 ....Princeton NJ 08540	800-444-4672		464
Opmedic Group Inc			
1361 Beaumont Ave Ste 301.......Mount-royal QC H3P2W3	888-776-2732	514-345-8535	417
OPPD (Omaha Public Power District)			
444 S 16th St Mall ....Omaha NE 68102	800-331-5666	402-536-4131	
Oppenheimer Cos Inc			
877 W Main Ste 700.............Boise ID 83702	800-727-9939	208-343-4883	297-8
OppenheimerFunds Inc			
225 Liberty St ....New York NY 10281	800-525-7048		524
OPT (Oceanside Photo and Telescope)			
918 Mission Ave ....Oceanside CA 92054	800-483-6287	760-400-0164	179
Optex Inc			
13661 Benson Ave Bldg C ....Chino CA 91710	800-966-7839	909-993-5770	688
Optical Cable Corp (OCC)			
5290 Concourse Dr ....Roanoke VA 24019	800-622-7711	540-265-0690	809
NASDAQ: OCC			
Optical Dynamics Corp			
1950 Production Ct ....Louisville KY 40299	800-587-2743	502-671-2020	
Optical Gaging Products Inc			
850 Hudson Ave ....Rochester NY 14621	800-647-4243	585-544-0450	540
Optical Society of America (OSA)			
2010 Massachusetts Ave NW ....Washington DC 20036	800-766-4672	202-223-8130	49-8
OptiCare PC			
87 Grandview Ave ....Waterbury CT 06708	800-225-5393	203-574-2020	539
Opti-Com Mfg Network Co Inc			
259 Plauche St ....New Orleans LA 70123	800-345-8774	504-736-0331	811
Opticote Inc			
10455 Seymour ....Franklin Park IL 60131	800-248-6784	847-678-8900	482
Opti-Craft			
17311 NE Halsey ....Portland OR 97230	800-288-8048	503-256-5330	
Optima Stantron			
1775 MacLeod Dr ....Lawrenceville GA 30043	800-821-0019	770-496-4000	254
Optimae LifeServices Inc			
301 W Burlington Ave ....Fairfield IA 52556	800-735-2942	641-472-1684	362
Optimal Engineering Systems			
6901 Woodley Ave ....Van Nuys CA 91406	888-777-1826	818-222-9200	357
Optimetra Inc			
1710 Chapel Hills Dr ....Colorado Springs CO 80920	800-758-9710		225
Optimist International			
4494 Lindell Blvd ....Saint Louis MO 63108	800-500-8130	314-371-6000	48-15
Optimum Health Institute			
6970 Central Ave ....Lemon Grove CA 91945	800-993-4325	619-464-3346	702
Optimum Logistic Solutions			
3540 Seven Bridges Dr Ste 300 ....Woodridge IL 60517	800-356-0595	630-350-0595	627
Optimum Solutions Corp			
170 Earle Ave ....Lynbrook NY 11563	800-227-0672	516-247-5300	177
OPTIO LLC			
390 Spaulding Ave SE ....Ada MI 49301	888-981-3282		196
Option Advisor			
5151 Pfeiffer Rd Ste 250.............Cincinnati OH 45242	800-448-2080	513-589-3800	527-9
OptionsXpress Inc			
311 W Monroe Ste 1000.............Chicago IL 60606	888-280-8020	312-630-3300	169
Optiwave Systems Inc			
7 Capella Ct ....Ottawa ON K2E7X1	866-576-6784	613-224-4700	179
Optovue Inc			
2800 Bayview Dr ....Fremont CA 94538	866-344-8948		
Opus Agency			
9000 SW Nimbus Ave ....Beaverton OR 97008	888-887-8908	971-223-0777	195
Opus Bank			
19900 MacArthur Blvd 12th Fl.............Irvine CA 92612	855-678-7226	949-250-9800	359-2
Opus Framing Ltd			
3445 Cornett Rd ....Vancouver BC V5M2H3	800-663-6953	604-435-9991	531
Opus Hotel			
322 Davie St ....Vancouver BC V6B5Z6	866-642-6787		378
OPW Engineered Systems			
2726 Henkle Dr ....Lebanon OH 45036	800-547-9393*	513-932-9114	616
*Cust Svc			
OPW Fuel Management Systems			
6900 Santa Fe Dr ....Hodgkins IL 60525	800-547-9393	708-485-4200	201
Oracle Corp			
500 Oracle Pkwy ....Redwood Shores CA 94065	800-392-2999*	800-633-0738	178-1
*NYSE: ORCL ■ *Sales*			
Oracle Information Rights Management			
500 Oracle Pkwy ....Redwood Shores CA 94065	800-633-0738		
Oracle Magazine			
500 Oracle Pkwy ....Redwood Shores CA 94065	800-392-2999	650-506-7000	455-7
Oracle Packaging			
220 E Polo Rd ....Winston-Salem NC 27105	800-634-3645	888-260-3947	544
Oradell Animal Hospital Inc			
580 Winters Ave ....Paramus NJ 07652	800-624-1883	201-262-0010	789
Oral Health America			
180 N Michigan Ave Ste 1150 ....Chicago IL 60601	800-523-3438	312-836-9900	48-17
Oral Roberts University			
7777 S Lewis Ave ....Tulsa OK 74171	800-678-8876	918-495-6161	166
Oral Roberts University Library			
7777 S Lewis Ave ....Tulsa OK 74171	800-678-8876	918-495-6723	433-6
Orange & Rockland Utilities Inc			
390 W Rte 59 ....Spring Valley NY 10977	877-434-4100*		782
*Cust Svc			
Orange Belt Stages			
PO Box 949 ....Visalia CA 93279	800-266-7433	559-733-4408	755
Orange Chamber of Commerce			
1940 N Tustin St ....Orange CA 92865	888-676-1040	714-538-3581	139
Orange City Area Health System			
1000 Lincoln Cir SE ....Orange City IA 51041	800-808-6264	712-737-4984	373-3

	Toll-Free	Phone	Class
Orange Coast Magazine			
3701 Birch St Ste 100.............Newport Beach CA 92660	800-397-8179	949-862-1133	455-22
Orange Coast Memorial Medical Ctr (OCMMC)			
9920 Talbert Ave ....Fountain Valley CA 92708	877-597-4777	714-378-7000	373-3
Orange County			
200 Dailey Dr ....Orange VA 22960	866-803-8641	540-661-4550	337
Orange County Community College			
115 S St ....Middletown NY 10940	866-694-4700	845-344-6222	162
Orange County Convention Ctr (OCCC)			
9800 International Dr ....Orlando FL 32819	800-345-9845	407-685-9800	205
Orange County Industrial Plastics Inc			
4811 E La Palma Ave ....Anaheim CA 92807	800-974-6247		599
Orange County Public Schools			
445 W Amelia St ....Orlando FL 32801	800-378-9264	407-317-3200	681
Orange County Regional History Ctr			
65 E Central Blvd ....Orlando FL 32801	800-965-2030	407-836-8500	517
Orange County Rural Electric Membership Corp			
7133 N State Rd 337 PO Box 208.......Orleans IN 47452	888-337-5900	812-865-2229	245
Orange County Transportation Authority			
550 S Main St PO Box 14184.............Orange CA 92863	800-600-9191	714-560-6282	466
Orange County's Credit Union			
PO Box 11777 ....Santa Ana CA 92711	888-354-6228	714-755-5900	219
Orange Fence & Supply			
205 Boston Post Rd ....Orange CT 06477	844-703-4267	203-904-2272	
Orange Julius of America			
7505 Metro Blvd ....Minneapolis MN 55439	866-793-7582	952-830-0200	666
Orange Line Oil Company Inc			
404 E Commercial St ....Pomona CA 91767	800-492-6864	909-623-0533	575
Orange Regional Medical Ctr			
707 E Main St ....Middletown NY 10940	888-321-6762	845-343-2424	373-3
Orange Research Inc			
140 Cascade Blvd ....Milford CT 06460	800-989-5657	203-877-5657	201
Orange Tree Employment Screening			
7275 Ohms Ln ....Minneapolis MN 55439	800-886-4777		631
Orangeburg County Chamber of Commerce			
155 Riverside Dr SW PO Box 328.............Orangeburg SC 29116	800-545-6153	803-534-6821	139
Orangeburg County Library (OCL)			
510 Louis St ....Orangeburg SC 29115	800-922-2594	803-531-4636	433-3
Orangeburg Pecan Company Inc			
761 Russell St ....Orangeburg SC 29115	800-845-6970		276
Orangevale Chamber of Commerce			
9267 Greenback Ln Ste B-91 ....Orangevale CA 95662	800-962-1106	916-988-0175	139
OraSure Technologies Inc			
220 E First St ....Bethlehem PA 18015	800-869-3538	610-882-1820	231
NASDAQ: OSUR			
ORBCOMM			
22970 Indian Creek Dr Ste 300.........Sterling VA 20166	800-672-2666*	703-433-6300	677
*Cust Svc			
ORBIS Corp			
1055 Corporate Center Dr ....Oconomowoc WI 53066	800-999-8683	800-890-7292	199
ORBIS International Inc			
520 Eigth Ave 12th Fl ....New York NY 10018	800-672-4787		48-5
Orbitel Communications LLC			
21116 N John Wayne Pkwy Ste B-9 ....Maricopa AZ 85239	800-998-8084	520-568-8890	386
ORC (Opinion Research Corp)			
902 Carnegie Ctr Ste 220 ....Princeton NJ 08540	800-444-4672		464
Orchard Hiltz & McCliment Inc (OHM)			
34000 Plymouth Rd ....Livonia MI 48150	888-522-6711	734-522-6711	261
Orchard Software Corp			
701 Congressional Blvd Ste 360 ....Carmel IN 46032	800-856-1948	317-573-2633	177
Orchard Supply Hardware			
6450 Via del Oro ....San Jose CA 95119	800-952-5210	408-281-3500	363
Orchards Inn of Sedona			
254 Hwy N 89 A ....Sedona AZ 86336	855-474-7719		378
Orchestra Hall			
1111 Nicollet Mall ....Minneapolis MN 55403	800-292-4141	612-371-5600	568
Orchestra New England			
PO Box 200123 ....New Haven CT 06520	800-595-4849	203-777-4690	569-3
Orchestre Symphonique de Montreal			
1600 Saint-Urbain St ....Montreal QC H2X0S1	888-842-9951	514-842-9951	569-3
Orcon Corp			
1570 Atlantic St ....Union City CA 94587	800-227-0505*	510-476-2124	596
*General			
Order Sons of Italy in America (OSIA)			
219 E St NE ....Washington DC 20002	800-552-6742	202-547-2900	48-14
Oreck Corp			
1400 Salem Rd ....Cookeville TN 38506	800-289-5888		783
Oregon			
Crime Victims Service Div			
1162 Ct St NE ....Salem OR 97301	877-877-9392	503-378-4400	338-38
Dept of Transportation			
355 Capitol St NE MS 11 ....Salem OR 97301	888-275-6368	503-986-4000	338-38
Energy Dept			
550 Capitol St NE ....Salem OR 97301	800-221-8035	503-378-4040	338-38
Environmental Quality Dept			
700 NE Multnomah St ....Portland OR 97204	800-452-4011	503-229-5696	338-38
Finance & Corporate Securities Div			
350 Winter St NE Rm 410 PO Box 14480 ....Salem OR 97309	866-814-9710	503-378-4140	338-38
Financial Fraud/Consumer Protection Section			
1162 Ct St NE ....Salem OR 97301	877-877-9392	503-378-4400	338-38
Fish & Wildlife Dept (ODFW)			
4034 Fairview Industrial Dr SE ....Salem OR 97302	800-720-6339	503-947-6000	338-38
Insurance Div			
3225 State St ....Salem OR 97309	866-814-9710	503-378-4140	338-38
Legislative Assembly			
900 Ct St NE ....Salem OR 97301	800-332-2313		338-38
Military Dept			
1776 Militia Way SE PO Box 14350......Salem OR 97309	800-452-7500	503-584-3980	338-38
Parks & Recreation Dept (OPRD)			
725 Summer St NE Ste C ....Salem OR 97301	800-551-6949	503-986-0707	338-38
Revenue Dept			
955 Ctr St NE ....Salem OR 97301	800-356-4222	503-378-4988	338-38
State Hospital			
2600 Ctr St NE ....Salem OR 97301	800-544-7078	503-945-2800	373-5
Student Assistance Commission			
1500 Valley River Dr Ste 100 ....Eugene OR 97401	800-452-8807	541-687-7400	721

	Toll-Free	Phone	Class
Veterans' Affairs Dept			
700 Summer St NE ....Salem OR 97301	800-828-8801	503-373-2000	338-38
Vocational Rehabilitation Services Office (OVRS)			
700 Summer St NE Ste 150 ....Salem OR 97310	800-692-9666	503-373-2085	338-38
Oregon Aero Inc			
34020 Skyway Dr ....Scappoose OR 97056	800-888-6910	503-543-7399	525
Oregon Assn of Realtors			
2110 Mission St SE ....Salem OR 97308	800-252-9115	503-362-3645	652
Oregon Bankers Assn			
777 13th St SE Ste 130..............Salem OR 97301	800-677-1116	503-581-3522	138
Oregon Catholic Press (OCP)			
5536 NE Hassalo St ....Portland OR 97213	877-596-1653	503-281-1191	633-3
Oregon Caves National Monument			
19000 Caves Hwy ....Cave Junction OR 97523	877-245-9022	541-592-2100	560
Oregon Cherry Growers Inc			
1520 Woodrow NE ....Salem OR 97301	800-367-2536	503-364-8421	315-3
Oregon Coast Aquarium			
2820 SE Ferry Slip Rd ....Newport OR 97365	800-452-7888	541-867-3474	40
Oregon Coast Magazine			
88906 Hwy 101 N Ste 2 ....Florence OR 97439	800-348-8401	541-997-8401	455-22
Oregon College of Art & Craft			
8245 SW Barnes Rd ....Portland OR 97225	800-390-0632	503-297-5544	166
Oregon Convention Ctr			
777 NE Martin Luther King Jr Blvd			
................................Portland OR 97232	800-791-2250	503-235-7575	205
Oregon Dental Assn			
PO Box 3710 ....Wilsonville OR 97070	800-452-5628	503-218-2010	227
Oregon Education Magazine (OEA)			
6900 SW Atlanta St Bldg 1 ....Portland OR 97223	800-858-5505	503-684-3300	455-8
Oregon Employment Dept			
875 Union St NE ....Salem OR 97311	877-345-3484	503-451-2400	259
Oregon Food Bank			
7900 NE 33rd Dr ....Portland OR 97211	800-777-7427	503-282-0555	48-5
Oregon Garden, The			
879 W Main St PO Box 155 ....Silverton OR 97381	877-674-2733	503-874-8100	97
Oregon Health & Science University (OHSU)			
Bone Marrow Transplant Clinic			
3181 SW Sam Jackson Pk Rd			
CB569 ....Portland OR 97239	800-452-1369	503-494-8500	764
School of Medicine			
3101 SW Sam Jackson Pk Rd			
L-109 ....Portland OR 97239	800-775-5460	503-494-7800	167-2
Oregon Institute of Technology			
3201 Campus Dr ....Klamath Falls OR 97601	800-422-2017	541-885-1000	166
Oregon Lions Sight & Hearing Foundation			
1010 NW 22nd Ave Ste 144 ....Portland OR 97210	800-635-4667	503-413-7399	269
Oregon Medical Assn (OMA)			
11740 SW 68th Pkwy Ste 100 ......Portland OR 97223	877-605-3229	503-619-8000	472
Oregon Museum of Science & Industry			
1945 SE Water Ave ....Portland OR 97214	800-955-6674	503-797-4000	517
Oregon Mutual Insurance Co			
PO Box 808 ....McMinnville OR 97128	800-888-2141	503-472-2141	390-4
Oregon Nurses Assn (ONA)			
18765 SW Boones Ferry Rd ....Tualatin OR 97062	800-634-3552	503-293-0011	529
Oregon Parks & Recreation Department			
Depoe Bay Whale Watching Center			
119 SW Hwy 101 ....Depoe Bay OR 97341	800-551-6949	541-765-3304	561
Oregon Potato Co			
PO Box 3110 ....Pasco WA 99302	800-336-6311	509-545-4545	296-18
Oregon Public Broadcasting Inc (OPB)			
7140 SW Macadam Ave ....Portland OR 97219	800-241-8123	503-244-9900	628
Oregon Shakespeare Festival			
15 S Pioneer St ....Ashland OR 97520	800-219-8161	541-482-2111	744
Oregon Society of CPA's			
10206 SW Laurel St ....Beaverton OR 97005	800-255-1470	503-641-7200	529
Oregon State Bar Assn			
16037 SW Upper Boones Ferry Rd .....Tigard OR 97224	800-452-8260	503-620-0222	72
Oregon State Bar Bulletin, The			
16037 SW Upper Boones Ferry Rd			
PO Box 231935. ....Tigard OR 97281	800-452-8260	503-620-0222	455-15
Oregon state Parks			
Devil's Lake State Recreation Area			
1452 NE Sixth Dr ....Lincoln City OR 97367	800-551-6949	541-994-2002	561
Oregon State University			
104 Kerr Admin Bldg ....Corvallis OR 97331	800-291-4192	541-737-4411	166
Oregon State University Press			
1500 Jefferson St ....Corvallis OR 97331	800-426-3797*	541-737-3166	633-4
*Orders			
Oregon Symphony Orchestra			
921 SW Washington St Ste 200 ......Portland OR 97205	800-228-7343	503-228-4294	569-3
Oregon Veterans' Home			
700 Veterans Dr ....The Dalles OR 97058	800-846-8460	541-296-7190	788
Oregon Veterinary Medical Assn			
1880 Lancaster Dr NE Ste 118 ....Salem OR 97305	800-235-3502	503-399-0311	790
Oregon-California Trails Assn			
524 S Osage St PO Box 1019......Independence MO 64051	888-811-6282	816-252-2276	48-23
Oregonian			
1320 SW Broadway ....Portland OR 97201	800-723-3638*	503-221-8100	528-2
*News Rm			
Orelube Corp, The			
20 Sawgrass Dr ....Bellport NY 11713	800-645-9124	631-205-9700	537
Organ Supply Industries Inc			
2320 W 50th St ....Erie PA 16506	800-458-0289	814-835-2244	523
Organic Valley Family of Farms			
1 Organic Way ....LaFarge WI 54639	888-444-6455		297-7
Organizational Dynamics Inc			
790 Boston Rd Ste 201. ....Billerica MA 01821	800-634-4636	978-671-5454	194
Organo Gold International Inc			
5505 Hovander Rd ....Ferndale WA 98248	877-674-2661		461
Orgill Inc			
3742 Tyndale Dr ....Memphis TN 38125	800-347-2860	901-754-8850	350
Orgill Singer			
8360 W Sahara Ave Ste 110 ....Las Vegas NV 89117	800-745-3065	702-796-9100	48-20
Orica USA Inc			
33101 E Quincy Ave ....Watkins CO 80137	800-800-3855	303-268-5000	268
Oriental Institute Museum			
1155 E 58th St			
University of Chicago ....Chicago IL 60637	800-791-9354	773-702-9514	517
Oriental Trading Company Inc			
5455 S 90th St ....Omaha NE 68127	800-875-8480	402-596-1200	457
Original Cake Candle Co, The			
102 Sundale Rd ....Norwich OH 43767	888-444-2253	740-872-3248	122
Original Impressions LLC			
12900 SW 89th Ct ....Miami FL 33176	888-853-8644	305-233-1322	623
Original Lincoln Logs Ltd			
5 Riverside Dr PO Box 135.......Chestertown NY 12817	800-833-2461		106
Original Parts Group Inc (OPGI)			
1770 Saturn Way ....Seal Beach CA 90740	800-243-8355	562-594-1000	54
OriginClear Inc			
5645 W Adams Blvd ....Los Angeles CA 90016	877-999-6645	323-939-6645	532
OriginLab Corp			
1 Roundhouse Plz Ste 303 ......Northampton MA 01060	800-969-7720	413-586-2013	177
Origins Natural Resources Inc			
767 Fifth Ave ....New York NY 10153	800-674-4467*		214
*Cust Svc			
Orion Development Group			
177 Beach 116th St Ste 4 ......Rockaway Park NY 11694	800-510-2117	718-474-4600	194
Orion Food Systems LLC			
2930 W Maple ....Sioux Falls SD 57107	800-648-6227	800-336-1320	392
Orion Instruments LLC			
2105 Oak Villa Blvd ....Baton Rouge LA 70815	866-556-7466	225-906-2343	201
Orion Magazine			
187 Main St ....Great Barrington MA 01230	888-909-6568	413-528-4422	455-19
Orion Registrar Inc			
7850 Vance Dr ....Arvada CO 80003	800-446-0674	303-456-6010	461
Orion Systems Integrators LLC			
333 Thornall St 7th Fl. ....Edison NJ 08837	877-456-9922		804
Oristech Inc			
Po Box 310069 ....New Braunfels TX 78131	800-929-9078	830-620-7422	225
Oritani Bank			
370 Pascack Rd			
PO Box 1329. ....Washington Township NJ 07676	888-674-8264	201-664-5400	70
NASDAQ: ORIT			
ORKIN LLC			
2170 Piedmont Rd NE ....Atlanta GA 30324	877-250-1652		573
Orland Square			
288 Orland Sq ....Orland Park IL 60462	877-746-6642	708-349-1646	458
Orlando Baking Company Inc			
7777 Grand Ave ....Cleveland OH 44104	800-362-5504	216-361-1872	296-1
Orlando International Airport			
1 Jeff Fuqua Blvd ....Orlando FL 32827	800-327-1390	407-825-2001	27
Orlando North, Seminole County Tourism			
1515 International Pkwy			
Ste 1013......................Lake Mary FL 32746	800-800-7832	407-665-2900	206
Orlando Regional Medical Ctr (ORMC)			
1414 Kuhl Ave ....Orlando FL 32806	800-424-6998	321-841-5111	373-3
Orlando Sentinel			
633 N Orange Ave ....Orlando FL 32801	800-974-7488	407-420-5000	528-2
Orleans Las Vegas Hotel & Casino			
4500 W Tropicana Ave ....Las Vegas NV 89103	800-675-3267	702-365-7111	133
ORMC (Orlando Regional Medical Ctr)			
1414 Kuhl Ave ....Orlando FL 32806	800-424-6998	321-841-5111	373-3
ORMCO Corp			
1717 W Collins Ave ....Orange CA 92867	800-854-1741*	714-516-7400	228
*Cust Svc			
Ormec Systems Corp			
19 Linden Park ....Rochester NY 14625	800-656-7632	585-385-3520	203
Ornamental Moulding & Millwork			
3804 Comanche Rd ....Archdale NC 27263	800-779-1135		
Ornim Inc			
125 Washington St Ste #7 ....Foxboro MA 02035	866-811-6384		738
OROCAL GOLD NUGGET CO			
1720 Bird St ....Oroville CA 95965	800-367-6225	530-533-5065	408
Oroville Area Chamber of Commerce			
1789 Montgomery St ....Oroville CA 95965	800-655-4653	530-538-2542	139
Orphan Foundation of America (OFA)			
23811 Chagrin Blvd Ste 210.........Cleveland OH 44122	800-950-4673	571-203-0270	48-6
Orpheum Theatre			
409 S 16th St ....Omaha NE 68102	866-434-8587	402-345-0202	568
Orr Safety Corp			
11601 Interchange Dr ....Louisville KY 40229	800-726-6789	502-774-5791	675
Orrick			
666 Fifth Ave ....New York NY 10103	866-342-5259	212-506-5000	427
Orscheln Farm & Home LLC			
1800 Overcenter Dr PO Box 698.......Moberly MO 65270	800-498-5090	800-577-2580	276
ORT American Inc			
75 Maiden Ln 10th Fl ....New York NY 10038	800-519-2678	212-505-7700	48-5
Orthman Manufacturing Inc			
75765 Rd 435 PO Box B. ....Lexington NE 68850	800-658-3270	308-324-4654	273
Ortho Computer Systems Inc			
1107 Buckeye Ave ....Ames IA 50010	800-678-4644	515-233-1026	177
Ortho Development Corp			
12187 S Business Pk Dr ....Draper UT 84020	800-429-8339	801-553-9991	475
Ortho-Clinical Diagnostics Inc			
1001 US Rt 202 N ....Raritan NJ 08869	800-828-6316		474
Orthodent Ltd			
311 Viola Ave ....Oshawa ON L1H3A7	800-267-8463	905-436-3133	414
Orthodox Union (OU)			
11 Broadway ....New York NY 10004	855-505-7500	212-563-4000	48-20
Orthofix Inc			
1720 Bray Central Dr ....McKinney TX 75069	800-527-0404	469-742-2500	475
Orthopedic Designs North America Inc			
5912 Breckenridge Pkwy Ste F. ....Tampa FL 33610	888-635-8535		473
ORTIG (Old Republic National Title Insurance Co)			
400 Second Ave S ....Minneapolis MN 55401	800-328-4441	612-371-1111	390-6
Ortman Fluid Power			
1400 North 30th St Ste 20 ....Quincy IL 62301	844-759-4922	217-277-0321	223
Orvis International Travel			
178 Conservation Way ....Sunderland VT 05250	800-547-4322	888-235-9763	706
Oryx Midstream Services LLC			
4000 N Big Spring Ste 400. ....Midland TX 79705	844-394-0841	432-684-4272	532
OSA (Optical Society of America)			
2010 Massachusetts Ave NW ......Washington DC 20036	800-766-4672	202-223-8130	49-8
Osage County			
900 S St Paul Ave ....Pawhuska OK 74056	888-287-3150	918-287-3535	337
Osage Hills State Park			
2131 Osage Hills State Pk Rd ......Pawhuska OK 74056	800-622-6317	918-336-4141	561

	Toll-Free	Phone	Class
OSBA (Ohio State Bar Assn)			
1700 Lake Shore Dr .... Columbus OH 43204	**800-282-6556**	614-487-2050	72
Osborn International			
5401 Hamilton Ave .... Cleveland OH 44114	**800-720-3358***	216-361-1900	103
*Cust Svc			
Osborne Industries Inc			
120 N Industrial Ave .... Osborne KS 67473	**800-255-0316**	785-346-2192	273
Osborne Partners Capital Management LLC			
580 California St			
Ste 1900 .... San Francisco CA 94104	**800-362-7734**	415-362-5637	400
Osborne Wood Products Inc			
4618 Hwy 123 .... Toccoa GA 30577	**800-849-8876**		
Oscar Scherer State Park			
1843 S Tamiami Trl .... Osprey FL 34229	**800-326-3521**	941-483-5956	561
Oscar Wilson Engines & Parts Inc			
826 Lone Star Dr .... O Fallon MO 63366	**800-873-6722**	636-978-1313	385
Osceola Electric Co-op Inc			
1102 Egret Dr PO Box 127 .... Sibley IA 51249	**888-754-2519**	712-754-2519	245
Oscor Inc			
3816 DeSoto Blvd .... Palm Harbor FL 34683	**800-726-7267***	727-937-2511	250
*Cust Svc			
OSF Global Services Inc			
6655 Blvd Pierre Bertrand 204-14			
.... Quebec City QC G2K1M1	**888-548-4344**		627
OSF HealthCare			
800 NE Glen Oak Ave .... Peoria IL 61603	**888-627-5673**	877-574-5678	
OSF Healthcare System			
800 NE Glen Oak Ave .... Peoria IL 61603	**877-574-5678**		
OSF Hospice			
2265 W Altorfer Dr .... Peoria IL 61615	**800-673-5288**		370
OSF Saint Anthony Medical Ctr			
5666 E State St .... Rockford IL 61108	**800-343-3185**	815-226-2000	373-3
OSF Saint Francis Medical Ctr			
530 NE Glen Oak Ave .... Peoria IL 61637	**888-627-5673**	309-655-2000	373-3
OSF Saint Mary Medical Ctr			
3333 N Seminary St .... Galesburg IL 61401	**877-795-0416**	309-344-3161	373-3
OSG Tap & Die Inc			
676 E Fullerton Ave .... Glendale Heights IL 60139	**800-837-2223**	630-790-1400	491
Osgood Textile Company Inc			
333 Park St .... West Springfield MA 01089	**888-674-6638**	413-737-6488	258
OSHA (Occupational Safety & Health Administration)			
200 Constitution Ave NW .... Washington DC 20210	**800-321-6742**	202-693-1999	339-14
OSHA Up-to-Date Newsletter			
1121 Spring Lake Dr .... Itasca IL 60143	**800-621-7615***	630-285-1121	527-8
*Cust Svc			
Oshkosh Coil Spring Inc			
3575 N Main St .... Oshkosh WI 54901	**800-638-8360**	920-235-7620	490
Oshkosh Northwestern Co			
224 State St .... Oshkosh WI 54901	**800-924-6168**	920-235-7700	633-8
Oshkosh Public Library			
106 Washington Ave .... Oshkosh WI 54901	**800-236-0850**	920-236-5205	433-3
Oshkosh Truck Corp			
2307 Oregon St .... Oshkosh WI 54903	**800-392-9921**	920-235-9150	513
Osi Environmental Inc			
300 Fayal Rd .... Eveleth MN 55734	**800-777-8542**		
OSI Systems Inc			
12525 Chadron Ave .... Hawthorne CA 90250	**800-579-1639**	310-978-0516	692
NASDAQ: OSIS			
OSIA (Order Sons of Italy in America)			
219 E St NE .... Washington DC 20002	**800-552-6742**	202-547-2900	48-14
Osmose Inc			
2475 George Urban Blvd Ste 160 .... Depew NY 14043	**800-877-7653**	770-632-6700	813
Osprey Valley Resorts			
18821 Main St .... Alton ON L7K1R1	**800-833-1561**	519-927-9034	703
Ossid Corp			
4000 College Rd .... Battleboro NC 27809	**800-334-8369**	252-446-6177	543
Ossining Union Free School District			
190 Croton Ave .... Ossining NY 10562	**877-769-7447**	914-941-7700	681
Ossur			
27412 Aliso Viejo Pkwy .... Aliso Viejo CA 92656	**800-233-6263**		111
Ostbye & Anderson Inc			
10055 51st Ave N .... Minneapolis MN 55442	**866-553-1515**		408
Osteohealth Co			
1 Luitpold Dr .... Shirley NY 11967	**800-874-2334**	631-924-4000	579
Osteomed Corp			
3885 Arapaho Rd .... Addison TX 75001	**800-456-7779***	972-677-4600	474
*Cust Svc			
Osterhout Free Library			
71 S Franklin St .... Wilkes-Barre PA 18701	**800-732-0999**	570-823-0156	433-3
Osthoff Resort, The			
101 Osthoff Ave PO Box 151 ..... Elkhart Lake WI 53020	**800-876-3399**	855-671-6870	665
Oswald Companies			
1100 Superior Ave Ste 1500 .... Cleveland OH 44114	**855-467-9253**	216-367-8787	389
Oswego County Opportunities Inc			
239 Oneida St .... Fulton NY 13069	**877-342-7618**	315-598-4717	48-15
Otc Global Holdings			
5151 San Felipe Ste 2200 .... Houston TX 77056	**877-737-8511**	713-358-5450	359-3
Otero County			
13 W Third St Rm 210 .... La Junta CO 81050	**800-438-3752**	719-383-3020	337
Otero County Electric Cooperative Inc			
404 Burro Ave PO Box 227 .... Cloudcroft NM 88317	**800-548-4660**	575-682-2521	245
Otesaga, The			
60 Lake St .... Cooperstown NY 13326	**800-348-6222**	607-547-9931	665
Otis College of Art & Design			
9045 Lincoln Blvd .... Los Angeles CA 90045	**800-527-6847**	310-665-6820	164
Otis-Magie Insurance Agency Inc			
332 W Superior St Ste 700 .... Duluth MN 55802	**800-241-2425**	218-722-7753	389
Otomix Inc			
747 Glasgow Ave .... Inglewood CA 90301	**800-701-7867**	310-215-6100	301
OTS			
3924 Clock Pointe Trl .... Stow OH 44224	**877-445-2058**		41
Otsego Club			
696 M-32 E Main St PO Box 556 .... Gaylord MI 49734	**800-752-5510**	989-732-5181	665
Otsego Electric Co-op Inc (OEC)			
PO Box 128 .... Hartwick NY 13348	**844-843-6842**	607-293-6622	
Otsuka America Pharmaceutical Inc			
2440 Research Blvd .... Rockville MD 20850	**800-562-3974**	301-424-9055	578
Ottawa Citizen			
1101 Baxter Rd PO Box 5020 .... Ottawa ON K2C3M4	**800-267-6100**	613-829-9100	528-1

	Toll-Free	Phone	Class
Ottawa City Hall			
110 Laurier Ave W .... Ottawa ON K1P1J1	**866-261-9799**	613-580-2400	336
Ottawa Regional Cancer Foundation The			
1500 Alta Vista Dr .... Ottawa ON K1G3Y9	**855-247-3527**	613-247-3527	305
Ottawa Senators			
1000 Palladium Dr .... Ottawa ON K2V1A5	**800-444-7367**	613-599-0250	712
Ottawa Sun			
1101 Baxter Rd .... Ottawa ON K2C3M4	**855-786-8812**	613-829-9100	528-1
Ottawa Tourism & Convention Authority			
150 Elgin St Ste 1405 .... Ottawa ON K2P1L4	**800-363-4465**	613-237-5150	206
Ottawa University			
1001 S Cedar St .... Ottawa KS 66067	**800-755-5200***	785-242-5200	166
*Admissions			
Ottawa University Phoenix			
10020 N 25th Ave .... Phoenix AZ 85021	**800-235-9586**	602-371-1188	166
Ottawa-AM 1200 (Sports)			
87 George St .... Ottawa ON K1N9H7	**877-670-1200**	613-789-2486	641-76
Otter Tail Corp			
4334 18th Ave SW PO Box 9156 .... Fargo ND 58106	**866-410-8780**	701-232-6414	359-3
NASDAQ: OTTR			
Otter Tail County			
520 Fir Ave W .... Fergus Falls MN 56537	**800-232-9077**	218-998-8000	337
Otter Tail Power Co			
215 S Cascade St .... Fergus Falls MN 56537	**800-257-4044**	218-739-8200	782
Otter Tail Telcom			
230 W Lincoln Ave .... Fergus Falls MN 56537	**800-247-2706**	218-826-6161	116
Otterbein College			
1 S Grove St .... Westerville OH 43081	**800-488-8144***	614-823-1500	166
*Admissions			
Otterbein senior lifestyle choices			
580 N SR 741 .... Lebanon OH 45036	**888-513-9131**	513-933-5400	668
Otterbine Barebo Inc			
3840 Main Rd E .... Emmaus PA 18049	**800-237-8837**	610-965-6018	321
Otto Brehm Inc			
PO Box 249 .... Yonkers NY 10710	**800-272-6886**	914-968-6100	297-11
Otto Engineering Inc			
2 E Main St .... Carpentersville IL 60110	**888-234-6886**	847-428-7171	725
Ottobock North America			
11501 Alterra Pky Ste 600 .... Austin TX 78758	**800-328-4058**		473
Ottosen Propeller & Accessories Inc			
105 S 28th St .... Phoenix AZ 85034	**800-528-7551**	602-275-8514	765
Ottumwa Courier			
213 E Second St .... Ottumwa IA 52501	**800-532-1504**	641-684-4611	528-2
Ottumwa Regional Health Ctr			
1001 Pennsylvania Ave .... Ottumwa IA 52501	**800-933-6742**	641-684-2300	373-3
O-two Medical Technologies Inc			
7575 Kimbel St .... Mississauga ON L5S1C8	**800-387-3405**	905-677-9410	250
OTZ Telephone Co-op Inc			
PO Box 324 .... Kotzebue AK 99752	**800-478-3111**	907-442-3114	731
OU (Orthodox Union)			
11 Broadway .... New York NY 10004	**855-505-7500**	212-563-4000	48-20
Ouachita Baptist University			
410 Ouachita St .... Arkadelphia AR 71998	**800-342-5628***	870-245-5000	166
*Admissions			
Ouachita County Medical Ctr (OCMC)			
PO Box 797 .... Camden AR 71711	**877-836-2472**	870-836-1000	373-3
Ouachita Electric Co-op Corp			
700 Bradley Ferry Rd PO Box 877 .... Camden AR 71711	**877-252-4538**	870-836-5791	245
Ouachita Technical College			
1 College Cir .... Malvern AR 72104	**800-337-0266**	501-337-5000	162
Our Lady of Fatima Retreat House			
5353 E 56th St .... Indianapolis IN 46226	**800-382-9836**	317-545-7681	669
Our Lady of Lourdes Medical Ctr			
1600 Haddon Ave .... Camden NJ 08103	**888-568-7337**	856-757-3500	373-3
Our Lady of the Lake University			
411 SW 24th St .... San Antonio TX 78207	**800-436-6558**	210-434-6711	166
Our Sunday Visitor Inc			
200 Noll Plz .... Huntington IN 46750	**800-348-2440**	260-356-8400	633-8
OutboundEngine			
98 San Jacinto Blvd Ste 1300 .... Austin TX 78701	**800-562-7315**		195
Outdoor Amusement Business Assn Inc (OABA)			
1035 S Semoran Blvd			
Ste 1045A .... Winter Park FL 32792	**800-517-6222**	407-848-4958	611
Outdoor Ch			
43445 Business Pk Dr Ste 103 ...... Temecula CA 92590	**800-770-5750**	951-699-6991	735
NASDAQ: OUTD			
Outdoor Photographer Magazine			
25 Braintree Hill Office Pk			
Ste 404 .... Braintree MA 02184	**800-283-4410***	617-706-9110	455-14
*Cust Svc			
Outer Banks Visitors Bureau			
1 Visitor Ctr Cir .... Manteo NC 27954	**877-629-4386**	252-473-2138	206
OuterBox Inc			
325 S Main St 3rd Fl .... Akron OH 44308	**866-647-9218**		
Outerlink Corp			
187 Ballardvale St Ste A260 .... Wilmington MA 01887	**877-688-3770**	978-284-6070	677
Outfest-Los Angeles Gay & Lesbian Film Festival			
3470 Wilshire Blvd Ste 935 .... Los Angeles CA 90010	**800-726-7147**	213-480-7088	282
outlaw 1013 KTXR, The			
3000 E Chestnut Expy .... Springfield MO 65802	**855-586-8852***	417-862-3751	641-103
*General			
Outlets at Anthem			
4250 W Anthem Way .... Phoenix AZ 85086	**888-482-5834**	623-465-9500	458
Outreach Communications			
2801 Glenda St .... Haltom City TX 76117	**800-982-3760**	817-288-7200	224
Outreach Healthcare Inc			
269 W Renner Pkwy .... Richardson TX 75080	**800-793-0081**		362
Outreach International			
129 W Lexington PO Box 210 ...... Independence MO 64050	**888-833-1235**	816-833-0883	48-5
Outrigger Enterprises Group			
2375 Kuhio Ave .... Honolulu HI 96815	**866-956-4262**		378
Outrigger Hotels Hawaii			
Outrigger Resorts & Resorts			
2375 Kuhio Ave .... Honolulu HI 96815	**800-688-7444**	866-956-4262	378
Outrigger Reef on the Beach			
2169 Kalia Rd .... Honolulu HI 96815	**800-688-7444**	808-923-3111	665
Outrigger Waikiki on the Beach			
2335 Kalakaua Ave .... Honolulu HI 96815	**800-688-7444**	808-923-0711	378

	Toll-Free	Phone	Class
Outside Magazine			
400 Market St ....Santa Fe NM 87501	888-909-2382*	505-989-7100	455-14
*General			
Outstart Inc			
745 Atlantic Ave 4th Fl ....Boston MA 02111	877-971-9171	617-897-6800	39
Outward Bound			
910 Jackson St Ste 140 ....Golden CO 80401	866-467-7651		761
Ovarian Cancer Research Fund Alliance			
1101 14th St NW Ste 850..........Washington DC 20005	866-399-6262	202-331-1332	472
Ovation Instore			
57-13 49th Pl ....Maspeth NY 11378	800-553-2202	718-628-2600	233
Overcomers in Christ			
PO Box 34460 ....Omaha NE 68134	866-573-0966		48-21
Overcomers Outreach			
PO Box 922950 ....Sylmar CA 91392	800-310-3001	818-833-1803	48-21
Overeaters Anonymous Inc (OA)			
PO Box 44020 ....Rio Rancho NM 87174	866-505-4966	505-891-2664	48-21
Overhead Door Company of Sacramento Inc			
6756 Franklin Blvd ....Sacramento CA 95823	800-929-3667	916-421-3747	189-2
Overhead Door Corp			
2501 S State Hwy 121 Bus			
Ste 200...................Lewisville TX 75067	800-275-3290	469-549-7100	234
Overhill Farms Inc			
2727 E Vernon Ave ....Vernon CA 90058	800-859-6406	323-582-9977	296-36
NYSE: OFI			
Overit			
435 New Scotland Ave ....Albany NY 12208	888-978-8147	518-465-8829	7
Overland Park Convention & Visitors Bureau			
9001 W 110th St Ste 100 ....Overland Park KS 66210	800-262-7275	913-491-0123	206
Overland Park Regional Medical Ctr			
10500 Quivira Rd ....Overland Park KS 66215	800-849-0829	913-541-5000	373-3
Overland Rentals Inc			
1901 N State Hwy 360			
Ste 340...................Grand Prairie TX 75050	844-943-7368*	800-944-7368	177
*Sales			
Overland Sheepskin Company Inc			
2096 Nutmeg Ave ....Fairfield IA 52556	800-683-7526	641-472-8434	157-5
Overlook Medical Ctr			
99 Beauvoir Ave ....Summit NJ 07902	800-619-4024	908-522-2000	373-3
Overly Manufacturing Co			
574 W Otterman St ....Greensburg PA 15601	800-979-7300	724-834-7300	489
OvernightPrints			
7582 S Las Vegas Blvd Ste 487 ....Las Vegas NV 89213	888-677-2000		
Overseas Adventure Travel			
347 Congress St ....Boston MA 02210	800-221-0814		755
Overseas Private Investment Corp (OPIC)			
1100 New York Ave NW ....Washington DC 20527	800-225-5722	202-336-8400	339-19
Overseas Shipholding Group Inc			
302 Knights Run Ave Ste 1200 ....Tampa FL 33602	800-851-9677	813-209-0600	313
Overstockcom Inc			
6350 South 3000 East ....Salt Lake City UT 84121	800-843-2446*	801-947-3100	786
NASDAQ: OSTK ■ *Cust Svc			
Overton Brooks Veterans Affairs Medical Ctr			
510 E Stoner Ave ....Shreveport LA 71101	800-863-7441	318-221-8411	373-8
Ovid Technologies Inc			
333 Seventh Ave 20th Fl........New York NY 10001	800-950-2035	646-674-6300	386
OVMA (Ohio Veterinary Medical Assn)			
3168 Riverside Dr ....Columbus OH 43221	800-662-6862	614-486-7253	790
OW Lee Company Inc			
1822 E Francis St ....Ontario CA 91761	800-776-9533		319-4
Owatonna Area Chamber of Commerce & Tourism			
320 Hoffman Dr ....Owatonna MN 55060	800-423-6466	507-451-7970	139
Owatonna Public Library			
105 N Elm St ....Owatonna MN 55060	800-657-3864	507-444-2460	433-3
Owen Community Bank			
279 E Morgan St ....Spencer IN 47460	800-690-2095	812-829-2095	359-2
Owen Electric Co-op Inc			
8205 Hwy 127 N PO Box 400 ....Owenton KY 40359	800-372-7612	502-484-3471	245
Owen Equipment Co			
13101 NE Whitaker Way ....Portland OR 97230	800-992-3656	503-255-9055	357
Owen Industries Inc			
501 Ave H ....Carter Lake IA 51510	800-831-9252	712-347-5500	490
Owens & Assoc Investigations			
8765 Aero Dr Ste 306.........San Diego CA 92123	800-297-1343		399
Owens & Minor Inc			
9120 Lockwood Blvd ....Mechanicsville VA 23116	800-488-8850	804-723-7000	473
NYSE: OMI			
Owens Community College			
Findlay			
3200 Bright Rd ....Findlay OH 45840	800-466-9367		162
Toledo			
30335 Oregon Rd ....Perrysburg OH 43551	800-466-9367	567-661-7357	162
Owensboro Community & Technical College			
4800 New Hartford Rd ....Owensboro KY 42303	866-755-6282	270-686-4400	795
Owensboro Daviess County Convention & Visitors Bureau			
215 E Second St ....Owensboro KY 42303	800-489-1131	270-926-1100	206
Owensboro Federal Credit Union			
717 Harvard Dr PO Box 1189.......Owensboro KY 42302	800-264-1054	270-683-1054	219
Owensboro Grain Co			
822 E Second St ....Owensboro KY 42303	800-874-0305	270-926-2032	296-29
Owensboro Health (OMHS)			
811 E Parish Ave PO Box 20007......Owensboro KY 42303	877-888-6647	270-691-8040	373-3
Owl Magazine			
10 Lower Spadina Ave Ste 400.........Toronto ON M5V2Z2	800-551-6957	416-340-2700	455-6
Owl Wire & Cable Inc			
3127 Seneca Tpke ....Canastota NY 13032	800-765-9473	315-697-2011	808
Owner-Operator Independent Drivers Assn Inc (OOIDA)			
1 NW OOIDA Dr ....Grain Valley MO 64029	800-444-5791	816-229-5791	49-21
OX Paper Tube & Core Inc			
331 Maple Ave ....Hanover PA 17331	800-414-2476		125
Oxfam America			
226 Cswy St 5th Fl.............Boston MA 02114	800-776-9326	617-482-1211	48-5
Oxford Alloys Inc			
2632 Tee Dr ....Baton Rouge LA 70814	800-562-3355	225-273-4800	357
Oxford Bank			
PO Box 129 ....Addison IL 60101	800-236-2442	630-629-5000	70
Oxford Biomedical Research Inc			
2165 Avon Industrial Dr			
................Rochester Hills MI 48309	800-692-4633	248-852-8815	231

	Toll-Free	Phone	Class
Oxford Convention & Visitors Bureau			
102 Ed Perry Blvd ....Oxford MS 38655	800-758-9177	662-232-2367	206
Oxford Financial Group Ltd			
11711 N Meridian St Ste 600 ....Carmel IN 46032	800-722-2289	317-843-5678	400
Oxford Global Resources Inc			
100 Cummings Ctr Ste 206L ....Beverly MA 01915	800-536-3562	978-922-7502	717
Oxford Graduate School Inc			
500 Oxford Dr ....Dayton TN 37321	800-933-6188	423-775-6596	166
Oxford Health Plans LLC			
48 Monroe Tpke ....Trumbull CT 06611	800-444-6222	203-459-9100	390-3
Oxford Hills Chamber of Commerce			
4 Western Ave ....South Paris ME 04281	800-871-7741	207-743-2281	139
Oxford Hotel			
1600 17th St ....Denver CO 80202	800-228-5838	303-628-5400	378
Oxford Life Insurance Co			
2721 N Central Ave ....Phoenix AZ 85004	800-308-2318*	602-263-6666	390-2
*Cust Svc			
Oxford Suites Boise			
1426 S Entertainment Ave ....Boise ID 83709	888-322-8001*	208-322-8000	378
*General			
Oxford Suites Spokane Valley			
15015 E Indiana Ave ....Spokane Valley WA 99216	866-668-7848	509-847-1000	378
Oxford Valley Mall			
225 W Washington St ....Indianapolis IN 46204	800-461-3439	317-636-1600	458
Oxnard Convention & Visitors Bureau			
2775 N Ventura Rd Ste 204 ....Oxnard CA 93036	800-269-6273	805-385-7545	206
Oyster Consulting LLC			
4128 Innslake Dr ....Glen Allen VA 23060	888-965-5401	804-965-5400	
Oyster Point Hotel, The			
146 Bodman Pl ....Red Bank NJ 07701	800-345-3484	732-530-8200	378
OZ Systems Inc			
2201 E Lamar Blvd Ste 260 ....Arlington TX 76006	888-727-3366		
O-Z/Gedney			
9377 W Higgins Rd ....Rosemont IL 60018	800-621-1506	847-268-6000	811
Ozark Area Chamber of Commerce			
294 Painter Ave ....Ozark AL 36360	800-582-8497	334-774-9321	139
Ozark Border Electric Co-op			
3281 S Westwood ....Poplar Bluff MO 63901	800-392-0567	573-785-4631	245
Ozark Folk Ctr State Park			
1032 Park Ave ....Mountain View AR 72560	800-264-3655	870-269-3851	561
Ozark Guidance Center Inc			
2400 S 40th St ....Springdale AR 72762	800-234-7052	479-750-2020	722
Ozark Motor Lines Inc			
3934 Homewood Rd ....Memphis TN 38118	800-264-4100	901-251-9711	775
Ozark National Scenic Riverways			
404 Watercress Dr PO Box 490 ....Van Buren MO 63965	877-444-6777	573-323-4236	560
Ozark Regional Transit			
2423 E Robinson Ave ....Springdale AR 72764	800-865-5901	479-756-5901	108
Ozarka College			
218 College Dr ....Melbourne AR 72556	800-821-4335	870-368-7371	162
Ozarka Water Co			
729 SW Third St ....Oklahoma City OK 73109	800-310-8474	405-235-8474	
Ozarks Coca-Cola Dr Pepper Bottling Co			
1777 N Packer Rd ....Springfield MO 65803	866-223-4498	417-865-9900	98
Ozarks Electric Co-op Inc			
3641 W Wedington Dr ....Fayetteville AR 72704	800-521-6144	479-521-2900	245
Ozarks Medical Ctr			
1100 N Kentucky Ave ....West Plains MO 65775	800-356-5395	417-256-9111	373-3
OZZ Electric Inc			
20 Floral Pkwy ....Concord ON L4K4R1	844-699-6100	416-637-7237	

P

	Toll-Free	Phone	Class
P & F Industries Inc			
445 Broadhollow Rd ....Melville NY 11747	800-327-9403	631-694-9800	754
NASDAQ: PFIN			
P A Landers Inc			
351 Winter St ....Hanover MA 02339	800-660-6404	781-826-8818	186
P J Noyes Company Inc			
89 Bridge St ....Lancaster NH 03584	800-522-2469		297-8
P K W Associates Inc			
705 E Ordnance Rd Ste 108 ....Baltimore MD 21226	888-358-3900	443-773-1000	225
P M Industrial Supply Co			
9613 Canoga Ave ....Chatsworth CA 91311	800-382-3684	818-341-9180	349
P T. M. Corp			
6560 Bethuy Rd ....Fair Haven MI 48023	800-486-2212	586-725-2211	60
P V Rentals Ltd			
5810 S Rice Ave ....Houston TX 77081	800-275-7878	713-667-0665	126
P1 Group Inc			
2151 Haskell Ave Bldg 1...........Lawrence KS 66046	800-376-2911	785-843-2910	189-10
P3 Inc 213 Hwy 35 ....Red Bank NJ 07701	866-222-5169		180
Paasche Airbrush Co			
4311 N Normandy Ave ....Chicago IL 60634	800-621-1907*		43
*Sales			
PABCO Gypsum			
37851 Cherry St ....Newark CA 94560	877-449-7786	510-792-9555	346
Pabst Brewing Co, The			
10635 Santa Monica Blvd			
Ste 350..................Los Angeles CA 90025	800-947-2278		102
Pac Tec			
12365 Haynes St ....Clinton LA 70722	877-554-2544		604
PACC (Peabody Area)			
Chamber of Commerce			
49 Walnut St 1st Fl...........Peabody MA 01960	888-287-9400	978-531-0384	
PACCAR Leasing Corp			
777 106th Ave NE ....Bellevue WA 98004	800-759-2979	425-468-7877	773
Pace Computer Solutions Inc			
10500 Little Patuxent Pkwy			
Ste 310..................Columbia MD 21044	888-225-7223	443-539-0290	
Pace Products Inc			
4510 W 89th St Ste 110 ....Prairie Village KS 66207	888-389-8203		46

Name / Address	City	State	ZIP	Toll-Free	Phone	Class
Pace Tech Inc 2040 Calumet St	Clearwater	FL	33765	**800-722-3024**	727-442-8118	474
Pace University 1 Pace Plz	New York	NY	10038	**866-722-3338**	212-346-1200	166
Birnbaum Library 1 Pace Plz	New York	NY	10038	**800-498-2071**	212-346-1332	433-6
Pleasantville/Briarcliff 861 Bedford Rd	Pleasantville	NY	10570	**866-722-3338**	914-773-3200	166
Pace-Edwards 2400 Commercial Rd	Centralia	WA	98531	**800-338-3697**	360-736-9991	120
Pacesetter Claims Service Inc 2871 N Hwy 167	Catoosa	OK	74015	**888-218-4880**	918-665-8887	389
Pacesetter Steel Service Inc 1045 Big Shanty Rd	Kennesaw	GA	30144	**800-749-6505**	770-919-8000	490
Pacific Aerospace & Electronics Inc 434 Olds Stn Rd	Wenatchee	WA	98801	**855-285-5200**	509-667-9600	617
Pacific Bag Inc 15300 Woodinville Redmond Rd NE Ste A	Woodinville	WA	98072	**800-562-2247**	425-455-1128	65
Pacific Building Maintenance Inc 2646 Palma Dr Ste 320	Ventura	CA	93003	**800-300-4094**	805-642-0214	104
Pacific Building Systems (PBS) 2100 N Pacific Hwy *General	Woodburn	OR	97071	**800-727-7844***	503-981-9581	105
Pacific Cataract & Laser Institute 2517 NE Kresky Ave	Chehalis	WA	98532	**800-888-9903**	360-748-8632	793
Pacific Choice Seafoods Co 16797 SE 130th Ave	Clackamas	OR	97015	**800-882-0212**	707-442-2981	296-13
Pacific Coast Container Inc 432 Estudillo Ave	San Leandro	CA	94577	**800-458-4788**	510-346-6100	646
Pacific Coast Feather Co 1964 Fourth Ave S	Seattle	WA	98134	**888-297-1778**		741
Pacific Coast Fruit Co 201 NE Second Ave	Portland	OR	97232	**800-423-4945**	503-234-6411	297-7
Pacific Coast Jet Charter Inc 10600 White Rock Rd	Rancho Cordova	CA	95670	**800-655-3599**	916-631-6507	13
Pacific Coast Lighting 20238 Plummer St	Chatsworth	CA	91311	**800-709-9004**	818-886-9751	438
Pacific Coast Producers 631 N Cluff Ave	Lodi	CA	95240	**877-618-4776**	209-367-8800	296-20
Pacific Coast Valuations 740 Corporate Ctr Dr	Pomona	CA	91768	**888-623-4001**		648
Pacific College Oriental Med Inc 7445 Mission Valley Rd Ste 105	San Diego	CA	92108	**800-729-0941**	619-574-6909	166
Pacific Color Graphics 440 Boulder Ct 100d	Pleasanton	CA	94566	**888-551-1482**	925-600-3006	623
Pacific Combustion Engineering Co 2107 Border Ave	Torrance	CA	90501	**800-342-4442**	310-212-6300	419
Pacific Continental Corp 111 W Seventh Ave PO Box 10727 *NASDAQ: PCBK*	Eugene	OR	97440	**877-231-2265**	541-686-8685	70
Pacific Disaster Ctr 1305 N Holopono St Ste 2	Kihei	HI	96753	**888-808-6688**	808-891-0525	664
Pacific Ethanol Corp 400 Capitol Mall Ste 2060 *NASDAQ: PEIX*	Sacramento	CA	95814	**866-508-4969**	916-403-2123	145
Pacific Fibre & Rope Company Inc 903 Flint St	Wilmington	CA	90744	**800-825-7673**	310-834-4567	208
Pacific Food Importers Inc 18620 80th Ct S Bldg F	Kent	WA	98032	**800-225-4029**	206-682-2740	359-3
Pacific Gas & Electric Co 77 Beale St *Cust Svc	San Francisco	CA	94105	**800-743-5000***	415-973-7000	782
Pacific Grain Products International Inc 351 Hanson Way PO Box 2060 *Cust Svc	Woodland	CA	95776	**800-333-0110***	530-631-5786	296-23
Pacific Guardian Life Insurance Company Ltd 1440 Kapiolani Blvd Ste 1700	Honolulu	HI	96814	**800-367-5354**	808-955-2236	390-2
Pacific Handy Cutter Inc 17819 Gillette Ave *Cust Svc	Irvine	CA	92614	**800-229-2233***	714-662-1033	222
Pacific Health Laboratories Inc 800 Lanidex Plz Ste 220 *General	Parsippany	NJ	07054	**877-363-8769***	732-739-2900	794
Pacific Inn 600 Marina Dr	Seal Beach	CA	90740	**866-466-0300**	562-493-7501	378
Pacific Inn Resort & Conference Centre 1160 King George Hwy	Surrey	BC	V4A4Z2	**800-667-2248**	604-535-1432	378
Pacific Institute 12101 Tukwila Int'l Blvd Ste 330	Seattle	WA	98168	**800-426-3660**	206-628-4800	760
Pacific International Rice Mills Inc 845 Kentucky Ave	Woodland	CA	95695	**800-747-4764**	530-661-6028	296-23
Pacific Investment Management Company LLC 840 Newport Ctr Dr	Newport Beach	CA	92660	**800-387-4626**	949-720-6000	400
Pacific Life Insurance Co 700 Newport Ctr Dr	Newport Beach	CA	92660	**800-800-7646**	949-219-3011	390-2
Pacific Lutheran Theological Seminary 2770 Marin Ave	Berkeley	CA	94708	**800-235-7587**		167-3
Pacific Lutheran University 1010 122nd St S	Tacoma	WA	98444	**800-274-6758**	253-531-6900	166
Pacific Marine Credit Union (PMCU) 1278 Rocky Point Dr	Oceanside	CA	92056	**800-736-4500**	760-631-8700	219
Pacific Medical Inc 1700 N Chrisman Rd	Tracy	CA	95304	**800-726-9180**		475
Pacific Metallurgical Inc 925 Fifth Ave S	Kent	WA	98032	**800-428-9436**		482
Pacific Modern Homes Inc (PMHI) 9723 Railroad St	Elk Grove	CA	95624	**800-395-1011**		106
Pacific Mutual Holding Co 700 Newport Ctr Dr	Newport Beach	CA	92660	**800-347-7787**	949-219-3011	359-4
Pacific Northwest College of Art 511 NW Broadway	Portland	OR	97209	**888-390-7499**	503-226-4391	166
Pacific Northwest Inlander 1227 W Summit Pkwy	Spokane	WA	99201	**866-444-3066**	509-325-0634	528-5
Pacific Northwest National Laboratory (PNNL) 902 Battelle Blvd PO Box 999	Richland	WA	99352	**888-375-7665**	509-375-2121	664
Pacific NW Federal Credit Union (PNWFCU) 12106 NE Marx St	Portland	OR	97220	**866-692-8669**	503-256-5858	219
Pacific Oaks College 55 W Eureka St	Pasadena	CA	91103	**877-314-2380**		166
Pacific Packaging Products Inc 24 Industrial Way	Wilmington	MA	01887	**800-777-0300**	978-657-9100	555
Pacific Palms Conference Resort 1 Industry Hills Pkwy *Cust Svc	City of Industry	CA	91744	**800-524-4557***	626-810-4455	665
Pacific Paper Tube Inc 1025 98th Ave	Oakland	CA	94603	**888-377-8823**	510-562-8823	125
Pacific Polymers Inc 12271 Monarch St	Garden Grove	CA	92841	**800-888-8340**	714-898-0025	3
Pacific Power & Light 825 NE Multnomah St *Cust Svc	Portland	OR	97232	**888-221-7070***	503-813-6666	782
Pacific Press 1350 N Kings Rd *Cust Svc	Nampa	ID	83687	**800-765-6955***	208-465-2500	633-9
Pacific Press Technologies 714 Walnut St	Mount Carmel	IL	62863	**800-851-3586**	618-262-8666	454
Pacific Records 523 N Hunter St	Stockton	CA	95202	**888-823-5467**	209-320-6600	798-1
Pacific Repertory Theater PO Box 222035	Carmel	CA	93922	**866-622-0709**	831-622-0700	569-4
Pacific Resources for Education & Learning 1136 Union Mall 9th Fl	Honolulu	HI	96813	**800-377-4773**	808-441-1300	242
Pacific Rim Mechanical 7655 Convoy Ct	San Diego	CA	92111	**800-891-4822**	858-974-6500	14
Pacific School of Religion 1798 Scenic Ave	Berkeley	CA	94709	**800-999-0528**	510-848-0528	167-3
Pacific Seacraft PO Box 189	Washington	NC	27889	**800-561-3357**	252-948-1421	90
Pacific Service Federal Credit Union PO Box 8191	Walnut Creek	CA	94596	**888-858-6878**	925-296-6200	219
Pacific Software Publishing Inc 1404 140th Pl NE	Bellevue	WA	98007	**800-232-3989**		180
Pacific Source Inc PO Box 2323	Woodinville	WA	98072	**888-343-1515**		191-3
Pacific Specialty Insurance Co 3601 Haven Ave	Menlo Park	CA	94025	**800-962-1172**		390-4
Pacific States Felt & Mfg Company Inc 23850 Clawiter Rd	Hayward	CA	94545	**800-566-8866**	510-783-0277	326
Pacific Steel & Recycling 1401 Third St NW	Great Falls	MT	59404	**800-889-6264**	406-771-7222	490
Pacific Terrace Hotel 610 Diamond St	San Diego	CA	92109	**800-344-3370**	858-581-3500	378
Pacific Title Archives 10717 Vanowen St	North Hollywood	CA	91605	**800-968-9111**	818-760-4223	511
Pacific Transit System 216 N Second St	Raymond	WA	98577	**800-833-6388**	360-875-9418	108
Pacific Union College 1 Angwin Ave	Angwin	CA	94508	**800-862-7080**	707-965-6336	166
Pacific University 2043 College Way *Admissions	Forest Grove	OR	97116	**800-677-6712***	503-352-2007	166
Pacific University Library 2043 College Way	Forest Grove	OR	97116	**800-677-6712**	503-352-1400	433-6
Pacifica Hotels 39 Argonaut	Aliso Viejo	CA	92656	**800-720-0223**	805-957-0095	648
PacifiCorp 825 NE Multnomah St	Portland	OR	97232	**888-221-7070**	503-813-5000	782
Package Pavement Company Inc PO Box 408	Stormville	NY	12582	**800-724-8193**	845-221-2224	46
Package Right Corp 811 Development Dr	Tipton	IN	46072	**800-964-3794**		
Package Steel Systems Inc 15 Harback Rd	Sutton	MA	01590	**800-225-7242**	508-865-5871	105
Packaging Corp of America 1955 W Field Ct *NYSE: PKG*	Lake Forest	IL	60045	**800-456-4725**		100
Packaging Distribution Services Inc (PDS) 2308 Sunset Rd	Des Moines	IA	50321	**800-747-2699**	515-243-3156	555
Packaging Inc 7200 93rd Ave N Ste 190	Brooklyn Park	MN	55445	**800-328-6650**	952-935-3421	490
Packaging Machinery Manufacturers Institute (PMMI) 4350 N Fairfax Dr Ste 600	Arlington	VA	22203	**888-275-7664**	703-243-8555	49-13
Packaging Material Direct Inc 30405 Solon Rd Ste 9	Solon	OH	44139	**800-456-2467**		686
Packaging Services of Maryland Inc 16461 Elliott Pkwy	Williamsport	MD	21795	**800-223-6255**	301-223-6200	545
Packaging Specialties Inc 300 Lake Rd	Medina	OH	44256	**800-344-9271**	330-723-6000	198
Packaging Systems International Inc 4990 Acoma St	Denver	CO	80216	**800-525-6110**	303-296-4445	543
Packard Transport Inc 24021 S Municipal Dr PO Box 380	Channahon	IL	60410	**800-467-9260**	815-467-9260	466
Packer Engineering Inc 420 N Main St	Montgomery	IL	60538	**866-264-4126**	630-701-7703	261
Packer Thomas 6601 Westford Pl Ste 101	Canfield	OH	44406	**800-943-4278**	330-533-9777	2
Packerland Rent-a-mat Inc 12580 W Rohr Ave	Butler	WI	53007	**800-472-9339**	262-781-5321	131
Packing House 900 E Layton Ave	Milwaukee	WI	53207	**800-727-9477**	414-483-5054	667
PackLatecom Inc 100 Four Falls Corporate Ctr Ste 104	West Conshohocken	PA	19428	**877-472-2552**		386
Packless Metal Hose Inc PO Box 20668	Waco	TX	76702	**800-347-4859**	254-666-7700	14
PACO Pumps Inc 902 Koomey Rd	Brookshire	TX	77423	**800-955-5847**	281-994-2700	637
Paco Steel & Engineering Corp 19818 S Alameda St	Rancho Dominguez	CA	90221	**800-421-1473**	310-537-6375	490
Pacon Corp 2525 N Casaloma Dr	Appleton	WI	54912	**800-333-2545**		550
Pacrim Hospitality Services Inc 30 Damascus Rd	Bedford	NS	B4A0C1	**800-561-7666**		194

Name / Address	City	State	ZIP	Toll-Free	Phone	Class
Pactiv Corp 1900 W Field Ct	Lake Forest	IL	60045	888-828-2850	847-482-2000	557
Pad Print Machinery of Vermont Inc 201 Tennis Way	East Dorset	VT	05253	800-272-7764	802-362-0844	624
Padco Inc 2220 Elm St SE	Minneapolis	MN	55414	800-328-5513	612-378-7270	103
PADF (Pan American Development Foundation) 1889 F St NW 2nd Fl	Washington	DC	20006	877-572-4484	202-458-3969	48-5
Padgett Business Services 160 Hawthorne Pk	Athens	GA	30606	800-723-4388		2
Padgett Services 140 Mountain Brook Dr	Canton	GA	30115	888-323-0777	678-880-1600	
PADI (Professional Assn of Diving Instructors Internatio) 30151 Tomas St *Sales	Rancho Santa Margarita	CA	92688	800-729-7234*	949-858-7234	48-22
PADI Americas 30151 Tomas St	Rancho Santa Margarita	CA	92688	800-527-8378	949-858-7234	510
Padre Island National Seashore PO Box 181300	Corpus Christi	TX	78480	800-343-2368	361-949-8068	560
Page & Assoc Inc 1979 Lakeside Pkwy Ste 200	Tucker	GA	30084	800-252-5282		791
Page 1 Solutions LLC 1726 Cole Blvd Ste 150	Lakewood	CO	80401	800-916-3886	303-233-3886	4
Pageplus Cellular 9700 NW 112th Ave	Miami	FL	33178	800-550-2436		386
Paging Network of Canada Inc 1-1685 Tech Ave	Mississauga	ON	L4W0A7	800-216-0888		41
Paige Electric Company LP 1160 Springfield Rd	Union	NJ	07083	800-327-2443	908-687-2722	246
Paine College 1235 15th St	Augusta	GA	30901	800-476-7703	706-821-8200	166
Paint & Decorating Retailers Assn (PDRA) 1401 Triad Ctr Dr	Saint Peters	MO	63376	800-737-0107	636-326-2636	49-18
Paint Creek State Park 280 Taylor Rd	Bainbridge	OH	45612	866-644-6727	937-981-7061	561
Painted Pony Petroleum Ltd 736 Sixth Ave SW Ste 1800	Calgary	AB	T2P3T7	866-975-0440	403-475-0440	535
Painters Supply & Equipment Co 25195 Brest Rd	Taylor	MI	48180	800-589-8100	734-946-8119	546
Painting & Decorating Contractors of America (PDCA) 2316 Millpark Dr *Cust Svc	Maryland Heights	MO	63043	800-332-7322*	314-514-7322	49-3
Paisano Publications LLC 28210 Dorothy Dr	Agoura Hills	CA	91301	800-323-3484	818-889-8740	633-9
Pak Mail Centers of America Inc 8601 W Cross Dr Ste F5 *Cust Svc	Littleton	CO	80123	800-778-6665*	303-971-0088	113
Pak West Paper & Packaging 4042 W Garry Ave	Santa Ana	CA	92704	800-927-7299	714-557-7420	544
Pakistan International Airlines Corp (PIA) 1200 New Jersey Ave SE	Washington	DC	20590	800-578-6786		25
PakSense Inc 6223 N Discovery Pl	Boise	ID	83713	877-832-0720	208-489-9010	201
PaLA (Pennsylvania Library Assn) 220 Cumberland Pkwy Ste 10	Mechanicsburg	PA	17055	800-622-3308	717-766-7663	434
Pala Casino Resort & Spa 11154 Hwy 76	Pala	CA	92059	877-946-7252	760-510-5100	665
Pala Mesa Resort 2001 Old Hwy 395	Fallbrook	CA	92028	800-722-4700	760-728-5881	665
Palace Casino 158 Howard Ave	Biloxi	MS	39530	800-725-2239	228-386-2315	132
Palace Hotel 2 New Montgomery St	San Francisco	CA	94105	866-716-8136	415-512-1111	378
Palace Station Hotel & Casino 2411 W Sahara Ave *Resv	Las Vegas	NV	89102	800-634-3101*	702-367-2411	133
Palace, The 601 Vine St	Cincinnati	OH	45202	800-942-9000	513-381-6006	667
Paladin Data Systems Corp 19362 Powder Hill Pl NE	Poulsbo	WA	98370	800-532-8448	360-779-2400	177
Palisade Corp 130 E Seneca St Ste 505	Ithaca	NY	14850	800-432-7475	607-277-8000	178-1
Pall Corp 2200 Northern Blvd *NYSE: PLL*	East Hills	NY	11548	800-645-6532	516-484-5400	385
Pall Life Sciences 600 S Wagner Rd	Ann Arbor	MI	48103	800-521-1520	734-665-0651	418
PALLAB (Physician's Automated Laboratory Inc) 9830 Brimhall Rd	Bakersfield	CA	93312	800-675-2271	661-829-2260	417
Pallet Consultants Corp 810 NW 13th Ave	Pompano Beach	FL	33069	888-782-2909	954-946-2212	547
Pallet Masters Inc 655 E Florence Ave	Los Angeles	CA	90001	800-675-2579	323-758-6559	547
Pallet Services Inc 201 E Fairhaven Ave	Burlington	WA	98233	800-769-2245	360-776-1130	200
PalletOne Inc 1470 US Hwy 17 S	Bartow	FL	33830	800-771-1148	863-533-1147	547
Pallett Valo LLP 77 City Ctr Dr Ste 300	Mississauga	ON	L5B1M5	800-323-3781	905-273-3300	427
Palliser Furniture Upholstery Ltd 70 Lexington Pk	Winnipeg	MB	R2G4H2	866-444-0777		469
Palm 5800 Universal Blvd Hard Rock Hotel	Orlando	FL	32819	866-333-7256	407-503-7256	667
Palm Beach Atlantic University PO Box 24708	West Palm Beach	FL	33416	888-468-6722	561-803-2000	166
Palm Beach Community College *Lake Worth* 4200 Congress Ave	Lake Worth	FL	33461	866-576-7222	561-868-3350	162
Palm Beach Gardens 3160 PGA Blvd	Palm Beach Gardens	FL	33410	866-576-7222	561-207-5340	162
Palm Beach County Public Library System 3650 Summit Blvd	West Palm Beach	FL	33406	888-780-4962	561-233-2600	433-3
Palm Beach County School District, The 3300 Forest Hill Blvd	West Palm Beach	FL	33406	866-930-8402	561-434-8000	681
Palm Beach Daily Business Review 324 Datura St Ste 140	West Palm Beach	FL	33401	800-777-7300	561-820-2060	455-5
Palm Beach Illustrated Magazine 1000 N Dixie Hwy Ste C	West Palm Beach	FL	33401	800-308-7346	561-659-6160	455-22
Palm Beach Motoring Accessories Inc 7744 SW Jack James Dr	Stuart	FL	34997	800-869-3011	772-286-2701	54
Palm Beach Newspapers Inc PO Box 24700	West Palm Beach	FL	33416	800-432-7595	561-820-4100	633-8
Palm Beach Post 2751 S Dixie Hwy	West Palm Beach	FL	33405	800-432-7595	561-820-4100	528-2
Palm Mountain Resort & Spa 155 S BelaRdo Rd	Palm Springs	CA	92262	800-622-9451	760-325-1301	665
Palm Restaurant 250 W 50 th St	New York	NY	10019	866-333-7256	212-333-7256	667
Palm Restaurant 200 S Broad St	Philadelphia	PA	19102	866-333-7256	215-546-7256	667
Palm Restaurant 6100 Westheimer Rd	Houston	TX	77057	866-333-7256	713-977-2544	667
Palm restaurant, The 100 Oliver St Lbby Level	Boston	MA	02110	866-333-7256	617-867-9292	667
Palm Springs Desert Resorts Convention & Visitors Authority 70-100 Hwy 111	Rancho Mirage	CA	92270	800-967-3767	760-770-9000	206
Palm Springs International Airport 3200 E Tahquitz Canyon Way	Palm Springs	CA	92262	800-847-4389	760-318-3800	27
Palm Springs Life Magazine 303 N Indian Canyon	Palm Springs	CA	92262	800-775-7256	760-325-2333	455-22
Palmer Asphalt Co 196 W Fifth St PO Box 58	Bayonne	NJ	07002	800-352-9898	201-339-0855	46
Palmer Holland Inc 25000 Country Club Blvd Ste 444	North Olmsted	OH	44070	800-635-4822	440-686-2300	146
Palmer Inn, The 3499 Rt One S	Princeton	NJ	08540	800-688-0500	609-452-2500	378
Palmer Investigative Services 624 W Gurley St Ste A	Prescott	AZ	86304	800-280-2951	928-778-2951	399
Palmer Manufacturing 18 N Bechtle Ave	Springfield	OH	45504	800-457-5456	937-323-6339	490
Palmer Moving & Storage 24660 Dequindre Rd	Warren	MI	48091	800-521-3954	586-834-3400	516
Palmer Paving Corp 25 Blanchard St	Palmer	MA	01069	800-244-8354	413-283-8354	188-4
Palmer Theological Seminary 588 N Gulph Rd	King Of Prussia	PA	19406	800-220-3287	610-896-5000	167-3
Palmer-Donavin Manufacturing Co 1200 Steelwood Rd	Columbus	OH	43212	800-589-4412	800-652-1234	191-3
Palmetto Brick Co 3501 BrickyaRd Rd	Wallace	SC	29596	800-922-4423		150
Palmetto Cooperative Services LLC 7440 Broad River Rd	Irmo	SC	29063	800-235-4290		623
Palmetto Dunes Resort 4 Queens Folly Rd	Hilton Head Island	SC	29928	866-380-1778		665
Palmetto GBA LLC 17 Technology Cir AG-905	Columbia	SC	29203	800-833-4455	803-735-1034	177
Palmetto Health 1400 Pickens St	Columbia	SC	29202	800-238-1884	803-296-3100	370
Palmetto State Transportation Company Inc 1050 Pk W Blvd	Greenville	SC	29611	800-269-0175	864-672-3800	775
Palms Casino Resort 4321 W Flamingo Rd	Las Vegas	NV	89103	866-942-7777	702-942-7777	133
Palms Resort 2500 N Ocean Blvd	Myrtle Beach	SC	29577	800-300-1198	843-626-8334	665
Palms West Hospital (PWH) 13001 Southern Blvd	Loxahatchee	FL	33470	877-549-9337	561-798-3300	373-3
Palms, The 3025 Collins Ave	Miami Beach	FL	33140	800-550-0505	305-534-0505	665
Palmyra Bologna Company Inc 230 N College St	Palmyra	PA	17078	800-282-6336	717-838-6336	296-26
Palo Alto Airport 1925 Embarcadero Rd	Palo Alto	CA	94303	866-638-2344	408-918-7700	27
Palo Alto Networks Inc 4401 Great America Pkwy	Santa Clara	CA	95054	866-898-9087	408-753-4000	
Palo Pinto County PO Box 219	Palo Pinto	TX	76484	844-769-4976	940-659-1277	337
Palomar Pomerado Health 15615 Pomerado Rd	Poway	CA	92064	800-628-2880	858-613-4000	352
Palomino Inc 545 King St W	Toronto	ON	M5V1M1	866-360-0360	416-964-7333	179
Palos Sports Inc 11711 S Austin Ave	Alsip	IL	60803	800-233-5484	708-396-2555	707
Paltech Enterprises Inc 2560 Bing Miller Ln	Urbana	IA	52345	800-949-1006	319-443-2700	497
PAM Transportation Services Inc 297 W Henri De Tonti Blvd *NASDAQ: PTSI*	Tontitown	AR	72770	800-879-7261	479-361-9111	775
Pamarco 171 E Marquardt Dr *Sales	Wheeling	IL	60090	800-323-7735*	847-459-6000	673
PAMED (Pennsylvania Medical Society) 777 E Park Dr PO Box 8820	Harrisburg	PA	17105	800-228-7823	717-558-7750	390-5
Pampered Chef Ltd 1 Pampered Chef Ln	Addison	IL	60101	888-687-2433		365
Pan Abode Cedar Homes Inc 1100 Maple Ave SW	Renton	WA	98057	800-782-2633	425-255-8260	106
Pan American Development Foundation (PADF) 1889 F St NW 2nd Fl	Washington	DC	20006	877-572-4484	202-458-3969	48-5
Pan American Screw Inc 630 Reese Dr SW *Cust Svc	Conover	NC	28613	800-951-2222*	828-466-0060	278
Pan American Travel Services 320 East 900 South	Salt Lake City	UT	84111	800-364-4359	801-364-4300	767
Pan Pacific Hotel Vancouver 999 Canada Pl Ste 300	Vancouver	BC	V6C3B5	800-937-1515	604-662-8111	378
Pan Pacific Seattle 2125 Terry Ave	Seattle	WA	98121	877-324-4856	206-264-8111	378
Pan Pacific Whistler Mountainside 4320 Sundial Crescent	Whistler	BC	V0N1B4	888-905-9995	604-905-2999	665
Panacore Corp 2015 E Eighth St Ste 242	Odessa	TX	79761	877-726-2267		

Alphabetical Section

Name	Address	City	State	Zip	Toll-Free	Phone	Class
Panama City Beaches Chamber of Commerce	309 Richard Jackson Blvd	Panama City Beach	FL	32407	**800-224-4853**	850-235-1159	139
Panamax Inc	1690 Corporate Cir	Petaluma	CA	94954	**800-472-5555**	707-283-5900	253
Pan-American Life Insurance Co	601 Poydras St *Life Ins	New Orleans	LA	70130	**877-939-4550***		390-2
Panaram International	126 Greylock Ave	Belleville	NJ	07109	**800-872-8695**	973-751-1100	361
Panasonic Avionics Corp	26200 Enterprise Way	Lake Forest	CA	92630	**877-627-2300**	949-672-2000	52
Panasonic Corp of North America	1 Panasonic Way *Cust Svc	Secaucus	NJ	07094	**800-211-7262***	877-826-6538	52
Panavise Products Inc	7540 Colbert Dr	Reno	NV	89511	**800-759-7535**	775-850-2900	693
Panavision Inc	6219 DeSoto Ave	Woodland Hills	CA	91367	**800-260-1846**	818-316-1000	587
Panda Express	1717 Walnut Grove Ave	Rosemead	CA	91770	**800-877-8988**	626-312-5401	666
Panda Inn	506 Horton Plz	San Diego	CA	92101	**800-877-8988**		
Panda Inn	111 E Wilson Ave	Glendale	CA	91206	**800-877-8988**		
Panda Travel	1017 Kapahulu Ave	Honolulu	HI	96816	**800-303-6702**	808-738-3898	767
Pandel Inc	21 River Dr	Cartersville	GA	30120	**800-537-3868**	770-382-1034	363
Panduit Corp	17301 Ridgeland Ave	Tinley Park	IL	60477	**888-506-5400**	708-532-1800	810
Panef Inc	5700 W Douglas Ave	Milwaukee	WI	53218	**800-448-1247**	414-464-7200	575
Panel Processing Inc	120 N Industrial Hwy	Alpena	MI	49707	**800-433-7142**		814
Panelfold Inc	10700 NW 36th Ave	Miami	FL	33167	**800-433-3222**	305-688-3501	286
Panera Bread Co	3630 S Geyer Rd *NASDAQ: PNRA*	Saint Louis	MO	63127	**800-301-5566**	314-984-1000	68
Panhandle Co-op Assn	401 S Beltline Hwy W *Cust Svc	Scottsbluff	NE	69361	**800-732-4546***	308-632-5301	276
Panhandle Royalty Co	5400 N Grand Blvd Grand Ctr Bldg Ste 300	Oklahoma City	OK	73112	**800-884-4225**	405-948-1560	534
Panhandle Telecommunication Systems Inc (PTSI)	2222 NW Hwy 64	Guymon	OK	73942	**800-562-2556**	580-338-2556	731
Pannier Corp	207 Sandusky St	Pittsburgh	PA	15212	**877-726-6437**	412-323-4900	492
Pannier Graphics	345 Oak Rd	Gibsonia	PA	15044	**800-544-8428**	724-265-4900	697
Pan-O-Gold Baking Co	444 E St Germain	Saint Cloud	MN	56304	**800-444-7005**	320-251-9361	296-1
Panola College	1109 W Panola St	Carthage	TX	75633	**800-252-9152**	903-693-2000	162
Panola Partnership Inc	150-A Public Sq	Batesville	MS	38606	**888-872-6652**	662-563-3126	139
Panola-Harrison Electric Co-op	410 E Houston St	Marshall	TX	75670	**800-972-1093**	903-935-7936	245
Panora Cooperative Telephone Association Inc	114 E Main St	Panora	IA	50216	**800-205-1110**	641-755-2424	116
Panorama Balloon Tours	2683 Via De La Valle 625G	Del Mar	CA	92014	**800-455-3592**	760-271-3467	755
Panorama City	1751 Cir Ln SE	Lacey	WA	98503	**800-999-9807**	360-456-0111	668
Panoramic Inc	1500 N Parker Dr	Janesville	WI	53545	**800-333-1394**	608-754-8850	101
Pan-Osten Co	6944 Louisville Rd	Bowling Green	KY	42101	**800-472-6678**	270-783-3900	286
Pantages Hotel	200 Victoria St	Toronto	ON	M5B1V8	**855-852-1777**	416-362-1777	378
Pantages Theatre	6233 Hollywood Blvd	Los Angeles	CA	90028	**800-430-8903**		568
Pantagraph	PO Box 2907	Bloomington	IL	61702	**800-747-7323**	309-829-9000	528-2
Panzer Nursery Inc	17980 W Baseline Rd	Beaverton	OR	97006	**888-212-5327**	503-645-1185	368
PAOC (Pentecostal Assemblies of Canada, The)	2450 Milltower Ct	Mississauga	ON	L5N5Z6	**800-779-7262**	905-542-7400	48-20
Paoli Inc	201 E Martin St	Orleans	IN	47452	**800-472-8669**		319-1
Papa Gino's Inc	600 Providence Hwy	Dedham	MA	02026	**800-727-2446**	781-329-1946	666
Papa John's International Inc	2002 Papa John's Blvd *NASDAQ: PZZA*	Louisville	KY	40299	**877-547-7272**	502-261-7272	666
Papa Murphy's International Inc	8000 NE Pkwy Dr Ste 350	Vancouver	WA	98662	**877-777-5062**		666
Papco Inc	4920 Southern Blvd	Virginia Beach	VA	23462	**800-899-0747**	757-499-5977	575
Paper Pak Industries (PPI)	1941 N White Ave	La Verne	CA	91750	**888-293-6529**	909-392-1750	297-9
Paper Store Inc	20 Main St	Acton	MA	01720	**844-480-7100**		562
Paper Systems Inc	185 S Pioneer Blvd	Springboro	OH	45066	**888-564-6774**	937-746-6841	550
Paper Tigers, The	2201 Waukegan Rd Ste 180	Bannockburn	IL	60015	**800-621-1774**	847-919-6500	656
Paper Transport Inc	1250 Mid Valley Dr	De Pere	WI	54115	**800-317-3650**		775
Paperclip Software Inc	1 University Plz	Hackensack	NJ	07601	**800-929-3503**	201-525-1221	178-1
Papercone Corp	3200 Fern Valley Rd	Louisville	KY	40213	**800-626-5308**	502-961-9493	263
PaperDirect Inc	1005 E Woodmen Rd	Colorado Springs	CO	80920	**800-272-7377**	800-338-3346	549
Papers Inc	206 S Main St	Milford	IN	46542	**800-733-4111**	574-658-4111	633-8
PaperWise Inc	3171 E Sunshine	Springfield	MO	65804	**888-828-7505**	417-886-7505	177
PAR Excellence Systems Inc	11500 Northlake Dr	Cincinnati	OH	45249	**800-888-7279**	513-936-9744	177
Par Pharmaceutical Cos Inc	6 Ram Ridge Rd *NASDAQ: ENDP*	Chestnut Ridge	NY	10977	**800-828-9393**	800-462-3636	579
PAR Technology Corp	8383 Seneca Tpke *NYSE: PAR*	New Hartford	NY	13413	**800-448-6505**	315-738-0600	610
Para Systems Inc	*Minuteman UPS* 1455 LeMay Dr	Carrollton	TX	75007	**800-238-7272**	972-446-7363	253
Para-Chem Southern Inc	863 SE Main St PO Box 127	Simpsonville	SC	29681	**800-763-7272**	864-967-7691	3
Par-A-Dice Hotel	21 Blackjack Blvd	East Peoria	IL	61611	**800-727-2342**	309-699-7711	378
Paradigm Design Associates Inc	4 Center Rd Unit 5	Old Saybrook	CT	06475	**800-495-3295**		521
Paradigm Imaging Group Inc	3010 Red Hill Ave	Costa Mesa	CA	92626	**888-221-7226**	714-432-7226	623
Paradise Chamber of Commerce	5550 Sky Way Ste 1	Paradise	CA	95969	**800-247-9889**	530-877-9356	139
Paradise Inc	1200 W MLK Jr Blvd *OTC: PARF*	Plant City	FL	33563	**800-330-8952**		296-8
Paradise Island Vacations	1000 S Pine Island Rd Ste 800 *Resv	Plantation	FL	33324	**888-877-7525***	954-809-2100	766
Paradise Point State Recreation Site	PO Box 1345	Port Orford	OR	97465	**800-551-6949**		561
Paragon Casino Resort	711 Paragon Pl	Marksville	LA	71351	**800-946-1946**		133
Paragon Development Systems Inc (PDS)	13400 Bishops Ln Ste 190	Brookfield	WI	53005	**800-966-6090**	262-569-5300	174
Paragon Furniture Management Inc	2224 E Randol Mill Rd	Arlington	TX	76011	**800-451-8546**	817-633-3242	320
Paragon Industries Inc	2011 S Town E Blvd	Mesquite	TX	75149	**800-876-4328**	972-288-7557	318
Paragon International Inc	2885 N Berkeley Lake Rd Ste 17	Duluth	GA	30096	**800-526-1095**		392
Paragon Laboratories	20433 Earl St	Torrance	CA	90503	**800-231-3670**	310-370-1563	794
Paragon Medical Inc	8 Matchett Industrial Park Dr	Pierceton	IN	46562	**800-225-6975**	574-594-2140	473
Paragon Sporting Goods Corp	867 Broadway 18th St	New York	NY	10003	**800-961-3030**	212-255-8889	707
Paragon Steel Enterprises LLC	4211 County Rd 61	Butler	IN	46721	**800-411-5677**	260-868-1100	490
Paragon Supply Co	160 Reaser Ct	Elyria	OH	44035	**800-726-8041**	440-365-8040	186
Parallax Inc	599 Menlo Dr Ste 100	Rocklin	CA	95765	**888-512-1024**	916-624-8333	621
Parallax Press	2236 Sixth St	Berkeley	CA	94710	**800-863-5290**	510-540-6411	196
Parametric Technology Corp (PTC)	140 Kendrick St *NASDAQ: PTC*	Needham	MA	02494	**800-613-7535**	781-370-5000	178-5
Parametrix Inc	1002 15th St SW	Auburn	WA	98001	**888-863-5128**		
Paramount Apparel International Inc	1 Paramount Dr	Bourbon	MO	65441	**866-274-4287**	573-732-4411	155-8
Paramount Beauty Distributing Associates Inc	41 Mercedes Way Unit 34	Edgewood	NY	11717	**800-755-7475**	631-242-3737	
Paramount Builders Inc	501 Central Dr	Virginia Beach	VA	23454	**888-340-9002**	757-340-9000	363
Paramount Chemical Specialties Inc	14750 NE 95th St	Redmond	WA	98052	**877-846-7826**	425-882-2673	151
Paramount Coffee Co	5133 W Grand River Ave	Lansing	MI	48906	**800-968-1222**		
Paramount Convention Services Inc	5015 Fyler Ave	Saint Louis	MO	63139	**800-883-6578**	314-621-6677	184
Paramount Cosmetics Inc	93 Entin Rd Ste 4	Clifton	NJ	07014	**800-522-9880**	973-472-2323	214
Paramount Graphics Inc	6075 Pkwy North Dr Ste D	Cumming	GA	30040	**800-714-8071**		
Paramount Health Care	1901 Indian Wood Cir	Maumee	OH	43537	**800-462-3589**	419-887-2525	390-3
Paramount Hotel	808 SW Taylor St	Portland	OR	97205	**855-215-0160**	503-223-9900	378
Paramount Industries Inc	304 N Howard St	Croswell	MI	48422	**800-521-5405**	810-679-2551	438
Paramount Pictures Corp	5555 Melrose Ave	Los Angeles	CA	90038	**844-392-9033**		
Paramount WorkPlace	1374 EW Maple Rd	Walled Lake	MI	48390	**800-725-4408**	248-960-0909	39
Parasec Inc	2804 Gateway Oaks Dr Ste 200 PO Box 160568 *General	Sacramento	CA	95833	**800-533-7272***		631
Paratech Ambulance Service	9401 W Brown Deer Rd	Milwaukee	WI	53224	**866-525-8888**	414-358-1111	30
Paratransit Services	4810 Auto Ctr Way	Bremerton	WA	98312	**800-933-3468**		
Parchem Trading Ltd	415 Huguenot St	New Rochelle	NY	10801	**800-282-3982**	914-654-6800	231
Parents Helping Parents (PHP)	1400 Parkmoor Ave Ste 100	San jose	CA	95126	**855-727-5775**	408-727-5775	48-6
Parents of Murdered Children (POMC)	4960 Ridge Ave Ste 2	Cincinnati	OH	45209	**888-818-7662**	513-721-5683	48-6
Parenty Reitmeier Inc	605 Des Meurons St	Winnipeg	MB	R2H2R1	**877-445-3737**	204-237-3737	317
PARI Respiratory Equipment Inc	2412 PARI Way	Midlothian	VA	23112	**800-327-8632**		
Paric Corp	77 Westport Plz Ste 250	St. Louis	MO	63146	**800-500-4320**	636-561-9500	194

Name / Address	Toll-Free	Phone	Class
Paris Business Products 800 Highland Dr .... Westampton NJ 08060 *Cust Svc	800-523-6454*	609-265-9200	110
Paris Farmers' Union PO Box D .... South Paris ME 04281	800-639-3603	207-743-8976	276
Paris Gourmet of New York Inc 145 Grand St .... Carlstadt NJ 07072	800-727-8791		297-8
Paris Junior College 2400 Clarksville St .... Paris TX 75460	800-232-5804	903-785-7661	162
Paris-Henry County Chamber of Commerce 2508 Eastwood St .... Paris TN 38242	800-345-1103	731-642-3431	139
Park 'N Fly 2060 Mt Paran Rd Ste 207 ...... Atlanta GA 30327 *Cust Svc	800-325-4863*		558
Park 100 Foods Inc 326 E Adams St .... Tipton IN 46072	800-854-6504	765-675-3480	296-26
Park City Chamber of Commerce/Convention & Visitors Bureau 1850 Sidewinder Dr Ste 320 ... Park City UT 84060	800-453-1360	435-649-6100	206
Park Community Federal Credit Union PO Box 18630 .... Louisville KY 40261	800-626-2870	502-968-3681	216
Park County 1002 Sheridan Ave .... Cody WY 82414	800-786-2844	307-527-8510	337
Park County Travel Council (PCTC) 836 Sheridan Ave PO Box 2454 .... Cody WY 82414	800-393-2639	307-587-2297	206
Park Electric Co-op Inc 5706 US Hwy 89 S PO Box 1119 .. Livingston MT 59047	888-298-0657	406-222-3100	245
Park Lane Jewelry 100 E Commerce Dr .... Schaumburg IL 60173	800-621-0088		409
PARK MGM 3770 Las Vegas Blvd S ...... Las Vegas NV 89109	800-311-8999	702-730-7777	665
Park National Bank 50 N Third St PO Box 3500 ...... Newark OH 43058 NYSE: PRK	888-791-8633	740-349-8451	359-2
Park Place Technologies Inc 5910 Landerbrook Dr .... Cleveland OH 44124	877-778-8707		177
Park Place Volvo 3515 Inwood Rd .... Dallas TX 75209	888-437-0906	855-272-5915	
Park Printing Inc 2801 California St NE ...... Minneapolis MN 55418	800-789-3877	612-789-4333	623
Park Seed Co 1 Parkton Ave .... Greenwood SC 29647 *Orders	800-845-3369*		690
Park Shore Resort 600 Neapolitan Way .... Naples FL 34103	855-923-8197		665
Park Shore Waikiki Hotel 2586 Kalakaua Ave .... Honolulu HI 96815	866-536-7975	808-954-7426	378
Park To Fly 1900 Jetport Dr Exit 8 off S R 528 (Beachline) ..... Orlando FL 32809	888-851-8875	407-851-8875	558
Park University 8700 NW River Pk Dr .... Parkville MO 64152	800-745-7275	816-741-2000	166
Park Vista Resort Hotel 705 Cherokee OrchaRd Rd PO Box 30 .... Gatlinburg TN 37738 *Sales	800-227-5622*	865-436-9211	378
Parkallen Restaurant 7018-109th St NW .... Edmonton AB T6H3C1	855-822-6854	587-520-6401	
Parkdale Mills Inc 531 Cotton Blossom Cir .... Gastonia NC 28054	800-331-1843	704-874-5000	740-9
Parke County Rural Electric Membership Corp 119 W High St .... Rockville IN 47872	800-537-3913	765-569-3133	245
Parke-Bell Ltd Inc 709 W 12th St .... Huntingburg IN 47542	800-457-7456	812-683-3707	114
Parker Fluid Connectors Group 6035 Parkland Blvd .... Cleveland OH 44124 *General	800-272-7537*	216-896-3000	369
Parker Furniture 10375 SW Beaverton-Hillsdale Hwy .... Beaverton OR 97005	866-515-9673	503-644-0155	321
Parker Hannifin Corp Automation Actuator Div 135 Quadral Dr .... Wadsworth OH 44281	800-272-7537	877-321-4736	223
Parker Hannifin Corp Brass Products Div 6035 Parkland Blvd .... Otsego MI 49078	800-272-7537	269-694-9411	785
Parker Hannifin Corp Cylinder Div 500 S Wolf Rd .... Des Plaines IL 60016	800-272-7537	847-298-2400	223
Parker Hannifin Corp Daedal Div 1140 Sandy Hill Rd .... Irwin PA 15642	800-245-6903	724-861-8200	540
Parker Hannifin Corp Electromechanical Automation Div 5500 Business Pk Dr .... Rohnert Park CA 94928	800-358-9068	707-584-7558	203
Parker Hannifin Corp Finite Filtratio & Separation Div 500 Glaspie St .... Oxford MI 48371	800-521-4357	248-628-6400	18
Parker Hannifin Corp General Valve Div 26 Clinton Dr Unit 103 .... Hollis NH 03049	800-272-7537		785
Parker Hannifin Corp Hydraulic Valve Div 520 Ternes Ave .... Elyria OH 44035	800-272-7537	440-366-5200	784
Parker Hannifin Corp Pneumatic Div 8676 E M 89 .... Richland MI 49083	877-321-4736	269-629-5000	785
Parker Hannifin Corp Skinner Valve Div 95 Edgewood Ave .... New Britain CT 06051	800-825-8305	860-827-2300	785
Parker Hannifin Corp Veriflo Div 250 Canal Blvd .... Richmond CA 94804	800-272-7537	510-235-9590	201
Parker Instrumentation Group 6035 Parkland Blvd .... Cleveland OH 44124	800-272-7537	216-896-3000	223
Parker Laboratories Inc 286 Eldridge Rd .... Fairfield NJ 07004	800-631-8888	973-276-9500	474
Parker Majestic Inc 300 N Pike Rd .... Sarver PA 16055	866-572-7537	724-352-1551	453
Parker McCrory Manufacturing Co 2000 Forest Ave .... Kansas City MO 64108	800-662-1038	816-221-2000	203
Parker Powis Inc 775 Heinz Ave .... Berkeley CA 94710	800-321-2463	510-848-2463	92
Parker Rose Design Inc 10075 Mesa Rim Rd Ste A ...... San Diego CA 92121	800-403-2711		41
Parker Smith & Feek Inc 2233 112th Ave NE .... Bellevue WA 98004 *Cust Svc	800-457-0220*		389
Parker Steel Co 1625 Indian Wood Cir .... Maumee OH 43537	800-333-4140	419-473-2481	490
Parker University 2540 Walnut Hill Ln .... Dallas TX 75229	800-637-8337	972-438-6932	759
Parkersburg News 519 Juliana St .... Parkersburg WV 26101	800-642-1997	304-485-1891	528-2
ParkerVision Inc 7915 Baymeadows Way ...... Jacksonville FL 32256 NASDAQ: PRKR	800-532-8034	904-732-6100	643
Parkhill Smith & Cooper Inc 4222 85th St .... Lubbock TX 79423	800-400-6646	806-473-2200	261
Parking Panda Corp 3422 Fait Ave .... Baltimore MD 21224	800-232-6415		558
Parking Solutions Inc 353 W Nationwide Blvd .... Columbus OH 43215	888-469-7690	614-469-7000	558
Parkinson's Disease Foundation (PDF) 1359 Broadway .... New York NY 10018	800-457-6676	212-923-4700	48-17
Parkland College 2400 W Bradley Ave .... Champaign IL 61821	888-467-6065	217-351-2200	162
Parkland College Theatre 2400 W Bradley Ave .... Champaign IL 61821	800-346-8089	217-351-2528	568
Parkland Health Ctr 1101 W Liberty St .... Farmington MO 63640	800-734-3944	573-756-6451	373-3
Parkland Plastics Inc 104 Yoder Dr PO Box 339 ...... Middlebury IN 46540	800-835-4110	574-825-4336	657
Parkline Inc PO Box 65 .... Winfield WV 25213	800-786-4855	304-586-2113	105
Parkplace 111 Emerson St .... Denver CO 80218	844-431-9875	615-564-8666	668
Parkridge East Hospital 941 Spring Creek Rd .... Chattanooga TN 37412	800-605-1527	423-894-7870	373-3
Parks Bros Farm Inc 6733 Parks Rd .... Van Buren AR 72956	800-334-5770	479-410-2217	368
Parks Canada 30 Victoria St .... Gatineau QC J8X0B3	888-773-8888	819-420-9486	559
Parksite Inc 1563 Hubbard Ave .... Batavia IL 60510	800-338-3355		191-3
Parkson Corp 1401 W Cyperess Creek Rd .... Fort Lauderdale FL 33309	888-727-5766		385
Parkview Hospital 2200 Randallia Dr .... Fort Wayne IN 46805	888-737-9311	260-373-4000	373-3
Parkview Medical Ctr 400 W 16th St .... Pueblo CO 81003	800-543-4046	719-584-4000	373-3
Parkville Insurances Services Inc 15242 E Whittier Blvd PO Box 1275 .... Whittier CA 90603	800-350-2702	562-945-2702	389
Parkway Chevrolet Inc 25500 Tomball Pkwy .... Tomball TX 77375	888-929-4556		513
Parkway Clinical Laboratories Inc 3494 Progress Dr .... Bensalem PA 19020	800-327-2764	215-245-5112	417
Parkway Electric Inc 11952 James St .... Holland MI 49424	800-574-9553		782
Parkway Inn 125 N Jackson St PO Box 494 .... Jackson WY 83001	800-247-8390		378
Parkway Properties Inc 188 E Capitol St Ste 1000 ...... Jackson MS 39201 NYSE: PKY	800-748-1667	601-948-4091	651
Parlec Inc 101 Perinton Pkwy .... Fairport NY 14450	800-866-5872	585-425-4400	357
Parmalat Canada Ltd 405 the W Mall 10th Fl .... Toronto ON M9C5J1	800-563-1515		296-27
Parman Energy Corp 7101 Cockrill Bend Blvd .... Nashville TN 37209	800-727-7920	615-350-7920	316
Parmed Pharmaceuticals Inc 4220 Hyde Pk Blvd .... Niagara Falls NY 14305	800-727-6331		238
Parnassus Investments 1 Market St Steuart Tower Ste 1600 .... San Francisco CA 94105	800-999-3505	415-778-0200	686
Parr Instrument Co 211 53rd St .... Moline IL 61265	800-872-7720	309-762-7716	419
Parr Moto 13120 Westlinks Ter Blvd Unit 4 .... Fort Myers FL 33913	866-772-1381		6
Parr Richey Frandsen Patterson Kruse LLP Capital Ctr N 251 N Illinois St Ste 1800 .... Indianapolis IN 46204	888-337-7766	317-269-2500	427
Parrish & Heimbecker Ltd (P&H) 201 Portage Ave Ste 1400 ...... Winnipeg MB R3B3K6	800-665-8937	204-956-2030	275
Parrish Medical Ctr 951 N Washington Ave .... Titusville FL 32796	800-227-9954	321-268-6111	373-3
Parrish Tire Company Inc 5130 Indiana Ave .... Winston-Salem NC 27106	800-849-8473	336-767-0202	62-5
Parsec Financial Management Inc 6 Wall St .... Asheville NC 28801	888-877-1012	828-255-0271	194
Parsley Energy Inc 303 Colorado St Ste 3000 .... Austin TX 78701	855-214-5200	737-704-2300	532
Parsons Capital Management Inc 10 Weybosset St Ste 1000 ...... Providence RI 02903	888-521-2440	401-521-2440	400
Parsons New School for Design 65 Fifth Ave .... New York NY 10011 *Admissions	800-252-0852*	212-229-8989	166
Parter Medical Products Inc 17015 Kingsview Ave .... Carson CA 90746	800-666-8282	310-327-4417	419
Particle Dynamics International LLC 2629 S Hanley Rd .... Saint Louis MO 63144	800-452-4682	314-968-2376	578
Particle Measuring Systems Inc 5475 Airport Blvd .... Boulder CO 80301 *Cust Svc	800-238-1801*	303-443-7100	418
Partner Assessment Corp 2154 Torrance Blvd Ste 200 ..... Torrance CA 90501	800-419-4923		192
Partner Software Inc PO Box 748 .... Athens GA 30603	844-778-4717	706-612-9494	
PARTNERS A Tasteful Choice Co 20232 72nd Ave .... South Kent WA 98032	800-632-7477	253-867-1580	68
Partnership for a Drug-Free America 405 Lexington Ave Ste 1601 .... New York NY 10174	855-378-4373	212-922-1560	48-17
Partnersolve Llc 30 Southville Rd .... Southborough MA 01772	855-445-2837		
Parton Lumber Company Inc 251 Parton Rd .... Rutherfordton NC 28139	800-624-1501	828-287-4257	679

				Toll-Free	Phone	Class
Parts Central Inc						
3243 Whitfield St	Macon	GA	31204	**800-226-9396**	478-745-0878	61
PartsBase Inc						
905 Clint Moore Rd	Boca Raton	FL	33487	**888-322-6896***	561-953-0700	765
*Cust Svc						
Party City Corp						
25 Green Pond Rd Ste 1	Rockaway	NJ	07866	**800-727-8924**	973-453-8600	562
Partylite Gifts Inc						
59 Armstrong Rd	Plymouth	MA	02360	**888-999-5706**	508-830-3100	365
Par-Way Tryson Co						
107 Bolte Ln	Saint Clair	MO	63077	**800-844-4554**	636-629-4545	296-30
Pasadena Convention & Visitors Bureau						
300 E Green St	Pasadena	CA	91101	**800-307-7977**	626-795-9311	206
Pasadena Convention Center						
300 E Green St	Pasadena	CA	91101	**800-307-7977**	626-793-2122	568
Pasco						
2600 S Hanley Rd Ste 450	Saint Louis	MO	63144	**800-489-3300**	314-781-2212	295
Pasco County						
7530 Little Rd	New Port Richey	FL	34654	**800-368-2411**	727-847-2411	337
Pasco Specialty & Manufacturing Inc						
11156 Wright Rd	Lynwood	CA	90262	**800-737-2726**	310-537-7782	608
Pasco-Hernando State College						
10230 Ridge Rd	New Port Richey	FL	34654	**855-669-7472**	727-847-2727	162
Pasco-Hernando Community College						
11415 Ponce de Leon Blvd	Brooksville	FL	34601	**855-669-7472**	352-796-6726	162
Pasek Corp						
9 W Third St	South Boston	MA	02127	**800-628-2822**	617-269-7110	689
PASNAP (Pennsylvania Assn of Staff Nurses & Allied Profess)						
1 Fayette St Ste 475	Conshohocken	PA	19428	**800-500-7850**	610-567-2907	529
Paso Fino Horse Assn						
4047 Iron Works Pkwy Ste 1	Lexington	KY	40511	**800-844-1409**	859-825-6000	48-3
Paso Robles Inn						
1103 Spring St	Paso Robles	CA	93446	**800-676-1713**	805-238-2660	378
Pason Systems Inc						
6130 Third St SE	Calgary	AB	T2H1K4	**877-255-3158**	403-301-3400	178-10
TSX: PSI						
Passaic Valley Water Commission						
1525 Main Ave	Clifton	NJ	07011	**877-772-7077**	973-340-4300	782
Passavant Retirement Community						
401 S Main St	Zelienople	PA	16063	**888-498-7753**	724-452-5400	668
Passenger Vessel Assn (PVA)						
103 Oronoco St Ste 200	Alexandria	VA	22314	**800-807-8360**	703-518-5005	49-21
Passero Assoc						
242 West Main St Ste 100	Rochester	NY	14614	**800-836-0365**	585-325-1000	261
Passport Corp						
16 West St	Warwick	NY	10990	**800-926-6736**		178-1
Passport Program-western						
925 Euclid Ave Ste 600	Cleveland	OH	44115	**800-626-7277**	216-621-0303	362
Passport Services Regional Offices						
Boston Agency						
10 Cswy St						
Tip O'Neill Federal Bldg Rm 247	Boston	MA	02222	**877-487-2778**		339-15
Connecticut Agency						
850 Canal St	Stamford	CT	06902	**877-487-2778**		339-15
Honolulu Agency						
300 Ala Moana Blvd Ste I-330	Honolulu	HI	96850	**877-487-2778**		339-15
Los Angeles Agency						
11000 Wilshire Blvd						
Ste 1000	Los Angeles	CA	90024	**877-487-2778**		339-15
New Orleans Agency						
365 Canal St Ste 1300	New Orleans	LA	70130	**877-487-2778**		339-15
New York Agency						
376 Hudson St	New York	NY	10014	**877-487-2778**		339-15
Seattle Agency						
300 Fifth Ave Ste 600	Seattle	WA	98104	**877-487-2778**		
Washington (DC) Agency						
600 19th St NW	Washington	DC	20006	**877-487-2778**		339-15
Passy-Muir Inc						
4521 Campus Dr Pmb 273	Irvine	CA	92612	**800-634-5397**	949-833-8255	475
Pastel Journal						
4700 E Galbraith Rd	Cincinnati	OH	45236	**800-422-2550**	513-531-2222	455-2
Pastorelli Food Products Inc						
162 N Sangamon St	Chicago	IL	60607	**800-767-2829**	312-666-2041	296-36
Pat Milliken Ford						
9600 Telegraph Rd	Redford	MI	48239	**855-803-3131***		
*Sales						
Pat O'Brien's International Inc						
718 St Peter St	New Orleans	LA	70116	**800-597-4823**	504-525-4823	666
Patagonia						
259 W Santa Clara St	Ventura	CA	93001	**800-638-6464***	805-643-8616	157-4
*Cust Svc						
Patene Building Supplies Ltd						
641 Speedvale Ave W	Guelph	ON	N1K1E6	**800-265-8319**	519-824-4030	191-1
Patent Trademark & Copyright Law Daily						
1801 S Bell St	Arlington	VA	22202	**800-372-1033**		527-7
Paternity Testing Corp (PTC)						
300 Portland St	Columbia	MO	65201	**888-837-8323**	573-442-9948	416
Paterson Pacific Parchment Co						
625 Greg St	Sparks	NV	89431	**800-678-8104**	775-353-3000	555
Path-2 Ventures LLC						
223 E Blvd	Charlotte	NC	28203	**888-692-1057**		461
Pathfinder Bancorp Inc						
214 W First St	Oswego	NY	13126	**800-811-5620**	315-343-0057	359-2
NASDAQ: PBHC						
Pathfinder Group						
Park Lane Terr 502 - 5657 Spring Garden Rd						
PO Box 142	Halifax	NS	B3J3R4	**800-200-7284**	902-425-2445	47
PathLogic						
1166 National Dr Ste 80	Sacramento	CA	95834	**844-603-3071**	866-863-1496	417
Pathology & Cytology Laboratories Inc						
290 Big Run Rd	Lexington	KY	40503	**800-264-0514**	859-278-9513	414
Pathology Group of The Mid South						
7550 Wolf River Blvd Ste 200	Germantown	TN	38138	**877-608-2756**	901-542-6800	
Pathology Laboratories Inc						
1946 N 13th St Ste 301	Toledo	OH	43604	**800-281-8804**	419-255-4600	414
Pathway Health						
11240 Stillwater Blvd N	Lake Elmo	MN	55042	**877-777-5463**		196
Pathways Home Health Hospice						
585 N Mary Ave	Sunnyvale	CA	94085	**888-755-7855**		

				Toll-Free	Phone	Class
Patient Advocate Foundation Inc						
700 Thimble Shoals Blvd						
Ste 200	Newport News	VA	23606	**800-532-5274**		305
PatientKeeper Inc						
880 Winter St Ste 300	Waltham	MA	02451	**888-994-2443**	781-373-6100	474
Patients Rights Council (PRC)						
PO Box 760	Steubenville	OH	43952	**800-958-5678**	740-282-3810	48-8
Patina						
141 S Grand Ave	Los Angeles	CA	90012	**866-972-8462**		
Patina Restaurant Group						
141 S Grand Ave	Los Angeles	CA	90012	**866-972-8462**		666
Patioshoppers Inc						
41188 Sandalwood Cir	Murrieta	CA	92562	**800-940-6123**	951-696-1700	321
Patrick Henry Community College						
645 Patriot Ave	Martinsville	VA	24112	**855-874-6692**	276-638-8777	162
Patrick Industries Inc						
107 W Franklin St PO Box 638	Elkhart	IN	46515	**800-331-2151**	574-294-7511	115
NASDAQ: PATK						
Patrick Industries Inc Patrick Metals Div						
5020 Lincolnway E	Mishawaka	IN	46544	**800-922-9692**	574-255-9692	483
Patrick James Inc						
780 W Shaw Ave	Fresno	CA	93704	**888-427-6003**	559-224-5500	157-3
Patriot National Bancorp Inc						
900 Bedford St	Stamford	CT	06901	**888-728-7468**		359-2
NASDAQ: PNBK						
Patriot Properties Inc						
123 Pleasant St	Marblehead	MA	01945	**800-527-9991**	781-586-9670	651
Patriot Rail Company LLC						
10060 Skinner Lake Dr	Jacksonville	FL	32246	**855-258-4514**	904-423-2540	645
Patriot Staffing & Services Llc						
47 Eggert Ave	Metuchen	NJ	08840	**888-412-6999**		566
Patriot Technologies Inc						
5108 Pegasus Ct Ste F	Frederick	MD	21704	**888-417-9899**	301-695-7500	177
Patriot Transportation Holding Inc						
200 West Forsyth St 7th Fl	Jacksonville	FL	32202	**877-704-1776**		775
NASDAQ: PATI						
Patriot-News						
2020 Technology Pkwy						
Ste 300	Mechanicsburg	PA	17050	**800-692-7207**	717-255-8100	528-2
Patriots Theater						
Memorial Dr	Trenton	NJ	08608	**866-847-7682**	609-984-8484	568
Patten & Patten Inc						
520 Lookout St	Chattanooga	TN	37403	**800-757-3480**	423-756-3480	194
Patten Industries Inc						
635 West Lake St	Elmhurst	IL	60126	**877-688-6812**	630-279-4400	357
Patten Monument Co						
3980 W River Dr NE	Comstock Park	MI	49321	**800-627-5371**	800-233-4472	45
Patten University						
2100 Franklin St Ste 350	Oakland	CA	94612	**866-841-1986**		166
Pattern Insight Inc						
465 Fairchild Dr Ste 209	Mountain View	CA	94043	**866-582-2655**		177
Patterson Dental Supply Inc						
1031 Mendota Heights Rd	Saint Paul	MN	55120	**800-328-5536**		473
NASDAQ: PDCO						
Patterson Office Supplies						
3310 N Duncan Rd	Champaign	IL	61822	**800-637-1140**	217-351-5400	110
Patterson-Schwartz & Assoc Inc						
7234 Lancaster Pk Ste 100A	Hockessin	DE	19707	**877-456-4663**	302-234-5270	648
Patti Engineering Inc						
2110 E Walton Blvd Ste A	Auburn Hills	MI	48326	**800-852-0994**	248-364-3200	261
Patuxent Cos						
2124 Priest Bridge Dr Ste 18	Crofton	MD	21114	**800-628-4942**	410-793-0181	189-16
Patz & Hall Wine Co						
851 Napa Vly Corporate Way Ste A	Napa	CA	94558	**877-265-6700**	707-931-2440	442
Paul Brown Stadium						
1 Paul Brown Stadium	Cincinnati	OH	45202	**866-621-8383**	513-455-4800	716
Paul C Buff Inc						
2725 Bransford Ave	Nashville	TN	37204	**800-443-5542**	615-383-3982	438
Paul D Camp Community College						
100 N College Dr PO Box 737	Franklin	VA	23851	**855-877-3918**	757-569-6700	162
Hobbs Suffolk						
271 Kenyon Rd	Suffolk	VA	23434	**855-877-3918**	757-925-6300	162
Paul Davis Systems Canada Ltd						
38 Crockford Blvd	Toronto	ON	M1R3C2	**800-661-5975**	416-299-8890	192
Paul deLima Co Inc						
7546 Morgan Rd	Liverpool	NY	13090	**800-962-8864**	315-457-3725	296-7
Paul Fredrick Menstyle						
223 W Poplar St	Fleetwood	PA	19522	**800-247-1417**	610-944-0909	157-3
Paul H Gesswein & Co						
255 Hancock Ave	Bridgeport	CT	06605	**800-544-2043**	203-366-5400	406
Paul Laurence Dunbar House						
219 N Paul Laurence Dunbar St	Dayton	OH	45402	**800-860-0148**	937-224-7061	50-3
Paul Mueller Co						
1600 W Phelps St	Springfield	MO	65802	**800-683-5537**	417-575-9000	385
OTC: MUEL						
Paul Smith's College						
7833 New York 30	Paul Smiths	NY	12970	**800-421-2605***	518-327-6227	166
*Admissions						
Paul Stuart Inc						
Madison Ave & 45th St	New York	NY	10017	**800-678-8278***	212-682-0320	157-4
*Orders						
Paulding-Putman Electric Co-op						
910 N Williams St	Paulding	OH	45879	**800-686-2357**	419-399-5015	245
Pauli Systems Inc						
1820 Walters Ct	Fairfield	CA	94533	**800-370-1115**	707-429-2434	295
Pauline Books & Media						
50 St Paul's Ave	Boston	MA	02130	**800-876-4463***	617-522-8911	633-3
*Sales						
Paulson Investment Company Inc						
2141 W North Ave 2nd Fl	Chicago	IL	60647	**855-653-3444**	503-243-6000	
Pavco Inc						
1935 John Crosland Jr Dr	Charlotte	NC	28208	**800-321-7735***	704-496-6800	145
*Orders						
Pavilion Financial Corp						
1001 Corydon Ave Ste 300	Winnipeg	MB	R3M0B6	**866-954-5101**	204-954-5101	687
Pavliks Com						
80 Bell Farm Rd	Barrie	ON	L4M5K5	**877-728-5457**	705-726-2966	180
Pawleys Plantation						
70 Tanglewood Dr	Pawleys Island	SC	29585	**877-283-2122**		665

Listing	Toll-Free	Phone	Class
Pawling Corp 32 Nelson Hill Rd PO Box 200 .... Wassaic NY 12592	800-431-3456		672
Pawnee County 715 Broadway .... Larned KS 67550	800-211-4401	620-285-3721	337
PAWS (Performing Animal Welfare Society) 11435 Simmerhorn Rd .... Galt CA 95632	800-513-6560	209-745-2606	48-3
Pawtucket Public Library 13 Summer St .... Pawtucket RI 02860	800-359-3090	401-725-3714	433-3
Pax World Fund Family 30 Penhallow St Ste 400 .... Portsmouth NH 03801	800-767-1729	603-431-8022	524
Paxton & Vierling Steel Co 501 Ave H .... Carter Lake IA 51510	800-831-9252	712-347-5500	478
Paxton Co 1111 Ingleside Rd .... Norfolk VA 23502	800-234-7290	757-853-6781	765
Paxton Van Lines Inc 5300 Port Royal Rd .... Springfield VA 22151	800-336-4536	703-321-7600	516
Pay Plus Benefits Inc 1110 N Ctr Pkwy Ste B .... Kennewick WA 99336	888-531-5781	509-735-1143	627
Payce Inc 1220B E Joppa Rd Ste 324 .... Towson MD 21286	800-729-5910	443-279-9000	729
Paycom 7501 W Memorial Rd .... Oklahoma City OK 73142	800-580-4505		729
Payden & Rygel 333 S Grand Ave .... Los Angeles CA 90071	800-572-9336	213-625-1900	400
Payless ShoeSource Inc 3231 SE Sixth Ave .... Topeka KS 66607	877-474-6379		301
Payne Engineering Co PO Box 70 .... Scott Depot WV 25560 *Orders	800-331-1345*	304-757-7353	203
Payne Theological Seminary 1230 Wilberforce Clifton Rd .... Wilberforce OH 45384	888-816-8933	937-376-2946	167-3
PayneGroup Inc 1111 Third Ave Ste 2200 .... Seattle WA 98101	888-467-2963	206-344-8966	196
PayNet Inc 5750 Old Orchard Rd Ste 250 .... Skokie IL 60077	866-825-3400		464
Pay-O-Matic Corp 160 Oak Dr .... Syosset NY 11791	888-545-6311		141
Payroll 1 34100 Woodward Ave Ste 250 .... Birmingham MI 48009	888-999-7291		
Payroll Masters 855 Bordeaux Way .... Napa CA 94558	800-963-1428	707-226-1428	2
Payscape Advisors 729 Lambert Dr NE .... Atlanta GA 30324	888-351-6565		507
Payson Casters Inc 2323 N Delaney Rd .... Gurnee IL 60031	800-323-4552	847-336-6200	349
Payson Roundup Newspaper 708 N Beeline Hwy .... Payson AZ 85541	800-253-9405	928-474-5251	528-3
Payspan Inc 7751 Belfort Pkwy Ste 200 .... Jacksonville FL 32256	877-331-7154		178-1
Payworks Inc 1565 Willson Pl .... Winnipeg MB R3T4H1	866-788-3500		729
PB Hoidale Company Inc 3801 W Harry .... Wichita KS 67213	800-362-0784	316-942-1361	786
PBA (Professional Beauty Assn) 15825 N 71st St Ste 100. .... Scottsdale AZ 85254	800-468-2274	480-281-0424	49-18
PBA Health 6300 Enterprise Rd .... Kansas City MO 64120	800-333-8097	816-245-5700	231
Pbbs Equipment Corp N59W16500 Greenway Cir .... Menomonee Falls WI 53051	800-236-9620	262-252-7575	608
PBCVB (Pine Bluff Convention & Visitors Bureau) 1 Convention Ctr Plz .... Pine Bluff AR 71601	800-536-7660	870-536-7600	206
PBEC (Polk-Burnett Electric Co-op) 1001 State Rd 35 .... Centuria WI 54824	800-421-0283	715-646-2191	245
PBI Market Equipment Inc 2667 Gundry Ave .... Signal Hill CA 90755	800-421-3753	562-595-4785	300
PBI/Gordon Corp 1217 W 12th St .... Kansas City MO 64101	800-821-7925	816-421-4070	280
PBK Bank Inc 120 Frontier Blvd .... Stanford KY 40484	877-230-3711	606-365-7098	70
PBM Corp 20600 Chagrin Blvd Ste 450. .... Cleveland OH 44122	800-341-5809	216-283-7999	39
PBM Graphics Inc 3700 S Miami Blvd .... Durham NC 27703	800-849-8100	919-544-6222	623
PBM Inc 1070 Sandy Hill Rd .... Irwin PA 15642	800-967-4726	724-863-0550	785
PBS (Public Broadcasting Service) 2100 Crystal Dr .... Arlington VA 22202	866-864-0828	703-739-5000	734
PBS (Pacific Building Systems) 2100 N Pacific Hwy .... Woodburn OR 97071 *General	800-727-7844*	503-981-9581	105
PBS Supply Company Inc 7013 S 216th St .... Kent WA 98032	877-727-7515	253-395-5550	530
PC Connection Inc 730 Milford Rd Rt 101A .... Merrimack NH 03054 NASDAQ: PCCC	888-213-0607	603-683-2000	179
PC Connection Inc MacConnection Div 730 Milford Rd .... Merrimack NH 03054	888-213-0260		179
PC Guardian Anti-Theft Products Inc 2171 E Francisco Blvd Ste G .... San Rafael CA 94901	800-453-4195	415-259-3103	180
PC Mall Inc 2555 W 190th St .... Torrance CA 90504 NASDAQ: PCMI	800-555-6255	310-354-5600	179
PC Richard & Son Inc 150 Price Pkwy .... Farmingdale NY 11735	800-696-2000	631-773-4900	35
PC/Nametag 124 Horizon Dr .... Verona WI 53593	877-626-3824	888-354-7868	178-8
PCA Engineering Inc 57 Cannonball Rd PO Box 196. .... Pompton Lakes NJ 07442	800-666-7221	973-616-4501	261
PCB Group Inc 3425 Walden Ave .... Depew NY 14043	800-828-8840	716-684-0001	253
PCE Pacific Inc 22011 26th Ave SE .... Bothell WA 98021	800-321-4723	425-487-9600	357
PCF (Prevent Cancer Foundation) 1600 Duke St Ste 500. .... Alexandria VA 22314	800-227-2732	703-836-4412	48-17
PCGH (University of Toledo Medical Center, The) 7007 Powers Blvd .... Parma OH 44129	855-292-4292	440-743-3000	373-3
PCI (Phoenix Cable Inc) 10801 N 24th Ave Ste 115-116 .... Phoenix AZ 85029	833-807-3855	602-870-8870	
Pcm Networking 2121 W First St .... Fort Myers FL 33901	866-726-6381	239-334-1615	180
PCMA (Professional Convention Management Assn) 35 E Wacker Dr Ste 500 .... Chicago IL 60601	877-827-7262	312-423-7262	49-12
PCO Services Corp 5840 Falbourne St .... Mississauga ON L5R4B5	800-800-6754	905-502-9700	573
PCOM (Philadelphia College of Osteopathic Medicine) 4170 City Ave .... Philadelphia PA 19131 *Admissions	800-999-6998*	215-871-6100	795
PCR (Mid-Atlantic PenFed Realty Berkshire Hathaway Home) 3050 Chain Bridge Rd .... Fairfax VA 22030	866-225-5778	703-691-7653	651
PCRM (Physicians Committee for Responsible Medicine) 5100 Wisconsin Ave NW Ste 400. .... Washington DC 20016	866-416-7276	202-686-2210	49-8
PCS Co 34488 Doreka Dr. .... Fraser MI 48026	800-521-0546	586-294-7780	752
PCTC (Park County Travel Council) 836 Sheridan Ave PO Box 2454 .... Cody WY 82414	800-393-2639	307-587-2297	206
PCTEL Inc 471 Brighton Dr .... Bloomingdale IL 60108 NASDAQ: PCTI	800-323-9122	630-372-6800	178-7
PDA (Presbyterian Disaster Assistance) 100 Witherspoon St .... Louisville KY 40202	800-728-7228		48-5
PDA (Property Damage Appraisers Inc) 6100 SW Blvd Ste 200 .... Fort Worth TX 76109	800-749-7324		310
PDC (Petroleum Development Corp) 120 Genesis Blvd PO Box 26 .... Bridgeport WV 26330 NASDAQ: PDCE	800-624-3821	303-860-5800	532
PDC Facilities Inc 700 Walnut Ridge Dr .... Hartland WI 53029	800-545-5998	262-367-7700	186
PDCA (Painting & Decorating Contractors of America) 2316 Millpark Dr .... Maryland Heights MO 63043 *Cust Svc	800-332-7322*	314-514-7322	49-3
PDEMC (Pee Dee Electric Membership Corp) 575 US Hwy 52 S .... Wadesboro NC 28170	800-992-1626	704-694-2114	245
PDF (Parkinson's Disease Foundation) 1359 Broadway .... New York NY 10018	800-457-6676	212-923-4700	48-17
PDI 100 American Metro Blvd Ste 201 .... Hamilton NJ 08619	800-242-7494	215-525-5207	195
PDI 4200 Oakleys Ct .... Richmond VA 23223	800-225-4838	804-737-9880	725
PDI Financial Group 601 N Lynndale Dr .... Appleton WI 54914	800-234-7341	920-739-2303	686
PDK (Phi Delta Kappa International) 408 N Union St .... Bloomington IN 47407	800-766-1156	812-339-1156	48-16
PDMA (Product Development & Management Assn) 330 N Wabash Ave Ste 2000. .... Chicago IL 60611	800-232-5241	312-321-5145	49-12
PdMA Corp 5909-C Hampton Oaks Pkwy .... Tampa FL 33610	800-476-6463	813-621-6463	201
PDQ Manufacturing 2754 Creek Hill Rd .... Leola PA 17540	800-441-9692	717-656-4281	349
PDQ Manufacturing Inc 1698 Scheuring Rd .... De Pere WI 54115	800-227-3373	920-983-8333	385
PDRA (Paint & Decorating Retailers Assn) 1401 Triad Ctr Dr .... Saint Peters MO 63376	800-737-0107	636-326-2636	49-18
PDS (Personnel Data Systems Inc) 470 Norristown Rd .... Blue Bell PA 19422	800-243-8737	610-238-4600	178-1
PDS (Packaging Distribution Services Inc) 2308 Sunset Rd .... Des Moines IA 50321	800-747-2699	515-243-3156	555
PDS (Paragon Development Systems Inc) 13400 Bishops Ln Ste 190 .... Brookfield WI 53005	800-966-6090	262-569-5300	174
PDS Gaming Corp 6280 Annie Oakley Dr .... Las Vegas NV 89120	800-479-3612	702-736-0700	216
PDX Inc 101 Jim Wright Fwy S Ste 200 .... Fort Worth TX 76108	800-433-5719		
Pea River Electric Co-op 1311 W Roy Parker Rd PO Box 969 .... Ozark AL 36361	800-264-7732	334-774-2545	245
Peabody Area (PACC) *Chamber of Commerce* 49 Lowell St 1st Fl .... Peabody MA 01960	888-287-9400	978-531-0384	
Peabody Essex Museum 161 Essex St East India Sq .... Salem MA 01970	866-745-1876	978-745-9500	517
Peabody Institute of the Johns Hopkins University *Peabody Conservatory of Music* 1 E Mt Vernon Pl .... Baltimore MD 21202	800-368-2521	667-208-6500	166
Peabody Memphis, The 149 Union Ave .... Memphis TN 38103	800-732-2639	901-529-4000	378
Peabody Office Furniture Corp 234 Congress St .... Boston MA 02110	800-263-2387	617-542-1902	320
Peace Action 8630 Fenton St .... Silver Spring MD 20910	800-228-1228	301-565-4050	48-5
Peace Bridge Duty Free Inc 1 Peace Bridge Plz .... Fort Erie ON L2A5N1	800-361-1302		241
Peace Corps 1111 20th St NW .... Washington DC 20526	800-424-8580	202-692-1040	339-19
Peace Corps Regional Offices *Atlanta Regional Office* 1111 20th St NW .... Washington DC 20526	855-855-1961	202-692-2250	339-19
Chicago Regional Office 230 S Dearborn St Ste 2020. .... Chicago IL 60604	800-424-8580	312-353-4990	339-19
Dallas Regional Office 1100 Commerce St Ste 427 .... Dallas TX 75242	855-855-1961		339-19
Denver Regional Office 1111 20th St NW .... Washington DC 20526	855-855-1961		339-19
Los Angeles Regional Office 2361 Rosecrans Ave Ste 155 .... El Segundo CA 90245	800-424-8580	310-356-1100	339-19
Mid-Atlantic Regional Office 1525 Wilson Blvd Ste 100 .... Arlington VA 22209	800-424-8580	202-692-1040	339-19
New York Regional Office 201 Varick St Ste 1025. .... New York NY 10014	800-424-8580	212-352-5440	339-19
Northwest Regional Office 1601 Fifth Ave Ste 605. .... Seattle WA 98101	800-424-8580	206-553-5490	339-19
San Francisco Regional Office 1301 Clay St Ste 620-N .... Oakland CA 94612	800-424-8580	510-452-8444	339-19
Peace River Chamber of Commerce 10006 96 Ave PO Box 6599 .... Peace River AB T8S1S4	888-525-4423	780-624-4166	137
Peace River Electric Cooperative Inc 210 Metheny Rd PO Box 1310 ....Wauchula FL 33873	866-201-1814	800-282-3824	245

Name / Address	City	State	ZIP	Toll-Free	Phone	Class
PeaceHealth Laboratories 123 International Way	Springfield	OR	97477	**800-826-3616**	541-341-8010	414
PeaceHealth St Joseph Medical Ctr 2901 Squalicum Pkwy	Bellingham	WA	98225	**800-541-7209**	360-734-5400	373-3
Peach State Labs Inc (PSL) 180 Burlington Rd PO Box 1087	Rome	GA	30162	**800-634-1653**	706-291-8743	145
Peach Trader Inc 6286 Dawson Blvd	Norcross	GA	30093	**888-949-9613**	404-752-6715	786
Peachtree Planning Corp 5040 Roswell Rd NE	Atlanta	GA	30342	**800-366-0839**	404-260-1600	113
Peak Financial Management Inc The Wellesley Office Park 20 William St Ste 135	Wellesley	MA	02481	**877-567-9500**	781-487-9500	400
Peak Technical Services Inc 583 Epsilon Dr	Pittsburgh	PA	15238	**888-888-7325**	412-696-1080	717
Peak Technologies Inc 10330 Old Columbia Rd	Columbia	MD	21046	**800-926-9212**		174
Peaklogix Inc 14409 Justice Rd	Midlothian	VA	23113	**800-849-6332**		186
Peaks Resort & Golden Door Spa 136 Country Club Dr	Telluride	CO	81435	**800-789-2220**		665
Peapack-Gladstone Bank 500 Hills Dr Ste 300 PO Box 700 *NASDAQ: PGC*	Bedminster	NJ	07921	**800-742-7595**	908-234-0700	359-2
Pearl City Nursing Home 919 Lehua Ave	Pearl City	HI	96782	**800-596-0026**	808-453-1919	788
Pearl Harbor Federal Credit Union (PHFCU) 94-449 Ukee St	Waipahu	HI	96797	**800-987-5583**		219
Pearl Hotel Waikiki 415 Nahua St	Honolulu	HI	96815	**855-518-3455**	808-922-1616	
Pearl Meat Packing Company Inc 27 York Ave	Randolph	MA	02368	**800-462-3022**	781-228-5100	471
Pearl River Community College 101 Hwy 11 N	Poplarville	MS	39470	**877-772-2338**	601-403-1000	162
Pearl River Valley Electric Power Assn 1422 Hwy 13 N PO Box 1217	Columbia	MS	39429	**855-277-8372**	601-736-2666	245
Pearpoint Inc 72055 Corporate Way	Thousand Palms	CA	92276	**800-688-8094**	760-343-7350	201
Pearrygin Lake State Park 561 Bear Creek Rd	Winthrop	WA	98862	**888-226-7688**	509-996-2370	
Pearson Dental Supplies Inc 13161 Telfair Ave	Sylmar	CA	91342	**800-535-4535**	818-362-2600	473
Pearson Education School Div 1900 E Lake Ave	Glenview	IL	60025	**800-348-4474**		633-2
Pearson Engineering Associates Inc 8825 N 23rd Ave Ste 11	Phoenix	AZ	85021	**866-747-9754**	602-264-0807	261
Pearson Inc 1330 Ave of the Americas 7th Fl	New York	NY	10019	**877-311-0948**		
Pearson Packaging Systems 8120 W Sunset Hwy	Spokane	WA	99224	**800-732-7766**		543
Pearson's Candy Co 2140 W Seventh St *Cust Svc	Saint Paul	MN	55116	**800-328-6507***	651-698-0356	296-8
Peavey Electronics Corp 5022 Hartley Peavey Dr	Meridian	MS	39305	**877-732-8391**	601-483-5365	52
Pechanga Resort & Casino 45000 Pechanga Pkwy	Temecula	CA	92592	**877-711-2946**	951-693-1819	665
Pecora Corp 165 Wambold Rd	Harleysville	PA	19438	**800-523-6688**	215-723-6051	3
Pedal Valves Inc 13625 River Rd	Luling	LA	70070	**800-431-3668**	985-785-9997	606
Peddinghaus Corp 300 N Washington Ave	Bradley	IL	60915	**800-786-2448**	815-937-3800	453
Pedernales Electric Co-op Inc PO Box 1	Johnson City	TX	78636	**888-554-4732**	830-868-7155	245
Pediatric Home Respiratory Services Inc 2800 Cleveland Ave N	Roseville	MN	55113	**800-225-7477**	651-642-1825	362
Pediatrix Medical Group Inc 1301 Concord Terr	Sunrise	FL	33323	**800-243-3839**	954-384-0175	461
Pedigree Technologies 4776 28th Ave S Ste 101	Fargo	ND	58104	**844-407-9307**	800-470-6581	804
Pedorthic Footwear Assn (PFA) 2025 M St NW Ste 800	Washington	DC	20036	**800-673-8447**	202-367-1145	48-17
Pedowitz Group, The 810 Mayfield Rd	Milton	GA	30009	**855-738-6584**		195
Pee Dee Electric Co-op Inc PO Box 491	Darlington	SC	29540	**866-747-0060**	843-665-4070	245
Pee Dee Electric Membership Corp (PDEMC) 575 US Hwy 52 S	Wadesboro	NC	28170	**800-992-1626**	704-694-2114	245
Peeco 7050 West Ridge Rd	Fairview	PA	16415	**800-235-9382**	814-474-5561	452
Peek 'n Peak Resort 1405 Olde Rd	Clymer	NY	14724	**800-772-6906**	716-355-4141	665
Peelle Co 34 E Main St Ste 372	Smithtown	NY	11787	**800-787-5020**	905-846-4545	234
PeelMaster Packaging Corp 6153 W Mulford St Unit C	Niles	IL	60714	**855-966-6200**		
Peer Bearing Co 2200 Norman Dr S	Waukegan	IL	60085	**800-433-7337**	847-578-1000	75
Peer Foods Group Inc 1200 W 35th St	Chicago	IL	60609	**800-365-5644**	773-475-2375	296-26
Peerless Chain Co 1416 E Sanborn St	Winona	MN	55987	**800-533-8056**	507-457-9100	674
Peerless Electric 1401 W Market St	Warren	OH	44485	**800-676-3651**	330-399-3651	515
Peerless Electronics Inc 700 Hicksville Rd	Bethpage	NY	11714	**800-285-2121**	516-594-3500	246
Peerless Food Equipment 500 S Vandenmark Rd	Sidney	OH	45365	**877-795-7377**	937-492-4158	298
Peerless Inc 79 Perry St	Buffalo	NY	14203	**800-234-3033**	716-852-4784	111
Peerless Industrial Group PO Box 949	Clackamas	OR	97015	**800-547-6806**	800-873-1916	674
Peerless Manufacturing Co US Hwy 82 E	Shellman	GA	39886	**800-225-4617**	229-679-5353	273
Peerless Network Inc 222 S Riverside Plz Ste 2730	Chicago	IL	60606	**888-380-2721**	312-506-0920	386
Peerless Pottery Inc 319 S Fifth St	Rockport	IN	47635	**866-457-5785**	812-649-9920	607
Peerless Premier Appliance Co 119 S 14th St	Belleville	IL	62222	**800-858-5844**		36
Peerless Products Inc 2403 S Main St	Fort Scott	KS	66701	**866-420-4000**	620-223-4610	234
Peerless Pump Co 2005 Dr Martin Luther King Jr St	Indianapolis	IN	46202	**800-879-0182**	317-925-9661	637
Peerless Steel Corp 2450 Austin	Troy	MI	48083	**800-482-3947**	248-528-3200	490
Peerless Tire Co 5000 Kingston St	Denver	CO	80239	**800-999-7810**		54
Peery Hotel 110 West 300 South	Salt Lake City	UT	84101	**800-331-0073**	801-521-4300	378
Peet Frate Line Inc 650 S Eastwood Dr PO Box 1129	Woodstock	IL	60098	**800-435-6909**	815-338-5500	775
Pegasus International Hotel 501 Southard St	Key West	FL	33040	**800-397-8148**	305-294-9323	378
Pegasus Logistics Group Inc 306 Airline Dr Ste 100	Coppell	TX	75019	**800-997-7226**	469-671-0300	447
Pegasus Solutions Co 14000 N Pima Rd Ste 200	Scottsdale	AZ	85260	**800-843-4343**	480-624-6000	334
PegEx Inc 2693 Research Park Dr Ste 201	Fitchburg	WI	53711	**888-681-9616**		192
Peg-Perego USA Inc 3625 Independence Dr *Cust Svc	Fort Wayne	IN	46808	**800-671-1701***	260-482-8191	64
PEI (Photofabrication Engineering Inc) 500 Fortune Blvd	Milford	MA	01757	**800-253-8518**	508-478-2025	
PEI-Genesis 2180 Hornig Rd	Philadelphia	PA	19116	**800-675-1214**	215-673-0400	246
Peirce College 1420 Pine St	Philadelphia	PA	19102	**888-467-3472**	215-545-6400	166
Peirce-Phelps Inc 516 E Township Line Rd Blue Bell	Philadelphia	PA	19131	**800-222-2096**	215-879-7217	38
Pekin Insurance (FAIA) 2505 Court St	Pekin	IL	61558	**800-322-0160**	309-346-1161	390-4
Pekin Life Insurance Co 2505 Ct St *OTC: PKIN*	Pekin	IL	61558	**800-322-0160**		390-2
Peking Noodle Co Inc 1514 N San Fernando Rd	Los Angeles	CA	90065	**877-735-4648**	323-223-2023	296-31
Pelco 3500 Pelco Way	Clovis	CA	93612	**800-289-9100**	559-292-1981	643
Pelican Grand Beach Resort 2000 N Ocean Blvd	Fort Lauderdale	FL	33305	**800-525-6232**	954-568-9431	378
Pelican Products Inc 147 N Main St	South Deerfield	MA	01373	**800-542-7344**	413-665-2163	199
Pelican Rope Works Inc 4001 W Carriage Dr	Santa Ana	CA	92704	**800-464-7673**	714-545-0116	208
Pelivan Transit 333 S Oak St PO Box B	Big Cabin	OK	74332	**800-482-4594**	918-783-5793	108
Pella Co-op Electric Assn 2615 Washington St	Pella	IA	50219	**800-619-1040**	641-628-1040	245
Pella Corp 102 Main St *Cust Svc	Pella	IA	50219	**877-473-5527***	641-621-1000	236
Pellettieri Rabstein & Altman 100 Nassau Pk Blvd	Princeton	NJ	08540	**800-432-5297**	609-520-0900	427
Pembina Pipeline Corp 585 Eighth Ave SW *TSE: PPL*	Calgary	AB	T2P1G1	**888-428-3222**	403-231-7500	404
Pembroke Hospital 199 Oak St	Pembroke	MA	02359	**800-222-2237**	781-829-7000	373-5
Pembroke Management Ltd 1002 Sherbrooke St W Ste 1700	Montreal	QC	H3A3S4	**800-667-0716**	514-848-1991	791
Pembroke Regional Hospital 705 MacKay St	Pembroke	ON	K8A1G8	**866-996-0991**	613-732-2811	373-2
Pemex Procurement International Inc 10344 Sam Houston Park Dr	Houston	TX	77064	**888-254-1487**	713-430-3100	532
Pemiscot-Dunklin Electric Co-op Hwy 412 W PO Box 509	Hayti	MO	63851	**800-558-6641**	573-757-6641	245
Pemko Mfg Company Inc 4226 Transport St	Ventura	CA	93003	**800-283-9988**	805-642-2600	326
PEN Products 2010 E New York St	Indianapolis	IN	46201	**800-736-2550**	317-955-6800	626
Penasco Valley Telephone Cooperative Inc (PVT) 4011 W Main St	Artesia	NM	88210	**800-505-4844**		731
Pencco Inc 831 Bartlett Rd PO Box 600	San Felipe	TX	77473	**800-864-1742**	979-885-0005	144
Penco Products Inc 1820 Stonehenge Dr	Greenville	NC	27858	**800-562-1000**		319-1
PendaForm Corp 2344 W Wisconsin St	Portage	WI	53901	**800-356-7704**	608-742-5301	60
Pender Memorial Hospital 507 E Fremont St	Burgaw	NC	28425	**888-815-5188**	910-259-5451	373-3
Pendle Hill 338 Plush Mill Rd	Wallingford	PA	19086	**800-742-3150**	610-566-4507	669
Pendleton Grain Growers Inc 1000 SW Dorian St PO Box 1248	Pendleton	OR	97801	**800-422-7611**	541-278-5035	275
Pendleton Woolen Mills Inc 220 NW Broadway	Portland	OR	97209	**800-760-4844**	503-226-4801	155-5
PendoPharm Inc 6111 Royalmount Ave *Cust Svc	Montreal	QC	H4P2T4	**866-926-7653***	514-340-5045	477
Pendu Manufacturing Inc 718 N Shirk Rd	New Holland	PA	17557	**800-233-0471**	717-354-4348	816
Pengo Corp 500 E Hwy 10 *Cust Svc	Laurens	IA	50554	**800-599-0211***	712-845-2540	190
Pengrowth Energy Corp 222 Third Ave SW Ste 1600 *TSX: PGF*	Calgary	AB	T2P0B4	**800-223-4122**	403-233-0224	671
Penguin Group (USA) Inc 375 Hudson St *Sales	New York	NY	10014	**800-847-5515***	212-366-2000	633-2

	Toll-Free	Phone	Class

Penguin Point Franchise Systems Inc
2691 E US 30 .... Warsaw IN 46580 | 800-557-5755 | 574-267-3107 | 666
Penguin Random House
1745 Broadway .... New York NY 10019 | 800-733-3000 | 212-782-9000 | 633-2
Penguins
1001 Fifth Ave .... Pittsburgh PA 15219 | 800-642-7367 | 412-642-1300 | 712
Peniel Solutions LLC
3885 Crestwood Pkwy Ste 275 .... Duluth GA 30096 | 866-878-2490 | | 113
Peninsula Airways Inc
6100 Boeing Ave .... Anchorage AK 99502 | 800-448-4226 | 907-771-2500 | 25
Peninsula Asset Management Inc
1111 Third Ave W Ste 340 .... Bradenton FL 34205 | 800-269-6417 | | 400
Peninsula Beverly Hills
9882 S Santa Monica Blvd .... Beverly Hills CA 90212 | 800-462-7899 | 310-551-2888 | 378
Peninsula Chicago
108 E Superior St .... Chicago IL 60611 | 866-288-8889 | 312-337-2888 | 378
Peninsula Daily News
305 W First St PO Box 1330 .... Port Angeles WA 98362 | 800-826-7714 | 360-452-2345 | 528-2
Peninsula Hospital
1501 Trousdale Dr .... Burlingame CA 94010 | 800-559-9960 | 650-696-5400 | 373-3
Peninsula Light Co
13315 Goodnough Dr NW .... Gig Harbor WA 98332 | 888-809-8021 | 253-857-5950 | 245
Peninsula New York
700 Fifth Ave .... New York NY 10019 | 800-262-9467 | 212-956-2888 | 378
Peninsula Regional Medical Ctr
100 E Carroll St .... Salisbury MD 21801 | 800-543-7780 | 410-546-6400 | 373-3
Penmor Lithographers Inc
8 Lexington St PO Box 2003 .... Lewiston ME 04241 | 800-339-1341 | | 623
Penn Air & Hydraulics Corp
580 Davies Dr .... York PA 17402 | 888-631-7638 | | 637
Penn Aluminum International Inc
1117 N Second St .... Murphysboro IL 62966 | 800-445-7366* | 618-684-2146 | 483
*All
Penn Color Inc
400 Old Dublin Pk .... Doylestown PA 18901 | 866-617-7366 | 215-345-6550 | 546
Penn Commercial Inc
242 Oak Spring Rd .... Washington PA 15301 | 888-309-7484 | 724-222-5330 | 795
Penn Emblem Co
10909 Dutton Rd .... Philadelphia PA 19154 | 800-793-7366 | | 258
Penn Fibre Plastics
2434 Bristol Rd .... Bensalem PA 19020 | 800-662-7366* | | 596
*Cust Svc
Penn Fishing Tackle Manufacturing Co
7 Science Ct .... Columbia SC 29203 | 800-892-5444 | | 706
Penn Foster Career School
925 Oak St .... Scranton PA 18515 | 800-275-4410 | 570-342-7701 | 795
Penn Inc
306 S 45th Ave .... Phoenix AZ 85043 | 800-289-7366 | | 706
Penn Line Service Inc
300 Scottdale Ave .... Scottdale PA 15683 | 800-448-9110* | 724-887-9110 | 188-10
*All
Penn Machine Co
106 Stn St .... Johnstown PA 15905 | 800-736-6872 | 814-288-1547 | 591
Penn Mutual
600 Dresher Rd .... Horsham PA 19044 | 800-523-0650* | 215-956-8000 | 390-2
*Cust Svc
Penn Mutual Life Insurance Co
600 Dresher Rd .... Horsham PA 19044 | 800-523-0650* | 215-956-8000 | 390-2
*Cust Svc
Penn National Insurance Co
2 N Second St PO Box 2361 .... Harrisburg PA 17101 | 800-388-4764 | 717-234-4941 | 390-4
Penn State Health
500 University Dr .... Hershey PA 17033 | 800-243-1455 | 717-531-6955 | 764
Penn State Milton S Hershey Medical Ctr
500 University Dr .... Hershey PA 17033 | 800-731-3032 | 717-531-6955 | 373-3
Penn Stater Conference Ctr Hotel
215 Innovation Blvd .... State College PA 16803 | 800-233-7505 | 814-863-5000 | 376
Penn Treaty Network America Insurance Co
3440 Lehigh St .... Allentown PA 18103 | 800-362-0700 | | 390-2
Penn United Technology Inc
799 N Pike Rd .... Cabot PA 16023 | 866-572-7537 | 724-352-1507 | 752
Penn Veterinary Supply Inc
53 Industrial Cir .... Lancaster PA 17601 | 800-233-0210 | 717-656-4121 | 789
Penn Virginia Corp
100 Matsonford Rd Ste 200 .... Radnor PA 19087 | 877-316-5288 | 610-687-8900 | 532
NASDAQ: PVAC
Penn's View Hotel
14 N Front St .... Philadelphia PA 19106 | 800-331-7634 | 215-922-7600 | 378
Penna State Education Assn Harrisburg (PSEA)
400 N Third St PO Box 1724 .... Harrisburg PA 17105 | 800-944-7732 | 717-255-7000 | 472
Penncorp Servicegroup Inc
600 N Second St Ste 401 .... Harrisburg PA 17101 | 800-544-9050 | 717-234-2300 | 631
PennEngineering & Manufacturing Corp
5190 Old Easton Rd .... Danboro PA 18916 | 800-237-4736 | 215-766-8853 | 278
Pennichuck Corp
25 Manchester St .... Merrimack NH 03054 | 800-553-5191 | 603-882-5191 | 782
NASDAQ: PNNW
Pennswood Village
1382 Newtown-Langhorne Rd .... Newtown PA 18940 | 888-454-1122 | 215-968-9110 | 668
Pennsylvania
Attorney General
Strawberry Sq 16th Fl. .... Harrisburg PA 17120 | 800-385-1044 | 717-787-3391 | 338-39
Banking Dept
17 N Second St Ste 1300 .... Harrisburg PA 17101 | 800-722-2657 | 717-783-4721 | 338-39
Community & Economic Development Dept
400 N St 4th Fl. .... Harrisburg PA 17120 | 866-466-3972 | | 338-39
Consumer Advocate
555 Walnut St
5th Fl Forum Pl .... Harrisburg PA 17101 | 800-684-6560 | 717-783-5048 | 338-39
Driver & Vehicle Services Bureau
1101 S Front St .... Harrisburg PA 17104 | 800-932-4600 | 800-265-0921 | 338-39
Higher Education Assistance Agency
1200 N Seventh St .... Harrisburg PA 17102 | 800-213-9827 | | 721
Insurance Dept
1326 Strawberry Sq .... Harrisburg PA 17120 | 877-881-6388 | 717-787-2317 | 338-39
Public Utility Commission
400 N St Keystone Bldg
PO Box 3265 .... Harrisburg PA 17120 | 800-692-7380 | 717-783-1740 | 338-39

State Ethics Commission
Rm 309 Finance Bldg
PO Box 11470 .... Harrisburg PA 17108 | 800-932-0936 | 717-783-1610 | 265
State Parks
Rachel Carson State Office Bldg 400 Market St
PO Box 8551 .... Harrisburg PA 17105 | 888-727-2757 | 717-787-6640 | 338-39
Transportation Dept
400 N St .... Harrisburg PA 17120 | 800-932-4600 | 717-787-2838 | 338-39
Victims Compensation Assistance Program
PO Box 1167 .... Harrisburg PA 17108 | 800-233-2339 | 717-783-5153 | 338-39
Vital Records Div
PO Box 1528 .... New Castle PA 16103 | 844-228-3516 | 800-254-5164 | 338-39
Vocational Rehabilitation Office (OVR)
1521 N Sixth St .... Harrisburg PA 17102 | 800-442-6351 | 717-787-5244 | 338-39
Workers Compensation Bureau
1171 S Cameron St Rm 324. ...... Harrisburg PA 17104 | 800-482-2383 | 717-783-5421 | 338-39
Pennsylvania Assn of Realtors
500 North 12th St Ste 100 .... Lemoyne PA 17043 | 800-555-3390 | | 652
Pennsylvania Assn of Staff Nurses & Allied Professionals (PASNAP)
1 Fayette St Ste 475 .... Conshohocken PA 19428 | 800-500-7850 | 610-567-2907 | 529
Pennsylvania Bar Assn
100 South St .... Harrisburg PA 17101 | 800-932-0311 | 717-238-6715 | 72
Pennsylvania Chamber of Business & Industry
417 Walnut St .... Harrisburg PA 17101 | 800-225-7224 | 717-255-3252 | 140
Pennsylvania College of Art & Design
204 N Prince St .... Lancaster PA 17603 | 800-689-0379 | 717-396-7833 | 164
Pennsylvania College of Technology
1 College Ave .... Williamsport PA 17701 | 800-367-9222* | 570-326-3761 | 795
*Admissions
Pennsylvania Convention Ctr
1101 Arch St .... Philadelphia PA 19107 | 800-428-9000 | 215-418-4700 | 205
Pennsylvania Correctional Industries
PO Box 47 .... Camp Hill PA 17011 | 877-673-3724* | 717-425-7292 | 626
*General
Pennsylvania Dutch Candies
1250 Slate Hill Rd .... Camp Hill PA 17011 | 800-233-7082 | | 296-8
Pennsylvania Institute of Technology (PIT)
800 Manchester Ave .... Media PA 19063 | 800-422-0025* | 610-892-1500 | 795
*Admissions
Pennsylvania Library Assn (PaLA)
220 Cumberland Pkwy
Ste 10 .... Mechanicsburg PA 17055 | 800-622-3308 | 717-766-7663 | 434
Pennsylvania Manufacturers Assn Co
380 Sentry Pkwy .... Blue Bell PA 19422 | 800-222-2749 | | 390-4
Pennsylvania Medical Society
777 E Pk Dr .... Harrisburg PA 17111 | 800-228-7823 | 855-726-3348 | 472
Pennsylvania Medical Society (PAMED)
777 E Park Dr PO Box 8820 .... Harrisburg PA 17105 | 800-228-7823 | 717-558-7750 | 390-5
Pennsylvania Real Estate Investment Trust
200 S Broad St 3rd Fl .... Philadelphia PA 19102 | 866-875-0700 | 215-875-0700 | 651
NYSE: PEI
Pennsylvania State Athletic Commission
2601 N Third St .... Harrisburg PA 17110 | 877-868-3772 | |
Pennsylvania State Employees Credit Union
1 Innovation Way .... Harrisburg PA 17110 | 800-237-7328 | 717-255-1760 | 219
Pennsylvania State University
201 Shields Bldg .... University Park PA 16802 | 800-279-8495 | 814-865-4700 | 166
Altoona
3000 Ivyside Pk .... Altoona PA 16601 | 800-848-9843 | 814-949-5466 | 166
Beaver
100 University Dr .... Monaca PA 15061 | 877-564-6778 | 724-773-3500 | 162
DuBois 1 College Pl .... Du Bois PA 15801 | 800-346-7627 | 814-375-4700 | 162
Fayette
2201 University Dr .... Lemont Furnace PA 15456 | 877-568-4130 | 724-430-4100 | 162
Harrisburg
777 W Harrisburg Pk .... Middletown PA 17057 | 800-222-2056 | 717-948-6000 | 166
Hazleton
76 University Dr .... Hazleton PA 18202 | 800-279-8495 | 570-450-3000 | 162
Mont Alto
1 Campus Dr .... Mont Alto PA 17237 | 800-392-6173 | 717-749-6000 | 162
Shenango
147 Shenango Ave .... Sharon PA 16146 | 888-275-7009 | 724-983-2803 | 162
Pennsylvania State University at Erie
Behrend College
4701 College Dr .... Erie PA 16563 | 866-374-3378 | 814-898-6000 | 166
Pennsylvania State University Press
820 N University Dr
USB1 Ste C. .... University Park PA 16802 | 800-326-9180 | 814-865-1327 | 633-4
Pennsylvania Tool & Gages Inc
PO Box 534 .... Meadville PA 16335 | 877-827-8285 | 814-336-3136 | 752
Pennsylvania Trust Co
5 Radnor Corp Ctr Ste 450 .... Radnor PA 19087 | 800-975-4316 | 610-975-4300 | 686
Pennyrile Forest State Resort Park
20781 Pennyrile Lodge Rd
.... Dawson Springs KY 42408 | 800-325-1711 | 270-797-3421 | 561
Pennyrile Rural Electric Co-op Corp
2000 Harrison St
PO Box 2900. .... Hopkinsville KY 42241 | 800-297-4710* | 270-886-2555 | 245
*Cust Svc
Penobscot Marine Museum
5 Church St PO Box 498. .... Searsport ME 04974 | 800-268-8030 | 207-548-2529 | 517
Penobscot McCrum LLC
28 Pierce St .... Belfast ME 04915 | 800-435-4456 | 207-338-4360 | 296-21
Penray Cos Inc
440 Denniston Ct .... Wheeling IL 60090 | 800-373-6729 | 800-323-6329 | 145
Penrod Co
272 Bendix Rd Ste 550 .... Virginia Beach VA 23452 | 800-537-3497 | 757-498-0186 | 191-2
Penrose Hospital
2222 N Nevada Ave .... Colorado Springs CO 80907 | 800-398-2045 | 719-776-5000 | 373-3
Pensacola Christian College
250 Brent Ln .... Pensacola FL 32503 | 800-722-4636 | 850-478-8496 | 166
Pensacola Convention & Visitors Bureau
1401 E Gregory St .... Pensacola FL 32502 | 800-874-1234 | 850-434-1234 | 206
Pensacola Greyhound Track
951 Dog Track Rd .... Pensacola FL 32506 | 800-345-3997 | 850-455-8595 | 638
Pensacola Gulf Coast Regional Airport
2430 Airport Blvd Ste 225 .... Pensacola FL 32504 | 800-874-6580 | 850-436-5000 | 27
Pensacola Junior College
1000 College Blvd .... Pensacola FL 32504 | 888-897-3605 | 850-484-1000 | 162

	Toll-Free	Phone	Class

Warrington
5555 W Hwy 98 .... Pensacola FL 32507 | 888-897-3605 | 850-484-2200 | 162

Pension Benefit Guaranty Corp
1200 K St NW .... Washington DC 20005 | 800-400-7242* | 202-326-4000 | 339-19
*Cust Svc

Pension Rights Ctr
1350 Connecticut Ave NW
Ste 206 .... Washington DC 20036 | 866-735-7737 | 202-296-3776 | 48-6

Penske Vehicle Services Inc
1225 E Maple Rd .... Troy MI 48083 | 877-210-5290 | 248-729-5400 | 194

Penta Laboratories (PL)
7868 Deering Ave .... Canoga Park CA 91304 | 800-421-4219 | 818-882-3872 | 417

Pentacle Theater
324 52nd Ave NW .... Salem OR 97304 | 800-333-0774 | 503-364-7200 | 568

Pentagon 2000 Software Inc
15 West 34 St 5th Fl .... New York NY 10001 | 800-643-1806 | 212-629-7521 | 178-1

Pentagon Federal Credit Union
2930 Eisenhower Ave .... Alexandria VA 22314 | 800-247-5626 | | 219

Pentair
7433 Harwin Dr .... Houston TX 77036 | 800-545-6258 | | 201

Pentair
1101 Myers Pkwy .... Ashland OH 44805 | 855-274-8948 | | 637

Pentair Ltd
1351 Rt 55 .... Lagrangeville NY 12450 | 888-711-7487 | 845-463-7200 | 706

Pentair Residential Filtration LLC
20580 Enterprise Ave .... Brookfield WI 53008 | 888-784-9065 | 262-784-4490 | 91

Pentair Water Pool & Spa
1620 Hawkins Ave .... Sanford NC 27330 | 800-831-7133 | | 637

Pentax Imaging Co
633 17th St Ste 2600 .... Denver CO 80202 | 800-877-0155 | 303-799-8000 | 173-6

Pentecostal Assemblies of Canada, The (PAOC)
2450 Milltower Ct .... Mississauga ON L5N5Z6 | 800-779-7262 | 905-542-7400 | 48-20

Pentecostal Theological Seminary
900 Walker St NE .... Cleveland TN 37311 | 800-228-9126 | 423-478-1131 | 167-3

Pentecostals of Alexandria, The
2817 Rapides Ave .... Alexandria LA 71301 | 800-376-2422 | 318-487-8976 | 95

Pentel of America Ltd
2715 Columbia St .... Torrance CA 90503 | 855-528-4101 | 760-200-0547 | 567

PenTeleData
540 Delaware Ave PO Box 197 .... Palmerton PA 18071 | 800-281-3564 | | 225

Pentron Clinical Technologies LLC
1717 W Collins Ave .... Orange CA 92867 | 800-551-0283 | 714-516-7557 | 228

Pentwater Wire Products Inc (PWP)
474 Carroll St PO Box 947 .... Pentwater MI 49449 | 877-869-6911 | 231-869-6911 | 286

Pentz Design Pattern & Foundry
14823 Main St NE .... Duvall WA 98019 | 800-411-6555 | 425-788-6490 | 490

People for the American Way (PFAW)
2000 M St NW Ste 400 ...... Washington DC 20036 | 800-326-7329 | 202-467-4999 | 48-7

People for the Ethical Treatment of Animals (PETA)
501 Front St .... Norfolk VA 23510 | 800-566-9768 | 757-622-7382 | 48-3

People Lease Inc
689 Towne Ctr Blvd .... Ridgeland MS 39157 | 800-723-3025 | 601-987-3025 | 627

People Magazine
Time & Life Bldg 1271 Avenue of the Americas
28th Fl .... New York NY 10020 | 800-541-9000 | 212-522-3347 | 455-11

People Plus Industrial Inc
1095 Nebo Rd .... Madisonville KY 42431 | 888-825-1500 | 270-825-8939 | 260

People's Energy Co-op
1775 Lake Shady Ave S .... Oronoco MN 55960 | 800-214-2694 | 507-367-7000 | 245

People's Securities Inc
850 Main St .... Bridgeport CT 06604 | 800-894-0300 | | 686

People's United Bank
850 Main St Bridgeport Ctr. .... Bridgeport CT 06604 | 800-772-1090 | 203-338-7171 | 70

Peoplefit Health & Fitness Center
237 Lexington St .... Woburn MA 01801 | 855-784-4663 | 781-932-9332 | 353

Peoples Bancorp Inc
138 Putnam St .... Marietta OH 45750 | 800-374-6123 | 740-373-3155 | 359-2
NASDAQ: PEBO

Peoples Bancorp of North Carolina Inc
518 W 'C' St .... Newton NC 28658 | 800-948-7195 | 828-464-5620 | 359-2
NASDAQ: PEBK

Peoples Financial Services Corp
82 Franklin Ave .... Hallstead PA 18822 | 888-868-3858 | 570-879-2175 | 70
NASDAQ: PFIS

Peoples Gas Light & Coke Co
200 E Randolph St .... Chicago IL 60601 | 866-556-6001* | 312-744-7000 | 782
*Cust Svc

Peoples Savings Bank (PSB)
414 N Adams PO Box 248 .... Wellsburg IA 50680 | 877-508-2265 | 641-869-3721 | 70

PeopleStrategy Inc
5883 Glenridge Dr Ste 200 .... Atlanta GA 30328 | 855-488-4100 | | 178-1

People-to-People Health Foundation
255 Carter Hall Ln .... Millwood VA 22646 | 800-544-4673 | 540-837-2100 | 48-5

Peoria Area Convention & Visitors Bureau
456 Fulton St Ste 300. .... Peoria IL 61602 | 800-747-0302 | 309-676-0303 | 206

Peoria County
324 Main St Rm 101. .... Peoria IL 61602 | 800-843-6154 | 309-672-6059 | 337

PEP Filters Inc
322 Rolling Hill Rd .... Mooresville NC 28117 | 800-243-4583 | 704-662-3133 | 801

PEPCO (Professional Electric Products Co)
33210 Lakeland Blvd .... Eastlake OH 44095 | 800-872-7000 | 440-946-3790 | 246

Pepco Sales of Dallas Inc
11310 Gemini Ln .... Dallas TX 75229 | 877-737-2699 | 972-823-8700 | 608

Pepin Distributing Co
4121 N 50th St .... Tampa FL 33610 | 800-331-2829 | 813-626-6176 | 81-1

Pepin Manufacturing Inc
1875 Hwy 61 S .... Lake City MN 55041 | 800-291-6505 | 651-345-5655 | 474

Pepose Vision Institute PC
1815 Clarkson Rd .... Chesterfield MO 63017 | 877-862-2020 | 636-728-0111 | 474

Pepperball Technologies Inc
6540 Lusk Blvd Ste C137 .... San Diego CA 92121 | 877-887-3773 | 858-638-0236 | 757

Pepperdine University
24255 Pacific Coast Hwy .... Malibu CA 90263 | 800-413-0848 | 310-506-4000 | 166

Pepperell Braiding Company Inc
22 Lowell St .... Pepperell MA 01463 | 800-343-8114 | | 592

Pepperidge Farm Inc
595 Westport Ave .... Norwalk CT 06851 | 888-737-7374* | | 296-1
*PR

	Toll-Free	Phone	Class

Peppermill Hotel & Casino
2707 S Virginia St .... Reno NV 89502 | 800-648-6992 | 775-826-2121 | 133

Pepsi Bottling Ventures LLC
4141 Parklake Ave Ste 600 .... Raleigh NC 27612 | 800-662-8792 | 919-865-2300 | 296-37

PepsiCo Inc
700 Anderson Hill Rd .... Purchase NY 10577 | 800-433-2652* | 914-253-2000 | 185
NYSE: PEP ■ *PR

Pepsi-Cola Bottling Company of Yuba City Inc
750 Sutter St .... Yuba City CA 95991 | 800-433-2652 | |

Peptides International Inc
11621 Electron Dr .... Louisville KY 40299 | 800-777-4779 | 502-266-8787 | 231

Per Mar Security
1910 E Kimberly Rd .... Davenport IA 52807 | 800-473-7627 | 563-359-3200 | 688

Perantinides & Nolan Company LPa
80 S Summit St Ste 300 .... Akron OH 44308 | 800-253-5452 | 330-253-5454 | 427

Percepties Corp
9737 Cogdill Rd Ste 200 .... Knoxville TN 37932 | 800-448-8544 | | 178-12

Percival Scientific Inc
505 Research Dr .... Perry IA 50220 | 800-695-2743 | | 419

Percussion Software Inc
600 Unicorn Pk Dr .... Woburn MA 01801 | 800-283-0800 | 781-438-9900 | 178-1

Perdido Beach Resort
27200 Perdido Beach Blvd .... Orange Beach AL 36561 | 800-634-8001 | 251-981-9811 | 665

Perdue Farms Inc
31149 Old Ocean City Rd .... Salisbury MD 21804 | 800-473-7383 | 410-543-3000 | 615

Perdue Inc
5 W Forsyth St Ste 100. .... Jacksonville FL 32202 | 800-732-5857 | 904-737-5858 | 361

Peregrine Pharmaceuticals Inc
14282 Franklin Ave Ste 100 .... Tustin CA 92780 | 800-987-8256 | 714-508-6000 | 85
NASDAQ: CDMO

Peregrine Surgical Ltd
51 Britain Dr .... New Britain PA 18901 | 877-348-0456 | 215-348-0456 | 474

Perennial Public Power District
2122 S Lincoln Ave .... York NE 68467 | 800-289-0288 | 402-362-3355 | 245

Perfect Commerce Inc
1 Compass Way Ste 120. .... Newport News VA 23606 | 877-871-3788* | 757-766-8211 | 39
*Sales

Perfect Fit Placement Inc
1253 Berlin Tpke .... Berlin CT 06037 | 800-290-2168 | 860-828-3127 |

Perfect Shutters Inc
12213 Rte 173 .... Hebron IL 60034 | 800-548-3336 | 815-648-2401 | 695

Perfect Turf Inc
622 Sandpebble Dr .... Schaumburg IL 60193 | 888-796-8873 | | 597

PerfectData Corp
1323 Conshohocken Rd ...... Plymouth Meeting PA 19462 | 800-973-7332 | | 530

PerfectForms Inc
2035 Corte Del Nogal Ste 165 .... Carlsbad CA 92011 | 866-900-8588 | | 174

Perfection Clutch Co
100 Perfection Way .... Timmonsville SC 29161 | 800-258-8312 | 843-326-5544 | 60

Perforated Tubes Inc
4850 Fulton St E .... Ada MI 49301 | 888-869-5736 | 616-942-4550 | 490

Performance Contracting Group Inc
16400 College Blvd .... Lenexa KS 66219 | 800-255-6886 | 913-888-8600 | 189-10

Performance Inc
1 Performance Way .... Chapel Hill NC 27514 | 800-727-2453* | | 707
*Cust Svc

Performance Office Papers
21565 Hamburg Ave .... Lakeville MN 55044 | 800-458-7189 | | 110

Performance Stamping Company Inc
20 Lake Marian Rd .... Carpentersville IL 60110 | 800-935-0393 | 847-426-2233 | 481

Performing Animal Welfare Society (PAWS)
11435 Simmerhorn Rd .... Galt CA 95632 | 800-513-6560 | 209-745-2606 | 48-3

Pergo Inc
3128 Highwoods Blvd Ste 100 .... Raleigh NC 27604 | 800-337-3746 | 919-773-6000 | 291

Perillo Tours
577 Chestnut Ridge Rd .... Woodcliff Lake NJ 07677 | 800-431-1515 | 201-307-1234 | 755

Perio Sciences LLC
11700 Preston Rd Ste 660 .... Dallas TX 75230 | 800-915-8110 | | 473

Periodical Publishers' Service Bureau
653 W Fallbrook Ave Ste 101 .... Fresno CA 93711 | 888-206-0350 | | 317

Peripheral Dynamics Inc
5150 Campus Dr .... Plymouth Meeting PA 19462 | 800-523-0253 | 610-825-7090 | 173-7

PerkinElmer Inc
940 Winter St .... Waltham MA 02451 | 800-762-4000 | 781-663-6050 | 253
NYSE: PKI

Perkins Coie LLP
1201 Third Ave Ste 4900 .... Seattle WA 98101 | 888-720-8382 | 206-359-8000 | 427

Perkins Investment Management LLC
311 S Wacker Dr Ste 6000 .... Chicago IL 60606 | 866-922-0355 | |

Perkins Oil Company Inc
4707 Pflaum Rd .... Madison WI 53718 | 800-634-9937 | 608-221-4736 | 537

Perkinson Reprographics Inc
735 E Brill St .... Phoenix AZ 85006 | 888-330-8782 | 602-393-3131 | 623

Perkiomen School
200 Seminary St .... Pennsburg PA 18073 | 866-966-9998 | 215-679-9511 | 618

Perley-Halladay Assn Inc
1037 Andrew Dr .... West Chester PA 19380 | 800-248-5800 | 610-296-5800 | 798-2

Perlick Corp
8300 W Good Hope Rd .... Milwaukee WI 53223 | 800-558-5592 | 414-353-7060 | 660

Perma-Bound
617 E Vandalia Rd .... Jacksonville IL 62650 | 800-637-6581 | 217-243-5451 | 92

Permadur Industries Inc
186 Rt 206 S .... Hillsborough NJ 08844 | 800-392-0146 | 908-359-9767 | 385

Perma-Fix Environmental Services Inc
8302 Dunwoody Pl Ste 250 .... Atlanta GA 30350 | 800-365-6066 | 770-587-9898 | 663
NASDAQ: PESI

Perma-Glaze Inc
1638 Research Loop Rd Ste 160. .... Tucson AZ 85710 | 800-332-7397 | | 189-11

Perma-Seal Waterproofing
513 Rogers St .... Downers Grove IL 60515 | 800-421-7325 | | 186

Permatile Concrete Products Co
100 Beacon Rd .... Bristol VA 24203 | 800-662-5332 | 276-669-5332 | 135

PermaTreat Pest & Termite Control
501 Lafayette Blvd .... Fredericksburg VA 22401 | 866-737-6287 | 540-373-6655 | 192

Permatron Group
2020 Touhy Ave .... Elk Grove Village IL 60007 | 800-882-8012 | 847-434-1421 | 17

Perma-Type Company Inc
83 NW Dr .... Plainville CT 06062 | 800-243-4234 | 860-747-9999 | 475

	Toll-Free	Phone	Class
Permco Inc 1500 Frost Rd . . . . Streetsboro OH 44241	800-626-2801	330-626-2801	636
Permobil Inc 300 Duke Dr . . . . Lebanon TN 37090	800-736-0925	615-547-1889	473
Perpetual Energy Inc 605 5 Ave SW Ste 3200 . . . . Calgary AB T2P3H5	800-811-5522	403-269-4400	532
Perrigo Co 515 Eastern Ave . . . . Allegan MI 49010 *NYSE: PRGO*	800-719-9260	269-673-8451	579
Perry Baromedical Corp 3750 Prospect Ave . . . . Riviera Beach FL 33404	800-741-4376	561-840-0395	474
Perry County 333 Seventh St PO Box 721 . . . . Tell City IN 47586	888-343-6262	812-547-7933	337
Perry County 25 W Main St PO Box 37 . . . . New Bloomfield PA 17068	800-852-2102	717-582-2131	337
Perry County 105 N Main St PO Box 207. . . . . . . New Lexington OH 43764	800-282-6556	740-342-3156	337
Perry Group International 1 Market Plz Ste 3600. . . . . San Francisco CA 94105	800-580-3950		377
Perry Johnson Registrars Inc 755 W Big Beaver Rd Ste 1340. . . . . . . Southfield MI 48084	800-800-7910	248-358-3388	194
Perry Technical Institute 2011 W Washington Ave . . . . Yakima WA 98903	888-528-8586	509-453-0374	162
Perry's Ice Cream Company Inc 1 Ice Cream Plz . . . . Akron NY 14001	800-873-7797	716-542-5492	296-25
Persante Health Care Inc 200 E Park Dr Ste 600 . . . . Mt Laurel NJ 08054	800-753-3779		
Pershing County 398 Main St PO Box 89 . . . . Lovelock NV 89419	877-368-7828	775-273-2401	337
Persimmon Press Inc PO Box 297 . . . . Belmont CA 94002	800-910-5080	650-802-8325	130
Person & Covey Inc 616 Allen Ave . . . . Glendale CA 91201	800-423-2341		214
Person County Schools 304 S Morgan St . . . . Roxboro NC 27573	866-724-6650	336-599-2191	681
Personal Capital Corp 1 Circle Star Way 1st Fl . . . . San Carlos CA 94070	855-855-8005		400
Personal Finance Newsletter 7600A Leesburg Pk W Bldg Ste 300. . . . . Falls Church VA 22043	800-832-2330	703-394-4931	527-9
PersonalizeDx 2980 Scott St . . . . Vista CA 92081	855-739-5669		414
Personal-Touch Home Care Inc 186-18 Hillside Ave . . . . Jamaica NY 11432	888-275-4147	718-468-2500	362
Personnel Data Systems Inc (PDS) 470 Norrittown Rd . . . . Blue Bell PA 19422	800-243-8737	610-238-4600	178-1
Personnel Management Inc PO Box 6657 . . . . Shreveport LA 71136	800-259-4126	318-869-4555	627
Persons Majestic Mfg Co PO Box 370 . . . . Huron OH 44839	800-772-2453	419-433-9057	514
Perspectives Ltd 20 N Clark St Ste 2650 . . . . Chicago IL 60602	800-866-7556		460
Perstorp Polyols Inc 600 Matzinger Rd . . . . Toledo OH 43612 *Cust Svc	800-537-0280*	419-729-5448	144
PerSys Medical Co 5310 Elm St . . . . Houston TX 77081	888-737-7978		473
Peru *Consulate General* 3450 Wilshire Blvd . . . . Los Angeles CA 90010	855-303-7378	213-252-5910	257
Peru State College 600 Hoyt St PO Box 10. . . . . Peru NE 68421	800-742-4412	402-872-3815	166
Peru State College Library 600 Hoyt St PO Box 10. . . . . Peru NE 68421	800-742-4412	402-872-3815	433-6
Pest Shield Pest Control Inc 15329 Tradesman . . . . San Antonio TX 78249	888-728-8237	210-525-8823	573
Pet Health Pharmacy 12012 N 111th Ave . . . . Youngtown AZ 85363	800-742-0516		237
Pet Industry Joint Advisory Council (PIJAC) 1220 19th St NW Ste 400. . . . . Washington DC 20036	800-553-7387	202-452-1525	49-4
Pet Safe International 10427 Electric Ave . . . . Knoxville TN 37932 *Cust Svc	800-732-2677*	865-777-5404	574
Pet Supermarket Inc 1100 International Pkwy . . . . Sunrise FL 33323	866-434-1990	954-351-0834	574
Pet Valu Canada Inc 225 Royal Crest Crt . . . . Markham ON L3R9X6	800-845-4759	905-946-1200	574
PETA (People for the Ethical Treatment of Animals) 501 Front St . . . . Norfolk VA 23510	800-566-9768	757-622-7382	48-3
PETCO Animal Supplies Inc 9125 Rehco Rd . . . . San Diego CA 92121	877-738-6742	858-453-7845	574
Pete's Road Service Inc 2230 E Orangethorpe Ave . . . . Fullerton CA 92831	800-352-8349		
Pete's Tire Barns Inc 114 New Athol Rd . . . . Orange MA 01364	800-239-1833	978-544-8811	750
Peter Dag Portfolio Strategy & Management, The 65 Lake Front Dr . . . . Akron OH 44319	800-833-2782	330-644-2782	527-9
Peter Glenn Ski & Sports 2901 W Oakland Pk Blvd . . . . Fort Lauderdale FL 33311	800-818-0946	954-484-3606	707
Peter J Jaensch Immigration 2198 Main St . . . . Sarasota FL 34237	800-870-3676	941-366-9841	427
Peter Lang Publishing Inc 29 Broadway . . . . New York NY 10006	800-770-5264	212-647-7706	633-2
Peter Lougheed Ctr 3500 26th Ave NE . . . . Calgary AB T1Y6J4	800-282-9911	403-943-4555	373-2
Peter Pan Bus Lines PO Box 1776 . . . . Springfield MA 01102	800-343-9999		107
Peter Paul Electronics Co Inc 480 John Downey Dr . . . . New Britain CT 06051	800-825-8377	860-229-4884	784
Peter Pepper Products Inc (PPP) 17929 S Susana Rd PO Box 5769 . . . . . . Compton CA 90224	800-496-0204		587
Peter Thomas Roth Labs LLC 460 Park Ave 16th Fl . . . . New York NY 10022	800-787-7546	212-581-5800	214
Peter White Public Library 217 N Front St . . . . Marquette MI 49855	800-992-9012	906-228-9510	433-3
Peter's Choice Nutrition Center 4879 Fountain Ave . . . . Los Angeles CA 90029	888-324-9904		297-8
Petersburg Fisheries PO Box 1147 . . . . Petersburg AK 99833	877-772-4294	907-772-4294	296-13
Petersen Aluminum Corp 1005 Tonne Rd . . . . Elk Grove Village IL 60007	800-323-1960	800-722-2523	693
Petersen Inc 1527 North 2000 West . . . . Ogden UT 84404	800-410-6789	801-732-2000	357
PetersenDean Roofing & Solar 39300 Civic Center Dr Ste 300. . . . . Fremont CA 94538	877-552-4418		46
Peterson Machine Tool Inc 1100 N Union St . . . . Council Grove KS 66846	800-835-3528	620-767-6721	385
Peterson Manufacturing Co 4200 E 135th St . . . . Grandview MO 64030	800-821-3490	816-765-2000	437
Peterson Steel Corp 61 W Mountain St . . . . Worcester MA 01606	800-325-3245	508-853-3630	490
Peterson Tractor Co 955 Marina Blvd . . . . San Leandro CA 94577	800-590-5945	510-357-6200	274
Petit Jean Electric Co-op 270 Quality Dr PO Box 37. . . . . Clinton AR 72031	800-786-7618	501-745-2493	245
Petland Inc 250 Riverside St . . . . Chillicothe OH 45601	800-221-5935	740-775-2464	574
Petmate 2300 E Randol Mill Rd . . . . Arlington TX 76011	877-738-6283		574
PetMed Express Inc 1441 SW 29th Ave . . . . Pompano Beach FL 33069 *NASDAQ: PETS*	800-738-6337	954-979-5995	574
Petoskey Area Visitors Bureau 401 E Mitchell St . . . . Petoskey MI 49770	800-845-2828	231-348-2755	206
Petra 3602 West Lake Rd . . . . Erie PA 16505	866-906-2931	814-838-7197	667
Petra Manufacturing Co 6600 W Armitage Ave . . . . Chicago IL 60707	800-888-7387	773-622-1475	683
Petro Plastics Company Inc 450 S Ave . . . . Garwood NJ 07027	800-486-4738	908-789-1200	595
PetroCard Systems Inc 730 Central Ave S . . . . Kent WA 98032	800-950-3835	253-852-2777	575
Petrocco Farms 14110 Brighton Rd . . . . Brighton CO 80601	888-876-2207	303-659-6498	10-9
Petroleum Development Corp (PDC) 120 Genesis Blvd PO Box 26 . . . . Bridgeport WV 26330 *NASDAQ: PDCE*	800-624-3821	303-860-5800	532
Petroleum Heat & Power Co Inc 9 W Broad St 3rd Fl . . . . Stamford CT 06902	800-645-4328		
Petroleum Traders Corp 7120 Pointe Inverness Way . . . . Fort Wayne IN 46804	800-348-3705		575
PetroLiance LLC 739 N State St . . . . Elgin IL 60123	800-628-7231	877-738-7699	575
PETsMART Inc 19601 N 27th Ave . . . . Phoenix AZ 85027 *NASDAQ: PETM ■ *Cust Svc*	800-738-1385*	623-580-6100	574
Pettibone Michigan 1100 Superior Ave . . . . Baraga MI 49908	800-467-3884	906-353-4800	468
Pettigrew & Sons Casket Co 6151 Power Inn Rd . . . . Sacramento CA 95824	800-852-1701	916-383-0777	134
Petz Enterprises LLC 7575 W Linne Rd . . . . Tracy CA 95304 *Sales	800-345-4337*	209-835-2720	
Pevco Sys Intl Inc 1401 Tangier Dr . . . . Baltimore MD 21220	800-296-7382	410-931-8800	591
PF Chang's China Bistro 7676 E Pinnacle Peak Rd . . . . Scottsdale AZ 85255	866-732-4264	480-888-3000	666
PF Chang's China Bistro 7676 E Pinnacle Peak Rd . . . . Scottsdale AZ 85255	844-737-7333	480-888-3000	
PF Chang's China Bistro 7676 E Pinnacle Peak Rd . . . . Scottsdale AZ 85255	844-737-7333	480-888-3000	
PF Chang's China Bistro 7676 E Pinnacle Peak Rd . . . . Scottsdale AZ 85255	844-737-7333	480-888-3000	
PF Chang's China Bistro 7676 E Pinnacle Peak Rd . . . . Scottsdale AZ 85255	844-737-7333	480-888-3000	
PF Chang's China Bistro 7676 E Pinnacle Peak Rd . . . . Scottsdale AZ 85255	844-737-7333	480-888-3000	
PFA (Pedorthic Footwear Assn) 2025 M St NW Ste 800. . . . . Washington DC 20036	800-673-8447	202-367-1145	48-17
Pfaltzgraff Co PO Box 21769 . . . . York PA 17402	800-999-2811		726
PFAW (People for the American Way) 2000 M St NW Ste 400. . . . . Washington DC 20036	800-326-7329	202-467-4999	48-7
Pfeiffer University 48380 Hwy 52 N . . . . Misenheimer NC 28109	800-338-2060	704-463-1360	166
PFERD Milwaukee Brush Company Inc 30 Jytek Dr . . . . Leominster MA 01453	800-342-9015	978-840-6420	103
Pfister Hotel 424 E Wisconsin Ave . . . . Milwaukee WI 53202	800-558-8222	414-273-8222	378
Pfizer Animal Health 5 Giralda Farms . . . . Madison NJ 07940	888-963-8471		578
Pfizer Canada Inc 17300 TransCanada Hwy . . . . Kirkland QC H9J2M5	800-463-6001	514-695-0500	578
Pfizer Inc 235 E 42nd St . . . . New York NY 10017 *NYSE: PFE*	800-879-3477	212-733-2323	578
Pfizer Inc Animal Health Group 235 E 42nd St . . . . New York NY 10017	800-879-3477	212-733-2323	580
PFSweb Inc 505 Millennium Dr Ste 500 . . . . Allen TX 75013 *NASDAQ: PFSW*	888-330-5504	972-881-2900	461
PFT Alexander Inc 3250 E Grant St . . . . Signal Hill CA 90755	800-696-1331	562-595-1741	246
PG (Procter & Gamble Co) 1 Procter & Gamble Plz . . . . Cincinnati OH 45202 *NYSE: PG*	800-503-4611	513-983-1100	185
PG & E Corp 77 Beale St 24th Fl . . . . San Francisco CA 94105 *NYSE: PCG*	800-743-5000	415-267-7000	359-5
PG Life Link Inc 167 Gap Way . . . . Erlanger KY 41018	800-287-4123	859-283-5900	253
PG Publishing Co 34 Blvd of the Allies . . . . Pittsburgh PA 15222 *Cust Svc	800-228-6397*	412-263-1100	633-8
PGA National Resort & Spa 400 Ave of the Champions . . . . Palm Beach Gardens FL 33418	800-863-2819	561-227-2547	665

	Toll-Free	Phone	Class
PGA of America			
100 Ave of the Champions			
.... Palm Beach Gardens FL 33418	800-477-6465	561-624-8400	48-22
PGT			
1070 Technology Dr .... Nokomis FL 34275	800-282-6019	941-480-1600	234
PGW (Philadelphia Gas Works)			
800 W Montgomery Ave .... Philadelphia PA 19122	800-242-1776	215-235-1000	782
P&H (Parrish & Heimbecker Ltd)			
201 Portage Ave Ste 1400 ......Winnipeg MB R3B3K6	800-665-8937	204-956-2030	275
Phadia US Inc			
4169 Commercial Ave .... Portage MI 49002	800-346-4364	269-492-1940	231
Phantom Laboratory Inc, The			
2727 SR- 29 .... Greenwich NY 12834	800-525-1190	518-692-1190	664
PharmaCentra LLC			
105 Industrial Dr .... Americus GA 31719	866-395-0088		
Pharmaceutical Assoc Inc			
1700 Perimeter Rd .... Greenville SC 29605	888-233-2334	864-277-7282	231
Pharmacists Mutual Insurance Co			
808 US Hwy 18 West PO Box 370 ...Algona IA 50511	800-247-5930*		390-4
*General			
Pharmacists Society of the State of New York			
210 Washington Ave Ext ...... Albany NY 12203	800-632-8822	518-869-6595	581
Pharmacommunications Group Inc			
100 Renfrew Dr ....Markham ON L3R9R6	800-267-5409	905-477-3100	238
Pharmacy Providers of OK (PPOK)			
3000 E Memorial Rd ....Edmond OK 73013	877-557-5707		
Pharmalucence Inc			
29 Dunham Rd .... Billerica MA 01821	800-221-7554	781-275-7120	231
Pharmasave Drugs (National) Ltd			
8411 - 200th St Ste 201 .... Langley BC V2Y0E7	800-661-6106	604-455-2400	231
Pharmascience Inc			
6111 Royalmount Ave Ste 100 ... Montreal QC H4P2T4	866-853-1178	514-340-9800	231
Pharmavite LLC			
8510 Balboa Blvd Ste 100 ...Northridge CA 91325	800-423-2405	818-221-6200	
PharmEcology Associates LLC			
1001 Fannin ....Houston TX 77002	877-247-7430		192
PharMethod Inc			
1170 Wheeler Way ....Langhorne PA 19047	877-200-0736	215-354-1212	195
Pharmetics Inc			
3695 AutoRt Des Laurentides .... Laval QC H7L3H7	877-472-4433	450-682-8580	231
Phase One Inc			
200 Broadhollow Rd Ste 312 ... Melville NY 11747	888-742-7366	631-757-0400	587
Phase Technology			
6400 Youngerman Cir ....Jacksonville FL 32244	888-742-7385	904-777-0700	52
PHCC (Plumbing-Heating-Cooling Contractors NA)			
180 S Washington St			
Ste 100 .... Falls Church VA 22046	800-533-7694	703-237-8100	49-3
PHD Inc			
9009 Clubridge Dr .... Fort Wayne IN 46809	800-624-8511	260-747-6151	223
Phelan Hallinan & Schmieg LLP			
400 Fellowship Rd Ste 100........ Mount Laurel NJ 08054	800-382-8746		427
Phelps Sungas Inc			
224 Cross Rd ....Geneva NY 14456	800-458-1085	315-789-3285	316
Phenopath Laboratories PLLC			
551 North 34th St Ste 100 ...... Seattle WA 98103	888-927-4366	206-374-9000	414
PHF (Phoenix House Foundation Inc)			
164 W 74th St ....New York NY 10023	888-671-9392	646-505-2018	722
PHFCU (Pearl Harbor Federal Credit Union)			
94-449 Ukee St .... Waipahu HI 96797	800-987-5583		219
PHH Mortgage Corp			
3000 Leadenhall Rd ....Mount Laurel NJ 08054	800-210-8849		507
Phi Alpha Theta			
National History Honor Society			
4202 E Fowler Ave SOC 107 .... Tampa FL 33620	800-394-8195		48-16
Phi Delta Kappa International (PDK)			
408 N Union St .... Bloomington IN 47407	800-766-1156	812-339-1156	48-16
Phi Delta Theta			
2 S Campus Ave .... Oxford OH 45056	888-373-9855	513-523-6345	48-16
PHI Inc			
2001 SE Evangeline Thwy			
PO Box 90808 .... Lafayette LA 70508	866-815-7101	337-235-2452	358
NASDAQ: PHII			
Phi Kappa Phi Foundation			
7576 Goodwood Blvd .... Baton Rouge LA 70806	800-804-9880	225-388-4917	305
Phi Kappa Psi			
5395 Emerson Way ....Indianapolis IN 46226	800-486-1852	317-632-1852	48-16
Phi Kappa Sigma International Fraternity Inc			
2 Timber Dr .... Chester Springs PA 19425	800-344-7335	610-469-3282	48-16
Phi Mu Alpha Sinfonia Fraternity of America Inc			
10600 Old State Rd .... Evansville IN 47711	800-473-2649	812-867-2433	48-16
Phi Mu Fraternity			
400 Westpark Dr .... Peachtree City GA 30269	888-744-6824	770-632-2090	48-16
Phi Sigma Kappa International			
2925 E 96th St ....Indianapolis IN 46240	888-846-6851	317-573-5420	48-16
Phi Sigma Pi National Honor Fraternity Inc			
2119 Ambassador Cir .... Lancaster PA 17603	800-366-1916	717-299-4710	48-16
Phi Theta Kappa International Honor Society			
1625 Eastover Dr ....Jackson MS 39211	800-946-9995		48-16
Phibro Animal Health Corp			
300 Frank W Burr Blvd Ste 21 .... Teaneck NJ 07666	800-223-0434	201-329-7300	143
Phifer Inc			
4400 Kauloosa Ave			
PO Box 1700................Tuscaloosa AL 35401	800-633-5955	205-345-2120	412
Phil Long Dealerships			
1020 Motor City Dr .... Colorado Springs CO 80905	866-644-1378		57
Philadelphia College of Osteopathic Medicine (PCOM)			
4170 City Ave ....Philadelphia PA 19131	800-999-6998*	215-871-6100	795
*Admissions			
Philadelphia Consolidated Holding Corp			
231 Saint Asaph's Rd			
Ste 100 .... Bala Cynwyd PA 19004	888-647-8639	610-617-7900	390-4
Philadelphia Contributionship Insurance Co			
212 S Fourth St ....Philadelphia PA 19106	888-627-1752*	215-627-1752	390-4
*Cust Svc			
Philadelphia Gas Works (PGW)			
800 W Montgomery Ave ....Philadelphia PA 19122	800-242-1776	215-235-1000	782
Philadelphia Inquirer			
801 Market St Ste 300			
PO Box 8263 ....Philadelphia PA 19107	800-341-3413	215-854-2000	528-2
Philadelphia International Airport			
8000 Essington Ave ....Philadelphia PA 19153	800-514-0301	215-937-6937	27
Philadelphia Reserve Supply Co			
200 Mack Dr ....Croydon PA 19021	800-347-7726	215-785-3141	191-4
Philadelphia University			
4201 Henry Ave ....Philadelphia PA 19144	800-951-7287*	215-951-2800	166
*Admissions			
Philander Smith College			
900 Daisy Bates Dr .... Little Rock AR 72202	800-446-6772	501-370-5221	166
Philharmonic Ctr for the Arts			
5833 Pelican Bay Blvd ....Naples FL 34108	800-597-1900	239-597-1111	568
Philip Crosby Assoc			
306 Dartmouth St ....Boston MA 02116	877-276-7295		194
Philippi-Hagenbuch Inc			
7424 W Plank Rd .... Peoria IL 61604	800-447-6464	309-697-9200	487
Philippines			
Consulate General			
30 N Michigan Ave Ste 2100 .... Chicago IL 60602	888-259-7838	312-332-6458	257
Consulate General			
556 Fifth Ave ....New York NY 10036	866-589-1878	212-764-1330	257
Philips Healthcare			
22100 Bothell Everett Hwy ....Bothell WA 98021	888-744-5477		473
Philips Lighting Co			
200 Franklin Sq Dr .... Somerset NJ 08873	800-555-0050		436
Philips Luminaire			
776 S Green St .... Tupelo MS 38804	800-234-1890		438
Philips Medical Systems			
3000 Minuteman Rd ....Andover MA 01810	800-934-7372	978-687-1501	381
Phillip's Flower Shops Inc			
524 N Cass Ave .... Westmont IL 60559	800-356-7257	630-719-5200	292
Phillips & Company Securities Inc			
1300 SW Fifth Ave Ste 2100 ....Portland OR 97201	800-572-4765	503-224-0858	686
Phillips & Johnston Inc			
21w179 Hill Ave .... Glen Ellyn IL 60137	877-411-8823	630-469-8150	490
Phillips & Jordan Inc			
10201 Parkside Dr Ste 300............ Knoxville TN 37922	800-955-0876	865-688-8342	189-5
Phillips & Temro Industries			
9700 W 74th St ....Eden Prairie MN 55344	800-328-6108	952-941-9700	60
Phillips & Webster Pllc Attys			
17410 133rd Ave NE Ste 301 .... Woodinville WA 98072	800-708-6000	425-482-1111	427
Phillips Academy			
180 Main St ....Andover MA 01810	877-445-5477	978-749-4000	618
Phillips Bros Electrical Contractors Inc			
235 Sweet Spring Rd ....Glenmoore PA 19343	800-220-5051		189-4
Phillips Buick-Pontiac-Gmc Truck Inc			
2160 US Hwy 441 .... Fruitland Park FL 34731	888-664-7454	352-728-1212	57
Phillips Community College			
1000 Campus Dr PO Box 785...........Helena AR 72342	800-582-6953	870-338-6474	162
Phillips Corp			
7390 Coca Cola Dr ....Hanover MD 21076	800-878-4242	410-564-2929	491
Phillips Distributing Corp			
3010 Nob Hill Rd .... Madison WI 53713	800-236-7269	608-222-9177	81-3
Phillips Distribution Inc			
3000 E Houston St ....San Antonio TX 78219	800-580-2397	210-227-2397	555
Phillips Exeter Academy			
20 Main St ....Exeter NH 03833	800-245-2525	603-772-4311	618
Phillips Group			
501 Fulling Mill Rd .... Middletown PA 17057	800-538-7500	717-944-0400	531
Phillips Machine Service Inc			
367 George St .... Beckley WV 25801	800-733-1521	304-255-0537	385
Phillips Manufacturing Co			
4949 S 30th St ....Omaha NE 68107	800-822-5055	402-339-3800	234
Phillips Mushroom Farms Inc			
1011 Kaolin Rd .... Kennett Square PA 19348	800-722-8818		10-6
Phillips Plywood Company Inc			
13599 Desmond St .... Pacoima CA 91331	800-649-6410*	818-897-7736	609
*Cust Svc			
Phillips Syrup Corp			
28025 Ranney Pkwy .... Westlake OH 44145	800-350-8443	440-835-8001	296-15
Phillips Theological Seminary			
901 N Mingo Rd .... Tulsa OK 74116	800-843-4675	918-610-8303	167-3
Phillips, Hager & North Investment Management Ltd			
200 Burrard St 20th Fl .... Vancouver BC V6C3N5	800-661-6141		524
Philosophy Inc			
3809 E Watkins .... Phoenix AZ 85034	800-568-3151		214
Philotechnics Ltd			
201 Renovare Blvd .... Oak Ridge TN 37830	888-723-9278	865-483-1551	271
Phoebe Putney Memorial Hospital			
417 W Third Ave ....Albany GA 31701	866-514-0015	229-312-1000	373-3
Phoenician, The			
6000 E Camelback Rd .... Scottsdale AZ 85251	800-888-8234	480-941-8200	665
Phoenix AMD International Inc			
41 Butler Ct .... Bowmanville ON L1C4P8	800-661-7313		360
Phoenix American Inc			
2401 Kerner Blvd .... San Rafael CA 94901	866-895-5050		216
Phoenix Cable Inc (PCI)			
10801 N 24th Ave Ste 115-116 ...... Phoenix AZ 85029	833-807-3855	602-870-8870	
Phoenix Children's Hospital			
1919 E Thomas Rd .... Phoenix AZ 85016	888-908-5437	602-546-1000	373-1
Phoenix College			
1202 W Thomas Rd .... Phoenix AZ 85013	800-266-7845	602-285-7777	162
Phoenix Company of Chicago Inc, The			
22 Great Hill Rd .... Naugatuck CT 06770	800-323-9562	203-729-9090	
Phoenix Controls			
75 Discovery Way ....Acton MA 01720	800-340-0007	978-795-3400	202
Phoenix Environmental Laboratories Inc			
587 Middle Tpke E .... Manchester CT 06040	800-827-5426	860-645-3513	738
Phoenix Flower Shops			
5733 E Thomas Rd Ste 4 ...... Scottsdale AZ 85251	888-311-0404	480-289-4000	292
Phoenix Footwear Group Inc			
5937 Darwin Ct Ste 109 ...... Carlsbad CA 92008	877-282-1168*	760-602-9688	301
*OTC: PXFG ■ *Investor Rel			
Phoenix Forging Company Inc			
800 Front St .... Catasauqua PA 18032	800-444-3674	610-264-2861	481
Phoenix Grand Hotel Salem			
201 Liberty St SE .... Salem OR 97301	877-540-7800	503-540-7800	378
Phoenix Home Care Inc			
3033 S Kansas Expy ....Springfield MO 65807	855-881-7442	417-881-7442	362

	Toll-Free	Phone	Class
Phoenix House Foundation Inc (PHF)			
164 W 74th St ....New York NY 10023	**888-671-9392**	646-505-2018	722
Phoenix Integration Inc			
1715 Pratt Dr Ste 2000...........Blacksburg VA 24060	**800-500-1936**	540-961-7215	
Phoenix International Freight Services Ltd			
1996-2018 CH Robinson Worldwide			
.....................Eden Prairie MN 55347	**855-229-6128**	855-350-0014	311
Phoenix Leasing Inc			
2401 Kerner Blvd ....San Rafael CA 94901	**866-895-5050**		216
Phoenix Magazine			
15169 N Scottsdale Ste 310 ....Scottsdale AZ 85254	**866-481-6970**	480-664-3960	455-22
Phoenix Manufacturing Inc			
3655 E Roeser Rd ....Phoenix AZ 85040	**800-325-6952***	602-437-4833	14
*Cust Svc			
Phoenix Metals Co			
4685 Buford Hwy ....Norcross GA 30071	**800-241-2290**	770-447-4211	490
Phoenix Park 'n Swap			
3801 E Washington St ....Phoenix AZ 85034	**800-772-0852**	602-273-1250	271
Phoenix Park Hotel			
520 N Capitol St ....Washington DC 20001	**800-824-5419**	202-638-6900	378
Phoenix Pharmaceuticals Inc			
330 Beach Rd ....Burlingame CA 94010	**800-988-1205**	650-558-8898	231
Phoenix Seminary			
4222 E Thomas Rd Ste 400 ....Phoenix AZ 85018	**888-443-1020**	602-850-8000	167-3
Phoenix Sky Harbor International Airport			
3400 E Sky Harbor Blvd Ste 3300........Phoenix AZ 85034	**800-781-1010**	602-273-3300	27
Phoenix Society for Burn Survivors Inc			
1835 RW Berends Dr SW ....Grand Rapids MI 49519	**800-888-2876**	616-458-2773	48-17
Phoenix Symphony			
1 N First St Ste 200 ....Phoenix AZ 85004	**800-776-9080**	602-495-1117	569-3
Phoenix Technologies Ltd			
915 Murphy Ranch Rd ....Milpitas CA 95035	**800-677-7305**	408-570-1000	178-12
Phoenix Transportation Services LLC			
335 E Yusen Dr ....Georgetown KY 40324	**800-860-0889**	502-863-0108	775
Phoenix Tube Company Inc			
1185 Win Dr ....Bethlehem PA 18017	**800-526-2124**	610-865-5337	490
Phoenix USA Inc			
51 E Borden St ....Cookeville TN 38501	**800-786-8785**		
Phone Ware Inc			
8902 Activity Rd ....San Diego CA 92126	**800-243-8329**	858-459-3000	317
Phonio Ear Inc			
2080 Lakeville Hwy ....Petaluma CA 94954	**800-227-0735**	707-769-1110	475
Photo Researchers Inc			
307 Fifth Ave 3rd Fl ....New York NY 10016	**800-833-9033**	212-758-3420	589
Photofabrication Engineering Inc (PEI)			
500 Fortune Blvd ....Milford MA 01757	**800-253-8518**	508-478-2025	
Photronics Inc			
15 Secor Rd ....Brookfield CT 06804	**800-292-9396**	203-775-9000	692
NASDAQ: PLAB			
PHP (Parents Helping Parents)			
1400 Parkmoor Ave Ste 100...........San jose CA 95126	**855-727-5775**	408-727-5775	48-6
Phunware Inc			
7800 Shoal Creek Blvd ....Austin TX 78757	**855-521-8485**		177
PHX Energy Services Corp			
1400-250 2 St SW ....Calgary AB T2P0C1	**800-909-9819**	403-543-4466	532
Phygen LLC			
2301 Dupont Ave Ste 110..............Irvine CA 92612	**800-939-7008**	949-752-7885	475
Phyle Inventory Control Specialists Inc			
4150 Grange Hall Rd ....Holly MI 48442	**888-303-8482**		392
Physician Insurers Assn of America (PIAA)			
2275 Research Blvd Ste 250..........Rockville MD 20850	**800-688-2421**	301-947-9000	49-9
Physician's Automated Laboratory Inc (PALLAB)			
9830 Brimhall Rd ....Bakersfield CA 93312	**800-675-2271**	661-829-2260	417
Physicians Committee for Responsible Medicine (PCRM)			
5100 Wisconsin Ave NW			
Ste 400..................Washington DC 20016	**866-416-7276**	202-686-2210	49-8
Physicians Laboratory Services Inc			
4840 "F" St ....Omaha NE 68117	**800-642-1117**	402-731-4145	414
Physicians Mutual Insurance Co			
2600 Dodge St ....Omaha NE 68131	**800-228-9100**	402-633-1000	390-2
Physicians Plus Insurance Corp			
2650 Novation Pkwy ....Madison WI 53713	**800-545-5015**	608-282-8900	390-3
Physicians Weight Loss Centers of America Inc			
395 Springside Dr ....Akron OH 44333	**800-205-7887**		805
Physio-Control Inc			
11811 Willows Rd NE ....Redmond WA 98052	**800-442-1142**	425-867-4000	250
Physmark Inc			
101 E Pk Blvd Ste 600 ....Plano TX 75074	**800-922-7060**	972-231-8000	179
PIA (Pakistan International Airlines Corp)			
1200 New Jersey Ave SE ....Washington DC 20590	**800-578-6786**		25
PIA (Pittsburgh Institute of Aeronautics)			
5 Allegheny County Airport			
.....................West Mifflin PA 15122	**800-444-1440**	412-346-2100	795
PIA/GATF (Printing Industries of America/Graphic Arts Techni)			
200 Deer Run Rd ....Sewickley PA 15143	**800-910-4283**	412-741-6860	49-16
PIAA (Physician Insurers Assn of America)			
2275 Research Blvd Ste 250..........Rockville MD 20850	**800-688-2421**	301-947-9000	49-9
Piad Precision Casting Corp			
112 Industrial Pk Rd ....Greensburg PA 15601	**800-441-9858**	724-838-5500	308
Piantedosi Baking Company Inc			
240 Commercial St ....Malden MA 02148	**800-339-0080**	781-321-3400	296-1
Pibbs Industries			
133-15 32nd Ave ....Flushing NY 11354	**800-551-5020**	718-445-8046	76
PIC Business Systems Inc			
5119 Beckwith Blvd Ste 106........San Antonio TX 78249	**800-742-7378**		177
Pic Design Corp			
86 Benson Rd PO Box 1004 ....Middlebury CT 06762	**800-243-6125**	203-758-8272	616
PIC Skate			
22 Village Dr ....Riverside RI 02915	**800-882-3448**	401-490-9334	706
PIC USA			
100 Bluegrass Commons Blvd			
Ste 2200...................Hendersonville TN 37075	**800-325-3398**		10-5
Piccadilly Circus Pizza			
1007 Okoboji Ave PO Box 188 ....Milford IA 51351	**800-338-4340**		666
Picco Engineering			
8611 Jane St Ste 200.............Concord ON L4K2M6	**888-772-0773**	905-760-9688	261
Pick N Save			
6950 W State St ....Wauwatosa WI 53213	**800-576-4377**	414-475-7181	
Pick Your Part Auto Wrecking Inc			
1235 S Beach Blvd ....Anaheim CA 92804	**800-962-2277**		54
Pickaway County District Public Library			
1160 North Court St ....Circleville OH 43113	**800-733-2767**	740-477-1644	433-3
Pickens Snodgrass Koch & Company PC			
3001 Medlin Dr Ste 100.............Arlington TX 76015	**800-424-5790**	817-664-3000	2
Pickens-Kane Moving Co			
410 N Milwaukee Ave ....Chicago IL 60610	**888-871-9998**	312-942-0330	516
Pickett County			
1 Courthouse Sq Ste 200 ....Byrdstown TN 38549	**888-406-4704**	931-864-3798	337
Pickett State Park			
4605 Pickett Pk Hwy ....Jamestown TN 38556	**877-260-0010**	931-879-5821	561
PickPoint			
3149 Skyway Ct Ste 101..............Fremont CA 94539	**800-636-1288**	925-924-1700	473
Pickrel Schaeffer & Ebeling			
40 N Main St - Kettering Tower ....Dayton OH 45423	**800-908-4490**	937-223-1130	427
Pickwick Co			
4200 Thomas Dr SW ....Cedar Rapids IA 52404	**800-397-9797**		693
Pickwick Electric Co-op			
672 HWY 142 ....Selmer TN 38375	**800-372-8258**	731-645-3411	245
PICO Holdings Inc			
7979 Ivanhoe Ave Ste 300 ....La Jolla CA 92037	**888-389-3222**	858-456-6022	359-4
NASDAQ: PICO			
Pics Telecom International Corp			
1920 Lyell Ave ....Rochester NY 14606	**800-521-7427**	585-295-2000	730
Piedmont Baptist College			
420 S Broad St ....Winston-Salem NC 27101	**800-937-5097***	336-725-8344	166
*Admissions			
Piedmont College			
165 Central Ave ....Demorest GA 30535	**800-277-7020**	706-776-0103	166
Piedmont Community Health Plan Inc			
2512 Langhorne Rd ....Lynchburg VA 24501	**800-400-7247**	434-947-4463	389
Piedmont Electric Membership Corp			
2500 No 86 PO Box 1179..........Hillsborough NC 27278	**800-222-3107**	919-732-2123	
Piedmont Gardens			
110 41st St ....Oakland CA 94611	**800-496-8126**	510-596-2600	668
Piedmont Medical Ctr			
222 S Herlong Ave ....Rock Hill SC 29732	**800-222-4218**	803-329-1234	373-3
Piedmont Natural Gas			
4720 Piedmont Row Dr			
PO Box 33068..................Charlotte NC 28233	**800-752-7504**	704-364-3120	782
NYSE: PNY			
Piedmont Technical College			
620 N Emerald Rd ....Greenwood SC 29646	**800-868-5528**		795
Piedmont Truck Tires Inc			
PO Box 18228 ....Greensboro NC 27419	**800-274-8473**	336-668-0091	750
Pier 1 Imports Inc			
100 Pier 1 Pl ....Fort Worth TX 76102	**800-245-4595**	817-252-8000	361
NYSE: PIR			
Pier 1 Kids			
100 Pier 1 Pl ....Fort Worth TX 76102	**800-433-4035**	817-252-8000	321
Pier 5 Hotel			
711 Eastern Ave ....Baltimore MD 21202	**866-583-4162**	410-539-2000	378
Pier House Resort Caribbean Spa			
1 Duval St ....Key West FL 33040	**800-723-2791**	305-296-4600	665
Pieratt's			
110 Mt Tabor Rd ....Lexington KY 40517	**855-743-7288**	859-268-6000	35
Pierce College			
Puyallup			
1601 39th Ave SE ....Puyallup WA 98374	**877-353-6763**	253-840-8400	162
Pierce County Library System			
3005 112th St E ....Tacoma WA 98446	**800-346-0995**	253-548-3300	433-3
Pierce County Security Inc			
2002 99th St E ....Tacoma WA 98445	**800-773-4432**	253-535-4433	689
Pierce Distribution Services Co			
PO Box 15600 ....Loves Park IL 61132	**800-466-7397**		447
Pierce Mfg Inc			
2600 American Dr PO Box 2017..........Appleton WI 54912	**888-974-3723***	920-832-3000	513
*Cust Svc			
Pierce Pacific Manufacturing Inc			
4424 NE 158th PO Box 30509 ....Portland OR 97294	**800-760-3270**	503-808-9110	190
Pierce Pepin Co-op Services			
W7725 US Hwy 10 PO Box 420 ....Ellsworth WI 54011	**800-924-2133**	715-273-4355	245
Pierce Transit			
3701 96th St SW PO Box 99070........Lakewood WA 98499	**800-562-8109**	253-581-8000	466
Pierre Area Chamber of Commerce			
800 W Dakota Ave ....Pierre SD 57501	**800-962-2034**	605-224-7361	139
Pigeon Forge Dept of Tourism			
PO Box 1390 ....Pigeon Forge TN 37868	**800-251-9100**	865-453-8574	206
Piggly Wiggly Carolina Company Inc			
176 Croghan Spur Rd Ste 301 ....Charleston SC 29407	**800-243-9880**	843-554-9880	344
PIJAC (Pet Industry Joint Advisory Council)			
1220 19th St NW Ste 400...........Washington DC 20036	**800-553-7387**	202-452-1525	49-4
Pike County			
506 Broad St ....Milford PA 18337	**866-681-4947**	570-296-7613	337
Pike County Chamber of Commerce			
201 Broad St Ste 2 ....Milford PA 18337	**877-345-0691**	570-296-8700	
Pike Industries Inc			
3 Eastgate Pk Rd ....Belmont NH 03220	**800-283-0803**	603-527-5100	188-4
Pike Lumber Company Inc			
PO Box 247 ....Akron IN 46910	**800-356-4554**	574-893-4511	679
Pike Outlets, The			
1126 Queens Hwy ....Long Beach CA 90802	**877-225-5337**		
Pikes Peak Community College			
Centennial			
5675 S Academy Blvd ....Colorado Springs CO 80906	**800-456-6847**	719-502-2000	162
Downtown Studio			
100 W Pikes Peak Ave ......Colorado Springs CO 80903	**800-456-6847**	719-502-2000	162
Rampart Range			
11195 Hwy 83 ....Colorado Springs CO 80921	**800-456-6847**	719-502-2000	162
Pikeville College			
147 Sycamore St ....Pikeville KY 41501	**866-232-7700**	606-218-5250	166
Pilat			
460 US Hwy 22 W			
Ste 408 ....Whitehouse Station NJ 08889	**800-338-9701**		
Pilgrim Bank			
2401 S Jefferson Ave ....Mount Pleasant TX 75455	**877-303-3111**	903-575-2150	70
Pilgrim Home & Hearth Alliance LLC			
5600 Imhoff Dr Ste G ....Concord CA 94520	**800-227-1044**		

				Toll-Free	Phone	Class
Pilgrim Psychiatric Ctr						
998 Crooked Hill Rd	West Brentwood	NY	11717	**800-597-8481**	631-761-3500	373-5
Pilgrim Tours & Travel Inc						
3071 Main St PO Box 268	Morgantown	PA	19543	**800-322-0788**	610-286-0788	755
Pillar Induction Co						
21905 Gateway Rd	Brookfield	WI	53045	**800-558-7733**	262-317-5300	318
Pillar Technology Group LLC						
301 E Liberty St Ste 700	Ann Arbor	MI	48104	**888-374-5527**		804
Piller Inc						
45 Turner Rd	Middletown	NY	10941	**800-597-6937**		515
Pilling Surgical						
2917 Weck Dr	Research Triangle Park	NC	27709	**866-246-6990***	919-544-8000	474
*Cust Svc						
Pilot Travel Centers LLC						
5508 Lonas Dr	Knoxville	TN	37939	**800-562-6210**	865-938-1439	324
Pilot Tribune						
PO Box 1187	Storm Lake	IA	50588	**800-447-1985**	712-732-3130	528-2
Pima Community College						
401 N Bonita Ave	Tucson	AZ	85709	**800-860-7462**	520-206-2733	162
West 2202 W Anklam Rd	Tucson	AZ	85709	**800-860-7462**	520-206-6600	162
Pima County Public Library						
101 N Stone Ave	Tucson	AZ	85701	**877-705-5437**	520-791-4010	433-3
Pima Medical Institute						
3350 E Grant Rd Ste 200	Tucson	AZ	85716	**888-556-7334**	520-326-1600	505
PIMCO Institutional Funds						
PO Box 219024	Kansas City	MO	64121	**800-927-4648**		524
Pimlico Race Course						
5201 Park Heights Ave	Baltimore	MD	21215	**800-638-1859**	410-542-9400	133
Pinchin Group, The						
2470 Milltower Ct	Mississauga	ON	L5N7W5	**855-746-2446**	905-363-0678	
Pindler & Pindler Inc						
11910 Poindexter Ave	Moorpark	CA	93021	**800-669-6002**	805-531-9090	194
Pine Bluff Convention & Visitors Bureau (PBCVB)						
1 Convention Ctr Plz	Pine Bluff	AR	71601	**800-536-7660**	870-536-7600	206
Pine Bluff Cotton Belt Federal Credit Union						
1703 River Pines Blvd	Pine Bluff	AR	71601	**888-249-1904**	870-535-6365	219
Pine Butte Guest Ranch						
351 S Fork Rd	Choteau	MT	59422	**877-812-3698**	800-628-6860	239
Pine County						
635 Northridge Dr NW	Pine City	MN	55063	**800-450-7463**	320-591-1400	337
Pine Crest Inn						
85 Pine Crest Ln	Tryon	NC	28782	**800-633-3001**	828-859-9135	378
Pine Grove Furnace State Park						
1100 Pine Grove Rd	Gardners	PA	17324	**888-727-2757**	717-486-7174	561
Pine Hall Brick Co						
2701 Shorefair Dr	Winston-Salem	NC	27105	**800-334-8689**		150
Pine Manor College						
400 Heath St	Chestnut Hill	MA	02467	**800-762-1357**	617-731-7104	166
Pine Mountain State Resort Park						
1050 State Pk Rd	Pineville	KY	40977	**800-325-1712**		561
Pine Needles Lodge & Golf Club						
PO Box 88	Southern Pines	NC	28388	**800-747-7272**	910-692-7111	665
Pine Pointe Hospice & Palliative Care						
6261 Peak Rd	Macon	GA	31210	**800-211-1084**	478-633-5660	370
Pine Rest Christian Mental Health Services						
300 68th St SE PO Box 165	Grand Rapids	MI	49501	**800-678-5500**	616-455-5000	373-5
Pine Ridge Winery LLC						
5901 Silverado Trl	Napa	CA	94558	**800-575-9777**		80-3
Pine Run Community						
777 Ferry Rd	Doylestown	PA	18901	**800-992-8992**	215-345-9000	668
Pine State Trading Co						
100 Enterprise Ave	Gardiner	ME	04345	**800-452-4633**		81-1
Pineapple Hospitality Co						
155 108th Ave NE	Bellevue	WA	98004	**866-866-7977**		703
Pinehurst Southern Pines Aberdeen Area						
165 NE Broad St	Southern Pines	NC	28387	**800-346-5362**	910-692-6926	206
Pineland Telephone Cooperative Inc						
30 S Rountree St	Metter	GA	30439	**800-247-1266**	912-685-2121	386
Pinellas County						
333 Chestnut St	Clearwater	FL	33756	**800-806-5154**	727-464-3485	337
Pines at Davidson						
400 Avinger Ln	Davidson	NC	28036	**877-574-8203**	704-896-1100	668
Pines Bach						
122 W Washington Ave Ste 900	Madison	WI	53703	**866-443-8661**	608-807-0752	427
Pines Resort, The						
103 Shore Rd	Digby	NS	B0V1A0	**800-667-4637**		665
Pines Technology						
30505 Clemens Rd	Westlake	OH	44145	**800-207-2840**	440-835-5553	492
Pinestar Technology Inc						
1000 E Jamestown Rd	Jamestown	PA	16134	**800-682-2226**	724-932-2121	
Pinestone Resort						
4252 County Rd Ste 21	Haliburton	ON	K0M1S0	**800-461-0357**	705-457-1800	665
Ping Inc						
2201 W Desert Cove Ave						
PO Box 82000	Phoenix	AZ	85071	**800-474-6434**	602-687-5000	706
Pinnacle Business Finance Inc						
914 A St Ste 200	Tacoma	WA	98402	**800-566-1993**	253-284-5600	216
Pinnacle Business Systems Inc						
3824 S Blvd St Ste 200	Edmond	OK	73013	**800-311-0757**		225
Pinnacle Communications Corp						
19821 Executive Park Cir	Germantown	MD	20874	**800-644-9101**	301-601-0777	386
Pinnacle Corp, The						
201A E Abram St	Arlington	TX	76010	**800-325-3535**	817-795-5555	179
Pinnacle Entertainment Inc						
3980 Howard Hughes Pkwy	Las Vegas	NV	89169	**877-764-8750**	702-541-7777	132
NYSE: PNK						
Pinnacle Health Hospital at Community General						
4300 Londonderry Rd	Harrisburg	PA	17109	**888-782-5678**	717-652-3000	373-3
Pinnacle Inn Resort						
301 Pinnacle Inn Rd	Beech Mountain	NC	28604	**800-405-7888**	828-387-2231	665
Pinnacle Management Systems Inc						
2140 East Southlake Blvd						
Ste L-803	Southlake	TX	76092	**888-975-1119**	703-382-9161	194
Pinnacle Staffing Inc						
PO Box 17589	Greenville	SC	29606	**888-297-4212**		717
Pinnacle West Capital Corp						
400 N Fifth St	Phoenix	AZ	85004	**800-457-2983**	602-250-1000	359-5
NYSE: PNW						
PinnacleCart Inc						
3320 W Cheryl Dr Ste B200	Phoenix	AZ	85051	**800-506-0398**		225
Pinnacles National Monument						
5000 Hwy 146	Paicines	CA	95043	**877-444-6777**	831-389-4485	560
Pinnacol Assurance						
7501 E Lowry Blvd	Denver	CO	80230	**800-873-7242**	303-361-4000	390-4
Pinpoint Technologies						
17802 Irvine Blvd Ste 215	Tustin	CA	92780	**866-603-7770**	714-505-7600	461
Pintoresco Advisors LLC						
466 Foothill Blvd						
Ste 333	La Canada Flintridge	CA	91011	**866-217-1140**	213-223-2070	70
Pinyon Environmental Inc						
3222 S Vance St Unit 200	Lakewood	CO	80227	**888-641-7337**	303-980-5200	461
Pioneer Bank						
21 Second St	Troy	NY	12180	**866-873-9573**	518-274-4800	71
Pioneer Broach Co						
6434 Telegraph Rd	Los Angeles	CA	90040	**800-621-1945**	323-728-1263	453
Pioneer Clubs						
123 E Elk	Carol Stream	IL	60188	**800-694-2582**		148
Pioneer Construction Company Inc						
550 Kirtland St SW	Grand Rapids	MI	49507	**800-861-0874**	616-247-6966	186
Pioneer Credit Recovery Inc						
26 Edward St	Arcade	NY	14009	**800-836-2442**	585-492-1234	160
Pioneer Electric Co-op						
300 Herbert St	Greenville	AL	36037	**800-239-3092**	334-382-6636	245
Pioneer Electric Co-op						
344 W US Rt 36	Piqua	OH	45356	**800-762-0997**	937-773-2523	245
Pioneer Electronics (USA) Inc						
1925 E Dominguez St	Long Beach	CA	90810	**800-421-1404**	310-952-2000	52
Pioneer Golf Inc						
609 Castle Ridge Rd Ste 335	Austin	TX	78746	**800-262-5725**	512-327-2680	755
Pioneer Hi-Bred International Inc						
PO Box 1000	Johnston	IA	50131	**800-247-6803**	515-535-3200	10-4
Pioneer Long Distance Inc						
PO Box 539	Kingfisher	OK	73750	**888-782-2667**		731
Pioneer Magnetics						
1745 Berkeley St	Santa Monica	CA	90404	**800-269-6426**	310-829-6751	392
Pioneer Metal Finishing LLC						
486 Globe Ave	Green Bay	WI	54304	**877-721-1100**		479
Pioneer Mfg						
4529 Industrial Pkwy	Cleveland	OH	44135	**800-877-1500**	216-671-5500	546
Pioneer Natural Resources Co						
5205 N O'Connor Blvd Ste 200	Irving	TX	75039	**888-234-6372**	972-444-9001	532
NYSE: PXD						
Pioneer Paper Stock						
155 Irving Ave N	Minneapolis	MN	55405	**800-821-8512**	612-374-2280	656
Pioneer Steel Corp						
7447 Intervale St	Detroit	MI	48238	**800-999-9440**	313-933-9400	490
Pioneer Telephone Assn Inc						
PO Box 707	Ulysses	KS	67880	**800-308-7536**	620-356-3211	731
Pioneer Telephone Co-op Inc						
202 W Broadway Ave						
PO Box 539	Kingfisher	OK	73750	**888-782-2667**		731
Pioneer Tool & Forge Inc						
101 Sixth St	New Kensington	PA	15068	**800-359-6408**	724-337-4700	754
Pioneer Transfer LLC						
2034 S St Aubin St						
PO Box 2567	Sioux City	IA	51106	**800-325-4650**	712-274-2946	311
Pioneer Wholesale Co						
500 W Bagley Rd	Berea	OH	44017	**888-234-5400**	440-234-5400	44
Pioneer/Eclipse Corp						
1 Eclipse Rd	Sparta	NC	28675	**800-367-3550***	336-372-8080	385
*Cust Svc						
Pioneers Medical Ctr						
100 Pioneers Medical Center Dr	Meeker	CO	81641	**800-332-1168**	970-878-5047	362
Pioneers Volunteer						
1801 California St Ste 225	Denver	CO	80202	**800-872-5995**	303-571-1200	48-15
Pipe & Tube Supply Inc						
1407 N Cypress	North Little Rock	AR	72114	**800-770-8823**	501-372-6556	385
Pipeline & Hazardous Materials Safety Administration						
Office of Hazardous Materials Safety						
1200 New Jersey Ave SE	Washington	DC	20590	**800-467-4922**	202-366-4433	339-16
Piper Jaffray Cos						
800 Nicollet Mall Ste 1000	Minneapolis	MN	55402	**800-333-6000**		686
NYSE: PJC						
Piper Products Inc						
300 S 84th Ave	Wausau	WI	54401	**800-544-3057**	715-842-2724	298
Pipestone Publishing Co						
PO Box 277	Pipestone	MN	56164	**800-325-6440**	507-825-3333	633-8
Pipestone Veterinary Clinic LLC						
1300 Hwy 75 S PO Box 188	Pipestone	MN	56164	**800-658-2523**	507-825-4211	789
Piping & Equipment Inc						
9100 Canniff St	Houston	TX	77017	**888-889-9683**	713-947-9393	384
Piping Technology & Products Inc						
3701 Holmes Rd PO Box 34506	Houston	TX	77051	**866-746-9172**	713-731-0030	591
Pipkins Inc						
14515 N Outer 40 Rd						
Ste 130	Chesterfield	MO	63017	**800-469-6106**	314-469-6106	177
Piranha Marketing Inc						
4440 S Rural Rd Bldg F	Tempe	AZ	85282	**800-275-2643**	480-858-0008	195
PIREL Inc						
1315 Rue Gay-Lussac	Boucherville	QC	J4B7K1	**800-449-5199**	450-449-5199	180
Pismo Coast Village RV Resort						
165 S Dolliver St	Pismo Beach	CA	93449	**888-782-3224**	805-755-5406	
PIT (Pennsylvania Institute of Technology)						
800 Manchester Ave	Media	PA	19063	**800-422-0025***	610-892-1500	795
*Admissions						
Pitmar Tours						
7549 140th St Ste 9	Surrey	BC	V3W5J9	**877-596-9670**	604-596-9670	755
Pitney Bowes Group 1 Software						
4200 Parliament Pl Ste 600	Lanham	MD	20706	**800-367-6950**	301-731-2300	178-1
Pitney Bowes inc						
3001 Summer St	Stamford	CT	06926	**844-256-6444**	203-356-5000	461
Pitt Ohio Express						
15 27th St	Pittsburgh	PA	15222	**800-366-7488***	412-232-3015	775
*Cust Svc						
Pitt Plastics Inc						
1400 Atkinson Ave	Pittsburg	KS	66762	**800-835-0366**	620-231-4337	66

Name / Address	City	State	ZIP	Toll-Free	Phone	Class
Pittcon 300 Penn Ctr Blvd Ste 332	Pittsburgh	PA	15235	**800-825-3221**	412-825-3220	184
Pittenger & Anderson Inc 5533 S 27th St Ste 201	Lincoln	NE	68512	**800-897-1588**	402-328-8800	400
Pittsburg State University 1701 S Broadway St	Pittsburg	KS	66762	**800-854-7488**	620-235-4251	166
Pittsburg Wholesale Groceries Inc 727 Kennedy St	Oakland	CA	94606	**800-200-4244**		344
Pittsburgh City Hall 414 Grant St City-County Bldg	Pittsburgh	PA	15219	**800-932-0313**	412-255-2883	336
Pittsburgh Foundation, The 5 PPG Pl Ste 250	Pittsburgh	PA	15222	**800-392-6900**	412-391-5122	303
Pittsburgh Institute of Aeronautics (PIA) 5 Allegheny County Airport	West Mifflin	PA	15122	**800-444-1440**	412-346-2100	795
Pittsburgh International Airport Landside Terminal 4th Fl Mezz PO Box 12370	Pittsburgh	PA	15231	**888-429-5377**	412-472-3500	27
Pittsburgh Pirates 115 Federal St PO Box 7000	Pittsburgh	PA	15212	**800-289-2827**	412-321-2827	709
Pittsburgh Supercomputing Ctr 300 S Craig St	Pittsburgh	PA	15213	**800-221-1641**	412-268-4960	664
Pittsburgh Symphony Orchestra 600 Penn Ave	Pittsburgh	PA	15222	**800-743-8560**	412-392-4900	569-3
Pittsburgh Technical College (PTI) 1111 McKee Rd	Oakdale	PA	15071	**800-784-9675**	412-809-5100	795
Pittsburgh Theological Seminary 616 N Highland Ave	Pittsburgh	PA	15206	**800-451-4194**	412-362-5610	167-3
Pittsburgh Tribune-Review 503 Martindale St Ste 300	Pittsburgh	PA	15212	**800-909-8742**	412-321-6460	528-2
Pittsylvania County Schools 39 Bank St SE PO Box 232	Chatham	VA	24531	**888-440-6520**	434-432-2761	681
Pitzer College 1050 N Mills Ave PO Box A-202	Claremont	CA	91711	**800-748-9371**	909-621-8129	166
Pizza Boli's 3 Greenwood Pl Ste 208	Pikesville	MD	21208	**800-234-2654**		666
Pizza Factory Inc 49430 Rd 426	Oakhurst	CA	93644	**800-654-4840**	559-683-3377	666
Pizza Inn Inc 3551 Plano Pkwy *NASDAQ: RAVE*	The Colony	TX	75050	**077-574-9924**		666
Pizza Pro Inc 2107 N Second St PO Box 1285	Cabot	AR	72023	**800-777-7554**	501-605-1175	666
Pizza Ranch Inc 204 19th St SE	Orange City	IA	51041	**800-321-3401**		666
PJ Keating Co 998 Reservoir Rd	Lunenburg	MA	01462	**800-441-4119**	978-582-5200	188-4
PJ Noah PetSalon 27762 Antonio Pkwy Ste L1-622	Ladera Ranch	CA	92694	**855-577-7669**		789
PJ's Auto Parts Inc 2708 W Main Rd	Caledonia	NY	14423	**800-946-5787**	716-538-2391	54
PK (Promise Keepers) PO Box 11798	Denver	CO	80211	**866-776-6473**		48-20
P&K Research 6323 N Avondale Ave	Chicago	IL	60631	**800-747-5522**	773-774-3100	664
PK Safety Supply 1829 Clement Ave Ste 200	Alameda	CA	94501	**800-829-9580**	510-337-8880	675
PK4 Media 2250 E Maple Ave	El Segundo	CA	90245	**888-320-6281**		386
PKM Electric Co-op Inc 406 N Minnesota St	Warren	MN	56762	**800-552-7366**	218-745-4711	245
PKWare Inc 201 E Pittsburgh Ave Ste 400	Milwaukee	WI	53204	**866-583-1795**	414-289-9788	178-12
PL (Penta Laboratories) 7868 Deering Ave	Canoga Park	CA	91304	**800-421-4219**	818-882-3872	417
PLA (Public Library Assn) 50 E Huron St	Chicago	IL	60611	**800-545-2433**	312-280-5752	49-11
Placement Strategies Inc 6965 El Camino Real Ste 105-200	Carlsbad	CA	92009	**866-445-0710**	909-597-0668	260
Placentia Chamber of Commerce 117 N Main St	Placentia	CA	92870	**844-730-0418**	714-528-1873	139
Placer County Library 350 Nevada St	Auburn	CA	95603	**800-488-4308**	530-886-4500	433-3
Placer Title Co 189 Fulweiler Ave	Auburn	CA	95603	**800-317-8407**	530-887-2410	390-6
Placon Corp 6096 McKee Rd	Madison	WI	53719	**800-541-1535**	608-271-5634	598
Plaid Enterprises Inc 3225 Westech Dr	Norcross	GA	30092	**800-842-4197**		43
Plainfield Correctional Facility 727 Moon Rd	Plainfield	IN	46168	**800-451-6028**	317-839-2513	213
Plainfield Re-Entry Educational Facility 501 W Main St	Plainfield	IN	46168	**800-677-9800**		
Plains All American Pipeline LP 333 Clay St Ste 1600 *NYSE: PAA* ■ *Mktg	Houston	TX	77002	**800-708-5071***	713-646-4100	593
Plains Cotton Co-op Assn 3301 E 50th St PO Box 2827	Lubbock	TX	79408	**800-333-8011**	806-763-8011	275
Plains Dairy Products 300 N Taylor St	Amarillo	TX	79107	**800-365-5608**	806-374-0385	297-4
Plains Grain & Agronomy LLC 109 Third Ave	Enderlin	ND	58027	**800-950-2219**	701-437-2400	10-3
Plains Midstream Canada 607 Eighth Ave SW Ste 1400	Calgary	AB	T2P0A7	**866-343-5182**	403-298-2100	
Plains Regional Medical Ctr 2100 N ML King Blvd	Clovis	NM	88101	**800-923-6980**	505-769-2141	373-3
Plains Reporter PO Box 1447	Williston	ND	58802	**800-950-2165**	701-572-2165	528-4
PlainsCapital Bank 325 N Saint Paul St Ste 800	Dallas	TX	75201	**866-762-8392**		359-2
Plainview Milk Products Co-Op 130 Second St SW	Plainview	MN	55964	**800-356-5606**	507-534-3872	296-3
Plan Administrators Inc 1300 Enterprise Dr	De Pere	WI	54115	**800-236-7400**		194
Plan B Technologies Inc 185 Admiral Cochrane Dr Ste 150	Annapolis	MD	21401	**888-925-1602**	301-860-1006	
Plan USA 155 Plan Way	Warwick	RI	02886	**800-556-7918**	401-738-5600	48-6
Planar Systems Inc 1195 NW Compton Dr *NASDAQ: PLNR*	Beaverton	OR	97006	**866-475-2627**	503-748-1100	173-4
Planemasters Ltd 32 W 611 Tower Rd DuPage Airport	West Chicago	IL	60185	**800-994-6400**	630-513-2100	13
PLANET (Professional Landcare Network) 950 Herndon Pkwy Ste 450	Herndon	VA	20170	**800-395-2522**	703-736-9666	48-2
Planet Bike 2402 Vondron Rd	Madison	WI	53718	**866-256-8510**		707
Planet Forward LLC 800 Hillgrove Ave Ste 201	Western Springs	IL	60558	**888-845-2539**		260
Planet Hollywood Resort & Casino 3667 Las Vegas Blvd S	Las Vegas	NV	89109	**866-919-7472**		665
Planetree Inc 130 Division St	Derby	CT	06418	**800-222-2818**	203-732-1365	529
Planit Measuring Co, The 94 Lkshore Rd E Unit C	Mississauga	ON	L5G1E3	**800-933-5136**	905-271-7010	317
Planit Solutions Inc 3800 Palisades Dr	Tuscaloosa	AL	35405	**800-280-6932**	205-556-9199	178-5
Planned Administrators Inc PO Box 6927	Columbia	SC	29260	**800-768-4375**	803-462-0151	389
Planned Parenthood Action Fund Inc 1110 Vermont Ave NW	Washington	DC	20005	**800-430-4907**	202-973-4800	611
Planned Parenthood Federation of America 434 W 33rd St	New York	NY	10001	**800-230-7526**	212-541-7800	48-6
Planned Parenthood of Indiana & Kentucky 200 S Meridian St PO Box 397	Indianapolis	IN	46206	**800-230-7526**		352
Planned Systems International Inc 10632 Lttle Patuxent Pkwy	Columbia	MD	21044	**800-275-7749**	410-964-8000	180
Planners Network Inc, The 43418 Business Park Dr	Temecula	CA	92590	**866-676-6288**		
Plano Centre 1520 K Ave	Plano	TX	75074	**800-613-3222**	972-422-0296	205
Plano City Hall 1520 K Ave	Plano	TX	75074	**800-832-5452**	972-941-7000	336
Plano Convention & Visitors Bureau 2000 E Spring Creek Pkwy	Plano	TX	75074	**800-817-5266**	972-941-5840	206
Plano Public Library System 5024 Custer Rd	Plano	TX	75023	**800-473-5707**	972-769-4200	433-3
Plantation Inn & Golf Resort 9301 W Fort Island Trl	Crystal River	FL	34429	**800-632-6262**	352-795-4211	665
Planters Cotton Oil Mill Inc 2901 Planters Dr	Pine Bluff	AR	71601	**800-264-7070**	870-534-3631	296-29
Planters Inn 112 N Market St	Charleston	SC	29401	**800-845-7082**	843-722-2345	378
Plantronics Inc 345 Encinal St *NYSE: PLT*	Santa Cruz	CA	95060	**800-544-4660**	831-426-5858	730
Plants of the Southwest 3095 Agua Fria Rd	Santa Fe	NM	87507	**800-788-7333**	505-438-8888	323
Plantscape Inc 3101 Liberty Ave	Pittsburgh	PA	15201	**800-303-1380**	412-281-6352	392
Planview Inc 12301 Research Blvd Research Park Plz Ste 101	Austin	TX	78759	**800-856-8600**	512-346-8600	178-1
Plaquemine Lock State Historic Site 57730 Main St	Plaquemine	LA	70764	**877-987-7158**	225-687-7158	517
Plaquemines Parish School Board 557 F Edward Hebert Blvd	Belle Chasse	LA	70037	**877-453-2721**	504-595-6400	681
Plascore Inc 615 N Fairview	Zeeland	MI	49464	**800-630-9257**	616-772-1220	692
Plaskolite Inc 1770 Joyce Ave	Columbus	OH	43219	**800-848-9124**	614-294-3281	596
Plasma Ruggedized Solutions Inc 2284 Ringwood Ave Ste A	San Jose	CA	95131	**800-994-7527**	408-954-8405	479
Plasser American Corp 2001 Myers Rd PO Box 5464	Chesapeake	VA	23324	**800-388-4825**	757-543-3526	646
Plas-Tanks Industries Inc 39 Standen Dr	Hamilton	OH	45015	**800-247-6709**	513-942-3800	199
Plastatech Engineering Ltd 725 Morley Dr	Saginaw	MI	48601	**800-892-9358**	989-754-6500	191-4
Plasteak Inc 3489 Sawmill Rd	Copley	OH	44321	**800-320-1841**	330-668-2587	186
Plasti Dip International 3920 Pheasant Ridge Dr	Blaine	MN	55449	**800-969-5432**		592
Plastic Card Systems Inc 31 Pierce St	Northborough	MA	01532	**800-742-2273**	508-351-6210	173-6
Plastic Components Inc N 116 W 18271 Morse Dr	Germantown	WI	53022	**877-253-1496**	262-253-0353	600
Plastic Development Co Inc 75 Palmer Industrial Rd PO Box 4007	Williamsport	PA	17701	**800-451-1420**		374
Plastic Film Corporation of America Inc 1287 Naperville Dr	Romeoville	IL	60446	**800-654-6589**	630-887-0800	599
Plastic Forming Company Inc 20 S Bradley Rd	Woodbridge	CT	06525	**800-732-2060**	203-397-1338	199
Plastic Package Inc 4600 Beloit Dr	Sacramento	CA	95838	**800-356-6900**	916-921-3399	343
Plastic Recycling of Iowa Falls Inc 10252 Hwy 65	Iowa Falls	IA	50126	**800-338-1438**	641-648-5073	657
Plastic Safety Systems Inc 2444 Baldwin Rd	Cleveland	OH	44104	**800-662-6338**		674
Plasticolors Inc 2600 Michigan Ave PO Box 816	Ashtabula	OH	44005	**888-661-7675**	440-997-5137	143
Plasticrest Products Inc 4519 W Harrison St	Chicago	IL	60624	**800-828-2163**	773-826-2163	286
Plastics Color & Compounding Inc 14201 Paxton Ave	Calumet City	IL	60409	**800-922-9936**		601-2
Plastikon Industries Inc 688 Sandoval Way	Hayward	CA	94544	**800-370-0858**	510-400-1010	604
Plastipak Inc 150 Industriel Blvd	Boucherville	QC	J4B2X3	**800-387-7452**	450-650-2200	597

Company / Address	City	State	ZIP	Toll-Free	Phone	Class
Plastpro Inc 5200 W Century Blvd 9F	Los Angeles	CA	90045	**800-779-0561**	310-693-8600	604
Plastronics Socket Co Inc 2601 Texas Dr *Cust Svc	Irving	TX	75062	**800-582-5822***	972-258-2580	253
Platform Computing Inc 3760 14th Ave	Markham	ON	L3R3T7	**877-528-3676**	905-948-8448	178-1
Platinum Control Technologies Corp 2822 W Fifth St	Fort Worth	TX	76107	**877-374-1115**	817-529-6485	535
Platinum Hotel 211 E Flamingo Rd *General	Las Vegas	NV	89169	**877-211-9211***	702-365-5000	378
Platinum Personnel 1475 Ellis St	Kelowna	BC	V1Y2A3	**800-652-1511**	250-979-7200	260
Platinum Vault Inc 10554 Norwalk Blvd	Santa Fe Springs	CA	90670	**888-671-2888**	562-903-1494	196
Plato Woodwork Inc 200 Third St SW	Plato	MN	55370	**800-328-5924**		115
Platt & Labonia Co 70 Stoddard Ave	North Haven	CT	06473	**800-505-9099**	203-239-5681	693
Platt Electric Supply 10605 SW Allen Blvd	Beaverton	OR	97005	**800-257-5288**	503-641-6121	246
Platt Luggage Inc 4051 W 51st St	Chicago	IL	60632	**800-222-1555**	773-838-2000	451
Plattco Corp 7 White St	Plattsburgh	NY	12901	**800-352-1731**	518-563-4640	784
Platts 2 Penn Plz 25th Fl	New York	NY	10121	**800-752-8878**	212-904-3070	633-9
Playback Now Inc 3139 Campus Dr Ste 700	Norcross	GA	30071	**800-241-7785**	770-447-0616	461
PlayCore Inc 544 Chestnut St	Chattanooga	TN	37402	**877-762-7563**		345
Player's Club Resort 35 Deallyon Ave	Hilton Head Island	SC	29928	**800-497-7529**	843-785-3355	665
Playhouse Square 1501 Euclid Ave Ste 200	Cleveland	OH	44115	**866-546-1353**	216-771-4444	568
Playmobil USA Inc 26 Commerce Dr	Cranbury	NJ	08512	**800-351-8697**	609-409-1263	757
Playscripts 7 Penn Plz Ste 904	New York	NY	10001	**866-639-7529**		786
Playwell Group, The 4743 Iberia Ave Ste C	Dallas	TX	75207	**800-726-1816**		707
Playworld Systems Inc 1000 Buffalo Rd	Lewisburg	PA	17837	**800-233-8404**	570-522-9800	345
Plaza Art 633 Middleton St	Nashville	TN	37203	**866-668-6714**		45
Plaza Artist Materials & Picture Framing 1120 19th St NW	Washington	DC	20036	**866-668-6714**		45
Plaza Fleet Parts Inc 1520 S Broadway	Saint Louis	MO	63104	**800-325-7618**	314-231-5047	61
Plaza Group Inc 10375 Richmond Ave Ste 1620	Houston	TX	77042	**800-876-3738**	713-266-0707	146
Plaza Home Mortgage Inc 4820 Eastgate Mall Ste 100	San Diego	CA	92121	**866-260-2529**	858-346-1208	507
Plaza Hotel & Casino 1 Main St	Las Vegas	NV	89101	**800-634-6575**	702-386-2110	378
Plaza Hotel, The 5th Ave at Central Park S	New York	NY	10019	**866-940-9361**	212-759-3000	377
Plaza Resort & Spa 600 N Atlantic Ave	Daytona Beach	FL	32118	**844-284-2685**		665
Plaza Resort Club 121 W St	Reno	NV	89501	**800-628-5974**	775-786-2200	378
Plaza Suites Silicon Valley 3100 Lakeside Dr	Santa Clara	CA	95054	**800-345-1554**	408-748-9800	378
Plaza Tire Service 2075 Corporate Cr PO Box 2048	Cape Girardeau	MO	63702	**800-334-5036**		62-5
Plaza Travel 16530 Ventura Blvd Ste 106	Encino	CA	91436	**800-347-4447**	818-990-4053	770
Pleasant Holidays LLC 2404 Townsgate Rd	Westlake Village	CA	91361	**800-742-9244**	818-991-3390	766
Pleasant Trucking 2250 Industrial Dr	Connellsville	PA	15425	**800-245-2402**		775
Pleasant View Gardens Inc 7316 Pleasant St	Loudon	NH	03307	**866-862-2974**	603-435-8361	323
Pleiger Plastics Co PO Box 1271	Washington	PA	15301	**800-753-4437**	724-228-2244	604
Pleora Technologies Inc 340 Terry Fox Dr Ste 300	Kanata	ON	K2K3A2	**888-687-6877**	613-270-0625	664
Plexus Corp 1 Plexus Way PO Box 156 *NASDAQ: PLXS*	Neenah	WI	54957	**877-733-7260**	920-722-3451	621
PLF (Public Lands Foundation) PO Box 7226	Arlington	VA	22207	**866-985-9636**	703-790-1988	48-13
PLH Products Inc 6655 Knott Ave	Buena Park	CA	90620	**800-946-6001**	714-739-6600	786
PLI (Practising Law Institute) 1177 Ave of the Americas 2nd Fl	New York	NY	10036	**800-260-4754**	212-824-5700	49-10
Plibrico Co 1010 N Hooker St	Chicago	IL	60622	**800-255-8793**	312-337-9000	659
Plitek LLC 69 Rawls Rd	Des Plaines	IL	60018	**800-966-1250**		604
Pln & Associates Inc 15400 Jennings Ln Ste 300	Bowie	MD	20721	**800-699-0299**	301-390-4635	461
PLRB (Property Loss Research Bureau) 3025 Highland Pkwy Ste 800	Downers Grove	IL	60515	**888-711-7572**	630-724-2200	49-9
Plum Grove Inc 2160 Stoningtone Ave	Hoffman Estates	IL	60169	**866-738-3702**	847-882-4020	623
Plumas County Visitors Bureau 550 Crescent St	Quincy	CA	95971	**800-326-2247**	530-283-6345	206
Plumas-Sierra Rural Electric Co-op 73233 State Rt 70	Portola	CA	96122	**800-555-2207**	530-832-4261	245
Plumb Supply Co 1622 NE 51st Ave	Des Moines	IA	50313	**800-483-9511**	515-262-9511	608
Plumbers Supply Co 1000 E Main St	Louisville	KY	40206	**800-626-5133**	502-582-2261	608
Plumbing Distributors Inc 1025 Old Norcross Rd	Lawrenceville	GA	30046	**800-262-9231**	770-963-9231	608
Plumbing Industry Board Trade Education Committee 3711 47th Ave	Long Island	NY	11101	**800-638-7442**	718-752-9630	413
Plumbing-Heating-Cooling Contractors NA (PHCC) 180 S Washington St Ste 100	Falls Church	VA	22046	**800-533-7694**	703-237-8100	49-3
Plump Jack's Squaw Valley Inn 1920 Squaw Valley Rd PO Box 2407	Olympic Valley	CA	96146	**800-323-7666**	530-583-1576	378
Plumrose USA Inc 1901 Butterfield Rd Ste 305	Downers Grove	IL	60515	**800-526-4909**	732-624-4040	471
Plunkett's Pest Control 40 NE 52nd Way	Fridley	MN	55421	**866-906-1780**		573
PlusOne Solutions Inc 3501 Quadrangle Blvd Ste 120	Orlando	FL	32817	**877-943-0100**	407-359-5929	196
Ply Gem 5020 Weston Pkwy Ste 400	Cary	NC	27513	**800-786-2726**	888-975-9436	693
PlymKraft Inc 479 Export Cir	Newport News	VA	23601	**800-992-0854**	757-595-0364	208
Plymold 615 Centennial Dr	Kenyon	MN	55946	**800-759-6653**		319-1
Plymouth Community Chamber of Commerce 850 W Ann Arbor Trl	Plymouth	MI	48170	**800-477-4747**	734-453-1540	139
Plymouth Rubber Company Inc 960 Turnpike St	Canton	MA	02021	**800-458-0336**		
Plymouth State University 17 High St	Plymouth	NH	03264	**800-842-6900**	603-535-2237	166
Plymouth Technology Inc 2925 Waterview Dr	Rochester Hills	MI	48309	**800-535-5053**	248-537-0081	608
Plymouth Tube Co 29W150 Warrenville Rd *Mktg	Warrenville	IL	60555	**800-323-9506***	630-393-3550	488
Plymouth Village 900 Salem Dr	Redlands	CA	92373	**800-391-4552**	909-793-9195	668
Plywood Supply Inc 7036 NE 175th St	Kenmore	WA	98028	**888-774-9663**	425-485-8585	609
PM Construction Co Inc PO Box 728	Saco	ME	04072	**800-646-0068**	207-282-7697	186
PMA (Polyurethane Manufacturers Assn) 6737 W Washington St Ste 1420	Milwaukee	WI	53214	**800-937-8461**	414-431-3094	49-13
PMA Canada Ltd 231 Oak Park Blvd Ste 400	Oakville	ON	L6H7S8	**800-667-9463**	905-257-2116	41
PMC Biogenix Inc 1231 Pope St	Memphis	TN	38108	**800-641-2152**	901-325-4930	
PMC Commercial Trust 17950 Preston Rd Ste 600 *NASDAQ: CMCT*	Dallas	TX	75252	**800-486-3223**	972-349-3200	216
PMC Engineering LLC 11 Old Sugar Hollow Rd	Danbury	CT	06810	**800-869-5747**	203-792-8686	201
PMC Lenco 10240 Deer Pk Rd *Cust Svc	Waverly	NE	68462	**877-789-5844***	402-786-2000	
PMC Specialties Group Inc 501 Murray Rd	Cincinnati	OH	45217	**800-543-2466**		144
PMCU (Pacific Marine Credit Union) 1278 Rocky Point Dr	Oceanside	CA	92056	**800-736-4500**	760-631-8700	219
PMHI (Pacific Modern Homes Inc) 9723 Railroad St	Elk Grove	CA	95624	**800-395-1011**		106
PMI (Project Management Institute) 14 Campus Blvd	Newtown Square	PA	19073	**866-276-4764**	610-356-4600	49-12
PMI Mortgage Insurance Co 3003 Oak Rd *OTC: PMI*	Walnut Creek	CA	94597	**800-288-1970**		359-4
PML (OneAmerica Financial Partners Inc) PO Box 368	Indianapolis	IN	46206	**800-249-6269**	317-285-1877	390-2
PMMI (Packaging Machinery Manufacturers Institute) 4350 N Fairfax Dr Ste 600	Arlington	VA	22203	**888-275-7664**	703-243-8555	49-13
PMOLink LLC 2001 Lakeshore Dr	Mandeville	LA	70448	**800-401-5701**	985-674-5968	196
PMP Corp 25 Security Dr *Cust Svc	Avon	CT	06001	**800-243-6628***	860-677-9656	493
PMS Systems Corp 26707 Agoura Rd Ste 201	Calabasas	CA	91302	**800-755-3968**	310-450-2566	178-5
PNBC (Progressive National Baptist Convention Inc) 601 50th St NE	Washington	DC	20019	**800-876-7622**	202-396-0558	48-20
PNC Bank 1 PNC Plz 300 Fifth Ave 29th Fl	Pittsburgh	PA	15222	**888-762-2265**	412-762-2000	70
PNC Bank Art Ctr Exit 116 Garden State Pkwy	Holmdel	NJ	07733	**800-745-3000**		568
PNC Bank NA 249 Fifth Ave 1 PNC Plaza	Pittsburgh	PA	15222	**888-762-2265**	412-762-2000	70
Pneumatic & Hydraulic Systems Company Inc 1338 Petroleum Pkwy	Broussard	LA	70518	**877-836-1999**	337-839-1999	357
PneumRx 530 Logue Ave	Mountain View	CA	94043	**800-226-7625**	650-625-8910	474
Pneutek 17 Friars Dr	Hudson	NH	03051	**800-431-8665**	603-883-1660	754
PNK (River City) LLC 777 River City Casino Blvd	Saint Louis	MO	63125	**888-578-7289**		376
PNM Resources Inc Alvarado Sq *NYSE: PNM*	Albuquerque	NM	87158	**888-342-5766**	505-241-2700	359-5
PNNL (Pacific Northwest National Laboratory) 902 Battelle Blvd PO Box 999	Richland	WA	99352	**888-375-7665**	509-375-2121	664
PNWFCU (Pacific NW Federal Credit Union) 12106 NE Marx St	Portland	OR	97220	**866-692-8669**	503-256-5858	219
PNY Technologies Inc 100 Jefferson Rd	Parsippany	NJ	07054	**800-769-0143**	973-515-9700	288
Poblocki Sign Company LLC 922 S 70th St	Milwaukee	WI	53214	**800-776-7064**	414-453-4010	697
Pocahontas County PO Box 275	Marlinton	WV	24954	**800-336-7009**		337
Pocock Racing Shells 615 80th St SW	Everett	WA	98203	**888-762-6251**	425-438-9048	694
Pocomoke State Forest 580 Taylor Ave	Annapolis	MD	21401	**877-620-8367**		561

Alphabetical Section

Name / Address	Toll-Free	Phone	Class
Pocono Manor Golf Resort & Spa 1 Manor Dr Rt 314 .... Pocono Manor PA 18349	800-233-8150	800-944-8392	665
Pocono Mountains Vacation Bureau 1004 W Main St .... Stroudsburg PA 18360	800-722-9199	570-421-5791	206
Pocono Raceway Long Pond Rd PO Box 500 .... Long Pond PA 18334	800-722-3929	570-646-2300	512
Pocono Record 511 Lenox St .... Stroudsburg PA 18360	800-530-6310	570-421-3000	528-2
Podiatry Insurance Company of America 3000 Meridian Blvd Ste 400 .... Franklin TN 37067	800-251-5727	615-984-2005	390-5
Poe Ted (Rep R - TX) 2132 Rayburn Bldg .... Washington DC 20515	866-425-6565	202-225-6565	
Pohly Co 867 Boylston St 5th Fl .... Boston MA 02116	800-383-0888	617-451-1700	633-9
Point Alliance Inc 20 Adelaide St E Ste 500 .... Toronto ON M5C2T6	855-947-6468		180
Point Loma Nazarene University 3900 Lomaland Dr .... San Diego CA 92106 *Admissions	800-733-7770*	619-849-2200	166
Point Park University 201 Wood St .... Pittsburgh PA 15222 *Admissions	800-321-0129*	412-391-4100	166
Point Pelee National Park of Canada 407 Monarch Ln RR 1 .... Leamington ON N8H3V4	888-773-8888	519-322-2365	559
Point Plaza Suites & Conference Hotel 950 J Clyde Morris Blvd .... Newport News VA 23601	800-841-1112	757-599-4460	378
Point Reyes National Seashore 1 Bear Valley Rd .... Point Reyes Station CA 94956	877-874-2478	415-464-5100	560
Point, The PO Box 1327 .... Saranac Lake NY 12983	800-255-3530	518-891-5674	665
Pointe Coupee Electric Membership Corp 2506 False River Dr PO Box 160 .... New Roads LA 70760	800-738-7232	225-638-3751	245
Pointe Hilton at Squaw Peak Resort 7677 N 16th St .... Phoenix AZ 85020	800-685-0550	602-997-2626	665
Pointe Hilton Resort at Tapatio Cliffs 11111 N Seventh St .... Phoenix AZ 85020	800-947-9784	602-866-7500	665
Pointe Scientific Inc 5449 Research Dr PO Box 87188 .... Canton MI 48188	800-445-9853	734-487-8300	231
Points of Light Foundation & Volunteer Ctr National Network 1400 'I' St NW Ste 800 .... Washington DC 20005	866-545-5307	202-729-8000	48-5
Poisoned Pen Bookstore 4014 N Goldwater Blvd .... Scottsdale AZ 85251	888-560-9919	480-947-2974	95
Pokagon State Park 450 Ln 100 Lake James .... Angola IN 46703	800-677-9800		
Polack Corp, The 1400 Keystone Ave .... Lansing MI 48911	800-392-8759	517-272-1400	531
Polar Beverages 1001 Southbridge St .... Worcester MA 01610 *Cust Svc	800-734-9800*		80-2
Polar Communications 110 Fourth St E PO Box 270 .... Park River ND 58270	800-284-7222	701-284-7221	
Polar King International Inc 4424 New Haven Ave .... Fort Wayne IN 46803	800-752-7178	260-428-2530	14
Polar Service Centers 7600 E Sam Houston Pkwy N .... Houston TX 77049	800-955-8558	281-459-6400	774
Polar Tank Trailer Inc 12810 County Rd 17 .... Holdingford MN 56340	800-826-6589	320-746-2255	774
Polar ware 502 Hgwy 67 .... Kiel WI 53402	800-237-3655		487
Police & Fire Federal Credit Union 901 Arch St .... Philadelphia PA 19107	800-228-8801	215-931-0300	219
Policemen's Annuity & Benefit Fund of Chicago 221 North LaSalle St Ste 1626 .... Chicago IL 60601	800-656-6606	312-744-3891	389
Policy Research Associates Inc 345 Delaware Ave .... Delmar NY 12054	800-311-4246	518-439-7415	141
Polish American Congress 5711 N Milwaukee Ave .... Chicago IL 60646	800-621-3723	773-763-9944	48-14
Polish American Cultural Ctr Museum 308 Walnut St .... Philadelphia PA 19106	800-422-1275	215-922-1700	517
Politics & Prose Bookstore 5015 Connecticut Ave NW .... Washington DC 20008	800-722-0790	202-364-1919	95
Polk Audio Inc 5601 Metro Dr .... Baltimore MD 21215	800-377-7655	410-358-3600	52
Polk County 111 Court Ave Administration Bldg .... Des Moines IA 50309	800-848-0869	515-286-3000	337
Polk County Rural Public Power District 115 W Third St PO Box 465 .... Stromsburg NE 68666	888-242-5265	402-764-4381	245
Polk County Travel & Tourism 20 E Mills St PO Box 308 .... Columbus NC 28722	800-440-7848	828-894-2324	206
Polk-Burnett Electric Co-op (PBEC) 1001 State Rd 35 .... Centuria WI 54824	800-421-0283	715-646-2191	245
Pollard Friendly Ford Co 3301 S Loop 289 .... Lubbock TX 79423	866-239-3735		
Pollock Paper & Packaging 1 Pollock Pl .... Grand Prairie TX 75050 *Cust Svc	800-843-7320*	972-263-2126	555
Pollock Printing Company Inc 928 Sixth Ave S .... Nashville TN 37203	800-349-1205	615-255-0526	623
Pollstar 4697 W Jacquelyn Ave .... Fresno CA 93722	800-344-7383	559-271-7900	455-9
Pollution Control Corp 500 W Country Club Rd .... Chickasha OK 73018	800-966-1265		196
Pollution Probe 150 Ferrand Dr Ste 208 .... Toronto ON M3C3E5	877-926-1907	416-926-1907	48-13
POLY (POLY Languages Institute Inc) 5757 Wilshire Blvd Ste 510 .... Los Angeles CA 90036	877-738-5787	323-933-9399	422
Poly Expert Inc 850 ave Munck .... Laval QC H7S1B1	877-384-5060		365
POLY Languages Institute Inc (POLY) 5757 Wilshire Blvd Ste 510 .... Los Angeles CA 90036	877-738-5787	323-933-9399	422
Poly Molding LLC 96 Fourth Ave .... Haskell NJ 07420	800-229-7161	973-835-7161	597
Poly Tech Diamond Co 4 E St PO Box 6 .... North Attleboro MA 02761	800-365-7659	508-695-3561	
Poly-America 2000 W Marshall Dr .... Grand Prairie TX 75051	800-527-3322	972-337-7100	66
Polycom Inc 4750 Willow Rd .... Pleasanton CA 94588	800-765-9266		730
PolyConversions Inc 505 Condit Dr .... Rantoul IL 61866	888-893-3330	217-893-3330	572
Polygon Co 103 Industrial Pk Dr PO Box 176 .... Walkerton IN 46574	800-918-9261	574-586-3145	598
Polygon Network PO Box 4806 .... Dillon CO 80435	800-221-4435		392
Polyguard Products Inc PO Box 755 .... Ennis TX 75120	800-541-4994	972-875-8421	740-2
PolyJohn Enterprises Corp 2500 Gaspar Ave .... Whiting IN 46394	800-292-1305		
Polymedco Inc 510 Furnace Dock Rd .... Cortlandt Manor NY 10567	800-431-2123	914-739-5400	231
Polymer Industries LLC 10526 Alabama Hwy 40 PO Box 32 ...... Henagar AL 35978	877-489-0039	256-657-5197	597
Polymer Resources Ltd 656 New Britain Ave .... Farmington CT 06032	800-243-5176		592
Polymer Solutions Inc 2903-C Commerce St .... Blacksburg VA 24060	877-961-4341		317
Polynesian Adventure Tours Inc 2880 Kilihau St .... Honolulu HI 96819	800-622-3011	808-833-3000	755
Polynesian Cultural Ctr 55-370 Kamehameha Hwy .... Laie HI 96762	800-367-7060	808-293-3005	517
Polynesian Resort, The 615 Ocean Shores Blvd NW ...... Ocean Shores WA 98569	800-562-4836	360-289-3361	665
PolyOne Corp 33587 Walker Rd .... Avon Lake OH 44012 NYSE: POL	866-765-9663	440-930-1000	601-2
Poly-Pak Industries Inc 125 Spagnoli Rd .... Melville NY 11747	800-969-1993	631-293-6767	66
PolyPeptide Laboratories Inc 365 Maple Ave .... Torrance CA 90503	800-338-4965	310-782-3569	231
Polysciences Inc 400 Valley Rd .... Warrington PA 18976 *Cust Svc	800-523-2575*	215-343-6484	231
Polyspede Electronics Company Inc 6770 Twin Hills Ave .... Dallas TX 75231	888-476-5944	214-363-7245	515
Polytechnic University Long Island 105 Maxess Rd .... Melville NY 11747 *Admissions	877-503-7659*	631-755-4300	166
Polytron Corp 4400 Wyland Dr .... Elkhart IN 46516	888-228-0246	574-522-0246	203
Polyurethane Manufacturers Assn (PMA) 6737 W Washington St Ste 1420 ...... Milwaukee WI 53214	800-937-8461	414-431-3094	49-13
Polyvinyl Films Inc PO Box 753 .... Sutton MA 01590	800-343-6134	508-865-3558	596
PolyVision Corp 10700 Abbotts Bridge Rd Ste 100 .... Johns Creek GA 30097	888-325-6351	678-542-3100	173-1
POM Inc 200 S Elmira Ave .... Russellville AR 72802	800-331-7275	479-968-2880	493
POMC (Parents of Murdered Children) 4960 Ridge Ave Ste 2 .... Cincinnati OH 45209	888-818-7662	513-721-5683	48-6
POMCO 2425 James St .... Syracuse NY 13206	855-247-0353	315-432-9171	389
Pomeroy IT Solutions Inc 1020 Petersburg Rd .... Hebron KY 41048	800-846-8727	859-586-0600	180
Pomona Capital 780 Third Ave 46th Fl .... New York NY 10017	800-992-0180		
Pompanoosuc Mills 3184 Rte 5 S .... East Thetford VT 05043	800-841-6671		360
Pomps Tire Service Inc 1123 Cedar St .... Green Bay WI 54301	800-236-8911	920-435-8301	750
Ponca City Area Chamber of Commerce 420 E Grand Ave .... Ponca City OK 74601	866-763-8092	580-765-4400	139
Ponca City Tourism 420 E Grand Ave PO Box 1109 .... Ponca City OK 74602	866-763-8092	580-765-4400	206
Pontarelli Limousine Service 5584 N Northwest Hwy .... Chicago IL 60630	800-322-5466	312-494-6700	440
Pontchartrain 2031 St Charles Ave .... New Orleans LA 70130	800-708-6652		378
Ponte Vedra Inn & Club 200 Ponte Vedra Blvd ...... Ponte Vedra Beach FL 32082	800-234-7842	866-748-8083	665
Pontiac Correctional Ctr 700 W Lincoln St .... Pontiac IL 61764	800-275-7877	815-842-2816	213
Pontiac Regional Chamber of Commerce 402 N Telegraph Rd .... Pontiac MI 48341	800-477-3172	248-335-9600	139
Pontifical College Josephinum 7625 N High St .... Columbus OH 43235	888-252-5812	614-885-5585	167-3
PONY Baseball/Softball Inc 1951 Pony Pl PO Box 225 .... Washington PA 15301	800-853-2414	724-225-1060	48-22
Pony Express National Museum 914 Penn St .... Saint Joseph MO 64503	800-530-5930	816-279-5059	517
Poole & Kent Corp 4530 Hollins Ferry Rd .... Baltimore MD 21227	800-468-0851	410-247-2200	189-10
Poolmaster Inc 770 Del Paso Rd .... Sacramento CA 95834	800-854-1492	916-567-9800	706
Pope Scientific Inc 351 N Dekora Woods Blvd .... Saukville WI 53080	844-400-7673		
Poplar Bluff Regional Medical Ctr 2620 N Westwood Blvd .... Poplar Bluff MO 63901	855-444-7276	573-785-7721	373-3
Poplar Springs Hospital 350 Poplar Dr .... Petersburg VA 23805	866-546-2229	804-733-6874	373-5
Popular Mechanics Magazine 300 W 57th St .... New York NY 10019	800-333-4948		
Population Connection 2120 L St NW Ste 500 .... Washington DC 20037	800-767-1956	202-332-2200	48-5
Population Reference Bureau (PRB) 1875 Connecticut Ave NW Ste 520 .... Washington DC 20009	800-877-9881	202-483-1100	48-7
Population-Environment Balance Inc 2000 P St NW Ste 600 .... Washington DC 20036	800-866-6269	202-955-5700	48-7
Por La Mar Nursery 905 S Patterson Ave .... Santa Barbara CA 93111	800-733-5286	805-699-4500	
Porex Technologies Corp 500 Bohannon Rd .... Fairburn GA 30213 *Cust Svc	800-241-0195*	770-964-1421	604

	Toll-Free	Phone	Class
Pork checkoff			
1776 NW 114th St . . . . .Des Moines IA 50325	800-456-7675	515-223-2600	455-1
Porsche Cars North America Inc			
980 Hammond Dr Ste 1000 . . . . .Atlanta GA 30328	800-505-1041	770-290-3500	59
Port Angeles Coast Guard Air Station			
Ediz Hook Rd . . . . .Port Angeles WA 98362	800-982-8813	360-417-5840	158
Port Arthur Convention & Visitors Bureau			
3401 Cultural Ctr Dr . . . . .Port Arthur TX 77642	800-235-7822	409-985-7822	206
Port Canaveral			
445 Challanger Rd . . . . .Cape Canaveral FL 32920	888-767-8226	321-783-7831	614
Port Everglades			
1850 Eller Dr . . . . .Fort Lauderdale FL 33316	800-421-0188	954-523-3404	614
Port Freeport			
1001 N Gulf Blvd . . . . .Freeport TX 77541	800-362-5743	979-233-2667	614
Port of Anacortes			
100 Commercial Ave . . . . .Anacortes WA 98221	800-874-4434	360-293-3134	614
Port of Anchorage			
632 W Sixth Ave . . . . .Anchorage AK 99501	877-650-8400	907-343-6543	614
Port of Astoria			
10 Pier 1 Bldg Ste 308 . . . . .Astoria OR 97103	800-860-4093	503-741-3300	614
Port of Baltimore			
Maryland Port Administration			
401 E Pratt St . . . . .Baltimore MD 21202	800-638-7519*		614
General			
Port of Brownsville			
1000 Foust Rd . . . . .Brownsville TX 78521	800-378-5395	956-831-4592	614
Port of Corpus Christi			
222 Power St . . . . .Corpus Christi TX 78401	800-580-7110	361-882-5633	614
Port of Duluth			
Duluth Seaway Port Authority			
1200 Port Terminal Dr . . . . .Duluth MN 55802	800-232-0703	218-727-8525	614
Port of Everett			
2911 Bond St Ste 202. . . . . .Everett WA 98201	800-729-7678	425-259-3164	614
Port of Jacksonville			
Jacksonville Port Authority			
2831 Talleyrand Ave			
PO Box 3005 . . . . .Jacksonville FL 32206	800-874-8050	904-357-3000	614
Port of New Orleans			
1350 Port of New Orleans Pl			
. . . . .New Orleans LA 70130	800-776-6652	504-522-2551	614
Port of Pensacola			
700 S Barracks St . . . . .Pensacola FL 32502	800-711-1712	850-436-5070	614
Port of Portland			
7200 NE Airport Way . . . . .Portland OR 97218	800-547-8411	503-415-6000	614
Port of San Diego			
3165 Pacific Hwy . . . . .San Diego CA 92101	800-854-2757	619-686-6200	614
Port of San Francisco			
Pier 1 The Embarcadero . . . . .San Francisco CA 94111	800-479-5314	415-274-0400	614
Port of Seattle			
2711 Alaskan Way . . . . .Seattle WA 98111	800-426-7817	206-728-3000	614
Port of Stockton			
2201 W Washington St . . . . .Stockton CA 95203	800-344-3213	209-946-0246	614
Port of Vancouver			
3103 NW Lower River Rd . . . . .Vancouver WA 98660	800-475-8012	360-693-3611	614
Port of Vancouver			
100 The Pointe 999 Canada Pl . . . . . .Vancouver BC V6C3T4	888-767-8826	604-665-9000	614
Port Orange-South Daytona Chamber of Commerce			
3431 S Ridgewood Ave . . . . .Port Orange FL 32129	800-848-3984	386-761-1601	139
Port Orchard Chamber of Commerce			
1014 Bay St Ste 8. . . . . .Port Orchard WA 98366	800-475-7526	360-876-3505	139
Port Panama City			
1 Seaport Dr . . . . .Panama City FL 32401	855-347-8371		
Port Plastics Inc			
15325 Fairfield Ranch Rd			
Ste 150. . . . . .Chino Hills CA 91709	800-800-0039	480-813-6118	599
Port Townsend Marine Science Ctr			
532 Battery Way . . . . .Port Townsend WA 98368	800-566-3932	360-385-5582	517
Portable Buildings Inc			
3235 Bay Rd .Milford DE 19963	800-205-5030	302-335-1300	186
Portable Church Industries Inc			
1923 Ring Dr . . . . .Troy MI 48083	800-939-7722		196
Portable Technology Solutions LLC			
221 David Ct . . . . .Calverton NY 11933	877-640-4152		177
Porta-Bote International			
1074 Independence Ave . . . . .Mountain View CA 94043	800-227-8882	650-961-5334	90
Porta-Fab Corp			
18080 Chesterfield Airport Rd			
. . . . .Chesterfield MO 63005	800-325-3781	636-537-5555	105
Portage County			
449 S Meridian St 1st Fl. . . . . .Ravenna OH 44266	800-772-3799	330-297-9422	337
Portage County Business Council			
5501 Vern Holmes Dr . . . . .Stevens Point WI 54481	800-333-6668	715-344-1940	139
Portage County District Library			
10482 S St . . . . .Garrettsville OH 44231	800-500-5179	330-527-4378	433-3
Portage Electric Products Inc			
7700 Freedom Ave NW . . . . .North Canton OH 44720	888-464-7374	330-499-2727	202
Porta-King Building Systems			
4133 Shoreline Dr . . . . .Earth City MO 63045	800-284-5346		186
Porter & Chester Institute Inc, The			
670 Lordship Blvd . . . . .Stratford CT 06615	800-870-6789	203-375-4463	148
Porter Capital Corp			
2112 First Ave N . . . . .Birmingham AL 35203	800-737-7344	205-322-5442	272
Porter Consulting Engineers PC			
552 State St . . . . .Meadville PA 16335	800-541-5941	814-337-4447	261
Porter Inc			
2200 W Monroe St . . . . .Decatur IN 46733	800-736-7685	260-724-9111	90
Porter Instrument Company Inc			
245 Township Line Rd			
PO Box 907. . . . . .Hatfield PA 19440	888-723-4001	215-723-4000	201
Porter Precision Products Inc			
2734 Banning Rd . . . . .Cincinnati OH 45239	800-543-7041	513-923-3777	752
Porter Truck Sales LP			
135 McCarty St . . . . .Houston TX 77029	800-956-2408	713-672-2400	513
PorterCorp			
4240 136th Ave . . . . .Holland MI 49424	800-354-7721	616-399-1963	105
Portico Healthnet			
1600 University Ave W			
Ste 211 . . . . .Saint Paul MN 55104	866-489-4899	651-489-2273	461

	Toll-Free	Phone	Class
Portland Bolt & Manufacturing Company Inc			
3441 NW Guam St . . . . .Portland OR 97210	800-547-6758	503-227-5488	350
Portland Community College			
Sylvania			
12000 SW 49th Ave . . . . .Portland OR 97219	866-922-1010	503-244-6111	162
Portland General Electric			
121 SW Salmon St . . . . .Portland OR 97204	800-542-8818	503-464-8000	782
NYSE: POR			
Portland Harbor Hotel			
468 Fore St . . . . .Portland ME 04101	888-798-9090	207-775-9090	378
Portland International Airport			
7000 NE Airport Way . . . . .Portland OR 97218	800-547-8411	503-460-4234	27
Portland Investment Counsel Inc			
1375 Kerns Rd . . . . .Burlington ON L7P4V7	888-710-4242	905-331-4242	
Portland Opera			
211 SE Caruthers St . . . . .Portland OR 97214	866-739-6737	503-241-1407	569-2
Portland Public Library			
5 Monument Sq . . . . .Portland ME 04101	800-848-5800	207-871-1700	433-3
Portland Regency Hotel			
20 Milk St .Portland ME 04101	800-727-3436	207-774-4200	378
Portland State University			
1825 SW Broadway PO Box 751. . . . . . . .Portland OR 97201	800-547-8887	503-725-3000	166
Portland Teachers Credit Union			
PO Box 3750 . . . . .Portland OR 97208	800-527-3932	503-228-7077	219
Portnoff Law Associates Ltd			
2700 Horizon Dr Ste 100 . . . . . . .King of Prussia PA 19406	866-211-9466		427
Port-O-Call Hotel			
1510 Boardwalk . . . . .Ocean City NJ 08226	800-334-4546	609-399-8812	378
Portofino Hotel & Yacht Club			
260 Portofino Way . . . . .Redondo Beach CA 90277	800-468-4292	310-379-8481	378
Portofino Inn & Suites Anaheim			
1831 S Harbor Blvd . . . . .Anaheim CA 92802	800-398-3963*	714-782-7600	378
Resv			
Portofino Spa at Portofino Island Resort			
10 Portofino Dr . . . . .Pensacola Beach FL 32561	877-523-2016		703
Portola Plaza Hotel			
2 Portola Plz . . . . .Monterey CA 93940	888-222-5851	831-649-4511	378
Portrait Express			
441 N Water St . . . . .Silverton OR 97381	800-228-3759	503-873-6365	586
Portraits International			
10835 Rockley Rd . . . . .Houston TX 77099	888-838-1495	281-879-8444	586
Ports Petroleum Company Inc			
1337 Blachleyville Rd			
PO Box 1046. . . . . .Wooster OH 44691	800-562-0373	330-264-1885	324
Portsmouth Daily Times			
637 Sixth St . . . . .Portsmouth OH 45662	800-582-7277	740-353-3101	528-2
Portsmouth Regional Hospital			
333 Borthwick Ave . . . . .Portsmouth NH 03801	800-685-8282	603-436-5110	373-3
Posca Bros Dental Laboratory Inc			
641 W Willow St . . . . .Long Beach CA 90806	800-537-6722	562-427-1811	414
Posey Co 5635 Peck Rd . . . . .Arcadia CA 91006	800-447-6739	626-443-3143	475
Positech Corp			
191 N Rush Lake Rd . . . . .Laurens IA 50554	800-831-6026	712-841-4548	468
POSitive Software Co			
604 W Kennewick Ave . . . . .Kennewick WA 99336	800-735-6860	509-371-0600	175
Positronic Industries Inc			
423 N Campbell Ave			
PO Box 8247. . . . . .Springfield MO 65801	800-641-4054	417-866-2322	253
Posner Industries Inc			
8641 Edgeworth Dr . . . . .Capitol Heights MD 20743	888-767-6377	301-350-1000	490
Post & Nickel			
144 N 14th St . . . . .Lincoln NE 68508	877-667-6107	402-476-3432	157-5
Post Glover Resistors Inc			
1369 Cox Rd . . . . .Erlanger KY 41018	800-537-6144*	859-283-0778	253
Cust Svc			
Post Hotel, The			
200 Pipestone Rd PO Box 69 . . . . .Lake Louise AB T0L1E0	800-661-1586	403-522-3989	378
Post Ranch Inn			
Hwy 1 PO Box 219 . . . . .Big Sur CA 93920	800-527-2200	831-667-2200	703
Post University			
800 Country Club Rd . . . . .Waterbury CT 06723	800-345-2562	203-596-4500	166
Postal Connections of America			
6136 Frisco Sq Blvd Ste 400 . . . . .Frisco TX 75034	800-767-8257		310
Postal Presort Inc			
820 W Second St N . . . . .Wichita KS 67203	800-235-3033	316-262-3333	5
PostalAnnex+ Inc			
7580 Metropolitan Dr Ste 200 . . . . .San Diego CA 92108	800-456-1525	619-563-4800	113
PostcardMania			
2145 Sunnydale Blvd Bldg 101 . . . . . . .Clearwater FL 33765	800-628-1804		365
Post-Journal			
15 W Second St . . . . .Jamestown NY 14701	866-756-9600	716-487-1111	528-2
Postler & Jaeckle Corp			
615 S Ave . . . . .Rochester NY 14620	800-724-4252	585-546-7450	189-10
PostNet International Franchise Corp			
1819 Wazee St . . . . .Denver CO 80202	800-841-7171	303-771-7100	113
Postpartum Support International			
6706 SW 54th Ave . . . . .Portland OR 97219	800-944-4773	503-894-9453	48-17
Post-Register			
PO Box 1800 . . . . .Idaho Falls ID 83403	800-574-6397	208-522-1800	528-2
Post-Standard			
220 S Warren St . . . . .Syracuse NY 13202	866-447-3787	315-470-0011	528-2
Post-Star			
76 Lawrence St . . . . .Glens Falls NY 12801	800-724-2543	518-792-3131	528-2
Posty Cards			
1600 Olive St . . . . .Kansas City MO 64127	800-821-7968	816-231-2323	130
Pot O' Gold Cinema Advertising			
11555 Central Pkwy . . . . .Jacksonville FL 32224	800-446-5330	904-744-7478	
Potamkin Automotive			
6200 NW 167th . . . . .Miami Lakes FL 33014	855-799-9965		57
Potawatomi Inn			
Pokagan State Pk 6 Ln 100A Lk James			
. . . . .Angola IN 46703	877-768-2928	260-833-1077	665
Potluck Press			
920 S Bayview St . . . . .Seattle WA 98134	877-818-5500	206-328-1300	130
Potomac Conference Corp of Seventh Day Adventists			
606 Greenville Ave . . . . .Staunton VA 24401	800-732-1844	540-886-0771	48-20
Potomac Electric Corp			
1 Westinghouse Plz . . . . .Boston MA 02136	877-737-2662		

Name	Address	City	State	Zip	Toll-Free	Phone	Class
Potomac Mills	2700 Potomac Mills Cir	Woodbridge	VA	22192	**877-746-6642**	317-636-1600	458
Potomac State College	101 Ft Ave	Keyser	WV	26726	**800-262-7332**	304-788-6800	162
Potomac Supply Corp	1398 Kinsale Rd *Sales	Kinsale	VA	22488	**800-365-3900***	804-472-2527	547
Potter Distributing Inc	4037 Roger B Chaffee Blvd	Grand Rapids	MI	49548	**800-748-0568**	616-531-6860	38
Potter Electric Signal Company Inc	5757 Phantom Dr Ste 125	Hazelwood	MO	63042	**800-325-3936**	314-878-4321	283
Potter-Roemer	17451 Hurley St	City of Industry	CA	91744	**800-366-3473**	626-336-4561	674
Poudre Valley Rural Electric Assn Inc	7649 Rea Pkwy	Fort Collins	CO	80528	**800-432-1012**	970-226-1234	245
Poughkeepsie Journal	85 Civic Ctr Plz	Poughkeepsie	NY	12601	**800-765-1120**	845-437-4800	528-2
Pounding Mill Quarry Corp	171 St Clair S Crossing	Bluefield	VA	24605	**888-661-7625**	276-326-1145	501-5
Poverty Point National Monument	c/o Poverty Point State Pk PO Box 276	Epps	LA	71237	**888-926-5492**	318-926-5492	560
Poverty Point Reservoir State Park	1500 Poverty Pt Pkwy	Delhi	LA	71232	**800-474-0392**	318-878-7536	561
Poverty Point State Historic Site	6859 Hwy 577	Pioneer	LA	71266	**888-926-5492**	318-926-5492	561
Powder River Energy Corp (PRE)	221 Main St PO Box 930	Sundance	WY	82729	**800-442-3630**		245
Powder River Transportation	1700 U S 14	Gillette	WY	82716	**888-970-7233**		108
Powel House	244 S Third St	Philadelphia	PA	19106	**877-426-8056**	215-627-0364	50-3
Powell Electronics Inc	200 Commodore Dr	Swedesboro	NJ	08085	**800-235-7880**	856-241-8000	246
Powell Industries Inc	8550 Mosely Dr *NASDAQ: POWL*	Houston	TX	77075	**800-480-7273**	713-944-6900	725
Powell River General Hospital	5000 Joyce Ave	Powell River	BC	V8A5R3	**800-567-8911**	604-485-3211	373-2
Powell's Books Inc	7 NW Ninth Ave	Portland	OR	97209	**800-878-7323**	503-228-0540	95
Powell's City of Books	1005 W Burnside St	Portland	OR	97209	**800-878-7323**	503-228-4651	95
Power & Motoryacht Magazine	10 Bokum Rd	Essex	CT	06426	**800-284-8036**	860-767-3200	455-4
Power & Telephone Supply Company Inc	2673 Yale Ave *Cust Svc	Memphis	TN	38112	**800-238-7514***	901-866-3300	246
Power 1051	32 Ave of the Americas	New York	NY	10013	**800-585-1051**	212-377-7900	641-71
Power Engineering Corp	PO Box 766	Wilkes-Barre	PA	18703	**800-626-0903**	570-823-8822	261
Power Grid Engineering LLC	100 Colonial Ctr Pkwy Ste 400	Lake Mary	FL	32746	**877-819-1171**	321-244-0170	188
Power Motive Corp	5000 Vasquez Blvd	Denver	CO	80216	**800-627-0087**	303-355-5900	357
Power Organics	301 S Old Stage Rd PO Box 1626	Mount Shasta	CA	96067	**877-769-3795**	530-926-6684	794
Power Service Products Inc	PO Box 1089	Weatherford	TX	76086	**800-643-9089**	817-599-9486	534
Power Wellness	851 Oak Creek Dr	Lombard	IL	60148	**877-888-2988**	630-570-2600	461
Power Worker's Union, The	244 Eglinton Ave E	Toronto	ON	M4P1K2	**800-958-8798**	416-481-4491	413
PowerChord Inc	360 Central Ave 5th Fl	St Petersburg	FL	33701	**800-350-0981**	727-823-1530	
Powercon Corp	PO Box 477	Severn	MD	21144	**800-638-5055**	410-551-6500	725
Powered By Search Inc	505 Consumers Rd Ste 507	Toronto	ON	M2J4V8	**866-611-5535**	416-840-9044	224
Powerex Inc	173 Pavilion Ln	Youngwood	PA	15697	**800-451-1415**	724-925-7272	692
Powerfilm Inc	2337 230th St	Ames	IA	50014	**888-354-7773**	515-292-7606	692
Powernail Co	1300 Rose Rd	Lake Zurich	IL	60047	**800-323-1653**	847-847-3000	754
Powers Fasteners Inc	2 Powers Ln	Brewster	NY	10509	**800-524-3244**		491
PowerScore Inc	57 Hasell St	Charleston	SC	29401	**800-545-1750**		759
Powersmiths International Corp	10 Devon Rd	Brampton	ON	L6T5B5	**800-747-9627**	905-791-1493	762
Powersteering Software Inc	401 Congress Ave Ste 1850	Austin	TX	78701	**866-390-9088**	617-492-0707	178-7
Powrmatic Inc	PO Box 439	Finksburg	MD	21048	**800-966-9100**	410-833-9100	356
Pozas Bros Trucking Company Inc	8130 Enterprise Dr	Newark	CA	94560	**800-874-8383**	510-742-9939	775
PP Systems International Inc	110 Haverhill Rd Ste 301	Amesbury	MA	01913	**866-211-9346**	978-834-0505	250
PPA (Professional Photographers of America Inc)	229 Peachtree St NE Ste 2200	Atlanta	GA	30303	**800-786-6277**	404-522-8600	48-4
PPAI (Promotional Products Assn International)	3125 Skyway Cir N	Irving	TX	75038	**888-426-7724**	972-252-0404	49-18
PPC Mechanical Seals	2769 Mission Dr	Baton Rouge	LA	70805	**800-731-7325**	225-356-4333	326
PPG Industries Inc	17451 Von Karman Ave	Irvine	CA	92614	**800-544-3338**	949-474-0400	546
PPI (Paper Pak Industries)	1941 N White Ave	La Verne	CA	91750	**888-293-6529**	909-392-1750	297-9
PPL Electric Utilities Corp	827 Hausman Rd *NYSE: PPL* ■ *Cust Svc	Allentown	PA	18104	**800-342-5775***	800-358-6623	782
PPL Global LLC	2 N Ninth St *NYSE: PPL*	Allentown	PA	18101	**800-345-3085**	610-774-5151	782
PPOK (Pharmacy Providers of OK)	3000 E Memorial Rd	Edmond	OK	73013	**877-557-5707**		

Name	Address	City	State	Zip	Toll-Free	Phone	Class
PPP (Peter Pepper Products Inc)	17929 S Susana Rd PO Box 5769	Compton	CA	90224	**800-496-0204**		587
PPPL (Princeton Plasma Physics Laboratory)	PO Box 451	Princeton	NJ	08543	**800-772-2222**	609-243-2000	664
PPS Parking & Transportation Inc	1800 E Garry Ave Ste 107	Santa Ana	CA	92705	**800-701-3763**	949-223-8707	
Prab Inc	5944 E Kilgore Rd	Kalamazoo	MI	49048	**800-968-7722**	269-382-8200	207
Practical Horseman Magazine	656 Quince OrchaRd Rd Ste 600	Gaithersburg	MD	20878	**800-365-5548**		455-14
Practice Concepts	2706 Harbor Blvd	Costa Mesa	CA	92626	**877-778-2020**	714-545-5110	317
Practice Technology Inc	1312 E Robinson St	Orlando	FL	32801	**866-974-3946**	407-228-4400	177
Practice Velocity LLC	8777 Velocity Dr	Machesney Park	IL	61115	**866-995-9863**		
Practicon Inc	1112 Sugg Pkwy	Greenville	NC	27834	**800-959-9505**	252-752-5183	228
Practising Law Institute (PLI)	1177 Ave of the Americas 2nd Fl	New York	NY	10036	**800-260-4754**	212-824-5700	49-10
Prader-Willi Syndrome Assn (USA)	8588 Potter Park Dr Ste 500	Sarasota	FL	34238	**800-926-4797**		48-17
Pragma Systems Inc	13809 Research Blvd Ste 675	Austin	TX	78750	**800-224-1675**	512-219-7270	178-12
Prairie Band Casino & Resort	12305 150th Rd	Mayetta	KS	66509	**888-727-4946**	785-966-7777	133
Prairie College	350 Fifth Ave NE PO Box 4000	Three Hills	AB	T0M2N0	**800-661-2425**	403-443-5511	780
Prairie Farms Dairy Inc	1100 N Broadway St	Carlinville	IL	62626	**800-654-2547**	217-854-2547	296-27
Prairie Knights Casino & Resort	7932 Hwy 24	Fort Yates	ND	58538	**800-425-8277**	701-854-7777	133
Prairie Lakes Area Education Agency	1235 Fifth Ave S	Fort Dodge	IA	50501	**800-669-2325**	515-574-5500	681
Prairie Lakes Hospital & Care Ctr	401 Ninth Ave NW	Watertown	SD	57201	**877-917-7547**	605-882-7000	373-3
Prairie Land Electric Co-op Inc	14935 US Hwy 36	Norton	KS	67654	**800-577-3323**	785-877-3323	245
Prairie Meadows	1 Prairie Meadows Dr	Altoona	IA	50009	**800-325-9015**	515-967-1000	133
Prairie Public Broadcasting	207 N Fifth St	Fargo	ND	58102	**800-359-6900**	701-241-6900	736-29
Prairie Public Broadcasting Inc	207 N Fifth St	Fargo	ND	58102	**800-359-6900**	701-241-6900	628
Prairie Valley School Div No 208	3080 Albert St N PO Box 1937	Regina	SK	SKS4P3E1	**877-266-1666**	306-949-3366	
Prairie View A & M University	700 University Dr PO Box 519	Prairie View	TX	77446	**877-241-1752**	936-261-3311	166
Prairie Wetlands Learning Ctr	602 State Hwy 210 E	Fergus Falls	MN	56537	**800-344-9453**		
Pran Systems	399 Jacquard St Ste 100	Quebec	QC	G1N4J6	**866-688-7726**	418-688-7726	
Prasco LLC	6125 Commerce Ct	Mason	OH	45040	**866-525-0688**	513-618-3333	231
Pratt & Whitney Canada Inc	1000 Marie-Victorin Blvd	Longueuil	QC	J4G1A1	**800-268-8000**	450-677-9411	21
Pratt Community College	348 NE SR-61	Pratt	KS	67124	**800-794-3091**	620-672-5641	162
Pratt Industries USA	1800C Sarasota Pkwy	Conyers	GA	30013	**800-835-2088**	770-918-5678	544
Praxair Inc	39 Old Ridgebury Rd *NYSE: PX*	Danbury	CT	06810	**800-772-9247**	203-837-2000	143
PRB (Population Reference Bureau)	1875 Connecticut Ave NW Ste 520	Washington	DC	20009	**800-877-9881**	202-483-1100	48-7
PRC (Patients Rights Council)	PO Box 760	Steubenville	OH	43952	**800-958-5678**	740-282-3810	48-8
PRCA (Professional Rodeo Cowboys Assn)	101 Pro Rodeo Dr	Colorado Springs	CO	80919	**800-234-7722**	719-593-8840	48-22
PRE (Powder River Energy Corp)	221 Main St PO Box 930	Sundance	WY	82729	**800-442-3630**		245
Precept Medical Products Inc	370 Airport Rd	Arden	NC	28704	**800-438-5827**	828-681-0209	572
PreCheck Inc	2500 E T C Jester Blvd	Houston	TX	77008	**800-999-9861**		362
Precise Flight Inc	63354 Powell Butte Hwy	Bend	OR	97701	**800-547-2558**		22
Precision Abrasives	3176 Abbott Rd	Orchard Park	NY	14127	**800-722-3967**		1
Precision Assoc Inc	3800 N Washington Ave	Minneapolis	MN	55412	**800-394-6590**	612-333-7464	673
Precision Auto Care Inc	748 Miller Dr SE *OTC: PACI*	Leesburg	VA	20175	**866-944-8863**		62-5
Precision BioLogic Inc	140 Eileen Stubbs Ave	Dartmouth	NS	B3B0A9	**800-267-2796**	902-468-6422	473
Precision Countertops Inc	26200 SW 95th Ave Ste 303	Wilsonville	OR	97070	**800-548-4445**	503-692-6660	115
Precision Devices Inc	8840 N Greenview Dr	Middleton	WI	53562	**800-274-9825**		
Precision Dynamics Corp	27770 N Entertainment Dr Ste 200	Valencia	CA	91355	**800-847-0670**	661-257-0233	475
Precision Electronic Glass Inc	1013 Hendee Rd	Vineland	NJ	08360	**800-982-4734**	856-691-2234	331
Precision Fabrics Group Inc	301 N Elm St Ste 600	Greensboro	NC	27401	**800-284-8001**		740-1
Precision Foods Inc	11457 Olde Cabin Rd Ste 100	Saint Louis	MO	63141	**800-442-5242**	314-567-7400	296-37
Precision H20 Inc	6328 E Utah Ave	Spokane	WA	99212	**800-425-2098**	509-536-9214	1
Precision Hose	2200 Centre Park Ct	Stone Mountain	GA	30087	**877-850-2662**	770-413-5680	295

				Toll-Free	Phone	Class
Precision IBC Inc 8054 Mcgowin Dr	Fairhope	AL	36532	**800-544-7069**	251-990-6789	686
Precision Kidd Steel Company Inc 1 Quality Way	Aliquippa	PA	15001	**800-945-5003**	724-378-7670	693
Precision Laboratories Inc 1429 S Shields Dr	Waukegan	IL	60085	**800-323-6280**	847-596-3001	145
Precision Metal Works 6901 Preston Hwy	Louisville	KY	40219	**877-511-9695**		752
Precision Opinion Inc 101 Convention Center Dr Plaza 125	Las Vegas	NV	89109	**800-780-2790**	702-483-4000	
Precision Optics Corp Inc 22 E Broadway *OTC: PEYE*	Gardner	MA	01440	**800-447-2812**	978-630-1800	381
Precision Parts & Remanufacturing Co 4411 SW 19th St	Oklahoma City	OK	73108	**800-654-3846**	405-681-2592	247
Precision Products Inc 316 Limit St *Cust Svc	Lincoln	IL	62656	**800-225-5891***	217-735-1590	428
Precision Shooting Equipment Inc 2727 N Fairview Ave	Tucson	AZ	85705	**800-477-7789**	520-884-9065	706
Precision Specialties Co 1201 E Pecan St	Sherman	TX	75090	**800-527-3295**		406
Precision Steel Warehouse Inc 3500 Wolf Rd	Franklin Park	IL	60131	**800-323-0740**	847-455-7000	490
Precision Tank & Equipment Company Inc 3503 Conover Rd	Virginia	IL	62691	**800-258-4197**	217-452-7228	273
Precision Thermoplastic Components Inc PO Box 1296	Lima	OH	45802	**800-860-4505**	419-227-4500	604
Precision Time Systems Inc 5433 Main St	Shallotte	NC	28470	**877-416-6660**	910-253-9850	406
Precision Walls Inc 1230 NE MaynaRd Rd	Cary	NC	27513	**800-849-9255**	919-832-0380	189-9
Precisionform Inc 148 W Airport Rd	Lititz	PA	17543	**800-233-3821**	717-560-7610	617
Precix Inc 744 Bellville Ave	New Bedford	MA	02745	**800-225-8505**	508-998-4000	673
Preco Electronics Inc 10335 W Emerald St	Boise	ID	83704	**866-977-7326**	208-323-1000	470
Precor Inc 20031 142nd Ave NE	Woodinville	WA	98072	**800-786-8404**	425-486-9292	267
Predator Trucking Co 3181 Trumbull Ave	McDonald	OH	44437	**800-235-5624**	330-530-0712	775
Preferred Bank Los Angeles 601 S Figueroa St 29th Fl *NASDAQ: PFBC*	Los Angeles	CA	90017	**888-673-1808**	213-891-1188	70
Preferred CommunityChoice PPO 218 W Sixth St	Tulsa	OK	74119	**800-884-4776**	918-594-5200	390-3
Preferred Employers Insurance Co PO Box 85478 *Cust Svc	San Diego	CA	92186	**888-472-9001***	866-472-9602	390-4
Preferred Homecare Infusion LLC 4601 E Hilton Ave Ste 100	Phoenix	AZ	85034	**800-636-2123**	480-446-9010	362
Preferred Hotel Group *Preferred Hotels & Resorts Worldwide Inc* 311 S Wacker Dr Ste 1900	Chicago	IL	60606	**800-650-1281**	312-913-0400	378
Preferred Meal Systems Inc 5240 St Charles Rd *Cust Svc	Berkeley	IL	60163	**800-886-6325***		296-36
Preferred Medical Marketing Corp 15720 Brixham Hill Ave Ste 460	Charlotte	NC	28277	**800-543-8176**	704-543-8103	177
Preferred Mental Health Management Inc 7309 E 21st St N Ste 110	Wichita	KS	67206	**800-819-9571**	316-262-0444	460
Preferred Mutual Insurance Co 1 Preferred Way	New Berlin	NY	13411	**800-333-7642**	607-847-6161	390-4
Preferred Strategies LLC 2425 Porter St Ste 20	Soquel	CA	95073	**888-232-7337**		177
PreferredOne Administrative Services Inc 6105 Golden Hills Dr	Golden Valley	MN	55416	**800-451-9597**	763-847-4000	461
Prelco Inc 94 Blvd Cartier	RiviŠre-du-Loup	QC	G5R2M9	**800-463-1325**	418-862-2274	329
Preload Inc 125 Kennedy Dr Ste 500	Hauppauge	NY	11788	**888-773-5623**	631-231-8100	
Prelude Systems Inc 5095 Ritter Rd Ste 112	Mechanicsburg	PA	17055	**800-579-1047**		177
Premera Blue Cross Blue 7001 220th St SW Bldg 1 *Cust Svc	Mountlake Terrace	WA	98043	**855-629-0987***		390-3
Premier Alaska Tours Inc 1900 Premier Ct	Anchorage	AK	99502	**888-486-8725**	907-279-0001	755
Premier Aluminum LLC 3633 S Memorial Dr	Racine	WI	53403	**800-254-9261**	262-554-2100	490
Premier America Credit Union 19867 Prairie St PO Box 2178	Chatsworth	CA	91313	**800-772-4000**	818-772-4000	219
Premier Coach Company Inc 946 Rte 7 S	Milton	VT	05468	**800-532-1811**	802-655-4456	107
Premier Colors Inc 100 Industrial Dr	Union	SC	29379	**800-245-6944**	864-427-0338	145
Premier Concrete Products 5102 Galveston Rd	Houston	TX	77017	**800-575-7293**	713-641-2727	183
Premier Dental Products Co 1710 Romano Dr	Plymouth Meeting	PA	19462	**888-670-6100**	610-239-6000	228
Premier Die Casting Co 1177 Rahway Ave	Avenel	NJ	07001	**800-394-3006**	732-634-3000	308
Premier Direct Marketing Inc 5051 Commerce Crossings Dr	Louisville	KY	40229	**800-737-0205**	502-367-6441	195
Premier Equipment LLC 2025 US Hwy 14 W	Huron	SD	57350	**800-627-5469**		274
Premier Golf 4355 River Green Pkwy	Duluth	GA	30096	**866-260-4409**	770-291-4202	766
Premier Inc 12255 El Camino Real	San Diego	CA	92130	**877-777-1552**	858-481-2727	352
Premier Jets 2140 NE 25th Ave	Hillsboro	OR	97124	**800-635-8583**	503-640-2927	13
Premier Malt Products Inc 88 Market St *Cust Svc	Saddle Brook	NJ	07663	**800-521-1057***	586-443-3355	459

				Toll-Free	Phone	Class
Premier Members Credit Union 5505 Arapahoe Ave	Boulder	CO	80303	**800-468-0634**	303-657-7000	219
Premier Pyrotechnics Inc 25255 Hwy K	Richland	MO	65556	**888-647-6863**	417-322-6595	45
Premier Realty Group 2 N Sewalls Point Rd	Stuart	FL	34996	**800-915-8517**	772-287-1777	648
Premier Safety & Service Inc 2 Industrial Pk Dr	Oakdale	PA	15071	**800-828-1080**	724-693-8699	385
Premier Subaru LLC 150 N Main St	Branford	CT	06405	**888-690-6710**	203-481-0687	57
Premier Tech Chronos 1 Premier Ave	Rivere-du-Loup	QC	G5R6C1	**866-571-7354**	418-868-8324	680
Premier Tours 1120 South St	Philadelphia	PA	19147	**800-545-1910**		755
Premier Valley Bank 255 E River Pk Cir Ste 180	Fresno	CA	93720	**877-438-2002**	559-438-2002	70
Premiere Credit of North America LLC PO Box 19309	Indianapolis	IN	46219	**866-808-7118**		160
Premio Foods Inc 50 Utter Ave	Hawthorne	NJ	07506	**800-864-7622**		
Premium Rx National LLC 15809 Crabbs Branch Way	Rockville	MD	20855	**877-862-7796**	301-230-0908	
Premix Marbletite 1259 NW 21st St	Pompano Beach	FL	33069	**800-432-5097**	954-917-7665	1
Prentke Romich Co 1022 Heyl Rd	Wooster	OH	44691	**800-262-1984**	330-262-1984	202
Presby's Inspired Life 2000 Joshua Rd	Lafayette Hill	PA	19444	**877-977-3729**	610-834-1001	48-20
Presbyterian Childrens Services Inc 1220 N Lindbergh Blvd	St. Louis	MO	63132	**800-383-8147**	314-989-9727	48-20
Presbyterian Church (USA) 100 Witherspoon St	Louisville	KY	40202	**888-728-7228**	502-569-5000	48-20
Presbyterian College 503 S Broad St	Clinton	SC	29325	**800-476-7272**		166
Presbyterian Disaster Assistance (PDA) 100 Witherspoon St	Louisville	KY	40202	**800-728-7228**		48-5
Presbyterian Homes Inc, The 2109 Sandy Ridge Rd	Colfax	NC	27235	**800-225-9573**	336-886-6553	48-15
Presbyterian Hospital 1100 Central Ave SE	Albuquerque	NM	87106	**888-977-2333**	505-841-1234	373-3
Presbyterian Kaseman Hospital 8300 Constitution Ave NE	Albuquerque	NM	87110	**800-356-2219**	505-291-2000	373-3
Presbyterian SeniorCare-Westminster Place 1215 Hulton Rd	Oakmont	PA	15139	**877-772-6500**	412-828-5600	448
Presbyterians Today Magazine 100 Witherspoon St	Louisville	KY	40202	**800-728-7228**	800-872-3283	455-18
Prescolite Inc 701 Millennium Blvd	Greenville	SC	29607	**888-777-4832**	864-678-1000	438
Prescott Chamber of Commerce 117 W Goodwin St	Prescott	AZ	86303	**800-266-7534**	928-445-2000	139
Prescott College 220 Grove Ave	Prescott	AZ	86301	**877-350-2100**		166
Prescott National Cemetery 500 Hwy 89 N	Prescott	AZ	86301	**800-535-1117**	928-717-7569	136
Prescott Valley Chamber of Commerce 3001 N Main St Ste 2A	Prescott Valley	AZ	86314	**800-355-0843**	928-772-8857	139
Prescription Solutions 3515 Harbor Blvd	Costa Mesa	CA	92626	**800-788-4863**		582
Presentation College 1500 N Main St	Aberdeen	SD	57401	**800-437-6060**	605-225-1634	166
Presentation Concepts Corp 6517 Basile Rowe	East Syracuse	NY	13057	**888-262-7596**	315-437-1314	45
Preservation Technologies LP 111 Thomson Park Dr	Cranberry Township	PA	16066	**800-416-2665**	724-779-2111	321
Presidential Aviation 1725 NW 51st Pl Ft Lauderdale Executive Airport	Fort Lauderdale	FL	33309	**888-772-8622**	954-772-8622	13
Presidential Online Bank 4520 East-West Hwy	Bethesda	MD	20814	**800-383-6266**	301-652-0700	70
Presidio County PO Box 879	Marfa	TX	79843	**888-368-4689**		
Presidio Group, The 6967 S River Gate Dr Ste 200	Salt Lake City	UT	84047	**800-924-1404**	801-924-1400	194
Presidio Networked Solutions Inc 7601 Ora Glen Dr Ste 100	Greenbelt	MD	20770	**800-452-6926**	301-313-2000	180
Presley Tours Inc 16 Presley Pk Dr PO Box 58	Makanda	IL	62958	**800-621-6100**	618-549-0704	755
Presque Isle Electric & Gas Co-op PO Box 308	Onaway	MI	49765	**800-423-6634**	989-733-8515	245
Presque Isle State Park 301 Peninsula Dr Ste 1	Erie	PA	16505	**888-727-2757**	814-833-7424	561
Press Democrat 427 Mendocino Ave	Santa Rosa	CA	95401	**800-675-5056**	707-546-2020	528-2
Press Ganey Associates Inc 404 Columbia Pl	South Bend	IN	46601	**800-232-8032**		194
Press-A-Print International LLC 1463 Commerce Way	Idaho Falls	ID	83401	**888-880-0004**		
Presscut Industries Inc 1730 Briercroft Ct	Carrollton	TX	75006	**800-442-4924**	972-389-0615	326
Pressed Juicery LLC 1550 17th St	Santa Monica	CA	90404	**855-755-8423**		
Pressed4Time Inc 50 Mendon St	Upton	MA	01568	**800-423-8711**	508-879-5966	425
Press-Enterprise Inc 3185 Lackawanna Ave	Bloomsburg	PA	17815	**888-484-6345**	570-387-1234	633-8
Pressley Ridge 5500 Corporate Dr Ste 400	Pittsburgh	PA	15237	**888-777-0820**	412-872-9400	48-6
Pressman Toy Corp 3701 W Plano Pkwy Ste 100 *Cust Svc	Plano	TX	75075	**800-800-0298***	855-258-8214	757
Press-Republican 170 Margaret St PO Box 459	Plattsburgh	NY	12901	**800-288-7323**	518-561-2300	528-2
Press-Seal Gasket Corp 2424 W State Blvd	Fort Wayne	IN	46808	**800-348-7325**	260-436-0521	326
Presstek Inc 55 Executive Dr *NASDAQ: PRST*	Hudson	NH	03051	**800-422-3616**	603-595-7000	776

Name / Address	City	State	Zip	Toll-Free	Phone	Class
Presteligence Inc 8328 Cleveland Ave NW	Canton	OH	44720	**888-438-6050**		180
Prestera Trucking 19129 US Rt 52	South Point	OH	45680	**855-761-7943**	740-894-4770	775
Prestige Accommodations International 1231 E Dyer Rd Ste 240	Santa Ana	CA	92705	**800-321-6338**	714-957-9100	184
Prestige Financial Services Inc 351 W Opportunity Way	Draper	UT	84020	**888-822-7422**		217
Prestige Graphics Inc 9630 Ridgehaven Ct Ste B	San Diego	CA	92123	**800-383-9361**	858-560-8213	531
Prestige Harbourfront Resort & Convention Centre 251 Harbourfront Dr NE	Salmon Arm	BC	V1E2W7	**877-737-8443**	250-833-5800	378
Prestige Maintenance USA Ltd 1808 Tenth St Ste 300	Plano	TX	75074	**800-321-4773**	972-578-9801	192
Prestige Medical Corporation International 8600 Wilbur Ave	Northridge	CA	91324	**800-762-3333**	818-993-3030	473
Prestige Travel & Cruises Inc 6175 Spring Mountain Rd	Las Vegas	NV	89146	**800-758-5693**	702-251-5552	766
Prestini Corp 351 E Patagonia Hwy Ste 4 *General	Nogales	AZ	85621	**800-528-6569***	520-287-4931	523
Presto Products Co 670 N Perkins St PO Box 2399	Appleton	WI	54912	**800-558-3525**		66
Presto Tape Inc 1626 Bridgewater Rd	Bensalem	PA	19020	**800-331-1373**	215-245-8555	727
Prestolite Wire Corp 200 Galleria Officentre Ste 212	Southfield	MI	48034	**800-498-3132**	248-355-4422	809
Preston Industries Inc 6600 W Touhy Ave	Niles	IL	60714	**800-229-7569**	847-647-0611	419
Presto-X Co 10421 Portal Rd Ste 101	La Vista	NE	68128	**800-759-1942**		573
Pretzelmaker 5555 Glenridge Connector Ste 850	Atlanta	GA	30342	**877-639-2361**		666
Pretzels Inc 123 Harvest Rd PO Box 503	Bluffton	IN	46714	**800-456-4838**	260-824-4838	296-9
Prevent Blindness America 211 W Wacker Dr Ste 1700	Chicago	IL	60606	**800-331-2020**		48-17
Prevent Cancer Foundation (PCF) 1600 Duke St Ste 500	Alexandria	VA	22314	**800-227-2732**	703-836-4412	48-17
Prevention Magazine 733 Third Ave	Emmaus	PA	10017	**800-813-8070**		455-13
Preventure Inc 2000 Nooseneck Hill Rd	Coventry	RI	02816	**888-321-4326**		702
Preverco Inc 285 Rue De Rotterdam	Saint-augustin-de-desmaures	QC	G3A2E5	**877-667-2725**	418-878-8930	363
Prevost Car Inc 35 boul Gagnon	Sainte-Claire	QC	G0R2V0	**877-773-8678**	418-883-3391	513
Prevue Pet Products Inc 224 N Maplewood Ave	Chicago	IL	60612	**800-243-3624**	312-243-3624	574
Prezacor Inc 170 Cold Soil Rd	Princeton	NJ	08540	**855-792-3335**		738
Price Books & Forms Inc 531 E Sierra Madre Ave	Glendora	CA	91741	**800-423-8961**	909-594-8942	633-2
Price Bros Equipment Co 619 S Washington St	Wichita	KS	67211	**877-957-9577**		
Price County 126 Cherry St	Phillips	WI	54555	**800-362-9472**	715-339-3325	337
Price Electric Co-op 508 N Lake Ave PO Box 110	Phillips	WI	54555	**800-884-0881**	715-339-2155	245
PRICE Futures Group Inc, The 141 West Jackson Blvd Ste 1340A	Chicago	IL	60604	**800-769-7021**	312-264-4300	686
Price Pfister Inc 19701 Da Vinci St	Lake Forest	CA	92610	**800-732-8238**	949-672-4000	605
Price Steel Ltd 13500 156 St	Edmonton	AB	T5V1L3	**800-661-6789**	780-447-9999	478
Pricelinecom LLC 800 Connecticut Ave	Norwalk	CT	06854	**800-774-2354**		51
PriceWaiter LLC 426 Market St	Chattanooga	TN	37421	**855-671-9889**		386
PricewaterhouseCoopers LLP 300 Madison Ave	New York	NY	10017	**800-993-9971**	646-471-4000	2
Pricon Inc 1831 W Lincoln Ave	Anaheim	CA	92801	**800-660-1831**	714-758-8832	225
Pride International Inc 5847 San Felipe St Ste 3300	Houston	TX	77057	**877-736-3772**	713-789-1400	535
Pride Mobility Products Corp 182 Susquehanna Ave	Exeter	PA	18643	**800-800-8586**		475
Pride Products Corp 4333 Veterans Memorial Hwy	Ronkonkoma	NY	11779	**800-898-5550**	631-737-4444	786
Pride Transport Inc 5499 W 2455 S	Salt Lake City	UT	84120	**800-877-1320**	801-972-8890	775
Priefert Manufacturing 2630 S Jefferson Ave PO box 1540	Mount Pleasant	TX	75455	**800-527-8616**	903-572-1741	311
Prier Products Inc 4515 E 139th St	Grandview	MO	64030	**800-362-1463**	800-362-9055	606
Priester Aviation 1061 S Wolf Rd	Wheeling	IL	60090	**888-323-7887**	847-537-1133	24
Priester Pecan Company Inc 208 Old Fort Rod E	Fort Deposit	AL	36032	**800-277-3226**	334-227-4301	296-28
Primal Essence Inc 1351 Maulhardt Ave	Oxnard	CA	93030	**877-774-6253**		
Primary Color Inc 9239 Premier Row	Dallas	TX	75247	**800-581-9555**	214-630-8800	683
Primary Freight Services Inc 6545 Caballero Blvd	Buena Park	CA	90620	**800-635-0013**	310-635-3000	311
Prima-Temp Inc 2820 Wilderness Pl Ste C	Boulder	CO	80301	**866-398-1032**		261
Prime Concepts Group Inc 1807 S Eisenhower St	Wichita	KS	67209	**800-946-7804**	316-942-1111	195
Prime Inc 2740 N Mayfair PO Box 4208 *Cust Svc	Springfield	MO	65803	**800-321-4552***	417-521-3950	775
Prime Management Services 3416 Primm Ln	Birmingham	AL	35216	**866-609-1599**	205-823-6106	47

Name / Address	City	State	Zip	Toll-Free	Phone	Class
Prime Rate Premium Finance Corp 2141 Enterprise Dr PO Box 100507 *Cust Svc	Florence	SC	29501	**800-777-7458***	843-669-0937	217
Prime Therapeutics Inc 1305 Corporate Ctr Dr	Eagan	MN	55121	**800-858-0723**	612-777-4000	582
PrimeArray Systems Inc 127 Riverneck Rd	Chelmsford	MA	01824	**800-433-5133**	978-654-6250	176
PrimeNet Direct Mktg Solutions LLC 7320 Bryan Dairy Rd	Largo	FL	33777	**800-826-2869**	727-447-6245	5
Primepak Co 133 Cedar Ln	Teaneck	NJ	07666	**800-786-5613**	201-836-5060	599
Primera Technology Inc 2 Carlson Pkwy N	Plymouth	MN	55447	**800-797-2772**	763-475-6676	173-6
Primeritus Financial Services Inc 440 Metroplex Dr	Nashville	TN	37211	**888-833-4238**		392
Primex Plastics Corp 1235 N 'F' St	Richmond	IN	47374	**800-222-5116**	765-966-7774	596
Primm Valley Resort & Casino 31900 S Las Vegas Blvd	Primm	NV	89019	**800-926-4455**		665
Primorigen Biosciences Inc 510 Charmany Dr	Madison	WI	53719	**866-372-7442**	608-441-8332	85
Primrose Oil Company Inc 11444 Denton Dr	Dallas	TX	75229	**800-275-2772**		537
Primrose School Franchising Co 3660 Cedarcrest Rd	Acworth	GA	30101	**800-745-0677**	770-529-4100	148
Prince Albert National Park of Canada Northern Prairies Field Unit PO Box 100 *Campground Resv	Waskesiu Lake	SK	S0J2Y0	**877-737-3783***	306-663-4522	559
Prince Castle Inc 355 E Kehoe Blvd	Carol Stream	IL	60188	**800-722-7853**	630-462-8800	298
Prince Corp 8351 County Rd H	Marshfield	WI	54449	**800-777-2486**		574
Prince Edward Island National Park of Canada 2 Palmers Ln *Campground Resv	Charlottetown	PE	C1A5V8	**800-663-7192***	902-672-6350	559
Prince Edward Island Tourism PO Box 2000	Charlottetown	PE	C1A7N8	**800-463-4734**	902-368-4000	769
Prince George Hotel, The 1725 Market St	Halifax	NS	B3J3N9	**800-565-1567**	902-425-1986	378
Prince George's Hospital Ctr 3001 Hospital Dr	Cheverly	MD	20785	**800-463-6295**	301-618-2000	373-3
Prince Lionheart Inc 2421 Westgate Rd	Santa Maria	CA	93455	**800-544-1132**	805-922-2250	64
Prince Preferred Guest Program 100 Holomoana St	Honolulu	HI	96815	**800-774-6234**		377
Prince Resorts Hawaii 100 Holomoana St	Honolulu	HI	96815	**888-977-4623**	808-956-1111	665
Prince William County-Greater Manassas Chamber of Commerce 9720 Capital Ct Ste 203	Manassas	VA	20110	**877-867-3853**	703-368-6600	139
Prince William Hospital 8700 Sudly Rd	Manassas	VA	20110	**800-526-7101**	703-369-8000	373-3
Prince William Regional Chamber of Commerce 9720 Capital Ct Ste 203	Manassas	VA	20110	**877-867-3853**	703-368-6600	139
Princess Bayside Beach Hotel & Golf Ctr 4801 Coastal Hwy *General	Ocean City	MD	21842	**888-622-9743***	410-723-2900	378
Princess Cruises 24844 Rockefeller Ave	Santa Clarita	CA	91355	**800-774-6237**	661-753-0000	220
Princess House Inc 470 Miles Standish Blvd *Sales	Taunton	MA	02780	**800-622-0039***	508-823-0711	365
Princeton Excess & Surplus Lines Insurance Co 555 College Rd E	Princeton	NJ	08543	**800-544-2378**	609-243-4200	390-4
Princeton HealthCare System 905 Herrontown Rd	Princeton	NJ	08540	**866-460-4776**	609-497-3300	362
Princeton Insurance Co 746 Alexander Rd PO Box 5322	Princeton	NJ	08540	**800-334-0588**	609-452-9404	390-4
Princeton Packet, The 300 Witherspoon St PO Box 350	Princeton	NJ	08542	**888-747-1122**	609-924-3244	633-8
Princeton Plasma Physics Laboratory (PPPL) PO Box 451	Princeton	NJ	08543	**800-772-2222**	609-243-2000	664
Princeton Public Schools 25 Valley Rd	Princeton	NJ	08540	**800-322-8174**	609-806-4200	
Princeton Review Inc, The Cochituate Pl 24 Prime Pkwy Ste 201	Natick	MA	01760	**800-273-8439**	508-663-5050	242
Princeton University 33 Washington Rd	Princeton	NJ	08544	**877-609-2273**	609-258-3000	166
Princeton University Press 41 William St	Princeton	NJ	08540	**800-777-4726**	609-258-4900	633-4
Principal Financial Services Inc 711 High St	Des Moines	IA	50392	**800-986-3343**		304
Principal Technical Services Inc 9960 Research Dr Ste 200	Irvine	CA	92618	**888-787-3711**		717
Principia College 13201 Clayton Rd	St. Louis	MO	63131	**800-277-4648**	618-374-2131	166
Principle Business Enterprises Inc PO Box 129	Dunbridge	OH	43414	**800-467-3224**	419-352-1551	554
Prinsco Inc 1717 16th St NE	Willmar	MN	56201	**800-992-1725**	320-222-6800	596
Print Direction Inc 1600 Indian Brook Way	Norcross	GA	30093	**877-435-1672**	770-446-6446	623
Print Magazine 10151 Carver Rd Ste 200	Blue Ash	OH	45242	**877-860-9145**	513-531-2690	455-5
Print NW 9914 32nd Ave S	Lakewood	WA	98499	**800-826-8260**	253-284-2300	623
Print Papa 1920 Lafayette St Ste L	Santa Clara	CA	95050	**800-657-7181**	408-567-9553	623
Print Services & Distribution Assn (PSDA) 330 N Wabash Ave Ste 2000	Chicago	IL	60611	**800-230-0175**		48-9
Print Source Inc, The 404 S Tracy St	Wichita	KS	67209	**800-535-9498**	316-945-7052	683
Print Works 3850 98 St NW	Edmonton	AB	T6E3L2	**888-452-8921**	780-452-8921	623
Printco Graphics Inc 14112 Industrial Rd	Omaha	NE	68144	**888-593-1080**	402-593-1080	225

	City	State	ZIP	Toll-Free	Phone	Class
Printed Systems						
1265 Gillingham Rd	Neenah	WI	54956	**800-352-2332***		412
*Sales						
PrintEdd Products Ltd						
2641 Forum Dr	Grand Prairie	TX	75052	**800-367-6728**	972-660-3800	110
Printek Inc						
1517 Townline Rd	Benton Harbor	MI	49022	**800-368-4636**	269-925-3200	173-6
Printers & Stationers Inc						
113 N Ct St	Florence	AL	35630	**800-624-5334**	256-764-8061	531
Printfection LLC						
3700 Quebec St Unit 100-136	Denver	CO	80207	**866-459-7990**		195
PrintFleet						
1000 Gardiners Rd Ste 202	Kingston	ON	K7K2X5	**866-382-8320**	613-549-3221	
Printing House Ltd, The						
1403 Bathurst St	Toronto	ON	M5R3H8	**800-874-0870**	416-536-6113	343
Printing Images Inc						
12266 Wilkins Ave A	Rockville	MD	20852	**866-685-4356**	301-984-1140	623
Printing Industries of America/Graphic Arts Technical Foundation (PIA/GATF)						
200 Deer Run Rd	Sewickley	PA	15143	**800-910-4283**	412-741-6860	49-16
Printing Prep Inc						
707 Washington St	Buffalo	NY	14203	**877-878-7114**	716-852-5011	776
PrintingForLesscom Inc						
100 PFL Way	Livingston	MT	59047	**800-930-6040**		623
Printmail Systems Inc						
23 Friends Ln	Newtown	PA	18940	**800-910-4844**	215-860-4250	225
Print-O-Stat Inc						
1011 W Market St	York	PA	17404	**800-711-8014**	717-854-7821	723
Print-O-Tape Inc						
755 Tower Rd	Mundelein	IL	60060	**800-346-6311**	847-362-1476	412
PrintPlacecom						
1130 Ave H E	Arlington	TX	76011	**877-405-3949**	817-701-3555	623
Printronix Inc						
6440 Oak Canyon Ste 200	Irvine	CA	92618	**800-665-6210**	714-368-2300	173-6
Printswell Inc						
135 Cahaba Valley Pkwy	Pelham	AL	35124	**800-476-4723**		
Prior Lake-Savage Area Public School District 719						
4540 Tower St SE	Prior Lake	MN	55372	**855-346-1650**	952-226-0000	681
Priority Business Services Inc						
19712 MacArthur Blvd Ste 110	Irvine	CA	92612	**800-710-8775**	949-222-1122	
Priority Capital Inc						
174 Green St	Melrose	MA	02176	**800-761-2118**	781-321-8778	216
Priority Express Courier						
5 Chelsea Pkwy	Boothwyn	PA	19061	**800-526-4646**	610-364-3300	542
Priority Health						
1231 E Beltline NE	Grand Rapids	MI	49525	**800-942-0954**	616-942-0954	390-3
Priority Management Systems Inc						
1595 Cliveden Ave Unit 7	Delta	BC	V3M6M2	**800-437-1032**	604-214-7772	760
Priority Wire & Cable Inc						
PO Box 398	North Little Rock	AR	72115	**800-945-5542***	501-372-5444	246
*General						
Pri-Pak Inc						
2000 Schenley Pl	Greendale	IN	47025	**800-274-7632**		88
Prism Medical Inc						
485 Millway Ave Unit 2	Concord	ON	L4K3V4	**877-304-5438**	416-260-2145	474
Prism Plastics Products Inc						
Hwy 65 PO Box 446	New Richmond	WI	54017	**877-246-7535**	715-246-7535	604
Prism Visual Software Inc						
1 Sagamore Hl Dr Ste 2B	Port Washington	NY	11050	**800-260-2793**	516-944-5920	225
Prisma Graphic Corp						
2937 E Broadway Rd	Phoenix	AZ	85040	**800-379-5777**	602-243-5777	623
Pristech Products Inc						
6952 Fairgrounds Pkwy Ste 107	San Antonio	TX	78238	**800-432-8722**	210-520-8051	172
Pritchett Controls Inc						
6980 Muirkirk Meadows Dr	Beltsville	MD	20705	**877-743-2363**	301-470-7300	189-10
Pritchett LLC						
8150 N Central Expy Ste 1350	Dallas	TX	75206	**800-992-5922**	214-239-9600	194
Pritchett Trucking Inc						
1050 SE Sixth St PO Box 311	Lake Butler	FL	32054	**800-486-7504**	386-496-2630	775
Pritikin Longevity Ctr & Spa						
8755 NW 36th St	Doral	FL	33178	**800-327-4914**	888-988-7168	702
Privacy Rights Clearinghouse						
3100 Fifth Ave Ste B	San Diego	CA	92103	**800-269-0271**	619-298-3396	48-10
Private Capital Management						
8889 Pelican Bay Blvd Ste 500	Naples	FL	34108	**800-763-0337**	239-254-2500	787
Private Eyes Inc						
2700 Ygnacio Valley Rd Ste 100	Walnut Creek	CA	94598	**877-292-3331**	925-927-3333	399
Priviti Capital Corp						
850 444 Fifth Ave S W	Calgary	AB	T2P2T8	**855-333-9943**	403-263-9943	524
PRL Aluminum						
14760 Don Julian Rd	City Of Industry	CA	91746	**877-775-2586**		490
PRL Glass Systems Inc						
251 Mason Way	City Of Industry	CA	91746	**800-433-7044**	626-961-5890	191-1
PRN Health Services Inc						
4321 W College Ave Ste 200	Appleton	WI	54914	**888-830-8811**		260
Pro Farmer						
6612 Chancellor Dr Ste 300	Cedar Falls	IA	50613	**800-772-0023***	319-277-1278	527-13
*Cust Svc						
Pro Orthopedic Devices Inc						
2884 E Ganley Rd	Tucson	AZ	85706	**800-523-5611**	520-294-4401	475
Pro Performance Sports LLC						
2081 Faraday Ave	Carlsbad	CA	92008	**877-225-7275**		707
Pro Petroleum Inc						
4985 N Sloan Ln	Las Vegas	NV	89115	**877-791-4900**		575
Pro Products LLC						
7201 Engle Rd	Fort Wayne	IN	46804	**866-357-5063**	260-490-5970	801
Pro Security Group						
541 N Valley Mills Dr	Waco	TX	76710	**855-753-7766**	254-753-7766	689
Pro Star Sports Inc						
1133 Winchester Ave	Kansas City	MO	64126	**800-821-8482**	816-241-9737	267
Pro Tapes & Specialties Inc						
621 Rte One S	North Brunswick	NJ	08902	**800-345-0234**	732-346-0900	727
Pro Tec Equipment Inc						
4837 W Grand River Ave	Charlotte	MI	48813	**800-292-1225**		
PrO Unlimited Inc						
301 Yamato Rd Ste 3199	Boca Raton	FL	33431	**800-291-1099**		729
Proa Medical Inc						
2512 Artesia Blvd Ste 305-C	Redondo Beach	CA	90278	**800-899-3385**		473
Proactive Management Consulting LLC						
2700 Cumberland Pkwy SE	Atlanta	GA	30339	**877-319-2198**	770-319-7468	196
Proactive Sports Inc						
1200 SE Second Ave	Canby	OR	97013	**800-369-8642**	503-263-8583	707
Proair LLC						
28731 County Rd 6	Elkhart	IN	46514	**800-338-8544**	574-264-5494	14
ProAssurance Corp						
100 Brookwood Pl	Birmingham	AL	35209	**800-282-6242**	205-877-4400	359-4
NYSE: PRA						
Pro-cad Software Ltd						
12 Elbow River Rd	Calgary	AB	T3Z2V2	**888-477-6223**	403-216-3375	177
ProCare Rx						
1267 Professional Pkwy	Gainesville	GA	30507	**800-377-1037**		804
Proceedings of the IEEE Magazine						
445 Hoes Ln	Piscataway	NJ	08855	**800-678-4333**	732-562-5478	455-21
Procel Temporary Services						
2447 Pacific Coast Hwy Ste 207	Hermosa Beach	CA	90254	**800-338-9905**	310-372-0560	260
Process Equipment Inc						
2770 Welborn St PO Box 1607	Pelham	AL	35124	**888-663-2028**	205-663-5330	18
Process Software Corp						
959 Concord St	Framingham	MA	01701	**800-722-7770**	508-879-6994	178-12
Processed Metals Innovators LLC						
600 21st Ave	Bloomer	WI	54724	**888-877-7277**	715-568-1700	478
Proco Products Inc						
PO Box 590	Stockton	CA	95201	**800-344-3246**	209-943-6088	672
ProCo Sound Inc						
5278 Lovers Ln	Portage	MI	49002	**800-253-7360**		490
ProComp Software Consultants Inc						
4629 Aicholtz Rd	Cincinnati	OH	45244	**800-783-1668**	513-685-5245	179
Procter & Gamble Co (PG)						
1 Procter & Gamble Plz	Cincinnati	OH	45202	**800-503-4611**	513-983-1100	185
NYSE: PG						
Proctor Engineering Group Ltd						
418 Mission Ave	San Rafael	CA	94901	**888-455-5742**	415-451-2480	261
Pro-data Computer Services Inc						
2809 S 160th St Ste 401	Omaha	NE	68130	**800-228-6318**	402-697-7575	175
Prodata Systems Inc						
11007 Slater Ave NE	Kirkland	WA	98033	**866-582-7485**	425-296-4168	39
Prodco International Inc						
9408 Boul du Golf	Montreal	QC	H1J3A1	**888-577-6326**	514-324-9796	689
Pro-Dex Inc						
2361 McGaw Ave	Irvine	CA	92614	**800-562-6204**		359-3
NASDAQ: PDEX						
Prodigy Diabetes Care LLC						
2701-A Hutchison McDonald Rd PO Box 481928	Charlotte	NC	28269	**800-366-5901**		474
Produce Source Partners						
13167 Telcourt Rd	Ashland	VA	23005	**800-344-4728**	804-262-8300	297-7
Producers Co-op Assoc						
300 E Buffalo St	Girard	KS	66743	**800-442-2809**	620-724-8241	445
Producers Financial						
5350 Tomah Dr Ste 3800	Colorado Springs	CO	80918	**800-985-5549**	719-535-0739	400
Producers Livestock Marketing Assn						
4809 S 114th St	Omaha	NE	68137	**800-257-4046**	402-597-9189	444
Producers Peanut Company Inc						
PO Box 250	Suffolk	VA	23434	**800-847-5491**	757-539-7496	296-32
Producers Rice Mill Inc						
PO Box 1248	Stuttgart	AR	72160	**800-369-7675**	870-673-4444	296-23
Product Design & Development Magazine						
199 E Badger Rd Ste 201	Madison	WI	53713	**800-869-6882**	973-920-7000	455-21
Product Development & Management Assn (PDMA)						
330 N Wabash Ave Ste 2000	Chicago	IL	60611	**800-232-5241**	312-321-5145	49-12
Product Safety Consulting Inc (PSC)						
605 Country Club Dr Ste I & J	Bensenville	IL	60106	**877-804-3066**	630-238-0188	196
Production Equipment Co						
401 Liberty St	Meriden	CT	06450	**800-758-5697**	203-235-5795	468
Production Management Industries LLC						
9761 Hwy 90 E	Morgan City	LA	70380	**888-229-3837**	985-631-3837	535
Production Press Inc						
307 E Morgan St	Jacksonville	IL	62650	**800-231-3880**	217-243-3353	623
Production Products Co						
6176 E Molloy Rd	East Syracuse	NY	13057	**800-800-6652**	315-431-7200	617
Production Tool Supply						
8655 E Eight Mile Rd	Warren	MI	48089	**800-366-3600**		384
Productivity Inc						
375 Bridgeport Ave 3rd Fl	Shelton	CT	06484	**800-966-5423**	203-225-0451	760
Products Engineering Corp						
2645 Maricopa St	Torrance	CA	90503	**800-923-6255**	310-787-4500	491
Proenergy Services LLC						
2001 ProEnergy Blvd	Sedalia	MO	65301	**844-367-4948**		461
Professional Ambulance & Oxygen Service Inc						
31 Smith Pl	Cambridge	MA	02138	**800-653-3640**	617-492-2700	30
Professional Assn of Diving Instructors International (PADI)						
30151 Tomas St	Rancho Santa Margarita	CA	92688	**800-729-7234***	949-858-7234	48-22
*Sales						
Professional Bank Services Inc						
6200 Dutchmans Ln Ste 305	Louisville	KY	40205	**800-523-4778**	502-451-6633	194
Professional Beauty Assn (PBA)						
15825 N 71st St Ste 100	Scottsdale	AZ	85254	**800-468-2274**	480-281-0424	49-18
Professional Building Systems Inc						
72 E Market St	Middleburg	PA	17842	**800-837-4552**		106
Professional Coaters Inc						
100 Commerce Park Dr	Cabot	AR	72023	**800-962-0344**		813
Professional Convention Management Assn (PCMA)						
35 E Wacker Dr Ste 500	Chicago	IL	60601	**877-827-7262**	312-423-7262	49-12
Professional Electric Products Co (PEPCO)						
33210 Lakeland Blvd	Eastlake	OH	44095	**800-872-7000**	440-946-3790	246
Professional Landcare Network (PLANET)						
950 Herndon Pkwy Ste 450	Herndon	VA	20170	**800-395-2522**	703-736-9666	48-2
Professional Liability Underwriting Society						
5353 Wayzata Blvd Ste 600	Minneapolis	MN	55416	**800-845-0778**	952-746-2580	49-9
Professional Photographers of America Inc (PPA)						
229 Peachtree St NE Ste 2200	Atlanta	GA	30303	**800-786-6277**	404-522-8600	48-4

Name / Address	Toll-Free	Phone	Class
Professional Plastics Inc 1810 E Valencia Dr . . . Fullerton CA 92831	800-878-0755	714-446-6500	597
Professional Research Consultants Inc 11326 P St . . . Omaha NE 68137	800-428-7455	402-592-5656	194
Professional Rodeo Cowboys Assn (PRCA) 101 Pro Rodeo Dr . . . Colorado Springs CO 80919	800-234-7722	719-593-8840	48-22
Professional Service Industries Inc (PSI) 1901 S Meyers Rd Ste 400 . . . Oakbrook Terrace IL 60181	800-548-7901	630-691-1490	261
Professional Shorthand Reporters Inc (PSR) 601 Poydras St Ste 1615 . . . New Orleans LA 70130	800-536-5255	504-529-5255	443
Professional Staff Management Inc 6801 Lake Plaza Dr Ste D-405 . . . Indianapolis IN 46220	800-967-5515	317-816-7007	627
Professional Tennis Registry PO Box 4739 . . . Hilton Head Island SC 29938	800-421-6289	843-785-7244	48-22
Professional Travel Inc 25000 Great Northern Corporate Ctr Ste 170 . . . Cleveland OH 44070	800-247-0060	440-734-8800	766
Proffitt & Goodson Inc Old Kingston Pl 4800 Old Kingston Pk Ste 200 . . . Knoxville TN 37919	866-776-3355	865-584-1850	229
Proficio 1555 Faraday Ave . . . Carlsbad CA 92008	800-779-5042		627
Profile Bank 45 Wakefield St PO Box 1808 . . . Rochester NH 03866	800-554-8969	603-332-2610	70
Profile Food Ingredients LLC 1151 Timber Dr . . . Elgin IL 60123	877-632-1700	847-622-1700	357
Profit Recovery Partners 2995 Red Hill Ave . . . Costa Mesa CA 92626	877-484-7776		
Profit Sharing/401(k) Council of America (PSCA) 20 N Wacker Dr Ste 3700 . . . Chicago IL 60606	866-614-8407	312-419-1863	49-12
Profitable Investing 9201 Corporate Blvd . . . Rockville MD 20850	800-211-8566		527-9
Proflowerscom 4840 Eastgate Mall . . . San Diego CA 92121	800-580-2913	800-565-6609	292
ProForma 8800 E Pleasant Valley Rd . . . Independence OH 44131	800-825-1525	216-520-8400	623
Progenics Pharmaceuticals Inc 1 World Trade Ctr 47th Fl Ste I . . . New York NY 10591 *NASDAQ: PGNX*	866-644-7188	646-975-2500	85
Program Planning Professionals 1340 Eisenhower Pl . . . Ann Arbor MI 48108	877-728-2331	734-741-7770	194
Programmer's Paradise Inc 1157 Shrewsbury Ave . . . Shrewsbury NJ 07702	800-599-4388	732-389-8950	174
Progress Instruments Inc 807 NW Commerce Dr . . . Lees Summit MO 64086	800-580-9881	816-524-4442	621
Progress Printing Co 2677 Waterlick Rd . . . Lynchburg VA 24502	800-572-7804		623
Progress Rail Services 1600 Progress Dr PO Box 1037 . . . Albertville AL 35950	800-476-8769	256-505-6600	682
Progress Software Corp 14 Oak Pk . . . Bedford MA 01730 *NASDAQ: PRGS*	800-477-6473	781-280-4000	178-1
Progressive Communications Corp 18 E Vine St . . . Mount Vernon OH 43050	800-772-5333	740-397-5333	633-8
Progressive Corp, The 6300 Wilson Mills Rd PO Box W33 . . . Mayfield Village OH 44143	888-806-9598	440-461-5000	390-4
Progressive Dynamics Inc 507 Industrial Rd . . . Marshall MI 49068	800-848-0558	269-781-4241	253
Progressive Employer Services 6407 Parkland Dr . . . Sarasota FL 34243	888-925-2990	941-925-2990	627
Progressive Impressions 1 Hardman Dr . . . Bloomington IL 61701	800-664-0444		633-9
Progressive Mktg Products Inc 2620 Palisades Dr . . . Corona CA 92882	800-368-9700	714-632-7100	194
Progressive National Baptist Convention Inc (PNBC) 601 50th St NE . . . Washington DC 20019	800-876-7622	202-396-0558	48-20
Progressive Plastics Inc 14801 Emery Ave . . . Cleveland OH 44135	800-252-0053	216-252-5595	98
Progressive Produce Co 5790 Peachtree St . . . Los Angeles CA 90040	800-900-0757	323-890-8100	297-7
Project Consulting Services Inc 3300 W Esplanade Ave S Ste 500 . . . Metairie LA 70002	855-468-7473	504-833-5321	196
Project Inform 273 Ninth St . . . San Francisco CA 94103	877-435-7443	415-558-8669	48-17
Project Management Institute (PMI) 14 Campus Blvd . . . Newtown Square PA 19073	866-276-4764	610-356-4600	49-12
Project Safe Neighborhoods (PSN) *Office of Justice Programs* 810 Seventh St NW . . . Washington DC 20531	888-744-6513	202-616-6500	197
Projection Presentation Technology 5803 Rolling Rd . . . Springfield VA 22152	800-377-7650	703-912-1334	264-2
Projections Unlimited Inc 15311 Varrenca Pkwy . . . Irvine CA 92618 *Cust Svc	800-551-4405*	714-544-2700	246
Prolifics 24025 Park Sorrento Ste 405 . . . Calabasas CA 91302	800-458-3313		178-2
Prolifiq Software Inc 8585 SW Watson Ave Ste 200 . . . Beaverton OR 97008	800-840-7183	503-684-1415	179
Prolitec Inc 1235 W Canal St . . . Milwaukee WI 53233	844-247-7599		261
ProLiteracy Worldwide 1320 Jamesville Ave . . . Syracuse NY 13210	800-448-8878	315-422-9121	48-5
ProLogis 4545 Airport Way . . . Denver CO 80239 *NYSE: PLD*	800-566-2706	400-320-2015	651
Pro-mail Associates Inc 22404 66th Ave S . . . Kent WA 98032	855-867-5081	253-867-5081	195
Promark Technology Inc 10900 Pump House Rd Ste B . . . Annapolis Junction MD 20701	800-634-0255	240-280-8030	174
ProMed Molded Products Inc 15600 Medina Rd . . . Plymouth MN 55447	855-331-3800	763-331-3800	
ProMedica 2142 N Cove Blvd . . . Toledo OH 43606	866-865-4677	419-291-5437	373-3
Promega Corp 2800 Woods Hollow Rd . . . Madison WI 53711	800-356-9526	608-274-4330	231
Promera Health 61 Accord Park Dr . . . Norwell MA 02061	888-878-9058		362
Prometheus Laboratories Inc 9410 Carroll Pk Dr . . . San Diego CA 92121	888-892-8391		578
Prometric 1501 S Clinton St . . . Baltimore MD 21224	866-776-6387	443-455-8000	244
Promiles Software Development 1900 Texas Ave . . . Bridge City TX 77611	800-324-8588		177
Promise Keepers (PK) PO Box 11798 . . . Denver CO 80211	866-776-6473		48-20
Promise Technology Inc 580 Cottonwood Dr . . . Milpitas CA 95035 *Sales	800-888-0245*	408-228-1400	621
Promodel Corp 3400 Bath Pk Ste 200 . . . Bethlehem PA 18017	888-900-3090	801-223-4600	178-10
Promotion Fulfillment Center 311 21st St . . . Camanche IA 52730	800-493-7063		
Promotional Products Assn International (PPAI) 3125 Skyway Cir N . . . Irving TX 75038	888-426-7724	972-252-0404	49-18
PROMPT Ambulance Central Inc 9835 Express Dr . . . Highland IN 46322	800-633-3590	219-934-1010	30
Prompton State Park c/o Lackawanna . . . North Abington Township PA 18414	888-727-2757	570-945-3239	561
Pronk Technologies Inc 8933 Lankershim Blvd . . . Sun Valley CA 91352	800-609-9802	818-768-5600	474
Propak Systems Ltd 440 East Lake Rd NE . . . Airdrie AB T4A2J8	800-408-4434	403-912-7000	261
Propel Tax PO Box 100350 . . . San Antonio TX 78201	877-324-8445		194
Property Damage Appraisers Inc (PDA) 6100 SW Blvd Ste 200 . . . Fort Worth TX 76109	800-749-7324		310
Property Loss Research Bureau (PLRB) 3025 Highland Pkwy Ste 800 . . . Downers Grove IL 60515	888-711-7572	630-724-2200	49-9
Property Owners Exchange Inc 6630 Baltimore National Pk Ste 208 . . . Catonsville MD 21228	800-869-3200	410-719-0100	631
Property Panorama Inc 9475 Pinecone Dr . . . Mentor OH 44060	877-299-6306	440-290-2200	177
Property-Owners Insurance Co PO Box 30660 . . . Lansing MI 48909	800-288-8740	517-323-1200	390-2
Propet USA Inc 2415 W Valley Hwy N . . . Auburn WA 98001	800-877-6738	253-854-7600	301
ProPetro Services Inc 1706 S Midkiff Rd Bldg B PO Box 873 . . . Midland TX 79701	800-221-1037	432-688-0012	536
ProPhase Labs Inc 621 Shady Retreat Rd . . . Doylestown PA 18901 *NASDAQ: PRPH*	800-505-2653	215-345-0919	578
Propper Mfg Company Inc 36-04 Skillman Ave . . . Long Island NY 11101 *Cust Svc	800-832-4300*	718-392-6650	474
Proserv Anchor Crane Group 455 Aldine Bender Rd . . . Houston TX 77060	800-835-2223	281-405-9048	468
Proshot Concrete Inc 4158 Musgrove Dr . . . Florence AL 35630	800-633-3141	256-263-0445	189-3
Proskauer Rose LLP 11 Times Sq . . . New York NY 10036	866-444-3272	212-969-3000	427
Prosoco Inc 3741 Greenway Cir . . . Lawrence KS 66046	800-255-4255		151
Prosource Fitness Equipment 6503 Hilburn Dr . . . Raleigh NC 27613	877-781-8077	919-781-8077	623
ProSource Solutions LLC 4199 Kinross Lakes Pkwy Ste 150 . . . Richfield OH 44286	866-549-0279		196
Prospect Medical Holdings Inc 3415 S Sepulveda Blvd 9th Fl . . . Los Angeles CA 90034	800-708-3230	310-943-4500	461
Prospects Influential Inc 1313 E Maple St Ste 548 . . . Bellingham WA 98225	800-352-2282		7
Prosperity Bank 1301 N Mechanic . . . El Campo TX 77437 *NYSE: PB ■ *Cust Svc	800-531-1401*		359-2
Prostar Computer Inc 837 Lawson St . . . City of Industry CA 91748	888-576-4742	626-839-6472	174
Prosthetic Design Inc 700 Harco Dr . . . Clayton OH 45315	800-459-0177		475
Prostrollo Motor Sales Inc 500 Fourth St NE . . . Huron SD 57350	866-466-4515		57
Pro-Tec Fire Services Ltd 2129 S Oneida St . . . Green Bay WI 54304	800-242-6352		63
Pro-tech Security Sales 1313 W Bagley Rd . . . Berea OH 44017	800-888-4002	440-239-0100	237
Protech Systems Group 3350 Players Club Pkwy . . . Memphis TN 38125	800-459-5100	901-767-7550	177
Protect-All Inc 109 Badger Pkwy . . . Darien WI 53114	888-432-8526		550
Protected Investors of America Inc 235 Montgomery St Ste 1050 . . . San Francisco CA 94104	800-786-2559		194
protection One Alarm Monitoring 1035 N Third St Ste 101 . . . Lawrence KS 66044	800-438-4357	785-371-1884	688
Protective Insurance Co 111 Congressional Blvd Ste 500 . . . Carmel IN 46032	800-644-5501		390-5
Protective Life Corp 2801 Hwy 280 S . . . Birmingham AL 35223 *NYSE: PL*	800-866-9933	844-733-5433	359-4
Protectoseal Co 225 W Foster Ave . . . Bensenville IL 60106	800-323-2268	630-595-0800	124
Protein Sciences Corp 1000 Research Pkwy . . . Meriden CT 06450	800-488-7099	203-686-0800	85
Protek Cargo 1568 Airport Blvd . . . Napa CA 94558	800-439-1426	707-254-9627	707
Protel Inc 4150 Kidron Rd . . . Lakeland FL 33811	800-925-8882	863-644-5558	730
Protelus 11000 NE 33rd Pl Ste 320 . . . Bellevue WA 98004	800-585-0207		464

Alphabetical Section

	Toll-Free	Phone	Class
Protestant Episcopal Theological Seminary in Virginia 3737 Seminary Rd, Alexandria VA 22304	800-941-0083	703-370-6600	167-3
Proteus Inc 1830 N Dinuba Blvd, Visalia CA 93291	888-776-9998	559-733-5423	681
Protide Pharmaceuticals Inc 505 Oakwood Rd Ste 200, Lake Zurich IL 60047	800-552-3569	847-726-3100	578
Protocol Driven Healthcare Inc 40 Morristown Rd Ste 2D, Bernardsville NJ 07924	888-816-4006	515-277-1376	461
Protocol Networks Inc 15 Shore Dr, Johnston RI 02919	877-676-0146		180
Protogate Inc 12225 World Trade Dr, San Diego CA 92128	877-473-0190	858-451-0865	225
Protravel International Inc 515 Madison Ave 10th Fl, New York NY 10022	800-227-1059	212-755-4550	766
Provantage Corp 7249 Whipple Ave NW, North Canton OH 44720	800-336-1166	330-494-8715	174
Provell Inc 855 Village Center Dr Ste 116, North Oaks MN 55127	800-624-2946	952-258-2000	461
Provia Door Inc 2150 SR- 39, Sugarcreek OH 44681 *General	800-669-4711*	403-555-5555	235
Providence Centralia Hospital 914 S Scheuber Rd, Centralia WA 98531 *Help Line	877-736-2803*	360-736-2803	373-3
Providence College 1 Cunningham Sq, Providence RI 02918 *Admissions	800-721-6444*	401-865-1000	166
Providence College & Seminary 10 College Crescent, Otterburne MB R0A1G0	800-668-7768	204-433-7488	167-3
Providence Health & Services 9205 SW Barnes Rd, Portland OR 97225	800-562-8964	503-216-1234	373-3
Providence Hospice of Seattle 2811 S 102nd St Ste 200, Tukwila WA 98168	888-782-4445	206-320-4000	370
Providence Journal 75 Fountain St, Providence RI 02902	888-697-7656	401-277-7303	528-2
Providence Life Services 18601 N Creek Dr, Tinley Park IL 60477	800-509-2800	708-342-8100	668
Providence Medford Medical Ctr 1111 Crater Lake Ave, Medford OR 97504	877-541-0588	541-732-5000	373-3
Providence Medical Ctr 8929 Parallel Pkwy, Kansas City KS 66112	800-281-7777	913-596-4000	373-3
Providence Mountains State Recreation Area 1416 Ninth St, Sacramento CA 95814	800-777-0369		561
Providence Mutual Fire Insurance Co 340 E Ave, Warwick RI 02886	877-763-1800	401-827-1800	390-4
Providence Portland Medical Ctr 4805 NE Glisan St, Portland OR 97213	800-833-8899	503-215-1111	373-3
Providence Sacred Heart Medical Ctr 101 W Eigth Ave, Spokane WA 99204	800-442-8534	888-294-8455	373-3
Providence Saint Joseph Medical Ctr 501 S Buena Vista St, Burbank CA 91505	800-750-7703	818-843-5111	373-3
Providence Sound Home Care & Hospice 4200 Sixth Ave SE Ste 201, Lacey WA 98503	800-869-7062		370
Providence St Mary Medical Ctr 401 W Poplar St, Walla Walla WA 99362	877-215-7833	509-525-3320	373-3
Providence Warwick Convention & Visitors Bureau 10 Memorial Blvd, Providence RI 02903	800-233-1636	401-456-0200	206
Provident Bank 3756 Central Ave, Riverside CA 92506 *NASDAQ: PROV*	800-442-5201	951-686-6060	359-2
Provident Central Credit Union 303 Twin Dolphin Dr, Redwood City CA 94065	800-632-4600	650-508-0300	219
Provident Savings Bank FSB 3756 Central Ave, Riverside CA 92506	800-442-5201	951-686-6060	70
Provident Travel 11309 Montgomery Rd, Cincinnati OH 45249	800-354-8108	513-247-1100	383
Providge Consulting 2207 Concord Pk Ste 537, Wilimington DE 19803	888-927-6583		177
Provimi North America Inc 10 Nutrition Way PO Box 69, Brookville OH 45309	800-257-3788		445
Provision Ministry Group 2050 MAIN ST Ste 400, Irvine CA 92614	800-597-9931		681
Provista 250 E John Carpenter Fwy, Irving TX 75062	888-538-4662		317
Provo City Library 550 N University Ave, Provo UT 84601	800-914-8931	801-852-6650	433-3
Proxibid Inc 4411 S 96 St, Omaha NE 68127	877-505-7770	402-505-7770	
Proxim Wireless Corp 1561 Buckeye Dr, Milpitas CA 95035 *OTC: PRXM*	800-229-1630	408-383-7600	730
Proximity Hotel 704 Green Valley Rd, Greensboro NC 27408	800-379-8200	336-379-8200	132
Proximo Consulting Services Inc 2500 Plaza Five, Jersey City NJ 07311	800-236-9250		177
Prozyme Inc 3832 Bay Ctr Pl, Hayward CA 94545	800-457-9444	510-638-6900	231
PRSA (Public Relations Society of America) 33 Maiden Ln 11th Fl, New York NY 10038	800-350-0111	212-460-1400	49-18
Prudential Financial Inc 751 Broad St, Newark NJ 07102 *NYSE: PRU*	800-843-7625	973-802-6000	400
Prudential Overall Supply PO Box 11210, Santa Ana CA 92711	800-767-5536	949-250-4855	441
Pryor Products 1819 Peacock Blvd, Oceanside CA 92056	800-854-2280	760-724-8244	474
PS Business Parks Inc 701 Western Ave, Glendale CA 91201 *NYSE: PSB* ■ *Cust Svc	888-782-6110*	818-244-8080	651
PS Energy Group Inc 4480 N Shallowford Rd Ste 100, Dunwoody GA 30338	800-334-7548	770-350-3000	782
Ps Websolutions Inc 906 Carriage Path SE Ste 106, Smyrna GA 30082	877-571-7829		177
PSA Airlines Inc 3400 Terminal Dr, Vandalia OH 45377 *Resv	800-235-0986*		25
PSA healthcare 400 Interstate N Pkwy SE Ste 1600, Atlanta GA 30339	800-408-4442	770-441-1580	362
PSB (Peoples Savings Bank) 414 N Adams PO Box 248, Wellsburg IA 50680	877-508-2265	641-869-3721	70
PSB Industries Inc PO Box 1318, Erie PA 16512	800-829-1119	814-453-3651	385
PSC 5151 San Felipe Ste 1100, Houston TX 77056	800-726-1300		192
PSC (Product Safety Consulting Inc) 605 Country Club Dr Ste I & J, Bensenville IL 60106	877-804-3066	630-238-0188	196
PSCA (Profit Sharing/401(k) Council of America) 20 N Wacker Dr Ste 3700, Chicago IL 60606	866-614-8407	312-419-1863	49-12
PSDA (Print Services & Distribution Assn) 330 N Wabash Ave Ste 2000, Chicago IL 60611	800-230-0175		48-9
PSEA (Penna State Education Assn Harrisburg) 400 N Third St PO Box 1724, Harrisburg PA 17105	800-944-7732	717-255-7000	472
PSEG (Public Service Enterprise Group Inc) 80 Park Plz, Newark NJ 07102	800-436-7734		782
PSF Industries Inc 65 S Horton St, Seattle WA 98134 *General	800-426-1204*	206-622-1252	189-10
PSI (Professional Service Industries Inc) 1901 S Meyers Rd Ste 400, Oakbrook Terrace IL 60181	800-548-7901	630-691-1490	261
PSI Services LLC 611 N Brand Blvd 1st Fl, Glendale CA 91505	800-367-1565		
PSI Upsilon Fraternity 3003 E 96th St, Indianapolis IN 46240	800-394-1833	317-571-1833	48-16
PSL (Peach State Labs Inc) 180 Burlington Rd PO Box 1087, Rome GA 30162	800-634-1653	706-291-8743	145
PSN (Project Safe Neighborhoods) *Office of Justice Programs* 810 Seventh St NW, Washington DC 20531	888-744-6513	202-616-6500	197
PSPrint LLC 2861 Mandela Pkwy, Oakland CA 94608	800-511-2009		623
PSR (Professional Shorthand Reporters Inc) 601 Poydras St Ste 1615, New Orleans LA 70130	800-536-5255	504-529-5255	443
Psychemedics Corp 289 Great Rd Ste 200, Acton MA 01720 *NASDAQ: PMD*	800-628-8073	877-517-2033	85
Psychiatric Institute of Washington 4228 Wisconsin Ave NW, Washington DC 20016	800-369-2273	202-885-5600	373-5
Psychology Software Tools Inc Sharpsburg Business Park 311 23rd St Ext Ste 200, Sharpsburg PA 15215	888-540-9664	412-449-0078	
Psychology Today 115 E 23 St 9th Fl, New York NY 10010	800-931-2237	212-260-7210	455-11
Psychotherapy Networker 5135 MacArthur Blvd NW, Washington DC 20016	888-851-9498		455-16
PsyMax Solutions LLC 25550 Chagrin Blvd Ste 100, Cleveland OH 44122	866-774-2273	216-896-9991	194
PTC (Paternity Testing Corp) 300 Portland St, Columbia MO 65201	888-837-8323	573-442-9948	416
PTC (Parametric Technology Corp) 140 Kendrick St, Needham MA 02494 *NASDAQ: PTC*	800-613-7535	781-370-5000	178-5
PTC Alliance Copperleaf Corporate Ctr 6051 Wallace Rd Ext Ste 200, Wexford PA 15090	800-274-8823	412-299-7900	488
Ptc Select LLC 2450 N Knoxville Ave, Peoria IL 61604	800-225-2320	309-685-8400	175
PTI (Pittsburgh Technical College) 1111 McKee Rd, Oakdale PA 15071	800-784-9675	412-809-5100	795
PTI Technologies Inc 501 Del Norte Blvd, Oxnard CA 93030	800-331-2701	805-604-3700	385
PTR Baler & Compactor Co 2207 E Ontario St, Philadelphia PA 19134	800-523-3654		468
PTSI (Panhandle Telecommunication Systems Inc) 2222 NW Hwy 64, Guymon OK 73942	800-562-2556	580-338-2556	731
Pubco Corp 3830 Kelley Ave, Cleveland OH 44114	800-878-3399	216-881-5300	111
Public Belt Railroad Commission 4822 Tchoupitulas St, New Orleans LA 70115 *Cust Svc	800-524-3421*	504-896-7410	647
Public Broadcasting Council of Central New York 506 Old Liverpool Rd PO Box 2400, Syracuse NY 13220	800-451-9269	315-453-2424	628
Public Broadcasting Northwest Pennsylvania 8425 Peach St, Erie PA 16509	800-727-8854	814-864-3001	628
Public Broadcasting Service (PBS) 2100 Crystal Dr, Arlington VA 22202	866-864-0828	703-739-5000	734
Public Consulting Group Inc 148 State St, Boston MA 02109	800-210-6113		194
Public Employee Magazine 1625 L St NW, Washington DC 20036	800-792-0045	855-237-2631	455-12
Public Interest Network 1543 Wazee St Ste 400, Denver CO 80202	800-401-6511	303-573-5995	305
Public Lands Foundation (PLF) PO Box 7226, Arlington VA 22207	866-985-9636	703-790-1988	48-13
Public Library Assn (PLA) 50 E Huron St, Chicago IL 60611	800-545-2433	312-280-5752	49-11
Public Opinion 77 N Third St, Chambersburg PA 17201	800-782-0661	717-264-6161	528-2
Public Radio 895 800 Tucker Dr, Tulsa OK 74104	888-594-5947	918-631-2577	641-112
Public Relations Society of America (PRSA) 33 Maiden Ln 11th Fl, New York NY 10038	800-350-0111	212-460-1400	49-18

	Toll-Free	Phone	Class
Public Service Enterprise Group Inc (PSEG)			
80 Park Plz ....Newark NJ 07102	800-436-7734		782
Public Service Enterprise Group Inc			
80 Park Plz ....Newark NJ 07102	800-436-7734*	973-430-7000	359-5
NYSE: PEG ■ *Cust Svc			
Public Storage Inc			
701 Western Ave .... Glendale CA 91201	800-567-0759*	818-244-8080	798-3
NYSE: PSA ■ *Cust Svc			
Public Technology Inc			
1420 Prince St Ste 200 .... Alexandria VA 22314	866-664-6368	202-626-2400	49-7
Public Welfare Foundation			
1200 U St NW .... Washington DC 20009	800-275-7934	202-965-1800	305
Public Works Commission of The City of Fayetteville North Carolina			
955 Old Wilmington Rd			
PO Box 1089. ....Fayetteville NC 28301	877-687-7921	910-483-1382	782
Publication Printers Corp			
2001 S Platte River Dr ......Denver CO 80223	888-824-0303	303-936-0303	623
Publications & Communications Inc			
13552 Hwy 183 N Ste A .... Austin TX 78750	800-678-9724	512-250-9023	633-9
Publications International Ltd			
7373 N Cicero Ave .... Lincolnwood IL 60712	800-777-5582*	847-676-3470	633-2
*General			
Publicis Touchpoint Solutions Inc			
1000 Floral Vale Blvd Ste 400 ....Yardley PA 19067	800-672-0676	215-525-9800	4
Publick House Historic Resort			
277 Main St Rt 131.............Sturbridge MA 01566	800-782-5425*	508-347-3313	378
*Cust Svc			
Publipage Inc			
2055 Rue Peel .... Montreal QC H3A1V4	800-544-8614	514-286-1550	7
Publishers Press Inc			
100 Frank E Simon Ave ....Shepherdsville KY 40165	800-627-5801	502-955-6526	622
Publix Super Markets Inc			
3300 Publix Corporate Pkwy .... Lakeland FL 33811	800-242-1227*	863-688-1188	344
*PR			
PubMed			
US National Library of Medicine			
8600 Rockville Pike .... Bethesda MD 20894	888-346-3656		355
PUC Inc			
500 Second Line E			
PO Box 9000........... Sault Ste Marie ON P6B4K1	800-400-2255	705-759-6500	
Pucel Enterprises Inc			
1440 E 36th St ....Cleveland OH 44114	800-336-4986	216-881-4604	468
Pueblo Bonito Golf & Spa Resorts			
4350 La Jolla Village Dr .... San Diego CA 92122	800-990-8250	858-642-2050	377
Pueblo Chieftain			
825 W Sixth St ....Pueblo CO 81003	800-279-6397	719-544-3520	528-2
Pueblo Community College			
900 W Orman Ave ....Pueblo CO 81004	888-642-6017	719-549-3200	162
Puente Hills Mall			
1600 Azusa Ave .... City of Industry CA 91748	800-743-3463	626-912-8777	458
Puerto Rico			
Paseo La Princesa ....Old San Juan PR 00902	800-866-7827	787-721-2400	770
Puerto Rico Convention Center			
500 Tanca Ste 402 ....San Juan PR 00901	800-875-4765	787-725-2110	206
Puerto Rico Farm Credit Aca			
PO Box 363649 ....San Juan PR 00936	800-981-3323	787-753-0579	216
Puffin Inn			
4400 SpenaRd Rd ....Anchorage AK 99517	800-478-3346	907-243-4044	378
Puget Energy			
10885 NE Fourth St ....Bellevue WA 98004	888-225-5773		
Puget Sound Educational Service District			
800 Oakesdale Ave SW ....Renton WA 98057	800-664-4549	425-917-7600	681
Puget Sound Energy Inc			
10885 NE Fourth St ....Bellevue WA 98004	888-225-5773	425-452-1234	782
Puget Sound Rope Corp			
1012 Second St ....Anacortes WA 98221	888-525-8488	360-293-8488	208
Pulaski County			
143 Third St NW Ste 1 ....Pulaski VA 24301	800-211-5540	540-980-7705	337
Pulaski County			
100 N Main St Ste 202 ....Somerset KY 42501	877-655-7154	606-678-4853	337
Pulaski County			
137 StRobert Bld Ste A ....St. Robert MO 65584	877-858-8687	573-336-6355	
Pulaski County Chamber of Commerce			
4440 Cleburne Blvd ....Dublin VA 24084	866-256-8864	540-674-1991	139
PULSE			
1301 McKinney St Ste 2500 ....Houston TX 77010	800-420-2122	832-214-0100	69
Pulse Communications Inc			
2900 Towerview Rd ....Herndon VA 20171	800-381-1997*	703-471-2900	730
*Cust Svc			
PulseTech Products Corp			
1100 S Kimball Ave ....Southlake TX 76092	800-580-7554	817-329-6099	74
Puma 10 Lyberty Way ....Westford MA 01886	888-565-7862*	978-698-1000	301
*General			
Puma Industries Inc			
1992 Airways Blvd ....Memphis TN 38114	888-848-1668	901-744-7979	172
Pumping Solutions Inc			
1906 S Quaker Ridge Pl ....Ontario CA 91761	800-603-0399		606
Punch & Associates Inc			
7701 France Ave S Ste 300............ Edina MN 55435	800-241-5552	952-224-4350	524
Punchbowl Inc			
50 Speen St Ste 202 .... Framingham MA 01701	877-570-4340	508-589-4486	107
Punchkick Interactive Inc			
150 N Michigan Ave Ste 3900 .... Chicago IL 60601	800-549-4104		195
Purafil Inc			
2654 Weaver Way ....Doraville GA 30340	800-222-6367	770-662-8545	18
Purchase College			
735 Anderson Hill Rd ....Purchase NY 10577	800-553-8118	914-251-6000	166
Purchasing Magazine			
225 Wyman St ....Waltham MA 02451	888-393-5000		455-5
Purdue Pharma			
575 Granite Ct ....Pickering ON L1W3W8	800-387-5349	905-420-6400	231
Purdue University			
Schleman Hall			
475 Stadium Mall Dr. ....West Lafayette IN 47907	800-743-3333	765-494-1776	166
Purdue University Press			
504 W State St Stewart Ctr 370			
...............West Lafayette IN 47907	800-247-6553*	765-494-4600	633-4
*Orders			
Purdy Corp			
101 Prospect Ave ....Cleveland OH 44115	800-547-0780		349
Pure & Secure LLC			
4120 NW 44th St .... Lincoln NE 68524	800-875-5915*	402-467-9300	801
*Cust Svc			
Pure Auto LLC			
164 Market St Ste 250 ....Charleston SC 29401	877-860-7873		386
PURE Storage Inc			
650 Castro St Ste 400............Mountain View CA 94041	800-379-7873	650-290-6088	173-8
Pure Sweet Honey Farm Inc			
514 Commerce Pkwy ....Verona WI 53593	800-355-9601		
Pure-Flo Water Co			
7737 Mission Gorge Rd .... Santee CA 92071	800-787-3356*	619-448-5120	800
*Cust Svc			
Puregas LLC			
226 Commerce St ....Broomfield CO 80020	800-521-5351	303-427-3700	111
Purestream Services			
2401 Foothill Dr ....Salt Lake City UT 84109	855-778-7342	801-869-4455	534
Puritan Manufacturing Inc			
1302 Grace St ....Omaha NE 68110	800-331-0487	402-341-3753	693
Puritan of Cape Cod			
408 Main St ....Hyannis MA 02601	800-924-0606	508-775-2400	157-2
PuriTec			
4705 S Durango Dr Ste 100-102 .... Las Vegas NV 89147	888-491-4100	610-268-5420	17
Purity Wholesale Grocers Inc			
5300 Broken Sound Blvd NW .... Boca Raton FL 33487	800-323-6838	561-994-9360	297-8
PuroClean			
6001 Hiatus Rd Ste 13 .... Tamarac FL 33321	800-775-7876		
Purolator Inc			
5995 Avebury Rd .... Mississauga ON L5R3T8	888-744-7123	905-712-8101	542
Purple Communications Inc			
595 Menlo Dr .... Rocklin CA 95765	800-900-9478		386
Pursuit			
100 Gopher St PO Box 1140. .... Banff AB T1L1J3	866-606-6700	403-762-6700	755
Pursuit Boats			
3901 St Lucie Blvd .... Fort Pierce FL 34946	800-947-8778	772-465-6006	90
Purves & Assoc Insurance			
500 Fourth St ....Davis CA 95616	800-681-2025	530-756-5561	389
Putnam County			
117 Putnam Dr Ste A .... Eatonton GA 31024	800-253-1077	706-485-5826	337
Putnam County			
130 Orie Griffin Blvd ....Palatka FL 32177	800-426-9975	386-329-0808	337
Putnam Family of Funds			
PO Box 41203 ....Providence RI 02940	800-225-1581		524
Putnam Investments			
30 Dan Rd PO Box 8383 .... Canton MA 02021	888-478-8626	617-292-1000	400
Putnam Lexus			
390 Convention Way .... Redwood City CA 94063	888-231-8005	650-363-8500	57
Putnam Valley School District Inc			
146 Peekskill Hollow Rd .... Putnam Valley NY 10579	800-666-5327	845-528-8143	681
Putney School			
418 Houghton Brook Rd .... Putney VT 05346	800-999-9080	802-387-5566	618
Putzmeister America			
1733 90th St .... Sturtevant WI 53177	800-553-3414		190
Puyallup Public Library			
333 S Meridian .... Puyallup WA 98371	844-821-8911	253-841-4321	433-3
PVA (Passenger Vessel Assn)			
103 Oronoco St Ste 200 .... Alexandria VA 22314	800-807-8360	703-518-5005	49-21
PVA Consulting Group Inc			
20865 Ch de la Cote Nord			
Ste 200 ....Boisbriand QC J7E4H5	877-970-1970	450-970-1970	461
PVA Tepla America Inc			
251 Corporate Terr ....Corona CA 92879	800-527-5667*	951-371-2500	203
*Sales			
PVG Asset Management Corp			
24918 Genesee Trl Rd ....Golden CO 80401	800-777-0818		400
PVH 200 Madison Ave .... New York NY 10016	888-203-1112	212-381-3500	155-11
NYSE: PVH			
PVI Industries LLC			
3209 Galvez Ave .... Fort Worth TX 76111	800-784-8326	817-335-9531	91
PVS Chemicals Inc			
10900 Harper Ave .... Detroit MI 48213	800-932-8860	313-921-1200	145
PVT (Penasco Valley Telephone Cooperative Inc)			
4011 W Main St ....Artesia NM 88210	800-505-4844		731
PW Minor & Son Inc			
3 Tread Easy Ave ....Batavia NY 14020	800-333-4067		301
PW Stephens Inc			
15201 Pipeline Ln			
Unit B .... Huntington Beach CA 92649	800-750-7733	714-892-2028	663
PWH (Palms West Hospital)			
13001 Southern Blvd ....Loxahatchee FL 33470	877-549-9337	561-798-3300	373-3
PWP (Pentwater Wire Products Inc)			
474 Carroll St PO Box 947............Pentwater MI 49449	877-869-6911	231-869-6911	286
PWR LLC			
6402 Deere Rd .... Syracuse NY 13206	800-342-0878	315-701-0210	762
Pybus Point Lodge			
PO Box 33497 ....Juneau AK 99803	800-947-9287	907-790-4866	665
Pyramid Consulting Inc			
11100 Atlantis Pl .... Alpharetta GA 30022	877-248-0024	678-514-3500	225
Pyramid Interiors Distributors Inc			
PO Box 181058 ....Memphis TN 38181	800-456-0592	901-375-4197	191-3
Pyramid Point Post-Acute Rehabilitation Ctr			
8530 Township Line Rd ....Indianapolis IN 46260	800-861-0086	317-876-9955	448
Pyromation Inc			
5211 Industrial Rd .... Fort Wayne IN 46825	800-837-6805	260-484-2580	201
Pyronics Inc			
17700 Miles Rd ....Cleveland OH 44128	800-883-9218	216-662-8800	318

	Toll-Free	Phone	Class
Q			

	Toll-Free	Phone	Class
Q 1043 32 Ave of the Americas .... New York NY 10013	**888-872-1043**	212-377-7900	641-71
Q Center 1405 N Fifth Ave .... Saint Charles IL 60174	**877-774-4627**	630-377-3100	31
Q102 111 Presidential Blvd Ste 100 .... Bala Cynwyd PA 19004	**800-521-1021**	610-784-3333	641
QACVB (Quincy Area Convention & Visitors Bureau) 532 Gardner Expy .... Quincy IL 62301	**800-978-4748**	217-214-3700	206
Qantas Airways Cargo 6555 W Imperial Hwy .... Los Angeles CA 90045 *General	**800-227-0290***	310-665-2280	12
Qantas Airways Ltd 6080 Ctr Dr Ste 400 .... Los Angeles CA 90045	**800-227-4500**	310-726-1400	25
QBE Farmers Union Insurance 5619 DTC Pkwy Ste 300 ...... Greenwood Village CO 80111	**800-347-1961**	303-337-5500	390-4
QBE Holdings Inc Wall St Plz 88 Pine St .... New York NY 10005	**800-362-5448**	212-422-1212	390-4
QC Holdings Inc 8208 Melrose Dr .... Lenexa KS 66214 OTC: QCCO	**866-660-2243**		141
QCA Systems Ltd #101-6951 72nd St .... Delta BC V4G0A2	**877-940-0868**	604-940-0868	
QCI Asset Management 40A Grove St .... Pittsford NY 14534	**800-836-3960**	585-218-2060	400
QCSS Inc 21925 Field Pkwy Ste 210 .... Deer Park IL 60010	**888-229-7046**	847-229-7046	317
QED Inc 1661 W Third Ave .... Denver CO 80223	**800-700-5011**	303-825-5011	246
QEP Co Inc 1001 Broken Sound Pkwy NW Ste A .... Boca Raton FL 33487 OTC: QEPC ■ *Sales	**800-777-8665***	561-994-5550	753
QHR Technologies Inc 1620 Dickson Ave Ste 300 .... Kelowna BC V1Y9Y2	**855-550-5004**		177
QlikTech International AB 150 N Radnor Chester Rd Ste E220 ... Radnor PA 19087 NASDAQ: QLIK	**888-828-9768**		178-10
QMI (Quality Mfg Company Inc) PO Box 616 .... Winchester KY 40392	**866-460-6459**	859-744-0420	452
QMS (Quality Management Solutions LLC) 146 Lowell St Ste 300B .... Wakefield MA 01889	**800-645-6430**		196
QNB Corp 15 N Third St PO Box 9005 .... Quakertown PA 18951 OTC: QNBC	**800-491-9070**	215-538-5600	70
QPI (Quality Perforating Inc) 166 Dundaff St .... Carbondale PA 18407	**800-872-7373**	570-282-4344	486
QSA ToolWorks LLC 3100 47th Ave .... Long Island NY 11101	**800-784-7018**	516-935-9151	178-7
QSC Audio Products LLC 1675 MacArthur Blvd .... Costa Mesa CA 92626	**800-854-4079**	714-754-6175	52
QSI (Quality Systems Inc) 18111 Von Karman Ave Ste 700 .... Irvine CA 92612 NASDAQ: QSII ■ *Cust Svc	**800-888-7955***	949-255-2600	178-10
Qst Consultations Ltd 11275 Edgewater Dr .... Allendale MI 49401	**866-757-4751**		231
QST Magazine 225 Main St .... Newington CT 06111	**888-277-5289**	860-594-0200	455-14
Quad Cities Convention & Visitors Bureau 1601 River Dr Ste 110 .... Moline IL 61265	**800-747-7800**	309-277-0937	206
Quad Cities Realty 1053 Ripon Ave .... Lewiston ID 83501	**877-798-7798**	208-798-7798	648
Quad City Bank & Trust 3551 Seventh St .... Moline IL 61265 NASDAQ: QCRH	**866-676-0551**	309-736-3580	359-2
Quad-City Peterbilt Inc 8100 N Fairmount St .... Davenport IA 52806	**888-774-1618**		513
Quad-City Times 500 E Third St .... Davenport IA 52801	**800-437-4641**	563-383-2200	528-2
Quadel Consulting 1200 G St NW Ste 700 .... Washington DC 20005	**866-640-1019**	202-789-2500	194
Quadra Chemicals Ltd 3901 Fixtessier .... Vaudreuil-Dorion QC J7V5V5	**800-665-6553**		146
Quadra Tech Inc 864 E Jenkins Ave .... Columbus OH 43207	**800-443-2766**		198
Quadramed Inc 12110 Sunset Hills Rd Ste 600 .... Reston VA 20190	**800-393-0278**	703-709-2300	177
Quadrant 4 System Corp 1501 E Woodfield Rd Ste 205 S .... Schaumburg IL 60173	**855-995-7367**		
Quadrant Engineering Plastic Products USA 2120 Fairmont Ave PO Box 14235 .... Reading PA 19612	**800-366-0300**	610-320-6600	598
Quadratec Inc 1028 Saunders Ln .... West Chester PA 19380	**800-745-6037**		786
Quadrex Corp PO Box 3881 .... Woodbridge CT 06525 *Sales	**800-275-7033***	203-393-3112	332
Quail Lodge Resort & Golf Club 8205 Valley Greens Dr .... Carmel CA 93923	**866-675-1101**		665
Quaker Chemical Corp 901 E Hector St .... Conshohocken PA 19428 NYSE: KWR	**800-523-7010**	610-832-4000	145
Quaker Funds 1180 W Swedesford Rd Ste 150 .... Berwyn PA 19312	**800-220-8888**	610-455-2200	400
Quaker Heights Nursing Home Inc 514 High St .... Waynesville OH 45068	**800-319-1317**	513-897-6050	370

	Toll-Free	Phone	Class
Quaker Oats Co 555 W Monroe St .... Chicago IL 60661	**800-367-6287**	312-821-1000	296-36
Quaker Window Products Inc 504 S Hwy 63 S .... Freeburg MO 65035	**800-347-0438**		234
Qualaroo Inc 122 E Houston St .... San Antonio TX 78205	**888-449-3364**		386
Quala-Tel Enterprises 9925 Business Park Ave Ste A ...... San Diego CA 92131	**800-442-1504**	858-577-2900	195
Qualchoice of Arkansas Inc 12615 Chenal Pkwy Ste 300 .... Little Rock AR 72211	**800-235-7111**		
Qualcomm Stadium 9449 Friars Rd .... San Diego CA 92108	**800-400-7115**	858-694-3900	716
QualCorp Inc 27240 Turnberry Ln Ste 200 .... Valencia CA 91355	**888-367-6775**	661-799-0033	804
Qual-Craft Industries PO Box 559 .... Stoughton MA 02072	**800-231-5647**		349
Qualex Consulting Services Inc 1111 Kane Concourse Ste 320 .... Bay Harbor Islands FL 33154	**877-887-4727**		180
Quali Tech Inc 318 Lake Hazeltine Dr .... Chaska MN 55318	**800-328-5870**	952-448-5151	445
Qualicaps Inc 6505 Franz Warner Pkwy .... Whitsett NC 27377	**800-227-7853**	336-449-3900	578
Qualico Steel Co Inc 7797 E State Hwy 52 .... Webb AL 36376	**866-234-5382**	334-793-1290	478
Qualis Health PO Box 33400 .... Seattle WA 98133	**800-949-7536**	206-364-9700	373-3
QualiTest Ltd 1 Post Rd 3rd Fl .... Fairfield CT 06824	**877-882-9540**		392
Quality Administration LLC 610 Indian Trail Ct .... Smithville MO 64089	**866-902-2090**	816-532-2090	
Quality Air Heating & Cooling Inc 3395 Kraft Ave SE .... Grand Rapids MI 49512	**800-723-8431**	713-830-9600	
Quality Bioresources Inc 1015 N Austin St .... Seguin TX 78155	**888-674-7224**	830-372-4797	414
Quality Built LLC 401 SE 12th St Ste 200 .... Fort Lauderdale FL 33316	**800-547-5125**	954-358-3500	194
Quality Craft Ltd 17750-65A Ave Ste 301 .... Surrey BC V3S5N4	**800-663-2252**	604-575-5550	290
Quality Customs Broker Inc 4464 S Whitnall Ave .... Saint Francis WI 53235	**888-813-4647**	414-482-9447	311
Quality Dining Inc 4220 Edison Lakes Pkwy .... Mishawaka IN 46545	**800-589-3820**	574-271-4600	666
Quality Distribution Inc 4041 Pk Oaks Blvd Ste 200 .... Tampa FL 33610 NASDAQ: QLTY	**800-282-2031**		775
Quality Edge Inc 2712 Walkent Dr NW .... Walker MI 49544	**888-784-0878**		488
Quality Enclosures Inc 2025 Porter Lake Dr .... Sarasota FL 34240	**800-881-0051**	941-378-0051	320
Quality Filtration LLC 5215 Linbar Dr Ste 204 .... Nashville TN 37211	**877-377-7702**		
Quality Food Centers 10116 NE 8th .... Bellevue WA 98004	**800-576-4377**	425-455-0870	
Quality Forms 4317 W US Rt 36 .... Piqua OH 45356	**866-773-4595**	937-773-4595	110
Quality Gold Inc 500 Quality Blvd .... Fairfield OH 45014	**800-354-9833**		410
Quality Group Inc, The 5825 Glenridge Dr NE Bldg 3 Ste 101 .... Atlanta GA 30328	**800-772-3071**	404-843-9525	
Quality Hotel-airport 7228 Wminster Hwy .... Richmond BC V6X1A1	**877-244-3051**	604-244-3051	378
Quality Industries Inc 130 Jones Blvd .... La Vergne TN 37086	**800-745-8613**	615-793-3000	693
Quality Inn & Suites Naples Golf Resort 4100 Golden Gate Pkwy .... Naples FL 34116	**800-277-0017**	239-455-1010	665
Quality Inn & Suites Plano East - Richardson 1600 N Central Expy .... Plano TX 75074	**877-386-4383**	972-578-8555	378
Quality Inn Halifax Airport 60 Sky Blvd .... Goffs NS B2T1K3	**800-667-3333**	902-873-3000	378
Quality Liquid Feeds Inc PO Box 240 .... Dodgeville WI 53533	**800-236-2345**	608-935-2345	276
Quality Management Solutions LLC (QMS) 146 Lowell St Ste 300B .... Wakefield MA 01889	**800-645-6430**		196
Quality Manufacturing Inc 969 Labore Industrial Ct .... Saint Paul MN 55110	**800-243-5473**	651-483-5473	697
Quality Mat Co 6550 Tram Rd .... Beaumont TX 77713	**800-227-8159**	409-722-4594	131
Quality Meats & Seafoods 700 Center St .... West Fargo ND 58078	**800-342-4250**	701-282-0202	471
Quality Media Resources Inc 10929 SE 23rd St .... Bellevue WA 98004	**800-800-5129**		461
Quality Metal Products Inc 720 Orange Rd .... Dallas PA 18612	**888-251-2805**	570-333-4248	693
Quality Metals Inc 2575 Doswell Ave .... St Paul MN 55108	**800-328-4893**	651-645-5875	
Quality Mfg Company Inc (QMI) PO Box 616 .... Winchester KY 40392	**866-460-6459**	859-744-0420	452
Quality of Life Health Services Inc 1411 Piedmont Cutoff .... Gadsden AL 35903	**888-490-0131**	256-492-0131	373-3
Quality Perforating Inc (QPI) 166 Dundaff St .... Carbondale PA 18407	**800-872-7373**	570-282-4344	486
Quality Plywood Specialties Inc 13000 Automobile Blvd .... Clearwater FL 33762	**888-722-1181**	727-572-0500	191-3
Quality Progress ASQ 600 N Plankinton Ave PO Box 3005 .... Milwaukee WI 53201 *Cust Svc	**800-248-1946***	414-272-8575	455-21
Quality Solutions Inc 128 N First St .... Colwich KS 67030	**888-328-2454**	316-721-3656	261
Quality Systems Inc (QSI) 18111 Von Karman Ave Ste 700 ...... Irvine CA 92612 NASDAQ: QSII ■ *Cust Svc	**800-888-7955***	949-255-2600	178-10
Quality Tool Inc 1220 Energy Park Dr .... Saint Paul MN 55108	**866-997-4647**	651-646-7433	693
Quality Transportation 36-40 37th St Ste 201 .... Long Island NY 11101	**800-677-2838**	212-308-6333	311

	Toll-Free	Phone	Class
Qualstar Corp 3990-B Heritage Oak Ct . . . . Simi Valley CA 93063 *NASDAQ: QBAK*	800-468-0680	805-583-7744	173-8
Qualtech Inc 1880 Leon-Harmel St . . . . Quebec QC G1N4K3	888-339-3801	418-686-3802	296
Quam-Nichols Company Inc 234 E Marquette Rd . . . . Chicago IL 60637	800-633-3669	773-488-5800	52
Quanex Building Products 2270 Woodale Dr . . . . Mounds View MN 55112	800-233-4383	763-231-4000	497
Quanex Building Products Corp 1900 W Loop S Ste 1500 . . . . Houston TX 77027 *Cust Svc	888-475-0633*	713-961-4600	235
Quanta Services Inc 1360 Post Oak Blvd Ste 2100 . . . . Houston TX 77056 *NYSE: PWR*	800-872-0615	713-629-7600	188-1
Quantech Corp 369 Lexington Ave . . . . New York NY 10016	833-256-8367	212-323-2660	804
Quantiam Technologies Inc 1651 - 94 St NW . . . . Edmonton AB T6N1E6	877-461-0707	780-462-0707	664
Quantimetrix Corp 2005 Manhattan Beach Blvd . . . . Redondo Beach CA 90278	800-624-8380	310-536-0006	231
Quantros Inc 691 S Milpitas Blvd Ste 100 . . . . Milpitas CA 95035	877-782-6876		
Quantum Audio Designs Inc PO Box 130 . . . . Benton MO 63736	888-545-4404	573-545-4404	522
Quantum Corp 224 Airport Pkwy Ste 300 . . . . San Jose CA 95110 *NYSE: QTM* ■ *Tech Supp	800-677-6268*	408-944-4000	173-8
Quantum Corporate Funding Ltd 1140 Ave of the Americas 16th Fl . . . . New York NY 10036	800-352-2535	212-768-1200	272
Quantum Dental Technologies Inc 748 Briar Hill Ave . . . . Toronto ON M6B1L3	866-993-9910		228
Quantum Inc PO Box 2791 . . . . Eugene OR 97402	800-448-1448	541-345-5556	297
Quantum Management Services Ltd 2000 McGill College Ave Ste 1800 . . . . Montreal QC H3A3H3	800-978-2688	514-842-5555	729
Quantum Marine Stabilizers 3790 SW 30th Ave . . . . Fort Lauderdale FL 33312	800-807-8360	954-587-4205	261
Quantum/ATL 141 Innovation Dr . . . . Irvine CA 92617	800-677-6268	949-856-7800	173-8
Quantum3D Inc 1759 McCarthy Blvd . . . . Milpitas CA 95035	888-747-1020	408-600-2500	173-2
QuantumDigital Inc 8702 Cross Park Dr . . . . Austin TX 78754	800-637-7373		5
Quark Inc 1800 Grant St . . . . Denver CO 80203 *Cust Svc	800-676-4575*		178-8
Quarq Technology Inc 3100 First Ave . . . . Spearfish SD 57783	800-660-6853	605-642-2226	707
Quartz Mountain Resort & Conference Ctr 22469 Lodge Rd . . . . Lone Wolf OK 73655	877-999-5567	580-563-2424	665
Quartzdyne Inc 4334 West Links Dr . . . . Salt Lake City UT 84120	800-222-3611	801-839-1000	253
Quasius Investment Corp 4200 W Cypress St Ste 375 . . . . Tampa FL 33607	888-422-9786	813-249-2514	
Quatech Inc 5675 Hudson Industrial Pkwy . . . . Hudson OH 44236	800-553-1170	330-655-9000	621
Quatred LLC 532 Fourth Range Rd . . . . Pembroke NH 03275	888-395-8534		41
Quebec 41 Boul Comtois . . . . Louiseville QC J5V2H8	888-693-3506	819-228-2731	
Quebec Inn 7175 Blvd Hamel Ouest . . . . Quebec QC G2G1B6	800-567-5276	418-872-9831	378
Quebec Port Authority 150 Dalhousie St PO Box 80 Stn Haute-Ville . . . . Quebec QC G1R4M8	800-465-1213	418-648-3640	614
Queen Anne Hotel 1590 Sutter St . . . . San Francisco CA 94109	800-227-3970	415-441-2828	378
Queen City Printers Inc 701 Pine St . . . . Burlington VT 05401	800-639-8099	802-864-4566	623
Queen CutleryCom 507 Chestnut St . . . . Titusville PA 16354 *Sales	800-222-5233*	814-827-3673	222
Queen Wilhelmina State Park 3877 Arkansas 88 . . . . Mena AR 71953	888-287-2757	479-394-2863	561
Queen's College Faculty of Theology 210 Prince Philip Dr . . . . Saint John's NL A1B3R6	877-753-0116	709-753-0116	167-3
Queen's University 99 University Ave . . . . Kingston ON K7L3N6	800-267-7837	613-533-2000	780
Queens College 65-30 Kissena Blvd . . . . Flushing NY 11367	888-888-0606	718-997-5000	166
Queens Hospital Ctr 82-68 164th St . . . . Jamaica NY 11432	888-692-6116	718-883-3000	373-3
Queens University of Charlotte 1900 Selwyn Ave . . . . Charlotte NC 28274	800-849-0202	704-337-2212	166
Queensborough National Bank & Trust Co 113 E Broad St PO Box 467 . . . . Louisville GA 30434	800-236-2442	478-625-2000	775
Queenstown Bank of Maryland 7101 Main St PO Box 120 . . . . Queenstown MD 21658	888-827-4300	410-827-8881	70
Quest Companies Inc 8011 N Point Blvd Ste 201 . . . . . . Winston-Salem NC 27106	800-467-9409		7
Quest Controls Inc 208 Ninth St Dr W . . . . Palmetto FL 34221	800-373-6331		
Quest Corp of America 17220 Camelot Ct . . . . Land O' Lakes FL 34638	866-662-6273		
Quest Diagnostics at Nichols Institute 33608 Ortega Hwy . . . . San Juan Capistrano CA 92675	800-642-4657	949-728-4000	417
Quest Diagnostics Inc 3 Giralda Farms . . . . Madison NJ 07940 *NYSE: DGX*	800-222-0446	201-393-5000	417
Quest Engineering Inc 2300 Edgewood Ave S . . . . Minneapolis MN 55426	800-328-4853	952-546-4441	357
Quest Software Inc 5 Polairis Way . . . . Aliso Viejo CA 92656	800-306-9329	949-754-8000	178-1
Questar Assessment Inc 5550 Upper 147th St W . . . . Apple Valley MN 55124 *OTC: QUSA* ■ *Cust Svc	800-800-2598*	952-997-2700	243
Questar Capital Corp 5701 Golden Hills Dr . . . . Minneapolis MN 55416	888-446-5872		686
Questco 100 Commercial Cir . . . . Conroe TX 77304	800-256-7823	936-756-1980	729
Questel Orbit 1725 Duke St Ste 625 . . . . Alexandria VA 22314	800-456-7248		631
Questex LLC 275 Grove St Ste 2-130 . . . . Newton MA 02466	888-552-4346	617-219-8300	527-13
Questionmark Corp 5 Hillandale Ave . . . . Stamford CT 06902	800-863-3950	203-358-3950	177
Questor Technology Inc 1121 940 - Sixth Ave SW . . . . Calgary AB T2P3T1	844-477-8669	403-571-1530	535
QuestSoft Corp 23441 S Pointe Dr Ste 220 . . . . Laguna Hills CA 92653	800-575-4632		35
Queue Inc 703 Post Rd . . . . Fairfield CT 06824	800-232-2224		178-3
Quick Color Solutions Inc 829 Knox Rd . . . . Mc Leansville NC 27301	877-698-0951	336-698-0951	623
Quick Crete Products 731 Parkridge Ave . . . . Norco CA 92860	866-703-3434		191-1
Quick Fuel Fleet Services Inc 11815 W Bradley Rd . . . . Milwaukee WI 53224	800-522-6287		316
Quick Tab II Inc 241 Heritage Dr . . . . Tiffin OH 44883	800-332-5081	419-448-6622	623
Quicken Loans Arena 1 Ctr Ct . . . . Cleveland OH 44115	888-894-9424	216-420-2000	716
Quickie Manufacturing Corp 1150 Taylor Ln . . . . Riverton NJ 08077	800-257-5751		
Quickmill Inc 760 Rye St . . . . Peterborough ON K9J6W9	800-295-0509	705-745-2961	489
QuickStart 5910 Courtyard Dr Ste 170 . . . . Austin TX 78731	866-991-3924		177
Quidel Corp 10165 McKellar Ct . . . . San Diego CA 92121 *NASDAQ: QDEL*	800-874-1517	858-552-1100	231
Quiel Bros Sign Co 272 S 'I' St . . . . San Bernardino CA 92410	800-874-7446	909-885-4476	697
Quik Stop Markets Inc 4567 Enterprise St . . . . Fremont CA 94538	888-200-6211	510-657-8500	204
Quik Travel Staffing Inc 175 E Olive Ave Ste 101 . . . . Burbank CA 91502	800-554-7501	800-554-2230	260
Quikbook 381 Park Ave S . . . . New York NY 10016	800-789-9887	212-779-7666	375
QUIKRETE Cos 3490 Piedmont Rd Ste 1300 . . . . Atlanta GA 30305	800-282-5828	404-634-9100	183
Quiksilver Inc 15202 Graham St . . . . Huntington Beach CA 92649 *NYSE: ZQK*	800-435-9917		155-3
Quikstik Labels 220 Broadway . . . . Everett MA 02149	800-225-3496	617-389-7570	412
Quiktrak Inc 9700 SW Nimbus Ave . . . . Beaverton OR 97008	800-927-8725		41
QuikTrip Corp 4705 S 129th E Ave . . . . Tulsa OK 74134	800-441-0253	918-615-7700	204
Quilter's Newsletter Magazine 741 Corporate Cir Ste A . . . . Golden CO 80401	800-477-6089	303-215-5600	455-14
Quiltmaker Magazine 741 Corporate Cir Ste A . . . . Golden CO 80401	800-388-7023	800-881-6634	455-14
Quimby House Inn 109 Cottage St . . . . Bar Harbor ME 04609	800-344-5811	207-288-5811	378
Quincy Area Convention & Visitors Bureau (QACVB) 532 Gardner Expy . . . . Quincy IL 62301	800-978-4748	217-214-3700	206
Quincy College 1250 Hancock St . . . . Quincy MA 02169	800-698-1700	617-984-1700	162
Plymouth 36 Cordage Pk Cir . . . . Plymouth MA 02360	800-698-1700	508-747-0400	162
Quincy Herald-Whig 130 S Fifth St . . . . Quincy IL 62301	800-373-9444	217-223-5100	528-2
Quincy Mutual Fire Insurance Co 57 Washington St . . . . Quincy MA 02169	800-899-1116		390-4
Quincy Newspapers Inc 130 S Fifth St . . . . Quincy IL 62301	800-373-9444	217-223-5100	633-8
Quincy Street Inc 13350 Quincy St . . . . Holland MI 49424	800-784-6290	616-399-3330	471
Quinnipiac University 275 Mt Carmel Ave . . . . Hamden CT 06518 *Admissions	800-462-1944*	203-582-8600	166
Quinnipiac University School of Law 275 Mt Carmel Ave . . . . Hamden CT 06518	800-462-1944	203-582-3400	167-1
Quintess Collection LLC 11101 W 120th Ave Ste 200 . . . . Broomfield CO 80021	800-895-4301		376
Quintessence Publishing Co 4350 Chandler Dr . . . . Hanover Park IL 60133	800-621-0387	630-736-3600	776
Quintevents LLC 9300 Harris Corners Pkwy Ste 120 . . . . Charlotte NC 28269	866-834-8663		195
Quirch Foods Co 7600 NW 82nd Pl . . . . Miami FL 33166	800-458-5252	305-691-3535	297-9
Quirks Enterprises Inc 4662 Slater Rd . . . . Eagan MN 55122	800-827-0676	651-379-6200	7
Quiznos Corp 7595 Technology Way Ste 200 . . . . Denver CO 80237	866-486-2783	720-359-3300	666
QUMAS 66 York St . . . . Jersey City NJ 07302 *Sales	800-577-1545*	973-805-8600	178-10
QVC Inc 1200 Wilson Dr . . . . West Chester PA 19380	800-367-9444	484-701-1000	735
Qwest Investment Management Corp 750 West Pender St Ste 802 . . . . Vancouver BC V6C2T8	866-602-1142	604-601-5804	524

R

Name / Address	City	State	Zip	Toll-Free	Phone	Class
R & B Wagner Inc PO Box 423	Butler	WI	53007	**888-243-6914**	414-214-0444	591
R & B Wholesale Distributors Inc 2350 S Milliken Ave	Ontario	CA	91761	**800-627-7539**	909-230-5400	38
R & D Batteries Inc 3300 Corporate Ctr Dr PO Box 5007	Burnsville	MN	55306	**800-950-1945**	952-890-0629	74
R & D Computers Inc 3190 Reps Miller Rd Ste 390	Norcross	GA	30071	**800-350-3071**	770-416-0103	585
R & D Systems Inc 614 McKinley Pl NE	Minneapolis	MN	55413	**800-343-7475**	612-379-2956	231
R & D Transportation Services Inc 4036 Adolfo Rd	Camarillo	CA	93012	**800-966-7114**	805-529-7511	311
R & K Industrial Products Co 1945 Seventh St	Richmond	CA	94801	**800-842-7655**	510-234-7212	672
R & M Office Furniture 9615 Oates Dr	Sacramento	CA	95827	**800-660-1756**	916-362-1756	320
R & R Limousine 4403 Kiln Ct	Louisville	KY	40218	**800-582-5576**	502-458-1862	440
R & R Trucking Inc 302 Thunder Rd PO Box 545	Duenweg	MO	64841	**800-625-6885**	417-623-6885	775
R & S/Godwin Truck Body Co LLC 5168 US Hyw 23 S PO Box 420	Ivel	KY	41642	**800-826-7413**	606-874-2151	513
R C Mc Lean & Assoc Inc 210 N Tustin Ave	Santa Ana	CA	92705	**800-883-7243**	714-347-1000	443
R E I Consultants Inc PO Box 286	Beaver	WV	25813	**800-999-0105**	304-255-2500	192
R H K Hydraulic Cylinder Services Inc 13111 159th St	Edmonton	AB	T5V1H6	**800-406-3111**	780-452-2876	392
R J Schinner Company Inc 16950 W Lincoln Ave	New Berlin	WI	53151	**800-234-1460**	262-797-7180	786
R K Allen Oil Inc 36002 AL Hwy 21	Talladega	AL	35161	**800-445-5823**	256-362-4261	575
R Kidd Fuels Corp 1172 Twinney Dr	Newmarket	ON	L3Y9E2	**866-274-2315**		575
R N Croft Financial Group Inc 218 Steeles Ave E	Thornhill	ON	L3T1A6	**877-249-2884**	905-695-7777	400
R O I Media Solutions LLC 11500 W Olympic Blvd Ste 400	Los Angeles	CA	90064	**866-211-2580**		5
R R Floody Co 5065 27th Ave	Rockford	IL	61109	**800-678-6639**	815-399-1931	357
R Seelaus & Company Inc 25 Deforest Ave Ste 304	Summit	NJ	07901	**800-922-0584**		686
R W Mercer Co 2322 Brooklyn Rd PO Box 180	Jackson	MI	49204	**877-763-7237**	517-787-2960	186
R W Rog & Company Inc 630 Johnson Ave Ste 103	Bohemia	NY	11716	**877-218-0085**	631-218-0077	194
R2 Unified Technologies 980 N Federal Hwy Ste 410	Boca Raton	FL	33432	**866-464-7381**	561-515-6800	196
R2c Group Inc 207 NW Park Ave	Portland	OR	97209	**866-402-1124**		
RA Miller Industries Inc 14500 168th Ave PO Box 858	Grand Haven	MI	49417	**888-845-9450**	616-842-9450	643
RAB (Radio Adv Bureau) 125 W 55th St 5th Fl	New York	NY	10019	**800-232-3131**		49-18
RAB Lighting 170 Ludlow Ave	Northvale	NJ	07647	**888-722-1000**	201-784-8600	438
Raba-Kistner Consultants Inc 12821 W Golden Ln	San Antonio	TX	78249	**866-722-2547**	210-699-9090	189-15
Rabbinical Assembly 3080 Broadway	New York	NY	10027	**866-907-2761**		
Rabbit Air 125 N Raymond Ave Ste 308	Pasadena	CA	91103	**888-866-8862**	562-861-4688	45
Rabbit Hill Inn 48 Lower Waterford Rd PO Box 55	Lower Waterford	VT	05848	**800-626-3215**	802-748-5168	378
Rabo Bank 1026 E Grand Ave	Arroyo Grande	CA	93420	**800-942-6222**	805-473-7710	70
Rabun Gap-Nacoochee School 339 Nacoochee Dr	Rabun Gap	GA	30568	**800-543-7467**	706-746-7467	618
Raccoon Mountain Caverns 319 W Hills Dr	Chattanooga	TN	37419	**800-823-2267**	423-821-9403	50-5
Raccoon Valley Electric Co-op 28725 Hwy 30 PO Box 486	Glidden	IA	51443	**800-253-6211**	712-659-3649	245
Race Face Components Inc 100 Braid St	New Westminster	BC	V3L3P4	**800-527-9244**	604-527-9996	155-1
RaceTrac Petroleum Inc 3225 Cumberland Blvd Ste 100	Atlanta	GA	30339	**888-636-5589**	770-431-7600	324
Racine County 730 Wisconsin Ave 1st Fl North end	Racine	WI	53403	**800-242-4202**	262-636-3121	337
Racine County Convention & Visitors Bureau 14015 Washington Ave	Sturtevant	WI	53177	**800-272-2463**	262-884-6400	206
RACO Mfg & Engineering Company Inc 1400-62nd St	Emeryville	CA	94608	**800-722-6999**		
RACVB (Ridgecrest Area Convention & Visitors Bureau) 643 N China Lake Blvd Ste C	Ridgecrest	CA	93555	**800-847-4830**	760-375-8202	206
RAD Data Communications Ltd 900 Corporate Dr	Mahwah	NJ	07430	**800-444-7234**	201-529-1100	730
Rada Manufacturing Co PO Box 838	Waverly	IA	50677	**800-311-9691**	319-352-5454	222
Radar Inc 22214 20TH Ave SE Ste 101	Bothell	WA	98021	**800-282-2524**		246
Rad-Comm Systems Corp 2931 Portland Dr	Oakville	ON	L6H5S4	**800-588-5229**	905-829-8290	406
Radford University 801 E Main St *Admissions	Radford	VA	24142	**800-890-4265***	540-831-5371	166
Radiac Abrasives Inc 1015 S College Ave	Salem	IL	62881	**800-851-1095**	618-548-4200	1
Radian Group Inc 1500 Market St	Philadelphia	PA	19102	**800-523-1988**		390-5
Radiancy Inc 40 Ramland Rd S Ste 200	Orangeburg	NY	10962	**888-661-2220**	845-398-1647	473
Radiant Communications Corp 1600-1050 W Pender St *TSX: RCN*	Vancouver	BC	V6E4T3	**888-219-2111**		803
Radiant Electric Co-op Inc PO Box 390	Fredonia	KS	66736	**800-821-0956**	620-378-2161	245
RADIANT GLOBAL LOGISTICS 405 114th Ave SE 3rd Fl	Bellevue	WA	98004	**800-843-4784**	425-462-1094	447
Radiant Networks 13000 Middletown Industrial Blvd Ste D	Louisville	KY	40223	**866-411-9526**	502-379-4800	
Radiant Pools Div Trojan Leisure Products LLC 440 N Pearl St	Albany	NY	12207	**866-697-5870**	518-434-4161	724
Radiant Technologies Inc 2835 Pan American Fwy NE	Albuquerque	NM	87107	**800-289-7176**	505-842-8007	256
Radianta Inc 320 Goddard Ste 100	Irvine	CA	92618	**866-467-9695**		804
Radio Adv Bureau (RAB) 125 W 55th St 5th Fl	New York	NY	10019	**800-232-3131**		49-18
Radio America 1100 N Glebe Rd Ste 900	Arlington	VA	22201	**800-807-4703**	703-302-1000	640
Radio Communications Co 8035 Chapel Hill Rd	Cary	NC	27513	**800-508-7580**	919-467-2421	194
Radio Flyer Inc 6515 W Grand Ave	Chicago	IL	60707	**800-621-7613**	773-637-7100	757
Radio Kansas 815 N Walnut Ste 300	Hutchinson	KS	67501	**800-723-4657**		641
Radio North 2682 Garfield Rd N Ste 22	Traverse City	MI	49686	**800-274-8255**		643
Radio Research Consortium Inc (RRC) PO Box 1309	Olney	MD	20830	**800-543-7300**	301-774-6686	628
Radiocat 32-A Mellor Ave	Baltimore	MD	21228	**800-323-9729**		789
Radiodetection Corp 154 Portland Rd	Bridgton	ME	04009	**877-247-3797**	207-647-9495	248
Radiofrequency Safety International (RSI) 543 Main St	Kiowa	KS	67070	**888-830-5648**		196
Radiological Society of North America (RSNA) 820 Jorie Blvd	Oak Brook	IL	60523	**800-381-6660**	630-571-2670	49-8
Radiology Business Management Assn (RBMA) 9990 Fairfax Blvd Ste 430	Fairfax	VA	22030	**888-224-7262**	703-621-3355	49-8
Radionet 2 Pillsbury St 6th Fl	Concord	NH	03301	**800-639-4131**	603-228-8910	641
Radiophone Engineering Inc 534 W Walnut St	Springfield	MO	65806	**800-369-2929**	417-862-6653	246
RadioU PO Box 1887	Westerville	OH	43086	**877-272-3468**		641
Radisson 11340 Blondo S Ste 100	Omaha	NE	68164	**888-288-8889**	800-615-7253	665
Radisson Chicago-O'Hare Hotel 1450 E Touhy Ave	Des Plaines	IL	60018	**888-201-1718**	888-288-8889	378
Radisson Hotel & Suites 100 W Michigan	Kalamazoo	MI	49007	**888-288-8889**		
Radisson Hotel Bloomington Mall of America 1700 American Blvd E *Resv	Bloomington	MN	55425	**800-967-9033***	952-854-8700	378
Radisson Hotel Gateway Seattle-Tacoma Airport 18118 International Blvd	Seattle	WA	98188	**888-288-8889**		
Radisson Resort Parkway 2900 PkwyBlvd	Kissimmee	FL	34747	**800-333-3333**	407-396-7000	665
RadiSys Corp 5445 NE Dawson Creek Dr *NASDAQ: RSYS*	Hillsboro	OR	97124	**800-950-0044**	503-615-1100	621
Radius Professional HDD Tools 2525 Ranger Hwy PO Box 3106	Weatherford	TX	76088	**800-892-9114**		534
Radnor Financial Advisors Inc 485 Devon Park Dr Ste 119	Wayne	PA	19087	**888-271-9922**	610-975-0280	400
Radon Control Systems Inc 160 US Rt 1	Freeport	ME	04032	**800-698-9655**	207-865-9200	35
RadView Software Inc 991 Hwy 22 West Ste 200	Bridgewater	NJ	08807	**888-723-8439**	908-526-7756	178-12
Radware Inc 575 Corporate Dr Lobby 2	Mahwah	NJ	07430	**888-234-5763**	400-920-2910	178-11
Radwell International Ltd 1 Millennium Dr	Willingboro	NJ	08046	**800-884-5500**	609-288-9393	
Rady Children's Hospital (RCH) 3020 Children's Way 3rd Fl	San Diego	CA	92123	**800-788-9029**	858-576-1700	373-1
Radyne Corp 211 W Boden St	Milwaukee	WI	53207	**800-236-8360**	414-481-8360	318
RAE Corp 4615 Prime Pkwy	McHenry	IL	60050	**800-323-7049**	815-385-3500	515
RAE Systems 3775 North First St	San Jose	CA	95134	**877-723-2878**	408-952-8200	201
Raft River Rural Electric Co-op Inc 155 N Main St PO Box 617	Malta	ID	83342	**800-342-7732**	208-645-2211	245
Ragan Communications Inc 316 N Michigan Ave Ste 400	Chicago	IL	60601	**800-878-5331**	312-960-4100	527-2
Ragland Mills Inc 14079 Hammer Rd	Neosho	MO	64850	**888-549-8014**	417-451-2510	445
Rail Car Service Co 584 Fairground Rd	Mercer	PA	16137	**800-521-2151**	724-662-3660	646
Rail Europe Inc 44 S Broadway 11th Fl	White Plains	NY	10601	**800-361-7245**	914-682-2999	770
Railhead Corp 12549 S Laramie Ave	Alsip	IL	60803	**800-235-1782**	708-844-5500	765
Railinc Corp 7001 Weston Pkwy Ste 200	Cary	NC	27513	**877-724-5462**	919-651-5000	
Railroad Pass Hotel & Casino 2800 S Boulder Hwy	Henderson	NV	89002	**800-654-0877**	702-294-5000	133
Railroad Retirement Board 844 N Rush St	Chicago	IL	60611	**877-772-5772**	312-751-4300	339-19
Rails Co 101 Newark Way	Maplewood	NJ	07040	**800-217-2457**	973-763-4320	765
Railserve Inc 1691 Phoenix Blvd Ste 250	Atlanta	GA	30349	**800-345-7245**	770-996-6838	647

		Toll-Free	Phone	Class

Company		Toll-Free	Phone	Class
Rails-to-Trails Conservancy (RTC) 2121 Ward Ct NW 5th Fl .... Washington DC 20037		800-944-6847	202-331-9696	48-13
Rain & Hail LLC 9200 Northpark Dr Ste 100 .... Johnston IA 50131		800-776-4045	515-559-1200	
Rainbow Advertising Lp 3904 W Vickery Blvd .... Fort Worth TX 76107		800-645-7377	817-738-3838	7
Rainbow Grocery Co-op Inc 1745 Folsom St .... San Francisco CA 94103		877-720-2667	415-863-0620	344
Rainbow International 1010 N University Park Dr .... Waco TX 76707		855-724-6269	254-756-5463	152
Rainbow Light 125 McPherson St .... Santa Cruz CA 95060		800-475-1890	831-429-9089	477
Rainbow Lodge 2011 Ella Blvd .... Houston TX 77008		866-861-8666	713-861-8666	667
Rainbow Trout Ranch (RTR) 1484 FDR 250 PO Box 458 .... Antonito CO 81120		800-633-3397	719-376-2440	239
Raindance Spa at the Lodge at Sonoma Renaissance Resort 1325 Broadway .... Sonoma CA 95476		866-263-0758	707-935-6600	703
Rainforest Action Network (RAN) 425 Bush St Ste 300 .... San Francisco CA 94108		800-368-1819	415-398-4404	48-13
Rainier Industries Ltd 18375 Olympic Ave S .... Tukwila WA 98188		800-869-7162	425-251-1800	728
RainMaker Securities LLC 11390 W Olympic Blvd Ste 380 .... Los Angeles CA 90064		888-333-1091		687
RAINN (Rape Abuse & Incest National Network) 2000 L St NW Ste 406 .... Washington DC 20036		800-656-4673	202-544-1034	48-6
Rainwater, Holt & Sexton PA 801 Technology Dr .... Little Rock AR 72223		800-434-4800	501-868-2500	427
Rainwise Inc 18 River Field Rd .... Trenton ME 04605		800-762-5723	207-288-5169	406
Rainy River Community College 1501 Hwy 71 .... International Falls MN 56649		800-456-3996	218-285-7722	162
Raj, The 1734 Jasmine Ave .... Fairfield IA 52556		800-248-9050	641-472-9580	702
Rajkowski Hansmeier Ltd 11 Seventh Ave N .... Saint Cloud MN 56303		800-445-9617	320-251-1055	427
Rakuten Marketing 215 Park Ave S 2nd Fl .... New York NY 10003		888-880-8430	646-943-8200	7
Rakutencom Shopping 85 Enterprise St .... Aliso Viejo CA 92656		800-800-0800	949-389-2000	786
Ralco Nutrition Inc 1600 Hahn Rd .... Marshall MN 56258		800-533-5306		445
Raleigh America Inc 6004 S 190th St Ste 101 .... Kent WA 98032		800-222-5527		82
Raleigh County 215 Main St .... Beckley WV 25801		800-509-6568	304-255-9178	337
Raleigh USA 6004 S 190th St Ste 101 .... Kent WA 98032		800-222-5527	253-395-1100	82
Raleigh-Durham International Airport PO Box 80001 .... Raleigh NC 27623		800-252-7522	919-840-2123	27
Raley's 500 W Capitol Ave .... Sacramento CA 95605		800-925-9989	916-373-3333	344
Ralls County Electric Co-op 17594 Hwy 19 PO Box 157 .... New London MO 63459		877-985-8711	573-985-8711	245
Rally Education 22 Railroad Ave .... Glen Head NY 11545		888-997-2559		
Rally House & Kansas Sampler 9750 Quivira Rd .... Lenexa KS 66215		800-645-5409		786
Rallyorgorg 995 Market St 2nd Fl .... San Francisco CA 94105		888-648-2220		386
Ralph Friedland & Bros 17 Industrial Dr .... Keyport NJ 07735		800-631-2162	732-290-9800	87
Ralph H Johnson VA Medical Center 109 Bee St .... Charleston SC 29401		888-878-6884	843-577-5011	373-8
Ralph Pill Electrical Supply Co 50 Von Hillern St .... Boston MA 02125		800-897-1769	617-265-8800	246
Ralph Rosenberg Court Reporters Inc 1001 Bishop St Ste 2460 .... Honolulu HI 96813		888-524-5888		443
Ralph Wilson Stadium 1 Bills Dr .... Orchard Park NY 14127		877-228-4257	716-648-1800	716
Ralphs Grocery Co 1014 Vine St .... Cincinnati OH 45202 *Cust Svc		800-576-4377*		344
Ralphs-pugh Company Inc 3931 Oregon St .... Benicia CA 94510		800-486-0021	707-745-6222	207
Ralston Metal Products Ltd 50 Watson Rd S .... Guelph ON N1L1E2		800-265-7611		478
Ram Welding Company Inc 93 Rado Dr .... Naugatuck CT 06770		800-927-6485	203-729-2289	478
Rama Corp 600 W Esplanade Ave .... San Jacinto CA 92583		800-472-5670	951-654-7351	14
Ramada Inn Airport 2275 Marina Mile Blvd STATE Rd 84 .... Fort Lauderdale FL 33312		800-509-9854	954-584-4000	377
Ramapo Sales & Marketing Inc 4760 Goer Dr Ste F .... North Charleston SC 29406		800-866-9173		195
Ramblin Express Transportation 3465 Astrozon Pl .... Colorado Springs CO 80910		800-772-6254	719-590-8687	108
Ramco Systems Corp 3150 Brunswick Pk Ste 130 .... Lawrenceville NJ 08648		800-472-6261	609-620-4800	225
Ramius Corp 283 Blvd Alexandre Tach, Ste F2014 .... Gatineau QC J9A1L8		888-932-2299	613-230-3808	
Ramos Oil Company Inc 1515 S River Rd .... West Sacramento CA 95691 *Cust Svc		800-477-7266*	916-371-2570	575
Rampart Brokerage Corp 1983 Marcus Ave Ste C130 ...... New Hyde Park NY 11042		800-772-6727	516-538-7000	389
Rampart Supply Inc 1801 N Union Blvd .... Colorado Springs CO 80909		800-748-1837	719-482-7333	608
Ramsey County 15 W Kellogg Blvd .... Saint Paul MN 55102		866-520-7225	651-266-8000	337
Ramsey Winch Company Inc 1600 N Garnett Rd .... Tulsa OK 74116		800-777-2760	918-438-2760	190
Ramtech Bldg Systems Inc 1400 Hwy 287 S .... Mansfield TX 76063		800-568-9376	817-473-9376	186
Ramtron International Corp 1850 Ramtron Dr .... Colorado Springs CO 80921 *NASDAQ: RMTR*		800-541-4736	719-481-7000	692
RAN (Rainforest Action Network) 425 Bush St Ste 300 .... San Francisco CA 94108		800-368-1819	415-398-4404	48-13
Ranac 11650 Lantern Rd Ste 111 .... Fishers IN 46038		888-335-0427		180
Ranch at Steamboat 1800 Ranch Rd .... Steamboat Springs CO 80487		888-686-8075	970-879-3000	378
Ranch Inn 45 E Pearl St .... Jackson WY 83001		800-348-5599	307-733-6363	378
Rancho Bernardo Inn 17550 Bernardo Oaks Dr .... San Diego CA 92128		877-517-9340	858-675-8500	667
Rancho de los Caballeros 1551 S Vulture Mine Rd .... Wickenburg AZ 85390		800-684-5030	928-684-5484	665
Rancho Los Amigos National Rehabilitation Ctr 7601 E Imperial Hwy .... Downey CA 90242		877-726-2461	562-385-7111	373-6
Rancho Santa Fe Protective Services Inc 1991 Vlg Pk Way Ste 100 .... Encinitas CA 92024		800-303-8877		689
Rancho Valencia Resort 5921 Valencia Cir PO Box 9126 .... Rancho Santa Fe CA 92067		800-548-3664	858-756-1123	665
Rancho Viejo Resort & Country Club 1 Rancho Viejo Dr .... Rancho Viejo TX 78575		800-531-7400	956-350-4000	665
RAND Corp 1776 Main St .... Santa Monica CA 90401		877-584-8642	310-393-0411	630
Rand Graphics Inc 500 S Florence St .... Wichita KS 67209		800-435-7263	316-942-1218	623
Rand McNally 9855 Woods Dr PO Box 7600 .... Skokie IL 60077		800-333-0136		633-1
Randall Bearings Inc 1046 Greenlawn Ave PO Box 1258 .... Lima OH 45802		800-626-7071	419-223-1075	481
Randall Bros Inc 665 Marietta St NW .... Atlanta GA 30313 *Cust Svc		800-476-4539*	404-892-6666	497
Randall Foods Inc PO Box 2669 .... Huntington Park CA 90255		800-427-2632	323-261-6565	615
Randall Mfg LLC 722 Church Rd .... Elmhurst IL 60126		800-323-7424	630-782-0001	604
Randall Museum 199 Museum Way .... San Francisco CA 94114		866-807-7148	415-554-9600	517
Randall S Miller & Associates PC 43252 Woodward Ave Ste 180 .... Bloomfield Hills MI 48302		844-322-6558	248-335-9200	41
Randall-Reilly Publishing Co 3200 Rice Mine Rd NE .... Tuscaloosa AL 35406 *Cust Svc		800-633-5953*	205-349-2990	633-9
Randolph Area Chamber of Commerce PO Box 391 .... Mount Freedom NJ 07970		800-366-3922	973-361-3462	139
Randolph Austin Company Inc 2119 FM 1626 PO Box 988 .... Manchaca TX 78652		800-531-5263	512-282-1590	637
Randolph College 2500 Rivermont Ave .... Lynchburg VA 24503 *Admissions		800-745-7692*	434-947-8000	166
Randolph County 1302 N Randolph Ave .... Elkins WV 26241		800-422-3304	304-636-2780	337
Randolph County 372 Hwy JJ .... Huntsville MO 65259		844-277-6555		337
Randolph Electric Membership Corp 879 McDowell Rd PO Box 40 .... Asheboro NC 27204		800-672-8212	336-625-5177	245
Randolph Packing Co 275 Roma Jean Pkwy .... Streamwood IL 60107		800-451-1607	630-830-3100	296-26
Randolph Savings Bank 129 N Main St .... Randolph MA 02368		877-963-2100	781-963-2100	70
Randolph-Brooks Federal Credit Union PO Box 2097 .... Universal City TX 78148		800-580-3300	210-945-3300	219
Randolph-Macon Academy 200 Academy Dr .... Front Royal VA 22630		800-272-1172	540-636-5200	618
Randolph-Macon College PO Box 5005 .... Ashland VA 23005		800-888-1762	804-752-7200	166
Rane Corp 10802 47th Ave W .... Mukilteo WA 98275		877-764-0093	425-355-6000	52
R-Anell Custom Homes Inc 235 Anthony Grave Rd .... Crouse NC 28033 *Cust Svc		800-951-5511*	574-533-7100	503
Rangam Consultants Inc 270 Davidson Ave Ste 103 .... Somerset NJ 08873		877-388-1858	908-704-8843	225
Rangen Inc 115 13th Ave S .... Buhl ID 83316 *Cust Svc		800-657-6446*	208-543-6421	445
Ranger Construction Industries Inc 101 Sansbury's Way .... West Palm Beach FL 33411		800-969-9402	561-793-9400	188-4
Rangers Die Casting Co 10828 S Alameda St .... Lynwood CA 90262		877-386-9969	310-764-1800	490
Rankin County Chamber of Commerce 101 Service Dr .... Brandon MS 39043		800-987-8280	601-825-2268	139
Ran-Pro Farms Inc PO Box 300 .... Tyler TX 75710		800-749-6266	903-593-7381	
Ransom & Randolph Co 3535 Briarfield Blvd .... Maumee OH 43537		800-800-7496	419-865-9497	659
Rapat Corp 919 Odonnel St .... Hawley MN 56549		800-325-6377	218-483-3344	207
Rape Abuse & Incest National Network (RAINN) 2000 L St NW Ste 406 .... Washington DC 20036		800-656-4673	202-544-1034	48-6
Raphael Kansas City 325 Ward Pkwy .... Kansas City MO 64112		800-821-5343	816-756-3800	378
Rapid City Convention & Visitors Bureau 444 Mt Rushmore Rd N .... Rapid City SD 57701		800-487-3223	605-718-8484	206
Rapid City Journal 507 Main St .... Rapid City SD 57701		800-843-2300	605-394-8300	528-2
Rapid City Regional Airport 4550 Terminal Rd Ste 102 .... Rapid City SD 57703		888-279-2135	605-393-9924	27
Rapid Displays 4300 W 47th St .... Chicago IL 60632		800-356-5775	773-927-1091	233
Rapid Engineering Inc 1100 7-Mile Rd NW .... Comstock Park MI 49321		800-536-3461	616-784-0500	318
Rapid Focus Security LLC 268 Summer St 2nd Fl .... Boston MA 02210		855-793-1337		689

	Toll-Free	Phone	Class
Rapid Industries			
4003 Oaklawn Dr ....Louisville KY 40219	800-727-4381	502-968-3645	207
Rapid Insight Inc			
53 Technology Ln Ste 112 ....Conway NH 03818	888-585-6511		177
Rapid Line Industries Inc			
455 N Ottawa St ....Joliet IL 60432	877-444-9955	815-727-4362	111
Rapid Response Monitoring Services Inc			
400 W Division St ....Syracuse NY 13204	800-558-7767		689
RAPIDS Wholesale Equipment Co			
6201 S Gateway Dr ....Marion IA 52302	800-472-7431	319-447-1670	300
Rappahannock Community College			
Glenns			
12745 College Dr ....Glenns VA 23149	800-836-9381	804-758-6700	162
Warsaw 52 Campus Dr ....Warsaw VA 22572	800-836-9381	804-333-6700	162
Raptim Humanitarian Travel			
6420 Inducon Dr W Ste A........Sanborn NY 14132	800-272-7846	716-754-9232	767
Raritan Bay Medical Ctr			
530 New Brunswick Ave ....Perth Amboy NJ 08861	800-701-0710	732-442-3700	373-3
Raritan Computer Inc			
400 Cottontail Ln ....Somerset NJ 08873	800-724-8090	732-764-8886	253
Raritan Valley Community College			
PO Box 3300 ....Somerville NJ 08876	888-326-4058	908-526-1200	162
Rasansky Law Firm			
2525 McKinnon Ave Ste 550 ....Dallas TX 75201	877-405-4313	214-651-6100	633-6
OTC: ATTY			
Rasmussen College Inc			
4400 W 78th St 6th Fl.........Bloomington MN 55345	800-852-0929	952-545-2000	166
Rasmussen Equipment Co			
3333 West 2100 South ....Salt Lake City UT 84119	800-453-8032	801-972-5588	357
RateHubca			
411 Richmond St E Ste 208 ....Toronto ON M5A3S5	800-679-9622		464
Raulerson Hospital			
1796 Hwy 441 N ....Okeechobee FL 34972	877-549-9337	863-763-2151	373-3
Ravalli County Fair			
100 Old Corvallis Rd ....Hamilton MT 59840	800-225-6779	406-363-3411	638
Rave Mobile Safety			
492 Old Connecticut Path			
2nd Fl..................Framingham MA 01701	888-605-7164	508-848-2484	177
Raven Industries Inc			
205 E Sixth St ....Sioux Falls SD 57104	800-243-5435	605-336-2750	596
NASDAQ: RAVN			
Ravenswood Winery Inc			
18701 Gehricke Rd ....Sonoma CA 95476	888-669-4679		80-3
Ravine Gardens State Park			
1600 Twigg St ....Palatka FL 32177	800-326-3521	386-329-3721	561
Rawah Ranch			
11447 N County Rd 103 ....Glendevey CO 82063	800-510-7071		239
Rawson Inc			
2010 McAllister ....Houston TX 77092	800-779-1414		246
Raxco Software Inc			
6 Montgomery Village Ave			
Ste 500..........Gaithersburg MD 20879	800-546-9728*	301-527-0803	178-12
Tech Supp			
Ray L Hellwig Plumbing & Heating Inc			
1301 Laurelwood Rd ....Santa Clara CA 95054	800-631-7013	408-727-5612	189-10
Ray Products Company Inc			
1700 Chablis Ave ....Ontario CA 91761	800-423-7859		598
Raybestos Powertrain LLC			
711 Tech Dr ....Crawfordsville IN 47933	800-729-7763		60
Raybourn Group International			
9100 PuRdue Rd Ste 200 ....Indianapolis IN 46268	800-362-2546	317-328-4636	47
Rayco Industries Inc			
1502 Valley Rd ....Richmond VA 23222	800-505-7111	804-321-7111	490
Raymarine Inc			
9 Townsend W ....Nashua NH 03063	800-539-5539	603-324-7900	525
Raymon H Mulford Library			
3000 Arlington Ave ....Toledo OH 43614	800-321-8383	419-383-4225	433-1
Raymond Bldg Supply Corp			
7751 Bayshore Rd ....North Fort Myers FL 33917	877-731-7272	239-731-8300	191-3
Raymond Corp			
22 S Canal St ....Greene NY 13778	800-235-7200*	607-656-2311	468
General			
Raymond Excavating Co Inc			
800 Gratiot Blvd ....Marysville MI 48040	800-837-6770	810-364-6881	189-5
Raymond F Kravis Ctr for the Performing Arts			
701 Okeechobee Blvd ....West Palm Beach FL 33401	800-572-8471	561-832-7469	568
Raymond Handling Concepts Corp			
41400 Boyce Rd ....Fremont CA 94538	800-675-2500	510-745-7500	264-3
Raymond James Financial Inc			
880 Carillon Pkwy ....Saint Petersburg FL 33716	800-248-8863	727-567-1000	686
NYSE: RJF			
Raymond James Ltd			
2200-925 W Georgia St Cathedral Pl			
..................Vancouver BC V6C3L2	888-545-6624	604-659-8000	400
Raymond James (USA) Ltd			
925 West Georgia St Ste 2100 ....Vancouver BC V6C3L2	844-654-7357		687
Raymond Vineyard			
849 Zinfandel Ln ....Saint Helena CA 94574	800-525-2659	707-963-3141	80-3
Raymour & Flanigan Furniture			
PO Box 220 ....Liverpool NY 13088	866-383-4484*	315-453-2500	321
Consumer Assistance			
Rayner Covering Systems Inc			
665 Schneider Dr................South Elgin IL 60177	800-648-0757	847-695-2264	604
Raynor Garage Doors			
1101 E River Rd ....Dixon IL 61021	800-472-9667	815-288-1431	234
Raypak Inc			
2151 Eastman Ave ....Oxnard CA 93030	800-438-4328	805-278-5300	356
Raytech Industries			
475 Smith St ....Middletown CT 06457	800-243-7163*	860-632-2020	1
Cust Svc			
Rayven Inc			
431 Griggs St N ....Saint Paul MN 55104	800-878-3776*	651-642-1112	624
Cust Svc			
RB Royal Industries Inc			
1350 S Hickory St ....Fond du Lac WI 54937	800-892-1550	920-921-1550	617
RBB Innovations			
2-258 Queen St E ....Sault Sainte Marie ON P6A1Y7	800-796-7864	705-942-9053	177
RBC Bearings Inc			
102 Willenbrock Rd ....Oxford CT 06478	800-390-3300		616
RBC Capital Markets			
200 Bay St S Tower 10th Fl............Toronto ON M5J2T6	800-769-2511		
RBC Dain Rauscher Inc			
60 S Sixth St ....Minneapolis MN 55402	800-933-9946		686
RBC Insurance Services			
PO Box 789 ....Greenville SC 29602	800-551-8354	864-609-8111	390-2
RBC Royal Bank			
1127 D,carie Blvd ....Saint-Laurent QC H4L3M8	800-769-2599		70
RBC Trust Company (Delaware) Ltd			
4550 New Linden Hill Rd			
Ste 200..........Wilmington DE 19808	800-441-7698	302-892-6976	70
RBCM (Royal British Columbia Museum)			
675 Belleville St ....Victoria BC V8W9W2	888-447-7977	250-356-7226	517
RBG (Royal Botanical Gardens)			
680 Plains Rd W ....Burlington ON L7T4H4	800-694-4769	905-527-1158	97
RBI Corp			
10201 Cedar Ridge Dr ....Ashland VA 23005	800-444-7370	804-550-2210	357
RBMA (Radiology Business Management Assn)			
9990 Fairfax Blvd Ste 430..............Fairfax VA 22030	888-224-7262	703-621-3355	49-8
RBMA (Reed Brennan Media Associates)			
628 Virginia Dr ....Orlando FL 32803	800-708-7311	407-894-7300	317
RBN Energy LLC			
2323 S Shepherd Dr Ste 1010 ....Houston TX 77019	888-400-9838		461
RBS Bulk Systems Inc			
9910 -48 St SE ....Calgary AB T2C2R2	800-882-5930	403-248-1530	314
Rbx Inc			
PO Box 2118 ....Springfield MO 65802	877-450-2200	800-245-5507	775
RC Fine Foods			
PO Box 236 ....Belle Mead NJ 08502	800-526-3953	908-359-5500	296-11
RC Smith Co			
14200 Southcross Dr W ....Burnsville MN 55306	800-747-7648	952-854-0711	286
RCH (Rady Children's Hospital)			
3020 Children's Way 3rd Fl ....San Diego CA 92123	800-788-9029	858-576-1700	373-1
RCI (Resort Condominiums International)			
9998 N Michigan Rd ....Carmel IN 46032	800-338-7777	317-805-8000	748
RCI (Records Consultants Inc)			
12829 Wetmore Rd ....San Antonio TX 78247	877-363-4127	210-366-4127	392
RCI (Retail Confectioners International)			
3029 E Sunshine St Ste A..........Springfield MO 65804	800-545-5381	417-883-2775	49-6
RCI Custom Products			
801 N East St Ste 2A................Frederick MD 21701	800-546-4724	301-620-9130	203
RCMA (Religious Conference Management Assn Inc)			
7702 Woodland Dr Ste 120 ....Indianapolis IN 46278	800-221-8235	317-632-1888	49-12
RCMC (Rush-Copley Medical Ctr)			
2000 Ogden Ave ....Aurora IL 60504	866-426-7539	630-978-6200	373-3
RCMP Heritage Ctr			
5907 Dewdney Ave ....Regina SK S4T0P4	866-567-7267	306-522-7333	517
RCP (Rubbermaid Commercial Products)			
3124 Valley Ave ....Winchester VA 22601	800-347-9800	540-667-8700	604
RCP Block & Brick Inc			
8240 Broadway ....Lemon Grove CA 91945	800-794-4727	619-460-7250	183
RCS Innovations			
7075 W Parkland Ct ....Milwaukee WI 53223	800-373-6873	414-354-6900	8
RD Legal Funding LLC			
45 Legion Dr ....Cresskill NJ 07626	800-565-5177		402
RDA Corp			
303 International Cir			
Ste 340..................Hunt Valley MD 21030	888-441-1278	410-308-9300	177
RDC (Roche Diagnostics Corp)			
9115 Hague Rd PO Box 50457........Indianapolis IN 46250	800-428-5076*		231
Cust Svc			
Rdk Truck Sales Inc			
3214 Adamo Dr ....Tampa FL 33605	877-735-4636	813-241-0711	513
RDO Equipment Co			
700 Seventh St S ....Fargo ND 58103	800-247-4650	877-444-7363	274
RDS Solutions LLC			
99 Grayrock Rd ....Clinton NJ 08809	888-473-7435		196
RE Lewis Refrigeration Inc			
803 S Lincoln St PO Box 92............Creston IA 50801	800-264-0767*	641-782-8183	661
Cust Svc			
RE/MAX International Inc			
5075 S Syracuse St ....Denver CO 80237	800-525-7452*	303-770-5531	648
Cust Svc			
RE/MAX Quebec Inc			
1500 rue Cunard ....Laval QC H7S2B7	800-361-9325	450-668-7743	648
REA Energy Co-op Inc			
75 Airport Rd ....Indiana PA 15701	800-211-5667	724-349-4800	245
Rea Magnet Wire Company Inc			
3400 E Coliseum Blvd Ste 200........Fort Wayne IN 46805	800-732-9473		
Reach Resort			
1435 Simonton St ....Key West FL 33040	888-318-4317	305-296-5000	665
ReachForce Inc			
2711 W Anderson Ln Ste 200........Austin TX 78757	844-254-5405		
Reaction Audio Visual LLC			
30400 Esperanza ....Rancho Santa Margarita CA 92618	877-273-6887		
Readerlink Distribution Services LLC			
1420 Kensington Rd Ste 300 ....Oak Brook IL 60523	800-549-5389	708-547-4400	96
Reading Area Community College			
10 S Second St ....Reading PA 19603	800-626-1665	610-372-4721	162
Reading Is Fundamental Inc (RIF)			
1825 Connecticut Ave NW			
Ste 400................Washington DC 20009	877-743-7323	202-536-3400	48-11
Reading Precast Inc			
5494 Pottsville Pk ....Leesport PA 19533	800-724-4881		183
Reading Rock Inc			
4600 Devitt Dr ....Cincinnati OH 45246	800-482-6466	513-874-2345	183
Reading Truck Body Inc			
201 Hancock Blvd ....Reading PA 19611	800-458-2226*		513
All			
Ready Pac Produce Inc			
4401 Foxdale Ave ....Irwindale CA 91706	800-800-7822		296-33
Ready Set Work LLC (RSW)			
1487 Dunwoody Dr Ste 200 ....West Chester PA 19380	877-507-3706		
Ready Technologies Inc			
101 Capitol Way N Ste 301........Olympia WA 98501	877-892-9104	360-413-9800	261
Reagan Wireless Corp			
720 S Powerline Rd			
Ste D..........Deerfield Beach FL 33442	877-724-3266	954-596-2355	246

	Toll-Free	Phone	Class
Reagent Chemical & Research Inc			
115 Rt 202 .... Ringoes NJ 08551	**800-231-1807**	908-284-2800	146
Real Estate Buyer's Agent Council (REBAC)			
430 N Michigan Ave .... Chicago IL 60611	**800-648-6224**		49-17
Real Estate Express			
12977 N 40 Dr Ste 108 .... Saint Louis MO 63141	**866-739-7277**		648
Real Estate Institute of Bc			
1750 - 355 Burrard St .... Vancouver BC V6C2G8	**800-667-2166**	604-685-3702	648
Real Estate Institute of Canada			
5407 Eglinton Ave W Unit 208 .... Toronto ON M9C5K6	**800-542-7342**	416-695-9000	652
Real Estate One Inc			
25800 NW Hwy .... Southfield MI 48075	**800-521-0508**	248-208-2900	648
Real Floors Inc			
1791 Williams Dr .... Marietta GA 30066	**800-728-2690**	770-590-7334	361
Real Goods Solar			
833 W S Boulder Rd .... Louisville CO 80027	**888-567-6527**		616
NASDAQ: RSGE			
Real Hip-Hop Network			
1717 Pennsylvania Ave NW			
Ste 1020 .... Washington DC 20006	**888-742-9993**		
Real Living First Service Realty			
13155 SW 42nd St Ste 200 .... Miami FL 33175	**800-899-8477**	305-551-9400	648
Real Living Real Estate LLC			
77 E Nationwide Blvd .... Columbus OH 43215	**800-274-7653**	949-794-7900	
Real Story Group, The			
3470 Olney-Laytonsville Rd			
Ste 131 .... Olney MD 20832	**800-325-6190**	617-340-6464	461
Real Time Measurements Inc			
4615 - 112th Ave SE Ste 125 .... Calgary AB T2C5J3	**866-720-3444**	403-720-3444	535
RealCapitalMarketscom LLC			
5780 Fleet St Ste 130 .... Carlsbad CA 92008	**888-546-5281**		
RealityCheck Inc			
2033 N Geyer Rd .... Saint Louis MO 63131	**866-751-2094**	314-909-9095	464
RealSTEEL			
1684 Medina Rd .... Medina OH 44256	**866-965-2688**		180
Realstreet Staffing			
2500 Wallington Way			
Ste 208 .... Marriottsville MD 21104	**877-480-8002**	410-480-8002	461
Realtime Software Corp			
24 Deane Rd .... Bernardston MA 01337	**800-323-1143**	847-803-1100	178-1
Realtor Magazine			
430 N Michigan Ave .... Chicago IL 60611	**800-874-6500**		455-5
Realtors Assn of New Mexico			
2201 Bros Rd .... Santa Fe NM 87505	**800-224-2282**	505-982-2442	652
Realty Executives International Inc			
645 E Missouri Ave Ste 210 .... Phoenix AZ 85020	**800-252-3366**	480-239-2038	648
Realty Income Corp			
11995 El Camino Real .... San Diego CA 92130	**877-924-6266**	858-284-5000	651
NYSE: O			
RealtyBid International Inc			
3225 Rainbow Dr Ste 248 .... Rainbow City AL 35906	**877-518-5600**		392
Reason Magazine			
3415 S Sepulveda Blvd			
Ste 400 .... Los Angeles CA 90034	**888-732-7668***	310-391-2245	455-17
*Cust Svc			
Reason Public Policy Institute			
3415 S Sepulveda Blvd			
Ste 400 .... Los Angeles CA 90034	**888-732-7668**	310-391-2245	630
Reaxis Inc			
941 Robinson Hwy .... Mcdonald PA 15057	**800-426-7273**		387
REBAC (Real Estate Buyer's Agent Council)			
430 N Michigan Ave .... Chicago IL 60611	**800-648-6224**		49-17
Re-Bath LLC			
16879 N 75th Ave Ste 101 .... Peoria AZ 85382	**800-426-4573**		189-11
Rebco Inc			
1171-1225 Madison Ave .... Paterson NJ 07509	**800-777-0787**	973-684-0200	234
Rebel State Historic Site			
1260 Hwy 1221 .... Marthaville LA 71450	**888-677-3600**	318-472-6255	561
Rebi (CRB)			
430 N Michigan Ave .... Chicago IL 60611	**800-621-8738**		49-17
Reboot Computer Services Inc			
70-11 Austin St Ste 3L .... Forest Hills NY 11375	**866-228-6286**		
Reborn Cabinets			
2981 E La Palma Ave .... Anaheim CA 92806	**888-273-2676**	714-630-2220	321
Rebuilding Together Inc			
1899 L St NW Ste 1000 .... Washington DC 20036	**800-473-4229**		48-5
REC (Rural Electric Co-op)			
13942 Hwy 76 PO Box 609 .... Lindsay OK 73052	**800-259-3504**	405-756-3104	245
Reco Equipment Inc			
41245 Reco Rd .... Belmont OH 41245	**800-686-7326**	740-782-1314	190
RECON Dynamics LLC			
18323 Bothell Everett Hwy			
Ste 330 .... Bothell WA 98012	**877-480-3551**		689
Recon Logistics LLC			
384 Inverness Pkwy Ste 270 .... Englewood CO 80112	**866-424-7153**		311
Recon Management Services Inc			
1907 Ruth St .... Sulphur LA 70663	**888-301-4662**	337-583-4662	627
Reconditioned Systems Inc (RSI)			
235 S 56th St .... Chandler AZ 85226	**800-280-5000**		319-1
Record			
4324 Phil Hargett Ct PO Box 3099 .... Monroe NC 28111	**800-438-1937***	704-289-9212	253
*Sales			
Record Play Tek Inc			
110 E Vistula St .... Bristol IN 46507	**800-809-5233**	574-848-5233	52
Record, The			
160 King St E .... Kitchener ON N2G4E5	**800-265-8261**	519-894-2231	528-1
Record-Courier			
1050 W Main St .... Kent OH 44240	**800-560-9657**	330-541-9400	528-2
Record-Courier			
1050 W Main St .... Kent OH 44240	**800-560-9657**	330-541-9400	528-4
Recording for the Blind & Dyslexic (RFB&D)			
20 Roszel Rd .... Princeton NJ 08540	**800-221-4792**		48-17
Record-Journal			
500 South Broad St 2nd Fl .... Meriden CT 06450	**800-228-6915**	203-235-1661	528-2
Recordnetcom			
530 E Market St .... Stockton CA 95202	**800-606-9741**	209-943-6568	528-2
Records Consultants Inc (RCI)			
12829 Wetmore Rd .... San Antonio TX 78247	**877-363-4127**	210-366-4127	392

	Toll-Free	Phone	Class
Recordtrak Inc			
651 Allendale Rd			
PO Box 61591 .... King Of Prussia PA 19406	**800-355-7400**		
Recovery Partners LLC			
4151 N Marshall Way Ste 12 .... Scottsdale AZ 85251	**866-661-5203**		
Recreation Vehicle Industry Assn (RVIA)			
1896 Preston White Dr .... Reston VA 20191	**800-336-0154**	703-620-6003	49-21
Recreational Equipment Inc (REI)			
6750 S 228th St .... Kent WA 98032	**800-426-4840***	253-395-3780	707
*Orders			
Recreationgov			
1849 C St NW .... Washington DC 20240	**877-444-6777**	202-208-4743	197
National Recreation Reservation Service			
PO Box 140 .... Ballston Spa NY 12020	**877-444-6777**	518-885-3639	768
Recreatives Industries Inc			
60 Depot St .... Buffalo NY 14206	**800-255-2511**	716-855-2226	29
Recruitmilitary LLC			
422 W Loveland Ave .... Loveland OH 45140	**800-226-0841**	513-683-5020	260
Recursion Software Inc			
2591 Dallas Pkwy Ste 200 .... Frisco TX 75034	**800-727-8674**	972-731-8800	179
Recycled Paper Greetings Inc			
111 N Canal St Ste 700 .... Chicago IL 60606	**800-777-3331**		130
Red Angus Assn of America			
4201 N IH- 35 .... Denton TX 76207	**800-422-2117**	940-387-3502	48-2
Red Bud Industries			
200 B & E Industrial Dr .... Red Bud IL 62278	**800-851-4612***	618-282-3801	492
*Cust Svc			
Red Carpet Charters			
4820 SW 20th .... Oklahoma City OK 73128	**888-878-5100**	405-672-5100	107
Red Clay Interactive			
22 Buford Village Way Ste 221 .... Buford GA 30518	**866-251-2800**	770-297-2430	225
Red Devil Inc			
1437 S Boulder .... Tulsa OK 74119	**800-423-3845**		3
Red Diamond Inc			
400 Park Ave .... Moody AL 35004	**800-292-4651**	205-577-4000	296-7
Red Dot Corp			
1209 W Corsicana St .... Athens TX 75751	**800-657-2234***		105
*Cust Svc			
Red Ewald Inc			
2669 US 181 .... Karnes City TX 78118	**800-242-3524**	830-780-3304	602
Red Fleet State Park			
8750 North Hwy 191 .... Vernal UT 84078	**800-322-3770**	435-789-4432	561
Red Gold Inc			
120 E Oak St .... Orestes IN 46063	**800-772-5726**	765-754-7527	296-20
Red Hat Inc			
1801 Varsity Dr .... Raleigh NC 27606	**888-733-4281**	919-754-3700	178-12
NYSE: RHT			
Red Hat Society Store			
431 S Acacia Ave .... Fullerton CA 92831	**866-386-2850**	714-738-0001	529
Red Hill Patrick Henry National Memorial			
1250 Red Hill Rd .... Brookneal VA 24528	**800-514-7463**	434-376-2044	560
Red Hot & Blue Restaurants Inc			
1600 Wilson Blvd .... Arlington VA 22209	**888-509-7100**	703-276-7427	666
Red Hot & Blue Restaurants Inc			
200 Old Mill Bottom Rd S .... Annapolis MD 21401	**888-509-7100**	410-626-7427	667
Red Inn			
15 Commercial St .... Provincetown MA 02657	**866-473-3466**	508-487-7334	667
Red Label Vacations Inc			
5450 Explorer Dr Ste 100 .... Mississauga ON L4W5N1	**866-573-3824**	905-283-6020	767
Red Lake Electric Co-op Inc			
412 International Dr			
PO Box 430 .... Red Lake Falls MN 56750	**800-245-6068**	218-253-2168	245
Red Lake Gaming Enterprises Inc			
PO Box 543 .... Red Lake MN 56671	**888-679-2501**	218-679-2111	132
Red Lion Hotels Corp			
201 W N River Dr Ste 100 .... Spokane WA 99201	**800-733-5466***		378
*NYSE: RLH ■ *Resv*			
Red Lion Templin's Hotel on the River			
414 E First Ave .... Post Falls ID 83854	**800-733-5466**	208-773-1611	665
Red River Commodities Inc			
501 42nd St N .... Fargo ND 58102	**800-437-5539**		690
Red River Computer Company Inc			
21 Water St Ste 500 .... Claremont NH 03743	**800-769-3060**	603-448-8880	121
Red River Specialties Inc			
1324 N Hearne Ave Ste 120 .... Shreveport LA 71107	**800-256-3344**	318-425-5944	276
Red River Valley Co-op Power Assn			
109 Second Ave E .... Halstad MN 56548	**800-788-7784**	218-456-2139	245
Red Rock Distributing Co			
1 NW 50th St .... Oklahoma City OK 73118	**800-323-7109**	405-677-3373	447
Red Rock Resort Spa & Casino			
11011 W Charleston Blvd .... Las Vegas NV 89135	**866-767-7773**	702-797-7777	378
Red Spot Interactive			
1001 Jupiter Park Dr .... Jupiter FL 33458	**800-401-7931**		461
Red Star Oil			
802 Purser Dr .... Raleigh NC 27603	**800-774-6033**	919-772-1944	447
Red Thread			
300 E River Dr .... East Hartford CT 06108	**800-635-4874**	860-528-9981	320
Red Wind Casino			
12819 Yelm Hwy .... Olympia WA 98513	**866-946-2444**		133
Red Wing Shoe Company Inc			
314 Main St .... Red Wing MN 55066	**800-733-9464***	844-314-6246	301
*Cust Svc			
Red Wing Software Inc			
491 Hwy 19 .... Red Wing MN 55066	**800-732-9464**	651-388-1106	178-1
RedBuilt LLC			
200 E Mallard Dr .... Boise ID 83706	**866-859-6757**		
Redco Foods Inc			
1 Hansen Is .... Little Falls NY 13365	**800-556-6674**	315-823-1300	296-40
Redd Paper Co			
3851 Ctr Loop .... Orlando FL 32808	**800-961-6656**	407-299-6656	549
Reddy Ice Holdings Inc			
8750 N Central Expy Ste 1800 ...... Dallas TX 75231	**800-683-4423**	214-526-6740	379
OTC: RDDYQ			
Redeemer University College			
777 Garner Rd E .... Ancaster ON L9K1J4	**877-779-0913**	905-648-2131	780
Redemptorist, The			
1 Liguori Dr .... Liguori MO 63057	**800-325-9521**	636-464-2500	48-20
Redeye Distribution Inc			
449a Trollingwood Rd .... Haw River NC 27258	**877-733-3931**		

	Toll-Free	Phone	Class
Redfin 9890 S Maryland Pkwy .... Las Vegas NV 89183	844-759-7732	877-973-3346	5
Redhawk Network Security LLC 62958 Layton Ave Ste One .... Bend OR 97701	866-605-6328		
Redi Bag USA 135 Fulton Ave .... New Hyde Park NY 11040	800-517-2247	516-746-0600	98
Redico Inc 1850 S Lee Ct .... Buford GA 30518	800-242-3920		661
Redi-Direct Marketing Inc 107 Little Falls Rd .... Fairfield NJ 07004	800-635-5833	973-808-4500	365
Rediker Software Inc 2 Wilbraham Rd .... Hampden MA 01036	800-213-9860	413-566-3463	177
Redland Brick Inc 15718 Clear Spring Rd ...... Williamsport MD 21795	800-366-2742	301-223-7700	150
Redlands Chamber of Commerce 47 N First St .... Redlands CA 92373	800-966-6428	909-793-2546	139
Redlands Community College 1300 S Country Club Rd .... El Reno OK 73036	866-415-6367	405-262-2552	162
Redlands Community Hospital Foundation PO Box 3391 .... Redlands CA 92373	888-397-4999	909-335-5500	373-3
RedLegg 319 1/2 State St Ste A. .... Geneva IL 60134	877-811-5040		196
Redman Equipment & Mfg Co 19800 Normandie Ave .... Torrance CA 90502	888-733-2602	310-329-1134	91
Redman Technologies Inc 10172-108 St .... Edmonton AB T5J1L3	866-425-0022		
Redmonk 95 High St Ste 206 .... Portland ME 04101	866-733-6665		461
Redneck Trailer Supplies 2100 NW By-Pass .... Springfield MO 65803	877-973-3632	417-864-5210	774
RedRick Technologies Inc 21624 Adelaide Rd ...... Mount Brydges ON N0L1W0	800-340-9511		473
Redspin A Division of CynergisTek 11410 Jollyville Rd Ste 2201 .... Austin TX 78759	800-721-9177		177
Redstone Federal Credit Union 220 Wynn Dr NW .... Huntsville AL 35893	800-234-1234	256-837-6110	219
RedTail Solutions Inc 69 Milk St Ste 100 .... Westborough MA 01581	866-764-7601	508-983-1900	225
Redwood Credit Union PO Box 6104 .... Santa Rosa CA 95406	800-479-7928	707-545-4000	217
Redwood Trust Inc 1 Belvedere Pl Ste 300 .... Mill Valley CA 94941 NYSE: RWT	866-269-4976	415-389-7373	507
Reeb Millwork Corp 7475 Henry Clay Blvd .... Liverpool NY 13088	800-862-8622	315-451-6699	497
Reebok International Ltd 1895 JW Foster Blvd .... Canton MA 02021	866-870-1743	781-401-5000	301
Reece Museum 363 Stout Dr .... Johnson City TN 37614	855-590-3878	423-439-4392	517
Reed 28 Sword St .... Auburn MA 01501	800-343-6068	508-753-6530	454
Reed Brennan Media Associates (RBMA) 628 Virginia Dr .... Orlando FL 32803	800-708-7311	407-894-7300	317
Reed College 3203 SE Woodstock Blvd .... Portland OR 97202 *Admissions	800-547-4750*	503-777-7511	166
Reed Group 10355 Westmoor Dr Ste 210 ...... Westminster CO 80021	800-347-7443		
Reed Manufacturing Co 1425 W Eigth St .... Erie PA 16502	800-456-1697	814-452-3691	753
Reed Mfg Co Inc 1321 S Veterans Blvd .... Tupelo MS 38804	800-466-1154	662-842-4472	155-10
Reeder Distributors Inc 5450 Wilbarger St .... Fort Worth TX 76119	800-722-3103	817-429-5957	575
Reedley College 995 N Reed Ave .... Reedley CA 93654	877-253-7122	559-638-3641	162
Reeds Family Outdoor Outfitters 522 Minnesota Ave NW .... Walker MN 56484	800-346-0019		707
Reeds Jewelers Inc PO Box 2229 .... Wilmington NC 28402 *Orders	877-406-3266*		409
Reedsville Co-op Assn Inc PO Box 460 .... Reedsville WI 54230	800-236-4047	920-754-4321	276
Reef Industries Inc 9209 Almeda Genoa Rd .... Houston TX 77075	800-231-6074	713-507-4200	595
Reef Resort 2101 S Ocean Blvd .... Myrtle Beach SC 29577 *Cust Svc	800-845-1212*	843-448-1765	665
Reese Enterprises Inc 16350 Asher Ave .... Rosemount MN 55068	800-328-0953	651-423-1126	234
Reese Pharmaceutical Co 10617 Frank Ave .... Cleveland OH 44106	800-321-7178		238
Reeve Store Equipment Co 9131 Bermudez St .... Pico Rivera CA 90660	800-927-3383	562-949-2535	286
Reeves Construction Co Inc 101 Sheraton Ct .... Macon GA 31210	800-743-0593	478-474-9092	188-4
Reeves-Wiedeman Co Inc 14861 W 100th St .... Lenexa KS 66215	800-365-0024	913-492-7100	608
Reference & User Services Assn (RUSA) 50 E Huron St .... Chicago IL 60611	800-545-2433	312-280-4398	49-11
Referentia Systems Inc 155 Kapalulu Pl Ste 200 .... Honolulu HI 96819	800-569-6255	808-840-8500	177
Reflexite Corp 120 Darling Dr .... Avon CT 06001	800-654-7570	860-676-7100	740-2
Reflexite North America 315 S St .... New Britain CT 06051	800-654-7570	860-223-9297	674
Reformed Church in America 4500 60th St SE .... Grand Rapids MI 49512	800-722-9977	616-698-7071	48-20
Reformed Theological Seminary 5422 Clinton Blvd .... Jackson MS 39209	800-543-2703	601-923-1600	167-3
Refrigerated Food Express Inc 57 Littlefield St .... Avon MA 02322	800-342-8822	508-587-4600	775
Refrigeration Sales Corp 9450 Allen Dr .... Valley View OH 44125	866-894-8200	216-525-8200	608
Refrigeration Service Engineers Society (RSES) 1666 Rand Rd .... Des Plaines IL 60016	800-297-5660	847-297-6464	49-3
RefrigiWear Inc 54 Breakstone Dr .... Dahlonega GA 30533 *Cust Svc	800-645-3744*	706-864-5757	155-5
Refugees International (RI) 2001 S St NW Ste 700 .... Washington DC 20009	800-733-8433	202-828-0110	48-5
RefWorks LLC 7200 Wisconsin Ave Ste 601 .... Bethesda MD 20814	800-843-7751	301-961-6700	386
Regal Beloit Canada 320 Superior Blvd .... Mississauga ON L5T2N7	800-563-0949	905-670-4770	111
Regal Entertainment Group 7132 Regal Ln .... Knoxville TN 37918 NASDAQ: RGC ■ *Cust Svc	877-835-5734*	865-922-1123	743
Regal Marine Industries Inc 2300 Jetport Dr .... Orlando FL 32809	800-877-3425	407-851-4360	90
Regal Plastic Supply Co 111 E Tenth Ave .... North Kansas City MO 64116	800-627-2102	816-421-6290	599
Regal Press 79 Astor Ave .... Norwood MA 02062	800-447-3425	781-769-3900	623
Regal Travel 615 Piikoi St Ste 104 .... Honolulu HI 96814	800-799-0865	808-566-7620	766
Regal Ware Inc 1675 Reigle Dr .... Kewaskum WI 53040	800-800-2850	262-626-2121	484
Regal-Beloit Corp 200 State St .... Beloit WI 53511 NYSE: RBC	800-672-6495	608-364-8800	616
Regal-Beloit Corp Durst Div PO Box 298 .... Beloit WI 53512	800-356-0775	608-365-2563	705
Regalia Manufacturing Co 2018 Fourth Ave .... Rock Island IL 61201	800-798-7471	309-788-7471	772
Regalix Inc 1121 San Antonio Rd Ste B200 .... Palo Alto CA 94303	888-683-4875	631-230-2629	195
Regence Blue Cross Blue Shield of Oregon PO Box 1071 .... Portland OR 97207	888-734-3623	888-675-6570	390-3
Regence BlueCross BlueShield of Utah 2890 E Cottonwood Pkwy ...... Salt Lake City UT 84121 *Cust Svc	800-624-6519*	888-367-2119	390-3
Regency Centers 1 Independent Dr Ste 114 .... Jacksonville FL 32202 NYSE: REG	800-950-6333	904-598-7000	651
Regency Fairbanks Hotel 95 Tenth Ave .... Fairbanks AK 99701	800-478-1320	907-459-2700	378
Regency Lighting Co 9261 Jordan Ave .... Chatsworth CA 91311	800-284-2024		246
Regency Limousine Inc 331 Danbury Rd .... Wilton CT 06897	800-243-5606	203-762-7780	440
Regency Seating Inc 2375 Romig Rd .... Akron OH 44320	866-816-9822	330-848-3700	321
Regency Suites Calgary 610 Fourth Ave SW .... Calgary AB T2P0K1	800-468-4044	403-231-1000	378
Regency Suites Hotel Midtown Atlanta 975 W Peachtree St .... Atlanta GA 30309	800-642-3629	404-876-5003	378
Regent College 5800 University Blvd .... Vancouver BC V6T2E4	800-663-8664	604-224-3245	167-3
Regent Group Inc 4501 Forbes Blvd Ste 100 .... Lanham MD 20706	888-354-6309	301-459-8020	527-6
Regent Products Corp 8999 Palmer St .... River Grove IL 60171	800-583-1002	708-583-1000	360
Regent University Library 1000 Regent University Dr .... Virginia Beach VA 23464	888-249-1822	757-352-4916	433-6
Regents Point 19191 Harvard Ave .... Irvine CA 92612 *General	800-347-3735*	949-988-0849	668
Regina Leader Post 1964 Park St PO Box 2020 .... Regina SK S4P3G4	800-667-9999	306-781-5211	528-1
Regional Acceptance Corp 1424 E Fire Tower Rd .... Greenville NC 27858	877-722-7299	252-321-7700	217
Regional Hospital of Scranton 746 Jefferson Ave .... Scranton PA 18510	800-654-5988	570-770-3000	373-3
Regional Medical Ctr of San Jose (RMCSJ) 225 N Jackson Ave .... San Jose CA 95116	800-307-7135	408-259-5000	373-3
Regional Medical Ctr, The 3000 St Matthews Rd .... Orangeburg SC 29118	800-476-3377	803-395-2200	373-3
Regional Transportation Authority 175 W Jackson Blvd Ste 1550 .... Chicago IL 60604	800-232-0502	312-913-3200	466
Regional Transportation Commission of Southern Nevada (RTC) 600 S Grand Central Pkwy Ste 350 .... Las Vegas NV 89106	800-228-3911	702-676-1500	466
Regional Transportation District (RTD) 1961 Stout St .... Denver CO 80202	800-366-7433	303-628-9000	466
Regions Bank 1900 Fifth Ave N .... Birmingham AL 35203	800-734-4667		70
Regions Financial Corp 1900 Fifth Ave N .... Birmingham AL 35203 NYSE: RF	866-688-0658		359-2
Regions Mortgage Inc 215 Forrest St .... Hattiesburg MS 39401	800-986-2462		507
Regis College 235 Wellesley St .... Weston MA 02493	866-438-7344	781-768-7000	166
Regis Corp 7201 Metro Blvd .... Minneapolis MN 55439 NYSE: RGS	888-888-7778	952-947-7777	77
Regis Corp MasterCuts Div 7201 Metro Blvd .... Minneapolis MN 55439	877-857-2070	952-947-7777	77
Regis Corp Pro-Cuts Div 7201 Metro Blvd .... Minneapolis MN 55439	877-857-2070		77
Regis Corp SmartStyle Div 7201 Metro Blvd .... Minneapolis MN 55439	800-737-3535		77
Regis Technologies Inc 8210 Austin Ave .... Morton Grove IL 60053	800-323-8144	847-967-6000	578
Regis University 3333 Regis Blvd .... Denver CO 80221 *Admissions Colorado Springs 7450 Campus Dr Ste 100 .. Colorado Springs CO 80920	800-388-2366* 800-568-8932	303-458-4100	166 166
Register Tapes Unlimited Inc 1445 Langham Creek .... Houston TX 77084	800-247-4793	281-206-2500	4
Registercom Inc 575 Eighth Ave 8th Fl .... New York NY 10018	888-734-4783		395
Register-Guard 3500 Chad Dr .... Eugene OR 97408	800-377-7428	541-485-1234	528-2

Name / Address	Toll-Free	Phone	Class
Register-Herald 801 N Kanawha St ... Beckley WV 25801	800-950-0250	304-255-4400	528-2
Register-Star 364 Warren St ... Hudson NY 12534	800-836-4069	518-828-1616	528-2
Regitar USA Inc 2575 Container Dr ... Montgomery AL 36109	877-734-4827	334-244-1885	350
Rego-fix Tool Corp 7752 Moller Rd ... Indianapolis IN 46268	800-999-7346	317-870-5959	357
Regupol America 11 Ritter Way ... Lebanon PA 17042	800-537-8737		291
Rehabilitation Hospital of Indiana 4141 Shore Dr ... Indianapolis IN 46254	866-510-2273	317-329-2000	373-6
Rehau Inc 1501 EdwaRds Ferry Rd NE ... Leesburg VA 20176	800-247-9445	703-777-5255	235
Rehmann Group 5800 Gratiot St Ste 201 ... Saginaw MI 48638	866-799-9580	989-799-9580	2
Rehoboth Beach Convention Ctr 229 Rehoboth Ave ... Rehoboth Beach DE 19971	888-743-3628	302-644-2288	206
Rehoboth Beach-Dewey Beach Chamber of Commerce 501 Rehoboth Ave ... Rehoboth Beach DE 19971	800-441-1329	302-227-2233	139
Rehrig Pacific Co 4010 E 26th St ... Los Angeles CA 90058	800-421-6244	323-262-5145	199
REI 1700 45th St E ... Sumner WA 98352	800-426-4840	253-863-5550	64
REI (Recreational Equipment Inc) 6750 S 228th St ... Kent WA 98032 *Orders	800-426-4840*	253-395-3780	707
REI Adventures PO Box 1938 ... Sumner WA 98390	800-622-2236		755
Reichhold Inc 2400 Ellis Rd ... Durham NC 27703	800-448-3482	919-990-7500	601-2
Reid Jones McRorie & Williams Inc (RJMW) 2200 Executive St PO Box 669248 ... Charlotte NC 28208	800-785-2604		389
Reidler Decal Corp 264 Industrial Pk Rd PO Box 8 ... Saint Clair PA 17970	800-628-7770		412
Reiff & Nestor Co 50 Reiff St ... Lykens PA 17048	800-521-3422	717-453-7113	491
Reigstad & Associates Inc 192 W Ninth St ... Saint Paul MN 55102	800-355-8414	651-292-1123	261
Reiko Wireless Inc 55 Mall Dr ... Commack NY 11725	888-797-3456	631-913-6700	731
Reilly Financial Advisors 7777 Alvarado Rd Ste 116 ... La Mesa CA 91942	800-682-3237		
Reily Foods Co 400 Poydras St 10th Fl ... New Orleans LA 70130	800-535-1961		296-7
Reimagine Office Furnishings 1212 N 39th St Ste 200 ... Tampa FL 33605	877-763-4400		321
Reimers Electra Steam Inc 4407 Martinsburg Pk ... Clear Brook VA 22624	800-872-7562	540-662-3811	356
Reindl Bindery Company Inc W194 N11381 McCormick Dr ... Germantown WI 53022	800-878-1121	262-293-1444	92
Reindl Printing Inc 1300 Johnson St ... Merrill WI 54452	800-236-9637	715-536-9537	623
Reinhardt College 7300 Reinhardt College Cir ... Waleska GA 30183	877-346-4273	770-720-5526	166
Reinhardt Corp 3919 State Hwy 23 ... West Oneonta NY 13861	800-421-2867	607-432-6633	316
Reinhart Partners Inc 1500 W Market St ... Mequon WI 53092	800-969-1159	262-241-2020	
Reinke Mfg Co Inc 5325 Reinke Rd ... Deshler NE 68340	866-365-7381	402-365-7251	273
Reinsurance Group of America Inc 16600 Swingley Ridge Rd ... Chesterfield MO 63017 NYSE: RGA	800-985-4326	636-736-7000	359-4
Reis Inc 530 Fifth Ave 5th Fl ... New York NY 10036 NASDAQ: REIS	800-366-7347		464
Rejoice Radio PO Box 18000 ... Pensacola FL 32523	800-726-1191	850-479-6570	641-78
Rejuvenation Inc 2550 NW Nicolai St ... Portland OR 97210	888-401-1900	503-238-1900	438
RelaDyne LLC 8280 Montgomery Rd Ste 101 ... Cincinnati OH 45236	888-830-3156	513-489-6000	
Relais International 1690 Woodward Dr Ste 215 ... Ottawa ON K2C3R8	888-294-5244	613-226-5571	178-12
Relate Corp 5141 Verdugo Way Ste C ... Camarillo CA 93012	800-428-3708		180
Relay Specialties Inc 17 Raritan Rd ... Oakland NJ 07436	800-526-5376		203
Relco Systems Inc 7310 Chestnut Ridge Rd ... Lockport NY 14094	800-262-1020	716-434-8100	775
Relevancy Group, The 505 Congress St Ste 602 ... Boston MA 02210	877-972-6886		464
Relevant Radio 1496 Bellevue St Ste 202 PO Box 10707 ... Green Bay WI 54311	877-291-0123		640
Reliability Center 501 Westover Ave ... Hopewell VA 23860	800-457-0645	804-458-0645	261
Reliable Carriers Inc 41555 Koppernick Rd ... Canton MI 48187	800-521-6393	734-453-6677	466
Reliable Factory Supply Co PO Box 340 ... Thomaston CT 06787	800-288-8464		360
Reliable Life Insurance Co 100 King St W PO Box 557 ... Hamilton ON L8N3K9	800-465-0661	905-523-5587	390-2
Reliable Racing Supply Inc 643 Glen St ... Queensbury NY 12804	800-223-4448	518-793-5677	707
Reliable Tire Co 805 N Blackhorse Pk ... Blackwood NJ 08012 *All	800-342-3426*		750
Reliable Wholesale Lumber Inc 7600 Redondo Cir ... Huntington Beach CA 92648	877-795-4638	714-848-8222	191-3
Reliance Connects 61 W Mesquite Blvd ... Mesquite NV 89027	866-894-4657	702-346-5211	386
Reliance Controls Corp 2001 Young Ct ... Racine WI 53404	800-634-6155	262-634-6155	725
Reliance Standard Life Insurance 2001 Market St Ste 1500 ... Philadelphia PA 19103	800-351-7500	267-256-3500	390-2
Reliant Energy Retail Services LLC 1201 Fannin St ... Houston TX 77002	866-660-4900	866-222-7100	782
Relias 111 Corning Rd Ste 250 ... Atlanta GA 30326 *Cust Svc	800-688-2421*	404-262-5476	633-9
Religious Conference Management Assn Inc (RCMA) 7702 Woodland Dr Ste 120 ... Indianapolis IN 46278	800-221-8235	317-632-1888	49-12
Relin, Goldstein & Crane LLP 28 E Main St Ste 1800 ... Rochester NY 14614	888-984-2351		427
Relios Inc 6815 Academy Pkwy W NE ... Albuquerque NM 87109	800-827-6543	505-345-5304	408
Reliv International Inc 136 Chesterfield Industrial Blvd ... Chesterfield MO 63005 NASDAQ: RELV	800-735-4887	636-537-9715	365
RELO Direct Inc 161 N Clark St Ste 1200 ... Chicago IL 60601	800-621-7356	312-384-5900	662
Relton Corp 317 Rolyn Pl ... Arcadia CA 91007 *Cust Svc	800-423-1505*	323-681-2551	753
Rely Services Inc 957 N Plum Grove Rd Ste B ... Schaumburg IL 60173	866-735-9328	847-310-8750	195
REMC (Okefenoke Rural Electric Membership Corp) 14384 Cleveland St PO Box 602 ... Nahunta GA 31553	800-262-5131	912-462-5131	245
REMC (Kosciusko Rural Electric Membership Corporation) 370 S 250 E ... Warsaw IN 46582	800-790-7362	574-267-6331	245
Remco Products Corp 4735 W 106th St ... Zionsville IN 46077	800-585-8619	317-876-9856	296
Remcon Plastics Inc 208 Chestnut St ... Reading PA 19602	800-360-3636		595
Remediation Services Inc 2735 S Tenth St PO Box 587 ... Independence KS 67301	800-335-1201		663
Reminger 101 W Prospect Ave Ste 1400 ... Cleveland OH 44115	800-486-1311	216-687-1311	427
Remington Arms Company Inc 870 Remington Dr PO Box 700 ... Madison NC 27025	800-243-9700	336-548-8700	284
Remington College Cleveland 14445 Broadway Ave ... Cleveland OH 44125	800-208-1950		
Remington College Honolulu 1111 Bishop St Ste 400 ... Honolulu HI 96813	800-208-1950	808-942-1000	
Remington Park Race Track 1 Remington Pl ... Oklahoma City OK 73111	866-456-9880	405-424-1000	638
Remo Inc 28101 Industry Dr ... Valencia CA 91355	800-525-5134	661-294-5600	523
Remote Access Technology Inc 61 Atlantic St ... Dartmouth NS B2Y4P4	877-356-2728	902-434-4405	364
Remote Operations Co 200 Pakerland Dr ... Green Bay WI 54303	888-837-4466	920-437-4466	180
Remstar International Inc 41 Eisenhower Dr ... Westbrook ME 04092	800-639-5805		384
Rena Ware International Inc 15885 NE 28th St ... Bellevue WA 98008	800-721-5156	425-881-6141	484
Renaissance Ctr Detroit River ... Detroit MI 48243	800-983-4240		
Renaissance Esmeralda Resort 44-400 Indian Wells Ln ... Indian Wells CA 92210	888-236-2427	760-773-4444	665
Renaissance Group 981 Worcester St ... Wellesley MA 02482	800-514-2667		389
Renaissance Orlando Resort at SeaWorld 6677 Sea Harbor Dr ... Orlando FL 32821	800-327-6677	407-351-5555	665
Renaissance Resort at World Golf Village 500 S Legacy Trl ... Saint Augustine FL 32092	888-740-7020	904-940-8000	665
Renaissance Vinoy Resort & Golf Club 501 Fifth Ave NE ... Saint Petersburg FL 33701	800-468-3571	727-894-1000	665
Renasant Corp 209 Troy St ■ ... Tupelo MS 38804 NASDAQ: RNST ■ *Cust Svc	800-680-1601*		359-2
Renbor Sales Solutions Inc 256 Thornway Ave ... Thornhill ON L4J7X8	855-257-2537	416-671-3555	392
Renco Corp 116 Third Ave N ... Minneapolis MN 55401	800-359-8181	612-338-6124	580
Renco Electronics Inc 595 International Pl ... Rockledge FL 32955	800-645-5828	321-637-1000	246
Rencor Controls Inc 21 Sullivan Pkwy ... Fort Edward NY 12828	866-472-7030	518-747-4171	357
Rend Lake College 468 N Ken Gray Pkwy ... Ina IL 62846	800-369-5321	618-437-5321	162
Rendigs, Fry, Kiely & Dennis LLP 600 Vine St Ste 2650 ... Cincinnati OH 45202	800-274-2330	513-381-9200	427
Rene Of Paris 9135 Independence Ave ... Chatsworth CA 91311 *Sales	800-353-7363*		347
Renee's Garden 6060 Graham Hill Rd ... Felton CA 95018	888-880-7228	831-335-7228	690
ReNew Life Formulas Inc 2076 Sunnydale Blvd ... Clearwater FL 33765	800-830-1800		297-11
Renew Plastics PO Box 480 ... Luxemburg WI 54217	800-666-5207	920-845-2326	657
Renfro Corp 661 Linville Rd PO Box 908 ... Mount Airy NC 27030	800-334-9091	336-719-8000	155-9
Reni Publishing Inc 150 Third St SW ... Winter Haven FL 33880	800-274-2812		623
Renkert Oil 3817 Main St PO Box 246 ... Morgantown PA 19543	800-423-6457	610-286-8012	575
Renkus-heinz Inc 19201 Cook St ... Foothill Ranch CA 92610	855-411-2364	949-588-9997	52
Rennco LLC 300 Elm St ... Homer MI 49245	800-409-5225		786
Rennoc Corp 645 Pine St ... Greenville OH 45331	800-372-7100		155-5
Reno Gazette-Journal PO Box 22000 ... Reno NV 89520	800-970-7366	775-788-6397	528-2
RENO Refractories Inc 601 Reno Dr ... Morris AL 35116	800-741-7366		659
RENO Refractories Inc Reftech Div 601 Reno Dr ... Morris AL 35116 *General	800-741-7366*		659
Renodis Inc 476 Robert St N ... Saint Paul MN 55101	866-200-8986	651-556-1200	447

				Toll-Free	Phone	Class

Renoir Staffing Services Inc
1301 Marina Vlg Pkwy Ste 350 .... Alameda CA 94501 — **866-672-3709** — — 260

Renold Ajax Inc
100 Bourne St .... Westfield NY 14787 — **800-251-9012** — 716-326-3121 — 616

Renold Jeffrey
2307 Maden St .... Morristown TN 37813 — **800-251-9012** — — 207

Reno-Sparks Convention Ctr
4590 S Virginia St .... Reno NV 89502 — **800-367-7366** — 775-827-7600 — 205

Renova Lighting Systems Inc
36 Bellair Ave .... Warwick RI 02886 — **800-635-6682** — 401-737-6700 — 438

Renovator's Supply Inc
Renovators Old ML .... Millers Falls MA 01349 — **800-659-2211** — 413-423-3300 — 349

RenoWorks Software Inc
2816 21 St NE .... Calgary AB T2E6Z2 — **877-980-3880** — 403-296-3880 — 177

Rensselaer Polytechnic Institute
110 Eighth St .... Troy NY 12180 — **800-433-4723** — 518-276-6000 — 166

Rent-A-Center Inc
5501 Headquarters Dr .... Plano TX 75024 — **800-422-8186** — — 264-2
NASDAQ: RCII

Rental Research Services Inc
7525 Mitchell Rd Ste 301 .... Eden Prairie MN 55344 — **800-328-0333** — 952-935-5700 — 631

Rentals Inc
3585 Engineering Dr .... Norcross GA 30092 — **888-501-7368** — — 386

Rent-A-PC Inc
265 Oser Ave .... Hauppauge NY 11788 — **800-888-8686** — 631-273-8888 — 264-1

RentPath LLC
950 East Paces Ferry Rd NE
Ste 2600 .... Atlanta GA 30326 — **800-216-1423** — 678-421-3000 — 633-9

Renville-Sibley Co-op Power Assn
103 Oak St PO Box 68 .... Danube MN 56230 — **800-826-2593** — 320-826-2593 — 245

RenWeb School Management Software
820 SW Wilshire Blvd .... Burleson TX 76028 — **866-800-6593** — — 619

Repaircliniccom Inc
48600 Michigan Ave .... Canton MI 48188 — **800-269-2609** — 734-495-3079 — 350

Repligen Corp
41 Seyon St .... Waltham MA 02453 — **800-622-2259*** — 781-250-0111 — 85
NASDAQ: RGEN ▥ *Sales

Reporting Systems Inc
2200 Rimland Dr Ste 305 .... Bellingham WA 98226 — **844-752-6066**

Repros Therapeutics Inc
2408 Timberloch Pl
Ste B-7 .... The Woodlands TX 77380 — **800-895-6554** — 281-719-3400 — 85
NASDAQ: RPRX

Republic Bancorp Inc
601 W Market St .... Louisville KY 40202 — **888-540-5363** — 502-584-3600 — 359-2
NASDAQ: RBCAA

Republic Finance
7031 Commerce Cir .... Baton Rouge LA 70809 — **800-317-7662** — 225-927-0005 — 217

Republic Financial Corp
5251 DTC Pkwy Ste 300 .... Greenwood Village CO 80111 — **800-596-3608** — 303-751-3501 — 216

Republic First Bancorp Inc
50 S 16th St Ste 2400 .... Philadelphia PA 19102 — **888-875-2265** — — 359-2
NASDAQ: FRBK

Republic Metals Corp
12900 NW 38th Ave .... Miami FL 33054 — **888-685-8505** — 305-685-8505 — 409

Republic Mortgage Insurance Co
101 N Cherry St Ste 101 .... Winston-Salem NC 27101 — **800-999-7642** — — 390-5

Republic Plumbing Supply Company Inc
890 Providence Hwy .... Norwood MA 02062 — **800-696-3900** — — 608

Republic Powdered Metals Inc
2628 Pearl Rd .... Medina OH 44256 — **800-382-1218** — — 546

Republic Storage Systems LLC
1038 Belden Ave NE .... Canton OH 44705 — **800-477-1255*** — 330-438-5800 — 286
*Sales

Republic Western Insurance Co
2721 N Central Ave .... Phoenix AZ 85004 — **800-528-7134*** — — 390-4
*Claims

Republic, The
2980 N National Rd Ste A .... Columbus IN 47201 — **800-876-7811** — 812-372-7811 — 528-2

Republican National Committee (RNC)
310 First St SE .... Washington DC 20003 — **800-445-5768** — 202-863-8500 — 612

Republican-American Inc
389 Meadow St .... Waterbury CT 06702 — **800-992-3232** — 203-574-3636 — 633-8

Reputation Rhino LLC
300 Park Ave 12th Fl .... New York NY 10022 — **888-975-3331** — — 386

ReQuest Inc
100 Saratoga Village Blvd
Ste 45 .... Ballston Spa NY 12020 — **800-236-2812*** — 518-899-1254 — 52
*Sales

RES Exhibit Services LLC
435 Smith St .... Rochester NY 14608 — **800-482-4049** — 585-546-2040 — 7

Rescar Inc
1101 31st St Ste 250 .... Downers Grove IL 60515 — **800-851-5196** — 630-963-1114 — 647

Resco Plastics Inc
93783 Newport Ln .... Coos Bay OR 97420 — **800-266-5097** — 541-269-5485 — 657

Resco Products Inc
2 Penn Ctr W Ste 430 .... Pittsburgh PA 15276 — **888-283-5505** — — 658

Rescuecom Corp
2560 Burnet Ave .... Syracuse NY 13206 — **800-737-2837** — — 310

Research & Diagnostic Antibodies
2645 W Cheyenne Ave .... North Las Vegas NV 89032 — **800-858-7322** — 702-638-7800 — 231

Research & Innovative Technology Administration (RITA)
1200 New Jersey Ave SE ..... Washington DC 20590 — **800-853-1351** — 202-366-7582 — 339-16
Bureau of Transportation Statistics
1200 New Jersey Ave SE ..... Washington DC 20590 — **855-368-4200** — — 339-16
Office of Research, Development & Technology Programs
1200 New Jersey Ave SE ..... Washington DC 20590 — **800-853-1351** — — 339-16

Research Assoc Inc
27999 Clemens Rd .... Cleveland OH 44145 — **800-255-9693** — 440-892-9439 — 399

Research Institute on Addictions (RIA)
1021 Main St .... Buffalo NY 14203 — **800-729-6686** — 716-887-2566 — 664

Research into Action Inc
3934 NE Mlking Jr Blvd Ste 300 .... Portland OR 97212 — **888-492-9100** — 503-287-9136 — 196

Research Products Corp
1015 E Washington Ave .... Madison WI 53703 — **800-334-6011** — 608-257-8801 — 17

Research Technology International Inc
4700 W Chase Ave .... Lincolnwood IL 60712 — **800-323-7520*** — 847-677-3000 — 587
*Sales

Research to Prevent Blindness Inc (RPB)
360 Lexington Ave 22nd Fl ...... New York NY 10017 — **800-621-0026** — 212-752-4333 — 48-17

Research Triangle Institute
3040 Cornwallis Rd
PO Box 12194 .... Research Triangle Park NC 27709 — **800-334-8571** — 919-541-6000 — 664

Reser's Fine Foods Inc
15570 SW Jenkins Rd .... Beaverton OR 97006 — **800-333-6431** — 503-643-6431 — 296-33

Reserve Casino Hotel
321 Gregory St .... Central City CO 80427 — **800-924-6646** — 303-582-0800 — 133

Reserve Officers Assn of the US (ROA)
1 Constitution Ave NE .... Washington DC 20002 — **800-809-9448** — 202-479-2200 — 48-19

Reserve Petroleum Co
6801 Broadway Ext Ste 300 ...... Oklahoma City OK 73116 — **800-690-6903** — 405-848-7551 — 532

Reserve Telephone Company Inc
3750 Nicole St .... Paulina LA 70763 — **888-611-6111** — 985-536-1111 — 731

ReserveAmerica Holdings Inc
2480 Meadowvale Blvd
Ste 120 .... Mississauga ON L5N8M6 — **877-444-6777** — — 768

Reshape Medical
100 Calle Iglesia .... San Clemente CA 92672 — **844-937-7374** — — 473

Residence & Conference Centre - Toronto
1760 Finch Ave E .... Toronto ON M2J5G3 — **877-225-8664** — 416-491-8811 — 378

Residential Mortgage LLC
100 Calais Dr .... Anchorage AK 99503 — **888-357-2707** — 907-222-8800 — 507

Resilite Sports Products
PO Box 764 .... Sunbury PA 17801 — **800-843-6287** — — 706

Resina West Inc
27455 Bostik Ct .... Temecula CA 92590 — **800-207-4804** — 951-296-6585 — 298

Resinall Corp
PO Box 195 .... Severn NC 27877 — **800-421-0561** — — 601-2

ResMed Inc
9001 Spectrum Ctr Blvd .... San Diego CA 92123 — **800-424-0737** — 858-836-5000 — 474
NYSE: RMD

Resolute Forest Products
111 Robert-Bourassa Blvd
Ste 5000 .... Montreal QC H3C2M1 — **800-361-2888** — 514-875-2160

Resolute Systems Inc
1550 N Prospect Ave .... Milwaukee WI 53202 — **800-776-6060** — 414-276-4774 — 41

RESOLVE Partners LLC
2733 Horse Pen Creek Rd
Ste 101 .... Greensboro NC 27410 — **866-921-5388** — 336-217-1005

Resort at Squaw Creek
400 Squaw Creek Rd
PO Box 3333 .... Olympic Valley CA 96146 — **800-327-3353** — 530-583-6300 — 665

Resort Condominiums International (RCI)
9998 N Michigan Rd .... Carmel IN 46032 — **800-338-7777** — 317-805-8000 — 748

Resort Data Processing Inc
211 Eagle Rd .... Avon CO 81620 — **877-779-3717** — 970-845-1140 — 177

Resort Semiahmoo
9565 Semiahmoo Pkwy .... Blaine WA 98230 — **855-917-3767** — 360-318-2000 — 665

Resorts Casino Hotel
1133 Boardwalk .... Atlantic City NJ 08401 — **800-334-6378** — — 665

Resource & Financial Management Systems Inc
3073 Palisades Ct .... Tuscaloosa AL 35405 — **800-701-7367** — — 177

Resource Connection Inc
161 S Main St .... Middleton MA 01949 — **800-649-5228** — 978-777-9333 — 184

Resource Development Corp
280 Daines St Ste 200 .... Birmingham MI 48009 — **800-360-7222** — 248-646-2300 — 39

Resource Management Inc
281 Main St Ste 5 .... Fitchburg MA 01420 — **800-508-0048*** — — 627
*Cust Svc

Resource Management Service LLC
31 Inverness Ctr Pkwy
Ste 360 .... Birmingham AL 35242 — **800-995-9516** — — 302

Respironics Novametrix LLC
5 Technology Dr .... Wallingford CT 06492 — **800-345-6443** — 724-387-4000 — 250

Response Envelope Inc
1340 S Baker Ave .... Ontario CA 91761 — **800-750-0046** — 909-923-5855 — 263

Restaurant & Stores Equipment Co
230 West 700 South .... Salt Lake City UT 84101 — **800-877-0087** — 801-364-1981 — 300

Restaurant Technologies Inc
2250 Pilot Knob Rd
Ste 100 .... Mendota Heights MN 55120 — **888-796-4997** — 651-796-1600 — 300

Restaurants Unlimited Inc
411 First Ave S Ste 200 .... Seattle WA 98104 — **877-855-6106** — 206-634-0550 — 666

Reston Hospital Ctr
1850 Town Ctr Pkwy .... Reston VA 20190 — **888-327-8882*** — 703-689-9000 — 373-3
*General

Restonic Mattress Corp
737 Main St .... Buffalo NY 14203 — **800-898-6075** — — 469

Restoration Hardware Inc
2900 N MacArthur Dr Ste 100 .... Tracy CA 95376 — **800-910-9836** — — 361

RESUMate Inc
2500 Packard St Ste 200 .... Ann Arbor MI 48104 — **800-530-9310*** — 734-477-9402 — 178-10
*Cust Svc

Resume Solutions
1033 Bay St Ste 317 .... Toronto ON M5S3A5 — **866-361-1290** — 416-361-1290 — 41

Retail Computer Group LLC, The
8194 Traphagen St NW .... Massillon OH 44646 — **800-944-0917** — — 521

Retail Confectioners International (RCI)
3029 E Sunshine St Ste A .... Springfield MO 65804 — **800-545-5381** — 417-883-2775 — 49-6

Retail Pro International LLC
400 Plaza Dr Ste 200 .... Folsom CA 95630 — **800-738-2457** — 916-605-7200 — 178-10
OTC: RTPRQ

Retail Solutions Providers Assn (RSPA)
9920 Couloak Dr Unit 120 .... Charlotte NC 28216 — **800-782-2693** — — 49-18

Retif Oil & Fuel Inc
527 Destrehan Ave .... Harvey LA 70058 — **800-349-9000** — — 575

Retirement Advantage Inc, The
47 Park Pl Ste 850 .... Appleton WI 54914 — **888-872-2364** — — 461

Retractable Technologies Inc
511 Lobo Ln .... Little Elm TX 75068 — **888-806-2626** — 972-294-1010 — 475
NYSE: RVP

Rettew Assoc Inc
3020 Columbia Ave .... Lancaster PA 17603 — **800-738-8395** — 717-394-3721 — 261

Reuland Electric Co
17969 E Railroad St .... Industry CA 91748 — **888-964-6411**

REV GROUP Inc
52216 State Rd 15 .... Bristol IN 46507 — **888-522-1126** — 574-848-1126 — 120

				Toll-Free	Phone	Class
Revcor Inc 251 E Edwards Ave	Carpentersville	IL	60110	**800-323-8261**		18
Revelation Software 99 Kinderkamack Rd	Westwood	NJ	07675	**800-262-4747**	201-594-1422	178-2
Revels Tractor Company Inc 2217 N Main St	Fuquay Varina	NC	27526	**800-849-5469**	919-552-5697	274
Revent Inc 100 Ethel Rd W	Piscataway	NJ	08854	**800-822-9642**	732-777-9433	296
Revention Inc 1315 W Sam Houston Pkwy North Ste 100	Houston	TX	77043	**877-738-7444**		196
RevenueAds Affiliate Network 322 NE Second St 2nd Fl	Oklahoma City	OK	73104	**800-441-1136**	405-455-9053	
Reverb Music LLC 3316 N Lincoln Ave	Chicago	IL	60657	**888-686-7872**	773-525-7773	522
Revere Control Systems Inc 2240 Rocky Ridge Rd	Birmingham	AL	35216	**800-536-2525**	205-824-0004	725
Revere Copper Products Inc 1 Revere Pk	Rome	NY	13440	**800-448-1776**		483
Revere Hotel Boston Common 200 Stuart St	Boston	MA	02116	**855-673-8373**	617-482-1800	703
Reverse Logistics Trends Inc 2300 Lakeview Pkwy Ste 700	Alpharetta	GA	30009	**866-801-6332**	801-331-8949	
Revestor 505 Montgomery St 11th Fl	San Francisco	CA	94111	**800-569-2674**		
Review & Herald Publishing Assn 55 W Oak Ridge Dr	Hagerstown	MD	21740	**800-456-3991**	301-393-3000	633-9
Reviva Inc 5130 Main St NE	Fridley	MN	55421	**877-357-7634**	763-535-8900	
Revlon Consumer Products Corp 1501 Williamsboro St	Oxford	NC	27565	**800-473-8566**	212-527-4000	214
Revlon Foundation Inc 237 Park Ave *Cust Svc	New York	NY	10017	**800-473-8566***		304
Revlon Inc 237 Park Ave *NYSE: REV*	New York	NY	10017	**800-473-8566**	212-527-4000	359-3
Revman International Inc 350 Fifth Ave 70th Fl	New York	NY	10118	**800-237-0658**		
Revo America Inc 850 Freeport Pkwy Ste 100	Coppell	TX	75019	**866-625-7386**		
Revolution Eyewear Inc 2853 Eisenhower St Ste 100	Carrollton	TX	75007	**800-986-0010**		237
REVShare Corp 32836 Wolf Store Rd	Temecula	CA	92592	**800-819-9945**		195
Rewards Network 2 N Riverside Plz Ste 200	Chicago	IL	60606	**866-844-3753**	866-559-3463	215
Rex Art Co 3160 SW 22 St	Miami	FL	33145	**800-739-2782**	305-445-1413	45
Rex Black Consulting Services Inc 31520 Beck Rd	Bulverde	TX	78163	**866-438-4830**	830-438-4830	180
Rex Healthcare 4420 Lake Boone Trl	Raleigh	NC	27607	**800-624-3004**	919-784-3100	373-3
Rex Heat Treat 951 W Eigth St PO Box 270	Lansdale	PA	19446	**800-220-4739**	215-855-1131	482
Rex Lumber Co 840 Main St	Acton	MA	01720	**800-343-0567**	978-263-0055	814
Rex Moore Electrical Contractors & Engineers 6001 Outfall Cir	Sacramento	CA	95828	**800-266-1922**	916-372-1300	189-4
Rex Supply Co 3715 Harrisburg Blvd	Houston	TX	77003	**800-369-0669**		384
Rexarc Inc 35 E Third St	West Alexandria	OH	45381	**877-739-2721**	937-839-4604	785
Rexel Inc 14951 Dallas Pkwy PO Box 9085	Dallas	TX	75254	**888-739-3577**	972-387-3600	246
Reyers 40 S Water Ave *Cust Svc	Sharon	PA	16146	**800-245-1550***	724-981-2200	301
Reynolda House Museum of American Art 2250 Reynolda Rd	Winston-Salem	NC	27106	**888-663-1149**	336-758-5150	517
Reynolds & Reynolds Co 1 Reynolds Way	Dayton	OH	45430	**800-767-0080**	937-485-2000	178-10
Reynolds Plantation 100 Linger Longer Rd	Greensboro	GA	30642	**800-800-5250**	706-467-0600	665
Reynolds Smith & Hills Inc 10748 Deerwood Pk Blvd	Jacksonville	FL	32256	**800-741-2014**	904-256-2500	261
Reynolds, Mirth, Richards & Farmer LLP Manulife Pl 10180-101 St Ste 3200	Edmonton	AB	T5J3W8	**800-661-7673**	780-425-9510	427
Reynolds-Alberta Museum 6426 40 Ave PO Box 6360	Wetaskiwin	AB	T9A2G1	**800-661-4726**	780-312-2065	517
RF Cook Manufacturing Co 4585 Allen Rd	Stow	OH	44224	**800-430-7536**	330-923-9797	453
RF Industries 7610 Miramar Rd *NASDAQ: RFIL*	San Diego	CA	92126	**800-233-1728**	858-549-6340	253
RF Ougheltree & Associates LLC 300 Executive Dr Ste 350	West Orange	NJ	07052	**800-388-0215**		
RFB&D (Recording for the Blind & Dyslexic) 20 Roszel Rd	Princeton	NJ	08540	**800-221-4792**		48-17
RG Shakour Inc 254 Tpke Rd	Westborough	MA	01581	**800-661-2030**		238
Rgh Enterprises Inc 1810 Summit Commerce Pk	Twinsburg	OH	44087	**800-307-5930**	330-963-6998	473
RGHS (Rochester Regional Health) 1425 Portland Ave	Rochester	NY	14621	**877-922-5465**	585-922-4000	373-3
RGIS LLC 2000 E Taylor Rd	Auburn Hills	MI	48326	**800-551-9130**	248-651-2511	317
RGS (Ruffed Grouse Society) 451 McCormick Rd	Coraopolis	PA	15108	**888-564-6747**	412-262-4044	48-3
RH White Construction Company Inc 41 Central St PO Box 404	Auburn	MA	01501	**800-876-3837**	508-832-3295	188-10
RHA Health Services Inc 17 Church St	Asheville	NC	28801	**866-742-2428**	828-232-6844	461
Rheem Mfg Company Air Conditioning Div 5600 Old Greenwood Rd	Fort Smith	AR	72903	**800-268-6966**	479-646-4311	14
RheTech Inc 1500 E N Territorial Rd	Whitmore Lake	MI	48189	**800-869-1230**	734-769-0585	601-2
Rhino Medical Staffing 2000 E Lamar Blvd Ste 250	Arlington	TX	76006	**866-267-4466**	817-795-2295	505
Rhode Island *Child Support Services* 77 Dorrance St	Providence	RI	02903	**800-745-5555**	401-458-4400	338-40
Children Youth & Families Dept 101 Friendship St	Providence	RI	02903	**800-742-4453**	401-528-3502	338-40
Housing & Mortgage Finance Corp 44 Washington St	Providence	RI	02903	**800-427-5560**	401-457-1234	338-40
Tourism Div 315 Iron Horse Way Ste 101	Providence	RI	02908	**800-556-2484**	401-278-9100	338-40
Rhode Island Airport Corp 2000 Post Rd Warwick	Warwick	RI	02886	**888-268-7222**	401-691-2000	27
Rhode Island Bar Assn 115 Cedar St	Providence	RI	02903	**877-659-0801**	401-421-5740	72
Rhode Island Blood Ctr 405 Promenade St	Providence	RI	02908	**800-283-8385**	401-453-8360	89
Rhode Island College 600 Mt Pleasant Ave	Providence	RI	02908	**800-669-5760**	401-456-8000	166
Rhode Island Public Interest Research Group (RIPIRG) 11 S Angell St Ste 150	Providence	RI	02906	**800-838-6554**	401-608-1201	
Rhode Island School of Design 2 College St	Providence	RI	02903	**800-364-7473**	401-454-6100	164
Rhode Island State Employees Credit Union 160 Francis St	Providence	RI	02903	**855-322-7428**	401-751-7440	219
Rhodes College 2000 N Pkwy	Memphis	TN	38112	**800-844-5969**	901-843-3700	166
Rhodes College Barret Library 2000 N Pkwy	Memphis	TN	38112	**800-844-5969**	901-843-3000	433-6
Rhodes International Inc PO Box 25487 *Cust Svc	Salt Lake City	UT	84125	**800-876-7333***	801-972-0122	296-16
Rhododendron Species Botanical Garden 2525 S 336th St PO Box 3798	Federal Way	WA	98063	**877-242-2528**	253-838-4646	97
Rhona Hoffman Gallery 1338 W Lake St	Chicago	IL	60607	**800-525-5562**	312-280-1212	42
Rhythm City Casino 7077 Elmore Ave	Davenport	IA	52807	**844-852-4386**	563-328-8000	133
Rhythm Tech 29 Beechwood Ave	New Rochelle	NY	10801	**800-726-2279**	914-636-6900	523
RI (Refugees International) 2001 S St NW Ste 700	Washington	DC	20009	**800-733-8433**	202-828-0110	48-5
RIA (Research Institute on Addictions) 1021 Main St	Buffalo	NY	14203	**800-729-6686**	716-887-2566	664
Ria Compliance Consultants Inc 11640 Arbor St Ste 100	Omaha	NE	68144	**877-345-4034**		196
Rialto Chamber of Commerce 120 N Riverside Ave	Rialto	CA	92376	**800-597-4955**	909-875-5364	139
Ribbon Technology Corp 825 Taylor Stn Rd	Gahanna	OH	43230	**800-848-0477**	614-864-5444	808
Ribelin Sales Inc 3857 Miller Pk Dr	Garland	TX	75042	**800-374-1594**	972-272-1594	146
Rice Fruit Co 2760 Carlisle Rd	Gardners	PA	17324	**800-627-3359**	717-677-8131	315-3
Rice Lake Weighing Systems Inc 230 W Coleman St	Rice Lake	WI	54868	**800-472-6703**		635
Rice Memorial Hospital 301 Becker Ave SW	Willmar	MN	56201	**800-543-7709**	320-235-4543	373-3
Rice Packaging Inc 356 Somers Rd	Ellington	CT	06029	**800-367-6725**	860-872-8341	101
Rice University 6100 Main St	Houston	TX	77005	**866-294-4633**	713-348-0000	166
RiceTec Inc 1925 FM 2917 PO Box 1305	Alvin	TX	77511	**877-580-7423**	281-393-3532	296-23
Rich Mountain Electric Co-op Inc 515 Janssen PO Box 897	Mena	AR	71953	**877-828-4074**	479-394-4140	245
Rich Ranch 939 Cottonwood Lakes Rd	Seeley Lake	MT	59868	**800-532-4350**	406-677-2317	239
Richard Carlton Consulting Inc 1941 Rollingwood Dr	Fairfield	CA	94534	**800-325-2747**	707-422-4053	196
Richard H Hutchings Psychiatric Ctr 620 Madison St	Syracuse	NY	13210	**800-597-8481**	315-426-3600	373-5
Richard L Roudebush VA Medical Ctr 1481 W Tenth St	Indianapolis	IN	46202	**888-878-6889**	317-554-0000	373-8
Richard Rodgers Theatre 226 W 46th St	New York	NY	10036	**866-755-3075**	212-221-1211	742
Richard Wolf Medical Instruments Corp 353 Corporate Woods Pkwy	Vernon Hills	IL	60061	**800-323-9653**		250
Richards Graphic Communications Inc 2700 Van Buren St	Bellwood	IL	60104	**866-827-3686**	708-547-6000	776
Richards Industries Inc 3170 Wasson Rd *Cust Svc	Cincinnati	OH	45209	**800-543-7311***	513-533-5600	591
Richards Maple Products Inc 545 Water St	Chardon	OH	44024	**800-352-4052**		296-39
Richardson Convention & Visitors Bureau 411 W Arapaho Rd Ste 105	Richardson	TX	75080	**888-690-7287**	972-744-4034	206
Richardson Electronics Ltd 40 W 267 Keslinger Rd PO Box 393 *NASDAQ: RELL* ■ *Sales	LaFox	IL	60147	**800-348-5580***	630-208-2200	246
Richardson Public Library 900 Civic Ctr Dr	Richardson	TX	75080	**800-735-2989**	972-744-4350	433-3
Richards-Wilcox Inc 600 S Lake St	Aurora	IL	60506	**800-253-5668**		207
Richland Community College 1 College Pk	Decatur	IL	62521	**800-899-4722**	217-875-7200	162
Richland Correctional Institution 1001 Olivesburg Rd	Mansfield	OH	44905	**800-686-4208**	419-526-2100	213
Richland Hospital Inc, The 333 E Second St	Richland Center	WI	53581	**888-467-7485**	608-647-6321	373-3
Richline Group Inc 6701 Nob Hill Rd	Tamarac	FL	33321	**800-327-1808**	954-718-3200	
Richmond American Homes Inc 4350 S Monaco St	Denver	CO	80237	**888-402-4663**	303-773-1100	649
RICHMOND CITY HALL 450 Civic Ctr Plz	Richmond	CA	94804	**800-833-2900**	510-620-6555	433-3
Richmond Community College PO Box 1189	Hamlet	NC	28345	**800-908-9946**	910-410-1700	162

	City	State	Zip	Toll-Free	Phone	Class
Richmond Gear						
PO Box 238	Liberty	SC	29657	**800-934-2727***	864-843-9231	705
*Sales						
Richmond International Forest Products Inc						
4050 Innslake Dr Ste 100	Glen Allen	VA	23060	**800-767-0111**	804-747-0111	191-3
Richmond Metropolitan Convention & Visitors Bureau						
401 N Third St	Richmond	VA	23219	**800-370-9004**	804-782-2777	206
Richmond National Battlefield Park						
3215 E Broad St	Richmond	VA	23223	**866-733-7768**	804-226-1981	517
Richmond Times-Dispatch						
PO Box 85333	Richmond	VA	23293	**800-468-3382**	804-649-6000	633-8
Richmond University Medical Ctr						
355 Bard Ave	Staten Island	NY	10310	**800-422-8798**	718-818-1234	373-3
Richmond/Wayne County Convention & Tourism Bureau						
5701 National Rd E	Richmond	IN	47374	**800-828-8414**	765-935-8687	206
Richmor Aviation Inc						
1142 Rte 9H PO Box 423	Hudson	NY	12534	**800-331-6101**	518-828-9461	63
Rick Johnson & Associates of Colorado						
1649 Downing St	Denver	CO	80218	**800-530-2300**	303-296-2200	399
Rickard Circular Folding Co						
325 N Ashland Ave	Chicago	IL	60607	**800-747-1389**	312-243-6300	92
Ricks Barbecue						
2347 US-43	Leoma	TN	38468	**800-544-5864**	931-852-2324	186
Ricochet Fuel Distributors Inc						
1201 Royal Pkwy	Euless	TX	76040	**800-284-2540**		316
Ricon Corp						
7900 Nelson Rd	Panorama City	CA	91402	**800-322-2884**	818-267-3000	256
Riddle Memorial Hospital						
1068 W Baltimore Pk	Media	PA	19063	**866-225-5654**	484-227-9400	373-3
Rideau Inc						
473 Deslauriers	Montreal	QC	H4N1W2	**800-363-6464**		461
Rideout Memorial Hospital						
726 Fourth St	Marysville	CA	95901	**888-923-3800**	530-749-4300	373-3
Rider University						
2083 Lawrenceville Rd	Lawrenceville	NJ	08648	**800-257-9026**	609-896-5000	166
Westminster Choir College						
101 Walnut Ln	Princeton	NJ	08540	**800-962-4647**	609-921-7100	166
Ridewell Corp						
PO Box 4586	Springfield	MO	65808	**877-434-8088**	417-833-4565	60
Ridge Behavioral Health System						
3050 Rio Dosa Dr	Lexington	KY	40509	**800-753-4673**	859-269-2325	373-5
Ridge Tahoe						
400 Ridge Club Dr PO Box 5790	Stateline	NV	89449	**800-334-1600**	775-588-3553	665
Ridgecrest Area Convention & Visitors Bureau (RACVB)						
643 N China Lake Blvd Ste C	Ridgecrest	CA	93555	**800-847-4830**	760-375-8202	206
Ridgeview Institute Inc						
3995 S Cobb Dr	Smyrna	GA	30080	**844-350-8800**		
Ridgeview Medical Ctr (RMC)						
500 S Maple St	Waconia	MN	55387	**800-967-4620**	952-442-2191	373-3
Ridgewater College						
Hutchinson						
2 Century Ave SE	Hutchinson	MN	55350	**800-722-1151**	320-234-8500	795
Willmar						
2101 15th Ave NW PO Box 1097	Willmar	MN	56201	**800-722-1151**	320-222-5200	795
Ridgewood Savings Bank						
71-02 Forest Ave	Ridgewood	NY	11385	**800-250-4832**	718-240-4800	70
Ridg-U-Rak Inc						
120 S Lake St	North East	PA	16428	**866-479-7225**	814-725-8751	286
Riechmann Transport Inc						
3328 W Chain of Rocks Rd	Granite City	IL	62040	**800-844-4225**	618-797-6700	775
Riedell Shoes Inc						
122 Cannon River Ave	Red Wing	MN	55066	**800-698-6893**	651-388-8251	706
Rieders, Travis, Humphrey, Waters & Dohrmann						
161 W Third St	Williamsport	PA	17701	**800-326-9259**	570-323-8711	427
Riegel Consumer Products						
51 Riegel Rd	Johnston	SC	29832	**800-845-3251**	803-275-2541	741
Riekes Equipment Co						
6703 L St	Omaha	NE	68117	**800-856-0931**	402-593-1181	384
Riel House National Historic Site of Canada						
330 River Rd	Winnipeg	MB	R2M3Z8	**888-773-8888**	519-826-5391	559
Riester						
3344 E Camelback Rd	Phoenix	AZ	85018	**844-602-3344**		7
RIF (Reading Is Fundamental Inc)						
1825 Connecticut Ave NW						
Ste 400	Washington	DC	20009	**877-743-7323**	202-536-3400	48-11
Rife Resources Ltd						
400 144 - Fourth Ave SW	Calgary	AB	T2P3N4	**888-257-1873**	403-221-0800	532
Rig-Chem Inc						
132 Thompson Rd	Houma	LA	70363	**800-375-7208**	985-873-7208	535
Rigel Pharmaceuticals Inc						
1180 Veterans Blvd	South San Francisco	CA	94080	**800-414-3627**	650-624-1100	85
NASDAQ: RIGL						
Riggins Inc						
3938 S Main Rd	Vineland	NJ	08360	**800-642-9148**	856-825-7600	316
Right at Home Inc						
6464 Center St Ste 150	Omaha	NE	68106	**877-697-7537**	402-697-7537	310
Right Systems Inc						
2600 Willamette Dr NE Ste C	Lacey	WA	98516	**800-571-1717**	360-956-0414	225
Righteous Babe						
341 Delaware Ave	Buffalo	NY	14202	**800-664-3769**	716-852-8020	653
Rightway Gate Inc						
5858 Edison Pl	Carlsbad	CA	92008	**888-398-4703**	760-736-3700	224
Rigid Hitch Inc						
3301 W Burnsville Pkwy	Burnsville	MN	55337	**800-624-7630***		758
*Cust Svc						
Rigidized Metals Corp						
658 Ohio St	Buffalo	NY	14203	**800-836-2580**	716-849-4760	490
RigNet Inc						
15115 Park Row Ste 300	Houston	TX	77084	**800-638-8844**	281-674-0100	224
Ri-go Lift Truck Ltd						
175 Courtland Ave	Concord	ON	L4K4T2	**855-211-9673**	647-846-8475	357
Rihm Kenworth (RK)						
425 Concord St S	South St.Paul	MN	55075	**800-988-8235**	651-646-7833	
Riiser Energy						
709 S 20th Ave	Wausau	WI	54401	**800-570-8024**	715-845-7272	324
RIM Logistics Ltd						
200 N Gary Ave	Roselle	IL	60172	**888-275-0937**	630-595-0610	447
Rimex Supply Ltd						
9726 186th St	Surrey	BC	V4N3N7	**800-663-9883**	604-888-0025	111
Rimkus Consulting Group Inc						
8 Greenway Plz Ste 500	Houston	TX	77046	**800-580-3228**		196
Rimrock Foundation						
1231 N 29th St	Billings	MT	59101	**800-227-3953**	406-248-3175	722
Rimrock Resort Hotel, The						
300 Mountain Ave PO Box 1110	Banff	AB	T1L1J2	**888-746-7625**	403-762-3356	665
Ringdale Inc						
101 Halmar Cove	Georgetown	TX	78628	**888-288-9080**	512-288-9080	176
Ringling College of Art & Design						
2700 N Tamiami Trl	Sarasota	FL	34234	**800-255-7695**	941-351-5100	164
Ringside SteakHouse						
2165 W Burnside St	Portland	OR	97210	**800-688-4142**	503-223-1513	667
Ringwood State Park						
1304 Sloatsburg Rd	Ringwood	NJ	07456	**800-852-7899**	973-962-7031	561
Rink Systems Inc						
1103 Hershey St	Albert Lea	MN	56007	**800-944-7930**	507-373-9175	14
Rinker Materials Corp Concrete Pipe Div						
8311 W Carder Ct	Littleton	CO	80125	**800-909-7763**	303-791-1600	183
Rio Grande Co						
201 Santa Fe Dr	Denver	CO	80223	**800-935-8420**	303-825-2211	191-1
Rio Grande Electric Cooperative Inc						
778 E US Hwy 90						
PO Box 1509	Brackettville	TX	78832	**800-749-1509**	830-563-2444	245
Rio Grande Wild & Scenic River						
PO Box 129	Big Bend National Park	TX	79834	**800-839-7238**	432-477-2251	560
Rio Salado College						
2323 W 14th St	Tempe	AZ	85281	**855-622-2332**	480-517-8000	162
RioCan Real Estate Investment Trust						
2300 Yonge St Ste 500						
PO Box 2386	Toronto	ON	M4P1E4	**800-465-2733**	416-866-3033	650
TSE: REI.UN.CA						
Riotel Group						
250 Ave du Phare Est	Matane	QC	G4W3N4	**877-566-2651**	418-566-2651	703
Rip city radio 620						
13333 SW 68th Pkwy Ste 310	Tigard	OR	97223	**844-289-7234**	503-323-6400	641-109
Rip Griffin Truck Travel Ctr Inc						
4710 Fourth St	Lubbock	TX	79416	**800-333-9330**	806-795-8785	324
Ripcho Studio						
7630 Lorain Ave	Cleveland	OH	44102	**800-686-7427**	216-631-0664	586
RIPIRG (Rhode Island Public Interest Research Group)						
11 S Angell St Ste 150	Providence	RI	02906	**800-838-6554**	401-608-1201	
Ripley Co						
46 Nooks Hill Rd	Cromwell	CT	06416	**800-528-8665**	860-635-2200	753
Ripley's Believe It or Not! Museum						
901 N Ocean Blvd	Myrtle Beach	SC	29577	**800-905-4228**	843-448-2331	517
Ripley's Believe It or Not! Museum						
19 San Marco Ave	Saint Augustine	FL	32084	**800-226-6545**	904-824-1606	517
Ripon College						
300 Seward St PO Box 248	Ripon	WI	54971	**800-947-4766***		166
*Admissions						
RIS Media Inc						
69 E Ave	Norwalk	CT	06851	**800-724-6000**	203-855-1234	648
RISC Networks Inc						
81 Broadway St Ste C	Asheville	NC	28801	**866-808-1227**		196
Risdall Adv Agency						
2685 Long Lake Rd Ste 100	Roseville	MN	55113	**888-747-3255**	651-286-6700	4
Rise Broadband						
61 Inverness Dr E Ste 250	Englewood	CO	80112	**844-411-7473**		
Rishi Tea LLC						
185 S 33rd Ct	Milwaukee	WI	53208	**866-747-4483**	414-747-4001	297-8
Rising Results Inc						
201 Edward Curry Ave						
Ste 202	Staten Island	NY	10314	**800-837-4648**	718-370-8300	400
Rising Star Casino Resort						
777 Rising Star Dr	Rising Sun	IN	47040	**800-472-6311**	812-438-1234	133
Risk Management Assn (RMA)						
1801 Market St Ste 300	Philadelphia	PA	19103	**800-677-7621***	215-446-4000	49-2
*Cust Svc						
RiskWatch (RWI)						
1237 N Gulfstream Ave	Sarasota	FL	34236	**800-360-1898**		178-10
RISO Inc						
800 District Ave Ste 390	Burlington	MA	01803	**800-942-7476***	978-777-7377	173-6
*General						
RITA (Research & Innovative Technology Administration)						
1200 New Jersey Ave SE	Washington	DC	20590	**800-853-1351**	202-366-7582	339-16
Ritchie Engineering Company Inc						
10950 Hampshire Ave S	Bloomington	MN	55438	**800-769-8370**	952-943-1300	
Rite Aid Corp						
30 Hunter Ln	Camp Hill	PA	17011	**800-748-3243**	717-761-2633	237
NYSE: RAD						
Rite-Hite Corp						
8900 N Arbon Dr	Milwaukee	WI	53224	**800-456-0600**	414-355-2600	674
Ritrama						
800 Kasota Ave SE	Minneapolis	MN	55414	**800-328-5071**		3
RITTAL North America LLC						
Woodfield Corporate Ctr 425 N Martingale Rd						
Ste 400	Schaumburg	IL	60173	**800-477-4000**	847-240-4600	811
Rittenhouse Book Distributors Inc						
511 Feheley Dr	King of Prussia	PA	19406	**800-345-6425***	610-277-1414	96
*Cust Svc						
Rittenhouse Hotel						
210 W Rittenhouse Sq	Philadelphia	PA	19103	**800-635-1042**	215-546-9000	378
Ritz Camera & Image						
2 Bergen Tpke	Ridgefield Park	NJ	07660	**855-622-7489***		119
*Cust Svc						
Ritz-Carlton Dallas						
2121 McKinney Ave	Dallas	TX	75201	**800-960-7082***	214-922-0200	378
*Resv						
Ritz-Carlton Half Moon Bay						
1 Miramontes Pt Rd	Half Moon Bay	CA	94019	**800-241-3333***	650-712-7000	665
*General						
Ritz-Carlton Hotel Co LLC, The						
4445 Willard Ave Ste 800	Chevy Chase	MD	20815	**800-241-3333**	301-547-4700	665
Ritz-Carlton Hotel Co LLC, The						
10400 Fernwood Rd	Bethesda	MD	20817	**800-542-8680**	301-380-3000	703
Ritz-Carlton Hotel Company LLC, The						
8301 Hollister Ave	Santa Barbara	CA	93117	**800-952-2027**	805-968-0100	665

Name / Address	City	State	Zip	Toll-Free	Phone	Class
Ritz-Carlton Kapalua 1 Ritz-Carlton Dr Kapalua *Resv	Maui	HI	96761	**800-262-8440***	808-669-6200	665
Ritz-Carlton Laguna Niguel, The 1 Ritz Carlton Dr	Dana Point	CA	92629	**800-542-8680**	949-240-2000	665
Ritz-Carlton Lodge Reynolds Plantation 1 Lake Oc1e Trl	Greensboro	GA	30642	**877-231-7916**	706-467-0600	665
Ritz-Carlton Naples Golf Resort 2600 Tiburon Dr *Resv	Naples	FL	34109	**877-231-7916***	239-593-2000	665
Ritz-Carlton Orlando Grande Lakes 4012 Central Florida Pkwy	Orlando	FL	32837	**866-922-6882**	407-206-2400	665
Ritz-Craft Corp of Pennsylvania Inc 15 Industrial Pk Rd	Mifflinburg	PA	17844	**800-326-9836**	570-966-1053	503
RivalHealth LLC 1121 Situs Ct Ste 190	Raleigh	NC	27606	**888-949-1001**	919-803-6709	386
Rivco Products Inc 440 S Pine St	Burlington	WI	53105	**888-801-8222**	262-763-8222	514
River Bend Business Products 304 Downtown Plz	Fairmont	MN	56031	**800-783-3877**	507-235-3800	316
River Bend Industries 2421 16th Ave S	Moorhead	MN	56560	**800-365-3070**		199
River City Bank PO Box 15247 *OTC: RCBC* ■ *Cust Svc	Sacramento	CA	95851	**800-564-7144***	916-567-2899	70
River City Brass Band Inc 500 Grant St Ste 2720	Pittsburgh	PA	15219	**800-292-7222**	412-434-7222	569-3
River Heights Chamber of Commerce 5782 Blackshire Path	Inver Grove Heights	MN	55076	**800-625-6079**	651-451-2266	139
River Oaks Ctr 96 River Oaks Ctr Dr	Calumet City	IL	60409	**877-746-6642**	317-636-1600	458
River Oaks Hospital 1525 River Oaks Rd W	New Orleans	LA	70123	**800-366-1740**		373-3
River Parishes Hospital 500 Rue De Sante	Laplace	LA	70068	**800-231-5275**	985-652-7000	373-3
River Park Hospital 1230 Sixth Ave	Huntington	WV	25701	**800-621-2673**	304-526-9111	373-5
River Rock Casino Resort 8811 River Rd	Richmond	BC	V6X3P8	**866-748-3718**	604-247-8900	665
River Rock Entertainment Authority 3250 Hwy 128 E	Geyserville	CA	95441	**877-883-7777**	707-857-2777	450
River Walk 110 Broadway Ste 500	San Antonio	TX	78204	**800-417-4139**	210-227-4262	50-6
River West Meeting Associates Inc 3616 N Lincoln Ave	Chicago	IL	60613	**888-534-5292**	773-755-3000	461
River's Edge Resort Cottages 4200 Boat St	Fairbanks	AK	99709	**800-770-3343**	907-474-0286	378
Riverdale Mills Corp 130 Riverdale St	Northbridge	MA	01534	**800-762-6374**	508-234-8715	279
Riveredge Nature Ctr 4458 W Hawthorne Dr PO Box 26	Newburg	WI	53060	**800-287-8098**	262-375-2715	50-5
Riveredge Resort Hotel 17 Holland St	Alexandria Bay	NY	13607	**800-365-6987**	315-482-9917	378
Riverhead Bldg Supply Corp 1093 Pulaski St	Riverhead	NY	11901	**800-378-3650**	631-727-3650	191-3
Riverland Community College 1900 Eigth Ave NW	Austin	MN	55912	**800-247-5039**	507-433-0600	162
Riverland Energy Co-op N28988 State Rd 93 PO Box 277	Arcadia	WI	54612	**800-411-9115**	608-323-3381	245
RiverMead Retirement Community 150 RiverMead Rd	Peterborough	NH	03458	**800-200-5433**	603-924-0062	668
RiverPoint Group LLC 2200 E Devon Ave Ste 385	Des Plaines	IL	60018	**800-297-5601**	847-233-9600	180
Rivers Club Inc 301 Grant St	Pittsburgh	PA	15219	**800-433-5079**		
Rivers Oceans & Mountains Adventures Inc (ROAM) 24-622 Front St	Nelson	BC	V1L4B7	**888-639-1114**		755
Riverside City Public Library 3581 Mission Inn Ave	Riverside	CA	92501	**888-225-7377**	951-826-5201	433-3
Riverside Convention & Visitors Bureau 3750 University Ave Ste 175	Riverside	CA	92501	**800-600-7080**	951-222-4700	206
Riverside Foods Inc 2520 Wilson St	Two Rivers	WI	54241	**800-678-4511**	920-793-4511	296-14
Riverside Ford 2625 Ludington St	Escanaba	MI	49829	**877-774-3171**	906-786-1130	57
Riverside Ford Inc 2089 Riverside Dr *Sales	Macon	GA	31204	**800-395-6210***	478-464-2900	57
Riverside Forest Products Inc 2912 Professional Pkwy PO Box 211663	Augusta	GA	30907	**888-855-8733**	706-855-5500	191-3
Riverside Health System 701 Town Ctr Dr Ste 1000	Newport News	VA	23606	**800-759-1001**	757-534-7000	352
Riverside Manufacturing Co 301 Riverside Dr	Moultrie	GA	31768	**800-841-8677**	229-985-5210	155-18
Riverside Marine Inc 600 Riverside Dr	Essex	MD	21221	**800-448-6872**	410-335-1500	90
Riverside Mattress Co 225 Dunn Rd	Fayetteville	NC	28312	**888-288-5195**	910-483-0461	469
Riverside Methodist Hospital 3535 Olentangy River Rd	Columbus	OH	43214	**800-837-7555**	614-566-4378	373-3
Riverside Military Academy 2001 Riverside Dr	Gainesville	GA	30501	**800-462-2338**	770-532-6251	618
Riverside Regional Convalescent Ctr 1000 Old Denbigh Blvd	Newport News	VA	23602	**800-759-1001**	757-875-2000	448
Riverside Transit Agency (RTA) 1825 Third St PO Box 59968	Riverside	CA	92517	**800-800-7821**	951-565-5000	466
Riverside-San Bernardino County Indian Health Inc (RSBCIH) 11555 1/2 Potrero Rd	Banning	CA	92220	**800-732-8805**	951-849-4761	352
Riverstone Billings Inn 880 N 29th St	Billings	MT	59101	**800-231-7782**	406-252-6800	378
RiverStone Group Inc 1701 Fifth Ave	Moline	IL	61265	**800-906-2489**	309-757-8250	182
Rivertown Newspaper Group 2760 N Service Dr PO Box 15	Red Wing	MN	55066	**800-535-1660**	651-388-8235	633-8
Rivervalley Behavioral Health Hospital 1100 Walnut St PO Box 1637	Owensboro	KY	42302	**800-737-0696**	270-689-6800	722
Riverview Hospital 395 Westfield Rd	Noblesville	IN	46060	**800-523-6001**	317-773-0760	373-3
Riverview Intermediate Unit Number 6 Administrative Services 270 Mayfield Rd	Clarion	PA	16214	**800-672-7123**	814-226-7103	681
Riverview Plaza Hotel 64 S Water St	Mobile	AL	36602	**800-321-2211**	251-438-4000	378
Riverview Psychiatric Ctr 250 Arsenal St 11 State House Stn	Augusta	ME	04332	**888-261-6684**	207-624-4600	373-5
Riverwalk Casino Hotel 1046 Warrenton Rd	Vicksburg	MS	39180	**866-615-9125**	601-634-0100	450
Rivier College 420 S Main St	Nashua	NH	03060	**800-447-4843**	603-888-1311	166
Riviera Advisors Inc PO Box 41446	Long Beach	CA	90853	**800-635-9063**		193
Riviera Finance 220 Ave I	Redondo Beach	CA	90277	**800-872-7484**	310-540-3993	272
Riviera Hotel 1431 Robson St	Vancouver	BC	V6G1C1	**888-699-5222**	604-685-1301	378
Riviera Telephone Co 103 S 8th PO Box 997	Riviera	TX	78379	**877-296-3232**	361-296-3232	386
RJ Marshall Co 26776 W 12-Mile Rd *Cust Svc	Southfield	MI	48034	**888-514-8600***	248-353-4100	720
RJ Thomas Mfg Company Inc PO Box 946	Cherokee	IA	51012	**800-762-5002**	712-225-5115	319-4
RJE Business Interiors Inc 623 Broadway St	Cincinnati	OH	45202	**800-236-8232**	513-641-3700	392
RJM Sales Inc 454 Park Ave	Scotch Plains	NJ	07076	**800-752-9055**	908-322-7880	357
RJMW (Reid Jones McRorie & Williams Inc) 2200 Executive St PO Box 669248	Charlotte	NC	28208	**800-785-2604**		389
RJN Group Inc 200 W Front St	Wheaton	IL	60187	**800-227-7838**	630-682-4700	192
RJR Fashion Fabrics 2610 Columbia St Ste B	Torrance	CA	90503	**800-422-5426**	310-222-8782	707
RK (Rihm Kenworth) 425 Concord St S	South St.Paul	MN	55075	**800-988-8235**	651-646-7833	
RK Mechanical Inc 3800 Xanthia St	Denver	CO	80238	**877-576-9696**	303-355-9696	189-10
RKA Petroleum Companies Inc 28340 Wick Rd	Romulus	MI	48174	**866-509-3288**	800-875-3835	575
RKI Inc 2301 Central Pkwy	Houston	TX	77092	**800-346-8988**	713-688-4414	468
Rl Deppmann Co 20929 Bridge St	Southfield	MI	48033	**800-589-6120**	248-354-3710	637
RL Drake Co 710 Pleasant Valley Dr	Springboro	OH	45066	**800-276-4523**	937-746-4556	643
RL Winston Rod Co 500 S Main St	Twin Bridges	MT	59754	**866-946-7637**	406-684-5674	
RLE Technologies Inc 104 Racquette Dr	Fort Collins	CO	80524	**800-518-1519**	970-484-6510	689
RLI Corp 9025 N Lindbergh Dr *NYSE: RLI* ■ *Cust Svc	Peoria	IL	61615	**800-331-4929***	309-692-1000	359-4
RLI Insurance Co 9025 N Lindbergh Dr	Peoria	IL	61615	**800-331-4929**	309-692-1000	390-4
Rlj Financial Services Inc 1788 Mitchell Rd Ste 102	Ceres	CA	95307	**800-240-1050**	209-538-7758	138
RLM Communications Inc 1027 E Manchester Rd	Spring Lake	NC	28390	**877-223-1345**	910-223-1350	179
RLR Management Consulting Inc 77806 Flora Rd Ste D	Palm Desert	CA	92211	**888-757-7330**	760-200-4800	193
RLTV 5525 Research Park Dr	Baltimore	MD	21228	**800-754-8464**		116
R&M Materials Handling Inc 4501 Gateway Blvd	Springfield	OH	45502	**800-955-9967**	937-328-5100	357
RMA (Risk Management Assn) 1801 Market St Ste 300 *Cust Svc	Philadelphia	PA	19103	**800-677-7621***	215-446-4000	49-2
RMA Group Inc 12130 Santa Margarita Ct	Rancho Cucamonga	CA	91730	**800-480-4808**	909-989-1751	261
RMC (Ridgeview Medical Ctr) 500 S Maple St	Waconia	MN	55387	**800-967-4620**	952-442-2191	373-3
RMCF (Rocky Mountain Chocolate Factory Inc) 265 Turner Dr *NASDAQ: RMCF* ■ *Cust Svc	Durango	CO	81303	**888-525-2462***	970-247-4943	123
RMCSJ (Regional Medical Ctr of San Jose) 225 N Jackson Ave	San Jose	CA	95116	**800-307-7135**	408-259-5000	373-3
RME360 4805 Independence Pkwy Ste 250	Tampa	FL	33634	**888-383-8770**		5
RMF (Rocky Mountain Fabrication) 1125 West 2300 North PO Box 16409	Salt Lake City	UT	84116	**888-763-5307**	801-596-2400	91
RMF Engineering Inc 5520 Research Pk Dr Ste 300	Baltimore	MD	21228	**800-938-5760**	410-576-0505	261
RMF Printing Technologies Inc 50 Pearl St	Lancaster	NY	14086	**800-828-7999**	716-683-7500	623
RMH (Ross Memorial Hospital) 10 Angeline St N	Lindsay	ON	K9V4M8	**800-510-7365**	705-324-6111	373-2
RMLEB (Rocky Mountain Lions Eye Bank) 1675 Aurora Crt Ste El2049 PO Box 6026	Aurora	CO	80045	**800-444-7479**	720-848-3937	269
RMO Inc (Rocky Mountain Orthodontics Inc) 650 W Colfax Ave	Denver	CO	80204	**800-525-6375**	303-592-8200	228
RMP (Robert Mann Packaging Inc) 340 El Camino Real S Bldg 36	Salinas	CA	93901	**800-345-6766**		100
RMPB (Rocky Mountain Public Broadcasting Network) 1089 Bannock St	Denver	CO	80204	**800-274-6666**	303-892-6666	628
Rmx Global Logistics 141 Union Blvd Ste 450	Evergreen	CO	80439	**888-824-7365**		311
RNC (Republican National Committee) 310 First St SE	Washington	DC	20003	**800-445-5768**	202-863-8500	612
RNC Genter Capital Management 11601 Wilshire Blvd 25th Fl	Los Angeles	CA	90025	**800-877-7624**	310-477-6543	400
RnR RV Ctr 23203 E Knox Ave	Liberty Lake	WA	99019	**866-386-4875**		57

Name / Address	City	State	ZIP	Toll-Free	Phone	Class
ROA (Reserve Officers Assn of the US) 1 Constitution Ave NE	Washington	DC	20002	**800-809-9448**	202-479-2200	48-19
Road America N 7390 Hwy 67	Elkhart Lake	WI	53020	**800-365-7223**	920-892-4576	512
Road Atlanta Raceway 5300 Winder Hwy	Braselton	GA	30517	**800-849-7223**	770-967-6143	512
Road Machinery Co 926 S Seventh St	Phoenix	AZ	85034	**800-989-7121**		
Roadrunner Transportation Systems Inc 4900 S Pennsylvania Ave	Cudahy	WI	53110	**800-831-4394**	414-615-1500	647
NYSE: RRTS						
Roadtec Inc 800 Manufacturers Rd PO Box 180515	Chattanooga	TN	37405	**800-272-7100**	423-265-0600	190
Roadtex Transportation Corp 13 Jensen Dr	Somerset	NJ	08873	**800-762-3839**		775
ROAM (Rivers Oceans & Mountains Adventures Inc) 24-622 Front St	Nelson	BC	V1L4B7	**888-639-1114**		755
Roam Mobility Holdings Inc 60 James St 3rd fl	St. Catharines	ON	L2R7E7	**800-282-1376**	613-995-8210	224
Roaman's 2300 SE Ave	Indianapolis	IN	46201	**800-840-6214**	317-266-3300	457
Roane Alliance 1209 N Kentucky St	Kingston	TN	37763	**800-386-4686**	865-376-2093	337
Roane State Community College 276 Patton Ln	Harriman	TN	37748	**800-343-9104**	865-354-3000	162
Roanoke College 221 College Ln	Salem	VA	24153	**800-388-2276***	540-375-2270	166
*Admissions						
Roanoke Electric Co-op 518 NC 561 W	Aulander	NC	27805	**800-433-2236**		245
Roanoke (Independent City) 210 Reserve Ave SW	Roanoke	VA	24016	**800-956-4237**	540-853-2000	337
Roanoke Times 201 W Campbell Ave SW	Roanoke	VA	24011	**800-346-1234**	540-981-3340	528-2
Roanoke Valley Chamber of Commerce 260 Premier Blvd	Roanoke Rapids	NC	27870	**800-280-3999**	252-537-3513	139
Roanoke Valley Convention & Visitors Bureau 101 Shenandoah Ave NE	Roanoke	VA	24016	**800-635-5535**	540-342-6025	206
Roaring Brook Ranch & Tennis Resort Rte 9N S	Lake George	NY	12845	**800-882-7665**	518-668-5767	665
RoArk Group Inc, The 1600 N 35th St	Rogers	AR	72756	**800-569-2616**	479-636-1686	623
Roasterie Inc, The 1204 W 27th St	Kansas City	MO	64108	**800-376-0245**	816-931-4000	344
Robbers Cave State Park Hwy 2 N	Wilburton	OK	74578	**800-654-8240**	918-465-2565	561
Robbie Manufacturing Inc 10810 Mid America Ave	Lenexa	KS	66219	**800-255-6328**	913-492-3400	597
Robbinex Inc 41 Stuart St	Hamilton	ON	L8L1B5	**888-762-2463**	905-523-7510	317
Robbins Arroyo LLP 600 B St Ste 1900	San Diego	CA	92101	**800-350-6003**		427
Robbins Inc 4777 Eastern Ave	Cincinnati	OH	45226	**800-543-1913**		679
Robbins LLC 3415 Thompson St	Muscle Shoals	AL	35661	**800-633-3312**	256-383-5441	749
Robbins Mfg Co 1003 E 131st Ave	Tampa	FL	33612	**888-558-8199**	813-971-3030	813
Robern Inc 701 N Wilson Ave	Bristol	PA	19007	**800-877-2376**	215-826-9800	319-2
Roberson Motors Inc 3100 Ryan Dr SE	Salem	OR	97301	**888-281-6220**	503-363-4117	57
Roberson Museum & Science Ctr 30 Front St	Binghamton	NY	13905	**888-269-5325**	607-772-0660	517
Robert Allen Fabrics Inc 225 Foxboro Blvd	Foxboro	MA	02035	**800-333-3777**	508-339-9151	590
Robert B Greenblatt MD Library *Medical College of Georgia* 1439 Lny Walker Blvd	Augusta	GA	30912	**800-715-4225**	706-721-3441	433-1
Robert Bearden Inc 2601 Industrial Pk Dr PO Box 870	Cairo	GA	39828	**888-298-6928**	229-377-6928	775
Robert Bosch Tool Corp 1800 W Central Rd	Mount Prospect	IL	60056	**877-267-2499**		754
Robert Busse & Company Inc 75 Arkay Dr	Hauppauge	NY	11788	**800-645-6526**	631-435-4711	
Robert Dietrick Co Inc PO Box 605	Fishers	IN	46038	**866-767-1888**	317-842-1991	384
Robert E Nolan Company Inc 92 Hopmeadow St	Weatogue	CT	06089	**800-653-1941**	877-736-6526	194
Robert e Webber Institute for Worship Studies, The (IWS) 4001 Hendricks Ave	Jacksonville	FL	32207	**800-282-2977**	904-264-2172	681
Robert H Wager Co 570 Montroyal Rd	Rural Hall	NC	27045	**800-562-7024**	336-969-6909	784
Robert Half International Inc 2884 Sand Hill Rd Ste 200	Menlo Park	CA	94025	**855-432-0924**		
NYSE: RHI						
Robert Half International Inc Accountemps Div 2884 Sand Hill Rd Ste 200	Menlo Park	CA	94025	**888-744-9202**	650-234-6000	717
Robert J Dole VA Medical Center 5500 E Kellogg St	Wichita	KS	67218	**888-878-6881**	316-685-2221	373-3
Robert Kaufman Company Inc PO Box 59266	Los Angeles	CA	90059	**800-877-2066**	310-538-3482	590
Robert Mann Packaging Inc (RMP) 340 El Camino Real S Bldg 36	Salinas	CA	93901	**800-345-6766**		100
Robert Moreno Insurance Services 2260 Savi Ranch Pkwy PO Box 87023	Yorba Linda	CA	92887	**800-815-7647**	714-738-1383	389
Robert Morris College						
Chicago 401 S State St	Chicago	IL	60605	**800-762-5960**	312-935-6800	166
DuPage 905 Meridian Lake Dr	Aurora	IL	60504	**800-762-5960***	630-375-8100	166
*Admissions						
Orland Park 82 Orland Square Dr	Orland Park	IL	60462	**800-762-5960**		166
Robert Morris University 6001 University Blvd	Moon Township	PA	15108	**800-762-0097**		166
Robert Morris University Institute of Culinary Arts 401 S State St	Chicago	IL	60605	**800-762-5960**	312-935-5460	163
Robert N Karpp Company Inc 480 E First St	Boston	MA	02127	**800-244-5886**	617-269-5880	191-2
Robert Packer Hospital 1 Guthrie Sq	Sayre	PA	18840	**888-448-8474**	570-888-6666	373-3
Robert Treat Hotel 50 Pk Pl	Newark	NJ	07102	**800-569-2300**	973-622-1000	378
Robert W Baird & Company Inc 777 E Wisconsin Ave PO Box 672	Milwaukee	WI	53202	**800-792-2473**	414-765-3500	686
Robert Wood Johnson Foundation PO Box 2316	Princeton	NJ	08543	**877-843-7953**		305
Robert Wood Johnson University Hospital 1 Robert Wood Johnson Pl	New Brunswick	NJ	08901	**888-637-9584**	732-828-3000	373-3
Robert Wood Johnson University Hospital at Rahway (RWJUHR) 865 Stone St	Rahway	NJ	07065	**800-443-4605**	732-381-4200	373-3
Roberts Company Inc 180 Franklin St	Framingham	MA	01702	**800-729-1482**		
Roberts Dairy Co 2901 Cuming St	Omaha	NE	68131	**800-779-4321**	402-344-4321	297-4
Roberts Hawaii Inc 680 Iwilei Rd Ste 700	Honolulu	HI	96817	**800-831-5541**	808-523-7750	755
Roberts Wesleyan College 2301 Westside Dr	Rochester	NY	14624	**800-777-4792***	585-594-6000	166
*Admissions						
Roberts-Gordon Inc 1250 William St PO Box 44	Buffalo	NY	14240	**800-828-7450**	716-852-4400	356
Robertshaw Industrial Products 1602 Mustang Dr	Maryville	TN	37801	**800-228-7429**	865-981-3100	201
Robertson County 523 S Brown St	Springfield	TN	37172	**866-355-6134**	615-384-0202	337
Robertson Furniture Company Inc 890 Elberton St	Toccoa	GA	30577	**800-241-0713**	706-886-1494	319-1
Robertson Heating Supply Co 2155 W Main St	Alliance	OH	44601	**800-433-9532**	330-821-9180	608
Robertson Inc 1185 Corporate Dr Unit 1	Burlington	ON	L7L5V5	**800-268-5090**	905-332-7776	278
Robinson Industries Inc 3051 W Curtis Rd	Coleman	MI	48618	**877-465-4055**	989-465-6111	544
Robishaw Engineering Inc 10106 Mathewson Ln	Houston	TX	77043	**800-877-1706**	713-468-1706	694
RoboVent 37900 Mound Rd	Sterling Heights	MI	48310	**888-298-4214**	586-698-1800	
Robson Communities 9532 E Riggs Rd	Sun Lakes	AZ	85248	**800-732-9949**		649
Robson Forensic Inc 354 N Prince St	Lancaster	PA	17603	**800-813-6736**	717-293-9050	194
Robstown High School 609 W Hwy 44	Robstown	TX	78380	**800-446-3142**	361-387-5999	681
Robyn Inc 7717 W Britton Rd	Oklahoma City	OK	73132	**877-211-9711**		623
Rochdale Village Inc 169-65 137th Ave	Jamaica	NY	11434	**800-275-8777**	718-276-5700	651
Roche Diagnostics Corp (RDC) 9115 Hague Rd PO Box 50457	Indianapolis	IN	46250	**800-428-5076***		231
*Cust Svc						
Roche Palo Alto LLC 4300 Hacienda Dr	Pleasanton	CA	94588	**888-545-2443**	925-730-8000	85
Rochester College 800 W Avon Rd	Rochester Hills	MI	48307	**800-521-6010**	248-218-2011	166
Rochester Community & Technical College 851 30th Ave SE	Rochester	MN	55904	**800-247-1296**	507-285-7210	162
Rochester Convention & Visitors Bureau 30 Civic Ctr Dr SE Ste 200	Rochester	MN	55904	**800-634-8277**	507-288-4331	206
Rochester Gas & Electric Corp 89 E Ave	Rochester	NY	14649	**800-743-2110**		782
Rochester Gauges Inc of Texas 11616 Harry Hines Blvd	Dallas	TX	75229	**800-821-1829**	972-241-2161	201
Rochester Homes Inc 1345 N Lucas St	Rochester	IN	46975	**800-860-4554**		106
Rochester International Airport (RST) 7600 Helgerson Dr SW	Rochester	MN	55902	**800-227-4672**	507-282-2328	27
Rochester Mayor's 201 Fourth St SE	Rochester	MN	55904	**800-657-3858**	507-328-2700	336
Rochester Midland Corp 333 Hollenbeck St	Rochester	NY	14621	**800-836-1627**	585-336-2200	145
Rochester Psychiatric Ctr 1111 Elmwood Ave	Rochester	NY	14620	**800-310-1160**	585-454-1490	373-5
Rochester Regional Health (RGHS) 1425 Portland Ave	Rochester	NY	14621	**877-922-5465**	585-922-4000	373-3
Rochester Shoe Tree Company Inc 1 Cedar Ln	Ashland	NH	03217	**866-627-3800**		
Rock & Gem Magazine 290 Maple Ct Ste 232	Ventura	CA	93003	**866-377-4666**	805-644-3824	455-14
Rock 'N Learn Inc 105 Commercial Cir	Conroe	TX	77304	**800-348-8445**	936-539-2731	243
Rock 923 | WKRR 192 E Lewis St	Greensboro	NC	27406	**800-762-5923**	336-274-8042	641
Rock County 51 S Main St	Janesville	WI	53545	**800-924-3570**	608-757-5660	337
Rock Creek Outfitters 1530 Riverside Dr	Chattanooga	TN	37406	**888-707-6708**	423-266-8200	707
Rock Creek Resort 6380 US Hwy 212	Red Lodge	MT	59068	**800-667-1119**	406-446-1111	665
Rock Hill Mechanical Corp 524 Clark Ave	Saint Louis	MO	63122	**877-966-7792**	314-966-0600	189-10
Rock Island Argus 1724 Fourth Ave	Rock Island	IL	61201	**800-660-2472**	309-786-6441	528-2
Rock Island State Park 82 Beach Rd	Rock Island	TN	38581	**800-713-6065**	931-686-2471	561
Rock of Ages Corp 558 Graniteville Rd	Graniteville	VT	05654	**800-421-0166**	802-476-3115	720
Rock River Valley Blood Ctr 3065 N Perryville Rd Ste 105	Rockford	IL	61114	**877-778-2299***	815-965-8751	89
*General						
Rock Springs National Bank 200 Second St PO Box 880	Rock Springs	WY	82902	**800-469-8801**	307-362-8801	69

Name	Address	City	State	ZIP	Toll-Free	Phone	Class
Rock Springs Run State Reserve	30601 CR 433	Sorrento	FL	32776	**800-326-3521**	407-884-2008	561
Rock Valley College	3301 N Mulford Rd	Rockford	IL	61114	**800-973-7821**	815-921-7821	162
Rock View Resort	1049 Parkview Dr	Hollister	MO	65672	**800-375-9530**	417-334-4678	378
Rock Wool Manufacturing Co	8610 Spruiell St PO Box 506	Leeds	AL	35094	**800-874-7625**	205-699-6121	388
Rockbestos-Surprenant Cable Corp	20 Bradley Pk Rd	East Granby	CT	06026	**800-327-7625**	860-653-8300	809
Rockbridge County	150 S Main St	Lexington	VA	24450	**800-420-1663**	540-463-4361	337
Rocket Communications Inc	81 Langton St Ste 12	San Francisco	CA	94103	**844-897-6253**	415-863-0101	
Rocket Jewelry Packaging & Displays	375 Executive Blvd Ste W-4	Elmsford	NY	10523	**800-762-5521**	718-292-5370	199
Rocket Media Inc	3335 E Baseline Rd	Gilbert	AZ	85234	**800-339-7305**		195
Rockford Area Convention & Visitors Bureau	102 N Main St	Rockford	IL	61101	**800-521-0849**	815-963-8111	206
Rockford Art Museum	711 N Main St	Rockford	IL	61103	**800-521-0849**	815-968-2787	517
Rockford College	5050 E State St	Rockford	IL	61108	**800-892-2984**	815-226-4000	166
Rockford Institute	928 N Main St	Rockford	IL	61103	**800-383-0680**	815-964-5053	630
Rockford Memorial Hospital	2400 N Rockton Ave	Rockford	IL	61103	**800-756-4147**	815-971-5000	373-3
Rockford Mercantile Agency Inc	2502 S Alpine Rd	Rockford	IL	61108	**800-369-6116**	815-229-3328	392
Rockford Process Control Inc	2020 Seventh St	Rockford	IL	61104	**800-228-3779**	815-966-2000	349
Rockford Systems Inc	4620 Hydraulic Rd *Cust Svc	Rockford	IL	61109	**800-922-7533***	815-874-7891	203
Rockhill-York County Convention & Visitors Bureau	452 S Anderson Rd	Rock Hill	SC	29730	**888-702-1320**	803-329-5200	206
Rockhurst University	1100 Rockhurst Rd	Kansas City	MO	64110	**800-842-6776**	816-501-4000	166
Rocking Horse Ranch Resort	600 State Rt 44/55	Highland	NY	12520	**800-647-2624**	844 402 3211	665
Rockingham Steel Inc	2565 John Wayland Hwy	Harrisonburg	VA	22803	**800-738-1742**	540-433-3000	490
Rock-It Cargo USA Inc	5343 W Imperial Hwy Ste 900	Los Angeles	CA	90045	**800-973-1727**	310-410-0935	311
Rockland Community College	145 College Rd	Suffern	NY	10901	**800-722-7666**	845-574-4000	162
Rockland County	11 New Hempstead Rd	New City	NY	10956	**800-662-1220**	845-638-5100	337
Rockland Federal Credit Union	241 Union St	Rockland	MA	02370	**800-562-7328**	781-878-0232	219
Rockland Immunochemicals Inc	PO Box 326	Gilbertsville	PA	19525	**800-656-7625**	610-369-1008	231
Rocklin Area Chamber of Commerce	3700 Rocklin Rd	Rocklin	CA	95677	**800-228-3380**	916-624-2548	139
Rocklin Park Hotel	5450 China Garden Rd	Rocklin	CA	95677	**888-630-9400**	916-630-9400	378
Rockmount Ranch Wear Manufacturing Co	1626 Wazee St	Denver	CO	80202	**800-776-2566**	303-629-7777	155-19
Rockport Company Inc	1220 Washington St	Newton	MA	02465	**800-828-0545**	781-401-5000	301
Rockport Technology Group Inc	5 Industrial Way Ste 2C	Salem	NH	03079	**800-399-7053**	603-681-0333	180
Rockview Dairies Inc	7011 Stewart & Gray Rd	Downey	CA	90241	**800-423-2479**	562-927-5511	297-4
Rockville Correctional Facility	811 W 50 N	Rockville	IN	47872	**800-451-6028**	765-569-3178	213
Rockwell Collins Inc	400 Collins Rd NE *NYSE: COL*	Cedar Rapids	IA	52498	**888-721-3094**	319-295-1000	525
Rockwell Farms	332 Rockwell Farms Rd	Rockwell	NC	28138	**800-635-6576**		368
Rockwell Laser Industries Inc	7754 Camargo Rd	Cincinnati	OH	45243	**800-945-2737**	513-272-9900	539
Rockwell Medical Inc	30142 Wixom Rd *NASDAQ: RMTI*	Wixom	MI	48393	**800-449-3353**	248-960-9009	250
Rockwood Retaining Walls Inc	7200 Hwy 63 N	Rochester	MN	55906	**800-535-2375**	888-288-4045	183
Rockwood Retirement Community	2903 E 25th Ave	Spokane	WA	99223	**800-727-6650**	509-536-6650	668
Rocky Brands Inc	39 E Canal St *NASDAQ: RCKY*	Nelsonville	OH	45764	**877-795-2410**	740-753-3130	301
Rocky Mount Cord Co	381 N Grace St *Orders	Rocky Mount	NC	27804	**800-342-9130***	252-977-9130	208
Rocky Mount Museum	200 Hyder Hill Rd PO Box 160	Piney Flats	TN	37686	**888-538-1791**	423-538-7396	517
Rocky Mountain Chocolate Factory Inc (RMCF)	265 Turner Dr *NASDAQ: RMCF* ■ *Cust Svc	Durango	CO	81303	**888-525-2462***	970-247-4943	123
Rocky Mountain College	1511 Poly Dr	Billings	MT	59102	**800-877-6259**	406-657-1000	166
Rocky Mountain Fabrication (RMF)	1125 West 2300 North PO Box 16409	Salt Lake City	UT	84116	**888-763-5307**	801-596-2400	91
Rocky Mountain Hardware Inc	1020 Airport Way	Hailey	ID	83333	**888-788-2013**	208-788-2013	349
Rocky Mountain Health Plans	2775 Crossroads Blvd PO Box 10600	Grand Junction	CO	81502	**800-843-0719**		390-3
Rocky Mountain Lions Eye Bank (RMLEB)	1675 Aurora Crt Ste El2049 PO Box 6026	Aurora	CO	80045	**800-444-7479**	720-848-3937	269
Rocky Mountain Orthodontics Inc (RMO Inc)	650 W Colfax Ave	Denver	CO	80204	**800-525-6375**	303-592-8200	228
Rocky Mountain Public Broadcasting Network (RMPB)	1089 Bannock St	Denver	CO	80204	**800-274-6666**	303-892-6666	628
Rocky Mountain Tissue Bank	2993 S Peoria St Ste 390	Aurora	CO	80014	**800-424-5169**	303-337-3330	541
Rocky Rococo	105 E Wisconsin Ave	Oconomowoc	WI	53066	**800-888-7625**	262-569-5580	666
Rocky Top Furniture Inc	8957 Lexington Rd	Lancaster	KY	40444	**800-332-1143**	859-548-2828	321
Roco Rescue	7077 Exchequer Dr	Baton Rouge	LA	70809	**800-647-7626**	225-755-7626	461
Rodale Institute	611 Siegfriedale Rd	Kutztown	PA	19530	**800-432-1565**	610-683-1400	664
Rodbat Security Services	8125 Somerset Blvd	Paramount	CA	90723	**877-676-3228**	562-806-9098	689
Rodd Hotels & Resorts	PO Box 432	Charlottetown	PE	C1A7K7	**800-565-7633**	902-892-7448	
Rodda Paint Co	6107 N Marine Dr	Portland	OR	97203	**800-452-2315**	503-521-4300	546
Rodgers & Hammerstein Organization, The	229 W 28th St 11th Fl	New York	NY	10001	**800-400-8160**	212-541-6600	511
Rodney Strong Vineyards	11455 Old Redwood Hwy	Healdsburg	CA	95448	**800-678-4763**	707-431-1533	80-3
Roe Dental Laboratory Inc	7165 E Pleasant Valley Rd	Independence	OH	44131	**800-228-6663**	216-663-2233	414
Roeder Implement Inc	2550 Rockdale Rd	Dubuque	IA	52003	**800-557-1184**	563-557-1184	274
Roehl & Yi Investment Advisors LLC	450 Country Club Rd Ste 200	Eugene	OR	97401	**888-683-4343**	541-683-2085	686
Roehl Transport Inc	1916 E 29th St PO Box 750	Marshfield	WI	54449	**800-826-8367**	715-591-3795	775
Roesch Inc	100 N 24th St	Belleville	IL	62222	**800-423-6243**		479
Roffman Miller Assoc Inc	1835 Market St Ste 500	Philadelphia	PA	19103	**800-995-1030**	215-981-1030	400
Rogan Corp	3455 Woodhead Dr	Northbrook	IL	60062	**800-584-5662**	847-498-2300	604
Roger Dean Chevrolet West Palm Beach	2235 Okeechobee Blvd	West Palm Beach	FL	33409	**877-827-4705**	561-594-1478	57
Roger Sipe CPA Firm LLC	5742 Coventry Ln	Fort Wayne	IN	46804	**888-747-3272**	260-432-9996	2
Roger Smith Hotel	501 Lexington Ave	New York	NY	10017	**800-445-0277**	212-755-1400	378
Roger Ward Inc	17275 Green Mtn Rd *General	San Antonio	TX	78247	**888-909-3147***	210-655-8623	775
Roger Williams University	1 Old Ferry Rd	Bristol	RI	02809	**800-458-7144**	401-254-3500	166
Roger Williams University Ralph R Papitto School of Law	10 Metacom Ave	Bristol	RI	02809	**800-633-2727**	401-254-4500	167-1
Rogers Bros Corp	100 Orchard St	Albion	PA	16401	**800-441-9880**	814-756-4121	774
Rogers Communications Inc	333 Bloor St E 9th Fl *TSX: RCI.B*	Toronto	ON	M4W1G9	**888-221-1687**	877-490-9481	731
Rogers Corp	1 Technology Dr	Rogers	CT	06263	**800-237-2267**	860-774-9605	601-2
Rogers Machinery Company Inc	14650 SW 72nd Ave PO Box 230429	Portland	OR	97224	**800-394-6151**	503-639-0808	172
Rogers Memorial Hospital Inc	34700 Valley Rd	Oconomowoc	WI	53066	**800-767-4411**	262-646-4411	373-5
Rogers Printing Inc	PO Box 215	Ravenna	MI	49451	**800-622-5591**	231-853-2244	623
Rogers State University	1701 W Will Rogers Blvd	Claremore	OK	74017	**800-256-7511**	918-343-7546	166
Rogers State University Pryor	421 S Elliott St	Pryor	OK	74361	**800-256-7511**	918-825-6117	162
Rogers Supply Company Inc	PO Box 740	Champaign	IL	61824	**800-252-0406**	217-356-0166	661
Rogers-Lowell Area Chamber of Commerce	317 W Walnut St	Rogers	AR	72756	**800-364-1240**	479-636-1240	139
Rogue Community College	3345 Redwood Hwy	Grants Pass	OR	97527	**800-411-6508**	541-956-7500	162
Rogue Valley Manor	1200 Mira Mar Ave	Medford	OR	97504	**800-848-7868**	541-857-7214	668
Rogue Wave Software Inc	5500 Flatiron Pkwy	Boulder	CO	80301	**800-487-3217**	303-473-9118	178-2
Rohrer Corp	717 Seville Rd PO Box 1009	Wadsworth	OH	44282	**800-243-6640**	330-335-1541	604
Roi Consulting Ll Llc	176 Logan St Ste 22	Noblesville	IN	46060	**866-465-6470**		196
Ro-Lab American Rubber Co Inc	8830 W Linne Rd	Tracy	CA	95304	**800-298-2066**	209-836-0965	369
Roland D Kelly Infiniti Inc	155 Andover St Rt 114	Danvers	MA	01923	**855-885-3559**		57
Roland DGA Corp	15363 Barranca Pkwy	Irvine	CA	92618	**800-542-2307**	949-727-2100	173-6
Roland Machinery Co	816 N Dirksen Pkwy	Springfield	IL	62702	**800-252-2926**	217-789-7711	357
Roland's Electric Inc	307 Suburban Ave	Deer Park	NY	11729	**800-981-8010**	631-242-8080	782
Rolf C Hagen Corp	305 Forbes Blvd *Cust Svc	Mansfield	MA	02048	**800-724-2436***	508-339-9531	574
Rolf Institute of Structural Integration	5055 Chaparral Ct Ste 103	Boulder	CO	80301	**800-530-8875**	303-449-5903	48-17
Rolf Prima Wheel Systems	940 Wilson St	Eugene	OR	97402	**888-308-7700**	541-868-1715	514
Roll Call	1625 Eye St NW Ste 200	Washington	DC	20006	**800-432-2250**	202-650-6500	527-7
Roll Shutter Systems Inc	21633 N 14th Ave	Phoenix	AZ	85027	**800-551-7655**	623-869-7057	695
Roll'n Oilfield Industries Ltd	305 5208 ? 53 Ave	Red Deer	AB	T4N5K2	**800-662-7139**	403-343-1710	536
Rolla Area Chamber of Commerce	1311 KingsHwy	Rolla	MO	65401	**888-809-3817**	573-364-3577	139
Roll-A-Way Conveyor Inc	2335 Delaney Rd	Gurnee	IL	60031	**800-747-9024**	847-336-5033	207

	Toll-Free	Phone	Class
Roll-A-Way Inc			
1661 Glenlake Ave ....Itasca IL 60143	866-749-5424		695
Rolled Alloys Inc			
125 W Sterns Rd ....Temperance MI 48182	800-521-0332	734-847-0561	490
Rolled Steel Products Corp			
2187 Garfield Ave ....Los Angeles CA 90040	800-400-7833	323-723-8836	490
Roller Bearing Company of America			
400 Sullivan Way ....West Trenton NJ 08628	800-390-3300	609-882-5050	75
Rollex Corp			
800 Chasa Ave ....Elk Grove Village IL 60007	800-251-3300*		693
*Cust Svc			
Rolling Hills Electric Co-op Inc			
3075B US Hwy 24 PO Box 339..........Beloit KS 67420	800-530-5572	785-534-1601	245
Rolling Meadows Library			
3110 Martin Ln ....Rolling Meadows IL 60008	800-232-3798	847-259-6050	434
Rolling Oaks Mall			
6909 N Loop 1604 E ....San Antonio TX 78247	877-746-6642	317-636-1600	458
Rolling Shield Inc			
9875 NW 79th Ave ....Hialeah Gardens FL 33016	800-474-9404	305-436-6661	695
Rollins College			
1000 Holt Ave ....Winter Park FL 32789	800-799-2586	407-646-2000	166
Rollins Moving & Storage Inc			
1900 E Leffel Ln ....Springfield OH 45505	800-826-8094	937-325-2484	545
Rolls-Royce Engine Services Inc			
7200 Earhart Rd ....Oakland CA 94621	888-255-4766	510-613-1000	24
Rollstock Inc			
5720 Brighton Ave ....Kansas City MO 64130	800-295-2949	616-570-0430	543
Rollx Vans			
6591 Hwy 13 W ....Savage MN 55378	800-956-6668	952-890-7851	62-7
Rolta Tusc Inc			
333 E Butterfield Rd Ste 900. .....Lombard IL 60148	800-755-8872	630-960-2909	180
Roma Italian Restaurant			
3 President Dr ....Dover DE 19901	800-711-5882	302-678-1041	667
Romac Industries Inc			
21919 20th Ave SE ....Bothell WA 98021	800-426-9341	425-951-6200	591
Romac Supply Company Inc			
7400 Bandini Blvd ....Commerce CA 90040	800-777-6622		725
Roman Meal Company Inc			
PO Box 2781 ....Fargo ND 58108	866-245-8921		297-8
Romanoff International Supply Corp			
9 Deforest St ....Amityville NY 11701	800-221-7448*		406
*Cust Svc			
Romanza			
2707 S Virginia St			
Peppermill Hotel Casino.................Reno NV 89502	866-821-9996	775-826-2121	667
Romar Transportation Systems Inc			
3500 S Kedzie Ave ....Chicago IL 60632	800-621-5416	773-376-8800	311
Rome Specialty Company Inc Rosco Div			
501 W Embargo St ....Rome NY 13440	800-794-8357	315-337-8200	706
Rome Tool & Die Company Inc			
113 Hemlock St ....Rome GA 30161	800-241-3369	706-234-6743	752
Romeo Community School District			
316 N Main St ....Romeo MI 48065	888-427-6818	586-752-0200	681
Romero Mazda			
1307 Kettering Dr ....Ontario CA 91761	888-317-2233	909-390-8484	57
Romet Ltd			
1080 Matheson Blvd E ....Mississauga ON L4W2V2	800-387-3201	905-624-1591	406
Ron Jon Surf Shop			
3850 S Banana River Blvd ....Cocoa Beach FL 32931	888-757-8737	321-799-8888	707
Ron Kendall Masonry Inc			
101 Benoist Farms Rd ....West Palm Beach FL 33411	866-844-1404	561-793-5924	189-7
Ronald Blue & Company LLC			
300 Colonial Center Pkwy			
Ste 300 ....Roswell GA 30076	800-841-0362	770-280-6000	400
Ronald McDonald House			
Akron 245 Locust St ....Akron OH 44302	800-262-0333	330-253-5400	372
Albany 139 S Lake Ave ....Albany NY 12208	866-244-8464	518-438-2655	372
Albuquerque			
1011 Yale Ave NE ....Albuquerque NM 87106	877-842-8960	505-842-8960	372
Ann Arbor			
1600 Washington Hts ....Ann Arbor MI 48104	800-544-8684	734-994-4442	372
Las Vegas			
2323 Potosi St ....Las Vegas NV 89146	888-248-1561	702-252-4663	372
Phoenix			
501 E Roanoke Ave ....Phoenix AZ 85004	877-333-2978	602-264-2654	372
Seattle			
5130 40th Ave NE ....Seattle WA 98105	866-987-9330	206-838-0600	372
Wilmington			
1901 Rockland Rd ....Wilmington DE 19803	888-656-4847	302-656-4847	372
Winston-Salem			
419 S Hawthorne Rd ....Winston-Salem NC 27103	855-227-7435	336-723-0228	372
Ronald McDonald House Charities?			
110 N Carpenter St ....Chicago IL 60607	888-236-6167	630-623-7048	
Ronald Reagan Bldg & International Trade Ctr			
1300 Pennsylvania Ave NW ....Washington DC 20004	800-984-3775	202-312-1300	817
Ronald Reagan Presidential Library & Museum			
40 Presidential Dr ....Simi Valley CA 93065	800-410-8354	805-522-2977	433-2
Ronan Engineering Co			
21200 Oxnard St ....Woodland Hills CA 91367	800-327-6626		201
Rooftop Media Inc			
188 Spear St Ste 250 ....San Francisco CA 94105	800-860-0293	612-492-1197	116
Rook Security			
11350 N Meridian St Ste 600 ....Carmel IN 46032	888-712-9531		196
Room & Board Inc			
4600 Olson Memorial Hwy ....Golden Valley MN 55422	800-301-9720	763-521-4431	319-2
Roosevelt & Cross Inc			
1 Exchange Plz 55 Broadway			
22nd Fl ....New York NY 10006	800-348-3426	212-344-2500	686
Roosevelt Field Mall			
630 Old Country Rd ....Garden City NY 11530	877-746-6642	516-742-8001	458
Roosevelt Hotel			
45 E 45th St ....New York NY 10017	877-322-8228	212-661-9600	378
Roosevelt Paper Co			
1 Roosevelt Dr ....Mount Laurel NJ 08054	800-523-3470	856-303-4100	549
Roosevelt University			
430 S Michigan Ave ....Chicago IL 60605	877-277-5978*	312-341-3500	166
*Admissions			
Albert A Robin			
1400 N Roosevelt Blvd ....Schaumburg IL 60173	877-277-5978*	847-619-7300	166
*Admissions			
Root Candles Co			
623 W Liberty St ....Medina OH 44256	800-289-7668	330-723-4359	122
Root Inc			
5470 Main St ....Sylvania OH 43560	800-852-1315		196
Root-Lowell Manufacturing Co			
1000 Foreman Rd ....Lowell MI 49331	800-748-0098		273
Roper Pump Co			
3475 Old Maysville Rd ....Commerce GA 30529	800-944-6769*	706-335-5551	637
*Sales			
Roplast Industries Inc			
3155 S Fifth Ave ....Oroville CA 95965	800-767-5278	530-532-9500	66
Roppe Corp			
1602 N Union St ....Fostoria OH 44830	800-537-9527	419-435-8546	291
Rosalind Franklin University of Medicine & Science Learning Resource Ctr			
3333 Green Bay Rd ....North Chicago IL 60064	800-244-1177	847-578-3000	433-1
Rosamond Gifford Zoo at Burnet Park			
1 Conservation Pl ....Syracuse NY 13204	800-724-5006	315-435-8511	818
Rosario Resort & Spa			
1400 Rosario Rd ....Eastsound WA 98245	800-562-8820	360-376-2222	665
Rosback Co			
125 Hawthorne Ave ....Saint Joseph MI 49085	800-542-2420	269-983-2582	625
Rosco Laboratories Inc			
52 Harbor View Ave ....Stamford CT 06902	800-767-2669	203-708-8900	718
Roscoe Co			
3535 W Harrison St ....Chicago IL 60624	888-476-7263*	773-722-5000	441
*Cust Svc			
Roscoe Medical Inc			
21973 Commerce Pkwy ....Strongsville OH 44149	800-376-7263	440-572-1962	194
Roscoe Village			
600 N Whitewoman St ....Coshocton OH 43812	800-877-1830	740-622-7644	517
Rose Displays Ltd			
500 Narragansett Park Dr ....Pawtucket RI 02861	888-452-9528		194
Rose Hotel			
807 Main St ....Pleasanton CA 94566	800-843-9540	925-846-8802	378
Rose Medical Ctr			
4567 E Ninth Ave ....Denver CO 80220	877-647-7440	303-320-2121	373-3
Rose Packing Company Inc			
65 S Barrington Rd ....South Barrington IL 60010	800-323-7363	847-381-5700	471
Rose Printing Company Inc			
2503 Jackson Bluff Rd ....Tallahassee FL 32304	800-227-3725	850-576-4151	622
Rose Products & Services Inc			
545 Stimmel Rd ....Columbus OH 43223	800-264-1568	614-443-7647	405
Rose State College			
6420 SE 15th St ....Midwest City OK 73110	866-621-0987	405-733-7372	162
Roseau Electric Co-op Inc			
1107 Third St NE ....Roseau MN 56751	888-847-8840	218-463-1543	245
Rosebud Electric Co-op Inc			
512 Rosebud Ave PO Box 439 ....Gregory SD 57533	888-464-9304	605-835-9624	245
Rosebud Wood Products			
701 SE 12th St ....Madison SD 57042	800-256-4561	605-256-4561	115
Roseburg Forest Products Co			
PO Box 1088 ....Roseburg OR 97470	800-245-1115	541-679-3311	679
Roseburg National Cemetery			
913 NW Garden Valley Blvd ....Roseburg OR 97471	800-535-1117	541-677-3152	136
Rosedale on Robson Suite Hotel			
838 Hamilton St ....Vancouver BC V6B6A2	800-661-8870	604-689-8033	378
Rosedale Technical Institute			
215 Beecham Dr Ste 2 ....Pittsburgh PA 15205	800-521-6262		148
Rosedown Plantation State Historic Site			
12501 Hwy 10 ....Saint Francisville LA 70775	888-376-1867	225-635-3332	50-3
Rose-Hulman Institute of Technology			
5500 Wabash Ave ....Terre Haute IN 47803	800-248-7448*	812-877-1511	166
*Admissions			
Rosellen Suites at Stanley Park			
2030 Barclay St ....Vancouver BC V6G1L5	888-317-6648	604-689-4807	378
Rosemont College			
1400 Montgomery Ave ....Rosemont PA 19010	888-521-0983*	610-527-0200	166
*Admissions			
Rosen Centre Hotel			
9840 International Dr ....Orlando FL 32819	800-204-7234	407-996-9840	378
Rosen Hotels & Resorts Inc			
9840 International Dr ....Orlando FL 32819	800-204-7234	407-996-9840	378
Rosen Plaza Hotel			
9700 International Dr ....Orlando FL 32819	800-366-9700	407-996-9700	378
Rosen Publishing Group Inc, The			
29 E 21st St ....New York NY 10010	800-237-9932		633-2
Rosen Shingle Creek			
9939 Universal Blvd ....Orlando FL 32819	866-996-9939	407-996-9939	378
Rosen's Diversified Inc			
1120 Lake Ave PO Box 933 ....Fairmont MN 56031	800-345-0293	507-238-6001	359-3
Rosenbaum Family House			
30 Family House Dr			
PO Box 8228 ....Morgantown WV 26506	855-988-2273	304-598-6094	371
Rosencrantz-Bemis Water Well Co			
1105 Hwy 281 Bypass ....Great Bend KS 67530	800-466-2467	620-793-5512	189-15
Rosenn, Jenkins & Greenwald LLP			
15 S Franklin St ....Wilkes-Barre PA 18711	800-888-4754	570-826-5600	427
Rosenthal Automotive Organization			
750 North Gelbe Rd ....Arlington VA 22203	877-446-4543		
Rosetta Stone Ltd			
1919 N Lynn St 7th Fl............Arlington VA 22209	800-788-0822		681
NYSE: RST			
Roseville Medical Ctr			
1 Medical Plz ....Roseville CA 95661	800-866-7724	916-781-1000	373-3
Roseville Public Library			
225 Taylor St ....Roseville CA 95678	800-984-4636	916-774-5221	433-3
Rosewood Care Center Holding Co			
100 Rosewood Village Dr ....Swansea IL 62226	800-213-0154	618-236-1391	138
Rosewood Hotels & Resorts			
500 Crescent Ct Ste 300 ....Dallas TX 75201	888-767-3966	214-880-4200	378
Ross & Matthews PC			
3650 Lovell Ave ....Fort Worth TX 76107	800-458-6982		427
Ross & Wallace Paper Products Inc			
204 Old Covington Hwy ....Hammond LA 70403	800-854-2300		65
Ross Controls			
1250 Stephenson Hwy ....Troy MI 48083	800-438-7677	248-764-1800	785

				Toll-Free	Phone	Class
Ross Group Inc 2730 Indian Ripple Rd	Dayton	OH	45440	**800-734-9304**		225
Ross Industries Inc 5321 Midland Rd	Midland	VA	22728	**800-336-6010**	540-439-3271	298
Ross Memorial Hospital (RMH) 10 Angeline St N	Lindsay	ON	K9V4M8	**800-510-7365**	705-324-6111	373-2
Ross Metals Corp 54 W 47th St	New York	NY	10036	**800-334-7191**		483
Ross Neely Systems Inc 1500 Second St	Birmingham	AL	35214	**800-561-3357**	205-798-1137	775
Ross Optical Industries Inc 1410 Gail Borden Pl	El Paso	TX	79935	**800-880-5417**	915-595-5417	540
Ross Realty Investments Inc 3325 S University Dr Ste 210	Davie	FL	33328	**800-370-4202**	954-452-5000	648
Ross Simons Jewelers Inc 9 Ross Simons Dr	Cranston	RI	02920	**800-835-0919**		409
Ross Sinclaire & Associates LLC 700 Walnut St Ste 600	Cincinnati	OH	45202	**800-543-1831**	513-381-3939	686
Rostra Precision Controls Inc 2519 Dana Dr *Cust Svc	Laurinburg	NC	28352	**800-782-3379***	910-276-4854	525
Roswell Bookbinding Co 2614 N 29th Ave	Phoenix	AZ	85009	**888-803-8883**	602-272-9338	92
Roswell Chamber of Commerce 131 W Second St	Roswell	NM	88201	**877-849-7679**	575-623-5695	139
Roswell Livestock Auction Sales Inc 900 N Garden PO Box 2041	Roswell	NM	88202	**800-748-1541**	575-622-5580	444
Roswell Park Cancer Institute Elm and Carlton St	Buffalo	NY	14263	**877-275-7724**	716-845-2300	373-7
Rotary Forms Press Inc 835 S High St	Hillsboro	OH	45133	**800-654-2876**	937-393-3426	110
Rotary International 1 Rotary Ctr 1560 Sherman Ave	Evanston	IL	60201	**866-976-8279**	847-866-3000	
Rotary Multiforms Inc 1340 E 11 Mile Rd	Madison Heights	MI	48071	**800-762-5644**	586-558-7960	623
Rotek Inc 1400 S Chillicothe Rd PO Box 312	Aurora	OH	44202	**800-221-8043**	330-562-4000	75
Roth 3847 Crum Rd	Youngstown	OH	44515	**800-872-7684**		189-10
Roth Living 11300 W 47th St	Minnetonka	MN	55343	**800-363-3818**	952-933-4428	38
Roth Pump Co PO Box 4330	Rock Island	IL	61204	**888-444-7684**	309-787-1791	637
Rothbury Farms PO Box 202	Grand Rapids	MI	49501	**877-684-2879**		296-1
Rothe Development Inc 4614 Sinclair Rd	San Antonio	TX	78222	**800-229-5209**	210-648-3131	738
Rothenberger USA 7130 Clinton Rd	Loves Park	IL	61111	**800-545-7698**	815-397-0260	453
Rothman Furniture Stores Inc 2101 E Terra Ln	O'Fallon	MO	63366	**877-704-0002**		
Rotochopper Inc 217 West St PO Box 295	Saint Martin	MN	56376	**800-663-7574**	320-548-3586	
RotoMetrics Group 800 Howerton Ln	Eureka	MO	63025	**800-325-3851**	636-587-3600	752
Roton Products Inc 660 E Elliott Ave	Kirkwood	MO	63122	**800-467-6866**	314-821-4400	
Rotonics Manufacturing Inc 6940 O St Ste 100	Lincoln	NE	68510	**888-422-8683**	402-467-5221	199
Rotor Clip Company Inc 187 Davidson Ave *Cust Svc	Somerset	NJ	08873	**800-557-6867***	732-469-7333	326
Rottler Mfg 8029 S 200th St	Kent	WA	98032	**800-452-0534**	253-872-7050	453
Rouge Valley Ajax & Pickering 580 Harwood Ave S	Ajax	ON	L1S2J4	**866-752-6989**	905-683-2320	373-2
Rough Notes Company Inc, The 11690 Technology Dr	Carmel	IN	46032	**800-428-4384**	317-582-1600	455-5
Rough Rider Industries 3303 E Main Ave PO Box 5521	Bismarck	ND	58506	**800-732-0557**		626
Rough River Dam State Resort Park 450 Lodge Rd	Falls of Rough	KY	40119	**800-325-1713**	270-257-2311	561
Round Butte Seed Growers Inc 505 C St	Culver	OR	97734	**866-385-7001**	541-546-5222	323
Round Lake Area Chamber of Commerce & Industry 2007 Civic Ctr Way	Round Lake Beach	IL	60073	**800-334-7661**	847-546-2002	139
Round Sky Inc 848 N Rainbow Blvd Ste 326	Las Vegas	NV	89107	**855-826-6284**		317
Rounds Mike (Sen R - SD) 502 Hart Senate Office Bldg	Washington	DC	20510	**844-875-5268**	202-224-5842	
Rountree Transport & Rigging Inc 2640 N Ln Ave	Jacksonville	FL	32254	**800-342-5036**	904-781-1033	775
Roush Enterprise 12447 Levan	Livonia	MI	48150	**800-215-9658**	734-779-7006	60
Rousseau Metal Inc 105 Ave De Gasp Ouest	St Jean-Port-Joli	QC	G0R3G0	**866-463-4270**	418-598-3381	349
Roux Assoc Inc 209 Shafter St	Islandia	NY	11749	**800-322-7689**	631-232-2600	193
Rovi Corp 1990 Post Oak Blvd Ste 2300	Houston	TX	77056	**877-745-6591**	713-963-1200	641-46
Rowan Regional Medical Ctr (RRMC) 612 Mocksville Ave	Salisbury	NC	28144	**888-844-0080**	704-210-5000	373-3
Rowan University 201 Mullica Hill Rd *Admissions	Glassboro	NJ	08028	**877-787-6926***	856-256-4200	166
Rowe Machinery & Automation Inc 76 Hinckley Rd	Clinton	ME	04927	**800-247-2645**	207-426-2351	492
Rowell Chemical Corp 15 Salt Creek Ln Ste 205	Hinsdale	IL	60521	**888-261-7963**	630-920-8833	146
Rowland Medical Library University of Mississippi 2500 N State St	Jackson	MS	39216	**800-621-8099**	601-984-1231	433-1
Rowland Transportation Inc 40824 Messick Rd	Dade City	FL	33525	**800-338-1146**	352-567-2002	314
Rowlands Sales Company Inc Butler Industrial Pk	Hazleton	PA	18201	**800-582-6388**	570-455-5813	357
Rowley Chapman & Barney Ltd 63 E Main St Ste 501	Mesa	AZ	85201	**888-476-8411**	480-833-1113	427
Rowman & Littlefield Publishers Inc 4501 Forbes Blvd Ste 200	Lanham	MD	20706	**800-462-6420**	301-459-3366	633-2
Rowmark Inc 2040 Industrial Dr	Findlay	OH	45840	**800-243-3339**	419-425-2407	595
Roxbury Correctional Institution 18701 Roxbury Rd	Hagerstown	MD	21746	**800-464-0764**	240-420-3000	
Roy Anderson Corp 11400 Reichold Rd	Gulfport	MS	39503	**800-688-4003**	228-896-4000	186
Roy Bros Inc 764 Boston Rd *Cust Svc	Billerica	MA	01821	**800-225-0830***	978-667-1921	775
Roy E Hanson Jr Mfg 1600 E Washington Blvd	Los Angeles	CA	90021	**800-421-9395**	213-747-7514	91
Roy Miller Freight Lines LLC 3165 E Coronado St	Anaheim	CA	92806	**800-336-5673**	714-632-5511	314
Roy O Martin 2189 Memorial Dr PO Box 1110	Alexandria	LA	71301	**800-299-5174**	318-448-0405	
Roy's Wood Products Inc 329 Thrush Ln	Lugoff	SC	29078	**800-727-1590**	803-438-1590	115
Royal & SunAlliance Insurance Co of Canada (RSA) 18 York St Ste 800	Toronto	ON	M5J2T8	**800-268-8406**	416-366-7511	390-4
Royal Alexandra Hospital 10240 Kingsway Ave	Edmonton	AB	T5H3V9	**800-332-1414**	780-735-4111	373-2
Royal Alliance Assoc Inc 1 World Financial Ctr 15th Fl	New York	NY	10281	**800-821-5100**		686
Royal Aloha Vacation Club 1505 Dillingham Blvd Ste 212	Honolulu	HI	96817	**800-367-5212**	808-847-8050	748
Royal Bank of Canada 200 Bay St 9th Fl S Twr *TSX: RY*	Toronto	ON	M5J2J5	**800-769-2599**	416-955-7806	70
Royal Bearing Inc 17719 NE Sandy Blvd	Portland	OR	97230	**800-279-0992**	503-231-0992	384
Royal Botanical Gardens (RBG) 680 Plains Rd W	Burlington	ON	L7T4H4	**800-694-4769**	905-527-1158	97
Royal British Columbia Museum (RBCM) 675 Belleville St	Victoria	BC	V8W9W2	**888-447-7977**	250-356-7226	517
Royal Business Forms Inc 3301 Ave E E	Arlington	TX	76011	**800-255-9303**		110
Royal Camp Services Ltd 7111 - 67 St	Edmonton	AB	T6B3L7	**877-884-2267**	780-463-8000	774
Royal Canadian Military Institute 426 University Ave	Toronto	ON	M5G1S9	**800-585-1072**	416-597-0286	517
Royal Caribbean International 1050 Caribbean Way	Miami	FL	33132	**800-327-6700**	305-539-6000	220
Royal Chemical Co 1755 Enterprise Pkwy Ste 600	Twinsburg	OH	44087	**844-462-7692**		
Royal Coachman Worldwide 88 Ford Rd Ste 26	Denville	NJ	07834	**800-472-7433**	973-400-3200	440
Royal College of Dental Surgeons of Ontario 6 Crescent Rd	Toronto	ON	M4W1T1	**800-565-4591**	416-961-6555	165
Royal Conservatory of Music The 273 Bloor St W	Toronto	ON	M5S1W2	**800-462-3815**	416-408-2824	623
Royal Consumer Information Products Inc 1160 US 22 *Sales	Bridgewater	NJ	08807	**888-261-4555***	908-864-4851	111
Royal Crest Dairy Inc 350 S Pearl St	Denver	CO	80209	**888-226-6455**	303-777-2227	296-27
Royal Cup PO Box 170971	Birmingham	AL	35217	**800-366-5836**		497
Royal Garden at Waikiki Hotel 440 Olohana St	Honolulu	HI	96815	**800-428-1932**	855-421-4785	378
Royal Group, The 71 Royal Group Crescent	Woodbridge	ON	L4H1X9	**800-263-2353**	905-264-0701	235
Royal Hawaiian 2259 Kalakaua Ave	Honolulu	HI	96815	**866-716-8110**	808-923-7311	665
Royal Holiday Beach Resort 1988 Beach Blvd *Resv	Biloxi	MS	39531	**800-874-0402***	228-388-7553	378
Royal Lahaina Resort 2780 Kekaa Dr	Lahaina	HI	96761	**800-222-5642**	808-661-3611	665
Royal Manufacturing 14635 Chrisman Rd	Houston	TX	77039	**800-826-0074**	281-442-3400	374
Royal Mouldings Ltd 135 Bearcreek Rd PO Box 610	Marion	VA	24354	**800-368-3117**	276-783-8161	309
Royal Neighbor Magazine 230 16th St	Rock Island	IL	61201	**800-627-4762**	309-788-4561	455-10
Royal Oak Foundation, The 35 W 35th St Ste 1200	New York	NY	10001	**800-913-6565**	212-480-2889	48-13
Royal Pacific Resort at Universal Orlando - A Loews Hotel 6300 Hollywood Way	Orlando	FL	32819	**800-235-6397**	407-503-3000	665
Royal Palms Resort & Spa 5200 E Camelback Rd	Phoenix	AZ	85018	**800-672-6011**	602-840-3610	665
Royal Park Hotel-brookshire & The Commons 600 E University Dr	Rochester	MI	48307	**800-339-2761**	248-652-2600	378
Royal Roads University 2005 Sooke Rd	Victoria	BC	V9B5Y2	**800-788-8028**	250-391-2511	780
Royal Sea Cliff Kona by Outrigger 75-6040 Alii Dr	Kailua-Kona	HI	96740	**866-956-4262**	808-322-7222	665
Royal Sonesta Hotel Boston 40 Edwin H Land Blvd	Cambridge	MA	02142	**800-766-3782**	617-806-4200	378
Royal Sonesta Hotel New Orleans 300 Bourbon St	New Orleans	LA	70130	**800-766-3782**	504-586-0300	378
Royal Sonesta Hotel New Orleans 300 Bourbon St	New Orleans	LA	70130	**800-766-3782**	504-586-0300	378
Royal Textile Mills Inc 929 Firetower Rd	Yanceyville	NC	27379	**800-334-9361**		155-1
Royal Tire Inc 3955 Roosevelt Rd	St. Cloud	MN	56301	**877-454-7070**	320-763-9618	750
Royal Trucking Co 1323 Eshman Ave N PO Box 387	West Point	MS	39773	**800-321-1293**		775
Royal Tyrrell Museum PO Box 7500	Drumheller	AB	T0J0Y0	**888-440-4240**	403-823-7707	517
Royal University Hospital 103 Hospital Dr	Saskatoon	SK	S7N0W8	**800-458-1179**	306-655-1000	373-2
Royale Management Services Inc 2319 N Andrews Ave	Fort Lauderdale	FL	33311	**800-382-1040**	954-563-1269	461
Royalton Hotel 44 W 44th St	New York	NY	10036	**800-606-6090**	212-869-4400	378

				Toll-Free	Phone	Class
Royce & Assoc LLC						
745 Fifth Ave	New York	NY	10151	**800-221-4268**		400
Royer Corp						
805 East St	Madison	IN	47250	**800-457-8997**	812-265-3133	707
Roylco Inc						
3251 Abbeville Hwy						
PO Box 13409	Anderson	SC	29624	**800-362-8656**	864-296-0043	243
Roysons Corp						
40 Vanderhoof Ave	Rockaway	NJ	07866	**888-769-7667**	973-625-5570	290
Rozelle Cosmetics						
4260 Loop Rd	Westfield	VT	05874	**800-451-4216**		214
RP Design Web Services						
17 Meriden Ave Ste 2A	Southington	CT	06489	**800-847-3475**	203-271-7991	177
RPB (Research to Prevent Blindness Inc)						
360 Lexington Ave 22nd Fl	New York	NY	10017	**800-621-0026**	212-752-4333	48-17
RPI Media Inc						
265 Racine Dr Ste 201	Wilmington	NC	28403	**800-736-0321**	910-763-2100	652
Rpl Supplies Inc						
141 Lanza Ave Bldg 3A	Garfield	NJ	07026	**800-524-0914**	973-767-0880	174
RPM International Inc						
2628 Pearl Rd	Medina	OH	44256	**800-776-4488**	330-273-5090	546
NYSE: RPM						
RPP Corp						
12 Ballard Way	Lawrence	MA	01843	**800-232-2239**	978-689-2800	673
RR Bowker LLC						
630 Central Ave	New Providence	NJ	07974	**888-269-5372**	908-795-3500	633-2
R&R Contracting Inc						
5201 N Washington St	Grand Forks	ND	58203	**800-872-5975**	701-772-7667	188
RR Donnelley						
111 S Wacker Dr	Chicago	IL	60606	**800-742-4455**		622
RR Donnelley Response Marketing Services						
4101 Winfield Rd	Warrenville	IL	60555	**800-722-9001**	630-963-9494	5
R&R Products Inc						
3334 E Milber St	Tucson	AZ	85714	**800-528-3446**	520-889-3593	385
RR. Donnelley & Sons Co (RRD)						
35 West Wacker Dr	Chicago	IL	60601	**800-742-4455**		5
RRC (Radio Research Consortium Inc)						
PO Box 1309	Olney	MD	20830	**800-543-7300**	301-774-6686	628
RRC Assoc						
4770 Baseline Rd Ste 360	Boulder	CO	80303	**888-449-4772**	303-449-6558	464
RRD (RR. Donnelley & Sons Company)						
35 West Wacker Dr	Chicago	IL	60601	**800-742-4455**		5
RRMC (Rowan Regional Medical Ctr)						
612 Mocksville Ave	Salisbury	NC	28144	**888-844-0080**	704-210-5000	373-3
RS (IEEE Reliability Society)						
IEEE Operations Ctr						
445 Hoes Ln	Piscataway	NJ	08854	**800-678-4333**	732-981-0060	49-19
RS Braswell Company Inc						
485 S Cannon Blvd	Kannapolis	NC	28083	**888-628-3550**	704-933-2269	765
RS Corcoran Co						
500 N Vine St	New Lenox	IL	60451	**800-637-1067**	815-485-2156	637
RS Electronics Inc						
34443 Schoolcraft Rd	Livonia	MI	48150	**866-600-6040**	734-525-1155	246
RS Hughes Company Inc						
1162 Sonora Ct	Sunnyvale	CA	94086	**877-774-8443**	408-739-3211	384
RS Owens & Co						
5535 N Lynch Ave	Chicago	IL	60630	**800-282-6200**	773-282-6000	772
RSA (Royal & SunAlliance Insurance Co of Canada)						
18 York St Ste 800	Toronto	ON	M5J2T8	**800-268-8406**	416-366-7511	390-4
RSA Security Inc						
174 Middlesex Tpke	Bedford	MA	01730	**800-995-5095**	781-515-5000	178-12
RSBCIH (Riverside-San Bernardino County Indian Health Inc)						
11555 1/2 Potrero Rd	Banning	CA	92220	**800-732-8805**	951-849-4761	352
RSDC of Michigan LLC						
1775 Holloway Dr	Holt	MI	48842	**877-881-7732**		478
RSES (Refrigeration Service Engineers Society)						
1666 Rand Rd	Des Plaines	IL	60016	**800-297-5660**	847-297-6464	49-3
R-S-H Engineering Inc						
909 N 18th St Ste 200	Monroe	LA	71201	**888-340-4884**	318-323-4009	261
RSI (Reconditioned Systems Inc)						
235 S 56th St	Chandler	AZ	85226	**800-280-5000**		319-1
RSI (Radiofrequency Safety International)						
543 Main St	Kiowa	KS	67070	**888-830-5648**		196
RSI Insurance Brokers Inc						
4000 Westerly Pl Ste 110	Newport Beach	CA	92660	**800-828-5273**	714-546-6616	389
RSNA (Radiological Society of North America)						
820 Jorie Blvd	Oak Brook	IL	60523	**800-381-6660**	630-571-2670	49-8
RSPA (Retail Solutions Providers Assn)						
9920 Couloak Dr Unit 120	Charlotte	NC	28216	**800-782-2693**		49-18
RSR Group Inc						
4405 Metric Dr	Winter Park	FL	32792	**800-541-4867**	407-677-1000	706
RST (Rochester International Airport)						
7600 Helgerson Dr SW	Rochester	MN	55902	**800-227-4672**	507-282-2328	27
RSVP Direct Inc						
550 Northgate Pkwy	Wheeling	IL	60090	**866-507-5182**	847-215-9054	457
RSVP Publications						
6730 W Linebaugh Ave Ste 201	Tampa	FL	33625	**800-360-7787**	813-960-7787	310
RSVP Vacations LLC						
9200 Sunset Blvd Ste 500	West Hollywood	CA	90069	**800-328-7787**	310-432-2300	755
RSW (Ready Set Work LLC)						
1487 Dunwoody Dr Ste 200	West Chester	PA	19380	**877-507-3706**		
RT Vanderbilt Company Inc						
30 Winfield St	Norwalk	CT	06855	**800-243-6064***	203-853-1400	144
*Cust Svc						
RTA (Riverside Transit Agency)						
1825 Third St PO Box 59968	Riverside	CA	92517	**800-800-7821**	951-565-5000	466
RTC (Regional Transportation Commission of Southern Nev)						
600 S Grand Central Pkwy						
Ste 350	Las Vegas	NV	89106	**800-228-3911**	702-676-1500	466
RTC (Rails-to-Trails Conservancy)						
2121 Ward Ct NW 5th Fl	Washington	DC	20037	**800-944-6847**	202-331-9696	48-13
RTD (Regional Transportation District)						
1961 Stout St	Denver	CO	80202	**800-366-7433**	303-628-9000	466
RTEC (Rural Transit Enterprises Coordinated Inc)						
100 E Main St	Mount Vernon	KY	40456	**800-321-7832**	606-256-9835	108
RTM Consulting Inc (RTMC)						
4335 Ferguson Dr Ste 210	Cincinnati	OH	45245	**855-786-2555**		461
RTMC (RTM Consulting Inc)						
4335 Ferguson Dr Ste 210	Cincinnati	OH	45245	**855-786-2555**		461
RTN Federal Credit Union						
600 Main St	Waltham	MA	02452	**800-338-0221**	781-736-9900	219
RTP Co 580 E Front St	Winona	MN	55987	**800-433-4787**	507-454-6900	601-2
RTR (Rainbow Trout Ranch)						
1484 FDR 250 PO Box 458	Antonito	CO	81120	**800-633-3397**	719-376-2440	239
RTR Financial Services Inc						
2 Teleport Dr Ste 302	Staten Island	NY	10311	**855-399-4787**	718-668-2881	251
RTS Financial Service						
9300 Metcalf Ste 301	Overland Park	KS	66212	**877-242-4390**	844-206-6123	272
RTS Packaging LLC						
504 Thrasher St	Norcross	GA	30071	**800-558-6984**		101
RTT Mobile Interpretation						
901 Woodland St	Nashville	TN	37206	**855-894-4788**		
RTW Inc						
PO Box 390327	Minneapolis	MN	55439	**800-789-2242***	952-893-0403	390-4
*Sales						
RUAN Transportation Management Systems						
666 Grand Ave 3200 Ruan Ctr	Des Moines	IA	50309	**866-782-6669**		289
Ruane Cunniff & Goldfarb Inc						
9 W 57th St Ste 5000	New York	NY	10019	**800-686-6884**		400
RubbAir Door Div Eckel Industries Inc						
100 Groton Shirley Rd	Ayer	MA	01432	**800-966-7822**	978-772-0480	235
Rubbermaid Commercial Products (RCP)						
3124 Valley Ave	Winchester	VA	22601	**800-347-9800**	540-667-8700	604
Rubberset Co						
101 W Prospect Ave	Cleveland	OH	44115	**800-345-4939**		103
Rubenstein Bros Inc						
102 St Charles Ave	New Orleans	LA	70130	**800-725-7823**	504-581-6666	157-3
Rubicon Minerals Corp						
121 King St W Ste 830	Toronto	ON	M5H3T9	**844-818-1776**	416-766-2804	500
OTC: RBYCF						
Rubio's Restaurants Inc						
1902 Wright Pl Ste 300	Carlsbad	CA	92008	**800-354-4199**	760-929-8226	666
Ruby Falls						
1720 S Scenic Hwy	Chattanooga	TN	37409	**800-755-7105**	423-821-2544	50-5
Ruby Stein Wagner						
300 Leo-pariseau Ste 1900	Montreal	QC	H2X4B5	**866-842-3911**	514-842-3911	2
Rudd Equipment Co						
4344 Poplar Level Rd	Louisville	KY	40213	**800-527-2282**	502-456-4050	357
Rudolph Brothers						
6550 Oley Speaks Way	Canal Winchester	OH	43110	**800-600-9508**	800-375-0605	707
Rudolph Foods Company Inc						
6575 Bellefontaine Rd	Lima	OH	45804	**800-241-7675**	419-648-3611	296-9
Rudolph Technologies Inc						
16 Jonspin Rd	Wilmington	MA	01887	**877-467-8365**	973-691-1300	470
NASDAQ: RTEC						
Rudy's Texas Bar-B-Q LLC						
2780 N Expressway 77-83a	Brownsville	TX	78526	**877-609-3337**	956-542-2532	
Rues Principales						
870 De Salaberry Ave Ste 309	Quebec	QC	G1R2T9	**877-694-9944**	418-694-9944	
Ruf Strategic Solutions						
1533 E Spruce St	Olathe	KS	66061	**800-829-8544**		464
Ruffed Grouse Society (RGS)						
451 McCormick Rd	Coraopolis	PA	15108	**888-564-6747**	412-262-4044	48-3
Rug Doctor LP						
4701 Old Shepard Pl	Plano	TX	75093	**800-784-3628**		264-2
Rugg Manufacturing Corp						
554 Willard St	Leominster	MA	01453	**800-633-8772**		428
Ruggie Wealth Management						
2100 Lake Eustis Dr	Tavares	FL	32778	**888-343-2711**	352-343-2700	461
Ruiz Foods Inc						
PO Box 37	Dinuba	CA	93618	**800-477-6474**		296-36
Rumble Tuff Inc						
865 N 1430 W	Orem	UT	84057	**855-228-8388**	801-609-8168	319-2
Rumpke						
10795 Hughes Rd	Cincinnati	OH	45251	**800-582-3107**		799
Rumsey Electric Co						
15 Colwell Ln	Conshohocken	PA	19428	**800-462-2402**	610-832-9000	246
Run Consultants LLC						
925 North Point Pkwy Ste 160	Alpharetta	GA	30005	**866-457-2193**		260
Rundle-Spence Mfg Co						
2075 S Moorland Rd	New Berlin	WI	53151	**800-783-6060**	262-782-3000	608
Runner's Edge Inc, The						
3195 N Federal Hwy	Boca Raton	FL	33431	**888-361-1950**	561-361-1950	707
Runza National Inc						
PO Box 6042	Lincoln	NE	68506	**800-929-2394**	402-423-2394	
Runzheimer International						
1 Runzheimer Pk	Waterford	WI	53185	**800-558-1702**	262-971-2200	193
Rupe's Hydraulics Sales & Service						
725 N Twin Oaks Valley Rd	San Marcos	CA	92069	**800-354-7873**	760-744-9350	785
Rural Development						
1400 Independence Ave SW	Washington	DC	20250	**800-414-1226**	202-720-9540	339-1
Rural Electric Convenience Co-op Co						
3973 W State Rt 104 PO Box 19	Auburn	IL	62615	**800-245-7322**	217-438-6197	245
Rural Electric Co-op (REC)						
13942 Hwy 76 PO Box 609	Lindsay	OK	73052	**800-259-3504**	405-756-3104	245
Rural Health Resource Ctr						
525 S Lake Ave Ste 320	Duluth	MN	55802	**800-997-6685**	218-727-9390	447
Rural Mutual Insurance Company Inc						
1241 John Q Hammons Dr	Madison	WI	53717	**800-362-7881**	608-836-5525	390-4
Rural Resources Community Action						
956 S Main St	Colville	WA	99114	**800-538-7659**	509-684-8421	148
Rural Telephone Service Company Inc						
PO Box 158	Lenora	KS	67645	**877-625-7872**	785-567-4281	731
Rural Transit Enterprises Coordinated Inc (RTEC)						
100 E Main St	Mount Vernon	KY	40456	**800-321-7832**	606-256-9835	108
Rural/Metro Corp						
9221 E Via de Ventura	Scottsdale	AZ	85258	**800-352-2309**		30
Ruritan National						
5451 Lyons Rd PO Box 487	Dublin	VA	24084	**877-787-8727**	540-674-5431	48-15
RUSA (Reference & User Services Assn)						
50 E Huron St	Chicago	IL	60611	**800-545-2433**	312-280-4398	49-11
Rusch Inc						
2917 Weck Dr						
PO Box 12600	Research Triangle Park	NC	27709	**866-246-6990**	919-544-8000	475

Alphabetical Section

	City	State	ZIP	Toll-Free	Phone	Class
Rush Enterprises Inc 555 IH 35 S Ste 500 *NASDAQ: RUSHA*	New Braunfels	TX	78130	**800-973-7874**	830-626-5200	264-3
Rush Gears Inc 550 Virginia Dr	Fort Washington	PA	19034	**800-523-2576**		705
Rush Shelby Energy Inc 2777 S 840 W PO Box 55 *General	Manilla	IN	46150	**800-706-7362***	765-544-2600	245
Rush Truck Ctr - Lubbock 4515 Ave A	Lubbock	TX	79404	**888-987-2458**	806-686-3600	513
Rush-Copley Medical Ctr (RCMC) 2000 Ogden Ave	Aurora	IL	60504	**866-426-7539**	630-978-6200	373-3
Rushmore Cave 13622 Hwy 40	Keystone	SD	57751	**800-344-8826**	605-255-4384	50-5
Rushmore Forest Products 23848 Hwy 385 PO Box 619	Hill City	SD	57745	**866-466-5254**	605-574-2512	679
Rushmore View Inn 522 Hwy 16A	Keystone	SD	57751	**800-888-2603**		
Rusken Packaging Inc 64 Walnut St NW	Cullman	AL	35055	**800-232-8108**	256-734-0092	101
Russ Bassett Co 8189 Byron Rd	Whittier	CA	90606	**800-350-2445**	562-945-2445	286
Russ' Restaurants Inc 390 E Eigth St	Holland	MI	49423	**800-521-1778**	616-396-6571	666
Russel Metals Inc 6600 Financial Dr *TSE: RUS*	Mississauga	ON	L5N7J6	**800-268-0750**	905-819-7777	490
Russelectric Inc 99 Industrial Pk Rd	Hingham	MA	02043	**800-225-5250**	781-749-6000	725
Russell Food Equipment Ltd 1255 Venables St	Vancouver	BC	V6A3X6	**800-663-0707**	604-253-6611	14
Russell Investments 1301 Second Ave 18th Fl	Seattle	WA	98101	**800-426-7969**	206-505-7877	400
Russell Reynolds Assoc Inc 277 Park Ave Ste 3800	New York	NY	10166	**800-259-0470**	212-351-2000	266
Russell Sage College 651st St *Admissions	Troy	NY	12180	**888-837-9724***	518-244-2217	166
Russell Standard Corp 285 Kappa Dr Ste 300 *General	Pittsburgh	PA	15238	**800-323-3053***		46
Russell Stover Candies Inc 4900 Oak St	Kansas City	MO	64112	**800-477-8683**	800-777-4004	296-8
Russian National Tourist Office 224 W 30th St Ste 701	New York	NY	10001	**877-221-7120**	646-473-2233	770
Russin Lumber Corp 21 Leonards Dr	Montgomery	NY	12549	**800-724-0010**	845-457-4000	191-3
Rust College 150 Rust Ave	Holly Springs	MS	38635	**888-886-8492**	662-252-8000	166
Rustler Lodge 10380 East Hwy 210 PO Box 8030	Alta	UT	84092	**888-532-2582**	801-742-2200	665
Rust-Oleum Corp 11 E Hawthorn Pkwy	Vernon Hills	IL	60061	**800-323-3584**	847-367-7700	546
Ruston/Lincoln Chamber of Commerce 2111 N Trenton St	Ruston	LA	71270	**800-392-9032**	318-255-2031	139
Rusty Parrot Lodge & Spa PO Box 1657	Jackson	WY	83001	**800-458-2004**	307-733-2000	665
Rutan Poly Industries Inc 39 Siding Pl	Mahwah	NJ	07430	**800-872-1474**	201-529-1474	297-8
Rutgers Organics Corp 201 Struble Rd	State College	PA	16801	**888-469-2188**	814-238-2424	143
Rutgers the State University of New Jersey *School of Law Camden* 217 N Fifth St	Camden	NJ	08102	**800-466-7561**	856-225-6375	167-1
Rutgers University Press 106 Somerset St 3rd Fl	New Brunswick	NJ	08901	**800-848-6224**	848-445-7762	633-4
Ruth Eckerd Hall 1111 McMullen Booth Rd	Clearwater	FL	33759	**800-875-8682**	727-791-7060	568
Ruth Lilly Medical Library 975 W Walnut St IB 100	Indianapolis	IN	46202	**877-952-1988**	317-274-7182	433-1
Rutherford B Hayes Presidential Ctr Spiegel Grove	Fremont	OH	43420	**800-998-7737**	419-332-2081	433-2
Rutherford Controls Int'l Corp 210 Shearson Crescent	Cambridge	ON	N1T1J6	**800-265-6630**	519-621-7651	349
Rutherford County Chamber of Commerce 501 Memorial Blvd	Murfreesboro	TN	37129	**800-716-7560**	615-278-2326	139
Rutherford County Chamber of Commerce 162 N Main St	Rutherfordton	NC	28139	**866-478-4646**	828-287-3090	139
Rutherford Electric Membership Corp 186 Hudlow Rd PO Box 1569	Forest City	NC	28043	**800-521-0920**	828-245-1621	245
Rutherford Institute PO Box 7482	Charlottesville	VA	22906	**800-225-1791**	434-978-3888	48-8
Rutherford Regional Health System 288 S Ridgecrest Ave	Rutherfordton	NC	28139	**800-542-4225**	828-286-5000	373-3
Rutland Herald PO Box 668	Rutland	VT	05702	**800-498-4296**		528-2
Rutland Plastic Technologies 10021 Rodney St	Pineville	NC	28134	**800-438-5134**	704-553-0046	601-2
Rutland Region Chamber of Commerce 50 Merchants Row	Rutland	VT	05701	**800-756-8880**	802-773-2747	337
Ruttger's Bay Lake Lodge 25039 Tame Fish Lake Rd PO Box 400	Deerwood	MN	56444	**800-450-4545**	218-678-2885	665
RVIA (Recreation Vehicle Industry Assn) 1896 Preston White Dr	Reston	VA	20191	**800-336-0154**	703-620-6003	49-21
RVing Women (RVW) 879 N Plaza Dr Ste B103	Apache Junction	AZ	85120	**888-557-8464**	480-671-6226	48-23
RVM Enterprises Inc 40 Rector St 17th Fl	New York	NY	10006	**800-525-7915**		395
RVW (RVing Women) 879 N Plaza Dr Ste B103	Apache Junction	AZ	85120	**888-557-8464**	480-671-6226	48-23
RW Beckett Corp PO Box 1289	Elyria	OH	44036	**800-645-2876**	440-327-1060	356
RW Sauder Inc 570 Furnace Hills Pk	Lititz	PA	17543	**800-233-0413**	717-626-2074	297-10
RW Screw Products Inc 999 Oberlin Rd SW	Massillon	OH	44647	**866-797-2739**	330-837-9211	617
RW. Lynch Company Inc 2333 San Ramon Vly Blvd	San Ramon	CA	94583	**800-594-8940**	925-837-3877	5
RWDSU 30 E 29th St	New York	NY	10016	**866-781-4430**	212-684-5300	413
RWH Trucking Inc 2970 Old Oakwood Rd	Oakwood	GA	30566	**800-256-8119**		775
RWI (RiskWatch) 1237 N Gulfstream Ave	Sarasota	FL	34236	**800-360-1898**		178-10
RWJUHR (Robert Wood Johnson University Hospital at Rahway) 865 Stone St	Rahway	NJ	07065	**800-443-4605**	732-381-4200	373-3
RWM Casters Co PO Box 668	Gastonia	NC	28053	**800-634-7704**		349
Rx Optical 1700 S Park St	Kalamazoo	MI	49001	**800-792-2737**	269-342-0003	539
Rx Systems Inc 121 Point West Blvd	St. Charles	MO	63301	**800-922-9142**		544
RX Worldwide Meetings Inc 3060 Communications Pkwy Ste 200	Plano	TX	75093	**800-562-1713**	214-291-2920	184
Rxcom 101 Jim Wright Fwy S Ste 200	Fort Worth	TX	76108	**800-433-5719**	817-246-6760	237
Rxusa Inc 81 Seaview Blvd	Port Washington	NY	11050	**800-764-3648**	516-467-2500	237
Ryan FireProtection Inc 9740 E 148th St	Noblesville	IN	46060	**800-409-7606**		606
Ryan Herco Products Corp 3010 N San Fernando Blvd	Burbank	CA	91504	**800-848-1141**	818-841-1141	599
Ryantech Cloud Services 60 E Rio Salado Pkwy 9th Fl	Tempe	AZ	85281	**866-804-9040**		225
Rycon Construction Inc 2525 Liberty Ave	Pittsburgh	PA	15222	**800-883-1901**	412-392-2525	186
Rydell Chevrolet Inc 18600 Devonshire St	Northridge	CA	91324	**866-697-5167**		513
Ryder Material Handling 210 Annagem Blvd	Mississauga	ON	L5T2V5	**800-268-2125**		357
Ryder System Inc 11690 NW 105th St *NYSE: R*	Miami	FL	33178	**800-297-9337**	305-500-3726	773
Rydex Funds 805 King Farm Blvd Ste 600 *Cust Svc	Rockville	MD	20850	**800-820-0888***	301-296-5100	524
Ryerson University 350 Victoria St	Toronto	ON	M5B2K3	**866-592-8882**	416-979-5000	780
Ryman Auditorium 116 Fifth Ave N	Nashville	TN	37219	**800-733-6779**	615-458-8700	568
Rymax Marketing Services Inc 19 Chapin Rd Bldg B PO Box 2024	Pine Brook	NJ	07058	**866-796-2911**		
Rynone Mfg Corp PO Box 128	Sayre	PA	18840	**800-839-1654**	570-888-5272	115
Ryobi Technologies Inc 1428 Pearman Dairy Rd	Anderson	SC	29625	**800-525-2579**		350
Ryokan College 11965 Venice Blvd Ste 304	Los Angeles	CA	90066	**866-796-5261**	310-390-7560	166
Rytec Corp 1 Cedar Pkwy	Jackson	WI	53037	**800-628-1909**	262-677-9046	234

S

	City	State	ZIP	Toll-Free	Phone	Class
S & C Electric Co 6601 N Ridge Blvd	Chicago	IL	60626	**800-621-5546**	773-338-1000	725
S & D Coffee Inc 300 Concord Pkwy *Cust Svc	Concord	NC	28027	**800-933-2210***		296-7
S & H Express Inc 400 Mulberry St	York	PA	17403	**800-637-9782**	717-848-5015	447
S & M Machine Service Inc 109 E Highland Dr	Oconto Falls	WI	54154	**800-323-1579**	920-846-8130	453
S & M Moving Systems Inc 12128 Burke St	Santa Fe Springs	CA	90670	**800-528-4561**	562-567-2100	516
S & ME Inc 3201 Spring Forest Rd *Cust Svc	Raleigh	NC	27616	**800-849-2517***	919-872-2660	192
S & s Industrial Equipment & Supply Company Inc 7 Chelten Way	Trenton	NJ	08638	**800-282-3506**	609-695-3800	357
S & S Technology 10625 Telge Rd	Houston	TX	77095	**800-231-1747**	281-815-1300	381
S & S Tire 1475 Jingle Bell Ln	Lexington	KY	40509	**800-685-6794**	859-252-0151	54
S & S Transport Inc PO Box 12579	Grand Forks	ND	58208	**800-726-8022**		775
S & S Worldwide Inc 75 Mill St *Orders	Colchester	CT	06415	**800-243-9232***	860-537-3451	457
S & S X-Ray Products Inc 10625 Telge Rd	Houston	TX	77095	**800-231-1747**	281-815-1300	693
S Abraham & Sons Inc (SAS) 4001 3 Mile Rd NW PO Box 1768 *General	Grand Rapids	MI	49534	**800-477-5455***	616-453-6358	297-8
S Freedman & Sons Inc 3322 Pennsy Dr	Landover	MD	20785	**800-545-7277**	301-322-5000	555
S K C Communication Products Inc 8320 Hedge Ln Terr	Shawnee Mission	KS	66227	**800-882-7779**	913-422-4222	246
S Parker Hardware Manufacturing Corp PO Box 9882	Englewood	NJ	07631	**800-772-7537**	201-569-1600	349
S R C Corp PO Box 30676	Salt Lake City	UT	84130	**800-888-4545**	801-268-4500	276
S R Snodgrass AC 2009 Mackenzie Way Ste 340	Cranberry Township	PA	16066	**800-580-7738**	724-934-0344	2
SA (Sexaholics Anonymous) PO Box 3565	Brentwood	TN	37024	**866-424-8777**	615-370-6062	48-21
SA Comunale Company Inc 2900 Newpark Dr	Barberton	OH	44203	**800-776-7181**	330-706-3040	189-13

Alphabetical Section

		Toll-Free	Phone	Class

SA Day Mfg Co Inc
1489 Niagara St .... Buffalo NY 14213 — **800-747-0030** — 716-881-3030 — 145

SA Recycling LLC
2411 N Glassell St .... Orange CA 92865 — **800-468-7272** — 714-637-4913 — 682

SA Scientific Ltd
4919 Golden Quail .... San Antonio TX 78240 — **800-272-2710** — 210-699-8800

SAA (Society of American Archivists)
17 North State St Ste 1425 .... Chicago IL 60602 — **866-722-7858** — 312-606-0722 — 48-4

SAA (Sex Addicts Anonymous)
PO Box 70949 .... Houston TX 77270 — **800-477-8191** — 713-869-4902 — 48-21

SAA (Society for American Archaeology)
900 Second St NE Ste 12 .... Washington DC 20002 — **800-759-5219** — 202-789-8200 — 49-5

Saba Software Inc
2400 Bridge Pkwy .... Redwood Shores CA 94065 — **877-722-2101** — 650-581-2500 — 178-3
TSX: SABA

Sabert Corp
2288 Main St Ext .... Sayreville NJ 08872 — **800-722-3781** — 544

Sabian Ltd
219 Main St .... Meductic NB E6H2L5 — **800-817-2242** — 506-272-2019 — 523

Sabine County
Chamber Of Commerce
1555 Worth St PO Box 717 ...... Hemphill TX 75948 — **800-986-5336** — 409-787-2732 — 337

Sablan Gregorio (Rep D - MP)
2411 Rayburn House Office Bldg
.... Washington DC 20515 — **877-446-3465** — 202-225-2646 — 341-1

Sable Systems International
3840 N Commerce St ...... North Las Vegas NV 89032 — **866-217-6760** — 800-330-0465 — 201

Sabra Dipping Co LLC
2420 49th St .... Astoria NY 11103 — **888-957-2272** — 296-37

Sabre Companies LLC, The
1891 New Scotland Rd .... Slingerlands NY 12159 — **800-349-2799** — 518-514-1572 — 192

Sabre Industries Inc
8653 E Hwy 67 .... Alvarado TX 76009 — **866-254-3707** — 817-852-1700 — 261

Sabre Solution, The
200 E 31st St .... Savannah GA 31401 — **888-494-7200** — 912-355-7200 — 180

SABRE Strategic Partners
5025 Orbitor Dr Bldg 3
Ste 300 .... Mississauga ON L4W4Y5 — **800-314-3346** — 905-206-0900 — 390-2

SAC (Speech-Language and Audiology Canada)
1 Nicholas St Ste 1000 .... Ottawa ON K1N7B7 — **800-259-8519** — 613-567-9968 — 48-1

SAC (Smith Affiliated Capital)
800 Third Ave 12th Fl .... New York NY 10022 — **888-387-3298** — 212-644-9440 — 402

Sac & Fox Casino Inc
1322 US Hwy 75 .... Powhattan KS 66527 — **800-990-2946**

SAC Federal Credit Union (SAFCU)
11515 S 39th St .... Bellevue NE 68123 — **800-228-0392** — 402-292-8000 — 219

Sac Osage Electric Co-op Inc
4815 E Hwy 54
PO Box 111. .... El Dorado Springs MO 64744 — **800-876-2701** — 417-876-2721 — 245

SACA Technologies LLC
5101 E La Palma Ave
Ste 200 .... Anaheim Hills CA 92807 — **888-603-9033** — 714-777-3222

Sachs Waldman PC
1000 Farmer St .... Detroit MI 48226 — **800-638-6722** — 313-965-3464 — 427

Sackett & Assoc
1055 Lincoln Ave .... San Jose CA 95125 — **800-913-3000** — 408-295-7755 — 427

Sacor Financial Inc
1911 Douglas Blvd 85-126 .... Roseville CA 95661 — **866-556-0231** — 392

Sacramento Bag Manufacturing Co
440 N Pioneer Ave Ste 300. .... Woodland CA 95776 — **800-287-2247** — 530-662-6130 — 67

Sacramento Bee
PO Box 15779 .... Sacramento CA 95852 — **800-284-3233*** — 800-222-7463 — 528-2
*Cust Svc

Sacramento City College
3835 Freeport Blvd .... Sacramento CA 95822 — **800-700-4144** — 916-558-2351 — 162

Sacramento Computer Power Inc
829 W Stadium Ln .... Sacramento CA 95834 — **800-441-1412**

Sacramento Convention & Visitors Bureau
1608 'I' St .... Sacramento CA 95814 — **800-292-2334** — 916-808-7777 — 206

Sacramento Kings
1 Sports Pkwy .... Sacramento CA 95834 — **800-231-8750** — 916-928-0000 — 710-1

Sacramento Public Library
828 'I' St .... Sacramento CA 95814 — **800-561-4636** — 916-264-2700 — 433-3

Sacred Heart Hospital
900 W Clairemont Ave .... Eau Claire WI 54701 — **888-445-4554** — 715-717-4121 — 373-3

Sacred Heart Hospital of Pensacola
5151 N Ninth Ave .... Pensacola FL 32504 — **800-874-1026** — 850-416-7000 — 373-3

Sacred Heart Medical Ctr
1255 Hilyard St .... Eugene OR 97401 — **800-288-7444** — 541-686-7300 — 373-3

Saddleback Educational Publishing
151 Kalmus Drive J-1 .... Costa Mesa CA 92626 — **888-735-2225** — 714-640-5200

Saddleback Memorial Medical Ctr
24451 Health Ctr Dr .... Laguna Hills CA 92653 — **800-553-6537** — 949-837-4500 — 373-3

Sadoff & Rudoy Industries LLP
240 W Arndt St .... Fond du Lac WI 54936 — **877-972-3633*** — 920-921-2070 — 682
*General

SAE (Sigma Alpha Epsilon Fraternity)
1856 Sheridan Rd .... Evanston IL 60201 — **800-233-1856** — 847-424-3031 — 48-16

SAE (Society of Automotive Engineers Inc)
400 Commonwealth Dr .... Warrendale PA 15096 — **877-606-7323** — 724-776-4841 — 49-21

SAE Circuits Colorado Inc
4820 N 63rd St .... Boulder CO 80301 — **800-234-9001** — 303-530-1900 — 621

Saebo Inc
2709 Water Ridge Pkwy
Ste 100 Six LakePointe Plz........... Charlotte NC 28217 — **888-284-5433** — 473

SAEC (South Alabama Electric Co-op)
PO Box 449 .... Troy AL 36081 — **800-556-2060** — 334-566-2060 — 245

SAES Pure Gas Inc
4175 Santa Fe Rd ...... San Luis Obispo CA 93401 — **800-934-3628** — 805-541-9299 — 385

SAF (Santa Fe Municipal Airport)
121 Aviation Dr .... Santa Fe NM 87504 — **866-773-2587** — 505-955-2900 — 27

SAF (Society of American Florists)
1601 Duke St .... Alexandria VA 22314 — **800-336-4743** — 703-836-8700 — 49-4

SAF (Society of American Foresters)
10100 Laureate way .... Bethesda MD 20814 — **866-897-8720** — 301-897-8720 — 48-2

Safari Circuits Inc
411 Washington St .... Otsego MI 49078 — **888-694-7230** — 269-694-9471 — 176

Safari Micro Inc
2185 W Pecos Rd .... Chandler AZ 85224 — **888-446-4770** — 196

Safari West Wildlife Preserve & Tent Camp
3115 Porter Creek Rd .... Santa Rosa CA 95404 — **800-616-2695** — 707-579-2551 — 818

Safariland LLC
13386 International Pkwy .... Jacksonville FL 32218 — **800-347-1200** — 904-741-5400 — 572

Safas Corp
2 Ackerman Ave .... Clifton NJ 07011 — **800-472-6854** — 973-772-5252 — 597

Safco Products Co
9300 West Research Center Rd ... New Hope MN 55428 — **800-328-3020*** — 888-971-6225 — 319-1
*Cust Svc

SAFCU (SAC Federal Credit Union)
11515 S 39th St .... Bellevue NE 68123 — **800-228-0392** — 402-292-8000 — 219

Safe & Civil Schools
2451 Willamette St .... Eugene OR 97405 — **800-323-8819** — 541-345-1442 — 242

Safe Auto Insurance Co
4 Easton Oval PO Box 182109 .... Columbus OH 43219 — **800-723-3288** — 614-231-0200 — 390-4

SAFE Credit Union
3720 Madison Ave ...... North Highlands CA 95660 — **800-733-7233** — 916-979-7233 — 219

Safe Federal Credit Union
201 N 12th St .... West Columbia SC 29169 — **800-763-8600**

Safe Home Security Inc
1125 Middle St Ste 201 .... Middletown CT 06457 — **800-833-3211**

Safeamerica Credit Union
6001 Gibraltar Dr .... Pleasanton CA 94588 — **800-972-0999** — 925-734-4111 — 219

Safeguard Business Systems Inc
8585 N Stemmons Fwy Ste 600 N .... Dallas TX 75247 — **800-523-2422** — 855-778-3124 — 142

Safeguard Chemical Corp
411 Wales Ave .... Bronx NY 10454 — **800-536-3170** — 718-585-3170 — 280

SafeGuard Health Enterprises Inc
95 Enterprise Ste 100 .... Aliso Viejo CA 92656 — **800-880-1800** — 949-425-4300 — 390-3

Safeguard Products Inc
2710 Division Hwy .... New Holland PA 17557 — **800-433-1819** — 717-354-4586 — 237

Safeguard Properties Inc
7887 Safeguard Cir .... Valley View OH 44125 — **800-852-8306** — 216-520-1334 — 507

Safeguard Security & Communications Inc
8454 N 90th St .... Scottsdale AZ 85258 — **800-426-6060** — 480-609-6200 — 689

Safelite Group Inc
2400 Farmers Dr .... Columbus OH 43235 — **877-664-8931** — 62-2

Safetec of America Inc
887 Kensington Ave .... Buffalo NY 14215 — **800-456-7077** — 716-895-1822 — 151

Safe-T-Gard Corp
4975 Miller St Unit B .... Wheat Ridge CO 80033 — **800-356-9026*** — 303-763-8900 — 572
*Cust Svc

Safety Analysis & Forensic Engineering
5665 Hollister Ave .... Goleta CA 93117 — **800-426-7866** — 805-964-0676 — 664

Safety Components International Inc
40 Emery St .... Greenville SC 29605 — **800-896-6926** — 864-240-2600 — 674

Safety Harbor Resort & Spa
105 North Bayshore Dr .... Safety Harbor FL 34695 — **888-237-8772** — 665

Safety Products Inc
3517 Craftsman Blvd .... Lakeland FL 33803 — **800-248-6860** — 863-665-3601 — 675

Safety Seal Piston Ring Co
4000 Airport Rd .... Marshall TX 75672 — **800-962-3631*** — 903-938-9241 — 128
*Sales

Safety Services Co
2626 S Roosevelt St .... Tempe AZ 85282 — **877-894-2566*** — 877-754-9578 — 760
*Cust Svc

Safety Speed Cut Mfg Co Inc
13943 Lincoln St NE .... Ham Lake MN 55304 — **800-772-2327** — 763-755-1600 — 816

Safety Supply South Inc
100 Centrum Dr .... Irmo SC 29063 — **800-522-8344*** — 675
*Cust Svc

Safety Technology International Inc
2306 Airport Rd .... Waterford MI 48327 — **800-888-4784** — 248-673-9898 — 604

Safety Training Seminars
598 Vermont St .... San Francisco CA 94107 — **800-470-9026** — 415-437-1600 — 138

Safety-Kleen Corp
2600 N Central Expwy Ste 400 .... Richardson TX 75080 — **800-669-5740** — 972-265-2000 — 663

Safeware Inc
3200 HubbaRd Rd .... Landover MD 20785 — **800-331-6707*** — 301-683-1234 — 675
*Cust Svc

Safeway Foods Inc
MS 10501 PO Box 29093......... Phoenix AZ 85038 — **877-723-3929**

Safeway Insurance Group
790 Pasquinelli Dr .... Westmont IL 60559 — **800-273-0300** — 630-887-8300 — 390-4

Safeway Sign Co
9875 Yucca Rd .... Adelanto CA 92301 — **800-637-7233** — 697

SAFH (Sutter Auburn Faith Community Hospital)
11815 Education Sty .... Auburn CA 95602 — **800-478-8837** — 530-888-4500 — 373-3

Saf-T-Cab Inc
PO Box 2587 .... Fresno CA 93745 — **800-344-7491** — 559-268-5541 — 513

Saf-T-Gard International Inc
205 Huehl Rd .... Northbrook IL 60062 — **800-548-4273** — 847-291-1600 — 675

SAG (Screen Actors Guild)
5757 Wilshire Blvd .... Los Angeles CA 90036 — **800-724-0767** — 323-954-1600 — 413

Sagamore Health Network
11555 N Meridian St Ste 600.......... Carmel IN 46032 — **800-364-3469** — 317-573-2886 — 390-3

Sagamore Insurance Co
111 Congressional Blvd Ste 500 .... Carmel IN 46032 — **800-317-9402** — 390-4

Sagamore, The
110 Sagamore Rd .... Bolton Landing NY 12814 — **866-384-1944** — 518-644-9400 — 665

Sage 271 17th St NW .... Atlanta GA 30363 — **800-368-2405** — 866-996-7243 — 178-1

Sage College of Albany
140 New Scotland Ave .... Albany NY 12208 — **888-837-9724*** — 518-292-1730 — 166
*Admissions

Sage Microsystems Inc
18 N Village Ave .... Exton PA 19341 — **800-724-7400** — 610-524-1300 — 177

Sage Publications Inc
2455 Teller Rd .... Thousand Oaks CA 91320 — **800-818-7243** — 805-499-9774 — 633-2

Sagebrush Steakhouse
129 Fast Ln .... Mooresville NC 28117 — **877-704-5939** — 704-660-5939 — 666

SagePoint Financial Inc
2800 N Central Ave Ste 2100 .... Phoenix AZ 85004 — **800-552-3319** — 686

Sager Electronics Inc
19 Lorena Dr .... Middleboro MA 02346 — **800-724-3780** — 508-947-8888 — 246

Sager's Seafood Plus Inc
4802 Bridal Wreath Dr .... Richmond TX 77406 — **800-929-3474** — 297-5

SageRider Inc
12950 S Kirkwood Ste 160 .... Stafford TX 77477 — **877-219-4730**

Name / Address	City	State	ZIP	Toll-Free	Phone	Class
Sagestone Spa & Salon						
Red Mountain Resort						
1275 East Red Mtn Cir	Ivins	UT	84738	**877-246-4453**	435-673-4905	702
Saginaw Chippewa Tribal College						
2274 Enterprise Dr	Mount Pleasant	MI	48858	**800-225-8172**	989-775-4123	165
Saginaw Control & Engineering Inc						
95 Midland Rd	Saginaw	MI	48638	**800-234-6871**	989-799-6871	811
Saginaw News						
203 S Washington Ave	Saginaw	MI	48607	**877-611-6397**	989-752-7171	528-2
Saginaw Pipe Company Inc						
1980 Hwy 31 S PO Box 8	Saginaw	AL	35137	**800-433-1374**	205-664-3670	490
Saginaw Valley State University						
7400 Bay Rd	University Center	MI	48710	**800-968-9500**	989-964-4200	166
Saginaw Valley State University Zahnow Library						
7400 Bay Rd	University Center	MI	48710	**800-968-9500**	989-964-4240	433-6
Saguaro Lake Ranch						
13020 Bush Hwy	Mesa	AZ	85215	**800-868-5617**	480-984-2194	665
Saguaro Resources Ltd						
3000 500 - Fourth Ave SW	Calgary	AB	T2P2V6	**855-835-4434**	403-453-3040	532
Saguenay-Lac-Saint-Jean Integrated Health & Social Services Ctr						
930 Jacques-Cartier St E	Chicoutimi	QC	G7H7K9	**800-370-4980**	418-545-4980	373-2
Sahlen Packing Company Inc						
318 Howard St	Buffalo	NY	14206	**800-466-8165**	716-852-8677	296-26
Sahouri Insurance						
8200 Grnsburg Dr Ste 1550	Mclean	VA	22102	**855-242-6660**	703-883-0500	389
SAI Systems International Inc						
5 Research Dr	Shelton	CT	06484	**877-724-4748**	203-929-0790	
SAIC Inc (Science Application International Corp Inc)						
1710 SAIC Dr	McLean	VA	22102	**866-400-7242**	866-955-7242	178-5
SAIL Magazine						
10 Bokum Rd	Essex	CT	06426	**800-745-7245**	860-767-3200	455-4
Saint Agnes HealthCare						
900 S Caton Ave	Baltimore	MD	21229	**800-875-8750**	410-368-6000	373-3
Saint Alexius Hospital						
Broadway Campus						
3933 S Broadway	Saint Louis	MO	63118	**800-245-1431**	314-865-7000	373-3
Saint Alphonsus Regional Medical Ctr						
1055 N Curtis Rd	Boise	ID	83706	**877-401-3627**	208-367-2121	373-3
Saint Ambrose University						
518 W Locust St	Davenport	IA	52803	**800-383-2627***	563-333-6000	166
*Admissions						
Saint Andrew's College						
15800 Yonge St	Aurora	ON	L4G3H7	**877-378-1899**	905-727-3178	618
Saint Anne's Hospital						
795 Middle St	Fall River	MA	02721	**800-488-5959**	508-674-5600	373-3
Saint Anselm College						
100 St Anselm Dr	Manchester	NH	03102	**888-426-7356**	603-641-7000	166
Saint Anthony College of Nursing Health Sciences Center						
5658 E State St	Rockford	IL	61108	**800-977-8449**	815-282-7900	166
Saint Anthony's Hospice						
2410 S Green St	Henderson	KY	42420	**866-380-2326**	270-826-2326	370
Saint Anthony's Medical Ctr						
10010 Kennerly Rd	Saint Louis	MO	63128	**800-554-9550**	314-525-1000	373-3
Saint Augustine's College						
1315 Oakwood Ave	Raleigh	NC	27610	**800-948-1126***	919-516-4000	166
*Admissions						
Saint Barnabas Medical Ctr						
94 Old Short Hills Rd	West Orange	NJ	07052	**888-724-7123**	973-322-5000	373-3
Saint Bernard State Park						
501 St Bernard Pkwy	Braithwaite	LA	70040	**888-677-7823**	504-682-2101	561
Saint Clair County Library System						
210 McMorran Blvd	Port Huron	MI	48060	**877-987-7323**	810-987-7323	433-3
Saint Cloud Area Convention & Visitors Bureau						
1411 W St Germain St						
Ste 104	Saint Cloud	MN	56301	**800-264-2940**	320-251-4170	206
Saint Cloud Times						
3000 Seventh St N	Saint Cloud	MN	56303	**877-424-4921**	320-255-8700	528-2
Saint Cloud/Greater Osceola Chamber of Commerce						
1200 New York Ave	Saint Cloud	FL	34769	**800-000-0000**	407-892-3671	139
Saint Croix Electric Cooperative						
1925 Ridgeway St PO Box 160	Hammond	WI	54015	**800-924-3407**	715-796-7000	245
Saint Croix Press Inc						
1185 S Knowles Ave	New Richmond	WI	54017	**800-826-6622**	715-246-5811	633-9
Saint Croix State Park						
30065 St Croix Pk Rd	Hinckley	MN	55037	**888-646-6367**	320-384-6591	561
Saint Elizabeth Hospital						
1506 S Oneida St	Appleton	WI	54915	**800-223-7332**	920-738-2000	373-3
Saint Francis Hospital & Medical Ctr						
114 Woodland St	Hartford	CT	06105	**800-993-4312**	860-714-4000	373-3
Saint Francis Medical Ctr						
211 Saint Francis Dr	Cape Girardeau	MO	63703	**888-216-3293**	573-331-3000	373-3
Saint Francis Xavier University						
PO Box 5000	Antigonish	NS	B2G2W5	**877-867-7839***	902-863-3300	780
*Admissions						
Saint Gregory's University						
1900 W MacArthur St	Shawnee	OK	74804	**888-784-7347***	405-878-5100	166
*Admissions						
Saint James Mercy Hospital						
411 Canisteo St	Hornell	NY	14843	**800-346-2211**	607-324-8000	373-3
Saint Joe State Park						
2800 Pimville Rd	Park Hills	MO	63601	**877-422-6766**	573-431-1069	
Saint John's Hospital						
800 E Carpenter St	Springfield	IL	62769	**855-228-4438**	217-544-6464	373-3
Saint John's Northwestern Military Academy						
1101 Genesee St	Delafield	WI	53018	**800-752-2338**		618
Saint John's Preparatory School						
2280 Watertower Rd						
PO Box 4000	Collegeville	MN	56321	**800-525-7737**	320-363-3315	618
Saint John's University						
8000 Utopia Pkwy	Queens	NY	11439	**888-978-5646**	718-990-2000	166
Saint John's University Alcuin Library						
2835 Abbey Plz	Collegeville	MN	56321	**800-544-1489**	320-363-2122	433-6
Saint Joseph Area Chamber of Commerce						
3003 Frederick Ave	Saint Joseph	MO	64506	**800-748-7856**	816-232-4461	139
Saint Joseph Convention & Visitors Bureau						
911 Frederick Ave	Saint Joseph	MO	64501	**800-785-0360**	816-233-6688	206
Saint Joseph Hospital						
700 Broadway	Fort Wayne	IN	46802	**800-258-0974**	260-425-3000	373-3
Saint Joseph Medical Ctr						
2500 Bernville Rd	Reading	PA	19605	**800-969-5007**	610-378-2000	373-3
Saint Joseph Mercy Ann Arbor						
5301 McAuley Dr	Ypsilanti	MI	48197	**866-522-8268**	734-712-3456	373-3
Saint Joseph Mercy Oakland						
44405 Woodward Ave	Pontiac	MI	48341	**800-396-1313**	248-858-3000	373-3
Saint Joseph Regional Medical Ctr						
415 Sixth St	Lewiston	ID	83501	**800-678-2511**	208-743-2511	373-3
Saint Joseph Regional Medical Ctr Mishawaka						
5215 Holy Cross Pkwy	Mishawaka	IN	46545	**800-274-1314**	574-335-5000	373-3
Saint Joseph's College of Maine						
278 Whites Bridge Rd	Standish	ME	04084	**800-338-7057***	207-893-7746	166
*Admissions						
Saint Joseph's Healthcare Hamilton						
50 Charlton Ave E	Hamilton	ON	L8N4A6	**800-461-2156**	905-522-1155	373-2
Saint Joseph's Hospital						
555 E Market St	Elmira	NY	14901	**800-952-2662**	607-733-6541	373-3
Saint Joseph's Hospital Health Ctr						
301 Prospect Ave	Syracuse	NY	13203	**888-785-6371**	315-448-5111	373-3
Saint Joseph's Lifecare Ctr						
99 Wayne Gretzky Pkwy	Brantford	ON	N3S6T6	**888-699-7817**	519-751-7096	373-2
Saint Joseph's University						
5600 City Ave	Philadelphia	PA	19131	**888-232-4295**	610-660-1000	166
Saint Jude Children's Research Hospital						
262 Danny Thomas Pl	Memphis	TN	38105	**800-822-6344**	901-595-1040	764
Saint Jude Medical Ctr						
101 E Valencia Mesa Dr	Fullerton	CA	92835	**800-378-4189**	714-871-3280	373-3
Saint Lawrence Seaway Development Corp						
1200 New Jersey Ave SE	Washington	DC	20590	**800-785-2779**	202-366-0091	339-16
Saint Lawrence University						
23 Romoda Dr	Canton	NY	13617	**800-285-1856***	315-229-5261	166
*Admissions						
Saint Leo University						
33701 State Rd 52	Saint Leo	FL	33574	**800-334-5532**	352-588-8200	166
Palatka Ctr						
33701 State Rd 52 PO Box 6665	Saint Leo	FL	33574	**800-334-5532**	352-588-8200	166
Saint Louis Children's Hospital						
1 Children's Pl	Saint Louis	MO	63110	**800-427-4626**	314-454-6000	373-1
Saint Louis Christian College						
1360 Grandview Dr	Florissant	MO	63033	**800-887-7522***	314-837-6777	161
*Admissions						
Saint Louis College of Pharmacy						
4588 Parkview Pl	Saint Louis	MO	63110	**800-278-5267**	314-367-8700	166
Saint Louis County Library (SLCL)						
1640 S Lindbergh Blvd	St. Louis	MO	63131	**800-473-0060**	314-994-3300	433-3
Saint Louis Paper & Box Co						
3843 Garfield Ave	Saint Louis	MO	63113	**800-779-7901**	314-531-7900	555
Saint Louis Public Library (SLPL)						
1301 Olive St	Saint Louis	MO	63103	**800-916-8938**	314-241-2288	433-3
Saint Louis Science Ctr						
5050 Oakland Ave	Saint Louis	MO	63110	**800-456-7572**	314-289-4400	517
Saint Louis Symphony Orchestra						
718 N Grand Blvd	Saint Louis	MO	63103	**800-232-1880**	314-533-2500	569-3
Saint Louis University						
221 N Grand Blvd	Saint Louis	MO	63103	**800-758-3678**	314-977-7288	166
Saint Louis University School of Law						
3700 Lindell Blvd	Saint Louis	MO	63108	**800-758-3678**	314-977-2766	167-1
Saint Louis University School of Medicine						
1 N Grand	Saint Louis	MO	63103	**800-758-3678**		167-2
Saint Louis Zoological Park						
1 Government Dr	Saint Louis	MO	63110	**800-966-8877**	314-781-0900	818
Saint Lucie Medical Ctr						
1800 SE Tiffany Ave	Port Saint Lucie	FL	34952	**800-382-3522**	772-335-4000	373-3
Saint Luke's Home Care & Hospice						
3100 Broadway St Ste 1000	Kansas City	MO	64111	**888-303-7576**	816-756-1160	370
Saint Luke's Hospital & Regional Trauma Ctr						
4401 Wornall Rd	Kansas City	MO	64111	**866-261-5915**	816-932-2000	373-3
Saint Luke's Hospital of New Bedford						
101 Page St	New Bedford	MA	02740	**800-497-1727**	508-997-1515	373-3
Saint Luke's Medical Ctr						
1800 E Van Buren St	Phoenix	AZ	85006	**800-446-2279**	602-251-8100	373-3
Saint Luke's Regional Medical Ctr						
2720 Stone Park Blvd	Sioux City	IA	51104	**800-352-4660**	712-279-3500	373-3
Saint Mark Village						
2655 Nebraska Ave	Palm Harbor	FL	34684	**800-706-4513**	727-785-2580	668
Saint Mark's Hospital						
1200 East 3900 South	Salt Lake City	UT	84124	**800-370-1983**	801-268-7111	373-3
Saint Martin's University						
5300 Pacific Ave SE	Lacey	WA	98503	**800-368-8803***	360-438-4311	166
*Admissions						
Saint Mary Mercy Hospital						
36475 Five-Mile Rd	Livonia	MI	48154	**800-464-7492**	734-655-4800	373-3
Saint Mary's College						
Le Mans Hall	Notre Dame	IN	46556	**800-551-7621***	574-284-4587	166
*Admissions						
Saint Mary's College of California						
1928 St Mary's Rd	Moraga	CA	94556	**800-800-4762***	925-631-4000	166
*Admissions						
Saint Mary's College of Maryland						
47645 College Dr	Saint Marys City	MD	20686	**800-492-7181***	240-895-2000	166
*Admissions						
Saint Mary's Health Care System						
1230 Baxter St	Athens	GA	30606	**800-233-7864**	706-389-3000	373-3
Saint Mary's Hospital						
2251 N Shore Dr	Rhinelander	WI	54501	**800-578-0840***	715-361-2000	373-3
*Cust Svc						
Saint Mary's River State Park						
c/o Pt Lookout State Pk						
11175 Pt Lookout Rd	Scotland	MD	20687	**800-830-3974**	301-872-5688	561
Saint Mary's School						
900 Hillsborough St	Raleigh	NC	27603	**800-948-2557**	919-424-4000	618
Saint Mary's University						
1 Camino Santa Maria	San Antonio	TX	78228	**800-367-7868***	210-436-3126	166
*Admissions						
Saint Mary-Corwin Medical Ctr						
1008 Minnequa Ave	Pueblo	CO	81004	**800-228-4039**	719-557-4000	373-3
Saint Mary-of-the-Woods College						
3301 St Mary Rd						
	Saint Mary Of The Woods	IN	47876	**800-926-7692**	812-535-5106	166

Alphabetical Section

	Toll-Free	Phone	Class
Saint Meinrad Archabbey 200 Hill Dr . . . . Saint Meinrad IN 47577	800-682-0988	812-357-6585	669
Saint Michael's College 1 Winooski Pk . . . . Colchester VT 05439	800-762-8000	802-654-2000	166
Saint Michael's Hospital 30 Bond St . . . . Toronto ON M5B1W8	866-797-0000	416-360-4000	373-2
Saint Michael's Hospital 900 Illinois Ave . . . . Stevens Point WI 54481	800-420-2622	715-346-5000	373-3
Saint Michael's University School (SMUS) 3400 Richmond Rd . . . . Victoria BC V8P4P5	800-661-5199	250-592-2411	618
Saint Michaels Harbour Inn & Marina 101 N Harbor Rd . . . . Saint Michaels MD 21663	800-955-9001	410-745-9001	378
Saint Norbert College 100 Grant St . . . . De Pere WI 54115 *Admissions	800-236-4878*	920-403-3005	166
Saint Paul City Hall 15 W Kellogg Blvd . . . . Saint Paul MN 55102	800-895-1999	651-266-8989	336
Saint Paul College 235 Marshall Ave . . . . Saint Paul MN 55102	800-227-6029	651-846-1600	795
Saint Paul Foundation, The 101 Fifth St E Ste 2400 . . . . Saint Paul MN 55101	800-875-6167	651-224-5463	303
Saint Paul Hotel 350 Market St . . . . Saint Paul MN 55102	800-292-9292	651-292-9292	378
Saint Paul University 223 Main St . . . . Ottawa ON K1S1C4	800-637-6859	613-236-1393	780
Saint Peter's Health Care Services 315 S Manning Blvd . . . . Albany NY 12208	800-432-7876	518-525-1550	373-3
Saint Peter's Seminary 1040 Waterloo St N . . . . London ON N6A3Y1	888-548-9649	519-432-1824	167-3
Saint Regis Aspen Resort, The 315 E Dean St . . . . Aspen CO 81611	888-627-7198	970-920-3300	665
Saint Regis Culvert Inc 202 Morrell St . . . . Charlotte MI 48813	800-527-4604	517-543-3430	693
Saint Regis Hotel 602 Dunsmuir St . . . . Vancouver BC V6B1Y6	800-770-7929	604-681-1135	378
Saint Tammany Parish Tourist & Convention Commission 68099 Hwy 59 . . . . Mandeville LA 70471	800-634-9443	985-892-0520	206
Saint Thomas Aquinas College 125 Rt 340 . . . . Sparkill NY 10976	800-262-3257	845-398-4000	166
Saint Thomas Hospital 4220 HaRding Rd . . . . Nashville TN 37205	800-400-5800	615-222-2111	373-3
Saint Thomas Hospital 444 N Main St . . . . Akron OH 44310	800-237-8662	330-375-3000	373-3
Saint Thomas University 16401 NW 37th Ave . . . . Miami Gardens FL 33054	800-367-9010	305-628-6546	166
Saint Thomas University School of Law 16401 NW 37th Ave . . . . Miami Gardens FL 33054	800-245-4569	305-623-2310	167-1
Saint Vincent College 300 Fraser Purchase Rd . . . . Latrobe PA 15650	800-782-5549	724-532-6600	166
Saint Vincent Hospital-Worcester Medical Ctr 123 Summer St . . . . Worcester MA 01608	877-633-2368	508-363-5000	373-3
Saint Vincent Women's Hospital 8111 Township Line Rd . . . . Indianapolis IN 46260	800-582-8258	317-415-8111	373-7
Saint Vincent's Hospital 810 St Vincent's Dr . . . . Birmingham AL 35205	800-965-7231	205-939-7000	373-3
Saint Vincent's Medical Ctr 2800 Main St . . . . Bridgeport CT 06606	877-255-7847	203-576-6000	373-3
Saint Xavier University 3700 W 103rd St . . . . Chicago IL 60655	800-462-9288	773-298-3000	166
Sakatah Lake State Park 50499 Sakatah Lake State Pk Rd . . . . Waterville MN 56096	888-646-6367	507-698-7850	561
Sakura Finetek USA Inc 1750 W 214th St . . . . Torrance CA 90501	800-725-8723	310-972-7800	418
Sakura Restaurant 1175 W Rt 66 . . . . Flagstaff AZ 86001	888-288-8889		
Saladmaster Inc 4300 Amon Carter Blvd Ste 100 . . . . Arlington TX 76018	800-765-5795	817-633-3555	484
Saleen Automotive Inc 2735 Wardlow Rd . . . . Corona CA 92882	800-888-8945		59
Salem Area Chamber of Commerce 713 E State St . . . . Salem OH 44460	800-644-6292	330-337-3473	139
Salem Chamber of Commerce 265 Essex St . . . . Salem MA 01970	800-392-6100	978-744-0004	139
Salem College 601 S Church St . . . . Winston-Salem NC 27101 *Admissions	800-327-2536*	336-721-2600	166
Salem Conference Ctr 200 Commercial St SE . . . . Salem OR 97301 *Sales	877-589-1700*	503-589-1700	205
Salem Convention & Visitors Assn 181 High St NE . . . . Salem OR 97301	800-874-7012	503-581-4325	206
Salem Five & Savings Bank 210 Essex St . . . . Salem MA 01970 *Cust Svc	800-850-5000*	978-745-5555	70
Salem Hospital 665 Winter St SE . . . . Salem OR 97301	800-876-1718		373-3
Salem International University 223 West Main St . . . . Salem WV 26426	800-283-4562	304-326-1109	166
Salem Tools Inc 1602 Midland Rd . . . . Salem VA 24153	800-390-4348		385
Salem Veterans Affairs Medical Ctr 1970 Roanoke Blvd . . . . Salem VA 24153	888-982-2463	540-982-2463	373-8
Salem Witch Museum 19 1/2 Washington Sq N . . . . Salem MA 01970	800-392-6100	978-744-1692	517
Salem-Keizer Public Schools 2450 Lancaster Dr NE . . . . Salem OR 97305	877-293-1090	503-399-3000	681
Salem-Republic Rubber Co 475 W California Ave . . . . Sebring OH 44672	800-686-4199	877-425-5079	369
Sales Benchmark Index 2021 McKinney Ave Ste 550 . . . . Dallas TX 75201	888-556-7338		5
Sales Concepts Inc 610 Hembree Pkwy . . . . Roswell GA 30076	800-229-2328	678-624-9229	461
Sales Leader 2222 Sedwick Dr . . . . Durham NC 27713	800-223-8720		527-10
Sales Readiness Group Inc 8015 SE 28th St Ste 200 . . . . Mercer Island WA 98040	800-490-0715	206-905-8756	195
SalesforceCom Foundation The Landmark @ One Market Ste 300 . . . . San Francisco CA 94105	800-667-6389		305
Salesnet 6340 Sugarloaf Pkwy Ste 200 . . . . Duluth GA 30097	866-732-8632		39
Salice America Inc 2123 Crown Centre Dr . . . . Charlotte NC 28227	800-222-9652	704-841-7810	349
Salin Bank 8455 Keystone Xing . . . . Indianapolis IN 46240	800-320-7536	317-452-8000	681
Salina Area Chamber of Commerce 120 W Ash St . . . . Salina KS 67401	877-725-4625	785-827-9301	139
Salina Journal PO Box 740 . . . . Salina KS 67402	800-827-6363	785-823-6363	528-2
Salina Public Library 301 W Elm St . . . . Salina KS 67401	800-362-2642	785-825-4624	433-3
Salina Vortex Corp 1725 Vortex Ave . . . . Salina KS 67401	888-829-7821		
Saline County 200 N Main St Ste 117 . . . . Benton AR 72015	800-438-6233	501-303-5630	337
Salisbury Bancorp Inc 5 Bissell St PO Box 1868 . . . . Lakeville CT 06039 NASDAQ: SAL	800-222-9801	860-435-9801	359-2
Salisbury University 1200 Camden Ave . . . . Salisbury MD 21801	888-543-0148	410-543-6000	166
Salisbury University Blackwell Library 1101 Camden Ave . . . . Salisbury MD 21801	888-543-0148	410-543-6130	433-6
Salish Kootenai College PO Box 70 . . . . Pablo MT 59855	877-752-6553	406-275-4800	165
Salish Lodge & Spa 6501 Railroad Ave DE . . . . Snoqualmie WA 98065	800-272-5474	425-888-2556	665
Salishan Lodge & Golf Resort PO Box 118 . . . . Gleneden Beach OR 97388	800-452-2300		665
Salit Steel Ltd 7771 Stanley Ave . . . . Niagara Falls ON L2E6V6	800-263-7110	905-354-5691	490
Salix Pharmaceuticals Inc 8510 Colonnade Ctr Dr . . . . Raleigh NC 27615	800-508-0024	919-862-1000	578
Sallie Mae 12061 Bluemont Way . . . . Reston VA 20190 *Cust Svc	888-272-5543*	703-810-3000	217
Sally Beauty Company Inc 3001 Colorado Blvd . . . . Denton TX 76210	800-777-5706	940-898-7500	76
Salmon River Electric Co-op Inc 1130 Main St PO Box 384 . . . . Challis ID 83226	877-806-2283	208-879-2283	245
Salon Marrow Dyckman Newman & Broudy LLP 292 Madison Ave . . . . New York NY 10017	888-317-8676		443
Salon Service Group Inc 1520 E Evergreen . . . . Springfield MO 65803	800-933-5733	417-761-7309	77
Salon Services & Supplies Inc 740 SW 34th St . . . . Renton WA 98057	800-251-4247	425-251-8840	77
Salsbury Industries Inc 1010 E 62nd St . . . . Los Angeles CA 90001	800-624-5299	323-846-6700	286
SALT Group, The 1845 Sidney Baker St . . . . Kerrville TX 78028	888-257-1266	830-257-1290	729
Salt Lake City International Airport 776 N Terminal Dr PO Box 145550 . . . . Salt Lake City UT 84116	800-595-2442	801-575-2400	27
Salt Lake Community College Grand Theatre 1575 S State St . . . . Salt Lake City UT 84115	800-524-9400	801-957-3322	568
Salt River Electric Co-op Corp 111 W Brashear Ave . . . . Bardstown KY 40004	800-221-7465	502-348-3931	245
Salt River Project (SRP) 1521 N Project Dr . . . . Tempe AZ 85281	800-258-4777	602-236-5900	782
Salt Springs State Park c/o Lackawanna . . . . . . North Abington Township PA 18414	888-727-2757	570-945-3239	561
Salt Water Sportsman Magazine 460 N Orlando Ave Ste 200 . . . . Winter Park FL 32789	800-759-2127	407-628-4802	455-20
Salter Bus Lines Inc 212 Hudson Ave . . . . Jonesboro LA 71251	800-223-8056	318-259-2522	107
Salter Labs 100 Sycamore Rd . . . . Arvin CA 93203	800-421-0024	661-854-3166	474
Salus Group Benefits Inc 37525 Mound Rd . . . . Sterling Heights MI 48310	866-991-9907		260
Salvatore's Hospitality 6461 Transit Rd . . . . Buffalo NY 14043	877-456-4097	716-635-9000	378
Salve Regina University McKillop Library 100 Ochre Pt Ave . . . . Newport RI 02840	800-388-6139	401-341-2291	433-6
Sam Clar Office Furniture Inc 1221 Diamond Way . . . . Concord CA 94520	800-726-2527		321
Sam Hatfield Realty Inc 4470 Mansford Rd . . . . Winchester TN 37398	866-959-7474	931-968-0500	648
Sam Hausman Meat Packer Inc 4261 Beacon . . . . Corpus Christi TX 78403	800-364-5521	361-883-5521	471
Sam Houston Electric Co-op Inc 1157 E Church St . . . . Livingston TX 77351	800-458-0381	936-327-5711	245
Sam Houston Jones State Park 107 Sutherland Rd . . . . Lake Charles LA 70611	888-677-7264	337-855-2665	561
Sam Houston State University 1903 University Ave . . . . Huntsville TX 77340	866-232-7528	936-294-1111	166
Sam's Town Hotel & Gambling Hall 5111 Boulder Hwy . . . . Las Vegas NV 89122	800-897-8696	702-456-7777	133
Samaritan Hospice 5 Eves Dr Ste 300 . . . . Marlton NJ 08053	800-229-8183	856-596-1600	370
Samaritan Medical Ctr 830 Washington St . . . . Watertown NY 13601	877-888-6138	315-785-4000	373-3
Samarkand, The 2550 Treasure Dr . . . . Santa Barbara CA 93105	800-510-2020	805-687-0701	668
Sambazon 209 Avenida Fabricante Ste 200 . . . . San Clemente CA 92672	877-726-2296		297-7
Samford University 800 Lakeshore Dr . . . . Birmingham AL 35229 *Admissions	800-888-7218*	205-726-3673	166
Samford University Cumberland School of Law 800 Lakeshore Dr . . . . Birmingham AL 35229	800-888-7213	205-726-2011	
SAMHSA (Substance Abuse & Mental Health Services Administr) 1 Choke Cherry Rd . . . . Rockville MD 20857	877-726-4727	240-276-2000	339-9
Sammons Trucking 3665 W Broadway . . . . Missoula MT 59808	800-548-9276	406-728-2600	775

	Toll-Free	Phone	Class
Samoset Resort			
220 Warrenton St .... Rockport ME 04856	800-341-1650	207-594-2511	665
Sampco Inc			
651 W Washington Blvd Ste 300 .... Chicago IL 60661	800-767-0689	312-346-1506	297-9
SAMPE (Society for the Advancement of Material & Process)			
21680 Gateway Center Dr Ste 300 .... Diamond Bar CA 91765	800-562-7360	626-521-9460	49-19
Sampson Community College			
PO Box 318 .... Clinton NC 28329	844-319-3640	910-592-8081	162
Sampson Correctional Institution			
700 NW Blvd Hwy 421N .... Clinton NC 28328	800-368-1985	910-592-2151	213
Sampson Regional Medical Ctr			
607 Beaman St .... Clinton NC 28328	800-827-5312	910-592-8511	373-3
Sampson-Bladen Oil Co Inc			
510 Commerce St PO Box 469 ...... Clinton NC 28329	800-849-4177	910-592-4177	324
SAMS (Society of Accredited Marine Surveyors Inc)			
7855 Argyle Forest Blvd Ste 203 .... Jacksonville FL 32244	800-344-9077	904-384-1494	48-1
Sams Technical Publishing			
9850 E 30th St .... Indianapolis IN 46229 *Cust Svc	800-428-7267*		633-2
Samsill Corp			
5740 Hartman Rd .... Fort Worth TX 76119	800-255-1100	817-536-1906	86
Samson Rope Technologies Inc			
2090 Thornton Rd .... Ferndale WA 98248 *Cust Svc	800-227-7673*	360-384-4669	208
Samson Technologies Inc			
45 Gilpin Ave .... Hauppauge NY 11788	800-372-6766	631-784-2200	511
Samsung Telecommunications America LLP			
1301 E Lookout Dr .... Richardson TX 75082	800-726-7864	972-761-7000	730
Samtec Inc			
520 Park E Blvd PO Box 1147 ...... New Albany IN 47151	800-726-8329	812-944-6733	253
Samuel A Ramirez & Co Inc			
61 Broadway Ste 2924 .... New York NY 10006	800-888-4086		686
Samuel Cabot Inc			
100 Hale St .... Newburyport MA 01950	800-877-8246	978-465-1900	546
Samuel French Inc			
45 W 25th St .... New York NY 10010	866-598-8449	212-206-8990	95
Samuel Merritt College			
370 Hawthorne Ave .... Oakland CA 94609 *Admissions	800-607-6377*	510-869-6576	166
Samuels Diamonds			
9607 Research Blvd Ste 100 Bldg F .... Austin TX 78759	877-388-1836		409
Samy's Camera Inc			
431 S Fairfax Ave .... Los Angeles CA 90036	800-321-4726	323-938-2420	119
San Angelo Chamber of Commerce			
418 W Ave B .... San Angelo TX 76903	800-252-1381	325-655-4136	206
San Angelo Standard Times Inc			
34 W Harris .... San Angelo TX 76901	800-588-1884	325-659-8100	633-8
San Antonio Convention & Visitors Bureau			
203 S St Marys St Ste 200 ...... San Antonio TX 78205	800-447-3372	210-207-6700	206
San Antonio International Airport (SAT)			
9800 Airport Blvd Rm 2041 ..... San Antonio TX 78216	800-237-6639	210-207-3411	27
San Antonio Missions National Historical Park			
2202 Roosevelt Ave .... San Antonio TX 78210	866-945-7920	210-534-8833	560
San Benito County			
450 Fourth St .... Hollister CA 95023	800-503-9230	831-636-4029	337
San Benito Public Library			
401 North Sam Houston Blvd ...... San Benito TX 78586	800-444-1187	956-361-3860	433-3
San Bernard Electric Co-op Inc			
309 W Main St .... Bellville TX 77418	800-364-3171	979-865-3171	245
San Bernardino Area Chamber of Commerce			
PO Box 658 .... San Bernardino CA 92402	800-928-5091	909-885-7515	139
San Bernardino County			
777 E Rialto Ave ...... San Bernardino CA 92415	888-818-8988	909-387-8306	337
San Carlos Hotel			
150 E 50th St .... New York NY 10022	800-722-2012	212-755-1800	378
San Diego Chargers			
4020 Murphy Canyon Rd .... San Diego CA 92123	877-242-7437	858-874-4500	711-2
San Diego Christian College			
200 Riverview Pkwy .... Santee CA 92071	800-676-2242	619-201-8700	166
San Diego City Hall			
202 C St .... San Diego CA 92101	866-470-1308	619-533-4000	336
San Diego Concierge			
4422 Glacier Ave E .... San Diego CA 92120	800-979-9091	619-280-4121	375
San Diego County Credit Union			
6545 Sequence Dr .... San Diego CA 92121	877-732-2848		219
San Diego Daily Transcript			
2131 Third Ave .... San Diego CA 92101	800-697-6397	619-232-4381	528-2
San Diego East County Chamber of Commerce			
201 S Magnolia Ave .... El Cajon CA 92020	800-402-8765	619-440-6161	139
San Diego Eye Bank (SDEB)			
9246 Lightwave Ave Ste 120 ...... San Diego CA 92123	800-393-2265	858-694-0400	269
San Diego Gas & Electric Co			
101 Ash St .... San Diego CA 92101	800-411-7343	619-696-2000	782
San Diego Natural History Museum			
1788 El Prado PO Box 121390 ...... San Diego CA 92101	877-946-7797	619-232-3821	517
San Diego Plastics Inc			
2220 Mckinley Ave .... National City CA 91950	800-925-4855	619-477-4855	599
San Diego Public Library			
820 E St .... San Diego CA 92101	866-470-1308	619-236-5800	433-3
San Diego Supercomputer Ctr (SDSC)			
9500 Gilman Dr .... La Jolla CA 92093	800-451-4515	858-534-5000	664
San Diego Union-Tribune			
350 Camino De La Reina .... San Diego CA 92108	800-244-6397	619-299-3131	528-2
San Diego Zoo Safari Park			
15500 San Pasqual Valley Rd ..... Escondido CA 92027 *Cust Svc	877-363-6237*	760-747-8702	818
San Dimas Chamber of Commerce			
246 E Bonita Ave .... San Dimas CA 91773	800-371-5465	909-592-3818	139
San Francisco Chronicle			
901 Mission St ...... San Francisco CA 94103	866-732-4766	415-777-1111	528-2
San Francisco Conservatory of Music			
50 Oak St ...... San Francisco CA 94102	800-999-8219	415-864-7326	166
San Francisco Federal Credit Union			
770 Golden Gate Ave ...... San Francisco CA 94102	800-852-7598	415-775-5377	219
San Francisco International Airport			
PO Box 8097 ...... San Francisco CA 94128	800-435-9736	650-821-8211	27
San Francisco Magazine			
243 Vallejo St ...... San Francisco CA 94111	866-736-2499	404-443-1180	455-22
San Francisco Music Box Co			
5370 W 95th St ...... Prairie Village KS 66207	800-227-2190		327
San Francisco Opera			
301 Van Ness Ave ...... San Francisco CA 94102	800-308-2898	415-861-4008	569-2
San Francisco Theological Seminary			
105 Seminary Rd .... San Anselmo CA 94960	800-447-8820	415-451-2800	167-3
San Francisco Travel Assn			
201 Third St Ste 900 ...... San Francisco CA 94103	855-847-6272	415-974-6900	206
San Francisco VA Medical Ctr			
4150 Clement St ...... San Francisco CA 94121	877-487-2838	415-221-4810	373-8
San Gabriel Valley Medical Ctr			
438 W Las Tunas Dr .... San Gabriel CA 91776	888-214-3874	626-289-5454	373-3
San Isabel Electric inc			
781 E Industrial Blvd .... Pueblo West CO 81007	800-279-7432	719-547-2160	245
San Jamar Inc			
555 Koopman Ln .... Elkhorn WI 53121	800-248-9826	262-723-6133	14
San Joaquin Delta College			
5151 Pacific Ave .... Stockton CA 95207	800-835-4611	209-954-5151	162
San Jose Convention & Visitors Bureau			
408 Almaden Blvd .... San Jose CA 95110	800-726-5673		206
San Jose Convention Ctr			
408 Almaden Blvd .... San Jose CA 95110	800-726-5673	408-792-4511	205
San Jose Ctr for the Performing Arts			
255 S Almaden Blvd .... San Jose CA 95113	800-726-5673	408-288-2800	568
San Jose Original Joe's			
301 S First St .... San Jose CA 95113	888-841-7030	408-292-7030	
San Jose Public Library			
150 E San Fernando St .... San Jose CA 95113	800-735-2929	408-808-2000	433-3
San Juan Airlines Co			
4167 Mitchell Way .... Bellingham WA 98226	800-874-4434		13
San Juan College			
4601 College Blvd .... Farmington NM 87402	866-426-1233	505-326-3311	162
San Juan County			
350 Ct St 2nd Fl ....Friday Harbor WA 98250	800-762-3716	360-378-2163	337
San Luis Obispo Chamber of Commerce			
1039 Chorro St .... San Luis Obispo CA 93401	800-634-1414	805-781-2777	139
San Luis Obispo County			
1055 Monterey St .... San Luis Obispo CA 93408	800-834-4636	805-781-5000	337
San Luis Resort Spa & Conference Ctr, The			
5222 Seawall Blvd .... Galveston Island TX 77551 *Cust Svc	800-445-0090*	409-744-1500	665
San Luis Valley Rural Electric Co-op			
3625 US Hwy 160 W .... Monte Vista CO 81144	800-332-7634	719-852-3538	245
San Manuel Indian Bingo & Casino			
777 San Manuel Blvd .... Highland CA 92346	800-359-2464		133
San Marcos Academy			
2801 Ranch Rd 12 .... San Marcos TX 78666 *Admissions	800-428-5120*	512-353-2400	618
San Mateo County Convention & Visitors Bureau			
111 Anza Blvd Ste 410 .... Burlingame CA 94010	800-288-4748	650-348-7600	206
San Mateo County Times			
4 N Second St Ste 800 .... San Jose CA 95113	800-870-6397	408-920-5000	528-2
San Mateo County Transit District			
1250 San Carlos Ave PO Box 3006 .... San Carlos CA 94070	800-660-4287	650-508-6200	466
San Miguel Power Assn Inc			
170 W Tenth Ave .... Nucla CO 81424	800-864-7256	970-864-7311	245
San Patricio Electric Co-op Inc			
402 E Sinton St .... Sinton TX 78387	888-740-2220	361-364-2220	245
San Sebastian Winery			
157 King St ....Saint Augustine FL 32084	888-352-9463	904-826-1594	50-7
Sanctuary Beach Resort Monterey Bay			
3295 Dunes Rd ....Marina CA 93933	855-693-6583	831-883-9478	703
Sanctuary on Camelback Mountain			
5700 E McDonald Dr .... Paradise Valley AZ 85253	855-245-2051	855-421-3522	665
Sand Dunes Resort Hotel			
201 74th Ave N ...... Myrtle Beach SC 29572	800-726-3783		665
Sand Mountain Electric Co-op			
402 Main St W ....Rainsville AL 35986	877-843-2512	256-638-2153	245
Sandals Resorts International			
4950 SW 72nd Ave .... Miami FL 33155	888-726-3257	305-284-1300	665
Sandata Technologies Inc			
26 Harbor Park Dr ...... Port Washington NY 11050 *Sales	800-544-7263*	516-484-4400	178-11
Sandelman & Associates			
257 La Paloma Ste 1 .... San Clemente CA 92672	888-897-7881		664
Sanderling Resort & Spa			
1461 Duck Rd .... Duck NC 27949	800-701-4111	855-412-7866	665
Sanders Ford Inc			
1135 Lejeune Blvd .... Jacksonville NC 28540 *General	888-897-8527*	910-455-1911	513
Sanderson-MacLeod Inc			
1199 S Main St PO Box 50 .... Palmer MA 01069	866-522-3481	413-283-3481	103
Sandestin Golf & Beach Resort			
9300 Emerald Coast Pkwy W ...... Sandestin FL 32550	800-277-0800	850-267-8000	665
Sandhills Community College			
3395 Airport Rd .... Pinehurst NC 28374	800-338-3944	910-692-6185	162
Sandhills Publishing			
120 W Harvest Dr .... Lincoln NE 68521	800-331-1978	402-479-2181	633-9
Sandia National Laboratories - New Mexico (SNL)			
1515 Eubank SE .... Albuquerque NM 87123	800-783-5337	505-844-8066	664
Sandia Resort & Casino			
30 Rainbow Rd NE .... Albuquerque NM 87113	800-526-9366	505-796-7500	133
SanDisk Corp			
601 McCarthy Blvd ....Milpitas CA 95035 *NASDAQ: SNDK*	866-726-3475	408-801-1000	288
Sandler O'Neill + Partners LP			
1251 Avenue of the Americas 6th Fl .... New York NY 10020	800-635-6851	212-466-7800	686
Sandler Partners			
1200 Artesia Blvd Ste 305 ...... Hermosa Beach CA 90254	800-825-1055	310-796-1393	224
Sandlin Homes			
5137 Davis Blvd .... Fort Worth TX 76180	800-821-4663	817-281-3509	187
Sandmeyer Steel Co			
10001 Sandmeyer Ln ....Philadelphia PA 19116	800-523-3663	215-464-7100	719
Sandridge Food Corp (SFC)			
133 Commerce Dr .... Medina OH 44256	800-627-2523	330-725-2348	296-33

	Toll-Free	Phone	Class
Sands Casino Resort Bethlehem			
77 Sands Blvd ....Bethlehem PA 18015	**877-726-3777**		378
Sands Expo & Convention Ctr			
201 Sands Ave ....Las Vegas NV 89169	**800-265-2235**	702-733-5556	205
Sands Ocean Club Resort			
9550 Shore Dr ....Myrtle Beach SC 29572	**888-999-8485***		378
*General			
Sands Regency Casino Hotel			
345 N Arlington Ave ....Reno NV 89501	**800-233-4939***	775-348-2200	378
*Resv			
Sandstone Asset Management Inc			
101 6 St SW ....Calgary AB T2P5K7	**866-318-6140**	403-218-6125	524
Sandusky County Convention & Visitor's Bureau (SCCVB)			
712 N St Ste 102 ....Fremont OH 43420	**800-255-8070**	419-332-4470	206
Sandusky Electric Inc			
1513 Sycamore Line ....Sandusky OH 44870	**800-356-1243**	419-625-4915	246
Sandusky Lee Corp			
16125 Widmere Rd PO Box 517 ......Arvin CA 93203	**800-886-8688***	661-854-5551	286
*Cust Svc			
Sandy Sansing Chevrolet			
6200 Pensacola Blvd ....Pensacola FL 32505	**877-776-3459**	850-659-6923	57
Sandy Spring Bancorp Inc			
17801 Georgia Ave ....Olney MD 20832	**800-399-5919**	301-774-6400	359-2
NASDAQ: SASR			
Sanexen Environmental Services Inc			
9935 rue de Chﬁteauneuf Entrance 1			
Ste 200 ....Brossard QC J4Z3V4	**800-263-7870**	450-466-2123	
Sanford Aircraft			
701 Rod Sullivan Rd ....Sanford NC 27330	**800-237-6902**	919-708-5549	63
Sanford Herald, The			
217 E First St ....Sanford FL 32771	**800-955-8770**	407-322-2611	528-2
Sanford-Brown			
1345 Mendota Heights Rd			
..................Mendota Heights MN 55120	**888-247-4238**	651-905-3400	795
Sanford-Brown College			
Boston 126 Newbury St ....Boston MA 02116	**877-809-2444**	617-578-7100	795
Sanibel & Captiva Islands Chamber of Commerce			
1159 Cswy Rd ....Sanibel FL 33957	**800-851-5088**	239-472-1080	139
Sanibel Harbour Marriott Resort & Spa			
17260 Harbour Pt Dr ....Fort Myers FL 33908	**800-767-7777**	239-466-4000	665
Sanibel Inn			
937 E Gulf Dr ....Sanibel FL 33957	**866-565-5480**	239-472-3181	378
SaniServ Inc			
451 E County Line Rd ....Mooresville IN 46158	**800-733-8073**	317-831-7030	298
Sanofi Pasteur Inc			
Discovery Dr ....Swiftwater PA 18370	**800-822-2463***	570-839-7187	85
*Orders			
Sanofi-Aventis Canada			
2905 PI Louis R Renaud ....Laval QC H7V0A3	**800-265-7927**	514-956-6200	85
S-Anon International Family Groups Inc			
PO Box 111242 ....Nashville TN 37222	**800-210-8141**	615-833-3152	48-21
Santa Barbara City College			
721 Cliff Dr ....Santa Barbara CA 93109	**877-232-3919**	805-965-0581	162
Santa Barbara Control Systems			
5375 Overpass Rd ....Santa Barbara CA 93111	**800-621-2279**	805-683-8833	406
Santa Barbara Inn			
901 E Cabrillo Blvd ....Santa Barbara CA 93103	**800-231-0431**	805-966-2285	378
Santa Barbara News-Press Publishing Co			
715 Anacapa St ....Santa Barbara CA 93101	**800-654-3292**	805-564-5200	633-8
Santa Barbara Public Library			
40 E Anapamu St ....Santa Barbara CA 93101	**800-354-9660**	805-962-7653	433-3
Santa Barbara Speakers Bureau (SBSB)			
500 E Montecito St ....Santa Barbara CA 93103	**800-676-1266**	805-966-9222	
Santa Barbara Visitors Bureau & Film Commission			
1601 Anacapa St ....Santa Barbara CA 93101	**800-676-1266**	805-966-9222	206
Santa Clara Convention Ctr			
5001 Great America Pkwy ......Santa Clara CA 95054	**800-272-6822**	408-748-7000	205
Santa Clara Convention/Visitors Bureau			
1390 Madison St ....Santa Clara CA 95050	**800-272-6822**	408-244-8244	206
Santa Clara County Library			
14600 Winchester Blvd ....Los Gatos CA 95032	**800-286-1991**	408-293-2326	433-3
Santa Clara Valley Medical Ctr			
751 S Bascom Ave ....San Jose CA 95128	**800-814-4351**	408-885-5000	373-3
Santa Clara Valley Transportation Authority (VTA)			
3331 N First St ....San Jose CA 95134	**800-894-9908**	408-321-2300	466
Santa Cruz Chamber of Commerce			
611 Ocean St Ste 1............Santa Cruz CA 95060	**866-282-5900**	831-457-3713	139
Santa Cruz County Conference & Visitors Council			
303 Water St Ste 100 ....Santa Cruz CA 95060	**800-833-3494**	831-425-1234	206
Santa Cruz Sentinel Inc			
207 Church St ....Santa Cruz CA 95060	**800-952-2335**	831-423-4242	528-3
Santa Fe Convention Ctr			
201 W Marcy St ....Santa Fe NM 87501	**800-777-2489**	505-955-6200	206
Santa Fe Extruders & Printing			
15315 Marquardt Ave ....Santa Fe Springs CA 90670	**800-645-0626**		
Santa Fe Municipal Airport (SAF)			
121 Aviation Dr ....Santa Fe NM 87504	**866-773-2587**	505-955-2900	27
Santa Fe Opera, The			
301 Opera Dr ....Santa Fe NM 87506	**800-280-4654**	505-986-5900	569-2
Santa Fe University of Art & Design			
1600 St Michaels Dr ....Santa Fe NM 87505	**800-456-2673**		166
Santa Maria Inn			
801 S Broadway ....Santa Maria CA 93454	**800-462-4276**	805-928-7777	378
Santa Monica Civic Auditorium			
1855 Main St ....Santa Monica CA 90401	**866-728-3229**	310-458-8551	205
Santa Monica Convention & Visitors Bureau			
1920 Main St Ste B.............Santa Monica CA 90405	**800-544-5319**	310-319-6263	206
Santa Monica Mountains National Recreation Area			
401 W Hillcrest Dr ....Thousand Oaks CA 91360	**888-275-8747**	805-370-2300	560
Santa Rosa County Chamber of Commerce			
5247 Stewart St ....Milton FL 32570	**800-239-8732**	850-623-2339	139
Santander			
PO Box 12646 ....Reading PA 19612	**877-768-2265***		70
*Cust Svc			
Santee Electric Co-op Inc			
424 Sumter Hwy ....Kingstree SC 29556	**800-922-1604**	843-355-6187	245
Santie Oil Co			
126 Larcel Dr ....Sikeston MO 63801	**800-748-7788**	314-436-3569	138

	Toll-Free	Phone	Class
Santillana USA Publishing Co			
2023 NW 84th Ave ....Doral FL 33122	**800-245-8584**	305-591-9522	633-2
Santinelli International Inc			
325 Oser Ave ....Hauppauge NY 11788	**800-644-3343**		452
Santora CPA Group			
220 Continental Dr			
Ste 112 Christiana Executive Campus .....Newark DE 19713	**800-347-0116**	302-737-6200	2
Sapiens International Corp			
4000 CentreGreen Way Ste 150 .....Cary NC 27513	**888-281-1167**	919-405-1500	178-10
NASDAQ: SPNS			
Sapient Corp			
131 Dartmouth St ....Boston MA 02116	**866-796-6860**	617-621-0200	804
Sapp Bros Petroleum Inc			
9915 S 148th St ....Omaha NE 68138	**800-233-4059**	402-895-2202	575
Sapp Bros Truck Stops Inc			
9915 S 148th St ....Omaha NE 68138	**800-233-4059**	402-895-7038	324
Sarah Bush Lincoln Health Ctr (SBLHC)			
1000 Health Ctr Dr PO Box 372 ......Mattoon IL 61938	**800-345-3191**	217-258-2525	373-3
Sarah Lawrence College			
1 Mead Way ....Bronxville NY 10708	**800-888-2858**	914-337-0700	166
Saranac Glove Co			
999 Lombardi Ave ....Green Bay WI 54304	**800-727-2622**	920-435-3737	155-7
Sarasota Herald-Tribune			
1741 Main St ....Sarasota FL 34236	**866-284-7102**	941-953-7755	528-2
Sarasota Jungle Gardens			
3701 Bay Shore Rd ....Sarasota FL 34234	**877-681-6547**	941-355-5305	818
Sarasota Memorial Hospital			
1700 S Tamiami Trl ....Sarasota FL 34239	**800-764-8255**	941-917-9000	373-3
Sarasota Opera			
61 N Pineapple Ave ....Sarasota FL 34236	**866-951-0111**	941-366-8450	569-2
Sarasota Orchestra			
709 N Tamiami Trl ....Sarasota FL 34236	**866-508-0611**	941-953-4252	569-3
Sarasota-Bradenton International Airport			
6000 Airport Cir ....Sarasota FL 34243	**800-711-1712**	941-359-2770	27
Saratoga Convention & Tourism Bureau			
60 Railroad Pl Ste 301 ......Saratoga Springs NY 12866	**855-424-6073**	518-584-1531	206
Saratoga County Chamber of Commerce			
28 Clinton St ....Saratoga Springs NY 12866	**855-765-7873**	518-584-3255	139
Saratoga Eagle Sales & Service Inc			
45 Duplainville Rd ....Saratoga Springs NY 12866	**800-310-5099**	518-581-7377	81-1
Saratoga Gaming & Raceway			
342 Jefferson St			
PO Box 356...............Saratoga Springs NY 12866	**800-727-2990**	518-584-2110	638
Saratoga Hilton			
534 Broadway ....Saratoga Springs NY 12866	**800-445-8667**	518-584-4000	378
Saratoga Honda			
3402 Rt 9 ....Saratoga Springs NY 12866	**888-658-2303**		57
Saratoga Liquor Company Inc			
3215 James Day Ave ....Superior WI 54880	**800-472-6923**	715-394-4487	442
SARCOM Inc AEP Colloids Div			
6299 Rt 9N ....Hadley NY 12835	**800-848-0658**	518-696-9900	146
Sargent & Greenleaf Inc			
1 Security Dr ....Nicholasville KY 40356	**800-826-7652**	859-885-9411	349
Sargent Art Inc			
100 E Diamond Ave ....Hazleton PA 18201	**800-424-3596**		43
Sargent Controls & Aerospace			
5675 W Burlingame Rd ....Tucson AZ 85743	**800-230-0359**	520-744-1000	223
Sargent County			
355 Main St ....Forman ND 58032	**866-634-8387**	701-724-6241	337
Sargent Manufacturing Co			
100 Sargent Dr ....New Haven CT 06511	**800-727-5477**		349
Sargento Foods Inc			
1 Persnickety Pl ....Plymouth WI 53073	**800-243-3737**	920-893-8484	296-5
Sartori			
107 Pleasant View Rd ....Plymouth WI 53073	**800-558-5888***		296-5
*Cust Svc			
SAS (S Abraham & Sons Inc)			
4001 3 Mile Rd NW			
PO Box 1768.................Grand Rapids MI 49534	**800-477-5455***	616-453-6358	297-8
*General			
SAS (Scandinavian Airlines System)			
301 Rt 17 N Ste 500 ....Rutherford NJ 07070	**800-221-2350**	800-437-5807	25
SAS Institute Inc			
100 SAS Campus Dr ....Cary NC 27513	**800-727-0025**	919-677-8000	178-1
Sas Safety Corp			
3031 Gardenia Ave ....Long Beach CA 90807	**800-262-0200**	562-427-2775	475
SAS Shoemakers			
1717 SAS Dr ....San Antonio TX 78224	**877-782-7463**		301
SASCO Electric			
2750 Moore Ave ....Fullerton CA 92833	**800-477-4422**	714-870-0217	189-4
Sashco Inc			
720 S Rochester Ave Ste D..........Ontario CA 91761	**800-600-3232**	909-937-8222	189-6
Saskatchewan Health Research Foundation			
324-111 Research Dr ....Saskatoon SK S7N3R2	**800-975-1699**	306-975-1680	231
Saskatchewan Indian Gaming Authority			
250 - 103 C Packham Ave ....Saskatoon SK S7N4K4	**800-306-6789**	306-477-7777	133
Saskatchewan Roughrider Football Club			
1910 Piffles Taylor Way			
PO Box 1966.......................Regina SK S4P3E1	**888-474-3377**	306-569-2323	711-1
Saskatoon Business College Ltd			
221 Third Ave N ....Saskatoon SK S7K2H7	**800-679-7711**	306-244-6333	162
Saskatoon City Hospital			
701 Queen St ....Saskatoon SK S7K0M7	**855-655-7612**	306-655-8000	373-2
Saskatoon Inn Hotel & Conference Centre			
2002 Airport Dr ....Saskatoon SK S7L6M4	**800-667-8789**	306-242-1440	
Sassy Inc			
2305 Breton Industrial Pk Dr ....Kentwood MI 49508	**800-323-6336**	800-433-9560	64
SAT (San Antonio International Airport)			
9800 Airport Blvd Rm 2041.....San Antonio TX 78216	**800-237-6639**	210-207-3411	27
Satchidananda Ashram Yogaville (SAYVA)			
108 Yogaville Way ....Buckingham VA 23921	**800-858-9642***	434-969-3121	669
*Resv			
Satellite Broadcasting & Communications Assn (SBCA)			
1730 M St NW Ste 600.............Washington DC 20036	**800-541-5981**	202-349-3620	49-14
Satellite Hotel			
411 Lakewood Cir ....Colorado Springs CO 80910	**800-423-8409**	719-596-6800	378
Satellite Industries Inc			
2530 Xenium Ln N ....Minneapolis MN 55441	**800-328-3332**		503

	Toll-Free	Phone	Class
Satellite Logistics Group Inc			
12621 Featherwood Ste 390 . . . . Houston TX 77034	**877-795-7540**	281-902-5500	311
Satellite Management Services Inc			
4529 E Bwy Rd . . . . Phoenix AZ 85040	**800-788-8388**	602-386-4444	224
Satellite Receivers Ltd/Cash Depot			
1740 Cofrin Dr Ste 2 . . . . Green Bay WI 54302	**800-776-8834**	920-432-5777	116
SATISFYD			
47 E Chicago Ave Ste 360 . . . . Naperville IL 60540	**800-562-9557**		196
Satmetrix Systems Inc			
1100 Park Pl Ste 210 . . . . San Mateo CA 94403	**866-943-3760**		177
Sato America Inc			
10350A Nations Ford Rd . . . . Charlotte NC 28273	**888-871-8741**	704-644-1650	173-6
Saturday Evening Post, The			
1100 Waterway Blvd . . . . Indianapolis IN 46202	**800-829-5576**	317-634-1100	455-11
Saturn Fasteners Inc			
425 S Varney St . . . . Burbank CA 91502	**800-947-9414**	818-846-7145	349
Saturn Industries Inc			
157 Union Tpke . . . . Hudson NY 12534	**800-775-1651**	518-828-9956	127
Saturn Systems Inc			
314 W Superior St Ste 1015 . . . . Duluth MN 55802	**888-638-4335**	218-623-7200	177
Saturna Capital Corp			
1300 N State St . . . . Bellingham WA 98225	**888-732-6262**	360-734-9900	400
Saucony Inc			
191 Spring St . . . . Lexington MA 02420	**800-282-6575**		301
Sauder Village			
22611 SR 2 . . . . Archbold OH 43502	**800-590-9755**	419-446-2541	517
Sauder Woodworking Co			
502 Middle St . . . . Archbold OH 43502	**800-523-3987***	419-446-2711	319-2
*Cust Svc			
Sault College			
443 Northern Ave . . . . Sault Sainte Marie ON P6A5L3	**800-461-2260**	705-759-6700	162
Sault Sainte Marie Convention			
225 E Portage Ave . . . . Sault Sainte Marie MI 49783	**800-647-2858**	906-632-3366	206
Saunders Archery Co			
1874 14th Ave PO Box 1707 . . . . Columbus NE 68601	**800-228-1408***	402-564-7176	706
*Cust Svc			
Saunders Manufacturing Co			
65 Nickerson Hill Rd . . . . Readfield ME 04355	**800-341-4674**	207-512-2550	486
Sause Bros			
3710 NW Front Ave . . . . Portland OR 97210	**800-488-4167**	503-222-1811	463
Savage Arms Inc			
100 Springdale Rd . . . . Westfield MA 01085	**800-243-3220**	413-568-7001	284
Savanna Portage State Park			
55626 Lake Pl . . . . McGregor MN 55760	**888-646-6367**	218-426-3271	561
Savannah Area Convention & Visitors Bureau			
101 E Bay St . . . . Savannah GA 31401	**877-728-2662**	912-644-6400	206
Savannah Civic Ctr			
301 W Oglethorp Ave . . . . Savannah GA 31401	**800-337-1101**	912-651-6550	568
Savannah College of Art & Design			
342 Bull St . . . . Savannah GA 31402	**800-869-7223**	912-525-5100	164
Savannah College of Art & Design			
Atlanta			
1600 Peachtree St PO Box 77300 . . . . Atlanta GA 30357	**877-722-3285**	404-253-2700	164
Savannah Distributing Co Inc			
2425 W Gwinnett St . . . . Savannah GA 31415	**800-551-0777***	912-233-1167	81-1
*General			
Savannah Morning News			
1375 Chatham Pkwy . . . . Savannah GA 31405	**800-533-1150**	912-236-9511	528-2
Savant Manufacturing Inc			
2930 Hwy 383 PO Box 520 . . . . Kinder LA 70648	**800-326-6880**	337-738-5896	349
Save America's Forests			
4 Library Ct SE . . . . Washington DC 20003	**800-729-1363**	202-544-9219	48-13
Save the Manatee Club (SMC)			
500 N Maitland Ave . . . . Maitland FL 32751	**800-432-5646**	407-539-0990	48-3
Savers Property & Casualty Insurance Co			
11880 College Blvd			
Ste 500 . . . . Overland Park KS 66210	**800-825-9489**	913-339-5000	
Sawmill Creek Resort			
400 Sawmill Creek Dr . . . . Huron OH 44839	**800-729-6455**	419-433-3800	665
Sawnee Electric Membership Corp			
543 Atlantic Hwy . . . . Cumming GA 30028	**800-635-9131**	770-887-2363	245
Sawyer County			
10610 Main St Ste 10 . . . . Hayward WI 54843	**877-699-4110**	715-634-4866	337
Sawyer Nursery Inc			
5401 Port Sheldon St . . . . Hudsonville MI 49426	**888-378-7800**		292
Saxon Shoes			
11800 W Broad St Ste 2750 . . . . Richmond VA 23233	**800-686-5616***	804-285-3473	301
*General			
Sayers Group LLC			
825 Corporate Woods Pkwy . . . . . Vernon Hills IL 60061	**800-323-5357**		180
Saylor Beall Mfg Company Inc			
400 N Kibbee St PO Box 40 . . . . Saint Johns MI 48879	**800-248-9001**	989-224-2371	172
SAYVA (Satchidananda Ashram Yogaville)			
108 Yogaville Way . . . . Buckingham VA 23921	**800-858-9642***	434-969-3121	669
*Resv			
SB One Bank			
100 Enterprise Dr Ste 700 . . . . Rockaway NJ 07866	**800-511-9900**	973-383-2211	359-2
NASDAQ: SBBX			
SB Whistler & Sons Inc			
PO Box 270 . . . . Medina NY 14103	**800-828-1010**	585-318-4630	752
SBA (Small Business Administration)			
409 Third St SW . . . . Washington DC 20416	**800-827-5722**	202-205-6600	339-19
SBA Communications Corp			
5900 Broken Sound Pkwy NW . . . . . . Boca Raton FL 33487	**800-487-7483**	561-995-7670	170
NASDAQ: SBAC			
SBA Materials Inc			
9430-H San Mateo Blvd NE . . . . Albuquerque NM 87113	**800-498-9608**		
SBAA (Spina Bifida Assn)			
1600 Wilson Blvd Ste 800 . . . . Arlington VA 22209	**800-621-3141**	202-944-3285	48-17
Sbar's Inc			
14 Sbar Blvd . . . . Moorestown NJ 08057	**800-989-7227**	856-234-8220	44
SBC (Southern Baptist Convention)			
901 Commerce St . . . . Nashville TN 37203	**866-722-5433**	615-244-2355	48-20
SBCA (Satellite Broadcasting & Communications Assn)			
1730 M St NW Ste 600 . . . . Washington DC 20036	**800-541-5981**	202-349-3620	49-14
SBCC (South Baldwin Chamber of Commerce)			
112 W Laurel Ave PO Box 1117 . . . . Foley AL 36535	**877-461-3712**	251-943-3291	139
Sbeeg Holdings Licensing LLC			
5900 Wilshire Blvd 30th Fl . . . . Los Angeles CA 90036	**800-411-0305**	323-655-8000	
SBIA (Small Business Investor Alliance)			
1100 H St NW Ste 1200 . . . . Washington DC 20005	**800-471-6153**	202-628-5055	611
SBL (Society of Biblical Literature)			
The Luce Ctr			
825 Houston Mill Rd. . . . . Atlanta GA 30329	**866-727-9955**	404-727-3100	48-20
SBLHC (Sarah Bush Lincoln Health Ctr)			
1000 Health Ctr Dr PO Box 372 . . . . Mattoon IL 61938	**800-345-3191**	217-258-2525	373-3
SBLI (Savings Bank Mutual Life Insurance Company of Mass)			
1 Linscott Rd . . . . Woburn MA 01801	**888-630-5000**		
SBS (Storage Battery Systems Inc)			
N56 W16665 Ridgewood Dr			
. . . . Menomonee Falls WI 53051	**800-554-2243**	262-703-5800	246
SBSB (Santa Barbara Speakers Bureau)			
500 E Montecito St . . . . Santa Barbara CA 93103	**800-676-1266**	805-966-9222	
SBSO (South Bend Symphony Orchestra)			
127 N Michigan St . . . . South Bend IN 46601	**800-537-6415**	574-232-6343	569-3
SCA (Society of Cardiovascular Anesthesiologists)			
8735 W Higgins Rd Ste 300 . . . . Chicago IL 60631	**800-283-6296**	855-658-2828	49-8
SCA (Student Conservation Assn)			
689 River Rd PO Box 550 . . . . Charlestown NH 03603	**888-722-9675**	603-543-1700	48-13
SCAA (Specialty Coffee Assn of America)			
117 W Fourth St Ste 300 . . . . Santa Ana CA 92701	**800-995-9019**	562-624-4100	49-6
Scala Inc			
7 Great Valley Pkwy Ste 300 . . . . Malvern PA 19355	**888-722-5296**	610-363-3350	
Scalamandre Silks Inc			
350 Wireless Blvd . . . . Hauppauge NY 11788	**800-932-4361**	631-467-8800	740-1
Scalar Decisions Inc			
1 Toronto St 3rd Fl . . . . Toronto ON M5C2V6	**866-364-5588**	416-202-0020	177
Scale Auto Magazine			
21027 Crossroads Cir . . . . Waukesha WI 53186	**800-533-6644***	262-796-8776	455-14
*Cust Svc			
ScaleGrid			
2225 E Bayshore Rd . . . . Palo Alto CA 94303	**866-449-2478**		
ScaleMatrix Inc			
5775 Kearny Villa Rd . . . . San Diego CA 92123	**888-349-9994**		
Scales Air Compressor Corp			
110 Voice Rd . . . . Carle Place NY 11514	**877-798-0454**	516-248-9096	172
SCAN (Sports Cardiovascular & Wellness Nutritionists)			
230 Washington Ave Extn Ste 101 . . . Albany NY 12203	**800-249-2875***	518-254-6730	49-8
*General			
SCAN Health Plan			
3800 Kilroy Airport Way			
Ste 100 . . . . Long Beach CA 90806	**800-247-5091**	562-989-5100	351
SCANA Corp			
220 Operation Way . . . . Cayce SC 29033	**800-251-7234**	803-217-9000	359-5
NYSE: SCG			
Scandinavian Airlines System (SAS)			
301 Rt 17 N Ste 500 . . . . Rutherford NJ 07070	**800-221-2350**	800-437-5807	25
Scania USA Inc			
121 Interpark Blvd Ste 601 . . . . San Antonio TX 78216	**800-272-2642**	210-403-0007	513
Scan-Optics Inc			
169 Progress Dr . . . . Manchester CT 06042	**800-543-8681**	860-645-7878	178-8
ScanSource Inc			
6 Logue Ct . . . . Greenville SC 29615	**800-944-2432**	864-288-2432	174
NASDAQ: SCSC			
Scantibodies Laboratory Inc			
9336 Abraham Way . . . . Santee CA 92071	**800-279-9181**	619-258-9300	231
Scantron Corp			
34 Parker . . . . Irvine CA 92618	**800-722-6876**	949-639-7500	173-7
SCB Distributors			
15608 New Century Dr . . . . Gardena CA 90248	**800-729-6423**	310-532-9400	96
SCC Soft Computer Inc			
5400 Tech Data Dr . . . . Clearwater FL 33760	**800-763-8352**	727-789-0100	180
SCCA (Sports Car Club of America)			
6700 SW Topeka Blvd . . . . Topeka KS 66619	**800-770-2055**		48-18
SCCVB (Sandusky County Convention & Visitor's Bureau)			
712 N St Ste 102 . . . . Fremont OH 43420	**800-255-8070**	419-332-4470	206
SCDAA (Sickle Cell Disease Assn of America)			
3700 Koppers St Ste 570 . . . . Baltimore MD 21202	**800-421-8453**	410-528-1555	48-17
Scelzi Equipment Inc			
1030 W Gladstone St . . . . Azusa CA 91702	**800-858-2883**	626-334-0573	513
Scenic Airlines Inc			
1265 Airport Rd . . . . Boulder City NV 89005	**800-634-6801**	702-638-3300	755
Scenic Rivers Energy Co-op			
231 N Sheridan St . . . . Lancaster WI 53813	**800-236-2141**	608-723-2121	245
SCG (Southern Connecticut Gas)			
60 Marsh Hill Rd . . . . Orange CT 06477	**866-268-2887**		782
SC&H Group LLC			
910 Ridgebrook Rd . . . . Sparks MD 21152	**800-832-3008**	410-403-1500	2
Schaefer Brush Manufacturing Company Inc			
1101 S Prairie Ave . . . . Waukesha WI 53186	**800-347-3501**	262-547-3500	582
Schaefer Systems International Inc			
10021 Westlake Dr . . . . Charlotte NC 28241	**800-876-6000**	704-944-4500	199
Schaeffer Mfg Company Inc			
102 Barton St . . . . Saint Louis MO 63104	**800-325-9962***	314-865-4100	537
*Cust Svc			
Schaeffer's Investment Research Inc			
5151 Pfeiffer Rd Ste 250 . . . . Cincinnati OH 45242	**800-448-2080**	513-589-3800	633-9
Schaeffler Group USA Inc			
308 Springhill Farm Rd . . . . Fort Mill SC 29715	**800-361-5841**	803-548-8500	75
Schaff Piano Supply Co			
451 Oakwood Rd . . . . Lake Zurich IL 60047	**800-747-4266**	847-438-4556	523
Scharine Group, The			
4213 N Scharine Rd . . . . Whitewater WI 53190	**800-472-2880**	608-883-2880	186
Schatten Properties Management Company Inc			
1514 S St . . . . Nashville TN 37212	**800-892-1315**	615-329-3011	649
Schatz Bearing Corp			
10 Fairview Ave . . . . Poughkeepsie NY 12601	**800-554-1406**	845-452-6000	75
Schawbel Corp			
26 Crosby Dr . . . . Bedford MA 01730	**866-753-3837**	781-541-6900	37
Schecter Guitar Research Inc			
10953 Pendleton St . . . . Sun Valley CA 91352	**800-660-6621**	818-846-2700	523
Scheeser Buckley Mayfield Inc			
1540 Corporate Woods Pkwy . . . . Uniontown OH 44685	**800-451-0221**	330-896-4664	261
Schenck Business Solutions			
200 E Washington St . . . . Appleton WI 54911	**800-236-2246**	920-731-8111	2
Schenck Trebel Corp			
535 Acorn St . . . . Deer Park NY 11729	**800-873-2357**	631-242-4010	680

Alphabetical Section

	Toll-Free	Phone	Class
Schendel Pest Services			
1035 SE Quincy St ....Topeka KS 66612	800-591-7378	785-232-9357	573
Schenectady County			
Newyork			
620 State St ....Schenectady NY 12305	877-846-7369	518-388-4220	337
Schenker Inc			
150 Albany Ave ....Freeport NY 11520	800-843-1687	516-377-3000	311
Schenker of Canada Ltd			
5935 Airport Rd 10th Fl ......Mississauga ON L4V1W5	800-461-3686	905-676-0676	311
Schetky Northwest Sales Inc			
8430 NE Killingsworth St ....Portland OR 97220	800-255-8341	503-607-3137	513
Schick Shadel Hospital			
12101 Ambaum Blvd SW ....Seattle WA 98146	800-272-8464		722
Schindler Elevator Corp			
20 Whippany Rd ....Morristown NJ 07960	800-225-3123	973-397-6500	256
Schlagel Inc			
491 N Emerson ....Cambridge MN 55008	800-328-8002	763-689-5991	273
Schlager Group Inc			
325 N Saint Paul Ste 3425 ....Dallas TX 75201	888-416-5727		94
Schlegel Systems Inc			
1555 Jefferson Rd ....Rochester NY 14623	888-924-7694	585-427-7200	326
Schlenner Wenner & Co			
630 Roosevelt Rd ....Saint Cloud MN 56301	877-616-0286	320-251-0286	2
Schlessman Seed Co			
11513 US Rt 250 ....Milan OH 44846	888-534-7333	419-499-2572	690
Schleuniger Inc			
87 Colin Dr ....Manchester NH 03103	877-902-1470*	603-668-8117	454
Tech Supp			
Schlichter, Bogard & Denton			
100 S Fourth St Ste 900 ....St. Louis MO 63102	800-873-5297	314-621-6115	427
Schlitterbahn Beach Waterpark			
90 Park Rd Hwy 100 ......South Padre Island TX 78597	888-852-2489	956-772-7873	
Schlueter Co			
320 N Main St ....Janesville WI 53545	800-359-1700	608-755-5444	298
Schlumberger Wireline & Testing			
210 Schlumberger Dr ....Sugar Land TX 77478	800-272-7328	281-285-4551	535
Schmidt Bros Inc			
420 N Hallett Ave ....Swanton OH 43558	800-200-7318	419-826-3671	186
Schmidt Machine Co			
7013 Ohio 199 ......Upper Sandusky OH 43351	866-368-3814	419-294-3814	274
Schmidt-Goodman Office Products			
1920 N Broadway ....Rochester MN 55906	800-247-0663	507-282-3870	321
Schmiede Corp			
1865 Riley Creek Rd			
PO Box 1630 ....Tullahoma TN 37388	800-535-1851	931-455-4801	452
Schnadig International Corp			
4200 Tudor Ln ....Greensboro NC 27410	800-468-8730		319-2
Schneck Medical Ctr			
411 W Tipton St ....Seymour IN 47274	800-234-9222	812-522-2349	373-3
Schneider Corp			
8901 Otis Ave ....Indianapolis IN 46216	866-973-7100		261
Schneider Electric			
10350 Ormsby Pk Pl Ste 400 ......Louisville KY 40223	866-907-8664	502-429-3800	461
Schneider Laboratories Inc			
2512 W Cary St ....Richmond VA 23220	800-785-5227	804-353-6778	738
Schneider National Inc			
3101 S Packerland Dr			
PO Box 2545 ....Green Bay WI 54306	800-558-6767	920-592-2000	447
Schneider Optics Century Div			
7701 Haskell Ave ....Van Nuys CA 91406	800-228-1254	818-766-3715	587
Schneider Packaging Equipment Company Inc			
5370 Guy Young Rd ....Brewerton NY 13029	800-829-9266	315-676-3035	543
Schneiderman & Sherman			
23938 Research Dr			
Ste 300 ....Farmington Hills MI 48335	866-867-7688	248-539-7400	427
Schnuck Markets Inc			
11420 Lackland Rd ....Saint Louis MO 63146	800-264-4400	314-994-4400	344
Schoepfle Garden			
12882 Diagonal Rd ....La Grange OH 44050	800-526-7275	440-458-5121	97
Schoharie County			
284 Main St PO Box 429 ....Schoharie NY 12157	800-227-3552	518-295-8347	337
Schoharie Crossing State Historic Site			
129 Schoharie St PO Box 140 ......Fort Hunter NY 12069	800-456-2267	518-829-7516	561
Scholars Inn Gourmet Cafe			
717 N College Ave ....Bloomington IN 47404	800-765-3466	812-332-1892	667
Scholarship America			
1 Scholarship Way ....Saint Peter MN 56082	800-537-4180	507-931-1682	48-11
Scholastic Book Fairs Inc			
1080 Greenwood Blvd ....Lake Mary FL 32746	800-874-4809	573-632-1687	96
Scholastic Coach & Athletic Director Magazine			
557 Broadway ....New York NY 10012	800-724-6527*	212-343-6100	455-8
General			
School Annual Publishing Co			
2568 Park Ctr Blvd ....State College PA 16801	800-436-6030		633-2
School District of The Chathams			
58 Meyersville Rd ....Chatham NJ 07928	800-225-5425	973-457-2500	681
School Employees Retirement System of Ohio			
300 E Broad St Ste 100 ....Columbus OH 43215	800-878-5853	614-222-5853	524
School Innovations & Advocacy Inc			
5200 Golden Foothill Pkwy			
...............El Dorado Hills CA 95762	877-954-4357	800-487-9234	461
School Law News			
360 Hiatt Dr ......Palm Beach Gardens FL 33418	800-341-7874		527-4
School Nurse Supply Co			
1690 Wright Blvd ....Schaumburg IL 60193	800-485-2737		681
School Nutrition Assn (SNA)			
700 S Washington St Ste 300 ......Alexandria VA 22314	800-877-8822	703-739-3900	49-6
School of the Art Institute of Chicago			
36 S Wabash Ave ....Chicago IL 60603	800-232-7242*	312-629-6100	166
Admissions			
School of the Museum of Fine Arts			
230 The Fenway ....Boston MA 02115	800-643-6078*	617-369-3626	166
Admissions			
School of Visual Arts			
209 E 23rd St ....New York NY 10010	800-436-4204	212-592-2000	164
School Photo Marketing			
200 D Campus Dr ....Morganville NJ 07751	877-543-9742	732-431-0440	195

	Toll-Free	Phone	Class
School Specialty Inc			
PO Box 1579 ....Appleton WI 54912	888-388-3224	419-589-1600	243
OTC: SCOO			
School Webmasters			
2846 E Nora St ....Mesa AZ 85213	888-750-4556	602-750-4556	177
SchoolCity Inc			
2900 Lakeside Dr Ste 270. ......Santa Clara CA 95054	800-343-6572		177
SchoolDocs LLC			
5944 Luther Ln Ste 600 ....Dallas TX 75225	866-311-2293		386
Schools Financial Credit Union			
1485 Response Rd Ste 126. ......Sacramento CA 95815	800-962-0990	916-569-5400	219
School-Tech Inc			
745 State Cir ....Ann Arbor MI 48108	800-521-2832		345
Schott Textiles Inc			
2850 Gilchrist Rd ....Akron OH 44305	877-661-2121	330-794-2121	590
Schramm Inc			
800 E Virginia Ave ....West Chester PA 19380	888-737-9438	610-696-2500	533
Schreiber Foods International Inc			
600 E Crescent Ave			
Ste 103 ....Upper Saddle River NJ 07458	800-631-7070	201-327-3535	297-11
Schreiber Translations Inc			
51 Monroe St Ste 101. ......Rockville MD 20850	800-822-3213	301-424-7737	763
Schreiner University			
2100 Memorial Blvd ....Kerrville TX 78028	800-343-4919	830-792-7217	166
Schreiner's Iris Gardens			
3625 Quinaby Rd NE ....Salem OR 97303	800-525-2367	503-393-3232	97
Schroder Investment Management North America Inc (SIMNA)			
7 Bryant Pk ....New York NY 10018	800-730-2932	212-641-3800	686
Schroeder America			
5620 Business Pk ....San Antonio TX 78218	877-404-2488	210-662-8200	661
Schroeder Industries LLC			
580 W Pk Rd ....Leetsdale PA 15056	800-722-4810	724-318-1100	207
Schroeder's Flowerland Inc			
1530 S Webster Ave ....Green Bay WI 54301	800-236-4769	920-436-6363	292
Schroer Manufacturing Co			
511 Osage Ave ....Kansas City KS 66105	800-444-1579	913-281-1500	418
Schroeter Goldmark & Bender Ps			
810 Third Ave ....Seattle WA 98104	800-809-2234	206-622-8000	443
Schuette Mfg & Steel Sales Inc			
5028 Hwy 42 ....Manitowoc WI 54220	800-626-6409	920-758-2491	273
Schuff Steel Inc			
1920 Ledo Rd ....Albany GA 31707	866-252-4628	229-883-4506	478
Schulmerich Carillons Inc			
Carillon Hill ....Sellersville PA 18960	800-772-3557	215-257-2771	523
Schultz Collins Lawson Chambers Inc			
455 Market St Ste 1250 ......San Francisco CA 94105	877-291-2205	415-291-3000	400
Schultz Lubricants Inc			
164 Shrewsbury St ....West Boylston MA 01583	800-262-3962	508-835-4446	537
Schumacher & Seiler Inc			
10 W Aylesbury Rd ....Timonium MD 21093	800-992-9356	410-465-7000	608
Schumacher Clinical Partners			
200 Corporate Blvd ....Lafayette LA 70508	800-893-9698		352
Schumacher Electric Corp			
801 E Business Ctr Dr ....Mount Prospect IL 60056	800-621-5485		253
Schumacher Elevator Co			
1 Schumacher Way ....Denver IA 50622	800-779-5438	319-984-5676	256
Schust Engineering Inc			
701 North St ....Auburn IN 46706	800-686-9297		189-12
Schuster Electronics Inc			
11320 Grooms Rd ....Cincinnati OH 45242	800-521-1358		246
Schuyler Mansion State Historic Site			
32 Catherine St ....Albany NY 12202	800-456-2267	518-434-0834	561
Schuylkill Chamber of Commerce			
91 S Progress Ave ....Pottsville PA 17901	800-755-1942	570-622-1942	139
Schwaab Inc			
11415 W Burleigh St ....Milwaukee WI 53222	800-935-9877	414-771-4150	465
Schwan's Co			
115 W College Dr ....Marshall MN 56258	800-533-5290	507-532-3274	296-36
Schwank Infrared Radiant Heaters			
2 Schwank Way at Hwy 56N ......Waynesboro GA 30830	877-446-3727		356
Schwarz			
8338 Austin Ave ....Morton Grove IL 60053	800-323-4903		555
Schwebel Baking Co			
PO Box 6018 ....Youngstown OH 44501	800-860-2867	330-783-2860	296-1
Schweizer Emblem Co			
1022 Busse Hwy ....Park Ridge IL 60068	800-942-5215*	847-292-1022	258
Cust Svc			
Schwend Inc			
28945 Johnston Rd ....Dade City FL 33523	800-243-7757	352-588-2220	774
Schwerdtle Stamp Co			
166 Elm St ....Bridgeport CT 06604	800-535-0004	203-330-2750	465
SCI			
180 Attwell Dr Ste 600 ....Toronto ON M9W6A9	866-773-7735	416-401-3011	314
SCI (Service Communications Inc)			
15223 NE 90th St ....Redmond WA 98052	800-488-0468	425-278-0300	179
SciCan Ltd			
701 Technology Dr ....Canonsburg PA 15317	800-572-1211	724-820-1600	473
SciClone Pharmaceuticals Inc			
950 Tower Ln Ste 900 ....Foster City CA 94404	800-724-2566	650-358-3456	578
NASDAQ: SCLN			
Science Application International Corp Inc (SAIC Inc)			
1710 SAIC Dr ....McLean VA 22102	866-400-7242	866-955-7242	178-5
Science Applications International Corp			
10260 Campus Pt Dr ....San Diego CA 92121	800-760-4332	866-955-7242	664
Science Magazine			
1200 New York Ave NW ....Washington DC 20005	866-434-2227	202-326-6500	455-19
Science Museum of Minnesota			
120 W Kellogg Blvd ....Saint Paul MN 55102	800-221-9444	651-221-9444	517
Science News			
1719 North St NW ....Washington DC 20036	800-552-4412*	202-785-2255	455-19
Cust Svc			
ScienceCare Inc			
21410 N 19th Ave Ste 126 ....Phoenix AZ 85027	800-417-3747		541
Scientech Inc			
5649 Arapahoe Ave ....Boulder CO 80303	800-525-0522	303-444-1361	680
Scientific Equipment & Furniture Assn (SEFA)			
65 Hilton Ave ....Garden City NY 11530	877-294-5424	516-294-5424	49-19

	Toll-Free	Phone	Class
Scientific Industries Inc 70 Orville Dr ... Bohemia NY 11716	888-850-6208	631-567-4700	418
Scientific Learning Corp 300 Frank H Ogawa Plz Ste 600 ... Oakland CA 94612 *OTC: SCIL*	888-665-9707	510-444-3500	178-3
Scientific Protein Laboratories Inc 700 E Main St ... Waunakee WI 53597	800-334-4775	608-849-5944	477
Scientist, The 478 Bay St Ste A213 ... Midland ON L4R1K9	888-781-0328	705-528-6888	455-19
Sciforma Corp 4880 Stevens Creek Blvd Ste 102 ... San Jose CA 95129 *Sales	800-533-9876*	408-354-0144	178-1
SCIMEDX Corp 100 Ford Rd ... Denville NJ 07834	800-221-5598	973-625-8822	231
Scion Medical Technologies LLC 90 Oak St ... Newton MA 02464	888-582-6211		738
Scion Steel Inc 21555 Mullin Ave ... Warren MI 48089	800-288-2127	586-755-4000	719
Scioto Sign Company Inc 6047 US Rt 68 N ... Kenton OH 43326	800-572-4686	419-673-1261	697
Scioto Trail State Park 144 Lake Rd ... Chillicothe OH 45601	866-644-6727	740-887-4818	561
Sci-Port Discovery Ctr 820 Clyde Fant Pkwy ... Shreveport LA 71101	877-724-7678	318-424-3466	517
Scivantage Inc 499 Washington Blvd 11th Fl ... Jersey City NJ 07310	866-724-8268	646-452-0050	174
Scleroderma Foundation 300 Rosewood Dr Ste 105 ... Danvers MA 01923	800-722-4673	978-463-5843	48-17
Score 726 E Anaheim St ... Wilmington CA 90744	800-626-7774		155-18
SCORE Assn 1175 Herndon Pkwy Ste 900 ... Herndon VA 20170	800-634-0245		49-12
Scorpion Design Inc 28480 Ave Stanford Ste 100 ... Valencia CA 91355	866-622-5648		180
Scosche Industries Inc PO Box 2901 ... Oxnard CA 93034	800-363-4490		253
Scot Forge Co 8001 Winn Rd PO Box 8 ... Spring Grove IL 60081	800-435-6621	847-587-1000	481
Scotchman Industries Inc 180 E Hwy 14 ... Philip SD 57567	800-843-8844	605-859-2542	491
Scotiabank 250 Vesey St 23rd & 24th fl ... New York NY 10281	877-294-3435	212-225-5000	686
Scotland County PO Box 489 ... Laurinburg NC 28353	800-913-6109	910-277-2406	337
Scotland Memorial Hospital 500 Lauchwood Dr ... Laurinburg NC 28352	800-557-9249	910-291-7000	373-3
Scotsman Ice Systems 775 Corporate Woods Pkwy ... Vernon Hills IL 60061 *Cust Svc	800-726-8762*	847-215-4500	660
Scotsman Inn West 5922 W Kellogg St ... Wichita KS 67209	800-950-7268	316-943-3800	378
Scott & White Health Plan 2401 S 31st St ... Temple TX 76508	800-321-7947	254-298-3000	390-3
Scott & White Medical Center 2401 S 31st St ... Temple TX 76508	800-792-3710	254-724-2111	373-3
Scott Community College 500 Belmont Rd ... Bettendorf IA 52722	888-336-3907	563-441-4001	162
Scott Construction Inc 560 Munroe Ave ... Lake Delton WI 53940	800-843-1556	608-254-2555	188-4
Scott County Library System 1615 Weston Ct ... Shakopee MN 55379	877-772-8346	952-707-1770	433-3
Scott Danahy Naylon Company Inc (SDN) 300 Spindrift Dr ... Williamsville NY 14221	800-728-6362	716-633-3400	389
Scott Electric 1000 S Main St PO Box S ... Greensburg PA 15601	800-442-8045	724-834-4321	246
Scott Enterprises Inc 2225 Downs Dr 6th Fl Exce stes ... Erie PA 16509	877-866-3445	814-868-9500	386
Scott Fetzer Company Scot Laboratories Div 16841 Pk Cir Dr ... Chagrin Falls OH 44023	800-486-7268	440-543-3033	151
Scott Fly Rod Co 2355 Air Pk Way ... Montrose CO 81401	800-728-7208	970-249-3180	706
Scott Health & Safety 4320 Goldmine Rd PO Box 569 ... Monroe NC 28110	800-247-7257	704-291-8300	572
Scott Industrial Systems Inc 4433 Interpoint Blvd ... Dayton OH 45424	800-416-6023	937-233-8146	468
Scott Industries Inc 1573 Hwy 136 W PO Box 7 ... Henderson KY 42419	800-951-9276	270-831-2037	388
Scott Insurance 1301 Old Graves Mill Rd ... Lynchburg VA 24502	800-365-0101	434-832-2100	390-4
Scott Logistics Corp PO Box 391 ... Rome GA 30162	800-893-6689	706-234-1184	311
Scott Phil (R) 109 State St Pavilion Office Bldg ... Montpelier VT 05609	800-649-6825	802-828-3333	
Scott Resort & Spa, The 4925 N Scottsdale Rd ... Scottsdale AZ 85251 *Resv	800-528-7867*		703
Scott Sheldon LLC 1375 S Main St Ste 203 ... North Canton OH 44720	844-835-2527	234-347-0689	461
Scott Tim (Sen R - SC) 717 Hart Senate Office Bldg ... Washington DC 20510	855-425-6324	202-224-6121	341-1
Scott USA Inc PO Box 2030 ... Sun Valley ID 83353	800-292-5874	208-622-1000	706
Scott's Liquid Gold Inc 4880 Havana St ... Denver CO 80239 *OTC: SLGD*	800-447-1919	303-373-4860	151
Scottdel Inc 400 Church St ... Swanton OH 43558	800-446-2341	419-825-2341	131
Scotts Miracle-Gro Co 14111 Scottslawn Rd ... Marysville OH 43041 *NYSE: SMG *Cust Svc	800-543-8873*	937-644-0011	280
Scottsdale Camelback Resort 6302 E Camelback Rd ... Scottsdale AZ 85251	800-891-8585	480-947-3300	665
Scottsdale Community College 9000 E Chaparral Rd ... Scottsdale AZ 85256	800-784-2433	480-423-6000	162
Scottsdale Convention & Visitors Bureau 4343 N Scottsdale Rd Ste 170 ... Scottsdale AZ 85251	800-782-1117	480-421-1004	206
Scottsdale Plaza Resort 7200 N Scottsdale Rd ... Scottsdale AZ 85253	800-832-2025	480-948-5000	665
Scottsdale Stadium 7408 E Osborn Rd ... Scottsdale AZ 85251	877-229-5042	480-312-2586	716
Scout shop PO Box 7143 ... Charlotte NC 28241	800-323-0736		786
Scouting Magazine 1325 W Walnut Hill Ln PO Box 152079 ... Irving TX 75015	800-323-0732	972-580-2000	455-10
Scovill Fasteners Inc 1802 Scovill Dr ... Clarkesville GA 30523 *Cust Svc	888-726-8455*	706-754-1000	590
SCPPD (South Central Public Power District) 275 S Main St PO Box 406 ... Nelson NE 68961	800-557-5254	402-225-2351	245
Scranton Mfg Company Inc 101 State St PO Box 336 ... Scranton IA 51462	800-831-1858	712-652-3396	273
Scranton Times-Tribune 149 Penn Ave ... Scranton PA 18503	800-228-4637	570-348-9100	528-2
SCREC (Sullivan County Rural Electric Co-op Inc) 5675 Rt 87 PO Box 65 ... Forksville PA 18616	800-570-5081	570-924-3381	245
Screen Actors Guild (SAG) 5757 Wilshire Blvd ... Los Angeles CA 90036	800-724-0767	323-954-1600	413
Screen Graphics of Florida Inc 1801 N Andrews Ave ... Pompano Beach FL 33069	800-346-4420		683
Screen Works 2201 W Fulton St ... Chicago IL 60612 *Cust Svc	800-294-8111*	312-243-8265	718
Screeningone Inc 2233 W 190th St ... Torrance CA 90504	888-327-6511		218
ScreenScape Networks Inc 133 Queen St 3rd Fl ... Charlottetown PE C1A4B3	877-666-1975		7
Scribendi Inc 405 Riverview Dr Ste 304 ... Chatham ON N7M0N3	877-351-1626	519-351-1626	
Scribner Cohen & Company SC 400 E Mason St Ste 300 ... Milwaukee WI 53202	888-730-0045	414-271-1700	2
Scripps College 1030 Columbia Ave ... Claremont CA 91711	800-770-1333	909-621-8149	166
Scripps Green Hospital 9898 Genesee Ave ... La Jolla CA 92037	800-727-4777	858-554-9100	373-3
Scripps Health 4275 Campus Pt Ct ... San Diego CA 92121	800-727-4777		352
Scripps Memorial Hospital-La Jolla 9888 Genesee Ave ... La Jolla CA 92037	800-727-4777		373-3
Scripps Mercy Hospital 4077 Fifth Ave ... San Diego CA 92103	800-727-4777	619-294-8111	373-3
Script Care Inc 6380 Folsom Dr ... Beaumont TX 77706	800-880-9988		582
ScriptLogic Corp 6000 Broken Sound Pkwy NW ... Boca Raton FL 33487	800-306-9329	561-886-2400	178-12
Scruggs Company Inc PO Box 2065 ... Valdosta GA 31604	800-230-7263	229-242-2388	188-4
SCS (Structural Component Systems Inc) 1255 Front St ... Fremont NE 68026	800-844-5622	402-721-5622	187
SCS Engineers 3900 Kilroy Airport Way Ste 100 ... Long Beach CA 90806	800-326-9544	562-426-9544	261
SCTC (Society of Communications Technology Consultants) 230 Washington Ave Ext Ste 101 ... Albany NY 12203	800-782-7670		49-20
SCTE (Society of Cable Telecommunications Engineers) 140 Philips Rd ... Exton PA 19341	800-542-5040	610-363-6888	49-19
Scuba Com Inc 1752 Langley Ave ... Irvine CA 92614	800-347-2822	949-221-9300	707
Scully Signal Co 70 Industrial Way ... Wilmington MA 01887	800-272-8559	617-692-8600	201
SD Ireland Co 193 Industrial Ave ... Williston VT 05495	800-339-4565	802-863-6222	183
Sda Consulting Inc 3011 183rd St # 377 ... Homewood IL 60430	800-823-2990		180
SDEB (San Diego Eye Bank) 9246 Lightwave Ave Ste 120 ... San Diego CA 92123	800-393-2265	858-694-0400	269
SDI Presence LLC 33 W Monroe Ste 400 ... Chicago IL 60603	888-968-7734	312-580-7500	689
SDI Technologies Inc 1299 Main St ... Rahway NJ 07065	800-333-3092		52
SDL 2550 N First St Ste 301 ... San Jose CA 95131	800-933-6910	408-743-3600	
SDMS (Society of Diagnostic Medical Sonography) 2745 Dallas Pkwy ... Plano TX 75093	800-229-9506	214-473-8057	49-8
SDN (Scott Danahy Naylon Company Inc) 300 Spindrift Dr ... Williamsville NY 14221	800-728-6362	716-633-3400	389
SDNA (South Dakota Nurses Assn) PO Box 1015 ... Pierre SD 57501	888-425-3032	605-945-4265	529
SDPB (South Dakota Public Broadcasting) 555 N Dakota St PO Box 5000 ... Vermillion SD 57069	800-456-0766	605-677-5861	628
SDSC (San Diego Supercomputer Ctr) 9500 Gilman Dr ... La Jolla CA 92093	800-451-4515	858-534-5000	664
SDT North America Inc 1532 Ontario St ... Cobourg ON K9A4R5	800-667-5325	905-377-1313	357
SEA (Software Engineering of America Inc) 1230 Hempstead Tpke ... Franklin Square NY 11010	800-272-7322	516-328-7000	178-12
Sea Breeze Inc 441 Rt 202 ... Towaco NJ 07082	800-732-2733		296-15
Sea Cloud Cruises Inc 282 Grand Ave Ste 3 ... Englewood NJ 07631	888-732-2568	201-227-9404	220
Sea Crest Resort & Conference Ctr 350 Quaker Rd ... North Falmouth MA 02556	800-225-3110	508-540-9400	665
Sea Eagle Boats Inc 19 N Columbia St Ste 1 ... Port Jefferson NY 11777	800-748-8066	631-791-1799	706
Sea Grill Restaurant 19 W 49th St ... New York NY 10020	866-972-8462		
Sea Gull Lighting Products LLC A Generations Brands Co 301 W Washington St ... Riverside NJ 08075	800-347-5483	800-519-4092	438
SEA Ltd 7349 Worthington-Galena Rd ... Columbus OH 43085	800-782-6851		461
Sea Magazine 1782 Crown St Ste C ... Irvine CA 92614	800-873-7327	949-660-6150	455-4
Sea Mar Community Health Ctr 1040 S Henderson St ... Seattle WA 98108	855-289-4503	206-763-5277	352

Name / Address				Toll-Free	Phone	Class
Sea Mist Resort 1200 S Ocean Blvd	Myrtle Beach	SC	29577	800-793-6507	843-448-1551	665
Sea Palms Golf & Tennis Resort 5445 Frederica Rd	Saint Simons Island	GA	31522	800-841-6268	912-638-3351	665
Sea Pearl Seafood Company Inc 14120 Shell Belt Rd	Bayou La Batre	AL	36509	800-872-8804	251-824-2129	392
Sea Pines Resort, The 32 Greenwood Dr	Hilton Head Island	SC	29928	866-561-8802	843-785-3333	649
Sea Ranch Lodge 60 Sea Walk Dr PO Box 44	The Sea Ranch	CA	95497	800-732-7262	707-785-2371	378
Sea Tow Services International Inc 1560 Youngs Ave PO Box 1178	Southold	NY	11971	800-473-2869	877-568-1672	463
Sea Trail Corp 75A Clubhouse Rd	Sunset Beach	NC	28468	888-321-9048	910-287-1100	649
Sea View Hotel 9909 Collins Ave	Bal Harbour	FL	33154	800-447-1010	305-866-4441	378
Seaboard Asphalt Products Co 3601 Fairfield Rd	Baltimore	MD	21226	800-536-0332	410-355-0330	46
Seaboard Corp 9000 W 67th St NYSE: SEB	Shawnee Mission	KS	66202	866-676-8886	913-676-8800	185
Seaboard Folding Box Co Inc 100 Simplex Dr PO Box 650	Westminster	MA	01473	800-225-6313	978-342-8921	101
Seaboard Foods 9000 W 67th St Ste 200	Shawnee Mission	KS	66202	800-262-7907	913-261-2600	10-5
Seaboard International Forest Products LLC 22F Cotton Rd	Nashua	NH	03063	800-669-6800	603-881-3700	191-3
Seaboard Marine 8001 NW 79th Ave	Miami	FL	33166	866-676-8886	305-863-4444	313
Seaborn Health Care 8918 78th Ave	Seminole	FL	33777	800-335-6176	727-398-1710	392
Seacoast Banking Corp of Florida PO Box 9012 NASDAQ: SBCF ■ *All	Stuart	FL	34995	800-706-9991*	772-287-4000	359-2
SEACOR Holdings Inc 2200 Eller Dr PO Box 13038 NYSE: CKH	Fort Lauderdale	FL	33316	800-516-6203	954-523-2200	663
Seacrest Oceanfront Resort on the South Beach 803 S Ocean Blvd	Myrtle Beach	SC	29577	888-889-4037		665
SeaDream Yacht Club 601 Brickell Key Dr Ste 1050	Miami	FL	33131	800-707-4911	305-631-6110	220
Seafarers International Union 5201 Auth Way	Camp Springs	MD	20746	800-252-4674	301-899-0675	413
Seagull Book & Tape Inc 1720 S Redwood Rd	Salt Lake City	UT	84104	800-999-6257	877-324-8551	95
Seagull Scientific Inc 15325 SE 30th Pl Ste 100	Bellevue	WA	98007	800-758-2001	425-641-1408	
Seal Methods Inc 11915 Shoemaker Ave	Santa Fe Springs	CA	90670	800-423-4777	562-944-0291	326
Sealco Data Center Services Ltd 1751 INTERNATIONAL Pkwy Ste 115	Richardson	TX	75081	800-283-5567	972-234-5567	104
Sealed Air Corp Packaging Products Div 301 Mayhill St	Saddle Brook	NJ	07663	800-648-9093	201-712-7000	544
Sealed Unit Parts Company Inc 2230 Landmark Pl	Allenwood	NJ	08720	800-333-9125	732-223-6644	14
Sealing Devices Inc 4400 Walden Ave *Cust Svc	Lancaster	NY	14086	800-727-3257*	716-684-7600	326
Sealing Equipment Products Co Inc 123 Airpark Industrial Rd	Alabaster	AL	35007	800-633-4770		326
Seaman Corp 1000 Venture Blvd	Wooster	OH	44691	800-927-8578	330-262-1111	740-2
Seaman Paper Co of Massachusetts 51 Main St	Otter River	MA	01436	800-784-7783	978-632-1513	553
SEAMARK Asset Management Ltd 810-1801 Hollis St	Halifax	NS	B3J3N4	888-303-5055	902-423-9367	524
SeaMates International Inc 316 Main St PO Box 436	East Rutherford	NJ	07073	800-541-4538	201-896-8899	194
Seamen's Bank 221 Commercial St PO Box 659	Provincetown	MA	02657	855-227-5347	508-487-0035	70
Seaport Hotel & World Trade Ctr 1 Seaport Ln	Boston	MA	02210	877-732-7678	617-385-4000	378
Search Company International 7700 E Arapahoe Rd Ste 220	Centennial	CO	80112	800-727-2120	303-863-1800	631
Search Network Ltd 1503 42nd St Ste 210	West Des Moines	IA	50266	800-383-5050	515-223-1153	631
Search Results Saint-Gobain High-Performance Refractories 4702 Rt 982	Latrobe	PA	15650	800-438-7237	724-539-6000	249
Searcher: The Magazine for Database Professionals 143 Old Marlton Pk	Medford	NJ	08055	800-300-9868	609-654-6266	455-7
Searchwide Inc 680 Commerce Dr Ste 220	Woodbury	MN	55082	888-386-6390	651-275-1370	193
Searcy Denney Scarola Barnhart Po Box 3626	West Palm Beach	FL	33402	800-780-8607	561-686-6300	427
Searing Industries Inc 8901 Arrow Rt	Rancho Cucamonga	CA	91730	800-874-4412	909-948-3030	490
SEARK (Southeast Arkansas College) 1900 Hazel St	Pine Bluff	AR	71603	888-732-7582	870-543-5900	162
Searles Valley Minerals 9401 Indian Creek Pkwy Ste 1000	Overland Park	KS	66210	800-637-2775	913-344-9500	501-1
Sears Manufacturing Co PO Box 3667 *Cust Svc	Davenport	IA	52808	800-553-3013*	563-383-2800	685
Sears Roebuck & Co 3333 Beverly Rd	Hoffman Estates	IL	60179	800-349-4358	847-286-2500	229
SEAS Education 955 Wallace Knob Ste 1	Mountain Home	AR	72654	877-221-7327		
Seaside Civic & Convention Ctr 415 First Ave	Seaside	OR	97138	800-394-3303	503-738-8585	205
Seaside Golf Vacations 218 Main St	North Myrtle Beach	SC	29582	877-732-6999		766
Seaside Inn 541 E Gulf Dr	Sanibel Island	FL	33957	866-717-2323		378
Seasons Restaurant at Highland Lake Inn 86 Lilly Pad Ln	Flat Rock	NC	28731	800-635-5101	828-696-9094	703
Seastrom Mfg Company Inc 456 Seastrom St	Twin Falls	ID	83301	800-634-2356	208-737-4300	349
Seat of the Soul Foundation PO Box 3310	Ashland	OR	97520	877-733-4279	541-482-1515	48-20
SEA-TAC (Seattle-Tacoma International Airport) 17801 International Blvd PO Box 68727	Seattle	WA	98158	800-544-1965	206-787-5388	27
Seats Inc 1515 Industrial St	Reedsburg	WI	53959	800-443-0615	608-524-8261	685
Seattle Aquarium 1483 Alaskan Way Pier 59	Seattle	WA	98101	800-853-1964	206-386-4300	40
Seattle Cancer Care Alliance 825 Eastlake Ave E PO Box 19023	Seattle	WA	98109	800-804-8824	206-606-7222	764
Seattle Children's Hospital 4800 Sand Pt Way NE	Seattle	WA	98105	866-987-2000	206-987-2000	373-1
Seattle Lighting Fixture Co 222 Second Ave Ext S *Cust Svc	Seattle	WA	98104	800-689-1000*	206-622-4736	361
Seattle Manufacturing Corp 6930 Salashan Pkwy	Ferndale	WA	98248	800-426-6251	360-366-5534	572
Seattle Opera 1020 John St *Sales	Seattle	WA	98109	800-426-1619*	206-389-7600	569-2
Seattle Pacific University 3307 Third Ave W	Seattle	WA	98119	800-366-3344	206-281-2000	166
Seattle Post-Intelligencer 200 First Ave W Ste 230	Seattle	WA	98119	800-542-0820	206-448-8030	528-2
Seattle Public Library 1000 Fourth Ave	Seattle	WA	98104	800-829-3676	206-386-4636	433-3
Seattle Repertory Theatre (SRT) 155 Mercer St PO Box 900923	Seattle	WA	98109	877-900-9285	206-443-2210	569-4
Seattle Seahawks 12 Seahawks Way	Renton	WA	98056	888-635-4295		711-2
Seattle SuperSonics 1201 Third Ave Ste 1000	Seattle	WA	98101	800-743-7021	206-281-5800	710-1
Seattle Symphony 200 University St	Seattle	WA	98101	866-833-4747	206-215-4700	569-3
Seattle Theatre Group 911 Pine St	Seattle	WA	98101	877-784-4849	206-467-5510	716
Seattle University 901 12th Ave	Seattle	WA	98122	800-426-7123	206-296-6000	166
Seattle University Lemieux Library 901 12th Ave	Seattle	WA	98122	800-426-7123	206-296-6210	433-6
Seattle's Best Coffee LLC PO Box 3717	Seattle	WA	98124	800-611-7793		159
Seattle's Convention & Visitors Bureau 701 Pike St Ste 800	Seattle	WA	98101	866-732-2695	206-461-5800	206
Seattle-Tacoma International Airport (SEA-TAC) 17801 International Blvd PO Box 68727	Seattle	WA	98158	800-544-1965	206-787-5388	27
Seaway Manufacturing Corp 2250 E 33rd St	Erie	PA	16510	800-458-2244	814-898-2255	234
Seaway Printing Company Inc 1609 Western Ave	Green Bay	WI	54303	800-622-3255	920-468-1500	623
Sebago USA LLC 9341 Courtland Dr	Rockford	MI	49351	866-699-7367		301
Sebasco Harbor Resort 29 Keynon Rd	Phippsburg	ME	04562	800-225-3819	877-420-1701	665
Sebastian County 35 S Sixth St Rm 105	Fort Smith	AR	72901	800-637-9314	479-782-5065	337
Sebastiani Vineyards Inc 389 Fourth St E	Sonoma	CA	95476	855-232-2338	707-933-3230	80-3
Sebewaing Tool & Engineering Co 415 Union St	Sebewaing	MI	48759	800-453-2207	989-883-2000	349
Sebring International Raceway 113 Midway Dr	Sebring	FL	33870	800-626-7223	863-655-1442	512
SEC (Shelby Electric Co-op) 1355 IL-128 state PO Box 560	Shelbyville	IL	62565	800-677-2612	217-774-3986	245
SEC (Securities & Exchange Commission) 100 F St NE	Washington	DC	20549	800-732-0330	202-942-8088	339-19
Sechrist Industries Inc 4225 E La Palma Ave	Anaheim	CA	92807	800-732-4747	714-579-8400	474
SECNAP Network Security Corp 3250 W Commercial Blvd Ste 345	Fort Lauderdale	FL	33309	844-638-7328	561-999-5000	
SECO (Southeast Electric Co-op Inc) 110 S Main St	Ekalaka	MT	59324	888-485-8762	406-775-8762	245
Seco Tools 2805 Bellingham Dr	Troy	MI	48083	800-832-8326	248-528-5200	491
Seco-Larm USA Inc 16842 Millikan Ave	Irvine	CA	92606	800-662-0800	949-857-0811	688
Second Amendment Foundation 12500 NE Tenth Pl	Bellevue	WA	98005	800-426-4302	425-454-7012	48-8
Second Cup Ltd 6303 Airport Rd	Mississauga	ON	L4V1R8	877-212-1818		159
Second Street Grill 200 E Fremont St	Las Vegas	NV	89101	800-634-6460	702-385-3232	667
Secova Inc 3090 Bristol St Ste 200	Costa Mesa	CA	92626	877-632-8122		194
SECPA (Southeast Colorado Power Assn) 27850 Harris Rd	La Junta	CO	81050	800-332-8634	719-384-2551	245
Secret Garden Spa at the Prince of Wales Hotel 6 Picton St	Niagara-on-the-Lake	ON	L0S1J0	888-669-5566	905-468-3246	703
Secretary of Agriculture 1400 Independence Ave SW	Washington	DC	20250	800-832-1355	202-720-3631	339-1
Secretary of Education 400 Maryland Ave SW	Washington	DC	20202	800-872-5327	202-401-3000	339-7
Secretary of Health & Human Services 200 Independence Ave SW	Washington	DC	20201	877-696-6775		
Secretary of Labor 200 Constitution Ave NW	Washington	DC	20210	866-487-2365	202-693-6000	339-14
Secretary of Transportation 1200 New Jersey Ave SE	Washington	DC	20590	855-368-4200		339-16
Secretary of Veterans Affairs 810 Vermont Ave NW	Washington	DC	20420	844-698-2311		339-18
Board of Veterans' Appeals 810 Vermont Ave NW	Washington	DC	20420	800-923-8387		339-18

Name / Address	City	State	ZIP	Toll-Free	Phone	Class
Center for Women Veterans						
810 Vermont Ave NW	Washington	DC	20420	**800-827-1000**		339-18
SECU (State Employees' Credit Union)						
PO Box 29606	Raleigh	NC	27626	**888-732-8562**	919-857-2150	219
Secura Insurance Cos						
PO Box 819	Appleton	WI	54912	**800-558-3405**	920-739-3161	390-4
Securance Consulting						
13904 Monroes Business Park	Tampa	FL	33635	**877-578-0215**		180
Secure Technology Alliance						
191 Clarkville Rd	Princeton Junction	NJ	08550	**800-556-6828**		49-2
Securitas Security Services USA Inc						
2 Campus Dr	Parsippany	NJ	07054	**800-555-0906**	973-267-5300	688
Securitech Inc						
8230 E Broadway Blvd	Tucson	AZ	85710	**888-792-4473**	520-721-0305	631
Securities & Exchange Commission (SEC)						
100 F St NE	Washington	DC	20549	**800-732-0330**	202-942-8088	339-19
Securities & Exchange Commission Regional Offices						
Los Angeles Regional Office						
5670 Wilshire Blvd 11th Fl	Los Angeles	CA	90036	**800-732-0330**	323-965-3998	339-19
Securities Center Inc, The						
245 E St	Chula Vista	CA	91910	**800-244-1718**	619-426-3550	686
Securities Law Daily						
1801 S Bell St	Arlington	VA	22202	**800-372-1033**		527-7
Securities Service Network Inc						
9729 Cogdill Rd Ste 301	Knoxville	TN	37932	**866-843-4635**		686
Securitron Magnalock Corp						
10027 S 51st St Ste 102	Phoenix	AZ	85044	**800-624-5625***	623-582-4626	349
*Sales						
Security 101 LLC						
2465 Mercer Ave Ste 101	West Palm Beach	FL	33401	**888-909-4101**		689
Security America Inc						
3412 Chesterfield Ave	Charleston	WV	25304	**888-832-6732**	304-925-4747	689
Security Benefit Group of Cos						
1 Security Benefit Pl	Topeka	KS	66636	**800-888-2461**	785-438-3000	359-4
Security Corp						
22325 Roethel Dr	Novi	MI	48375	**877-374-5700**		688
Security Credit Services LLC						
2653 W Oxford Loop Ste 108	Oxford	MS	38655	**866-699-7889**		402
Security Defense Systems Corp						
160 Park Ave	Nutley	NJ	07110	**800-325-6339**		688
Security Door Controls Inc						
801 Avenida Acaso	Camarillo	CA	93012	**800-413-8783**	805-494-0622	349
Security Engineered Machinery Company Inc						
5 Walkup Dr PO Box 1045	Westborough	MA	01581	**800-225-9293***	508-366-1488	111
*Sales						
Security Federal Bank (SFB)						
238 Richland Ave W	Aiken	SC	29801	**866-851-3000**	803-641-3000	71
Security Finance Corp						
181 Security Pl	Spartanburg	SC	29304	**800-395-8195**	864-582-8193	217
Security First Corp						
29811 Santa Margarita Pkwy						
Ste 600	Rancho Santa Margarita	CA	92688	**888-884-7152**	949-858-7525	84
Security Funds						
1 Security Benefit Pl	Topeka	KS	66636	**800-888-2461**	785-438-3000	524
Security Industry Assn (SIA)						
8405 Colesville Rd						
Ste 500	Silver Spring	MD	20910	**866-817-8888**	301-804-4700	49-4
Security Life Insurance Co of America						
10901 Red Cir Dr	Minnetonka	MN	55343	**800-328-4667**	717-397-2751	390-2
Security Mutual Life Insurance Co of New York						
100 Court St PO Box 1625	Binghamton	NY	13901	**800-927-8846**	800-346-7171	390-2
Security National Financial Corp (SNFC)						
5300 South 360 West	Salt Lake City	UT	84123	**800-574-7117**	801-264-1060	390-2
NASDAQ: SNFCA						
Security Service Federal Credit Union						
16211 La Cantera Pkwy	San Antonio	TX	78256	**800-527-7328**	210-476-4000	219
Security Signal Devices Inc						
1740 N Lemon St	Anaheim	CA	92801	**800-888-0444**		688
Security Square Mall						
6901 Security Blvd	Baltimore	MD	21244	**800-977-2769**	410-265-6000	458
Security Van Lines LLC						
100 W Airline Dr	Kenner	LA	70062	**800-794-5961**		775
SecurTek Monitoring Solutions Inc						
70-1st Ave N	Yorkton	SK	S3N1J7	**844-321-2712**	877-777-7591	
Securus Technologies Inc						
14651 Dallas Pkwy	Dallas	TX	75254	**800-844-6591**	972-734-1111	731
Seda France Inc						
10200 McKalla Pl Ste 400	Austin	TX	78758	**800-474-0854**	512-206-0105	96
Sedgwick County						
525 N Main St	Wichita	KS	67203	**800-527-0709**	316-660-9222	337
SEDL 4700 Mueller Blvd	Austin	TX	78723	**800-476-6861**	512-476-6861	664
SEDONA Corp						
1003 W Ninth Ave 2nd Fl	King Of Prussia	PA	19406	**800-815-3307**	610-337-8400	177
Sedona Rouge Hotel & Spa						
2250 W SR- 89A	Sedona	AZ	86336	**866-312-4111**	928-203-4111	378
See Water Inc						
22220 Opportunity Way Ste 101	Riverside	CA	92518	**888-733-9283**	951-487-8073	201
See World Satellites Inc						
1321 Wayne Ave	Indiana	PA	15701	**800-435-2808**	724-463-3200	116
See's Candies Inc						
210 El Camino Real	South San Francisco	CA	94080	**800-877-7337***	650-761-2490	296-8
*Cust Svc						
Seedway LLC						
1734 Railroad Pl	Hall	NY	14463	**800-836-3710**	585-526-6391	690
Seeker Rod Co						
700 N Batavia Unit B	Orange	CA	92868	**800-373-3537**	714-769-1700	
Seelbach Hilton Louisville						
500 S Fourth St	Louisville	KY	40202	**800-333-3399**	502-585-3200	378
Seelye Plastics Inc						
9700 Newton Ave S	Bloomington	MN	55431	**800-328-2728**		599
SeeMore Putter Co, The						
277 Mallory Sta Ste 119	Franklin	TN	37067	**800-985-8170**	615-435-8015	707
SeePoint Technology LLC						
2619 Manhattan Beach Blvd						
	Redondo Beach	CA	90278	**888-587-1777**	310-725-9660	610
SEER Technology Inc						
2681 Parleys Way Ste 201	Salt Lake City	UT	84109	**877-505-7337**	801-746-7888	418
SEFA (Scientific Equipment & Furniture Assn)						
65 Hilton Ave	Garden City	NY	11530	**877-294-5424**	516-294-5424	49-19
Sefar Printing Solutions Inc						
111 Calumet St	Depew	NY	14043	**800-995-0531**	716-683-4050	740-3
Segall Bryant & Hamill						
540 W Madison St Ste 1900	Chicago	IL	60661	**800-836-4265**	312-474-1222	400
Segway Inc						
14 Technology Dr	Bedford	NH	03110	**866-473-4929**	603-222-6000	513
SEI 1 Freedom Vly Dr	Oaks	PA	19456	**800-342-5734**	610-676-1000	524
NASDAQ: SEIC						
SEI (Software Engineering Institute)						
4500 Fifth Ave	Pittsburgh	PA	15213	**888-201-4479**	412-268-5800	664
SEI (Stephenson Equipment Inc)						
7201 Paxton St	Harrisburg	PA	17111	**800-325-6455**	717-564-3434	264-3
SEI (System Engineering International Inc)						
5115 Pegasus Ct Ste Q	Frederick	MD	21704	**800-765-4734**	301-694-9601	782
SEIA (Signature Estate & Investment Advisors LLC)						
2121 Ave Of The Stars						
Ste 1600	Los Angeles	CA	90067	**800-723-5115**	310-712-2323	400
Seico Security Systems						
132 Court St	Pekin	IL	61554	**800-272-0316**	309-347-3200	689
Seidel Tanning Corp						
1306 E Meinecke Ave	Milwaukee	WI	53212	**800-826-6379**	414-562-4030	431
Seiko Corp of America						
1111 MacArthur Blvd	Mahwah	NJ	07430	**800-545-2783***	201-529-5730	153
*Cust Svc						
Seiko Instruments USA Inc (SII)						
21221 S Western Ave Ste 250	Torrance	CA	90501	**800-688-0817**	310-517-7700	173-6
Seiko Instruments USA Inc						
21221 S Western Ave Ste 250	Torrance	CA	90501	**800-688-0817***	310-517-7700	153
*Sales						
Seiler Instrument & Mfg Company Inc						
3433 Tree Court Industrial Blvd						
	Saint Louis	MO	63122	**800-489-2282**	314-968-2282	540
Seitz LLC						
212 Industrial Ln	Torrington	CT	06790	**800-261-2011**	860-489-0476	600
Seiu Local 503						
488 E 11th Ave Ste B100	Eugene	OR	97401	**800-452-2146**	541-342-1055	413
Seize The Deal LLC						
1851 N Greenville Ave						
Ste 100	Richardson	TX	75081	**866-210-0881**		386
SEK Genetics						
9525 70th Rd	Galesburg	KS	66740	**800-443-6389**		11-2
Sekisui Voltek LLC						
100 Shepard St	Lawrence	MA	01843	**800-225-0668**	978-685-2557	597
Seko						
1100 Arlington Heights Rd						
Ste 600	Itasca	IL	60143	**800-228-2711**	630-919-4800	447
Selas Heat Technology Company LLC						
130 Keystone Dr	Montgomeryville	PA	18936	**800-523-6500**	215-646-6600	318
Selbysoft Inc						
8326 Woodland Ave E	Puyallup	WA	98371	**800-454-4434**		177
Selco Community Credit Union						
299 E 11th Ave	Eugene	OR	97401	**800-445-4483**	541-686-8000	219
Seldovia Native Association Inc						
101 W Benson Blvd Ste 302	Anchorage	AK	99503	**844-868-8006**	907-868-8006	
Select Engineered Systems						
7991 W 26th Ave	Hialeah	FL	33016	**800-342-5737**	305-823-5410	689
Select Group Real Estate Inc						
409 Century Park Dr	Yuba City	CA	95991	**800-992-3883**		
Select Medical Corp						
4714 Gettysburg Rd	Mechanicsburg	PA	17055	**888-735-6332**	717-972-1100	461
Select Portfolio Management Inc						
120 Vantis	Aliso Viejo	CA	92656	**800-445-9822**	949-975-7900	400
Select Portfolio Servicing Inc						
PO Box 65250	Salt Lake City	UT	84165	**800-258-8602**		217
Select Publishing Inc						
6417 Normandy Ln	Madison	WI	53719	**800-278-5670**	608-277-5787	365
Select Technical Staffing Inc						
1025 S 108th St	West Allis	WI	53214	**888-476-9331**	414-476-9331	
Select-A-Ticket Inc						
25 Rt 23 S	Riverdale	NJ	07457	**800-735-3288**	973-839-6100	745
Selected Funds						
PO Box 8243	Boston	MA	02266	**800-243-1575**		524
Selected Independent Funeral Homes						
500 Lake Cook Rd Ste 205	Deerfield	IL	60015	**800-323-4219**	847-236-9401	49-4
Selection Management Systems Inc						
155 Tri County Pkwy Ste 150	Cincinnati	OH	45246	**800-325-3609**		
Selective Enterprises Inc						
10701 Texland Blvd	Charlotte	NC	28273	**800-334-1207**	704-588-3310	360
Selective Insurance Group Inc						
40 Wantage Ave	Branchville	NJ	07890	**800-777-9656**	973-948-3000	359-4
NASDAQ: SIGI						
Selective Service System						
1515 Wilson Blvd	Arlington	VA	22209	**888-655-1825**	847-688-6888	339-19
Selective Service System Regional Offices						
Region 1						
PO Box 94638	Palatine	IL	60094	**888-655-1825**	847-688-6888	339-19
Region 2						
PO Box 94638	Palatine	IL	60094	**888-655-1825**	847-688-6888	339-19
Select-O-Hits Inc						
1981 Fletcher Creek Dr	Memphis	TN	38133	**800-346-0723**	901-388-1190	520
Selectpath Benefits & Financial Inc						
310-700 Richmond St	London	ON	N6A5C7	**888-327-5777**	519-675-1177	389
Selectquote Insurance Services						
595 Market St 10th Fl	San Francisco	CA	94105	**800-670-3213**		389
SelecTransportation Resources LLC						
9550 N Loop E	Houston	TX	77029	**800-299-4200**	713-672-4115	786
Selee Corp						
700 Shepherd St	Hendersonville	NC	28792	**800-842-3818**	828-697-2411	144
SELEX Inc						
11300 W 89th St	Overland Park	KS	66214	**800-765-0861**	913-495-2600	525
Self Opportunity Inc						
808 Office Park Cir	Lewisville	TX	75057	**800-594-7036**	214-222-1500	194
Self Storage Assn (SSA)						
1901 N Beauregard St Ste 106	Alexandria	VA	22311	**888-735-3784**	703-575-8000	49-21
Self-Employed America Magazine						
PO Box 241	Annapolis Junction	MD	20701	**800-649-6273**		455-5
Selfhelp Community Services						
520 Eigth Ave 5th Fl	New York	NY	10018	**866-735-1234**	212-971-7600	362

	Toll-Free	Phone	Class
Selkirk Canada Corp			
375 Green Rd . . . . Stoney Creek ON L8E4A5	800-263-9308	905-662-6600	183
Selkirk College			
301 Frank Beinder Way . . . . Castlegar BC V1N4L3	888-953-1133	250-365-7292	166
Sell My Timeshare Now LLC			
383 Central Ave Ste 260 . . . . Dover NH 03820	877-815-4227	603-516-0200	386
Sellars			
6565 North 60th St . . . . Milwaukee WI 53223	800-237-8454		740-6
Selling Power Magazine			
1140 International Pkwy . . . . Fredericksburg VA 22406	800-752-7355	540-752-7000	455-5
Sellstrom Manufacturing Co			
2050 Hammond Dr . . . . Schaumburg IL 60173	800-323-7402	847-358-2000	572
SEM (Society for Experimental Mechanics Inc)			
7 School St . . . . Bethel CT 06801	800-627-8258	203-790-6373	49-19
SEM (Society for Ethnomusicology)			
Indiana University			
800 E Third St . . . . Bloomington IN 47405	800-933-9330	812-855-6672	48-4
SEMA Equipment Inc			
11555 Hwy 60 Blvd . . . . Wanamingo MN 55983	800-569-1377	507-824-2256	274
Semasys Inc			
4480 Blalock Rd . . . . Houston TX 77041	800-231-1425*		286
*Cust Svc			
SEMCO ENERGY Gas Co			
1411 Third St Ste A . . . . Port Huron MI 48060	800-624-2019		576
Semiconductor Equipment & Materials International			
3081 Zenker Rd . . . . San Jose CA 95134	877-746-7788	408-943-6900	49-19
Seminary of the southwest (SSW)			
501 E 32nd PO Box 2247 . . . . Austin TX 78705	800-252-5400	512-472-4133	167-3
Seminole Casino Immokalee			
506 S First St . . . . Immokalee FL 34142	800-218-0007		133
Seminole Feed			
335 NE Watula Ave PO Box 940 . . . . Ocala FL 34470	800-683-1881	352-732-4143	445
Seminole Hard Rock Hotel & Casino Hollywood			
1 Seminole Way . . . . Hollywood FL 33314	866-502-7529		665
Seminole Hard Rock Hotel & Casino Tampa (SHRH & C)			
5223 N Orient Rd . . . . Tampa FL 33610	866-388-4263*	813-627-7625	133
*General			
Seminole State College			
2701 Boren Blvd PO Box 351 . . . . Seminole OK 74868	877-738-6365	405-382-9950	162
Semling-Menke Company Inc			
PO Box 378 . . . . Merrill WI 54452	800-333-2206	715-536-9411	236
Semonin Realtors			
600 N Hurstbourne Pkwy			
Ste 200 . . . . Louisville KY 40222	800-548-1650	502-425-4760	648
Sempra Energy Corp			
101 Ash St . . . . San Diego CA 92101	800-411-7343	619-696-2000	359-5
NYSE: SRE			
Senate House State Historic Site			
296 Fair St . . . . Kingston NY 12401	800-456-2267	845-338-2786	561
Senator Inn & Spa of Augusta			
284 Western Ave . . . . Augusta ME 04330	877-772-2224	207-622-5804	703
SENCO			
4270 Ivy Pointe Blvd . . . . Cincinnati OH 45245	800-543-4596*		754
*Tech Supp			
SencorpWhite			
400 Kidds Hill Rd . . . . Hyannis MA 02601	800-571-8822	508-771-9400	
Sendec Corp			
72 Perinton Pkwy . . . . Fairport NY 14450	800-295-8000	855-294-3800	203
Sen-Dure Products Inc			
6785 NW 17th Ave . . . . Fort Lauderdale FL 33309	800-394-5112	954-973-1260	91
Seneca Consulting Group Inc			
111 Smithtown Byp Ste 112 . . . . Hauppauge NY 11788	866-487-4157	631-577-4092	464
Seneca County Chamber of Commerce			
2020 Rt 5 & 20 W . . . . Seneca Falls NY 13148	800-732-1848	315-568-2906	139
Seneca Foods Corp			
3736 S Main St . . . . Marion NY 14505	800-622-6757	315-926-8100	296-20
NASDAQ: SENEA			
Seneca Fouts Memorial State Natural Area			
Hood River . . . . Hood River OR 97031	800-551-6949		561
Seneca Niagara Casino			
310 Fourth St . . . . Niagara Falls NY 14303	877-873-6322	716-299-1100	133
Seneca Tank Inc			
5585 NE 16th St . . . . Des Moines IA 50313	800-362-2910	515-262-5900	57
Senergy Petroleum LLC			
622 S 56th Ave . . . . Phoenix AZ 85043	800-964-0076	602-272-6795	575
Senet Inc			
100 Market St Ste 302 . . . . Portsmouth NH 03801	877-807-5755		406
Senior Housing Companies			
208 35th St Dr SE Ste 500 . . . . Cedar Rapids IA 52403	800-366-6716		
Senior Lifestyle			
303 E Upper Wacker Dr Ste 2400 . . . . Chicago IL 60601	877-315-0914		668
Senior Market Sales Inc (SMS)			
8420 W Dodge Rd Ste 510 . . . . Omaha NE 68114	800-786-5566	402-397-3311	389
Senior Marketing Specialist			
801 Gray Oak Dr . . . . Columbia MO 65201	800-689-2800		195
Senior Softball USA			
9823 Old Winery Pl Ste 12 . . . . Sacramento CA 95827	800-327-0074	916-326-5303	48-22
Senior Whole Health LLC (SWH)			
58 Charles St . . . . Cambridge MA 02141	888-794-7268	617-494-5353	352
Seniorsplus			
8 Falcon Rd . . . . Lewiston ME 04240	800-427-1241	207-795-4010	668
Sennheiser Electronics Corp			
1 Enterprise Dr . . . . Old Lyme CT 06371	877-736-6434	860-434-9190	246
Seno Jewelry LLC			
259 W 30th St 10th Fl . . . . New York NY 10001	888-660-2910	212-619-4552	410
Sensidyne Inc			
16333 Bay Vista Dr . . . . Clearwater FL 33760	800-451-9444	727-530-3602	201
Sensient Technologies Corp			
777 E Wisconsin Ave . . . . Milwaukee WI 53202	800-558-9892	414-271-6755	296-15
NYSE: SXT			
Sensitech Inc			
800 Cummings Ctr Ste 258x . . . . Beverly MA 01915	800-843-8367	978-927-7033	171
Senske Services			
400 N Quay St . . . . Kennewick WA 99336	877-944-4007	509-374-5000	573
Sensormatic Electronics Corp			
6600 Congress Ave . . . . Boca Raton FL 33487	800-327-1765	561-912-6000	688
SensorMedics Corp			
22745 Savi Ranch Pkwy . . . . Yorba Linda CA 92887	800-231-2466	714-283-2228	250
SensoryEffects Flavor Co			
231 Rock Industrial Park Dr . . . . Bridgeton MO 63044	800-422-5444	314-291-5444	296-37
Sensus			
8601 Six Forks Rd Ste 700 . . . . Raleigh NC 27615	800-638-3748	919-845-4000	201
Sentara Careplex Hospital			
3000 Coliseum Dr . . . . Hampton VA 23666	800-736-8272	757-736-1000	373-3
Sentara Leigh Hospital			
830 Kempsville Rd . . . . Norfolk VA 23502	800-237-4822	757-261-6000	373-3
Sentara Martha Jefferson Hospital (MJH)			
500 Martha Jefferson Dr			
. . . . Charlottesville VA 22911	888-652-6663	434-654-7000	373-3
Sentara Virginia Beach General Hospital			
1060 First Colonial Rd . . . . Virginia Beach VA 23454	800-736-8272	757-395-8000	373-3
Sentinel			
12100 E Iliff Ave Ste 102 . . . . Aurora CO 80014	855-269-4484	303-750-7555	528-4
Sentinel Bldg Systems Inc			
237 S Fourth St PO Box 348. . . . . Albion NE 68620	800-327-0790	402-395-5076	307
Sentinel Development Solutions Inc			
4015 Beltline Rd Ste 100 . . . . Addison TX 75001	877-395-8976	515-564-0585	804
Sentinel Hotel			
614 SW 11th Ave . . . . Portland OR 97205	888-246-5631	503-224-3400	378
Sentinel Power Services Inc			
7517 E Pine St . . . . Tulsa OK 74115	800-831-9550	918-359-0350	528-3
Sentinel Process Systems			
3265 Sunset Ln . . . . Hatboro PA 19040	800-345-3569		330
Sentinel Systems Corp			
1620 Kipling St . . . . Lakewood CO 80215	800-456-9955	303-242-2000	528-3
Sentinel Technologies Inc			
2550 Warrenville Rd . . . . Downers Grove IL 60515	800-769-4343	630-769-4300	175
Sentinel, The			
457 E N St . . . . Carlisle PA 17013	800-829-5570	717-243-2611	528-2
Sentinel, The			
300 W Sixth St . . . . Hanford CA 93230	888-606-0605	559-582-0471	528-2
Sentran LLC			
4355 Lowell St . . . . Ontario CA 91761	888-545-8988	909-605-1544	361
Sentry BioPharma Services Inc			
4605 Decatur Blvd Ameriplex Pk			
. . . . Indianapolis IN 46241	866-757-7400	317-856-5889	579
Sentry Group			
900 Linden Ave . . . . Rochester NY 14625	800-828-1438*	585-381-4900	688
*Cust Svc			
Sentry Insurance A Mutual Co			
1800 N Point Dr			
PO Box 8032. . . . . Stevens Point WI 54481	800-473-6879		390-4
Sentry Insurance Co			
2 Technology Park Dr . . . . Westford MA 01886	800-373-6879	978-392-7119	390-4
Sentry Investments Inc			
Commerce Court W 199 Bay St Ste 2700			
PO Box 108. . . . . Toronto ON M5L1E2	888-246-6656	416-861-8729	524
Sentry Security LLC			
339 Egidi Dr . . . . Wheeling IL 60090	888-272-7080	847-353-7200	689
Sentry Technology Corp			
1881 Lakeland Ave . . . . Ronkonkoma NY 11779	800-645-4224		688
OTC: SKVY			
Sentry Watch Inc			
1705 Holbrook St . . . . Greensboro NC 27403	800-632-4961		689
Senvoy LLC			
18055 NE San Rafael St . . . . Portland OR 97230	866-373-6869	503-234-7722	311
SEO com LLC			
14870 S Pony Express Rd			
Ste 100 . . . . Bluffdale UT 84065	800-351-9081		7
SEOP			
1621 Alton Pkwy Ste 150 . . . . Irvine CA 92606	877-231-1557		7
Sephora USA Inc			
525 Market St			
1st Market Twr 32nd Fl . . . . San Francisco CA 94105	877-737-4672*		214
*Cust Svc			
SEPLSO (Southeastern Public Library System of Oklahoma)			
401 N Second St . . . . McAlester OK 74501	800-562-9520	918-426-0456	433-3
SEPM (Society for Sedimentary Geology)			
4111 S Darlington Ste 100 . . . . Tulsa OK 74135	800-865-9765	918-610-3361	49-19
Sepp Leaf Products Inc			
381 Park Ave S Ste 1301 . . . . New York NY 10016	800-971-7377	212-683-2840	44
Septagon Construction			
113 E Third St . . . . Sedalia MO 65301	800-733-5999	660-827-2115	186
Sequachee Valley Electric Co-op			
512 Cedar Ave PO Box 31 . . . . South Pittsburg TN 37380	800-923-2203	423-837-8605	245
Sequatchie Concrete Service Inc			
406 Cedar Ave . . . . South Pittsburg TN 37380	800-824-0824	423-837-7913	183
Sequence Controls Inc			
150 Rosamond St . . . . Carleton ON K7C1V2	800-663-1833	613-257-7356	203
Sequenom Inc			
3595 John Hopkins Ct . . . . San Diego CA 92121	877-821-7266	858-202-9000	85
NASDAQ: SQNM			
Sequent Energy Management			
1200 Smith St . . . . Houston TX 77002	866-581-8074	832-397-1700	
Sequins International Inc			
60-01 31st Ave . . . . Woodside NY 11377	800-221-5801	718-204-0002	740-5
Sequoia Fund Inc			
767 Fifth Ave Ste 4701 . . . . New York NY 10153	800-686-6884		524
Sequoyah Bay State Park			
6237 E 100th St N . . . . Wagoner OK 74467	800-622-6317	918-683-0878	561
SeraCare Life Sciences Inc			
37 Birch St . . . . Milford MA 01757	800-676-1881	508-244-6400	89
NASDAQ: SRLS			
Serco Inc			
1818 Library St Ste 1000 . . . . Reston VA 20190	866-628-6458	703-939-6000	24
Serengeti Systems Inc			
1108 Lavaca St Ste 110 PMB 431 . . . . Austin TX 78701	800-634-3122	512-345-2211	178-12
Serenity Lane			
1 Serenity Ln PO Box 8549. . . . . Coburg OR 97408	800-543-9905	541-687-1110	722
Sererra Consulting Group LLC			
4590 MacArthur Blvd			
Ste 500 . . . . Newport Beach CA 92660	877-276-3774		196
Serfilco Ltd			
2900 MacArthur Blvd . . . . Northbrook IL 60062	800-323-5431	847-559-1777	637
Serigraph Inc			
3801 E Decorah Rd . . . . West Bend WI 53095	800-279-6060	262-335-7200	683

Name / Address	City	State	Zip	Toll-Free	Phone	Class
Serta Mattress 3 Golf Ctr Ste 392	Hoffman Estates	IL	60169	**888-557-3782**	888-708-1466	469
Serti Informatique Inc 7555 Beclard St	Montreal	QC	H1J2S5	**800-361-6615**	514-493-1909	196
Sertoma International 1912 E Meyer Blvd	Kansas City	MO	64132	**800-593-5646**	816-333-8300	48-5
Servall Co 6761 E 10 Mile Rd	Center Line	MI	48015	**800-856-9874**		38
SERVE 5900 Summit Ave Ste 201	Browns Summit	NC	27214	**800-755-3277**	336-315-7400	664
Server Products Inc 3601 Pleasant Hill Rd PO Box 98	Richfield	WI	53076	**800-558-8722**	262-628-5100	298
Server Technology Inc 1040 Sandhill Dr	Reno	NV	89521	**800-835-1515**	775-284-2000	176
Service 800 2190 W Wayzata Blvd	Minneapolis	MN	55356	**800-475-3747**	952-475-3747	
Service by Air Inc 222 Crossways Pk Dr	Woodbury	NY	11797	**800-243-5545**		12
Service Communications Inc (SCI) 15223 NE 90th St	Redmond	WA	98052	**800-488-0468**	425-278-0300	179
Service Companies Inc, The 14750 NW 77th Ct Ste 100	Miami Lakes	FL	33016	**800-385-8800**	305-681-8800	392
Service Construction Supply Inc PO Box 13405	Birmingham	AL	35202	**866-729-4968**	205-252-3158	191-3
Service Corp International 1929 Allen Pkwy *NYSE: SCI*	Houston	TX	77019	**800-758-5804**	713-522-5141	508
Service Electric Cable TV & Communications 2260 Ave A	Bethlehem	PA	18017	**800-232-9100**	610-865-9100	116
Service Electric Supply Inc 15424 Oakwood Dr	Romulus	MI	48174	**800-426-7575**	734-229-9100	246
Service Employees International Union 1800 Massachusetts Ave NW	Washington	DC	20036	**800-424-8592**	202-730-7000	413
Service Express Inc 3854 Broadmoor Ave SE	Grand Rapids	MI	49512	**800-940-4484**	800-940-5585	
Service Graphics LLC 8350 Allison Ave	Indianapolis	IN	46268	**800-884-9876**	317-471-8246	683
Service Ideas Inc 2354 Ventura Dr	Woodbury	MN	55125	**800-328-4493**	651-730-8800	300
Service King Collision Repair Centers 2375 N Glenville Dr	Richardson	TX	75080	**844-611-5068**	972-960-7595	62-4
Service Objects Inc 27 E Cota St Ste 500	Santa Barbara	CA	93101	**800-694-6269**		
Service Spring Corp 6615 Maumee Western Rd	Maumee	OH	43537	**800-752-8522**	419-838-6081	714
Service Steel Aerospace Corp 4609 70th St E	Fife	WA	98424	**800-426-9794**	253-627-2910	490
ServiceMaster Clean 3839 Forrest Hill Irene Rd *General	Memphis	TN	38125	**844-319-5401***		152
Servo Products Co 34940 Lakeland Blvd	Eastlake	OH	44095	**800-521-7359**	440-942-9999	453
Servpro Industries Inc 801 Industrial Blvd	Gallatin	TN	37066	**800-826-9586**	615-451-0200	152
SESAC Inc 55 Music Sq E	Nashville	TN	37203	**800-826-9996**	615-320-0055	48-4
Sesame Software 5201 Great America Pkwy Ste 320	Santa Clara	CA	94160	**866-474-7575**	408-550-7999	260
SESRC (Social & Economic Sciences Research Ctr) *Washington State University* Wilson Hall Rm 133 PO Box 644014	Pullman	WA	99164	**800-932-5393**	509-335-1511	664
Sessions Specialty Co 5090 Styers Ferry Rd	Lewisville	NC	27023	**800-763-0077**	336-766-2880	146
Set & Service Resources LLC 5400 Glenwood Ave Ste 310	Raleigh	NC	27615	**866-867-5571**		260
Set Solutions Inc 1800 W Loop S Ste 700	Houston	TX	77027	**888-353-0574**	713-956-6600	174
SETA (Southeast Tissue Alliance) 6241 NW 23rd St Ste 400	Gainesville	FL	32653	**866-432-1164**	352-248-2114	541
Setai, The 2001 Collins Ave	Miami Beach	FL	33139	**888-625-7500**	305-520-6000	378
Setco Sales Co 5880 Hillside Ave	Cincinnati	OH	45233	**800-543-0470**	513-941-5110	453
Setcom Corp 3019 Alvin DeVane Blvd Ste 560	Austin	TX	78741	**800-645-1285**	650-965-8020	643
Setel 1165 s Sixth st	Macclenny	FL	32063	**800-662-0716**	904-259-1300	386
SETEL UC 720 Cool Springs Blvd Ste 520	Franklin	TN	37067	**800-743-1340**	615-874-6000	782
Sethness Products Co 3422 W Touhy Ave	Lincolnwood	IL	60712	**888-772-1880**	847-329-2080	296-15
Setina Manufacturing Company Inc 2926 Yelm Hwy SE	Olympia	WA	98501	**800-426-2627**	360-491-6197	392
Seton Hall University 400 S Orange Ave	South Orange	NJ	07079	**800-992-4723**	973-761-9332	166
Seton Hill University 1 Seton Hill Dr	Greensburg	PA	15601	**800-826-6234**	724-838-4255	166
Seton Home Study School 1350 Progress Dr	Front Royal	VA	22630	**800-542-1066**	540-636-9990	681
Seton Hotel 144 E 40th St	New York	NY	10016	**866-697-3866**	212-889-5301	461
Seton Medical Ctr 1900 Sullivan Ave	Daly City	CA	94015	**833-427-7436**	650-992-4000	373-3
Setra Systems Inc 159 Swanson Rd	Boxborough	MA	01719	**800-257-3872**	978-263-1400	470
Settle & Pou PC 3333 Lee Pkwy 8th Fl	Dallas	TX	75219	**800-538-4661**	214-520-3300	427
Settlers Life Insurance Co 1969 Lee Hwy	Bristol	VA	24201	**800-523-2650**	276-645-4300	390-2
Seva Foundation 1786 Fifth St	Berkeley	CA	94710	**877-764-7382**	510-845-7382	305
Seven Oaks Capital Assoc LLC 7854 Anselmo Ln PO Box 82360	Baton Rouge	LA	70810	**800-511-4588**	225-757-1919	272
Seven Pines National Cemetery 400 E Williamsburg Rd	Sandston	VA	23150	**800-535-1117**	804-795-2031	136
Seven Springs Mountain Resort 777 Waterwheel Dr	Champion	PA	15622	**800-452-2223**	814-352-7777	665
Seventh Generation Inc 60 Lake St	Burlington	VT	05401	**800-456-1191**	802-658-3773	151
Seventh Mountain Resort 18575 SW Century Dr	Bend	OR	97702	**877-765-1501**	541-382-8711	665
Seventh-day Adventist World Church 12501 Old Columbia Pk	Silver Spring	MD	20904	**800-226-1119**	301-680-6000	48-20
Severn Bancorp Inc 200 Westgate Cir Ste 200 *NASDAQ: SVBI*	Annapolis	MD	21401	**800-752-5854**	410-260-2000	70
Seward Convention & Visitors Bureau 2001 Seward Hwy	Seward	AK	99664	**800-257-7760**	907-224-8051	206
Seward County Community College 1801 N Campus Ave PO Box 1137	Liberal	KS	67905	**800-373-9951**	620-624-1951	162
Seward Motor Freight PO Box 126	Seward	NE	68434	**800-786-4469**	402-643-4503	775
Sewickley Valley Hospital 720 Blackburn Rd	Sewickley	PA	15143	**800-400-6180**	877-771-4847	373-3
Sex Addicts Anonymous (SAA) PO Box 70949	Houston	TX	77270	**800-477-8191**	713-869-4902	48-21
Sexaholics Anonymous (SA) PO Box 3565	Brentwood	TN	37024	**866-424-8777**	615-370-6062	48-21
Seymour Johnson Air Force Base 1510 Wright Bros Ave	Seymour Johnson AFB	NC	27531	**800-525-0102**	919-722-0027	495-1
Seymour of Sycamore Inc 917 Crosby Ave	Sycamore	IL	60178	**800-435-4482**	815-895-9101	546
Seyon Lodge State Park 1 National Life Dr	Vermont	VT	05620	**888-409-7579**	802-584-3829	561
SFASU (Stephen F Austin State University Steen Library) 1936 N St	Nacogdoches	TX	75962	**800-765-1534**	936-468-3401	433-6
SFB (Security Federal Bank) 238 Richland Ave W	Aiken	SC	29801	**866-851-3000**	803-641-3000	71
SFC (Sandridge Food Corp) 133 Commerce Dr	Medina	OH	44256	**800-627-2523**	330-725-2348	296-33
SFE Investment Counsel Inc 801 S Figueroa St Ste 2100	Los Angeles	CA	90017	**800-445-6320**	213-612-0220	686
SFS intec Inc Spring St & Van Reed Rd	Wyomissing	PA	19610	**800-234-4533**	610-376-5751	617
SFSP (Society of Financial Service Professionals) 19 Campus Blvd Ste 100	Newtown Square	PA	19073	**800-392-6900**	610-526-2500	49-9
SG Wholesale Roofing Supplies 1101 E Sixth St *Cust Svc	Santa Ana	CA	92701	**800-464-2461***	714-568-1900	191-4
SGH (Southwest General Hospital) 7400 Barlite Blvd	San Antonio	TX	78224	**877-898-6080**	210-921-2000	373-3
SGH Golf Inc 6805 Mt Vernon Ave	Cincinnati	OH	45227	**800-284-8884**	513-984-0414	766
SGIA (Specialty Graphic Imaging Assn) 10015 Main St	Fairfax	VA	22031	**888-385-3588**	703-385-1335	49-16
SGNA (Society of Gastroenterology Nurses & Assoc Inc) 401 N Michigan Ave	Chicago	IL	60611	**800-245-7462**	312-321-5165	49-8
SGS North America Inc 201 State Rt 17 N	Rutherford	NJ	07070	**800-645-5227**	201-508-3000	359-3
SH (Shive-Hattery Inc) 316 Second St SE Ste 500 PO Box 1599	Cedar Rapids	IA	52406	**800-798-0227**	319-362-0313	261
SH. Coleman Library *FAMU Libraries* 1500 S Martin Luther King Blvd	Tallahassee	FL	32307	**800-540-6754**	850-599-3370	433-6
Shackford Head State Park 106 Hogan Ave	Bangor	ME	04401	**800-400-6856**	207-941-4014	561
Shade Systems Inc 4150 SW 19th St	Ocala	FL	34474	**800-609-6066**	352-237-0135	295
Shader Bros Corp 6325 Edgewater Dr	Orlando	FL	32810	**866-762-4888**		
Shades of Green on Walt Disney World Resort 1950 W Magnolia Palm Dr	Lake Buena Vista	FL	32830	**888-593-2242**	407-824-3400	378
Shadin LP 6831 Oxford St	St Louis Park	MN	55426	**800-328-0584**	952-927-6500	525
Shadow Mountain Resort & Club 45-750 San Luis Rey	Palm Desert	CA	92260	**800-472-3713**	760-346-6123	665
Shafer's Tour & Charter 500 N St	Endicott	NY	13760	**800-287-8986**	607-797-2006	107
Shaffstall Corp 8531 Bash St	Indianapolis	IN	46250	**800-357-6250**	317-842-2077	173-8
Shaker Group Inc, The 862 Albany Shaker Rd	Latham	NY	12110	**800-267-0314**	518-786-9286	447
Shaker International 3201 Entp Pkwy Ste 360	Cleveland	OH	44122	**888-485-7633**		461
Shaker Village of Pleasant Hill 3501 Lexington Rd	Harrodsburg	KY	40330	**800-734-5611**	859-734-5411	517
Shakespeare Fishing Tackle Co 7 Science Ct *Cust Svc	Columbia	SC	29203	**800-466-5643***	803-754-7000	706
Shakespeare Monofilaments & Specialty Polymers 6111 Shakespeare Rd	Columbia	SC	29223	**800-845-2110**	803-754-7011	604
Shakespeare Theatre 516 Eigth St SE	Washington	DC	20003	**877-487-8849**	202-547-3230	569-4
Shaklee Corp 4747 Willow Rd	Pleasanton	CA	94588	**800-742-5533**	925-924-2000	365
Shambhala Mountain Ctr 151 Shambhala Wy	Red Feather Lakes	CO	80545	**888-788-7221**	970-881-2184	669
Shamokin Filler Company Inc PO Box 568	Shamokin	PA	17872	**800-577-8008**	570-644-0437	190
Shamrock Communications Inc 149 Penn Ave	Scranton	PA	18503	**800-228-4637**	570-348-9100	639
Shamrock Foods 3900 E Camelback Rd Ste 300	Phoenix	AZ	85018	**800-289-3663**	602-477-2500	296-27
Shamrock Scientific Specialty Systems Inc 34 Davis Dr	Bellwood	IL	60104	**800-323-0249**		412
Shamrock Steel Sales Inc 238 W County Rd S	Odessa	TX	79763	**800-299-2317**	432-337-2317	490
Shanahan's LP 13139 80th Ave	Surrey	BC	V3W3B1	**888-591-5999**	604-591-5111	497

	Toll-Free	Phone	Class
Shands Hospital at the University of Florida			
1600 SW Archer Rd ....Gainesville FL 32608	855-483-7546	352-265-0111	373-3
Shane Co			
9790 E Arapahoe Rd ....Greenwood Village CO 80112	866-467-4263	303-799-4700	409
Shanks Extracts Inc			
350 Richardson Dr ....Lancaster PA 17603	800-346-3135	717-393-4441	297-8
Shannon Diversified Inc			
1360 E Locust St ....Ontario CA 91761	800-794-2345		104
Shanty Creek Resort			
5780 Shanty Creek Rd ....Bellaire MI 49615	800-678-4111	231-533-8621	665
Shape LLC			
2105 Corporate Dr ....Addison IL 60101	800-367-5811	630-620-8394	762
Share Corp			
7821 N Faulkner Rd ....Milwaukee WI 53224	800-776-7192		151
Share Our Strength			
1730 M St NW Ste 700..............Washington DC 20036	800-969-4767	202-393-2925	48-5
SHARE Pregnancy & Infant Loss Support Inc			
402 Jackson St ....Saint Charles MO 63301	800-821-6819	636-947-6164	48-21
shared logic group inc, The			
6904 Spring Vly Dr Ste 305 ....Holland OH 43528	877-865-0083	419-865-0083	177
Shared Service Systems Inc			
1725 S 20th St ....Omaha NE 68108	800-228-9976	402-536-5300	473
ShareSquared Inc			
2155 Verdugo Blvd ....Montrose CA 91020	800-445-1279		180
Sharetracker			
PO Box 20 ....Ashland MO 65010	888-628-3088		464
Sharf Woodward & Associates Inc			
5900 Sepulveda Blvd ....Van Nuys CA 91411	877-482-6687	818-989-2200	260
Shari's Restaurant & Pies			
9400 SW Gemini Dr ....Beaverton OR 97008	800-433-5334	503-605-4299	666
Sharkey Howes & Javer Inc			
720 S Colorado Blvd			
Ste 600 S Twr ....Denver CO 80246	800-557-9380	303-639-5100	194
Sharon Public Library			
90 S Main St ....Sharon MA 02067	800-825-3260	781-784-1578	433-3
Sharonville Convention Ctr			
11355 Chester Rd ....Sharonville OH 45246	800-294-3179	513-771-7744	205
Sharp Bros Seed Co			
1005 S Sycamore ....Healy KS 67850	800-462-8483	620-398-2231	690
Sharp Electronics Corp			
1 Sharp Plz ....Mahwah NJ 07430	800-237-4277	201-529-8200	52
Sharp Energy Inc			
648 Ocean Hwy ....Pocomoke City MD 21851	888-742-7740		316
Sharp Health Plan			
4305 University Ave Ste 200..........San Diego CA 92105	800-359-2002	619-228-2300	390-3
Sharp Healthcare			
8695 Spectrum Ctr Blvd ....San Diego CA 92123	800-827-4277	858-499-4000	352
Sharp Innovations Inc			
3113 Main St Bldg B, Main Level			
..............Conestoga PA 17516	888-575-8977	717-290-6760	804
Shasta Beverages Inc			
26901 Industrial Blvd ....Hayward CA 94545	800-834-9980	510-783-4070	80-2
Shasta County			
1643 Market St ....Redding CA 96099	800-735-2922	530-225-5730	337
Shasta Public Library			
1100 Parkview Ave ....Redding CA 96001	800-735-2922	530-245-7250	433-3
Shattuck-Saint Mary's School			
1000 Shumway Ave ....Faribault MN 55021	800-421-2724	507-333-1500	618
Shaw Air Force Base			
20 FW/SEF 517 Lance Ave			
Ste 215 ....Shaw AFB SC 29152	800-235-7776	803-895-1971	495-1
Shaw Communications Inc			
630 Third Ave SW ....Calgary AB T2P4L4	888-472-2222	403-750-4500	116
TSE: SJR.B			
Shaw Glass Company Inc			
55 Bristol Dr ....South Easton MA 02375	800-225-0430		
Shaw Industries Inc			
616 E Walnut Ave ....Dalton GA 30722	800-441-7429		131
Shaw University			
118 E S St ....Raleigh NC 27601	800-214-6683*	919-546-8275	166
*Admissions			
Shaw/Stewart Lumber Co			
645 Johnson St NE ....Minneapolis MN 55413	800-233-0101	612-378-1520	497
Shawano Country Chamber of Commerce			
1263 S Main St ....Shawano WI 54166	800-235-8528	715-524-2139	139
Shawnee Community College			
8364 Shawnee College Rd ....Ullin IL 62992	800-481-2242	618-634-3200	162
Shawnee Milling Company Inc			
201 S Broadway PO Box 1567 ....Shawnee OK 74802	800-654-2600	405-273-7000	296-23
Shawnee Mountain Ski Area			
401 Hollow Rd ....East Stroudsburg PA 18301	800-233-4218	570-421-7231	31
Shawnee State University			
940 Second St ....Portsmouth OH 45662	800-959-2778	740-351-3221	166
Shawnee Telephone Co			
PO Box 69 ....Equality IL 62934	800-461-3956	618-276-4211	731
SHDR (Stanley Hunt DuPree & Rhine)			
7701 Airport Ctr Dr ....Greensboro NC 27409	800-930-2441	800-768-4873	193
Shea Concrete Products Inc			
87 Haverhill Rd ....Amesbury MA 01913	800-696-7432	978-388-1509	765
Sheaff Brock Investment Advisors LLC			
8801 River Crossing Blvd			
Ste 100 ....Indianapolis IN 46240	866-575-5700	317-705-5700	400
Shealy's Truck Ctr Inc			
1340 Bluff Rd ....Columbia SC 29201	800-951-8580	803-771-0176	513
Sheboygan Paint Co (SPC)			
1439 N 25th St PO Box 417..........Sheboygan WI 53081	800-773-7801	920-458-2157	546
Sheboygan Press			
632 Center Ave ....Sheboygan WI 53081	800-686-3900	920-843-9656	528-2
Shee Atika Inc			
315 Lincoln St Ste 300..............Sitka AK 99835	800-478-3534	907-747-3534	113
Sheetz Inc			
5700 Sixth Ave ....Altoona PA 16602	800-487-5444	814-941-5106	204
Sheffield Metals International Inc			
5467 Evergreen Pkwy ....Sheffield Village OH 44054	800-283-5262	440-934-8500	490
Shelburne Farms			
1611 Harbor Rd ....Shelburne VT 05482	800-286-6022	802-985-8686	48-13
Shelby County			
612 Ct St ....Harlan IA 51537	800-735-3942	712-755-3831	337
Shelby County Alabama			
200 W College St ....Columbiana AL 35051	800-272-4263	205-670-6550	337
Shelby County Chamber of Commerce			
501 N Harrison St ....Shelbyville IN 46176	800-318-4083	317-398-6647	139
Shelby Electric Co-op (SEC)			
1355 IL-128 state			
PO Box 560..............Shelbyville IL 62565	800-677-2612	217-774-3986	245
Shelby Energy Co-op Inc			
620 Old Finchville Rd ....Shelbyville KY 40065	800-292-6585	502-633-4420	245
Shelby Materials			
157 E Rampart St PO Box 242 ....Shelbyville IN 46176	800-548-9516		182
Shelby Systems Inc			
7345 Goodlett Farms Pkwy ....Cordova TN 38016	800-877-0222	901-757-2372	177
Shelby Williams Industries Inc			
810 West Hwy 25/70 ....Newport TN 37821	800-873-3252*	423-623-0031	319-3
*General			
Sheldahl Inc			
1150 Sheldahl Rd ....Northfield MN 55057	800-927-3580	507-663-8000	692
Sheldon Museum of Art			
PO Box 880300 ....Lincoln NE 68588	800-833-6747	402-472-2461	517
Shell Canada Ltd			
400 Fourth Ave SW ....Calgary AB T2P0J4	877-656-3111	403-691-3111	532
Shell Chemical Co			
910 Louisiana St ....Houston TX 77002	855-697-4355		144
Shell Island Ocean Front Suites			
2700 N Lumina Ave ....Wrightsville Beach NC 28480	800-689-6765	910-256-8696	703
Shell Oil Co			
910 Louisanna St ....Houston TX 77002	888-467-4355	713-241-6161	532
Shell Point Village			
15101 Shell Pt Blvd ....Fort Myers FL 33908	800-780-1131*	239-466-1131	668
*Mktg			
Shelly Automotive Group			
Irvine BMW			
9881 Research Dr ....Irvine CA 92618	888-853-7429		57
Shelly Co 80 Pk Dr ....Thornville OH 43076	888-743-5590		
SheltAir Aviation Services Fort Lauderdale			
4860 NE 12th Ave ....Fort Lauderdale FL 33334	800-700-2210	954-771-2210	63
Shelton State			
Community College			
9500 Old Greensboro Rd ....Tuscaloosa AL 35405	877-838-2778	205-391-2211	162
Shelton-Mason County Chamber of Commerce			
215 W Railroad Ave PO Box 2389 ....Shelton WA 98584	800-576-2021	360-426-2021	139
Shenandoah Life Insurance Co			
2301 Brambleton Ave ....Roanoke VA 24015	800-848-5433	540-985-4400	390-2
Shenandoah National Park			
3655 US Hwy 211E ....Luray VA 22835	800-732-0911	540-999-3500	560
Shenandoah Telecommunications Co			
500 Shentel Way ....Edinburg VA 22824	800-743-6835	540-984-5224	359-3
NASDAQ: SHEN			
Shenandoah University			
1460 University Dr ....Winchester VA 22601	800-432-2266	540-665-4581	166
Shenandoah Valley Westminster-Canterbury			
300 Westminster-Canterbury Dr			
..............Winchester VA 22603	800-492-9463	540-665-5914	668
Shenango Advanced Ceramics LLC			
606 McCleary Ave ....New Castle PA 16101	888-283-5505		
Shenvalee Golf Resort			
9660 Fairway Dr ....New Market VA 22844	888-339-3181	540-740-3181	665
Shepherd Caster			
203 Kerth St ....Saint Joseph MI 49085	800-253-0868	269-983-7351	349
Shepherd CE Company Inc			
2221 Canada Dry St ....Houston TX 77023	800-324-6733	713-924-4300	596
Shepherd Electric Supply			
7401 Pulaski Hwy ....Baltimore MD 21237	800-253-1777*	410-866-6000	246
*Sales			
Shepherd University			
301 N King St ....Shepherdstown WV 25443	800-344-5231	304-876-5000	166
Shepherdsville-Bullitt County Tourist & Convention Commission			
395 Paroquet Springs Dr ....Shepherdsville KY 40165	800-526-2068	502-543-8687	206
Sheplers Inc			
6501 W Kellogg Dr ....Wichita KS 67209	888-835-4004	316-946-3786	157-5
Sheppard Air Force Base			
419 G Ave Ste 1 ....Sheppard AFB TX 76311	877-676-1847	940-676-2511	495-1
Sheppard Motors			
2300 W Seventh Ave ....Eugene OR 97402	877-362-1865*	541-343-8811	57
*Sales			
Sheppard Pratt Health System (SPHS)			
6501 N Charles St ....Baltimore MD 21285	800-627-0330	410-938-3000	373-5
Sheraton Agoura Hills Hotel			
30100 Agoura Rd ....Agoura Hills CA 91301	866-716-8134	818-707-1220	703
Sheraton Colonial Hotel & Golf Club Boston North			
1 Audubon Rd ....Wakefield MA 01880	866-716-8133	781-245-9300	378
Sheraton Denver Tech Center Hotel			
7007 S Clinton St ....Greenwood Village CO 80112	800-525-3177	303-799-6200	703
Sheraton Fishermans Wharf (San Francisco, CA)			
2500 Mason St ....San Francisco CA 94133	866-716-8134	415-362-5500	703
Sheraton Gateway Hotel Los Angeles			
6101 W Century Blvd ....Los Angeles CA 90045	888-627-7104	310-642-1111	378
Sheraton Gunter Hotel			
205 E Houston St ....San Antonio TX 78205	866-716-8134	210-227-3241	703
Sheraton Lake Buena Vista			
12205 S Apopka Vineland Rd ....Orlando FL 32836	800-325-3535	407-239-0444	703
Sheraton Oklahoma City Hotel			
1 N Broadway ....Oklahoma City OK 73102	888-627-8416	405-235-2780	377
Sheraton Old San Juan Hotel			
100 Brumbaugh St ....San Juan PR 00901	888-627-8185	787-289-1914	376
Sheraton Phoenix Downtown Hotel			
340 N Third St ....Phoenix AZ 85004	866-716-8134	602-262-2500	703
Sheraton Raleigh Hotel			
421 S Salisbury St ....Raleigh NC 27601	888-627-8319	919-834-9900	703
Sheraton Sand Key Resort			
1160 Gulf Blvd ....Clearwater Beach FL 33767	800-456-7263	727-595-1611	665
Sheraton Suites Calgary Eau Claire			
255 Barclay Parade SW ....Calgary AB T2P5C2	866-716-8134	403-266-7200	378
Sheraton Washington North Hotel			
4095 Powder Mill Rd ....Beltsville MD 20705	888-627-8646	301-937-4422	703
Sheraton Wild Horse Pass Resort & Spa			
5594 W Wild Horse Pass Blvd ....Phoenix AZ 85226	866-837-4156	602-225-0100	665

	Toll-Free	Phone	Class
Sheridan College 3059 Coffeen Ave PO Box 1500 .... Sheridan WY 82801	800-913-9139	307-674-6446	162
Gillette 300 West Sinclair .... Gillette WY 82718	800-913-9139	307-686-0254	162
Sheridan County 224 S Main St Ste B-2 .... Sheridan WY 82801	800-565-4502	307-674-2500	337
Sheridan County Chamber of Commerce 1898 Fort Rd .... Sheridan WY 82801	800-453-3650	307-672-2485	139
Sheridan Group 11311 McCormick Rd Ste 260 .... Hunt Valley MD 21031	800-352-2210	410-785-7277	622
Sheridan Healthcare Inc 1613 NW 136th Ave Ste 200............ Sunrise FL 33323	800-437-2672		461
Shermag Inc 3035 Boul Industriel .... Sherbrooke QC J1L2T9	800-567-3419	819-566-1515	319-2
Sherman & Reilly Inc 400 W 33rd St .... Chattanooga TN 37410 *Sales	800-251-7780*	423-756-5300	468
Sherman Bros Trucking 32921 Diamond Hill Dr PO Box 706........................ Harrisburg OR 97446	800-547-8980	541-995-7751	775
Sherman Clay & Company Inc 1111 Bayhill Dr Ste 450 .... San Bruno CA 94066	888-562-4069		522
Shermeta, Adams & Von Allmen PC 1030 Doris Rd Ste 200............ Auburn Hills MI 48326	800-451-7992	248-519-1700	427
Shernoff Bidart Darras & Echeverria LLP 600 S Indian Hill Blvd .... Claremont CA 91711	800-458-3386	909-621-4935	427
Sherpa Digital Media Inc 509 Seaport Ct .... Redwood City CA 94063	866-989-7794		5
Sherrill-Lubinski Corp 240 Tamal Vista Blvd ....Corte Madera CA 94925	800-548-6881	415-927-8400	177
Sherritt International Corp 1133 Yonge St .... Toronto ON M4T2Y7 *TSE: S*	800-704-6698	416-924-4551	500
Sherrod Vans Inc 3151 Industrial Blvd ....Waycross GA 31503	800-824-6333		62-7
Sherry Matthews Inc 200 S Congress Ave .... Austin TX 78704	877-478-4397	512-478-4397	4
Sherry Mfg Co Inc 3287 NW 65th St .... Miami FL 33147	800-741-4750	305-693-7000	155-3
Sherry-Netherland Hotel 781 Fifth Ave ....New York NY 10022	877-743-7710	212-355-2800	378
Sherwin-Williams Automotive Finishes 4440 Warrensville Ctr Rd .... Warrensville Heights OH 44128	800-798-5872		546
Sherwood 2200 N Main St .... Washington PA 15301	888-508-2583	724-225-8000	784
Sherwood Oaks 100 Norman Dr ....Cranberry Township PA 16066	800-642-2217	724-776-8100	668
Sherwood Windows Ltd 37 Iron St .... Toronto ON M9W5E3	800-770-5256	416-675-3262	349
Shetler Moving & Storage Inc 1253 E Diamond Ave .... Evansville IN 47711	800-321-5069	812-421-7750	775
SHI (Software House International) 290 Davidson Ave ....Somerset NJ 08873	888-764-8888		174
Shibuya Hoppmann Corp 13129 Airpark Dr Ste 120..............Elkwood VA 22718 *Cust Svc	800-368-3582*	540-829-2564	543
Shick Tube Veyor Corp 4346 Clary Blvd .... Kansas City MO 64130	877-744-2587	816-861-7224	207
Shiel Medical Laboratory Inc 292 63 Flushing Ave Brooklyn Navy Yard Bldg .... Brooklyn NY 11205	800-553-0873	718-552-1000	414
Shield Air Solutions Inc 3708 Greenhouse Rd ....Houston TX 77084	800-237-2095	281-944-4300	14
Shield Engineering Inc 4301 Taggart Creek Rd .... Charlotte NC 28208	800-395-5220	704-394-6913	261
Shields Bag & Printing Co 1009 Rock Ave ....Yakima WA 98902	800-541-8630	509-248-7500	66
SHIFT Energy Inc 1 Germain St 18th Fl................Saint John NB E2L4V1	855-744-3860		
ShiftCentral Inc 210 John St Ste 100................. Moncton NB E1C0B8	866-551-5533		5
ShiftWise Inc 200 SW Market St Ste 700 ....Portland OR 97201	866-399-2220		804
Shilo Inn Suites Salem 3304 Market St .... Salem OR 97301	800-222-2244	503-581-4001	378
Shiloh Industries Corp 880 Steel Dr .... Valley City OH 44280	800-414-3627	330-558-2600	487
Shimadzu Medical Systems 20101 S Vermont Ave ....Torrance CA 90502 *General	800-477-1227*	310-217-8855	381
Shimadzu Precision Instruments inc 7102 Riverwood Dr ....Columbia MD 21046	800-477-1227	410-381-1227	
Shimadzu Scientific Instruments Inc 7102 Riverwood Dr ....Columbia MD 21046	800-477-1227	410-381-1227	418
Shimpo 1701 Glenlake Ave ....Itasca IL 60143	800-842-1479	630-924-7138	190
SHINE Medical Technologies Inc 101 E Milwaukee St Ste 600...........Janesville WI 53545	877-512-6554	608-210-1060	
Shin-Etsu Silicones of America 1150 Damar Dr ....Akron OH 44305	800-544-1745	330-630-9860	144
Shipley Energy 415 Norway St ....York PA 17403	800-839-1849	717-848-4100	316
Shippensburg University 1871 Old Main Dr .... Shippensburg PA 17257	800-822-8028	717-477-1231	166
Shippers Express INC 1651 Kerr Dr ....Jackson MS 39204	800-647-2480	601-948-4251	775
Shipshewana/LaGrange County Convention & Visitors Bureau 350 S Van Buren St Ste H..........Shipshewana IN 46565	800-254-8090	260-768-4008	206
Shirtcliff Oil Co PO Box 6003 .... Myrtle Creek OR 97457	800-422-0536	541-863-5268	324
Shive-Hattery Inc (SH) 316 Second St SE Ste 500 PO Box 1599...................Cedar Rapids IA 52406	800-798-0227	319-362-0313	261
Shively Bros Inc 2919 S Grand Travers St PO Box 1520.........................Flint MI 48501	800-530-9352	810-232-7401	384
Shively Labs 188 Harrison Rd PO Box 389 ....Bridgton ME 04009	888-744-8359	207-647-3327	643
Shivvers Inc 614 W English St ....Corydon IA 50060	800-245-9093	641-872-1005	273
Sho-Air International 5401 Argosy Ave .... Huntington Beach CA 92649	800-227-9111	949-476-9111	311
Shoalwater Bay Casino 4112 State Hwy 105 .... Tokeland WA 98590	866-992-3675	360-267-2048	132
Shoco Oil Inc 5135 E 74th Ave ....Commerce CO 80037	800-854-5553	303-289-1677	575
Shoe Carnival Inc 7500 E Columbia St .... Evansville IN 47715 *NASDAQ: SCVL* ■ *Cust Svc	800-430-7463*	812-867-6471	301
Shoe Sensation Inc 253 America Pl ....Jeffersonville IN 47130	844-891-3070		301
Shoe Show of Rocky Mountain Inc 2201 Trinity Church Rd ....Concord NC 28027 *Cust Svc	888-557-4637*	704-782-4143	301
Shofu Dental Corp 1225 Stone Dr ....San Marcos CA 92078	800-827-4638	760-736-3277	474
Shoney's Restaurants Inc 1717 Elm Hill Pk Ste B1 .... Nashville TN 37210	800-708-3558		666
Shook & Fletcher Insulation Co 4625 Valleydale Rd ....Birmingham AL 35242	888-829-2575	205-991-7606	191-4
Shook & Stone Attorneys at Law 710 S Fourth St .... Las Vegas NV 89101	888-662-2013	702-385-2220	427
Shook Hardy & Bacon LLP 2555 Grand Blvd .... Kansas City MO 64108	855-380-7584	816-474-6550	427
Shooting Star Casino 777 SE Casino Rd .... Mahnomen MN 56557	800-453-7827		450
Shop 'n Save 10461 Manchester Rd ....Kirkwood MO 63122	800-428-6974	314-984-0322	344
Shop at North Bridge, The 520 N Michigan Ave ....Chicago IL 60611	800-977-6255	312-327-2300	
Shop Floor Automations Inc 5360 Jackson Dr ....La Mesa CA 91942	877-611-5825	619-461-4000	225
Shopko LLC 700 Pilgrim Way .... Green Bay WI 54304	800-791-7333	920-429-2211	229
Shopletcom 39 Broadway Ste 2030 ....New York NY 10006	800-757-3015		786
Shopper Local 2327 Englert Dr .... Durham NC 27713	877-251-4592		413
Shoppes at Bel Air, The 3299 Bel Air Mall ....Mobile AL 36606	800-275-8777	251-478-1893	458
Shopping Centers Today 1221 Ave of the Americas ....New York NY 10020	888-427-2885	646-728-3800	527-13
ShopRite PO Box 7812 .... Edison NJ 08818	800-746-7748		344
Shops at Woodlake 725 Woodlake Rd .... Kohler WI 53044	855-444-2838	920-459-1713	458
Shopsmith Inc 6530 Poe Ave ....Dayton OH 45414 *OTC: SSMH* ■ *Cust Svc	800-543-7586*	937-898-6070	754
Shop-Vac Corp 2323 Reach Rd PO Box 3307 .... Williamsport PA 17701	844-807-7711	570-326-0502	385
Shore Acres State Park 725 Summer St NE Ste C .... Salem OR 97301	800-551-6949	541-888-3732	
Shore Memorial Hospital 20480 Market St PO Box 430..........Onancock VA 23417	800-834-7035	757-302-2100	373-3
Shore Morgan Young 300 W Wilson Bridge Rd ....Worthington OH 43085	800-288-2117	614-888-2117	686
Shoreline Community College 16101 Greenwood Ave N ....Shoreline WA 98133	866-427-4747	206-546-4101	162
Shoreline Container Inc 4450 N 136th Ave PO Box 1993......... Holland MI 49422	800-968-2088	616-399-2088	100
Shorewest Realtors Inc 17450 W N Ave .... Brookfield WI 53008	800-434-7350	262-827-4200	648
Shorr Packaging Inc 800 N Commerce St .... Aurora IL 60504	888-885-0055	630-978-1000	555
Short Freight Lines Inc 459 S River Rd PO Box 357 ....Bay City MI 48707	800-248-0625	989-893-3505	775
Short Hills Tours 46 Chatham Rd ....Short Hills NJ 07078	800-348-6871	973-467-2113	755
Short-Elliott-Hendrickson Inc 3535 Vadnais Ctr Dr .... Saint Paul MN 55110	800-325-2055	651-490-2000	261
Shorter University 315 Shorter Ave ....Rome GA 30165	800-868-6980	706-233-7319	166
Shoshone County 700 Bank St .... Wallace ID 83873	800-325-7940	208-752-3331	337
SHOWA 579 Edison St .... Menlo GA 30731	800-241-0323		431
Showplace Wood Products Inc 1 Enterprise St ....Harrisburg SD 57032	877-512-2500	605-743-2200	115
SHPTV (Smoky Hills Public Television) 604 Elm St ....Bunker Hill KS 67626	800-337-4788	785-483-6990	628
Shreveport-Bossier Convention & Tourist Bureau 629 Spring St ....Shreveport LA 71101	800-551-8682	318-222-9391	206
SHRH & C (Seminole Hard Rock Hotel & Casino Tampa) 5223 N Orient Rd .... Tampa FL 33610 *General	866-388-4263*	813-627-7625	133
Shrine of Our Lady of La Leche 27 Ocean Ave ....Saint Augustine FL 32084	800-342-6529	904-824-2809	50-1
Shriners Hospitals for Children 2900 N Rocky Point Dr .... Tampa FL 33607	800-361-7256	514-842-4464	373-1
Shriners Hospitals for Children 2900 N Rocky Pt Dr .... Tampa FL 33607	800-237-5055	813-281-0300	352
Shriners Hospitals for Children Boston 51 Blossom St ....Boston MA 02114	800-255-1916	617-722-3000	373-1
Shriners Hospitals for Children Erie 1645 W Eigth St .... Erie PA 16505	800-873-5437	814-875-8700	373-1
Shriners Hospitals for Children Galveston 2900 Rocky Pt Dr .... Tampa FL 33607	844-739-0849	813-281-0300	373-1
Shriners Hospitals for Children Greenville 950 W Faris Rd .... Greenville SC 29605	800-361-7256	864-271-3444	373-1
Shriners Hospitals for Children Lexington 1900 Richmond Rd ....Lexington KY 40502	800-668-4634	859-266-2101	373-1
Shriners Hospitals for Children Los Angeles 3160 Geneva St ....Los Angeles CA 90020	888-486-5437	864-240-8155	373-1
Shriners Hospitals for Children Philadelphia 3551 N Broad St ....Philadelphia PA 19140	800-281-4050	215-430-4000	373-1

	Toll-Free	Phone	Class
Shriners Hospitals for Children Salt Lake City Fairfax Rd & Virginia St ....Salt Lake City UT 84103	800-313-3745	801-536-3500	373-1
Shriners Hospitals for Children Tampa 12502 N Pine Dr .... Tampa FL 33612	800-237-5055	813-972-2250	373-1
SHRM (Society for Human Resource Management) 1800 Duke St .... Alexandria VA 22314	800-283-7476	703-548-3440	49-12
SHRM Global Forum 1800 Duke St .... Alexandria VA 22314	800-283-7476	703-548-3440	171
SHSMD (Society for Healthcare Strategy & Market Developme) 155 N Wacker Dr Ste 400 ....Chicago IL 60606	800-242-2626	312-422-3888	49-8
Shuert Technologies LLC 6600 Dobry Rd ....Sterling Heights MI 48314	877-748-3781	586-254-4590	
Shui Spa at Crowne Pointe Historic Inn 82 Bradford St ....Provincetown MA 02657	877-276-9631	508-487-6767	703
Shula's Steak House 4860 W Kennedy Blvd .... Tampa FL 33609	800-888-7012	813-286-4366	667
Shuman Plastics Inc 35 Neoga St .... Depew NY 14043	800-803-6242	716-685-2121	601-2
Shumsky Enterprises Inc 811 E Fourth St .... Dayton OH 45402	800-223-2203	937-223-2203	4
Shur-Co Inc 2309 Shur-Lok St PO Box 713 ....Yankton SD 57078	800-474-8756	605-665-6000	728
Shure Inc 5800 W Touhy Ave .... Niles IL 60714	800-257-4873	847-600-2000	52
Shure Manufacturing Corp 1901 W Main St ....Washington MO 63090	800-227-4873	636-390-7100	319-1
SHURflo Pump Mfg Company Inc 5900 Katella Ave .... Cypress CA 90630	800-854-3218	562-795-5200	637
Shurtape Technologies LLC 1712 Eigth St Dr SE .... Hickory NC 28602	888-442-8273	828-322-2700	727
Shuster's Bldg Components 2920 Clay Pk .... Irwin PA 15642	800-676-0640	724-446-7000	497
Shutter Mill Inc 8517 S Perkins Rd .... Stillwater OK 74074	800-416-6455	405-377-6455	695
Shutters on the Beach 1 Pico Blvd ....Santa Monica CA 90405	866-527-6612	310-458-0030	
Shuttleworth Inc 10 Commercial Rd ....Huntington IN 46750	800-444-7412	260-356-8500	207
SI Holdings 3267 Bee Caves Rd Ste 107 .... Austin TX 78746	866-551-4646		395
SIA (Survivors of Incest Anonymous) PO Box 190 .... Benson MD 21018	877-742-9761		
SIA (Security Industry Assn) 8405 Colesville Rd Ste 500 ....Silver Spring MD 20910	866-817-8888	301-804-4700	49-4
SIAM (Society for Industrial & Applied Mathematics) 3600 Market St 6th Fl.............Philadelphia PA 19104	800-447-7426	215-382-9800	49-19
Sibley State Park 800 Sibley Pk Rd .... New London MN 56273	888-646-6367	320-354-2055	561
SICB (Society for Integrative & Comparative Biology) 1313 Dolley Madison Blvd Ste 402 ......McLean VA 22101	800-955-1236	703-790-1745	49-19
Sickle Cell Disease Assn of America (SCDAA) 3700 Koppers St Ste 570 ....Baltimore MD 21202	800-421-8453	410-528-1555	48-17
SICO America Inc 7525 Cahill Rd ....Minneapolis MN 55439	800-328-6138	952-941-1700	319-3
SID (Society for Information Display) 1475 S Bascom Ave # 114 .... Campbell CA 95008	800-350-0111	408-879-3901	48-9
Side Effects Software Inc 123 Front St W Ste 1401 .... Toronto ON M5J2M2	888-504-9876	416-504-9876	179
Sidel Systems Usa Inc 12500 El Camino Real ....Atascadero CA 93422	800-668-5003	805-462-1250	357
Sidewinder Conversions 44658 Yale Rd W .... Chilliwack BC V2R0G5	888-266-2299	604-792-2082	62-7
Sidney Transportation Services 777 W Russell Rd PO Box 946 .... Sidney OH 45365	800-743-6391	937-498-2323	681
Sidran Inc 1050 Venture Ct Ste 100............. Carrollton TX 75006	800-969-5015	214-352-7979	155-19
Sidwell Co Inc 2570 Foxfield Rd Ste 300 ....Saint Charles IL 60174	877-743-9355	630-549-1000	723
Sieben Polk PA 2600 Eagan Woods Dr Ste 50.............Eagan MN 55121	800-620-1829	651-304-6708	427
Siebert Cisneros Shank & Co LLC 100 Wall St 18th Fl.................New York NY 10005	800-334-6800	646-775-4850	686
Siegel Display Products 300 Sixth Ave N ....Minneapolis MN 55401	800-626-0322	612-340-1493	232
Siegers Seed Co 13031 Reflections Dr .... Holland MI 49424	800-962-4999	616-786-4999	276
Siegfried USA LLC 33 Industrial Pk Rd ....Pennsville NJ 08070 *Cust Svc	877-763-8630*	856-678-3601	477
Siegwerk USA Co 3535 SW 56th St .... Des Moines IA 50321	800-728-8200	515-471-2100	387
Sielox LLC 170 E Ninth Ave .... Runnemede NJ 08078	800-424-2126	856-939-9300	688
Siemens Canada Ltd 1550 Appleby Line ....Burlington ON L7L6X7	800-236-2967	905-319-3600	730
Siemens Corp 300 New Jersey Ave Ste 1000........ Washington DC 20001	800-743-6367		185
Siemens Financial Services Inc 170 Wood Ave S ....Iselin NJ 08830	800-327-4443	732-590-6500	216
Siemens Power Transmission & Distribution Inc 7000 Siemens Rd .... Wendell NC 27591	800-347-6659	919-365-2200	616
Siemens Product Lifecycle Management Software Inc 5800 Granite Pkwy Ste 600.............Plano TX 75024	800-498-5351	972-987-3000	178-10
Siemer Milling Co 111 W Main St .... Teutopolis IL 62467	800-826-1065	217-857-3131	296-23
Siemon Co 101 Siemon Co Dr ....Watertown CT 06795	866-548-5814	860-945-4200	809
Siena Heights University 1247 E Siena Heights Dr .... Adrian MI 49221	800-521-0009	517-263-0731	166
Siena Hotel 1505 E Franklin St ....Chapel Hill NC 27514	800-223-7379	919-929-4000	378
Sierra Bancorp 86 N Main St PO Box 1930.......... Porterville CA 93257 *NASDAQ: BSRR*	888-454-2265	559-782-4900	359-2
Sierra Club Canada 412-1 Nicholas St .... Ottawa ON K1N7B7	888-810-4204	613-241-4611	48-13
Sierra College *Nevada County* 250 Sierra College Dr ....Grass Valley CA 95945	800-242-4004	530-274-5300	162
Sierra Community College 5100 Sierra College Blvd .... Rocklin CA 95677	800-242-4004	916-624-3333	162
Sierra Converting Corp 1400 Kleppe Ln .... Sparks NV 89431	800-332-8221		
Sierra Creative Systems Inc 15700 Texaco Ave ....Paramount CA 92723	800-961-4877	562-232-8100	804
Sierra Donor Services 3940 Industrial Blvd ....West Sacramento CA 95833	877-401-2546		541
Sierra Electronics 690 E Glendale Ave Ste 9B PO Box 1545. .... Sparks NV 89432	800-874-7515	775-359-1121	246
Sierra Energy 1020 Winding Creek Rd Ste #100 ....Roseville CA 95678	800-576-2264	916-218-1600	575
Sierra Forest Products 13575 Benson Ave ....Chino CA 91710	800-548-3975	909-591-9442	
Sierra Group, The 588 N Gulph Rd # 110 ....King Of Prussia PA 19406	800-973-7687	610-992-0288	194
Sierra Instruments Inc 5 Harris Ct Bldg L................. Monterey CA 93940	800-866-0200	831-373-0200	201
Sierra Magazine 85 Second St 2nd Fl.........San Francisco CA 94105	866-338-1015	415-977-5500	455-19
Sierra Monitor Corp 1991 Tarob Ct .... Milpitas CA 95035 *OTC: SRMC*	888-509-1970	408-262-6611	470
Sierra Nevada College 999 Tahoe Blvd ....Incline Village NV 89451	866-412-4636	775-831-1314	166
Sierra Receivables Management Inc 2500 Goodwater Ave ....Redding CA 96002	800-237-3205	530-224-1360	160
Sierra Select Distributors 4320 Roseville Rd .... North Highlands CA 95660	800-793-7334		
Sierra Tucson Inc 39580 S Lago Del Oro Pkwy ....Tucson AZ 85739	800-842-4487	520-624-4000	722
Sierra Volkswagen Inc 510 E Norris Dr .... Ottawa IL 61350	877-854-2771	815-401-0663	57
Sift Media (US) Inc 120 E 23rd St 4th Fl ....New York NY 10010	855-253-8392		526
SIG Mfg Company Inc 401 S Front St .... Montezuma IA 50171 *Sales	800-247-5008*	641-623-5154	757
SIG SAUER Inc 72 Pease Blvd .... Newington NH 03801	866-345-6744	603-610-3000	284
SightLife 221 Yale Ave N Ste 450 .... Seattle WA 98109	800-847-5786	206-682-8500	269
Sigler 3100 S Riverside Dr PO Box 887 ....Ames IA 50010	800-750-6997	515-232-6997	623
Sigma Alpha Epsilon Fraternity (SAE) 1856 Sheridan Rd .... Evanston IL 60201	800-233-1856	847-424-3031	48-16
Sigma Breakthrough Technologies Inc 123 N Edward Gary 2nd Fl ....San Marcos TX 78666	888-752-7070	512-353-7489	461
Sigma Business Solutions Inc 55 York St .... Toronto ON M5J1R7	855-594-1991		804
Sigma Chi Fraternity 1714 Hinman Ave .... Evanston IL 60201	877-829-5500	877-471-5410	48-16
Sigma Design 5521 Jackson St .... Alexandria LA 71303 *Sales	888-990-0900*	318-449-9900	178-8
Sigma Electronics Inc 1027 Commercial Ave ....East Petersburg PA 17520	866-569-2681	717-569-2926	253
Sigma Gamma Rho Sorority Inc 1000 Southhill Dr Ste 200 ....Cary NC 27513	888-747-1922	919-678-9720	48-16
Sigma Phi Epsilon Fraternity 310 S Blvd .... Richmond VA 23220	800-767-1901	804-353-1901	48-16
Sigma Solutions Inc 607 E Sonterra Blvd Ste 250.........San Antonio TX 78258	800-567-5964	210-348-9876	225
Sigma Stretch Film Corp Page & Schuyler Aves Bldg 8....... Lyndhurst NJ 07071	800-672-9727	201-507-9100	597
Sigma Theta Tau International 550 W N St ....Indianapolis IN 46202	888-634-7575	317-634-8171	48-16
Sigma Xi Scientific Research Society 3106 E NC Hwy 54 PO Box 13975. ....Research Triangle Park NC 27709	800-243-6534	919-549-4691	48-16
Sigma-Aldrich Corp 3050 Spruce St .... Saint Louis MO 63103 *NASDAQ: SIAL*	800-325-3010	314-771-5765	145
Sigman Janssen Stack Sewall & Pitz 303 S Memorial Dr .... Appleton WI 54911	800-775-1441	920-731-5201	427
SigmaTron International Inc 2201 Landmeier Rd ....Elk Grove Village IL 60007 *NASDAQ: SGMA*	800-700-9095	847-956-8000	621
Sign Biz Inc 24681 La Plz Ste 270 ....Dana Point CA 92629	800-633-5580	949-234-0408	196
Sign Builders Inc 4800 Jefferson Ave PO Box 28380. .... Birmingham AL 35228	800-222-7330		697
Sign Designs Inc 204 Campus Way .... Modesto CA 95352	800-421-7446	209-524-4484	697
Sign Resource Inc 6135 District Blvd ....Maywood CA 90270	800-423-4283	323-771-2098	697
Signa Engineering Corp 2 Northpoint Dr Ste 700.............Houston TX 77060	800-987-3331	281-774-1000	261
Signal Industrial Products Corp 1601 Cowart St ....Chattanooga TN 37408	800-728-1326	423-756-4980	350
Signal Magazine 4400 Fair Lakes Ct .... Fairfax VA 22033	800-336-4583	703-631-6100	455-5
Signal Point Systems Inc 1270 Shiloh Rd Ste 100 .... Kennesaw GA 30144	800-814-6502	770-499-0439	186
Signal Securities Inc 700 Throckmorton St .... Fort Worth TX 76102	800-957-4256	817-877-4256	196
Signal Transformer Company Inc 500 Bayview Ave ....Inwood NY 11096	866-239-5777	516-239-5777	253
Signal Travel & Tours Inc 219 E Main St .... Niles MI 49120	800-811-1522	269-684-2880	767
Signalfire Wireless Telemetry Inc 43 Broad St .... Hudson MA 01749	800-772-0878	978-212-2868	641-9

Company / Address	City	State	ZIP	Toll-Free	Phone	Class
Signalisation Ver-Mac Inc 1781 Bresse	Quebec	QC	G2G2V2	**888-488-7446**	418-654-1303	406
Signal-Tech 4985 Pittsburgh Ave	Erie	PA	16509	**877-547-9900**	814-835-3000	196
Signator Investors Inc 197 Clarendon St C-8	Boston	MA	02116	**800-543-6611**		400
Signature Bank 565 Fifth Ave 12th Fl *NASDAQ: SBNY*	New York	NY	10017	**866-744-5463**	646-822-1500	70
Signature Breads Inc 100 Justin Dr	Chelsea	MA	02150	**888-602-6533**		296-1
Signature Estate & Investment Advisors LLC (SEIA) 2121 Ave Of The Stars Ste 1600	Los Angeles	CA	90067	**800-723-5115**	310-712-2323	400
Signature Eyewear Inc 498 N Oak St *OTC: SEYE*	Inglewood	CA	90302	**800-765-3937**	310-330-2700	538
Signature Graphics Inc 1000 Signature Dr	Porter	IN	46304	**800-356-3235**	219-926-4994	343
Signature Hardware 2700 Crescent Spring Pk	Erlanger	KY	41017	**866-855-2284**		349
Signature Inc 5115 Parkcenter Ave	Dublin	OH	43017	**800-398-0518**	614-766-5101	194
Signature Services Corp 2705 Hawes Ave	Dallas	TX	75235	**800-929-5519**	214-353-2661	299
Signcraft Screenprint Inc 100 A J Harle Dr	Galena	IL	61036	**800-733-5150**	815-777-3030	683
Signe's Bakery & Cafe 93 Arrow Rd	Hilton Head Island	SC	29928	**866-807-4463**	843-785-9118	667
Signet Inc 1801 Shelby Oaks Dr Ste 12	Memphis	TN	38134	**800-654-3889**		195
Signet Marking Devices 3121 Red Hill Ave	Costa Mesa	CA	92626	**800-421-5150**		465
Signifi Solutions Inc 2100 Matheson Blvd E Ste 100	Mississauga	ON	L4W5E1	**877-744-6434**	905-602-7707	177
Signix Inc 1110 Market St Ste 402	Chattanooga	TN	37402	**877-890-5350**		521
Signs by Tomorrow USA Inc 8681 Robert Fulton Dr	Columbia	MD	21046	**800-765-7446**	410-312-3600	697
Signs Now 5368 Dixie Hwy Ste 1	Waterford	MI	48329	**800-356-3373**	248-596-8600	697
Signtech Electrical Adv Inc 4444 Federal Blvd	San Diego	CA	92102	**877-885-1135**	619-527-6100	697
Signtronix 1445 W Sepulveda Blvd	Torrance	CA	90501	**800-729-4853**		697
Signum Group LLC 1200 Stephenson Hwy	Troy	MI	48083	**844-854-3282**		461
Sign-ups & Banners Corp 2764 W T C Jester Blvd	Houston	TX	77018	**877-682-7979**	713-682-7979	623
SII (Seiko Instruments USA Inc) 21221 S Western Ave Ste 250	Torrance	CA	90501	**800-688-0817**	310-517-7700	173-6
SII Investments Inc 5555 W Grande Market Dr	Appleton	WI	54913	**800-426-5975**	866-275-4422	686
Sika Corp 201 Polito Ave	Lyndhurst	NJ	07071	**800-933-7452**	201-933-8800	145
Sika Sarnafil Inc 100 Dan Rd	Canton	MA	02021	**800-451-2504**	781-828-5400	46
Sikich LLP 1415 W Diehl Rd Ste 400	Naperville	IL	60563	**877-279-1900**	630-566-8400	2
Silberline Mfg Company Inc 130 Lincoln Dr PO Box B	Tamaqua	PA	18252	**800-348-4824**	570-668-6050	143
Silbrico Corp 6300 River Rd	Hodgkins	IL	60525	**800-323-4287**	708-354-3350	498
Silent Knight 7550 Meridian Cir Ste 100	Maple Grove	MN	55369	**800-328-0103**	763-493-6400	283
Silex Technology America Inc 167 W 7065 S Ste 330	Midvale	UT	84047	**866-765-8761**	801-748-1199	
Silgan Holdings Inc 4 Landmark Sq Ste 400 *NASDAQ: SLGN*	Stamford	CT	06901	**800-732-0330**	203-975-7110	124
Silgan Plastics Corp 14515 N Outer Forty Ste 210	Chesterfield	MO	63017	**800-274-5426**		98
Silicon Laboratories Inc 400 W Cesar Chavez St *NASDAQ: SLAB*	Austin	TX	78701	**877-444-3032**	512-416-8500	692
Silicon Valley Assn of Realtors 19400 Stevens Creek Blvd Ste 100	Cupertino	CA	95014	**877-699-6787**	408-200-0100	648
Silicon Valley Bank (SVB) 3003 Tasman Dr	Santa Clara	CA	95054	**800-579-1639**	408-654-7400	70
Silicon Valley Staffing 2336 Harrison St	Oakland	CA	94612	**877-660-6000**	510-923-9898	717
Silicone Specialties Inc 430 S Rockford Ave	Tulsa	OK	74120	**888-243-0672**	918-587-5567	350
Silipos Inc 7049 Williams Rd	Niagara Falls	NY	14304	**800-229-4404**	716-283-0700	578
Silkworm Inc 102 S Sezmore Dr	Murphysboro	IL	62966	**800-826-0577**	618-687-4077	683
Silliman Associates Inc Thomas 425 N Lee St	Alexandria	VA	22314	**800-454-5554**	703-548-4100	461
Silvanus Products 40 Merchant St	Sainte Genevieve	MO	63670	**800-822-2788**		592
Silver & Archibald LLP 997 S Milledge Ave	Athens	GA	30605	**877-526-6281**	706-548-8122	427
Silver Airways Corp 1100 Lee Wagener Blvd Ste 201	Fort Lauderdale	FL	33315	**844-674-5837**	801-401-9100	25
Silver City-Grant County Chamber of Commerce 201 N Hudson St	Silver City	NM	88061	**800-548-9378**	575-534-1700	139
Silver Cloud Hotel Seattle Broadway 1100 Broadway	Seattle	WA	98122	**800-590-1801**	206-325-1400	378
Silver Cloud Inn Seattle-Lake Union 1150 Fairview Ave N *General	Seattle	WA	98109	**800-330-5812***	206-447-9500	378
Silver Cloud Inn University District 5036 25th Ave NE	Seattle	WA	98105	**800-205-6940**	206-526-5200	378
Silver Creek Financial ServicesInc 175 Hwy 82	Lostine	OR	97857	**866-569-0020**	541-569-2272	729
Silver Diner Development LLC 12276 Rockville Pk	Rockville	MD	20852	**866-561-0518**	301-770-0333	666
Silver Eagle Distributors LP 7777 Washington Ave	Houston	TX	77007	**855-332-2110**	713-869-4361	81-1
Silver Edge Co-op 39999 Hilton Rd	Edgewood	IA	52042	**800-632-5953**	563-928-6419	276
Silver Fox Tours & Motorcoaches 3 Silver Fox Dr	Millbury	MA	01527	**800-342-5998**	508-865-6000	755
Silver Golub & Teitell LLP 184 Atlantic St	Stamford	CT	06901	**866-248-8744**	203-325-4491	
Silver King Hotel 1485 Empire Ave	Park City	UT	84060	**888-667-2775**	435-649-5500	378
Silver King Refrigeration Inc 1600 Xenium Ln N	Minneapolis	MN	55441	**800-328-3329**	763-923-2441	660
Silver Lake College 2406 S Alverno Rd	Manitowoc	WI	54220	**800-236-4752**	920-686-6175	166
Silver Lake Resort Ltd 7751 Black Lake Rd *General	Kissimmee	FL	34747	**800-226-6090***	407-397-2828	
Silver Legacy Resort & Casino 407 N Virginia St	Reno	NV	89501	**800-687-8733**	775-325-7401	133
Silver Legacy Resort Casino 407 N Virginia St	Reno	NV	89501	**800-687-8733**	775-329-4777	686
Silver Reef Casino 4876 Haxton Way	Ferndale	WA	98248	**866-383-0777**	360-383-0777	132
Silver Saddle Ranch & Club Inc 20751 Aristotle Dr	California City	CA	93505	**888-430-8728**	760-373-8617	649
Silver Smith Hotel & Suites 10 S Wabash Ave	Chicago	IL	60603	**800-979-0084**	312-372-7696	378
Silver Springs Bottled Water Company Inc PO Box 926	Silver Springs	FL	34489	**800-556-0334**		297-11
Silver Star Cadillac 3601 Auto Mall Dr *Cust Svc	Thousand Oaks	CA	91362	**877-813-1334***	805-267-3200	57
Silver Star Meats Inc 1720 Middletown Rd	McKees Rocks	PA	15136	**800-548-1321**	412-777-4460	296-26
Silver Strong & Associates 3 Tice Rd	Franklin Lakes	NJ	07417	**800-962-4432**		
Silver Towne LP 120 E Union City Pk PO Box 424	Winchester	IN	47394	**800-788-7481**	765-584-7481	327
Silverado Stages Inc 2239 N Black Canyon Hwy	Phoenix	AZ	85009	**888-383-8109**		755
SilverBirch Hotels & Resorts 1640 - 1188 W Georgia St	Vancouver	BC	V6E4A2	**800-431-0070**	604-646-2447	378
Silverdale Beach Hotel 3073 NW Bucklin Hill Rd	Silverdale	WA	98383	**800-544-9799**	360-698-1000	378
Silvergate Bank 4275 Executive Sq Ste 800	La Jolla	CA	92037	**800-595-5856**	858-362-6300	70
Silverhawk Aviation Inc 1751 W Kearney Ave	Lincoln	NE	68524	**800-479-5851**	402-475-8600	63
Silverleaf Resorts Inc 1221 Riverbend Dr Ste 120	Dallas	TX	75247	**800-544-8468**	214-631-1166	748
SilverStone Group 11516 Miracle Hills Dr Ste 100	Omaha	NE	68154	**800-288-5501**	402-964-5400	389
Silverton Hotel & Casino 3333 Blue Diamond Rd	Las Vegas	NV	89139	**866-722-4608**	702-263-7777	133
Silvestri Studio Inc 8125 Beach St	Los Angeles	CA	90001	**800-647-8874**	323-277-4420	462
Silvi Concrete Products Inc 355 Newbold Rd	Fairless Hills	PA	19030	**800-426-6273**	215-295-0777	182
Silvon Software Inc 900 Oakmont Ln Ste 400	Westmont	IL	60559	**800-874-5866**	630-655-3313	178-1
SIM (Society for Information Management) 1120 Rte 73 Ste 200	Mount Laurel	NJ	08054	**800-387-9746**	312-527-6734	48-9
Sim USA Inc PO Box 7900	Charlotte	NC	28241	**800-521-6449**		48-20
Simacor LLC 10700 Hwy 55 Ste 170	Plymouth	MN	55441	**888-284-4415**	763-544-4415	180
Simark Controls Ltd 10509 46 St SE	Calgary	AB	T2C5C2	**800-565-7431**	403-236-0580	357
Simba Information 11200 Rockville Pk Ste 504	Rockville	MD	20852	**888-297-4622**	240-747-3096	633-9
Simco Drilling Equipment Inc PO Box 448	Osceola	IA	50213	**800-338-9925**	641-342-2166	190
Simco Electronics 3131 Jay St	Santa Clara	CA	95054	**866-299-6029**	408-734-9750	738
SIMKAR Corp 700 Ramona Ave	Philadelphia	PA	19120	**800-523-3602**	215-831-7700	438
Simmons College 300 The Fenway	Boston	MA	02115	**800-345-8468**	617-521-2000	166
Simmons College Beatley Library 300 The Fenway	Boston	MA	02115	**800-831-4284**	617-521-2780	433-6
Simmons Hanly Conroy LLC 230 W Monroe Ste 2221	Chicago	IL	60606	**877-438-6610**		443
Simmons Knife & Saw 400 Regency Dr	Glendale Heights	IL	60139	**800-252-3381**	630-912-2880	261
Simmons-Boardman Publishing Corp 55 Broad St 26th Fl	New York	NY	10004	**800-257-5091**	212-620-7200	633-9
Simmons-rockwell Inc 784 County Rd 64	Elmira	NY	14903	**888-520-2213**	607-796-5555	57
Simms Fishing Products Corp 101 Evergreen Dr	Bozeman	MT	59715	**800-217-4667**	406-585-3557	706
SIMNA (Schroder Investment Management North America Inc) 7 Bryant Pk	New York	NY	10018	**800-730-2932**	212-641-3800	686
Simon & Assoc Inc 3200 Commerce St	Blacksburg	VA	24060	**800-763-4234**	540-951-4234	261
Simon & Schuster Interactive 1230 Ave of the Americas	New York	NY	10020	**800-223-2336**	212-698-7000	633-1
Simon Metals LLC 2202 E River St	Tacoma	WA	98421	**800-562-8464**	253-272-9364	682
Simon Roofing & Sheet Metal Corp 70 Karago Ave	Youngstown	OH	44512	**800-523-7714**	330-629-7663	46
Simon Wiesenthal Ctr 1399 Roxbury Dr	Los Angeles	CA	90035	**800-900-9036**	310-553-9036	48-8

Name / Address	City	State	ZIP	Toll-Free	Phone	Class
Simonds International 135 Intervale Rd	Fitchburg	MA	01420	**800-343-1616**		678
Simoniz USA 201 Boston Tpke	Bolton	CT	06043	**800-227-5536**		151
Simons Trucking Inc 920 Simon Dr PO Box 8	Farley	IA	52046	**800-373-2580**	563-744-3304	775
Simonsen Industries Inc 500 Iowa 31	Quimby	IA	51049	**800-831-4860**	712-445-2211	273
Simonson Properties Co 535 First St NE	Saint Cloud	MN	56304	**888-843-8789**	320-252-9385	363
Simonton Court Historic Inn & Cottages 320 Simonton St	Key West	FL	33040	**800-944-2687**		378
Simonton Windows Inc 5020 Weston Pkwy Ste 400	Cary	NC	27513	**800-746-6686**		
Simpay 1210 Northbrook Dr	Trevose	PA	19006	**866-253-2227**		251
Simple Verity Inc 1218 Third Ave	Seattle	WA	98101	**855-583-7489**	617-905-7467	392
Simplex Inc 5300 Rising Moon Rd	Springfield	IL	62711	**800-637-8603**		253
Simplicity Consulting Inc 6710 108th Ave NE Ste 354	Kirkland	WA	98033	**888-252-0385**		196
Simplicity Manufacturing Inc PO Box 702	Milwaukee	WI	53201	**800-837-6836**		428
Simply Healthcare Plans Inc 1701 Ponce De Leon Blvd Ste 300	Coral Gables	FL	33134	**877-577-9042**	305-408-5890	194
Simply Orange Juice Co 2659 Orange Ave	Apopka	FL	32703	**800-871-2653**		296-20
Simply Whispers 50 Perry Ave	Attleboro	MA	02703	**800-451-5700**	508-455-0864	414
Simpson College 701 N 'C' St	Indianola	IA	50125	**800-362-2454**	515-961-6251	166
Simpson Door Co 400 Simpson Ave	Mccleary	WA	98557	**800-746-7766**		679
Simpson Gumpertz & Heger Inc 41 Seyon St Bldg 1 Ste 500	Waltham	MA	02453	**800-729-7429**	781-907-9000	261
Simpson Mfg Company Inc 5956 W Las Positas Blvd *NYSE: SSD*	Pleasanton	CA	94588	**800-925-5099**	925-560-9000	15
Simpson Norton Corp 4144 S Bullard Ave	Goodyear	AZ	85338	**877-859-8676**	623-932-5116	274
Simpson Strong-Tie Company Inc 5956 W Las Positas Blvd	Pleasanton	CA	94588	**800-925-5099**	925-560-9000	349
Simpson University 2211 College View Dr	Redding	CA	96003	**888-974-6776**	530-224-5600	166
Simpson's Eggs Inc 5015 Hwy 218 E	Monroe	NC	28110	**800-726-1330**	704-753-1478	10-7
Sims Bark Company Inc 1765 Spring Valley Rd	Tuscumbia	AL	35674	**800-346-3216**	256-381-8323	679
Sims Brothers Recycling 1011 S Prospect St	Marion	OH	43302	**800-536-7465**	740-387-9041	682
Sims Cab Depot 200 Moulinette Rd	Long Sault	ON	K0C1P0	**800-225-7290**	613-534-2289	478
Sims Recycling Solutions Holdings Inc 1600 Harvester Rd	West Chicago	IL	60185	**800-270-8220**	630-231-6060	782
Sim-Tex LP 20880 FM 362 Rd	Waller	TX	77484	**866-829-8939**	713-450-3940	490
Simulations Plus Inc 42505 Tenth St W *NASDAQ: SLP*	Lancaster	CA	93534	**888-266-9294**	661-723-7723	178-10
Simunition Ltd 65 Sandscreen Rd	Avon	CT	06001	**800-465-8255**	860-404-0162	461
Sinai Hospital of Baltimore 2401 W Belvedere Ave	Baltimore	MD	21215	**800-876-1175**	410-601-9000	373-3
Sinclair & Rush Inc 123 Manufacturers Dr	Arnold	MO	63010	**800-526-6273**	636-282-6800	596
Sindel, Sindel & Noble PC 8000 Maryland Ave Ste 910	Saint Louis	MO	63105	**866-489-5504**	314-499-1282	427
Singapore Airlines KrisFlyer 380 World Way Ste 336B	Los Angeles	CA	90045	**800-742-3333**	310-647-6144	26
Singapore Airlines Ltd 222 N Sepulveda Blvd Ste 1600	El Segundo	CA	90245	**800-742-3333**	310-647-1922	25
Singer Lewak Greenbaum & Goldstein LLP 10960 Wilshire Blvd 7th Fl	Los Angeles	CA	90024	**877-754-4557**	310-477-3924	2
Singer Sewing Co 1714 Heil Quaker Blvd Ste 130	La Vergne	TN	37086	**800-474-6437**	615-213-0880	37
Singing Machine Company Inc, The 6601 Lyons Rd Bldg A-7 *OTC: SMDM*	Coconut Creek	FL	33073	**866-670-6888**	954-596-1000	246
Single Source Technologies Inc 2600 Superior Ct	Auburn Hills	MI	48326	**800-336-7283**	248-232-6232	357
SinglePoint Solutions 210 Townepark Cir Ste 200	Louisville	KY	40243	**877-774-4840**	502-212-4017	
Sinopec Daylight Energy Ltd 112-4th Ave SW Sun Life Plz E Tower Ste 2700	Calgary	AB	T2P0H3	**877-266-6901**	403-266-6900	532
Sintel Inc 18437 171st Ave	Spring Lake	MI	49456	**800-394-8276**	616-842-6960	452
Sioux Automation Ctr Inc 877 First Ave NW	Sioux Center	IA	51250	**866-722-1488**	712-722-1488	274
Sioux Chief Manufacturing Company Inc 14940 Thunderbird Rd	Kansas City	MO	64147	**800-821-3944**		
Sioux City Convention Ctr 801 Fourth St	Sioux City	IA	51101	**800-593-2228**	712-279-4800	205
Sioux City Foundry Co 801 Div St	Sioux City	IA	51102	**800-831-0874**	712-252-4181	307
Sioux City Journal 515 Pavonia St	Sioux City	IA	51101	**800-397-3530**	712-293-4300	528-2
Sioux Falls Arena 1201 NW Ave	Sioux Falls	SD	57104	**800-338-3177**	605-367-7288	716
Sioux Falls Convention & Visitors Bureau 200 N Phillips Ave Ste 102	Sioux Falls	SD	57104	**800-333-2072**	605-275-6060	206
Sioux Falls Seminary 2100 S Summit	Sioux Falls	SD	57105	**800-440-6227**	605-336-6588	167-3
Sioux Steel Co 196 1/2 E Sixth St	Sioux Falls	SD	57104	**800-557-4689**	605-336-1750	273
Sioux Tools Inc 250 Snap-on Dr *Orders	Murphy	NC	28906	**800-722-7290***	828-835-9765	754
Sioux Valley-Southwestern Electric Co-op Inc 47092 SD Hwy 34 PO Box 216	Colman	SD	57017	**800-234-1960**	605-534-3535	245
Siouxland Chamber of Commerce 101 Pierce St	Sioux City	IA	51101	**800-228-7903**	712-255-7903	139
Sioux-Preme Packing Co 4241 US 75th Ave *General	Sioux Center	IA	51250	**800-735-7675***		471
SIPA (Specialized Information Publishers Assn) 8229 Boone Blvd Ste 260	Vienna	VA	22182	**800-356-9302**	703-992-9339	49-14
SIPC (SouthEastern Illinois Electric Cooperative Inc) 100 Cooperative Way PO Box 1001	Carrier Mills	IL	62917	**800-833-2611**	618-273-2611	245
Sir Francis Drake Hotel 450 Powell St	San Francisco	CA	94102	**800-795-7129**	415-392-7755	378
Sir Speedy Inc 26722 Plaza Dr	Mission Viejo	CA	92691	**800-854-8297**	949-348-5000	623
Sir Winston's Restaurant & Lounge 1126 Queens Hwy	Long Beach	CA	90802	**877-342-0742**	562-499-1739	667
SIRCHIE Finger Print Laboratories Inc 100 Hunter Pl	Youngsville	NC	27596	**800-356-7311**		84
Sirius XM Canada Inc 135 Liberty St 4th Fl	Toronto	ON	M6K1A7	**888-539-7474**	416-408-6000	731
Sirmilik National Park PO Box 300	Pond Inlet	NU	X0A0S0	**888-773-8888**	867-899-8092	
Sirsi Corp 3300 N Ashton Blvd Ste 500	Lehi	UT	84043	**800-288-8020**		177
SIRVA Inc 1 Parkview Plz	Oakbrook Terrace	IL	60181	**800-341-5648**	630-570-3050	662
SIS (Software Information Systems Inc) 165 Barr St	Lexington	KY	40507	**800-337-6914**	859-977-4747	180
Sisbarro Dealerships 425 W Boutz Rd	Las Cruces	NM	88005	**800-215-8021**	575-524-7707	57
Siskin Steel & Supply Co Inc 1901 Riverfront Pkwy	Chattanooga	TN	37408	**800-756-3671**	423-756-3671	490
Siskinds LLP 680 Waterloo St PO Box 2520	London	ON	N6A3V8	**877-672-2121**	519-672-2121	427
Siskiyou Corp 110 SW Booth St	Grants Pass	OR	97526	**877-313-6418**	541-479-8697	418
Sisters Network Inc 2922 Rosedale St	Houston	TX	77004	**866-781-1808**	713-781-0255	48-21
Sisters of Charity Hospital of Buffalo 2157 Main St	Buffalo	NY	14214	**800-698-4543**	716-862-1000	373-3
Sisters of Charity Hospital, St Joseph Campus 2605 Harlem Rd	Cheektowaga	NY	14225	**800-698-4543**	716-891-2400	373-3
SISU Inc 7635 N Fraser Way Ste 102	Burnaby	BC	V5J0B8	**800-663-4163**	604-420-6610	578
Sit 'n Sleep 14300 S Main St	Gardena	CA	90248	**877-262-4006**	310-604-8903	321
Sita World Travel Inc 16250 Ventura Blvd	Encino	CA	91436	**800-421-5643**	818-990-9530	766
Site Tech Systems 2513 N Oak St Ste 305	Myrtle Beach	SC	29577	**800-470-2895**	843-808-9716	461
Siteman Cancer Ctr 4921 Parkview Pl	Saint Louis	MO	63110	**800-600-3606**	314-362-5196	664
Sitex Corp 1300 Commonwealth Dr	Henderson	KY	42420	**800-278-3537**	270-827-3537	441
Sitrick & Co 11999 San Vicente Blvd PH	Los Angeles	CA	90049	**800-288-8809**	310-788-2850	632
SIU School of Medicine PO Box 19620	Springfield	IL	62794	**800-342-5748**	217-545-8000	167-2
Sivaco Wire Group 800 Rue Ouellette	Marieville	QC	J3M1P5	**800-876-9473**	450-658-8741	808
Six Flags Great Adventure 1 Six Flags Blvd	Jackson	NJ	08527	**800-772-2287**	732-928-1821	32
Six Flags New England 1623 Main St	Agawam	MA	01001	**800-370-7488**	413-786-9300	32
Six Flags Wild Safari 1 Six Flags Blvd	Jackson	NJ	08527	**800-772-2287**	732-928-1821	32
Six Robblees' Inc 11010 Tukwila International Blvd	Tukwila	WA	98168	**800-275-7499**	206-767-7970	61
SIX Safety Systems Inc 250031 Mountain View Trl	Calgary	AB	T3Z3S3	**888-918-9440**	403-288-9440	
Six States Distributors Inc 247 West 1700 South *Cust Svc	Salt Lake City	UT	84115	**800-453-5703***	801-488-4666	61
Sixth Floor Museum 411 Elm St	Dallas	TX	75202	**888-485-4854**	214-747-6660	517
Sixthman LTD 437 Memorial Dr SE Ste A10	Atlanta	GA	30312	**877-749-8462**	404-525-0222	755
Sixty Hotels 206 Spring St 4th Fl	New York	NY	10012	**877-431-0400**		703
Sizemore Inc 2116 Walton Way	Augusta	GA	30904	**800-445-1748**	706-736-1456	688
S-j Transportation Co Inc PO Box 169	Woodstown	NJ	08098	**800-524-2552**	856-769-2741	775
SJE-Rhombus 22650 County Hwy 6 PO Box 1708	Detroit Lakes	MN	56502	**800-746-6287**	218-847-1317	201
SJF Material Handling Equipment 211 Baker Ave	Winsted	MN	55395	**800-598-5532**	320-485-2824	385
SJH Regional Medical Ctr (SJHRMC) 1505 W Sheman Ave	Vineland	NJ	08360	**800-770-7547**	856-641-8000	373-3
SJHRMC (SJH Regional Medical Ctr) 1505 W Sheman Ave	Vineland	NJ	08360	**800-770-7547**	856-641-8000	373-3
SJMH (Stonewall Jackson Memorial Hospital) 230 Hospital Plz	Weston	WV	26452	**866-637-0471**	304-269-8000	373-3
SK Food Group Inc 4600 37th Ave SW	Seattle	WA	98126	**800-722-6290**	206-935-8100	365
SK Textile Inc 1 Knollcrest Dr	Cincinnati	OH	45237	**800-888-9112**		258
Skagit Valley Casino Resort 5984 N Darrk Ln	Bow	WA	98232	**877-275-2448**		133
Skagit Valley College 2405 E College Way	Mount Vernon	WA	98273	**877-385-5360**	360-416-7600	162

	Toll-Free	Phone	Class
Skagit Valley Herald			
1000 E College Way .... Mount Vernon WA 98273	800-683-3300	360-424-3251	528-2
Skagway Visitor Information			
245 Broadway PO Box 1029 .... Skagway AK 99840	888-762-1898	907-983-2854	206
Skamania County			
240 NW Vancouver Ave			
PO Box 790. .... Stevenson WA 98648	800-375-5283	509-427-3770	337
Skamania Lodge			
1131 SW Skamania Lodge Way .... Stevenson WA 98648	800-221-7117	509-314-4177	376
Skate One			
30 S La Patera Ln .... Santa Barbara CA 93117	800-288-7528	805-964-1330	706
SKB Corp			
434 W Levers Pl ....Orange CA 92867	800-410-2024*	714-637-1252	451
*Sales			
Skechers USA Inc			
228 Manhattan Beach Blvd			
....................Manhattan Beach CA 90266	800-746-3411*	310-318-3100	301
NYSE: SKX ■ *Cust Svc			
Ski Bromont			
150 Champlain ....Bromont QC J2L1A2	866-276-6668	450-534-2200	378
Skidmore College			
815 N Broadway ....Saratoga Springs NY 12866	800-867-6007	518-580-5000	166
Skidmore Owings & Merrill LLP (SOM)			
224 S Michigan Ave Ste 1000 .... Chicago IL 60604	866-296-2688	312-554-9090	261
Skier's Choice Inc			
1717 Henry G Ln St .... Maryville TN 37801	800-320-2779	865-983-9924	90
Skilled Care Pharmacy Inc			
6175 HI Tek Ct ....Mason OH 45040	800-334-1624	513-459-7455	579
Skillforce Inc			
405 Williams Ct Ste 106......... Baltimore MD 21220	866-581-8989		260
Skillpath Seminars			
6900 Squibb Rd .... Mission KS 66202	800-873-7545		195
SkillSoft PLC			
107 NE Blvd ....Nashua NH 03062	877-545-5763	603-324-3000	760
SkillsUSA			
14001 James Monroe Hwy .... Leesburg VA 20176	800-321-8422	703-777-8810	48-11
Skinner & Kennedy Co			
9451 Natural Bridge Rd .... Saint Louis MO 63134	800-426-3094	314-426-2800	623
Skinner Transfer Corp			
PO Box 438 ....Reedsburg WI 53959	800-356-9350	608-524-2326	775
skoah Inc			
4800 Kingsway Ave Ste 309 ....Burnaby BC V5H4J2	888-697-5624	604-901-4780	
Skokie Chamber of Commerce			
5002 Oakton St PO Box 106 .... Skokie IL 60077	800-526-8441	847-673-0240	139
Skoler, Abbott & Presser PC			
1 Monarch Pl Ste 2000............Springfield MA 01144	800-274-6774	413-737-4753	427
Skolnik Industries Inc			
4900 S Kilbourn Ave .... Chicago IL 60632	800-441-8780	773-735-0700	198
SKS Bottle & Packaging Inc			
2600 Seventh Ave Bldg 60 W .... Watervliet NY 12189	800-880-6990	518-880-6980	384
Skuttle Manufacturing Co			
101 Margaret St ....Marietta OH 45750	800-848-9786	740-373-9169	14
Sky & Telescope Magazine			
90 Sherman St ....Cambridge MA 02140	800-253-0245	617-864-7360	455-19
Sky Bird Travel & Tours			
24701 Swanson .... Southfield MI 48033	888-759-2473	248-372-4800	16
Sky Bright			
65 Aviation Dr ....Gilford NH 03249	800-639-6012	603-528-6818	63
Sky High Marketing			
3550 E Post Rd .... Las Vegas NV 89120	800-246-7447	702-436-0867	195
Sky I T Group LLC			
330 Seventh Ave ....New York NY 10001	866-641-6017	212-868-7800	196
Sky Publishing Corp			
90 Sherman St ....Cambridge MA 02140	800-253-0245	617-864-7360	633-9
Sky Ranch 24657 CR 448 .... Van TX 75790	800-962-2267		148
Sky Sox Stadium			
4385 Tutt Blvd			
Security Service Field......... Colorado Springs CO 80922	866-698-4253	719-597-1449	716
Sky Ute Casino			
14324 US Hwy 172 N ....Ignacio CO 81137	888-842-4180	970-563-7777	133
Skycom Avionics Inc			
2441 Aviation Rd .... Waukesha WI 53188	800-443-4490	262-521-8180	57
Skyhawks Sports Academy Inc			
9425 N Nevada Ste 210 .... Spokane WA 99218	800-804-3509	509-466-6590	
Skyjack Inc			
55 Campbell Rd ....Guelph ON N1H1B9	800-265-2738		
Skyland Travel Inc			
100-445 Sixth Ave W .... Vancouver BC V5Y1L3	888-685-6888	604-685-6885	
Skyline			
3355 Discovery Rd ....St Paul MN 55121	800-328-2725	651-234-6592	392
Skyline Corp			
2520 By-Pass Rd ....Elkhart IN 46514	800-348-7469	574-294-6521	120
NYSE: SKY			
Skyline Displays Bay Area Inc			
44111 Fremont Blvd ....Fremont CA 94538	800-328-2725	510-490-9900	8
Skyline Medical Ctr			
3441 Dickerson Pk .... Nashville TN 37207	800-242-5662	615-769-2000	373-3
Skyline Membership Corp			
1200 NC Hwy 194 N ....West Jefferson NC 28694	800-759-2226		731
Skyline Products			
2903 Delta Dr .... Colorado Springs CO 80910	800-759-9046		693
Skyline Properties South Inc			
50 116th Ave SE Ste 120 .... Bellevue WA 98004	800-753-6156	425-455-2065	648
Skylink Travel			
980 Ave of the Americas .... New York NY 10018	800-247-6659	212-573-8980	16
Skyservice Airlines Inc			
9785 Ryan Ave ....Dorval QC H9P1A2	888-985-1402	514-636-3300	13
Skystone Partner			
635 W Seventh St Ste 107 .... Cincinnati OH 45203	800-883-0801	513-241-6778	317
SkyTel Corp			
PO Box 2469 ....Jackson MS 39225	800-759-8737*		731
*Cust Svc			
Skytop Lodge 1 Skytop .... Skytop PA 18357	800-345-7759	855-345-7759	665
Skywalker AV Supply			
1760 West Terra Ln ....O'Fallon MO 63366	800-844-9555	636-272-8025	246
Skyway West			
3644 Beach Ave .... Roberts Creek BC V0N2W2	877-771-1077	604-482-1228	
Skyweb Networks			
2710 State St ....Saginaw MI 48602	866-575-9932	989-792-8681	180
SkyWest Airlines			
444 S River Rd .... Saint George UT 84790	800-778-4838	435-634-3000	25
Skyworks LLC			
100 Thielman Dr ....Buffalo NY 14206	877-601-5438	716-822-5438	264-3
Skyy Consulting Inc			
1335 Fourth St Ste 200.........Santa Monica CA 90401	877-897-3473		
SL Power Electronics Inc			
6050 King Dr Bldg A. .... Ventura CA 93003	800-235-5929	805-486-4565	253
SLA (Special Libraries Assn)			
331 S Patrick St .... Alexandria VA 22314	866-446-6069	703-647-4900	49-11
Slack & Davis LLP			
2705 Bee Caves Rd Ste 220 .... Austin TX 78746	800-455-8686	512-795-8686	427
Slack Inc			
6900 Grove Rd ....Thorofare NJ 08086	800-257-8290	856-848-1000	633-9
Slade Gorton Company Inc			
225 Southampton St .... Boston MA 02118	800-225-1573	617-442-5800	297-5
Slant Fin Corp			
100 Forest Dr ....Greenvale NY 11548	800-875-2389	516-484-2600	14
Slay Industries Inc			
1441 Hampton Ave .... Saint Louis MO 63139	800-852-7529	314-647-7529	447
SLC Meter LLC			
595 Bradford St ....Pontiac MI 48340	800-433-4332	248-625-0667	384
SLCL (Saint Louis County Library)			
1640 S Lindbergh Blvd .... St. Louis MO 63131	800-473-0060	314-994-3300	433-3
SlickEdit Inc			
3000 Aerial Ctr Pkwy			
Ste 120 ....Morrisville NC 27560	800-934-3348	919-473-0070	178-2
Slippery Rock University			
1 Morrow Way .... Slippery Rock PA 16057	800-929-4778	724-738-9000	166
SLM Corp			
12061 Bluemont Way ....Reston VA 20190	888-272-5543*	703-810-3000	217
NASDAQ: SLM *Cust Svc			
SLM Manufacturing Corp			
215 Davidson Ave ....Somerset NJ 08873	800-526-3708	732-469-7500	596
SLMP LLC			
407 Interchange St .... Mckinney TX 75071	800-442-3573	972-436-1010	473
Sloan Implement Co			
120 N Business 51 .... Assumption IL 62510	800-745-4020	217-226-4411	274
Sloan Management Review			
77 Massachusetts Ave E60-100 .... Cambridge MA 02139	800-876-5764	617-253-7170	455-5
Sloan Valve Co			
10500 Seymour Ave .... Franklin Park IL 60131	800-982-5839	847-671-4300	605
Slope Electric Co-op Inc			
116 E 12th St PO Box 338 ...... New England ND 58647	800-559-4191	701-579-4191	245
SLPL (Saint Louis Public Library)			
1301 Olive St .... Saint Louis MO 63103	800-916-8938	314-241-2288	433-3
Sly Inc			
8300 Dow Cir ....Strongsville OH 44136	800-334-2957	440-891-3200	18
SM Arnold Inc			
7901 Michigan Ave .... Saint Louis MO 63111	800-325-7865*	314-544-4103	103
*Cust Svc			
Small Business Administration (SBA)			
409 Third St SW ....Washington DC 20416	800-827-5722	202-205-6600	339-19
Small Business Administration Regional Offices			
Region 6			
4300 Amon Carter Blvd			
Ste 108. ....Fort Worth TX 76155	800-274-2812	817-684-5581	339-19
Small Business Investor Alliance (SBIA)			
1100 H St NW Ste 1200 ....Washington DC 20005	800-471-6153	202-628-5055	611
Small Planet Foods Inc			
106 Woodworth St ....Sedro Woolley WA 98284	800-624-4123	360-855-0100	296-18
SMART (Special Military Active Retired Travel Club)			
600 University Office Blvd			
Ste 1A. ....Pensacola FL 32504	800-354-7681	850-478-1986	48-23
SMART (Suburban Mobility Authority for Regional Transport)			
535 Griswold St Ste 600............... Detroit MI 48226	866-962-5515	313-223-2100	466
Smart & Final Inc			
600 Citadel Dr ....Commerce CA 90040	800-894-0511	323-869-7500	344
Smart Business Network Inc			
835 Sharon Dr Ste 200 ....Cleveland OH 44145	800-988-4726		528-3
Smart Cabling Solutions Inc			
1250 N Winchester St .... Olathe KS 66061	877-390-9501	913-390-9501	224
Smart Care Equipment Solutions			
370 Wabasha St N .... St. Paul MN 55102	800-822-2302	651-250-5555	392
Smart Choice Communications LLC			
16 W 45th St ....New York NY 10036	800-217-3096	212-660-7300	386
Smart City Networks			
5795 W Badura Ave Ste 110 .... Las Vegas NV 89118	888-446-6911	702-943-6000	731
Smart Eye Care Ctr			
255 Western Ave ....Augusta ME 04330	800-459-5800	207-622-5800	237
Smart Furniture Inc			
430 Market St .... Chattanooga TN 37402	888-467-6278	423-267-7007	321
Smart Industries Corp			
1626 Delaware Ave .... Des Moines IA 50317	800-553-2442	515-265-9900	322
SMART Modular Technologies Inc			
39870 Eureka Dr ....Newark CA 94560	800-956-7627	510-623-1231	173-1
NASDAQ: SMOD			
Smart Power Systems Inc			
1760 Stebbins Dr ....Houston TX 77043	800-882-8285	713-464-8000	253
SMART Recovery			
7304 Mentor Ave Ste F ....Mentor OH 44060	866-951-5357	440-951-5357	48-21
SMART Technologies Inc			
3636 Research Rd NW .... Calgary AB T2L1Y1	888-427-6278	403-245-0333	173-1
TSX: SMA			
Smart Union (SMWIA)			
1750 New York Ave NW 6th Fl ...... Washington DC 20006	800-457-7694	202-662-0800	49-3
Smart Warehousing LLC			
18905 Kill Creek Rd .... Edgerton KS 66021	800-591-2097		
SmarTek21 LLC			
12910 Totem Lake Blvd NE			
Ste 200. ....Kirkland WA 98034	888-221-9578		
SmarTire Systems Inc			
6900 Graybar Rd Ste 2110 .... Richmond BC V3W0A5	800-247-2725	440-329-9000	60
SmartIT Staffing Inc			
6500 Technology Ctr Dr			
Ste 300. ....Indianapolis IN 46278	800-336-4466	317-634-0211	260

	Toll-Free	Phone	Class
Smartpak Equine LLC			
40 Grissom Rd Ste 500 . . . . .Plymouth MA 02360	**888-752-5171**	774-773-1000	365
Smartronix Inc			
44150 Smartronix Way . . . . .Hollywood MD 20636	**866-442-7767**	301-373-6000	177
SmartScrubs LLC			
3400 E Mcdowell Rd . . . . .Phoenix AZ 85008	**800-800-5788**		473
Smartware Computer Services			
2821 S Bay St Ste B . . . . .Eustis FL 32726	**800-796-5000**	352-483-4350	175
SMC (Southwestern Michigan College)			
58900 Cherry Grove Rd . . . . .Dowagiac MI 49047	**800-456-8675**		162
SMC (Save the Manatee Club)			
500 N Maitland Ave . . . . .Maitland FL 32751	**800-432-5646**	407-539-0990	48-3
SMC Business Councils			
600 Cranberry Woods Dr			
Ste 190 . . . . .Cranberry Township PA 16066	**800-553-3260**	412-371-1500	138
SMCC (Southern Maine Community College)			
2 Ft Rd . . . . .South Portland ME 04106	**877-282-2182**	207-741-5500	795
SME (Society of Mfg Engineers)			
1 SME Dr . . . . .Dearborn MI 48128	**800-733-4763***	313-425-3000	49-13
*Cust Svc			
SME (Society for Mining Metallurgy & Exploration Inc)			
12999 E Adam Aircraft Cir . . . . . . .Englewood CO 80112	**800-763-3132**	303-948-4200	49-13
SMH (Southeast Missouri Hospital)			
1701 Lacey St . . . . .Cape Girardeau MO 63701	**800-800-5123**	573-334-4822	373-3
SMI (Spring Manufacturers Institute)			
2001 Midwest Rd Ste 106. . . . . .Oak Brook IL 60523	**866-482-5569**	630-495-8588	49-13
Smile Train Inc			
633 Third Ave 9th Fl . . . . .New York NY 10017	**800-932-9541**	212-689-9199	48-5
Smith			
5306 Hollister Rd . . . . .Houston TX 77040	**800-468-7866**	713-430-3000	246
Smith & Butterfield Co Inc			
2800 Lynch Rd . . . . .Evansville IN 47711	**800-321-6543**	812-422-3261	531
Smith & Greene Co			
19015 66th Ave S .Kent WA 98032	**800-232-8050**		300
Smith & Nephew Inc			
1450 E Brooks Rd . . . . .Memphis TN 38116	**800-238-7538***	901-396-2121	475
*Cust Svc			
Smith & Nephew Inc Endoscopy Div			
150 Minuteman Rd . . . . .Andover MA 01810	**800-343-5717**	978-749-1000	474
Smith & Richardson Manufacturing Co			
PO Box 589 . . . . .Geneva IL 60134	**800-426-0876**	630-232-2581	617
Smith & Wesson Academy			
299 Page Blvd . . . . .Springfield MA 01104	**800-331-0852**	850-850-1250	761
Smith & Wesson Corp			
2100 Roosevelt Ave . . . . .Springfield MA 01104	**800-331-0852***	413-781-8300	284
*Cust Svc			
Smith Affiliated Capital (SAC)			
800 Third Ave 12th Fl . . . . .New York NY 10022	**888-387-3298**	212-644-9440	402
Smith Anglin Financial LLC			
14755 Preston Rd Ste 700 . . . . .Dallas TX 75254	**800-301-8486**	972-267-1244	
Smith College			
7 College Ln . . . . .NorthHampton MA 01063	**800-383-3232**	413-584-2700	166
Smith Dray Line			
320 Frontage Rd . . . . .Greenville SC 29611	**877-203-7048**		516
Smith Equipment Mfg Co			
2601 Lockheed Ave . . . . .Watertown SD 57201	**866-931-9730***	605-882-3200	806
*Cust Svc			
Smith Fork Ranch			
45362 Needle Rock Rd . . . . .Crawford CO 81415	**855-539-1492**	970-921-3454	239
Smith Gardens Inc			
4164 Meridian St Ste 400. . . . . .Bellingham WA 98226	**800-755-6256**	360-733-4671	368
Smith Graham & Co			
600 Travis St			
6900 JPMorgan Chase Tower . . . . .Houston TX 77002	**800-739-4470**	713-227-1100	400
Smith Hartvigsen PLLC			
257 E 200 S Ste 500. . . . . .Salt Lake City UT 84111	**877-825-2064**	801-413-1600	427
Smith McDonald Corp			
1270 Niagara St . . . . .Buffalo NY 14213	**800-753-8548**		604
SMITH Mfg Company Inc			
1610 S Dixie Hwy . . . . .Pompano Beach FL 33060	**800-653-9311**	954-941-9744	82
Smith Motors Inc of Hammond			
6405 Indianapolis Blvd . . . . .Hammond IN 46320	**877-392-2689**	219-845-4000	57
Smith Plantation Home			
935 Alpharetta St . . . . .Roswell GA 30075	**800-776-7935**	770-641-3978	50-3
Smith Power Products Inc			
3065 W California Ave . . . . .Salt Lake City UT 84104	**800-658-5352**	801-415-5000	384
Smith Protective Services Inc			
1801 Royal Ln Ste 250 . . . . .Dallas TX 75229	**800-631-1384**	214-631-4444	689
Smith Ranch Homes			
400 Deer Valley Rd . . . . .San Rafael CA 94903	**800-772-6264**	415-491-4918	668
Smith Southwestern Inc			
1850 N Rosemont .Mesa AZ 85205	**800-783-3909**	480-854-9545	292
Smith System Driver Improvement Institute Inc			
2301 E Lamar Blvd Ste 250 . . . . .Arlington TX 76006	**800-777-7648**	817-652-6969	162
Smith Systems Transportation Inc (SST)			
PO Box 2455 . . . . .Scottsbluff NE 69361	**800-897-5571**		311
Smith Village Home Furnishings			
34 N Main St .Jacobus PA 17407	**800-242-1921**	717-428-1921	321
Smith, Sovik, Kendrick & Sugnet PC			
250 S Clinton St Ste 600 . . . . .Syracuse NY 13202	**800-675-0011**	315-474-2911	427
Smith-Edwards-Dunlap Co			
2867 E Allegheny Ave . . . . .Philadelphia PA 19134	**800-829-0020**	215-425-8800	622
Smithereen Pest Management Services			
7400 N Melvina Ave . . . . .Niles IL 60714	**800-336-3500**	847-647-0010	573
Smiths Detection			
2202 Lakeside Blvd . . . . .Edgewood MD 21040	**800-297-0955**	410-510-9100	470
Smiths Medical Respiratory Support Products			
5200 Upper Metro Pl Ste 200 . . . . .Dublin OH 43017	**800-258-5361**	214-618-0218	475
Smithsonian Air & Space Magazine			
PO Box 37012 . . . . .Washington DC 20013	**800-766-2149***	202-633-6070	455-19
*Cust Svc			
Smithsonian Folkways Recordings			
600 Maryland Ave SW Ste 200 . . . . .Washington DC 20024	**800-410-9815**	202-633-6450	653
Smithsonian Magazine			
600 Maryland Ave Se 6001 . . . . .Washington DC 20024	**800-766-2149**	202-633-6090	455-11
Smitty's Canada Inc			
501 18th Ave SW Ste 500. . . . . .Calgary AB T2S0C7	**800-927-0366**	403-229-3838	666
Smitty's Supply Inc			
63399 Hwy 51 N PO Box 530. . . . . .Roseland LA 70456	**800-256-7575**	985-748-3247	537

	Toll-Free	Phone	Class
SMO (Southern Maryland Oil Co Inc)			
109 N Maple Ave .La Plata MD 20646	**888-222-3720**		575
Smoke Magazine			
26 Broadway . . . . .New York NY 10004	**800-766-2633**		455-14
Smoker Craft			
PO Box 65 . . . . .New Paris IN 46553	**866-719-7873**		90
Smoker Smith & Associates PC			
339 W Governor Rd Ste 202. . . . . .Hershey PA 17033	**888-277-1040**	717-533-5154	2
Smoky Hills Public Television (SHPTV)			
604 Elm St .Bunker Hill KS 67626	**800-337-4788**	785-483-6990	628
Smoky Mountain Knife Works Inc			
2320 Winfield Dunn Pkwy			
PO Box 4430. . . . . .Sevierville TN 37876	**800-251-9306**		
Smoky Mountain Visitors Bureau			
7906 E Lamar Alexander Pkwy . . . . .Townsend TN 37882	**800-525-6834**	865-448-6134	206
Smoll & Banning CPA's LLC			
2410 Central Ave . . . . .Dodge City KS 67801	**800-499-8881**	620-225-6100	2
Smooth-On Inc			
2000 St John St .Easton PA 18042	**800-762-0744**	610-252-5800	43
Smp Communications Corp			
7626 E Greenway Rd Ste 100 . . . . .Scottsdale AZ 85260	**888-796-3342**	480-905-4100	511
SMPS (Society for Marketing Professional Services)			
123 North Pitt St Ste 400 . . . . .Alexandria VA 22314	**800-292-7677**	703-549-6117	49-18
SMS (Senior Market Sales Inc)			
8420 W Dodge Rd Ste 510 . . . . .Omaha NE 68114	**800-786-5566**	402-397-3311	389
SMS Data Products Group Inc			
1751 Pinnacle Dr 12th Fl . . . . .McLean VA 22102	**800-331-1767**		180
SMS Productions Inc			
1340 Charwood Rd Ste g . . . . .Hanover MD 21076	**800-289-7671**	301-953-0011	623
SMT Inc 7300 ACC Blvd . . . . .Raleigh NC 27617	**888-214-4804**	919-782-4804	693
Smugglers' Notch Resort			
4323 Vermont Rt 108 S . . . . .Jeffersonville VT 05464	**800-451-8752**	802-644-8851	665
SMUS (Saint Michael's University School)			
3400 Richmond Rd . . . . .Victoria BC V8P4P5	**800-661-5199**	250-592-2411	618
SMWIA (Smart Union)			
1750 New York Ave NW 6th Fl . . . . . . .Washington DC 20006	**800-457-7694**	202-662-0800	49-3
Smyth Cos Inc			
1085 Snelling Ave N . . . . .Saint Paul MN 55108	**800-473-3464**	651-646-4544	412
SNA (School Nutrition Assn)			
700 S Washington St Ste 300. . . . . .Alexandria VA 22314	**800-877-8822**	703-739-3900	49-6
SNAC International			
1600 Wilson Blvd Ste 650 . . . . .Arlington VA 22209	**800-628-1334**	703-836-4500	49-6
SNAME (Society of Naval Architects & Marine Engineers)			
601 Pavonia Ave . . . . .Jersey City NJ 07306	**800-798-2188**	201-798-4800	49-21
SNAP (Survivors Network of Those Abused by Priests)			
PO Box 6416 . . . . .Chicago IL 60680	**877-762-7432**	312-455-1499	48-21
Snap-on Credit LLC			
950 Technology Way Ste 301 . . . . .Libertyville IL 60048	**877-777-8455**		216
Snap-on Inc			
2801 80th St .Kenosha WI 53143	**877-762-7664**	262-656-5200	753
NYSE: SNA			
Snap-Tite Autoclave Engineers Div			
8325 Hessinger Dr . . . . .Erie PA 16509	**800-458-0409**	814-838-5700	91
SNC Mfg Company Inc			
101 West Waukau Ave . . . . .Oshkosh WI 54902	**800-558-3325**	920-231-7370	253
Snell & Wilmer LLP			
1 Arizona Ctr 400 E Van Buren St			
Ste 1900 . . . . .Phoenix AZ 85004	**800-322-0430**	602-382-6000	427
Snethkamp Chrysler Dodge Jeep Ram			
11600 Telegraph Rd . . . . .Redford MI 48239	**888-455-6146**	313-429-0013	513
SNFC (Security National Financial Corp)			
5300 South 360 West . . . . .Salt Lake City UT 84123	**800-574-7117**	801-264-1060	390-2
NASDAQ: SNFCA			
Snipp Interactive Inc			
530 Richmond St W Rear Lower Level			
. . . . .Toronto ON M5V1K4	**888-997-6477**		
SNL (Sandia National Laboratories - New Mexico)			
1515 Eubank SE . . . . .Albuquerque NM 87123	**800-783-5337**	505-844-8066	664
Snohomish County			
3000 Rockefeller Ave . . . . .Everett WA 98201	**800-584-3578**	425-388-3411	337_
Snorkel			
2009 Roseport Rd . . . . .Elwood KS 66024	**800-255-0317**	785-989-3000	468
Snow College			
150 College Ave PO Box 1037 . . . . .Ephraim UT 84627	**800-848-3399**	435-283-7000	162
Snow Goer Magazine			
10405 Sixth Ave N Ste 210 . . . . .Plymouth MN 55441	**800-710-5249**	763-383-4400	455-20
Snowbasin Ski Resort			
3925 E Snowbasin Rd . . . . .Huntsville UT 84317	**888-437-5488**	801-620-1100	665
SnowBear Ltd			
259 Third Concession rd . . . . .Princeton ON N0J1V0	**800-337-2327**		478
Snowbird Mountain Lodge			
4633 Santeetlah Rd . . . . .Robbinsville NC 28771	**800-941-9290**	828-479-3433	378
Snowbird Ski & Summer Resort			
Hwy 210 PO Box 929000 . . . . .Snowbird UT 84092	**800-453-3000**	801-742-2222	665
Snowdale State Park			
501 S 439 . . . . .Salina OK 74361	**800-622-6317**	918-434-2651	561
Snowfire			
100 Vs Rt 2 .Waterbury VT 05676	**800-287-5606**	802-244-5606	57
Snowline Engineering			
4261 Business Dr . . . . .Cameron Park CA 95682	**800-361-6083**	530-677-2675	261
Snowshoe Mountain Resort			
10 Snowshoe Dr . . . . .Snowshoe WV 26209	**877-441-4386**		665
Snowy Owl Inn			
41 Village Rd . . . . .Waterville Valley NH 03215	**800-766-9969**	603-236-8383	378
Snyder Chevrolet			
524 N Perry St . . . . .Napoleon OH 43545	**800-569-3957**	567-341-4132	57
Snyder Manufacturing Corp			
1541 W Cowles St . . . . .Long Beach CA 90813	**800-395-6478**	562-432-2038	151
Snyder of Berlin			
1313 Stadium Dr .Berlin PA 15530	**888-257-8042**		296-35
Snyder Paper Corp			
250 26th St Dr SE PO Box 758 . . . . .Hickory NC 28603	**800-222-8562**	828-328-2501	555
Snyder Tire			
401 Cadiz Rd . . . . .Steubenville OH 43953	**800-967-8473**	740-264-5543	750
Snyder's of Hanover			
1250 York St PO Box 6917 . . . . .Hanover PA 17331	**800-233-7125**	717-632-4477	296-9
So Cal. Sandbags Inc			
12620 Bosley Ln . . . . .Corona CA 92883	**800-834-8682**	951-277-3404	384

	City	State	ZIP	Toll-Free	Phone	Class
SOAR (Soar Corp)						
5200 Constitution Ave NE	Albuquerque	NM	87110	**866-616-4450**	505-268-6110	653
Soar Corp (SOAR)						
5200 Constitution Ave NE	Albuquerque	NM	87110	**866-616-4450**	505-268-6110	653
Soaring Eagle Casino & Resort						
6800 E Soaring Eagle Blvd						
	Mount Pleasant	MI	48858	**888-732-4537**	989-775-5777	133
Sobel & Company LLC						
293 Eisenhower Pkwy Ste 290	Livingston	NJ	07039	**800-471-2468**	973-994-9494	2
Sobel Westex Inc						
2670 Western Ave	Las Vegas	NV	89109	**855-697-6235**		360
Sobeys Inc						
115 King St	Stellarton	NS	B0K1S0	**800-723-3929**	902-752-8371	344
Soboba Casino						
23333 Soboba Rd	San Jacinto	CA	92583	**866-476-2622**	951-665-1000	450
Social & Economic Sciences Research Ctr (SESRC)						
Washington State University						
Wilson Hall Rm 133						
PO Box 644014	Pullman	WA	99164	**800-932-5393**	509-335-1511	664
Social Security Administration (SSA)						
6401 Security Blvd	Baltimore	MD	21235	**800-772-1213**	410-965-8904	339-19
Social Security Administration Regional Offices						
Region 4						
61 Forsyth St SW Ste 23T29	Atlanta	GA	30303	**800-772-1213**		339-19
Social Strategy1						
5000 Sawgrass Village Cir						
Ste 30	Ponte Vedra Beach	FL	32082	**877-771-3366**		386
Social Studies School Service						
10200 Jefferson Blvd	Culver City	CA	90232	**800-421-4246**	310-839-2436	95
Social Work pr.n. Inc						
10680 Barkley Ste 100	Overland Park	KS	66212	**800-595-9648**	913-648-2984	260
SocialCode LLC						
151 W 26th St 9th Fl	New York	NY	10001	**844-608-4610**		5
Society for American Archaeology (SAA)						
900 Second St NE Ste 12	Washington	DC	20002	**800-759-5219**	202-789-8200	49-5
Society for Ethnomusicology (SEM)						
Indiana University						
800 E Third St	Bloomington	IN	47405	**800-933-9330**	812-855-6672	48-4
Society for Experimental Mechanics Inc (SEM)						
7 School St	Bethel	CT	06801	**800-627-8258**	203-790-6373	49-19
Society for Healthcare Strategy & Market Development (SHSMD)						
155 N Wacker Dr Ste 400	Chicago	IL	60606	**800-242-2626**	312-422-3888	49-8
Society for Human Resource Management (SHRM)						
1800 Duke St	Alexandria	VA	22314	**800-283-7476**	703-548-3440	49-12
Society for Imaging Science & Technology (IS&T)						
7003 Kilworth Ln	Springfield	VA	22151	**800-654-2240**	703-642-9090	49-16
Society for Industrial & Applied Mathematics (SIAM)						
3600 Market St 6th Fl	Philadelphia	PA	19104	**800-447-7426**	215-382-9800	49-19
Society for Information Display (SID)						
1475 S Bascom Ave # 114	Campbell	CA	95008	**800-350-0111**	408-879-3901	48-9
Society for Information Management (SIM)						
1120 Rte 73 Ste 200	Mount Laurel	NJ	08054	**800-387-9746**	312-527-6734	48-9
Society for Integrative & Comparative Biology (SICB)						
1313 Dolley Madison Blvd Ste 402	McLean	VA	22101	**800-955-1236**	703-790-1745	49-19
Society for Marketing Professional Services (SMPS)						
123 North Pitt St Ste 400	Alexandria	VA	22314	**800-292-7677**	703-549-6117	49-18
Society for Mining Metallurgy & Exploration Inc (SME)						
12999 E Adam Aircraft Cir	Englewood	CO	80112	**800-763-3132**	303-948-4200	49-13
Society for Protective Coatings (SSPC)						
40 24th St 6th Fl	Pittsburgh	PA	15222	**877-281-7772**	412-281-2331	49-13
Society for Sedimentary Geology (SEPM)						
4111 S Darlington Ste 100	Tulsa	OK	74135	**800-865-9765**	918-610-3361	49-19
Society for Social Work Leadership in Health Care						
100 N 20th St 4th Fl	Philadelphia	PA	19103	**866-237-9542**		49-15
Society for the Advancement of Material & Process Engineering (SAMPE)						
21680 Gateway Center Dr						
Ste 300	Diamond Bar	CA	91765	**800-562-7360**	626-521-9460	49-19
Society for Vascular Surgery (SVS)						
633 N St Clair St 22nd Fl	Chicago	IL	60611	**800-258-7188**	312-334-2300	49-8
Society of Accredited Marine Surveyors Inc (SAMS)						
7855 Argyle Forest Blvd						
Ste 203	Jacksonville	FL	32244	**800-344-9077**	904-384-1494	48-1
Society of American Archivists (SAA)						
17 North State St Ste 1425	Chicago	IL	60602	**866-722-7858**	312-606-0722	48-4
Society of American Florists (SAF)						
1601 Duke St	Alexandria	VA	22314	**800-336-4743**	703-836-8700	49-4
Society of American Foresters (SAF)						
10100 Laureate way	Bethesda	MD	20814	**866-897-8720**	301-897-8720	48-2
Society of Automotive Engineers Inc (SAE)						
400 Commonwealth Dr	Warrendale	PA	15096	**877-606-7323**	724-776-4841	49-21
Society of Biblical Literature (SBL)						
The Luce Ctr						
825 Houston Mill Rd	Atlanta	GA	30329	**866-727-9955**	404-727-3100	48-20
Society of Cable Telecommunications Engineers (SCTE)						
140 Philips Rd	Exton	PA	19341	**800-542-5040**	610-363-6888	49-19
Society of Cardiovascular Anesthesiologists (SCA)						
8735 W Higgins Rd Ste 300	Chicago	IL	60631	**800-283-6296**	855-658-2828	49-8
Society of Communications Technology Consultants (SCTC)						
230 Washington Ave Ext Ste 101	Albany	NY	12203	**800-782-7670**		49-20
Society of Diagnostic Medical Sonography (SDMS)						
2745 Dallas Pkwy	Plano	TX	75093	**800-229-9506**	214-473-8057	49-8
Society of Financial Service Professionals (SFSP)						
19 Campus Blvd Ste 100	Newtown Square	PA	19073	**800-392-6900**	610-526-2500	49-9
Society of Gastroenterology Nurses & Assoc Inc (SGNA)						
401 N Michigan Ave	Chicago	IL	60611	**800-245-7462**	312-321-5165	49-8
Society Of Hospital Medicine						
190 N Independence Mall W	Philadelphia	PA	19106	**800-843-3360**		
Society of Mfg Engineers (SME)						
1 SME Dr	Dearborn	MI	48128	**800-733-4763***	313-425-3000	49-13
*Cust Svc						
Society of Naval Architects & Marine Engineers (SNAME)						
601 Pavonia Ave	Jersey City	NJ	07306	**800-798-2188**	201-798-4800	49-21
Society of Petroleum Engineers (SPE)						
222 Palisades Creek Dr	Richardson	TX	75080	**800-456-6863**	972-952-9393	48-12
Society of Professional Journalists (SPJ)						
3909 N Meridian St	Indianapolis	IN	46208	**800-331-1212**	317-927-8000	49-14
Society of Saint Andrew (SoSA)						
3383 Sweet Hollow Rd	Big Island	VA	24526	**800-333-4597**	434-299-5956	48-5
Society of Teachers of Family Medicine (STFM)						
11400 Tomahawk Creek Pkwy						
Ste 240	Leawood	KS	66211	**800-274-7928**	913-906-6000	49-8
Society of Thoracic Surgeons (STS)						
633 N St Clair St Ste 2320	Chicago	IL	60611	**877-865-5321**	312-202-5800	49-8
Society of Vacuum Coaters (SVC)						
71 Pinon Hill Pl NE	Albuquerque	NM	87122	**800-443-8817**	505-856-7188	49-13
Society of Women Engineers (SWE)						
130 E Randolph St Ste 3500	Chicago	IL	60601	**877-793-4636**	312-596-5223	49-19
Society's Assets Inc						
5200 Washington Ave Ste 225	Racine	WI	53406	**800-378-9128**	262-637-9128	362
Socorro Electric Co-op Inc						
215 Manzanares Ave PO Box H	Socorro	NM	87801	**800-351-7575**	575-835-0560	245
Socratic Technologies Inc						
2505 Mariposa St	San Francisco	CA	94110	**800-576-2728**	415-430-2200	664
Sodexho						
9801 Washingtonian Blvd	Gaithersburg	MD	20878	**888-763-3967**	301-987-4000	299
Sofia Hotel						
150 W Broadway	San Diego	CA	92101	**800-826-0009**	619-234-9200	378
Soft Science						
2101 CityWest Blvd	Houston	TX	77042	**888-507-6387**	281-861-0832	
Soft Surroundings						
2280 Schuetz Rd						
Ste 100	Maryland Heights	MO	63146	**800-240-7076***		
*Cust Svc						
Softchalk LLC						
22 S Auburn Ave	Richmond	VA	23221	**877-638-2425**		177
Softech & Associates Inc						
1570 Corporate Dr Ste B	Costa Mesa	CA	92626	**877-638-3241**	714-427-1122	180
Softechnologies Inc						
1504 W Northwest Blvd	Spokane	WA	99205	**866-873-9799**		
Softeq Development Corp						
1155 Dairy Ashford Ste 125	Houston	TX	77079	**888-552-5001**	281-552-5000	
Softerware Inc						
132 Welsh Rd Ste 140	Horsham	PA	19044	**800-220-8111**	215-628-0400	177
Softlayer Technologies Inc						
4849 Alpha Rd	Dallas	TX	75244	**866-398-7638***	214-442-0600	225
*Sales						
Soft-Lite LLC						
10250 Philipp Pkwy	Streetsboro	OH	44241	**800-551-1953**	330-528-3400	235
Softomato LLC						
901 N Pitt St Ste 325	Alexandria	VA	22314	**877-243-8735**		526
Softplan Systems Inc						
8118 Isabella Ln	Brentwood	TN	37027	**800-248-0164**	615-370-1121	177
SoftPress Systems Inc						
3020 Bridgeway Ste 408	Sausalito	CA	94965	**800-853-6454**	415-331-4820	178-8
Softrock-FM 989 (AC)						
83 E Shaw Ave Ste 150	Fresno	CA	93710	**800-606-7625**	559-230-4300	641-40
SoftThinks USA Inc						
11940 Jollyville Rd Ste 225-S	Austin	TX	78759	**800-305-1754**		804
Software AG USA						
11700 Plaza America Dr Ste 700	Reston	VA	20190	**877-724-4965**	703-860-5050	178-1
Software Answers Inc						
6770 W Snowville Rd Ste 200	Cleveland	OH	44141	**800-638-5212**	440-526-0095	
Software Engineering Institute (SEI)						
4500 Fifth Ave	Pittsburgh	PA	15213	**888-201-4479**	412-268-5800	664
Software Engineering of America Inc (SEA)						
1230 Hempstead Tpke	Franklin Square	NY	11010	**800-272-7322**	516-328-7000	178-12
Software Engineering Services Corp						
1311 Ft Crook Rd S	Bellevue	NE	68005	**800-244-1278**	402-292-8660	664
Software House International (SHI)						
290 Davidson Ave	Somerset	NJ	08873	**888-764-8888**		174
Software Information Systems Inc (SIS)						
165 Barr St	Lexington	KY	40507	**800-337-6914**	859-977-4747	180
Software Pursuits Inc						
1900 S Norfolk St	San Mateo	CA	94403	**800-367-4823**	650-372-0900	178-12
Software Technology Group						
555 S 300 E	Salt Lake City	UT	84111	**888-595-1001**	801-595-1000	180
SOG Specialty Knives & Tools LLC						
6521 212th St SW	Lynnwood	WA	98036	**888-405-6433**	425-771-6230	360
Sogetel Inc						
111 rue du 12-Novembre	Nicolet	QC	J3T1S3	**866-764-3835**	819-293-6125	386
SoHo Metropolitan Hotel						
318 Wellington St W	Toronto	ON	M5V3T4	**866-764-6638**	416-599-8800	378
Soil & Water Conservation Society (SWCS)						
945 SW Ankeny Rd	Ankeny	IA	50023	**800-843-7645**	515-289-2331	48-13
Sokol & Co						
5315 Dansher Rd	Countryside	IL	60525	**800-328-7656***		296-1
*Cust Svc						
Sol Jewelry Designs Inc						
550 S Hill St Ste 1020	Los Angeles	CA	90013	**888-323-7772**	213-622-7772	409
Solacom Technologies Inc						
84 Jean-Proulx	Gatineau	QC	J8Z1W1	**888-765-2266**		
Solage Calistoga						
755 Silverado Trl	Calistoga	CA	94515	**866-942-7442**		703
Solano Coalition for Better Health						
744 Empire St Ste 210	Fairfield	CA	94533	**800-978-7547**		362
Solano County Fair						
900 Fairgrounds Dr	Vallejo	CA	94589	**800-700-2482**	707-551-2000	638
Solano County Library						
1150 Kentucky St	Fairfield	CA	94533	**866-572-7587**		434
Solar Atmospheres Inc						
1969 Clearview Rd	Souderton	PA	18964	**800-347-3236**	215-721-1502	482
Solar Industries Inc						
4940 S Alvernon Way PO Box 27337	Tucson	AZ	85706	**800-449-2323**	520-519-8258	191-3
Solar Solutions & Distribution LLC						
2500 W Fifth Ave	Denver	CO	80204	**855-765-3478**	303-948-6300	692
Solaris Paper Inc						
13415 Carmenita Rd	Santa Fe Springs	CA	90670	**888-998-4778**		
Solarus						
440 E Grand Ave	Wisconsin Rapids	WI	54494	**800-421-9282**	715-421-8111	731
Solatube International Inc						
2210 Oak Ridge Way	Vista	CA	92081	**888-765-2882**	760-477-1120	692
Solco Plumbing Supply Inc						
413 Liberty Ave	Brooklyn	NY	11207	**800-273-6632**		
Soldiers Delight Natural Environment Area						
5100 Deer Park Rd	Owings Mills	MD	21117	**800-830-3974**	410-461-5005	561

Company	Address	City	State	ZIP	Toll-Free	Phone	Class
Solebury School	6832 Phillips Mill Rd	New Hope	PA	18938	**800-675-6900**	215-862-5261	618
Soliant Consulting Inc	14 N Peoria St 2H	Chicago	IL	60607	**800-582-0170**	312-850-3830	177
Soliant LLC	1872 Hwy 9 Bypass	Lancaster	SC	29720	**800-288-9401**	803-285-9401	596
Solid Border	1806 Turnmill St	San Antonio	TX	78248	**800-213-8175**		180
Solid Concepts Inc	28309 Ave Crocker	Valencia	CA	91355	**888-311-1017**	661-295-4400	452
Solid Gospel 1270	PO Box 307	Elkhart	IN	46515	**800-522-9376**	574-875-5166	641
Solid Waste Assn of North America (SWANA)	1100 Wayne Ave Ste 700	Silver Spring	MD	20910	**800-467-9262**	301-585-2898	527-5
SolidBoss Worldwide Inc	200 Veterans Blvd	South Haven	MI	49090	**888-258-7252**	269-637-6356	749
SolidWorks Corp	300 Baker Ave	Concord	MA	01742	**800-693-9000**	978-371-5011	178-10
Solisco Inc	120 10e Rue	Scott	QC	G0S3G0	**800-463-4188**	418-387-8908	623
Solitude Mountain	12000 Big Cottonwood Canyon	Solitude	UT	84121	**800-748-4754**	801-534-1400	665
Solmax International Inc	2801 Marie-Victorin Blvd	Varennes	QC	J3X1P7	**800-571-3904**	450-929-1234	146
Solo Printing Inc	7860 NW 66th St	Miami	FL	33166	**800-325-0118**	305-594-8699	623
Soloflex Inc	1281 NE 25th Ave Ste I	Hillsboro	OR	97124	**800-547-8802**		267
Solomon Corp	103 W Main	Solomon	KS	67480	**800-234-2867**	785-655-2191	616
Solomon Pond Mall	601 Donald Lynch Blvd	Marlborough	MA	01752	**877-746-6642**	508-303-6255	458
Solomon R Guggenheim Museum	1071 Fifth Ave	New York	NY	10128	**800-329-6109**	212-423-3500	517
Solon Manufacturing Co	425 Center St	Chardon	OH	44024	**800-323-9717**	440-286-7149	490
Solta Medical Inc	25881 Industrial Blvd	Hayward	CA	94545	**877-782-2286**		250
Solutek Corp	94 Shirley St	Boston	MA	02119	**800-403-0770**	617-445-5335	145
Solutioninc Technologies Ltd	5692 Bloomfield St	Halifax	NS	B3K1T2	**888-496-2221**	902-420-0077	363
Solutions 21	152 Wabash St	Pittsburgh	PA	15220	**866-765-2121**		461
Solutions AE Inc	236 Auburn Ave	Atlanta	GA	30303	**888-562-4441**		461
SolutionsIQ Inc	6801 185th Ave NE Ste 200	Redmond	WA	98052	**800-235-4091**	425-451-2727	180
SolutionStream	249 N 1200 E	Lehi	UT	84043	**800-314-3451**		395
Solvents & Chemicals Inc	1904 Mykawa Rd	Pearland	TX	77581	**800-622-3990**	281-485-5377	146
SOM (Skidmore Owings & Merrill LLP)	224 S Michigan Ave Ste 1000	Chicago	IL	60604	**866-296-2688**	312-554-9090	261
SOMA Medical Assessments	8800 Dufferin St Ste 105	Vaughan	ON	L4K0C5	**877-664-7662**	905-881-8855	
Somagen Diagnostics Inc	9220 25th Ave	Edmonton	AB	T6N1E1	**800-661-9993**	780-702-9500	473
Somers Cove Marina	715 Broadway	Crisfield	MD	21817	**800-967-3474**	410-968-0925	561
Somerset Capital Group Ltd	612 Wheelers Farms Rd	Milford	CT	06461	**877-282-9922**	203-701-5100	264-2
Somerset Community College	808 Monticello St	Somerset	KY	42501	**877-629-9722**	606-679-8501	162
Somerset County	11440 Ocean Hwy PO Box 243	Princess Anne	MD	21853	**800-521-9189**	410-651-2968	337
Somerset County	20 Grove St PO Box 3000	Somerville	NJ	08876	**800-246-0527**	908-231-7000	337
Somerset Door & Column Co	174 Sagamore St	Somerset	PA	15501	**800-242-7916**	814-444-9427	497
Somerset Fine Arts	PO Box 869 *Sales	Fulshear	TX	77441	**800-444-2540***		633-10
Somerset Inn	2601 W Big Beaver Rd	Troy	MI	48084	**800-228-8769**	248-643-7800	378
Somerset Rural Electric Co-op	223 Industrial Pk Rd	Somerset	PA	15501	**800-443-4255**	814-445-4106	245
Somerset Trust Co	151 W Main St PO Box 777	Somerset	PA	15501	**800-972-1651**	814-443-9200	70
Somerset Welding & Steel Inc	10558 Somerset Pk	Somerset	PA	15501	**800-777-2671**	814-444-3400	513
Somerset-Pulaski County Chamber of Commerce	445 S Hwy 27 Ste 101	Somerset	KY	42501	**877-629-9722**	606-679-7323	139
Sommer Electric Corp	818 Third St NE	Canton	OH	44704	**800-766-6373**		246
Sommer Metalcraft Corp	315 Poston Dr	Crawfordsville	IN	47933	**888-876-6637**		480
Sonalysts Inc	215 Waterford Pkwy N	Waterford	CT	06385	**800-526-8091**	860-442-4355	261
SonarMed Inc	12220 N Meridian St Ste 150	Carmel	IN	46032	**866-853-3684**	317-489-3161	250
Sonesta Hotel & Suites Coconut Grove	2889 McFarlane Rd	Miami	FL	33133	**800-766-3782**	305-529-2828	378
Sonetics Corp	7340 SW Durham Rd	Portland	OR	97224	**800-833-4558**		643
Songwriters Guild of America	210 Jamestown Park Rd Ste 100	Brentwood	TN	37027	**800-524-6742**	615-742-9945	48-4
Soniat House	1133 Chartres St	New Orleans	LA	70116	**800-544-8808**	504-522-0570	378
Sonic Air Systems Inc	1050 Beacon St	Brea	CA	92821	**800-827-6642**	714-255-0124	18
Sonic Corp	300 Johnny Bench Dr *NASDAQ: SONC*	Oklahoma City	OK	73104	**877-828-7868**	405-225-5000	666
Sonic Drive-in Restaurants	300 Johnny Bench Dr	Oklahoma City	OK	73104	**877-828-7868**	405-225-5000	666
Sonic Innovations Inc	2501 Cottontail Ln	Somerset	NJ	08873	**888-678-4327**	888-423-7834	475
Sonicor Inc	82 Otis St	West Babylon	NY	11704	**800-864-5022**	631-920-6555	777
Sonics & Materials Inc	53 Church Hill Rd *OTC: SIMA*	Newtown	CT	06470	**800-745-1105**	203-270-4600	777
SonicWALL Inc	2001 Logic Dr	San Jose	CA	95124	**888-557-6642**	408-745-9600	176
Sonnenalp Resort of Vail	20 Vail Rd	Vail	CO	81657	**800-654-8312**	970-476-5656	665
Sonobond Ultrasonics Inc	1191 McDermott Dr	West Chester	PA	19380	**800-323-1269**	610-696-4710	806
Sonoco	1 N Second St *NYSE: SON*	Hartsville	SC	29550	**800-377-2692**		597
Sonoma County Transit	355 W Robles Ave	Santa Rosa	CA	95407	**800-345-7433**	707-576-7433	466
Sonoma Developmental Ctr	15000 Arnold Dr	Eldridge	CA	95431	**800-862-0007**	707-938-6000	230
Sonoma Graphic Products Inc	961 Stockton Ave	San Jose	CA	95110	**800-250-4252**	408-294-2072	597
Sonoma Outfitters	2412 Magowan Dr	Santa Rosa	CA	95405	**800-290-1920**		707
Sonoma Raceway	29355 Arnold Dr Hwy 37 & 121	Sonoma	CA	95476	**800-870-7223**	707-938-8448	512
Sonoma Technical Support Services	505-8840 210th St Ste 342	Langley	BC	V1M2Y2	**866-898-3123**		196
Sonora Regional Medical Ctr (SRMC)	1000 Greenly Rd *Compliance	Sonora	CA	95370	**877-336-3566***	209-536-5000	373-3
Sonos	614 Chapala St	Santa Barbara	CA	93101	**800-680-2345**	805-965-3001	180
SonoSite Inc	21919 30th Dr SE *NASDAQ: SONO*	Bothell	WA	98021	**888-482-9449**	425-951-1200	381
Sons of Norway	1455 West Lake St	Minneapolis	MN	55408	**800-945-8851**	612-827-3611	48-14
Sonstegard Foods Co	5005 S Bur Oak Pl	Sioux Falls	SD	57108	**800-533-3184**		615
Sony Corp of America	550 Madison Ave	New York	NY	10022	**800-282-2848**	212-833-6800	52
Sony Creative Software	8215 Greenway Blvd Ste 400	Middleton	WI	53562	**800-577-6642**	608-203-7620	178-9
Sony Electronics Inc	1 Sony Dr *Cust Svc	Park Ridge	NJ	07656	**800-222-7669***	201-930-1000	52
Sooner Pipe LLC	1331 Lamar St Ste 970	Houston	TX	77010	**800-888-9161**	713-759-1200	384
Sopark Corp	3300 S Park Ave	Buffalo	NY	14218	**866-576-7275**	716-822-0434	621
Sophie Station Suites	1717 University Ave	Fairbanks	AK	99709	**800-528-4916**		378
Sophos Inc	3 Van de Graaff Dr 2nd Fl	Burlington	MA	01803	**866-866-2802**		178-1
SOR Inc	14685 W 105th St	Lenexa	KS	66215	**800-676-6794**	913-888-2630	201
Sorbothane Inc	2144 State Rt 59	Kent	OH	44240	**800-838-3906**	330-678-9444	326
Sorenson Media Inc	25 East Scenic Pointe Dr Ste 100	Draper	UT	84020	**888-767-3676**	801-501-8650	540
Sorin Group USA Inc	14401 W 65th Way	Arvada	CO	80004	**800-289-5759**	303-424-0129	474
Sorrento Electronics Inc	4949 Greencraig Ln	San Diego	CA	92123	**800-252-1180**	858-522-8300	470
Sorrento Hotel	900 Madison St	Seattle	WA	98104	**800-426-1265**	206-622-6400	667
sortimat Technology	5655 Meadowbrook Industrial Ct	Rolling Meadows	IL	60008	**800-385-6805**	847-925-1234	
SOS (Store Opening Solutions)	800 Middle Tennessee Blvd	Murfreesboro	TN	37129	**877-388-9262**		447
SOS Children's Villages-USA	1620 I St NW Ste 900 *General	Washington	DC	20006	**888-767-4543***	202-347-7920	48-6
SoSA (Society of Saint Andrew)	3383 Sweet Hollow Rd	Big Island	VA	24526	**800-333-4597**	434-299-5956	48-5
Sotech Nitram Inc	1695 Boul Laval	Laval	QC	H7S2M2	**877-664-8726**	450-975-2100	311
Sotheby's International Realty	38 E 61st St	New York	NY	10065	**866-899-4747**	212-606-7660	648
Sothys USA Inc	1500 NW 94th Ave	Miami	FL	33172	**800-325-0503**	305-594-4222	238
Soucy Holding Inc	5450 Saint-Roch St	Drummondville	QC	J2B6W3	**844-474-4740**	819-474-9008	60
Soudan Underground Mine State Park	1302 McKinley Park Rd	Soudan	MN	55782	**888-646-6367**	218-300-7000	561
Sound Com Corp	227 Depot St	Berea	OH	44017	**800-628-8739**	440-234-2604	52
Sound Imaging Inc	7580 Trade St	San Diego	CA	92121	**866-530-7850**		474
Sound Shore Fund	3 Canal Plz	Portland	ME	04101	**800-754-8758**		524
Sound Shore Management Inc	8 Sound Shore Dr Ste 180	Greenwich	CT	06830	**800-551-1980**	203-629-1980	400
Soundcoat Co	1 Burt Dr	Deer Park	NY	11729	**800-394-8913**	631-242-2200	388
Soundview Executive Book Summaries	511 School House Rd Ste 300	Kennett Square	PA	19348	**800-786-6279**	484-730-1270	196
Source Data Products Inc	18350 Mt Langley St	Fountain Valley	CA	92708	**800-333-2669**	714-593-0387	196
Source Intelligence LLC	1921 Palomar Oaks Way Ste 205	Carlsbad	CA	92008	**877-916-6337**		192
Source Media Inc	1 State St Plz 27th Fl	New York	NY	10004	**800-221-1809**	212-803-8200	633-9
Source North America Corp	510 S Westgate	Addison	IL	60101	**800-621-5524**	847-364-9000	576
Source Technologies	4205B Westinghouse Commons Dr	Charlotte	NC	28273	**800-922-8501**	704-969-7500	178-1

				Toll-Free	Phone	Class
Source2						
1245 W Fairbanks Ave	Winter Park	FL	32789	**800-557-6704**	407-893-3711	260
Sourcebooks Inc						
1935 Brookdale Rd Ste 139	Naperville	IL	60563	**800-432-7444**	630-961-3900	633-2
SourceLink LLC						
500 Pk Blvd Ste 1425	Itasca	IL	60143	**866-947-6872**		5
Soutex Inc						
357 Rue Jackson	Quebec	QC	G1N4C4	**800-463-2839**	418-871-2455	261
South African Airways						
1200 S Pine Island Rd Ste 650	Plantation	FL	33324	**800-722-9675**	954-769-5000	25
South Alabama Electric Co-op (SAEC)						
PO Box 449	Troy	AL	36081	**800-556-2060**	334-566-2060	245
South Arkansas Arboretum						
PO Box 7010	El Dorado	AR	71731	**888-287-2757**		561
South Arkansas Community College						
PO Box 7010	El Dorado	AR	71731	**800-955-2289**	870-862-8131	162
South Baldwin Chamber of Commerce (SBCC)						
112 W Laurel Ave PO Box 1117	Foley	AL	36535	**877-461-3712**	251-943-3291	139
South Bay Correctional Facility						
600 US Hwy 27 S	South Bay	FL	33493	**800-574-5729**	561-992-9505	213
South Bay Expressway LP						
1129 La Media Rd	San Diego	CA	92154	**888-889-1515**	619-661-7070	414
South Bay Hospital						
4016 Sun City Ctr Blvd	Sun City Center	FL	33573	**888-499-1293**	813-634-3301	373-3
South Baylo University						
1126 N Brookhurst St	Anaheim	CA	92801	**888-642-2956**	714-533-1495	166
South Beach Marina Inn & Vacation Rentals						
232 S Sea Pines Dr	Hilton Head Island	SC	29928	**800-367-3909**	843-671-6498	378
South Beach State Park						
5580 S Coast Hwy	Newport	OR	97366	**800-452-5687**	800-551-6949	561
South Bend Medical Foundation						
530 N Lafayette Blvd	South Bend	IN	46601	**800-544-0925**	574-234-4176	417
South Bend Symphony Orchestra (SBSO)						
127 N Michigan St	South Bend	IN	46601	**800-537-6415**	574-232-6343	569-3
South Bend Tribune						
225 W Colfax Ave	South Bend	IN	46626	**800-220-7378**	574-235-6464	528-2
South Bend/Mishawaka Convention & Visitors Bureau						
101 N Michigan St Ste 300	South Bend	IN	46601	**800-519-0577**		206
South Boston Speedway						
1188 James D Hagood Hwy PO Box 1066	South Boston	VA	24592	**877-440-1540**	434-572-4947	512
South Carolina						
Child Support Enforcement Office						
3150 Harden St Ext PO Box 1469	Columbia	SC	29203	**800-768-5858**	803-898-9282	338-41
Commerce Dept						
1201 Main St Ste 1600	Columbia	SC	29201	**800-868-7232**	803-737-0400	338-41
Education Lottery						
PO Box 11949 *Help Line	Columbia	SC	29211	**866-736-9819***	803-737-2002	
Social Services Dept						
1535 Confederate Ave	Columbia	SC	29202	**800-616-1309**	803-898-7601	338-41
State Government Information						
1301 Gervais St Ste 710	Columbia	SC	29201	**866-340-7105**	803-771-0131	338-41
State Ports Authority						
176 Concord St	Charleston	SC	29401	**800-845-7106**	843-723-8651	614
Vocational Rehabilitation Dept						
1410 Boston Ave PO Box 15	West Columbia	SC	29171	**800-832-7526**	803-896-6500	338-41
South Carolina Aquarium						
100 Aquarium Wharf	Charleston	SC	29401	**800-722-6455**	843-577-3474	40
South Carolina Assn of Realtors						
3780 Fernandina Rd	Columbia	SC	29210	**800-233-6381**	803-772-5206	652
South Carolina Assn of Veterinarians						
PO Box 11766	Columbia	SC	29211	**800-441-7228**	803-254-1027	790
South Carolina Bar						
950 Taylor St	Columbia	SC	29201	**877-797-2227**	803-799-6653	72
South Carolina Chamber of Commerce						
1301 Gervais St Ste 1100	Columbia	SC	29201	**800-799-4601**	803-799-4601	140
South Carolina Dental Assn						
120 Stonemark Ln	Columbia	SC	29210	**800-327-2598**	803-750-2277	227
South Carolina Education Association, The						
421 Zimalcrest Dr	Columbia	SC	29210	**800-422-7232**	803-772-6553	529
South Carolina Educational Television Commission (ETV)						
1101 George Rogers Blvd	Columbia	SC	29201	**800-922-5437**	803-737-3200	628
South Carolina Elastic Co						
201 S Carolina Elastic Rd	Landrum	SC	29356	**800-845-6700**	864-457-3388	740-5
South Carolina Federal Credit Union						
PO Box 190012	North Charleston	SC	29419	**800-845-0432**	843-797-8300	219
South Carolina Medical Assn						
132 Westpark Blvd	Columbia	SC	29210	**800-327-1021**	803-798-6207	472
South Carolina Press Assn						
106 Outlet Pointe Blvd PO Box 11429	Columbia	SC	29210	**888-727-7377**	803-750-9561	620
South Carolina State Library						
1500 Senate St	Columbia	SC	29201	**888-221-4643**	803-734-8666	
South Carolina State University						
300 College St NE *Admissions	Orangeburg	SC	29117	**800-260-5956***	803-536-7000	166
South Central Arkansas Electric Co-op						
4818 Hwy 8 W PO Box 476	Arkadelphia	AR	71923	**800-814-2931**	870-246-6701	245
South Central College						
Faribault						
1225 Third St	Faribault	MN	55021	**800-422-0391**	507-332-5800	162
Mankato						
1920 Lee Blvd	North Mankato	MN	56003	**800-722-9359**	507-389-7200	162
South Central Electric Assn						
71176 Tiell Dr PO Box 150	Saint James	MN	56081	**888-805-7232**	507-375-3164	245
South Central Indiana Rural Electric Membership Corp						
300 Morton Ave	Martinsville	IN	46151	**800-264-7362**	765-342-3344	245
South Central Library System						
4610 S Biltmore Ln	Madison	WI	53718	**855-516-7257**	608-246-7970	433-3
South Central Power Company Inc						
2780 Coon Path Rd	Lancaster	OH	43130	**800-282-5064**	740-653-4422	245
South Central Public Power District (SCPPD)						
275 S Main St PO Box 406	Nelson	NE	68961	**800-557-5254**	402-225-2351	245
South Charlotte Nissan						
9215 S Blvd	Charlotte	NC	28273	**888-411-1423**	704-552-9191	57
South Coast Plaza						
3333 Bristol St	Costa Mesa	CA	92626	**800-782-8888**		458
South College						
3904 Lonas Dr	Knoxville	TN	37909	**877-557-2575**	865-251-1800	795
South College-Asheville						
140 Sweeten Creek Rd	Asheville	NC	28803	**800-207-7847**	828-398-2500	795
South Dakota						
Arts Council						
711 E Wells Ave	Pierre	SD	57501	**800-952-3625**		
Child Support Div						
700 Governors Dr	Pierre	SD	57501	**800-286-9145**	605-773-3641	338-42
Consumer Protection Div						
1302 E Hwy 14 Ste 3	Pierre	SD	57501	**800-300-1986**	605-773-4400	338-42
Department of Health						
600 E Capitol Ave Robert Hayes Bldg	Pierre	SD	57501	**800-738-2301**	605-773-3361	338-42
Personnel Bureau						
500 E Capitol Ave	Pierre	SD	57501	**877-573-7347**	605-773-3148	338-42
Rehabilitation Services Div						
500 E Capitol Ave	Pierre	SD	57501	**877-873-8500**	605-773-3318	338-42
Social Services Dept						
700 Governors Dr	Pierre	SD	57501	**800-597-1603**	605-773-3165	338-42
Tourism Office						
711 E Wells Ave	Pierre	SD	57501	**800-732-5682**	605-773-3301	338-42
South Dakota Assn of Realtors						
204 N Euclid Ave	Pierre	SD	57501	**800-227-5877**	605-224-0554	652
South Dakota Chamber of Commerce & Industry						
108 N Euclid Ave	Pierre	SD	57501	**800-742-8112**	605-224-6161	140
South Dakota Dental Assn						
804 N Euclid Ave Ste 103	Pierre	SD	57501	**866-551-8023**	605-224-9133	227
South Dakota Lions Eye Bank						
4501 W 61st St N	Sioux Falls	SD	57107	**800-245-7846**	605-373-1008	269
South Dakota Newspaper Services						
1125 32nd Ave	Brookings	SD	57006	**800-658-3697**		620
South Dakota Nurses Assn (SDNA)						
PO Box 1015	Pierre	SD	57501	**888-425-3032**	605-945-4265	529
South Dakota Public Broadcasting (SDPB)						
555 N Dakota St PO Box 5000	Vermillion	SD	57069	**800-456-0766**	605-677-5861	628
South Dakota School of Mines & Technology						
501 E St Joseph St	Rapid City	SD	57701	**800-544-8162**	605-394-2414	166
South Dakota State Library						
800 Governors Dr	Pierre	SD	57501	**800-423-6665**	605-773-3131	433-5
South Dakota State University						
PO Box 2201	Brookings	SD	57007	**800-952-3541**	605-688-4121	166
South Dakota State University Briggs Library						
1300 N Campus Dr	Brookings	SD	57007	**800-786-2038**	605-688-5106	433-6
South Florida Sun-Sentinel						
200 E Las Olas Blvd *Cust Svc	Fort Lauderdale	FL	33301	**800-548-6397***	954-356-4000	528-2
South Jersey Healthcare HospiceCare						
2848 S Delsea Dr Bldg 1	Vineland	NJ	08360	**800-770-7547**		370
South Kentucky Rural Electrical Co-op						
925 N Main St PO Box 910	Somerset	KY	42502	**800-264-5112**	606-678-4121	245
South Miami Hospital						
6200 SW 73rd St	Miami	FL	33143	**800-228-6557**	786-662-4000	373-3
South Mountain Community College						
7050 S 24th St	Phoenix	AZ	85042	**855-622-2332**	602-243-8000	162
South Mountain Restoration Ctr						
10058 S Mountain Rd	South Mountain	PA	17261	**800-932-0313**		
South Padre Island Convention & Visitors Bureau						
7355 Padre Blvd	South Padre Island	TX	78597	**800-767-2373**	956-761-6433	206
South Pier Inn on the Canal						
701 Lake Ave S	Duluth	MN	55802	**800-430-7437**	218-786-9007	378
South Plains Electric Co-op Inc						
PO Box 1830	Lubbock	TX	79408	**800-658-2655**	806-775-7766	245
South Plains Implement						
1645 FM 403 PO Box 752	Brownfield	TX	79316	**800-725-5435**	806-637-3594	274
South Point Hotel & Casino						
9777 Las Vegas Blvd S	Las Vegas	NV	89183	**866-796-7111**	866-791-7626	378
South River Electric Membership Corp						
17494 US 421 S PO Box 931	Dunn	NC	28335	**800-338-5530**	910-892-8071	245
South Seas Island Resort						
5400 Plantation Rd	Captiva	FL	33924	**866-565-5089**	239-472-5111	665
South Shore Harbour Resort & Conference Center						
2500 S Shore Blvd	League City	TX	77573	**800-442-5005**	281-334-1000	
South Shore Harbour Resort & Conference Ctr						
2500 S Shore Blvd *Resv	League City	TX	77573	**800-442-5005***	281-334-1000	665
South Shore Music Circus						
130 Sohier St	Cohasset	MA	02025	**800-514-3849**	781-383-9850	568
South Shore Plaza						
250 Granite St	Braintree	MA	02184	**877-746-6642**	781-843-8200	458
South Sioux City Convention & Visitors Bureau						
4401 Dakota Ave	South Sioux City	NE	68776	**866-494-1307**	402-494-1307	206
South st Paul Steel Supply Company Inc						
200 Hardman Ave N	South Saint Paul	MN	55075	**800-456-7777**	651-451-6666	490
South Suburban College						
15800 S State St	South Holland	IL	60473	**800-609-8056**	708-596-2000	162
South Texas Blood & Tissue Ctr						
6211 IH-10 W	San Antonio	TX	78201	**800-292-5534**	210-731-5555	89
South Texas Money Management Ltd						
700 N Saint Mary's Ste 100	San Antonio	TX	78205	**800-805-1385**	210-824-8916	400
South Texas Veterans Health Care System						
7400 Merton Minter St	San Antonio	TX	78229	**800-209-7377**	210-617-5300	373-8
South Toledo Bend State Park						
120 Bald Eaglel Rd	Anacoco	LA	71403	**888-398-4770**	337-286-9075	561
South University						
Montgomery						
5355 Vaughn Rd	Montgomery	AL	36116	**866-629-2962**	334-395-8800	166
South University Columbia						
9 Science Ct	Columbia	SC	29203	**800-688-0932**	803-799-9082	166
South University Savannah						
709 Mall Blvd	Savannah	GA	31406	**800-688-0932**	912-201-8000	166
South University West Palm Beach						
9801 Belvedere Rd University Ctr	West Palm Beach	FL	33411	**800-688-0932**	561-273-6500	166
South Western Communications Inc						
4871 Rosebud Ln	Newburgh	IN	47630	**800-903-8432**	812-477-6495	246
Southampton Inn						
91 Hill St	SoutHampton	NY	11968	**800-832-6500**	631-283-6500	378

Name / Address	City	State	ZIP	Toll-Free	Phone	Class
Southbend Inc						
1100 Old Honeycutt Rd	Fuquay Varina	NC	27526	**800-755-4777**	919-762-1000	298
Southco						
210 N Brinton Lake Rd	Concordville	PA	19331	**877-821-0666**	610-459-4000	349
Southco Distributing Co						
2201 S John St	Goldsboro	NC	27530	**800-969-3172**	919-735-8012	297-8
Southdale Ctr						
10 Southdale Ctr	Edina	MN	55435	**877-746-6642**	952-925-7874	458
Southdata Inc						
201 Technology Ln	Mt Airy	NC	27030	**800-549-4722**		177
Southeast Arkansas College (SEARK)						
1900 Hazel St	Pine Bluff	AR	71603	**888-732-7582**	870-543-5900	162
Southeast Colorado Power Assn (SECPA)						
27850 Harris Rd	La Junta	CO	81050	**800-332-8634**	719-384-2551	245
Southeast Community College						
Beatrice						
4771 W Scott Rd	Beatrice	NE	68310	**800-233-5027**	402-228-3468	162
Lincoln 8800 'O' St	Lincoln	NE	68520	**800-642-4075**	402-471-3333	162
Milford 600 State St	Milford	NE	68405	**800-933-7223**	402-761-2131	795
Southeast Electric Co-op Inc (SECO)						
110 S Main St	Ekalaka	MT	59324	**888-485-8762**	406-775-8762	245
Southeast Fabricators Inc						
7301 University Blvd E	Cottondale	AL	35453	**800-932-3227**	205-556-3227	478
Southeast Industrial Equipment Inc						
12200 Steele Creek Rd	Charlotte	NC	28273	**866-696-9125**	704-399-9700	468
Southeast Kentucky Community & Technical College						
Cumberland						
700 College Rd	Cumberland	KY	40823	**888-274-7322**	606-589-2145	162
Middlesboro Campus						
1300 Chichester Ave	Middlesboro	KY	40965	**888-274-7322**	606-242-2145	162
Whitesburg						
2 Long Ave	Whitesburg	KY	41858	**888-274-7322**	606-633-0279	162
Southeast Milk Inc						
PO Box 3790	Belleview	FL	34420	**800-598-7866**		296-27
Southeast Missouri Hospital (SMH)						
1701 Lacey St	Cape Girardeau	MO	63701	**800-800-5123**	573-334-4822	373-3
Southeast Missourian						
301 Broadway St	Cape Girardeau	MO	63701	**800-879-1210**	573-335-6611	528-2
Southeast Technical Institute						
2320 N Career Ave	Sioux Falls	SD	57107	**800-247-0789**	605-367-8355	795
Southeast Tissue Alliance (SETA)						
6241 NW 23rd St Ste 400	Gainesville	FL	32653	**866-432-1164**	352-248-2114	541
Southeastern Aluminum Products Inc						
4925 Bulls Bay Hwy	Jacksonville	FL	32219	**800-243-8200***	904-781-8200	234
*Sales						
Southeastern Asset Management Inc						
6410 Poplar Ave Ste 900	Memphis	TN	38119	**800-445-9469**	901-761-2474	400
Southeastern Baptist Theological Seminary						
120 S Wingate St	Wake Forest	NC	27587	**800-284-6317**	919-556-3101	167-3
Southeastern Community College South						
335 Messenger Rd	Keokuk	IA	52632	**866-722-4692**	319-524-3221	162
Southeastern Correctional Institution						
5900 B I S Rd	Lancaster	OH	43130	**800-237-3454**	740-653-4324	213
Southeastern Electric Co-op Inc						
1514 E Hwy 70 PO Box 1370	Durant	OK	74702	**866-924-1315**	580-924-2170	245
Southeastern Equipment Company Inc						
10874 E Pike Rd	Cambridge	OH	43725	**800-798-5438**	740-432-6303	357
Southeastern Freight Lines Inc						
420 Davega Rd	Lexington	SC	29073	**800-637-7335**	803-794-7300	775
Southeastern Illinois College						
3575 College Rd	Harrisburg	IL	62946	**866-338-2742**	618-252-5400	162
SouthEastern Illinois Electric Cooperative Inc (SIPC)						
100 Cooperative Way						
PO Box 1001	Carrier Mills	IL	62917	**800-833-2611**	618-273-2611	245
Southeastern Indiana Rural Electric Membership Corp						
712 S Buckeye St	Osgood	IN	47037	**800-737-4111**	812-689-4111	245
Southeastern Louisiana University						
500 Western Ave	Hammond	LA	70402	**800-222-7358**	985-549-2062	166
Southeastern Metals Mfg Company Inc						
11801 Industry Dr	Jacksonville	FL	32218	**800-874-0335**	904-757-4200	234
Southeastern Oklahoma State University						
1405 N Fourth St	Durant	OK	74701	**800-435-1327**	580-745-2000	166
Southeastern Paperboard Inc						
100 S Harris Rd	Piedmont	SC	29673	**800-229-7372**	864-277-7353	550
Southeastern Public Library System of Oklahoma (SEPLSO)						
401 N Second St	McAlester	OK	74501	**800-562-9520**	918-426-0456	433-3
Southeastern University						
1000 Longfellow Blvd	Lakeland	FL	33801	**800-500-8760**	863-667-5000	166
Southeastern Wholesale Tire Co						
4721 Trademark Dr	Raleigh	NC	27610	**800-849-9215***		750
*General						
Southern Adventist University						
4881 Taylor Cir	Collegedale	TN	37315	**800-768-8437**	423-236-2000	166
Southern Air Inc						
2655 Lakeside Dr	Lynchburg	VA	24501	**800-743-1214**	434-385-6200	189-10
Southern Arizona Veterans Healthcare System						
3601 S Sixth Ave	Tucson	AZ	85723	**800-470-8262**	520-792-1450	373-8
Southern Arkansas University						
100 E University St	Magnolia	AR	71753	**800-332-7286**	870-235-4000	166
Southern Assn of Colleges & Schools						
1866 Southern Ln	Decatur	GA	30033	**888-413-3669**	404-679-4500	49-5
Southern Audio Services						
14763 Florida Blvd	Baton Rouge	LA	70819	**800-843-8823***	888-651-1203	52
*Cust Svc						
Southern Baptist Convention (SBC)						
901 Commerce St	Nashville	TN	37203	**866-722-5433**	615-244-2355	48-20
Southern Baptist Theological Seminary						
2825 Lexington Rd	Louisville	KY	40280	**800-626-5525**		167-3
Southern Biotechnology Assoc Inc						
160A Oxmoor Blvd	Birmingham	AL	35209	**800-722-2255**	205-945-1774	231
Southern Bleacher Company Inc						
801 Fifth St	Graham	TX	76450	**800-433-0912**	940-549-0733	106
Southern California Boiler Inc						
5331 Business Dr	Huntington Beach	CA	92649	**800-775-2645**	714-891-0701	187
Southern California Edison Co						
2244 Walnut Grove Ave	Rosemead	CA	91770	**800-655-4555**	626-302-1212	782
Southern California Gas Co						
555 W Fifth St	Los Angeles	CA	90013	**800-427-2200**	909-305-8261	782
Southern California Regional Rail Authority						
700 S Flower St Ste 2600	Los Angeles	CA	90017	**800-371-5465**	213-452-0200	466
Southern California Seminary						
2075 E Madison Ave	El Cajon	CA	92019	**888-389-7244**		166
Southern Co						
30 Ivan Allen Jr Blvd NW	Atlanta	GA	30308	**800-754-9452***	404-506-5000	782
*Cust Svc						
Southern Columbiana County Regional Chamber of Commerce						
529 Market St PO Box 94	East Liverpool	OH	43920	**800-804-0468**	330-385-0845	139
Southern Communications Services Inc						
5555 Glenridge Connector						
Ste 500	Atlanta	GA	30342	**800-818-5462**		731
Southern Company Inc						
3101 Carrier St	Memphis	TN	38116	**800-264-7626**	901-345-2531	533
Southern Company of NLR Inc, The						
1201 N Cypress St	North Little Rock	AR	72114	**800-482-5493**	501-376-6333	786
Southern Components Inc						
7360 Julie Frances Dr	Shreveport	LA	71129	**800-256-2144**	318-687-3330	812
Southern Connecticut Gas (SCG)						
60 Marsh Hill Rd	Orange	CT	06477	**866-268-2887**		782
Southern Connecticut State University						
501 Crescent St	New Haven	CT	06515	**888-500-7278**	203-392-5200	166
Southern Controls Inc						
3511 Wetumpka Hwy	Montgomery	AL	36110	**800-392-5770**		246
Southern Copper & Supply Company Inc						
875 Yeager Pkwy	Pelham	AL	35124	**800-289-2728**	205-664-9440	490
Southern Data Systems Inc						
1245 Land O Lakes Dr	Roswell	GA	30075	**888-425-6151**	770-993-7103	225
Southern Film Extruders Inc						
2319 English Rd	High Point	NC	27262	**800-334-6101**	336-885-8091	596
Southern First Bancshares Inc						
100 Verdae Blvd Ste 100	Greenville	SC	29607	**877-679-9646**	864-679-9000	70
Southern Folger Detention Equipment Co						
4634 S Presa St	San Antonio	TX	78223	**888-745-0530**	210-533-1231	688
Southern Foods Inc						
3500 Old Battleground Rd	Greensboro	NC	27410	**800-642-3768**		
Southern FS Inc						
2002 E Main St PO Box 728	Marion	IL	62959	**800-492-7684**	618-993-2833	276
Southern Fulfillment Services LLC						
1650 90th Ave	Vero Beach	FL	32966	**800-891-2120**	772-226-3500	457
Southern Glove Mfg Company Inc						
749 AC Little Dr	Newton	NC	28658	**800-222-1113***	828-464-4884	155-7
*Cust Svc						
Southern Grouts & Mortars Inc						
1502 SW Second Pl	Pompano Beach	FL	33069	**800-641-9247**		3
Southern Healthcare Agency Inc						
PO Box 320999	Flowood	MS	39232	**800-880-2772**	601-933-0037	260
Southern Illinois Electric Co-op						
7420 US Hwy 51 S	Dongola	IL	62926	**800-762-1400**	618-827-3555	245
Southern Illinois Healthcare						
1239 E Main St	Carbondale	IL	62902	**866-744-2468**	618-457-5200	352
Southern Illinois University						
Edwardsville						
1 Hairpin Dr	Edwardsville	IL	62026	**888-328-5168**	618-650-5555	166
Southern Illinois University Edwardsville						
Lovejoy Library						
30 Hairpin Dr						
Campus Box 1063	Edwardsville	IL	62026	**888-328-5168**	618-650-4636	433-6
Southern Illinois University School of Law						
1209 W Chautauqua Rd	Carbondale	IL	62901	**800-739-9187**	618-453-8858	167-1
Southern Illinoisan						
710 N Illinois Ave	Carbondale	IL	62901	**800-228-0429**	618-529-5454	528-2
Southern Imperial Inc						
1400 Eddy Ave	Rockford	IL	61103	**800-747-4665***	815-877-7041	286
*Cust Svc						
Southern Indiana Rehabilitation Hospital						
3104 Blackiston Blvd	New Albany	IN	47150	**800-737-7090**	812-941-8300	373-6
Southern Indiana Rural Electric Co-op Inc						
1776 Tenth St PO Box 219	Tell City	IN	47586	**800-323-2316**	812-547-2316	245
Southern Ionics Inc						
201 Commerce St	West Point	MS	39773	**800-953-3585**	912-647-0301	143
Southern Iowa Electric Co-op Inc						
22458 Hwy 2 PO Box 70	Bloomfield	IA	52537	**800-607-2027**	641-664-2277	245
Southern Kentucky Rehabilitation Hospital						
1300 Campbell Ln	Bowling Green	KY	42104	**800-989-5775**	270-782-6900	373-6
Southern Living Magazine						
2100 Lakeshore Dr	Birmingham	AL	35209	**877-262-5866**	205-445-6000	455-22
Southern Living Magazine						
2100 Lakeshore Dr	Birmingham	AL	35209	**800-366-4712**	866-772-7083	455-22
Southern Maine Community College (SMCC)						
2 Ft Rd	South Portland	ME	04106	**877-282-2182**	207-741-5500	795
Southern Maryland Oil Co Inc (SMO)						
109 N Maple Ave	La Plata	MD	20646	**888-222-3720**		575
Southern Methodist University						
6425 Boaz Ln	Dallas	TX	75205	**800-323-0672**	214-768-2000	166
Southern Methodist University Dedman School of Law						
3300 University Blvd Ste 331	Dallas	TX	75205	**888-768-5291**	214-768-2550	167-1
Southern Michigan Bank & Trust						
51 W Pearl St PO Box 309	Coldwater	MI	49036	**800-379-7628**	517-279-5500	70
Southern Missouri Bancorp Inc						
531 Vine St	Poplar Bluff	MO	63901	**855-452-7272**	573-778-1800	359-2
NASDAQ: SMBC						
Southern Motor Carriers Rate Conference Inc						
500 Westpark Dr	Peachtree City	GA	30269	**800-845-8090**	770-486-5800	476
Southern Nazarene University						
6729 NW 39th Expy	Bethany	OK	73008	**800-648-9899**	405-789-6400	166
Southern New Hampshire University						
2500 N River Rd	Manchester	NH	03106	**800-668-1249**	603-668-2211	166
Southern Ocean County Chamber of Commerce						
265 W Ninth St	Ship Bottom	NJ	08008	**800-292-6372**	609-494-7211	139
Southern Oregon University						
1250 Siskiyou Blvd Britt Hall	Ashland	OR	97520	**800-482-7672**	541-552-6411	166
Southern Park Mall						
7401 Market St	Youngstown	OH	44512	**877-746-6642**	317-636-1600	458
Southern Petroleum Lab Inc						
8850 Interchange Dr	Houston	TX	77054	**877-775-5227**	713-660-0901	738
Southern Pine Electric Power Assn						
110 Risher St PO Box 60	Taylorsville	MS	39168	**800-231-5240**	601-785-6511	245

	Toll-Free	Phone	Class
Southern Poverty Law Ctr (SPLC)			
400 Washington Ave .... Montgomery AL 36104	**888-414-7752**	334-956-8200	48-8
Southern Public Power District (SPPD)			
4550 W Husker Hwy			
PO Box 1687 .... Grand Island NE 68803	**800-652-2013**	308-384-2350	245
Southern Pump & Tank Co			
4800 N Graham St .... Charlotte NC 28269	**800-477-2826***	704-596-4373	384
*Cust Svc			
Southern Refrigeration Corp			
3140 Shenandoah Ave .... Roanoke VA 24017	**800-763-4433**	540-342-3493	661
Southern Research			
2000 Ninth Ave S .... Birmingham AL 35205	**800-967-6774**	205-581-2000	664
Southern Research Company Inc			
2850 Centenary Blvd .... Shreveport LA 71104	**888-772-6952**	318-227-9700	399
Southern Rubber Company Inc			
2209 Patterson St .... Greensboro NC 27407	**800-333-7325**	336-299-2456	326
Southern Spring & Stamping Inc			
401 Sub Stn Rd .... Venice FL 34285	**800-450-5882**	941-488-2276	714
Southern State Community College			
North			
1850 Davids Dr .... Wilmington OH 45177	**877-644-6562**	937-382-6645	162
South 12681 US Rt 62 .... Sardinia OH 45171	**877-644-6562**	937-695-0307	162
Southern States Chemical Co			
1600 E President St .... Savannah GA 31404	**888-337-8922**	912-232-1101	280
Southern States Co-op Inc			
6606 W Broad St .... Richmond VA 23230	**866-372-8272**	804-281-1000	276
Southern States Frederick Co-op Inc			
500 E South St .... Frederick MD 21701	**866-633-5747**	301-663-6164	276
Southern States Packaging Co			
PO Box 650 .... Spartanburg SC 29304	**800-621-2051**		545
Southern University & A & M College			
156 Elton C Harrison Dr			
PO Box 9757 .... Baton Rouge LA 70813	**800-256-1531***	225-771-5180	166
*Admissions			
Southern University Law Ctr			
2 Roosevelt Steptoe Dr .... Baton Rouge LA 70813	**800-537-1135**	225-771-6297	167-1
Southern University Museum of Art (SUSLA)			
3050 Martin Luther King Jr Dr			
.... Shreveport LA 71107	**800-458-1472**	318-670-6000	517
Southern Vermont Cable Co			
PO Box 166 .... Bondville VT 05340	**800-544-5931**		116
Southern Vermont College			
982 Mansion Dr .... Bennington VT 05201	**800-378-2782**	802-442-5427	166
Southern Virginia University			
1 University Hill Dr .... Buena Vista VA 24416	**800-229-8420**	540-261-8400	166
Southern Weaving Co			
1005 W Bramlett Rd .... Greenville SC 29611	**800-849-8962**	864-233-1635	740-5
Southern Wesleyan University			
907 Wesleyan Dr .... Central SC 29630	**800-282-8798**	864-644-5000	166
Southern West Virginia Convention & Visitors Bureau			
1406 Harper Rd .... Beckley WV 25801	**800-847-4898**	304-252-2244	206
Southern Wire			
8045 Metro Rd .... Olive Branch MS 38654	**800-238-0333**		490
Southernmost Illinois Tourism Bureau			
PO Box 378 .... Anna IL 62906	**800-248-4373**	618-833-9928	206
Southfield Dodge Chrysler Jeep Ram			
28100 Telegraph Rd .... Southfield MI 48034	**888-714-1015***	248-354-2950	57
*Sales			
SouthFirst Bancshares Inc			
126 N Norton Ave PO Box 167 .... Sylacauga AL 35150	**800-239-1492**	256-245-4365	359-2
OTC: SZBI			
Southlake Regional Health Ctr			
596 Davis Dr .... Newmarket ON L3Y2P9	**800-445-1822**	905-895-4521	373-2
Southland Printing Company Inc			
213 Airport Dr .... Shreveport LA 71107	**800-241-8662**	318-221-8662	623
Southland Safety LLC			
1409 Kilgore Dr .... Henderson TX 75652	**866-723-3719**	903-657-8669	196
Southland Steel Fabricators Inc			
251 Greensburg St .... Greensburg LA 70441	**800-738-7734**	225-222-4141	478
Southland Tube Inc			
3525 Richard Arrington Blvd N			
.... Birmingham AL 35234	**800-543-9024**	205-251-1884	488
Southmedic Inc			
50 Alliance Blvd .... Barrie ON L4M5K3	**800-463-7146**	705-726-9383	475
SouthPark Mall			
4400 Sharon Rd .... Charlotte NC 28211	**888-726-5930**	704-364-4411	458
Southside Bancshares Inc			
1201 S Beckham Ave .... Tyler TX 75701	**877-639-3511**	903-531-7111	359-2
NASDAQ: SBSI			
Southside Electric Co-op Inc			
2000 W Virgina Ave .... Crewe VA 23930	**800-552-2118**	434-645-7721	245
Southside Virginia Community College			
109 Campus Dr .... Alberta VA 23821	**888-220-7822**	434-949-1000	162
Southwark Metal Mfg Company Inc			
2800 Red Lion Rd .... Philadelphia PA 19114	**800-523-1052**	215-735-3401	693
Southwest Airlines Air Cargo			
2702 Love Field Dr .... Dallas TX 75235	**800-533-1222**		12
Southwest Airlines Co			
2702 Love Field Dr PO Box 36611 ...... Dallas TX 75235	**800-435-9792**	214-792-4000	25
NYSE: LUV			
Southwest Art Magazine			
10901 W 120th Ave Ste 340 .... Broomfield CO 80021	**877-212-1938**	303-442-0427	455-2
Southwest Baptist University			
1600 University Ave .... Bolivar MO 65613	**800-526-5859**		166
Southwest Binding & Laminating			
109 Millwell Ct .... Maryland Heights MO 63043	**800-325-3628**	314-739-4400	86
SouthWest Capital Bank			
622 Douglas Ave .... Las Vegas NM 87701	**800-748-2406**	505-425-7565	70
Southwest Florida International Airport			
11000 Terminal Access Rd			
Ste 8671 .... Fort Myers FL 33913	**800-359-6786**	239-590-4800	27
Southwest Freightlines			
11991 Transpark Dr .... El Paso TX 79927	**800-776-5799***	915-860-8592	775
*General			
Southwest Gas Corp			
5241 Spring Mtn Rd			
PO Box 98510 .... Las Vegas NV 89193	**877-860-6020**	702-876-7237	782
NYSE: SWX			

	Toll-Free	Phone	Class
Southwest Gas Corp Northern Nevada Div			
400 Eagle Stn Ln .... Carson City NV 89701	**877-860-6020**		782
Southwest Gas Corp Southern Arizona Div			
PO Box 98512 .... Las Vegas NV 89193	**877-860-6020**		782
Southwest Gas Corp Southern California Div			
13471 Mariposa Rd .... Victorville CA 92395	**877-860-6020**		782
Southwest Gas Corp Southern Nevada Div			
5241 Spring Mtn Rd .... Las Vegas NV 89150	**877-860-6020**	702-876-7011	782
Southwest General Hospital (SGH)			
7400 Barlite Blvd .... San Antonio TX 78224	**877-898-6080**	210-921-2000	373-3
Southwest Georgia Financial Corp			
201 First St SE .... Moultrie GA 31768	**888-683-2265**	229-985-1120	359-2
NYSE: SGB			
Southwest Institute of Healing Arts			
1100 E Apache Blvd .... Tempe AZ 85281	**888-504-9106**	480-994-9244	795
Southwest Iowa Rural Electric Co-op			
1801 Grove Ave .... Corning IA 50841	**888-220-4869**	641-322-3165	245
Southwest Louisiana Convention & Visitors Bureau			
1205 N Lakeshore Dr .... Lake Charles LA 70601	**800-456-7952**	337-436-9588	206
Southwest Louisiana Electric Membership Corp			
3420 NE Evangeline Thwy .... Lafayette LA 70509	**888-275-3626**	337-896-5384	245
Southwest Materials Handling Company Inc			
4719 Almond St .... Dallas TX 75247	**866-674-6067**	214-630-1375	357
Southwest Medical Assoc Inc			
638 E Market St PO Box 2168 .... Rockport TX 78382	**800-929-4854**	361-729-0646	717
Southwest Minnesota State University			
1501 State St .... Marshall MN 56258	**800-642-0684**		166
Southwest Mississippi Electric Power Assn			
18671 Hwy 61 PO Box 5 .... Lorman MS 39096	**800-287-8564**		245
Southwest Missouri Bank			
2417 S Grand Ave .... Carthage MO 64836	**800-943-8488**	417-358-1770	70
Southwest Oilfield Products Inc			
10340 Wallisville Rd .... Houston TX 77013	**800-392-4600**	713-675-7541	533
Southwest Public Power District			
221 S Main St PO Box 289 .... Palisade NE 69040	**800-379-7977**	308-285-3295	245
Southwest Rural Electric Assn			
700 N Broadway PO Box 310 .... Tipton OK 73570	**800-256-7973**	580-667-5281	245
Southwest Tennessee Community College			
5983 Macon Cove PO Box 780 .... Memphis TN 38134	**877-717-7822**	901-333-5000	162
Southwest Tennessee Electric Membership Corp			
1009 E Main St .... Brownsville TN 38012	**800 772 0472**	731 772 1322	245
Southwest Texas Electric Co-op Inc			
101 E Gillis St PO Box 677 .... Eldorado TX 76936	**800-643-3980**	325-853-2544	245
Southwest Virginia Community College			
724 Community College Rd .... Cedar Bluff VA 24609	**855-877-3944**	276-964-2555	162
Southwest Washington Convention & Visitors Bureau			
1220 Main S Ste 220 .... Vancouver WA 98660	**877-600-0800**	360-750-1553	206
Southwest Wisconsin Technical College (SWTC)			
1800 Bronson Blvd .... Fennimore WI 53809	**800-362-3322**	608-822-3262	795
Southwestern Adventist University			
100 W Hillcrest Dr .... Keene TX 76059	**800-433-2240***	817-645-3921	166
*Admissions			
Southwestern Assemblies of God University			
1200 Sycamore St .... Waxahachie TX 75165	**888-937-7248**	972-937-4010	166
Southwestern Baptist Theological Seminary			
PO Box 22740 .... Fort Worth TX 76122	**877-467-9287**	817-923-1921	167-3
Southwestern Christian College			
PO Box 10 .... Terrell TX 75160	**800-925-9357**	972-524-3341	166
Southwestern Christian University			
7210 NW 39th Expy PO Box 340 .... Bethany OK 73008	**888-418-9272**	405-789-7661	166
Southwestern College			
900 Otay Lakes Rd .... Chula Vista CA 91910	**866-262-9881**	619-421-6700	162
Southwestern College			
100 College St .... Winfield KS 67156	**800-846-1543**		166
Southwestern Community College			
1501 W Townline St .... Creston IA 50801	**800-247-4023**	641-782-7081	162
Southwestern Community College			
447 College Dr .... Sylva NC 28779	**800-447-4091**	828-339-4000	162
Southwestern Controls			
6720 Sands Point Dr Ste 100 .... Houston TX 77074	**800-444-9368**	713-777-2626	223
Southwestern Electric Cooperative Inc			
525 US Rt 40 .... Greenville IL 62246	**800-637-8667**		245
Southwestern Energy Co			
10000 Energy Dr .... Spring TX 77389	**866-322-0801**	832-796-1000	782
NYSE: SWN			
Southwestern Illinois College			
2500 Carlyle Ave .... Belleville IL 62221	**800-222-5131**	618-235-2700	162
Southwestern Industries Inc			
2615 Homestead Pl .... Rancho Dominguez CA 90220	**800-421-6875**	310-608-4422	453
Southwestern Michigan College (SMC)			
58900 Cherry Grove Rd .... Dowagiac MI 49047	**800-456-8675**		162
Niles Area 2229 US 12 .... Niles MI 49120	**800-456-8675**		162
Southwestern Michigan Tourism Council			
2300 Pipestone Rd .... Benton Harbor MI 49022	**800-764-2836**	269-925-6301	206
Southwestern Petroleum Corp			
PO Box 961005 .... Fort Worth TX 76161	**800-877-9372**		537
Southwestern University			
PO Box 770 .... Georgetown TX 78627	**800-252-3166**	512-863-1200	166
Southwestern Wire Inc			
PO Box CC .... Norman OK 73070	**800-348-9473**	405-447-6900	808
Southwestern/Great American			
2451 Atrium Way .... Nashville TN 37214	**888-602-7867***		96
*Cust Svc			
Southwire Co			
1 Southwire Dr .... Carrollton GA 30119	**800-444-1700**	770-832-4242	483
Southworth Products Corp			
PO Box 1380 .... Portland ME 04104	**800-743-1000**	207-878-0700	468
Sovereign Pharmaceuticals Ltd			
7590 Sand St .... Fort Worth TX 76118	**877-248-0228**	817-284-0429	578
Sovereign Systems LLC			
3930 E Jones Bridge Rd Ste 300 ...... Norcross GA 30092	**844-727-3622**		
Soybean Digest			
7900 International Dr			
Ste 300 .... Minneapolis MN 55425	**800-722-5334***	952-851-4667	455-1
*Cust Svc			
Spa at Big Cedar Lodge			
190 Top of the Rock Rd .... Ridgedale MO 65739	**800-225-6343**	417-339-5201	703

	Toll-Free	Phone	Class
Spa at Kingsmill Resort			
1010 Kingsmill Rd .... Williamsburg VA 23185	**800-965-4772**	757-253-8230	703
Spa at Le Merigot JW Marriott Beach Hotel Santa Monica			
1740 Ocean Ave .... Santa Monica CA 90401	**888-236-2427**	310-395-9700	703
Spa at Pebble Beach			
1518 Cypress Dr .... Pebble Beach CA 93953	**800-654-9300**	831-649-7615	703
Spa at Peninsula Beverly Hills			
9882 S Santa Monica Blvd .... Beverly Hills CA 90212	**800-462-7899**	310-551-2888	702
Spa at Pinehurst Resort			
80 Carolina Vista Dr .... Pinehurst NC 28374	**800-487-4653**	910-235-8320	703
Spa at the Broadmoor			
1 Lake Ave .... Colorado Springs CO 80906	**800-634-7711**	719-634-7711	703
Spa at the Chattanoogan			
1201 Broad St .... Chattanooga TN 37402	**800-619-0018**	423-756-3400	703
Spa at the Equinox Resort			
3567 Main St .... Manchester Village VT 05254	**800-362-4747**		703
Spa at the Fairmont Inn Sonoma Mission Inn			
100 Boyes Blvd .... Sonoma CA 95476	**866-540-4499**	707-938-9000	703
Spa at the Hotel Hershey			
100 Hotel Rd .... Hershey PA 17033	**877-772-9988**	717-520-5888	703
Spa at the Norwich Inn			
607 W Thames St .... Norwich CT 06360	**800-275-4772**	860-425-3500	703
Spa at the Saddlebrook Resort			
5700 Saddlebrook Way .... Wesley Chapel FL 33543	**800-729-8383**	813-907-4419	703
Spa at the Sagamore			
110 Sagamore Rd .... Bolton Landing NY 12814	**866-384-1944**	518-743-6081	703
Spa at the Sanderling Resort			
1461 Duck Rd .... Duck NC 27949	**855-412-7866**		703
Spa at The Setai			
2001 Collins Ave .... Miami Beach FL 33139	**888-625-7500**		702
Spa at White Oaks Conference Resort			
253 Taylor Rd .... Niagara-on-the-Lake ON L0S1J0	**800-263-5766**	905-641-2599	703
Spa Manufacturers			
6060 Ulmerton Rd .... Clearwater FL 33760	**877-530-9493**	727-530-9493	374
Spa Resort Casino			
401 E Amado Rd .... Palm Springs CA 92262	**888-999-1995**		133
Spa Resort, The			
401 E Amado Rd .... Palm Springs CA 92262	**888-999-1995**	760-883-1060	665
Spa Terre at LaPlaya Beach & Golf Resort			
9891 Gulf Shore Dr .... Naples FL 34108	**800-237-6883**	239-597-3123	703
Spa Terre at Paradise Point Resort			
1404 Vacation Rd .... San Diego CA 92109	**800-344-2626**	858-581-5998	703
Spa Terre at the Inn & Spa at Loretto			
211 Old Santa Fe Trl .... Santa Fe NM 87501	**800-727-5531**	505-984-7997	703
Spa Toccare at Borgata Hotel Casino			
1 Borgata Way .... Atlantic City NJ 08401	**877-448-5833**	609-317-7235	703
Space Coast Credit Union			
8045 N Wickham Rd			
PO Box 419001 .... Melbourne FL 32941	**800-447-7228**	321-752-2222	219
Space Coast Jet Ctr			
7003 Challenger Ave .... Titusville FL 32780	**800-559-5473**	321-267-8355	63
Space Optics Research Labs LLC			
7 Stuart Rd .... Chelmsford MA 01824	**800-552-7675**	978-250-8640	406
Space Science & Engineering Ctr			
University of Wisconsin-Madison			
1225 W Dayton St .... Madison WI 53706	**866-391-1753**	608-263-6750	664
Space Systems/Loral			
3825 Fabian Way .... Palo Alto CA 94303	**800-332-6490**	650-852-4000	643
SpaceGuard Products Inc			
711 S Commerce Dr .... Seymour IN 47274	**800-841-0680**	812-523-3044	286
Spacelabs Health Care			
35301 SE Center St .... Snoqualmie WA 98065	**800-522-7025**	425-396-3300	250
Spacesaver Corp			
1450 Janesville Ave .... Fort Atkinson WI 53538	**800-492-3434**	800-255-8170	286
Spader Business Management			
2101 W 41st St Ste 49 .... Sioux Falls SD 57105	**800-772-3377**		196
SpaHalekulani at the Halekulani Hotel			
2199 Kalia Rd .... Honolulu HI 96815	**800-367-2343**	808-931-5322	703
Spalding			
PO Box 90015 .... Bowling Green KY 42103	**855-253-4533**		706
Spalding Hardware Ltd			
1616 10 Ave SW .... Calgary AB T3C0J5	**800-837-0850**		349
Spalding Rehabilitation Hospital			
900 Potomac St .... Aurora CO 80011	**800-367-3309**	303-367-1166	373-6
Spalding University			
851 S Fourth St .... Louisville KY 40203	**800-896-8941**	502-585-9911	166
Spal-Usa Inc			
1731 SE Oralabor Rd .... Ankeny IA 50021	**800-345-0327**		54
Span-America Medical Systems Inc			
70 Commerce Ctr .... Greenville SC 29615	**800-888-6752**	864-288-8877	475
NASDAQ: SPAN			
Spangler Candy Co			
400 N Portland St PO Box 71 .... Bryan OH 43506	**888-636-4221***	419-636-4221	296-8
*Sales			
Spanish Cove			
11 Palm Ave .... Yukon OK 73099	**800-965-2683**		668
Spanish-American Translating			
330 Eagle Ave .... West Hempstead NY 11552	**800-870-5790**	516-481-3339	763
Spark Energy Gas LP			
2105 Citywest Blvd .... Houston TX 77042	**877-547-7275**		325
Sparkhound Inc			
11207 Proverbs Ave .... Baton Rouge LA 70816	**866-217-1500**	225-216-1500	180
Sparkle Solutions LP			
100 Courtland Ave .... Concord ON L4K3T6	**866-660-2282**	905-660-2282	35
Sparks Belting Co			
3800 Stahl Dr SE .... Grand Rapids MI 49546	**800-451-4537**	616-949-2750	369
Sparks Marketing Corp			
2828 Charter Rd .... Philadelphia PA 19154	**800-925-7727**	215-676-1100	286
Sparks Regional Medical Ctr (SRMC)			
1001 Towson Ave .... Fort Smith AR 72901	**800-285-1131**	479-441-4000	373-3
Sparling Instruments Company Inc			
4097 N Temple City Blvd .... El Monte CA 91731	**800-800-3569***	626-444-0571	493
*Sales			
Sparrow Health System			
1215 E Michigan Ave .... Lansing MI 48912	**800-772-7769**	517-364-1000	373-3
Sparta Systems Inc			
2000 Waterview Dr Ste 300 .... Holmdel NJ 08691	**888-261-5948**	609-807-5100	177

	Toll-Free	Phone	Class
Spartan Chemical Company Inc			
1110 Spartan Dr .... Maumee OH 43537	**800-537-8990**	419-531-5551	145
Spartan College of Aeronautics & Technology			
8820 E Pine St .... Tulsa OK 74115	**800-331-1204***	918-836-6886	795
*Admissions			
Spartan Distributors			
487 W Div St .... Sparta MI 49345	**800-822-2216**	616-887-7301	274
Spartan Energy Corp			
850 - Second St SW Ste 500 .... Calgary AB T2P0R8	**866-567-3105**	403-355-8920	532
Spartan Graphics Inc			
200 Applewood Dr .... Sparta MI 49345	**800-747-4477**	616-887-8243	623
Spartan Showcase Inc			
c/o Prock Operations Inc			
321 E Hardy St .... St James MO 65559	**800-325-0775**		
Spartan Technology			
125 Venture Blvd .... Spartanburg SC 29306	**877-727-8260**		
Spartanburg Community College			
800 Brisack Rd PO Box 4386 .... Spartanburg SC 29305	**866-591-3700**	864-592-4800	795
Spartanburg Convention & Visitors Bureau			
298 Magnolia St .... Spartanburg SC 29306	**800-374-8326**	864-594-5050	206
Spartanburg Methodist College			
1000 Powell Mill Rd .... Spartanburg SC 29301	**800-772-7286**	864-587-4000	162
Spartanburg Regional Medical Ctr (SRMC)			
101 E Wood St .... Spartanburg SC 29303	**800-318-2596**	864-560-6000	373-3
Spartanburg Steel Products Inc			
1290 New Cut Rd PO Box 6428 ...... Spartanburg SC 29304	**888-974-7500**	864-585-5211	487
Sparus			
3175 Corners N Ct .... Peachtree Corners GA 30071	**800-241-5057**		461
Spatial Insights Inc			
4938 Hampden Ln .... Bethesda MD 20814	**800-347-5291**		535
Spaulding Composites Co			
55 Nadeau Dr .... Rochester NH 03867	**800-801-0560**	603-332-0555	595
Spaulding Rehabilitation Hospital			
125 Nashua St .... Boston MA 02114	**888-774-0055**	617-573-7000	373-6
SPC (Sheboygan Paint Company)			
1439 N 25th St PO Box 417 .... Sheboygan WI 53081	**800-773-7801**	920-458-2157	546
SPE (Society of Petroleum Engineers)			
222 Palisades Creek Dr .... Richardson TX 75080	**800-456-6863**	972-952-9393	48-12
Speak Inc Speakers Bureau			
10680 Treena St Ste 230 .... San Diego CA 92131	**800-677-3324**	858-228-3771	704
SpeakerCraft Inc			
940 Columbia Ave .... Riverside CA 92507	**800-448-0976**	951-781-3030	173-5
Speakers Unlimited			
PO Box 27225 .... Columbus OH 43227	**888-333-6676**	614-864-3703	704
Speakman Co			
400 Anchor Mill Rd .... New Castle DE 19720	**800-537-2107**		605
Spearfish Canyon Resort			
10619 Roughlock Falls Rd .... Lead SD 57754	**877-975-6343**	605-584-3435	665
Spears Manufacturing Co			
PO Box 9203 .... Sylmar CA 91392	**800-862-1499**	818-364-1611	604
SPEC (Systems & Processes Engineering Corp)			
4120 Commercial Ctr Dr Ste 500 .... Austin TX 78744	**800-789-7732**	512-479-7732	
SPEC Building Materials Corp			
2840 Roe Ln .... Kansas City KS 66103	**866-585-7785**	913-384-0804	191-4
Spec Ops Inc			
319 Business Ln .... Ashland VA 23005	**800-774-3854**	804-752-4790	261
Spec Personnel LLC			
25 Walls Dr .... Fairfield CT 06824	**888-788-7732**		
Spec's Wines Spirits & Finer Foods			
2410 Smith St .... Houston TX 77006	**888-526-8787**	713-526-8787	442
Specco Industries Inc			
13087 Main St .... Lemont IL 60439	**800-441-6646**	630-257-5060	145
Special Counsel Inc			
10151 Deerwood Park Blvd			
Bldg 400 3rd Fl .... Jacksonville FL 32256	**800-737-3436**	904-737-3436	717
Special Libraries Assn (SLA)			
331 S Patrick St .... Alexandria VA 22314	**866-446-6069**	703-647-4900	49-11
Special Metals Corp			
4317 Middle Settlement Rd .... New Hartford NY 13413	**800-334-8351**	315-798-2900	483
Special Metals Inc			
2009 S Broadway .... Moore OK 73160	**800-727-7177**		490
Special Military Active Retired Travel Club (SMART)			
600 University Office Blvd			
Ste 1A .... Pensacola FL 32504	**800-354-7681**	850-478-1986	48-23
Special Olympics Inc			
1133 19th St NW .... Washington DC 20036	**800-700-8585**	202-628-3630	48-22
Specialized Bicycle Components			
15130 Concord Cir .... Morgan Hill CA 95037	**877-808-8154**	408-779-6229	82
Specialized Information Publishers Assn (SIPA)			
8229 Boone Blvd Ste 260 .... Vienna VA 22182	**800-356-9302**	703-992-9339	49-14
Specialized Printed Forms Inc			
352 Ctr St .... Caledonia NY 14423	**800-688-2381**	585-538-2381	110
Special-Lite Inc			
PO Box 6 .... Decatur MI 49045	**800-821-6531**	269-423-7068	234
Specialty Bolt & Screw Inc			
235 Bowles Rd .... Agawam MA 01001	**800-322-7878**	413-789-6700	350
Specialty Coffee Assn of America (SCAA)			
117 W Fourth St Ste 300 .... Santa Ana CA 92701	**800-995-9019**	562-624-4100	49-6
Specialty Design & Mfg Co			
PO Box 4039 .... Reading PA 19606	**800-720-0867**	610-779-1357	752
Specialty Foods Group Inc			
6 Dublin Ln .... Owensboro KY 42301	**800-238-0020**	270-926-2324	296-26
Specialty Graphic Imaging Assn (SGIA)			
10015 Main St .... Fairfax VA 22031	**888-385-3588**	703-385-1335	49-16
Specialty Hearse & Ambulance Sale Corp			
60 Engineers Ln E .... Farmingdale NY 11735	**800-349-6102***	516-349-7700	57
*General			
Specialty Laboratories Inc			
27027 Tourney Rd .... Valencia CA 91355	**800-421-7110***	661-799-6543	417
*Sales			
Specialty Loose Leaf Inc			
1 Cabot St .... Holyoke MA 01040	**800-227-3623**	413-532-0106	548-2
Specialty Manufacturing Co			
5858 Centerville Rd .... Saint Paul MN 55127	**800-549-4473**	651-653-0599	785
Specialty Motors Inc			
25060 Ave Tibbitts .... Valencia CA 91355	**800-232-2612**	661-257-7388	515
Specialty Pipe & Tube Inc			
PO Box 516 .... Mineral Ridge OH 44440	**800-842-5839**	330-505-8262	490

Name / Address	City	State	ZIP	Toll-Free	Phone	Class
Specialty Plastic Fabricators Inc						
9658 196th St	Mokena	IL	60448	**800-747-9509**	708-479-5501	199
Specialty Products & Insulation Co (SPI)						
1650 Manheim Pk Ste 202	Lancaster	PA	17601	**800-788-7764**	855-519-4044	191-4
Specialty Retailers Inc						
2425 W Loop	South Houston	TX	77027	**800-743-8730**		157-4
Specialty Surgical Products Inc						
1131 US Hwy 93 N	Victor	MT	59875	**888-878-0811**	406-961-0102	473
Specialty Tires of America Inc						
1600 Washington St	Indiana	PA	15701	**800-622-7327**	724-349-9010	749
Specialty Tools & Fasteners Distributors Assn (STAFDA)						
500 Elm Grove Rd Ste 210						
PO Box 44	Elm Grove	WI	53122	**800-352-2981**	262-784-4774	49-18
Specialty Vehicle Institute of America (SVIA)						
2 Jenner St Ste 150	Irvine	CA	92618	**800-887-2887**	949-727-3727	49-21
Specific Impulse Inc						
2601 Blanding Ave Ste 401	Alameda	CA	94501	**800-470-0043**	510-251-2330	180
Specification Rubber Products Inc						
1568 First St N	Alabaster	AL	35007	**800-633-3415**	205-663-2521	326
Specified Technologies Inc						
210 Evans Way	Somerville	NJ	08876	**800-992-1180**	908-526-8000	146
Specmo Enterprises						
1200 E Avis Dr	Madison Heights	MI	48071	**800-545-7910**		54
Speco Inc						
3946 Willow Rd	Schiller Park	IL	60176	**800-541-5415**	847-678-4240	357
Speco Technologies						
200 New Hwy	Amityville	NY	11701	**800-645-5516**	631-957-8700	38
Spectator, The						
44 Frid St	Hamilton	ON	L8N3G3	**800-263-6902**	905-526-3333	528-1
Spectera Inc						
6220 Old Dobbin Ln						
Liberty 6 Ste 200	Columbia	MD	21045	**800-638-3120**		390-3
Spectra Co						
2510 Supply St	Pomona	CA	91767	**800-375-1771**		377
Spectra Colors Corp						
25 Rizzolo Rd	Kearny	NJ	07032	**800-527-8588**	201-997-0606	146
Spectra Integrated Systems Inc						
8100 Arrowridge Blvd	Charlotte	NC	28273	**800-443-7561**	704-525-7099	246
Spectra Merchandising International Inc						
4230 N Normandy Ave	Chicago	IL	60634	**800-777-5331**	773-202-8408	246
Spectra Precision Inc						
10355 Westmoor Dr Ste 100	Westminster	CO	80021	**888-527-3771**		
Spectra Services Inc						
6359 Dean Pkwy	Ontario	NY	14519	**800-955-7732**	585-265-4320	418
Spectrachem						
10 Dell Glen Ave	Lodi	NJ	07644	**800-524-2806**	973-253-3553	387
Spectra-Kote Corp						
301 E Water St	Gettysburg	PA	17325	**800-241-4626**	717-334-3177	550
Spectranetics Corp						
9965 Federal Dr	Colorado Springs	CO	80921	**800-231-0978**	719-447-2000	423
NASDAQ: SPNC						
SpectraSensors Inc						
4333 W Sam Houston Pkwy N	Houston	TX	77043	**800-619-2861**	713-300-2700	201
Spectrolab Inc						
12500 Gladstone Ave	Sylmar	CA	91342	**800-936-4888**	818-365-4611	692
Spectronics Corp						
956 Brush Hollow Rd	Westbury	NY	11590	**800-274-8888**	516-333-4840	201
Spectrum Brands						
3001 Deming Way	Middleton	WI	53562	**800-566-7899**	608-275-3340	280
Spectrum Control Inc						
8031 Avonia Rd	Fairview	PA	16415	**855-294-3800**		
Spectrum Data Inc						
131 N Third St	Oregon	IL	61061	**800-733-6567**		225
Spectrum Glass Co						
PO Box 646	Woodinville	WA	98072	**800-426-3120**	425-483-6699	329
Spectrum Health Blodgett Campus						
100 Michigan St NE	Grand Rapids	MI	49503	**866-989-7999**	616-774-7444	373-3
Spectrum Health Systems Inc						
10 Mechanic St Ste 302	Worcester	MA	01608	**800-464-9555**	508-792-5400	48-15
Spectrum Healthcare Resources Inc						
12647 Olive Blvd Ste 600	Saint Louis	MO	63141	**800-325-3982**		461
Spectrum Industries Inc						
925 First Ave	Chippewa Falls	WI	54729	**800-235-1262**	715-723-6750	286
Spectrum Laboratories Inc						
18617 Broadwick St	Rancho Dominguez	CA	90220	**800-634-3300**	310-885-4600	418
Spectrum Laboratory Products Inc						
14422 S San Pedro St	Gardena	CA	90248	**800-772-8786***	310-516-8000	477
*General						
Spectrum Products						
7100 Spectrum Ln	Missoula	MT	59808	**800-791-8056**		
Spectrum Signal Processing by Vecima						
2700 Production Way Ste 300	Burnaby	BC	V5A4X1	**800-663-8986**	604-676-6700	621
Spectrum Systems Inc						
3410 W Nine-Mile Rd	Pensacola	FL	32526	**800-432-6119**	850-944-3392	418
Speech-Language & Audiology Canada (SAC)						
1 Nicholas St Ste 1000	Ottawa	ON	K1N7B7	**800-259-8519**	613-567-9968	48-1
Speed Consulting LLC						
500 Cantrell St	Waxahachie	TX	75165	**800-256-7140**		461
Speed Skating Canada						
2781 Lancaster Rd	Ottawa	ON	K1B1A7	**877-572-4772**	902-425-5450	138
Speed Sport						
142 F S Cardigan Way	Mooresville	NC	28117	**866-455-2531**	704-790-0136	455-3
Speed Trader 1717 Rt 6	Carmel	NY	10512	**800-874-3039**	845-531-2487	
Speedie & Assoc Inc						
3331 E Wood St	Phoenix	AZ	85040	**800-628-6221**	602-997-6391	738
Speedling Inc						
4447 Old 41 Hwy S	Ruskin	FL	33570	**800-881-4769***		368
*Cust Svc						
Speedway LLC						
500 Speedway Dr	Enon	OH	45323	**800-643-1948***	937-864-3000	324
*Cust Svc						
Speedway Motors						
340 Victory Ln	Lincoln	NE	68528	**800-736-3733**	800-979-0122	786
Speedway Redi Mix Inc						
1201 N Taylor Rd	Garrett	IN	46738	**800-227-5649**	260-357-6885	182
Speedy Automated Mailers Inc						
2200 Queen St Ste 15	Bellingham	WA	98229	**800-678-4775**	360-676-4775	5
Speidel						
34 Branch Ave	Providence	RI	02904	**800-441-2200**	401-519-2000	407
Spellman Hardwoods Inc						
4645 N 43rd Ave	Phoenix	AZ	85031	**800-624-5401**	602-272-2313	191-3
Spelman College						
350 Spelman Ln SW	Atlanta	GA	30314	**800-982-2411***	404-681-3643	166
*Admissions						
Spence Engineering Company Inc						
150 Coldenham Rd	Walden	NY	12586	**800-398-2493**	845-778-5566	784
Spence Law Firm LLC						
15 S Jackson St	Jackson	WY	83001	**800-967-2117**	307-733-7290	427
Spencer Cos Inc						
2600 Memorial Pkwy S	Huntsville	AL	35801	**800-633-2910**	256-533-1150	575
Spencer Fabrications Inc						
29511 County Rd 561	Tavares	FL	32778	**866-277-3623**	352-343-0014	693
Spencer Recovery Centers Inc						
1316 S Coast Hwy	Laguna Beach	CA	92651	**800-334-0394**		722
Spencer Reed Group Inc						
5700 W 112th St Ste 110	Overland Park	KS	66211	**800-477-5035**	913-663-4400	266
Spencer Savings Bank SLA						
611 River Dr	Elmwood Park	NJ	07407	**800-363-8115**	973-772-6700	70
Spencer Turbine Co						
600 Day Hill Rd	Windsor	CT	06095	**800-232-4321**	860-688-8361	18
Spenco Medical Corp						
PO Box 2501	Waco	TX	76702	**800-877-3626**		475
Sperry & Rice Mfg Company LLC						
9146 US Hwy 52	Brookville	IN	47012	**800-541-9277**	765-647-4141	673
Sperry Automatics Company Inc						
1372 New Haven Rd PO Box 717	Naugatuck	CT	06770	**800-923-3709**	203-729-4589	617
Sperry Rail Inc						
46 Shelter Rock Rd	Danbury	CT	06810	**800-525-8913**	203-791-4500	41
Sperry Software Inc						
12443 San Jose Blvd						
Ste 503	Jacksonville	FL	32223	**800-878-1645**		521
SPFPA (International Union Security Police & Fire Profess)						
25510 Kelly Rd	Roseville	MI	48066	**800-228-7492**	586-772-7250	413
SPG International						
11230 Harland Dr	Covington	GA	30014	**877-503-4774**	770-787-9830	286
Sphere 3D Corp						
240 Matheson Blvd E	Mississauga	ON	L4Z1X1	**800-406-7325**	416-749-5999	180
SPHS (Sheppard Pratt Health System)						
6501 N Charles St	Baltimore	MD	21285	**800-627-0330**	410-938-3000	373-5
SPI (Specialty Products & Insulation Co)						
1650 Manheim Pk Ste 202	Lancaster	PA	17601	**800-788-7764**	855-519-4044	191-4
SPI Pharma						
Rockwood Office Pk 503 Carr Rd						
Ste 210	Wilmington	DE	19809	**800-789-9755**	302-576-8567	477
SPI/Mobile Pulley Works Inc						
905 S Ann St	Mobile	AL	36605	**866-334-6325**	251-653-0606	261
Spice Hunter Inc						
2000 W Broad St	Richmond	VA	23220	**800-444-3061**		296-37
Spice World Inc						
8101 Presidents Dr	Orlando	FL	32809	**800-433-4979**	407-851-9432	296-37
Spiced Pear						
117 Memorial Blvd	Newport	RI	02840	**866-793-5664**	401-847-2244	667
Spicers Paper Inc						
12310 Slauson Ave	Santa Fe Springs	CA	90670	**800-774-2377**	562-698-1199	549
Spider Staging Corp						
365 Upland Dr	Tukwila	WA	98188	**877-774-3370**	206-575-6445	489
Spike 1352 W Main	Tremonton	UT	84337	**800-821-4474**		274
Spilltech Environmental Inc						
1627 Odonoghue St	Mobile	AL	36615	**800-228-3877**		604
Spilman Thomas & Battle PLLC						
300 Kanawha Blvd E	Charleston	WV	25301	**800-967-8251**	304-340-3800	427
Spin Master Ltd						
450 Front St W	Toronto	ON	M5V1B6	**800-622-8339**	416-364-6002	757
Spina Bifida Assn (SBAA)						
1600 Wilson Blvd Ste 800	Arlington	VA	22209	**800-621-3141**	202-944-3285	48-17
Spindrift Inn						
652 Cannery Row	Monterey	CA	93940	**800-841-1879**	831-646-8900	378
Spindustry Systems Inc						
1370 NW 114th St Ste 300	Des Moines	IA	50325	**877-225-4200**	515-225-0920	
SpinGo Solutions Inc						
14193 S Minuteman Dr Ste 100	Draper	UT	84020	**877-377-4646**		386
Spinnaker Coating Inc						
518 E Water St	Troy	OH	45373	**800-543-9452**	937-332-6500	550
Spira Data Corp						
707 Seventh Ave SW Ste 1000	Calgary	AB	T2P3H6	**855-666-6353**	403-263-6475	386
Spiral Binding Company Inc						
1 Maltese Dr	Totowa	NJ	07511	**800-631-3572**		86
Spiralock Corp						
25235 Dequindre Rd	Madison Heights	MI	48071	**800-521-2688**	586-949-0440	491
Spirax Sarco Inc						
1150 Northpoint Blvd	Blythewood	SC	29016	**800-883-4411**	803-714-2000	201
Spire 2828 Dauphin St	Mobile	AL	36606	**800-837-3374**	251-476-8052	782
Spire Consulting Group LLC						
114 W Seventh St Ste 1300	Austin	TX	78701	**855-216-0812**	512-637-0845	196
Spire Inc 65 Bay St	Boston	MA	02125	**877-350-8837**	617-350-8837	343
Spire Investment Partners LLC						
7901 Jones Branch Dr	Mclean	VA	22102	**888-737-8907**	703-748-5800	400
Spire Technologies Inc						
2140 SW Jefferson St Ste 300	Portland	OR	97201	**800-481-7332**	503-222-3086	196
Spirit AeroSystems Inc						
3801 S Oliver St	Wichita	KS	67210	**800-501-7597**	316-526-9000	20
Spirit Airlines Inc						
2800 Executive Way	Miramar	FL	33025	**800-772-7117**	954-447-7828	25
NASDAQ: SAVE						
Spirit Lake Casino & Resort						
7889 Hwy 57	Saint Michael	ND	58370	**800-946-8238**	701-766-4747	
Spirit Manufacturing Inc						
3000 Nestle Rd	Jonesboro	AR	72401	**800-258-4555**	870-935-1107	267
Spiritual Life Ctr						
7100 E 45th St N	Wichita	KS	67226	**800-348-2440**	316-744-0167	669
SPJ (Society of Professional Journalists)						
3909 N Meridian St	Indianapolis	IN	46208	**800-331-1212**	317-927-8000	49-14
Splash Lagoon Water Pk Resort						
8091 Peach St	Erie	PA	16509	**866-377-5274**		

	Toll-Free	Phone	Class
Splash!events Inc			
210 Hillsdale Ave .... San Jose CA 95136	**866-204-6000**	408-287-8600	184
SPLC (Southern Poverty Law Ctr)			
400 Washington Ave .... Montgomery AL 36104	**888-414-7752**	334-956-8200	48-8
SPLICE Software Inc			
425 78 Ave SW .... Calgary AB T2V5K5	**855-677-5423**	403-720-8326	
Split Rock Creek State Park			
50th Ave .... Jasper MN 56144	**888-646-6367**	507-348-7908	561
Split Rock Resort			
100 Moseywood Rd .... Lake Harmony PA 18624	**800-255-7625**	570-722-9111	665
Spok Inc			
6850 Versar Ctr Ste 420 ....Springfield VA 22151	**888-878-5009**	800-611-8488	731
Spokane Art Supply Inc			
1303 N Monroe St ....Spokane WA 99201	**800-556-5568**	509-327-6622	45
Spokane Community College			
1810 N Greene St ....Spokane WA 99217	**800-248-5644**	509-533-7000	162
Spokane Convention & Visitors Bureau			
Main Level River Park Sq 808 W Main Ave			
....Spokane WA 99201	**800-662-0084**	509-624-1341	206
Spokane County			
1116 W Broadway Ave ....Spokane WA 99260	**800-562-6000**	509-477-2265	337
Spokane Falls Community College			
3410 W Ft George Wright Dr ....Spokane WA 99224	**888-509-7944**	509-533-3500	162
Spokane Hardware Supply Inc			
2001 E Trent Ave ....Spokane WA 99202	**800-888-1663**	509-535-1663	349
Spokane International Airport			
9000 W Airport Dr ....Spokane WA 99224	**800-776-5263**	509-455-6455	27
Spokane Public Radio			
2319 N Monroe St ....Spokane WA 99201	**800-328-5729**	509-328-5729	641-101
Spokane Symphony			
PO Box 365 ....Spokane WA 99210	**800-899-1482**	509-624-1200	569-3
Spokane Valley Chamber of Commerce			
9507 E Sprague Ave .... Spokane Valley WA 99206	**866-475-1436**	509-924-4994	139
Sponseller Group Inc			
1600 Timberwolf Dr ....Holland OH 43528	**800-776-1625**	419-861-3000	261
Spoon River College (SRC)			
23235 N County Hwy 22 ....Canton IL 61520	**800-334-7337**	309-647-4645	162
Spoon River Electric Co-op Inc (SREC)			
930 S Fifth Ave PO Box 340 ....Canton IL 61520	**877-404-2572**	309-647-2700	245
Sport Fishing Magazine			
460 N Orlando Ave Ste 200 ...... Winter Park FL 32789	**800-879-0496**		455-20
Sport Obermeyer Ltd USA Inc			
115 AABC .... Aspen CO 81611	**800-525-4203**	970-925-5060	155-5
Sport-Haley Inc			
10367 Brockwood Rd .... Dallas TX 75238	**800-627-9211**		
SportPharma Inc			
3 Terminal Rd .... New Brunswick NJ 08901	**800-872-0101**	732-545-3130	794
Sports Afield Magazine			
15621 Chemical Ln .... Huntington Beach CA 92649	**800-451-4788**	714-373-4910	455-20
Sports Business Daily			
120 W Morehead St Ste 310...... Charlotte NC 28202	**800-829-9839**	704-973-1410	455-20
Sports Car Club of America (SCCA)			
6700 SW Topeka Blvd .... Topeka KS 66619	**800-770-2055**		48-18
Sports Cardiovascular & Wellness Nutritionists (SCAN)			
230 Washington Ave Extn Ste 101 .... Albany NY 12203	**800-249-2875***	518-254-6730	49-8
*General			
Sports Empire			
PO Box 6169 .... Lakewood CA 90714	**800-255-5258**	562-920-2350	766
Sports Imports Inc			
4000 Pkwy Ln ....Hilliard OH 43026	**800-556-3198**		
Sports Leisure Vacations			
9812 Old Winery Pl Ste 1 .... Sacramento CA 95827	**800-951-5556**	916-361-2051	755
Sports Promotion Network			
2895 125th St .... Grand Prairie TX 75050	**800-460-9989**	866-780-6151	707
Sports Spectrum Magazine			
640 Plaza Dr Ste 110 ...... Highlands Ranch CO 80129	**866-821-2971**	704-821-2971	455-20
Sports Travel Inc			
60 Main St PO Box 50 .... Hatfield MA 01038	**800-662-4424**	413-247-7678	755
Sports Turf Managers Assn (STMA)			
805 New Hampshire Ste E .... Lawrence KS 66044	**800-323-3875**	785-843-2549	48-22
SportsEngine			
807 Broadway St NE Ste 300 ....Minneapolis MN 55413	**888-379-1035***		
*Sales			
Sportservice Corp			
40 Fountain Plz ....Buffalo NY 14202	**800-828-7240**	716-858-5000	299
Sportsmen's Lodge Hotel			
12825 Ventura Blvd ....Studio City CA 91604	**800-821-8511**	818-769-4700	703
SportsPlay Equipment Inc			
5642 Natural Bridge Ave .... Saint Louis MO 63120	**800-727-8180**	314-389-4140	345
Spotnails			
1100 Hicks Rd ....Rolling Meadows IL 60008	**800-873-2239**	847-259-1620	808
SpotOn Inc			
300 California St 4th Fl. ...... San Francisco CA 94104	**877-814-4102**		386
Spotts Fain PC			
411 E Franklin St Ste 600 .... Richmond VA 23219	**866-788-1190**	804-697-2000	41
Spotwave Wireless Inc			
500 Van Buren St PO Box 550 .... Kemptville ON K0G1J0	**866-704-9750**	613-591-1662	731
SPPD (Southern Public Power District)			
4550 W Husker Hwy			
PO Box 1687....................... Grand Island NE 68803	**800-652-2013**	308-384-2350	245
Spradling International Inc			
200 Cahaba Vly Pkwy PO Box 1668 .... Pelham AL 35124	**800-333-0955**	205-985-4206	590
Sprague Energy			
185 International Dr Ste 200........ Portsmouth NH 03801	**800-225-1560**	603-431-1000	575
Sprague Pest Solutions			
2725 Pacific Ave Ste 200 .... Tacoma WA 98402	**800-272-4988**	253-272-4400	573
Spray Enclosure Technologies			
1427 N Linden Ave .... Rialto CA 92376	**800-535-8196**		693
Spraying Systems Co			
PO Box 7900 .... Wheaton IL 60189	**800-800-6509**	630-665-5000	485
Sprayway Inc			
1005 S Westgate Ave .... Addison IL 60101	**800-332-9000**	630-628-3000	145
Sprecher + Schuh			
15910 International Plaza Dr ....Houston TX 77032	**877-721-5913**	281-442-9000	203
Spreedly Inc			
733 Foster St .... Durham NC 27701	**888-727-7750**		386
Spring Arbor Distributors			
1 Ingram Blvd .... La Vergne TN 37086	**800-395-4340**	615-793-5000	96

	Toll-Free	Phone	Class
Spring Arbor University			
106 E Main St .... Spring Arbor MI 49283	**800-968-9103***	517-750-6504	166
*Admissions			
Spring Creek Ranch			
1600 N East Butte Rd			
PO Box 4780..........................Jackson WY 83001	**800-443-6139**	307-733-8833	378
Spring Creek Youth Services Ctr			
3190 E Las Vegas St .... Colorado Springs CO 80906	**800-388-5515**	719-390-2700	411
Spring Dynamics Inc			
7378 Research Dr ....Almont MI 48003	**888-274-8432**	810-798-2622	715
Spring Engineers Inc			
9740 Tanner Rd ....Houston TX 77041	**800-899-9488**	713-690-9488	715
Spring Glen Fresh Foods Inc			
314 Spring Glen Dr .... Ephrata PA 17522	**800-641-2853**	717-733-2201	296-19
Spring Grove Cemetery			
4521 Spring Grove Ave .... Cincinnati OH 45232	**888-853-2230**	513-681-7526	508
Spring Harbor Hospital			
123 Andover Rd ....Westbrook ME 04092	**888-524-0080**	207-761-2200	373-5
Spring Hill College			
4000 Dauphin St ....Mobile AL 36608	**800-742-6704***	251-380-4000	166
*Admissions			
Spring Hill Mall			
1072 Spring Hill Mall .... West Dundee IL 60118	**800-718-8788**	847-428-2200	458
Spring House Estates			
728 Norristown Rd ....Lower Gwynedd PA 19002	**888-365-2287**	267-460-6116	668
Spring Manufacturers Institute (SMI)			
2001 Midwest Rd Ste 106............ Oak Brook IL 60523	**866-482-5569**	630-495-8588	49-13
Spring Mountain Vineyards			
2805 Spring Mtn Rd .... Saint Helena CA 94574	**877-769-4637**	707-967-4188	315-5
Springboard Nonprofit Consumer Credit Management			
4351 Latham St .... Riverside CA 92501	**888-425-3453**		392
Springer Electric Co-op Inc			
408 Maxwell Ave PO Box 698..........Springer NM 87747	**800-288-1353**	575-483-2421	245
Springfield Armory			
420 W Main St ....Geneseo IL 61254	**800-680-6866**	309-944-5631	284
Springfield City Library			
220 State St .... Springfield MA 01103	**800-852-3133**	413-263-6828	433-3
Springfield College			
263 Alden St .... Springfield MA 01109	**800-343-1257***	413-748-3136	166
*Admissions			
Springfield College in Illinois - Benedictine University			
1500 N Fifth St .... Springfield IL 62702	**800-635-7289**	217-525-1420	162
Springfield Convention & Visitors Bureau			
109 N Seventh St .... Springfield IL 62701	**800-545-7300**	217-789-2360	206
Springfield Electric Supply Co			
700 N Ninth St .... Springfield IL 62702	**800-747-2101**	217-788-2100	246
Springfield Hospital Ctr			
6655 Sykesville Rd .... Sykesville MD 21784	**800-333-7564**	410-970-7000	373-5
Springfield Missouri Convention & Visitors Bureau			
815 E St Louis St Ste 100............Springfield MO 65806	**800-678-8767**	417-881-5300	206
Springfield Museums			
21 Edwards St .... Springfield MA 01103	**800-625-7738**	413-263-6800	517
Springfield News-Sun			
202 N Limestone St .... Springfield OH 45503	**800-441-6397**	937-328-0300	528-2
Springfield Public School District #186			
1900 West Monroe St .... Springfield IL 62704	**877-632-7753**	217-525-3006	681
Springfield ReManufacturing Corp			
4727 E Kearney ....Springfield MO 65803	**800-531-7134**		262
Spring-Green Lawn Care Corp			
11909 Spaulding School Dr .... Plainfield IL 60585	**800-435-4051**	815-436-8777	573
Springs Window Fashions LP			
7549 Graber Rd .... Middleton WI 53562	**877-792-0002**	608-836-1011	360
Springville Museum of Art			
126 E 400 S ....Springville UT 84663	**800-833-6667**	801-489-2727	517
Sprott Global Resource Investments Ltd			
1910 Palomar Point Way Ste 200 ..... Carlsbad CA 92008	**800-477-7853**		687
Sprott Inc			
Royal Bank Plz South Twr 200 Bay St			
Ste 2600 .... Toronto ON M5J2J1	**855-943-8099**	416-943-8099	
Sproule Associates Ltd			
900 N Tower Sun Life Plz 140 Fourth Ave SW			
....Calgary AB T2P3N3	**877-777-6135**	403-294-5500	261
Sprout Pharmaceuticals Inc			
4208 Six Forks Rd .... Raleigh NC 27609	**844-746-5745**	919-882-0850	238
SPROUT Wellness Solutions Inc			
366 Adelaide St W Ste 301 .... Toronto ON M5V1R9	**866-535-5027**		224
Spruce			
9 Cornell Rd Latham ....New York NY 12110	**800-777-8231**		174
SPX Cooling Technologies			
7401 W 129th St .... Overland Park KS 66213	**800-462-7539**	913-664-7400	91
SPX Corp			
13515 Ballantyne Corporate Pl			
....Charlotte NC 28277	**877-247-3797**	704-752-4400	185
NYSE: SPXC			
SPX Corp OTC Div			
655 Eisenhower Dr ....Owatonna MN 55060	**800-533-6127**	507-455-7000	752
Spx Flow			
611 Sugar Creek Rd .... Delavan WI 53115	**800-252-5200**		563
SPX Transformer Solutions Inc			
400 S Prairie Ave .... Waukesha WI 53186	**800-835-2732**		762
SPY Inc			
2070 Las Palmas Dr .... Carlsbad CA 92011	**800-779-3937**		
Sqrrl Data Inc			
125 Cambridgepark Dr Ste 401 ....Cambridge MA 02140	**800-395-9683**	617-902-0784	
Square 1 Art LLC			
5470 Oakbrook Pkwy Ste E.......... Norcross GA 30093	**888-332-3294**	678-906-2291	623
Square Books			
160 Courthouse Sq .... Oxford MS 38655	**800-648-4001**	662-236-2262	95
Square One Mall			
1201 Broadway .... Saugus MA 01906	**877-746-6642**	781-233-8787	458
Squaw Valley USA			
PO Box 2007 ....Olympic Valley CA 96146	**800-403-0206**		665
S&R Truck Tire Center Inc			
1402 Truckers Blvd .... Jeffersonville IN 47130	**800-488-2670**	812-282-4799	54
SRAM Corp			
1333 N Kingsbury St 4th Fl ....Chicago IL 60622	**800-346-2928**	312-664-8800	82
SRC (Spoon River College)			
23235 N County Hwy 22 ....Canton IL 61520	**800-334-7337**	309-647-4645	162

Name / Address	Toll-Free	Phone	Class
SRC (Syracuse Research Corp) 7502 Round Pond Rd ... North Syracuse NY 13212	800-724-0451	315-452-8000	664
SRC Holdings Corp 531 S Union Ave ... Springfield MO 65802	800-327-2253	417-862-2337	262
SREC (Spoon River Electric Co-op Inc) 930 S Fifth Ave PO Box 340 ... Canton IL 61520	877-404-2572	309-647-2700	245
Sri Quality Sys 300 Northpointe Cir #304 ... Seven Fields PA 16046	800-549-6709	724-934-9000	196
SriLankan Airlines 379 Thornall St 6th Fl. ... Edison NJ 08837	877-915-2652	732-205-0017	25
SRMC (Sparks Regional Medical Ctr) 1001 Towson Ave ... Fort Smith AR 72901	800-285-1131	479-441-4000	373-3
SRMC (Spartanburg Regional Medical Ctr) 101 E Wood St ... Spartanburg SC 29303	800-318-2596	864-560-6000	373-3
SRMC (Sonora Regional Medical Ctr) 1000 Greenly Rd ... Sonora CA 95370 *Compliance	877-336-3566*	209-536-5000	373-3
SRP (Salt River Project) 1521 N Project Dr ... Tempe AZ 85281	800-258-4777	602-236-5900	782
SRT (Seattle Repertory Theatre) 155 Mercer St PO Box 900923 ... Seattle WA 98109	877-900-9285	206-443-2210	569-4
SS & C Technologies Inc 80 Lamberton Rd ... Windsor CT 06095	800-234-0556	860-298-4500	178-11
SS Nesbitt & Co Inc 3500 Blue Lake Dr ... Birmingham AL 35243	800-422-3223	205-262-2700	390-4
SSA (Self Storage Assn) 1901 N Beauregard St Ste 106 ... Alexandria VA 22311	888-735-3784	703-575-8000	49-21
SSA (Social Security Administration) 6401 Security Blvd ... Baltimore MD 21235	800-772-1213	410-965-8904	339-19
SSA Consultants Inc 9331 Bluebonnet Blvd ... Baton Rouge LA 70810	800-634-2758	225-769-2676	461
SSA Marine 1131 SW Klickitat Way ... Seattle WA 98134	800-422-3505	206-623-0304	463
SSAI (Support Systems Associates Inc) Marina Towers 709 S Harbor City Blvd Ste 350 ... Melbourne FL 32901	877-234-7724		
Ssci 3065 Kent Ave ... West Lafayette IN 47906	800-375-2179	765-463-0112	194
SSgA Funds 1 Lincoln St ... Boston MA 02111	800-997-7327	617-786-3000	524
SSIT (IFFF Society on Social Implications of Technology) IEEE Operations Ctr 445 and 501 Hoes Ln ... Piscataway NJ 08854	800-678-4333	732-981-0060	49-19
SSJCPL (Stockton-San Joaquin County Public Library) 605 N El Dorado St ... Stockton CA 95202	866-805-7323	209-937-8416	433-3
SSM Health 1000 N Lee PO Box 205 ... Oklahoma City OK 73102	866-203-5846	405-272-7279	352
SSM Health St Anthony 1000 N Lee St ... Oklahoma City OK 73101	800-227-6964	405-272-7000	373-3
SSMB Pacific Holding Company Inc 1755 Adams Ave ... San Leandro CA 94577	866-572-2525	510-836-6100	359-2
SSMC (Sutter Solano Medical Ctr) 300 Hospital Dr ... Vallejo CA 94589	800-866-7724	707-554-4444	373-3
SSPC (Society for Protective Coatings) 40 24th St 6th Fl. ... Pittsburgh PA 15222	877-281-7772	412-281-2331	49-13
SSPR Public Relations Agency 150 N Upper Wacker Dr Ste 2010. ... Chicago IL 60606	800-287-2279		632
SSR Mining Inc 999 W Hastings St Ste 1180. ... Vancouver BC V6C2W2 NASDAQ: SSRM	888-338-0046	604-689-3846	500
SSS Co 71 University Ave ... Atlanta GA 30315	800-237-3843	404-521-0857	578
SST (Smith Systems Transportation Inc) PO Box 2455 ... Scottsbluff NE 69361	800-897-5571		311
SST Group Inc 309 Laurelwood Rd Ste 20 ... Santa Clara CA 95054	800-944-6281	408-350-3450	473
SSW (Seminary of the southwest) 501 E 32nd PO Box 2247 ... Austin TX 78705	800-252-5400	512-472-4133	167-3
St Agnes Hospital 430 E Div St ... Fond du Lac WI 54935	800-922-3400	920-929-2300	373-3
St Albert & District Chamber of Commerce 71 St Albert Trl ... Saint Albert AB T8N6L5	800-207-9410	780-458-2833	137
St Andrews Blockhouse National Historic Site of Canada 30 Victoria St ... Gatineau QC J8X0B3	888-773-8888	819-420-9486	559
St Andrews University 1700 Dogwood Mile ... Laurinburg NC 28352	800-763-0198	910-277-5555	166
S&T Bancorp Inc 800 Philadelphia St ... Indiana PA 15701 NASDAQ: STBA	800-325-2265	724-349-1800	359-2
St Clair County Regional Educational Service Agency 499 Range Rd ... Marysville MI 48040	800-294-9229	810-364-8990	681
St Croix Forge 5195 Scandia Trl ... Forest Lake MN 55025	866-668-7642	651-287-8289	481
St Elizabeth's Medical Ctr 736 Cambridge St ... Brighton MA 02135	800-488-5959	617-789-3000	352
St Ignatius College Prep 2001 37th Ave ... San Francisco CA 94116	888-225-5427	415-731-7500	681
S-T Industries Inc 301 Armstrong Blvd N PO Box 517. ... Saint James MN 56081	800-326-2039	507-375-3211	491
St James Hotel 406 Main St ... Red Wing MN 55066	800-252-1875		378
St John Diakon Hospice 1201 N Church St ... Hazleton PA 18202	877-666-5784		370
St John Providence 28000 Dequindre ... Warren MI 48092	866-501-3627	586-573-5000	373-3
St John Providence Health System 28000 Dequindre ... Warren MI 48092	866-501-3627		373-3
ST JOHNS RIVER STATE COLLEGE 5001 St Johns Ave ... Palatka FL 32177	888-757-2293	386-312-4200	162
St Julien Hotel & Spa 900 Walnut St ... Boulder CO 80302	877-303-0900	720-406-9696	378
St Lawrence County Chamber of Commerce 101 Main St ... Canton NY 13617	877-228-7810	315-386-4000	139
St Louis County 100 N Fifth Ave W ... Duluth MN 55802	800-450-9278	218-726-2450	337
St Louis Pipe & Supply Inc 17740 Edison Ave ... Chesterfield MO 63005	800-737-7473	636-391-2500	490
St Luke's College 2800 Pierce St Ste 410 ... Sioux City IA 51104	800-352-4660	712-279-3149	505
St Luke's Des Peres Hospital 2345 Dougherty Ferry Rd ... Saint Louis MO 63122	888-457-5203	314-966-9100	373-3
St Mary's Healthcare System for Children 29-01 216th St ... Bayside NY 11360	888-543-7697	718-281-8800	
St Mary's of Michigan (STMH) 800 S Washington Ave ... Saginaw MI 48601	877-738-6672	989-907-8115	373-3
St Moritz Bldg Services Inc 4616 Clairton Blvd ... Pittsburgh PA 15236	800-218-9159	412-885-2100	152
St Paul Flight Ctr 270 Airport Rd ... Saint Paul MN 55107	800-368-0107	651-227-8108	63
St Petersburg General Hospital 6500 38th Ave N ... Saint Petersburg FL 33710	800-733-0610	727-384-1414	373-3
St Raphael Academy 123 Walcott St ... Pawtucket RI 02860	800-498-0045	401-723-8100	148
St Regis 88 W Paces Ferry Rd ... Atlanta GA 30305	877-787-3447	404-563-7900	665
St Renatus LLC 1000 Centre Ave ... Fort Collins CO 80526	888-686-2314	970-282-0156	231
St Vincent's College 2800 Main St ... Bridgeport CT 06606	800-873-1013		166
STA (Student Transportation Inc) 3349 Hwy 138 Bldg A Ste C ... Wall NJ 07719	888-942-2250	732-280-4200	109
Sta International 1400 Old Country Rd Ste 411. ... Westbury NY 11590	866-970-9882		216
Staab Battery Manufacturing Co 931 S 11th St ... Springfield IL 62703	800-252-8625		
STAAR Surgical Co 1911 Walker Ave ... Monrovia CA 91016 NASDAQ: STAA	800-352-7842	626-303-7902	538
Stabila Inc 332 Industrial Dr PO Box 402. ... South Elgin IL 60177	800-869-7460		753
Stackbin Corp 29 Powderhill Rd ... Lincoln RI 02865 *Sales	800-333-1603*		198
Stack-On Products Co 1360 N Old Rand Rd ... Wauconda IL 60084	800-323-9601		486
Stacy Furniture & Design 1900 S Main St ... Grapevine TX 76051	800-403-6077	817-424-8800	321
Stafast Products Inc 505 Lake Shore Blvd ... Painesville OH 44077	800-782-3278	440-357-5546	278
STAFDA (Specialty Tools & Fasteners Distributors Assn) 500 Elm Grove Rd Ste 210 PO Box 44. ... Elm Grove WI 53122	800-352-2981	262-784-4774	49-18
Staff One Inc 8111 LBJ Fwy ... Dallas TX 75251	800-771-7823		627
Staffing Resource Group Inc, The 405 Reo St Ste 255. ... Tampa FL 33609	877-774-7742		260
Stafford Printing Co 2707 Jefferson Davis Hwy ... Stafford VA 22554	800-774-6831	540-659-4554	623
Stafford-Smith Inc 3414 S Burdick St ... Kalamazoo MI 49001	800-968-2442	269-343-1240	661
Stage Neck Inn 8 Stage Neck Rd Rt 1A PO Box 70. ... York Harbor ME 03911	800-222-3238	207-363-3850	665
Stagecraft Industries Inc 5051 N Lagoon Ave ... Portland OR 97217	800-727-2673	503-286-1600	45
Stageright Corp 495 Pioneer Pkwy ... Clare MI 48617	800-438-4499	989-386-7393	321
Stahancyk Kent & Hook 2400 SW Fourth Ave ... Portland OR 97201	877-673-7632	503-222-9115	443
Stahl Specialty Co 111 E Pacific ... Kingsville MO 64061	800-821-7852	816-597-3322	308
STAHL/A Scott Fetzer Co 3201 W Old Lincoln Way ... Wooster OH 44691	800-277-8245	330-264-7441	513
Stahls Inc 6353 14 Mile Rd ... Sterling Heights MI 48312	800-521-5255		
Staker Parson Cos 2350 S 1900 W ... Ogden UT 84401	888-672-7766	801-731-1111	188-4
Staley Inc 8101 Fourche Rd ... Little Rock AR 72209	877-708-7532	800-280-9675	189-4
Stallings Crop Insurance Corp PO Box 6100 ... Lakeland FL 33807	800-721-7099	863-647-2747	389
Stamats Communications Inc 615 Fifth St SE ... Cedar Rapids IA 52401	800-553-8878	319-364-6167	633-9
Stambaugh Auditorium 1000 Fifth Ave ... Youngstown OH 44504	866-516-2269	330-747-5175	568
Stamford City Hall 888 Washington Blvd 10th Fl ... Stamford CT 06901	800-864-2742	203-977-4150	336
Stamford Suites 720 Bedford St ... Stamford CT 06901	866-394-4365	203-359-7300	378
Stampede Meat Inc 7351 S 78th Ave ... Bridgeview IL 60455	800-353-0933		296-26
Stampin Up 12907 S 3600 W ... Riverton UT 84065 *Cust Svc	800-782-6787*		
Stamprite 154 S Larch St ... Lansing MI 48912	800-328-1988	517-487-5071	465
Stampscom Inc 1990 E Grand Ave ... El Segundo CA 90245 NASDAQ: STMP	855-889-7867		178-1
Stan Houston Equipment Co 501 S Marion Rd ... Sioux Falls SD 57106	800-952-3033	605-336-3727	357
Stan Hywet Hall & Gardens 714 N Portage Path ... Akron OH 44303	888-836-5533	330-836-5533	517
Stan White Realty & Construction 2506 S Croatan Hwy ... Nags Head NC 27959	800-338-3233	252-441-1515	648
Stanadyne Corp 92 Deerfield Rd ... Windsor CT 06095	888-336-3473	860-525-0821	60
Stanbury Uniforms Inc 108 Stanbury Industrial Dr PO Box 100. ... Brookfield MO 64628	800-826-2246		155-18
Standard & Poor's Corp 55 Water St ... New York NY 10041	877-772-5436	212-438-1000	633-2
Standard Air & Lite Corp 2406 Woodmere Dr ... Pittsburgh PA 15205	800-472-2458	412-920-6505	608

				Toll-Free	Phone	Class
Standard Alloys & Mfg PO Box 969	Port Arthur	TX	77640	**800-231-8240**	409-983-3201	637
Standard Bag Manufacturing Co 1800 SW Merlo Dr	Beaverton	OR	97003	**800-654-1395**		
Standard Beverage Corp 2416 E 37th St N	Wichita	KS	67219	**800-999-8797**		81-3
Standard Digital Imaging 4426 S 108th St	Omaha	NE	68137	**800-642-8062**	402-592-1292	240
Standard Duplicating Machines Corp 10 Connector Rd	Andover	MA	01810	**800-526-4774**	978-470-1920	112
Standard Electric Supply Co 222 N Emmber Ln PO Box 651	Milwaukee	WI	53233	**800-776-8222**	414-272-8100	246
Standard Equipment Company Inc 75 Beauregard St	Mobile	AL	36602	**800-239-3442**	251-432-1705	765
Standard Filter Corp 5928 Balfour Ct	Carlsbad	CA	92008	**800-634-5837**	760-929-8559	18
Standard Furniture Mfg Company Inc 801 Hwy 31 S *General	Bay Minette	AL	36507	**877-788-1899***	251-937-6741	319-2
Standard Imaging Inc 3120 Deming Way	Middleton	WI	53562	**800-261-4446**	608-831-0025	635
Standard Knapp Inc 63 Pickering St *Cust Svc	Portland	CT	06480	**800-628-9565***	860-342-1100	543
Standard Locknut Inc 1045 E 169th St	Westfield	IN	46074	**800-783-6887**	317-867-0100	452
Standard Meat Company LP 5105 Investment Dr	Dallas	TX	75236	**866-859-6313**	214-561-0561	296-26
Standard Motor Products Inc 37-18 Northern Blvd *NYSE: SMP*	Long Island	NY	11101	**800-895-1085**	718-392-0200	247
Standard Motors Ltd 44 Second Ave NW	Swift Current	SK	S9H3V6	**866-334-8985**		57
Standard Parking Corp 200 E Randolph St Ste 7700	Chicago	IL	60611	**888-700-7275**	312-274-2000	558
Standard Publishing Co 4050 Lee Vance Dr	Colorado Springs	CO	80918	**800-323-7543**		633-9
Standard Roofing Co 516 N McDonough St PO Box 1309	Montgomery	AL	36102	**800-239-5705**	334-265-1262	189-12
Standard Security Life Insurance Co of New York 485 Madison Ave 14th Fl	New York	NY	10022	**800-477-0087**	212-355-4141	390-2
Standard Textile Company Inc 1 Knollcrest Dr	Cincinnati	OH	45237	**800-999-0400**	513-761-9255	475
Standard-Examiner 332 Standard Way	Ogden	UT	84404	**888-221-7070**	801-625-4200	528-2
Standards Council of Canada 270 Albert St Ste 200	Ottawa	ON	K1P6N7	**800-844-6790**	613-238-3222	464
Standex Electronics Inc 4538 Camberwell Rd	Cincinnati	OH	45209	**866-782-6339**	513-871-3777	253
Standex International Corp Consumer Group 11 Keewaydin Dr *NYSE: SXI*	Salem	NH	03079	**800-514-5275**	603-893-9701	633-3
Standex International Corp Custom Hoists Div 771 County Rd 30A W	Ashland	OH	44805	**800-837-4668**	419-368-4721	223
Standing Stone Inc 49 Richmondville Ave	Westport	CT	06880	**800-648-9877**		
Stanford Federal Credit Union 1860 Embarcadero Rd	Palo Alto	CA	94303	**888-723-7328**	650-723-2509	219
Stanford Shopping Ctr 660 Stanford Shopping Ctr	Palo Alto	CA	94304	**800-284-8273**	650-617-8200	458
Stanford University 450 Serra Mall	Stanford	CA	94305	**877-407-9529**	650-723-2091	166
Stanford University Green Library 557 Escondido Mall	Stanford	CA	94305	**800-521-0600**	650-723-1493	433-6
Stanion Wholesale Electric Co 812 S Main St PO Box F	Pratt	KS	67124	**866-782-6466**	620-672-5678	246
Stanislaus Credit Control Service Inc 914-14th St	Modesto	CA	95354	**800-838-7227**	209-523-1813	160
Stanislaus Farm Supply Co 624 E Service Rd	Modesto	CA	95358	**800-323-0725**	209-538-7070	276
Stanislaus Food Products Co 1202 D St	Modesto	CA	95354	**800-327-7201**		296-20
Stanley Access Technologies 65 Scott Swamp Rd	Farmington	CT	06032	**800-722-2377**	860-677-2861	234
Stanley Assembly Technologies Div 5335 Avion Pk Dr	Cleveland	OH	44143	**877-787-7830**	440-461-5500	754
Stanley Consultants Inc 225 Iowa Ave	Muscatine	IA	52761	**800-553-9694**	563-264-6600	261
Stanley Creations Inc 1414 Willow Ave	Melrose Park	PA	19027	**800-220-1414**	215-635-6207	408
Stanley Hotel 333 Wonderview Ave	Estes Park	CO	80517	**800-976-1377**	970-577-4000	378
Stanley Hunt DuPree & Rhine (SHDR) 7701 Airport Ctr Dr	Greensboro	NC	27409	**800-930-2441**	800-768-4873	193
Stanley Jay s & Assoc 5313 Mcclanahan Dr Ste G5	North Little Rock	AR	72116	**888-758-4728**	501-758-8029	507
Stanley Korshak 500 Crescent Ct Ste 100	Dallas	TX	75201	**855-479-9539**		157-4
Stanley Martin Cos 11111 Sunset Hills Rd Ste 200	Reston	VA	20190	**800-446-4807**	703-964-5000	649
Stanley Tools Inc 701 E Joppa Rd	Towson	MD	21286	**800-262-2161**		753
Stanley Vidmar Storage Technologies 11 Grammes Rd	Allentown	PA	18103	**800-523-9462**		286
Stanly Community College 141 College Dr	Albemarle	NC	28001	**877-275-4219**	704-982-0121	795
Stansberry & Assoc Investment Research LLC 1217 Saint Paul St	Baltimore	MD	21202	**888-261-2693**		400
Stansteel Asphalt Plant Products 12700 Shelbyville Rd	Louisville	KY	40243	**800-826-0223**	502-245-1977	637
Stant Corp 1620 Columbia Ave	Connersville	IN	47331	**800-822-3121**	765-825-3121	604
Stanton County Public Power District 807 Douglas St	Stanton	NE	68779	**877-439-2300**	402-439-2228	245
Stanton's Sheet Music 330 S Fourth St	Columbus	OH	43215	**800-426-8742**	614-224-4257	522
Staplcotn Co-op Assn Inc 214 W Market St	Greenwood	MS	38930	**800-293-6231**	662-453-6231	275
Staples Business Advantage 500 Staples Dr	Framingham	MA	01702	**877-826-7755**		530
Staples Promotional Products 7500 W 110th St	Overland Park	KS	66210	**800-369-4669**	913-319-3100	9
Stapleton Technologies Inc 1350 W 12th St	Long Beach	CA	90813	**800-266-0541**	562-437-0541	145
Stapleton-Spence Packing Co 1530 The Alameda Ste 320	San Jose	CA	95126	**800-297-8815**	408-297-8815	296-20
Staplex Co 777 Fifth Ave *Cust Svc	Brooklyn	NY	11232	**800-221-0822***	718-768-3333	111
Star 6688 93rd Ave N	Minneapolis	MN	55445	**800-419-7827**	763-561-4655	392
Star 929 265 Hegeman Ave	Colchester	VT	05446	**866-865-7827**	802-655-0093	641
STAR Academy 12279 Brady Dr	Custer	SD	57730	**800-265-9684**	605-673-2521	411
Star Beacon PO Box 2100	Ashtabula	OH	44005	**800-554-6768**	440-998-2323	528-2
Star Bldg Systems 8600 S I-35	Oklahoma City	OK	73149	**800-879-7827**		105
Star Casualty Insurance Company Inc PO Box 451037	Miami	FL	33134	**877-782-7210**		389
Star Cutter Co 23461 Industrial Pk Dr	Farmington	MI	48335	**877-635-3488**	248-474-8200	491
Star Distributors Inc 460 Frontage Rd	West Haven	CT	06516	**877-922-3501**	203-932-3636	81-1
STAR Financial Group Inc PO Box 11409 *OTC: SFIGA*	Fort Wayne	IN	46858	**888-395-2447**		70
Star Fleet Inc 915 S Main St	Middlebury	IN	46540	**877-805-9547**		775
Star Furniture Company Inc 16666 Barker Springs Rd	Houston	TX	77084	**800-364-6661**	281-492-6661	321
Star Group LP 2187 Atlantic St *NYSE: SGU*	Stamford	CT	06902	**800-960-7546**	203-328-7310	316
Star Island Corp, The 30 Middle St	Portsmouth	NH	03801	**800-441-4620**	603-430-6272	239
Star Island Resort 5000 Ave of the Stars	Kissimmee	FL	34746	**800-513-2820**	407-997-8000	378
Star Leasing Co 4080 Business Pk Dr	Columbus	OH	43204	**888-771-1004**	614-278-9999	773
Star Lumber & Supply 325 S W St	Wichita	KS	67213	**800-797-9556**	316-942-2221	363
Star Micronics America Inc 1150 King George's Post Rd	Edison	NJ	08837	**800-782-7636**	732-623-5500	173-6
Star Milling Co 24067 Water St	Perris	CA	92570	**800-733-6455**	951-657-3143	445
Star Multi Care Services Inc 115 Broad Hollow Rd Ste 275	Melville	NY	11747	**877-920-0600**	631-424-7827	362
Star Nail Products Inc 29120 Ave Paine	Valencia	CA	91355	**800-762-6245**	661-257-7827	214
Star One Federal Credit Union PO Box 3643	Sunnyvale	CA	94088	**866-543-5202**	408-543-5202	219
Star Pipe LLC 4018 Westhollow Pkwy	Houston	TX	77082	**800-999-3009**	281-558-3000	591
Star Rentals Inc 1919 Fourth Ave S	Seattle	WA	98134	**800-825-7880**	206-622-7880	264-3
Star Sales & Distributing Corp 29 Commerce Way	Woburn	MA	01801	**800-222-8118**	781-933-8830	191-2
Star Services 4663 Halls Mill Rd	Mobile	AL	36693	**800-661-9050**	251-661-4050	606
Star Transportation Inc PO Box 100925 *Cust Svc	Nashville	TN	37224	**800-333-3060***	615-256-4336	775
Star Truck Rentals Inc 3940 Eastern Ave SE	Grand Rapids	MI	49508	**800-748-0468**	616-243-7033	773
Starboard Cruise Services Inc 8400 NW 36th St	Miami	FL	33166	**800-540-4785**	786-845-7300	241
Starborn Industries Inc 45 Mayfield Ave	Edison	NJ	08837	**800-596-7747**		349
Starbucks Coffee Co 2401 Utah Ave S	Seattle	WA	98134	**800-782-7282**	206-447-1575	159
Starco Impex 2710 S 11th St	Beaumont	TX	77701	**866-740-9601**		344
Star-Gazette 310 E Church St PO Box 285	Elmira	NY	14902	**800-836-8970**	607-734-5151	528-2
Stark & Stark 993 Lenox Dr Bldg 2	Lawrenceville	NJ	08648	**800-535-3425**	609-896-9060	427
Stark State College of Technology 6200 Frank Ave NW	North Canton	OH	44720	**800-797-8275**	330-494-6170	795
Starkey Hearing Technologies 6700 Washington Ave S	Eden Prairie	MN	55344	**800-328-8602**	888-251-9340	475
Starkey Hearing Trechnologies 2476 Argentia Rd Ste 301	Mississauga	ON	L5N6M1	**888-282-1086**		
Starkey International Institute for Household Management 1350 Logan St	Denver	CO	80203	**800-888-4904**	303-832-5510	149
Starkweather & Shepley Inc 60 Catamore Blvd	East Providence	RI	02914	**800-854-4625**	401-435-3600	389
Star-Ledger, The 1 Star Ledger Plz	Newark	NJ	07102	**800-501-2100**	973-877-4141	528-2
Starlight Theatre 4600 Starlight Rd	Kansas City	MO	64132	**800-776-1730**	816-363-7827	568
Starline Inc 1300 W Henry St	Sedalia	MO	65301	**800-280-6660**	660-827-6640	707
Starlite Limousines LLC PO Box 13542	Scottsdale	AZ	85267	**877-474-4847**	480-422-3619	440
Starmark Cabinetry 600 E 48th St N	Sioux Falls	SD	57104	**800-594-9444**		115
Starmark International Inc 210 S Andrews Ave	Fort Lauderdale	FL	33301	**888-280-9630**	954-874-9000	195
Starnet Data Design Inc 2659 Townsgate Rd Ste 227	Westlake Village	CA	91361	**800-779-0587**	805-371-0585	196

			Toll-Free	Phone	Class

Starplex Scientific Inc
50 A Steinway Blvd ....Etobicoke ON M9W6Y3 **800-665-0954** 416-674-7474 474

Starr Commonwealth
13725 Starr Commonwealth Rd ....Albion MI 49224 **800-837-5591** 517-629-5591 48-15

STARR Life Sciences Corp
333 Allegheney Ave Ste 300 ....Oakmont PA 15139 **866-978-2779** 418

Starr Transit Inc
2531 E State St ....Trenton NJ 08619 **800-782-7703** 609-587-0626 107

Starrett Tru-Stone Technologies Div
1101 Prosper Dr PO Box 430 ....Waite Park MN 56387 **800-959-0517** 320-251-7171 720

Starrett Webber Gage Div
24500 Detroit Rd ....Cleveland OH 44145 **800-255-3924** 440-835-0001 491

Star-Seal
6596 New Peachtree Rd ....Atlanta GA 30340 **800-779-6066** 770-455-6551 576

Starside Security & Investigation Inc
1930 S Brea Canyon Rd
Ste 220 ....Diamond Bar CA 91765 **888-478-2774** 909-396-9999 399

Startec Global Communications Corp
11300 Rockville Pk Ste 900 ....Rockville MD 20852 **800-827-3374** 301-610-4300 731

Startech Computing Inc
1755 Old W Main St ....Red Wing MN 55066 **888-385-0607** 651-385-0607 180

STARTEL
16 Goodyear B-125 ....Irvine CA 92618 **800-782-7835**

Star-Tribune
170 Star Ln ....Casper WY 82604 **866-981-6397** 307-266-0500 528-2

StartWire
10 Water St Ste 150 ....Lebanon NH 03766 **800-572-9470** 260

Starvation Creek State Park
Historic Columbia River Hwy State Trl
...................................Cascade Locks OR 97014 **800-551-6949**

Starving Students Moving & Storage Co
1850 Sawtelle Blvd Ste 300 ....Los Angeles CA 90025 **888-931-6683** 516

Starwest Botanicals Inc
11253 Trade Ctr Dr ....Rancho Cordova CA 95742 **888-273-4372*** 916-638-8100 477
*General

Starwood Hotels & Resorts Worldwide Inc
Westin Hotels & Resorts
1111 Westchester Ave ....White Plains NY 10604 **888-625-5144** 914-640-8100 378

State & Federal Communications Inc
80 S Summit St Ste 100 ....Akron OH 44308 **888-452-9669** 330-761-9960 776

State Auto Property & Casualty Insurance Co
518 E Broad St ....Columbus OH 43215 **800-444-9950** 614-464-5000 390-4

State Bank
175 N Leroy St ....Fenton MI 48430 **800-535-0517** 810-629-2263 70

State Bank & Trust
3100 13th Ave S ....Fargo ND 58103 **800-450-8949** 701-298-1500

State Bank of Waterloo
PO Box 148 ....Waterloo IL 62298 **800-383-8000** 618-939-7194 70

State Bar Assn of North Dakota
504 N Washington St
PO Box 2136........................Bismarck ND 58502 **800-472-2685** 701-255-1404 72

State Bar of Arizona
4201 N 24th St Ste 100 ....Phoenix AZ 85016 **866-482-9227** 602-252-4804 72

State Bar of Georgia
104 Marietta St NW Ste 100 ....Atlanta GA 30303 **800-334-6865** 404-527-8700 72

State Bar of Michigan
306 Townsend St ....Lansing MI 48933 **800-968-1442** 517-346-6300 72

State Bar of Montana
PO Box 577 ....Helena MT 59624 **877-880-1335**

State Bar of Nevada
1211 S Maryland Pkwy ....Las Vegas NV 89104 **800-254-2797** 702-382-2200 72

State Bar of New Mexico
5121 Masthead St NE
PO Box 92860.................Albuquerque NM 87109 **800-876-6227** 505-797-6000 72

State Bar of Texas
1414 Colorado St ....Austin TX 78701 **800-204-2222** 512-427-1463 72

State Compensation Insurance Fund
333 Bush St ....San Francisco CA 94104 **866-721-3498** 390-4

State Education Resource Ctr
25 Industrial Park Rd ....Middletown CT 06457 **800-842-8678** 860-632-1485 434

State Electric Supply Company Inc
2010 Second Ave ....Huntington WV 25703 **800-624-3417*** 304-523-7491 246
*Cust Svc

State Employees Credit Union of Maryland Inc
971 Corporate Blvd ....Linthicum MD 21090 **800-879-7328** 410-487-7328 219

State Employees Federal Credit Union
700 Patroon Creek Blvd
Patroon Creek Corporate Ctr............Albany NY 12206 **800-727-3328** 518-452-8234 219

State Employees' Credit Union (SECU)
PO Box 29606 ....Raleigh NC 27626 **888-732-8562** 919-857-2150 219

State Fair & Exposition
1001 Beulah Ave ....Pueblo CO 81004 **800-876-4567** 719-404-2018 716

State Fair Community College
3201 W 16th St ....Sedalia MO 65301 **877-311-7322** 660-530-5800 162

State Farm Financial Services FSB
PO Box 2316 ....Bloomington IL 61702 **877-734-2265** 70

State Farm Fire & Casualty Co
1 State Farm Plz ....Bloomington IL 61710 **800-782-8332** 390-4

State Farm Insurance
333 First Commerce Dr ....Aurora ON L4G8A4 **877-659-1570** 390-4

State Farm Mutual Funds
PO Box 219548 ....Kansas City MO 64121 **800-447-4930** 524

State Historical Society of Missouri, The
1020 Lowry St ....Columbia MO 65201 **800-747-6366** 573-882-1187 517

State Industrial Products
3100 Hamilton Ave ....Cleveland OH 44114 **877-747-6986** 216-861-7114 151

State Library of Ohio
274 E First Ave Ste 100 ....Columbus OH 43201 **800-686-1532** 614-644-7061 433-5

State Life Insurance Co
1 American Sq PO Box 368 ....Indianapolis IN 46206 **800-537-6442*** 317-285-1877 390-2
*Cust Svc

State Museum of Pennsylvania, The
300 N St ....Harrisburg PA 17120 **800-654-5984** 717-787-4980 517

State of California
Morro Bay State Park
Morro Bay State Park Rd ....Morro Bay CA 93442 **800-777-0369** 805-772-2560 561

State of Michigan
Island Lake Recreation Area
12950 E Grand River Ave ....Brighton MI 48116 **800-447-2757** 810-229-7067

North Higgins Lake State Park
11747 N Higgins Lake Dr ....Roscommon MI 48653 **800-447-2757** 989-821-6125

State of South Dakota
Lake Cochrane Recreation Area
3454 Edgewater Dr ....Gary SD 57237 **800-710-2267** 605-882-5200

State of The Art Inc
2470 Fox Hill Rd ....State College PA 16803 **800-458-3401**

State of the Heart Hospice
1350 N Broadway ....Greenville OH 45331 **800-417-7535** 937-548-2999 370

State Parks of Arkansas
Herman Davis State Park
Corner of Ark 18 Baltimore St ....Manila AR 72442 **888-287-2757** 561

State Pipe & Supply Inc
9615 S Norwalk Blvd ....Santa Fe Springs CA 90670 **800-733-6410** 562-695-5555 490

State Plaza Hotel
2117 E St NW ....Washington DC 20037 **866-868-7774** 202-861-8200 378

State Steel Supply Co
208 Ct St ....Sioux City IA 51101 **800-831-0862** 712-277-4000

State Supply Co
597 Seventh St E ....Saint Paul MN 55130 **877-775-7705** 651-774-5985 606

State Teachers Retirement System of Ohio
275 E Broad St ....Columbus OH 43215 **888-227-7877** 524

State Theatre
15 Livingston Ave ....New Brunswick NJ 08901 **800-432-9382** 732-247-7200 568

State Training School
3211 Edgington Ave ....Eldora IA 50627 **800-362-2178** 641-858-5402 411

State Universities Retirement System of Illinois
1901 Fox Dr ....Champaign IL 61820 **800-275-7877** 217-378-8800 400

State University of New York
Brockport
350 New Campus Dr ....Brockport NY 14420 **888-800-0029** 585-395-2751 166
Canton 34 Cornell Dr ....Canton NY 13617 **800-388-7123** 315-386-7011 162
College of Agriculture & Technology at Cobleskill
106 Suffolk Cir ....Cobleskill NY 12043 **800-295-8988** 518-255-5525 166
College of Environmental Science & Forestry
1 Forestry Dr ....Syracuse NY 13210 **800-777-7373*** 315-470-6500 166
*Admissions
College of Technology at Alfred
10 Upper College Dr ....Alfred NY 14802 **800-425-3733** 607-587-4215 162
Delhi 2 Main St ....Delhi NY 13753 **800-963-3544** 607-746-4000 162
Empire State College
1 Union Ave ....Saratoga Springs NY 12866 **800-847-3000** 518-587-2100 166
Geneseo 1 College Cir ....Geneseo NY 14454 **866-245-5211*** 585-245-5571 166
*Admitting
Maritime College
6 Pennyfield Ave Fort Schuyler.........Bronx NY 10465 **888-800-0029** 718-409-7200 166
New Paltz 1 Hawk Dr ....New Paltz NY 12561 **877-696-7411** 845-257-3212 166
Plattsburgh
101 Broad St ....Plattsburgh NY 12901 **888-673-0012*** 518-564-2040 166
*Admissions
Potsdam
44 Pierrpont Ave ....Potsdam NY 13676 **877-768-7326*** 315-267-2180 166
*Admissions
University at Buffalo
12 Capen Hall ....Buffalo NY 14260 **888-822-3648** 716-645-2450 166

State University of New York Press (SUNY)
22 Corporate Woods Blvd 3rd Fl ......Albany NY 12211 **866-430-7869** 518-472-5000 633-4

State University of New York Upstate Medical University
766 Irving Ave ....Syracuse NY 13210 **800-736-2171** 315-464-4570 167-2

State University of New York Upstate Medical University Tissue Typing Laboratory
750 E Adams St ....Syracuse NY 13210 **877-464-5540** 315-464-4775 416

State University of New York, The (SUNY)
State University Plz ....Albany NY 12246 **800-342-3811** 518-320-1888 781

State Volunteer Mutual Insurance Co (SVMIC)
101 W Pk Dr Ste 300 ....Brentwood TN 37027 **800-342-2239** 615-377-1999 390-5

Statehouse Convention Ctr
101 S Spring St PO Box 3232 ....Little Rock AR 72201 **800-844-4781** 501-376-4781 205

Staten Island Advance
950 W FingerboaRd Rd ....Staten Island NY 10305 **800-675-8645** 718-981-1234 528-2

Statera Inc
5619 DTC Pkwy Ste 900.......Greenwood Village CO 80111 **866-697-0266**

States Industries LLC
PO Box 41150 ....Eugene OR 97404 **800-626-1981** 541-688-7871 609

States Recovery Systems Inc
2491 Sunrise Blvd ....Rancho Cordova CA 95670 **800-211-1435** 916-631-7085 160

Statesman Journal
280 Church St NE ....Salem OR 97301 **800-874-7012** 503-399-6611 528-2

Statesville Brick Co
391 BrickyaRd Rd ....Statesville NC 28677 **800-522-4716** 704-872-4123 150

Stateville Correctional Ctr
16830 S Broadway St PO Box 112 ....Joliet IL 60434 **800-526-0844** 815-727-3607 213

Static Control Components Inc
3010 Lee Ave PO Box 152 ....Sanford NC 27331 **800-488-2426** 919-774-3808 174

Station Casinos Inc
1505 S Pavilion Ctr Dr ....Las Vegas NV 89135 **800-634-3101*** 702-495-3000 132
*Resv

Stationers Inc
100 Industrial Ln ....Huntington WV 25702 **800-862-7200** 304-528-2780 531

Stavis Seafoods Inc
212 Northern Ave Ste 305...............Boston MA 02210 **800-390-5103** 617-897-1200 297-5

Stavola Contracting
PO Box 482 ....Red Bank NJ 07701 **800-359-1424** 732-542-2328 46

Stay Aspen Snowmass
255 Gold Rivers Ct Ste 300 ....Basalt CO 81621 **888-649-5982** 970-429-5037 375

Steadyhand Investment Funds LP
1747 W Third Ave ....Vancouver BC V6J1K7 **888-888-3147** 524

Steam Bros Inc
2400 Vermont Ave ....Bismarck ND 58504 **800-767-5064** 701-222-1263 152

Steamboat Grand Resort Hotel & Conference Ctr
2300 Mt Werner Cir ....Steamboat Springs CO 80487 **877-269-2628** 970-871-5500 665

Steamboat Ski & Resort Corp
2305 Mt Werner Cir ....Steamboat Springs CO 80487 **877-237-2628** 970-879-6111 665

Steamtown National Historic Site
150 S Washington Ave ....Scranton PA 18503 **888-693-9391** 570-340-5200 560

Stearns ElectricAssn
900 E Kraft Dr ....Melrose MN 56352 **800-962-0655** 320-256-4241 245

Stearns Packaging Corp
4200 Sycamore Ave ....Madison WI 53714 **800-655-5008** 608-246-5150 151

Alphabetical Section

	Toll-Free	Phone	Class
Steel Ceilings Inc			
451 E Coshocton St ....Johnstown OH 43031	800-848-0496	740-967-1063	489
Steel City Corp			
190 N Meridian Rd ....Youngstown OH 44501	800-321-0350	330-792-7663	486
Steel Grip Inc			
1501 E Voorhees St ....Danville IL 61832	800-223-1595	217-442-6240	572
Steel House Inc			
3644 Eastham Dr ....Culver City CA 90232	888-978-3354		5
Steel King Industries Inc			
2700 Chamber St ....Stevens Point WI 54481	800-826-0203	715-341-3120	468
Steel of West Virginia Inc			
17th St & Second Ave ....Huntington WV 25703	800-624-3492	304-696-8200	719
Steel Service Corp			
2260 Flowood Dr PO Box 321425 ......Jackson MS 39232	800-844-9222	601-939-9222	307
Steel Supply Co, The			
5101 Newport Dr ....Rolling Meadows IL 60008	800-323-7571		490
Steel Unlimited Inc			
456 W Valley Blvd ....Rialto CA 92376	800-544-6453	909-873-1222	490
Steel Warehouse Company Inc			
2722 W Tucker Dr ....South Bend IN 46619	800-348-2529	574-236-5100	490
Steelcase Inc			
901 44th St SE ....Grand Rapids MI 49508	888-783-3522	800-333-9939	319-1
NYSE: SCS			
SteelCloud Inc			
20110 Ashbrook Pl Ste 270 ....Ashburn VA 20147	800-296-3866	703-674-5500	176
OTC: SCLD			
Steele Canvas Basket Corp			
201 William St PO Box 6267 IMCN ......Chelsea MA 02150	800-541-8929	617-889-0202	728
Steele Capital Management Inc			
788 Main St #200 ....Dubuque IA 52001	800-397-2097	563-588-2097	524
Steele County			
PO Box 296 ....Finley ND 58230	800-584-7077	701-524-2152	337
Steele Law Firm p C The			
949 County Rt 53 ....Oswego NY 13126	877-496-2687	315-216-4721	427
Steele Solutions Inc			
9909 S 57th St ....Franklin WI 53132	888-542-5099	414-367-5099	478
Steele Truck Ctr Inc			
2150 Rockfill Rd ....Fort Myers FL 33916	888-806-4839	239-334-7300	57
Steele-Waseca Co-op Electric (SWCE)			
2411 W Bridge St PO Box 485 ......Owatonna MN 55060	800-526-3514	507-451-7340	245
Steelhead LNG Corp			
650 - 669 Howe St ....Vancouver BC V6C0B4	855-860-8744	604-235-3800	532
Steelman Industries Inc			
2800 Hwy 135 North ....Kilgore TX 75662	800-287-6633	903-984-3061	318
Steelman Transportation			
2160 N Burton ....Springfield MO 65803	800-488-6287	417-831-6300	775
Steere Enterprises Inc			
285 Commerce St ....Tallmadge OH 44278	800-875-4926	330-633-4926	600
Steering Group Inc, The			
1078 Dixie Belle Ct ....Lawrenceville GA 30045	866-290-8123	800-405-3068	461
Stefanini TechTeam Inc			
27100 W Eleven-Mile Rd ....Southfield MI 48034	800-522-4451		180
Steffes Corp			
3050 Hwy 22 N ....Dickinson ND 58601	888-783-3337	701-483-5400	478
Steico Industries Inc			
1814 Ord Way ....Oceanside CA 92056	800-444-3515	760-438-8015	591
Steiff North America			
24 Albion Rd Ste 220 ....Lincoln RI 02865	888-978-3433	401-312-0080	757
Stein Eriksen Lodge			
7700 Stein Way ....Park City UT 84060	800-453-1302	435-649-3700	665
Stein Hospice			
1200 Sycamore Line ....Sandusky OH 44870	800-625-5269	419-625-5269	370
Steinaker State Park			
4335 N Hwy 191 ....Vernal UT 84078	800-322-3770	435-789-4432	561
Steiner Electric Co			
1250 Touhy Ave ....Elk Grove Village IL 60007	800-783-4637	847-228-0400	246
Steiner Industries			
5801 N Tripp Ave ....Chicago IL 60646	800-621-4515	773-588-3444	572
Steinhafels			
W 231 N 1013 County Hwy F ......Waukesha WI 53186	866-351-4600*	262-436-4600	321
*Cust Svc			
Steinhart Aquarium			
California Academy of Sciences			
55 Music Concourse Dr			
Golden Gate Park ....San Francisco CA 94118	800-794-7576	415-379-8000	40
Steinwall Inc			
1759 116th Ave NW ....Coon Rapids MN 55448	800-229-9199	763-767-7060	604
Steinway & Sons			
1 Steinway Pl ....Long Island NY 11105	800-783-4692	718-721-2600	523
Stellar Group			
2900 Hartley Rd ....Jacksonville FL 32257	800-488-2900	904-260-2900	186
Stellar Technology Inc			
237 Commerce Dr ....Amherst NY 14228	800-274-1846	716-250-1900	452
StellArt			
2012 Waltzer Rd ....Santa Rosa CA 95403	866-621-1987	707-569-1378	130
Stemco LP			
300 Industrial Blvd			
PO Box 1989 ....Longview TX 75606	800-527-8492	903-758-9981	60
Stenograph LLC			
1500 Bishop Ct ....Mount Prospect IL 60056	800-323-4247	847-803-1400	177
Stens Corp			
2424 Cathy Ln ....Jasper IN 47546	800-457-7444	812-482-2526	428
Step Up For Students			
PO Box 54429 ....Jacksonville FL 32245	877-735-7837		305
Step2 Co			
10010 Aurora-Hudson Rd ....Streetsboro OH 44241	800-347-8372*	866-429-5200	64
*Cust Svc			
Stepan Co			
22 W Frontage Rd ....Northfield IL 60093	800-745-7837*	847-446-7500	145
*Cust Svc			
Stephen F Austin State University			
1936 N St PO Box 13051 ....Nacogdoches TX 75962	800-257-9558	936-468-2504	166
Stephen F Austin State University Steen Library (SFASU)			
1936 N St ....Nacogdoches TX 75962	800-765-1534	936-468-3401	433-6
Stephen Mack Middle School			
11810 Old River Rd ....Rockton IL 61072	800-252-2873	815-624-2611	681
Stephen Miller Gallery			
800 Santa Cruz Ave ....Menlo Park CA 94025	888-566-8833	650-327-5040	360

	Toll-Free	Phone	Class
Stephens College			
1200 E Broadway ....Columbia MO 65215	800-876-7207	573-442-2211	166
Stephens Inc			
111 Ctr St ....Little Rock AR 72201	800-643-9691	501-377-2000	686
Stephens Manufacturing Co			
711 W Fourth St ....Tompkinsville KY 42167	800-626-0200	270-487-6774	190
Stephenson Equipment Inc (SEI)			
7201 Paxton St ....Harrisburg PA 17111	800-325-6455	717-564-3434	264-3
Stereotaxis Inc			
4320 Forest Park Ave ....Saint Louis MO 63108	866-646-2346	314-678-6100	381
NASDAQ: STXS			
Stericycle Inc			
28161 N Keith Dr ....Lake Forest IL 60045	866-783-9816	847-367-5910	799
NASDAQ: SRCL			
Sterigenics			
2015 Spring Rd Ste 650 ....Oak Brook IL 60523	800-472-4508	630-928-1700	777
Sterilite Corp			
PO Box 524 ....Townsend MA 01469	800-225-1046		603
STERIS Corp			
5960 Heisley Rd ....Mentor OH 44060	800-548-4873	440-354-2600	474
NYSE: STE			
Sterling Bldg Systems			
PO Box 8005 ....Wausau WI 54402	800-455-0545		106
Sterling Business Forms			
PO Box 2486 ....White City OR 97503	800-759-3676*		110
*Cust Svc			
Sterling College			
125 W Cooper ....Sterling KS 67579	800-346-1017	620-278-2173	166
Sterling College			
PO Box 72 ....Craftsbury Common VT 05827	800-648-3591	802-586-7711	795
Sterling Computer Corp			
600 Stevens Port Dr			
Ste 200 ....Dakota Dunes SD 57049	877-242-4074	605-242-4000	717
Sterling Cruises & Travel			
8700 W Flagler St ....Miami FL 33174	800-435-7967	305-592-2522	766
Sterling Cut Glass Company Inc			
5020 Olympic Blvd ....Erlanger KY 41018	800-543-1317	859-283-2333	360
Sterling Electric Inc			
7997 Allison Ave ....Indianapolis IN 46268	800-654-6220*	317-872-0471	515
*Cust Svc			
Sterling Federal Bank			
PO Box 617 ....Sterling IL 61081	800-353-0888	815-626-0614	
Sterling Fibers Inc			
5005 Sterling Way ....Pace FL 32571	800-342-3779*	850-994-5311	601-2
*Cust Svc			
Sterling Hotel			
1300 H St ....Sacramento CA 95814	800-365-7660	916-448-1300	378
Sterling Mutuals Inc			
1090 University Ave 2nd Fl..............Windsor ON N9A5S4	800-354-4956		400
Sterling Plumbing			
444 Highland Dr ....Kohler WI 53044	888-783-7546*	920-457-4441	607
*Cust Svc			
Sterling Publishing Company Inc			
1166 Avenue of the Americas			
17th Fl ....New York NY 10036	800-367-9692*	212-532-7160	633-2
*Cust Svc			
Sterling Stores			
1305 First Ave SW ....Austin MN 55912	800-803-1503	507-433-4586	238
Sterling-Clark-Lurton Corp			
PO Box 130 ....Norwood MA 02062	800-225-9872	781-762-5400	546
Stern & Stern Industries Inc			
188 Thacher St PO Box 556 ....Hornell NY 14843	800-664-7415	607-324-4485	740-3
Stern Oil Company Inc			
PO Box 218 ....Freeman SD 57029	800-477-2744	605-925-7999	575
Stertil-Koni USA Inc			
200 Log Canoe Cir ....Stevensville MD 21666	800-336-6637	410-643-9001	194
Stetson University			
421 N Woodland Blvd Unit 8378 ......DeLand FL 32723	800-688-0101*	386-822-7100	166
*Admissions			
Stetson University DuPont-Ball Library			
421 N Woodland Blvd ....DeLand FL 32723	800-688-0101	386-822-7183	433-6
Steuben County Rural Electric Membership Corp			
1212 S Wayne St ....Angola IN 46703	888-233-9088	260-665-3563	245
Steuben County Tourism Bureau			
430 N Wayne St Ste 1B ....Angola IN 46703	888-665-5668	260-665-5386	206
Steuben Rural Electric Co-op Inc			
9 Wilson Ave ....Bath NY 14810	800-843-3414	607-776-4161	245
Steuben Trust Co			
1 Steuben Sq ....Hornell NY 14843	866-783-8236	607-324-5010	70
Steve Foley Cadillac			
100 Skokie Blvd ....Northbrook IL 60062	877-223-9671*	866-664-4037	126
*Sales			
Steve Hopkins Inc			
2499 Auto Mall Pkwy ....Fairfield CA 94533	877-873-3913	707-427-1000	513
Steve Landers Toyota			
10825 Colonel Glenn Rd ....Little Rock AR 72204	866-584-3844		513
Steve Millen Sportparts Inc			
3176 Airway Ave ....Costa Mesa CA 92626	866-250-5542		57
Steve's Music			
51 Rue Saint-antoine O St W ......Montreal QC H2Z1G9	877-978-3837	514-878-2216	522
Steven Barclay Agency			
12 Western Ave ....Petaluma CA 94952	888-965-7323	707-773-0654	704
Steven Engineering Inc			
230 Ryan Way ......South San Francisco CA 94080	800-258-9200	650-588-9200	246
Steven Restivo Event Services LLC			
805 Fourth St Ste 8..............San Rafael CA 94901	800-310-6563	415-456-6455	184
Steven Schaefer Associates Inc			
10411 Medallion Dr ....Cincinnati OH 45241	800-542-3302	513-542-3300	261
Stevens Aviation Inc			
600 Delaware St ....Greenville SC 29605	800-359-7838		63
Stevens Business Service Inc			
92 Bolt St Ste 1..............Lowell MA 01852	800-769-0375	978-458-2500	160
Stevens County			
215 S Oak St ....Colville WA 99114	800-833-6388	509-684-3751	337
Stevens Creek Software			
PO Box 2126 ....Cupertino CA 95015	800-823-4279	408-725-0424	178-9
Stevens Henager College			
1890 S 1350 W ....Ogden UT 84401	800-622-2640		162

				Toll-Free	Phone	Class
Stevens Industries Inc						
704 W Main St	Teutopolis	IL	62467	**800-637-1609**	217-540-3100	286
Stevens Institute of Technology						
Castle Pt on the Hudson	Hoboken	NJ	07030	**800-458-5323**	201-216-5194	166
Stevens Marine Inc						
9180 SW Burnham St	Tigard	OR	97223	**800-225-7023**	503-620-7023	90
Stevens Sausage Company Inc						
3411 Stevens Sausage Rd	Smithfield	NC	27577	**800-338-0561**	919-934-3159	615
Stevens Transport						
PO Box 279010	Dallas	TX	75227	**800-233-9369**	866-551-0337	775
Stevens Water Monitoring Systems						
12067 NE Glenn Widing Dr Ste 106	Portland	OR	97220	**800-452-5272**	503-445-8000	540
Stevens Worldwide Van Lines						
527 W Morley Dr	Saginaw	MI	48601	**877-490-0713**	800-678-3836	516
Stevenson & Vestal						
2347 W Hanford Rd	Burlington	NC	27215	**800-535-3636**		195
Steward Health Care (TSLH)						
Tempe Saint Luke's Hospital						
1500 S Mill Ave	Tempe	AZ	85281	**877-351-9355**	480-784-5500	
Stewart Business Systems LLC						
105 Connecticut Dr	Burlington	NJ	08016	**800-322-5584**		
Stewart Directories Inc						
50314 Kings Point Dr PO Box 326	Frisco	NC	27936	**800-311-0786**		633-6
Stewart EFI LLC						
45 Old Waterbury Rd	Thomaston	CT	06787	**800-393-5387**	860-283-8213	487
Stewart Enterprises Inc						
1333 S Clearview Pkwy	New Orleans	LA	70121	**877-239-3264**	713-522-5141	508
NASDAQ: STEI						
Stewart Filmscreen Corp						
1161 W Sepulveda Blvd	Torrance	CA	90502	**800-762-4999**	310-784-5300	587
Stewart Information Services Corp						
1980 Post Oak Blvd Ste 800	Houston	TX	77056	**800-729-1900**	713-625-8100	390-6
NYSE: STC						
Stewart REI Data Inc						
1980 Post Oak Blvd Ste 800	Houston	TX	77056	**800-729-1900**	212-922-0050	390-6
Stewart School of Cosmetology						
604 NW Ave	Sioux Falls	SD	57104	**800-537-2625**	605-336-2775	77
Stewart Systems						
808 Stewart Ave	Plano	TX	75074	**800-966-5808**	972-422-5808	207
Stewart Title Guaranty Co						
1980 Post Oak Blvd Ste 800	Houston	TX	77056	**800-729-1900**	713-625-8100	390-6
STFM (Society of Teachers of Family Medicine)						
11400 Tomahawk Creek Pkwy Ste 240	Leawood	KS	66211	**800-274-7928**	913-906-6000	49-8
Stg International Inc						
4900 Seminary Rd Ste 1100	Alexandria	VA	22311	**855-507-0660**	703-578-6030	180
STI Electronics Inc						
261 Palmer Rd	Madison	AL	35758	**888-650-3006**	256-461-9191	385
Sti Polymer Inc						
5618 Clyde Rhyne Dr	Sanford	NC	27330	**800-874-5878**		3
Stic-adhesive Products Company Inc						
3950 Medford St	Los Angeles	CA	90063	**800-854-6813**	323-268-2956	707
Stickkcom LLC						
109 S Fifth St	New York	NY	11249	**866-578-4255**	347-394-4964	386
Stidham Trucking Inc						
PO Box 308	Yreka	CA	96097	**800-827-9500**	530-842-4161	186
Stifel Financial Corp						
501 N Broadway	Saint Louis	MO	63102	**800-679-5446**		686
NYSE: SF						
Stifel Nicolaus & Co Inc						
501 N Broadway	Saint Louis	MO	63102	**800-679-5446**	314-317-6900	686
Stihl Inc						
536 Viking Dr	Virginia Beach	VA	23452	**800-467-8445***	757-486-9100	754
*Cust Svc						
Stillman Banccorp NA						
PO Box 150	Stillman Valle	IL	61084	**866-546-8273**	815-645-2000	70
Stillman College						
3601 Stillman Blvd	Tuscaloosa	AL	35401	**800-841-5722**	205-349-4240	166
Stillwater Chamber of Commerce						
409 S Main St	Stillwater	OK	74075	**800-593-5573**	405-372-5573	139
Stillwater Public Library						
1107 S Duck St	Stillwater	OK	74074	**800-829-3676**	405-372-3633	433-3
Stillwater State Park						
44 Stillwater Rd	Groton	VT	05046	**888-409-7579**	802-584-3822	561
Stillwater Technologies Inc						
1040 S Dorset	Troy	OH	45373	**800-338-7561**	937-440-2500	452
Stilson Products						
15935 Sturgeon St	Roseville	MI	48066	**888-400-5978**	586-778-1100	491
Stimple & Ward Co						
3400 Babcock Blvd	Pittsburgh	PA	15237	**800-792-6457**	412-364-5200	515
Stimson Lumber Co						
520 SW Yamhill St Ste 700	Portland	OR	97204	**800-445-9758**	503-701-6510	679
Stimwave Technologies Inc						
1310 Park Central Blvd S	Pompano Beach	FL	33064	**800-965-5134**	786-565-3342	738
Stinnett & Assoc LLC						
8811 S Yale Ave Ste 300	Tulsa	OK	74137	**888-808-1795**		2
STMA (Sports Turf Managers Assn)						
805 New Hampshire Ste E	Lawrence	KS	66044	**800-323-3875**	785-843-2549	48-22
STMH (St Mary's of Michigan)						
800 S Washington Ave	Saginaw	MI	48601	**877-738-6672**	989-907-8115	373-3
Stock & Option Solutions Inc						
6399 San Ignacio Ave Ste 100	San Jose	CA	95119	**888-767-0199**	408-979-8700	461
Stock Drive Products/Sterling Instrument						
2101 Jericho Tpke	New Hyde Park	NY	11040	**800-737-7436**	800-819-8900	616
Stock Equipment Co						
16490 Chillicothe Rd	Chagrin Falls	OH	44023	**888-742-1249**	440-543-6000	273
Stock Seed Farms						
28008 Mill Rd	Murdock	NE	68407	**800-759-1520**	402-867-3771	690
Stock Transportation						
60 Columbia Way Ste 800	Markham	ON	L3R0C9	**888-952-0878**	905-940-9977	109
Stock Yards						
1040 E Main St	Louisville	KY	40206	**800-625-9066**	502-625-1790	359-2
NASDAQ: SYBT						
Stock Yards Packing Co Inc						
2500 S Pacific Hwy PO Box 9100	Medford	OR	97501	**888-842-6111**		296-26
StockCap						
123 Manufacturers Dr	Arnold	MO	63010	**800-827-2277**	636-282-6800	154

				Toll-Free	Phone	Class
Stockman's Casino						
1560 W Williams Ave	Fallon	NV	89406	**855-423-2117**		
Stockton-San Joaquin County Public Library (SSJCPL)						
605 N El Dorado St	Stockton	CA	95202	**866-805-7323**	209-937-8416	433-3
Stockwatch						
700 W Georgia St PO Box 10371	Vancouver	BC	V7Y1J6	**800-268-6397**	604-687-1500	403
Stockyards Hotel						
109 E Exchange Ave	Fort Worth	TX	76164	**800-423-8471**	817-625-6427	378
Stoelting LLC 502 Hwy 67	Kiel	WI	53042	**800-558-5807**	920-894-2293	298
Stoever Glass & Company Inc						
30 Wall St	New York	NY	10005	**800-223-3881**	212-952-1910	400
Stoffel Equipment Company Inc						
7764 N 81st St	Milwaukee	WI	53223	**800-354-7502**	414-354-7500	357
Stoller Fisheries						
1301 18th St PO Box B	Spirit Lake	IA	51360	**800-831-5174**	712-336-1750	296-14
Stoller USA						
4001 W Sam Houston Pkwy N Ste 100	Houston	TX	77043	**800-539-5283**	713-461-1493	280
Stoltzfus RV's & Marine						
1335 Wilmington Pk	West Chester	PA	19382	**866-755-8858**		90
Stone Belt Freight Lines Inc						
101 W Dillman Rd	Bloomington	IN	47403	**800-264-2340**	812-824-6741	314
Stone Castle Hotel & Conference Ctr, The						
3050 Green Mtn Dr	Branson	MO	65616	**800-677-6906**	417-335-4700	378
Stone Coast Fund Services LLC						
2 Portland Sq	Portland	ME	04101	**888-699-2680**	207-699-2680	195
Stone Mountain State Park						
3042 Frank Pkwy	Roaring Gap	NC	28668	**877-722-6762**	919-707-9300	561
Stonebridge Press Inc						
25 Elm St	Southbridge	MA	01550	**800-536-5836**	508-764-4325	633-8
Stonefield Beach State Recreation Site						
95330 US-101	Florence	OR	97439	**800-551-6949**		561
Stoneham Savings Bank						
80 Montvale Ave	Stoneham	MA	02180	**888-402-2265**		70
Stonehill College						
320 Washington St	Easton	MA	02357	**888-694-4554**	508-565-1373	166
Stoneleigh Recovery Associates Llc						
PO Box 1479	Lombard	IL	60148	**866-724-2330**		141
Stoneridge Shopping Ctr						
1 Stoneridge Mall	Pleasanton	CA	94588	**877-746-6642**	317-636-1600	458
Stonewall Jackson Hotel & Conference Ctr						
24 S Market St	Staunton	VA	24401	**866-880-0024**	540-885-4848	378
Stonewall Jackson Memorial Hospital (SJMH)						
230 Hospital Plz	Weston	WV	26452	**866-637-0471**	304-269-8000	373-3
Stonewall Resort						
940 Resort Dr	Roanoke	WV	26447	**888-278-8150**	304-269-7400	665
Stoney Creek Inn						
101 Mariner's Way	East Peoria	IL	61611	**800-659-2220**	309-694-1300	378
Stonhard Inc						
1000 E Park Ave	Maple Shade	NJ	08052	**800-854-0310***	800-257-7953	291
*Cust Svc						
Stop & Shop Supermarket Co						
1385 Hancock St	Quincy	MA	02169	**800-767-7772**	781-397-0006	344
Stoptech Ltd						
365 Industrial Dr	Harrison	OH	45030	**800-537-0102**	513-202-5500	195
Storage Battery Systems Inc (SBS)						
N56 W16665 Ridgewood Dr	Menomonee Falls	WI	53051	**800-554-2243**	262-703-5800	246
Storage Engine Inc						
1 Sheila Dr	Tinton Falls	NJ	07724	**866-734-8899**	732-747-6995	176
Stor-All Storage						
1375 W Hillsboro Blvd	Deerfield Beach	FL	33442	**877-786-7255**	954-421-7888	798-3
Store Decor Co, The						
5050 Boyd Blvd	Rowlett	TX	75088	**800-831-3267**	972-475-4404	343
Store Opening Solutions (SOS)						
800 Middle Tennessee Blvd	Murfreesboro	TN	37129	**877-388-9262**		447
Store Supply Warehouse LLC						
9801 Page Ave	St Louis	MO	63132	**800-823-0004**	314-427-8887	786
Storer Coachways						
3519 McDonald Ave	Modesto	CA	95358	**800-621-3383**	209-521-8250	107
Storey Publishing LLC						
210 Mass Moca Way	North Adams	MA	01247	**800-827-7444**	413-346-2100	633-2
Stork Craft Manufacturing Inc						
12033 Riverside Way Ste 200	Richmond	BC	V6W1G3	**877-274-0277**	604-274-5121	319-2
Stork News of America Inc						
1305 Hope Mills Rd Ste A	Fayetteville	NC	28304	**800-633-6395**	910-426-1357	310
Storm Internet Services Inc						
1760 Courtwood Crescent	Ottawa	ON	K2C2B5	**866-257-8676**	613-567-6585	225
Storm Products Inc						
165 S 800 W	Brigham City	UT	84302	**800-369-4402**	435-723-0403	706
StormHarbour Securities LP						
140 E 45th St Two Grand Central Tower 33rd Fl	New York	NY	10017	**800-662-2739**	212-905-2500	686
Stormont-Vail Regional Health Ctr						
1500 SW Tenth Ave	Topeka	KS	66604	**800-432-2951**	785-354-6000	373-3
Stornoway Diamond Corp						
1111 St-Charles Ouest Tour Ouest Ste 400	Longueuil	QC	J4K5G4	**877-331-2232**	450-616-5555	501-3
TSX: SWY						
Storopack Inc						
12007 S Woodruff Ave	Downey	CA	90241	**800-829-1491**	562-803-5582	597
Storr Tractor Co						
3191 Rt 22	Branchburg	NJ	08876	**800-526-3802**	908-722-9830	428
Stott Outdoor Advertising						
PO Box 7209	Chico	CA	95927	**888-342-7868**		8
Stoughton Trailers LLC						
416 S Academy St	Stoughton	WI	53589	**800-227-5391**	608-873-2500	774
Stowe Mountain Resort						
5781 Mountain Rd	Stowe	VT	05672	**800-253-4754**	802-253-3000	665
Stoweflake Mountain Resort & Spa						
1746 Mountain Rd PO Box 369	Stowe	VT	05672	**800-253-2232**	802-253-7355	665
Strafford Publications Inc						
PO Box 13729	Atlanta	GA	30324	**800-926-7926**	404-881-1141	633-9
Straight A Tours & Travel						
6881 Kingspointe Pkwy Ste 18	Orlando	FL	32819	**800-237-5440**	407-896-1242	755
Straight North LLC						
1001 W 31st St	Downers Grove	IL	60515	**866-353-3953**		7

Alphabetical Section

Name / Address	Toll-Free	Phone	Class
Strait Music Co 2428 W Ben White Blvd ......Austin TX 78704	800-725-8877	512-476-6927	522
Stranahan Theater 4645 Heatherdowns Blvd ......Toledo OH 43614	866-381-7469	419-381-8851	568
Strand Book Store Inc 828 Broadway ......New York NY 10003	800-366-3664	212-473-1452	95
Strand Diagnostics LLC 5770 Decatur Blvd Ste A...Indianapolis IN 46241	888-924-6779	317-455-2100	417
Strand Lighting 10911 Petal St ......Dallas TX 75238	800-733-0564	214-647-7880	438
Strand Theatre 619 Louisiana Ave ......Shreveport LA 71101	800-313-6373	318-226-1481	568
Strange's Florist Inc 3313 Mechanicsville Pk ......Richmond VA 23223	800-421-4070	804-321-2200	292
Strata Health Solutions Inc 933 - 17 Ave SW Ste 600 ......Calgary BC T2T5R6	866-556-5005		179
Strata Information Group 3935 Harney St Ste 203 ......San Diego CA 92110	800-776-0111		
Strata Oil & Gas Inc 10010 - 98 St PO Box 7770 ......Peace River AB T8S1T3	877-237-5443	403-237-5443	532
Strata Products Worldwide LLC 8995 Roswell Rd Ste 200 ...Sandy Springs GA 30350	800-691-6601	770-321-2500	359-3
Stratacache 2 Emmet St Ste 200 ......Dayton OH 45405	800-244-8915	937-224-0485	180
Stratagem Inc 10922 N Cedarburg Rd ......Mequon WI 53092	800-228-4422	262-532-2700	225
Stratagraph Inc 125 Raggio Rd ......Scott LA 70583	800-256-1147		534
Stratasys Inc 7665 Commerce Way ......Eden Prairie MN 55344 *NASDAQ: SSYS*	800-937-3010	952-937-3000	261
Strategic Distribution Inc 1414 Radcliffe St Ste 300 ......Bristol PA 19007	800-322-2644	215-633-1900	384
Strategic Finance Magazine 10 Paragon Dr Ste 1 ......Montvale NJ 07645	800-638-4427	201-573-9000	455-5
Strategic Financial Alliance Inc, The 2200 Century Pkwy Ste 500 ......Atlanta GA 30345	888-447-2444	678-954-4000	400
Strategic Information Resources Inc 155 Brookdale Dr ......Springfield MA 01104	800-332-9479	800-813-4381	218
Strategy Companion Corp 3240 El Camino Real Ste 120 ......Irvine CA 92602	800-905-6792	714-460-8398	179
Strategy Institute 401 Richmond St W Ste 401 ......Toronto ON M5V3A8	866-298-9343		464
Strater Hotel 699 Main Ave ......Durango CO 81301	800-247-4431	970-247-4431	378
Stratford Court 45 Katherine Blvd ......Palm Harbor FL 34684	888-434-4648	727-787-1500	668
Stratford General Hospital 46 General Hospital Dr ......Stratford ON N5A2Y6	888-275-1102	519-272-8210	373-2
Stratford Homes LP 402 S Weber Ave ......Stratford WI 54484	800-448-1524	715-687-3133	106
Stratford University School of Culinary Arts 7777 Leesburg Pk ......Falls Church VA 22043	800-444-0804	703-821-8570	163
Strathcona Hotel 60 York St ......Toronto ON M5J1S8	800-268-8304	416-363-3321	378
Strathcona Hotel, The 919 Douglas St ......Victoria BC V8W2C2	800-663-7476	250-383-7137	378
Stratix 4920 Avalon Ridge Pkwy ......Norcross GA 30071	800-883-8300	770-326-7580	173-7
StratMar Retail Services 109 Willett Ave ......Port Chester NY 10573	800-866-2399		
Stratos Global Corp 6550 Rock Spring Dr Ste 650 ......Bethesda MD 20817	800-563-2255	301-214-8800	677
Stratosphere Tower Hotel & Casino 2000 S Las Vegas Blvd ......Las Vegas NV 89104	800-998-6937	702-380-7777	133
Stratton Equity Co-op Co Inc 98 Colorado Ave PO Box 25 ......Stratton CO 80836	800-438-7070	719-348-5326	275
Stratton Hats Inc 3200 Randolph St ......Bellwood IL 60104	877-453-3777	708-544-5220	155-8
STRATTON MOUNTAIN RESORT 5 Village Lodge Rd ......Stratton Mountain VT 05155	800-787-2886	802-297-4211	665
Stratton Seed Co 1530 Hwy 79 S ......Stuttgart AR 72160	800-264-4433	870-673-4433	690
Stratton Veterans Affairs Medical Ctr 113 Holland Ave ......Albany NY 12208	800-223-4810	518-626-5000	373-8
Stratus Properties Inc 212 Lavaca St Ste 300 ......Austin TX 78701 *NYSE: STRS*	800-690-0315	512-478-5788	649
Stratus Technologies 111 Powdermill Rd ......Maynard MA 01754	800-787-2887	978-461-7000	178-12
Strawbridge Studios Inc 3616 Hillsborough Rd PO Box 3005 ......Durham NC 27705	800-326-9080	919-226-3000	623
Strayer University 4710 Auth Pl Ste 100 ......Suitland MD 20746	888-311-0355		166
Strayer University Alexandria 2730 Eisenhower Ave ......Alexandria VA 22314	888-311-0355		166
Strayer University Arlington 2121 15th St N ......Arlington VA 22201	888-478-7293	703-892-5100	166
Strayer University Fredericksburg 150 Riverside Pkwy Ste 100 ......Fredericksburg VA 22406	888-311-0355	540-374-4300	166
Stream Gas & Electric Ltd 1950 Stemmons Fwy Ste 3000 ......Dallas TX 75207	866-447-8732		782
Streamlight Inc 30 Eagleville Rd ......Eagleville PA 19403	800-523-7488	610-631-0600	438
Streamline Health Solutions Inc 10200 Alliance Rd Ste 200 ......Cincinnati OH 45242 *NASDAQ: STRM*	800-878-5269	888-997-8732	39
StreamSend 78 York St ......Sacramento CA 95814	877-439-4078	916-326-5407	392
Streamwood Behavioral Health Ctr 1400 E Irving Pk Rd ......Streamwood IL 60107	800-272-7790	630-837-9000	373-1
Streamworks LLC 3640 Pheasant Ridge Dr NE ......Blaine MN 55449	800-328-5680		
Streater Inc 411 S First Ave ......Albert Lea MN 56007	800-527-4197		286
Streator Dependable Manufacturing Co 1705 N Shabbona St ......Streator IL 61364	800-795-0551	815-672-0551	468
Streck Inc 7002 S 109th St ......Omaha NE 68128	800-228-6090	402-333-1982	231
Streimer Sheet Metal Works Inc 740 N Knott St ......Portland OR 97227	888-288-3828	503-288-9393	693
Strem Chemicals Inc 7 Mulliken Way ......Newburyport MA 01950	800-647-8736	978-499-1600	146
Stremicks Heritage Foods 4002 Westminster Ave ......Santa Ana CA 92703 *Orders	800-321-5960*	714-775-5000	296-27
Stretch Boards 983 Tower Pl ......Santa Cruz CA 95062	800-480-4754	831-479-7309	707
Stretch-N-Grow PO Box 7599 ......Seminole FL 33775	800-348-0166		310
Stria Inc 4300 Resnik Ct ......Bakersfield CA 93313	877-839-8952		196
Strick Trailers LLC 301 N Polk St ......Monroe IN 46772 *Sales	888-552-3055*	260-692-6121	
Stric-Lan Companies LLC 104 Sable St ......Duson LA 70529	800-749-4586	337-984-7850	535
Strictly Business Computer Systems Inc 848 Fourth Ave Ste 200 ......Huntington WV 25701	888-529-0401		176
Stride Rite Corp 191 Spring St ......Lexington MA 02421 *Cust Svc	800-299-6575*	617-824-6000	301
Stride Tool Inc Imperial Div 30333 Emerald Vly Pkwy ......Glenwillow OH 44139	888-467-8665	440-247-4600	753
Strider 6-6150 Hwy 7 Ste 400 ......Woodbridge ON L4H0R6	800-314-8895	416-502-8895	195
Stripes Convenience Stores 3200 Hackberry Rd ......Irving TX 75063 *NYSE: SUSS*	800-255-0711		204
Strippit Inc/LVD 12975 Clarence Ctr Rd ......Akron NY 14001	800-828-1527	716-542-4511	454
Strom Aviation Inc 109 S Elm St ......Waconia MN 55387	800-356-6440	952-544-3611	627
Strong Enterprises Inc 11236 Satellite Blvd ......Orlando FL 32837	800-344-6319	407-859-9317	572
Strong Memorial Hospital *Stem Cell Transplantation Ctr* 601 Elmwood Ave ......Rochester NY 14642	888-661-6162	585-275-2100	
University of Rochester Medical Ctr 601 Elmwood Ave ......Rochester NY 14642	800-999-6673	585-275-2100	373-3
Strong Travel Services Inc 8235 Douglas Ave Ste 1040 ......Dallas TX 75225	800-747-5670	214-361-0027	767
Stronghaven Inc 5090 McDougall Dr SW ......Atlanta GA 30336	800-331-7835	404-699-1952	100
Strouds Run State Park 2045 Morse Rd ......Columbus OH 43229	800-945-3543	740-592-2302	561
Structall Building Systems Inc 350 Burbank Rd ......Oldsmar FL 34677	800-969-3706		234
Structural Component Systems Inc (SCS) 1255 Front St ......Fremont NE 68026	800-844-5622	402-721-5622	187
Structural Concepts Corp 888 Porter Rd ......Muskegon MI 49441	800-433-9489	231-798-8888	286
Structural Wood Corp 4000 Labore Rd ......Saint Paul MN 55110	800-652-9058	651-426-8111	812
Structural Wood Systems 321 Dohrimier St ......Greenville AL 36037	800-553-0661	334-382-6534	812
Structure House 3017 Pickett Rd ......Durham NC 27705	800-553-0052	855-736-4009	702
Structures Unlimited Inc 166 River Rd ......Bow NH 03304	800-225-3895	603-645-6539	693
Struktol Company of America Inc PO Box 1649 ......Stow OH 44224	800-327-8649	330-928-5188	144
Stryker Corp 2825 Airview Blvd ......Kalamazoo MI 49002 *NYSE: SYK*	800-616-1406	269-385-2600	474
Stry-Lenkoff Co 1100 W Broadway ......Louisville KY 40203	800-626-8247	502-587-6804	110
STS (Society of Thoracic Surgeons) 633 N St Clair St Ste 2320 ......Chicago IL 60611	877-865-5321	312-202-5800	49-8
STS Component Solutions LLC 2910 SW 42 Ave ......Palm City FL 34990	888-777-2960		22
Stuart C Irby Co 815 Irby St ......Jackson MS 39201	866-687-4729	713-476-0788	188-10
Stuart Hall School 235 W Frederick St PO Box 210 ......Staunton VA 24402	888-306-8926	540-885-0356	618
Stuart Jet Ctr LLC 2501 Aviation Way ......Stuart FL 34996	877-735-9538	772-288-6700	63
Stuart Maue Mitchell & James Ltd 3840 McKelvey Rd ......St. Louis MO 63044	800-291-9940		195
Stuart-Martin County Chamber of Commerce 1650 S Kanner Hwy ......Stuart FL 34994	800-962-2873	772-287-1088	139
Stubbe's Precast 30 Muir Line ......Harley ON N0E1E0	866-355-2183	519-424-2183	
Stubbs & Perdue PA 9208 Falls of Neuse Rd Ste 201 ......Raleigh NC 27615	800-348-9404		443
StubHub 199 Fremont St 4th Fl ......San Francisco CA 94105	866-788-2482		
Stuckey's Corp 8555 16th St Ste 850 ......Silver Spring MD 20910	800-423-6171	301-585-8222	666
Studebaker National Museum 201 Chapin St ......South Bend IN 46601	888-391-5600	574-235-9714	517
Student Advantage LLC 280 Summer St ......Boston MA 02210	800-333-2920		383
Student Agencies Foundation Inc 409 College Ave ......Ithaca NY 14850	800-631-8405	607-272-2000	305
Student Book Store 421 E Grand River Ave ......East Lansing MI 48823	800-968-1111	517-351-4210	95
Student Conservation Assn (SCA) 689 River Rd PO Box 550 ......Charlestown NH 03603	888-722-9675	603-543-1700	48-13
Student Tours Inc 60 West Ave ......Vineyard Haven MA 02568	800-331-7093	508-693-5078	755
Student Transportation Inc (STA) 3349 Hwy 138 Bldg A Ste C ......Wall NJ 07719	888-942-2250	732-280-4200	109
Student Travel Services Inc 2431 Solomons Island Rd Ste 302 ......Annapolis MD 21061	800-648-4849	410-787-9500	755

Name / Address	City	State	Zip	Toll-Free	Phone	Class
Student Veterans of America PO Box 77673	Washington	DC	20013	866-320-3826	202-223-4710	305
Studentcitycom Inc 8 Essex Ctr Dr	Peabody	MA	01960	888-777-4642		766
Studio Desgraff 2831 rue King Ouest	Sherbrooke	QC	J1L1C6	800-292-5110	819-823-8024	395
Stueve Siegel Hanson LLP 460 Nichols Rd Ste 200	Kansas City	MO	64112	800-714-0360	816-714-7100	427
Stuller Settings Inc PO Box 87777	Lafayette	LA	70598	800-877-7777		406
Stupp Bros Inc 3800 Weber Rd	Saint Louis	MO	63125	800-535-9999	314-638-5000	478
Stupp Corp 12555 Ronaldson Rd	Baton Rouge	LA	70807	800-535-9999	225-775-8800	488
Sturbridge Host Hotel & Conference Ctr 366 Main St	Sturbridge	MA	01566	800-582-3232	508-347-7393	378
Sturdisteel Co PO Box 2655	Waco	TX	76702	800-433-3116		319-3
Sturdy Corp 1822 Carolina Beach Rd	Wilmington	NC	28401	800-721-3282	910-763-2500	203
Sturm Foods Inc PO Box 287	Manawa	WI	54949	800-347-8876	920-596-2511	297-11
Sturtevant Inc 348 Circuit St	Hanover	MA	02339	800-992-0209	781-829-6501	111
Stuttering Foundation of America 3100 Walnut Grove Rd Ste 603	Memphis	TN	38111	800-992-9392	901-452-7343	48-17
StVincent Health 2001 W 86th St	Indianapolis	IN	46260	866-338-2345	317-338-2345	448
Styberg Engineering 1600 Gold St PO Box 788	Racine	WI	53401	800-240-7275		616
Styer Transportation Co 7870 215th St W	Lakeville	MN	55044	800-548-9149	952-469-4491	775
Stylex PO Box 5038	Delanco	NJ	08075	800-257-5742		319-1
Stylmark Inc 6536 Main St NE	Fridley	MN	55432	800-328-2495		286
Suarez Corp Industries 7800 Whipple Ave NW	North Canton	OH	44720	800-764-0008	330-494-5504	195
Subaru of America Inc 2235 Marlton Pike W	Cherry Hill	NJ	08002	800-782-2783	856-488-8500	59
Subco Foods Inc 4350 S Taylor Dr	Sheboygan	WI	53081	800-473-0757	920-457-7761	296-16
Substance Abuse & Mental Health Services Administration (SAMHSA) 1 Choke Cherry Rd	Rockville	MD	20857	877-726-4727	240-276-2000	339-9
Center for Mental Health Services 1 Choke Cherry Ln	Rockville	MD	20857	877-726-4727		339-9
Center for Substance Abuse Prevention 1 Choke Cherry Rd	Rockville	MD	20857	877-726-4727	240-276-2420	339-9
Center for Substance Abuse Treatment 5600 Fishers Ln PO Box 2345	Rockville	MD	20857	877-726-4727	240-276-2130	339-9
Subsurface Constructors Inc 110 Angelica St	Saint Louis	MO	63147	800-242-9425	314-421-2460	189-5
Suburban Collection 1810 Maplelawn Dr	Troy	MI	48084	877-471-7100		57
Suburban Hospital 8600 Old Georgetown Rd	Bethesda	MD	20814	800-456-4543	301-896-3100	373-3
Suburban Life Publications 1101 W 31st St Ste 100	Downers Grove	IL	60515	800-397-9397	630-368-1100	633-8
Suburban Mobility Authority for Regional Transportation (SMART) 535 Griswold St Ste 600	Detroit	MI	48226	866-962-5515	313-223-2100	466
Suburban Press & Metro Press 1550 Woodville Rd	Millbury	OH	43447	800-300-6158	419-836-2221	528-4
Suburban Propane LP 240 Rt 10 W PO Box 206	Whippany	NJ	07981	800-776-7263	973-503-9252	316
Suburban Transit Corp 750 Somerset St	New Brunswick	NJ	08901	800-222-0492	732-249-1100	108
Suburban Wheel Cover Co 1420 Landmeier Rd	Elk Grove Village	IL	60007	800-635-8126	847-758-0388	54
Success Motivation International Inc 4567 Lakeshore Dr *Sales	Waco	TX	76710	800-876-2389*	254-776-7551	365
Successories Inc 1040 Holland Dr	Boca Raton	FL	33487	800-535-2773		310
Succor Creek State Natural Area 1298 Lake Owyhee Dam Rd	Adrian	OR	97901	800-551-6949		561
Suddath Cos 815 S Main St	Jacksonville	FL	32207	800-395-7100	904-352-2577	516
Suddenlink Communications 6151 Paluxy Dr	Tyler	TX	75703	877-694-9474		116
Sudenga Industries Inc 2002 Kingbird Ave	George	IA	51237	888-783-3642	712-475-3301	273
Sudjam LLC 520 E Broadway Ste 202	Glendale	CA	91205	800-555-1234	818-206-1145	177
Suffolk University 8 Ashburton Pl	Boston	MA	02108	800-678-3365	617-573-8460	166
Sugar Creek Foods International 301 N El Paso St	Russellville	AR	72801	800-445-2715		296-25
Sugar Creek Packing Co 2101 Kenskill Ave	Washington Court House	OH	43160	800-848-8205	740-335-7440	296-26
Sugar Foods Corp 950 Third Ave Ste 21	New York	NY	10022	800-732-8963	212-753-6900	297-11
Sugarbush Resort & Inn 1840 Sugarbush Access Rd	Warren	VT	05674	800-537-8427	802-583-6300	665
Sugarloaf/USA 5092 Access Rd	Carrabassett Valley	ME	04947	800-843-5623	207-237-2000	665
Sugino Corp 1380 Hamilton Pkwy	Itasca	IL	60143	888-784-4661	630-250-8585	357
SUHM Spring Works Inc 14650 Heathrow Forest Pkwy	Houston	TX	77032	800-338-6903	713-224-9293	295
Suite 66 366 Adelaide St W Ste 600	Toronto	ON	M5V1R9	866-779-3486	416-628-5565	8
Suites at Fisherman's Wharf 2655 Hyde St	San Francisco	CA	94109	800-227-3608	415-771-0200	378
Suites Hotel in Canal Park, The 325 Lake Ave S	Duluth	MN	55802	800-794-1716	218-727-4663	378
Sukhi's Gourmet Indian Foods 25823 Clawiter Rd	Hayward	CA	94545	888-478-5447		
Sukup Manufacturing Co 1555 255th St PO Box 677	Sheffield	IA	50475	866-427-4422	641-892-4222	273
Sukut Construction Inc 4010 W Chandler Ave	Santa Ana	CA	92704	888-785-8801		188-4
Sul Ross State University E Hwy 90	Alpine	TX	79832	888-722-7778	432-837-8011	166
Sullivan County 245 Muncy St PO Box 157	Laporte	PA	18626	800-369-3599	570-946-5201	337
Sullivan County 100 N St	Monticello	NY	12701	800-320-2617	845-794-3000	337
Sullivan County Community College 112 College Rd	Loch Sheldrake	NY	12759	800-577-5243	845-434-5750	162
Sullivan County Rural Electric Co-op Inc (SCREC) 5675 Rt 87 PO Box 65	Forksville	PA	18616	800-570-5081	570-924-3381	245
Sullivan Curtis Monroe 1920 Main St	Irvine	CA	92614	800-427-3253	949-250-7172	389
Sullivan Tire Co Inc 41 Accord Park Dr	Norwell	MA	02061	877-855-4826	781-982-1550	62-5
Sullivan University 3101 BaRdstown Rd	Louisville	KY	40205	800-844-1354	502-456-6505	166
Sullivan-Palatek Inc 1201 W US Hwy 20	Michigan City	IN	46360	800-438-6203	219-874-2497	172
Sully-Miller Contracting Co Inc 135 S State Collage Blvd Ste 400	Brea	CA	92821	800-300-4240	714-578-9600	188-4
Sulphur Springs & Quitman 1040 Gilmer St	Sulphur Springs	TX	75482	866-435-1307		
Sultana Distribution Services Inc 600 Food Ctr Dr	Bronx	NY	10474	877-617-5500	718-617-5500	297-3
Sumitomo Corp of America 300 Madison Ave	New York	NY	10017	877-980-3283	212-207-0700	359-3
Sumitomo Machinery Corp of America 4200 Holland Blvd	Chesapeake	VA	23323	800-762-9256	757-485-3355	705
Summa Barberton Hospital 155 Fifth St NE	Barberton	OH	44203	888-905-6071	330-615-3000	373-3
Summer Infant Inc 1275 Park E Dr	Woonsocket	RI	02895	800-268-6237		782
Summit Account Resolution 12201 Champlin Dr	Champlin	MN	55316	888-822-7509	888-222-0793	392
Summit Aviation Inc 4200 Summit Bridge Rd	Middletown	DE	19709	800-441-9343	302-834-5400	24
Summit Bank 2969 Broadway	Oakland	CA	94611	800-380-9333	510-839-8800	70
Summit Behavioral Healthcare 1101 Summit Rd	Cincinnati	OH	45237	800-372-8862	513-948-3600	373-5
Summit Canyon Mountaineering 205 sixth St	Glenwood Springs	CO	81601	800-360-6994	970-945-6994	707
Summit Chemical Co 235 S Kresson St	Baltimore	MD	21224	800-227-8664	410-522-0661	280
Summit Christian College 2025 21st St	Gering	NE	69341	888-305-8083	308-632-6933	166
Summit Electric Supply Co 2900 Stanford NE	Albuquerque	NM	87107	800-824-4400	505-346-9000	246
Summit Food Service Distributors Inc 580 Industrial Rd	London	ON	N5V1V1	800-265-9267	519-453-3410	299
Summit Funding Group Inc 4680 Pkwy Dr Ste 300	Mason	OH	45040	866-489-1222	513-489-1222	264-1
Summit Golf Brands Inc 8 W 40th St 2nd Fl	New York	NY	10018	800-926-8010		441
Summit Holding Southeast Inc PO Box 600	Gainesville	GA	30503	800-971-2667	678-450-5825	359-4
Summit Hut 5045 E Speedway Blvd	Tucson	AZ	85712	800-499-8696	520-325-1554	707
Summit Lodge & Spa 4359 Main St	Whistler	BC	V0N1B4	888-913-8811	604-932-2778	378
Summit Medical Ctr 350 Hawthorne Ave	Oakland	CA	94609	800-478-8837	510-655-4000	373-3
Summit Motorsports Park 1300 Ohio 18	Norwalk	OH	44857	800-729-6455	800-230-3030	512
Summit Plastics Inc 107 S Laurel St	Summit	MS	39666	800-790-7117	601-276-7500	596
Summit Technical Services Inc 355 Centerville Rd	Warwick	RI	02886	800-643-7372	401-736-8323	627
Summit Trailer Sales Inc 1 Summit Plz	Summit Station	PA	17979	800-437-3729	570-754-3511	774
Summit Training Source 4170 Embassy Dr	Grand Rapids	MI	49546	800-447-3177		33
Summit, The 65 Steiner Ave	Akron	OH	44301	877-411-3662	330-761-3099	641-2
Summitt Trucking LLC 1800 Progress Way	Clarksville	IN	47129	866-999-7799	812-285-7777	775
Sumner School District 1202 Wood Ave	Sumner	WA	98390	866-548-3847	253-891-6000	681
Sumner-Cowley Electric Co-op Inc 2223 N A St PO Box 220	Wellington	KS	67152	888-326-3356	620-326-3356	245
Sumter Electric Membership Corp 1120 Felder St	Americus	GA	31709	800-342-6978	229-924-8041	245
Sun & Ski Sports 10560 Bissonnet St Ste 100	Houston	TX	77099	866-786-3869	281-340-5000	707
Sun Chemical Corp 35 Waterview Blvd	Parsippany	NJ	07054	800-543-2323	973-404-6000	387
Sun Chronicle PO Box 600	Attleboro	MA	02703	800-323-4673	508 222 7000	528-2
Sun Coast Resources Inc 6405 Cavalcade St Bldg 1	Houston	TX	77028	800-677-3835	713-844-9600	575
Sun Control Products Window Shades 1908 Second St SW	Rochester	MN	55902	800-533-0010	507-282-2620	87
Sun Country Airlines Inc 1300 Mendota Heights Rd	Mendota Heights	MN	55120	800-359-6786	651-681-3900	25
Sun Drilling Products Corp 503 Main St	Belle Chasse	LA	70037	800-962-6490	504-393-2778	537
Sun Ergoline Inc 1 Walter Kratz Dr	Jonesboro	AR	72401	888-771-0996		436
Sun Life Assurance Company of Canada 1 Sun Life Executive Pk PO Box 9106	Wellesley Hills	MA	02481	800-786-5433	781-237-6030	390-2

Name	Toll-Free	Phone	Class
Sun Life Financial Inc 150 King St W .... Toronto ON M5H1J9 *TSX: SLF*	877-786-5433	416-979-9966	359-4
Sun Magazine 8815 Conroy Windermere Rd Ste 130 .... Orlando FL 32835	888-218-9968	407-477-2815	455-11
Sun Mountain Lodge 604 Patterson Lake RD .... Winthrop WA 98862	800-572-0493	509-996-2211	665
Sun National Bank 350 Fellowship Rd Ste 101 .... Mount Laurel NJ 08054	800-786-9066		70
Sun News 914 Frontage Rd E .... Myrtle Beach SC 29578	800-568-1800	843-626-8555	528-2
Sun Orchard Inc 1198 W Fairmont Dr .... Tempe AZ 85282	800-505-8423		296-20
Sun Packaging Technologies Inc 2200 NW 32nd St Ste 1700 .... Pompano Beach FL 33069	800-866-0322	954-978-3080	357
Sun River Electric Co-op Inc 310 First Ave S PO Box 309 .... Fairfield MT 59436	800-452-7516	406-467-2527	245
Sun Valley Floral Farms Inc 3160 Upper Bay Rd .... Arcata CA 95521	800-747-0396		368
Sun Valley Resort 1 Sun Valley Rd .... Sun Valley ID 83353	800-786-8259	208-622-4111	665
Sun Valley/Ketchum Chamber & Visitors Bureau 491 Sun Valley Rd .... Ketchum ID 83340	800-634-3347	208-726-3423	139
Sun Viking Lodge 2411 S Atlantic Ave .... Daytona Beach Shores FL 32118	800-874-4469	386-252-6252	378
Sunbelt Marketing Investment Corp 3255 S Sweetwater Rd .... Lithia Springs GA 30122	800-257-5566	770-739-3740	608
Sunbelt Rentals Inc 2341 Deerfield Dr .... Fort Mill SC 29715 *General	800-667-9328*	704-348-2676	264-3
Sunbelt Transformer Ltd 1922 S Martin Luther King Jr Dr .... Temple TX 76504	800-433-3128	254-771-3777	249
Sunburst Shutters 6480 W Flamingo Rd Ste D .... Las Vegas NV 89103	877-786-2877	702-367-1600	695
Sunbury Motor Co 943 N Fourth St .... Sunbury PA 17801	866-440-7854	570-286-7746	513
Suncast Corp 701 N Kirk Rd .... Batavia IL 60510	800-444-3310	800-846-2345	319-2
Sunchaser Vacation Villas 5129 Riverview Gate Rd .... Fairmont Hot Springs BC V0B1L1 *Resv	877-451-1250*	250-345-4545	748
Suncoast Communities Blood Bank 1760 Mound St .... Sarasota FL 34236	866-972-5663	941-954-1600	89
Suncoast Hotel & Casino 9090 Alta Dr .... Las Vegas NV 89145	877-677-7111	702-636-7111	378
Suncoast Post-Tension LP 509 N Sam Houston Pkwy E Ste 400 .... Houston TX 77060	800-847-8886	281-668-1840	189-3
Suncor Energy Inc 150 - 6 Ave SW PO Box 2844 .... Calgary AB T2P3E3 *NYSE: SU*	800-558-9071	403-296-8000	532
Sundance Beach 7127 Hollister Ave Ste 25A-323 .... Goleta CA 93117	877-968-0036		707
Sundance Institute 1825 Three Kings Dr .... Park City UT 84060	888-285-7790	801-328-3456	511
Sundance Trail Guest Ranch 17931 Red Feather Lakes Rd .... Red Feather Lakes CO 80545	800-357-4930	970-224-1222	239
Sunday River Ski Resort 15 S Ridge Rd PO Box 4500 .... Newry ME 04261	800-543-2754	207-824-3500	665
Sundial Boutique Hotel 4340 Sundial Crescent .... Whistler BC V0N1B4	800-661-2321	604-932-2321	378
Sundowner Trailers Inc 9805 S State Hwy 48 .... Coleman OK 73432	800-654-3879	580-937-4255	758
Sundt Construction 2620 S 55th St .... Tempe AZ 85282	800-280-3000	480-293-3000	189-2
Sundt Construction Inc 2015 W River Rd Ste 101 .... Tucson AZ 85704	800-467-5544	520-750-4600	186
Sunflower Group 14001 Marshall Dr .... Lenexa KS 66215	800-288-5085		
SunGard Availability Services 680 E Swedesford Rd .... Wayne PA 19087	800-468-7483	484-582-2000	393
Sun-Journal PO Box 4400 .... Lewiston ME 04243	800-482-0759	207-784-5411	528-2
Sunland Group Inc 1033 La Posada Dr Ste 370 .... Austin TX 78752	866-732-8500	512-494-0208	261
Sunland Park Racetrack & Casino 1200 Futurity Dr .... Sunland Park NM 88063	800-572-1142	575-874-5200	638
Sunnen Products Co 7910 Manchester Ave .... Saint Louis MO 63143	800-325-3670	314-781-2100	453
Sunny 1079 Radio *Palm Beach Broadcasting* 701 Northpoint Pkwy Ste 500 .... West Palm Beach FL 33407	800-919-1079	561-616-4777	641-115
Sunny Land Tours Inc 21 Old Kings Rd N Ste B-212 .... Palm Coast FL 32137	800-783-7839	386-449-0059	755
Sunnyland Farms Inc PO Box 8200 .... Albany GA 31706	800-999-2488		457
Sunnyland Outdoor & Casual Furniture 7879 Spring Valley Rd Ste 125 .... Dallas TX 75254	877-239-3716	972-239-3716	321
Sunoco Inc 1735 Market St .... Philadelphia PA 19103 *NYSE: SUN*	800-786-6261		532
Sunovion Pharmaceuticals Inc 84 Waterford Dr .... Marlborough MA 01752	888-394-7377	508-481-6700	231
Sunquest Information Systems Inc 3300 E Sunrise Dr .... Tucson AZ 85718	877-239-6337	520-570-2000	
Sunrich LLC 3824 SW 93rd St PO Box 128 .... Hope MN 56046	800-297-5997	507-451-6030	80-1
Sunrider International 1625 Abalone Ave .... Torrance CA 90501 *Orders	888-278-6743*	310-781-3808	365
Sunrise Chamber of Commerce 6800 Sunset Strip .... Sunrise FL 33313	800-273-1614	954-835-2428	139
Sunrise Home Health Services 3200 Broadway Blvd Ste 260 .... Garland TX 75043	800-296-7823	972-278-1414	362
Sunrise Medical Inc 2842 Business Park Ave .... Fresno CA 93727	800-333-4000		475
Sunrise Medical Laboratories Inc 250 Miller Pl .... Hicksville NY 11801 *Cust Svc	800-782-0282*	631-435-1515	417
Sunrise Mfg Inc 2665 Mercantile Dr .... Rancho Cordova CA 95742	800-748-6529	916-635-6262	497
Sunrise Senior Living LLC 7902 Westpark Dr .... McLean VA 22102 *NYSE: SRZ*	888-434-4648	703-273-7500	449
Sunrise Specialty Co 930 98th Ave .... Oakland CA 94603	800-444-4280	510-729-7277	607
Sunriver Resort 17600 Center Dr .... Sunriver OR 97707	800-547-3922	855-420-8206	665
Sunset Beach Resort 3287 W Gulf Dr .... Sanibel Island FL 33957	866-565-5091	239-472-1700	665
Sunset Farm Foods Inc 1201 Madison Hwy .... Valdosta GA 31601	800-882-1121	229-242-3389	392
Sunset Inn Travel Apartments 1111 Burnaby St .... Vancouver BC V6E1P4	800-786-1997	604-688-2474	378
Sunset Marquis Hotel & Villas 1200 N Alta Loma Rd .... West Hollywood CA 90069	800-858-9758	310-657-1333	378
Sunset Printing 4522 Rosemead Blvd .... Pico Rivera CA 90660	800-427-8980		
Sunset Publishing Corp 80 Willow Rd .... Menlo Park CA 94025	800-777-0117	650-321-3600	633-9
Sunset Station Hotel & Casino 1301 W Sunset Rd .... Henderson NV 89014	888-786-7389	702-547-7777	378
Sunset Transportation Inc 11325 Concord Village Ave .... St Louis MO 63123	800-849-6540		311
Sunshine Artist Magazine 4075 LB McLeod Rd Ste E .... Orlando FL 32811	800-597-2573	800-331-0038	455-2
Sunshine Business Class 150 Kingswood Dr .... Mankato MN 56001	800-873-7681		130
Sunshine Makers Inc 15922 Pacific Coast Hwy .... Huntington Harbour CA 92649	800-228-0709	562-795-6000	151
Sunshine Mills Inc 500 Sixth St SW .... Red Bay AL 35582	800-633-3349	256-356-9541	574
Sunshine Minting Inc 7600 Mineral Dr Ste 700 .... Coeur d'Alene ID 83815	800-274-5837	208-772-9592	408
Sunstar Americas Inc 4635 W Foster Ave .... Chicago IL 60630	888-777-3101		228
Sunstate Federal Credit Union (Inc) PO Box 1162 .... Gainesville FL 32627	877-786-7828	352-381-5200	219
Sunstream Hotels & Resorts 6231 Estero Blvd .... Fort Myers Beach FL 33931	844-652-3696	239-765-4111	377
Sunsweet Growers Inc 901 N Walton Ave .... Yuba City CA 95993	800-417-2253	530-674-5010	296-18
Suntrust Bank PO Box 4418 .... Atlanta GA 30302 *NYSE: STI*	800-786-8787		70
SunTrust Banks Inc 303 Peachtree St NE .... Atlanta GA 30308 *NYSE: STI*	800-786-8787	404-588-7711	359-2
SunTrust Mortgage Inc 1001 Semmes Ave .... Richmond VA 23224	800-634-7928		507
SunTrust Robinson Humphrey Capital Markets 3333 Peachtree Rd NE .... Atlanta GA 30326	800-634-7928	404-926-5000	686
Sunwest Aviation Ltd 217 Aero Ct NE .... Calgary AB T2E7C6	888-291-4566	403-275-8121	23
Sunwest Silver Company Inc 324 Lomas Blvd NW .... Albuquerque NM 87102	800-771-3781	505-243-3781	292
SUNY (State University of New York Press) 22 Corporate Woods Blvd 3rd Fl .... Albany NY 12211	866-430-7869	518-472-5000	633-4
SUNY (State University of New York, The) State University Plz .... Albany NY 12246	800-342-3811	518-320-1888	781
Supelco Inc 595 N Harrison Rd .... Bellefonte PA 16823	800-247-6628	814-359-2147	418
Super Color Digital LLC 16761 Hale Ave .... Irvine CA 92606	800-979-4446		623
Super Glue Corp 3281 E Guasti Rd Ste 260 .... Ontario CA 91761	800-538-3091	909-987-0550	3
Super H Mart Inc 2550 Pleasant Hill Rd .... Duluth GA 30096	877-427-7386	678-543-4000	344
Super Holiday Tours 116 Gatlin Ave .... Orlando FL 32806	800-327-2116		755
Super Products LLC 17000 W Cleveland Ave .... New Berlin WI 53151	800-837-9711	262-784-7100	385
Super Shoe Stores Inc 601 Dual Hwy .... Hagerstown MD 21740	866-842-7510	301-739-2130	301
Super Sky Products Inc 10301 N Enterprise Dr .... Mequon WI 53092	800-558-0467	262-242-2000	234
Super Store Industries 16888 McKinley Ave PO Box 549 .... Lathrop CA 95330	888-292-8004	209-858-2010	297-8
Superb Internet Corp 999 Bishop St Ste 1850 .... Honolulu HI 96813	888-354-6128	808-544-0387	803
Superbag Corp 9291 Baythrone Dr .... Houston TX 77041	888-842-1177	713-462-1173	66
Superchips Inc 1790 E Airport Blvd .... Sanford FL 32773	888-227-2447	407-585-7000	173-2
Supercuts 7201 Metro Blvd .... Minneapolis MN 55439	877-857-2070		77
SuperFlow Technologies Group 4747 Centennial Blvd .... Colorado Springs CO 80919	800-471-7701	719-471-1746	470
SuperGlass Windshield Repair Inc 6220 Hazeltine National Dr Ste 118 .... Orlando FL 32822	866-557-7497	407-240-1920	62-2
Superheat Fgh Services Inc 313 Garnet St .... New Lenox IL 60451	888-508-3226		224
Superior Air Parts Inc 621 S Royal Ln Ste 100 .... Coppell TX 75019	800-420-4727		525
Superior Aluminum Products Inc 555 E Main St PO Box 430 .... Russia OH 45363	800-548-8656	937-526-4065	489
Superior Auto Sales Inc 5201 Camp Rd .... Hamburg NY 14075	866-439-9637	716-649-6695	513
Superior Boiler Works Inc 3524 E Fourth St .... Hutchinson KS 67501	800-444-6693	620-662-6693	91

	Toll-Free	Phone	Class
Superior Carriers Inc			
711 Jory Blvd Ste 101-N ....Oak Brook IL 60523	800-654-7707	630-573-2555	775
Superior Clay Corp			
6566 Superior Rd SE ....Uhrichsville OH 44683	800-848-6166	740-922-4122	150
Superior Dairy Inc			
4719 Navarre Rd SW ....Canton OH 44706	800-597-5460	330-477-4515	296-27
Superior Die Set Corp			
900 West Drexel Ave ....Oak Creek WI 53154	800-558-6040	414-764-4900	752
Superior Die Tool & Machine Co			
2301 Fairwood Ave ....Columbus OH 43207	800-292-2181	614-444-2181	752
Superior Environmental Corp			
1128 Franklin Ct ....Marne MI 49435	877-667-4142		193
Superior Essex Communications LP			
6120 Powers Ferry Rd Ste 150 ....Atlanta GA 30339	800-551-8948	770-657-6000	730
Superior Essex Inc			
6120 Powers Ferry Rd ....Atlanta GA 30339	800-551-8948	770-657-6000	808
Superior Freight Services Inc			
1230 Trapp Rd ....Saint Paul MN 55121	800-298-4305	952-854-5053	311
Superior Gearbox Co			
803 W Hwy 32 ....Stockton MO 65785	800-346-5745	417-276-5191	705
Superior Graphite			
10 S Riverside Plz Ste 1470 ....Chicago IL 60606	800-325-0337*	312-559-2999	127
*Cust Svc			
Superior Group Inc			
250 International Dr ....Williamsville NY 14221	800-568-8310		359-3
superior group of companies(SGC)			
10055Seminole Blvd ....Seminole FL 33772	800-727-8643*	727-397-9611	155-18
NASDAQ: SGC ▪ *Cust Svc			
Superior Industries LLC			
315 E State Hwy 28 PO Box 684 ....Morris MN 56267	800-321-1558	320-589-2406	207
Superior Metal Technologies LLC			
9850 E 30th St ....Indianapolis IN 46229	800-654-9850	317-897-9850	295
Superior Mfg Group			
5655 W 73rd St ....Chicago IL 60638	800-621-2802	708-458-4600	291
Superior Motors Inc			
282 John C Calhoun Dr ....Orangeburg SC 29115	877-375-4759		513
Superior Nut Co Inc			
225 Monsignor O'Brien Hwy ....Cambridge MA 02141	800-295-4093	617-876-3808	296-28
Superior Oil Co Inc			
1402 N Capitol Ave Ste 100 ....Indianapolis IN 46202	800-553-5480	317-781-4400	599
Superior Packaging Solutions			
26858 Almond Ave ....Redlands CA 92374	844-792-2626		557
Superior Plus Energy Services Inc			
1870 S Winton Rd Ste 200 ....Rochester NY 14618	855-804-3835		
Superior Plus Income Fund			
1400 840-7 Ave SW ....Calgary AB T2P3G2	866-490-7587	403-218-2951	404
Superior Press Inc			
9440 Norwalk Blvd ....Santa Fe Springs CA 90670	888-590-7998*		86
*Cust Svc			
Superior Products Inc			
3786 Ridge Rd ....Cleveland OH 44144	800-651-9490	216-651-9400	617
Superior Shores Resort			
1521 Superior Shores Dr ....Two Harbors MN 55616	800-242-1988	218-834-5671	665
Superior Software Inc			
16055 Ventura Blvd Ste 650 ....Encino CA 91436	800-421-3264	818-990-1135	178-1
Superior Tank Company Inc			
9500 Lucas Ranch Rd ....Rancho Cucamonga CA 91730	800-221-8265		765
Superior Technical Resources Inc			
250 International Dr ....Williamsville NY 14221	800-568-8310	716-929-1400	717
Superior Tire & Rubber Corp			
1818 Pennsylvania Ave W PO Box 308 ....Warren PA 16365	800-289-1456*	814-723-2370	749
*Cust Svc			
Superior Tool Co			
100 Hayes Dr Unit C ....Cleveland OH 44131	800-533-3244*	216-398-8600	753
*Cust Svc			
Superior Trailer Sales Co			
501 Hwy 80 ....Sunnyvale TX 75182	800-637-0324	972-226-3893	513
Superior Vision			
939 Elkridge Landing Rd Ste 200 ....Linthicum MD 21090	800-243-1401	410-752-0121	
Superior Water Light & Power			
2915 Hill Ave PO Box 519 ....Superior WI 54880	800-227-7957	715-394-2200	782
Superior/Douglas County Convention & Visitors Bureau			
305 Harborview Pkwy ....Superior WI 54880	800-942-5313	715-392-7151	206
Superior-Douglas County Chamber of Commerce			
205 Belknap St ....Superior WI 54880	800-942-5313	715-394-7716	139
Superlite Block Co Inc			
4150 W Turney Ave ....Phoenix AZ 85019	800-366-7877	602-352-3500	183
Supermarket Systems Inc			
6419 Bannington Rd ....Charlotte NC 28226	800-553-1905	704-542-6000	661
Supermercado Mi Tierra LLC			
9520 International Blvd ....Oakland CA 94603	800-225-9902	510-567-8617	344
SuperShuttle International Inc			
14500 N Northsight Blvd Ste 329 ....Scottsdale AZ 85260	800-258-3826	480-609-3000	440
SuperTalk 997 WTN			
10 Music Cir E ....Nashville TN 37203	800-618-7445	615-321-1067	641-69
SUPERVALU Inc			
11840 Valley View Rd ....Eden Prairie MN 55344	877-322-8228*	952-828-4000	297-8
NYSE: SVU ▪ *Cust Svc			
Superwinch Inc			
359 Lake Rd ....Dayville CT 06241	800-323-2031		190
Supply Technologies LLC			
6065 Parkland Blvd ....Cleveland OH 44124	800-695-8650	440-947-2100	350
Support Services of America Inc			
12440 Firestone Blvd Ste 312 ....Norwalk CA 90650	888-564-0005	562-868-3550	152
Support Systems Associates Inc (SSAI)			
Marina Towers 709 S Harbor City Blvd Ste 350 ....Melbourne FL 32901	877-234-7724		
Supportcom Inc			
1200 Crossman Ave Ste 210-240 ....Sunnyvale CA 94089	877-493-2778	650-556-9440	178-7
NASDAQ: SPRT			
Supreme Corp			
325 Spence Rd ....Conover NC 28613	888-604-6975	828-322-6975	740-9
Supreme Corp			
2581 E Kercher Rd ....Goshen IN 46528	800-642-4889*		513
*All			
Supreme Oil Co			
2109 W Monte Vista Rd ....Phoenix AZ 85009	800-752-7888		535
Supreme Petroleum Inc			
1200 Progress Rd PO Box 1246 ....Smithfield VA 23434	800-924-5823	757-934-0550	
Suquamish Clearwater Casino Resort			
15347 Suquamish Way NE ....Suquamish WA 98392	800-375-6073	360-598-8700	450
Sur La Table			
PO Box 840 ....Brownsburg IN 46112	800-243-0852		361
Surdna Foundation			
330 Madison Ave 25th Fl ....New York NY 10016	800-421-9512	212-557-0010	305
Sure Winner Foods Inc			
2 Lehner Rd ....Saco ME 04072	800-640-6447	207-282-1258	297-4
Surefire LLC			
18300 Mt Baldy Cir ....Fountain Valley CA 92708	800-828-8809		74
Surefit Inc			
8000 Quarry Rd Ste C ....Alburtis PA 18011	888-796-0500		741
SurePayroll			
2350 Ravine Way Ste 100 ....Glenview IL 60025	877-954-7873	847-676-8420	566
Surety Group Inc			
12890 Lebanon Rd ....Mt. Juliet TN 37122	800-486-8211	844-432-6637	390-5
Surety LLC			
12020 Sunrise Vly Dr Ste 250 ....Reston VA 20191	800-298-3115	703-476-6030	178-7
Surf & Sand Resort			
1555 S Coast Hwy ....Laguna Beach CA 92651	877-741-5908	888-579-8544	378
Surf & Sand Resort			
1555 S Coast Hwy ....Laguna Beach CA 92651	877-741-5908	877-751-5493	703
Surf Assoc East Inc			
1701 N Federal Hwy ....Fort Lauderdale FL 33305	800-528-9061	954-564-0202	
Surf Line Hawaii Ltd			
411 Puuhale Rd ....Honolulu HI 96819	800-847-5267	808-847-5985	155-3
Surface Combustion Inc			
1700 Indian Wood Cir ....Maumee OH 43537	800-537-8980	419-891-7150	318
Surfsand Resort			
148 W Gower Rd ....Cannon Beach OR 97110	800-547-6100	503-436-2274	378
Surge Resources			
920 Candia Rd ....Manchester NH 03109	800-787-4387	603-623-0007	461
Surgical Staff Inc			
120 St Matthews Ave ....San Mateo CA 94401	800-339-9599	650-558-3999	717
Surprise Valley Electrification Corp (SVEC)			
516 US Hwy 395 E ....Alturas CA 96101	866-843-2667	530-233-3511	245
Surrex Solutions Corp			
300 N Sepulveda Blvd Ste 1020 ....El Segundo CA 90245	866-308-2628	310-640-3000	196
Surrey Board of Trade			
14439 104th Ave Ste 101 ....Surrey BC V3R1M1	866-848-7130	604-581-7130	137
Surrey Honda			
15291 Fraser Hwy ....Surrey BC V3R3P3	888-549-3080		
Surry-Yadkin Electric Membership Corp			
510 S Main St ....Dobson NC 27017	800-682-5903	336-356-8241	245
Surveillance Specialties Ltd			
600 Research Dr ....Wilmington MA 01887	800-354-2616		41
Survey & Ballot Systems Inc			
7653 Anagram Dr ....Eden Prairie MN 55344	800-974-8099	952-974-2300	177
Survey Service Inc			
1911 Sheridan Dr ....Buffalo NY 14223	800-507-7969	716-876-6450	464
Survival Strategies Inc			
335 N Third St ....Burbank CA 91502	800-834-0357	818-276-1000	196
Survival Systems Training Ltd			
40 Mt Hope Ave ....Dartmouth NS B2Y4K9	800-788-3888	902-465-3888	447
Survivors Network of Those Abused by Priests (SNAP)			
PO Box 6416 ....Chicago IL 60680	877-762-7432	312-455-1499	48-21
Survivors of Incest Anonymous (SIA)			
PO Box 190 ....Benson MD 21018	877-742-9761		
Susan G Komen for the Cure			
5005 LBJ Fwy Ste 250 ....Dallas TX 75244	877-465-6636		48-17
Susan Schein Automotive			
3171 Pelham Pkwy ....Pelham AL 35124	800-845-1578	205-664-1491	57
SUSLA (Southern University Museum of Art)			
3050 Martin Luther King Jr Dr ....Shreveport LA 71107	800-458-1472	318-670-6000	517
Susquehanna County			
75 Public Ave ....Montrose PA 18801	800-932-0313	570-278-4600	337
Susquehanna University			
514 University Ave ....Selinsgrove PA 17870	800-326-9672	570-374-0101	166
Sussex County Chamber of Commerce			
120 Hampton House Rd ....Newton NJ 07860	844-256-7328	973-579-1811	139
Sussex County Community College			
1 College Hill Rd ....Newton NJ 07860	800-848-4555	973-300-2100	162
Sussex Rural Electric Co-op			
64 County Rt 639 PO Box 346 ....Sussex NJ 07461	877-504-6463	973-875-5101	245
Sussman Automatic Corp			
43-20 34th St ....Long Island NY 11101	800-727-8326	718-937-4500	91
Suter Company Inc			
258 May St ....Sycamore IL 60178	800-435-6942	815-895-9186	296-36
Sutherland Lumber Co			
4000 Main St ....Kansas City MO 64111	800-821-2252	816-756-3000	363
Sutphen Corp PO Box 158 ....Amlin OH 43002	800-726-7030	614-889-1005	513
Sutter Auburn Faith Community Hospital (SAFH)			
11815 Education St ....Auburn CA 95602	800-478-8837	530-888-4500	373-3
Sutter County			
433 Second St ....Yuba City CA 95991	800-371-3177	530-822-7134	337
Sutter General Hospital			
2801 L St ....Sacramento CA 95816	800-478-8837	916-454-2222	373-3
Sutter Health			
2200 River Plz ....Sacramento CA 95833	888-888-6044	916-733-8800	352
Sutter Medical Ctr of Santa Rosa			
3325 Chanate Rd ....Santa Rosa CA 95404	800-651-5111	707-576-4006	373-3
Sutter Memorial Hospital			
5151 F St ....Sacramento CA 95819	800-478-8837	916-454-3333	373-3
Sutter Solano Medical Ctr (SSMC)			
300 Hospital Dr ....Vallejo CA 94589	800-866-7724	707-554-4444	373-3
Suttle			
1001 East Hwy 212 ....Hector MN 55342	800-852-8662	320-848-6711	730
Sutton Alliance LLC			
515 Rockaway Ave ....Valley Stream NY 11581	866-435-6600	516-837-6100	648
Suzuki Association of The Americas Inc			
1900 Folsom St Ste 101 ....Boulder CO 80302	888-378-9854	303-444-0948	138

					Toll-Free	Phone	Class

Suzuki Musical Instrument Corp
PO Box 710459 . . . . Santee CA 92072 **800-854-1594*** 619-258-1896 523
*Cust Svc

SVA
1221 John Q Hammons Dr . . . . Madison WI 53717 **800-279-2616** 608-831-8181 2

Svam International Inc
233 E Shore Rd Ste 201 . . . . Great Neck NY 11023 **800-903-6716** 180

SVB (Silicon Valley Bank)
3003 Tasman Dr . . . . Santa Clara CA 95054 **800-579-1639** 408-654-7400 70

SVC (Society of Vacuum Coaters)
71 Pinon Hill Pl NE . . . . Albuquerque NM 87122 **800-443-8817** 505-856-7188 49-13

SVEC (Surprise Valley Electrification Corp)
516 US Hwy 395 E . . . . Alturas CA 96101 **866-843-2667** 530-233-3511 245

Svi Inc
440 Mark Leany Dr . . . . Henderson NV 89011 **800-784-8726**

SVIA (Specialty Vehicle Institute of America)
2 Jenner St Ste 150 . . . . Irvine CA 92618 **800-887-2887** 949-727-3727 49-21

SVMIC (State Volunteer Mutual Insurance Co)
101 W Pk Dr Ste 300 . . . . Brentwood TN 37027 **800-342-2239** 615-377-1999 390-5

SVS (Society for Vascular Surgery)
633 N St Clair St 22nd Fl . . . . Chicago IL 60611 **800-258-7188** 312-334-2300 49-8

SVS Vision
140 Macomb Pl . . . . Mount Clemens MI 48043 **800-787-4600** 586-468-7612 539

SVT 7699 Lochlin Dr . . . . Brighton MI 48116 **888-697-8832** 800-521-4188

SW Steakhouse
3131 Las Vegas Blvd S . . . . Las Vegas NV 89109 **888-320-7123** 702-770-7000 667

Swag, The
2300 Swag Rd . . . . Waynesville NC 28785 **800-789-7672** 828-926-0430 378

Swan 200 Swan Ave . . . . Centralia IL 62801 **800-325-7008** 608

Swan & Sons-Morss Company Inc
309 E Water St PO Box 179 . . . . Elmira NY 14901 **877-407-1657** 607-734-6283 389

Swan Lake Resort & Campground
17463 County Hwy 29 . . . . Fergus Falls MN 56537 **800-697-4626** 218-736-4626 121

Swan Products LLC
1201 Delaware Ave . . . . Marion OH 43302 **800-800-4673** 369

SWANA (Solid Waste Assn of North America)
1100 Wayne Ave Ste 700 . . . . Silver Spring MD 20910 **800-467-9262** 301-585-2898 527-5

Swank Motion Pictures Inc
10795 Watson Rd . . . . St Louis MO 63127 **888-389-3622** 314-984-6000 511

Swans Candles
16524 Tilley Rd S . . . . Tenino WA 98589 **888-848-7926** 122

Swanson Group Inc
2695 Glendale Valley Rd
PO Box 250 . . . . Glendale OR 97442 **800-331-0831** 541-832-1121 446

Swanson Health Products Inc
PO Box 2803 . . . . Fargo ND 58108 **800-824-4491** 701-356-2700 794

Swany America Corp
115 Corp Dr . . . . Johnstown NY 12095 **888-234-5450** 518-725-3333 155-7

Swarco Industries Inc
PO Box 89 . . . . Columbia TN 38402 **800-216-8781** 931-388-5900 672

Swarovski North America Ltd
1 Kenney Dr . . . . Cranston RI 02920 **800-289-4900** 401-463-6400 333

Swarthmore College
500 College Ave . . . . Swarthmore PA 19081 **800-667-3110*** 610-328-8300 166
*Admissions

Swarthout Coaches Inc
115 Graham Rd . . . . Ithaca NY 14850 **800-772-7267** 607-257-2277 107

Swartz Kitchens & Baths
5550 Allentown Blvd (Rt 22) . . . . Harrisburg PA 17112 **800-652-0111** 717-652-7111 321

SWCA Inc
3033 N Central Ave Ste 145 . . . . Phoenix AZ 85012 **800-828-8517** 602-274-3831 192

SWCE (Steele-Waseca Co-op Electric)
2411 W Bridge St PO Box 485 . . . . Owatonna MN 55060 **800-526-3514** 507-451-7340 245

SWCS (Soil & Water Conservation Society)
945 SW Ankeny Rd . . . . Ankeny IA 50023 **800-843-7645** 515-289-2331 48-13

SWE (Society of Women Engineers)
130 E Randolph St Ste 3500 . . . . Chicago IL 60601 **877-793-4636** 312-596-5223 49-19

Swearingen Software Inc
PO Box 23018 . . . . Beaumont TX 77720 **800-992-1767** 180

Swedish Medical Ctr
501 E Hampden Ave . . . . Englewood CO 80113 **866-779-3347** 303-788-5000 373-3

Swedish-American Chamber of Commerce Inc New York Chapter
570 Lexington Ave 20th Fl . . . . New York NY 10022 **800-862-2793** 212-838-5530 138

SwedishAmerican Hospital
1401 E State St . . . . Rockford IL 61104 **800-322-4724** 779-696-4400 373-3

Sweed Machinery Inc
653 Second Ave PO Box 228 . . . . Gold Hill OR 97525 **800-888-1352*** 541-855-1512 492
*Sales

Sweeney Buick
7997 Market St . . . . Youngstown OH 44512 **866-560-9470** 513

Sweeney Law Firm
8109 Lima Rd . . . . Fort Wayne IN 46818 **866-793-6339** 260-420-3137 427

Sweepster Inc
2800 N Zeeb Rd . . . . Dexter MI 48130 **800-456-7100** 103

Sweet Adelines International
9110 S Toledo Ave . . . . Tulsa OK 74137 **800-992-7464** 918-622-1444 48-18

Sweet Briar College
134 Chappel Rd . . . . Sweet Briar VA 24595 **800-381-6142*** 434-381-6100 166
*Admissions

Sweet Candy Co Inc
3780 W Directors Row . . . . Salt Lake City UT 84104 **800-669-8669** 801-886-1444 296-8

Sweet Mfg Company Inc
2000 E Leffel Ln . . . . Springfield OH 45505 **800-334-7254*** 937-325-1511 207
*Cust Svc

Sweetlake Chemical Ltd
446 Heights Blvd . . . . Houston TX 77007 **888-752-1998** 713-827-8707

Sweetwater Sound Inc
5501 US Hwy 30 W . . . . Fort Wayne IN 46818 **800-222-4700** 260-432-8176 522

Sweetwater Valley Oil Company Inc
1236 New Hwy 68 . . . . Sweetwater TN 37874 **800-362-4519** 423-337-6671 577

Swenson Spreader Co
127 Walnut St . . . . Lindenwood IL 61049 **888-825-7323** 815-393-4455 190

SWH (Senior Whole Health LLC)
58 Charles St . . . . Cambridge MA 02141 **888-794-7268** 617-494-5353 352

SWH Supply Co
242 E Main St . . . . Louisville KY 40202 **800-321-3598** 502-589-9287 661

Swibco Inc
4810 Venture Rd . . . . Lisle IL 60532 **877-794-2261** 630-968-8900 757

Swift Aviation
Sky Harbor International Airport 2710 E Old Tower
. . . . Phoenix AZ 85034 **866-704-9274** 602-273-3770 63

Swift Communications Inc
580 Mallory Way . . . . Carson City NV 89701 **800-551-5691** 775-283-5500 528-3

Swift Glass Company Inc
131 W 22nd St . . . . Elmira Heights NY 14903 **800-537-9438** 607-733-7166 331

Swift Print Communication
1248 Research Blvd . . . . Saint Louis MO 63132 **800-545-1141** 314-991-4300 623

Swift Transportation Company Inc
2200 S 75th Ave . . . . Phoenix AZ 85043 **800-800-2200** 602-269-9700 775
NYSE: SWFT

Swiger Coils Systems Inc
4677 Mfg Rd . . . . Cleveland OH 44135 **800-321-3310** 216-362-7500 515

Swintec Corp
320 W Commercial Ave . . . . Moonachie NJ 07074 **800-225-0867** 201-935-0115 111

Swire Coca-Cola USA
12634 S 265 W . . . . Draper UT 84020 **800-497-2653** 801-816-5300 81-2

Swisher Electric Co-op Inc
401 SW Second St PO Box 67 . . . . Tulia TX 79088 **800-530-4344** 806-995-3567 245

Swisher Mower & Machine Company Inc
1602 Corporate Dr . . . . Warrensburg MO 64093 **800-222-8183** 660-747-8183 428

Swiss Knife Shop
10 Northern Blvd Ste 8 . . . . Amherst NH 03031 **866-438-7947** 603-732-0069 195

Swiss Precision Instruments Inc
11450 Markon Dr . . . . Garden Grove CA 92841 **888-774-8200** 714-799-1555 385

Swisslog
10825 E 47th Ave . . . . Denver CO 80239 **800-525-1841** 303-371-7770 207

Switzerland Tourism
608 Fifth Ave Ste 202 . . . . New York NY 10020 **800-794-7795** 212-757-5944 770

SWTC (Southwest Wisconsin Technical College)
1800 Bronson Blvd . . . . Fennimore WI 53809 **800-362-3322** 608-822-3262 795

Sycuan Casino & Resort
5469 Casino Way . . . . El Cajon CA 92019 **800-279-2826*** 619-445-6002 133
*General

Sydneys Closet
11840 Dorsett Rd . . . . Maryland Heights MO 63043 **888-479-3639** 314-344-5066 157-6

Sydnor Hydro Inc
2111 Magnolia St . . . . Richmond VA 23223 **844-339-6334** 804-643-2725 801

Syfan USA Corp
1622 Twin Bridges Rd . . . . Everetts NC 27825 **888-597-9326** 597

SYGMA Network Inc
5550 Blazer Pkwy Ste 300 . . . . Dublin OH 43017 **877-441-1144** 297-8

Sykes Enterprises Inc
400 N Ashley Dr . . . . Tampa FL 33602 **800-867-9537** 180
NASDAQ: SYKE

Sylvan Inc
90 Glade Dr . . . . Kittanning PA 16201 **866-352-7520** 724-543-3900 10-6

Sylvan Learning Centers
4 N Park Dr Ste 500 . . . . Hunt Valley MD 21030 **888-338-2283** 800-627-4276 242

Sylvania Steel Corp
4169 Holland Sylvania Rd . . . . Toledo OH 43623 **800-435-0986*** 419-885-3838 490
*General

Symantec Corp
350 Ellis St . . . . Mountain View CA 94043 **800-441-7234** 650-527-8000 178-12
NASDAQ: SYMC

Symbolist
1090 Texan Trl . . . . Grapevine TX 76051 **800-498-6885** 195

Symco Group
5012 Bristol Industrial Way . . . . Buford GA 30518 **800-878-8002** 770-451-8002 174

Symetra Life Insurance Co
777 108th Ave NE Ste 1200 . . . . Bellevue WA 98004 **800-574-0233** 425-256-8000 390-2

Symmetricom Inc
2300 Orchard Pkwy . . . . San Jose CA 95131 **888-367-7966** 408-433-0910 730
NASDAQ: MCHP

Symmons Industries Inc
31 Brooks Dr . . . . Braintree MA 02184 **800-796-6667** 605

Symons Capital Management Inc
650 Washington Rd Ste 800 . . . . Pittsburgh PA 15228 **888-344-7740** 412-344-7690 237

Symphony Ctr
220 S Michigan Ave . . . . Chicago IL 60604 **800-223-7114*** 312-294-3000 568
*Cust Svc

Symphony Nova Scotia
6101 University Ave
Dalhousie Arts Ctr . . . . Halifax NS B3H4R2 **800-874-1669** 902-494-3820 569-3

Symphony Silicon Valley
345 S First St . . . . San Jose CA 95113 **800-736-7401** 408-286-2600

Symposia Medicus
399 Taylor Blvd Ste 201 . . . . Pleasant Hill CA 94523 **800-327-3161** 925-969-1789 242

Synagro Technologies Inc
435 Williams Ct Ste 100 . . . . Baltimore MD 21220 **800-370-0035** 799

Synaptec Software Inc
4155 E Jewell Ave Ste 600 . . . . Denver CO 80222 **800-569-3377** 303-320-4420 35

Synchronoss Technologies Inc
200 Crossing Blvd . . . . Bridgewater NJ 08807 **866-620-3940** 224
OTC: SNCR

Syncsort Inc
50 Tice Blvd . . . . Woodcliff Lake NJ 07677 **877-700-0970** 178-12

Syndesi Solutions
115 West Market St . . . . Athens AL 35611 **877-744-0568**

Syndicate Sales Inc
PO Box 756 . . . . Kokomo IN 46903 **800-428-0515** 765-457-7277 604

Syndication Networks Corp
8700 Waukegan Rd Ste 250 . . . . . . Morton Grove IL 60053 **800-743-1988** 847-583-9000 642

Synemed Inc
4562 E Second St Ste A . . . . Benicia CA 94510 **800-777-0650** 707-745-8386 474

Synergent
2 Ledgeview Dr . . . . Westbrook ME 04092 **800-341-0180** 207-773-5671 317

Synergex International Corp
2330 Gold Meadow Way . . . . Gold River CA 95670 **800-366-3472** 916-635-7300 178-10

Synergon Solutions Inc
1335 Gateway Dr . . . . Melbourne FL 32901 **800-820-6103** 321-728-2674 225

Synergy Associates LLC
550 Clydesdale Trl . . . . Medina MN 55340 **888-763-9920** 180

Synergy Co of Utah LLC, The
2279 S Resource Blvd . . . . Moab UT 84532 **800-723-0277** 664

Synergy Direct Response
130 E Alton Ave . . . . Santa Ana CA 92707 **888-902-6166** 195

	Toll-Free	Phone	Class
Synergy Resources Inc 3500 Sunrise Hwy Bldg 100 Ste 201 ....Great River NY 11739	**866-896-6347**	631-665-2050	174
Synerion North America Inc 7420 Airport Rd Ste 101 ...... Mississauga ON L4T4E5	**877-816-8463**		177
Synexus 11500 Northlake Dr Ste 320 .... Cincinnati OH 45249	**855-427-8839**	513-247-5500	664
SYNEXXUS Inc 2425 Wilson Blvd Ste 400 .... Arlington VA 22201	**866-707-4594**		261
SYNNEX Canada 200 Ronson Dr ....Etobicoke ON M9W5Z9	**800-268-1220**	416-240-7012	174
Synnex Corp 44201 Nobel Dr ....Fremont CA 94538 *NYSE: SNX ■ *Cust Svc*	**800-756-1888***	510-656-3333	174
Synopsys Inc 700 E Middlefield Rd ....Mountain View CA 94043 *NASDAQ: SNPS*	**800-541-7737**	500-501-1000	178-10
Synovis Life Technologies Inc 2575 University Ave W .... Saint Paul MN 55114 *NASDAQ: SYNO*	**800-255-4018**	651-796-7300	475
Synovis Micro Companies Alliance Inc 439 Industrial Ln ....Birmingham AL 35211	**800-510-3318**	205-941-0111	473
Synovus Financial Corp 1111 Bay Ave Ste 400 .... Columbus GA 31901 *NYSE: SNV*	**888-796-6887**	706-649-2311	359-2
Syntec LLC 438 Lavender Dr ....Rome GA 30165	**800-526-8428**		131
Syntelli Solutions Inc 13925 Ballantyne Corporate Pl Ste 260 ....Charlotte NC 28277	**877-796-8355**		174
Syntrio 500 Lake Cook Rd Ste 350 .... Deerfield IL 60015	**888-289-6670**	415-951-7913	39
Synutra Ingredients 2275 Research Blvd Ste 500 .... Rockville MD 20850	**866-405-2350**	301-840-3888	794
Synventive Molding Solutions Inc 10 Centennial Dr .... Peabody MA 01960	**800-367-5662**	978-750-8065	385
Sypris Electronics LLC 10421 University Center Dr .... Tampa FL 33612	**800-937-9220**	813-972-6000	253
Sypris Solutions Inc 101 Bullitt Ln Ste 450 ....Louisville KY 40222 *NASDAQ: SYPR*	**800-508-9119**	502-329-2000	253
Syracuse Research Corp (SRC) 7502 Round Pond Rd .... North Syracuse NY 13212	**800-724-0451**	315-452-8000	664
Syracuse Scenery & Stage Lighting Company Inc 101 Monarch Dr ....Liverpool NY 13088	**800-453-7775**	315-453-8096	718
Syracuse Stamping Co 1054 S Clinton St .... Syracuse NY 13202	**800-581-5555**	315-476-5306	487
Syracuse University 900 S Crouse Ave .... Syracuse NY 13244	**800-782-5867**	315-443-3611	166
Sysazzle Inc 15815 S 46th St Ste 116. .... Phoenix AZ 85048	**800-862-9545**		717
Sysco Central Ohio Inc 2400 Harrison Rd .... Columbus OH 43204	**800-735-3341**	614-771-3801	297-8
Sysco Corp 5710 Pan Am Ave ....Boise ID 83716	**800-747-9726**	208-345-9500	297-8
Sysco Grand Rapids 3700 Sysco Ct SE ....Grand Rapids MI 49512	**800-669-6967**	616-949-3700	297-8
Syscon Inc 94 McFarland Blvd ....Northport AL 35476	**888-797-2661**	205-758-2000	180
Sysmex America Inc 577 Aptakisic Rd ....Lincolnshire IL 60069	**800-379-7639**	800-462-1262	473
SYSPRO 959 S Coast Dr Ste 100 .... Costa Mesa CA 92626	**800-369-8649**	714-437-1000	178-1
Systec Conveyor Corp 10010 Conveyor Dr ....Indianapolis IN 46235	**800-578-1755**		
Systech Corp 16510 Via Esprillo .... San Diego CA 92127	**800-800-8970**	858-674-6500	176
Systel Business Equipment Company Inc 2604 Fort Bragg Rd ....Fayetteville NC 28303	**800-849-5900**	910-321-7700	112
System Automation Corp 7110 Samuel Morse Dr .... Columbia MD 21046	**800-839-4729**	301-837-8000	178-10
System Concepts Inc 15900 N 78th St .... Scottsdale AZ 85260	**800-553-2438**	480-951-8011	177
System Engineering International Inc (SEI) 5115 Pegasus Ct Ste Q. .... Frederick MD 21704	**800-765-4734**	301-694-9601	782
System Innovators Inc 10550 Deerwood Pk Blvd Ste 700 ....Jacksonville FL 32256	**800-963-5000**		178-10
System Sensor 3825 Ohio Ave ....Saint Charles IL 60174 *Tech Supp*	**800-736-7672***	630-377-6580	253
Systematics Inc 1025 Saunders Ln .... West Chester PA 19380	**800-222-9353**		806
Systemax Inc 11 Harbor Pk Dr ... Port Washington NY 11050 *NYSE: SYX*	**800-344-6783**	516-608-7000	173-2
Systems & Processes Engineering Corp (SPEC) 4120 Commercial Ctr Dr Ste 500 .... Austin TX 78744	**800-789-7732**	512-479-7732	
Systems Engineering Technologies Corp 6121 Lincolnia Rd Ste 200 .... Alexandria VA 22312	**800-385-8977**	703-941-7887	177
Systems House, The 1033 Rte 46 E Ste A202 .... Clifton NJ 07013	**800-637-5556**	973-777-8050	225
Systems Plus Computers Inc 12 Centerra Pkwy Ste 20. .... Lebanon NH 03766	**800-388-8486**	603-643-5800	196
Systemtec Inc 246 Stoneridge Dr Ste 301 ....Columbia SC 29210	**888-900-1655**	803-806-8100	177
Systron Donner Inertial 355 Lennon Ln .... Walnut Creek CA 94598	**866-234-4976**	925-979-4400	525
Syvantis Technologies LLC 13822 Bluestem Ct .... Baxter MN 56425	**800-450-8908**		196
Szarka Financial Management 29691 Lorain Rd .... North Olmsted OH 44070	**800-859-8095**	440-779-1430	461

T

	Toll-Free	Phone	Class
T & A Supply Company Inc 6821 S 216th St Bldg A PO Box 927 .... Kent WA 98032	**800-562-2857**	253-872-3682	360
T & C Industries Inc *Royal Basket Trucks Inc* 201 Badger Pkwy .... Darien WI 53114	**800-426-6447**	262-882-1227	693
T & E Industries Inc 215 Watchung Ave ....Orange NJ 07050 *Sales*	**800-245-7080***	973-672-5454	326
T & R Electric Supply Company Inc 308 SW Third St .... Colman SD 57017	**800-843-7994**	605-534-3555	762
T & S Brass & Bronze Works Inc PO Box 1088 .... Travelers Rest SC 29690 *Cust Svc*	**800-476-4103***	864-834-4102	605
T & t Staff Management Inc 511 Executive Ctr Blvd .... El Paso TX 79902	**800-598-1647**	915-771-0393	627
T & T Trucking Inc 11396 N Hwy 99 ....Lodi CA 95240 *Cust Svc*	**800-692-3457***	209-931-6000	775
T A. Pelsue Co 2500 S Tejon St ....Englewood CO 80110	**800-525-8460**		762
T Bruce Sales Inc 9 Carbaugh St .... West Middlesex PA 16159	**800-944-0738**	724-528-9961	478
T Cook's 5200 E Camelback Rd ....Phoenix AZ 85018	**800-672-6011**	602-808-0766	667
T G H Aviation 2389 Rickenbacker Way .... Auburn CA 95602	**800-843-4976**	530-823-6204	57
T Marzetti Co 380 Polaris Pkwy Ste 400. ....Westerville OH 43082	**800-999-1835**		296-19
T Marzetti Company Allen Milk Div 1709 Frank Rd ....Columbus OH 43223	**800-999-1835**		
T R C Hydraulics Inc 7 Mosher Dr .... Dartmouth NS B3B1E5	**800-668-9000**	902-468-4605	452
T R Toppers Inc 320 Fairchild ....Pueblo CO 81001	**800 748 4635**	719 948 4902	296-0
T Rowe Price Assoc Inc 100 E Pratt St .... Baltimore MD 21202	**800-638-7890**	410-345-2000	400
T Tech Inc 510 Guthridge Ct ....Norcross GA 30092	**800-370-1530**	770-455-0676	489
T3 Expo LLC 8 Lakeville Business Pk .... Lakeville MA 02347	**888-698-3397**		184
T3 Software Builders Inc 1708 Chester Mill Rd .... Silver Spring MD 20906	**800-281-4879**	301-260-9504	395
TAB Computer Systems Inc 29 Bissell St .... East Hartford CT 06118	**888-822-4435**	860-289-8850	
TAB Products Co 605 Fourth St ....Mayville WI 53050	**888-466-8228**		530
Tabata US.A. Inc 2380 Mira Mar Ave .... Long Beach CA 90815	**800-482-2282**	562-498-3708	707
TABB Inc PO Box 10 .... Chester NJ 07930	**800-887-8222**		631
Taber Extrusions LP 915 S Elmira Ave .... Russellville AR 72802	**800-563-6853**	479-968-1021	483
Taber Industries 455 Bryant St ....North Tonawanda NY 14120	**800-333-5300**	716-694-4000	470
Table Mountain Casino 8184 Table Mountain Rd .... Friant CA 93626	**800-541-3637**	559-822-7777	133
Tack Room Too Inc 201 Lee St SW .... Tumwater WA 98501	**800-258-2581**	360-357-4268	707
Taco Cabana Inc 8918 Tesoro Dr Ste 200 ....San Antonio TX 78217	**800-580-8668**	210-804-0990	666
Taco Inc 1160 Cranston St .... Cranston RI 02920	**888-778-2733**	401-942-8000	356
Taco Metals Inc 50 NE 179th St .... Miami FL 33162	**800-653-8568**	305-652-8566	490
Tacoma Electric Supply Inc 1311 S Tacoma Way .... Tacoma WA 98409	**800-422-0540**	253-475-0540	246
Tacoma General Hospital 315 MLK Jr Way .... Tacoma WA 98405	**800-552-1419**	253-403-1000	373-3
Tacoma Inc 328 E Church St .... Martinsville VA 24112	**800-352-9417**	276-666-9417	666
Tacoma Mall 4502 S Steele St .... Tacoma WA 98409	**877-746-6642**	253-475-4566	458
Tacoma Regional Convention & Visitor Bureau 1516 Commerce St .... Tacoma WA 98402	**800-272-2662**	253-627-2836	206
Tacoma Rubber Stamp & Sign 919 Market St .... Tacoma WA 98402	**800-544-7281**	253-383-5433	465
Tacoma Screw Products Inc 2001 Center St .... Tacoma WA 98409	**800-562-8192**	253-572-3444	452
Tacoma Symphony 901 Broadway Ste 600 .... Tacoma WA 98402	**800-291-7593**	253-272-7264	569-3
Taconic 136 Coonbrook Rd PO Box 69 .... Petersburg NY 12138	**800-833-1805**	518-658-3202	740-2
Tactician Corp 305 N Main St ....Andover MA 01810	**800-927-7666**	978-475-4475	195
Tadiran Batteries 2001 Marcus Ave Ste 125E. ..... New Hyde Park NY 11042	**800-537-1368**	516-621-4980	74
Tadych's Econofoods 1600 Stephenson .... Iron Mountain MI 49801	**877-295-4558**	906-774-1911	344
Taft College 29 Cougar Ct ....Taft CA 93268	**800-379-6784**	661-763-7700	162
TAG (Tube Art Group) 11715 SE Fifth St ....Bellevue WA 98005	**800-562-2854**	206-223-1122	697
Tag-A-Long Expeditions 452 N Main St ....Moab UT 84532	**800-453-3292**	435-259-8946	755
Tahitian Noni International 333 W Riverpark Dr ....Provo UT 84604 *Cust Svc*	**800-445-2969***	801-234-1000	296-11
Tahoe Biltmore Lodge & Casino 5 NV-28 .... Crystal Bay NV 89402	**800-245-8667**		377
Tahoe Mountain Sports 11200 Donner Pass Rd Ste 5e .... Truckee CA 96161	**866-891-9177**		707

Name / Address	City	State	ZIP	Toll-Free	Phone	Class
Taiga Building Products 800-4710 Kingsway	Burnaby	BC	V5H4M2	**800-663-1470**	604-438-1471	279
Tailhook Assn 9696 Businesspark Ave	San Diego	CA	92131	**800-322-4665**	858-689-9223	48-19
Tailored Chemical Products Inc 700 12th St Dr NW	Hickory	NC	28601	**800-627-1687**	828-322-6512	3
Tailored Living LLC 19000 MacArthur Blvd Ste 100	Irvine	CA	92612	**866-675-8819**		360
Taitron Components Inc 28040 W Harrison Pkwy *NASDAQ: TAIT*	Valencia	CA	91355	**800-247-2232**	661-257-6060	246
Taiyo Yuden (USA) Inc 10 N Martingale Rd Ste 575	Schaumburg	IL	60173	**800-348-2496**	630-237-2405	253
Taj Boston 15 Arlington St	Boston	MA	02116	**866-969-1825**	617-536-5700	378
Taj Campton Place 340 Stockton St	San Francisco	CA	94108	**866-969-1825**	415-781-5555	378
TAJ Technologies Inc 1168 Northland Dr	Mendota Heights	MN	55120	**877-825-2801**	651-688-2801	717
Takagi Industrial Company USA Inc 500 Wald	Irvine	CA	92618	**888-882-5244**	949-770-7171	15
Takara Belmont USA Inc 101 Belmont Dr	Somerset	NJ	08873	**877-283-1289**		76
Take 3 Trailers Inc 1808 Hwy 105	Brenham	TX	77833	**866-428-2533**	979-337-9568	758
Takeda Canada Inc 435 N Service Rd W Ste 101	Oakville	ON	L6M4X8	**888-367-3331**	905-469-9333	85
Talbert Manufacturing Inc 1628 W State Rd 114	Rensselaer	IN	47978	**888-489-1731**		774
Talbot County 11 N Washington St County Courthouse	Easton	MD	21601	**800-339-3403**	410-822-2611	337
Talbot County Board of Commissioners 74 W Monroe St PO Box 155	Talbotton	GA	31827	**800-486-7642**	706-665-3220	337
Talbot County Tourism Office 11 S Harrison St	Easton	MD	21601	**800-690-5080**	410-770-8000	206
Talbott Recovery Campus 5448 Yorktowne Dr	Atlanta	GA	30349	**800-445-4232**	877-345-3301	722
Talent Curve 14 Bridle Path	Pittsboro	NC	27312	**866-494-0248**		461
TalentLens Inc 19500 Bulverde Rd	San Antonio	TX	78259	**888-298-6227**		260
TalentMap 245 Menten Pl Ste 301	Ottawa	ON	K2H9E8	**888-641-1113**	613-248-3417	461
Taliesin 5607 County Hwy C	Spring Green	WI	53588	**877-588-7900**	608-588-7090	50-3
Talisma Corporation Pvt Ltd 5201 Congress Ave	Boca Raton	FL	33487	**866-397-2537**	561-923-2500	39
Talk O'Texas Brands Inc 1610 Roosevelt St	San Angelo	TX	76905	**800-749-6572**	325-655-6077	296-20
TalkPoint Holdings LLC 100 William St Ste 100	New York	NY	10038	**866-323-8660**		176
Talladega Castings & Machine Co Inc 228 N Ct St	Talladega	AL	35160	**800-766-6708**	256-362-5550	307
Talladega College 627 W Battle St	Talladega	AL	35160	**866-540-3956**	256-761-6100	166
Talladega Machinery & Supply Co Inc 301 N Johnson Ave PO Box 736 *Cust Svc	Talladega	AL	35161	**800-289-8672***	256-362-4124	307
Tallahassee Community College 444 Appleyard Dr	Tallahassee	FL	32304	**800-538-9784**	850-201-6200	162
Tallahassee Museum of History & Natural Science 3945 Museum Dr	Tallahassee	FL	32310	**800-628-2866**	850-575-8684	517
Tallan Inc 175 Capital Blvd Ste 401	Rocky Hill	CT	06067	**800-677-3693**	860-633-3693	177
Tallapoosa River Electric Co-op 15163 US Hwy 431 S PO Box 675	Lafayette	AL	36862	**800-332-8732**	334-864-9331	245
Tallgrass Restoration LLC 2221 Hammond Dr	Schaumburg	IL	60173	**877-699-8300**	847-925-9830	196
Talton Communications Inc 910 Ravenwood Dr	Selma	AL	36701	**800-685-1840**	334-877-0704	620
TALX Corp 11432 Lackland Dr	Saint Louis	MO	63146	**800-888-8277**	314-214-7000	39
T-A-M (Trace-A-Matic Inc) 21125 Enterprise Ave	Brookfield	WI	53045	**877-375-0217**	262-797-7300	617
Tam International Inc 4620 Southerland Rd	Houston	TX	77092	**800-462-7617**	713-462-7617	533
Tamarac Inc 701 Fifth Ave 14th Fl	Seattle	WA	98104	**866-525-8811**		400
Tamarack Habilitation Technologies Inc 1670 94th Ln NE	Blaine	MN	55449	**866-795-0057**	763-795-0057	475
Tamco Inc 1466 Delberts Dr	Monongahela	PA	15063	**800-826-2672**	724-258-6622	753
Tamiment Resort & Conference Ctr Bushkill Falls Rd	Tamiment	PA	18371	**800-233-8105**	570-588-6652	665
Tampa Armature Works Inc (TAW) 6312 78th St	Riverview	FL	33578	**800-333-9449**	813-621-5661	515
Tampa Bay & Co 401 E Jackson St Ste 2100	Tampa	FL	33602	**877-230-0078**	813-223-1111	206
Tampa Bay Downs Inc 11225 Racetrack Rd	Tampa	FL	33626	**800-200-4434**	813-855-4401	638
Tampa Bay Fisheries Inc 3060 Gallagher Rd	Dover	FL	33527	**800-732-3663**	813-752-8883	296-14
Tampa Convention Ctr 333 S Franklin St	Tampa	FL	33602	**866-790-4111**	813-274-8511	205
Tampa International Airport 4160 George J Bean Pkwy PO Box 22287	Tampa	FL	33607	**866-289-9673**	813-870-8700	27
Tampa Marriott Waterside Hotel & Marina 700 S Florida Ave	Tampa	FL	33602	**888-268-1616**	813-221-4900	703
Tampa Museum of Art 120 W Gasparilla Plz	Tampa	FL	33602	**866-790-4111**	813-274-8211	517
Tampa Port Authority 1101 Channelside Dr	Tampa	FL	33602	**800-741-2297**	813-905-7678	614
Tamwood International College 300-909 Burrard St	Vancouver	BC	V6Z2N2	**866-533-0123**	604-899-4480	422
Tandberg Data 10225 Westmoor Dr Ste 125	Westminster	CO	80021	**800-392-2983**	303-442-4333	173-8
Tandus Centiva 311 Smith Industrial Blvd PO Box 1147	Dalton	GA	30722	**800-248-2878**	706-259-9711	131
Tangata 2002 N Main St	Santa Ana	CA	92706	**866-972-8462**		
Tangent Inc 191 Airport Blvd	Burlingame	CA	94010	**800-342-9388**	650-342-9388	173-2
Tanger Factory Outlet Centers Inc 3200 Northline Ave Ste 360 *NYSE: SKT*	Greensboro	NC	27408	**800-720-6728**	336-292-3010	651
Tanger Outlet Ctr San Marcos 4015 S IH-35 Ste 319	San Marcos	TX	78666	**800-408-8424**	512-396-7446	458
Tangerine Travel Ltd 16017 Juanita Woodinville Way NE Ste 201	Bothell	WA	98011	**800-678-8202**	425-822-2333	767
Tangible Solutions Inc 1320 Matthews Township Pkwy Ste 201	Matthews	NC	28105	**800-393-9886**	704-940-4200	180
Tango Consulting Group LLC 31 James Vincent Dr	Clinton	CT	06413	**877-567-6045**	860-669-9380	196
Tango Management Consulting LLC 6225 N State Hwy 161 Ste 300	Irving	TX	75038	**855-938-2646**		180
Tangoe 169 Lackawanna Ave	Parsippany	NJ	07054	**844-484-5041**		178-7
Tanimura & Antle Inc PO Box 4070	Salinas	CA	93912	**800-772-4542**		10-9
Tanita Corp of America Inc 2625 S Clearbrook Dr	Arlington Heights	IL	60005	**800-826-4828**	847-640-9241	680
Tankmaster Rentals L T D Poplar St Ste 117	Red Deer	AB	T4E1B4	**877-342-1105**	403-342-1105	
Tanks-A-Lot Ltd 1810 Yellowhead Trail NE	Edmonton	AB	T6S1B4	**800-661-5667**	780-472-8265	765
Tanner Electric Co 45710 SE North Bend Way	North Bend	WA	98045	**800-472-0208**	425-888-0623	245
Tanner Industries Inc 735 Davisville Rd	Southampton	PA	18966	**800-643-6226**	215-322-1238	146
Tanner Research Inc 825 S Myrtle Ave	Monrovia	CA	91016	**877-325-2223**	626-471-9700	174
Tanner Systems Inc 625 19th Ave NE PO Box 488	Saint Joseph	MN	56374	**800-461-6454**	320-363-1800	143
Tanque Verde Ranch 14301 E Speedway	Tucson	AZ	85748	**800-234-3833**	520-296-6275	239
Tantalus Resort Lodge 4200 Whistler Way	Whistler	BC	V0N1B4	**888-806-2299**	604-932-4146	665
Tan-Tar-A Resort Golf Club & Spa 494 Tantara Dr PO Box 188TT *Resv	Osage Beach	MO	65065	**800-826-8272***	573-348-3131	665
TanTara Transportation Corp 2420 Stewart Rd	Muscatine	IA	52761	**800-650-0292**	563-262-8621	775
Taos Mountain 121 Daggett Dr	San Jose	CA	95134	**888-826-7686**	408-588-1200	461
Taos Ski Valley Inc 116 Sutton Pl	Taos Ski Valley	NM	87525	**800-776-1111**	575-776-2291	31
Tap Packaging Solutions 2160 Superior Ave	Cleveland	OH	44114	**800-827-5679**	216-781-6000	556
TAP Plastics Inc 6475 Sierra Ln	Dublin	CA	94568	**800-894-0827**	925-829-4889	603
Tapatio Springs Golf Resort & Conference Ctr 1 Resort Way	Boerne	TX	78006	**855-627-2243**		665
Tapco Group 29797 Beck Rd	Wixom	MI	48393	**800-521-7567**	248-668-6400	695
Tape & Label Converters Inc 8231 Allport Ave	Santa Fe Springs	CA	90670	**888-285-2462**	562-945-3486	412
Tapecon Inc 10 Latta Rd	Rochester	NY	14612	**800-333-2407**	585-621-8400	412
TAPEMARK Co 1685 Marthaler Ln	St Paul	MN	55118	**800-535-1998**	651-455-1611	412
Tapeswitch Corp 100 Schmitt Blvd	Farmingdale	NY	11735	**800-234-8273**	631-630-0442	725
Tapmatic Corp 802 S Clearwater Loop *General	Post Falls	ID	83854	**800-854-6019***	208-773-8048	491
TAPPI (Technical Assn of the Pulp & Paper Industry) 15 Technology Pkwy S *Sales	Norcross	GA	30092	**800-332-8686***	770-446-1400	49-13
Tapscott's 1403 E 18th St	Owensboro	KY	42303	**800-626-1922**	270-684-2308	293
TAR (Tennessee Assn of Realtors) 901 19th Ave S	Nashville	TN	37212	**877-321-1477**	615-321-1477	652
Tara Pearls 10 W 46th Ste 600	New York	NY	10036	**888-575-8272**		410
Target Corp 1000 Nicollet Mall *NYSE: TGT* ■ *Cust Svc	Minneapolis	MN	55403	**800-440-0680***	612-304-6073	229
Targeted Job Fairs Inc 4441 Glenway Ave	Cincinnati	OH	45205	**800-695-1939**		260
Targus Inc 1211 N Miller St	Anaheim	CA	92806	**877-482-7487**	714-765-5555	451
Tarkett Inc 1001 Yamaska St E	Farnham	QC	J2N1J7	**800-363-9276**	450-293-3173	291
Tarleton State University PO Box T-0030	Stephenville	TX	76402	**800-687-8236**	254-968-9125	166
Taro Pharmaceutical Industries Ltd 126 E Dr	Brampton	ON	L6T1C1	**800-268-1975**	905-791-8276	578
Taro Pharmaceuticals USA Inc 3 Skyline Dr	Hawthorne	NY	10532	**800-544-1449**	914-345-9001	579
Tarr LLC 2946 NE Columbia Blvd	Portland	OR	97211	**800-422-5069**	503-288-5294	146
Tarryall River Ranch 270015 County Rd 77	Lake George	CO	80827	**800-408-8407**		239
Tarrytown House Estate & Conference Ctr 49 E Sunnyside Ln	Tarrytown	NY	10591	**800-553-8118**	914-591-8200	226
TASC Technical Services LLC 73 Newton Rd	Plaistow	NH	03865	**877-304-8272**		195
Task Force Tips Inc 3701 Innovation Way	Valparaiso	IN	46383	**800-348-2686**	219-462-6161	283
Taskstream LLC 71 W 23rd St	New York	NY	10010	**800-311-5656**	212-868-2700	225

		Toll-Free	Phone	Class
Tasler Inc 1804 Tasler Dr	Webster City IA 50595	800-482-7537	515-832-5200	547
Tasty Baking Co 4300 S 26th St	Philadelphia PA 19112	800-248-2789	215-221-8500	296-1
Tate Andale Inc 1941 Lansdowne Rd	Baltimore MD 21227	800-296-8283	410-247-8700	591
Tate Inc 7510 Montevideo Rd	Jessup MD 20794	800-231-7788	410-799-4200	489
Tatro Plumbing Company Inc 1285 Acraway Ste 300	Garden City KS 67846	888-828-7648	620-277-2167	189-10
Tattered Cover Book Store Inc 1628 16th St	Denver CO 80202	800-833-9327	303-436-1070	95
Tatung Company of America Inc 2850 El Presidio St	Long Beach CA 90810	800-827-2850	310-637-2105	173-4
Tau Beta Pi Assn 1512 Middle Dr	Knoxville TN 37996	877-829-5500	865-546-4578	48-16
Tauck World Discovery 10 Norden Pl	Norwalk CT 06855	800-468-2825	203-899-6500	755
Taurus International Mfg Inc 16175 NW 49th Ave	Miami Lakes FL 33014	800-327-3776		284
Tavaero Jet Charter 7930 Airport Blvd	Houston TX 77061	800-343-3771	713-643-5387	13
Tavis Corp 3636 State Hwy 49 S	Mariposa CA 95338	800-842-6102	209-966-2027	406
Tavistock Restaurants LLC 4705 S Apopka Vineland Rd Ste 210	Orlando FL 32819	800-424-2753	407-909-7101	666
TAW (Tampa Armature Works Inc) 6312 78th St	Riverview FL 33578	800-333-9449	813-621-5661	515
TaxMatrix 1011 Mumma Rd	Lemoyne PA 17043	855-788-3375		
Taycom Business Solutions Inc 719 Griswold Ave Ste 820	Detroit MI 48226	866-482-9266	313-967-7857	2
Taycor LLC 6065 Bristol Pkwy	Culver City CA 90230	800-322-9738	310-895-7704	216
Taylor 750 N Blackhawk Blvd	Rockton IL 61072	800-255-0626		298
Taylor & Francis Group 6000 Broken Sound Pkwy NW Ste 300	Boca Raton FL 33487	877-622-5543	207-017-6000	633-2
Taylor & Hill Inc 9941 Ruwlett Rd	Houston TX 77075	800-318-0231	713-941-2671	260
Taylor & Messick Inc 325 Walt Messick Rd	Harrington DE 19952	800-237-1272	302-398-3729	517
Taylor & Syfan Consulting Engineers Inc 684 Clarion Ct	San Luis Obispo CA 93401	800-579-3881	805-547-2000	261
Taylor Bldg Products 631 N First St	West Branch MI 48661	800-248-3600	989-345-5110	234
Taylor County 224 S Second St	Medford WI 54451	800-362-4802	715-748-1456	337
Taylor County RECC 625 W Main St PO Box 100	Campbellsville KY 42719	800-931-4551	270-465-4101	245
Taylor Electric Co-op N1831 State Hwy 13	Medford WI 54451	800-862-2407	715-678-2411	245
Taylor Enterprises Inc (TEI) 2586 Southport Rd	Spartanburg SC 29302	800-922-3149	864-573-9518	575
Taylor Farms Inc 150 Main St	Salinas CA 93901	877-323-7374		297-7
Taylor Freezer Sales Company Inc 2032 Atlantic Ave	Chesapeake VA 23324	800-768-6945	757-545-7900	661
Taylor Freezers of California 221 Harris Ct	South San Francisco CA 94080	877-978-4800		405
Taylor Hospital 175 E Chester Pk	Ridley Park PA 19078	800-254-3258	610-595-6000	373-3
Taylor Made Products *Taylor Made Group* 167 N Main St	Gloversville NY 12078	800-628-5188		
Taylor Products Company Inc 2205 Jothi Ave	Parsons KS 67357	888-882-9567	620-421-5550	543
Taylor Technologies Inc 31 Loveton Cir	Sparks MD 21152 *Cust Svc		800-837-8548*	410-472-4340	801
Taylor Truck Line Inc 31485 Northfield Blvd	Northfield MN 55057	800-962-5994	507-645-4531	775
Taylor University 236 W Reade Ave	Upland IN 46989	800-882-3456	765-998-2751	166
Fort Wayne 915 W Rudisill Blvd	Fort Wayne IN 46807 *General	800-882-3456*	260-744-8790	166
Taylor University College & Seminary 11525 23rd Ave	Edmonton AB T6J4T3	800-567-4988	780-431-5200	167-3
Taylor Valve Technology Inc 8300 SW 8th	Oklahoma City OK 73128	800-805-3401	405-787-0145	784
Taylor Wellons Politz & Duhe Aplc 8550 United Plaza Blvd Ste 101	Baton Rouge LA 70809	877-850-1047	225-387-9888	427
Taylor, Porter, Brooks & Phillips LLP 450 Laurel St Ste 800	Baton Rouge LA 70801	800-310-7029	225-387-3221	
Taylor-Dunn Manufacturing Co 2114 W Ball Rd	Anaheim CA 92804	800-688-8680		468
Taylor-Winfield Inc 3200 Innovation Pl	Youngstown OH 44509	800-523-4899	330-259-8500	806
TB Wood's Inc 440 N Fifth Ave	Chambersburg PA 17201	888-829-6637	717-264-7161	616
TBayTel 1060 Lithium Dr	Thunder Bay ON P7B6G3	800-264-9501	807-623-4400	224
TBC (Tom Barrow Co) 2800 Plant Atkinson Rd	Atlanta GA 30339	800-229-8226	404-351-1010	14
Tbm Consulting Group Inc 4400 Ben Franklin Blvd	Durham NC 27704	800-438-5535	919-471-5535	194
TBN (Trinity Broadcasting Network) PO Box A	Santa Ana CA 92711	888-731-1000	714-832-2950	735
TBS (Trachte Bldg Systems Inc) 314 Wilburn Rd	Sun Prairie WI 53590	800-356-5824		105
TBT (Transco Business Technologies) 34 Leighton Rd	Augusta ME 04330	800-322-0003	800-452-4657	112
TCAG (Center for Association Growth, The) 1926 Waukegan Rd Ste 300	Glenview IL 60025	800-492-6462	847-657-6700	47
TCC (Customer Communicator, The) 712 Main St Ste 187B	Boonton NJ 07005	800-232-4317	973-265-2300	527-2
TCF National Bank 801 Marquette Ave	Minneapolis MN 55402	800-343-6145	612-823-2265	70
TCI (Teachers' Curriculum Institute) 2440 W El Camino Real Ste 400	Mountain View CA 94040	800-497-6138		
TCI Aluminum/North Inc 2353 Davis Ave	Hayward CA 94545	800-824-6197	510-786-3750	490
TCI Scales Inc PO Box 1648	Snohomish WA 98291	800-522-2206	425-353-4384	680
TCIA (Tree Care Industry Assn) 136 Harvey Rd Ste 101	Londonderry NH 03053	800-733-2622	603-314-5380	48-13
TCM (Turner Classic Movies Inc) 1050 Techwood Dr NW	Atlanta GA 30318	844-356-7875		
TCR Industries 26 Centerpointe Dr Ste 120	La Palma CA 90623	877-827-1444	714-521-5222	146
Tcs of America Enterprises Llc PO Box 219	Brookline NH 03033	888-423-7820		196
Tct Computing Group Inc Po Box 402	Bel Air MD 21014	866-828-6372	410-893-5800	193
TCT Ministries Inc 11717 N Rt 37 PO Box 1010	Marion IL 62959	800-232-9855	618-997-4700	735
TCU (Teachers Credit Union) PO Box 1395	South Bend IN 46624	800-552-4745	574-284-6247	219
TCVB (Tyler Convention & Visitors Bureau) 315 N Broadway Ave	Tyler TX 75702	800-235-5712	903-592-1661	206
TD Bank NA 1701 Rt 70 E	Cherry Hill NJ 08034	888-751-9000	856-751-2739	70
TD Banknorth Massachusetts 295 Park Ave	Worcester MA 01609 *Cust Svc	800-747-7000*	508-752-2584	70
TDA (Tennessee Dental Assn) 660 Bakers Bridge Ave Ste 300	Franklin TN 37067	800-824-9722	615-628-0208	227
TDC (Discovery Ctr) 1944 N Winery Ave	Fresno CA 93703	800-946-3039	559-251-5533	518
TDECU (Texas Dow Employees Credit Union) 1001 FM 2004	Lake Jackson TX 77566	800-839-1154	979-297-1154	219
TDS (Texas Disposal Systems Inc) 12200 Carl Rd	Creedmoor TX 78610	800-375-8375	512-421-1300	799
TDS Telecommunications Corp 525 Junction Rd	Madison WI 53717	866-571-6662	608-664-4000	731
Te21 Inc 1184 Clements Ferry Rd Ste G	Charleston SC 29492	866-982-8321	843-579-2520	196
Teach Away Inc 147 Liberty St	Toronto ON M6K3G3	855-483-2242	416-628-1386	260
Teach For America 315 W 36th St 7th Fl	New York NY 10018	800-832-1230	212-279-2080	49-5
Teacher Created Resources 6421 Industry Way	Westminster CA 92683	888-343-4335		243
Teacher Magazine 6935 Arlington Rd Ste 100	Bethesda MD 20814	800-346-1834	301-280-3100	455-8
Teachers Credit Union (TCU) PO Box 1395	South Bend IN 46624	800-552-4745	574-284-6247	219
Teachers Federal Credit Union (TFCU) 2410 N Ocean Ave	Farmingville NY 11738	800-341-4333	631-698-7000	219
Teachers of English to Speakers of Other Languages (TESOL) 700 S Washington St Ste 200	Alexandria VA 22314	888-547-3369	703-836-0774	49-5
Teachers on Reserve LLC 604 Sonora Ave	Glendale CA 91201	800-457-1899		260
Teachers' Curriculum Institute (TCI) 2440 W El Camino Real Ste 400	Mountain View CA 94040	800-497-6138		
Teaching & Mentoring Communities (TMC) PO Box 2579	Laredo TX 78044	888-836-5151	956-722-5174	49-5
Teal's Express Inc 22411 Teal Dr PO Box 6010	Watertown NY 13601	800-836-0369		775
Teal-Jones Group, The 17897 Triggs Rd	Surrey BC V4N4M8	888-995-8325	604-587-8700	679
Team Connection Inc 615 Alton Pl	High Point NC 27263	800-535-3975		707
Team Health Inc 265 Brookview Ctr Way Ste 400	Knoxville TN 37919	800-342-2898	865-693-1000	717
Team IA Inc 212 Palmetto Park Blvd	Lexington SC 29072	888-483-2642	803-356-7676	804
Team Inc 200 Hermann Dr	Alvin TX 77511 *NYSE: TISI*	800-662-8326	281-331-6154	535
Team Quality Services Inc 4483 County Rd 19 Ste B	Auburn IN 46706	866-568-8326	260-572-0060	461
Team Velocity Marketing LLC 13825 Sunrise Valley Dr	Herndon VA 20171	877-832-6848		7
TeamBonding 298 Tosca Dr	Stoughton MA 02072	888-398-8326		317
TeamQuest Corp 1 TeamQuest Way	Clear Lake IA 50428	800-551-8326	641-357-2700	178-12
Teamwork Newsletter 2222 Sedwick Dr	Durham NC 27713	800-223-8720		527-2
TeamWorld Inc 498 Conklin Ave	Binghamton NY 13903	800-797-1005	607-770-1005	34
Teaneck Public Library 840 Teaneck Rd	Teaneck NJ 07666	800-245-1377	201-837-4171	433-3
TEC (Telephone Electronics Corp) 700 W St	Jackson MS 39201	800-832-2515	601-353-9118	386
Tec Laboratories Inc 7100 Tec Labs Way SW	Albany OR 97321	800-482-4464	541-926-4577	231
Tech 24 410 E Washington St	Greenville SC 29601	888-774-4950		
Tech Center Inc 265 S Main St	Akron OH 44308	800-990-8083	330-762-6212	193
Tech Credit Union 10951 Broadway	Crown Point IN 46307	800-276-8324	219-663-5120	219
Tech Data Corp 5350 Tech Data Dr	Clearwater FL 33760 *NASDAQ: TECD*	800-237-8931	727-539-7429	174
Tech Friends inc PO Box 16480	Jonesboro AR 72403	866-933-6386	870-933-6386	
Tech Hero 200 E Robinson St Ste 425	Orlando FL 32801	800-900-8324		180

	Toll-Free	Phone	Class

Tech International
200 E Coshocton St ....Johnstown OH 43031 — 800-336-8324 — 740-967-9015 — 749

Tech Lighting LLC
7400 Linda Ave ....Skokie IL 60077 — 800-522-5315 — 847-410-4400 — 438

Tech Museum of Innovation
201 S Market St ....San Jose CA 95113 — 800-411-7245 — 408-294-8324 — 517

Tech Networks of Boston
574 Dorchester Ave ....Boston MA 02127 — 888-527-9333 — 617-269-0299 — 41

Tech Packaging Inc
13241 Bartram Pk Blvd
Ste 601 ....Jacksonville FL 32258 — 866-453-8324 — 904-288-6403 — 545

Tech Pharmacy Services Inc
12503 Exchange Dr Ste 536 ....Stafford TX 77477 — 800-378-9020 — — 583

Tech Transport Inc
PO Box 431 ....Milford NH 03055 — 800-641-5300

Tech West Vacuum Inc
2625 N Argyle Ave ....Fresno CA 93727 — 800-428-7139 — 559-291-1650 — 473

Tech4Learning Inc
10981 San Diego Mission Rd
Ste 120 ....San Diego CA 92108 — 877-834-5453 — 619-563-5348 — 457

Techne Corp
614 McKinley Pl NE ....Minneapolis MN 55413 — 800-343-7475 — 612-379-8854 — 231
NASDAQ: TECH

Techneal Inc
2100 S Reservoir St ....Pomona CA 91766 — 800-545-6325 — 909-465-6325 — 531

Technetics Group
3125 Damon Way ....Burbank CA 91505 — 800-618-4701 — 818-841-9667 — 604

Technical Assn of the Pulp & Paper Industry (TAPPI)
15 Technology Pkwy S ....Norcross GA 30092 — 800-332-8686* — 770-446-1400 — 49-13
*Sales

Technical Assurance Inc
38112 Second St ....Willoughby OH 44094 — 866-953-3147 — 440-953-3147 — 196

Technical Cable Concepts Inc
350 Lear Ave ....Costa Mesa CA 92626 — 800-832-2225 — 714-835-1081 — 116

Technical Chemical Co
3327 Pipeline Rd ....Cleburne TX 76033 — 800-527-0885 — 817-645-6088 — 145

Technical Communications Corp
100 Domino Dr ....Concord MA 01742 — 800-952-4082 — 978-287-5100 — 730
NASDAQ: TCCO

Technical Communities Inc
1111 Bayhill Dr Ste 400 ....San Bruno CA 94066 — 888-665-2765 — 650-624-0525 — 195

Technical Consumer Products Inc
325 Campus Dr ....Aurora OH 44202 — 800-324-1496 — 330-995-6111 — 436

Technical Gas Products Inc
66 Leonardo Dr ....North Haven CT 06473 — 800-847-0745 — — 575

Technical Instrument San Francisco
1826 Rollins Rd ....Burlingame CA 94010 — 866-800-9797 — 650-651-3000 — 473

Technical Systems Integration Inc
816 Greenbrier Cir Ste 208 ....Chesapeake VA 23320 — 800-566-8744 — 757-424-5793 — 256

Technical Toolboxes Ltd
3801 Kirby Dr Ste 520 ....Houston TX 77098 — 866-866-6766 — 713-630-0505 — 177

Technical Transportation Inc
1701 W Northwest Hwy Ste 100 ....Grapevine TX 76051 — 800-852-8726 — — 447

Techni-Car Inc
450 Commerce Blvd ....Oldsmar FL 34677 — 800-886-0022 — 813-855-0022 — 62-5

Techni-Cast Corp
11220 Garfield Ave ....South Gate CA 90280 — 800-923-4585 — 562-923-4585 — 308

Technicote Westfield Inc
222 Mound Ave ....Miamisburg OH 45342 — 800-358-4448 — — 548-1

Technidrill Systems Inc
429 Portage Blvd ....Kent OH 44240 — 844-313-7012 — 330-678-9980 — 453

Techniform Industries Inc
2107 Hayes Ave ....Fremont OH 43420 — 800-691-2816 — 419-332-8484 — 595

Technigraph Corp
850 W Third St ....Winona MN 55987 — 800-421-4772 — 507-454-3830 — 683

Techni-Tool Inc
1547 N Trooper Rd PO Box 1117 ......Worcester PA 19490 — 800-832-4866* — — 350
*Cust Svc

Techno-Aide Inc
7117 Centennial Blvd ....Nashville TN 37209 — 800-251-2629 — 615-350-7030 — 474

Technolab International Corp
2020 NE 163 St ....Miami FL 33162 — 888-382-2851 — 305-433-2973 — 196

Technology Funding Inc
460 St Michael's Dr Ste 1000 ....Santa Fe NM 87505 — 800-821-5323 — — 787

Technology Futures Inc (TFI)
13740 Research Blvd (N Hwy 183)
Ste C-1 ....Austin TX 78750 — 800-835-3887 — 512-258-8898 — 196

Technology Integration Group (TIG)
7810 Trade St ....San Diego CA 92121 — 800-858-0549 — — 176

Technology Marketing Corp
1 Technology Plz ....Norwalk CT 06854 — 800-243-6002* — 203-852-6800 — 633-2
*Cust Svc

Technology Service Corp
251 18th St S Ste 705 ....Arlington VA 22202 — 800-324-7700 — 256-705-2222 — 664

Technology Solutions Provider Inc (TSPI)
11490 Commerce Park Dr Ste 200 ......Reston VA 20191 — 877-455-8774 — — 196

Technomart RGA Inc
401 Washington Ave Ste 1101 ....Baltimore MD 21204 — 800-877-6555 — 410-828-6555 — 400

TechnoServe
1120 19th St NW 8th Fl ....Washington DC 20036 — 800-999-6757 — 202-785-4515 — 48-5

TechSmith Corp
2405 Woodlake Dr ....Okemos MI 48864 — 800-517-3001 — 517-381-2300 — 178-8

Techspeed Inc
280 SW Moonridge Pl ....Portland OR 97225 — 800-750-4066 — 503-291-0027 — 180

TechStar
802 W 13th St ....Deer Park TX 77536 — 866-542-0205

TechTarget
275 Grove St ....Newton MA 02466 — 888-274-4111 — 617-431-9200 — 633-10

Techtonic Group Llc
2000 Central Ave ....Boulder CO 80301 — 866-382-8280 — 303-223-3468

Tecinfo Communication LLC
601 N Deer Creek Dr E ....Leland MS 38756 — 800-863-5415 — 662-686-9009 — 175

Teck Resources Ltd
501 N Riverpoint Blvd Ste 300 ......Spokane WA 99202 — 866-225-0198 — 800-432-3206 — 730

Tecnicard Inc
3191 Coral Way Ste 800 ....Miami FL 33145 — 800-317-6020 — 305-442-0018 — 225

Tecnico Corp
831 Industrial Ave ....Chesapeake VA 23324 — 800-786-2207* — 757-545-4013 — 694
*General

Teco Diagnostics
1268 N Lakeview Ave ....Anaheim CA 92807 — 800-222-9880 — 714-463-1111 — 231

Tecom Industries Inc
375 Conejo Ridge Ave ....Thousand Oaks CA 91361 — 866-840-8550 — 805-267-0100 — 643

Tecon Services Inc
515 Garden Oaks Blvd ....Houston TX 77018 — 800-245-1728 — 713-691-2700 — 188

TECO-Westinghouse Motor Co
5100 N IH-35 ....Round Rock TX 78681 — 800-451-8798 — 512-255-4141 — 705

Tecplot Inc
3535 Factoria Blvd SE Ste 550 ....Bellevue WA 98006 — 800-763-7005 — 425-653-1200 — 177

TECSys Development Inc
1600 Tenth St ....Plano TX 75074 — 800-695-1258 — 972-881-1553 — 180

TECSYS Inc
1 Place Alexis Nihon Ste 800 ......Montreal QC H3Z3B8 — 800-922-8649 — 514-866-0001 — 178-1

Tectonic Engineering & Surveying Consultants PC
70 Pleasant Hill Rd ....Mountainville NY 10953 — 800-829-6531 — — 261

Tectum Inc
105 S Sixth St ....Newark OH 43055 — 888-977-9691 — 740-345-9691 — 814

Tedia Company Inc
1000 Tedia Way ....Fairfield OH 45014 — 800-787-4891 — 513-874-5340 — 144

Teeco Products Inc
16881 Armstrong Ave ....Irvine CA 92606 — 800-854-3463 — 949-261-6295 — 384

Teeter Irrigation Inc
2729 W Oklahoma ....Ulysses KS 67880 — 800-524-5497 — 620-353-1111 — 274

TEGAM Inc 10 Tegam Way ....Geneva OH 44041 — 800-666-1010 — 440-466-6100 — 248

TEI (Taylor Enterprises Inc)
2586 Southport Rd ....Spartanburg SC 29302 — 800-922-3149 — 864-573-9518 — 575

Tejas Logistics System
PO Box 1339 ....Waco TX 76703 — 800-535-9786 — 254-753-0301 — 798-1

Tekelec
5200 Paramount Pkwy ....Morrisville NC 27560 — 800-633-0738 — — 730
NASDAQ: TKLC

Tekla Inc
1075 Big Shanty Rd NW Ste 175 ......Kennesaw GA 30144 — 877-835-5265 — 770-426-5105 — 174

Tekmasters Llc
4437 brookfield corporate Dr
Ste 201A..........................Chantilly VA 20151 — 855-856-7877 — 703-349-1110

Teknor Apex Co
505 Central Ave ....Pawtucket RI 02861 — 800-556-3864 — 401-725-8000 — 601-3

Tekra Corp
16700 W Lincoln Ave ....New Berlin WI 53151 — 800-448-3572 — — 599

Tekran Instruments Corp
230 Tech Ctr Dr ....Knoxville TN 37912 — 888-383-5726 — 865-688-0688 — 418

Teksavers Inc
2120 Grand Ave Pkwy ....Austin TX 78728 — 866-832-6188 — — 180

TekScape inc
131 West 35th St 5th Fl ....New York NY 10001 — 855-835-7227 — — 196

Teksouth Corp
1420 Northbrook Dr Ste 220 ....Gardendale AL 35071 — 800-842-1470 — 205-631-1500

TEKsystems Inc
7437 Race Rd ....Hanover MD 21076 — 888-519-0776 — 410-540-7700 — 717

Tektronix Component Solutions Inc
2905 SW Hocken Ave ....Beaverton OR 97005 — 800-833-9200 — — 392

Tekworks Inc
13000 Gregg St Ste B ....Poway CA 92064 — 877-835-9675 — 858-668-1705 — 176

Tel Electronics Inc
313 South 740 East Ste 1 ....American Fork UT 84003 — 800-748-5022 — — 730

Tel Star Cablevision Inc
1295 Lourdes Rd ....Metamora IL 61548 — 888-842-0258 — — 116

TeL Systems
7235 Jackson Rd ....Ann Arbor MI 48103 — 800-686-7235 — 734-761-4506 — 246

Tel Tec Security Systems Inc
5020 Lisa Marie Ct ....Bakersfield CA 93313 — 800-292-9227 — 661-397-5511 — 196

TelAlaska Inc
201 E 56th St ....Anchorage AK 99518 — 888-570-1792 — 907-563-2003 — 731

Telax Voice Solutions
365 Evans Ave Ste 302.............Toronto ON M8Z1K2 — 888-808-3529 — 416-207-0630 — 732

Telco IQ
4300 Forbes Blvd Ste 210 ....Lanham MD 20706 — 877-835-2647 — 202-595-1500 — 386

Telco Systems Inc
15 Berkshire Rd ....Mansfield MA 02048 — 800-227-0937 — 781-255-2120 — 730

Telcobuy com L L C
60 Weldon Pkwy ....St. Louis MO 63043 — 877-350-0191 — — 246

Telcoe Federal Credit Union
820 Lousiana St ....Little Rock AR 72201 — 800-482-9009 — 501-375-5321 — 219

Tele Atlas North America Inc
11 Lafayette St ....Lebanon NH 03766 — 844-394-2020

Tele Business USA
1945 Techny Rd Ste 3..............Northbrook IL 60062 — 877-315-8353 — — 732

Tel-e Technologies
7 Kodiak Crescent ....Toronto ON M3J3E5 — 800-661-2340 — 416-631-1300 — 5

Telebyte Communications Inc
6816 50 Ave ....Red Deer AB T4N4E3 — 800-565-1849 — 403-346-9966 — 224

Telebyte Inc
355 Marcus Blvd ....Hauppauge NY 11788 — 800-835-3298 — 631-423-3232 — 176

TeleCommunication Systems Inc
275 W St Ste 400 ....Annapolis MD 21401 — 800-810-0827 — 410-263-7616 — 224
NASDAQ: TSYS

Telecon Inc
7 450 rue du Mile-End ....Montreal QC H2R2Z6 — 800-465-0349 — 514-644-2333 — 186

Telecorp Products Inc
2000 E Oakley Park Rd
Ste 101 ....Walled Lake MI 48390 — 800-634-1012 — 248-960-1000 — 174

Telect Inc
22425 E Appleway Ave
Ste 11 ....Liberty Lake WA 99019 — 800-551-4567* — 509-926-6000 — 730
*Cust Svc

TeleDevelopment Services Inc
149 Kensington Crt ....Broadview Heights OH 44147 — 888-788-4441

Teledyne Advanced Pollution Instrumentation
9480 Carroll Pk Dr ....San Diego CA 92121 — 800-324-5190 — 858-657-9800 — 201

Teledyne Brown Engineering Inc
300 Sparkman Dr ....Huntsville AL 35805 — 800-933-2091 — 256-726-1000 — 261

Teledyne Lighting & Display Products
5005 McConnell Ave ....Los Angeles CA 90066 — 800-563-4020 — 805-373-4545 — 437

Teledyne Monitor Labs Inc (TML)
35 Inverness Dr E ....Englewood CO 80112 — 800-422-1499 — 303-792-3300 — 201

	Toll-Free	Phone	Class
Teleflex Medical			
2917 Weck Dr			
PO Box 12600.......... Research Triangle Park NC 27709	**866-246-6990**	919-544-8000	60
Teleflex Medical OEM			
50 Plantation Dr .... Jaffrey NH 03452	**800-548-6600**	603-532-7706	474
Teleflora Inc			
11444 Olympic Blvd ....Los Angeles CA 90064	**800-493-5610**		294
Telegramcom			
100 Front St 5th Fl .... Worcester MA 01608	**800-678-6680**	508-793-9100	633-8
Telegraph			
113 S Peoria Ave ....Dixon IL 61021	**800-798-4085**	815-284-2224	528-2
Telegraph Herald			
801 Bluff St .... Dubuque IA 52001	**800-553-4801**	563-588-5611	528-2
Telegraph, The			
PO Box 278 .... Alton IL 62002	**866-299-9256**	618-463-2500	528-2
Telegraph, The			
1675 Montpelier Ave .... Macon GA 31201	**800-679-6397**	478-744-4200	528-2
Telegraph-Journal			
210 Crown St PO Box 2350 .... Saint John NB E2L3V8	**888-295-8665**		528-1
Telelatino Network Inc (TLN)			
5125 Steeles Ave W .... Toronto ON M9L1R5	**800-551-8401**	416-744-8200	735
Telemedia Inc			
750 West Lake Cook Rd Rd			
Ste 250 ....Buffalo Grove IL 60089	**800-837-8872**	847-808-4000	760
Telemundo 39			
4805 Amon Carter Blvd .... Fort Worth TX 76155	**877-266-8365**		736-21
Telenet Marketing Solutions			
1915 New Jimmy Daniel Rd .... Athens GA 30606	**877-282-2345**	706-353-1940	317
Telepath Corp			
49111 Milmont Dr .... Fremont CA 94538	**800-292-1700**	510-656-5600	643
Telephone & Data Systems Inc			
30 N La Salle St Ste 4000............. Chicago IL 60602	**877-337-1575**	312-630-1900	359-3
NYSE: TDS			
Telephone Doctor Inc			
30 Hollenberg Ct ....Bridgeton MO 63044	**800-882-9911**	314-291-1012	196
Telephone Electronics Corp (TEC)			
700 W St .... Jackson MS 39201	**800-832-2515**	601-353-9118	386
Telephone Service Co			
2 Willipie St .... Wapakoneta OH 45895	**800-743-5707**	419-739-2200	731
Telepress Global			
19241 62nd Ave S .... Kent WA 98032	**800-234-4466**		
TeleProviders Inc			
23461 S Pointe Dr Ste 185 ...... Laguna Hills CA 92653	**888-999-4244**		461
Telerent Leasing Corp			
4191 Fayetteville Rd .... Raleigh NC 27603	**800-626-0682**	919-772-8604	38
Telerhythmics LLC			
60 Market Center Dr ....Collierville TN 38017	**888-333-1003**		588
Telesource Services LLC			
1450 Highwood E .... Pontiac MI 48340	**800-525-4300**	248-335-3000	246
Telesouth Communications Inc			
6311 Ridgewood Rd ....Jackson MS 39211	**888-808-8637**	601-957-1700	639
Telestream Inc			
848 Gold Flat Rd Ste 1 .... Nevada City CA 95959	**877-681-2088**	530-470-1300	178-8
TeleTech Holdings Inc			
9197 S Peoria St ....Englewood CO 80112	**800-835-3832***	303-397-8100	732
*NASDAQ: TTEC ■ *General*			
Tele-Track			
40 Pacifica Ste 900..................... Irvine CA 92618	**800-729-6981**	949-214-1000	218
Telex Communications Inc			
12000 Portland Ave S .... Burnsville MN 55337	**877-863-4169**	877-863-4166	52
Telfair County			
91 Telfair Ave .... McRae GA 31055	**800-829-4933**	800-436-7442	337
Telgian Holdings Inc			
10230 S 50th Pl Ste 100............. Phoenix AZ 85044	**877-835-4426**	480-753-5444	189-10
Telics			
3440 Lakemont Blvd ....Fort Mill SC 29708	**800-424-1454**		
Teligent Inc			
105 Lincoln Ave .... Buena NJ 08310	**800-656-0793**		731
Telkonet Inc			
10200 W Innovation Dr Ste 300 .... Milwaukee WI 53226	**888-703-9398***	414-223-0473	176
*OTC: TKOI ■ *Sales*			
Tellurex Corp			
1462 International Dr .... Traverse City MI 49686	**877-774-7468**	231-947-0110	692
Telosa Software Inc			
610 Cowper St .... Palo Alto CA 94301	**800-676-5831**		
Telpar Inc			
121 Broadway Ste 201 ....Dover NH 03820	**800-872-4886**	603-750-7237	173-6
TelSpan Inc			
101 W Washington St E Tower			
Ste 1200 ....Indianapolis IN 46204	**800-800-1729**		386
Telus			
630 Ren,-L,vesque Blvd W .... Montreal QC H3B1S6	**877-999-4669**	514-665-3050	803
Temecula Creek Inn			
44501 Rainbow Canyon Rd .... Temecula CA 92592	**888-976-3404**	855-774-8535	665
Temo Sunrooms Inc			
20400 Hall Rd ....Clinton Township MI 48038	**800-344-8366**		105
Temp-Air Inc			
3700 W Preserve Blvd .... Burnsville MN 55337	**800-836-7432**		14
Tempco Electric Heater Corp			
607 N Central Ave ....Wood Dale IL 60191	**888-268-6396**	630-350-2252	318
Tempe Tourism Office			
222 S Mill Ave Ste 120................. Tempe AZ 85281	**866-914-1052**	480-894-8158	206
Temperature Systems Inc			
5001 Voges Rd .... Madison WI 53718	**800-366-0930**	608-271-7500	608
Temple College			
2600 S First St ....Temple TX 76504	**800-460-4636***	254-298-8300	162
*Admissions			
Temporary Solutions Inc			
10550 Linden Lake Plz Ste 200 .... Manassas VA 20109	**888-222-0457**	703-361-2220	717
Temps Plus Inc			
268 N Lincoln Ave Ste 12 ....Corona CA 92882	**888-288-0808**		260
Temptronic Corp			
41 Hampden Rd ....Mansfield MA 02048	**800-558-5080***	781-688-2300	418
*Tech Support			
Tempur-Pedic North America LLC			
1000 Tempur Way ....Lexington KY 40511	**800-821-6621**		
Ten-8 Fire Equipment Inc			
2904 59th Ave Dr E .... Bradenton FL 34203	**877-989-7660**	941-756-7779	513

	Toll-Free	Phone	Class
TenAsys Corp			
1400 NW Compton Dr Ste 301......... Hillsboro OR 97006	**877-277-9189**	503-748-4720	
Tencarva Machinery Company Inc			
12200 Wilfong Ct ....Midlothian VA 23112	**800-849-5764**	804-639-4646	384
TenCate Geosynthetics North America			
365 S Holland Dr ....Pendergrass GA 30567	**888-795-0808**	706-693-2226	740-3
TenCate Grass America			
1131 Broadway St ....Dayton TN 37321	**800-251-1033**	423-775-0792	601-1
TenCate Protective Fabrics USA			
6501 Mall Blvd ....Union City GA 30291	**800-241-8630**		740-3
Tender Corp			
106 Burndy Rd ....Littleton NH 03561	**800-258-4696**	603-444-5464	280
Tenenbaum's Vacation Stores Inc			
300 Market St .... Kingston PA 18704	**800-545-7099**	570-288-8747	766
Tenenz Inc			
9655 Penn S Ave ....Minneapolis MN 55431	**800-888-5803**		623
Tenere Inc			
700 Kelly Ave .... Dresser WI 54009	**866-836-3734**	715-294-1577	
Tenet Healthcare Corp			
1445 Ross Ave .... Dallas TX 75202	**800-743-6333**	469-893-2000	352
NYSE: THC			
Tennant Co			
701 N Lilac Dr ....Minneapolis MN 55422	**800-553-8033***	763-540-1200	385
*NYSE: TNC ■ *Cust Svc*			
Tenneco Inc			
500 N Field Dr .... Lake Forest IL 60045	**866-839-3259**	847-482-5000	60
NYSE: TEN			
Tennessee State Government			
Obion County			
1604B W Reelfoot Ave .... Union City TN 38261	**800-222-8754**	731-884-2133	337
Tennessean			
1100 Broadway .... Nashville TN 37203	**800-342-8237**	615-259-8000	528-2
Tennessee			
Administrative Office of the Cts			
511 Union St Ste 600............... Nashville TN 37219	**800-448-7970**	615-741-2687	338-43
Child Support Services Div			
400 Deaderick St .... Nashville TN 37243	**800-838-6911**	615-313-4880	338-43
Consumer Affairs Div			
500 James Robertson Pkwy .... Nashville TN 37243	**800-342-8385**	615-741-4737	338-43
Department of Financial Institutions			
312 Rosa L Parks Ave 2nd Fl .... Nashville TN 37243	**800-231-7831**	615-741-2236	338-43
Housing Development Agency			
502 Deaderick St			
Andrew Jackson Bldg 3rd Fl........ Nashville TN 37243	**800-228-8432**	615-815-2200	338-43
Human Services Dept			
400 Deaderick St .... Nashville TN 37248	**866-311-4287**	615-313-4700	338-43
Insurance Div			
500 James Robertson Pkwy .... Nashville TN 37243	**800-342-4029**	615-741-2241	338-43
Labor & Workforce Development Dept			
220 French Landing Dr .... Nashville TN 37243	**844-224-5818**		259
Lottery			
1 Century Pl 26 Century Blvd Ste 200			
PO Box 291869 .... Nashville TN 37214	**800-826-4311**	615-324-6500	
Mental Health & Developmental Disabilities Dept			
500 Deaderick St .... Nashville TN 37243	**800-560-5767**		338-43
Securities Div			
500 James Robertson Pkwy			
8th Fl .... Nashville TN 37243	**800-863-9117**	615-741-2947	338-43
Student Assistance Corp			
404 James Robertson Pkwy			
Ste 1510...................... Nashville TN 37243	**800-342-1663**	615-741-1346	721
Supreme Court			
511 Union St			
Nashville City Ctr Ste 600 .... Nashville TN 37219	**800-448-7970**	615-741-2687	338-43
Vital Records Div			
Andrew Johnson Twr 710 James Robertson Pkwy			
1st Fl .... Nashville TN 37243	**855-809-0072**	615-741-1763	
Workers Compensation Div			
220 French Landing Dr .... Nashville TN 37243	**844-224-5818**	615-741-6642	338-43
Tennessee Aquarium			
1 Broad St .... Chattanooga TN 37402	**800-262-0695**		40
Tennessee Assn of Realtors (TAR)			
901 19th Ave S .... Nashville TN 37212	**877-321-1477**	615-321-1477	652
Tennessee Baptist Convention			
PO Box 682789 ....Franklin TN 37068	**800-558-2090**	615-373-2255	48-20
Tennessee Bar Assn			
221 Fourth Ave N Ste 400............ Nashville TN 37219	**800-899-6993**	615-383-7421	72
Tennessee Commerce Bank			
381 Mallory Stn Rd Ste 207 .... Franklin TN 37067	**877-275-3342**		70
Tennessee Dental Assn (TDA)			
660 Bakers Bridge Ave Ste 300........ Franklin TN 37067	**800-824-9722**	615-628-0208	227
Tennessee Farmers Co-op			
180 Old Nashville Hwy .... La Vergne TN 37086	**800-366-2667**	615-793-8011	276
Tennessee Fitness Spa			
299 Natural Bridge Pk Rd ....Waynesboro TN 38485	**800-235-8365**	931-722-5589	702
Tennessee Rehabilitative Initiative in Correction (TRICOR)			
240 Great Cir Rd Ste 310 .... Nashville TN 37228	**800-958-7426**	615-741-5705	626
Tennessee State Employees Association			
627 Woodland St .... Nashville TN 37206	**800-251-8732**	615-256-4533	529
Tennessee State Museum			
505 Deaderick St .... Nashville TN 37243	**800-407-4324**	615-741-2692	517
Tennessee State University			
3500 John A Merritt Blvd			
PO Box 9609................... Nashville TN 37209	**888-463-6878***	615-963-5000	166
*Admissions			
Tennessee Steel Haulers Inc			
PO Box 78189 .... Nashville TN 37207	**800-776-4004**	615-271-2400	775
Tennessee Technological University			
1 William L Jones Dr .... Cookeville TN 38505	**800-255-8881**	931-372-3888	166
Tennessee Temple University			
1815 Union Ave .... Chattanooga TN 37404	**800-553-4050**	423-493-4100	166
Tennessee Valley Electric Co-op			
590 Florence Rd .... Savannah TN 38372	**866-925-4916**	731-925-4916	245
Tennessee Valley Printing Company Inc			
PO Box 2213 .... Decatur AL 35609	**888-353-4612**	256-353-4612	633-8
Tennessee Veterinary Medical Assn			
PO Box 803 ....Fayetteville TN 37334	**800-697-3587**	931-438-0070	790
Tennessee Wesleyan College			
204 E College St .... Athens TN 37303	**844-742-5898**	423-745-7504	166

	Toll-Free	Phone	Class

Alphabetical Section

Tennessee/DCI Donor Services
1600 Hayes St . . . . Nashville TN 37203 — **877-401-2517** — — 541

Tennis Canada
285 Rue Gary-carter . . . . Montreal QC H2R2W1 — **866-338-2685** — 514-273-1515

Tennsco Corp
201 Tennsco Dr PO Box 1888 . . . . Dickson TN 37056 — **866-446-8686*** — — 319-1
*Cust Svc

Tensas Parish
201 Hancock St PO Box 78. . . . . . Saint Joseph LA 71366 — **800-256-6660** — 318-766-3921 — 337

Tension Envelope Corp
819 E 19th St . . . . Kansas City MO 64108 — **800-388-5122** — — 263

TenStep Inc
181 Waterman St . . . . Marietta GA 30060 — **877-536-8434** — 770-795-9097 — 461

Tenzing Consulting LLC
2100 Georgetowne Dr Ste 302 . . . . . . Sewickley PA 15143 — **877-980-5300** — 724-940-4060 — 196

Teo Technologies Inc
11609 49th Pl W . . . . Mukilteo WA 98275 — **800-524-0024** — 425-349-1000 — 730

TEOCO Corp
12150 Monument Dr Ste 400 . . . . Fairfax VA 22033 — **888-868-3626** — 703-322-9200 — 787

Teracai
217 Lawrence Rd E . . . . North Syracuse NY 13212 — **800-913-9459** — 315-883-3500

Teraco Inc
2080 Commerce Dr . . . . Midland TX 79703 — **800-687-3999**

Teradata Corp
10000 Innovation Dr . . . . Dayton OH 45342 — **866-548-8348** — — 225
NYSE: TDC

Teradyne Inc Assembly Test Div
600 Riverpark Dr . . . . North Reading MA 01864 — **800-837-2396** — 978-370-2700 — 248

TeraGo Networks Inc
55 Commerce Vly Dr W Ste 800 . . . . Thornhill ON L3T7V9 — **866-837-2461** — 866-837-2465 — 224

Teragren
1920 S Proforma Ave . . . . Ontario CA 91761 — **800-929-6333** — 206-842-9477 — 290

TeraMach Technologies Inc
1130 Morrison Dr Ste 105 . . . . Ottawa ON K2H9N6 — **877-226-6549** — 613-226-7775 — 180

TERATECH Corp
77 Terrace Hall Ave . . . . Burlington MA 01803 — **866-837-2766** — 781-270-4143 — 474

Terex Corp Crane Div
202 Raleigh St . . . . Wilmington NC 28412 — **877-794-5284** — 910-395-8500 — 468

Terex-Telelect Inc
500 Oakwood Rd PO Box 1150. . . . . . . Watertown SD 57201 — **800-982-8975** — 605-882-4000 — 468

Terminal Corp, The
1657 A S Highland Ave . . . . Baltimore MD 21224 — **800-560-7207** — — 311

Terminal Railroad Assn of Saint Louis
1017 Olive St 5th Fl . . . . Saint Louis MO 63101 — **866-931-0498** — 618-451-8400 — 647

Terminix International Company LP
860 Ridge Lake Blvd . . . . Memphis TN 38120 — **877-837-6464** — — 573

Terminix Service Inc
3612 Fernandina Rd . . . . Columbia SC 29210 — **877-855-4093** — — 573

TernPro
320 Westlake Ave 4th Fl . . . . Seattle WA 98109 — **888-483-8779** — — 392

Terra Community College
2830 Napoleon Rd . . . . Fremont OH 43420 — **800-334-3886** — 419-334-8400 — 162

Terra Dotta LLC
501 W Franklin St Ste 105 . . . . Chapel Hill NC 27516 — **877-368-8277** — — 177

Terra Nova Steel & Iron (Ontario) Inc
3595 Hawkestone Rd . . . . Mississauga ON L5C2V1 — **877-427-0269** — 905-273-3872 — 490

Terra Remote Sensing Inc
1962 Mills Rd . . . . Sidney BC V8L5Y3 — **800-814-4212** — 250-656-0931 — 723

Terracap Group
100 Sheppard Ave E Ste 502 . . . . Toronto ON M2N6N5 — **800-363-3207** — 416-222-9345 — 524

Terraces at Los Altos, The
373 Pine Ln . . . . Los Altos CA 94022 — **800-230-2976** — 650-948-8291 — 668

Terraces at Phoenix, The
7550 N 16th St . . . . Phoenix AZ 85020 — **800-836-4281** — 602-906-4024 — 668

Terraces of Los Gatos
800 Blossom Hill Rd . . . . Los Gatos CA 95032 — **800-673-1982** — 408-356-1006 — 668

Terracon
18001 W 106th St . . . . Olathe KS 66061 — **800-593-7777** — 913-599-6886 — 261

Terracor Business Solutions
677 St Mary's Rd . . . . Winnipeg MB R2M3M6 — **877-942-0005** — 204-477-5342 — 177

Terraine Inc
310 S Harrington St . . . . Raleigh NC 27603 — **800-531-1242** — — 395

TERRAMAI
8400 Agate Rd . . . . White City OR 97503 — **800-220-9062** — — 41

Terranea Resort & Spa
100 Terranea Way . . . . Rancho Palos Verdes CA 90275 — **866-547-3066** — 310-265-2800 — 377

Terrapin Systems LLC
9841 Washingtonian Blvd
Ste 200 . . . . Gaithersburg MD 20878 — **866-837-7797** — 301-530-9106

Terrazzo & Marble Supply Company of Illinois
77 Wheeling Rd . . . . Wheeling IL 60090 — **800-762-7253**

Terre Haute Regional Hospital (THRH)
3901 S Seventh St . . . . Terre Haute IN 47802 — **866-270-2311** — 812-232-0021 — 373-3

Terre Hill Silo Company Inc
PO Box 10 . . . . Terre Hill PA 17581 — **800-242-1509** — 717-445-3100 — 183

Terrebonne General Medical Ctr (TGMC)
8166 Main St . . . . Houma LA 70360 — **888-850-6270** — 985-873-4141 — 373-3

Terroco Industries Ltd
27212 Twp Rd 391 . . . . Red Deer AB T4N5E1 — **800-670-1100** — 403-346-1171 — 535

Terry Laboratories Inc
7005 Technology Dr . . . . Melbourne FL 32904 — **800-367-2563** — 321-259-1630 — 477

Terry Precision Bicycles for Women Inc
47 Maple St . . . . Burlington VT 05401 — **800-289-8379** — — 82

Terry Thompson Chevrolet Olds
1402 US Hwy 98 . . . . Daphne AL 36526 — **800-287-9309** — 251-626-0631 — 57

Terryberry Co
2033 Oak Industrial Dr NE . . . . . . Grand Rapids MI 49505 — **800-253-0882** — 616-458-1391 — 408

Terry-Durin Co
409 Seventh Ave SE . . . . Cedar Rapids IA 52401 — **800-332-8114** — 319-364-4106 — 246

Terumo Cardiovascular Systems Corp
6200 Jackson Rd . . . . Ann Arbor MI 48103 — **800-262-3304** — 734-663-4145 — 474

Terumo Medical Corp
2101 Cottontail Ln . . . . Somerset NJ 08873 — **800-283-7866** — 732-302-4900 — 474

Tesa Tape Inc
5825 Carnegie Blvd . . . . Charlotte NC 28209 — **800-426-2181** — 704-554-0707 — 727

Tesco Industries LP
1035 E Hacienda . . . . Bellville TX 77418 — **800-699-5824** — — 319-3

Tesko Enterprises
7350 W Montrose Ave . . . . Norridge IL 60706 — **800-621-4514** — 708-452-0045 — 286

Tesla
3500 Deer Creek Rd . . . . Palo Alto CA 94304 — **888-518-3752** — 650-681-5000 — 59

TESOL (Teachers of English to Speakers of Other Languages)
700 S Washington St Ste 200. . . . . . . Alexandria VA 22314 — **888-547-3369** — 703-836-0774 — 49-5

TESSCO Technologies Inc
11126 McCormick Rd . . . . Hunt Valley MD 21031 — **800-472-7373** — 410-229-1000 — 246
NASDAQ: TESS

Test com Inc
3558 Lee Rd . . . . Shaker Heights OH 44120 — **877-502-8600** — — 521

Test Inc 2323 Fourth St . . . . Peru IL 61354 — **800-659-4659** — 815-224-1650 — 738

Test Mark Industries Inc
995 North Market St . . . . East Palestine OH 44413 — **800-783-3227** — — 190

TestAmerica Laboratories Inc
4625 E Cotton Ctr Blvd Ste 189 . . . . Phoenix AZ 85040 — **866-785-5227** — 602-437-3340 — 738

Testcountry
10123 Carroll Canyon Rd . . . . San Diego CA 92131 — **800-656-0745** — 858-784-6904 — 738

Testing Machines Inc
40 McCullough Dr . . . . .New Castle DE 19720 — **800-678-3221*** — 302-613-5600 — 470
*General

Testor Corp
11 Hawthorn Pkwy . . . . .Vernon Hills IL 60061 — **800-837-8677** — 815-962-6654 — 757

Teters Floral Products Inc
1425 S Lillian Ave . . . . Bolivar MO 65613 — **800-999-5996** — 417-326-7654 — 293

Teton County
PO Box 1727 . . . . Jackson WY 83001 — **800-368-8683** — 307-733-4430 — 337

Teton Mountain Lodge & Spa
3385 Cody Ln . . . . Teton Village WY 83025 — **800-631-6271** — 307-201-6066 — 378

Tetra Corporate Services LLC
6995 Union Park Ctr
Ste 360 . . . . .Salt Lake City UT 84047 — **800-417-0548** — 801-566-2600 — 264-3

Tetra Medical Supply Corp
6364 W Gross Pt Rd . . . . Niles IL 60714 — **800-621-4041*** — 847-647-0590 — 473
*Cust Svc

Tetrad Computer Applications Ltd
1465 Slater Rd PO Box 5007 . . . . Vancouver BC V6G2T3 — **800-663-1334** — 604-685-2295 — 177

Tetrasoft Inc
16647 Chesterfield Grove Rd
Ste 120 . . . . Chesterfield MO 63005 — **866-314-7557** — 636-530-7638 — 179

Tetrault Insurance Agency Inc
4317 Acushnet Ave . . . . New Bedford MA 02745 — **800-696-9991** — 508-995-8365 — 389

Teva
123 N Leroux St . . . . Flagstaff AZ 86001 — **800-367-8382*** — 928-779-5938 — 301
*General

Teva Pharmaceutical USA
1090 Horsham Rd . . . . .North Wales PA 19454 — **800-545-8800** — 215-591-3000 — 579
NYSE: TEVA

Tevet LLC
85 Spring St S . . . . Mosheim TN 37818 — **866-886-8527** — 678-905-1300 — 201

Texans Credit Union
777 E Campbell Rd . . . . Richardson TX 75081 — **800-843-5295** — 972-348-2000 — 219

Texarkana College
2500 North Robison Rd . . . . Texarkana TX 75599 — **877-275-4377** — 903-838-4541 — 162

Texas
Aging & Disability Services
701 W 51st St . . . . Austin TX 78751 — **888-388-6332** — 512-438-3011 — 338-44
Agriculture Dept
PO Box 12847 . . . . Austin TX 78711 — **800-835-5832*** — 512-463-7476 — 338-44
*Cust Svc
Arts Commission
920 Colorado Ste 501
PO Box 13406 . . . . Austin TX 78701 — **800-252-9415** — 512-463-5535 — 338-44
Assistive & Rehabilitation Services Dept
4800 N Lamar Blvd 3rd Fl . . . . Austin TX 78756 — **800-252-7009** — 512-377-0500 — 338-44
Banking Dept
2601 N Lamar Blvd . . . . Austin TX 78705 — **877-276-5554** — 512-475-1300 — 338-44
Comptroller of Public Accounts
111 E 17th St . . . . Austin TX 78774 — **800-252-5555** — 512-463-4444 — 338-44
Crime Victims Services Div
PO Box 12198 . . . . Austin TX 78711 — **800-983-9933** — 512-936-1200 — 338-44
General Land Office
1700 N Congress Ave Ste 935 . . . . Austin TX 78701 — **800-998-4456** — 512-463-5001 — 338-44
Governor PO Box 12428 . . . . Austin TX 78711 — **800-843-5789** — 512-463-2000 — 338-44
Information Resources Dept
300 W 15th St Ste 1300 . . . . Austin TX 78701 — **855-275-3471** — 512-475-4700 — 338-44
Insurance Dept
333 Guadalupe St PO Box 149104 . . . . Austin TX 78714 — **800-578-4677** — — 338-44
Licensing & Regulation Dept
920 Colorado . . . . Austin TX 78701 — **800-803-9202** — 512-463-6599 — 338-44
Medical Board
PO Box 2018 . . . . Austin TX 78768 — **800-248-4062*** — 512-305-7010 — 338-44
*Cust Svc
Motor Vehicle Div
4000 Jackson Ave . . . . Austin TX 78731 — **888-368-4689** — — 338-44
Parks & Wildlife Dept
4200 Smith School Rd . . . . Austin TX 78744 — **800-792-1112** — 512-389-4800 — 338-44
Public Utility Commission
PO Box 13326 . . . . Austin TX 78711 — **888-782-8477** — 512-936-7000 — 338-44
Railroad Commission
1701 N Congress Ave PO Box 12967. . . . Austin TX 78711 — **877-228-5740** — 512-463-7058 — 338-44
Vital Statistics Bureau
1100 W 49th St PO Box 12040. . . . . . . Austin TX 78756 — **888-963-7111** — — 338-44
Workers Compensation Commission
7551 Metro Ctr Dr Ste 100. . . . . Austin TX 78744 — **800-252-7031*** — — 338-44
*Cust Svc

Texas A & M University
Rudder Tower Ste 205. . . . . College Station TX 77843 — **888-890-5667** — 979-845-8901 — 166
Galveston
200 Seawolf Pkwy . . . . .Galveston TX 77554 — **877-322-4443** — 409-740-4428 — 166
Kingsville
700 University Blvd MSC 128 . . . . . .Kingsville TX 78363 — **800-726-8192** — 361-593-2111 — 166
Texarkana
7101 University Ave . . . . .Texarkana TX 75503 — **866-791-9120** — 903-223-3000 — 166

Texas A & M University Press
John H Lindsey Bldg 4354 TAMU
. . . . College Station TX 77843 — **800-826-8911*** — 979-845-1436 — 633-4
*Orders

Name / Address	City	State	ZIP	Toll-Free	Phone	Class
Texas Art Supply 2001 Montrose Blvd	Houston	TX	77006	**800-888-9278**	713-526-5221	45
Texas Assn of Realtors 1115 San Jacinto Blvd Ste 200	Austin	TX	78701	**800-873-9155**	512-480-8200	652
Texas Association of School Business Officials 6611 Boeing Dr	El Paso	TX	79925	**800-338-6531**	512-462-1711	
Texas Bank & Trust 300 E Whaley PO Box 3188	Longview	TX	75606	**800-263-7013**	903-237-5500	
Texas Bar Journal 1414 Colorado St	Austin	TX	78701	**800-204-2222**	512-463-1463	455-15
Texas Basket Co 100 Myrtle Dr	Jacksonville	TX	75766	**800-657-2200**	903-586-8014	200
Texas Book Festival 610 Brazos St Ste 200	Austin	TX	78701	**800-222-8733**	512-477-4055	281
Texas Capital Bank 2000 McKinney Ave Ste 700	Dallas	TX	75201	**877-839-2265**	214-932-6600	70
Texas Children's Hospital 6621 Fannin St	Houston	TX	77030	**800-364-5437**	832-824-1000	373-1
Texas Christian University TCU PO Box 297043	Fort Worth	TX	76129	**800-828-3764**	817-257-7490	166
Texas Christian University Mary Couts Burnett Library 2800 S University Dr	Fort Worth	TX	76129	**866-321-7428**	817-257-7000	433-6
Texas Coffee Co Inc 3297 S M L King Jr Pkwy	Beaumont	TX	77705	**800-259-3400**	409-835-3434	296-7
Texas College 2404 N Grand Ave	Tyler	TX	75702	**800-306-6299**	903-593-8311	166
Texas Crushed Stone Co 5300 S IH-35 PO Box 1000	Georgetown	TX	78627	**800-772-8272**	512-930-0106	501-5
Texas Ctr for Infectious Diseases 2303 SE Military Dr	San Antonio	TX	78223	**800-839-5864**	210-534-8857	373-7
Texas Dental Assn 1946 S IH-35 Ste 400	Austin	TX	78704	**800-832-1145**	512-443-3675	227
Texas Disposal Systems Inc (TDS) 12200 Carl Rd	Creedmoor	TX	78610	**800-375-8375**	512-421-1300	799
Texas Dow Employees Credit Union (TDECU) 1001 FM 2004	Lake Jackson	TX	77566	**800-839-1154**	979-297-1154	219
Texas Electric Co-ops Inc 1122 Colorado St 24th Fl	Austin	TX	78701	**800-301-2860**	512-454-0311	245
Texas Enterprises 5005 E Seventh St	Austin	TX	78702	**800-545-4412**	512-385-2167	575
Texas Farm Bureau PO Box 2689	Waco	TX	76702	**800-488-7872**	254-772-3030	455-1
Texas Fish & Game Magazine 247 Airtex Dr	Houston	TX	77090	**800-725-1134**	281-227-3001	526
Texas Gauge & Control Inc 7575 Dillon St	Houston	TX	77061	**800-914-0009**	713-641-2282	357
Texas Health Resources 612 E Lamar Blvd	Arlington	TX	76011	**877-847-9355**		352
Texas Healthcare PLLC 2821 Lackland Rd Ste 300	Fort Worth	TX	76116	**877-238-6200**	817-378-3640	373-3
Texas Heat Treating Inc 155 Texas Ave	Round Rock	TX	78664	**800-580-5884**	512-255-5884	482
Texas Hospital Insurance Exchange 8310 N Capital of Texas Hwy Ste 250	Austin	TX	78731	**800-792-0060**	512-451-5775	390-5
Texas Instruments Inc 12500 TI Blvd *NASDAQ: TXN* ■ *Cust Svc	Dallas	TX	75243	**800-336-5236***	972-995-2011	692
Texas Jet Inc 200 Texas Way	Fort Worth	TX	76106	**800-776-4547**	817-624-8438	
Texas Lawyers Insurance Exchange (TLIE) 1801 S MoPac Ste 300	Austin	TX	78746	**800-252-9332**	512-480-9074	390-5
Texas Legal Services Center Inc 2101 S IH 35 Frontage Rd	Austin	TX	78741	**888-343-4414**	800-622-2520	427
Texas Life Insurance Co 900 Washington PO Box 830	Waco	TX	76703	**800-283-9233**	254-752-6521	390-2
Texas Lime Co 15865 Farm Rd 1434 PO Box 851	Cleburne	TX	76033	**800-772-8000**	817-641-4433	439
Texas Lutheran University 1000 W Ct St	Seguin	TX	78155	**800-771-8521**	830-372-8050	166
Texas Medical Assn 401 W 15th St	Austin	TX	78701	**800-880-1300**	512-370-1300	472
Texas Memorial Museum 2400 Trinity St	Austin	TX	78705	**800-687-4132**	512-471-1604	517
Texas Methodist Foundation 11709 Boulder Ln Ste 100	Austin	TX	78726	**800-933-5502**	512-331-9971	305
Texas Motor Speedway 3545 Lone Star Cir	Fort Worth	TX	76177	**800-805-8721**	817-215-8510	638
Texas Motorplex 7500 W Hwy 287	Ennis	TX	75119	**800-668-6775**	972-878-2641	512
Texas Mutual Insurance Co 6210 E Hwy 290	Austin	TX	78723	**888-532-5246**	512-224-3800	390-4
Texas Orthopedic Hospital 7401 Main St	Houston	TX	77030	**866-783-4549**	713-799-8600	373-7
Texas Parks & Wildlife Department 4200 Smith School Rd	Austin	TX	78744	**800-792-1112**	512-389-4800	561
Texas Pharmacy Assn 3200 Steck Ave Ste 370	Austin	TX	78757	**800-505-5463**	512-836-8350	581
Texas Pipe & Supply Co Inc 2330 Holmes Rd	Houston	TX	77051	**800-233-8736**	713-799-9235	490
Texas Pneumatics Systems Inc 2404 Superior Dr	Arlington	TX	76013	**800-211-9690**	817-794-0068	20
Texas Presbyterian Foundation 6100 Colwell Blvd Ste 250	Irving	TX	75039	**800-955-3155**	214-522-3155	48-20
Texas Press Assn 305 S Congress Ave	Austin	TX	78704	**800-749-4793**	512-477-6755	7
Texas Process Equipment Co 5215 Ted St	Houston	TX	77040	**800-828-4114**	713-460-5555	384
Texas Public Radio (TPR) 8401 Datapoint Dr Ste 800	San Antonio	TX	78229	**800-622-8977**	210-614-8977	628
Texas Refinery Corp 840 N Main St	Fort Worth	TX	76164	**800-827-0711**	817-332-1161	537
Texas Republican Party 1108 Lavaca Ste 500	Austin	TX	78701	**800-525-5555**	512-477-9821	612-2
Texas Roadhouse Inc 6040 Dutchmans Ln Ste 400 *NASDAQ: TXRH*	Louisville	KY	40205	**800-839-7623**	502-426-9984	666
Texas Scottish Rite Hospital for Children 2222 Welborn St	Dallas	TX	75219	**800-421-1121**	214-559-5000	373-1
Texas Sports Hall of Fame 1108 S University Parks Dr	Waco	TX	76706	**800-567-9561**	254-756-1633	519
Texas State Technical College (TSTC) *Abilene* 650 E Hwy 80	Abilene	TX	79601	**800-852-8784**	325-672-7091	162
Harlingen 1902 N Loop 499	Harlingen	TX	78550	**800-852-8784**	956-364-4000	162
Sweetwater 300 Homer K Taylor Dr	Sweetwater	TX	79556	**877-450-3595**	325-235-7300	162
Texas State University *San Marcos* 601 University Dr *Admissions	San Marcos	TX	78666	**866-294-0987***	512-245-2340	166
Texas Station Gambling Hall & Hotel 2101 Texas Star Ln *Resv	North Las Vegas	NV	89032	**800-654-8888***	702-631-1000	133
Texas Steakhouse 711 Sutters Creek Blvd	Rocky Mount	NC	27804	**855-220-7228**		
Texas Tech University PO Box 45005	Lubbock	TX	79409	**888-270-3369**	806-742-1480	166
Texas Tech University Press 608 N Knoxville Ave Ste120 Grantham Bldg	Lubbock	TX	79415	**800-832-4042**	806-742-2982	633-4
Texas Transplant Institute 7700 Floyd Curl Dr	San Antonio	TX	78229	**800-298-7824**	210-575-3817	764
Texas United Pipe Inc 11627 N Houston Rosslyn Rd *Sales	Houston	TX	77086	**800-966-8741***	281-448-9463	592
Texas Vet Lab Inc 1702 N Bell St	San Angelo	TX	76903	**800-284-8403**	325-653-4505	580
Texas Veterinary Medical Assn 8104 Exchange Dr	Austin	TX	78754	**800-711-0023**	512-452-4224	790
Texas Wesleyan University 1201 Wesleyan St	Fort Worth	TX	76105	**800-580-8980**	817-531-4444	166
Texas Wesleyan University School of Law 1515 Commerce St	Fort Worth	TX	76102	**800-733-9529**	817-212-4000	167-1
Texas Woman's University 304 Admin Dr PO Box 425589	Denton	TX	76204	**866-809-6130**	940-898-3188	166
Texas-New Mexico Power Co (TNMP) 577 N Garden Ridge Blvd	Lewisville	TX	75067	**888-866-7456**	972-420-4189	782
TexLoc Ltd 4700 Lone Star Blvd	Fort Worth	TX	76106	**800-423-6551**	817-625-5081	636
Texoma Medical Ctr 5016 S US Hwy 75	Denison	TX	75020	**800-256-0943**	903-416-4000	373-3
Textile Care Services Inc 225 Wood Lake Dr SE	Rochester	MN	55904	**800-422-0945**		441
Textile Rental Services Assn (TRSA) 1800 Diagonal Rd Ste 200	Alexandria	VA	22314	**877-770-9274**	703-519-0029	49-4
Textile Rubber & Chemical Co Inc 1300 Tiarco Dr SW	Dalton	GA	30721	**800-727-8453**	706-277-1300	601-3
Tex-Tube Co 1503 N Post Oak Rd	Houston	TX	77055	**800-839-7473**	713-686-4351	488
Textured Coatings Of America 2422 E 15th St	Panama City	FL	32405	**800-454-0340**		546
Tezzaron Semiconductor Corp 7600 Chevy Chase Dr Bldg 2 Ste 300	Austin	TX	78752	**844-839-7364**	630-505-0404	
TF Hudgins Inc 4405 Directors Row	Houston	TX	77092	**800-582-3834**	713-682-3651	384
TF System The Vertical ICF Inc 3030c Holmgren Way	Green Bay	WI	54304	**800-360-4634**	920-983-9960	693
TFB (Fauquier Bank, The) 10 Courthouse Sq	Warrenton	VA	20186	**800-638-3798**	540-347-2700	70
TFC (Franchise Co, The) 14502 N Dale Mabry Ste 200	Tampa	FL	33618	**800-294-5591**		461
TFCU (Teachers Federal Credit Union) 2410 N Ocean Ave	Farmingville	NY	11738	**800-341-4333**	631-698-7000	219
TFI (Technology Futures Inc) 13740 Research Blvd (N Hwy 183) Ste C-1	Austin	TX	78750	**800-835-3887**	512-258-8898	196
TFP nutrition 915 S Fredonia St	Nacogdoches	TX	75964	**800-392-3110**	936-564-3711	574
TFS Capital LLC 10 N High St Ste 500	West Chester	PA	19380	**888-837-4446**		524
TFT Inc 2991 N Osage Dr PO Box 445	Tulsa	OK	74127	**800-303-7982**	918-834-2366	478
TGMC (Terrebonne General Medical Ctr) 8166 Main St	Houma	LA	70360	**888-850-6270**	985-873-4141	373-3
TGP (Grocery People Ltd, The) 14505 Yellowhead Trl	Edmonton	AB	T5L3C4	**800-461-9401**	780-447-5700	297-8
TGR Industrial Services 8777 Tallyho Rd Bldg 1	Houston	TX	77061	**800-625-9288**	713-636-2288	
TH Properties 345 Main St Ste 112 *Sales	Harleysville	PA	19438	**800-225-5847***	215-513-4270	187
Thaddeus Stevens College of Technology (TSCT) 750 E King St	Lancaster	PA	17602	**800-842-3832**	717-299-7701	795
Thales ATM 23501 W 84th St	Shawnee	KS	66227	**800-624-7497**	913-422-2600	525
Thales Communications Inc 22605 Gateway Ctr Dr	Clarksburg	MD	20871	**800-258-4420**	240-864-7000	643
Thales e-Security Inc 2200 N Commerce Pkwy Ste 200	Weston	FL	33326	**888-744-4976**	954-888-6200	178-12
Tharo Systems Inc 2866 Nationwide Pkwy	Brunswick	OH	44212	**800-878-6833**	330-273-4408	174
Thayer Hotel 674 Thayer Rd	West Point	NY	10996	**800-247-5047**	845-446-4731	378
Thayer Scale 91 Schoosett St	Pembroke	MA	02359	**855-784-2937**	781-826-8101	680
Thayers Natural Remedies 65 Adams Rd	Easton	CT	06612	**888-842-9371**		794
The Greater New Braunfels Chamber of Commerce Inc 390 S Seguin St	New Braunfels	TX	78130	**800-572-2626**	830-625-2385	139
The Milledgeville-Baldwin Convention & Visitors Bureau 200 W Hancock St	Milledgeville	GA	31061	**800-653-1804**	478-452-4687	206
The Savings Bank Mutual Life Insurance Company of Massachusetts (SBLI) 1 Linscott Rd	Woburn	MA	01801	**888-630-5000**		

Name / Address	City	State	ZIP	Toll-Free	Phone	Class
Theatre Development Fund 1501 Broadway 21st Fl	New York	NY	10036	**888-424-4685**	212-221-0885	745
Theatre For A New Audience 154 Christopher St Ste 3D	New York	NY	10014	**866-811-4111**	212-229-2819	744
Theda Care at Home 3000 E College Ave	Appleton	WI	54915	**800-984-5554**	920-969-0919	370
Theda Clark Medical Ctr 130 Second St	Neenah	WI	54956	**800-236-3122**	920-729-3100	373-3
TheMART 222 Merchandise Mart Plz Ste 470	Chicago	IL	60654	**800-677-6278**		205
Themlsonline Com Inc 11150 Commerce Dr N	Champlin	MN	55316	**866-657-6654**	763-576-8286	648
Theodore Presser Co 588 North Gulph Rd	King of Prussia	PA	19406	**800-854-6764**	610-592-1222	633-7
Theprinterscom 3500 E College Ave	State College	PA	16801	**800-359-2097**		343
TheraCare 116 W 32nd St 8th Fl	New York	NY	10001	**800-505-7000**	212-564-2350	352
Therapedic International 103 College Rd E 2nd Fl	Princeton	NJ	08540	**800-314-4433**	609-720-0700	469
Therapeutic Solutions International Inc 4093 Oceanside Blvd Ste B	Oceanside	CA	92056	**877-468-4877**		
Therapy Support Inc 2803 N Oak Grove Ave	Springfield	MO	65803	**877-885-4325**	417-447-0987	473
TheraTest Laboratories Inc 1120 Dupage Ave	Lombard	IL	60148	**800-441-0771**		474
TheraTogs Inc 305 Society Dr Ste 3-C	Telluride	CO	81435	**888-634-0495**		194
There & Back Again Travel 35 E Broad St	Savannah	GA	31401	**800-782-8222**	912-920-8222	767
Theriault's PO Box 151	Annapolis	MD	21404	**800-966-3655**	410-224-3655	51
Therm Air Sales Corp 1413 41st St NW PO Box 9004	Fargo	ND	58106	**800-726-7520**	701-282-9500	608
Thermafiber Inc 3711 W Mill St	Wabash	IN	46992	**888-834-2371**	260-563-2111	388
Thermal Care Inc 5680 W Jarvis Ave	Niles	IL	60714	**888-828-7387**	847-966-2260	14
Thermal Circuits Inc 1 Technology Way	Salem	MA	01970	**800-808-4328**	978-745-1162	318
Thermal Corp 1264 Slaughter Rd	Madison	AL	35758	**800-633-2962**	256-837-1122	608
Thermal Dynamics 82 Benning St	West Lebanon	NH	03784	**800-752-7621**	603-298-5711	453
Thermal Engineering Corp 2741 The Blvd	Columbia	SC	29209	**800-331-0097**	803-783-0750	318
Thermal Engineering of Arizona Inc 2250 W Wetmore Rd	Tucson	AZ	85705	**866-832-7278**	520-888-4000	426
Thermal Equipment Corp 2030 E University Dr	Rancho Dominguez	CA	90220	**800-548-4422**	310-328-6600	318
Thermal Product Solutions 3827 Riverside Rd	Riverside	MI	49084	**800-873-4468**	269-849-2700	318
Thermal Windows & Doors 3700 Haney C	Murrysville	PA	15668	**800-245-1540**	724-325-6100	235
Therma-Stor LLC 4201 Lien Rd	Madison	WI	53704	**800-533-7533**	608-237-8400	606
Therma-Tru Corp 1750 Indian Wood Cir	Maumee	OH	43537	**800-537-8827**	419-891-7400	234
Thermedx LLC 31200 Solon Rd Unit 1	Solon	OH	44139	**888-542-9276**	440-542-0883	473
Thermionics Laboratory 1842 Sabre St	Hayward	CA	94545	**800-962-2310**	510-732-1755	172
Thermo Fisher Scientific 46360 Fremont Blvd	Fremont	CA	94538	**800-232-3342**	866-356-0354	231
Thermo Fisher Scientific 8365 Valley Pk	Middletown	VA	22645	**800-528-0494**	866-356-0354	231
Thermo Fluids Inc 4301 W Jefferson St	Phoenix	AZ	85043	**800-350-7565**		682
Thermo Scientific 12076 Santa Fe Dr PO Box 14428	Lenexa	KS	66215	**800-255-6730**	913-888-0939	231
Thermodyn Corp 3550 Silica Rd	Sylvania	OH	43560	**800-654-6518**	419-841-7782	673
Thermo-Fab Corp 76 Walker Rd	Shirley	MA	01464	**888-494-9777**	978-425-2311	598
ThermoGenesis Corp 2711 Citrus Rd *NASDAQ: KOOL*	Rancho Cordova	CA	95742	**800-783-8357**	916-858-5100	419
Thermopatch Corp 2204 Erie Blvd E	Syracuse	NY	13224	**800-252-6555**	315-446-8110	739
Thermoplastic Processes Inc 1268 Valley Rd	Stirling	NJ	07980	**888-554-6400**	908-561-3000	596
Thermos Co 475 N Martingale Rd Ste 1100	Schaumburg	IL	60173	**800-243-0745**	847-439-7821	603
ThermoSafe Brands 3930 N Ventura Dr Ste 450	Arlington Heights	IL	60004	**800-323-7442**	847-398-0110	597
Thermoseal 2350 Campbell Rd	Sidney	OH	45365	**800-990-7325**	937-498-2222	326
Thermoseal Glass Corp 400 Water St	Gloucester City	NJ	08030	**800-456-7788**	856-456-3109	329
ThermoServ 3901 Pipestone Rd	Dallas	TX	75212	**800-635-5559**	214-631-0307	597
Thermosoft International Corp 701 corporate Woods Pkwy	Vernon Hills	IL	60061	**800-308-8057**	847-279-3800	317
ThermoSpas Hot Tubs 10 Research Pkwy Ste 300	Wallingford	CT	06492	**800-876-0158**		374
Thermotron Industries Co 291 Kollen Pk Dr	Holland	MI	49423	**800-409-3449**	616-393-4580	385
Thermo-Twin Industries Inc 1155 Allegheny Ave	Oakmont	PA	15139	**800-641-2211**	412-826-1000	234
Thermwell Products Co 420 Rt 17 S	Mahwah	NJ	07430	**800-526-5265**	201-684-4400	388
Thermwood Corp 904 Buffaloville Rd *OTC: TOOD* ■ *Mktg	Dale	IN	47523	**800-533-6901***	812-937-4476	816
Thern Inc 5712 Industrial Pk Rd PO Box 347	Winona	MN	55987	**800-843-7648**	507-454-2996	468
TheStreetcom Inc 14 Wall St 15th Fl *NASDAQ: TST*	New York	NY	10005	**800-562-9571**	212-321-5000	403
Theta Delta Chi Inc 214 Lewis Wharf	Boston	MA	02110	**800-999-1847**	804-344-4300	48-16
Theta Tau Professional Engineering Fraternity 1011 San Jacinto Ste 205	Austin	TX	78701	**800-264-1904**	512-472-1904	48-16
Thetford Corp 7101 Jackson Ave PO Box 1285	Ann Arbor	MI	48106	**800-521-3032**	734-769-6000	606
Thetford Corp Recreational Vehicle Group 2901 E Bristol St Ste B	Elkhart	IN	46514	**800-831-1076**	574-266-7980	606
Thetubestore Inc 120 Lancing Dr	Hamilton	ON	L8W3A1	**877-570-0979**	905-570-0979	317
Thibaut Inc 480 Frelinghuysen Ave	Newark	NJ	07114	**800-223-0704**	973-643-1118	797
Thibodaux Regional Medical Ctr (TRMC) 602 N Acadia Rd	Thibodaux	LA	70301	**800-822-8442**	985-447-5500	373-3
Thiel College 75 College Ave	Greenville	PA	16125	**800-248-4435**	724-589-2000	166
Thiele Technologies 315 27th Ave NE	Minneapolis	MN	55418	**800-932-3647**	612-782-1200	543
Thillens Inc 4242 N Elston Ave	Chicago	IL	60618	**888-539-4446**	773-539-4444	399
Think Cp Technologies 16812 Hale Ave	Irvine	CA	92606	**800-726-2477**	949-833-3222	173-8
ThinkDirect Marketing Group Inc 8285 Bryan Dairy Rd Ste 150	Largo	FL	33773	**800-325-3155**	727-369-2700	392
Thinkfun Inc 1321 Cameron St	Alexandria	VA	22314	**800-468-1864**	703-549-4999	756
ThinkTV 110 S Jefferson St	Dayton	OH	45402	**800-247-1614**	937-220-1600	628
Thinkway Toys Inc 8885 Woodbine Ave	Markham	ON	L3R5G1	**800-535-5754**	905-470-8883	756
Third Federal Savings & Loan Assn of Cleveland 7007 Broadway Ave	Cleveland	OH	44105	**888-844-7333**	800-844-7333	70
Third Millennium Ministries 316 Live Oaks Blvd	Casselberry	FL	32707	**877-443-6455**	407-830-0222	48-20
Thirstystone Resources Inc 1304 Corporate Dr	Gainesville	TX	76240	**800-829-6888**	940-668-6793	292
Thirty-One Gifts 3425 Morse Crossing	Columbus	OH	43219	**866-443-8731**		365
This Week Community Newspapers 7801 N Central Dr PO Box 608	Lewis Center	OH	43035	**888-837-4342**	740-888-6000	633-8
Thomas Aquinas College 10000 Ojai Rd	Santa Paula	CA	93060	**800-634-9797**	805-525-4417	166
Thomas C Wilson Inc 21-11 44th Ave	Long Island	NY	11101	**800-230-2636**	718-729-3360	754
Thomas College 180 W River Rd *Admissions	Waterville	ME	04901	**800-339-7001***	207-859-1111	166
Thomas Conveyor Co 555 N Burleson Blvd	Burleson	TX	76028	**800-433-2217**	817-295-7151	207
Thomas Creative Apparel Inc 1 Harmony Pl	New London	OH	44851	**800-537-2575**	419-929-1506	155-13
Thomas E Creek Veterans Affairs Medical Ctr 6010 Amarillo Blvd W	Amarillo	TX	79106	**800-687-8262**	806-355-9703	373-8
Thomas Edison State College 101 W State St	Trenton	NJ	08608	**888-442-8372**	609-777-5680	166
Thomas Engineering Inc 575 W Central Rd	Hoffman Estates	IL	60192	**800-634-9910**	847-358-5800	385
Thomas George Associates Ltd 10 Larkfield Rd	East Northport	NY	11731	**800-443-8338**	631-261-8800	389
Thomas H Lee Partners LP 100 Federal St	Boston	MA	02110	**877-456-3427**	617-227-1050	404
Thomas Hospital 750 Morphy Ave	Fairhope	AL	36532	**800-422-2027**	251-928-2375	373-3
Thomas Jefferson School of Law 1155 Island Ave	San Diego	CA	92101	**877-318-6901**	619-297-9700	167-1
Thomas Jefferson University 1020 Walnut St	Philadelphia	PA	19107	**800-533-3669**	215-955-6000	166
Thomas Jefferson University Hospital 111 S 11th St	Philadelphia	PA	19107	**800-533-3669**	215-955-6000	373-3
Thomas M Cooley Law School 300 S Capitol Ave	Lansing	MI	48933	**800-243-2586**	517-371-5140	167-1
Thomas More College 333 Thomas More Pkwy	Crestview Hills	KY	41017	**800-825-4557**	859-344-3332	166
Thomas Nelson Inc 501 Nelson Pl PO Box 141000	Nashville	TN	37214	**800-251-4000**		633-3
Thomas Publishing Co 5 Penn Plz	New York	NY	10001	**800-733-1127**	212-695-0500	633-2
Thomas Reprographics 600 N Central Expy	Richardson	TX	75080	**800-877-3776**	972-231-7227	240
Thomas Scientific 1654 High Hill Rd PO Box 99	Swedesboro	NJ	08085	**800-345-2100**		419
Thomas Transcription Services Inc PO Box 26613	Jacksonville	FL	32226	**888-878-2889**	904-751-5058	476
Thomas University 1501 Millpond Rd	Thomasville	GA	31792	**800-538-9784**	229-226-1621	166
Thomaston Savings Bank 203 Main St PO Box 907 *General	Thomaston	CT	06787	**855-344-1874***	860-283-1874	70
Thomasville Medical Ctr 207 Old Lexington Rd	Thomasville	NC	27360	**888-844-0080**	336-472-2000	373-3
Thombert Inc 316 E Seventh St N	Newton	IA	50208	**800-433-3572**		604
Thompson Hine LLP 127 Public Sq 3900 Key Ctr	Cleveland	OH	44114	**877-257-3382**	216-566-5500	427
Thompson Industrial Services LLC 104 N Main	Sumter	SC	29150	**800-849-8040**	803-773-8005	606
Thompson Information Services 4340 E-West Hwy Ste 300 *Cust Svc	Bethesda	MD	20814	**800-677-3789***	202-872-3611	633-9
Thompson Mahogany Co 7400 Edmund St	Philadelphia	PA	19136	**877-589-6637**		679
Thompson Olde Inc 3250 Camino Del Sol	Oxnard	CA	93030	**800-827-1565**	805-983-0388	360

Name / Address	City	State	Zip	Toll-Free	Phone	Class
Thompson Pump & Mfg Company Inc 4620 City Ctr Dr PO Box 291370	Port Orange	FL	32129	**800-767-7310**	386-767-7310	637
Thompson Rivers University (TRU) 805 TRU Way	Kamloops	BC	V2C0C8	**800-663-1663**	250-828-5000	780
Thompson Siegel & Walmsley Inc 6806 Paragon Pl Ste 300	Richmond	VA	23230	**800-697-1056**	804-353-4500	400
Thompson Technologies 200 Galleria Pkwy Ste 1100	Atlanta	GA	30339	**888-794-7947**	770-794-8380	717
Thoms Proestler Co 8001 TPC Rd	Rock Island	IL	61204	**800-747-1234**	309-787-1234	297-8
Thomsen Group LLC 1303 43rd St	Kenosha	WI	53140	**800-558-4018**		296
Thomson CenterWatch Inc 100 N Washington St Ste 301 *Cust Svc	Boston	MA	02114	**800-765-9647***	617-948-5100	633-10
Thomson Elite 800 Corporate Pointe Ste 150 *Cust Svc	Los Angeles	CA	90230	**800-354-8337***	424-243-2100	178-10
Thomson Reuters 7322 Newman Blvd *Cust Svc	Dexter	MI	48130	**800-968-8900***		178-1
Thomson Reuters 22 Thomson Pl	Boston	MA	02210	**888-216-1929**	617-856-2000	386
Thomson Reuters DT Tax & Acctg 3333 Graham Blvd Ste 222	Montreal	QC	H3R3L5	**800-663-7829**	514-733-8355	180
Thomson Safaris 14 Mt Auburn St	Watertown	MA	02472	**800-235-0289**	800-262-6255	632
Thomson-Hood Veterans Ctr 100 Veterans Dr	Wilmore	KY	40390	**800-928-4838**	859-858-2814	788
Thomson-Macconnell Cadillac Inc 2820 Gilbert Ave	Cincinnati	OH	45206	**877-472-0738**	888-838-1071	513
Thomson-Shore Inc 7300 W Joy Rd	Dexter	MI	48130	**800-706-4545**	734-426-3939	622
Thor Travel Services Inc 12202 Airport Way Ste 150	Broomfield	CO	80021	**800-825-1071**	303-439-4100	767
Thoratec Corp 6035 Stoneridge Dr	Pleasanton	CA	94588	**800-528-2577**	925-847-8600	250
Thor-Lo Inc 2210 Newton Dr	Statesville	NC	28677	**888-846-7567**	704-872-6522	155-9
Thornburg Investment Management Funds 2300 N Ridgetop Rd	Santa Fe	NM	87506	**800-533-9337**	505-984-0200	524
Thorneloe University 935 Ramsey Lake Rd *General	Sudbury	ON	P3E2C6	**866-846-7635***	705-673-1730	780
Thornmark Asset Management Inc 119 Spadina Ave Ste 701	Toronto	ON	M5V2L1	**877-204-6201**	416-204-6200	193
Thoro'Bred Inc 5020 E La Palma Ave	Anaheim	CA	92807	**800-854-6059**	714-779-2581	481
Thoroughbred Direct Intermodal Services 5165 Campus Dr Ste 400	Plymouth Meeting	PA	19462	**877-250-2902**		447
Thoroughbred Owners & Breeders Assn (TOBA) PO Box 910668	Lexington	KY	40591	**888-606-8622**	859-276-2291	48-3
Thoroughbred Racing Associations of North America Inc (TRA) 420 Fair Hill Dr	Elkton	MD	21921	**866-847-8772**	410-392-9200	
Thoroughbred Software International Inc 285 Davidson Ave Ste 302	Somerset	NJ	08873	**800-524-0430**	732-560-1377	178-2
Thorp Reed & Armstrong LLP 301 Grant St 14th Fl	Pittsburgh	PA	15219	**800-949-3120**	412-394-7711	427
Thorsnes Bartolotta McGuire 2550 Fifth Ave 11th Fl	San Diego	CA	92103	**800-577-2922**	619-236-9363	427
Thought Technology Ltd 2180 Belgrave Ave	Montreal	QC	H4A2L8	**800-361-3651**	514-489-8251	738
Thousand Hills Golf Resort 245 S Wildwood Dr	Branson	MO	65616	**877-262-0430**	417-336-5873	665
Thousand Pines Christian Camp & Conference Center 359 Thousnd Pines Rd	Crestline	CA	92325	**888-423-2267**	909-338-2705	239
Thread Check Inc 390 Oser Ave	Hauppauge	NY	11788	**800-767-7633**	631-231-1515	491
Three Bars Cattle & Guest Ranch 9500 Wycliffe Perry Creek Rd	Cranbrook	BC	V1C7C7	**877-426-5230**	250-426-5230	239
Three D Graphics Inc 11340 W Olympic Blvd Ste 352	Los Angeles	CA	90064	**800-913-0008**	310-231-3330	178-8
Three D Metals Inc 5462 Innovation Dr	Valley City	OH	44280	**800-362-9905**	330-220-0451	490
Three Hands Corp 13259 Ralston Ave	Sylmar	CA	91342	**800-443-5443**	818-833-1200	360
Three Island Crossing State Park 1083 S Three Island Park Dr	Glenns Ferry	ID	83623	**888-922-6743**	208-366-2394	561
Three Lakes Information Bureau 1704 Superior St PO Box 268	Three Lakes	WI	54562	**800-972-6103**	715-546-3344	206
Three Notch Electric Membership Corp PO Box 295	Donalsonville	GA	39845	**800-239-5377**	229-524-5377	245
Three Rivers Community College 2080 Three Rivers Blvd	Poplar Bluff	MO	63901	**877-879-8722**	573-840-9600	162
Three Rivers Electric Co-op 1324 E Main St PO Box 918	Linn	MO	65051	**800-892-2251**	573-644-9000	245
Three Rivers Planning & Development District Inc 75 S Main St PO Box 690	Pontotoc	MS	38863	**877-489-6911**	662-489-2415	461
Threshold Communications 16541 Redmond Way Ste 245C	Redmond	WA	98052	**844-844-1382**	206-812-6200	224
THRH (Terre Haute Regional Hospital) 3901 S Seventh St	Terre Haute	IN	47802	**866-270-2311**	812-232-0021	373-3
Thrifty White Stores 6055 Nathan Lane N Ste 200	Plymouth	MN	55442	**800-642-3275**	763-513-4300	237
Thrive Networks Inc 836 North St Bldg 300 Ste 3201	Tewksbury	MA	01876	**866-205-2810**	978-461-3999	620
Thrivent Financial for Lutherans 4321 N BallaRd Rd	Appleton	WI	54919	**800-847-4836**		390-2
ThriveOn Inc 210 S 20th St	New Ulm	MN	56073	**855-767-2571**		196
Thumann Inc 670 Dell Rd	Carlstadt	NJ	07072	**800-358-0761**	201-935-3636	297-9
Thumb Cellular Ltd Partnership PO Box 650	Pigeon	MI	48755	**800-443-5057**		731
Thumbs-Up Telemarketing Inc 11861 Westline Industrial Dr Ste 600	Saint Louis	MO	63146	**800-410-2016**		732
Thunder Airlines Ltd 310 Hector Dougall Way	Thunder Bay	ON	P7E6M6	**800-803-9943**		13
Thunder Bay Regional Health Sciences Centre 980 Olvier Rd	Thunder Bay	ON	P7B6V4	**800-465-5003**	807-684-6000	373-2
Thunder Tech Inc 3635 Perkins Ave Studio 5 SW	Cleveland	OH	44114	**888-321-8422**	216-391-2255	7
Thunder Valley Casino 1200 Athens Ave	Lincoln	CA	95648	**877-468-8777**	916-408-7777	133
Thunderbird School of Global Management 1 Global Pl	Glendale	AZ	85306	**800-848-9084**	602-978-7000	681
Thune John (Sen R - SD) 511 Dirksen Senate Office Bldg	Washington	DC	20510	**866-850-3855**	202-224-2321	
Thybar Corp 913 S Kay Ave	Addison	IL	60101	**800-666-2872**	630-543-5300	693
Thyme on the Creek 1345 28th St	Boulder	CO	80302	**866-866-8086**	303-443-3850	667
Thyssen Krupp Hearn 59 I- Dr	Wentzville	MO	63385	**877-854-7178**	636-332-1772	194
ThyssenKrupp Elevator 9280 Crestwyn Hills Dr	Memphis	TN	38125	**877-230-0303**	901-261-1800	359-3
ThyssenKrupp Materials NA 22355 W 11 Mile Rd	Southfield	MI	48033	**800-926-2600**	248-233-5600	490
Ti Ba Enterprises Inc 25 Hytec Cir	Rochester	NY	14606	**800-836-8422**	585-247-1212	473
TIA (Tire Industry Assn) 1532 Pointer Ridge Pl Ste G	Bowie	MD	20716	**800-876-8372**	301-430-7280	49-4
TIAW (International Alliance for Women) 1101 Pennsylvania Ave NW 3rd Fl	Washington	DC	20004	**888-712-5200**		48-24
Ticket Source Inc 5516 E Mockingbird Ln Ste 100	Dallas	TX	75206	**800-557-6872**	214-821-9011	745
TicketBiscuit LLC 5120 Cyrus Cir Ste 101	Birmingham	AL	35242	**866-757-8330**	205-757-8330	386
Ticketscom Inc 555 Anton Blvd 11th Fl	Costa Mesa	CA	92626	**800-352-0212**	714-327-5400	745
TicketWeb Inc 807 S Jackson Rd *Cust Svc	Pharr	TX	78577	**866-777-8932***	866-468-3399	745
Tickfaw State Park 27225 Patterson Rd	Springfield	LA	70462	**888-981-2020**	225-294-5020	561
Tickle Pink Inn at Carmel Highlands 155 Highland Dr	Carmel	CA	93923	**800-635-4774**	831-624-1244	378
Ticona LLC 8040 Dixie Hwy	Florence	KY	41042	**800-833-4882**	859-372-3244	601-2
Tidel Engineering Inc 2025 W Belt Line Rd Ste 114	Carrollton	TX	75006	**800-678-7577**	972-484-3358	56
Tideland Electric Membership Corp 25831 Hwy 264 E	Pantego	NC	27860	**800-637-1079**	252-943-3046	245
Tides Canada Foundation 400-163 W Hastings St	Vancouver	BC	V6B1H5	**866-843-3722**	604-647-6611	305
Tidewater Barge Lines Inc 6305 NW Old Lower River Rd	Vancouver	WA	98660	**800-562-1607**	360-693-1491	314
Tidewater Community College						
Chesapeake 1428 Cedar Rd	Chesapeake	VA	23322	**800-371-0898**	757-822-5100	162
Norfolk 121 College Pl	Norfolk	VA	23510	**800-371-0898**	757-822-1110	162
Portsmouth 7000 College Dr	Portsmouth	VA	23703	**800-371-0898**	757-822-2124	162
Virginia Beach 1700 College Crescent	Virginia Beach	VA	23453	**800-371-0898**	757-822-7100	162
Tidewater Grill 1060 Charleston Town Ctr	Charleston	WV	25389	**888-456-3463**	304-345-2620	667
Tidewater Inc 6002 Rogerdale Rd Ste 600 *NYSE: TDW*	Houston	TX	77072	**800-678-8433**	713-470-5300	463
Tidewater Inn & Conference Ctr 101 E Dover St	Easton	MD	21601	**800-237-8775**	410-822-1300	378
Tidewell Hospice 5955 Rand Blvd	Sarasota	FL	34238	**800-959-4291**	941-552-7500	370
TIDI Products LLC 570 Enterprise Dr	Neenah	WI	54956	**800-521-1314**		475
Tie Down Engineering Inc 255 Villanova Dr SW	Atlanta	GA	30336	**800-241-1806**	404-344-0000	478
Tier One LLC 31 Pecks Ln	Newtown	CT	06470	**877-251-2228**		452
Tier1 Inc 2403 Sidney St Ste 225	Pittsburgh	PA	15203	**888-284-0202**	412-381-9201	177
Tietex International 3010 N Blackstock Rd	Spartanburg	SC	29301	**800-843-8390**	864-574-0500	740-6
Tiffany & Co 727 Fifth Ave *NYSE: TIF* ■ *Orders	New York	NY	10022	**800-526-0649***	212-755-8000	409
Tiffen Company LLC 90 Oser Ave	Hauppauge	NY	11788	**800-645-2522**	631-273-2500	587
Tiffin Metal Products Co 450 Wall St	Tiffin	OH	44883	**800-537-0983**		349
Tiffin University 155 Miami St	Tiffin	OH	44883	**800-968-6446**	419-447-6442	166
Tift Regional Medical Ctr 1641 Madison Ave	Tifton	GA	31794	**800-648-1935**	229-382-7120	373-3
Tifton-Tift County Chamber of Commerce 100 Central Ave	Tifton	GA	31794	**800-550-8438**	229-382-6200	139
TIG (Technology Integration Group) 7810 Trade St	San Diego	CA	92121	**800-858-0549**		176
Tiger Button Company Inc 307 W 38th St	New York	NY	10018	**800-223-2754**	212-594-0570	590
Tiger Financial News Network 601 Cleveland St Ste 618	Clearwater	FL	33755	**877-518-9190**	727-467-9190	640
Tiger Lines LLC Lodi 927 Black Diamond Way	Lodi	CA	95241	**800-967-8443**		775
Tiger Schulmann's Karate Ctr 485 Blvd	Elmwood Park	NJ	07407	**800-867-1218**		148
Tiger Supplies Inc 27 Selvage St	Irvington	NJ	07111	**888-844-3765**		786

	Toll-Free	Phone	Class

TigerDirect Inc
7795 W Flagler St Ste 35 .... Miami FL 33144 — **800-800-8300** — 174

Tihati Productions Ltd
3615 Harding Ave Ste 507 .... Honolulu HI 96816 — **877-846-5554** — 808-735-0292 — 569-4

TII Network Technologies Inc
141 Rodeo Dr .... Edgewood NY 11717 — **888-844-4720** — 631-789-5000 — 636
NASDAQ: TIII

Tilcon Connecticut Inc
PO Box 1357 .... New Britain CT 06050 — **888-845-2666** — 860-224-6010 — 46

Tilcon NY Inc
162 Old Mill Rd .... West Nyack NY 10994 — **800-872-7762** — 845-358-4500 — 501-5

Tillamook Bay Community College
4301 Third St .... Tillamook OR 97141 — **888-306-8222** — 503-842-8222 — 162

Tillamook County Creamery Assn Inc
4185 Hwy 101 N .... Tillamook OR 97141 — **800-542-7290** — 503-815-1300 — 296-5

Tillamook People's Utility District
1115 Pacific Ave .... Tillamook OR 97141 — **800-422-2535** — 503-842-4100 — 245

Tillar-Wenstrup Advisors LLC
1065 E Centerville Sta Rd .... Centerville OH 45459 — **800-207-1143** — 937-428-9700 — 524

Tilley Chemical Company Inc
501 Chesapeake Park Plz .... Baltimore MD 21220 — **800-638-6968** — 410-574-4500 — 146

Tilson HR Inc
1530 American Way Ste 200........ Greenwood IN 46143 — **800-276-3976** — 317-885-3838 — 627

Tim Hortons Inc
874 Sinclair Rd .... Oakville ON L6K2Y1 — **888-601-1616** — 905-845-6511 — 666
NYSE: QSR

Timber Products Co
305 S Fourth St PO Box 269. ...... Springfield OR 97477 — **800-954-4340** — 541-995-0780 — 191-3

Timberland Bancorp Inc
624 Simpson Ave .... Hoquiam WA 98550 — **800-562-8761** — 360-533-4747 — 359-2
NASDAQ: TSBK

Timberland Co, The
200 Domain Dr .... Stratham NH 03885 — **888-802-9947** — 301
NYSE: VFC

Timberland Homes Inc
1201 37th St NW .... Auburn WA 98001 — **800-488-5036** — 253-735-3435 — 106

Timberland Regional Library
415 Tumwater Blvd SW .... Tumwater WA 98501 — **877-284-6237** — 360-943-5001 — 433-3

Timberlane Inc
150 Domorah Dr .... Montgomeryville PA 18936 — **800-250-2221** — 215-616-0600 — 361

Timberlawn Mental Health System
4600 Samuell Blvd .... Dallas TX 75228 — **800-426-4944** — 214-381-7181 — 373-5

Timberline Lodge
27500 E Timberline Rd .... Government Camp OR 97028 — **800-547-1406** — 503-272-3311 — 665

Timberwolf Tours Inc
51404 Range Rd 264 Ste 34 .... Spruce Grove AB T7Y1E4 — **888-467-9697** — 780-470-4966 — 755

Timco Rubber
125 Blaze Industrial Pkwy
PO Box 35135. .... Berea OH 44017 — **800-969-6242** — 216-267-6242

Time 4 Learning
6300 NE First Ave
Ste 203. .... Fort Lauderdale FL 33334 — **888-771-0914**

Time Definite Services Inc
1360 Madeline Ln Ste 300 .... Elgin IL 60124 — **800-466-8040** — 311

Time Hotels
224 W 49th St ....New York NY 10019 — **877-846-3692** — 212-246-5252 — 378

Time Mark Corp
11440 E Pine St .... Tulsa OK 74116 — **800-862-2875** — 918-438-1220 — 203

Time Trak Systems Inc
933 Pine Grove ....Port Huron MI 48060 — **888-484-6387** — 810-984-1313 — 177

Time Warner Inc
1 Time Warner Ctr ....New York NY 10019 — **866-463-6899** — 212-484-8000 — 185
NYSE: TWX

Timely Inc
10241 Norris Ave ....Pacoima CA 91331 — **800-247-6242** — 818-492-3500 — 286

TimeMed Labeling Systems Inc
144 Tower Dr .... Burr Ridge IL 60527 — **800-323-4840*** — 630-986-1800 — 550
*Cust Svc

Time-O-Matic Inc
1015 Maple St .... Danville IL 61832 — **800-637-2645** — 217-442-0611 — 203

Times
401 Market St ....Shreveport LA 71101 — **866-979-6397** — 318-459-3200 — 528-2

Times Colonist
2621 Douglas St .... Victoria BC V8T4M2 — **800-663-6384** — 250-380-5211 — 528-1

Times Fiber Communications Inc
358 Hall Ave PO Box 384 .... Wallingford CT 06492 — **800-677-2288** — 434-432-1800 — 808

Times Herald Inc
639 S Chester Rd PO Box 591 .... Swarthmore PA 19081 — **888-933-4233** — 610-272-2500 — 633-8

Times Herald-Record
40 Mulberry St PO Box 2046 .... Middletown NY 10940 — **888-620-1700** — 845-341-1100 — 528-2

Times Microwave Systems Inc
PO Box 5039 .... Wallingford CT 06492 — **800-867-2629** — 203-949-8400 — 253

Times of Acadiana
1100 Bertrand Dr .... Lafayette LA 70506 — **877-289-2216** — 337-289-6300 — 528-4

Times Printing Company Inc
100 Industrial Dr ....Random Lake WI 53075 — **800-236-4396** — 920-994-4396 — 623

Times Record
3600 Wheeler Ave .... Fort Smith AR 72901 — **888-274-4051** — 479-785-7700 — 528-2

Times Reporter
629 Wabash Ave NW ....New Philadelphia OH 44663 — **800-686-5577** — 330-364-5577 — 528-2

Times Union Ctr
51 S Pearl St .... Albany NY 12207 — **866-308-3394** — 518-487-2000 — 716

Times, The
601 W 45th Ave .... Munster IN 46321 — **866-301-3331** — 219-933-3200 — 528-2

Timesavers Inc
11123 89th Ave N .... Maple Grove MN 55369 — **800-537-3611** — 763-488-6600 — 385

Times-Call, The
350 Terry St .... Longmont CO 80501 — **800-279-8537** — 303-776-2244 — 528-2

Times-Citizen Communications Inc
406 Stevens St PO Box 640 .... Iowa Falls IA 50126 — **800-798-2691** — 641-648-2521 — 633-8

Times-Mail
813 16th St .... Bedford IN 47421 — **800-782-4405** — 812-275-3355 — 528-2

Times-News
PO Box 548 .... Twin Falls ID 83303 — **800-658-3883** — 208-733-0931 — 528-2

Times-News
PO Box 490 ....Hendersonville NC 28793 — **800-849-8050** — 828-692-0505 — 528-2

Times-News, The
707 S Main St .... Burlington NC 27215 — **800-488-0085** — 336-227-0131 — 633-8

Times-Picayune
3800 Howard Ave .... New Orleans LA 70125 — **800-925-0000** — 504-826-3279 — 528-2

Times-Standard
930 Sixth St .... Eureka CA 95501 — **800-564-5630** — 707-441-0500 — 528-2

Times-Transcript
939 Main St .... Moncton NB E1C8P3 — **800-561-7166** — 528-1

Times-Tribune, The
201 N Kentucky Ave .... Corbin KY 40701 — **877-629-9722** — 606-528-2464 — 528-2

TimeValue Software
22 Mauchly .... Irvine CA 92618 — **800-426-4741*** — 949-727-1800 — 178-11
*Sales

Timeware Inc
9329 Ravenna Rd Ste D .... Twinsburg OH 44087 — **866-936-2420** — 330-963-2700 — 177

Timex Group USA Inc
555 Christian Rd PO Box 310 ..... Middlebury CT 06762 — **800-448-4639** — 888-727-2931 — 153

Timken Co
4500 Mount Pleasant St NW ....North Canton OH 44706 — **800-223-1954** — 330-438-3000 — 75
NYSE: TKR

Timmins & District Hospital
700 Ross Ave E .... Timmins ON P4N8P2 — **888-340-3003** — 705-267-2131 — 373-2

Timpte Inc
1827 Industrial Dr .... David City NE 68632 — **888-256-4884** — 402-367-3056 — 774

Tims Ford State Park
570 Tims Ford Dr .... Winchester TN 37398 — **800-471-5295** — 931-962-1183 — 561

Tindall Corp
2273 Hayne St .... Spartanburg SC 29301 — **800-849-4521** — 864-576-3230 — 183

Tingley Rubber Corp
1551 S Washington Ave
Ste 403. .... Piscataway NJ 08854 — **800-631-5498*** — 572
*Cust Svc

Tingue
535 N Midland Ave ....Saddle Brook NJ 07663 — **800-829-3864** — 201-796-4490 — 590

Tintri Inc
2570 W El Camino Real .... Mountain View CA 94040 — **855-484-6874** — 650-209-3900 — 173-8

Tioga County Visitors Bureau
2053 Rt 660 .... Wellsboro PA 16901 — **888-846-4228** — 570-724-0635 — 206

Tioga Pipe Supply Company Inc
2450 Wheatsheaf Ln ....Philadelphia PA 19137 — **800-523-3678** — 215-831-0700 — 490

TIP Rural Electric Co-op
612 W Des Moines St PO Box 534 ...... Brooklyn IA 52211 — **800-934-7976** — 641-522-9221 — 245

Tip Top Canning Co
505 S Second St PO Box 126 .... Tipp City OH 45371 — **800-352-2635** — 937-667-3713 — 296-20

Tip Top Poultry Inc
327 Wallace Rd .... Marietta GA 30062 — **800-241-5230** — 770-973-8070 — 615

TIPAC (Title Industry PAC)
1800 M St NW Ste 300S............ Washington DC 20036 — **800-787-2582** — 202-296-3671 — 611

Tipco Punch Inc
1 Coventry Rd ....Brampton ON L6T4B1 — **800-544-8444** — 905-791-9811 — 357

Tipmont REMC
403 S Main St .... Linden IN 47955 — **800-726-3953** — 245

Tippecanoe County Public Library
627 S St .... Lafayette IN 47901 — **800-542-7818** — 765-429-0100 — 433-3

Tipper Tie Inc
2000 Lufkin Rd .... Apex NC 27539 — **800-331-2905** — 919-362-8811 — 154

Tips Inc
2402 Williams Dr .... Georgetown TX 78628 — **800-242-8477** — 512-863-3653 — 177

Tipton & Hurst Inc
1801 N Grant St .... Little Rock AR 72207 — **800-666-3333** — 501-666-3333 — 292

Tipton County
220 Hwy 51 N Ste 2 .... Covington TN 38019 — **800-342-1003** — 901-476-0207 — 337

Tire Centers LLC
310 Inglesby Pkwy .... Duncan SC 29334 — **800-603-2430** — 864-329-2700 — 750

Tire Industry Assn (TIA)
1532 Pointer Ridge Pl Ste G .... Bowie MD 20716 — **800-876-8372** — 301-430-7280 — 49-4

Tire Rack
7101 Vorden Pkwy .... South Bend IN 46628 — **888-541-1777** — 574-287-2345 — 750

Tire Warehouse
200 Holleder Pkwy ....Rochester NY 14615 — **800-876-6676** — 54

Tire's Warehouse Inc
240 Teller St .... Corona CA 92879 — **800-655-8851** — 951-808-0111 — 750

Tire-Rama Inc
1429 Grand Ave .... Billings MT 59102 — **800-828-1642** — 406-245-3161 — 750

Tires Plus Total Car Care
2021 Sunnydale Blvd .... Clearwater FL 33765 — **844-338-0739** — 727-330-3684 — 62-5

TIRR Memorial Hermann Hospital
1333 Moursund St .... Houston TX 77030 — **800-447-3422** — 713-799-5000 — 373-6

Tishcon Corp
50 Sylvester St .... Westbury NY 11590 — **800-848-8442** — 516-333-3050 — 794

Titan Air Inc
13901 16th St .... Osseo WI 54758 — **800-242-9398** — 715-597-2050 — 693

Titan America Inc
1151 Azalea Garden Rd ....Norfolk VA 23502 — **800-468-7622** — 757-858-6500 — 182

Titan Global Distribution
11973 Westline Industrial Dr
Ste 200 .... Saint Louis MO 63143 — **800-325-4074** — 314-817-0051 — 447

Titan International Inc
2701 Spruce St .... Quincy IL 62301 — **800-872-2327** — 217-228-6011 — 60
NYSE: TWI

Titan Laboratories
1380 Zuni St PO Box 40567 .... Denver CO 80204 — **800-848-4826** — 575

Titan Logix Corp
4130 - 93 St .... Edmonton AB T6E5P5 — **877-462-4085** — 780-462-4085 — 201

Titan Tire Co
2345 E Market St .... Des Moines IA 50317 — **800-872-2327** — 515-265-9200 — 749

Titeflex Corp
603 Hendee St .... Springfield MA 01139 — **800-765-2525** — 413-739-5631 — 369

Title Guaranty of Hawaii Inc
235 Queen St .... Honolulu HI 96813 — **800-222-3229** — 808-533-6261 — 390-6

Title Industry PAC (TIPAC)
1800 M St NW Ste 300S............ Washington DC 20036 — **800-787-2582** — 202-296-3671 — 611

Title Resources Guaranty Co (TRGC)
8111 LBJ Fwy Ste 1200 .... Dallas TX 75251 — **800-526-8018** — 390-6

Titlemax of South Carolina Inc
15 Bull St .... Savannah GA 31401 — **888-485-3629** — 400

Titonka Bancshares Inc
PO Box 309 .... Titonka IA 50480 — **866-985-3247** — 515-928-2142 — 359-2

TiVo Inc 2160 Gold St .... Alviso CA 95002 — **877-367-8486** — 408-519-9100 — 116
NASDAQ: TIVO

Name / Address	City	State	ZIP	Toll-Free	Phone	Class
Tivoli Lodge 386 Hanson Ranch Rd	Vail	CO	81657	**800-451-4756**	970-476-5615	378
Tizbi Inc 800 Saint Mary's St Ste 402	Raleigh	NC	27605	**888-729-0951**		177
TJ Cope Inc 11500 Norcom Rd	Philadelphia	PA	19154	**800-483-3473**	800-882-5543	811
TJ Hale Co W 139 N 9499 Hwy 145	Menomonee Falls	WI	53051	**800-236-4253**	262-255-5555	286
TJ Samson Community Hospital 1301 N Race St	Glasgow	KY	42141	**800-651-5635**	270-651-4444	373-3
Tjernlund Products Inc 1601 Ninth St	White Bear Lake	MN	55110	**800-255-4208**	651-426-2993	18
TJX Cos Inc 770 Cochituate Rd *NYSE: TJX*	Framingham	MA	01701	**800-926-6299**	508-390-1000	157-4
TK Stanley Inc 6739 Hwy 184	Waynesboro	MS	39367	**800-477-2855**		535
T-I Irrigation Co 151 E Hwy 6 AB Rd PO Box 1047	Hastings	NE	68902	**800-330-4264**	402-462-4128	273
TLC Vision Corp 50 Burnhamthorpe Rd W Ste 101	Mississauga	ON	L5B3C2	**877-852-2020**		793
TLIE (Texas Lawyers Insurance Exchange) 1801 S MoPac Ste 300	Austin	TX	78746	**800-252-9332**	512-480-9074	390-5
TLN (Telelatino Network Inc) 5125 Steeles Ave W	Toronto	ON	M9L1R5	**800-551-8401**	416-744-8200	735
TLX Inc 7944 E Beck Ln Ste 200	Scottsdale	AZ	85260	**800-520-7493**	480-609-8888	180
TM Group Inc, The 27555 Executive Dr Ste 100	Farmington Hills	MI	48331	**888-482-2864**	248-489-0707	
TM Smith Tool International Corp 360 Hubbard Ave	Mount Clemens	MI	48043	**800-521-4894**	586-468-1465	491
TMA Systems LLC 5100 E Skelly Dr Ste 900	Tulsa	OK	74135	**800-862-1130**	918-858-6600	178-11
TMC (Teaching & Mentoring Communities) PO Box 2579	Laredo	TX	78044	**888-836-5151**	956-722-5174	49-5
TMC (Tufts Medical Ctr) 800 Washington St	Boston	MA	02111	**866-220-3699**	617-636-5000	373-3
TMC (Tulane Medical Ctr) 1415 Tulane Ave	New Orleans	LA	70112	**800-588-5800**	504-988-5263	373-3
TMG Co 43 Woodstock St	Roswell	GA	30075	**800-720-1563**		2
TMI Coatings Inc 3291 Terminal Dr	Saint Paul	MN	55121	**800-328-0229**	651-452-6100	189-8
TMI Hospitality 4850 32nd Ave S	Fargo	ND	58104	**800-210-8223**	701-235-1060	703
TMI LLC 5350 Campbells Run Rd	Pittsburgh	PA	15205	**800-888-9750**		604
TMI Systems Design Corp 50 S Third Ave W	Dickinson	ND	58601	**800-456-6716**	701-456-6716	319-3
TML (Teledyne Monitor Labs Inc) 35 Inverness Dr E	Englewood	CO	80112	**800-422-1499**	303-792-3300	201
TMNG (Management Network Group Inc) 7300 College Blvd Ste 302 *NASDAQ: CRTN*	Overland Park	KS	66210	**800-690-6903**	913-345-9315	196
TMP Technologies 1200 Northland Ave	Buffalo	NY	14215	**866-728-1932**	716-895-6100	597
TMS (Tube City IMS Corp) 12 Monongahela Ave *NYSE: TMS*	Glassport	PA	15045	**800-860-2442**	412-678-6141	682
TMS (Minerals Metals & Materials Society, The) 5700 Corporate Dr Ste 750	Pittsburgh	PA	15237	**800-759-4867**	724-776-9000	49-13
TMW Systems Inc 21111 Chagrin Blvd	Beachwood	OH	44122	**800-401-6682**	216-831-6606	178-10
TNCI (Trans National Communications International Inc) 2 Charlesgate W	Boston	MA	02215	**800-800-8400**	617-369-1000	731
Tnemec Company Inc 6800 Corporate Dr	Kansas City	MO	64120	**800-863-6321**	816-483-3400	546
TNMP (Texas-New Mexico Power Co) 577 N Garden Ridge Blvd	Lewisville	TX	75067	**888-866-7456**	972-420-4189	782
TNNA (National NeedleArts Assn, The) 1100-H Brandywine Blvd	Zanesville	OH	43701	**800-889-8662**	740-455-6773	48-18
TNR Technical Inc 301 Central Park Dr *OTC: TNRK*	Sanford	FL	32771	**800-346-0601**	407-321-3011	74
Toa Canada Corp 6150 Kennedy Rd Unit 3	Mississauga	ON	L5T2J4	**800-263-7639**	905-564-3570	246
TOASTnet 4841 Monroe St Ste 307	Toledo	OH	43623	**888-862-7863**	419-292-2200	397
TOBA (Thoroughbred Owners & Breeders Assn) PO Box 910668	Lexington	KY	40591	**888-606-8622**	859-276-2291	48-3
Tocco Financial Services Inc 1647 N Swan Rd	Tucson	AZ	85712	**877-881-1149**	520-881-1149	686
Toccoa Falls College 107 Kincaid Dr *General	Toccoa Falls	GA	30598	**888-785-5624***	706-886-7299	161
Today's Business Computers 213 E Black Horse Pk	Pleasantville	NJ	08232	**800-371-5132**	609-645-5132	177
Today's Christian Woman Magazine 465 Gundersen Dr *Orders	Carol Stream	IL	60188	**877-247-4787***	630-260-6200	455-18
Todd, Bremer & Lawson Inc 560 S Herlong Ave	Rock Hill	SC	29732	**877-427-6544**		
Todd-Wadena Electric Co-op 550 Ash Ave NE PO Box 431	Wadena	MN	56482	**800-321-8932**	218-631-3120	245
Tofurky PO Box 176	Hood River	OR	97031	**800-508-8100**		
Tog Shop Inc 30 Tozer Rd	Beverly	MA	01915	**800-767-6666**		
Togus National Cemetery VA Regional Office Ctr	Togus	ME	04330	**800-535-1117**	508-563-7113	136
Tokatee Klootchman State Natural Site 93111 Hwy 101 N	Florence	OR	97439	**800-551-6949**		561
Tokio Marine America 1221 Ave Ste 1500	New York	NY	10020	**800-628-2796**	212-297-6600	390-4
Toledo Edison Co PO Box 3687	Akron	OH	44309	**800-447-3333**		782
Toledo Engineering Co Inc 3400 Executive Pkwy PO Box 2927	Toledo	OH	43606	**800-654-4567**	419-537-9711	261
Toledo Mud Hens Baseball Club Inc 406 Washington St	Toledo	OH	43604	**800-736-9520**	419-725-4367	709
Toledo Museum of Art 2445 Monroe St	Toledo	OH	43620	**800-644-6862**	419-255-8000	517
Toledo Opera 425 Jefferson Ave Ste 601	Toledo	OH	43604	**866-860-9048**	419-255-7464	569-2
Toledo Physical Education Supply Inc 5101 Advantage Dr	Toledo	OH	43612	**800-225-7749**	419-726-8122	707
Toll Bros Inc 250 Gibraltar Rd *NYSE: TOL*	Horsham	PA	19044	**855-897-8655**	215-938-8000	649
Toll Gas & Welding Supply 3005 Niagara Ln N	Plymouth	MN	55447	**877-865-5427**	763-551-5300	357
Toll House Hotel 140 S Santa Cruz Ave	Los Gatos	CA	95030	**800-238-6111**	408-395-7070	703
Tol-O-Matic Inc 3800 County Rd 116	Hamel	MN	55340	**800-328-2174**	763-478-8000	223
Tolunay-Wong Engineers Inc 10710 S Sam Houston Pkwy W	Houston	TX	77031	**888-887-9932**		
Tom Barrow Co (TBC) 2800 Plant Atkinson Rd	Atlanta	GA	30339	**800-229-8226**	404-351-1010	14
Tom Duffy Co 5200 Watt Ct Ste B	Fairfield	CA	94534	**800-479-5671**		290
Tom Hassenfritz Equipment Co 1300 W Washington St	Mount Pleasant	IA	52641	**800-634-4885**	319-385-3114	274
Tom Hopkins International 465 E Chilton Dr Ste 4	Chandler	AZ	85255	**800-528-0446**	480-949-0786	196
Tom James Co 263 Seaboard Ln	Franklin	TN	37067	**800-236-9023**	615-771-0795	155-11
Tom Johnson Investment Management Inc 201 Robert S Kerr Ave	Oklahoma City	OK	73102	**888-404-8546**	405-236-2111	400
Tom Lee Music Ltd 929 Granville St	Vancouver	BC	V6Z1L3	**888-886-6533**	604-685-8471	522
Tom McCall & Assoc Inc 20180 Governors Hwy Ste 100	Olympia Fields	IL	60461	**800-715-5474**	708-747-5707	194
Tom Sturgis Pretzels Inc 2267 Lancaster Pk	Reading	PA	19607	**800-817-3834**	610-775-0335	296-9
Tom's of Maine Inc 302 Lafayette Ctr	Kennebunk	ME	04043	**800-367-8667**		214
Tomah Convention & Visitors Bureau 310 N Superior Ave PO Box 625	Tomah	WI	54660	**800-948-6624**	608-372-2166	206
Tomah Veterans Affairs Medical Ctr 500 E Veterans St	Tomah	WI	54660	**800-872-8662**	608-372-3971	373-8
Tombigbee Electric Co-op 7686 Hwy 43	Guin	AL	35563	**800-621-8069**	205-468-3325	245
Tombigbee State Park 264 Cabin Dr	Tupelo	MS	38804	**800-467-2757**	662-842-7669	561
Tomco2 Systems 3340 Rosebud Rd	Loganville	GA	30052	**800-832-4262**	770-979-8000	801
Tommy Tape 378 Four Rod Rd	Berlin	CT	06037	**888-866-8273**	860-378-0111	727
Tompkins Cortland Community College 170 N St	Dryden	NY	13053	**888-567-8211**	607-844-8211	162
Tompkins County 320 N Tioga St	Ithaca	NY	14850	**800-268-7869**		
Tompkins County Chamber of Commerce 904 E Shore Dr	Ithaca	NY	14850	**888-568-9816**	607-273-7080	139
Tompkins County Public Library 101 E Green St	Ithaca	NY	14850	**800-772-7267**	607-272-4557	433-3
Tompkins Industries Inc 1912 E 123rd	Olathe	KS	66061	**800-255-1008**	913-764-8088	349
Tompkins International 6870 Perry Creek Rd	Raleigh	NC	27616	**800-789-1257**	919-876-3667	194
Tompkins Trust Co PO Box 460 *NYSE: TMP*	Ithaca	NY	14851	**888-273-3210**	607-273-3210	70
Toms Truck Ctr Inc 909 N Grand Ave	Santa Ana	CA	92701	**800-638-1015**		57
Tomson Steel Co (Inc) PO Box 940	Middletown	OH	45042	**800-837-3001**		490
TOMY International Inc 2015 Spring Rd Ste 700	Oak Brook	IL	60523	**800-704-8697**	630-573-7200	757
Tone Software Inc 1735 S Brookhurst St	Anaheim	CA	92804	**800-833-8663**	714-991-9460	177
Tonertype of Florida LLC 5313 Johns Rd Ste 210	Tampa	FL	33634	**888-916-1300**	813-915-1300	387
Tongass Trading Co 201 Dock St	Ketchikan	AK	99901	**800-235-5102**	907-225-5101	229
Toni & Guy USA Inc 2311 Midway Rd	Carrollton	TX	75006	**800-256-9391**		77
Tonix Corp 40910 Encyclopedia Cir	Fremont	CA	94538	**800-227-2072**	510-651-8050	155-3
Tonner Doll Co PO Box 4410	Kingston	NY	12402	**800-794-2107**	845-339-9537	757
Tony Packo's 1902 Front St	Toledo	OH	43605	**866-472-2567**	419-691-1953	667
Toobs Inc 347 Quintana Rd	Morro Bay	CA	93442	**800-795-8662**		706
Tool Smith Company Inc 1300 Fourth Ave S	Birmingham	AL	35233	**800-317-8665**	205-323-2576	385
Tool Technology Distributors Inc 3110 Osgood Ct	Fremont	CA	94539	**800-335-8437**	510-656-8220	357
Tool-Flo Mfg Inc 7803 Hansen Rd	Houston	TX	77061	**800-345-2815**	713-941-1080	453
Tools for Bending Inc 194 W Dakota Ave *Cust Svc	Denver	CO	80223	**800-873-3305***	303-777-7170	454
Toolwire Inc 7031 Koll Ctr Pkwy Ste 220	Pleasanton	CA	94566	**866-935-8665**	925-227-8500	39
Tootsie Roll Industries Inc 7401 S Cicero Ave *NYSE: TR*	Chicago	IL	60629	**866-972-6879**	773-838-3400	296-8
Top Air Sprayers 601 S Broad St	Kalida	OH	45853	**800-322-6301**	419-532-3121	273
Top Flight Inc 1300 Central Ave	Chattanooga	TN	37408	**800-777-3740**	423-266-8171	263

	Toll-Free	Phone	Class
Top Producer Systems Inc 10651 Shellbridge Way Ste 155 .... Richmond BC V6X2W8	800-821-3657		179
Top Promotions Inc 8831 S Greenview Dr ...... Middleton WI 53562	800-344-2968	608-836-9111	683
Top Rank Inc 3980 Howard Hughes Pkwy Ste 580 ...... Las Vegas NV 89119	800-943-0087		181
Topa Insurance Corp 24025 Park Sorrento Ste 300 ...... Calabasas CA 91302	877-353-8672	310-201-0451	390-4
Topaz Lighting Corp 925 Waverly Ave ...... Holtsville NY 11742	800-666-2852		361
Topco Assoc LLC 7711 Gross Pt Rd ...... Skokie IL 60077	888-423-0139	847-745-2396	297-8
Topcon Medical Systems Inc 111 Bauer Dr ...... Oakland NJ 07436	800-223-1130	201-599-5100	381
Topeka Capital-Journal 616 SE Jefferson St ...... Topeka KS 66607	800-777-7171	785-295-1111	528-2
Topica Inc 1 Post St Ste 875 ...... San Francisco CA 94104	888-728-2465	415-344-0800	7
Topnotch at Stowe Resort & Spa 4000 Mountain Rd ...... Stowe VT 05672	800-451-8686		665
Topp Industries Inc 420 N State Rd 25 PO Box 420. ..Rochester IN 46975	800-354-4534	574-223-3681	597
Topps Company Inc 1 Whitehall St ...... New York NY 10004	800-489-9149	212-376-0300	296-6
Topps Safety Apparel Inc 2516 E State Rd 14 ...... Rochester IN 46975	800-348-2990	574-223-4311	155-18
TOPS Club Inc 4575 S Fifth St ...... Milwaukee WI 53207	800-932-8677	414-482-4620	48-17
Torah Umesorah-National Society for Hebrew Day Schools 620 Foster Ave ...... Brooklyn NY 11230	800-788-3942	212-227-1000	49-5
Torchmark Corp 3700 S Stonebridge Dr ...... McKinney TX 75070 *NYSE: TMK*	877-577-3899	972-569-4000	359-4
Torke Coffee Roasting Company Inc 3455 Paine Ave ...... Sheboygan WI 53081	800-242-7671		296-7
Tornado Alley Turbo 300 Airport Rd ...... Ada OK 74820	877-359-8284	580-332-3510	765
Tornado Spectral Systems 555 Richmond St W Ste 402. ...... Toronto ON M5V3B1	800-227-9770	416-361-3444	406
Tornatech Inc 7075 Place Robert-Joncas Ste 132 ...... Saint-laurent QC H4M2Z2	800-363-8448	514-334-0523	203
Toro Co 8111 Lyndale Ave ...... Bloomington MN 55420 *NYSE: TTC*	888-384-9939		428
Toro Co Commercial Products Div 8111 Lyndale Ave ...... Bloomington MN 55420 *Cust Svc*	800-348-2424*	952-888-8801	428
Toro Co Irrigation Div 5825 Jasmine St ...... Riverside CA 92504	800-654-1882		273
Toronto Blue Jays 1 Blue Jays Way Ste 3200 ...... Toronto ON M5V1J1	888-654-6529	416-341-1000	709
Toronto Convention & Visitors Assn 207 Queen's Quay W Ste 405 PO Box 126. ...... Toronto ON M5J1A7	800-499-2514	416-203-2600	206
Toronto International Film Festival Inc Reitman Sq 350 King St W ...... Toronto ON M5V3X5	888-599-8433		282
Toronto Star 1 Yonge St ...... Toronto ON M5E1E6	800-268-9756	416-869-4949	528-1
Toronto Stock Exchange 130 King St W The Exchange Tower ...... Toronto ON M5X1J2	888-873-8392	416-947-4670	687
Toronto Sun 333 King St E ...... Toronto ON M5A3X5	888-786-7821	416-947-2222	528-1
Toronto Transit Commission (TTC) 1900 Yonge St ...... Toronto ON M4S1Z2	800-223-6192	416-393-4000	466
Torrance Memorial Home Health & Hospice 3330 Lomita Blvd ...... Torrance CA 90505	800-906-9909	310-784-3739	370
Torrance Memorial Medical Ctr 3330 Lomita Blvd ...... Torrance CA 90505	800-551-1300	310-325-9110	373-3
Torray Fund 7501 Wisconsin Ave Ste 750 W ...... Bethesda MD 20814	800-443-3036	301-493-4600	524
Torrey Pines State Natural Reserve 9th St ...... Sacramento CA 95814	866-240-4655	916-653-6995	561
Tortoise Energy Capital Corp 11550 Ash St Ste 300 ...... Leawood KS 66211 *NYSE: TTP*	866-362-9331	913-981-1020	787
Toshiba America Inc 1251 Ave of the Americas 41st Fl. ...... New York NY 10020	800-457-7777	212-596-0600	52
Toshiba America Information Systems Inc 9740 Irvine Blvd ...... Irvine CA 92618 *Cust Svc*	800-457-7777*	949-583-3000	173-2
Toshiba International Corp 13131 W Little York Rd ...... Houston TX 77041	800-231-1412	713-466-0277	515
Tosoh Bioscience Inc 6000 Shoreline Ct Ste 101 ...... South San Francisco CA 94080	800-248-6764	650-615-4970	473
TOSS Corp 1253 Worcester Rd ...... Framingham MA 01701	888-884-8677	508-820-2990	180
Total Contentz 540 Millers Run Rd Ste 200 ...... Morgan PA 15064	888-722-5688	805-522-5900	
Total Energy Services Ltd 2550 300-5th Ave SW Ste 2550 ...... Calgary AB T2P3C4 *NYSE: TOT*	877-818-6825	403-216-3939	536
Total Filtration Services Inc 2725 Commerce Pkwy ...... Auburn Hills MI 48326	800-331-3118	248-377-4004	384
Total Insight LLC 310 Main Ave Way SE ...... Hickory NC 28602	877-226-9950	828-485-5000	782
Total Lubricants USA 5 N Stiles St ...... Linden NJ 07036	800-323-3198	908-862-9300	537
Total Maintenance Solutions 3540 Rutherford Rd ...... Taylors SC 29687	800-476-2212	864-268-2891	606
TOTAL Marketing LLC 1751 River Run Ste 200 ...... Ft Worth TX 76107	800-998-5269	817-560-3970	195
Total Merchant Concepts Inc 12300 NE Fourth Plain Rd A ...... Vancouver WA 98682	888-249-9919	360-253-5934	531
Total Plastics Inc 3316 Pagosa Ct ...... Indianapolis IN 46226	800-382-4635	317-543-3540	598
Total Printing Systems 201 S Gregory St ...... Newton IL 62448	800-465-5200		623
Total Quality Logistics Inc (TQL) 4289 Ivy Pointe Blvd ...... Cincinnati OH 45245	800-580-3101	513-831-2600	311
Total Seal Inc 22642 N 15th Ave ...... Phoenix AZ 85027	800-874-2753	623-587-7400	128
Total Seminars LLC 12550 Fuqua Ste 150 ...... Houston TX 77034	877-687-2768	281-922-4166	759
Total Solutions Inc 1626 County Line Rd ...... Madison AL 35756	866-413-4111	256-721-3987	177
Total Technologies Ltd 9710 Research Dr ...... Irvine CA 92618	800-669-4885	949-465-0200	253
Total Telcom Inc 540 1632 Dickson Ave ...... Kelowna BC V1Y7T2	877-860-3762	250-860-3762	731
Total Wine & More 6600 Rockledge Dr ...... Bethesda MD 20817	855-328-9463		344
Totalcomp Scales & Components 99 Reagent Ln ...... Fair Lawn NJ 07410	800-631-0347	201-797-2718	361
Totelcom Communications LLC 6100 Hwy 16 S PO Box 290 ...... De Leon TX 76444	800-261-5911	254-893-1000	224
Totem Ocean Trailer Express Inc 32001 32nd Ave S Ste 200 ...... Federal Way WA 98001	800-426-0074	253-449-8100	312
Toter Inc PO Box 5338 ...... Statesville NC 28677	800-424-0422		199
Toto Tours 1326 W Albion Ave ...... Chicago IL 60626	800-565-1241	773-274-8686	755
Toto USA Inc 1155 Southern Rd ...... Morrow GA 30260	888-295-8134	770-282-8686	607
Totten Tubes Inc 500 Danlee St ...... Azusa CA 91702	800-882-3748		490
TouchAmerica 1403 S Third St Ext ...... Mebane NC 27302	800-678-6824	919-732-6968	76
TouchLogic Corp 30 Kinnear Ct Ste 202. ...... Richmond Hill ON L4B1K8	877-355-4774		386
Touchstone Medical Imaging LLC 1431 Perrone Way ...... Franklin TN 37069	877-275-9077	615-661-9200	
Touchstorm LLC 450 Lexington Ave 4th Fl ...... New York NY 10017	877-794-6101		386
TouchSystems Corp 2222 W Rundberg Ln Ste 200. ...... Austin TX 78758	800-320-5944	512-846-2424	610
Tougaloo College 500 W County Line Rd ...... Tougaloo MS 39174 *Admissions*	888-424-2566*	601-977-7700	166
Tough Traveler Ltd 1012 State St ...... Schenectady NY 12307 *Cust Svc*	800-468-6844*	518-377-8526	64
Tour Edge Golf Manufacturing Inc 1301 Pierson Dr ...... Batavia IL 60510	800-515-3343	630-584-4777	767
Touring & Tasting 125 S Quarantina St ...... Santa Barbara CA 93103	800-850-4370	805-965-2813	442
Tourism Abbotsford Society 34561 Delair Rd ...... Abbotsford BC V2S2E1	888-332-2229	604-859-1721	341
Tourism Calgary 200 238 11th Ave SE ...... Calgary AB T2G0X8	800-661-1678	403-263-8510	206
Tourism Council of Frederick County Inc 151 S East St ...... Frederick MD 21701	800-999-3613	301-600-2888	206
Tourism New Brunswick PO Box 6000 ...... Fredericton NB E3B5H1	800-561-0123		769
Tourism Richmond South Twr 5811 Cooney Rd Ste 205 ...... Richmond BC V6X3M1	877-247-0777	604-821-5474	767
Tourism Saskatchewan 1621 Albert St ...... Regina SK S4P2S5	877-237-2273	306-787-9600	769
Tourism Saskatoon 202 Fourth Ave N ...... Saskatoon SK S7K0K1	800-567-2444	306-242-1206	770
Tourism Winnipeg 1 Lombard Pl Ste 810. ...... Winnipeg MB R3B0X3	855-734-2489	204-943-1970	769
Tourmaline Oil Corp 250 Sixth Ave SW Ste 3700 ...... Calgary AB T2P3H7	877-504-4252	403-266-5992	532
Touvelle State Recreation Site Table Rock Rd ...... Central Point OR 97502	800-551-6949		561
Tower Federal Credit Union 7901 Sandy Spring Rd ...... Laurel MD 20707	800-787-8328	301-497-7000	219
Tower Innovations 3266 Tower Dr ...... Newburgh IN 47630	800-664-8222	812-853-0595	170
Tower Travel Management 53 Ogden Ave ...... Clarendon Hills IL 60514	800-542-9700		766
Towers at the Kahler Grand, The 20 Second Ave SW ...... Rochester MN 55902	800-940-6811	507-208-1409	378
Towmaster Inc 61381 US Hwy 12 ...... Litchfield MN 55355	800-462-4517	320-693-7900	774
Town & Country Hospital 6001 Webb Rd ...... Tampa FL 33615	866-463-7449	813-888-7060	373-3
Town & Country Inn 20 State RT 2 ...... Shelburne NH 03581 *General*	800-325-4386*	603-466-3315	378
Town & Country Inn & Conference Ctr 2008 Savannah Hwy ...... Charleston SC 29407	800-334-6660	843-571-1000	378
Town & Country Resort Hotel 500 Hotel Cir N ...... San Diego CA 92108	800-772-8527	619-291-7131	665
Town Fair Tire Company Inc 460 Coe Ave ...... East Haven CT 06512	800-972-2245		54
Town Food Service Equipment Co 72 Beadel St ...... Brooklyn NY 11222	800-221-5032	718-388-5650	298
Town Inn Suites 620 Church St ...... Toronto ON M4Y2G2	800-387-2755	416-964-3311	378
Town Pump Inc 600 S Main St ...... Butte MT 59701	800-823-4931	406-497-6700	324
Town Talk Inc 6310 Cane Run Rd ...... Louisville KY 40258	800-626-2220		155-8
Towne Technologies Inc 6-10 Bell Ave PO Box 460 ...... Somerville NJ 08876	800-837-2515	908-722-9500	479
Townes Tele-Communications Inc 120 E First St ...... Lewisville AR 71845	800-255-1975	870-921-4224	386
Townley Engineering & Manufacturing Company Inc 10551 SE 110th St Rd ...... Candler FL 32111	800-342-9920	352-687-3001	637

Company / Address	City	State	ZIP	Toll-Free	Phone	Class
Towns County 1411 Jack Dayton Cir	Young Harris	GA	30582	**800-984-1543**	706-896-4966	337
Townsend Farms Inc 23400 NE Townsend Way	Fairview	OR	97024	**800-875-5291**	503-666-1780	296-21
Townsend Press 439 Kelley Dr	West Berlin	NJ	08091	**800-772-6410**	856-753-0554	633-2
Townsend Security 724 Columbia St Nw	Olympia	WA	98501	**800-357-1019**	360-359-4400	225
Towson University 8000 York Rd	Towson	MD	21252	**866-301-3375**	410-704-2113	166
Toxics Law Reporter 1801 S Bell St	Arlington	VA	22202	**800-372-1033**		527-5
Toxikon Corp 15 Wiggins Ave	Bedford	MA	01730	**800-458-4141**	781-275-3330	738
Toy Industry Assn 1115 Broadway Ste 400	New York	NY	10010	**800-541-1345**	212-675-1141	49-4
Toyo Ink America LLC 1225 N Michael Dr *General	Wood Dale	IL	60191	**866-969-8696***	630-930-5100	387
Toyo Tires 6261 Katella Ave Ste 2B	Cypress	CA	90630	**800-678-3250**		749
Toyoda Machinery USA Inc 316 W University Dr	Arlington Heights	IL	60004	**800-257-2985**	847-253-0340	453
Toyota Canada Inc 1 Toyota Pl *Cust Svc	Scarborough	ON	M1H1H9	**888-869-6828***		59
Toyota Ctr 1510 Polk St	Houston	TX	77002	**866-446-8849**	713-758-7200	716
Toyota Financial Services 19001 S Western Ave *Cust Svc	Torrance	CA	90501	**800-874-8822***	212-715-7386	217
Toyota Motor Manufacturing Indiana Inc 4000 S Tulip Tree Dr	Princeton	IN	47670	**888-696-8211**	812-387-2266	
Toyota Motor Sales USA Inc 19001 S Western Ave *Cust Svc	Torrance	CA	90501	**800-331-4331***	310-468-4000	59
Toyota Motor Sales USA Inc Lexus Div 19001 S Western Ave *Cust Svc	Torrance	CA	90501	**800-255-3987***		59
Toyota Sunnyvale 898 W El Camino Real	Sunnyvale	CA	94087	**888-210-0091**	408-338-0063	57
Toys 'R' Us (Canada) Ltd 2777 Langstaff Rd	Concord	ON	L4K4M5	**800-869-7787**		756
TP Orthodontics Inc 100 Ctr Plz	La Porte	IN	46350	**800-348-8856**	219-785-2591	228
TP Trucking LLC 5630 Table Rock Rd	Central Point	OR	97502	**800-292-4399**		775
TPC Advance Technology Inc 18525 Gale Ave	City Of Industry	CA	91748	**800-560-8222**	626-810-4337	473
TPI Corp PO Box 4973	Johnson City	TN	37602	**800-682-3398**		15
TPL (Trust for Public Land) 116 New Montgomery St 4th Fl	San Francisco	CA	94105	**800-714-5263**	415-495-4014	48-13
TPL Communications 3825 Foothill Blvd	La Crescenta	CA	91214	**800-447-6937**	323-256-3000	643
TPM Life Insurance Co 1850 William Penn Way Ste 202	Lancaster	PA	17601	**800-555-3122**	717-394-7156	389
TPR (Texas Public Radio) 8401 Datapoint Dr Ste 800	San Antonio	TX	78229	**800-622-8977**	210-614-8977	628
TQL (Total Quality Logistics Inc) 4289 Ivy Pointe Blvd	Cincinnati	OH	45245	**800-580-3101**	513-831-2600	311
TR International Trading Company Inc 1218 Third Ave Ste 2100	Seattle	WA	98101	**800-761-7717**	206-505-3500	146
TR Miller Mill Company Inc 215 Deer St PO Box 708	Brewton	AL	36427	**800-633-6740**	251-867-4331	679
TRA (Thoroughbred Racing Associations of North America) 420 Fair Hill Dr	Elkton	MD	21921	**866-847-8772**	410-392-9200	
Trabert & Hoeffer 111 E Oak St	Chicago	IL	60611	**800-539-3573**	312-787-1654	409
TRAC Media Services 2030 E Speedway Blvd Ste 210	Tucson	AZ	85719	**888-299-1866**	520-299-1866	628
Trace-A-Matic Inc (T-A-M) 21125 Enterprise Ave	Brookfield	WI	53045	**877-375-0217**	262-797-7300	617
Trachte Bldg Systems Inc (TBS) 314 Wilburn Rd	Sun Prairie	WI	53590	**800-356-5824**		105
Tracie Martyn Salon 101 Fifth AVE 11th Fl	New York	NY	10003	**866-862-7896**	212-206-9333	702
Trackers Earth Portland 4617 SE Milwaukie Ave	Portland	OR	97202	**800-522-0255**	503-345-3312	138
TrackMaster 2083 Old Middlefield Way Ste 206	Mountain View	CA	94043	**800-334-3800**	650-316-1020	638
TRACO 71 Progress Ave	Cranberry Township	PA	16066	**800-992-4444**	724-776-7000	234
TRACOM Group, The 6675 S Kenton St Ste 118	Centennial	CO	80111	**800-221-2321**	303-470-4900	193
Tractor Supply Co 5401 Virginia Way *NASDAQ: TSCO*	Brentwood	TN	37027	**877-718-6750**	615-440-4000	274
trade associates group Ltd 900 W Bliss St	Chicago	IL	60642	**800-621-8350**	773-871-1300	321
Trade Manage Capital Inc PO Box 295	Waldwick	NJ	07463	**800-221-5676**	201-587-2424	177
Trade Products Corp 12124 Popes Head Rd	Fairfax	VA	22030	**888-352-3580**	703-502-9000	320
Trade Service Company LLC 13280 Evening Creek Dr S Ste 200	San Diego	CA	92128	**800-854-1527**		224
Trademark Co, The 344 Maple Ave W PO Box 151	Vienna	VA	22180	**800-906-8626**		317
Trademark Media Corp 2400 Webberville Rd	Austin	TX	78702	**800-916-1224**	512-459-7000	7
Trademark Transportation Inc 739 Vandalia St	Saint Paul	MN	55114	**800-646-2550**	651-646-2500	311
Trader's Library LLC 6310 Stevens Forest Rd Ste 200	Columbia	MD	21046	**800-272-2855**	410-964-0026	686
Tradescape Inc 520 S El Camino Real Ste 640	San Mateo	CA	94402	**800-697-6068**		196
TradeStation Group Inc 8050 SW Tenth St Ste 2000	Plantation	FL	33324	**800-871-3577**	954-652-7000	178-10
Trading Direct 160 Broadway 7th Fl East Bldg	New York	NY	10038	**800-925-8566**	212-766-0230	686
Trading Places International 25510 Commercentre Dr Ste 100	Lake Forest	CA	92630	**800-365-7617**		
Tradition Asiel Securities Inc 255 Greenwich St 4th Fl	New York	NY	10007	**866-220-5771**	212-791-4500	686
Traditional Door Design & Millwork Ltd 261 Regina Rd	Woodbridge	ON	L4L8M3	**877-226-9930**	416-747-1992	234
Traffic Control Service Inc 2435 Lemon Ave	Signal Hill	CA	90755	**800-763-3999**		264-3
Traffic Group Inc, The 9900 Franklin Sq Dr	Baltimore	MD	21236	**800-583-8411**	410-931-6600	461
Traffic Management Inc 8862 W 35W Service Dr NE	Minneapolis	MN	55449	**888-726-9559**	763-544-3455	194
Trail King Industries Inc 300 E Norway	Mitchell	SD	57301	**800-843-3324**		774
Trailer Bridge Inc 10405 New Berlin Rd E *OTC: TRBRQ*	Jacksonville	FL	32226	**800-554-1589**	904-751-7100	312
Trailer Transit Inc 1130 E US 20	Porter	IN	46304	**800-423-3647**	219-926-2111	775
Trailercraft Inc 222 W 92nd Ave	Anchorage	AK	99515	**800-478-3238**	907-563-3238	513
Trailiner Corp 2169 E Blaine St	Springfield	MO	65803	**800-833-8209**	417-866-7258	774
Trailways Transportation System Inc 3554 Chain Bridge Rd Ste 202	Fairfax	VA	22030	**877-467-3346**	703-691-3052	107
Trainertainment LLC PO Box 2168	Keller	TX	76248	**800-860-8474**	817-886-4840	461
Training Magazine 27020 Noble Rd	Excelsior	MN	55331	**877-865-9361**	847-559-7596	455-5
Training Modernization Group Inc 9737 Peppertree Rd	Spotsylvania	VA	22553	**866-855-6449**	540-295-9313	196
Trainworld Associates LLC 751 Mcdonald Ave	Brooklyn	NY	11218	**800-541-7010**	718-436-7072	756
TRAK Microwave Corp 4726 Eisenhower Blvd	Tampa	FL	33634	**888-283-8444**	813-901-7200	253
Tramex Travel Inc 4505 Spicewood Springs Rd Ste 200	Austin	TX	78759	**800-527-3039**		766
Trans National Communications International Inc (TNCI) 2 Charlesgate W	Boston	MA	02215	**800-800-8400**	617-369-1000	731
Trans1 Inc 3804 Park Ave Ste C	Wilmington	NC	28403	**888-526-1879**		
TransAct Technologies Inc 1 Hamden Ctr 2319 Whitney Ave Ste 3B *NASDAQ: TACT*	Hamden	CT	06518	**800-243-8941**		173-6
Transaction Network Services Inc 10740 Parkridge Blvd Ste 100	Reston	VA	20191	**866-523-0661**	703-453-8300	215
Transam Travel Inc 7013 Backlick Crt	Springfield	VA	22151	**800-822-7600**	703-998-7676	16
Transamerica 4333 Edgewood Rd NE	Cedar Rapids	IA	52499	**800-852-4678**	319-355-8511	390-5
Transamerica Occidental Life Insurance Co 1150 S Olive St *Cust Svc	Los Angeles	CA	90015	**800-852-4678***	213-742-2111	390-2
Transat AT Inc 300 Leo-Pariseau St Ste 600 *TSE: TRZ*	Montreal	QC	H2X4C2	**800-387-0825**	514-987-1616	766
Transaver LLC 108 Washington St	Manlius	NY	13104	**800-698-8629**	315-399-1200	311
Trans-Border Global Freight Systems Inc 2103 Rt 9	Round Lake	NY	12151	**800-493-9444**	518-785-6000	311
Trans-Bridge Lines Inc 2012 Industrial Dr	Bethlehem	PA	18017	**800-556-3815**	610-868-6001	108
TransCanada Pipelines Ltd 450 First St SW	Calgary	AB	T2P5H1	**800-661-3805**	403-920-2000	325
Trans-Carriers Inc 5135 US Hwy 78	Memphis	TN	38118	**800-999-7383**	901-368-2900	775
Transcat Inc 35 Vantage Pt Dr *NASDAQ: TRNS*	Rochester	NY	14624	**800-800-5001**	585-352-9460	201
TransChemical Inc 419 De Soto Ave	Saint Louis	MO	63147	**888-873-6481**	314-231-6905	146
Transco Business Technologies (TBT) 34 Leighton Rd	Augusta	ME	04330	**800-322-0003**	800-452-4657	112
Transco Industries Inc 5534 NE 122nd Ave	Portland	OR	97230	**800-545-9991**	503-256-1955	207
Transco Railway Products Inc 200 N LaSalle St Ste 1550	Chicago	IL	60601	**800-472-4592**	312-427-2818	646
TransCon Builders Inc 25250 Rockside Rd	Cleveland	OH	44146	**800-451-2608**	440-439-2100	649
Trans-Continental Systems Inc 10801 Evendale Dr	Cincinnati	OH	45241	**800-525-8726**	513-769-4774	644
TransCore 150 Fourth Ave N Ste 1200	Nashville	TN	37219	**800-923-4824**	615-988-9993	261
TransCore Link Logistics Corp 6660 Kennedy Rd Ste 205	Mississauga	ON	L5T2M9	**800-263-6149**		311
Transcosmos America Inc 879 W 190th St Ste 410	Gardena	CA	90248	**844-630-2224**		
Transcript Pharmacy Inc 2506 Lakeland Dr Ste 201	Jackson	MS	39232	**866-420-4041**		237
Transducer Techniques Inc 42480 Rio Nedo	Temecula	CA	92590	**800-344-3965**	951-719-3965	361
Transentric 1400 Douglas St Ste 0840	Omaha	NE	68179	**800-877-0328**	402-544-6000	178-10
Transfer Express Inc 7650 Tyler Blvd	Mentor	OH	44060	**800-622-2280**	440-918-1900	623
Transforce Inc 5520 Cherokee Ave Ste 200	Alexandria	VA	22312	**800-308-6989**		717
TransGuardian Inc St Vincent Jewelry Ctr 650 S Hill St Ste 519	Los Angeles	CA	90014	**877-570-7447**	213-622-5877	

	Toll-Free	Phone	Class
TRANSInternational System Inc			
130 E Wilson Bridge Rd			
Ste 150 ....Worthington OH 43085	**800-340-7540**	614-891-4942	311
Transit Systems Inc			
999 Old Eagle School Rd Ste 114 .... Wayne PA 19087	**800-626-1257**		311
Transition Networks Inc			
10900 Red Cir Dr ....Minnetonka MN 55343	**800-526-9267**	952-941-7600	176
Transitions Optical Inc			
9251 Belcher Rd ....Pinellas Park FL 33782	**800-533-2081**	727-545-0400	538
Translationscom Inc			
3 Park Ave 39th Fl ....New York NY 10016	**800-688-7205**	212-689-1616	179
Trans-Lux Corp			
26 Pearl St ....Norwalk CT 06850	**800-243-5544**	203-853-4321	173-4
OTC: TNLX			
Trans-Lux Fair-Play Inc			
1700 Delaware Ave .... Des Moines IA 50317	**800-247-0265**	515-265-5305	173-4
Transmedia			
719 Battery St .... San Francisco CA 94111	**800-229-7234**	415-956-3118	642
Transoft Solutions Inc			
13575 Commerce Pkwy Ste 250....... Richmond BC V6V2L1	**888-244-8387**	604-244-8387	174
Transource Computers Corp			
2405 W Utopia Rd ....Phoenix AZ 85027	**800-486-3715**	623-879-8882	173-2
Transpara Corp			
4715 W Culpepper Dr ....Phoenix AZ 85087	**866-994-5747**	925-218-6983	
Transparent Container Company Inc			
625 Thomas Dr ....Bensenville IL 60106	**888-449-8520**		
Transparent Language Inc			
12 Murphy Dr ....Nashua NH 03062	**800-538-8867**		178-3
Trans-Phos Inc			
4201 Bonnie Mine Rd ....Mulberry FL 33860	**800-940-1575**		775
Transpo Electronics Inc			
2150 Brengle Ave ....Orlando FL 32808	**800-327-6903**		247
Transport Distribution Co			
PO Box 306 ....Joplin MO 64802	**800-866-7709**	417-624-3814	775
Transport Inc			
2225 Main Ave SE ....Moorhead MN 56560	**800-598-7267**	218-236-6300	775
Transport Jacques Auger Inc			
860 Archimede St ....Levis QC G6V7M5	**800-387-3835**	418-835-9266	476
Transportation Alliance Bank Inc			
4185 Harrison Blvd Ste 200 ....Ogden UT 84403	**800-355-3063**		70
Transportation Management Assoc Inc			
344 Oak Grove Church Rd ....Mocksville NC 27028	**800-745-8292**		311
Transportation Research Corp			
4305 Business Dr ....Cameron Park CA 95682	**888-676-7770**	530-676-7770	646
Transportation Security Administration			
Federal Air Marshal Service			
601 S 12th St ....Arlington VA 22202	**866-289-9673**		339-10
TransPro Freight Systems Ltd			
8600 Escarpment Way ....Milton ON L9T0M1	**800-268-6857**	905-693-0699	476
Trans-Tel Central Inc (TTC)			
2805 Broce Dr ....Norman OK 73072	**800-729-4636**	405-447-5025	782
Transtelco Corp			
500 W Overland Ave Ste 301 ....El Paso TX 79901	**877-918-3526**		
TransUnion LLC			
555 W Adams St ....Chicago IL 60661	**866-922-2100**		218
Transwest			
20770 I-76 Frontage Rd ....Brighton CO 80603	**800-289-3161**	303-289-3161	57
Transwestern Commercial Services			
1900 W Loop S Ste 1300 ....Houston TX 77027	**800-531-8182**	713-270-7700	651
TransWood Carriers Inc			
PO Box 189 ....Omaha NE 68101	**888-346-8092**		775
TransWorks			
2720 Dupont Commerce Crt			
Ste 230 ....Fort Wayne IN 46825	**888-325-6510**		178-10
TransWorld Network Corp			
255 Pine Ave N ....Oldsmar FL 34677	**800-253-0665**	813-891-4700	386
Transworld Systems Inc			
PO Box 15618 ....Wilmington DE 19850	**888-446-4733**	877-282-1250	160
TransX Group of Cos			
2595 Inkster Blvd ....Winnipeg MB R3C2E6	**877-558-9444**	204-632-6694	311
Transylvania University			
300 N Broadway ....Lexington KY 40508	**800-872-6798**	859-233-8242	166
Tranter Inc			
1900 Old Burk Hwy ....Wichita Falls TX 76306	**800-414-6908**		91
Tranzon LLC			
2100 Club Dr Ste 100................Gadsden AL 35901	**866-872-6966**	256-413-2902	41
Trapp Family Lodge			
700 Trapp Hill Rd PO Box 1428 ....Stowe VT 05672	**800-826-7000**	802-253-8511	665
Traulsen & Company Inc			
4401 Blue Mound Rd ....Fort Worth TX 76106	**800-825-8220**		14
Travaasa Hana			
5031 Hana Hwy ....Hana HI 96713	**855-868-7282**	808-248-8211	665
Travcoa			
100 N Sepulveda Blvd			
Ste 1700 ....El Segundo CA 90245	**800-992-2003**	310-649-7104	755
Travel & Transport Inc			
2120 S 72nd St ....Omaha NE 68124	**800-228-2545**	402-399-4500	766
Travel + Leisure Magazine			
225 Liberty St ....New York NY 10281	**800-888-8728**		455-20
Travel Agent Magazine			
757 Third Ave ....New York NY 10017	**855-424-6247**	212-895-8200	455-22
Travel Berkley Springs			
127 Fairfax St ....Berkeley Springs WV 25411	**800-447-8797**	304-258-9147	767
Travel Destinations Management Group Inc			
110 Painters Mill Rd ....Owings Mills MD 21117	**800-635-7307**	410-363-3111	766
Travel Goods Association			
301 N Harrison St Ste 412 ....Princeton NJ 08540	**877-842-1938**		138
Travel Impressions Ltd			
465 Smith St ....Farmingdale NY 11735	**800-284-0044**	631-845-8000	766
Travel Institute			
945 Concord St ....Framingham MA 01701	**800-542-4282**	781-237-0280	48-23
Travel Insured International			
855 Winding Brook Dr			
PO Box 6503................Glastonbury CT 06033	**800-243-3174**		390-7
Travel Leaders Group LLC			
?119 West 40th? St ....New ?York NY 10018	**800-448-3090**	763-744-3700	782
Travel Manitoba			
155 Carlton St 7th Fl ....Winnipeg MB R3C3H8	**800-665-0040**	204-927-7800	769

	Toll-Free	Phone	Class
Travel One Inc			
8009 34th Ave S 15th Fl...........Minneapolis MN 55425	**800-247-1311**	952-854-2551	767
Travel Portland			
Pioneer Courthouse Sq			
701 SW Sixth Ave...................Portland OR 97204	**877-678-5263**	503-275-9750	206
Travel Society Inc			
650 S Cherry St Ste 200 ....Denver CO 80246	**800-926-6031**	303-321-0900	767
Travel Turf Inc			
7540 Windsor Dr Ste 202 ....Allentown PA 18195	**800-222-4432**	610-391-9094	767
Travel Weekly Crossroads Magazine			
100 Lighting Way ....Secaucus NJ 07094	**800-635-1666**	201-902-2000	455-21
TravelCenters of America			
24601 Ctr Ridge Rd Ste 200 ....Westlake OH 44145	**800-632-9240**	440-808-9100	324
Travelclick			
7 Times Sq 38th Fl ....New York NY 10036	**866-674-4549**	212-817-4800	194
Travelennium Inc			
556 Colonial Rd ....Memphis TN 38117	**800-844-4924**	901-767-0761	766
Travelers Cos Inc			
385 Washington St ....Saint Paul MN 55102	**800-328-2189**	651-310-7911	359-4
NYSE: TRV			
Travelers Motor Club			
720 NW 50th St ....Oklahoma City OK 73154	**800-654-9208**	405-848-1711	53
Travelers Transportation Services Inc			
195 Heart Lake Rd S ....Brampton ON L6W3N6	**800-265-8789**	905-457-8789	311
Travelex International Inc			
2061 N Barrington Rd ....Hoffman Estates IL 60169	**800-882-0499**	847-882-0400	767
Travelex Worldwide Money			
122 E 42nd St Ste 2800 ....New York NY 10168	**800-228-9792**	516-300-1622	69
Travelhost Magazine			
10701 N Stemmons Fwy ....Dallas TX 75220	**800-527-1782**	972-556-0541	455-22
Traveline Travel Agencies Inc			
4074 Erie St ....Willoughby OH 44094	**888-700-8747**	440-602-8020	766
Travelink Inc			
404 BNA Dr #650 ....Nashville TN 37217	**800-821-4671**	615-367-4900	317
Travel-On Ltd			
9000 Virginia Manor Rd			
Ste 201 ....Beltsville MD 20705	**800-333-6778**	240-387-4000	767
Travelpro USA			
700 Banyan Trl ....Boca Raton FL 33431	**800-741-7471**	561-998-2824	451
TravelSmith Outfitters			
75 Aircraft RD ....Southington CT 06489	**800-770-3387**		457
TravelStore Inc			
11601 Wilshire Blvd ....Los Angeles CA 90025	**800-850-3224**	310-575-5540	766
TRAVELVIDEOSTOREcom Inc			
5420 Boran Dr ....Tampa FL 33610	**800-288-5123**	813-630-9778	767
Travers Printing Inc			
32 Mission St ....Gardner MA 01440	**800-696-0530**	978-632-0530	623
Travers Tool Company Inc			
128-15 26th Ave ....Flushing NY 11354	**800-221-0270***	718-886-7200	384
*Cust Svc			
Traverse City Convention & Visitors Bureau			
101 W Grandview Pkwy ....Traverse City MI 49684	**800-940-1120**	231-947-1120	206
Traverse City Record-Eagle			
120 W Front St ....Traverse City MI 49684	**800-968-8273**	231-946-2000	528-2
Traverse Electric Co-op Inc			
1618 Broadway PO Box 66............Wheaton MN 56296	**800-927-5443**	320-563-8616	245
Travis Body & Trailer Inc			
13955 FM529 ....Houston TX 77041	**800-535-4372**	713-466-5888	774
Travis Federal Credit Union			
1 Travis Way ....Vacaville CA 95687	**800-877-8328**	707-449-4000	219
Travisco			
7210 Clinton Hwy PO Box 670............Powell TN 37849	**800-247-7606**		471
Trayer Engineering Corp			
898 Pennsylvania Ave ....San Francisco CA 94107	**800-377-1774**	415-285-7770	261
Traylor Bros Inc			
835 N Congress Ave ....Evansville IN 47715	**866-895-1491**	812-477-1542	188-4
TRC			
1300 Virginia Dr			
Ste 200 ....Fort Washington PA 19034	**800-275-2827**	215-641-2200	464
Treasure Chest Casino			
5050 Williams Blvd ....Kenner LA 70065	**800-298-0711**	504-443-8000	133
Treasure Health			
1201 SE Indian St ....Stuart FL 34997	**800-299-4677**	772-403-4500	370
Treasure Island Hotel & Casino			
3300 Las Vegas Blvd S ....Las Vegas NV 89109	**800-288-7206**	702-894-7111	665
Treasure Island Resort & Casino			
5734 Sturgeon Lake Rd ....Welch MN 55089	**800-222-7077**		
Tredegar Corp			
1100 Boulders Pkwy ....North Chesterfield VA 23225	**800-411-7441**	804-330-1000	359-3
NYSE: TG			
Tree Care Industry Assn (TCIA)			
136 Harvey Rd Ste 101 ....Londonderry NH 03053	**800-733-2622**	603-314-5380	48-13
Tree Island Industries			
3933 Boundary Rd ....Richmond BC V6V1T8	**800-663-0955**	604-524-3744	483
Tree Island Steel			
12459 Arrow Rt ....Rancho Cucamonga CA 91739	**800-255-6974**	909-594-7511	808
Treeland Garden Center & Nursery			
1000 Huntington Tpke ....Bridgeport CT 06610	**800-243-0232**	203-372-3511	323
Treeline Associates Inc			
5300 Lakewood Rd ....Whitehall MI 49461	**888-231-8039**	248-814-7151	
Treeline Well Services Inc			
750 333 - 11th Ave SW ....Calgary AB T2R1L9	**844-344-7447**	403-266-2868	190
Treetops Resort			
3962 Wilkinson Rd ....Gaylord MI 49735	**866-348-5249**	989-732-6711	665
Trefethen Vineyards Winery Inc			
1160 Oak Knoll Ave ....Napa CA 94558	**866-895-7696**	707-255-7700	80-3
Treflie Capital Management			
35 Ezekills Holw ....Sag Harbor NY 11963	**866-236-3363**	631-725-2500	400
Trego County			
216 N Main St ....WaKeeney KS 67672	**877-962-7248**	785-743-5785	337
Trehel Corp			
935 S Main St Ste 300			
PO Box 6688. ....Greenville SC 29601	**800-319-7006**	864-654-6582	186
Trek Inc			
11601 Maple Ridge Rd ....Medina NY 14103	**800-367-8735**	585-798-3140	248
Trelleborg Coated Systems US Inc			
1886 Prairie Way ....Louisville CO 80027	**800-344-0714**	303-469-1357	740-1
Tremco Inc Roofing Div			
3735 Green Rd ....Beachwood OH 44122	**800-852-6013**	216-292-5000	3

Company / Address	Toll-Free	Phone	Class
Tremont Chicago 100 E Chestnut St ....Chicago IL 60611	888-627-8281	312-751-1900	378
Trempealeau County 36245 Main St ....Whitehall WI 54773	877-538-2311	715-538-2311	337
Trench Plate Rental Co 13217 Laureldale Ave ....Downey CA 90242	800-821-4478		23
Trend 660 American Ave Ste 203 ....King Of Prussia PA 19406	877-330-9900	610-783-4650	225
TREND Enterprises Inc 300 Ninth Ave SW ....New Brighton MN 55112 *Cust Svc	800-860-6762*	651-631-2850	243
Trendex Inc 240 E Maryland Ave ....Saint Paul MN 55117	800-328-9200	651-489-4655	86
TrendMicro Inc 10101 N De Anza Blvd ....Cupertino CA 95014	800-228-5651	408-257-1500	178-12
Trends International LLC 5188 W 74th St ....Indianapolis IN 46268	866-406-7771	317-388-1212	328
Trendware International Inc 20675 Manhattan Pl ....Torrance CA 90501	888-326-6061	310-961-5500	176
Trendway Corp 13467 Quincy St PO Box 9016.........Holland MI 49422	800-968-5344	616-399-3900	319-1
Trent University 1600 W Bank Dr ....Peterborough ON K9J7B8	888-739-8885	705-748-1011	780
Trenton City Hall 319 E State St ....Trenton NJ 08608	800-221-0051	609-989-3000	336
Trenton Psychiatric Hospital PO Box 7500 ....West Trenton NJ 08628	800-382-6717	609-633-1500	373-5
Trevecca Nazarene University 333 Murfreesboro Rd ....Nashville TN 37210	888-210-4868	615-248-1200	166
Trew Industrial Wheels Inc 310 Wilhagan Rd ....Nashville TN 37217	888-977-8739	615-360-9100	54
Trex Enterprises Corp 10455 Pacific Ctr Ct ....San Diego CA 92121	800-626-5885	858-646-5300	664
Trez Capital LP 1550 - 1185 W Georgia St ....Vancouver BC V6E4E6	877-689-0821	604-689-0821	524
TRGC (Title Resources Guaranty Co) 8111 LBJ Fwy Ste 1200 ....Dallas TX 75251	800-526-8018		390-6
Tri County Ford 4032 Commerce Pkwy ....Buckner KY 40010	800-945-2520	502-241-7333	57
TRI MAP International Inc 119 Val Dervin Pkwy Ste 5 ....Stockton CA 95206	888-687-4627	209-234-0100	254
Tri Star Freight System Inc 5407 Mesa Dr ....Houston TX 77028	800-229-1095	713-631-1095	775
Tri Star Metals LLC 375 Village Dr ....Carol Stream IL 60188	800-541-2294	630-462-7600	490
Tri State Distribution Inc 600 Vista Dr ....Sparta TN 38583	800-392-9824		473
Tri State Wholesale Flooring Inc 3900 W 34th St N ....Sioux Falls SD 57107	800-353-3080	605-336-3080	131
Tri Tool Inc 3041 Sunrise Blvd ....Rancho Cordova CA 95742	800-345-5015	916-288-6100	617
Triad Financial Services Inc 4336 Pablo Oaks Ct ....Jacksonville FL 32224	800-522-2013		217
Triad Freightliner of Tennessee LLC 841 Eastern Star Rd ....Kingsport TN 37663	800-451-1508		57
Triad Guaranty Insurance Corp 101 S Stratford Rd ......Winston-Salem NC 27104 *Cust Svc	888-691-8074*	336-723-1282	390-5
Triad Isotopes Inc 4205 Vineland Rd Ste L1 ....Orlando FL 32811	866-310-0086	407-455-6700	231
Triad Products Co 1801 W 'B' St ....Hastings NE 68901 *General	888-253-4227*	402-462-2181	604
Triangle Brick Co 6523 NC Hwy 55 ....Durham NC 27713	800-672-8547	919-544-1796	150
Triangle C Dude Ranch 3737 Hwy 26 ....Dubois WY 82513	800-661-4928	307-455-2225	239
Triangle Fastener Corp 1925 Preble Ave ....Pittsburgh PA 15233 *General	800-486-1832*	412-321-5000	350
Triangle Package Machinery Co 6655 W Diversey Ave ....Chicago IL 60707	800-621-4170	773-889-0200	543
Triangle Suspension Systems Inc 200 E Maloney Rd ....Du Bois PA 15801	800-458-6077		60
Triangle Tech Inc *Du Bois* 225 Tannery Row Rd ....Falls Creek PA 15840	800-874-8324	814-371-2090	795
Erie 2000 Liberty St ....Erie PA 16502	800-874-8324	814-453-6016	795
Greensburg 222 E Pittsburgh St ....Greensburg PA 15601	800-874-8324	724-832-1050	795
Triangle X-ray Co 4900 Thornton Rd Ste 117 ....Raleigh NC 27616	866-763-9729	919-876-6156	473
Trianon Old Naples 955 Seventh Ave S ....Naples FL 34102	877-482-5228	239-435-9600	378
Triathlete Sports 186 Exchange St ....Bangor ME 04401	800-635-0528	207-990-2013	707
Tri-Basin Natural Resources District 1723 Burlington St ....Holdrege NE 68949	877-995-6688	308-995-6688	196
Tri-boro Shelving & Partition Corp 300 Dominion Dr ....Farmville VA 23901	800-633-3070	434-315-5600	321
Tribridge 4830 W Kennedy Blvd Ste 890 ....Tampa FL 33609	877-744-1360		178-1
Tribune Direct Marketing Inc 505 Northwest Ave ....Northlake IL 60164	800-545-9657		5
Tribune Newspapers of Snohomish County 127 Ave C Ste B PO Box 499 ..Snohomish WA 98291	877-894-4663	360-568-4121	528-4
Tribune Review Publishing Co 622 Cabin Hill Dr ....Greensburg PA 15601	800-524-5700	724-834-1151	633-8
Tribune, The 3825 S Higuera St ......San Luis Obispo CA 93401	800-477-8799	805-781-7800	528-2
Tribune-Democrat 425 Locust St ....Johnstown PA 15907	855-255-5975	814-532-5050	528-2
Tribune-Star PO Box 149 ....Terre Haute IN 47808	800-783-8742	812-231-4200	528-2
Tricerat Inc 11500 Cronridge Dr Ste 100........Owings Mills MD 21117	800-582-5167	410-715-4226	179
Tri-Cities Visitor & Convention Bureau 7130 W Grandridge Blvd Ste B........Kennewick WA 99336	800-254-5824	509-735-8486	206
Tri-City Electrical Contractors Inc 430 W Dr ....Altamonte Springs FL 32714	800-768-2489	407-788-3500	189-4
Tri-City Herald 333 W Canal Dr ....Kennewick WA 99336	800-874-0445	509-582-1500	528-2
Trickle Up Program Inc 104 W 27th St 12th Fl. ....New York NY 10001	866-246-9980	212-255-9980	48-5
TriCo Bancshares 63 Constitution Dr ....Chico CA 95973 *NASDAQ: TCBK*	800-922-8742	530-898-0300	359-2
Tricolor Inc 1111 W Mockingbird Ln Ste 1500 ....Dallas TX 75247	888-253-0423		
Tricomm Services Corp 1247 N Church St Ste 12 ....Moorestown NJ 08057	800-872-2401	856-914-9001	782
Tri-Con Inc 7076 W Port Arthur Rd PO Box 20555. ....Beaumont TX 77705	800-876-7102	409-835-2237	575
TRICOR (Tennessee Rehabilitative Initiative in Correction) 240 Great Cir Rd Ste 310 ....Nashville TN 37228	800-958-7426	615-741-5705	626
TRICOR Insurance Inc 230 W Cherry St ....Lancaster WI 53813	877-468-7426	608-723-6441	389
Tricor Metals Inc 3225 W Old Lincoln Way ....Wooster OH 44691	800-421-5141	330-264-3299	295
Tricor Print Communications Inc 7931 NE Halsey St Ste 101............Portland OR 97213	800-635-7778	503-255-5595	623
Tricorbraun Winepak 2280 Cordelia Rd ....Fairfield CA 94534	800-374-6594		333
TriCore Reference Laboratories 1001 Woodward Pl NE ....Albuquerque NM 87102	800-245-3296	505-938-8888	414
Tri-County Electric 995 Mile 46 Rd PO Box 880 ....Hooker OK 73945	800-522-3315	580-652-2418	245
Tri-County Electric Co-op PO Box 159 ....Lancaster MO 63548	888-457-3734	660-457-3733	245
Tri-County Electric Co-op 6473 Old State Rd ....Saint Matthews SC 29135	877-874-1215	803-874-1215	245
Tri-County Electric Co-op Inc 3906 Broadway St ....Mount Vernon IL 62864	800-244-5151	618-244-5151	245
Tri-County Electric Co-op Inc 600 NW Pkwy ....Azle TX 76020	800-367-8232	817-444-3201	245
Tri-County Electric Membership Corp PO Box 487 ....Gray GA 31032	866-254-8100	478-986-8100	245
Tri-County Electric Membership Corp 405 College St ....Lafayette TN 37083	800-369-2111	615-666-2111	245
Tri-County Mall 11700 Princeton Pk ....Cincinnati OH 45246	866-905-4675	513-671-0120	458
Tri-County Rural Electric Co-op Inc 22 N Main St PO Box 526. ....Mansfield PA 16933	800-343-2559	570-662-2175	245
Tri-County Technical College 7900 Hwy 76 ....Pendleton SC 29670	866-269-5677	864-646-8361	795
Tricycle Inc 1293 Riverfront Pkwy Ste 1293-B ....Chattanooga TN 37402	800-808-4809		804
Trident Medical Ctr 9330 Medical Plaza Dr ....Charleston SC 29406	866-492-9085	843-797-7000	373-3
Trident Steel Corp 12825 Flushing Meadows Dr Ste 110 ....St. Louis MO 63131	800-777-9687	314-822-0500	490
Trident Technical College (TTC) 7000 Rivers Ave PO Box 118067. ......North Charleston SC 29406	877-349-7184	843-574-6111	795
Trident Technologies Inc 8885 Rehco Rd ....San Diego CA 92121	800-326-4010	619-688-9600	608
Tri-Dim Filter Corp 93 Industrial Dr ....Louisa VA 23093	800-458-9835	540-967-2600	18
Tri-Ed Distribution Inc 135 Crossways Pk Dr W ....Woodbury NY 11797	888-874-3336	516-941-2800	246
Triflo International Inc 1000 FM 830 ....Willis TX 77318	800-332-0993	936-856-8551	357
Tri-Gas & Oil Company Inc 3941 Federalsburg Hwy PO Box 465. ....Federalsburg MD 21632	800-638-7802	410-754-8184	325
Trijicon Inc 49385 Shafer Ave PO Box 930059 ....Wixom MI 48393	800-338-0563	248-960-7700	707
Tri-Land 1 E Oak Hill Dr Ste 302. ....Westmont IL 60559	800-441-7032	708-531-8210	648
TriLeaf Crop 10845 Olive Blvd Ste 260 ....Saint Louis MO 63141	800-652-5552	314-997-6111	261
TriLink BioTechnologies Inc 9955 Mesa Rim Rd ....San Diego CA 92121	800-863-6801	858-546-0004	738
Tri-Lite Inc 1642 N Besly Ct ....Chicago IL 60642	800-322-5250	773-384-7765	438
Trilithic Inc 9710 Pk Davis Dr ....Indianapolis IN 46235	800-344-2412	317-895-3600	248
Trillium Asset Management LLC 2 Financial Ctr 60 S St Ste 1100. ....Boston MA 02111	800-548-5684	617-423-6655	524
Trillium Community Health Plan Inc 1800 Millrace Dr ....Eugene OR 97403	877-600-5472	541-485-2155	390-3
Trimaco LLC 2300 Gateway Centre Blvd Ste 200 ....Morrisville NC 27560	800-325-7356	919-674-3460	728
Trimark Corp PO Box 350 ....New Hampton IA 50659	800-447-0343	641-394-3188	349
TriMark USA Inc 505 Collins St ....South Attleboro MA 02703	800-755-5580	508-399-2400	300
Trimble Navigation Ltd 935 Stewart Dr ....Sunnyvale CA 94085 *NASDAQ: TRMB*	800-538-7800	408-481-8000	525
Trimco/Builders Brass Works 3528 Emery St ....Los Angeles CA 90023	800-637-8746	323-262-4191	349
Trimedyne Inc 15091 Bake Pkwy ....Irvine CA 92618 *OTC: TMED*	800-733-5273	949-559-5300	423
Trimfoot Co LLC 115 Trimfoot Terr ....Farmington MO 63640	800-325-6116		301
TrimJoist Corp 5146 Hwy 182 E ....Columbus MS 39702	800-844-8281	662-327-7950	815
TrimMaster 4860 N Fifth St Hwy ....Temple PA 19560	800-356-4237	610-921-0203	739

Alphabetical Section

	Toll-Free	Phone	Class
TriNet Group Inc 1100 San Leandro Blvd Ste 300 . . . . San Leandro CA 94577	888-874-6388	510-352-5000	627
Trinidad State Junior College 600 Prospect St . . . . Trinidad CO 81082	800-621-8752	719-846-5011	162
Trinity Bible College 50 Sixth Ave N . . . . Ellendale ND 58436	800-523-1603	701-349-3621	161
Trinity Biotech PLC 5919 Farnsworth Ct . . . . Carlsbad CA 92008 *NASDAQ: TRIB*	800-331-2291	760-929-0500	231
Trinity Broadcasting Network (TBN) PO Box A . . . . Santa Ana CA 92711	888-731-1000	714-832-2950	735
Trinity Business Furniture 6089 Kennedy Rd . . . . Trinity NC 27370	855-311-6660	336-472-6660	321
Trinity College of Florida 2430 Welbilt Blvd . . . . Trinity FL 34655	800-388-0869	727-376-6911	161
Trinity Episcopal School for Ministry 311 Eleventh St . . . . Ambridge PA 15003	800-874-8754	724-266-3838	167-3
Trinity Fiduciary Partners LLC 325 S Mesquite St Ste 104 . . . . Arlington TX 76010	877-334-1283		524
Trinity Green Services LLC 751 Hebron Pkwy Ste 225 . . . . Lewisville TX 75057	888-243-3605	214-446-9500	464
Trinity Health 1 Burdick Expy W PO Box 5020 . . . . Minot ND 58702	800-862-0005	701-857-5000	373-3
Trinity Hospital Saint Joseph's 1 W Burdick Expy . . . . Minot ND 58701	800-247-1316	701-857-5000	373-3
Trinity International University 2065 Half Day Rd . . . . Deerfield IL 60015	800-822-3225	847-945-8800	166
Trinity International University South Florida 8190 W SR 84 . . . . Davie FL 33324	800-822-3225	954-382-6400	166
Trinity Lutheran Seminary 2199 E Main St . . . . Columbus OH 43209	866-610-8571	614-235-4136	167-3
Trinity Marine Products Inc 2525 N Stemmons Fwy . . . . Dallas TX 75207	877-876-5463	214-631-4420	694
Trinity Mining Service 109 48th St . . . . Pittsburgh PA 15201	800-264-2583	412-682-4700	646
Trinity Rail Group LLC 2525 N Stemmons Fwy . . . . Dallas TX 75207	800-631-4420	214-631-4420	646
Trinity Sterile Inc 201 Kiley Dr . . . . Salisbury MD 21801	800-829-8384		592
Trinity Trailer Manufacturing Inc 7533 S Federal Way . . . . Boise ID 83716	800-235-6577	208-336-3666	774
Trinity University 125 Michigan Ave NE . . . . Washington DC 20017 *Admissions	800-492-6882*	202-884-9000	166
Trinity University 1 Trinity Pl . . . . San Antonio TX 78212	800-874-6489	210-999-7011	166
Trinity Valley Community College *Palestine* PO Box 2530 . . . . Palestine TX 75802	866-882-2937	903-729-0256	162
Trinity Valley Electric Co-op Inc (TVEC) 1800 E HWY 243 . . . . Kaufman TX 75142	800-766-9576	972-932-2214	245
Trinity Western University 7600 Glover Rd . . . . Langley BC V2Y1Y1	888-468-6898	604-888-7511	780
Trintech Inc 15851 Dallas Pkwy Ste 900 . . . . Addison TX 75001	800-416-0075	972-701-9802	178-1
Trio Pac Inc 386 Mcarthur . . . . Saint-Laurent QC H4T1X8	888-565-6722	514-733-7793	
Trion Inc 101 McNeill Rd . . . . Sanford NC 27330	800-884-0002	919-775-2201	18
Trion Industries Inc 297 Laird St . . . . Wilkes-Barre PA 18702	800-444-4665		286
Triple B Forwarders Inc 1511 Glen Curtis St . . . . Carson CA 90746	800-228-8465	310-604-5840	311
Triple Creek Ranch 5551 W Fork Rd . . . . Darby MT 59829	800-654-2943	406-821-4600	665
Triple Crown Nutrition Inc 315 Lake St E Ste 300. . . . . Wayzata MN 55391	800-451-9916		445
Triple Crown Products Inc 814 Ela Ave . . . . Waterford WI 53185	800-619-1110	262-534-7878	683
Triple Crown Services 2720 Dupont Commerce Ct . . . . . . Fort Wayne IN 46825	800-325-6510	260-416-3600	644
Triple J Wilderness Ranch 91 Mortimer Rd PO Box 310. . . . . Augusta MT 59410	800-826-1300	406-562-3653	239
Triple Play Products LLC 120 Getty Ave . . . . Paterson NJ 07503	800-829-1625	646-484-8112	64
Triple/S Dynamics Inc 1031 S Haskell Ave PO Box 151027. . . . . . . Dallas TX 75315	800-527-2116	214-828-8600	468
Triple-S Steel Supply LLC 6000 Jensen Dr . . . . Houston TX 77026	800-231-1034	713-697-7105	490
Triplett Office Essentials Corp 3553 109th St . . . . Urbandale IA 50322	800-437-5034	515-270-9150	531
Tripmasters 5640 Nicholson Ln Ste 215 . . . . Rockville MD 20852	800-430-0484	202-349-7579	16
Trippnt Inc 8830 NE 108th St . . . . Kansas City MO 64157	800-874-7768	816-792-2604	604
Tripwire Inc 101 SW Main St Ste 1500 . . . . Portland OR 97204 *General	800-874-7947*	503-276-7500	178-12
Tri-Rail 800 NW 33rd St . . . . Pompano Beach FL 33064	800-874-7245	954-783-6030	
Trisoft Technologies Inc 14429 Independence Dr . . . . Plainfield IL 60544	866-364-7031		461
Trissential LLC 1905 E Wayzata Blvd Ste 333 . . . . Wayzata MN 55391	888-595-7970		
TriStar Inc 3740 E La Salle St . . . . Phoenix AZ 85040	800-800-1714		
Tri-Star Plastics Corp 906 Boston Tpke . . . . Shrewsbury MA 01545	800-874-7827		
Tristar Southern Hills Medical Ctr 391 Wallace Rd . . . . Nashville TN 37211	800-242-5662	615-781-4000	373-3
Tri-Starr Investigations Inc 3525 Hwy 138 SW Rockdale County. . . . . Stockbridge GA 30281	800-849-9841	770-388-9841	41
Tri-state Adjustments Inc 3439 E Ave S PO Box 3219 . . . . La Crosse WI 54602	800-562-3906	608-788-8683	160
Tri-State Armature & Electrical Works Inc 330 GE Patterson Ave . . . . Memphis TN 38126	800-238-7654	901-527-8412	246

	Toll-Free	Phone	Class
Tri-State Better Business Bureau 3101 N Green River Rd Ste 410 . . . . Evansville IN 47715	800-359-0979	812-473-0202	79
Tri-State Bible College 506 Margaret St . . . . South Point OH 45680	800-333-3243	740-377-2520	161
Tri-State Electric Membership Corp (TSEMC) 2310 Blue Ridge Dr . . . . Blue Ridge GA 30513	800-351-1111	706-492-3251	245
Tri-state Fabricators Inc 1146 Ferris Rd . . . . Amelia OH 45102	888-523-1488	513-752-5005	606
Tri-State Financial Press LLC 109 N Fifth St . . . . Saddle Brook NJ 07663	800-866-6375		623
Tri-state Forest Products Inc 2105 Sheridan Ave . . . . Springfield OH 45505	800-949-6325	937-323-6325	191-3
Tri-state Home Services 82A Wormans Mill Ct . . . . Frederick MD 21701	844-202-2126		606
Tri-State Pumps Inc 1162 Chastain Rd . . . . Liberty SC 29657	800-868-4631	864-843-8100	707
Tri-State Surgical Supply & Equipment Ltd 409 Hoyt St . . . . Brooklyn NY 11231	800-899-8741	718-624-1000	473
Tri-State Travel 4349 Industrial Pk Dr . . . . Galena IL 61036	800-779-4869	815-777-0820	755
Tri-State Utility Products Inc 1030 Atlanta Industrial Dr . . . . Marietta GA 30066	800-282-7985	770-427-3119	246
Triton Systems Inc 21405 B St . . . . Long Beach MS 39560	866-787-4866	228-575-3100	253
Triumph Group 899 Cassatt Rd Ste 210 . . . . Berwyn PA 19312	800-889-4422	610-251-1000	617
Triumph Group Inc 1550 Liberty Ridge Dr Ste 100 . . . . Wayne PA 19087 *NYSE: TGI*	800-863-1083	610-251-1000	24
Triumph Learning 136 Madison Ave . . . . New York NY 10016	800-338-6519	800-586-9940	633-2
Triumph Sunshine mills Inc 500 Sixth St SW . . . . Red Bay AL 35582	800-705-2111	256-356-9541	574
Triumph Twist Drill Co Inc 1 SW Seventh St . . . . Chisholm MN 55719	800-942-1501	218-263-3891	753
Triumvirate Environmental 61 Innerbelt Rd . . . . Somerville MA 02143	800-966-9282	617-628-8098	799
TriZetto Corp 3300 Rider Trail S . . . . Earth City MO 63045	800-969-3666	314-802-6700	177
TRMC (Thibodaux Regional Medical Ctr) 602 N Acadia Rd . . . . Thibodaux LA 70301	800-822-8442	985-447-5500	373-3
TRN (TRN) PO Box 3755 . . . . Central Point OR 97502	888-383-3733		642
Trocaire College 360 Choate Ave . . . . Buffalo NY 14220	877-616-6633	716-826-1200	162
Trois-Rivieres Tourism 1457 rue Notre-Dame Ctr . . . . Trois-Rivieres QC G9A4X4	800-313-1123	819-375-1122	770
Trojan Battery Co 12380 Clark St . . . . Santa Fe Springs CA 90670 *Cust Svc	800-423-6569*	562-236-3000	74
Trojan Inc 198 Trojan St . . . . Mount Sterling KY 40353	800-264-0526		436
Trojan Professional Services Inc 14410 Cerritos Ave . . . . Los Alamitos CA 90720	800-451-9723		224
Tronair Inc 1740 Eber Rd . . . . Holland OH 43528	800-426-6301	419-866-6301	22
Trophy Nut Company Inc 320 N Second St . . . . Tipp City OH 45371	800-729-6887	937-667-8478	296-28
Trophyland USA Inc 7001 W 20th Ave . . . . Hialeah FL 33014	800-327-5820	305-823-4830	772
Tropic Oil Company Inc 10002 NW 89th Ave . . . . Miami FL 33178	866-645-3835	305-888-4611	575
Tropical Cheese Industries Inc 450 Fayette St PO Box 1357. . . . . . . Perth Amboy NJ 08861	888-874-4928	732-442-4898	296-5
Tropical Ford 9900 S Orange Blossom Trial . . . . Orlando FL 32837 *Sales	877-241-0502*	407-851-3800	57
Tropical Winds Oceanfront Hotel 1398 N Atlantic Ave . . . . Daytona Beach FL 32118	800-245-6099	386-258-1016	378
Tropicana Entertainment 2831 Boardwalk . . . . Atlantic City NJ 08401 *OTC: TPCA*	800-843-8767		665
Tropicana Express 2121 S Casino Dr . . . . Laughlin NV 89029	800-243-6846	702-298-4200	133
Tropicana Field 1 Tropicana Dr . . . . Saint Petersburg FL 33705	888-326-7297	727-825-3137	716
Tropicana Inn & Suites 1540 S Harbor Blvd . . . . Anaheim CA 92802	800-828-4898	714-635-4082	378
Tropicana Resort & Casino 3801 Las Vegas Blvd S . . . . Las Vegas NV 89109 *Resv	800-462-8767*	702-739-2222	665
Trotter & Morton Ltd 5711 1 St SE . . . . Calgary AB T2H1H9	800-355-9401	403-255-7535	186
Trotters Restaurant 2008 Savannah Hwy . . . . Charleston SC 29401	800-334-6660	843-571-1000	667
Trout Unlimited (TU) 1300 N 17th Ave Ste 500 . . . . Arlington VA 22209	800-834-2419	703-522-0200	48-3
Trouw Nutrition 115 Executive Dr . . . . Highland IL 62249	800-365-1357	618-654-2070	445
Troxler Electronic Laboratories Inc 3008 E Cornwallis Rd PO Box 12057. . . . . . . Research Triangle Park NC 27709	877-876-9537	919-549-8661	201
Troy Public Library 510 W Big Beaver Rd . . . . Troy MI 48084	800-649-7377	248-524-3538	433-3
Troy Sunshade Co 607 Riffle Ave . . . . Greenville OH 45331	800-833-8769	937-548-2466	728
Troy University 600 University Ave . . . . Troy AL 36082 *Montgomery* 231 Montgomery St PO Box 4419 . . . . Montgomery AL 36104	800-551-9716 888-357-8843	334-670-3100	166 166
Troy-CSL Lighting Inc 14508 Nelson Ave . . . . City of Industry CA 91744	800-533-8769	626-336-4511	438
Troyer Foods Inc 17141 State Rd 4 . . . . Goshen IN 46528	800-876-9377	574-533-0302	297-10
Troy-Miami County Public Library 419 W Main St . . . . Troy OH 45373	866-657-8556	937-339-0502	433-3

Company	Toll-Free	Phone	Class
TRSA (Textile Rental Services Assn) 1800 Diagonal Rd Ste 200 .... Alexandria VA 22314	877-770-9274	703-519-0029	49-4
TRU (Thompson Rivers University) 805 TRU Way .... Kamloops BC V2C0C8	800-663-1663	250-828-5000	780
Tru Tech Corp 20 Vaughan Vly Blvd .... Vaughan ON L4H0B1	888-760-0099	905-856-0096	497
TRU TECH Systems Inc 24550 N River Rd PO Box 46965.......... Mount Clemens MI 48043	877-878-8324	586-469-2700	453
Tru Vue Inc 9400 W 55th St ....McCook IL 60525	800-621-8339	708-485-5080	329
Truck Center Companies 10550 I St PO Box 27379..............Omaha NE 68127	800-777-2440		126
Truck Equipment Service Co 800 Oak St .... Lincoln NE 68521	800-869-0363	402-476-3225	774
Truck Sales & Service Inc PO Box 262 .... Midvale OH 44653	800-282-6100	740-922-3412	57
Truck Utilities Inc 2370 English St .... Saint Paul MN 55109	800-869-1075	651-484-3305	513
Truckers Helper LLC, The 630 S Wickham Rd ....Melbourne FL 32904	800-875-7435	321-956-7331	177
Truckin Movers Corp 1031 Harvest St .... Durham NC 27704	800-334-1651	919-682-2300	516
Truck-Lite Company Inc 310 E Elmwood Ave ....Falconer NY 14733 *Cust Svc	800-562-5012*		437
Trudell Medical Group Ltd 758 Third St .... London ON N5V5J7	800-757-4881	519-685-8800	473
Trudiligence LLC 3190 S Wadsworth Blvd Ste 260 .. Lakewood CO 80227	800-580-0474	303-692-8445	218
True Blue Inc PO Box 2910 .... Tacoma WA 98401 NYSE: TBI	800-610-8920	253-383-9101	717
True Fitness Technology 865 Hoff Rd ....O'Fallon MO 63366	800-426-6570	888-491-2307	267
True Manufacturing Co 2001 E Terra Ln ....O'Fallon MO 63366	800-325-6152	636-240-2400	660
True North Energy LLC 5565 Airport Hwy .... Toledo OH 43615	888-245-9336	419-868-6800	324
True Temper Sports 8275 Tournament Dr Ste 200 .... Memphis TN 38125	800-355-8783		706
Truc Value Co 8600 W Bryn Mawr Ave ....Chicago IL 60631	800-897-3112	773-695-5000	363
TrueAccord Corp 303 Second St S Ste 750 .... San Francisco CA 94107	866-611-2731		392
TrueCloud 2147 E Baseline Rd .... Tempe AZ 85283	866-990-8783		196
TrueNet Communications Corp 7666 Blanding Blvd ....Jacksonville FL 32244	800-285-2028	904-777-9052	261
Truett-McConnell College 100 Alumni Dr ....Cleveland GA 30528	800-226-8621	706-865-2134	166
Tru-Flex Metal Hose Corp 2391 S St Rd 263 PO Box 247............. West Lebanon IN 47991	800-255-6291	765-893-4403	591
TruGreen ChemLawn 860 Ridge Lake Blvd .... Memphis TN 38120	866-369-9539		573
Truheat Inc 700 Grand St .... Allegan MI 49010	800-879-6199		318
Truitt Bros Inc 1105 Front St NE .... Salem OR 97301	800-547-8712		296-20
Truity Credit Union PO Box 1358 ....Bartlesville OK 74005	800-897-6991	877-744-2835	219
Truliant Federal Credit Union 3200 Truliant Way .... Winston-Salem NC 27103	800-822-0382	336-659-1955	219
Truline Corp 9390 Redwood St .... Las Vegas NV 89139	800-634-6489	702-362-7495	775
Tru-Link Fence Co 5009 West Lake St .... Melrose Park IL 60610	800-568-9300	847-568-9300	279
Trulioo 1055 W Hastings Ste 1200.......... Vancouver BC V6B1L1	888-773-0179		224
Trulite Glass & Aluminum Solutions LLC 800 Fairway Dr Ste 200 .... Deerfield Beach FL 33441	800-432-8132		478
Trulock Tool Co 113 Drayton St .... Whigham GA 39897	800-293-9402	229-762-4678	295
Truly Nolen of America Inc 3636 E Speedway Blvd ....Tucson AZ 85716	800-468-7859	855-534-9139	573
Truman Arnold Cos 701 S Robison Rd ....Texarkana TX 75501	800-235-5343	903-794-3835	575
Truman Medical Ctr 2301 Holmes St .... Kansas City MO 64108	800-318-2596	816-404-1000	352
Truman Medical Ctr Hospital Hill 2301 Holmes St .... Kansas City MO 64108	800-318-2596	816-404-1000	373-3
Truman State University 100 E Normal St .... Kirksville MO 63501	800-892-7792	660-785-4000	166
TruMarx Data Partners Inc 30 S Wacker Dr Ste 2200 ....Chicago IL 60606	844-878-6279		
Trumbull Industries Inc 400 Dietz Rd NE ....Warren OH 44482	800-477-1799	330-392-1551	1
Trump International Hotel & Tower 725 Fifth Ave ....New York NY 10022	888-448-7867	312-588-8000	378
Trump Soho New York 725 Fifth Ave ....New York NY 10022	855-878-6700		703
TRUMPF Group 111 Hyde Rd .... Farmington CT 06032	800-306-1077	860-255-6000	424
Trusco Inc 12527 Porr Rd ....Doylestown OH 44230	800-847-5841	330-658-2027	812
Trust Bank 600 E Main St PO Box 158...............Olney IL 62450	800-766-3451	618-395-4311	70
Trust for Public Land (TPL) 116 New Montgomery St 4th Fl .... San Francisco CA 94105	800-714-5263	415-495-4014	48-13
Trustco Bank Corp NY PO Box 1082 .... Schenectady NY 12301 NASDAQ: TRST	800-670-3110	518-377-3311	359-2
Trusted Advisor Associates Llc 193 Zeppi Ln .... West Orange NJ 07052	855-878-7801		461
Trustile 1780 E 66th Ave ....Denver CO 80229	888-286-3931		236
Trustmark Insurance Co 400 Field Dr .... Lake Forest IL 60045	888-246-9949	847-615-1500	390-2
Trustmark National Bank 248 E Capitol St PO Box 291 ....Jackson MS 39201 NASDAQ: TRMK ■ *Cust Svc	800-243-2524*	601-208-5111	359-2
TruTech LLC PO Box 6849 ....Marietta GA 30065	844-492-5974		573
Truth Hardware Inc 700 W Bridge St ....Owatonna MN 55060 *Cust Svc	800-866-7884*	507-451-5620	349
TruTouch Technologies Inc 73 Carriage Way ....Sudbury MA 01776	866-721-6221	909-703-5963	579
Truwest Credit Union PO Box 3489 .... Scottsdale AZ 85271	855-878-9378	480-441-5900	507
Trydor Industries (Canada) Ltd 19275 - 25th Ave .... Surrey BC V3Z3X1	800-567-8558	604-542-4773	786
Tryiton Eyewear LLC 147 Post Rd E .... Westport CT 06880	888-896-3885	203-544-0770	539
Tryon Trucking Inc PO Box 68 .... Fairless Hills PA 19030	800-523-5254	215-295-6622	775
TS Distributors Inc 4404 Windfern Rd .... Houston TX 77041	800-392-3655		349
TSC Apparel LLC 12080 Mosteller Rd .... Cincinnati OH 45241	800-543-7230	513-771-1138	156
TSCT (Thaddeus Stevens College of Technology) 750 E King St ....Lancaster PA 17602	800-842-3832	717-299-7701	795
TSE Industries Inc 4370 112th Terr N .... Clearwater FL 33762	800-237-7634	727-573-7676	604
TSEMC (Tri-State Electric Membership Corp) 2310 Blue Ridge Dr .... Blue Ridge GA 30513	800-351-1111	706-492-3251	245
TSI Global Cos 700 Fountain Lakes Blvd .... Saint Charles MO 63301	800-875-5605	636-949-8889	730
TSI Inc 500 CaRdigan Rd .... Shoreview MN 55126	800-874-2811	651-483-0900	201
TSI Power Corp 1103 W Pierce Ave .... Antigo WI 54409	800-874-3160	715-623-0636	253
TSLH (Steward Health Care) Tempe Saint Luke's Hospital 1500 S Mill Ave .... Tempe AZ 85281	877-351-9355	480-784-5500	
TSN Inc 4001 Salazar Way .... Frederick CO 80504 *General	888-997-5959*	303-530-0600	555
TSO3 Inc 2505 Dalton Ave .... Quebec QC G1P3S5	866-715-0003	418-651-0003	475
TSPI (Technology Solutions Provider Inc) 11490 Commerce Park Dr Ste 200 ....Reston VA 20191	877-455-8774		196
TST/Impreso Inc 652 Southwestern Blvd .... Coppell TX 75019	800-527-2878	972-462-0100	548-1
TSTA Advocate Magazine 316 W 12th St .... Austin TX 78701	877-275-8782	512-476-5355	455-8
TSTC (Texas State Technical College) Abilene 650 E Hwy 80 ....Abilene TX 79601	800-852-8784	325-672-7091	162
TT Electronics 1645 Wallace Dr .... Carrollton TX 75006	800-341-4747	972-323-2200	692
TTC (Toronto Transit Commission) 1900 Yonge St .... Toronto ON M4S1Z2	800-223-6192	416-393-4000	466
TTC (Trans-Tel Central Inc) 2805 Broce Dr .... Norman OK 73072	800-729-4636	405-447-5025	782
TTC (Trident Technical College) 7000 Rivers Ave PO Box 118067.......... North Charleston SC 29406	877-349-7184	843-574-6111	795
TTG Consultants 4727 Wilshire Blvd .... Los Angeles CA 90010	800-736-8840	323-936-6600	461
TTHE TERMO CO 3275 Cherry Ave .... Long Beach CA 90807	888-260-4715	562-595-7401	532
TTI Inc 2441 NE Pkwy .... Fort Worth TX 76106 *Sales	800-225-5884*	817-740-9000	246
TTX Co 101 N Wacker Dr ....Chicago IL 60606	800-889-4357	312-853-3223	264-5
TU (Trout Unlimited) 1300 N 17th St Ste 500 .... Arlington VA 22209	800-834-2419	703-522-0200	48-3
Tu.c.s. Cleaning Service Inc 166 Central Ave ....Orange NJ 07050	800-992-5998	973-673-0700	152
Tub Springs State Wayside Tub Springs State Wayside .... Ashland OR 97520	800-551-6949		561
Tubby's 31920 Groesbeck Hwy .... Fraser MI 48026	800-752-0644		666
Tube Art Group (TAG) 11715 SE Fifth St ....Bellevue WA 98005	800-562-2854	206-223-1122	697
Tube City IMS Corp (TMS) 12 Monongahela Ave ....Glassport PA 15045 NYSE: TMS	800-860-2442	412-678-6141	682
Tube Methods Inc 416 Depot St .... Bridgeport PA 19405	800-220-2123	610-279-7700	488
Tubelite Inc 4878 Mackinaw Trl ....Reed City MI 49677	800-866-2227	616-808-2505	234
Tubular Fabricators Industry Inc 600 W Wythe St ....Petersburg VA 23803	800-526-0178		591
Tubular Products Co 1400 Red Hollow Rd ....Birmingham AL 35215	800-456-8823	205-856-1300	
Tubular Steel Inc 1031 Executive Pkwy Dr .... Saint Louis MO 63141	800-388-7491	314-851-9200	490
Tucker Company Worldwide Inc 900 Dudley Ave ....Cherry Hill NJ 08002	800-229-7780	856-317-9600	311
Tucker County Convention & Visitors Bureau 410 William Ave ....Davis WV 26260	800-782-2775	304-259-5315	206
Tucows Inc 96 Mowat Ave .... Toronto ON M6K3M1 NASDAQ: TC	800-371-6992	416-535-0123	396
Tucson International Airport 7250 S Tucson Blvd ....Tucson AZ 85756	866-289-9673	520-573-8100	27
Tucson Medical Ctr 5301 E Grant Rd ....Tucson AZ 85712	800-526-5353	520-327-5461	373-3
Tuesday Morning Corp 6250 LBJ Fwy .... Dallas TX 75240 NASDAQ: TUES	800-457-0099	972-387-3562	327
TUFF SHED Inc 1777 S Harrison St Ste 100 .... Denver CO 80210	800-289-8833	303-474-5510	

Name	Address	City	State	Zip	Toll-Free	Phone	Class
Tuff Torq Corp	5943 Commerce Blvd	Morristown	TN	37814	**866-572-3441**	423-585-2000	428
Tuffaloy Products Inc	1400 S Batesville Rd	Greer	SC	29650	**800-521-3722**	864-879-0763	806
TuffStuff Fitness Equipment Inc	13971 Norton Ave	Chino	CA	91710	**888-884-8275**	909-629-1600	353
Tuffy Assoc Corp	7150 Granite Cir	Toledo	OH	43617	**800-228-8339**	419-865-6900	62-5
Tuffy Security Products Inc	25733 Rd H	Cortez	CO	81321	**800-348-8339**		57
Tuftco Corp	2318 S Holtzclaw Ave	Chattanooga	TN	37408	**800-288-3826**	423-698-8601	739
Tufts Associated Health Plans	705 Mt Auburn St	Watertown	MA	02472	**800-462-0224**	617-972-9400	390-3
Tufts Library	46 Broad St	Weymouth	MA	02188	**888-283-3757**	781-337-1402	433-3
Tufts Medical Ctr (TMC)	800 Washington St	Boston	MA	02111	**866-220-3699**	617-636-5000	373-3
Tugboat Inn	80 Commercial St PO Box 267	Boothbay Harbor	ME	04538	**800-248-2628**	207-633-4434	378
Tukaiz LLC	2917 N Latoria Ln	Franklin Park	IL	60131	**800-543-2674**	847-455-1588	7
Tulalip Resort Casino	10200 Quil Ceda Blvd	Tulalip	WA	98271	**888-272-1111**		703
Tulane Medical Ctr (TMC)	1415 Tulane Ave	New Orleans	LA	70112	**800-588-5800**	504-988-5263	373-3
Tulane University	6823 St Charles Ave *Admissions	New Orleans	LA	70118	**800-873-9283***	504-865-5000	166
Tulane University School of Medicine	1430 Tulane Ave	New Orleans	LA	70112	**800-588-5800**	504-988-5462	
Tulare County Library System	200 W Oak Ave	Visalia	CA	93291	**866-290-8681**	559-713-2700	433-3
Tulco Oils Inc	5240 E Pine	Tulsa	OK	74115	**800-375-2347**	918-838-3354	575
Tulip City Air Service Inc	1581 S Washington Ave	Holland	MI	49423	**800-748-0515**	616-392-7831	13
Tulloch Engineering Inc	200 Main St	Thessalon	ON	P0R1L0	**800-797-2997**	705-842-3372	256
Tulsa City Hall	175 E Second St Ste 690	Tulsa	OK	74103	**800-522-6543**	918-596-2100	336
Tulsa Convention & Visitors Bureau	1 W Third St Ste 100	Tulsa	OK	74103	**800-558-3311**		206
Tulsa Convention Ctr	100 Civic Ctr	Tulsa	OK	74103	**800-678-7177**	918-894-4350	205
Tulsa Metro Chamber	1 W Third St Ste 100	Tulsa	OK	74103	**888-424-9411**	918-585-1201	139
Tulsa Opera	1610 S Boulder Ave	Tulsa	OK	74119	**866-298-2530**	918-582-4035	569-2
Tulsa Welding School Inc	2545 E 11th St	Tulsa	OK	74104	**800-331-2934**	918-856-6416	738
Tulsa World	315 S Boulder Ave	Tulsa	OK	74103	**800-897-3557**	918-583-2161	528-2
Tulsair Beechcraft Inc	3207 N Sheridan Rd	Tulsa	OK	74115	**800-331-4071**	918-835-7651	24
Tumbleweed Inc	2301 River Rd	Louisville	KY	40206	**866-719-3892**	502-893-0323	666
Tumbling River Ranch	3715 Pk County Rd 62 PO Box 30	Grant	CO	80448	**800-654-8770**	303-838-5981	239
Tundra Lodge Resort & Waterpark	865 Lombardi Ave	Green Bay	WI	54304	**877-886-3725**	920-405-8700	665
Tundra Process Solutions Ltd	7523 Flint Rd SE	Calgary	AB	T2H1G3	**800-265-1166**	403-255-5222	111
Tunica MS	13625 Hwy 61 N	Tunica Resorts	MS	38664	**888-488-6422**		206
Tunnel Duty Free Shop Inc	465 Goyeau St	Windsor	ON	N9A1H1	**800-669-2105**	519-252-2713	241
Tuohy Furniture Corp	42 St Albans Pl *Cust Svc	Chatfield	MN	55923	**800-533-1696***	507-867-4280	319-1
Tuolumne County Chamber of Commerce	222 S Shepherd St	Sonora	CA	95370	**877-532-4212**	209-532-4212	139
Tupelo Furniture Market	1879 N Coley Rd	Tupelo	MS	38801	**800-844-0841**	662-842-4442	
Tupelo National Battlefield	2680 Natchez Trace Pkwy	Tupelo	MS	38804	**800-305-7417**	662-680-4025	560
Turbo 2 n 1 Grip	46460 Continental Dr	Chesterfield	MI	48047	**800-530-9878**	586-598-3948	707
Turbo International Inc	2151 Las Palmas Dr Ste E	Carlsbad	CA	92011	**800-238-8726**	760-476-1444	786
Turbo Parts LLC	767 Pierce Rd Ste 2	Clifton Park	NY	12065	**800-446-4776**	518-885-3199	54
Turbo Refrigerating	1000 W Ormsby Ave	Louisville	KY	40210	**800-853-8648**	502-635-3000	660
Turbotec Products Inc	651 Day Hill Rd	Windsor	CT	06095	**800-394-1633**	860-731-4200	295
Turbotek Computer Corp	70 Zachary Rd Ste 3	Manchester	NH	03109	**800-573-5393**	603-666-3062	180
Turf Paradise Racetrack	1501 W Bell Rd	Phoenix	AZ	85023	**800-639-8783**	602-942-1101	638
Turfgrass Producers International	444 E Roosevelt Rd Ste 346	Lombard	IL	60148	**800-405-8873**	847-649-5555	138
Turkey *Consulate General*	1990 Post Oak Blvd Ste 1300	Houston	TX	77056	**888-566-7656**	713-622-5849	257
Turkey Hill Dairy Inc	2601 River Rd	Conestoga	PA	17516	**800-693-2479**	717-872-5461	296-25
Turks & Caicos Islands Tourism Office	225 W 35th St Ste 1200	New York	NY	10001	**800-241-0824**	646-375-8830	770
Turlock Chamber of Commerce	115 S Golden State Blvd	Turlock	CA	95380	**800-834-0401**	209-632-2221	139
Turner Classic Movies Inc (TCM)	1050 Techwood Dr NW	Atlanta	GA	30318	**844-356-7875**		
Turner County	PO Box 191	Ashburn	GA	31714	**800-436-7442**		337
Turner County Stockyard	1315 US Hwy 41 S	Ashburn	GA	31714	**800-344-9808**	229-567-3371	444
Turner Dairy Farms Inc	1049 Jefferson Rd	Pittsburgh	PA	15235	**800-892-1039**	412-372-2211	296-25
Turner Gas Company Inc	2825 W 500 S	Salt Lake City	UT	84104	**800-932-4277**		
Turner Industries Group LLC	8687 United Plaza Blvd	Baton Rouge	LA	70809	**800-288-6503**	225-922-5050	188-9
Turner Investment Partners Inc	1205 Westlakes Dr Ste 100	Berwyn	PA	19312	**800-224-6312**	484-329-2300	400
Turner-Fairbank Highway Research Ctr	6300 Georgetown Pk	McLean	VA	22101	**800-424-9071**		664
Turning Point Hospital	3015 Veterans Pkwy PO Box 1177	Moultrie	GA	31776	**800-342-1075**	229-985-4815	722
Turning Point of Tampa	6227 Sheldon Rd	Tampa	FL	33615	**800-397-3006**	813-882-3003	722
Turning Stone Resort Casino LLC	5218 Patrick Rd	Verona	NY	13478	**800-771-7711**	315-361-7711	133
Turn-key Medical Inc	365 SW Fifth Ave	Meridian	ID	83642	**877-484-9549**		
Turpin Sales & Marketing Inc	330 Cold Spring Ave	West Springfield	MA	01089	**877-377-7573**		461
Turret Steel Industries Inc	105 Pine St	Imperial	PA	15126	**800-245-4800**	724-218-1014	490
Turtle Bay Exploration Park	840 Auditorium Dr	Redding	CA	96001	**800-887-8532**	530-243-8850	517
Turtle Bay Resort	57-091 Kamehameha Hwy	Kahuku	HI	96731	**866-475-2567**	808-293-6000	665
Turtle Cay Resort	600 Atlantic Ave	Virginia Beach	VA	23451	**888-989-7788**	757-437-5565	665
Turtle Magazine	1100 Waterway Blvd	Indianapolis	IN	46202	**800-558-2376**	317-634-1100	455-6
Turtle Mountain Community College	10145 BIA Rd 7	Belcourt	ND	58316	**800-827-1100**	701-477-7862	165
Turtle-Top Inc	67819 State Rd 15	New Paris	IN	46553	**800-296-2105**		59
Tuscaloosa News	315 28th Ave	Tuscaloosa	AL	35401	**800-888-8639**	205-345-0505	528-2
Tuscaloosa VA Medical Ctr	3701 Loop Rd E	Tuscaloosa	AL	35404	**888-269-3045**	205-554-2000	373-8
Tuscany Suites & Casino	255 E Flamingo Rd *Resv	Las Vegas	NV	89169	**877-887-2261***	702-893-8933	378
Tusculum College	60 Shiloh Rd	Greeneville	TN	37743	**800-729-0256**	423-636-7300	166
Tuskegee University	1200 W Montgomery Rd *Admissions	Tuskegee	AL	36088	**800-622-6531***	334-727-8011	166
Tutco Inc	500 Gould Dr	Cookeville	TN	38506	**877-262-4533**	931-432-4141	14
Tuthill Corp	8500 S Madison St	Burr Ridge	IL	60527	**800-634-2695**	630-382-4900	637
Tuthill Corp Plastics Group	2050 Sunnydale Blvd	Clearwater	FL	33765	**800-634-2695**	727-446-8593	600
Tuthill Transfer Systems	8500 S Madison	Burr Ridge	IL	60527	**800-825-6937**	260-747-7529	635
Tuthill Vacuum & Blower Systems	4840 W Kearney St	Springfield	MO	65803	**800-825-6937**	417-865-8715	18
Tuthill Vacuum Systems	4840 W Kearney St	Springfield	MO	65803	**800-634-2695**	417-865-8715	172
Tuttle Law Print Inc	414 Quality Ln	Rutland	VT	05701	**800-776-7682**		623
Tuttle Publishing	364 Innovation Dr *Sales	North Clarendon	VT	05759	**800-526-2778***	802-773-8930	633-2
Tvc Marketing	3200 W Wilshire Blvd	Oklahoma City	OK	73116	**800-227-6459**	405-843-2722	195
TVEC (Trinity Valley Electric Co-op Inc)	1800 E HWY 243	Kaufman	TX	75142	**800-766-9576**	972-932-2214	245
TVL Inc	901 16th St W	North Vancouver	BC	V7P1R2	**800-263-0000**		
T-w Transport Inc	7405 S Hayford Rd	Cheney	WA	99004	**800-356-4070**		775
Tweed Museum of Art	1201 ordean Ct	Duluth	MN	55812	**866-999-6995**	218-726-8222	517
Tweetsie Railroad Inc	300 Tweetsie Railroad Ln	Blowing Rock	NC	28605	**800-526-5740**	828-264-9061	31
Twenty-First Century Assoc	266 Summit Ave	Hackensack	NJ	07601	**888-760-5052**	201-678-1144	160
Twentynine Palms Chamber of Commerce	73484 Twentynine Palms Hwy	Twentynine Palms	CA	92277	**800-442-2283**	760-367-3445	139
Twin Bridges State Park	14801 Hwy 137 S	Fairland	OK	74343	**800-622-6317**	918-540-2545	561
Twin Cities & Western Railroad	2925 12th St E	Glencoe	MN	55336	**800-290-8297**	320-864-7200	645
Twin Cities Public Television Inc	172 E Fourth St	Saint Paul	MN	55101	**866-229-1300**	651-222-1717	628
Twin City EDM	7940 Rancher Rd NE	Fridley	MN	55432	**800-397-0338**	763-783-7808	452
Twin County Regional Hospital	200 Hospital Dr	Galax	VA	24333	**800-295-3342**	276-236-8181	373-3
Twin Falls Area Chamber of Commerce	2015 Neilsen Point Pl	Twin Falls	ID	83301	**866-894-6325**	208-733-3974	139
Twin Falls County	2469 Wright Ave	Twin Falls	ID	83301	**800-377-3529**	208-736-4004	337
Twin Falls School District 411	201 Main Ave W	Twin Falls	ID	83301	**800-726-0003**	208-733-6900	681
Twin Harbors Beach State Park	3120 Hwy 105	Westport	WA	98595	**888-226-7688**	360-268-9717	
Twin Lakes State Park	6685 Twin Lakes Rd	Rockwell City	IA	50579	**800-361-8072**		
Twin Lakes Telephone Co-op	200 Telephone Ln *Cust Svc	Gainesboro	TN	38562	**800-644-8582***	931-268-2151	731
Twin Oaks Hammocks	138 Twin Oaks Rd	Louisa	VA	23093	**800-688-8946**	540-894-5125	319-4
Twin Oaks Software Development Inc	1463 Berlin Tpke	Berlin	CT	06037	**866-278-6750**	860-829-6000	177

Name / Address	City	State	ZIP	Toll-Free	Phone	Class
Twin Pine Casino						
22223 Hwy 29 PO Box 789	Middletown	CA	95461	**800-564-4872**	707-987-0197	377
Twin River Casino						
100 Twin River Rd	Lincoln	RI	02865	**877-827-4837**	401-475-8505	638
Twin Rivers Unified School District						
3222 Winona Way	North Highlands	CA	95660	**800-260-0659**	916-566-1628	681
Twin Technologies Inc						
11 Computer Dr W	Albany	NY	12205	**800-439-4821**		196
Twin Valleys Public Power District						
PO Box 160	Cambridge	NE	69022	**800-658-4266**		245
Twinhead Corp						
48303 Fremont Blvd	Fremont	CA	94538	**800-995-8946***		173-2
*Sales						
Twinlab Corp						
4800 T-Rex Ave	Boca Raton	FL	33431	**800-645-5626**		794
TwinWest Chamber of Commerce						
10700 Old County Rd 15	Plymouth	MN	55441	**800-649-5397**	763-450-2220	139
Twitchell Corp						
4031 Ross Clark Cir	Dothan	AL	36303	**800-633-7550***	334-792-0002	740-2
*General						
Two Bunch Palms Resort & Spa						
67425 Two Bunch Palms Trl	Desert Hot Springs	CA	92240	**800-472-4334**	760-329-8791	665
Two Guys Relocation Systems Inc						
3571 Pacific Hwy	San Diego	CA	92101	**800-896-4897**	619-296-7995	516
Two Men & A Truck International Inc						
3400 Belle Chase Way	Lansing	MI	48911	**800-345-1070**	517-394-7210	516
TWP Inc						
2831 Tenth St	Berkeley	CA	94710	**800-227-1570**	510-548-4434	684
TXU Electric						
PO Box 65764	Dallas	TX	75262	**800-242-9113**	972-791-2888	782
Tyco SimplexGrinnell						
50 Technology Dr	Westminster	MA	01441	**800-746-7539**	978-731-2500	283
Tyger Scientific Inc						
324 Stokes Ave	Ewing	NJ	08638	**888-329-8990**	609-434-0143	231
TYGH Capital Management Inc						
1211 S W Fifth Ave Ste 2100	Portland	OR	97204	**800-972-0150**	503-972-0150	400
TYK America Inc						
301 BrickyaRd Rd	Clairton	PA	15025	**800-569-9359**	412-384-4259	659
Tyler Area Chamber of Commerce						
315 N Broadway Ave	Tyler	TX	75702	**800-235-5712**	903-592-1661	139
Tyler Convention & Visitors Bureau (TCVB)						
315 N Broadway Ave	Tyler	TX	75702	**800-235-5712**	903-592-1661	206
Tyler County						
100 Bluff St Rm 110	Woodville	TX	75979	**800-256-6848**	409-283-2281	337
Tyler Equipment Corp						
251 Shaker Rd	East Longmeadow	MA	01028	**800-292-6351**	413-525-6351	357
Tyler Junior College						
PO Box 9020	Tyler	TX	75711	**800-687-5680**	903-510-2523	162
Tyler Pipe Co						
11910 CR 492	Tyler	TX	75706	**800-527-8478**	903-882-5511	307
Tyler Technologies Inc						
5949 Sherry Ln Ste 1400	Dallas	TX	75225	**800-431-5776**		178-10
NYSE: TYL						
Tylok International Inc						
1061 E 260th St	Euclid	OH	44132	**800-321-0466**	216-261-7310	591
Tymco Inc						
225 E Industrial Blvd PO Box 2368	Waco	TX	76703	**800-258-9626**	254-799-5546	513
Tyndale House Publishers Inc						
351 Executive Dr	Carol Stream	IL	60188	**800-323-9400**		633-3
Tyndall Air Force Base						
555 Suwannee Rd Rm 140-A-1	Tyndall AFB	FL	32403	**800-356-5273**	850-283-1110	495-1
Tyndall Federal Credit Union						
PO Box 59760	Panama City	FL	32412	**888-896-3255**	850-769-9999	216
TYR Sport						
1790 Apollo Ct	Seal Beach	CA	90740	**800-252-7878**	714-897-0799	155-16
Tyson Foods Inc						
PO Box 219	Kings Mountains	NC	28086	**800-233-6332**	479-290-6397	615
NYSE: TSN						
Tyson Pet Products Inc						
812 Third St NW	Independence	IA	50644	**877-303-9247**		
Tyson Prepared Foods Inc						
2200 Don Tyson Pkwy	Springdale	AR	72762	**800-233-6332**	479-290-4000	296-26

U

Name / Address	City	State	ZIP	Toll-Free	Phone	Class
U hotel Fifth Avenue						
373 Fifth Ave	New York	NY	10016	**800-315-4642**	212-213-3388	703
U S Employees O C Federal Credit Union						
PO Box 44000	Oklahoma City	OK	73144	**800-227-6366**	405-685-6200	219
U S Monitor						
86 Maple Ave	New City	NY	10956	**800-767-7967**	845-634-1331	5
U s Nameplate Co						
2100 Hwy 30 W PO Box 10	Mount Vernon	IA	52314	**800-553-8871**	319-895-8804	697
U S Risk Insurance Group Inc						
10210 N Central Expy	Dallas	TX	75231	**800-926-9155**	214-265-7090	389
U W Provision Company Inc						
PO Box 620038	Middleton	WI	53562	**800-832-0517**	608-836-7421	297-9
U.S. Department of Education						
Region 6						
1999 Bryan St Ste 1510	Dallas	TX	75202	**877-521-2172**	214-661-9600	339-7
UAB Comprehensive Cancer Ctr						
University of Alabama at Birmingham						
1824 Sixth Ave S	Birmingham	AL	35294	**800-822-0933**	205-934-4011	664
UAMS Medical Ctr						
4301 W Markham St	Little Rock	AR	72205	**877-467-6560**	501-686-7000	373-3
UBS AG						
1285 Ave of the Americas	New York	NY	10019	**877-827-8001**	212-713-2000	70
UC Davis Cancer Ctr						
2315 Stockton Blvd	Sacramento	CA	95817	**800-362-5566**	530-752-1011	373-7
UC Irvine Healthcare						
101 the City Dr S	Orange	CA	92868	**877-824-3627**	714-456-7890	373-3
UCare Minnesota						
500 Stinson Blvd NE						
PO Box 52	Minneapolis	MN	55413	**866-457-7144**	612-676-6500	48-17
UCB Pharma Inc						
1950 Lake Pk Dr	Smyrna	GA	30080	**800-477-7877**	770-970-7500	578
UCC (United Church of Christ)						
700 Prospect Ave	Cleveland	OH	44115	**866-822-8224**	216-736-2100	48-20
Uchee Pines Lifestyle Center						
30 Uchee Pines Rd	Seale	AL	36875	**877-824-3374**	334-855-4764	702
UCIT Online Security						
6441 Northam Dr	Mississauga	ON	L4V1J2	**866-756-7847**	905-405-9898	689
UCLA (University of California)						
Berkeley						
110 Sproul Hall MC Ste 5800	Berkeley	CA	94720	**866-740-1260**	510-642-6000	166
UCM (United Color Manufacturing Inc)						
PO Box 480	Newtown	PA	18940	**800-852-5942**	215-860-2165	145
UCS (Union of Concerned Scientists)						
2 Brattle Sq	Cambridge	MA	02238	**800-666-8276**	617-547-5552	48-13
UDL Laboratories Inc						
1718 Northrock Ct	Rockford	IL	61103	**800-848-0462**		579
UFC (United Farmers Co-op)						
705 E Fourth St PO Box 461	Winthrop	MN	55396	**866-998-3266**	507-647-6600	10
UFCW (United Food & Commercial Workers International Uni)						
1775 K St NW	Washington	DC	20006	**800-551-4010**	202-223-3111	413
UFFC-S (IEEE Ultrasonics Ferroelectrics & Frequency Contro)						
445 Hoes Ln	Piscataway	NJ	08854	**800-678-4333**	732-981-0060	49-19
UFG						
118 Second Ave SE						
PO Box 73909	Cedar Rapids	IA	52407	**800-895-6253**	319-399-5700	390-4
NASDAQ: UFCS						
UFP Technologies Inc						
172 E Main St	Georgetown	MA	01833	**800-372-3172**	978-352-2200	597
NASDAQ: UFPT						
UFPI (Universal Forest Products Inc)						
2801 E Beltline Ave NE	Grand Rapids	MI	49525	**800-598-9663**	616-364-6161	679
NASDAQ: UFPI						
UGC (United Guaranty Corp)						
230 N Elm St	Greensboro	NC	27401	**877-642-4642**		390-5
UGI (United-Guardian Inc)						
230 Marcus Blvd PO Box 18050	Hauppauge	NY	11788	**800-645-5566**	631-273-0900	477
NASDAQ: UG						
U-Haul International Inc						
2727 N Central Ave	Phoenix	AZ	85004	**800-528-0361**		773
Uhl Company Inc						
9065 Zachary Ln N	Maple grove	MN	55369	**800-815-3820**	763-425-7226	392
UHMS (Undersea & Hyperbaric Medical Society)						
21 W Colony Pl Ste 280	Durham	NC	27705	**877-533-8467**	919-490-5140	48-17
UIC (Universal Instruments Corp)						
33 Broome Corporate Pk	Conklin	NY	13748	**800-842-9732**	607-779-7522	691
UIH (Universal Insurance Holding Inc)						
1110 W Commerical Blvd						
Ste 100	Fort Lauderdale	FL	33309	**800-509-5586**		390-4
NYSE: UVE						
Uintah County						
204 East 100 North	Vernal	UT	84078	**800-966-4680**	435-781-0770	337
UK (Underwater Kinetics)						
13400 Danielson St	Poway	CA	92064	**800-852-7483**	858-513-9100	706
Ukrainian National Association Inc (UNA)						
2200 Rt 10	Parsippany	NJ	07054	**800-253-9862**		48-14
Ukrainian National Federal Credit Union						
215 Second Ave	New York	NY	10003	**866-859-5848**		219
UL EHS Sustainability						
5000 Meridian Blvd Ste 600	Franklin	TN	37067	**888-202-3016**	615-367-4404	39
UL LLC 1559 King St	Enfield	CT	06082	**800-903-5660**	860-749-8371	738
Ulbrich Stainless Steels & Special Metals Inc (USSM)						
57 Dodge Ave	North Haven	CT	06473	**800-243-1676**	203-239-4481	719
ULC (Universal Lending Corp)						
6775 E Evans Ave	Denver	CO	80224	**800-758-4063**		507
ULI (Urban Land Institute)						
1025 Thomas Jefferson St NW						
Ste 500W	Washington	DC	20007	**800-321-5011***	202-624-7000	48-8
*Orders						
U-line Corp						
8900 N 55th St	Milwaukee	WI	53223	**800-779-2547**	414-354-0300	786
Ulla Popken Ltd						
777 Dulaney Valley Rd Ste 263	Towson	MD	21204	**800-245-8552**		
ULLICO Casualty Co						
1625 I St NW	Washington	DC	20006	**800-431-5425**		390-5
ULLICO Inc						
1625 Eye St NW	Washington	DC	20006	**800-431-5425**		359-4
Ullman Oil Inc						
PO Box 23399	Chagrin Falls	OH	44023	**800-543-5195**	440-543-5195	575
Ulster County						
244 Fair St	Kingston	NY	12401	**800-342-5826**		
Ulster County Community College						
Cottekill Rd	Stone Ridge	NY	12484	**800-724-0833**	845-687-5000	162
ULTA Beauty						
1000 Remington Blvd Ste 120	Bolingbrook	IL	60440	**866-983-8582**	630-410-4800	214
Ulteig Engineers Inc						
3350 38th Ave S	Fargo	ND	58104	**888-858-3441**	701-280-8500	261
Ultimate Lead Systems Inc						
401 Frnt St	Berea	OH	44017	**800-323-0550**	440-826-1908	5
Ultimate Software Group Inc						
2000 Ultimate Way	Weston	FL	33326	**800-432-1729**	954-331-7000	178-1
NASDAQ: ULTI						
Ultimate Support Systems Inc						
5836 Wright Dr	Loveland	CO	80538	**800-525-5628**	970-776-1920	523
Ultimate Washer Inc						
711 Commerce Way Ste 1	Jupiter	FL	33458	**866-858-4982**	561-741-7022	637
Ultra Clean Technologies Corp						
1274 Hgwy 77	Bridgeton	NJ	08302	**800-791-9111**	856-451-2176	146
Ultra Electronics Flightline Systems Inc						
7625 Omni Tech Pl	Victor	NY	14564	**888-959-9001**	585-924-4000	643
Ultra Electronics-DNE Technologies Inc						
50 Barnes Industrial Pk N	Wallingford	CT	06492	**800-370-4485**	203-265-7151	643
UltraBac Software						
15015 Main St Ste 200	Bellevue	WA	98007	**866-554-8562**	425-644-6000	178-12
Ultracraft Co						
6163 Old 421 Rd	Liberty	NC	27298	**800-262-4046**		115

Name / Address	City	State	ZIP	Toll-Free	Phone	Class
Ultraex Inc						
2633 Barrington Ct	Hayward	CA	94545	**800-882-1000**	510-723-3760	317
Ultrafabrics LLC						
303 S Broadway	Tarrytown	NY	10591	**877-309-6648**	914-460-1730	740-3
Ultraflote LLC						
3640 W 12th St	Houston	TX	77008	**800-821-6825**	713-461-2100	91
Ultrafryer Systems Inc						
302 Spencer Ln	San Antonio	TX	78201	**800-545-9189**		298
Ultralife Batteries Inc						
2000 Technology Pkwy	Newark	NY	14513	**800-332-5000**	315-332-7100	74
NASDAQ: ULBI						
Ultra-Poly Corp						
102 Demi Rd PO Box 330	Portland	PA	18351	**800-932-0619**	570-897-7500	604
UltraStaff						
1818 Memorial Dr Ste 200	Houston	TX	77007	**800-522-7707**	713-522-7100	717
Ultra-tech Enterprises Inc						
4701 Taylor Rd	Punta Gorda	FL	33950	**800-293-2001**		479
Ultratech Inc						
3050 Zanker Rd	San Jose	CA	95134	**800-222-1213**	408-321-8835	691
NASDAQ: UTEK						
Ultryx PO Box 1841	Las Vegas	NV	89125	**866-485-8799**	702-940-6900	804
UMA (United Motorcoach Assn)						
113 SW St 4th Fl	Alexandria	VA	22314	**800-424-8262**	703-838-2929	49-21
Uman Pharma Inc						
100 De L'Industrie Blvd	Candiac	QC	J5R1J1	**877-444-9989**	450-444-9989	231
U-mark Inc						
102 Iowa Ave	Belleville	IL	62220	**866-383-6275**	618-235-7500	387
UMass Hotel at the Campus Ctr						
1 Campus Ctr Way	Amherst	MA	01003	**877-822-2110**	413-549-6000	378
UMass Memorial Medical Care						
Bone Marrow Transplant						
55 Lake Ave N	Worcester	MA	01655	**855-862-7763**	508-334-1000	
UMass Memorial Medical Ctr						
Memorial Campus						
119 Belmont St	Worcester	MA	01605	**800-225-8885**	508-334-1000	373-3
University Campus						
55 Lake Ave N	Worcester	MA	01655	**800-225-8885**	508-334-1000	373-3
UMB Bank NA						
1010 Grand Blvd	Kansas City	MO	64106	**800-821-2171**	816-860-7000	70
UMCES (University of Maryland Ctr for Environmental Scien)						
2020 Horn Pt Rd	Cambridge	MD	21613	**866-842-2520**	410-228-9250	664
UMCP (University Medical Ctr at Princeton)						
253 Witherspoon St	Princeton	NJ	08540	**877-932-8935**	609-497-4304	373-3
UmeVoice Inc						
1435 Technology Ln Ste B4	Petaluma	CA	94954	**888-230-3300**	707-939-8607	178-7
UMF Medical						
1316 Eisenhower Blvd	Johnstown	PA	15904	**800-638-5322**	814-266-8726	319-3
UMHC (University of Miami Hospital & Clinics)						
Sylvester Comprehensive Cancer Ctr						
1475 NW 12th Ave	Miami	FL	33136	**800-545-2292**	305-243-1000	764
UMIAQ LLC						
6700 Arctic Spur Rd	Anchorage	AK	99518	**800-226-0009**	907-677-8220	41
UMP 730AM 1039FM, The						
3280 Peachtree Rd Ste 2300	Atlanta	GA	30305	**866-485-9867**		641
Umpqua Bank						
PO Box 1820	Roseburg	OR	97470	**866-486-7782**	800-452-1929	70
Umpqua Community College						
1140 Umpqva College Rd						
PO Box 967	Roseburg	OR	97470	**800-820-5161**	541-440-4600	162
Umpqua Dairy Products Co						
1686 SE N St PO Box 1306	Grants Pass	OR	97526	**800-222-6455**	541-672-2638	296-27
Umpqua Investments Inc						
1 SW Columbia St Ste 300	Portland	OR	97258	**866-486-7782**	800-452-1929	359-2
NASDAQ: UMPQ						
Umpqua Lighthouse State Park						
Umpqua Lighthouse State Park	Reedsport	OR	97467	**800-551-6949**	541-271-4118	561
UMSL (University of Missouri)						
Columbia						
104 Jesse Hall	Columbia	MO	65211	**800-856-2181**	573-882-6333	166
Umstead Hotel & Spa						
100 Woodland Pond	Cary	NC	27513	**866-877-4141**	919-447-4000	378
UMW (Utah Metal Works Inc)						
805 Everett Ave	Salt Lake City	UT	84116	**877-221-0099**		656
UNA (Ukrainian National Association Inc)						
2200 Rt 10	Parsippany	NJ	07054	**800-253-9862**		48-14
Unarco Material Handling Inc						
701 16th Ave E	Springfield	TN	37172	**800-862-7261**		286
Uncle Milton Industries Inc						
29209 Canwood St Ste 120	Agoura	CA	91301	**800-869-7555***	818-707-0800	757
*General						
Uncle Ray's LLC						
14245 Birwood St	Detroit	MI	48238	**800-800-3286**	313-834-0800	296-35
UNC-TV (University of North Carolina Ctr for Public Televi)						
10 TW Alexander Dr						
PO Box 14900	Research Triangle Park	NC	27709	**800-906-5050**	919-549-7000	628
UNC-TV Ch 4 (PBS)						
10 TW Alexander Dr						
PO Box 14900	Research Triangle Park	NC	27709	**800-906-5050**	919-549-7000	736
Underground Construction Company Inc						
5145 Industrial Way	Benicia	CA	94510	**800-227-2314**	707-746-8800	188-10
Undersea & Hyperbaric Medical Society (UHMS)						
21 W Colony Pl Ste 280	Durham	NC	27705	**877-533-8467**	919-490-5140	48-17
Underwater Kinetics (UK)						
13400 Danielson St	Poway	CA	92064	**800-852-7483**	858-513-9100	706
Underwood Transfer Company LLC						
940 W Troy Ave	Indianapolis	IN	46225	**800-428-2372**	317-783-9235	775
Uneeda Enterprizes Inc						
640 Chestnut Ridge Rd Spring Valley						
	New York	NY	10977	**800-431-2494**	845-426-2800	1
UNFCU (United Nations Federal Credit Union)						
24-01 44th Rd Ct Sq Pl	Long Island	NY	11101	**800-891-2471**	347-686-6000	219
Unger Co						
12401 Berea Rd	Cleveland	OH	44111	**800-321-1418**	216-252-1400	544
Ungerboeck Systems International Inc						
100 Ungerboeck Pk	O'fallon	MO	63368	**800-400-4052**	636-300-5606	180
Unibank For Savings						
49 Church St	Whitinsville	MA	01588	**800-578-4270**	508-234-8112	70
Unibilt Industries Inc						
8005 Johnson Stn Rd PO Box 373	Vandalia	OH	45377	**800-777-9942**		106
Unicell Body Co						
571 Howard St	Buffalo	NY	14206	**800-628-8914***	716-853-8628	513
*Cust Svc						
Unicep Packaging Inc						
1702 Industrial Dr	Sandpoint	ID	83864	**800-354-9396**	208-265-9696	545
Unicircuit Inc						
8192 Southpark Ln	Littleton	CO	80120	**800-648-6449**	303-730-0505	621
Unico American Corp						
23251 Mulholland Dr	Woodland Hills	CA	91364	**800-669-9800**		390-4
Unicoi State Park & Lodge						
1788 Hwy 356 Rd	Helen	GA	30545	**800-573-9659**		561
UNICOM						
565 Brea Canyon Rd Ste A	Walnut	CA	91789	**800-346-6668**	626-964-7873	176
Unicorn HRO LLC						
25B Hanover Rd	Florham Park	NJ	07932	**800-368-8149**		39
Unicorp						
291 Cleveland St	Orange	NJ	07050	**800-526-1389**	973-674-1700	349
Unicover Corp						
1 Unicover Ctr	Cheyenne	WY	82008	**800-443-4225***	307-771-3000	457
*Cust Svc						
Uniden America Corp						
4700 Amon Carter Blvd	Fort Worth	TX	76155	**800-297-1023***	817-858-3300	730
*Cust Svc						
Unified Brands						
1055 Mendell Davis Dr	Jackson	MS	39272	**888-994-7636**		385
Unified Grocers Inc						
5200 Sheila St	Commerce	CA	90040	**800-724-7762**	323-264-5200	297-8
Unified Industries Inc						
6551 Loisdale Ct Ste 400	Springfield	VA	22150	**800-666-1642**	703-922-9800	261
Unified Systems Group Inc						
1235 64th Ave SE Ste 4a	Calgary	AB	T2H2J7	**866-892-8988**	403-686-8088	174
Unifor						
301 Laurier Ave W	Ottawa	ON	K1P6M6	**877-230-5201**	613-230-5200	413
Uniform & Textile Service Assn (UTSA)						
1300 N 17th St Ste 750	Arlington	VA	22209	**800-996-3426**	703-247-2600	49-4
Uniform Commercial Code Law Letter						
610 Opperman Dr	Eagan	MN	55123	**800-328-4880***	651-687-7000	527-13
*Cust Svc						
Unigen Corp						
45388 Warm Springs Blvd	Fremont	CA	94539	**800-826-0808**	510-668-2088	621
UNIGLOBE Travel USA LLC						
18662 MacArthur Blvd Ste 100	Irvine	CA	92612	**877-438-4338**	949-623-9000	767
Unilux Inc						
59 N Fifth St	Saddle Brook	NJ	07663	**800-522-0801**	201-712-1266	470
Unimark Products						
2016 Unimark 9818 Pflumm Rd	Lenexa	KS	66215	**800-255-6356***	913-649-2424	176
*Cust Svc						
Unimax						
121 S Eighth St	Minneapolis	MN	55402	**800-886-0390**		177
Union Bank Co, The						
105 Progressive Dr	Columbus Grove	OH	45830	**800-837-8111**	419-659-2141	359-2
NASDAQ: UBOH						
Union Bank of California NA						
400 California St 1st Fl	San Francisco	CA	94104	**800-238-4486**	415-765-3434	70
Union Bankshares Inc						
20 Lower Main St	Morrisville	VT	05661	**866-862-1891**	802-888-6600	359-2
NASDAQ: UNB						
Union City Chamber of Commerce						
3939 Smith St	Union City	CA	94587	**800-945-2288**	510-952-9637	139
Union College						
310 College St	Barbourville	KY	40906	**800-489-8646**	606-546-4151	166
Union College						
3800 S 48th St	Lincoln	NE	68506	**800-228-4600***	402-486-2504	166
*Admissions						
Union County						
1103 S First St	Clayton	NM	88415	**800-390-7858**	575-374-9253	337
Union County						
1106 K Ave	La Grande	OR	97850	**800-735-1232**	541-963-1001	337
Union County						
210 W Main St	Union	SC	29379	**800-273-5066**	864-429-1600	337
Union County Chamber of Commerce						
135 W Main St	Union	SC	29379	**877-202-8755**	864-427-9039	139
Union County Electric Co-op Inc						
122 W Main St	Elk Point	SD	57025	**888-356-3395**	605-356-3395	245
Union Eyecare Centers						
4750 Beidler Rd	Willoughby	OH	44094	**800-443-9699**	216-986-9700	539
Union for Reformed Judaism						
633 Third Ave	New York	NY	10017	**855-875-1800**	212-650-4000	48-20
Union Hospital						
1606 N Seventh St	Terre Haute	IN	47804	**800-355-2470**	812-238-7000	373-3
Union Hospital 659 Blvd	Dover	OH	44622	**800-541-6664**	330-343-3311	373-3
Union Institute & University						
440 E McMillan St	Cincinnati	OH	45206	**800-486-3116**	513-861-6400	166
Union Metal Corp						
1432 Maple Ave NE PO Box 73028	Canton	OH	44705	**800-327-0097**	330-456-7653	478
Union of American Physicians & Dentists						
180 Grand Ave Ste 1380	Oakland	CA	94612	**800-622-0909**	510-839-0193	413
Union of Concerned Scientists (UCS)						
2 Brattle Sq	Cambridge	MA	02238	**800-666-8276**	617-547-5552	48-13
Union Pacific Corp						
1400 Douglas St	Omaha	NE	68179	**888-870-8777**	402-544-5000	359-3
NYSE: UNP						
Union Pacific Railroad Co						
1400 Douglas St	Omaha	NE	68179	**888-870-8777**		644
Union Pacific Railroad Employees' Health Systems						
1040 North 2200 West	Salt Lake City	UT	84116	**800-547-0421**	801-595-4300	390-3
Union Power Co-op						
1525 N Rocky River Rd	Monroe	NC	28110	**800-922-6840**	704-289-3145	245
Union Rural Electric Co-op Inc						
15461 US 36E	Marysville	OH	43040	**800-642-1826**	937-642-1826	245
Union Standard Equipment Co						
801 E 141st St	Bronx	NY	10454	**877-282-7333**	718-585-0200	298
Union Standard Insurance Co						
122 W Carpenter Fwy Ste 350	Irving	TX	75039	**800-444-0049**	972-719-2400	390-4
Union Station						
50 Massachusetts Ave	Washington	DC	20002	**800-331-0008**	202-289-1908	50-6
Union Theological Seminary & Presbyterian School of Christian Education						
3401 Brook Rd	Richmond	VA	23227	**800-229-2990**	804-355-0671	167-3

Alphabetical Section

	Toll-Free	Phone	Class
Union University			
1050 Union University Dr .... Jackson TN 38305	800-338-6466	731-661-5210	166
Unipunch Products Inc			
311 Fifth St NW .... Clear Lake WI 54005	800-828-7061		752
Unique Broadband Systems Ltd			
400 Spinnaker Way .... Vaughan ON L4K5Y9	877-669-8533	905-669-8533	643
Unique Business Systems Corp			
2901 Ocean Park Blvd # 215			
.... Santa Monica CA 90405	800-669-4827	310-396-3929	177
Unique Carpets Ltd			
7360 Jurupa Ave .... Riverside CA 92504	800-547-8266	951-352-8125	131
Unique Communications Inc			
3650 Coral Ridge Dr .... Coral Springs FL 33065	800-881-8182	954-735-4002	246
Unique Employment Services Inc			
4646 Corona Dr Ste 100 .... Corpus Christi TX 78411	800-824-8367	361-852-6392	260
Unique Functional Products Corp			
135 Sunshine Ln .... San Marcos CA 92069	800-854-1905	760-744-1610	758
Unique Industries Inc			
4750 League Island Blvd .... Philadelphia PA 19112	800-888-0559	215-336-4300	328
Unique Lighting Systems Inc			
1240 Simpson Way .... Escondido CA 92029	800-955-4831		762
Unique Management Services Inc			
119 E Maple St .... Jeffersonville IN 47130	800-879-5453	812-280-2147	160
Uniroyal Engineered Products LLC			
501 S Water St .... Stoughton WI 53589	800-873-8800		
UniSea Inc			
15400 NE 90th St .... Redmond WA 98073	800-535-8509	425-881-8181	296-14
Unisearch Inc			
1780 Barnes Blvd SW .... Tumwater WA 98512	800-722-0708	360-956-9500	631
Unisec Inc			
2555 Nicholson St .... San Leandro CA 94577	800-982-4587		688
Uniserve Communications			
333 Terminal Ave Ste 330 .... Vancouver BC V6A4C1	844-395-3900	604-395-3900	
Unishippers Assn Inc			
746 E Winchester Ste 200 .... Salt Lake City UT 84107	800-999-8721		542
Unisource Manufacturing Inc			
8040 NE 33rd Dr .... Portland OR 97211	800-234-2566	503-281-4673	452
Unisource NTC			
1336 Moorpark Rd Ste 159 .... Thousand Oaks CA 91360	800-736-8470	747-226-0978	461
Unistar-Sparco Computers Inc			
7089 Ryburn Dr .... Millington TN 38053	800-840-8400	901-872-2272	457
Unit Chemical Corp			
7360 Commercial Way .... Henderson NV 89015	800-879-8648	702-564-6454	151
Unit Corp			
7130 S Lewis Ave Ste 1000 .... Tulsa OK 74136	800-722-3612	918-493-7700	536
NYSE: UNT			
Unitarian Universalist Service Committee (UUSC)			
689 Massachusetts Ave .... Cambridge MA 02139	800-388-3920	617-868-6600	48-5
UNITE HERE			
275 Seventh Ave .... New York NY 10001	800-452-4155	212-265-7000	413
Unitech Services Group			
295 Parker St .... Springfield MA 01151	800-344-3824	413-543-6911	441
United Airlines Cargo			
PO Box 66100 .... Chicago IL 60666	800-822-2746		12
United Aluminum Corp			
100 United Dr .... North Haven CT 06473	800-243-2515	203-239-5881	490
United American Insurance Co			
PO Box 8080 .... McKinney TX 75070	800-755-2137		390-2
United Animal Health			
4310 State Rd 38 W .... Sheridan IN 46069	800-382-9909	317-758-4495	445
United Bakery Equipment Co Inc			
15815 W 110th St .... Lenexa KS 66219	888-823-2253	913-541-8700	298
United Bancorp Inc			
201 S Fourth St .... Martins Ferry OH 43935	888-275-5566	740-633-0445	359-2
NASDAQ: UBCP			
United Bank			
11185 Fairfax Blvd .... Fairfax VA 22030	800-327-9862	703-219-4850	70
United Behavioral Health Inc			
425 Market St 27th Fl .... San Francisco CA 94105	800-888-2998	415-547-5000	460
United Blood Services			
6210 E Oak St PO Box 1867 .... Scottsdale AZ 85252	800-288-2199	480-946-4201	89
Farmington			
475 E 20th St Ste A .... Farmington NM 87401	888-804-9913		89
New Mexico			
1515 University Blvd NE .... Albuquerque NM 87102	800-333-8037*		89
General			
United Blood Services Arizona			
Chandler			
1989 W Elliot Rd Ste 32 .... Chandler AZ 85224	877-827-4376		89
United Blood Services of Arizona			
San Luis Obispo			
4119 Broad St Ste 100 ...... San Luis Obispo CA 93401	877-827-4376	805-543-4290	89
United Blood Services of Colorado			
146 Sawyer Dr .... Durango CO 81303	800-288-2199	970-385-4601	89
United Blood Services of Mississippi			
Tupelo			
4326 S Eason Blvd .... Tupelo MS 38801	800-844-8870	662-842-8871	89
United Blood Services of Montana			
Billings			
1444 Grand Ave .... Billings MT 59102	800-365-4450	406-248-9168	89
United Blood Services of New Mexico			
1515 University Blvd NE .... Albuquerque NM 87102	800-333-8037		89
Albuquerque			
1515 University Blvd NE .... Albuquerque NM 87102	800-333-8037		89
United Blood Services of North Dakota			
Bismarck 3231 S 11th St .... Fargo ND 58104	800-917-4929	701-293-9453	89
United Blood Services of Texas			
El Paso			
424 S Mesa Hills .... El Paso TX 79912	877-827-4376	915-544-5422	89
Lubbock 2523 48th St .... Lubbock TX 79413	800-333-6920	806-797-6804	89
McAllen			
1400 S Sixth St .... McAllen TX 78501	888-827-4376*	956-213-7500	89
General			
San Angelo			
2020 W Beauregard Ave .... San Angelo TX 76901	800-756-0024*	877-464-4376	89
General			
United Brass Works Inc			
714 S Main St .... Randleman NC 27317	800-334-3035	336-498-2661	784
United Brotherhood of Carpenters & Joiners of America			
101 Constitution Ave NW .... Washington DC 20001	800-530-5090	202-546-6206	413
United Chemi-Con Inc			
9801 W Higgins Rd .... Rosemont IL 60018	800-344-4539	847-696-2000	253
United Church of Christ (UCC)			
700 Prospect Ave .... Cleveland OH 44115	866-822-8224	216-736-2100	48-20
United Collection Bureau Inc			
5620 Southwyck Blvd .... Toledo OH 43614	866-209-0622		160
United Color Manufacturing Inc (UCM)			
PO Box 480 .... Newtown PA 18940	800-852-5942	215-860-2165	145
United Commercial Travellers			
1801 Watermark Dr Ste 100 .... Columbus OH 43215	800-848-0123	614-228-3276	455-10
United Community Bank			
PO Box 309 .... Four Oaks NC 27524	877-963-6257	919-963-2177	70
United Companies			
2273 River Rd .... Grand Junction CO 81505	800-321-0807	970-243-4900	182
United Consulting Group Ltd			
625 Holcomb Bridge Rd .... Norcross GA 30071	800-266-0990	770-209-0029	256
United Contractors Midwest Inc			
3151 Robbins Rd			
PO Box 13420 .... Springfield IL 62791	800-381-5497	217-546-6192	188-4
United CoolAir Corp			
491 E Princess St .... York PA 17403	877-905-1111	717-843-4311	14
United Coop			
N7160 Raceway Rd .... Beaver Dam WI 53916	800-924-2991	920-887-1756	344
United Cooperative Services			
3309 N Main St PO Box 16 .... Cleburne TX 76033	800-342-6239	817-556-4000	245
United Country Real Estate Inc			
2820 NW Barry Rd .... Kansas City MO 64154	800-999-1020		648
United Dairy Farmers			
3955 Montgomery Rd .... Cincinnati OH 45212	866-837-4833*	513-396-8700	296-27
General			
United Dairy Inc			
300 N Fifth St .... Martins Ferry OH 43935	800-252-1542	740-633-1451	296-27
United Data Technologies Inc			
8825 NW 21st Terr .... Doral FL 33172	800-882-9919	305-882-0435	620
United Displaycraft			
333 E Touhy Ave .... Des Plaines IL 60018	877-632-8767*	847-375-3800	233
General			
United Drill Bushing Corp			
12200 Woodruff Ave .... Downey CA 90241	800-486-3466	562-803-1521	491
United Electric Supply Inc			
10 Bellecor Dr .... New Castle DE 19720	800-322-3374	302-322-3333	782
United Electrical Sales Ltd			
4496 SW 36th St .... Orlando FL 32811	800-432-5126	407-246-1992	246
United Engine & Machine Company Inc			
1040 Corbett St .... Carson City NV 89706	800-648-7970	775-882-7790	128
United Envelope LLC			
150 Industrial Park Dr .... Mount Pocono PA 18344	800-752-4012	570-839-1600	
United Equipment Accessories Inc			
2103 E Bremer Ave Hwy .... Waverly IA 50677	800-394-9986		
United Farmers Co-op (UFC)			
705 E Fourth St PO Box 461 .... Winthrop MN 55396	866-998-3266	507-647-6600	10
United Financial Bancorp Inc			
95 Elm St PO Box 9020 .... West Springfield MA 01090	866-959-2265	413-787-1700	70
NASDAQ: UBNK			
United Financial Services Group Inc			
325 Chestnut St Ste 3000 .... Philadelphia PA 19106	800-626-0787	215-238-0300	
United Fire Equipment Co			
335 N Fourth Ave .... Tucson AZ 85705	800-362-0150	520-622-3639	675
United Food & Commercial Workers International Union (UFCW)			
1775 K St NW .... Washington DC 20006	800-551-4010	202-223-3111	413
United Food & Commercial Workers Union Local 555			
7095 SW Sandburg St .... Tigard OR 97281	800-452-8329	503-684-2822	413
United Ford Parts & Distribtion Ctr Inc			
12007 E 61st St .... Broken Arrow OK 74012	800-800-9001	918-317-6800	513
United Freezer & Storage Co			
650 N Meridian Rd .... Youngstown OH 44509	800-716-1416	330-792-1739	798-2
United Guaranty Corp (UGC)			
230 N Elm St .... Greensboro NC 27401	877-642-4642		390-5
United Heartland Inc			
PO Box 3026 .... Milwaukee WI 53201	866-206-5851		390-4
United Heritage Life Insurance Co			
PO Box 7777 .... Meridian ID 83680	800-657-6351	208-493-6100	390-2
United Hospital			
333 N Smith Ave .... Saint Paul MN 55102	800-869-1320	651-241-8000	373-3
United Hospital Ctr			
327 Medical pk Dr .... Bridgeport WV 26330	800-607-8888	681-342-1000	373-3
United Illuminating Co			
157 Church St .... New Haven CT 06510	800-722-5584*	203-499-2000	782
Cust Svc			
United Insurance Holdings Corp			
360 Central Ave			
Ste 900 .... Saint Petersburg FL 33701	800-861-4370	800-295-8016	390-2
NASDAQ: UIHC			
United Laboratories Inc			
320 37th Ave .... Saint Charles IL 60174	800-323-2594		145
United Lutheran Seminary Gatteysburg			
61 Seminary Rdg .... Gettysburg PA 17325	800-658-8437	717-334-6286	167-3
United Lutheran Seminary Philadelphia			
7301 Germantown Ave .... Philadelphia PA 19119	800-286-4616	215-248-4616	167-3
United Materials LLC			
3374 Walden Ave Ste 120 .... Depew NY 14043	888-918-6483	716-213-5832	182
United Methodist News Service			
810 12th Ave S .... Nashville TN 37203	800-251-8140	615-742-5470	526
United Methodist Publishing House			
201 Eigth Ave S .... Nashville TN 37203	800-672-1789	615-749-6000	633-3
United Microelectronics Corp			
488 De Guigne Dr .... Sunnyvale CA 94085	800-990-1135	408-523-7800	692
NYSE: UMC			
United Mobile Homes Inc			
3499 Rt 9 N Ste 3C .... Freehold NJ 07728	800-504-0670	732-577-9997	651
NYSE: UMH			
United Motorcoach Assn (UMA)			
113 SW St 4th Fl .... Alexandria VA 22314	800-424-8262	703-838-2929	49-21
United National Group			
3 Bala Plz E Ste 300 .... Bala Cynwyd PA 19004	800-333-0352	610-664-1500	390-4
United National Insurance Co			
3 Bala Plz E Ste 300 .... Bala Cynwyd PA 19004	800-333-0352	610-664-1500	390-4

	Toll-Free	Phone	Class
United Nations Federal Credit Union (UNFCU)			
24-01 44th Rd Ct Sq Pl .... Long Island NY 11101	**800-891-2471**	347-686-6000	219
United Network for Organ Sharing (UNOS)			
700 N Fourth St .... Richmond VA 23219	**888-894-6361**	804-782-4800	48-17
United Notions Inc			
13800 Hutton St .... Dallas TX 75234	**800-527-9447**	972-484-8901	590
United of Omaha Life Insurance Co			
Mutual of Omaha Plz .... Omaha NE 68175	**866-688-7957**		390-2
United Pacific Pet			
12060 Cabernet Dr .... Fontana CA 92337	**800-979-3333**	951-360-8550	574
United Paramount Tax Group Inc			
4025 Woodland Park Blvd			
Ste 310 .... Arlington TX 76013	**888-829-8829**	817-983-0099	2
United Parcel Service Inc (UPS)			
55 Glenlake Pkwy NE .... Atlanta GA 30328	**800-742-5877***	404-828-6000	542
NYSE: UPS ■ *Cust Svc			
United Performance Metals			
3475 Symmes Rd .... Hamilton OH 45015	**888-282-3292**	513-860-6500	719
United Personnel Services Inc			
289 Bridge St .... Springfield MA 01103	**800-363-8200**	413-736-0800	260
United Pet Care LLC			
6232 N Seventh St Ste 202 .... Phoenix AZ 85014	**877-872-8800**	602-266-5303	789
United Pharmacal Company of Missouri Inc			
3705 Pear St .... Saint Joseph MO 64503	**800-254-8726**	816-233-8800	574
United Pioneer Co			
2777 Summer St Ste 206 .... Stamford CT 06905	**800-466-9823**		572
United Plastic Fabricating Inc			
165 Flagship Dr .... North Andover MA 01845	**800-638-8265**		601-1
United Power Inc			
500 Co-op Way .... Brighton CO 80603	**800-468-8809**	303-659-0551	245
United Producers Inc			
8351 N High St Ste 250 .... Columbus OH 43235	**800-456-3276**		444
United Propane Gas			
4200 Cairo Rd .... Paducah KY 42001	**800-782-7743**		
United Record Pressing LLC			
453 Allied Dr .... Nashville TN 37211	**866-407-3165**	615-259-9396	622
United Rentals			
3266 E Washington St .... Phoenix AZ 85233	**844-873-4948**	602-267-3898	264-3
United Rentals Inc			
224 Selleck St .... Stamford CT 06902	**800-877-3687**	203-622-3131	264-3
NYSE: URI			
United Road Services Inc			
10701 Middlebelt Rd .... Romulus MI 48174	**800-221-5127**		775
United Salt Corp			
4800 San Felipe St .... Houston TX 77056	**800-554-8658**	713-877-2600	501-1
United Security Bancshares			
2126 Inyo St .... Fresno CA 93721	**888-683-6030**	559-248-4943	70
NASDAQ: UBFO			
United Security Bancshares Inc			
PO Box 249 .... Thomasville AL 36784	**866-546-8273**	334-636-5424	359-2
United Security Inc			
4295 Arthur Kill Rd .... Staten Island NY 10309	**800-874-6434**	718-967-6820	
United Service Organizations (USO)			
2111 Wilson Blvd Ste 1200 ...... Arlington VA 22201	**800-876-7469**	888-484-3876	48-19
United Services Automobile Assn (USAA)			
10750 McDermott Fwy .... San Antonio TX 78288	**800-531-8722**		185
United Soybean Board (USB)			
16305 Swingley Ridge Rd			
Ste 150 .... Chesterfield MO 63017	**800-989-8721**	636-530-1777	48-2
United Staffing Solutions (USS)			
111 Broadway 3rd Fl .... New York NY 10006	**800-972-9725**		
United States Aviation			
4141 N Memorial Dr .... Tulsa OK 74115	**800-897-5387**	918-836-7345	63
United States Brass & Copper			
1401 Brook Dr .... Downers Grove IL 60515	**800-821-2854**		490
United States Department of Labor (DOL)			
Office of Workers' Compensation Programs			
200 Constitution Ave			
Ste S3524. .... Washington DC 20210	**866-487-2365**		339-14
United States District Court			
Western District of Michigan			
110 Michigan St NW			
399 Federal Bldg .... Grand Rapids MI 49503	**800-290-2742**	616-456-2381	340-2
United States District Court, Central District			
312 N Spring St .... Los Angeles CA 90012	**800-676-6856**	213-894-1565	340-2
United States Drug Testing Laboratories (USDTL)			
1700 S Mt Prospect Rd .... Des Plaines IL 60018	**800-235-2367**	847-375-0770	415
United States Information Systems Inc (USIS)			
35 W Jefferson Ave .... Pearl River NY 10965	**866-222-3778**	845-358-7755	782
United States Patent & Trademark Office			
PO Box 1450 .... Alexandria VA 22313	**800-786-9199**	571-272-5600	339-2
United States Sports Academy, The			
1 Academy Dr .... Daphne AL 36526	**800-223-2668**	251-626-3303	166
United States Steel Corp			
600 Grant St .... Pittsburgh PA 15219	**866-433-4801**	412-433-1121	261
NYSE: X			
United Stations Radio Network			
1065 Ave of the Americas			
3rd Fl .... New York NY 10018	**866-989-1975**	212-869-1111	640
United Steel Products Inc			
33-40 127th Pl .... Flushing NY 11368	**888-683-2516**		
United Sugars Corp			
7803 Glenroy Rd Ste 300 .... Bloomington MN 55439	**800-984-3585**	952-896-0131	297-11
United Suppliers Inc			
30473 260th St PO Box 538 .... Eldora IA 50627	**800-782-5123**	641-858-2341	276
United Systems & Software Inc			
300 Colonial Center Pkwy			
Ste 150 .... Lake Mary FL 32746	**800-522-8774**	407-875-2120	177
United Textile Company Inc			
14275 Catalina St .... San Leandro CA 94577	**800-233-0077***	510-276-2288	506
*General			
United Therapeutics Corp			
1040 Spring St .... Silver Spring MD 20910	**877-864-8437**	301-608-9292	578
NASDAQ: UTHR			
United Titanium Inc			
3450 Old Airport Rd .... Wooster OH 44691	**800-321-4938**	330-264-2111	308
United Tool & Stamping Co of North Carolina Inc			
2817 Enterprise Ave .... Fayetteville NC 28306	**800-883-6087**	910-323-8588	693

	Toll-Free	Phone	Class
United Treating & Distribution LLC			
338 E Washington Ave .... Muscle Shoals AL 35661	**877-248-0944**	256-248-0944	
United Underwriters Inc			
PO Box 971000 .... Orem UT 84097	**866-686-4833**	801-226-2662	389
United Utilities Inc			
5450 A St .... Anchorage AK 99518	**800-478-2020**	907-561-1674	731
United Van Lines Inc			
1 United Dr .... St. Louis MO 63026	**877-740-3040**	636-343-3900	516
United Way of America			
701 N Fairfax St .... Alexandria VA 22314	**800-892-2757**	703-836-7100	48-5
United Window & Door			
24-36 Fadem Rd .... Springfield NJ 07081	**800-848-4550**		478
United World Life Insurance Co			
3300 Mutual of Omaha Plz .... Omaha NE 68175	**866-688-7957**		390-2
United-Bilt Homes Inc			
8500 Line Ave .... Shreveport LA 71106	**800-551-8955**	318-861-4572	187
United-Guardian Inc (UG)			
230 Marcus Blvd PO Box 18050 .. Hauppauge NY 11788	**800-645-5566**	631-273-0900	477
NASDAQ: UG			
UnitedHealth Group Inc			
9900 Bren Rd E .... Minnetonka MN 55343	**800-328-5979**	952-936-1300	390-3
NYSE: UNH			
Unitel Inc PO Box 165 .... Unity ME 04988	**888-760-1048**	207-948-3900	731
UniteU Technologies Inc			
12 Pine Cone Dr .... Pittsford NY 14534	**866-386-4838**		224
Unitil Corp			
6 Liberty Ln W .... Hampton NH 03842	**800-852-3339**	603-772-0775	359-5
NYSE: UTL			
Unitrends Software Corp			
200 Wheeler Rd 2nd fl .... Burlington MA 01803	**866-359-5411**	803-454-0300	173-8
Unitron LP			
10925 Miller Rd PO Box 38902 ...... Dallas TX 75238	**800-527-1279**	214-340-8600	515
Unitus Community Credit Union			
PO Box 1937 .... Portland OR 97207	**800-452-0900**	503-227-5571	219
Unity Bancorp Inc			
64 Old Hwy 22 .... Clinton NJ 08809	**800-618-2265**	908-730-7630	359-2
NASDAQ: UNTY			
Unity College			
90 Quaker Hill Rd .... Unity ME 04988	**800-624-1024**	207-948-3131	166
Unity Health Insurance			
840 Carolina St .... Sauk City WI 53583	**800-362-3308**	608-644-3430	390-3
Unity Hospice			
2366 Oak Ridge Cir .... De Pere WI 54115	**800-990-9249**	920-338-1111	370
Unity Hospice			
700 S Clinton St Ste 210 .... Chicago IL 60607	**888-949-1188**	312-427-6000	370
Unity Lake State Recreation Site			
725 Summer St NE Ste C .... Salem OR 97301	**800-551-6949**	541-932-4453	561
Univar Canada Ltd			
9800 Van Horne Way .... Richmond BC V6X1W5	**855-888-8648**		146
Univar USA Inc			
17425 NE Union Hill Rd .... Redmond WA 98052	**855-888-8648**	425-889-3400	146
Univenture Inc			
16710 Square Dr .... Marysville OH 43040	**800-992-8262**	937-645-4600	604
Univera Healthcare			
205 Pk Club Ln .... Buffalo NY 14221	**877-883-9577**	716-847-1480	390-3
Univers Workplace Benefits Inc			
897 12th St .... Hammonton NJ 08037	**800-343-0240**		400
Universal Audio Inc			
1700 Green Hills Rd .... Scotts Valley CA 95066	**877-698-2834**	831-440-1176	52
Universal Bearings Inc			
431 North Birkey Dr PO Box 38 .... Bremen IN 46506	**800-824-7743**		
Universal Brush Manufacturing Co			
16200 Dixie Hwy .... Markham IL 60428	**800-323-3474**	708-331-1700	103
Universal City Development Partners Ltd			
1000 Universal Studios Plz .... Orlando FL 32819	**800-447-0672**	407-363-8000	31
Universal Display & Fixtures Co			
726 E Hwy 121 .... Lewisville TX 75057	**800-235-0701**	972-221-5157	233
Universal Enterprises Inc			
8625 SW Cascade Ave .... Beaverton OR 97008	**800-547-5740**	503-644-8723	359-2
Universal Environmental Services LLC			
411 Dividend Dr .... Peachtree City GA 30269	**800-988-7977**		537
Universal Fabric Structures Inc			
2200 Kumry Rd .... Telford PA 18951	**800-634-8368**	215-529-9921	728
Universal Fibers Inc			
PO Box 8930 .... Bristol VA 24203	**800-457-4759**	276-669-1161	740-9
Universal Forest Products Inc (UFPI)			
2801 E Beltline Ave NE .... Grand Rapids MI 49525	**800-598-9663**	616-364-6161	679
NASDAQ: UFPI			
Universal Hospital Services Inc			
6625 W 78th St Ste 300 .... Minneapolis MN 55439	**800-847-7368**	952-893-3200	264-4
Universal Image			
PO Box 77090 .... Winter Garden FL 34787	**800-553-5499**	407-352-5302	588
Universal Industries Inc			
5800 Nordic Dr .... Cedar Falls IA 50613	**800-553-4446**	319-277-7501	207
Universal Instruments Corp (UIC)			
33 Broome Corporate Pk .... Conklin NY 13748	**800-842-9732**	607-779-7522	691
Universal Insurance Holding Inc (UIH)			
1110 W Commerical Blvd			
Ste 100 .... Fort Lauderdale FL 33309	**800-509-5586**		390-4
NYSE: UVE			
Universal Labeling Systems			
3501 Eigth Ave S .... Saint Petersburg FL 33711	**877-236-0266**	727-327-2123	543
Universal Lending Corp (ULC)			
6775 E Evans Ave .... Denver CO 80224	**800-758-4063**		507
Universal Logistics Holdings Inc			
12755 E Nine Mile Rd .... Warren MI 48089	**800-233-9445**	586-920-0100	775
NASDAQ: UACL			
Universal Machine & Engineering Corp			
645 Old Reading Pk .... Stowe PA 19464	**800-879-2477**	610-323-1810	385
Universal Manufacturing Co			
405 Diagonal St PO Box 190 .... Algona IA 50511	**800-343-3557**	515-295-3557	60
OTC: UFMG			
Universal Metals LLC			
805 Chicago St .... Toledo OH 43611	**800-853-8890**	419-726-0850	490
Universal Mfg Co Inc			
5030 Mackey S .... Overland Park KS 66203	**800-524-5860**	913-815-6230	757
Universal Orlando			
6000 Universal Blvd .... Orlando FL 32819	**877-801-9720**	407-363-8000	32

	Toll-Free	Phone	Class

Universal Overall Co
1060 W Van Buren St ....Chicago IL 60607 — 800-621-3344* — 312-226-3336 — 155-18
*Cust Svc

Universal Plastic Mold Inc
13245 Los Angeles St ....Baldwin Park CA 91706 — 888-893-1587 — — 600

Universal Protective Packaging Inc
61 Texaco Rd ....Mechanicsburg PA 17050 — 800-544-6649 — 717-766-1578 — 597

Universal Remote Control Inc
500 Mamaroneck Ave ....Harrison NY 10528 — 800-901-0800 — — 246

Universal Security Instruments Inc
11407 Cronhill Dr ....Owings Mills MD 21117 — 800-390-4321 — 410-363-3000 — 688
NYSE: UUU

Universal Service Administrative Co
2000 L St NW Ste 200 ....Washington DC 20036 — 888-203-8100 — — 731

Universal Steel America Houston Inc
1230 E Richey Rd ....Houston TX 77073 — 866-988-3800 — 281-821-7400 — 490

Universal Studios Hollywood
100 Universal City Plz ....Universal City CA 91608 — 800-864-8377 — 818-622-9841 —

Universal Studios Hollywood
100 Universal City Plz ....Universal City CA 91608 — 800-864-8377 — — 31

Universal Valve Company Inc
478 Schiller St ....Elizabeth NJ 07206 — 800-223-0741 — 908-351-0606 — 785

Universal Wilde
26 Dartmouth St ....Westwood MA 02090 — 866-825-5515 — 781-251-2700 — 5

Universal Wire Cloth Co
16 N Steel Rd ....Morrisville PA 19067 — 800-523-0575 — 215-736-8981 — 684

Universal's Islands of Adventure
6000 Universal Studios Plz ......Orlando FL 32819 — 877-801-9720 — 407-363-8000 — 32

Universitas Foundation of Canada
1035 Wilfrid-Pelletier Ave
Ste 500 ....Quebec QC G1W0C5 — 877-710-7377 — 418-651-8975 — 305

Universite de Moncton
Edmundston
165 Blvd Hebert ....Edmundston NB E3V2S8 — 888-736-8623 — 506-737-5051 — 780
Shippagan Campus
218 Blvd JD Gauthier ....Shippagan NB E8S1P6 — 800-363-8336 — 506-336-3400 — 780

Universite de Sherbrooke
2500 boul de l'Universite ....Sherbrooke QC J1K2R1 — 800-267-8337 — 819-821-8000 — 780

Universite du Quebec a Trois-Rivieres
3351 Boul des Forges CP 500
...................Trois-Rivieres QC G9A5H7 — 800-365-0922 — 819-376-5011 — 780

Universite Sainte Anne
1695 RI I ....Pointe-de-l'Eglise NS B0W1M0 — 888-338-8337 — 902-769-2114 — 780

University Art Museum
1250 N Bellflower Blvd ....Long Beach CA 90840 — 800-437-2934 — 562-985-5761 — 517

University at Albany
1400 Washington Ave ....Albany NY 12222 — 800-293-7869 — 518-442-3300 — 166

University Behavioral Ctr
2500 Discovery Dr ....Orlando FL 32826 — 800-999-0807 — 407-281-7000 — 373-5

University Book Store, The
711 State St ....Madison WI 53703 — 800-993-2665 — 608-257-3784 — 95

University Games Corp
2030 Harrison St ....San Francisco CA 94110 — 800-347-4818 — 415-503-1600 — 757

University Health Care System
1350 Walton Way ....Augusta GA 30901 — 866-591-2502 — 706-722-9011 — 373-3

University Hospital SUNY Upstate Medical University
750 E Adams St ....Syracuse NY 13210 — 877-464-5540 — 315-464-5540 — 373-3

University Hospitals of Cleveland
11100 Euclid Ave ....Cleveland OH 44106 — 866-844-2273 — 216-844-1000 — 373-3

University Inn Seattle
4140 Roosevelt Way NE ....Seattle WA 98105 — 800-733-3855 — 206-632-5055 — 378

University Libraries
1155 Union Cir Ste 305190 ....Denton TX 76203 — 877-872-0264 — 940-565-2411 — 433-6

University Medical Ctr at Princeton (UMCP)
253 Witherspoon St ....Princeton NJ 08540 — 877-932-8935 — 609-497-4304 — 373-3

University Moving & Storage Co
23305 Commerce Dr ......Farmington Hills MI 48335 — 800-448-6683 — 248-615-7000 — 186

University of Akron
277 E Buchtel Ave ....Akron OH 44325 — 800-655-4884* — 330-972-7100 — 166
*Admissions

University of Akron School of Law
150 University Ave ....Akron OH 44325 — 800-655-4884 — 330-972-7331 — 167-1

University of Akron Wayne College
1901 Smucker Rd ....Orrville OH 44667 — 800-221-8308 — 330-683-2010 — 162

University of Alabama
PO Box 870132 ....Tuscaloosa AL 35487 — 800-933-2262* — 205-348-6010 — 166
*Admissions
Birmingham
1720 second Ave S ....Birmingham AL 35294 — 800-421-8743 — 205-934-4011 — 166
Huntsville
301 Sparkman Dr ....Huntsville AL 35899 — 800-824-2255 — 256-824-1000 — 166

University of Alabama System
401 Queen City Ave ....Tuscaloosa AL 35401 — 866-362-9476 — 205-348-5861 — 781

University of Alaska Anchorage
3211 Providence Dr ....Anchorage AK 99508 — 888-822-8973 — 907-786-1800 — 166

University of Alaska Anchorage Kenai Peninsula College
156 College Rd ....Soldotna AK 99669 — 877-262-0330 — — 162

University of Alaska Anchorage Kodiak College
117 Benny Benson Dr ....Kodiak AK 99615 — 800-486-7660 — 907-486-4161 — 162

University of Alaska Fairbanks
Signers' Hall 2nd Fl
PO Box 757480................Fairbanks AK 99775 — 800-478-1823 — 907-474-7500 — 166
Bristol Bay
527 Seward St PO Box 1070 ....Dillingham AK 99576 — 800-478-5109 — 907-842-5109 — 166
Northwest
400 E Front St PO Box 400............Nome AK 99762 — 800-478-2202 — 907-443-2201 — 162

University of Alaska Museum of the North
907 Yukon Dr ....Fairbanks AK 99775 — 866-478-2721 — 907-474-7505 — 517

University of Alaska Press
1760 Wwood Wy PO Box 756240......Fairbanks AK 99709 — 888-252-6657 — 907-474-5831 — 633-4

University of Alaska Southeast
11066 Auke Lake Way ....Juneau AK 99801 — 877-465-4827 — 907-796-6000 — 166

University of Alaska Southeast Ketchikan
2600 Seventh Ave ....Ketchikan AK 99901 — 877-465-6400 — 907-225-6177 — 162

University of Alaska Southeast Sitka
1332 Seward Ave ....Sitka AK 99835 — 800-478-6653 — — 162

University of Alberta
Augustana
4901-46th Ave ....Camrose AB T4V2R3 — 800-661-8714 — 780-679-1100 — 780

University of Arkansas
232 Silas Hunt Hall ....Fayetteville AR 72701 — 800-377-8632* — 479-575-5346 — 166
*Admissions
Little Rock
2801 S University Ave ....Little Rock AR 72204 — 800-482-8892 — 501-569-3000 — 166
Monticello
PO Box 3600 ....Monticello AR 71656 — 800-844-1826 — 870-460-1026 — 166
Pine Bluff
1200 N University Dr ....Pine Bluff AR 71601 — 800-264-6585* — 870-575-8000 — 166
*Admissions

University of Arkansas Community College Rich Mountain
1100 College Dr ....Mena AR 71953 — 800-612-7440 — 479-394-7622 — 162

University of Bridgeport
126 Park Ave ....Bridgeport CT 06604 — 800-392-3582 — 203-576-4000 — 166

University of British Columbia
2016-1874 E Mall ....Vancouver BC V6T1Z1 — 877-272-1422 — 604-822-9836 — 780

University of California (UCLA)
Berkeley
110 Sproul Hall MC Ste 5800 ....Berkeley CA 94720 — 866-740-1260 — 510-642-6000 — 166
Davis 1 Shields Ave ....Davis CA 95616 — 800-242-4723 — 530-752-1011 — 166
Riverside
900 University Ave ....Riverside CA 92521 — 800-426-2586 — 951-827-3411 — 166
San Diego
9500 Gilman Dr ....La Jolla CA 92093 — 800-207-1710 — 858-534-2230 — 166
Santa Barbara
1210 Cheadle Hall ....Santa Barbara CA 93106 — 888-488-8272 — 805-893-8000 — 166
Santa Cruz
1156 High St ....Santa Cruz CA 95064 — 800-933-7584 — 831-459-2131 — 166

University of California Davis School of Medicine
4610 X St ....Sacramento CA 95817 — 800-282-3284 — 916-734-7131 — 167-2

University of California Irvine
Library PO Box 19557 ....Irvine CA 92623 — 800-843-2763 — 949-824-6836 — 433-6

University of California Press
2120 Berkeley Way ....Berkeley CA 94704 — 800-343-4499 — — 633-4

University of California System
1111 Franklin St 6th Fl...........Oakland CA 94607 — 800-888-8267 — 510-987-9074 — 781

University of Central Florida
4000 Central Florida Blvd ....Orlando FL 32816 — 800-272-7252 — 407-823-2000 — 166

University of Charleston
2300 MacCorkle Ave SE ......Charleston WV 25304 — 800-995-4682* — 304-357-4800 — 166
*Admissions

University of Chicago Medical Ctr
5841 S Maryland Ave ....Chicago IL 60637 — 888-824-0200 — 773-702-1000 — 373-3

University of Chicago Press
1427 E 60th St ....Chicago IL 60637 — 800-621-2736* — 773-702-1234 — 633-4
*Sales

University of Chicago Press Journals Div
1427 E 60th St ....Chicago IL 60637 — 877-705-1878 — 773-702-1234 — 633-9

University of Cincinnati
2600 Clifton Ave
PO Box 210091................Cincinnati OH 45221 — 866-397-3382 — 513-556-1100 — 166

University of Cincinnati Clermont College
4200 Clermont College Dr ....Batavia OH 45103 — 866-446-2822 — 513-732-5200 — 162

University of Cincinnati Langsam Library
PO Box 210033 ....Cincinnati OH 45221 — 866-397-3382 — 513-556-1515 — 433-6

University of Colorado
Colorado Springs
PO Box 7150 ....Colorado Springs CO 80933 — 800-990-8227 — 719-262-3000 — 166

University of Colorado at Colorado Springs
Kraemer Family Library
1420 Austin Bluffs Pkwy
PO Box 7150 ....Colorado Springs CO 80918 — 800-990-8227 — 719-255-3295 — 433-6

University of Connecticut
Babbidge Library
369 Fairfield Rd ....Storrs CT 06269 — 888-603-9635 — 860-486-2219 — 433-6

University of Connecticut Health Ctr
John Dempsey Hospital
263 Farmington Ave ....Farmington CT 06030 — 800-535-6232 — 860-679-2000 — 373-3

University of Dallas
1845 E Northgate Dr ....Irving TX 75062 — 800-628-6999* — 972-721-5266 — 166
*Admissions

University of Dayton
300 College Pk ....Dayton OH 45469 — 800-837-7433 — 937-229-4411 — 166

University of Delaware
210 S College Ave ....Newark DE 19716 — 844-237-1338 — 302-831-2792 — 166

University of Denver
2199 S University Blvd ....Denver CO 80208 — 800-525-9495 — 303-871-2036 — 166

University of Detroit Mercy
4001 W McNichols Rd ....Detroit MI 48221 — 800-635-5020* — 313-993-1000 — 166
*Admissions

University of Dubuque
2000 University Ave ....Dubuque IA 52001 — 800-722-5583 — 563-589-3000 — 166

University of Evansville
1800 Lincoln Ave ....Evansville IN 47722 — 800-423-8633 — 812-488-2000 — 166

University of Findlay
1000 N Main St ....Findlay OH 45840 — 800-472-9502 — 419-422-8313 — 166

University of Florida
219 Grinter Hall
PO Box 115500................Gainesville FL 32611 — 866-876-4472 — 352-392-3261 — 166

University of Florida Levin College of Law
309 Village Dr
PO Box 117620................Gainesville FL 32611 — 877-429-1297 — 352-273-0804 — 167-1

University of Florida Libraries
PO Box 117001................Gainesville FL 32611 — 877-351-2377 — 352-392-0342 — 433-6

University of Georgia Library
320 S Jackson St ....Athens GA 30602 — 877-314-5560 — 706-542-0621 — 433-6

University of Guelph
50 Stone Rd E ....Guelph ON N1G2W1 — 877-674-1610 — 519-824-4120 — 780

University of Hartford
200 Bloomfield Ave ....West Hartford CT 06117 — 800-947-4303 — 860-768-4296 — 166

University of Hawai?i Maui College
310 W Kaahumanu Ave ....Kahului HI 96732 — 800-479-6692 — 808-984-3267 — 162

University of Hawaii
Hilo 200 W Kawili St ....Hilo HI 96720 — 800-897-4456* — 808-974-7414 — 166
*Admissions
Manoa
2600 Campus Rd Rm 001 ....Honolulu HI 96822 — 800-823-9771* — 808-956-8975 — 166
*Admissions

Name / Address	City	State	ZIP	Toll-Free	Phone	Class
West Oahu						
96-129 Ala Ike	Pearl City	HI	96782	**866-299-8656**	808-454-4700	166
University of Hawaii Federal Credit Union						
PO Box 22070	Honolulu	HI	96823	**800-927-3397**	808-983-5500	219
University of Hawaii Foundation, The						
2444 Dole St Bachman Hall 105	Honolulu	HI	96822	**866-846-4262**	808-956-8849	219
University of Hawaii Press						
2840 Kolowalu St	Honolulu	HI	96822	**888-847-7377**	808-956-8255	633-4
University of Houston						
Victoria						
3007 N Ben Wilson St	Victoria	TX	77901	**877-970-4848**	361-570-4848	166
University of Houston Law Ctr						
4604 Calhoun Rd	Houston	TX	77204	**800-252-9690**	713-743-2100	167-1
University of Idaho						
875 Perimeter Dr	Moscow	ID	83844	**888-884-3246**	208-885-6111	166
University of Idaho College of Law						
709 Deakin St Rm 117	Moscow	ID	83844	**888-884-3246**	208-885-6111	167-1
University of Illinois						
Springfield						
1 University Plz						
MS UHB 1080	Springfield	IL	62703	**888-977-4847**	217-206-4847	166
University of Illinois Press						
1325 S Oak St	Champaign	IL	61820	**866-244-0626**	217-333-0950	633-4
University of Indianapolis						
1400 E Hanna Ave	Indianapolis	IN	46227	**800-232-8634**	317-788-3368	166
University of Iowa						
107 Calvin Hall	Iowa City	IA	52242	**800-553-4692**	319-335-3847	166
University of Iowa College of Law						
130 Byington Rd	Iowa City	IA	52242	**800-553-4692**	319-335-3500	167-1
University of Iowa Hospitals & Clinics						
200 Hawkins Dr	Iowa City	IA	52242	**800-777-8442**		
University of Iowa Roy J & Lucille A Carver College of Medicine						
200 CMAB	Iowa City	IA	52242	**800-725-8460**	319-335-6707	167-2
University of Judaism						
15600 Mulholland Dr	Los Angeles	CA	90077	**888-853-6763**	310-476-9777	166
University of Kansas Health system						
3901 Rainbow Blvd	Kansas City	KS	66160	**844-323-1227**	913-588-1227	373-3
University of Kansas Health System St Francis Campus						
1700 SW Seventh St	Topeka	KS	66606	**855-578-3726**	785-295-8000	373-3
University of Kansas School of Law						
1535 W 15th St	Lawrence	KS	66045	**866-220-3654**	785-864-4550	167-1
University of Kentucky						
800 Rose St	Lexington	KY	40536	**866-900-4685**	859-257-9000	166
University of La Verne						
1950 Third St	La Verne	CA	91750	**800-876-4858***	909-593-3511	166
*Admissions						
University of Library						
302 Buchtel Common	Akron	OH	44325	**800-425-7668**	330-972-5355	433-6
University of Louisiana						
Lafayette						
611 McKinley St	Lafayette	LA	70504	**800-752-6553**	337-482-1000	166
Monroe						
700 University Ave	Monroe	LA	71209	**800-372-5127***	318-342-5430	166
*Admissions						
University of Louisville						
2301 S Third St	Louisville	KY	40292	**800-334-8635**	502-852-5555	166
University of Louisville Hospital						
530 S Jackson St	Louisville	KY	40202	**800-891-0947**	502-562-3000	373-3
University of Louisville School of Medicine						
323 E Chestnut St	Louisville	KY	40292	**800-334-8635**	502-852-5193	167-2
University of Maine						
5713 Chadbourne Hall	Orono	ME	04469	**877-486-2364***	207-581-1110	166
*Admissions						
Augusta						
46 University Dr	Augusta	ME	04330	**877-862-1234**	207-621-3000	166
Farmington						
111 S St	Farmington	ME	04938	**800-871-7741**	207-778-7000	166
Fort Kent						
23 University Dr	Fort Kent	ME	04743	**888-879-8635***	207-834-7500	166
*Admissions						
Machias						
116 O'Brien Ave	Machias	ME	04654	**888-468-6866***	207-255-1200	166
*Admissions						
University of Manitoba						
65 Chancellors Cir						
500 University Ctr.	Winnipeg	MB	R3T2N2	**800-224-7713***	204-474-8880	780
*Admissions						
University of Mary						
7500 University Dr	Bismarck	ND	58504	**800-288-6279***	701-255-7500	166
*Admissions						
University of Mary Hardin-Baylor						
900 College St	Belton	TX	76513	**800-727-8642**	254-295-8642	166
University of Mary Washington						
1301 College Ave	Fredericksburg	VA	22401	**800-468-5614***	540-654-2000	166
*Admissions						
University of Maryland						
7569 Baltimore Ave	College Park	MD	20742	**800-422-5867***	301-405-1000	166
*Admissions						
Baltimore County						
1000 Hilltop Cir	Baltimore	MD	21250	**800-810-0271**	410-455-1000	166
University of Maryland Ctr for Environmental Science (UMCES)						
2020 Horn Pt Rd	Cambridge	MD	21613	**866-842-2520**	410-228-9250	664
University of Maryland Greenebaum Cancer Ctr						
22 S Greene St	Baltimore	MD	21201	**800-888-8823**	410-328-7904	764
University of Maryland Medical System						
22 S Greene St	Baltimore	MD	21201	**800-492-5538**	410-328-8667	352
University of Massachusetts						
Boston						
100 Morrissey Blvd Campus Ctr	Boston	MA	02125	**800-767-1833**	617-287-6100	166
Lowell						
1 University Ave	Lowell	MA	01854	**800-480-3190**	978-934-4000	166
University of Massachusetts Press						
671 N Pleasant St	Amherst	MA	01003	**800-562-0112**	413-545-2217	633-4
University of Memphis Cecil C Humphreys School of Law						
3715 Central Ave	Memphis	TN	38152	**800-872-3728**	901-678-2421	167-1
University of Memphis McWherter Library						
126 Ned R McWherter Library	Memphis	TN	38152	**866-670-6147**	901-678-2201	433-6
University of Miami Hospital & Clinics (UMHC)						
Sylvester Comprehensive Cancer Ctr						
1475 NW 12th Ave	Miami	FL	33136	**800-545-2292**	305-243-1000	764
University of Michigan						
Flint 303 E Kearsley St	Flint	MI	48502	**800-942-5636**	734-764-1817	166
University of Michigan Dearborn						
Mardigian Library						
4901 Evergreen Rd	Dearborn	MI	48128	**877-619-6650**	313-593-5000	433-6
University of Michigan Press						
839 Greene St	Ann Arbor	MI	48104	**866-804-0002**	734-764-4388	633-4
University of Minnesota						
200 Oak St SE Ste 500	Minneapolis	MN	55455	**800-775-2187**	612-624-3333	48-11
Crookston						
2900 University Ave						
170 Owen Hall	Crookston	MN	56716	**800-862-6466**	218-281-8569	166
Duluth						
1049 University Dr	Duluth	MN	55812	**800-232-1339**	218-726-8000	166
Morris 600 E Fourth St	Morris	MN	56267	**800-992-8863**	888-866-3382	166
Twin Cities						
3 Morrill Hall						
100 Church St SE	Minneapolis	MN	55455	**800-752-1000**	612-625-2008	166
University of Minnesota Crookston						
UMC Library						
2900 University Ave	Crookston	MN	56716	**800-862-6466**	218-281-8399	433-6
University of Minnesota Duluth						
Kathryn A. Martin Library						
416 Library Dr	Duluth	MN	55812	**866-999-6995**	218-726-8102	433-6
University of Minnesota Medical Ctr Fairview - University Campus						
500 Harvard St	Minneapolis	MN	55455	**800-688-5252**	612-273-3000	373-3
University of Mississippi						
PO Box 1848	University	MS	38677	**800-891-4596**	662-915-7211	166
Williams Library						
1 Library Loop	University	MS	38677	**800-891-4596**	662-915-7091	433-6
University of Mississippi School of Medicine						
2500 N State St	Jackson	MS	39216	**888-815-2005**	601-984-1080	167-2
University of Missouri (UMSL)						
Columbia						
104 Jesse Hall	Columbia	MO	65211	**800-856-2181**	573-882-6333	166
Kansas City						
5100 Rockhill Rd	Kansas City	MO	64110	**800-775-8652**	816-235-1000	166
Saint Louis						
1 University Blvd	Saint Louis	MO	63121	**888-462-8675***	314-516-5000	166
*Admissions						
University of Missouri Kansas City						
Nichols Library						
800 E 51st St	Kansas City	MO	64110	**800-775-8652**	816-235-1000	433-6
University of Missouri System						
321 University Hall	Columbia	MO	65211	**800-225-6075**	573-882-2011	781
University of Missouri-Kansas City School of Medicine						
2411 Holmes St	Kansas City	MO	64108	**800-735-2466**	816-235-1111	167-2
University of Mobile						
5735 College Pkwy	Mobile	AL	36613	**800-946-7267**	251-675-5990	166
University of Moncton						
18 Ave Antonine-Maillet	Moncton	NB	E1A3E9	**800-331-9283**	506-858-4088	517
University of Montana						
32 Campus Dr	Missoula	MT	59812	**800-462-8636***	406-243-6266	166
*Admissions						
Western						
710 S Atlantic St	Dillon	MT	59725	**877-683-7331***	406-683-7011	166
*Admissions						
University of Montana Missoula						
Mansfield Library						
32 Campus Dr	Missoula	MT	59812	**800-240-4939**	406-243-2053	433-6
University of Nebraska						
Kearney						
2504 Ninth Ave	Kearney	NE	68849	**800-532-7639**	308-865-8441	166
Lincoln 1410 Q St	Lincoln	NE	68588	**800-742-8800**	402-472-2023	166
Omaha 6001 Dodge St	Omaha	NE	68182	**800-858-8648**	402-554-2800	166
University of Nebraska Medical Ctr McGoogan Library of Medicine						
986705 Nebraska Medical Ctr	Omaha	NE	68198	**866-800-5209**	402-559-4006	433-1
University of Nebraska School of Medicine						
985527 Nebraska Medical Ctr	Omaha	NE	68198	**800-626-8431**	402-559-2259	167-2
University of Nebraska System						
3835 Holdrege St Varner Hall	Lincoln	NE	68583	**800-542-1602**	402-472-2111	781
University of Nebraska-Lincoln						
1400 R St	Lincoln	NE	68588	**800-242-3766**	402-472-7211	517
University of Nevada						
Las Vegas						
4505 S Maryland Pkwy	Las Vegas	NV	89154	**800-331-3103**	702-895-3011	166
Reno 1664 N Virginia St	Reno	NV	89557	**866-263-8232**	775-784-1110	166
University of New Brunswick						
100 Tucker Pk Rd						
PO Box 4400	Fredericton	NB	E2L4L5	**888-895-3344**	506-453-4666	780
University of New England						
11 Hills Beach Rd	Biddeford	ME	04005	**800-477-4863***	207-283-0171	166
*Admissions						
Westbrook College						
716 Stevens Ave	Portland	ME	04103	**800-477-4863***	207-797-7261	166
*Admissions						
University of New Hampshire						
3 Garrison Ave	Durham	NH	03824	**800-313-5327**	603-862-1234	166
University of New Haven						
300 Boston Post Rd	West Haven	CT	06516	**800-342-5864**	203-932-7319	166
University of New Mexico (UNM)						
1 University of New Mexico	Albuquerque	NM	87131	**800-225-5866**	505-277-0111	166
Gallup 200 College Rd	Gallup	NM	87301	**800-225-5866**	505-863-7500	166
Valencia						
280 La Entrada	Los Lunas	NM	87031	**800-225-5866**	505-925-8580	162
University of New Orleans						
2000 Lakeshore Dr	New Orleans	LA	70148	**800-256-5866***	504-280-6000	166
*Admissions						
University of North Alabama						
1 Harrison Plz	Florence	AL	35632	**800-825-5862**	256-765-4608	166
University of North Carolina						
Asheville						
1 University Hts	Asheville	NC	28804	**800-531-9842**	828-251-6481	166
Chapel Hill						
Jackson Hall CB 2200	Chapel Hill	NC	27599	**800-962-8519**	919-966-3621	166
Pembroke PO Box 1510	Pembroke	NC	28372	**800-949-8627**	910-521-6000	166

	Toll-Free	Phone	Class
Wilmington			
601 S College Rd .... Wilmington NC 28403	**800-596-2880**	910-962-3000	166
University of North Carolina Ctr for Public Television (UNC-TV)			
10 TW Alexander Dr			
PO Box 14900........... Research Triangle Park NC 27709	**800-906-5050**	919-549-7000	628
University of North Carolina Press			
116 S Boundary St ....Chapel Hill NC 27514	**800-848-6224**	919-966-3561	633-4
University of North Dakota			
PO Box 8357 ....Grand Forks ND 58202	**800-225-5863**	701-777-3000	166
University of North Dakota School of Medicine & Health Sciences			
1301 N Columbia Rd Stop 9037			
................................Grand Forks ND 58202	**800-225-5863**	701-777-5046	167-2
University of North Florida			
4567 St Johns Bluff Rd S ....Jacksonville FL 32224	**866-697-7150**	904-620-1000	166
University of North Texas			
PO Box 311277 ....Denton TX 76203	**800-868-8211**	940-565-2681	166
University of North Texas Health Science Ctr			
3500 Camp Bowie Blvd .... Fort Worth TX 76107	**800-687-7580**	817-735-2000	416
University of North Texas Press			
1155 Union Cir Ste 311336 ....Denton TX 76203	**800-826-8911**	940-565-2142	633-4
University of Northern British Columbia			
3333 University Way .... Prince George BC V2N4Z9	**800-627-9931**	250-960-5555	780
University of Northern Colorado			
501 20th St CB 92 .... Greeley CO 80639	**888-700-4862***	970-351-2881	166
*Admissions			
University of Northern Iowa			
1222 W 27th St .... Cedar Falls IA 50614	**800-772-2037***	319-273-2311	166
*Admissions			
University of Oklahoma			
1000 Asp Ave .... Norman OK 73019	**800-234-6868**	405-325-0311	166
University of Oregon			
1585 E 13th Ave ....Eugene OR 97403	**800-232-3825***	541-346-1000	166
*Admissions			
University of Oregon Bookstore Inc			
895 E 13th Ave ....Eugene OR 97401	**800-352-1733**	541-346-4331	95
University of Ottawa			
550 Cumberland St .... Ottawa ON K1N6N5	**877-868-8292**	613-562-5800	780
University of Ottawa Faculty of Medicine			
451 Smyth Rd .... Ottawa ON K1H8M5	**877-868-8292**	613-562-5700	167-2
University of Pennsylvania			
3451 Walnut St ....Philadelphia PA 19104	**800-537-5487**	215-898-5000	166
University of Pennsylvania Press			
3902 Spruce St ....Philadelphia PA 19104	**800-537-5487***	215-898-6261	633-4
*Cust Svc			
University of Pittsburgh			
4227 Fifth Ave .... Pittsburgh PA 15260	**877-999-3223**	412-624-4141	166
Bradford			
300 Campus Dr ....Bradford PA 16701	**800-872-1787**	814-362-7555	166
Greensburg			
150 Finoli Dr .... Greensburg PA 15601	**888-843-4563**	724-837-7040	166
Johnstown			
157 Blackington Hall ....Johnstown PA 15904	**800-765-4875**	814-269-7050	166
Titusville			
504 E Main St .... Titusville PA 16354	**888-878-0462**		162
University of Pittsburgh Medical Ctr (UPMC)			
Horizon			
110 N Main St .... Greenville PA 16125	**888-447-1122**	724-588-2100	373-3
Passavant			
9100 Babcock Blvd .... Pittsburgh PA 15237	**800-533-8762**	412-367-6700	373-3
Shadyside			
5230 Centre Ave .... Pittsburgh PA 15232	**800-533-8762**	412-623-2121	373-3
South Side			
2000 Mary St .... Pittsburgh PA 15203	**800-533-8762**	412-488-5550	373-3
University of Portland			
5000 N Willamette Blvd ....Portland OR 97203	**888-627-5601**	503-943-7147	166
University of Providence			
1301 20th St S ....Great Falls MT 59405	**800-856-9544***		166
*Admissions			
University of Puget Sound			
1500 N Warner St .... Tacoma WA 98416	**800-396-7191**	253-879-3100	166
University of Redlands			
1200 E Colton Ave PO Box 3080 .... Redlands CA 92373	**800-455-5064**	909-793-2121	166
University of Regina			
3737 Wascana Pkwy .... Regina SK S4S0A2	**800-644-4756**	306-585-4111	780
University of Richmond			
28 Westhampton Way .... Richmond VA 23173	**800-700-1662**	804-289-8000	166
Westhampton College			
28 Westhampton Way			
....................University Of Richmond VA 23173	**800-700-1662**	804-289-8000	166
University of Rio Grande			
218 N College Ave ....Rio Grande OH 45674	**800-282-7201**		166
University of Rochester			
252 Elmwood Ave ....Rochester NY 14627	**888-822-2256***	585-275-2121	166
*Admissions			
University of Rochester School of Medicine & Dentistry			
601 Elmwood Ave ....Rochester NY 14642	**888-661-6162**	585-275-0017	167-2
University of Saint Francis			
180 Remsen St ....Brooklyn Heights NY 11201	**800-356-8329**	718-522-2300	166
University of Saint Mary			
4100 S Fourth St .... Leavenworth KS 66048	**800-752-7043**	913-682-5151	166
University of Saint Thomas			
3800 Montrose Blvd ....Houston TX 77006	**800-856-8565**	713-522-7911	166
University of Saint Thomas			
2115 Summit Ave .... Saint Paul MN 55105	**800-328-6819**	651-962-5000	166
University of Saint Thomas O'Shaughnessy-Frey Library			
2115 Summit Ave .... Saint Paul MN 55105	**800-328-6819**	651-962-5494	433-6
University of Saint Thomas School of Law			
1000 LaSalle Ave ....Minneapolis MN 55403	**800-328-6819**	651-962-4892	167-1
University of San Diego			
5998 Alcala Pk .... San Diego CA 92110	**800-248-4873**	619-260-4600	166
University of San Diego School of Law			
5998 Alcala Pk .... San Diego CA 92110	**800-248-4873**	619-260-4528	167-1
University of San Francisco			
2130 Fulton St .... San Francisco CA 94117	**800-854-1385***	415-422-5555	166
*Admissions			
University of Saskatchewan			
1121 College Dr .... Saskatoon SK S7N0W3	**877-653-8501**	306-966-8970	167-3
Saint Thomas More College			
1437 College Dr .... Saskatoon SK S7N0W6	**800-667-2019**	306-966-8900	780
University of Sciences & Arts of Oklahoma			
1727 W Alabama Ave .... Chickasha OK 73018	**800-933-8726**	405-224-3140	166
University of Scranton			
800 Linden St St Thomas Hall .... Scranton PA 18510	**888-727-2686**	570-941-7400	166
University of Sioux Falls			
1101 W 22nd St ....Sioux Falls SD 57105	**800-888-1047**	605-331-6600	166
University of South Alabama			
2500 Meisler Hall ....Mobile AL 36688	**800-872-5247**	251-460-6141	166
University of South Carolina			
1601 Greene St ....Columbia SC 29208	**800-868-5872**	803-777-7000	166
Aiken			
471 University Pkwy .... Aiken SC 29801	**866-254-2366**	803-648-6851	166
Beaufort			
801 Carteret St ....Beaufort SC 29902	**866-455-4753**	843-521-4100	166
Sumter 200 Miller Rd ....Sumter SC 29150	**888-872-7868**	803-775-8727	166
Union 401 E Main St ....Union SC 29379	**800-768-5566**	864-429-8728	162
Upstate			
800 University Way ....Spartanburg SC 29303	**800-277-8727**	864-503-5246	166
University of South Carolina Press			
1600 Hampton St 5th Fl ....Columbia SC 29208	**800-768-2500***	803-777-5243	633-4
*Orders			
University of South Dakota			
414 E Clark St .... Vermillion SD 57069	**877-269-6837**	605-677-5341	166
University of South Dakota Foundation			
1110 N Dakota St PO Box 5555 .... Vermillion SD 57069	**800-521-3575**	605-677-6703	781
University of South Dakota School of Law			
414 E Clark St .... Vermillion SD 57069	**877-269-6837**	605-677-5443	167-1
University of South Florida			
Sarasota-Manatee			
8350 N Tamiami Trl ....Sarasota FL 34243	**866-974-1222**	941-359-4200	166
University of Southern California			
Doheny Memorial Library			
3550 Trousdale Pkwy			
University Pk Campus ....Los Angeles CA 90089	**800-775-7330**	213-740-4039	433-6
University of Southern Indiana			
8600 University Blvd .... Evansville IN 47712	**800-467-1965**	812-464-1765	166
University of Southern Maine			
96 Falmouth St ....Portland ME 04103	**800-800-4876**	207-780-4141	166
Gorham 37 College Ave .... Gorham ME 04038	**800-800-4876**	207-780-5670	166
Lewiston-Auburn College			
51 Westminster St .... Lewiston ME 04240	**800-800-4876**	207-753-6500	166
University of Southern Maine Arboretum			
PO Box 9300 ....Portland ME 04104	**800-800-4876**		97
University of Southern Mississippi			
118 College Dr .... Hattiesburg MS 39406	**800-446-0892**	601-266-1000	166
University of St Francis			
500 Wilcox St .... Joliet IL 60435	**800-735-7500**		166
University of Tennessee			
Chattanooga			
615 McCallie Ave ....Chattanooga TN 37403	**800-882-6627**	423-425-4111	166
Martin			
554 University St .... Martin TN 38238	**800-829-8861**	731-881-7020	166
University of Tennessee Health Science Ctr			
Health Sciences Library & Biocommunications Ctr			
877 Madison Ave ....Memphis TN 38103	**877-747-0004**	901-448-5634	433-1
University of Tennessee Knoxville			
Hodges Library			
1015 Volunteer Blvd ....Knoxville TN 37996	**800-426-9119**	865-974-4351	433-6
University of Texas			
Dallas			
International Ctr 800 W Campbell Rd SSB34			
...............................Richardson TX 75080	**800-889-2443**	972-883-4189	166
Ex-Student's Association			
2110 San Jacinto Blvd .... Austin TX 78712	**866-974-7220**	512-840-5700	
Permian Basin			
4901 E University Blvd ....Odessa TX 79762	**866-552-8872***	432-552-2020	166
*Admissions			
San Antonio			
6900 N Loop 1604 W ....San Antonio TX 78249	**800-669-0919**	210-458-4011	166
Tyler			
3900 University Blvd ....Tyler TX 75799	**800-888-9537**	903-566-7000	166
University of Texas Medical Branch			
301 University Blvd ....Galveston TX 77555	**800-228-1841**	409-772-2618	167-2
University of Texas Medical Branch Hospitals			
301 University Blvd ....Galveston TX 77555	**800-201-0527**	409-772-1011	373-3
University of Texas Press			
3001 Lake Austin Blvd			
2-200 Stop E4800..................... Austin TX 78703	**800-252-3206***	512-471-7233	633-4
*Sales			
University of Texas Southwestern Medical Ctr at Dallas Library, The			
5323 Harry Hines Blvd .... Dallas TX 75390	**866-645-6455**	214-648-2001	433-1
University of Texas Southwestern Medical Ctr Dallas			
Hematopoietic Cell Transplant Program			
5323 Harry Hines Blvd ....Dallas TX 75390	**866-645-6455**	214-648-3111	764
Southwestern Medical School			
5323 Harry Hines Blvd ....Dallas TX 75390	**866-648-2455**	214-648-3111	167-2
University of Texas System			
601 Colorado St .... Austin TX 78701	**866-882-2034**	512-499-4200	781
University of the Arts			
320 S Broad St ....Philadelphia PA 19102	**800-616-2787**	215-717-6049	164
University of the Cumberlands			
6178 College Station Dr ....Williamsburg KY 40769	**800-343-1609**	606-539-4201	166
University of the Incarnate Word			
4301 Broadway St Ste 285 ....San Antonio TX 78209	**800-749-9673***	210-829-6000	166
*Admissions			
University of the Ozarks			
415 N College Ave .... Clarksville AR 72830	**800-264-8636***	479-979-1227	166
*Admissions			
University of the Pacific			
3601 Pacific Ave .... Stockton CA 95211	**800-959-2867**	209-946-2211	166
University of the Sciences in Philadelphia			
600 S 43rd St ....Philadelphia PA 19104	**888-857-6264**	215-596-8800	166
University of the South			
735 University Ave .... Sewanee TN 37383	**800-522-2234**	931-598-1238	166
University of Toledo			
2801 W Bancroft .... Toledo OH 43606	**800-586-5336**	419-530-4636	166
University of Toledo Carlson Library			
2801 W Bancroft MS 507............... Toledo OH 43606	**800-586-5336**	419-530-2324	433-6

Alphabetical Section

				Toll-Free	Phone	Class
University of Toledo Medical Center, The (PCGH)						
7007 Powers Blvd	Parma	OH	44129	855-292-4292	440-743-3000	373-3
University of Toledo Medical Center, The						
3000 Arlington Ave	Toledo	OH	43614	800-586-5336	419-383-4000	373-3
University of Tulsa						
800 S Tucker Rd	Tulsa	OK	74104	800-331-3050	918-631-2307	166
University of Utah Hospital						
Miner's Hospital						
50 N Medical Dr Rm 1B295	Salt Lake City	UT	84132	800-824-2073*	866-864-6377	764
*General						
University of Utah School of Medicine						
30 N 1900 E	Salt Lake City	UT	84132	844-988-7284	801-581-7201	167-2
University of Vermont						
85 S Prospect St	Burlington	VT	05405	800-499-0113	802-656-3131	166
University of Vermont College of Medicine						
89 Beaumont Ave						
E-126 Given Bldg	Burlington	VT	05405	800-571-0668	802-656-2156	167-2
University of Vermont Medical Center, The (FAHC)						
111 Colchester Ave	Burlington	VT	05401	800-358-1144	802-847-0000	373-3
University of Virginia Health System						
1215 Lee St	Charlottesville	VA	22908	800-251-3627	434-924-0211	373-3
University of Virginia Press						
210 Sprigg Ln						
PO Box 400318	Charlottesville	VA	22904	800-831-3406*	434-924-3469	633-4
*Orders						
University of Virginia School of Law						
580 Massie Rd	Charlottesville	VA	22903	877-307-0158	434-924-7354	167-1
University of Virginia's College at Wise						
1 College Ave	Wise	VA	24293	888-282-9324*	276-328-0102	166
*Admissions						
University of Washington School of Law						
William H Gates Hall						
PO Box 353020	Seattle	WA	98195	866-866-0158	206-543-4078	167-1
University of West Alabama						
100 US 11	Livingston	AL	35470	888-636-8800*		166
*Admissions						
University of West Florida Center for Fine & Performing Arts						
11000 University Pkwy Bldg 82	Pensacola	FL	32514	800-263-1074	850-474-2000	568
University of Wisconsin (UWEC)						
Eau Claire						
Schofield Hall 111 105 Garfield Ave						
	Eau Claire	WI	54701	800-949-8932	715-836-5415	166
La Crosse						
328 Front St	La Crosse	WI	54601	800-382-2150	608-785-8000	166
Madison						
702 W Johnson St Ste 1101	Madison	WI	53715	800-442-6459	608-262-3961	166
Marathon County						
518 S Seventh Ave	Wausau	WI	54401	888-367-8962	715-261-6100	162
Milwaukee						
PO Box 413	Milwaukee	WI	53201	800-442-6459	414-229-1122	166
Parkside 900 Wood Rd	Kenosha	WI	53141	800-742-2858	262-595-2345	166
Platteville						
1 University Plz	Platteville	WI	53818	800-362-5515	608-342-1125	166
Richland						
1200 Hwy 14 W	Richland Center	WI	53581	800-947-3529	608-647-6186	162
Sheboygan						
1 University Dr	Sheboygan	WI	53081	800-442-6459*	920-459-6600	162
*Help Line						
Stout						
802 S Broadway	Menomonie	WI	54751	800-447-8688*	715-232-1232	166
*Admissions						
Washington County						
400 S University Dr	West Bend	WI	53095	800-240-0276	262-335-5200	162
University of Wisconsin Eau Claire						
McIntyre Library						
105 Garfield Ave	Eau Claire	WI	54702	877-267-1384	715-836-3715	433-6
University of Wisconsin Hospital & Clinics						
600 Highland Ave	Madison	WI	53792	800-323-8942	608-263-6400	373-3
University of Wisconsin Law School						
975 Bascom Mall	Madison	WI	53706	866-301-1753	608-262-2240	167-1
University of Wisconsin Oshkosh						
Polk Library						
801 Elmwood Ave	Oshkosh	WI	54901	800-574-5041	920-424-4333	
University of Wisconsin System						
1220 Linden Dr						
1720 Van Hise Hall	Madison	WI	53706	800-442-6461	608-262-2321	781
University of Wyoming						
1000 E University Ave	Laramie	WY	82071	800-342-5996*	307-766-1121	166
*Admissions						
University of Wyoming Libraries						
1000 E University Ave Dept 3334	Laramie	WY	82071	800-442-6757	307-766-3190	433-6
University Park Mall						
6501 N Grape Rd	Mishawaka	IN	46545	877-746-6642	574-277-2223	458
University Place						
310 SW Lincoln St	Portland	OR	97201	866-845-4647	503-725-4926	378
University Press Books (UPB)						
2430 Bancroft Way	Berkeley	CA	94704	800-676-8722	510-548-0585	95
University Press of America						
4501 Forbes Blvd Ste 200	Lanham	MD	20706	800-462-6420	301-459-3366	633-2
University Press of Florida						
15 NW 15th St	Gainesville	FL	32603	800-226-3822*	352-392-1351	633-4
*Sales						
University Press of Kentucky						
663 S Limestone St	Lexington	KY	40508	800-537-5487*	859-257-8400	633-4
*Sales						
University Press of Mississippi						
3825 Ridgewood Rd	Jackson	MS	39211	800-737-7788	601-432-6205	633-4
University Press of New England (UPNE)						
1 Ct St Ste 250	Lebanon	NH	03766	800-421-1561*	603-448-1533	633-4
*Orders						
University Products Inc						
517 Main St	Holyoke	MA	01040	800-628-1912	413-532-3372	556
Univest Corp of Pennsylvania						
14 N Main St PO Box 64197	Souderton	PA	18964	877-723-5571		359-2
NASDAQ: UVSP						
Univex Corp						
3 Old Rockingham Rd	Salem	NH	03079	800-258-6358	603-893-6191	298
Uniweld Products Inc						
2850 Ravenswood Rd	Fort Lauderdale	FL	33312	800-323-2111	954-584-2000	806

				Toll-Free	Phone	Class
Uniworld Boutique River Cruise Collection						
17323 Ventura Blvd	Encino	CA	91316	800-257-2407	818-382-7820	221
Unlimited Systems Corp Inc						
9530 Padgett St	San Diego	CA	92126	800-275-6354	858-537-5010	173-3
UNM (University of New Mexico)						
1 University of New Mexico	Albuquerque	NM	87131	800-225-5866	505-277-0111	166
Unmetric Inc						
2001 Victoria Rd	Mundelein	IL	60060	855-558-5588		464
Uno Langmann Ltd						
2117 Granville St	Vancouver	BC	V6H3E9	800-730-8825	604-736-8825	42
UNOS (United Network for Organ Sharing)						
700 N Fourth St	Richmond	VA	23219	888-894-6361	804-782-4800	48-17
Unruh Fire						
100 Industrial Dr	Sedgwick	KS	67135	800-856-7080		
UnumProvident Corp						
1 Fountain Sq	Chattanooga	TN	37402	800-262-0018	423-294-1011	359-4
Unverferth Mfg Company Inc						
601 S Broad St	Kalida	OH	45853	800-322-6301	419-532-3121	273
UOP LLC						
25 E Algonquin Rd	Des Plaines	IL	60017	800-877-6184	847-391-2000	143
Office for Victims of Crime						
350 E 500 S Ste 200	Salt Lake City	UT	84111	800-621-7444	801-238-2360	
Up Communications Services LLC						
103 SE Atlantic St	Tullahoma	TN	37388	877-667-0968		392
Up With Paper						
6049 Hi-Tek Ct	Mason	OH	45040	800-852-7677	513-759-7473	130
Up With People						
6830 Broadway	Denver	CO	80221	877-264-8856	303-460-7100	48-15
UPB (University Press Books)						
2430 Bancroft Way	Berkeley	CA	94704	800-676-8722	510-548-0585	95
Upchurch Scientific Inc						
619 Oak St	Oak Harbor	WA	98277	800-426-0191	360-679-2528	418
UpCurve Cloud						
10801 National blvd 410						
Ste 410	Los Angeles	CA	90064	888-898-4787		196
UpCurve Cloud						
2815 Manor Rd Ste 201	Austin	TX	78722	800-775-8378		
UPI Energy LP						
105 Silvercreek Pkwy N Ste 200	Guelph	ON	N1H8M1	800-396-2667	519-821-2667	324
Upland Software Inc						
Frost Tower 401 Congress Ave						
Ste 2950	Austin	TX	78701	855-944-7526		782
UPMC (University of Pittsburgh Medical Ctr)						
Horizon						
110 N Main St	Greenville	PA	16125	888-447-1122	724-588-2100	373-3
UPMC Pinnacle Lancaster						
250 College Ave	Lancaster	PA	17603	877-456-9617	717-291-8211	373-3
UPMC Pinnacle Memorial						
325 S Belmont St	York	PA	17405	800-436-4326	717-843-8623	373-3
UPMC Presbyterian						
200 Lothrop St	Pittsburgh	PA	15213	877-986-9862	412-647-8762	373-3
UPNE (University Press of New England)						
1 Ct St Ste 250	Lebanon	NH	03766	800-421-1561*	603-448-1533	633-4
*Orders						
Upper Cumberland Electric Membership Corp						
138 Gordonsville Hwy	South Carthage	TN	37030	800-261-2940	615-735-2940	245
Upper Deck Co LLC						
5909 Sea Otter Pl	Carlsbad	CA	92010	800-873-7332*		757
*Cust Svc						
Upper Iowa University						
605 Washington St PO Box 1857	Fayette	IA	52142	800-553-4150*	563-425-5200	166
*Admissions						
Upper Room Chapel & Museum						
1908 Grand Ave	Nashville	TN	37212	800-972-0433	615-340-7200	517
Upper Valley Medical Ctr (UVMC)						
3130 N County Rd 25-A	Troy	OH	45373	866-608-3463	937-440-4000	373-3
UPS (United Parcel Service Inc)						
55 Glenlake Pkwy NE	Atlanta	GA	30328	800-742-5877*	404-828-6000	542
NYSE: UPS ■ *Cust Svc						
UPS Capital Business Credit						
35 Glenlake Pkwy NE	Atlanta	GA	30328	877-263-8772		70
UPS Store, The						
6060 Cornerstone Ct W	San Diego	CA	92121	800-789-4623	858-455-8800	310
UPS Strategic Enterprise Fund						
55 Glenlake Pkwy NE						
Bldg 1 4th Fl	Atlanta	GA	30328	800-742-5877		787
UPS Supply Chain Solutions						
12380 Morris Rd	Alpharetta	GA	30005	800-742-5727	913-693-6151	447
Upsher-Smith Laboratories Inc						
6701 Evenstad Dr	Maple Grove	MN	55369	800-654-2299	763-315-2000	578
Upstate New York Transplant Services Inc						
110 Broadway	Buffalo	NY	14203	800-227-4771	716-853-6667	269
Upstate Pharmacy Ltd						
1900 N America Dr	West Seneca	NY	14224	800-314-4655	716-675-3784	
Upstate Shredding LLC						
1 Recycle Dr Tioga Industrial Pk	Owego	NY	13827	800-245-3133	607-687-7777	682
Upton County Sheriff						
PO Box 27	Rankin	TX	79778	800-680-9052	432-693-2422	337
Urania Engineering Company Inc						
198 S Poplar St	Hazleton	PA	18201	800-533-1985	570-455-7531	349
Urban Alternative						
PO Box 4000	Dallas	TX	75208	800-800-3222	214-943-3868	48-20
Urban Barn Ltd						
4085 Marine Way Ste 1	Burnaby	BC	V5J5E2	844-456-2200	604-456-2200	321
Urban Decay						
833 W 16th St	Newport Beach	CA	92663	800-784-8722		214
Urban Institute						
2100 M St NW	Washington	DC	20037	866-518-3874	202-833-7200	630
Urban Land Institute (ULI)						
1025 Thomas Jefferson St NW						
Ste 500W	Washington	DC	20007	800-321-5011*	202-624-7000	48-8
*Orders						
Urban Outfitters Inc						
30 Industrial Pk Blvd	Trenton	SC	29847	800-282-2200		157-4
Urban Web Design						
102-19 Dallas Rd	Victoria	BC	V8V5A6	877-889-2573	250-380-1296	225
Urologix Inc						
14405 21st Ave N	Minneapolis	MN	55447	800-475-1403	763-475-1400	474

	Toll-Free	Phone	Class
Ursinus College			
601 E Main St PO Box 1000 .... Collegeville PA 19426	**877-448-3282**	610-409-3200	166
Ursula of Switzerland Inc			
31 Mohawk Ave .... Waterford NY 12188	**800-826-4041**		155-20
Ursuline College			
2550 Lander Rd .... Pepper Pike OH 44124	**888-778-5463**	440-449-4200	166
Us Adventure Rv			
5120 N Brady St .... Davenport IA 52806	**877-768-4678**		23
US Air Force Academy (USAFA)			
2304 Cadet Dr			
Ste 3100 .... Air Force Academy CO 80840	**800-443-9266**	719-333-1110	496
US Airconditioning Distributors			
16900 Chestnut St .... City of Industry CA 91748	**800-937-7222**		608
US Alliance Federal Credit Union			
411 Theodore Fremd Ave Ste 350 .... Rye NY 10580	**800-431-2754**		219
US Apple Assn			
8233 Old Courthouse Rd Ste 200 .... Vienna VA 22182	**800-781-4443**	703-442-8850	48-2
US Army War College			
122 Forbes Ave .... Carlisle PA 17013	**800-453-0992**	717-245-3131	339-4
Us Art Company Inc			
66 Pacella Park Dr .... Randolph MA 02368	**800-872-7826**		519
US Bancorp			
800 Nicollet Mall .... Minneapolis MN 55402	**800-872-2657**	651-466-3000	359-2
NYSE: USB			
US Bankruptcy Court			
Alaska			
605 W Fourth Ave Ste 138 .... Anchorage AK 99501	**800-859-8059**	907-271-2655	340-1
Arizona			
230 N First Ave Ste 101 .... Phoenix AZ 85003	**800-556-9230**	602-682-4000	340-1
Arkansas			
300 W Second St .... Little Rock AR 72201	**800-676-6856**	501-918-5500	340-1
California Southern			
325 W F St .... San Diego CA 92101	**800-676-6856**	619-557-5620	340-1
Connecticut			
450 Main St 7th Fl .... Hartford CT 06103	**800-676-6856**	860-240-3675	340-1
Eastern District of Washington			
904 W Riverside Ave Ste 304 .... Spokane WA 99201	**800-519-2549**	509-458-5300	340-1
Florida Northern			
110 E Park Ave Ste 100 .... Tallahassee FL 32301	**888-765-1752**	850-521-5001	340-1
Georgia Northern			
75 Spring St SW .... Atlanta GA 30303	**800-676-6856**	404-215-1000	340-1
Georgia Southern			
125 Bull St .... Savannah GA 31401	**800-676-6856**	912-650-4100	340-1
Louisiana Eastern			
500 Poydras St Ste B-601 .... New Orleans LA 70130	**800-676-6856**	504-589-7878	340-1
Louisiana Western			
300 Fannin St Ste 2201 .... Shreveport LA 71101	**866-721-2105**	318-676-4267	340-1
Michigan Eastern			
211 W Fort St Ste 1820 .... Detroit MI 48226	**800-676-6856**	313-234-0065	340-1
Michigan Western			
1 Div Ave N Rm 200 .... Grand Rapids MI 49503	**800-859-7375**	616-456-2693	340-1
Minnesota			
300 S Fourth St			
301 US Courthouse .... Minneapolis MN 55415	**866-260-7337**	612-664-5260	340-1
Missouri Eastern			
111 S Tenth St 4th Fl .... Saint Louis MO 63102	**866-803-9517**	314-244-4500	340-1
Montana 400 N Main St .... Butte MT 59701	**888-888-2530**	406-497-1240	340-1
New York Eastern			
271 Cadman Plz E .... Brooklyn NY 11201	**800-676-6856**	347-394-1700	340-1
Northern District of Iowa			
111 Seventh Ave SE 6th Fl .... Cedar Rapids IA 52401	**866-222-8029**	319-286-2200	340-1
Oklahoma Western			
215 Dean A McGee Ave .... Oklahoma City OK 73102	**800-676-6856**	405-609-5700	340-1
Oregon			
1001 SW Fifth Ave Ste 700 .... Portland OR 97204	**800-676-6856**	503-326-1500	340-1
Pennsylvania Middle			
197 S Main St .... Wilkes-Barre PA 18701	**877-298-2053**	570-831-2500	340-1
Pennsylvania Western			
5414 US Steel Tower			
600 Grant St .... Pittsburgh PA 15219	**800-676-6856**	412-644-2700	340-1
Puerto Rico			
300 Recinto Sur St .... San Juan PR 00901	**866-222-8029**	787-977-6000	340-1
Tennessee Western			
200 Jefferson Ave Ste 413 .... Memphis TN 38103	**800-406-0190**	901-328-3500	340-1
Texas Northern			
1100 Commerce St Rm 1254 .... Dallas TX 75242	**800-442-6850**	214-753-2000	340-1
West Virginia Southern			
300 Virginia St E Rm 3200 .... Charleston WV 25301	**800-685-1111**	304-347-3003	340-1
Wisconsin Eastern			
US Federal Courthouse			
517 E Wisconsin Ave Rm 126 ...... Milwaukee WI 53202	**877-781-7277**	414-297-3291	340-1
Wyoming			
2120 Capitol Ave Ste 6004 .... Cheyenne WY 82001	**800-676-6856**	307-433-2200	340-1
US Beverage Net Inc			
225 W Jefferson St .... Syracuse NY 13202	**888-298-3641**		296
US Biathlon Assn			
49 Pineland Dr Ste 301-A ...... New Gloucester ME 04260	**800-242-8456***	207-688-6500	48-22
General			
US Bronze Sign Co			
811 Second Ave .... New Hyde Park NY 11040	**800-872-5155**	516-352-5155	772
US Button Corp			
328 Kennedy Dr .... Putnam CT 06260	**800-243-1842**	860-928-2707	590
US Catholic Magazine			
205 W Monroe .... Chicago IL 60606	**800-328-6515***	312-236-7782	455-18
Cust Svc			
US Cellular Corp (USCC)			
8410 W Bryn Mawr Ave Ste 700 .... Chicago IL 60631	**888-944-9400**	773-399-8900	731
NYSE: USM			
US Census Bureau Regional Offices			
Atlanta			
101 Marietta St NW Ste 3200 .... Atlanta GA 30303	**800-424-6974**	404-730-3832	339-2
Boston			
4 Copley Pl Ste 301 .... Boston MA 02117	**800-562-5721**	617-424-4501	339-2
Chicago			
1111 W 22nd St Ste 400 ...... Oak Brook IL 60523	**800-865-6384**	630-288-9200	339-2
Denver			
6950 W Jefferson Ave Ste 250 .... Lakewood CO 80235	**800-852-6159**	303-264-0202	339-2
Los Angeles			
15350 Sherman Way Ste 400 ...... Van Nuys CA 91406	**800-992-3530**	818-267-1700	339-2
New York			
32 Old Slip 9th Fl .... New York NY 10005	**800-991-2520**	212-584-3400	339-2
Philadelphia			
100 S Independence Mall W			
Ste 410 .... Philadelphia PA 19106	**800-262-4236**	215-717-1800	339-2
US Chamber of Commerce			
1615 H St NW .... Washington DC 20062	**800-638-6582**	202-659-6000	140
US Chemical & Plastics			
600 Nova Dr SE .... Massillon OH 44646	**800-321-0672**	330-830-6000	60
US Chess Federation			
PO Box 3967 .... Crossville TN 38557	**800-903-8723***	931-787-1234	455-14
Sales			
US Chrome Corp			
175 Garfield Ave .... Stratford CT 06615	**800-637-9019**		479
US Citizenship & Immigration Services Regional Offices			
70 Kimball Ave .... South Burlington VT 05403	**800-767-1833**		339-10
US Coachways Inc			
100 St Mary's Ave Ste 2B .... Staten Island NY 10305	**800-359-5991**	718-477-4242	440
US Coast Guard			
Law Enforcement Office			
2100 Second St SW .... Washington DC 20593	**800-982-8813**		339-10
National Maritime Ctr			
100 Forbes Dr .... Martinsburg WV 25404	**888-427-5662**	304-433-3400	339-10
US Coast Guard Academy			
15 Mohegan Ave .... New London CT 06320	**800-883-8724**	860-444-8444	166
US Coast Guard Air Station Detroit			
1461 N Perimeter Rd			
Selfridge ANGB .... Selfridge MI 48045	**800-424-8802**	586-239-6700	158
US Commission on Civil Rights			
1331 Pennsylvania Ave NW			
Ste 1150 .... Washington DC 20425	**800-552-6843**	202-376-7700	339-19
US Commission on Civil Rights Regional Offices			
Central Regional Office			
400 State Ave Ste 908 .... Kansas City KS 66101	**800-552-6843**	913-551-1400	339-19
Eastern Regional Office			
624 Ninth St NW .... Washington DC 20425	**800-552-6843**	202-376-7700	339-19
Midwestern Regional Office			
55 W Monroe St Ste 410 .... Chicago IL 60603	**800-552-6843**	312-353-8311	339-19
Southern Regional Office			
61 Forsyth St SW Ste 1840 T .... Atlanta GA 30303	**800-552-6843**	404-562-7000	339-19
US Conference of Catholic Bishops (USCCB)			
3211 Fourth St NE .... Washington DC 20017	**866-582-0943**	202-541-3000	48-20
US Curling Assn (USCA)			
5525 Clem's Way .... Stevens Point WI 54482	**888-287-5377**	715-344-1199	48-22
US Customs & Border Protection			
1300 Pennsylvania Ave NW .... Washington DC 20229	**877-227-5511**	703-526-4200	339-10
US Dataworks Inc			
14090 SW Fwy Ste 300 .... Sugar Land TX 77478	**888-254-8821**	281-504-8000	178-10
OTC: UDWK			
US Department of Veterans Affairs			
Office of Research & Development			
810 Vermont Ave NW .... Washington DC 20420	**844-698-2311**	800-827-1000	339-18
US Dept of Labor Women's Bureau			
200 Constitution Ave NW			
Rm S-3002 .... Washington DC 20210	**800-827-5335**	202-693-6710	197
US Diamond Wheel Co			
101 Kendall Pt Dr .... Oswego IL 60543	**800-223-0457**	800-851-1095	498
US Digital Corp			
1400 NE 136th Ave .... Vancouver WA 98684	**800-736-0194**	360-260-2468	178-10
US Digital Media Inc			
1929 W Lone Cactus Dr .... Phoenix AZ 85027	**877-992-3766**	623-587-4900	543
US District Court Alabama Northern			
1729 Fifth Ave N .... Birmingham AL 35203	**800-676-6856**	205-278-1700	340-2
US District Court Colorado			
901 19th St .... Denver CO 80294	**800-359-8699**	303-844-3433	340-2
US District Court for the District of Alaska			
222 W Seventh Ave Ste 4 .... Anchorage AK 99513	**866-243-3814**	907-677-6100	340-2
US District Court Georgia Northern			
75 Spring St SW .... Atlanta GA 30303	**800-827-2982**	404-215-1600	340-2
US District Court Mississippi Southern			
501 E Court St Ste 2500 .... Jackson MS 39201	**866-517-7682**	601-965-4439	340-2
US District Court Missouri Western			
400 E Ninth St .... Kansas City MO 64106	**800-466-9302**	816-512-5000	340-2
US District Court Nebraska			
111 S 18th Plz Ste 1152 .... Omaha NE 68102	**866-220-4381**	402-661-7350	340-2
US District Court Nevada			
333 Las Vegas Blvd S .... Las Vegas NV 89101	**800-676-6856**	702-464-5400	340-2
US District Court North Carolina Western			
401 W Trade St .... Charlotte NC 28202	**866-851-1605**	704-350-7400	340-2
US District Court Northern District Of Florida			
111 N Adams St .... Tallahassee FL 32301	**800-676-6856**	850-521-3501	340-2
US District Court Ohio Northern			
801 W Superior Ave .... Cleveland OH 44113	**800-355-8498**	216-357-7000	340-2
US District Court Oklahoma Northern			
333 W Fourth St .... Tulsa OK 74103	**866-213-1957**	918-699-4700	340-2
US District Court Oklahoma Western			
200 NW Fourth St Rm 1210 .... Oklahoma City OK 73102	**888-609-6953**	405-609-5000	340-2
US District Court Vermont			
11 Elmwood Ave Rm 506 .... Burlington VT 05401	**800-837-8718**	802-951-6301	340-2
US Ecology			
300 E Mallard Dr Ste 300 .... Boise ID 83706	**800-590-5220**	208-331-8400	663
NASDAQ: ECOL			
US Election Assistance Commission			
1201 New York Ave NW Ste 300 ...... Washington DC 20005	**866-747-1471**	202-566-3100	339-19
US Energy Corp			
877 N Eigth W .... Riverton WY 82501	**800-776-9271**	307-856-9271	500
NASDAQ: USEG			
US Equestrian Federation Inc			
4047 Iron Works Pkwy .... Lexington KY 40511	**800-633-2472**	859-258-2472	48-22
US Farm Data Inc			
10824 Old Mill Rd Ste 8 .... Omaha NE 68154	**800-960-6267**		
US Figure Skating Assn (USFSA)			
20 First St .... Colorado Springs CO 80906	**800-332-9256**	719-635-5200	48-22
US Fish & Wildlife Service (USFWS)			
1849 C St NW .... Washington DC 20240	**800-344-9453**		339-12
US Fish & Wildlife Service Regional Offices			
Southeast Region			
1875 Century Blvd 3rd Fl .... Atlanta GA 30345	**800-364-4263**	404-679-4000	339-12

	Toll-Free	Phone	Class
US Fund for UNICEF 125 Maiden Ln .... New York NY 10038	800-367-5437		48-5
US General Services Administration (GSA) 1275 First St NW .... Washington DC 20405	800-424-5210	202-208-7642	339-19
US General Services Administration 1800 F St NW .... Washington DC 20405	800-488-3111		339-19
US Geological Survey (USGS) 12201 Sunrise Valley Dr ...... Reston VA 20192	888-275-8747	703-648-6723	339-12
Ask USGS 12201 Sunrise Valley Dr ...... Reston VA 20192	888-275-8747	703-648-5953	339-12
US Global Investors Inc 7900 Callaghan Rd .... San Antonio TX 78229 *NASDAQ: GROW*	800-873-8637	210-308-1234	400
US Golf Assn (USGA) 77 Liberty Corner Rd .... Far Hills NJ 07931 *Orders*	800-336-4446*	908-234-2300	48-22
US Government Printing Office Bookstore (GPO) 732 N Capitol St NW ...... Washington DC 20401	866-512-1800	202-512-1800	341
US Grant, The 326 Broadway .... San Diego CA 92101	866-716-8136	619-232-3121	378
US Health & Human Services Department *Region 9* 90 Seventh St Ste 4-100 ...... San Francisco CA 94103	800-368-1019		339-9
Us Health Connect Inc 500 Office Ctr Dr ...... Fort Washington PA 19034	800-889-4944		162
US Immigration & Customs Enforcement (ICE) 425 'I' St NW .... Washington DC 20536	866-347-2423		339-10
US Institute of Peace 2301 Constitution Ave NW ...... Washington DC 20037	800-868-8064	202-457-1700	339-19
US Lawns Inc 6700 Forum Dr Ste 150 ...... Orlando FL 32821	800-875-2967	407-246-1630	421
US Learning Inc 516 Tennessee St Ste 219 ...... Memphis TN 38103	800-647-9166	901-767-0000	760
US Legal Support Inc 363 N Sam Houston Pkwy E Ste 1200 .... Houston TX 77060	800-567-8757	713-653-7100	443
US Marshals Service 401 Courthouse Sq ...... Alexandria VA 22314 *General*	800-336-0102*	202-307-9100	339-13
US Merchant Marine Academy 300 Steamboat Rd ...... Kings Point NY 11024	866-546-4778	516-726-5800	166
Us Micro Corp 7000 HighInds Pkwy SE ...... Smyrna GA 30082	888-876-4276	770-437-0706	174
US Mint 801 Ninth St NW ...... Washington DC 20220 *Cust Svc*	800-872-6468*	202-354-7462	339-17
Denver 320 W Colfax Ave ...... Denver CO 80204	800-642-6116	303-405-4761	339-17
San Francisco 155 Hermann St ...... San Francisco CA 94102	800-872-6468	415-575-8000	339-17
West Point (NY) 1063 NY 218 ...... West Point NY 10996	800-872-6468	845-446-6200	339-17
US Naval Academy 121 Blake Rd ...... Annapolis MD 21402 *Admissions*	888-249-7707*	410-293-1000	496
US Naval Institute 291 Wood Rd ...... Annapolis MD 21402	800-233-8764	410-268-6110	48-19
US News & World Report 1050 Thomas Jefferson St NW ...... Washington DC 20007	800-836-6397	202-955-2000	455-17
US News University Connection LLC 9417 Princess Palm Ave ...... Tampa FL 33619	866-442-6587		386
US PAACC (US Pan Asian American Chamber of Commerce) 1329 18th St NW ...... Washington DC 20036	800-696-7818	202-296-5221	48-14
US Pan Asian American Chamber of Commerce (US PAACC) 1329 18th St NW ...... Washington DC 20036	800-696-7818	202-296-5221	48-14
US Parole Commission 5550 Friendship Blvd Rm 420 ...... Chevy Chase MD 20815	888-585-9103	202-346-7000	339-13
US Passports & International Travel *Chicago Passport Agency* 101 W Congress Pkwy 9th Fl ...... Chicago IL 60605	877-487-2778		339-15
San Francisco Passport Agency 450 Golden Gate Ave 3rd Fl Ste 3-2501 ...... San Francisco CA 94102	877-487-2778		339-15
US Pharmacist Magazine 160 Chubb Ave Ste 304 ...... Lyndhurst NJ 07071	800-825-4696		455-16
US Pharmacopeia (USP) 12601 Twinbrook Pkwy ...... Rockville MD 20852	800-227-8772	301-881-0666	49-8
US Physical Therapy 1300 W Sam Houston Pkwy S Ste 300 ...... Houston TX 77042 *NYSE: USPH*	800-580-6285	713-297-7000	351
US Pipe & Foundry Co 2 Chase Corporate Dr Ste 200 ...... Birmingham AL 35244	866-347-7473		307
US Plastic Corp 1390 Newbrecht Rd ...... Lima OH 45801	800-537-9724	419-228-2242	199
US Postal Service (USPS) 475 L'Enfant Plz W SW ...... Washington DC 20260 *Cust Svc*	800-275-8777*	202-268-2000	339-19
Us Postal Service Federal Credit Union 7905 Malcolm Rd Ste 311 ...... Clinton MD 20735	800-877-7328	301-856-5000	
US Premium Beef LLC (USPB) 12200 N Ambassador Dr PO Box 20103 ...... Kansas City MO 64163	866-877-2525	816-713-8800	296-26
US Professional Tennis Assn (USPTA) 11961 Performance Dr ...... Orlando FL 32827	800-877-8248		48-22
US Ring Binder 6800 Arsenal St ...... Saint Louis MO 63139	800-888-8772	314-645-7880	86
US Robotics Corp 1300 E Woodfield Dr Ste 506 ...... Schaumburg IL 60173	877-710-0884	847-874-2000	173-3
US Rowing Assn 2 Wall St ...... Princeton NJ 08540	800-314-4769	609-924-1578	48-22
US Rubber Corp 211 E Loop 336 ...... Conroe TX 77301	800-872-3587		
US Sailing Assn 15 Maritime Dr PO Box 1260 ...... Portsmouth RI 02871	800-877-2451	401-683-0800	48-22
US Security Assoc Inc 200 Mansell Ct 5th Fl ...... Roswell GA 30076	800-730-9599	770-625-1500	689
US Shipping Corp 399 Thornall St 8th Fl ...... Edison NJ 08837	866-942-6592	732-635-1500	312
US Silica Co 8490 Progress Dr Ste 300 ...... Frederick MD 21701	800-243-7500	304-258-2500	501-4
US Special Delivery Inc 821 E Blvd ...... Kingsford MI 49802	800-821-6389	906-774-1931	681
US Synchronized Swimming 1 Olympic Plz ...... Colorado Springs CO 80909	800-775-8762	317-237-5700	48-22
US Tool Grinding Inc 2000 Progress Dr ...... Farmington MO 63640	800-222-1771	573-431-3856	453
US Trotting Assn (USTA) 750 Michigan Ave ...... Columbus OH 43215	877-800-8782	614-224-2291	48-22
US Tsubaki Inc 301 E Marquardt Dr ...... Wheeling IL 60090	800-323-7790	847-459-9500	616
US Vision Inc 1 Harmon Dr Glen Oaks Industrial Pk. ...... Glendora NJ 08029	866-435-7111	856-228-1000	539
US WorldMeds LLC 4010 Dupont Cir Ste L-07 ...... Louisville KY 40207	888-900-8796	502-815-8000	238
US Xpress Enterprises Inc 4080 Jenkins Rd ...... Chattanooga TN 37421	800-251-6291	423-510-3000	775
US. Bankcard Services Inc 17171 E Gale Ave Ste 110 ...... City Of Industry CA 91745	888-888-8872		251
US. Department of Education *Office of Career, Technical, and Adult Education* 550 12th St SW 11th Fl ...... Washington DC 20202	800-872-5327	202-245-7700	339-7
US. Department of Veterans Affairs 325 E 'H' St ...... Iron Mountain MI 49801	800-215-8262	906-774-3300	373-8
US. Eagle Federal Credit Union (USNMFCU) 3939 Osuna Rd NE PO Box 129 ...... Albuquerque NM 87109	888-342-8766	505-342-8888	219
US. Energy Development Corp 2350 N Forest Rd ...... Getzville NY 14068	800-636-7606	716-636-0401	536
US. Facilities Inc 30 N 41 St Ste 400 ...... Philadelphia PA 19104	800-236-6241		192
US. Fleet Forces Command 1562 Mitscher Ave Ste 250 ...... Norfolk VA 23551	800-473-3549	757-836-3630	495-4
US. Kids Golf LLC 3040 Northwoods Pkwy ...... Norcross GA 30071	888-387-5437	770-441-3077	707
US. National Ski Hall of Fame 610 Palms Ave ...... Ishpeming MI 49849	800-648-0720	906-485-6323	519
US. Quality Furniture Services Inc 8920 Winkler Dr ...... Houston TX 77017	800-774-8700		321
USA 800 Inc 9808 E 66th Terr ...... Kansas City MO 64133	800-821-7539	816-358-1303	732
USA Baby 793 Springer Dr ...... Lombard IL 60148	800-767-9464	630-652-0600	321
USA Baseball 403 Blackwell St ...... Durham NC 27701	855-420-5910	919-474-8721	48-22
USA Basketball 5465 Mark Dabling Blvd ...... Colorado Springs CO 80918	888-284-5383	719-590-4800	48-22
USA Communications 124 Main St PO Box 389 ...... Shellsburg IA 52332	800-248-8007	319-436-2224	116
USA Communications Inc 920 E 56th St Ste B. ...... Kearney NE 68847	877-234-0102		386
USA Container Company Inc 1776 S Second St ...... Piscataway NJ 08854	888-752-7722		198
USA for UNHCR 1775 K St NW Ste 580 ...... Washington DC 20006	800-770-1100	202-296-1115	48-5
USA Gymnastics 201 S Capitol Ave Ste 300 ...... Indianapolis IN 46225	800-345-4719	317-237-5050	48-22
USA Hockey 1775 Bob Johnson Dr ...... Colorado Springs CO 80906	800-566-3288	800-383-1379	48-22
USA Risk Group Inc 2418 Airport Rd Ste 2A. ...... Barre VT 05641	800-872-7475		461
USA Swimming 1 Olympic Plz ...... Colorado Springs CO 80909	800-356-2722	719-866-4578	48-22
USA Technologies Inc 100 Deerfield Ln Ste 140 ...... Malvern PA 19355	800-633-0340		251
USA Today 7950 Jones Branch Dr ...... McLean VA 22108 *Cust Svc*	800-872-0001*	703-854-3400	528-3
USA Track & Field Inc (USATF) 132 E Washington St Ste 800 ...... Indianapolis IN 46204	800-222-8733	317-261-0500	48-22
USA Water Polo 2124 Main St Ste 240 ...... Huntington Beach CA 92648	888-712-2166	714-500-5445	48-22
USA Water Ski 1251 Holy Cow Rd ...... Polk City FL 33868	800-533-2972	863-324-4341	48-22
USA Workers Injury Network 1250 S Capital of Texas Hwy Bldg 3 Ste 500 ...... Austin TX 78746 *Cust Svc*	800-872-0020*		390-4
USAA (United Services Automobile Assn) 10750 McDermott Fwy ...... San Antonio TX 78288	800-531-8722		185
USAA (USAA Life Insurance Co) 9800 Fredericksburg Rd ...... San Antonio TX 78288	800-531-8000	210-531-8722	390-2
USAA FSB (USAAFSB) 10750 McDermott Fwy ...... San Antonio TX 78288	800-531-8722		70
USAA Investment Management 9800 Fredericksburg Rd PO Box 659453. ...... San Antonio TX 78288	800-531-8722		400
USAA Life Insurance Co (USAA) 9800 Fredericksburg Rd ...... San Antonio TX 78288	800-531-8000	210-531-8722	390-2
USAA Property & Casualty Insurance Group 9800 Fredericksburg Rd ...... San Antonio TX 78288	800-531-8722	210-531-8722	390-4
USAA Real Estate Co 9830 Colonnade Blvd Ste 600 ...... San Antonio TX 78230	800-531-8182		651
USAAFSB (USAA FSB) 10750 McDermott Fwy ...... San Antonio TX 78288	800-531-8722		70
USAFA (US Air Force Academy) 2304 Cadet Dr Ste 3100 ...... Air Force Academy CO 80840	800-443-9266	719-333-1110	496
USAFact Inc 6240 Box Springs Blvd ...... Riverside CA 92507	800-547-0263	951-656-7800	260
USANA Health Sciences Inc 3838 West PkwyBlvd ...... Salt Lake City UT 84120 *NYSE: USNA*	888-950-9595	801-954-7100	794

Alphabetical Section

Listing	Toll-Free	Phone	Class
US-Analytics 600 E Las Colinas Blvd Ste 2222 ....Irving TX 75039 *General	877-828-8727*	214-630-0081	180
USATF (USA Track & Field Inc) 132 E Washington St Ste 800 ....Indianapolis IN 46204	800-222-8733	317-261-0500	48-22
U-Save Auto Rental of America Inc 1052 Highland Colony Pkwy Ste 204 ....Ridgeland MS 39157 *General	800-438-2300*	601-713-4333	126
USB (United Soybean Board) 16305 Swingley Ridge Rd Ste 150 ....Chesterfield MO 63017	800-989-8721	636-530-1777	48-2
USC Consulting Group LLC 3000 Bayport Dr Ste 1010 ....Tampa FL 33607	800-888-8872		196
USCA (US Curling Assn) 5525 Clem's Way ....Stevens Point WI 54482	888-287-5377	715-344-1199	48-22
USCC (US Cellular Corp) 8410 W Bryn Mawr Ave Ste 700 ....Chicago IL 60631 NYSE: USM	888-944-9400	773-399-8900	731
USCCB (US Conference of Catholic Bishops) 3211 Fourth St NE ....Washington DC 20017	866-582-0943	202-541-3000	48-20
USDA (Department of Agriculture) 1400 Independence Ave SW ....Washington DC 20250	844-433-2774	202-720-3631	339-1
USDiagnostics Inc 2 Parade St ....Huntsville AL 35806	888-669-4337	256-534-4881	
USDM Life Sciences 535 Chapala St ....Santa Barbara CA 93101	888-231-0816		180
USDTL (United States Drug Testing Laboratories) 1700 S Mt Prospect Rd ....Des Plaines IL 60018	800-235-2367	847-375-0770	415
Used-Car-Partscom Inc 1980 Highland Pk ....Fort Wright KY 41017	800-288-7415	859-344-1925	224
USENIX Assn 2560 Ninth St Ste 215 ....Berkeley CA 94710	800-397-3342	510-528-8649	48-9
USFS (Forest Service) 1400 Independence Ave SW ....Washington DC 20050	800-832-1355	202-205-8333	339-1
USFSA (US Figure Skating Assn) 20 First St ....Colorado Springs CO 80906	800-332-9256	719-635-5200	48-22
USFWS (US Fish & Wildlife Service) 1849 C St NW ....Washington DC 20240	800-344-9453		339-12
USG Corp 550 W Adams St ....Chicago IL 60661 NYSE: USG	800-874-4968	312 436-4000	340
USGA (US Golf Assn) 77 Liberty Corner Rd ....Far Hills NJ 07931 *Orders	800-336-4446*	908-234-2300	48-22
USGS (US Geological Survey) 12201 Sunrise Valley Dr ....Reston VA 20192	888-275-8747	703-648-6723	339-12
USGS Education USGS National Ctr 12201 Sunrise Vly Dr ....Reston VA 20192	800-228-0975	703-648-5953	
USHEALTH Group Inc 300 Burnett St Ste 200 ....Fort Worth TX 76102	800-387-9027		390-6
Usherwood Office Technology Inc 1005 W Fayette St ....Syracuse NY 13204	800-724-2119	315-472-0050	41
Ushio America Inc 5440 Cerritos Ave ....Cypress CA 90630	800-326-1960	714-236-8600	436
uShip Inc 205 E Riverside Dr ....Austin TX 78704	800-698-7447		386
USIS (United States Information Systems Inc) 35 W Jefferson Ave ....Pearl River NY 10965	866-222-3778	845-358-7755	782
USL Pharma 301 S Cherokee St ....Denver CO 80223	800-654-2299	303-607-4500	579
USM Inc 1700 Markley St 100 ....Norristown PA 19401	800-355-4000		186
USNMFCU (US. Eagle Federal Credit Union) 3939 Osuna Rd NE PO Box 129 ....Albuquerque NM 87109	888-342-8766	505-342-8888	219
USNR 1981 Schurman Way PO Box 310 ....Woodland WA 98674	800-289-8767	360-225-8267	679
USO (United Service Organizations) 2111 Wilson Blvd Ste 1200 ....Arlington VA 22201	800-876-7469	888-484-3876	48-19
USP (US Pharmacopeia) 12601 Twinbrook Pkwy ....Rockville MD 20852	800-227-8772	301-881-0666	49-8
USP Structural Connectors Inc 703 Rogers Dr ....Montgomery MN 56069	800-328-5934		
USPB (US Premium Beef LLC) 12200 N Ambassador Dr PO Box 20103 ....Kansas City MO 64163	866-877-2525	816-713-8800	296-26
USPS (US Postal Service) 475 L'Enfant Plz W SW ....Washington DC 20260 *Cust Svc	800-275-8777*	202-268-2000	339-19
USPTA (US Professional Tennis Assn) 11961 Performance Dr ....Orlando FL 32827	800-877-8248		48-22
US-Reports Inc 5802 Wright Dr ....Loveland CO 80538	800-223-2310		461
USS (United Staffing Solutions) 111 Broadway 3rd Fl. ....New York NY 10006	800-972-9725		
USS Kidd Veterans Memorial & Museum 305 S River Rd ....Baton Rouge LA 70802	800-638-0594	225-342-1942	50-4
USS Lexington Museum on the Bay 2914 N Shoreline Blvd ....Corpus Christi TX 78402	800-523-9539	361-888-4873	517
USS Missouri Memorial Assn Inc 63 Cowpens St ....Honolulu HI 96818	877-644-4896	808-455-1600	50-4
USSM (Ulbrich Stainless Steels & Special Metals Inc) 57 Dodge Ave ....North Haven CT 06473	800-243-1676	203-239-4481	719
USS-POSCO Industries 900 Loveridge Rd ....Pittsburg CA 94565	800-877-7672		719
USTA (US Trotting Assn) 750 Michigan Ave ....Columbus OH 43215	877-800-8782	614-224-2291	48-22
USWired Inc 2107 N First St Ste 250 ....San Jose CA 95131	877-879-4733	408-432-1144	180
UTA (Utah Transit Authority) PO Box 30810 ....Salt Lake City UT 84130	888-743-3882	801-262-5626	466
Utah *Aging & Adult Services Div* 195 N 1950 W ....Salt Lake City UT 84116	877-424-4640	801-538-3910	338-45
Child & Family Services Div 195 N 1950 W ....Salt Lake City UT 84116	855-323-3237	801-538-4100	338-45
Community & Economic Development Dept 60 E S Temple 3rd Fl ....Salt Lake City UT 84111	855-204-9046	801-538-8680	338-45
Consumer Protection Div 160 E Broadway 2nd Fl PO Box 146704 ....Salt Lake City UT 84111	800-721-7233	801-530-6601	
Environmental Quality Dept 195 North 1950 West ....Salt Lake City UT 84116	800-458-0145	801-536-4400	338-45
Governor 350 N State St Ste 200 PO Box 142220 ....Salt Lake City UT 84114	800-705-2464	801-538-1000	338-45
Health Dept PO Box 141010 ....Salt Lake City UT 84114	888-222-2542	801-538-6003	338-45
Higher Education Assistance Authority PO Box 145110 ....Salt Lake City UT 84114	877-336-7378	801-321-7294	721
Higher Education System 60 S 400 W ....Salt Lake City UT 84101	877-336-7378	801-321-7294	338-45
Housing Corp 2479 S Lake Park Blvd ....West Valley City UT 84120	800-284-6950	801-902-8200	338-45
Labor Commission PO Box 146600 ....Salt Lake City UT 84114	800-530-5090	801-530-6800	338-45
Lieutenant Governor Utah State Capitol Complex Ste 220 PO Box 142325 ....Salt Lake City UT 84114	800-995-8683	801-538-1041	338-45
Motor Vehicle Div PO Box 30412 ....Salt Lake City UT 84130	800-368-8824	801-297-7780	338-45
Occupational & Professional Licensing Div PO Box 146741 ....Salt Lake City UT 84111	866-275-3675	801-530-6628	338-45
Office for Victims of Crime 350 E 500 S Ste 200 ....Salt Lake City UT 84111	800-621-7444	801-238-2360	338-45
Office of Tourism 300 N State St ....Salt Lake City UT 84114	800-200-1160	801-538-1900	338-45
Parks & Recreation Div 1594 W N Temple Ste 116 ....Salt Lake City UT 84116	800-322-3770	801-538-7220	338-45
Public Service Commission 160 E 300 S ....Salt Lake City UT 84111	866-772-8824	801-530-6716	
Securities Div 160 E 300 S 2nd Fl. ....Salt Lake City UT 84111	800-721-7233	801-530-6600	338-45
Tax Commission 210 N 1950 W ....Salt Lake City UT 84134	800-662-4335	801-297-2200	338-45
Veterans' Affairs Office 550 Foothills Dr Ste 105 ....Salt Lake City UT 84113	800-894-9497	801-326-2372	338-45
Vital Records & Statistics Office 288 N 1460 W PO Box 141012 ....Salt Lake City UT 84114	888-222-2542		
Utah Assn of Realtors 230 W Towne Ridge Pkwy Ste 500 ....Sandy UT 84070	800-594-8933	801-676-5200	652
Utah Business Magazine 90 South 400 West Ste 650 ....Salt Lake City UT 84101	888-414-5566	801-568-0114	455-5
Utah Imaging Associates Inc 1433 N 1075 W Ste 104 ....Farmington UT 84025	800-475-3698		414
Utah League of Cities & Towns, The 50 South 600 East Ste 150 ....Salt Lake City UT 84102	800-852-8528	801-328-1601	
Utah Medical Products Inc 7043 S 300 W ....Midvale UT 84047 NASDAQ: UTMD	866-754-9789	801-566-1200	474
Utah Metal Works Inc (UMW) 805 Everett Ave ....Salt Lake City UT 84116	877-221-0099		656
Utah State Bar 645 S 200 E ....Salt Lake City UT 84111	877-752-2611	801-531-9077	72
Utah State Library 250 N 1950 W Ste A ....Salt Lake City UT 84116	800-662-9150	801-715-6777	433-5
Utah State University 1600 Old Main Hill ....Logan UT 84322	800-488-8108	435-797-1000	166
Utah System of Higher Education 60 South 400 West ....Salt Lake City UT 84101	800-418-8757	801-321-7200	781
Utah Transit Authority (UTA) PO Box 30810 ....Salt Lake City UT 84130	888-743-3882	801-262-5626	466
Utah Valley Convention & Visitors Bureau 220 West Center St Ste 100 ....Provo UT 84601	800-222-8824	801-851-2100	206
Utah Valley State College 800 West University Pkwy ....Orem UT 84058	800-952-8220	801-863-8000	162
Utak Laboratories Inc 25020 Ave Tibbitts ....Valencia CA 91355	800-235-3442	661-294-3935	231
UTC RETAIL Inc 100 Rawson Rd ....Victor NY 14564	800-349-0546		610
Ute Mountain Casino 3 Weeminuche Dr ....Towaoc CO 81334	800-258-8007	970-565-8800	133
Ute Water Conservancy District 2190 H 1/4 Rd ....Grand Junction CO 81505	866-768-1732	970-242-7491	799
UTEX Industries Inc 10810 Katy Fwy Ste 100 ....Houston TX 77043	800-359-9230	713-467-1000	326
Utica Boilers Inc PO Box 4729 ....Utica NY 13504	800-325-5479	866-847-6656	356
Utica College 1600 Burrstone Rd ....Utica NY 13502 *Admissions	800-782-8884*	315-792-3111	166
Utica First Insurance Co 5981 Airport Rd ....Oriskany NY 13424	800-456-4556	315-736-8211	390-4
Utica National Insurance Group 180 Genesee St ....New Hartford NY 13413	800-274-1914	315-734-2000	390-2
Utilant LLC 475 Ellicott St Ste 5 ....Buffalo NY 14203	888-884-5268		177
Utility Notification Center of Colorado 16361 Table Mtn Pkwy ....Golden CO 80403	800-922-1987	303-232-1991	305
Utility Service Company Inc 535 Courtney Hodges Blvd ....Perry GA 31069	855-526-4413	478-987-0303	192
Utility Trailer Mfg Co 17295 E Railroad St ....City of Industry CA 91748	800-874-6807	626-965-1541	774
Utilityone Inc PO Box 3027 ....York PA 17402	800-388-9088	717-840-4200	196
Utne Reader Magazine 1503 SW 42nd St ....Topeka KS 66609 *Cust Svc	800-736-8863*	612-338-5040	455-11
Utrecht Art Supplies PO Box 1769 ....Galesburg IL 61402	888-336-3114	609-409-8001	43
UTSA (Uniform & Textile Service Assn) 1300 N 17th St Ste 750 ....Arlington VA 22209	800-996-3426	703-247-2600	49-4

Alphabetical Section

	Toll-Free	Phone	Class
UTXL Inc			
10771 NW Ambassador Dr ....Kansas City MO 64153	**800-351-2821**	816-891-7770	311
UTZ Quality Foods Co			
900 High St ....Hanover PA 17331	**800-367-7629**	717-637-6644	296-35
UUSC (Unitarian Universalist Service Committee)			
689 Massachusetts Ave ....Cambridge MA 02139	**800-388-3920**	617-868-6600	48-5
UV Pure Technologies Inc			
60 Venture Dr Unit 19................Toronto ON M1B3S4	**888-407-9997**	416-208-9884	104
UVA Health System			
501 Sunset Ln ....Culpeper VA 22701	**866-608-4749**	540-829-4100	373-3
Uvex Safety Inc			
900 Douglas Pk ....Smithfield RI 02917	**800-682-0839***		572
*General			
UVMC (Upper Valley Medical Ctr)			
3130 N County Rd 25-A ....Troy OH 45373	**866-608-3463**	937-440-4000	373-3
UVP Inc 2066 W 11th St ....Upland CA 91786	**800-452-6788***	909-946-3197	436
*Cust Svc			
UW Medicine Eastside Hospital & Specialty			
3100 Northup Way ....Bellevue WA 98004	**877-520-5000**		373-3
UWEC (University of Wisconsin)			
Eau Claire			
Schofield Hall 111 105 Garfield Ave			
..................Eau Claire WI 54701	**800-949-8932**	715-836-5415	166

V

	Toll-Free	Phone	Class
V & J Holding Cos Inc			
6933 W Brown Deer Rd ....Milwaukee WI 53223	**800-384-6972**	414-365-9003	666
V & S Midwest Carriers Corp			
2001 Hyland Ave ....Kaukauna WI 54130	**800-876-4330**		775
V2Soft Inc			
300 Enterprise Ct			
Ste 100...................Bloomfield Hills MI 48302	**866-982-7638**	248-904-1700	
VA (Department of Veterans Affairs)			
810 Vermont Ave NW ....Washington DC 20420	**800-827-1000***	202-461-7600	339-18
*Cust Svc			
VA Central Iowa Health Care System			
3600 30th St ....Des Moines IA 50310	**800-294-8387**	515-699-5999	373-8
VA Greater Los Angeles Healthcare System			
11301 Wilshire Blvd ....Los Angeles CA 90073	**800-952-4852**	310-478-3711	373-8
VA Hudson Valley Health Care System			
Montrose Campus			
2094 Albany Post Rd ....Montrose NY 10548	**800-269-8749**	914-737-4400	373-8
VA Medical Ctr			
4500 S Lancaster Rd ....Dallas TX 75216	**800-849-3597**	214-742-8387	373-8
VA Medical Ctr			
2400 Hospital Rd ....Tuskegee AL 36083	**800-214-8387**	334-727-0550	373-8
VA Nebraska-Western Iowa Health Care System			
600 S 70th St ....Lincoln NE 68510	**866-851-6052**	402-489-3802	373-8
VA Oakland Regional Benefit Office			
1301 Clay St N Tower ....Oakland CA 94612	**877-696-6775**		339-9
VA Puget Sound Health Care System - Seattle Div			
1660 S Columbian Way ....Seattle WA 98108	**800-329-8387**	206-762-1010	764
VA San Diego Healthcare System			
3350 La Jolla Village Dr ....San Diego CA 92161	**800-331-8387**	858-552-8585	373-8
VA Sierra Nevada Health Care System			
975 Kirman Ave ....Reno NV 89502	**888-838-6256**	775-786-7200	373-8
Vacation Internationale			
1417 116th Ave NE ....Bellevue WA 98004	**800-444-6633**	425-454-8429	748
Vacationcom Inc			
1650 King St Ste 450 ....Alexandria VA 22314	**800-843-0733**	703-740-4100	767
Vacationer RV Resort			
1581 E Main St ....El Cajon CA 92021	**877-626-4409**		377
Vacations To Go Inc			
5851 San Felipe St Ste 500 ....Houston TX 77057	**800-338-4962**	713-974-2121	767
Vacco Industries Inc			
10350 Vacco St ....South El Monte CA 91733	**800-874-7113**	626-443-7121	591
Vac-Con Inc			
969 Hall Park Dr ....Green Cove Spgs FL 32043	**888-920-2945**	904-493-4969	
Vacudyne Inc			
375 E Joe Orr Rd ....Chicago Heights IL 60411	**800-459-9591**	708-757-5200	385
VAC-U-MAX			
69 William St ....Belleville NJ 07109	**800-822-8629**	973-759-4600	
Vaderstad Industries Inc			
PO Box 123 ....Langbank SK S0G2X0	**800-667-4295**	306-538-2221	273
Vail Marriott Mountain Resort			
715 W Lionshead Cir ....Vail CO 81657	**800-648-0720**	970-476-4444	703
Vail Mountain Lodge & Spa, The			
352 E Meadow Dr ....Vail CO 81657	**888-794-0410**	970-476-0700	703
Vail Racquet Club			
4695 Vail Racquet Club Dr ....Vail CO 81657	**800-428-4840**	970-476-4840	702
Vail Resorts Management Co			
390 Interlocken Crescent			
Ste 1000...................Broomfield CO 80021	**800-842-8062**	303-404-1800	665
NYSE: MTN			
Vaisala Inc			
10-D Gill St ....Woburn MA 01801	**888-824-7252**	781-933-4500	470
Val's Distributing Co			
6124 E 30th St N ....Tulsa OK 74115	**800-274-9987**	918-835-9987	297-5
Valair Aviation			
7301 NW 50th St ....Oklahoma City OK 73132	**800-299-8546**	405-789-5000	20
Valassis Communications Inc			
19975 Victor Pkwy ....Livonia MI 48152	**800-437-0479**	734-591-3000	623
NYSE: VCI			
Valcom Consulting Group Inc			
85 Albert St ....Ottawa ON K1P6A4	**866-561-5580**	613-594-5200	261
Valcom Inc			
5614 Hollins Rd ....Roanoke VA 24019	**800-825-2661**	540-563-2000	730
Valdosta Daily Times			
PO Box 968 ....Valdosta GA 31603	**800-600-4838**	229-244-1880	528-2
Valdosta State University			
1500 N Patterson St ....Valdosta GA 31698	**800-618-1878**	229-333-5800	166

	Toll-Free	Phone	Class
Valence Technology Inc			
1807 W Braker Ln Ste 500 ....Austin TX 78758	**888-825-3623**	512-527-2900	74
Valencia College			
PO Box 3028 ....Orlando FL 32802	**800-590-3428**	407-299-5000	162
Valeo Pharma Inc			
16667 Hymus Blvd Kirkland ....Kirkland QC H9H4R9	**888-694-0865**	514-694-0150	231
Valerie Wilson Travel Inc			
475 Park Ave S ....New York NY 10016	**800-776-1116**	212-532-3400	766
Valeritas Inc			
750 Rt 202 S Ste 600 ....Bridgewater NJ 08807	**855-384-8848**	908-927-9920	473
Valero LP			
1 Valero Way? ....San Antonio TX 78249	**800-333-3377**	210-246-2000	593
Valiant Products Corp			
2727 Fifth Ave W ....Denver CO 80204	**800-347-2727***	303-892-1234	441
*Cust Svc			
Valiant Steel & Equipment Inc			
6455 Old Peachtree Rd ....Norcross GA 30071	**800-939-9905**	770-417-1235	490
Valiant TMs			
6555 Hawthorne Dr ....Windsor ON N8T3G6	**888-497-5537**	519-974-5200	535
VALIC (Variable Annuity Life Insurance Co)			
2929 Allen Pkwy ....Houston TX 77019	**800-448-2542**		390-2
Valid8 com Inc			
500 W Cummings Pk Ste 6550..........Woburn MA 01801	**855-482-5438**	781-938-1221	177
Validar Inc			
800 Maynard Ave S Ste 401 ....Seattle WA 98134	**888-784-2929**	206-264-9151	178-1
Valient Market Research Inc			
PO Box 335 ....Exton PA 19341	**844-332-7082**		
Valin Corp			
555 E California Ave ....Sunnyvale CA 94086	**800-774-5630**	408-730-9850	357
Valle Verde			
900 Calle de los Amigos ......Santa Barbara CA 93105	**800-750-5089**	805-883-4000	668
Vallejo Convention & Visitors Bureau			
289 Mare Island Way ....Vallejo CA 94590	**866-921-9277***	707-642-3653	206
*General			
Vallejo Times Herald			
420 Virginia St Ste 2A ....Vallejo CA 94590	**800-600-1141**	707-644-1141	528-2
Valley Blox Inc			
210 Stone Spring Rd ....Harrisonburg VA 22801	**800-648-6725**	540-434-6725	183
Valley Chevrolet Inc			
601 Kidder St ....Wilkes-Barre PA 18702	**877-207-9214**	570-821-2772	513
Valley City State University			
101 College St SW ....Valley City ND 58072	**800-532-8641**	701-845-7990	166
Valley Electric Assn Inc			
800 E Hwy 372 PO Box 237 ....Pahrump NV 89048	**800-742-3330**	775-727-5312	245
Valley Electric Supply Corp			
1361 N State Rd PO Box 724 ....Vincennes IN 47591	**800-825-7877**	812-882-7860	246
Valley Express Llc			
6003 State Rd 76 ....Oshkosh WI 54904	**800-594-4744**	920-231-1677	311
Valley First Credit Union			
PO Box 1411 ....Modesto CA 95353	**877-549-4567**	209-549-8500	219
Valley Flowers Inc			
3675 Foothill Rd ....Carpinteria CA 93013	**800-549-5500**	805-684-6651	292
Valley Forge Christian College			
1401 Charlestown Rd ....Phoenixville PA 19460	**800-432-8322**	610-935-0450	166
Valley Forge Medical Ctr & Hospital			
1033 W Germantown Pk ....Norristown PA 19403	**888-539-8500**	610-539-8500	722
Valley Forge Military Academy & College			
1001 Eagle Rd ....Wayne PA 19087	**800-234-8362**	610-989-1300	162
Valley Health System			
223 N Van Dien Ave ....Ridgewood NJ 07450	**800-825-5391**	201-447-8000	373-3
Valley Hospice Inc			
380 Summit Ave ....Steubenville OH 43952	**877-467-7423**	740-859-5660	370
Valley Internet Inc			
102 Maple St E ....Fayetteville TN 37334	**888-433-1924**	931-433-1921	41
Valley Litho Supply Inc			
1047 Haugen Ave ....Rice Lake WI 54868	**800-826-6781**		357
Valley National Bancorp			
1455 Valley Rd ....Wayne NJ 07470	**800-522-4100**	973-305-8800	359-2
NYSE: VLY			
Valley National Bank			
615 Main Ave ....Passaic NJ 07055	**800-522-4100**	973-777-6768	70
Valley News			
24 Interchange Dr ....West Lebanon NH 03784	**800-874-2226**	603-298-8711	528-2
Valley News Dispatch			
210 Fourth Ave ....Tarentum PA 15084	**800-909-8742**		528-2
Valley Office Systems			
2050 First St ....Idaho Falls ID 83401	**800-610-2865**	208-529-2777	179
Valley Offset Printing Inc			
160 S Sheridan Ave ....Valley Center KS 67147	**888-895-7913**	316-755-0061	623
Valley Power Systems Inc			
425 S Hacienda Blvd ....City of Industry CA 91745	**800-924-4265**	626-333-1243	765
Valley Proteins Inc			
151 Valpro Dr ....Winchester VA 22603	**800-871-3406**	540-877-2590	445
Valley River Inn			
1000 Vly River Way ....Eugene OR 97401	**800-543-8266**	541-743-1000	378
Valley Rural Electric Co-op Inc			
10700 Fairgrounds Rd			
PO Box 477..................Huntingdon PA 16652	**800-432-0680**	814-643-2650	245
Valley Supply & Equipment Company Inc			
1109 Middle River Rd ....Baltimore MD 21220	**800-633-5077**	888-890-8165	23
Valley Telephone Co-op Inc			
752 E Maley St ....Willcox AZ 85643	**800-421-5711**	520-384-2231	731
Valley View Casino Ctr			
3500 Sports Arena Blvd ....San Diego CA 92110	**888-929-7849**	619-224-4171	716
Valley Yellow Pages			
1850 N Gateway Blvd ....Fresno CA 93727	**800-350-8887**	559-251-8888	633-6
Valmont Industries Inc			
1 Valmont Plz ....Omaha NE 68154	**800-825-6668**	402-963-1000	273
NYSE: VMI			
Valor Oil			
1200 Alsop Ln ....Owensboro KY 42303	**844-468-2567**		575
Valparaiso University			
1700 Chapel Dr ....Valparaiso IN 46383	**888-468-2576**	219-464-5011	166
Valparaiso University Law			
656 S Greenwich St ....Valparaiso IN 46383	**888-825-7652**	219-465-7829	167-1
Valtim Inc			
1095 Venture Dr ....Forest VA 24551	**800-230-2857**	434-525-3004	461

	Toll-Free	Phone	Class
Valtra Inc			
8750 Pioneer Blvd . . . . .Santa Fe Springs CA 90670	800-989-5244	562-949-8625	384
Valuation Management Group LLC			
1640 Powers Ferry Rd SE Bldg 15			
Ste 100 . . . . .Marietta GA 30067	866-799-7488	678-483-4420	648
Value Creation Inc			
1100 635 - Eighth Ave SW . . . . .Calgary AB T2P3M3	855-908-8800	403-539-4500	532
Value Drug Co			
195 Theater Dr . . . . .Duncansville PA 16635	800-252-3786		
Value Drug Mart Assoc Ltd			
16504 - 121A Ave . . . . .Edmonton AB T5V1J9	888-554-8258	780-453-1701	238
Value Line Asset Management			
551 Fifth Ave 3rd Fl . . . . .New York NY 10176	800-634-3583	212-907-1500	400
Value Payment Systems LLC			
2207 Crestmoor Rd Ste 200 . . . . .Nashville TN 37215	888-877-0450		
ValueClick Media			
530 E Montecito St . . . . .Santa Barbara CA 93103	877-361-3316	805-879-1600	7
ValuSource LLC			
4575 Galley Rd			
Ste 200E . . . . .Colorado Springs CO 80915	800-825-8763	719-548-4900	177
Valvoline LLC			
100 Valvoline Way . . . . .Lexington KY 40509	800-832-6825	859-357-7777	537
Van Air Systems Inc			
2950 Mechanic St . . . . .Lake City PA 16423	800-840-9906	814-774-2631	385
Van Ausdall & Farrar Inc			
6430 E 75th St . . . . .Indianapolis IN 46250	800-467-7474	317-634-2913	530
Van Bergen & Greener Inc			
1818 Madison St . . . . .Maywood IL 60153	800-621-3889	708-343-4700	247
Van Bortel Aircraft Inc			
4912 S Collins . . . . .Arlington TX 76018	800-759-4295	817-468-7788	765
Van Bortel Subaru			
6327 Rt 96 . . . . .Victor NY 14564	888-902-7961	585-924-5230	57
Van Buren State Park			
12259 Township Rd 218 . . . . .Van Buren OH 45889	866-644-6727	419-832-7662	561
Van Cleef & Arpels Inc			
744 Fifth Ave . . . . .New York NY 10019	877-826-2533	212-896-9284	409
Van Dam Inc			
The VanDam Bldg 121 W 27 St . . . . . . .New York NY 10011	800-863-6537	212-929-0416	
Van De Pol Enterprises Inc			
4895 S Airport Way . . . . .Stockton CA 95206	800-379-0306	209-465-3421	324
Van Diest Supply Oo			
1434 220th St PO Box 610 . . . . .Webster City IA 50595	800-779-2424	515-832-2366	280
Van Doren Sales Inc			
10 NE Cascade Ave . . . . .East Wenatchee WA 98802	866-886-1837	509-886-1837	298
Van Dyk Group Inc, The			
12800 Long Beach Blvd . . . . .Beach Haven NJ 08008	800-222-0131	609-492-1511	389
Van Dyke Supply Co			
39771 Sd Hwy 34 . . . . .Woonsocket SD 57385	800-279-7985	704-279-7985	457
Van Galder Bus Co			
715 S Pearl St . . . . .Janesville WI 53548	800-747-0994	888-970-7233	107
Van Horn Aviation LLC			
1000 E Vista Del Cerro Dr . . . . .Tempe AZ 85281	800-326-1534	480-483-4202	20
VAN HORN CHEVROLET OF PLYMOUTH			
3008 Eastern Ave . . . . .Plymouth WI 53073	800-236-1415	920-893-6361	57
Van Horn Inc			
PO Box 380 . . . . .Cerro Gordo IL 61818	800-252-1615	217-677-2131	276
Van Horn Metz & Company Inc			
201 E Elm St . . . . .Conshohocken PA 19428	800-523-0424	610-828-4500	146
Van Meter Industrial Inc			
850 32nd Ave SW . . . . .Cedar Rapids IA 52404	800-247-1410		246
Van Ru Credit Corp			
1350 E Touhy Ave Ste 300E . . . . .Des Plaines IL 60018	800-468-2678		160
Van Well Nursery			
2821 Grant Rd . . . . .East Wenatchee WA 98802	800-572-1553	509-886-8189	293
Van Wezel Performing Arts Ctr			
777 N Tamiami Trl . . . . .Sarasota FL 34236	800-826-9303	941-953-3368	568
Van Zyverden Inc			
8079 Van Zyverden Rd . . . . .Meridian MS 39305	800-332-2852	601-679-8274	293
Vanadium Group Corp			
134 Three Degree Rd . . . . .Pittsburgh PA 15237	800-685-0354	412-367-6060	261
Vance Air Force Base			
246 Brown Pkwy Ste 102 . . . . .Enid OK 73703	866-966-1020	580-213-7522	495-1
Vance Birthplace State Historic Site			
911 Reems Creek Rd . . . . .Weaverville NC 28787	800-767-1560	828-645-6706	50-3
Vance Bros Inc			
5201 Brighton PO Box 300107 . . . . . . .Kansas City MO 64130	800-821-8549	816-923-4325	46
Vance-Granville Community College			
South PO Box 39 . . . . .Creedmoor NC 27522	877-823-2378	919-528-4737	162
Warren County			
PO Box 207 . . . . .Warrenton NC 27536	877-823-2378	252-257-1900	162
Vancouver Aquarium Marine Science Ctr			
845 Avison Way . . . . .Vancouver BC V6G3E2	800-931-1186	604-659-3474	40
Vancouver Convention & Exposition Centre (VCEC)			
1055 Canada Pl . . . . .Vancouver BC V6C0C3	866-785-8232	604-689-8232	205
Vancouver Door Company Inc			
203 Fifth St NW . . . . .Puyallup WA 98371	800-999-3667	253-845-9581	236
Vancouver International Airport (YVR)			
Airport Postal Outlet			
PO Box 23750 . . . . .Richmond BC V7B1Y7	800-461-9999	604-207-7077	27
Vancouver School of Theology			
The University of British Columbia			
6015 Walter Gage Rd . . . . .Vancouver BC V6T1Z1	866-822-9031	604-822-9031	167-3
Vancouver Sun			
200 Granville St Ste 1. . . . . .Vancouver BC V6C3N3	866-372-3707	604-605-2000	528-1
Vander Haag's Inc			
3809 Fourth Ave W . . . . .Spencer IA 51301	888-940-5030	712-262-7000	61
Vanderbilt Beach Resort			
9225 Gulf Shore Dr N . . . . .Naples FL 34108	800-243-9076	239-597-3144	665
Vanderbilt Grace			
41 Mary St . . . . .Newport RI 02840	888-826-4255	401-846-6200	378
Vanderbilt Minerals Corp			
30 Winfield St .Norwalk CT 06855	800-243-6064	203-853-1400	501-3
Vanderbilt Mortgage & Finance Inc			
500 Alcoa Trl . . . . .Maryville TN 37804	800-970-7250		507
Vanderbilt University			
2201 W End Ave . . . . .Nashville TN 37240	800-288-0432	615-322-7311	166
Vanderbilt University Medical Ctr			
1215 21st Ave S . . . . .Nashville TN 37232	877-936-8422	615-322-5000	373-3
Vanderbilt University Press			
2014 Broadway . . . . .Nashville TN 37203	800-627-7377	615-322-3585	633-4
Vanderbilt University School of Medicine			
2215 Garland Ave . . . . .Nashville TN 37232	866-263-8263	615-322-6109	167-2
VanDyke Software Inc			
4848 Tramway Ridge Dr NE			
Ste 101 . . . . .Albuquerque NM 87111	800-952-5210	505-332-5700	178-12
Vango Graphics Inc			
1371 S Inca St . . . . .Denver CO 80223	877-722-6168	303-722-6109	343
Vanguard Brokerage Services			
PO Box 1110 . . . . .Valley Forge PA 19482	800-992-8327	610-669-1000	686
Vanguard East			
1172 Azalea Garden Rd . . . . .Norfolk VA 23502	800-221-1264		9
Vanguard Furniture Co Inc			
109 Simpson St . . . . .Conover NC 28613	800-968-1702	828-328-5631	319-2
Vanguard Group			
455 Devon Pk Dr .Wayne PA 19087	877-662-7447	610-669-1000	400
Vanguard Integrity Professionals Inc			
6625 S Eastern Ave Ste 100 . . . . .Las Vegas NV 89119	877-794-0014	702-794-0014	180
Vanguard Products Group Inc			
720 Brooker Creek Blvd Ste 223. . . . . . . .Oldsmar FL 34677	877-477-4874	813-855-9639	689
Vanguard Resources Inc			
6500 Hwy 281 N . . . . .Spring Branch TX 78070	800-211-8848	210-495-1950	
Vanguard Systems Inc			
2901 Dutton Mill Rd Ste 220 . . . . .Aston PA 19014	800-445-1418		386
Vanguard Trucks Centers			
700 Ruskin Dr . . . . .Forest Park GA 30297	866-216-7925	800-783-5353	54
Vanguard University of Southern California			
55 Fair Dr . . . . .Costa Mesa CA 92626	800-722-6279*	714-556-3610	166
*Admissions			
Vanilla Forums Inc			
388 Rue Saint-Jacques Ste 800 . . . . .Montreal QC H2Y1S1	866-845-0815		386
Vanir Construction Management Inc			
4540 Duckhorn Dr Ste 300 . . . . .Sacramento CA 95834	888-912-1201	916-575-8888	461
Vanity Fair Magazine			
1 World Trade Ctr . . . . .New York NY 10007	800-365-0635		455-11
Van-Kam Freightways Ltd			
10155 Grace Rd . . . . .Surrey BC V3V3V7	800-663-2161	604-582-7451	314
Vans Inc			
15700 Shoemaker Ave . . . . .Santa Fe Springs CA 90670	855-909-8267		301
Vantage Credit Union (VCU)			
PO Box 4433 . . . . .Bridgeton MO 63044	800-522-6009	314-298-0055	219
Vantage Health Plan Inc			
130 Desiard St Ste 300. . . . . .Monroe LA 71201	888-823-1910	318-361-0900	352
Vantage Mobility International (VMI)			
5202 S 28th Pl .Phoenix AZ 85040	855-864-8267		62-7
Vantage Solutions Llc			
1035 W Lake St Ste 205 . . . . .Chicago IL 60607	877-816-4818	312-440-0602	443
Vantage Sourcing LLC			
4930 W St Hwy 52 . . . . .Taylor AL 36305	866-580-4562		317
Vantage Trailers Inc			
29335 Hwy Blvd .Katy TX 77494	800-826-8245		774
Vanteon Corp			
250 Cross Keys Office Pk			
Bldg 250 .Fairport NY 14450	888-506-5677	585-419-9555	261
VanTran Industries Inc			
7711 Imperial Dr . . . . .Waco TX 76712	800-433-3346	254-772-9740	762
Varel International Energy Services Inc			
1625 W Crosby Dr Ste 124. . . . . .Carrollton TX 75006	800-827-3526	972-242-1160	190
Varflex Corp			
512 West Court St . . . . .Rome NY 13440	800-648-4014	315-336-4400	811
VARGO 3709 Pkwy Ln . . . . .Hilliard OH 43026	877-876-6384	614-876-1163	357
Variable Annuity Life Insurance Co (VALIC)			
2929 Allen Pkwy .Houston TX 77019	800-448-2542		390-2
Varian Medical Systems Inc			
3100 Hansen Way . . . . .Palo Alto CA 94304	800-544-4636	650-493-4000	381
NYSE: VAR			
Variant Microsystems			
4128 Business Ctr Dr . . . . .Fremont CA 94538	800-827-4268	510-440-2870	531
Variety Distributors Inc			
609 Seventh St . . . . .Harlan IA 51537	800-274-1095	712-755-2184	328
Variform Inc			
5020 Weston Pkwy Ste 400 . . . . .Cary NC 27513	800-800-2244	888-975-9436	191-4
Varscona Hotel			
8208 106th St . . . . .Edmonton AB T6E6R9	866-465-8150	780-434-6111	378
Vartek Services Inc			
4770 Hempstead Station Dr . . . . .Dayton OH 45459	800-954-2524		174
Varvid			
705 Sunset Pond Ln . . . . .Bellingham WA 98225	855-827-8434		5
Vasamed Inc			
7615 Golden Triangle Dr			
Ste A. .Eden Prairie MN 55344	800-695-2737		474
Vascular Solutions Inc			
6464 Sycamore Ct . . . . .Minneapolis MN 55369	877-979-4300	763-656-4300	474
VasoHealthcare			
Revolution Mill Studios 1150 Revolution Mill Dr St			
. . . . .Greensboro NC 27405	877-900-8276	336-398-8276	
Vasomedical Inc			
180 Linden Ave . . . . .Westbury NY 11590	800-455-3327	516-997-4600	250
OTC: VASO			
Vassar College			
124 Raymond Ave . . . . .Poughkeepsie NY 12604	800-827-7270	845-437-7000	166
Vatterott College Berkeley			
8580 Evans Ave . . . . .Berkeley MO 63134	888-202-2636		795
Vatterott College Joplin			
809 Illinois Ave .Joplin MO 64801	866-200-1898	888-202-2636	795
Vatterott College South County			
12900 Maurer Industrial Dr . . . . .Saint Louis MO 63127	866-312-8276	888-202-2636	795
Vatterott College Springfield			
3850 S Campbell . . . . .Springfield MO 65807	888-202-2636		
Vaughan & Bushnell Manufacturing Co			
11414 Maple Ave . . . . .Hebron IL 60034	800-435-6000		753
Vaughan Chamber of Commerce			
25 Edilcan Dr Ste 2. . . . . .Vaughan ON L4K3S4	888-943-8937	905-761-1366	137
Vaughan Company Inc			
364 Monte-Elma Rd . . . . .Montesano WA 98563	888-249-2467	360-249-4042	637
Vaughan Mills			
1 Bass Pro Mills Dr . . . . .Vaughan ON L4K5W4	800-998-6844	905-879-2110	

Name / Address	City	State	Zip	Toll-Free	Phone	Class
Vaughan Nelson Investment Management LP 600 Travis St Ste 6300	Houston	TX	77002	**888-888-8676**	713-224-2545	524
Vaughn College of Aeronautics & Technology 86-01 23rd Ave	East Elmhurst	NY	11369	**866-682-8446**	718-429-6600	166
Vaughn Manufacturing Corp 26 Old Elm St PO Box 5431	Salisbury	MA	01952	**800-282-8446**	978-462-6683	36
VAWC (Virginia American Water Co) 2223 Duke St	Alexandria	VA	22314	**800-452-6863**	703-706-3879	782
Vawter Financial Ltd 1161 Bethel Rd Ste 304	Columbus	OH	43220	**800-955-1575**	614-451-1002	194
VBA (Vermont Bar Assn) 35-37 Ct St PO Box 100	Montpelier	VT	05601	**800-639-7036**	802-223-2020	72
VBCVB (Virginia Beach Convention & Visitor Bureau) 2101 Parks Ave Ste 500	Virginia Beach	VA	23451	**800-700-7702**	757-385-4700	206
Vbrick Systems Inc 12 Beaumont Rd	Wallingford	CT	06492	**866-827-4251**		730
VBT 426 Industrial Ave Ste 120	Williston	VT	05495	**800-245-3868**		755
VCEC (Vancouver Convention & Exposition Centre) 1055 Canada Pl	Vancouver	BC	V6C0C3	**866-785-8232**	604-689-8232	205
VCF Films Inc 1100 Sutton Ave	Howell	MI	48843	**888-905-7680**	517-546-2300	596
VCI Emergency Vehicle 43 Jefferson Ave	Berlin	NJ	08009	**800-394-2162**	856-768-2162	400
VCU (Vantage Credit Union) PO Box 4433	Bridgeton	MO	63044	**800-522-6009**	314-298-0055	219
Vdara Hotel & Spa 2600 W Harmon Ave	Las Vegas	NV	89158	**866-745-7111**	702-590-2111	376
VDN (Voice & Data Networks Inc) 4218 Park Glen Rd	St. Louis Park	MN	55416	**800-246-7999**	952-946-5353	521
VDx Veterinary Diagnostics Inc 2019 Anderson Rd Ste C	Davis	CA	95616	**877-753-4285**	530-753-4285	789
Vecellio & Grogan Inc PO Box 2438	Beckley	WV	25802	**800-255-6575**	304-252-6575	188-4
Vector Networks Inc 541 Tenth St Unit 123	Atlanta	GA	30318	**800-330-5035**	770-622-2850	179
Vector Planning & Services Inc 591 Camino De La Reina Ste 300	San Diego	CA	92108	**888-522-5491**	619-297-5656	177
Vector Security Inc 2000 Ericsson Dr	Warrendale	PA	15086	**800-832-8575**		688
Vectorply Corp 3500 Lakewood Dr	Phenix City	AL	36867	**800-577-4521**	334-291-7704	740-1
VectorVest Inc 20472 Chartwell Ctr Dr Ste D	Cornelius	NC	28031	**800-130-1519**	888-658-7638	400
Vectra Bank Colorado NA 2000 S Colorado Blvd Ste 2-1200	Denver	CO	80222	**800-232-8948**	720-947-7700	70
Vectra Fitness Inc 7901 S 190th St	Kent	WA	98032	**800-283-2872**	425-291-9550	267
Vectren Corp 211 NW Riverside Dr *NYSE: VVC*	Evansville	IN	47708	**800-227-1376**	812-491-4000	359-5
Vectus Inc 18685 Main St 101 PMB 360	Huntington Beach	CA	92648	**866-483-2887**		386
Vedder Transportation Group 400 Riverside Rd	Abbotsford	BC	V2S4P4	**866-857-1375**		314
Vee Bar Guest Ranch 38 Vee Bar Ranch Rd	Laramie	WY	82070	**800-483-3227**	307-745-7036	239
Vee Neal Aviation Inc 148 Aviation Ln Ste 109	Latrobe	PA	15650	**800-278-2710**	724-539-4533	63
Veeco Instruments Inc 1 Terminal Dr *NASDAQ: VECO*	Plainview	NY	11803	**888-724-9511**	516-677-0200	691
Veeder-Root 125 Powder Forest Dr	Simsbury	CT	06070	**888-262-7539**	860-651-2700	201
Veenstra & Kimm Inc 3000 Westown Pkwy	West Des Moines	IA	50266	**800-241-8000**	515-225-8000	261
Veetronix Inc 1311 W Pacific Ave *General	Lexington	NE	68850	**800-445-0007***	308-324-6661	810
Vegas PBS 3050 E Flamingo	Las Vegas	NV	89121	**877-727-4483**	702-799-1010	736-39
VEGAScom LLC 2370 Corporate Cir 3rd Fl	Henderson	NV	89074	**866-983-4279**		
Vegetable Juices Inc 7400 S Narragansett *General	Bedford Park	IL	60638	**888-776-9752***	708-924-9500	296-20
Vehicle Safety Mfg LLC 408 Central Ave *General	Newark	NJ	07107	**800-832-7233***	973-643-3000	437
VehSmart Inc 12180 Ridgecrest Rd Ste 412	Victorville	CA	92395	**855-834-7627**		643
VEITS Group LLC 7610 Olentangy River Rd Ste 200	Columbus	OH	43235	**877-834-8702**	614-467-5414	225
Veka Inc 100 Veka Dr	Fombell	PA	16123	**800-654-5589**	724-452-1000	235
Velaro Inc 8174 Lark Brown Rd Ste 201	Elkridge	MD	21075	**800-983-5276**		804
Velcro USA Inc 406 Brown Ave	Manchester	NH	03103	**800-225-0180**	603-669-4880	590
Veldkamp's Flowers 9501 W Colfax Ave	Lakewood	CO	80215	**800-247-3730**	303-232-2673	292
Vellano Bros Inc 7 Hemlock St	Latham	NY	12110	**800-342-9855**	518-785-5537	384
Vellumoid Inc 54 Rockdale St	Worcester	MA	01606	**800-609-5558**	508-853-2500	326
Velsicol Chemical LLC 10400 W Higgins Rd Ste 700 *Cust Svc	Rosemont	IL	60018	**877-847-8351***	847-813-7888	144
VELUX America Inc 450 Old BrickyaRd Rd PO Box 5001	Greenwood	SC	29648	**800-888-3589**	803-396-5700	489
Velvac Inc 2405 S Calhoun Rd	New Berlin	WI	53151	**800-783-8871**	262-786-0700	60
Vendant Inc 4845 Pearl East Cir Ste 101	Bouler	CO	80301	**800-714-4900**	720-378-4420	178-12
Vendini Inc 660 Market St	San Francisco	CA	94104	**800-901-7173**		187
Vendio Services Llc 1510 Fashion Island Blvd	San Mateo	CA	94403	**866-269-9549**		178-7
Vendome Copper & Brass Works Inc 729 Franklin St	Louisville	KY	40202	**888-384-5161**	502-587-1930	298
Vendome Group LLC 216 E 45th St 6th Fl	New York	NY	10017	**800-519-3692**		633-9
Vendors Exchange International Inc 8700 Brookpark Rd	Cleveland	OH	44129	**800-321-2311**	216-432-1800	461
Venetian Resort Hotel & Casino 3355 Las Vegas Blvd S	Las Vegas	NV	89109	**866-659-9643**	702-414-1000	665
Vengroff Williams & Assoc Inc (VWA) 2099 S State College Bvld	Anaheim	CA	92806	**800-238-9655**	714-889-6200	160
Venice Consulting Group 212 Marine St Ste 100	Santa Monica	CA	90405	**855-202-0824**		196
Venkel Ltd 5900 Shepherd Mountain Cove	Austin	TX	78730	**800-950-8365**	512-794-0081	246
Vensai Technologies 2450 Atlanta Hwy Ste 1002	Cumming	GA	30040	**866-849-4057**	770-888-4804	196
VENSURE Employer Services Inc 4140 E Baseline Rd Ste 201	Mesa	AZ	85206	**800-409-8958**		359-3
Vent-A-Hood Ltd PO Box 830426	Richardson	TX	75083	**800-331-2492**	972-235-5201	693
Ventamatic Ltd 100 Washington Rd	Mineral Wells	TX	76067	**800-433-1626**	940-325-7887	15
Ventana Inn 48123 Hwy 1	Big Sur	CA	93920	**800-628-6500**	831-667-2331	665
Ventana Medical Systems Inc 1910 Innovation Pk Dr	Tucson	AZ	85755	**800-227-2155**	520-887-2155	474
Ventas Inc 353 N Clark St Ste 3300 *NYSE: VTR*	Chicago	IL	60654	**877-483-6827**	312-660-3800	650
Ventec Life Systems 19021 120th Ave NE Ste E101	Bothell	WA	98011	**844-640-4357**	844-698-6276	
Ventura County Medical Ctr 3291 Loma Vista Rd	Ventura	CA	93003	**888-285-5012**	805-652-6000	373-3
Ventura Foods LLC 40 Pointe Dr	Brea	CA	92821	**800-421-6257**	714-257-3700	296-30
Ventura Visitors & Convention Bureau 101 S California St	Ventura	CA	93001	**800-333-2989**	805-648-2075	206
Ventura Youth Correctional Facility 3100 Wright Rd	Camarillo	CA	93010	**866-232-5627**	805-485-7951	411
Venture Communications Cooperative Inc 218 Commercial Ave SE PO Box 157	Highmore	SD	57345	**800-932-0637**	605-852-2224	49-17
Venture Lighting International Inc 32000 Aurora Rd	Solon	OH	44139	**800-451-2606**	440-248-3510	436
Venture Solutions Inc 1170 Grey Fox Rd	Arden Hills	MN	55112	**800-728-2615**	651-494-1740	195
VentureOut 575 Pierce St Ste 604	San Francisco	CA	94117	**888-431-6789**	415-626-5678	755
Venus Swimwear 11711 Marco Beach Dr	Jacksonville	FL	32224	**800-366-7946**	904-645-6000	155-16
Vera Bradley Designs 2208 Production Rd	Fort Wayne	IN	46808	**800-975-8372**	260-482-4673	348
Verbatim Americas LLC 8210 University Executive Park Dr	Charlotte	NC	28262	**800-538-8589**	704-547-6500	654
Verbatim Solutions LLC 5200 S Highland Dr Ste 201	Salt Lake City	UT	84117	**800-573-5702**		763
Verdanza Hotel 8020 Calle Tartak	Carolina	PR	00979	**800-625-0312**	787-253-9000	132
Verdigris Valley Electric Co-op 8901 E 146th St N	Collinsville	OK	74021	**800-870-5948**	918-371-2584	245
Verdin Co, The 444 Reading Rd	Cincinnati	OH	45202	**800-543-0488**		153
Verendrye Electric Co-op Inc 615 Hwy 52	Velva	ND	58790	**800-472-2141**	701-338-2855	245
Verican Inc 227 E Florida Ave	Hemet	CA	92543	**800-888-0470**	415-296-7300	177
Verichem Laboratories Inc 90 Narragansett Ave	Providence	RI	02907	**800-552-5859**	401-461-0180	738
Vericon Resources Inc 3295 River Exchange Dr Ste 405	Norcross	GA	30092	**800-795-3784**	770-457-9922	399
Veridex LLC 700 US Hwy Rt 202 S	Raritan	NJ	08869	**877-837-4339**		474
Verified Credentials Inc 20890 Kenbridge Ct	Lakeville	MN	55044	**800-473-4934**	952-985-7202	631
Verified Label & Print Inc 7905 Hopi Pl	Tampa	FL	33634	**800-764-6110**	813-290-7721	623
Verigent LLC 149 Plantation Ridge Dr Ste 100	Mooresville	NC	28117	**877-637-6422**	704-658-3285	606
Verint Video Solutions 330 S Service Rd	Melville	NY	11747	**800-483-7468**		688
Veris Industries Inc 16640 SW 72nd Ave	Portland	OR	97224	**800-354-8556**	503-598-4564	406
Verisk Analytics 545 Washington Blvd *NASDAQ: VRSK*	Jersey City	NJ	07310	**800-888-4476**	201-469-3000	461
Verisma Systems Inc 510 W Third St Ste 200	Pueblo	CO	81003	**866-390-7404**	719-546-1849	
Verisurf Software Inc 4907 E Landon Dr	Anaheim	CA	92807	**888-713-7201**	714-970-1683	177
VerisVisalign 920 S Broad St	Lansdale	PA	19446	**888-458-3747**	267-649-8001	
VeriTainer Corp 1127 Pope St	St. Helena	CA	94574	**844-344-8796**	707-967-0944	689
Veritas Press 1805 Olde Homestead Ln	Lancaster	PA	17601	**800-922-5082**	717-519-1974	531
Veri-Tax 30 Executive Pk Ste 200	Irvine	CA	92614	**800-969-5100**		461
Veritext LLC 290 W Mt Pleasant Ave Ste 3200	Livingston	NJ	07039	**800-567-8658**		443
Verity Credit Union PO Box 75974	Seattle	WA	98175	**800-444-4589**	206-440-9000	219
Verity International Ltd 200 King St W Ste 1301	Toronto	ON	M5H3T4	**877-623-2396**	416-862-8422	194

	Toll-Free	Phone	Class
Verity Professionals			
8000 Avalon Blvd Ste 100 . . . . Alpharetta GA 30009	888-367-3110	404-920-6400	461
Verizon Business			
1 Verizon Way . . . . Basking Ridge NJ 07920	877-297-7816*	202-789-1432	731
*Cust Svc			
Verizon Communications Inc			
140 W St . . . . New York NY 10007	800-837-4966	202-789-1432	731
NYSE: VZ			
Verizon Credit Inc			
201 N Tampa St . . . . Tampa FL 33602	800-483-7988	202-789-1432	216
Verizon Wireless			
180 Washington Valley Rd . . . . Bedminster NJ 07921	800-922-0204	908-306-7000	731
Vermeer Mid Atlantic Inc			
10900 Carpet St . . . . Charlotte NC 28273	800-768-3444	704-588-3238	786
Vermeer Midsouth Inc			
1200 Vermeer Cv . . . . Cordova TN 38018	800-264-4123		385
Vermilion Community College			
1900 E Camp St . . . . Ely MN 55731	800-657-3608		162
Vermillion County			
255 S Main St . . . . Newport IN 47966	800-340-8155	765-492-5345	337
Vermont			
Aging & Disabilities Dept			
280 State Dr HC2 South . . . . Waterbury VT 05671	888-405-5005	802-241-2401	338-46
Children & Families Dept			
280 State Dr HC 1 N . . . . Waterbury VT 05671	800-786-3214	802-241-2100	338-46
Consumer Assistance Program			
146 University Pl . . . . Burlington VT 05405	800-649-2424	802-656-3183	338-46
Crime Victim Services Ctr			
58 S Main St Ste 1 . . . . Waterbury VT 05676	800-750-1213	802-241-1250	
Emergency Management Office			
45 State Dr . . . . Waterbury VT 05671	800-347-0488	802-244-8721	338-46
Executive Office of Governor			
109 State St . . . . Montpelier VT 05609	800-649-6825	802-828-3333	
Motor Vehicles Dept			
120 State St . . . . Montpelier VT 05603	888-998-3766	802-828-2000	338-46
Office of Veteran Affairs			
118 State St . . . . Montpelier VT 05620	888-666-9844	802-828-3379	338-46
Vocational Rehabilitation Div			
HC 2 S 280 State Dr . . . . Waterbury VT 05671	866-879-6757	802-447-2781	338-46
Vermont Bar Assn (VBA)			
35-37 Ct St PO Box 100 . . . . Montpelier VT 05601	800-639-7036	802-223-2020	72
Vermont Convention Bureau			
60 Main St Ste 100 . . . . Burlington VT 05401	877-264-3503	802-860-0606	206
Vermont Electric Co-op Inc			
42 Wescom Rd . . . . Johnson VT 05656	800-832-2667	802-635-2331	245
Vermont Energy Investment Corp			
128 Lakeside Ave Ste 401 . . . . Burlington VT 05401	800-639-6069	802-658-6060	461
Vermont Garden Park			
1100 Dorset St . . . . South Burlington VT 05403	800-538-7476	802-863-5251	97
Vermont Gas Systems Inc			
85 Swift St . . . . South Burlington VT 05403	800-639-8081	802-863-4511	324
Vermont Law School			
168 Chelsea St PO Box 96 . . . . South Royalton VT 05068	800-227-1395	802-831-1239	167-1
Vermont Maple Sugar Co			
37 Industrial Park Dr . . . . Morrisville VT 05661	800-828-2376		123
Vermont Medical Society			
134 Main St . . . . Montpelier VT 05601	800-640-8767	802-223-7898	472
Vermont Mutual Insurance Co			
89 State St PO Box 188 . . . . Montpelier VT 05601	800-451-5000	802-223-2341	390-4
Vermont NEA Today Magazine			
10 Wheelock St . . . . Montpelier VT 05602	800-649-6375	802-223-6375	455-8
Vermont Public Television (VPT)			
204 Ethan Allen Ave . . . . Colchester VT 05446	800-639-7811	802-655-4800	628
Vermont Railway Inc			
1 Railway Ln . . . . Burlington VT 05401	800-639-3088	802-658-2550	647
Vermont State Nurses Assn (VSNA)			
4 Carmichael St Ste 111 Rm 215 . . . . . . Essex VT 05452	877-810-5972		529
Vermont Structural Slate Company Inc			
3 Prospect St PO Box 98 . . . . Fair Haven VT 05743	800-343-1900	802-265-4933	720
Vermont Student Assistance Corp (VSAC)			
10 E Allen St PO Box 2000 . . . . Winooski VT 05404	800-642-3177		721
Vermont Systems Inc			
12 Market Pl . . . . Essex Junction VT 05452	877-883-8757	802-879-6993	178-10
Vermont Technical College			
PO Box 500 . . . . Randolph Center VT 05061	800-442-8821	802-728-1000	795
Vermont Teddy Bear Company Inc			
6655 Shelburne Rd . . . . Shelburne VT 05482	800-988-8277	802-985-3001	757
Vernier Software & Technology LLC			
13979 SW Millikan Way . . . . Beaverton OR 97005	800-387-2474	503-277-2299	418
Vernon College			
4400 College Dr . . . . Vernon TX 76384	866-336-9371	940-552-6291	162
Vernon Electric Co-op			
110 Saugstad Rd . . . . Westby WI 54667	800-447-5051	608-634-3121	245
Vernon Jubilee Hospital			
2101 32nd St . . . . Vernon BC V1T5L2	800-224-9376	250-545-2211	373-2
Vernon Tool Company Ltd			
1170 Trademark Dr Ste 101 . . . . Reno NV 89521	866-571-1066	775-673-2200	453
Verologix LLC			
18100 Von Karman Ave Ste 850 . . . . Irvine CA 92612	800-403-8041		196
Veros Real Estate Solutions LLC			
2333 N Broadway Ste 350 . . . . Santa Ana CA 92706	866-458-3767	714-415-6300	177
Versa Press Inc			
1465 Springbay Rd . . . . East Peoria IL 61611	800-447-7829		622
VersaCold Logistics Services			
3371 No 6 Rd . . . . Richmond BC V6V1P6	877-207-1950	604-258-0350	314
Versacom			
1501 McGill College Ave 6th Fl . . . . . . Montreal QC H3A3M8	866-320-1950	514-397-1950	
Versalogic Corp			
4211 W 11th Ave . . . . Eugene OR 97402	800-824-3163	541-485-8575	173-2
Versasuite			
10601 Pecan Park Blvd . . . . Austin TX 78750	800-903-8774		225
Versatile Mobile Systems			
4900 Ritter Rd Ste 100 . . . . Mechanicsburg PA 17055	800-262-1622		225
NYSE: CVE			
Verso Corp			
6775 Lenox Ctr Ct . . . . Memphis TN 38115	877-837-7606		
NYSE: VRS			
Verspeeten Cartage Ltd			
274129 Wallace Line . . . . Ingersoll ON N5C3J7	800-265-6701	519-425-7881	59
Vertafore Inc			
5 Waterside Crossing . . . . Windsor CT 06095	800-444-4813		178-10
Vertellus Specialties Inc			
201 N Illinois St Ste 1800 . . . . Indianapolis IN 46204	800-777-3536	317-247-8141	145
Vertex Companies Inc, The			
400 Libbey Pkwy . . . . Weymouth MA 02189	888-298-5162	781-952-6000	192
Vertex Inc			
1041 Old Cassatt Rd . . . . Berwyn PA 19312	800-355-3500	610-640-4200	178-1
Vertex Systems Inc			
2550 Corporate Exchange Dr			
Ste 104 . . . . Columbus OH 43231	866-981-2600	614-318-7100	
Vertical Alliance Group Inc			
1730 Galleria Oaks . . . . Texarkana TX 75503	877-792-3866	903-792-3866	242
Vertical Communications Inc			
3910 Freedom Cr Ste 103 . . . . Santa Clara CA 95054	800-914-9985*	408-404-1600	178-7
OTC: VRCC ■ *Sales			
Vertical Flight Society, The			
2701 Prosperity Ave Ste 210 . . . . Fairfax VA 22031	855-247-4685	703-684-6777	49-21
Vertical Management Systems Inc			
15440 Laguna Canyon Rd Ste 160 . . . . . . Irvine CA 92618	800-867-4357		177
Vertical Vision Financial Marketing LLC			
1201 Roberts Blvd			
Bldg A Ste 150 . . . . Kennesaw GA 30144	866-984-1585		5
Vertigraph Inc			
12959 Jupiter Rd Ste 252 . . . . Dallas TX 75238	800-989-4243	214-340-9436	461
Vertisoft			
990 Boul Pierre-roux E . . . . Victoriaville QC G6T0K9	877-368-3241		180
VertitechIT Inc			
4 Open Sq Way Ste 310 . . . . Holyoke MA 01040	855-638-9879		627
Vescio Threading Co			
14002 Anson Ave . . . . Santa Fe Springs CA 90670	800-361-4218	562-802-1868	452
Vesco Oil Corp			
16055 W 12-Mile Rd . . . . Southfield MI 48076	800-527-5358		575
Vessel Metrics LLC			
Soveral Harbor 2401 PGA Blvd			
Ste 155 . . . . Palm Beach Gardens FL 33410	888-214-1710		386
Vested Business Brokers Inc			
50 Karl Ave # 102 . . . . Smithtown NY 11787	877-735-5224	631-265-7300	524
Vestra Resources Inc			
5300 Aviation Dr . . . . Redding CA 96002	877-983-7872	530-223-2585	302
Veteran's Truck Line Inc			
800 Black Hawk Dr . . . . Burlington WI 53105	800-456-9476	262-539-3400	359-2
Veterans Affairs Health Care System			
1 Veterans Dr . . . . Minneapolis MN 55417	866-414-5058	612-725-2000	373-8
Veterans Affairs Medical Ctr			
508 Fulton St . . . . Durham NC 27705	888-878-6890	919-286-0411	373-8
Veterans Affairs Medical Ctr			
150 S Huntington Ave . . . . Jamaica Plain MA 02130	800-273-8255		373-8
Veterans Affairs Medical Ctr			
1310 24th Ave S . . . . Nashville TN 37212	800-228-4973	615-327-4751	373-8
Veterans Affairs Medical Ctr			
6439 Garners Ferry Rd . . . . Columbia SC 29209	888-651-2683	803-776-4000	373-8
Veterans Affairs Medical Ctr			
2215 Fuller Rd . . . . Ann Arbor MI 48105	800-361-8387	734-769-7100	373-8
Veterans Affairs Medical Ctr			
1100 Tunnel Rd . . . . Asheville NC 28805	800-932-6408	828-298-7911	373-8
Veterans Affairs Medical Ctr			
10 N Greene St . . . . Baltimore MD 21201	800-463-6295	410-605-7000	373-8
Veterans Affairs Medical Ctr			
940 Belmont St . . . . Brockton MA 02301	800-865-3384	508-583-4500	373-8
Veterans Affairs Medical Ctr			
3495 Bailey Ave . . . . Buffalo NY 14215	800-532-8387	716-834-9200	373-8
Veterans Affairs Medical Ctr			
820 S Damen Ave . . . . Chicago IL 60612	888-569-5282	312-569-8387	373-8
Veterans Affairs Medical Ctr			
2002 Holcombe Blvd . . . . Houston TX 77030	800-553-2278	713-791-1414	373-8
Veterans Affairs Medical Ctr			
1700 S Lincoln Ave . . . . Lebanon PA 17042	800-409-8771		373-8
Veterans Affairs Medical Ctr			
1030 Jefferson Ave . . . . Memphis TN 38104	800-636-8262	901-523-8990	373-8
Veterans Affairs Medical Ctr			
1201 NW 16th St . . . . Miami FL 33125	888-276-1785	305-324-4455	373-8
Veterans Affairs Medical Ctr			
79 Middleville Rd . . . . Northport NY 11768	800-877-6976	631-261-4400	373-8
Veterans Affairs Medical Ctr			
921 NE 13th St . . . . Oklahoma City OK 73104	866-835-5273	405-456-1000	373-8
Veterans Affairs Medical Ctr			
4101 Woolworth Ave . . . . Omaha NE 68105	800-451-5796	402-346-8800	373-8
Veterans Affairs Medical Ctr			
830 Chalkstone Ave . . . . Providence RI 02908	866-590-2976	401-273-7100	373-8
Veterans Affairs Medical Ctr			
500 Foothill Dr . . . . Salt Lake City UT 84148	800-613-4012	801-582-1565	373-8
Veterans Affairs Medical Ctr			
601 Hwy 6 W . . . . Iowa City IA 52246	866-687-7382	319-338-0581	373-8
Veterans Affairs Medical Ctr			
1601 Kirkwood Hwy . . . . Wilmington DE 19805	800-450-8262	302-994-2511	373-8
Veterans Affairs Medical Ctr			
10000 Bay Pines Blvd . . . . Bay Pines FL 33744	888-820-0230	727-398-6661	373-8
Veterans Affairs Medical Ctr			
13000 Bruce B Downs Blvd . . . . Tampa FL 33612	888-716-7787	813-972-2000	373-8
Veterans Affairs Medical Ctr			
2121 Lake Ave . . . . Fort Wayne IN 46805	800-360-8387	260-426-5431	
Veterans Affairs Medical Ctr			
1500 Weiss St . . . . Saginaw MI 48602	877-222-8387	989-497-2500	373-8
Veterans Affairs Medical Ctr			
718 Smyth Rd . . . . Manchester NH 03104	800-892-8384	603-624-4366	373-8
Veterans Affairs Medical Ctr			
800 Irving Ave . . . . Syracuse NY 13210	800-792-4334	315-425-4400	373-8
Veterans Affairs Medical Ctr			
100 Emancipation Dr . . . . Hampton VA 23667	800-488-8244	757-722-9961	373-8
Veterans Affairs Medical Ctr			
2500 Overlook Terr . . . . Madison WI 53705	888-478-8321	608-256-1901	373-8
Veterans Affairs Puget Sound Medical Ctr			
1660 S Columbian Way . . . . Seattle WA 98108	800-329-8387	206-762-1010	373-8
Veterans Benefits Administration			
810 Vermont Ave NW . . . . Washington DC 20420	800-827-1000		339-18
Veterans Health Administration			
810 Vermont Ave NW . . . . Washington DC 20420	844-698-2311		339-18

			Toll-Free	Phone	Class

Gulf War Veterans Information
810 Vermont Ave NW .... Washington DC 20420 — 800-313-2232 — 339-18

Veterans Health Care System of the Ozarks
1100 N College Ave .... Fayetteville AR 72703 — 800-691-8387 — 479-443-4301 — 373-8

Veterans Home
1200 E 18th St .... Hastings MN 55033 — 877-838-3803 — 651-539-2400 — 788

Veterans Home of California-Barstow
100 E Veterans Pkwy .... Barstow CA 92311 — 800-746-0606 — 760-252-6200 — 788

Veterans Home of California-Chula Vista
700 E Naples Ct .... Chula Vista CA 91911 — 800-952-5626 — 788

Veterans of Foreign Wars of the US (VFW)
406 W 34th St .... Kansas City MO 64111 — 800-963-3180 — 816-756-3390 — 48-19

Veterinary Pet Insurance Inc
PO Box 2344 .... Brea CA 92822 — 800-872-7387 — 390-1

Veterinary Pharmacies of America Inc (VPA)
4802 N Sam Houston Pkwy W
Ste 100 .... Houston TX 77066 — 877-838-7979 — 580

VetJobs Inc
PO Box 71445 .... Marietta GA 30007 — 877-838-5627 — 770-993-5117 — 260

Vetoquinol Canada Inc
2000 Ch Georges .... Lavaltrie QC J5T3S5 — 800-363-1700 — 450-586-2252 — 580

Vet-Stem Inc
12860 Danielson Ct Ste B. ...... Poway CA 92064 — 888-387-8361 — 858-748-2004 — 789

VetStrategy
30 Whitmore Rd .... Woodbridge ON L4L7Z4 — 866-901-6471 — 461

Vetstreet
780 Township Line Rd .... Yardley PA 19067 — 888-799-8387 — 215-493-0621 — 386

Vetter Senior Living
20220 Harney St .... Elkhorn NE 68022 — 800-388-4264 — 402-895-3932 — 461

Vetter Stone Co (VSC)
23894 Third Ave .... Mankato MN 56001 — 800-878-2850 — 507-345-4568 — 720

vFinance Inc
1200 N Federal Hwy 400 ... Boca Raton FL 33432 — 800-487-0577

V-fluence Interactive
4579 Laclede Ave Ste 275 ...... St. Louis MO 63108 — 877-835-8362 — 225

VFUC (Visions Federal Credit Union)
24 McKinley Ave .... Endicott NY 13760 — 800-242-2120 — 607-754-7900 — 219

VFW (Veterans of Foreign Wars of the US)
406 W 34th St .... Kansas City MO 64111 — 800-963-3180 — 816-756-3390 — 48-19

V&H Inc
1505 S Central Ave .... Marshfield WI 54449 — 800-826-2308 — 715-486-8800 — 57

Vi 71 S Wacker Dr .... Chicago IL 60606 — 800-421-1442 — 312-803-8800 — 668

VIA Metropolitan Transit
800 W Myrtle St .... San Antonio TX 78212 — 866-362-4200 — 210-362-2000 — 466

VIA Rail Canada Inc
3 Place Ville Marie Ste 500. .... Montreal QC H3B2C9 — 888-842-7245 — 514-871-6000 — 645

Viable Solutions Inc
7802 Kingspointe Pkwy Ste 206 .... Orlando FL 32819 — 800-679-7626 — 407-249-9600

Viair Corp 15 Edelman .... Irvine CA 92618 — 800-618-1994 — 949-585-0011 — 782

ViaSat Inc
6155 El Camino Real .... Carlsbad CA 92009 — 855-463-9333 — 760-476-2200 — 677
NASDAQ: VSAT

ViaTech Publishing Solutions
1440 Fifth Ave .... Bay Shore NY 11706 — 800-645-8558 — 631-968-8500 — 86

Viatran Corp
3829 Forest Pkwy Ste 500 .... Wheatfield NY 14120 — 800-688-0030 — 716-629-3800 — 253

Vibac SPA
12250 Industrial Blvd .... Montreal QC H1B5M5 — 800-557-0192 — 514-640-0250 — 727

Vibra Screw Inc
755 Union Blvd .... Totowa NJ 07512 — 800-243-7677 — 973-256-7410 — 468

Vibrant Corp
8330A Washington Pl NE .... Albuquerque NM 87113 — 800-410-3048 — 505-314-1488 — 738

Viceroy Santa Monica
1819 Ocean Ave .... Santa Monica CA 90401 — 888-622-4567 — 310-260-7500 — 378

Vi-Chem Corp
55 Cottage Grove St SW .... Grand Rapids MI 49507 — 800-477-8501 — 616-247-8501 — 601-2

Vicon Industries Inc
135 Fell Ct .... Hauppauge NY 11788 — 800-645-9116* — 631-952-2288 — 643
*NYSE: VII ■ *Sales*

Viconics Technologies Inc
7262 Marconi 3rd fl .... Montreal QC H2R2Z5 — 800-563-5660 — 514-321-5660 — 406

Victaulic Co
4901 Kesslersville Rd .... Easton PA 18040 — 800-742-5842* — 610-559-3300 — 591
*Sales

Victor L Phillips Co
4100 Gardner Ave .... Kansas City MO 64120 — 800-878-9290 — 816-241-9290 — 357

Victor Printing Inc
1 Victor Way .... Sharon PA 16146 — 800-443-2845 — 110

Victor Settings Inc
25 Brook Ave .... Maywood NJ 07607 — 800-322-9008 — 201-845-4433 — 406

Victor Technology LLC
175 E Crossroads Pkwy .... Bolingbrook IL 60440 — 800-628-2420 — 630-754-4400 — 118

Victor Valley Community College
18422 Bear Valley Rd .... Victorville CA 92392 — 877-741-8532 — 760-245-4271 — 162

Victoria Advocate
PO Box 1518 .... Victoria TX 77902 — 800-234-8108 — 361-575-1451 — 528-2

Victoria College
2200 E Red River St .... Victoria TX 77901 — 877-843-4369 — 361-573-3291 — 162

Victoria Cruises Inc
57-08 39th Ave .... Woodside NY 11377 — 800-348-8084* — 212-818-1680 — 221
*Cust Svc

Victoria Inn Winnipeg
1808 Wellington Ave .... Winnipeg MB R3H0G3 — 877-842-4667 — 204-786-4801 — 378

Victoria Regent Hotel, The
1234 Wharf St .... Victoria BC V8W3H9 — 800-663-7472 — 250-386-2211 — 378

Victoria Theatre
138 N Main St .... Dayton OH 45402 — 888-228-3630 — 937-228-3630 — 568

Victoria's Secret Stores
4 Limited Pkwy .... Reynoldsburg OH 43068 — 800-411-5116 — 157-6

Victorian Trading Co
15600 W 99th St .... Lenexa KS 66219 — 800-700-2035* — 913-438-3995 — 457
*Cust Svc

Victory Electric Co-op Assn Inc
3230 N 14th Ave .... Dodge City KS 67801 — 800-279-7915 — 620-227-2139 — 245

Victory Enterprises Inc
5200 30th St SW .... Davenport IA 52802 — 800-670-5716 — 563-884-4444 — 180

Victory Funds
4900 Tiedeman Rd 4th Fl .... Brooklyn OH 43219 — 877-660-4400 — 216-898-2400 — 524

Victory Furniture
2512 Santa Monica Blvd .... Santa Monica CA 90404 — 800-953-2000 — 310-264-1046 — 321

Victory Refrigeration Inc
110 Woodcrest Rd .... Cherry Hill NJ 08003 — 800-523-5008 — 856-428-4200 — 660

Victory White Metal Co
3027 E 55th St .... Cleveland OH 44127 — 800-635-5050 — 216-271-1400 — 483

VictorystoreCom Inc
5200 SW 30th St .... Davenport IA 52802 — 866-241-2295 — 866-241-2294 — 623

Vicwest Corp
1296 S Service Rd W .... Oakville ON L6L5T7 — 800-265-6583 — 905-825-2252 — 489

VIDA Diagnostics Inc
2500 Crosspark Rd W150 BioVentures Ctr
.... Coralville IA 52241 — 855-900-8432 — 804

Video Display Corp
1868 Tucker Industrial Rd .... Tucker GA 30084 — 800-241-5005* — 770-938-2080 — 173-4
*OTC: VIDE ■ *Cust Svc*

Video King Gaming Systems (VKGS LLC)
2717 N 118 Cir Ste 210 .... Omaha NE 68164 — 800-635-9912 — 402-951-2970 — 322

Video Symphony Entertraining Inc
266 E Magnolia Blvd .... Burbank CA 91502 — 888-370-7589 — 818-557-6500 — 511

Videojet Technologies Inc
1500 Mittel Blvd .... Wood Dale IL 60191 — 800-843-3610* — 630-860-7300 — 385
*Cust Svc

Videoland Inc
6808 Hornwood Dr .... Houston TX 77074 — 800-877-2900 — 35

Videomaker Magazine
1350 E Ninth St PO Box 4591 .... Chico CA 95927 — 800-284-3226 — 530-891-8410 — 455-9

VideoMining Corp
403 S Allen St Ste 101 .... State College PA 16801 — 800-898-9950 — 177

Videotex Systems Inc
10255 Miller Rd .... Dallas TX 75238 — 800-888-4336 — 972-231-9200 — 178-8

Vie de France Yamazaki Inc
2070 Chain Bridge Rd Ste 500 .... Vienna VA 22182 — 800-446-4404* — 703-442-9205 — 68
*General

Viejas Casino
5000 Willows Rd .... Alpine CA 91901 — 800-847-6537 — 619-445-5400 — 133

Viejas Outlet Ctr
5005 Willows .... Alpine CA 91901 — 877-303-2695 — 619-659-2070 — 458

Vienna Sausage Manufacturing Co
2501 N Damen Ave .... Chicago IL 60647 — 800-366-3647 — 773-278-7800 — 296-26

Vietnam Women's Memorial Foundation Inc
1735 Connecticut Ave NW
3rd Fl .... Washington DC 20009 — 866-822-8963 — 50-4

Vigilante Electric Co-op Inc
225 E Bannack St .... Dillon MT 59725 — 800-221-8271

Vigilistics Inc
711 Grand Ave Ste 290. .... San Rafael CA 94901 — 888-235-7540 — 949-900-8380 — 804

Vignette Corp
1301 S Mopac Expy Ste 100. .... Austin TX 78746 — 800-540-7292 — 512-741-4300 — 178-1

VIH Aviation Group
1962 Canso Rd .... North Saanich BC V8L5V5 — 866-844-4354 — 250-656-3987 — 358

VIH Logging Ltd
1962 Canso Rd .... North Saanich BC V8L5V5 — 866-844-4354 — 250-656-3987 — 358

Vi-Jon Labs Inc
8800 Page Ave .... Saint Louis MO 63114 — 800-227-1863 — 314-427-1000 — 214

Viking Acoustical Corp
21480 Heath Ave .... Lakeville MN 55044 — 800-328-8385 — 952-469-3405 — 319-1

Viking Client Services Inc
7500 Office Ridge Cir
Ste 100 .... Eden Prairie MN 55344 — 800-767-7895 — 952-944-7575 — 392

Viking Corp
210 N Industrial Pk Dr .... Hastings MI 49058 — 800-968-9501 — 269-945-9501 — 283

Viking Drill & Tool Inc
355 State St .... Saint Paul MN 55107 — 800-328-4655 — 651-227-8911 — 491

Viking Electric Supply Inc
451 Industrial Blvd W .... Minneapolis MN 55413 — 800-435-3345 — 612-627-1300 — 246

Viking Engineering & Development Inc
5750 Main St N .... Fridley MN 55432 — 800-545-5112* — 763-571-2400 — 816
*Sales

Viking Forest Products LLC
7615 Smetana Rd .... Eden Prairie MN 55344 — 800-733-3801 — 952-941-6512 — 191-3

Viking Materials Inc
3225 Como Ave SE .... Minneapolis MN 55414 — 800-682-3942* — 612-617-5800 — 490
*General

Viking Pools
121 Crawford Rd PO Box 96. .... Williams CA 95987 — 800-854-7665 — 724

Viking Range Corp
111 Front St .... Greenwood MS 38930 — 888-845-4641 — 662-455-1200 — 298

Viking Recreational Vehicles LLC
580 W Burr Oak St
PO Box 549. .... Centreville MI 49032 — 888-422-2582

Viking River Cruises
5700 Canoga Ave Ste 200 .... Woodland Hills CA 91367 — 877-668-4546* — 818-227-1234 — 221
*Cust Svc

Viking Trailways
201 Glendale Av .... Joplin MO 64804 — 877-467-3346 — 108

Viktor Incentives & Meetings
4020 Copper View Ste 130 .... Traverse City MI 49684 — 800-748-0478 — 231-947-0882 — 383

Villa Gardens
842 E Villa St .... Pasadena CA 91101 — 800-958-4552 — 626-463-5330 — 668

Villa Julie College
1525 Green Spring Valley Rd .... Stevenson MD 21153 — 877-468-6852 — 410-486-7001 — 166

Villa Lighting Supply Inc
2929 Chouteau Ave .... Saint Louis MO 63103 — 800-325-0963 — 392

Villa Marin
100 Thorndale Dr .... San Rafael CA 94903 — 888-926-2030 — 415-492-2408 — 668

Villa Roma Resort & Conference Ctr
356 Villa Roma Rd .... Callicoon NY 12723 — 800-533-6767 — 845-887-4880 — 665

Village Automotive Group
75-95 N Beacon St .... Boston MA 02135 — 888-707-5524

Village Green Cos
28411 Northwestern Hwy
Ste 400 .... Southfield MI 48034 — 866-396-1105

Village Inn
400 W 48th Ave .... Denver CO 80216 — 800-800-3644 — 303-294-0609 — 666

Village Latch Inn
101 Hill St PO Box 3000. .... SouthHampton NY 11968 — 800-545-2824 — 631-283-2160 — 378

Village Nurseries
1589 N Main St .... Orange CA 92867 — 800-542-0209 — 323

				Toll-Free	Phone	Class
Village on the Green						
500 Village Pl	Longwood	FL	32779	**888-541-3443***	407-682-0230	668
*Mktg						
Village Vacances Valcartier						
1860 Valcartier Blvd	Valcartier	QC	G0A4S0	**888-384-5524**	418-844-2200	32
Villages of Lake Sumter Inc						
1000 Lake Sumter Landing	The Villages	FL	32162	**800-245-1081**	352-753-2270	649
Villagio Inn & Spa						
6481 Washington St	Yountville	CA	94599	**800-351-1133**	707-944-8877	378
Villas by the Sea Resort						
1175 N Beachview Dr	Jekyll Island	GA	31527	**800-841-6262**	912-635-2521	665
Villas of Grand Cypress Golf Resort						
1 N Jacaranda	Orlando	FL	32836	**877-330-7377**	407-239-4700	665
Villaume Industries Inc						
2926 Lone Oak Cir	Eagan	MN	55121	**800-488-3610***	651-454-3610	812
*Cust Svc						
Villere's Florist						
750 Martin Behrman Ave	Metairie	LA	70005	**800-845-5373**	504-833-3716	292
Villeroy & Boch USA Inc						
3A S Middlesex Ave	Monroe Township	NJ	08331	**800-536-2284**		361
Vimco Inc						
300 Hansen Access Rd	King Of Prussia	PA	19406	**800-468-4626***	610-768-0500	191-1
*Cust Svc						
Vimich Traffic Logistics						
12201 Tecumseh Rd	Tecumseh	ON	N8N1M3	**800-284-1045**		447
Vin Devers Inc						
5570 Monroe St	Sylvania	OH	43560	**888-847-9535**	419-885-5111	57
Vincennes University						
1002 N First St	Vincennes	IN	47591	**800-742-9198**	812-888-4313	162
Jasper 850 College Ave	Jasper	IN	47546	**800-809-8852**	812-482-3030	162
Vincent Printing Company Inc						
1512 Sholar Ave	Chattanooga	TN	37406	**800-251-7262**		683
Vincit Group, The						
412 Georgia Ave Ste 300	Chattanooga	TN	37403	**888-484-6248**		354
Vining Sparks IBG LP						
775 Ridge Lake Blvd	Memphis	TN	38120	**800-829-0321**	901-766-3000	686
Vinson Guard Service Inc						
955 Howard Ave	New Orleans	LA	70113	**800-441-7899**	504-529-2260	689
Vinson Process Controls Company LP						
2747 Highpoint Oaks Dr	Lewisville	TX	75067	**800-420-6571**	972-459-8200	357
Vintage Air Inc						
18865 Goll St	San Antonio	TX	78266	**800-862-6658**	210-654-7171	660
Vintage House						
6541 Washington St	Yountville	CA	94599	**800-351-1133***		378
*Cust Svc						
Vintners Inn						
4350 Barnes Rd	Santa Rosa	CA	95403	**800-421-2584**	707-575-7350	378
Vinylplex Inc						
1800 Atkinson Ave	Pittsburg	KS	66762	**877-779-7473**	620-231-8290	592
Vinyltech Corp						
201 S 61st Ave	Phoenix	AZ	85043	**800-255-3924**	602-233-0071	592
Viox Services Inc						
15 W Voorhees St	Cincinnati	OH	45215	**888-846-9462**	513-948-8469	271
VIPdesk Connect Inc						
908 King St Ste 400W	Alexandria	VA	22314	**844-874-3472**		392
VIRA Insight LLC						
120 Dividend Dr Ste 100	Coppell	TX	75019	**800-305-8472**		286
Viracon Inc						
800 Pk Dr	Owatonna	MN	55060	**800-533-2080**	507-451-9555	329
Virco Manufacturing Corp						
2027 Harpers Way	Torrance	CA	90501	**800-448-4726***	310-533-0474	319-3
NASDAQ: VIRC ■ *Cust Svc						
Virgin Atlantic Airways Ltd						
75 N Water St	Norwalk	CT	06854	**888-747-7474**	120-375-0200	25
Virgin Atlantic Cargo						
78 N Boundary Rd	Jamaica	NY	11430	**800-828-6822**	516-775-2600	12
Virgin Mobile USA Inc						
10 Independence Blvd	Warren	NJ	07059	**888-322-1122**		731
Virgin River Casino Corp						
100 Pioneer Blvd	Mesquite	NV	89027	**877-438-2929**		377
Aging & Rehabilitative Services Dept						
8004 Franklin Farms Dr	Richmond	VA	23229	**800-552-5019**	804-662-7000	338-47
Virginia						
Aging Dept						
1610 Forest Ave Ste 100	Henrico	VA	23229	**800-552-3402**	804-662-9333	338-47
Community College System						
300 Arboretum Pl Ste 200	Richmond	VA	23236	**844-897-9096**		338-47
Criminal Injuries Compensation Fund (CICF)						
PO Box 26927	Richmond	VA	23261	**800-552-4007**		338-47
Employment Commission						
703 E Main St	Richmond	VA	23219	**866-832-2363**		259
Health Professions Dept						
9960 Mayland Dr Ste 300	Henrico	VA	23233	**800-533-1560**	804-367-4400	338-47
Housing Development Authority						
601 S Belvidere St	Richmond	VA	23220	**877-843-2123**		338-47
Information Technologies Agency (VITA)						
11751 Meadowville Ln	Chester	VA	23836	**866-637-8482**		338-47
Social Services Dept						
801 E Main St	Richmond	VA	23219	**800-552-3431**	804-726-7000	338-47
State Corp Commission						
1300 E Main St PO Box 1197	Richmond	VA	23218	**800-552-7945**	804-371-9967	338-47
State Parks Div						
600 E Main St 24th Fl	Richmond	VA	23219	**800-933-7275***	804-692-0403	338-47
*Resv						
Vital Records Div						
2001 Maywill St PO Box 1000	Richmond	VA	23230	**877-572-6333**	804-662-6200	338-47
Workers Compensation Commission						
333 E Franklin St	Richmond	VA	23219	**877-664-2566**		338-47
Virginia 529						
9001 Arboretum Pkwy	Richmond	VA	23236	**888-567-0540**		721
Virginia American Water Co (VAWC)						
2223 Duke St	Alexandria	VA	22314	**800-452-6863**	703-706-3879	782
Virginia Aquarium & Marine Science Center						
717 General Booth Blvd	Virginia Beach	VA	23451	**800-822-3224**	757-385-3474	517
Virginia Baptist Hospital						
3300 Rivermont Ave	Lynchburg	VA	24503	**866-749-4455**	434-200-3000	373-3
Virginia Beach Convention & Visitor Bureau (VBCVB)						
2101 Parks Ave Ste 500	Virginia Beach	VA	23451	**800-700-7702**	757-385-4700	206
Virginia Beach Resort Hotel & Conference Ctr						
2800 Shore Dr	Virginia Beach	VA	23451	**800-468-2722**		665
Virginia College						
Birmingham						
488 Palisades Blvd	Birmingham	AL	35209	**800-584-7290**	205-802-1200	795
Virginia Commonwealth University						
910 W Franklin St	Richmond	VA	23284	**800-841-3638**	804-828-0100	166
Virginia Commonwealth University Cabell Library						
901 Park Ave PO Box 842033	Richmond	VA	23284	**844-352-7399**	804-828-1111	433-6
Virginia Commonwealth University School of Medicine						
1101 E Marshall St						
PO Box 980565	Richmond	VA	23298	**800-332-8813**	804-828-9629	167-2
Virginia Cook Realtors						
5950 Sherry Ln Ste 100	Dallas	TX	75225	**877-975-2665**	214-696-8877	
Virginia Credit Union						
7500 Boulders View Dr	Richmond	VA	23225	**800-285-5051**	804-323-6000	219
Virginia Episcopal School						
400 VES Rd	Lynchburg	VA	24503	**800-937-3582**	434-385-3607	618
Virginia Historical Society Museum of Virginia History						
428 N Blvd	Richmond	VA	23220	**800-473-0060**	804-340-1800	517
Virginia International Terminals Inc						
7737 Hampton Blvd	Norfolk	VA	23505	**800-541-2431***	757-440-7000	463
*General						
Virginia Journal of Education						
116 S Third St	Richmond	VA	23219	**800-552-9554**	804-648-5801	455-8
Virginia Marti College of Art & Design						
11724 Detroit Ave	Lakewood	OH	44107	**800-473-4350**		164
Virginia Medical News						
2924 Emerywood Pkwy Ste 300	Richmond	VA	23294	**800-746-6768**		455-16
Virginia Military Institute						
319 Letcher Ave	Lexington	VA	24450	**800-767-4207**	540-464-7211	166
Virginia Mirror Co Inc						
300 Moss St S	Martinsville	VA	24112	**800-368-3011**	276-632-9816	329
Virginia Museum of Transportation						
303 Norfolk Ave	Roanoke	VA	24016	**800-578-4111**	540-342-5670	517
Virginia Peninsula Chamber of Commerce						
21 Enterprise Pkwy Ste 100	Hampton	VA	23666	**800-462-3204**	757-262-2000	139
Virginia Plastics Co Inc						
3453 Aerial Way Dr SW	Roanoke	VA	24018	**877-351-1699**	540-981-9700	811
Virginia Press Services Inc						
11529 Nuckols Rd	Glen Allen	VA	23059	**800-849-8717**	804-521-7570	620
Virginia Society of CPA's						
4309 Cox Rd	Glen Allen	VA	23060	**800-733-8272**	804-270-5344	2
Virginia State Bar						
707 E Main St Ste 1500	Richmond	VA	23219	**800-552-7977**	804-775-0500	72
Virginia State University						
1 Hayden Dr	Petersburg	VA	23806	**800-871-7611***	804-524-5000	166
*Admissions						
Virginia Transformer Corp						
220 Glade View Dr	Roanoke	VA	24012	**800-882-3944**	540-345-9892	762
Virginia Union University						
1500 N Lombardy St	Richmond	VA	23220	**800-368-3227**	804-342-3570	166
Virginia Veterinary Medical Assn (VVMA)						
3801 Westerre Pkwy Ste D	Henrico	VA	23233	**800-937-8862**	804-346-2611	790
Virginia Wesleyan College						
1584 Wesleyan Dr	Norfolk	VA	23502	**800-737-8684**	757-455-3200	166
Virginia West Electric Supply Co (WVES)						
250 12-th St W	Huntington	WV	25704	**800-624-3433**	304-525-0361	246
Virginia Western Community College						
3094 Colonial Ave	Roanoke	VA	24015	**855-874-6690**	540-857-8922	162
Virginian Lodge						
750 W Broadway PO Box 1052	Jackson Hole	WY	83001	**800-262-4999**	307-733-2792	378
Virginian Suites						
1500 Arlington Blvd	Arlington	VA	22209	**866-371-1446**	703-522-9600	378
Virnig Manufacturing Inc						
101 Gateway Dr NE	Rice	MN	56367	**800-648-2408**		190
Virtela Technology Services Inc						
5680 Greenwood Plz Blvd						
	Greenwood Village	CO	80111	**877-803-9629**	720-475-4000	176
Virtexco Corp						
977 Norfolk Sq	Norfolk	VA	23502	**800-766-1082**	757-466-1114	186
Virtua Health						
303 Lippincott Dr 4th Fl	Marlton	NJ	08053	**888-847-8823**	609-914-6000	352
Virtual Images						
425 S Rockefeller Ave	Ontario	CA	91761	**800-924-5401**		88
Virtual Training Company Inc						
5395 Main St	Stephens City	VA	22655	**888-316-5374**	540-869-8686	177
VirtualBank						
PO Box 109638	Palm Beach Gardens	FL	33410	**877-998-2265**		70
VirtualPBXcom Inc						
111 N Market St Ste 402	San Jose	CA	95113	**888-825-0800**	408-414-7646	
Virtucom Inc						
5060 Avalon Ridge Pkwy Ste 300	Norcross	GA	30071	**800-890-2611**	770-908-8100	174
Virtuoso						
505 Main St Ste 5	Fort Worth	TX	76102	**800-401-4274**	817-870-0300	767
Virtus Investment Partners Inc						
100 Pearl St 9th Fl	Hartford	CT	06103	**800-243-1574**	413-775-6091	
Visalia Chamber of Commerce						
222 N Garden St Ste 300	Visalia	CA	93291	**800-728-0724**	559-734-5876	139
Visalia Convention & Visitors Bureau						
PO Box 2734	Visalia	CA	93279	**800-524-0303**	559-334-0141	206
Visalia Convention Ctr						
303 E Acequia Ave	Visalia	CA	93291	**800-640-4888**	559-713-4000	205
Visalia Medical Lab						
5400 W Hillsdale Ave	Visalia	CA	93291	**800-486-2362**	559-738-7500	417
Visara International Inc						
2700 Gateway Centre Blvd						
Ste 600	Morrisville	NC	27560	**888-334-4380**	919-882-0200	176
Viscount Gort Hotel						
1670 Portage Ave	Winnipeg	MB	R3J0C9	**800-665-1122**	204-775-0451	378
Viscount Suite Hotel						
4855 E Broadway Blvd	Tucson	AZ	85711	**800-527-9666***	520-745-6500	378
*Resv						
Vishay Intertechnology Inc						
63 Lancaster Ave	Malvern	PA	19355	**800-567-6098**	610-644-1300	692
NYSE: VSH						
Visible Systems Corp						
201 Spring St	Lexington	MA	02421	**888-850-9911***	781-778-0200	178-1
*Sales						

Name / Address	City	State	Zip	Toll-Free	Phone	Class
Vision Capital Management Inc 1 SW Columbia Ste 915	Portland	OR	97258	**800-707-5335**		
Vision Council, The 225 Reinekers Ln Ste 700	Alexandria	VA	22314	**866-826-0290**	703-548-4560	49-4
Vision Envelope Inc 2451 Executive St	Charlotte	NC	28208	**800-200-9797**		623
Vision Financial Corp PO Box 506	Keene	NH	03431	**800-793-0223**		390-5
Vision Graphics Inc 5610 Boeing Dr	Loveland	CO	80538	**800-833-4263**	970-679-9000	623
Vision Solutions Inc 15300 Barranca Pkwy	Irvine	CA	92618	**800-683-4667**	949-253-6500	178-12
Vision Source LP 23824 Hwy 59 N Ste 101	Kingwood	TX	77339	**888-558-2020**	281-312-1111	237
Vision Technologies Inc 530 McCormick Dr Ste G	Glen Burnie	MD	21061	**866-746-1122**	410-424-2183	177
Vision-Ease Lens Inc 7000 Sunwood Dr NW *Cust Svc	Ramsey	MN	55303	**800-328-3449***	320-251-8140	538
Visions Federal Credit Union (VFUC) 24 McKinley Ave	Endicott	NY	13760	**800-242-2120**	607-754-7900	219
Visions Services 500 Greenwich St 3rd Fl	New York	NY	10013	**888-245-8333**	212-625-1616	121
Visionworks of America Inc 175 E Houston St	San Antonio	TX	78205	**800-669-1183**		539
Visit Dothan Alabama 3311 Ross Clark Cir	Dothan	AL	36303	**888-449-0212**	334-794-6622	206
Visit Duluth 21 W Superior St Ste 100	Duluth	MN	55802	**800-438-5884**	218-722-4011	206
Visit Jacksonville 208 N Laura St Ste 1	Jacksonville	FL	32202	**800-733-2668**	904-798-9111	206
Visit Rochester 45 E Ave Ste 400	Rochester	NY	14604	**800-677-7282**	585-279-8300	206
Visit Salt Lake 90 SW Temple	Salt Lake City	UT	84101	**800-541-4955**	801-534-4900	206
Visit Sarasota County 1777 Main St Ste 302	Sarasota	FL	34236	**800-522-9799**	941-955-0991	206
Visit St Petersburg Clearwater 13805 58th St N Ste 2-200	Clearwater	FL	33760	**877-352-3224**	727-464-7200	206
Visit Topeka Inc 618 S Kansas Ave	Topeka	KS	66603	**800-235-1030**	785-234-1030	206
VisitErie 208 E Bayfront Pkwy Ste 103	Erie	PA	16507	**800-524-3743**	814-454-1000	206
Visiting Nurse Assn 12565 W Ctr Rd Ste 100	Omaha	NE	68144	**800-456-8869**	402-342-5566	370
Visiting Nurse Assn of Morris County (Inc) 175 South St	Morristown	NJ	07960	**800-938-4748**	973-539-1216	362
Visiting Nurse Assn of Ohio 2500 E 22nd St	Cleveland	OH	44115	**877-698-6264**	216-931-1300	370
Visiting Nurse Assn of the Treasure Coast 1110 35th Ln	Vero Beach	FL	32960	**800-749-5760**	772-567-5551	370
Visiting Nurse Assns of America (VNAA) 1800 Diagonal Rd Ste 600	Alexandria	VA	22314	**888-866-8773**	571-527-1520	49-8
Visiting Nurse Assocation of Greater St Louis *Hospice Care* 2029 Woodland Pkwy Ste 105	Maryland Heights	MO	63146	**800-392-4740**	314-918-7171	370
Viskase Cos Inc 333 E Butterfield Rd Ste 40	Lombard	IL	60148	**800-323-8562**	630-874-0700	544
VIST Financial Corp 1240 Broadcasting Rd *NASDAQ: VIST*	Wyomissing	PA	19610	**888-238-3330**	610-208-0966	359-2
Vista Auto 21501 Ventura Blvd	Woodland Hills	CA	91364	**888-887-6530**	888-442-8817	57
Vista del Monte 3775 Modoc Rd	Santa Barbara	CA	93105	**800-736-1333**	805-687-0793	668
Vista Electronics Inc 27525 Newhall Ranch Rd	Valencia	CA	91355	**800-847-8299**	661-294-9820	511
Vista Grande Villa 2251 Springport Rd	Jackson	MI	49202	**800-889-8499**	517-787-0222	668
Vista International Packaging LLC 1126 88th Pl	Kenosha	WI	53143	**800-558-4058**		296-26
Vista Medical Ctr 1324 N Sheridan Rd	Waukegan	IL	60085	**800-843-2464**	847-360-3000	373-3
Vista Metals Inc 65 Ballou Blvd	Bristol	RI	02809	**800-431-4113**	401-253-1772	490
Vista Verde Guest & Ski Ranch PO Box 770465	Steamboat Springs	CO	80477	**800-526-7433**	970-879-3858	239
VistaPharm Inc 630 Central Ave	New Providence	NJ	07974	**877-437-8567**		231
Vistar Corp 12650 E Arapahoe Rd	Centennial	CO	80112	**800-880-9900**	303-662-7100	297-8
Vistar Eye Center 2802 Brandon Ave	Roanoke	VA	24015	**866-615-5454**	540-855-5100	539
VistaVu Solutions Inc 30 Springborough Blvd SW Ste 214	Calgary	AB	T3H0N9	**888-300-2727**	403-263-2727	179
Visual Communications Group Inc 1548 Cliff Rd E	Burnsville	MN	55337	**800-566-4162**		511
Visual Departures Ltd 48 Sheffield Business Pk	Ashley Falls	MA	01222	**800-628-2003**		587
Visual Learning Systems Inc PO Box 8226	Missoula	MT	59807	**866-968-7857**		177
Visual Marketing Inc 154 W Erie St	Chicago	IL	60654	**800-662-8640**	312-664-9177	233
Visual Pak Co 1909 S Waukegan Rd	Waukegan	IL	60085	**877-689-0001**		
Visual Retail Plus 540 Hudson St	Hackensack	NJ	07601	**888-767-4004**		
Visualware Inc 937 Sierra Dr PO Box 668	Turlock	CA	95380	**866-847-9273**	209-262-3491	177
Vita Food Products Inc 2222 West Lake St	Chicago	IL	60612	**800-989-8482**	312-738-4500	296-13
Vita Plus Corp 2514 Fish Hatchery Rd	Madison	WI	53713	**800-362-8334**	608-256-1988	445
Vitac Corp 8300 E Maplewood Ave Ste 310	Greenwood Village	CO	80111	**800-278-4822**	724-514-4111	

Name / Address	City	State	Zip	Toll-Free	Phone	Class
Vitacostcom Inc 5400 Broken Sound Blvd NW Ste 500	Boca Raton	FL	33487	**800-381-0759**		237
VitaDigestcom 20687-2 Amar Rd Ste 258	Walnut	CA	91789	**877-848-2168**		344
Vital Images Inc 5850 Opus Pkwy Ste 300	Minnetonka	MN	55343	**800-208-3005**	952-487-9500	178-10
VitalAire Canada Inc 6990 Creditview Rd Unit 6	Mississauga	ON	L5N8R9	**888-629-0202**		474
Vitamin Shoppe Inc 2101 91st St *NYSE: VSI*	North Bergen	NJ	07047	**800-223-1216**	201-868-5959	237
Vitaminerals Inc 1815 Flower St	Glendale	CA	91201	**800-432-1856**	818-500-8718	296-11
Vita-Mix Corp 8615 Usher Rd	Cleveland	OH	44138	**800-848-2649**	440-235-4840	37
Vita-Pakt Citrus Products 203 E Badillo St	Covina	CA	91723	**888-684-8272**	626-332-1101	
VITAS Healthcare Corp 201 S Biscayne Blvd Ste 400	Miami	FL	33131	**800-873-5198**	305-374-4143	370
VITAS Healthcare Corp of California 2675 N Mayfair Rd Ste 500	Wauwatosa	WI	53226	**866-418-4827**	414-257-2600	370
VITAS Healthcare Corp of California 9655 Granite Ridge Dr Ste 300	San Diego	CA	92123	**866-418-4827**	858-499-8901	370
VITAS Healthcare Corp of San Gabriel Cities 1343 N Grand Ave	Covina	CA	91724	**866-418-4827**		370
VitaSound Audio Inc 2880 Zanker Rd Ste 203	San Jose	CA	95134	**888-667-7205**		250
Vitasoy USA Inc 57 Russell St	Woburn	MA	01801	**800-848-2769**		296-8
Vitelity Communications 317 Inverness Way S Ste 140	Englewood	CO	80112	**888-898-4835**		
Viterbo University 900 Viterbo Dr	La Crosse	WI	54601	**800-848-3726**	608-796-3000	166
Vitran Express Inc 1201 Creditstone Rd	Concord	ON	L4K0C2	**800-263-0791**	416-798-4965	775
Vitro Seating Products Inc 201 Madison St *Cust Svc	Saint Louis	MO	63102	**800-325-7093***	314-241-2265	319-1
VIVA Health Inc 1222 14th Ave S	Birmingham	AL	35205	**800-633-1542**	205-939-1718	389
Vivax-Metrotech Corp 3251 Olcott St	Santa Clara	CA	95054	**800-446-3392**	408-734-1400	470
Viviano Flower Shop 32050 Harper Ave	Saint Clair Shores	MI	48082	**800-848-4266**	586-293-0227	292
Vivienne Tam 580 Eighth Ave 17th Fl	New York	NY	10018	**877-659-7994**		277
Vivint Solar Inc 1800 W Ashton Blvd	Lehi	UT	84043	**877-404-4129**	801-216-3927	192
Vivitar Corp 195 Carter Dr	Edison	NJ	08817	**800-592-9541**	732-248-1306	587
Vivosonic Inc 5535 Eglinton Ave W Ste 222	Toronto	ON	M9C5K5	**877-255-7685**	416-231-9997	474
Vivus Inc 1172 Castro St *NASDAQ: VVUS*	Mountain View	CA	94040	**800-607-0088**	650-934-5200	578
Viwintech Window & Door Inc 2400 Irvin Cobb Dr	Paducah	KY	42003	**800-788-1050**		592
ViWinTech Windows & Door 2400 Irvin Cobb Dr	Paducah	KY	42003	**800-788-1050**		
VJ Technologies Inc 89 Carlough Rd	Bohemia	NY	11716	**800-858-9729**	631-589-8800	738
VJV IT 96 Linwood Plz	Fort Lee	NJ	07024	**800-614-7561**		627
VKGS LLC (Video King Gaming Systems) 2717 N 118 Cir Ste 210	Omaha	NE	68164	**800-635-9912**	402-951-2970	322
VKI Technologies Inc 3200 2E Rue	Saint-hubert	QC	J3Y8Y7	**800-567-2951**	450-676-0504	159
VLN Partners LLC 661 Andersen Dr	Pittsburgh	PA	15220	**877-856-3311**	412-381-0183	174
VMI (Vantage Mobility International) 5202 S 28th Pl	Phoenix	AZ	85040	**855-864-8267**		62-7
VNA 154 Hindman Rd	Butler	PA	16001	**877-862-6659**	724-282-6806	370
VNA (VNA Hospice Care) 2029 Woodland Pkwy Ste 105	Maryland Heights	MO	63146	**800-392-4740**	314-918-7171	370
VNA & Hospice of Northern California 1900 Powell St Ste 300	Emeryville	CA	94608	**800-698-1273**	510-450-8596	370
VNA & Hospice of Southern California 150 W First St Ste 270	Claremont	CA	91711	**888-357-3574**	909-624-3574	370
VNA Hospice & Home Health of Lackawanna County 301 Delaware Ave	Olyphant	PA	18447	**800-936-7671**	570-383-5180	370
VNA Hospice Care (VNA) 2029 Woodland Pkwy Ste 105	Maryland Heights	MO	63146	**800-392-4740**	314-918-7171	370
VNA of Central Jersey (VNACJ) 176 Riverside Ave	Red Bank	NJ	07701	**800-862-3330**		370
VNAA (Visiting Nurse Assns of America) 1800 Diagonal Rd Ste 600	Alexandria	VA	22314	**888-866-8773**	571-527-1520	49-8
VNACJ (VNA of Central Jersey) 176 Riverside Ave	Red Bank	NJ	07701	**800-862-3330**		370
Vocalink Global 405 W First St Unit A	Dayton	OH	45402	**877-492-7754**		763
Vocantas Inc 2934 Baseline Rd Ste 301	Ottawa	ON	K2H1B2	**877-271-8853**	613-271-8853	179
Vocera Communications Inc 525 RACE St Ste 150	San Jose	CA	95126	**800-473-3971**		177
Vogelsang USA 7966 State Rt 44	Ravenna	OH	44266	**800-984-9400**	330-296-3820	637
Vogt Ice 1000 W Ormsby Ave	Louisville	KY	40210	**800-853-8648**	502-635-3000	660
Vogue Fabrics 618 Hartrey Ave	Evanston	IL	60202	**800-433-4313**		270
Vogue Flowers & Gifts Ltd 1114 N Blvd	Richmond	VA	23230	**800-923-1010**	804-353-9600	292
Vogue Optical 5 Brackley Pt Rd	Charlottetown	PE	C1A6X8	**866-594-3937**	902-566-3326	539

Company	Toll-Free	Phone	Class
Voice & Data Networks Inc (VDN) 4218 Park Glen Rd ...... St. Louis Park MN 55416	800-246-7999	952-946-5353	521
Voice Pro Inc 2055 Lee Rd ...... Cleveland OH 44118	800-261-0104	216-932-8040	760
Voicecom 5900 Windward Pkwy Ste 500 ...... Alpharetta GA 30005	888-468-3554		731
Voices of September 11th 161 Cherry St ...... New Canaan CT 06840	866-505-3911	203-966-3911	48-5
VoIP Innovations Inc 8 Penn Ctr W Ste 101 ...... Pittsburgh PA 15276	877-478-6471		386
Volckening 6700 Third Ave ...... Brooklyn NY 11220	800-221-0876	718-836-4000	298
Volk Optical Inc 7893 Enterprise Dr ...... Mentor OH 44060	800-345-8655	440-942-6161	539
Volk Packaging Corp 11 Morin St ...... Biddeford ME 04005	800-341-0208		
Volkswagen of America Inc 3800 Hamlin Rd ...... Auburn Hills MI 48326	800-822-8987		59
Vollrath Co LLC, The 1236 N 18th St ...... Sheboygan WI 53081	800-624-2051	920-457-4851	300
Vollwerth & Co 200 Hancock St PO Box 239 ...... Hancock MI 49930	800-562-7620	906-482-1550	296-26
Volpi Foods 5263 Northrup Ave ...... St Louis MO 63110	800-288-3439	314-772-8550	296-10
Volt VIEWtech Inc 4761 E Hunter Ave ...... Anaheim CA 92807	888-396-9927	714-695-3377	461
VoltDelta Resources Inc 3750 Monroe Ave Ste 4B ...... Pittsford NY 14534	866-436-1169		
Volume Transportation Inc 2261 Plunkett Rd ...... Conyers GA 30012	800-879-5565	770-482-1400	775
Volunteer State Community College 1480 Nashville Pk ...... Gallatin TN 37066	888-335-8722	615-452-8600	162
Volunteers of America 1660 Duke St ...... Alexandria VA 22314	800-899-0089	703-341-5000	48-5
Volusia County 123 W Indiana Ave ...... DeLand FL 32720	800-955-8771	386-736-5920	337
Volvo Cars of North America 1 Volvo Dr ...... Rockleigh NJ 07647 *Cust Svc	800-458-1552*	201-768-7300	59
Volvo Penta of the Americas Inc 1300 Volvo Penta Dr ...... Chesapeake VA 23320	800-522-1959	757-436-2800	262
Vomela Co, The 274 E Fillmore Ave ...... Saint Paul MN 55107	800-645-1012	651-228-2200	697
Von Maur Inc 6565 Brady St ...... Davenport IA 52806	877-866-6287	563-388-2200	229
Von Paris Enterprises Inc 8691 Larkin Rd ...... Savage MD 20763	800-866-6355	410-888-8500	516
Von Rabenau Media Corp 332 S Michigan Ave 9th fl ...... Chicago IL 60654	800-229-1967	312-849-2220	455-21
Von Roll Isola USA 200 Von Roll Dr ...... Schenectady NY 12306	800-654-7652	518-344-7100	498
Vonage Holdings Corp 23 Main St ...... Holmdel NJ 07733 NYSE: VG	877-862-2562	732-528-2600	731
Vooner Flogard Corp 4729 Stockholm Ct ...... Charlotte NC 28273	800-345-7879	704-552-9314	295
Voorhees College 213 Wiggins Dr PO Box 678 ...... Denmark SC 29042	866-685-9904	803-780-1234	166
Voorhees Pediatric Facility 1304 Laurel Oak Rd ...... Voorhees NJ 08043	888-873-5437	856-346-3300	448
Voorwood Co 2350 Barney St ...... Anderson CA 96007	800-826-0089	530-365-3311	816
Vornado Realty Trust 888 Seventh Ave ...... New York NY 10019 NYSE: VNO	800-294-1322	212-894-7000	651
Vorwerk USA Company LP 3255 E Thousand Oaks Blvd Unit B ...... Thousand Oaks CA 91362	888-867-9375		
Voss Lighting PO Box 22159 ...... Lincoln NE 68542	866-292-0529	402-328-2281	246
Voss Signs LLC 112 Fairgrounds Dr ...... Manlius NY 13104	800-473-0698	315-682-6418	683
Voto Manufacturers Sales Co 500 N Third St PO Box 1299 ...... Steubenville OH 43952	800-848-4010	740-282-3621	384
VOX Data 1155 Metcalfe St 18th Fl. ...... Montreal QC H3B2V6	800-861-9599	514-871-1920	732
Vox Mobile 6100 Rockside Woods Blvd Ste 100 ...... Independence OH 44131	800-536-9030		
Voyager Systems Inc 360 Rt 101 ...... Bedford NH 03110	800-634-1966	603-472-5172	180
Voyages Michel Barrette 100 Rue Saint-joseph ...... Alma QC G8B7A6	800-263-3078	418-668-3078	770
Voyageur Transportation Services 573 Admiral Ct ...... London ON N5V4L3	855-263-7163	519-455-4580	107
Voyageurs National Park 360 Hwy 11 E ...... International Falls MN 56649	888-381-2873	218-283-6600	560
VPA (Veterinary Pharmacies of America Inc) 4802 N Sam Houston Pkwy W Ste 100 ...... Houston TX 77066	877-838-7979		580
VPI Corp 3123 S Ninth St ...... Sheboygan WI 53081 *Orders	800-874-4240*	920-458-4664	596
VPOP Technologies Inc 1772J Avenida de los Arboles Ste 374 ...... Thousand Oaks CA 91362 *Sales	888-811-8767*	805-529-9374	803
VPT (Vermont Public Television) 204 Ethan Allen Ave ...... Colchester VT 05446	800-639-7811	802-655-4800	628
VRC Inc 696 W Bagley Rd ...... Berea OH 44017	800-872-1012	440-243-6666	752
Vsa Inc 6929 Seward Ave ...... Lincoln NE 68507	800-888-2140	402-467-3668	246
VSAC (Vermont Student Assistance Corp) 10 E Allen St PO Box 2000 ...... Winooski VT 05404	800-642-3177		721
VSC (Vetter Stone Co) 23894 Third Ave ...... Mankato MN 56001	800-878-2850	507-345-4568	720
VSE Corp 2550 Huntington Ave ...... Alexandria VA 22303 NASDAQ: VSEC	800-455-4873	703-960-4600	261
VSM Abrasives 1012 E Wabash St ...... O'Fallon MO 63366 *Cust Svc	800-737-0176*	636-272-7432	1
VSNA (Vermont State Nurses Assn) 4 Carmichael St Ste 111 Rm 215 ...... Essex VT 05452	877-810-5972		529
VT Halter Marine Inc 900 Bayou Casotte Pkwy ...... Pascagoula MS 39581	800-639-2715	228-696-6756	694
V-T Industries Inc 1000 Industrial Pk ...... Holstein IA 51025	800-827-1615	712-368-4381	595
VTA (Santa Clara Valley Transportation Authority) 3331 N First St ...... San Jose CA 95134	800-894-9908	408-321-2300	466
VTech Communications Inc 9590 SW Gemini Dr Ste 120 ...... Beaverton OR 97008	800-595-9511	503-596-1200	730
VTech Electronics North America LLC 1155 W Dundee St Ste 130 ...... Arlington Heights IL 60004	800-521-2010	847-400-3600	757
V-Technologies LLC 675 W Johnson Ave ...... Cheshire CT 06410	800-462-4016		521
VTS Investigations LLC 7 S State St ...... Elgin IL 60123	800-538-4464		399
Vulcan Corp 30 Garfield Pl Ste 1040 ...... Cincinnati OH 45202 *Sales	800-447-1146*	513-621-2850	672
Vulcan Inc 410 E Berry Ave ...... Foley AL 36535	888-846-2728	251-943-7000	153
Vulcan Industries Inc 300 Display Dr ...... Moody AL 35004	888-444-4417	205-640-2400	233
Vulcan Materials Co 1200 Urban Ctr Dr PO Box 385014 ...... Birmingham AL 35238 NYSE: VMC	800-615-4331	205-298-3000	501-5
Vulcan Materials Company Western Div 1200 Urban Center Dr ...... Birmingham AL 35242 NYSE: VMC	800-615-4331	205-298-3000	501-5
Vulsay Industries Ltd 35 Regan Rd ...... Brampton ON L7A1B2	800-468-1760	905-846-2200	88
Vutec Corp 11711 W Sample Rd ...... Coral Springs FL 33065	800-770-4700		587
Vuzix Corp 2166 Brighton Henrietta Town Line Rd ...... Rochester NY 14623	800-436-7838	585-359-5900	539
VVMA (Virginia Veterinary Medical Assn) 3801 Westerre Pkwy Ste D ...... Henrico VA 23233	800-937-8862	804-346-2611	790
VWA (Vengroff Williams & Assoc Inc) 2099 S State College Bvld ...... Anaheim CA 92806	800-238-9655	714-889-6200	160
VWR International 100 Matsonford Rd Bldg 1 Ste 200 ...... Radnorpa PA 19087	800-932-5000	610-431-1700	473
Vyrian Inc 4660 Sweetwater Blvd Ste 200 ...... Sugar Land TX 77479	866-874-0598		
Vyse Gelatin Co 5010 Rose St ...... Schiller Park IL 60176	800-533-2152	847-678-4780	344
Vystar Credit Union 1802 Kernan Blvd S ...... Jacksonville FL 32246	800-445-6289	904-777-6000	219

W

Company	Toll-Free	Phone	Class
W & H Co-op Oil Co 407 13th St N ...... Humboldt IA 50548	800-392-3816	515-332-2782	324
W & H Systems Inc 120 Asia Pl ...... Carlstadt NJ 07072	800-966-6993	201-933-7840	207
W & W Steel Co 1730 W Reno Ave ...... Oklahoma City OK 73106	800-222-1868	405-235-3621	478
W A Baum Company Inc 620 Oak St ...... Copiague NY 11726	888-281-6061	631-226-3940	474
W a m s Inc 1800 E Lambert Ave Ste 155 ...... Brea CA 92821	800-421-7151		177
W Atlee Burpee Co 300 Park Ave ...... Warminster PA 18974 *Cust Svc	800-333-5808*	215-674-4900	690
W Ca Logistics LLC 643 Bodey Cir ...... Urbana OH 43078	800-860-7838	937-653-6382	195
W L Gore & Associates Inc 551 Papermill Rd ...... Newark DE 19711	888-914-4673	410-506-7787	740-2
W L Halsey Grocery Company Inc PO Box 6485 ...... Huntsville AL 35824	800-621-0240	256-772-9691	297-8
W M Sprinkman Corp 404 Pilot Ct ...... Waukesha WI 53188	800-816-1610		385
W Montreal Hotel 901 Victoria Sq ...... Montreal QC H2Z1R1	888-627-7081	514-395-3100	667
W N. Morehouse Truck Line Inc 4010 Dahlman Ave ...... Omaha NE 68107	800-228-9378	402-733-2200	681
W New York- Union Square 201 Park Ave S ...... New York NY 10003	877-822-0000	212-253-9119	377
W O W Logistics Co 3040 W Wisconsin Ave ...... Appleton WI 54914	800-236-3565	920-734-9924	798-1
W R. Vernon Produce Co 1035 N Cherry St PO Box 4054 ...... Winston-Salem NC 27101	800-222-6406	336-725-9741	297-7
W/M Display Group 1040 W 40th St ...... Chicago IL 60609	800-443-2000	773-254-3700	286
W3health Solutions LLC 115 Franklin TurnPk Ste 352 ...... Mahwah NJ 07430	888-934-3258	201-701-0240	804
Wabash College 410 W Wabash Ave PO Box 352 ...... Crawfordsville IN 47933	800-345-5385	765-361-6326	166
Wabash County 221 S Miami St ...... Wabash IN 46992	800-346-2110	260-563-7171	337
Wabash Electric Supply Inc 1400 N Wabash St ...... Wabash IN 46992	800-552-7777	260-563-4146	246
Wabash Telephone Co-op Inc 210 S Church St PO Box 299 ...... Louisville IL 62858	877-878-2120	618-665-3311	731

Listing	Toll-Free	Phone	Class
Wabash Valley Correctional Facility 6908 S Old US Hwy 41 PO Box 500 .... Carlisle IN 47838	800-677-9800		213
Wabash Valley Manufacturing Inc 505 E Main St ....Silver Lake IN 46982	800-253-8619	260-352-2102	319-4
Wabash Valley Service Company Inc 909 N Court St .... Grayville IL 62844	888-869-8127	618-375-2311	276
WABCO Locomotive Products 1001 Air Brake Ave .... Wilmerding PA 15148 *Cust Svc	877-922-2627*	412-825-1000	646
Wabtec Corp 1001 Air Brake Ave .... Wilmerding PA 15148 NYSE: WAB ■ *Cust Svc	877-922-2627*	412-825-1000	646
Wachovia Bank 3800 Wilshire Blvd Ste 110e ....Los Angeles CA 90010	800-225-5935	213-739-8579	70
Wachs Water Services 801 Asbury Dr ....Buffalo Grove IL 60089	800-525-5821		392
Wachters' Organic Sea Products Corp 550 Sylvan St .... Daly City CA 94014	800-682-7100	650-757-9851	794
Wacker Chemical Corp 3301 Sutton Rd .... Adrian MI 49221	888-922-5374	517-264-8500	144
Wacker Neuson N 92 W 15000 Anthony Ave .... Menomonee Falls WI 53051	800-770-0957	262-255-0500	190
Waco Convention & Visitors Bureau 100 Washington Ave .... Waco TX 76701	800-321-9226	254-750-5810	206
Waco Tribune-Herald 900 Franklin Ave .... Waco TX 76701	800-678-8742	254-757-5757	528-2
Wacoal America 50 Polito Ave ....Lyndhurst NJ 07071	800-922-6250	201-933-8400	155-17
Wacoal Europe 65 Sprague St .... Hyde Park MA 02136	800-733-8964	617-361-7559	155-17
Wacom Technology Corp 1311 SE Cardinal Ct .... Vancouver WA 98683	800-922-6613	360-896-9833	173-1
Waddell & Reed Financial Inc 6300 Lamar Ave .... Overland Park KS 66201 NYSE: WDR	888-923-3355	913-236-2000	400
Wade College 1950 N Stemmons Fwy LB 562 Ste 4080 .... Dallas TX 75207	800-624-4850	214-637-3530	795
Wade Tours Inc 797 Burdeck St .... Schenectady NY 12306	800-955-9233	518-355-4500	755
Wade-Trim Group Inc 500 Griswold Ave Ste 2500 .... Detroit MI 48226	800-482-2864	313-961-3650	261
WAFB-TV Ch 9 (CBS) 844 Government St .... Baton Rouge LA 70802	888-677-2900	225-215-4700	736-8
Waggoners Trucking 5220 Midland Rd .... Billings MT 59101	800-999-9097	406-248-1919	775
Wagman Metal Products Inc 400 S Albemarle St .... York PA 17403	800-233-9461	717-854-2120	295
Wagner College 1 Campus Rd .... Staten Island NY 10301 *Admissions	800-221-1010*	718-390-3400	166
Wagner Oil Co 500 Commerce St Ste 600 .... Fort Worth TX 76102	800-457-5332	817-335-2222	532
Wagner Spray Tech Corp 1770 Fernbrook Ln ....Plymouth MN 55447	800-328-8251	763-553-7000	172
Wago Corp N120 W19129 Freistadt Rd .... Germantown WI 53022	800-346-7245	262-255-6222	203
Wahkiakum County 64 Main St PO Box 157 .... Cathlamet WA 98612	800-359-1506	360-795-3558	337
Wahl Clipper Corp 2900 Locust St .... Sterling IL 61081	800-767-9245		214
Wahl Media Inc 580 Packetts Landing .... Fairport NY 14450	888-924-5633		
Wahlco Inc 2722 S Fairview St .... Santa Ana CA 92704	800-423-5432	714-979-7300	452
WAIglobal 411 Eagleview Blvd Ste 100 .... Exton PA 19341	800-877-3340	484-875-6600	61
Waikiki Parc Hotel 2233 Helumoa Rd .... Honolulu HI 96815	800-422-0450	808-921-7272	378
Waikiki Resort Hotel 2460 Koa Ave .... Honolulu HI 96815	800-367-5116	808-922-4911	378
Waisman Ctr University of Wisconsin 1500 Highland Ave .... Madison WI 53705	888-428-8476	608-263-1656	664
WAKA-TV Ch 8 (CBS) 3020 Eastern Blvd .... Montgomery AL 36116	800-467-0401	334-271-8888	736-48
Wake Correctional Ctr 1000 Rock Quarry Rd .... Raleigh NC 27610	866-719-0108	919-733-7988	213
Wake Electric 100 S Franklin St PO Box 1229 ....Wake Forest NC 27588	800-474-6300		245
Wake Forest University 2825 University Pkwy .... Winston-Salem NC 27105	888-758-3322	336-758-2410	
Wakefern Food Corp 600 York St .... Elizabeth NJ 07207	800-746-7748	908-527-3300	297-8
Wakefield's Inc 1212 Quintard Ave .... Anniston AL 36201	800-333-1552		157-2
Wako Chemicals USA Inc 1600 Bellwood Rd .... Richmond VA 23237	800-992-9256	804-271-7677	231
Wakunaga of America Company Ltd 23501 Madero .... Mission Viejo CA 92691	800-421-2998	949-855-2776	794
WAKW-FM 933 (Rel) 6275 Collegevue Pl PO Box 24126 .... Cincinnati OH 45224	888-542-9393	513-542-9259	641-24
WALA-TV Ch 10 (Fox) 1501 Satchel Paige Dr .... Mobile AL 36606	800-876-8810	251-434-1010	736-47
Walch Education 40 Walch Dr ....Portland ME 04103	800-558-2846	207-772-2846	633-2
Walden Farms 1209 W St Georges Ave .... Linden NJ 07036	800-229-1706		296-19
Walden Galleria 1 Walden Galleria ....Buffalo NY 14225	800-297-5009	716-681-7600	458
Waldinger Corp 2601 Bell Ave ....Des Moines IA 50321	800-473-4934	515-284-1911	189-14
Waldo County 137 Church St .... Belfast ME 04915	800-244-5211	207-338-1710	337
Waldoch Crafts Inc 13821 Lake Dr NE .... Forest Lake MN 55025	800-328-9259	800-878-8635	62-7
Waldon Mfg LLC 201 W Oklahoma Ave ....Fiarview OK 73737	866-283-2759	580-227-3711	468
Waldorf College 106 S Sixth St ....Forest City IA 50436	800-292-1903	641-585-2450	166
Wale Apparatus Co Inc 400 Front St ....Hellertown PA 18055	800-334-9253	610-838-7047	332
Walgreen Co 200 Wilmot Rd .... Deerfield IL 60015 *Cust Svc	800-925-4733*	847-940-2500	237
Walgreens Health Services 1411 Lake Cook Rd .... Deerfield IL 60015	800-207-2568		582
Walker Advertising 20101 Hamilton Ave Ste 375 ....Torrance CA 90502	800-492-5537		
Walker County 101 S Duke St PO Box 445 .... La Fayette GA 30728	800-424-8666	706-638-1437	337
Walker Honda 6677 Coliseum Blvd .... Alexandria LA 71303	888-726-1687		
Walker Industries Holdings Ltd 2800 Thorold Townline Rd ....Niagara Falls ON L2E6S4	866-694-9360	905-227-4142	186
Walker Information Inc 301 Pennsylvania Pkwy ....Indianapolis IN 46280	800-334-3939	317-843-3939	464
Walker Magnetics Group Inc 20 Rockdale St .... Worcester MA 01606	800-962-4638	508-853-3232	491
Walker MS Inc 20 Third Ave ....Somerville MA 02143	800-528-2787	617-776-6700	80-1
Walker Process Equipment 840 N Russell Ave .... Aurora IL 60506	800-992-5537	630-892-7921	801
Walker Tool & Die Inc 2411 Walker Ave NW ....Grand Rapids MI 49544	877-925-5378	616-735-6660	752
Walker's Furniture Inc 3808 N Sullivan Rd Bldg 22-C .... Spokane Valley WA 99216	866-667-6655	509-535-1995	321
Walker, Morgan & Kinard 135 E Main St ....Lexington SC 29072	800-922-8411	803-675-5942	427
Walking Adventures International 14612 NE Fourth Plain Rd Ste A .... Vancouver WA 98682	800-779-0353		755
WalkMed Infusion LLC 6555 S Kenton St Ste 304 ....Centennial CO 80111	800-578-0555	303-420-9569	474
Wall Street Financial Group Inc 255 Woodcliff Dr .... Fairport NY 14450	800-303-9255		
Wall Street Inn, The 9 S William St .... New York NY 10004	877-747-1500	212-747-1500	
Wall Street Journal, The 1211 Ave of the Americas .... New York NY 10036 *General	800-568-7625*	212-416-2000	528-3
Walla Walla Community College 500 Tausick Way .... Walla Walla WA 99362	877-992-9922	509-522-2500	162
Walla Walla University 204 S College Ave ....College Place WA 99324	800-541-8900	509-527-2327	166
Walla Walla Valley Chamber of Commerce 29 E Sumach St PO Box 644 .... Walla Walla WA 99362	866-826-9422	509-525-0850	139
Wallace & Carey 5445-8 St NE .... Calgary AB T2K5R9	800-661-1504	403-275-7360	447
Wallace Community College 1141 Wallace Dr ....Dothan AL 36303	800-543-2426	334-983-3521	162
Wallace Community College Selma 3000 Earl Goodwin Pkwy .... Selma AL 36703	855-428-8313	334-876-9227	795
Wallace Cranes 71 N Bacton Hill Rd .... Malvern PA 19355	800-553-5438	610-647-1400	357
Wallace Hardware Company Inc 5050 S Davy Crockett Pkwy PO Box 6004 .... Morristown TN 37815	800-776-0976		350
Wallace State Community College 801 Main St .... Hanceville AL 35077	866-350-9722	256-352-8000	162
Wallace Welch & Willingham 300 First Ave S 4th Fl .... Saint Petersburg FL 33701	800-783-5085	727-522-7777	389
Wallach & Company Inc 107 W Federal St .... Middleburg VA 20118	800-237-6615	540-687-3166	390-7
Wallco Inc 53 E Jackson St # 55 .... Wilkes-Barre PA 18701	800-392-5526	570-823-6181	692
Waller Truck Company Inc 400 S McCleary Rd ....Excelsior Springs MO 64024	800-821-2196	816-629-3400	775
Wallick & Volk Mortgage 222 E 18th St ....Cheyenne WY 82001	800-280-8655	307-634-5941	217
Wallingford Buick GMC 1122 Old N Colony Rd .... Wallingford CT 06492 *Cust Svc	866-582-4487*	888-765-9107	57
Wallingford Coffee Mills 11401 Rockfield Ct .... Cincinnati OH 45241	800-533-3690	513-771-3131	80-2
Wallis Companies 106 E Washington St .... Cuba MO 65453	800-467-6652	573-885-2277	324
Walls 360 5054 Bond St .... Las Vegas NV 89118	888-244-9969		392
Wal-Mart Stores Inc 702 SW Eighth St ....Bentonville AR 72716 NYSE: WMT ■ *Cust Svc	800-925-6278*	479-273-4000	229
Walmartcom 1919 Davis St .... San Leandro CA 94577	800-925-6278	479-273-1329	229
Walnut Hollow Farm Inc 1409 State Rd 23 ....Dodgeville WI 53533	800-395-5995	608-935-2341	279
Walnut Street Theatre 825 Walnut St ....Philadelphia PA 19107	800-982-2787	215-574-3550	568
Walpole Inc 269 NW Ninth St ....Okeechobee FL 34972	800-741-6500	863-763-5593	775
Walpole Woodworkers Inc 767 E St .... Walpole MA 02081 *Cust Svc	800-343-6948*	508-668-2800	319-4
Walsh Group Inc 929 W Adams St .... Chicago IL 60607	800-957-1842	312-563-5400	186
Walsh University 2020 E Maple St ....North Canton OH 44720 *Admissions	800-362-9846*	330-499-7090	166
Walsworth Publishing Co 306 N Kansas Ave ....Marceline MO 64658	800-972-4968	660-376-3543	633-2

Name / Address	Toll-Free	Phone	Class
Walt Disney World Dolphin 1500 Epcot Resorts Blvd ....Lake Buena Vista FL 32830	888-828-8850	407-934-4000	665
Walt Disney World Swan 1200 Epcot Resorts Blvd ....Lake Buena Vista FL 32830	888-828-8850	407-934-4000	665
Walt Whitman House State Historic Site 330 Mickle Blvd ....Camden NJ 08103	800-843-6420		561
Waltek Inc 14310 Sunfish Lake Blvd ....Ramsey MN 55303	800-937-9496	763-427-3181	306
Walter B Jones Alcohol & Drug Abuse Treatment Ctr 2577 W Fifth St ....Greenville NC 27834	800-422-1884	252-830-3426	722
Walter Haas & Sons Inc 123 W 23rd St ....Hialeah FL 33010	800-552-3845	305-883-2257	697
Walter Meier Mfg Inc 427 New Sanford Rd ....La Vergne TN 37086	800-274-6848		753
Walter P Moore 1301 Mckinney St Ste 1100 ....Houston TX 77010	800-364-7300	713-630-7300	261
Walter Snyder Printer Inc 691 River St ....Troy NY 12180	888-272-9774	518-272-8881	623
Walter USA Inc N22 W23855 Ridgeview Pkwy W ....Waukesha WI 53188	800-945-5554		491
Walters State Community College 500 S Davy Crockett Pkwy ....Morristown TN 37813	800-225-4770	423-585-2600	162
Walters Wholesale Electric Co 2825 Temple Ave ....Signal Hill CA 90755 *Support	833-993-3266*	562-988-3100	246
Walthall Oil Company Inc 2510 Allen Rd ....Macon GA 31216	800-633-5685	478-781-1234	575
Waltham Services Inc 817 Moody St ....Waltham MA 02453	866-974-7378	781-893-1810	573
Walton Press (WP) 402 Mayfield Dr ....Monroe GA 30655	800-354-0235	770-267-2596	551
Walton-De Funiak Library 3 Cir Dr ....DeFuniak Springs FL 32435	800-342-0141	850-892-3624	433-3
Walts Mailing Service Ltd 9610 E First Ave ....Spokane Valley WA 99206	888-549-2006	509-924-5939	5
WALZ Label & Mailing Systems 624 High Point Ln ....East Peoria IL 61611	877-971-1500	309-698-1500	531
WAMC/Northeast Public Radio 318 Central Ave ....Albany NY 12206	800-323-9262	518-465-5233	628
WAMC-FM 903 (NPR) 318 Central Ave ....Albany NY 12206	800-323-9262	518-465-5233	641-3
Wang Theatre 270 Tremont St ....Boston MA 02116	800-982-2787		568
Wanke Cascade Co 6330 N Cutter Cir ....Portland OR 97217	800-365-5053	503-289-8609	360
Wantman Group Inc 2035 Vista Pkwy Ste 100 ....West Palm Beach FL 33411	866-909-2220	561-687-2220	
WAPE-FM 951 (CHR) 8000 Belfort Pkwy Ste 100 ....Jacksonville FL 32256	800-475-9595	904-245-8500	641-51
WAPT-TV Ch 16 (ABC) 7616 Ch 16 Way ....Jackson MS 39209	800-441-1948	601-922-1607	736-36
Wapusk National Park PO Box 127 ....Churchill MB R0B0E0	888-773-8888	204-675-8863	559
WAQY-FM 1021 (CR) 45 Fisher Ave ....East Longmeadow MA 01028	800-242-3142	413-525-4141	641
Ward Aluminum Casting Co 642 Growth Ave ....Fort Wayne IN 46808	800-648-9918	260-426-8700	308
Ward Cedar Log Homes 37 Bangor St PO Box 72 ....Houlton ME 04730 *Cust Svc	800-341-1566*		106
Ward Manufacturing LLC 117 Gulick St ....Blossburg PA 16912	800-248-1027	570-638-2131	608
Ward's Food Systems Inc 5133 Lincoln Rd Ext ....Hattiesburg MS 39402	800-748-9273	601-268-9273	666
Warde Medical Laboratory (WML) 300 W Textile Rd ....Ann Arbor MI 48108	800-760-9969	734-214-0300	414
Ward-Kraft Inc 2401 Cooper St ....Fort Scott KS 66701	800-821-4021	620-223-5500	110
Warehouse Home Furnishings Distributors Inc 1851 Telfair St PO Box 1140 ....Dublin GA 31021	800-456-0424		321
Warehouse Skateboards Inc 1638 Military Cutoff Rd ....Wilmington NC 28403	877-791-9795		707
Warm Co 5529 186th Pl SW ....Lynnwood WA 98037	800-234-9276	425-248-2424	740-1
Warner Bros Television Production Inc 4000 Warner Blvd ....Burbank CA 91522	800-462-8855	818-954-1853	511
Warner Electric 449 Gardner St ....South Beloit IL 61080	800-825-6544		616
Warner Manufacturing Co 13435 Industrial Pk Blvd ....Plymouth MN 55441	800-444-0606	763-559-4740	753
Warner Music Group 1633 Broadway ....New York NY 10019	800-820-1653	212-275-2000	653
Warner Pacific College 2219 SE 68th Ave ....Portland OR 97215	800-804-1510	503-517-1020	166
Warner Southern College 13895 Hwy 27 ....Lake Wales FL 33859	800-309-9563		166
Warner Vineyards Inc 706 S Kalamazoo St ....Paw Paw MI 49079	800-756-5357	269-657-3165	80-3
Warp Bros Flex-O-Glass Inc 4647 W Augusta Blvd ....Chicago IL 60651	800-621-3345	773-261-5200	544
Warrantech Corp Inc 2200 Hwy 121 ....Bedford TX 76021	800-833-8801	817-785-6601	366
Warranty Group Inc, The 175 W Jackson 11th Fl ....Chicago IL 60604	800-621-2130	312-356-3000	390-5
Warranty Life Services Inc 4152 Meridian St Ste 105-29 ....Bellingham WA 98226	888-927-7269		392
Warren Co, The 2201 Loveland Ave ....Erie PA 16506	800-562-0357		295
Warren Communications News Inc 2115 Ward Ct NW ....Washington DC 20037	800-771-9202	202-872-9200	633-9
Warren County 220 N Commerce Ave Ste 100 ....Front Royal VA 22630	800-248-6342	540-636-4600	337
Warren County 406 Justice Dr ....Lebanon OH 45036	800-282-0253	513-695-1358	337
Warren County 125 N Monroe St Ste 11 ....Williamsport IN 47993	800-622-4941	765-762-3510	337
Warren County Rural Electric Membership Corp 15 Midway St PO Box 37 ....Williamsport IN 47993	800-872-7319	765-762-6114	245
Warren County Visitors Bureau 22045 Rt 6 ....Warren PA 16365	800-624-7802	814-726-1222	206
Warren Electric Co-op Inc (WEC) 320 E Main St PO Box 208 ....Youngsville PA 16371	800-364-8640	814-563-7548	245
Warren Equities Inc 27 Warren Way ....Providence RI 02905	866-867-4075	401-781-9900	359-3
Warren General Hospital 2 Crescent Pk W ....Warren PA 16365	800-777-9441	814-723-3300	373-3
Warren Gibson Ltd 206 Church St S PO Box 100 ....Alliston ON L9R1T9	800-461-4374	705-435-4342	476
Warren Hospital 185 Roseberry St ....Phillipsburg NJ 08865	800-220-8116	908-859-6700	373-3
Warren Oil Company Inc PO Box 1507 ....Dunn NC 28335	800-779-6456	910-892-6456	575
Warren Printing & Mailing Inc 5000 Eagle Rock Blvd ....Los Angeles CA 90041	888-468-6976	323-258-2621	623
Warren Properties Inc PO Box 469114 ....Escondido CA 92046	800-831-0804		651
Warren Resources Inc 1114 Ave of the Americas 34th Fl ....New York NY 10036 *NASDAQ: WRES*	877-587-9494	212-697-9660	532
Warren Rural Electric Co-op Corp 951 Fairview Ave ....Bowling Green KY 42101	866-319-3234	270-842-6541	245
Warren State Hospital 33 Main Dr ....North Warren PA 16365	800-932-0313		
Warren Transport Inc 210 Beck Ave ....Waterloo IA 50701	800-526-3053		775
Warren Wilson College 701 Warren Wilson Rd ....Swannanoa NC 28778 *Admissions	800-934-3536*		166
Warrior Custom Golf 15 Mason Ste A ....Irvine CA 92618	800-600-5113	866-436-6722	707
Warsaw Chemical Company Inc Argonne Rd PO Box 858 ....Warsaw IN 46580	800-548-3396	574-267-3251	151
Wartburg College 100 Wartburg Blvd ....Waverly IA 50677	800-772-2085	319-352-8264	166
Wartburg Theological Seminary 333 Wartburg Pl ....Dubuque IA 52003	800-225-5987	563-589-0200	167-3
Warwick Denver Hotel 1776 Grant St ....Denver CO 80203	800-203-3232	303-861-2000	378
Warwick Melrose Hotel 3015 Oak Lawn Ave ....Dallas TX 75219	800-521-7172	214-521-5151	378
Warwick New York Hotel 65 W 54th St ....New York NY 10019	800-203-3232	212-247-2700	378
Warwick Seattle Hotel 401 Lenora St ....Seattle WA 98121	800-426-9280	206-443-4300	378
Warwick Valley Telephone Co 47 Main St PO Box 592 ....Warwick NY 10990 *Cust Svc	800-952-7642*	845-986-8080	731
Wasatch Academy 120 S 100 W ....Mount Pleasant UT 84647	800-634-4690	435-462-1400	618
Wasco Electric Co-op Inc PO Box 1700 ....The Dalles OR 97058	800-341-8580	541-296-2740	245
Wasco Products Inc 85 Spencer Dr Unit A PO Box 559 ....Wells ME 04090	800-388-0293		329
WASH Multifamily Laundry Systems 100 N Sepulveda Blvd 12th Fl ....El Segundo CA 90245 *General	800-421-6897*		38
Wash Tub, The 2208 NW Loop 410 ....San Antonio TX 78230 *Cust Svc	866-493-8822*	210-493-8822	62-1
Washburn County PO Box 639 ....Shell Lake WI 54871	800-469-6562	800-367-3306	337
Washburn University 1700 SW College Ave ....Topeka KS 66621	800-736-9060	785-670-1010	166
Washington *Aging & Disability Services Administration* 4450 Tenth Ave SE ....Lacey WA 98503	800-422-3263	360-725-2300	338-48
Child Support Div PO Box 11520 ....Tacoma WA 98411	800-457-6202	360-664-5321	338-48
Employment Security Dept 212 Maple Park Ave SE ....Olympia WA 98501	800-318-6022	360-902-9500	259
Financial Institutions Dept PO Box 41200 ....Olympia WA 98504	877-746-4334	360-902-8703	338-48
Historical Society 1911 Pacific Ave ....Tacoma WA 98402	888-238-4373	253-272-3500	338-48
Housing Finance Commission 1000 Second Ave Ste 2700 ....Seattle WA 98104	800-767-4663	206-464-7139	338-48
Indeterminate Sentence Review Board 4317 Sixth Ave SE ....Olympia WA 98504	866-948-9266	360-407-2400	338-48
Natural Resources Dept 1111 Washington St SE PO Box 47000 ....Olympia WA 98504	800-258-5990	360-902-1000	338-48
Public Disclosure Commission 711 Capitol Way Ste 206 PO Box 40908 ....Olympia WA 98504	877-601-2828	360-753-1111	265
Revenue Dept PO Box 47478 ....Olympia WA 98504	800-647-7706	360-705-6714	338-48
Secretary of State PO Box 40220 ....Olympia WA 98504	800-822-1065	360-902-4151	338-48
Securities Div PO Box 9033 ....Olympia WA 98507	877-746-4334	360-902-8760	338-48
Social & Health Services Dept PO Box 45131 ....Olympia WA 98504	800-737-0617	360-902-8400	338-48
State Parks & Recreation Commission 1111 Israel Rd SW ....Tumwater WA 98501 *Campground Resv	888-226-7688*	360-725-9770	338-48
Utilities & Transportation Commission 1300 S Evergreen Pk Dr SW PO Box 47250 ....Olympia WA 98504	888-333-9882	360-664-1160	338-48
Veterans Affairs Dept 1102 Quince St SE PO Box 41150 ....Olympia WA 98504	800-562-0132	360-725-2200	338-48
Vocational Rehabilitation Div PO Box 45340 ....Olympia WA 98504	800-637-5627	360-725-3636	338-48
Washington & Jefferson College 60 S Lincoln St ....Washington PA 15301	888-926-3529	724-222-4400	166

Name	Address	City	State	ZIP	Toll-Free	Phone	Class
Washington & Lee University	204 W Washington St	Lexington	VA	24450	**800-221-3943**	540-458-8710	166
Washington Adventist University	7600 Flower Ave	Takoma Park	MD	20912	**800-835-4212**	301-891-4000	166
Washington Assn of Realtors	128 Tenth Ave SW PO Box 719 *General	Olympia	WA	98501	**800-562-6024***	360-943-3100	652
Washington Chain & Supply Inc	2901 Utah Ave S PO Box 3645	Seattle	WA	98124	**800-851-3429**	206-623-8500	765
Washington College	300 Washington Ave	Chestertown	MD	21620	**800-422-1782**	410-778-2800	166
Washington Correctional Industries	801 88th Ave SE	Tumwater	WA	98501	**800-628-4738**	360-725-9100	626
Washington County	280 N College Ave Ste 300	Fayetteville	AR	72701	**800-563-0012**	479-444-1711	337
Washington County Chamber of Commerce, The	1 S Potomac St	Hagerstown	MD	21740	**800-520-6685**	301-739-2015	139
Washington County Community College	1 College Dr	Calais	ME	04619	**800-210-6932**	207-454-1000	
Washington County Library	8595 Central Pk Pl	Woodbury	MN	55125	**800-657-3750**	651-275-8500	433-3
Washington County Visitors Assn	12725 SW Millikan Way Ste 210	Beaverton	OR	97005	**800-537-3149**	503-644-5555	206
Washington Court Hotel	525 New Jersey Ave NW	Washington	DC	20001	**800-321-3010**	202-628-2100	378
Washington DC Accommodations	2201 Wisconsin Ave NW Ste C-120	Washington	DC	20007	**800-503-3330**	202-289-2220	375
Washington DC Convention & Tourism Corp	901 Seventh St NW 4th Fl	Washington	DC	20001	**800-422-8644**	202-789-7000	206
Washington Dental Service	9706 Fourth Ave NE	Seattle	WA	98115	**800-367-4104**	206-522-1300	390-3
Washington Duke Inn & Golf Club	3001 Cameron Blvd	Durham	NC	27705	**800-443-3853**	919-490-0999	378
Washington Education Assn Inc	32032 Weyerhaeuser Way S PO Box 9100	Federal Way	WA	98001	**800-622-3393**	253-941-6700	49-5
Washington Electric Co-op	40 Church St	East Montpelier	VT	05651	**800-932-5245**	802-223-5245	245
Washington Electric Cooperative Inc	440 Highland Ridge Rd	Marietta	OH	45750	**877-594-9324**	740-373-2141	245
Washington Electric Membership Corp	258 N Harris St	Sandersville	GA	31082	**800-552-2577**	478-552-2577	245
Washington Express Service LLC	12240 Indian Creek Ct Ste 100	Beltsville	MD	20705	**800-939-5463**	301-210-0899	542
Washington Federal Inc	425 Pike St *NASDAQ: WAFD*	Seattle	WA	98101	**800-324-9375**	206-624-7930	359-2
Washington Floral Service Inc	2701 S 35th St	Tacoma	WA	98409	**800-351-5515**	253-472-8343	292
Washington Hospital Ctr	110 Irving St NW	Washington	DC	20010	**855-546-1686**	202-877-7000	373-3
Washington Internet Daily	2115 Ward Ct NW	Washington	DC	20037	**800-771-9202**	202-872-9200	527-3
Washington Jefferson LLC	318 W 51st St	New York	NY	10019	**888-567-7550**	212-246-7550	377
Washington Lawyer Magazine	1101 K St NW Ste 200	Washington	DC	20005	**877-333-2227**	202-737-4700	455-15
Washington Local Schools	3505 W Lincolnshire Blvd	Toledo	OH	43606	**800-462-3589**	419-473-8251	186
Washington Metropolitan Area Transit Authority	600 Fifth St NW	Washington	DC	20001	**800-523-7009**	202-637-7000	466
Washington Mills Electro Minerals Co	20 N Main St	North Grafton	MA	01536	**800-828-1666**	508-839-6511	1
Washington Missourian	14 W Main St PO Box 336	Washington	MO	63090	**888-239-7701**	636-239-7701	528-4
Washington National Insurance Co	11825 N Pennsylvania St	Carmel	IN	46032	**866-595-2255**		390-2
Washington Parish	909 Pearl St	Franklinton	LA	70438	**800-375-7570**	985-839-7825	337
Washington Pavilion	301 S Main	Sioux Falls	SD	57104	**877-927-4728**	605-367-6000	517
Washington Plaza Hotel	10 Thomas Cir NW	Washington	DC	20005	**800-424-1140**	202-842-1300	378
Washington Post	1301 K St NW	Washington	DC	20071	**800-627-1150**	202-334-6100	528-2
Washington Real Estate Investment Trust (WRIT)	1775 I St NW *NYSE: WRE*	Washington	DC	20006	**800-565-9748**	202-774-3200	651
Washington Speakers Bureau	1663 Prince St	Alexandria	VA	22314	**833-972-8255**		631
Washington Square Hotel	103 Waverly Pl	New York	NY	10011	**800-222-0418**	212-777-9515	378
Washington Square Mall	10202 E Washington St	Indianapolis	IN	46229	**800-283-9490**	317-636-1600	458
Washington State Bar Assn	1325 Fourth Ave Ste 600	Seattle	WA	98101	**800-945-9722**	206-443-9722	72
Washington State Bar News	1325 Fourth Ave Ste 600	Seattle	WA	98101	**800-945-9722**		455-15
Washington State Capital Museum	211 21st Ave SW	Olympia	WA	98501	**888-238-4373**		
Washington State Employees Credit Union	330 Union Ave SE	Olympia	WA	98501	**800-562-0999**	360-943-7911	219
Washington State Library	PO Box 40220	Olympia	WA	98504	**800-822-1065**	360-902-4151	433-5
Washington State Medical Assn	2001 Sixth Ave Ste 2700	Seattle	WA	98121	**800-552-0612**	206-441-9762	472
Washington State Nurses Assn (WSNA)	575 Andover Pk W Ste 101	Seattle	WA	98188	**800-231-8482**	206-575-7979	529
Washington State Reformatory	16550 177th Ave SE PO Box 777	Monroe	WA	98272	**800-483-8314**	360-794-2600	213
Washington State University	PO Box 641040	Pullman	WA	99164	**888-468-6978**	509-335-3564	166
Spokane	310 N Riverpoint Blvd PO Box 1495	Spokane	WA	99210	**866-766-0767**	509-358-7978	166
Washington State Veterinary Medical Assn	8024 Bracken Pl SE	Snoqualmie	WA	98065	**800-399-7862**	425-396-3191	790

Name	Address	City	State	ZIP	Toll-Free	Phone	Class
Washington Trust Bancorp Inc	23 Broad St *NASDAQ: WASH*	Westerly	RI	02891	**800-475-2265**		359-2
Washington University in Saint Louis	1 Brookings Dr	Saint Louis	MO	63130	**800-638-0700**	314-935-5000	166
Washington-Saint Tammany Electric Co-op	950 Pearl St PO Box 697	Franklinton	LA	70438	**866-672-9773**	985-839-3562	245
Washtenaw Community College	4800 E Huron River Dr PO Box 1610	Ann Arbor	MI	48106	**800-218-4341**	734-973-3300	162
Washtenaw County	PO Box 8645	Ann Arbor	MI	48107	**800-440-7548**	734-222-6850	337
Wasserstrom Co	477 S Front St	Columbus	OH	43215	**866-634-8927**	614-228-6525	300
Waste Industries USA Inc	3301 Benson Dr Ste 601	Raleigh	NC	27609	**800-647-9946**	919-325-3000	799
Waste Management Inc	1001 Fannin St Ste 4000 *NYSE: WM*	Houston	TX	77002	**800-633-7871**	713-512-6200	799
Wastecorp Inc	PO Box 70	Grand Island	NY	14072	**888-829-2783**		637
Watanabe Floral Inc	1607 Hart St	Honolulu	HI	96817	**888-832-9360**	808-832-9360	292
WatchGuard Technologies Inc	505 Fifth Ave S Ste 500 *Sales	Seattle	WA	98104	**800-734-9905***	206-613-6600	176
Water Country USA	176 Water Country Pkwy	Williamsburg	VA	23185	**800-343-7946**		32
Water Environment Federation (WEF)	601 Wythe St	Alexandria	VA	22314	**800-666-0206**	703-684-2400	48-13
Water Furnace International Inc	9000 Conservation Way	Fort Wayne	IN	46809	**800-222-5667**	260-478-5667	356
Water Pik Inc	1730 E Prospect Rd	Fort Collins	CO	80553	**800-525-2774**		228
Water Street	131 N Water St	Edgartown	MA	02539	**800-225-6005**	508-627-7000	667
Water's Edge Resort & Spa	1525 Boston Post Rd PO Box 688	Westbrook	CT	06498	**800-222-5901**	860-399-5901	665
Waterbury Button Co	1855 Peck Ln	Cheshire	CT	06410	**800-928-1812**		590
Waterbury Ctr State Park	177 Reservoir Rd	Waterbury Center	VT	05677	**800-837-4261**	802-244-1226	561
Waterco USA Inc	1864 Tobacco Rd *General	Augusta	GA	30906	**800-277-4150***	706-793-7291	801
Waterfield Technologies Inc	1 W Third St Ste 1115	Tulsa	OK	74103	**800-324-0936**	918-858-6400	141
Waterford Retirement Residence	2431 Bank St	Ottawa	ON	K1V8R9	**877-688-4929**	613-737-0811	378
Waterford Township Public Library	5168 Civic Ctr Dr	Waterford	MI	48329	**800-773-2587**	248-674-4831	433-3
Waterford Wedgwood USA Inc	1330 Campus Pkwy	Wall	NJ	07753	**877-720-3486**		361
Waterford, The	601 Universe Blvd	Juno Beach	FL	33408	**888-335-1678**	561-627-3800	668
Waterfront Hotel	10 Washington St	Oakland	CA	94607	**888-842-5333**	510-836-3800	378
Water-Jel Technologies LLC	50 Broad St	Carlstadt	NJ	07072	**800-693-1171**	201-806-3040	473
Waterloo Cedar Falls Courier	PO Box 540	Waterloo	IA	50701	**800-798-1730**	800-798-1717	528-2
Waterloo Convention & Visitor Bureau	500 Jefferson St	Waterloo	IA	50701	**800-728-8431**	319-233-8350	206
Waterloo Industries Inc	1500 Waterloo Dr *Cust Svc	Sedalia	MO	65301	**800-833-8851***	800-558-5528	486
Watermark Capital Partners LLC	150 North Riverside Plz Ste 4200	Chicago	IL	60606	**800-321-2211**	847-482-8600	194
Watermark Learning Inc	7300 Metro Blvd Ste 207	Minneapolis	MN	55439	**800-646-9362**	952-921-0900	194
Waterous Co	125 Hardman Ave	South Saint Paul	MN	55075	**800-488-1228**	651-450-5000	637
Waters Corp	34 Maple St *NYSE: WAT*	Milford	MA	01757	**800-252-4752**	508-478-2000	418
Watersaver Company Inc	5870 E 56th Ave	Commerce	CO	80022	**800-525-2424**	303-289-1818	596
Waterstone Group Inc, The	1145 W Main Ave Ste 209	De Pere	WI	54115	**800-291-3836**	920-964-0333	260
Watertech Whirlpool Bath & Spa	2507 Plymouth Rd	Johnson City	TN	37601	**800-289-8827**		374
Waterton Lakes Lodge Resort	101 Clematis Ave PO Box 4	Waterton Park	AB	T0K2M0	**888-985-6343**	403-859-2150	665
Watertown Daily Times	260 Washington St	Watertown	NY	13601	**800-642-6222**	315-782-1000	528-2
Watertown Public Library	100 S Water St	Watertown	WI	53094	**800-829-3676**	920-262-4090	433-3
Waterville Valley Resort	1 Ski Area Rd PO Box 540	Waterville Valley	NH	03215	**800-468-2553**	603-236-8311	665
Waterworks Operating Company LLC	60 Backus Ave	Danbury	CT	06810	**800-899-6757**	203-546-6000	605
Watkins College of Art & Design	2298 Rose Parks Blvd	Nashville	TN	37228	**866-887-6395**	615-383-4848	164
Watkins Mfg Corp	1280 Pk Ctr Dr	Vista	CA	92081	**800-999-4688**		374
Watlow Winona	1241 Bundy Blvd	Winona	MN	55987	**800-928-5692**	507-454-5300	202
Watson Bowman Acme Corp	95 Pineview Dr	Amherst	NY	14228	**800-677-4922**		
Watson Foods Company Inc	301 Heffernan Dr	West Haven	CT	06516	**800-388-3481**	203-932-3000	296-16
Watson Label Products	10616 Trenton Ave	Saint Louis	MO	63132	**800-678-6715**	314-493-9300	623
Watson Rice	301 Rte 17 N 4th Fl	Rutherford	NJ	07070	**800-945-5985**	201-460-4590	2

Name	Address	City	State	ZIP	Toll-Free	Phone	Class
Watson-Marlow Inc	37 Upton Technology Pk	Wilmington	MA	01887	**800-282-8823**		
Watsontown Trucking Company Inc	60 Belford Blvd	Milton	PA	17847	**800-344-0313**	570-522-9820	775
Watsonville Public Library	275 Main St Ste 100	Watsonville	CA	95076	**800-281-7275**	831-768-3400	433-3
Watt Printing Co	4544 Hinckley Industrial Pkwy	Cleveland	OH	44109	**800-273-2170**	216-398-2000	623
Watts Radiant Inc	1630 E Bradford Pkwy Ste B	Springfield	MO	65804	**800-276-2419**		14
Watts Towers of Simon Rodia State Historic Park	1765 E 107th St	Los Angeles	CA	90002	**866-240-4655**	213-847-4646	561
Waukesha County	515 W Moreland Blvd Rm 120	Waukesha	WI	53188	**800-247-5645**	262-548-7010	337
Waukesha County Freeman	801 N Barstow St PO Box 7	Waukesha	WI	53187	**800-762-6219**	262-542-2501	528-2
Waukesha Foundry Company Inc	1300 Lincoln Ave	Waukesha	WI	53186	**800-727-0741**	262-542-0741	307
Waukesha Memorial Hospital	725 American Ave	Waukesha	WI	53188	**800-326-2011**	262-928-1000	373-3
Waupaca Elevator Co Inc	1726 N Ballard Rd Ste 1	Appleton	WI	54911	**800-238-8739**		256
Waupaca Foundry Inc	1955 Brunner Dr PO Box 249	Waupaca	WI	54981	**800-669-6820**	715-258-6611	307
Wausau Central Wisconsin Convention & Visitors Bureau (CWCVB)	219 Jefferson St	Wausau	WI	54403	**888-948-4748**	715-355-8788	206
Wausau Chemical Corp	2001 N River Dr	Wausau	WI	54403	**800-950-6656**	715-842-2285	144
Wausau Daily Herald	800 Scott St	Wausau	WI	54403	**800-477-4838**	715-842-2101	528-2
Wausau Homes Inc	PO Box 8005	Wausau	WI	54402	**800-455-0545**	715-359-7272	106
Wausau Tile Inc	PO Box 1520	Wausau	WI	54402	**800-388-8728**	715-359-3121	183
WaUSAu Window & Wall Systems	7800 International Dr	Wausau	WI	54401	**877-678-2983**	715-845-2161	478
WAV Inc	2380 Prospect Dr	Aurora	IL	60502	**800-678-2419**	630-818-1000	176
WAVA-FM 1051 (Rel)	1735 N Lynn St Ste 500	Arlington	VA	22209	**888-293-9282**	703-807-2266	641
Wave Direct	9 Del Prado Blvd N Ste B	Cape Coral	FL	33909	**888-550-9918**	239-574-8181	5
Wavedivision Holdings LLC	401 Parkplace Ctr Ste 103	Kirkland	WA	98033	**844-910-8519**	425-576-8200	731
Waveline Direct Inc	192 Hempt Rd	Mechanicsburg	PA	17050	**800-257-8830**	717-795-8830	623
Waverly Plastics Company Inc	1001 Industrial St PO Box 801	Waverly	IA	50677	**800-454-6377**		66
WAVE-TV Ch 3 (NBC)	725 S Floyd St	Louisville	KY	40203	**800-223-2579**	502-585-2201	736-43
WAVV-FM 1011	11800 Tamiami Trl E	Naples	FL	34113	**866-310-9288**	239-775-9288	641-68
Wawa Inc	260 W Baltimore Pk	Media	PA	19063	**800-444-9292**	610-358-8000	204
Waxman Industries Inc	24460 Aurora Rd *OTC: WXMN*	Bedford Heights	OH	44146	**800-201-7298**	440-439-1830	608
WAXN-TV Ch 64	1901 N Tryon St	Charlotte	NC	28206	**855-336-0360**	704-335-4786	736-16
Way to Happiness Foundation International, The	201 E Broadway	Glendale	CA	91205	**800-255-7906**	818-254-0600	305
Wayland Academy	101 N University Ave *Admissions	Beaver Dam	WI	53916	**800-860-7725***	920-356-2120	618
Wayland Baptist University	1900 W Seventh St	Plainview	TX	79072	**800-588-1928**	806-291-1000	166
Wayland Baptist University Anchorage	7801 E 32 Ave	Anchorage	AK	99504	**800-588-1928**	907-333-2277	166
Wayland Free Public Library	41 Cochituate Rd	Wayland	MA	01778	**800-592-2000**	508-358-2311	433-3
Waymouth Farms Inc	5300 Boone Ave	New Hope	MN	55428	**800-527-0094**	763-533-5300	296-8
Wayne Combustion Systems	801 Glasgow Ave	Fort Wayne	IN	46803	**855-929-6327**	260-425-9200	356
Wayne County	925 Court St	Honesdale	PA	18431	**800-321-9973**	570-253-5970	337
Wayne County	26 Church St	Lyons	NY	14489	**800-527-6510**	315-946-5400	337
Wayne County Boot Camp	PO Box 182	Clifton	TN	38425	**855-876-7283**	931-676-3345	213
Wayne County Chamber of Commerce	308 N Williams St	Goldsboro	NC	27530	**800-849-6222**	919-734-2241	139
Wayne County Convention & Visitors Bureau	428 W Liberty St	Wooster	OH	44691	**800-362-6474**		206
Wayne Farms LLC	4110 Continental Dr	Oakwood	GA	30566	**800-392-0844**		10-7
Wayne Hummer Investments LLC	222 S Riverside Pz 28th Fl	Chicago	IL	60606	**800-621-4477**	866-943-4732	686
Wayne Independent	220 Eigth St	Honesdale	PA	18431	**800-598-5002**	570-253-3055	528-2
Wayne Mills Co Inc	130 W Berkley St	Philadelphia	PA	19144	**800-220-8053**	215-842-2134	740-5
Wayne Oil Company Inc	1301 Wayne Memorial Dr	Goldsboro	NC	27534	**800-641-2816**	919-735-2021	532
Wayne Pipe & Supply Inc	6040 Innovation Blvd	Fort Wayne	IN	46818	**800-552-3697**	260-423-9577	608
Wayne Reaves Software & Websites Inc	6211 Thomaston Rd	Macon	GA	31220	**888-477-9707**		
Wayne Savings Bancshares Inc	1908 Cleveland Rd *NASDAQ: WAYN*	Wooster	OH	44691	**800-414-1103**	330-264-5767	359-2
Wayne State College	1111 Main St	Wayne	NE	68787	**800-228-9972**	402-375-7000	166
Wayne State University	42 W Warren	Detroit	MI	48202	**877-978-4636**	313-577-3577	166
Wayneco Inc	800 Hanover Rd	York	PA	17408	**800-233-9313**	717-225-4413	321
Wayne-Dalton Corp	1 Door Dr PO Box 67	Mount Hope	OH	44660	**800-827-3667**	330-674-7015	234
Waynesburg College	51 W College St *Admissions	Waynesburg	PA	15370	**800-225-7393***	724-627-8191	166
Waynesville Inn Golf & Country Club, The	176 Country Club Dr	Waynesville	NC	28786	**800-627-6250**	828-456-3551	665
Wayne-White Counties Electric Co-op	1501 W Main St	Fairfield	IL	62837	**888-871-7695**	618-842-2196	245
Waypoint Consulting	1450 E Boot Rd	West Chester	PA	19380	**866-826-7075**		
Wayside Furniture Inc	1367 Canton Rd	Akron	OH	44312	**877-499-3968**	330-733-6221	321
WAYZ-FM 1047 (Ctry)	10960 John Wayne Dr	Greencastle	PA	17225	**888-950-1047**	717-597-9200	641
WB Bottle Supply Company Inc	3400 S Clement Ave	Milwaukee	WI	53207	**800-738-3931**	414-482-4300	332
WB Mason Company Inc	59 Centre St	Brockton	MA	02303	**888-926-2766**		321
WBANA (Wild Blueberry Assn of North America)	PO Box 100	Old Town	ME	04468	**800-341-1758**	207-570-3535	48-2
WBAP-AM 820 (N/T)	3090 Olive St Ste 400	Dallas	TX	75219	**800-288-9227**	214-526-2400	641
WBAY-TV Ch 2 (ABC)	115 S Jefferson St	Green Bay	WI	54301	**800-261-9229**	920-432-3331	736-32
WBEN-AM 930 (N/T)	500 Corporate Pkwy Ste 200	Amherst	NY	14226	**800-616-9236**	716-843-0600	641
WBG (Wright Business Graphics)	18440 NE San Rafael St	Portland	OR	97230	**800-547-8397**		110
WBG (World Bank Group, The)	1818 H St NW	Washington	DC	20433	**800-645-7247**	202-473-1000	778
WBGL-FM 917 (Rel)	4101 Fieldstone Rd PO Box 111 *Cust Svc	Champaign	IL	61822	**800-475-9245***	217-359-8232	641-20
WBHM-FM 903 (NPR)	650 11th St S	Birmingham	AL	35233	**800-444-9246**	205-934-2606	641-14
WBHY-FM 885 (Rel)	PO Box 1328	Mobile	AL	36633	**888-473-8488**	251-473-8488	641-67
WBI Energy	1250 W Century Ave	Bismarck	ND	58503	**877-924-4677**	701-530-1095	325
WBI Holdings Inc	1250 W Century Ave *General	Bismarck	ND	58503	**877-924-4677***		325
WBIQ-TV Ch 10 (PBS)	2112 11th Ave S Ste 400	Birmingham	AL	35205	**800-239-5233**	205-328-8756	736-10
WBNX-TV Ch 55 (CW)	2690 State Rd	Cuyahoga Falls	OH	44223	**800-282-0515**	330-922-5500	736
WBRE-TV Ch 28 (NBC)	62 S Franklin St	Wilkes-Barre	PA	18701	**800-367-9222**	570-823-2828	736
WBRZ 2 abc	1650 Highland Rd	Baton Rouge	LA	70802	**800-726-6409**	225-383-1111	736-8
WBUR-FM 909 (NPR)	890 Commonwealth Ave	Boston	MA	02215	**800-909-9287**	617-353-0909	641-16
WBZT-AM 1230 (N/T)	3071 Continental Dr	West Palm Beach	FL	33407	**800-889-0267**	561-616-6600	641-115
WCAU NBC 10	10 Monument Rd	Bala Cynwyd	PA	19004	**800-847-9228**	610-668-5510	736
WCBB-TV Ch 10 (PBS)	1450 Lisbon St	Lewiston	ME	04240	**800-884-1717**		736
WCBD-TV Ch 2 (NBC)	210 W Coleman Blvd	Mount Pleasant	SC	29464	**800-861-5255**	843-884-2222	736
WCBE-FM 905 (NPR)	540 Jack Gibbs Blvd	Columbus	OH	43215	**800-241-0421**	614-365-5555	641-28
WCEC (Wharton County Electric Co-op Inc)	1815 E Jackson St	El Campo	TX	77437	**800-460-6271**	979-543-6271	245
WCF Insurance	*Workers' Compensation Fund* 100 W Towne Ridge Pkwy	Sandy	UT	84070	**800-446-2667**	385-351-8000	338-45
WCG	915 Fort St 5th Fl	Victoria	BC	V8V3K3	**888-562-9283**	250-389-0699	
WCH (Women's & Children's Hospital)	4600 Ambassador Caffery Pkwy	Lafayette	LA	70508	**888-569-8331**	337-521-9100	373-7
WCHS-TV Ch 8 (ABC)	1301 Piedmont Rd	Charleston	WV	25301	**888-696-9247**	304-346-5358	736-15
WCI Communities Inc	24301 Walden Ctr Dr	Bonita Springs	FL	34134	**800-924-4005**	239-498-8200	649
WCIA-TV Ch 3 (CBS)	PO Box 20	Champaign	IL	61824	**800-676-3382**	217-356-8333	736
WCIC-FM 915 (Rel)	3902 W Baring Trace	Peoria	IL	61615	**877-692-9242**	309-692-9242	641-79
WCKT-FM 1071 (Ctry)	13320 Metro Pkwy Ste 1	Fort Myers	FL	33966	**800-827-1071**	239-225-4300	
WCLK-FM 919	111 James P Brawley Dr SW	Atlanta	GA	30314	**888-448-3925**	404-880-8284	641-9
WCLV	1375 Euclid Ave Idea Ctr	Cleveland	OH	44115	**877-399-3307**	216-916-6100	642
WCNY-FM 913 (NPR)	506 Old Liverpool Rd	Liverpool	NY	13088	**800-451-9269**	315-453-2424	641
WCNY-TV Ch 24 (PBS)	506 Old Liverpool Rd PO Box 2400	Syracuse	NY	13220	**800-638-5163**	315-453-2424	736-76
WCOL-FM 923 (Ctry)	2323 W Fifth Ave Ste 200	Columbus	OH	43204	**800-899-9265**	614-486-6101	641-28
Wcp Solutions	6703 S 234th St Ste 120	Kent	WA	98032	**877-398-3030**		548-1
WCPX-TV Ch 38 (I)	333 S Desplaines St Ste 101	Chicago	IL	60661	**888-467-2988**	212-757-3100	736-17
WCQR-FM 883 (Rel)	2312 Oak St	Gray	TN	37615	**888-477-5676**	423-477-5676	641
WCQS-FM 881 (NPR)	73 Broadway	Asheville	NC	28801	**866-448-3881**	828-210-4800	641-100
WCR (Women's Council of REALTORS)	430 N Michigan Ave	Chicago	IL	60611	**800-245-8512**		49-17
WCSH-TV Ch 6 (NBC)	1 Congress Sq	Portland	ME	04101	**800-464-1213**	207-828-6666	736-59
WCU (Western Carolina University)	1 University Dr	Cullowhee	NC	28723	**877-928-4968**	828-227-7211	166

Name / Address	City	State	ZIP	Toll-Free	Phone	Class
WCVE-TV Ch 23 (PBS)						
23 Sesame St	Richmond	VA	23235	**800-476-8440**	804-320-1301	736-61
WCWC (Western Canada Wilderness Committee)						
46 E Sixth Ave	Vancouver	BC	V5T1J4	**800-661-9453**	604-683-8220	48-13
WD-40 Co						
1061 Cudahy Pl	San Diego	CA	92110	**800-448-9340**	619-275-1400	537
NASDAQ: WDFC						
WDAE-AM 620 (Sports)						
4002 W Gandy Blvd	Tampa	FL	33611	**888-546-4620**	813-832-1000	641-108
WDAM-TV Ch 7 (NBC)						
PO Box 16269	Hattiesburg	MS	39404	**800-844-9326**	601-544-4730	736
WDCX-FM 995 (Rel)						
625 Delaware Ave Ste 308	Buffalo	NY	14202	**800-684-2848**	716-883-3010	641-18
WDEL-AM 1150 (N/T)						
2727 Shipley Rd	Wilmington	DE	19810	**800-544-1150**	302-478-2700	641-116
WDIO-TV Ch 10 (ABC)						
10 Observation Rd	Duluth	MN	55811	**800-477-1013**	218-727-6864	736-25
WDKS-FM 1061 (CHR)						
117 SE Fifth St	Evansville	IN	47708	**888-454-5477**	812-425-4226	641-37
WDKY-TV Ch 56 (Fox)						
836 Euclid Ave Ste 201	Lexington	KY	40502	**888-404-5656**	859-269-5656	736-40
WDL Systems						
220 Chatham Business Dr	Pittsboro	NC	27312	**800-548-2319***	919-545-2500	174
*Sales						
WDRM-FM 1021						
26869 Peoples Rd	Madison	AL	35756	**866-302-0102**	256-309-2400	641
WDRV-FM 971 (CR)						
875 N Michigan Ave Ste 1510	Chicago	IL	60611	**800-899-0089**	312-274-9710	641-23
WDSE-TV Ch 8 (PBS)						
632 Niagara Ct	Duluth	MN	55811	**800-563-9373**	218-788-2831	736-25
WDSU-TV Ch 6 (NBC)						
846 Howard Ave	New Orleans	LA	70113	**888-925-4127**	504-679-0600	736-50
WDUZ-AM 1400 (Sports)						
810 Victoria St	Green Bay	WI	54302	**855-724-1075**	920-468-4100	641-42
WDWS-AM 1400 (N/T)						
15 Main St	Champaign	IL	61820	**800-223-9397**	217-351-5300	641-20
We Are Alexander						
1227 Washington Ave	Saint Louis	MO	63103	**844-922-0002**		
WE Aubuchon Company Inc						
95 Aubuchon Dr	Westminster	MA	01473	**800-431-2712**	978-874-0521	363
We Check Inc						
301 Moodie Dr Ste 320	Ottawa	ON	K2H9C4	**877-889-0602**		
We Energies						
231 W Michigan St PO Box 2046	Milwaukee	WI	53203	**800-242-9137**	414-221-2345	782
We Raise Foundation						
1 Pierce Pl Ste 250E	Itasca	IL	60143	**800-762-6748**	630-766-9066	48-20
WE Yoder Inc						
41 S Maple St	Kutztown	PA	19530	**800-889-5149**	610-683-7383	188-8
Weaber Inc						
1231 Mt Wilson Rd	Lebanon	PA	17042	**800-745-9663**	717-867-2212	497
Wealth Conservancy Inc, The						
1525 Spruce St Ste 300	Boulder	CO	80302	**888-440-1919**	303-444-1919	400
Wealthfront Inc						
541 Cowper St	Palo Alto	CA	94301	**844-995-8437**		
Wealthsimple Inc						
860 Richmond St W 3rd Fl	Toronto	ON	M6J1C9	**855-255-9038**		
WEAO-TV Ch 49 (PBS)						
1750 Campus Ctr Dr	Kent	OH	44240	**800-554-4549**	330-677-4549	736
Weather Ch Inc, The						
300 I N Pkwy	Atlanta	GA	30339	**866-843-0392**	770-226-0000	735
Weather Shield Manufacturing Inc						
1 Weather Shield Plz PO Box 309	Medford	WI	54451	**800-222-2995**	715-748-2100	236
Weatherall Printing Co						
1349 Cliff Gookin Blvd	Tupelo	MS	38801	**800-273-6043**	662-842-5284	623
Weatherbank Inc						
1015 Waterwood Pkwy Ste J	Edmond	OK	73034	**800-687-3562**	405-359-0773	70
Weatherby Inc						
1605 Commerce Way	Paso Robles	CA	93446	**800-227-2016**	805-227-2600	284
Weatherford Chamber of Commerce						
401 Ft Worth St	Weatherford	TX	76086	**888-594-3801**	817-596-3801	139
Weatherford College						
225 College Pk Dr	Weatherford	TX	76086	**800-287-5471**	817-594-5471	162
Weatherford International Inc						
515 Post Oak Blvd Ste 600	Houston	TX	77027	**866-398-0010**	713-693-4000	533
NYSE: WFT						
Weathermatic						
3301 W Kingsley Rd	Garland	TX	75041	**888-484-3776**	972-278-6131	428
Weathers Auto Supply Inc						
23308 Airpark Dr	Petersburg	VA	23803	**888-572-2886**	804-861-1076	54
Weathervane Seafood Restaurant						
306 US Rt 1	Kittery	ME	03904	**800-914-1774**	207-439-0330	666
Weaver Bros Inc						
2230 Spar Ave	Anchorage	AK	99501	**800-478-4600**	907-278-4526	775
Weaver-Bailey Contractors Inc						
PO Box 60	El Paso	AR	72045	**800-253-3385**	501-796-2301	189-3
Weavertown Environmental Group						
2 Dorrington Rd	Carnegie	PA	15106	**800-746-4850**		187
WEB (Worldwide Employee Benefits Network Inc)						
11520 N Central Expy Ste 201	Dallas	TX	75243	**888-795-6862**		49-12
Web Advanced						
36 Discovery Ste 150	Irvine	CA	92618	**888-261-7414**		
Web Equipment						
464 Central Rd	Fredericksburg	VA	22401	**800-225-3858**	540-657-5855	190
Web Presence Architects LLC						
10113 Meadowneck Ct	Silver Spring	MD	20910	**888-873-6218**		
Webb Financial Group						
8120 Penn Ave S Ste 177	Bloomington	MN	55431	**800-927-9322**	952-837-3200	400
Webb Institute						
298 Crescent Beach Rd	Glen Cove	NY	11542	**866-708-9322**	516-671-2213	166
Webb School						
PO Box 488	Bell Buckle	TN	37020	**888-733-9322**	931-389-9322	618
Webb Wheel Products Inc						
2310 Industrial Dr SW	Cullman	AL	35055	**800-633-3256**	256-739-6660	60
Webb; County Appraisal Distric						
3302 Clark Blvd	Laredo	TX	78043	**800-252-9121**	956-718-4091	41
WebBank Corp						
215 S State St Ste 1000	Salt Lake City	UT	84111	**888-881-3789**	801-456-8350	217
Webber International University						
1201 N Scenic Hwy	Babson Park	FL	33827	**800-741-1844**		166
WEBCARGO Inc						
800 Pl Victoria Ste 2603 Tour de la bourse CP 329	Montreal	QC	H4Z1G8	**866-905-0123**	514-905-5223	365
Webcom						
12808 Grand Bay Pkwy W	Jacksonville	FL	32258	**800-338-1771**	904-680-6600	804
WEBE-FM 108 (AC)						
2 Lafayette Sq	Bridgeport	CT	06604	**800-932-3108**	203-333-9108	641-104
Weber County						
2380 Washington Blvd Ste 350	Ogden	UT	84401	**800-407-2757**	801-399-8454	337
Weber County Library						
2464 Jefferson Ave	Ogden	UT	84401	**866-678-5342**	801-337-2632	433-3
Weber Insurance Corp						
505 Corporate Dr W	Langhorne	PA	19047	**888-860-0400**	215-860-0400	389
Weber Logistics						
13530 Rosecrans Ave	Santa Fe Springs	CA	90670	**855-469-3237**		447
Weber State University						
3848 Harrison Blvd	Ogden	UT	84408	**800-848-7770**	801-626-6000	166
Davis						
2750 University Park Blvd	Layton	UT	84041	**800-848-7770**	801-395-3555	166
Stewart Library						
3921 Central Campus Dr Dept 2901	Ogden	UT	84408	**877-306-3140**	801-626-6403	433-6
Weber's Inn						
3050 Jackson Rd	Ann Arbor	MI	48103	**800-443-3050***	734-769-2500	378
*Resv						
Weber-Knapp Co						
441 Chandler St	Jamestown	NY	14701	**800-828-9254**	716-484-9135	349
Weber-Stephen Products Co						
200 E Daniels Rd	Palatine	IL	60067	**800-446-1071***		36
*Cust Svc						
WebEyeCare Inc						
10 Canal St Ste 302	Bristol	PA	19007	**888-536-7480**		365
WebiMaxcom						
2 Aquarium Loop Dr Ste 140	Camden	NJ	08103	**888-932-4629**	856-840-8301	195
WebLinc LLC						
22 S Third St 2nd Fl	Philadelphia	PA	19106	**855-227-0511**		
Weblocom Inc						
2075 Blvd Robert-Bourassa	Montreal	QC	H3A2L1	**866-381-3395**	514-364-3636	
Webroot Software Inc						
2560 55th St	Boulder	CO	80301	**800-772-9383**	303-442-3813	178-12
Websense Inc						
10240 Sorrento Valley Rd	San Diego	CA	92121	**800-723-1166**	858-320-8000	178-7
NASDAQ: WBSN						
Website Magazine Inc						
999 E Touhy Ave	Des Plaines	IL	60018	**800-817-1518**	773-628-2779	526
Webster City Federal Bancorp						
820 Des Moines St	Webster City	IA	50595	**866-519-4004**	515-832-3071	359-2
NASDAQ: WCFB						
Webster Electric Co-op						
1240 Spur Dr	Marshfield	MO	65706	**800-643-4305**	417-859-2216	245
Webster Financial Corp						
PO Box 10305	Waterbury	CT	06726	**800-325-2424**		359-2
NYSE: WBS						
Webster First Federal Credit Union						
271 Greenwood St	Worcester	MA	01607	**800-962-4452**	508-949-1043	71
Webster Industries Inc						
95 Chestnut Ridge Rd	Montvale	NJ	07645	**800-955-2374**	800-999-2374	66
Webster Industries Inc						
325 Hall St	Tiffin	OH	44883	**800-243-9327**	419-447-8232	207
Webstone Company Inc						
1 Appian Way	Worcester	MA	01610	**800-225-9529**		608
WEC (Warren Electric Co-op Inc)						
320 E Main St PO Box 208	Youngsville	PA	16371	**800-364-8640**	814-563-7548	245
Wecsys LLC						
8825 Xylon Ave N	Minneapolis	MN	55445	**888-493-2797**	763-504-1069	75
Wedding Experience						
2307 Douglas Rd Ste 400	Coral Gables	FL	33145	**866-223-9672**	305-421-1260	226
Wedding Shoppe Inc, The						
1196 Grand Ave	Saint Paul	MN	55105	**877-294-4991**	651-298-1144	157-6
Wedgewood Hotel						
845 Hornby St	Vancouver	BC	V6Z1V1	**800-663-0666**	604-689-7777	378
Wedgewood Resort Hotel						
212 Wedgewood Dr	Fairbanks	AK	99701	**800-528-4916**		378
WEDU-TV Ch 3 (PBS)						
1300 N Blvd	Tampa	FL	33607	**800-354-9338**	813-254-9338	736-77
Weecycle Environmental Consulting Inc						
1208 Commerce Ct Ste 5B	Lafayette	CO	80026	**800-875-7033**	303-413-0452	738
Weed USA Inc						
5780 Harrow Glen Ct	Galena	OH	43021	**800-933-3758**	740-548-3881	706
Weekends Only Inc						
349 Marshall Ave 3rd Fl	Saint Louis	MO	63119	**855-803-5888**	314-447-1500	321
Weeks-Lerman Group						
58-38 Page Pl	Maspeth	NY	11378	**800-544-5959**	718-803-5000	530
Weetabix Co Inc						
300 Nickerson Rd	Marlborough	MA	01752	**800-343-0590**		296-4
WEF (Water Environment Federation)						
601 Wythe St	Alexandria	VA	22314	**800-666-0206**	703-684-2400	48-13
WEG (West Essex Graphics Inc)						
305 Fairfield Ave	Fairfield	NJ	07004	**800-221-5859**		776
Wege Pretzel Co						
PO Box 334	Hanover	PA	17331	**800-888-4646**		296-9
Wegmans Food Markets Inc						
1500 Brooks Ave PO Box 30844	Rochester	NY	14603	**800-934-6267**	585-328-2550	344
WEHT-TV						
800 Marywood Dr	Henderson	KY	42420	**800-879-8542**	800-879-8549	736
WEI (Wieland Electric Inc)						
49 International Rd	Burgaw	NC	28425	**800-943-5263**	910-259-5050	246
Weibel 1 Winemaster Way	Lodi	CA	95240	**800-932-9463**	209-365-9463	80-3
Weichert Realtors						
1625 Rt 10 E	Morris Plains	NJ	07950	**800-401-0486**	973-984-1400	648
Weidenhammer Systems Corp						
935 Berkshire Blvd	Reading	PA	19610	**866-497-2227**	610-378-1149	177
Weidmuller Inc						
821 Southlake Blvd	Richmond	VA	23236	**800-849-9343***	804-794-2877	810
*Cust Svc						
Weidner Ctr for the Performing Arts						
2420 Nicolet Dr University of Wisconsin at Green Bay	Green Bay	WI	54311	**800-895-0071**	920-465-2726	568

	Toll-Free	Phone	Class
Weightech 1649 Country Elite Dr — Waldron AR 72958	800-457-3720	479-637-4182	360
Weil Co, The 11236 El Camino Real Ste 200 — San Diego CA 92130	800-355-9345	858-724-6040	400
Weiler Corp 1 Wildwood Dr — Cresco PA 18326 *Cust Svc	800-835-9999*	570-595-7495	103
Weinbrenner Shoe Co Inc 108 S Polk St — Merrill WI 54452 *General	800-569-6817*	715-536-5521	301
Weingarten Realty Investors 2600 Citadel Plaza Dr Ste 125 — Houston TX 77008 NYSE: WRI	800-688-8865	713-866-6000	651
Weingartz Supply Co 46061 Van Dyke Ave — Utica MI 48317	855-669-7278	586-731-7240	323
WEIQ-TV Ch 42 (PBS) 2112 11th Ave S Ste 400 — Birmingham AL 35205	800-239-5233	205-328-8756	736-10
Weis Markets 1000 S Second St PO Box 471 — Sunbury PA 17801 NYSE: WMK	866-999-9347		344
Weiser 19701 Da Vinci — Lake Forest CA 92610	800-677-5625		349
WEKU-FM 889 (Clas) 521 Lancaster Ave 102 Perkins Bldg-EKU — Richmond KY 40475	800-621-8890		641
Wel Companies Inc 1625 S Broadway PO Box 5610 — De Pere WI 54115	800-333-4415		775
Weland Clinical Laboratories PC 1911 First Ave SE — Cedar Rapids IA 52402	800-728-1503	319-366-1503	414
Welch & Rushe Inc 391 Prince George's Blvd — Upper Marlboro MD 20774	800-683-3852	301-430-6000	186
Welch Allyn Inc 4341 State St Rd — Skaneateles Falls NY 13153	800-535-6663		250
Welch Allyn Monitoring Inc 8500 SW Creekside Pl — Beaverton OR 97008 *Cust Svc	800-289-2500*	503-530-7500	250
Welch Group LLC, The 3940 Montclair Rd — Birmingham AL 35213	800-709-7100	205-879-5001	524
Welch Packaging Group 1020 Horman St — Elkhart IN 46516	800-246-2475	574-295-2460	100
Welcome Wagon 5830 Coral Ridge Dr — Coral Springs FL 33076	800-779-3526		5
Weld Mold Co 750 Rickett Rd — Brighton MI 48116	800-521-9755	810-229-9521	806
Weldaloy Products Co 24011 Hoover Rd — Warren MI 48089	888-935-3256	586-758-5550	
Weldangrind Ltd 10323 174 St NW — Edmonton AB T5S1H1	866-226-2414	780-484-3030	752
Welder Training & Testing Institute 1144 N Graham St — Allentown PA 18109	800-923-9884	610-820-9551	795
Weldmac Manufacturing Co 1451 N Johnson Ave — El Cajon CA 92020	800-252-1533	619-440-2300	452
Weldon Williams & Lick Inc 711 N A St — Fort Smith AR 72901	800-242-4995	479-783-4113	623
Welk Resort Branson 8860 Lawrence Welk Dr — Escondido CA 92026	800-505-9355	417-336-3575	665
Welk Resort San Diego 8860 Lawrence Welk Dr — Escondido CA 92026 *Resv	800-932-9355*	760-749-3000	665
Well Spa at Miramonte Resort 45000 Indian Wells Ln — Indian Wells CA 92210	800-237-2926	760-837-1652	703
Well Spouse Assn 63 W Main St Ste H — Freehold NJ 07728	800-838-0879	732-577-8899	48-6
Wella Corp 4500 Park Granada — Calabasas CA 91302	800-422-2336		214
WellAware 3424 Paesanos Pkwy Ste 200 — San Antonio TX 78231	855-935-5292	210-816-4600	386
WellCare 8735 Henderson Rd — Tampa FL 33634	800-960-2530	813-290-6208	390-3
WellCare Health Plans Inc PO Box 31372 — Tampa FL 33631	866-530-9491		390-3
WellCare of Georgia Inc 8725 Henderson Rd — Tampa FL 33634	800-919-8807		389
Wellesley Volkswagen 231 Linden St — Wellesley MA 02482 *Sales	888-602-6905*	781-237-3553	
Welles-Turner Memorial Library 2407 Main St — Glastonbury CT 06033	800-411-9671	860-652-7719	433-3
Welligent Inc 5005 Colley Ave — Norfolk VA 23508	888-317-5960		177
Wellington Hotel 871 Seventh Ave — New York NY 10019	800-652-1212	212-247-3900	378
Wellington Resort 551 Thames St — Newport RI 02840	800-228-2968	401-849-1770	378
Wellness Coaches 725 Skippack Pk Ste 300 — Blue Bell PA 19422	866-894-1300		
Wells & Drew Cos 3414 Galilee Rd — Jacksonville FL 32207	800-342-8636		623
Wells Bloomfield Industries 10 Sunnen Dr — Saint Louis MO 63143	888-356-5362		298
Wells Cargo Inc 1503 W McNaughton St — Elkhart IN 46514	800-348-7553	574-264-9661	774
Wells College 170 Main St — Aurora NY 13026 *Admissions	800-952-9355*	315-364-3266	166
Wells Concrete 210 Inspiration Ln PO Box 656 — Albany MN 56307	800-658-7049		183
Wells County Public Library 200 W Washington St — Bluffton IN 46714	800-824-6111	260-824-1612	433-3
Wells Enterprises Inc 1 Blue Bunny Dr — Le Mars IA 51031 *All	800-942-3800*	712-546-4000	296-25
Wells Fargo 420 Montgomery St — San Francisco CA 94104 NYSE: WFC	800-877-4833		216
Wells Fargo Bank 5622 Third St — Katy TX 77493	800-864-8377	281-391-2101	70
Wells Fargo Bank Iowa NA 666 Walnut St — Des Moines IA 50309	800-864-8377	515-245-3131	70
Wells Fargo Bank Minnesota South NA 21 First St SW — Rochester MN 55902	800-864-8377	507-285-2800	70
Wells Fargo Bank Nebraska NA 1919 Douglas St — Omaha NE 68102	800-864-8377	402-536-2022	70
Wells Fargo Bank Texas NA 707 Castroville Rd — San Antonio TX 78237	800-864-8377	210-856-6224	70
Wells Fargo Education Financial Services PO Box 5185 — Sioux Falls SD 57117	800-658-3567		217
Wells Fargo Home Mortgage 2840 Ingersoll Ave — Des Moines IA 50312	800-401-1957	515-237-5196	507
Wells Johnson Co 8000 S Kolb Rd — Tucson AZ 85756	800-528-1597	520-298-6069	474
Wells Lamont Industry Group 6640 W Touhy Ave — Niles IL 60714	800-247-3295		155-7
Wells Printing Company Inc 6030 Perimeter Pkwy — Montgomery AL 36116	800-264-4958	334-281-3449	623
Wells-Gardner Electronics Corp 9500 W 55th St Ste A — McCook IL 60525 NYSE: WGA	800-336-6630	708-290-2100	173-4
Wellstar Douglas Hospital 8954 Hospital Dr — Douglasville GA 30134	888-800-5094	770-949-1500	373-3
Wellstar Kennestone Hospital 677 Church St — Marietta GA 30060	888-800-5094	770-793-5000	373-3
Welocalize Inc 241 E Fourth St Ste 207 — Frederick MD 21701	800-370-9515	301-668-0330	194
WEMU-FM 891 (NPR) PO Box 980350 — Ypsilanti MI 48198	888-299-8910	734-487-2229	641
Wenatchee Valley College 1300 Fifth St — Wenatchee WA 98801	877-982-4968	509-682-6800	162
Wenatchee World 14 N Mission St — Wenatchee WA 98801	800-572-4433	509-663-5161	528-2
Wendell August Forge Inc 2074 Leesburg-Grove City Rd — Mercer PA 16137	866-354-5192	724-748-9501	327
Wendell's Inc 6601 Bunker Lake Blvd NW — Ramsey MN 55303	800-936-3355	763-576-8200	465
WEND-FM 1065 (Alt) 801 Wood Ridge Ctr Dr — Charlotte NC 28217	800-934-1065	704-714-9444	641-22
Wendy's International Inc 1 Dave Thomas Blvd — Dublin OH 43017	800-952-5210	614-764-3100	666
Wenger Corp 555 Pk Dr PO Box 448 — Owatonna MN 55060	800-493-6437	507-455-4100	523
WENH-TV Ch 11 (PBS) 268 Mast Rd — Durham NH 03824	800-639-8408	603-868-1100	736
Wenner Bread Products Inc 33 Rajon Rd — Bayport NY 11705	800-869-6262	631-563-6262	296-1
Wentworth Institute of Technology 550 Huntington Ave — Boston MA 02115	800-556-0610	617-989-4590	166
Wentworth Printing Corp 101 N 12th St — West Columbia SC 29169	800-326-0784		623
Wentworth-Douglass Hospital 789 Central Ave — Dover NH 03820	877-201-7100	603-742-5252	373-3
WENZ-FM 1079 (Urban) 2510 St Clair Ave NE — Cleveland OH 44114	800-440-1079	216-579-1111	641-25
Werk-Brau Company Inc 2800 Fostoria Ave — Findlay OH 45840	800-537-9561		
Werner Co 93 Werner Rd — Greenville PA 16125	888-523-3371		420
Werner Electric Supply Co 2341 Industrial Dr — Neenah WI 54956	800-236-5026	920-729-4500	246
Werner Enterprises Inc 14507 Frontier Rd — Omaha NE 68138 NASDAQ: WERN	800-228-2240	402-895-6640	775
Werner G Smith Inc 1730 Train Ave — Cleveland OH 44113 *General	800-535-8343*	216-861-3676	296-12
WERN-FM 887 (NPR) 821 University Ave — Madison WI 53706	800-747-7444		641-60
Werres Corp 807 E South St — Frederick MD 21701	800-638-6563		384
Wert Bookbinding Inc 9975 Allentown Blvd — Grantville PA 17028 *Cust Svc	800-344-9378*	717-469-0629	92
WERU-FM 899 (Var) 1186 Acadia Hwy — East Orland ME 04431	800-643-6273	207-469-6600	641
Werzalit of America Inc 40 Holly Ave — Bradford PA 16701	800-999-3730	814-362-3881	497
WesBanco Inc 1 Bank Plz — Wheeling WV 26003 NASDAQ: WSBC	800-328-3369	304-234-9000	70
Wesbury United Methodist Community 31 N Park Ave — Meadville PA 16335	877-937-2879	814-332-9000	48-20
Wesco Cedar Inc PO Box 520 — Creswell OR 97426	800-547-2511	541-688-5020	191-4
Wescom Credit Union 123 S Marengo Ave PO Box 7058 — Pasadena CA 91101	888-493-7266	626-535-1000	219
Wes-Garde Components Group Inc 100 Shield St — West Hartford CT 06110	800-554-8866	860-527-7705	246
Weslaco Area Chamber of Commerce 301 W Railroad — Weslaco TX 78596	800-700-2443	956-968-2102	139
Wesley Homes 815 S 216th St — Des Moines WA 98198	866-937-5390	206-824-5000	668
Wesley Medical Ctr 550 N Hillside St — Wichita KS 67214	800-362-0288	316-962-2000	373-3
Wesley Towers 700 Monterey Pl — Hutchinson KS 67502	888-663-9175	620-663-9175	668
Wesleyan College 4760 Forsyth Rd — Macon GA 31210	800-447-6610	478-757-5219	166
Wesleyan University 70 Wyllys Ave — Middletown CT 06459	800-288-2020	860-685-2000	166
Wesleyan University Olin Library 252 Church St — Middletown CT 06459	800-421-1561	860-685-2660	433-6
Wesleyan University Press 215 Long Ln — Middletown CT 06459	800-421-1561	860-685-7711	633-4
Wesspur Tree Equipment 2121 Iron St — Bellingham WA 98225	800-268-2141	360-734-5242	428

Name / Address	City	State	ZIP	Toll-Free	Phone	Class
West American Rubber Co LLC						
1337 Braden Ct	Orange	CA	92868	**800-245-8748**	714-532-3355	673
West Bancorp Inc						
PO Box 65020	West Des Moines	IA	50265	**800-810-2301**	515-222-2300	359-2
NASDAQ: WTBA						
West Baton Rouge Museum						
845 N Jefferson Ave	Port Allen	LA	70767	**888-881-6811**	225-336-2422	517
West Baton Rouge Parish						
PO Box 757	Port Allen	LA	70767	**800-654-9701**	225-383-4755	337
West Bend Area Chamber of Commerce						
304 S Main St	West Bend	WI	53095	**888-338-8666**	262-338-2666	139
West Bend Housewares LLC						
2845 Wingate St	West Bend	WI	53095	**866-290-1851**		37
West Bend Mutual Insurance Co						
1900 S 18th Ave	West Bend	WI	53095	**800-236-5010**	262-334-5571	390-4
West Branch Area Chamber of Commerce						
422 W Houghton Ave	West Branch	MI	48661	**800-755-9091**	989-345-2821	206
West Canadian Digital Imaging Inc						
200 - 1601 Ninth Ave SE	Calgary	AB	T2G0H4	**800-267-2555**	403-245-2555	343
West Carroll Parish						
PO Box 1078	Oak Grove	LA	71263	**800-256-6660**	318-428-3281	337
West Central Electric Co-op Inc						
204 Main St PO Box 17	Murdo	SD	57559	**800-242-9232**	605-669-2472	245
West Central Illinois Educational Telecommunications Corp						
PO Box 6248	Springfield	IL	62708	**800-232-3605**	217-483-7887	628
West Central Steel Inc						
110 19th St NW PO Box 1178	Willmar	MN	56201	**800-992-8853**		490
West Central Tribune						
PO Box 839	Willmar	MN	56201	**800-450-1150**	320-235-1150	528-2
West Central Wireless						
3389 Knickerbocker Rd	San Angelo	TX	76904	**800-695-9016**		731
West Chester University						
700 S High St	West Chester	PA	19383	**877-315-2165**	610-436-1000	166
West Coast Aviation Services						
19711 Campus Dr Ste 150	Santa Ana	CA	92707	**800-352-6153**	949-852-8340	13
West Coast Connection						
1725 Main St Ste 215	Weston	FL	33326	**800-767-0227**	954-888-9780	755
West Coast Construction						
9021 Rancho Park Ct	Rancho Cucamonga	CA	91730	**800-491-2032**		
West Coast Differentials						
2429 Mercantile Dr Ste A	Rancho Cordova	CA	95742	**800-510-0950**	916-635-0950	54
West Coast Distributing Inc						
Commerce Pl 350 Main St	Boston	MA	02148	**800-235-3730**	781-665-9393	10-9
West Coast General Hospital						
3949 Port Alberni Hwy	Port Alberni	BC	V9Y4S1	**800-317-7878**	250-731-1370	373-2
West Coast Green Institute						
760 Market St Ste 1028	San Francisco	CA	94102	**800-724-4880**	415-955-1935	386
West Coast Industries Inc						
10 Jackson St	San Francisco	CA	94111	**800-243-3150**	415-621-6656	319-1
West Coast Shoe Co						
52828 NW Shoe Factory Ln						
PO Box 607	Scappoose	OR	97056	**800-326-2711**	503-543-7114	301
West Coast Trends						
17811 Jamestown Ln	Huntington Beach	CA	92647	**800-736-4568**	714-843-9288	706
West Corp						
11808 Miracle Hills Dr	Omaha	NE	68154	**800-232-0900***		732
*Sales						
West End Gallery Ltd						
12308 Jasper Ave	Edmonton	AB	T5N3K5	**855-488-4892**	780-488-4892	42
West Essex Graphics Inc (WEG)						
305 Fairfield Ave	Fairfield	NJ	07004	**800-221-5859**		776
West Florida Electric Co-op						
5282 Peanut Rd	Graceville	FL	32440	**800-342-7400**	850-263-3231	245
West Group						
610 Opperman Dr	Eagan	MN	55123	**800-328-4880***	651-687-7000	633-2
*Cust Svc						
West Hills College						
Coalinga						
300 Cherry Ln	Coalinga	CA	93210	**800-266-1114**	559-934-2000	162
Lemoore						
555 College Ave	Lemoore	CA	93245	**800-266-1114**	559-925-3000	162
West Hollywood Chamber of Commerce						
8272 Santa Monica Blvd	West Hollywood	CA	90046	**800-345-8683**	323-650-2688	139
West Hollywood Marketing Corp						
1017 N La Cienega Blvd						
Ste 400	West Hollywood	CA	90069	**800-368-6020**	310-289-2525	206
West Islip Public Library						
3 Higbie Ln	West Islip	NY	11795	**866-833-1122**	631-661-7080	433-3
West Kentucky Community & Technical College						
4810 Alben Barkley Dr						
PO Box 7380	Paducah	KY	42001	**855-469-5282**	270-554-9200	162
West Kentucky Rural Electric Co-op Corp						
PO Box 589	Mayfield	KY	42066	**877-495-7322**	270-247-1321	245
West Liberty Foods LLC						
228 W Second St	West Liberty	IA	52776	**888-511-4500**	319-627-6000	615
West Marine Inc						
500 Westridge Dr	Watsonville	CA	95076	**800-262-8464**	831-728-2700	765
NASDAQ: WMAR						
West Monroe Partners LLC						
222 W Adams St	Chicago	IL	60606	**800-828-6708**	312-602-4000	194
West Music Inc						
1212 Fifth St	Coralville	IA	52241	**800-373-2000**	319-351-2000	522
West Nottingham Academy						
1079 Firetower Rd	Colora	MD	21917	**866-381-3684**	410-658-5556	618
West Oregon Electric Co-op Inc						
652 Rose Ave PO Box 69	Vernonia	OR	97064	**800-777-1276**	503-429-3021	245
West Pasco Chamber of Commerce						
5443 Main St	New Port Richey	FL	34652	**800-851-8754**	727-842-7651	139
West Penetone Corp						
700 Gotham Pkwy	Carlstadt	NJ	07072	**800-631-1652**	201-567-3000	151
West Penn Allegheny Health System						
4800 Friendship Ave	Pittsburgh	PA	15224	**800-994-6610**		352
West Penn Power Co						
800 Cabin Hill Dr	Greensburg	PA	15601	**800-686-0021**		186
West Pharmaceutical Services Inc						
101 Gordon Dr	Lionville	PA	19341	**800-345-9800**	610-594-2900	475
NYSE: WST						
West Point Underwriters LLC						
7785 66th St	Pinellas Park	FL	33781	**800-688-6213**	727-507-7565	389
West Press Printing & Copying						
1663 W Grant Rd	Tucson	AZ	85745	**888-637-0337**	520-624-4939	623
West River Electric Assn Inc						
1200 W Fourth Ave PO Box 412	Wall	SD	57790	**888-279-2135**		245
West River Telecommunications Co-op						
PO Box 467	Hazen	ND	58545	**800-748-7220**	701-748-2211	731
West Shore Community College						
PO Box 277	Scottville	MI	49454	**800-848-9722**	231-845-6211	162
West Side Telecommunications						
1449 Fairmont Rd	Morgantown	WV	26501	**800-296-9113**	304-983-2211	196
West Side Unlimited						
4201 16th Ave SW	Cedar Rapids	IA	52404	**800-373-2957**	319-390-4466	359-2
West Springfield Auto Parts						
92 Blandin Ave	Framingham	MA	01702	**800-615-2392**	508-879-6932	786
West Star Aviation Inc						
796 Heritage Way	Grand Junction	CO	81506	**800-255-4193**	970-243-7500	24
West Suburban Bank						
711 Westmore Meyers Rd	Lombard	IL	60148	**800-258-4009**	630-652-2000	70
West Suburban Chamber of Commerce						
9440 Joliet Rd Ste B	Hodgkins	IL	60525	**800-796-9696**	708-387-7550	139
West Suburban Hospital Medical Ctr						
3 Erie Ct	Oak Park	IL	60302	**866-938-7256**	708-383-6200	373-3
West Texas A & M University						
2501 Fourth Ave	Canyon	TX	79016	**877-656-2065**	806-651-2020	166
West Texas Rural TelephoneCo-op Inc						
PO Box 1737	Hereford	TX	79045	**888-440-4331**	806-364-3331	731
West University Travel						
3622 University Blvd	Houston	TX	77005	**800-256-0640**	713-665-4767	767
West Valley Construction Company Inc						
580 McGlincey Ln	Campbell	CA	95008	**800-588-5510**		188-10
West Valley Medical Ctr						
1717 Arlington Ave	Caldwell	ID	83605	**866-270-2311**	208-459-4641	373-3
West Virginia						
Children & Families Bureau						
350 Capitol St Rm 730	Charleston	WV	25301	**800-352-6513**	304-558-0628	338-49
Community Development Div						
1900 Kanawha Blvd E	Charleston	WV	25311	**800-982-3386**	304-558-2234	338-49
Consumer Protection Div						
812 Quarrier St						
1st Fl PO Box 1789	Charleston	WV	25301	**800-368-8808**	304-558-8986	338-49
Crime Victims Compensation Fund						
1900 Kanawha Blvd E Rm W-334	Charleston	WV	25305	**877-562-6878**	304-347-4850	338-49
Department of veterans assistance						
1900 Kanawha Blvd E						
bldg 5 Rm 205	Charleston	WV	25305	**888-838-2332**	304-558-3661	338-49
Development Office						
1900 Kanawah Blvd E	Charleston	WV	25305	**800-982-3386**	304-558-2234	338-49
Ethics Commission						
210 Brooks St Ste 300	Charleston	WV	25301	**866-558-0664**	304-558-0664	265
Higher Education Policy Commission						
1018 Kanawha Blvd E Ste 700	Charleston	WV	25301	**888-825-5707**	304-558-2101	721
Housing Development Fund						
5710 MacCorkle Ave SE	Charleston	WV	25304	**800-933-9843**	304-391-8600	338-49
Insurance Commission						
900 Pennsylvania Ave	Charleston	WV	25302	**888-879-9842**	304-558-3354	338-49
Lottery						
900 Pennsylvania Ave						
PO Box 2067	Charleston	WV	25302	**800-982-2274**	304-558-0500	450
Motor Vehicles Div						
5707 Maccorkle Ave SE						
PO Box 17020	Charleston	WV	25317	**800-642-9066**	304-926-3802	338-49
Office of Technology						
1900 Kanawha Blvd ECapitol Complex						
Bldg 5 10th Fl	Charleston	WV	25304	**877-558-9966**	304-558-5472	338-49
Public Service Commission						
201 Brooke St PO Box 812	Charleston	WV	25301	**800-344-5113**	304-340-0300	338-49
Secretary of State						
1900 Kanawha Blvd E						
Bldg 1 Ste 157K	Charleston	WV	25305	**866-767-8683**	304-558-6000	338-49
Securities Div						
1900 Kanawha Blvd E						
Bldg 1 Rm W-100	Charleston	WV	25305	**877-982-9148**	304-558-2251	338-49
State Government Information						
100 Dee Dr	Charleston	WV	25311	**888-558-7002**	304-558-7000	338-49
Tourism Div						
90 MacCorkle Ave SW	South Charleston	WV	25303	**800-225-5982**	304-558-2200	338-49
Treasurer						
1900 Kanawha Blvd E						
Bldg 1 Ste E-145	Charleston	WV	25305	**800-422-7498**	304-558-5000	338-49
West Virginia Assn of Realtors						
2110 Kanawha Blvd E	Charleston	WV	25311	**800-445-7600**	304-342-7600	652
West Virginia Correctional Industries						
617 Leon Sullivan Way	Charleston	WV	25301	**800-525-5381**	304-558-6054	626
West Virginia Junior College						
Charleston						
1000 Virginia St E	Charleston	WV	25301	**800-924-5208**	304-345-2820	795
West Virginia Junior College - Bridgeport						
176 Thompson Dr	Bridgeport	WV	26330	**800-470-5627**	304-842-4007	795
West Virginia Library Commission						
1900 Kanawha Blvd E	Charleston	WV	25305	**800-642-9021**	304-558-2041	433-5
West Virginia Nurses Assn (WVNA)						
PO Box 1946	Charleston	WV	25327	**800-400-1226**	304-417-1497	529
West Virginia Press Association						
3422 Pennsylvania Ave	Charleston	WV	25302	**800-235-6881**	304-342-1011	620
West Virginia School Journal						
1558 Quarrier St	Charleston	WV	25311	**800-642-8261**	304-346-5315	455-8
West Virginia State Bar						
2000 Deitrick Blvd	Charleston	WV	25311	**866-989-8227**	304-553-7220	72
West Virginia State Medical Assn						
4307 MacCorkle Ave SE	Charleston	WV	25364	**800-257-4747**	304-925-0342	455-16
West Virginia State Museum						
1900 Kanawha Blvd E	Charleston	WV	25305	**800-946-9471**	304-558-0220	517
West Virginia State University						
117 Ferrell Hall PO Box 368	Institute	WV	25112	**800-987-2112**	304-766-3000	166
West Virginia University						
PO Box 6009	Morgantown	WV	26506	**800-344-9881**	304-293-2121	166
Institute of Technology						
405 Fayette Pk	Montgomery	WV	25136	**888-554-8324**	304-442-1000	166

Name	Address	City	State	ZIP	Toll-Free	Phone	Class
Parkersburg	300 Campus Dr	Parkersburg	WV	26104	**800-982-9887**	304-424-8000	162
West Virginia University School of Medicine	1 Medical Center Dr PO Box 9100	Morgantown	WV	26506	**800-543-5650**	304-293-0111	167-2
West Virginia Wesleyan College	59 College Ave *Admitting	Buckhannon	WV	26201	**800-722-9933***	304-473-8000	166
West Wind Inn	3345 W Gulf Dr	Sanibel	FL	33957	**800-824-0476**	239-472-1541	665
West Window Corp	226 Industrial Pk Dr	Martinsville	VA	24112	**800-446-4167**	276-638-2394	234
Westak Inc	1116 Elko Dri	Sunnyvale	CA	94089	**800-893-7825**	408-734-8686	621
Westar Energy Inc	818 S Kansas Ave *NYSE: WR*	Topeka	KS	66612	**800-383-1183**		359-5
Westbrook Engineering	23501 Mound Rd	Warren	MI	48091	**800-899-8182**	586-759-3100	357
Westbury National Show Systems Ltd	772 Warden Ave	Toronto	ON	M1L4T7	**855-752-1372**	416-752-1371	184
Westcare Management Inc	3155 River Rd S Ste 100	Salem	OR	97302	**800-541-3732**		194
Westchester County Tourism & Film	148 Martine Ave Ste 104	White Plains	NY	10601	**800-833-9282**	914-995-8500	206
Westchester Modular Homes Inc	30 Reagans Mill Rd	Wingdale	NY	12594	**800-832-3888**	845-832-9400	106
Westchester Toyota	2167 Central Park Ave	Yonkers	NY	10710	**888-224-4595**		57
Westchester, The	125 Westchester Ave	White Plains	NY	10601	**877-746-6642**	914-421-1333	458
West-Com Nurse Call Systems Inc	2200 Cordelia Rd	Fairfield	CA	94534	**800-761-1180**	707-428-5900	174
Westcon Comstor	520 White Plains Rd	Tarrytown	NY	10591	**877-642-7750**	914-829-7000	174
West-Con Co-op	520 Co Rd 9	Holloway	MN	56249	**800-368-3310**	320-394-2171	276
Westcon Group Inc	520 White Plains Rd	Tarrytown	NY	10591	**800-527-9516**	914-829-7000	174
WestEd	730 Harrison St	San Francisco	CA	94107	**877-493-7833**	415-565-3000	664
Westell Technologies Inc	750 N Commons Dr *NASDAQ: WSTL*	Aurora	IL	60504	**800-323-6883**	630-898-2500	730
Westerbeke Corp	150 John Hancock Rd Miles Standish Industrial Pk	Taunton	MA	02780	**800-582-7846**	508-823-7677	262
Westerly Hospital	25 Wells St	Westerly	RI	02891	**800-933-5960**	401-596-6000	373-3
Western & Southern Financial Group	400 Broadway	Cincinnati	OH	45202	**877-367-9734**		359-4
Western & Southern Life Insurance Co	400 Broadway	Cincinnati	OH	45202	**800-926-1993**		390-2
Western Agcredit	PO Box 95850	South Jordan	UT	84095	**800-824-9198**	801-571-9200	216
Western Aircraft Inc	4300 S Kennedy St	Boise	ID	83705	**800-333-3442**	208-338-1800	63
Western Bagel Baking Corp	7814 Sepulveda Blvd	Van Nuys	CA	91405	**800-555-0882**	818-786-5847	344
Western Bee Supplies Inc	5 Ninth Ave E	Polson	MT	59860	**800-548-8440**	406-883-2918	279
Western Bus Sales Inc	30355 SE Hwy 212	Boring	OR	97009	**800-258-2473**	503-905-0002	57
Western Canada Lottery Corp	125 Garry St 10th Fl	Winnipeg	MB	R3C4J1	**800-665-3313**		
Western Canada Wilderness Committee (WCWC)	46 E Sixth Ave	Vancouver	BC	V5T1J4	**800-661-9453**	604-683-8220	48-13
Western Carolina University (WCU)	1 University Dr	Cullowhee	NC	28723	**877-928-4968**	828-227-7211	166
Western Communications Inc	1777 Chandler Ave	Bend	OR	97702	**800-503-3933**	541-382-1811	633-8
Western Concord Manufacturing Ltd	880 Cliveden Ave	Vancouver	BC	V3M5R5	**800-663-6208**	604-525-1061	597
Western Co-op Electric Assn Inc	635 S 13th St	WaKeeney	KS	67672	**800-456-6720**	785-743-5561	245
Western Copper Corp	1040 W Georgia St 1st Fl	Vancouver	BC	V6E4H1	**888-966-9995**	604-684-9497	500
Western Digital Corp	3355 Michelson Dr Ste 100 *NASDAQ: WDC*	Irvine	CA	92612	**800-832-4778**	949-672-7000	173-8
Western Drug	3604 San Fernando Rd	Glendale	CA	91204	**800-891-3661**	818-956-6691	473
Western Enterprises Inc	875 Bassett Rd	Westlake	OH	44145	**800-783-7890**		806
Western Excelsior Corp	901 Grand Ave	Mancos	CO	81328	**800-833-8573**		
Western Express Inc	7135 Centennial Pl	Nashville	TN	37209	**800-316-7160**	877-986-8855	775
Western Exterminator Co	305 N Crescent Way	Anaheim	CA	92801	**800-698-2440**	714-239-2800	573
Western Forestry & Conservation Assn	4033 SW Canyon Rd	Portland	OR	97221	**888-722-9416**	503-226-4562	48-12
Western Forge & Flange Co	687 County Rd 2201	Cleveland	TX	77327	**800-352-6433**	281-727-7060	481
Western Fraternal Life Assn (WFLA)	1900 First Ave NE	Cedar Rapids	IA	52402	**877-935-2467**	319-363-2653	390-2
Western Hoist Inc	1839 Cleveland Ave	National City	CA	91950	**888-994-6478**	619-474-3361	468
Western Horseman Magazine	2112 Montgomery St	Fort Worth	TX	76107	**800-877-5278**	817-737-6397	455-14
Western Hydro Corp	3449 Enterprise Ave	Hayward	CA	94545	**800-972-5945**	510-783-9166	385
Western Illinois Electrical Co-op	524 N Madison St PO Box 338	Carthage	IL	62321	**800-576-3125**	217-357-3125	245
Western Illinois University	1 University Cir *Admissions	Macomb	IL	61455	**877-742-5948***	309-298-1414	166
Malpass Library	1 University Cir	Macomb	IL	61455	**800-413-6544**	309-298-2762	433-6
Quad Cities	3300 River Dr	Moline	IL	61265	**877-742-5948**	309-762-9481	166
Western Implement Co Inc	2919 North Ave	Grand Junction	CO	81504	**800-338-6639**	970-242-7960	274
Western Institutional Review Board Inc	1019 39th Ave SE Ste 120	Puyallup	WA	98374	**800-562-4789**	360-252-2500	529
Western International Securities Inc	70 S Lake Ave Ste 700	Pasadena	CA	91101	**888-793-7717**		686
Western Iowa Power Co-op	809 Iowa 39	Denison	IA	51442	**800-253-5189**	712-263-2943	245
Western Iowa Tech Community College	4647 Stone Ave	Sioux City	IA	51102	**800-352-4649**	712-274-6400	795
Western Kentucky University	1906 College Heights Blvd *Admissions	Bowling Green	KY	42101	**800-495-8463***	270-745-0111	166
Western Land Services Inc	1100 Conrad Industrial Dr	Ludington	MI	49431	**800-968-4840**		
Western Living Magazine (WL)	2608 Granville St Ste 560	Vancouver	BC	V6H3V3	**800-363-3272**	604-877-7732	455-11
Western Missouri Correctional Ctr	609 E Pence Rd	Cameron	MO	64429	**800-726-7390**	816-632-1390	213
Western Museum of Mining & Industry	225 N Gate Blvd	Colorado Springs	CO	80921	**800-752-6558**	719-488-0880	517
Western National Mutual Insurance Co	5350 W 78th St	Edina	MN	55439	**800-862-6070**	952-835-5350	390-4
Western Nebraska Community College	1601 E 27th St	Scottsbluff	NE	69361	**800-348-4435**	308-635-3606	162
Western Nevada Supply Co	950 S Rock Blvd	Sparks	NV	89431	**800-648-1230**	775-359-5800	608
Western New England College	1215 Wilbraham Rd	Springfield	MA	01119	**800-782-6665**	413-782-3111	166
Western New Mexico University	1000 W College St PO Box 680 *Admissions	Silver City	NM	88061	**800-872-9668***		166
Western Oilfields Supply Co	3404 State Rd	Bakersfield	CA	93308	**800-742-7246**	661-399-9124	264-3
Western Oklahoma State College	2801 N Main St	Altus	OK	73521	**800-662-1113**	580-477-2000	162
Western Ophthalmics Corp	19019 36th Ave W Ste G	Lynnwood	WA	98036	**800-426-9938**	425-672-9332	540
Western Oregon University	345 Monmouth Ave N *Admissions	Monmouth	OR	97361	**877-877-1593***	503-838-8000	166
Western Oregon University Hamersly Library	345 N Monmouth Ave	Monmouth	OR	97361	**877-877-1593**	503-838-8418	433-6
Western Outdoors Magazine	185 Avenida La Pata	San Clemente	CA	92673	**800-290-2929**	949-366-0030	455-22
Western Pacific Storage Systems Inc	300 E Arrow Hwy	San Dimas	CA	91773	**800-732-9777**		286
Western Partitions Inc	26055 SW Canyon Creek Rd	Wilsonville	OR	97070	**800-783-0315**	503-620-1600	189-9
Western Pest Services Inc	800 Lanidex Plz	Parsippany	NJ	07054	**877-250-3857**		573
Western Pioneer Inc	4601 Shilshole Ave NW	Seattle	WA	98107	**800-426-6783**	206-789-1930	312
Western Pioneer Sales Co	6631 Calle Eva Miranda	Glendale	CA	91702	**800-640-4535**	818-244-1466	300
Western Plastic Products Inc	8441 Monroe Ave	Stanton	CA	90680	**800-453-1881**		9
Western Power Sports Inc	601 E Gowen Rd	Boise	ID	83716	**800-999-3388**	208-376-8400	707
Western Reflections	261 Commerce Way *Cust Svc	Gallatin	TN	37066	**800-507-8302***	615-451-9700	438
Western Research Institute	365 N Ninth St	Laramie	WY	82072	**888-463-6974**	307-721-2011	664
Western Reserve Group, The	1685 Cleveland Rd PO Box 36	Wooster	OH	44691	**800-362-0426**		390-4
Western Security Bank	2812 First Ave N	Billings	MT	59101	**800-983-5537**	406-371-8200	70
Western Seminary	5511 SE Hawthorne Blvd	Portland	OR	97215	**877-517-1800**	503-517-1800	167-3
Western State College of Colorado	600 N Adams St *Admissions	Gunnison	CO	81231	**800-876-5309***	970-943-2119	166
Western State Hospital	9601 Steilacoom Blvd SW	Tacoma	WA	98498	**877-501-2233**	253-582-8900	373-5
Western States Envelope & Label Co	4480 N 132nd St	Butler	WI	53007	**800-558-0514**	262-781-5540	263
Western States Petroleum Inc	450 S 15th Ave	Phoenix	AZ	85007	**800-220-1353**	602-252-4011	575
Western States Ticket Service	143 W McDowell Rd	Phoenix	AZ	85003	**800-326-0331**	602-254-3300	745
Western States Weeklies Inc	PO Box 600600	San Diego	CA	92160	**800-628-9466**	619-280-2985	633-8
Western Sugar Co-op	7555 E Hampden Ave Ste 520	Denver	CO	80231	**800-523-7497**	303-830-3939	296-38
Western Syrup Co	13766 Milroy Pl	Santa Fe Springs	CA	90670	**800-521-3888**	562-921-4485	296-15
Western Technical College	400 Seventh St N	La Crosse	WI	54601	**800-322-9982**	608-785-9200	795
Western Technologies Inc	3737 E Broadway Rd	Phoenix	AZ	85040	**800-580-3737**	602-437-3737	192
Western Telematic Inc	5 Sterling	Irvine	CA	92618	**800-854-7226**	949-586-9950	173-3
Western Texas College	6200 College Ave	Snyder	TX	79549	**888-468-6982**	325-573-8511	162
Western Theological Seminary	101 E 13th St	Holland	MI	49423	**800-392-8554**	616-392-8555	167-3
Western Trailer Co	251 W Gowen Rd	Boise	ID	83716	**888-344-2539**	208-344-2539	774
Western Truck Parts & Equip Co	3707 Airport Way S	Seattle	WA	98134	**800-255-7383**	206-624-7383	61
Western Tube & Conduit Corp	2001 E Dominguez St	Long Beach	CA	90810	**800-310-8823**		

Name / Address	City	State	ZIP	Toll-Free	Phone	Class
Western Union Holdings Inc						
12500 E Belford Ave *NYSE: WU* ■ *Cust Svc	Englewood	CO	80112	**800-325-6000***	720-332-1000	69
Western United Electric Supply Corp						
100 Bromley Business Pkwy	Brighton	CO	80603	**800-748-3116**	303-659-2356	786
Western United Life Assurance Co						
929 W Sprague Ave PO Box 2290 *General	Spokane	WA	99210	**800-247-2045***	509-835-2500	390-2
Western University Canada						
King's University College 266 Epworth Ave	London	ON	N6A2M3	**800-265-4406**	519-433-3491	780
Western Upper Peninsula Convention & Visitor Bureau						
1200 E US 2	Ironwood	MI	49938	**800-522-5657**	906-932-4850	206
Western Veterinary Conference						
2425 E Oquendo Rd	Las Vegas	NV	89120	**866-800-7326**	702-739-6698	789
Western Village Inn & Casino						
815 Nichols Blvd	Sparks	NV	89434	**800-648-1170**		133
Western Washington University						
516 High St	Bellingham	WA	98225	**800-261-7331**	360-650-3000	166
Western Window Systems						
2200 E Riverview Dr	Phoenix	AZ	85034	**877-268-1300**		234
Western Wood Preserving Co						
1310 Zehnder St	Sumner	WA	98390	**800-472-7714**	253-863-8191	813
Western Wyoming Community College						
2500 College Dr	Rock Springs	WY	82901	**800-226-1181**	307-382-1600	162
Westerra Credit Union						
3700 E Alameda Ave	Denver	CO	80209	**800-858-7212**	303-321-4209	219
Westerville Public Library						
126 S State St	Westerville	OH	43081	**800-816-0662**	614-882-7277	433-3
Westex Inc						
122 W 22nd St	Oak Brook	IL	60523	**866-493-7839**	773-523-7000	740-7
Westfalia Technologies Inc						
3655 Sandhurst Dr	York	PA	17406	**800-673-2522**	717-764-1115	207
Westfield Bank						
2 Park Cir	Westfield Ctr	OH	44251	**800-368-8930**		
Westfield Board of Education Inc						
302 Elm St	Westfield	NJ	07090	**800-355-2583**	908-789-4401	681
Westfield Financial Inc						
141 Elm St *NASDAQ: WNEB*	Westfield	MA	01085	**800-995-5734**	413-568-1911	359-2
Westfield Industries Ltd						
74 Hwy 205 E	Rosenort	MB	R0G1W0	**866-467-7207**	204-746-2396	273
Westfield Shoppingtown Annapolis						
2002 Annapolis Mall	Annapolis	MD	21401	**800-805-2339**	410-266-5432	458
Westfield Steel Inc						
530 State Rd 32 W	Westfield	IN	46074	**800-622-4984**		490
Westgate Branson Woods						
2201 Roark Valley Rd	Branson	MO	65616	**877-253-8572**	417-334-2324	378
Westgate Hotel, The						
1055 Second Ave	San Diego	CA	92101	**800-522-1564**	619-238-1818	667
Westgate Painted Mountain Country Club						
6302 E McKellips Rd	Mesa	AZ	85215	**888-433-3707**	480-654-3611	378
Westglow Resort & Spa						
224 Westglow Cir	Blowing Rock	NC	28605	**800-562-0807**	828-295-4463	703
West-Herr Automotive Group Inc						
3448 McKinley Pkwy	Blasdell	NY	14219	**800-643-2112**	716-926-8150	57
Westin Atlanta Perimeter North, The						
7 Concourse Pkwy NE	Atlanta	GA	30328	**888-627-8407**	770-395-3900	377
Westin Automotive Products Inc						
5200 N Irwindale Ave Ste 220	Irwindale	CA	91706	**800-345-8476**	626-960-6762	61
Westin Casuarina Las Vegas Hotel Casino & Spa						
160 E Flamingo Rd	Las Vegas	NV	89109	**866-837-4215**	702-836-5900	
Westin Kierland Resort & Spa						
6902 E Greenway Pkwy	Scottsdale	AZ	85254	**800-354-5892**	480-624-1000	703
Westin Michigan Avenue Hotel						
909 N Michigan Ave	Chicago	IL	60611	**888-627-8385**	312-943-7200	377
Westin Resort & Spa						
4090 Whistler Way	Whistler	BC	V0N1B4	**888-627-8979**	604-905-5000	703
Westin Reston Heights, The						
11750 Sunrise Vly Dr	Reston	VA	20191	**888-627-8344**	703-391-9000	377
WestJet Airlines Ltd						
22 Aerial Pl NE *TSE: WJA*	Calgary	AB	T2E3J1	**888-937-8538**	403-444-2600	25
Westlake Chemical Corp						
2801 Post Oak Blvd Ste 600 *NYSE: WLK*	Houston	TX	77056	**888-953-3623**	713-960-9111	601-2
Westlake Hospital						
1225 West Lake St	Melrose Park	IL	60160	**800-570-8809**	708-681-3000	373-3
Westlake Plastics Co						
PO Box 127	Lenni	PA	19052	**800-999-1700**	610-459-1000	600
Westland Chamber of Commerce						
36900 Ford Rd	Westland	MI	48185	**800-737-4859**	734-326-7222	139
Westland Corp						
1735 S Maize Rd	Wichita	KS	67209	**800-247-1144**	316-721-1144	752
Westland Sales						
PO Box 427	Clackamas	OR	97015	**800-356-0766**	503-655-2563	38
Westlaw Court Express						
1333 H St NW	Washington	DC	20005	**877-362-7387**	202-423-2163	631
West-Lite Supply Company Inc						
12951 166th St	Cerritos	CA	90703	**800-660-6678**	562-802-0224	246
Westlog Aviation						
311 Cove Rd	Brookings	OR	97415	**800-761-5183**	541-469-7911	30
Westman Communications Group						
1906 Park Ave	Brandon	MB	R7B0R9	**800-665-3337**	204-725-4300	224
Westmark Hotels Inc						
300 Elliott Ave W	Seattle	WA	98119	**800-544-0970**		378
Westminster College						
501 Westminster Ave *Admissions	Fulton	MO	65251	**800-475-3361***	573-592-5251	166
Westminster College						
319 S Market St	New Wilmington	PA	16172	**800-942-8033**	724-946-8761	166
Westminster College						
1840 South 1300 East	Salt Lake City	UT	84105	**800-748-4753**	801-832-2200	166
Westminster Communities of Florida						
4449 Meandering Way	Tallahassee	FL	32308	**800-948-1881**	850-878-1136	668
Westminster Manor						
1700 21st Ave W	Bradenton	FL	34205	**877-382-9036**	941-748-4161	668
Westminster Public Library						
7392 Irving St	Westminster	CO	80030	**800-424-1554**	303-430-2400	433-3

Name / Address	City	State	ZIP	Toll-Free	Phone	Class
Westminster School District						
14121 Cedarwood St	Westminster	CA	92683	**888-491-6603**	714-894-7311	681
Westminster Theological Seminary						
2960 Church Rd	Glenside	PA	19038	**800-373-0119**	215-887-5511	167-3
Westminster Theological Seminary in California						
1725 Bear Vly Pkwy	Escondido	CA	92027	**888-480-8474**	760-480-8474	167-3
Westminster Towers						
70 W Lucerne Cir	Orlando	FL	32801	**877-382-9036**	800-948-1881	668
Westminster Towers						
1330 India Hook Rd	Rock Hill	SC	29732	**800-345-6026**	803-328-5000	668
Westminster Village						
1175 Mckee Rd	Dover	DE	19904	**800-382-1385**	302-744-3600	668
Westminster-Canterbury of Lynchburg						
501 VES Rd	Lynchburg	VA	24503	**800-962-3520**	434-386-3500	668
Westminster-Canterbury on Chesapeake Bay						
3100 Shore Dr	Virginia Beach	VA	23451	**800-753-2918**		668
Westminster-Canterbury Richmond						
1600 Westbrook Ave	Richmond	VA	23227	**800-445-9904**	804-264-6000	668
Westmont College						
955 La Paz Rd *Admissions	Santa Barbara	CA	93108	**800-777-9011***	805-565-6000	166
Westmor Industries LLC						
3 Development Dr	Morris	MN	56267	**800-992-8981**	320-589-2100	198
Westmoreland Coal Co						
9540 S Maroon Cir Ste 300 *NASDAQ: WLBA*	Englewood	CO	80112	**855-922-6463**	303-922-6463	499
Westmoreland County Community College						
145 Pavilion Ln	Youngwood	PA	15697	**800-262-2103**	724-925-4000	162
Weston & Sampson Inc						
5 Centennial Dr	Peabody	MA	01960	**800-726-7766**	978-532-1900	261
Weston Hurd LLP						
The Tower at Erieview 1301 E Ninth St Ste 1900	Cleveland	OH	44114	**800-336-4952**	216-241-6602	
Westpac Banking Corp Americas Div						
575 Fifth Ave 39th Fl	New York	NY	10017	**888-269-2377**	212-551-1800	70
WestPark Capital Inc						
1900 Ave of the Stars Ste 310	Los Angeles	CA	90067	**800-811-3487**	310-843-9300	686
Westport Country Playhouse						
25 Powers Ct	Westport	CT	06880	**888-927-7529**	203-227-4177	568
Westside Regional Medical Ctr						
8201 W Broward Blvd	Plantation	FL	33324	**800-523-5658**	954-473-6600	373-3
Westward Look Resort						
245 E Ina Rd	Tucson	AZ	85704	**800-722-2500**	520-297-1151	665
Westward Parts Services Ltd						
6517 - 67 St	Red Deer	AB	T4P1A3	**888-937-7278**	403-347-2200	111
Westway Ford						
801 W Airport Fwy	Irving	TX	75062	**844-877-9037**		57
Westwood College Atlanta Northlake						
2309 Parklake Dr NE	Atlanta	GA	30345	**866-552-7536**		795
Westwood Lodge Hospital						
45 Clapboardtree St	Westwood	MA	02090	**800-222-2237**	781-762-7764	373-5
Wet 'n Wild Emerald Pointe						
3910 S Holden Rd	Greensboro	NC	27406	**800-555-5900**	336-852-9721	32
Wet 'n Wild Orlando						
6200 International Dr *General	Orlando	FL	32819	**800-992-9453***	407-351-1800	32
WETA-TV Ch 26 (PBS)						
3939 Campbell Ave	Arlington	VA	22206	**800-662-2386**	703-998-2600	736
WeTip Inc						
PO Box 1296	Rancho Cucamonga	CA	91730	**800-782-7463**	909-987-5005	48-8
Wetland Studies & Solutions Inc						
5300 Wellington Branch Dr	Gainesville	VA	20155	**800-247-1812**	703-679-5600	261
Wetsel Inc						
961 N Liberty St *Cust Svc	Harrisonburg	VA	22802	**800-572-4018***	540-434-6753	690
WETS-FM 895 (NPR)						
PO Box 70630	Johnson City	TN	37614	**888-895-9387**	423-439-6440	641-52
Wetzel County Chamber of Commerce						
201 Main St PO Box 271	New Martinsville	WV	26155	**800-834-2070**	304-455-3825	139
Weyco Group Inc						
333 W Estabrook Blvd *NASDAQ: WEYS*	Glendale	WI	53212	**866-454-0449**	414-908-1880	301
Weyerhaeuser Co						
33663 Weyerhaeuser Way S *NYSE: WY*	Federal Way	WA	98003	**800-525-5440**	253-924-2345	185
WEZN-FM 999 (AC)						
440 Wheelers Farm Rd Ste 302	Milford	CT	06461	**800-330-9999**	203-783-8200	641
WF Meyers Co						
1008 13th St	Bedford	IN	47421	**800-457-4055**	812-275-4485	453
WF Young Inc						
302 Benton Dr	East Longmeadow	MA	01028	**800-628-9653**	413-526-9999	578
WF. Taylor Company Inc						
11545 Pacific Ave	Fontana	CA	92337	**800-397-4583**	951-360-6677	3
WFAE-FM 907 (NPR)						
8801 JM Keynes Dr Ste 91 *Cust Svc	Charlotte	NC	28262	**800-876-9323***	704-549-9323	641-22
WFAN-AM 66 (Rel)						
345 Hudson St 10th Fl	New York	NY	10014	**866-540-9326**		
WFCA (World Floor Covering Assn)						
2211 Howell Ave	Anaheim	CA	92806	**800-624-6880**	714-978-6440	49-4
WFHN-FM 1071 (CHR)						
22 Sconticut Neck Rd	Fairhaven	MA	02719	**877-854-9467**	508-999-6690	641
WFIE-TV Ch 14 (NBC)						
1115 Mt Auburn Rd	Evansville	IN	47720	**800-832-0014**	812-426-1414	736-28
WFIU-FM 1037						
1229 E Seventh St	Bloomington	IN	47405	**877-285-9348**	812-855-1357	641
WFIV-FM 1053						
517 Watt Rd	Knoxville	TN	37934	**800-352-9250**	865-675-4105	641-54
WFLA (Western Fraternal Life Assn)						
1900 First Ave NE	Cedar Rapids	IA	52402	**877-935-2467**	319-363-2653	390-2
WFLA-TV Ch 8 (NBC)						
PO Box 1410	Tampa	FL	33601	**800-338-0808**	813-228-8888	736-77
WFM (William Fox Munroe Inc)						
3 E Lancaster Ave	Shillington	PA	19607	**800-344-2402**	610-775-4521	343
WFMJ-TV Ch 21 (NBC)						
101 W Boardman St	Youngstown	OH	44503	**800-488-9365**	330-744-8611	736-86
WFMV-FM 953						
2440 Milwood Ave	Columbia	SC	29205	**888-953-9830**	803-939-9530	

		Toll-Free	Phone	Class

WFMY News 2
1615 Phillips Ave .... Greensboro NC 27405 — 800-593-3692 — 212-975-3247 — 736

WFP (World Food Program USA)
1725 Eye St NW Ste 510 .... Washington DC 20006 — 888-454-0555 — 202-627-3737 — 48-5

WFPG-FM 969 (AC)
950 Tilton Rd Ste 200 .... Northfield NJ 08225 — 800-969-9374 — 609-645-9797 — 641

WFRV-TV Ch 5 (CBS)
1181 E Mason St .... Green Bay WI 54301 — 800-236-5550 — 920-437-5411 — 736-32

WFSQ-FM 915 (Clas)
1600 Red Barber Plz .... Tallahassee FL 32310 — 855-937-8123 — 850-645-7200 — 641-107

WFSU-FM 889 (NPR)
1600 Red Barber Plz .... Tallahassee FL 32310 — 855-937-8123 — 850-645-7200 — 641-107

WFTS-TV Ch 28 (ABC)
4045 N Himes Ave .... Tampa FL 33607 — 877-833-2828 — 813-354-2828 — 736-77

WFUV 907 (Var)
441 E Fordham Rd
Fordham University .... Bronx NY 10458 — 877-938-8907 — 718-817-4550 — 641

WFWI
2915 Maples Rd .... Fort Wayne IN 46816 — 800-333-1190 — 260-447-5511

WFXG-TV Ch 54 (Fox)
3933 Washington Rd .... Augusta GA 30907 — 866-974-0487 — 706-650-5400 — 736-5

WG Bill Hefner Veterans Affairs Medical Ctr
1601 Brenner Ave .... Salisbury NC 28144 — 800-469-8262 — 704-638-9000 — 373-8

WGBF-FM 1031 (Rock)
20 NW Third St 600 .... Evansville IN 47708 — 888-900-9423 — 812-425-4226 — 641-37

WGBH-FM 897 (NPR)
1 Guest St .... Boston MA 02135 — 800-492-1111 — 617-300-2000 — 641-16

WGBH-TV Ch 2 (PBS)
1 Guest St .... Brighton MA 02135 — 800-492-1111 — 617-300-2000 — 736

WGCL-TV Ch 46 (CBS)
425 14th St NW .... Atlanta GA 30318 — 800-949-6397 — 404-327-3194 — 736-4

WGGS-TV Ch 16 (Ind)
3409 Rutherford Rd Ext .... Taylors SC 29687 — 800-849-3683* — 864-244-1616 — 736
*General

WGGY-FM 1013
305 Hwy 315 .... Pittston PA 18640 — 800-570-1013 — 570-883-1111 — 641

WGH
5589 Greenwich Rd
Ste 200 .... Virginia Beach VA 23462 — 800-552-9935 — 757-671-1000 — 641-72

WGHP-TV Ch 8 (Fox)
2005 Francis St .... High Point NC 27263 — 800 808 6397 — 336 841 8888 — 736

WGL Holdings Inc
101 Constitution Ave NW .... Washington DC 20080 — 800-645-3751 — 703-750-2000 — 359-5
NYSE: WGL

WGMD-FM 927 (N/T)
PO Box 530 .... Rehoboth Beach DE 19971 — 800-518-9292 — 302-945-2050 — 641

WGOK Gospel 900
2800 Dauphin St Ste 104 .... Mobile AL 36606 — 866-992-5660 — 251-423-9900 — 641-67

WG&R Furniture Co
900 Challenger Dr .... Green Bay WI 54311 — 888-947-7782 — 920-469-4880 — 321

WGRD-FM 979 (Rock)
50 Monroe Ave NW Ste 500 .... Grand Rapids MI 49503 — 800-947-3979 — 616-451-4800 — 641-41

WGTS-FM 919 (Rel)
7600 Flower Ave .... Takoma Park MD 20912 — 800-700-1094 — 301-891-4200 — 641

WGVU-FM 885 (NPR)
301 W Fulton St .... Grand Rapids MI 49504 — 800-442-2771 — 616-331-6666 — 641-41

WGVU-TV Ch 35 (PBS)
301 W Fulton St .... Grand Rapids MI 49504 — 800-442-2771 — 616-331-6666 — 736-31

WH Bagshaw Company Inc
1 Pine St Ext .... Nashua NH 03060 — 800-343-7467 — 603-883-7758 — 385

WHAD-FM 907 (NPR)
310 W Wisconsin Ave Ste 750-E ...... Milwaukee WI 53203 — 800-486-8655 — 414-227-2040 — 641-63

WHAM-TV Ch 13 (ABC)
4225 W Henrietta Rd .... Rochester NY 14623 — 800-322-3632 — 585-334-8700 — 736-63

Wharf Resources USA Inc
10928 Wharf Rd .... Lead SD 57754 — 800-567-6223 — 605-584-1441 — 500

Wharton County Electric Co-op Inc (WCEC)
1815 E Jackson St .... El Campo TX 77437 — 800-460-6271 — 979-543-6271 — 245

Wharton County Junior College
911 Boling Hwy .... Wharton TX 77488 — 800-561-9252 — 979-532-4560 — 162
Sugar Land
14004 University Blvd .... Sugar Land TX 77479 — 800-561-9252 — 281-243-8447 — 162

Wharton County Library
1920 N Fulton St .... Wharton TX 77488 — 800-244-5492 — 979-532-8080 — 433-3

Wharton Ctr for the Performing Arts
Michigan State University .... East Lansing MI 48824 — 800-942-7866 — 517-432-2000 — 568

Wharton Group
101 S Livingston Ave .... Livingston NJ 07039 — 800-521-2725 — 973-992-5775 — 389

Wharton Independent School District
2100 N Fulton St .... Wharton TX 77488 — 800-818-3453 — 979-532-3612 — 681

WHAS-AM 840 (N/T)
4000 One Radio Dr .... Louisville KY 40218 — 800-444-8484 — 502-479-2222 — 641-58

WHBM (White House/Black Market)
11215 Metro Pkwy .... Fort Myers FL 33966 — 888-550-5559 — 239-277-6200 — 157-6

WHCF-FM 885 (Rel)
PO Box 5000 .... Bangor ME 04402 — 800-947-2577 — 207-947-2751 — 641-11

WHDH TV 7NEWS
7 Bulfinch Pl .... Boston MA 02114 — 800-280-8477 — 855-247-4265 — 736-12

Wheat Belt Public Power District
11306 Rd 32 PO Box 177 .... Sidney NE 69162 — 800-261-7114 — 308-254-5871 — 245

Wheat Foods Council
51 Red Fox Ln Unit D .... Ridgway CO 81432 — 800-970-2254 — — 49-6

Wheat Montana Farms Inc
10778 US Hwy 287 .... Three Forks MT 59752 — 800-535-2798 — 406-285-3614 — 297-1

Wheatland Electric Co-op Inc
101 S Main St .... Scott City KS 67871 — 800-762-0436 — 620-872-5885 — 245

Wheatland Rural Electric Assn
2154 S St PO Box 1209 ...... Wheatland WY 82201 — 800-344-3351 — 307-322-2125 — 245

Wheatland Tube Co
700 S Dock St .... Sharon PA 16146 — 800-257-8182 — — 488

Wheatmark Inc
2030 E Speedway Blvd Ste 106 .... Tucson AZ 85719 — 888-934-0888 — 520-798-0888 — 633-2

Wheaton College
26 E Main St .... Norton MA 02766 — 800-394-6003* — 508-286-8200 — 166
*Admissions

Wheaton College
501 College Ave .... Wheaton IL 60187 — 800-222-2419 — 630-752-5000 — 166

Wheaton Franciscan - Saint Joseph
5000 W Chambers St .... Milwaukee WI 53210 — 800-914-6601 — 414-447-2000 — 373-3

Wheaton Franciscan Healthcare
3801 Spring St .... Racine WI 53405 — 877-304-6332 — 262-687-4011 — 373-3
All Saints
3801 Spring St .... Racine WI 53405 — 877-304-6332 — 262-687-4011 — 373-3

Wheaton Van Lines Inc
8010 Castleton Rd .... Indianapolis IN 46250 — 800-932-7799 — 800-248-7962 — 516

Wheel & Sprocket Inc
5722 S 108th St .... Hales Corners WI 53130 — 866-995-9918 — 414-529-6600 — 707

Wheeled Coach Industries Inc
2737 Forsyth Rd .... Winter Park FL 32792 — 800-932-7077 — 407-677-7777 — 513

Wheeler Lumber LLC
9330 James Ave S .... Bloomington MN 55431 — 800-328-3986 — 952-929-7854 — 191-3

Wheeler Mfg Co Inc
107 Main Ave PO Box 629 .... Lemmon SD 57638 — 800-843-1937 — — 408

Wheeler Opera House
320 E Hyman Ave .... Aspen CO 81611 — 866-449-0464 — 970-920-5770 — 568

Wheeler-Rex Inc
3744 Jefferson Rd PO Box 688 .... Ashtabula OH 44005 — 800-321-7950 — 440-998-2788 — 753

Wheeling & Lake Erie Railway Co
100 E First St .... Brewster OH 44613 — 800-837-5622 — 330-767-3401 — 647

Wheeling Convention & Visitors Bureau
1401 Main St .... Wheeling WV 26003 — 800-828-3097 — 304-233-7709 — 206

Wheeling Hospital
1 Medical Pk .... Wheeling WV 26003 — 800-626-0023 — 304-243-3000 — 373-3

Wheeling Island Gaming Inc
1 S St1 St .... Wheeling WV 26003 — 877-946-4373 — 304-232-5050 — 133

Wheeling Jesuit University
316 Washington Ave .... Wheeling WV 26003 — 800-624-6992 — 304-243-2000 — 166

Wheelock College
200 The Riverway .... Boston MA 02215 — 800-734-5212 — 617-879-2206 — 166

Wheelwright Museum of the American Indian
704 Camino Lejo .... Santa Fe NM 87505 — 800-607-4636 — 505-982-4636 — 517

Where Chicago Magazine
1165 N Clark St Ste 302 .... Chicago IL 60610 — 800-680-4035 — 312-642-1896 — 455-22

Whetstone Valley Electric Co-op
1101 E Fourth Ave .... Milbank SD 57252 — 800-568-6631 — 605-432-5331 — 245

WHIL-FM 913 (NPR)
920 Paul W Bryant Dr
Bryant Denny Stadium Rm N460 ...... Tuscaloosa AL 35487 — 800-654-4262 — 205-348-6644 — 641-67

Whirl Air Flow Corp
20055 177th St .... Big Lake MN 55309 — 800-373-3461 — 763-262-1200 — 207

Whirlpool Canada
200-6750 Century Ave ...... Mississauga ON L5N0B7 — 800-807-6777 — 905-821-6400 — 38

Whirlpool Corp
2000 N M-63 .... Benton Harbor MI 49022 — 800-253-1301 — 269-923-5000 — 36
NYSE: WHR

Whirlpool Corp North American Region
2000 N M-63 .... Benton Harbor MI 49022 — 800-253-1301 — 269-923-5000 — 36

Whirlpool Foundation
2000 N M-63 .... Benton Harbor MI 49022 — 800-952-9245 — 269-923-5000 — 304

Whirlwind Steel
8234 Hansen Rd .... Houston TX 77075 — 800-324-9992 — 713-946-7140 — 105

Whisper Knits Inc
9303 Monroe Rd Ste N .... Charlotte NC 28270 — 866-695-7022 — 704-489-6105

Whistler Blackcomb Mountain Ski Resort
4545 Blackcomb Way .... Whistler BC V0N1B4 — 800-766-0449 — 604-932-3434 — 665

Whistler Group Inc
13016 N Walton Blvd .... Bentonville AR 72712 — 800-531-0004* — 479-273-6012 — 525
*Cust Svc

Whitacre Greer Fireproofing Inc
1400 S Mahoning Ave .... Alliance OH 44601 — 800-947-2837* — 330-823-1610 — 150
*Cust Svc

Whitaker Buick Co
131 19th St SW .... Forest Lake MN 55025 — 877-324-8885 — — 57

Whitaker House/Anchor Distributors
1030 Hunt Vly Cir .... New Kensington PA 15068 — 800-444-4484* — 724-334-7000 — 633-3
*General

Whitaker Oil Co
1557 Marietta Rd NW .... Atlanta GA 30318 — 888-895-3506 — 404-355-8220 — 146

White Aluminum Products LLC
2101 US Hwy 441 .... Leesburg FL 34748 — 888-474-5884 — — 490

White Bison Inc
5585 Erindale Dr
Ste 203 .... Colorado Springs CO 80918 — 877-871-1495 — 719-548-1000 — 48-21

White Bros Trucking Co
4N793 School Rd .... Wasco IL 60183 — 800-323-4762 — 630-584-3810 — 775

White Buffalo Club
160 W Gill Ave .... Jackson WY 83001 — 888-256-8182 — 307-734-4900 — 427

White Cap Industries Inc
1723 S Ritchie St .... Santa Ana CA 92705 — 800-944-8322 — 714-258-3300 — 191-3

White Coffee Corp
18-35 Steinway Pl .... Astoria NY 11105 — 800-221-0140 — 718-204-7900 — 296-7

White Construction Inc
3900 E White Ave .... Clinton IN 47842 — 800-355-9401

White Conveyors Inc
10 Boright Ave .... Kenilworth NJ 07033 — 800-524-0273 — 908-686-5700 — 207

White County
110 N Main St .... Monticello IN 47960 — 800-272-9829 — 574-583-7032 — 337

White County Chamber of Commerce
122 N Main St .... Cleveland GA 30528 — 800-392-8279 — 706-865-5356 — 139

White County Rural Electric Membership Corp
302 N Sixth St .... Monticello IN 47960 — 800-844-7161 — 574-583-7161 — 245

White Electrical Construction Co
1730 Chattahoochee Ave .... Atlanta GA 30318 — 888-519-4483 — 404-351-5740 — 189-4

White Elephant Inn & Cottages
50 Easton St .... Nantucket MA 02554 — 800-475-2637 — 508-228-2500 — 378

White Flower Farm Inc
30 Irene St .... Torrington CT 06790 — 800-411-6159* — 860-496-9624 — 323
*Cust Svc

White Glove Placement Inc
85 Bartlett St .... Brooklyn NY 11206 — 866-387-8100 — 718-387-8181 — 717

White House/Black Market (WHBM)
11215 Metro Pkwy .... Fort Myers FL 33966 — 888-550-5559 — 239-277-6200 — 157-6

White Knight Engineered Products
9525 Monroe Rd Ste N .... Charlotte NC 28270 — 888-743-4700 — 704-542-6876 — 572

White Memorial Medical Ctr
1720 Cesar E Chavez Ave .... Los Angeles CA 90033 — 800-806-0993 — 323-268-5000 — 373-3

Alphabetical Section

Name / Address	City	State	Zip	Toll-Free	Phone	Class
White Mountain Adventures						
131 Eagle Crescent PO Box 4259	Banff	AB	T1L1A6	**800-408-0005**	403-760-4403	755
White Mountain Hotel & Resort						
87 Fairway Dr PO Box 1828	North Conway	NH	03860	**800-533-6301**	603-356-7100	665
White Mountains Community College (WMCC)						
2020 Riverside Dr	Berlin	NH	03570	**800-445-4525**	603-752-1113	162
White Mountains Insurance Group Ltd						
80 S Main St	Hanover	NH	03755	**866-295-3762**	603-640-2200	359-4
NYSE: WTM						
White Oaks Resort & Spa						
253 Taylor Rd SS4	Niagara-on-the-Lake	ON	L0S1J0	**800-263-5766***	905-688-2550	376
*Resv						
White Oaks Wealth Advisors Inc						
80 S Eighth St IDS Ctr Ste 1725	Minneapolis	MN	55402	**800-596-3579**	612-455-6900	194
White Paper Co						
9990 River Way	Delta	BC	V4G1M9	**888-840-7300**	604-951-3900	549
White Pine County						
801 Clark St	Ely	NV	89301	**800-884-4072**	775-293-6509	337
White Plains Honda						
344 Central Ave	White Plains	NY	10606	**888-683-1716**	888-671-0343	57
White River Distributors Inc						
720 Ramsey	Batesville	AR	72501	**800-548-7219**	870-793-2374	480
White River Electric Assn (WREA)						
PO Box 958	Meeker	CO	81641	**800-922-1987**	970-878-5041	245
White River Junction Veterans Affairs Medical Ctr						
215 N Main St	White River Junction	VT	05009	**866-687-8387**	802-295-9363	373-8
White River State Park						
302 W Washington St Rm E418	Indianapolis	IN	46204	**800-665-9056**	317-233-2434	561
White River Valley Electric Co-op Inc						
2449 State Hwy 76 E	Branson	MO	65616	**800-879-4056**	417-335-9335	245
White Rock Products Corp						
141-07 20th Ave Ste 403	Whitestone	NY	11357	**800-969-7625**	718-746-3400	80-2
White Sands Federal Credit Union						
2190 E Lohman Ave	Las Cruces	NM	88001	**800-658-9933**	575-647-4500	70
White Stallion Ranch						
9251 W Twin Peaks Rd	Tucson	AZ	85743	**888-977-2624**	520-297-0252	239
White Star Tours						
26 E Lancaster Ave	Reading	PA	19607	**800-437-2323**	610-775-5000	755
White's Electronics Inc						
1011 Pleasant Valley Rd	Sweet Home	OR	97386	**800-547-6911***	541-367-6121	470
*Sales						
White's Farm Supply Inc						
4154 State Rt 31	Canastota	NY	13032	**800-633-4443**	315-697-2214	357
White's Inc						
4614 Navigation Blvd PO Box 2344	Houston	TX	77011	**800-231-9559**	713-928-2632	274
Whitecap Canada Inc						
200 Yorkland Blvd Ste 920	Toronto	ON	M2J5C1	**855-393-9977**		395
Whitecap Resources Inc						
3800 525 - Eighth Ave SW	Calgary	AB	T2P1G1	**866-590-5289**	403-266-0767	532
Whiteface Club & Resort						
373 Whiteface Inn Ln	Lake Placid	NY	12946	**800-422-6757**	518-523-2551	665
Whitehall Hotel						
105 E Delaware Pl	Chicago	IL	60611	**800-948-4255**	312-944-6300	378
Whitehall Printing Co						
4244 Corporate Sq	Naples	FL	34104	**800-321-9290**		622
Whitesell Corp						
2703 Avalon Ave	Muscle Shoals	AL	35662	**855-227-4515***		484
*General						
Whiteside County						
200 E Knox St	Morrison	IL	61270	**800-460-5657**	815-772-5100	337
Whitewater Valley Rural Electric Membership Corp						
101 Brownsville Ave	Liberty	IN	47353	**800-529-5557**	765-458-5171	245
WhiteWave Foods Co						
12002 Airport Way	Broomfield	CO	80021	**888-820-9283**	303-635-4000	296-27
Whiting Corp						
26000 Whiting Way	Monee	IL	60449	**800-861-5744**		468
Whiting Petroleum Corp						
1700 Broadway Ste 2300	Denver	CO	80290	**800-723-4608**	303-837-1661	532
NYSE: WLL						
Whitlam Label Company Inc						
24800 Sherwood Ave	Center Line	MI	48015	**800-755-2235**	586-757-5100	412
Whitlock Group						
12820 W Creekk Pkwy	Richmond	VA	23238	**800-726-9843**	804-273-9100	246
Whitman College						
345 Boyer Ave	Walla Walla	WA	99362	**877-462-9448***	509-527-5111	166
*Admissions						
Whitmore Manufacturing Co						
930 Whitmore Dr	Rockwall	TX	75087	**800-699-6318**	972-771-1000	546
Whitney Bailey Cox & Magnani LLC						
300 E Joppa Rd Ste 200	Baltimore	MD	21286	**800-673-9312**	410-512-4500	
Whitney Bank						
228 St Charles Ave	New Orleans	LA	70130	**800-844-4450**	504-586-7456	70
Whitney Hotel, The						
610 Poydras St	New Orleans	LA	70130	**844-581-4222**	504-581-4222	378
Whitney Museum of American Art						
945 Madison Ave	New York	NY	10021	**800-944-8639**	212-570-3600	517
Whitney Tool Company Inc						
906 R St	Bedford	IN	47421	**800-536-1971**	812-275-4491	453
Whittet-Higgins Co						
33 Higginson Ave PO Box 8	Central Falls	RI	02863	**800-323-7790**	401-728-0700	616
Whittier College						
13406 E Philadelphia St	Whittier	CA	90602	**800-299-4898**	562-907-4200	166
Whittier Hospital Medical Ctr						
9080 Colima Rd	Whittier	CA	90605	**800-613-4291**	562-945-3561	373-3
Whittier Wood Products						
3787 W First Ave PO Box 2827	Eugene	OR	97402	**800-653-3336**	541-687-0213	319-2
Whitworth College						
300 W Hawthorne Rd	Spokane	WA	99251	**800-533-4668***	509-777-1000	166
*Admissions						
WHKY-TV Ch 14 (Ind)						
526 Main Ave SE PO Box 1059	Hickory	NC	28602	**800-899-4897**	828-322-1290	736
WHMB-TV Ch 40 (Ind)						
10511 Greenfield Ave	Noblesville	IN	46060	**800-535-5542**	317-773-5050	736
WHMC-FM 901 (NPR)						
1041 George Rogers Blvd	Columbia	SC	29201	**800-922-5437**	803-737-3200	641-27
WHMC-TV Ch 23 (PBS)						
1041 George Rogers Blvd	Columbia	SC	29201	**800-277-3245**	803-737-3200	736-20
WHNT-TV Ch 19 (CBS)						
200 Holmes Ave	Huntsville	AL	35801	**800-533-8819**	256-533-1919	736-35
WhoKnows						
585 Broadway St	Redwood City	CA	94063	**800-348-5031**		386
Whole Foods Market Inc						
550 Bowie St	Austin	TX	78703	**888-992-6227**	512-477-4455	354
Wholesale Interiors Inc						
971 Supreme Dr	Bensenville	IL	60106	**800-517-0717**		320
WHO-TV Ch 13 (NBC)						
1801 Grand Ave	Des Moines	IA	50309	**800-777-8398**	515-242-3500	736-24
WHPT-FM 1025 (CR)						
11300 Fourth St N Ste 300	Saint Petersburg	FL	33716	**800-771-1025**	727-579-2000	641-108
WHUR-FM 963 (Urban AC)						
529 Bryant St NW	Washington	DC	20059	**800-221-9487**	202-432-9487	641-114
WHUT-TV Ch 32 (PBS)						
2222 Fourth St NW	Washington	DC	20059	**800-683-1899**	202-806-3200	736-82
WHY (World Hunger Year Inc)						
505 Eigth Ave Ste 2100	New York	NY	10018	**800-548-6479**	212-629-8850	48-5
WI (Wilderness Inquiry)						
808 14th Ave SE	Minneapolis	MN	55414	**800-728-0719**	612-676-9400	48-23
WIBC-FM 931 (N/T)						
40 Monument Cir Ste 400	Indianapolis	IN	46204	**800-571-9422**	317-266-9422	641-49
Wichita Area Technical College						
301 S Grove St	Wichita	KS	67211	**866-296-4031**	316-677-9400	795
Wichita Convention & Visitors Bureau						
515 Main St Ste 115	Wichita	KS	67202	**800-288-9424**	316-265-2800	206
Wichita Eagle, The						
825 E Douglas Ave	Wichita	KS	67202	**800-200-8906**	316-268-6000	528-2
Wichita Falls CVB						
1000 Fifth St	Wichita Falls	TX	76301	**800-799-6732**		568
Wichita Kenworth Inc						
5115 N Broadway	Wichita	KS	67219	**800-825-5558**	316-838-0867	513
Wichita State University						
1845 Fairmount St	Wichita	KS	67260	**800-362-2594***	316-978-3456	166
*Admissions						
Wick Buildings						
405 Walter Rd	Mazomanie	WI	53560	**855-438-9425**		503
Wickaninnish Inn						
500 Osprey Ln PO Box 250	Tofino	BC	V0R2Z0	**800-333-4604**	250-725-3100	378
Wicklander Zulawski & Associates Inc						
4932 Main St	Downers Grove	IL	60515	**800-222-7789**		461
Wicks Pies Inc						
217 Greenville Ave	Winchester	IN	47394	**800-642-5880**		68
Wicks Pipe Organ Co						
416 Pine St	Highland	IL	62249	**877-654-2191***	618-654-2191	523
*Cust Svc						
WICN-FM 905 (NPR)						
50 Portland St	Worcester	MA	01608	**855-752-0700**	508-752-0700	641-47
Wicomico County Convention & Visitors Bureau						
8480 Ocean Hwy	Delmar	MD	21875	**800-332-8687**	410-548-4914	206
WICU-TV Ch 12 (NBC)						
3514 State St	Erie	PA	16508	**800-454-8812**	814-454-5201	736-27
WideBand Corp						
401 W Grand St	Gallatin	MO	64640	**888-663-3050**	660-663-3000	176
Widener University						
1 University Pl	Chester	PA	19013	**888-943-3637***	610-499-4000	166
*Admissions						
WidePoint Corp						
7926 Jones Branch Dr Ste 520	Mclean	VA	22102	**877-919-5943***	703-349-5644	
*Sales						
Wider Church Ministries						
700 Prospect Ave	Cleveland	OH	44115	**866-822-8224**	216-736-3200	48-20
Wider Opportunities for Women (WOW)						
1001 Connecticut Ave NW Ste 930	Washington	DC	20036	**800-260-5956**	202-464-1596	48-24
Wiederkehr Wine Cellars Inc						
3324 Swiss Family Dr	Wiederkehr Village	AR	72821	**800-622-9463**	479-468-9463	442
Wieland						
10785 Rose Ave	New Haven	IN	46774	**888-943-5263**	260-627-3686	319-3
Wieland Electric Inc (WEI)						
49 International Rd	Burgaw	NC	28425	**800-943-5263**	910-259-5050	246
Wiers Farm Inc						
4465 St Rt 103 S PO Box 385	Willard	OH	44890	**800-777-6243**	419-935-0131	10-9
Wiese Industries						
1501 Fifth St	Perry	IA	50220	**800-568-4391**	515-465-9854	273
Wieser Concrete Products Inc						
W3716 US Hwy 10	Maiden Rock	WI	54750	**800-325-8456**	715-647-2311	183
Wig America Co						
27317 Industrial Blvd	Hayward	CA	94545	**800-338-7600**	510-887-9579	347
Wigwam Mills Inc						
3402 Crocker Ave	Sheboygan	WI	53082	**800-558-7760**	855-275-0356	155-9
Wika Instrument Corp						
1000 Wiegand Blvd	Lawrenceville	GA	30043	**888-945-2872**		201
Wilbur Curtis Company Inc						
6913 Acco St	Montebello	CA	90640	**800-421-6150**	323-837-2300	298
Wilco Farmers						
200 Industrial Way	Mount Angel	OR	97362	**800-382-5339**		276
Wilco Inc						
3502 W Harry	Wichita	KS	67213	**800-767-7593**		
Wilco Marsh Buggies & Draglines Inc						
1304 Macarthur Ave	Harvey	LA	70058	**800-253-0869**	504-341-3409	190
Wilcom Inc						
73 Daniel Webster Hwy PO Box 508	Belmont	NH	03220	**800-222-1898**	603-524-2622	643
Wilcox County						
103 N Broad St	Abbeville	GA	31001	**866-694-5824**	229-467-2737	337
Wilcox Memorial Hospital (WMH)						
3-3420 Kuhio Hwy	Lihue	HI	96766	**877-709-9355**	808-245-1100	373-3
Wilcox Travel Sandals						
1550 Hendersonville Rd Ste 214	Asheville	NC	28803	**800-294-5269**	828-254-0746	
Wilcoxon Research Inc						
20511 Seneca Meadows Pkwy	Germantown	MD	20876	**800-945-2696**	301-330-8811	2
Wild 949						
340 Townsend St 4th Fl	San Francisco	CA	94107	**888-333-9490**	415-975-5555	641-96

Company	Toll-Free	Phone	Class
Wild Animal Baby Magazine 11100 Wildlife Ctr Dr Reston VA 20190	800-822-9919		455-6
Wild Animal Safari 1300 Oak Grove Rd Pine Mountain GA 31822	800-367-2751	706-663-8744	818
Wild Blueberry Assn of North America (WBANA) PO Box 100 Old Town ME 04468	800-341-1758	207-570-3535	48-2
Wild Dunes Resort 5757 Palm Blvd Isle of Palms SC 29451	866-359-5593		665
Wild Flavors Inc 1261 Pacific Ave Erlanger KY 41018	800-263-5286	859-342-3600	296-15
Wild Rice Electric Co-op Inc 502 N Main PO Box 438 Mahnomen MN 56557	800-244-5709	218-935-2517	245
Wild Wings LLC 2101 S Hwy 61 Lake City MN 55041	800-445-4833		457
Wilderness Inquiry (WI) 808 14th Ave SE Minneapolis MN 55414	800-728-0719	612-676-9400	48-23
Wilderness Press c/o Keen Communications 2204 First Ave S Ste 102 Birmingham AL 35233	800-443-7227		633-2
Wilderness Travel 1102 Ninth St Berkeley CA 94710	800-368-2794	510-558-2488	755
Wildland Adventures Inc 3516 NE 155th St Lake Forest Park WA 98155	800-345-4453	206-365-0686	755
Wildlife Sanctuary of Northwest Florida PO Box 1092 Pensacola FL 32591	800-435-7353	850-433-9453	818
Wildlife West Nature Park 87 North Frontage Rd Edgewood NM 87015	877-981-9453	505-281-7655	818
Wildwoods Convention Ctr 4501 Boardwalk Wildwood NJ 08260	800-992-9732	609-729-9000	205
Wiley College 711 Wiley Ave Marshall TX 75670 *Admissions	800-658-6889*	903-927-3300	166
Wiley Publishing Inc 111 River St Hoboken NJ 07030	800-225-5945	201-748-6000	633-2
Wiley Sanders Truck Lines Inc PO Box 707 Troy AL 36081	800-392-8017		483
Wiley X Inc 7800 Patterson Pass Rd Livermore CA 94550	800-776-7842	925-243-9810	539
Wiley's Waterski Pro Shop 1417 S Trenton St Seattle WA 98108	800-962-0785	206-762-1300	706
Wilheit Packaging LLC 1527 May Dr Gainesville GA 30507	800-727-4421	770-532-4421	447
Wilkerson 222 S Main St Stuttgart AR 72160	800-631-1999		409
Wilkes & McHugh P A 1 N Dale Mabry Hwy Ste 800 Tampa FL 33609	800-255-5070		443
Wilkes Community College 1328 S Collegiate Dr PO Box 120 Wilkesboro NC 28697	866-222-1548	336-838-6100	162
Wilkes University 84 West South St Wilkes-Barre PA 18766	800-945-5378		166
Wilkins-Rogers Inc 27 Frederick Rd Ellicott City MD 21043 *Cust Svc	877-438-4338*	410-465-5800	296-23
Will Rogers Memorial Ctr 3401 W Lancaster Ave Fort Worth TX 76107	800-433-5747		
Will Rogers Memorial Museum 1720 W Will Rogers Blvd Claremore OK 74017	800-324-9455	918-341-0719	517
Will Vision & Laser Centers 8100 NE Pkwy Dr Ste 125 Vancouver WA 98662	877-542-3937		793
Willamette Stone State Heritage Site 11321 SW Terwilliger Blvd Portland OR 97219	800-551-6949		561
Willamette University 900 State St Salem OR 97301	877-542-2787	503-370-6303	166
Willamette University College of Law 245 Winter St SE Salem OR 97301	844-232-7228	503-370-6282	167-1
Willamette Valley Co 1075 Arrowsmith St Eugene OR 97402	800-333-9826	541-484-9621	546
Willamette Valley Hospice 1015 Third St NW Salem OR 97304	800-555-2431	503-588-3600	370
Willamette Valley Vineyards Inc 8800 Enchanted Way SE Turner OR 97392 *NASDAQ: WVVI* ■ *Sales	800-344-9463*	503-588-9463	80-3
Willamette View 12705 SE River Rd Portland OR 97222	800-446-0670	503-654-6581	668
Willard Bay State Park 900 W 650 N Ste A Willard UT 84340	800-322-3770	435-734-9494	561
Willbanks Metals Inc 1155 NE 28th St Fort Worth TX 76106	800-772-2352	817-625-6161	490
Willdan 2401 E Katella Ave Ste 300 Anaheim CA 92806	800-424-9144	714-940-6300	261
Willey Honda 2215 S 500 W Bountiful UT 84010 *Sales	888-431-4490*		57
William & Mary 400 Landrum Dr Williamsburg VA 23187	800-462-3683	757-221-3072	433-6
William B Meyer Inc 255 Long Beach Blvd Stratford CT 06615	800-727-5985	203-375-5801	681
William Blair & Company LLC 222 W Adams St Chicago IL 60606	800-621-0687	312-236-1600	686
William Carey University 498 Tuscan Ave Hattiesburg MS 39401	800-962-5991	601-318-6051	166
William E Walter Inc 1917 Howard Ave Flint MI 48503	800-681-3320	810-232-7459	189-10
William F Renk & Sons Inc 6809 Wilburn Rd Sun Prairie WI 53590	800-289-7365		10-4
William Fox Munroe Inc (WFM) 3 E Lancaster Ave Shillington PA 19607	800-344-2402	610-775-4521	343
William G Satterlee & Sons Inc 12475 Rt 119 Hwy N Rochester Mills PA 15771	800-942-2214	724-397-2400	316
William H Harvey 4334 S 67th St Omaha NE 68117	800-321-9532	402-331-1175	326
William H Sadlier Inc 9 Pine St New York NY 10005 *OTC: SADL*	800-221-5175		633-2
William J Rish Recreational Park 6773 Cape San Blas Rd Port St Joe FL 32456	800-470-8101		560
William Jessup University 2121 University Ave Rocklin CA 95765	800-355-7522	916-577-2200	166

Company	Toll-Free	Phone	Class
William Jewell College 500 College Hill WJC Liberty MO 64068	888-253-9355	816-781-7700	166
William K Walthers Inc 5601 W Florist Ave Milwaukee WI 53218	800-877-7171	414-527-0770	757
William M Tugman State Park 72549 Hwy 101 Lakeside OR 97449	800-551-6949		561
William Marvy Company Inc 1540 St Clair Ave Saint Paul MN 55105	800-874-2651	651-698-0726	76
William Mitchell College of Law 875 Summit Ave Saint Paul MN 55105	888-962-5529	651-227-9171	167-1
William Morrow & Co 10 E 53rd St New York NY 10022	800-242-7737	212-207-7000	633-2
William Paterson University 300 Pompton Rd Wayne NJ 07470	877-978-3923	973-720-2000	166
William Penn Assn 709 Brighton Rd Pittsburgh PA 15233	800-848-7366	412-231-2979	389
William Penn Life Insurance Co of New York 100 Quentin Roosevelt Blvd Garden City NY 11530	800-346-4773		390-2
William Penn University 201 Trueblood Ave Oskaloosa IA 52577	800-779-7366		166
William S Hein & Company Inc 1285 Main St Buffalo NY 14209	800-828-7571	716-882-2600	633-2
William V MacGill & Co 1000 N Lombard Rd Lombard IL 60148	800-323-2841	630-889-0500	473
William Woods University 1 University Ave Fulton MO 65251 *Admissions	800-995-3159*	573-592-4221	166
Williams & Williams Real Estate Auctions 7120 S Lewis Ave Ste 200 Tulsa OK 74136	800-801-8003	913-541-8084	648
Williams Baptist College 60 W Fulbright St Walnut Ridge AR 72476	800-722-4434	870-886-6741	166
Williams College 880 Main St Williamstown MA 01267	877-374-7526	413-597-3131	166
Williams Comfort Products 250 W Laurel St Colton CA 92324	866-677-8444	909-825-0993	356
Williams Companies Inc 1 Williams Ctr Tulsa OK 74172 *NYSE: WMB*	800-945-5426	918-573-2000	359-3
Williams Engineering Canada Inc 10065 Jasper Ave Ste 200 Edmonton AB T5J3B1	800-263-2393	780-409-5300	256
Williams Financial Group Inc 2711 N Haskell Ave Cityplace Tower Ste 2900 Dallas TX 75204	800-225-3650	972-661-8700	687
Williams Gun Sight Co 7389 Lapeer Rd Davison MI 48423	800-530-9028	810-653-2131	284
Williams International 2280 E W Maple Rd PO Box 200 Walled Lake MI 48390	800-859-3544	248-624-5200	21
Williams Nationalease Ltd 400 W Northtown Rd Normal IL 61761	800-779-8785	309-452-1110	57
Williams Partners LP 1 Williams Ctr Tulsa OK 74172 *NYSE: WPZ*	800-600-3782	918-573-2000	325
Williams Performing Arts Ctr *Abilene Christian University* 1600 Campus Ct Abilene TX 79601	800-460-6228	325-674-2199	568
Williams Records Management 1925 E Vernon Ave Los Angeles CA 90058 *Cust Svc	888-478-3453*	323-234-3453	225
Williams Sausage Company Inc 5132 Old Troy Hickman Rd Union City TN 38261	800-844-4242	731-885-5841	297-9
Williams Supply Inc 210 Seventh St Roanoke VA 24016	800-533-6969	540-343-9333	246
Williams White & Co 600 River Dr Moline IL 61265	877-797-7650		454
Williams, Charles & Scott Ltd 2171 Jericho Tpke LL1 Commack NY 11725	800-652-4445	631-462-1553	160
Williams, Turner & Holmes PC 744 Horizon Crt Ste 115 Grand Junction CO 81506	800-548-6528	970-242-6262	427
Williamsburg Destination Marketing Committee 421 N Boundary St Williamsburg VA 23185	800-368-6511	757-229-6511	206
Williamsburg (Independent City) 401 Lafayette St Williamsburg VA 23185	800-275-2355	757-220-6100	337
Williamsburg Landing 5700 Williamsburg Landing Dr Williamsburg VA 23185	800-554-5517	757-565-6505	668
Williamsburg Travel Management Companies 570 W Crossville Rd Ste 102 Roswell GA 30075	800-952-9922	770-650-5515	770
Williamson ARH Hospital 260 Hospital Dr South Williamson KY 41503 *General	888-654-0015*	606-237-1700	373-3
Williamson Cadillac 7815 SW 104th St Miami FL 33156	877-228-6093	877-579-0775	58
Williamson County Tourism Bureau 1602 Sioux Dr Marion IL 62959 *General	800-433-7399*	618-997-3690	206
Williamson Law Book Co 790 Canning Pkwy Victor NY 14564	800-733-9522	585-924-3400	178
Williamson-Dickie Mfg Co 509 W Vickery Blvd Fort Worth TX 76104	866-411-1501		155-18
Williamsport Area School District 2780 W Fourth St Williamsport PA 17701	888-448-4642	570-327-5500	681
Williamsport Sun-Gazette 252 W Fourth St Williamsport PA 17701	800-339-0289	570-326-1551	528-2
Williams-Sonoma Inc 3250 Van Ness Ave San Francisco CA 94109 *NYSE: WSM*	800-838-2589	415-421-7900	361
Willington Nameplate 11 Middle River Dr Stafford Springs CT 06076	877-967-4743		479
Willingway Hospital 311 Jones Mill Rd Statesboro GA 30458	800-242-9455	912-764-6236	722
Willis College of Business & Technology 85 O'Connor St Ottawa ON K1P5M6	877-233-1128	613-233-1128	162
Willis Group Holdings Ltd 200 Liberty St 3rd Fl New York NY 10281 *NASDAQ: WSH*	800-234-8596	212-915-8888	389
Williston State College 1410 University Ave PO Box 1326 Williston ND 58802	888-863-9455	701-774-4200	162

Name / Address	City	State	ZIP	Toll-Free	Phone	Class
Willo Products Company Inc 714 Willo Industrial Dr SE	Decatur	AL	35601	**800-633-3276**	256-353-7161	234
Willoughby Industries Inc 5105 W 78th St	Indianapolis	IN	46268	**800-428-4065**		
Willow Creek Press Inc 9931 Hwy 70 W PO Box 147 *Cust Svc	Minocqua	WI	54548	**800-850-9453***		130
Willow Creek Rehabilitation & Care Ctr 1165 Easton Ave	Somerset	NJ	08873	**800-486-0027**	732-246-4100	448
Willow Stream Spa at Fairmont Scottsdale Princess 7575 E Princess Dr	Scottsdale	AZ	85255	**800-908-9540**	480-585-2732	703
Willow Stream Spa at the Fairmont Banff Springs 405 Spray Ave	Banff	AB	T1L1J4	**800-404-1772**	403-762-1772	703
Willow Stream Spa at the Fairmont Empress 633 Humboldt St	Victoria	BC	V8W1A6	**866-854-7444**	250-995-4650	703
Willow Valley Lakes Manor 300 Willow Vly Lakes Dr	Willow Street	PA	17584	**800-770-5445**	717-464-0800	668
Willows Chamber of Commerce 118 W Sycamore	Willows	CA	95988	**855-233-6362**	530-934-8150	139
Willows Historic Palm Springs Inn 412 W Tahquitz Canyon Way	Palm Springs	CA	92262	**800-966-9597**	760-320-0771	378
Willows Lodge 14580 NE 145th St	Woodinville	WA	98072	**877-424-3930**	425-424-3900	378
Willows, The 1 Lyman St	Westborough	MA	01581	**800-464-8060**	508-366-4730	668
Willsie Cap & Gown Co 1220 S 13th St	Omaha	NE	68108	**800-234-4696**	402-341-6536	155-13
Willson International Ltd 2345 Argentia Rd Ste 201	Mississauga	ON	L5N8K4	**800-754-1918**	905-363-1133	447
Wilmer Service Line 515 W Sycamore St	Coldwater	OH	45828	**800-494-5637**		110
Wilmington & Beaches CVB 505 Nutt St Unit A	Wilmington	NC	28401	**877-406-2356**	910-341-4030	206
Wilmington College of Ohio 1870 Quaker Way	Wilmington	OH	45177	**800-341-9318**	937-382-6661	166
Wilmington Fibre Specialty Co 700 Washington St	New Castle	DE	19720	**800-220-5132**	302-328-7525	595
Wilmington Health 1202 Medical Center Dr	Wilmington	NC	28401	**800-334-3053**	910-341-3300	
Wilmington Instrument Company Inc 332 N Fries Ave	Wilmington	CA	90744	**800-544-2843**	310-834-1133	201
Wilmington National Cemetery 2011 Market St	Wilmington	NC	28403	**800-535-1117**	910-815-4877	136
Wilmington Treatment Ctr 2520 Troy Dr	Wilmington	NC	28401	**866-783-6605**		722
Wilmington University 320 N DuPont Hwy *Admissions	New Castle	DE	19720	**877-967-5464***		166
Wilshire Assoc Inc 1299 Ocean Ave Ste 700	Santa Monica	CA	90401	**855-626-8281**	310-451-3051	400
Wilshire Enterprises Inc 100 Eagle Rock Ave Ste 100 *OTC: WLSE*	East Hanover	NJ	07936	**888-697-3962**	973-585-7770	532
Wilshire Mutual Funds Inc PO Box 219512	Kansas City	MO	64121	**888-200-6796**		524
Wilson Air Ctr 2930 Winchester Rd Memphis International Airport	Memphis	TN	38118	**800-464-2992**	901-345-2992	63
Wilson Bus Lines Inc 203 Patriots Rd PO Box 415	East Templeton	MA	01438	**800-253-5235**	978-632-3894	107
Wilson College 1015 Philadelphia Ave *Admissions	Chambersburg	PA	17201	**800-421-8402***	717-264-4141	166
Wilson Consulting Group 100 Old Schoolhouse Rd	Mechanicsburg	PA	17055	**800-837-2265**	717-591-3070	196
Wilson Industrial Sales Co Inc 5063 South 1000 West PO Box 297	Rensselaer	IN	47978	**800-633-5427**	219-866-6900	146
Wilson Learning Corp 8000 W 78th St Ste 200	Edina	MN	55439	**800-328-7937**	952-944-2880	760
Wilson Lines of Minnesota Inc 2131 Second Ave *General	Newport	MN	55055	**800-525-3333***	651-459-2384	775
Wilson Manufacturing Co 4725 Green Park Rd	Saint Louis	MO	63123	**800-634-5248**	314-416-8900	693
Wilson of Wallingford Inc 221 Rogers Ln	Wallingford	PA	19086	**888-607-2621**	610-566-7600	316
Wilson Quarterly Magazine 1300 Pennsylvania Ave NW *Orders	Washington	DC	20004	**888-947-9018***	202-691-4122	455-11
Wilson Sporting Goods Co 8750 W Bryn Mawr Ave	Chicago	IL	60631	**800-874-5930**	800-800-9936	706
Wilson Tool International Inc 12912 Farnham Ave	White Bear Lake	MN	55110	**800-328-9646**	651-286-6000	693
Wilson Trailer Co 4400 S Lewis Blvd	Sioux City	IA	51106	**800-798-2002**	712-252-6500	774
Wilson Trophy Co 1724 Frienza Ave	Sacramento	CA	95815	**800-635-5005**	916-927-9733	772
Wilson Trucking Corp 137 Wilson Blvd	Fishersville	VA	22939	**866-645-7405**	540-949-3200	775
Wilsonart International Inc 2400 Wilson Pl *Cust Svc	Temple	TX	76504	**800-433-3222***	254-207-7000	595
Wilson-Davis & Company Inc 236 S Main	Salt Lake City	UT	84101	**800-621-1571**	801-532-1313	686
Wilson-Hurd Mfg Co 311 Winton St PO Box 8028	Wausau	WI	54403	**800-950-5013**		
Wilsons Leather Inc 7401 Boone Ave N	Brooklyn Park	MN	55428	**800-967-6270**	763-391-4000	157-5
Wiltern Theatre 3790 Wilshire Blvd	Los Angeles	CA	90010	**800-348-8499**	213-388-1400	568
Wilton Armetale Co 903 Square St	Mount Joy	PA	17552	**800-779-4586**	717-653-4444	484
Wilton Industries Inc 2240 W 75th St	Woodridge	IL	60517	**800-794-5866**	630-963-7100	484
Wimmer Cookbooks 4650 Shelby Air Dr	Memphis	TN	38118	**800-548-2537**		633-2
Wimmer's Meat Products Inc 126 W Grant St *Cust Svc	West Point	NE	68788	**800-762-9865***	402-372-2437	296-26
WIN Energy Rural Electric Membership Corp 3981 S US Hwy 41	Vincennes	IN	47591	**800-882-5140**	812-882-5140	245
WIN Home Inspection 3326 Aspen Grove Dr	Franklin	TN	37067	**800-309-6753**		364
Winbco Tank Co 1200 E Main St PO Box 618	Ottumwa	IA	52501	**800-822-1855**		91
Winchester Equipment Co 121 Indian Hollow Rd	Winchester	VA	22603	**800-323-3581**		357
Winchester Systems Inc 101 Billerica Ave Bldg 5 *Cust Svc	Billerica	MA	01862	**800-325-3700***	781-265-0200	176
Winchuck State Recreation Site 1655 Hwy 101 N	Brookings	OR	97415	**800-551-6949**		561
WinCo Foods Inc 8200 W Fairview Ave	Boise	ID	83704	**888-674-6854**	208-377-9840	344
Winco Inc 5516 SW First Ln	Ocala	FL	34474	**800-237-3377**	352-854-2929	319-3
WinCraft Inc 960 E Mark St PO Box 888	Winona	MN	55987	**800-533-8006**	507-454-5510	328
WinCup 4640 Lewis Rd	Stone Mountain	GA	30083	**800-292-2877**	770-771-5861	597
Wind River Financial Inc 65 Buttonwood Ct	Madison	WI	53718	**866-356-0837**		
Wind River Ranch PO Box 3410	Estes Park	CO	80517	**800-523-4212**	970-586-4212	239
Wind River Systems Inc 500 Wind River Way	Alameda	CA	94501	**800-545-9463**	510-748-4100	178-12
Windemere Hotel & Conference Center 2047 S Hwy 92	Sierra Vista	AZ	85635	**800-825-4656**	520-459-5900	376
Windermere Relocation Inc 5424 Sand Point Way NE	Seattle	WA	98105	**866-740-9589**	206-527-3801	662
Windham Manufacturing Company Inc 8520 Forney Rd	Dallas	TX	75227	**888-965-0093**	214-388-0511	452
Windings Inc 208 N Valley St PO Box 566	New Ulm	MN	56073	**800-795-8533**	507-359-2034	452
Windmill Health Products 10 Henderson Dr	West Caldwell	NJ	07006	**800-822-4320**	973-575-6591	794
Window & Door Factory, The 5595 Magnatron Ste C	San Diego	CA	92111	**855-230-6558**		
Window Gang 405 Arendell St	Morehead City	NC	28557	**800-849-2308**	252-726-1463	152
Window Rama Enterprises Inc 71 Heartland Blvd	Edgewood	NY	11717	**800-897-7262**	631-667-8088	191-3
Windsor Arms Hotel 18 St Thomas St	Toronto	ON	M5S3E7	**877-999-2767**	416-971-9666	378
Windsor Court Hotel 300 Gravier St	New Orleans	LA	70130	**888-596-0955**	504-523-6000	378
Windsor Factory Supply Ltd 730 N Service Rd	Windsor	ON	N8X3J3	**800-387-2659**	519-966-2202	384
Windsor Inc 4533 Pacific Blvd	Vernon	CA	90058	**888-494-6376**	323-282-9000	157-6
Windsor K,,rcher Group 1351 W Stanford Ave	Englewood	CO	80110	**800-444-7654**	303-762-1800	385
Windsor Star, The 300 Ouellette Ave	Windsor	ON	N9A7B4	**800-265-5647**	888-394-9296	528-1
Windsor Symphony Orchestra 121 University Ave	West Windsor	ON	N9A5P4	**888-327-8327**	519-973-1238	569-3
Windsor Vineyards 205 Concourse Blvd	Santa Rosa	CA	95403	**800-289-9463**		315-5
Windsor Windows & Doors 900 S 19th St	West Des Moines	IA	50265	**800-218-6186**	515-223-6660	236
Windsor-Bertie Area Chamber of Commerce 121 Granville St PO Box 572	Windsor	NC	27983	**800-334-5010**	252-794-4277	139
Windstar Cruises 2101 Fourth Ave Ste 210 *Resv	Seattle	WA	98121	**800-258-7245***	206-733-2970	220
Windstar Lines Inc 1903 US Hwy 71 N	Carroll	IA	51401	**888-494-6378**	712-792-4221	186
Wine & Spirits Shippers Assn Inc (WSSA) 11800 Sunrise Vly Dr *General	Reston	VA	20191	**800-368-3167***		49-6
Wine Appreciation 450 Taraval St Ste 201	South San Francisco	CA	94116	**800-231-9463**	650-866-3020	
Wine Club, The 1431 S Village Way	Santa Ana	CA	92705	**800-966-5432**	714-835-6485	442
Wine Spectator Magazine 825 Eighth Ave *Orders	New York	NY	10019	**800-752-7799***	212-684-4224	455-14
Winebow Inc 75 Chestnut Ridge Rd	Montvale	NJ	07645	**800-859-0689**	201-445-0620	81-3
Winebrenner Theological Seminary 950 N Main St	Findlay	OH	45840	**800-992-4987**	419-434-4200	167-3
Winecom Inc 222 Sutter St Ste 450	San Francisco	CA	94108	**800-592-5870**		442
Winegard Co 3000 Kirkwood St *Cust Svc	Burlington	IA	52601	**800-288-8094***	319-754-0600	643
Winery at Wolf Creek 2637 Cleveland Massillon Rd	Norton	OH	44203	**800-436-0426**	330-666-9285	50-7
WineShop At Home 525 Airpark Rd	Napa	CA	94558	**800-946-3746**	707-253-0200	442
Winfield Associates Inc 700 W St Clair Ave Ste 404	Cleveland	OH	44113	**888-322-2575**	216-241-2575	791
Winfree Business Growth Advisors 10808 Ward Ave	Louisville	KY	40223	**800-616-9260**	502-253-0700	461
Wing Enterprises Inc 1198 N Spring Creek	Springville	UT	84663	**866-872-5901**	801-489-3684	420
Wing Hing Foods Inc 2539 E Philadelphia St	Ontario	CA	91761	**855-734-2742**	909-627-7312	344
Wing Luke Asian Museum 719 S King St	Seattle	WA	98104	**800-961-6119**	206-623-5124	517
Wingate by Wyndham Calgary Hotel 400 Midpark Way SE	Calgary	AB	T2X3S4	**800-228-1000**	403-514-0099	703
Wingate Healthcare 63 Kendrick St	Needham	MA	02494	**800-946-4283**		4

	Toll-Free	Phone	Class
Wingate University			
220 N Camden Rd ....Wingate NC 28174	**800-755-5550**	704-233-8000	166
Wingfield J e & Associates PC			
700 Fifth St NW Ste 300 ....Washington DC 20001	**800-338-5954**	202-789-8000	443
Wingfoot Commercial Tire Systems LLC			
1000 S 21st St ....Fort Smith AR 72901	**800-643-7330**	479-788-6400	62-5
Wingra Stone Co			
2975 Kapec Rd PO Box 44284 ....Madison WI 53744	**800-249-6908**	608-271-5555	183
Wings Financial Credit Union			
14985 Glazier Ave Ste 100 ....Apple Valley MN 55124	**800-692-2274**		219
Wings Tours Inc			
11350 McCormick Rd Ste 904 .... Hunt Valley MD 21031	**800-869-4647**	410-771-0925	755
Wingstop Restaurants Inc			
908 Audelia Rd Ste 100 ....Richardson TX 75081	**877-411-9464**		666
WinHolt Equipment Group			
141 Eileen Way ....Syosset NY 11791	**800-444-3595**	516-222-0335	468
Winkler Inc			
535 E Medcalf St ....Dale IN 47523	**800-621-3843**	812-937-4421	297-8
Winland Electronics Inc			
1950 Excel Dr ....Mankato MN 56001	**800-635-4269**		201
NYSE: WEX			
Winn Technology Group Inc			
523 Palm Harbor Blvd .... Palm Harbor FL 34683	**800-444-5622**		195
Winn Transportation			
1831 Westwood Ave ....Richmond VA 23227	**800-296-9466**	804-358-9466	107
Winnebago Industries Inc			
605 W Crystal Lake Rd			
PO Box 152...................Forest City IA 50436	**800-643-4892**	641-585-3535	120
NYSE: WGO			
Winneconne News			
908 E Main St ....Winneconne WI 54986	**800-545-5026**	920-582-4541	528-3
Winnemucca Convention & Visitors Authority			
50 W Winnemucca Blvd ....Winnemucca NV 89445	**800-962-2638**	775-623-5071	206
Winner International LLC			
32 W State St ....Sharon PA 16146	**800-258-2321**	724-981-1152	688
Winner Livestock Auction Co			
31690 Livestock Barn Rd ....Winner SD 57580	**800-201-0451**	605-842-0451	444
Winner's Cir Resort			
550 Via de la Valle ....Solana Beach CA 92075	**800-874-8770**	858-755-6666	665
Winners Sports Haven			
600 Long Wharf Dr ....New Haven CT 06511	**800-468-2260**		133
Winning Technologies Great Lakes LLC			
147 Triad Ctr W ....O Fallon MO 63366	**877-379-8279**		180
Winnipeg Folk Festival			
203-211 Bannatyne Ave ....Winnipeg MB R3B3P2	**866-301-3823**	204-231-0096	716
Winnipeg Free Press			
1355 Mountain Ave ....Winnipeg MB R2X3B6	**800-542-8900**	204-697-7000	528-1
Winnipeg Richardson International Airport			
2000 Wellington Ave ....Winnipeg MB R3H1C2	**855-500-6589**	204-987-9402	27
Winnsboro State Bank & Trust Co			
3875 Front St ....Winnsboro LA 71295	**866-205-4026**	318-435-7535	70
win-OMT Software Inc			
280 - 1630 Ness Ave ....Winnipeg MB R3J3X1	**888-665-0501**	204-786-3994	394
Winona National Bank			
204 Main St PO Box 499 ....Winona MN 55987	**800-546-4392**	507-454-8800	359-2
Winona State University			
175 W Mark St ....Winona MN 55987	**800-342-5978**	507-457-5000	166
Winpak Ltd			
100 Salteaux Crescent ....Winnipeg MB R3J3T3	**800-841-2600**	204-889-1015	544
TSE: WPK			
Winship Cancer Institute of Emory University			
1365 Clifton Rd NE ....Atlanta GA 30322	**888-946-7447**	404-778-1900	764
Winslow BMW			
730 N Cir Dr .... Colorado Springs CO 80909	**877-367-7357**	719-473-1373	57
Winston Flowers			
131 Newbury St ....Boston MA 02116	**800-457-4901**		292
Winston Industries LLC			
2345 Carton Dr ....Louisville KY 40299	**800-234-5286**	502-495-5400	298
Winston Packaging			
8095 N Point Blvd .... Winston-Salem NC 27106	**800-558-8952**	336-759-0051	623
Winston/Royal Guard Corp			
1604 Cherokee Trace ...... White Oak TX 75693	**800-527-8465**	903-757-7341	533
Winston-Salem Convention & Visitors Bureau			
200 Brookstown Ave ...... Winston-Salem NC 27101	**866-728-4200**	336-728-4200	206
Winston-Salem Journal			
418 N Marshall St .... Winston-Salem NC 27101	**800-642-0925**	336-727-7211	528-2
Winston-Salem State University			
601 S ML King Jr Dr .... Winston-Salem NC 27110	**800-257-4052***	336-750-2000	166
*Admissions			
Winsupply Inc			
3110 Kettering Blvd ....Dayton OH 45439	**800-677-4380**	937-294-5331	608
Winter Gardens Quality Foods Inc			
304 Commerce St PO Box 339....... New Oxford PA 17350	**800-242-7637**	717-624-4911	296-36
Winter Hill Bank			
342 Broadway ....Somerville MA 02145	**800-444-4300**	617-666-8600	70
Winter Park Chamber of Commerce			
151 W Lyman Ave .... Winter Park FL 32789	**877-972-4262***	407-644-8281	139
*Help Line			
Winter Park Resort			
85 Parsenn Rd .... Winter Park CO 80482	**800-903-7275***	970-726-5514	375
*Resv			
Winter Quarters State Historic Site			
4929 Hwy 608 ....Newellton LA 71357	**888-677-9468**	888-677-2784	561
WinterBell Co			
2018 Brevard Rd ....High Point NC 27263	**800-685-2957**	336-887-2651	557
Wintersilks LLC			
PO Box 196 ....Jessup PA 18434	**800-648-7455**	800-718-3687	457
Winterthur Museum & Country Estate			
5105 Kennett Pk ....Winterthur DE 19735	**800-448-3883**	302-888-4600	517
Winward International Inc			
3089 Whipple Rd ....Union City CA 94587	**800-888-8898**	510-487-8686	292
WINZ-AM 940 (N/T)			
7601 Riviera Blvd ....Miramar FL 33023	**844-289-7234**		
WIOD-AM 610 (N/T)			
7601 Riviera Blvd ....Miramar FL 33023	**866-610-6397**	954-862-2000	641-65
Wipaire Inc			
1700 Henry Ave .... South St. Paul MN 55075	**888-947-2473**	651-451-1205	525
Wipe-Tex International Corp			
110 E 153rd St ....Bronx NY 10451	**800-643-9607**	718-665-0013	506

	Toll-Free	Phone	Class
Wire Belt Company of America			
154 Harvey Rd .... Londonderry NH 03053	**800-922-2637***	603-644-2500	207
*Cust Svc			
Wire Rope Industries Ltd			
5501 Trans-Canada Hwy .... Pointe-claire QC H9R1B7	**800-565-5501**	514-697-9711	490
Wired News			
Wired 520 Third St			
Ste 305 ....San Francisco CA 94107	**800-769-4733**		396
Wireless Analytics LLC			
230 N St ....Danvers MA 01923	**888-588-5550**	978-762-0900	224
Wireless Watchdogs LLC			
317 Isis Ave Ste 102............. Inglewood CA 90301	**866-522-0688**	310-622-0688	2
Wireless Zone LLC			
795 Brook St ....Rocky Hill CT 06067	**888-881-2622**	800-411-2355	35
Wiremasters Inc			
1788 N Pt Rd ....Columbia TN 38401	**800-635-5342**	615-791-0281	246
Wirerope Works Inc			
100 Maynard St .... Williamsport PA 17701	**800-541-7673***	570-326-5146	808
*Cust Svc			
WIS International			
9265 Sky Park Ct Ste 100........... San Diego CA 92123	**800-268-6848**	858-565-8111	398
Wisco Industries Inc			
736 Janesville St ....Oregon WI 53575	**800-999-4726**	608-835-3106	36
Wisco Products Inc			
109 Commercial St ....Dayton OH 45402	**800-367-6570**	937-228-2101	693
Wisco Supply Inc			
815 S Saint Vrain St ....El Paso TX 79901	**800-947-2689**	915-544-8294	606
Wiscolift Inc			
W6396 Speciality Dr .... Greenville WI 54942	**800-242-3477**	920-757-8832	490
Wisconsin			
Crime Victims Services Office			
17 W Main St PO Box 7857 ......Madison WI 53703	**800-446-6564**	608-266-1221	338-50
Department of Safety & Professional Services			
1400 E Washington Ave Rm 112 ......Madison WI 53703	**877-617-1565**	608-266-2112	338-50
Ethics Board			
212 E Washington Ave 3rd Fl ....Madison WI 53707	**866-868-3947**	608-266-8005	265
Historical Society			
816 State St ....Madison WI 53706	**888-936-7463**		
Housing & Economic Development Authority			
201 W Washington Ave Ste 700......Madison WI 53703	**800-334-6873**	608-266-7884	338-50
Insurance Commission			
125 S Webster St ....Madison WI 53707	**800-236-8517**	608-266-3585	338-50
Legislature			
State Capitol ....Madison WI 53702	**800-362-9472**	608-266-9960	338-50
Natural Resources Dept			
101 S Webster St PO Box 7921 ....Madison WI 53707	**888-936-7463**	608-266-2621	338-50
Public Instruction Dept			
125 S Webster St PO Box 7841 ....Madison WI 53707	**800-441-4563**	608-266-3390	338-50
Public Service Commission			
4822 Madison Yards Way			
N Tower 6th Fl ....Madison WI 53705	**888-816-3831**	608-266-5481	338-50
State Patrol Div			
4802 Sheboygan Ave			
Rm 551 PO Box 7912...............Madison WI 53707	**844-847-1234**		338-50
Teacher Education & Licensing Bureau			
125 S Webster St ....Madison WI 53703	**800-441-4563**	608-266-3390	338-50
Veterans Affairs Dept			
201 W Washington Ave			
PO Box 7843 ....Madison WI 53707	**800-947-8387**	608-266-1311	338-50
Vital Records Office			
1 W Wilson St ....Madison WI 53703	**800-947-3529**	608-266-1865	338-50
Vocational Rehabilitation Div			
201 E Washington Ave			
PO Box 7852 ....Madison WI 53707	**800-442-3477**	608-261-0050	338-50
Wisconsin Aviation Inc			
1741 River Dr .... Watertown WI 53094	**800-657-0761**	920-261-4567	63
Wisconsin Box Company Inc			
929 Townline Rd .... Wausau WI 54402	**800-876-6658**	715-842-2248	200
Wisconsin Dells Visitors & Convention Bureau			
701 Superior St			
PO Box 390...................Wisconsin Dells WI 53965	**800-223-3557**	608-254-8088	206
Wisconsin Dental Assn			
6737 W Washington St			
Ste 2360 .... West Allis WI 53214	**800-364-7646**	414-276-4520	227
Wisconsin Educational Communications Board			
3319 W Beltline Hwy .... Madison WI 53713	**800-422-9707**	608-264-9600	628
Wisconsin Film & Bag Inc			
3100 E Richmond St ....Shawano WI 54166	**800-765-9224**	715-524-2565	66
Wisconsin Historical Museum			
30 N Carroll St ....Madison WI 53703	**888-999-1669**	608-264-6555	517
Wisconsin Hospital Association Inc			
5510 Research Park Dr ....Fitchburg WI 53711	**800-782-8581**	608-274-1820	138
Wisconsin Indianhead Technical College			
New Richmond Campus			
1019 S Knowles Ave .... New Richmond WI 54017	**800-243-9482**	715-246-6561	795
Rice Lake Campus			
1900 College Dr ....Rice Lake WI 54868	**800-243-9482**	715-234-7082	795
Superior Campus			
600 N 21 St ....Superior WI 54880	**800-243-9482**	715-394-6677	795
Wisconsin Lift Truck Corp			
3125 Intertech Dr .... Brookfield WI 53045	**800-634-9010**	262-781-8010	357
Wisconsin Machine Tool Corp			
3225 Gateway Rd Ste 100............ Brookfield WI 53045	**800-243-3078**	262-317-3048	453
Wisconsin Manufacturers & Commerce			
PO Box 352 ....Madison WI 53701	**800-236-5414**	608-258-3400	140
Wisconsin Maritime Museum			
75 Maritime Dr ....Manitowoc WI 54220	**866-724-2356**	920-684-0218	517
Wisconsin Power & Light Co			
4902 N Biltmore Ln PO Box 77007...... Madison WI 53718	**800-255-4268**		782
Wisconsin Public Radio (WPR)			
821 University Ave .... Madison WI 53706	**800-747-7444**		628
Wisconsin Public Service Corp			
PO Box 19001 .... Green Bay WI 54307	**800-450-7260**		782
Wisconsin Public Television (WPT)			
821 University Ave .... Madison WI 53706	**800-422-9707**	608-263-2121	628
Wisconsin Realtors Assn			
4801 Forest Run Rd Ste 201 ...... Madison WI 53704	**800-279-1972**	608-241-2047	652
Wisconsin Reinsurance Corp			
2810 City View Dr .... Madison WI 53707	**800-939-9473**	608-242-4500	390-4

	Toll-Free	Phone	Class
Wisconsin State Journal			
1901 Fish Hatchery Rd .... Madison WI 53713	800-362-8333	608-252-6200	528-2
Wisconsin State Medical Society			
330 E Lakeside St PO Box 1109 ..... Madison WI 53701	866-442-3800		472
Wisconsin Steel & Tube Corp			
1555 N Mayfair Rd .... Milwaukee WI 53226	800-279-8335	414-453-4441	490
Wisconsin Veterans Home			
N2665 County Rd QQ .... King WI 54946	877-944-6667	715-258-5586	788
Wisconsin Veterinary Medical Assn (WVMA)			
2801 Crossroads Dr Ste 1200 .... Madison WI 53718	888-254-5202	608-257-3665	790
Wise Business Forms Inc			
555 McFarland 400 Dr .... Alpharetta GA 30004	888-815-9473	770-442-1060	110
Wise Consulting Associates Inc			
54 Scott Adam Rd Ste 206 .... Hunt Valley MD 21030	800-654-4550	410-628-0100	447
Wise Electric Co-op Inc			
1900 N Trinity St .... Decatur TX 76234	888-627-9326	940-627-2167	245
Wise Foods Inc			
228 Rasely St Ste 75. .... Berwick PA 18603	888-759-4401*	570-759-4000	296-35
*Cust Svc			
Wiseco Piston Inc			
7201 Industrial Pk Blvd .... Mentor OH 44060	800-321-1364	440-951-6600	128
Wiseway Motor Freight Inc			
PO Box 838 .... Hudson WI 54016	800-876-1660		775
WISH List			
46-E Peninsula Ctr			
Ste 385 .... Rolling Hills Estates CA 90274	888-310-4504		48-7
Wist Office Products Co			
107 W Julie Dr .... Tempe AZ 85283	800-999-9478	480-921-2900	531
Wistar Institute			
3601 Spruce St .... Philadelphia PA 19104	800-724-6633	215-898-3700	664
WITF-FM 895 (NPR)			
4801 Lindle Rd .... Harrisburg PA 17111	800-366-9483	717-704-3000	641-44
WITI (Women in Technology International)			
11500 Olympic Blvd Ste 400 ....Los Angeles CA 90064	800-334-9484	818-788-9484	49-19
Witmer's Construction Inc			
39821 Salem Unity Rd .... Salem OH 44460	888-427-2150	330-427-2611	274
Witt Industries Inc			
4600 Mason-Montgomery Rd .... Mason OH 45040	800-543-7417		657
Witt Lincoln			
588 Camino Del Rio North .... San Diego CA 92108	877-937-3301	888-668-9787	57
Witt Printing Company Inc			
301 Oak St .... El Dorado Springs MO 64744	800-641-4342	417-876-4721	110
Witt/Kieffer Ford Hadelman & Lloyd			
2015 Spring Rd Ste 510 .... Oak Brook IL 60523	888-281-1370	630-990-1370	266
Wittek Golf Supply Co Inc			
300 Bond St .... Elk Grove Village IL 60007	800-869-1800		706
Wittenberg University			
200 W Ward St .... Springfield OH 45504	800-677-7558	937-327-6314	166
WITV-TV Ch 7 (PBS)			
1041 George Rogers Blvd .... Columbia SC 29201	800-277-3245	803-737-3200	736
WIVB-TV Ch 4 (CBS)			
2077 Elmwood Ave .... Buffalo NY 14207	800-794-3687	716-874-4410	736-13
WIX Filtration Products			
1 Wix Way PO Box 1967............ Gastonia NC 28053	800-949-6698	704-864-6711	60
Wixon Inc			
1390 E Bolivar Ave .... Saint Francis WI 53235	800-841-5304	414-769-3000	296
Wizards of the Coast Inc			
PO Box 707 .... Renton WA 98057	800-324-6496	425-226-6500	757
Wizcom Technologies Inc			
33 Boston Post Rd W Ste 320....... Marlborough MA 01752	888-777-0552	508-251-5388	173-7
WIZN-FM 1067			
450 Weaver St .... Winooski VT 05404	888-873-9496	802-860-2440	641-118
WJHL-TV Ch 11 (CBS)			
338 E Main St .... Johnson City TN 37601	800-861-5255	423-926-2151	736-37
WJMZ-FM 1073 (Urban)			
220 N Main St Ste 402 .... Greenville SC 29601	800-767-1073	864-235-1073	641-43
WJOY-AM 1230 (Nost)			
70 Joy Dr .... South Burlington VT 05403	800-554-9890	802-658-1230	641
WJQK-FM			
425 Centerstone Ct .... Zeeland MI 49464	866-931-9936	616-931-9930	641
WJYI-AM 1340 (Rel)			
5407 W McKinley Ave .... Milwaukee WI 53208	800-256-6102	414-978-9000	641-63
WKBW-TV Ch 7 (ABC)			
7 Broadcast Plz .... Buffalo NY 14202	888-373-7888	716-845-6100	736-13
WKCQ-FM 981 (Ctry)			
2000 Whittier St .... Saginaw MI 48601	800-262-0098	989-752-8161	641
WKDQ 995			
20 NW Third St Ste 600 .... Evansville IN 47708	877-437-5995	812-425-4226	
WKLB-FM 1025 (Ctry)			
55 Morrissey Blvd .... Boston MA 02125	888-819-1025	617-822-9600	641-16
WKNO			
7151 Cherry Farms Rd .... Cordova TN 38016	877-717-7822	901-729-8765	736
WKNO-FM 911 (NPR)			
7151 Cherry Farms Rd .... Cordova TN 38016	800-766-9566	901-325-6544	641-62
WKRC-TV Ch 12 (CBS)			
1906 Highland Ave .... Cincinnati OH 45219	877-889-5610	513-763-5500	736-18
WKSU-FM 897 (NPR)			
1613 E Summit St .... Kent OH 44242	800-672-2132	330-672-3114	641
WKYC-TV Ch 3 (NBC)			
1333 Lakeside Ave E .... Cleveland OH 44114	877-790-7370	216-344-3333	736-19
WKYL-FM 1021 (NAC)			
102 Perkins Bldg			
521 Lancaster Ave............... Richmond KY 40475	800-621-8890		641-88
WL (Western Living Magazine)			
2608 Granville St Ste 560.......... Vancouver BC V6H3V3	800-363-3272	604-877-7732	455-11
Wlav			
60 Monroe Ctr Ste 300........... Grand Rapids MI 49503	800-882-9528	616-774-8461	
WLBT-TV Ch 3 (NBC)			
715 S Jefferson St .... Jackson MS 39201	800-792-6067	601-948-3333	736-36
WLBZ-TV Ch 2 (NBC)			
329 Mt Hope Ave .... Bangor ME 04401	800-244-6306	207-942-4821	736-7
WLDE FUN 1017			
347 W Berry Ste 600. .... Fort Wayne IN 46802	888-450-1017	260-423-3676	641-39
Wlh Consulting Inc			
1417 Capri Ln .... Weston FL 33326	800-392-0745		
WLLL-AM 930 (Rel)			
PO Box 11375 .... Lynchburg VA 24506	888-224-9809*	434-385-9555	641
*Cust Svc			

	Toll-Free	Phone	Class
WLMB-TV Ch 40 (Ind)			
825 Capital Commons Dr .... Toledo OH 43615	800-218-5740	419-720-9562	736-78
WLOS-TV Ch 13 (ABC)			
110 Technology Dr .... Asheville NC 28803	800-419-6356	828-684-1340	736-3
WLPB-TV Ch 27 (PBS)			
7733 Perkins Rd .... Baton Rouge LA 70810	800-272-8161	225-767-5660	736-8
WLRH Huntsville 893 FM			
UAH Campus John Wright Dr........ Huntsville AL 35899	800-239-9574	256-895-9574	641-48
WLTR-FM 913 (NPR)			
1041 George Rogers Blvd .... Columbia SC 29201	800-922-5437	803-737-3200	641-27
WLUK-TV Ch 11 (Fox)			
787 Lombardi Ave .... Green Bay WI 54304	800-242-8067	920-494-8711	736-32
WM Barr & Company Inc			
PO Box 1879 .... Memphis TN 38101	800-238-2672	901-775-0100	546
WMCC (White Mountains Community College)			
2020 Riverside Dr .... Berlin NH 03570	800-445-4525	603-752-1113	162
WMF Americas Inc			
2121 Eden Rd .... Millville NJ 08332	800-966-3009	704-882-3898	360
WMH (Wilcox Memorial Hospital)			
3-3420 Kuhio Hwy .... Lihue HI 96766	877-709-9355	808-245-1100	373-3
WMIT-FM 1069 (Rel)			
3 Porters Cove Rd .... Asheville NC 28805	800-330-9648	828-285-8477	641
WMK Inc			
4199 Kinross Lakes Pkwy .... Richfield OH 44286	877-275-4912	234-312-2000	57
WML (Warde Medical Laboratory)			
300 W Textile Rd .... Ann Arbor MI 48108	800-760-9969	734-214-0300	414
WMPI-FM 1053 (Ctry)			
22 E McClain Ave .... Scottsburg IN 47170	800-441-1053	812-752-3688	641
WMPV-TV Ch 21 (TBN)			
1668 W I-65 Service Rd S .... Mobile AL 36693	855-826-2255	251-661-2101	
WMTW-TV Ch 8 (ABC)			
4 Ledgeview Dr .... Westbrook ME 04092	800-248-6397	207-835-3888	736
WMU (Woman's Missionary Union)			
100 Missionary Rdg ....Birmingham AL 35242	800-968-7301	205-991-8100	48-20
WMUM-FM 897 (NPR)			
243 Carey Salem Rd .... Cochran GA 31014	800-222-4788	478-301-5760	641
WMXJ-FM 1027 (Oldies)			
20450 NW Second Ave .... Miami FL 33169	800-924-1027	305-521-5240	641-65
WMZQ-FM 987 (Ctry)			
1801 Rockville Pk .... Rockville MD 20852	800-505-0098	240-747-2700	641
WN (World Neighbors Inc)			
4127 NW 122nd St ....Oklahoma City OK 73120	800-242-6387	405-752-9700	48-5
WNBC-TV Ch 4 (NBC)			
30 Rockefeller Plz .... New York NY 10112	866-639-7244	212-664-4444	736-51
WNC Supply LLC			
37841 N 16th St .... Phoenix AZ 85086	800-538-5108	623-594-4602	624
WNCI-FM 979 (CHR)			
2323 W Fifth Ave Ste 200 .... Columbus OH 43204	844-289-7234		
WNCW-FM 887			
PO Box 804 .... Spindale NC 28160	800-245-8870	828-287-8000	641
WNDV-FM 929 (CHR)			
3371 Cleveland Rd Ste 300 .... South Bend IN 46628	800-242-0100	574-273-9300	641-66
WNED			
140 Lower Terr PO Box 1263 .... Buffalo NY 14202	800-678-1873	716-845-7000	641-18
WNED-TV Ch 17 (PBS)			
Horizons Plz PO Box 1263 .... Buffalo NY 14240	800-678-1873	716-845-7000	736-13
WNEM-TV 5 (CBS)			
107 N Franklin St .... Saginaw MI 48607	800-522-9636	989-755-8191	736
WNEP-TV Ch 16 (ABC)			
16 Montage Mtn Rd .... Moosic PA 18507	800-982-4374	570-346-7474	736
WNET-TV Ch 13 (PBS)			
450 W 33rd St .... New York NY 10001	800-468-9913	212-560-1313	736-51
WNIN-FM 883 (NPR)			
405 Carpenter St .... Evansville IN 47708	855-888-9646	812-423-2973	641-37
WNIN-TV Ch 9 (PBS)			
405 Carpenter St .... Evansville IN 47708	855-888-9646	812-423-2973	736-28
WNIT Public Television			
300 W Jefferson Blvd .... South Bend IN 46601	877-411-3662	574-675-9648	736-73
WNJU-TV Ch 47 (Tele)			
2200 Fletcher Ave 6th Fl. .... Fort Lee NJ 07024	877-478-3536		736
WO Grubb Steel Erection Inc			
5120 Jefferson Davis Hwy .... Richmond VA 23234	866-964-7822	804-271-9471	189-14
Wo Stinson & Son Ltd			
4726 Bank St .... Ottawa ON K1T3W7	800-267-9714	613-822-7400	316
WOAI-AM 1200 (N/T)			
6222 Interstate 10 .... San Antonio TX 78201	800-383-9624	210-736-9700	641-94
WOCN (Wound Ostomy & Continence Nurses Society)			
1120 Rt 73 Ste 200............. Mount Laurel NJ 08054	888-224-9626		49-8
Woeber Mustard Manufacturing Co			
1966 Commerce Cir			
PO Box 388..................... Springfield OH 45501	800-548-2929		297-8
WOGB-FM 1031 (AC)			
810 Victoria St .... Green Bay WI 54302	800-236-3771	920-468-4100	641-42
WOGL-FM 981 (Oldies)			
555 E City Ave Ste 330........... Bala Cynwyd PA 19004	800-942-8998		641
WOI-TV Ch 5 (ABC)			
3903 Westown Pkwy .... West Des Moines IA 50266	800-858-5555	515-457-9645	736
Wojan Window & Door Corp			
217 Stover Rd .... Charlevoix MI 49720	800-632-9827		478
Wojanis Inc			
1001 Montour W Ind Pk .... Coraopolis PA 15108	800-345-9024	724-695-1415	357
WOKO-FM 989 (Ctry)			
70 Joy Dr .... South Burlington VT 05403	800-354-9890	802-862-9890	641
WOKQ-FM 975 (Ctry)			
292 Middle Rd PO Box 576 .... Dover NH 03821	877-975-1037	603-749-9750	641
Wolf Gordon Inc			
33-00 47th Ave .... Long Island NY 11101	800-347-0550		546
Wolf Organization, The			
20 W Market St .... York PA 17401	800-388-9653		200
Wolf Ridge Ski Resort			
578 Vly View Cir .... Mars Hill NC 28754	800-817-4111	828-689-4111	665
Wolf Robotics LLC			
4600 Innovation Dr .... Fort Collins CO 80525	866-965-3911	970-225-7600	489
Wolf Technology Group Inc			
1 Chick Springs Rd Ste 112 ...... Greenville SC 29609	833-482-6435		
Wolf Trap Foundation for the Performing Arts			
1645 Trap Rd .... Vienna VA 22182	877-965-3872	703-255-1900	568

	Toll-Free	Phone	Class
Wolf X-Ray Corp			
100 W Industry Ct ....Deer Park NY 11729	800-356-9729*	631-242-9729	381
*Cust Svc			
Wolfe Industrial Auctions Inc			
9801 Hansonville Rd ....Frederick MD 21702	800-443-9580	301-898-0340	41
Wolferman's			
2500 S Pacific Hwy PO Box 9100........Medford OR 97501	800-999-0169		296-1
Wolfgang Candy Co			
50 E Fourth Ave ....York PA 17404	800-248-4273	717-843-5536	296-8
Wolseley Canada Inc			
880 Laurentian Dr ....Burlington ON L7N3V6	800-282-1376	905-335-7373	111
Wolters Kluwer Financial Services Inc			
100 S Fifth St Ste 700.............Minneapolis MN 55402	800-552-9408	612-656-7700	178-10
Wolverine Mutual Insurance Co			
1 Wolverine Way ....Dowagiac MI 49047	800-733-3320	269-782-3451	389
Wolverine Power Systems Inc			
3229 80th Ave ....Zeeland MI 49464	800-485-8068	616-879-0040	515
Woman's Hospital			
100 Woman's Wy ....Baton Rouge LA 70815	800-620-8474	225-927-1300	373-7
Woman's Life Insurance Society			
1338 Military St PO Box 5020.......Port Huron MI 48061	800-521-9292	810-985-5191	390-2
Woman's Missionary Union (WMU)			
100 Missionary Rdg ....Birmingham AL 35242	800-968-7301	205-991-8100	48-20
Women & Infants Hospital of Rhode Island			
101 Dudley St ....Providence RI 02905	800-711-7011	401-274-1100	373-7
Women in Military Service for America Memorial Foundation Inc			
Dept 560 ....Washington DC 20042	800-222-2294	703-533-1155	48-19
Women in Technology International (WITI)			
11500 Olympic Blvd Ste 400 ....Los Angeles CA 90064	800-334-9484	818-788-9484	49-19
Women's & Children's Hospital (WCH)			
4600 Ambassador Caffery Pkwy ....Lafayette LA 70508	888-569-8331	337-521-9100	373-7
Women's & Children's Hospital of Buffalo			
219 Bryant St ....Buffalo NY 14222	800-462-7653	716-878-7000	373-1
Women's Bureau			
200 Constitution Ave NW			
Rm S3002.....................Washington DC 20210	800-827-5335	202-693-6710	339-14
US Department of Labor			
200 Constitution Ave NW			
Rm S-3002....................Washington DC 20210	800-827-5335	202-693-6710	339-14
Women's Bureau Regional Offices			
Region 1			
JFK Federal Bldg Rm 525-A..........Boston MA 02203	800-827-5335	617-565-1988	339-14
Region 2			
201 Varick St Rm 602.............New York NY 10014	800-827-5335	646-264-3789	339-14
Region 3			
The Curtis Ctr Ste 631 E West			
170 S Independence Mall West ....Philadelphia PA 19106	800-827-5335	866-487-2365	339-14
Region 5			
230 S Dearborn St Rm 1022.........Chicago IL 60604	800-827-5335	312-353-6985	339-14
Region 7			
2300 Main St Ste 1050.......Kansas City MO 64108	800-827-5335	816-285-7233	339-14
Region 8			
1999 Broadway Ste 1620			
PO Box 46550 ....Denver CO 80201	800-827-5335	303-844-1286	339-14
Region 9			
90 Seventh St Ste 2650 ....San Francisco CA 94103	800-827-5335	866-487-2365	339-14
Region 10			
300 Fifth Ave Ste 1230...........Seattle WA 98104	800-827-5335	206-757-6740	339-14
Women's Council of REALTORS (WCR)			
430 N Michigan Ave ....Chicago IL 60611	800-245-8512		49-17
Women's International Pharmacy Inc			
PO Box 6468 ....Madison WI 53716	800-279-5708		457
Women's Sports Foundation			
1899 Hempstead Tpke			
Ste 400 Eisenhower Pk ....East Meadow NY 11554	800-227-3988	516-542-4700	48-22
Women's Wear Daily Magazine			
475 Fifth Ave 3rd Fl ....New York NY 10017	866-401-7801	212-213-1900	455-11
WOMX-FM 105.1 (AC)			
1800 Pembrook Dr Ste 400 ....Orlando FL 32810	877-919-1051	407-919-1000	641-75
Wonder View Inn & Suites			
50 Eden St PO Box 25 ....Bar Harbor ME 04609	888-439-8439	207-288-3358	378
Wonderland Amusement Park			
2601 Dumas Dr ....Amarillo TX 79107	800-383-4712	806-383-0832	32
Wonderlic Inc			
400 Lakeview Pkwy Ste 200 ....Vernon Hills IL 60061	877-605-9496	847-680-4900	633-10
Wonders of Wildlife			
500 W Sunshine St ....Springfield MO 65807	888-222-6060		818
Wonderware Corp			
26561 Rancho Pkwy S ....Lake Forest CA 92630	800-966-3371	949-727-3200	178-10
Won-Door Corp			
1865 South 3480 West ....Salt Lake City UT 84104	800-453-8494	801-973-7500	234
Wood & Tait LLC			
64-5249 Kauakea Rd PO Box 6180......Kamuela HI 96743	800-774-8585	808-885-5090	399
Wood County			
1 Courthouse Sq ....Bowling Green OH 43402	866-860-4140	419-354-9000	337
Wood County			
PO Box 1796 ....Quitman TX 75783	800-253-8014	903-763-2711	337
Wood County Electric Co-op Inc			
501 S Main St ....Quitman TX 75783	800-762-2203	903-763-2203	245
Wood County Hospital			
950 W Wooster St ....Bowling Green OH 43402	800-288-4470	419-354-8900	373-3
Wood Preservers Inc			
15939 Historyland Hwy PO Box 158.. Warsaw VA 22572	800-368-2536	804-333-4022	813
Wood Pro Inc			
421 Washington St PO Box 363 ....Auburn MA 01501	800-786-5577	508-832-9888	746
Wood Tobe-Coburn School			
8 E 40th St ....New York NY 10016	800-394-9663	212-686-9040	795
Woodard & Curran			
41 Hutchins Dr ....Portland ME 04102	800-426-4262	207-774-2112	261
Woodbine Entertainment Group Inc			
555 Rexdale Blvd PO Box 156 ....Toronto ON M9W5L2	888-675-7223	416-675-7223	638
Woodburn Nursery & Azaleas			
13009 McKee School Rd NE ......Woodburn OR 97071	888-634-2232*	503-634-2231	368
*Sales			
Woodbury County Rural Electric Co-op Assn			
1495 Humboldt Ave ....Moville IA 51039	800-469-3125	712-873-3125	245
Woodbury Pewterers Inc			
860 Main St S ....Woodbury CT 06798	800-648-2014		698
Woodbury Technologies Inc			
1725 East 1450 South ....Clearfield UT 84015	800-408-8857	801-773-7157	196
Woodbury University			
7500 Glenoaks Blvd ....Burbank CA 91510	800-784-9663	818-767-0888	166
Woodcliff Hotel & Spa			
199 Woodcliff Dr ....Fairport NY 14450	800-365-3065	585-381-4000	665
WOODCO USA			
773 McCarty Dr ....Houston TX 77029	800-496-6326	713-672-9491	357
Woodcraft Supply LLC			
1177 Rosemar Rd ....Parkersburg WV 26105	800-535-4482		45
Woodford Manufacturing Co			
2121 Waynoka Rd ....Colorado Springs CO 80915	800-621-6032*	719-574-0600	605
*Sales			
Woodford Oil Company Inc			
13th St PO Box 567 ....Elkins WV 26241	800-927-3688	304-636-2688	316
Woodforest National Bank			
PO Box 7889 ....Spring TX 77387	877-968-7962	832-375-2000	70
Wood-Fruitticher Grocery Company Inc			
2900 Alton Rd ....Birmingham AL 35210	800-328-0026	205-836-9663	297-8
Woodgrain Distribution			
80 Shelby St ....Montevallo AL 35115	800-756-0199	205-665-2546	309
Woodgrain Millworks Inc			
300 NW 16th St ....Fruitland ID 83619	888-783-5485	208-452-3801	497
Woodhill Supply Inc			
4665 Beidler Rd ....Willoughby OH 44094	800-362-6111	440-269-1100	608
Woodland Aviation Inc			
25170 Aviation Ave ....Davis CA 95616	800-442-1333	530-759-6037	63
Woodland Chamber of Commerce			
400 Court St ....Woodland CA 95695	888-843-2636	530-662-7327	139
Woodland Healthcare			
1325 Cottonwood St ....Woodland CA 95695	844-274-8497		
Woodland Paper Inc			
50785 Pontiac Trl ....Wixom MI 48393	800-979-9919	248-926-5550	550
Woodland Public Library			
250 First St ....Woodland CA 95695	800-321-2752	530-661-5980	433-3
Woodlands Inn, The			
1073 Hwy 315 ....Wilkes-Barre PA 18702	888-221-6039		
Woodlands Resort & Conference Ctr, The			
2301 N Millbend Dr ....The Woodlands TX 77380	800-433-2624*	281-367-1100	376
*Resv			
Woodlawn Cemetery Inc, The			
Webster Ave & E 233rd St ....Bronx NY 10470	877-496-6352	718-920-0500	508
Woodlawn National Cemetery			
1825 Davis St ....Elmira NY 14901	877-907-8585	607-732-5411	136
Woodloch Pines Inc			
731 Welcome Lake Rd ....Hawley PA 18428	800-966-3562	570-685-8000	378
WOODMARK HOTEL			
1200 Carillon Pt ....Kirkland WA 98033	800-822-3700	425-822-3700	378
Woodmen Life			
1700 Farnam St ....Omaha NE 68102	800-225-3108	402-342-1890	455-10
Woodmont Investment Counsel LLC			
401 Commerce St Ste 5400 ....Nashville TN 37219	800-278-8003	615-297-6144	400
Woodridge Park District			
2600 Center Dr ....Woodridge IL 60517	800-713-7415	630-353-3300	31
Woodruff Electric Co-op			
PO Box 1619 ....Forrest City AR 72336	888-559-6400	870-633-2262	245
Woodruff Energy			
73 Water St PO Box 777 ....Bridgeton NJ 08302	800-557-1121		316
Woods Equipment Co			
2606 S Illinois Rt 2 PO Box 1000.........Oregon IL 61061	800-319-6637	815-732-2141	273
Woods Rogers PLC			
10 S Jefferson St Ste 1400 ....Roanoke VA 24011	800-552-4529	540-983-7600	427
Woods, The			
Mountain Lake Rd PO Box 5.. Hedgesville WV 25427	800-248-2222	304-754-7977	665
Woodshop News			
10 Bokum Rd ....Essex CT 06426	800-444-7686	860-767-8227	455-14
Woodsmith Magazine			
2200 Grand Ave ....Des Moines IA 50312	800-333-5075*		455-14
*Cust Svc			
Woodson & Bozeman Inc			
3870 New Getwell Rd ....Memphis TN 38118	800-876-4243	901-362-1500	38
Woodstock Inn & Resort			
14 The Green ....Woodstock VT 05091	800-448-7900	802-332-6853	665
Woodstream Corp			
69 N Locust St ....Lititz PA 17543	800-800-1819*	717-626-2125	280
*All			
Woodsville Guaranty Savings Bank			
10 Pleasant St PO Box 266........Woodsville NH 03785	800-564-2735	603-747-2735	70
Woodward Communications Inc			
801 Bluff St ....Dubuque IA 52001	800-553-4801		641
Woodward Resource Ctr			
1251 334th St ....Woodward IA 50276	888-229-9223	515-438-2600	230
Woodway USA			
W229 N591 Foster Ct ....Waukesha WI 53186	800-966-3929	262-548-6235	267
Woody Bogler Trucking Co			
PO Box 229 ....Rosebud MO 63091	800-899-4120	573-764-3700	775
Woolaroc Ranch Museum & Wildlife Preserve			
1925 Woolaroc Ranch Rd ....Bartlesville OK 74003	888-966-5276	918-336-0307	517
Woolrich Inc			
2 Mill St ....Woolrich PA 17779	800-995-1299	570-769-6464	155-5
Woolverton Printing Co			
6714 Chancellor Dr ....Cedar Falls IA 50613	800-670-7713	319-277-2616	623
Wooster Area Chamber of Commerce			
377 W Liberty St ....Wooster OH 44691	800-414-1103	330-262-5735	139
Wooster Brush Co			
604 Madison Ave ....Wooster OH 44691	800-392-7246	330-264-4440	103
Wooster Products Inc			
1000 Spruce St PO Box 6005..........Wooster OH 44691	800-321-4936	330-264-2844	489
Worcester County			
1 W Market St Rm 1103 ....Snow Hill MD 21863	800-852-0335	410-632-1194	337
Worcester Envelope Co			
22 Millbury St ....Auburn MA 01501	800-343-1398		263
Worcester Skilled Care Ctr			
59 Acton St ....Worcester MA 01604	800-946-4283	508-791-3147	448
Word Among Us Inc			
9639 Doctor Perry Rd ....Ijamsville MD 21754	800-775-9673	301-874-1700	95
Worden Bros Inc			
4905 Pine Cone Dr ....Durham NC 27707	800-776-4940	919-408-0542	178-1

	Toll-Free	Phone	Class
Worden Company Inc 199 E 17th St . . . . .Holland MI 49423	800-748-0561	616-392-1848	319-3
Work 'n Gear Stores 2300 Crown Colony Dr Ste 300 . . . . .Quincy MA 02169	800-987-0218		157-5
Workers' Credit Union 815 Main St PO Box 900 . . . . .Fitchburg MA 01420	800-221-4020	978-345-1021	219
WorkersCompensationcom LLC PO Box 2432 .Sarasota FL 34230	866-927-2667	941-366-3791	392
Workforce Alliance Inc 1951 N Military Trl Ste D. . . . . .West Palm Beach FL 33409	800-204-2418	561-340-1060	260
Workincom Inc 2255 Green Vista Dr Ste 402 . . . . .Sparks NV 89431	800-774-8671	775-336-3366	260
Working Machines Corp 2170 Dwight Way . . . . .Berkeley CA 94704	877-648-4808	510-704-1100	180
Working Solutions 1820 Preston Pk Blvd Ste 2000 . . . . .Plano TX 75093	866-857-4800	972-964-4800	732
Worklife Balance com 7742 Spalding Dr Ste 356 . . . . .Atlanta GA 30092	877-644-0064	770-997-7881	461
Workman Publishing 225 Varick St . . . . .New York NY 10014	800-722-7202	212-254-5900	633-2
Workplace Answers LLC 3701 Executive Ctr Dr Ste 201 . . . . .Austin TX 78731	866-861-4410		400
Workplace Law Report 1801 S Bell St . . . . .Arlington VA 22202	800-372-1033		527-7
Workplace Resource LLC 4400 NE Loop 410 Ste 130. . . . . . . .San Antonio TX 78218	800-580-3000	512-472-7300	321
Workplace Systems Inc 562 Mammoth Rd . . . . .Londonderry NH 03053	800-258-9700	603-622-3727	319-1
Works Computing Inc 1801 American Blvd E Ste 12 . . . . . .Bloomington MN 55425	866-222-4077	952-746-1580	173-3
Workshare 208 Utah St Ste 350 . . . . .San Francisco CA 94103	888-404-4246	415-590-7700	177
Worksman Trading Corp 94-15 100th St . . . . .Ozone Park NY 11416	800-962-2453	718-322-2000	82
Worksoft Inc 15851 Dallas Pkwy Ste 855 . . . . .Addison TX 75001	866-836-1773	214-239-0400	178-10
Workspace com Inc 10451 Mill Run Cir Ste 400 . . . . . . .Owings Mills MD 21117	888-245-9168		521
Worktank Enterprises LLC 400 E Pine St Ste 301 . . . . .Seattle WA 98122	877-975-8265		
World Agricultural Outlook Board 1400 Independence Ave SW . . . . . . .Washington DC 20250	800-949-3964	202-720-6030	339-1
World Animal Protection 450 Seventh Ave 31st Fl . . . . .New York NY 10123	800-883-9772	646-783-2200	48-3
World Bank Group, The (WBG) 1818 H St NW . . . . .Washington DC 20433	800-645-7247	202-473-1000	778
World Book Inc 180 N LaSalle St Ste 900 . . . . .Chicago IL 60601	800-967-5325	312-729-5800	633-2
World Cat 1090 W St James St . . . . .Tarboro NC 27886	866-485-8899		90
World Chamber of Commerce Directory Inc 446 E 29th St Ste 1029. . . . . .Loveland CO 80538	888-883-3231	970-663-3231	633-6
World Class Lighting 14350 60th St N . . . . .Clearwater FL 33760	877-499-6753	727-524-7661	361
World Class Plastics Inc 7695 SR- 708 . . . . .Russells Point OH 43348	800-954-3140	937-843-4927	604
World Concern 19303 Fremont Ave N . . . . .Seattle WA 98133	800-755-5022	206-546-7201	48-5
World Currency USA Inc 16 W Main St Ste C . . . . .Marlton NJ 08053	888-593-7927		687
World Data Products Inc 1105 Xenium Ln N Ste 200. . . . . .Plymouth MN 55441	888-210-7636		176
World Dryer Corp 5700 McDermott Dr . . . . .Berkeley IL 60163	800-323-0701	708-449-6950	37
World Electronics Sales & Service Inc 3000 Kutztown Rd . . . . .Reading PA 19605	800-523-0427	610-939-9800	253
World Emblem International Inc 1500 NE 131 St . . . . .Miami FL 33161	800-766-0448		
World Floor Covering Assn (WFCA) 2211 Howell Ave . . . . .Anaheim CA 92806	800-624-6880	714-978-6440	49-4
World Food Program USA (WFP) 1725 Eye St NW Ste 510. . . . . .Washington DC 20006	888-454-0555	202-627-3737	48-5
World Fuel Services Corp 9800 NW 41st St Ste 400 . . . . .Miami FL 33178 *NYSE: INT*	800-345-3818	305-428-8000	575
World Health 7222 Edgemont Blvd NW . . . . .Calgary AB T3A2X7	866-278-4131	403-239-4048	353
World Hunger Year Inc (WHY) 505 Eigth Ave Ste 2100 . . . . .New York NY 10018	800-548-6479	212-629-8850	48-5
World Kitchen LLC 1200 S Antrim Way . . . . .Greencastle PA 17225	800-999-3436		360
World Learning 1 Kipling Rd PO Box 676 . . . . .Brattleboro VT 05302	800-257-7751	802-257-7751	48-5
World Learning International Development Programs 1015 15th St NW 7th Fl . . . . .Washington DC 20005	800-345-2929	202-408-5420	48-11
World Literature Crusade 640 Chapel Hills Dr . . . . .Colorado Springs CO 80920	800-423-5054	719-260-8888	48-20
World Micro Components Inc 205 Hembree Park Dr Ste 105 . . . . .Roswell GA 30076	800-400-5026	770-698-1900	246
World Music Supply 2414 W Seventh St . . . . .Muncie IN 47302	800-867-4611	765-213-6085	522
World Neighbors Inc (WN) 4127 NW 122nd St . . . . .Oklahoma City OK 73120	800-242-6387	405-752-9700	48-5
World Nutrition Inc 9449 N 90th St Ste 116 . . . . .Scottsdale AZ 85258	800-548-2710		
World of Coca-Cola Atlanta 121 Baker St NW . . . . .Atlanta GA 30313	888-855-5701	404-676-5151	517
World Policy Institute (WPI) 220 Fifth Ave 9th Fl . . . . .New York NY 10001	800-207-8354	212-481-5005	630
World Publishing Co 315 S Boulder Ave . . . . .Tulsa OK 74103	800-444-6552	918-583-2161	633-8
World Relief 7 E Baltimore St . . . . .Baltimore MD 21202	800-535-5433	443-451-1900	48-5
World Spice Inc 223 E Highland Pkwy . . . . .Roselle NJ 07203	800-234-1060		296-37
World Travel Holdings (WTH) 100 Fordham Rd Bldg C . . . . .Wilmington MA 01887	877-958-7447	617-424-7990	766
World Travel Services LLC 7645 E 63rd St Ste 101. . . . . .Tulsa OK 74133	800-324-4987	918-743-8856	767
World Vision Inc 34834 Weyerhaeuser Way S PO Box 9716. . . . . .Federal Way WA 98001	888-511-6548	800-777-5777	48-5
World Wide Concessions Inc 1950 Old Cuthbert Rd Ste M. . . . . .Cherry Hill NJ 08034	888-377-7666	856-933-9900	697
World Wide Fittings Inc 7501 N Natchez Ave . . . . .Niles IL 60714	800-393-9894	847-588-2200	591
World Wide Group LLC 5507 Nesconset Hwy Ste 10. . . . . . . .Mount Sanai NY 11766	800-790-4519		148
World Wildlife Fund (WWF) 1250 24th St NW PO Box 97180 . . . . . .Washington DC 20090	800-225-5993	202-293-4800	48-3
World Wildlife Fund Canada (WWF) 410 Adelaide St W Ste 400 . . . . .Toronto ON M5V1S8	800-267-2632	416-489-8800	48-3
World's Best 1801 W Waco Dr . . . . .Waco TX 76707	800-437-0940	254-753-7301	155-3
World's Finest Chocolate Inc 4801 S Lawndale . . . . .Chicago IL 60632	888-821-8452		296-8
World*Class Learning Materials PO Box 639 . . . . .Candler NC 28715	800-638-6470		243
World, The 403 US Rt 302-Berlin . . . . .Barre VT 05641	800-639-9753	802-479-2582	528-4
Worldata 3000 N Military Trl . . . . .Boca Raton FL 33431	800-331-8102	561-393-8200	6
WorldatWork 14040 N Northsight Blvd . . . . .Scottsdale AZ 85260	877-951-9191		49-12
WorldClass Travel Network 7831 Southtown Ctr Ste A . . . . .Bloomington MN 55431	800-234-3576	952-835-8636	767
Worldly Voices PO Box 218435 . . . . .Nashville TN 37221	800-286-4237	615-321-8802	653
WorldMark the Club 9805 Willows Rd . . . . .Redmond WA 98052	800-565-0370		748
WORLDPAC Inc 37137 Hickory St . . . . .Newark CA 94560	800-888-9982		61
WorldPantrycom Inc 790 Tennessee St . . . . .San Francisco CA 94107	866-972-6879		392
Worlds of Fun & Oceans of Fun 4545 NE Worlds of Fun Dr . . . . .Kansas City MO 64161	800-434-7894	816-454-4545	32
Worldscom Inc 11 Royal Rd . . . . .Brookline MA 02445	800-315-2580	617-725-8900	178-8
WorldStrides 218 W Water St Ste 400 . . . . .Charlottesville VA 22902 *General	800-999-7676*		755
WorldTEK Event & Travel Management 100 Beard Sawmill Rd Ste 601 . . . . .Shelton CT 06484	800-233-5989	203-772-0470	767
Worldview Travel 101 W Fourth St Ste 400 . . . . .Santa Ana CA 92701	800-627-8726	714-540-7400	
Worldwatch Institute 1776 Massachusetts Ave NW . . . . . . .Washington DC 20036	877-539-9946	202-452-1999	630
Worldwide Court Reporters 3000 Weslayan St Ste 235 . . . . .Houston TX 77027	800-745-1101		392
Worldwide Employee Benefits Network Inc (WEB) 11520 N Central Expy Ste 201 . . . . .Dallas TX 75243	888-795-6862		49-12
Worldwide Express 2323 Victory Ave Ste 1600 . . . . .Dallas TX 75219	800-758-7447		542
Worldwide Golf Shops 1421 Village Way . . . . .Santa Ana CA 92705	888-216-5252	714-972-3695	706
Worldwide Sign Systems 446 N Cecil St . . . . .Bonduel WI 54107	800-874-3334		697
Worldwide Steel Buildings PO Box 588 . . . . .Peculiar MO 64078	800-825-0316		105
Worley & Obetz Inc 85 White Oak Rd PO Box 429. . . . . .Manheim PA 17545	800-697-6891	717-665-6891	316
Wormser Corp 150 Coolidge Ave . . . . .Englewood NJ 07631	800-546-4040	800-666-9676	155-14
Wormsloe State Historic Site 7601 Skidaway Rd . . . . .Savannah GA 31406	800-864-7275	912-353-3023	561
Worrell Corp 305 S Post Rd . . . . .Indianapolis IN 46219	800-297-9599		292
Worship Network PO Box 428 . . . . .Safety Harbor FL 34695	800-728-8723		735
Wort Hotel 50 N Glenwood . . . . .Jackson WY 83001 *Cust Svc	800-322-2727*	307-733-2190	378
Worth & Company Inc 6263 Kellers Church Rd . . . . .Pipersville PA 18947	800-220-5130	267-362-1100	189-10
Worth Co, The 214 Sherman Ave PO Box 88 . . . . . .Stevens Point WI 54481	800-944-1899	715-344-6081	706
Worth Higgins & Assoc Inc 8770 Park Central Dr . . . . .Richmond VA 23227	800-883-7768	804-264-2304	174
Worthington Biochemical Corp 730 Vassar Ave . . . . .Lakewood NJ 08701	800-445-9603	732-942-1660	231
Worthington Direct Holdings LLC 6301 Gaston Ave Ste 670 . . . . .Dallas TX 75214	800-599-6636		359-3
Worthington Industries 200 Old Wilson Bridge Rd . . . . .Columbus OH 43085 *NYSE: WOR*	800-944-2255	614-438-3210	483
Worthington Steel Co 200 W Old Wilson Bridge Rd . . . . .Columbus OH 43085	800-944-3733	614-438-3210	719
Worx Group LLC, The 18 Waterbury Rd . . . . .Prospect CT 06712	800-732-8090	203-758-3311	180
WOUC-TV Ch 44 (PBS) 35 S College St . . . . .Athens OH 45701	800-456-2044	740-593-1771	736
Wound Ostomy & Continence Nurses Society (WOCN) 1120 Rt 73 Ste 200. . . . . .Mount Laurel NJ 08054	888-224-9626		49-8
WOW (Wider Opportunities for Women) 1001 Connecticut Ave NW Ste 930 . . . . .Washington DC 20036	800-260-5956	202-464-1596	48-24
WOWK-TV Ch 13 (CBS) 555 Fifth Ave . . . . .Huntington WV 25701	800-333-7636	304-525-1313	736
WOWO-AM 1190 (N/T) 2915 Maples Rd . . . . .Fort Wayne IN 46816	800-333-1190	260-447-5511	641-39
Wozniak Industries Inc Commercial Forged Products Div 5757 W 65th St . . . . .Bedford Park IL 60638	800-637-2695	708-458-1220	481
WP (Walton Press) 402 Mayfield Dr . . . . .Monroe GA 30655	800-354-0235	770-267-2596	551

	Toll-Free	Phone	Class
WP Carey & Company LLC			
50 Rockefeller Plz ....New York NY 10020	800-972-2739	212-492-1100	651
NYSE: WPC			
WPBT-TV Ch 2 (PBS)			
14901 NE 20th Ave ....Miami FL 33181	800-222-9728	305-949-8321	736-44
WPCV-FM 975 (Ctry)			
404 W Lime St ....Lakeland FL 33815	800-227-9797	863-682-8184	641
WPGC-FM 955			
1015 Half St SE Ste 200 .....Washington DC 20003	877-955-5267		641
WPI (World Policy Institute)			
220 Fifth Ave 9th Fl ....New York NY 10001	800-207-8354	212-481-5005	630
WPLM-FM 991			
17 Columbus Rd ....Plymouth MA 02360	877-327-9991	508-746-1390	641
WPLN-FM 903 (NPR)			
630 Mainstream Dr ....Nashville TN 37228	877-760-2903	615-760-2903	641-69
WPNE-FM 893 (NPR)			
2420 Nicolet Dr ....Green Bay WI 54311	800-654-6228	920-465-2444	641-42
WPPX-TV Ch 61			
3901 B Main St Ste 301 ......Philadelphia PA 19127	888-467-2988		
WPR (Wisconsin Public Radio)			
821 University Ave ....Madison WI 53706	800-747-7444		628
WPRO-FM 923 (CHR)			
1502 Wampanoag Trl .....East Providence RI 02915	800-638-0092	401-433-4200	641
WPST-FM 945 (AC)			
619 Alexander Rd 3rd Fl ....Princeton NJ 08540	800-248-9778	609-419-0300	641
WPT (Wisconsin Public Television)			
821 University Ave ....Madison WI 53706	800-422-9707	608-263-2121	628
WPTD-TV Ch 16 (PBS)			
110 S Jefferson St ....Dayton OH 45402	800-247-1614	937-220-1600	736-22
WPX Delivery Solutions			
3320 W Valley Hwy N Ste 111 ......Auburn WA 98001	800-562-1091	253-876-2760	542
WPXD-TV Ch 31 (I)			
26935 W 11 Mile Rd ....Southfield MI 48033	888-467-2988	212-757-3100	736
WPXN-TV Ch 31 (I)			
810 Seventh Ave 30th Fl........New York NY 10019	888-467-2988	212-757-3100	736-51
WPXW			
6199 Old Arrington Ln ....Fairfax Station VA 22039	888-467-2988		
WQBE-FM 975 (Ctry)			
817 Suncrest Pl ....Charleston WV 25303	800-222-3697	304-344-9700	641-21
WQED Multimedia			
4802 Fifth Ave ....Pittsburgh PA 15213	855-700-9733	412-622-1300	736-57
WQED-FM 893 (Clas)			
4802 Fifth Ave ....Pittsburgh PA 15213	855-700-9733	412-622-1300	641-83
WQFL-FM 1009 (Rel)			
PO Box 2118 ....Omaha NE 68103	888-937-2471		641
WQHT-FM 971 (Urban)			
395 Hudson St 7th Fl ....New York NY 10014	800-223-9797	212-229-9797	641-71
WQLN-FM 913 (NPR)			
8425 Peach St ....Erie PA 16509	800-727-8854	814-864-3001	641-35
WQLN-TV Ch 54 (PBS)			
8425 Peach St ....Erie PA 16509	800-727-8854	814-864-3001	736-27
WQOK K975			
8001 Creedmoor Rd Ste 101 ....Raleigh NC 27613	800-321-5975	919-848-9736	
WR Berkley Corp			
475 Steamboat Rd ....Greenwich CT 06830	800-238-6225	203-629-3000	359-4
NYSE: WRB			
WR Case & Sons Cutlery Co			
50 Owens Way PO Box 4000 ....Bradford PA 16701	800-523-6350		222
WR Grace & Co			
7500 Grace Dr ....Columbia MD 21044	800-638-6014	410-531-4000	145
NYSE: GRA			
WR Hambrecht & Co			
909 Montgomery St 3rd Fl ....San Francisco CA 94133	855-753-6484*	415-551-8600	686
Cust Svc			
Wragtime Air Freight Inc			
596 W 135th St ....Gardena CA 90248	800-586-9701		775
Wrangell Harbor			
PO Box 531 ....Wrangell AK 99929	800-347-4462	907-874-3736	614
Wrap-On Company LLC			
11756 S Austin Ave ....Alsip IL 60803	800-621-6947	708-496-2150	808
WRAZ FOX 50			
2619 Western Blvd ....Raleigh NC 27606	877-369-5050	919-595-5050	736-60
WRBS-FM 951 (Rel)			
3500 Commerce Dr ....Baltimore MD 21227	800-965-9324	410-247-4100	641-10
WREA (White River Electric Assn)			
PO Box 958 ....Meeker CO 81641	800-922-1987	970-878-5041	245
Wren Assoc Ltd			
124 Wren Pkwy ....Jefferson City MO 65109	800-881-2249	573-893-2249	604
Wright & Lato			
2100 Felver Ct ....Rahway NJ 07065	800-724-1855	973-674-8700	408
Wright Business Graphics (WBG)			
18440 NE San Rafael St ....Portland OR 97230	800-547-8397		110
Wright Express Corp			
97 Darling Ave ....South Portland ME 04106	800-761-7181	207-773-8171	215
NYSE: WEX			
Wright Global Graphics			
5115 Prospect St ....Thomasville NC 27360	800-678-9019	336-472-4200	412
Wright Group, The			
6428 Airport Rd ....Crowley LA 70526	800-201-3096	337-783-3096	578
Wright Implement Company LLC			
3225 Carter Rd ....Owensboro KY 42301	800-252-3904	270-683-3606	111
Wright Investors' Service			
440 Wheelers Farms Rd ....Milford CT 06461	800-232-0013		400
Wright Line LLC			
160 Gold Star Blvd ....Worcester MA 01606	800-225-7348	508-852-4300	319-1
Wright Medical Group Inc			
1023 Cherry Rd ....Memphis TN 38117	800-238-7117	901-867-9971	475
NASDAQ: WMGI			
Wright Medical Technology Inc			
5677 Airline Rd ....Arlington TN 38002	800-238-7117	901-867-9971	475
Wright State University			
3640 Colonel Glenn Hwy ....Dayton OH 45435	800-247-1770*	937-775-5740	166
Admissions			
Wright State University Lake			
7600 Lake Campus Dr ....Celina OH 45822	800-237-1477	419-586-0300	162
Wright Tool Co			
1 Wright Dr PO Box 512 ....Barberton OH 44203	800-321-2902	330-848-0600	349
Wright Transportation Inc			
2333 Dauphin Island Pkwy ....Mobile AL 36605	800-342-4598	251-432-6390	775
Wright's Media			
2407 Timberloch Pl Ste B.........The Woodlands TX 77380	877-652-5295		633-9
Wright-Hennepin Co-op Electric Assn			
6800 Electric Dr PO Box 330 ....Rockford MN 55373	800-943-2667	763-477-3000	245
Wright-Patt Credit Union Inc			
2455 Executive Pk Blvd			
PO Box 286.......................Fairborn OH 45324	800-762-0047	937-912-7000	219
Wright-Patterson Air Force Base			
5030 Patterson Pkwy			
...................Wright-Patterson AFB OH 45433	800-225-5288	937-257-1110	495-1
Wright-Pierce			
11 Bowdoin Mill Is Ste 140 ....Topsham ME 04086	888-621-8156	207-725-8721	261
Wrightsoft Corp			
131 Hartwell Ave ....Lexington MA 02421	800-225-8697		225
Wrisco Industries Inc			
355 Hiatt Dr Ste B..........Palm Beach Gardens FL 33418	800-627-2646	561-626-5700	490
WRIT (Washington Real Estate Investment Trust)			
1775 I St NW ....Washington DC 20006	800-565-9748	202-774-3200	651
NYSE: WRE			
Writer's Digest			
4700 E Galbraith Rd ....Cincinnati OH 45236	800-283-0963*	513-531-2690	455-21
Cust Svc			
Writer's Digest Shop			
4700 E Galbraith Rd ....Cincinnati OH 45236	800-759-0963*	513-531-2690	93
Cust Svc			
WRKF-FM 893 (NPR)			
3050 Vly Creek Dr ....Baton Rouge LA 70808	855-893-9753	225-926-3050	641-12
WRNR-FM 1031			
179 Admiral Cochrane Dr ....Annapolis MD 21401	877-762-1031	410-626-0103	641-8
WROQ-FM 1011 (CR)			
25 Garlington Rd ....Greenville SC 29615	888-257-0058	864-271-9200	641-43
Wrought Washer Manufacturing Inc			
2100 S Bay St ....Milwaukee WI 53207	800-558-5217	414-744-0771	481
WRQN-FM 935 (Oldies)			
3225 Arlington Ave ....Toledo OH 43614	866-240-1935	419-725-5700	641-110
WRTI-FM 901 (NPR)			
1509 Cecil B Moore Ave			
3rd Fl ....Philadelphia PA 19121	866-809-9784	215-204-8405	641-80
WRVM-FM 1027 (Rel)			
PO Box 212 ....Suring WI 54174	888-225-9786	920-842-2900	641
WS Badcock Corp (WSBC)			
PO Box 497 ....Mulberry FL 33860	800 223 2625		321
WS Emerson Co Inc			
15 Acme Rd ....Brewer ME 04412	800-789-6120	207-989-3410	156
WS Hampshire Inc			
365 Keyes Ave ....Hampshire IL 60140	800-541-0251	847-683-4400	720
WS Packaging Group Inc			
2571 S Hemlock Rd ....Green Bay WI 54229	800-236-3424	800-818-5481	412
WSBC (WS Badcock Corp)			
PO Box 497 ....Mulberry FL 33860	800-223-2625		321
WSBT-TV Ch 22 (CBS)			
1301 E Douglas Rd ....Mishawaka IN 46545	877-634-7181	574-232-6397	736
WSCI-FM 893 (NPR)			
1041 George Rogers Blvd ....Columbia SC 29201	800-922-5437	803-737-3200	641
WSEE-TV Ch 35 (CBS)			
3514 State St ....Erie PA 16508	866-571-4553	814-454-5201	736-27
WSF Industries Inc			
7 Hackett Dr ....Tonawanda NY 14150	800-874-8265	716-692-4930	478
WSFS Financial Corp			
500 Delaware Ave ....Wilmington DE 19801	888-973-7226	302-792-6000	359-2
NASDAQ: WSFS			
WSGL-FM 1047 (AC)			
10915 K-Nine Dr ....Bonita Springs FL 34135	888-725-2345	239-495-8383	641
WSHA-FM 889 (Jazz)			
118 E S St ....Raleigh NC 27601	800-241-0421	919-546-8430	641-85
WSHU 5151 Park Ave			
...................................Fairfield CT 06825	800-937-6045	203-365-6604	641
WSI			
20 Carlson Ct Ste 100 ....Mississauga ON M9W7K6	888-678-7588	905-678-7588	310
WSKY 1230 AM			
292 S Pine St PO Box 444 ....Spartanburg SC 29302	888-989-2299		641-100
WSLQ-FM 991 (AC)			
3934 Electric Rd SW ....Roanoke VA 24018	800-410-9936	540-387-0234	641-90
WSNA (Washington State Nurses Assn)			
575 Andover Pk W Ste 101...........Seattle WA 98188	800-231-8482	206-575-7979	529
WSOC-TV Ch 9 (ABC)			
1901 N Tryon St ....Charlotte NC 28206	855-336-0360	704-338-9999	736-16
WSOS Community Action Commission Inc			
109 S Front St ....Fremont OH 43420	800-775-9767	419-334-8911	8
WSPA-TV Ch 7 (CBS)			
250 International Dr ....Spartanburg SC 29303	866-946-6349	864-576-7777	736-3
WSRE-TV Ch 23 (PBS)			
1000 College Blvd ....Pensacola FL 32504	800-239-9773	850-484-1200	736
WSSA (Wine & Spirits Shippers Assn Inc)			
11800 Sunrise Vly Dr ....Reston VA 20191	800-368-3167*		49-6
General			
WSTW-FM 937 (CHR)			
2727 Shipley Rd ....Wilmington DE 19810	800-544-9370	302-478-2700	641-116
Davis			
2750 University Park Blvd ....Layton UT 84041	800-848-7770	801-395-3555	166
WSUN-FM 971 (Alt)			
11300 Fourth St N			
Ste 300 ....Saint Petersburg FL 33716	877-327-9797	727-579-2000	641-108
WSVH 911 FM			
13040 Abercorn St Ste 8............Savannah GA 31419	877-472-1227	912-344-3565	641-97
WSYR-AM 570 (N/T)			
500 Plum St Ste 400................Syracuse NY 13204	844-289-7234	315-472-9797	641-106
WTB Financial Corp			
PO Box 2127 ....Spokane WA 99210	800-788-4578		359-2
WTBY-TV Ch 54 (TBN)			
111 E 15th St ....New York NY 10003	800-201-5200	714-731-1000	736-51
WTFM-FM 985 (AC)			
222 Commerce St ....Kingsport TN 37660	888-633-5452	423-246-9578	641
WTH (World Travel Holdings)			
100 Fordham Rd Bldg C ....Wilmington MA 01887	877-958-7447	617-424-7990	766
WTP Inc PO Box 937 ....Coloma MI 49038	800-521-0731	269-468-3399	727
WTSU-FM 899			
Troy University Wallace Hall ....Troy AL 36082	800-800-6616		641
WTTS-FM 923 (AAA)			
400 One City Centre ....Bloomington IN 47404	800-923-9887	812-332-3366	641

				Toll-Free	Phone	Class
WTVN-AM 610 (N/T)						
2323 W Fifth Ave Ste 200	Columbus	OH	43221	**844-289-7234**		641-28
WTVP-TV Ch 47 (PBS)						
101 State St	Peoria	IL	61602	**800-837-4747**	309-677-4747	736-54
WTVT-TV Ch 13 (Fox)						
3213 W Kennedy Blvd	Tampa	FL	33609	**800-334-9888**	813-876-1313	736-77
WTXF-TV Ch 29 (Fox)						
330 Market St	Philadelphia	PA	19106	**800-220-6397**	215-925-2929	736-55
WUAL-FM 915 (NPR)						
920 Paul W Bryant Dr						
PO Box 870370	Tuscaloosa	AL	35487	**800-654-4262**	205-348-8620	641-113
Wulftec International Inc						
209 Wulftec St	Ayer's Cliff	QC	J0B1C0	**877-985-3832**	819-838-4232	543
WUMB-FM 919 (Folk)						
100 Morrissey Blvd	Boston	MA	02125	**800-573-2100**	617-287-6900	641-16
WUNC-FM 915 (NPR)						
120 Friday Center Dr	Chapel Hill	NC	27517	**800-962-9862**	919-445-9150	641
WUOM-FM 917 (NPR)						
535 W William St Ste 110	Ann Arbor	MI	48103	**888-258-9866**	734-764-9210	641-7
WUOT-FM 919 (NPR)						
209 Communications Bldg						
University of Tennessee	Knoxville	TN	37996	**888-266-9868**	865-974-5375	641-54
Wurth						
1640 Mims Ave SW	Birmingham	AL	35211	**800-272-6486**	205-925-7601	609
Wurth Revcar Fasteners Inc						
3845 Thirlane Rd	Roanoke	VA	24019	**800-542-5762**		350
Wurth USA Inc						
93 Grant St	Ramsey	NJ	07446	**800-987-8487**	201-825-2710	61
WUSF						
4202 E Fowler Ave TVB 100	Tampa	FL	33620	**800-741-9090**	813-974-8700	641-108
WUSF Public Broadcasting						
4202 E Fowler Ave TVB100	Tampa	FL	33620	**800-741-9090**	813-974-8700	641-9
WUSF-TV Ch 16 (PBS)						
4202 E Fowler Ave	Tampa	FL	33620	**800-654-3703**	813-974-4000	736-77
WUWF-FM 881 (NPR)						
11000 University Pkwy	Pensacola	FL	32514	**800-239-9893**	850-474-2787	641-78
WVCY-TV Ch 30 (Ind)						
3434 W Kilbourn Ave	Milwaukee	WI	53208	**800-729-9829**	414-935-3000	736-45
WVES (Virginia West Electric Supply Co)						
250 12-th St W	Huntington	WV	25704	**800-624-3433**	304-525-0361	246
Housing Development Fund						
5710 MacCorkle Ave SE	Charleston	WV	25304	**800-933-9843**	304-391-8600	338-49
WVMA (Wisconsin Veterinary Medical Assn)						
2801 Crossroads Dr Ste 1200	Madison	WI	53718	**888-254-5202**	608-257-3665	790
WVMA (Wyoming Veterinary Medical Assn)						
2001 Capitol Ave	Cheyenne	WY	82001	**800-272-1813**		790
WVNA (West Virginia Nurses Assn)						
PO Box 1946	Charleston	WV	25327	**800-400-1226**	304-417-1497	529
WVOM-FM 1039 (N/T)						
184 Target Industrial Cir	Bangor	ME	04401	**800-966-1039**	207-947-9100	641-11
WVPE-FM 881 (NPR)						
2424 California Rd	Elkhart	IN	46514	**888-399-9873**	574-674-9873	641
WVPS-FM 1079 (NPR)						
365 Troy Ave	Colchester	VT	05446	**800-639-2192**	802-655-9451	641
WVTF-FM 891 (NPR)						
3520 Kingsbury Ln	Roanoke	VA	24014	**800-856-8900**	540-989-8900	641-90
WVTM-TV Ch 13 (NBC)						
1732 Valley View Dr	Birmingham	AL	35209	**844-248-7698**	205-933-1313	736-10
WW Grainger Inc						
100 Grainger Pkwy	Lake Forest	IL	60045	**888-361-8649**	847-535-1000	246
NYSE: GWW						
WW Norton & Company Inc						
500 Fifth Ave	New York	NY	10110	**800-233-4830**	212-354-5500	633-2
WWF (World Wildlife Fund Canada)						
410 Adelaide St W Ste 400	Toronto	ON	M5V1S8	**800-267-2632**	416-489-8800	48-3
WWF (World Wildlife Fund)						
1250 24th St NW PO Box 97180	Washington	DC	20090	**800-225-5993**	202-293-4800	48-3
WWKA-FM 923 (Ctry)						
4192 N John Young Pkwy	Orlando	FL	32804	**866-438-0220**	407-424-9236	641-75
WWMT-TV Ch 3 (CBS)						
590 W Maple St	Kalamazoo	MI	49008	**800-875-3333**		736
WWNO-FM 899 (NPR)						
University of New Orleans						
2000 Lakeshore Dr	New Orleans	LA	70148	**800-286-7002**	504-280-7000	641-70
WXCY-FM 1037						
707 Revolution St	Havre de Grace	MD	21078	**800-788-9929**	410-939-1100	641
WXEL-FM 907 (NPR)						
3401 S Congress Ave	Boynton Beach	FL	33426	**800-915-9935**	561-737-8000	641-115
WXEL-TV Ch 42 (PBS)						
PO Box 6607	West Palm Beach	FL	33405	**800-915-9935**	561-737-8000	736-83
WXGL-FM 1073 (AC)						
11300 Fourth St N						
Ste 300	Saint Petersburg	FL	33716	**800-242-1073**	727-579-2000	641-108
WXKR-FM 945 (CR)						
3225 Arlington Ave	Toledo	OH	43614	**866-240-9945**	419-725-5700	641-110
WXYZ-TV Ch 7 (ABC)						
20777 W 10-Mile Rd	Southfield	MI	48037	**800-825-0770**	248-827-7777	736
Wyatt Transfer Inc						
3035 Bells Rd PO Box 24326	Richmond	VA	23224	**800-552-5708**	804-743-3800	775
Wyatt-Quarles Seed Co						
730 US Hwy 70 W	Garner	NC	27529	**800-662-7591**	919-772-4243	274
Wycliffe Bible Translators						
11221 John Wycliffe Blvd	Orlando	FL	32832	**800-992-5433**	407-852-3600	48-20
Wyffels Hybrids Inc						
13344 US Hwy 6	Geneseo	IL	61254	**800-369-7833**	309-944-8334	10-4
WYFF-TV Ch 4 (NBC)						
505 Rutherford St	Greenville	SC	29609	**800-453-9933**	864-242-4404	736-3
Wylie Spray Center						
702 E 40th St	Lubbock	TX	79404	**888-249-5162**	806-763-1335	273
Wyndham Hotel Group						
Travelodge						
1910 Eigth Ave NE	Aberdeen	SD	57041	**800-525-4055***	605-229-8058	378
*Resv						
Wyndham Vacation Resorts						
6277 Sea Harbor Dr	Orlando	FL	32821	**800-251-8736**		378
Wyndham Lake Buena Vista						
1850 Hotel Plaza Blvd	Lake Buena Vista	FL	32830	**800-624-4109**	407-828-4444	378
Wyndham Vacation Rentals						
14 Sylvan Way	Parsippany	NJ	07054	**800-467-3529**		665
Wyndham Vacation Resorts King Cotton Villas						
1 King Cotton Rd	Edisto Beach	SC	29438	**800-251-8736**	843-869-2561	665
Wynne Transport Service Inc						
2222 N 11th St PO Box 8700	Omaha	NE	68110	**800-383-9330**	402-342-4001	775
Wyo-Ben Inc						
1345 Discovery Dr	Billings	MT	59102	**800-548-7055***	406-652-6351	501-2
*Cust Svc						
Wyoming						
Aging Div						
2300 Capitol Ave 4th Fl	Cheyenne	WY	82002	**800-442-2766**	307-777-7995	338-51
Business Council						
214 W 15th St	Cheyenne	WY	82002	**800-262-3425**	307-777-2800	338-51
Health Dept						
401 Hathaway Bldg	Cheyenne	WY	82002	**866-571-0944**	307-777-7656	338-51
Highway Patrol (WHP)						
5300 Bishop Blvd	Cheyenne	WY	82009	**800-442-9090**	307-777-4301	338-51
Insurance Dept						
106 E Sixth Ave	Cheyenne	WY	82001	**800-438-5768**	307-777-7401	338-51
Tourism Div						
5611 High Plains Rd	Cheyenne	WY	82007	**800-225-5996**	307-777-7777	338-51
Wyoming Assn of Realtors						
777 Overland Trl Ste 220	Casper	WY	82601	**800-676-4085**	307-237-4085	652
Wyoming County						
143 N Main St	Warsaw	NY	14569	**800-527-1757**	585-786-8810	337
Wyoming Medical Ctr						
1233 E Second St	Casper	WY	82601	**800-822-7201**	307-577-7201	373-3
Wyoming Public Television						
2660 Peck Ave	Riverton	WY	82501	**800-495-9788**	307-856-6944	628
Wyoming Seminary						
201 N Sprague Ave	Kingston	PA	18704	**800-325-3252**	570-270-2100	618
Wyoming State Bar						
4124 Laramie St	Cheyenne	WY	82001	**855-445-8058**	307-632-9061	72
Wyoming Tribune-Eagle						
702 W Lincolnway	Cheyenne	WY	82001	**800-561-6268**	307-634-3361	528-2
Wyoming Veterinary Medical Assn (WVMA)						
2001 Capitol Ave	Cheyenne	WY	82001	**800-272-1813**		790
WYOU-TV Ch 22 (CBS)						
62 S Franklin St	Wilkes-Barre	PA	18701	**855-241-5144**	570-961-2222	736
Wyrulec Co						
3978 US Hwy 26/85	Torrington	WY	82240	**800-628-5266**	307-837-2225	245
Wyse Meter Solutions Inc						
RPO Newmarket Ct PO Box 95530	Newmarket	ON	L3Y8J8	**866-681-9465**		392
WYSE Technology Inc						
3471 N First St	San Jose	CA	95134	**800-800-9973**	408-473-1200	173-2
Wysong Inc						
4820 US 29 N	Greensboro	NC	27405	**800-299-7664**	336-621-3960	454
Wyvern Consulting Ltd						
10 N Main St	Yardley	PA	19067	**800-946-4626**		689
WyzAnt Inc						
1714 N Damen Ave Ste 3N	Chicago	IL	60647	**877-999-2681**		386
WZBT-FM 911 (Alt)						
300 N Washington St						
Gettysburg College	Gettysburg	PA	17325	**800-431-0803**	717-337-6315	641
WZVN-TV Ch 26 (ABC)						
3719 Central Ave	Fort Myers	FL	33901	**888-232-8635**	239-939-2020	736-49
WZZK-FM 1047 (Ctry)						
2700 Corporate Dr Ste 115	Birmingham	AL	35242	**866-998-1047**	205-916-1100	641-14

X

				Toll-Free	Phone	Class
X1065						
8000 Belfort Pkwy	Jacksonville	FL	32256	**800-460-6394**	904-245-8500	641-51
Xactware Solutions Inc						
1100 W Traverse Pkwy	Lehi	UT	84043	**800-424-9228***	801-764-5900	178-11
*Sales						
Xamax Industries Inc						
63 Silvermine Rd	Seymour	CT	06483	**888-926-2988**	203-888-7200	553
Xante Corp						
2800 Dauphin St Ste 100	Mobile	AL	36606	**800-926-8839**	251-473-6502	173-6
Xantech						
1800 S McDowell Blvd	Petaluma	CA	94954	**800-472-5555***	707-283-5900	52
*Sales						
Xanterra Parks & Resorts						
6312 S Fiddlers Green Cir						
Ste 600-N	Greenwood Village	CO	80111	**800-236-7916**	303-600-3400	271
Xanterra South Rim LLC						
10 Albright St PO Box 699	Grand Canyon	AZ	86023	**800-843-8723**	928-638-2631	375
Xantrex Technology Inc						
3700 Gilmore Way	Burnaby	BC	V5G4M1	**800-670-0707**	604-422-8595	253
XAP Corp						
3534 Hayden Ave	Culver City	CA	90232	**800-468-6927**	310-842-9800	178-7
Xavier University						
3800 Victory Pkwy	Cincinnati	OH	45207	**800-344-4698**	513-745-3000	166
Xavier University Library						
3800 Victory Pkwy	Cincinnati	OH	45207	**888-468-4509**	513-745-3881	433-6
Xcel Energy Inc						
414 Nicollet Mall	Minneapolis	MN	55401	**800-328-8226**	612-330-5500	782
NYSE: XEL						
Xcel HR						
7361 Calhoun Pl Ste 600	Rockville	MD	20855	**800-776-0076**		260
X-Cel Optical Company Inc						
806 S Benton Dr	Sauk Rapids	MN	56379	**800-747-9235***	320-251-8404	538
*General						
Xcitex Inc						
25 First St Ste 105	Cambridge	MA	02141	**800-780-7836**		643
XEcom Inc						
1145 Nicholson Rd Ste 200	Newmarket	ON	L3Y9C3	**877-932-6640**	416-214-5606	225
Xerces Society, The						
628 NE Broadway Ste 200	Portland	OR	97232	**855-232-6639**		
Xeris Pharmaceuticals Inc						
180 N LaSalle St Ste 1810	Chicago	IL	60601	**844-445-5704**		231

	Toll-Free	Phone	Class
Xerox Corp 201 Merritt 7 .... Norwalk CT 06856 *NYSE: XRX*	800-327-9753	888-242-9098	585
Xerox Financial Services Inc 800 Long Ridge Rd .... Stamford CT 06904	800-275-9376	888-242-9098	216
Xerox Foundation 45 Glover Ave .... Norwalk CT 06856	800-275-9376		304
Xetus Corp 1325 Howard Ave Ste 527 .... Burlingame CA 94010	877-469-3887	650-237-1225	251
XF Enterprises Inc 500 S Taylor Ste 301 PO Box 229 .... Amarillo TX 79101	800-783-5616	806-367-5810	580
X-Gen Pharmaceuticals Inc 300 Daniels Zenker Dr .... Horseheads NY 14845	866-390-4411		579
Xilinx Inc 2100 Logic Dr .... San Jose CA 95124 *NASDAQ: XLNX*	800-594-5469	408-559-7778	692
Xiologix 8050 SW Warm Springs St Ste 100 .... Tualatin OR 97062	888-492-6843	503-691-4364	225
XIOtech Corp 9950 Federal Dr Ste 100. .... Colorado Springs CO 80921	866-472-6764	719-388-5500	178-12
XipLink Inc 4200 St Laurent Blvd Ste 1010 ...... Montreal QC H2W2R2	855-408-2483	514-848-9640	
XKS Unlimited Inc 850 Fiero Ln .... San Luis Obispo CA 93401	800-444-5247	805-544-7864	54
XL Brands 198 Nexus Dr .... Dalton GA 30721	800-367-4583	706-272-5800	145
Xlibris Corp 1663 Liberty Dr Ste 200 .... Bloomington IN 47403	888-795-4274		623
XLPrint USA LLC 213 Rose Ave Ste 1. .... Venice CA 90291	866-275-1290	310-829-7684	804
XO Communications Inc 13865 Sunrise Vly Dr .... Herndon VA 20171	866-349-0134	703-547-2000	731
XOJET Inc 2000 Sierra Point Pkwy .... Brisbane CA 94005	877-599-6538		
XP Power 990 Benicia Ave .... Sunnyvale CA 94085	800-253-0490	408-732-7777	246
Xplane Corp 811 SW Sixth Ave Ste 500 .... Portland OR 97204	855-548-4343		343
XPO Logistics Inc 6005 Perimeter Dr .... Dublin OH 43016	800-837-7584	614-923-1400	447
XpressBet LLC 200 Racetrack Rd Bldg 26. .... Washington PA 15301	866-889-7737		
Xs Sight Systems Inc 2401 Ludelle St .... Fort Worth TX 76105	888-744-4880	817-536-0136	707
XSYS Inc 653 Steele Dr .... Valparaiso IN 46385	888-810-9797		
Xtek Inc 11451 Reading Rd .... Cincinnati OH 45241	888-332-9835	513-733-7800	452
Xtel Communications Inc 401 Rt 73 n .... Marlton NJ 08053	800-438-9835	856-596-4000	386
XTO Energy Inc 810 Houston St .... Fort Worth TX 76102	800-299-2800	817-870-2800	532
XTRAC LLC 245 Summer St .... Boston MA 02210	855-975-3569		386
XtremeEDA Corp 200-25 Holland Ave .... Ottawa ON K1Y4R9	800-586-0280		
Xybernet Inc 10640 Scripps Ranch Blvd .... San Diego CA 92131 *Cust Svc	800-228-9026*	858-530-1900	178-10
Xyron Inc 15820 N 90th St Ste 6 .... Scottsdale AZ 85258	800-793-3523		483
XYZ Two Way Radio Inc 275 20th St .... Brooklyn NY 11215	800-535-3377	718-499-2007	440

Y

	Toll-Free	Phone	Class
Y101 FM KWYE-FM 1071 W Shaw Ave .... Fresno CA 93711	800-345-9101	559-490-5800	641-40
Y107 (KTXY-FM) 3215 Lemone Industrial Blvd Ste 200. .... Columbia MO 65201	800-500-1079	573-441-1079	641
Y-12 Federal Credit Union 501 Lafayette Dr .... Oak Ridge TN 37830	800-482-1043	865-482-1043	219
Y94 iHeartMedia 500 Plum St Ste 400. .... Syracuse NY 13204	844-289-7234	315-472-9797	641-106
Yachats Ocean Road State Natural Site 5580 S Coast Hwy .... Newport OR 97366	800-551-6949		561
Yachting Magazine 460 N Orlando Ave .... Winter Park FL 32789	800-999-0869		455-4
Yacktman Asset Management Co 6300 Bridgepoint Pkwy Bldg 1 Ste 320 .... Austin TX 78730	800-835-3879	512-767-6700	400
Yadkin County Chamber of Commerce 205 S Jackson St PO Box 1840. .... Yadkinville NC 27055	877-492-3546	336-679-2200	139
Yaffe Cos Inc, The 1200 S G St .... Muskogee OK 74403	800-759-2333	918-687-7543	682
Yager Museum of Art & Culture, The Hartwick College PO Box 4022. .... Oneonta NY 13820	888-427-8942	607-431-4000	
Yak PO Box 71055 Laurier W PO .... Ottawa ON K2P2L9	877-925-4925		731
Yakima Bait Company Inc PO Box 310 .... Granger WA 98932	800-527-2711	509-854-1311	706
Yakima Convention Ctr 10 N Eigth St .... Yakima WA 98901	800-221-0751	509-575-6062	205
Yakima County 128 N Second St Rm 323 .... Yakima WA 98901	800-572-7354	509-574-1430	337
Yakima Federal Savings & Loan Assn 118 E Yakima Ave .... Yakima WA 98901	800-331-3225	509-248-2634	70

	Toll-Free	Phone	Class
Yakima Herald-Republic PO Box 9668 .... Yakima WA 98909	800-343-2799	509-248-1251	528-2
Yale Appliance 296 Freeport St .... Dorchester MA 02122	800-565-6435	617-825-9253	35
Yale Divinity School Admissions Office 409 Prospect St .... New Haven CT 06511	877-725-3334	203-432-5360	167-3
Yale Residential Security Products Inc 100 Yale Ave .... Lenoir City TN 37771	800-438-1951		349
Yale Security Inc 1902 Airport Rd .... Monroe NC 28110	800-438-1951		349
YALSA (Young Adult Library Services Assn) 50 E Huron St .... Chicago IL 60611	800-545-2433	312-280-4390	49-11
Yamada Enterprises 16552 Burke Ln .... Huntington Beach CA 92647	800-444-4594		
Yamaha Electronics Corp 6660 Orangethorpe Ave .... Buena Park CA 90620	800-292-2982	866-430-2652	52
Yamaha Motor Corp USA 6555 Katella Ave .... Cypress CA 90630 *Cust Svc	800-962-7926*		514
Yamato Corp 1775 S Murray Blvd .... Colorado Springs CO 80916	800-538-1762	719-591-1500	680
Yamazen Inc 735 E Remington Rd .... Schaumburg IL 60173	800-882-8558		384
Yampa Valley Electric Assn Inc 2211 Elk River Rd .... Steamboat Springs CO 81626	888-873-9832	970-879-1160	245
Yankee Barn Homes 131 Yankee Barn Rd .... Grantham NH 03753	800-258-9786		106
Yankee Candle Company Inc PO Box 110 .... South Deerfield MA 01373	877-803-6890	413-665-8306	327
Yankee Inn 461 Pittsfield Lenox Rd .... Lenox MA 01240	800-835-2364	413-499-3700	378
Yankee Magazine 1121 Main St PO Box 520 .... Dublin NH 03444	800-288-4284	603-563-8111	455-22
Yankee Publishing Inc PO Box 520 .... Dublin NH 03444	800-729-9265	603-563-8111	633-9
Yankton Ag Service 114 Mulberry St .... Yankton SD 57078	800-456-5528	605-665-3691	276
Yankton Press & Dakotan 319 Walnut St PO Box 56. .... Yankton SD 57078	800-743-2968	605-665-7811	633-8
YAP (Youth Advocate Programs Inc) 2007 N Third St PO Box 950 .... Harrisburg PA 17102	800-324-5794	717-232-7580	
Yarde Metals Inc 45 Newell St .... Southington CT 06489	800-444-9494	860-406-6061	488
Yardley Products Corp 10 W College Ave .... Yardley PA 19067	800-457-0154	215-493-2700	349
Yark Automotive Group Inc 6019 W Central Ave .... Toledo OH 43615	866-390-8894		513
Yarmouth Regional Hospital (YRH) 60 Vancouver St .... Yarmouth NS B5A2P5	800-460-2110	902-742-3541	373-2
Yarmouth Resort 343 Main St Rt 28 .... West Yarmouth MA 02673	877-838-3524	508-775-5155	378
Yaskawa America Inc 2121 Norman Dr S .... Waukegan IL 60085	800-927-5292	847-887-7000	203
Yates County 417 Liberty St .... Penn Yan NY 14527	866-212-5160	315-536-5120	337
Yates-American Machine Company Inc 2880 Kennedy Dr .... Beloit WI 53511	800-752-6377	608-364-6333	816
Yavapai College 1100 E Sheldon St .... Prescott AZ 86301 *Verde Valley* 601 Black Hills Dr .... Clarkdale AZ 86324	800-922-6787 800-922-6787	928-445-7300 928-634-7501	162 162
Yavapai County 1015 Fair St .... Prescott AZ 86305	800-659-7149	928-771-3200	337
Yavapai Regional Medical Ctr 1003 Willow Creek Rd .... Prescott AZ 86301	877-843-9762	928-445-2700	373-3
Yazoo County PO Box 186 .... Yazoo City MS 39194	800-381-0662	662-746-1815	337
Yazoo Mills Inc PO Box 369 .... New Oxford PA 17350 *Cust Svc	800-242-5216*	717-624-8993	125
Yazoo Valley Electric Power Assn 2255 Gordon Ave .... Yazoo City MS 39194	800-281-5098	662-746-4251	245
YDR (York Daily Record) 1891 Loucks Rd .... York PA 17408	800-559-3520	717-771-2000	528-2
Yeck Bros Co 2222 Arbor Blvd .... Moraine OH 45439	800-417-2767	937-294-4000	5
Yellow Medicine County 415 Ninth Ave .... Granite Falls MN 56241	800-366-4812	320-564-3325	337
Yellowhead Helicopters Ltd 3010 Selwyn Rd .... Valemount BC V0E2Z0	888-566-4401		358
YELLOWPAGEScom LLC 208 S Akard .... Dallas TX 75202	866-329-7118		396
Yellowstone Baptist College 1515 S Shiloh Rd .... Billings MT 59106	800-487-9950	406-656-9950	166
Yellowstone Public Radio 1500 University Dr .... Billings MT 59101	800-441-2941	406-657-2941	641-13
Yellowstone Valley Electric Co-op 150 Co-op Way .... Huntley MT 59037	800-736-5323	406-348-3411	245
Yenkin-Majestic Paint Corp 1920 Leonard Ave .... Columbus OH 43219	800-848-1898	614-253-8511	546
Yeo & Yeo 5300 Bay Rd Ste 100 .... Saginaw MI 48604	800-968-0010	989-793-9830	
Yesterday USA Radio Networks, The 2001 Plymouth Rock Dr .... Richardson TX 75081	800-624-2272	972-889-9872	640
Yesware Inc 75 Kneeland St 1st Fl .... Boston MA 02111	855-937-9273		386
Yetter Manufacturing Inc 109 S McDonough St PO Box 358. .... Colchester IL 62326	800-447-5777	309-776-4111	273
Yingling Aircraft Inc 2010 Airport Rd .... Wichita KS 67209	800-835-0083	316-943-3246	765
YK International Co 3246 W Montrose Ave .... Chicago IL 60618	800-266-5254	773-583-5270	347
YMCA (YMCA of the USA) 101 N Wacker Dr .... Chicago IL 60606	800-872-9622	312-977-0031	48-6
YMCA of the USA (YMCA) 101 N Wacker Dr .... Chicago IL 60606	800-872-9622	312-977-0031	48-6

	Toll-Free	Phone	Class
Yodle Inc 330 W 34th St 18th Fl. . . . . New York NY 10001	877-276-5104		394
Yogo Inn 211 E Main St . . . . Lewistown MT 59457	800-860-9646	406-535-8721	378
Yokogawa Corp of America 12530 W Airport Blvd . . . . Sugar Land TX 77478	800-888-6400	281-340-3800	248
Yokohama Tire Corp 601 S Acacia Ave . . . . Fullerton CA 92831	800-423-4544	714-870-3800	749
Yolo County 625 Ct St Rm B01. . . . . Woodland CA 95695	800-433-5060	530-666-8150	337
Yolo County Library 226 Buckeye St . . . . Woodland CA 95695	800-755-6864	530-666-8005	433-3
Yolo Federal Credit Union 266 W Main St . . . . Woodland CA 95695	877-965-6328	530-668-2700	219
Yonex Corp 20140 S Western Ave . . . . Torrance CA 90501	800-449-6639	424-201-4800	706
York Barbell Co Inc 3300 BoaRd Rd . . . . York PA 17406 *Cust Svc	800-358-9675*	717-767-6481	267
York Bldg Products Co 950 Smile Way . . . . York PA 17404	800-673-2408	717-848-2831	183
York Building Services Inc 99 Grand St Ste 3 . . . . Moonachie NJ 07074	855-443-9675		256
York College 1125 E Eigth St . . . . York NE 68467	800-950-9675	402-363-5600	166
York County Community College 112 College Dr . . . . Wells ME 04090	800-580-3820	207-646-9282	162
York County Public Library 8500 George Washington Memorial Hwy . . . . Yorktown VA 23692	800-552-7945	757-890-3377	433-3
York County Transportation Authority 1230 Roosevelt Ave . . . . York PA 17404	800-632-9063	717-846-5562	466
York Daily Record (YDR) 1891 Loucks Rd . . . . York PA 17408	800-559-3520	717-771-2000	528-2
York Electric Cooperative Inc 1385 E Alexander Love Hwy PO Box 150. . . . . York SC 29745	800-582-8810	803-684-4248	245
York Ford Inc 1481 Bwy . . . . Saugus MA 01906	888-705-6229	781-231-1945	57
York Metal Fabricators Inc 27 NE 26th St . . . . Oklahoma City OK 73105	800-255-4703	405-528-7495	693
York Solutions 1 Westbrook Corporate Ctr Ste 910 . . . . Westchester IL 60154	877-700-9675	708-531-8362	717
York Sunday News 1891 Loucks Rd . . . . York PA 17408	888-629-4095	717-767-6397	528-4
York Technical College 452 S Anderson Rd . . . . Rock Hill SC 29730	800-922-8324	803-327-8000	162
York University 4700 Keele St . . . . Toronto ON M3J1P3	800-426-2255	416-736-2100	780
York Wallcoverings Inc 750 Linden Ave . . . . York PA 17404	800-375-9675	717-846-4456	797
York Water Co, The 130 E Market St . . . . York PA 17401 NASDAQ: YORW	800-750-5561	717-845-3601	782
Yorkston Oil Company Inc 2801 Roeder Ave . . . . Bellingham WA 98225	800-401-2201	360-734-2201	575
Yosemite Sierra Visitors Bureau 40637 Hwy 41 . . . . Oakhurst CA 93644	800-613-0709	559-683-4636	206
Youghiogheny Scenic & Wild River c/o Deep Creek Lake Recreation Area 898 State Pk Rd . . . . Swanton MD 21561	800-248-1893	301-387-5563	561
YouMail Inc 43 Corporate Pk Ste 200. . . . . Irvine CA 92606	800-374-0013		180
Young Adult Library Services Assn (YALSA) 50 E Huron St . . . . Chicago IL 60611	800-545-2433	312-280-4390	49-11
Young America Corp 10 S Fifth St 7th Fl . . . . Minneapolis MN 55402	800-533-4529		732
Young America's Foundation 11480 Commerce Park Dr Ste 600 . . . . Reston VA 20191	800-872-1776	703-318-9608	48-7
Young Bros Stamp Works Inc 1415 Howard Ave PO Box 75 . . . . Muscatine IA 52761	800-553-8248		
Young Children Magazine 1313 L St NW Ste 500 PO Box 97156. . . . . Washington DC 20005	800-424-2460	202-232-8777	455-8
Young Corp 3231 Utah Ave S . . . . Seattle WA 98134	800-321-9090	206-624-1071	190
Young Dental Manufacturing LLC 13705 Shoreline Ct E . . . . Earth City MO 63045	800-325-1881		228
Young Electric Sign Co 2401 Foothill Dr . . . . Salt Lake City UT 84109	866-779-8357	801-464-4600	697
Young Fashions Inc 11111 Coursey Blvd . . . . Baton Rouge LA 70816	800-824-4154	225-766-1010	590
Young Harris College PO Box 116 . . . . Young Harris GA 30582	800-241-3754	706-379-3111	162
Young Industries Inc 16 Painter St . . . . Muncy PA 17756	800-546-3165	570-546-3165	207
Young Israel of New Rochelle 1149 N Ave . . . . New Rochelle NY 10804	888-942-3638	914-636-2215	48-20
Young Living Essential Oils 3125 Executive Pkwy . . . . Lehi UT 84043	866-203-5666	801-418-8900	794
Young Manufacturing Inc 2331 N 42nd St . . . . Grand Forks ND 58203	800-451-9884	701-772-5541	481
Young Mfg Company Inc 521 S Main St PO Box 167 . . . . Beaver Dam KY 42320	800-545-6595	270-274-3306	497
Young Presidents' Organization (YPO) 600 E Las Colinas Blvd Ste 1100 . . . . Irving TX 75039	800-773-7976	972-587-1500	49-12
Young Transportation & Tours 843 Riverside Dr . . . . Asheville NC 28804	800-622-5444	828-258-0084	107
Young's Commercial Transfer 2075 W Scranton Ave PO Box 871. . . . . Porterville CA 93257	800-289-1639	559-784-6651	775
Young's Market Company LLC 500 S Central Ave . . . . Los Angeles CA 90013	800-627-2777	213-612-1248	81-3
Young's Plant Farm 863 Airport Rd . . . . Auburn AL 36830	800-304-8609		368
Younger Optics 2925 California St . . . . Torrance CA 90503	800-366-5367	310-783-1533	538
Youngsoft Inc 49197 Wixom Tech Dr . . . . Wixom MI 48393	888-470-4553	248-675-1200	177

	Toll-Free	Phone	Class
Youngstown State University 1 University Plz . . . . Youngstown OH 44555 *Admissions	877-468-6978*	330-941-3000	166
Your 949 FM 7601 Riviera Blvd . . . . Miramar FL 33023	877-599-2946	954-862-2000	641
Your Big Backyard Magazine 11100 Wildlife Ctr Dr . . . . Reston VA 20190	800-822-9919		455-6
Your Church Magazine 465 Gundersen Dr . . . . Carol Stream IL 60188	877-247-4787	630-260-6200	455-5
Your Selling Team 100 Spectrum Ctr Dr Ste 700 . . . . Irvine CA 92618	888-387-8002		732
YourAmigo Inc 4708 Del Valle Pkwy . . . . Pleasanton CA 94566	800-816-7054	510-813-1355	196
YourAreaCode LLC 6242 28th St Ste B . . . . Grand Rapids MI 49546	888-244-7751	616-622-2000	365
Yourga Trucking Inc 145 JH Yourga Pl PO Box 607 . . . . Wheatland PA 16161	800-245-1722	724-981-3600	775
Youth Advocate Programs Inc (YAP) 2007 N Third St PO Box 950 . . . . Harrisburg PA 17102	800-324-5794	717-232-7580	
Youth For Understanding USA 6400 Goldsboro Rd Ste 100 . . . . Bethesda MD 20817	800-424-3691	800-833-6243	48-11
Youth Frontiers Inc 6009 Excelsior Blvd . . . . Minneapolis MN 55416	888-992-0222	952-922-0222	196
Youth Home Inc 20400 Colonel Glenn Rd . . . . Little Rock AR 72210	800-728-6452	501-821-5500	722
Youth Villages Inner Harbour 4685 Dorsett Shoals Rd . . . . Douglasville GA 30135	800-255-8657	770-852-6300	373-1
YouVisit 20533 Biscayne Blvd Ste 1322 . . . . Aventura FL 33180	866-585-7158		386
YP LLC 611 N Brand Blvd Ste 500 . . . . Glendale CA 91203	866-570-8863		5
YPO (Young Presidents' Organization) 600 E Las Colinas Blvd Ste 1100 . . . . Irving TX 75039	800-773-7976	972-587-1500	49-12
YRC Worldwide Inc 10990 Roe Ave . . . . Overland Park KS 66211 NASDAQ: YRCW	800-846-4300	913-696-6100	359-3
YRH (Yarmouth Regional Hospital) 60 Vancouver St . . . . Yarmouth NS B5A2P5	800-460-2110	902-742-3541	373-2
YSI Inc 1700-1725 Brannum Ln . . . . Yellow Springs OH 45387 *Cust Svc	800-765-4974*	937-767-7241	201
Y-Tex Corp 1825 Big Horn Ave . . . . Cody WY 82414	800-443-6401	307-587-5515	280
Yucaipa Valley Water District PO Box 730 . . . . Yucaipa CA 92399	800-304-2226	909-797-5117	782
Yucca Telecom 201 W Second St . . . . Portales NM 88130	866-239-6858	575-226-2255	246
Yucca Valley Chamber of Commerce 56711 29 Palms Hwy . . . . Yucca Valley CA 92284	855-365-6558	760-365-6323	139
Yukon 2nd Ave & Lambert St PO Box 2703. . . . . Whitehorse YT Y1A2C6	800-661-0494		769
Yum! Brands Inc 1441 Gardiner Ln . . . . Louisville KY 40213 NYSE: YUM	800-225-5532	502-874-1000	666
Yuma Civic Ctr 1440 W Desert Hills Dr . . . . Yuma AZ 85365	866-966-0220	928-373-5040	205
Yuma Convention & Visitors Bureau 201 N Fourth Ave . . . . Yuma AZ 85364	800-293-0071	928-783-0071	206
Yuma County 198 S Main St . . . . Yuma AZ 85364	800-253-0883	928-373-1010	337
YVR (Vancouver International Airport) Airport Postal Outlet PO Box 23750. . . . . Richmond BC V7B1Y7	800-461-9999	604-207-7077	27
Y-W Electric Assn Inc 250 Main Ave PO Box Y . . . . Akron CO 80720	800-660-2291	970-345-2291	245
YWCA (YWCA USA) 2025 M St NW Ste 550 . . . . Washington DC 20036	888-872-9259	202-467-0801	48-6
YWCA USA (YWCA) 2025 M St NW Ste 550 . . . . Washington DC 20036	888-872-9259	202-467-0801	48-6

Z

	Toll-Free	Phone	Class
Z Communications Inc 14118 Stowe Dr Ste B. . . . . Poway CA 92064	877-808-1226	858-621-2700	253
Z Gallerie Inc 1855 W 139th St . . . . Gardena CA 90249	800-358-8288	310-630-1200	361
Z57 Internet Solutions 10045 Mesa Rim Rd . . . . San Diego CA 92121	800-899-8148		225
Z92 FM 10714 Mockingbird Dr . . . . Omaha NE 68127	800-955-9230		641-74
Zachary & Elizabeth Fisher House 111 Rockville Pk Ste 420 . . . . Rockville MD 20850	888-294-8560		371
Zachary Confections Inc 2130 IN-28 . . . . Frankfort IN 46041 *Cust Svc	800-445-4222*		296-8
Zachys Wine & Liquor Inc 16 E Pkwy . . . . Scarsdale NY 10583	800-723-0241	914-874-8000	442
Zack Electronics Inc 1075 Hamilton Rd . . . . Duarte CA 91010	800-466-0449	626-303-0655	246
Zacky Farms 13200 Crossroads Pkwy N Ste 250 . . . . City of Industry CA 91746	800-888-0235	562-641-2020	297-10
Zadro Products Inc 5422 Argosy Ave . . . . Huntington Beach CA 92649	800-468-4348	714-892-9200	604
ZAGG Inc 3855 South 500 West Ste J . . . . Salt Lake City UT 84115	800-700-9244	801-263-0699	604
Zale Corp *Zales Jewelers Div* 901 W Walnut Hill Ln . . . . Irving TX 75038 *Cust Svc	800-311-5393*	972-580-4000	409

Company / Address	City	State	ZIP	Toll-Free	Phone	Class
Zane State College 1555 Newark Rd	Zanesville	OH	43701	**800-686-8324**	740-454-2501	795
Zaner Group LLC 150 S Wacker Dr Ste 2350	Chicago	IL	60606	**800-621-1414**	312-930-2703	169
Zaner-Bloser Inc 1201 Dublin Rd	Columbus	OH	43215	**800-421-3018**	614-486-0221	633-2
Zanesville City School Board 1701 Blue Ave	Zanesville	OH	43701	**866-280-7377**	740-454-9751	681
Zanesville Times Recorder 3871 Gorsky Dr Unit G1	Zanesville	OH	43701	**877-424-0214**	740-452-4561	528-2
Zanesville-Muskingum County Chamber of Commerce 205 N Fifth St	Zanesville	OH	43701	**800-743-2303**	740-455-8282	139
ZapLabs LLC 2000 Powell St Ste 700 *NASDAQ: ZIPR*	Emeryville	CA	94608	**800-225-5947**	510-735-2600	648
Zapposcom 400 E Stewart Ave	Las Vegas	NV	89101	**800-927-7671**		457
ZAPS Technologies Inc 4314 SW Research Way	Corvallis	OR	97333	**866-390-9387**		418
Zasio Enterprises Inc 401 W Front St Ste 305	Boise	ID	83702	**800-513-1000**		177
ZBA Inc 94 Old Camplain Rd	Hillsborough	NJ	08844	**800-750-4239**	908-359-2070	173-7
ZE PowerGroup Inc 130 - 5920 No Two Rd	Richmond	BC	V7C4R9	**866-944-1469**	604-244-1469	193
ZeaVision LLC 716-I Crown Industrial Ct	Chesterfield	MO	63005	**866-833-2800**	314-628-1000	344
Zebra Books *Kensington Publishing Corp* 119 West 40th St	New York	NY	10018	**800-221-2647**	212-407-1500	633-2
Zebra Print Solutions 9401 Globe Ctr Dr	Morrisville	NC	27560	**800-545-8835**	919-314-3700	623
Zebra Technologies Corp 475 Half Day Rd Ste 500 *NASDAQ: ZBRA*	Lincolnshire	IL	60069	**800-423-0422**	847-634-6700	173-6
Zebulon Pike Youth Services Ctr 1427 W Rio Grande	Colorado Springs	CO	80906	**800-970-3468**	719-633-8713	411
zedSuite 210 Water St Ste 400	St. John's	NL	A1C1A9	**877-722-1177**	709-722-7213	196
Zee Medical Inc 22 Corporate Pk	Irvine	CA	92606	**800-435-7763**		473
Zeeland Lumber & Supply Co 146 E Washington	Zeeland	MI	49464	**888-772-2119**	616-772-2119	191-3
Zehnder America Inc 6 Merrill Industrial Dr Ste 7	Hampton	NH	03842	**888-778-6701**	603-601-8544	606
Zeigler Beverages LLC 1513 N Broad St *Sales	Lansdale	PA	19446	**800-854-6123***	215-855-5161	296-20
Zeigler Bros Inc 400 GaRdner Stn Rd	Gardners	PA	17324	**800-841-6800**	717-677-6181	445
Zeigler Chevrolet Inc 13153 Dunnings Hwy	Claysburg	PA	16625	**877-364-4817**		57
Zeiser Wilbert Vault Inc 750 Howard St	Elmira	NY	14904	**800-472-4335**	607-733-0568	191-1
Zeks Compressed Air Solutions 1302 Goshen Pkwy	West Chester	PA	19380	**800-888-2323**	610-692-9100	172
Zen Ventures LLC 3939 S Sixth St Ste 201	Klamath Falls	OR	97603	**888-936-2278**		804
Zenith Cutter Co 5200 Zenith Pkwy	Loves Park	IL	61111	**800-223-5202**	815-282-5200	491
Zenith Insurance Co PO Box 9055	Van Nuys	CA	91409	**800-440-5020**	818-713-1000	390-4
Zenith Products Corp 400 Lukens Dr	New Castle	DE	19720	**800-892-3986**		319-2
Zenith Specialty Bag Company Inc 17625 E Railroad St PO Box 8445	City of Industry	CA	91748	**800-962-2247**	626-912-2481	65
Zenoss Inc 11305 Four Points Dr Bldg 1 Ste 300	Austin	TX	78726	**888-936-6770**		177
Zentech Manufacturing Inc 6980 Tudsbury Rd	Baltimore	MD	21244	**800-871-7838**	443-348-4500	253
ZEP Inc 1310 Seaboard Industrial Blvd NW *NYSE: ZEP*	Atlanta	GA	30318	**877-428-9937**	404-352-1680	151
Zephyr Egg Co Inc 4622 Gall Blvd	Zephyrhills	FL	33542	**800-333-4415**	813-782-1521	10-7
Zephyr Mfg Company Inc 200 Mitchell Rd	Sedalia	MO	65301	**800-821-7197**	660-827-0352	103
Zephyr-Tec Corp 9651 Business Ctr Dr Ste C	Rancho Cucamonga	CA	91730	**877-493-7497**	909-481-9991	177
Zepp Labs Inc 75 E Santa Clara St 6th Fl	San Jose	CA	95113	**866-400-9377**		
Zepto Metrix Corp 872 Main St *Cust Svc	Buffalo	NY	14202	**800-274-5487***	716-882-0920	231
Zerion Group PO Box 940411	Maitland	FL	32794	**877-872-1726**		317
Zero International Inc 415 Concord Ave	Bronx	NY	10455	**800-635-5335**	718-585-3230	326
Zero Manufacturing Inc 500 W 200 N	North Salt Lake	UT	84054	**800-959-5050**	801-298-5900	451
Zero Technologies LLC 7 Neshaminy Interplex Ste 116	Trevose	PA	19053	**800-503-2939**		
Zero-Max Inc 13200 Sixth Ave N	Plymouth	MN	55441	**800-533-1731**	763-546-4300	616
Zeta Phi Beta Sorority Inc 1734 New Hampshire Ave NW	Washington	DC	20009	**800-393-2503**	202-387-3103	48-16
Zeta Psi Fraternity of North America 15 S Henry St	Pearl River	NY	10965	**800-477-1847**	845-735-1847	48-16
Zetec Inc 8226 Bracken Pl SE Ste 100	Snoqualmie	WA	98065	**800-643-1771**	425-974-2700	248

Company / Address	City	State	ZIP	Toll-Free	Phone	Class
Zia's Italian Restaurant 20 Main St	Toledo	OH	43605	**888-456-3463**		
Zibiz Corp 50 Alexander Ct	Ronkonkoma	NY	11779	**888-263-6005**		
Ziebart International Corp 1290 E Maple Rd	Troy	MI	48083	**800-877-1312**	248-588-4100	62-1
Zieger & Sons Inc 6215 Ardleigh St	Philadelphia	PA	19138	**800-752-2003**	215-438-7060	293
Ziegler Capital Markets Investment Services 200 S Wacker	Chicago	IL	60606	**800-797-4272**	414-978-6400	686
Ziegler Chemical & Mineral Corp 600 Prospect Ave	Piscataway	NJ	08854	**888-213-7500**	732-752-4111	498
Zierick Manufacturing Corp 131 Radio Cr	Mount Kisco	NY	10549	**800-882-8020**	914-666-2911	810
Ziff Davis LLC 28 E 28th St	New York	NY	10016	**800-289-0429**	212-503-3500	455-7
Zimmer Biomet 1800 W Ctr St PO Box 708	Warsaw	IN	46580	**800-613-6131**	574-267-6131	475
Zimmer Radio Group 3215 Lemone Industrial Blvd Ste 200	Columbia	MO	65201	**800-455-1099**	573-875-1099	639
Zimmerman Metals Inc 201 E 58th Ave	Denver	CO	80216	**800-247-4202**	303-294-0180	478
Zingle Inc 2270 Camino Vida Roble Ste K	Carlsbad	CA	92011	**877-946-4536**		224
Zinkan Enterprises Inc 1919 Case Pkwy N	Twinsburg	OH	44087	**800-229-6801**		145
Zions Bank 1 S Main St	Salt Lake City	UT	84133	**800-974-8800**	801-974-8800	70
Zippertubing Co 7150 W Erie St	Chandler	AZ	85226	**855-289-1874**		596
Zippo Manufacturing Co 33 Barbour St	Bradford	PA	16701	**888-442-1932**	814-368-2700	222
ZirMed Inc 888 W Market St *Support	Louisvill	KY	40202	**877-494-7633***	866-347-5653	
Zito Media LP 102 S Main St PO Box 665	Coudersport	PA	16915	**800-365-6988**		
Zix Corp 2711 N Haskell Ave Ste 2300-LB *NASDAQ: ZIXI*	Dallas	TX	75204	**888-771-4049**	214-370-2000	178-12
Z-Law Software Inc 80 Upton Ave PO Box 40602	Providence	RI	02940	**800-526-5588**	401-331-3002	177
ZLB Behring LLC 1020 First Ave PO Box 61501	King of Prussia	PA	19406	**800-683-1288**	610-878-4000	578
Z-Medica Corp 4 Fairfield Blvd	Wallingford	CT	06492	**800-343-8656**	203-294-0000	473
Zodax Inc 14040 Arminta St	Panorama City	CA	91402	**800-800-3443**	818-785-5626	
Zodiac Pool Systems Inc 2620 Commerce Way	Vista	CA	92081	**800-822-7933**		801
Zoeller Co 3649 Kane Run Rd *OTC: ZOLR*	Louisville	KY	40211	**800-928-7867**	502-778-2731	637
Zogenix Inc 12400 High Bluff Dr Ste 650	San Diego	CA	92130	**866-964-3649**	858-259-1165	578
ZOLL Medical Corp 269 Mill Rd	Chelmsford	MA	01824	**800-348-9011**	978-421-9655	250
Zonar Systems LLC 18200 Cascade Ave S	Seattle	WA	98188	**877-843-3847**	206-878-2459	525
Zone Alarm 800 Bridge Pkwy	Redwood City	CA	94065	**877-966-5221**	415-633-4500	178-7
Zonic Design & Imaging Llc 875 Mahler Rd Ste 238	Burlingame	CA	94010	**877-349-6642**	415-643-3700	
Zontec Inc 1389 Kemper Meadow Dr	Cincinnati	OH	45240	**866-955-0088**	513-648-9695	180
Zoocheck Canada 788 1/2 O'Connor Dr	Toronto	ON	M4B2S6	**888-801-3222**	416-285-1744	48-3
Zookbinders Inc 151-K S Pfingsten Rd	Deerfield	IL	60015	**800-810-5745**		623
Zortec International 25 Century Blvd Ste 103	Nashville	TN	37214	**800-361-7005**	615-361-7000	178-2
ZTEST Electronics Inc 523 Mcnicoll Ave	North York	ON	M2H2C9	**866-393-4891**	416-297-5155	621
ZTR Control Systems Inc 8050 County Rd 101 E	Minneapolis	MN	55379	**855-724-5987**		418
Zuercher Technologies LLC 4509 W 58th St	Sioux Falls	SD	57108	**877-229-2205**	605-274-6061	174
Zuken USA 238 Littleton Rd Ste 100	Westford	MA	01886	**800-447-7332**	978-692-4900	178-5
Zumar Industries Inc 9719 Santa Fe Springs Rd	Santa Fe Springs	CA	90670	**800-654-7446**	562-941-4633	697
Zumiez Inc 6300 Merrill Creek Pkwy Ste B *NASDAQ: ZUMZ*	Everett	WA	98203	**877-828-6929**	425-551-1500	157-2
Zurich American Insurance Co 1299 Zurich Way	Schaumburg	IL	60196	**800-382-2150**		390-5
Zurn Industries LLC 511 W Freshwater Way	Milwaukee	WI	53204	**855-663-9876**		597
Zygo Corp Laurel Brook Rd *NASDAQ: ZIGO*	Middlefield	CT	06455	**800-994-6669**	860-347-8506	540
Zymo Research Corp 17062 Murphy Ave	Irvine	CA	92614	**888-882-9682**	949-679-1190	531
ZymoGenetics Inc 1201 Eastlake Ave E	Seattle	WA	98102	**800-332-2056**	206-442-6600	85
ZyQuest Inc 1385 W Main Ave	De Pere	WI	54115	**800-992-0533**	920-499-0533	180
ZyXEL Communications Inc 1130 N Miller St	Anaheim	CA	92806	**800-255-4101**	714-632-0882	173-3

Classified Section

Listings in the Classified Section are organized alphabetically under subject headings denoting a business or organization type. These headings are fully outlined in the Index to Classified Headings located at the back of this book. "See" and "See Also" references are included in this section to help locate appropriate subject categories. Alphabetizing is on a word-by-word rather than letter-by-letter basis. For a detailed explanation of the scope and arrangement of listings in Toll-Free Phone Book USA, please refer to "How To Use This Directory" at the beginning of this book. An explanation of individual page elements is also provided under the "Sample Entry" on the back inside cover of the book.

1 — ABRASIVE PRODUCTS

				Toll-Free	Phone
Basic Carbide Corp					
900 Main St	Lowber	PA	15660	800-426-4291	724-446-1630
Bullard Abrasives Inc					
6 Carol Dr	Lincoln	RI	02865	800-227-4469	401-333-3000
Comco Inc 2151 N Lincoln St	Burbank	CA	91504	800-796-6626	818-841-5500
Composition Materials Company Inc					
249 Pepes Farm Rd	Milford	CT	06460	800-262-7763	203-874-6500
Diamond Products Inc					
333 Prospect	Elyria	OH	44035	800-321-5336	
Equipment Development Company Inc					
100 Thomas Johnson Dr	Frederick	MD	21702	800-638-3326	
Ervin Industries Inc					
3893 Research Pk Dr	Ann Arbor	MI	48108	800-748-0055	734-769-4600
Formax Manufacturing Corp					
168 Wealthy St SW	Grand Rapids	MI	49503	800-242-2833	616-456-5458
Gemtex Abrasives					
234 Belfield Rd	Toronto	ON	M9W1H3	800-387-5100	416-245-5605
Hermes Abrasives Ltd					
524 Viking Dr	Virginia Beach	VA	23452	800-464-8314	757-486-6623
Kennametal Inc					
2879 Aero Pk Dr	Traverse City	MI	49686	800-662-2131	231-946-2100
NYSE: KMT					
Marvel Abrasive Products Inc					
6230 S Oak Park Ave	Chicago	IL	60638	800-621-0673	
Micro Surface Finishing Products Inc					
1217 W Third St	Wilton	IA	52778	800-225-3006	563-732-3240
Norton Sandblasting Equipment					
1006 Executive Blvd	Chesapeake	VA	23320	800-366-4341	757-548-4842
Precision Abrasives					
3176 Abbott Rd	Orchard Park	NY	14127	800-722-3967	
Precision H2O Inc					
6328 E Utah Ave	Spokane	WA	99212	800-425-2098	509-536-9214
Premix Marbletite					
1259 NW 21st St	Pompano Beach	FL	33069	800-432-5097	954-917-7665
Radiac Abrasives Inc					
1015 S College Ave	Salem	IL	62881	800-851-1095	618-548-4200
Raytech Industries					
475 Smith St	Middletown	CT	06457	800-243-7163*	860-632-2020
Cust Svc					
Trumbull Industries Inc					
400 Dietz Rd NE	Warren	OH	44482	800-477-1799	330-392-1551
Uneeda Enterprizes Inc					
640 Chestnut Ridge Rd Spring Valley	New York	NY	10977	800-431-2494	845-426-2800
VSM Abrasives					
1012 E Wabash St	O'Fallon	MO	63366	800-737-0176*	636-272-7432
Cust Svc					
Washington Mills Electro Minerals Co					
20 N Main St	North Grafton	MA	01536	800-828-1666	508-839-6511

2 — ACCOUNTING FIRMS

				Toll-Free	Phone
Accounts Payable Chexs Inc					
1829 Ranchlands Blvd NW	Calgary	AB	T3G2A7	888-437-0624	403-247-8913
ACU Serve Corp					
2020 Front St Ste 205	Cuyahoga Fls	OH	44221	800-887-8965	330-923-5258
Adserts Inc					
14750 W Capitol Dr	Brookfield	WI	53005	800-346-6919	
Ahola Corp, The					
6820 West Snowville Rd	Brecksville	OH	44141	800-727-2849	
Altera Payroll Inc					
2400 Northside Crossing	Macon	GA	31210	877-474-6060	478-477-6060
Andrews Hooper Pavlik Plc					
5300 Gratiot Rd	Saginaw	MI	48638	888-754-8478	989-497-5300
Armanino LLP					
12657 Alcosta Blvd Ste 500	San Ramon	CA	94583	844-582-8883	
Bauman Associates Ltd					
PO Box 1225	Eau Claire	WI	54702	888-952-2866	715-834-2001
Berdon LLP					
360 Madison Ave 8th Fl	New York	NY	10017	800-372-1033	212-832-0400
Bolden Lipkin PC					
3993 Huntingdon Pk	Huntingdon Valley	PA	19006	888-947-3750	215-947-3750
Bonadio Group, The					
171 Sully's Trl Ste 201	Pittsford	NY	14534	877-917-3077	585-381-1000

				Toll-Free	Phone
Bookkeeping Express Enterprises LLC					
671 N Glebe Rd Ste 1610	Arlington	VA	22203	844-629-8797	
Cachet Financial Services					
175 S Lake Ave Ste 200	Pasadena	CA	91101	855-591-9865	
Certipay					
199 Ave B NW Ste 270	Winter Haven	FL	33881	800-422-3782	863-299-2400
CIS Group					
55 Castonguay St Ste 301	St-jerome	QC	J7Y2H9	888-432-1550	450-432-1550
Clark Nuber PS					
10900 NE Fourth St Ste 1400	Bellevue	WA	98004	800-504-8747*	425-454-4919
General					
Clark Schaefer Hackett & Co					
1 E Fourth St Ste 1200	Cincinnati	OH	45202	800-772-8144	513-241-3111
CliftonLarsonAllen - CLA					
301 SW Adams St Ste 1000	Peoria	IL	61602	888-529-2648	309-671-4500
Clinic Service Corp					
3464 S Willow St	Denver	CO	80231	800-929-5395	303-755-2900
Complete Payroll Processing Inc					
7488 SR- 39 Po Box 190	Perry	NY	14530	888-237-5800	585-237-5800
Contingent Workforce Solutions Inc					
2430 Meadowpine Blvd Ste 101	Mississauga	ON	L5N6S2	866-837-8630	
ECS Financial Services Inc					
3400 Dundee Rd	Northbrook	IL	60062	800-826-7070	847-291-1333
Farmers Insurance Group of Companies					
6301 Owensmouth Ave	Woodland Hills	CA	91367	888-327-6335	
First Financial Bank					
PO Box 2122	Terre Haute	IN	47802	800-511-0045	812-238-6000
Freyberg Hinkle Ashland Powers & Stowell SC CPA					
15420 W Capitol Dr	Brookfield	WI	53005	800-413-8799	262-784-6210
Glass Jacobson Financial Group					
10711 Red Run Blvd Ste 101	Owings Mills	MD	21117	800-356-7666	410-356-1000
Gompers & Assoc PLLC					
117 Edgington Ln	Wheeling	WV	26003	844-805-9844	304-242-9300
Grant Bennett Accountants					
1375 Exposition Blvd Ste 230	Sacramento	CA	95815	888-763-7323	916-922-5109
Gross Mendelsohn & Associates PA					
36 S Charles St 18th fl	Baltimore	MD	21201	800-899-4623	410-685-5512
Hacker Johnson & Smith PA					
500 N Wshore Blvd Ste 1000	Tampa	FL	33609	800-366-7126	813-286-2424
Hill Barth & King LLC					
6603 Summit Dr	Canfield	OH	44406	800-733-8613	330-758-8613
Honegger Ringger & Company Inc					
1905 N Main St	Bluffton	IN	46714	888-853-5906	260-824-4107
Honkamp Krueger & Company PC					
2345 JFK Rd PO Box 699	Dubuque	IA	52004	888-556-0123	563-556-0123
HR&P					
9621 W Sam Houston Pkwy N Ste 100	Houston	TX	77064	877-880-4477	281-880-6525
IC. System Inc					
PO Box 64378	St. Paul	MN	55164	800-443-4123	
Investment Planning Counsel					
5015 Spectrum Way Ste 200	Mississauga	ON	L4W0E4	877-212-9799	905-212-9799
Jobe Hastings & Assoc CPA's					
745 S Church St Ste 105	Murfreesboro	TN	37133	866-207-2384	615-893-7777
Kahn Litwin Renza & Company Ltd					
951 N Main St	Providence	RI	02904	888-557-8557	401-274-2001
Keystone Payroll					
355-C Colonnade Blvd	State College	PA	16803	877-717-2272	814-234-2272
Lazer Grant Inc					
309 Mcdermot Ave	Winnipeg	MB	R3A1T3	800-220-0005	204-942-0300
Lenning & Company Inc					
13924 Seal Beach Blvd Ste C	Seal Beach	CA	90740	800-200-4829	562-594-9729
Lewis & Knopf CPA's PC					
5206 Gateway Centre Ste 100	Flint	MI	48507	877-244-1787	810-238-4617
LSL CPA's & Advisors					
1611 e Fourth st	Santa Ana	CA	92701	800-821-5184	714-569-1000
M & K CPA's PLLC					
363 N Sam Houston Pkwy E Ste 650	Houston	TX	77060	866-770-5931	832-242-9950
Massachusetts Society of Certified Public Accountants					
105 Chauncy St 10th Fl	Boston	MA	02111	800-392-6145	617-556-4000
Mauldin & Jenkins Certified Public Accountants LLC					
200 Galleria Pkwy SE	Atlanta	GA	30339	800-277-0080	770-955-8600
MBAF 1450 Brickell Ave 18th Fl	Miami	FL	33131	800-239-3843	305-373-5500
Mcswain & Co PS					
612 Woodland Sq Loop SE Ste 300	Lacey	WA	98503	800-282-1301	360-357-9304
Medical Billing Concepts Inc (MBC)					
16001 Ventura Blvd Ste 135	Encino	CA	91436	866-351-2852	
Medical Management Specialists					
4100 Embassy Dr SE Ste 200	Grand Rapids	MI	49546	888-707-2684	616-975-1845
Michael J Liccar & Co					
231 S La Salle St	Chicago	IL	60604	800-922-6604	312-922-6600

Accounting Firms (Cont'd)

	Toll-Free	Phone
Michael R Rubenstein & Assoc		
12527 New Brittany Blvd .... Fort Myers FL 33907	888-616-1222	239-489-4443
Moore & Neidenthal Inc		
3034 N Wooster Ave .... Dover OH 44622	866-364-7774	330-364-7774
Moore Stephens Lovelace PA		
255 S Orange Ave Ste 600 .... Orlando FL 32801	800-683-5401	407-740-5400
Nearman Maynard Vallez		
205 Brandywine Blvd Ste 200 .... Fayetteville GA 30214	800-288-0293	
Packer Thomas		
6601 Westford Pl Ste 101 .... Canfield OH 44406	800-943-4278	330-533-9777
Padgett Business Services		
160 Hawthorne Pk .... Athens GA 30606	800-723-4388	
Payroll 1		
34100 Woodward Ave Ste 250 .... Birmingham MI 48009	888-999-7291	
Payroll Masters		
855 Bordeaux Way .... Napa CA 94558	800-963-1428	707-226-1428
Pickens Snodgrass Koch & Company PC		
3001 Medlin Dr Ste 100 .... Arlington TX 76015	800-424-5790	817-664-3000
PricewaterhouseCoopers LLP		
300 Madison Ave .... New York NY 10017	800-993-9971	646-471-4000
Rehmann Group		
5800 Gratiot St Ste 201 .... Saginaw MI 48638	866-799-9580	989-799-9580
Roger Sipe CPA Firm LLC		
5742 Coventry Ln .... Fort Wayne IN 46804	888-747-3272	260-432-9996
Ruby Stein Wagner		
300 Leo-pariseau Ste 1900 .... Montreal QC H2X4B5	866-842-3911	514-842-3911
S R Snodgrass AC		
2009 Mackenzie Way Ste 340 .... Cranberry Township PA 16066	800-580-7738	724-934-0344
Santora CPA Group		
220 Continental Dr Ste 112 Christiana Executive Campus .... Newark DE 19713	800-347-0116	302-737-6200
SC&H Group LLC		
910 Ridgebrook Rd .... Sparks MD 21152	800-832-3008	410-403-1500
Schenck Business Solutions		
200 E Washington St .... Appleton WI 54911	800-236-2246	920-731-8111
Schlenner Wenner & Co		
630 Roosevelt Rd .... Saint Cloud MN 56301	877-616-0286	320-251-0286
Scribner Cohen & Company SC		
400 E Mason St Ste 300 .... Milwaukee WI 53202	888-730-0045	414-271-1700
Sikich LLP		
1415 W Diehl Rd Ste 400 .... Naperville IL 60563	877-279-1900	630-566-8400
Singer Lewak Greenbaum & Goldstein LLP		
10960 Wilshire Blvd 7th Fl .... Los Angeles CA 90024	877-754-4557	310-477-3924
Smith Anglin Financial LLC		
14755 Preston Rd Ste 700 .... Dallas TX 75254	800-301-8486	972-267-1244
Smoker Smith & Associates PC		
339 W Governor Rd Ste 202 .... Hershey PA 17033	888-277-1040	717-533-5154
Smoll & Banning CPA's LLC		
2410 Central Ave .... Dodge City KS 67801	800-499-8881	620-225-6100
Sobel & Company LLC		
293 Eisenhower Pkwy Ste 290 .... Livingston NJ 07039	800-471-2468	973-994-9494
Stinnett & Assoc LLC		
8811 S Yale Ave Ste 300 .... Tulsa OK 74137	888-808-1795	
SVA 1221 John Q Hammons Dr .... Madison WI 53717	800-279-2616	608-831-8181
Taycom Business Solutions Inc		
719 Griswold Ave Ste 820 .... Detroit MI 48226	866-482-9266	313-967-7857
TMG Co 43 Woodstock St .... Roswell GA 30075	800-720-1563	
United Paramount Tax Group Inc		
4025 Woodland Park Blvd Ste 310 .... Arlington TX 76013	888-829-8829	817-983-0099
Virginia Society of CPA's		
4309 Cox Rd .... Glen Allen VA 23060	800-733-8272	804-270-5344
Watson Rice		
301 Rte 17 N 4th Fl .... Rutherford NJ 07070	800-945-5985	201-460-4590
Wireless Watchdogs LLC		
317 Isis Ave Ste 102 .... Inglewood CA 90301	866-522-0688	310-622-0688
Yeo & Yeo		
5300 Bay Rd Ste 100 .... Saginaw MI 48604	800-968-0010	989-793-9830

3   ADHESIVES & SEALANTS

	Toll-Free	Phone
Aabbitt Adhesives Inc		
2403 N Oakley .... Chicago IL 60647	800-222-2488	
Adhesives Research Inc		
400 Seaks Run Rd PO Box 100 .... Glen Rock PA 17327	800-445-6240	717-235-7979
Arlon Graphics		
2811 S Harbor Blvd .... Santa Ana CA 92704	800-232-7161	714-540-2811
Atlas Minerals & Chemicals Inc		
1227 Valley Rd .... Mertztown PA 19539	800-523-8269*	610-682-7171
*Cust Svc		
Avery Dennison Corp		
207 Goode Ave .... Glendale CA 91203	888-567-4387*	626-304-2000
NYSE: AVY ■ *Cust Svc		
BASF Corp/Bldg Systems		
889 Valley Pk Dr .... Shakopee MN 55379	800-433-9517*	952-496-6000
*Cust Svc		
Bestolife Corp		
2777 Stemmons Fwy Ste 1800 .... Dallas TX 75207	855-243-9164	214-583-0271
Bonstone Materials Corp		
707 Swan Dr .... Mukwonago WI 53149	800-425-2214	262-363-9877
CFC International Inc		
500 State St .... Chicago Heights IL 60411	800-393-4505	708-891-3456
Chase Corp 26 Summer St .... Bridgewater MA 02324	800-323-4182	781-332-0700
NYSE: CCF		
Colloid Environmental Technologies Co (CETCO)		
2870 Forbs Ave .... Hoffman Estates IL 60192	800-527-9948	847-851-1899
Custom Bldg Products		
13001 Seal Beach Blvd .... Seal Beach CA 90740	800-272-8786	562-598-8808
DAP Products Inc		
2400 Boston St Ste 200 .... Baltimore MD 21224	800-543-3840*	888-327-8477
*Cust Svc		
Devcon Inc 30 Endicott St .... Danvers MA 01923	800-626-7226	855-489-7262
Dymax Corp		
318 Industrial Ln .... Torrington CT 06790	877-396-2963	860-482-1010
Eclectic Products Inc		
1075 Arrowsmith St PO Box 2280 .... Eugene OR 97402	800-693-4667	

	Toll-Free	Phone
Elmer's Products Inc		
1 Easton Oval .... Columbus OH 43219	888-435-6377	
Euclid Chemical Co		
19218 Redwood Rd .... Cleveland OH 44110	800-321-7628	216-531-9222
Foster Construction Products Inc		
1105 S Frontenac Rd .... Aurora IL 60504	800-231-9541	
Fox Industries Inc		
3100 Falls Cliff Rd .... Baltimore MD 21211	888-760-0369	410-646-8405
Franklin International		
2020 Bruck St .... Columbus OH 43207	800-877-4583	614-443-0241
Geocel Corp 2504 Marina Dr .... Elkhart IN 46514	800-348-7615	
H B Fuller Construction Products Inc		
1105 S Frontenac Rd .... Aurora IL 60504	800-832-9002	
HB Fuller Co		
1200 Willow Lake Blvd PO Box 64683 .... St. Paul MN 55164	888-423-8553	651-236-5900
NYSE: FUL		
Henkel Corp 1 Henkel Way .... Rocky Hill CT 06067	800-243-4874*	860-571-5100
*Cust Svc		
Hercules Chemical Company Inc		
111 S St .... Passaic NJ 07055	800-221-9330	
Houghton International Inc		
945 Madison Ave PO Box 930 .... Valley Forge PA 19482	888-459-9844	610-666-4000
Inovex Industries Inc		
45681 Oakbrook Ct Ste 102 .... Sterling VA 20166	888-374-3366	703-421-9778
IPS Corp 455 W Victoria St .... Compton CA 90220	800-888-8312	310-898-3300
ITW Polymers Sealants North America		
111 S Nursery R .... Irving TX 75060	800-878-7876*	972-438-9111
*Hotline		
Lapolla Industries Inc		
15402 Vantage Pkwy E Ste 322 .... Houston TX 77032	888-452-7655	281-219-4700
OTC: LPAD		
Laticrete International Inc		
91 Amity Rd .... Bethany CT 06524	800-243-4788	203-393-0010
Lord Corp 111 Lord Dr .... Cary NC 27511	877-275-5673	919-468-5979
MAPEI Corp		
1144 E Newport Ctr Dr .... Deerfield Beach FL 33442	800-426-2734	954-246-8888
Morgan Adhesives Co		
4560 Darrow Rd .... Stow OH 44224	866-262-2822	330-688-1111
Nylok Corp 15260 Hallmark Dr .... Macomb MI 48042	800-826-5161	586-786-0100
Pacific Polymers Inc		
12271 Monarch St .... Garden Grove CA 92841	800-888-8340	714-898-0025
Para-Chem Southern Inc		
863 SE Main St PO Box 127 .... Simpsonville SC 29681	800-763-7272	864-967-7691
Pecora Corp		
165 Wambold Rd .... Harleysville PA 19438	800-523-6688	215-723-6051
Red Devil Inc 1437 S Boulder .... Tulsa OK 74119	800-423-3845	
Ritrama		
800 Kasota Ave SE .... Minneapolis MN 55414	800-328-5071	
Southern Grouts & Mortars Inc		
1502 SW Second Pl .... Pompano Beach FL 33069	800-641-9247	
Sti Polymer Inc		
5618 Clyde Rhyne Dr .... Sanford NC 27330	800-874-5878	
Super Glue Corp		
3281 E Guasti Rd Ste 260 .... Ontario CA 91761	800-538-3091	909-987-0550
Tailored Chemical Products Inc		
700 12th St Dr NW .... Hickory NC 28601	800-627-1687	828-322-6512
Tremco Inc Roofing Div		
3735 Green Rd .... Beachwood OH 44122	800-852-6013	216-292-5000
WF. Taylor Company Inc		
11545 Pacific Ave .... Fontana CA 92337	800-397-4583	951-360-6677

4   ADVERTISING AGENCIES

SEE ALSO Public Relations Firms

	Toll-Free	Phone
Alesco Data Group LLC		
5276 Summerlin Commons Way .... Fort Myers FL 33907	800-701-6531	239-275-5006
All-Ways Adv Co		
1442 Broad St .... Bloomfield NJ 07003	800-255-9291	973-338-0700
Anderson Partners Advertising		
444 Regency Pkwy Dr Ste 311 .... Omaha NE 68114	800-551-9737	402-341-4807
Aspen Marketing Services		
1240 N Ave .... West Chicago IL 60185	800-848-0212	630-293-9600
CBC Advertising		
56 Industrial Park Rd Ste 103 .... Saco ME 04072	800-222-2682	207-283-9191
Cooper Smith Advertising		
3500 Granite Cir .... Toledo OH 43617	800-215-8812	419-470-5900
DW Green Co 8100 S Priest Dr .... Tempe AZ 85284	800-253-7146	480-491-8483
Fahlgren Mortine		
4030 Easton Stn Ste 300 .... Columbus OH 43219	800-731-8927	614-383-1500
Ideal Adv & Printing		
116 N Winnebago St .... Rockford IL 61101	800-208-0294	815-965-1713
Imagemakers Inc		
514 Lincoln Ave PO Box 368 .... Wamego KS 66547	888-865-8511	
Innis Maggiore Group Inc		
4715 Whipple Ave NW .... Canton OH 44718	800-460-4111	330-492-5500
Intermark Group		
101 25th St N .... Birmingham AL 35203	800-624-9239	
Interpublic Group		
909 Third Ave .... New York NY 10036	800-908-5395	212-704-1200
NYSE: IPG		
Iris Group Inc, The		
1675 Faraday Ave .... Carlsbad CA 92008	800-347-1103	760-431-1103
J&L Marketing		
2100 Nelson Miller Pkwy .... Louisville KY 40223	800-651-5508	
Korey Kay & Partners		
130 Fifth Ave .... New York NY 10011	800-264-8590	212-620-4300
Kuno Creative Group LLC		
36901 American Wy Ste 2A .... Avon OH 44011	800-303-0806	
Launch Agency LP		
4100 Midway Rd Ste 2110 .... Carrollton TX 75007	866-427-5013	972-818-4100
McKee Wallwork Cleveland LLC		
1030 18th St NW .... Albuquerque NM 87104	888-821-2999	
Mindgrub Technologies LLC		
1215 E Ft Ave Ste 200 .... Baltimore MD 21230	855-646-3472	410-988-2444
Mower Boston's One-Stop B2B Marketing Agency		
134 Rumford Ave Ste 307 .... Newton MA 02466	800-553-6477	781-818-4201

Classified Section

	Toll-Free	Phone
NAS Recruitment Communications		
9700 Rockside Rd Ste 170 . . . . .Cleveland OH 44125	866-627-7327	216-503-9001
Neathawk Dubuque & Packett (NDP)		
2912 W Leigh St .Richmond VA 23230	800-847-2674	804-783-8140
Page 1 Solutions LLC		
1726 Cole Blvd Ste 150 . . . . .Lakewood CO 80401	800-916-3886	303-233-3886
R2c Group Inc		
207 NW Park Ave .Portland OR 97209	866-402-1124	
Register Tapes Unlimited Inc		
1445 Langham Creek . . . . .Houston TX 77084	800-247-4793	281-206-2500
Risdall Adv Agency		
2685 Long Lake Rd Ste 100 . . . . .Roseville MN 55113	888-747-3255	651-286-6700
Sherry Matthews Inc		
200 S Congress Ave . . . . .Austin TX 78704	877-478-4397	512-478-4397
Shumsky Enterprises Inc		
811 E Fourth St . . . . .Dayton OH 45402	800-223-2203	937-223-2203
Streamworks LLC		
3640 Pheasant Ridge Dr NE . . . . .Blaine MN 55449	800-328-5680	

ADVERTISING DISPLAYS

SEE Displays - Point-of-Purchase ; Displays - Exhibit & Trade Show ; Signs

5   ADVERTISING SERVICES - DIRECT MAIL

	Toll-Free	Phone
A M Solutions		
100 Interstate Blvd . . . . .Edgerton WI 53534	800-410-6245	
Accurate Mailings Inc		
215 O'Neill Ave . . . . .Belmont CA 94002	800-732-3290	650-508-8885
Action Mailing Corp		
3165 W Heartland Dr . . . . .Liberty MO 64068	866-990-9001	816-415-9000
Acxiom 301 E Dave Ward Dr . . . . .Conway AR 72032	888-322-9466	501-342-7799
NASDAQ: ACXM		
Adzzup		
2600 N Central Ave Ste 1700 . . . . .Phoenix AZ 85004	888-723-9987	
Agency Revolution 698 NW . . . . .Bend OR 97701	800-606-0477	
AKA Direct 2415 N Ross Ave . . . . . .Portland OR 97227	800-647-8587	
AKT Enterprises		
6424 Forest City Rd . . . . .Orlando FL 32810	877-306-3651	
Amazing Mail-print Ctr		
2130 S Seventh Ave Ste 170. . . . . .Phoenix AZ 85007	888-681-1214	
Ballantine Corp		
55 Lane Rd . . . . .Fairfield NJ 07004	800-669-6801	973-305-1500
BIGMPG Design/Marketing		
811 E Vienna Ave . . . . .Milwaukee WI 53212	866-332-3919	
BlueSpire Strategic Marketing		
7650 Edinborough Way Ste 500 . . . . . . .Minneapolis MN 55435	800-727-6397	
Boostability Inc		
2600 W Executive Pkwy Ste 200. . . . . .Lehi UT 84043	800-261-1537	
Brandpoint 850 Fifth St S . . . . .Hopkins MN 55343	877-374-5270	
Bridgcom		
11388 W Olympic Blvd . . . . .Los Angeles CA 90064	855-455-5522	323-510-3860
Brierley & Partners		
5465 Legacy Dr Ste 300 . . . . .Plano TX 75024	800-899-8700	214-760-8700
Bulldog Solutions LLC		
7600 N Capital of Texas Hwy Bldg C		
Ste 250 . . . . .Austin TX 78731	877-402-9199	
Cactus Mailing Co		
16020 N 77th St . . . . .Scottsdale AZ 85260	888-633-7939	
Cardlytics Inc		
675 Ponce de Leon Ave NE Ste 6000 . . . . . .Atlanta GA 30308	888-798-5802	866-269-1020
Catawba Print & Mail Inc		
1215 15th St Dr NE . . . . .Hickory NC 28601	800-632-9513	
Centron Data Services Inc		
1175 Devin Dr . . . . .Norton Shores MI 49441	800-732-8787*	
Cust Svc		
Comark Direct		
507 S Main St . . . . .Ft. Worth TX 76104	888-742-0405	
Data-Graphics Inc		
240 Hartford Ave . . . . .Newington CT 06111	800-639-4316	
DataSphere Technologies Inc		
3350 161st Ave SE . . . . .Bellevue WA 98008	866-912-7090	
DirectMailcom		
5351 Ketch Rd . . . . .Prince Frederick MD 20678	866-284-5816	301-855-1700
Dp Murphy Company Inc		
945 Grand Blvd . . . . .Deer Park NY 11729	800-424-8724	631-673-9400
DropThought Inc		
2755 Great America Way Ste 425 . . . . . .Santa Clara CA 95054	855-437-6776	
DynamiCard Inc		
215 S Hickory St Ste 220 . . . . .Escondido CA 92025	800-928-7670	
Edmunds & Associates Inc		
301 Tilton Rd .Northfield NJ 08225	888-336-6999*	609-645-7333
Sales		
eLocal Listing		
25240 Hancock Ave Ste 410. . . . . .Murrieta CA 92563	800-285-0484	
Encore Image Group Inc		
1445 W Sepulveda Blvd . . . . .Torrance CA 90509	800-729-4853	
EQ Inc 1235 Bay St Ste 401. . . . . .Toronto ON M5R3K4	888-597-8889	
Focus Direct LLC		
9707 Broadway . . . . .San Antonio TX 78217	800-555-1551	210-805-9185
Funnel Science Internet Marketing LLC		
1802 N Carson St . . . . .Carson City NV 89701	877-301-0001	
GRAHAM OLESON		
525 Communication Cir . . . . .Colorado Springs CO 80905	800-776-7336	
Gregory Welteroth Advertising Inc		
356 Laurens Rd . . . . .Montoursville PA 17754	866-294-5765	570-433-3366
Haines & Company Inc		
8050 Freedom Ave . . . . .North Canton OH 44720	800-843-8452	
Harte-Hanks Inc		
9601 McAllister Fwy Ste 610 . . . . .San Antonio TX 78216	800-456-9748	210-829-9000
NYSE: HHS		
Haystak Digital Marketing LLC		
1514 Broadway Ste 201 . . . . .Fort Myers FL 33901	866-292-0194	
Headrick Companies Inc, The		
1 Freedom Sq . . . . .Laurel MS 39440	800-933-1365	601-649-1977

	Toll-Free	Phone
Heritage Co, The		
2402 Wildwood Ave . . . . .Sherwood AR 72120	800-643-8822	501-835-5000
HEROweb Marketing & Design Inc		
1976 Garden Ave . . . . .Eugene OR 97403	888-257-2567	541-746-6418
Hkm Direct Market Communications Inc		
5501 Cass Ave .Cleveland OH 44102	800-860-4456*	216-651-9500
General		
HouseLens Inc		
150 Fourth Ave N 20th Fl . . . . .Nashville TN 37219	888-552-3851	
IMS inc 245 Commerce Blvd . . . . .Liverpool NY 13088	800-466-4189	
infoGroup Inc		
1020 E First St .Papillion NE 68046	866-414-7848	402-836-5290
International Delivery Solutions		
7340 S Howell Ave . . . . .Oak Creek WI 53154	877-437-8722	
JLS Mailing Services		
672 Crescent St . . . . .Brockton MA 02302	866-557-6245	
justClick media Inc		
16782-B Red Hill Ave . . . . .Irvine CA 92606	866-623-8777	
L & m Mail Service Inc		
2452 Truax Blvd . . . . .Eau Claire WI 54703	800-507-7070	715-836-0138
LeadingResponse LLC		
4805 Independence Pkwy . . . . .Tampa FL 33634	800-660-2550	
LeadRival		
1207 S White Chapel Blvd Ste 250. . . . . . .Southlake TX 76092	800-332-8017	
Lemon Peak		
500 W Putnam Ave Ste 400 . . . . .Greenwich CT 06830	888-253-7348	
Level Agency		
235 Fort Pitt Blvd . . . . .Pittsburgh PA 15222	877-733-8625	
Lewis Direct Marketing		
325 E Oliver St . . . . .Baltimore MD 21202	800-533-5394	410-539-5100
Lexinet Corp, The		
701 N Union St . . . . .Council Grove KS 66846	800-767-1577	620-767-7000
Mailing Services of Pittsburgh Inc		
155 Commerce Dr . . . . .Freedom PA 15042	800-876-3211	724-774-3244
Mailing Systems Inc (MSI)		
2431 Mercantile Dr Ste A . . . . .Rancho Cordova CA 95742	877-577-2647	916-631-7400
Mailings Unlimited		
116 Riverside Industrial Pkwy . . . . .Portland ME 04103	800-773-7417	207-347-5000
Market Data Retrieval		
6 Armstrong Rd . . . . .Shelton CT 06484	800-333-8802	203-926-4800
Marketing Resource Group Inc (MRG)		
225 S Washington Sq . . . . .Lansing MI 48933	800-928-2086	517-372-4400
MarketLeverage LLC		
6314 Brookside Plz Ste 301 . . . . .Kansas City MO 64113	888-653-8372	
Mediacom Communications Corp		
1 Mediacom Way . . . . .Mediacom Park NY 10918	855-633-4226	
Meridian Display & Merchandising Inc		
162 York Ave E .St Paul MN 55117	800-786-2501	
Mint Magazine Inc		
6960 Bonneval Rd Ste 102 . . . . .Jacksonville FL 32216	888-620-3877	
Mobivity Inc		
58 W Buffalo Ste 200 . . . . .Chandler AZ 85225	877-282-7660	
Money Mailer LLC		
12131 Western Ave . . . . .Garden Grove CA 92841	800-468-5865	714-889-3800
News America Marketing		
1185 Ave of the Americas 27 . . . . .New York NY 10036	800-462-0852	212-782-8000
Next Day Flyers		
8000 Haskell Ave . . . . .Van Nuys CA 91406	855-898-9870	
Numero Uno Web Solutions Inc		
3300 Hwy 7 Ste 908 . . . . .Concord ON L4K4M3	855-736-9778	905-669-1708
Oohology 908 S Eighth St . . . . .Louisville KY 40203	855-664-6564	502-416-0143
Postal Presort Inc		
820 W Second St N . . . . .Wichita KS 67203	800-235-3033	316-262-3333
PowerChord Inc		
360 Central Ave 5th Fl . . . . .St Petersburg FL 33701	800-350-0981	727-823-1530
PrimeNet Direct Mktg Solutions LLC		
7320 Bryan Dairy Rd . . . . .Largo FL 33777	800-826-2869	727-447-6245
QuantumDigital Inc		
8702 Cross Park Dr . . . . .Austin TX 78754	800-637-7373	
R O I Media Solutions LLC		
11500 W Olympic Blvd Ste 400 . . . . . . .Los Angeles CA 90064	866-211-2580	
Redfin		
9890 S Maryland Pkwy . . . . .Las Vegas NV 89183	844-759-7732	877-973-3346
RevenueAds Affiliate Network		
322 NE Second St 2nd Fl . . . . .Oklahoma City OK 73104	800-441-1136	405-455-9053
RME360		
4805 Independence Pkwy Ste 250 . . . . .Tampa FL 33634	888-383-8770	
RR Donnelley Response Marketing Services		
4101 Winfield Rd . . . . .Warrenville IL 60555	800-722-9001	630-963-9494
RR. Donnelley & Sons Co (RRD)		
35 West Wacker Dr . . . . .Chicago IL 60601	800-742-4455	
RSVP Publications		
6730 W Linebaugh Ave Ste 201 . . . . .Tampa FL 33625	800-360-7787	813-960-7787
Sales Benchmark Index		
2021 McKinney Ave Ste 550. . . . . .Dallas TX 75201	888-556-7338	
Sherpa Digital Media Inc		
509 Seaport Ct . . . . .Redwood City CA 94063	866-989-7794	
ShiftCentral Inc		
210 John St Ste 100 . . . . .Moncton NB E1C0B8	866-551-5533	
SocialCode LLC		
151 W 26th St 9th Fl. . . . . .New York NY 10001	844-608-4610	
SourceLink LLC		
500 Pk Blvd Ste 1425 . . . . .Itasca IL 60143	866-947-6872	
Speedy Automated Mailers Inc		
2200 Queen St Ste 15. . . . . .Bellingham WA 98229	800-678-4775	360-676-4775
Steel House Inc		
3644 Eastham Dr . . . . .Culver City CA 90232	888-978-3354	
Tension Envelope Corp		
819 E 19th St . . . . .Kansas City MO 64108	800-388-5122	
Tribune Direct Marketing Inc		
505 Northwest Ave . . . . .Northlake IL 60164	800-545-9657	
U S Monitor 86 Maple Ave . . . . .New City NY 10956	800-767-7967	845-634-1331
Ultimate Lead Systems Inc		
401 Frnt St . . . . .Berea OH 44017	800-323-0550	440-826-1908
Universal Wilde		
26 Dartmouth St . . . . .Westwood MA 02090	866-825-5515	781-251-2700
Varvid		
705 Sunset Pond Ln . . . . .Bellingham WA 98225	855-827-8434	

	City	State	Zip	Toll-Free	Phone
Vertical Vision Financial Marketing LLC					
1201 Roberts Blvd Bldg A Ste 150	Kennesaw	GA	30144	**866-984-1585**	
Wahl Media Inc					
580 Packetts Landing	Fairport	NY	14450	**888-924-5633**	
Walts Mailing Service Ltd					
9610 E First Ave	Spokane Valley	WA	99206	**888-549-2006**	509-924-5939
Wave Direct					
9 Del Prado Blvd N Ste B	Cape Coral	FL	33909	**888-550-9918**	239-574-8181
Welcome Wagon					
5830 Coral Ridge Dr	Coral Springs	FL	33076	**800-779-3526**	
Yeck Bros Co					
2222 Arbor Blvd	Moraine	OH	45439	**800-417-2767**	937-294-4000
YP LLC					
611 N Brand Blvd Ste 500	Glendale	CA	91203	**866-570-8863**	

6 ADVERTISING SERVICES - MEDIA BUYERS

	City	State	Zip	Toll-Free	Phone
Allan Hackel Organization					
1330 Ctr St	Newton Center	MA	02459	**800-970-2499**	617-965-4400
Backchannelmedia Inc					
105 S St	Boston	MA	02111	**800-676-0823**	
Media Brokers International Inc					
555 N Point Ctr E Ste 700	Alpharetta	GA	30022	**866-514-1620**	
Media Space Solutions					
5600 Rowland Rd Ste 170	Minnetonka	MN	55343	**888-672-2100**	
Parr Moto					
13120 Westlinks Ter Blvd Unit 4	Fort Myers	FL	33913	**866-772-1381**	
Worldata					
3000 N Military Trl	Boca Raton	FL	33431	**800-331-8102**	561-393-8200

7 ADVERTISING SERVICES - ONLINE

	City	State	Zip	Toll-Free	Phone
Access To Media					
432 Front St	Chicopee	MA	01013	**866-612-0034**	413-206-0715
Active Network					
10182 Telesis Ct Ste 100	San Diego	CA	92121	**888-543-7223**	858-964-3800
Adler Display					
7140 Windsor Blvd	Baltimore	MD	21244	**855-552-3537**	
Adstrategies Inc					
101 Bay St Ste 201	Easton	MD	21601	**888-456-2450**	
Advance Notice Inc					
24 Winter St	Peabody	MA	01960	**800-992-0313**	
Agency Mabu					
1003 Gateway Ave	Bismarck	ND	58503	**800-568-9346**	701-250-0728
Alamo Tee's & Advertising					
12814 Cogburn	San Antonio	TX	78249	**888-562-3800**	210-699-3800
AMCI					
5353 Grosvenor Blvd	Los Angeles	CA	90066	**855-486-5527**	
Apex Advertising Inc					
2959 Old Tree Dr	Lancaster	PA	17603	**800-666-5556**	717-396-7100
Atlas Advertising LLC					
1128 Grant St	Denver	CO	80203	**800-543-4402**	303-292-3300
Austin Williams					
80 Arkay Dr Ste 220	Hauppauge	NY	11788	**877-386-6035**	631-498-5756
Banner Marketing					
16201 E Indiana Ave Ste 3240	Spokane Valley	WA	99216	**800-843-9271**	509-922-7828
Barnes Advertising Corp					
1580 Fairview Rd	Zanesville	OH	43701	**800-458-1410**	740-453-6836
Big Frey Promotional Products					
420 Lake Cook Rd Ste 117	Deerfield	IL	60015	**800-888-1636**	
Blade Creative Branding Inc					
15 Gervais Dr Ste 103	Toronto	ON	M3C1Y8	**800-392-5233**	416-467-4770
Blast Radius					
509 Richards St	Vancouver	BC	?V6B2Z6	**866-473-6800**	604-647-6500
Blue Zebra Appointment Setting					
25 Pequot Ave Ste A	Port Washington	NY	11050	**800-755-0094**	
BOC Partners Inc					
1030 South Ave W Ste 1	Westfield	NJ	07090	**877-310-8445**	
Bolin Marketing & Advertising					
2523 Wayzata Blvd Ste 300	Minneapolis	MN	55405	**800-876-6264**	612-374-1200
Brunet-Garcia Advertising Inc					
1510 Hendricks Ave	Jacksonville	FL	32207	**866-346-1977**	904-346-1977
Burkhart Advertising Inc					
1335 Mishawaka Ave	South Bend	IN	46615	**800-777-8122**	574-233-2101
Catalpha Advertising & Design Inc					
6801 Loch Raven Blvd	Towson	MD	21286	**888-337-0066**	410-337-0066
Central Address Systems Inc					
10303 Crown Point Ave	Omaha	NE	68134	**800-482-7705**	402-964-9998
Chrisad Inc					
11 Professional Ctr Pkwy	San Rafael	CA	94903	**800-505-4150**	415-924-8575
Chumney & Associates					
660 US-1 2nd Fl	North Palm Beach	FL	33408	**877-816-7347**	561-768-5818
City of Com, The					
1559 S Brownlee Blvd	Corpus Christi	TX	78404	**888-785-0500**	
Commission Junction Inc					
530 E Montecito St	Santa Barbara	CA	93103	**800-761-1072**	805-730-8000
Concerto Marketing Group Inc					
128 Hastings St W	Vancouver	BC	V6B1G8	**877-873-2738**	604-642-5901
Confluent Translations LLC					
340 Mansfield Ave	Pittsburgh	PA	15220	**888-539-9077**	412-539-1410
Conversant LLC					
30699 Russell Ranch Rd					
Ste 250	Westlake Village	CA	91362	**877-361-3316**	818-575-4500
NASDAQ: VCLK					
Conway Marketing Communications					
6400 Baum Dr	Knoxville	TN	37919	**800-882-7875**	865-588-5731
Creative Outdoor Advertising					
2402 Stouffville Rd	Stouffville	ON	L4A2J4	**800-661-6088**	
Crouch Group Inc, The					
300 N Carroll Blvd Ste 103	Denton	TX	76201	**888-211-0273**	940-383-1990
Cyphers Agency Inc, The					
1682 Village Green	Crofton	MD	21114	**888-412-7469**	
Daniels & Roberts Inc					
209 N Seacrest Blvd	Boynton Beach	FL	33435	**800-488-0066**	561-241-0066
Datamine Internet Marketing Solutions Inc					
330 S Lake St	Gary	IN	46403	**877-328-2646**	219-939-9987
Davco Advertising Inc					
89 N Kinzer Rd PO Box 288	Kinzers	PA	17535	**800-283-2826**	717-442-4155
Decker Advertising					
99 Citizens Dr	Glastonbury	CT	06033	**800-777-3677**	860-659-1311
Dexter Solutions					
3493 Lamar Ave	Memphis	TN	38118	**800-641-3398**	
Dogwood Productions Inc					
757 Government St	Mobile	AL	36602	**800-254-9903**	251-476-0858
DoublePositive					
1111 Light St Ste 350	Baltimore	MD	21230	**888-376-7484**	410-332-0464
eCreative Group Inc					
1827 First St W Ste B PO Box 66	Independence	IA	50644	**877-334-5115**	319-334-5115
Evo Exhibits					
399 Wegner Dr	West Chicago	IL	60185	**888-404-4224**	630-520-0710
F p i s Inc 220 Story Rd	Ocoee	FL	34761	**800-346-5977**	407-656-8818
Gift Card Partners Inc					
47 Pine Plain Rd	Wellesley	MA	02482	**800-413-9101**	
Grafik Marketing Communications Ltd					
625 N Washington St Ste 302	Alexandria	VA	22314	**800-750-9772**	703-299-4500
Graystone Group Advertising					
2710 N ave	Bridgeport	CT	06604	**800-544-0005**	203-549-0060
HelloWorld					
3000 Town Ctr Ste 2100	South Field	MI	48075	**877-837-7493**	
Interline Creative Group					
553 North N Ct Ste 160	Palatine	IL	60067	**800-222-1208**	847-358-4848
Ion 948 W Seventh Ave W	Vancouver	BC	V5Z1C3	**888-336-2466**	604-682-6787
Jobelephantcom Inc					
5443 Fremontia Ln	San Diego	CA	92115	**800-311-0563**	619-795-0837
LiveWorld Inc					
4340 Stevens Creek Blvd Ste 101	San Jose	CA	95129	**800-301-9507**	
Madwire					
3420 E Harmony Rd Bldg 5 3rd Fl	Fort Collins	CO	80528	**888-872-3734***	855-773-8171
*Sales					
Marco Corp, The					
470 Hardy Rd	Brantford	ON	N3V6T1	**888-636-6161**	
MarketLauncher Inc					
PO Box 916582	Longwood	FL	32791	**800-901-3803**	
MatchCraft Inc					
2701 Ocean Park Blvd Ste 220	Santa Monica	CA	90405	**888-502-7238**	310-314-3320
MBI Direct Mail					
710 W New Hampshire Ave	Deland	FL	32720	**800-359-4780**	386-736-9998
Mediabidscom Inc					
448 Main St	Winsted	CT	06098	**800-545-1135***	
*Cust Svc					
Merz Group, The					
1570 Mcdaniel Dr	West Chester	PA	19380	**800-600-9900**	610-429-3160
MMA Creative Inc					
480 Neal St Ste 201	Cookeville	TN	38501	**800-499-2332**	931-528-8852
Monticello Corp, The					
PO Box 190645	Atlanta	GA	31119	**866-701-1561**	404-478-6413
Naylor LLC					
5950 NW First Pl	Gainesville	FL	32607	**800-369-6220**	
Overit 435 New Scotland Ave	Albany	NY	12208	**888-978-8147**	518-465-8829
Prospects Influential Inc					
1313 E Maple St Ste 548	Bellingham	WA	98225	**800-352-2282**	
Publipage Inc					
2055 Rue Peel	Montreal	QC	H3A1V4	**800-544-8614**	514-286-1550
Quest Companies Inc					
8011 N Point Blvd Ste 201	Winston-Salem	NC	27106	**800-467-9409**	
Quirks Enterprises Inc					
4662 Slater Rd	Eagan	MN	55122	**800-827-0676**	651-379-6200
Rainbow Advertising Lp					
3904 W Vickery Blvd	Fort Worth	TX	76107	**800-645-7377**	817-738-3838
Rakuten Marketing					
215 Park Ave S 2nd Fl	New York	NY	10003	**888-880-8430**	646-943-8200
RES Exhibit Services LLC					
435 Smith St	Rochester	NY	14608	**800-482-4049**	585-546-2040
Riester 3344 E Camelback Rd	Phoenix	AZ	85018	**844-602-3344**	
ScreenScape Networks Inc					
133 Queen St 3rd Fl	Charlottetown	PE	C1A4B3	**877-666-1975**	
SEO com LLC					
14870 S Pony Express Rd Ste 100	Bluffdale	UT	84065	**800-351-9081**	
SEOP 1621 Alton Pkwy Ste 150	Irvine	CA	92606	**877-231-1557**	
Straight North LLC					
1001 W 31st St	Downers Grove	IL	60515	**866-353-3953**	
StratMar Retail Services					
109 Willett Ave	Port Chester	NY	10573	**800-866-2399**	
Team Velocity Marketing LLC					
13825 Sunrise Valley Dr	Herndon	VA	20171	**877-832-6848**	
Texas Press Assn					
305 S Congress Ave	Austin	TX	78704	**800-749-4793**	512-477-6755
Thunder Tech Inc					
3635 Perkins Ave Studio 5 SW	Cleveland	OH	44114	**888-321-8422**	216-391-2255
Topica Inc					
1 Post St Ste 875	San Francisco	CA	94104	**888-728-2465**	415-344-0800
Trademark Media Corp					
2400 Webberville Rd	Austin	TX	78702	**800-916-1224**	512-459-7000
Tukaiz LLC					
2917 N Latoria Ln	Franklin Park	IL	60131	**800-543-2674**	847-455-1588
ValueClick Media					
530 E Montecito St	Santa Barbara	CA	93103	**877-361-3316**	805-879-1600
Walker Advertising					
20101 Hamilton Ave Ste 375	Torrance	CA	90502	**800-492-5537**	

8 ADVERTISING SERVICES - OUTDOOR ADVERTISING

	City	State	Zip	Toll-Free	Phone
Above All Advertising Inc					
9080 Activity Rd Ste A	San Diego	CA	92126	**866-552-2683**	858-549-2226
BriteVision Media LLC					
475 14th St Ste 200	Oakland	CA	94612	**877-479-7777**	
Grand Image Inc 560 Main St	Hudson	MA	01749	**888-973-2622**	978-212-3037

Impac International
11445 Pacific Ave . . . . Fontana CA 92337 **800-227-9591** 951-685-9660
Kegerreis Outdoor Advertising LLC
1310 Lincoln Way East . . . . Chambersburg PA 17202 **800-745-4166** 717-263-6700
Kubin-Nicholson
KN 8440 N 87th St . . . . Milwaukee WI 53224 **800-858-9557** 414-586-4300
Lamar Adv Co
5321 Corporate Blvd . . . . Baton Rouge LA 70808 **800-235-2627** 225-926-1000
NASDAQ: LAMR
MediaChoice LLC
3701 Bee Caves Rd . . . . Austin TX 78746 **888-567-2424** 512-693-9905
RCS Innovations
7075 W Parkland Ct . . . . Milwaukee WI 53223 **800-373-6873** 414-354-6900
Skyline Displays Bay Area Inc
44111 Fremont Blvd . . . . Fremont CA 94538 **800-328-2725** 510-490-9900
Spec Personnel LLC
25 Walls Dr . . . . Fairfield CT 06824 **888-788-7732**
Stott Outdoor Advertising
PO Box 7209 . . . . Chico CA 95927 **888-342-7868**
Suite 66
366 Adelaide St W Ste 600 . . . . Toronto ON M5V1R9 **866-779-3486** 416-628-5565
WSOS Community Action Commission Inc
109 S Front St . . . . Fremont OH 43420 **800-775-9767** 419-334-8911

9	ADVERTISING SPECIALTIES

SEE ALSO Smart Cards ; Trophies, Plaques, Awards ; Signs

			Toll-Free	Phone

ADG Promotional Products
2300 Main St . . . . Hugo MN 55038 **800-852-5208**
Airmate Co Inc
16280 County Rd D . . . . Bryan OH 43506 **800-544-3614** 419-636-3184
Alexander Mfg Co
12978 Tesson Ferry Rd . . . . Sappington MO 63128 **800-258-2743*** 800-467-5343
*General
Americanna Co
101 Industrial . . . . Lakeville MA 02347 **888-747-5550*** 508-747-5550
*Cust Svc
Amsterdam Printing & Litho Corp
166 Wallins Corners Rd . . . . Amsterdam NY 12010 **800-833-6231***
*Cust Svc
Atlas Match LLC
1801 S Airport Cir . . . . Euless TX 76040 **800-628-2426** 817-354-7474
Bergamot Inc
820 E Wisconsin St . . . . Delavan WI 53115 **800-922-6733*** 262-728-5572
*Cust Svc
Brown & Bigelow Inc
345 Plato Blvd E . . . . Saint Paul MN 55107 **800-628-1755*** 651-293-7000
*Cust Svc
Churchwell Co
814 S Edgewood Ave . . . . Jacksonville FL 32205 **877-537-6166** 904-356-5721
EBSCO Creative Concepts
3500 Blue Lake Dr Ste 150 . . . . Birmingham AL 35243 **800-756-7023** 205-980-6789
Geiger 70 Mt Hope Ave . . . . Lewiston ME 04240 **888-953-9340**
Hit Promotional Products Inc
7150 Bryan Dairy Rd . . . . Largo FL 33777 **800-237-6305** 727-541-5561
Instant Imprints
6615 Flanders Dr Ste B. . . . . San Diego CA 92121 **800-542-3437** 858-642-4848
Marco Promotional Products
2640 Commerce Dr . . . . Harrisburg PA 17110 **877-545-9322**
Marietta Hospitality
37 Huntington St . . . . Cortland NY 13045 **800-950-7772** 607-753-6746
Maryland Match Corp
605 Alluvion St . . . . Baltimore MD 21230 **800-423-0013** 410-752-8164
Mid-America Merchandising Inc
204 W Third St . . . . Kansas City MO 64105 **800-333-6737** 816-471-5600
Myron Corp 205 Maywood Ave . . . . Maywood NJ 07607 **877-803-3358**
National Pen Corp (NPC)
12121 Scripps Summit Dr . . . . San Diego CA 92131 **888-672-7370**
Nationwide Adv Specialty Co
854 Angliana Ave . . . . Lexington KY 40508 **800-683-5697** 817-382-1616
Newton Manufacturing Co
854 Angliana Ave . . . . Lexington KY 40508 **855-754-8123** 641-316-0500
Norscot Group Inc
1000 W Donges Bay Rd . . . . Mequon WI 53092 **800-653-3313** 262-241-3313
Staples Promotional Products
7500 W 110th St . . . . Overland Park KS 66210 **800-369-4669** 913-319-3100
Vanguard East
1172 Azalea Garden Rd . . . . Norfolk VA 23502 **800-221-1264**
Western Plastic Products Inc
8441 Monroe Ave . . . . Stanton CA 90680 **800-453-1881**

	AGRICULTURAL CHEMICALS

	AGRICULTURAL MACHINERY & EQUIPMENT

SEE Farm Machinery & Equipment - Mfr ;
Farm Machinery & Equipment - Whol

10	AGRICULTURAL PRODUCTS

SEE ALSO Horticultural Products Growers ; Seed Companies ; Horse Breeders ; Fruit Growers

			Toll-Free	Phone

United Farmers Co-op (UFC)
705 E Fourth St PO Box 461. . . . . Winthrop MN 55396 **866-998-3266** 507-647-6600

10-1 Cattle Ranches, Farms, Feedlots (Beef Cattle)

			Toll-Free	Phone

Agri Beef Co
1555 Shoreline Dr Ste 320 . . . . Boise ID 83702 **800-657-6305** 208-338-2500

AzTx Cattle Co
311 E Park Ave . . . . Hereford TX 79045 **800-999-5065** 806-364-8871
Bar G Feed Yard
275 FM 1057 Rd . . . . Summerfield TX 79085 **800-569-3736** 806-357-2241
Boise Valley Feeders LLC
1555 Shoreline Dr Ste 320 . . . . Boise ID 83702 **800-657-6305** 208-338-2605
Dinklage Feedyards
PO Box 274 . . . . Sidney NE 69162 **888-343-5940** 308-254-5940
Friona Industries
500 S Taylor St Ste 601 . . . . Amarillo TX 79101 **800-658-6014** 806-374-1811
JR Simplot Co PO Box 27 . . . . Boise ID 83707 **800-832-8893** 208-336-2110

10-2 Dairy Farms

			Toll-Free	Phone

Kreider Farms
1461 Lancaster Rd . . . . Manheim PA 17545 **888-665-4415** 717-665-4415
Marburger Farm Dairy Inc
1506 Mars Evans City Rd . . . . Evans City PA 16033 **800-331-1295** 724-538-4800

10-3 General Farms

			Toll-Free	Phone

Agrex Inc
10975 Grandview Dr St Ste 200 . . . . Overland Park KS 66210 **800-523-8181** 913-851-6300
Amana Colonies 622 46th Ave . . . . Amana IA 52203 **800-579-2294** 319-622-7622
DM Camp & Sons
31798 Merced Ave . . . . Bakersfield CA 93308 **800-826-0200** 661-399-5511
Farmers Win Coop (FFC)
110 N Jefferson . . . . Fredericksburg IA 50630 **800-562-8389** 563-237-5324
FarmTek
1395 John Fitch Blvd . . . . South Windsor CT 06074 **800-327-6835*** 860-528-1119
*Sales
Gold-Eagle Co-op
PO Box 280 . . . . Goldfield IA 50542 **800-825-3331**
Plains Grain & Agronomy LLC
109 Third Ave . . . . Enderlin ND 58027 **800-950-2219** 701-437-2400

10-4 Grain Farms

			Toll-Free	Phone

Country Pride Co-op (CPC)
201 S Monroe PO Box 529. . . . . Winner SD 57580 **888-325-7743** 605-842-2711
Golden Grain Energy LLC
1822 43rd St SW . . . . Mason City IA 50401 **888-443-2676** 641-423-8500
Hoegemeyer Hybrids Inc
1755 Hoegemeyer Rd . . . . Hooper NE 68031 **800-245-4631** 402-654-3399
Moews Seed Co
Route 89 S of Jct 89 & 71
PO Box 214. . . . . Granville IL 61326 **800-663-9795** 815-339-2201
Morrow County Grain Growers Inc (MCGG)
350 N Main St . . . . Lexington OR 97839 **800-452-7396** 541-989-8221
Pioneer Hi-Bred International Inc
PO Box 1000 . . . . Johnston IA 50131 **800-247-6803** 515-535-3200
William F Renk & Sons Inc
6809 Wilburn Rd . . . . Sun Prairie WI 53590 **800-289-7365**
Wyffels Hybrids Inc
13344 US Hwy 6 . . . . Geneseo IL 61254 **800-369-7833** 309-944-8334

10-5 Hog Farms

			Toll-Free	Phone

Cargill Inc
15407 McGinty Rd W . . . . Wayzata MN 55391 **800-227-4455**
Hog Slat Inc
PO Box 300 . . . . Newton Grove NC 28366 **800-949-4647** 910-594-0219
PIC USA
100 Bluegrass Commons Blvd
Ste 2200 . . . . Hendersonville TN 37075 **800-325-3398**
Seaboard Foods
9000 W 67th St Ste 200 . . . . Shawnee Mission KS 66202 **800-262-7907** 913-261-2600
Tyson Foods Inc
PO Box 219 . . . . Kings Mountains NC 28086 **800-233-6332** 479-290-6397
NYSE: TSN

10-6 Mushroom Growers

			Toll-Free	Phone

Monterey Mushrooms Inc
260 Westgate Dr . . . . Watsonville CA 95076 **800-333-6874** 831-763-5300
Phillips Mushroom Farms Inc
1011 Kaolin Rd . . . . Kennett Square PA 19348 **800-722-8818**
Sylvan Inc 90 Glade Dr . . . . Kittanning PA 16201 **866-352-7520** 724-543-3900

10-7 Poultry & Eggs Production

			Toll-Free	Phone

Amick Farms Inc
2079 Batesburg Hwy . . . . Batesburg SC 29006 **800-926-4257** 803-532-1400
Cobb-Vantress Inc
PO Box 1030 . . . . Siloam Springs AR 72761 **800-748-9719** 479-524-3166
Culver Duck Farms Inc
12215 CR 10 . . . . Middlebury IN 46540 **800-825-9225** 574-825-9537
Echo Lake Farm Produce Co
PO Box 279 . . . . Burlington WI 53105 **800-888-3447**
Foster Farms Inc
PO Box 306 . . . . Livingston CA 95334 **800-255-7227**
Maple Leaf Farms Inc
PO Box 167 . . . . Leesburg IN 46538 **800-348-2812**

				Toll-Free	Phone
Michael Foods Inc					
301 Carlson Pkwy Ste 400	Minnetonka	MN	55305	800-328-5474	952-258-4000
Perdue Farms Inc					
31149 Old Ocean City Rd	Salisbury	MD	21804	800-473-7383	410-543-3000
Simpson's Eggs Inc					
5015 Hwy 218 E	Monroe	NC	28110	800-726-1330	704-753-1478
Tyson Foods Inc					
PO Box 219	Kings Mountains	NC	28086	800-233-6332	479-290-6397
NYSE: TSN					
Wayne Farms LLC					
4110 Continental Dr	Oakwood	GA	30566	800-392-0844	
Zephyr Egg Co Inc					
4622 Gall Blvd	Zephyrhills	FL	33542	800-333-4415	813-782-1521

10-8 Tree Nuts Growers

				Toll-Free	Phone
Green Valley Pecan Co					
1625 E Sahuarita Rd	Sahuarita	AZ	85629	800-533-5269	520-791-2852
Mauna Loa Macadamia Nut Corp					
16-701 Macadamia Rd	Keaau	HI	96749	888-628-6256*	808-966-8618
*Cust Svc					
Sunnyland Farms Inc					
PO Box 8200	Albany	GA	31706	800-999-2488	

10-9 Vegetable Farms

				Toll-Free	Phone
Barnes Farming Corp					
7840 Old Bailey Hwy	Spring Hope	NC	27882	800-367-2799	
Bolthouse Farms					
7200 E Brundage Ln	Bakersfield	CA	93307	800-467-4683	661-366-7209
Bonipak					
1850 W Stowell Rd	Santa Maria	CA	93458	800-328-8816	
Buurma Farms Inc					
3909 Kok Rd	Willard	OH	44890	888-428-8762	419-935-6411
Caruso Inc 3465 Hauck Rd	Cincinnati	OH	45241	800-759-7659	513-860-9200
Christopher Ranch					
305 Bloomfield Ave	Gilroy	CA	95020	800-779-1156	408-847-1100
CROPP Co-op 1 Organic Way	LaFarge	WI	54639	888-444-6455	
D'Arrigo Bros Company of California Inc					
PO Box 850	Salinas	CA	93902	800-995-5939*	831-455-4500
*Cust Svc					
Earthbound Farm					
1721 San Juan Hwy	San Juan Bautista	CA	95045	800-690-3200	831-623-7880
Fresh Express Inc					
PO Box 80599	Salinas	CA	93912	800-242-5472*	
*Cust Svc					
Greenheart Farms Inc					
902 Zenon Way	Arroyo Grande	CA	93420	800-549-5531	805-481-2234
Grimmway Farms Inc					
PO Box 81498	Bakersfield	CA	93380	800-301-3101	
Harris Farms Inc					
27366 W Oakland Ave	Coalinga	CA	93210	800-311-6211	559-884-2859
Hartung Bros Inc					
708 Heartland Trl Ste 2000	Madison	WI	53717	800-362-2522	608-829-6000
Nash Produce Co					
6160 S N Carolina 58	Nashville	NC	27856	800-334-3032	
Petrocco Farms					
14110 Brighton Rd	Brighton	CO	80601	888-876-2207	303-659-6498
Tanimura & Antle Inc					
PO Box 4070	Salinas	CA	93912	800-772-4542	
West Coast Distributing Inc					
Commerce Pl 350 Main St	Boston	MA	02148	800-235-3730	781-665-9393
Wiers Farm Inc					
4465 St Rt 103 S PO Box 385	Willard	OH	44890	800-777-6243	419-935-0131

11 AGRICULTURAL SERVICES

11-1 Crop Preparation Services

				Toll-Free	Phone
Central Prairie Co-op					
225 S Broadway	Sterling	KS	67579	800-861-3207	620-278-2141
Fresh Express Inc					
PO Box 80599	Salinas	CA	93912	800-242-5472*	
*Cust Svc					
Haines City Citrus Growers Assn (HCCGA)					
8 Railroad Ave PO Box 337	Haines City	FL	33844	800-327-6676*	863-422-1174
*Sales					
Index Fresh Inc					
18184 Slover Ave	Bloomington	CA	92316	800-352-6931	909-877-0999
Mann Packing Co PO Box 690	Salinas	CA	93902	800-285-1002	
Mariani Packing Company Inc					
500 Crocker Dr	Vacaville	CA	95688	800-231-1287	707-452-2800

11-2 Livestock Improvement Services

				Toll-Free	Phone
Accelerated Genetics					
E 10890 Penny Ln	Baraboo	WI	53913	800-451-9275	608-356-8357
COBA/Select Sires Inc					
1224 Alton Darby Creek Rd	Columbus	OH	43228	800-837-2621	614-878-5333
Cobb-Vantress Inc					
PO Box 1030	Siloam Springs	AR	72761	800-748-9719	479-524-3166
Dairy One 730 Warren Rd	Ithaca	NY	14850	800-344-2697	607-257-1272
Genex Co-op Inc/CRI					
PO Box 469	Shawano	WI	54166	888-333-1783	715-526-2141
Hagyard-Davidson-McGee Assoc PSC					
4250 Iron Works Pk	Lexington	KY	40511	888-323-7798	859-255-8741
SEK Genetics 9525 70th Rd	Galesburg	KS	66740	800-443-6389	

12 AIR CARGO CARRIERS

				Toll-Free	Phone
Aeronet Worldwide					
42 Corporate Pk	Irvine	CA	92606	800-552-3869	949-474-3000
Air Creebec Inc					
101 Fecteau St	Val-d'or	QC	J9P0G4	800-567-6567	819-825-8375
Air North Charter & Training Ltd					
150 Condor Rd	Whitehorse	YT	Y1A0M7	800-661-0407	867-668-2228
Ameriflight Inc					
1515 W 20th St PO Box 612763	DFW Airport	TX	75261	800-800-4538	
Amerijet International Inc					
2800 S Andrews Ave	Fort Lauderdale	FL	33316	800-927-6059	954-320-5300
Atlas Air Worldwide Holdings Inc					
2000 Westchester Ave	Purchase	NY	10577	866-434-1617	914-701-8000
NASDAQ: AAWW					
Cathay Pacific Cargo					
6040 Avion Dr Ste 338	Los Angeles	CA	90045	800-628-6960	310-417-0052
Cayman Airways Cargo Services					
6103 NW 72nd Ave	Miami	FL	33166	800-252-2746	305-526-3190
Delta Air Lines Inc					
PO Box 20559	Atlanta	GA	30320	800-352-2737	
Kalitta Flying Service					
818 Willow Run Airport	Ypsilanti	MI	48198	800-521-1590	734-484-0088
Lynden Air Cargo LLC					
6441 S Airpark Pl	Anchorage	AK	99502	888-243-7248	907-243-7248
MartinAire Aviation LLC					
4553 Glenn Curtiss Dr	Addison	TX	75001	866-557-1861	972-349-5700
Qantas Airways Cargo					
6555 W Imperial Hwy	Los Angeles	CA	90045	800-227-0290*	310-665-2280
*General					
Service by Air Inc					
222 Crossways Pk Dr	Woodbury	NY	11797	800-243-5545	
Southwest Airlines Air Cargo					
2702 Love Field Dr	Dallas	TX	75235	800-533-1222	
United Airlines Cargo					
PO Box 66100	Chicago	IL	60666	800-822-2746	
Virgin Atlantic Cargo					
78 N Boundary Rd	Jamaica	NY	11430	800-828-6822	516-775-2600

13 AIR CHARTER SERVICES

SEE ALSO Helicopter Transport Services ; Aviation - Fixed-Base Operations

				Toll-Free	Phone
Aero Air LLC					
2050 NE 25th Ave	Hillsboro	OR	97124	800-448-2376	503-640-3711
Air Charter Team					
4151 N Mulberry Dr Ste 250	Kansas City	MO	64116	800-205-6610	816-283-3280
Air Palm Springs					
145 N Gene Autry Trl Ste 14	Palm Springs	CA	92262	800-760-7774	
Airbus Helicopters Canada					
1100 Gilmore Rd PO Box 250	Fort Erie	ON	L2A5M9	800-267-4999	905-871-7772
American Air Charter Inc					
577 Bell Ave	Chesterfield	MO	63005	888-532-2710	636-532-2707
Avstar Aviation Ltd					
12 N Haven Ln	East Northport	NY	11731	800-575-2359	631-499-0048
Berry Aviation Inc					
1807 Airport Dr	San Marcos	TX	78666	800-229-2379	
Charter Flight Inc					
1928 S Blvd	Charlotte	NC	28208	800-521-3148	
Chrysler Aviation Inc (CAI)					
7120 Hayvenhurst Ave Ste 309	Van Nuys	CA	91406	800-995-0825	818-989-7900
Clay Lacy Aviation					
7435 Valjean Ave	Van Nuys	CA	91406	800-423-2904	818-989-2900
Era Helicopters LLC					
600 Airport Service Rd					
PO Box 6550	Lake Charles	LA	70606	888-503-8172	337-478-6131
Exec Air Montana Inc					
2430 Airport Rd	Helena	MT	59601	800-513-2190	406-442-2190
Executive Jet					
4556 Airport Rd	Cincinnati	OH	45226	877-356-5387	513-979-6600
Fair Wind Air Charter					
2525 SE Witham Field Hangar 7	Stuart	FL	34996	800-989-9665	
Flightstar Corp					
7 Airport Rd Willard Airport	Savoy	IL	61874	800-747-4777	217-351-7700
Hop-A-Jet					
5525 NW 15th Ave Ste 150	Fort Lauderdale	FL	33309	800-556-6633	954-771-5779
International Jet Aviation Services					
8511 Aviator Ln	Centennial	CO	80112	800-858-5891	303-790-0414
JetSuite					
18952 MacArthur Blvd	Irvine	CA	92612	866-779-7770	
KaiserAir Inc					
8735 Earhart Rd	Oakland	CA	94621	800-538-2625	510-569-9622
Life Flight Network LLC					
22285 Yellow Gate Ln NE	Aurora	OR	97002	800-232-0911	503-678-4364
LR Services					
602 Hayden Cir	Allentown	PA	18109	888-675-9650	610-266-2500
Mayo Aviation Inc					
7735 S Peoria St	Englewood	CO	80112	800-525-0194	303-792-4020
Million Air Interlink Inc					
8501 Telephone Rd	Houston	TX	77061	888-589-9059	713-640-4000
New England Life Flight Inc					
Robins St Hangar 1727 Hanscom Air Force Base					
	Bedford	MA	01730	800-233-8998	781-863-2213
Ohio Medical Transportation Inc					
2827 W Dblin Granville Rd	Columbus	OH	43235	877-633-3598	614-734-8001
Pacific Coast Jet Charter Inc					
10600 White Rock Rd	Rancho Cordova	CA	95670	800-655-3599	916-631-6507
Planemasters Ltd					
32 W 611 Tower Rd DuPage Airport	West Chicago	IL	60185	800-994-6400	630-513-2100
Premier Jets					
2140 NE 25th Ave	Hillsboro	OR	97124	800-635-8583	503-640-2927

			Toll-Free	Phone

Presidential Aviation
1725 NW 51st Pl Ft Lauderdale Executive Airport
. . . . Fort Lauderdale FL 33309 **888-772-8622** 954-772-8622
Priester Aviation
1061 S Wolf Rd . . . . Wheeling IL 60090 **888-323-7887** 847-537-1133
San Juan Airlines Co
4167 Mitchell Way . . . . Bellingham WA 98226 **800-874-4434**
Skyservice Airlines Inc
9785 Ryan Ave . . . . Dorval QC H9P1A2 **888-985-1402** 514-636-3300
Tavaero Jet Charter
7930 Airport Blvd . . . . Houston TX 77061 **800-343-3771** 713-643-5387
Thunder Airlines Ltd
310 Hector Dougall Way . . . . Thunder Bay ON P7E6M6 **800-803-9943**
Tulip City Air Service Inc
1581 S Washington Ave . . . . Holland MI 49423 **800-748-0515** 616-392-7831
West Coast Aviation Services
19711 Campus Dr Ste 150 . . . . Santa Ana CA 92707 **800-352-6153** 949-852-8340

AIR CONDITIONING EQUIPMENT - AUTOMOTIVE

AIR CONDITIONING EQUIPMENT - WHOL

SEE Plumbing, Heating, Air Conditioning Equipment & Supplies - Whol

14   AIR CONDITIONING & HEATING EQUIPMENT - COMMERCIAL/INDUSTRIAL

SEE ALSO Air Conditioning & Heating Equipment - Residential ; Refrigeration Equipment - Mfr

			Toll-Free	Phone

Absolut Aire Inc
5496 N Riverview Dr . . . . Kalamazoo MI 49004 **800-804-4000** 269-382-1875
ACS Group, The
2900 S 160th St . . . . New Berlin WI 53151 **800-423-3183** 262-641-8600
Aqua Cal Inc
2737 24th St N . . . . Saint Petersburg FL 33713 **800-786-7751** 727-823-5642
Arctic Industries Inc
9731 NW 114th Way . . . . Miami FL 33178 **800-325-0123**
Armstrong International Inc
2081 SE Ocean Blvd 4th Fl . . . . Stuart FL 34996 **866-738-5125** 772-286-7175
Auer Steel & Heating Supply Co
2935 W Silver Spring Dr . . . . Milwaukee WI 53209 **800-242-0406** 414-463-1234
Blissfield Manufacturing Co
626 Depot St . . . . Blissfield MI 49228 **800-626-1772*** 517-486-2121
*Cust Svc
Brainerd Compressor
3034 Sandbrook St . . . . Memphis TN 38116 **800-228-4138**
Brooks Automation Inc Polycold Systems
3800 Lakeville Hwy . . . . Petaluma CA 94954 **800-698-6149** 707-769-7000
Bry-Air Inc 10793 SR 37 W . . . . Sunbury OH 43074 **877-427-9247** 740-965-2974
CEI Enterprises Inc
245 WoodwaRd Rd SE . . . . Albuquerque NM 87102 **800-545-4034**
Central Products LLC
7750 Georgetown Rd . . . . Indianapolis IN 46268 **800-215-9293**
ClimateMaster Inc
7300 SW 44th St . . . . Oklahoma City OK 73179 **800-299-9747** 405-745-6000
Cold Shot Chillers
14020 InterDr W . . . . Houston TX 77032 **800-473-9178** 281-227-8400
Colmac Coil Manufacturing Inc
370 N Lincoln St PO Box 571 . . . . Colville WA 99114 **800-845-6778** 509-684-2595
DeHumidification Technologies LP
6609 Ave U . . . . Houston TX 77011 **866-736-8348** 713-939-1166
DiversiTech Corp
6650 Sugarloaf Pkwy Ste 100 . . . . Duluth GA 30097 **800-995-2222** 678-542-3600
Dometic Corp
2320 Industrial Pkwy . . . . Elkhart IN 46516 **800-544-4881** 574-294-2511
Doucette Industries Inc (DII)
20 Leigh Dr . . . . York PA 17406 **800-445-7511** 717-845-8746
Drink More Water Store
7595-A Rickenbacker Dr . . . . Gaithersburg MD 20879 **800-697-2070**
DRISTEEM Corp
14949 Technology Dr . . . . Eden Prairie MN 55344 **800-328-4447** 952-949-2415
Duro Dyne Corp
81 Spence St . . . . Bay Shore NY 11706 **800-899-3876** 631-249-9000
Fidelity Engineering Corp
25 Loveton Cir PO Box 2500 . . . . Sparks MD 21152 **800-787-6000** 410-771-9400
Friedrich
10001 Reunion Pl Ste 500 . . . . San Antonio TX 78216 **800-541-6645** 210-546-0500
Hastings HVAC Inc
3606 Yost Ave PO Box 669 . . . . Hastings NE 68902 **800-228-4243*** 402-463-9821
*Cust Svc
Henry Technologies
701 S Main St . . . . Chatham IL 62629 **800-964-3679** 217-483-2406
Howden Buffalo Inc
7909 Parklane Rd Ste 300 . . . . Columbia SC 29223 **866-757-0908** 803-741-2700
International Environmental Corp (IEC)
PO Box 2598 . . . . Oklahoma City OK 73101 **800-264-5329** 405-605-5000
ITW Vortec
10125 Carver Rd . . . . Cincinnati OH 45242 **800-441-7475** 513-891-7485
Layton Manufacturing Corp
825 Remsen Ave . . . . Brooklyn NY 11236 **800-545-8002** 718-498-6000
Lintern Corp 8685 Stn St . . . . Mentor OH 44060 **800-321-3638** 440-255-9333
Lomanco Inc
2101 W Main St . . . . Jacksonville AR 72076 **800-643-5596** 501-982-6511
Maradyne Corp
4540 W 160th St . . . . Cleveland OH 44135 **800-537-7444** 216-362-0755
Master-Bilt Products
908 Hwy 15 N . . . . New Albany MS 38652 **800-647-1284** 662-534-9061
Mee Industries Inc
16021 Adelante St . . . . Irwindale CA 91702 **800-732-5364** 626-359-4550
Munters Corp
210 Sixth St PO Box 6428 . . . . Fort Myers FL 33907 **800-843-5360** 239-936-1555
Munters Corp DHI
79 Monroe St . . . . Amesbury MA 01913 **800-843-5360*** 978-241-1100
*Sales

Niagara Blower Co Inc
91 Sawyer Ave . . . . Tonawanda NY 14150 **800-426-5169** 716-875-2000
Nordyne Inc
8000 Phoenix Pkwy . . . . O'Fallon MO 63368 **800-422-4328** 636-561-7300
Pacific Rim Mechanical
7655 Convoy Ct . . . . San Diego CA 92111 **800-891-4822** 858-974-6500
Packless Metal Hose Inc
PO Box 20668 . . . . Waco TX 76702 **800-347-4859** 254-666-7700
Phoenix Manufacturing Inc
3655 E Roeser Rd . . . . Phoenix AZ 85040 **800-325-6952*** 602-437-4833
*Cust Svc
Polar King International Inc
4424 New Haven Ave . . . . Fort Wayne IN 46803 **800-752-7178** 260-428-2530
Proair LLC
28731 County Rd 6 . . . . Elkhart IN 46514 **800-338-8544** 574-264-5494
Rama Corp
600 W Esplanade Ave . . . . San Jacinto CA 92583 **800-472-5670** 951-654-7351
Rheem Mfg Company Air Conditioning Div
5600 Old Greenwood Rd . . . . Fort Smith AR 72903 **800-268-6966** 479-646-4311
Rink Systems Inc
1103 Hershey St . . . . Albert Lea MN 56007 **800-944-7930** 507-373-9175
Ritchie Engineering Company Inc
10950 Hampshire Ave S . . . . Bloomington MN 55438 **800-769-8370** 952-943-1300
Russell Food Equipment Ltd
1255 Venables St . . . . Vancouver BC V6A3X6 **800-663-0707** 604-253-6611
San Jamar Inc
555 Koopman Ln . . . . Elkhorn WI 53121 **800-248-9826** 262-723-6133
Sealed Unit Parts Company Inc
2230 Landmark Pl . . . . Allenwood NJ 08720 **800-333-9125** 732-223-6644
Shield Air Solutions Inc
3708 Greenhouse Rd . . . . Houston TX 77084 **800-237-2095** 281-944-4300
Skuttle Manufacturing Co
101 Margaret St . . . . Marietta OH 45750 **800-848-9786** 740-373-9169
Slant Fin Corp
100 Forest Dr . . . . Greenvale NY 11548 **800-875-2389** 516-484-2600
Temp-Air Inc
3700 W Preserve Blvd . . . . Burnsville MN 55337 **800-836-7432**
Thermal Care Inc
5680 W Jarvis Ave . . . . Niles IL 60714 **888-828-7387** 847-966-2260
Tom Barrow Co (TBC)
2800 Plant Atkinson Rd . . . . Atlanta GA 30339 **800-229-8226** 404-351-1010
Traulsen & Company Inc
4401 Blue Mound Rd . . . . Fort Worth TX 76106 **800-825-8220**
Tutco Inc 500 Gould Dr . . . . Cookeville TN 38506 **877-262-4533** 931-432-4141
United CoolAir Corp
491 E Princess St . . . . York PA 17403 **877-905-1111** 717-843-4311
Watts Radiant Inc
1630 E Bradford Pkwy Ste B . . . . Springfield MO 65804 **800-276-2419**

15   AIR CONDITIONING & HEATING EQUIPMENT - RESIDENTIAL

SEE ALSO Air Conditioning & Heating Equipment - Commercial/Industrial

			Toll-Free	Phone

Airefco Inc
18755 SW Teton Ave PO Box 1349 . . . . Tualatin OR 97062 **800-869-1349** 503-692-3210
Allied Air Enterprises
215 Metropolitan Dr . . . . West Columbia SC 29170 **800-448-5872**
Amana Appliances Inc
2800 220th Trl . . . . Amana IA 52204 **800-843-0304*** 319-622-5511
*Cust Svc
Bard Mfg Co Inc
1914 Randolph Dr . . . . Bryan OH 43506 **800-563-5660** 419-636-1194
Evans Tempcon Michigan LLC
701 Ann St NW . . . . Grand Rapids MI 49504 **800-878-7147** 616-361-2681
Friedrich
10001 Reunion Pl Ste 500 . . . . San Antonio TX 78216 **800-541-6645** 210-546-0500
HDT Global
30500 Aurora Rd Ste 100 . . . . Solon OH 44139 **800-969-8527** 216-438-6111
Kim Hotstart Manufacturing Co
5723 E Alki Ave . . . . Spokane WA 99212 **800-224-5550** 509-536-8660
Lennox Industries Inc
2100 Lake Pk Blvd . . . . Richardson TX 75080 **800-953-6669***
*Cust Svc
Lennox International Inc
2140 Lake Pk Blvd . . . . Richardson TX 75080 **800-953-6669** 972-497-5000
NYSE: LII
Modine Manufacturing Co
1500 De Koven Ave . . . . Racine WI 53403 **800-828-4328** 262-636-1200
NYSE: MOD
National System of Garage Ventilation Inc
714 N Church St PO Box 1186 . . . . Decatur IL 62525 **800-728-8368** 217-423-7314
Nortek Inc
50 Kennedy Plz . . . . Providence RI 02903 **800-422-4328**
NASDAQ: NTK
Simpson Mfg Company Inc
5956 W Las Positas Blvd . . . . Pleasanton CA 94588 **800-925-5099** 925-560-9000
NYSE: SSD
Takagi Industrial Company USA Inc
500 Wald . . . . Irvine CA 92618 **888-882-5244** 949-770-7171
TPI Corp PO Box 4973 . . . . Johnson City TN 37602 **800-682-3398**
Ventamatic Ltd
100 Washington Rd . . . . Mineral Wells TX 76067 **800-433-1626** 940-325-7887
Whirlpool Corp
2000 N M-63 . . . . Benton Harbor MI 49022 **800-253-1301** 269-923-5000
NYSE: WHR

16   AIR FARE CONSOLIDATORS

			Toll-Free	Phone

Brazilian Travel Service (BTS)
16 W 46th St 2nd Fl . . . . New York NY 10036 **800-342-5746** 212-764-6161
C & H International
4751 Wilshire Blvd Ste 201 . . . . Los Angeles CA 90010 **800-833-8888** 323-933-2288
Centrav Inc
511 E Travelers Trl . . . . Burnsville MN 55337 **800-874-2033** 952-886-7650

				Toll-Free	Phone
GTT Global 600 Data Dr Ste 101	Plano	TX	75075	**800-485-6828**	972-490-3394
International Travel Systems Inc					
64 Madison Ave	Wood-Ridge	NJ	07075	**800-258-0135**	201-727-0470
Mill Run Tours					
424 Madison Ave 12th Fl	New York	NY	10017	**855-645-5868**	
Sky Bird Travel & Tours					
24701 Swanson	Southfield	MI	48033	**888-759-2473**	248-372-4800
Skylink Travel					
980 Ave of the Americas	New York	NY	10018	**800-247-6659**	212-573-8980
Transam Travel Inc					
7013 Backlick Crt	Springfield	VA	22151	**800-822-7600**	703-998-7676
Tripmasters					
5640 Nicholson Ln Ste 215	Rockville	MD	20852	**800-430-0484**	202-349-7579

17   AIR PURIFICATION EQUIPMENT - HOUSEHOLD

SEE ALSO Appliances - Small - Mfr

				Toll-Free	Phone
Air Quality Engineering Inc					
7140 Northland Dr N	Brooklyn Park	MN	55428	**888-883-3273**	763-531-9823
Airguard Industries Inc					
100 River Ridge Cir	Jeffersonville	IN	47130	**866-247-4827**	
Dayton Reliable Air Filter Inc					
2294 N Moraine Dr	Dayton	OH	45439	**800-699-0747***	
*Orders					
Gaylord Industries Inc					
10900 SW Avery St	Tualatin	OR	97062	**800-547-9696**	503-691-2010
General Filters Inc					
43800 Grand River Ave	Novi	MI	48375	**866-476-5101**	
Home Care Industries Inc ALFCO Div					
1 Lisbon St	Clifton	NJ	07013	**800-325-1908***	973-365-1600
*Cust Svc					
Indoor Purification Systems Inc					
Surround Air Div					
334 N Marshall Way Ste C	Layton	UT	84041	**888-812-1516**	801-547-1162
Koch Filter Corp					
625 W Hill St	Louisville	KY	40208	**800-757-5624**	502-634-4796
Permatron Group					
2020 Touhy Ave	Elk Grove Village	IL	60007	**800-882-8012**	847-434-1421
PuriTec					
4705 S Durango Dr Ste 100-102	Las Vegas	NV	89147	**888-491-4100**	610-268-5420
Rena Ware International Inc					
15885 NE 28th St	Bellevue	WA	98008	**800-721-5156**	425-881-6171
Research Products Corp					
1015 E Washington Ave	Madison	WI	53703	**800-334-6011**	608-257-8801
Spencer Turbine Co					
600 Day Hill Rd	Windsor	CT	06095	**800-232-4321**	860-688-8361
Tjernlund Products Inc					
1601 Ninth St	White Bear Lake	MN	55110	**800-255-4208**	651-426-2993

18   AIR PURIFICATION EQUIPMENT - INDUSTRIAL

				Toll-Free	Phone
AAF International Corp					
10300 Ormsby Pk Pl Ste 600	Louisville	KY	40223	**888-223-2003**	502-637-0011
Acme Engineering & Manufacturing Corp					
PO Box 978	Muskogee	OK	74402	**800-382-2263**	918-682-7791
Advantec MFS Inc					
6723 Sierra Ct Ste A	Dublin	CA	94568	**800-334-7132**	925-479-0625
Aget Manufacturing Co					
1408 E Church St	Adrian	MI	49221	**800-832-2438**	517-263-5781
Air Quality Engineering Inc					
7140 Northland Dr N	Brooklyn Park	MN	55428	**888-883-3273**	763-531-9823
Airflow Systems Inc					
11221 Pagemill Rd	Dallas	TX	75243	**800-818-6185**	214-503-8008
Airguard Industries Inc					
100 River Ridge Cir	Jeffersonville	IN	47130	**866-247-4827**	
Airmaster Fan Co					
9229 S Meridian Rd	Clarklake	MI	49234	**800-410-3267**	517-764-2300
American Fan Company Inc					
2933 Symmes Rd	Fairfield	OH	45014	**866-771-6266**	513-874-2400
Anguil Environmental Systems Inc					
8855 N 55th St	Milwaukee	WI	53223	**800-488-0230**	414-365-6400
Beckett Air Inc					
37850 Beckett Pkwy	North Ridgeville	OH	44039	**800-831-7839**	440-327-9999
Cleanroom Systems					
7000 Performance Dr	North Syracuse	NY	13212	**800-825-3268**	315-452-7400
CUNO Inc 400 Research Pkwy	Meriden	CT	06450	**800-243-6894**	203-237-5541
Donaldson Company Inc					
1400 W 94th St	Bloomington	MN	55431	**800-365-1331**	952-887-3131
NYSE: DCI					
Dustex Corp					
100 Chastain Ctr Blvd Ste 195	Kennesaw	GA	30144	**800-647-6167**	770-429-5575
Filtration Group Inc					
912 E Washington St	Joliet	IL	60433	**877-603-1003**	815-726-4600
Flanders Corp					
531 Flanders Filters Rd	Washington	NC	27889	**800-637-2803**	252-946-8081
OTC: FLDR					
Fuel Tech Inc					
27601 Bella Vista Pkwy	Warrenville	IL	60555	**800-666-9688***	630-845-4500
NASDAQ: FTEK ■ *General					
Gaylord Industries Inc					
10900 SW Avery St	Tualatin	OR	97062	**800-547-9696**	503-691-2010
General Filters Inc					
43800 Grand River Ave	Novi	MI	48375	**866-476-5101**	
Great Lakes Filters					
301 Arch Ave	Hillsdale	MI	49242	**800-521-8565**	
Greenheck Fan Corp					
1100 Greenheck Dr PO Box 410	Schofield	WI	54476	**800-355-5354**	715-359-6171
Hartzell Fan Inc					
910 S Downing St	Piqua	OH	45356	**800-336-3267**	937-773-7411
Home Care Industries Inc ALFCO Div					
1 Lisbon St	Clifton	NJ	07013	**800-325-1908***	973-365-1600
*Cust Svc					

				Toll-Free	Phone
Honeyville Metal Inc					
4200 S 900 West	Topeka	IN	46571	**800-593-8377**	
Houston Service Industries Inc					
7901 Hansen Rd	Houston	TX	77061	**800-725-2291**	713-947-1623
Howden Buffalo Inc					
7909 Parklane Rd Ste 300	Columbia	SC	29223	**866-757-0908**	803-741-2700
King Engineering Corp					
3201 S State St	Ann Arbor	MI	48106	**800-242-8871***	734-662-5691
*Cust Svc					
Koch Filter Corp					
625 W Hill St	Louisville	KY	40208	**800-757-5624**	502-634-4796
McIntire Co 745 Clark Ave	Bristol	CT	06010	**800-437-9247**	860-585-0050
Midwesco Filter Resources Inc					
309 N Braddock St	Winchester	VA	22601	**800-336-7300**	540-773-4780
NAO Inc					
1284 E Sedgley Ave	Philadelphia	PA	19134	**800-523-3495***	215-743-5300
*Cust Svc					
National Filter Media Corp					
691 North 400 West	Salt Lake City	UT	84103	**800-777-4248**	801-363-6736
New York Blower Co					
7660 Quincy St	Willowbrook	IL	60527	**800-208-7918**	630-794-5700
Parker Hannifin Corp Finite Filtratio & Separation Div					
500 Glaspie St	Oxford	MI	48371	**800-521-4357**	248-628-6400
Process Equipment Inc					
2770 Welborn St PO Box 1607	Pelham	AL	35124	**888-663-2028**	205-663-5330
Purafil Inc					
2654 Weaver Way	Doraville	GA	30340	**800-222-6367**	770-662-8545
Revcor Inc					
251 E Edwards Ave	Carpentersville	IL	60110	**800-323-8261**	
Sly Inc 8300 Dow Cir	Strongsville	OH	44136	**800-334-2957**	440-891-3200
Sonic Air Systems Inc					
1050 Beacon St	Brea	CA	92821	**800-827-6642**	714-255-0124
Spencer Turbine Co					
600 Day Hill Rd	Windsor	CT	06095	**800-232-4321**	860-688-8361
Standard Filter Corp					
5928 Balfour St	Carlsbad	CA	92008	**800-634-5837**	760-929-8559
Tjernlund Products Inc					
1601 Ninth St	White Bear Lake	MN	55110	**800-255-4208**	651-426-2993
Tri-Dim Filter Corp					
93 Industrial Dr	Louisa	VA	23093	**800-458-9835**	540-967-2600
Trion Inc 101 McNeill Rd	Sanford	NC	27330	**800-884-0002**	919-775-2201
Tuthill Vacuum & Blower Systems					
4840 W Kearney St	Springfield	MO	65803	**800-825-6937**	417-865-8715

19   AIR TRAFFIC CONTROL SERVICES

The Federal Aviation Administration (a US government agency) and NAV CANADA (a private, not-for-profit Canadian firm) provide air traffic services nationwide in the US and Canada, respectively. The types of services provided include aircraft routing, approach and departure instruction, and weather information.

				Toll-Free	Phone
Federal Aviation Administration (FAA)					
800 Independence Ave SW	Washington	DC	20591	**866-835-5322**	
Federal Aviation Administration Northwest Mountain Region					
1601 Lind Ave SW	Renton	WA	98057	**800-220-5715**	425-227-2001
FlightAware					
Eleven Greenway Plz Ste 2900	Houston	TX	77046	**800-713-8570**	713-877-9010
NAV CANADA					
77 Metcalfe St PO Box 3411 Stn D	Ottawa	ON	K1P5L6	**800-876-4693**	613-563-5588

20   AIRCRAFT

SEE ALSO Airships

				Toll-Free	Phone
AeroVironment Inc					
181 W Huntington Dr Ste 202	Monrovia	CA	91016	**888-833-2148**	626-357-9983
NASDAQ: AVAV					
Airbus Helicopters Inc					
2701 Forum Dr	Grand Prairie	TX	75052	**800-873-0001**	972-641-0000
Bombardier Aerospace					
400 Cote-Vertu Ouest	Dorval	QC	H4S1Y9	**866-855-5001***	514-855-5000
*General					
Bombardier Learjet					
1 Learjet Way	Wichita	KS	67209	**888-227-1428**	316-946-2287
Cirrus Design Corp					
4515 Taylor Cir	Duluth	MN	55811	**800-279-4322**	218-727-2737
Dassault Falcon Jet Corp					
PO Box 2000	South Hackensack	NJ	07606	**800-527-2463**	201-440-6700
Diamond Aircraft Industries Inc					
1560 Crumlin Sideroad	London	ON	N5V1S2	**888-359-3220**	519-457-4000
Lockheed Martin Corp					
6801 Rockledge Dr	Bethesda	MD	20817	**866-562-2363**	301-897-6000
NYSE: LMT					
Mooney Aircraft Corp					
165 Al Mooney Rd	Kerrville	TX	78028	**800-456-3033**	
Skycom Avionics Inc					
2441 Aviation Rd	Waukesha	WI	53188	**800-443-4490**	262-521-8180
Spirit AeroSystems Inc					
3801 S Oliver St	Wichita	KS	67210	**800-501-7597**	316-526-9000
Texas Pneumatics Systems Inc					
2404 Superior Dr	Arlington	TX	76013	**800-211-9690**	817-794-0068
Valair Aviation					
7301 NW 50th St	Oklahoma City	OK	73132	**800-299-8546**	405-789-5000
Van Horn Aviation LLC					
1000 E Vista Del Cerro Dr	Tempe	AZ	85281	**800-326-1534**	480-483-4202

21   AIRCRAFT ENGINES & ENGINE PARTS

				Toll-Free	Phone
AAR Corp					
1100 N Wood Dale Rd	Wood Dale	IL	60191	**800-422-2213**	630-227-2000
NYSE: AIR					

			Toll-Free	Phone

Abipa Canada Inc
3700 Ave des Grandes Tourelles .... Boisbraind QC J7H0A1 **877-963-6888** 450-963-6888
Action Aircraft
10570 Olympic Dr .... Dallas TX 75220 **800-909-7616** 214-351-1284
Aimpoint Inc
7309 Gateway Ct .... Manassas VA 20109 **877-246-7646** 703-263-9795
Avtron Aerospace Inc
7900 E Pleasant Valley Rd .... Cleveland OH 44131 **800-783-7871** 216-750-5152
Beacon Industries Inc
12300 Old Tesson Rd .... Saint Louis MO 63128 **800-454-7159** 314-487-7600
Blackcomb Helicopters
9960 Heliport Rd .... Whistler BC V0N1B0 **800-330-4354** 604-938-1700
Continental Motors Inc
2039 Broad St .... Mobile AL 36615 **800-326-0089** 251-436-8292
Dart Aerospace Ltd
1270 Aberdeen St .... Hawkesbury ON K6A1K7 **800-556-4166** 613-632-3336
Engine Components Inc (ECI)
9503 Middlex .... San Antonio TX 78217 **800-324-2359** 210-820-8101
Flight Dimensions International Inc
4835 Cordell Ave Ste 150 .... Bethesda MD 20814 **866-235-6870** 301-634-8201
Gama Aviation LLC
2 Corporate Dr Ste 1050 .... Shelton CT 06484 **800-468-1110** 203-337-4600
Garsite LLC
539 S Tenth St .... Kansas City KS 66105 **888-427-7483** 913-342-5600
Global Filtration Inc
9207 Emmott St .... Houston TX 77040 **888-717-0888** 713-856-9800
Hartzell Engine Technologies LLC
2900 Selma Hwy .... Montgomery AL 36108 **877-359-5355** 334-386-5400
Imagine Air Jet Services LLC
460 Briscoe Blvd Ste 210 .... Lawrenceville GA 30046 **877-359-4242**
Insight Technology Inc
9 Akira Way .... Londonderry NH 03053 **866-509-2040** 603-626-4800
Institute For Natural Resources
PO Box 5757 .... Concord CA 94524 **877-246-6336** 925-609-2820
Kalitta Charters LLC
843 Willow Run Airport .... Ypsilanti MI 48198 **800-525-4882** 734-544-3400
Moeller Mfg Company Inc Aircraft Div
30100 Beck Rd .... Wixom MI 48393 **800-321-8010** 248-960-3999
Navhouse Corp 10 Loring Dr .... Bolton ON L7E1J9 **877-628-6667** 905-857-8102
Pratt & Whitney Canada Inc
1000 Marie-Victorin Blvd .... Longueuil QC J4G1A1 **800-268-8000** 450-677-9411
Williams International
2280 E W Maple Rd PO Box 200 .... Walled Lake MI 48390 **800-859-3544** 248-624-5200
XOJET Inc
2000 Sierra Point Pkwy .... Brisbane CA 94005 **877-599-6538**

22   AIRCRAFT PARTS & AUXILIARY EQUIPMENT

SEE ALSO Precision Machined Products

			Toll-Free	Phone

AAR Corp
1100 N Wood Dale Rd .... Wood Dale IL 60191 **800-422-2213** 630-227-2000
NYSE: AIR
Advanced Technology Co
2858 E Walnut St .... Pasadena CA 91107 **800-447-2442** 626-449-2696
Aereon Corp
16310 Bratton Ln Bldg 3 Ste 350 .... Austin TX 78728 **800-475-9473** 512-836-9473
Aerospace Products International (API)
2871 Business Pk Dr .... Memphis TN 38118 **888-274-2497** 901-365-3470
Arkwin Industries Inc
686 Main St .... Westbury NY 11590 **800-284-2551** 516-333-2640
Aviation Ground Equipment Corp
53 Hanse Ave .... Freeport NY 11520 **800-758-0044** 516-546-0003
CEF Industries Inc
320 S Church St .... Addison IL 60101 **800-888-6419** 630-628-2299
CRS Jet Spares Inc
6701 NW 12th Ave .... Fort Lauderdale FL 33309 **800-338-5387** 954-972-2807
Curtiss-Wright Corp
10 Waterview Blvd 2nd Fl .... Parsippany NJ 07054 **855-449-0995** 973-541-3700
NYSE: CW
Esterline Interface Technologies
600 W Wilbur Ave .... Coeur d'Alene ID 83815 **800-444-5923** 208-765-8000
FletchAir Inc
103 Turkey Run Ln .... Comfort TX 78013 **800-329-4647** 830-995-5900
General Electrodynamics Corporation Inc
8000 Calendar Rd .... Arlington TX 76001 **800-551-6038** 817-572-0366
Global Ground Support LLC
540 Old Hwy 56 .... Olathe KS 66061 **888-780-0303** 913-780-0300
Hartzell Propeller Inc
1 Propeller Pl .... Piqua OH 45356 **800-942-7767** 937-778-4200
Honeywell Aerospace
1944 E Sky Harbor Cir .... Phoenix AZ 85034 **800-601-3099**
L-3 Communications Integrated Systems
600 Third Ave .... New York NY 10016 **877-282-1168** 903-455-3450
LEKTRO Inc
1190 SE Flightline Dr .... Warrenton OR 97146 **800-535-8767** 503-861-2288
Middle River Aircraft Systems (MRAS)
103 Chesapeake Park Plz .... Baltimore MD 21220 **877-432-3272** 410-682-1500
MSA Aircraft Products Inc
10000 Iota Dr .... San Antonio TX 78217 **800-695-1212** 210-590-6100
Precise Flight Inc
63354 Powell Butte Hwy .... Bend OR 97701 **800-547-2558**
Shimadzu Precision Instruments inc
7102 Riverwood Dr .... Columbia MD 21046 **800-477-1227** 410-381-1227
STS Component Solutions LLC
2910 SW 42 Ave .... Palm City FL 34990 **888-777-2960**
Tronair Inc 1740 Eber Rd .... Holland OH 43528 **800-426-6301** 419-866-6301

23   AIRCRAFT RENTAL

SEE ALSO Aviation - Fixed-Base Operations

			Toll-Free	Phone

Apple Discount Drugs
404 N Fruitland Blvd .... Salisbury MD 21801 **800-424-8401** 410-749-8401

Argus Supply Co
46400 Continental Dr .... Chesterfield MI 48047 **800-873-0456** 800-332-0435
Armour Transportation Systems Inc
689 Edinburgh Dr .... Moncton NB E1E2L4 **800-561-7987** 506-857-0205
ATT Metrology Services Inc
30210 SE 79th St Ste 100 .... Issaquah WA 98027 **888-320-7011** 425-867-5356
Bartha Visual
600 N Cassady Ave .... Columbus OH 43219 **800-513-1209** 800-363-2698
Bigrentz Inc
1063 Mcgaw Ave Ste 200 .... Irvine CA 92614 **855-999-5438** 888-325-5172
Compact Power Equipment Centers LLC
PO Box 40 .... Fort Mill SC 29716 **888-266-7228**
eLease Funding Inc
550 First Ave N .... St. Petersburg FL 33701 **800-499-2577** 727-209-1200
JA. Riggs Tractor Company Inc
9125 I-30 .... Little Rock AR 72209 **800-759-3140** 501-570-3100
LEAF Commercial Capital Inc
1 Commerce Sq 2005 Market St
14th Fl .... Philadelphia PA 19103 **800-819-5556**
Moncton Flight College
1719 Champlain St .... Dieppe NB E1A7P5 **800-760-4632** 506-857-3080
Northern Jet Management
5500 44th St SE .... Grand Rapids MI 49512 **800-462-7709** 616-336-4800
Sunwest Aviation Ltd
217 Aero Ct NE .... Calgary AB T2E7C6 **888-291-4566** 403-275-8121
Tankmaster Rentals L T D
Poplar St Ste 117 .... Red Deer AB T4E1B4 **877-342-1105** 403-342-1105
Trench Plate Rental Co
13217 Laureldale Ave .... Downey CA 90242 **800-821-4478**
Us Adventure Rv
5120 N Brady St .... Davenport IA 52806 **877-768-4678**
Valley Supply & Equipment Company Inc
1109 Middle River Rd .... Baltimore MD 21220 **800-633-5077** 888-890-8165

24   AIRCRAFT SERVICE & REPAIR

			Toll-Free	Phone

AAR Corp
1100 N Wood Dale Rd .... Wood Dale IL 60191 **800-422-2213** 630-227-2000
NYSE: AIR
Barfield Inc 4101 NW 29th St .... Miami FL 33142 **800-321-1039** 305-894-5300
Cutter Aviation
2802 E Old Tower Rd .... Phoenix AZ 85034 **800-234-5382** 602-273-1237
Duncan Aviation Inc
3701 Aviation Rd .... Lincoln NE 68524 **800-228-4277** 402-475-2611
Elliott Aviation Inc
6601 74th Ave PO Box 100 .... Milan IL 61264 **800-447-6711** 309-799-3183
Emteq Inc
5349 S Emmer Dr .... New Berlin WI 53151 **888-679-6170** 262-679-6170
Jet Aviation
112 Charles A Lindbergh Dr .... Teterboro NJ 07608 **800-538-0832** 201-288-8400
Kfs Inc 1840 W Airfield Dr .... Dallas TX 75261 **800-364-4115** 817-488-4115
McKinley Air Transport Inc
5430 Lauby Rd Bldg 4 .... Canton OH 44720 **800-225-6446*** 330-499-3316
*General
Million Air Interlink Inc
8501 Telephone Rd .... Houston TX 77061 **888-589-9059** 713-640-4000
Priester Aviation
1061 S Wolf Rd .... Wheeling IL 60090 **888-323-7887** 847-537-1133
Rolls-Royce Engine Services Inc
7200 Earhart Rd .... Oakland CA 94621 **888-255-4766** 510-613-1000
Serco Inc
1818 Library St Ste 1000 .... Reston VA 20190 **866-628-6458** 703-939-6000
Summit Aviation Inc
4200 Summit Bridge Rd .... Middletown DE 19709 **800-441-9343** 302-834-5400
T G H Aviation
2389 Rickenbacker Way .... Auburn CA 95602 **800-843-4976** 530-823-6204
Triumph Group Inc
1550 Liberty Ridge Dr Ste 100 .... Wayne PA 19087 **800-863-1083** 610-251-1000
NYSE: TGI
Tulsair Beechcraft Inc
3207 N Sheridan Rd .... Tulsa OK 74115 **800-331-4071** 918-835-7651
West Star Aviation Inc
796 Heritage Way .... Grand Junction CO 81506 **800-255-4193** 970-243-7500

25   AIRLINES - COMMERCIAL

SEE ALSO Air Cargo Carriers ; Airlines - Frequent Flyer Programs ; Air Charter Services

			Toll-Free	Phone

Aeroflot Russian International Airlines
358 Fifth Ave Ste 1103 .... New York NY 10001 **866-879-7647**
Air India
570 Lexington Ave 15th Fl .... New York NY 10022 **800-223-7776**
Air Sunshine PO Box 37698 .... San Juan PR 00937 **800-435-8900** 954-434-8900
All Nippon Airways Company Ltd
2050 W 190th St Ste 100 .... Torrance CA 90504 **800-235-9262**
American Airlines Inc
4333 Amon Carter Blvd .... Fort Worth TX 76155 **800-433-7300** 817-963-1234
Bearskin Airlines
1475 W Walsh St .... Thunder Bay ON P7E4X6 **800-465-2327**
Bering Air
1470 Sepalla Dr PO Box 1650 .... Nome AK 99762 **800-478-5422** 907-443-5464
Bulloch & Bulloch Inc
309 Cash Memorial Blvd .... Forest Park GA 30297 **800-339-8177** 404-762-5063
Cape Air 660 Barnstable Rd .... Hyannis MA 02601 **800-227-3247** 508-771-6944
Czech Airlines
147 West 35th St Ste 1505 .... New York NY 10119 **855-359-2932**
Delta Air Lines Inc
1030 Delta Blvd .... Atlanta GA 30354 **800-221-1212** 404-715-2600
NYSE: DAL
El Al Israel Airlines Inc
15 E 26th St .... New York NY 10010 **800-223-6700** 212-852-0600
EVA Airways
200 N Sepulveda Blvd Ste 1600 .... El Segundo CA 90245 **800-695-1188** 310-362-6600

Classified Section

			Toll-Free	Phone
Great Lakes Aviation Ltd				
1022 Airport Pkwy ....Cheyenne WY	82001		800-554-5111	307-432-7000
OTC: GLUX				
Hawaiian Airlines Inc				
3375 Koapaka St Ste G350 ....Honolulu HI	96819		800-367-5320	808-835-3700
Kenmore Air Harbor Inc				
6321 NE 175th St ....Kenmore WA	98028		866-435-9524	425-486-1257
Korean Air				
6101 W Imperial Hwy ....Los Angeles CA	90045		800-438-5000	310-417-5200
Malaysia Airlines				
100 N Sepulveda Blvd Ste 1710 ....El Segundo CA	90245		800-552-9264*	310-535-9288
*Resv				
New England Airlines Inc				
56 Airport Rd ....Westerly RI	02891		800-243-2460	401-596-2460
Pakistan International Airlines Corp (PIA)				
1200 New Jersey Ave SE ....Washington DC	20590		800-578-6786	
Peninsula Airways Inc				
6100 Boeing Ave ....Anchorage AK	99502		800-448-4226	907-771-2500
PSA Airlines Inc				
3400 Terminal Dr ....Vandalia OH	45377		800-235-0986*	
*Resv				
Qantas Airways Ltd				
6080 Ctr Dr Ste 400 ....Los Angeles CA	90045		800-227-4500	310-726-1400
Scandinavian Airlines System (SAS)				
301 Rt 17 N Ste 500 ....Rutherford NJ	07070		800-221-2350	800-437-5807
Silver Airways Corp				
1100 Lee Wagener Blvd Ste 201 ....Fort Lauderdale FL	33315		844-674-5837	801-401-9100
Singapore Airlines Ltd				
222 N Sepulveda Blvd Ste 1600 ....El Segundo CA	90245		800-742-3333	310-647-1922
Skyservice Airlines Inc				
9785 Ryan Ave ....Dorval QC	H9P1A2		888-985-1402	514-636-3300
SkyWest Airlines				
444 S River Rd ....Saint George UT	84790		800-778-4838	435-634-3000
South African Airways				
1200 S Pine Island Rd Ste 650 ....Plantation FL	33324		800-722-9675	954-769-5000
Southwest Airlines Co				
2702 Love Field Dr PO Box 36611 ....Dallas TX	75235		800-435-9792	214-792-4000
NYSE: LUV				
Spirit Airlines Inc				
2800 Executive Way ....Miramar FL	33025		800-772-7117	954-447-7828
NASDAQ: SAVE				
SriLankan Airlines				
379 Thornall St 6th Fl. ....Edison NJ	08837		877-915-2652	732-205-0017
Sun Country Airlines Inc				
1300 Mendota Heights Rd ....Mendota Heights MN	55120		800-359-6786	651-681-3900
Virgin Atlantic Airways Ltd				
75 N Water St ....Norwalk CT	06854		888-747-7474	120-375-0200
WestJet Airlines Ltd				
22 Aerial Pl NE ....Calgary AB	T2E3J1		888-937-8538	403-444-2600
TSE: WJA				

26   AIRLINES - FREQUENT FLYER PROGRAMS

			Toll-Free	Phone
British Airways Executive Club				
PO Box 300743 ....Jamaica NY	11430		800-452-1201	
Continental Airlines Inc				
900 Grand Plaza Dr ....Houston TX	77067		800-621-7467	713-952-1630
Czech Airlines OK Plus				
147 W 35th St Ste 1505 ....New York NY	10001		855-359-2932	
Hawaiian Airlines HawaiianMiles				
PO Box 30008 ....Honolulu HI	96820		877-426-4537	
Icelandair North America				
1900 Crown Colony Dr ....Quincy MA	02169		800-223-5500	
Kuwait Airways Oasis Club				
400 Kelby St ....Fort Lee NJ	07024		800-458-9248	201-582-9222
Miles & More				
PO Box 946 ....Santa Clarita CA	91380		800-581-6400	
Singapore Airlines KrisFlyer				
380 World Way Ste 336B ....Los Angeles CA	90045		800-742-3333	310-647-6144

27   AIRPORTS

SEE ALSO Ports & Port Authorities
Listings for airports in the US and Canada are organized by states and provinces, and then by city names within those groupings.

			Toll-Free	Phone
Mobile Regional Airport				
8400 Airport Blvd ....Mobile AL	36608		800-357-5373	251-633-4510
Calgary International Airport				
2000 Airport Rd NE ....Calgary AB	T2E6W5		877-254-7427	403-735-1200
Flagstaff Pulliam Airport				
6200 S Pulliam Dr ....Flagstaff AZ	86001		800-463-1389	928-213-2930
Phoenix Sky Harbor International Airport				
3400 E Sky Harbor Blvd Ste 3300 ....Phoenix AZ	85034		800-781-1010	602-273-3300
Tucson International Airport				
7250 S Tucson Blvd ....Tucson AZ	85756		866-289-9673	520-573-8100
Fort Smith Regional Airport				
6700 McKennon Blvd Ste 200 ....Fort Smith AR	72903		800-992-7433	479-452-7000
Hot Springs Memorial Field				
525 Airport Rd ....Hot Springs AR	71913		800-992-7433	501-321-6750
Bill & Hillary Clinton National Airport				
1 Airport Dr ....Little Rock AR	72202		800-897-1910	501-372-3439
Vancouver International Airport (YVR)				
Airport Postal Outlet PO Box 23750 ....Richmond BC	V7B1Y7		800-461-9999	604-207-7077
Fresno Yosemite International Airport				
5175 E Clinton Way ....Fresno CA	93727		866-275-7772	559-621-4500
Long Beach Airport LGB				
4100 Donald Douglas Dr ....Long Beach CA	90808		800-331-1212	562-570-2600
Palm Springs International Airport				
3200 E Tahquitz Canyon Way ....Palm Springs CA	92262		800-847-4389	760-318-3800
Palo Alto Airport				
1925 Embarcadero Rd ....Palo Alto CA	94303		866-638-2344	408-918-7700
San Francisco International Airport				
PO Box 8097 ....San Francisco CA	94128		800-435-9736	650-821-8211

			Toll-Free	Phone
Denver International Airport				
8500 Pena Blvd ....Denver CO	80249		800-247-2336	303-342-2000
Fort Lauderdale Executive Airport				
5101 NW 21st Ave ....Fort Lauderdale FL	33309		800-955-8770	954-828-4955
Fort Lauderdale/Hollywood International Airport				
100 Aviation Blvd ....Fort Lauderdale FL	33315		866-682-2258	954-359-1200
Southwest Florida International Airport				
11000 Terminal Access Rd Ste 8671 ....Fort Myers FL	33913		800-359-6786	239-590-4800
Key West International Airport				
3491 S Roosevelt Blvd ....Key West FL	33040		800-327-1390	305-809-5200
Miami International Airport				
4200 NW 36th St 4th Fl ....Miami FL	33166		800-825-5642	305-876-7000
Orlando International Airport				
1 Jeff Fuqua Blvd ....Orlando FL	32827		800-327-1390	407-825-2001
Pensacola Gulf Coast Regional Airport				
2430 Airport Blvd Ste 225 ....Pensacola FL	32504		800-874-6580	850-436-5000
Sarasota-Bradenton International Airport				
6000 Airport Cir ....Sarasota FL	34243		800-711-1712	941-359-2770
Tampa International Airport				
4160 George J Bean Pkwy PO Box 22287 ....Tampa FL	33607		866-289-9673	813-870-8700
Hartsfield-Jackson Atlanta International Airport				
6000 N Terminal Pkwy Ste 4000 ....Atlanta GA	30320		800-897-1910	404-530-6600
Kahului Airport				
1 Kahului Airport Rd ....Kahului HI	96732		800-321-3712	808-872-3830
Kona International Airport				
73-200 Kupipi St ....Kailua-Kona HI	96740		800-321-3712	808-327-9520
O'Hare International Airport				
Dept of Aviation				
PO Box 66142 ....Chicago IL	60666		800-832-6352	773-686-3700
Greater Rockford Airport				
60 Airport Dr ....Rockford IL	61109		800-517-2000	815-969-4000
Du Page Airport Authority				
2700 International Dr Ste 200 ....West Chicago IL	60185		800-208-5690	630-584-2211
Des Moines International Airport				
5800 Fleur Dr ....Des Moines IA	50321		877-686-0029	515-256-5050
Midcontinent Airport				
2173 Air Cargo Rd ....Wichita KS	67209		800-628-6800	316-946-4700
Blue Grass Airport				
4000 Terminal Dr ....Lexington KY	40510		800-800-4000	859-425-3100
Bangor International Airport				
287 Godfrey Blvd ....Bangor ME	04401		866-359-2264	207-992-4600
Winnipeg Richardson International Airport				
2000 Wellington Ave ....Winnipeg MB	R3H1C2		855-500-6589	204-987-9402
Baltimore/Washington International Thurgood Marshall Airport (BWI)				
PO Box 8766 ....Baltimore MD	21240		800-435-9294	410-859-7111
Coleman A Young International Airport				
11499 Conner ....Detroit MI	48213		800-874-9426	313-628-2146
Duluth International Airport				
4701 Grinden Dr ....Duluth MN	55811		855-787-2227	218-727-2968
Rochester International Airport (RST)				
7600 Helgerson Dr SW ....Rochester MN	55902		800-227-4672	507-282-2328
Jackson International Airport				
100 International Dr Ste 300 ....Jackson MS	39208		800-227-7368	601-939-5631
Lambert Saint Louis International Airport				
10701 Lambert International Blvd				
PO Box 10212 ....Saint Louis MO	63145		855-787-2227	314-426-8000
Newark Liberty International Airport				
3 Brewster Rd ....Newark NJ	07114		888-397-4636	973-961-6000
Santa Fe Municipal Airport (SAF)				
121 Aviation Dr ....Santa Fe NM	87504		866-773-2587	505-955-2900
Buffalo Niagara International Airport				
4200 Genesee St ....Cheektowaga NY	14225		877-359-2642	716-630-6000
Long Island MacArthur Airport				
100 Arrival Ave Ste 100 ....Ronkonkoma NY	11779		888-542-4776	631-467-3300
Asheville Regional Airport				
61 Terminal Dr Ste 1 ....Fletcher NC	28732		866-719-3910	828-684-2226
Raleigh-Durham International Airport				
PO Box 80001 ....Raleigh NC	27623		800-252-7522	919-840-2123
Hector International Airport				
2801 32nd Ave NW ....Fargo ND	58102		800-451-5333	701-241-8168
Cincinnati-Northern Kentucky International Airport				
PO Box 752000 ....Cincinnati OH	45275		800-990-8841	859-767-3151
Akron-Canton Airport				
5400 Lauby Rd NW ....North Canton OH	44720		888-434-2359	330-499-4221
Eugene Airport				
28801 Douglas Dr ....Eugene OR	97402		800-741-5097	541-682-5430
Portland International Airport				
7000 NE Airport Way ....Portland OR	97218		800-547-8411	503-460-4234
Lehigh Valley International Airport				
3311 Airport Rd ....Allentown PA	18109		800-359-5842	610-266-6000
Philadelphia International Airport				
8000 Essington Ave ....Philadelphia PA	19153		800-514-0301	215-937-6937
Pittsburgh International Airport				
Landside Terminal 4th Fl Mezz				
PO Box 12370 ....Pittsburgh PA	15231		888-429-5377	412-472-3500
Rhode Island Airport Corp				
2000 Post Rd Warwick ....Warwick RI	02886		888-268-7222	401-691-2000
Greenville-Spartanburg Airport (GSP)				
2000 GSP Dr Ste 1 ....Greer SC	29651		800-331-1212	864-877-7426
Myrtle Beach International Airport				
1100 Jetport Rd ....Myrtle Beach SC	29577		800-778-4838	843-448-1589
Rapid City Regional Airport				
4550 Terminal Rd Ste 102 ....Rapid City SD	57703		888-279-2135	605-393-9924
Metropolitan Nashville Airport Authority				
1 Terminal Dr Ste 501 ....Nashville TN	37214		800-628-6800	615-275-1675
Dallas-Fort Worth International Airport (DFW)				
2400 Aviation Dr PO Box 619428 ....Dallas TX	75261		800-252-7522	972-973-3112
El Paso International Airport				
6701 Convair Rd ....El Paso TX	79925		800-288-1784	915-780-4749
Midland International Air & Space Port				
9506 Laforce Blvd PO Box 60305 ....Midland TX	79706		800-973-2867	432-560-2200
San Antonio International Airport (SAT)				
9800 Airport Blvd Rm 2041 ....San Antonio TX	78216		800-237-6639	210-207-3411
Salt Lake City International Airport				
776 N Terminal Dr				
PO Box 145550 ....Salt Lake City UT	84116		800-595-2442	801-575-2400
Seattle-Tacoma International Airport (SEA-TAC)				
17801 International Blvd PO Box 68727 ....Seattle WA	98158		800-544-1965	206-787-5388

			Toll-Free	Phone
Spokane International Airport				
9000 W Airport Dr	Spokane WA	99224	**800-776-5263**	509-455-6455

28   AIRSHIPS

SEE ALSO Aircraft

			Toll-Free	Phone
Cameron Balloons US				
PO Box 3672	Ann Arbor MI	48106	**866-423-6178**	734-426-5525
ILC Dover Inc				
1 Moonwalker Rd	Frederica DE	19946	**800-631-9567**	302-335-3911

29   ALL-TERRAIN VEHICLES

SEE ALSO Sporting Goods

			Toll-Free	Phone
American Honda Motor Company Inc				
1919 Torrance Blvd	Torrance CA	90501	**800-999-1009**	310-783-3170
Cycle Country Access Corp				
205 N Depot St PO Box 107	Fox Lake WI	53933	**800-841-2222***	
*Sales				
Ontario Drive & Gear Ltd (ODG)				
220 Bergey Ct	New Hamburg ON	N3A2J5	**877-274-6288**	519-662-2840
Recreatives Industries Inc				
60 Depot St	Buffalo NY	14206	**800-255-2511**	716-855-2226
Yamaha Motor Corp USA				
6555 Katella Ave	Cypress CA	90630	**800-962-7926***	
*Cust Svc				

30   AMBULANCE SERVICES

			Toll-Free	Phone
Acadian Ambulance Service Inc				
PO Box 98000	Lafayette LA	70509	**800-259-3333**	
Air Trek Inc				
28000 A-5 Airport Rd	Punta Gorda FL	33982	**800-247-8735**	941-639-7855
American Medical Response (AMR)				
6200 S Syracuse Way Ste 200	Greenwood Village CO	80111	**877-244-4890**	303-495-1200
Emergency Ambulance Service Inc				
3200 E Birch St Ste A	Brea CA	92821	**800-400-0689**	714-990-1331
Emergycare Inc 1926 Peach St	Erie PA	16502	**800-814-1038**	814-870-1010
Global Air Response				
5919 Approach Rd	Sarasota FL	34238	**800-631-6565**	
Lifenet Inc				
6225 St Michaels Dr	Texarkana TX	75503	**800-832-6395**	903-832-8531
MedjetAssist				
3500 Colonnade Pkwy Ste 500				
PO Box 43099	Birmingham AL	35243	**800-527-7478**	205-595-6626
Mercy Flights Inc				
2020 Milligan Way	Medford OR	97504	**800-903-9000**	541-858-2600
Mission Ambulance				
1055 E Third St	Corona CA	92879	**800-899-9100**	
Mobile Life Support Services Inc				
3188 Us Rt 9w	New Windsor NY	12553	**800-209-8815**	845-562-4368
MTS Ambulance				
2431 Greenup Ave	Ashland KY	41101	**800-598-3458**	606-324-3286
NES Health 39 Main St	Tiburon CA	94920	**800-394-6376**	
On Time Transport Inc				
135 E Highland Pkwy	Roselle NJ	07203	**800-858-8463**	908-298-9500
Paratech Ambulance Service				
9401 W Brown Deer Rd	Milwaukee WI	53224	**866-525-8888**	414-358-1111
Professional Ambulance & Oxygen Service Inc				
31 Smith Pl	Cambridge MA	02138	**800-653-3640**	617-492-2700
PROMPT Ambulance Central Inc				
9835 Express Dr	Highland IN	46322	**800-633-3590**	219-934-1010
Rural/Metro Corp				
9221 E Via de Ventura	Scottsdale AZ	85258	**800-352-2309**	
Skyservice Airlines Inc				
9785 Ryan Ave	Dorval QC	H9P1A2	**888-985-1402**	514-636-3300
Westlog Aviation				
311 Cove Rd	Brookings OR	97415	**800-761-5183**	541-469-7911

31   AMUSEMENT PARK COMPANIES

SEE ALSO Circus, Carnival, Festival Operators

			Toll-Free	Phone
Georgia Public Library				
1800 Century Pl NE Ste 150	Atlanta GA	30345	**800-248-6701**	404-235-7200
iFly USA LLC				
31310 Alvarado-Niles Rd	Union City CA	94587	**800-759-3861**	510-489-4359
International Training Inc				
1321 SE Decker Ave	Stuart FL	34994	**888-778-9073**	207-729-4201
Island Windjammers Inc				
165 Shaw Dr	Acworth GA	30102	**877-772-4549**	
Lisle Park District				
1825 Short St	Lisle IL	60532	**800-526-0854**	630-964-3410
Ober Gatlinburg Inc				
1001 Pkwy Ste 2	Gatlinburg TN	37738	**800-251-9202**	865-436-5423
Q Center				
1405 N Fifth Ave	Saint Charles IL	60174	**877-774-4627**	630-377-3100
Shawnee Mountain Ski Area				
401 Hollow Rd	East Stroudsburg PA	18301	**800-233-4218**	570-421-7231
Splash Lagoon Water Pk Resort				
8091 Peach St	Erie PA	16509	**866-377-5274**	
Taos Ski Valley Inc				
116 Sutton Pl	Taos Ski Valley NM	87525	**800-776-1111**	575-776-2291
Tweetsie Railroad Inc				
300 Tweetsie Railroad Ln	Blowing Rock NC	28605	**800-526-5740**	828-264-9061
Universal City Development Partners Ltd				
1000 Universal Studios Plz	Orlando FL	32819	**800-447-0672**	407-363-8000
Universal Studios Hollywood				
100 Universal City Plz	Universal City CA	91608	**800-864-8377**	

			Toll-Free	Phone
Woodridge Park District				
2600 Center Dr	Woodridge IL	60517	**800-713-7415**	630-353-3300

32   AMUSEMENT PARKS

			Toll-Free	Phone
Adventuredome				
2880 Las Vegas Blvd S	Las Vegas NV	89109	**866-456-8894**	702-691-5861
Adventureland Park				
3200 Adventureland Dr	Altoona IA	50009	**800-532-1286**	515-266-2121
Darien Lake Theme Park Resort				
9993 Allegheny Rd PO Box 91	Darien Center NY	14040	**866-640-0652**	585-599-4641
Disney's California Adventure				
1313 S Disneyland Dr	Anaheim CA	92802	**800-225-2024**	714-781-7290
Dollywood				
2700 Dollywood Parks Blvd	Pigeon Forge TN	37863	**800-365-5996**	
Dutch Wonderland				
2249 Lincoln Hwy E	Lancaster PA	17602	**866-386-2839**	717-291-1888
Grand Harbor Resort & Waterpark				
350 Bell St	Dubuque IA	52001	**866-690-4006**	563-690-4000
Hersheypark				
100 Hershey Pk Dr	Hershey PA	17033	**844-330-1813**	717-534-3900
Holiday World & Splashin' Safari				
452 E Christmas Blvd	Santa Claus IN	47579	**877-463-2645**	812-937-4401
Knoebels Amusement Resort				
391 Knoebels Blvd	Elysburg PA	17824	**800-487-4386**	570-672-2572
Knott's Berry Farm				
8039 Beach Blvd	Buena Park CA	90620	**800-742-6427**	714-220-5200
Lagoon & Pioneer Village				
375 N Lagoon Dr	Farmington UT	84025	**800-748-5246**	801-451-8000
LEGOLAND California				
1 Legoland Dr	Carlsbad CA	92008	**877-534-6526**	888-690-5346
Schlitterbahn Beach Waterpark				
90 Park Rd Hwy 100	South Padre Island TX	78597	**888-852-2489**	956-772-7873
Six Flags Great Adventure				
1 Six Flags Blvd	Jackson NJ	08527	**800-772-2287**	732-928-1821
Six Flags New England				
1623 Main St	Agawam MA	01001	**800-370-7488**	413-786-9300
Six Flags Wild Safari				
1 Six Flags Blvd	Jackson NJ	08527	**800 772-2207**	732-920-1821
Universal Orlando				
6000 Universal Blvd	Orlando FL	32819	**877-801-9720**	407-363-8000
Universal's Islands of Adventure				
6000 Universal Studios Plz	Orlando FL	32819	**877-801-9720**	407-363-8000
Village Vacances Valcartier				
1860 Valcartier Blvd	Valcartier QC	G0A4S0	**888-384-5524**	418-844-2200
Water Country USA				
176 Water Country Pkwy	Williamsburg VA	23185	**800-343-7946**	
Wet 'n Wild Emerald Pointe				
3910 S Holden Rd	Greensboro NC	27406	**800-555-5900**	336-852-9721
Wet 'n Wild Orlando				
6200 International Dr	Orlando FL	32819	**800-992-9453***	407-351-1000
*General				
Wonderland Amusement Park				
2601 Dumas Dr	Amarillo TX	79107	**800-383-4712**	806-383-0832
Worlds of Fun & Oceans of Fun				
4545 NE Worlds of Fun Dr	Kansas City MO	64161	**800-434-7894**	816-454-4545

33   ANIMATION COMPANIES

SEE ALSO Motion Picture & Television Production ; Motion Picture Production - Special Interest

			Toll-Free	Phone
Keith Watson Productions Inc				
350 NW 39th Ave	Gainesville FL	32609	**800-584-1709**	352-264-8814
Medcom Inc 6060 Phyllis Dr	Cypress CA	90630	**800-541-0253**	800-877-1443
NestFamily				
1461 S Beltline Rd Ste 500	Coppell TX	75019	**800-634-4298**	972-402-7100
Summit Training Source				
4170 Embassy Dr	Grand Rapids MI	49546	**800-447-3177**	

34   APPAREL FINDINGS

			Toll-Free	Phone
Agron Inc				
2440 S Sepulveda Blvd Ste 201	Los Angeles CA	90064	**800-966-7697**	
Eric Javits				
21-35 44th Rd	Long Island City NY	11101	**855-208-6200***	800-374-4287
*Consumer Info				
TeamWorld Inc				
498 Conklin Ave	Binghamton NY	13903	**800-797-1005**	607-770-1005

35   APPLIANCE & HOME ELECTRONICS STORES

SEE ALSO Home Improvement Centers ; Department Stores ; Furniture Stores ; Computer Stores

			Toll-Free	Phone
ABC Appliance Inc				
1 Silverdome Industrial Pk	Pontiac MI	48343	**800-981-3866**	
Absocold PO Box 1545	Richmond IN	47374	**800-843-3714**	
Air Cleaning Technologies Inc				
1300 W Detroit	Broken Arrow OK	74012	**800-351-1858**	918-251-8000
Audio Direct				
2004 E Irvington Rd Ste 264	Tucson AZ	85714	**888-628-3467***	
*Cust Svc				
Best Buy Company Inc				
7601 Penn Ave S	Richfield MN	55423	**888-237-8289**	612-291-1000
NYSE: BBY				
BrandsMart USA Corp				
3200 SW 42nd St	Hollywood FL	33312	**800-432-8579**	
Carey Sales & Services Inc				
3141-47 Frederick Ave	Baltimore MD	21229	**800-848-7748**	410-945-7878

				Toll-Free	Phone
Conn's Inc 3295 College St	Beaumont	TX	77701	**800-511-5750***	409-832-1696
NASDAQ: CONN ■ *Cust Svc*					
EarthLinked Technologies Inc					
4151 S Pipkin Rd	Lakeland	FL	33811	**866-211-6102**	863-701-0096
Harco Company Ltd					
5610 McAdam Rd	Mississauga	ON	L4Z1P1	**800-387-9503**	905-890-1220
Interbond Corp of America					
3200 SW 42nd St	Fort Lauderdale	FL	33312	**800-432-8579**	
Mintie Corp					
1114 San Fernando Rd	Los Angeles	CA	90065	**800-964-6843**	323-225-4111
NOVA of California					
6323 Maywood Ave	Los Angeles	CA	90255	**800-835-6682**	323-277-6266
PC Richard & Son Inc					
150 Price Pkwy	Farmingdale	NY	11735	**800-696-2000**	631-773-4900
Pieratt's 110 Mt Tabor Rd	Lexington	KY	40517	**855-743-7288**	859-268-6000
QuestSoft Corp					
23441 S Pointe Dr Ste 220	Laguna Hills	CA	92653	**800-575-4632**	
Radon Control Systems Inc					
160 US Rt 1	Freeport	ME	04032	**800-698-9655**	207-865-9200
Sparkle Solutions LP					
100 Courtland Ave	Concord	ON	L4K3T6	**866-660-2282**	905-660-2282
Synaptec Software Inc					
4155 E Jewell Ave Ste 600	Denver	CO	80222	**800-569-3377**	303-320-4420
Videoland Inc					
6808 Hornwood Dr	Houston	TX	77074	**800-877-2900**	
Wine Appreciation					
450 Taraval St Ste 201	South San Francisco	CA	94116	**800-231-9463**	650-866-3020
Wireless Zone LLC					
795 Brook St	Rocky Hill	CT	06067	**888-881-2622**	800-411-2355
Yale Appliance					
296 Freeport St	Dorchester	MA	02122	**800-565-6435**	617-825-9253

36   APPLIANCES - MAJOR - MFR

SEE ALSO Air Conditioning & Heating Equipment - Residential

				Toll-Free	Phone
Anaheim Manufacturing Co					
25300 Al Moen Dr	North Olmsted	OH	44070	**800-767-6293***	
Cust Svc					
AO Smith Water Products Co					
500 Tennessee Waltz Pkwy	Ashland City	TN	37015	**800-527-1953**	866-362-9898
Atlanta Attachment Company Inc					
362 Industrial Pk Dr	Lawrenceville	GA	30045	**877-206-5116**	770-963-7369
Bock Water Heaters Inc					
110 S Dickinson St	Madison	WI	53703	**800-794-2491**	608-257-2225
Bradford White Corp					
725 Talamore Dr	Ambler	PA	19002	**800-523-2931**	215-641-9400
Brown Stove Works Inc					
1422 Carolina Ave PO Box 2490	Cleveland	TN	37320	**800-251-7485***	423-476-6544
All					
Char-Broil					
1442 Belfast Ave	Columbus	GA	31902	**800-241-7548**	
CookTek LLC					
156 N Jefferson St Ste 300	Chicago	IL	60661	**888-266-5835**	312-563-9600
Ecosmart					
3315 N West 167th St	Miami Gardens	FL	33056	**877-474-6473**	
Electric Heater Co					
45 Seymour St	Stratford	CT	06615	**800-647-3165**	203-378-2659
Electrolux Appliances					
PO Box 212237	Augusta	GA	30907	**877-435-3287**	
Fisher & Paykel Appliances Inc					
5900 Skylab Rd	Huntington Beach	CA	92647	**888-936-7872**	
In-Sink-Erator 4700 21st St	Racine	WI	53406	**800-558-5712**	262-554-5432
LG Electronics USA Inc					
1000 Sylvan Ave	Englewood Cliffs	NJ	07632	**800-243-0000***	201-816-2000
Tech Supp					
Lochinvar Corp					
300 Maddox Simpson Pkwy	Lebanon	TN	37090	**800-722-2101**	615-889-8900
Maytag Appliances					
403 W Fourth St N	Newton	IA	50208	**800-344-1274***	
Cust Svc					
Miele Inc					
9 Independence Way	Princeton	NJ	08540	**800-843-7231**	609-419-9898
Millenia Products Group					
1345 Norwood Ave	Itasca	IL	60143	**800-822-0092**	630-741-7900
Peerless Premier Appliance Co					
119 S 14th St	Belleville	IL	62222	**800-858-5844**	
Sharp Electronics Corp					
1 Sharp Plz	Mahwah	NJ	07430	**800-237-4277**	201-529-8200
Vaughn Manufacturing Corp					
26 Old Elm St PO Box 5431	Salisbury	MA	01952	**800-282-8446**	978-462-6683
Weber-Stephen Products Co					
200 E Daniels Rd	Palatine	IL	60067	**800-446-1071***	
Cust Svc					
Whirlpool Corp					
2000 N M-63	Benton Harbor	MI	49022	**800-253-1301**	269-923-5000
NYSE: WHR					
Whirlpool Corp North American Region					
2000 N M-63	Benton Harbor	MI	49022	**800-253-1301**	269-923-5000
Wisco Industries Inc					
736 Janesville St	Oregon	WI	53575	**800-999-4726**	608-835-3106

37   APPLIANCES - SMALL - MFR

SEE ALSO Air Purification Equipment - Household ; Vacuum Cleaners - Household

				Toll-Free	Phone
Abatement Technologies					
605 Satellite Blvd Ste 300	Suwanee	GA	30024	**800-634-9091**	678-889-4200
Aerus LLC 300 E Valley Dr	Bristol	VA	24201	**800-243-9078**	
Andis Co					
1800 Renaissance Blvd	Sturtevant	WI	53177	**800-558-9441**	
Broan-NuTone LLC					
926 W State St	Hartford	WI	53027	**800-558-1711***	262-673-4340
Cust Svc					

				Toll-Free	Phone
Bunn-O-Matic Corp					
1400 Stevenson Dr	Springfield	IL	62703	**800-637-8606**	217-529-6601
Cadet Mfg Company Inc					
2500 W Fourth Plain Blvd	Vancouver	WA	98660	**800-442-2338**	360-693-2505
City of Chula Vista					
276 Fourth Ave	Chula Vista	CA	91910	**877-478-5478**	619-691-5047
Conair Corp					
1 Cummings Point Rd	Stamford	CT	06902	**800-326-6247**	203-351-9000
OTC: CNGA					
Craftmade 650 S Royal Ln	Coppell	TX	75019	**800-486-4892**	
OTC: CRFT					
Cuisinart 1 Cummings Pt Rd	Stamford	CT	06902	**800-726-0190**	203-975-4609
El Electronics LLC					
1800 Shames Dr	Westbury	NY	11590	**877-346-3837**	516-334-0870
Fan-Tastic Vent Corp					
2083 S Almont Ave	Imlay City	MI	48444	**800-521-0298**	810-724-3818
Hamilton Beach/Proctor-Silex Inc					
4421 Waterfront Dr	Glen Allen	VA	23060	**800-851-8900***	804-273-9777
Cust Svc					
Hunter Fan Co					
7130 Goodlett Farms Pkwy Ste 400	Memphis	TN	38016	**888-830-1326**	901-743-1360
Jarden Consumer Solutions					
2381 Executive Ctr Dr	Boca Raton	FL	33431	**800-777-5452**	561-912-4100
KAZ Inc 250 Tpke Rd	Southborough	MA	01772	**800-477-0457**	
King Electrical Manufacturing Co					
9131 Tenth Ave S	Seattle	WA	98108	**800-603-5464**	206-762-0400
KitchenAid Div					
553 Benson Rd	Benton Harbor	MI	49022	**800-422-1230**	
Lasko Metal Products Inc					
820 Lincoln Ave	West Chester	PA	19380	**800-233-0268**	610-692-7400
LG Electronics USA Inc					
1000 Sylvan Ave	Englewood Cliffs	NJ	07632	**800-243-0000***	201-816-2000
Tech Supp					
Marley Engineered Products					
470 Beauty Spot Rd E	Bennettsville	SC	29512	**800-452-4179**	843-479-4006
National Presto Industries Inc					
3925 N Hastings Way	Eau Claire	WI	54703	**800-877-0441**	715-839-2121
NYSE: NPK					
Nesco/American Harvest					
1700 Monroe St PO Box 237	Two Rivers	WI	54241	**800-288-4545***	920-793-1368
Cust Svc					
Schwabel Corp 26 Crosby Dr	Bedford	MA	01730	**866-753-3837**	781-541-6900
Sharp Electronics Corp					
1 Sharp Plz	Mahwah	NJ	07430	**800-237-4277**	201-529-8200
Singer Sewing Co					
1714 Heil Quaker Blvd Ste 130	La Vergne	TN	37086	**800-474-6437**	615-213-0880
Vita-Mix Corp					
8615 Usher Rd	Cleveland	OH	44138	**800-848-2649**	440-235-4840
West Bend Housewares LLC					
2845 Wingate St	West Bend	WI	53095	**866-290-1851**	
World Dryer Corp					
5700 McDermott Dr	Berkeley	IL	60163	**800-323-0701**	708-449-6950

38   APPLIANCES - WHOL

				Toll-Free	Phone
Almo Corp					
2709 Commerce Way	Philadelphia	PA	19154	**800-345-2566**	215-698-4000
Aves Audio Visual Systems Inc					
PO Box 500	Sugar Land	TX	77487	**800-365-2837**	281-295-1300
Blodgett Supply Co Inc					
100 Ave D PO Box 759	Williston	VT	05495	**888-888-3424**	802-864-9831
Bursma Electronic Distributing Inc					
2851 Buchanan Ave SW	Grand Rapids	MI	49548	**800-777-2604**	616-831-0080
C & L Supply Co PO Box 578	Vinita	OK	74301	**800-256-6411**	
DAS Inc 724 Lawn Rd	Palmyra	PA	17078	**866-622-7979**	717-964-3642
Electrical Distributing Inc					
4600 NW St Helens Rd	Portland	OR	97210	**800-877-4229**	503-226-4044
Felix Storch Inc					
770 Garrison Ave	Bronx	NY	10474	**800-932-4267**	718-893-3900
Helen of Troy Ltd					
1 Helen of Troy Plz	El Paso	TX	79912	**800-487-7273**	
NASDAQ: HELE					
Home Entertainment Distribution Inc					
120 Shawmut Rd	Canton	MA	02021	**888-567-7557**	
MD.M. Commercial Enterprises Inc					
1102 A1a N Ste 205	Ponte Vedra	FL	32082	**800-359-6741**	
Midwest Sales & Service Inc					
917 S Chapin St	South Bend	IN	46601	**800-772-7262**	574-287-3365
Molok North America Ltd					
179 Norpark Ave	Mount Forest	ON	N0G2L0	**877-558-5576**	519-323-9909
Peirce-Phelps Inc					
516 E Township Line Rd Blue Bell	Philadelphia	PA	19131	**800-222-2096**	215-879-7217
Potter Distributing Inc					
4037 Roger B Chaffee Blvd	Grand Rapids	MI	49548	**800-748-0568**	616-531-6860
R & B Wholesale Distributors Inc					
2350 S Milliken Ave	Ontario	CA	91761	**800-627-7539**	909-230-5400
Roth Living					
11300 W 47th St	Minnetonka	MN	55343	**800-363-3818**	952-933-4428
Servall Co					
6761 E 10 Mile Rd	Center Line	MI	48015	**800-856-9874**	
Speco Technologies					
200 New Hwy	Amityville	NY	11701	**800-645-5516**	631-957-8700
Telerent Leasing Corp					
4191 Fayetteville Rd	Raleigh	NC	27603	**800-626-0682**	919-772-8604
WASH Multifamily Laundry Systems					
100 N Sepulveda Blvd 12th Fl	El Segundo	CA	90245	**800-421-6897***	
General					
Westland Sales PO Box 427	Clackamas	OR	97015	**800-356-0766**	503-655-2563
Whirlpool Canada					
200-6750 Century Ave	Mississauga	ON	L5N0B7	**800-807-6777**	905-821-6400
Woodson & Bozeman Inc					
3870 New Getwell Rd	Memphis	TN	38118	**800-876-4243**	901-362-1500

39   APPLICATION SERVICE PROVIDERS (ASPS)

Application Service Providers rent, deliver, license, manage, and/or host proprietary and/ or third-party business software ("applications") and/or computer services to multiple users (customers). Included here are companies that host software applications as well as companies that provide the equipment necessary to do so.

				Toll-Free	Phone
AllMeds Inc					
151 Lafayette Dr Ste 401	Oak Ridge	TN	37830	**888-343-6337**	865-482-1999
Ariba Inc 807 11th Ave	Sunnyvale	CA	94089	**866-772-7422**	
NYSE: SAP					
Avanade Inc 818 Stewart St	Seattle	WA	98101	**844-282-6233**	206-239-5600
Baillio's Inc					
5301 Menaul Blvd NE	Albuquerque	NM	87110	**800-540-7511**	505-395-5611
BizLand Inc					
70 BlanchaRd Rd	Burlington	MA	01803	**800-249-5263**	
Chemical Safety Corp					
5901 Christie Ave	Emeryville	CA	94608	**888-594-1100**	510-594-1000
CliniComp International					
9655 Towne Ctr Dr	San Diego	CA	92121	**800-350-8202**	858-546-8202
Connectria Hosting					
10845 Olive Blvd 300	Saint Louis	MO	63141	**800-781-7820**	314-587-7000
Crexendo Inc 1615 S 52nd St	Tempe	AZ	85281	**866-621-6111**	602-714-8500
OTC: CXDO					
Digital River Inc					
10380 Bren Rd W	Minnetonka	MN	55343	**800-598-7450**	
NASDAQ: DRIV					
DigitalWork Inc					
14300 N Northsight Blvd Ste 206	Scottsdale	AZ	85260	**877-496-7571**	
E-Builder Inc					
1800 NW 69 Ave Ste 201	Plantation	FL	33313	**800-580-9322**	954-556-6701
eGain Corp					
1252 Borregas Ave	Sunnyvale	CA	94089	**888-603-4246**	408-636-4500
NASDAQ: EGAN					
Emdeon Business Services LLC					
3055 Lebanon Pk	Nashville	TN	37214	**800-735-8254**	615-932-3000
ePlus Inc					
13595 Dulles Technology Dr	Herndon	VA	20171	**888-482-1122**	703-984-8400
NASDAQ: PLUS					
FinancialCAD Corp					
13450 102nd Ave Ste 1750	Surrey	BC	V3T5X3	**800-304-0702**	604-957-1200
Internap Network Services Corp					
250 Williams St Ste E-100	Atlanta	GA	30303	**877-843-7627**	404-302-9700
NASDAQ: INAP					
IntraLinks Inc					
150 E 42nd St	New York	NY	10017	**888-546-5383**	212-543-7700
Journyx Inc					
7600 Burnet Rd Ste 300	Austin	TX	78757	**800-755-9878**	512-834-8888
Kleinschmidt Inc					
450 Lake Cook Rd	Deerfield	IL	60015	**800-824-2330**	847-945-1000
Mobile Smith					
5400 Trinity Rd Ste 208	Raleigh	NC	27607	**855-516-2413**	
Oracle Corp					
500 Oracle Pkwy	Redwood Shores	CA	94065	**800-392-2999***	800-633-0738
NYSE: ORCL ■ *Sales					
Outstart Inc					
745 Atlantic Ave 4th Fl	Boston	MA	02111	**877-971-9171**	617-897-6800
Paramount WorkPlace					
1374 EW Maple Rd	Walled Lake	MI	48390	**800-725-4408**	248-960-0909
PBM Corp					
20600 Chagrin Blvd Ste 450	Cleveland	OH	44122	**800-341-5809**	216-283-7999
Perfect Commerce Inc					
1 Compass Way Ste 120	Newport News	VA	23606	**877-871-3788***	757-766-8211
*Sales					
Prodata Systems Inc					
11007 Slater Ave NE	Kirkland	WA	98033	**866-582-7485**	425-296-4168
Radware Inc					
575 Corporate Dr Lobby 2	Mahwah	NJ	07430	**888-234-5763**	400-920-2910
Resource Development Corp					
280 Daines St Ste 200	Birmingham	MI	48009	**800-360-7222**	248-646-2300
Salesnet					
6340 Sugarloaf Pkwy Ste 200	Duluth	GA	30097	**866-732-8632**	
Streamline Health Solutions Inc					
10200 Alliance Rd Ste 200	Cincinnati	OH	45242	**800-878-5269**	888-997-8732
NASDAQ: STRM					
Syntrio					
500 Lake Cook Rd Ste 350	Deerfield	IL	60015	**888-289-6670**	415-951-7913
Talisma Corporation Pvt Ltd					
5201 Congress Ave	Boca Raton	FL	33487	**866-397-2537**	561-923-2500
TALX Corp					
11432 Lackland Dr	Saint Louis	MO	63146	**800-888-8277**	314-214-7000
Toolwire Inc					
7031 Koll Ctr Pkwy Ste 220	Pleasanton	CA	94566	**866-935-8665**	925-227-8500
UL EHS Sustainability					
5000 Meridian Blvd Ste 600	Franklin	TN	37067	**888-202-3016**	615-367-4404
Unicorn HRO LLC					
25B Hanover Rd	Florham Park	NJ	07932	**800-368-8149**	

40   AQUARIUMS - PUBLIC

SEE ALSO Zoos & Wildlife Parks ; Botanical Gardens & Arboreta

				Toll-Free	Phone
Adventure Aquarium					
1 Riverside Dr	Camden	NJ	08103	**844-474-3474**	
Aquarium du Quebec					
1675 des Hotels Ave	Quebec	QC	G1W4S3	**866-659-5264**	418-659-5264
Florida Aquarium					
701 Channelside Dr	Tampa	FL	33602	**800-353-4741**	813-273-4000
Key West Aquarium					
1 Whitehead St	Key West	FL	33040	**888-544-5927**	
Marineland of Florida					
9600 Ocean Shore Blvd	Saint Augustine	FL	32080	**877-933-3402**	904-471-1111
Marinelife Ctr of Juno Beach					
14200 US Hwy 1 Loggerhead Pk	Juno Beach	FL	33408	**800-843-5451**	561-627-8280

				Toll-Free	Phone
National Aquarium in Baltimore					
501 E Pratt St	Baltimore	MD	21202	**800-628-9944**	410-576-3800
Newport Aquarium					
1 Aquarium Way	Newport	KY	41071	**800-406-3474**	
Oregon Coast Aquarium					
2820 SE Ferry Slip Rd	Newport	OR	97365	**800-452-7888**	541-867-3474
Seattle Aquarium					
1483 Alaskan Way Pier 59	Seattle	WA	98101	**800-853-1964**	206-386-4300
South Carolina Aquarium					
100 Aquarium Wharf	Charleston	SC	29401	**800-722-6455**	843-577-3474
Steinhart Aquarium					
California Academy of Sciences					
55 Music Concourse Dr					
Golden Gate Park	San Francisco	CA	94118	**800-794-7576**	415-379-8000
Tennessee Aquarium					
1 Broad St	Chattanooga	TN	37402	**800-262-0695**	
Vancouver Aquarium Marine Science Ctr					
845 Avison Way	Vancouver	BC	V6G3E2	**800-931-1186**	604-659-3474

41   ARBITRATION SERVICES - LEGAL

				Toll-Free	Phone
Alliance Abroad Group					
1645 E Sixth St Ste 100	Austin	TX	78702	**866-622-7623**	512-457-8062
Americall 1502 Tacoma Ave S	Tacoma	WA	98402	**800-964-3556**	253-272-4111
Annuvia Inc					
1725 Clay St Ste 100	San Francisco	CA	94109	**866-364-7940**	
Anresco Inc					
1375 Van Dyke Ave	San Francisco	CA	94124	**800-359-0920**	415-822-1100
Arbitration Forums Inc					
3350 Buschwood Pk Dr Ste 295	Tampa	FL	33618	**800-967-8889***	813-931-4004
*Cust Svc					
Arcturus Advisors					
4320 Dunewood Pl	Fernandina Beach	FL	32034	**866-593-2207**	
Balasa Dinverno Foltz LLC					
500 Park Blvd Ste 1400	Itasca	IL	60143	**800-840-4740**	630-875-4900
Brunswick School Inc					
100 Maher Ave	Greenwich	CT	06830	**800-546-9425**	203-625-5800
CareerCurve LLC					
5005 Rockside Rd Ste 600 076	Cleveland	OH	44131	**800-314-8230**	216-406-5542
CIR Law Offices International LLP					
2650 Camino Del Rio N Ste 308	San Diego	CA	92108	**800-496-8909**	858-496-8909
Clean Air Engineering Inc					
500 W Wood St	Palatine	IL	60067	**800-553-5511**	847-991-3300
Council of Better Business Bureaus Inc					
Dispute Resolution Services & Mediation Training					
4200 Wilson Blvd Ste 800	Arlington	VA	22203	**855-748-4600**	703-276-0100
David A Noyes & Co					
209 S LaSalle St	Chicago	IL	60604	**800-669-3732**	312-782-0400
EmpXtrack					
150 Motor Pkwy Ste 401	Hauppauge	NY	11788	**888-840-2682**	
Estabrook Capital Management LLC					
900 Third Ave Ste 1004	New York	NY	10022	**888-447-7443**	212-605-5595
Eurofase Inc					
33 W Beaver Creek Rd	Richmond Hill	ON	L4B1L8	**800-660-5391**	905-695-2055
Family Credit Management					
111 N Wabash Ste 1410	Chicago	IL	60602	**877-322-8319**	800-994-3328
Farris Vaughan Wills & Murphy					
700 W Georgia St Pacific Centre S 25th Fl					
PO Box 10026	Vancouver	BC	V7Y1B3	**877-684-9151**	604-684-9151
Fasken Martineau DuMoulin LLP					
333 Bay St Bay Adelaide Ctr Ste 2400					
PO Box 20	Toronto	ON	M5H2T6	**800-268-8424**	416-366-8381
Florida Council Against Sexual Violence Inc					
1820 E Park Ave Ste 100	Tallahassee	FL	32301	**888-956-7273**	850-297-2000
Florida Surplus Lines Service Office					
1441 Maclay Commerce Dr	Tallahassee	FL	32312	**800-562-4496**	850-224-7676
Global Imaging Inc					
2011 Cherry St Ste 116	Louisville	CO	80027	**800-787-9801**	303-673-9773
Gokeyless 3646 Cargo Rd	Vandalia	OH	45377	**877-439-5377**	937-890-2333
Guidesoft Inc					
5875 Castle Creek Pkwy Ste 400	Indianapolis	IN	46250	**877-256-6948**	317-578-1700
J P. King Auction Company Inc					
414 Broad St	Gadsden	AL	35901	**800-558-5464**	
JAMS/Endispute					
500 N State College Blvd 14th Fl	Orange	CA	92868	**800-352-5267**	714-939-1300
Jeffrey Byrne & Assoc					
4042 Central St	Kansas City	MO	64111	**800-222-9233**	816-237-1999
JS Paluch Company Inc					
3708 River Rd Ste 400	Franklin Park	IL	60131	**800-621-5197**	847-678-9300
Judicate West					
1851 E First St Ste 1600	Santa Ana	CA	92705	**800-488-8805**	714-834-1340
July Business Services					
215 Mary Ave Ste 302	Waco	TX	76701	**888-333-5859**	
JumpSport Inc					
2055 S Seventh St Ste A	San Jose	CA	95112	**888-567-5867**	408-213-2551
Kaufman Company Inc					
19 Walkhill St	Norwood	MA	02062	**800-338-8023**	781-255-1000
Living Color Enterprises Inc					
6850 NW 12th Ave	Fort Lauderdale	FL	33309	**800-878-9511**	954-970-9511
Loeb Equipment & Appraisal Co					
4131 S State St	Chicago	IL	60609	**800-560-5632**	773-548-4131
McDonald Carano LLP					
2300 W Sahara Ave Ste 1200	Las Vegas	NV	89102	**800-872-3862**	702-873-4100
Medicount Management Inc					
10361 Spartan Dr	Cincinnati	OH	45215	**800-962-1484**	513-772-4465
Mega Group Inc					
720-1st Ave N	Saskatoon	SK	S7K6R9	**800-265-9030**	306-242-7366
Merchant Law Group LLP					
2401 Saskatchewan Dr Saskatchewan Dr Plz					
	Regina	SK	S4P4H8	**888-567-7777**	306-359-7777
Middleton & Company Inc					
600 Atlantic Ave 18th Fl	Boston	MA	02210	**800-357-5101**	617-357-5101
Miller Thomson LLP					
Scotia Plz 40 King St W Ste 5800	Toronto	ON	M5H3S1	**888-762-5559**	416-595-8500
Missouri Protection & Advocacy Services					
925 S Country Club Dr	Jefferson City	MO	65109	**800-392-8667**	573-659-0678

	Toll-Free	Phone
National Arbitration & Mediation (NAM)		
990 Stewart Ave 1st Fl .... Garden City NY 11530	800-358-2550	
Nines Hotel, The		
525 SW Morrison .... Portland OR 97204	877-229-9995	
Notus Career Management		
5 Centerpointe Dr Ste 400 .... Lake Oswego OR 97035	800-431-1990	503-443-1113
O'connor Company Inc		
16910 W 116th St .... Lenexa KS 66219	888-800-3540	913-894-8788
OneTouch Direct LLC		
4902 W Sligh Ave .... Tampa FL 33634	866-948-4005	
Ontellus 1010 Lamar 18th Fl ..... Houston TX 77002	800-467-9181	
OTS 3924 Clock Pointe Trl .... Stow OH 44224	877-445-2058	
Paging Network of Canada Inc		
1-1685 Tech Ave .... Mississauga ON L4W0A7	800-216-0888	
Parker Rose Design Inc		
10075 Mesa Rim Rd Ste A .... San Diego CA 92121	800-403-2711	
PMA Canada Ltd		
231 Oak Park Blvd Ste 400 .... Oakville ON L6H7S8	800-667-9463	905-257-2116
Promotion Fulfillment Center		
311 21st St .... Camanche IA 52730	800-493-7063	
Quatred LLC		
532 Fourth Range Rd .... Pembroke NH 03275	888-395-8534	
Quiktrak Inc		
9700 SW Nimbus Ave .... Beaverton OR 97008	800-927-8725	
Randall S Miller & Associates PC		
43252 Woodward Ave Ste 180 ..... Bloomfield Hills MI 48302	844-322-6558	248-335-9200
Resolute Systems Inc		
1550 N Prospect Ave .... Milwaukee WI 53202	800-776-6060	414-276-4774
RESOLVE Partners LLC		
2733 Horse Pen Creek Rd Ste 101 ..... Greensboro NC 27410	866-921-5388	336-217-1005
Resume Solutions		
1033 Bay St Ste 317 .... Toronto ON M5S3A5	866-361-1290	416-361-1290
RVM Enterprises Inc		
40 Rector St 17th Fl .... New York NY 10006	800-525-7915	
SOMA Medical Assessments		
8800 Dufferin St Ste 105 .... Vaughan ON L4K0C5	877-664-7662	905-881-8855
Sperry Rail Inc		
46 Shelter Rock Rd .... Danbury CT 06810	800-525-8913	203-791-4500
Spotts Fain PC		
411 E Franklin St Ste 600 .... Richmond VA 23219	866-788-1190	804-697-2000
Surveillance Specialties Ltd		
600 Research Dr .... Wilmington MA 01887	800-354-2616	
Tech Networks of Boston		
574 Dorchester Ave .... Boston MA 02127	888-527-9333	617-269-0299
TERRAMAI 8400 Agate Rd .... White City OR 97503	800-220-9062	
Tranzon LLC		
2100 Club Dr Ste 100 .... Gadsden AL 35901	866-872-6966	256-413-2902
Tri-Starr Investigations Inc		
3525 Hwy 138 SW Rockdale County ..... Stockbridge GA 30281	800-849-9841	770-388-9841
UMIAQ LLC		
6700 Arctic Spur Rd .... Anchorage AK 99518	800-226-0009	907-677-8220
Usherwood Office Technology Inc		
1005 W Fayette St .... Syracuse NY 13204	800-724-2119	315-472-0050
Valley Internet Inc		
102 Maple St E .... Fayetteville TN 37334	888-433-1924	931-433-1921
Webb; County Appraisal Distric		
3302 Clark Blvd .... Laredo TX 78043	800-252-9121	956-718-4091
Wolfe Industrial Auctions Inc		
9801 Hansonville Rd .... Frederick MD 21702	800-443-9580	301-898-0340
Xerces Society, The		
628 NE Broadway Ste 200 .... Portland OR 97232	855-232-6639	

ARCHITECTS

SEE Engineering & Design

ART - COMMERCIAL

SEE Graphic Design

42   ART DEALERS & GALLERIES

	Toll-Free	Phone
Airway Surgical Appliances Ltd		
189 Colonnade Rd .... Nepean ON K2E7J4	800-267-3476	613-723-4790
Gallery 78 Inc		
796 Queen St .... Fredericton NB E3B1C6	888-883-8322	506-454-5192
Heffel Gallery Ltd		
2247 Granville St .... Vancouver BC V6H3G1	800-528-9608	604-732-6505
Inuit Gallery of Vancouver Ltd		
206 Cambie St Gastown .... Vancouver BC V6B2M9	888-615-8399	604-688-7323
Masters Gallery Ltd		
2115 Fourth St SW .... Calgary AB T2S1W8	866-245-0616	403-245-2064
Mayberry Fine Art Inc		
212 Mcdermot Ave .... Winnipeg MB R3B0S3	877-871-9261	204-255-5690
Meyer Gallery		
225 Canyon Rd Ste 14 .... Santa Fe NM 87501	800-779-7387	505-983-1434
Odon Wagner Gallery		
196 Davenport Rd .... Toronto ON M5R1J2	800-551-2465	416-962-0438
Rhona Hoffman Gallery		
1338 W Lake St .... Chicago IL 60607	800-525-5562	312-280-1212
Uno Langmann Ltd		
2117 Granville St .... Vancouver BC V6H3E9	800-730-8825	604-736-8825
West End Gallery Ltd		
12308 Jasper Ave .... Edmonton AB T5N3K5	855-488-4892	780-488-4892

43   ART MATERIALS & SUPPLIES - MFR

SEE ALSO Pens, Pencils, Parts

	Toll-Free	Phone
Adco Industries		
11333 Pagemill Rd .... Dallas TX 75243	800-527-4609	214-217-7800
Alvin & Company Inc		
1335 Blue Hills Ave .... Bloomfield CT 06002	800-444-2584	860-243-8991

	Toll-Free	Phone
American Art Clay Co (AMACO)		
6060 Guion Rd .... Indianapolis IN 46254	800-374-1600	317-244-6871
American Metalcraft Inc		
3708 N River Rd Ste 800 .... Franklin Park IL 60131	800-333-9133	708-345-1177
Ampersand Art Supply		
1235 S Loop 4 Ste 400 .... Buda TX 78610	800-822-1939	512-322-0278
Artist Brand Canvas		
2448 Loma Ave .... South El Monte CA 91733	888-579-2704*	626-579-2740
*Orders		
Badger Air Brush Co		
9128 Belmont Ave .... Franklin Park IL 60131	800-247-2787	847-678-3104
Chartpak Inc 1 River Rd .... Leeds MA 01053	800-628-1910	413-584-5446
DecoArt Inc 49 Cotton Ave .... Stanford KY 40484	800-367-3047	606-365-3193
Duncan Enterprises		
5673 E Shields Ave .... Fresno CA 93727	800-438-6226	559-291-4444
Gare Inc 165 Rosemont St .... Haverhill MA 01832	888-289-4273	978-373-9131
Georgie's Ceramic & Clay Company Inc		
756 NE Lombard St .... Portland OR 97211	800-999-2529	503-283-1353
Golden Artists Colors Inc		
188 Bell Rd .... New Berlin NY 13411	800-959-6543	607-847-6154
Jack Richeson & Company Inc		
557 Marcella Dr .... Kimberly WI 54136	800-233-2404	920-738-0744
Martin/F Weber Co		
2727 Southampton Rd .... Philadelphia PA 19154	800-876-8076	215-677-5600
National Artcraft Supply Co		
300 Campus Dr .... Aurora OH 44202	888-937-2723	330-562-3500
Paasche Airbrush Co		
4311 N Normandy Ave .... Chicago IL 60634	800-621-1907*	
*Sales		
Plaid Enterprises Inc		
3225 Westech Dr .... Norcross GA 30092	800-842-4197	
Sargent Art Inc		
100 E Diamond Ave .... Hazleton PA 18201	800-424-3596	
Smooth-On Inc		
2000 St John St .... Easton PA 18042	800-762-0744	610-252-5800
Testor Corp		
11 Hawthorn Pkwy .... Vernon Hills IL 60061	800-837-8677	815-962-6654
Utrecht Art Supplies		
PO Box 1769 .... Galesburg IL 61402	888-336-3114	609-409-8001

44   ART MATERIALS & SUPPLIES - WHOL

	Toll-Free	Phone
CWI Gifts & Crafts		
77 Cypress St SW .... Reynoldsburg OH 43068	800-666-5858	740-964-6210
D&L Art Glass Supply		
1440 W 52nd Ave .... Denver CO 80221	800-525-0940	303-449-8737
Darice Inc		
13000 Darice Pkwy .... Strongsville OH 44149	866-432-7423	
Hobby Lobby		
7717 SW 44th St .... Oklahoma City OK 73179	800-888-0321	405-745-1275
Pioneer Wholesale Co		
500 W Bagley Rd .... Berea OH 44017	888-234-5400	440-234-5400
Sbar's Inc 14 Sbar Blvd .... Moorestown NJ 08057	800-989-7227	856-234-8220
Sepp Leaf Products Inc		
381 Park Ave S Ste 1301 .... New York NY 10016	800-971-7377	212-683-2840

45   ART SUPPLY STORES

	Toll-Free	Phone
Aaron Bros		
8000 Bent Branch Dr .... Irving TX 75063	877-372-6370	
AC Moore Arts & Crafts Inc		
130 AC Moore Dr .... Berlin NJ 08009	888-226-6673	
NASDAQ: ACMR		
Accord Carton 6155 W 115th St .... Alsip IL 60803	800-648-6780	
Alabama Art Supply Inc		
1006 23rd St S .... Birmingham AL 35205	800-749-4741*	205-322-4741
*Cust Svc		
All Copy Products LLC		
4141 Colorado Blvd .... Denver CO 80216	800-332-2352	303-295-0741
All in One Poster Co		
8521 Whitaker St .... Buena Park CA 90621	800-273-0307	714-521-7720
Alpina Manufacturing LLC		
6460 W Cortland St .... Chicago IL 60707	800-915-2828	773-202-8887
AmeriWater Inc		
1303 Stanley Ave .... Dayton OH 45404	800-535-5585	937-461-8833
Arizona Art Supply		
4025 N 16th St .... Phoenix AZ 85016	877-264-9514	602-264-9514
Art Supply Warehouse		
6672 Westminster Blvd .... Westminster CA 92683	800-854-6467	714-891-3626
Blaine's Art Supply		
1025 Photo Ave .... Anchorage AK 99503	866-561-4278	907-561-5344
Cashman Equipment Co		
3300 St Rose Pkwy .... Henderson NV 89052	800-937-2326	702-649-8777
Congdon's Aids To Daily Living Ltd		
10550 - Mayfield Rd .... Edmonton AB T5P4X4	800-252-9368	780-483-1762
Controls Corporation of America		
1501 Harpers Rd .... Virginia Beach VA 23454	800-225-0473	757-422-8330
Crime Alert 690 Lenfest Rd .... San Jose CA 95133	800-367-1094	
Dick Blick Co PO Box 1267 .... Galesburg IL 61402	800-447-8192*	309-343-6181
*Orders		
Excelleris Technologies Inc		
200-3500 Gilmore Way .... Burnaby BC V5C2W7	866-728-4777*	604-658-2111
*Support		
Fastframe USA Inc		
212 Marine St Ste 100 .... Santa Monica CA 90405	800-631-4964	
Flax Art & Design		
Fort Mason Ctr 2 Marina Blvd		
Bldg D. .... San Francisco CA 94123	844-352-9278	415-530-3510
Georgie's Ceramic & Clay Company Inc		
756 NE Lombard St .... Portland OR 97211	800-999-2529	503-283-1353
Haber Vision LLC		
15710 W Colfax Ave Ste 204 .... Golden CO 80401	800-621-4381	303-459-2220

				Toll-Free	Phone

Herweck's Art & Drafting Supplies
300 Broadway St .... San Antonio TX 78205 **800-725-1349** 210-227-1349

Imaging Office Systems Inc
4505 E Park 30 Dr .... Columbia City IN 46725 **800-878-7731** 260-248-9696

Kanson Electronics Inc
245 Forrest Ave .... Hohenwald TN 38462 **800-233-9354** 931-796-3050

Lantana Communications Corp
1700 Tech Centre Pkwy Ste 100 .... Arlington TX 76014 **800-345-4211**

Legend Data Systems Inc
18024 72nd Ave S .... Kent WA 98032 **866-371-1670** 425-251-1670

Masterman's LLP 11 C St .... Auburn MA 01501 **800-525-3313**

Michaels Stores Inc
8000 Bent Branch Dr .... Irving TX 75063 **800-642-4235***
*Cust Svc

Model Electronics Inc
615 E Crescent Ave .... Ramsey NJ 07446 **800-433-9657**

Omnipure Filter Company Inc
1904 Industrial Way .... Caldwell ID 83605 **800-398-0833** 208-454-2597

Patten Monument Co
3980 W River Dr NE .... Comstock Park MI 49321 **800-627-5371** 800-233-4472

Plaza Art
633 Middleton St .... Nashville TN 37203 **866-668-6714**

Plaza Artist Materials & Picture Framing
1120 19th St NW .... Washington DC 20036 **866-668-6714**

Premier Pyrotechnics Inc
25255 Hwy K .... Richland MO 65556 **888-647-6863** 417-322-6595

Presentation Concepts Corp
6517 Basile Rowe .... East Syracuse NY 13057 **888-262-7596** 315-437-1314

Quality Filtration LLC
5215 Linbar Dr Ste 204 .... Nashville TN 37211 **877-377-7702**

Rabbit Air
125 N Raymond Ave Ste 308 .... Pasadena CA 91103 **888-866-8862** 562-861-4688

Rex Art Co 3160 SW 22 St .... Miami FL 33145 **800-739-2782** 305-445-1413

Spokane Art Supply Inc
1303 N Monroe St .... Spokane WA 99201 **800-556-5568** 509-327-6622

Stagecraft Industries Inc
5051 N Lagoon Ave .... Portland OR 97217 **800-727-2673** 503-286-1600

Stewart Business Systems LLC
105 Connecticut Dr .... Burlington NJ 08016 **800-322-5584**

Texas Art Supply
2001 Montrose Blvd .... Houston TX 77006 **800-888-9278** 713-526-5221

Woodcraft Supply LLC
1177 Rosemar Rd .... Parkersburg WV 26105 **800-535-4482**

46　ASPHALT PAVING & ROOFING MATERIALS

				Toll-Free	Phone

Atlas Roofing Corp
2322 Valley Rd .... Meridian MS 39307 **800-478-0258*** 601-483-7111
*Cust Svc

Baker Rock Resources
21880 SW Farmington Rd .... Beaverton OR 97007 **800-340-7625** 503-642-2531

Brewer Co 1354 US Hwy 50 .... Milford OH 45150 **800-394-0017** 513-576-6300

Capitol Aggregates Ltd
2330 N Loop 1604 W .... San Antonio TX 78248 **855-422-7244** 210-871-6100

CertainTeed Corp
750 E Swedesford Rd .... Valley Forge PA 19482 **800-782-8777*** 610-341-7000
*Prod Info

Crafco Inc
420 N Roosevelt Ave .... Chandler AZ 85226 **800-528-8242** 602-276-0406

CRH Americas Inc
900 Ashwood Pkwy Ste 700 .... Atlanta GA 30338 **800-241-7074** 770-522-5600

Dalrymple Gravel & Contracting Company Inc
2105 S Broadway .... Pine City NY 14871 **800-957-3130** 607-737-6200

Dalton Enterprises Inc
131 Willow St .... Cheshire CT 06410 **800-851-5606** 203-272-3221

Dewitt Products Co
5860 Plumer Ave .... Detroit MI 48209 **800-962-8599*** 313-554-0575
*Cust Svc

Fields Company LLC
2240 Taylor Way .... Tacoma WA 98421 **800-627-4098**

Gardner-Gibson PO Box 5449 .... Tampa FL 33675 **800-237-1155** 813-248-2101

Garland Company Inc
3800 E 91st St .... Cleveland OH 44105 **800-321-9336** 216-641-7500

Glenn O Hawbaker Inc
1952 Waddle Rd Ste 203 .... State College PA 16803 **800-221-1355** 814-237-1444

Heely-Brown Company Inc
1280 Chattahoochee Ave .... Atlanta GA 30318 **800-241-4628** 404-352-0022

Henry Co
909 N Sepulveda Blvd Ste 650 ...... El Segundo CA 90245 **800-598-7663** 310-955-9200

HRI Inc
1750 W College Ave .... State College PA 16801 **877-474-9999** 814-238-5071

Innovative Metals Company Inc (IMETCO)
4648 S Old Peachtree Rd .... Norcross GA 30071 **800-646-3826** 770-908-1030

Karnak Corp, The
330 Central Ave .... Clark NJ 07066 **800-526-4236** 732-388-0300

Koppers Inc
436 Seventh Ave .... Pittsburgh PA 15219 **800-385-4406** 412-227-2001
NYSE: KOP

Malarkey Roofing Products
PO Box 17217 .... Portland OR 97217 **800-545-1191** 503-283-1191

Neyra Industries
10700 Evendale Dr .... Cincinnati OH 45241 **800-543-7077** 513-733-1000

Pace Products Inc
4510 W 89th St Ste 110 .... Prairie Village KS 66207 **888-389-8203**

Package Pavement Company Inc
PO Box 408 .... Stormville NY 12582 **800-724-8193** 845-221-2224

Palmer Asphalt Co
196 W Fifth St PO Box 58 .... Bayonne NJ 07002 **800-352-9898** 201-339-0855

PetersenDean Roofing & Solar
39300 Civic Center Dr Ste 300 .... Fremont CA 94538 **877-552-4418**

Pike Industries Inc
3 Eastgate Pk Rd .... Belmont NH 03220 **800-283-0803** 603-527-5100

Russell Standard Corp
285 Kappa Dr Ste 300 .... Pittsburgh PA 15238 **800-323-3053***
*General

				Toll-Free	Phone

Seaboard Asphalt Products Co
3601 Fairfield Rd .... Baltimore MD 21226 **800-536-0332** 410-355-0330

Sika Sarnafil Inc 100 Dan Rd .... Canton MA 02021 **800-451-2504** 781-828-5400

Simon Roofing & Sheet Metal Corp
70 Karago Ave .... Youngstown OH 44512 **800-523-7714** 330-629-7663

Stavola Contracting
PO Box 482 .... Red Bank NJ 07701 **800-359-1424** 732-542-2328

Tilcon Connecticut Inc
PO Box 1357 .... New Britain CT 06050 **888-845-2666** 860-224-6010

Vance Bros Inc
5201 Brighton PO Box 300107 .... Kansas City MO 64130 **800-821-8549** 816-923-4325

Vulcan Materials Co
1200 Urban Ctr Dr PO Box 385014 ...... Birmingham AL 35238 **800-615-4331** 205-298-3000
NYSE: VMC

47　ASSOCIATION MANAGEMENT COMPANIES

				Toll-Free	Phone

Allen Press Inc
810 E Tenth St PO Box 1897 .... Lawrence KS 66044 **800-627-0932** 785-843-1234

Applied Measurement Professionals Inc (AMP)
18000 W 105th St .... Olathe KS 66061 **800-345-6559** 913-895-4600

Association Headquarters Inc
1120 Rt 73 Ste 200 .... Mount Laurel NJ 08054 **877-777-6753**

Center for Assn Resources Inc
1901 N Roselle Rd Ste 920 .... Schaumburg IL 60195 **888-705-1434**

Center for Association Growth, The (TCAG)
1926 Waukegan Rd Ste 300 .... Glenview IL 60025 **800-492-6462** 847-657-6700

CM Services Inc
800 Roosevelt Rd Bldg C Ste 312 ...... Glen Ellyn IL 60137 **800-613-6672** 630-858-7337

Grassley Group, The (FMCI)
600 State St Ste A .... Cedar Falls IA 50613 **866-619-5580**

J Edgar Eubanks & Assoc
1 Windsor Cove Ste 305 .... Columbia SC 29223 **800-445-8629** 803-252-5646

LoBue & Majdalany Management Group
572B Ruger St PO Box 29920 ...... San Francisco CA 94129 **800-820-4690** 415-561-6110

NeuStar Inc
21575 Ridgetop Cir .... Sterling VA 20166 **855-638-2677** 571-434-5400

Pathfinder Group
Park Lane Terr 502 - 5657 Spring Garden Rd
PO Box 142 .... Halifax NS B3J3R4 **800-200-7284** 902-425-2445

Prime Management Services
3416 Primm Ln .... Birmingham AL 35216 **866-609-1599** 205-823-6106

Raybourn Group International
9100 PuRdue Rd Ste 200 .... Indianapolis IN 46268 **800-362-2546** 317-328-4636

48　ASSOCIATIONS & ORGANIZATIONS - GENERAL

SEE ALSO Political Parties (Major) ; Political Action Committees ; Performing Arts Organizations

48-1 Accreditation & Certification Organizations

				Toll-Free	Phone

Accrediting Commission of Career Schools & Colleges of Technology (ACCSCT)
2101 Wilson Blvd Ste 302 .... Arlington VA 22201 **800-842-0229** 703-247-4212

Accrediting Council for Independent Colleges & Schools (ACICS)
750 First St NE Ste 980 .... Washington DC 20002 **800-258-3826** 202-336-6780

Advanced California (NAAS)
1510 Robert St Ste 103 .... Boise ID 83705 **888-413-3669**

American Assn for Accreditation of Ambulatory Surgery Facilities Inc (AAAASF)
5101 Washington St Ste 2F PO Box 9500 ... Gurnee IL 60031 **888-545-5222** 847-775-1985

American Board of Internal Medicine (ABIM)
510 Walnut St Ste 1700 .... Philadelphia PA 19106 **800-441-2246** 215-446-3590

American Culinary Federation Inc (ACF)
180 Ctr Pl Way .... Saint Augustine FL 32095 **800-624-9458** 904-824-4468

American National Standards Institute (ANSI)
25 W 43rd St 4th fl .... New York NY 10036 **800-374-3818** 212-642-4900

American Osteopathic Assn (AOA)
142 E Ontario St .... Chicago IL 60611 **800-621-1773** 888-626-9262

Association for Assessment & Accreditation of Laboratory Animal Care International
5283 Corporate Dr Ste 203 .... Frederick MD 21703 **800-926-0066** 301-696-9626

Association for Biblical Higher Education (AABC)
5850 T G Lee Blvd Ste 130 .... Orlando FL 32822 **800-525-1611** 407-207-0808

Canadian Assn of Occupational Therapists (CAOT)
1125 Colonel By Dr .... Ottawa ON K1S5R1 **800-434-2268** 613-523-2268

Canadian Dental Association
1815 Alta Vista Dr .... Ottawa ON K1G3Y6 **866-521-2322** 613-523-7114

Canadian Information Processing Society (CIPS)
5090 Explorer Dr Ste 801 .... Mississauga ON L4W4T9 **877-275-2477** 905-602-1370

Certified Financial Planner Board of Standards Inc
1425 K St NW Ste 500 .... Washington DC 20005 **800-487-1497** 202-379-2200

COLA
9881 Broken Land Pkwy Ste 200 ...... Columbia MD 21046 **800-981-9883** 410-381-6581

Commission on Accreditation for Dietetics Education (CADE)
120 S Riverside Plz Ste 2000 .... Chicago IL 60606 **800-877-1600** 312-899-0040

Commission on Accreditation for Law Enforcement Agencies (CALEA)
13575 Heathcote Blvd Ste 320 ...... Gainesville VA 20155 **877-789-6904** 703-352-4225

Commission on Accreditation in Physical Therapy Education (CAPTE)
1111 North Fairfax St .... Alexandria VA 22314 **800-999-2782** 703-706-3245

Commission on Accreditation of Rehabilitation Facilities International (CARF)
6951 E Southpoint Rd .... Tucson AZ 85756 **888-281-6531** 520-325-1044

Community Health Accreditation Program Inc (CHAP)
1275 K St NW Ste 800 .... Washington DC 20005 **800-656-9656** 202-862-3413

Council of the Section of Legal Education & Admissions to the Bar
321 N Clark St 21st Fl .... Chicago IL 60654 **800-238-2667** 312-988-6738

Council on Academic Accreditation in Audiology & Speech-Language Pathology
2200 Research Blvd .... Rockville MD 20850 **800-498-2071** 301-296-5700

Council on Accreditation (COA)
45 Broadway 29th fl .... New York NY 10006 **866-262-8088** 212-797-3000

Council on Chiropractic Education Commission on Accreditation
8049 N 85th Way .... Scottsdale AZ 85258 **888-443-3506** 480-443-8877

Council on Occupational Education
7840 Roswell Rd Bldg 300 Ste 325 ...... Atlanta GA 30350 **800-917-2081** 770-396-3898

Organization / Address	City	State	Zip	Toll-Free	Phone
Engineers Canada 180 Elgin St Ste 1100	Ottawa	ON	K2P2K3	**877-408-9273**	613-232-2474
Joint Commission on Accreditation of Healthcare Organizations (JCAHO) 1 Renaissance Blvd	Oakbrook Terrace	IL	60181	**800-994-6610**	630-792-5000
National Accrediting Commission of Cosmetology Arts & Sciences (NACCAS) 4401 Ford Ave Ste 1300	Alexandria	VA	22302	**877-212-5752**	703-600-7600
National Certification Commission for Acupuncture & Oriental Medicine (NCCAOM) 2025 M St NW Ste 800	Washington	DC	20036	**888-381-1140**	202-381-1140
North Central Assn Commission on Accreditation & School Improvement (NCA CASI) 9115 Westside Pkwy	Alpharetta	GA	30009	**888-413-3669**	
North Central Assn Higher Learning Commission 230 S LaSalle St	Chicago	IL	60604	**800-621-7440**	312-263-0456
Society of Accredited Marine Surveyors Inc (SAMS) 7855 Argyle Forest Blvd Ste 203	Jacksonville	FL	32244	**800-344-9077**	904-384-1494
Society of American Foresters (SAF) 10100 Laureate way	Bethesda	MD	20814	**866-897-8720**	301-897-8720
Southern Assn of Colleges & Schools 1866 Southern Ln	Decatur	GA	30033	**888-413-3669**	404-679-4500
Speech-Language & Audiology Canada (SAC) 1 Nicholas St Ste 1000	Ottawa	ON	K1N7B7	**800-259-8519**	613-567-9968

48-2 Agricultural Organizations

Organization / Address	City	State	Zip	Toll-Free	Phone
Agricultural Retailers Assn (ARA) 1156 15th St NW Ste 500	Washington	DC	20005	**800-535-6272**	202-457-0825
American Angus Assn (AAA) 3201 Frederick Ave	Saint Joseph	MO	64506	**800-821-5478**	816-383-5100
American Dairy Science Assn (ADSA) 1111 N Dunlap Ave	Savoy	IL	61874	**888-670-2250**	217-356-5146
American Egg Board (AEB) 8755 W Higgins Rd Ste 300	Chicago	IL	60631	**888-549-2140**	847-296-7043
American Farm Bureau Federation 600 Maryland Ave SW Ste 1000-W	Washington	DC	20024	**800-327-6287**	202-406-3600
American Farmland Trust (AFT) 1200 18th St	Washington	DC	20036	**800-431-1499**	202-331-7300
American Forest & Paper Assn (AF&PA) 1111 19th St NW Ste 800	Washington	DC	20036	**800-878-8878**	202-463-2700
American Forest Foundation (AFF) 2000 M St NW Ste 550	Washington	DC	20036	**800-325-2954**	202-765-3660
American Seed Trade Assn (ASTA) 1701 Duke St Ste 275	Alexandria	VA	22304	**888-890-7333**	703-837-8140
American Society for Horticultural Science (ASHS) 1018 Duke St	Alexandria	VA	22314	**800-331-1600**	703-836-4606
American Society of Agronomy (ASA) 5585 Guilford Rd	Madison	WI	53711	**866-359-9161**	608-273-8080
American Society of Landscape Architects (ASLA) 636 'I' St NW	Washington	DC	20001	**888-999-2752**	202-898-2444
American Soybean Assn (ASA) 12125 Woodcrest Executive Dr Ste 100	Saint Louis	MO	63141	**800-688-7692**	314-576-1770
American-International Charolais Assn (AICA) 11700 NW Plaza Cir	Kansas City	MO	64153	**800-270-7711**	816-464-5977
Breg Inc 2885 Loker Ave E	Carlsbad	CA	92010	**800-897-2734**	
Cotton Inc 6399 Weston Pkwy	Cary	NC	27513	**800-334-5868**	919-678-2220
Crop Science Society of America (CSSA) 677 S Segoe Rd	Madison	WI	53711	**800-755-2751**	608-273-8080
CropLife America 1156 15th St NW	Washington	DC	20005	**800-266-9432**	202-296-1585
Dairy Management Inc (DMI) 10255 W Higgins Rd Ste 900	Rosemont	IL	60018	**800-853-2479**	
Decatur Co-op Assn 305 S York Ave	Oberlin	KS	67749	**800-886-2293**	785-475-2234
Farmer's Co-op Assn 110 S Keokuk Wash Rd	Keota	IA	52248	**877-843-4893**	641-636-3748
Golf Course Superintendents Assn of America (GCSAA) 1421 Research Pk Dr	Lawrence	KS	66049	**800-472-7878**	785-841-2240
Herb Growing & Marketing Network (HGMN) PO Box 245	Silver Spring	PA	17575	**800-753-9199**	717-393-3295
Hohman Assoc Inc (HAI) 6951 W Little York	Houston	TX	77040	**800-324-0978**	713-896-0978
Holstein Assn USA Inc 1 Holstein Pl PO Box 808	Brattleboro	VT	05302	**800-952-5200*** *Orders	802-254-4551
International Society of Arboriculture (ISA) PO Box 3129	Champaign	IL	61826	**888-472-8733**	217-355-9411
Irrigation Assn (IA) 6540 Arlington Blvd	Falls Church	VA	22042	**800-362-8774**	703-536-7080
Livestock Marketing Assn (LMA) 10510 N Ambassador Dr	Kansas City	MO	64153	**800-821-2048**	816-891-0502
Mid-Kansas Co-op (MKC) PO Box D	Moundridge	KS	67107	**800-864-4428**	
Mohair Council of America 233 W Twohig Rd	San Angelo	TX	76903	**800-583-3161**	325-655-3161
National Cattlemen's Beef Assn (NCBA) 9110 E Nichols Ave Ste 300	Centennial	CO	80112	**866-233-3872**	303-694-0305
National Christmas Tree Assn (NCTA) 16020 Swingley Ridge Rd Ste 300	Chesterfield	MO	63017	**800-975-5920**	
National Council of Farmer Co-ops (NCFC) 50 F St NW Ste 900	Washington	DC	20001	**800-344-2626**	202-626-8700
National Crop Insurance Services (NCIS) 8900 Indian Creek Pkwy Ste 600	Overland Park	KS	66210	**800-951-6247**	913-685-2767
National Farmers Organization (NFO) 528 Billy Sunday Rd Ste 100 PO Box 2508	Ames	IA	50010	**800-247-2110**	515-292-2000
National FFA Organization 6060 FFA Dr	Indianapolis	IN	46268	**800-772-0939**	317-802-6060
National Grange 1616 H St NW	Washington	DC	20006	**888-447-2643**	202-628-3507
National Renderers Association Inc (NRA) 500 Montgomery St Ste 310	Alexandria	VA	22314	**800-366-2563**	703-683-0155
National Turkey Federation (NTF) 1225 New York Ave NW Ste 400	Washington	DC	20005	**866-536-7593**	202-898-0100
National Woodland Owners Assn (NWOA) 374 Maple Ave E Ste 310	Vienna	VA	22180	**800-476-8733**	703-255-2300
North American Limousin Foundation (NALF) 6 Inverness Ct E Ste 260	Englewood	CO	80112	**888-320-8747**	303-220-1693
Professional Landcare Network (PLANET) 950 Herndon Pkwy Ste 450	Herndon	VA	20170	**800-395-2522**	703-736-9666
Red Angus Assn of America 4201 N IH- 35	Denton	TX	76207	**800-422-2117**	940-387-3502
Shelburne Farms 1611 Harbor Rd	Shelburne	VT	05482	**800-286-6022**	802-985-8686
Society of American Foresters (SAF) 10100 Laureate way	Bethesda	MD	20814	**866-897-8720**	301-897-8720
United Producers Inc 8351 N High St Ste 250	Columbus	OH	43235	**800-456-3276**	
United Soybean Board (USB) 16305 Swingley Ridge Rd Ste 150	Chesterfield	MO	63017	**800-989-8721**	636-530-1777
US Apple Assn 8233 Old Courthouse Rd Ste 200	Vienna	VA	22182	**800-781-4443**	703-442-8850
Wild Blueberry Assn of North America (WBANA) PO Box 100	Old Town	ME	04468	**800-341-1758**	207-570-3535

48-3 Animals & Animal Welfare Organizations

Organization / Address	City	State	Zip	Toll-Free	Phone
African Wildlife Foundation (AWF) 1100 New Jersey Ave SE Ste 900	Washington	DC	20003	**888-494-5354**	202-939-3333
American Animal Hospital Assn (AAHA) 12575 W Bayaud Ave	Lakewood	CO	80228	**800-252-2242**	303-986-2800
American Assn of Equine Practitioners (AAEP) 4075 Iron Works Pkwy	Lexington	KY	40511	**800-443-0177**	859-233-0147
American Buckskin Registry Assn Inc (ABRA) 1141 Hartnell Ave	Redding	CA	96002	**800-458-4283**	530-223-1420
American Horse Council (AHC) 1616 H St NW 7th Fl	Washington	DC	20006	**800-443-0177**	202-296-4031
American Humane Assn (AHA) 63 Inverness Dr E	Englewood	CO	80112	**800-227-4645**	
American Morgan Horse Assn (AMHA) 4066 Shelburne Rd Ste 5	Shelburne	VT	05482	**888-436-3700**	802-985-4944
American Quarter Horse Assn (AQHA) 1600 Quarter Horse Dr	Amarillo	TX	79104	**800-291-7323**	806-376-4811
American Rabbit Breeders Assn (ARBA) PO Box 5667	Bloomington	IL	61702	**800-753-9448**	309-664-7500
American Society for the Prevention of Cruelty to Animals (ASPCA) 424 E 92nd St	New York	NY	10128	**800-582-5979**	212-876-7700
Appaloosa Horse Club (ApHC) 2720 W Pullman Rd	Moscow	ID	83843	**888-304-7768**	208-882-5578
Atlantic Salmon Federation (ASF) PO Box 5200	Saint Andrews	NB	E5B3S8	**800-565-5666**	506-529-1033
Bat Conservation International (BCI) 500 N Capital of Texas Hwy	Austin	TX	78746	**800-538-2287**	512-327-9721
Bird Studies Canada 115 Front St PO Box 160	Port Rowan	ON	N0E1M0	**888-448-2473**	519-586-3531
Canadian Federation of Humane Societies (CFHS) 30 Concourse Gate Ste 102	Ottawa	ON	K2E7V7	**888-678-2347**	613-224-8072
Canadian Kennel Club (CKC) 200 Ronson Dr Ste 400	Etobicoke	ON	M9W5Z9	**800-250-8040**	416-675-5511
Canadian Peregrine Foundation 25 Crouse Rd Unit 20	Toronto	ON	M1R5P8	**888-709-3944**	416-481-1233
Certified Horsemanship Assn (CHA) 1795 Alysheba Way Ste 7102	Lexington	KY	40509	**800-399-0138**	859-259-3399
Defenders of Wildlife 1130 17th St NW	Washington	DC	20036	**800-385-9712**	202-682-9400
Delta Waterfowl PO Box 3128	Bismarck	ND	58502	**888-987-3695**	701-222-8857
Dian Fossey Gorilla Fund International 800 Cherokee Ave SE	Atlanta	GA	30315	**800-851-0203**	404-624-5881
Friends of Animals Inc (FOA) 777 Post Rd Ste 205	Darien	CT	06820	**800-321-7387**	203-656-1522
Fund for Animals, The 200 West 57th St	New York	NY	10019	**866-482-3708**	
Humane Society of the US (HSUS) 1255 23rd St NW Ste 450	Washington	DC	20037	**866-720-2676**	202-452-1100
In Defense of Animals (IDA) 3010 Kerner Blvd	San Rafael	CA	94901	**800-705-0425**	415-448-0048
International Fund for Animal Welfare (IFAW) 290 Summer St	Yarmouth Port	MA	02675	**800-932-4329**	508-744-2000
International Society for Animal Rights (ISAR) PO Box F	Clarks Summit	PA	18411	**888-589-6397**	570-586-2200
Jane Goodall Institute for Wildlife Research Education (JGI) 1595 Spring Hill Rd Ste 550	Vienna	VA	22182	**800-592-5263**	703-682-9220
Mountain Lion Foundation PO Box 1896	Sacramento	CA	95812	**800-319-7621**	916-442-2666
National Anti-Vivisection Society (NAVS) 53 W Jackson Blvd Ste 1552	Chicago	IL	60604	**800-888-6287**	312-427-6065
National Disaster Search Dog Foundation 6800 Wheeler Canyon Rd	Ojai	CA	93023	**888-459-4376**	805-646-1015
National Wild Turkey Federation (NWTF) 770 Augusta Rd PO Box 530	Edgefield	SC	29824	**800-843-6983*** *Cust Svc	803-637-3106
National Wildlife Federation (NWF) 11100 Wildlife Ctr Dr	Reston	VA	20190	**800-822-9919**	703-438-6000
Paso Fino Horse Assn 4047 Iron Works Pkwy Ste 1	Lexington	KY	40511	**800-844-1409**	859-825-6000
People for the Ethical Treatment of Animals (PETA) 501 Front St	Norfolk	VA	23510	**800-566-9768**	757-622-7382
Performing Animal Welfare Society (PAWS) 11435 Simmerhorn Rd	Galt	CA	95632	**800-513-6560**	209-745-2606
Ruffed Grouse Society (RGS) 451 McCormick Rd	Coraopolis	PA	15108	**888-564-6747**	412-262-4044
Save the Manatee Club (SMC) 500 N Maitland Ave	Maitland	FL	32751	**800-432-5646**	407-539-0990
Thoroughbred Owners & Breeders Assn (TOBA) PO Box 910668	Lexington	KY	40591	**888-606-8622**	859-276-2291
Trout Unlimited (TU) 1300 N 17th St Ste 500	Arlington	VA	22209	**800-834-2419**	703-522-0200
World Animal Protection 450 Seventh Ave 31st Fl	New York	NY	10123	**800-883-9772**	646-783-2200
World Wildlife Fund (WWF) 1250 24th St NW PO Box 97180	Washington	DC	20090	**800-225-5993**	202-293-4800
World Wildlife Fund Canada (WWF) 410 Adelaide St W Ste 400	Toronto	ON	M5V1S8	**800-267-2632**	416-489-8800

	Toll-Free	Phone
Zoocheck Canada		
788 1/2 O'Connor Dr ....Toronto ON M4B2S6	888-801-3222	416-285-1744

48-4 Arts & Artists Organizations

	Toll-Free	Phone
Actors' Equity Assn		
1560 Broadway ....New York NY 10036	866-270-4232	212-869-8530
American Assn of Museums (AAM)		
1575 Eye St NW Ste 400........Washington DC 20005	866-226-2150	202-289-1818
American Ceramic Society (ACerS)		
600 N Cleveland Ave Ste 210 ....Westerville OH 43082	866-721-3322	614-890-4700
American Craft Council		
1224 Marshall St Ste 200........Minneapolis MN 55413	800-836-3470	612-206-3100
American Federation of Musicians of the US & Canada (AFM)		
1501 Broadway Ste 600 ....New York NY 10036	800-762-3444	212-869-1330
American Film Institute (AFI)		
2021 N Western Ave ....Los Angeles CA 90027	866-234-3378	323-856-7600
American Guild of Musical Artists (AGMA)		
1430 Broadway 14th Fl........New York NY 10018	800-543-2462	212-265-3687
American Guild of Organists (AGO)		
475 Riverside Dr Ste 1260 ....New York NY 10115	855-631-0759	212-870-2310
American Guild of Variety Artists (AGVA)		
363 Seventh Ave 17th Fl........New York NY 10001	800-331-0890	212-675-1003
American Institute of Architects (AIA)		
1735 New York Ave NW ....Washington DC 20006	800-242-3837*	202-626-7300
*Orders		
American Institute of Graphic Arts (AIGA)		
164 Fifth Ave ....New York NY 10010	800-548-1634	212-807-1990
American Musicological Society (AMS)		
6010 College Stn ....Brunswick ME 04011	888-421-1442	212-992-6340
American Society of Cinematographers (ASC)		
1782 N Orange Dr ....Hollywood CA 90028	800-448-0145	323-969-4333
Association of Film Commissioners International (AFCI)		
9595 Wilshire Blvd Ste 900 ....Beverly Hills CA 90212	888-765-5777	323-461-2324
Association of Performing Arts Presenters		
1211 Connecticut Ave NW Ste 200........Washington DC 20036	888-820-2787	202-833-2787
Bix Beiderbecke Memorial Society		
PO Box 3688 ....Davenport IA 52808	888-249-5487	563-324-7170
Broadway League, The		
729 Seventh Ave 5th Fl........New York NY 10019	866-442-9878	212-764-1122
Chamber Music America (CMA)		
305 Seventh Ave 5th Fl........New York NY 10001	888-221-9836	212-242-2022
Choristers Guild		
2834 W Kingsley Rd ....Garland TX 75041	800-246-7478	469-398-3606
Clowns of America International (COAI)		
PO Box 122 ....Eustis FL 32727	877-816-6941	352-357-1676
Drum Corps International (DCI)		
110 W Washington St Ste C ....Indianapolis IN 46204	800-495-7469*	317-275-1212
*Orders		
Educational Theatre Assn (EDTA)		
2343 Auburn Ave ....Cincinnati OH 45219	800-848-2263	513-421-3900
Glass Art Society (GAS)		
6512 23rd Ave NW Ste 329 ....Seattle WA 98117	800-636-2377	206-382-1305
International Interior Design Assn (IIDA)		
222 Merchandise Mart Plz Ste 567........Chicago IL 60654	888-799-4432	312-467-1950
Motion Picture & Television Fund		
23388 Mulholland Dr ....Woodland Hills CA 91364	855-760-6783	
National Academy of Recording Arts & Sciences		
3030 Olympic Blvd ....Santa Monica CA 90404	800-423-2017	310-392-3777
Professional Photographers of America Inc (PPA)		
229 Peachtree St NE Ste 2200 ....Atlanta GA 30303	800-786-6277	404-522-8600
Screen Actors Guild (SAG)		
5757 Wilshire Blvd ....Los Angeles CA 90036	800-724-0767	323-954-1600
SESAC Inc 55 Music Sq E ....Nashville TN 37203	800-826-9996	615-320-0055
Society for Ethnomusicology (SEM)		
Indiana University 800 E Third St ....Bloomington IN 47405	800-933-9330	812-855-6672
Society of American Archivists (SAA)		
17 North State St Ste 1425 ....Chicago IL 60602	866-722-7858	312-606-0722
Songwriters Guild of America		
210 Jamestown Park Rd Ste 100 ....Brentwood TN 37027	800-524-6742	615-742-9945

48-5 Charitable & Humanitarian Organizations

	Toll-Free	Phone
ACDI/VOCA		
50 F St NW Ste 1000 ....Washington DC 20001	800-929-8622	202-638-4661
Action Against Hunger		
247 W 37th St 10th Fl........New York NY 10018	877-777-1420	212-967-7800
Adventist Community Services		
12501 Old Columbia Pk ....Silver Spring MD 20904	877-227-2702	301-680-6438
Adventist Development & Relief Agency (ADRA)		
12501 Old Columbia Pk ....Silver Spring MD 20904	800-424-2372	
Africare Inc 440 R St NW ....Washington DC 20001	800-429-9493	202-462-3614
America's Second Harvest		
35 E Wacker Dr Ste 2000 ....Chicago IL 60601	800-771-2303	
American Anti-Slavery Group, The		
198 Tremont St ....Boston MA 02116	800-884-0719	617-426-8161
American Battlefield Trust		
Civil War Trust, The		
1156 15th St NW Ste 900........Washington DC 20005	888-606-1400	202-367-1861
American Friends Service Committee (AFSC)		
1501 Cherry St ....Philadelphia PA 19102	800-621-4000	215-241-7000
American Jewish World Service (AJWS)		
45 West 36th St ....New York NY 10018	800-889-7146	212-792-2900
American Lebanese Syrian Associated Charities (ALSAC)		
262 Danny Thomas Pl ....Memphis TN 38105	800-822-6344	901-578-2000
American Red Cross		
2025 E St NW ....Washington DC 20006	800-257-7575	202-303-4498
American Refugee Committee (ARC)		
430 Oak Grove St Ste 204........Minneapolis MN 55403	800-875-7060	612-872-7060
AmeriCares Foundation		
88 Hamilton Ave ....Stamford CT 06902	800-486-4357	203-658-9500
Amigos de las Americas		
1800 W Loop S Ste 1325 ....Houston TX 77027	800-231-7796	

	Toll-Free	Phone
Amnesty International USA (AIUSA)		
5 Penn Plz 16th Fl ....New York NY 10001	866-273-4466	800-266-3789
Association of Fundraising Professionals (AFP)		
4300 Wilson Blvd Ste 300 ....Arlington VA 22203	800-666-3863	703-684-0410
Bread for the World		
425 Third St SW Ste 1200 ....Washington DC 20024	800-822-7323*	202-639-9400
*Cust Svc		
CARE USA 151 Ellis St NE ....Atlanta GA 30303	800-521-2273	404-681-2552
Catholic Charities USA		
2050 Ballenger Ave Ste 400 ....Alexandria VA 22314	800-919-9338	703-549-1390
Catholic Medical Mission Board (CMMB)		
100 Wall St 9th Fl........New York NY 10005	800-678-5659	212-242-7757
Catholic Relief Services (CRS)		
228 W Lexington St ....Baltimore MD 21201	800-235-2772	410-625-2220
Children International		
2000 E Red Bridge Rd ....Kansas City MO 64131	800-888-3089	816-942-2000
Christian Appalachian Project		
485 Ponderosa Dr PO Box 1768........Paintsville KY 41240	800-755-5322	
Christian Reformed World Relief Committee (CRWRC)		
2850 Kalamazoo Ave SE ....Grand Rapids MI 49560	800-552-7972	616-241-1691
Church World Service		
28606 Phillips St PO Box 968 ....Elkhart IN 46515	800-297-1516	574-264-3102
Church World Service Emergency Response Program		
475 Riverside Dr Ste 700 ....New York NY 10115	888-297-2767	212-870-2061
Community Health Charities		
1199 N Fairfax St ....Alexandria VA 22314	800-654-0845	703-528-1007
Compassion International		
12290 Voyager Pkwy ....Colorado Springs CO 80921	800-336-7676	719-487-7000
Concern America		
2015 N Broadway ....Santa Ana CA 92706	800-266-2376	714-953-8575
Council on Foundations		
2121 Crystal Dr Ste 700 ....Arlington VA 22202	800-673-9036	703-879-0600
Direct Relief International		
6100 Wallace Becknell Rd ....Santa Barbara CA 93117	800-676-1638	805-964-4767
Doctors Without Borders USA Inc		
40 Rector St 16th Fl........New York NY 10006	888-392-0392	212-679-6800
Enterprise Community Partners Inc		
10227 Wincopin Cir ....Columbia MD 21044	800-624-4298	410-964-1230
Episcopal Migration Ministries (EMM)		
815 Second Ave ....New York NY 10017	800-334-7626	212-716-6000
Episcopal Relief & Development		
815 Second Ave ....New York NY 10017	800-334-7626	855-312-4325
Evangelical Council for Financial Accountability (ECFA)		
440 W Jubal Early Dr Ste 130........Winchester VA 22601	800-323-9473	540-535-0103
Feed the Children (FTC)		
PO Box 36 ....Oklahoma City OK 73101	800-627-4556	405-942-0228
Food for the Poor Inc (FFP)		
6401 Lyons Rd ....Coconut Creek FL 33073	800-427-9104	954-427-2222
Foundation for International Community Assistance (FINCA)		
1201 15th St NW 8th fl........Washington DC 20005	855-903-4622	202-682-1510
Freedom from Hunger		
1460 Drew Ave Ste 300 ....Davis CA 95618	800-708-2555	530-758-6200
Goodwill Industries International Inc		
15810 Indianola Dr ....Rockville MD 20855	800-741-0197	800-466-3945
Guttmacher Institute (AGI)		
125 Maiden Ln 7th Fl........New York NY 10038	800-355-0244	212-248-1111
Habitat for Humanity International Inc		
121 Habitat St ....Americus GA 31709	800-422-4828	229-924-6935
Heifer International		
1 World Ave ....Little Rock AR 72202	800-422-0474	501-907-2600
Holy Family Memorial		
2300 Western Ave PO Box 1450........Manitowoc WI 54221	800-994-3662	920-320-2011
HOPE Worldwide		
4231 Balboa Ave Ste 330 ....San Diego CA 92117	866-551-7327	610-254-8800
Housing Assistance Council (HAC)		
1025 Vermont Ave NW Ste 606........Washington DC 20005	866-234-2689	202-842-8600
Hunger Project, The		
5 Union Sq W ....New York NY 10003	800-228-6691	212-251-9100
Independent Order of Foresters (IOF)		
789 Don Mills Rd ....Toronto ON M3C1T9	800-828-1540	416-429-3000
INMED Partnerships for Children		
21240 Ridgetop Cir Ste 115........Ashburn VA 20147	800-552-7096	571-293-9849
Interchurch Medical Assistance Inc (IMA)		
1730 M St NW Ste 1100........Washington DC 20036	877-241-7952	202-888-6200
International Aid Inc		
17011 W Hickory St ....Spring Lake MI 49456	800-968-7490	616-846-7490
International Medical Corps (IMC)		
1919 Santa Monica Blvd Ste 400 ....Santa Monica CA 90404	800-481-4462	310-826-7800
International Orthodox Christian Charities (IOCC)		
110 W Rd Ste 360........Towson MD 21204	877-803-4622	410-243-9820
Lutheran Disaster Response		
8765 W Higgins Rd ....Chicago IL 60631	800-638-3522	
Make-A-Wish Foundation of America		
4742 N 24th St Ste 400 ....Phoenix AZ 85016	800-722-9474	602-279-9474
MAP International		
4700 Glynco Pkwy ....Brunswick GA 31525	800-225-8550	912-265-6010
Medical Care Development International (MCDI)		
8401 Colesville Rd Ste 425 ....Silver Spring MD 20910	800-427-7566	301-562-1920
Medical Teams International (MTI)		
PO Box 10 ....Portland OR 97207	800-959-4325	503-624-1000
Mennonite Central Committee (MCC)		
21 S 12th St PO Box 500 ....Akron PA 17501	888-563-4676	717-859-1151
Mennonite Disaster Service (MDS)		
583 Airport Rd ....Lititz PA 17543	800-241-8111	717-735-3536
MENTOR/National Mentoring Partnership		
201 South St Ste 615 ....Boston MA 02111	877-333-2464	703-224-2200
Mercy-USA for Aid & Development Inc (M-USA)		
44450 Pinetree Dr Ste 201 ....Plymouth MI 48170	800-556-3729	734-454-0011
Michigan Municipal League		
1675 Green Rd PO Box 1487 ....Ann Arbor MI 48105	800-653-2483	734-662-3246
NAEIR (NAEIR) 560 McClure St ....Galesburg IL 61401	800-562-0955	309-343-0704
National Benevolent Assn (NBA)		
733 Union Blvd Ste 300 ....St. Louis MO 63108	866-262-2669	314-993-9000
National Peace Corps Assn (NPCA)		
1900 L St NW Ste 610 ....Washington DC 20036	800-336-1616	202-293-7728
North American Mission Board SBC		
4200 N Pt Pkwy ....Alpharetta GA 30022	800-634-2462	770-410-6000

Classified Section

Organization / Address	City	State	ZIP	Toll-Free	Phone
Operation USA 7421 Beverly Blvd PH	Los Angeles	CA	90036	**800-678-7255**	323-413-2353
ORBIS International Inc 520 Eigth Ave 12th Fl	New York	NY	10018	**800-672-4787**	
Oregon Food Bank 7900 NE 33rd Dr	Portland	OR	97211	**800-777-7427**	503-282-0555
ORT American Inc 75 Maiden Ln 10th Fl	New York	NY	10038	**800-519-2678**	212-505-7700
Outreach International 129 W Lexington PO Box 210	Independence	MO	64050	**888-833-1235**	816-833-0883
Oxfam America 226 Cswy St 5th Fl	Boston	MA	02114	**800-776-9326**	617-482-1211
Pan American Development Foundation (PADF) 1889 F St NW 2nd Fl	Washington	DC	20006	**877-572-4484**	202-458-3969
Peace Action 8630 Fenton St	Silver Spring	MD	20910	**800-228-1228**	301-565-4050
People-to-People Health Foundation 255 Carter Hall Ln	Millwood	VA	22646	**800-544-4673**	540-837-2100
Points of Light Foundation & Volunteer Ctr National Network 1400 'I' St NW Ste 800	Washington	DC	20005	**866-545-5307**	202-729-8000
Population Connection 2120 L St NW Ste 500	Washington	DC	20037	**800-767-1956**	202-332-2200
Presbyterian Disaster Assistance (PDA) 100 Witherspoon St	Louisville	KY	40202	**800-728-7228**	
ProLiteracy Worldwide 1320 Jamesville Ave	Syracuse	NY	13210	**800-448-8878**	315-422-9121
Rebuilding Together Inc 1899 L St NW Ste 1000	Washington	DC	20036	**800-473-4229**	
Refugees International (RI) 2001 S St NW Ste 700	Washington	DC	20009	**800-733-8433**	202-828-0110
Sertoma International 1912 E Meyer Blvd	Kansas City	MO	64132	**800-593-5646**	816-333-8300
Share Our Strength 1730 M St NW Ste 700	Washington	DC	20036	**800-969-4767**	202-393-2925
Smile Train Inc 633 Third Ave 9th Fl	New York	NY	10017	**800-932-9541**	212-689-9199
Society of Saint Andrew (SoSA) 3383 Sweet Hollow Rd	Big Island	VA	24526	**800-333-4597**	434-299-5956
TechnoServe 1120 19th St NW 8th Fl	Washington	DC	20036	**800-999-6757**	202-785-4515
Trickle Up Program Inc 104 W 27th St 12th Fl	New York	NY	10001	**866-246-9980**	212-255-9980
Unitarian Universalist Service Committee (UUSC) 689 Massachusetts Ave	Cambridge	MA	02139	**800-388-3920**	617-868-6600
United Way of America 701 N Fairfax St	Alexandria	VA	22314	**800-892-2757**	703-836-7100
US Fund for UNICEF 125 Maiden Ln	New York	NY	10038	**800-367-5437**	
USA for UNHCR 1775 K St NW Ste 580	Washington	DC	20006	**800-770-1100**	202-296-1115
Voices of September 11th 161 Cherry St	New Canaan	CT	06840	**866-505-3911**	203-966-3911
Volunteers of America 1660 Duke St	Alexandria	VA	22314	**800-899-0089**	703-341-5000
World Concern 19303 Fremont Ave N	Seattle	WA	98133	**800-755-5022**	206-546-7201
World Food Program USA (WFP) 1725 Eye St NW Ste 510	Washington	DC	20006	**888-454-0555**	202-627-3737
World Hunger Year Inc (WHY) 505 Eigth Ave Ste 2100	New York	NY	10018	**800-548-6479**	212-629-8850
World Learning 1 Kipling Rd PO Box 676	Brattleboro	VT	05302	**800-257-7751**	802-257-7751
World Neighbors Inc (WN) 4127 NW 122nd St	Oklahoma City	OK	73120	**800-242-6387**	405-752-9700
World Relief 7 E Baltimore St	Baltimore	MD	21202	**800-535-5433**	443-451-1900
World Vision Inc 34834 Weyerhaeuser Way S PO Box 9716	Federal Way	WA	98001	**888-511-6548**	800-777-5777

48-6 Children & Family Advocacy Organizations

Organization / Address	City	State	ZIP	Toll-Free	Phone
Adoption ARC Inc 4247 Locust St Apt 16	Philadelphia	PA	19104	**888-558-6561**	215-748-1441
Advocacy Center for Persons With Disabilities 2728 Centerview Dr Ste 102	Tallahassee	FL	32301	**800-342-0823**	850-488-9071
Alliance for Children & Families Inc 11700 West Lake Pk Dr	Milwaukee	WI	53224	**800-221-3726**	
Alliance for Retired Americans 815 16th St NW 4th Fl	Washington	DC	20006	**888-373-6497**	202-637-5399
American Academy of Pediatrics (AAP) 141 NW Pt Blvd	Elk Grove Village	IL	60007	**800-433-9016**	847-434-4000
American Coalition for Fathers & Children (ACFC) 1718 M St NW Ste 1187	Washington	DC	20036	**800-978-3237**	
American Humane Assn (AHA) 63 Inverness Dr E	Englewood	CO	80112	**800-227-4645**	
American Society on Aging (ASA) 575 Market St Ste 2100	San Francisco	CA	94105	**800-537-9728**	415-974-9600
Association for Couples in Marriage Enrichment (ACME) PO Box 21374	Winston-Salem	NC	27120	**800-634-8325**	
Blue Grass Regional Mental Health-Mental Retardation Board Inc 1351 Newtown Pk Bldg 1	Lexington	KY	40511	**800-928-8000**	859-253-1686
Buckner International 700 N Pearl St Ste 1200	Dallas	TX	75201	**800-442-4800**	214-758-8000
Cal Farley's PO Box 1890	Amarillo	TX	79174	**800-687-3722**	
Child Find Canada 212-2211 McPhillips St	Winnipeg	MB	R2V3M5	**800-387-7962**	204-339-5584
Child Lures Prevention 5166 Shelburne Rd	Shelburne	VT	05482	**800-552-2197**	802-985-8458
Childhelp USA 4350 E Camelback Rd Bldg F250	Phoenix	AZ	85018	**800-422-4453**	480-922-8212
Children Awaiting Parents Inc (CAP) 595 Blossom Rd Ste 306	Rochester	NY	14610	**888-835-8802**	585-232-5110
Children Inc 4205 Dover Rd	Richmond	VA	23221	**800-538-5381**	804-359-4562
Children of the Night 14530 Sylvan St	Van Nuys	CA	91411	**800-551-1300**	818-908-4474
Children's Defense Fund (CDF) 25 E St NW	Washington	DC	20001	**800-233-1200**	202-628-8787
Christian Foundation for Children & Aging (CFCA) 1 Elmwood Ave	Kansas City	KS	66103	**800-875-6564**	913-384-6500
DePelchin Children's Ctr 4950 Memorial Dr	Houston	TX	77007	**888-730-2335**	713-730-2335
Envision Inc 610 N Main St	Wichita	KS	67203	**888-425-7072**	316-440-1500
Experience Works Inc 4401 Wilson Blvd Ste 1100	Arlington	VA	22203	**866-397-9757**	703-522-7272
Family Research Council (FRC) 801 G St NW	Washington	DC	20001	**800-225-4008**	202-393-2100
Find the Children 2656 29th St Ste 203	Santa Monica	CA	90405	**888-477-6721**	310-314-3213
First Candle 49 Locust Ave Ste 104	New Canaan	CT	06840	**800-221-7437**	120-396-6130
Focus on the Family 8605 Explorer Dr *Sales	Colorado Springs	CO	80920	**800-232-6459***	719-531-3400
Girls Inc 120 Wall St 18th Fl	New York	NY	10005	**800-374-4475**	212-509-2000
Human Life International (HLI) 4 Family Life Ln *Orders	Front Royal	VA	22630	**800-549-5433***	540-635-7884
Jewish Board of Family & Children Services (JBFCS) 135 W 50th St	New York	NY	10020	**888-523-2769**	212-582-9100
Kansas Children's Service League (KCSL) 3545 SW Fifth St	Topeka	KS	66606	**877-530-5275**	785-274-3100
Leading Age 2519 Connecticut Ave NW	Washington	DC	20008	**866-898-2624**	202-783-2242
May Institute Inc 41 Pacella Pk Dr	Randolph	MA	02368	**800-778-7601**	781-440-0400
MENTOR/National Mentoring Partnership 201 South St Ste 615	Boston	MA	02111	**877-333-2464**	703-224-2200
MOPS International 2370 S Trenton Way *General	Denver	CO	80231	**888-910-6677***	303-733-5353
Mothers Against Drunk Driving (MADD) 511 E John Carpenter Fwy Ste 700	Irving	TX	75062	**877-275-6233**	
National CASA Assn (CASA) 100 W Harrison St North Tower Ste 500	Seattle	WA	98119	**800-628-3233**	206-270-0072
National Child Care Assn (NCCA) 1325 G St NW Ste 500	Washington	DC	20005	**866-536-1945**	
National Council on Family Relations (NCFR) 1201 W River Pkwy Ste 200	Minneapolis	MN	55454	**888-781-9331**	
National Council on the Aging (NCOA) 1901 L St NW 4th Fl	Washington	DC	20036	**800-677-1116**	571-527-3900
National Ctr for Missing & Exploited Children (NCMEC) 699 Prince St	Alexandria	VA	22314	**800-843-5678**	703-274-3900
National Domestic Violence Hotline (NDVH) PO Box 161810	Austin	TX	78716	**800-799-7233**	512-794-1133
National Family Caregivers Assn (NFCA) 10400 Connecticut Ave Ste 500	Kensington	MD	20895	**800-896-3650**	301-942-6430
National Resource Center on Native American Aging (NRCNAA) 1301 N Columbia Rd Ste E231 PO Box 9037	Grand Forks	ND	58202	**800-896-7628**	701-777-3720
National Resource Ctr on Domestic Violence (NRCDV) 6400 Flank Dr Ste 1300	Harrisburg	PA	17112	**800-799-7233**	
National Runaway Switchboard (NRS) 3141 N Lincoln Ave	Chicago	IL	60657	**800-786-2929**	773-880-9860
National Urban Technology Ctr 25 Broadway 9th Fl	New York	NY	10004	**800-998-3212**	212-528-7350
National WIC Assn (NWA) 2001 S St NW Ste 580	Washington	DC	20009	**866-782-6246**	202-232-5492
North American Council on Adoptable Children (NACAC) 970 Raymond Ave Ste 106	Saint Paul	MN	55114	**877-823-2237**	651-644-3036
Orphan Foundation of America (OFA) 23811 Chagrin Blvd Ste 210	Cleveland	OH	44122	**800-950-4673**	571-203-0270
Parents Helping Parents (PHP) 1400 Parkmoor Ave Ste 100	San jose	CA	95126	**855-727-5775**	408-727-5775
Parents of Murdered Children (POMC) 4960 Ridge Ave Ste 2	Cincinnati	OH	45209	**888-818-7662**	513-721-5683
Pension Rights Ctr 1350 Connecticut Ave NW Ste 206	Washington	DC	20036	**866-735-7737**	202-296-3776
Plan USA 155 Plan Way	Warwick	RI	02886	**800-556-7918**	401-738-5600
Planned Parenthood Federation of America 434 W 33rd St	New York	NY	10001	**800-230-7526**	212-541-7800
Pressley Ridge 5500 Corporate Dr Ste 400	Pittsburgh	PA	15237	**888-777-0820**	412-872-9400
Promise Keepers (PK) PO Box 11798	Denver	CO	80211	**866-776-6473**	
Rape Abuse & Incest National Network (RAINN) 2000 L St NW Ste 406	Washington	DC	20036	**800-656-4673**	202-544-1034
SOS Children's Villages-USA 1620 I St NW Ste 900 *General	Washington	DC	20006	**888-767-4543***	202-347-7920
Well Spouse Assn 63 W Main St Ste H	Freehold	NJ	07728	**800-838-0879**	732-577-8899
YMCA of the USA (YMCA) 101 N Wacker Dr	Chicago	IL	60606	**800-872-9622**	312-977-0031
YWCA USA (YWCA) 2025 M St NW Ste 550	Washington	DC	20036	**888-872-9259**	202-467-0801

48-7 Civic & Political Organizations

Organization / Address	City	State	ZIP	Toll-Free	Phone
Americans for Fair Taxation PO Box 4929	Clearwater	FL	33758	**800-324-7829**	
Americans for Peace Now (APN) 1101 14th St NW 6th Fl	Washington	DC	20005	**877-429-0678**	202-728-1893
Americans United for Separation of Church & State 518 C St NE	Washington	DC	20002	**800-875-3707**	202-466-3234
Center for Democracy & Technology (CDT) 1401 K St NW Ste 200	Washington	DC	20005	**800-869-4499**	202-637-9800
Citizens Committee for the Right to Keep & Bear Arms (CCRKBA) Liberty Park 12500 NE Tenth Pl	Bellevue	WA	98005	**800-486-6963**	425-454-4911
Close Up Foundation 1330 Braddock Pl Ste 400	Alexandria	VA	22314	**800-256-7387**	703-706-3300

Classified Section

	Toll-Free	Phone

Community Assns Institute (CAI)
6402 Arlington Blvd Ste 500 . . . . Falls Church VA 22042 — **888-224-4321** — 703-970-9220

Congress Watch
215 Pennsylvania Ave SE . . . . Washington DC 20003 — **800-289-3787** — 202-546-4996

Constitutional Rights Foundation
601 S Kingsley Dr . . . . Los Angeles CA 90005 — **800-488-4273** — 213-487-5590

Council of Canadians
170 Laurier Ave W Ste 700 . . . . Ottawa ON K1P5V5 — **800-387-7177** — 613-233-2773

Evangelicals for Social Action (ESA)
PO Box 367 . . . . Wayne PA 19087 — **800-650-6600** — 484-384-2988

Federation for American Immigration Reform (FAIR)
25 Massachusetts Ave NW Ste 330 . . . . Washington DC 20001 — **877-627-3247** — 202-328-7004

Foreign Policy Assn (FPA)
470 Park Ave S . . . . New York NY 10016 — **800-628-5754** — 212-481-8100

FreedomWorks
400 North Capitol St NW Ste 765 . . . . Washington DC 20001 — **888-564-6273** — 202-783-3870

Girls Nation
American Legion Auxiliary
8945 N Meridian St . . . . Indianapolis IN 46260 — **800-504-4098** — 317-569-4500

Judicial Watch Inc
425 Third St SW Ste 800 . . . . Washington DC 20024 — **888-593-8442**

Junior Chamber International (JCI)
15645 Olive Blvd . . . . Chesterfield MO 63017 — **800-905-5499** — 636-449-3100

National Association of Town Watch (NATW)
308 E Lancaster Ave Ste 115 . . . . Wynnewood PA 19096 — **800-648-3688**

National Committee to Preserve Social Security & Medicare (NCPSSM)
10 G St NE Ste 600 . . . . Washington DC 20002 — **800-966-1935** — 202-216-0420

National Federation of Republican Women (NFRW)
124 N Alfred St . . . . Alexandria VA 22314 — **800-373-9688** — 703-548-9688

OMB Watch
1742 Connecticut Ave NW . . . . Washington DC 20009 — **866-544-7573** — 202-234-8494

People for the American Way (PFAW)
2000 M St NW Ste 400 . . . . Washington DC 20036 — **800-326-7329** — 202-467-4999

Population Reference Bureau (PRB)
1875 Connecticut Ave NW Ste 520 . . . . Washington DC 20009 — **800-877-9881** — 202-483-1100

Population-Environment Balance Inc
2000 P St NW Ste 600 . . . . Washington DC 20036 — **800-866-6269** — 202-955-5700

WISH List
46-E Peninsula Ctr
Ste 385 . . . . Rolling Hills Estates CA 90274 — **888-310-4504**

Young America's Foundation
11480 Commerce Park Dr Ste 600 . . . . Reston VA 20191 — **800-872-1776** — 703-318-9608

48-8 Civil & Human Rights Organizations

	Toll-Free	Phone

American Civil Liberties Union (ACLU)
125 Broad St 18th Fl . . . . New York NY 10004 — **877-867-1025** — 212-549-2500

American-Arab Anti Discrimination Committee (ADC)
1990 M St NW Ste 610 . . . . Washington DC 20036 — **800-253-3931** — 202-244-2990

Americans for Effective Law Enforcement (AELE)
841 W Touhy Ave . . . . Park Ridge IL 60068 — **800-763-2802** — 847-685-0700

Anti-Defamation League (ADL)
605 Third Ave . . . . New York NY 10158 — **866-386-3235** — 212-885-7700

Asian American Legal Defense & Education Fund (AALDEF)
99 Hudson St 12th Fl . . . . New York NY 10013 — **800-966-5946** — 212-966-5932

Center for Individual Rights (CIR)
1100 Connecticut Ave NW Ste 625 . . . . Washington DC 20036 — **877-426-2665** — 202-833-8400

Corporate Accountability International
10 Milk St Ste 610 . . . . Boston MA 02108 — **800-688-8797** — 617-695-2525

Disability Rights Ctr Inc
18 Low Ave . . . . Concord NH 03301 — **800-834-1721** — 603-228-0432

Human Rights Campaign
1640 Rhode Island Ave NW . . . . Washington DC 20036 — **800-777-4723** — 202-628-4160

Institute for Health Freedom
1825 K St NW Ste 1200 . . . . Washington DC 20006 — **800-433-5255** — 202-534-3700

Lambda Legal Defense & Education Fund
120 Wall St 19th Fl . . . . New York NY 10005 — **866-542-8336** — 212-809-8585

Media Watch PO Box 618 . . . . Santa Cruz CA 95061 — **800-631-6355** — 831-423-6355

Medicare Rights Ctr (MRC)
520 Eigth Ave N Wing 3rd Fl . . . . New York NY 10018 — **800-333-4114*** — 212-869-3850
*Hotline

NA for the Advancement of Colored People (NAACP)
4805 Mt Hope Dr . . . . Baltimore MD 21215 — **877-622-2798** — 410-580-5777

National Abortion Federation (NAF)
1755 Massachusetts Ave NW . . . . Washington DC 20036 — **800-772-9100** — 202-667-5881

National Council on Crime & Delinquency (NCCD)
1970 Broadway Ste 500 . . . . Oakland CA 94612 — **800-306-6223** — 510-208-0500

National Crime Prevention Council (NCPC)
2345 Crystal Dr Ste 500 . . . . Arlington VA 22202 — **800-627-2911** — 443-292-4565

National Ctr for Juvenile Justice (NCJJ)
3700 S Water St Ste 200 . . . . Pittsburgh PA 15203 — **800-851-3420** — 412-227-6950

National Ctr for Victims of Crime, The
2000 M St NW Ste 480 . . . . Washington DC 20036 — **800-394-2255** — 202-467-8700

National Freedom of Information Coalition
344 Hearnes Ctr . . . . Columbia MO 65211 — **866-682-6663** — 573-882-4856

National Organization for the Reform of Marijuana Laws (NORML)
1600 K St NW Ste 501 . . . . Washington DC 20006 — **888-420-8932** — 202-483-5500

National Organization for Victim Assistance (NOVA)
510 King St Ste 424 . . . . Alexandria VA 22314 — **800-879-6682** — 703-535-6682

Patients Rights Council (PRC)
PO Box 760 . . . . Steubenville OH 43952 — **800-958-5678** — 740-282-3810

Rutherford Institute
PO Box 7482 . . . . Charlottesville VA 22906 — **800-225-1791** — 434-978-3888

Second Amendment Foundation
12500 NE Tenth Pl . . . . Bellevue WA 98005 — **800-426-4302** — 425-454-7012

Simon Wiesenthal Ctr
1399 Roxbury Dr . . . . Los Angeles CA 90035 — **800-900-9036** — 310-553-9036

Southern Poverty Law Ctr (SPLC)
400 Washington Ave . . . . Montgomery AL 36104 — **888-414-7752** — 334-956-8200

Urban Land Institute (ULI)
1025 Thomas Jefferson St NW
Ste 500W . . . . Washington DC 20007 — **800-321-5011*** — 202-624-7000
*Orders

WeTip Inc
PO Box 1296 . . . . Rancho Cucamonga CA 91730 — **800-782-7463** — 909-987-5005

48-9 Computer & Internet Organizations

	Toll-Free	Phone

Association for Computing Machinery (ACM)
2 Penn Plz Ste 701 . . . . New York NY 10121 — **800-342-6626** — 212-626-0500

Association for the Advancement of Artificial Intelligence (AAAI)
445 Burgess Dr Ste 100 . . . . Menlo Park CA 94025 — **800-548-4664** — 650-328-3123

Association of Service & Computer Dealers International (ASCDI)
131 NW First Ave . . . . Delray Beach FL 33444 — **800-393-2505** — 561-266-9016

Canarie
45 O'Connor St Ste 500 . . . . Ottawa ON K1P1A4 — **800-959-5525** — 613-943-5454

Consortium for School Networking (CoSN)
1025 Vermont Ave NW Ste 1010 . . . . Washington DC 20005 — **866-267-8747** — 202-861-2676

Entertainment Software Assn (ESA)
601 Massachusetts Ave NW Ste 300 . . . . Washington DC 20001 — **800-949-3660** — 202-223-2400

Institute for Certification of Computing Professionals (ICCP)
2400 E Devon Ave Ste 281 . . . . Des Plaines IL 60018 — **800-843-8227** — 847-299-4227

International Webmasters Assn (IWA)
119 E Union St Ste A . . . . Pasadena CA 91103 — **866-607-1773** — 626-449-3709

National Urban Technology Ctr
25 Broadway 9th Fl . . . . New York NY 10004 — **800-998-3212** — 212-528-7350

Open Group
44 Montgomery St Ste 960 . . . . San Francisco CA 94104 — **800-433-6611** — 415-374-8280

Print Services & Distribution Assn (PSDA)
330 N Wabash Ave Ste 2000 . . . . Chicago IL 60611 — **800-230-0175**

Society for Information Display (SID)
1475 S Bascom Ave # 114 . . . . Campbell CA 95008 — **800-350-0111** — 408-879-3901

Society for Information Management (SIM)
1120 Rte 73 Ste 200 . . . . Mount Laurel NJ 08054 — **800-387-9746** — 312-527-6734

USENIX Assn
2560 Ninth St Ste 215 . . . . Berkeley CA 94710 — **800-397-3342** — 510-528-8649

48-10 Consumer Interest Organizations

	Toll-Free	Phone

Accuracy in Media Inc (AIM)
4350 EW Hwy Ste 555 . . . . Bethesda MD 20814 — **800-787-4567** — 202-364-4401

American Council on Science & Health (ACSH)
110 E 42nd St Ste 1300 . . . . New York NY 10017 — **866-905-2694** — 212-362-7044

Consumers' Research Council of America (CRCA)
2020 Pennsylvania Ave NW Ste 300-A . . . . Washington DC 20006 — **877-774-6337** — 202-835-9698

Council of Better Business Bureaus Inc Wise Giving Alliance
4200 Wilson Blvd Ste 800 . . . . Arlington VA 22203 — **800-248-4040** — 703-276-0100

Funeral Consumers Alliance
33 Patchen Rd . . . . South Burlington VT 05403 — **800-765-0107** — 802-865-8300

Insurance Information Institute Inc (III)
110 William St . . . . New York NY 10038 — **877-263-7995** — 212-346-5500

National Committee for Quality Assurance (NCQA)
1100 13th St . . . . Washington DC 20005 — **888-275-7585** — 202-955-3500

National Consumers League (NCL)
1701 K St NW Ste 1200 . . . . Washington DC 20006 — **800-388-2227** — 202-835-3323

NeighborWorks America
999 N Capitol St NE Ste 900 . . . . Washington DC 20002 — **800-438-5547** — 202-760-4000

Privacy Rights Clearinghouse
3100 Fifth Ave Ste B . . . . San Diego CA 92103 — **800-269-0271** — 619-298-3396

48-11 Educational Associations & Organizations

	Toll-Free	Phone

A Better Chance Inc
253 W 35th St 6th Fl . . . . New York NY 10001 — **800-562-7865** — 646-346-1310

American Council of the Blind (ACB)
2200 Wilson Blvd Ste 650 . . . . Arlington VA 22201 — **800-424-8666** — 202-467-5081

American Indian College Fund
8333 Greenwood Blvd . . . . Denver CO 80221 — **800-776-3863** — 303-426-8900

Archaeological Institute of America (AIA)
44 Beacon St . . . . Boston MA 02108 — **877-524-6300** — 617-353-9361

Astronomical Society of the Pacific
390 Ashton Ave . . . . San Francisco CA 94112 — **800-335-2624** — 415-337-1100

Braille Institute of America Inc
741 North Vermont Ave . . . . Los Angeles CA 90029 — **800-272-4553** — 323-663-1111

Challenger Ctr for Space Science Education
422 First St SE 3rd Fl . . . . Washington DC 20003 — **800-969-5747*** — 202-827-1580
*General

College Board
45 Columbus Ave . . . . New York NY 10023 — **800-927-4302** — 212-713-8000

College Parents of America (CPA)
2200 Wilson Blvd Ste 102-396 . . . . Arlington VA 22201 — **888-761-6702**

Comstar Enterprises Inc
PO Box 6698 . . . . Springdale AR 72766 — **800-533-2343** — 479-361-2111

Education Development Ctr Inc (EDC)
55 Chapel St . . . . Newton MA 02458 — **800-225-4276** — 617-969-7100

Facing History & Ourselves
16 HuRd Rd . . . . Brookline MA 02445 — **800-856-9039** — 617-232-1595

FIRST 200 Bedford St . . . . Manchester NH 03101 — **800-871-8326** — 603-666-3906

Foundation Ctr
32 Old Slip 24th Fl . . . . New York NY 10005 — **800-424-9836** — 212-620-4230

Future Business Leaders of America-Phi Beta Lambda Inc (FBLA-PBL)
1912 Assn Dr . . . . Reston VA 20191 — **800-325-2946**

Graduate Management Admission Council (GMAC)
11921 Freedom Dr Ste 300 . . . . Reston VA 20190 — **866-505-6559** — 703-668-9600

Great Books Foundation
35 E Wacker Dr Ste 400 . . . . Chicago IL 60601 — **800-222-5870** — 312-332-5870

Institute of Consumer Financial Education
PO Box 34070 . . . . San Diego CA 92163 — **800-685-1111** — 619-239-1401

Institute of General Semantics (IGS)
72-11 Austin St . . . . Forest Hills NY 11375 — **800-346-1359** — 212-729-7973

Intercollegiate Studies Institute (ISI)
3901 Centerville Rd . . . . Wilmington DE 19807 — **800-526-7022** — 302-652-4600

International Montessori Council & The Montessori Foundation
19600 E State Rd 64 . . . . Bradenton FL 34212 — **800-655-5843** — 941-729-9565

Junior Achievement of Canada (JACAN)
161 Bay St 27th Fl . . . . Toronto ON M5J2S1 — **800-265-0699** — 416-622-4602

				Toll-Free	Phone
Junior State of America (JSA)					
111 Anza Blvd Ste 109	Burlingame	CA	94010	800-334-5353	650-347-1600
Linguistic Society of America (LSA)					
1325 18th St NW Ste 211	Washington	DC	20036	800-726-0479	202-835-1714
Mu Phi Epsilon					
1611 County Rd B West Ste 320	Saint paul	MN	55113	888-259-1471	
Music for All					
39 W Jackson Pl Ste 150	Indianapolis	IN	46225	800-848-2263	317-636-2263
National Head Start Assn (NHSA)					
1651 Prince St	Alexandria	VA	22314	866-677-8724	703-739-0875
National Honor Society (NHS)					
1904 Assn Dr	Reston	VA	20191	800-253-7746	703-860-0200
Reading Is Fundamental Inc (RIF)					
1825 Connecticut Ave NW Ste 400	Washington	DC	20009	877-743-7323	202-536-3400
Scholarship America					
1 Scholarship Way	Saint Peter	MN	56082	800-537-4180	507-931-1682
SkillsUSA					
14001 James Monroe Hwy	Leesburg	VA	20176	800-321-8422	703-777-8810
University of Minnesota					
200 Oak St SE Ste 500	Minneapolis	MN	55455	800-775-2187	612-624-3333
World Learning International Development Programs					
1015 15th St NW 7th Fl	Washington	DC	20005	800-345-2929	202-408-5420
Youth For Understanding USA					
6400 Goldsboro Rd Ste 100	Bethesda	MD	20817	800-424-3691	800-833-6243

48-12 Energy & Natural Resources Organizations

				Toll-Free	Phone
Air & Waste Management Assn (A&WMA)					
436 Seventh Ave Ste 2100	Pittsburgh	PA	15219	800-270-3444	412-232-3444
Alliance to Save Energy (ASE)					
1850 M St NW Ste 600	Washington	DC	20036	800-862-2086	202-857-0666
American Association of Petroleum Geologists (AAPG)					
1444 S Boulder Ave PO Box 979	Tulsa	OK	74119	800-364-2274	918-584-2555
American Institute of Mining Metallurgical & Petroleum Engineers (AIME)					
12999 E Adam Aircraft Cir	Englewood	CO	80112	888-702-0049	303-325-5185
American Oil Chemists Society (AOCS)					
2710 S Boulder PO Box 17190	Urbana	IL	61802	866-535-2730	217-359-2344
American Public Gas Assn (APGA)					
201 Massachusetts Ave NE Ste C-4	Washington	DC	20002	800-927-4204	202-464-2742
American Water Works Assn (AWWA)					
6666 W Quincy Ave	Denver	CO	80235	800-926-7337	303-794-7711
Association of Energy Service Cos (AESC)					
14531 Fm 529 Ste 250	Houston	TX	77095	800-692-0771	713-781-0758
Edison Electric Institute (EEI)					
701 Pennsylvania Ave NW	Washington	DC	20004	800-649-1202	202-508-5000
Independent Petroleum Assn of America (IPAA)					
1201 15th St NW Ste 300	Washington	DC	20005	800-433-2851	202-857-4722
Institute of Clean Air Cos (ICAC)					
1730 M St NW Ste 206	Washington	DC	20036	800-631-9505	202-478-6188
National Ground Water Assn (NGWA)					
601 Dempsey Rd	Westerville	OH	43081	800-551-7379	614-898-7791
National Ocean Industries Assn (NOIA)					
1120 G St NW Ste 900	Washington	DC	20005	800-558-9994	202-347-6900
National Propane Gas Assn (NPGA)					
1899 L St NW Ste 350	Washington	DC	20036	800-328-1111	202-466-7200
Society of Petroleum Engineers (SPE)					
222 Palisades Creek Dr	Richardson	TX	75080	800-456-6863	972-952-9393
Western Forestry & Conservation Assn					
4033 SW Canyon Rd	Portland	OR	97221	888-722-9416	503-226-4562

48-13 Environmental Organizations

				Toll-Free	Phone
Adirondack Council					
103 Hand Ave Ste 3	Elizabethtown	NY	12932	877-873-2240	518-873-2240
American Farmland Trust (AFT)					
1200 18th St	Washington	DC	20036	800-431-1499	202-331-7300
American Rivers					
1101 14th St NW Ste 1400	Washington	DC	20005	877-347-7550	202-347-7550
American Shore & Beach Preservation Assn (ASBPA)					
5460 Beaujolais Ln	Fort Myers	FL	33919	800-331-1600	239-489-2616
Appalachian Mountain Club (AMC)					
5 Joy St	Boston	MA	02108	800-262-4455*	617-523-0655
*Orders					
Audubon Naturalist Society					
8940 Jones Mill Rd	Chevy Chase	MD	20815	888-744-4723	301-652-9188
Beyond Pesticides					
701 E St SE Ste 200	Washington	DC	20003	866-260-6653	202-543-5450
Canadian Parks & Wilderness Society (CPAWS)					
250 City Ctr Ave Ste 506	Ottawa	ON	K1R6K7	800-333-9453	613-569-7226
Canadian Wildlife Federation (CWF)					
350 Michael Cowpland Dr	Kanata	ON	K2M2W1	800-563-9453	613-599-9594
Clean Water Action					
4455 Connecticut Ave NW	Washington	DC	20008	800-657-3864	202-895-0420
Co-op America					
1612 K St NW Ste 600	Washington	DC	20006	800-584-7336	202-872-5307
Conservation International (CI)					
2011 Crystal Dr Ste 500	Arlington	VA	22202	800-406-2306	703-341-2400
Earth Share					
7735 Old Georgetown Rd Ste 900	Bethesda	MD	20814	800-875-3863	240-333-0300
Earthwatch Institute					
114 Western Ave	Boston	MA	02134	800-776-0188	978-461-0081
Ecojustice Canada					
131 Water St Ste 214	Vancouver	BC	V6B4M3	800-926-7744	604-685-5618
Environmental Defense					
257 Park Ave S	New York	NY	10010	800-505-0703	212-505-2100
Environmental Information Assn (EIA)					
6935 Wisconsin Ave Ste 306	Chevy Chase	MD	20815	888-343-4342	301-961-4999
Environmental Law Institute (ELI)					
2000 L St NW Ste 620	Washington	DC	20036	800-433-5120	202-939-3800
Forest Landowners Assn (FLA)					
950 Glenn Dr Ste 150	Folsom	CA	95630	800-325-2954	404-325-2954
Freshwater Society					
2500 Shadywood Rd	Excelsior	MN	55331	888-471-9773	952-471-9773

				Toll-Free	Phone
Friends of the Earth					
1717 Massachusetts Ave NW Ste 600	Washington	DC	20036	877-843-8687	202-783-7400
Friends of the River					
1418 20th St Ste 100	Sacramento	CA	95811	888-464-2477	916-442-3155
Grand Canyon Trust					
2601 N Fort Valley Rd	Flagstaff	AZ	86001	800-827-5722	928-774-7488
Greater Yellowstone Coalition (GYC)					
215 S Wallace Ave	Bozeman	MT	59715	800-775-1834	406-586-1593
Greenpeace Canada					
33 Cecil St	Toronto	ON	M5T1N1	800-320-7183	416-597-8408
Greenpeace USA					
702 H St NW Ste 300	Washington	DC	20001	800-326-0959	202-462-1177
Historic New England					
141 Cambridge St	Boston	MA	02114	800-722-2256	617-227-3956
Izaak Walton League of America (IWLA)					
707 Conservation Ln	Gaithersburg	MD	20878	800-453-5463	301-548-0150
National Arbor Day Foundation					
100 Arbor Ave	Nebraska City	NE	68410	888-448-7337	402-474-5655
National Audubon Society (NAS)					
225 Varick St	New York	NY	10014	800-274-4201	212-979-3000
National Council for Air & Stream Improvement Inc (NCASI)					
PO Box 13318	Research Triangle Park	NC	27709	888-448-2473	919-941-6400
National Parks Conservation Assn (NPCA)					
1300 19th St NW Ste 300	Washington	DC	20036	800-628-7275	202-223-6722
National Trust for Canada, The					
190 Bronson Ave	Ottawa	ON	K1R6H4	866-964-1066	613-237-1066
National Trust for Historic Preservation					
1785 Massachusetts Ave NW	Washington	DC	20036	800-944-6847	202-588-6000
Nature Conservancy					
4245 N Fairfax Dr Ste 100	Arlington	VA	22203	800-628-6860*	703-841-5300
*Cust Svc					
Nature Conservancy of Canada					
36 Eglinton Ave W Ste 400	Toronto	ON	M4R1A1	800-465-8005	416-932-3202
Ocean Conservancy					
1300 19th St NW 8th Fl	Washington	DC	20036	800-519-1541	202-429-5609
Pollution Probe					
150 Ferrand Dr Ste 208	Toronto	ON	M3C3E5	877-926-1907	416-926-1907
Public Lands Foundation (PLF)					
PO Box 7226	Arlington	VA	22207	866-985-9636	703-790-1988
Rails-to-Trails Conservancy (RTC)					
2121 Ward Ct NW 5th Fl	Washington	DC	20037	800-944-6847	202-331-9696
Rainforest Action Network (RAN)					
425 Bush St Ste 300	San Francisco	CA	94108	800-368-1819	415-398-4404
Royal Oak Foundation, The					
35 W 35th St Ste 1200	New York	NY	10001	800-913-6565	212-480-2889
Save America's Forests					
4 Library Ct SE	Washington	DC	20003	800-729-1363	202-544-9219
Seldovia Native Association Inc					
101 W Benson Blvd Ste 302	Anchorage	AK	99503	844-868-8006	907-868-8006
Shelburne Farms					
1611 Harbor Rd	Shelburne	VT	05482	800-286-6022	802-985-8686
Sierra Club Canada					
412-1 Nicholas St	Ottawa	ON	K1N7B7	888-810-4204	613-241-4611
Soil & Water Conservation Society (SWCS)					
945 SW Ankeny Rd	Ankeny	IA	50023	800-843-7645	515-289-2331
Student Conservation Assn (SCA)					
689 River Rd PO Box 550	Charlestown	NH	03603	888-722-9675	603-543-1700
Tree Care Industry Assn (TCIA)					
136 Harvey Rd Ste 101	Londonderry	NH	03053	800-733-2622	603-314-5380
Trust for Public Land (TPL)					
116 New Montgomery St 4th Fl	San Francisco	CA	94105	800-714-5263	415-495-4014
Union of Concerned Scientists (UCS)					
2 Brattle Sq	Cambridge	MA	02238	800-666-8276	617-547-5552
Water Environment Federation (WEF)					
601 Wythe St	Alexandria	VA	22314	800-666-0206	703-684-2400
Western Canada Wilderness Committee (WCWC)					
46 E Sixth Ave	Vancouver	BC	V5T1J4	800-661-9453	604-683-8220

48-14 Ethnic & Nationality Organizations

				Toll-Free	Phone
American Folklore Society (AFS)					
800 E Third St	Bloomington	IN	47405	866-315-9403	812-856-2379
American Hellenic Educational Progressive Assn (AHEPA)					
1909 Q St NW Ste 500	Washington	DC	20009	855-473-3512	202-232-6300
First Nations Development Institute					
2217 Princess Anne St Ste 111-1	Fredericksburg	VA	22401	888-371-3686	540-371-5615
National Congress of American Indians (NCAI)					
1516 P St NW	Washington	DC	20005	800-388-2227	202-466-7767
National Slovak Society of the USA (NSS)					
351 Vly Brook Rd	McMurray	PA	15317	800-488-1890	724-731-0094
Order Sons of Italy in America (OSIA)					
219 E St NE	Washington	DC	20002	800-552-6742	202-547-2900
Polish American Congress					
5711 N Milwaukee Ave	Chicago	IL	60646	800-621-3723	773-763-9944
Sons of Norway					
1455 West Lake St	Minneapolis	MN	55408	800-945-8851	612-827-3611
Ukrainian National Association Inc (UNA)					
2200 Rt 10	Parsippany	NJ	07054	800-253-9862	
US Pan Asian American Chamber of Commerce (US PAACC)					
1329 18th St NW	Washington	DC	20036	800-696-7818	202-296-5221

48-15 Fraternal & Social Organizations

				Toll-Free	Phone
American Mensa Ltd					
1229 Corporate Dr W	Arlington	TX	76006	800-666-3672	817-607-0060
Association of Junior Leagues International Inc (AJLI)					
80 Maiden Ln Ste 305	New York	NY	10038	800-955-3248	212-951-8300
Boy Scouts of America (BSA)					
1325 W Walnut Hill Ln PO Box 152079	Irving	TX	75015	800-323-0732	972-580-2000
Civitan International					
PO Box 130744	Birmingham	AL	35213	800-248-4826	205-591-8910

Organization	Address	City	State	ZIP	Toll-Free	Phone
Cosmopolitan International	PO Box 7351	Lancaster	PA	17604	**800-648-4331**	717-295-7142
DeMolay International	10200 NW Ambassabor Dr	Kansas City	MO	64153	**800-336-6529***	816-891-8333
*Orders						
Fraternal Order of Police (FOP)	701 Marriott Dr	Nashville	TN	37214	**800-451-2711**	615-399-0900
Girl Scouts of the USA	420 Fifth Ave	New York	NY	10018	**800-478-7248**	212-852-8000
Independent Order of Odd Fellows	422 N Trade St	Winston-Salem	NC	27101	**800-235-8358**	336-725-5955
International Assn of Lions Clubs	300 W 22nd St	Oak Brook	IL	60523	**800-710-7822**	630-571-5466
Key Club International	3636 Woodview Trace	Indianapolis	IN	46268	**800-549-2647**	317-875-8755
Knights of Columbus	1 Columbus Plz	New Haven	CT	06510	**800-380-9995***	203-752-4000
*Cust Svc						
Lutheran Social Services of Illinois	1001 E Touhy Ave Ste 50	Des Plaines	IL	60018	**888-671-0300**	847-635-4600
Masonic Service Assn of North America (MSANA)	8120 Fenton St Ste 203	Silver Spring	MD	20910	**855-476-4010**	301-588-4010
Moose International Inc	155 S International Dr	Mooseheart	IL	60539	**800-668-5901**	630-859-2000
National Exchange Club	3050 W Central Ave	Toledo	OH	43606	**800-924-2643**	419-535-3232
Optimist International	4494 Lindell Blvd	Saint Louis	MO	63108	**800-500-8130**	314-371-6000
Oswego County Opportunities Inc	239 Oneida St	Fulton	NY	13069	**877-342-7618**	315-598-4717
Pioneers Volunteer	1801 California St Ste 225	Denver	CO	80202	**800-872-5995**	303-571-1200
Presbyterian Homes Inc, The	2109 Sandy Ridge Rd	Colfax	NC	27235	**800-225-9573**	336-886-6553
Rotary International	1 Rotary Ctr 1560 Sherman Ave	Evanston	IL	60201	**866-976-8279**	847-866-3000
Ruritan National	5451 Lyons Rd PO Box 487	Dublin	VA	24084	**877-787-8727**	540-674-5431
Spectrum Health Systems Inc	10 Mechanic St Ste 302	Worcester	MA	01608	**800-464-9555**	508-792-5400
Starr Commonwealth	13725 Starr Commonwealth Rd	Albion	MI	49224	**800-837-5591**	517-629-5591
Up With People	6830 Broadway	Denver	CO	80221	**877-264-8856**	303-460-7100

48-16 Greek Letter Societies

Organization	Address	City	State	ZIP	Toll-Free	Phone
Alpha Epsilon Phi Sorority (AEPhi)	11 Lake Ave Ext Ste 1A	Danbury	CT	06811	**888-668-4293**	203-748-0029
Alpha Lambda Delta	6800 Pittsford-Palmyra Rd Ste 340	Fairport	NY	14450	**800-925-7421**	
Alpha Omega International Dental Fraternity	50 W Edmonston Dr	Rockville	MD	20852	**877-368-6326**	301-738-6400
Alpha Omicron Pi International	5390 Virginia Way	Brentwood	TN	37027	**855-230-1183**	615-370-0920
Alpha Tau Omega Fraternity (ATO)	1 N Pennsylvania St 12th Fl	Indianapolis	IN	46204	**800-798-9286**	317-684-1865
Beta Alpha Psi	220 Leigh Farm Rd	Durham	NC	27707	**800-362-5066**	919-402-4044
Beta Gamma Sigma Inc (BGS)	125 Weldon Pkwy	Maryland Heights	MO	63043	**800-337-4677**	314-432-5650
Delta Delta Delta Fraternity	2331 Brookhollow Plaza Dr	Arlington	TX	76006	**877-746-7333**	817-633-8001
Delta Gamma	3250 Riverside Dr Ste A-2	Columbus	OH	43221	**800-644-5414**	614-481-8169
Delta Sigma Theta Sorority Inc	1707 New Hampshire Ave NW	Washington	DC	20009	**866-615-6464**	202-986-2400
Delta Theta Phi	225 Hillsborough St Ste 432	Raleigh	NC	27603	**800-783-2600**	
Eta Sigma Gamma	2000 University Ave	Muncie	IN	47306	**800-715-2559**	765-285-2258
Gamma Beta Phi Society	5204 Kingston Pk Ste 31-33	Knoxville	TN	37919	**800-628-9920**	865-483-6212
International Fraternity of Phi Gamma Delta	1201 Red Mile Rd PO Box 4599	Lexington	KY	40544	**888-668-4293**	859-255-1848
Kappa Alpha Theta Fraternity	8740 Founders Rd	Indianapolis	IN	46268	**800-526-1870**	888-526-1870
Kappa Delta Pi	3707 Woodview Trace	Indianapolis	IN	46268	**800-284-3167**	317-871-4900
Kappa Delta Sorority	3205 Players Ln	Memphis	TN	38125	**800-536-1897**	901-748-1897
Kappa Kappa Gamma	PO Box 38	Columbus	OH	43216	**866-554-1870**	614-228-6515
National Fraternity of Kappa Delta Rho (KDR)	331 S Main St	Greensburg	PA	15601	**800-536-5371**	724-838-7100
National Kappa Kappa Iota Inc	1875 E 15th St	Tulsa	OK	74104	**800-678-0389**	918-744-0389
Omega Psi Phi Fraternity Inc	3951 Snapfinger Pkwy	Decatur	GA	30035	**800-829-4933**	404-284-5533
Phi Alpha Theta *National History Honor Society*	4202 E Fowler Ave SOC 107	Tampa	FL	33620	**800-394-8195**	
Phi Delta Kappa International (PDK)	408 N Union St	Bloomington	IN	47407	**800-766-1156**	812-339-1156
Phi Delta Theta	2 S Campus Ave	Oxford	OH	45056	**888-373-9855**	513-523-6345
Phi Kappa Psi	5395 Emerson Way	Indianapolis	IN	46226	**800-486-1852**	317-632-1852
Phi Kappa Sigma International Fraternity Inc	2 Timber Dr	Chester Springs	PA	19425	**800-344-7335**	610-469-3282
Phi Mu Alpha Sinfonia Fraternity of America Inc	10600 Old State Rd	Evansville	IN	47711	**800-473-2649**	812-867-2433
Phi Mu Fraternity	400 Westpark Dr	Peachtree City	GA	30269	**888-744-6824**	770-632-2090
Phi Sigma Kappa International	2925 E 96th St	Indianapolis	IN	46240	**888-846-6851**	317-573-5420
Phi Sigma Pi National Honor Fraternity Inc	2119 Ambassador Cir	Lancaster	PA	17603	**800-366-1916**	717-299-4710
Phi Theta Kappa International Honor Society	1625 Eastover Dr	Jackson	MS	39211	**800-946-9995**	
PSI Upsilon Fraternity	3003 E 96th St	Indianapolis	IN	46240	**800-394-1833**	317-571-1833
Sigma Alpha Epsilon Fraternity (SAE)	1856 Sheridan Rd	Evanston	IL	60201	**800-233-1856**	847-424-3031
Sigma Chi Fraternity	1714 Hinman Ave	Evanston	IL	60201	**877-829-5500**	877-471-5410
Sigma Gamma Rho Sorority Inc	1000 Southhill Dr Ste 200	Cary	NC	27513	**888-747-1922**	919-678-9720
Sigma Phi Epsilon Fraternity	310 S Blvd	Richmond	VA	23220	**800-767-1901**	804-353-1901
Sigma Theta Tau International	550 W N St	Indianapolis	IN	46202	**888-634-7575**	317-634-8171
Sigma Xi Scientific Research Society	3106 E NC Hwy 54 PO Box 13975	Research Triangle Park	NC	27709	**800-243-6534**	919-549-4691
Tau Beta Pi Assn	1512 Middle Dr	Knoxville	TN	37996	**877-829-5500**	865-546-4578
Theta Delta Chi Inc	214 Lewis Wharf	Boston	MA	02110	**800-999-1847**	804-344-4300
Theta Tau Professional Engineering Fraternity	1011 San Jacinto Ste 205	Austin	TX	78701	**800-264-1904**	512-472-1904
Zeta Phi Beta Sorority Inc	1734 New Hampshire Ave NW	Washington	DC	20009	**800-393-2503**	202-387-3103
Zeta Psi Fraternity of North America	15 S Henry St	Pearl River	NY	10965	**800-477-1847**	845-735-1847

48-17 Health & Health-Related Organizations

Organization	Address	City	State	ZIP	Toll-Free	Phone
Acoustic Neuroma Assn (ANA)	600 Peachtree Pkwy Ste 108	Cumming	GA	30041	**877-200-8211**	770-205-8211
Alliance for Lupus Research (ALA)	28 W 44th St Ste 501	New York	NY	10036	**800-867-1743**	212-218-2840
Alzheimer's Assn	225 N Michigan Ave 1st Fl	Chicago	IL	60601	**800-272-3900**	312-335-8700
American Assn of Acupunture & Oriental Medicine (AAAOM)	PO Box 162340	Sacramento	CA	95816	**866-455-7999**	916-443-4770
American Assn of Naturopathic Physicians (AANP)	818 18th St Ste 250	Washington	DC	20006	**866-538-2267**	202-237-8150
American Assn on Intellectual & Developmental Disabilities (AAIDD)	444 N Capitol St NW Ste 846	Washington	DC	20001	**800-424-3688**	202-387-1968
American Association of Drugless Practitioners (AADP)	2200 Market St Ste 803	Galveston	TX	77550	**888-764-2237**	409-621-2600
American Autoimmune Related Disease Assn (AARDA)	22100 Gratiot Ave	Eastpointe	MI	48021	**800-598-4668**	586-776-3900
American Botanical Council	6200 Manor Rd	Austin	TX	78723	**800-373-7105**	512-926-4900
American Brain Tumor Assn (ABTA)	2720 River Rd	Des Plaines	IL	60018	**800-886-2282**	847-827-9910
American Cancer Society (ACS)	250 William St NW	Atlanta	GA	30303	**800-227-2345**	404-315-1123
American Chronic Pain Assn (ACPA)	PO Box 850	Rocklin	CA	95677	**800-533-3231**	
American Council on Exercise (ACE)	4851 Paramount Dr	San Diego	CA	92123	**800-825-3636**	858-576-6500
American Diabetes Assn (ADA)	1701 N Beauregard St	Alexandria	VA	22311	**800-232-3472**	703-549-1500
American Epilepsy Society (AES)	342 N Main St	West Hartford	CT	06117	**888-233-2334**	860-586-7505
American Foundation for Suicide Prevention (AFSP)	120 Wall St 29th Fl	New York	NY	10005	**888-333-2377**	212-363-3500
American Foundation for the Blind (AFB)	1401 S Clark St Ste 730	Arlington	VA	22202	**800-232-5463**	212-502-7600
American Heart Assn (AHA)	7272 Greenville Ave	Dallas	TX	75231	**800-242-8721**	214-373-6300
American Holistic Nurses Assn (AHNA)	2900 SW Plass Ct	Topeka	KS	66611	**800-278-2462**	785-234-1712
American Kidney Fund (AKF)	6110 Executive Blvd Ste 1010	Rockville	MD	20852	**800-638-8299**	
American Liver Foundation (ALF)	39 Broadway	New York	NY	10006	**800-465-4837**	212-668-1000
American Lung Assn (ALA)	14 Wall St	New York	NY	10005	**800-586-4872**	212-315-8700
American Massage Therapy Assn (AMTA)	500 Davis St Ste 900	Evanston	IL	60201	**877-905-2700**	847-864-0123
American Parkinson Disease Assn (APDA)	135 Parkinson Ave	Staten Island	NY	10305	**800-223-2732**	718-981-8001
American Sleep Apnea Assn (ASAA)	6856 Eastern Ave NW Ste 203	Washington	DC	20012	**888-293-3650**	202-293-3650
American Tinnitus Assn (ATA)	522 SW Fifth Ave Ste 825	Portland	OR	97204	**800-634-8978**	503-248-9985
Anxiety Disorders Assn of America (ADAA)	8701 Georgia Ave Ste #412	Silver Spring	MD	20910	**800-922-8947**	240-485-1001
Arc of the US	1010 Wayne Ave Ste 650	Silver Spring	MD	20910	**800-433-5255**	301-565-3842
Arthritis Foundation	1330 W Peachtree St Ste 100	Atlanta	GA	30309	**800-283-7800**	404-872-7100
Associated Bodywork & Massage Professionals (ABMP)	25188 Genesee Trl Rd Ste 200	Golden	CO	80401	**800-458-2267**	303-674-8478
Association for Research & Enlightenment (ARE)	215 67th St	Virginia Beach	VA	23451	**800-333-4499**	757-428-3588
Asthma & Allergy Foundation of America (AAFA)	8201 Corporate Dr Ste 1000	Landover	MD	20785	**800-727-8462**	202-466-7643
Autism Research Institute (ARI)	4182 Adams Ave	San Diego	CA	92116	**866-366-3361**	619-281-7165
Autism Society of America (ASA)	4340 EW Hwy Ste 350	Bethesda	MD	20814	**800-328-8476**	301-657-0881
Beginnings For Parents	156 Wind Chime Ct Ste A	Raleigh	NC	27615	**800-541-4327**	919-715-4092
Better Hearing Institute (BHI)	1444 I St NW Ste 700	Washington	DC	20005	**800-639-3884**	202-449-1100
Brain Injury Assn of America	1608 Spring Hill Rd Ste 110	Vienna	VA	22182	**800-444-6443**	703-761-0750

				Toll-Free	Phone

Cancer Care Inc
275 Seventh Ave 22nd Fl . . . . New York NY 10001 **800-813-4673** 212-712-8400

Candlelighters Childhood Cancer Foundation
10920 Connecticut Ave Suuite A
PO Box 498. . . . . Kensington MD 20895 **800-366-2223** 301-962-3520

Canine Companions for Independence Inc (CCI)
2965 Dutton Ave PO Box 446. . . . . Santa Rosa CA 95402 **800-572-2275** 707-577-1700

Center for Practical Bioethics
1111 Main St Ste 500. Kansas City MO 64105 **800-344-3829** 816-221-1100

Children & Adults with Attention-Deficit/Hyperactivity Disorder (CHADD)
4601 Presidents Dr Ste 300 . . . . Lanham MD 20706 **800-233-4050**

Children's Organ Transplant Assn (COTA)
2501 W Cota Dr . . . . Bloomington IN 47403 **800-366-2682** 812-336-8872

Children's Tumor Foundation
120 Wall St 16th Fl. . . . . New York NY 10005 **800-323-7938** 212-344-6633

Children's Wish Foundation International
8615 Roswell Rd . . . . Atlanta GA 30350 **800-323-9474** 770-393-9474

Christopher Reeve Foundation
636 Morris Tpke Ste 3A . . . . Short Hills NJ 07078 **800-225-0292** 973-379-2690

Cleft Palate Foundation (CPF)
1504 E Franklin St Ste 102. . . . . Chapel Hill NC 27514 **800-242-5338** 919-933-9044

Compassion & Choices
PO Box 101810 . . . . Denver CO 80250 **800-247-7421**

Cornelia de Lange Syndrome Foundation Inc (CdLS)
302 W Main St Ste 100. . . . . Avon CT 06001 **800-753-2357** 860-676-8166

Creutzfeldt-Jakob Disease Foundation Inc
3610 W Market St Ste 110 . . . . Fairlawn OH 44333 **800-659-1991**

Crohn's & Colitis Foundation of America (CCFA)
733 Third Ave Ste 510 . . . . New York NY 10017 **800-932-2423**

Cystic Fibrosis Foundation
6931 Arlington Rd Ste 200 . . . . Bethesda MD 20814 **800-344-4823** 301-951-4422

Dental Lifeline Network
1800 15th St Ste 100 . . . . Denver CO 80202 **888-471-6334** 303-534-5360

Depression & Bipolar Support Alliance (DBSA)
730 N Franklin St Ste 501. . . . . Chicago IL 60610 **800-826-3632** 312-642-0049

Disability Rights Ctr Inc
18 Low Ave . . . . Concord NH 03301 **800-834-1721** 603-228-0432

Disabled & Alone/Life Services for the Handicapped
1440 Broadway 23rd Fl. . . . . New York NY 10018 **800-995-0066** 212-532-6740

Dystonia Medical Research Foundation
1 E Wacker Dr Ste 2810 . . . . Chicago IL 60601 **800-377-3978*** 312-755-0198
*General

Easter Seals
230 W Monroe St Ste 1800 . . . . Chicago IL 60606 **800-221-6827** 312-726-6200

ECRI Institute
5200 Butler Pk . . . . Plymouth Meeting PA 19462 **866-247-3004** 610-825-6000

El Paso Health
1145 Westmoreland Dr . . . . El Paso TX 79925 **877-532-3778** 915-532-3778

Endometriosis Assn
8585 N 76th Pl . . . . Milwaukee WI 53223 **800-992-3636** 414-355-2200

EngenderHealth
505 Ninth St NW Ste 601 . . . . Washington DC 20004 **800-564-2872** 202-902-2000

Epilepsy Foundation
8301 Professional Pl Ste 200 . . . . Landover MD 20785 **800-332-1000** 301-459-3700

FaithTrust Institute
2400 N 45th St Ste 101 . . . . Seattle WA 98103 **877-860-2255** 206-634-1903

Family Caregiver Alliance (FCA)
101 Montgomery St Ste 2150. . . . . .San Francisco CA 94104 **800-445-8106** 415-434-3388

Family of the Americas Foundation
5929 Talbot Rd . . . . Lothian MD 20711 **800-443-3395** 301-627-3346

Feingold Association of the US
11849 Suncatcher Dr . . . . Fishers IN 46037 **800-321-3287** 631-369-9340

First Candle
49 Locust Ave Ste 104 . . . . New Canaan CT 06840 **800-221-7437** 120-396-6130

Food Allergy & Anaphylaxis Network (FAAN)
11781 Lee Jackson Hwy Ste 160 . . . . Fairfax VA 22033 **800-929-4040** 703-691-3179

Foundation Fighting Blindness
11435 Cron Hill Dr . . . . Owings Mills MD 21117 **800-683-5555** 410-568-0150

Gay Men's Health Crisis (GMHC)
119 W 24th St . . . . New York NY 10011 **800-243-7692** 212-367-1000

Genetic Alliance Inc
4301 Connecticut Ave NW Ste 404. . . . . Washington DC 20008 **800-860-8747** 202-966-5557

Gift of Life Bone Marrow Foundation
800 Yamato Rd Ste 101 . . . . Boca Raton FL 33431 **800-962-7769** 561-982-2900

Glaucoma Research Foundation
251 Post St Ste 600 . . . . .San Francisco CA 94108 **800-826-6693** 415-986-3162

Guide Dog Foundation for the Blind Inc
371 E Jericho Tkpe . . . . Smithtown NY 11787 **800-548-4337** 631-930-9000

Guide Dogs for the Blind
350 Los Ranchitos Rd . . . . San Rafael CA 94903 **800-295-4050** 415-499-4000

Guide Dogs of America
13445 Glenoaks Blvd . . . . Sylmar CA 91342 **800-459-4843** 818-362-5834

Health Physics Society
1313 Dolley Madison Blvd Ste 402 . . . . Mclean VA 22101 **888-624-8373** 703-790-1745

Hearing Loss Assn of America
7910 Woodmont Ave Ste 1200 . . . . Bethesda MD 20814 **800-221-6827** 301-657-2248

Hepatitis Foundation International (HFI)
504 Blick Dr . . . . Silver Spring MD 20904 **800-891-0707** 301-622-4200

Herb Research Foundation (HRF)
4140 15th St . . . . Boulder CO 80304 **800-748-2617** 303-449-2265

Human Growth Foundation
997 Glen Cove Ave Ste 5 . . . . Glen Head NY 11545 **800-451-6434** 516-671-4041

Huntington's Disease Society of America (HDSA)
505 Eigth Ave Ste 902 . . . . New York NY 10018 **800-345-4372** 212-242-1968

Hysterectomy Educational Resources & Services Foundation (HERS)
422 Bryn Mawr Ave . . . . Bala Cynwyd PA 19004 **888-750-4377** 610-667-7757

Icahn School of Medicine at Mount Sinai
1 Gustave L Levy Pl . . . . New York NY 10029 **800-862-1674** 212-241-6500

Immune Deficiency Foundation (IDF)
40 W Chesapeake Ave Ste 308 . . . . Towson MD 21204 **800-296-4433**

International Assn for the Study of Pain (IASP)
111 Queen Anne N Ste 501 . . . . Seattle WA 98109 **866-574-2654** 206-283-0311

International OCD Foundation (OCF)
PO Box 961029 . . . . Boston MA 02196 **800-331-3131** 617-973-5801

JDRF (JDRF) 26 Broadway . . . . New York NY 10004 **800-533-2873** 212-785-9500

La Leche League International Inc (LLLI)
957 N Plum Grove Rd . . . . Schaumburg IL 60173 **800-525-3243** 847-519-7730

Lamaze International
2025 M St NW Ste 800. . . . . Washington DC 20036 **800-368-4404** 202-367-1128

Learning Disabilities Assn of America (LDA)
4156 Library Rd . . . . Pittsburgh PA 15234 **888-300-6710** 412-341-1515

Living Bank PO Box 6725 . . . . Houston TX 77027 **800-528-2971** 713-961-9431

Lupus Foundation of America Inc (LFA)
2000 L St NW Ste 410 . . . . Washington DC 20036 **800-558-0121** 202-349-1155

Lymphoma Research Foundation (LRF)
115 Broadway Ste 1301 . . . . New York NY 10006 **800-500-9976** 212-349-2910

Male Survivor
4768 BRdway Ste 527. New York NY 10034 **800-738-4181**

MCS Referral & Resources Inc
6101 Gentry Ln . . . . Baltimore MD 21210 **800-526-7234** 410-889-6666

MedicAlert Foundation International
5226 Pirrone Ct . . . . Salida CA 95368 **800-432-5378***
*Cust Svc

Medicare Rights Ctr (MRC)
520 Eigth Ave N Wing 3rd Fl . . . . New York NY 10018 **800-333-4114*** 212-869-3850
*Hotline

Mended Hearts Inc, The
8150 N Central Expy M2248. . . . . Dallas TX 75206 **888-432-7899** 214-296-9252

Mental Health America (MHA)
2000 N Beauregard St 6th Fl. . . . . Alexandria VA 22311 **800-969-6642*** 703-684-7722
*Help Line

Multiple Sclerosis Foundation (MSF)
6520 N Andrews Ave . . . . Fort Lauderdale FL 33309 **800-225-6495** 954-776-6805

Muscular Dystrophy Assn (MDA)
3300 E Sunrise Dr . . . . Tucson AZ 85718 **800-572-1717** 520-529-2000

Narcolepsy Network Inc
PO Box 2178 Ste A212. Lynnwood WA 98036 **888-292-6522** 401-667-2523

National Alliance for Hispanic Health
1501 16th St NW . . . . Washington DC 20036 **866-783-2645**

National Alliance on Mental Illness (NAMI)
3803 N Fairfax Dr Ste 100 . . . . Arlington VA 22203 **800-950-6264** 703-524-7600

National Association of People With AIDS (NAPWA)
8401 Colesville Rd Ste 505 . . . . Silver Spring MD 20910 **866-846-9366** 240-247-0880

National Breast Cancer Coalition (NBCC)
1101 17th St NW Ste 1300 . . . . Washington DC 20036 **800-622-2838** 202-296-7477

National Citizens' Coalition for Nursing Home Reform (NCCNHR)
National Consumer Voice for Quality Long-Term Care
1828 L St NW Ste 801 . . . . Washington DC 20036 **866-992-3668** 202-332-2275

National Coalition for Cancer Survivorship (NCCS)
8455 Colesville Rd Ste 930 . . . . Silver Spring MD 20910 **877-622-7937**

National Committee for Quality Assurance (NCQA)
1100 13th St . . . . Washington DC 20005 **888-275-7585** 202-955-3500

National Council on Alcoholism & Drug Dependence Inc (NCADD)
217 Broadway Ste 712 . . . . New York NY 10007 **800-622-2255** 212-269-7797

National Down Syndrome Congress (NDSC)
30 Mansell Ct Ste 108 . . . . Roswell GA 30076 **800-232-6372** 770-604-9500

National Down Syndrome Society (NDSS)
666 Broadway 8th Fl. . . . . New York NY 10012 **800-221-4602**

National Eating Disorders Assn
200 W 41st St Ste 1203 . . . . New York NY 10036 **800-931-2237** 212-575-6200

National Eye Institute
2318 Mill Rd Ste 1300 . . . . Alexandria VA 22314 **800-372-3937** 703-548-4560

National Federation of the Blind (NFB)
1800 Johnson St . . . . Baltimore MD 21230 **800-392-5671** 410-659-9314

National Fire Protection Assn (NFPA)
1 Batterymarch Pk . . . . Quincy MA 02169 **800-344-3555** 617-770-3000

National Gaucher Foundation (NGF)
5410 Edson Ln Ste 220 . . . . Rockville MD 20852 **800-504-3189**

National Hemophilia Foundation (NHF)
7 Penn Plz Ste 1204 . . . . New York NY 10001 **800-424-2634** 212-328-3700

National Industries for the Blind (NIB)
1310 Braddock Pl . . . . Alexandria VA 22314 **800-325-3535*** 703-310-0500
*Cust Svc

National Inhalant Prevention Coalition (NIPC)
PO Box 4117 . . . . Chattanooga TN 37405 **855-704-4400** 423-265-4662

National Kidney Foundation (NKF)
30 E 33rd St . . . . New York NY 10016 **800-622-9010** 212-889-2210

National Marfan Foundation (NMF)
22 Manhasset Ave . . . . .Port Washington NY 11050 **800-862-7326** 516-883-8712

National Marrow Donor Program (NMDP)
500 N Fifth St . . . . Minneapolis MN 55401 **800-627-7692**

National Multiple Sclerosis Society
733 Third Ave 3rd Fl. . . . . New York NY 10017 **800-344-4867** 212-986-3240

National Niemann-Pick Disease Foundation Inc (NNPDF)
401 Madison Ave Ste B PO Box 49. . . . . Fort Atkinson WI 53538 **877-287-3672** 920-563-0930

National Oral Health Information Clearinghouse (NIDCR)
1 NOHIC Way . . . . Bethesda MD 20892 **866-232-4528** 301-496-4261

National Organization for Albinism & Hypopigmentation (NOAH)
PO Box 959 . . . . East Hampstead NH 03826 **800-648-2310** 603-887-2310

National Organization for Rare Disorders (NORD)
55 Kenosia Ave . . . . Danbury CT 06810 **800-999-6673** 203-744-0100

National Organization of Circumcision Information Resource Centers (NOCIRC)
PO Box 2512 . . . . San Anselmo CA 94979 **800-727-8622** 415-488-9883

National Osteoporosis Foundation (NOF)
251 18th St S Ste 630 . . . . Arlington VA 22202 **800-231-4222** 202-223-2226

National Ovarian Cancer Coalition (NOCC)
2501 Oak Lawn Ave Ste 435. . . . . Dallas TX 75219 **888-682-7426**

National Pesticide Information Ctr (NPIC)
333 Weniger Hall . . . . Corvallis OR 97331 **800-858-7378**

National Psoriasis Foundation (NPF)
6600 SW 92nd Ave Ste 300 . . . . Portland OR 97223 **800-723-9166** 503-244-7404

National Rehabilitation Assn (NRA)
633 S Washington St . . . . Alexandria VA 22314 **888-258-4295** 703-836-0850

National Rehabilitation Information Ctr (NARIC)
8400 Corporate Dr Ste 500. . . . . Landover MD 20785 **800-346-2742** 301-459-5900

National Reye's Syndrome Foundation (NRSF)
426 N Lewis St . . . . Bryan OH 43506 **800-233-7393** 419-924-9000

National Rosacea Society (NRS)
196 James St . . . . Barrington IL 60010 **888-662-5874**

				Toll-Free	Phone
National Safety Council (NSC)					
1121 Spring Lake Dr	Itasca	IL	60143	**800-621-7615**	630-285-1121
National Spinal Cord Injury Assn (NSCIA)					
75-20 Astoria Blvd Ste 120	East Elmhurst	NY	11370	**800-962-9629**	718-512-0010
National Stroke Assn (NSA)					
9707 E Easter Ln	Centennial	CO	80112	**800-787-6537***	
*Cust Svc					
National Stuttering Assn (NSA)					
119 W 40th St 14th Fl.	New York	NY	10018	**800-937-8888**	212-944-4050
National Tay-Sachs & Allied Diseases Assn (NTSAD)					
2001 Beacon St Ste 204	Brighton	MA	02135	**800-906-8723**	617-277-4463
NISH 8401 Old Courthouse Rd	Vienna	VA	22182	**888-411-8424**	
NSF International					
789 N Dixboro Rd PO Box 130140	Ann Arbor	MI	48105	**800-673-6275**	734-769-8010
Oley Foundation					
214 Hun Memorial MC-28					
Albany Medical Ctr	Albany	NY	12208	**800-776-6539**	518-262-5079
Oral Health America					
180 N Michigan Ave Ste 1150	Chicago	IL	60601	**800-523-3438**	312-836-9900
Parkinson's Disease Foundation (PDF)					
1359 Broadway	New York	NY	10018	**800-457-6676**	212-923-4700
Partnership for a Drug-Free America					
405 Lexington Ave 1601	New York	NY	10174	**855-378-4373**	212-922-1560
Pedorthic Footwear Assn (PFA)					
2025 M St NW Ste 800	Washington	DC	20036	**800-673-8447**	202-367-1145
Phoenix Society for Burn Survivors Inc					
1835 RW Berends Dr SW	Grand Rapids	MI	49519	**800-888-2876**	616-458-2773
Postpartum Support International					
6706 SW 54th Ave	Portland	OR	97219	**800-944-4773**	503-894-9453
Prader-Willi Syndrome Assn (USA)					
8588 Potter Park Dr Ste 500	Sarasota	FL	34238	**800-926-4797**	
Prevent Blindness America					
211 W Wacker Dr Ste 1700	Chicago	IL	60606	**800-331-2020**	
Prevent Cancer Foundation (PCF)					
1600 Duke St Ste 500	Alexandria	VA	22314	**800-227-2732**	703-836-4412
Project Inform					
273 Ninth St	San Francisco	CA	94103	**877-435-7443**	415-558-8669
Recording for the Blind & Dyslexic (RFB&D)					
20 Roszel Rd	Princeton	NJ	08540	**800-221-4792**	
Research to Prevent Blindness Inc (RPR)					
360 Lexington Ave 22nd Fl	New York	NY	10017	**800-621-0026**	212-752-4333
Rolf Institute of Structural Integration					
5055 Chaparral Ct Ste 103	Boulder	CO	80301	**800-530-8875**	303-449-5903
Scleroderma Foundation					
300 Rosewood Dr Ste 105	Danvers	MA	01923	**800-722-4673**	978-463-5843
Sickle Cell Disease Assn of America (SCDAA)					
3700 Koppers St Ste 570	Baltimore	MD	21202	**800-421-8453**	410-528-1555
Spina Bifida Assn (SBAA)					
1600 Wilson Blvd Ste 800	Arlington	VA	22209	**800-621-3141**	202-944-3285
Stuttering Foundation of America					
3100 Walnut Grove Rd Ste 603	Memphis	TN	38111	**800-992-9392**	901-452-7343
Susan G Komen for the Cure					
5005 LBJ Fwy Ste 250	Dallas	TX	75244	**877-465-6636**	
TOPS Club Inc					
4575 S Fifth St	Milwaukee	WI	53207	**800-932-8677**	414-482-4620
UCare Minnesota					
500 Stinson Blvd NE PO Box 52	Minneapolis	MN	55413	**866-457-7144**	612-676-6500
Undersea & Hyperbaric Medical Society (UHMS)					
21 W Colony Pl Ste 280	Durham	NC	27705	**877-533-8467**	919-490-5140
United Network for Organ Sharing (UNOS)					
700 N Fourth St	Richmond	VA	23219	**888-894-6361**	804-782-4800
Well Spouse Assn					
63 W Main St Ste H	Freehold	NJ	07728	**800-838-0879**	732-577-8899

48-18 Hobby Organizations

				Toll-Free	Phone
Academy of Model Aeronautics (AMA)					
5161 E Memorial Dr	Muncie	IN	47302	**800-435-9262**	
American Contract Bridge League (ACBL)					
6575 Windchase Blvd	Horn Lake	MS	38637	**800-264-2743***	662-253-3100
*Sales					
American Craft Council					
1224 Marshall St Ste 200	Minneapolis	MN	55413	**800-836-3470**	612-206-3100
American Federation of Astrologers (AFA)					
6535 S Rural Rd	Tempe	AZ	85283	**888-301-7630**	480-838-1751
American Horticultural Society (AHS)					
7931 E Blvd Dr	Alexandria	VA	22308	**800-777-7931**	703-768-5700
American Radio Relay League (ARRL)					
225 Main St	Newington	CT	06111	**888-277-5289**	860-594-0200
American Rose Society (ARS)					
8877 Jefferson Paige Rd	Shreveport	LA	71119	**800-637-6534**	
Antique Automobile Club of America (AACA)					
501 W Governor Rd PO Box 417	Hershey	PA	17033	**800-452-9910**	717-534-1910
Barbershop Harmony Society					
110 Seventh Ave N	Nashville	TN	37203	**800-876-7464**	615-823-3993
Craft & Hobby Assn (CHA)					
319 E 54th St	Elmwood Park	NJ	07407	**800-822-0494**	201-835-1200
Experimental Aircraft Assn (EAA)					
3000 Poberezny Rd	Oshkosh	WI	54902	**800-236-4800**	920-426-4800
National Garden Clubs Inc (NGC)					
4401 Magnolia Ave	Saint Louis	MO	63110	**800-550-6007**	314-776-7574
National Gardening Assn (NGA)					
1100 Dorset St	South Burlington	VT	05403	**800-538-7476**	802-863-5251
National Genealogical Society (NGS)					
3108 Columbia Pk Ste 300	Arlington	VA	22204	**800-473-0060**	703-525-0050
National Model Railroad Assn (NMRA)					
4121 Cromwell Rd	Chattanooga	TN	37421	**800-654-2256**	423-892-2846
National NeedleArts Assn, The (TNNA)					
1100-H Brandywine Blvd	Zanesville	OH	43701	**800-889-8662**	740-455-6773
Sports Car Club of America (SCCA)					
6700 SW Topeka Blvd	Topeka	KS	66619	**800-770-2055**	
Sweet Adelines International					
9110 S Toledo Ave	Tulsa	OK	74137	**800-992-7464**	918-622-1444

48-19 Military, Veterans, Patriotic Organizations

				Toll-Free	Phone
Air Force Assn (AFA)					
1501 Lee Hwy	Arlington	VA	22209	**800-727-3337**	703-247-5800
American Legion Auxiliary					
8945 N Meridian St Ste 200	Indianapolis	IN	46260	**800-504-4098**	317-569-4500
American Legion, The					
700 N Pennsylvania St	Indianapolis	IN	46204	**800-433-3318***	317-630-1200
*Cust Svc					
American Logistics Assn (ALA)					
1101 Vermont Ave NW Ste 1002	Washington	DC	20005	**800-791-7146**	202-466-2520
American Society of Military Comptrollers (ASMC)					
415 N Alfred St	Alexandria	VA	22314	**800-462-5637**	703-549-0360
AMVETS 4647 Forbes Blvd	Lanham	MD	20706	**877-726-8387**	301-459-9600
Armed Forces Communications & Electronics Assn (AFCEA)					
4400 Fair Lakes Ct	Fairfax	VA	22033	**800-336-4583**	703-631-6100
Armed Services Mutual Benefit Assn (ASMBA)					
PO Box 160384	Nashville	TN	37216	**800-251-8434**	615-851-0800
Association of the US Army (AUSA)					
2425 Wilson Blvd	Arlington	VA	22201	**800-336-4570**	703-841-4300
Disabled American Veterans (DAV)					
3725 Alexandria Pk	Cold Spring	KY	41076	**877-426-2838**	859-441-7300
Enlisted Assn of the National Guard of the US (EANGUS)					
3133 Mt Vernon Ave	Alexandria	VA	22305	**800-234-3264**	703-519-3846
Fleet Reserve Assn (FRA)					
125 NW St	Alexandria	VA	22314	**800-372-1924**	703-683-1400
Marine Corps Assn (MCA)					
PO Box 1775	Quantico	VA	22134	**800-336-0291**	703-640-6161
Military Benefit Assn (MBA)					
14605 Avion Pkwy PO Box 221110	Chantilly	VA	20153	**800-336-0100**	703-968-6200
Military Officers Assn of America (MOAA)					
201 N Washington St	Alexandria	VA	22314	**800-234-6622**	
NA for Uniformed Services (NAUS)					
5535 Hempstead Way	Springfield	VA	22151	**800-842-3451**	703-750-1342
National Committee for Employer Support of the Guard & Reserve (ESGR)					
1555 Wilson Blvd Ste 319	Arlington	VA	22209	**800-336-4590**	
National Guard Educational Foundation (NGAUS)					
1 Massachusetts Ave NW	Washington	DC	20001	**888-226-4287**	202-789-0031
National Society Daughters of the American Revolution (DAR)					
1776 D St NW	Washington	DC	20006	**800-449-1776**	202-628-1776
Naval Enlisted Reserve Assn (NERA)					
6703 Farragut Ave	Falls Church	VA	22042	**800-776-9020**	
Naval Reserve Assn (NRA)					
1619 King St	Alexandria	VA	22314	**877-628-9411**	703-548-5800
Navy League of the US					
2300 Wilson Blvd	Arlington	VA	22201	**800-356-5760**	703-528-1775
Navy-Marine Corps Relief Society (NMCRS)					
875 N Randolph St Ste 225	Arlington	VA	22203	**800-654-8364**	703-696-4904
Non Commissioned Officers Assn (NCOA)					
9330 Corporate Dr Ste 708	Selma	TX	78154	**800-662-2620**	210-653-6161
Reserve Officers Assn of the US (ROA)					
1 Constitution Ave NE	Washington	DC	20002	**800-809-9448**	202-479-2200
Tailhook Assn					
9696 Businesspark Ave	San Diego	CA	92131	**800-322-4665**	858-689-9223
United Service Organizations (USO)					
2111 Wilson Blvd Ste 1200	Arlington	VA	22201	**800-876-7469**	888-484-3876
US Naval Institute					
291 Wood Rd	Annapolis	MD	21402	**800-233-8764**	410-268-6110
Veterans of Foreign Wars of the US (VFW)					
406 W 34th St	Kansas City	MO	64111	**800-963-3180**	816-756-3390
Women in Military Service for America Memorial Foundation Inc					
Dept 560	Washington	DC	20042	**800-222-2294**	703-533-1155

48-20 Religious Organizations

				Toll-Free	Phone
92nd St Young Men's & Young Women's Hebrew Assn					
1395 Lexington Ave	New York	NY	10128	**800-385-1689**	212-415-5500
American Baptist Assn (ABA)					
4605 N State Line Ave	Texarkana	TX	75503	**800-264-2482**	903-792-2783
American Baptist Churches USA					
PO Box 851	Valley Forge	PA	19482	**800-222-3872**	610-768-2000
American Theological Library Assn (ATLA)					
300 S Wacker Dr Ste 2100	Chicago	IL	60606	**888-665-2852**	312-454-5100
Antiochian Orthodox Christian Archdiocese of North America					
358 Mountain Rd	Englewood	NJ	07631	**888-421-1442**	201-871-1355
Archdiocese of Saint Paul & Minneapolis					
226 Summit Ave	Saint Paul	MN	55102	**877-290-1605**	651-291-4411
Arkansas Baptist Foundation					
10 Remington Dr	Little Rock	AR	72204	**800-838-2272**	501-376-4791
Assemblies of God (A/G)					
1445 N Boonville Ave	Springfield	MO	65802	**800-641-4310**	417-862-2781
Avant Ministries					
10000 N Oak Trafficway	Kansas City	MO	64155	**800-468-1892**	816-734-8500
B'nai B'rith International					
2020 K St NW 7th Fl	Washington	DC	20006	**888-388-4224**	202-857-6600
Baptist General Convention of Texas					
7557 Rambler Rd Ste 1200	Dallas	TX	75231	**888-244-9400**	
Baptist Missionary Assn of America (BMA)					
611 Locust Ave PO Box 878	Conway	AR	72034	**800-333-1442**	501-455-4977
Benny Hinn Ministries					
PO Box 162000	Irving	TX	75016	**888-377-7783**	
Bible League					
3801 Eagle Nest Dr	Crete	IL	60417	**866-825-4636**	
Billy Graham Evangelistic Assn					
1 Billy Graham Pkwy	Charlotte	NC	28201	**877-247-2426**	704-401-3200
Catholic Extension					
150 S Wacker Dr Ste 2000	Chicago	IL	60606	**800-842-7804**	
Catholic Supply of st Louis Inc					
6759 Chippewa St	Saint Louis	MO	63109	**800-325-9026**	314-644-0643
Catholic Transcript Inc, The					
467 Bloomfield Ave	Bloomfield	CT	06002	**800-726-2381**	860-286-2828

				Toll-Free	Phone
Child Evangelism Fellowship Inc					
17482 Hwy M	Warrenton	MO	63383	800-748-7710	636-456-4321
Christian & Missionary Alliance					
8595 Explorer Dr	Colorado Springs	CO	80920	800-700-2651	719-599-5999
Christian Business Men's Connection (CBMC)					
5746 Marlin Rd Ste 602 Osborne Ctr	Chattanooga	TN	37411	800-566-2262	423-698-4444
Christian Church (Disciples of Christ)					
130 E Washington St	Indianapolis	IN	46204	800-668-8016	317-635-3100
Christian Reformed Church in North America (CRC)					
2850 Kalamazoo Ave SE	Grand Rapids	MI	49560	800-272-5125	616-241-1691
Christophers, The					
5 Hanover Sq	New York	NY	10004	888-298-4050	212-759-4050
Church of God in Christ Inc					
930 Mason St	Memphis	TN	38126	877-746-8578	901-947-9300
Church of God Ministries					
1201 E Fifth St	Anderson	IN	46012	800-848-2464	765-642-0256
Church of God World Missions (COGWM)					
2490 Keith St	Cleveland	TN	37311	800-345-7492	
Church of Jesus Christ of Latter-Day Saints					
50 E N Temple St	Salt Lake City	UT	84150	800-453-3860	801-240-1000
Church of the Brethren					
1451 Dundee Ave	Elgin	IL	60120	800-323-8039	847-742-5100
Church Women United (CWU)					
475 Riverside Dr Ste 243	New York	NY	10115	800-298-5551	212-870-2347
Commons at Orlando Lutheran Towers, The					
300 E Church St	Orlando	FL	32801	800-859-1033	407-422-4103
Community of Christ					
1001 W Walnut St	Independence	MO	64050	800-825-2806	816-833-1000
Compassion Canada					
985 Adelaide St S	London	ON	N6E4A3	800-563-5437	519-668-0224
Crossworld 306 Bala Ave	Bala Cynwyd	PA	19004	888-785-0087	
Dare 2 Share Ministries International					
PO Box 745323	Arvada	CO	80006	800-462-8355	303-425-1606
Diocese of Rochester					
1150 Buffalo Rd	Roch	NY	14624	800-388-7177	585-328-3210
Diocese of St Augustine Inc					
11625 Old St Augustine	Jacksonville	FL	32258	800-775-4659	904-262-3200
Episcopal Church USA					
815 Second Ave	New York	NY	10017	800-334-6946	212-716-6000
Episcopal Diocese of West Texas					
111 Torcido Dr	San Antonio	TX	78209	888-824-5387	210-824-5387
Evangelical Church Alliance (ECA)					
205 W Broadway St PO Box 9	Bradley	IL	60915	888-855-6060	815-937-0720
Evangelical Fellowship of Canada (EFC)					
9821 Leslie St Ste 103	Richmond Hill	ON	L4B3Y4	866-302-3362	905-479-5885
Evangelical Free Church of America, The					
901 E 78th St	Minneapolis	MN	55420	800-745-2202	952-854-1300
Evangelical Lutheran Church in America (ELCA)					
8765 W Higgins Rd	Chicago	IL	60631	800-638-3522	773-380-2700
Evangelical Training Assn (ETA)					
1551 Regency Ct *General	Calumet City	IL	60409	800-369-8291*	
Fellowship Senior Living					
8000 Fellowship Rd	Basking Ridge	NJ	07920	877-824-4909	877-343-6059
First Church of Christ Scientist					
210 Massachusetts Ave	Boston	MA	02115	800-288-7155	617-450-2000
Franciscan Sisters of Chicago Inc					
11500 Theresa Dr	Lemont	IL	60439	800-524-6126	
General Assn of Regular Baptist Churches (GARBC)					
1300 N Meacham Rd	Schaumburg	IL	60173	888-588-1600	
Greater Atlanta Christian					
1575 Indian Trl Lilburn Rd	Norcross	GA	30093	800-450-1327	770-243-2000
Henderson Hills Baptist Church					
1200 E I 35 Frontage Rd	Edmond	OK	73034	877-901-4639	405-341-4639
Holy Cross Family Ministries					
518 Washington St	North Easton	MA	02356	800-299-7729	508-238-4095
IFCA International					
3520 Fairlane Ave SW	Grandville	MI	49418	800-347-1840	616-531-1840
International Bible Society (IBS) Biblica					
1820 Jet Stream Dr *Cust Svc	Colorado Springs	CO	80921	800-524-1588*	719-488-9200
International Church of the Foursquare Gospel (ICFG)					
1910 W Sunset Blvd PO Box 26902	Los Angeles	CA	90026	888-635-4234	213-989-4234
International Pentecostal Holiness Church (IPHC)					
PO Box 12609	Oklahoma City	OK	73157	888-474-2966	405-787-7110
Interserve USA					
PO Box 418	Upper Darby	PA	19082	800-809-4440	610-352-0581
InterVarsity Christian Fellowship/USA					
6400 Schroeder Rd	Madison	WI	53711	866-734-4823	608-274-9001
Jewish National Fund (JNF)					
42 E 69th St	New York	NY	10021	800-542-8733	212-879-9300
Jewish Reconstructionist Federation (JRF)					
101 Greenwood Ave	Jenkintown	PA	19046	877-226-7573	215-885-5601
Jewish United Fund/Jewish Federation of Metropolitan Chicago (JUF)					
30 S Wells St	Chicago	IL	60606	855-275-5237	312-346-6700
Jews for Jesus					
60 Haight St	San Francisco	CA	94102	800-366-5521	415-864-2600
Jimmy Swaggart Ministries (JSM)					
8919 World Ministry Blvd PO Box 262550 *Orders	Baton Rouge	LA	70810	800-288-8350*	225-768-8300
Kingsway Charities					
1119 Commonwealth Ave	Bristol	VA	24201	800-321-9234	276-466-3014
Lake Junaluska Assembly					
Lake Junaluska Conference Retreat Ctr 689 N Lakeshore Dr	Lake Junaluska	NC	28745	800-482-1442	828-452-2881
Lutheran Church Missouri Synod (LCMS)					
1333 S Kirkwood Rd	Saint Louis	MO	63122	888-843-5267	314-965-9000
Lutheran Home at Hollidaysburg, The					
916 Hickory St	Hollidaysburg	PA	16648	800-400-2285	814-696-4527
Lutheran Metropolitan Ministry					
The Richard Sering Ctr 4515 Superior Ave	Cleveland	OH	44103	800-917-2081	216-696-2715
Mission Aviation Fellowship (MAF)					
112 N Pilatus Ln	Nampa	ID	83687	800-359-7623	208-498-0800
Morris Cerullo World Evangelism					
3545 Aero Ct Frnt	San Diego	CA	92123	866-756-4200	

				Toll-Free	Phone
National Association of Congregational Christian Churches (NACCC)					
8473 S Howell Ave	Oak Creek	WI	53154	800-262-1620	414-764-1620
National Association of Free Will Baptists Inc (NAFWB)					
5233 Mt View Rd	Antioch	TN	37013	877-767-7659	615-731-6812
National Baptist Convention of America International Inc					
1000 S Fourth St	Louisville	KY	40203	844-610-6222	
National Baptist Convention USA Inc					
1700 Baptist World Ctr Dr	Nashville	TN	37207	866-531-3054	615-228-6292
Navigators of Canada					
11 St John'S Dr	Arva	ON	N0M1C0	866-202-6287	519-660-8300
Navigators, The					
3820 N 30th St PO Box 6000	Colorado Springs	CO	80934	866-568-7827	719-598-1212
New Hampshire Catholic Charities Inc					
215 Myrtle St	Manchester	NH	03104	800-562-5249	603-669-3030
Orgill Singer					
8360 W Sahara Ave Ste 110	Las Vegas	NV	89117	800-745-3065	702-796-9100
Orthodox Union (OU)					
11 Broadway	New York	NY	10004	855-505-7500	212-563-4000
Pentecostal Assemblies of Canada, The (PAOC)					
2450 Milltower Ct	Mississauga	ON	L5N5Z6	800-779-7262	905-542-7400
Potomac Conference Corp of Seventh Day Adventists					
606 Greenville Ave	Staunton	VA	24401	800-732-1844	540-886-0771
Presby's Inspired Life					
2000 Joshua Rd	Lafayette Hill	PA	19444	877-977-3729	610-834-1001
Presbyterian Childrens Services Inc					
1220 N Lindbergh Blvd	St. Louis	MO	63132	800-383-8147	314-989-9727
Presbyterian Church (USA)					
100 Witherspoon St	Louisville	KY	40202	888-728-7228	502-569-5000
Progressive National Baptist Convention Inc (PNBC)					
601 50th St NE	Washington	DC	20019	800-876-7622	202-396-0558
Promise Keepers (PK)					
PO Box 11798	Denver	CO	80211	866-776-6473	
Rabbinical Assembly					
3080 Broadway	New York	NY	10027	866-907-2761	
Redemptorist, The					
1 Liguori Dr	Liguori	MO	63057	800-325-9521	636-464-2500
Reformed Church in America					
4500 60th St SE	Grand Rapids	MI	49512	800-722-9977	616-698-7071
Seat of the Soul Foundation					
PO Box 3310	Ashland	OR	97520	877-733-4279	541-482-1515
Seventh-day Adventist World Church					
12501 Old Columbia Pk	Silver Spring	MD	20904	800-226-1119	301-680-6000
Sim USA Inc PO Box 7900	Charlotte	NC	28241	800-521-6449	
Society of Biblical Literature (SBL)					
The Luce Ctr 825 Houston Mill Rd	Atlanta	GA	30329	866-727-9955	404-727-3100
Southern Baptist Convention (SBC)					
901 Commerce St	Nashville	TN	37203	866-722-5433	615-244-2355
Tennessee Baptist Convention					
PO Box 682789	Franklin	TN	37068	800-558-2090	615-373-2255
Texas Presbyterian Foundation					
6100 Colwell Blvd Ste 250	Irving	TX	75039	800-955-3155	214-522-3155
Third Millennium Ministries					
316 Live Oaks Blvd	Casselberry	FL	32707	877-443-6455	407-830-0222
Union for Reformed Judaism					
633 Third Ave	New York	NY	10017	855-875-1800	212-650-4000
United Church of Christ (UCC)					
700 Prospect Ave	Cleveland	OH	44115	866-822-8224	216-736-2100
Urban Alternative					
PO Box 4000	Dallas	TX	75208	800-800-3222	214-943-3868
US Conference of Catholic Bishops (USCCB)					
3211 Fourth St NE	Washington	DC	20017	866-582-0943	202-541-3000
We Raise Foundation					
1 Pierce Pl Ste 250E	Itasca	IL	60143	800-762-6748	630-766-9066
Wesbury United Methodist Community					
31 N Park Ave	Meadville	PA	16335	877-937-2879	814-332-9000
Wider Church Ministries					
700 Prospect Ave	Cleveland	OH	44115	866-822-8224	216-736-3200
Woman's Missionary Union (WMU)					
100 Missionary Rdg	Birmingham	AL	35242	800-968-7301	205-991-8100
World Literature Crusade					
640 Chapel Hills Dr	Colorado Springs	CO	80920	800-423-5054	719-260-8888
Wycliffe Bible Translators					
11221 John Wycliffe Blvd	Orlando	FL	32832	800-992-5433	407-852-3600
Young Israel of New Rochelle					
1149 N Ave	New Rochelle	NY	10804	888-942-3638	914-636-2215

48-21 Self-Help Organizations

				Toll-Free	Phone
Al-Anon Family Group Inc					
1600 Corporate Landing Pkwy	Virginia Beach	VA	23454	888-425-2666	757-563-1600
Alcoholics Anonymous (AA)					
475 Riverside Dr 11th Fl	New York	NY	10115	800-437-3584	212-870-3400
Candlelighters Childhood Cancer Foundation					
10920 Connecticut Ave Suuite A PO Box 498	Kensington	MD	20895	800-366-2223	301-962-3520
Chemically Dependent Anonymous (CDA)					
PO Box 423	Severna Park	MD	21146	888-232-4673	
Co-Dependents Anonymous Inc (CODA)					
PO Box 33577	Phoenix	AZ	85067	888-444-2359	602-277-7991
Cocaine Anonymous World Services Inc (CA)					
PO Box 492000	Los Angeles	CA	90049	800-347-8998	310-559-5833
Compassionate Friends					
PO Box 3696	Oak Brook	IL	60522	877-969-0010	630-990-0010
Concerned United Birthparents Inc (CUB)					
PO Box 503475	San Diego	CA	92150	800-822-2777	
Concerns of Police Survivors Inc (COPS)					
846 Old S 5 PO Box 3199	Camdenton	MO	65020	800-784-2677	573-346-4911
Crystal Meth Anonymous (CMA)					
4470 W Sunset Blvd Ste 107 PO Box 555	Los Angeles	CA	90027	877-262-6691	
Debtors Anonymous (DA)					
PO Box 920888	Needham	MA	02492	800-421-2383	781-453-2743
DignityUSA PO Box 376	Medford	MA	02155	800-877-8797	202-861-0017
LifeRing Secular Recovery					
1440 Broadway Ste 312	Oakland	CA	94612	800-811-4142	970-227-6650

Organization / Address	City	State	Zip	Toll-Free	Phone
Marijuana Anonymous World Services (MAWS) PO Box 7807	Torrance	CA	90504	**800-766-6779**	
Overcomers in Christ PO Box 34460	Omaha	NE	68134	**866-573-0966**	
Overcomers Outreach PO Box 922950	Sylmar	CA	91392	**800-310-3001**	818-833-1803
Overeaters Anonymous Inc (OA) PO Box 44020	Rio Rancho	NM	87174	**866-505-4966**	505-891-2664
S-Anon International Family Groups Inc PO Box 111242	Nashville	TN	37222	**800-210-8141**	615-833-3152
Sex Addicts Anonymous (SAA) PO Box 70949	Houston	TX	77270	**800-477-8191**	713-869-4902
Sexaholics Anonymous (SA) PO Box 3565	Brentwood	TN	37024	**866-424-8777**	615-370-6062
SHARE Pregnancy & Infant Loss Support Inc 402 Jackson St	Saint Charles	MO	63301	**800-821-6819**	636-947-6164
Sisters Network Inc 2922 Rosedale St	Houston	TX	77004	**866-781-1808**	713-781-0255
SMART Recovery 7304 Mentor Ave Ste F	Mentor	OH	44060	**866-951-5357**	440-951-5357
Survivors Network of Those Abused by Priests (SNAP) PO Box 6416	Chicago	IL	60680	**877-762-7432**	312-455-1499
Survivors of Incest Anonymous (SIA) PO Box 190	Benson	MD	21018	**877-742-9761**	
TOPS Club Inc 4575 S Fifth St	Milwaukee	WI	53207	**800-932-8677**	414-482-4620
White Bison Inc 5585 Erindale Dr Ste 203	Colorado Springs	CO	80918	**877-871-1495**	719-548-1000

48-22 Sports Organizations

Organization / Address	City	State	Zip	Toll-Free	Phone
Adventure Cycling Assn 150 E Pine St PO Box 8308	Missoula	MT	59807	**800-755-2453**	406-721-1776
Aerobics & Fitness Association of America (AFAA) 1750 E Northrop Blvd Ste 200	Chandler	AZ	85286	**800-446-2322**	
Amateur Athletic Union of the US (AAU) 1910 Hotel Plaza Blvd	Lake Buena Vista	FL	32830	**800-228-4872**	407-934-7200
Amateur Trapshooting Assn (ATA) 601 W National Rd	Vandalia	OH	45377	**800-671-8042**	037 808 1638
American Bicycle Assn (ABA) 1645 W Sunrise Blvd	Gilbert	AZ	85233	**866-650-4867**	480-961-1903
American Canoe Assn (ACA) 503 Sophia St Ste 100	Fredericksburg	VA	22401	**888-229-3792**	540-907-4460
American Council on Exercise (ACE) 4851 Paramount Dr	San Diego	CA	92123	**800-825-3636**	858-576-6500
American Football Coaches Assn (AFCA) 100 Legends Ln	Waco	TX	76706	**877-557-5338**	254-754-9900
American Motorcyclist Assn (AMA) 13515 Yarmouth Dr	Pickerington	OH	43147	**800-262-5646**	614-856-1900
American Running Assn 4405 E W Hwy Ste 405	Bethesda	MD	20814	**800-776-2732**	301-913-9517
American Youth Soccer Organization (AYSO) 19750 S Vermont Ave Ste 200	Torrance	CA	90502	**800-872-2976**	
AMOA-National Dart Assn (NDA) 10070 W 190th Pl	Mokena	IL	60448	**800-808-9884**	
Babe Ruth League Inc 1770 Brunswick Pk PO Box 5000	Trenton	NJ	08638	**800-880-3142**	609-695-1434
Boat Owners Assn of the US 880 S Pickett St	Alexandria	VA	22304	**800-395-2628**	703-823-9550
Cross Country Ski Areas Assn (CCSAA) 259 Bolton Rd	Winchester	NH	03470	**877-779-2754**	603-239-4341
Disabled Sports USA (DS/USA) 451 Hungerford Dr Ste 100	Rockville	MD	20850	**800-543-2754**	301-217-0960
Fellowship of Christian Athletes (FCA) 8701 Leeds Rd	Kansas City	MO	64129	**800-289-0909**	816-921-0909
Hockey North America (HNA) 45570 Shepard Dr	Sterling	VA	20164	**800-446-2539**	703-430-8100
IDEA Inc 10455 Pacific Ctr Ct	San Diego	CA	92121	**800-999-4332**	858-535-8979
International Collegiate Licensing Assn (ICLA) 24651 Detroit Rd	Westlake	OH	44145	**877-887-2261**	440-892-4000
International Health Racquet & Sportsclub Assn (IHRSA) 70 Fargo St	Boston	MA	02210	**800-228-4772**	617-951-0055
International Professional Rodeo Assn (IPRA) 1412 S Agnew	Oklahoma City	OK	73108	**800-639-9002**	405-235-6540
Jockeys' Guild Inc 448 Lewis Hargett Cir Ste 220	Lexington	KY	40503	**866-465-6257**	859-523-5625
Little League Baseball Inc 539 US Rt 15 Hwy PO Box 3485	Williamsport	PA	17701	**800-811-7443**	570-326-1921
NA of Collegiate Directors of Athletics (NACDA) 24651 Detroit Rd	Westlake	OH	44145	**877-887-2261**	440-892-4000
National Aeronautic Association Hanger 7 Ste 202	Washington	DC	20001	**800-644-9777**	703-416-4888
National Alliance for Youth Sports 2050 Vista Pkwy	West Palm Beach	FL	33411	**800-729-2057**	561-684-1141
National Archery Association of the United States (NAA) 4065 Sinton Rd Ste 110	Colorado Springs	CO	80907	**800-775-8762**	719-866-4576
National Athletic Trainers Assn (NATA) 2952 N Stemmons Fwy Ste 200	Dallas	TX	75247	**800-879-6282**	214-637-6282
National Basketball Players Assn (NBPA) 1133 Avenue of Americas	New York	NY	10036	**800-955-6272**	212-655-0880
National Federation of State High School Assn (NFHS) PO Box 690 *Cust Svc	Indianapolis	IN	46206	**800-776-3462***	317-972-6900
National Football League Players (NFLPA) 1133 20th St NW	Washington	DC	20036	**800-372-2000**	
National Golf Foundation (NGF) 1150 S US Hwy 1 Ste 401	Jupiter	FL	33477	**800-733-6006**	561-744-6006
National Greyhound Assn (NGA) 729 Old US 40	Abilene	KS	67410	**800-366-1471**	785-263-4660
National Little Britches Rodeo Assn (NLBRA) 5050 Edison Ave Ste 105	Colorado Springs	CO	80915	**800-763-3694**	719-389-0333
National Senior Golf Assn (NSGA) 200 Perrine Rd Ste 201	Old Bridge	NJ	08857	**800-282-6772**	
National Soccer Coaches Assn of America (NSCAA) 800 Ann Ave	Kansas City	KS	66101	**800-458-0678**	913-362-1747
National Strength & Conditioning Assn (NSCA) 1885 Bob Johnson Dr	Colorado Springs	CO	80906	**800-815-6826**	719-632-6722
National Thoroughbred Racing Assn (NTRA) 2525 Harrodsburg Rd Ste 510	Lexington	KY	40504	**800-792-6872**	
National Youth Sports Coaches Assn (NYSCA) 2050 Vista Pkwy	West Palm Beach	FL	33411	**800-729-2057**	561-684-1141
PGA of America 100 Ave of the Champions	Palm Beach Gardens	FL	33418	**800-477-6465**	561-624-8400
PONY Baseball/Softball Inc 1951 Pony Pl PO Box 225	Washington	PA	15301	**800-853-2414**	724-225-1060
Professional Assn of Diving Instructors International (PADI) 30151 Tomas St *Sales	Rancho Santa Margarita	CA	92688	**800-729-7234***	949-858-7234
Professional Rodeo Cowboys Assn (PRCA) 101 Pro Rodeo Dr	Colorado Springs	CO	80919	**800-234-7722**	719-593-8840
Professional Tennis Registry PO Box 4739	Hilton Head Island	SC	29938	**800-421-6289**	843-785-7244
Senior Softball USA 9823 Old Winery Pl Ste 12	Sacramento	CA	95827	**800-327-0074**	916-326-5303
Special Olympics Inc 1133 19th St NW	Washington	DC	20036	**800-700-8585**	202-628-3630
Sports Turf Managers Assn (STMA) 805 New Hampshire Ste E	Lawrence	KS	66044	**800-323-3875**	785-843-2549
Thoroughbred Racing Associations of North America Inc (TRA) 420 Fair Hill Dr	Elkton	MD	21921	**866-847-8772**	410-392-9200
US Biathlon Assn 49 Pineland Dr Ste 301-A *General	New Gloucester	ME	04260	**800-242-8456***	207-688-6500
US Curling Assn (USCA) 5525 Clem's Way	Stevens Point	WI	54482	**888-287-5377**	715-344-1199
US Equestrian Federation Inc 4047 Iron Works Pkwy	Lexington	KY	40511	**800-633-2472**	859-258-2472
US Figure Skating Assn (USFSA) 20 First St	Colorado Springs	CO	80906	**800-332-9256**	719-635-5200
US Golf Assn (USGA) 77 Liberty Corner Rd *Orders	Far Hills	NJ	07931	**800-336-4446***	908-234-2300
US Professional Tennis Assn (USPTA) 11961 Performance Dr	Orlando	FL	32827	**800-877-8248**	
US Rowing Assn 2 Wall St	Princeton	NJ	08540	**800-314-4769**	609-924-1578
US Sailing Assn 15 Maritime Dr PO Box 1260	Portsmouth	RI	02871	**800-877-2451**	401-683-0800
US Synchronized Swimming 1 Olympic Plz	Colorado Springs	CO	80909	**800-775-8762**	317-237-5700
US Trotting Assn (USTA) 750 Michigan Ave	Columbus	OH	43215	**877-800-8782**	614-224-2291
USA Baseball 403 Blackwell St	Durham	NC	27701	**855-420-5910**	919-474-8721
USA Basketball 5465 Mark Dabling Blvd	Colorado Springs	CO	80918	**888-284-5383**	719-590-4800
USA Gymnastics 201 S Capitol Ave Ste 300	Indianapolis	IN	46225	**800-345-4719**	317-237-5050
USA Hockey 1775 Bob Johnson Dr	Colorado Springs	CO	80906	**800-566-3288**	800-383-1379
USA Swimming 1 Olympic Plz	Colorado Springs	CO	80909	**800-356-2722**	719-866-4578
USA Track & Field Inc (USATF) 132 E Washington St Ste 800	Indianapolis	IN	46204	**800-222-8733**	317-261-0500
USA Water Polo 2124 Main St Ste 240	Huntington Beach	CA	92648	**888-712-2166**	714-500-5445
USA Water Ski 1251 Holy Cow Rd	Polk City	FL	33868	**800-533-2972**	863-324-4341
Women's Sports Foundation 1899 Hempstead Tpke Ste 400 Eisenhower Pk	East Meadow	NY	11554	**800-227-3988**	516-542-4700

48-23 Travel & Recreation Organizations

Organization / Address	City	State	Zip	Toll-Free	Phone
Adirondack Mountain Club 814 Goggins Rd *Orders	Lake George	NY	12845	**800-395-8080***	518-668-4447
Alberta Hotel & Lodging Assn (AHLA) 2707 Ellwood Dr	Edmonton	AB	T6X0P7	**888-436-6112**	780-436-6112
America Outdoors 5816 Kingston Pk	Knoxville	TN	37919	**800-524-4814**	
American Camp Assn (ACA) 5000 State Rd 67 N	Martinsville	IN	46151	**800-428-2267**	765-342-8456
American Hiking Society (AHS) 8605 Second Ave	Silver Spring	MD	20910	**800-972-8608**	301-565-6704
American Park & Recreation Society (APRS) 22377 Belmont Ridge Rd	Ashburn	VA	20148	**800-765-3110**	703-858-0784
American Society of Travel Agents (ASTA) 675 N Washington St Ste 490	Alexandria	VA	22314	**800-275-2782**	703-739-2782
American Trails PO Box 491797	Redding	CA	96049	**866-363-7226**	530-605-4395
American Whitewater (AW) PO Box 1540	Cullowhee	NC	28723	**866-262-8429**	828-586-1930
Amusement & Music Operators Assn (AMOA) 380 Terra Cotta Rd Ste F	Crystal Lake	IL	60012	**800-937-2662**	815-893-6010
Appalachian Mountain Club (AMC) 5 Joy St *Orders	Boston	MA	02108	**800-262-4455***	617-523-0655
Appalachian Trail Conservancy (ATC) 799 Washington St PO Box 807 *Sales	Harpers Ferry	WV	25425	**888-287-8673***	304-535-6331
Association of Corporate Travel Executives (ACTE) 526 King St Ste 215	Alexandria	VA	22314	**800-228-3669**	703-683-5322
Back Country Horsemen of America (BCHA) 59 Rainbow Rd	East Granby	CT	06029	**888-893-5161**	860-586-7540
Bowling Proprietors' Assn of America (BPAA) 621 Six Flags Dr PO Box 5802	Arlington	TX	76011	**800-343-1329**	
Canadian Automobile Assn (CAA) 2151 Thurston Dr	Ottawa	ON	K1G6C9	**800-267-8713**	613-820-1890
Colorado Dude & Guest Ranch Assn (CDGRA) PO Box D	Shawnee	CO	80475	**866-942-3472**	

Classified Section

			Toll-Free	Phone

Cruise Lines International Assn (CLIA)
1201 F St NW Ste 250 . . . . Washington DC 20004 — 855-444-2542 — 202-759-9370
Dude Ranchers Assn
1122 12th St PO Box 2307 . . . . Cody WY 82414 — 866-399-2339 — 307-587-2339
Elderhostel Inc
11 Ave de Lafayette . . . . Boston MA 02111 — 800-454-5768
Escapees RV Club
100 Rainbow Dr . . . . Livingston TX 77351 — 888-757-2582
Family Campers & RVers (FCRV)
4804 Transit Rd Bldg 2 . . . . Depew NY 14043 — 800-245-9755
Family Motor Coach Assn (FMCA)
8291 Clough Pk . . . . Cincinnati OH 45244 — 800-543-3622 — 513-474-3622
Global Business Travel Assn, The (GBTA)
123 N Pitt St . . . . Alexandria VA 22314 — 888-574-6447 — 703-684-0836
Good Sam Club PO Box 6888 . . . . Englewood CO 80155 — 800-234-3450
Hostelling International USA - American Youth Hostels (HI-AYH)
8401 Colesville Rd Ste 600 . . . . Silver Spring MD 20910 — 888-449-8727 — 240-650-2100
International Airline Passengers Assn (IAPA)
PO Box 700188 . . . . Dallas TX 75370 — 800-821-4272 — 972-404-9980
International Assn of Fairs & Expositions, The (IAFE)
3043 E Cairo St . . . . Springfield MO 65802 — 800-516-0313 — 417-862-5771
Leave No Trace Ctr for Outdoor Ethics Inc
1830 17th St . . . . Boulder CO 80302 — 800-332-4100 — 303-442-8222
Lewis & Clark Trail Heritage Foundation
4201 Giant Springs Rd . . . . Great Falls MT 59405 — 888-701-3434 — 406-454-1234
Mountaineers, The
7700 Sand Pt Way NE . . . . Seattle WA 98115 — 800-573-8484 — 206-521-6000
National Club Assn (NCA)
1201 15th St NW Ste 450 . . . . Washington DC 20005 — 800-625-6221 — 202-822-9822
National Golf Course Owners Assn (NGCOA)
291 Seven Farms Dr 2nd Fl . . . . Charleston SC 29492 — 800-933-4262 — 843-881-9956
National Recreation & Park Assn (NSPR)
22377 Belmont Ridge Rd . . . . Ashburn VA 20148 — 800-626-6772
National Tour Assn (NTA)
546 E Main St . . . . Lexington KY 40508 — 800-682-8886 — 859-226-4444
North Country Trail Assn
229 E Main St . . . . Lowell MI 49331 — 866-445-3628 — 616-897-5987
Oregon-California Trails Assn
524 S Osage St PO Box 1019 . . . . Independence MO 64051 — 888-811-6282 — 816-252-2276
RVing Women (RVW)
879 N Plaza Dr Ste B103 . . . . Apache Junction AZ 85120 — 888-557-8464 — 480-671-6226
Special Military Active Retired Travel Club (SMART)
600 University Office Blvd Ste 1A . . . . Pensacola FL 32504 — 800-354-7681 — 850-478-1986
Travel Institute
945 Concord St . . . . Framingham MA 01701 — 800-542-4282 — 781-237-0280
Wilderness Inquiry (WI)
808 14th Ave SE . . . . Minneapolis MN 55414 — 800-728-0719 — 612-676-9400

48-24 Women's Organizations

			Toll-Free	Phone

Equal Rights Advocates (ERA)
1170 Market St Ste 700 . . . . San Francisco CA 94102 — 800-839-4372 — 415-621-0672
General Federation of Women's Clubs (GFWC)
1734 N St NW . . . . Washington DC 20036 — 800-443-4392 — 202-347-3168
Girls Inc
120 Wall St 18th Fl . . . . New York NY 10005 — 800-374-4475 — 212-509-2000
International Alliance for Women (TIAW)
1101 Pennsylvania Ave NW 3rd Fl . . . . . . Washington DC 20004 — 888-712-5200
National Organization for Women (NOW)
1100 H St NW 3rd Fl . . . . Washington DC 20005 — 855-212-0212 — 202-628-8669
Ninety-Nines Inc
4300 Amelia Earhart Rd . . . . Oklahoma City OK 73159 — 800-994-1929 — 405-685-7969
Wider Opportunities for Women (WOW)
1001 Connecticut Ave NW Ste 930 . . . . . . Washington DC 20036 — 800-260-5956 — 202-464-1596
Women's Sports Foundation
1899 Hempstead Tpke
Ste 400 Eisenhower Pk . . . . East Meadow NY 11554 — 800-227-3988 — 516-542-4700

49   ASSOCIATIONS & ORGANIZATIONS - PROFESSIONAL & TRADE

SEE ALSO Bar Associations - State; Library Associations - State & Province; Pharmacy Associations - State; Medical Associations - State; Realtor Associations - State; Labor Unions; Veterinary Medical Associations - State; Dental Associations - State; Nurses Associations - State

49-1 Accountants Associations

			Toll-Free	Phone

AGN International-North America
2851 S Parker Rd Ste 850 . . . . Aurora CO 80014 — 800-782-2272 — 303-743-7880
American Institute of Certified Public Accountants (AICPA)
1211 Ave of the Americas . . . . New York NY 10036 — 888-777-7077 — 212-596-6200
American Institute of Professional Bookkeepers (AIPB)
6001 Montrose Rd Ste 500 . . . . Rockville MD 20852 — 800-622-0121
Association of Certified Fraud Examiners (ACFE)
716 W Ave . . . . Austin TX 78701 — 800-245-3321 — 512-478-9000
Association of Government Accountants (AGA)
2208 Mt Vernon Ave . . . . Alexandria VA 22301 — 800-242-7211 — 703-684-6931
Association of Healthcare Internal Auditors (AHIA)
10200 W 44th Ave Ste 304 . . . . Wheat Ridge CO 80033 — 888-275-2442 — 303-327-7546
Construction Financial Management Assn (CFMA)
100 Village Blvd Ste 200 . . . . Princeton NJ 08540 — 888-421-9996 — 609-452-8000
CPA Auto Dealer Consultants Assn (CADCA)
1801 W End Ave Ste 800 . . . . Nashville TN 37203 — 800-231-2524 — 615-373-9880
Financial Acctg Standards Board (FASB)
401 Merritt 7 PO Box 5116 . . . . Norwalk CT 06856 — 800-748-0659 — 203-847-0700
Foundation for Acctg Education (FAE)
14 Wall St 19th Fl . . . . New York NY 10005 — 800-537-3635* — 212-719-8300
*General
Hospitality Financial & Technology Professionals (HFTP)
11709 Boulder Ln Ste 110 . . . . Austin TX 78726 — 800-646-4387 — 512-249-5333
Institute of Management Accountants Inc (IMA)
10 Paragon Dr Ste 1 . . . . Montvale NJ 07645 — 800-638-4427 — 201-573-9000

			Toll-Free	Phone

International Federation of Accountants (IFAC)
545 Fifth Ave 14th Fl . . . . New York NY 10017 — 888-272-2001 — 212-286-9344
National Acctg & Finance Council (NAFC)
American Trucking Assn
950 N Glebe Rd. . . . . Arlington VA 22203 — 800-517-7370 — 703-838-1700
National Association of Nonprofit Accountants & Consultants (NSA)
1801 W End Ave Ste 800 . . . . Nashville TN 37203 — 800-231-2524 — 615-373-9880
National CPA Health Care Advisors Assn (HCAA)
1801 W End Ave Ste 800 . . . . Nashville TN 37203 — 800-231-2524 — 615-373-9880
National Society of Accountants (NSA)
1010 N Fairfax St . . . . Alexandria VA 22314 — 800-966-6679 — 703-549-6400

49-2 Banking & Finance Professionals Associations

			Toll-Free	Phone

ABA Marketing Network
1120 Connecticut Ave NW . . . . Washington DC 20036 — 800-226-5377 — 202-663-5000
Accuplan Benefits Services
515 East 4500 South Ste G200 . . . . Salt Lake City UT 84107 — 800-454-2649 — 801-266-9900
America's Community Bankers (ACB)
1120 Connecticut Ave NW . . . . Washington DC 20036 — 800-226-5377
American Assn of Daily Money Managers (AADMM)
174 Crestview Dr . . . . Bellefonte PA 16823 — 877-326-5991
American Assn of Individual Investors (AAII)
625 N Michigan Ave Ste 1900 . . . . Chicago IL 60611 — 800-428-2244 — 312-280-0170
American Bankers Assn (ABA)
1120 Connecticut Ave NW . . . . Washington DC 20036 — 800-226-5377*
*Cust Svc
American Benefits Council
1501 M St NW Ste 600. . . . . Washington DC 20005 — 877-829-5500 — 202-289-6700
American Finance Assn (AFA)
101 Station Landing 350 Main St
Ste 300 . . . . Medford MA 02155 — 800-835-6770 — 781-388-8599
Bank Administration Institute (BAI)
115 S LaSalle St Ste 3300 . . . . Chicago IL 60603 — 800-224-9889* — 312-683-2464
*Cust Svc
Better Investing
PO Box 220 . . . . Royal Oak MI 48068 — 877-275-6242 — 248-583-6242
Certified Financial Planner Board of Standards Inc
1425 K St NW Ste 500 . . . . Washington DC 20005 — 800-487-1497 — 202-379-2200
CFA Institute
915 E High St . . . . Charlottesville VA 22902 — 800-247-8132 — 434-951-5499
Community Banking Advisory Network (CBAN)
1801 W End Ave Ste 800 . . . . Nashville TN 37203 — 800-231-2524 — 615-373-9880
Credit Union Executives Society (CUES)
5510 Research Pk Dr . . . . Madison WI 53711 — 800-252-2664 — 608-271-2664
Financial Industry Regulatory Authority (FINRA)
9509 Key W Ave . . . . Rockville MD 20850 — 800-321-6273 — 301-590-6500
Financial Managers Society (FMS)
100 W Monroe St Ste 810 . . . . Chicago IL 60603 — 800-275-4367* — 312-578-1300
*Cust Svc
Financial Planning Assn (FPA)
7535 E Hampden Ave Ste 600 . . . . Denver CO 80231 — 800-322-4237 — 303-759-4900
FINRA 1735 K St NW . . . . Washington DC 20006 — 800-289-9999 — 202-728-8000
Independent Community Bankers of America (ICBA)
1615 L St NW Ste 900 . . . . Washington DC 20036 — 800-422-8439 — 202-659-8111
Investments & Wealth Institute (IMCA)
5619 DTC Pkwy Ste 500. . . . . Greenwood Village CO 80111 — 800-250-9083 — 303-770-3377
Mortgage Bankers Assn (MBA)
1919 M St NW 5th Fl . . . . Washington DC 20036 — 800-793-6222 — 202-557-2700
NACHA - Electronic Payments Association
2550 Wasser Terr Ste 400 . . . . Herndon VA 20171 — 800-487-9180 — 703-561-1100
National Association of Federally-Insured Credit Unions (NAFCU)
3138 Tenth St N . . . . Arlington VA 22201 — 800-336-4644 — 703-522-4770
National Federation of Community Development Credit Unions (NFCDCU)
39 Broadway Ste 2140 . . . . New York NY 10006 — 800-437-8711 — 212-809-1850
National Futures Assn (NFA)
300 S Riverside Plz Ste 1800 . . . . Chicago IL 60606 — 800-621-3570 — 312-781-1300
National Investment Co Service Assn (NICSA)
8400 Westpark Dr 2nd Fl . . . . Mclean VA 22102 — 800-426-1122 — 508-485-1500
Risk Management Assn (RMA)
1801 Market St Ste 300 . . . . Philadelphia PA 19103 — 800-677-7621* — 215-446-4000
*Cust Svc
Secure Technology Alliance
191 Clarkville Rd . . . . Princeton Junction NJ 08550 — 800-556-6828

49-3 Construction Industry Associations

			Toll-Free	Phone

Air Conditioning Contractors of America (ACCA)
2800 S Shirlington Rd Ste 300 . . . . Arlington VA 22206 — 888-290-2220 — 703-575-4477
American Concrete Pavement Assn (ACPA)
5420 Old OrchaRd Rd Ste A-100 . . . . Skokie IL 60077 — 800-281-7899 — 847-966-2272
American Fence Association (AFA)
6404 Internationa Pkwy Ste 2250-A . . . . Plano TX 75093 — 800-822-4342
American Road & Transportation Builders Assn (ARTBA)
1219 28th St NW . . . . Washington DC 20007 — 800-636-2377 — 202-289-4434
American Society of Heating Refrigerating & Air-Conditioning Engineers Inc (ASHRAE)
1791 Tullie Cir NE . . . . Atlanta GA 30329 — 800-527-4723* — 404-636-8400
*Cust Svc
American Society of Home Inspectors (ASHI)
932 Lee St Ste 101 . . . . Des Plaines IL 60016 — 800-743-2744 — 847-759-2820
American Society of Professional Estimators (ASPE)
2525 Perimeter Pl Dr Ste 103 . . . . Nashville TN 37214 — 888-378-6283 — 615-316-9200
American Welding Society (AWS)
550 NW 42nd Ave . . . . Miami FL 33126 — 800-443-9353 — 305-443-9353
Asphalt Roofing Manufacturers Assn (ARMA)
529 14th St NW Ste 750 . . . . Washington DC 20045 — 800-247-6637 — 202-207-0917
Associated Builders & Contractors Inc (ABC)
4250 Fairfax Dr . . . . Arlington VA 22203 — 877-889-5627 — 202-595-1505
Associated General Contractors of America (AGC)
2300 Wilson Blvd Ste 300 . . . . Arlington VA 22201 — 800-242-1766 — 703-548-3118
Associated Locksmiths of America (ALOA)
3500 Easy St . . . . Dallas TX 75247 — 800-532-2562 — 214-819-9733
Association of the Wall & Ceiling Industries International (AWCI)
513 W Broad St Ste 210 . . . . Falls Church VA 22046 — 800-233-8990 — 703-538-1600

	Toll-Free	Phone
Brick Industry Assn (BIA)		
12007 Sunrise Valley Dr Ste 430 .... Reston VA 20191	866-644-1293	703-620-0010
Building Material Dealers Assn (BMDA)		
1006 SE Grand Ave Ste 301 .... Portland OR 97214	888-960-6329	503-208-3763
Ceilings & Interior Systems Construction Assn (CISCA)		
1010 Jorie Blvd Ste 30 .... Oak Brook IL 60523	866-560-8537	630-584-1919
Composite Panel Assn		
19465 Deerfield Ave Ste 306 .... Leesburg VA 20176	866-426-6767	703-724-1128
Construction Financial Management Assn (CFMA)		
100 Village Blvd Ste 200 .... Princeton NJ 08540	888-421-9996	609-452-8000
Electronic Security Assn Inc (ESA)		
6333 North State Hwy 161 Ste 350 .... Irving TX 75038	888-447-1689	972-807-6800
Interlocking Concrete Pavement Institute (ICPI)		
14801 Murdock St Ste 230 .... Chantilly VA 20151	800-241-3652	703-657-6900
International Assn of Electrical Inspectors (IAEI)		
901 Waterfall Way Ste 602 .... Richardson TX 75080	800-786-4234	972-235-1455
International Code Council (ICC)		
500 New Jersey Ave NW 6th Fl .... Washington DC 20001	888-422-7233	202-370-1800
International Masonry Institute (IMI)		
17101 Science Dr .... Bowie MD 20715	800-803-0295	301-291-2124
International Wood Products Assn (IWPA)		
4214 King St .... Alexandria VA 22302	855-435-0005	703-820-6696
Mason Contractors Assn of America (MCCA) (MCAA)		
1481 Merchant Dr .... Algonquin IL 60102	800-536-2225	224-678-9709
Mechanical Contractors Assn of America (MCAA)		
1385 Piccard Dr .... Rockville MD 20850	800-556-3653	301-869-5800
Monument Builders of North America (MBNA)		
136 S Keowee St .... Dayton OH 45402	800-233-4472	
NA of Women in Construction (NAWIC)		
327 S Adams St .... Fort Worth TX 76104	800-552-3506	817-877-5551
National Association of Tower Erectors (NATE)		
8 Second St SE .... Watertown SD 57201	888-882-5865	605-882-5865
National Concrete Masonry Assn		
13750 Sunrise Vly Dr .... Herndon VA 20171	877-343-6268	703-713-1900
National Council of Examiners for Engineering & Surveying (NCEES)		
280 Seneca Creek Rd .... Seneca SC 29678	800-250-3196	864-654-6824
National Electrical Contractors Assn (NECA)		
3 Bethesda Metro Ctr Ste 1100 .... Bethesda MD 20814	800-214-0585	301-657-3110
National Frame Builders Assn (NFBA)		
8735 W Higgins Rd Ste 300 .... Chicago IL 60631	800-557-6957	
National Hardwood Lumber Assn (NHLA)		
6830 Raleigh-LaGrange Rd .... Memphis TN 38134	800-933-0318	901-377-1818
National Insulation Assn (NIA)		
99 Canal Ctr Plz Ste 222 .... Alexandria VA 22314	877-968-7642	703-683-6422
National Kitchen & Bath Assn (NKBA)		
687 Willow Grove St .... Hackettstown NJ 07840	800-843-6522	
National Parking Assn (NPA)		
1112 16th St NW Ste 840 .... Washington DC 20036	800-647-7275	202-296-4336
National Precast Concrete Assn (NPCA)		
10333 N Meridian St Ste 272 .... Indianapolis IN 46290	800-366-7731	317-571-9500
National Ready Mixed Concrete Assn (NRMCA)		
900 Spring St .... Silver Spring MD 20910	888-846-7622	301-587-1400
National Roofing Contractors Assn (NRCA)		
10255 W Higgins Rd Ste 600 .... Rosemont IL 60018	800-323-9545*	847-299-9070
*Cust Svc		
National Stone Sand & Gravel Assn (NSSGA)		
1605 King St .... Alexandria VA 22314	800-342-1415	703-525-8788
National Wood Flooring Assn (NWFA)		
111 Chesterfield Industrial Blvd		
.... Chesterfield MO 63005	800-422-4556	636-519-9663
North American Bldg Material Distribution Assn (NBMDA)		
330 N Wabash Ave Ste 2000 .... Chicago IL 60611	888-747-7862	312-321-6845
Operative Plasterers' & Cement Masons' International Assn (OPCMIA)		
9700 Patuxent Woods Dr Ste 200 .... Columbia MD 21046	888-379-1558	301-623-1000
Painting & Decorating Contractors of America (PDCA)		
2316 Millpark Dr .... Maryland Heights MO 63043	800-332-7322*	314-514-7322
*Cust Svc		
Plumbing-Heating-Cooling Contractors NA (PHCC)		
180 S Washington St Ste 100 .... Falls Church VA 22046	800-533-7694	703-237-8100
Refrigeration Service Engineers Society (RSES)		
1666 Rand Rd .... Des Plaines IL 60016	800-297-5660	847-297-6464
Smart Union (SMWIA)		
1750 New York Ave NW 6th Fl .... Washington DC 20006	800-457-7694	202-662-0800

49-4 Consumer Sales & Service Professionals Associations

	Toll-Free	Phone
American Apparel & Footwear Assn (AAFA)		
740 sixth St NW 3rd & 4th Fl .... Washington DC 20001	800-520-2262	202-853-9080
American Gem Society (AGS)		
8881 W Sahara Ave .... Las Vegas NV 89117	866-805-6500	702-255-6500
American Gem Trade Assn (AGTA)		
3030 LBJ Fwy Ste 840 .... Dallas TX 75234	800-972-1162	214-742-4367
American Lighting Assn (ALA)		
2050 Stemmons Fwy Ste 10046 .... Dallas TX 75207	800-605-4448	214-698-9898
American Pet Products Manufacturers Assn (APPMA)		
255 Glenville Rd .... Greenwich CT 06831	800-452-1225	203-532-0000
American Rental Assn (ARA)		
1900 19th St .... Moline IL 61265	800-334-2177	309-764-2475
American Watchmakers-Clockmakers Institute (AWI)		
701 Enterprise Dr .... Harrison OH 45030	866-367-2924	513-367-9800
Association for Linen Management		
138 N Keeneland Dr Ste D .... Richmond KY 40475	800-669-0863	859-624-0177
Association of Pool & Spa Professionals (APSP)		
2111 Eisenhower Ave Ste 500 .... Alexandria VA 22314	800-323-3996	703-838-0083
Automotive Recyclers Assn (ARA)		
9113 Church St .... Manassas VA 20110	888-385-1005	571-208-0428
Awards & Personalization Assn (ARA)		
8735 W Higgins Rd Ste 300 .... Chicago IL 60631	800-344-2148	847-375-4800
Coin Laundry Assn (CLA)		
1s660 Midwest Rd Ste 205 .... Oakbrook Terrace IL 60181	800-570-5629	630-953-7920
Contact Lens Manufacturers Assn		
PO Box 29398 .... Lincoln NE 68529	800-344-9060	402-465-4122
Diamond Council of America (DCA)		
3212 W End Ave Ste 202 .... Nashville TN 37203	877-283-5669	615-385-5301
Diving Equipment & Marketing Assn (DEMA)		
3750 Convoy St Ste 310 .... San Diego CA 92111	800-862-3483	858-616-6408

	Toll-Free	Phone
Drycleaning & Laundry Institute		
14700 Sweitzer Ln .... Laurel MD 20707	800-638-2627	301-622-1900
Gemological Institute of America (GIA)		
5345 Armada Dr .... Carlsbad CA 92008	800-421-7250	760-603-4000
Home Furnishings Independents Assn (HFIA)		
500 Giuseppe Ct Ste 6 .... Roseville CA 95678	800-422-3778	
Independent Jewelers Organization (IJO)		
136 Old Post Rd .... Southport CT 06890	800-624-9252	
Institute of Inspection Cleaning & Restoration Certification (IICRC)		
4043 S E Ave .... Las Vegas NV 89119	844-464-4272	
International Cemetery Cremation & Funeral Assn (ICCFA)		
107 Carpenter Dr Ste 100 .... Sterling VA 20164	800-645-7700	703-391-8400
International Engraved Graphics Assn		
305 Plus Pk Blvd .... Nashville TN 37217	800-821-3138	
International Executive Housekeepers Assn (IEHA)		
1001 Eastwind Dr Ste 301 .... Westerville OH 43081	800-200-6342	614-895-7166
International Housewares Assn (IHA)		
6400 Shafer Ct Ste 650 .... Rosemont IL 60018	800-752-1052	847-292-4200
International Order of the Golden Rule (OGR)		
3520 Executive Ctr Dr Ste 300 .... Austin TX 78731	800-637-8030	512-334-5504
Jewelers of America (JA)		
52 Vanderbilt Ave 19th Fl .... New York NY 10017	800-223-0673	646-658-0246
Leather Industries of America (LIA)		
3050 K St NW Ste 400 .... Washington DC 20007	800-635-0617	202-342-8497
Manufacturing Jewelers & Suppliers of America Inc (MJSA)		
57 John L Dietsch Sq .... Attleboro MA 02763	800-444-6572	401-274-3840
National Cleaners Assn		
252 W 29th St .... New York NY 10001	800-888-1622*	212-967-3002
*General		
National Funeral Directors & Morticians Assn (NFDMA)		
6290 Shannon Pkwy .... Union City GA 30291	800-434-0958	770-969-0064
National Funeral Directors Assn (NFDA)		
13625 Bishop's Dr .... Brookfield WI 53005	800-228-6332	262-789-1880
National Home Furnishings Assn (NHFA)		
500 Giuseppe Ct Ste 6 .... Roseville CA 95678	800-422-3778	
National Pest Management Assn Inc (NPMA)		
10460 N St .... Fairfax VA 22030	800-678-6722	703-352-6762
National Shoe Retailers Assn (NSRA)		
7386 N La Cholla Blvd .... Tucson AZ 85741	800-673-8446	520-209-1710
National Sporting Goods Assn (NSGA)		
1601 Feehanville Dr Ste 300 .... Mount Prospect IL 60056	800-815-5422	847-296-6742
Pet Industry Joint Advisory Council (PIJAC)		
1220 19th St NW Ste 400 .... Washington DC 20036	800-553-7387	202-452-1525
Recreation Vehicle Industry Assn (RVIA)		
1896 Preston White Dr .... Reston VA 20191	800-336-0154	703-620-6003
Security Industry Assn (SIA)		
8405 Colesville Rd Ste 500 .... Silver Spring MD 20910	866-817-8888	301-804-4700
Selected Independent Funeral Homes		
500 Lake Cook Rd Ste 205 .... Deerfield IL 60015	800-323-4219	847-236-9401
Society of American Florists (SAF)		
1601 Duke St .... Alexandria VA 22314	800-336-4743	703-836-8700
Textile Rental Services Assn (TRSA)		
1800 Diagonal Rd Ste 200 .... Alexandria VA 22314	877-770-9274	703-519-0029
Tire Industry Assn (TIA)		
1532 Pointer Ridge Pl Ste G .... Bowie MD 20716	800-876-8372	301-430-7280
Toy Industry Assn		
1115 Broadway Ste 400 .... New York NY 10010	800-541-1345	212-675-1141
Uniform & Textile Service Assn (UTSA)		
1300 N 17th St Ste 750 .... Arlington VA 22209	800-996-3426	703-247-2600
Vision Council, The		
225 Reinekers Ln Ste 700 .... Alexandria VA 22314	866-826-0290	703-548-4560
World Floor Covering Assn (WFCA)		
2211 Howell Ave .... Anaheim CA 92806	800-624-6880	714-978-6440

49-5 Education Professionals Associations

	Toll-Free	Phone
American Assn of Family & Consumer Sciences (AAFCS)		
400 N Columbus St Ste 202 .... Alexandria VA 22314	800-424-8080	703-706-4600
American Assn of Physics Teachers (AAPT)		
1 Physics Ellipse .... College Park MD 20740	800-446-8923	301-209-3311
American Assn of School Administrators (AASA)		
801 N Quincy St Ste 700 .... Arlington VA 22203	800-771-1162	703-528-0700
American Assn of State Colleges & Universities (AASCU)		
1307 New York Ave NW 5th Fl .... Washington DC 20005	800-558-3417	202-293-7070
American Assn of Teachers of German (AATG)		
112 Haddontowne Ct Ste 104 .... Cherry Hill NJ 08034	800-835-6770	856-795-5553
American Assn of University Professors (AAUP)		
1133 Nineteenth St Ste 200 .... Washington DC 20036	800-424-2973	202-737-5900
American Assn of University Women (AAUW)		
1111 16th St NW .... Washington DC 20036	800-326-2289	202-785-7700
American Association of Collegiate Registrars & Admissions Officers (AACRAO)		
1 Dupont Cir NW Ste 520 .... Washington DC 20036	800-222-4922	202-293-9161
American Dental Education Assn (ADEA)		
1400 K St NW Ste 1100 .... Washington DC 20005	800-353-2237	202-289-7201
American Educational Research Assn (AERA)		
1430 K St NW Ste 1200 .... Washington DC 20005	800-893-7950	202-238-3200
American Library Assn (ALA)		
50 E Huron St .... Chicago IL 60611	800-545-2433	312-944-6780
American Medical Student Assn (AMSA)		
1902 Assn Dr .... Reston VA 20191	800-767-2266	703-620-6600
American School Counselor Assn (ASCA)		
1101 King St Ste 625 .... Alexandria VA 22314	800-306-4722	703-683-2722
American Sociological Assn (ASA)		
1307 New York Ave .... Washington DC 20005	800-524-9400	202-383-9005
Association for Advanced Training in the Behavioral Sciences (AATBS)		
5126 Ralston St .... Ventura CA 93003	800-472-1931	805-676-3030
Association for Career & Technical Education (ACTE)		
1410 King St .... Alexandria VA 22314	800-826-9972	703-683-3111
Association for Childhood Education International (ACEI)		
1101 16th St NW Ste 300 .... Washington DC 20036	800-423-3563	202-372-9986
Association for Continuing Higher Education (ACHE)		
1700 Asp Ave .... Norman OK 73072	800-807-2243	
Association for Supervision & Curriculum Development (ASCD)		
1703 North Beauregard St .... Alexandria VA 22311	800-933-2723	703-578-9600

				Toll-Free	Phone
Association of Christian Schools International (ACSI)					
731 Chapel Hills Dr	Colorado Springs	CO	80920	800-367-0798*	719-528-6906
*Cust Svc					
Association of Community College Trustees (ACCT)					
1101 17th St NW Ste 300	Washington	DC	20036	866-895-2228	202-775-4667
Association of Governing Boards of Universities & Colleges (AGB)					
1133 20th St NW Ste 300	Washington	DC	20036	800-356-6317	202-296-8400
Association of School Business Officials International (ASBO)					
11401 N Shore Dr	Reston	VA	20190	866-682-2729	
Association of Test Publishers					
601 Pennsylvania Ave NW Ste 900	Washington	DC	20004	866-240-7909	
Association of Universities for Research in Astronomy (AURA)					
1200 New York Ave NW Ste 350	Washington	DC	20005	888-624-8373	202-483-2101
Association of University Centers on Disabilities (AUCD)					
1100 Wayne Ave Ste 1000	Silver Spring	MD	20910	888-572-2249	301-588-8252
Business Professionals of America					
5454 Cleveland Ave	Columbus	OH	43231	800-334-2007	614-895-7277
Christian Schools International (CSI)					
3350 E Paris Ave SE	Grand Rapids	MI	49512	800-635-8288	616-957-1070
College & University Professional Assn for Hum Res (CUPA-HR)					
1811 Commons Pt Dr	Knoxville	TN	37932	877-287-2474	865-637-7673
College Music Society (CMS)					
312 E Pine St	Missoula	MT	59802	800-729-0235	406-721-9616
Conference on College Composition & Communication (CCCC)					
1111 W Kenyon Rd	Urbana	IL	61801	877-369-6283	217-328-3870
Council for Advancement & Support of Education (CASE)					
1307 New York Ave NW Ste 1000	Washington	DC	20005	800-554-8536*	202-328-5900
*Orders					
Council for Professional Recognition					
2460 16th St NW	Washington	DC	20009	800-424-4310	202-265-9090
Council of Administrators of Special Education (CASE)					
Osigian Office Centre 101 Katelyn Cir					
Ste E	Warner Robins	GA	31088	800-585-1753	478-333-6892
Council on International Educational Exchange (CIEE)					
300 Fore St	Portland	ME	04101	888-268-6245*	207-553-4000
*Cust Svc					
Educational Housing Services Inc					
55 Clark St	Brooklyn	NY	11201	800-385-1689	800-297-4694
Hispanic Assn of Colleges & Universities (HACU)					
8415 Datapoint Dr Ste 400	San Antonio	TX	78229	800-780-4228	210-692-3805
International Society for Technology in Education (ISTE)					
1530 Wilson Blvd Ste 730	Arlington	VA	22209	800-336-5191*	
*General					
Languages Canada					
27282 - 12B AVE	Aldergrove	BC	V4W2P6	888-277-0522	604-574-1532
MENC: NA for Music Education					
1806 Robert Fulton Dr	Reston	VA	20191	800-336-3768	703-860-4000
Modern Language Assn (MLA)					
26 Broadway 3rd Fl.	New York	NY	10004	800-323-4900	646-576-5000
MSDSonline					
222 Merchandise Mart Plz Ste 1750.	Chicago	IL	60654	888-362-2007	312-881-2000
Music Teachers NA (MTNA)					
441 Vine St Ste 3100	Cincinnati	OH	45202	888-512-5278	513-421-1420
NA of Colleges & Employers (NACE)					
62 Highland Ave	Bethlehem	PA	18017	800-544-5272	610-868-1421
National Art Education Assn (NAEA)					
1806 Robert Fulton Dr	Reston	VA	20191	800-299-8321	703-860-8000
National Association of Elementary School Principals (NAESP)					
1615 Duke St	Alexandria	VA	22314	800-386-2377	703-684-3345
National Association of State Boards of Education (NASBE)					
333 John Carlyle St Ste 530	Alexandria	VA	22314	800-899-6693	703-684-4000
National Catholic Educational Assn (NCEA)					
1005 N Glebe St Ste 525	Arlington	VA	22201	800-711-6232	571-257-0010
National Council for the Social Studies (NCSS)					
8555 16th St Ste 500	Silver Spring	MD	20910	800-683-0812*	301-588-1800
*Orders					
National Council of Teachers of English (NCTE)					
1111 W Kenyon Rd	Urbana	IL	61801	877-369-6283	217-328-3870
National Council of Teachers of Mathematics (NCTM)					
1906 Assn Dr	Reston	VA	20191	800-235-7566*	703-620-9840
*Orders					
National Council on Economic Education (NCEE)					
122 E 42nd St Ste 2600	New York	NY	10168	800-338-1192	212-730-7007
National Education Assn (NEA)					
1201 16th St NW	Washington	DC	20036	888-552-0624	202-833-4000
National Guild for Community Arts Education					
520 Eighth Ave Ste 302	New York	NY	10018	800-441-1414	212-268-3337
National Middle School Assn (NMSA)					
4151 Executive Pkwy Ste 300	Westerville	OH	43081	800-528-6672	614-895-4730
National Science Teachers Assn (NSTA)					
1840 Wilson Blvd	Arlington	VA	22201	800-722-6782*	703-243-7100
*Sales					
National Staff Development Council (NSDC)					
504 S Locust St	Oxford	OH	45056	800-727-7288	513-523-6029
North Central Assn Higher Learning Commission					
230 S LaSalle St	Chicago	IL	60604	800-621-7440	312-263-0456
Society for American Archaeology (SAA)					
900 Second St NE Ste 12	Washington	DC	20002	800-759-5219	202-789-8200
Southern Assn of Colleges & Schools					
1866 Southern Ln	Decatur	GA	30033	888-413-3669	404-679-4500
Teach For America					
315 W 36th St 7th Fl.	New York	NY	10018	800-832-1230	212-279-2080
Teachers of English to Speakers of Other Languages (TESOL)					
700 S Washington St Ste 200	Alexandria	VA	22314	888-547-3369	703-836-0774
Teaching & Mentoring Communities (TMC)					
PO Box 2579	Laredo	TX	78044	888-836-5151	956-722-5174
Torah Umesorah-National Society for Hebrew Day Schools					
620 Foster Ave	Brooklyn	NY	11230	800-788-3942	212-227-1000
Washington Education Assn Inc					
32032 Weyerhaeuser Way S					
PO Box 9100	Federal Way	WA	98001	800-622-3393	253-941-6700

49-6 Food & Beverage Industries Professional Associations

				Toll-Free	Phone
American Culinary Federation Inc (ACF)					
180 Ctr Pl Way	Saint Augustine	FL	32095	800-624-9458	904-824-4468

				Toll-Free	Phone
American Society for Nutrition (ASNS)					
9211 Corporate Blvd Ste 300	Rockville	MD	20850	800-627-8723	240-428-3650
Beer Institute					
440 First St NW Ste 350	Washington	DC	20001	800-379-2739	202-737-2337
Food Marketing Institute (FMI)					
2345 Crystal Dr Ste 800	Arlington	VA	22202	800-732-2639	202-452-8444
Institute of Food Technologists (IFT)					
525 W Van Buren St Ste 1000	Chicago	IL	60607	800-438-3663	312-782-8424
International Assn for Food Protection (IAFP)					
6200 Aurora Ave Ste 200W.	Des Moines	IA	50322	800-369-6337*	515-276-3344
*General					
International Assn of Culinary Professionals (IACP)					
45 Rockefeller Plz Ste 2000	New York	NY	10111	855-738-4227	
International Bottled Water Association (IBWA)					
1700 Diagonal Rd Ste 650	Alexandria	VA	22314	800-928-3711	703-683-5213
International Dairy-Deli-Bakery Assn (IDDBA)					
636 Science Dr	Madison	WI	53711	877-399-4925	608-310-5000
International Food Information Council Foundation (IFIC)					
1100 Connecticut Ave NW Ste 430.	Washington	DC	20036	888-723-3366	202-296-6540
National Beer Wholesalers Assn (NBWA)					
1101 King St Ste 600	Alexandria	VA	22314	800-300-6417	703-683-4300
National Grocers Assn (NGA)					
1005 N Glebe Rd Ste 250	Arlington	VA	22201	800-627-6667	703-516-0700
National Pork Producers Council (NPPC)					
122 C St NW Ste 875	Washington	DC	20001	800-952-4629	202-347-3600
National Restaurant Assn (NRA)					
2055 L St NW Ste 700	Washington	DC	20036	800-424-5156	202-331-5900
North American Millers Assn (NAMA)					
600 Maryland Ave SW Ste 825-W	Washington	DC	20024	800-633-5137	202-484-2200
Retail Confectioners International (RCI)					
3029 E Sunshine St Ste A.	Springfield	MO	65804	800-545-5381	417-883-2775
School Nutrition Assn (SNA)					
700 S Washington St Ste 300	Alexandria	VA	22314	800-877-8822	703-739-3900
SNAC international					
1600 Wilson Blvd Ste 650	Arlington	VA	22209	800-628-1334	703-836-4500
Specialty Coffee Assn of America (SCAA)					
117 W Fourth St Ste 300	Santa Ana	CA	92701	800-995-9019	562-624-4100
Wheat Foods Council					
51 Red Fox Ln Unit D	Ridgway	CO	81432	800-970-2254	
Wine & Spirits Shippers Assn Inc (WSSA)					
11800 Sunrise Vly Dr	Reston	VA	20191	800-368-3167*	
*General					

49-7 Government & Public Administration Professional Associations

				Toll-Free	Phone
American Assn of Motor Vehicle Administrators (AAMVA)					
4301 Wilson Blvd Ste 400	Arlington	VA	22203	800-221-9253	703-522-4200
American Correctional Assn (ACA)					
206 N Washington St Ste 200.	Alexandria	VA	22314	800-222-5646	703-224-0000
American Foreign Service Assn (AFSA)					
2101 E St NW	Washington	DC	20037	800-704-2372	202-338-4045
American Jail Assn (AJA)					
1135 Professional Ct	Hagerstown	MD	21740	800-211-2754	301-790-3930
American Public Works Assn (APWA)					
2345 Grand Blvd Ste 700	Kansas City	MO	64108	800-848-2792	816-472-6100
Association of Public Health Laboratories (APHL)					
8515 Georgia Ave Ste 700	Silver Spring	MD	20910	800-899-2278	240-485-2745
Association of Public-Safety Communications Officials International Inc					
351 N Williamson Blvd	Daytona Beach	FL	32114	888-272-6911	386-322-2500
Association of Social Work Boards (ASWB)					
400 S Ridge Pkwy Ste B	Culpeper	VA	22701	800-225-6880	540-829-6880
Association of State Wetland Managers					
32 Tandberg Trl Ste 2A	Windham	ME	04062	800-451-6027	207-892-3399
Commission on Accreditation for Law Enforcement Agencies (CALEA)					
13575 Heathcote Blvd Ste 320	Gainesville	VA	20155	877-789-6904	703-352-4225
Council of State Governments (CSG)					
2760 Research Pk Dr	Lexington	KY	40511	800-800-1910*	859-244-8000
*Sales					
Federation of State Medical Boards of the US Inc (FSMB)					
400 Fuller Wiser Rd Ste 300.	Euless	TX	76039	800-793-7939	817-868-4000
Federation of Tax Administrators (FTA)					
444 N Capitol St NW Ste 348	Washington	DC	20001	800-829-9188	202-624-5890
International Assn of Arson Investigators (IAAI)					
2111 Baldwin Ave # 203	Crofton	MD	21114	800-468-4224	410-451-3473
International Assn of Assessing Officers (IAAO)					
314 W Tenth St	Kansas City	MO	64105	800-616-4226	816-701-8100
International Assn of Chiefs of Police (IACP)					
44 Canal Ctr Plz Ste 200.	Alexandria	VA	22314	800-843-4227	703-836-6767
International Assn of Fire Chiefs (IAFC)					
4025 Fair Ridge Dr Ste 300	Fairfax	VA	22033	866-385-9110	703-273-0911
International Assn of Plumbing & Mechanical Officials (IAPMO)					
4755 E Philadelphia St	Ontario	CA	91761	877-427-6601	909-472-4100
International City/County Management Assn (ICMA)					
777 N Capitol St NE Ste 500.	Washington	DC	20002	800-745-8780	202-289-4262
International Institute of Municipal Clerks (IIMC)					
8331 Utica Ave Ste 200	Rancho Cucamonga	CA	91730	800-251-1639	909-944-4162
International Municipal Signal Assn (IMSA)					
165 E Union St PO Box 539	Newark	NY	14513	800-723-4672	315-331-2182
International Society of Fire Service Instructors (ISFSI)					
14001C St Germain Dr	Centreville	VA	20121	800-435-0005	
National American Indian Housing Council (NAIHC)					
122 C S NW Ste 350.	Washington	DC	20001	800-284-9165	202-789-1754
National Association of Clean Water Agencies (NACWA)					
1816 Jefferson Pl NW	Washington	DC	20036	888-267-9505	202-833-2672
National Board of Boiler & Pressure Vessel Inspectors					
1055 Crupper Ave	Columbus	OH	43229	877-682-8772	614-888-8320
National Conference of State Legislatures					
7700 E First Pl	Denver	CO	80230	800-659-2656	303-364-7700
National Council of State Housing Agencies (NCSHA)					
444 N Capitol St NW Ste 438	Washington	DC	20001	800-475-2098	202-624-7710
National Ctr for State Courts (NCSC)					
300 Newport Ave	Williamsburg	VA	23185	800-616-6164	757-259-1525
National Environmental Health Assn (NEHA)					
720 S Colorado Blvd Ste 1000-N	Denver	CO	80246	866-956-2258	303-756-9090
National Fire Protection Assn (NFPA)					
1 Batterymarch Pk	Quincy	MA	02169	800-344-3555	617-770-3000

Classified Section

			Toll-Free	Phone

National Institute of Governmental Purchasing Inc (NIGP)
151 Spring St . . . . Herndon VA 20170 **800-367-6447** 703-736-8900
National League of Cities (NLC)
660 North Capitol St NW . . . . Washington DC 20001 **877-827-2385**
National Sheriffs' Assn (NSA)
1450 Duke St . . . . Alexandria VA 22314 **800-424-7827** 703-836-7827
Public Technology Inc
1420 Prince St Ste 200 . . . . Alexandria VA 22314 **866-664-6368** 202-626-2400

49-8 Health & Medical Professionals Associations

			Toll-Free	Phone

Academy of General Dentistry (AGD)
211 E Chicago Ave Ste 900 . . . . Chicago IL 60611 **888-243-3368** 312-440-4300
Academy of Managed Care Pharmacy (AMCP)
100 N Pitt St Ste 400 . . . . Alexandria VA 22314 **800-827-2627** 703-683-8416
Academy of Osseointegration
85 W Algonquin Rd Ste 550 . . . . Arlington Heights IL 60005 **800-656-7736** 847-439-1919
Academy of Students of Pharmacy
American Pharmacists Assn
1100 15th St NW Ste 400 . . . . Washington DC 20005 **800-237-2742** 202-628-4410
America's Blood Centers (ABC)
725 15th St NW Ste 700 . . . . Washington DC 20005 **888-872-5663** 202-393-5725
American Academy of Audiology (AAA)
11730 Plaza America Dr Ste 300 . . . . Reston VA 20190 **800-222-2336** 703-226-1032
American Academy of Cosmetic Dentistry (AACD)
402 W Wilson St . . . . Madison WI 53703 **800-543-9220** 608-222-8583
American Academy of Dermatology (AAD)
9500 W Bryn Mawr Ave Ste 500 . . . . Rosemont IL 60018 **888-462-3376**
American Academy of Family Physicians (AAFP)
11400 Tomahawk Creek Pkwy . . . . Leawood KS 66211 **800-274-2237** 913-906-6000
American Academy of Neurology (AAN)
1080 Montreal Ave . . . . Saint Paul MN 55116 **800-879-1960** 651-695-1940
American Academy of Nurse Practitioners (AANP)
PO Box 12846 . . . . Austin TX 78711 **800-981-2491** 512-442-4262
American Academy of Ophthalmology
655 Beach St . . . . San Francisco CA 94109 **866-561-8558** 415-561-8500
American Academy of Orthopaedic Surgeons (AAOS)
6300 N River Rd . . . . Rosemont IL 60018 **800-346-2267** 847-823-7186
American Academy of Otolaryngology-Head & Neck Surgery (AAO-HNS)
1650 Diagonal Rd . . . . Alexandria VA 22314 **877-722-6467** 703-836-4444
American Academy of Pediatrics (AAP)
141 NW Pt Blvd . . . . Elk Grove Village IL 60007 **800-433-9016** 847-434-4000
American Academy of Periodontology (AAP)
737 N Michigan Ave Ste 800 . . . . Chicago IL 60611 **800-282-4867** 312-787-5518
American Assn for Cancer Research (AACR)
615 Chestnut St 17th Fl . . . . Philadelphia PA 19106 **866-423-3965** 215-440-9300
American Assn for Thoracic Surgery (AATS)
800 Cummings Ctr Ste 350-V . . . . Beverly MA 01915 **800-424-5249** 978-252-2200
American Assn of Colleges of Osteopathic Medicine (AACOM)
5550 Friendship Blvd Ste 310 . . . . Chevy Chase MD 20815 **800-356-7836** 301-968-4100
American Assn of Critical-Care Nurses (AACN)
101 Columbia . . . . Aliso Viejo CA 92656 **800-809-2273** 949-362-2000
American Assn of Endodontists (AAE)
211 E Chicago Ave Ste 1100 . . . . Chicago IL 60611 **800-872-3636** 312-266-7255
American Assn of Gynecological Laparoscopists (AAGL)
6757 Katella Ave . . . . Cypress CA 90630 **800-554-2245** 714-503-6200
American Assn of Medical Assistants (AAMA)
20 N Wacker Dr Ste 1575 . . . . Chicago IL 60606 **800-228-2262** 312-899-1500
American Assn of Medical Review Officers (AAMRO)
PO Box 12873 . . . . Research Triangle Park NC 27709 **800-489-1839** 919-489-5407
American Assn of Neurological Surgeons (AANS)
5550 Meadowbrook Dr . . . . Rolling Meadows IL 60008 **888-566-2267** 847-378-0500
American Assn of Neuromuscular & Electrodiagnostic Medicine (AANEM)
2621 Superior Dr NW . . . . Rochester MN 55901 **844-347-3277** 507-288-0100
American Assn of Neuroscience Nurses (AANN)
4700 West Lake Ave . . . . Glenview IL 60025 **888-557-2266** 847-375-4733
American Assn of Nurse Anesthetists (AANA)
222 S Prospect Ave . . . . Park Ridge IL 60068 **855-526-2262** 847-692-7050
American Assn of Oral & Maxillofacial Surgeons (AAOMS)
9700 W Bryn Mawr Ave . . . . Rosemont IL 60018 **800-822-6637** 847-678-6200
American Assn of Orthodontists (AAO)
401 N Lindbergh Blvd . . . . Saint Louis MO 63141 **800-424-2841** 314-993-1700
American Assn of Poison Control Centers (AAPCC)
3201 New Mexico Ave Ste 310 . . . . Washington DC 20016 **800-222-1222**
American Association for Homecare
2011 Crystal Dr Ste 725 . . . . Arlington VA 22202 **800-988-4484** 703-836-6263
American Association of Bioanalysts (AAB)
906 Olive St Ste 1200 . . . . Saint Louis MO 63101 **800-457-3332** 314-241-1445
American Autoimmune Related Disease Assn (AARDA)
22100 Gratiot Ave . . . . Eastpointe MI 48021 **800-598-4668** 586-776-3900
American Cancer Society (ACS)
250 William St NW . . . . Atlanta GA 30303 **800-227-2345** 404-315-1123
American Chiropractic Assn (ACA)
1701 Clarendon Blvd Ste 200 . . . . Arlington VA 22209 **800-986-4636** 703-276-8800
American College of Cardiology (ACC)
2400 N St NW . . . . Washington DC 20037 **800-253-4636*** 202-375-6000
*Cust Svc
American College of Chest Physicians (ACCP)
3300 Dundee Rd . . . . Northbrook IL 60062 **800-343-2227** 847-498-1400
American College of Emergency Physicians (ACEP)
1125 Executive Cir PO Box 619911 . . . . Dallas TX 75261 **800-798-1822** 972-550-0911
American College of Eye Surgeons/American Board of Eye Surgery (ACES)
334 E Lake Rd Ste 135 . . . . Palm Harbor FL 34685 **800-223-2233** 727-366-1487
American College of Foot & Ankle Surgeons (ACFAS)
8725 W Higgins Rd Ste 555 . . . . Chicago IL 60631 **800-421-2237** 773-693-9300
American College of Nurse-Midwives (ACNM)
8403 Colesville Rd Ste 1550 . . . . Silver Spring MD 20910 **800-468-3571** 240-485-1800
American College of Osteopathic Family Physicians (ACOFP)
330 E Algonquin Rd Ste 1 . . . . Arlington Heights IL 60005 **800-323-0794** 847-952-5100
American College of Physician Executives (ACPE)
400 N Ashley Dr Ste 400 . . . . Tampa FL 33602 **800-562-8088** 813-287-2000
American College of Physicians (ACP)
190 N Independence Mall W . . . . Philadelphia PA 19106 **800-523-1546** 215-351-2400
American College of Radiology (ACR)
1891 Preston White Dr . . . . Reston VA 20191 **800-227-5463** 703-648-8900

American College of Surgeons (ACS)
633 N St Clair St . . . . Chicago IL 60611 **800-621-4111** 312-202-5000
American Dental Assistants Assn (ADAA)
140 N Bloomingdale Rd . . . . Bloomingdale IL 60108 **877-874-3785** 312-541-1550
American Dental Assn (ADA)
211 E Chicago Ave . . . . Chicago IL 60611 **800-621-8099** 312-440-2500
American Dental Hygienists' Assn (ADHA)
444 N Michigan Ave Ste 3400 . . . . Chicago IL 60611 **800-243-2342** 312-440-8900
American Diabetes Assn (ADA)
1701 N Beauregard St . . . . Alexandria VA 22311 **800-232-3472** 703-549-1500
American Epilepsy Society (AES)
342 N Main St . . . . West Hartford CT 06117 **888-233-2334** 860-586-7505
American Federation for Aging Research (AFAR)
55 W 39th St 16th Fl . . . . New York NY 10018 **888-582-2327** 212-703-9977
American Gastroenterological Assn (AGA)
4930 Del Ray Ave . . . . Bethesda MD 20814 **800-227-7888** 301-654-2055
American Health Care Assn (AHCA)
1201 L St NW . . . . Washington DC 20005 **800-321-0343** 202-842-4444
American Health Information Management Assn (AHIMA)
233 N Michigan Ave 21st Fl . . . . Chicago IL 60601 **800-335-5535** 312-233-1100
American Healthcare Radiology Administrators (AHRA)
490-B Boston Post Rd Ste 200 . . . . Sudbury MA 01776 **800-334-2472** 978-443-7591
American Herbal Products Assn (AHPA)
8630 Fenton St Ste 918 . . . . Silver Spring MD 20910 **800-358-2104** 301-588-1171
American Hospital Assn (AHA)
155 N Wacker Dr . . . . Chicago IL 60606 **800-424-4301** 312-422-3000
American Institute of Ultrasound in Medicine (AIUM)
14750 Sweitzer Ln Ste 100 . . . . Laurel MD 20707 **800-638-5352** 301-498-4100
American Lung Assn (ALA)
14 Wall St . . . . New York NY 10005 **800-586-4872** 212-315-8700
American Medical Assn (AMA)
515 N State St . . . . Chicago IL 60610 **800-621-8335** 312-464-5000
American Medical Directors Assn (AMDA)
10500 Little Patuxent Pkwy Ste 210 . . . . Columbia MD 21044 **800-876-2632** 410-740-9743
American Medical Rehabilitation Providers Assn (AMRPA)
1710 N St NW . . . . Washington DC 20036 **888-346-4624** 202-223-1920
American Medical Technologists (AMT)
10700 W Higgins Rd Ste 150 . . . . Rosemont IL 60018 **800-275-1268** 847-823-5169
American Nephrology Nurses Assn (ANNA)
200 E Holly Ave . . . . Sewell NJ 08080 **888-600-2662** 856-256-2320
American Nurses Assn (ANA)
8515 Georgia Ave Ste 400 . . . . Silver Spring MD 20910 **800-274-4262** 301-628-5000
American Occupational Therapy Assn Inc (AOTA)
4720 Montgomery Ln PO Box 31220 . . . . Bethesda MD 20824 **800-877-1383** 301-652-2682
American Orthopaedic Society for Sports Medicine (AOSSM)
9400 W Higgins Rd Ste 300 . . . . Rosemont IL 60018 **877-321-3500** 847-292-4900
American Osteopathic Assn (AOA)
142 E Ontario St . . . . Chicago IL 60611 **800-621-1773** 888-626-9262
American Pharmacists Association
2215 Constitution Ave NW . . . . Washington DC 20037 **800-237-2742** 202-628-4410
American Physical Therapy Assn (APTA)
1111 North Fairfax St . . . . Alexandria VA 22314 **800-999-2782** 703-684-2782
American Podiatric Medical Assn (APMA)
9312 Old Georgetown Rd . . . . Bethesda MD 20814 **800-275-2762** 301-581-9200
American Psychiatric Nurses Assn (APNA)
1555 Wilson Blvd Ste 530 . . . . Arlington VA 22209 **866-243-2443** 703-243-2443
American Registry of Diagnostic Medical Sonographers (ARDMS)
1401 Rockville Pk Ste 600 . . . . Rockville MD 20852 **800-541-9754** 301-738-8401
American Roentgen Ray Society (ARRS)
44211 Slatestone Ct . . . . Leesburg VA 20176 **800-438-2777** 703-729-3353
American Society for Aesthetic Plastic Surgery, The (ASAPS)
11262 Monarch St . . . . Garden Grove CA 92841 **800-364-2147** 562-799-2356
American Society for Clinical Pathology (ASCP)
33 W Monroe St Ste 1600 . . . . Chicago IL 60603 **800-621-4142*** 312-541-4999
*Cust Svc
American Society for Colposcopy & Cervical Pathology (ASCCP)
152 W Washington St . . . . Hagerstown MD 21740 **800-787-7227** 301-733-3640
American Society for Dermatologic Surgery (ASDS)
5550 Meadowbrook Dr Ste 120 . . . . Rolling Meadows IL 60008 **800-714-1374** 847-956-0900
American Society for Gastrointestinal Endoscopy (ASGE)
1520 Kensington Rd Ste 202 . . . . Oak Brook IL 60523 **866-353-2743** 630-573-0600
American Society for Laser Medicine & Surgery Inc (ASLMS)
2100 Stewart Ave Ste 240 . . . . Wausau WI 54401 **877-258-6028** 715-845-9283
American Society for Microbiology (ASM)
1752 N St NW . . . . Washington DC 20036 **800-546-2416** 202-737-3600
American Society for Parenteral & Enteral Nutrition (ASPEN)
8630 Fenton St Ste 412 . . . . Silver Spring MD 20910 **800-727-4567** 301-587-6315
American Society for Therapeutic Radiology & Oncology (ASTRO)
8280 Willow Oaks Corporate Dr Ste 500 . . . . Fairfax VA 22031 **800-962-7876** 703-839-7312
American Society of Cataract & Refractive Surgery (ASCRS)
4000 Legato Rd Ste 700 . . . . Fairfax VA 22033 **877-996-4464** 703-591-2220
American Society of Clinical Hypnosis (ASCH)
140 N Bloomingdale Rd . . . . Bloomingdale IL 60108 **800-227-6963** 630-980-4740
American Society of Clinical Oncology (ASCO)
2318 Mill Rd Ste 800 . . . . Alexandria VA 22314 **888-282-2552** 571-483-1300
American Society of Consultant Pharmacists (ASCP)
1321 Duke St . . . . Alexandria VA 22314 **800-355-2727** 703-739-1300
American Society of Health-System Pharmacists (ASHP)
7272 Wisconsin Ave . . . . Bethesda MD 20814 **866-279-0681** 301-664-8700
American Society of PeriAnesthesia Nurses (ASPAN)
90 Frontage Rd . . . . Cherry Hill NJ 08034 **877-737-9696** 856-616-9600
American Society of Radiologic Technologists (ASRT)
15000 Central Ave SE . . . . Albuquerque NM 87123 **800-444-2778** 505-298-4500
American Society of Regional Anesthesia & Pain Medicine (ASRA)
4 Penn Ctr W Ste 401 . . . . Pittsburgh PA 15276 **855-795-2772** 412-471-2718
American Speech-Language-Hearing Assn (ASHA)
2200 Research Blvd . . . . Rockville MD 20850 **800-498-2071** 301-296-5700
American Urological Assn (AUA)
1000 Corporate Blvd . . . . Linthicum MD 21090 **866-746-4282** 410-689-3700
American Veterinary Medical Assn (AVMA)
1931 N Meacham Rd Ste 100 . . . . Schaumburg IL 60173 **800-248-2862** 847-925-8070
AORN Inc
2170 S Parker Rd Ste 400 . . . . Denver CO 80231 **800-755-2676** 303-755-6300
Arthroscopy Assn of North America (AANA)
9400 W Higgins Rd Ste 200 . . . . Rosemont IL 60018 **877-924-0305** 847-292-2262
Association for Applied Psychophysiology & Biofeedback (AAPB)
10200 W 44th Ave Ste 304 . . . . Wheat Ridge CO 80033 **800-477-8892** 303-422-8436

	Toll-Free	Phone
Association for Healthcare Documentation Integrity (AHDI)		
4230 Kiernan Ave Ste 130 ....Modesto CA 95356	800-982-2182	209-527-9620
Association for Professionals in Infection Control & Epidemiology Inc (APIC)		
1275 K St NW Ste 1000 ....Washington DC 20005	800-650-9883	202-789-1890
Association for Research in Vision & Ophthalmology (ARVO)		
12300 Twinbrook Pkwy Ste 250 ....Rockville MD 20852	888-503-1050	240-221-2900
Association for the Advancement of Medical Instrumentation (AAMI)		
4301 N Fairfax Dr Ste 301 ....Arlington VA 22203	800-332-2264	703-525-4890
Association for Vascular Access (AVA)		
5526 W 13400 S Ste 229 ....Herriman UT 84096	877-924-2821	801-792-9079
Association of Military Surgeons of the United States (AMSUS)		
9320 Old Georgetown Rd ....Bethesda MD 20814	800-761-9320	301-897-8800
Association of Nurses in AIDS Care (ANAC)		
3538 Ridgewood Rd ....Akron OH 44333	800-260-6780	330-670-0101
Association of Rehabilitation Nurses (ARN)		
4700 West Lake Ave ....Glenview IL 60025	800-229-7530	847-375-4710
Association of Reproductive Health Professionals (ARHP)		
1300 19th St NW Ste 200 ....Washington DC 20036	877-311-8972	202-466-3825
Association of Staff Physician Recruiters (ASPR)		
1000 Westgate Dr Ste 252 ....Saint Paul MN 55114	800-830-2777	
Association of Surgical Technologists (AST)		
6 W Dry Creek Cir Ste 200 ....Littleton CO 80120	800-637-7433	303-694-9130
Association of University Programs in Health Admin (AUPHA)		
2000 N 14th St Ste 780 ....Arlington VA 22201	877-275-6462	703-894-0941
Association of Women's Health Obstetric & Neonatal Nurses (AWHONN)		
2000 L St NW Ste 740 ....Washington DC 20036	800-673-8499	202-261-2400
Asthma & Allergy Foundation of America (AAFA)		
8201 Corporate Dr Ste 1000 ....Landover MD 20785	800-727-8462	202-466-7643
Canadian Academy of Sport Medicine (CASM)		
55 Metcalfe St 300 ....Ottawa ON K1P6L5	877-585-2394	613-748-5851
Canadian Assn of Emergency Physicians (CAEP)		
1785 Alta Vista Dr Ste 104 ....Ottawa ON K1G3Y6	800-463-1158	613-523-3343
Canadian Medical Assn (CMA)		
1867 Alta Vista Dr ....Ottawa ON K1G5W8	800-663-7336	613-731-9331
Canadian Veterinary Medical Assn (CVMA)		
339 Booth St ....Ottawa ON K1R7K1	800-567-2862	613-236-1162
Case Management Society of America (CMSA)		
6301 Ranch Dr ....Little Rock AR 72223	800-216-2672	501-225-2229
Catholic Health Assn of the US (CHA)		
4455 Woodson Rd ....Saint Louis MO 63134	800-230-7823	314-427-2500
Christian Medical & Dental Assn (CMDA)		
2604 Hwy 421 PO Box 7500 ....Bristol TN 37620	888-231-2637	423-844-1000
COLA		
9881 Broken Land Pkwy Ste 200 ....Columbia MD 21046	800-981-9883	410-381-6581
College of American Pathologists (CAP)		
325 Waukegan Rd ....Northfield IL 60093	800-323-4040	847-832-7000
Emergency Nurses Assn (ENA)		
915 Lee St ....Des Plaines IL 60016	800-900-9659	847-460-4000
Endocrine Society		
8401 Connecticut Ave Ste 900 ....Chevy Chase MD 20815	888-363-6274	301-941-0200
Federation of State Medical Boards of the US Inc (FSMB)		
400 Fuller Wiser Rd Ste 300 ....Euless TX 76039	800-793-7939	817-868-4000
Gerontological Society of America, The		
1220 L St NW Ste 901 ....Washington DC 20005	800-677-1116	202-842-1275
Gynecologic Oncology Group (GOG)		
1600 JFK Blvd Ste 1020 ....Philadelphia PA 19103	800-225-3053	215-854-0770
Health Industry Business Communications Council (HIBCC)		
2525 E Arizona Biltmore Cir Ste 127 ....Phoenix AZ 85016	800-755-5505	602-381-1091
Healthcare Financial Management Assn (HFMA)		
2 Westbrook Corporate Ctr Ste 700 ....Westchester IL 60154	800-252-4362	
Hospice Foundation of America (HFA)		
1707 L St NW Ste 220 ....Washington DC 20036	800-854-3402	202-457-5811
IDSA (IDSA)		
1300 Wilson Blvd Ste 300 ....Arlington VA 22209	888-463-6332	703-299-0200
Infusion Nurses Society (INS)		
315 Norwood Pk S ....Norwood MA 02062	800-694-0298	781-440-9408
Institute for Healthcare Improvement (IHI)		
20 University Rd 7th Fl ....Cambridge MA 02138	866-787-0831	617-301-4800
Institute for the Advancement of Human Behavior (IAHB)		
PO Box 5527 ....Santa Rosa CA 95402	800-258-8411	650-851-8411
Interamerican College of Physicians & Surgeons		
233 Broadway ....New York NY 10279	800-554-2245	212-777-3642
International Academy of Compounding Pharmacists (IACP)		
4638 Riverstone Blvd ....Missouri City TX 77459	800-927-4227	281-933-8400
International Chiropractors Assn (ICA)		
6400 Arlington Blvd Ste 800 ....Falls Church VA 22042	800-423-4690	703-528-5000
International Congress of Oral Implantologists (ICOI)		
55 Ln Rd Ste 305 ....Fairfield NJ 07004	800-442-0525	973-783-6300
International Society for Peritoneal Dialysis (ISPD)		
66 Martin St ....Milton ON L9T2R2	888-834-1001	905-875-2456
International Society of Refractive Surgery (ISRS)		
655 Beach St PO Box 7424. ....San Francisco CA 94109	866-561-8558	415-561-8581
International Transplant Nurses Society (ITNS)		
8735 W Higgins Rd Ste 300 ....Chicago IL 60631	800-776-8636	847-375-6340
ISPOR (ISPOR)		
505 Lawrence Sq Blvd S ....Lawrenceville NJ 08648	800-992-0643	609-586-4981
Lamaze International		
2025 M St NW Ste 800. ....Washington DC 20036	800-368-4404	202-367-1128
Medical Group Management Assn (MGMA)		
104 Inverness Terr E ....Englewood CO 80112	877-275-6462	303-799-1111
National Abortion Federation (NAF)		
1755 Massachusetts Ave NW ....Washington DC 20036	800-772-9100	202-667-5881
National Association of Neonatal Nurses (NANN)		
8735 W Higgins Rd Ste 300 ....Chicago IL 60631	800-451-3795	847-375-3660
National Community Pharmacists Assn (NCPA)		
100 Daingerfield Rd ....Alexandria VA 22314	800-544-7447	703-683-8200
National Council of State Boards of Nursing (NCSBN)		
111 E Wacker Dr Ste 2900 ....Chicago IL 60601	866-293-9600	312-525-3600
National Council on Problem Gambling Inc		
730 11th St NW Ste 601 ....Washington DC 20001	800-522-4700	202-547-9204
National Foundation for Infectious Diseases (NFID)		
4733 Bethesda Ave Ste 750 ....Bethesda MD 20814	800-708-5478	301-656-0003
National Hospice & Palliative Care Organization (NHPCO)		
1700 Diagonal Rd Ste 625 ....Alexandria VA 22314	800-658-8898*	703-837-1500
*Help Line		
National League for Nursing (NLN)		
61 Broadway 33rd Fl. ....New York NY 10006	800-669-1656	212-363-5555

	Toll-Free	Phone
National Medical Assn (NMA)		
8403 Colesville Rd Ste 920 ....Silver Spring MD 20910	800-662-0554	202-347-1895
National Nursing Staff Development Organization (NNSDO)		
330 N Wabash Ave Ste 2000. ....Chicago IL 60611	800-489-1995	312-321-5135
National Organization for Rare Disorders (NORD)		
55 Kenosia Ave ....Danbury CT 06810	800-999-6673	203-744-0100
North American Spine Society (NASS)		
7075 Veterans Blvd ....Burr Ridge IL 60527	877-774-6337	630-230-3600
Oncology Nursing Society (ONS)		
125 Enterprise Dr ....Pittsburgh PA 15275	866-257-4667	412-859-6100
Optical Society of America (OSA)		
2010 Massachusetts Ave NW ....Washington DC 20036	800-766-4672	202-223-8130
Physicians Committee for Responsible Medicine (PCRM)		
5100 Wisconsin Ave NW Ste 400 ....Washington DC 20016	866-416-7276	202-686-2210
Radiological Society of North America (RSNA)		
820 Jorie Blvd ....Oak Brook IL 60523	800-381-6660	630-571-2670
Radiology Business Management Assn (RBMA)		
9990 Fairfax Blvd Ste 430. ....Fairfax VA 22030	888-224-7262	703-621-3355
Society for Healthcare Strategy & Market Development (SHSMD)		
155 N Wacker Dr Ste 400 ....Chicago IL 60606	800-242-2626	312-422-3888
Society for Vascular Surgery (SVS)		
633 N St Clair St 22nd Fl ....Chicago IL 60611	800-258-7188	312-334-2300
Society of Cardiovascular Anesthesiologists (SCA)		
8735 W Higgins Rd Ste 300 ....Chicago IL 60631	800-283-6296	855-658-2828
Society of Diagnostic Medical Sonography (SDMS)		
2745 Dallas Pkwy ....Plano TX 75093	800-229-9506	214-473-8057
Society of Gastroenterology Nurses & Assoc Inc (SGNA)		
401 N Michigan Ave ....Chicago IL 60611	800-245-7462	312-321-5165
Society of Teachers of Family Medicine (STFM)		
11400 Tomahawk Creek Pkwy Ste 240 ....Leawood KS 66211	800-274-7928	913-906-6000
Society of Thoracic Surgeons (STS)		
633 N St Clair St Ste 2320 ....Chicago IL 60611	877-865-5321	312-202-5800
Sports Cardiovascular & Wellness Nutritionists (SCAN)		
230 Washington Ave Extn Ste 101 ....Albany NY 12203	800-249-2875*	518-254-6730
*General		
US Pharmacopeia (USP)		
12601 Twinbrook Pkwy ....Rockville MD 20852	800-227-8772	301-881-0666
Visiting Nurse Assns of America (VNAA)		
1800 Diagonal Rd Ste 600 ....Alexandria VA 22314	888-866-8773	571-527-1520
Wound Ostomy & Continence Nurses Society (WOCN)		
1120 Rt 73 Ste 200. ....Mount Laurel NJ 08054	888-224-9626	

49-9 Insurance Industry Associations

	Toll-Free	Phone
American Assn of Insurance Services Inc (AAIS)		
701 Warrenville Rd Ste 100 ....Lisle IL 60532	800-564-2247	630-681-8347
American Institute for CPCU & Insurance Institute of America (AICPCU/IIA)		
720 Providence Rd Ste 100 ....Malvern PA 19355	800-644-2101	610-644-2100
Associated Risk Managers (ARM)		
2850 Golf Rd ....Rolling Meadows IL 60008	800-735-5441	630-285-4324
Association for Advanced Life Underwriting (AALU)		
11921 Freedom Dr Ste 1100. ....Reston VA 20190	888-275-0092	703-641-9400
Association for Co-op Operations Research & Development (ACORD)		
1 Blue Hill Plz PO Box 1529. ....Pearl River NY 10965	800-444-3341	845-620-1700
Blue Cross & Blue Shield Assn		
225 N Michigan Ave ....Chicago IL 60601	888-630-2583	312-297-6000
Casualty Actuarial Society (CAS)		
4350 Fairfax Dr # 250 ....Arlington VA 22203	800-766-0070	703-276-3100
Coalition Against Insurance Fraud		
1012 14th St NW Ste 200 ....Washington DC 20005	800-835-6422	202-393-7330
CPCU Society		
720 Providence Rd ....Malvern PA 19355	800-932-2728	
GAMA International		
2901 Telestar Ct ....Falls Church VA 22042	800-345-2687*	
*Cust Svc		
Independent Insurance Agents & Brokers of America Inc (IIABA)		
127 S Peyton St ....Alexandria VA 22314	800-221-7917	703-683-4422
Institute for Business & Home Safety (IBHS)		
4775 E Fowler Ave ....Tampa FL 33617	866-657-4247	813-286-3400
Insurance Information Institute Inc (III)		
110 William St ....New York NY 10038	877-263-7995	212-346-5500
LIMRA International Inc		
300 Day Hill Rd ....Windsor CT 06095	800-235-4672	860-688-3358
LOMA		
2300 Windy Ridge Pkwy Ste 600 ....Atlanta GA 30339	800-275-5662	770-951-1770
NA of Insurance & Financial Advisors (NAIFA)		
2901 Telestar Ct ....Falls Church VA 22042	877-866-2432*	703-770-8100
*Sales		
National Crop Insurance Services (NCIS)		
8900 Indian Creek Pkwy Ste 600 ....Overland Park KS 66210	800-951-6247	913-685-2767
National Insurance Crime Bureau (NICB)		
1111 E Touhy Ave Ste 400 ....Des Plaines IL 60018	800-447-6282	847-544-7002
Physician Insurers Assn of America (PIAA)		
2275 Research Blvd Ste 250. ....Rockville MD 20850	800-688-2421	301-947-9000
Professional Liability Underwriting Society		
5353 Wayzata Blvd Ste 600 ....Minneapolis MN 55416	800-845-0778	952-746-2580
Property Loss Research Bureau (PLRB)		
3025 Highland Pkwy Ste 800 ....Downers Grove IL 60515	888-711-7572	630-724-2200
Society of Financial Service Professionals (SFSP)		
19 Campus Blvd Ste 100 ....Newtown Square PA 19073	800-392-6900	610-526-2500

49-10 Legal Professionals Associations

	Toll-Free	Phone
ABA Commission on Domestic Violence		
321 N Clark St ....Chicago IL 60654	800-285-2221	312-988-5000
American Academy of Psychiatry & the Law (AAPL)		
1 Regency Dr PO Box 30 ....Bloomfield CT 06002	800-331-1389	860-242-5450
American Association for Justice (AAJ)		
777 Sixth St NW Ste 200 ....Washington DC 20001	800-424-2725	202-965-3500
American Bar Assn (ABA)		
321 N Clark St ....Chicago IL 60654	800-285-2221	312-988-5000
American Immigration Lawyers Assn (AILA)		
918 F St NW ....Washington DC 20004	800-982-2839	202-216-2400

Organization	City	State	Zip	Toll-Free	Phone
American Land Title Assn (ALTA) 1800 M St NW Ste 300S	Washington	DC	20036	**800-787-2582**	202-296-3671
American Law Institute (ALI) 4025 Chestnut St	Philadelphia	PA	19104	**800-253-6397**	215-243-1600
American Society of International Law, The (ASIL) 2223 Massachusetts Ave NW	Washington	DC	20008	**800-828-7571**	202-939-6000
Association of Corporate Counsel (ACC) 1025 Connecticut Ave NW Ste 200	Washington	DC	20036	**877-647-3411**	202-293-4103
Battered Women's Justice Project 1801 Nicollet Ave S Ste 102	Minneapolis	MN	55403	**800-903-0111**	612-824-8768
Christian Legal Society (CLS) 8001 Braddock Rd Ste 300	Springfield	VA	22151	**800-225-4008**	703-642-1070
Commercial Law League of America (CLLA) 3005 Tollview Dr	Rolling Meadows	IL	60008	**800-978-2552**	312-240-1400
Environmental Law Institute (ELI) 2000 L St NW Ste 620	Washington	DC	20036	**800-433-5120**	202-939-3800
Food & Drug Law Institute (FDLI) 1155 15th St NW Ste 910	Washington	DC	20005	**800-956-6293**	202-371-1420
International Municipal Lawyers Assn (IMLA) 51 Monroe St Ste 404	Rockville	MD	20850	**800-942-7732**	202-466-5424
Lawyers' Committee for Civil Rights Under Law 1401 New York Ave NW Ste 400	Washington	DC	20005	**888-299-5227**	202-662-8600
National Council of Juvenile & Family Court Judges (NCJFCJ) Univ of Nevada PO Box 8970	Reno	NV	89507	**800-527-3223**	775-784-6012
National Court Reporters Assn (NCRA) 8224 Old Courthouse Rd	Vienna	VA	22182	**800-272-6272**	703-556-6272
National Legal Aid & Defender Assn (NLADA) 1140 Connecticut Ave NW Ste 900	Washington	DC	20036	**800-725-4513**	202-452-0620
Native American Rights Fund (NARF) 1506 Broadway	Boulder	CO	80302	**888-280-0726**	303-447-8760
Pension Rights Ctr 1350 Connecticut Ave NW Ste 206	Washington	DC	20036	**866-735-7737**	202-296-3776
Practising Law Institute (PLI) 1177 Ave of the Americas 2nd Fl	New York	NY	10036	**800-260-4754**	212-824-5700

49-11 Library & Information Science Associations

Organization	City	State	Zip	Toll-Free	Phone
American Assn of School Librarians (AASL) 50 E Huron St	Chicago	IL	60611	**800-545-2433**	312-280-4386
American Library Assn (ALA) 50 E Huron St	Chicago	IL	60611	**800-545-2433**	312-944-6780
American Theological Library Assn (ATLA) 300 S Wacker Dr Ste 2100	Chicago	IL	60606	**888-665-2852**	312-454-5100
Association for Library & Information Science Education (ALISE) 2150 N 107th St Ste 205	Seattle	WA	98133	**877-275-7547**	206-209-5267
Association for Library Collections & Technical Services (ALCTS) 50 E Huron St	Chicago	IL	60611	**800-545-2433**	312-280-5037
Association for Library Service to Children (ALSC) 50 E Huron St	Chicago	IL	60611	**800-545-2433**	312-280-2163
Association of College & Research Libraries (ACRL) 50 E Huron St	Chicago	IL	60611	**800-545-2433**	312-280-2519
Association of Specialized & Co-op Library Agencies (ASCLA) 50 E Huron St	Chicago	IL	60611	**800-545-2433**	312-280-4395
Library & Information Technology Assn (LITA) 50 E Huron St	Chicago	IL	60611	**800-545-2433**	312-280-4270
Library Leadership & Management Assn (LLAMA) 50 E Huron St	Chicago	IL	60611	**800-545-2433**	
Medical Library Assn (MLA) 65 E Wacker Pl Ste 1900	Chicago	IL	60601	**800-523-1850**	312-419-9094
Online Computer Library Ctr Inc (OCLC) 6565 Kilgour Pl	Dublin	OH	43017	**800-848-5878**	
Public Library Assn (PLA) 50 E Huron St	Chicago	IL	60611	**800-545-2433**	312-280-5752
Reference & User Services Assn (RUSA) 50 E Huron St	Chicago	IL	60611	**800-545-2433**	312-280-4398
Special Libraries Assn (SLA) 331 S Patrick St	Alexandria	VA	22314	**866-446-6069**	703-647-4900
Young Adult Library Services Assn (YALSA) 50 E Huron St	Chicago	IL	60611	**800-545-2433**	312-280-4390

49-12 Management & Business Professional Associations

Organization	City	State	Zip	Toll-Free	Phone
Academy of Management (AOM) 235 Elm Rd PO Box 3020	Briarcliff Manor	NY	10510	**800-633-4931**	914-923-2607
American Business Women's Assn (ABWA) 11050 Roe Ave Ste 200	Overland Park	KS	66211	**800-228-0007**	
American Chamber of Commerce Executives (ACCE) 4875 Eisenhower Ave Ste 250	Alexandria	VA	22304	**800-394-2223**	703-998-0072
American Society of Assn Executives (ASAE) 1575 'I' St NW	Washington	DC	20005	**888-950-2723**	202-626-2723
APQC 123 N Post Oak Ln Ste 300	Houston	TX	77024	**800-776-9676**	713-681-4020
ARMA International 11880 College Blvd Ste 450	Overland Park	KS	66210	**800-422-2762**	913-341-3808
Association for Corporate Growth (ACG) 125 S Wacker Dr Ste 3100	Chicago	IL	60606	**877-358-2220**	312-957-4260
Association for Mfg Technology (AMT) 7901 Westpark Dr	McLean	VA	22102	**800-524-0475**	703-893-2900
Association of Fundraising Professionals (AFP) 4300 Wilson Blvd Ste 300	Arlington	VA	22203	**800-666-3863**	703-684-0410
Business Forms Management Assn (BFMA) 3800 Old Cheney Rd Ste 101-285	Lincoln	NE	68516	**888-367-3078**	
Christian Leadership Alliance (CLA) 635 Camino De Los Mares Ste 216	San Clemente	CA	92673	**800-263-6317**	949-487-0900
Club Managers Assn of America (CMAA) CMAA - 1733 King St	Alexandria	VA	22314	**800-409-7755**	703-739-9500
Employee Assistance Professionals Assn Inc (EAPA) 4350 N Fairfax Dr Ste 740	Arlington	VA	22203	**800-937-8461**	703-387-1000
ESOP Assn 1726 M St NW Ste 501	Washington	DC	20036	**866-366-3832**	202-293-2971
Executive Women International (EWI) 3860 South 2300 East Ste 211	Salt Lake City	UT	84109	**877-439-4669**	801-355-2800
HR People & Strategy (HRPS) 1800 Duke St	Alexandria	VA	22314	**888-602-3270**	703-535-6056
Institute for Supply Management (ISM) 2055 Centennial Cir *Cust Svc	Tempe	AZ	85284	**800-888-6276***	480-752-6276
Institute of Management Consultants USA Inc (IMC USA) 2025 M St NW Ste 800	Washington	DC	20036	**800-221-2557**	800-793-4992
International Assn for Human Resource Information Management Inc (IHRIM) PO Box 1086	Burlington	MA	01803	**800-804-3983**	
International Assn of Business Communicators (IABC) 155 Montgomery St Ste 1210	San Francisco	CA	94104	**800-776-4222**	415-544-4700
International Assn of Venue Managers Inc (IAVM) 635 Fritz Dr Ste 100	Coppell	TX	75019	**800-935-4226**	972-906-7441
International Public Management Assn for Hum Res (IPMA-HR) 1617 Duke St	Alexandria	VA	22314	**800-381-8378**	703-549-7100
International Society for Performance Improvement (ISPI) PO Box 13035	Silver Spring	MD	20910	**800-825-7550**	301-587-8570
International Society of Certified Employee Benefits (ISCEBS) 18700 W Bluemond Rd PO Box 209	Brookfield	WI	53008	**888-334-3327**	262-786-8771
International Trademark Assn (INTA) 655 Third Ave 10th Fl	New York	NY	10017	**800-995-3579**	212-768-9887
Meeting Professionals International (MPI) 2711 Lyndon B Johnson Fwy Ste 600	Dallas	TX	75234	**866-318-2743**	972-702-3053
National Association of Parliamentarians (NAP) 213 S Main St	Independence	MO	64050	**888-627-2929**	816-833-3892
National Business Assn (NBA) 5151 Beltline Rd Ste 1150	Dallas	TX	75254	**800-456-0440**	972-458-0900
National Co-op Business Assn (NCBA) 1401 New York Ave NW Ste 1100	Washington	DC	20005	**800-356-9655**	202-638-6222
National Contract Management Assn (NCMA) 21740 Beaumeade Cir Ste 125	Ashburn	VA	20147	**800-344-8096**	571-382-0082
National Notary Assn (NNA) 9350 DeSoto Ave	Chatsworth	CA	91313	**800-876-6827**	
National Right to Work Committee (NRTWC) 8001 Braddock Rd Ste 500	Springfield	VA	22160	**800-325-7892**	
National Small Business Assn (NSBA) 1156 15th St NW Ste 1100	Washington	DC	20005	**800-345-6728**	
Product Development & Management Assn (PDMA) 330 N Wabash Ave Ste 2000	Chicago	IL	60611	**800-232-5241**	312-321-5145
Professional Convention Management Assn (PCMA) 35 E Wacker Dr Ste 500	Chicago	IL	60601	**877-827-7262**	312-423-7262
Profit Sharing/401(k) Council of America (PSCA) 20 N Wacker Dr Ste 3700	Chicago	IL	60606	**866-614-8407**	312-419-1863
Project Management Institute (PMI) 14 Campus Blvd	Newtown Square	PA	19073	**866-276-4764**	610-356-4600
Religious Conference Management Assn Inc (RCMA) 7702 Woodland Dr Ste 120	Indianapolis	IN	46278	**800-221-8235**	317-632-1888
SCORE Assn 1175 Herndon Pkwy Ste 900	Herndon	VA	20170	**800-634-0245**	
Society for Human Resource Management (SHRM) 1800 Duke St	Alexandria	VA	22314	**800-283-7476**	703-548-3440
WorldatWork 14040 N Northsight Blvd	Scottsdale	AZ	85260	**877-951-9191**	
Worldwide Employee Benefits Network Inc (WEB) 11520 N Central Expy Ste 201	Dallas	TX	75243	**888-795-6862**	
Young Presidents' Organization (YPO) 600 E Las Colinas Blvd Ste 1100	Irving	TX	75039	**800-773-7976**	972-587-1500

49-13 Manufacturing Industry Professional & Trade Associations

Organization	City	State	Zip	Toll-Free	Phone
American Boiler Manufacturers Assn (ABMA) 8221 Old Courthouse Rd Ste 380	Vienna	VA	22182	**800-227-1966**	703-356-7172
American Foundry Society (AFS) 1695 N Penny Ln	Schaumburg	IL	60173	**800-537-4237**	847-824-0181
American Galvanizers Assn (AGA) 6881 S Holly Cir Ste 108	Centennial	CO	80112	**800-468-7732**	720-554-0900
American Society for Quality (ASQ) 600 N Plankinton Ave	Milwaukee	WI	53203	**800-248-1946**	414-272-8575
ASM International 9639 Kinsman Rd	Materials Park	OH	44073	**800-336-5152**	440-338-5151
Association for Iron & Steel Technology (AIST) 186 Thorn Hill Rd	Warrendale	PA	15086	**800-759-4867**	724-814-3000
Association of Equipment Manufacturers (AEM) 6737 W Washington St Ste 2400	Milwaukee	WI	53214	**866-236-0442**	414-272-0943
Building Service Contractors Assn International (BSCAI) 401 N Michigan Ave Ste 2200	Chicago	IL	60611	**800-368-3414**	312-321-5167
Color Pigments Manufacturers Association Inc 1400 Crystal Dr Ste 630	Arlington	VA	22202	**888-233-9527**	571-348-5130
Copper Development Assn Inc 260 Madison Ave 16th Fl	New York	NY	10016	**800-232-3282**	212-251-7200
Crane Manufacturers Assn of America (CMAA) 8720 Red Oak Blvd Ste 201	Charlotte	NC	28217	**800-345-1815**	704-676-1190
Fabricators & Manufacturers Assn International (FMA) 833 Featherstone Rd	Rockford	IL	61107	**888-394-4362**	815-399-8700
INDA: Assn of the Nonwoven Fabrics Industry 1100 Crescent Green Ste 115 PO Box 1288	Cary	NC	27518	**800-628-2112**	919-459-3700
Industrial Fabrics Assn International (IFAI) 1801 County Rd 'B' W	Roseville	MN	55113	**800-225-4324**	651-222-2508
Institute of Caster & Wheel Manufacturers (ICWM) 8720 Red Oak Blvd Ste 201	Charlotte	NC	28217	**877-522-5431**	704-676-1190
Institute of Industrial & Systems Engineers (IIE) 3577 PkwyLn Ste 200 *Cust Svc	Norcross	GA	30092	**800-494-0460***	770-449-0461
Institute of Packaging Professionals (IoPP) 1833 Centre Point Cir Ste 123	Naperville	IL	60563	**800-432-4085**	630-544-5050
International Ground Source Heat Pump Assn (IGSHPA) Oklahoma State University 374 Cordell S	Stillwater	OK	74078	**800-626-4747**	405-744-5175
Material Handling Industry of America (MHIA) 8720 Red Oak Blvd Ste 201	Charlotte	NC	28217	**800-345-1815**	704-676-1190
Metals Service Ctr Institute (MSCI) 4201 Euclid Ave	Rolling Meadows	IL	60008	**800-634-2358**	847-485-3000
Minerals Metals & Materials Society, The (TMS) 5700 Corporate Dr Ste 750	Pittsburgh	PA	15237	**800-759-4867**	724-776-9000
NACE International: Corrosion Society 1440 S Creek Dr	Houston	TX	77084	**800-797-6223**	281-228-6200

			Toll-Free	Phone

National Council of Textile Organizations (NCTO)
1701 K St NW Ste 625 .... Washington DC 20006 **800-238-7192** 202-822-8028
National Electrical Manufacturers Assn (NEMA)
1300 N 17th St Ste 1752 .... Rosslyn VA 22209 **800-699-9277** 703-841-3200
National Glass Assn (NGA)
8200 Greensboro Dr Ste 302 .... McLean VA 22102 **866-342-5642** 703-442-4890
National Marine Electronics Assn (NMEA)
692 Ritchie Hwy Ste 104 .... Severna Park MD 21146 **800-808-6632** 410-975-9425
National Tooling & Machining Assn (NTMA)
6363 Oak Tree Blvd .... Independence OH 44131 **800-248-6862**
North American Assn of Food Equipment Manufacturers (NAFEM)
161 N Clark St Ste 2020 .... Chicago IL 60601 **888-493-5961** 312-821-0201
Packaging Machinery Manufacturers Institute (PMMI)
4350 N Fairfax Dr Ste 600 .... Arlington VA 22203 **888-275-7664** 703-243-8555
Polyurethane Manufacturers Assn (PMA)
6737 W Washington St Ste 1420 .... Milwaukee WI 53214 **800-937-8461** 414-431-3094
Society for Mining Metallurgy & Exploration Inc (SME)
12999 E Adam Aircraft Cir .... Englewood CO 80112 **800-763-3132** 303-948-4200
Society for Protective Coatings (SSPC)
40 24th St 6th Fl .... Pittsburgh PA 15222 **877-281-7772** 412-281-2331
Society of Mfg Engineers (SME)
1 SME Dr .... Dearborn MI 48128 **800-733-4763*** 313-425-3000
*Cust Svc
Society of Vacuum Coaters (SVC)
71 Pinon Hill Pl NE .... Albuquerque NM 87122 **800-443-8817** 505-856-7188
Spring Manufacturers Institute (SMI)
2001 Midwest Rd Ste 106 .... Oak Brook IL 60523 **866-482-5569** 630-495-8588
Technical Assn of the Pulp & Paper Industry (TAPPI)
15 Technology Pkwy S .... Norcross GA 30092 **800-332-8686*** 770-446-1400
*Sales

49-14 Media Professionals Associations

			Toll-Free	Phone

Accuracy in Media Inc (AIM)
4350 EW Hwy Ste 555 .... Bethesda MD 20814 **800-787-4567** 202-364-4401
American Radio Relay League (ARRL)
225 Main St .... Newington CT 06111 **888-277-5289** 860-594-0200
Association of Alternative Newsweeklies (AAN)
115615th St NW .... Washington DC 20005 **866-415-0704** 202-289-8484
National Newspaper Assn (NNA)
PO Box 7540 .... Columbia MO 65205 **800-829-4662** 217-241-1400
Satellite Broadcasting & Communications Assn (SBCA)
1730 M St NW Ste 600 .... Washington DC 20036 **800-541-5981** 202-349-3620
Society of Professional Journalists (SPJ)
3909 N Meridian St .... Indianapolis IN 46208 **800-331-1212** 317-927-8000
Specialized Information Publishers Assn (SIPA)
8229 Boone Blvd Ste 260 .... Vienna VA 22182 **800-356-9302** 703-992-9339

49-15 Mental Health Professionals Associations

			Toll-Free	Phone

American Academy of Addiction Psychiatry (AAAP)
400 Massasoit Ave
2nd Fl Ste 307 .... East Providence RI 02914 **800-263-6317** 401-524-3076
American Academy of Child & Adolescent Psychiatry (AACAP)
3615 Wisconsin Ave NW .... Washington DC 20016 **800-333-7636** 202-966-7300
American Academy of Psychiatry & the Law (AAPL)
1 Regency Dr PO Box 30 .... Bloomfield CT 06002 **800-331-1389** 860-242-5450
American Counseling Assn (ACA)
5999 Stevenson Ave .... Alexandria VA 22304 **800-347-6647** 703-823-9800
American Group Psychotherapy Assn (AGPA)
25 E 21st St 6th Fl .... New York NY 10010 **877-668-2472** 212-477-2677
American Mental Health Counselors Assn (AMHCA)
107 S W St Ste 779 .... Alexandria VA 22314 **800-326-2642** 703-548-6002
American Psychiatric Assn (APA)
1000 Wilson Blvd Ste 1825 .... Arlington VA 22209 **888-357-7924** 703-907-7300
American Psychiatric Nurses Assn (APNA)
1555 Wilson Blvd Ste 530 .... Arlington VA 22209 **866-243-2443** 703-243-2443
American Psychological Assn (APA)
750 First St NE .... Washington DC 20002 **800-374-2721** 202-336-5500
American Society for Adolescent Psychiatry (ASAP)
PO Box 3948 .... Parker CO 80134 **866-672-9060**
Arc of Stanly County, The
350 Pee Dee Ave Ste A .... Albemarle NC 28001 **800-230-7525** 704-986-1500
Association for Behavioral & Cognitive Therapies (ABCT)
305 Seventh Ave 16th Fl .... New York NY 10001 **800-685-2228** 212-647-1890
International Assn of Marriage & Family Counselors (IAMFC)
5999 Stevenson Ave .... Alexandria VA 22304 **800-347-6647**
International Society for Traumatic Stress Studies (ISTSS)
111 Deer Lake Rd Ste 100 .... Deerfield IL 60015 **877-469-7873** 847-480-9028
Lifespring Inc
460 Spring St .... Jeffersonville IN 47130 **800-456-2117** 812-280-2080
National Psychological Assn for Psychoanalysis (NPAP)
40 W 13th St .... New York NY 10011 **800-365-7006** 212-924-7440
Northern Arizona Regional Behavioral Health Authority Inc (NARBHA)
1300 S Yale St .... Flagstaff AZ 86001 **877-923-1400** 928-774-7128
Northwestern Counseling & Support Services Inc
107 Fisher Pond Rd .... Saint Albans VT 05478 **800-834-7793** 802-524-6554
Society for Social Work Leadership in Health Care
100 N 20th St 4th Fl .... Philadelphia PA 19103 **866-237-9542**

49-16 Publishing & Printing Professional Associations

			Toll-Free	Phone

Association of Directory Publishers (ADP)
PO Box 209 .... Traverse City MI 49685 **800-267-9002** 231-486-2182
Association of Magazine Media, The (MPA)
757 Third Ave 11th Fl .... New York NY 10017 **800-234-3368** 212-872-3700
Association of University Presses
28 W 36th St Ste 602 .... New York NY 10018 **800-678-2120** 212-989-1010
Copyright Clearance Ctr Inc (CCC)
222 Rosewood Dr .... Danvers MA 01923 **855-239-3415** 978-750-8400

Independent Book Publishers Assn, The (IBPA)
1020 Manhattan Beach Blvd
Ste 204 .... Manhattan Beach CA 90266 **800-327-5113** 310-546-1818
International Reprographic Assn (IRgA)
401 N Michigan Ave Ste 2200 .... Chicago IL 60611 **800-833-4742** 877-226-6839
National Information Standards Organization (NISO)
3600 Clipper Mill Rd Ste 302 .... Baltimore MD 21211 **877-375-2160** 301-654-2512
NPES: Assn for Suppliers of Printing Publishing & Converting Technologies
1899 Preston White Dr .... Reston VA 20191 **866-381-9839** 703-264-7200
Printing Industries of America/Graphic Arts Technical Foundation (PIA/GATF)
200 Deer Run Rd .... Sewickley PA 15143 **800-910-4283** 412-741-6860
Society for Imaging Science & Technology (IS&T)
7003 Kilworth Ln .... Springfield VA 22151 **800-654-2240** 703-642-9090
Specialty Graphic Imaging Assn (SGIA)
10015 Main St .... Fairfax VA 22031 **888-385-3588** 703-385-1335

49-17 Real Estate Professionals Associations

			Toll-Free	Phone

American Homeowners Foundation (AHF)
6776 Little Falls Rd .... Arlington VA 22213 **800-489-7776**
American Society of Appraisers (ASA)
555 Herndon Ave Ste 125 .... Herndon VA 20170 **800-272-8258** 703-478-2228
Appraisal Institute
550 W Van Buren St Ste 1000 .... Chicago IL 60607 **888-756-4624** 312-335-4100
Building Owners & Managers Assn International (BOMA)
1101 15th St NW Ste 800 .... Washington DC 20005 **800-426-6292** 202-408-2662
CCIM Institute
430 N Michigan Ave Ste 800 .... Chicago IL 60611 **800-621-7027** 312-321-4460
CoreNet Global Inc
260 Peachtree St NW Ste 1500 .... Atlanta GA 30303 **800-726-8111** 404-589-3200
Council of Residential Specialists
430 N Michigan Ave Ste 300 .... Chicago IL 60611 **800-462-8841** 312-321-4400
Institute of Real Estate Management (IREM)
430 N Michigan Ave .... Chicago IL 60611 **800-837-0706** 312-329-6000
National Apartment Assn (NAA)
4300 Wilson Blvd Ste 400 .... Arlington VA 22203 **800-632-3007** 703-518-6141
Real Estate Buyer's Agent Council (REBAC)
430 N Michigan Ave .... Chicago IL 60611 **800-648-6224**
Rebi (CRB) 430 N Michigan Ave .... Chicago IL 60611 **800-621-8738**
Venture Communications Cooperative Inc
218 Commercial Ave SE PO Box 157 .... Highmore SD 57345 **800-932-0637** 605-852-2224
Women's Council of REALTORS (WCR)
430 N Michigan Ave .... Chicago IL 60611 **800-245-8512**

49-18 Sales & Marketing Professional Associations

			Toll-Free	Phone

Advertising Council Inc
815 Second Ave 9th Fl .... New York NY 10016 **888-200-4005** 212-922-1500
American Assn of Franchisees & Dealers (AAFD)
PO Box 10158 .... Palm Desert CA 92255 **800-733-9858** 619-209-3775
American Booksellers Assn (ABA)
333 Westchester Ave Ste S202 .... White Plains NY 10604 **800-637-0037**
American International Automobile Dealers Assn (AIADA)
500 Montgomery St Ste 800 .... Alexandria VA 22314 **800-462-4232**
American Marketing Assn (AMA)
311 S Wacker Dr Ste 5800 .... Chicago IL 60606 **800-262-1150** 312-542-9000
Associated Equipment Distributors (AED)
650 E Algonquin Rd Ste 305 .... Schaumburg IL 60173 **800-388-0650** 630-574-0650
Association of Progressive Rental Organizations (APRO)
1504 Robin Hood Trl .... Austin TX 78703 **800-204-2776** 512-794-0095
Automotive Distribution Network
3085 Fountainside Dr Ste 210 .... Germantown TN 38138 **800-616-7587**
Brick Industry Assn (BIA)
12007 Sunrise Valley Dr Ste 430 .... Reston VA 20191 **866-644-1293** 703-620-0010
Business Technology Assn (BTA)
12411 Wornall Rd Ste 200 .... Kansas City MO 64145 **800-325-7219** 816-941-3100
Chain Drug Marketing Assn (CDMA)
43157 W Nine-Mile Rd PO Box 995 .... Novi MI 48376 **800-935-2362** 248-449-9300
Dairyamerica Inc
7815 N Palm Ave Ste 250 .... Fresno CA 93711 **800-722-3110** 559-251-0992
Direct Marketing Assn Inc (DMA)
1120 Ave of the Americas .... New York NY 10036 **855-422-0749** 212-768-7277
Food Marketing Institute (FMI)
2345 Crystal Dr Ste 800 .... Arlington VA 22202 **800-732-2639** 202-452-8444
HARDI Hydronic Heating & Cooling Council
445 Hutchinson Ave Ste 550 .... Columbus OH 43235 **888-253-2128** 614-345-4328
Health Industry Distributors Association (HIDA)
310 Montgomery St .... Alexandria VA 22314 **800-549-4432** 703-549-4432
International Franchise Assn (IFA)
1501 K St NW Ste 350 .... Washington DC 20005 **800-543-1038** 202-628-8000
International Sanitary Supply Assn (ISSA)
3300 Dundee Rd .... Northbrook IL 60062 **800-225-4772** 847-982-0800
Machinery Dealers National Assn (MDNA)
315 S Patrick St .... Alexandria VA 22314 **800-872-7807** 703-836-9300
Metals Service Ctr Institute (MSCI)
4201 Euclid Ave .... Rolling Meadows IL 60008 **800-634-2358** 847-485-3000
NA of Convenience Stores (NACS)
1600 Duke St 7th Fl .... Alexandria VA 22314 **800-966-6227*** 703-684-3600
*Cust Svc
NAMM (NAMM) 5790 Armada Dr .... Carlsbad CA 92008 **800-767-6266** 760-438-8001
National Art Materials Trade Assn
20200 Zion Ave .... Cornelius NC 28031 **800-349-1039** 704-892-6244
National Association of Chain Drug Stores (NACDS)
413 N Lee St .... Alexandria VA 22314 **800-678-6223** 703-549-3001
National Association of College Stores (NACS)
500 E Lorain St .... Oberlin OH 44074 **800-622-7498** 440-775-7777
National Association of Electrical Distributors (NAED)
1181 Corporate Lake Dr .... Saint Louis MO 63132 **888-791-2512** 314-991-9000
National Auctioneers Assn (NAA)
8880 Ballentine St .... Overland Park KS 66214 **877-657-1990** 913-541-8084
National Auto Auction Assn (NAAA)
5320 Spectrum Dr Ste D .... Frederick MD 21703 **800-232-5411** 301-696-0400

			Toll-Free	Phone
National Automobile Dealers Assn (NADA)				
8400 Westpark Dr	McLean VA	22102	800-252-6232	703-821-7000
National Electrical Manufacturers Representatives Assn (NEMRA)				
28 Deer St Ste 302	Portsmouth NH	03801	800-446-3672	914-524-8650
National Electronics Service Dealers Assn (NESDA)				
3608 Pershing Ave	Fort Worth TX	76107	800-946-0201	817-921-9061
National Independent Automobile Dealers Assn (NIADA)				
2521 Brown Blvd	Arlington TX	76006	800-682-3837	817-640-3838
National Independent Flag Dealers Assn (NIFDA)				
7984 S Chicago Ave	Chicago IL	60617	800-356-4085	773-768-8076
National Luggage Dealers Association (NLDA)				
1817 Elmdale Ave	Glenview IL	60026	800-411-0705	847-998-6869
National Mail Order Assn LLC (NMOA)				
2807 Polk St NE	Minneapolis MN	55418	800-992-1377	612-788-1673
National Marine Representatives Assn (NMRA)				
PO Box 360	Gurnee IL	60031	800-890-3819	847-662-3167
National Minority Supplier Development Council (NMSDC)				
1359 Broadway 10th Fl.	New York NY	10018	800-843-4898	212-944-2430
National Retail Federation (NRF)				
1101 New York Ave NW	Washington DC	20005	800-673-4692	202-783-7971
National Retail Hardware Assn (NRHA)				
5822 W 74th St	Indianapolis IN	46278	800-772-4424*	317-290-0338
*Cust Svc				
National School Supply & Equipment Assn (NSSEA)				
8380 Colesville Rd Ste 250	Silver Spring MD	20910	800-395-5550	301-495-0240
National Shoe Retailers Assn (NSRA)				
7386 N La Cholla Blvd	Tucson AZ	85741	800-673-8446	520-209-1710
North American Bldg Material Distribution Assn (NBMDA)				
330 N Wabash Ave Ste 2000.	Chicago IL	60611	888-747-7862	312-321-6845
NPTA Alliance				
330 N Wabash Ave Ste 2000.	Chicago IL	60611	800-355-6782	312-321-4092
Paint & Decorating Retailers Assn (PDRA)				
1401 Triad Ctr Dr	Saint Peters MO	63376	800-737-0107	636-326-2636
Professional Beauty Assn (PBA)				
15825 N 71st St Ste 100.	Scottsdale AZ	85254	800-468-2274	480-281-0424
Promotional Products Assn International (PPAI)				
3125 Skyway Cir N	Irving TX	75038	888-426-7724	972-252-0404
Public Relations Society of America (PRSA)				
33 Maiden Ln 11th Fl	New York NY	10038	800-350-0111	212-460-1400
Radio Adv Bureau (RAB)				
125 W 55th St 5th Fl.	New York NY	10019	800-232-3131	
Retail Solutions Providers Assn (RSPA)				
9920 Couloak Dr Unit 120	Charlotte NC	28216	800-782-2693	
Society for Marketing Professional Services (SMPS)				
123 North Pitt St Ste 400	Alexandria VA	22314	800-292-7677	703-549-6117
Specialty Tools & Fasteners Distributors Assn (STAFDA)				
500 Elm Grove Rd Ste 210 PO Box 44	Elm Grove WI	53122	800-352-2981	262-784-4774

49-19 Technology, Science, Engineering Professionals Associations

			Toll-Free	Phone
Acoustical Society of America (ASA)				
1305 Walt Whitman Rd Ste 300	Melville NY	11747	800-828-8840	516-576-2360
American Assn for Clinical Chemistry Inc (AACC)				
1850 K St NW Ste 625	Washington DC	20006	800-892-1400*	202-857-0717
*Cust Svc				
American Assn of Engineering Societies (AAES)				
1801 Alexander Bell Dr	Reston VA	20191	888-400-2237*	202-296-2237
*Orders				
American Assn of Pharmaceutical Scientists (AAPS)				
2107 Wilson Blvd Ste 700	Arlington VA	22201	877-998-2277	703-243-2800
American Chemical Society (ACS)				
1155 16th St NW	Washington DC	20036	800-227-5558	202-872-4600
American Council of Engineering Cos (ACEC)				
1015 15th St NW 8th Fl	Washington DC	20005	800-338-1391	202-347-7474
American Council of Independent Laboratories (ACIL)				
1875 I St NW Ste 500.	Washington DC	20006	800-368-1131	202-887-5872
American Council on Science & Health (ACSH)				
110 E 42nd St Ste 1300	New York NY	10017	866-905-2694	212-362-7044
American Geophysical Union (AGU)				
2000 Florida Ave NW	Washington DC	20009	800-966-2481	202-462-6900
American Indian Science & Engineering Society (AISES)				
2305 Renard SE Ste 200.	Albuquerque NM	87106	800-759-5219	505-765-1052
American Institute of Aeronautics & Astronautics Inc (AIAA)				
1801 Alexander Bell Dr Ste 500	Reston VA	20191	800-639-2422	703-264-7500
American Institute of Chemical Engineers (AIChE)				
120 Wall St 2nd Fl	New York NY	10005	800-242-4363*	203-702-7660
*Cust Svc				
American Institute of Physics				
1 Physics Ellipse	College Park MD	20740	800-892-8259	301-209-3100
American Institute of Professional Geologists (AIPG)				
1400 W 122nd Ave Ste 250	Westminster CO	80234	800-337-3140	303-412-6205
American Mathematical Society (AMS)				
201 Charles St	Providence RI	02904	800-321-4267*	401-455-4000
*Cust Svc				
American Meteorological Society (AMS)				
45 Beacon St	Boston MA	02108	800-824-0405	617-227-2425
American Nuclear Society (ANS)				
555 N Kensington Ave	La Grange Park IL	60526	800-323-3044	708-352-6611
American Physical Society (APS)				
1 Physics Ellipse	College Park MD	20740	866-918-1164	301-209-3200
American Society for Nondestructive Testing Inc (ASNT)				
1711 Arlingate Ln PO Box 28518	Columbus OH	43228	800-222-2768*	614-274-6003
*Orders				
American Society of Limnology & Oceanography (ASLO)				
5400 Bosque Blvd Ste 680	Waco TX	76710	800-929-2756	254-399-9635
American Statistical Assn (ASA)				
732 N Washington St	Alexandria VA	22314	888-231-3473	703-684-1221
AOAC International				
481 N Frederick Ave Ste 500	Gaithersburg MD	20877	800-379-2622	301-924-7077
Association of American Geographers (AAG)				
1710 16th St NW	Washington DC	20009	800-696-7353	202-234-1450
ASTM International				
100 Barr Harbor Dr				
PO Box C700	West Conshohocken PA	19428	800-814-1017	610-832-9500
Audio Engineering Society				
60 E 42nd St Rm 2520	New York NY	10165	800-541-7299	212-661-8528

			Toll-Free	Phone
Biotechnology Industry Organization				
1201 Maryland Ave SW Ste 900	Washington DC	20024	866-356-5155	202-962-9200
Center for Chemical Process Safety (CCPS)				
120 Wall St	New York NY	10005	800-242-4363	646-495-1371
Custom Electronic Design & Installation Assn (CEDIA)				
7150 Winton Dr Ste 300	Indianapolis IN	46268	800-669-5329	317-328-4336
Drug Chemical & Associated Technologies Assn (DCAT)				
1 Washington Blvd Ste 7	Robbinsville NJ	08691	800-640-3228	609-448-1000
Electronics Technicians Assn International (ETA)				
5 Depot St	Greencastle IN	46135	800-288-3824	765-653-8262
Entomological Society of America				
10001 Derekwood Ln Ste 100.	Lanham MD	20706	800-523-8635	301-731-4535
Federation of American Societies for Experimental Biology (FASEB)				
9650 Rockville Pk	Bethesda MD	20814	800-433-2732	301-634-7000
Genetics Society of America (GSA)				
9650 Rockville Pk	Bethesda MD	20814	866-486-4363	301-634-7300
Geological Society of America, The (GSA)				
3300 Penrose Pl PO Box 9140	Boulder CO	80301	800-472-1988	303-357-1000
IEEE Broadcast Technology Society (BTS)				
445 Hoes Ln	Piscataway NJ	08854	800-678-4333	732-562-5407
IEEE Computer Society				
2001 L St NW Ste 700	Washington DC	20036	800-272-6657	202-371-0101
IEEE Electromagnetic Compatibility Society (EMC)				
445 and 501 Hoes Ln	Piscataway NJ	08854	800-678-4333	732-981-0060
IEEE Geoscience & Remote Sensing Society				
3 Park Ave 17th Fl	New York NY	10016	800-678-4333	212-419-7900
IEEE Magnetics Society				
445 Hoes Ln PO Box 459	Piscataway NJ	08855	800-678-4333	908-981-0060
IEEE Microwave Theory & Techniques Society (MTT-S)				
5829 Bellanca Dr	Elkridge MD	21075	800-678-4333	410-796-5866
IEEE Nuclear & Plasma Sciences Society (NPSS)				
445 Hoes Ln	Piscataway NJ	08854	800-678-4333	732-981-0060
IEEE Product Safety Engineering Society				
445 Hoes Ln	Piscataway NJ	08854	800-678-4333	732-981-0060
IEEE Reliability Society (RS)				
IEEE Operations Ctr 445 Hoes Ln	Piscataway NJ	08854	800-678-4333	732-981-0060
IEEE Signal Processing Society				
445 Hoes Ln	Piscataway NJ	08854	800-678-4333	732-981-0060
IEEE Society on Social Implications of Technology (SSIT)				
IEEE Operations Ctr				
445 and 501 Hooc Ln	Piscataway NJ	08854	800-678-4333	732-981-0060
IEEE Technology & Engineering Management Society (IEEE TEMS)				
445 Hoes Ln	Piscataway NJ	08854	800-678-4333	732-981-0060
IEEE Ultrasonics Ferroelectrics & Frequency Control Society (UFFC-S)				
445 Hoes Ln	Piscataway NJ	08854	800-678-4333	732-981-0060
Institute for Operations Research & the Management Sciences (INFORMS)				
7240 Pkwy Dr Ste 300	Hanover MD	21076	800-446-3676	443-757-3500
International Society of Certified Electronics Technicians (ISCET)				
3608 Pershing Ave	Fort Worth TX	76107	800-946-0201	817-921-9101
Laser Institute of America (LIA)				
13501 Ingenuity Dr Ste 128	Orlando FL	32826	800-345-2737	407-380-1553
Mathematical Assn of America (MAA)				
1529 18th St NW	Washington DC	20036	800-331-1622	202-387-5200
MTM Assn for Standards & Research				
1111 E Touhy Ave Ste 280	Des Plaines IL	60018	844-300-5355	
National Academies				
500 Fifth St NW	Washington DC	20001	800-624-6242	202-334-2138
National Council on Radiation Protection & Measurements (NCRP)				
7910 Woodmont Ave Ste 400	Bethesda MD	20814	800-462-3683	301-657-2652
National Geographic Society				
1145 17th St NW	Washington DC	20036	800-647-5463	202-857-7000
National Society of Professional Engineers (NSPE)				
1420 King St	Alexandria VA	22314	888-285-6773	
New York Academy of Sciences				
250 Greenwich St 40th Fl	New York NY	10007	800-843-6927	212-298-8600
Scientific Equipment & Furniture Assn (SEFA)				
65 Hilton Ave	Garden City NY	11530	877-294-5424	516-294-5424
Semiconductor Equipment & Materials International				
3081 Zenker Rd	San Jose CA	95134	877-746-7788	408-943-6900
Society for Experimental Mechanics Inc (SEM)				
7 School St	Bethel CT	06801	800-627-8258	203-790-6373
Society for Industrial & Applied Mathematics (SIAM)				
3600 Market St 6th Fl	Philadelphia PA	19104	800-447-7426	215-382-9800
Society for Integrative & Comparative Biology (SICB)				
1313 Dolley Madison Blvd Ste 402	McLean VA	22101	800-955-1236	703-790-1745
Society for Sedimentary Geology (SEPM)				
4111 S Darlington Ste 100	Tulsa OK	74135	800-865-9765	918-610-3361
Society for the Advancement of Material & Process Engineering (SAMPE)				
21680 Gateway Center Dr Ste 300	Diamond Bar CA	91765	800-562-7360	626-521-9460
Society of Cable Telecommunications Engineers (SCTE)				
140 Philips Rd	Exton PA	19341	800-542-5040	610-363-6888
Society of Women Engineers (SWE)				
130 E Randolph St Ste 3500.	Chicago IL	60601	877-793-4636	312-596-5223
Women in Technology International (WITI)				
11500 Olympic Blvd Ste 400	Los Angeles CA	90064	800-334-9484	818-788-9484

49-20 Telecommunications Professionals Associations

			Toll-Free	Phone
Alliance for Telecommunications Industry Solutions (ATIS)				
1200 G St NW Ste 500	Washington DC	20005	800-649-1202	202-628-6380
Audiovisual & Integrated Experience Association (ICIA)				
11242 Waples Mill Rd Ste 200	Fairfax VA	22030	800-659-7469	703-273-7200
Communications Supply Service Assn (CSSA)				
5700 Murray St	Little Rock AR	72209	800-252-2772	501-562-7666
Enterprise Wireless Alliance (EWA)				
8484 Westpark Dr Ste 630	McLean VA	22102	800-482-8282	703-528-5115
Society of Communications Technology Consultants (SCTC)				
230 Washington Ave Ext Ste 101	Albany NY	12203	800-782-7670	

49-21 Transportation Industry Associations

			Toll-Free	Phone
Aircraft Owners & Pilots Assn (AOPA)				
421 Aviation Way	Frederick MD	21701	800-872-2672	301-695-2000

Classified Section

				Toll-Free	Phone
American Ambulance Assn (AAA)					
8400 Westpark Dr 2nd Fl	McLean	VA	22102	**800-523-4447**	703-610-9018
American Highway Users Alliance					
1920 L St NW Ste 525	Washington	DC	20036	**800-388-0650**	202-857-1200
American International Automobile Dealers Assn (AIADA)					
500 Montgomery St Ste 800	Alexandria	VA	22314	**800-462-4232**	
American Moving & Storage Assn (AMSA)					
1611 Duke St	Alexandria	VA	22314	**888-849-2672**	703-683-7410
American Traffic Safety Services Assn (ATSSA)					
15 Riverside Pkwy Ste 100	Fredericksburg	VA	22406	**800-272-8772**	540-368-1701
American Trucking Assn (ATA)					
950 N Glebe Rd Ste 210	Arlington	VA	22203	**800-282-5463**	703-838-1700
Association of American Railroads (AAR)					
425 Third St SW	Washington	DC	20024	**800-533-6644**	202-639-2100
Automatic Transmission Rebuilders Assn (ATRA)					
2400 Latigo Ave	Oxnard	CA	93030	**866-464-2872**	805-604-2000
Automotive Engine Rebuilders Assn (AERA)					
500 Coventry Ln Ste 180	Crystal Lake	IL	60014	**888-326-2372**	847-541-6550
Automotive Industry Action Group (AIAG)					
26200 Lahser Rd Ste 200	Southfield	MI	48033	**877-275-2424**	248-358-3570
Automotive Oil Change Assn (AOCA)					
330 N Wabash Ave Ste 2000	Chicago	IL	60611	**800-230-0702**	312-321-5132
Automotive Parts Remanufacturers Assn (APRA)					
4215 Lafayette Ctr Dr Ste 3	Chantilly	VA	20151	**877-734-4827**	703-968-2772
Automotive Recyclers Assn (ARA)					
9113 Church St	Manassas	VA	20110	**888-385-1005**	571-208-0428
Automotive Service Assn (ASA)					
1901 Airport Fwy	Bedford	TX	76021	**800-272-7467***	
*Cust Svc					
Coalition Against Bigger Trucks (CABT)					
109 NFairfax St 2nd Fl	Alexandria	VA	22314	**888-222-8123**	703-535-3131
Coalition for Auto Repair Equality (CARE)					
105 Oronoco St Ste 115	Alexandria	VA	22314	**800-229-5380**	703-519-7555
Community Transportation Assn of America (CTAA)					
1341 G St NW 10th Fl	Washington	DC	20005	**800-891-0590**	
General Aviation Manufacturers Association (GAMA)					
1400 K St NW Ste 801	Washington	DC	20005	**866-427-3287**	202-393-1500
Helicopter Assn International (HAI)					
1920 Ballenger Ave 4th Fl	Alexandria	VA	22314	**800-435-4976**	703-683-4646
Intelligent Transportation Society of America (ITS)					
1100 New Jersey Ave SE Ste 850	Washington	DC	20003	**800-374-8472**	202-484-4847
Intermodal Assn of North America (IANA)					
11785 Beltsville Dr Ste 1100	Calverton	MD	20705	**877-438-8442**	301-982-3400
International Air Transport Assn					
800 Pl Victoria PO Box 113	Montreal	QC	H4Z1M1	**800-716-6326**	514-874-0202
International Carwash Assn					
230 E Ohio St	Chicago	IL	60611	**888-422-8422**	
International Motor Coach Group Inc (IMG)					
12351 W 96th Ter	Lenexa	KS	66215	**888-447-3466**	
International Safe Transit Assn (ISTA)					
1400 Abbott Rd Ste 160	East Lansing	MI	48823	**888-299-2208**	517-333-3437
Jewelers Shipping Assn (JSA)					
125 Carlsbad St	Cranston	RI	02920	**800-688-4572**	401-943-6020
National Air Transportation Assn (NATA)					
4226 King St	Alexandria	VA	22302	**800-808-6282**	703-845-9000
National Automobile Dealers Assn (NADA)					
8400 Westpark Dr	McLean	VA	22102	**800-252-6232**	703-821-7000
National Business Aviation Assn (NBAA)					
1200 18th St NW Ste 400	Washington	DC	20036	**800-394-6222**	202-783-9000
National Motor Freight Traffic Assn (NMFTA)					
1001 N Fairfax St Ste 600	Alexandria	VA	22314	**866-411-6632**	703-838-1810
National Motorists Assn (NMA)					
402 W Second St	Waunakee	WI	53597	**800-882-2785**	608-849-6000
National Tank Truck Carriers Inc					
950 N Glebe Rd Ste 520	Arlington	VA	22203	**800-228-9290***	703-838-1960
*Resv					
National Truck Equipment Assn (NTEA)					
37400 Hills Tech Dr	Farmington Hills	MI	48331	**800-441-6832**	248-489-7090
National Waterways Conference Inc (NWC)					
4650 Washington Blvd Ste 608	Arlington	VA	22201	**866-371-1390**	703-243-4090
NATSO Inc					
1737 King St Ste 200	Alexandria	VA	22314	**800-956-9160**	703-549-2100
Owner-Operator Independent Drivers Assn Inc (OOIDA)					
1 NW OOIDA Dr	Grain Valley	MO	64029	**800-444-5791**	816-229-5791
Passenger Vessel Assn (PVA)					
103 Oronoco St Ste 200	Alexandria	VA	22314	**800-807-8360**	703-518-5005
Recreation Vehicle Industry Assn (RVIA)					
1896 Preston White Dr	Reston	VA	20191	**800-336-0154**	703-620-6003
Self Storage Assn (SSA)					
1901 N Beauregard St Ste 106	Alexandria	VA	22311	**888-735-3784**	703-575-8000
Society of Automotive Engineers Inc (SAE)					
400 Commonwealth Dr	Warrendale	PA	15096	**877-606-7323**	724-776-4841
Society of Naval Architects & Marine Engineers (SNAME)					
601 Pavonia Ave	Jersey City	NJ	07306	**800-798-2188**	201-798-4800
Specialty Vehicle Institute of America (SVIA)					
2 Jenner St Ste 150	Irvine	CA	92618	**800-887-2887**	949-727-3727
United Motorcoach Assn (UMA)					
113 SW St 4th Fl	Alexandria	VA	22314	**800-424-8262**	703-838-2929
Vertical Flight Society, The					
2701 Prosperity Ave Ste 210	Fairfax	VA	22031	**855-247-4685**	703-684-6777

50 ATTRACTIONS

SEE ALSO Art Dealers & Galleries ; Performing Arts Facilities ; Amusement Parks ; Presidential Libraries ; Special Collections Libraries ; Museums ; Museums - Children's ; Museums & Halls of Fame - Sports ; Planetariums ; Zoos & Wildlife Parks ; Botanical Gardens & Arboreta ; Aquariums - Public ; Parks - National - US ; Parks - National - Canada ; Parks - State ; Cemeteries - National

50-1 Churches, Cathedrals, Synagogues, Temples

				Toll-Free	Phone
Mesa Arizona Temple					
101 S LeSueur	Mesa	AZ	85204	**855-537-4357**	480-833-1211

				Toll-Free	Phone
National Shrine of Our Lady of the Snows					
442 S De Mazenod Dr	Belleville	IL	62223	**800-682-2879**	618-397-6700
Shrine of Our Lady of La Leche					
27 Ocean Ave	Saint Augustine	FL	32084	**800-342-6529**	904-824-2809

50-2 Cultural & Arts Centers

Colorado

				Toll-Free	Phone
Anderson Ranch Arts Center					
5263 Owl Creek Rd PO Box 5598	Snowmass Village	CO	81615	**800-525-6363**	970-923-3181

Georgia

				Toll-Free	Phone
Center for Puppetry Arts					
1404 Spring St NW	Atlanta	GA	30309	**800-642-3629**	404-873-3089

Maine

				Toll-Free	Phone
Maine Folklife Ctr					
5773 S Stevens Rm 112B	Orono	ME	04469	**800-753-9044**	207-581-1840

Nebraska

				Toll-Free	Phone
Gerald R Ford Conservation Ctr					
1326 S 32nd St	Omaha	NE	68105	**800-634-6932**	402-595-1180

Ohio

				Toll-Free	Phone
Contemporary Arts Ctr					
44 E Sixth St	Cincinnati	OH	45202	**800-644-6862**	513-345-8400

South Dakota

				Toll-Free	Phone
Dahl Arts Ctr					
713 Seventh St	Rapid City	SD	57701	**800-487-3223**	605-394-4101

Washington

				Toll-Free	Phone
Daybreak Star Ctr					
3801 W Government Way PO Box 99100	Seattle	WA	98199	**800-321-4321**	206-285-4425

West Virginia

				Toll-Free	Phone
Oglebay Institute's Stifel Fine Arts Ctr					
1330 National Rd	Wheeling	WV	26003	**800-624-6988**	304-242-7700

50-3 Historic Homes & Buildings

Alabama

				Toll-Free	Phone
Old Alabama Town					
301 Columbus St	Montgomery	AL	36104	**888-240-1850**	334-240-4500

Arizona

				Toll-Free	Phone
Cosanti Originals Inc					
6433 Doubletree Ranch Rd	Paradise Valley	AZ	85253	**800-752-3187**	480-948-6145

California

				Toll-Free	Phone
Marston House Museum & Gardens					
3525 Seventh Ave	San Diego	CA	92103	**800-577-6679**	619-297-9327

Georgia

				Toll-Free	Phone
Historic Roswell District					
617 Atlanta St	Roswell	GA	30075	**800-776-7935**	
Smith Plantation Home					
935 Alpharetta St	Roswell	GA	30075	**800-776-7935**	770-641-3978

Illinois

				Toll-Free	Phone
Jane Addams Hull-House Museum					
800 S Halsted St	Chicago	IL	60607	**800-625-2013**	312-413-5353

Indiana

				Toll-Free	Phone
Indiana Landmarks					
1201 Central Ave	Indianapolis	IN	46202	**800-450-4534**	317-639-4534

Iowa

				Toll-Free	Phone
Mathias Ham House Historic Site					
350 E Third St	Dubuque	IA	52001	**800-226-3369**	563-557-9545

Kentucky

					Toll-Free	Phone
Loudoun House						
209 Castlewood Dr	Lexington	KY	40505		**866-945-7920**	859-254-7024

Louisiana

					Toll-Free	Phone
Rosedown Plantation State Historic Site						
12501 Hwy 10	Saint Francisville	LA	70775		**888-376-1867**	225-635-3332

Minnesota

					Toll-Free	Phone
Alexander Ramsey House (ARH)						
265 S Exchange St	Saint Paul	MN	55102		**800-657-3773**	651-296-8760
Comstock Historic House						
506 Eigth St S	Moorhead	MN	56560		**800-657-3773**	218-291-4211
Glensheen Mansion						
3300 London Rd	Duluth	MN	55804		**888-454-4536**	218-726-8910
Historic Fort Snelling						
200 Tower Ave Ft Snelling History Ctr	Saint Paul	MN	55111		**800-657-3773**	612-726-1171
James J Hill House						
240 Summit Ave	Saint Paul	MN	55102		**888-727-8386**	651-297-2555

New York

					Toll-Free	Phone
Frank Lloyd Wright's Martin House Complex						
125 Jewett Pkwy	Buffalo	NY	14214		**877-377-3858**	716-856-3858

North Carolina

					Toll-Free	Phone
Vance Birthplace State Historic Site						
911 Reems Creek Rd	Weaverville	NC	28787		**800-767-1560**	828-645-6706

Ohio

					Toll-Free	Phone
Fort Meigs State Memorial						
29100 W River Rd	Perrysburg	OH	43551		**800-283-8916**	419-874-4121
Paul Laurence Dunbar House						
219 N Paul Laurence Dunbar St	Dayton	OH	45402		**800-860-0148**	937-224-7061

Pennsylvania

					Toll-Free	Phone
John Harris-Simon Cameron Mansion, The						
219 S Front St	Harrisburg	PA	17104		**800-732-0099**	717-233-3462
Powel House						
244 S Third St	Philadelphia	PA	19106		**877-426-8056**	215-627-0364

Rhode Island

					Toll-Free	Phone
Chateau-Sur-Mer						
474 Bellevue Ave	Newport	RI	02840		**800-326-6030**	401-847-1000
Hunter House						
424 Bellevue Ave	Newport	RI	02840		**800-326-6030**	401-847-1000

South Carolina

					Toll-Free	Phone
Fort Hill The John C Calhoun House						
Clemson University	Clemson	SC	29634		**800-777-1004**	864-656-3311
Gassaway Mansion						
106 Dupont Dr	Greenville	SC	29607		**888-912-7469**	864-271-0188
Old Exchange & Provost Dungeon						
122 E Bay St	Charleston	SC	29401		**888-763-0448**	843-727-2165

South Dakota

					Toll-Free	Phone
Corn Palace 604 N Main St	Mitchell	SD	57301		**800-289-7469**	605-995-8430

Virginia

					Toll-Free	Phone
Monticello						
556 Dettor Rd Ste 107	Charlottesville	VA	22903		**800-243-0743**	434-984-9822

Wisconsin

					Toll-Free	Phone
Taliesin						
5607 County Hwy C	Spring Green	WI	53588		**877-588-7900**	608-588-7090

50-4 Monuments, Memorials, Landmarks

					Toll-Free	Phone
African-American Civil War Memorial & Museum						
1925 Vermont Ave NW	Washington	DC	20001		**800-753-9222**	202-667-2667
Empire State Bldg						
350 Fifth Ave Ste 100	New York	NY	10118		**877-692-8439**	212-736-3100
Gateway Arch						
50 S Leonor K Sullivan Blvd	Saint Louis	MO	63102		**877-982-1410**	
Golden Gate Bridge						
Golden Gate Bridge Toll Plz Presidio Stn						
PO Box 9000	San Francisco	CA	94129		**877-229-8655**	415-921-5858
Illinois Vietnam Veterans Memorial						
Oak Ridge Cemetery	Springfield	IL	62702		**800-545-7300**	217-782-2717

					Toll-Free	Phone
Lincoln Boyhood National Memorial						
2916 E S St PO Box 1816	Lincoln City	IN	47552		**800-445-9667**	812-937-4541
Littleton Coin Company LLC						
1309 Mt Eustis Rd	Littleton	NH	03561		**800-645-3122**	
USS Kidd Veterans Memorial & Museum						
305 S River Rd	Baton Rouge	LA	70802		**800-638-0594**	225-342-1942
USS Missouri Memorial Assn Inc						
63 Cowpens St	Honolulu	HI	96818		**877-644-4896**	808-455-1600
Vietnam Women's Memorial Foundation Inc						
1735 Connecticut Ave NW 3rd Fl	Washington	DC	20009		**866-822-8963**	

50-5 Nature Centers, Parks, Other Natural Areas

					Toll-Free	Phone
Black Hills Caverns						
2600 Cavern Rd	Rapid City	SD	57702		**800-837-9358**	605-343-0542
Butterfly House - Faust Park, The						
15193 Olive Blvd	Chesterfield	MO	63017		**800-642-8842**	636-530-0076
Carson Hot Springs						
1500 Hot Springs Rd	Carson City	NV	89706		**888-917-3711**	775-885-8844
Cave & Mine Adventures/Sierra Nevada Recreation Corporation						
5350 Moaning Cave Rd	Vallecito	CA	95251		**866-762-2837**	209-736-2708
DeGraaf Nature Ctr						
600 Graafschap Rd	Holland	MI	49423		**888-535-5792**	616-355-1057
Devil's Den Preserve						
33 Pent Rd	Weston	CT	06883		**800-628-6860**	
El Dorado Nature Ctr						
7550 E Spring St	Long Beach	CA	90815		**800-662-8887**	562-570-1745
Genesee County Parks & Recreation						
5045 Stanley Rd	Flint	MI	48506		**800-648-7275**	810-736-7100
Hanauma Bay Nature Preserve						
100 Hanauma Bay Rd	Honolulu	HI	96825		**800-690-6200**	808-396-4229
Houston Arboretum & Nature Ctr						
4501 Woodway Dr	Houston	TX	77024		**866-510-7219**	713-681-8433
Katharine Ordway Preserve						
4245 N Fairfax Dr Ste 100	Arlington	VA	22203		**800-628-6860**	
Lava Hot Springs State Foundation						
430 E Main St PO Box 669	Lava Hot Springs	ID	83246		**800-423-8597**	208-776-5221
Linville Caverns Inc						
19929 US 221 N	Marion	NC	20752		**800-419-0540**	
Lost River Caverns						
726 Durham St PO Box M	Hellertown	PA	18055		**888-529-1907**	610-838-8767
Prairie Wetlands Learning Ctr						
602 State Hwy 210 E	Fergus Falls	MN	56537		**800-344-9453**	
Raccoon Mountain Caverns						
319 W Hills Dr	Chattanooga	TN	37419		**800-823-2267**	423-821-9403
Riveredge Nature Ctr						
4458 W Hawthorne Dr PO Box 26	Newburg	WI	53060		**800-287-8098**	262-375-2715
Ruby Falls						
1720 S Scenic Hwy	Chattanooga	TN	37409		**800-755-7105**	423-821-2544
Rushmore Cave 13622 Hwy 40	Keystone	SD	57751		**800-344-8826**	605-255-4384

50-6 Shopping/Dining/Entertainment Districts

					Toll-Free	Phone
Broadway at the Beach						
1325 Celebrity Cir	Myrtle Beach	SC	29577		**800-386-4662**	843-444-3200
Cooper Young Business Assn						
2120 Young Ave	Memphis	TN	38104		**800-342-3308**	901-276-7222
Great Lakes Crossing Outlets						
4000 Baldwin Rd	Auburn Hills	MI	48326		**877-746-7452**	248-454-5000
Hillcrest Historic District						
Markham & Kavanaugh	Little Rock	AR	72216		**877-637-0037**	501-371-0075
John's Pass Village & Boardwalk						
150 John's Pass Boardwalk Pl	Madeira Beach	FL	33708		**800-853-1536**	727-398-6577
Pike Outlets, The						
1126 Queens Hwy	Long Beach	CA	90802		**877-225-5337**	
Renaissance Ctr						
Detroit River	Detroit	MI	48243		**800-983-4240**	
River Walk						
110 Broadway Ste 500	San Antonio	TX	78204		**800-417-4139**	210-227-4262
Sierra Select Distributors						
4320 Roseville Rd	North Highlands	CA	95660		**800-793-7334**	
Union Station						
50 Massachusetts Ave	Washington	DC	20002		**800-331-0008**	202-289-1908
Universal Studios Hollywood						
100 Universal City Plz	Universal City	CA	91608		**800-864-8377**	818-622-9841

50-7 Wineries

The wineries listed in this category feature wine-tasting as an attraction.

					Toll-Free	Phone
Adams County Winery						
251 Peach Tree Rd	Orrtanna	PA	17353		**877-601-7936**	717-334-4631
Chateau Elan Winery						
100 Tour de France	Braselton	GA	30517		**800-233-9463**	678-425-0900
Chateau Morrisette Winery						
287 Winery Rd SW	Floyd	VA	24091		**866-695-2001**	540-593-2865
Chateau Ste Michelle Winery						
14111 NE 145th St	Woodinville	WA	98072		**800-267-6793**	425-488-1133
Columbia Winery						
14030 NE 145th St	Woodinville	WA	98072		**800-488-2347**	425-482-7490
Eola Hills Wine Cellars						
501 S Pacific Hwy 99 W	Rickreall	OR	97371		**800-291-6730**	503-623-2405
Honeywood Winery						
1350 Hines St SE	Salem	OR	97302		**800-726-4101**	503-362-4111
Huber's Orchard & Winery						
19816 Huber Rd	Borden	IN	47106		**800-345-9463**	812-923-9463
King Estate Winery						
80854 Territorial Rd	Eugene	OR	97405		**800-884-4441**	541-942-9874
Llano Estacado Winery						
3426 E FM 1585	Lubbock	TX	79404		**800-634-3854**	806-745-2258
Mazza Vineyards						
11815 E Lake Rd	North East	PA	16428		**800-796-9463**	

Classified Section

			Toll-Free	Phone
Nassau Valley Vineyards				
32165 Winery Way	Lewes DE	19958	800-425-2355	302-645-9463
Oliver Winery				
8024 N SR-37	Bloomington IN	47404	800-258-2783	812-876-5800
San Sebastian Winery				
157 King St	Saint Augustine FL	32084	888-352-9463	904-826-1594
Winery at Wolf Creek				
2637 Cleveland Massillon Rd	Norton OH	44203	800-436-0426	330-666-9285

51   AUCTIONS

			Toll-Free	Phone
ADESA Inc				
13085 Hamilton Crossing Blvd	Carmel IN	46032	800-923-3725	317-815-1100
Akron Auto Auction Inc				
2471 Ley Dr	Akron OH	44319	800-773-0033	330-773-8245
Bonhams & Butterfields				
220 San Bruno Ave	San Francisco CA	94103	800-223-2854	415-861-7500
Collectors Universe Inc				
PO Box 6280	Newport Beach CA	92658	800-325-1121	949-567-1234
eBay Inc 2065 Hamilton Ave	San Jose CA	95125	800-322-9266	408-376-7400
NASDAQ: EBAY				
Fasig-Tipton Co Inc				
2400 Newtown Pk	Lexington KY	40511	877-945-2020	859-255-1555
Gallery of History Inc				
3601 W Sahara Ave	Las Vegas NV	89102	800-425-5379	702-364-1000
Greater Rockford Auto Auction Inc (GRAA)				
5937 Sandy Hollow Rd	Rockford IL	61109	800-830-4722	815-874-7800
Harry Davis & Co				
1725 Blvd of Allies	Pittsburgh PA	15219	800-775-2289	412-765-1170
Henderson Auctions				
13340 Florida Blvd PO Box 336	Livingston LA	70754	800-334-7443	225-686-2252
Heritage Place Inc				
2829 S MacArthur	Oklahoma City OK	73128	888-343-9831	405-682-4551
iCollectorcom				
103-2071 Kingsway Ave	Port Coquitlam BC	V3C6N2	866-313-0123	604-941-2221
Insurance Auto Auctions Inc				
2 Westbrook Corporate Ctr 10th Fl	Westchester IL	60154	800-872-1501	708-492-7000
Ironplanet Inc				
3825 Hopyard Rd Ste 250	Pleasanton CA	94588	888-433-5426 *	925-225-8600
*Cust Svc				
Liquidity Services Inc				
1920 L St NW 6th Fl	Washington DC	20036	800-310-4604	202-467-6868
NASDAQ: LQDT				
Pricelinecom LLC				
800 Connecticut Ave	Norwalk CT	06854	800-774-2354	
Theriault's PO Box 151	Annapolis MD	21404	800-966-3655	410-224-3655

52   AUDIO & VIDEO EQUIPMENT

			Toll-Free	Phone
Alpine Electronics of America				
19145 Gramercy Pl	Torrance CA	90501	800-257-4631	310-326-8000
AmpliVox Sound Systems LLC				
3995 Commercial Ave	Northbrook IL	60062	800-267-5486	847-498-9000
Atlas Sound				
1601 Jack McKay Blvd	Ennis TX	75119	800-876-3333	
Audio America				
15132 Park Of Commerce Blvd	Jupiter FL	33478	800-432-8532	561-863-7704
Audio Command Systems				
694 Main St	Westbury NY	11590	800-382-2939	516-997-5800
Audiosears Corp 2 S St	Stamford NY	12167	800-533-7863	607-652-7305
Audiovox Corp				
180 Marcus Blvd	Hauppauge NY	11788	800-645-4994	631-231-7750
NASDAQ: VOXX				
Biamp Systems Inc				
9300 SW Gemini Dr	Beaverton OR	97008	800-826-1457	
Bob Reeves Brass Mouthpieces				
25574 Rye Canyon Rd Ste D	Valencia CA	91355	800-837-0980	661-775-8820
Bogen Communications International Inc				
50 Spring St	Ramsey NJ	07446	800-999-2809	201-934-8500
OTC: BOGN				
Bose Corp The Mountain	Framingham MA	01701	800-379-2073 *	508-766-1099
*Cust Svc				
Car Toys Inc				
400 Fairview Ave N Ste 900	Seattle WA	98109	888-227-8697	
City of Chula Vista				
276 Fourth Ave	Chula Vista CA	91910	877-478-5478	619-691-5047
Clarion Corp of America				
6200 Gateway Dr	Cypress CA	90630	800-347-8667	310-327-9100
Community Professional Loudspeakers				
333 E Fifth St	Chester PA	19013	800-523-4934	610-876-3400
Dana Innovations				
212 Avenida Fabricante	San Clemente CA	92672	800-582-7777	949-492-7777
DEI Holdings Inc 1 Viper Way	Vista CA	92081	800-876-0800	760-598-6200
OTC: DEI				
Eminence Speaker LLC				
838 Mulberry Pk PO Box 360	Eminence KY	40019	800-897-8373	502-845-5622
Encore Event Technologies				
1 N Arlington 1500 W Shure Dr				
Ste 175	Arlington Heights IL	60004	800-836-8361	
Extron Electronics				
1230 S Lewis St	Anaheim CA	92805	800-633-9876 *	714-491-1500
*Tech Supp				
FlexHead Industries Inc				
56 Lowland St	Holliston MA	01746	800-829-6975	508-893-9596
Ford Audio-Video Systems Inc				
4800 W I- 40	Oklahoma City OK	73128	800-654-6744	405-946-9966
Fujitsu Ten Corp of America				
19600 S Vermont Ave	Torrance CA	90502	800-233-2216	310-327-2151
FURMAN 1690 Corporate Cir	Petaluma CA	94954	877-486-4738	707-763-1010
Harman International Industries Inc				
400 Atlantic St 15th Fl	Stamford CT	06901	800-473-0602	203-328-3500
NYSE: HAR				

			Toll-Free	Phone
Interactive Digital Solutions Inc				
14701 Cumberland Rd Ste 400	Noblesville IN	46060	877-880-0022	
JBL Professional				
8500 Balboa Blvd	Northridge CA	91329	800-852-5776	800-397-1881
JVC Professional Products Co				
1700 Valley Rd	Wayne NJ	07470	800-252-5722	973-317-5000
Kenwood USA PO Box 22745	Long Beach CA	90810	800-536-9663	310-639-9000
KLH Audio Speakers				
984 Logan St Ste 301	Noblesville IN	46060	833-554-8326	
Klipsch LLC 137 Hempstead 278	Hope AR	71801	888-250-8561	
Koss Corp				
4129 N Port Washington Ave	Milwaukee WI	53212	800-872-5677	
NASDAQ: KOSS				
Law Enforcement Assoc Corp (LEA-AID)				
120 Penmarc Dr Ste 113	Raleigh NC	27603	800-354-9669	919-872-6210
OTC: LAWEQ				
Lectrosonics Inc				
PO Box 15900	Rio Rancho NM	87174	800-821-1121	505-892-4501
LifeSize Communications Inc				
1601 S Mopac Expwy Ste 100	Austin TX	78746	877-543-3749	512-347-9300
Logitech Inc 6505 Kaiser Dr	Fremont CA	94555	800-231-7717 *	510-795-8500
*Sales				
Lowell Manufacturing Co				
100 Integram Dr	Pacific MO	63069	800-325-9660	636-257-3400
McIntosh Laboratory Inc				
2 Chambers St	Binghamton NY	13903	800-538-6576	607-723-3512
Metra Electronics Corp				
460 Walker St	Holly Hill FL	32117	800-221-0932 *	386-257-1186
*Sales				
Mitsubishi Digital Electronics America Inc				
9351 Jeronimo Rd	Irvine CA	92618	800-332-2119	949-465-6000
Monster Cable Products Inc				
455 Valley Dr	Brisbane CA	94005	877-800-8989	415-840-2000
Omnitronics LLC				
6573 Cochran Rd	Solon OH	44139	800-762-9266	440-349-4900
Panasonic Avionics Corp				
26200 Enterprise Way	Lake Forest CA	92630	877-627-2300	949-672-2000
Panasonic Corp of North America				
1 Panasonic Way	Secaucus NJ	07094	800-211-7262 *	877-826-6538
*Cust Svc				
Peavey Electronics Corp				
5022 Hartley Peavey Dr	Meridian MS	39305	877-732-8391	601-483-5365
Phase Technology				
6400 Youngerman Cir	Jacksonville FL	32244	888-742-7385	904-777-0700
Pioneer Electronics (USA) Inc				
1925 E Dominguez St	Long Beach CA	90810	800-421-1404	310-952-2000
Polk Audio Inc				
5601 Metro Dr	Baltimore MD	21215	800-377-7655	410-358-3600
QSC Audio Products LLC				
1675 MacArthur Blvd	Costa Mesa CA	92626	800-854-4079	714-754-6175
Quam-Nichols Company Inc				
234 E Marquette Rd	Chicago IL	60637	800-633-3669	773-488-5800
Rane Corp 10802 47th Ave W	Mukilteo WA	98275	877-764-0093	425-355-6000
Record Play Tek Inc				
110 E Vistula St	Bristol IN	46507	800-809-5233	574-848-5233
Renkus-heinz Inc				
19201 Cook St	Foothill Ranch CA	92610	855-411-2364	949-588-9997
ReQuest Inc				
100 Saratoga Village Blvd Ste 45	Ballston Spa NY	12020	800-236-2812 *	518-899-1254
*Sales				
SDI Technologies Inc				
1299 Main St	Rahway NJ	07065	800-333-3092	
Sharp Electronics Corp				
1 Sharp Plz	Mahwah NJ	07430	800-237-4277	201-529-8200
Shure Inc 5800 W Touhy Ave	Niles IL	60714	800-257-4873	847-600-2000
Sony Corp of America				
550 Madison Ave	New York NY	10022	800-282-2848	212-833-6800
Sony Electronics Inc				
1 Sony Dr	Park Ridge NJ	07656	800-222-7669 *	201-930-1000
*Cust Svc				
Sound Com Corp 227 Depot St	Berea OH	44017	800-628-8739	440-234-2604
Southern Audio Services				
14763 Florida Blvd	Baton Rouge LA	70819	800-843-8823 *	888-651-1203
*Cust Svc				
Telex Communications Inc				
12000 Portland Ave S	Burnsville MN	55337	877-863-4169	877-863-4166
Toshiba America Inc				
1251 Ave of the Americas 41st Fl	New York NY	10020	800-457-7777	212-596-0600
Universal Audio Inc				
1700 Green Hills Rd	Scotts Valley CA	95066	877-698-2834	831-440-1176
Xantech				
1800 S McDowell Blvd	Petaluma CA	94954	800-472-5555 *	707-283-5900
*Sales				
Yamaha Electronics Corp				
6660 Orangethorpe Ave	Buena Park CA	90620	800-292-2982	866-430-2652

53   AUTO CLUBS

			Toll-Free	Phone
AAA Chicago Motor Club				
975 Meridian Lake Dr	Aurora IL	60504	866-968-7222	
AAA Club Alliance Inc				
3201 Meijer Dr	Toledo OH	43617	800-763-9900	419-843-1212
AAA Colorado				
4100 E Arkansas Ave	Denver CO	80222	866-625-3601	303-753-8800
AAA East Penn				
1020 W Hamilton St	Allentown PA	18101	800-222-4357	
AAA Hawaii				
1130 N Nimitz Hwy Ste A-170	Honolulu HI	96817	800-736-2886	877-440-6943
AAA Michigan				
1 Auto Club Dr	Dearborn MI	48126	800-222-6424	
AAA Minnesota/Iowa				
600 W Travelers Trl	Burnsville MN	55337	800-222-1333	952-707-4500
AAA MountainWest				
2100 11th Ave	Helena MT	59601	800-332-6119	406-447-8100
AAA Nebraska 815 N 98th St	Omaha NE	68114	800-222-6327	402-390-1000

	Toll-Free	Phone
AAA New York		
1415 Kellum Pl .... Garden City NY 11530	**855-374-1821**	
AAA North Penn		
1035 N Washington Ave .... Scranton PA 18509	**800-222-4357**	570-348-2511
AAA Northway		
112 Railroad St .... Schenectady NY 12305	**866-222-7283**	518-374-4696
AAA Ohio Auto Club		
90 E Wilson Bridge Rd .... Worthington OH 43085	**888-222-6446**	614-431-7901
AAA Oklahoma 2121 E 15th St .... Tulsa OK 74104	**800-222-2582**	918-748-1000
AAA Southern Pennsylvania		
2840 Eastern Blvd .... York PA 17402	**800-222-1469**	717-600-8700
AAA Utica & Central New York		
409 Court St .... Utica NY 13502	**800-222-4357**	
AAA Western & Central New York		
100 International Dr .... Williamsville NY 14221	**800-836-2582**	716-633-9860
AARP Motoring Plan		
601 E St NW .... Washington DC 20049	**800-555-1121**	
Auto Club of America Corp (ACA)		
9411 N Georgia St .... Oklahoma City OK 73120	**800-411-2007**	405-751-4430
Automobile Club of Southern California		
2601 S Figueroa St .... Los Angeles CA 90007	**800-400-4222**	213-741-3686
BP MotorClub		
PO Box 4441 .... Carol Stream IL 60197	**800-334-3300**	
Brickell Financial Services Motor Club Inc		
7300 Corporate Ctr Dr .... Miami FL 33126	**800-262-7262**	305-392-4300
CAA Club Group		
60 Commerce Valley Dr E .... Thornhill ON L3T7P9	**866-988-8878**	905-771-3000
CAA Maritimes Ltd		
378 Westmorland Rd .... Saint John NB E2J2G4	**800-471-1611**	506-634-1400
CAA North & East Ontario		
PO Box 8350 .... Ottawa ON K1G3T2	**800-267-8713**	613-820-1890
CAA Stoney Creek		
75 Centennial Pkwy N .... Hamilton ON L8E2P2	**877-544-0445**	905-664-8000
Canadian Automobile Assn (CAA)		
2151 Thurston Dr .... Ottawa ON K1G6C9	**800-267-8713**	613-820-1890
National Automobile Club (NAC)		
373 Vintage Park Dr Ste E....... Foster City CA 94404	**800-622-2136**	
National Motor Club of America Inc (NMC)		
130 E John Carpenter Fwy .... Irving TX 75062	**800-523-4582**	
Travelers Motor Club		
720 NW 50th St .... Oklahoma City OK 73154	**800-654-9208**	405-848-1711

54 AUTO SUPPLY STORES

	Toll-Free	Phone
A 1 Auto Recyclers		
7804 S Hwy 79 .... Rapid City SD 57702	**800-456-0715**	605-348-8442
Advance Auto Parts Inc		
5008 Airport Rd .... Roanoke VA 24012	**877-238-2623**	
NYSE: AAP		
Air Lift Co 2727 Snow Rd .... Lansing MI 48917	**800-248-0892**	517-322-2144
Ats All Tire Supply Co		
6600 Long Point Rd Ste 101.......... Houston TX 77055	**888-339-6665**	
AutoZone Inc 123 S Front St ...... Memphis TN 38103	**800-288-6966**	901-495-6500
NYSE: AZO		
Bap-Geon Import Auto Parts		
3403 Gulf Fwy .... Houston TX 77003	**888-868-2281**	713-227-1544
Bavarian Autosport Inc		
275 Constitution Ave .... Portsmouth NH 03801	**800-535-2002**	603-427-2002
Beck/Arnley Worldparts Inc		
2375 Midway Ln .... Smyrna TN 37167	**888-464-2325**	
Bill Smith Auto Parts		
400 Ash St Ste 100................... Danville IL 61832	**800-252-3005**	217-442-0156
BMW of Manhattan Inc		
555 W 57th St .... New York NY 10019	**877-855-4607**	212-586-2269
Bowditch Ford Inc		
11291 Jefferson Ave .... Newport News VA 23601	**866-399-2616**	757-595-2211
Briggs Auto Group Inc		
2312 Stagg Hill Rd .... Manhattan KS 66502	**800-257-4004**	785-537-8330
CEC Industries Ltd		
599 Bond St .... Lincolnshire IL 60069	**800-572-4168**	847-821-1199
Chris Alston Chassisworks Inc		
8661 Younger Creek Dr .... Sacramento CA 95828	**800-722-2269**	916-388-0288
Cumberland Truck Parts		
15 Sylmar Rd .... Nottingham PA 19362	**800-364-6995**	610-932-1152
Custom Truck Accessories Inc		
13408 Hwy 65 NE .... Ham Lake MN 55304	**800-333-1282**	763-757-5326
Delco Diesel Services Inc		
1100 S Agnew Ave .... Oklahoma City OK 73108	**800-256-0395**	405-232-3595
Duncan Systems Inc		
29391 Old US Hwy 33 .... Elkhart IN 46516	**800-551-9149**	
Jack's Tire & Oil Inc		
1795 N Main St .... Logan UT 84341	**866-804-8473**	435-752-7897
JE Adams Industries Ltd		
1025 63rd Ave SW .... Cedar Rapids IA 52404	**800-553-8861**	319-363-0237
JohnDow Industries Inc		
151 Snyder Ave .... Barberton OH 44203	**800-433-0708**	330-753-6895
KOI Auto Parts		
2701 Spring Grove Ave .... Cincinnati OH 45225	**800-354-0408**	513-357-2400
Meridian Auto Parts		
10211 Pacific Mesa Blvd Ste 404...... San Diego CA 92121	**800-874-1974**	
Minor Tire & Wheel Company Inc		
3512 Sixth Ave SE .... Decatur AL 35603	**800-633-3936**	256-353-4957
Momo Automotive Accessories Inc		
1161 N Knollwood Cir .... Anaheim CA 92801	**800-749-6666**	949-380-7556
Myers Brothers of Kansas City Inc		
1210 W 28th St .... Kansas City MO 64108	**800-264-2404**	816-931-5501
NORD Drivesystems		
800 Nord Dr .... Waunakee WI 53597	**888-314-6673**	
Northland Auto & Truck Accessories		
1106 S 29th St W .... Billings MT 59102	**800-736-5302**	406-245-0595
O'Reilly Auto Parts		
233 S Patterson .... Springfield MO 65802	**888-327-7153**	417-862-6708
NASDAQ: ORLY		
Original Parts Group Inc (OPGI)		
1770 Saturn Way .... Seal Beach CA 90740	**800-243-8355**	562-594-1000

	Toll-Free	Phone
Palm Beach Motoring Accessories Inc		
7744 SW Jack James Dr .... Stuart FL 34997	**800-869-3011**	772-286-2701
Peerless Tire Co		
5000 Kingston St .... Denver CO 80239	**800-999-7810**	
Phoenix USA Inc		
51 E Borden St .... Cookeville TN 38501	**800-786-8785**	
Pick Your Part Auto Wrecking Inc		
1235 S Beach Blvd .... Anaheim CA 92804	**800-962-2277**	
PJ's Auto Parts Inc		
2708 W Main Rd .... Caledonia NY 14423	**800-946-5787**	716-538-2391
S & S Tire		
1475 Jingle Bell Ln .... Lexington KY 40509	**800-685-6794**	859-252-0151
S&R Truck Tire Center Inc		
1402 Truckers Blvd .... Jeffersonville IN 47130	**800-488-2670**	812-282-4799
Spal-Usa Inc		
1731 SE Oralabor Rd .... Ankeny IA 50021	**800-345-0327**	
Specmo Enterprises		
1200 E Avis Dr .... Madison Heights MI 48071	**800-545-7910**	
Suburban Wheel Cover Co		
1420 Landmeier Rd .... Elk Grove Village IL 60007	**800-635-8126**	847-758-0388
Tire Warehouse		
200 Holleder Pkwy .... Rochester NY 14615	**800-876-6676**	
Town Fair Tire Company Inc		
460 Coe Ave .... East Haven CT 06512	**800-972-2245**	
Trew Industrial Wheels Inc		
310 Wilhagan Rd .... Nashville TN 37217	**888-977-8739**	615-360-9100
Turbo Parts LLC		
767 Pierce Rd Ste 2 .... Clifton Park NY 12065	**800-446-4776**	518-885-3199
Vanguard Trucks Centers		
700 Nunkin Dr .... Forest Park GA 30297	**866-216-7925**	800-783-5353
Weathers Auto Supply Inc		
23308 Airpark Dr .... Petersburg VA 23803	**888-572-2886**	804-861-1076
West Coast Differentials		
2429 Mercantile Dr Ste A .... Rancho Cordova CA 95742	**800-510-0950**	916-635-0950
XKS Unlimited Inc		
850 Fiero Ln .... San Luis Obispo CA 93401	**800-444-5247**	805-544-7864

55 AUTOMATIC MERCHANDISING EQUIPMENT & SYSTEMS

SEE ALSO Food Service

	Toll-Free	Phone
Affiliated Control Equipment Inc		
640 Wheat Ln .... Wood Dale IL 60191	**800-942-8753**	630-595-4680
AIR-serv Group LLC		
1370 Mendota Heights Rd ...... Mendota Heights MN 55120	**800-247-8363**	
AVS Companies		
750 Morse Ave .... Elk Grove Village IL 60007	**800-441-0009**	847-439-9400
Bastian Solutions (BMH)		
10585 N Meridian St 3rd Fl .... Indianapolis IN 46290	**800-772-0464**	317-575-9992
Betson Enterprises Inc		
303 Patterson Plank Rd .... Carlstadt NJ 07072	**800-524-2343**	201-438-1300
Birmingham Vending Co		
540 Second Ave N .... Birmingham AL 35204	**800-288-7635**	205-324-7526
Coin Acceptors Inc		
300 Hunter Ave .... Saint Louis MO 63124	**800-325-2646**	314-725-0100
Coinstar Inc		
1800 114th Ave SE .... Bellevue WA 98004	**800-928-2274**	425-943-8000
Glacier Water Services Inc		
1385 Park Center Dr .... Vista CA 92081	**800-452-2437**	
OTC: GWSV		
Harcourt Outlines Inc		
7765 S 175 W PO Box 128............... Milroy IN 46156	**800-428-6584**	

56 AUTOMATIC TELLER MACHINES (ATMS)

	Toll-Free	Phone
Accu-time Systems Inc		
420 Somers Rd .... Ellington CT 06029	**800-355-4648**	860-870-5000
Diebold Nixdorf Inc		
5995 Mayfair Rd .... North Canton OH 44720	**800-999-3600**	330-490-4000
NYSE: DBD		
Electronic Cash Systems Inc (ECS)		
29883 Santa Margarita Pkwy		
.... Rancho Santa Margarita CA 92688	**888-327-2860**	949-888-8580
Everi Holdings Inc (GCA)		
7250 S Tenaya Way Ste 100 .... Las Vegas NV 89113	**800-833-7110**	702-855-3000
NYSE: EVRI		
Tidel Engineering Inc		
2025 W Belt Line Rd Ste 114 .... Carrollton TX 75006	**800-678-7577**	972-484-3358

57 AUTOMOBILE DEALERS & GROUPS

SEE ALSO Automobile Sales & Related Services - Online

	Toll-Free	Phone
A C Nelson Rv World		
11818 L St .... Omaha NE 68137	**888-655-2332**	402-333-1122
Alamo City Chverolet		
9400 San Pedro Ave .... San Antonio TX 78216	**866-635-6971**	210-987-2134
Alberic Colon Auto Sales		
551 Marginal JF Kennedy .... San Juan PR 00920	**888-510-0718**	877-292-4610
America's Car-Mart Inc		
802 Southeast Plaza Ave Ste 200 ...... Bentonville AR 72712	**866-819-9944**	
NASDAQ: CRMT		
American Augers Inc		
135 US Rt 42 .... West Salem OH 44287	**800-324-4930**	419-869-7107
Ancira Winton Chevrolet		
6111 Bandera Rd .... San Antonio TX 78238	**800-299-5286***	210-681-4900
*General		
Arrow Truck Sales Inc		
3200 Manchester Trfy .... Kansas City MO 64129	**800-311-7144**	816-923-5000
Art Morrison Enterprises Inc		
5301 Eighth St E .... Fife WA 98424	**888-640-0516**	253-922-7188
Asheville Chevrolet Inc		
205 Smokey Park Hwy .... Asheville NC 28806	**866-921-1073**	828-348-7326

	Toll-Free	Phone

Astoria Ford
710 W Marine Dr .... Astoria OR 97103 — **888-760-9303** — 503-325-6411

Atlantic British Ltd
Halfmoon Light Industrial Pk 6 Enterprise Ave
.... Clifton Park NY 12065 — **800-533-2210** — 518-664-6169

Auto Credit Express (ACE)
3271 Five Points Dr Ste 200 .... Auburn Hills MI 48326 — **888-535-2277**

Auto Lenders Liquidation Center
104 Rt 73 .... Voorhees NJ 08043 — **888-305-5968**

Autoland 170 Rt 22 E .... Springfield NJ 07081 — **877-813-7239*** — 973-467-2900
*Sales

AutoRevo LTD
3820 American Dr Ste 110 .... Plano TX 75075 — **888-311-7386***
*Support

Banner Equipment Company Inc
1370 Bungalow Rd .... Morris IL 60450 — **800-621-4625**

Barry Bunker Chevrolet Inc
1307 N Wabash Ave .... Marion IN 46952 — **866-603-8625*** — 866-726-5519
*Sales

Bartow Ford Co
2800 US Hwy 98 N .... Bartow FL 33830 — **800-533-0425**

Baskin Auto Truck & Tractor Inc
1844 Hwy 51 S .... Covington TN 38019 — **877-476-2626** — 901-476-2626

Bates Ford 1673 W Main St .... Lebanon TN 37087 — **888-834-4671**

Bayway Lincoln-mercury Inc
12333 Gulf Fwy .... Houston TX 77034 — **888-356-1895** — 866-956-0972

Bell Ford Inc
2401 W Bell Rd .... Phoenix AZ 85023 — **800-688-1776** — 602-457-2144

Bergstrom of Kaukauna
2929 Lawe St .... Kaukauna WI 54130 — **866-939-0130**

Biggers Chevrolet
1385 E Chicago St .... Elgin IL 60120 — **866-431-1555** — 847-742-9000

Birchwood automative group
35D-3965 Portage Ave .... Winnipeg MB R3K2H7 — **866-990-6237** — 204-831-4214

BMW of Darien 140 Ledge Rd .... Darien CT 06820 — **855-349-6240** — 203-656-1804

Bob Davidson Ford Lincoln
1845 E Joppa Rd .... Baltimore MD 21234 — **877-885-7890** — 410-661-6400

Bob Stall Chevrolet
7601 Alvarado Rd .... La Mesa CA 91942 — **800-295-2695** — 619-458-3231

Bommarito Automotive Group
15736 Manchester Rd .... Ellisville MO 63011 — **800-367-2289** — 636-391-7200

Brasher Motor Company of Weimar Inc
1700 I- 10 .... Weimar TX 78962 — **800-783-1746** — 979-725-8515

Brighton Ford Inc
8240 W Grand River .... Brighton MI 48114 — **888-644-9991** — 810-227-1171

Brown Automotive Group LP
4300 S Georgia .... Amarillo TX 79110 — **888-388-6728** — 806-353-7211

Buchanan Automotive Group
707 S Washington Blvd .... Sarasota FL 34236 — **888-349-4989**

Buckeye Nissan Inc
3820 Pkwy Ln .... Hilliard OH 43026 — **800-686-4391** — 614-771-2345

Bus Andrews Truck Equipment Inc
2828 N E Ave .... Springfield MO 65803 — **800-273-0733** — 417-869-1541

Byerly Ford
4041 Dixie Hwy .... Louisville KY 40216 — **888-436-0819** — 502-448-1661

Cable-Dahmer Chevrolet Inc
1834 S Noland Rd .... Independence MO 64055 — **866-650-1809**

Callaway Cars Inc
3 High St .... Old Lyme CT 06371 — **866-927-9400** — 860-434-9002

Capital Ford Inc
4900 Capital Blvd .... Raleigh NC 27616 — **877-659-2496** — 919-790-4600

Capitol Chevrolet Montgomery
711 Eastern Blvd .... Montgomery AL 36117 — **800-410-1137*** — 334-223-4458
*Sales

Car City Motor Company Inc
3100 S US Hwy 169 .... Saint Joseph MO 64503 — **800-525-7008** — 816-233-9149

CarMax Inc
12800 Tuckahoe Creek Pkwy .... Richmond VA 23238 — **800-519-1511**
NYSE: KMX

Carolina International Trucks Inc
1619 Bluff Rd .... Columbia SC 29201 — **800-868-4923**

Charles Gabus Ford Inc
4545 Merle Hay Rd .... Des Moines IA 50310 — **800-934-2287*** — 515-270-0707
*Sales

Checkered Flag Motor Car Corp
5225 Virginia Beach Blvd .... Virginia Beach VA 23462 — **866-414-7820** — 757-687-3486

Chenoweth Ford Inc
1564 E Pike St .... Clarksburg WV 26301 — **877-289-8348*** — 800-344-1108
*Sales

Chino Hills Ford
4480 Chino Hills Pkwy .... Chino CA 91710 — **866-261-0153**

Coffman Truck Sales
1149 West Lake St .... Aurora IL 60507 — **800-255-7641** — 630-892-7093

College Station Ford
1351 Earl Rudder Freeway Fwy .... College Station TX 77845 — **888-508-0241** — 979-431-3382

Cook Truck Equipment & Tools
3701 Harlee Ave .... Charlotte NC 28208 — **800-241-4210** — 704-392-4138

Cooper Motors Inc
985 York St .... Hanover PA 17331 — **866-414-2809**

Coral Springs Auto Mall
9400 W Atlantic Blvd .... Coral Springs FL 33071 — **800-353-8660** — 954-369-1016

Courtesy Chevrolet
1233 E Camelback Rd .... Phoenix AZ 85014 — **877-295-4648** — 602-235-0255

Courtesy Chrysler Jeep Dodge
9207 Adamo Dr E .... Tampa FL 33619 — **866-343-9730**

Criswell Automotive
503 Quince Orchard Rd .... Gaithersburg MD 20878 — **888-672-7559**

Crown Motors Ltd
196 Regent Blvd .... Holland MI 49423 — **800-466-7000** — 616-396-5268

DCH Honda of Nanuet
10 NY-304 .... Nanuet NY 10954 — **888-495-8660** — 845-367-7050

Dean Team Automotive Group Inc
15121 Manchester Rd .... Ballwin MO 63011 — **888-699-0663** — 636-227-0100

Dearth Chrysler Dodge Jeep Ram
520 Eigth St .... Monroe WI 53566 — **877-495-5321** — 866-949-3653

Dellenbach Motors
3111 S College Ave .... Fort Collins CO 80525 — **866-963-5689**

DeMontrond 888 I- 45 S .... Conroe TX 77304 — **888-843-6583*** — 281-443-2500
*Sales

Dick Brantmeier Ford Inc
3624 Kohler Memorial Dr .... Sheboygan WI 53082 — **800-498-6111** — 920-458-6111

Dick Masheter Ford Inc
1090 S Hamilton Rd .... Columbus OH 43227 — **888-839-9646**

Don Beyer Motors Inc
1231 W Broad St .... Falls Church VA 22046 — **855-892-6528** — 855-844-0659

Don Johnson Motors
2101 Central Blvd .... Brownsville TX 78520 — **888-653-0794** — 956-546-2288

Don McGill Toyota Inc
11800 Katy Fwy .... Houston TX 77079 — **866-938-0767** — 281-496-2000

Dothan Chrysler-Dodge Inc
4074 Ross Clark Cir NW .... Dothan AL 36303 — **877-674-9574** — 334-794-0606

DriveTime Corp
4020 E Indian School Rd .... Phoenix AZ 85018 — **888-418-1212**

Durocher Auto Sales Inc
4651 Rt 9 .... Plattsburgh NY 12901 — **877-215-8954** — 518-563-3587

Earnhardt Auto Centers
7300 W Orchid Ln .... Chandler AZ 85226 — **888-378-7711** — 480-926-4000

Ed Martin Inc
3800 E 96th St .... Indianapolis IN 46240 — **800-211-5410** — 317-846-3800

El Camino Store, The
420 Athena Dr .... Athens GA 30601 — **888-685-5987**

Erhard BMW of Bloomfield
1845 S Telegraph .... Bloomfield Hills MI 48302 — **888-481-4058** — 248-642-6565

F C Kerbeck & Sons
100 Rt 73 N .... Palmyra NJ 08065 — **855-846-1500*** — 855-581-5700
*General

Fairway Lincoln
10101 Abercorn St .... Savannah GA 31406 — **888-716-2924** — 888-762-8050

First Truck Centre Inc
11313 170 St .... Edmonton AB T5M3P5 — **888-882-8530** — 780-413-8800

Fletch's Inc
825 Charlevoix Ave PO Box 265 .... Petoskey MI 49770 — **888-764-0308** — 231-347-9651

Ford of Montebello Inc
2747 Via Campo .... Montebello CA 90640 — **888-313-2305** — 323-358-2880

FordDirect
1740 US Hwy 60 PO Box 700 .... Republic MO 65738 — **888-578-8478** — 417-732-2626

Fordham Auto Sales Inc
236 W Fordham Rd .... Bronx NY 10468 — **800-407-1153**

Frank Kent Cadillac Inc
3500 W Loop 820 S .... Fort Worth TX 76116 — **877-558-5468**

Frederick Motor Co, The
1 Waverley Dr .... Frederick MD 21702 — **800-734-9118**

Freightliner Northwest
277 Stewart Rd SW .... Pacific WA 98047 — **800-523-8014**

Freightliner of Hartford Inc
222 Roberts St .... East Hartford CT 06108 — **800-453-6967**

Frontier Ford
3701 Stevens Creek Blvd .... Santa Clara CA 95051 — **844-480-0574**

Gateway Truck & Refrigeration
921 Fournie Ln .... Collinsville IL 62234 — **800-449-2131** — 618-345-0123

Germain Motor Co
Mercedes-Benz of Easton
4300 Morse Crossing .... Columbus OH 43219 — **855-217-5986**

GERZENY'S RV NOKOMIS
2110 N Tamiami Trl .... Nokomis FL 34275 — **800-262-2182** — 941-966-2182

Gilroy Chevrolet
6720 Auto Mall Dr .... Gilroy CA 95020 — **800-237-6318** — 408-427-3708

Gladstone Dodge Chrysler Jeep RAM
5610 North Oak Trafficway .... Gladstone MO 64118 — **866-695-2043** — 816-455-3500

Graff Truck Centers Inc
1401 S Saginaw St .... Flint MI 48503 — **888-870-4203** — 810-239-8300

Gray Chevrolet Cadillac
1245 N Ninth St .... Stroudsburg PA 18360 — **866-505-3058**

Gulf Coast Autoplex Inc
414 W Fred&Ruth Zingler Dr .... Jennings LA 70546 — **888-526-2391**

Gunn Automotive Group
227 Broadway .... San Antonio TX 78205 — **888-452-2856** — 210-472-2501

H & H Chevrolet LLC
4645 S 84 St .... Omaha NE 68127 — **855-866-1733**

HARPER CHEVROLET-BUICK-GMC
200 Hwy 531 .... Minden LA 71055 — **800-259-0395** — 318-268-3320

Harte Nissan
165 W Service Rd .... Hartford CT 06120 — **866-687-8971** — 860-549-2800

Harvey Cadillac Co
2600 28th St SE .... Grand Rapids MI 49512 — **877-845-1557*** — 616-949-1140
*Sales

Headquarter Toyota
5895 NW 167th St .... Miami FL 33015 — **800-549-0947** — 305-600-4663

Herb Chambers Chevrolet
90 Andover St Rt 114 .... Danvers MA 01923 — **877-907-1965** — 978-774-2000

Herb Gordon Nissan
3131 Automobile Blvd .... Silver Spring MD 20904 — **877-345-9869**

Herson's Inc
15525 Frederick Rd .... Rockville MD 20855 — **888-203-8318** — 301-279-8600

Holler Classic
1150 N Orlando Ave .... Sanford FL 32789 — **866-937-1398** — 407-645-4969

Holman Cadillac Co
1200 Rt 73 S .... Mount Laurel NJ 08054 — **866-865-6973** — 877-209-6052

Honda of Santa Monica
1720 Santa Monica Blvd .... Santa Monica CA 90404 — **800-269-2031**

Honda World
10645 Studebaker Rd .... Downey CA 90241 — **888-458-9404** — 562-929-7000

Horwith Trucks Inc
PO Box 7 .... NorthHampton PA 18067 — **800-220-8807** — 610-261-2220

James Wood Motors
2111 US Hwy 287 S .... Decatur TX 76234 — **866-232-6058** — 940-539-9143

John Watson Chevrolet
3535 Wall Ave .... Ogden UT 84401 — **866-647-9930** — 801-394-2611

Joyce Honda
3166 State Rte 10 .... Denville NJ 07834 — **844-332-5955**

Keeler Motor Car Co
1111 Troy Schenectady Rd .... Latham NY 12110 — **800-474-4197** — 518-785-4197

Ken Fowler Motors
1265 Airport Pk Blvd .... Ukiah CA 95482 — **800-287-0107** — 707-468-0101

			Toll-Free	Phone

Kenworth Northwest Inc
20220 International Blvd S .... SeaTac WA 98198 **800-562-0060** 206-433-5911

Kenworth of Indianapolis Inc
2929 S Holt Rd .... Indianapolis IN 46241 **800-827-8421** 317-247-8421

Keyes Toyota
5855 Van Nuys Blvd .... Van Nuys CA 91401 **844-781-4304**

Knippelmier Chevrolet Inc
1811 E Hwy 62 E .... Blanchard OK 73010 **877-644-7255**

Kolosso Toyota
3000 W Wisconsin Ave .... Appleton WI 54914 **877-756-2297** 920-738-3666

La Beau Bros Inc
295 N Harrison Ave .... Kankakee IL 60901 **800-747-9519** 815-933-5519

La Belle Dodge Chrysler Jeep Inc
501 S Main St .... Labelle FL 33935 **800-226-1193** 863-675-2701

La Mesa Rv Ctr Inc
7430 Copley Pk Pl .... San Diego CA 92111 **800-496-8778***
*Sales 858-874-8000

Lafontaine Honda
2245 S Telegraph Rd .... Dearborn MI 48124 **866-567-5088**

Lancaster Toyota Inc
5270 Manheim Pk .... East Petersburg PA 17520 **888-424-1295**

Land Rover of Calgary
175 Glendeer Cir SE .... Calgary AB T2H2V4 **866-274-4080**

Landmark Lincoln-Mercury Inc
5000 S Broadway .... Englewood CO 80113 **888-318-9692** 303-761-1560

Les Stanford Chevrolet Inc
21730 Michigan Ave .... Dearborn MI 48124 **800-836-0972** 313-769-3140

Lia Auto Group, The
1258 Central Ave .... Albany NY 12205 **855-212-7985**

Lithia Motors Inc
360 E Jackson St .... Medford OR 97501 **866-318-9660**
NYSE: LAD

Loeber Motors Inc
4255 W Touhy Ave .... Lincolnwood IL 60712 **888-211-4485** 847-675-1000

Lordco Parts Ltd
22866 Dewdney Trunk Rd .... Maple Ridge BC V2X3K6 **877-591-1581** 604-467-1581

Mac Haik Auto Group
11711 Katy Fwy .... Houston TX 77079 **866-721-8619**

Maclean Assoc LLC
1700 Boston Post Rd .... Guilford CT 06437 **877-819-6922*** 866-924-4854
*Sales

Marshal Mlze Ford Inc
5348 Hwy 153 .... Chattanooga TN 37343 **888-633-5038**

Marty Franich Ford Lincoln
550 Auto Ctr Dr .... Watsonville CA 95076 **888-442-9037**

Matt Blatt Inc
501 Delsea Dr N .... Glassboro NJ 08028 **877-462-5288** 856-881-0005

Matthews Currie Ford Company Inc
130 N Tamiami Trl .... Nokomis FL 34275 **855-491-3131** 800-248-2378

McDevitt Trucks Inc
1 Mack Ave .... Manchester NH 03108 **800-370-6225**

McGrath Auto
1548 Collins Rd NE .... Cedar Rapids IA 52402 **855-495-3118**

McGrath Ford Hyundai BMW
4001 First Ave SE .... Cedar Rapids IA 52402 **855-795-7289** 319-366-4000

Mercedes-Benz of San Francisco
500 Eigth St .... San Francisco CA 94103 **877-554-6016** 415-673-2000

Mercedes-Benz of Seattle
2025 Airport Way S .... Seattle WA 98134 **855-263-5688** 206-467-9999

Michael's Volkswagen of Bellevue
15000 SE Eastgate Way .... Bellevue WA 98007 **888-480-5424** 425-641-2002

Mike Reed Chevrolet
1559 E Oglethorpe .... Hinesville GA 31313 **877-228-3943**

Mission Golf Cars
18865 Redland Rd .... San Antonio TX 78259 **800-324-7868** 210-545-7868

Mission Valley Ford Truck Sales Inc
780 E Brokaw Rd .... San Jose CA 95112 **888-284-7471** 408-933-2300

Modern Chevrolet of Winston-Salem
5955 University Pkwy .... Winston-Salem NC 27105 **888-306-0825*** 336-793-5943
*General

Molle Toyota Inc
601 West 103rd St .... Kansas City MO 64114 **888-510-7705** 816-942-5200

Motorcars International
3015 E Cairo St .... Springfield MO 65802 **866-970-6800** 417-831-9999

Muzi Motors Inc
557 Highland Ave .... Needham Heights MA 02494 **800-296-9440**

Nalley Lexus Smyrna
2750 Cobb Pkwy SE .... Smyrna GA 30080 **877-454-4206**

National Tire & Wheel
5 Garden Ct .... Wheeling WV 26003 **800-847-3287**

Nationwide Lift Trucks Inc
3900 N 28th Terr .... Hollywood FL 33020 **800-327-4431** 954-922-4645

Nextran Corp
1986 W Beaver St .... Jacksonville FL 32209 **800-347-6225** 904-354-3721

NFI Inc Dba Harrisonburg Honda Mitsubishi Hyundai
2885 S Main St .... Harrisonburg VA 22801 **800-433-1987** 540-433-1467

Nitrous Express Inc
5411 Seymour Hwy .... Wichita Falls TX 76310 **888-463-2781** 940-767-7694

Norman Frede Chevrolet Co
16801 Feather Craft Ln .... Houston TX 77058 **888-307-1703** 281-486-2200

Norris Ford
901 Merritt Blvd .... Baltimore MD 21222 **888-205-0310*** 410-285-0200
*Sales

North Bay Nissan Inc
1250 Auto Ctr Dr .... Petaluma CA 94952 **855-540-5697**

Northway Toyota
727 New Loudon Rd .... Latham NY 12110 **877-800-5098** 518-213-5686

Northwest Chevrolet
35108 92nd Ave S .... McKenna WA 98558 **855-216-5183*** 855-234-9884
*Sales

O Neill's Chevrolet & Buick Inc
5 W Main St .... Avon CT 06001 **844-315-0960** 860-269-3637

O'Gara Coach Company LLC
8833 W Olympic Blvd .... Beverly Hills CA 90211 **888-291-5533** 877-588-8862

Park Place Volvo
3515 Inwood Rd .... Dallas TX 75209 **888-437-0906** 855-272-5915

Pat Milliken Ford
9600 Telegraph Rd .... Redford MI 48239 **855-803-3131***
*Sales

Phil Long Dealerships
1020 Motor City Dr .... Colorado Springs CO 80905 **866-644-1378**

Phillips Buick-Pontiac-Gmc Truck Inc
2160 US Hwy 441 .... Fruitland Park FL 34731 **888-664-7454** 352-728-1212

Pollard Friendly Ford Co
3301 S Loop 289 .... Lubbock TX 79423 **866-239-3735**

Potamkin Automotive
6200 NW 167th .... Miami Lakes FL 33014 **855-799-9965**

Premier Subaru LLC
150 N Main St .... Branford CT 06405 **888-690-6710** 203-481-0687

Prostrollo Motor Sales Inc
500 Fourth St NE .... Huron SD 57350 **866-466-4515**

Putnam Lexus
390 Convention Way .... Redwood City CA 94063 **888-231-8005** 650-363-8500

Riverside Ford
2625 Ludington St .... Escanaba MI 49829 **877-774-3171** 906-786-1130

Riverside Ford Inc
2089 Riverside Dr .... Macon GA 31204 **800-395-6210*** 478-464-2900
*Sales

RnR RV Ctr
23203 E Knox Ave .... Liberty Lake WA 99019 **866-386-4875**

Roberson Motors Inc
3100 Ryan Dr SE .... Salem OR 97301 **888-281-6220** 503-363-4117

Roger Dean Chevrolet West Palm Beach
2235 Okeechobee Blvd .... West Palm Beach FL 33409 **877-827-4705** 561-594-1478

Roland D Kelly Infiniti Inc
155 Andover St Rt 114 .... Danvers MA 01923 **855-885-3559**

Romero Mazda
1307 Kettering Dr .... Ontario CA 91761 **888-317-2233** 909-390-8484

Rosenthal Automotive Organization
750 North Gelbe Rd .... Arlington VA 22203 **877-446-4543**

Sandy Sansing Chevrolet
6200 Pensacola Blvd .... Pensacola FL 32505 **877-776-3459** 850-659-6923

Saratoga Honda
3402 Rt 9 .... Saratoga Springs NY 12866 **888-658-2303**

Seneca Tank Inc
5585 NE 16th St .... Des Moines IA 50313 **800-362-2910** 515-262-5900

Shelly Automotive Group
Irvine BMW 9881 Research Dr .... Irvine CA 92618 **888-853-7429**

Sheppard Motors
2300 W Seventh Ave .... Eugene OR 97402 **877-362-1065*** 541-343-0011
*Sales

Sierra Volkswagen Inc
510 E Norris Dr .... Ottawa IL 61350 **877-854-2771** 815-401-0663

Silver Star Cadillac
3601 Auto Mall Dr .... Thousand Oaks CA 91362 **877-813-1334*** 805-267-3200
*Cust Svc

Simmons-rockwell Inc
784 County Rd 64 .... Elmira NY 14903 **888-520-2213** 607-796-5555

Sisbarro Dealerships
425 W Boutz Rd .... Las Cruces NM 88005 **800-215-8021** 575-524-7707

Smith Motors Inc of Hammond
6405 Indianapolis Blvd .... Hammond IN 46320 **877-392-2689** 219-845-4000

Snowfire 100 Us Rt 2 .... Waterbury VT 05676 **800-287-5606** 802-244-5606

Snyder Chevrolet
524 N Perry St .... Napoleon OH 43545 **800-569-3957** 567-341-4132

South Charlotte Nissan
9215 S Blvd .... Charlotte NC 28273 **888-411-1423** 704-552-9191

Southfield Dodge Chrysler Jeep Ram
28100 Telegraph Rd .... Southfield MI 48034 **888-714-1015*** 248-354-2950
*Sales

Specialty Hearse & Ambulance Sale Corp
60 Engineers Ln E .... Farmingdale NY 11735 **800-349-6102*** 516-349-7700
*General

Standard Motors Ltd
44 Second Ave NW .... Swift Current SK S9H3V6 **866-334-8985**

Steele Truck Ctr Inc
2150 Rockfill Rd .... Fort Myers FL 33916 **888-806-4839** 239-334-7300

Suburban Collection
1810 Maplelawn Dr .... Troy MI 48084 **877-471-7100**

Sulphur Springs & Quitman
1040 Gilmer St .... Sulphur Springs TX 75482 **866-435-1307**

Surrey Honda
15291 Fraser Hwy .... Surrey BC V3R3P3 **888-549-3080**

Susan Schein Automotive
3171 Pelham Pkwy .... Pelham AL 35124 **800-845-1578** 205-664-1491

Terry Thompson Chevrolet Olds
1402 US Hwy 98 .... Daphne AL 36526 **800-287-9309** 251-626-0631

Toms Truck Ctr Inc
909 N Grand Ave .... Santa Ana CA 92701 **800-638-1015**

Toyota Sunnyvale
898 W El Camino Real .... Sunnyvale CA 94087 **888-210-0091** 408-338-0063

Transwest
20770 I-76 Frontage Rd .... Brighton CO 80603 **800-289-3161** 303-289-3161

Tri County Ford
4032 Commerce Pkwy .... Buckner KY 40010 **800-945-2520** 502-241-7333

Triad Freightliner of Tennessee LLC
841 Eastern Star Rd .... Kingsport TN 37663 **800-451-1508**

Tropical Ford
9900 S Orange Blossom Trail .... Orlando FL 32837 **877-241-0502*** 407-851-3800
*Sales

Truck Sales & Service Inc
PO Box 262 .... Midvale OH 44653 **800-282-6100** 740-922-3412

V&H Inc
1505 S Central Ave .... Marshfield WI 54449 **800-826-2308** 715-486-8800

Van Bortel Subaru 6327 Rt 96 .... Victor NY 14564 **888-902-7961** 585-924-5230

VAN HORN CHEVROLET OF PLYMOUTH
3008 Eastern Ave .... Plymouth WI 53073 **800-236-1415** 920-893-6361

Village Automotive Group
75-95 N Beacon St .... Boston MA 02135 **888-707-5524**

Vin Devers Inc
5570 Monroe St .... Sylvania OH 43560 **888-847-9535** 419-885-5111

Vista Auto
21501 Ventura Blvd .... Woodland Hills CA 91364 **888-887-6530** 888-442-8817

Walker Honda
6677 Coliseum Blvd .... Alexandria LA 71303 **888-726-1687**

Name / Address	City	State	Zip	Toll-Free	Phone
Wallingford Buick GMC 1122 Old N Colony Rd *Cust Svc	Wallingford	CT	06492	**866-582-4487***	888-765-9107
Wellesley Volkswagen 231 Linden St *Sales	Wellesley	MA	02482	**888-602-6905***	781-237-3553
West-Herr Automotive Group Inc 3448 McKinley Pkwy	Blasdell	NY	14219	**800-643-2112**	716-926-8150
Westchester Toyota 2167 Central Park Ave	Yonkers	NY	10710	**888-224-4595**	
Western Bus Sales Inc 30355 SE Hwy 212	Boring	OR	97009	**800-258-2473**	503-905-0002
Westway Ford 801 W Airport Fwy	Irving	TX	75062	**844-877-9037**	
Whitaker Buick Co 131 19th St SW	Forest Lake	MN	55025	**877-324-8885**	
White Plains Honda 344 Central Ave	White Plains	NY	10606	**888-683-1716**	888-671-0343
Willey Honda 2215 S 500 W *Sales	Bountiful	UT	84010	**888-431-4490***	
Williams Nationalease Ltd 400 W Northtown Rd	Normal	IL	61761	**800-779-8785**	309-452-1110
Winslow BMW 730 N Cir Dr	Colorado Springs	CO	80909	**877-367-7357**	719-473-1373
Witt Lincoln 588 Camino Del Rio North	San Diego	CA	92108	**877-937-3301**	888-668-9787
WMK Inc 4199 Kinross Lakes Pkwy	Richfield	OH	44286	**877-275-4912**	234-312-2000
York Ford Inc 1481 Bwy	Saugus	MA	01906	**888-705-6229**	781-231-1945
Zeigler Chevrolet Inc 13153 Dunnings Hwy	Claysburg	PA	16625	**877-364-4817**	

AUTOMOBILE LEASING

SEE Credit & Financing - Consumer ; Credit & Financing - Commercial ; Fleet Leasing & Management

58 AUTOMOBILE SALES & RELATED SERVICES - ONLINE

SEE ALSO Automobile Dealers & Groups

Name / Address	City	State	Zip	Toll-Free	Phone
Autobytel Inc 18872 MacArthur Blvd *NASDAQ: AUTO*	Irvine	CA	92612	**888-422-8999**	949-225-4500
Automobile Consumer Services Inc 6249 Stewart Rd	Cincinnati	OH	45227	**800-223-4882**	513-527-7700
Automotive Information Ctr 18872 MacArthur Blvd	Irvine	CA	92612	**888-422-8999**	
AutoVIN Inc 13085 Hamilton Crossing Blvd	Carmel	IN	46032	**866-585-8080**	
Carscom 175 W Jackson Blvd Ste 800	Chicago	IL	60604	**888-246-6298**	312-601-5000
CarsDirectcom Inc 909 N Sepulveda Blvd 11th Fl *Cust Svc	El Segundo	CA	90245	**888-227-7347***	
Kelley Blue Book Company Inc 195 Technology Dr	Irvine	CA	92618	**800-258-3266**	949-770-7704
Williamson Cadillac 7815 SW 104th St	Miami	FL	33156	**877-228-6093**	877-579-0775

59 AUTOMOBILES - MFR

SEE ALSO Motor Vehicles - Commercial & Special Purpose ; Motorcycles & Motorcycle Parts & Accessories ; Snowmobiles ; All-Terrain Vehicles

Name / Address	City	State	Zip	Toll-Free	Phone
American Honda Motor Company Inc 1919 Torrance Blvd	Torrance	CA	90501	**800-999-1009**	310-783-3170
Audi of America 3800 Hamlin Rd	Auburn Hills	MI	48326	**888-237-2834**	
Bentley Motors Inc 2200 Ferdinand Porsche Dr	Herndon	VA	20171	**800-777-6923**	
BMW of North America LLC 300 Chestnut Ridge Rd	Woodcliff Lake	NJ	07677	**800-831-1117**	201-307-4000
Braun Industries Inc 1170 Production Dr	Van Wert	OH	45891	**877-344-9990**	
Canfield Equipment Service 21533 Mound Rd	Warren	MI	48091	**800-637-3956**	586-757-2020
Chrysler Group LLC 1000 Chrysler Dr *Cust Svc	Auburn Hills	MI	48326	**800-423-6343***	
DaimlerChrysler Corp Jeep Div PO Box 21-8004 *Cust Svc	Auburn Hills	MI	48321	**800-992-1997***	
Ferrara Fire Apparatus Inc PO Box 249	Holden	LA	70744	**800-443-9006**	225-567-7100
Ford Motor Co PO Box 6248 *NYSE: F*	Dearborn	MI	48126	**800-392-3673**	313-845-8540
Freightliner Specialty Vehicles Inc 2300 S 13th St	Clinton	OK	73601	**800-358-7624**	580-323-4100
General Motors Corp (GMC) 100 Renaissance Ctr *NYSE: GM*	Detroit	MI	48265	**800-462-8782**	313-556-5000
General Motors Corp Buick Motor Div 300 Renaissance Ctr *Cust Svc	Detroit	MI	48265	**877-825-8964***	800-521-7300
Glaval Bus 914 County Rd 1	Elkhart	IN	46514	**800-445-2825**	574-262-2212
Horton Emergency Vehicles 3800 McDowell Rd	Grove City	OH	43123	**800-282-5113**	614-539-8181
Hyundai Motor America 10550 Talbert Ave *Cust Svc	Fountain Valley	CA	92708	**800-633-5151***	714-965-3000
Land Rover North America Inc 555 MacArthur Blvd	Mahwah	NJ	07430	**800-637-6837**	
Lincoln Motor Co PO Box 6248	Dearborn	MI	48126	**800-521-4140**	
Mazda North American Operations 7755 Irvine Center Dr PO Box 19734 *Cust Svc	Irvine	CA	92623	**800-222-5500***	949-727-1990
Mercedes-Benz US. International Inc 1 Mercedes Dr	Vance	AL	35490	**888-286-8762**	205-507-2252
Mercedes-Benz USA LLC 1 Mercedes Dr *Cust Svc	Montvale	NJ	07645	**800-367-6372***	
Nissan Canada Inc (NCI) 5290 Orbitor Dr	Mississauga	ON	L4W4Z5	**800-387-0122**	
Nissan Motor Corp USA Infiniti Div 1 Nissan Way	Franklin	TN	37067	**800-662-6200**	
Nissan North America Inc 25 Vantage way	Nashville	TN	37228	**800-647-7261**	
Porsche Cars North America Inc 980 Hammond Dr Ste 1000	Atlanta	GA	30328	**800-505-1041**	770-290-3500
Saleen Automotive Inc 2735 Wardlow Rd	Corona	CA	92882	**800-888-8945**	
Subaru of America Inc 2235 Marlton Pike W	Cherry Hill	NJ	08002	**800-782-2783**	856-488-8500
Tesla 3500 Deer Creek Rd	Palo Alto	CA	94304	**888-518-3752**	650-681-5000
Toyota Canada Inc 1 Toyota Pl *Cust Svc	Scarborough	ON	M1H1H9	**888-869-6828***	
Toyota Motor Manufacturing Indiana Inc 4000 S Tulip Tree Dr	Princeton	IN	47670	**888-696-8211**	812-387-2266
Toyota Motor Sales USA Inc 19001 S Western Ave *Cust Svc	Torrance	CA	90501	**800-331-4331***	310-468-4000
Toyota Motor Sales USA Inc Lexus Div 19001 S Western Ave *Cust Svc	Torrance	CA	90501	**800-255-3987***	
Turtle-Top Inc 67819 State Rd 15	New Paris	IN	46553	**800-296-2105**	
Verspeeten Cartage Ltd 274129 Wallace Line	Ingersoll	ON	N5C3J7	**800-265-6701**	519-425-7881
Volkswagen of America Inc 3800 Hamlin Rd	Auburn Hills	MI	48326	**800-822-8987**	
Volvo Cars of North America 1 Volvo Dr *Cust Svc	Rockleigh	NJ	07647	**800-458-1552***	201-768-7300

60 AUTOMOTIVE PARTS & SUPPLIES - MFR

SEE ALSO Hose & Belting - Rubber or Plastics ; Gaskets, Packing, Sealing Devices ; Engines & Turbines ; Carburetors, Pistons, Piston Rings, Valves ; Motors (Electric) & Generators ; Electrical Equipment for Internal Combustion Engines

Name / Address	City	State	Zip	Toll-Free	Phone
Accuride Corp 7140 Office Cir *NYSE: ACW* ■ *Cust Svc	Evansville	IN	47715	**800-823-8332***	812-962-5000
Aer Mfg Inc PO Box 979	Carrollton	TX	75011	**800-753-5237**	972-417-2582
Alma Products Co 2000 Michigan Ave	Alma	MI	48801	**877-427-2624**	989-463-1151
AMBAC International Inc 910 Spears Creek Ct	Elgin	SC	29045	**800-628-6894**	
AP Exhaust Technologies Inc 300 Dixie Trial	Goldsboro	NC	27530	**800-277-2787**	919-580-2000
ArvinMeritor Inc 2135 W Maple Rd *NYSE: MTOR*	Troy	MI	48084	**800-535-5560**	248-435-1000
Atwood Mobile Products 1120 N Main St	Elkhart	IN	46514	**800-546-8759**	574-264-2131
Autocam Corp 4070 E Paris Ave	Kentwood	MI	49512	**800-747-6978**	616-698-0707
Baldwin Filters 4400 Hwy 30	Kearney	NE	68847	**800-822-5394**	
Beach Manufacturing Co PO Box 129	Donnelsville	OH	45319	**800-543-5942**	937-882-6372
Borla Performance Industries Inc 500 Borla Dr	Johnson City	TN	37604	**877-462-6752**	423-979-4000
Bushwacker Inc 6710 N Catlin Ave	Portland	OR	97203	**800-234-8920**	503-283-4335
Cardone Industries Inc 5501 Whitaker Ave *Cust Svc	Philadelphia	PA	19124	**800-777-4780***	800-777-4304
Carlisle Industrial Brake 1031 E Hillside Dr	Bloomington	IN	47401	**800-873-6361**	812-336-3811
Competition Cams Inc 3406 Democrat Rd	Memphis	TN	38118	**800-999-0853**	901-795-2400
Consolidated Metco Inc 5701 SE Columbia Way *Sales	Vancouver	WA	98661	**800-547-9473***	
Cummins Filtration 26 Century Blvd	Nashville	TN	37214	**800-777-7064**	615-367-0040
Cummins Inc 500 Jackson St PO Box 3005 *NYSE: CMI*	Columbus	IN	47201	**800-343-7357**	812-377-5000
CWC Textron 1085 W Sherman Blvd	Muskegon	MI	49441	**800-999-0853**	231-733-1331
Davco Technology LLC 1600 Woodland Dr PO Box 487	Saline	MI	48176	**800-328-2611**	734-429-5665
Dayton Parts LLC 3500 Industrial Rd PO Box 5795 *Cust Svc	Harrisburg	PA	17110	**800-225-2159***	717-255-8500
Dorman Products Inc 3400 E Walnut St *NASDAQ: DORM*	Colmar	PA	18915	**800-523-2492**	215-997-1800
Edelbrock Corp 2700 California St	Torrance	CA	90503	**800-739-3737**	310-781-2222
Federal-Mogul Corp 27300 W 11 Mile Rd *Cust Svc	Southfield	MI	48034	**800-325-8886***	248-354-7700
Firestone Industrial Products Co 250 W 96th St	Indianapolis	IN	46260	**800-888-0650**	800-247-4337

Classified Section

			Toll-Free	Phone
Flex-N-Gate Corp				
1306 E University Ave	Urbana IL	61802	**800-398-1496**	
Fontaine Fifth Wheel				
7574 Commerce Cir	Trussville AL	35173	**800-874-9780**	205-847-3250
Fontaine Truck Equipment Co				
7574 Commerce Cir	Trussville AL	35173	**800-874-9780**	205-661-4900
Griffin Thermal Products				
100 Hurricane Creek Rd	Piedmont SC	29673	**800-722-3723**	
Grote Industries Inc				
2600 Lanier Dr	Madison IN	47250	**800-628-0809**	812-273-1296
Hastings Manufacturing Co				
325 N Hanover St	Hastings MI	49058	**800-776-1088**	269-945-2491
Hayden Automotive				
1801 Waters Ridge Dr	Lewisville TX	75057	**888-505-4567**	
Hendrickson International				
800 S Frontage Rd	Woodridge IL	60517	**855-743-3733**	630-910-2800
Hennessy Industries Inc				
1601 JP Hennesey Dr	La Vergne TN	37086	**800-688-6359**	855-876-3864
Hopkins Manufacturing Corp				
428 Peyton St	Emporia KS	66801	**800-524-1458**	620-342-7320
Hutchens Industries Inc				
215 N Patterson Ave	Springfield MO	65802	**800-654-8824**	417-862-5012
HWH Corp 2096 Moscow Rd	Moscow IA	52760	**800-321-3494**	563-724-3396
Indian Head Industries Inc				
8530 Cliff Cameron Dr	Charlotte NC	28269	**800-527-1534**	704-547-7411
JASPER Engines & Transmissions				
815 Wernsing Rd PO Box 650	Jasper IN	47547	**800-827-7455**	812-482-1041
John Bean Co				
309 Exchange Ave	Conway AR	72032	**800-225-5786**	501-450-1500
KONI North America				
1961-A International Way	Hebron KY	41048	**800-965-5664**	859-586-4100
Lund International Holdings Inc				
4325 Hamilton Mill Rd Ste 400	Buford GA	30518	**800-241-7219**	
MacLean-Fogg Co				
1000 Allanson Rd	Mundelein IL	60060	**800-323-4536**	847-566-0010
MAHLE Industries Inc				
2020 Sanford St	Muskegon MI	49444	**888-255-1942**	231-722-1300
Marmon-Herrington Co				
13001 Magisterial Dr	Louisville KY	40223	**800-227-0727**	
Neapco Inc				
6735 Haggerty Rd	Belleville MI	48111	**800-821-2374**	734-447-1380
P T. M. Corp				
6560 Bethuy Rd	Fair Haven MI	48023	**800-486-2212**	586-725-2211
PendaForm Corp				
2344 W Wisconsin St	Portage WI	53901	**800-356-7704**	608-742-5301
Perfection Clutch Co				
100 Perfection Way	Timmonsville SC	29161	**800-258-8312**	843-326-5544
Phillips & Temro Industries				
9700 W 74th St	Eden Prairie MN	55344	**800-328-6108**	952-941-9700
Raybestos Powertrain LLC				
711 Tech Dr	Crawfordsville IN	47933	**800-729-7763**	
Ridewell Corp				
PO Box 4586	Springfield MO	65808	**877-434-8088**	417-833-4565
Roush Enterprise				
12447 Levan	Livonia MI	48150	**800-215-9658**	734-779-7006
SmarTire Systems Inc				
6900 Graybar Rd Ste 2110	Richmond BC	V3W0A5	**800-247-2725**	440-329-9000
Soucy Holding Inc				
5450 Saint-Roch St	Drummondville QC	J2B6W3	**844-474-4740**	819-474-9008
Stanadyne Corp				
92 Deerfield Rd	Windsor CT	06095	**888-336-3473**	860-525-0821
Standard Motor Products Inc				
37-18 Northern Blvd	Long Island NY	11101	**800-895-1085**	718-392-0200
NYSE: SMP				
Stemco LP				
300 Industrial Blvd PO Box 1989	Longview TX	75606	**800-527-8492**	903-758-9981
Steve Millen Sportparts Inc				
3176 Airway Ave	Costa Mesa CA	92626	**866-250-5542**	
Teleflex Medical				
2917 Weck Dr				
PO Box 12600	Research Triangle Park NC	27709	**866-246-6990**	919-544-8000
Tenneco Inc				
500 N Field Dr	Lake Forest IL	60045	**866-839-3259**	847-482-5000
NYSE: TEN				
Titan International Inc				
2701 Spruce St	Quincy IL	62301	**800-872-2327**	217-228-6011
NYSE: TWI				
Triangle Suspension Systems Inc				
200 E Maloney Rd	Du Bois PA	15801	**800-458-6077**	
Universal Manufacturing Co				
405 Diagonal St PO Box 190	Algona IA	50511	**800-343-3557**	515-295-3557
OTC: UFMG				
US Chemical & Plastics				
600 Nova Dr SE	Massillon OH	44646	**800-321-0672**	330-830-6000
Velvac Inc				
2405 S Calhoun Rd	New Berlin WI	53151	**800-783-8871**	262-786-0700
Webb Wheel Products Inc				
2310 Industrial Dr SW	Cullman AL	35055	**800-633-3256**	256-739-6660
WIX Filtration Products				
1 Wix Way PO Box 1967	Gastonia NC	28053	**800-949-6698**	704-864-6711

61   AUTOMOTIVE PARTS & SUPPLIES - WHOL

			Toll-Free	Phone
Ace Tool Co				
7337 Bryan Dairy Rd	Largo FL	33777	**800-777-5910**	727-544-6652
Advantage Truck Accessories Inc				
5400 S State Rd	Ann Arbor MI	48108	**800-773-3110**	
Allomatic Products Co				
102 Jericho Tpke				
Ste 104 Floral Pk	Floral Park NY	11001	**800-568-0330**	516-775-0330
Automotive Distributors Company Inc				
2981 Morse Rd	Columbus OH	43231	**800-421-5556**	
Automotive Mfg & Supply Co (AMSCO)				
90 Plant Ave	Hauppauge NY	11788	**800-645-5604**	631-435-1400
Automotive Parts Headquarters				
2959 Clearwater Rd	Saint Cloud MN	56301	**800-247-0339**	320-252-5411

			Toll-Free	Phone
Bendix Commercial Vehicle Systems LLC				
901 Cleveland St	Elyria OH	44035	**800-247-2725**	440-329-9000
CAM International LLC				
503 Space Park S	Nashville TN	37211	**800-251-8544**	
Carolina Rim & Wheel Co				
1308 Upper Asbury Ave	Charlotte NC	28206	**800-247-4337**	704-334-7276
Carolinas Auto Supply House Inc				
2135 Tipton Dr	Charlotte NC	28206	**800-438-4070**	704-334-4646
Champion Power Equipment				
12039 Smith Ave	Santa Fe Springs CA	90670	**877-338-0999**	
Custom Chrome Inc				
155 E Main Ave Ste 150	Morgan Hill CA	95037	**800-729-3332**	408-825-5000
Dero Bike Racks Inc				
504 Malcolm Ave SE Ste 100	Minneapolis MN	55414	**888-337-6729**	612-359-0689
Drive Train Industries Inc				
5555 Joliet St	Denver CO	80239	**800-525-6177**	303-292-5176
Eagle Parts & Products Inc				
1411 Marvin Griffin Rd	Augusta GA	30906	**888-972-9911**	706-790-6687
Enginetech Inc				
1205 W Crosby Rd	Carrollton TX	75006	**800-869-8711**	972-245-0110
Flowers Auto Parts Co				
935 Hwy 70 SE	Hickory NC	28602	**800-538-6272***	828-322-5414
*Cust Svc				
General Truck Parts & Equipment Co				
4040 W 40th St	Chicago IL	60632	**800-621-3914**	773-247-6900
GK Industries Ltd				
50 Precidio Ct	Brampton ON	L6S6E3	**800-463-8889**	905-799-1972
Harmonic Drive LLC				
247 Lynnfield St	Peabody MA	01960	**800-921-3332**	978-532-1800
Henderson Wheel & Warehouse Supply				
1825 South 300 West	Salt Lake City UT	84115	**800-748-5111**	801-486-2073
Instrument Sales & Service Inc				
16427 NE Airport Way	Portland OR	97230	**800-333-7976**	503-239-0754
InterAmerican Motor Corp (IMC)				
8901 Canoga Ave	Canoga Park CA	91304	**800-874-8925**	818-678-1200
JEGS Performance Auto Parts				
101 Jeg'S Pl	Delaware OH	43015	**800-345-4545**	614-294-5050
Kansas City Peterbilt Inc				
8915 Woodend Rd	Kansas City KS	66111	**800-489-1122**	913-441-2888
Keystone Automotive Operations Inc				
44 Tunkhannock Ave	Exeter PA	18643	**800-521-9999**	570-655-4514
L & M Radiator Inc				
1414 E 37th St	Hibbing MN	55746	**800-346-3500**	218-263-8993
LKQ Corp				
500 West Madison St Ste 2800	Chicago IL	60661	**877-557-2677**	
NASDAQ: LKQX				
London Machinery Inc				
15790 Robin's Hill Rd	London ON	N5V0A4	**800-265-1098**	519-963-2500
McGard LLC				
3875 California Rd	Orchard Park NY	14127	**800-444-5847**	716-662-8980
Mid America Motorworks				
17082 N US Hwy 45 PO Box 1368	Effingham IL	62401	**866-350-4543**	217-540-4200
Midwest Truck & Auto Parts Inc				
1001 W Exchange	Chicago IL	60609	**800-934-2727**	773-247-3400
Mighty Distributing System of America Inc				
650 Engineering Dr	Norcross GA	30092	**800-829-3900**	770-448-3900
Mile Marker International Inc				
2121 BLOUNT Rd	Pompano Beach FL	33069	**800-886-8647**	
Milliron Auto Parts				
2375 Springmill Rd	Mansfield OH	44903	**800-747-4566**	419-747-4566
Minnpar LLC				
5273 Program Ave	Mounds View MN	55112	**800-889-3382**	612-379-0606
Mutual Wheel Co Inc				
2345 Fourth Ave	Moline IL	61265	**800-798-6926**	309-757-1200
National Automotive Parts Assn (NAPA)				
2999 Circle 75 Pkwy	Atlanta GA	30339	**800-538-6272**	770-953-1700
NB.C. Truck Equipment Inc				
28130 Groesbeck Hwy	Roseville MI	48066	**800-778-8207**	586-774-4900
Northeast Battery & Alternator Inc				
240 Washington St	Auburn MA	01501	**800-441-8824**	508-832-2700
Northern Factory Sales Inc				
PO Box 660	Willmar MN	56201	**800-328-8900**	320-235-2288
NTP Distribution Inc				
27150 SW Kinsman Rd	Wilsonville OR	97070	**800-242-6987**	503-570-0171
OEM Systems LLC				
210 W Oklahoma Ave	Okarche OK	73762	**800-810-7252**	405-263-7488
Parts Central Inc				
3243 Whitfield St	Macon GA	31204	**800-226-9396**	478-745-0878
Plaza Fleet Parts Inc				
1520 S Broadway	Saint Louis MO	63104	**800-325-7618**	314-231-5047
Six Robblees' Inc				
11010 Tukwila International Blvd	Tukwila WA	98168	**800-275-7499**	206-767-7970
Six States Distributors Inc				
247 West 1700 South	Salt Lake City UT	84115	**800-453-5703***	801-488-4666
*Cust Svc				
Vander Haag's Inc				
3809 Fourth Ave W	Spencer IA	51301	**888-940-5030**	712-262-7000
WAlglobal				
411 Eagleview Blvd Ste 100	Exton PA	19341	**800-877-3340**	484-875-6600
Western Truck Parts & Equip Co				
3707 Airport Way S	Seattle WA	98134	**800-255-7383**	206-624-7383
Westin Automotive Products Inc				
5200 N Irwindale Ave Ste 220	Irwindale CA	91706	**800-345-8476**	626-960-6762
WORLDPAC Inc				
37137 Hickory St	Newark CA	94560	**800-888-9982**	
Wurth USA Inc 93 Grant St	Ramsey NJ	07446	**800-987-8487**	201-825-2710

62   AUTOMOTIVE SERVICES

SEE ALSO Gas Stations

			Toll-Free	Phone
Boyd Group Inc, The				
3570 Portage Ave	Winnipeg MB	R3K0Z8	**800-385-5451**	204-895-1244

62-1 Appearance Care - Automotive

	Toll-Free	Phone
Autobell Car Wash Inc 1521 E Third St . . . . .Charlotte NC 28204	800-582-8096	704-527-9274
Creative Colors International Inc 19015 S Jodi Rd Ste E . . . . Mokena IL 60448	800-933-2656	708-478-1437
Dr Vinyl & Assoc Ltd 1350 SE Hamblen Rd . . . . Lees Summit MO 64081 *General	800-531-6600*	816-525-6060
Fleetwash Inc 26 Law Dr . . . . Fairfield NJ 07004	800-847-3735	
Hoffman Car Wash & Hoffman Jiffy Lube 1757 Central Ave . . . . Albany NY 12205	877-446-3362	518-862-1658
Mister Car Wash 3101 E Speedway Blvd . . . . Tucson AZ 85716 *Cust Svc	866-254-3229*	520-327-5656
Precision Auto Care Inc 748 Miller Dr SE . . . . Leesburg VA 20175 OTC: PACI	866-944-8863	
Wash Tub, The 2208 NW Loop 410 . . . . San Antonio TX 78230 *Cust Svc	866-493-8822*	210-493-8822
Ziebart International Corp 1290 E Maple Rd . . . . Troy MI 48083	800-877-1312	248-588-4100

62-2 Glass Replacement - Automotive

	Toll-Free	Phone
All Star Glass Co Inc 1845 Morena Blvd . . . . .San Diego CA 92110	800-225-4184	619-275-3343
City Auto Glass Inc 116 S Concord Exchange . . . . .South Saint Paul MN 55075	888-552-4272	651-552-1000
Martin Glass Co 25 Ctr Plz . . . . .Belleville IL 62220	800-325-1946	618-277-1946
Safelite Group Inc 2400 Farmers Dr . . . . .Columbus OH 43235	877-664-8931	
SuperGlass Windshield Repair Inc 6220 Hazeltine National Dr Ste 118 . . . . Orlando FL 32822	866-557-7497	407-240-1920

62-3 Mufflers & Exhaust Systems Repair - Automotive

	Toll-Free	Phone
Midas International Corp 823 Donald Ross Rd . . . . .Juno Beach FL 33408	800-621-8545	630-438-3000
Monro Muffler Brake Inc 200 Holleder Pkwy . . . . Rochester NY 14615 NASDAQ: MNRO	800-876-6676	585-647-6400

62-4 Paint & Body Work - Automotive

	Toll-Free	Phone
CARSTAR Quality Collision Service 13750 W 108th St . . . . Lenexa KS 66215 *Cust Svc	800-227-7827*	913-696-0003
Colors on Parade 125 Daytona St PO Box 50940 . . . . Conway SC 29526 *Cust Svc	866-756-4207*	843-347-8818
Dent Wizard International 4710 Earth City Expy . . . . Bridgeton MO 63044	800-336-8949	
Gerber Collision & Glass 400 W Grand Ave . . . . .Elmhurst IL 60126	877-743-7237	847-679-0510
Gerber Collision & Glass 400 W Grand Ave . . . . .Elmhurst IL 60126 *General	877-743-7237*	630-628-5848
Maaco LLC 440 S Church St Ste 700 . . . . .Charlotte NC 28202	800-523-1180	
Mike Rose's Auto Body Inc 2260 Via de Marcardos . . . . .Concord CA 94520	855-340-1739	925-689-1739
Service King Collision Repair Centers 2375 N Glenville Dr . . . . Richardson TX 75080	844-611-5068	972-960-7595

62-5 Repair Service (General) - Automotive

	Toll-Free	Phone
All Tune & Lube International Inc *ATL International Inc* 8334 Veterans Hwy . . . . Millersville MD 21108 *Cust Svc	877-978-1758*	
Basin Tire & Auto Inc 2700 E Main St . . . . .Farmington NM 87402	800-832-9832	505-326-2231
Belle Tire Inc 1000 Enterprise Dr . . . . .Allen Park MI 48101	888-462-3553	313-271-9400
BERGEY'S AUTO DEALERSHIPS 462 Harleysville Pk . . . . .Souderton PA 18964	800-237-4397	215-723-6071
Bridgestone Americas Holding Inc 535 Marriott Dr . . . . Nashville TN 37214 *Cust Svc	877-201-2373*	615-937-1000
Evans Tire & Service Centers Inc 510 N Broadway . . . . .Escondido CA 92025	877-338-2678	
Express Oil Change & Tire Engineers 1880 S Pk Dr . . . . Hoover AL 35244	888-945-1771	205-940-2226
Fyda Freightliner Youngstown Inc 5260 76th Dr . . . . Youngstown OH 44515	800-837-3932	330-797-0224
Grease Monkey International 5575 DTC Pkwy Ste 100. . . . . .Greenwood Village CO 80111	800-822-7706	303-308-1660
Hunter Engineering Co 11250 Hunter Dr . . . . .Bridgeton MO 63044	800-448-6848	314-731-3020
Jack Williams Tire Co Inc PO Box 3655 . . . . .Scranton PA 18505	800-833-5051	
Jiffy Lube PO Box 4427 . . . . Houston TX 77210	800-344-6933	
Jubitz Corp 33 NE Middlefield Rd . . . . Portland OR 97211	800-523-0600	503-283-1111

	Toll-Free	Phone
Kansas City Peterbilt Inc 8915 Woodend Rd . . . . Kansas City KS 66111	800-489-1122	913-441-2888
Merlin 3815 E Main St Ste D . . . . .Saint Charles IL 60174	800-652-9900	630-513-8200
Mr Tire Auto Service Centers Inc 200 Holleder Pkwy . . . . .Rochester NY 14615	800-876-6676	
Parrish Tire Company Inc 5130 Indiana Ave . . . . .Winston-Salem NC 27106	800-849-8473	336-767-0202
Plaza Tire Service 2075 Corporate Cr PO Box 2048 . . . . .Cape Girardeau MO 63702	800-334-5036	
Precision Auto Care Inc 748 Miller Dr SE . . . . Leesburg VA 20175 OTC: PACI	866-944-8863	
Sullivan Tire Co Inc 41 Accord Park Dr . . . . .Norwell MA 02061	877-855-4826	781-982-1550
Techni-Car Inc 450 Commerce Blvd . . . . Oldsmar FL 34677	800-886-0022	813-855-0022
Tire-Rama Inc 1429 Grand Ave . . . . Billings MT 59102	800-828-1642	406-245-3161
Tires Plus Total Car Care 2021 Sunnydale Blvd . . . . Clearwater FL 33765	844-338-0739	727-330-3684
Tuffy Assoc Corp 7150 Granite Cir . . . . Toledo OH 43617	800-228-8339	419-865-6900
Wingfoot Commercial Tire Systems LLC 1000 S 21st St . . . . .Fort Smith AR 72901	800-643-7330	479-788-6400

62-6 Transmission Repair - Automotive

	Toll-Free	Phone
Lee Myles Auto Group 914 Fern Ave . . . . Reading PA 19607	800-533-6953	
Mister Transmission 9555 Yonge St Ste 204 . . . . .Richmond Hill ON L4C9M5	800-373-8432	905-884-1511

62-7 Van Conversions

	Toll-Free	Phone
Clock Mobility 6700 Clay Ave . . . . .Grand Rapids MI 49548	800-732-5625	616-698-9400
Foley Inc 855 Centennial Ave . . . . .Piscataway NJ 08854	888-417-6464	732-885-5555
Marathon Coach 91333 Coburg Industrial Way . . . . .Coburg OR 97408	800-234-9991	541-343-9991
Monaco Coach Corp 1031 US 224 E . . . . Decatur IN 46733	877-466-6226	
Rollx Vans 6591 Hwy 13 W . . . . .Savage MN 55378	800-956-6668	952-890-7851
Sherrod Vans Inc 3151 Industrial Blvd . . . . Waycross GA 31503	800-824-6333	
Sidewinder Conversions 44658 Yale Rd W . . . . .Chilliwack BC V2R0G5	888-266-2299	604-792-2082
Vantage Mobility International (VMI) 5202 S 28th Pl . . . . Phoenix AZ 85040	855-864-8267	
Waldoch Crafts Inc 13821 Lake Dr NE . . . . .Forest Lake MN 55025	800-328-9259	800-878-8635

63   AVIATION - FIXED-BASE OPERATIONS

SEE ALSO Air Cargo Carriers ; Air Charter Services ; Aircraft Service & Repair ; Aircraft Rental

	Toll-Free	Phone
Aero Industries Inc 5745 Huntsman Rd Richmond International Airport . . . . .Richmond VA 23250	800-845-1308	804-226-7200
Aircraft Specialists Inc 6005 Propeller Ln . . . . .Sellersburg IN 47172	800-776-5387	
Banyan Air Service 5360 NW 20th Terr . . . . Fort Lauderdale FL 33309	800-200-2031	954-491-3170
Basler Flight Service Wittman Regional Airport PO Box 2464 . . . . .Oshkosh WI 54903	800-564-6322	920-236-7827
Belshire Environmental Services Inc 25971 Towne Centre Dr . . . . .Foothill Ranch CA 92610	800-995-8220	949-460-5200
BMG Aviation Inc 984 S Kirby Rd . . . . .Bloomington IN 47403	888-457-3787	812-825-7979
Central Flying Service Inc 1501 Bond St . . . . Little Rock AR 72202	800-888-5387	501-375-3245
Columbia Air Services 175 Tower Ave Groton-New London Airport . . . . Groton CT 06340	800-787-5001	860-449-1400
Cook Aviation Inc 970 S Kirby Rd . . . . .Bloomington IN 47403	800-880-3499	812-825-2392
Corporate Air LLC 15 Allegheny County Airport . . . . .West Mifflin PA 15122	888-429-5377	412-469-6800
Crow Executive Air Inc 28331 Lemoyne Rd Toledo Metcalf Airport. . . . . .Millbury OH 43447	800-972-2769	567-200-0057
Eagle Aviation 2861 Aviation Way Columbia Metropolitan Airport . . . . .West Columbia SC 29170	800-849-3245	803-822-5555
Edmonton International Airport 1000 Airport Rd Edmonton International Airport Ste 1 . . . . .Edmonton AB T9E0V3	800-268-7134	780-890-8900
Edwards Jet Center 1691 Aviation Pl . . . . Billings MT 59105	866-353-8245	406-252-0508
Epps Aviation Inc 1 Aviation Way DeKalb Peachtree Airport . . . . .Atlanta GA 30341	800-241-6807	770-458-9851
Fargo Jet Center Inc 3802 20th St N . . . . Fargo ND 58102	800-770-0538	701-235-3600
Felts Field Aviation Inc 6205 E Rutter Ave . . . . Spokane WA 99212	800-676-5538	509-535-9011
Flight Light Inc 2708 47th Ave . . . . .Sacramento CA 95822	800-806-3548	
Grand Aire Express Inc 11777 W Airport Service Rd . . . . Swanton OH 43558	800-704-7263	

Classified Section (vertical left margin text)

				Toll-Free	Phone

Hunt Pan Am Aviation Inc
505 Amelia Earhart Dr ....Brownsville TX 78521 **800-888-7524** 956-542-9111

Inter-State Aviation
4800 Airport Complex N ....Pullman WA 99163 **800-653-8420** 509-332-6596

Interstate Aviation Inc
62 Johnson Ave ....Plainville CT 06062 **800-573-5519** 860-747-5519

Lane Aviation Corp
4389 International Gateway ....Columbus OH 43219 **800-848-6263** 614-237-3747

Loyd's Aviation
1601 Skyway Dr Ste 100
PO Box 80958. ....Bakersfield CA 93308 **800-284-1334** 661-393-1334

Maine Instrument Flight Inc
215 Winthrop St ....Augusta ME 04330 **888-643-3597** 207-622-1211

McCall Aviation
300 Deinhard Ln ....McCall ID 83638 **800-992-6559** 208-634-7137

Midwest Corporate Aviation
3512 N Webb Rd ....Wichita KS 67226 **800-435-9622** 316-636-9700

Millenium Aviation
2365 Bernville Rd ....Reading PA 19605 **800-366-9419** 610-372-4728

Miller Environmental Services Inc
401 Navigation Blvd ....Corpus Christi TX 78408 **800-929-7227** 361-289-9800

Million Air
4300 Westgrove Dr ....Addison TX 75001 **800-248-1602** 972-248-1600

National Jets
3495 SW Ninth Ave ....Fort Lauderdale FL 33315 **800-327-3710** 954-359-9900

Northeast Airmotive Inc
1011 Westbrook St ....Portland ME 04102 **877-354-7881** 207-774-6318

Pro-Tec Fire Services Ltd
2129 S Oneida St ....Green Bay WI 54304 **800-242-6352**

Richmor Aviation Inc
1142 Rte 9H PO Box 423 ....Hudson NY 12534 **800-331-6101** 518-828-9461

Sanford Aircraft
701 Rod Sullivan Rd ....Sanford NC 27330 **800-237-6902** 919-708-5549

SheltAir Aviation Services Fort Lauderdale
4860 NE 12th Ave ....Fort Lauderdale FL 33334 **800-700-2210** 954-771-2210

Silverhawk Aviation Inc
1751 W Kearney Ave ....Lincoln NE 68524 **800-479-5851** 402-475-8600

Sky Bright 65 Aviation Dr ....Gilford NH 03249 **800-639-6012** 603-528-6818

Skyservice Airlines Inc
9785 Ryan Ave ....Dorval QC H9P1A2 **888-985-1402** 514-636-3300

Space Coast Jet Ctr
7003 Challenger Ave ....Titusville FL 32780 **800-559-5473** 321-267-8355

St Paul Flight Ctr
270 Airport Rd ....Saint Paul MN 55107 **800-368-0107** 651-227-8108

Stevens Aviation Inc
600 Delaware St ....Greenville SC 29605 **800-359-7838**

Stuart Jet Ctr LLC
2501 Aviation Way ....Stuart FL 34996 **877-735-9538** 772-288-6700

Swift Aviation
Sky Harbor International Airport 2710 E Old Tower
....Phoenix AZ 85034 **866-704-9274** 602-273-3770

Texas Jet Inc
200 Texas Way ....Fort Worth TX 76106 **800-776-4547** 817-624-8438

Truman Arnold Cos
701 S Robison Rd ....Texarkana TX 75501 **800-235-5343** 903-794-3835

United States Aviation
4141 N Memorial Dr ....Tulsa OK 74115 **800-897-5387** 918-836-7345

Vee Neal Aviation Inc
148 Aviation Ln Ste 109 ....Latrobe PA 15650 **800-278-2710** 724-539-4533

Western Aircraft Inc
4300 S Kennedy St ....Boise ID 83705 **800-333-3442** 208-338-1800

Wilson Air Ctr
2930 Winchester Rd
Memphis International Airport ....Memphis TN 38118 **800-464-2992** 901-345-2992

Wisconsin Aviation Inc
1741 River Dr ....Watertown WI 53094 **800-657-0761** 920-261-4567

Woodland Aviation Inc
25170 Aviation Ave ....Davis CA 95616 **800-442-1333** 530-759-6037

64   BABY PRODUCTS

SEE ALSO Children's & Infants' Clothing ; Household Furniture ; Paper Products - Sanitary ; Toys, Games, Hobbies

				Toll-Free	Phone

Baby Jogger Co
8575 Magellan Pkwy Ste 1000 ....Richmond VA 23227 **800-241-1848**

Baby Trend Inc
1567 S Campus Ave ....Ontario CA 91761 **800-328-7363***
*Cust Svc

Ball Bounce & Sport Inc/Hedstrom Plastics
1 Hedstrom Dr ....Ashland OH 44805 **800-765-9665** 419-289-9310

Britax Child Safety Inc
....Fort Mill NC 29708 **888-427-4829** 704-409-1700

Cardinal Gates
79 Amlajack Way ....Newnan GA 30265 **800-318-3380** 770-252-4200

Central Specialties Ltd
220 Exchange Dr ....Crystal Lake IL 60014 **800-873-4370** 815-459-6000

Delta Children
114 W 26th St ....New York NY 10001 **800-377-3777**

Evenflo Company Inc
1801 Commerce Dr ....Piqua OH 45356 **800-233-5921**

Fisher-Price Inc
636 Girard Ave ....East Aurora NY 14052 **800-432-5437** 716-687-3000

Gerber Products Co
445 State St ....Fremont MI 49413 **800-284-9488**

Infantino LLC
4920 Carroll Canyon Rd Ste 200 ....San Diego CA 92121 **800-840-4916**

Kelty 6235 Lookout Rd ....Boulder CO 80301 **800-423-2320** 800-535-3589

KidCo Inc
1013 Technology Way ....Libertyville IL 60048 **800-553-5529** 847-549-8600

Kolcraft Enterprises Inc
10832 NC Hwy 211 E ....Aberdeen NC 28315 **800-453-7673*** 910-944-9345
*Cust Svc

Little Tikes Co, The
2180 Barlow Rd ....Hudson OH 44236 **800-321-0183***
*Cust Svc

Manhattan Toy
300 First Ave North Ste 200 ....Minneapolis MN 55401 **800-541-1345**

Peg-Perego USA Inc
3625 Independence Dr ....Fort Wayne IN 46808 **800-671-1701*** 260-482-8191
*Cust Svc

Prince Lionheart
2421 Westgate Rd ....Santa Maria CA 93455 **800-544-1132** 805-922-2250

REI 1700 45th St E ....Sumner WA 98352 **800-426-4840** 253-863-5550

Sassy Inc
2305 Breton Industrial Pk Dr ....Kentwood MI 49508 **800-323-6336** 800-433-9560

Step2 Co
10010 Aurora-Hudson Rd ....Streetsboro OH 44241 **800-347-8372*** 866-429-5200
*Cust Svc

Tough Traveler Ltd
1012 State St ....Schenectady NY 12307 **800-468-6844*** 518-377-8526
*Cust Svc

Triple Play Products LLC
120 Getty Ave ....Paterson NJ 07503 **800-829-1625** 646-484-8112

65   BAGS - PAPER

				Toll-Free	Phone

Bancroft Bag Inc
425 Bancroft Blvd ....West Monroe LA 71292 **800-551-4950** 318-387-2550

Bemis Company Inc
2301 Industrial Dr ....Neenah WI 54956 **800-544-4672** 920-527-5000
NYSE: BMS

Hood Packaging Corp
25 Woodgreen Pl ....Madison MS 39110 **800-321-8115** 601-853-7260

Pacific Bag Inc
15300 Woodinville Redmond Rd NE
Ste A. ....Woodinville WA 98072 **800-562-2247** 425-455-1128

Ross & Wallace Paper Products Inc
204 Old Covington Hwy ....Hammond LA 70403 **800-854-2300**

Weyerhaeuser Co
33663 Weyerhaeuser Way S ....Federal Way WA 98003 **800-525-5440** 253-924-2345
NYSE: WY

Zenith Specialty Bag Company Inc
17625 E Railroad St
PO Box 0445. ....City of Industry CA 91748 **800-962-2247** 626-912-2481

66   BAGS - PLASTICS

				Toll-Free	Phone

Admiral Packaging Inc
10 Admiral St ....Providence RI 02908 **800-556-6454** 401-274-7000

Ampac Packaging LLC
12025 Tricon Rd ....Cincinnati OH 45246 **800-543-7030** 513-671-1777

Apco Extruders Inc
180 National Rd ....Edison NJ 08817 **800-942-8725*** 732-287-3000
*Orders

Armand Manufacturing Inc
2399 Silver Wolf Dr ....Henderson NV 89011 **800-669-9811** 702-565-7500

Associated Bag Co
400 W Boden St ....Milwaukee WI 53207 **800-926-6100** 414-769-1000

Bag Makers Inc
6606 S Union Rd ....Union IL 60180 **800-458-9031**

Bemis Company Inc
2301 Industrial Dr ....Neenah WI 54956 **800-544-4672** 920-527-5000
NYSE: BMS

Clear View Bag Co
5 Burdick Dr ....Albany NY 12205 **800-458-7153** 518-458-7153

Colonial Bag Corp
205 E Fullerton Ave ....Carol Stream IL 60188 **800-445-7496** 630-690-3999

Enviro-Tote Inc
15 Industrial Dr ....Londonderry NH 03053 **800-868-3224** 603-647-7171

Heritage Bags
1648 Diplomat Dr ....Carrollton TX 75006 **800-527-2247**

International Poly Bag Inc
900 Park Center Dr Ste F & G. ....Vista CA 92081 **800-976-5922** 760-598-2468

Pacific Bag Inc
15300 Woodinville Redmond Rd NE
Ste A. ....Woodinville WA 98072 **800-562-2247** 425-455-1128

Pactiv Corp
1900 W Field Ct ....Lake Forest IL 60045 **888-828-2850** 847-482-2000

Pitt Plastics Inc
1400 Atkinson Ave ....Pittsburg KS 66762 **800-835-0366** 620-231-4337

Poly-America
2000 W Marshall Dr ....Grand Prairie TX 75051 **800-527-3322** 972-337-7100

Poly-Pak Industries Inc
125 Spagnoli Rd ....Melville NY 11747 **800-969-1993** 631-293-6767

Presto Products Co
670 N Perkins St PO Box 2399. ....Appleton WI 54912 **800-558-3525**

Roplast Industries Inc
3155 S Fifth Ave ....Oroville CA 95965 **800-767-5278** 530-532-9500

Shields Bag & Printing Co
1009 Rock Ave ....Yakima WA 98902 **800-541-8630** 509-248-7500

Superbag Corp
9291 Baythrone Dr ....Houston TX 77041 **888-842-1177** 713-462-1173

Waverly Plastics Company Inc
1001 Industrial St PO Box 801 ....Waverly IA 50677 **800-454-6377**

Webster Industries Inc
95 Chestnut Ridge Rd ....Montvale NJ 07645 **800-955-2374** 800-999-2374

Wisconsin Film & Bag Inc
3100 E Richmond St ....Shawano WI 54166 **800-765-9224** 715-524-2565

67   BAGS - TEXTILE

SEE ALSO Handbags, Totes, Backpacks ; Luggage, Bags, Cases

				Toll-Free	Phone

A Rifkin Co
1400 Sans Souci Pkwy ....Wilkes-Barre PA 18706 **800-458-7300*** 570-825-9551
*Cust Svc

				Toll-Free	Phone
Bulk Lift International Inc (BLI)					
1013 Tamarac Dr	Carpentersville	IL	60110	800-879-2247	847-428-6059
Fulton-Denver Co					
3500 Wynkoop St	Denver	CO	80216	800-521-1414	303-294-9292
GEM Group					
9 International Way	Lawrence	MA	01843	800-800-3200	978-691-2000
Halsted Corp					
51 Commerce Dr Ste 3	Cranbury	NJ	08512	800-843-5184	609-235-4444
HBD Inc					
3901 Riverdale Rd	Greensboro	NC	27406	800-403-2247	336-275-4800
Indian Valley Industries Inc					
PO Box 810	Johnson City	NY	13790	800-659-5111	607-729-5111
J & M Industries Inc					
300 Ponchatoula Pkwy	Ponchatoula	LA	70454	800-989-1002	985-386-6000
Langston Cos Inc					
1760 S Third St	Memphis	TN	38109	800-238-5798	
Menardi 1 Maxwell Dr	Trenton	SC	29847	800-321-3218	
NYP Corp 805 E Grand St	Elizabeth	NJ	07201	800-524-1052	908-351-6550
Sacramento Bag Manufacturing Co					
440 N Pioneer Ave Ste 300	Woodland	CA	95776	800-287-2247	530-662-6130

68   BAKERIES

				Toll-Free	Phone
Au Bon Pain					
19 Fid Kennedy Ave	Boston	MA	02210	800-825-5227	617-423-2100
Big Apple Bagels					
500 Lake Cook Rd Ste 475	Deerfield	IL	60015	800-251-6101	847-948-7520
Cheryl & Co					
646 McCorkle Blvd	Westerville	OH	43082	800-443-8124	
Collin Street Bakery Inc					
401 W Seventh Ave	Corsicana	TX	75110	800-267-4657*	
*Sales					
Cookies By Design Inc					
1865 Summit Ave Ste 605	Plano	TX	75074	800-945-2665	972-398-9536
Cookies From Home Inc					
1605 W University Dr Ste 106	Tempe	AZ	85281	800-543-8133	480-894-1944
Damascus Bakery Inc					
56 Gold St	Brooklyn	NY	11201	800-367-7482	718-855-1456
Daylight Donut Flour Company LLC					
11707 E 11th St	Tulsa	OK	74128	800-331-2245	918-438-0800
Dunkin' Donuts 130 Royall St	Canton	MA	02021	800-859-5339*	781-737-3000
*Cust Svc					
East Balt Inc					
1801 W 31st Pl	Chicago	IL	60608	800-621-8555	773-376-4444
Eleni's 205 E 42nd St	New York	NY	10017	888-435-3647	
Galasso's Inc					
10820 San Sevaine Way	Mira Loma	CA	91752	800-339-7494	951-360-1211
Gold Medal Bakery Inc					
1397 Bay St	Fall River	MA	02724	800-642-7568	508-674-5766
Gonnella Baking Co					
1117 E Wiley Rd	Schaumburg	IL	60173	800-322-8829	
Great American Cookie Company Inc					
3300 Chambers Rd	Horseheads	NY	14845	877-639-2361	
Great Harvest Bread Co					
28 S Montana St	Dillon	MT	59725	800-442-0424	406-683-6842
Hill & Valley Premium Bakery					
320 44th St	Rock Island	IL	61201	800-480-0055	309-793-0161
Honey Dew Assoc Inc					
2 Taunton St	Plainville	MA	02762	800-946-6393	508-699-3900
Hot Stuff Pizza					
2930 W Maple St	Sioux Falls	SD	57107	800-336-1320	605-336-6961
Krispy Kreme Doughnuts Corp					
PO Box 83	Winston-Salem	NC	27102	800-457-4779	336-725-2981
NYSE: KKD					
Maple Donuts Inc					
3455 E Market St	York	PA	17402	800-627-5348	717-757-7826
Panera Bread Co					
3630 S Geyer Rd	Saint Louis	MO	63127	800-301-5566	314-984-1000
NASDAQ: PNRA					
PARTNERS A Tasteful Choice Co					
20232 72nd Ave	South Kent	WA	98032	800-632-7477	253-867-1580
Vie de France Yamazaki Inc					
2070 Chain Bridge Rd Ste 500	Vienna	VA	22182	800-446-4404*	703-442-9205
*General					
Wicks Pies Inc					
217 Greenville Ave	Winchester	IN	47394	800-642-5880	

69   BANKING-RELATED SERVICES

				Toll-Free	Phone
Atm Merchant Systems					
1667 Helm Dr	Las Vegas	NV	89119	888-878-8166	702-837-8787
Automatic Funds Transfer Services					
151 S Landers St Ste C.	Seattle	WA	98134	800-275-2033	206-254-0975
Blackhawk Bank					
400 Broad St PO Box 719	Beloit	WI	53511	888-769-2600	608-364-8911
Bremer Financial Corp					
372 St Peter St	Saint Paul	MN	55102	800-908-2265	651-288-3751
Capital Farm Credit Aca					
7000 Woodway Dr	Waco	TX	76712	877-944-5500	254-776-7506
Civista Bank					
100 E Water St	Sandusky	OH	44870	888-645-4121	419-625-4121
Comdata Corp					
5301 Maryland Way	Brentwood	TN	37027	800-266-3282	615-370-7000
Community Bank					
505 E Colorado Blvd	Pasadena	CA	91101	800-788-9999	
Eagle Direct 1 Printer's Dr	Hermon	ME	04401	800-675-7669	207-848-7300
eCivis Inc					
418 N Fair Oaks Ave Ste 301	Pasadena	CA	91103	877-232-4847	
Emprise Financial Corp					
257 N Broadway St PO Box 2970	Wichita	KS	67202	800-201-7118*	316-383-4301
*Cust Svc					
Eureka Homestead					
1922 Veterans Memorial Blvd	Metairie	LA	70005	855-858-5179	504-834-0242

				Toll-Free	Phone
Fiserv Inc					
255 Fiserv Dr PO Box 979	Brookfield	WI	53008	800-872-7882*	262-879-5000
NASDAQ: FISV ■ *Sales					
Hawaii National Bank					
45 N King St	Honolulu	HI	96817	800-528-2273	808-528-7711
HomEquity Bank					
1881 Yonge St Ste 300	Toronto	ON	M4S3C4	866-522-2447	416-925-4757
Lockwood Advisors Inc					
760 Moore Rd	King Of Prussia	PA	19406	800-200-3033	
MoneyGram International Inc					
2828 N Harwood 1st Fl.	Dallas	TX	75201	800-666-3947	
NASDAQ: MGI					
Moneytree Inc					
6720 Ft Dent Way Ste 230	Seattle	WA	98188	877-613-6669	206-246-3500
NYCE Corp 400 Plaza Dr	Secaucus	NJ	07094	888-323-0310	904-438-6000
Oak Ridge Financial					
701 Xenia Ave S Ste 100	Minneapolis	MN	55416	800-231-8364	763-923-2200
OANDA Corp					
140 Broadway 46th Fl.	New York	NY	10005	800-826-8164	416-593-9436
PULSE					
1301 McKinney St Ste 2500	Houston	TX	77010	800-420-2122	832-214-0100
Rock Springs National Bank					
200 Second St PO Box 880	Rock Springs	WY	82902	800-469-8801	307-362-8801
Travelex Worldwide Money					
122 E 42nd St Ste 2800	New York	NY	10168	800-228-9792	516-300-1622
Western Union Holdings Inc					
12500 E Belford Ave	Englewood	CO	80112	800-325-6000*	720-332-1000
NYSE: WU ■ *Cust Svc					

70   BANKS - COMMERCIAL & SAVINGS

SEE ALSO Credit Unions ; Credit & Financing - Consumer ; Credit & Financing - Commercial ; Bank Holding Companies

				Toll-Free	Phone
1st Colonial Bancorp Inc					
1040 Haddon Ave	Collingswood	NJ	08108	800-500-1044	856-858-1100
OTC: FCOB					
1st Source Bank					
100 N Michigan St	South Bend	IN	46601	800-513-2360	574-235-2260
Alostar Bank					
3680 Grandview Pkwy Ste 200	Birmingham	AL	35243	877-738-6391	205-298-6391
Amalgamated Bank of New York					
275 Seventh Ave	New York	NY	10001	800-662-0860	
Amarillo National Bank					
410 S Taylor St	Amarillo	TX	79101	800-253-1031	806-378-8000
Amboy National Bank					
3590 US Hwy 9 S	Old Bridge	NJ	08857	800-942-6269	732-591-8700
Amegy Bank of Texas					
4400 Post Oak Pkwy	Houston	TX	77027	800-287-0301	713-235-8800
American Exchange Bank (AEB)					
510 W Main St PO Box 818	Henryetta	OK	74437	888-652-3321	918-652-3321
American National Bank					
PO Box 2139	Omaha	NE	68103	800-279-0007*	402-457-1077
*Cust Svc					
American Savings Bank FSB					
1001 Bishop St	Honolulu	HI	96813	800-272-2566	808-627-6900
Ameriserv Financial					
216 Franklin St PO Box 520	Johnstown	PA	15907	800-837-2265	
NASDAQ: ASRV					
AmTrust Bank					
1801 E Ninth St	Cleveland	OH	44114	888-696-4444	216-736-3480
Apple Bank for Savings					
122 E 42nd St	New York	NY	10168	800-824-0710	914-902-2775
Artisan's Bank					
2961 Centerville Rd	Wilmington	DE	19808	800-282-8255	302-658-6881
Asheville Savings Bank S S B					
PO Box 652	Asheville	NC	28802	800-222-3230	828-254-7411
Associated Banc-Corp					
310 W Wisconsin Ave Ste 400	Milwaukee	WI	53202	800-236-8866	920-491-7000
Associated Bank					
1305 Main St MS 7722	Stevens Point	WI	54481	800-236-8866	
Associated Bank Green Bay NA					
200 N Adams St	Green Bay	WI	54301	800-728-3501	920-433-3200
Associated Bank Illinois NA					
612 N Main St	Rockford	IL	61103	800-236-8866	815-987-3500
Athens State Bank					
6530 N State Rt 29	Springfield	IL	62707	800-367-7576	217-487-7766
Bancorp Bank					
409 Silverside Rd Ste 105	Wilmington	DE	19809	866-255-9831*	302-385-5000
NASDAQ: TBBK ■ *Cust Svc					
Bangor Savings Bank					
99 Franklin St	Bangor	ME	04401	877-226-4671	207-942-5211
Bank Financial					
6415 W 95th St	Chicago Ridge	IL	60415	800-894-6900	
Bank Leumi USA					
350 Madison Ave	New York	NY	10017	800-892-5430	917-542-2343
Bank of Albuquerque					
400 S Tijeras Ave North W Ste 150	Albuquerque	NM	87102	800-583-0709	505-855-0855
Bank of Louisiana					
300 St Charles Ave	New Orleans	LA	70130	866-392-9952	504-592-0600
Bank of Marin					
504 Tamalpais Dr	Corte Madera	CA	94925	800-654-5111	415-927-2265
NASDAQ: BMRC					
Bank of Montreal (BMO)					
100 King St W 1 First Canadian Pl 19th Fl	Toronto	ON	M5X1A1	800-340-5021	416-867-6785
NYSE: BMO					
Bank of Montreal					
3 Times Sq	New York	NY	10036	877-225-5266	
Bank of North Dakota					
1200 Memorial Hwy	Bismarck	ND	58504	800-472-2166	701-328-5600
Bank of Nova Scotia					
1 Liberty Plz 26th Fl	New York	NY	10006	800-472-6842	212-225-5000
TSE: BNS					
Bank of Oklahoma NA					
PO Box 2300	Tulsa	OK	74192	800-234-6181	918-588-6010

	City	State	ZIP	Toll-Free	Phone
Bank of Springfield 2600 Adlai Stevenson Dr	Springfield	IL	62703	**877-698-3278**	217-529-5555
Bank of Stockton PO Box 1110	Stockton	CA	95201	**800-941-1494**	209-929-1600
Bank of Sunset & Trust Co 863 Napoleon Ave	Sunset	LA	70584	**800-264-5578**	337-662-5222
Bank of the Sierra PO Box 1930 *Cust Svc	Porterville	CA	93258	**888-454-2265***	559-782-4900
Bank Of Utica 222 Genesee St *OTC: BKUT*	Utica	NY	13502	**800-442-1028**	315-797-2700
Bankers' Bank 7700 Mineral Point Rd	Madison	WI	53717	**800-388-5550**	608-833-5550
Bankwest 420 S Pierre St	Pierre	SD	57501	**800-253-0362**	605-224-7391
Banner Bank 10 S First Ave PO Box 907	Walla Walla	WA	99362	**800-272-9933**	509-527-3636
Banterra Corp 1404 US Rt 45 S	Eldorado	IL	62930	**877-541-2265**	618-273-9346
BB & T Corp 200 W Second St *NYSE: BBT*	Winston-Salem	NC	27101	**800-226-5228**	
Beneficial Mutual Savings Bank 530 Walnut St	Philadelphia	PA	19106	**800-784-8490**	888-742-5272
Berkshire Bank PO Box 1308	Pittsfield	MA	01202	**800-773-5601**	413-443-5601
Blue Ridge Bank & Trust Co 4240 Blue Ridge Blvd Ste 100	Kansas City	MO	64133	**800-569-4287**	816-358-5000
Blueharbor Bank 106 Corporate Park Dr	Mooresville	NC	28117	**877-322-8228**	704-662-7700
BMO Harris Bank 111 W Monroe St	Chicago	IL	60603	**888-340-2265**	773-682-7481
BNC National Bank 322 E Main Ave	Bismarck	ND	58501	**800-262-2265**	701-250-3000
Boiling Springs Savings Bank (BSSB) 25 Orient Way	Rutherford	NJ	07070	**888-388-7459**	201-939-5000
Branch Banking & Trust Company of South Carolina 301 College St	Greenville	SC	29601	**800-226-5228**	
Brotherhood Bank & Trust 756 Minnesota Ave	Kansas City	MO	66101	**855-522-6722**	913-321-4242
Burke & Herbert Bank & Trust Co 100 S Fairfax St	Alexandria	VA	22314	**877-440-0800**	703-751-7701
California Bank & Trust 11622 El Camino Real Ste 200	San Diego	CA	92130	**800-400-6080**	858-793-7400
Cambridge Savings Bank 1374 Massachusetts Ave	Cambridge	MA	02138	**888-418-5626**	617-441-4155
Canadian Imperial Bank of Commerce (CIBC) 199 Bay St Commerce Ct W *NYSE: CM*	Toronto	ON	M5L1A2	**800-465-2422**	
Cape Cod Five Cents Savings Bank 532 Rte 28 PO Box 20	Harwich Port	MA	02646	**800-678-1855**	508-430-0400
Capital City Bank 217 North Monroe St	Tallahassee	FL	32301	**888-671-0400**	850-402-7700
Capital One Auto Finance Inc PO Box 60511	City of Industry	CA	91716	**800-946-0332**	
Capital One FSB *Capital One Bank* 15000 Capital One Dr	Richmond	VA	23238	**877-383-4802**	
Capitol FSB 700 S Kansas Ave	Topeka	KS	66603	**888-822-7333**	785-235-1341
Carolina Trust Bank 901 E Main St *NASDAQ: CART*	Lincolnton	NC	28092	**877-983-5537**	704-735-1104
Casey State Bank 305-307 N Central Ave	Casey	IL	62420	**866-666-2754**	217-932-2136
CBT Bank 11 N Second St PO Box 171	Clearfield	PA	16830	**888-765-7551**	814-765-7551
Centerstate Banks Inc 42725 US Hwy 27	Davenport	FL	33837	**855-863-2265**	
Century National Bank 14 S Fifth St *Cust Svc	Zanesville	OH	43701	**800-548-3557***	740-454-2521
CharterBank 1233 OG Skinner Dr	West Point	GA	31833	**800-763-4444**	706-645-1391
Chase Bank 28 Liberty St	New York	NY	10005	**800-935-9935**	
Chinatrust Bank USA 801 S Figueroa St Ste 2300	Los Angeles	CA	90017	**888-308-0986**	310-791-2828
Citibank NA 399 Park Ave	New York	NY	10022	**800-627-3999**	
Citizen National Bank Of Bluffton, The 102 S Main St PO Box 88	Bluffton	OH	45817	**800-262-4663**	419-358-8040
Citizens Bank of Clovis 420 Wheeler	Texico	NM	88135	**844-657-3553**	575-482-3381
Citizens Bank of Massachusetts 28 State St	Boston	MA	02109	**800-610-7300**	
Citizens Bank of Mukwonago 301 N Rochester St PO Box 223	Mukwonago	WI	53149	**877-546-5868**	262-363-6500
Citizens Bank of Rhode Island 1 Citizens Plz *Cust Svc	Providence	RI	02903	**800-922-9999***	401-456-7000
Citizens Business Bank (CBB) 701 N Haven Ave *Cust Svc	Ontario	CA	91764	**888-222-5432***	909-980-4030
Citizens Financial Services 707 Ridge Rd	Munster	IN	46321	**800-205-3464**	219-836-5500
Citizens State Bank & Trust Co 203 N Douglas PO Box 518	Ellsworth	KS	67439	**800-472-3145**	785-472-3141
Citizens Trust Bank 1700 Third Ave N	Birmingham	AL	35203	**888-214-3099**	205-328-2041
City National Bank 400 N Roxbury Dr *Cust Svc	Beverly Hills	CA	90210	**800-773-7100***	310-888-6000
City National Bank of Florida 450 E Las Olas Blvd	Fort Lauderdale	FL	33301	**800-762-2489**	954-467-6667
City National Bank of New Jersey (CNB) 900 Broad St	Newark	NJ	07102	**877-350-3524**	973-624-0865
City National Bank of West Virginia 3601 McCorckle Ave	Charleston	WV	25304	**888-816-8064**	304-926-3324
Coast Capital Savings 800-9900 King George Blvd	Surrey	BC	V3T0K7	**888-517-7000**	250-483-7000

	City	State	ZIP	Toll-Free	Phone
College Savings Bank PO Box 3769	Princeton	NJ	08543	**800-888-2723**	
Colorado Fsb 8400 E Prentice Ave Ste 840	Greenwood Village	CO	80111	**877-484-2372**	303-793-3555
Columbia Bank 506 SW Coast Hwy *Cust Svc	Newport	OR	97365	**800-304-0050***	877-272-3678
Columbia Bank, The 7168 Columbia Gateway Dr	Columbia	MD	21046	**888-822-2265**	
Columbia Savings Bank 19-01 Rt 208 *Cust Svc	Fair Lawn	NJ	07410	**800-747-4428***	800-522-4167
Columbia State Bank PO Box 2156	Tacoma	WA	98401	**800-305-1905**	253-305-1900
Columbus Bank & Trust Co 1148 Broadway	Columbus	GA	31901	**800-334-9007**	706-649-4900
Comerica Bank 411 W Lafayette	Detroit	MI	48226	**800-292-1300**	313-222-4000
Comerica Bank-California 333 W Santa Clara St	San Jose	CA	95113	**800-522-2265**	408-556-5300
Comerica Bank-Texas 1717 Main St	Dallas	TX	75201	**800-925-2160**	
Commercial Bank 301 N State St PO Box 638 *OTC: CEFC*	Alma	MI	48801	**800-547-8531**	989-463-2185
Community Bank of Raymore PO Box 200	Raymore	MO	64083	**800-523-4175**	816-322-2100
Community Trust Bank NA 346 N Mayo Trl PO Box 2947	Pikeville	KY	41501	**800-422-1090**	606-432-1414
Conneaut Savings Bank 305 Main St PO Box 740	Conneaut	OH	44030	**888-453-2311**	440-599-8121
Cornhusker Bank 1101 Cornhusker Hwy	Lincoln	NE	68521	**877-837-4481**	402-434-2265
Country Bank for Savings 75 Main St	Ware	MA	01082	**800-322-8233**	413-967-6221
D L Evans Bank 397 N Overland PO Box 1188	Burley	ID	83318	**888-873-9777**	208-678-9076
DBS Bank Ltd 725 S Figueroa St	Los Angeles	CA	90017	**800-209-4555**	213-627-0222
Dedham Institution For Savings 55 Elm St PO Box 9107	Dedham	MA	02026	**888-289-0342**	781-329-6700
Deutsche Bank Canada (DB) 199 Bay St Commerce Ct W Ste 4700	Toronto	ON	M5L1E9	**800-735-7777**	416-682-8000
Dime Bank, The 820 Church St PO Box 509	Honesdale	PA	18431	**888-469-3463**	570-253-1902
Discover Bank PO Box 30416	Salt Lake City	UT	84130	**800-347-7000**	302-323-7810
Dollar Bank FSB 225 Forbes Ave	Pittsburgh	PA	15222	**800-828-5527**	
E*Trade Bank 671 N Glebe Rd	Arlington	VA	22203	**877-800-1208**	
East Boston Savings Bank 10 Meridian St	East Boston	MA	02128	**800-657-3272**	617-567-1500
Eastern Bank 1 Eastern Pl	Lynn	MA	01901	**800-327-8376**	800-333-7234
El Dorado Savings Bank 4040 El Dorado Rd	Placerville	CA	95667	**800-874-9779**	530-622-1492
Elmira Savings Bank 333 E Water St *NASDAQ: ESBK*	Elmira	NY	14901	**888-372-9299**	607-734-3374
Encore Bank 3003 Tamiami Trail N Ste 100	Naples	FL	34103	**800-472-3272**	239-919-5888
Enterprise Bank of SC 13497 Broxton Bridge Rd PO Box 8	Ehrhardt	SC	29081	**800-554-8969**	803-267-3191
Equitable Bank (MHC) 113 N Locust St	Grand Island	NE	68801	**877-821-5783**	308-382-3136
Essex Savings Bank PO Box 950	Essex	CT	06426	**877-377-3922**	860-767-4414
Euro Pacific Capital Inc 88 Post Rd W 2nd Fl	Westport	CT	06880	**800-727-7922**	203-662-9700
Exchange State Bank 3992 Chandler St PO Box 68	Carsonville	MI	48419	**888-488-9300**	810-657-9333
F&M Bank 50 Franklin St	Clarksville	TN	37040	**800-645-4199**	931-906-0005
Farm Bureau Bank 2165 Green Vista Dr Ste 204	Sparks	NV	89431	**800-492-3276**	775-673-4566
Fauquier Bank, The (TFB) 10 Courthouse Sq	Warrenton	VA	20186	**800-638-3798**	540-347-2700
Fidelity Bancshares Nc Inc PO Box 8	Fuquay Varina	NC	27526	**800-816-9608**	919-552-2242
Fidelity Bank 100 E English St	Wichita	KS	67201	**800-658-1637**	
Fidelity Bank & Trust 208 Second St SE PO Box 277	Dyersville	IA	52040	**800-403-8333**	563-875-7157
Fifth Third Bank Central Ohio 21 E State St	Columbus	OH	43215	**866-671-5353**	800-972-3030
First American Bank & Trust 2785 Hwy 20 W PO Box 550	Vacherie	LA	70090	**800-738-2265**	225-265-2265
First Bank Financial Centre (FBFC) 155 W Wisconsin Ave PO Box 1004	Oconomowoc	WI	53066	**888-569-9909**	262-569-9900
First Bank of Muleshoe 202 S 1st PO Box 565	Muleshoe	TX	79347	**888-653-9558**	806-272-4515
First Calgary Savings 510 16th Ave NE	Calgary	AB	T2E1K4	**866-923-4778**	
First Federal Bank Fsb 6900 N Executive Dr	Kansas City	MO	64120	**888-651-4759**	816-241-7800
First Federal Lakewood 14806 Detroit Ave	Lakewood	OH	44107	**800-966-7300**	216-529-2700
First Financial Bank PO Box 2122	Terre Haute	IN	47802	**800-511-0045**	812-238-6000
First Financial Bank 300 High St *Cust Svc	Hamilton	OH	45011	**877-322-9530***	513-867-4744
First Foundation Bank 18101 Von Karman Ave Ste 750	Irvine	CA	92612	**800-224-7931**	949-202-4100
First Hawaiian Bank 999 Bishop St	Honolulu	HI	96813	**888-844-4444**	808-525-6340
First Interstate Bank 401 N 31st St	Billings	MT	59101	**888-752-3341**	406-255-5000
First Jackson Bank 43243 US Hwy 72	Stevenson	AL	35772	**888-950-2265**	256-437-2107

Classified Section

				Toll-Free	Phone
First Mercantile Trust Co					
57 Germantown Ct 4th Fl	Cordova	TN	38018	**800-753-3682**	901-753-9080
First National Bank					
PO Box 578	Fort Collins	CO	80521	**800-883-8773**	970-495-9450
First National Bank Alaska					
101 W 36 Ave PO Box 100720	Anchorage	AK	99510	**800-856-4362**	907-777-4362
OTC: FBAK					
First National Bank Creston					
PO Box 445	Creston	IA	50801	**877-782-2195**	641-782-2195
First National Bank Jasper					
301 E Houston St	Jasper	TX	75951	**800-340-7167**	409-384-3486
First National Bank of Omaha					
1620 Dodge St	Omaha	NE	68197	**800-462-5266**	402-602-3022
First National Bank of Oneida, The					
18418 Alberta St PO Box 4699	Oneida	TN	37841	**866-546-8273**	423-569-8586
First National Bank of Santa Fe					
PO Box 609	Santa Fe	NM	87504	**888-912-2265**	505-992-2000
First National Bankers Bankshares Inc (FNBB)					
7813 Office Pk Blvd	Baton Rouge	LA	70809	**800-421-6182**	225-924-8015
First Palmetto Savings Bank Fsb					
PO Box 430	Camden	SC	29021	**800-922-7411**	803-432-2265
First Republic Bank					
111 Pine St	San Francisco	CA	94111	**800-392-1400**	415-392-1400
NYSE: FRC					
First Savings Bank					
2804 N Telshor Blvd	Las Cruces	NM	88011	**800-555-6895**	575-521-7931
First Security Bank of Missoula					
1704 Dearborn PO Box 4506	Missoula	MT	59801	**888-782-3115**	406-728-3115
First Security Bank of Sleepy Eye					
100 Main St E PO Box 469	Sleepy	MN	56085	**800-535-8440**	507-794-3911
First State Bank					
708 Azalea Dr PO Box 506	Waynesboro	MS	39367	**866-408-3582**	
First State Bank & Trust Co					
1005 E 23rd St	Fremont	NE	68025	**888-674-4344**	402-721-2500
First State Bank of Kansas City					
650 Kansas Ave	Kansas City	KS	66105	**800-883-1242**	913-371-1242
First Tennessee Bank					
165 Madison Ave	Memphis	TN	38103	**800-382-5465**	901-523-4883
First Texas Bank					
501 E Third St	Lampasas	TX	76550	**866-220-1598**	512-556-3691
First United Bank					
1400 W Main St	Durant	OK	74701	**800-924-4427**	580-924-2211
First Western Bank & Trust					
PO Box 1090	Minot	ND	58702	**800-688-2584**	701-852-3711
First-Knox National Bank					
1 S Main St PO Box 1270	Mount Vernon	OH	43050	**800-837-5266**	740-399-5500
Firstrust Savings Bank					
15 E Ridge Pk 4th Fl	Conshohocken	PA	19428	**800-220-2265**	610-238-5000
Flagstar Bank FSB					
5151 Corporate Dr	Troy	MI	48098	**800-945-7700**	248-312-5400
Fowler State Bank					
300 E Fifth St PO Box 511	Fowler	IN	47944	**800-439-3951**	765-884-1200
Garden State Community Bank (GSCB)					
36 Ferry St	Newark	NJ	07105	**877-786-6560**	973-589-8616
NYSE: NYCB					
Giantbankcom					
6300 NE First Ave	Fort Lauderdale	FL	33334	**877-446-4200**	
Glenwood State Bank					
5 E Minnesota Ave PO Box 197	Glenwood	MN	56334	**800-207-7333**	320-634-5111
Golden Valley Bank					
190 Cohasset Rd Ste 170	Chico	CA	95926	**800-472-3272**	530-894-1000
Great Western Bank					
6001 NW Radial Hwy	Omaha	NE	68104	**800-952-2043**	402-552-1200
Greenfield Savings Bank					
400 Main St PO Box 1537	Greenfield	MA	01302	**888-324-3191**	413-774-3191
Guaranty Bank					
4000 W Brown Deer Rd	Brown Deer	WI	53209	**800-235-4636**	
Guaranty State Bank & Trust Co Beloit Kansas, The					
201 S Mill St	Beloit	KS	67420	**888-738-8000**	785-738-3501
Guilford Savings Bank (GSB)					
PO Box 369	Guilford	CT	06437	**866-878-1480**	203-453-2015
Gulf Coast Bank					
4310 Johnston St	Lafayette	LA	70503	**800-722-5363**	337-989-1133
Hastings City Bank					
150 W Court St	Hastings	MI	49058	**888-422-2280**	
Heritage Group Inc					
1101 12th St	Aurora	NE	68818	**888-463-6611**	402-694-3136
Hickory Point Bank & Trust FSB					
PO Box 2548	Decatur	IL	62525	**800-872-0081***	217-875-3131
*Cust Svc					
Hills Bank & Trust Co					
131 Main St PO Box 70	Hills	IA	52235	**800-445-5725**	
Hocking Valley Bank					
7 W Stimson Ave	Athens	OH	45701	**888-482-5854**	740-592-4441
Home Savings & Loan Company of Youngstown					
275 W Federal St	Youngstown	OH	44503	**888-822-4751**	330-742-0500
HomeStreet Bank					
601 Union St Ste 2000	Seattle	WA	98101	**800-654-1075**	206-623-3050
Hometrust Bank, The					
PO Box 10	Asheville	NC	28802	**800-627-1632**	828-259-3939
Huntington National Bank					
41 S High St Huntington Ctr	Columbus	OH	43287	**800-480-2265**	614-480-8300
Illinois National Bank					
322 E Capitol	Springfield	IL	62701	**877-771-2316**	217-747-5500
Independence FSB					
1301 Ninth St NW	Washington	DC	20001	**888-922-6537**	
InsurBanc					
10 Executive Dr	Farmington	CT	06032	**866-467-2262**	860-677-9701
Inter-County Bakers Inc					
1095 Long Island Ave	Deer Park	NY	11729	**800-696-1350**	631-957-1350
Investors Bank					
101 Wood Ave S	Iselin	NJ	08830	**855-422-6548**	973-924-5100
NASDAQ: ISBC					
Iowa State Savings Bank					
401 W Adams St	Creston	IA	50801	**888-508-0142**	641-782-1000
Jeff Davis Bancshares Inc					
507 N Main St PO Box 730	Jennings	LA	70546	**800-789-5159**	337-824-3424
OTC: JDVB					

				Toll-Free	Phone
Jersey Shore State Bank					
300 Market St	Williamsport	PA	17701	**888-412-5772**	570-322-1111
Kearny FSB					
120 Passaic Ave	Fairfield	NJ	07004	**800-273-3406**	
Kennebec Savings Bank					
150 State St PO Box 50	Augusta	ME	04332	**888-303-7788**	207-622-5801
Kentucky Bank PO Box 157	Paris	KY	40362	**800-467-1939**	859-987-1795
Key Bank					
65 Dutch Hill Rd	Orangeburg	NY	10962	**800-539-2968***	845-398-2280
*Cust Svc					
Kingston National Bank					
2 N Main St PO Box 613	Kingston	OH	45644	**800-337-4562**	740-642-2191
Kirkwood Bank & Trust Co					
2911 N 14th St	Bismarck	ND	58503	**800-492-4955**	701-258-6550
Kish Bancorp Inc					
4255 E Main St PO Box 917	Belleville	PA	17004	**888-554-4748**	717-935-2191
OTC: KISB					
Labette Bank					
4th & Huston PO Box 497	Altamont	KS	67330	**800-711-5311**	620-784-5311
Laurentian Bank of Canada					
1981 McGill College Ave	Montreal	QC	H3A3K3	**800-252-1846**	514-284-4500
TSE: LB					
LCNB National Bank					
3209 W Galbraith Rd	Cincinnati	OH	45239	**800-344-2265**	513-932-1414
Legacy Bank					
1580 E Cheyenne Mtn Blvd	Colorado Springs	CO	80906	**866-627-0800**	719-579-9150
Liberty Bank 315 Main St	Middletown	CT	06457	**800-622-6732**	888-570-0773
Liberty Bank & Trust Co					
PO Box 60131	New Orleans	LA	70160	**800-883-3943**	504-240-5100
Liberty Savings Bank FSB					
3435 Airborne Rd Ste B	Wilmington	OH	45177	**800-436-6300**	
Luther Burbank Savings					
804 Fourth St	Santa Rosa	CA	95404	**888-205-6005**	707-578-9216
M&T Bank 345 Main St	Buffalo	NY	14203	**800-724-2440**	716-842-4470
NYSE: MTB					
Machias Savings Bank					
4 Ctr St PO Box 318	Machias	ME	04654	**800-982-7179**	207-255-3347
Main Source Bank					
201 N Broadway	Greensburg	IN	47240	**800-713-6083**	
Marquette Bank					
10000 W 151st St	Orland Park	IL	60462	**888-254-9500**	708-226-8026
Marquette Savings Bank					
920 Peach St	Erie	PA	16501	**866-672-3743**	814-455-4481
Maspeth Federal Savings					
56-18 69th St	Maspeth	NY	11378	**888-558-1300**	718-335-1300
Max Credit Union					
400 Eastdale Cir	Montgomery	AL	36117	**800-776-6776**	334-260-2600
MCNB Bank & Trust Co					
PO Box 549	Welch	WV	24801	**800-532-9553**	304-436-4112
Mechanics Savings Bank					
100 Minot Ave PO Box 400	Auburn	ME	04210	**877-886-1020**	207-786-5700
Merchants National Bank of Bangor Inc					
25 Broadway PO Box 227	Bangor	PA	18013	**877-678-6622**	610-588-0981
Meredith Village Savings Bank (MVSB)					
24 State Rt 25 PO Box 177	Meredith	NH	03253	**800-922-6872**	603-279-7986
Midamerica National Bancshares					
100 W Elm St	Canton	IL	61520	**877-647-5050**	309-647-5000
Middlesex Savings Bank					
120 Flanders Rd	Westborough	MA	01581	**877-463-6287**	508-653-0300
MidFirst Bank					
PO Box 76149	Oklahoma City	OK	73147	**888-643-3477**	405-767-7000
Midland National Bank					
527 Main St	Newton	KS	67114	**800-810-9457**	316-283-1700
Midwest Bank					
105 E Soo St PO Box 40	Parkers Prairie	MN	56361	**877-365-5155**	218-338-6054
Mifflinburg Bank & Trust Co (MBTC)					
250 E Chestnut St PO Box 186	Mifflinburg	PA	17844	**888-966-3131**	570-966-1041
Milford Bank 33 Broad St	Milford	CT	06460	**800-340-4862**	203-783-5700
Monroe Bank & Trust					
102 E Front St	Monroe	MI	48161	**800-321-0032**	734-241-3431
Montgomery Bank					
1 Montgomery Bank Plz PO Box 948	Sikeston	MO	63801	**800-455-2275**	573-471-2275
Mountain Valley Bank					
317 DAVIS Ave	Elkins	WV	26241	**800-555-3503**	304-637-2265
Murray Bank, The					
405 S 12th St	Murray	KY	42071	**877-965-1122**	270-753-5626
Mutual of Omaha Bank					
3333 Farnam St	Omaha	NE	68131	**866-351-5646**	877-471-7896
Nantucket Bank					
104 Pleasant St	Nantucket	MA	02554	**800-533-9313**	508-228-0580
National Australia Bank Americas					
245 Park Ave 28th Fl	New York	NY	10167	**866-706-0509**	212-916-9500
National Bank of Arizona					
6001 N 24th St	Phoenix	AZ	85016	**800-655-7622**	602-235-6000
National Bank of Blacksburg					
PO Box 90002	Blacksburg	VA	24062	**800-552-4123**	540-552-2011
National Bank, The					
852 Middle Rd	Bettendorf	IA	52722	**877-321-4347**	563-344-3935
National United					
PO Box 779	Gatesville	TX	76528	**877-628-2265**	254-865-2211
NBT Bank NA PO Box 351	Norwich	NY	13815	**800-628-2265**	607-337-2265
Nevada State Bank					
PO Box 990	Las Vegas	NV	89125	**800-727-4743**	702-383-0009
New Washington State Bank					
402 E Main St PO Box 10	New Washington	IN	47162	**800-883-0131**	812-293-3321
Newtown Savings Bank Foundation Inc					
39 Main St	Newtown	CT	06470	**800-461-0672**	203-426-2563
North American Savings Bank (NASB)					
12520 S 71 Hwy	Grandview	MO	64030	**800-677-6272**	816-765-2200
North Shore Bank FSB					
15700 W Bluemound Rd	Brookfield	WI	53005	**800-236-4672**	877-672-2265
Northern Trust Co					
50 S LaSalle St	Chicago	IL	60603	**888-289-6542**	312-630-6000
NASDAQ: NTRS					
Northfield Savings Bank (NSB)					
PO Box 7180	Barre	VT	05641	**800-672-2274**	

Name / Address	City	State	ZIP	Toll-Free	Phone
Northrim BanCorp Inc 3111 C St *NASDAQ: NRIM*	Anchorage	AK	99503	**800-478-3311**	907-562-0062
Northwest 100 Liberty St PO Box 128	Warren	PA	16365	**877-672-5678**	814-726-2140
Northwest Community Bank 86 Main St	Winsted	CT	06098	**800-455-6668**	860-379-7561
Ocean Bank 780 NW 42nd Ave	Miami	FL	33126	**877-688-2265**	305-442-2660
OceanFirst Bank 975 Hooper Ave	Toms River	NJ	08753	**888-623-2633**	732-240-4500
Ocwen Federal Bank FSB 1661 Worthington Rd Ste 100	West Palm Beach	FL	33409	**800-746-2936**	561-681-8000
Old National Bank 1 Main St PO Box 718	Evansville	IN	47705	**800-731-2265**	
OneUnited Bank 3683 Crenshaw Blvd	Los Angeles	CA	90016	**877-663-8648**	323-290-4848
Oritani Bank 370 Pascack Rd PO Box 1329 *NASDAQ: ORIT*	Washington Township	NJ	07676	**888-674-8264**	201-664-5400
Oxford Bank PO Box 129	Addison	IL	60101	**800-236-2442**	630-629-5000
Pacific Continental Corp 111 W Seventh Ave PO Box 10727 *NASDAQ: PCBK*	Eugene	OR	97440	**877-231-2265**	541-686-8685
PBK Bank Inc 120 Frontier Blvd	Stanford	KY	40484	**877-230-3711**	606-365-7098
People's United Bank 850 Main St Bridgeport Ctr	Bridgeport	CT	06604	**800-772-1090**	203-338-7171
Peoples Financial Services Corp 82 Franklin Ave *NASDAQ: PFIS*	Hallstead	PA	18822	**888-868-3858**	570-879-2175
Peoples Savings Bank (PSB) 414 N Adams PO Box 248	Wellsburg	IA	50680	**877-508-2265**	641-869-3721
Pilgrim Bank 2401 S Jefferson Ave	Mount Pleasant	TX	75455	**877-303-3111**	903-575-2150
Pintoresco Advisors LLC 466 Foothill Blvd Ste 333	La Canada Flintridge	CA	91011	**866-217-1140**	213-223-2070
PNC Bank 1 PNC Plz 300 Fifth Ave 29th Fl	Pittsburgh	PA	15222	**888-762-2265**	412-762-2000
PNC Bank NA 249 Fifth Ave 1 PNC Plaza	Pittsburgh	PA	15222	**888-762-2265**	412-762-2000
Preferred Bank Los Angeles 601 S Figueroa St 29th Fl *NASDAQ: PFBC*	Los Angeles	CA	90017	**888-673-1808**	213-891-1188
Premier Valley Bank 255 E River Pk Cir Ste 180	Fresno	CA	93720	**877-438-2002**	559-438-2002
Presidential Online Bank 4520 East-West Hwy	Bethesda	MD	20814	**800-383-6266**	301-652-0700
Profile Bank 45 Wakefield St PO Box 1808	Rochester	NH	03866	**800-554-8969**	603-332-2610
Provident Savings Bank FSB 3756 Central Ave	Riverside	CA	92506	**800-442-5201**	951-686-6060
QNB Corp 15 N Third St PO Box 9005 *OTC: QNBC*	Quakertown	PA	18951	**800-491-9070**	215-538-5600
Queenstown Bank of Maryland 7101 Main St PO Box 120	Queenstown	MD	21658	**888-827-4300**	410-827-8881
Rabo Bank 1026 E Grand Ave	Arroyo Grande	CA	93420	**800-942-6222**	805-473-7710
Randolph Savings Bank 129 N Main St	Randolph	MA	02368	**877-963-2100**	781-963-2100
RBC Royal Bank 1127 D,carie Blvd	Saint-Laurent	QC	H4L3M8	**800-769-2599**	
RBC Trust Company (Delaware) Ltd 4550 New Linden Hill Rd Ste 200	Wilmington	DE	19808	**800-441-7698**	302-892-6976
Regions Bank 1900 Fifth Ave N	Birmingham	AL	35203	**800-734-4667**	
Ridgewood Savings Bank 71-02 Forest Ave	Ridgewood	NY	11385	**800-250-4832**	718-240-4800
River City Bank PO Box 15247 *OTC: RCBC* ■ *Cust Svc	Sacramento	CA	95851	**800-564-7144***	916-567-2899
Royal Bank of Canada 200 Bay St 9th Fl S Twr *TSX: RY*	Toronto	ON	M5J2J5	**800-769-2599**	416-955-7806
Salem Five & Savings Bank 210 Essex St *Cust Svc	Salem	MA	01970	**800-850-5000***	978-745-5555
Santander PO Box 12646 *Cust Svc	Reading	PA	19612	**877-768-2265***	
Seamen's Bank 221 Commercial St PO Box 659	Provincetown	MA	02657	**855-227-5347**	508-487-0035
Severn Bancorp Inc 200 Westgate Cir Ste 200 *NASDAQ: SVBI*	Annapolis	MD	21401	**800-752-5854**	410-260-2000
Signature Bank 565 Fifth Ave 12th Fl *NASDAQ: SBNY*	New York	NY	10017	**866-744-5463**	646-822-1500
Silicon Valley Bank (SVB) 3003 Tasman Dr	Santa Clara	CA	95054	**800-579-1639**	408-654-7400
Silvergate Bank 4275 Executive Sq Ste 800	La Jolla	CA	92037	**800-595-5856**	858-362-6300
Somerset Trust Co 151 W Main St PO Box 777	Somerset	PA	15501	**800-972-1651**	814-443-9200
Southern First Bancshares Inc 100 Verdae Blvd Ste 100	Greenville	SC	29607	**877-679-9646**	864-679-9000
Southern Michigan Bank & Trust 51 W Pearl St PO Box 309	Coldwater	MI	49036	**800-379-7628**	517-279-5500
SouthWest Capital Bank 622 Douglas Ave	Las Vegas	NM	87701	**800-748-2406**	505-425-7565
Southwest Missouri Bank 2417 S Grand Ave	Carthage	MO	64836	**800-943-8488**	417-358-1770
Spencer Savings Bank SLA 611 River Dr	Elmwood Park	NJ	07407	**800-363-8115**	973-772-6700
STAR Financial Group Inc PO Box 11409 *OTC: SFIGA*	Fort Wayne	IN	46858	**888-395-2447**	
State Bank 175 N Leroy St	Fenton	MI	48430	**800-535-0517**	810-629-2263
State Bank & Trust 3100 13th Ave S	Fargo	ND	58103	**800-450-8949**	701-298-1500
State Bank of Waterloo PO Box 148	Waterloo	IL	62298	**800-383-8000**	618-939-7194
State Farm Financial Services FSB PO Box 2316	Bloomington	IL	61702	**877-734-2265**	
Steuben Trust Co 1 Steuben Sq	Hornell	NY	14843	**866-783-8236**	607-324-5010
Stillman Banccorp NA PO Box 150	Stillman Valle	IL	61084	**866-546-8273**	815-645-2000
Stoneham Savings Bank 80 Montvale Ave	Stoneham	MA	02180	**888-402-2265**	
Summit Bank 2969 Broadway	Oakland	CA	94611	**800-380-9333**	510-839-8800
Sun National Bank 350 Fellowship Rd Ste 101	Mount Laurel	NJ	08054	**800-786-9066**	
Suntrust Bank PO Box 4418 *NYSE: STI*	Atlanta	GA	30302	**800-786-8787**	
TCF National Bank 801 Marquette Ave	Minneapolis	MN	55402	**800-343-6145**	612-823-2265
TD Bank NA 1701 Rt 70 E	Cherry Hill	NJ	08034	**888-751-9000**	856-751-2739
TD Banknorth Massachusetts 295 Park Ave *Cust Svc	Worcester	MA	01609	**800-747-7000***	508-752-2584
Tennessee Commerce Bank 381 Mallory Stn Rd Ste 207	Franklin	TN	37067	**877-275-3342**	
Texas Bank & Trust 300 E Whaley PO Box 3188	Longview	TX	75606	**800-263-7013**	903-237-5500
Texas Capital Bank 2000 McKinney Ave Ste 700	Dallas	TX	75201	**877-839-2265**	214-932-6600
Third Federal Savings & Loan Assn of Cleveland 7007 Broadway Ave	Cleveland	OH	44105	**888-844-7333**	800-844-7333
Thomaston Savings Bank 203 Main St PO Box 907 *General	Thomaston	CT	06787	**855-344-1874***	860-283-1874
Tompkins Trust Co PO Box 460 *NYSE: TMP*	Ithaca	NY	14851	**888-273-3210**	607-273-3210
Transportation Alliance Bank Inc 4185 Harrison Blvd Ste 200	Ogden	UT	84403	**800-355-3063**	
Trust Bank 600 E Main St PO Box 158	Olney	IL	62450	**800-766-3451**	618-395-4311
UBS AG 1285 Ave of the Americas	New York	NY	10019	**877-827-8001**	212-713-2000
UMB Bank NA 1010 Grand Blvd	Kansas City	MO	64106	**800-821-2171**	816-860-7000
Umpqua Bank PO Box 1820	Roseburg	OR	97470	**866-486-7782**	800-452-1929
Unibank For Savings 49 Church St	Whitinsville	MA	01588	**800-578-4270**	508-234-8112
Union Bank of California NA 400 California St 1st Fl	San Francisco	CA	94104	**800-238-4486**	415-765-3434
United Bank 11185 Fairfax Blvd	Fairfax	VA	22030	**800-327-9862**	703-219-4850
United Community Bank PO Box 309	Four Oaks	NC	27524	**877-963-6257**	919-963-2177
United Financial Bancorp Inc 95 Elm St PO Box 9020 *NASDAQ: UBNK*	West Springfield	MA	01090	**866-959-2265**	413-787-1700
United Security Bancshares 2126 Inyo St *NASDAQ: UBFO*	Fresno	CA	93721	**888-683-6030**	559-248-4943
UPS Capital Business Credit 35 Glenlake Pkwy NE	Atlanta	GA	30328	**877-263-8772**	
USAA FSB (USAAFSB) 10750 McDermott Fwy	San Antonio	TX	78288	**800-531-8722**	
Valley National Bank 615 Main Ave	Passaic	NJ	07055	**800-522-4100**	973-777-6768
Vectra Bank Colorado NA 2000 S Colorado Blvd Ste 2-1200	Denver	CO	80222	**800-232-8948**	720-947-7700
VirtualBank PO Box 109638	Palm Beach Gardens	FL	33410	**877-998-2265**	
Wachovia Bank 3800 Wilshire Blvd Ste 110e	Los Angeles	CA	90010	**800-225-5935**	213-739-8579
Weatherbank Inc 1015 Waterwood Pkwy Ste J	Edmond	OK	73034	**800-687-3562**	405-359-0773
Wells Fargo Bank 5622 Third St	Katy	TX	77493	**800-864-8377**	281-391-2101
Wells Fargo Bank Iowa NA 666 Walnut St	Des Moines	IA	50309	**800-864-8377**	515-245-3131
Wells Fargo Bank Minnesota South NA 21 First St SW	Rochester	MN	55902	**800-864-8377**	507-285-2800
Wells Fargo Bank Nebraska NA 1919 Douglas St	Omaha	NE	68102	**800-864-8377**	402-536-2022
Wells Fargo Bank Texas NA 707 Castroville Rd	San Antonio	TX	78237	**800-864-8377**	210-856-6224
WesBanco Inc 1 Bank Plz *NASDAQ: WSBC*	Wheeling	WV	26003	**800-328-3369**	304-234-9000
West Suburban Bank 711 Westmore Meyers Rd	Lombard	IL	60148	**800-258-4009**	630-652-2000
Western Security Bank 2812 First Ave N	Billings	MT	59101	**800-983-5537**	406-371-8200
Westfield Bank 2 Park Cir	Westfield Ctr	OH	44251	**800-368-8930**	
Westpac Banking Corp Americas Div 575 Fifth Ave 39th Fl	New York	NY	10017	**888-269-2377**	212-551-1800
White Sands Federal Credit Union 2190 E Lohman Ave	Las Cruces	NM	88001	**800-658-9933**	575-647-4500
Whitney Bank 228 St Charles Ave	New Orleans	LA	70130	**800-844-4450**	504-586-7456
Winnsboro State Bank & Trust Co 3875 Front St	Winnsboro	LA	71295	**866-205-4026**	318-435-7535
Winter Hill Bank 342 Broadway	Somerville	MA	02145	**800-444-4300**	617-666-8600
Woodforest National Bank PO Box 7889	Spring	TX	77387	**877-968-7962**	832-375-2000
Woodsville Guaranty Savings Bank 10 Pleasant St PO Box 266	Woodsville	NH	03785	**800-564-2735**	603-747-2735
Yakima Federal Savings & Loan Assn 118 E Yakima Ave	Yakima	WA	98901	**800-331-3225**	509-248-2634
Zions Bank 1 S Main St	Salt Lake City	UT	84133	**800-974-8800**	801-974-8800

71   BANKS - FEDERAL RESERVE

				Toll-Free	Phone
Federal Reserve Bank of Atlanta					
1000 Peachtree St NE	Atlanta	GA	30309	**888-500-7390**	404-498-8500
New Orleans Branch					
525 St Charles Ave	New Orleans	LA	70130	**877-638-7003**	504-593-3200
Federal Reserve Bank of Cleveland					
1455 E Sixth St PO Box 6387	Cleveland	OH	44101	**877-372-2457**	216-579-2000
Cincinnati Branch					
150 E Fourth St	Cincinnati	OH	45202	**877-372-2457**	513-721-4787
Federal Reserve Bank of Dallas					
2200 N Pearl St	Dallas	TX	75201	**800-333-4460**	214-922-6000
El Paso Branch					
301 E Main St	El Paso	TX	79901	**800-333-4460**	915-521-5200
San Antonio Branch					
402 Dwyer Ave	San Antonio	TX	78204	**800-333-4460**	210-978-1200
Federal Reserve Bank of Kansas City					
1 Memorial Dr PO Box 1200	Kansas City	MO	64198	**800-333-1010**	816-881-2000
Denver Branch					
1 Memorial Dr	Kansas City	MO	64198	**888-851-1920**	
Oklahoma City Branch					
211 North Robinson					
2 Leadership Sq Ste 300	Oklahoma City	OK	73102	**800-333-1030**	405-270-8400
Federal Reserve Bank of Minneapolis					
90 Hennepin Ave	Minneapolis	MN	55401	**800-553-9656**	612-204-5000
Federal Reserve Bank of Philadelphia					
10 Independence Mall	Philadelphia	PA	19106	**866-574-3727**	215-574-6000
Federal Reserve Bank of Richmond					
Baltimore Branch					
502 S Sharp St	Baltimore	MD	21201	**800-446-7045**	410-576-3300
Federal Reserve Bank of Saint Louis					
1 Federal Reserve Bank Plz					
Broadway and Locust St	Saint Louis	MO	63102	**800-333-0810**	314-444-8444
Little Rock Branch					
111 Ctr St Ste 1000 Stephens Bldg	Little Rock	AR	72201	**877-372-2457**	501-324-8300
Federal Reserve Bank of San Francisco (FRBSF)					
101 Market St	San Francisco	CA	94105	**800-227-4133**	415-974-2000
Portland Branch					
101 Market St	San Francisco	CA	94105	**800-227-4133**	503-276-3000
Salt Lake City Branch					
101 Market St	San Francisco	CA	94105	**800-227-4133**	415-974-2000
First Shore Federal					
106-108 S Div St PO Box 4248	Salisbury	MD	21803	**800-634-6309**	410-546-1101
Lincoln FSB 1101 North St	Lincoln	NE	68508	**800-333-2158**	402-474-1400
Milford Federal Savings & Loan Assn					
246 Main St	Milford	MA	01757	**800-478-6990**	508-634-2500
Pioneer Bank 21 Second St	Troy	NY	12180	**866-873-9573**	518-274-4800
Security Federal Bank (SFB)					
238 Richland Ave W	Aiken	SC	29801	**866-851-3000**	803-641-3000
Sterling Federal Bank					
PO Box 617	Sterling	IL	61081	**800-353-0888**	815-626-0614
Webster First Federal Credit Union					
271 Greenwood St	Worcester	MA	01607	**800-962-4452**	508-949-1043

72   BAR ASSOCIATIONS - STATE

SEE ALSO Legal Professionals Associations

				Toll-Free	Phone
Alabama State Bar					
415 Dexter Ave	Montgomery	AL	36104	**800-392-5660**	334-269-1515
Arkansas Bar Assn					
2224 Cottondale Ln	Little Rock	AR	72202	**800-609-5668**	501-375-4606
Colorado Bar Assn					
1900 Grant St Ste 900	Denver	CO	80203	**800-332-6736**	303-860-1115
District of Columbia Bar, The					
1101 K St NW Ste 200	Washington	DC	20005	**877-333-2227**	202-737-4700
Florida Bar					
651 E Jefferson St	Tallahassee	FL	32399	**800-342-8060**	850-561-5600
Hawaii State Bar Assn (HSBA)					
1100 Alakea St Ste 1000	Honolulu	HI	96813	**800-932-0311**	808-537-1868
Idaho State Bar					
525 W Jefferson St	Boise	ID	83702	**800-221-3295**	208-334-4500
Illinois State Bar Assn					
424 S Second St	Springfield	IL	62701	**800-252-8908**	217-525-1760
Indiana State Bar Assn					
1 Indiana Sq Ste 530	Indianapolis	IN	46204	**800-266-2581**	317-639-5465
Iowa State Bar Assn					
625 E Ct Ave	Des Moines	IA	50309	**800-457-3729**	515-243-3179
Kansas Bar Assn					
1200 SW Harrison St	Topeka	KS	66612	**800-928-3111**	785-234-5696
Louisiana State Bar Assn (LSBA)					
601 St Charles Ave	New Orleans	LA	70130	**800-421-5722**	504-566-1600
Maine State Bar Assn					
124 State St	Augusta	ME	04330	**800-475-7523**	207-622-7523
Maryland State Bar Assn Inc					
520 W Fayette St	Baltimore	MD	21201	**800-492-1964**	410-685-7878
Minnesota State Bar Assn					
600 Nicollet Mall Ste 380	Minneapolis	MN	55402	**800-882-6722**	612-333-1183
Mississippi Bar					
643 N State St	Jackson	MS	39202	**800-682-6423**	601-948-4471
Missouri Bar, The					
326 Monroe St PO Box 119	Jefferson City	MO	65102	**888-253-6013**	573-635-4128
Nebraska State Bar Assn					
635 S 14th St Ste 200	Lincoln	NE	68501	**800-927-0117**	402-475-7091
New York State Bar Assn					
1 Elk St	Albany	NY	12207	**800-342-3661**	518-463-3200
North Carolina State Bar					
217 E Edenton St PO Box 25996	Raleigh	NC	27601	**800-662-7407**	919-828-4620
Ohio State Bar Assn (OSBA)					
1700 Lake Shore Dr	Columbus	OH	43204	**800-282-6556**	614-487-2050
Oklahoma Bar Assn					
1901 N Lincoln Blvd					
PO Box 53036	Oklahoma City	OK	73105	**800-522-8065**	405-416-7000

				Toll-Free	Phone
Oregon State Bar Assn					
16037 SW Upper Boones Ferry Rd	Tigard	OR	97224	**800-452-8260**	503-620-0222
Pennsylvania Bar Assn					
100 South St	Harrisburg	PA	17101	**800-932-0311**	717-238-6715
Rhode Island Bar Assn					
115 Cedar St	Providence	RI	02903	**877-659-0801**	401-421-5740
South Carolina Bar					
950 Taylor St	Columbia	SC	29201	**877-797-2227**	803-799-6653
State Bar Assn of North Dakota					
504 N Washington St PO Box 2136	Bismarck	ND	58502	**800-472-2685**	701-255-1404
State Bar of Arizona					
4201 N 24th St Ste 100	Phoenix	AZ	85016	**866-482-9227**	602-252-4804
State Bar of Georgia					
104 Marietta St NW Ste 100	Atlanta	GA	30303	**800-334-6865**	404-527-8700
State Bar of Michigan					
306 Townsend St	Lansing	MI	48933	**800-968-1442**	517-346-6300
State Bar of Montana					
PO Box 577	Helena	MT	59624	**877-880-1335**	
State Bar of Nevada					
1211 S Maryland Pkwy	Las Vegas	NV	89104	**800-254-2797**	702-382-2200
State Bar of New Mexico					
5121 Masthead St NE PO Box 92860	Albuquerque	NM	87109	**800-876-6227**	505-797-6000
State Bar of Texas					
1414 Colorado St	Austin	TX	78701	**800-204-2222**	512-427-1463
Tennessee Bar Assn					
221 Fourth Ave N Ste 400	Nashville	TN	37219	**800-899-6993**	615-383-7421
Utah State Bar					
645 S 200 E	Salt Lake City	UT	84111	**877-752-2611**	801-531-9077
Vermont Bar Assn (VBA)					
35-37 Ct St PO Box 100	Montpelier	VT	05601	**800-639-7036**	802-223-2020
Virginia State Bar					
707 E Main St Ste 1500	Richmond	VA	23219	**800-552-7977**	804-775-0500
Washington State Bar Assn					
1325 Fourth Ave Ste 600	Seattle	WA	98101	**800-945-9722**	206-443-9722
West Virginia State Bar					
2000 Deitrick Blvd	Charleston	WV	25311	**866-989-8227**	304-553-7220
Wyoming State Bar					
4124 Laramie St	Cheyenne	WY	82001	**855-445-8058**	307-632-9061

73   BASKETS, CAGES, RACKS, ETC - WIRE

SEE ALSO Pet Products

				Toll-Free	Phone
Bright Co-op Inc					
803 W Seale St	Nacogdoches	TX	75964	**800-562-0730**	936-564-8378
Glamos Wire Products Company Inc					
5561 N 152nd St	Hugo	MN	55038	**800-328-5062**	651-429-5386
InterMetro Industries Corp					
651 N Washington St	Wilkes-Barre	PA	18705	**800-992-1776***	570-825-2741
Cust Svc					
Lab Products Inc					
742 Sussex Ave	Seaford	DE	19973	**800-526-0469**	302-628-4300
Nashville Wire Products Manufacturing Co					
199 Polk Ave	Nashville	TN	37210	**800-448-2125**	615-743-2500
Riverdale Mills Corp					
130 Riverdale St	Northbridge	MA	01534	**800-762-6374**	508-234-8715

74   BATTERIES

				Toll-Free	Phone
Applied Energy Solutions LLC					
1 Technology Pl	Caledonia	NY	14423	**800-836-2132**	585-538-4421
C & D Technologies Inc					
1400 Union Meeting Rd PO Box 3053	Blue Bell	PA	19422	**800-543-8630**	215-619-2700
Cell-con Inc					
305 Commerce Dr Ste 300	Exton	PA	19341	**800-771-7139**	
Continental Battery Corp					
4919 Woodall St	Dallas	TX	75247	**800-442-0081**	214-631-5701
Crown Battery Manufacturing Co					
1445 Majestic Dr	Fremont	OH	43420	**800-487-2879**	419-334-7181
Douglas Battery Manufacturing Co					
500 Battery Dr	Winston-Salem	NC	27107	**800-368-4527**	
Duracell 14 Research Dr	Bethel	CT	06801	**800-551-2355**	
EnerSys 2366 Bernville Rd	Reading	PA	19605	**800-538-3627**	610-208-1991
NYSE: ENS					
Exide Technologies					
13000 Deerfield Pkwy Bldg 200	Milton	GA	30004	**888-563-6300**	678-566-9000
NASDAQ: XIDE					
Hawker Powersource Inc					
9404 Ooltewah Industrial Dr					
PO Box 808	Ooltewah	TN	37363	**800-238-8658**	423-238-5700
Industrial Battery & Charger Inc					
5831 Orr Rd	Charlotte	NC	28213	**800-833-8412**	704-597-7330
Mathews Assoc Inc					
220 Power Ct	Sanford	FL	32771	**800-871-5262**	407-323-3390
PulseTech Products Corp					
1100 S Kimball Ave	Southlake	TX	76092	**800-580-7554**	817-329-6099
R & D Batteries Inc					
3300 Corporate Ctr Dr PO Box 5007	Burnsville	MN	55306	**800-950-1945**	952-890-0629
Staab Battery Manufacturing Co					
931 S 11th St	Springfield	IL	62703	**800-252-8625**	
Surefire LLC					
18300 Mt Baldy Cir	Fountain Valley	CA	92708	**800-828-8809**	
Tadiran Batteries					
2001 Marcus Ave Ste 125E	New Hyde Park	NY	11042	**800-537-1368**	516-621-4980
TNR Technical Inc					
301 Central Park Dr	Sanford	FL	32771	**800-346-0601**	407-321-3011
OTC: TNRK					
Trojan Battery Co					
12380 Clark St	Santa Fe Springs	CA	90670	**800-423-6569***	562-236-3000
Cust Svc					
Ultralife Batteries Inc					
2000 Technology Pkwy	Newark	NY	14513	**800-332-5000**	315-332-7100
NASDAQ: ULBI					

				Toll-Free	Phone
Valence Technology Inc 1807 W Braker Ln Ste 500	Austin	TX	78758	**888-825-3623**	512-527-2900

75 BEARINGS - BALL & ROLLER

				Toll-Free	Phone
Accurate Bushing Company Inc 443 N Ave *Sales	Garwood	NJ	07027	**800-932-0076***	908-789-1121
AST Bearings 115 Main Rd	Montville	NJ	07045	**800-526-1250**	973-335-2230
Bearing Inspection Inc 4500 Mt Pleasant NW *Cust Svc	North Canton	OH	44720	**800-416-8881***	234-262-3000
Bearing Service Co of Pennsylvania 630 Alpha Dr RIDC Park	Pittsburgh	PA	15238	**800-783-2327**	412-963-7710
General Bearing Corp 44 High St *Sales	West Nyack	NY	10994	**800-431-1766***	845-358-6000
JTEKT Corp 29570 Clemens Rd *Cust Svc	Westlake	OH	44145	**800-263-5163***	440-835-1000
LSB Industries Inc 16 S Pennsylvania Ave *NYSE: LXU*	Oklahoma City	OK	73107	**800-657-4428**	405-235-4546
Nachi America Inc 715 Pushville Rd	Greenwood	IN	46143	**888-340-2747**	317-530-1001
Peer Bearing Co 2200 Norman Dr S	Waukegan	IL	60085	**800-433-7337**	847-578-1000
Roller Bearing Company of America 400 Sullivan Way	West Trenton	NJ	08628	**800-390-3300**	609-882-5050
Rotek Inc 1400 S Chillicothe Rd PO Box 312	Aurora	OH	44202	**800-221-8043**	330-562-4000
Schaeffler Group USA Inc 308 Springhill Farm Rd	Fort Mill	SC	29715	**800-361-5841**	803-548-8500
Schatz Bearing Corp 10 Fairview Ave	Poughkeepsie	NY	12601	**800-554-1406**	845-452-6000
Timken Co 4500 Mount Pleasant St NW *NYSE: TKR*	North Canton	OH	44706	**800-223-1954**	330-438-3000
Universal Bearings Inc 431 North Birkey Dr PO Box 38	Bremen	IN	46506	**800-824-7743**	
Wecsys LLC 8825 Xylon Ave N	Minneapolis	MN	55445	**888-493-2797**	763-504-1069

76 BEAUTY SALON EQUIPMENT & SUPPLIES

				Toll-Free	Phone
Belvedere USA Corp 1 Belvedere Blvd	Belvidere	IL	61008	**800-435-5491**	
Betty Dain Creations Inc 9701 NW 112 Ave Ste 10 *General	Miami	FL	33178	**800-327-5256***	305-769-3451
Burmax Co 28 Barretts Ave	Holtsville	NY	11742	**800-645-5118**	
Collins Manufacturing Co 2000 Bowser Rd	Cookeville	TN	38506	**800-292-6450**	931-528-5151
Jerdon Style 1820 N Glenville Dr Ste 124	Richardson	TX	75081	**800-223-3571**	
Living Earth Crafts 3210 Executive Ridge Dr	Vista	CA	92081	**800-358-8292**	760-597-2155
National Salon Resources Inc 3109 Louisiana Ave N	Minneapolis	MN	55427	**800-622-0003**	
Pibbs Industries 133-15 32nd Ave	Flushing	NY	11354	**800-551-5020**	718-445-8046
Sally Beauty Company Inc 3001 Colorado Blvd	Denton	TX	76210	**800-777-5706**	940-898-7500
Takara Belmont USA Inc 101 Belmont Dr	Somerset	NJ	08873	**877-283-1289**	
TouchAmerica 1403 S Third St Ext	Mebane	NC	27302	**800-678-6824**	919-732-6968
William Marvy Company Inc 1540 St Clair Ave	Saint Paul	MN	55105	**800-874-2651**	651-698-0726

77 BEAUTY SALONS

				Toll-Free	Phone
Adam Broderick Salon & Spa 89 Danbury Rd	Ridgefield	CT	06877	**800-438-3834**	203-431-3994
Aedes De Venustas 16A Orchard St	New York	NY	10002	**888-233-3715**	212-206-8674
Aromaland Inc 1326 Rufina Cir	Santa Fe	NM	87507	**800-933-5267**	505-438-0402
Ball Beauty Supplies 416 N Fairfax Ave	Los Angeles	CA	90036	**800-588-0244**	
Beauty Brands Inc 4600 Madison St Ste 400	Kansas City	MO	64112	**877-640-2248**	816-531-2266
Beauty Craft Supply & Equipment Co 11110 Bren Rd W	Minnetonka	MN	55343	**800-328-5010**	952-935-4420
Chella Professional Skin Care 507 Calle San Pablo	Camarillo	CA	93012	**877-424-3552**	805-383-7711
FintronX LED LLC 5995 Chapel Hill Rd Ste 119	Raleigh	NC	27607	**800-541-9082**	919-324-3960
Gadabout Inc 3501 E Kindale	Tucson	AZ	85716	**800-600-3662**	520-325-0000
Genesis Biosystems Inc 1500 Eagle Ct # 75057	Lewisville	TX	75057	**888-577-7335**	972-315-7888
Great Clips Inc 4400 W 78th St Ste 700	Minneapolis	MN	55435	**800-999-5959**	952-893-9088
Hair Club for Men LTD Inc 1515 S Federal Hwy Ste 401	Boca Raton	FL	33432	**800-251-2658**	561-361-7600
Holiday Hair 7201 Metro Blvd	Minneapolis	MN	55439	**800-345-7811**	
J D Beauty 5 Adams Ave	Hauppauge	NY	11788	**800-523-2889**	631-273-2800
Maka Beauty Systems 4042 W Kitty Hawk	Chandler	AZ	85226	**800-293-6252**	480-968-7980
Regis Corp 7201 Metro Blvd *NYSE: RGS*	Minneapolis	MN	55439	**888-888-7778**	952-947-7777
Regis Corp MasterCuts Div 7201 Metro Blvd	Minneapolis	MN	55439	**877-857-2070**	952-947-7777
Regis Corp Pro-Cuts Div 7201 Metro Blvd	Minneapolis	MN	55439	**877-857-2070**	
Regis Corp SmartStyle Div 7201 Metro Blvd	Minneapolis	MN	55439	**800-737-3535**	
Salon Service Group Inc 1520 E Evergreen	Springfield	MO	65803	**800-933-5733**	417-761-7309
Salon Services & Supplies Inc 740 SW 34th St	Renton	WA	98057	**800-251-4247**	425-251-8840
Stewart School of Cosmetology 604 NW Ave	Sioux Falls	SD	57104	**800-537-2625**	605-336-2775
Supercuts 7201 Metro Blvd	Minneapolis	MN	55439	**877-857-2070**	
Toni & Guy USA Inc 2311 Midway Rd	Carrollton	TX	75006	**800-256-9391**	

78 BETTER BUSINESS BUREAUS - CANADA

				Toll-Free	Phone
AAA of Minnesota & Iowa 600 W Travelers Trl	Burnsville	MN	55337	**800-222-1333**	
Better Business Bureau of Eastern Ontario & the Outaouais Inc 700 Industrial Ave Unit 505	Ottawa	ON	K1G0Y9	**877-859-8566**	613-237-4856
Better Business Bureau of Saskatchewan 980 Albert St	Regina	SK	S4R2P7	**888-352-7601**	306-352-7601
Better Business Bureau of Vancouver Island 220-1175 Cook St Ste 220	Victoria	BC	V8V4A1	**877-826-4222**	250-386-6348
Better Business Bureau Serving Mainland British Columbia 788 Beatty St Ste 404	Vancouver	BC	V6B2M1	**888-803-1222**	604-682-2711
Better Business Bureau Serving Western Ontario 190 Wortley Rd Ste 206	London	ON	N6C4Y7	**877-283-9222**	519-673-3222
Better Business Bureau Serving Winnipeg & Manitoba 1030B Empress St	Winnipeg	MB	R3G3H4	**800-385-3074**	204-989-9010
Florida Academy of Family Physicians (FAFP) 13241 Bartram Pk Blvd Ste 1321	Jacksonville	FL	32258	**800-223-3237**	904-726-0944
Kansas Bankers Assn 610 SW Corporate View	Topeka	KS	66615	**800-285-7878**	785-272-7836
MEA Energy Association 7825 Telegraph Rd	Bloomington	MN	55438	**800-542-6096**	651-289-9600
North Delta Planning & Development District 220 Power Dr	Batesville	MS	38606	**800-844-2433**	662-561-4100
Oates Energy Inc 14286 Beach Blvd Ste 12	Jacksonville	FL	32250	**800-717-9811**	
Rues Principales 870 De Salaberry Ave Ste 309	Quebec	QC	G1R2T9	**877-694-9944**	418-694-9944
SACA Technologies LLC 5101 E La Palma Ave Ste 200	Anaheim Hills	CA	92807	**888-603-9033**	714-777-3222
Society Of Hospital Medicine 190 N Independence Mall W	Philadelphia	PA	19106	**800-843-3360**	
Tennis Canada 285 Rue Gary-carter	Montreal	QC	H2R2W1	**866-338-2685**	514-273-1515
Texas Association of School Business Officials 6611 Boeing Dr	El Paso	TX	79925	**800-338-6531**	512-462-1711
Utah League of Cities & Towns, The 50 South 600 East Ste 150	Salt Lake City	UT	84102	**800-852-8528**	801-328-1601

79 BETTER BUSINESS BUREAUS - US

SEE ALSO Consumer Interest Organizations

				Toll-Free	Phone
Better Business Bureau Online *Council of Better Business Bureaus, The* 4200 Wilson Blvd Ste 800	Arlington	VA	22203	**800-459-8875**	703-276-0100
Better Business Bureau Inc 1000 Broadway Ste 625	Oakland	CA	94607	**866-411-2221**	510-844-2000
Better Business Bureau of Acadiana 4003 W Congress St	Lafayette	LA	70506	**800-557-7392**	337-981-3497
Better Business Bureau of Asheville/Western North Carolina 112 Executive Pk	Asheville	NC	28801	**800-452-2882**	828-253-2392
Better Business Bureau of Canton Region/West Virginia 1434 Cleveland Ave NW	Canton	OH	44703	**800-362-0494**	330-454-9401
Better Business Bureau of Central & Eastern Kentucky 1460 Newtown Pk	Lexington	KY	40511	**800-866-6668**	859-259-1008
Better Business Bureau of Central Alabama & the Wiregrass Area 2101 Highland Ave Ste 410	Birmingham	AL	35205	**800-824-5274**	205-558-2222
Better Business Bureau of Central East Texas 3600 Old BullaRd Rd Bldg 1	Tyler	TX	75701	**800-443-0131**	903-581-5704
Better Business Bureau of Central Illinois 8100 N University Peoria	Peoria	IL	61615	**800-763-4222**	309-688-3741
Better Business Bureau of Central Indiana 151 N Delaware St	Indianapolis	IN	46204	**866-463-9222**	317-488-2222
Better Business Bureau of Central Northeast Northwest & Southwest Arizona 4428 N 12th St	Phoenix	AZ	85014	**877-291-6222**	602-264-1721
Better Business Bureau of Central Ohio 1169 Dublin Rd	Columbus	OH	43215	**800-759-2400**	614-486-6336
Better Business Bureau of Central Oklahoma 17 S Dewey Ave	Oklahoma City	OK	73102	**800-654-7757**	405-239-6081
Better Business Bureau of Central Texas 1805 Rutherford Ln Ste 100	Austin	TX	78754	**800-621-0508**	512-445-2911
Better Business Bureau of Central Virginia 720 Moorefield Pk Dr Ste 300	Richmond	VA	23236	**800-533-5501**	804-648-0016
Better Business Bureau of Cincinnati 1 E Fourth St Ste 600	Cincinnati	OH	45202	**800-388-2222**	513-421-3015
Better Business Bureau of Dayton/Miami Valley 15 W Fourth St Ste 300	Dayton	OH	45402	**800-776-5301**	937-222-5825
Better Business Bureau of Eastern Massachusetts Maine Rhode Island & Vermont 290 Donald Lynch Blvd Ste 102	Marlborough	MA	01752	**800-422-2811**	508-652-4800
Better Business Bureau of Eastern Oklahoma 1722 S Carson Ave Ste 3200	Tulsa	OK	74119	**800-955-5100**	918-492-1266
Better Business Bureau of El Paso 720 Arizona Ave	El Paso	TX	79902	**800-621-0508**	915-577-0191

Classified Section

	Toll-Free	Phone
Better Business Bureau of Greater Iowa Quad Cities & Sioux Land Region		
2625 Beaver Ave .... Des Moines IA 50310	800-239-1642	515-243-8137
Better Business Bureau of Greater Kansas City		
8080 Ward Pkwy Ste 401 .... Kansas City MO 64114	877-606-0695	816-421-7800
Better Business Bureau of Greater Maryland		
502 S Sharp St Ste 1200 .... Baltimore MD 21201	800-579-6239	410-347-3990
Better Business Bureau of Heartland		
11811 P St .... Omaha NE 68137	800-649-6814	402-391-7612
Better Business Bureau of Kansas Inc		
11811 P St .... Omaha NE 68137	800-856-2417	402-391-7612
Better Business Bureau of Louisville Southern Indiana		
844 S Fourth St .... Louisville KY 40203	800-388-2222	502-583-6546
Better Business Bureau of Metro Washington DC & Eastern Pennsylvania		
1411 K St NW Ste 1000 .... Washington DC 20005	800-864-1224	202-393-8000
Better Business Bureau of Metropolitan Dallas & Northeast Texas		
1601 Elm St Ste 3838.................... Dallas TX 75201	800-444-0686	214-220-2000
Better Business Bureau of Metropolitan Houston		
1333 W Loop S Ste 1200 .... Houston TX 77027	800-876-7060	713-868-9500
Better Business Bureau of Middle Tennessee Inc		
201 Fourth Ave N Ste 100. .... Nashville TN 37219	800-615-9720	615-242-4222
Better Business Bureau of Minnesota & North Dakota		
220 River Ridge Cir S .... Burnsville MN 55337	800-646-6222	651-699-1111
Better Business Bureau of Northeast California		
3075 Beacon Blvd .... West Sacramento CA 95691	866-334-6272	916-443-6843
Better Business Bureau of Northeast Ohio		
2800 Euclid Ave 4th Fl .... Cleveland OH 44115	800-233-0361	216-241-7678
Better Business Bureau of Northern Colorado & East Central Wyoming		
8020 S County Rd 5 Ste 100 .... Fort Collins CO 80528	800-564-0371	970-484-1348
Better Business Bureau of Northern Indiana		
4011 Parnell Ave .... Fort Wayne IN 46805	800-552-4631	260-423-4433
Better Business Bureau of Northwest Florida		
912 E Gadsden St .... Pensacola FL 32501	800-729-9226	850-429-0002
Better Business Bureau of Northwest North Carolina		
500 W Fifth St Ste 202 .... Winston-Salem NC 27101	800-777-8348	336-725-8348
Better Business Bureau of Northwest Ohio & Southeast Michigan		
7668 King's Pt Rd .... Toledo OH 43617	800-743-4222	419-531-3116
Better Business Bureau of South Texas		
1333 W Loop S Ste 1200 .... Houston TX 77027	800-705-3994	713-868-9500
Better Business Bureau of Southeast Florida & the Caribbean		
4411 Beacon Cir Ste 4 .... West Palm Beach FL 33407	866-966-7226	561-842-1918
Better Business Bureau of Southeast Tennessee & Northwest Georgia		
508 N Market St .... Chattanooga TN 37405	800-548-4456	423-266-6144
Better Business Bureau of Southeast Texas		
550 Fannin St Ste 100 .... Beaumont TX 77701	800-685-7650	409-835-5348
Better Business Bureau of Southern Arizona		
434 S Williams Blvd Ste 102 .... Tucson AZ 85711	800-697-4733	520-888-5353
Better Business Bureau of Southern Nevada		
6040 S Jones Blvd .... Las Vegas NV 89118	800-449-8693	702-320-4500
Better Business Bureau of Southern Piedmont Carolinas		
9719 Northeast Pkwy .... Matthews NC 28105	800-432-1000	704-927-8611
Better Business Bureau of Southwest Louisiana Inc		
2309 E Prien Lake Rd .... Lake Charles LA 70601	800-542-7085	337-478-6253
Better Business Bureau of the Abilene Area		
3300 S 14th St Ste 307. .... Abilene TX 79605	800-705-3994	325-691-1533
Better Business Bureau of the Bakersfield Area		
1601 H St Ste 101 .... Bakersfield CA 93301	800-675-8118	661-322-2074
Better Business Bureau of the Denver-Boulder Metro Area		
1020 Cherokee St .... Denver CO 80204	800-356-6333	303-758-2100
Better Business Bureau of the Mid-South		
3693 Tyndale Dr .... Memphis TN 38125	800-222-8754	901-759-1300
Better Business Bureau of the Texas Panhandle		
600 S Tyler Ste 1300 .... Amarillo TX 79101	800-621-0508	806-379-6222
Better Business Bureau of the Tri-Parish Area		
801 Barrow St Ste 400 .... Houma LA 70360	800-533-5501	985-868-3456
Better Business Bureau of Upstate New York		
100 Bryant Woods S .... Amherst NY 14228	800-828-5000	716-881-5222
Better Business Bureau of Utah		
5673 S Redwood Rd .... Salt Lake City UT 84123	800-456-3907	801-892-6009
Better Business Bureau of West Florida		
2655 McCormick Dr .... Clearwater FL 33759	800-525-1447	727-535-5522
Better Business Bureau of Western Pennsylvania		
400 Holiday Dr Ste 220 .... Pittsburgh PA 15220	877-267-5222	
Better Business Bureau Serving Central & Western MA & Northeastern CT		
400 Grove St .... Worcester MA 01605	866-566-9222	508-755-3340
Better Business Bureau Serving Central California		
4201 W Shaw Ave Ste 107 .... Fresno CA 93722	800-675-8118	559-222-8111
Tri-State Better Business Bureau		
3101 N Green River Rd Ste 410 .... Evansville IN 47715	800-359-0979	812-473-0202

80 — BEVERAGES - MFR

SEE ALSO Breweries ; Water - Bottled

	Toll-Free	Phone
All Market Inc		
250 Park Ave S 7th Fl...................... New York NY 10003	877-848-2262	212-206-0763
Dot Com Holdings of Buffalo Inc		
1460 Military Rd .... Buffalo NY 14217	877-636-3673	

80-1 Liquor - Mfr

	Toll-Free	Phone
Anheuser-Busch Cos Inc		
1 Busch Pl .... Saint Louis MO 63118	800-342-5283	
Sunrich LLC		
3824 SW 93rd St PO Box 128 .... Hope MN 56046	800-297-5997	507-451-6030
Walker MS Inc		
20 Third Ave .... Somerville MA 02143	800-528-2787	617-776-6700

80-2 Soft Drinks - Mfr

	Toll-Free	Phone
Crystal Rock Holdings Inc		
1050 Buckingham St .... Watertown CT 06795	800-525-0070	860-945-0661
NYSE: CRVP		

	Toll-Free	Phone
Dr Pepper/Seven-Up Inc		
5301 Legacy Dr .... Plano TX 75024	800-696-5891	972-673-7000
Faygo Beverages Inc		
3579 Gratiot Ave .... Detroit MI 48207	800-347-6591	313-925-1600
Fiji Water		
11444 W Olympic Blvd 2nd Fl .... Los Angeles CA 90064	888-426-3454	310-312-2850
Great Plains Coca-Cola Bottling Company Inc		
600 N May Ave .... Oklahoma City OK 73107	800-753-2653	405-280-2000
Middlesboro Coca-Cola Bottling Works Inc		
1324 Cumberland Ave .... Middlesboro KY 40965	800-442-0102	877-692-4679
Pepsi-Cola Bottling Company of Yuba City Inc		
750 Sutter St .... Yuba City CA 95991	800-433-2652	
Polar Beverages		
1001 Southbridge St .... Worcester MA 01610	800-734-9800*	
Cust Svc		
Primal Essence Inc		
1351 Maulhardt Ave .... Oxnard CA 93030	877-774-6253	
Shasta Beverages Inc		
26901 Industrial Blvd .... Hayward CA 94545	800-834-9980	510-783-4070
Wallingford Coffee Mills		
11401 Rockfield Ct .... Cincinnati OH 45241	800-533-3690	513-771-3131
White Rock Products Corp		
141-07 20th Ave Ste 403 .... Whitestone NY 11357	800-969-7625	718-746-3400

80-3 Wines - Mfr

	Toll-Free	Phone
Barton Brescome Inc		
69 Defco Park Rd .... North Haven CT 06473	800-922-4840	203-239-4901
Beaulieu Vineyard		
1960 St Helena Hwy .... Rutherford CA 94573	800-373-5896	707-967-5200
Bronco Wine Co		
6342 Bystrum Rd .... Ceres CA 95307	855-874-2394	209-538-3131
Brotherhood Winery		
100 Brotherhood Plaza Dr		
PO Box 190. .... Washingtonville NY 10992	800-724-3960	845-496-3661
Clos du Bois		
19410 Geyserville Ave .... Geyserville CA 95441	800-222-3189*	
Sales		
Columbia Crest Winery		
178810 State Rt 221 PO Box 231 .... Paterson WA 99345	888-309-9463	509-875-4227
Domaine Chandon Inc		
1 California Dr .... Yountville CA 94599	888-242-6366	
Garvey Wholesale Beverage Inc		
2542 San Gabriel Blvd .... Rosemead CA 91770	800-287-2075	626-280-5244
Hogue Cellars 2800 Lee Rd .... Prosser WA 99350	800-565-9779	
Kendall-Jackson Wine Estates & Gardens		
5007 Fulton Rd .... Fulton CA 95439	800-769-3649	866-287-9818
Louis M Martini Winery		
254 S St Helena Hwy .... Saint Helena CA 94574	800-321-9463	707-968-3362
Magnotta Winery Corp		
271 Chrislea Rd .... Vaughan ON L4L8N6	800-461-9463	905-738-9463
Meier's Wine Cellars		
6955 Plainfield Rd .... Cincinnati OH 45236	800-229-9813	513-891-2900
Mendocino Wine Co		
501 ParDucci Rd .... Ukiah CA 95482	800-362-9463	707-463-5350
Michel-Schlumberger Partners LP		
4155 Wine Creek Rd .... Healdsburg CA 95448	800-447-3060	707-433-7427
Newlands Systems Inc		
602-30731 Simpson Rd .... Abbotsford BC V2T6Y7	877-855-4890	604-855-4890
Old Mill Winery		
403 S Broadway .... Geneva OH 44041	800-227-6972	
Pine Ridge Winery LLC		
5901 Silverado Trl .... Napa CA 94558	800-575-9777	
Ravenswood Winery Inc		
18701 Gehricke Rd .... Sonoma CA 95476	888-669-4679	
Raymond Vineyard		
849 Zinfandel Ln .... Saint Helena CA 94574	800-525-2659	707-963-3141
Rodney Strong Vineyards		
11455 Old Redwood Hwy .... Healdsburg CA 95448	800-678-4763	707-431-1533
Sebastiani Vineyards Inc		
389 Fourth St E .... Sonoma CA 95476	855-232-2338	707-933-3230
Trefethen Vineyards Winery Inc		
1160 Oak Knoll Ave .... Napa CA 94558	866-895-7696	707-255-7700
Warner Vineyards Inc		
706 S Kalamazoo St .... Paw Paw MI 49079	800-756-5357	269-657-3165
Weibel 1 Winemaster Way .... Lodi CA 95240	800-932-9463	209-365-9463
Willamette Valley Vineyards Inc		
8800 Enchanted Way SE .... Turner OR 97392	800-344-9463*	503-588-9463
*NASDAQ: WVVI ■ *Sales*		

81 — BEVERAGES - WHOL

81-1 Beer & Ale - Whol

	Toll-Free	Phone
Atlas Distributing Corp		
44 Southbridge St .... Auburn MA 01501	800-649-6221	508-791-6221
Blach Distributing Co		
131 W Main St .... Elko NV 89801	800-310-5099	775-738-7111
Buck Distributing Company Inc		
15827 Commerce Ct .... Upper Marlboro MD 20774	800-750-2825*	301-952-0400
Cust Svc		
Frank B Fuhrer Wholesale Co		
3100 E Carson St .... Pittsburgh PA 15203	800-837-2212	412-488-8844
Gambrinus Co, The		
14800 San Pedro 3rd Fl .... San Antonio TX 78232	800-596-6486	210-496-6525
Georgia Crown Distributing Co		
100 Georgia Crown Dr .... McDonough GA 30253	800-342-2350	770-302-3000
Iron City Distributing Co		
2670 Commercial Ave .... Mingo Junction OH 43938	800-759-2671*	740-598-4171
Cust Svc		
Koerner Distributors Inc		
1601 Pike Ave .... Effingham IL 62401	800-475-5162	

		Toll-Free	Phone
Labatt Breweries of Canada			
207 Queen's Quay W Ste 299 ....Toronto ON M5J1A7		**800-268-2337***	416-361-5050
*Cust Svc			
Maple City Ice Co Inc			
371 Cleveland Rd ....Norwalk OH 44857		**800-736-6091***	419-668-2531
*Cust Svc			
New Hampshire Distributors Inc			
65 Regional Dr ....Concord NH 03301		**800-519-9770**	603-224-9991
NKS Distributors Inc			
399 Churchmans Rd ....New Castle DE 19720		**800-310-5099**	302-322-1811
Pepin Distributing Co			
4121 N 50th St ....Tampa FL 33610		**800-331-2829**	813-626-6176
Pine State Trading Co			
100 Enterprise Ave ....Gardiner ME 04345		**800-452-4633**	
Saratoga Eagle Sales & Service Inc			
45 Duplainville Rd ......Saratoga Springs NY 12866		**800-310-5099**	518-581-7377
Savannah Distributing Co Inc			
2425 W Gwinnett St ....Savannah GA 31415		**800-551-0777***	912-233-1167
*General			
Silver Eagle Distributors LP			
7777 Washington Ave ....Houston TX 77007		**855-332-2110**	713-869-4361
Standard Beverage Corp			
2416 E 37th St N ....Wichita KS 67219		**800-999-8797**	
Star Distributors Inc			
460 Frontage Rd ....West Haven CT 06516		**877-922-3501**	203-932-3636

81-2 Soft Drinks - Whol

		Toll-Free	Phone
Atlas Distributing Corp			
44 Southbridge St ....Auburn MA 01501		**800-649-6221**	508-791-6221
Coca-Cola Consolidated			
4100 Coca-Cola Plz PO Box 31487 ......Charlotte NC 28211		**800-866-2653**	704-557-4000
NASDAQ: COKE			
Nor-Cal Beverage Company Inc			
2286 Stone Blvd ....West Sacramento CA 95691		**800-331-2059**	916-372-0600
Swire Coca-Cola USA			
12634 S 265 W ....Draper UT 84020		**800-497-2653**	801-816-5300

81-3 Wine & Liquor - Whol

		Toll-Free	Phone
Alabama Crown Distributing			
421 Industrial Ln ....Birmingham AL 35211		**800-548-1869**	205-941-1155
Badger Liquor Company Inc			
850 S Morris St ....Fond du Lac WI 54936		**800-242-9708**	920-923-8160
Badger West Wine & Spirits LLC			
5400 Old Town Hall Rd ....Eau Claire WI 54701		**800-472-6674**	715-836-8600
Beverage Distributors Co			
14200 E Moncrieff Pl ....Aurora CO 80011		**888-262-9787***	303-371-3421
*General			
Castle Brands Inc			
122 E 42nd St Ste 4700 ....New York NY 10168		**800-882-8140**	646-356-0200
NYSE: ROX			
Constellation Brands Inc			
207 High Pt Dr Bldg 100 ....Victor NY 14564		**888-724-2169**	
NYSE: STZ			
Frederick Wildman & Sons Ltd			
307 E 53rd St ....New York NY 10022		**800-733-9463***	212-355-0700
*General			
Georgia Crown Distributing Co			
100 Georgia Crown Dr ....McDonough GA 30253		**800-342-2350**	770-302-3000
NKS Distributors Inc			
399 Churchmans Rd ....New Castle DE 19720		**800-310-5099**	302-322-1811
Phillips Distributing Corp			
3010 Nob Hill Rd ....Madison WI 53713		**800-236-7269**	608-222-9177
Savannah Distributing Co Inc			
2425 W Gwinnett St ....Savannah GA 31415		**800-551-0777***	912-233-1167
*General			
Standard Beverage Corp			
2416 E 37th St N ....Wichita KS 67219		**800-999-8797**	
Winebow Inc			
75 Chestnut Ridge Rd ....Montvale NJ 07645		**800-859-0689**	201-445-0620
Young's Market Company LLC			
500 S Central Ave ....Los Angeles CA 90013		**800-627-2777**	213-612-1248

82   BICYCLES & BICYCLE PARTS & ACCESSORIES

SEE ALSO Toys, Games, Hobbies ; Sporting Goods

		Toll-Free	Phone
Cane Creek Cycling Components			
355 Cane Creek Rd ....Fletcher NC 28732		**800-234-2725**	828-684-3551
Haro Bicycles			
1230 Avenida Chelsea ....Vista CA 92081		**800-289-4276**	
Huffy Bicycle Co			
6551 Centerville Business Pkwy ....Centerville OH 45459		**800-872-2453**	937-865-2800
Raleigh America Inc			
6004 S 190th St Ste 101 ....Kent WA 98032		**800-222-5527**	
Raleigh USA			
6004 S 190th St Ste 101 ....Kent WA 98032		**800-222-5527**	253-395-1100
SMITH Mfg Company Inc			
1610 S Dixie Hwy ....Pompano Beach FL 33060		**800-653-9311**	954-941-9744
Specialized Bicycle Components			
15130 Concord Cir ....Morgan Hill CA 95037		**877-808-8154**	408-779-6229
SRAM Corp			
1333 N Kingsbury St 4th Fl ....Chicago IL 60622		**800-346-2928**	312-664-8800
Terry Precision Bicycles for Women Inc			
47 Maple St ....Burlington VT 05401		**800-289-8379**	
Worksman Trading Corp			
94-15 100th St ....Ozone Park NY 11416		**800-962-2453**	718-322-2000

83   BIO-RECOVERY SERVICES

Companies listed here provide services for managing and eliminating biohazard dangers that may be present after a death or injury. These services include cleaning, disinfecting, and deodorizing biohazard scenes resulting from accidents, homicides, suicides, natural deaths, and similar events.

		Toll-Free	Phone
Bio-Recovery Corp			
1863 Pond Rd Ste 4 ....Ronkonkoma NY 11779		**800-556-0621**	888-609-5735
Bio-Scene Recovery			
13191 Meadow St NE ....Alliance OH 44601		**877-380-5500**	330-823-5500
JP Maguire Assoc Inc			
266 Brookside Rd ....Waterbury CT 06708		**877-576-2484**	203-755-2297

84   BIOMETRIC IDENTIFICATION EQUIPMENT & SOFTWARE

		Toll-Free	Phone
Bio Medic Data Systems Inc			
1 Silas Rd ....Seaford DE 19973		**800-526-2637**	
Count Me In			
5955 Edmond St ....Las Vegas NV 89118		**866-514-5888**	
Crossmatch			
3950 RCA Blvd Ste 5001 ....Palm Beach Garden FL 33410		**866-725-3926**	561-622-1650
Honeywell Aerospace			
1944 E Sky Harbor Cir ....Phoenix AZ 85034		**800-601-3099**	
MorphoTrak Inc			
5515 E La Palma Ave Ste 100 ....Anaheim CA 92807		**800-346-2674**	714-238-2000
Security First Corp			
29811 Santa Margarita Pkwy			
Ste 600 ....Rancho Santa Margarita CA 92688		**888-884-7152**	949-858-7525
SIRCHIE Finger Print Laboratories Inc			
100 Hunter Pl ....Youngsville NC 27596		**800-356-7311**	

85   BIOTECHNOLOGY COMPANIES

SEE ALSO Medicinal Chemicals & Botanical Products ; Pharmaceutical Companies ; Pharmaceutical Companies - Generic Drugs ; Diagnostic Products

		Toll-Free	Phone
ACADIA Pharmaceuticals Inc			
3911 Sorrento Valley Blvd ....San Diego CA 92121		**800-901-5231**	858-558-2871
NASDAQ: ACAD			
AGC Biologics			
22021 20th Ave SE ....Bothell WA 98021		**800-845-6973**	425-485-1900
Alkermes Inc 852 Winter St ....Waltham MA 02451		**800-848-4876**	781-609-6000
NASDAQ: ALKS			
Alnylam Pharmaceuticals Inc			
300 Third St 3rd Fl ....Cambridge MA 02142		**866-330-0326**	617-551-8200
NASDAQ: ALNY			
American Bio Medica Corp (ABMC)			
122 Smith Rd ....Kinderhook NY 12106		**800-227-1243***	518-758-8158
OTC: ABMC ■ *General			
Amgen Canada Inc			
6775 Financial Dr Ste 100 ....Mississauga ON L5N0A4		**800-665-4273**	905-285-3000
Amgen Inc			
1 Amgen Ctr Dr ....Thousand Oaks CA 91320		**800-563-9798**	805-447-1000
Antibodies Inc PO Box 1560 ....Davis CA 95617		**800-824-8540**	
ArQule Inc			
19 Presidential Way ....Woburn MA 01801		**800-373-7827**	781-994-0300
NASDAQ: ARQL			
Astellas Pharma US Inc			
1 Astellas Way ....Northbrook IL 60062		**800-695-4321**	
AtriCure Inc			
6217 Centre Pk Dr ....West Chester OH 45069		**888-347-6403**	513-755-4100
NASDAQ: ATRC			
Bayer CropScience			
2 TW Alexander Dr .....Research Triangle Park NC 27709		**800-331-2867**	919-549-2000
BD Biosciences PharMingen			
10975 Torreyana Rd ....San Diego CA 92121		**800-848-6227**	858-812-8800
BioCryst Pharmaceuticals Inc			
2190 Pkwy Lake Dr ....Birmingham AL 35244		**800-361-0912**	205-444-4600
NASDAQ: BCRX			
Bioqual Corp			
4 Research Ct ....Rockville MD 20850		**800-208-3149**	240-404-7654
BioReliance Corp			
14920 Broschart Rd ....Rockville MD 20850		**800-553-5372**	301-738-1000
Celgene Corp 86 Morris Ave ....Summit NJ 07901		**888-771-0141**	908-673-9000
NASDAQ: CELG			
Colorado Serum Co			
4950 York St PO Box 16428...........Denver CO 80216		**800-525-2065***	303-295-7527
*Orders			
CombiMatrix Corp			
300 Goddard Ste 100 ....Irvine CA 92618		**800-710-0624**	949-753-0624
NASDAQ: CBMX			
Cook Biotech Inc			
1425 Innovation Pl ....West Lafayette IN 47906		**888-299-4224**	765-497-3355
Correvio Pharma Corp			
1441 Creekside Dr 6th Fl ....Vancouver BC V6J4S7		**800-330-9928**	604-677-6905
NASDAQ: CORV			
Covance Inc			
210 Carnegie Ctr ....Princeton NJ 08540		**888-268-2623**	609-452-4440
NYSE: CVD			
Cryolife Inc			
1655 Roberts Blvd NW ....Kennesaw GA 30144		**800-438-8285**	770-419-3355
NYSE: CRY			
Dendreon Corp			
1700 Saturn Way ....Seal Beach CA 90740		**877-256-4545**	
OTC: DNDNQ			
DexCom Inc			
6340 Sequence Dr ....San Diego CA 92121		**888-738-3646**	858-200-0200
NASDAQ: DXCM			

				Toll-Free	Phone
DUSA Pharmaceuticals Inc					
25 Upton Dr	Wilmington	MA	01887	877-533-3872	978-657-7500
NASDAQ: DUSA					
EMD Serono Inc					
1 Technology Pl	Rockland	MA	02370	800-283-8088	781-982-9000
Encore Medical Corp					
9800 Metric Blvd	Austin	TX	78758	800-456-8696	512-832-9500
Enzo Biochem Inc					
527 Madison Ave	New York	NY	10022	800-522-5052	212-583-0100
NYSE: ENZ					
Generex Biotechnology Corp					
4145 N Service Rd Ste 200	Burlington	ON	L7L6A3	800-391-6755	
OTC: GNBT					
Genomic Health Inc					
101 Galveston Dr	Redwood City	CA	94063	866-662-6897	650-556-9300
NASDAQ: GHDX					
Genzyme Corp					
500 Kendall St	Cambridge	MA	02142	800-745-4447	617-252-7500
Gilead Sciences Inc					
333 Lakeside Dr	Foster City	CA	94404	800-445-3235	650-574-3000
NASDAQ: GILD					
Grifols USA LLC					
2410 Lillyvale Ave	Los Angeles	CA	90032	888-474-3657	
Illumina Inc					
9885 Towne Centre Dr	San Diego	CA	92121	800-809-4566	858-202-4500
NASDAQ: ILMN					
Irvine Scientific					
2511 Daimler St	Santa Ana	CA	92705	800-577-6097	949-261-7800
Ivers-Lee Inc 31 Hansen S	Brampton	ON	L6W3H7	800-265-1009	905-451-5535
Lexicon Pharmaceuticals Inc					
8800 Technology Forest Pl	The Woodlands	TX	77381	855-828-4651	281-863-3000
NASDAQ: LXRX					
LifeCore Biomedical LLC					
3515 Lyman Blvd	Chaska	MN	55318	800-348-4368*	952-368-4300
*Cust Svc					
LiphaTech Inc					
3600 W Elm St	Milwaukee	WI	53209	888-331-7900	414-351-1476
Lundbeck Canada Inc					
2600 Alfred-Nobel Blvd Ste 400	Saint Laurent	QC	H4S0A9	800-586-2325	514-844-8515
Medicines Co					
8 Sylvan Way	Parsippany	NJ	07054	800-388-1183	973-290-6000
NASDAQ: MDCO					
Myriad Genetics Inc					
320 Wakara Way	Salt Lake City	UT	84108	800-469-7423	801-584-3600
NASDAQ: MYGN					
NE.T. Inc					
5651 Palmer Way Ste C	Carlsbad	CA	92010	800-888-4638	760-929-5980
Nordion 447 March Rd	Ottawa	ON	K2K1X8	800-465-3666	613-592-2790
NYSE: NDZ					
Nuo Therapeutics Inc					
207A Perry Pkwy Ste 1	Gaithersburg	MD	20877	866-298-6633	
OTC: NUOT					
Peregrine Pharmaceuticals Inc					
14282 Franklin Ave Ste 100	Tustin	CA	92780	800-987-8256	714-508-6000
NASDAQ: CDMO					
Primorigen Biosciences Inc					
510 Charmany Dr	Madison	WI	53719	866-372-7442	608-441-8332
Progenics Pharmaceuticals Inc					
1 World Trade Ctr 47th Fl Ste J	New York	NY	10591	866-644-7188	646-975-2500
NASDAQ: PGNX					
Protein Sciences Corp					
1000 Research Pkwy	Meriden	CT	06450	800-488-7099	203-686-0800
Psychemedics Corp					
289 Great Rd Ste 200	Acton	MA	01720	800-628-8073	877-517-2033
NASDAQ: PMD					
Repligen Corp 41 Seyon St	Waltham	MA	02453	800-622-2259*	781-250-0111
NASDAQ: RGEN ■ *Sales					
Repros Therapeutics Inc					
2408 Timberloch Pl Ste B-7	The Woodlands	TX	77380	800-895-6554	281-719-3400
NASDAQ: RPRX					
Rigel Pharmaceuticals Inc					
1180 Veterans Blvd	South San Francisco	CA	94080	800-414-3627	650-624-1100
NASDAQ: RIGL					
Roche Palo Alto LLC					
4300 Hacienda Dr	Pleasanton	CA	94588	888-545-2443	925-730-8000
Sanofi Pasteur Inc					
Discovery Dr	Swiftwater	PA	18370	800-822-2463*	570-839-7187
*Orders					
Sanofi-Aventis Canada					
2905 Pl Louis R Renaud	Laval	QC	H7V0A3	800-265-7927	514-956-6200
Sequenom Inc					
3595 John Hopkins Ct	San Diego	CA	92121	877-821-7266	858-202-9000
NASDAQ: SQNM					
Takeda Canada Inc					
435 N Service Rd W Ste 101	Oakville	ON	L6M4X8	888-367-3331	905-469-9333
ZymoGenetics Inc					
1201 Eastlake Ave E	Seattle	WA	98102	800-332-2056	206-442-6600

86   BLANKBOOKS & BINDERS

SEE ALSO Checks - Personal & Business

				Toll-Free	Phone
Abco Inc 1621 Wall St	Dallas	TX	75215	800-969-2226	214-565-1191
Advanced Looseleaf Technologies Inc					
1424 Somerset Ave	Dighton	MA	02715	800-339-6354	508-669-6354
Allison Payment Systems LLC					
2200 Production Dr	Indianapolis	IN	46241	800-755-2440	
American Thermoplastic Co (ATC)					
106 Gamma Dr	Pittsburgh	PA	15238	800-245-6600	
Avery Dennison Corp					
207 Goode Ave	Glendale	CA	91203	888-567-4387*	626-304-2000
NYSE: AVY ■ *Cust Svc					
Blackbourn					
200 Fourth Ave N	Edgerton	MN	56128	800-842-7550	
Colad Group 801 Exchange St	Buffalo	NY	14210	800-950-1755	716-961-1776
Continental Binder & Specialty Corp					
407 W Compton Blvd	Gardena	CA	90248	800-872-2897	310-324-8227

				Toll-Free	Phone
Data Management Inc					
537 New Britain Ave	Farmington	CT	06034	800-243-1969*	860-677-8586
*Orders					
Eckhart & Company Inc					
4011 W 54th St	Indianapolis	IN	46254	800-443-3791	317-347-2665
Federal Direct					
150 Clove Rd 5th Fl	Little Falls	NJ	07424	800-927-5123	973-667-9800
Fey Industries Inc					
200 Fourth Ave N	Edgerton	MN	56128	800-533-5340	507-442-4311
Formflex Inc					
PO Box 218	Bloomingdale	IN	47832	800-255-7659	
General Loose Leaf Bindery Co					
3811 Hawthorn Ct	Waukegan	IL	60087	800-621-0493	847-244-9700
Holum & Sons Company Inc					
740 Burr Oak Dr	Westmont	IL	60559	800-447-4479	630-654-8222
Kurtz Bros Company Inc					
400 Reed St PO Box 392	Clearfield	PA	16830	800-252-3811	814-765-6561
Leed Selling Tools Corp					
9700 Hwy 57	Evansville	IN	47725	855-687-5333	812-867-4340
NAPCO Inc 120 Trojan Ave	Sparta	NC	28675	800-854-8621	
Samsill Corp					
5740 Hartman Rd	Fort Worth	TX	76119	800-255-1100	817-536-1906
Southwest Binding & Laminating					
109 Millwell Ct	Maryland Heights	MO	63043	800-325-3628	314-739-4400
Spiral Binding Company Inc					
1 Maltese Dr	Totowa	NJ	07511	800-631-3572	
Superior Press Inc					
9440 Norwalk Blvd	Santa Fe Springs	CA	90670	888-590-7998*	
*Cust Svc					
Trendex Inc					
240 E Maryland Ave	Saint Paul	MN	55117	800-328-9200	651-489-4655
US Ring Binder					
6800 Arsenal St	Saint Louis	MO	63139	800-888-8772	314-645-7880
ViaTech Publishing Solutions					
1440 Fifth Ave	Bay Shore	NY	11706	800-645-8558	631-968-8500

87   BLINDS & SHADES

				Toll-Free	Phone
Budget Blinds Inc					
1927 N Glassell St	Orange	CA	92865	800-800-9250	949-404-1100
Carnegie Fabrics Llc					
110 N Ctr Ave	Rockville Centre	NY	11570	800-727-6770	516-678-6770
Comfortex Window Fashions Inc					
21 Elm St	Maplewood	NY	12189	800-843-4151*	
*Cust Svc					
Kenney Mfg Co					
1000 Jefferson Blvd	Warwick	RI	02886	800-753-6639*	401-739-2200
*Cust Svc					
Lafayette Venetian Blind Inc					
3000 Klondike Rd PO Box 2838	West Lafayette	IN	47996	800-342-5523	
Levolor Kirsch Window Fashions					
4110 Premier Dr	High Point	NC	27265	800-752-9677	336-812-8181
Mill Supply Div 266 Morse St	Hamden	CT	06517	888-585-9354*	203-777-7668
*General					
Ralph Friedland & Bros					
17 Industrial Dr	Keyport	NJ	07735	800-631-2162	732-290-9800
Sun Control Products Window Shades					
1908 Second St SW	Rochester	MN	55902	800-533-0010	507-282-2620
Warm Co 5529 186th Pl SW	Lynnwood	WA	98037	800-234-9276	425-248-2424

88   BLISTER PACKAGING

				Toll-Free	Phone
Adec Industries					
2700 Industrial Pkwy	Elkhart	IN	46516	866-730-3111	574-295-3167
Andex Industries Inc					
1911 Fourth Ave N	Escanaba	MI	49829	800-338-9882	
Helm Inc					
47911 Halyard Dr Ste 200	Plymouth	MI	48170	800-782-4356	
Innovated Packaging Company Inc					
38505 Cherry St Ste C	Newark	CA	94560	866-745-8180	510-745-8180
Nelson Packaging Company Inc					
1801 Reservoir Rd	Lima	OH	45804	888-229-3471	419-229-3471
Package Right Corp					
811 Development Dr	Tipton	IN	46072	800-964-3794	
Placon Corp 6096 McKee Rd	Madison	WI	53719	800-541-1535	608-271-5634
Pri-Pak Inc					
2000 Schenley Pl	Greendale	IN	47025	800-274-7632	
Virtual Images					
425 S Rockefeller Ave	Ontario	CA	91761	800-924-5401	
Visual Pak Co					
1909 S Waukegan Rd	Waukegan	IL	60085	877-689-0001	
Vulsay Industries Ltd					
35 Regan Rd	Brampton	ON	L7A1B2	800-468-1760	905-846-2200

89   BLOOD CENTERS

SEE ALSO Laboratories - Medical ; Laboratories - Drug-Testing ; Laboratories - Genetic Testing

The centers listed here are members of America's Blood Centers (ABC), the national network of non-profit, independent community blood centers. ABC members are licensed and regulated by the US Food & Drug Administration.

				Toll-Free	Phone
Belle Bonfils Memorial Blood Ctr					
717 Yosemite St	Denver	CO	80230	800-365-0006	303-341-4000
Blood Assurance Inc					
705 E Fourth St	Chattanooga	TN	37403	800-962-0628	423-756-0966
Blood Bank of Delmarva					
100 Hygeia Dr	Newark	DE	19713	800-548-4009	302-737-8405
Blood Bank of Hawaii					
2043 Dillingham Blvd	Honolulu	HI	96819	800-372-9966	808-845-9966

	Toll-Free	Phone
Blood Centers of the Pacific		
250 Bush St Ste 136 ....San Francisco CA 94104	**888-393-4483**	415-567-6400
Blood Ctr, The		
2609 Canal St ....New Orleans LA 70119	**800-862-5663**	504-524-1322
BloodCenter of Wisconsin		
638 N 18th St ....Milwaukee WI 53233	**877-232-4376**	414-933-5000
BloodSource 1608 Q St ....Sacramento CA 95811	**800-995-4420**	916-456-1500
Bloodworks Northwest		
921 Terry Ave ....Seattle WA 98104	**800-366-2831**	206-292-6500
Central California Blood Ctr		
4343 W Herndon Ave ....Fresno CA 93722	**800-649-5399**	559-389-5433
Central Illinois Community Blood Ctr		
1999 Wabash Ave ....Springfield IL 62703	**866-448-3253***	217-753-1530
*Help Line		
Central Pennsylvania Blood Bank		
8167 Adams Dr ....Hummelstown PA 17036	**800-771-0059**	717-566-6161
Coastal Bend Blood Ctr		
209 N Padre Island Dr ....Corpus Christi TX 78406	**800-299-4943**	361-855-4943
Community Blood Bank of Northwest Pennsylvania		
2646 Peach St ....Erie PA 16508	**877-842-0631**	814-456-4206
Community Blood Center (CBC)		
4040 Main St ....Kansas City MO 64111	**888-647-4040**	816-753-4040
Community Blood Ctr		
349 S Main St ....Dayton OH 45402	**800-388-4483**	
Community Blood Ctr		
4040 Main St ....Kansas City MO 64111	**888-647-4040**	816-753-4040
Community Blood Ctr Inc		
4406 W Spencer St ....Appleton WI 54914	**800-280-4102**	920-738-3131
Community Blood Ctr of the Ozarks		
220 W Plainview Rd ....Springfield MO 65810	**800-280-5337**	417-227-5000
Community Blood Services		
102 Chestnut Ridge Rd ....Montvale NJ 07645	**866-228-1500**	201-444-3900
Gulf Coast Regional Blood Ctr		
1400 La Concha Ln ....Houston TX 77054	**888-482-5663**	713-790-1200
Heartland Blood Centers		
1200 N Highland Ave ....Aurora IL 60506	**800-786-4483**	630-892-7055
Hemacare Corp		
15350 Sherman Way Ste 350 ....Van Nuys CA 91406	**877-310-0717**	877-397-3087
Hoxworth Blood Ctr University of Cincinnati Medical Ctr		
3130 Highland Ave MI 0055 ....Cincinnati OH 45267	**800-265-1515**	513-451-0910
Inland Northwest Blood Ctr		
210 W Cataldo Ave ....Spokane WA 99201	**800-423-0151**	509-624-0151
kentucky Blood center		
3121 Beaumont Centre Cir ....Lexington KY 40513	**800-775-2522**	859-276-2534
Lifeblood Mid-South Regional Blood Center		
1040 Madison Ave ....Memphis TN 38104	**888-543-3256**	901-399-8120
LifeServe Blood Ctr		
431 E Locust St ....Des Moines IA 50309	**800-287-4903**	
LifeShare Blood Centers		
8910 Linwood Ave ....Shreveport LA 71106	**800-256-4483**	318-222-7770
LifeShare Community Blood Services		
105 Cleveland St ....Elyria OH 44035	**800-317-5412**	440-322-5700
LifeSouth Community Blood Centers		
4039 Newberry Rd ....Gainesville FL 32607	**888-795-2707**	
Memorial Blood Centers (MBC)		
737 Pelham Blvd ....Saint Paul MN 55114	**888-448-3253***	
*Cust Svc		
Mississippi Blood Services		
115 Tree St ....Flowood MS 39232	**888-902-5663**	601-981-3232
Mississippi Valley Regional Blood Ctr		
5500 Lakeview Pkwy ....Davenport IA 52807	**800-747-5401**	
Nebraska Community Blood Bank		
100 N 84th St ....Lincoln NE 68505	**877-486-9414**	402-486-9414
New York Blood Ctr		
310 E 67th St ....New York NY 10065	**800-688-0900**	646-456-4281
Oklahoma Blood Institute (OBI)		
1001 N Lincoln Blvd ....Oklahoma City OK 73104	**866-708-4995**	405-278-3100
Rhode Island Blood Ctr		
405 Promenade St ....Providence RI 02908	**800-283-8385**	401-453-8360
Rock River Valley Blood Ctr		
3065 N Perryville Rd Ste 105 ....Rockford IL 61114	**877-778-2299***	815-965-8751
*General		
SeraCare Life Sciences Inc		
37 Birch St ....Milford MA 01757	**800-676-1881**	508-244-6400
NASDAQ: SRLS		
South Texas Blood & Tissue Ctr		
6211 IH-10 W ....San Antonio TX 78201	**800-292-5534**	210-731-5555
Suncoast Communities Blood Bank		
1760 Mound St ....Sarasota FL 34236	**866-972-5663**	941-954-1600
United Blood Services		
6210 E Oak St PO Box 1867 ....Scottsdale AZ 85252	**800-288-2199**	480-946-4201
Farmington		
475 E 20th St Ste A ....Farmington NM 87401	**888-804-9913**	
New Mexico		
1515 University Blvd NE ....Albuquerque NM 87102	**800-333-8037***	
*General		
United Blood Services Arizona		
Chandler		
1989 W Elliot Rd Ste 32 ....Chandler AZ 85224	**877-827-4376**	
United Blood Services of Arizona		
San Luis Obispo		
4119 Broad St Ste 100 ....San Luis Obispo CA 93401	**877-827-4376**	805-543-4290
United Blood Services of Colorado		
146 Sawyer Dr ....Durango CO 81303	**800-288-2199**	970-385-4601
United Blood Services of Mississippi		
Tupelo 4326 S Eason Blvd ....Tupelo MS 38801	**800-844-8870**	662-842-8871
United Blood Services of Montana		
Billings 1444 Grand Ave ....Billings MT 59102	**800-365-4450**	406-248-9168
United Blood Services of New Mexico		
1515 University Blvd NE ....Albuquerque NM 87102	**800-333-8037**	
Albuquerque		
1515 University Blvd NE ....Albuquerque NM 87102	**800-333-8037**	
United Blood Services of North Dakota		
Bismarck 3231 S 11th St ....Fargo ND 58104	**800-917-4929**	701-293-9453
United Blood Services of Texas		
El Paso 424 S Mesa Hills ....El Paso TX 79912	**877-827-4376**	915-544-5422
Lubbock 2523 48th St ....Lubbock TX 79413	**800-333-6920**	806-797-6804

	Toll-Free	Phone
McAllen 1400 S Sixth St ....McAllen TX 78501	**888-827-4376***	956-213-7500
*General		
San Angelo		
2020 W Beauregard Ave ....San Angelo TX 76901	**800-756-0024***	877-464-4376
*General		

90   BOATS - RECREATIONAL

	Toll-Free	Phone
Alpin Haus Ski Shop		
4850 State Hwy 30 N ....Amsterdam NY 12010	**888-454-3691**	518-843-4400
Alumaweld Boats Inc		
1601 Ave F ....White City OR 97503	**800-401-2628**	541-826-7171
Boston Whaler Inc		
100 Whaler Way ....Edgewater FL 32141	**877-294-5645**	
Cobalt Boats LLC		
1715 N Eigth St ....Neodesha KS 66757	**800-468-5764**	620-325-2653
Correct Craft Inc		
14700 Aerospace Pkwy ....Orlando FL 32832	**800-346-2092**	407-855-4141
Crestliner Inc		
9040 Quaday Ave NE ....Ostego MN 55330	**866-301-8544**	
Everglades Boats		
544 Air Pk Rd ....Edgewater FL 32132	**800-368-5647**	386-409-2202
Glastron 925 Frisbie St ....Cadillac MI 49601	**800-354-3141**	
Larson Boats LLC		
700 Paul Larson Memorial Dr ....Little Falls MN 56345	**800-220-6262***	320-632-5481
*General		
Lowe Boats		
2900 Industrial Dr ....Lebanon MO 65536	**800-641-4372**	417-532-9101
MasterCraft Boat Co		
100 Cherokee Cove Dr ....Vonore TN 37885	**800-443-8774**	845-676-7876
Pacific Seacraft		
PO Box 189 ....Washington NC 27889	**800-561-3357**	252-948-1421
Porta-Bote International		
1074 Independence Ave ....Mountain View CA 94043	**800-227-8882**	650-961-5334
Porter Inc 2200 W Monroe St ....Decatur IN 46733	**800-736-7685**	260-724-9111
Pursuit Boats		
3901 St Lucie Blvd ....Fort Pierce FL 34946	**800-947-8778**	772-465-6006
Regal Marine Industries Inc		
2300 Jetport Dr ....Orlando Fl 32809	**800-877-3425**	407-851-4360
Riverside Marine Inc		
600 Riverside Dr ....Essex MD 21221	**800-448-6872**	410-335-1500
Skier's Choice Inc		
1717 Henry G Ln St ....Maryville TN 37801	**800-320-2779**	865-983-9924
Smoker Craft PO Box 65 ....New Paris IN 46553	**866-719-7873**	
Stevens Marine Inc		
9180 SW Burnham St ....Tigard OR 97223	**800-225-7023**	503-620-7023
Stoltzfus RV's & Marine		
1335 Wilmington Pk ....West Chester PA 19382	**866-755-8858**	
World Cat		
1090 W St James St ....Tarboro NC 27886	**866-485-8899**	

91   BOILER SHOPS

	Toll-Free	Phone
Adamson Global Technology Corp		
13101 N Eron Church Rd ....Chester VA 23836	**800-525-7703**	804-748-6453
Aerofin Corp		
4621 Murray Pl PO Box 10819 ....Lynchburg VA 24506	**800-237-6346**	434-845-7081
API Heat Transfer Inc		
2777 Walden Ave ....Buffalo NY 14225	**877-274-4328**	716-684-6700
Arrow Tank & Engineering Co		
650 N Emerson St ....Cambridge MN 55008	**888-892-7769**	763-689-3360
AustinMohawk & Company Inc		
2175 Beechgrove Pl ....Utica NY 13501	**800-765-3110**	315-793-9390
Babcock & Wilcox Co		
13024 Ballantyne Corporate Pl		
Ste 700 ....Charlotte NC 28277	**800-222-2625**	704-625-4900
Babcock Power Inc		
6 Kimball Ln Ste 210 ....Lynnfield MA 01940	**800-523-0480**	978-646-3300
Chicago Boiler Co		
1300 Northwestern Ave ....Gurnee IL 60031	**800-522-7343***	847-662-4000
*Cust Svc		
Clawson Tank Co		
4701 White Lake Rd ....Clarkston MI 48346	**800-272-1367**	248-625-8700
Cleaver Brooks		
221 Law St ....Thomasville GA 31792	**800-250-5883**	229-226-3024
Eaton Metal Products Co		
4803 York St ....Denver CO 80216	**800-208-2657**	303-296-4800
Enerfab Inc		
4955 Spring Grove Ave ....Cincinnati OH 45232	**800-772-5066**	513-641-0500
Essick Air Products Inc		
5800 Murray St ....Little Rock AR 72209	**800-643-8341**	501-562-1094
Fafco Inc 435 Otterson Dr ....Chico CA 95928	**800-994-7652**	530-332-2100
Hammersmith Mfg & Sales Inc		
401 Central Ave ....Horton KS 66439	**800-375-8245**	785-486-2121
Harsco Industrial Air-X-Changers		
5616 S 129th E Ave ....Tulsa OK 74134	**800-404-3904**	918-619-8000
Hurst Boiler & Welding Company Inc		
100 Boilermaker Ln ....Coolidge GA 31738	**877-994-8778**	229-346-3545
ITT Standard		
175 Standard Pkwy ....Cheektowaga NY 14227	**800-447-7700**	800-281-4111
Mgs Inc		
178 Muddy Creek Church Rd ....Denver PA 17517	**800-952-4228**	
MiTek Industries Inc		
16023 Swingley Ridge Rd ....Chesterfield MO 63017	**800-325-8075**	314-434-1200
Modern Welding Company Inc		
2880 New Hartford Rd ....Owensboro KY 42303	**800-922-1932**	270-685-4400
Ohmstede 895 N Main St ....Beaumont TX 77704	**800-568-2328**	409-833-6375
Pentair Residential Filtration LLC		
20580 Enterprise Ave ....Brookfield WI 53008	**888-784-9065**	262-784-4490
PVI Industries LLC		
3209 Galvez Ave ....Fort Worth TX 76111	**800-784-8326**	817-335-9531
Redman Equipment & Mfg Co		
19800 Normandie Ave ....Torrance CA 90502	**888-733-2602**	310-329-1134

Classified Section

				Toll-Free	Phone
Rocky Mountain Fabrication (RMF)					
1125 West 2300 North PO Box 16409	Salt Lake City	UT	84116	888-763-5307	801-596-2400
Roy E Hanson Jr Mfg					
1600 E Washington Blvd	Los Angeles	CA	90021	800-421-9395	213-747-7514
Sen-Dure Products Inc					
6785 NW 17th Ave	Fort Lauderdale	FL	33309	800-394-5112	954-973-1260
Snap-Tite Autoclave Engineers Div					
8325 Hessinger Dr	Erie	PA	16509	800-458-0409	814-838-5700
SPX Cooling Technologies					
7401 W 129th St	Overland Park	KS	66213	800-462-7539	913-664-7400
Superior Boiler Works Inc					
3524 E Fourth St	Hutchinson	KS	67501	800-444-6693	620-662-6693
Superior Die Set Corp					
900 West Drexel Ave	Oak Creek	WI	53154	800-558-6040	414-764-4900
Sussman Automatic Corp					
43-20 34th St	Long Island	NY	11101	800-727-8326	718-937-4500
Tranter Inc					
1900 Old Burk Hwy	Wichita Falls	TX	76306	800-414-6908	
Ultraflote LLC					
3640 W 12th St	Houston	TX	77008	800-821-6825	713-461-2100
Winbco Tank Co					
1200 E Main St PO Box 618	Ottumwa	IA	52501	800-822-1855	

92   BOOK BINDING & RELATED WORK

SEE ALSO Printing Companies - Book Printers

				Toll-Free	Phone
360 Imaging Inc					
2 Concourse Pkwy Ste 140	Atlanta	GA	30328	866-360-6622	404-236-7700
Bindagraphics Inc					
2701 Wilmarco Ave	Baltimore	MD	21223	800-326-0300	410-362-7200
Booksource Inc					
1230 Macklind Ave	Saint Louis	MO	63110	800-444-0435	314-647-0600
Bound to Stay Bound Books Inc (BTSB)					
1880 W Morton Ave	Jacksonville	IL	62650	800-637-6586	217-245-5191
Contract Converting LLC					
W6580 Quality Ct	Greenville	WI	54942	800-734-0990	
David Dobbs Enterprises Inc					
4600 US Hwy 1 N	Saint Augustine	FL	32095	800-889-6368	904-824-6171
HF Group, The					
8844 Mayfield Rd	Chesterland	OH	44026	800-444-7534	440-729-2445
Library Binding Service (LBS)					
1801 Thompson Ave	Des Moines	IA	50316	800-247-5323	515-262-3191
Parker Powis Inc					
775 Heinz Ave	Berkeley	CA	94710	800-321-2463	510-848-2463
Perma-Bound					
617 E Vandalia Rd	Jacksonville	IL	62650	800-637-6581	217-243-5451
Reindl Bindery Company Inc					
W194 N11381 McCormick Dr	Germantown	WI	53022	800-878-1121	262-293-1444
Rickard Circular Folding Co					
325 N Ashland Ave	Chicago	IL	60607	800-747-1389	312-243-6300
Roswell Bookbinding Co					
2614 N 29th Ave	Phoenix	AZ	85009	888-803-8883	602-272-9338
Wert Bookbinding Inc					
9975 Allentown Blvd	Grantville	PA	17028	800-344-9378*	717-469-0629
*Cust Svc					

93   BOOK, MUSIC, VIDEO CLUBS

				Toll-Free	Phone
NetFlix Inc					
100 Winchester Cir	Los Gatos	CA	95032	866-579-7293	408-540-3700
NASDAQ: NFLX					
Writer's Digest Shop					
4700 E Galbraith Rd	Cincinnati	OH	45236	800-759-0963*	513-531-2690
*Cust Svc					

94   BOOK PRODUCERS

Book producers, or book packagers, work with authors, editors, printers, publishers, and others to provide all publication services except sales and order fulfillment. These publication services include editing of manuscripts, formatting of computer disks, producing books as a finished product, and helping the book publisher to develop marketing plans. Book producers listed here are members of the American Book Producers Association.

				Toll-Free	Phone
Guru Labs					
1148 W Legacy Crossing Blvd Ste 200	Centerville	UT	84014	800-833-3582	801-298-5227
Schlager Group Inc					
325 N Saint Paul Ste 3425	Dallas	TX	75201	888-416-5727	

95   BOOK STORES

				Toll-Free	Phone
Amazoncom Inc					
1200 12th Ave S Ste 1200	Seattle	WA	98144	800-201-7575*	206-266-1000
NASDAQ: AMZN *Cust Svc					
BarristerBooks Inc					
615 Florida St	Lawrence	KS	66044	866-808-5635	
Book Passage					
51 Tamal Vista Blvd	Corte Madera	CA	94925	800-999-7909	415-927-0960
BookPal LLC					
18101 Von Karman Ave Ste 120	Irvine	CA	92612	866-522-6657	
BookPeople 603 N Lamar	Austin	TX	78703	800-853-9757	512-472-5050
Books of Discovery					
2539 Spruce St	Boulder	CO	80302	800-775-9227	
Books on the Square					
471 Angell St	Providence	RI	02906	888-669-9660	401-331-9097

				Toll-Free	Phone
Books-A-Million Inc					
402 Industrial Ln	Birmingham	AL	35211	800-201-3550	205-942-3737
NASDAQ: BAMM					
Boston Consumers Checkbook					
185 Franklin St	Boston	MA	02110	888-382-1222	
Boulder Book Store					
1107 Pearl St	Boulder	CO	80302	800-244-4651	303-447-2074
Childrens Plus Inc					
1387 Dutch American Way	Beecher	IL	60401	800-230-1279	
Continental Book Company Inc					
6425 Washington St	Denver	CO	80229	800-364-0350	303-289-1761
Deseret Book Co					
45 W S Temple	Salt Lake City	UT	84101	800-453-4532	801-534-1515
East West Bookshop					
324 Castro St	Mountain View	CA	94041	800-909-6161	650-988-9800
Elliott Bay Book Co					
1521 Tenth Ave	Seattle	WA	98122	800-962-5311	206-624-6600
FJH Music Company Inc, The					
2525 Davie Rd Ste 360	Davie	FL	33317	800-262-8744	954-382-6061
Follett Corp					
3 Westbrook Corporate Ctr Ste 200	Westchester	IL	60154	800-365-5388	708-884-0000
Follett Higher Education Group					
3 Westbrook Corporate Ctr	Westchester	IL	60154	800-323-4506	
Horizon Books					
243 E Front St	Traverse City	MI	49684	800-587-2147	231-946-7290
Hosanna					
2421 Aztec Rd NE	Albuquerque	NM	87107	800-545-6552	505-881-3321
In The Line of Duty					
10786 Indian Head Industrial Blvd	Saint Louis	MO	63132	800-462-5232	314-890-8733
Indigo Books & Music Inc					
468 King St W Ste 500	Toronto	ON	M5V1L8	800-832-7569*	416-364-4499
TSX: IDG *Cust Svc					
Kalkomey Enterprises Inc					
14086 Proton Rd	Dallas	TX	75244	800-830-2268	214-351-0461
Keyano College					
8115 Franklin Ave	Fort Mcmurray	AB	T9H2H7	800-251-1408	780-791-4800
LibertyTree 100 Swan Way	Oakland	CA	94621	800-927-8733	510-632-1366
Loyola Press					
3441 North Ashland Ave	Chicago	IL	60657	800-621-1008	773-281-1818
Mastermind LP					
2134 Queen St E	Toronto	ON	M4E1E3	888-388-0000	416-699-3797
Matthews Book Co					
11559 Rock Island Ct	Maryland Heights	MO	63043	800-633-2665	314-432-1400
MCE Technologies LLC					
30 Hughes Ste 203	Irvine	CA	92618	800-500-0622	949-458-0800
McNally Robinson Booksellers Inc					
1120 Grant Ave	Winnipeg	MB	R3M2A6	800-561-1833	204-475-0483
Mountaineers Books					
1001 SW Klickitat Way Ste 201	Seattle	WA	98134	800-553-4453	206-223-6303
Mrs Nelsons Library Service					
1650 W Orange Grove Ave	Pomona	CA	91768	800-875-9911	909-865-8550
National Book Network Inc					
4501 Forbes Blvd Ste 200	Lanham	MD	20706	800-243-0495	301-459-3366
Northshire Information Inc					
4869 Main St	Manchester Center	VT	05255	800-437-3700	802-362-2200
Pentecostals of Alexandria, The					
2817 Rapides Ave	Alexandria	LA	71301	800-376-2422	318-487-8976
Poisoned Pen Bookstore					
4014 N Goldwater Blvd	Scottsdale	AZ	85251	888-560-9919	480-947-2974
Politics & Prose Bookstore					
5015 Connecticut Ave NW	Washington	DC	20008	800-722-0790	202-364-1919
Powell's Books Inc					
7 NW Ninth Ave	Portland	OR	97209	800-878-7323	503-228-0540
Powell's City of Books					
1005 W Burnside St	Portland	OR	97209	800-878-7323	503-228-4651
Samuel French Inc					
45 W 25th St	New York	NY	10010	866-598-8449	212-206-8990
Seagull Book & Tape Inc					
1720 S Redwood Rd	Salt Lake City	UT	84104	800-999-6257	877-324-8551
Social Studies School Service					
10200 Jefferson Blvd	Culver City	CA	90232	800-421-4246	310-839-2436
Square Books					
160 Courthouse Sq	Oxford	MS	38655	800-648-4001	662-236-2262
Strand Book Store Inc					
828 Broadway	New York	NY	10003	800-366-3664	212-473-1452
Student Book Store					
421 E Grand River Ave	East Lansing	MI	48823	800-968-1111	517-351-4210
Tattered Cover Book Store Inc					
1628 16th St	Denver	CO	80202	800-833-9327	303-436-1070
University Book Store, The					
711 State St	Madison	WI	53703	800-993-2665	608-257-3784
University of Oregon Bookstore Inc					
895 E 13th Ave	Eugene	OR	97401	800-352-1733	541-346-4331
University Press Books (UPB)					
2430 Bancroft Way	Berkeley	CA	94704	800-676-8722	510-548-0585
Word Among Us Inc					
9639 Doctor Perry Rd	Ijamsville	MD	21754	800-775-9673	301-874-1700

96   BOOKS, PERIODICALS, NEWSPAPERS - WHOL

				Toll-Free	Phone
21st Century Christian Inc					
PO Box 40526	Nashville	TN	37204	800-251-2477	615-383-3842
Advantage Mktg Inc					
14 W Main St	Ashland	OH	44805	800-670-7479	419-281-4762
Baker & Taylor Inc					
2550 W Tyvola Rd Ste 300	Charlotte	NC	28217	800-775-1800	
BMI Educational Services					
PO Box 800	Dayton	NJ	08810	800-222-8100	732-329-6991
Book Depot 67 Front St N	Thorold	ON	L2V1X3	800-801-7193	905-680-7230
Bookazine Company Inc					
75 Hook Rd	Bayonne	NJ	07002	800-221-8112	201-339-7777
Booksource Inc					
1230 Macklind Ave	Saint Louis	MO	63110	800-444-0435	314-647-0600
C2F Inc 6600 SW 111th Ave	Beaverton	OR	97008	800-544-8825	503-643-9050

			Toll-Free	Phone
Campus Text Inc				
7 Bala Ave Ste 203	Bala Cynwyd PA	19004	**888-606-8398**	610-664-6900
Choice Books LLC				
2387 Grace Chapel Rd	Harrisonburg VA	22801	**800-827-1894**	540-434-1827
Command Spanish Inc				
PO Box 1091	Petal MS	39465	**800-250-8637**	601-582-8378
Coppel Corp 503 Scaroni Rd	Calexico CA	92231	**800-220-7735**	
Direct Holdings Americas Inc				
8280 Willow Oaks Corporate Dr	Fairfax VA	22031	**800-950-7887**	
EBSCO Information Services				
10 Estes St	Ipswich MA	01938	**800-653-2726**	978-356-6500
Educational Development Corp				
5402 S 122nd E Ave	Tulsa OK	74146	**800-475-4522**	918-622-4522
NASDAQ: EDUC				
ePromos Promotional Products Inc				
113 Fifth Ave S Ste 1360	St Cloud NY	10271	**800-564-6216**	212-286-8008
Follett Corp				
1340 Ridgeview Dr	McHenry IL	60050	**877-899-8550**	815-759-1700
Follett Corp				
3 Westbrook Corporate Ctr Ste 200	Westchester IL	60154	**800-365-5388**	708-884-0000
General Pet Supply Inc				
7711 N 81st St	Milwaukee WI	53223	**800-433-9786**	414-365-3400
Independent Publishers Group				
814 N Franklin St	Chicago IL	60610	**800-888-4741***	312-337-0747
*Orders				
MBS Textbook Exchange Inc				
2711 W Ash St	Columbia MO	65203	**800-325-0530***	573-445-2243
*Cust Svc				
Midwest Library Service Inc				
11443 St Charles Rock Rd	Bridgeton MO	63044	**800-325-8833**	314-739-3100
Nebraska Book Co				
4700 S 19th St	Lincoln NE	68512	**800-869-0366**	402-421-7300
Neway Packaging Corp				
1973 E Via Arado	Rancho Dominguez CA	90220	**800-456-3929**	310-898-3400
Readerlink Distribution Services LLC				
1420 Kensington Rd Ste 300	Oak Brook IL	60523	**800-549-5389**	708-547-4400
Rittenhouse Book Distributors Inc				
511 Feheley Dr	King of Prussia PA	19406	**800-345-6425***	610-277-1414
*Cust Svc				
Saddleback Educational Publishing				
151 Kalmus Drive J-1	Costa Mesa CA	92626	**888-735-2225**	714-640-5200
SCB Distributors				
15608 New Century Dr	Gardena CA	90248	**800-729-6423**	310-532-9400
Scholastic Book Fairs Inc				
1080 Greenwood Blvd	Lake Mary FL	32746	**800-874-4809**	573-632-1687
Seda France Inc				
10200 McKalla Pl Ste 400	Austin TX	78758	**800-474-0854**	512-206-0105
Southwestern/Great American				
2451 Atrium Way	Nashville TN	37214	**888-602-7867***	
*Cust Svc				
Spring Arbor Distributors				
1 Ingram Blvd	La Vergne TN	37086	**800-395-4340**	615-793-5000

97   BOTANICAL GARDENS & ARBORETA

SEE ALSO Zoos & Wildlife Parks

			Toll-Free	Phone
Arboretum, The				
Arboretum Rd University of Guelph	Guelph ON	N1G2W1	**877-674-1610**	519-824-4120
Bellingrath Gardens & Home				
12401 Bellingrath Garden Rd	Theodore AL	36582	**800-247-8420**	251-973-2217
Boyce Thompson Arboretum				
37615 US Hwy 60	Superior AZ	85273	**877-763-5315**	520-689-2723
Brookgreen Gardens				
1931 Brookgreen Dr	Murrells Inlet SC	29576	**800-849-1931**	843-235-6000
Butchart Gardens, The				
800 Benvenuto Ave	Brentwood Bay BC	V8M1J8	**866-652-4422**	250-652-4422
Calgary Zoo Botanical Garden & Prehistoric Park				
1300 Zoo Rd NE	Calgary AB	T2E7V6	**800-588-9993**	403-232-9300
Callaway Gardens				
17800 Hwy 27	Pine Mountain GA	31822	**800-225-5292**	706-663-2281
Cedar Crest College				
100 College Dr	Allentown PA	18104	**800-360-1222***	610-437-4471
*Admissions				
Chimney Rock Park				
431 Main St	Chimney Rock NC	28720	**800-277-9611**	
Cincinnati Zoo & Botanical Garden				
3400 Vine St	Cincinnati OH	45220	**800-944-4776**	513-281-4700
Cornell Botanic Gardens				
1 Plantations Rd	Ithaca NY	14850	**800-269-8368**	607-255-2400
Earl Burns Miller Japanese Garden				
1250 Bellflower Blvd	Long Beach CA	90840	**800-985-8880**	562-985-8885
Edith J Carrier Arboretum & Botanical Gardens at James Madison University				
780 University Blvd MSC 3705	Harrisonburg VA	22807	**888-568-2586**	540-568-3194
Frederik Meijer Gardens & Sculpture Park				
1000 E Beltline Ave NE	Grand Rapids MI	49525	**877-975-3171**	616-957-1580
Gardens of the American Rose Ctr				
8877 Jefferson-Paige Rd	Shreveport LA	71119	**800-637-6534**	318-938-5402
Garvan Woodland Gardens				
550 Arkridge Rd PO Box 22240	Hot Springs AR	71903	**800-366-4664**	501-262-9300
Huntsville Botanical Garden				
4747 Bob Wallace Ave	Huntsville AL	35805	**877-930-4447**	256-830-4447
Idaho Botanical Garden				
2355 N Penitentiary Rd	Boise ID	83712	**877-527-8233**	208-343-8649
Japanese Garden				
611 SW Kingston Ave	Portland OR	97205	**800-955-8352**	503-223-1321
JC Raulston Arboretum				
4415 Beryl Rd Campus Box 7522	Raleigh NC	27695	**888-842-2442**	919-515-3132
Lady Bird Johnson Wildflower Ctr				
4801 La Crosse Ave	Austin TX	78739	**877-945-3357**	512-232-0100
Lakewold Gardens				
12317 Gravelly Lake Dr SW	Lakewood WA	98499	**888-858-4106**	253-584-4106
Lincoln Botanical Garden & Arboretum (BGA)				
c/o Landscape Services 1309 N 17th St	Lincoln NE	68588	**800-742-8800**	402-472-2679
Longue Vue House & Gardens				
7 Bamboo Rd	New Orleans LA	70124	**800-476-9137**	504-488-5488

			Toll-Free	Phone
Magnolia Plantation & Gardens				
3550 Ashley River Rd	Charleston SC	29414	**800-367-3517**	843-571-1266
Matthaei Botanical Gardens				
1800 N Dixboro Rd	Ann Arbor MI	48105	**800-666-8693**	734-647-7600
Missouri Botanical Garden				
4344 Shaw Blvd	Saint Louis MO	63110	**800-642-8842**	314-577-5100
Monticello				
556 Dettor Rd Ste 107	Charlottesville VA	22903	**800-243-0743**	434-984-9822
Niagara Parks Botanical Gardens				
7400 Portage Rd PO Box 150	Niagara Falls ON	L2E6T2	**877-642-7275**	
Oregon Garden, The				
879 W Main St PO Box 155	Silverton OR	97381	**877-674-2733**	503-874-8100
Polynesian Cultural Ctr				
55-370 Kamehameha Hwy	Laie HI	96762	**800-367-7060**	808-293-3005
Rhododendron Species Botanical Garden				
2525 S 336th St PO Box 3798	Federal Way WA	98063	**877-242-2528**	253-838-4646
Royal Botanical Gardens (RBG)				
680 Plains Rd W	Burlington ON	L7T4H4	**800-694-4769**	905-527-1158
Schoepfle Garden				
12882 Diagonal Rd	La Grange OH	44050	**800-526-7275**	440-458-5121
Schreiner's Iris Gardens				
3625 Quinaby Rd NE	Salem OR	97303	**800-525-2367**	503-393-3232
Shambhala Mountain Ctr				
151 Shambhala Wy	Red Feather Lakes CO	80545	**888-788-7221**	970-881-2184
Stan Hywet Hall & Gardens				
714 N Portage Path	Akron OH	44303	**888-836-5533**	330-836-5533
University of Southern Maine Arboretum				
PO Box 9300	Portland ME	04104	**800-800-4876**	
Vanderbilt University				
2201 W End Ave	Nashville TN	37240	**800-288-0432**	615-322-7311
Vermont Garden Park				
1100 Dorset St	South Burlington VT	05403	**800-538-7476**	802-863-5251
Winterthur Museum & Country Estate				
5105 Kennett Pk	Winterthur DE	19735	**800-448-3883**	302-888-4600

BOTTLES - GLASS

98   BOTTLES - PLASTICS

			Toll-Free	Phone
Alpha Packaging				
1555 Page Industrial Blvd	Saint Louis MO	63132	**800-421-4772**	314-427-4300
Colt's Plastics Co				
969 N Main St	Dayville CT	06241	**800-222-2658**	860-774-2301
Graham Packaging Co				
2401 Pleasant Valley Rd	York PA	17402	**800-777-0065**	717-849-8500
NEW Plastics Corp				
112 Fourth St	Luxemburg WI	54217	**800-666-5207**	920-845-2326
Nutrifaster Inc				
209 S Bennett St	Seattle WA	98108	**800-800-2641**	206-767-5054
Ozarks Coca-Cola Dr Pepper Bottling Co				
1777 N Packer Rd	Springfield MO	65803	**866-223-4498**	417-865-9900
Progressive Plastics Inc				
14801 Emery Ave	Cleveland OH	44135	**800-252-0053**	216-252-5595
Redi Bag USA				
135 Fulton Ave	New Hyde Park NY	11040	**800-517-2247**	516-746-0600
Silgan Plastics Corp				
14515 N Outer Forty Ste 210	Chesterfield MO	63017	**800-274-5426**	

99   BOWLING CENTERS

			Toll-Free	Phone
AMF Bowling Worldwide Inc				
7313 Bell Creek Rd	Mechanicsville VA	23111	**800-342-5263**	

100   BOXES - CORRUGATED & SOLID FIBER

			Toll-Free	Phone
Akers Packaging Service Inc				
2820 Lefferson Rd	Middletown OH	45044	**800-327-7308**	513-422-6312
American Environmental Container Corp				
2302 Lasso Ln	Lakeland FL	33801	**800-535-7946**	863-666-3020
Arrowhead Containers Inc				
4330 Clary Blvd	Kansas City MO	64130	**888-861-9225**	816-861-8050
Artistic Carton Co				
1975 Big Timber Rd	Elgin IL	60123	**800-735-7225**	847-741-0247
Arvco Container Corp				
845 Gibson St	Kalamazoo MI	49001	**800-968-9127**	269-381-0900
Atlas Container Corp				
8140 Telegraph Rd	Severn MD	21144	**800-394-4894**	410-551-6300
Beacon Container Corp				
700 W First St	Birdsboro PA	19508	**800-422-8383**	610-582-2222
Capitol City Container Corp				
8240 Zionsville Rd	Indianapolis IN	46268	**800-233-5145**	317-875-0290
Carolina Container Co				
909 Prospect St	High Point NC	27260	**800-627-0825**	336-883-7146
Colorado Container Corp				
4221 Monaco St	Denver CO	80216	**800-456-4725**	
Ferguson Supply & Box Manufacturing Co				
10820 Quality Dr	Charlotte NC	28278	**800-821-1023**	704-597-0310
Great Lakes Packaging Corp				
W 190 N 11393 Carnegie Dr	Germantown WI	53022	**800-261-4572**	262-255-2100
Great Northern Corp				
395 Stroebe Rd	Appleton WI	54914	**800-236-3671**	920-739-3671
Green Bay Packaging Inc				
1700 Webster Ct	Green Bay WI	54302	**800-236-8400**	920-433-5111
Key Container Corp				
21 Campbell St	Pawtucket RI	02861	**800-343-8811**	401-723-2000
Landaal Packaging Systems Inc				
3256 B Iron St	Burton MI	48529	**800-616-6619**	
Lawrence Paper Co				
2801 Lakeview Rd	Lawrence KS	66049	**800-535-4553**	

Boxes - Corrugated & Solid Fiber (Cont'd)

			Toll-Free	Phone
Lone Star Container Corp				
700 N Wildwood Dr	Irving TX	75061	800-552-6937	
Menasha Corp				
1645 Bergstrom Rd	Neenah WI	54956	800-558-5073	920-751-1000
Menasha Packaging Co				
1645 Bergstrom Rd	Neenah WI	54956	800-558-5073	920-751-1000
Minnesota Corrugated Box Inc				
2200 YH Hanson Ave	Albert Lea MN	56007	888-216-9454	
North American Container Corp				
1811 W Oak Pkwy Ste D	Marietta GA	30062	800-929-0610	770-431-4858
Packaging Corp of America				
1955 W Field Ct	Lake Forest IL	60045	800-456-4725	
NYSE: PKG				
Pactiv Corp				
1900 W Field Ct	Lake Forest IL	60045	888-828-2850	847-482-2000
Robert Mann Packaging Inc (RMP)				
340 El Camino Real S Bldg 36	Salinas CA	93901	800-345-6766	
Shoreline Container Inc				
4450 N 136th Ave PO Box 1993	Holland MI	49422	800-968-2088	616-399-2088
Stronghaven Inc				
5090 McDougall Dr SW	Atlanta GA	30336	800-331-7835	404-699-1952
Volk Packaging Corp				
11 Morin St	Biddeford ME	04005	800-341-0208	
Welch Packaging Group				
1020 Herman St	Elkhart IN	46516	800-246-2475	574-295-2460

101 BOXES - PAPERBOARD <CATID:101>

Products made by these companies include setup, folding, and nonfolding boxes.

			Toll-Free	Phone
Apex Paper Box Co				
5601 Walworth Ave	Cleveland OH	44102	800-438-2269*	216-631-6900
*Cust Svc				
Burd & Fletcher				
5151 E Geospace Dr	Independence MO	64056	800-821-2776	
Caraustar Industries Inc				
5000 Austell-Powder Springs Rd				
Ste 300	Austell GA	30106	800-858-1438	770-948-3100
Carton Service Inc				
First Quality Dr PO Box 702	Shelby OH	44875	800-533-7744*	419-342-5010
*General				
Complemar Partners				
500 Lee Rd	Rochester NY	14606	800-388-7254	585-647-5800
Dee Paper Box Company Inc				
100 Broomall St	Chester PA	19013	800-359-0041	610-876-9285
Diamond Packaging Company Inc				
111 Commerce Dr PO Box 23620	Rochester NY	14692	800-333-4079	585-334-8030
Hub Folding Box Co Inc				
774 Norfolk St	Mansfield MA	02048	800-334-1113	508-339-0005
Mafcote Industries Inc				
108 Main St	Norwalk CT	06851	800-526-4280*	203-847-8500
*Cust Svc				
Malnove Inc 13434 F St	Omaha NE	68137	800-228-9877	402-330-1100
Menasha Corp				
1645 Bergstrom Rd	Neenah WI	54956	800-558-5073	920-751-1000
MOD-PAC Corp				
1801 Elmwood Ave	Buffalo NY	14207	866-216-6193*	716-873-0640
NASDAQ: MPAC ■ *Cust Svc				
Pactiv Corp				
1900 W Field Ct	Lake Forest IL	60045	888-828-2850	847-482-2000
Panoramic Inc				
1500 N Parker Dr	Janesville WI	53545	800-333-1394	608-754-8850
Rice Packaging Inc				
356 Somers Rd	Ellington CT	06029	800-367-6725	860-872-8341
RTS Packaging LLC				
504 Thrasher St	Norcross GA	30071	800-558-6984	
Rusken Packaging Inc				
64 Walnut St NW	Cullman AL	35055	800-232-8108	256-734-0092
Seaboard Folding Box Co Inc				
100 Simplex Dr PO Box 650	Westminster MA	01473	800-225-6313	978-342-8921

102 BREWERIES <CATID:102>

SEE ALSO Malting Products

			Toll-Free	Phone
Abita Brewing Co				
21084 Hwy 36	Covington LA	70433	800-737-2311	985-893-3143
Boston Beer Co				
1 Design Ctr Pl Ste 850	Boston MA	02210	888-661-2337	617-368-5000
NYSE: SAM				
BridgePort Brewing Co				
1318 NW Northrup St	Portland OR	97209	888-834-7546	503-241-7179
Capital Brewery				
7734 Terr Ave	Middleton WI	53562	800-598-6352	608-836-7100
DL Geary Brewing Company Inc				
38 Evergreen Dr	Portland ME	04103	800-452-4633	207-878-2337
Jacob Leinenkugel Brewing Co				
124 E Elm St	Chippewa Falls WI	54729	888-534-6437*	715-723-5558
*General				
Keurig Dr Pepper Inc				
53 S Ave	Burlington MA	01803	866-901-2739	
Labatt Breweries of Canada				
207 Queen's Quay W Ste 299	Toronto ON	M5J1A7	800-268-2337*	416-361-5050
*Cust Svc				
Malt Products Corp				
88 Market St	Saddle Brook NJ	07663	800-526-0180	201-845-4420
McMenamins				
430 N Killingsworth	Portland OR	97217	800-669-8610	503-223-0109
Minhas Craft Brewery				
1208 14th Ave	Monroe WI	53566	800-233-7205	
Molson Coors Brewing Co				
1225 17th St Ste 3200	Denver CO	80202	800-645-5376	303-927-2337
NYSE: TAP				
Pabst Brewing Co, The				
10635 Santa Monica Blvd Ste 350	Los Angeles CA	90025	800-947-2278	

BROKERS

SEE Mortgage Lenders & Loan Brokers ; Securities Brokers & Dealers ; Electronic Communications Networks (ECNs) ; Commodity Contracts Brokers & Dealers ; Insurance Agents, Brokers, Services ; Real Estate Agents & Brokers

103 BRUSHES & BROOMS

SEE ALSO Art Materials & Supplies - Mfr

			Toll-Free	Phone
Abco Cleaning Products				
6800 NW 36th Ave	Miami FL	33147	888-694-2226	305-694-2226
Brush Research Mfg Company Inc				
4642 Floral Dr	Los Angeles CA	90022	800-572-6501	323-261-2193
Carlisle Sanitary Maintenance Products				
402 Black River St	Sparta WI	54656	800-654-8210	608-269-2151
Corona Brushes Inc				
5065 Savarese Cir	Tampa FL	33634	800-458-3483	813-885-2525
Detroit Quality Brush Mfg				
32165 Schoolcraft Rd	Livonia MI	48150	800-722-3037	734-525-5660
Felton Brush Inc				
7 Burton Dr	Londonderry NH	03053	800-258-9702	603-425-0200
Fuller Brush Co, The				
1 Fuller Way PO Box 729	Great Bend KS	67530	800-522-0499*	620-792-1711
*Cust Svc				
Gordon Brush Mfg Company Inc				
3737 Capitol Ave	City of Industry CA	90601	800-950-7950	323-724-7777
Greenwood Mop & Broom Inc				
312 Palmer St	Greenwood SC	29646	800-635-6849	864-227-8411
Harper Brush Works Inc				
400 N Second St	Fairfield IA	52556	800-223-7894	641-472-5186
Industrial Brush Company Inc				
105 Clinton Rd	Fairfield NJ	07004	800-241-9860	973-575-0455
Industries of the Blind Inc				
920 W Lee St	Greensboro NC	27403	800-909-7086	336-274-1591
Libman Co 220 N Sheldon St	Arcola IL	61910	877-818-3380	
Magnolia Brush Mfg Ltd				
1000 N Cedar st PO Box 932	Clarksville TX	75426	800-248-2261	903-427-2261
Mill-Rose Co 7995 Tyler Blvd	Mentor OH	44060	800-321-3533	440-255-9171
Osborn International				
5401 Hamilton Ave	Cleveland OH	44114	800-720-3358*	216-361-1900
*Cust Svc				
Padco Inc				
2220 Elm St SE	Minneapolis MN	55414	800-328-5513	612-378-7270
PFERD Milwaukee Brush Company Inc				
30 Jytek Dr	Leominster MA	01453	800-342-9015	978-840-6420
Quickie Manufacturing Corp				
1150 Taylor Ln	Riverton NJ	08077	800-257-5751	
Rubberset Co				
101 W Prospect Ave	Cleveland OH	44115	800-345-4939	
Sanderson-MacLeod Inc				
1199 S Main St PO Box 50	Palmer MA	01069	866-522-3481	413-283-3481
SM Arnold Inc				
7901 Michigan Ave	Saint Louis MO	63111	800-325-7865*	314-544-4103
*Cust Svc				
Sweepster Inc 2800 N Zeeb Rd	Dexter MI	48130	800-456-7100	
Universal Brush Manufacturing Co				
16200 Dixie Hwy	Markham IL	60428	800-323-3474	708-331-1700
Weiler Corp 1 Wildwood Dr	Cresco PA	18326	800-835-9999*	570-595-7495
*Cust Svc				
Wooster Brush Co				
604 Madison Ave	Wooster OH	44691	800-392-7246	330-264-4440
Zephyr Mfg Company Inc				
200 Mitchell Rd	Sedalia MO	65301	800-821-7197	660-827-0352

104 BUILDING MAINTENANCE SERVICES

SEE ALSO Cleaning Services

			Toll-Free	Phone
AHI Facility Services Inc (AHI)				
1253 Round Table Dr	Dallas TX	75247	800-472-5749	214-741-3714
Aid Maintenance Co				
300 Roosevelt Ave	Pawtucket RI	02860	800-886-6627	401-722-6627
Ambius Plants				
485 E Half Day Rd	Buffalo Grove IL	60089	800-581-9946	
Associated Building Maintenance Company Inc				
2140 Priest Bridge Ct Ste 3	Crofton MD	21114	800-721-9068	410-721-1818
Calico Building Services Inc				
15550-C Rockfield Blvd	Irvine CA	92618	800-576-7313	
Coastal Building Maintenance				
8651 NW 70th St	Miami FL	33166	800-357-7790	305-681-6100
Courtesy Building Services Inc				
2154 N Northwest Hwy Ste 214	Dallas TX	75220	800-479-3853	972-831-1444
Cristi Cleaning Service				
77 Trinity Pl	Hackensack NJ	07608	800-287-6173	201-883-1717
Cummins Facility Services				
5202 Marion Waldo Rd	Prospect OH	43342	800-451-5629	740-726-9800
Diamond H2O				
N1022 Quality Dr	Greenville WI	54942	800-236-8931	920-757-5440
DMS Facility Services				
1040 Arroyo Dr	South Pasadena CA	91030	800-443-8677	626-305-8500
Drayton Group				
2295 N Opdyke Rd Ste D	Auburn Hills MI	48326	888-655-4442	
Eagle Cleaning Service Inc				
525 Belview St	Bessemer AL	35020	877-864-5696	205-424-5252
Ecolo Odor Control Technologies Inc				
59 Penn Dr	Toronto ON	M9L2A6	800-667-6355	416-740-3900
FBG Service Corp				
407 S 27th Ave	Omaha NE	68131	800-777-8326	
HB Management Group Inc				
7100 Broadway Ste 6L	Denver CO	80221	866-440-1100	
Horizon Services Inc				
250 Governor St	East Hartford CT	06108	800-949-5323	

			Toll-Free	Phone
Merchants Building Maintenance				
606 Monterey Pass Rd	Monterey Park CA	91754	800-560-6700	
Pacific Building Maintenance Inc				
2646 Palma Dr Ste 320.	Ventura CA	93003	800-300-4094	805-642-0214
Sealco Data Center Services Ltd				
1751 INTERNATIONAL Pkwy Ste 115	Richardson TX	75081	800-283-5567	972-234-5567
Shannon Diversified Inc				
1360 E Locust St	Ontario CA	91761	800-794-2345	
UV Pure Technologies Inc				
60 Venture Dr Unit 19.	Toronto ON	M1B3S4	888-407-9997	416-208-9884
Vanguard Resources Inc				
6500 Hwy 281 N	Spring Branch TX	78070	800-211-8848	210-495-1950

105   BUILDINGS - PREFABRICATED - METAL

			Toll-Free	Phone
American Buildings Co				
1150 State Docks Rd	Eufaula AL	36027	888-307-4338	334-687-2032
Ceco Building Systems				
2400 Hwy 45 N	Columbus MS	39705	800-474-2326	662-243-6400
CEMCO				
263 N Covina Ln	City Of Industry CA	91744	800-775-2362	
Erect-A-Tube Inc PO Box 100	Harvard IL	60033	800-624-9219	815-943-4091
Four Seasons Solar Products LLC				
5005 Veterans Memorial Hwy	Holbrook NY	11741	800-368-7732	631-563-4000
Garco Bldg Systems				
2714 S Garfield Rd	Airway Heights WA	99001	800-941-2291	509-244-5611
Imperial Industries Inc				
505 Industrial Park Ave	Rothschild WI	54474	800-558-2945	715-359-0200
Kirby Bldg Systems Inc				
124 Kirby Dr	Portland TN	37148	800-348-7799	615-325-4165
Mesco Bldg Solutions				
5244 Bear Creek Ct	Irving TX	75061	800-556-3726	214-687-9999
Metl-Span LLC				
1720 Lakepointe Dr Ste 101	Lewisville TX	75057	877-585-9969	972-221-6656
Mid-West Steel Bldg Co				
7301 Fairview	Houston TX	77041	800-777-9378	713-466-7788
Morton Buildings Inc				
252 W Adams St PO Box 399	Morton IL	61550	800-447-7436	
Mueller Inc				
1913 Hutchins Ave	Ballinger TX	76821	877-268-3553	325-365-3555
NCI Bldg Systems Inc				
10943 N Sam Houston PkwyWest	Houston TX	77064	888-624-8677	281-897-7788
NYSE: NCS				
Pacific Building Systems (PBS)				
2100 N Pacific Hwy	Woodburn OR	97071	800-727-7844*	503-981-9581
General				
Package Steel Systems Inc				
15 Harback Rd	Sutton MA	01590	800-225-7242	508-865-5871
Parkline Inc PO Box 65	Winfield WV	25213	800-786-4855	304-586-2113
Porta-Fab Corp				
18080 Chesterfield Airport Rd	Chesterfield MO	63005	800-325-3781	636-537-5555
PorterCorp 4240 136th Ave	Holland MI	49424	800-354-7721	616-399-1963
Red Dot Corp				
1209 W Corsicana St	Athens TX	75751	800-657-2234*	
Cust Svc				
Star Bldg Systems				
8600 S I-35	Oklahoma City OK	73149	800-879-7827	
Temo Sunrooms Inc				
20400 Hall Rd	Clinton Township MI	48038	800-344-8366	
Trachte Bldg Systems Inc (TBS)				
314 Wilburn Rd	Sun Prairie WI	53590	800-356-5824	
Whirlwind Steel				
8234 Hansen Rd	Houston TX	77075	800-324-9992	713-946-7140
Worldwide Steel Buildings				
PO Box 588	Peculiar MO	64078	800-825-0316	

106   BUILDINGS - PREFABRICATED - WOOD

			Toll-Free	Phone
Acorn Deck House Co				
852 Main St	Acton MA	01720	800-727-3325	
Alfresco				
1085 Bixby Dr	Hacienda Heights CA	91745	888-383-8800	323-722-7900
Barden & Robeson Corp				
103 Kelly Ave	Middleport NY	14105	800-724-0141	716-735-3732
Blazer Industries Inc				
PO Box 489	Aumsville OR	97325	877-211-3437	503-749-1900
Deluxe Bldg Systems Inc				
499 W Third St	Berwick PA	18603	800-843-7372	570-752-5914
Design Homes Inc				
600 N Marquette Rd	Prairie du Chien WI	53821	800-627-9443	608-326-6041
Dickinson Homes Inc				
404 N Stephenson Ave Hwy US-2				
PO Box 2245.	Iron Mountain MI	49801	800-438-4687	906-774-2186
Dynamic Homes LLC				
525 Roosevelt Ave	Detroit Lakes MN	56501	800-492-4833	218-847-2611
Energy Panel Structures Inc				
603 N Van Gordon Ave	Graettinger IA	51342	800-967-2130	
Fleetwood Homes				
7007 Jurupa Ave	Riverside CA	92504	888-568-2080	
Flexospan Steel Buildings Inc				
253 Railroad St	Sandy Lake PA	16145	800-245-0396	
Homes by Keystone Inc				
13338 Midvale Rd PO Box 69.	Waynesboro PA	17268	800-890-7926	
Indaco Metal 3 American Way	Shawnee OK	74804	877-750-5614	405-273-9200
International Homes of Cedar Inc (IHC)				
PO Box 886	Woodinville WA	98072	800-767-7674	360-668-8511
KIT HomeBuilders West LLC				
1124 Garber St	Caldwell ID	83605	800-859-0347	208-454-5000
Lester Bldg Systems LLC				
1111 Second Ave S	Lester Prairie MN	55354	800-826-4439	320-395-2531
Lindal Cedar Homes Inc				
4300 S 104th Pl	Seattle WA	98178	800-426-0536*	206-725-0900
Prod Info				

			Toll-Free	Phone
Nationwide Custom Homes				
1100 Rives Rd	Martinsville VA	24115	800-216-7001	
New England Homes				
270 Ocean Rd	Greenland NH	03840	800-800-8831	603-436-8830
Nexus Corp				
10983 Leroy Dr	Northglenn CO	80233	800-228-9639	303-457-9199
Northeastern Log Homes Inc				
10 Ames Rd	Kenduskeag ME	04450	800-624-2797	207-884-7000
Original Lincoln Logs Ltd				
5 Riverside Dr PO Box 135	Chestertown NY	12817	800-833-2461	
Pacific Modern Homes Inc (PMHI)				
9723 Railroad St	Elk Grove CA	95624	800-395-1011	
Pan Abode Cedar Homes Inc				
1100 Maple Ave SW	Renton WA	98057	800-782-2633	425-255-8260
Professional Building Systems Inc				
72 E Market St	Middleburg PA	17842	800-837-4552	
Rochester Homes Inc				
1345 N Lucas St	Rochester IN	46975	800-860-4554	
Southern Bleacher Company Inc				
801 Fifth St	Graham TX	76450	800-433-0912	940-549-0733
Sterling Bldg Systems				
PO Box 8005	Wausau WI	54402	800-455-0545	
Stratford Homes LP				
402 S Weber Ave	Stratford WI	54484	800-448-1524	715-687-3133
Timberland Homes Inc				
1201 37th St NW	Auburn WA	98001	800-488-5036	253-735-3435
Unibilt Industries Inc				
8005 Johnson Stn Rd PO Box 373	Vandalia OH	45377	800-777-9942	
Ward Cedar Log Homes				
37 Bangor St PO Box 72.	Houlton ME	04730	800-341-1566*	
Cust Svc				
Wausau Homes Inc PO Box 8005	Wausau WI	54402	800-455-0545	715-359-7272
Westchester Modular Homes Inc				
30 Reagans Mill Rd	Wingdale NY	12594	800-832-3888	845-832-9400
Yankee Barn Homes				
131 Yankee Barn Rd	Grantham NH	03753	800-258-9786	

107   BUS SERVICES - CHARTER

			Toll-Free	Phone
A Yankee Line 370 W First St	Boston MA	02127	800-942-8890	617-268-8890
All West Coach Lines				
7701 Wilbur Way	Sacramento CA	95828	800-843-2121	888-970-7233
Anderson Coach & Travel				
1 Anderson Plz	Greenville PA	16125	800-345-3435	724-588-8310
Arrow Stage Lines				
720 E Norfolk Ave	Norfolk NE	68701	800-672-8302	402-371-3850
B & C Transportation Inc				
427 Continental Dr	Maryville TN	37804	877-812-2287	865-983-4653
Badger Bus 5501 Femrite Dr	Madison WI	53718	800-442-8259	608-255-1511
Bieber Transportation Group				
320 Fair St PO Box 180	Kutztown PA	19530	800-243-2374	610-683-7333
Blue Lakes Charters & Tours				
12154 N Saginaw Rd	Clio MI	48420	800-282-4287	810-686-4287
Boise-Winnemucca Stages Inc				
1230 W Bannock St	Boise ID	83702	800-448-5692	208-336-3300
Brown Coach Inc				
50 Venner Rd	Amsterdam NY	12010	800-424-4700	518-843-4700
Butler Motor Transit				
210 S Monroe St PO Box 1602.	Butler PA	16003	800-222-8750	724-282-1000
Citizen Auto Stage Co				
3594 E Lincoln St	Tucson AZ	85714	800-276-1528	520-622-8811
Coach Tours Ltd				
475 Federal Rd	Brookfield CT	06804	800-822-6224	203-740-1118
Colorado Charter Lines				
4960 Locust St	Commerce CO	80022	800-821-7491	303-287-0239
Conestoga Tours Inc				
1619 Manheim Pk	Lancaster PA	17601	800-538-2222	717-569-1111
Croswell Bus Lines Inc				
975 W Main St	Williamsburg OH	45176	800-782-8747	513-724-2206
DATTCO Inc 583 S St	New Britain CT	06051	800-229-4879	860-229-4878
Elite Coach 1685 W Main St	Ephrata PA	17522	800-722-6206	717-733-7710
Eyre Bus Service Inc				
13600 Triadelphia Rd PO Box 239	Glenelg MD	21737	800-321-3973	410-442-1330
Gold Coast Tours				
105 Gemini Ave	Brea CA	92821	800-638-6427	714-449-6888
Good Time Tours				
455 Corday St	Pensacola FL	32503	800-446-0886	850-476-0046
Gray Line Corporation Inc				
1900 16th St Ste 210	Denver CO	80202	800-472-9546	303-539-8502
Greyhound Canada Transportation Corp				
1111 International Blvd Ste 700	Burlington ON	L7L6W1	800-661-8747	
Hawkeye Stages Inc				
703 Dudley St	Decorah IA	52101	877-464-2954	
Kerrville Bus Co				
1430 E Houston St	San Antonio TX	78202	800-256-2757	210-226-7371
Lamers Bus Lines Inc				
2407 S Pt Rd	Green Bay WI	54313	800-236-1240	920-496-3600
Martz First Class Coach Company Inc				
4783 37th St N	Saint Petersburg FL	33714	800-282-8020	
Mid-America Charter Lines				
2513 E Higgins Rd	Elk Grove Village IL	60007	800-323-0312	847-437-3779
Northfield Lines Inc				
1034 Gemini Rd	Eagan MN	55121	888-670-8068	651-203-8888
Onondaga Coach Corp				
PO Box 277	Auburn NY	13021	800-451-1570	315-255-2216
Peter Pan Bus Lines				
PO Box 1776	Springfield MA	01102	800-343-9999	
Premier Coach Company Inc				
946 Rte 7 S	Milton VT	05468	800-532-1811	802-655-4456
Punchbowl Inc				
50 Speen St Ste 202	Framingham MA	01701	877-570-4340	508-589-4486
Red Carpet Charters				
4820 SW 20th	Oklahoma City OK	73128	888-878-5100	405-672-5100
Salter Bus Lines Inc				
212 Hudson Ave	Jonesboro LA	71251	800-223-8056	318-259-2522

				Toll-Free	Phone

Shafer's Tour & Charter
500 N St .... Endicott NY 13760 — 800-287-8986 — 607-797-2006

Silver Fox Tours & Motorcoaches
3 Silver Fox Dr .... Millbury MA 01527 — 800-342-5998 — 508-865-6000

Starr Transit Inc
2531 E State St .... Trenton NJ 08619 — 800-782-7703 — 609-587-0626

Storer Coachways
3519 McDonald Ave .... Modesto CA 95358 — 800-621-3383 — 209-521-8250

Swarthout Coaches Inc
115 Graham Rd .... Ithaca NY 14850 — 800-772-7267 — 607-257-2277

Trailways Transportation System Inc
3554 Chain Bridge Rd Ste 202 ... Fairfax VA 22030 — 877-467-3346 — 703-691-3052

Van Galder Bus Co
715 S Pearl St .... Janesville WI 53548 — 800-747-0994 — 888-970-7233

Voyageur Transportation Services
573 Admiral Ct .... London ON N5V4L3 — 855-263-7163 — 519-455-4580

Wilson Bus Lines Inc
203 Patriots Rd PO Box 415 ... East Templeton MA 01438 — 800-253-5235 — 978-632-3894

Winn Transportation
1831 Westwood Ave .... Richmond VA 23227 — 800-296-9466 — 804-358-9466

Young Transportation & Tours
843 Riverside Dr .... Asheville NC 28804 — 800-622-5444 — 828-258-0084

108 BUS SERVICES - INTERCITY & RURAL

SEE ALSO Mass Transportation (Local & Suburban) ; Bus Services - School

				Toll-Free	Phone

Colorado Valley Transit Inc
108 Cardinal Ln PO Box 940 ... Columbus TX 78934 — 800-548-1068 — 979-732-6281

GATRA 2 Oak St .... Taunton MA 02780 — 800-483-2500 — 508-823-8828

Geauga County Transit
12555 Merritt Rd .... Chardon OH 44024 — 888-287-7190* — 440-279-2150
*Cust Svc

Greyhound Canada Transportation Corp
1111 International Blvd Ste 700 ... Burlington ON L7L6W1 — 800-661-8747

Jefferson Partners LP
2100 E 26th St .... Minneapolis MN 55404 — 800-767-5333* — 612-359-3400
*Cust Svc

Ozark Regional Transit
2423 E Robinson Ave .... Springdale AR 72764 — 800-865-5901 — 479-756-5901

Pacific Transit System
216 N Second St .... Raymond WA 98577 — 800-833-6388 — 360-875-9418

Pelivan Transit
333 S Oak St PO Box B .... Big Cabin OK 74332 — 800-482-4594 — 918-783-5793

Powder River Transportation
1700 U S 14 .... Gillette WY 82716 — 888-970-7233

Ramblin Express Transportation
3465 Astrozon Pl .... Colorado Springs CO 80910 — 800-772-6254 — 719-590-8687

Rural Transit Enterprises Coordinated Inc (RTEC)
100 E Main St .... Mount Vernon KY 40456 — 800-321-7832 — 606-256-9835

Suburban Transit Corp
750 Somerset St .... New Brunswick NJ 08901 — 800-222-0492 — 732-249-1100

Trans-Bridge Lines Inc
2012 Industrial Dr .... Bethlehem PA 18017 — 800-556-3815 — 610-868-6001

Viking Trailways
201 Glendale Rd .... Joplin MO 64804 — 877-467-3346

109 BUS SERVICES - SCHOOL

				Toll-Free	Phone

Birnie Bus Service Inc
248 Otis St .... Rome NY 13441 — 800-734-3950 — 315-336-3950

Brown Bus Co
2111 E Sherman Ave .... Nampa ID 83686 — 800-574-1580 — 208-466-4181

Davidsmeyer Bus Service Inc
2513 E Higgins Rd ...... Elk Grove Village IL 60007 — 800-323-0312 — 847-437-3767

Dean Transportation Inc
4812 Aurelius Rd .... Lansing MI 48910 — 800-282-3326 — 517-319-8300

First Student Inc
600 Vine St .... Cincinnati OH 45202 — 800-844-5588 — 513-241-2200

John T Cyr & Sons Inc
153 Gilman Falls Ave .... Old Town ME 04468 — 800-244-2335 — 207-827-2335

Kobussen Buses Ltd
W914 County Rd CE .... Kaukauna WI 54130 — 800-447-0116 — 920-766-0606

Michael's Transportation Service Inc
140 Yolano Dr .... Vallejo CA 94589 — 800-295-2448* — 707-643-2099
*Cust Svc

Stock Transportation
60 Columbia Way Ste 800 ..... Markham ON L3R0C9 — 888-952-0878 — 905-940-9977

Student Transportation Inc (STA)
3349 Hwy 138 Bldg A Ste C ... Wall NJ 07719 — 888-942-2250 — 732-280-4200

110 BUSINESS FORMS

SEE ALSO Printing Companies - Commercial Printers

				Toll-Free	Phone

Ace Forms of Kansas Inc
2900 N Rotary Terr .... Pittsburg KS 66762 — 800-223-9287

Adams Investment Co
2500 Industrial Pkwy .... Dewey OK 74029 — 800-331-0920

Allison Payment Systems LLC
2200 Production Dr ...... Indianapolis IN 46241 — 800-755-2440

Amsterdam Printing & Litho Corp
166 Wallins Corners Rd ...... Amsterdam NY 12010 — 800-833-6231*
*Cust Svc

Apex Color
200 N Lee St .... Jacksonville FL 32204 — 800-367-6790

Bestforms Inc
1135 Avenida Acaso .... Camarillo CA 93012 — 800-350-0618 — 805-383-6993

Champion Industries Inc
PO Box 2968 .... Huntington WV 25728 — 800-624-3431 — 304-528-2791
OTC: CHMP

Curtis 1000 Inc
1725 Breckinridge Pkwy Ste 500 ... Duluth GA 30096 — 877-287-8715 — 678-380-9095

				Toll-Free	Phone

DATA Communications Management Corp (DCM)
9195 Torbram Rd .... Brampton ON L6S6H2 — 800-268-0128 — 905-791-3151

Data Papers Inc
468 Industrial Pk Rd .... Muncy PA 17756 — 800-233-3032

Data Source Inc
1400 Universal Ave .... Kansas City MO 64120 — 877-846-9120 — 816-483-3282

Datatel Resources Corp
1729 Pennsylvania Ave .... Monaca PA 15061 — 800-245-2688 — 724-775-5300

DFS 500 Main St .... Groton MA 01471 — 800-225-9528*
*General

Dupli-Systems Inc
8260 Dow Cir .... Strongsville OH 44136 — 800-321-1610 — 440-234-9415

Eastern Business Forms Inc
PO Box 10 .... Mauldin SC 29662 — 800-387-2648

Federal Direct
150 Clove Rd 5th Fl .... Little Falls NJ 07424 — 800-927-5123 — 973-667-9800

FedEx
3875 Airways Module H3 Dept 4634 ... Memphis TN 38116 — 800-463-3339

Flesh Co 2118 59th St ..... Saint Louis MO 63110 — 800-869-3330 — 314-781-4400

Forms Manufacturers Inc
312 E Forest Ave .... Girard KS 66743 — 800-835-0614

Freedom Graphic Systems Inc (FGS)
1101 S Janesville St .... Milton WI 53563 — 800-334-3540

Genoa Business Forms Inc
445 Park Ave .... Sycamore IL 60178 — 800-383-2801

Gulf Business Forms Inc
2460 IH 35 S .... San Marcos TX 78666 — 800-433-4853 — 512-353-8313

Highland Computer Forms Inc
1025 W Main St .... Hillsboro OH 45133 — 800-669-5213 — 937-393-4215

IBS Direct
431 Yerkes Rd .... King of Prussia PA 19406 — 800-220-1255 — 610-265-8210

Imperial Graphics Inc
3100 Walknet Dr NW ...... Grand Rapids MI 49544 — 800-777-2591

Kaye-Smith
4101 Oakesdale Ave SW .... Renton WA 98057 — 800-822-9987 — 425-228-8600

New Jersey Business Forms Manufacturing Co
55 W Sheffield Ave .... Englewood NJ 07631 — 800-466-6523 — 201-569-4500

Paris Business Products
800 Highland Dr .... Westampton NJ 08060 — 800-523-6454* — 609-265-9200
*Cust Svc

Patterson Office Supplies
3310 N Duncan Rd .... Champaign IL 61822 — 800-637-1140 — 217-351-5400

Performance Office Papers
21565 Hamburg Ave .... Lakeville MN 55044 — 800-458-7189

PrintEdd Products Ltd
2641 Forum Dr .... Grand Prairie TX 75052 — 800-367-6728 — 972-660-3800

Quality Forms 4317 W US Rt 36 ... Piqua OH 45356 — 866-773-4595 — 937-773-4595

Rotary Forms Press Inc
835 S High St .... Hillsboro OH 45133 — 800-654-2876 — 937-393-3426

Royal Business Forms Inc
3301 Ave E E .... Arlington TX 76011 — 800-255-9303

Specialized Printed Forms Inc
352 Ctr St .... Caledonia NY 14423 — 800-688-2381 — 585-538-2381

Sterling Business Forms
PO Box 2486 .... White City OR 97503 — 800-759-3676*
*Cust Svc

Stry-Lenkoff Co
1100 W Broadway .... Louisville KY 40203 — 800-626-8247 — 502-587-6804

Victor Printing Inc
1 Victor Way .... Sharon PA 16146 — 800-443-2845

Ward-Kraft Inc
2401 Cooper St .... Fort Scott KS 66701 — 800-821-4021 — 620-223-5500

Wilmer Service Line
515 W Sycamore St .... Coldwater OH 45828 — 800-494-5637

Wise Business Forms Inc
555 McFarland 400 Dr .... Alpharetta GA 30004 — 888-815-9473 — 770-442-1060

Witt Printing Company Inc
301 Oak St .... El Dorado Springs MO 64744 — 800-641-4342 — 417-876-4721

Wright Business Graphics (WBG)
18440 NE San Rafael St ...... Portland OR 97230 — 800-547-8397

111 BUSINESS MACHINES - MFR

SEE ALSO Calculators - Electronic ; Photocopying Equipment & Supplies ; Business Machines - Whol ; Computer Equipment

				Toll-Free	Phone

Aaxon Laundry Systems
6100 N Powerline Rd ...... Ft. Lauderdale FL 33309 — 800-826-1012 — 954-772-7100

Abbott 26531 Ynez Rd .... Temecula CA 92591 — 800-227-9902

ACR Supply Company Inc
4040 S Alston Ave .... Durham NC 27713 — 800-442-4044 — 919-765-8081

Amano Cincinnati Inc
140 Harrison Ave .... Roseland NJ 07068 — 800-526-2559 — 973-403-1900

Aurora Biomed Inc
1001 E Pender St .... Vancouver BC V6A1W2 — 800-883-2918 — 604-215-8700

Autometrix Precision Cutting Systems Inc
12098 Charles Dr .... Grass Valley CA 95945 — 800-635-3080 — 530-477-5065

Better Packages Inc
255 Canal St PO Box 711 ..... Shelton CT 06484 — 800-237-9151 — 203-926-3700

Biosafe Engineering
5750 W 80th St .... Indianapolis IN 46278 — 888-858-8099 — 317-858-8099

Brandt Tractor Ltd
Hwy 1 E PO Box 3856 .... Regina SK S4P3R8 — 888-227-2638 — 306-791-7777

Brother International Corp
100 Somerset Corporate Blvd ... Bridgewater NJ 08807 — 877-552-6255* — 908-704-1700
*Cust Svc

CCTF Corp 5407 - 53 Ave NW ... Edmonton AB T6B3G2 — 800-661-3633 — 780-463-8700

Con-tek Machine Inc
3575 Hoffman Rd E .... Saint Paul MN 55110 — 800-968-9801 — 651-779-6058

CRANE Merchandising Systems
3330 Crane Way PO Box 719 ... Williston SC 29853 — 800-628-8363 — 800-621-7278

Cubeit Portable Storage
100 Canadian Rd .... Scarborough ON M1R4Z5 — 844-897-3811

Cummins-Allison Corp
852 Feehanville Dr .... Mount Prospect IL 60056 — 800-786-5528 — 847-299-9550

				Toll-Free	Phone
Dynetics Engineering Corp					
515 Bond St	Lincolnshire	IL	60069	800-888-8110	847-541-7300
Elliot Equipment Corp					
1131 Country Club Rd	Indianapolis	IN	46234	800-823-7527	317-271-3065
Exocor Inc					
271 Ridley Rd	St. Catharines	ON	L2R6P7	888-317-2209	905-704-0603
Fabgroups Technologies Inc					
1100 Saint Amour	Saint-laurent	QC	H4S1J2	800-561-8910	514-331-3712
Fellowes Inc					
1789 Norwood Ave	Itasca	IL	60143	800-945-4545	630-893-1600
Fountain Industries Co					
922 E 14th St	Albert Lea	MN	56007	800-328-3594	507-373-2351
G & O Thermal Supply Co					
5435 N Northwest Hwy	Chicago	IL	60630	800-621-4997	773-763-1300
Groves Industrial Supply Inc					
7301 Pinemont Dr	Houston	TX	77040	800-343-8923	713-675-4747
Imaging Business Machines LLC (IBML)					
2750 Crestwood Blvd	Birmingham	AL	35210	877-627-8325	205-956-4071
International Business Machines Corp (IBM)					
1 New OrchaRd Rd	Armonk	NY	10504	800-426-4968	914-499-1900
NYSE: IBM					
J C Foodservice Inc					
415 S Atlantic Blvd	Monterey Park	CA	91754	800-328-6688	626-308-1988
Lathem Time Corp					
200 Selig Dr SW	Atlanta	GA	30336	800-241-4990	404-691-0400
Lynde-Ordway Company Inc					
3308 W Warner Ave	Santa Ana	CA	92704	800-762-7057	714-957-1311
Magnatech International Inc					
17 E Meadow Ave	Robesonia	PA	19551	800-523-8193	610-693-8866
Martin Yale Industries Inc					
251 Wedcor Ave	Wabash	IN	46992	800-225-5644	260-563-0641
MBM Corp (MBM)					
3134 Industry Dr	North Charleston	SC	29418	800-223-2508*	843-552-2700
*Cust Svc					
National Lift Truck Inc					
3333 Mt Prospect Rd	Franklin Park	IL	60131	800-469-6420	
Neopost Inc Canada					
150 Steelcase Rd W	Markham	ON	L3R3J9	800-636-7678	
Newbold Corp					
450 Weaver St	Rocky Mount	VA	24151	800-552-3282	540-489-4400
Nissei America Inc					
1480 N Hancock St	Anaheim	CA	92807	800-693-3231	714-693-3000
Noble Trade Inc					
7171 Jane St	Concord	ON	L4K1A7	800-529-9805	905-760-6800
Nordon Inc 1 Cabot Blvd E	Langhorne	PA	19047	800-544-0400	215-504-4700
Norsask Farm Equipment Ltd					
Hwy 16 E	North Battleford	SK	S9A2X6	888-446-8128	306-445-8128
Ossur					
27412 Aliso Viejo Pkwy	Aliso Viejo	CA	92656	800-233-6263	
Peerless Inc 79 Perry St	Buffalo	NY	14203	800-234-3033	716-852-4784
Pubco Corp					
3830 Kelley Ave	Cleveland	OH	44114	800-878-3399	216-881-5300
Puregas LLC					
226 Commerce St	Broomfield	CO	80020	800-521-5351	303-427-3700
Rapid Line Industries Inc					
455 N Ottawa St	Joliet	IL	60432	877-444-9955	815-727-4362
Regal Beloit Canada					
320 Superior Blvd	Mississauga	ON	L5T2N7	800-563-0949	905-670-4770
Rimex Supply Ltd					
9726 186th St	Surrey	BC	V4N3N7	800-663-9883	604-888-0025
Royal Consumer Information Products Inc					
1160 US 22	Bridgewater	NJ	08807	888-261-4555*	908-864-4851
*Sales					
Security Engineered Machinery Company Inc					
5 Walkup Dr PO Box 1045	Westborough	MA	01581	800-225-9293*	508-366-1488
*Sales					
Sharp Electronics Corp					
1 Sharp Plz	Mahwah	NJ	07430	800-237-4277	201-529-8200
Skyjack Inc 55 Campbell Rd	Guelph	ON	N1H1B9	800-265-2738	
Staplex Co 777 Fifth Ave	Brooklyn	NY	11232	800-221-0822*	718-768-3333
*Cust Svc					
Sturtevant Inc					
348 Circuit St	Hanover	MA	02339	800-992-0209	781-829-6501
Swintec Corp					
320 W Commercial Ave	Moonachie	NJ	07074	800-225-0867	201-935-0115
Tundra Process Solutions Ltd					
7523 Flint Rd SE	Calgary	AB	T2H1G3	800-265-1166	403-255-5222
Westward Parts Services Ltd					
6517 - 67 St	Red Deer	AB	T4P1A3	888-937-7278	403-347-2200
Wolseley Canada Inc					
880 Laurentian Dr	Burlington	ON	L7N3V6	800-282-1376	905-335-7373
Wright Implement Company LLC					
3225 Carter Rd	Owensboro	KY	42301	800-252-3904	270-683-3606

112　　BUSINESS MACHINES - WHOL

SEE ALSO Business Machines - Mfr ; Photocopying Equipment & Supplies ; Computer Equipment & Software - Whol

				Toll-Free	Phone
Adams Remco Inc					
2612 Foundation Dr	South Bend	IN	46628	800-627-2113	574-288-2113
Arkansas Power Steering & Hydraulics Inc					
900 Fiber Optic Dr	North Little Rock	AR	72117	800-734-9411	501-372-4828
Black Equipment Co Inc					
1187 Burch Dr	Evansville	IN	47725	866-414-7062	812-477-6481
Brahma Compression Ltd					
8825 Shepard Rd SE	Calgary	AB	T2C4N9	800-230-6056	403-287-6990
Canon Business Solutions-Central					
425 N Martingale Rd Ste 100	Schaumburg	IL	60173	844-443-4636	847-706-3400
Carr Business Systems					
130 Spagnoli Rd	Melville	NY	11747	800-720-2277	631-249-9880
Copiers Northwest Inc					
601 Dexter Ave N	Seattle	WA	98109	866-692-0700	206-282-1200
CRS Inc					
4851 White Bear Pkwy	Saint Paul	MN	55110	800-333-4949	651-294-2700

				Toll-Free	Phone
Daisy IT Supplies Sales & Service					
8575 Red Oak Ave	Rancho Cucamonga	CA	91730	800-266-5585	909-989-5585
Dieterich-Post Co					
616 Monterey Pass Rd	Monterey Park	CA	91754	800-955-3729	
Don-Nan					
3427 E Garden City Hwy 158	Midland	TX	79706	800-348-7742	
El Dorado Trading Group Inc					
760 San Antonio Rd	Palo Alto	CA	94303	800-227-8292	
FP Mailing Solutions					
140 N Mitchell Ct	Addison	IL	60101	800-341-6052	
Global Imaging Systems					
3903 Northdale Blvd Ste 200W.	Tampa	FL	33624	888-628-7834	813-960-5508
Huston-Patterson Corp					
123 W N St PO Box 260	Decatur	IL	62522	800-866-5692	
Illinois Wholesale Cash Register Inc					
2790 Pinnacle Dr	Elgin	IL	60124	800-544-5493	847-310-4200
Leyman Manufacturing Corp					
10335 Wayne Ave	Cincinnati	OH	45215	866-539-6261	513-891-6210
Mead O'brien Inc					
1429 Atlantic Ave	North Kansas City	MO	64116	800-892-2769	816-471-3993
Metro - Sales Inc					
1640 E 78th St	Minneapolis	MN	55423	800-862-7414	612-861-4000
Numeridex Inc					
632 S Wheeling Rd	Wheeling	IL	60090	800-323-7737	847-541-8840
Standard Duplicating Machines Corp					
10 Connector Rd	Andover	MA	01810	800-526-4774	978-470-1920
Systel Business Equipment Company Inc					
2604 Fort Bragg Rd	Fayetteville	NC	28303	800-849-5900	910-321-7700
Transco Business Technologies (TBT)					
34 Leighton Rd	Augusta	ME	04330	800-322-0003	800-452-4657

BUSINESS ORGANIZATIONS

SEE Chambers of Commerce - US - State ; Chambers of Commerce - US - Local ; Management & Business Professional Associations ; Chambers of Commerce - International ; Chambers of Commerce - Canadian

113　　BUSINESS SERVICE CENTERS

				Toll-Free	Phone
A & d Technical Supply Company Inc					
4320 S 89th St	Omaha	NE	68127	800-228-2753	402-592-4950
Aloha Petroleum Ltd					
1132 Bishop St Ste 1700	Honolulu	HI	96813	800-621-4654	808-522-9700
Alphanumeric Systems Inc					
3801 Wake Forest Rd	Raleigh	NC	27609	800-638-6556	919-781-7575
Aminian Business Services Inc					
50 Tesla	Irvine	CA	92618	888-800-5207	949-724-1155
Annex Brands Inc					
7580 Metropolitan Dr Ste 200	San Diego	CA	92108	877-722-5236	619-563-4800
Asi System Integration Inc					
48 W 37th St	New York	NY	10018	866-308-3920	
Core Bts Inc					
5875 Castle Creek Pkwy N Dr Ste 320	Indianapolis	IN	46250	855-267-3287	
Corporation Service Co					
2711 Centerville Rd Ste 400	Wilmington	DE	19808	866-403-5272	302-636-5400
Craters & Freighters					
331 Corporate Cir Ste J	Golden	CO	80401	800-736-3335	
Dollar Bill Copying					
611 Church St	Ann Arbor	MI	48104	877-738-9200	734-665-9200
Duncan-Parnell Inc					
900 S McDowell St	Charlotte	NC	28204	800-849-7708	704-372-7766
Elbar Duplicator Corp					
10526 Jamaica Ave	Richmond Hill	NY	11418	800-540-1123	718-441-1123
Galaxie Coffee Services					
110 Sea Ln	Farmingdale	NY	11735	800-564-9104	631-694-2688
Group O Inc 4905 77th Ave	Milan	IL	61264	800-752-0730*	309-736-8300
*Cust Svc					
Hackworth Reprographics					
1700 Liberty St	Chesapeake	VA	23324	800-676-2424	757-545-7675
Java Dave's Executive Coffee Service					
6239 E 15th St	Tulsa	OK	74112	800-725-7315	918-836-5570
Juran Institute Inc					
160 Main St	Southington	CT	06489	800-338-7726	
Kabel Business Services					
1454 30th St Ste 105	West Des Moines	IA	50266	800-300-9691	515-224-9400
Kal-blue Reprographics Inc					
914 E Vine St	Kalamazoo	MI	49001	800-522-0541	
Mej Personal Business Services Inc					
245 E 116th St	New York	NY	10029	866-418-3836	212-426-6017
Navis Pack & Ship Centers					
12742 E Caley Ave Ste 2 A	Centennial	CO	80111	800-344-3528	
New Jersey Legal Copy Inc					
501 King Ave	Cherry Hill	NJ	08002	800-426-7965	856-910-0202
Office Depot Inc					
2200 Old Germantown Rd	Delray Beach	FL	33445	800-937-3600	561-438-4800
NASDAQ: ODP					
Pak Mail Centers of America Inc					
8601 W Cross Dr Ste F5.	Littleton	CO	80123	800-778-6665*	303-971-0088
*Cust Svc					
Peachtree Planning Corp					
5040 Roswell Rd NE	Atlanta	GA	30342	800-366-0839	404-260-1600
Peniel Solutions LLC					
3885 Crestwood Pkwy Ste 275	Duluth	GA	30096	866-878-2490	
Postal Connections of America					
6136 Frisco Sq Blvd Ste 400	Frisco	TX	75034	800-767-8257	
PostalAnnex+ Inc					
7580 Metropolitan Dr Ste 200	San Diego	CA	92108	800-456-1525	619-563-4800
PostNet International Franchise Corp					
1819 Wazee St	Denver	CO	80202	800-841-7171	303-771-7100
Shee Atika Inc					
315 Lincoln St Ste 300	Sitka	AK	99835	800-478-3534	907-747-3534
Sir Speedy Inc					
26722 Plaza Dr	Mission Viejo	CA	92691	800-854-8297	949-348-5000

		Toll-Free	Phone
UPS Store, The			
6060 Cornerstone Ct W ....San Diego CA 92121		800-789-4623	858-455-8800

114 BUYER'S GUIDES - ONLINE

SEE ALSO Investment Guides - Online

		Toll-Free	Phone
Ace Mart - Downtown San Antonio			
1220 S St Mary's ....San Antonio TX 78210		888-898-8079	210-224-0082
Market America Inc			
1302 Pleasant Ridge Rd ....Greensboro NC 27409		866-420-1709	336-605-0040
Parke-Bell Ltd Inc			
709 W 12th St ....Huntingburg IN 47542		800-457-7456	812-683-3707

115 CABINETS - WOOD

SEE ALSO Carpentry & Flooring Contractors ; Household Furniture

		Toll-Free	Phone
Bloch Industries			
140 Commerce Dr ....Rochester NY 14623		800-499-7871	585-334-9600
Brentwood Corp			
453 Industrial Way PO Box 265 ....Molalla OR 97038		800-331-6013	503-829-7366
Cabinetry By Karman			
6000 S Stratler St ....Salt Lake City UT 84107		800-255-3581	801-268-3581
Canyon Creek Cabinet Co			
16726 Tye St SE ....Monroe WA 98272		800-228-1830	360-348-4600
Cardell Cabinetry			
3215 N Panam Expy ....San Antonio TX 78219		888-221-3872	
Conestoga Wood Specialties Inc			
245 Reading Rd ....East Earl PA 17519		800-964-3667	
Decore-ative Specialties Inc			
2772 S Peck Rd ....Monrovia CA 91016		800-729-7277	626-254-9191
Doormark Inc			
430 Goolsby Blvd ....Deerfield Beach FL 33442		888-969-0124	954-418-4700
Grabill Cabinet Company Inc			
13844 Sawmill Dr ....Grabill IN 46741		877-472-2782	260-376-1500
Grandview Products Co			
1601 Superior Dr ....Parsons KS 67357		800-247-9105	620-421-6950
Haas Cabinet Company Inc			
625 W Utica St ....Sellersburg IN 47172		800-457-6458	812-246-4431
Halabi Inc			
2100 Huntington Dr ....Fairfield CA 94533		800-660-4167	707-402-1600
Helmut Guenschel Inc			
10 Emala Ave ....Baltimore MD 21220		800-852-2525	410-686-5900
Huntwood Industries			
23800 E Apple Way ....Liberty Lake WA 99019		800-873-7350	509-924-5858
Jim Bishop Cabinets Inc			
5640 Bell Rd ....Montgomery AL 36116		800-410-2444	
Kraftmaid Cabinetry Inc			
15535 S State Ave PO Box 1055..........Middlefield OH 44062		888-562-7744	
Masco Cabinetry LLC			
5353 W US 223 ....Adrian MI 49221		866-850-8557	517-263-0771
Mastercraft Industries Inc			
777 South St ....Newburgh NY 12550		800-835-7812	845-565-8850
Medallion Cabinetry			
2222 Camden Ct ....Oak Brook IL 60523		800-543-4074	800-476-4181
Meridian Products			
124 Earland Dr Bldg 2 ....New Holland PA 17557		888-423-2804	717-355-7700
Mouser Custom Cabinetry			
2112 N Hwy 31 W ....Elizabethtown KY 42701		800-345-7537	270-737-7477
Norcraft cabinetry			
950 Blue Gentian Rd Ste 200 ....Eagan MN 55121		866-802-7892	
Northern Contours Inc			
1355 Mendota Heights Rd Ste 100..........Mendota Heights MN 55120		866-344-8132	651-695-1698
Patrick Industries Inc			
107 W Franklin St PO Box 638 ....Elkhart IN 46515		800-331-2151	574-294-7511
NASDAQ: PATK			
Plato Woodwork Inc			
200 Third St SW ....Plato MN 55370		800-328-5924	
Precision Countertops Inc			
26200 SW 95th Ave Ste 303..........Wilsonville OR 97070		800-548-4445	503-692-6660
Rosebud Wood Products			
701 SE 12th St ....Madison SD 57042		800-256-4561	605-256-4561
Roy's Wood Products Inc			
329 Thrush Ln ....Lugoff SC 29078		800-727-1590	803-438-1590
Rynone Mfg Corp PO Box 128 ....Sayre PA 18840		800-839-1654	570-888-5272
Showplace Wood Products Inc			
1 Enterprise St ....Harrisburg SD 57032		877-512-2500	605-743-2200
Starmark Cabinetry			
600 E 48th St N ....Sioux Falls SD 57104		800-594-9444	
Ultracraft Co			
6163 Old 421 Rd ....Liberty NC 27298		800-262-4046	

116 CABLE & OTHER PAY TELEVISION SERVICES

		Toll-Free	Phone
Areacall Inc			
7803 Stratford Rd ....Bethesda MD 20814		800-205-6268	301-657-2718
Big Bend Telephone Company Inc			
808 N Fifth St ....Alpine TX 79830		800-520-0092	844-592-4781
Broadnet Teleservices LLC			
1805 Shea Ctr Dr Ste 160..........Highlands Ranch CO 80129		877-579-4929	
Cable Connection, The			
52 Heppner Dr ....Carson City NV 89706		800-851-2961	775-885-1443
Cable One Inc			
210 E Earll Dr ....Phoenix AZ 85012		877-692-2253	602-364-6000
CableAmerica Corp			
7822 E Gray Rd ....Scottsdale AZ 85260		866-871-4492	480-315-1820
Capitol Connection			
4400 University Dr MSN 1D2..........Fairfax VA 22030		844-504-7161	703-993-3100
Cass Cable Tv Inc			
100 Redbud Rd ....Virginia IL 62691		800-252-1799	217-452-7725

		Toll-Free	Phone
Charter Communications Inc			
12405 Powerscourt Dr ....Saint Louis MO 63131		888-438-2427	314-965-0555
NASDAQ: CHTR			
Comcast Cable Communications LLC			
1701 John F Kennedy Blvd ....Philadelphia PA 19103		800-624-0331	215-665-1700
Country Cablevision Inc			
9449 State Hwy 197 S ....Burnsville NC 28714		800-722-4074	828-682-4074
Cox Communications Inc			
1400 Lake Hearn Dr ....Atlanta GA 30319		866-961-0027	404-843-5000
Custom Cable Corp			
242 Butler St ....Westbury NY 11590		800-832-3600	516-334-3600
Defender Inc			
3750 Priority Way S Dr ....Indianapolis IN 46240		800-860-0303	317-810-4720
DIRECTV Inc			
2230 E Imperial Hwy ....El Segundo CA 90245		800-531-5000*	
Cust Svc			
DISH Network LLC			
9601 S Meridian Blvd ....Englewood CO 80112		800-823-4929	
NASDAQ: DISH			
Fandango Inc			
12200 W Olympic Blvd Ste 400 ....Los Angeles CA 90064		855-646-2580	
Favorite Office Automation			
2011 W State St ....New Castle PA 16101		800-466-8338	724-658-8300
Fibercomm Lc			
1605 Ninth St ....Sioux City IA 51101		800-836-2472	712-224-2020
Giant Communications Inc			
418 W Fifth St Ste C ....Holton KS 66436		800-346-9084	785-362-9331
Green Earth Cleaning			
51 W 135th St ....Kansas City MO 64145		877-926-0895	816-926-0895
Hamilton Telecommunications			
1001 12th St ....Aurora NE 68818		800-821-1831	402-694-5101
High Power Technical Services Inc (HPTS)			
2230 Ampere Dr ....Louisville KY 40299		866-398-3474	502-271-2469
Inter Mountain Cable Inc			
20 Laynesville Rd PO Box 159 ....Harold KY 41635		800-635-7052	606-478-9406
Kincardine Cable TV Ltd			
223 Bruce Ave ....Kincardine ON N2Z2P2		800-265-3064	519-396-8880
Link Electronics Inc			
2137 Rust Ave ....Cape Girardeau MO 63703		800-776-4411	573-334-4433
Live Wire Net 4577 Pecos St ....Denver CO 80211		866-913-5221	303-458-5667
Mediacom Communications Corp			
100 Crystal Run Rd ....Middletown NY 10941		800-479-2082*	845-695-2600
General			
Midcontinent Communications			
PO Box 5010 ....Sioux Falls SD 57117		800-888-1300	605-274-9810
Multicom Inc			
1076 Florida Central Pkwy ....Longwood FL 32750		800-423-2594	407-331-7779
Otter Tail Telcom			
230 W Lincoln Ave ....Fergus Falls MN 56537		800-247-2706	218-826-6161
Panora Cooperative Telephone Association Inc			
114 E Main St ....Panora IA 50216		800-205-1110	641-755-2424
Phoenix Cable Inc (PCI)			
10801 N 24th Ave Ste 115-116 ....Phoenix AZ 85029		833-807-3855	602-870-8870
Polar Communications			
110 Fourth St E PO Box 270..........Park River ND 58270		800-284-7222	701-284-7221
Real Hip-Hop Network			
1717 Pennsylvania Ave NW Ste 1020..........Washington DC 20006		888-742-9993	
RLTV			
5525 Research Park Dr ....Baltimore MD 21228		800-754-8464	
Rooftop Media Inc			
188 Spear St Ste 250 ....San Francisco CA 94105		800-860-0293	612-492-1197
Satellite Receivers Ltd/Cash Depot			
1740 Cofrin Dr Ste 2..........Green Bay WI 54302		800-776-8834	920-432-5777
See World Satellites Inc			
1321 Wayne Ave ....Indiana PA 15701		800-435-2808	724-463-3200
Service Electric Cable TV & Communications			
2260 Ave A ....Bethlehem PA 18017		800-232-9100	610-865-9100
Shaw Communications Inc			
630 Third Ave SW ....Calgary AB T2P4L4		888-472-2222	403-750-4500
TSE: SJR.B			
Southern Vermont Cable Co			
PO Box 166 ....Bondville VT 05340		800-544-5931	
Suddenlink Communications			
6151 Paluxy Dr ....Tyler TX 75703		877-694-9474	
Technical Cable Concepts Inc			
350 Lear Ave ....Costa Mesa CA 92626		800-832-2225	714-835-1081
Tel Star Cablevision Inc			
1295 Lourdes Rd ....Metamora IL 61548		888-842-0258	
TiVo Inc 2160 Gold St ....Alviso CA 95002		877-367-8486	408-519-9100
NASDAQ: TIVO			
USA Communications			
124 Main St PO Box 389 ....Shellsburg IA 52332		800-248-8007	319-436-2224
Zito Media LP			
102 S Main St PO Box 665..........Coudersport PA 16915		800-365-6988	

117 CABLE REELS

		Toll-Free	Phone
American Reeling Devices Inc			
15 Airpark Vista Blvd ....Dayton NV 89403		800-354-7335*	
Sales			
Conductix 10102 F St ....Omaha NE 68127		800-521-4888	402-339-9300
Gleason Reel Corp			
600 S Clark St ....Mayville WI 53050		888-504-5151	920-387-4120
Hannay Reels Inc			
553 State Rt 143 ....Westerlo NY 12193		877-467-3357	518-797-3791

118 CALCULATORS - ELECTRONIC

		Toll-Free	Phone
Calculated Industries Inc			
4840 Hytech Dr ....Carson City NV 89706		800-854-8075	775-885-4900
Sharp Electronics Corp			
1 Sharp Plz ....Mahwah NJ 07430		800-237-4277	201-529-8200

	Toll-Free	Phone
Texas Instruments Inc		
12500 TI Blvd ....Dallas TX 75243	800-336-5236*	972-995-2011
*NASDAQ: TXN ■ *Cust Svc*		
Victor Technology LLC		
175 E Crossroads Pkwy ....Bolingbrook IL 60440	800-628-2420	630-754-4400

119   CAMERAS & RELATED SUPPLIES - RETAIL

	Toll-Free	Phone
Adorama Camera Inc		
42 W 18th St ....New York NY 10011	800-223-2500	212-741-0052
B & H Photo-Video-Pro Audio Corp		
420 Ninth Ave ....New York NY 10001	800-947-9954	212-444-6615
Beach Camera		
203 Rt 22 E ....Green Brook NJ 08812	800-572-3224	732-968-6400
CambridgeWorld		
34 Franklin Ave ....Brooklyn NY 11205	800-221-2253	718-858-5002
Camera Corner Inc		
PO Box 1899 ....Burlington NC 27216	800-868-2462	336-228-0251
Dodd Camera		
2077 E 30th St ....Cleveland OH 44115	855-544-1705	216-361-6800
Focus Camera Inc		
905 McDonald Ave ....Brooklyn NY 11218	800-221-0828	
Kenmore Camera Inc		
6708 NE 181st St PO Box 82467 ....Kenmore WA 98028	888-485-7447	425-485-7447
Ritz Camera & Image		
2 Bergen Tpke ....Ridgefield Park NJ 07660	855-622-7489*	
*Cust Svc		
Samy's Camera Inc		
431 S Fairfax Ave ....Los Angeles CA 90036	800-321-4726	323-938-2420

120   CAMPERS, TRAVEL TRAILERS, MOTOR HOMES

	Toll-Free	Phone
A & N Trailer Parts		
6028 S 118th E Ave ....Tulsa OK 74146	800-272-1898	918-461-8404
Coach House Inc		
3480 Technology Dr ....Nokomis FL 34275	800-235-0984	941-485-0984
Cruise America		
11 W Hampton Ave ....Mesa AZ 85210	800-671-8042	480-464-7300
Custom Fiberglass Mfg Corp		
Snugtop		
1711 Harbor Ave PO Box 121.............Long Beach CA 90813	800-768-4867	562-432-5454
Davidson-Kennedy Co		
800 Industrial Park Dr ....Marietta GA 30062	800-733-3434	770-427-9467
Dutchmen Mfg Inc		
2164 Caragana Ct PO Box 2164...............Goshen IN 46527	866-425-4369	574-537-0600
Exiss Aluminum Trailers Inc		
900 E Trailer Blvd ....El Reno OK 73036	800-256-6668	877-553-9477
Foretravel Motorcoach Inc		
1221 NW Stallings Dr ....Nacogdoches TX 75964	800-955-6226	936-564-8367
Four Wheel Campers		
1460 Churchill Downs Ave ....Woodland CA 95776	800-242-1442	530-666-1442
Gulf Stream Coach Inc		
503 S Oakland Ave PO Box 1005 ....Nappanee IN 46550	800-289-8787	
Jayco Inc 903 S Main St ....Middlebury IN 46540	800-283-8267*	574-825-5861
*Cust Svc		
Monaco Coach Corp		
1031 US 224 E ....Decatur IN 46733	877-466-6226	
New Horizons RV Corp		
2401 Lacy Dr ....Junction City KS 66441	800-235-3140	785-238-7575
Newell Coach Corp		
3900 N Main St ....Miami OK 74354	888-363-9355	918-542-3344
Newmar Corp		
355 Delaware St ....Nappanee IN 46550	800-731-8300	574-773-7791
Nu-Wa Industries Inc		
3701 Johnson Rd ....Chanute KS 66720	800-835-0676	620-431-2088
Pace-Edwards		
2400 Commercial Rd ....Centralia WA 98531	800-338-3697	360-736-9991
REV GROUP Inc		
52216 State Rd 15 ....Bristol IN 46507	888-522-1126	574-848-1126
Skyline Corp		
2520 By-Pass Rd ....Elkhart IN 46514	800-348-7469	574-294-6521
NYSE: SKY		
Viking Recreational Vehicles LLC		
580 W Burr Oak St PO Box 549 ....Centreville MI 49032	888-422-2582	
Winnebago Industries Inc		
605 W Crystal Lake Rd PO Box 152 ....Forest City IA 50436	800-643-4892	641-585-3535
NYSE: WGO		

121   CAMPGROUND OPERATORS

	Toll-Free	Phone
CanaDream Corp		
292154 Crosspointe Dr		
Rocky View County..............................Calgary AB T4A0V2	800-461-7368	403-291-1000
Glen Eden Corp		
25999 Glen Eden Rd ....Corona CA 92883	800-843-6833	951-277-4650
Hart Ranch Camping Resort Club		
23756 Arena Dr ....Rapid City SD 57702	800-605-4278	605-399-2582
Kampgrounds of America Inc (KOA)		
PO Box 30558 ....Billings MT 59114	888-562-0000	
Leisure Systems Inc		
502 TechneCenter Dr Ste D......................Milford OH 45150	866-928-9644	513-831-2100
Red River Computer Company Inc		
21 Water St Ste 500 ....Claremont NH 03743	800-769-3060	603-448-8880
Swan Lake Resort & Campground		
17463 County Hwy 29 ....Fergus Falls MN 56537	800-697-4626	218-736-4626
Visions Services		
500 Greenwich St 3rd Fl.........................New York NY 10013	888-245-8333	212-625-1616

122   CANDLES

SEE ALSO Gift Shops

	Toll-Free	Phone
Dadant & Sons Inc		
51 S Second St ....Hamilton IL 62341	888-922-1293	217-847-3324
General Wax & Candle Co		
6863 Beck Ave PO Box 9398 ....North Hollywood CA 91605	800-929-7867	818-765-5800
Knorr Beeswax Products Inc		
14906 Via De La Valle ....Del Mar CA 92014	800-807-2337	760-431-2007
Original Cake Candle Co, The		
102 Sundale Rd ....Norwich OH 43767	888-444-2253	740-872-3248
Root Candles Co		
623 W Liberty St ....Medina OH 44256	800-289-7668	330-723-4359
Swans Candles		
16524 Tilley Rd S ....Tenino WA 98589	888-848-7926	

123   CANDY STORES

	Toll-Free	Phone
Burdette Beckmann Inc		
5851 Johnson St ....Hollywood FL 33021	888-575-7413	954-983-4360
Candy Bouquet International Inc		
510 Mclean St ....Little Rock AR 72202	877-226-3901	501-375-9990
Comarco Products Inc		
501 Jackson St ....Camden NJ 08104	800-524-2128	
Efco Products		
136 Smith St ....Poughkeepsie NY 12601	800-284-3326	
Gardners Candies Inc		
2600 Adams Ave PO Box E.......................Tyrone PA 16686	800-242-2639	814-684-3925
Gertrude Hawk Chocolates Inc		
9 Keystone Pk ....Dunmore PA 18512	866-932-4295	800-822-2032
Good Earth Teasinc		
831 Almar Ave ....Santa Cruz CA 95060	888-625-8227	
Gorant Candies		
8301 Market St ....Youngstown OH 44512	800-572-4139	330-726-8821
Kilwins Quality Confections Inc (KQC)		
1050 Bay View Rd ....Petoskey MI 49770	888-454-5946	
Lammes Candies Since 1885 Inc		
PO Box 1885 ....Austin TX 78767	800-252-1885	512-310-2223
Rocky Mountain Chocolate Factory Inc (RMCF)		
265 Turner Dr ....Durango CO 81303	888-525-2462*	970-247-4943
*NASDAQ: RMCF ■ *Cust Svc*		
See's Candies Inc		
210 El Camino Real ....South San Francisco CA 94080	800-877-7337*	650-761-2490
*Cust Svc		
Tofurky PO Box 176 ....Hood River OR 97031	800-508-8100	
Vermont Maple Sugar Co		
37 Industrial Park Dr ....Morrisville VT 05661	800-828-2376	

124   CANS - METAL

SEE ALSO Containers - Metal (Barrels, Drums, Kegs)

	Toll-Free	Phone
BWAY Corp		
8607 Roberts Dr Ste 250 ....Atlanta GA 30350	800-527-2267	770-645-4800
Crown Holdings Inc		
1 Crown Way ....Philadelphia PA 19154	800-523-3644	215-698-5100
NYSE: CCK		
G3 Enterprises Inc		
502 E Whitmore Ave ....Modesto CA 95358	800-321-8747	
JL Clark Mfg Co		
923 23rd Ave ....Rockford IL 61104	877-482-5275	815-962-8861
JL Clark Mfg Co Lancaster Div		
303 N Plum St ....Lancaster PA 17602	877-482-5275	717-392-4125
KOR Water Inc		
95 Enterprise Ste 310 ....Aliso Viejo CA 92656	877-708-7567	714-708-7567
Protectoseal Co		
225 W Foster Ave ....Bensenville IL 60106	800-323-2268	630-595-0800
Silgan Holdings Inc		
4 Landmark Sq Ste 400 ....Stamford CT 06901	800-732-0330	203-975-7110
NASDAQ: SLGN		

125   CANS, TUBES, DRUMS - PAPER (FIBER)

	Toll-Free	Phone
Acme Spirally Wound Paper Products Inc		
4810 W 139th St PO Box 35320................Cleveland OH 44135	800-274-2797	216-267-2950
Caraustar Industries Inc		
5000 Austell-Powder Springs Rd		
Ste 300 ....Austell GA 30106	800-858-1438	770-948-3100
Greif Inc 425 Winter Rd ....Delaware OH 43015	877-781-9797	
NYSE: GEF		
Industrial Paper Tube Inc		
1335 E Bay Ave ....Bronx NY 10474	800-345-0960	
LCH Paper Tube & Core Co		
11930 Larc Industrial Blvd ....Burnsville MN 55337	800-472-3477	952-358-3587
OX Paper Tube & Core Inc		
331 Maple Ave ....Hanover PA 17331	800-414-2476	
Pacific Paper Tube Inc		
1025 98th Ave ....Oakland CA 94603	888-377-8823	510-562-8823
Yazoo Mills Inc		
PO Box 369 ....New Oxford PA 17350	800-242-5216*	717-624-8993
*Cust Svc		

126   CAR RENTAL AGENCIES

SEE ALSO Fleet Leasing & Management ; Truck Rental & Leasing

	Toll-Free	Phone
A Betterway Rent-a-car Inc		
1092 Roswell Rd ....Marietta GA 30067	800-527-0700	770-240-3305

Classified Section

			Toll-Free	Phone
ACE Rent A Car				
8639 W Washington St	Indianapolis IN	46241	**877-822-3872**	317-399-5247
Advantage Rent-A-Car				
1030 W Manchester Blvd	Inglewood CA	94010	**800-777-5500**	
Affiliated Car Rental				
105 Hwy 36	Eatontown NJ	07724	**800-367-5159**	
Auto Europe				
39 Commercial St	Portland ME	04101	**800-223-5555**	207-842-2000
Avis Rent A Car System Inc				
6 Sylvan Way	Parsippany NJ	07054	**800-331-1212**	973-496-3500
Budget Rent A Car System Inc				
6 Sylvan Way	Parsippany NJ	07054	**800-527-0700**	800-283-4382
Discount Car & Truck Rentals Ltd				
720 Arrow Rd	North York ON	M9M2M1	**866-742-5968**	416-744-7942
Dollar Rent A Car Inc				
5330 E 31st St	Tulsa OK	74135	**800-800-4000**	918-669-3000
Enterprise Rent-A-Car				
600 Corporate Pk Dr	Saint Louis MO	63105	**800-307-6666**	314-512-5000
Foss National Leasing				
125 Commerce Valley Dr W Ste 801	Markham ON	L3T7W4	**800-461-3677**	905-886-4244
Hale Trailer Brake & Wheel Inc				
76 Cooper Rd PO Box 1400	Voorhees NJ	08043	**800-232-6535**	856-768-1330
Hertz Global Holdings Inc				
225 Brae Blvd	Park Ridge NJ	07656	**800-654-3131**	201-307-2000
NYSE: HTZ				
Kemwel 39 Commercial St	Portland ME	04102	**800-678-0678**	207-842-2285
P V Rentals Ltd				
5810 S Rice Ave	Houston TX	77081	**800-275-7878**	713-667-0665
Steve Foley Cadillac				
100 Skokie Blvd	Northbrook IL	60062	**877-223-9671***	866-664-4037
*Sales				
Truck Center Companies				
10550 I St PO Box 27379	Omaha NE	68127	**800-777-2440**	
U-Save Auto Rental of America Inc				
1052 Highland Colony Pkwy Ste 204	Ridgeland MS	39157	**800-438-2300***	601-713-4333
*General				

127   CARBON & GRAPHITE PRODUCTS

			Toll-Free	Phone
Advance Carbon Products Inc				
2036 National Ave	Hayward CA	94545	**800-283-1249**	510-293-5930
Helwig Carbon Products Inc				
8900 W Tower Ave	Milwaukee WI	53224	**800-365-3113**	414-354-2411
Mersen USA BN Corp				
400 Myrtle Ave	Boonton NJ	07005	**800-526-0877***	
*General				
National Electrical Carbon				
251 Forrester Dr	Greenville SC	29607	**800-471-7842**	864-284-9728
Saturn Industries Inc				
157 Union Tpke	Hudson NY	12534	**800-775-1651**	518-828-9956
Superior Graphite				
10 S Riverside Plz Ste 1470	Chicago IL	60606	**800-325-0337***	312-559-2999
*Cust Svc				

128   CARBURETORS, PISTONS, PISTON RINGS, VALVES

SEE ALSO Automotive Parts & Supplies - Mfr ; Aircraft Engines & Engine Parts

			Toll-Free	Phone
Compressor Products International				
4410 Greenbriar Dr	Stafford TX	77477	**800-675-6646**	281-207-4600
Grover Corp				
2759 S 28th St	Milwaukee WI	53234	**800-776-3602**	414-716-5900
Hastings Manufacturing Co				
325 N Hanover St	Hastings MI	49058	**800-776-1088**	269-945-2491
IMPCO Technologies				
5757 Farinon Dr	San Antonio TX	78240	**800-325-4534**	210-495-9772
MAHLE Industries Inc				
2020 Sanford St	Muskegon MI	49444	**888-255-1942**	231-722-1300
Martin Wells Industries				
5886 Compton Ave PO Box 01406	Los Angeles CA	90001	**800-421-6000**	323-581-6266
Safety Seal Piston Ring Co				
4000 Airport Rd	Marshall TX	75672	**800-962-3631***	903-938-9241
*Sales				
Total Seal Inc				
22642 N 15th Ave	Phoenix AZ	85027	**800-874-2753**	623-587-7400
United Engine & Machine Company Inc				
1040 Corbett St	Carson City NV	89706	**800-648-7970**	775-882-7790
Wiseco Piston Inc				
7201 Industrial Pk Blvd	Mentor OH	44060	**800-321-1364**	440-951-6600

129   CARD SHOPS

SEE ALSO Gift Shops

			Toll-Free	Phone
Ad-venture Promotions LLC				
2625 Regency Rd	Lexington KY	40503	**800-218-5488**	859-263-4299
Design It Yourself Gift Baskets LLC				
7999 Hansen Rd Ste 204	Houston TX	77061	**800-589-7553**	713-944-3440
Future of Flight Foundation				
8415 Paine Field Blvd	Mukilteo WA	98275	**888-467-4777**	425-438-8100
Recycled Paper Greetings Inc				
111 N Canal St Ste 700	Chicago IL	60606	**800-777-3331**	

130   CARDS - GREETING - MFR

			Toll-Free	Phone
Amber Lotus Publishing				
PO Box 11329	Portland OR	97211	**800-326-2375**	503-284-6400
American Greetings Corp				
1 American Rd	Cleveland OH	44144	**800-777-4891***	216-252-7300
NYSE: AM ■ *Sales*				

			Toll-Free	Phone
AtticSalt Greetings Inc				
PO Box 5773	Topeka KS	66605	**888-345-6005**	
Avanti Press Inc				
155 W Congress St Ste 200	Detroit MI	48226	**800-228-2684**	313-961-0022
Bayview Press				
30 Knox St PO Box 153	Thomaston ME	04861	**800-903-2346**	207-354-9919
Blue Mountain Arts Inc				
PO Box 4549	Boulder CO	80306	**800-545-8573***	303-449-0536
*Sales				
Bonair Daydreams				
PO Box 1522	Wrightsville Beach NC	28480	**888-226-6247**	910-617-3887
DaySpring Cards Inc				
21154 Hwy 16 E	Siloam Springs AR	72761	**800-944-8000**	877-751-4347
Design Design Inc				
19 La Grave SE	Grand Rapids MI	49503	**800-334-3348**	866-935-2648
Fantus Paper Products PS. Greetings Inc				
5730 N Tripp Ave	Chicago IL	60646	**800-621-8823***	800-334-2141
*Sales				
Galison Publishing LLC				
28 W 44th St Ste 1411	New York NY	10036	**800-670-7441**	212-354-8840
Gallant Greetings Corp				
4300 United Pkwy	Schiller Park IL	60176	**800-621-4279**	847-671-6500
Gina B Designs Inc				
12700 Industrial Pk Blvd Ste 40	Plymouth MN	55441	**800-228-4856**	763-559-7595
Graphique De France				
9 State St	Woburn MA	01801	**800-444-1464***	
*Sales				
Great Arrow Graphics				
2495 Main St Ste 457	Buffalo NY	14214	**800-835-0490**	716-836-0408
Laughing Elephant				
3645 Interlake Ave N	Seattle WA	98103	**800-354-0400**	800-509-4166
Leanin' Tree Inc				
6055 Longbow Dr	Boulder CO	80301	**800-525-0656**	
Museum Facsimiles				
117 Fourth St	Pittsfield MA	01201	**877-499-0020**	413-499-0020
NobleWorks Inc				
500 Paterson Plank Rd	Union City NJ	07087	**800-346-6253**	201-420-0095
Northern Exposure Greeting Cards				
2194 Northpoint Pkwy	Santa Rosa CA	95407	**800-237-3524**	
Persimmon Press Inc				
PO Box 297	Belmont CA	94002	**800-910-5080**	650-802-8325
Posty Cards				
1600 Olive St	Kansas City MO	64127	**800-821-7968**	816-231-2323
Potluck Press				
920 S Bayview St	Seattle WA	98134	**877-818-5500**	206-328-1300
Recycled Paper Greetings Inc				
111 N Canal St Ste 700	Chicago IL	60606	**800-777-3331**	
StellArt 2012 Waltzer Rd	Santa Rosa CA	95403	**866-621-1987**	707-569-1378
Sunshine Business Class				
150 Kingswood Dr	Mankato MN	56001	**800-873-7681**	
Up With Paper 6049 Hi-Tek Ct	Mason OH	45040	**800-852-7677**	513-759-7473
Victorian Trading Co				
15600 W 99th St	Lenexa KS	66219	**800-700-2035***	913-438-3995
*Cust Svc				
Willow Creek Press Inc				
9931 Hwy 70 W PO Box 147	Minocqua WI	54548	**800-850-9453***	
*Cust Svc				

131   CARPETS & RUGS

SEE ALSO Tile - Ceramic (Wall & Floor) ; Flooring - Resilient
The companies listed here include carpet finishers and makers of mats and padding.

			Toll-Free	Phone
Artisans Inc PO Box 1059	Calhoun GA	30703	**800-311-8756**	
Atlas Carpet Mills Inc				
2200 Saybrook Ave	Los Angeles CA	90040	**800-272-8527**	323-724-9000
Barrett Carpet Mills Inc				
2216 Abutment Rd	Dalton GA	30721	**800-241-4064**	
Bentley Prince Street				
14641 E Don Julian Rd	City of Industry CA	91746	**800-423-4709**	
Blair Rubber Co				
5020 Panther Pkwy	Seville OH	44273	**800-321-5583**	
Bloomsburg Carpet Industries Inc				
4999 Columbia Blvd	Bloomsburg PA	17815	**800-233-8773**	570-784-9188
Brumlow Mills Inc				
734 S River St PO Box 1779	Calhoun GA	30701	**855-427-8656**	
Capel Inc 831 N Main St	Troy NC	27371	**800-334-3711**	
Dixie Group Inc				
475 Reed Rd PO Box 2007	Dalton GA	30722	**800-289-4811**	423-510-7000
NASDAQ: DXYN				
Dorsett Industries Inc				
1304 May St PO Box 805	Dalton GA	30721	**800-241-4035**	706-278-1961
Flex Foam 617 N 21st Ave	Phoenix AZ	85009	**800-266-3626**	602-252-5819
Forbo Flooring North America				
8 Maplewood Dr Humboldt Industrial Pk				
	Hazleton PA	18202	**800-842-7839**	
Fortune Contract Inc				
272 Kraft Dr	Dalton GA	30721	**800-359-4508**	
Garland Sales Inc				
PO Box 1870	Dalton GA	30720	**800-524-0361**	706-278-7880
Gilford Johnson Flooring				
1874 Defoor Ave NW	Atlanta GA	30325	**877-722-5545**	
Home Dynamix				
100 Porete Ave	North Arlington NJ	07031	**800-726-9290**	
Indian Summer Carpet Mills Inc				
601 Callahan Rd PO Box 3577	Dalton GA	30719	**800-824-4010**	706-277-6277
J & J Industries Inc				
818 J & J Dr PO Box 1287	Dalton GA	30721	**800-241-4586**	706-529-2100
Jaipur Living Inc				
1800 Cherokee pkwy	Acworth GA	30102	**888-676-7330**	404-351-2360
Johnsonite Inc				
16910 Munn Rd	Chagrin Falls OH	44023	**800-899-8916**	440-543-8916
KAS Inc 62 Veronica Ave	Somerset NJ	08873	**800-967-4254**	
Langhorne Carpet Co Inc				
201 W Lincoln Hwy PO Box 7175	Penndel PA	19047	**800-372-6274**	215-757-5155
Masland Carpets Inc				
716 Bill Myles Dr	Saraland AL	36571	**800-633-0468**	

				Toll-Free	Phone
Milliken & Co's Live Oak Plant					
300 Industrial Dr	La Grange	GA	30240	**800-241-8666**	
Mohawk Industries Inc					
160 S Industrial Blvd	Calhoun	GA	30703	**800-241-4494**	706-629-7721
NYSE: MHK					
Mohawk Industries Inc Lees Carpets Div					
160 S Industrial Blvd	Calhoun	GA	30701	**800-241-4494**	706-629-7721
Packerland Rent-a-mat Inc					
12580 W Rohr Ave	Butler	WI	53007	**800-472-9339**	262-781-5321
Quality Mat Co					
6550 Tram Rd	Beaumont	TX	77713	**800-227-8159**	409-722-4594
Scottdel Inc 400 Church St	Swanton	OH	43558	**800-446-2341**	419-825-2341
Shaw Industries Inc					
616 E Walnut Ave	Dalton	GA	30722	**800-441-7429**	
Syntec LLC 438 Lavender Dr	Rome	GA	30165	**800-526-8428**	
Tandus Centiva					
311 Smith Industrial Blvd PO Box 1147	Dalton	GA	30722	**800-248-2878**	706-259-9711
Tri State Wholesale Flooring Inc					
3900 W 34th St N	Sioux Falls	SD	57107	**800-353-3080**	605-336-3080
Unique Carpets Ltd					
7360 Jurupa Ave	Riverside	CA	92504	**800-547-8266**	951-352-8125

132   CASINO COMPANIES

SEE ALSO Games & Gaming

				Toll-Free	Phone
Boomtown Inc 2100 Garson Rd	Verdi	NV	89439	**800-648-3790**	775-345-6000
Century Casinos Inc					
2860 S Cir Dr Ste 350	Colorado Springs	CO	80906	**888-966-2257**	719-527-8300
NASDAQ: CNTY					
Colony Palms Hotel					
572 N Indian Canyon Dr	Palm Springs	CA	92262	**800-557-2187**	760-969-1800
Fond du Lac Band of Lake Superior Chippewa					
1720 Big Lake Rd	Cloquet	MN	55720	**888-888-6007**	218-879-4593
Four Winds Casino Resort					
11111 Wilson Rd	New Buffalo	MI	49117	**866-494-6371**	
Hotel Fusion					
140 Ellis St	San Francisco	CA	94102	**866-753-4244**	415-568-2525
Mille Lacs Band of Ojibwe					
43408 Oodena Dr	Onamia	MN	56359	**800-709-6445**	320-532-4181
Mountain High Resort					
24510 State Hwy 2	Wrightwood	CA	92397	**888-754-7878**	
Palace Casino 158 Howard Ave	Biloxi	MS	39530	**800-725-2239**	228-386-2315
Pinnacle Entertainment Inc					
3980 Howard Hughes Pkwy	Las Vegas	NV	89169	**877-764-8750**	702-541-7777
NYSE: PNK					
Proximity Hotel					
704 Green Valley Rd	Greensboro	NC	27408	**800-379-8200**	336-379-8200
Red Lake Gaming Enterprises Inc					
PO Box 543	Red Lake	MN	56671	**888-679-2501**	218-679-2111
Shoalwater Bay Casino					
4112 State Hwy 105	Tokeland	WA	98590	**866-992-3675**	360-267-2048
Silver Reef Casino					
4876 Haxton Way	Ferndale	WA	98248	**866-383-0777**	360-383-0777
Station Casinos Inc					
1505 S Pavilion Ctr Dr	Las Vegas	NV	89135	**800-634-3101***	702-495-3000
*Resv					
Verdanza Hotel					
8020 Calle Tartak	Carolina	PR	00979	**800-625-0312**	787-253-9000

133   CASINOS

SEE ALSO Games & Gaming
Listings for casinos are alphabetized by states.

				Toll-Free	Phone
Birmingham Race Course					
1000 John Rogers Dr	Birmingham	AL	35210	**800-998-8238**	205-838-7500
Deerfoot Inn & Casino					
1000 11500 35th St SE	Calgary	AB	T2Z3W4	**877-236-5225**	403-236-7529
Apache Greyhound Park					
3801 E Washington	Phoenix	AZ	85034	**800-772-0852**	480-982-2371
Casino Arizona at Salt River					
524 N 92nd St	Scottsdale	AZ	85256	**866-877-9897***	480-850-7777
*General					
Fort McDowell Casino					
10424 N Ft McDowell Rd	Fort Mcdowell	AZ	85264	**800-843-3678**	
River Rock Casino Resort					
8811 River Rd	Richmond	BC	V6X3P8	**866-748-3718**	604-247-8900
Barona Resort & Casino					
1932 Wildcat Canyon Rd	Lakeside	CA	92040	**888-722-7662**	619-443-2300
Eagle Mountain Casino					
681 S Reservation Rd PO Box 1659	Porterville	CA	93257	**800-903-3353**	
Fantasy Springs Resort Casino					
84-245 Indio Springs Pkwy	Indio	CA	92203	**800-827-2946***	760-342-5000
*Cust Svc					
Golden West Casino					
1001 S Union Ave	Bakersfield	CA	93307	**800-426-2537**	661-324-6936
Pala Casino Resort & Spa					
11154 Hwy 76	Pala	CA	92059	**877-946-7252**	760-510-5100
Pechanga Resort & Casino					
45000 Pechanga Pkwy	Temecula	CA	92592	**877-711-2946**	951-693-1819
San Manuel Indian Bingo & Casino					
777 San Manuel Blvd	Highland	CA	92346	**800-359-2464**	
Spa Resort Casino					
401 E Amado Rd	Palm Springs	CA	92262	**888-999-1995**	
Sycuan Casino & Resort					
5469 Casino Way	El Cajon	CA	92019	**800-279-2826***	619-445-6002
*General					
Table Mountain Casino					
8184 Table Mountain Rd	Friant	CA	93626	**800-541-3637**	559-822-7777
Thunder Valley Casino					
1200 Athens Ave	Lincoln	CA	95648	**877-468-8777**	916-408-7777
Viejas Casino					
5000 Willows Rd	Alpine	CA	91901	**800-847-6537**	619-445-5400

				Toll-Free	Phone
Bronco Billy's Casino					
233 E Bennett Ave	Cripple Creek	CO	80813	**877-989-2142**	719-689-2142
Dostal Alley Casino					
1 Dostal Alley	Central City	CO	80427	**888-949-2757**	303-582-1610
Double Eagle Hotel & Casino					
442 E Bennett Ave	Cripple Creek	CO	80813	**800-711-7234**	719-689-5000
Gilpin Casino, The					
111 Main St PO Box 50	Black Hawk	CO	80422	**800-522-4700**	
Lodge Casino					
240 Main St PO Box 50	Black Hawk	CO	80422	**800-522-4700**	
Midnight Rose Hotel & Casino					
256 E Bennett Ave	Cripple Creek	CO	80813	**800-635-5825**	
Reserve Casino Hotel					
321 Gregory St	Central City	CO	80427	**800-924-6646**	303-582-0800
Sky Ute Casino					
14324 US Hwy 172 N	Ignacio	CO	81137	**888-842-4180**	970-563-7777
Ute Mountain Casino					
3 Weeminuche Dr	Towaoc	CO	81334	**800-258-8007**	970-565-8800
Mohegan Sun Resort & Casino					
1 Mohegan Sun Blvd	Uncasville	CT	06382	**888-226-7711**	860-862-8150
Winners Sports Haven					
600 Long Wharf Dr	New Haven	CT	06511	**800-468-2260**	
Seminole Casino Immokalee					
506 S First St	Immokalee	FL	34142	**800-218-0007**	
Seminole Hard Rock Hotel & Casino Tampa (SHRH & C)					
5223 N Orient Rd	Tampa	FL	33610	**866-388-4263***	813-627-7625
*General					
Argosy Casino Alton					
1 Piasa St	Alton	IL	62002	**800-711-4263**	
Casino Queen					
200 S Front St	East Saint Louis	IL	62201	**800-777-0777**	618-874-5000
Hollywood Casino Joliet					
777 Hollywood Blvd	Joliet	IL	60436	**800-426-2537**	
Belterra Casino Resort					
777 Belterra Dr	Florence	IN	47020	**888-235-8377**	812-427-7777
Blue Chip Casino Inc					
777 Blue Chip Dr	Michigan City	IN	46360	**888-879-7711**	219-879-7711
Casino Aztar					
421 NW Riverside Dr	Evansville	IN	47708	**800-342-5386**	812-433-4000
Majestic Star Casino & Hotel					
1 Buffington Harbor Dr	Gary	IN	46406	**888-225-8259**	
Rising Star Casino Resort					
777 Rising Star Dr	Rising Sun	IN	47040	**800-472-6311**	812-438-1234
Ameristar Casino Hotel Council Bluffs					
2200 River Rd	Council Bluffs	IA	51501	**866-667-3386**	712-328-8888
Harrah's Council Bluffs					
1 Harrahs Blvd	Council Bluffs	IA	51501	**800-342-7724**	712-329-6000
Horseshoe Council Bluffs					
2701 23rd Ave	Council Bluffs	IA	51501	**800-895-0711**	712-323-2500
Meskwaki Bingo Hotel Casino					
1504 305th St	Tama	IA	52339	**800-728-4263**	
Prairie Meadows					
1 Prairie Meadows Dr	Altoona	IA	50009	**800-325-9015**	515-967-1000
Rhythm City Casino					
7077 Elmore Ave	Davenport	IA	52807	**844-852-4386**	563-328-8000
Prairie Band Casino & Resort					
12305 150th Rd	Mayetta	KS	66509	**888-727-4946**	785-966-7777
Sac & Fox Casino Inc					
1322 US Hwy 75	Powhattan	KS	66527	**800-990-2946**	
Belle of Baton Rouge Casino					
103 France St	Baton Rouge	LA	70802	**800-676-4847**	
Coushatta Casino Resort					
777 Coushatta Dr PO Box 1510	Kinder	LA	70648	**800-584-7263**	
DiamondJacks Casino Resort					
711 Diamond Jacks Blvd	Bossier City	LA	71111	**866-552-9629**	318-678-7777
Eldorado Resort Casino Shreveport					
451 Clyde Fant Pkwy	Shreveport	LA	71101	**877-602-0711**	318-220-0711
Harrah's New Orleans					
228 Poydras St	New Orleans	LA	70130	**800-427-7247**	
Hollywood Casino Baton Rouge					
1717 River Rd N	Baton Rouge	LA	70802	**800-447-6843**	225-709-7777
Isle of Capri Casino Hotel Lake Charles					
100 West Lake Ave	Westlake	LA	70669	**800-843-4753**	
Paragon Casino Resort					
711 Paragon Pl	Marksville	LA	71351	**800-946-1946**	
Treasure Chest Casino					
5050 Williams Blvd	Kenner	LA	70065	**800-298-0711**	504-443-8000
Pimlico Race Course					
5201 Park Heights Ave	Baltimore	MD	21215	**800-638-1859**	410-542-9400
MGM Grand Detroit					
1777 Third St	Detroit	MI	48226	**877-888-2121**	313-465-1400
MotorCity Casino Hotel					
2901 Grand River Ave	Detroit	MI	48201	**866-752-9622**	866-782-9622
Soaring Eagle Casino & Resort					
6800 E Soaring Eagle Blvd	Mount Pleasant	MI	48858	**888-732-4537**	989-775-5777
Black Bear Casino Resort					
1785 Hwy 210 PO Box 777	Carlton	MN	55718	**888-771-0777**	218-878-2327
Grand Casino Hinckley					
777 Lady Luck Dr	Hinckley	MN	55037	**800-472-6321**	
Grand Casino Mille Lacs					
777 Grand Ave PO Box 343	Onamia	MN	56359	**800-626-5825**	
Jackpot Junction Casino Hotel					
39375 County Hwy 24 PO Box 420	Morton	MN	56270	**800-946-2274**	
Mystic Lake Casino Hotel					
2400 Mystic Lake Blvd	Prior Lake	MN	55372	**800-262-7799**	866-832-6402
Ameristar Casino Hotel Vicksburg					
4116 Washington St	Vicksburg	MS	39180	**800-700-7770**	601-638-1000
Boomtown Casino Biloxi					
676 Bayview Ave	Biloxi	MS	39530	**800-627-0777**	228-435-7000
Fitzgeralds Casino & Hotel Tunica					
711 Lucky Ln	Robinsonville	MS	38664	**888-766-5825**	662-363-5825
Gold Strike Casino Resort					
1010 Casino Ctr Dr	Tunica Resorts	MS	38664	**888-245-7829***	662-357-1111
*Resv					
Golden Nugget Hotels & Casinos					
151 Beach Blvd	Biloxi	MS	39530	**800-777-7568**	228-435-5400
Hard Rock Hotel & Casino Biloxi					
777 Beach Blvd	Biloxi	MS	39530	**877-877-6256**	228-374-7625

				Toll-Free	Phone
Hollywood Casino Bay Saint Louis 711 Hollywood Blvd	Bay Saint Louis	MS	39520	**866-758-2591**	
IP Casino Resort & Spa 850 Bayview Ave *Resv	Biloxi	MS	39530	**888-946-2847***	228-436-3000
Island View Casino Resort PO Box 1600 *General	Gulfport	MS	39502	**877-774-8439***	228-314-2100
Aquarius Casino Resort 1900 S Casino Dr	Laughlin	NV	89029	**888-662-5825**	702-298-5111
Arizona Charlie's Boulder Casino & Hotel 4575 Boulder Hwy	Las Vegas	NV	89121	**888-236-9066**	702-951-5800
Atlantis Casino Resort 3800 S Virginia St	Reno	NV	89502	**800-723-6500**	775-825-4700
Binion's Gambling Hall & Hotel 128 E Fremont St	Las Vegas	NV	89101	**800-937-6537**	702-382-1600
Boulder Station Hotel & Casino 4111 Boulder Hwy	Las Vegas	NV	89121	**800-683-7777**	702-432-7777
Buffalo Bill's Resort & Casino 31900 Las Vegas Blvd S	Primm	NV	89019	**888-774-6668**	702-386-7867
California Hotel & Casino 12 E Ogden Ave	Las Vegas	NV	89101	**800-634-6505**	702-385-1222
Carson City Nugget 507 N Carson St	Carson City	NV	89701	**800-426-5239**	775-882-1626
Casino Royale Hotel 3411 Las Vegas Blvd S	Las Vegas	NV	89109	**800-854-7666**	702-737-3500
Circus Circus Hotel & Casino Reno 500 N Sierra St	Reno	NV	89503	**800-648-5010**	775-329-0711
Circus Circus Hotel Casino & Theme Park Las Vegas 2880 Las Vegas Blvd S *Resv	Las Vegas	NV	89109	**800-634-3450***	702-734-0410
Colorado Belle Hotel & Casino 2100 S Casino Dr *Resv	Laughlin	NV	89029	**877-460-0777***	702-298-4000
Don Laughlin's Riverside Resort & Casino 1650 Casino Dr	Laughlin	NV	89029	**800-227-3849**	702-298-2535
Edgewater Hotel & Casino 2020 S Casino Dr *Resv	Laughlin	NV	89029	**866-352-3553***	702-298-2453
El Cortez Hotel & Casino 600 E Fremont St	Las Vegas	NV	89101	**800-634-6703**	702-385-5200
Eldorado Hotel Casino 345 N Virginia St *Resv	Reno	NV	89501	**800-879-8879***	775-786-5700
Excalibur Hotel & Casino 3850 S Las Vegas Blvd	Las Vegas	NV	89109	**877-750-5464**	702-597-7777
Fiesta Rancho Casino Hotel 2400 N Rancho Dr *Resv	Las Vegas	NV	89130	**800-731-7333***	702-631-7000
Fremont Hotel & Casino 200 Fremont St	Las Vegas	NV	89101	**800-634-6460**	702-385-3232
Gold Coast Hotel & Casino 4000 W Flamingo Rd	Las Vegas	NV	89103	**800-331-5334**	702-367-7111
Gold Dust West Carson City 2171 E William St	Carson City	NV	89701	**877-519-5567**	775-885-9000
Gold Strike Hotel & Gambling Hall 1 Main St	Jean	NV	89019	**800-634-1359**	702-477-5000
Golden Nugget Laughlin 2300 S Casino Dr	Laughlin	NV	89029	**800-950-7700**	702-298-7111
Grand Sierra Resort & Casino 2500 E Second St	Reno	NV	89595	**800-501-2651**	775-789-2000
Green Valley Ranch Resort Casino & Spa 2300 Paseo Verde Pkwy *Resv	Henderson	NV	89052	**866-782-9487***	702-617-7777
Hooters Casino Hotel 115 E Tropicana Ave	Las Vegas	NV	89109	**866-584-6687**	702-739-9000
Luxor Hotel & Casino 3900 Las Vegas Blvd S *Resv	Las Vegas	NV	89119	**800-288-1000***	702-262-4000
Mandalay Bay Resort & Casino 3950 Las Vegas Blvd S	Las Vegas	NV	89119	**877-632-7800**	702-632-7777
MGM Grand Hotel & Casino 3799 Las Vegas Blvd S	Las Vegas	NV	89109	**877-880-0880**	702-891-1111
New York New York Hotel & Casino 3790 Las Vegas Blvd S	Las Vegas	NV	89109	**800-689-1797**	702-740-6969
Orleans Las Vegas Hotel & Casino 4500 W Tropicana Ave	Las Vegas	NV	89103	**800-675-3267**	702-365-7111
Palace Station Hotel & Casino 2411 W Sahara Ave *Resv	Las Vegas	NV	89102	**800-634-3101***	702-367-2411
Palms Casino Resort 4321 W Flamingo Rd	Las Vegas	NV	89103	**866-942-7777**	702-942-7777
PARK MGM 3770 Las Vegas Blvd S	Las Vegas	NV	89109	**800-311-8999**	702-730-7777
Peppermill Hotel & Casino 2707 S Virginia St	Reno	NV	89502	**800-648-6992**	775-826-2121
Railroad Pass Hotel & Casino 2800 S Boulder Hwy	Henderson	NV	89002	**800-654-0877**	702-294-5000
Red Rock Resort Spa & Casino 11011 W Charleston Blvd	Las Vegas	NV	89135	**866-767-7773**	702-797-7777
Sam's Town Hotel & Gambling Hall 5111 Boulder Hwy	Las Vegas	NV	89122	**800-897-8696**	702-456-7777
Silver Legacy Resort & Casino 407 N Virginia St	Reno	NV	89501	**800-687-8733**	775-325-7401
Silverton Hotel & Casino 3333 Blue Diamond Rd	Las Vegas	NV	89139	**866-722-4608**	702-263-7777
South Point Hotel & Casino 9777 Las Vegas Blvd S	Las Vegas	NV	89183	**866-796-7111**	866-791-7626
Stratosphere Tower Hotel & Casino 2000 S Las Vegas Blvd	Las Vegas	NV	89104	**800-998-6937**	702-380-7777
Suncoast Hotel & Casino 9090 Alta Dr	Las Vegas	NV	89145	**877-677-7111**	702-636-7111
Sunset Station Hotel & Casino 1301 W Sunset Rd	Henderson	NV	89014	**888-786-7389**	702-547-7777
Texas Station Gambling Hall & Hotel 2101 Texas Star Ln *Resv	North Las Vegas	NV	89032	**800-654-8888***	702-631-1000
Treasure Island Hotel & Casino 3300 Las Vegas Blvd S	Las Vegas	NV	89109	**800-288-7206**	702-894-7111
Tropicana Express 2121 S Casino Dr	Laughlin	NV	89029	**800-243-6846**	702-298-4200
Tuscany Suites & Casino 255 E Flamingo Rd *Resv	Las Vegas	NV	89169	**877-887-2261***	702-893-8933
Western Village Inn & Casino 815 Nichols Blvd	Sparks	NV	89434	**800-648-1170**	
Westin Casuarina Las Vegas Hotel Casino & Spa 160 E Flamingo Rd	Las Vegas	NV	89109	**866-837-4215**	702-836-5900
Casino NB 21 Casino Dr	Moncton	NB	E1G0R7	**877-859-7775**	
Harrah's Resort Atlantic City 777 Harrah's Blvd	Atlantic City	NJ	08401	**800-342-7724**	609-441-5000
Resorts Casino Hotel 1133 Boardwalk	Atlantic City	NJ	08401	**800-334-6378**	
Tropicana Entertainment 2831 Boardwalk *OTC: TPCA*	Atlantic City	NJ	08401	**800-843-8767**	
Camel Rock Casino 17486A Hwy 84/285	Santa Fe	NM	87506	**800-483-1040**	800-462-2635
Cities of Gold Casino 10-B Cities of Gold Rd	Santa Fe	NM	87506	**800-455-3313**	505-455-4232
Sandia Resort & Casino 30 Rainbow Rd NE	Albuquerque	NM	87113	**800-526-9366**	505-796-7500
Seneca Niagara Casino 310 Fourth St	Niagara Falls	NY	14303	**877-873-6322**	716-299-1100
Turning Stone Resort Casino LLC 5218 Patrick Rd	Verona	NY	13478	**800-771-7711**	315-361-7711
Prairie Knights Casino & Resort 7932 Hwy 24	Fort Yates	ND	58538	**800-425-8277**	701-854-7777
Caesars License Company LLC 377 Riverside Dr E	Windsor	ON	N9A7H7	**800-991-7777**	519-258-7878
Casino Niagara 5705 Falls Ave	Niagara Falls	ON	L2E6T3	**888-325-5788**	
Saskatchewan Indian Gaming Authority 250 - 103 C Packham Ave	Saskatoon	SK	S7N4K4	**800-306-6789**	306-477-7777
Emerald Downs 2300 Emerald Downs Dr PO Box 617	Auburn	WA	98001	**888-931-8400**	253-288-7000
Emerald Queen Casino (EQC) 2024 E 29th St	Tacoma	WA	98404	**888-831-7655**	253-594-7777
Lucky Eagle Casino 12888 188th Ave SW	Rochester	WA	98579	**800-720-1788**	360-273-2000
Northern Quest Resort & Casino 100 N Hayford Rd	Airway Heights	WA	99001	**877-871-6772**	
Red Wind Casino 12819 Yelm Hwy	Olympia	WA	98513	**866-946-2444**	
Skagit Valley Casino Resort 5984 N Darrk Ln	Bow	WA	98232	**877-275-2448**	
Wheeling Island Gaming Inc 1 S St1 St	Wheeling	WV	26003	**877-946-4373**	304-232-5050

134 CASKETS & VAULTS

SEE ALSO Mortuary, Crematory, Cemetery Products & Services

				Toll-Free	Phone
American Wilbert Vault Corp 4415 W Harrison PO Box 7245	Hillside	IL	60162	**800-328-5040**	708-366-3210
Batesville Casket Co 1 Batesville Blvd *Cust Svc	Batesville	IN	47006	**800-622-8373***	812-934-7500
Brown-Wilbert Inc 2280 Hamline Ave N	Saint Paul	MN	55113	**800-672-0709**	
Clark Grave Vault Co, The 375 E Fifth Ave	Columbus	OH	43201	**800-848-3570**	
Norwalk-Wilbert Vault Co 425 Harral Ave	Bridgeport	CT	06604	**800-826-9406**	203-366-5678
Pettigrew & Sons Casket Co 6151 Power Inn Rd	Sacramento	CA	95824	**800-852-1701**	916-383-0777

135 CEMENT

				Toll-Free	Phone
Ash Grove Cement Co 8900 Indian Creek Pkwy Ste 200 *OTC: ASHG*	Overland Park	KS	66210	**800-545-1882**	913-451-8900
California Portland Cement Co 2025 E Financial Way *Cust Svc	Glendora	CA	91741	**800-272-1891***	626-852-6200
Cemex USA 929 Gessner Rd Ste 1900 *NYSE: CX*	Houston	TX	77024	**800-999-8529**	713-650-6200
Continental Cement Company LLC 16401 Swingley Ridge Rd Ste 610	Chesterfield	MO	63017	**800-625-1144**	636-532-7440
Eagle Materials Inc 3811 Turtle Creek Blvd Ste 1100 *NYSE: EXP*	Dallas	TX	75219	**800-759-7625**	214-432-2000
EZG Manufacturing 1833 North Riverview Rd	Malta	OH	43758	**800-417-9272**	
Federal White Cement Ltd PO Box 1609 *Sales	Woodstock	ON	N4S0A8	**800-265-1806***	519-485-5410
Knife River Corp 3303 Rock Island Pl	Bismarck	ND	58504	**800-982-5339**	701-530-1380
Lafarge North America Inc 8700 W Bryn Mawr Ave Ste 300	Chicago	IL	60631	**800-451-8346**	773-372-1000
Lehigh Hanson Materials Ltd 12640 Inland Way *Orders	Edmonton	AB	T5V1K2	**800-252-9304***	780-420-2500
Permatile Concrete Products Co 100 Beacon Rd	Bristol	VA	24203	**800-662-5332**	276-669-5332
Titan America Inc 1151 Azalea Garden Rd	Norfolk	VA	23502	**800-468-7622**	757-858-6500

136   CEMETERIES - NATIONAL

SEE ALSO Historic Homes & Buildings ; Parks - National - US

			Toll-Free	Phone

Alton National Cemetery
600 Pearl St . . . . Alton IL   62003   **800-535-1117**   314-845-8320

Baltimore National Cemetery
5501 Frederick Ave . . . . Baltimore MD   21228   **800-535-1117**   410-644-9696

Camp Butler National Cemetery
5063 Camp Butler Rd . . . . Springfield IL   62707   **877-907-8585**   217-492-4070

Chattanooga National Cemetery
1200 Bailey Ave . . . . Chattanooga TN   37404   **877-907-8585**   423-855-6590

Cypress Hills National Cemetery
625 Jamaica Ave . . . . Brooklyn NY   11208   **800-535-1117**   631-454-4949

Eagle Point National Cemetery
2763 Riley Rd . . . . Eagle Point OR   97524   **800-535-1117**   541-826-2511

Florence National Cemetery
803 E National Cemetery Rd . . . . Florence SC   29506   **877-907-8585**   843-669-8783

Florida National Cemetery
6502 SW 102nd Ave . . . . Bushnell FL   33513   **877-907-8585**   352-793-7740

Fort Smith National Cemetery
522 Garland Ave . . . . Fort Smith AR   72901   **800-535-1117**   479-783-5345

Grafton National Cemetery
431 Walnut St . . . . Grafton WV   26354   **800-535-1117**   304-265-2044

Jefferson City National Cemetery
1024 E McCarty St . . . . Jefferson City MO   65101   **877-907-8585**   314-845-8320

Marietta National Cemetery
500 Washington Ave . . . . Marietta GA   30060   **866-236-8159**

Prescott National Cemetery
500 Hwy 89 N . . . . Prescott AZ   86301   **800-535-1117**   928-717-7569

Roseburg National Cemetery
913 NW Garden Valley Blvd . . . . Roseburg OR   97471   **800-535-1117**   541-677-3152

Seven Pines National Cemetery
400 E Williamsburg Rd . . . . Sandston VA   23150   **800-535-1117**   804-795-2031

Togus National Cemetery
VA Regional Office Ctr . . . . Togus ME   04330   **800-535-1117**   508-563-7113

Wilmington National Cemetery
2011 Market St . . . . Wilmington NC   28403   **800-535-1117**   910-815-4877

Woodlawn National Cemetery
1825 Davis St . . . . Elmira NY   14901   **877-907-8585**   607-732-5411

137   CHAMBERS OF COMMERCE - CANADIAN

Listings are organized by provinces and then are alphabetized within each province grouping according to the name of the city in which each chamber is located.

			Toll-Free	Phone

Alberta Chambers of Commerce
10025 - 102A Ave Ste 1808 . . . . Edmonton AB   T5J2Z2   **800-272-8854**   780-425-4180

Peace River Chamber of Commerce
10006 96 Ave PO Box 6599 . . . . Peace River AB   T8S1S4   **888-525-4423**   780-624-4166

St Albert & District Chamber of Commerce
71 St Albert Trl . . . . Saint Albert AB   T8N6L5   **800-207-9410**   780-458-2833

Comox Valley Chamber of Commerce
2040 Cliffe Ave . . . . Courtenay BC   V9N2L3   **888-357-4471**   250-334-3234

Surrey Board of Trade
14439 104th Ave Ste 101 . . . . Surrey BC   V3R1M1   **866-848-7130**   604-581-7130

Manitoba Chambers of Commerce, The
227 Portage Ave . . . . Winnipeg MB   R3B2A6   **877-444-5222**   204-948-0100

Barrie
Chamber of Commerce
121 Commerce Park Dr Unit A . . . . Barrie ON   L4N8X1   **888-220-2221**   705-721-5000

Belleville Chamber of Commerce
5 Moira St E . . . . Belleville ON   K8P2S3   **888-852-9992**   613-962-4597

Cambridge Chamber of Commerce
750 Hespeler Rd . . . . Cambridge ON   N3H5L8   **800-749-7560***   519-622-2221
*General

North Bay & District Chamber of Commerce
205 Main St E . . . . North Bay ON   P1B1B2   **888-249-8998**   705-472-8480

Greater Peterborough Chamber of Commerce
175 George St N . . . . Peterborough ON   K9J3G6   **877-640-4037**   705-748-9771

Vaughan Chamber of Commerce
25 Edilcan Dr Ste 2 . . . . Vaughan ON   L4K3S4   **888-943-8937**   905-761-1366

Chambre de Commerce du Quebec
555 boul Ren,-L,vesque W Ste 1100 . . . . Montreal QC   H2Z1B1   **800-361-5019**   514-844-9571

138   CHAMBERS OF COMMERCE - INTERNATIONAL

SEE ALSO Chambers of Commerce - Canadian
Included here are organizations that work to promote business and trade relationships between the United States and other countries.

			Toll-Free	Phone

Alberta Soccer
9023 111 Ave NW . . . . Edmonton AB   T5B0C3   **866-250-2200**   780-474-2200

Arizona Automobile Dealers Association
4701 N 24th St Ste B3 . . . . Phoenix AZ   85016   **800-678-3875**   602-468-0888

Aski Capital Inc
419 Notre Dame Ave . . . . Winnipeg MB   R3B1R3   **866-987-7180**   204-987-7180

Association of American Chambers of Commerce in Latin America
1615 H St NW . . . . Washington DC   20062   **800-638-6582**   202-463-5485

Australian-American Chamber of Commerce - San Francisco
PO Box 471285 . . . . San Francisco CA   94147   **800-662-4455**   415-485-6718

Burns Bog Conservation Society
7953 120 St . . . . Delta BC   V4C6P6   **888-850-6264**   604-572-0373

Canadian Bar Assn
500-865 Carling Ave . . . . Ottawa ON   K1S5S8   **800-267-8860**   613-237-2925

Canadian Finance & Leasing Association
15 Toronto St . . . . Toronto ON   M5C2E3   **877-213-7373**   416-860-1133

Canadian Mental Health Association
250 Dundas St W Ste 500 . . . . Toronto ON   M5T2Z5   **800-616-8816**   416-646-5557

Canadian Payroll Association
250 Bloor St E . . . . Toronto ON   M4W1E6   **800-387-4693**   416-487-3380

			Toll-Free	Phone

Canadian Society of Customs Brokers
55 Murray St Ste 320 . . . . Ottawa ON   K1N5M3   **800-668-6870**   613-562-3543

Carefirst Seniors & Community Services Association
3601 Victoria Park Ave . . . . Scarborough ON   M1W3Y3   **800-268-7708**   416-502-2323

Chinese Chamber of Commerce of Hawaii
8 S King St Ste 201 . . . . Honolulu HI   96813   **877-533-2444**   808-533-3181

Constructors Association of Western Pennsylvania
800 Cranberry Woods Dr
Ste 110 . . . . Cranberry Township PA   16066   **877-343-2297**   412-343-8000

Deaf Inter-link
100 rue St Francois Ste 206 . . . . Florissant MO   63031   **800-330-7062**   314-837-7757

Digital Health Canada
1100 - 151 Yonge St . . . . Toronto ON   M5C2W7   **844-220-3468**   647-775-8555

Eden i & r Inc 570 B St . . . . Hayward CA   94541   **888-886-9660**   510-537-2710

Electric Cooperatives of South Carolina Inc, The
808 Knox Abbott Dr . . . . Cayce SC   29033   **800-459-2141**   803-796-6060

Electronic Transactions Association, The
1101 16th St NW Ste 402. . . . . Washington DC   20036   **800-695-5509**   202-828-2635

Empire Building Services
1570 E Edinger Ave . . . . Santa Ana CA   92705   **888-296-2078**   714-836-7700

Flagship Fire Inc
1500 15th Ave dr e . . . . Palmetto FL   34221   **866-242-3307**   941-723-7230

Flashbanc LLC
185 NW spanish river blvd . . . . Boca Raton FL   33431   **800-808-1622**   561-278-8888

Florida Venture Forum Inc, The
707 W Azeele St . . . . Tampa FL   33606   **888-375-7136**   813-335-8116

French-American Chamber of Commerce in New York
1350 Broadway Ste 2101 . . . . New York NY   10018   **800-821-2241**   212-867-0123

Georgia Society of CPA's
6 Concourse Pkwy Ste 800. . . . . Atlanta GA   30328   **800-330-8889**   404-231-8676

Graphic Arts Association
1210 Northbrook Dr Ste 200. . . . . Trevose PA   19053   **800-475-6708**   215-396-2300

Health Unit Brant County
194 Ter Hill St . . . . Brantford ON   N3R1G7   **800-565-8603**   519-753-4937

Hive Modern Design
820 NW glisan st . . . . Portland OR   97209   **866-663-4483**   503-242-1967

Ibb Design Group
5798 Genesis Ct . . . . Frisco TX   75034   **800-355-9195**   214-618-6600

Iowa Soybean Association
4554 114th St . . . . Urbandale IA   50322   **800-383-1423**   515-251-8640

JJ Kane
1000 Lenola Rd Bldg 1 Ste 203 . . . . Maple Shade NJ   08052   **855-462-5263**

Kids Help Phone
300-439 University Ave . . . . Toronto ON   M5G1Y8   **800-268-3062**   416-586-5437

Lignite Energy Council
1016 E Owens Ave . . . . Bismarck ND   58502   **800-932-7117**   701-258-7117

Meclabs LLC
1300 Marsh Landing Pkwy
Ste 106 . . . . Jacksonville Beach FL   32250   **800-517-5531**

Mercer Engineering & Research
135 Osigian Blvd . . . . Warner Robins GA   31088   **877-650-6372**   478-953-6800

Michigan Bankers Assn
507 S Grand Ave . . . . Lansing MI   48933   **800-368-7764**   517-485-3600

Namgis First Nation
49 Atli St . . . . Alert Bay BC   V0N1A0   **888-962-6447**   250-974-5556

National Association of Federal Retirees
865 Shefford Rd . . . . Ottawa ON   K1J1H9   **855-304-4700**   613-745-2559

Nazcare Inc
599 White Spar Rd . . . . Prescott AZ   86303   **877-756-4090**   928-442-9205

Nbcot 150 Main St Ste 300 . . . . Gaithersburg MD   20878   **800-967-1139**   301-990-7979

Nebraska Bankers Association Inc
233 S 13th St Ste 700. . . . . Lincoln NE   68508   **800-593-3881**   402-474-1555

Nebraska Beef Council
1319 Central Ave . . . . Kearney NE   68848   **800-421-5326**   308-236-7551

Nebraska Farm Bureau Federation
5225 S 16th St . . . . Lincoln NE   68512   **800-742-4016**   402-421-4400

New Tech Network
1250 Main St Ste 100. Napa CA   94559   **800-856-7038**   707-253-6951

Nofa-ny Certified Organic LLC
840 Upper Front St . . . . Binghamton NY   13905   **800-853-2676**   607-724-9851

Ohio Contractors Association
1313 Dublin Rd . . . . Columbus OH   43215   **800-229-1388**   614-488-0724

Ohio Manufacturers' Association
33 N High St . . . . Columbus OH   43215   **800-662-4463**   614-224-5111

Ohio Motorcycle Dealers Association
655 Metro Pl S Ste 270 . . . . Dublin OH   43017   **800-686-9100**   614-766-9100

Ontario Association of Archiects
111 Moatfield Dr . . . . North York ON   M3B3L6   **800-565-2724**   416-449-6898

Ontario Dental Nurses & Assistants Association
869 Dundas St . . . . London ON   N5W2Z8   **800-461-4348**   519-679-2566

Oregon Bankers Assn
777 13th St SE Ste 130. . . . . Salem OR   97301   **800-677-1116**   503-581-3522

Rlj Financial Services Inc
1788 Mitchell Rd Ste 102. . . . . Ceres CA   95307   **800-240-1050**   209-538-7758

Rosewood Care Center Holding Co
100 Rosewood Village Dr . . . . Swansea IL   62226   **800-213-0154**   618-236-1391

Safety Training Seminars
598 Vermont St . . . . San Francisco CA   94107   **800-470-9026**   415-437-1600

Santie Oil Co
126 Larcel Dr . . . . Sikeston MO   63801   **800-748-7788**   314-436-3569

SMC Business Councils
600 Cranberry Woods Dr
Ste 190 . . . . Cranberry Township PA   16066   **800-553-3260**   412-371-1500

Speed Skating Canada
2781 Lancaster Rd . . . . Ottawa ON   K1B1A7   **877-572-4772**   902-425-5450

Suzuki Association of The Americas Inc
1900 Folsom St Ste 101 . . . . Boulder CO   80302   **888-378-9854**   303-444-0948

Swedish-American Chamber of Commerce Inc New York Chapter
570 Lexington Ave 20th Fl . . . . New York NY   10022   **800-862-2793**   212-838-5530

Trackers Earth Portland
4617 SE Milwaukie Ave . . . . Portland OR   97202   **800-522-0255**   503-345-3312

Travel Goods Association
301 N Harrison St Ste 412 . . . . Princeton NJ   08540   **877-842-1938**

Turfgrass Producers International
444 E Roosevelt Rd Ste 346 . . . . Lombard IL   60148   **800-405-8873**   847-649-5555

Ex-Student's Association
2110 San Jacinto Blvd . . . . Austin TX   78712   **866-974-7220**   512-840-5700

Classified Section

	Toll-Free	Phone

Wisconsin Hospital Association Inc
5510 Research Park Dr .... Fitchburg WI 53711 **800-782-8581** 608-274-1820

139   CHAMBERS OF COMMERCE - US - LOCAL

SEE ALSO Civic & Political Organizations
Chambers listed here represent areas with a population of 25,000 or more. Listings are organized by states and then are alphabetized within each state grouping according to the name of the city in which each chamber is located.

Alabama

			Toll-Free	Phone

Greater Limestone County Chamber of Commerce
101 S Beaty St .... Athens AL 35611 **866-953-6565** 256-232-2600
North Baldwin Chamber of Commerce
301 McMeans Ave .... Bay Minette AL 36507 **800-634-8104** 251-937-5665
Bessemer Area Chamber of Commerce
321 N 18th St .... Bessemer AL 35020 **888-423-7736** 205-425-3253
Cullman Area Chamber of Commerce
301 Second Ave SW .... Cullman AL 35055 **800-313-5114** 256-734-0454
Dothan Area Chamber of Commerce
102 Jamestown Blvd .... Dothan AL 36301 **800-221-1027** 334-792-5138
Eufaula/Barbour County Chamber of Commerce
333 E Broad St .... Eufaula AL 36027 **800-524-7529** 334-687-6664
South Baldwin Chamber of Commerce (SBCC)
112 W Laurel Ave PO Box 1117 .... Foley AL 36535 **877-461-3712** 251-943-3291
Gadsden & Etowah County Chamber
1 Commerce Sq .... Gadsden AL 35901 **800-659-2955** 256-543-3472
Greater Valley Area Chamber of Commerce
2102 S Broad Ave PO Box 205 .... Lanett AL 36863 **800-245-2244** 334-642-1411
Mobile Area Chamber of Commerce
451 Government St .... Mobile AL 36602 **800-422-6951** 251-433-6951
Ozark Area Chamber of Commerce
294 Painter Ave .... Ozark AL 36360 **800-582-8497** 334-774-9321
Greater Jackson County Chamber of Commerce, The
407 E Willow St .... Scottsboro AL 35768 **800-259-5508** 256-259-5500

Alaska

			Toll-Free	Phone

Juneau Chamber of Commerce
9301 Glacier Hwy Ste 110 .... Juneau AK 99801 **888-581-2201** 907-463-3488

Arizona

			Toll-Free	Phone

Chandler Chamber of Commerce
25 S Arizona Pl Ste 201 .... Chandler AZ 85225 **800-963-4571** 480-963-4571
Lake Havasu Area Chamber of Commerce
314 London Bridge Rd .... Lake Havasu City AZ 86403 **800-307-3610** 928-855-4115
Nogales-Santa Cruz County Chamber of Commerce
123 W Kino Pk .... Nogales AZ 85621 **800-508-7624** 520-287-3685
Prescott Chamber of Commerce
117 W Goodwin St .... Prescott AZ 86303 **800-266-7534** 928-445-2000
Prescott Valley Chamber of Commerce
3001 N Main St Ste 2A .... Prescott Valley AZ 86314 **800-355-0843** 928-772-8857
Graham County Chamber of Commerce
1111 Thatcher Blvd .... Safford AZ 85546 **888-837-1841** 928-428-2511

Arkansas

			Toll-Free	Phone

Conway Area Chamber of Commerce
900 Oak St .... Conway AR 72032 **800-750-8155** 501-327-7788
Jacksonville Chamber of Commerce
200 Dupree Dr .... Jacksonville AR 72076 **877-815-3111** 501-982-1511
Mountain Home Area Chamber of Commerce
1023 Hwy 62 .... Mountain Home AR 72653 **800-822-3536** 870-425-5111
Rogers-Lowell Area Chamber of Commerce
317 W Walnut St .... Rogers AR 72756 **800-364-1240** 479-636-1240

California

			Toll-Free	Phone

Atascadero Chamber of Commerce
6904 El Camino Real .... Atascadero CA 93422 **877-204-9830** 805-466-2044
Atwater Chamber of Commerce
1181 Third St .... Atwater CA 95301 **844-269-9688** 209-358-4251
Kern County Board of Trade
2101 Oak St .... Bakersfield CA 93301 **800-500-5376*** 661-868-5376
*General
Berkeley Chamber of Commerce
1834 University Ave .... Berkeley CA 94703 **800-847-4823** 510-549-7000
Burbank Chamber of Commerce
200 W Magnolia Blvd .... Burbank CA 91502 **800-495-5005** 818-846-3111
Carmichael Chamber of Commerce
6825 Fair Oaks Blvd Ste 100 .... Carmichael CA 95608 **800-991-6147** 916-481-1002
Chatsworth Chamber of Commerce
10038 Old Depot Plaza Rd .... Chatsworth CA 91311 **800-613-5903** 818-341-2428
Greater Concord Chamber of Commerce
2280 Diamond Blvd Ste 200 .... Concord CA 94520 **800-427-8686** 925-685-1181
San Diego East County Chamber of Commerce
201 S Magnolia Ave .... El Cajon CA 92020 **800-402-8765** 619-440-6161
Encinitas Chamber of Commerce
527 Encinitas Blvd .... Encinitas CA 92024 **800-953-6041** 760-753-6041
Garden Grove Chamber of Commerce
12866 Main St Ste 102 .... Garden Grove CA 92840 **800-959-5560** 714-638-7950
Lakeport Regional Chamber of Commerce
875 Lakeport Blvd .... Lakeport CA 95453 **866-525-3767** 707-263-5092
Lompoc Valley Chamber of Commerce & Visitors Bureau
PO Box 626 .... Lompoc CA 93438 **800-240-0999** 805-736-4567
Madera Chamber of Commerce
120 NE St .... Madera CA 93638 **800-872-7245** 559-673-3563
Malibu Chamber of Commerce
23805 Stuart Ranch Rd Ste 210 .... Malibu CA 90265 **800-442-4988** 310-456-9025

			Toll-Free	Phone

Monrovia Chamber of Commerce
620 S Myrtle Ave .... Monrovia CA 91016 **800-755-1515** 626-358-1159
Newark Chamber of Commerce
37101 Newark Blvd .... Newark CA 94560 **844-245-8925** 510-578-4500
Novato Chamber of Commerce
807 DeLong Ave .... Novato CA 94945 **800-897-1164** 415-897-1164
Orange Chamber of Commerce
1940 N Tustin St .... Orange CA 92865 **888-676-1040** 714-538-3581
Orangevale Chamber of Commerce
9267 Greenback Ln Ste B-91 .... Orangevale CA 95662 **800-962-1106** 916-988-0175
Oroville Area Chamber of Commerce
1789 Montgomery St .... Oroville CA 95965 **800-655-4653** 530-538-2542
Paradise Chamber of Commerce
5550 Sky Way Ste 1 .... Paradise CA 95969 **800-247-9889** 530-877-9356
Placentia Chamber of Commerce
117 N Main St .... Placentia CA 92870 **844-730-0418** 714-528-1873
El Dorado County Chamber of Commerce
542 Main St .... Placerville CA 95667 **800-457-6279** 530-621-5885
Redlands Chamber of Commerce
47 N First St .... Redlands CA 92373 **800-966-6428** 909-793-2546
Rialto Chamber of Commerce
120 N Riverside Ave .... Rialto CA 92376 **800-597-4955** 909-875-5364
Rocklin Area Chamber of Commerce
3700 Rocklin Rd .... Rocklin CA 95677 **800-228-3380** 916-624-2548
San Bernardino Area Chamber of Commerce
PO Box 658 .... San Bernardino CA 92402 **800-928-5091** 909-885-7515
San Dimas Chamber of Commerce
246 E Bonita Ave .... San Dimas CA 91773 **800-371-5465** 909-592-3818
San Luis Obispo Chamber of Commerce
1039 Chorro St .... San Luis Obispo CA 93401 **800-634-1414** 805-781-2777
Santa Cruz Chamber of Commerce
611 Ocean St Ste 1 .... Santa Cruz CA 95060 **866-282-5900** 831-457-3713
Tuolumne County Chamber of Commerce
222 S Shepherd St .... Sonora CA 95370 **877-532-4212** 209-532-4212
Turlock Chamber of Commerce
115 S Golden State Blvd .... Turlock CA 95380 **800-834-0401** 209-632-2221
Twentynine Palms Chamber of Commerce
73484 Twentynine Palms Hwy .... Twentynine Palms CA 92277 **800-442-2283** 760-367-3445
Union City Chamber of Commerce
3939 Smith St .... Union City CA 94587 **800-945-2288** 510-952-9637
Visalia Chamber of Commerce
222 N Garden St Ste 300 .... Visalia CA 93291 **800-728-0724** 559-734-5876
West Hollywood Chamber of Commerce
8272 Santa Monica Blvd .... West Hollywood CA 90046 **800-345-8683** 323-650-2688
Willows Chamber of Commerce
118 W Sycamore .... Willows CA 95988 **855-233-6362** 530-934-8150
Woodland Chamber of Commerce
400 Court St .... Woodland CA 95695 **888-843-2636** 530-662-7327
Yucca Valley Chamber of Commerce
56711 29 Palms Hwy .... Yucca Valley CA 92284 **855-365-6558** 760-365-6323

Colorado

			Toll-Free	Phone

Aspen Chamber Resort Assn
590 N Mill St .... Aspen CO 81611 **800-670-0792** 970-925-1940
Canon City Chamber of Commerce
403 Royal Gorge Blvd .... Canon City CO 81212 **800-876-7922** 719-275-2331
Fort Collins Area Chamber of Commerce
225 S Meldrum St .... Fort Collins CO 80521 **877-652-8607** 970-482-3746
Fort Morgan Area Chamber of Commerce
300 Main St .... Fort Morgan CO 80701 **800-354-8660** 970-867-6702
Grand Junction Area Chamber of Commerce
360 Grand Ave .... Grand Junction CO 81501 **800-352-5286** 970-242-3214
Greeley-Weld Chamber of Commerce
902 Seventh Ave .... Greeley CO 80631 **800-449-3866** 970-352-3566
Greater Pueblo Chamber of Commerce
302 N Santa Fe Ave .... Pueblo CO 81003 **800-233-3446** 719-542-1704

Connecticut

			Toll-Free	Phone

Greater Danbury Chamber of Commerce
39 West St .... Danbury CT 06810 **800-722-2936** 203-743-5565
Greater Meriden Chamber of Commerce
3 Colony St Ste 301 .... Meriden CT 06451 **877-283-8158** 203-235-7901
Greater New Haven Chamber of Commerce
900 Chapel St 10th Fl .... New Haven CT 06510 **800-953-4467** 203-787-6735
Greater New Milford Chamber of Commerce
11 Railroad St .... New Milford CT 06776 **800-998-2984** 860-354-6080

Delaware

			Toll-Free	Phone

Rehoboth Beach-Dewey Beach Chamber of Commerce
501 Rehoboth Ave .... Rehoboth Beach DE 19971 **800-441-1329** 302-227-2233

Florida

			Toll-Free	Phone

Lower Keys Chamber of Commerce
31020 Overseas Hwy .... Big Pine Key FL 33043 **800-872-3722** 305-872-2411
Bonita Springs Area Chamber of Commerce
25071 Chamber of Commerce Dr .... Bonita Springs FL 34135 **800-226-2943** 239-992-2943
Coral Springs Chamber of Commerce
11805 Heron Bay Blvd .... Coral Springs FL 33076 **800-816-1256** 954-752-4242
Citrus County Chamber of Commerce
28 NW US Hwy 19 .... Crystal River FL 34428 **800-665-6701** 352-795-3149
Greater Deerfield Beach Chamber of Commerce
1601 E Hillsboro Blvd .... Deerfield Beach FL 33441 **866-551-9805** 954-427-1050
Greater Fort Myers Chamber of Commerce
2310 Edwards Dr .... Fort Myers FL 33901 **800-366-3622** 239-332-3624
Greater Fort Walton Beach Chamber of Commerce
34 Miracle Strip Pkwy SE .... Fort Walton Beach FL 32548 **800-225-5797** 850-244-8191
Islamorada Chamber of Commerce
PO Box 915 .... Islamorada FL 33036 **800-322-5397** 305-664-4503

				Toll-Free	Phone
Kissimmee/Osceola County Chamber of Commerce					
1425 E Vine St	Kissimmee	FL	34744	**800-447-8206**	407-847-3174
Lake Wales Area Chamber of Commerce					
340 W Central Ave	Lake Wales	FL	33859	**800-365-6380**	863-676-3445
Greater Marathon Chamber of Commerce					
12222 Overseas Hwy	Marathon	FL	33050	**800-262-7284**	305-743-5417
Marco Island Chamber of Commerce					
1102 N Collier Blvd	Marco Island	FL	34145	**888-330-1422**	239-394-7549
Cocoa Beach Area Chamber of Commerce					
400 Fortenberry Rd	Merritt Island	FL	32952	**800-248-5955**	321-459-2200
Miami Beach Chamber of Commerce					
1920 Meridian Ave	Miami Beach	FL	33139	**800-501-0401**	305-674-1300
Santa Rosa County Chamber of Commerce					
5247 Stewart St	Milton	FL	32570	**800-239-8732**	850-623-2339
West Pasco Chamber of Commerce					
5443 Main St	New Port Richey	FL	34652	**800-851-8754**	727-842-7651
Niceville-Valparaiso Chamber of Commerce					
1055 E John Sims Pkwy	Niceville	FL	32578	**800-729-9226**	850-678-2323
Greater North Miami Chamber of Commerce					
13100 W Dixie Hwy	North Miami	FL	33161	**800-939-3848**	305-891-7811
Ocala-Marion County Chamber of Commerce					
310 SE Third St	Ocala	FL	34471	**800-466-5055**	352-629-8051
Panama City Beaches Chamber of Commerce					
309 Richard Jackson Blvd	Panama City Beach	FL	32407	**800-224-4853**	850-235-1159
Greater Pompano Beach Chamber of Commerce					
2200 E Atlantic Blvd	Pompano Beach	FL	33062	**888-939-5711**	954-941-2940
Port Orange-South Daytona Chamber of Commerce					
3431 S Ridgewood Ave	Port Orange	FL	32129	**800-848-3984**	386-761-1601
Saint Cloud/Greater Osceola Chamber of Commerce					
1200 New York Ave	Saint Cloud	FL	34769	**800-000-0000**	407-892-3671
Sanibel & Captiva Islands Chamber of Commerce					
1159 Cswy Rd	Sanibel	FL	33957	**800-851-5088**	239-472-1080
Stuart-Martin County Chamber of Commerce					
1650 S Kanner Hwy	Stuart	FL	34994	**800-962-2873**	772-287-1088
Sunrise Chamber of Commerce					
6800 Sunset Strip	Sunrise	FL	33313	**800-273-1614**	954-835-2428
Greater Winter Haven Area Chamber of Commerce					
401 Ave 'B' NW	Winter Haven	FL	33881	**800-260-9220**	863-293-2138
Winter Park Chamber of Commerce					
151 W Lyman Ave	Winter Park	FL	32789	**877-972-4262***	407-644-8281
*Help Line					

Georgia

				Toll-Free	Phone
Albany Area Chamber of Commerce					
225 W Broad Ave	Albany	GA	31701	**800-475-8700**	229-434-8700
Augusta Metro Chamber of Commerce					
1 Tenth St Ste 120	Augusta	GA	30901	**888-639-8188**	706-821-1300
Cartersville-Bartow County Chamber of Commerce					
122 W Main St PO Box 307	Cartersville	GA	30120	**800-527-9395**	770-382-1466
Chatsworth-Murray County Chamber of Commerce					
1001 Green Rd	Chatsworth	GA	30705	**800-969-9490**	706-695-6060
White County Chamber of Commerce					
122 N Main St	Cleveland	GA	30528	**800-392-8279**	706-865-5356
Greater Columbus Chamber of Commerce					
1200 Sixth Ave PO Box 1200	Columbus	GA	31902	**800-360-8552**	706-327-1566
Habersham County Chamber of Commerce					
668 Clarkesville St	Cornelia	GA	30531	**800-835-2559**	706-778-4654
Moultrie-Colquitt County Chamber of Commerce					
116 First Ave SE	Moultrie	GA	31768	**888-408-4748**	229-985-2131
Tifton-Tift County Chamber of Commerce					
100 Central Ave	Tifton	GA	31794	**800-550-8438**	229-382-6200

Hawaii

				Toll-Free	Phone
Hawaii Island Chamber of Commerce					
117 Keawe St	Hilo	HI	96720	**877-482-4411**	808-935-7178
Kailua Chamber of Commerce					
600 Kailua Rd Ste 107	Kailua	HI	96734	**888-261-7997**	808-261-7997

Idaho

				Toll-Free	Phone
Caldwell Chamber of Commerce					
704 Blaine St	Caldwell	ID	83605	**866-206-6944**	208-459-7493
Coeur d'Alene Area Chamber of Commerce					
105 N First St Ste 100	Coeur d'Alene	ID	83814	**877-782-9232**	208-664-3194
Sun Valley/Ketchum Chamber & Visitors Bureau					
491 Sun Valley Rd	Ketchum	ID	83340	**800-634-3347**	208-726-3423
Moscow Chamber of Commerce					
411 S Main St	Moscow	ID	83843	**866-770-2020**	208-882-1800
Greater Pocatello Chamber of Commerce					
324 S Main St	Pocatello	ID	83204	**800-632-0905**	208-233-1525
Twin Falls Area Chamber of Commerce					
2015 Neilsen Point Pl	Twin Falls	ID	83301	**866-894-6325**	208-733-3974

Illinois

				Toll-Free	Phone
Aurora Chamber of Commerce					
43 W Galena Blvd	Aurora	IL	60506	**866-947-8081**	630-256-3180
Des Plaines Chamber of Commerce & Industry					
1401 E Oakton St	Des Plaines	IL	60018	**800-933-2412**	847-824-4200
Glenview Chamber of Commerce					
2320 Glenview Rd	Glenview	IL	60025	**800-459-4250**	847-724-0900
Growth Assn of Southwestern Illinois					
5800 Godfrey Rd Alden Hall	Godfrey	IL	62035	**855-852-9460**	618-467-2280
West Suburban Chamber of Commerce					
9440 Joliet Rd Ste B	Hodgkins	IL	60525	**800-796-9696**	708-387-7550
Jacksonville Area Chamber of Commerce					
310 E State St	Jacksonville	IL	62650	**800-593-5678**	217-243-5678
McHenry Area Chamber of Commerce					
1257 N Green St	McHenry	IL	60050	**800-374-8373**	815-385-4300
Round Lake Area Chamber of Commerce & Industry					
2007 Civic Ctr Way	Round Lake Beach	IL	60073	**800-334-7661**	847-546-2002

				Toll-Free	Phone
Skokie Chamber of Commerce					
5002 Oakton St PO Box 106	Skokie	IL	60077	**800-526-8441**	847-673-0240

Indiana

				Toll-Free	Phone
Goshen Chamber of Commerce					
232 S Main St	Goshen	IN	46526	**800-307-4204**	574-533-2102
Greater Greenwood Chamber of Commerce					
65 Airport Pkwy	Greenwood	IN	46143	**800-462-7585**	317-888-4856
Dearborn County Chamber of Commerce					
320 Walnut St	Lawrenceburg	IN	47025	**800-322-8198**	812-537-0814
Madison Area Chamber of Commerce					
301 E Main St	Madison	IN	47250	**800-559-2956**	812-265-3135
Greater Monticello Chamber of Commerce					
116 N Main St	Monticello	IN	47960	**800-541-7906**	574-583-7220
Muncie-Delaware County Chamber of Commerce					
401 S High St	Muncie	IN	47305	**800-336-1373**	765-288-6681
One Southern Indiana					
4100 Charlestown Rd	New Albany	IN	47150	**800-521-2232**	812-945-0266
Noblesville Chamber of Commerce					
601 Conner St	Noblesville	IN	46060	**800-227-1376**	317-773-0086
Jennings County Chamber of Commerce					
203 N State St PO Box 340	North Vernon	IN	47265	**866-382-4968**	812-346-2339
Miami County Chamber of Commerce					
13 E Main St	Peru	IN	46970	**800-521-9945**	765-472-1923
Shelby County Chamber of Commerce					
501 N Harrison St	Shelbyville	IN	46176	**800-318-4083**	317-398-6647

Iowa

				Toll-Free	Phone
Ames Chamber of Commerce					
1601 Golden Aspen Dr Ste 110	Ames	IA	50010	**800-288-7470**	515-232-2310
Council Bluffs Area Chamber of Commerce					
149 W Broadway	Council Bluffs	IA	51503	**800-228-6878**	712-325-1000
Dubuque Area Chamber of Commerce					
300 Main St Ste 200	Dubuque	IA	52001	**800-798-4748**	563-557-9200
Siouxland Chamber of Commerce					
101 Pierce St	Sioux City	IA	51101	**800-228-7903**	712-255-7903

Kansas

				Toll-Free	Phone
Arkansas City Area Chamber of Commerce					
PO Box 795	Arkansas City	KS	67005	**800-794-4780**	620-442-0230
Emporia Area Chamber of Commerce					
719 Commercial St	Emporia	KS	66801	**800-279-3730**	620-342-1600
Hutchinson/Reno County Chamber of Commerce					
117 N Walnut St	Hutchinson	KS	67501	**800-691-4262**	620-662-3391
Manhattan Area Chamber of Commerce					
501 Poyntz Ave	Manhattan	KS	66502	**800-759-0134**	785-776-8829
Salina Area Chamber of Commerce					
120 W Ash St	Salina	KS	67401	**877-725-4625**	785-827-9301

Kentucky

				Toll-Free	Phone
Bowling Green Area Chamber of Commerce					
710 College St	Bowling Green	KY	42101	**866-330-2422**	270-781-3200
Danville-Boyle County Chamber of Commerce					
105 E Walnut St	Danville	KY	40422	**800-548-4229**	859-236-2805
Glasgow-Barren County Chamber of Commerce					
118 E Public Sq	Glasgow	KY	42141	**800-264-3161**	270-651-3161
Hopkinsville-Christian County Chamber of Commerce					
2800 Port Campbell Blvd	Hopkinsville	KY	42240	**800-842-9959**	270-885-9096
Oldham County Chamber of Commerce					
412 E Main St	LaGrange	KY	40031	**800-264-0521**	502-222-1635
Greater Lexington Chamber of Commerce Inc					
330 E Main St Ste 100	Lexington	KY	40507	**800-848-1224**	859-254-4447
Somerset-Pulaski County Chamber of Commerce					
445 S Hwy 27 Ste 101	Somerset	KY	42501	**877-629-9722**	606-679-7323

Louisiana

				Toll-Free	Phone
Houma-Terrebonne Chamber of Commerce					
6133 Louisiana 311	Houma	LA	70360	**800-649-7346**	985-876-5600
DeSoto Parish Chamber of Commerce					
115 N Washington Ave	Mansfield	LA	71052	**800-844-4646**	318-872-1310
Monroe Chamber of Commerce					
212 Walnut St Ste 100	Monroe	LA	71201	**888-677-5200**	318-323-3461
Natchitoches Area Chamber of Commerce					
780 Front St Ste 101	Natchitoches	LA	71457	**877-646-6689**	318-352-6894
Iberville Parish Chamber of Commerce					
23675 Church St	Plaquemine	LA	70764	**800-266-2692**	225-687-3560
Ruston/Lincoln Chamber of Commerce					
2111 N Trenton St	Ruston	LA	71270	**800-392-9032**	318-255-2031

Maine

				Toll-Free	Phone
Bar Harbor Chamber of Commerce					
2 Cottage St	Bar Harbor	ME	04609	**888-540-9990**	207-288-5103
Belfast Area Chamber of Commerce					
14 Main St	Belfast	ME	04915	**877-338-9015**	207-338-5900
Oxford Hills Chamber of Commerce					
4 Western Ave	South Paris	ME	04281	**800-871-7741**	207-743-2281

Maryland

				Toll-Free	Phone
Annapolis & Anne Arundel County Chamber of Commerce					
134 Holiday Ct Ste 316	Annapolis	MD	21401	**800-624-8887**	410-266-3960
Washington County Chamber of Commerce, The					
1 S Potomac St	Hagerstown	MD	21740	**800-520-6685**	301-739-2015

				Toll-Free	Phone
Charles County Chamber of Commerce 101 Centennial St Ste A	La Plata	MD	20646	**800-992-3194**	301-932-6500
Greater Ocean City Chamber of Commerce 12320 Ocean Gateway	Ocean City	MD	21842	**888-626-3386**	410-213-0552
Calvert County Chamber of Commerce PO Box 9	Prince Frederick	MD	20678	**800-972-4389**	410-535-2577

Massachusetts

				Toll-Free	Phone
Amherst Area Chamber of Commerce 28 Amity St	Amherst	MA	01002	**800-593-4052**	413-253-0700
Greater Boston Chamber of Commerce 265 Franklin St	Boston	MA	02110	**800-476-3094**	617-227-4500
Metro South Chamber of Commerce 60 School St	Brockton	MA	02301	**877-777-4414**	508-586-0500
Cape Cod Canal Regional Chamber of Commerce 70 Main St	Buzzards Bay	MA	02532	**888-332-2732**	508-759-6000
Cape Cod Chamber of Commerce 5 Shoot Flying Hill Rd	Centerville	MA	02632	**888-332-2732**	508-362-3225
Falmouth Chamber of Commerce 20 Academy Ln	Falmouth	MA	02540	**800-526-8532**	508-548-8500
Greater Lowell Chamber of Commerce 131 Merrimack St	Lowell	MA	01852	**800-338-0221**	978-459-8154
Marlborough Regional Chamber of Commerce 11 Florence St	Marlborough	MA	01752	**800-508-2265**	508-485-7746
Peabody Area (PACC) *Chamber of Commerce* 49 Lowell St 1st Fl	Peabody	MA	01960	**888-287-9400**	978-531-0384
Salem Chamber of Commerce 265 Essex St	Salem	MA	01970	**800-392-6100**	978-744-0004
Affiliated Chamber of Commerce of Greater Springfield 1441 Main St	Springfield	MA	01103	**888-283-3757**	413-787-1555
Blackstone Valley Chamber of Commerce 110 Church St	Whitinsville	MA	01588	**800-841-0919**	508-234-9090

Michigan

				Toll-Free	Phone
Battle Creek Area Chamber of Commerce 1 Riverwalk Ctr 34 W Jackson St Ste 3A	Battle Creek	MI	49017	**800-397-2240**	269-962-4076
Belleville Area Chamber of Commerce 248 Main St	Belleville	MI	48111	**800-692-2274**	734-697-7151
Detroit Regional Chamber 1 Woodward Ave Ste 1900	Detroit	MI	48226	**800-427-5100**	313-964-4000
Ferndale Chamber of Commerce 1938 Burdette St Ste 112	Ferndale	MI	48220	**800-495-5464**	248-542-2160
Midland Area *Chamber of Commerce* 300 Rodd St Ste 101	Midland	MI	48640	**800-999-3199**	989-839-9901
Monroe County Chamber of Commerce 1645 N Dixie Hwy Ste 20	Monroe	MI	48162	**855-386-1280**	734-384-3366
Macomb County Chamber 28 First St Ste B	Mount Clemens	MI	48043	**800-564-3136**	586-493-7600
Muskegon Area Chamber of Commerce 380 W Western Ste 202	Muskegon	MI	49440	**800-659-2955**	231-722-3751
Four Flags Area Chamber of Commerce 321 E Main St	Niles	MI	49120	**800-719-2188**	269-683-3720
Novi Chamber of Commerce, The 41875 W 11 Mile Rd Ste 201	Novi	MI	48375	**888-440-7325**	248-349-3743
Plymouth Community Chamber of Commerce 850 W Ann Arbor Trl	Plymouth	MI	48170	**800-477-4747**	734-453-1540
Pontiac Regional Chamber of Commerce 402 N Telegraph Rd	Pontiac	MI	48341	**800-477-3172**	248-335-9600
Blue Water Area Chamber of Commerce 512 McMorran Blvd	Port Huron	MI	48060	**800-361-0526**	810-985-7101
Westland Chamber of Commerce 36900 Ford Rd	Westland	MI	48185	**800-737-4859**	734-326-7222

Minnesota

				Toll-Free	Phone
Alexandria Lakes Area Chamber of Commerce 206 Broadway	Alexandria	MN	56308	**800-235-9441**	320-763-3161
Apple Valley Chamber of Commerce 14800 Galaxie Ave Ste 101	Apple Valley	MN	55124	**800-301-9435**	952-432-8422
Bemidji Area Chamber of Commerce 300 Bemidji Ave	Bemidji	MN	56601	**800-458-2223**	218-444-3541
Brainerd Lakes Area Chamber of Commerce 7393 State Hwy 371 PO Box 356	Brainerd	MN	56401	**800-450-2838**	218-829-2838
Burnsville Chamber of Commerce 350 W Burnsville Pkwy Ste 425	Burnsville	MN	55337	**800-521-6055**	952-435-6000
Cloquet Area Chamber of Commerce 225 Sunnyside Dr	Cloquet	MN	55720	**800-554-4350**	218-879-1551
Detroit Lakes Regional Chamber of Commerce 700 Summit Ave	Detroit Lakes	MN	56501	**800-542-3992**	218-847-9202
Eden Prairie Chamber of Commerce 11455 Viking Dr Ste 270	Eden Prairie	MN	55344	**800-932-8677**	952-944-2830
Grand Rapids Area Chamber of Commerce 1 NW Third St	Grand Rapids	MN	55744	**800-472-6366**	218-326-6619
River Heights Chamber of Commerce 5782 Blackshire Path	Inver Grove Heights	MN	55076	**800-625-6079**	651-451-2266
Owatonna Area Chamber of Commerce & Tourism 320 Hoffman Dr	Owatonna	MN	55060	**800-423-6466**	507-451-7970
TwinWest Chamber of Commerce 10700 Old County Rd 15	Plymouth	MN	55441	**800-649-5397**	763-450-2220
Leech Lake Area Chamber of Commerce 205 Minnesota Ave E	Walker	MN	56484	**800-833-1118**	218-547-1313

Mississippi

				Toll-Free	Phone
Monroe County Chamber of Commerce 124 W Commerce St	Aberdeen	MS	39730	**800-457-5351**	662-369-6488
Panola Partnership Inc 150-A Public Sq	Batesville	MS	38606	**888-872-6652**	662-563-3126
Rankin County Chamber of Commerce 101 Service Dr	Brandon	MS	39043	**800-987-8280**	601-825-2268
Brookhaven-Lincoln County Chamber of Commerce 230 S Whitworth Ave	Brookhaven	MS	39601	**800-613-4667**	601-833-1411
Clarksdale-Coahoma County Chamber of Commerce & Industrial Foundation 1540 DeSoto Ave PO Box 160	Clarksdale	MS	38614	**800-626-3764**	662-627-7337
Natchez-Adams County *Chamber of Commerce* 211 Main St	Natchez	MS	39120	**800-647-6724**	601-445-4611
Olive Branch Chamber of Commerce 9123 Pigeon Roost PO Box 608	Olive Branch	MS	38654	**800-948-3090**	662-895-2600
Greater Starkville Development Partnership 200 E Main St	Starkville	MS	39759	**800-649-8687**	662-323-3322

Missouri

				Toll-Free	Phone
Affton Chamber of Commerce 9815 Mackenzie Rd	Affton	MO	63123	**800-877-1234**	314-631-3100
Branson/Lakes Area Chamber of Commerce PO Box 1897	Branson	MO	65615	**800-214-3661**	417-334-4084
Independence Chamber of Commerce 210 W Truman Rd	Independence	MO	64050	**800-222-6400**	816-252-4745
Jefferson City Area Chamber of Commerce 213 Adams St	Jefferson City	MO	65101	**866-223-6535**	573-634-3616
Lebanon Area Chamber of Commerce 186 N Adams St	Lebanon	MO	65536	**888-588-5710**	417-588-3256
Lee's Summit Chamber of Commerce 220 SE Main St	Lees Summit	MO	64063	**888-816-5757**	816-524-2424
O'Fallon Chamber of Commerce 2145 Bryan Vly Commercial Dr	O'Fallon	MO	63366	**888-349-1897**	636-240-1818
Rolla Area Chamber of Commerce 1311 KingsHwy	Rolla	MO	65401	**888-809-3817**	573-364-3577
Saint Joseph Area Chamber of Commerce 3003 Frederick Ave	Saint Joseph	MO	64506	**800-748-7856**	816-232-4461

Montana

				Toll-Free	Phone
Billings Area Chamber of Commerce 815 S 27th St	Billings	MT	59101	**855-328-9116**	406-245-4111
Butte-Silver Bow Chamber of Commerce 1000 George St	Butte	MT	59701	**800-735-6814**	406-723-3177
Helena Area Chamber of Commerce 225 Cruse Ave	Helena	MT	59601	**800-743-5362**	406-442-4120

Nebraska

				Toll-Free	Phone
Kearney Area Chamber of Commerce 1007 Second Ave PO Box 607	Kearney	NE	68848	**800-227-8340**	308-237-3101
Greater Omaha Chamber of Commerce 1301 Harney St	Omaha	NE	68102	**800-852-2622**	402-346-5000

Nevada

				Toll-Free	Phone
Fallon Chamber of Commerce 85 N Taylor St	Fallon	NV	89406	**800-242-0478**	775-423-2544
Carson Valley Chamber of Commerce 1477 Hwy 395 N Ste A	Gardnerville	NV	89410	**800-727-7677**	775-782-8144
Las Vegas Chamber of Commerce 575 Symphony Park Ave Ste 100	Las Vegas	NV	89106	**800-468-7272**	702-641-5822

New Hampshire

				Toll-Free	Phone
Greater Concord Chamber of Commerce 49 S Main St Ste 104	Concord	NH	03301	**800-360-4839**	603-224-2508

New Jersey

				Toll-Free	Phone
Greater Atlantic City Chamber 12 S Virginia Ave	Atlantic City	NJ	08401	**800-123-4567**	609-345-4524
Fair Lawn Chamber of Commerce 12-45 River Rd	Fair Lawn	NJ	07410	**800-474-1299**	201-796-7050
Randolph Area Chamber of Commerce PO Box 391	Mount Freedom	NJ	07970	**800-366-3922**	973-361-3462
Sussex County Chamber of Commerce 120 Hampton House Rd	Newton	NJ	07860	**844-256-7328**	973-579-1811
Greater Paterson Chamber of Commerce 100 Hamilton Plz Ste 1201	Paterson	NJ	07505	**800-220-2892**	973-881-7300
Southern Ocean County Chamber of Commerce 265 W Ninth St	Ship Bottom	NJ	08008	**800-292-6372**	609-494-7211

New Mexico

				Toll-Free	Phone
Alamogordo Chamber of Commerce 1301 N White Sands Blvd	Alamogordo	NM	88310	**800-826-0294**	575-437-6120
Clovis/Curry County Chamber of Commerce 105 E Third St	Clovis	NM	88101	**800-261-7656**	575-763-3435
Grants/Cibola County Chamber of Commerce 100 N Iron Ave	Grants	NM	87020	**866-270-5110**	505-287-4802
Roswell Chamber of Commerce 131 W Second St	Roswell	NM	88201	**877-849-7679**	575-623-5695
Silver City-Grant County Chamber of Commerce 201 N Hudson St	Silver City	NM	88061	**800-548-9378**	575-534-1700

New York

				Toll-Free	Phone
Buffalo Niagara Partnership 665 Main St	Buffalo	NY	14203	**844-308-9165**	716-566-5400
St Lawrence County Chamber of Commerce 101 Main St	Canton	NY	13617	**877-228-7810**	315-386-4000

	Toll-Free	Phone
Greene County Chamber of Commerce 327 Main St PO Box 248 . . . . . . Catskill NY 12414	800-888-3586	518-943-4222
Chamber of Southern Saratoga County 58 Clifton Country Rd Ste 102 . . . Clifton Park NY 12065	800-766-9001	518-371-7748
Corning Area Chamber of Commerce 1 W Market St Ste 202 . . . . . . Corning NY 14830	866-463-6264	607-936-4686
Livingston County Chamber of Commerce 4635 Millennium Dr . . . . . . Geneseo NY 14454	800-538-7365	585-243-2222
Adirondack Regional Chambers of Commerce 136 Glen St Ste 3 . . . . . . Glens Falls NY 12801	888-516-7247	518-798-1761
Tompkins County Chamber of Commerce 904 E Shore Dr . . . . . . Ithaca NY 14850	888-568-9816	607-273-7080
Greater Liverpool Chamber of Commerce 314 Second St . . . . . . Liverpool NY 13088	800-388-2000	315-457-3895
Lewis County Chamber of Commerce 7576 S State St . . . . . . Lowville NY 13367	800-724-0242	315-376-2213
Herkimer County Chamber of Commerce 28 W Main St . . . . . . Mohawk NY 13407	877-984-4636	315-866-7820
Mount Vernon Chamber of Commerce 66 Mount Vernon Ave . . . . . . Mount Vernon NY 10550	888-868-2269	914-775-8127
Greater New York Chamber of Commerce 20 W 44th St 4th Fl . . . . . . New York NY 10036	800-344-6088	212-686-7220
Saratoga County Chamber of Commerce 28 Clinton St . . . . . . Saratoga Springs NY 12866	855-765-7873	518-584-3255
Seneca County Chamber of Commerce 2020 Rt 5 & 20 W . . . . . . Seneca Falls NY 13148	800-732-1848	315-568-2906

North Carolina

	Toll-Free	Phone
Archdale-Trinity Chamber of Commerce 213 Balfour Dr . . . . . . Archdale NC 27263	800-626-2672	336-434-2073
Asheville Area Chamber of Commerce 36 Montford Ave . . . . . . Asheville NC 28802	888-314-1041	828-258-6101
Black Mountain-Swannanoa Chamber of Commerce 201 E State St . . . . . . Black Mountain NC 28711	800-669-2301	828-669-2300
Blowing Rock Chamber of Commerce PO Box 406 . . . . . . Blowing Rock NC 28605	877-750-4636	828-295-7851
Chapel Hill-Carrboro Chamber of Commerce 104 S Estes Dr . . . . . . Chapel Hill NC 27515	800-694-9784	919-967-7075
Wayne County Chamber of Commerce 308 N Williams St . . . . . . Goldsboro NC 27530	800-849-8222	919-734-2241
Lincolnton-Lincoln County Chamber of Commerce 101 E Main St . . . . . . Lincolnton NC 28092	800-222-1167	704-735-3096
Mooresville-South Iredell Chamber of Commerce 149 E Iredell Ave . . . . . . Mooresville NC 28115	800-764-7113	704-664-3898
Carteret County Chamber of Commerce 801 Arendell St Ste 1 . . . . . . Morehead City NC 28557	800-622-6278	252-726-6350
Greater Mount Airy Chamber of Commerce 200 N Main St . . . . . . Mount Airy NC 27030	800-948-0949	336-786-6116
Greater Raleigh Chamber of Commerce PO Box 2978 . . . . . . Raleigh NC 27602	888-456-8535	919-664-7000
Roanoke Valley Chamber of Commerce 260 Premier Blvd . . . . . . Roanoke Rapids NC 27870	800-280-3999	252-537-3513
Rutherford County Chamber of Commerce 162 N Main St . . . . . . Rutherfordton NC 28139	866-478-4646	828-287-3090
Brunswick County Chamber of Commerce 114 Wall St . . . . . . Shallotte NC 28459	800-426-6644	910-754-6644
Chatham Chamber of Commerce 531 E Third St . . . . . . Siler City NC 27344	800-329-7466	919-742-3333
Moore County Chamber of Commerce 10677 Hwy 15-501 . . . . . . Southern Pines NC 28387	800-346-5362	910-692-3926
Jackson County Chamber of Commerce 773 W Main St . . . . . . Sylva NC 28779	800-962-1911	828-586-2155
Windsor-Bertie Area Chamber of Commerce 121 Granville St PO Box 572 . . . . . . Windsor NC 27983	800-334-5010	252-794-4277
Yadkin County Chamber of Commerce 205 S Jackson St PO Box 1840 . . . . . . Yadkinville NC 27055	877-492-3546	336-679-2200

North Dakota

	Toll-Free	Phone
Jamestown Area Chamber of Commerce 120 Second St SE PO Box 1530 . . . . . . Jamestown ND 58402	800-882-2500	701-252-4830

Ohio

	Toll-Free	Phone
Athens Area Chamber of Commerce 449 E State St Ste 1 . . . . . . Athens OH 45701	877-360-3608	740-594-2251
Logan County Chamber of Commerce 100 S Main St . . . . . . Bellefontaine OH 43311	877-360-3608	937-599-5121
Canton Regional Chamber of Commerce 222 Market Ave N . . . . . . Canton OH 44702	800-533-4302	330-456-7253
Carroll County Chamber of Commerce & Economic Development 61 N Lisbon St PO Box 277 . . . . . . Carrollton OH 44615	877-727-0103	330-627-4811
Greater Cleveland Partnership 1240 Huron Rd E Ste 300 . . . . . . Cleveland OH 44115	888-304-4769	216-621-3300
Cuyahoga Falls Chamber of Commerce (CFCC) 151 Portage Trl Ste 1 . . . . . . Cuyahoga Falls OH 44221	800-248-4040	330-929-6756
Southern Columbiana County Regional Chamber of Commerce 529 Market St PO Box 94 . . . . . . East Liverpool OH 43920	800-804-0468	330-385-0845
Lorain County Chamber of Commerce 226 Middle Ave . . . . . . Elyria OH 44035	800-633-4766	440-328-2550
Darke County Chamber of Commerce 209 E Fourth St . . . . . . Greenville OH 45331	800-396-0787	937-548-2102
Kettering-Moraine-Oakwood Area Chamber of Commerce 2977 Far Hills Ave . . . . . . Kettering OH 45419	800-621-8931	937-299-3852
Lima/Allen County Chamber of Commerce 144 S Main St Ste 100 . . . . . . Lima OH 45801	800-233-5462	419-222-6045
Marion Area Chamber of Commerce 267 W Ctr St Ste 100 . . . . . . Marion OH 43302	800-371-6688	740-387-2267
Milford-Miami Township Chamber of Commerce 745 Center St #302 . . . . . . Milford OH 45150	800-837-3200	513-831-2411
Napoleon/Henry County Chamber of Commerce 611 N Perry St . . . . . . Napoleon OH 43545	800-322-6849	419-592-1786
North Canton Area Chamber of Commerce 121 S Main St . . . . . . North Canton OH 44720	800-833-3722	330-499-5100
Salem Area Chamber of Commerce 713 E State St . . . . . . Salem OH 44460	800-644-6292	330-337-3473
Greater Lawrence County Area Chamber of Commerce 216 Collins Ave . . . . . . South Point OH 45680	800-408-1334	740-377-4550
Champaign County Chamber of Commerce 107 N Main St . . . . . . Urbana OH 43078	877-873-5764	937-653-5764
Adams County Travel & Visitors Bureau 509 E Main St . . . . . . West Union OH 45693	877-232-6764	937-544-5639
Wooster Area Chamber of Commerce 377 W Liberty St . . . . . . Wooster OH 44691	800-414-1103	330-262-5735
Zanesville-Muskingum County Chamber of Commerce 205 N Fifth St . . . . . . Zanesville OH 43701	800-743-2303	740-455-8282

Oklahoma

	Toll-Free	Phone
Edmond Area Chamber of Commerce 825 E Second St Ste 100 . . . . . . Edmond OK 73034	800-717-2601	405-341-2808
Greater Muskogee Area Chamber of Commerce PO Box 797 . . . . . . Muskogee OK 74402	866-381-6543	918-682-2401
Greater Oklahoma City Chamber of Commerce 123 Park Ave . . . . . . Oklahoma City OK 73102	800-225-5652	405-297-8900
Ponca City Area Chamber of Commerce 420 E Grand Ave . . . . . . Ponca City OK 74601	866-763-8092	580-765-4400
Stillwater Chamber of Commerce 409 S Main St . . . . . . Stillwater OK 74075	800-593-5573	405-372-5573
Tulsa Metro Chamber 1 W Third St Ste 100 . . . . . . Tulsa OK 74103	888-424-9411	918-585-1201

Oregon

	Toll-Free	Phone
Corvallis Area Chamber of Commerce 420 NW Second St . . . . . . Corvallis OR 97330	800-562-8526	541-757-1505
Grants Pass Chamber of Commerce 1995 NW Vine St . . . . . . Grants Pass OR 97526	800-547-5927	541-476-7717
La Grande-Union County Chamber of Commerce 102 Elm St . . . . . . La Grande OR 97850	800-848-9969	541-963-8588
Greater Newport Chamber of Commerce 555 SW Coast Hwy . . . . . . Newport OR 97365	800-262-7844	541-265-8801
Lake Oswego Chamber of Commerce 459 Third St Lk . . . . . . Oswego OR 97034	800-518-0760	503-636-3634

Pennsylvania

	Toll-Free	Phone
Greater Lehigh Valley Chamber of Commerce 840 Hamilton St Ste 205 . . . . . . Allentown PA 18101	800-845-7941	610-841-5800
Columbia Montour chamber of Commerce, The 238 Market St . . . . . . Bloomsburg PA 17815	800-342-5775	570-784-2522
Greater Chambersburg Chamber of Commerce 100 Lincoln Way E Ste A . . . . . . Chambersburg PA 17201	800-840-9081	717-264-7101
Exton Region Chamber of Commerce 185 Exton Square Mall . . . . . . Exton PA 19341	800-666-0191	610-363-7746
Lower Bucks County Chamber of Commerce 409 Hood Blvd . . . . . . Fairless Hills PA 19030	800-786-2234	215-943-7400
Harrisburg Regional Chamber 3211 N Front St Ste 201 . . . . . . Harrisburg PA 17110	877-883-8339	717-232-4099
Norwin Chamber of Commerce 321 Main St . . . . . . Irwin PA 15642	800-377-3539	724-863-0888
Greater Johnstown/Cambria County Chamber of Commerce 245 Market St Ste 100 . . . . . . Johnstown PA 15901	800-790-4522	814-536-5107
Clinton County Economic Partnership 212 N Jay St . . . . . . Lock Haven PA 17745	888-388-6991	570-748-5782
Pike County Chamber of Commerce 201 Broad St Ste 2 . . . . . . Milford PA 18337	877-345-0691	570-296-8700
Monroeville Area Chamber of Commerce 4268 Northern Pk . . . . . . Monroeville PA 15146	800-527-8941	412-856-0622
Schuylkill Chamber of Commerce 91 S Progress Ave . . . . . . Pottsville PA 17901	800-755-1942	570-622-1942
Greater Susquehanna Valley Chamber of Commerce 2859 N Susquehanna Trl PO Box 10 . . . . . . Shamokin Dam PA 17876	800-410-2880	570-743-4100
Chamber of Business & Industry of Centre County 200 Innovation Blvd Ste 150 . . . . . . State College PA 16803	877-234-5050	814-234-1829
Greater West Chester Chamber of Commerce 119 N High St . . . . . . West Chester PA 19380	800-210-8008	610-696-4046

South Carolina

	Toll-Free	Phone
Greater Aiken Chamber of Commerce 121 Richland Ave E PO Box 892 . . . . . . Aiken SC 29802	800-251-7234	803-641-1111
Kershaw County Chamber of Commerce 607 S Broad St . . . . . . Camden SC 29020	800-968-4037	803-432-2525
Greater Cayce West Columbia Chamber of Commerce 1006 12th St . . . . . . Cayce SC 29033	866-720-5400	803-794-6504
Georgetown County Chamber of Commerce 531 Front St . . . . . . Georgetown SC 29440	800-777-7705	843-546-8436
Greater Greenville Chamber of Commerce 24 Cleveland St . . . . . . Greenville SC 29601	866-485-5262	864-242-1050
Hilton Head Island Visitor & Convention Bureau, The 1 Chamber of Commerce Dr PO Box 5647 . . . . . . Hilton Head Island SC 29938	800-523-3373	843-785-3673
Lancaster County Chamber of Commerce PO Box 430 . . . . . . Lancaster SC 29721	800-532-0335	803-283-4105
Berkeley County Chamber of Commerce PO Box 968 . . . . . . Moncks Corner SC 29461	800-882-0337	843-761-8238
Myrtle Beach Area Chamber of Commerce 1200 N Oak St . . . . . . Myrtle Beach SC 29577	800-356-3016	843-626-7444
Newberry County Chamber of Commerce 1209 Caldwell St PO Box 396 . . . . . . Newberry SC 29108	800-288-2020	803-276-4274
Orangeburg County Chamber of Commerce 155 Riverside Dr SW PO Box 328 . . . . . . Orangeburg SC 29116	800-545-6153	803-534-6821
Union County Chamber of Commerce 135 W Main St . . . . . . Union SC 29379	877-202-8755	864-427-9039

Classified Section

Classified Section (sidebar)

South Dakota

				Toll-Free	Phone
Aberdeen Area Chamber of Commerce 516 S Main St	Aberdeen	SD	57401	800-874-9038	605-225-2860
Pierre Area Chamber of Commerce 800 W Dakota Ave	Pierre	SD	57501	800-962-2034	605-224-7361

Tennessee

				Toll-Free	Phone
Chattanooga Area Chamber of Commerce 811 Broad St	Chattanooga	TN	37402	877-756-1684	423-756-2121
Clarksville Area Chamber of Commerce 25 Jefferson St Ste 300	Clarksville	TN	37040	800-530-2487	931-647-2331
Cleveland/Bradley Chamber of Commerce 225 Keith St	Cleveland	TN	37311	800-533-9930	423-472-6587
Cookeville Area-Putnam County Chamber of Commerce 1 W First St	Cookeville	TN	38501	800-264-5541	931-526-2211
Crossville Cumberland County Chamber of Commerce 34 S Main St	Crossville	TN	38555	877-465-3861	931-484-8444
Fayetteville-Lincoln County Chamber of Commerce 208 S Elk Ave	Fayetteville	TN	37334	888-433-1238	931-433-6154
Rutherford County Chamber of Commerce 501 Memorial Blvd	Murfreesboro	TN	37129	800-716-7560	615-278-2326
Paris-Henry County Chamber of Commerce 2508 Eastwood St	Paris	TN	38242	800-345-1103	731-642-3431

Texas

				Toll-Free	Phone
Canyon Chamber of Commerce 1518 Fifth Ave	Canyon	TX	79015	800-999-9481	806-655-7815
Cleburne Chamber of Commerce 1511 W Henderson St	Cleburne	TX	76033	800-621-8566	817-645-2455
Eagle Pass Chamber of Commerce 400 E Garrison St	Eagle Pass	TX	78852	888-355-3224	830-773-3224
Fort Worth Chamber of Commerce 777 Taylor St Ste 900	Fort Worth	TX	76102	800-433-5747	817-336-2491
Harlingen Area Chamber of Commerce 311 E Tyler St	Harlingen	TX	78550	800-225-5345	956-423-5440
Cy-Fair Houston Chamber of Commerce 8711 Hwy 6 N Ste 120	Houston	TX	77095	800-403-6120	281-373-1390
Huntsville-Walker County Chamber of Commerce 1327 11th St	Huntsville	TX	77340	800-289-0389	936-295-8113
Greater Killeen Chamber of Commerce 1 Santa Fe Plz	Killeen	TX	76540	866-790-4769	254-526-9551
Laredo Chamber of Commerce, The 2310 San Bernardo	Laredo	TX	78040	800-292-2122	956-722-9895
McAllen Chamber of Commerce 1200 Ash Ave	McAllen	TX	78501	800-786-9199	956-682-2871
Mineral Wells Area Chamber of Commerce 511 E Hubbard St	Mineral Wells	TX	76067	800-252-6989	940-325-2557
Mission Chamber of Commerce 202 W Tom Landry St	Mission	TX	78572	800-827-8298	956-585-2727
The Greater New Braunfels Chamber of Commerce Inc 390 S Seguin St	New Braunfels	TX	78130	800-572-2626	830-625-2385
Odessa Chamber of Commerce 700 N Grant St Ste 200	Odessa	TX	79761	800-780-4678	432-332-9111
Lamar County Chamber of Commerce 1125 Bonham St	Paris	TX	75460	800-727-4789	903-784-2501
Greater San Antonio Chamber of Commerce 602 E Commerce St	San Antonio	TX	78205	888-828-8680	210-229-2100
North San Antonio Chamber of Commerce 12930 Country Pkwy	San Antonio	TX	78216	877-495-5888	210-344-4848
Tyler Area Chamber of Commerce 315 N Broadway Ave	Tyler	TX	75702	800-235-5712	903-592-1661
Weatherford Chamber of Commerce 401 Ft Worth St	Weatherford	TX	76086	888-594-3801	817-596-3801
Weslaco Area Chamber of Commerce 301 W Railroad	Weslaco	TX	78596	800-700-2443	956-968-2102

Vermont

				Toll-Free	Phone
Central Vermont Chamber of Commerce 33 Stewart Rd	Berlin	VT	05641	877-887-3678	802-229-5711
Brattleboro Area Chamber of Commerce 180 Main St	Brattleboro	VT	05301	877-254-4565	802-254-4565
Lake Champlain Regional Chamber of Commerce 60 Main St Ste 100	Burlington	VT	05401	877-686-5253	802-863-3489

Virginia

				Toll-Free	Phone
Annandale Chamber of Commerce 7263 Maple Pl Ste 207	Annandale	VA	22003	800-357-2110	703-256-7232
Danville Pittsylvania County Chamber of Commerce 8653 US Hwy 29 PO Box 99	Blairs	VA	24527	800-826-2355	434-836-6990
Pulaski County Chamber of Commerce 4440 Cleburne Blvd	Dublin	VA	24084	866-256-8864	540-674-1991
Greater Augusta Regional Chamber of Commerce 30 Ladd Rd PO Box 1107	Fishersville	VA	22939	866-922-2514	540-324-1133
Fredericksburg Regional Chamber of Commerce 2300 Fall Hill Ave Ste 240	Fredericksburg	VA	22401	888-338-0252	540-373-9400
Virginia Peninsula Chamber of Commerce 21 Enterprise Pkwy Ste 100	Hampton	VA	23666	800-462-3204	757-262-2000
Prince William County-Greater Manassas Chamber of Commerce 9720 Capital Ct Ste 203	Manassas	VA	20110	877-867-3853	703-368-6600
Prince William Regional Chamber of Commerce 9720 Capital Ct Ste 203	Manassas	VA	20110	877-867-3853	703-368-6600
Greater Williamsburg Chamber & Tourism Alliance 421 N Boundary St	Williamsburg	VA	23185	800-368-6511	757-229-6511

Washington

				Toll-Free	Phone
Grays Harbor Chamber of Commerce 506 Duffy St	Aberdeen	WA	98520	800-321-1924	360-532-1924
Auburn Area Chamber of Commerce 25 Second St NW	Auburn	WA	98001	800-395-0144	253-833-0700
Camas-Washougal Chamber of Commerce 422 NE Fourth Ave	Camas	WA	98607	844-262-1100	360-834-2472
Centralia-Chehalis Chamber of Commerce 500 NW Chamber of Commerce Way	Chehalis	WA	98532	800-525-3323	360-748-8885
Kent Chamber of Commerce 524 W Meeker St Ste 1	Kent	WA	98032	800-321-2808	253-854-1770
Greater Kirkland Chamber of Commerce 440 Central Way	Kirkland	WA	98033	800-501-7772	425-822-7066
Moses Lake Area Chamber of Commerce 324 S Pioneer Way	Moses Lake	WA	98837	800-992-6234	509-765-7888
Port Orchard Chamber of Commerce 1014 Bay St Ste 8	Port Orchard	WA	98366	800-475-7526	360-876-3505
Greater Renton Chamber of Commerce 625 S Fourth St	Renton	WA	98057	877-467-3686	425-226-4560
Greater Seattle Chamber of Commerce 1301 Fifth Ave Ste 1500	Seattle	WA	98101	866-978-2997	206-389-7200
Shelton-Mason County Chamber of Commerce 215 W Railroad Ave PO Box 2389	Shelton	WA	98584	800-576-2021	360-426-2021
Greater Spokane Inc 801 W Riverside Ave Ste 100	Spokane	WA	99201	800-776-5263	509-624-1393
Spokane Valley Chamber of Commerce 9507 E Sprague Ave	Spokane Valley	WA	99206	866-475-1436	509-924-4994
Walla Walla Valley Chamber of Commerce 29 E Sumach St PO Box 644	Walla Walla	WA	99362	866-826-9422	509-525-0850

West Virginia

				Toll-Free	Phone
Jefferson County Chamber of Commerce 201 E Washington St	Charles Town	WV	25414	800-624-0577	304-725-2055
Charleston Regional Chamber of Commerce 1116 Smith St	Charleston	WV	25301	800-792-4326	304-340-4253
Greater Greenbrier Chamber of Commerce 200 W Washington St Ste C	Lewisburg	WV	24901	855-453-4858	
Morgantown Area Chamber of Commerce 1029 University Ave Ste 101 *General	Morgantown	WV	26505	800-618-2525*	304-292-3311
Wetzel County Chamber of Commerce 201 Main St PO Box 271	New Martinsville	WV	26155	800-834-2070	304-455-3825
Greater Beloit Chamber of Commerce 500 Public Ave	Beloit	WI	53511	866-981-5969	608-365-8835
Chippewa Falls Area Chamber of Commerce 10 S Bridge St	Chippewa Falls	WI	54729	888-723-0024	715-723-0331
Fond du Lac Area Assn of Commerce 235 N National Ave	Fond du Lac	WI	54935	800-279-8811	920-921-9500
Greater Madison Chamber of Commerce PO Box 71	Madison	WI	53701	800-750-5437	608-256-8348
Manitowoc-Two Rivers Area Chamber of Commerce 1515 Memorial Dr	Manitowoc	WI	54220	866-727-5575	920-684-5575
Greater Menomonie Area Chamber of Commerce 342 E Main St	Menomonie	WI	54751	800-283-1862	715-235-9087
Metropolitan Milwaukee Assn of Commerce 756 N Milwaukee St	Milwaukee	WI	53202	855-729-1300	414-287-4100
Shawano Country Chamber of Commerce 1263 S Main St	Shawano	WI	54166	800-235-8528	715-524-2139
Portage County Business Council 5501 Vern Holmes Dr	Stevens Point	WI	54481	800-333-6668	715-344-1940
Superior-Douglas County Chamber of Commerce 205 Belknap St	Superior	WI	54880	800-942-5313	715-394-7716
West Bend Area Chamber of Commerce 304 S Main St	West Bend	WI	53095	888-338-8666	262-338-2666

Wyoming

				Toll-Free	Phone
Laramie Area Chamber of Commerce 800 S Third St	Laramie	WY	82070	866-876-1012	307-745-7339
Sheridan County Chamber of Commerce 1898 Fort Rd	Sheridan	WY	82801	800-453-3650	307-672-2485

140   CHAMBERS OF COMMERCE - US - STATE

				Toll-Free	Phone
US Chamber of Commerce 1615 H St NW	Washington	DC	20062	800-638-6582	202-659-6000
Arizona Chamber of Commerce & Industry 3200 N Central Ave Ste 1125	Phoenix	AZ	85012	866-275-5816	602-248-9172
Association of Washington Business PO Box 658	Olympia	WA	98507	800-521-9325	360-943-1600
Business Council of Alabama 2 N Jackson St PO Box 76	Montgomery	AL	36101	800-665-9647	334-834-6000
Business Council of New York State Inc 152 Washington Ave	Albany	NY	12210	800-358-1202	518-465-7511
California Chamber of Commerce 1215 K St Ste 1400 PO Box 1736	Sacramento	CA	95812	800-649-4921	916-444-6670
Delaware State Chamber of Commerce 1201 N Orange St Ste 200 PO Box 671	Wilmington	DE	19899	800-292-9507	302-655-7221
Georgia Chamber of Commerce 270 Peachtree St NW	Atlanta	GA	30303	800-241-2286	404-223-2264
Indiana Chamber of Commerce 115 W Washington St Ste 850-S	Indianapolis	IN	46204	800-824-6885	317-264-3110
Iowa Assn of Business & Industry 400 E Ct Ave Ste 100	Des Moines	IA	50309	800-383-4224	515-280-8000
Louisiana Assn of Business & Industry 3113 Vly Creek Dr PO Box 80258	Baton Rouge	LA	70898	888-816-5224	225-928-5388
Maine State Chamber of Commerce 125 Community Dr Ste 101	Augusta	ME	04330	800-546-7866	207-623-4568
Michigan Chamber of Commerce 600 S Walnut St	Lansing	MI	48933	800-748-0266	517-371-2100
Minnesota Chamber of Commerce 400 Robert St N Ste 1500	Saint Paul	MN	55101	800-821-2230	651-292-4650
Mississippi Economic Council PO Box 23276	Jackson	MS	39225	800-748-7626	601-969-0022

			Toll-Free	Phone

Montana Chamber of Commerce
900 GIBBON St PO Box 1730 . . . . Helena MT 59624 **888-442-6668** 406-442-2405

Pennsylvania Chamber of Business & Industry
417 Walnut St . . . . Harrisburg PA 17101 **800-225-7224** 717-255-3252

South Carolina Chamber of Commerce
1301 Gervais St Ste 1100 . . . . Columbia SC 29201 **800-799-4601** 803-799-4601

South Dakota Chamber of Commerce & Industry
108 N Euclid Ave . . . . Pierre SD 57501 **800-742-8112** 605-224-6161

Wisconsin Manufacturers & Commerce
PO Box 352 . . . . Madison WI 53701 **800-236-5414** 608-258-3400

141 CHECK CASHING SERVICES

			Toll-Free	Phone

Check Cashing Store (CCS)
6340 NW Fifth Way . . . . Fort Lauderdale FL 33309 **800-361-1407**

Check Cashing USA Inc
899 NW 37th Ave . . . . Miami FL 33125 **833-352-2274** 305-644-1840

FirstCash Inc
1600 W Seventh St . . . . Fort Worth TX 76102 **800-290-4598** 817-335-1100
NASDAQ: FCFS

Pay-O-Matic Corp 160 Oak Dr . . . . Syosset NY 11791 **888-545-6311**

Policy Research Associates Inc
345 Delaware Ave . . . . Delmar NY 12054 **800-311-4246** 518-439-7415

QC Holdings Inc
8208 Melrose Dr . . . . Lenexa KS 66214 **866-660-2243**
OTC: QCCO

Stoneleigh Recovery Associates Llc
PO Box 1479 . . . . Lombard IL 60148 **866-724-2330**

United Financial Services Group Inc
325 Chestnut St Ste 3000 . . . . Philadelphia PA 19106 **800-626-0787** 215-238-0300

Waterfield Technologies Inc
1 W Third St Ste 1115 . . . . Tulsa OK 74103 **800-324-0936** 918-858-6400

142 CHECKS - PERSONAL & BUSINESS

			Toll-Free	Phone

4Checkscom
8245 N Union Blvd . . . . Colorado Springs CO 80920 **800-995-9925**

Artistic Checks
PO Box 40003 . . . . Colorado Springs CO 80935 **800-824-3255**

Checks In The Mail Inc
2435 Goodwin Ln . . . . New Braunfels TX 78135 **800-733-4443**

Checks Unlimited
PO Box 19000 . . . . Colorado Springs CO 80935 **800-210-0468**

Safeguard Business Systems Inc
8585 N Stemmons Fwy Ste 600 N . . . . Dallas TX 75247 **800-523-2422** 855-778-3124

CHEMICALS - AGRICULTURAL

SEE Fertilizers & Pesticides

143 CHEMICALS - INDUSTRIAL (INORGANIC)

			Toll-Free	Phone

AIR LIQUIDE USA LLC
9811 Katy Fwy Ste 100 . . . . Houston TX 77024 **877-855-9533** 713-624-8000

Air Products & Chemicals Inc
7201 Hamilton Blvd . . . . Allentown PA 18195 **800-345-3148*** 610-481-4911
*NYSE: APD ■ *Prod Info*

Almatis Inc 501 W Pk Rd . . . . Leetsdale PA 15056 **800-643-8771** 412-630-2903

Americhem Inc
2000 Americhem Way . . . . Cuyahoga Falls OH 44221 **800-228-3476** 330-929-4213

Ampacet Corp
660 White Plains Rd . . . . Tarrytown NY 10591 **800-888-4267*** 914-631-6600
**Cust Svc*

Ashta Chemicals Inc
3509 Middle Rd . . . . Ashtabula OH 44004 **800-492-5082*** 440-997-5221
**Cust Svc*

BASF Corp
100 Campus Dr . . . . Florham Park NJ 07932 **800-526-1072** 973-245-6000

Cabot Corp
2 Seaport Ln Ste 1300 . . . . Boston MA 02210 **800-322-1236** 617-345-0100
NYSE: CBT

Calgon Carbon Corp
3000 GSK Dr . . . . Moon Township PA 15108 **800-422-7266*** 412-787-6700
*NYSE: CCC ■ *Cust Svc*

Carus Corp 315 Fifth St . . . . Peru IL 61354 **800-435-6856** 815-223-1500

Centrus Energy Corp
6903 Rockledge Dr . . . . Bethesda MD 20817 **800-273-7754** 301-564-3200
NYSE: LEU

Chemical Products Corp
102 Old Mill Rd . . . . Cartersville GA 30120 **877-210-9814*** 770-382-2144
**Cust Svc*

Dow Chemical Co
2030 Dow Ctr . . . . Midland MI 48674 **800-422-8193*** 989-636-1463
*NYSE: DWDP ■ *Cust Svc*

DuPont Titanium Technologies
1007 Market St . . . . Wilmington DE 19898 **800-441-7515** 302-774-1000

Elementis Specialties Inc
469 Old Trenton Rd . . . . East Windsor NJ 08512 **800-866-6800**

FMC Corp
2929 Walnut St . . . . Philadelphia PA 19104 **888-548-4486** 215-299-6000
NYSE: FMC

H E Anderson Company Inc
2025 Anderson Dr . . . . Muskogee OK 74403 **800-331-9620** 918-687-4426

Hawkins Inc
3100 E Hennepin Ave . . . . Minneapolis MN 55413 **800-328-5460** 612-331-6910
NASDAQ: HWKN

Horsehead Corp
4955 Steubenville Pk Ste 405 . . . . Pittsburgh PA 15205 **800-648-8897** 724-774-1020

Interstate Chemical Co Inc
2797 Freeland Rd . . . . Hermitage PA 16148 **800-422-2436** 724-981-3771

Jones Hamilton Co
30354 Tracy Rd . . . . Walbridge OH 43465 **888-858-4425** 419-666-9838

Kanto Corp
13424 N Woodrush Way . . . . Portland OR 97203 **866-609-5571** 503-283-0405

Keystone Aniline Corp
2501 W Fulton St . . . . Chicago IL 60612 **800-522-4393** 312-666-2015

LSB Industries Inc
16 S Pennsylvania Ave . . . . Oklahoma City OK 73107 **800-657-4428** 405-235-4546
NYSE: LXU

Martin Marietta Magnesia Specialties Inc
8140 Corporate Dr Ste 220 . . . . Baltimore MD 21236 **800-648-7400** 410-780-5500

NL Industries
16801 Greenspoint Pk Dr . . . . Houston TX 77060 **800-866-5600** 281-423-3300
NYSE: NL

Old Bridge Chemicals Inc
554 Waterworks Rd . . . . Old Bridge NJ 08857 **800-275-3924** 732-727-2225

OMYA Inc 62 Main St . . . . Proctor VT 05765 **800-451-4468** 802-459-3311

Phibro Animal Health Corp
300 Frank W Burr Blvd Ste 21 . . . . Teaneck NJ 07666 **800-223-0434** 201-329-7300

Plasticolors Inc
2600 Michigan Ave PO Box 816 . . . . Ashtabula OH 44005 **888-661-7675** 440-997-5137

Praxair Inc
39 Old Ridgebury Rd . . . . Danbury CT 06810 **800-772-9247** 203-837-2000
NYSE: PX

Rutgers Organics Corp
201 Struble Rd . . . . State College PA 16801 **888-469-2188** 814-238-2424

Silberline Mfg Company Inc
130 Lincoln Dr PO Box B . . . . Tamaqua PA 18252 **800-348-4824** 570-668-6050

Southern Ionics Inc
201 Commerce St . . . . West Point MS 39773 **800-953-3585** 912-647-0301

Tanner Systems Inc
625 19th Ave NE PO Box 488 . . . . Saint Joseph MN 56374 **800-461-6454** 320-363-1800

UOP LLC
25 E Algonquin Rd . . . . Des Plaines IL 60017 **800-877-6184** 847-391-2000

Vulcan Materials Co
1200 Urban Ctr Dr PO Box 385014 . . . . Birmingham AL 35238 **800-615-4331** 205-298-3000
NYSE: VMC

Westlake Chemical Corp
2801 Post Oak Blvd Ste 600 . . . . Houston TX 77056 **888-953-3623** 713-960-9111
NYSE: WLK

144 CHEMICALS - INDUSTRIAL (ORGANIC)

			Toll-Free	Phone

Ampacet Corp
660 White Plains Rd . . . . Tarrytown NY 10591 **800-888-4267*** 914-631-6600
**Cust Svc*

Bayer Inc 77 Belfield Rd . . . . Toronto ON M9W1G6 **800-622-2937** 416-248-0771

Cambrex Corp
1 Meadowlands Plz . . . . East Rutherford NJ 07073 **866-286-9133** 201-804-3000
NYSE: CBM

Celanese Corp 1601 W LBJ Fwy . . . . Dallas TX 75234 **800-627-9581** 972-443-4000
NYSE: CE

Chemstar Products Co
3915 Hiawatha Ave . . . . Minneapolis MN 55406 **800-328-5037** 612-722-0079

Chevron Phillips Chemical Company LP
10001 Six Pines Dr . . . . The Woodlands TX 77380 **800-231-1212** 832-813-4100

Dow Chemical Canada Inc (DCCI)
450 First St SW Ste 2100 . . . . Calgary AB T2P5H1 **800-447-4369** 403-267-3500

Dow Chemical Co
2030 Dow Ctr . . . . Midland MI 48674 **800-422-8193*** 989-636-1463
*NYSE: DWDP ■ *Cust Svc*

Dow Corning Corp
2200 W Salzburg Rd PO Box 994 . . . . Auburn MI 48611 **800-248-2481*** 989-496-4000
**Cust Svc*

DSM Resins Inc
31 Columbia Nitrogen Rd PO Box 2452 . . . . Augusta GA 30903 **800-277-9975** 706-849-6706

Eastman Chemical Co
200 S Wilcox Dr . . . . Kingsport TN 37660 **800-327-8626*** 423-229-2000
*NYSE: EMN ■ *Cust Svc*

First Chemical Corp
1001 Industrial Rd . . . . Pascagoula MS 39581 **877-243-6178** 228-762-0870

Huntsman Corp
500 Huntsman Way . . . . Salt Lake City UT 84108 **888-490-8484** 801-584-5700
NYSE: HUN

ICC Industries Inc
460 Park Ave . . . . New York NY 10022 **800-422-1720** 212-521-1700

Inolex Chemical Co
2101 S Swanson St . . . . Philadelphia PA 19148 **800-521-9891*** 215-271-0800
**Cust Svc*

Methanex Corp
1800 Waterfront Centre 200 Burrard St
. . . . Vancouver BC V6C3M1 **800-661-8851** 604-661-2600
TSX: MX

National Enzyme Co Inc
15366 US Hwy 160 . . . . Forsyth MO 65653 **800-825-8545** 417-546-4796

Niacet Corp
400 47th St . . . . Niagara Falls NY 14304 **800-828-1207** 716-285-1474

Oakwood Products Inc
1741 Old Dunbar Rd . . . . West Columbia SC 29172 **800-467-3386** 803-739-8800

Pencco Inc
831 Bartlett Rd PO Box 600 . . . . San Felipe TX 77473 **800-864-1742** 979-885-0005

Perstorp Polyols Inc
600 Matzinger Rd . . . . Toledo OH 43612 **800-537-0280*** 419-729-5448
**Cust Svc*

PMC Specialties Group Inc
501 Murray Rd . . . . Cincinnati OH 45217 **800-543-2466**

RT Vanderbilt Company Inc
30 Winfield St . . . . Norwalk CT 06855 **800-243-6064*** 203-853-1400
**Cust Svc*

Selee Corp
700 Shepherd St . . . . Hendersonville NC 28792 **800-842-3818** 828-697-2411

Shell Chemical Co
910 Louisiana St . . . . Houston TX 77002 **855-697-4355**

Shin-Etsu Silicones of America
1150 Damar Dr . . . . Akron OH 44305 **800-544-1745** 330-630-9860

		Toll-Free	Phone
Struktol Company of America Inc PO Box 1649 .... Stow OH 44224		800-327-8649	330-928-5188
Sun Chemical Corp 35 Waterview Blvd .... Parsippany NJ 07054		800-543-2323	973-404-6000
Sunoco Inc 1735 Market St .... Philadelphia PA 19103		800-786-6261	
NYSE: SUN			
Tedia Company Inc 1000 Tedia Way .... Fairfield OH 45014		800-787-4891	513-874-5340
Velsicol Chemical LLC 10400 W Higgins Rd Ste 700 ..... Rosemont IL 60018		877-847-8351*	847-813-7888
*Cust Svc			
Vulcan Materials Co 1200 Urban Ctr Dr PO Box 385014 ..... Birmingham AL 35238		800-615-4331	205-298-3000
NYSE: VMC			
Wacker Chemical Corp 3301 Sutton Rd .... Adrian MI 49221		888-922-5374	517-264-8500
Wausau Chemical Corp 2001 N River Dr .... Wausau WI 54403		800-950-6656	715-842-2285

CHEMICALS - MEDICINAL

145   CHEMICALS - SPECIALTY

		Toll-Free	Phone
ADA-ES Inc 640 Plz Dr Ste 270 .... Highlands Ranch CO 80129		888-822-8617	720-598-3500
NASDAQ: ADES			
Airosol Company Inc 1206 Illinois St .... Neodesha KS 66757		800-633-9576	620-325-2666
Akzo Nobel Chemicals Inc 10 Finderne Ave .... Bridgewater NJ 08807		888-331-6212	
Alex C Fergusson LLC (AFCO) 5000 Letterkenny Rd .... Chambersburg PA 17201		800-345-1329	
Alfa Aesar Co 26 Parkridge Rd .... Ward Hill MA 01835		800-343-0660	978-521-6300
American Polywater Corp 11222 60th St N .... Stillwater MN 55082		800-328-9384	651-430-2270
American Radiolabeled Chemicals Inc (ARC) 101 ARC Dr .... Saint Louis MO 63146		800-331-6661	314-991-4545
AMPAC Fine Chemicals (AFC) MS 1007 PO Box 1718. ......Rancho Cordova CA 95741		800-311-9668	916-357-6880
Anderson Chemical Co 325 S Davis .... Litchfield MN 55355		800-366-2477	320-693-2477
Angstrom Technologies Inc 7880 Foundation Dr .... Florence KY 41042		800-543-7358*	859-282-0020
*Cust Svc			
Apollo Chemical Company LLC 2001 Willow Springs Ln .... Burlington NC 27253		800-374-3827	336-226-1161
Arch Chemicals Inc 1200 Old Lower River Rd PO Box 800 .... Charleston TN 37310		800-638-8174	423-780-2724
NYSE: ARJ			
Athea Laboratories Inc 1900 W Cornell St .... Milwaukee WI 53209		800-743-6417	
Birchwood Laboratories Inc 7900 Fuller Rd .... Eden Prairie MN 55344		800-328-6156	952-937-7900
Brulin Holding Co 2920 Dr AJ Brown Ave .... Indianapolis IN 46205		800-776-7149	317-923-3211
Cabot Corp 2 Seaport Ln Ste 1300 .... Boston MA 02210		800-322-1236	617-345-0100
NYSE: CBT			
Cabot Microelectronics Corp 870 N Commons Dr .... Aurora IL 60504		800-811-2756	630-375-6631
NASDAQ: CCMP			
Cabot Specialty Fluids Inc Waterway Plz Two 10001 Woodlock Forest Dr Ste 275 .... The Woodlands TX 77380		800-322-1236	281-298-9955
Cambridge Isotope Laboratories Inc 3 Highwood Dr .... Tewksbury MA 01876		800-322-1174	
Chemtronics Inc 8125 Cobb Centre Dr .... Kennesaw GA 30152		800-645-5244	770-424-4888
Claire Manufacturing Co 1005 S Westgate Ave .... Addison IL 60101		800-252-4731*	630-543-7600
*Sales			
Columbian Chemicals Co 1800 W Oak Commons Ct .... Marietta GA 30062		800-235-4003	770-792-9400
Coral Chemical Co 1915 Industrial Ave .... Zion IL 60099		800-228-4646	847-246-6666
Cortec Corp 4119 White Bear Pkwy .... Saint Paul MN 55110		800-426-7832	651-429-1100
CRC Industries Inc 885 Louis Dr .... Warminster PA 18974		800-556-5074*	215-674-4300
*Cust Svc			
Diversified Chemical Technologies Inc (DCT) 15477 Woodrow Wilson St .... Detroit MI 48238		800-243-1424	313-867-5444
DOBER 11230 Katherine Crossing Ste 100. .... Woodridge IL 60517		800-323-4983	630-410-7300
Dover Chemical Corp 3676 Davis Rd NW .... Dover OH 44622		800-321-8805*	330-343-7711
*General			
DSM Desotech Inc 1122 St Charles St .... Elgin IL 60120		800-222-7189	847-697-0400
DuPont Chemical Solutions 1007 Market St .... Wilmington DE 19898		800-441-7515	302-774-1000
Dynaloy LLC 6445 Olivia Ln .... Indianapolis IN 46226		800-669-5709	317-788-5694
Elantas PDG Inc 5200 N Second St .... Saint Louis MO 63147		800-325-7492	314-621-5700
Fremont Industries Inc 4400 Vly Industrial Blvd N PO Box 67 ......Shakopee MN 55379		800-436-1238	952-445-4121
Genieco Inc 200 N Laflin St .... Chicago IL 60607		800-223-8217	312-421-2383
Gold Eagle Co 4400 S Kildare Ave .... Chicago IL 60632		800-367-3245	
Grace Davison 7500 Grace Dr .... Columbia MD 21044		800-638-6014	410-531-4000
Harcros 5200 Speaker Rd .... Kansas City KS 66106		800-424-9300	913-321-3131

		Toll-Free	Phone
Houghton Chemical Corp 52 Cambridge St .... Allston MA 02134		800-777-2466	617-254-1010
Kao Specialties Americas LLC 243 Woodbine St PO Box 2316 ...... High Point NC 27261		800-727-2214	336-884-2214
Kester Inc 800 W Thorndale Ave .... Itasca IL 60143		800-253-7837	630-616-4048
KIK Custom Products 2730 Middlebury St .... Elkhart IN 46516		800-479-6603	574-295-0000
KIK Pool Additives Inc 5160 E Airport Dr .... Ontario CA 91761		800-745-4536	909-390-9912
King Industries Inc 1 Science Rd .... Norwalk CT 06852		800-431-7900	203-866-5551
Kolene Corp 12890 Westwood Ave .... Detroit MI 48223		800-521-4182	313-273-9220
Koppers Inc 436 Seventh Ave .... Pittsburgh PA 15219		800-385-4406	412-227-2001
NYSE: KOP			
Leadership Performance Sustainability Laboratories 4647 Hugh Howell Rd .... Tucker GA 30084		800-241-8334	
Lubrizol Corp 29400 Lakeland Blvd .... Wickliffe OH 44092		800-380-5397	440-943-4200
NYSE: LZ			
McGean-Rohco Inc 2910 Harvard Ave .... Cleveland OH 44105		800-932-7006*	216-441-4900
*Orders			
Miller-Stephenson Chemical Co 55 Backus Ave .... Danbury CT 06810		800-992-2424*	203-743-4447
*Tech Supp			
Momar Inc 1830 Ellsworth Industrial Dr .... Atlanta GA 30318		800-556-3967	404-355-4580
Monroe Fluid Technology Inc 36 Draffin Rd .... Hilton NY 14468		800-828-6351	585-392-3434
Montello Inc 6106 E 32nd Pl Ste 100 .... Tulsa OK 74135		800-331-4628	
Nalco Co 1601 W Diehl Rd .... Naperville IL 60563		800-288-0879	630-305-1000
Northern Technologies International Corp (NTIC) 4201 Woodland Rd PO Box 69 .... Circle Pines MN 55014		800-328-2433	763-225-6600
NASDAQ: NTIC			
Nox-Crete Inc 1444 S 20th St .... Omaha NE 68108		800-669-2738	402-341-2080
OMNOVA Solutions Inc Performance Chemicals Div 165 S Cleveland Ave .... Mogadore OH 44260		888-253-5454	330-628-6536
Pacific Ethanol Corp 400 Capitol Mall Ste 2060 .... Sacramento CA 95814		866-508-4969	916-403-2123
NASDAQ: PEIX			
Pavco Inc 1935 John Crosland Jr Dr .... Charlotte NC 28208		800-321-7735*	704-496-6800
*Orders			
Peach State Labs Inc (PSL) 180 Burlington Rd PO Box 1087. ...... Rome GA 30162		800-634-1653	706-291-8743
Penray Cos Inc 440 Denniston Ct .... Wheeling IL 60090		800-373-6729	800-323-6329
Precision Laboratories Inc 1429 S Shields Dr .... Waukegan IL 60085		800-323-6280	847-596-3001
Premier Colors Inc 100 Industrial Dr .... Union SC 29379		800-245-6944	864-427-0338
PVS Chemicals Inc 10900 Harper Ave .... Detroit MI 48213		800-932-8860	313-921-1200
Quaker Chemical Corp 901 E Hector St .... Conshohocken PA 19428		800-523-7010	610-832-4000
NYSE: KWR			
Rochester Midland Corp 333 Hollenbeck St .... Rochester NY 14621		800-836-1627	585-336-2200
Royal Chemical Co 1755 Enterprise Pkwy Ste 600 ...... Twinsburg OH 44087		844-462-7692	
SA Day Mfg Co Inc 1489 Niagara St .... Buffalo NY 14213		800-747-0030	716-881-3030
Sigma-Aldrich Corp 3050 Spruce St .... Saint Louis MO 63103		800-325-3010	314-771-5765
NASDAQ: SIAL			
Sika Corp 201 Polito Ave .... Lyndhurst NJ 07071		800-933-7452	201-933-8800
Solutek Corp 94 Shirley St .... Boston MA 02119		800-403-0770	617-445-5335
Spartan Chemical Company Inc 1110 Spartan Dr .... Maumee OH 43537		800-537-8990	419-531-5551
Specco Industries Inc 13087 Main St .... Lemont IL 60439		800-441-6646	630-257-5060
Sprayway Inc 1005 S Westgate Ave .... Addison IL 60101		800-332-9000	630-628-3000
Stapleton Technologies Inc 1350 W 12th St .... Long Beach CA 90813		800-266-0541	562-437-0541
Stepan Co 22 W Frontage Rd .... Northfield IL 60093		800-745-7837*	847-446-7500
*Cust Svc			
Technical Chemical Co 3327 Pipeline Rd .... Cleburne TX 76033		800-527-0885	817-645-6088
United Color Manufacturing Inc (UCM) PO Box 480 .... Newtown PA 18940		800-852-5942	215-860-2165
United Laboratories Inc 320 37th Ave .... Saint Charles IL 60174		800-323-2594	
United Salt Corp 4800 San Felipe St .... Houston TX 77056		800-554-8658	713-877-2600
Vertellus Specialties Inc 201 N Illinois St Ste 1800. .... Indianapolis IN 46204		800-777-3536	317-247-8141
WR Grace & Co 7500 Grace Dr .... Columbia MD 21044		800-638-6014	410-531-4000
NYSE: GRA			
XL Brands 198 Nexus Dr .... Dalton GA 30721		800-367-4583	706-272-5800
Zinkan Enterprises Inc 1919 Case Pkwy N .... Twinsburg OH 44087		800-229-6801	

146   CHEMICALS & RELATED PRODUCTS - WHOL

		Toll-Free	Phone
Airgas Inc 259 N Radnor-Chester Rd Ste 100 ...... Radnor PA 19087		800-255-2165	610-687-5253
NYSE: ARG			
Americas Styrenics LLC 24 Waterway Ave Ste 1200 .... Woodlands TX 77380		844-512-1212	832-616-7800

				Toll-Free	Phone
Aramsco Inc					
1480 Grandview Ave	Paulsboro	NJ	08086	**800-767-6933**	856-686-7700
Barton Solvents Inc					
1920 NE Broadway Ave	Des Moines	IA	50313	**800-728-6488**	515-265-7998
Berryman Products Inc					
3800 E Randol Mill Rd	Arlington	TX	76011	**800-433-1704**	817-640-2376
Boral Material Technologies Inc					
45 NE Loop 410 Ste 700	San Antonio	TX	78216	**800-964-0951**	210-349-4069
Brenntag Canada Inc					
43 Jutland Rd	Toronto	ON	M8Z2G6	**866-516-9707**	416-243-9615
Brenntag North America Inc					
5083 Pottsville Pk	Reading	PA	19605	**877-363-5843**	610-926-6100
Brenntag Southwest Inc					
Industry Park W 17550	Citronelle	AL	36522	**800-732-0562**	903-759-7151
Brown Machine LLC					
330 N Ross St	Beaverton	MI	48612	**877-702-4142**	989-435-7741
Callahan Chemical Co					
Broad St & Filmore Ave	Palmyra	NJ	08065	**800-257-7967**	
Canada Colors & Chemicals Ltd					
175 Bloor St E Ste 1300 N Twr	Toronto	ON	M4W3R8	**800-461-1638**	416-443-5500
Coolant Control Inc					
5353 Spring Grove Ave	Cincinnati	OH	45217	**800-535-3885**	513-471-8770
Dar-tech Inc					
16485 Rockside Rd	Cleveland	OH	44137	**800-228-7347**	216-663-7600
DB Becker Company Inc					
46 Leigh St	Clinton	NJ	08809	**800-394-3991**	908-730-6010
Denso North America Inc					
9747 Whithorn Dr	Houston	TX	77095	**888-821-2300**	281-821-3355
DM Figley Company Inc					
10 Kelly Ct	Menlo Park	CA	94025	**800-292-9919**	650-329-8700
Dorsett & Jackson Inc					
3800 Noakes St	Los Angeles	CA	90023	**800-871-8365**	323-268-1815
Ellsworth Adhesives					
W129 N10825 Washington Dr	Germantown	WI	53022	**877-454-9224**	262-253-8600
ET Horn Co					
16050 Canary Ave	La Mirada	CA	90638	**800-442-4676**	714-523-8050
FDF Energy Services					
240 Jasmine Rd	Crowley	LA	70526	**800-252-3104**	337-783-8685
Gallade Chemical Inc					
1230 E St Gertrude Pl	Santa Ana	CA	92707	**888-830-9092**	714-546-9901
Conoral Air Service & Supply Company Inc					
1105 Zuni St	Denver	CO	80204	**877-782-8434**	303-092-7003
George S Coyne Chemical Co					
3015 State Rd	Croydon	PA	19021	**800-523-1230**	215-785-3000
Harcros 5200 Speaker Rd	Kansas City	KS	66106	**800-424-9300**	913-321-3131
Haviland Enterprises Inc					
421 Ann St NW	Grand Rapids	MI	49504	**800-456-1134**	
Hill Bros Chemical Co					
1675 N Main St	Orange	CA	92867	**800-994-8801**	714-998-8800
HM Royal Inc					
689 Pennington Ave	Trenton	NJ	08601	**800-257-9452**	609-396-9176
Homax Products Inc					
1835 Barkley Blvd Ste 101	Bellingham	WA	98226	**888-890-9029**	360-733-9029
Hubbard-Hall Inc					
563 S Leonard St	Waterbury	CT	06708	**800-331-6871**	866-441-5831
ICC Chemical Corp					
460 Park Ave	New York	NY	10022	**800-422-1720**	212-521-1700
Ideal Chemical & Supply Co					
4025 Air Park St	Memphis	TN	38118	**800-232-6776**	901-363-7720
Independent Chemical Corp					
79-51 Cooper Ave	Glendale	NY	11385	**800-892-2578**	718-894-0700
Industrial Chemicals Inc					
2042 Montreat Dr	Vestavia	AL	35216	**800-476-2042***	205-823-7330
*Cust Svc					
John R Hess & Company Inc					
400 Stn St PO Box 3615	Cranston	RI	02910	**800-828-4377**	401-785-9300
John R White Company Inc					
PO Box 10043	Birmingham	AL	35202	**800-245-1183**	205-595-8381
Kraft Chemical Co					
1975 N Hawthorne Ave	Melrose Park	IL	60160	**800-345-5200**	708-345-5200
LV Lomas Ltd					
99 Summerlea Rd	Brampton	ON	L6T4V2	**800-575-3382**	905-458-1555
McCullough & Assoc					
1746 NE Expy PO Box 29803	Atlanta	GA	30329	**800-969-1606**	404-325-1606
NuCo2 Inc					
2800 SE Marketplace	Stuart	FL	34997	**800-472-2855**	772-221-1754
Palmer Holland Inc					
25000 Country Club Blvd Ste 444	North Olmsted	OH	44070	**800-635-4822**	440-686-2300
Plaza Group Inc					
10375 Richmond Ave Ste 1620	Houston	TX	77042	**800-876-3738**	713-266-0707
Quadra Chemicals Ltd					
3901 Fixtessier	Vaudreuil-Dorion	QC	J7V5V5	**800-665-6553**	
Reagent Chemical & Research Inc					
115 Rt 202	Ringoes	NJ	08551	**800-231-1807**	908-284-2800
Ribelin Sales Inc					
3857 Miller Pk Dr	Garland	TX	75042	**800-374-1594**	972-272-1594
Rowell Chemical Corp					
15 Salt Creek Ln Ste 205	Hinsdale	IL	60521	**888-261-7963**	630-920-8833
SARCOM Inc AEP Colloids Div					
6299 Rt 9N	Hadley	NY	12835	**800-848-0658**	518-696-9900
Sessions Specialty Co					
5090 Styers Ferry Rd	Lewisville	NC	27023	**800-763-0077**	336-766-2880
Solmax International Inc					
2801 Marie-Victorin Blvd	Varennes	QC	J3X1P7	**800-571-3904**	450-929-1234
Solvents & Chemicals Inc					
1904 Mykawa Rd	Pearland	TX	77581	**800-622-3990**	281-485-5377
Specified Technologies Inc					
210 Evans Way	Somerville	NJ	08876	**800-992-1180**	908-526-8000
Spectra Colors Corp					
25 Rizzolo Rd	Kearny	NJ	07032	**800-527-8588**	201-997-0606
Strem Chemicals Inc					
7 Mulliken Way	Newburyport	MA	01950	**800-647-8736**	978-499-1600
Sweetlake Chemical Ltd					
446 Heights Blvd	Houston	TX	77007	**888-752-1998**	713-827-8707
Tanner Industries Inc					
735 Davisville Rd	Southampton	PA	18966	**800-643-6226**	215-322-1238
Tarr LLC					
2946 NE Columbia Blvd	Portland	OR	97211	**800-422-5069**	503-288-5294
TCR Industries					
26 Centerpointe Dr Ste 120	La Palma	CA	90623	**877-827-1444**	714-521-5222
Tilley Chemical Company Inc					
501 Chesapeake Park Plz	Baltimore	MD	21220	**800-638-6968**	410-574-4500
TR International Trading Company Inc					
1218 Third Ave Ste 2100	Seattle	WA	98101	**800-761-7717**	206-505-3500
TransChemical Inc					
419 De Soto Ave	Saint Louis	MO	63147	**888-873-6481**	314-231-6905
Ultra Clean Technologies Corp					
1274 Hgwy 77	Bridgeton	NJ	08302	**800-791-9111**	856-451-2176
Univar Canada Ltd					
9800 Van Horne Way	Richmond	BC	V6X1W5	**855-888-8648**	
Univar USA Inc					
17425 NE Union Hill Rd	Redmond	WA	98052	**855-888-8648**	425-889-3400
Van Horn Metz & Company Inc					
201 E Elm St	Conshohocken	PA	19428	**800-523-0424**	610-828-4500
Whitaker Oil Co					
1557 Marietta Rd NW	Atlanta	GA	30318	**888-895-3506**	404-355-8220
Wilson Industrial Sales Co Inc					
5063 South 1000 West PO Box 297	Rensselaer	IN	47978	**800-633-5427**	219-866-6900

147   CHILD CARE MONITORING SYSTEMS - INTERNET

				Toll-Free	Phone
Mississippi Action For Progress Inc (MAP)					
1751 Morson Rd	Jackson	MS	39209	**800-924-4615**	601-923-4100

148   CHILDREN'S LEARNING CENTERS

				Toll-Free	Phone
Abundant Life Christian Academy					
1494 Banks Rd	Margate	FL	33063	**800-948-6291**	954-979-2665
Autistic Treatment Center Inc					
10503 Metric Dr	Dallas	TX	75243	**877-666-2747**	972-644-2076
Bright Horizons Family Solutions LLC					
200 Talcott Ave S	Watertown	MA	02472	**800-324-4386**	617-673-8000
Centre for Skills Development & Training, The					
3350 S Service Rd	Burlington	ON	L7N3M6	**888-315-5521**	905-333-3499
Child Development Associates Inc					
100 Otay Lakoe Rd Ste 310	Bonita	CA	91902	**888-755-2445**	619-427-4411
Childcare Network					
3009 University Ave	Columbus	GA	31909	**866-521-5437**	706-819-6297
Competency & Credentialing Institute					
2170 S Parker Rd Ste 295	Denver	CO	80231	**888-257-2667**	
Computer Explorers					
12715 Telge Rd	Cypress	TX	77429	**800-531-5053**	
DePelchin Children's Ctr					
4950 Memorial Dr	Houston	TX	77007	**888-730-2335**	713-730-2335
FasTracKids International Ltd					
6900 E Belleview Ave					
Ste 100	Greenwood Village	CO	80111	**888-576-6888**	303-224-0200
Goddard Systems Inc					
1016 West Ninth Ave	King of Prussia	PA	19406	**800-463-3273**	877-256-7046
Golflogix Inc					
15685 N Greenway-Hayden Loop					
Ste 100A	Scottsdale	AZ	85260	**877-977-0162**	
Huntington Learning Centers Inc					
496 Kinderkamack Rd	Oradell	NJ	07649	**800-653-8400**	201-261-8400
KinderCare Learning Centers LLC					
650 NE Holladay St Ste 1400	Portland	OR	97232	**800-633-1488**	
Kumon North America Inc					
300 Frank W Burr Blvd Glenpointe Ctr E					
Ste 6	Teaneck	NJ	07666	**800-222-6284**	201-928-0444
Lad Lake Inc					
W350s1401 Waterville Rd PO Box 158	Dousman	WI	53118	**877-965-2131**	262-965-2131
New Horizon Kids Quest Inc					
3405 Annapolis Ln N Ste 100	Plymouth	MN	55447	**800-941-1007**	
Pioneer Clubs					
123 E Elk	Carol Stream	IL	60188	**800-694-2582**	
Porter & Chester Institute Inc, The					
670 Lordship Blvd	Stratford	CT	06615	**800-870-6789**	203-375-4463
Primrose School Franchising Co					
3660 Cedarcrest Rd	Acworth	GA	30101	**800-745-0677**	770-529-4100
Rosedale Technical Institute					
215 Beecham Dr Ste 2	Pittsburgh	PA	15205	**800-521-6262**	
Rural Resources Community Action					
956 S Main St	Colville	WA	99114	**800-538-7659**	509-684-8421
Sky Ranch 24657 CR 448	Van	TX	75790	**800-962-2267**	
St Raphael Academy					
123 Walcott St	Pawtucket	RI	02860	**800-498-0045**	401-723-8100
Tiger Schulmann's Karate Ctr					
485 Blvd	Elmwood Park	NJ	07407	**800-867-1218**	
World Wide Group LLC					
5507 Nesconset Hwy Ste 10	Mount Sanai	NY	11766	**800-790-4519**	

149   CIRCUS, CARNIVAL, FESTIVAL OPERATORS

				Toll-Free	Phone
Big Apple Circus (BAC)					
321 W 44th St Ste 400	New York	NY	10036	**888-541-3750**	212-257-2330
Feld Entertainment Inc					
8607 Westwood Ctr Dr	Vienna	VA	22182	**800-844-3545**	703-448-4000
Maryland Renaissance Festival					
PO Box 315	Crownsville	MD	21032	**800-296-7304**	410-266-7304
Starkey International Institute for Household Management					
1350 Logan St	Denver	CO	80203	**800-888-4904**	303-832-5510

150   CLAY PRODUCTS - STRUCTURAL

SEE ALSO Brick, Stone, Related Materials

				Toll-Free	Phone
Cherokee Brick & Tile Co Inc					
3250 Waterville Rd	Macon	GA	31206	**800-277-2745**	

	Toll-Free	Phone
Colloid Environmental Technologies Co (CETCO)		
2870 Forbs Ave .... Hoffman Estates IL 60192	800-527-9948	847-851-1899
General Shale Products LLC		
3015 Bristol Hwy .... Johnson City TN 37601	800-414-4661	423-282-4661
Henry Brick Co Inc		
3409 Water Ave .... Selma AL 36703	800-218-3906	334-875-2600
International Chimney Corp		
55 S Long St .... Williamsville NY 14221	800-828-1446	
Kinney Brick Co		
100 Prosperity Rd PO Box 1804 ...... Albuquerque NM 87103	800-464-4605	505-877-4550
Lee Brick & Tile Co		
3704 Hawkins Ave PO Box 1027 ...... Sanford NC 27330	800-672-7559	919-774-4800
Logan Clay Products Co		
201 S Walnut St .... Logan OH 43138	800-848-2141	
Ludowici Roof Tile Inc		
4757 Tile Plant Rd PO Box 69 ...... New Lexington OH 43764	800-945-8453*	740-342-1995
*Cust Svc		
Marion Ceramics Inc		
PO Box 1134 .... Marion SC 29571	800-845-4010	843-423-1311
McNear Brick & Block		
1 McNear BrickyaRd Rd		
PO Box 151380 .... San Rafael CA 94901	888-442-6811	415-453-7702
Palmetto Brick Co		
3501 BrickyaRd Rd .... Wallace SC 29596	800-922-4423	
Pine Hall Brick Co		
2701 Shorefair Dr .... Winston-Salem NC 27105	800-334-8689	
Redland Brick Inc		
15718 Clear Spring Rd .... Williamsport MD 21795	800-366-2742	301-223-7700
Statesville Brick Co		
391 BrickyaRd Rd .... Statesville NC 28677	800-522-4716	704-872-4123
Superior Clay Corp		
6566 Superior Rd SE .... Uhrichsville OH 44683	800-848-6166	740-922-4122
Triangle Brick Co		
6523 NC Hwy 55 .... Durham NC 27713	800-672-8547	919-544-1796
Whitacre Greer Fireproofing Inc		
1400 S Mahoning Ave .... Alliance OH 44601	800-947-2837*	330-823-1610
*Cust Svc		

151 CLEANING PRODUCTS

SEE ALSO Mops, Sponges, Wiping Cloths ; Brushes & Brooms

	Toll-Free	Phone
ABC Compounding Company Inc & Acme Wholesale		
6970 Jonesboro Rd .... Morrow GA 30260	800-795-9222	770-968-9222
Adco Inc 1909 W Oakridge .... Albany GA 31707	800-821-7556	
American Cleaning Solutions		
39-30 Review Ave PO Box 1943 ...... Long Island NY 11101	888-929-7587	718-392-8080
Arrow-Magnolia International		
2646 Rodney Ln .... Dallas TX 75229	800-527-2101	972-247-7111
Aztec International Inc		
3010 Henson Rd .... Knoxville TN 37921	800-369-5357	865-588-5357
BAF Industries Inc		
1451 Edinger Ave .... Tustin CA 92780	800-437-9893	714-258-8055
Buckeye International Inc		
2700 Wagner Pl .... Maryland Heights MO 63043	800-321-2583	314-291-1900
Bullen Cos		
1640 Delmar Dr PO Box 37 .... Folcroft PA 19032	800-444-8900	610-534-8900
Camco Chemical Co		
8145 Holton Dr .... Florence KY 41042	800-354-1001*	859-727-3200
*Cust Svc		
Canberra Corp		
3610 Holland Sylvania Rd .... Toledo OH 43615	800-832-8992	419-841-6616
Carroll Co		
2900 W Kingsley Rd .... Garland TX 75041	800-527-5722	
Cello Professional Products		
1354 Old Post Rd .... Havre de Grace MD 21078	800-638-4850	410-939-1234
Champion Chemical Co		
8319 S Greenleaf Ave .... Whittier CA 90602	800-424-9300	
Church & Dwight Company Inc		
469 N Harrison St .... Princeton NJ 08543	800-617-4220	
NYSE: CHD		
Clean Ones Corp		
317 SW Alder St Ste 350 .... Portland OR 97204	800-367-4587	
comFrank B Ross Co Inc		
970-H New Brunswick Ave .... Rahway NJ 07065	800-541-6752	732-669-0810
Correlated Products Inc		
5616 Progress Rd .... Indianapolis IN 46242	800-428-3266	317-243-3248
Damon Industries Inc		
12435 Rockhill Ave NE .... Alliance OH 44601	800-362-9850	330-821-5310
Dreumex USA 3445 BoaRd Rd .... York PA 17406	800-233-9382	717-767-6881
Dubois Chemicals		
3630 E Kemper Rd .... Cincinnati OH 45241	800-438-2647	
Dura Wax Co		
4101 W Albany St .... Mchenry IL 60050	800-435-5705	
Falcon Safety Products Inc		
25 Imclone Dr .... Branchburg NJ 08876	800-332-5266	908-707-4900
Fine Organics Corp		
420 Kuller Rd PO Box 2277 .... Clifton NJ 07015	800-526-7480	973-478-1000
Heritage-Crystal Clean Inc		
2175 Pt Blvd Ste 375 .... Elgin IL 60123	877-938-7948	847-836-5670
Hill Mfg Company Inc		
1500 Jonesboro Rd SE .... Atlanta GA 30315	800-445-5123	404-522-8364
Hillyard Chemical Company Inc		
302 N Fourth St PO Box 909 .... St. Joseph MO 64501	800-365-1555	816-233-1321
Impact Products LLC		
2840 Centennial Rd .... Toledo OH 43617	800-333-1541*	419-841-2891
*Cust Svc		
ITW Dymon 805 E Old 56 Hwy .... Olathe KS 66061	800-443-9536	913-829-6296
James Austin Co		
115 Downieville Rd PO Box 827 .... Mars PA 16046	800-245-1942	724-625-1535
Kay Chemical Co		
8300 Capital Dr .... Greensboro NC 27409	877-315-1115	844-880-8355
Koger/Air Corp		
PO Box 2098 .... Martinsville VA 24113	800-368-2096	276-638-8821
Leadership Performance Sustainability Laboratories		
4647 Hugh Howell Rd .... Tucker GA 30084	800-241-8334	

	Toll-Free	Phone
Malco Products Inc		
361 Fairview Ave PO Box 892 .... Barberton OH 44203	800-253-2526	330-753-0361
Maxim Technologies Inc		
1607 Derwent Way .... Delta BC V3M6K8	800-663-9925	
Meguiar's Inc		
17991 Mitchell S .... Irvine CA 92614	800-347-5700*	
*Cust Svc		
Micro Care Corp		
595 John Downey Dr .... New Britain CT 06051	800-638-0125	860-827-0626
Morga-Gallacher Inc		
8707 Millergrove Dr .... Santa Fe Springs CA 90670	877-647-6279	
National Chemical Laboratories Inc		
401 N Tenth St .... Philadelphia PA 19123	800-628-2436	215-922-1200
National Chemicals Inc		
105 Liberty St PO Box 32 .... Winona MN 55987	800-533-0027*	507-454-5640
*Cust Svc		
NCH Corp		
2727 Chemsearch Blvd .... Irving TX 75062	800-527-9919	972-438-0211
New Pig Corp 1 Pork Ave .... Tipton PA 16684	800-468-4647	814-684-0101
Nuvite Chemical Compounds Corp		
85 Jetson Ln .... Central Islip NY 11722	800-394-8351	718-383-8351
Ocean Bio-Chem Inc (OBCI)		
4041 SW 47th Ave .... Fort Lauderdale FL 33314	800-327-8583	954-587-6280
NASDAQ: OBCI		
Paramount Chemical Specialties Inc		
14750 NE 95th St .... Redmond WA 98052	877-846-7826	425-882-2673
Prosoco Inc		
3741 Greenway Cir .... Lawrence KS 66046	800-255-4255	
Safeguard Chemical Corp		
411 Wales Ave .... Bronx NY 10454	800-536-3170	718-585-3170
Safetec of America Inc		
887 Kensington Ave .... Buffalo NY 14215	800-456-7077	716-895-1822
Scott Fetzer Company Scot Laboratories Div		
16841 Pk Cir Dr .... Chagrin Falls OH 44023	800-486-7268	440-543-3033
Scott's Liquid Gold Inc		
4880 Havana St .... Denver CO 80239	800-447-1919	303-373-4860
OTC: SLGD		
Seventh Generation Inc		
60 Lake St .... Burlington VT 05401	800-456-1191	802-658-3773
Share Corp		
7821 N Faulkner Rd .... Milwaukee WI 53224	800-776-7192	
Simoniz USA 201 Boston Tpke .... Bolton CT 06043	800-227-5536	
Snyder Manufacturing Corp		
1541 W Cowles St .... Long Beach CA 90813	800-395-6478	562-432-2038
State Industrial Products		
3100 Hamilton Ave .... Cleveland OH 44114	877-747-6986	216-861-7114
Stearns Packaging Corp		
4200 Sycamore Ave .... Madison WI 53714	800-655-5008	608-246-5150
Sunshine Makers Inc		
15922 Pacific Coast Hwy .... Huntington Harbour CA 92649	800-228-0709	562-795-6000
Unit Chemical Corp		
7360 Commercial Way .... Henderson NV 89015	800-879-8648	702-564-6454
Warsaw Chemical Company Inc		
Argonne Rd PO Box 858 .... Warsaw IN 46580	800-548-3396	574-267-3251
WD-40 Co 1061 Cudahy Pl .... San Diego CA 92110	800-448-9340	619-275-1400
NASDAQ: WDFC		
West Penetone Corp		
700 Gotham Pkwy .... Carlstadt NJ 07072	800-631-1652	201-567-3000
ZEP Inc		
1310 Seaboard Industrial Blvd NW .... Atlanta GA 30318	877-428-9937	404-352-1680
NYSE: ZEP		

152 CLEANING SERVICES

SEE ALSO Bio-Recovery Services ; Building Maintenance Services

	Toll-Free	Phone
1-800-Water Damage		
1167 Mercer St .... Seattle WA 98109	800-928-3732	206-381-3041
Boston's Best Chimney Sweep		
76 Bacon St .... Waltham MA 02451	800-660-6708*	781-893-6611
*Cust Svc		
Braco Window Cleaning Service Inc		
1 Braco International Blvd .... Wilder KY 41076	800-969-4300	859-442-6000
Clean Power LLC		
124 N 121st St .... Milwaukee WI 53226	800-588-1608	414-302-3000
Cleaning Authority		
7230 Lee DeForest Dr .... Columbia MD 21046	888-658-0659	443-602-9154
CleanNet USA		
9861 Brokenland Pkwy Ste 208 .... Columbia MD 21046	800-735-8838	410-720-6444
Coverall Cleaning Concepts		
5201 Congress Ave Ste 275 .... Boca Raton FL 33487	800-537-3371	866-296-8944
Duraclean International Inc		
220 Campus Dr .... Arlington Heights IL 60004	800-251-7070	
Fish Window Cleaning Services Inc		
200 Enchanted Pkwy .... Manchester MO 63021	877-707-3474	636-779-1500
GCA Services Group		
1350 Euclid Ave Ste 1500 .... Cleveland OH 44115	800-422-8760	
Heaven's Best Carpet & Upholstery Cleaning		
PO Box 607 .... Rexburg ID 83440	800-359-2095	208-359-1106
Jan-Pro International Inc (JPI)		
2520 Northwinds Pkwy Ste 375 .... Alpharetta GA 30009	866-355-1064	678-336-1780
Maid Brigade USA/Minimaid Canada		
4 Concourse Pkwy Ste 200 .... Atlanta GA 30328	866-800-7470	800-722-6243
Maids International		
9394 W Dodge Rd Ste 140 .... Omaha NE 68114	800-843-6243	402-558-8600
Merry Maids		
3839 Forrest Hill-Irene Rd .... Memphis TN 38125	800-798-8000	
MPW Industrial Services Group Inc		
9711 Lancaster Ro SE .... Hebron OH 43025	800-827-8790	740-929-1614
Rainbow International		
1010 N University Park Dr .... Waco TX 76707	855-724-6269	254-756-5463
ServiceMaster Clean		
3839 Forrest Hill Irene Rd .... Memphis TN 38125	844-319-5401*	
*General		
Servpro Industries Inc		
801 Industrial Blvd .... Gallatin TN 37066	800-826-9586	615-451-0200

	Toll-Free	Phone
St Moritz Bldg Services Inc		
4616 Clairton Blvd ....Pittsburgh PA 15236	800-218-9159	412-885-2100
Steam Bros Inc		
2400 Vermont Ave ....Bismarck ND 58504	800-767-5064	701-222-1263
Support Services of America Inc		
12440 Firestone Blvd Ste 312..........Norwalk CA 90650	888-564-0005	562-868-3550
Tu.c.s. Cleaning Service Inc		
166 Central Ave ....Orange NJ 07050	800-992-5998	973-673-0700
Window Gang		
405 Arendell St ....Morehead City NC 28557	800-849-2308	252-726-1463

153 CLOCKS, WATCHES, RELATED DEVICES, PARTS

	Toll-Free	Phone
Bulova Corp		
Empire State Bldg 350 Fifth Ave ....New York NY 10118	800-228-5682	212-497-1875
Canterbury Designs		
5632 W Washington Blvd ....Los Angeles CA 90016	800-935-7111	323-936-7111
Capintec Inc		
7 Vreeland Rd ....Florham Park NJ 07932	800-631-3826	201-825-9500
Citizen Watch Co of America Inc		
1000 W 190th St ....Torrance CA 90502	800-321-1023	310-532-8463
E Gluck Corp		
60-15 Little Neck Pkwy ....Little Neck NY 11362	800-840-2933	718-784-0700
Milton Industries Inc		
4500 W Cortland ....Chicago IL 60639	855-464-6458	
Seiko Corp of America		
1111 MacArthur Blvd ....Mahwah NJ 07430	800-545-2783*	201-529-5730
*Cust Svc		
Seiko Instruments USA Inc		
21221 S Western Ave Ste 250..........Torrance CA 90501	800-688-0817*	310-517-7700
*Sales		
Timex Group USA Inc		
555 Christian Rd PO Box 310..........Middlebury CT 06762	800-448-4639	888-727-2931
Verdin Co, The		
444 Reading Rd ....Cincinnati OH 45202	800-543-0488	
Vulcan Inc 410 E Berry Ave ....Foley AL 36535	888-846-2728	251-943-7000

154 CLOSURES - METAL OR PLASTICS

	Toll-Free	Phone
AptarGroup Inc		
475 W Terra Cotta Ave Ste E ....Crystal Lake IL 60014	800-401-1957	815-477-0424
NYSE: ATR		
Caplugs LLC		
2150 Elmwood Ave ....Buffalo NY 14207	888-227-5847*	716-876-9855
*Cust Svc		
Essentra PLC		
7400 W Industrial Dr ....Forest Park IL 60130	800-847-0486	
Mila Displays Inc		
1315B Broadway Ste 108 ....Hewlett NY 11557	800-295-6452	516-791-2643
Silgan Holdings Inc		
4 Landmark Sq Ste 400 ....Stamford CT 06901	800-732-0330	203-975-7110
NASDAQ: SLGN		
StockCap		
123 Manufacturers Dr ....Arnold MO 63010	800-827-2277	636-282-6800
Tipper Tie Inc 2000 Lufkin Rd ....Apex NC 27539	800-331-2905	919-362-8811

155 CLOTHING & ACCESSORIES - MFR

SEE ALSO Footwear ; Leather Goods - Personal ; Personal Protective Equipment & Clothing ; Baby Products ; Clothing & Accessories - Whol ; Fashion Design Houses

155-1 Athletic Apparel

	Toll-Free	Phone
Bristol Products Corp		
700 Shelby St ....Bristol TN 37620	800-336-8775*	423-968-4140
*Orders		
Choi Bros Inc 3401 W Div St ....Chicago IL 60651	800-524-2464	773-489-2800
Columbia Sportswear Co		
14375 NW Science Park Dr ....Portland OR 97229	800-622-6953	503-985-4000
NASDAQ: COLM		
Cutter & Buck Inc		
701 N 34th St Ste 400 ....Seattle WA 98103	800-713-7810	888-338-9944
Dodger Industries		
2075 Stultz Rd PO Box 711 ....Martinsville VA 24112	800-436-3437*	
*Cust Svc		
Elite Sportswear LP		
2136 N 13th St ....Reading PA 19604	800-345-4087*	610-921-1469
*Cust Svc		
Gear for Sports Inc		
9700 Commerce Pkwy ....Lenexa KS 66219	800-255-1065	913-693-3200
MJ Soffe Co 1 Soffe Dr ....Fayetteville NC 28312	888-257-8673	
Race Face Components Inc		
100 Braid St ....New Westminster BC V3L3P4	800-527-9244	604-527-9996
Royal Textile Mills Inc		
929 Firetower Rd ....Yanceyville NC 27379	800-334-9361	

155-2 Belts (Leather, Plastics, Fabric)

	Toll-Free	Phone
Bent Gate Mountaineering		
1313 Washington Ave ....Golden CO 80401	877-236-8428	303-271-9382
Gem Dandy Inc		
200 W Academy St ....Madison NC 27025	800-334-5101	336-548-9624

155-3 Casual Wear (Men's & Women's)

	Toll-Free	Phone
Attraction Inc		
672 Rue du Parc ....Lac-Drolet QC G0Y1C0	800-567-6095	819-549-2477

	Toll-Free	Phone
Badger Sportswear Inc		
111 Badger Ln ....Statesville NC 28625	888-871-0990	704-871-0990
Big Dogs		
519 Lincoln County Pkwy ....Lincolnton NC 28092	800-244-3647	828-695-2800
Bobby Jones		
2625 N Berkeley Lake Rd NW		
Bldg 200 Ste 100 ....Duluth GA 30096	888-776-0076*	
*Cust Svc		
Columbia Sportswear Co		
14375 NW Science Park Dr ....Portland OR 97229	800-622-6953	503-985-4000
NASDAQ: COLM		
Crazy Shirts Inc		
99-969 Iwaena St ....Aiea HI 96701	800-771-2720	808-487-9919
Delta Apparel Inc		
2750 Premiere Pkwy Ste 100 ....Duluth GA 30097	800-285-4456	678-775-6900
NYSE: DLA		
Fruit of the Loom Inc		
1 Fruit of the Loom Dr		
PO Box 90015..........Bowling Green KY 42102	888-378-4829	270-781-6400
Quiksilver Inc		
15202 Graham St ....Huntington Beach CA 92649	800-435-9917	
NYSE: ZQK		
Sherry Mfg Co Inc		
3287 NW 65th St ....Miami FL 33147	800-741-4750	305-693-7000
Sport-Haley Inc		
10367 Brockwood Rd ....Dallas TX 75238	800-627-9211	
Surf Line Hawaii Ltd		
411 Puuhale Rd ....Honolulu HI 96819	800-847-5267	808-847-5985
Tonix Corp		
40910 Encyclopedia Cir ....Fremont CA 94538	800-227-2072	510-651-8050
Whisper Knits Inc		
9303 Monroe Rd Ste N ....Charlotte NC 28270	866-695-7022	704-489-6105
World's Best 1801 W Waco Dr ....Waco TX 76707	800-437-0940	254-753-7301

155-4 Children's & Infants' Clothing

	Toll-Free	Phone
Florence Eiseman company LLC		
1966 S Fourth St ....Milwaukee WI 53204	800-558-9013	
Gerber Childrenswear Inc		
7005 Pelham Rd Ste D ....Greenville SC 29615	800-642-4452	877-313-2114
New ICM 220 Sam Bishkin ....El Campo TX 77437	800-987-9008	979-578-0543

155-5 Coats (Overcoats, Jackets, Raincoats, etc)

	Toll-Free	Phone
Alpha Industries Inc		
14200 Park Meadow Dr		
Ste 110 S Tower ....Chantilly VA 20151	866-631-0719*	
*General		
Essex Manufacturing Inc		
PO Box 92864 ....Southlake TX 76092	888-643-7739	817-847-4555
Helly Hansen US Inc		
3703 I St NW ....Auburn WA 98001	800-435-5901	
London Fog 1615 Kellogg Dr ....Douglas GA 31535	877-588-8189	732-346-9009
MECA Sportswear		
1120 Townline Rd ....Tomah WI 54660	800-729-6322	608-374-6450
Pendleton Woolen Mills Inc		
220 NW Broadway ....Portland OR 97209	800-760-4844	503-226-4801
RefrigiWear Inc		
54 Breakstone Dr ....Dahlonega GA 30533	800-645-3744*	706-864-5757
*Cust Svc		
Rennoc Corp 645 Pine St ....Greenville OH 45331	800-372-7100	
Sport Obermeyer Ltd USA Inc		
115 AABC ....Aspen CO 81611	800-525-4203	970-925-5060
Sport-Haley Inc		
10367 Brockwood Rd ....Dallas TX 75238	800-627-9211	
Woolrich Inc 2 Mill St ....Woolrich PA 17779	800-995-1299	570-769-6464

155-6 Costumes

	Toll-Free	Phone
Costume Gallery		
700 Creek Rd ....Delanco NJ 08075	800-222-8125	609-386-6601
Costume Specialists Inc		
211 N Fifth St ....Columbus OH 43215	800-596-9357	614-464-2115
Curtain Call Costumes		
333 E Seventh Ave ....York PA 17404	888-808-0801	800-677-7053
Disguise 12120 Kear Pl ....Poway CA 92064	877-875-2557	858-391-3600

155-7 Gloves & Mittens

	Toll-Free	Phone
Carolina Glove Co		
116 Mclin Creek Rd PO Box 999 ....Conover NC 28613	800-335-1918	828-464-1132
Fownes Bros & Company Inc		
16 E 34th St ....New York NY 10016	800-345-6837*	
*All		
Gloves Inc		
1950 Collins Blvd ....Austell GA 30106	800-476-4568	770-944-9186
Guard-Line Inc		
215 S Louise St PO Box 1030 ....Atlanta TX 75551	800-527-8822	903-796-4111
Illinois Glove Co		
650 Anthony Trl ....Northbrook IL 60062	800-342-5458	847-291-1700
Kinco International		
4286 NE 185th Dr ....Portland OR 97230	800-547-8410*	
Magid Glove & Safety Manufacturing Co		
2060 N Kolmar Ave ....Chicago IL 60639	800-444-8010	773-384-2070
MCR Safety 5321 E Shelby Dr ....Memphis TN 38118	800-955-6887	901-795-5810
Midwest Quality Gloves Inc		
835 Industrial Rd ....Chillicothe MO 64601	800-821-3028	660-646-2165

				Toll-Free	Phone
Montpelier Glove Co Inc					
129 N Main St	Montpelier	IN	47359	**800-645-3931**	765-728-2481
North Star Glove Co					
2916 S Steele St	Tacoma	WA	98409	**800-423-1616**	253-627-7107
Saranac Glove Co					
999 Lombardi Ave	Green Bay	WI	54304	**800-727-2622**	920-435-3737
Southern Glove Mfg Company Inc					
749 AC Little Dr	Newton	NC	28658	**800-222-1113***	828-464-4884
*Cust Svc					
Swany America Corp					
115 Corp Dr	Johnstown	NY	12095	**888-234-5450**	518-725-3333
Wells Lamont Industry Group					
6640 W Touhy Ave	Niles	IL	60714	**800-247-3295**	

155-8 Hats & Caps

				Toll-Free	Phone
Ahead LLC					
270 Samuel Barnet Blvd	New Bedford	MA	02745	**800-282-2246**	508-985-9898
F & M Hat Co Inc					
103 Walnut St PO Box 40	Denver	PA	17517	**800-953-4287**	717-336-5505
MPC Promotions					
4300 Produce Rd PO Box 34336	Louisville	KY	40232	**800-331-0989**	502-451-4900
Paramount Apparel International Inc					
1 Paramount Dr	Bourbon	MO	65441	**866-274-4287**	573-732-4411
Stratton Hats Inc					
3200 Randolph St	Bellwood	IL	60104	**877-453-3777**	708-544-5220
Town Talk Inc					
6310 Cane Run Rd	Louisville	KY	40258	**800-626-2220**	

155-9 Hosiery & Socks

				Toll-Free	Phone
Holt Hosiery Mills Inc					
PO Box 1757	Burlington	NC	27216	**800-545-4658**	
Jefferies Socks					
2203 Tucker St	Burlington	NC	27215	**800-334-6831**	336-226-7315
Jockey International Inc					
2300 60th St PO Box 1417	Kenosha	WI	53140	**800-562-5391**	
Renfro Corp					
661 Linville Rd PO Box 908	Mount Airy	NC	27030	**800-334-9091**	336-719-8000
Thor-Lo Inc					
2210 Newton Dr	Statesville	NC	28677	**888-846-7567**	704-872-6522
Wigwam Mills Inc					
3402 Crocker Ave	Sheboygan	WI	53082	**800-558-7760**	855-275-0356

155-10 Jeans

				Toll-Free	Phone
Lee Jeans 9001 W 67th St	Merriam	KS	66202	**800-453-3348***	
*Cust Svc					
Reed Mfg Co Inc					
1321 S Veterans Blvd	Tupelo	MS	38804	**800-466-1154**	662-842-4472

155-11 Men's Clothing

				Toll-Free	Phone
After Six 118 W 20th St	New York	NY	10011	**800-444-8304**	646-638-9600
American Apparel LLC					
747 Warehouse St	Los Angeles	CA	90021	**888-747-0070**	213-488-0226
Anniston Sportswear Corp					
4305 McClellan Blvd PO Box 189	Anniston	AL	36206	**866-814-9253**	256-236-1551
Antigua Group Inc, The					
16651 N 84 Ave	Peoria	AZ	85382	**800-528-3133**	623-523-6000
Gitman Bros					
2309 Chestnut St	Ashland	PA	17921	**800-526-3929**	
Granite Knitwear Inc					
805 S Salberry Ave Hwy 52S	Granite Quarry	NC	28072	**800-476-9944***	704-279-5526
*Cust Svc					
H Freeman & Son Inc					
411 N Cranberry Rd	Westminster	MD	21157	**800-876-7700**	410-857-5774
Haggar Clothing Co					
11818 Harry Hines Blvd Ste 202	Dallas	TX	75234	**877-841-2219**	972-481-1579
Hardwick Clothes Inc					
3800 Old Tasso Rd	Cleveland	TN	37312	**800-251-6392**	
Hickey Freeman					
1155 N Clinton Ave	Rochester	NY	14621	**844-755-7344***	585-467-7021
*Cust Svc					
Hugo Boss Fashions Inc					
601 West 26th St Ste #M281	New York	NY	10001	**800-484-6267**	
Jos A Bank Clothiers Inc					
6380 Rogerdale Rd PO Box 1000	Houston	TX	77072	**800-285-2265***	
*Cust Svc					
Nautica Retail USA Inc					
40 W 57th St	New York	NY	10019	**866-376-4184**	
PVH 200 Madison Ave	New York	NY	10016	**888-203-1112**	212-381-3500
NYSE: PVH					
Tom James Co					
263 Seaboard Ln	Franklin	TN	37067	**800-236-9023**	615-771-0795

155-12 Neckwear

				Toll-Free	Phone
Carolina Mfg					
7025 Augusta Rd	Greenville	SC	29605	**800-845-2744**	
Echo Design Group					
10 E 40th St 16th Fl	New York	NY	10016	**800-327-3896***	212-686-8771
*General					

155-13 Robes (Ceremonial)

				Toll-Free	Phone
Academic Apparel					
20644 Superior St	Chatsworth	CA	91311	**800-626-5000**	818-886-8697
CM ALMY 28 Kaysal Ct	Armonk	NY	10504	**800-225-2569**	207-487-3232
Gaspard Inc					
200 N Janacek Rd	Brookfield	WI	53045	**800-784-6868**	262-784-6800
Jostens Inc					
3601 Minnesota Ave Ste 400	Minneapolis	MN	55435	**800-235-4774**	952-830-3300
Oak Hall Industries					
840 Union St	Salem	VA	24153	**800-223-0429**	540-387-0000
Thomas Creative Apparel Inc					
1 Harmony Pl	New London	OH	44851	**800-537-2575**	419-929-1506
Willsie Cap & Gown Co					
1220 S 13th St	Omaha	NE	68108	**800-234-4696**	402-341-6536

155-14 Sleepwear

				Toll-Free	Phone
Miss Elaine Inc					
8430 Valcour Ave	Saint Louis	MO	63123	**800-458-1422**	314-631-1900
Wormser Corp					
150 Coolidge Ave	Englewood	NJ	07631	**800-546-4040**	800-666-9676

155-15 Sweaters (Knit)

				Toll-Free	Phone
Binghamton Knitting Co Inc					
11 Alice St	Binghamton	NY	13904	**877-746-3368**	

155-16 Swimwear

				Toll-Free	Phone
Blue Sky Swimwear					
729 E International Speedway Blvd	Daytona Beach	FL	32118	**800-799-6445***	386-255-2590
*Orders					
Quiksilver Inc					
15202 Graham St	Huntington Beach	CA	92649	**800-435-9917**	
NYSE: ZQK					
TYR Sport 1790 Apollo Ct	Seal Beach	CA	90740	**800-252-7878**	714-897-0799
Venus Swimwear					
11711 Marco Beach Dr	Jacksonville	FL	32224	**800-366-7946**	904-645-6000

155-17 Undergarments

				Toll-Free	Phone
Cupid Foundations Inc					
475 Park Ave S	New York	NY	10016	**877-649-5283**	212-686-6224
Indera Mills Co					
350 W Maple St PO Box 309	Yadkinville	NC	27055	**800-334-8605**	
Jockey International Inc					
2300 60th St PO Box 1417	Kenosha	WI	53140	**800-562-5391**	
Leading Lady					
24050 Commerce Pk	Beachwood	OH	44122	**800-321-4804***	
*Cust Svc					
Wacoal America					
50 Polito Ave	Lyndhurst	NJ	07071	**800-922-6250**	201-933-8400
Wacoal Europe					
65 Sprague St	Hyde Park	MA	02136	**800-733-8964**	617-361-7559

155-18 Uniforms & Work Clothes

				Toll-Free	Phone
A+ School Apparel					
401 Knoss Ave	Star City	AR	71667	**800-227-3215**	
Action Sports Systems Inc					
617 Carbon City Rd PO Box 1442	Morganton	NC	28655	**800-631-1091**	828-584-8000
Algy Team Collection					
440 NE First Ave	Hallandale	FL	33009	**800-458-2549**	954-457-8100
Barco Uniforms					
350 W Rosecrans Ave	Gardena	CA	90248	**800-262-1559**	310-323-7315
Berne Apparel Co					
2501 East 850 North PO Box 530	Ossian	IN	46777	**800-843-7657**	888-772-3763
Blauer Mfg Co Inc					
20 Aberdeen St	Boston	MA	02215	**800-225-6715**	617-536-6606
Blue Generation Div of M Rubin & Sons Inc					
34-01 38th Ave	Long Island	NY	11101	**888-336-4687**	
Carhartt Inc					
5750 Mercury Dr	Dearborn	MI	48126	**800-833-3118**	313-271-8460
Choi Bros Inc 3401 W Div St	Chicago	IL	60651	**800-524-2464**	773-489-2800
DeMoulin Bros & Company Inc					
1025 S Fourth St	Greenville	IL	62246	**800-228-8134**	618-664-2000
Dennis Uniform Mfg Company Inc					
135 SE Hawthorne Blvd	Portland	OR	97214	**800-854-6951**	
Earl's Apparel Inc					
908 S Fourth St	Crockett	TX	75835	**800-527-3148**	936-544-5521
Elbeco Inc					
4418 Pottsville Pk	Reading	PA	19605	**800-468-4654**	610-921-0651
Encompass Group LLC					
615 Macon Rd	McDonough	GA	30253	**800-284-4540**	770-957-1211
Fechheimer Bros Company Inc					
4545 Malsbary Rd	Cincinnati	OH	45242	**800-543-1939**	513-793-5400
Gibson & Barnes					
1900 Weld Blvd Ste 140	El Cajon	CA	92020	**800-748-6693***	619-440-6977
*Sales					
Howard Uniform Co					
1915 Annapolis Rd	Baltimore	MD	21230	**800-628-8299**	410-727-3086

			Toll-Free	Phone
Key Industries Inc				
400 Marble Rd	Fort Scott KS	66701	800-835-0365	
Landau Uniforms				
8410 W Sandidge Rd	Olive Branch MS	38654	800-238-7513*	662-895-7200
*General				
LC King Mfg Company Inc				
24 Seventh St	Bristol TN	37620	800-826-2510	423-764-5188
Leventhal Ltd				
PO Box 564	Fayetteville NC	28302	800-847-4095*	
*General				
Lion Apparel Inc				
7200 Poe Ave Ste 400	Dayton OH	45414	800-548-6614	937-898-1949
Riverside Manufacturing Co				
301 Riverside Dr	Moultrie GA	31768	800-841-8677	229-985-5210
Score 726 E Anaheim St	Wilmington CA	90744	800-626-7774	
Stanbury Uniforms Inc				
108 Stanbury Industrial Dr				
PO Box 100	Brookfield MO	64628	800-826-2246	
Standard Textile Company Inc				
1 Knollcrest Dr	Cincinnati OH	45237	800-999-0400	513-761-9255
superior group of companies(SGC)				
10055Seminole Blvd	Seminole FL	33772	800-727-8643*	727-397-9611
NASDAQ: SGC ■ *Cust Svc				
Topps Safety Apparel Inc				
2516 E State Rd 14	Rochester IN	46975	800-348-2990	574-223-4311
Universal Overall Co				
1060 W Van Buren St	Chicago IL	60607	800-621-3344*	312-226-3336
*Cust Svc				
Williamson-Dickie Mfg Co				
509 W Vickery Blvd	Fort Worth TX	76104	866-411-1501	

155-19 Western Wear (Except Hats & Boots)

			Toll-Free	Phone
Rockmount Ranch Wear Manufacturing Co				
1626 Wazee St	Denver CO	80202	800-776-2566	303-629-7777
Sidran Inc				
1050 Venture Ct Ste 100	Carrollton TX	75006	800-969-5015	214-352-7979

155-20 Women's Clothing

			Toll-Free	Phone
Adrianna Papell				
500 Seventh Ave 10th Fl	New York NY	10018	800-325-9450	
Bari-Jay Fashions Inc				
1277 Bridge St Unit 1B	New Dundee ON	N0B2E0	800-735-5808	
bebe stores Inc				
400 Valley Dr	Brisbane CA	94005	877-232-3777	415-715-3900
Jones Apparel Group Inc Jones New York Collection Div				
1411 Broadway	New York NY	10018	888-880-8730	212-642-3860
Leon Max Inc				
3100 New York Dr	Pasadena CA	91107	888-334-4629	626-797-9991
Ursula of Switzerland Inc				
31 Mohawk Ave	Waterford NY	12188	800-826-4041	

156 CLOTHING & ACCESSORIES - WHOL

			Toll-Free	Phone
Alternative Apparel Inc				
1650 Indian Brook Way Bldg 200	Norcross GA	30093	877-747-2915	678-380-1890
Crew Outfitters Inc				
1001 Virginia Ave	Atlanta GA	30354	888-345-5353	
MediUSA				
6481 Franz Warner Pkwy	Whitsett NC	27377	800-633-6334	
Noamex Inc 625 Wortman Ave	Brooklyn NY	11208	800-640-5917	718-342-2278
TSC Apparel LLC				
12080 Mosteller Rd	Cincinnati OH	45241	800-543-7230	513-771-1138
WS Emerson Co Inc 15 Acme Rd	Brewer ME	04412	800-789-6120	207-989-3410

157 CLOTHING STORES

SEE ALSO Department Stores

157-1 Children's Clothing Stores

			Toll-Free	Phone
Base Camp Franchising				
39 E Eagle Ridge Dr Ste 100	North Salt Lake UT	84054	855-637-3211	
Children's Place Retail Stores Inc				
500 Plaza Dr	Secaucus NJ	07094	877-752-2387	201-558-2400
NASDAQ: PLCE				
Goldbug Inc				
511 16th St Ste 400	Denver CO	80202	800-942-9442	303-371-2535
Gymboree Corp				
500 Howard St	San Francisco CA	94105	877-449-6932	
NASDAQ: GYMB				

157-2 Family Clothing Stores

			Toll-Free	Phone
Bob's Stores Inc				
160 Corporate Ct	Meriden CT	06450	866-333-2627	203-379-2260
Dawahares Inc				
1845 Alexandria Dr	Lexington KY	40504	800-677-9108	859-278-0422
Foursome Inc				
3570 Vicksveurg Ln N Ste 100	Plymouth MN	55447	888-368-7766	763-473-4667
Halston LLC				
1201 W Fifth St 11th fl	Los Angeles CA	90017	844-425-7866	
Kittery Trading Post				
301 US 1	Kittery ME	03904	888-587-6246	603-334-1157

			Toll-Free	Phone
Marshalls Inc				
770 Cochituate Rd	Framingham MA	01701	888-627-7425	
Puritan of Cape Cod				
408 Main St	Hyannis MA	02601	800-924-0606	508-775-2400
Wakefield's Inc				
1212 Quintard Ave	Anniston AL	36201	800-333-1552	
Zumiez Inc				
6300 Merrill Creek Pkwy Ste B	Everett WA	98203	877-828-6929	425-551-1500
NASDAQ: ZUMZ				

157-3 Men's Clothing Stores

			Toll-Free	Phone
Carroll & Co				
425 N Canon Dr	Beverly Hills CA	90210	800-238-9400	310-273-9060
Destination XL Group Inc (DXL)				
555 Tpke St	Canton MA	02021	855-746-7395	
NASDAQ: DXLG				
Jos A Bank Clothiers Inc				
6380 Rogerdale Rd PO Box 1000	Houston TX	77072	800-285-2265*	
*Cust Svc				
Men's Wearhouse Inc				
6380 Rogerdale Rd	Houston TX	77072	877-986-9669	281-776-7000
NYSE: TLRD				
Miltons Inc				
250 Granite St	Braintree MA	02184	888-645-8667	781-848-1880
Patrick James Inc				
780 W Shaw Ave	Fresno CA	93704	888-427-6003	559-224-5500
Paul Fredrick Menstyle				
223 W Poplar St	Fleetwood PA	19522	800-247-1417	610-944-0909
Rubenstein Bros Inc				
102 St Charles Ave	New Orleans LA	70130	800-725-7823	504-581-6666

157-4 Men's & Women's Clothing Stores

			Toll-Free	Phone
Abercrombie & Fitch Co				
6301 Fitch Pass	New Albany OH	43054	866-681-3115	
NASDAQ: ANF				
American Eagle Outfitters Inc				
77 Hot Metal St	Pittsburgh PA	15203	888-232-4535*	412-432-3300
NYSE: AEO ■ *Cust Svc				
Bergdorf Goodman Inc				
754 Fifth Ave	New York NY	10019	888-774-2424*	212-753-7300
*Cust Svc				
Buckle Inc 2407 W 24th St	Kearney NE	68845	800-626-1255	308-236-8491
NYSE: BKE				
Burberry Ltd (New York)				
444 Madison Ave	New York NY	10022	877-217-4085	212-407-7100
Eddie Bauer LLC				
PO Box 7001	Groveport OH	43125	800-426-8020*	
*Orders				
Gap Inc 2 Folsom St	San Francisco CA	94105	800-333-7899	
NYSE: GPS				
J Crew Group Inc				
770 Broadway	New York NY	10003	800-562-0258	212-209-2500
John B Malouf Inc				
8201 Quaker Ave Ste 106	Lubbock TX	79424	800-658-9500	806-794-9500
Maurices Inc				
105 W Superior St	Duluth MN	55802	866-977-1542	218-727-8431
Oak Hall Inc				
6150 Poplar Ave Ste 146	Memphis TN	38119	844-625-4255	901-761-3580
Patagonia				
259 W Santa Clara St	Ventura CA	93001	800-638-6464*	805-643-8616
*Cust Svc				
Paul Stuart Inc				
Madison Ave & 45th St	New York NY	10017	800-678-8278*	212-682-0320
*Orders				
Specialty Retailers Inc				
2425 W Loop	South Houston TX	77027	800-743-8730	
Stanley Korshak				
500 Crescent Ct Ste 100	Dallas TX	75201	855-479-9539	
TJX Cos Inc				
770 Cochituate Rd	Framingham MA	01701	800-926-6299	508-390-1000
NYSE: TJX				
Urban Outfitters Inc				
30 Industrial Pk Blvd	Trenton SC	29847	800-282-2200	

157-5 Specialty Clothing Stores

Specialty clothing stores are those which sell a specific type of clothing, such as Western wear, uniforms, etc.

			Toll-Free	Phone
511 Inc 3201 N Airport Way	Manteca CA	95356	866-451-1726	
Dunham's Sports				
5000 Dixie Hwy	Waterford MI	48329	844-636-4109	
Hat World Corp				
7555 Woodland Dr	Indianapolis IN	46278	888-564-4287	
HorseLoverZ com				
254 N Cedar St	Hazleton PA	18201	877-804-7810	570-399-3469
Mark's Work Warehouse				
1035 64th Ave SE Ste 30	Calgary AB	T2H2J7	800-663-6275	403-255-9220
Mobile Nations LLC				
3151 E Thomas St	Inverness FL	34453	877-799-0143	
Modell's Sporting Goods				
498 Seventh Ave 20th Fl	New York NY	10018	800-275-6633	
Northwest Designs Ink Inc				
13456 SE 27th Pl Ste 200	Bellevue WA	98005	800-925-9327	
Overland Sheepskin Company Inc				
2096 Nutmeg Ave	Fairfield IA	52556	800-683-7526	641-472-8434
Post & Nickel 144 N 14th St	Lincoln NE	68508	877-667-6107	402-476-3432
Sheplers Inc				
6501 W Kellogg Dr	Wichita KS	67209	888-835-4004	316-946-3786

Classified Section

				Toll-Free	Phone
Wilsons Leather Inc					
7401 Boone Ave N	Brooklyn Park	MN	55428	800-967-6270	763-391-4000
Work 'n Gear Stores					
2300 Crown Colony Dr Ste 300	Quincy	MA	02169	800-987-0218	

157-6 Women's Clothing Stores

				Toll-Free	Phone
A'Gaci LLC					
12460 Network Blvd Ste 106	San Antonio	TX	78249	866-265-3036	
AnnTaylor Inc 7 Times Sq	New York	NY	10036	800-342-5266	212-541-3300
Avenue Stores Inc					
365 W Passaic St	Rochelle Park	NJ	07662	888-843-2836	201-845-0880
Bailey44 4700 S Boyle Ave	Vernon	CA	90058	844-894-8100	
Born Into It Inc					
112 Burlington St	Woburn	MA	01801	800-560-2840	781-491-0707
Capsmith Inc					
2240 Old Lake Mary Rd	Sanford	FL	32771	800-228-3889	407-328-7660
Cato Corp, The					
8100 Denmark Rd	Charlotte	NC	28273	800-758-2286	704-554-8510
Charlotte Russe Inc					
5910 Pacific Center Blvd	San Diego	CA	92121	888-211-7271	
Chico's FAS Inc					
11215 Metro Pkwy	Fort Myers	FL	33966	888-855-4986	
NYSE: CHS					
Claire's Accessories					
3 SW 129th Ave	Pembroke Pines	FL	33027	800-252-4737	954-433-3000
Close To My Heart					
1199 W 700 S	Pleasant Grove	UT	84062	888-655-6552	
David's Bridal Inc					
1001 Washington St	Conshohocken	PA	19428	844-400-3222	610-943-5000
Destination Maternity Corp					
232 Strawbridge Dr	Moorestown	NJ	08057	800-466-6223	
NASDAQ: DEST					
Drapers & Damons					
9 Pasteur Ste 200	Irvine	CA	92618	800-843-1174	
Express 1 Limited Pkwy	Columbus	OH	43230	888-397-1980	
NYSE: EXPR					
Forever 21 Inc					
2001 S Alameda St	Los Angeles	CA	90058	800-966-1355*	213-741-5100
*Cust Svc					
Henig Inc					
4135 Carmichael Rd	Montgomery	AL	36106	800-521-2037	334-277-7610
Henri Bendel Inc					
712 Fifth Ave	New York	NY	10019	866-875-7975	212-247-1100
Irresistibles					
7 Hawkes St	Marblehead	MA	01945	800-555-9865	781-631-8903
Lady Grace Stores Inc					
238 W Cummings Pk	Woburn	MA	01801	877-381-4629	
Lane Bryant Inc					
3344 Morse Crossing Rd	Columbus	OH	43219	866-886-4731*	954-970-2205
*Cust Svc					
Louis Vuitton NA Inc					
1 E 57th St	New York	NY	10022	866-884-8866*	212-758-8877
*Cust Svc					
New York & Co					
330 W 34th St	New York	NY	10001	800-961-9906	
NYDJ Apparel LLC					
5401 S Soto St	Vernon	CA	90058	800-407-6001	323-581-9040
Soft Surroundings					
2280 Schuetz Rd Ste 100	Maryland Heights	MO	63146	800-240-7076*	
*Cust Svc					
Sydneys Closet					
11840 Dorsett Rd	Maryland Heights	MO	63043	888-479-3639	314-344-5066
Ulla Popken Ltd					
777 Dulaney Valley Rd Ste 263	Towson	MD	21204	800-245-8552	
Victoria's Secret Stores					
4 Limited Pkwy	Reynoldsburg	OH	43068	800-411-5116	
Wedding Shoppe Inc, The					
1196 Grand Ave	Saint Paul	MN	55105	877-294-4991	651-298-1144
White House/Black Market (WHBM)					
11215 Metro Pkwy	Fort Myers	FL	33966	888-550-5559	239-277-6200
Windsor Inc					
4533 Pacific Blvd	Vernon	CA	90058	888-494-6376	323-282-9000

158 COAST GUARD INSTALLATIONS

				Toll-Free	Phone
Integrated Support Command Miami Beach					
100 MacArthur Cswy	Miami Beach	FL	33139	866-772-8724	305-535-4300
Milwaukee Coast Guard Base					
2420 S Lincoln Memorial Dr	Milwaukee	WI	53207	866-772-8724	414-747-7100
Port Angeles Coast Guard Air Station					
Ediz Hook Rd	Port Angeles	WA	98362	800-982-8813	360-417-5840
US Coast Guard Air Station Detroit					
1461 N Perimeter Rd Selfridge ANGB	Selfridge	MI	48045	800-424-8802	586-239-6700

159 COFFEE & TEA STORES

				Toll-Free	Phone
Caribou Coffee Company Inc					
3900 Lakebreeze Ave N	Minneapolis	MN	55429	888-227-4268	763-592-2200
NASDAQ: CBOU					
Coffee Beanery Ltd, The					
3429 Pierson Pl	Flushing	MI	48433	800-441-2255	810-733-1020
Dunkin' Donuts 130 Royall St	Canton	MA	02021	800-859-5339*	781-737-3000
*Cust Svc					
Hawaii Coffee Co					
1555 Kalani St	Honolulu	HI	96817	800-338-8353	808-847-3600
McNulty's Tea & Coffee Company Inc					
109 Christopher St	New York	NY	10014	800-356-5200	212-242-5351
Montana Coffee Traders Inc					
5810 Hwy 93 S	Whitefish	MT	59937	800-345-5282	406-862-7633
Royal Cup PO Box 170971	Birmingham	AL	35217	800-366-5836	

				Toll-Free	Phone
Seattle's Best Coffee LLC					
PO Box 3717	Seattle	WA	98124	800-611-7793	
Second Cup Ltd					
6303 Airport Rd	Mississauga	ON	L4V1R8	877-212-1818	
Starbucks Coffee Co					
2401 Utah Ave S	Seattle	WA	98134	800-782-7282	206-447-1575
VKI Technologies Inc					
3200 2E Rue	Saint-hubert	QC	J3Y8Y7	800-567-2951	450-676-0504

160 COLLECTION AGENCIES

				Toll-Free	Phone
Account Control Systems Inc					
85 Chestnut Ridge Rd Ste 113	Montvale	NJ	07645	800-482-8026	
Afni Inc 404 Brock Dr	Bloomington	IL	61701	866-377-8844	
Allied International Credit Corp					
16635 Young St Ste 26	Newmarket	ON	L3X1V6	877-451-2594	
American Accounts & Advisers					
PO Box 250	Cottage Grove	MN	55016	866-714-0489	651-287-6100
Amsher					
4524 Southlake Pkwy Ste 15	Birmingham	AL	35244	844-227-4627	205-322-4110
AR.M. Solutions Inc					
PO Box 2929	Camarillo	CA	93011	888-772-6468	
Asset Acceptance Capital Corp (AACC)					
28405 Van Dyke Ave	Warren	MI	48093	800-545-9931	586-939-9600
NASDAQ: AACC					
Atlantic Credit & Finance Inc					
3353 Orange Ave	Roanoke	VA	24012	800-888-9419	540-772-7800
Bonneville Collections					
6026 S Fashion Point Dr	Ogden	UT	84403	800-660-6138	801-621-7880
Brennan & Clark LLC					
721 E Madison Ste 200	Villa Park	IL	60181	800-858-7600	630-279-7600
CACi					
12855 Tesson Ferry Rd Ste 201	St. Louis	MO	63128	800-777-7971	
CBV Collection Services Ltd					
1490 Denison St Ste 100	Markham	ON	L3R9T7	866-877-9323	416-482-9323
CBY Systems Inc 33 S Duke St	York	PA	17401	800-717-4229	
Cedars Business Services LLC					
5230 Las Virgenes Ste 210	Calabasas	CA	91302	800-804-3353	818-224-3357
CMI Credit Mediators Inc					
414 Sansom St	Upper Darby	PA	19082	800-456-3328	610-352-5151
Collectcents Inc					
1450 Meyerside Dr 2nd Fl	Mississauga	ON	L5T2N5	800-256-8964	905-670-7575
Columbia Collectors Inc (CCI)					
1104 Main St Ste 311	Vancouver	WA	98660	800-694-7585	360-694-7585
Continental Service Group Inc					
200 Cross Keys Office Pk	Fairport	NY	14450	800-724-7500	585-421-1000
Credit Consulting Services Inc					
201 John St Ste E	Salinas	CA	93901	800-679-6888	831-424-0606
Credit Management LP					
4200 International Pkwy	Carrollton	TX	75007	800-377-7713	
Creditors Adjustment Bureau-LC Financial (CABLCF)					
14226 Ventura Blvd	Sherman Oaks	CA	91423	800-800-4523	818-990-4800
DataTicket Inc					
4600 Campus Dr Ste 200	Newport Beach	CA	92660	888-752-0512	949-752-6937
Encore Capital Group Inc					
3111 Camino Del Rio N Ste 1300	San Diego	CA	92108	877-445-4581	858-560-2600
NASDAQ: ECPG					
FMA Alliance Ltd					
80 Garden Ctr Ste 3	Broomfield	CO	80020	800-955-5598	281-931-5050
GC Services LP					
6330 Gulfton St	Houston	TX	77081	800-756-6524	713-777-4441
General Collection Company inc					
402 W Third St	Grand Island	NE	68802	888-603-1423	308-381-1423
General Revenue Corp					
4660 Duke Dr Ste 300	Mason	OH	45040	800-234-6258	
James, Stevens & Daniels Inc					
1283 College Park Dr	Dover	DE	19904	800-305-0773	302-735-4628
Johnson & Rountree Premium Inc					
6160 Lusk Blvd Ste C-203	San Diego	CA	92121	800-578-3300	858-259-5846
Keybridge Medical Revenue Management					
2348 Baton Rouge Ave	Lima	OH	45805	877-222-4114	
Kings Credit Services					
510 N Douty St	Hanford	CA	93230	800-366-0950	559-587-4200
Lamont, Hanley & Associates Inc					
1138 Elm St	Manchester	NH	03105	800-639-2204	603-625-5547
Matthews Pierce & Lloyd Inc					
830 Walker Rd Ste 12	Dover	DE	19904	800-267-4026	302-678-5500
Med Shield Inc					
2424 E 55th St	Indianapolis	IN	46220	800-272-5454	317-613-3700
Medco Services Inc					
7037 Madison Pk Ste 450	Huntsville	AL	35806	866-661-5739	
Merchants & Medical Credit Corporation Inc					
6324 Taylor Dr	Flint	MI	48507	800-562-0273	810-239-3030
MJ Altman Cos Inc					
205 S Magnolia Ave	Ocala	FL	34471	800-927-2655	352-732-1112
Monarch Recovery Management Inc					
3260 Tillman Dr Ste 75	Bensalem	PA	19020	800-220-0605	215-281-7500
Nationwide Credit Inc (NCI)					
PO Box 14581	Des Moines	IA	50306	800-456-4729	
NRA Group LLC					
2491 Paxton St	Harrisburg	PA	17111	800-360-9953	800-773-4503
Pioneer Credit Recovery Inc					
26 Edward St	Arcade	NY	14009	800-836-2442	585-492-1234
Premiere Credit of North America LLC					
PO Box 19309	Indianapolis	IN	46219	866-808-7118	
Recovery Partners LLC					
4151 N Marshall Way Ste 12	Scottsdale	AZ	85251	866-661-5203	
Sierra Receivables Management Inc					
2500 Goodwater Ave	Redding	CA	96002	800-237-3205	530-224-1360
Stanislaus Credit Control Service Inc					
914 14th St	Modesto	CA	95354	800-838-7227	209-523-1813
States Recovery Systems Inc					
2491 Sunrise Blvd	Rancho Cordova	CA	95670	800-211-1435	916-631-7085
Stevens Business Service Inc					
92 Bolt St 1	Lowell	MA	01852	800-769-0375	978-458-2500

				Toll-Free	Phone
Todd, Bremer & Lawson Inc					
560 S Herlong Ave	Rock Hill	SC	29732	**877-427-6544**	
Transworld Systems Inc					
PO Box 15618	Wilmington	DE	19850	**888-446-4733**	877-282-1250
Tri-state Adjustments Inc					
3439 E Ave S PO Box 3219	La Crosse	WI	54602	**800-562-3906**	608-788-8683
Twenty-First Century Assoc					
266 Summit Ave	Hackensack	NJ	07601	**888-760-5052**	201-678-1144
Unique Management Services Inc					
119 E Maple St	Jeffersonville	IN	47130	**800-879-5453**	812-280-2147
United Collection Bureau Inc					
5620 Southwyck Blvd	Toledo	OH	43614	**866-209-0622**	
Van Ru Credit Corp					
1350 E Touhy Ave Ste 300E	Des Plaines	IL	60018	**800-468-2678**	
Vengroff Williams & Assoc Inc (VWA)					
2099 S State College Bvld	Anaheim	CA	92806	**800-238-9655**	714-889-6200
Williams, Charles & Scott Ltd					
2171 Jericho Tpke LL1	Commack	NY	11725	**800-652-4445**	631-462-1553

161   COLLEGES - BIBLE

SEE ALSO

				Toll-Free	Phone
Alaska Bible College					
248 E Elmwood Ave	Palmer	AK	99645	**800-478-7884**	907-745-3201
Allegheny Wesleyan College					
2161 Woodsdale Rd	Salem	OH	44460	**800-292-3153**	330-337-6403
Baptist Bible College					
628 E Kearney St	Springfield	MO	65803	**800-228-5754**	
Baptist University of the Americas					
7838 Barlite Blvd	San Antonio	TX	78224	**800-721-1396**	210-924-4338
Barclay College					
607 N Kingman St	Haviland	KS	67059	**800-862-0226**	620-862-5252
Beulah Heights University					
892 Berne St SE	Atlanta	GA	30316	**888-777-2422**	404-627-2681
Boise Bible College					
8695 W Marigold St	Boise	ID	83714	**800-893-7755**	208-376-7731
Calvary Bible College & Theological Seminary					
15800 Calvary Rd	Kansas City	MO	64147	**800-326-3960**	816-322-3960
Central Christian College of the Bible					
911 E Urbandale Dr	Moberly	MO	65270	**888-263-3900**	660-263-3900
Cincinnati Christian University					
2700 Glenway Ave	Cincinnati	OH	45204	**800-949-4228**	513-244-8100
Clear Creek Baptist Bible College					
300 Clear Creek Rd	Pineville	KY	40977	**866-340-3196**	606-337-3196
College of Biblical Studies-Houston					
7000 Regency Sq Blvd Ste 110.	Houston	TX	77036	**844-227-9673**	713-785-5995
Columbia International University					
7435 Monticello Rd	Columbia	SC	29203	**800-777-2227**	803-754-4100
Crossroads Bible College					
601 North Shortridge Rd	Indianapolis	IN	46219	**800-822-3119**	317-789-8255
Crossroads College					
920 Mayowood Rd SW	Rochester	MN	55902	**800-456-7651**	507-288-4563
Crown College					
8700 College View Dr	Saint Bonifacius	MN	55375	**800-346-9252**	952-446-4100
Dallas Christian College					
2700 Christian Pkwy	Dallas	TX	75234	**800-688-1029**	972-241-3371
Davis College					
400 Riverside Dr	Johnson City	NY	13790	**800-331-4137**	607-729-1581
Emmaus Bible College					
2570 Asbury Rd	Dubuque	IA	52001	**800-397-2425**	563-588-8000
Florida Christian College					
1011 Bill Beck Blvd	Kissimmee	FL	34744	**888-468-6322**	407-847-8966
Grace Bible College					
1011 Aldon St SW PO Box 910	Grand Rapids	MI	49509	**800-968-1887**	616-538-2330
Grace University					
1311 S Ninth St	Omaha	NE	68108	**800-383-1422**	402-449-2800
Great Lakes Christian College					
6211 W Willow Hwy	Lansing	MI	48917	**800-937-4522***	517-321-0242
*Admissions					
Heritage Christian University					
3625 Helton Dr PO Box HCU	Florence	AL	35630	**800-367-3565**	256-766-6610
Hobe Sound Bible College					
PO Box 1065	Hobe Sound	FL	33475	**800-881-5534**	772-546-5534
Johnson University					
7900 Johnson Dr	Knoxville	TN	37998	**800-827-2122**	865-573-4517
Kentucky Mountain Bible College					
855 Hwy 541	Jackson	KY	41339	**800-879-5622**	606-693-5000
Kuyper College					
3333 E Beltline Ave NE	Grand Rapids	MI	49525	**800-511-3749**	616-222-3000
Lancaster Bible College					
901 Eden Rd	Lancaster	PA	17601	**800-544-7335**	717-569-7071
Life Pacific College					
1100 W Covina Blvd	San Dimas	CA	91773	**877-886-5433**	909-599-5433
Lincoln Christian College Seminary					
100 Campus View Dr	Lincoln	IL	62656	**888-522-5228**	217-732-3168
Manhattan Christian College					
1415 Anderson Ave	Manhattan	KS	66502	**877-246-4622**	785-539-3571
Mid-Atlantic Christian University					
715 N Poindexter St	Elizabeth City	NC	27909	**866-996-6228**	252-334-2000
Moody Bible Institute					
820 N La Salle St	Chicago	IL	60610	**800-967-4624**	312-329-4400
Multnomah University					
8435 NE Glisan St	Portland	OR	97220	**800-275-4672**	503-255-0332
Oak Hills Christian College					
1600 Oak Hills Rd SW	Bemidji	MN	56601	**888-751-8670**	218-751-8670
Saint Louis Christian College					
1360 Grandview Dr	Florissant	MO	63033	**800-887-7522***	314-837-6777
*Admissions					
Toccoa Falls College					
107 Kincaid Dr	Toccoa Falls	GA	30598	**888-785-5624***	706-886-7299
*General					
Tri-State Bible College					
506 Margaret St	South Point	OH	45680	**800-333-3243**	740-377-2520
Trinity Bible College					
50 Sixth Ave N	Ellendale	ND	58436	**800-523-1603**	701-349-3621

				Toll-Free	Phone
Trinity College of Florida					
2430 Welbilt Blvd	Trinity	FL	34655	**800-388-0869**	727-376-6911

162   COLLEGES - COMMUNITY & JUNIOR

SEE ALSO Colleges & Universities - Four-Year ; Colleges - Tribal ; Vocational & Technical Schools ; Colleges - Fine Arts
Institutions that offer academic degrees that can be transferred to a four-year college or university.

Alabama

				Toll-Free	Phone
Coastal Alabama Community College					
1900 Hwy 31 S	Bay Minette	AL	36507	**800-381-3722**	
Jefferson State Community College					
2601 Carson Rd	Birmingham	AL	35215	**800-239-5900**	205-853-1200
Calhoun Community College					
PO Box 2216	Decatur	AL	35609	**800-626-3628**	256-306-2500
Wallace Community College					
1141 Wallace Dr	Dothan	AL	36303	**800-543-2426**	334-983-3521
Bevill State Community College					
2631 Temple Ave N	Fayette	AL	35555	**800-648-3271**	205-932-3221
Gadsden State Community College					
1001 George Wallace Dr PO Box 227	Gadsden	AL	35902	**800-226-5563**	256-549-8200
Wallace State Community College					
801 Main St	Hanceville	AL	35077	**866-350-9722**	256-352-8000
Calhoun Community College					
Huntsville 102B Wynn Dr	Huntsville	AL	35805	**800-626-3628**	256-890-4701
Bevill State Community College					
Jasper 1411 Indiana Ave	Jasper	AL	35501	**800-648-3271**	205-387-0511
Marion Military Institute					
1101 Washington St	Marion	AL	36756	**800-664-1842**	334-683-2322
Bishop State Community College					
351 N Broad St	Mobile	AL	36603	**800-523-7000**	251-405-7000
Northwest-Shoals Community College					
Muscle Shoals					
800 George Wallace Blvd	Muscle Shoals	AL	35661	**800-645-8967**	256-331-5200
Northwest-Shoals Community College					
Phil Campbell					
2080 College Rd	Phil Campbell	AL	35581	**800-645-8967**	256-331-6200
Northeast Alabama Community College					
PO Box 159	Rainsville	AL	35986	**800-548-2546**	256-228-6001
Calhoun Community College					
Redstone Arsenal					
6250 Hwy 31 N	Tanner	AL	35671	**800-626-3628**	256-306-2500
Alabama Southern Community College					
30755 Hwy 43	Thomasville	AL	36784	**800-381-3722**	334-636-9642
Shelton State					
Community College					
9500 Old Greensboro Rd	Tuscaloosa	AL	35405	**877-838-2778**	205-391-2211

Alaska

				Toll-Free	Phone
University of Alaska Fairbanks					
Signers' Hall 2nd Fl PO Box 757480	Fairbanks	AK	99775	**800-478-1823**	907-474-7500
University of Alaska Southeast Ketchikan					
2600 Seventh Ave	Ketchikan	AK	99901	**877-465-6400**	907-225-6177
University of Alaska Anchorage Kodiak College					
117 Benny Benson Dr	Kodiak	AK	99615	**800-486-7660**	907-486-4161
University of Alaska Fairbanks					
Northwest					
400 E Front St PO Box 400	Nome	AK	99762	**800-478-2202**	907-443-2201
University of Alaska Southeast Sitka					
1332 Seward Ave	Sitka	AK	99835	**800-478-6653**	
University of Alaska Anchorage Kenai Peninsula College					
156 College Rd	Soldotna	AK	99669	**877-262-0330**	

Alberta

				Toll-Free	Phone
MacEwan College					
10700 104 Ave NW	Edmonton	AB	T5J4S2	**888-497-4622**	
Olds College 4500-50 St	Olds	AB	T4H1R6	**800-661-6537**	403-556-8281

Arizona

				Toll-Free	Phone
Mohave Community College					
Bullhead City					
3400 Hwy 95	Bullhead City	AZ	86442	**866-664-2832**	928-758-3926
Yavapai College					
Verde Valley					
601 Black Hills Dr	Clarkdale	AZ	86324	**800-922-6787**	928-634-7501
Mohave Community College					
North Mohave					
PO Box 980	Colorado City	AZ	86021	**800-678-3992**	928-875-2799
Central Arizona College					
8470 N Overfield Rd	Coolidge	AZ	85228	**800-237-9814**	520-494-5444
Cochise College					
4190 W Hwy 80	Douglas	AZ	85607	**800-966-7943**	520-364-7943
Coconino Community College					
Lonetree					
2800 S Lone Tree Rd	Flagstaff	AZ	86005	**800-350-7122**	928-527-1222
Northland Pioneer College					
PO Box 610	Holbrook	AZ	86025	**800-266-7845**	928-532-6111
Mohave Community College					
Lake Havasu					
1977 W Acoma Blvd	Lake Havasu City	AZ	86403	**866-664-2832**	928-855-7812
Mesa Community College					
1833 W Southern Ave	Mesa	AZ	85202	**866-532-4983**	480-461-7000
Mesa Community College					
Red Mountain					
7110 E McKellips Rd	Mesa	AZ	85207	**866-532-4983**	480-654-7200
GateWay Community College					
108 N 40th St	Phoenix	AZ	85034	**888-994-4433**	602-286-8000

College / Address	City	ST	ZIP	Toll-Free	Phone
Phoenix College 1202 W Thomas Rd	Phoenix	AZ	85013	800-266-7845	602-285-7777
South Mountain Community College 7050 S 24th St	Phoenix	AZ	85042	855-622-2332	602-243-8000
Yavapai College 1100 E Sheldon St	Prescott	AZ	86301	800-922-6787	928-445-7300
Scottsdale Community College 9000 E Chaparral Rd	Scottsdale	AZ	85256	800-784-2433	480-423-6000
Cochise College *Sierra Vista* 901 N Colombo Ave	Sierra Vista	AZ	85635	800-966-7943	520-515-0500
Rio Salado College 2323 W 14th St	Tempe	AZ	85281	855-622-2332	480-517-8000
Eastern Arizona College 615 N Stadium Ave	Thatcher	AZ	85552	800-678-3808	928-428-8472
Pima Community College 401 N Bonita Ave	Tucson	AZ	85709	800-860-7462	520-206-2733
Pima Community College West 2202 W Anklam Rd	Tucson	AZ	85709	800-860-7462	520-206-6600
Arizona Western College 2020 S Ave 8 E	Yuma	AZ	85366	888-293-0392	928-317-6000

Arkansas

College / Address	City	ST	ZIP	Toll-Free	Phone
NorthWest Arkansas Community College 1 College Dr	Bentonville	AR	72712	800-995-6922	479-636-9222
South Arkansas Community College PO Box 7010	El Dorado	AR	71731	800-955-2289	870-862-8131
East Arkansas Community College 1700 Newcastle Rd	Forrest City	AR	72335	877-797-3222	870-633-4480
North Arkansas College 1515 Pioneer Dr	Harrison	AR	72601	800-679-6622	870-743-3000
Phillips Community College 1000 Campus Dr PO Box 785	Helena	AR	72342	800-582-6953	870-338-6474
Ouachita Technical College 1 College Cir	Malvern	AR	72104	800-337-0266	501-337-5000
Ozarka College 218 College Dr	Melbourne	AR	72556	800-821-4335	870-368-7371
University of Arkansas Community College Rich Mountain 1100 College Dr	Mena	AR	71953	800-612-7440	479-394-7622
Arkansas State University Mountain Home 1600 S College St	Mountain Home	AR	72653	800-482-5964	870-508-6100
Arkansas State University Newport 7648 Victory Blvd	Newport	AR	72112	800-976-1676	870-512-7800
Crowley's Ridge College 100 College Dr	Paragould	AR	72450	800-264-1096	870-236-6901
Southeast Arkansas College (SEARK) 1900 Hazel St	Pine Bluff	AR	71603	888-732-7582	870-543-5900
Black River Technical College 1410 Hwy 304 E	Pocahontas	AR	72455	866-890-6933	870-248-4000
Mid-South Community College 2000 W Broadway	West Memphis	AR	72301	866-733-6722	870-733-6722

British Columbia

College / Address	City	ST	ZIP	Toll-Free	Phone
Okanagan College 1000 KLO Rd	Kelowna	BC	V1Y4X8	800-621-3038	250-762-5445

California

College / Address	City	ST	ZIP	Toll-Free	Phone
Cabrillo College 6500 Soquel Dr	Aptos	CA	95003	888-442-4551	831-479-6100
Cerro Coso Community College Bishop 4090 W Line St	Bishop	CA	93514	888-537-6932	760-872-1565
MiraCosta College *San Elijo* 3333 Manchester Ave	Cardiff	CA	92007	888-201-8480	760-944-4449
Southwestern College 900 Otay Lakes Rd	Chula Vista	CA	91910	866-262-9881	619-421-6700
West Hills College Coalinga 300 Cherry Ln	Coalinga	CA	93210	800-266-1114	559-934-2000
College of the Redwoods *Del Norte* 883 W Washington Blvd	Crescent City	CA	95531	800-641-0400	707-465-2300
Cerro Coso Community College *South Kern* 140 Methusa Ave	Edwards AFB	CA	93524	888-537-6932	661-258-8644
Cuyamaca College 900 Rancho San Diego Pkwy	El Cajon	CA	92019	800-234-1597	619-660-4275
College of the Redwoods 7351 Tompkins Hill Rd	Eureka	CA	95501	800-641-0400	707-476-4100
College of the Redwoods *Mendocino Coast* 440 Alger St	Fort Bragg	CA	95437	800-641-0400	707-962-2600
Coastline Community College 11460 Warner Ave	Fountain Valley	CA	92708	866-422-2645	714-546-7600
Glendale Community College 1500 N Verdugo Rd	Glendale	CA	91208	866-251-1977	818-240-1000
Sierra College *Nevada County* 250 Sierra College Dr	Grass Valley	CA	95945	800-242-4004	530-274-5300
Imperial Valley College 380 E Atten Rd PO Box 158	Imperial	CA	92251	800-336-1642	760-352-8320
Cerro Coso Community College *Kern River Valley* 5520 Lake Isabella Blvd	Lake Isabella	CA	93240	888-537-6932	760-379-5501
West Hills College Lemoore 555 College Ave	Lemoore	CA	93245	800-266-1114	559-925-3000
Long Beach City Colleges 4901 E Carson St	Long Beach	CA	90808	888-442-4551	562-938-4111
Foothill College 12345 El Monte Rd	Los Altos Hills	CA	94022	800-234-1597	650-949-7777
Cerro Coso Community College *Mammoth* 101 College Pkwy	Mammoth Lakes	CA	93546	888-537-6932	760-934-2875
Merced College 3600 M St	Merced	CA	95348	800-784-2433	209-384-6000
Monterey Peninsula College 980 Fremont St	Monterey	CA	93940	877-663-5433	831-646-4000
Napa Valley College 2277 Napa-Vallejo Hwy	Napa	CA	94558	800-826-1077	707-256-7000
College of Marin *Indian Valley* 1800 Ignacio Blvd	Novato	CA	94949	800-579-2878	415-883-2211
MiraCosta College Oceanside 1 Barnard Dr	Oceanside	CA	92056	888-201-8480	760-757-2121
Butte College 3536 Butte Campus Dr *Hum Res	Oroville	CA	95965	800-933-8322*	530-895-2511
Los Medanos College 2700 E Leland Rd	Pittsburg	CA	94565	800-677-6337	925-439-2181
Diablo Valley College 321 Golf Club Rd	Pleasant Hill	CA	94523	800-227-1060	925-685-1230
Feather River College 570 Golden Eagle Ave	Quincy	CA	95971	800-442-9799	530-283-0202
Chaffey College 5885 Haven Ave	Rancho Cucamonga	CA	91737	800-535-2421	909-652-6000
Reedley College 995 N Reed Ave	Reedley	CA	93654	877-253-7122	559-638-3641
Cerro Coso Community College *Indian Wells Valley* 3000 College Heights Blvd	Ridgecrest	CA	93555	888-537-6932	760-384-6100
Sierra Community College 5100 Sierra College Blvd	Rocklin	CA	95677	800-242-4004	916-624-3333
American River College 4700 College Oak Dr	Sacramento	CA	95841	800-700-4144	916-484-8011
Sacramento City College 3835 Freeport Blvd	Sacramento	CA	95822	800-700-4144	916-558-2351
City College of San Francisco 50 Phelan Ave	San Francisco	CA	94112	800-433-3243	415-239-3000
Mount San Jacinto College 1499 N State St	San Jacinto	CA	92583	800-624-5561	951-487-6752
Cuesta College PO Box 8106	San Luis Obispo	CA	93403	877-732-0436	805-546-3100
Santa Barbara City College 721 Cliff Dr	Santa Barbara	CA	93109	877-232-3919	805-965-0581
College of the Canyons 26455 Rockwell Canyon Rd	Santa Clarita	CA	91355	800-695-4858	661-259-7800
Allan Hancock College 800 S College Dr	Santa Maria	CA	93454	866-342-5242	805-922-6966
Columbia College 11600 Columbia College Dr	Sonora	CA	95370	888-722-2873	209-588-5100
Lake Tahoe Community College 1 College Dr	South Lake Tahoe	CA	96150	800-877-1466	530-541-4660
San Joaquin Delta College 5151 Pacific Ave	Stockton	CA	95207	800-835-4611	209-954-5151
Lassen Community College 478-200 Hwy 139 PO Box 3000	Susanville	CA	96130	800-461-9389	530-257-6181
Los Angeles Mission College 13356 Eldridge Ave	Sylmar	CA	91342	800-854-7771	818-364-7600
Taft College 29 Cougar Ct	Taft	CA	93268	800-379-6784	661-763-7700
El Camino College 16007 Crenshaw Blvd	Torrance	CA	90506	866-352-2646	310-532-3670
Victor Valley Community College 18422 Bear Valley Rd	Victorville	CA	92392	877-741-8532	760-245-4271
College of the Siskiyous 800 College Ave	Weed	CA	96094	888-397-4339	530-938-4461

Colorado

College / Address	City	ST	ZIP	Toll-Free	Phone
Colorado Mountain College Aspen 0255 Sage Way	Aspen	CO	81611	800-621-8559	970-925-7740
Community College of Aurora 16000 E Centretech Pkwy	Aurora	CO	80011	844-493-8255	303-360-4700
Pikes Peak Community College *Centennial* 5675 S Academy Blvd	Colorado Springs	CO	80906	800-456-6847	719-502-2000
Pikes Peak Community College *Downtown Studio* 100 W Pikes Peak Ave	Colorado Springs	CO	80903	800-456-6847	719-502-2000
Pikes Peak Community College *Rampart Range* 11195 Hwy 83	Colorado Springs	CO	80921	800-456-6847	719-502-2000
Colorado Northwestern Community College Craig 50 College Dr	Craig	CO	81625	800-562-1105	
Front Range Community College *Larimer* 4616 S Shields St	Fort Collins	CO	80526	888-800-9198	970-226-2500
Morgan Community College 920 Barlow Rd	Fort Morgan	CO	80701	800-622-0216	970-542-3100
Colorado Mountain College *Spring Valley* 3000 County Rd 114	Glenwood Springs	CO	81601	800-621-8559	970-945-7481
Aims Community College 5401 W 20th St	Greeley	CO	80634	800-301-5388	970-330-8008
Lamar Community College 2401 S Main St	Lamar	CO	81052	800-968-6920	719-336-2248
Arapahoe Community College 5900 S Santa Fe Dr	Littleton	CO	80160	888-800-9198	303-797-0100
Front Range Community College (FRCC) *Boulder County* 2190 Miller Dr	Longmont	CO	80501	888-800-9198	303-678-3722
Pueblo Community College 900 W Orman Ave	Pueblo	CO	81004	888-642-6017	719-549-3200
Colorado Northwestern Community College 500 Kennedy Dr	Rangely	CO	81648	800-562-1105	970-675-3335
Colorado Mountain College *Alpine* 1330 Bob Adams Dr	Steamboat Springs	CO	80487	800-621-8559	970-870-4444
Northeastern Junior College 100 College Ave	Sterling	CO	80751	800-626-4637	970-521-6600
Trinidad State Junior College 600 Prospect St	Trinidad	CO	81082	800-621-8752	719-846-5011

Connecticut

				Toll-Free	Phone
Asnuntuck Community College					
170 Elm St	Enfield	CT	06082	**800-501-3967**	860-253-3000
Capital Community College					
950 Main St	Hartford	CT	06103	**800-894-6126**	860-906-5000
Manchester Community College					
PO Box 1046	Manchester	CT	06045	**888-999-5545**	860-512-2800
Middlesex Community College					
100 Training Hill Rd	Middletown	CT	06457	**800-818-5501**	860-343-5800
Gateway Community College					
20 Church St	New Haven	CT	06510	**800-390-7723**	203-285-2000

Florida

				Toll-Free	Phone
Pasco-Hernando Community College					
11415 Ponce de Leon Blvd	Brooksville	FL	34601	**855-669-7472**	352-796-6726
Brevard Community College (BCC)					
Cocoa 1519 Clearlake Rd	Cocoa	FL	32922	**888-747-2802**	321-632-1111
Broward Community College					
North					
1000 Coconut Creek Blvd	Coconut Creek	FL	33066	**888-654-6482**	954-201-2240
Daytona Beach Community College					
1200 W International Speedway Blvd					
	Daytona Beach	FL	32114	**877-822-6669**	386-506-3000
Broward Community College					
Downtown Center					
111 E Las Olas Blvd	Fort Lauderdale	FL	33301	**888-654-6482**	954-201-7350
Indian River State College (IRSC)					
3209 Virginia Ave	Fort Pierce	FL	34981	**866-792-4772**	772-462-4772
Florida Community College at Jacksonville					
Downtown					
101 State St W	Jacksonville	FL	32202	**877-633-5950**	904-633-8100
Florida State College at Jacksonville					
Kent					
3939 Roosevelt Blvd	Jacksonville	FL	32205	**800-700-2795**	904-381-3400
Florida State College at Jacksonville					
South 11901 Beach Blvd	Jacksonville	FL	32246	**800-700-2795**	904-646-2111
Florida Keys Community College					
5901 College Rd	Key West	FL	33040	**866-567-2665**	305-296-9081
Palm Beach Community College					
Lake Worth					
4200 Congress Ave	Lake Worth	FL	33461	**866-576-7222**	561-868-3350
North Florida Community College					
325 NW Turner Davis Dr	Madison	FL	32340	**866-937-6322**	850-973-2288
Brevard Community College					
Melbourne					
3865 N Wickham Rd	Melbourne	FL	32935	**888-747-2802**	321-632-1111
Pasco-Hernado State College					
10230 Ridge Rd	New Port Richey	FL	34654	**855-669-7472**	727-847-2727
Valencia College					
PO Box 3028	Orlando	FL	32802	**800-590-3428**	407-299-5000
ST JOHNS RIVER STATE COLLEGE					
5001 St Johns Ave	Palatka	FL	32177	**888-757-2293**	386-312-4200
Brevard Community College					
Palm Bay					
250 Community College Pkwy	Palm Bay	FL	32909	**888-747-2802**	321-632-1111
Palm Beach Community College					
Palm Beach Gardens					
3160 PGA Blvd	Palm Beach Gardens	FL	33410	**866-576-7222**	561-207-5340
Gulf Coast Community College					
5230 W Hwy 98	Panama City	FL	32401	**800-311-3685**	850-769-1551
Pensacola Junior College					
1000 College Blvd	Pensacola	FL	32504	**888-897-3605**	850-484-1000
Pensacola Junior College					
Warrington 5555 W Hwy 98	Pensacola	FL	32507	**888-897-3605**	850-484-2200
Edison College					
Charlotte					
26300 Airport Rd	Punta Gorda	FL	33950	**800-749-2322**	941-637-5629
Tallahassee Community College					
444 Appleyard Dr	Tallahassee	FL	32304	**800-538-9784**	850-201-6200
Hillsborough Community College					
Dale Mabry					
4001 Tampa Bay Blvd	Tampa	FL	33614	**866-253-7077**	813-253-7000
Brevard Community College					
Titusville 1311 N US 1	Titusville	FL	32796	**888-747-2802**	321-632-1111

Georgia

				Toll-Free	Phone
Georgia Highlands College					
Cartersville					
5441 Hwy 20 NE	Cartersville	GA	30121	**800-332-2406**	678-872-8000
Middle Georgia College					
1100 Second St SE	Cochran	GA	31014	**800-548-4221**	478-934-6221
Andrew College					
501 College St	Cuthbert	GA	39840	**800-664-9250**	
Georgia Military College					
201 E Green St	Milledgeville	GA	31061	**800-342-0413**	478-387-4900
Georgia Highlands College					
Floyd 3175 Cedartown Hwy	Rome	GA	30161	**800-332-2406**	706-802-5000
East Georgia College					
131 College Cir	Swainsboro	GA	30401	**800-715-4255**	478-289-2000
Abraham Baldwin Agricultural College					
2802 Moore Hwy	Tifton	GA	31793	**800-733-3653**	229-391-5001
Young Harris College					
PO Box 116	Young Harris	GA	30582	**800-241-3754**	706-379-3111

Hawaii

				Toll-Free	Phone
University of Hawaii					
Hilo 200 W Kawili St	Hilo	HI	96720	**800-897-4456***	808-974-7414
*Admissions					
University of Hawaiʔi Maui College					
310 W Kaahumanu Ave	Kahului	HI	96732	**800-479-6692**	808-984-3267

				Toll-Free	Phone
Leeward Community College					
96-045 Ala Ike	Pearl City	HI	96782	**888-442-4551**	808-455-0011

Idaho

				Toll-Free	Phone
North Idaho College					
1000 W Garden Ave	Coeur d'Alene	ID	83814	**877-404-4536**	208-769-3300
College of Southern Idaho					
PO Box 1238	Twin Falls	ID	83303	**800-680-0274**	208-733-9554

Illinois

				Toll-Free	Phone
Southwestern Illinois College					
2500 Carlyle Ave	Belleville	IL	62221	**800-222-5131**	618-235-2700
Spoon River College (SRC)					
23235 N County Hwy 22	Canton	IL	61520	**800-334-7337**	309-647-4645
Kaskaskia College					
27210 College Rd	Centralia	IL	62801	**800-642-0859**	618-545-3090
Parkland College					
2400 W Bradley Ave	Champaign	IL	61821	**888-467-6065**	217-351-2200
City Colleges of Chicago					
226 W Jackson	Chicago	IL	60606	**866-908-7582**	312-553-2500
Harry S Truman College					
1145 W Wilson Ave	Chicago	IL	60640	**877-863-6339**	773-907-4000
Kennedy-King College					
6301 S Halsted St	Chicago	IL	60621	**800-798-8100**	773-602-5000
Malcolm X College					
1900 W Jackson	Chicago	IL	60612	**877-542-0285**	312-850-7000
McHenry County College					
8900 US Hwy 14	Crystal Lake	IL	60012	**888-977-4847**	815-455-3700
Danville Area Community College					
2000 E Main St	Danville	IL	61832	**877-342-3042**	217-443-3222
Richland Community College					
1 College Pk	Decatur	IL	62521	**800-899-4722**	217-875-7200
Elgin Community College					
1700 Spartan Dr	Elgin	IL	60123	**855-850-2525**	847-697-1000
Carl Sandburg College					
2400 Tom L Wilson Blvd	Galesburg	IL	61401	**877-236-1862**	309-344-2518
Southeastern Illinois College					
3575 College Rd	Harrisburg	IL	62946	**866-338-2742**	618-252-5400
Rend Lake College					
468 N Ken Gray Pkwy	Ina	IL	62846	**800-369-5321**	618-437-5321
Black Hawk College					
East 1501 State Hwy 78	Kewanee	IL	61443	**800-233-5671**	309-852-5671
Lincoln College					
300 Keokuk St	Lincoln	IL	62656	**800-569-0556**	217-732-3155
Kishwaukee College					
21193 Malta Rd	Malta	IL	60150	**888-656-7329**	815-825-2086
Black Hawk College					
Quad Cities 6600 34th Ave	Moline	IL	61265	**800-334-1311**	309-796-5000
Olney Central College					
305 NW St	Olney	IL	62450	**866-529-4322**	618-395-7777
Lincoln Trail College					
11220 State Hwy 1	Robinson	IL	62454	**866-582-4322**	618-544-8657
Rock Valley College					
3301 N Mulford Rd	Rockford	IL	61114	**800-973-7821**	815-921-7821
South Suburban College					
15800 S State St	South Holland	IL	60473	**800-609-8056**	708-596-2000
Lincoln Land Community College					
5250 Shepherd Rd PO Box 19256	Springfield	IL	62794	**800-727-4161**	217-786-2200
Springfield College in Illinois - Benedictine University					
1500 N Fifth St	Springfield	IL	62702	**800-635-7289**	217-525-1420
Shawnee Community College					
8364 Shawnee College Rd	Ullin	IL	62992	**800-481-2242**	618-634-3200

Indiana

				Toll-Free	Phone
Vincennes University					
Jasper 850 College Ave	Jasper	IN	47546	**800-809-8852**	812-482-3030
Vincennes University					
1002 N First St	Vincennes	IN	47591	**800-742-9198**	812-888-4313

Iowa

				Toll-Free	Phone
Des Moines Area Community College					
Ankeny 2006 S Ankeny Blvd	Ankeny	IA	50021	**800-362-2127**	515-964-6200
Scott Community College					
500 Belmont Rd	Bettendorf	IA	52722	**888-336-3907**	563-441-4001
Des Moines Area Community College					
Boone 1125 Hancock Dr	Boone	IA	50036	**800-362-2127**	515-432-7203
Northeast Iowa Community College					
Calmar					
1625 Hwy 150 S PO Box 400	Calmar	IA	52132	**800-728-2256**	563-562-3263
Des Moines Area Community College					
Carroll 906 N Grant Rd	Carroll	IA	51401	**800-622-3334**	712-792-1755
Kirkwood Community College					
6301 Kirkwood Blvd SW	Cedar Rapids	IA	52404	**800-332-2055**	319-398-5411
Iowa Western Community College					
Clarinda					
923 E Washington St	Clarinda	IA	51632	**800-521-2073**	712-542-5117
Clinton Community College					
1000 Lincoln Blvd	Clinton	IA	52732	**877-495-3320**	563-244-7001
Southwestern Community College					
1501 W Townline St	Creston	IA	50801	**800-247-4023**	641-782-7081
Des Moines Area Community College					
Urban/Des Moines					
1100 Seventh St	Des Moines	IA	50314	**800-622-3334**	515-244-4226
Iowa Lakes Community College					
300 S 18th St	Estherville	IA	51334	**800-242-5106**	712-362-2604
Iowa Central Community College					
2031 Quail Ave	Fort Dodge	IA	50501	**800-362-2793**	515-576-7201
Ellsworth Community College					
1100 College Ave	Iowa Falls	IA	50126	**800-322-9235**	641-648-4611

				Toll-Free	Phone
Southeastern Community College South					
335 Messenger Rd	Keokuk	IA	52632	866-722-4692	319-524-3221
Marshalltown Community College					
3700 S Ctr St	Marshalltown	IA	50158	866-622-4748	641-844-5708
North Iowa Area Community College					
500 College Dr	Mason City	IA	50401	888-466-4222	641-423-1264
Muscatine Community College					
152 Colorado St	Muscatine	IA	52761	888-336-3907	563-288-6001
Indian Hills Community College					
525 Grandview Ave	Ottumwa	IA	52501	800-726-2585	641-683-5111
Northeast Iowa Community College					
Peosta 8342 NICC Dr	Peosta	IA	52068	800-728-7367	563-556-5110
Northwest Iowa Community College					
603 W Park St	Sheldon	IA	51201	800-352-4907	712-324-5061
Hawkeye Community College					
1501 E Orange Rd	Waterloo	IA	50704	800-670-4769	319-296-2320

Kansas

				Toll-Free	Phone
Cowley County Community College & Area Vocational-Technical School					
PO Box 1147	Arkansas City	KS	67005	800-593-2222	620-442-0430
Colby Community College					
1255 S Range	Colby	KS	67701	888-634-9350	785-462-3984
Cloud County Community College					
2221 Campus Dr	Concordia	KS	66901	800-729-5101	785-243-1435
Dodge City Community College					
2501 N 14th Ave	Dodge City	KS	67801	800-367-3222	620-225-1321
Fort Scott Community College					
2108 S Horton St	Fort Scott	KS	66701	800-874-3722	620-223-2700
Garden City Community College					
801 N Campus Dr	Garden City	KS	67846	800-658-1696	620-276-7611
Barton County Community College					
245 NE 30th Rd	Great Bend	KS	67530	800-722-6842	620-792-2701
Hesston College					
325 S College Dr PO Box 3000	Hesston	KS	67062	800-995-2757	620-327-4221
Highland Community College (HCC)					
606 W Main	Highland	KS	66035	800-985-9781	785-442-6000
Hutchinson Community College & Area Vocational School					
1300 N Plum St	Hutchinson	KS	67501	800-289-3501	620-665-3500
Independence Community College					
1057 W College Ave PO Box 708	Independence	KS	67301	800-842-6063	620-331-4100
Allen County Community College					
1801 N Cottonwood St	Iola	KS	66749	800-444-0535	620-365-5116
Donnelly College					
608 N 18th St	Kansas City	KS	66102	800-908-9946	913-621-8700
Kansas City Kansas Community College					
7250 State Ave	Kansas City	KS	66112	800-640-0352	913-334-1100
Seward County Community College					
1801 N Campus Ave PO Box 1137	Liberal	KS	67905	800-373-9951	620-624-1951
Manhattan Area Technical College					
3136 Dickens	Manhattan	KS	66503	800-352-7575	785-587-2800
Neosho County Community College					
Ottawa 900 E Logan St	Ottawa	KS	66067	888-466-2588	785-242-2067
Johnson County Community College					
12345 College Blvd	Overland Park	KS	66210	866-896-5893	913-469-8500
Labette Community College					
200 S 14th St	Parsons	KS	67357	888-522-3883	620-421-6700
Pratt Community College					
348 NE SR-61	Pratt	KS	67124	800-794-3091	620-672-5641

Kentucky

				Toll-Free	Phone
Ashland Community & Technical College					
1400 College Dr	Ashland	KY	41101	800-928-4256	606-326-2000
Southeast Kentucky Community & Technical College					
Cumberland					
700 College Rd	Cumberland	KY	40823	888-274-7322	606-589-2145
Elizabethtown Community & Technical College					
600 College St Rd	Elizabethtown	KY	42701	877-246-2322	270-769-2371
Hazard Community & Technical College					
1 Community College Dr	Hazard	KY	41701	800-246-7521	606-436-5721
Hazard Community & Technical College					
Hazard Campus 101 Vo Tech Dr	Hazard	KY	41701	800-246-7521	606-436-5721
Henderson Community College					
2660 S Green St	Henderson	KY	42420	800-696-9958	270-827-1867
Hopkinsville Community College					
720 N Dr	Hopkinsville	KY	42240	866-534-2224	270-886-3921
Hazard Community & Technical College					
Lees College Campus Library					
601 Jefferson Ave	Jackson	KY	41339	800-246-7521	606-666-7521
Bluegrass Community & Technical College					
Cooper Campus					
470 Cooper Dr	Lexington	KY	40506	866-774-4872	859-246-6200
Jefferson Community & Technical College					
109 E Broadway	Louisville	KY	40202	855-246-5282	502-213-5333
Madisonville Community College					
2000 College Dr	Madisonville	KY	42431	866-227-4812	270-821-2250
Southeast Kentucky Community & Technical College					
Middlesboro Campus					
1300 Chichester Ave	Middlesboro	KY	40965	888-274-7322	606-242-2145
West Kentucky Community & Technical College					
4810 Alben Barkley Dr PO Box 7380	Paducah	KY	42001	855-469-5282	270-554-9200
Big Sandy Community & Technical College					
1 Bert T Combs Dr	Prestonsburg	KY	41653	888-641-4132	606-886-3863
Somerset Community College					
808 Monticello St	Somerset	KY	42501	877-629-9722	606-679-8501
Southeast Kentucky Community & Technical College					
Whitesburg 2 Long Ave	Whitesburg	KY	41858	888-274-7322	606-633-0279

Louisiana

				Toll-Free	Phone
Louisiana State University					
Alexandria					
8100 US Hwy 71 S	Alexandria	LA	71302	888-473-6417*	318-445-3672
*Admissions					

				Toll-Free	Phone
Baton Rouge Community College (BRCC)					
201 Community College Dr	Baton Rouge	LA	70806	866-217-9823	225-216-8000
Delta College of Arts & Technology					
7380 Exchange Pl	Baton Rouge	LA	70806	800-858-0551	225-928-7770
Elaine P Nunez Community College					
3710 Paris Rd	Chalmette	LA	70043	800-256-3000	504-278-7497
Louisiana State University					
Eunice PO Box 1129	Eunice	LA	70535	888-367-5783	337-457-7311
Louisiana Delta Community College					
7500 Millhaven Rd	Monroe	LA	71203	866-500-5322	318-345-9000

Maine

				Toll-Free	Phone
Washington County Community College					
1 College Dr	Calais	ME	04619	800-210-6932	207-454-1000
Kennebec Valley Community College					
92 Western Ave	Fairfield	ME	04937	800-528-5882	207-453-5000
York County Community College					
112 College Dr	Wells	ME	04090	800-580-3820	207-646-9282

Maryland

				Toll-Free	Phone
Baltimore City Community College					
2901 Liberty Heights Ave	Baltimore	MD	21215	888-203-1261	410-462-8300
Community College of Baltimore County					
Essex 7201 Rossville Blvd	Baltimore	MD	21237	877-557-2575	410-682-6000
Allegany College of Maryland					
12401 Willowbrook Rd SE	Cumberland	MD	21502	800-974-0203	301-784-5000
College of Southern Maryland					
Leonardtown					
22950 Hollywood Rd	Leonardtown	MD	20650	800-933-9177	240-725-5300
Garrett College					
687 Mosser Rd	McHenry	MD	21541	866-554-2773	301-387-3000
Cecil Community College					
1 Seahawk Dr	North East	MD	21901	866-966-1001	410-287-6060
College of Southern Maryland					
Prince Frederick					
115 J W Williams Rd	Prince Frederick	MD	20678	800-933-9177	443-550-6000
Carroll Community College					
1601 Washington Rd	Westminster	MD	21157	888-221-9748	410-386-8000

Massachusetts

				Toll-Free	Phone
Middlesex Community College					
590 Springs Rd	Bedford	MA	01730	800-818-3434	978-656-3370
Bunker Hill Community College					
Charlestown					
250 New Rutherford Ave	Boston	MA	02129	877-218-8829	617-228-2000
Fisher College 118 Beacon St	Boston	MA	02116	866-266-6007	617-236-8800
Massasoit Community College					
1 Massasoit Blvd	Brockton	MA	02302	800-434-6000	508-588-9100
North Shore Community College					
1 Ferncroft Rd	Danvers	MA	01923	800-841-2900	978-762-4000
Dean College 99 Main St	Franklin	MA	02038	877-879-3326	508-541-1508
Holyoke Community College					
303 Homestead Ave	Holyoke	MA	01040	800-325-3252	413-538-7000
Quincy College					
Plymouth 36 Cordage Pk Cir	Plymouth	MA	02360	800-698-1700	508-747-0400
Quincy College					
1250 Hancock St	Quincy	MA	02169	800-698-1700	617-984-1700
Massachusetts Bay Community College					
Wellesley Hills					
50 Oakland St	Wellesley Hills	MA	02481	800-233-3182	781-239-3000
Cape Cod Community College					
2240 Iyanough Rd	West Barnstable	MA	02668	877-846-3672	508-362-2131

Michigan

				Toll-Free	Phone
Alpena Community College (ACC)					
665 Johnson St	Alpena	MI	49707	888-468-6222	989-356-9021
Washtenaw Community College					
4800 E Huron River Dr PO Box 1610	Ann Arbor	MI	48106	800-218-4341	734-973-3300
Lake Michigan College					
2755 E Napier Ave	Benton Harbor	MI	49022	800-252-1562	269-927-1000
Bay Mills Community College					
12214 West Lakeshore Dr	Brimley	MI	49715	800-844-2622	906-248-3354
Glen Oaks Community College					
62249 Shimmel Rd	Centreville	MI	49032	888-994-7818	269-467-9945
Macomb Community College					
Center					
44575 Garfield Rd	Clinton Township	MI	48038	866-622-6621	586-445-7999
Henry Ford Community College					
5101 Evergreen Rd	Dearborn	MI	48128	800-585-4322	313-845-9600
Southwestern Michigan College (SMC)					
58900 Cherry Grove Rd	Dowagiac	MI	49047	800-456-8675	
Bay de Noc Community College					
2001 N Lincoln Rd	Escanaba	MI	49829	800-221-2001	906-786-5802
Gogebic Community College					
E 4946 Jackson Rd	Ironwood	MI	49938	800-682-5910	906-932-4231
Jackson Community College					
2111 Emmons Rd	Jackson	MI	49201	888-522-7344	517-787-0800
Kalamazoo Valley Community College					
Texas Township					
6767 W 'O' Ave PO Box 4070	Kalamazoo	MI	49003	800-221-2001	269-488-4400
Lansing Community College					
411 N Grand Ave	Lansing	MI	48933	800-644-4522	517-483-1957
Monroe County Community College					
1555 S Raisinville Rd	Monroe	MI	48161	877-937-6222	734-242-7300
Saginaw Chippewa Tribal College					
2274 Enterprise Dr	Mount Pleasant	MI	48858	800-225-8172	989-775-4123
Muskegon Community College					
221 S Quarterline Rd	Muskegon	MI	49442	866-711-4622	231-773-9131

	Toll-Free	Phone
Lake Michigan College		
Bertrand Crossing		
1905 Foundation Dr ....Niles MI 49120	800-252-1562	269-695-1391
Southwestern Michigan College		
Niles Area 2229 US 12 ....Niles MI 49120	800-456-8675	
North Central Michigan College		
1515 Howard St ....Petoskey MI 49770	888-298-6605	231-348-6605
Kirtland Community College		
10775 N St Helen Rd ....Roscommon MI 48653	866-632-9992	989-275-5000
West Shore Community College		
PO Box 277 ....Scottville MI 49454	800-848-9722	231-845-6211
Northwestern Michigan College		
1701 E Front St ....Traverse City MI 49686	800-748-0566	231-995-1000
Macomb Community College		
South 14500 E 12-Mile Rd ....Warren MI 48088	866-622-6621	586-445-7000

Minnesota

	Toll-Free	Phone
Riverland Community College		
1900 Eigth Ave NW ....Austin MN 55912	800-247-5039	507-433-0600
Normandale Community College		
9700 France Ave S ....Bloomington MN 55431	866-880-8740	952-487-8200
Central Lakes College		
Brainerd 501 W College Dr ....Brainerd MN 56401	800-933-0346	218-855-8199
North Hennepin Community College		
7411 85th Ave N ....Brooklyn Park MN 55445	800-818-0395	763-488-0391
Anoka-Ramsey Community College		
Cambridge 300 Polk St S ....Cambridge MN 55008	800-627-3529	763-433-1100
Fond du Lac Tribal & Community College		
2101 14th St ....Cloquet MN 55720	800-657-3712	218-879-0800
Anoka-Ramsey Community College		
11200 Mississippi Blvd NW ....Coon Rapids MN 55433	800-627-3529	763-433-1230
Minnesota State Community & Technical College		
Detroit Lakes		
900 Hwy 34 E ....Detroit Lakes MN 56501	877-450-3322	218-846-3700
Lake Superior College		
2101 Trinity Rd ....Duluth MN 55811	800-432-2884	218-733-7600
Northland Community & Technical College		
East Grand Forks		
2022 Central Ave NE ....East Grand Forks MN 56721	800-451-3441	218-773-3441
Vermilion Community College		
1900 E Camp St ....Ely MN 55731	800-657-3608	
Mesabi Range Community & Technical College		
1100 Industrial Pk Dr PO Box 648 ....Eveleth MN 55734	800-657-3860	218-741-3095
South Central College		
Faribault 1225 Third St ....Faribault MN 55021	800-422-0391	507-332-5800
Minnesota State Community & Technical College		
Fergus Falls		
712 Cascade St S ....Fergus Falls MN 56537	877-450-3322	
Itasca Community College		
1851 E US Hwy 169 ....Grand Rapids MN 55744	800-996-6422	218-327-4460
Hibbing Community College		
1515 E 25th St ....Hibbing MN 55746	800-224-4422	218-262-7200
Rainy River Community College		
1501 Hwy 71 ....International Falls MN 56649	800-456-3996	218-285-7722
Inver Hills Community College		
2500 80th St E ....Inver Grove Heights MN 55076	866-576-0689	651-450-3000
Minneapolis Community & Technical College		
1501 Hennepin Ave ....Minneapolis MN 55403	800-247-0911	612-659-6200
Minnesota State Community & Technical College		
Moorhead 1900 28th Ave S ....Moorhead MN 56560	800-426-5603	218-299-6500
South Central College		
Mankato 1920 Lee Blvd ....North Mankato MN 56003	800-722-9359	507-389-7200
Rochester Community & Technical College		
851 30th Ave SE ....Rochester MN 55904	800-247-1296	507-285-7210
Central Lakes College		
Staples 1830 Airport Rd ....Staples MN 56479	800-247-6836	218-894-5100
Northland Community & Technical College		
1101 US Hwy 1 E ....Thief River Falls MN 56701	800-959-6282	218-681-0701
Century College		
3300 Century Ave N ....White Bear Lake MN 55110	800-228-1978	651-779-3300
Minnesota West Community & Technical College		
1450 Collegeway ....Worthington MN 56187	800-657-3966	507-372-3400

Mississippi

	Toll-Free	Phone
Northeast Mississippi Community College		
101 Cunningham Blvd ....Booneville MS 38829	800-555-2154	662-728-7751
East Central Community College		
15738 Hwy 15 S PO Box 129 ....Decatur MS 39327	877-462-3222	601-635-2111
Mississippi Gulf Coast Community College (MGCCC)		
Jackson County 2300 Hwy 90 ....Gautier MS 39553	866-735-1122	228-497-9602
Holmes Community College		
PO Box 399 ....Goodman MS 39079	800-465-6374	662-472-2312
Mississippi Gulf Coast Community College		
Jefferson Davis		
2226 Switzer Rd ....Gulfport MS 39507	866-735-1122	228-896-3355
Meridian Community College		
910 Hwy 19 N ....Meridian MS 39307	800-622-8431	601-483-8241
Mississippi Gulf Coast Community College		
51 Main St PO Box 548 ....Perkinston MS 39573	866-735-1122	601-928-5211
Pearl River Community College		
101 Hwy 11 N ....Poplarville MS 39470	877-772-2338	601-403-1000
Hinds Community College		
501 E Main St PO Box 1100 ....Raymond MS 39154	800-446-3722	601-857-3212

Missouri

	Toll-Free	Phone
Metropolitan Community College Penn Valley		
3200 Broadway ....Kansas City MO 64111	866-676-6224	816-604-1000
AT. Still University of Health Sciences		
800 W Jefferson St ....Kirksville MO 63501	866-626-2878	660-626-2121
Moberly Area Community College		
101 College Ave ....Moberly MO 65270	800-622-2070	660-263-4110
Crowder College		
601 Laclede Ave ....Neosho MO 64850	866-238-7788	417-451-3223
Cottey College		
1000 W Austin Blvd ....Nevada MO 64772	888-526-8839	417-667-8181
Three Rivers Community College		
2080 Three Rivers Blvd ....Poplar Bluff MO 63901	877-879-8722	573-840-9600
State Fair Community College		
3201 W 16th St ....Sedalia MO 65301	877-311-7322	660-530-5800
East Central College		
1964 Prairie Dell Rd ....Union MO 63084	800-392-6848	636-583-5193

Montana

	Toll-Free	Phone
Dawson Community College		
300 College Dr ....Glendive MT 59330	800-821-8320	406-377-3396
Flathead Valley Community College		
777 Grandview Dr ....Kalispell MT 59901	800-313-3822	406-756-3822
Flathead Valley Community College		
Libby 225 Commerce Way ....Libby MT 59923	800-313-3822	406-293-2721
Miles Community College		
2715 Dickinson St ....Miles City MT 59301	800-541-9281	406-874-6100
Salish Kootenai College		
PO Box 70 ....Pablo MT 59855	877-752-6553	406-275-4800

Nebraska

	Toll-Free	Phone
Southeast Community College		
Beatrice 4771 W Scott Rd ....Beatrice NE 68310	800-233-5027	402-228-3468
Central Community College		
Grand Island		
3134 W Hwy 34 PO Box 4903 ....Grand Island NE 68802	877-222-0780	308-398-4222
Southeast Community College		
Lincoln 8800 'O' St ....Lincoln NE 68520	800-642-4075	402-471-3333
Nebraska Indian Community College		
PO Box 428 ....Macy NE 68039	844-440-6422	402-837-5078
McCook Community College		
1205 E Third St ....McCook NE 69001	800-658-4348	308-345-8100
Northeast Community College		
801 E Benjamin Ave PO Box 409 ....Norfolk NE 68702	800 348 9033	402-371-2020
North Platte Community College		
North 1101 Halligan Dr ....North Platte NE 69101	800-658-4308	308-535-3601
North Platte Community College		
South		
601 W State Farm Rd ....North Platte NE 69101	800-658-4348	
Metropolitan Community College		
PO Box 3777 ....Omaha NE 68103	800-228-9553	402-457-2400
Western Nebraska Community College		
1601 E 27th St ....Scottsbluff NE 69361	800-348-4435	308-635-3606

New Hampshire

	Toll-Free	Phone
White Mountains Community College (WMCC)		
2020 Riverside Dr ....Berlin NH 03570	800-445-4525	603-752-1113
Community College System of New Hampshire (CCSNH)		
26 College Dr ....Concord NH 03301	866-945-2255	603-230-3500
NHTI Concord's Community College		
31 College Dr ....Concord NH 03301	800-247-0179	603-271-6484
Lakes Region Community College (LRCC)		
379 Belmont Rd ....Laconia NH 03246	800-357-2992	603-524-3207
Manchester Community College		
1066 Front St ....Manchester NH 03102	800-924-3445	603-206-8000

New Jersey

	Toll-Free	Phone
Brookdale Community College		
765 Newman Springs Rd ....Lincroft NJ 07738	866-767-9512	732-842-1900
Sussex County Community College		
1 College Hill Rd ....Newton NJ 07860	800-848-4555	973-300-2100
Bergen Community College		
400 Paramus Rd ....Paramus NJ 07652	877-612-5381	201-447-7200
County College of Morris		
214 Ctr Grove Rd ....Randolph NJ 07869	888-726-3260	973-328-5000
Raritan Valley Community College		
PO Box 3300 ....Somerville NJ 08876	888-326-4058	908-526-1200
Cumberland County College		
3322 College Dr ....Vineland NJ 08360	800-792-8670	856-691-8600

New Mexico

	Toll-Free	Phone
University of New Mexico (UNM)		
1 University of New Mexico ....Albuquerque NM 87131	800-225-5866	505-277-0111
New Mexico State University		
Carlsbad		
1500 University Dr ....Carlsbad NM 88220	888-888-2199	575-234-9200
Clovis Community College (CCC)		
417 Schepps Blvd ....Clovis NM 88101	800-769-1409	575-769-2811
Northern New Mexico College		
921 Paseo de Onate ....Espanola NM 87532	800-477-3632	505-747-2100
San Juan College		
4601 College Blvd ....Farmington NM 87402	866-426-1233	505-326-3311
New Mexico Junior College		
1 Thunderbird Cir ....Hobbs NM 88240	800-657-6260	505-392-4510
Doña Ana Community College (DACC)		
2800 N Sonoma Ranch Blvd ....Las Cruces NM 88011	800-903-7503	575-528-7000
New Mexico State University (NMSU)		
MSC-3A PO Box 30001 ....Las Cruces NM 88003	800-662-6678*	575-646-3121
Admissions		
Luna Community College		
366 Luna Dr ....Las Vegas NM 87701	800-588-7232	505-454-2500
University of New Mexico		
Valencia 280 La Entrada ....Los Lunas NM 87031	800-225-5866	505-925-8580

Classified Section

	Toll-Free	Phone
Eastern New Mexico University Roswell		
52 University Blvd ....Roswell NM 88203	800-243-6687	575-624-7000

New York

	Toll-Free	Phone
State University of New York		
College of Technology at Alfred		
10 Upper College Dr ....Alfred NY 14802	800-425-3733	607-587-4215
Cayuga Community College		
197 Franklin St ....Auburn NY 13021	866-598-8883	315-255-1743
Genesee Community College		
1 College Rd ....Batavia NY 14020	866-225-5422	585-343-0055
Broome Community College		
901 Front St ....Binghamton NY 13905	800-836-0689	607-778-5000
State University of New York		
Brockport		
350 New Campus Dr ....Brockport NY 14420	888-800-0029	585-395-2751
Bronx Community College		
2155 University Ave ....Bronx NY 10453	866-888-8777	718-289-5100
Trocaire College		
360 Choate Ave ....Buffalo NY 14220	877-616-6633	716-826-1200
State University of New York		
Canton 34 Cornell Dr ....Canton NY 13617	800-388-7123	315-386-7011
State University of New York		
Delhi 2 Main St ....Delhi NY 13753	800-963-3544	607-746-4000
Tompkins Cortland Community College		
170 N St ....Dryden NY 13053	888-567-8211	607-844-8211
Herkimer County Community College		
100 Reservoir Rd ....Herkimer NY 13350	844-464-4375	315-866-0300
Jamestown Community College		
525 Falconer St ....Jamestown NY 14702	800-388-8557	716-338-1000
Sullivan County Community College		
112 College Rd ....Loch Sheldrake NY 12759	800-577-5243	845-434-5750
Orange County Community College		
115 S St ....Middletown NY 10940	866-694-4700	845-344-6222
Clinton Community College		
136 Clinton Pt Dr ....Plattsburgh NY 12901	800-552-1160	518-562-4200
Adirondack Community College		
640 Bay Rd ....Queensbury NY 12804	888-786-9235	518-743-2200
Monroe Community College		
1000 E Henrietta Rd ....Rochester NY 14623	800-875-6269	585-292-2000
Niagara County Community College		
3111 Saunders Settlement Rd ....Sanborn NY 14132	800-875-6269	716-614-6222
North Country Community College		
23 Santanoni Ave ....Saranac Lake NY 12983	888-879-6222	518-891-2915
Ulster County Community College		
Cottekill Rd ....Stone Ridge NY 12484	800-724-0833	845-687-5000
Rockland Community College		
145 College Rd ....Suffern NY 10901	800-722-7666	845-574-4000
Hudson Valley Community College		
80 Vandenburgh Ave ....Troy NY 12180	877-325-4822	518-629-4822
Mohawk Valley Community College		
1101 Sherman Dr ....Utica NY 13501	800-733-6822	315-792-5400
Jefferson Community College		
1220 Coffeen St ....Watertown NY 13601	888-435-6522	315-786-2200

North Carolina

	Toll-Free	Phone
Brunswick Community College		
50 College Rd ....Bolivia NC 28422	800-754-1050	910-755-7300
Central Piedmont Community College		
1201 Elizabeth Ave ....Charlotte NC 28204	877-530-8815	704-330-2722
Sampson Community College		
PO Box 318 ....Clinton NC 28329	844-319-3640	910-592-8081
Vance-Granville Community College		
South PO Box 39 ....Creedmoor NC 27522	877-823-2378	919-528-4737
College of the Albemarle		
PO Box 2327 ....Elizabeth City NC 27906	800-335-9050	252-335-0821
Alamance Community College		
PO Box 8000 ....Graham NC 27253	877-667-7533	336-578-2002
Richmond Community College		
PO Box 1189 ....Hamlet NC 28345	800-908-9946	910-410-1700
Coastal Carolina Community College		
444 Western Blvd ....Jacksonville NC 28546	800-908-9946	910-455-1221
Lenoir Community College		
231 Hwy 58 S PO Box 188 ....Kinston NC 28502	866-866-2362	252-527-6223
Davidson County Community College		
PO Box 1287 ....Lexington NC 27293	800-233-4050	336-249-8186
Louisburg College		
501 N Main St ....Louisburg NC 27549	800-775-0208	919-496-2521
Sandhills Community College		
3395 Airport Rd ....Pinehurst NC 28374	800-338-3944	910-692-6185
Central Carolina Community College		
1105 Kelly Dr ....Sanford NC 27330	800-682-8353	919-775-5401
Johnston Community College		
245 College Rd ....Smithfield NC 27577	800-510-9132	919-934-3051
Mayland Community College		
200 Mayland Dr PO Box 547 ....Spruce Pine NC 28777	800-462-9526	828-765-7351
Southwestern Community College		
447 College Dr ....Sylva NC 28779	800-447-4091	828-339-4000
Vance-Granville Community College		
Warren County PO Box 207 ....Warrenton NC 27536	877-823-2378	252-257-1900
Halifax Community College		
100 College Dr ....Weldon NC 27890	800-228-8443	252-536-2551
Wilkes Community College		
1328 S Collegiate Dr PO Box 120 ....Wilkesboro NC 28697	866-222-1548	336-838-6100
Martin Community College		
1161 Kehukee Pk Rd ....Williamston NC 27892	800-488-4101	252-792-1521

North Dakota

	Toll-Free	Phone
Turtle Mountain Community College		
10145 BIA Rd 7 ....Belcourt ND 58316	800-827-1100	701-477-7862
Bismarck State College		
1500 Edwards Blvd ....Bismarck ND 58501	800-445-5073	701-224-5400

	Toll-Free	Phone
Minot State University Bottineau		
105 Simrall Blvd ....Bottineau ND 58318	800-542-6866	701-228-5451
Lake Region State College		
1801 College Dr N ....Devils Lake ND 58301	800-443-1313	701-662-1600
Cankdeska Cikana Community College		
PO Box 269 ....Fort Totten ND 58335	888-783-1463	701-766-4415
North Dakota State College of Science		
800 Sixth St N ....Wahpeton ND 58076	800-342-4325	701-671-2401
Williston State College		
1410 University Ave PO Box 1326 ....Williston ND 58802	888-863-9455	701-774-4200

Ohio

	Toll-Free	Phone
Kent State University		
Ashtabula 3300 Lake Rd W ....Ashtabula OH 44004	800-988-5368	440-964-3322
University of Cincinnati Clermont College		
4200 Clermont College Dr ....Batavia OH 45103	866-446-2822	513-732-5200
Wright State University Lake		
7600 Lake Campus Dr ....Celina OH 45822	800-237-1477	419-586-0300
Cincinnati State Technical & Community College		
3520 Central Pkwy ....Cincinnati OH 45223	877-569-0115	513-569-1500
Columbus State Community College		
550 E Spring St ....Columbus OH 43215	800-621-6407	614-287-2400
Lorain County Community College		
1005 N Abbe Rd ....Elyria OH 44035	800-995-5222	440-365-5222
Owens Community College		
Findlay 3200 Bright Rd ....Findlay OH 45840	800-466-9367	
Terra Community College		
2830 Napoleon Rd ....Fremont OH 43420	800-334-3886	419-334-8400
Cuyahoga Community College		
Eastern		
4250 Richmond Rd ....Highland Hills OH 44122	800-954-8742	216-987-2024
Kent State University		
800 E Summit St PO Box 5190 ....Kent OH 44242	800-988-5368	330-672-3000
Lakeland Community College		
7700 Clocktower Dr ....Kirtland OH 44094	800-589-8520	440-525-7000
Buckeye Career Ctr		
545 University Dr NE ....New Philadelphia OH 44663	800-227-1665	330-339-2288
University of Akron Wayne College		
1901 Smucker Rd ....Orrville OH 44667	800-221-8308	330-683-2010
Miami University		
501 E High St ....Oxford OH 45056	866-426-4643	513-529-1809
Cuyahoga Community College		
Western		
11000 Pleasant Valley Rd ....Parma OH 44130	800-954-8742	216-987-2800
Owens Community College		
Toledo 30335 Oregon Rd ....Perrysburg OH 43551	800-466-9367	567-661-7357
Edison Community College		
1973 Edison Dr ....Piqua OH 45356	888-442-4551	937-778-8600
Southern State Community College		
South 12681 US Rt 62 ....Sardinia OH 45171	877-644-6562	937-695-0307
Southern State Community College		
North 1850 Davids Dr ....Wilmington OH 45177	877-644-6562	937-382-6645

Oklahoma

	Toll-Free	Phone
Western Oklahoma State College		
2801 N Main St ....Altus OK 73521	800-662-1113	580-477-2000
Redlands Community College		
1300 S Country Club Rd ....El Reno OK 73036	866-415-6367	405-262-2552
Rose State College		
6420 SE 15th St ....Midwest City OK 73110	866-621-0987	405-733-7372
Oklahoma State University		
Oklahoma City		
900 N Portland Ave ....Oklahoma City OK 73107	800-560-4099	405-947-4421
Rogers State University Pryor		
421 S Elliott St ....Pryor OK 74361	800-256-7511	918-825-6117
Seminole State College		
2701 Boren Blvd PO Box 351 ....Seminole OK 74868	877-738-6365	405-382-9950
Oklahoma State University		
219 Student Union Bldg ....Stillwater OK 74078	800-852-1255	405-744-5000
Murray State College		
1 Murray Campus ....Tishomingo OK 73460	800-342-0698	580-371-2371
Northern Oklahoma College		
1220 E Grand St PO Box 310 ....Tonkawa OK 74653	800-522-0188	580-628-6200

Ontario

	Toll-Free	Phone
Loyalist College		
Wallbridge-Loyalist Rd ....Belleville ON K8N5B9	800-992-5866	613-969-1913
Fleming College		
200 Albert St S ....Lindsay ON K9V5E6	866-353-6464	705-324-9144
Willis College of Business & Technology		
85 O'Connor St ....Ottawa ON K1P5M6	877-233-1128	613-233-1128
Sault College		
443 Northern Ave ....Sault Sainte Marie ON P6A5L3	800-461-2260	705-759-6700
College of Nurses of Ontario		
101 Davenport Rd ....Toronto ON M5R3P1	800-387-5526	416-928-0900
Institute of Corporate Directors		
2701 - 250 Yonge St ....Toronto ON M5B2L7	877-593-7741	416-593-7741

Oregon

	Toll-Free	Phone
Clatsop Community College		
1653 Jerome Ave ....Astoria OR 97103	855-252-8767	503-325-0910
Lane Community College		
4000 E 30th Ave ....Eugene OR 97405	800-321-2211	541-463-3000
Lane Community College		
3149 Oak St ....Florence OR 97439	800-222-3290	541-997-8444
Rogue Community College		
3345 Redwood Hwy ....Grants Pass OR 97527	800-411-6508	541-956-7500
Blue Mountain Community College		
2411 NW Carden Ave PO Box 100 ....Pendleton OR 97801	888-441-7232	541-276-1260

			Toll-Free	Phone
Portland Community College *Sylvania* 12000 SW 49th Ave	Portland OR	97219	**866-922-1010**	503-244-6111
Umpqua Community College 1140 Umpqva College Rd PO Box 967	Roseburg OR	97470	**800-820-5161**	541-440-4600
Tillamook Bay Community College 4301 Third St	Tillamook OR	97141	**888-306-8222**	503-842-8222

Pennsylvania

			Toll-Free	Phone
NanoHorizons Inc 270 Rolling Ridge Dr Ste 100	Bellefonte PA	16823	**866-584-6235**	814-355-4700
Northampton Community College 3835 Green Pond Rd	Bethlehem PA	18020	**877-543-0998**	610-861-5300
Harcum College 750 Montgomery Ave	Bryn Mawr PA	19010	**800-537-3000**	610-525-4100
Butler County Community College 107 College Dr	Butler PA	16002	**888-826-2829**	724-287-8711
Pennsylvania State University *DuBois* 1 College Pl	Du Bois PA	15801	**800-346-7627**	814-375-4700
Us Health Connect Inc 500 Office Ctr Dr	Fort Washington PA	19034	**800-889-4944**	
Harrisburg Area Community College *Gettysburg* 731 Old Harrisburg Rd	Gettysburg PA	17325	**800-222-4222**	717-337-3855
Harrisburg Area Community College 1 HACC Dr	Harrisburg PA	17110	**800-222-4222**	717-780-2300
Pennsylvania State University *Hazleton* 76 University Dr	Hazleton PA	18202	**800-279-8495**	570-450-3000
Harrisburg Area Community College *Lebanon* 735 Cumberland St	Lebanon PA	17042	**800-222-4222**	717-270-4222
Pennsylvania State University *Fayette* 2201 University Dr	Lemont Furnace PA	15456	**877-568-4130**	724-430-4100
Community College of Beaver County 1 Campus Dr	Monaca PA	15061	**800-335-0222**	724-775-8561
Pennsylvania State University *Beaver* 100 University Dr	Monaca PA	15061	**877-564-6778**	724-773-3500
Pennsylvania State University *Mont Alto* 1 Campus Dr	Mont Alto PA	17237	**800-392-6173**	717-749-6000
Luzerne County Community College 1333 S Prospect St	Nanticoke PA	18634	**800-377-5222**	
University of Pittsburgh 4227 Fifth Ave	Pittsburgh PA	15260	**877-999-3223**	412-624-4141
Reading Area Community College 10 S Second St	Reading PA	19603	**800-626-1665**	610-372-4721
Lehigh Carbon Community College 4525 Education Pk Dr *General	Schnecksville PA	18078	**800-414-3975***	610-799-2121
Pennsylvania State University *Shenango* 147 Shenango Ave	Sharon PA	16146	**888-275-7009**	724-983-2803
University of Pittsburgh *Titusville* 504 E Main St	Titusville PA	16354	**888-878-0462**	
Pennsylvania State University 201 Shields Bldg	University Park PA	16802	**800-279-8495**	814-865-4700
Valley Forge Military Academy & College 1001 Eagle Rd	Wayne PA	19087	**800-234-8362**	610-989-1300
Westmoreland County Community College 145 Pavilion Ln	Youngwood PA	15697	**800-262-2103**	724-925-4000

Prince Edward Island

			Toll-Free	Phone
Holland College 140 Weymouth St	Charlottetown PE	C1A4Z1	**800-446-5265**	902-566-9510

Quebec

			Toll-Free	Phone
College Merici 755 Grande All,e Ouest	Quebec QC	G1S1C1	**800-208-1463**	418-683-1591

Rhode Island

			Toll-Free	Phone
Community College of Rhode Island *Flanagan* 1762 Louisquisset Pk	Lincoln RI	02865	**800-494-8100**	401-333-7000
Community College of Rhode Island *Liston* 1 Hilton St	Providence RI	02905	**800-494-8100**	401-455-6000

Saskatchewan

			Toll-Free	Phone
Saskatoon Business College Ltd 221 Third Ave N	Saskatoon SK	S7K2H7	**800-679-7711**	306-244-6333

South Carolina

			Toll-Free	Phone
Northeastern Technical College 1201 Chesterfield Hwy	Cheraw SC	29520	**800-921-7399**	843-921-6900
Midlands Technical College PO Box 2408	Columbia SC	29202	**800-922-8038**	803-738-1400
University of South Carolina 1601 Greene St	Columbia SC	29208	**800-868-5872**	803-777-7000
Aiken Technical College 2276 J Davis Hwy	Graniteville SC	29829	**800-246-6198**	803-593-9231
Greenville Technical College *Barton* 506 S Pleasantburg Dr *All	Greenville SC	29607	**800-723-0673***	864-250-8000
York Technical College 452 S Anderson Rd	Rock Hill SC	29730	**800-922-8324**	803-327-8000
Spartanburg Methodist College 1000 Powell Mill Rd	Spartanburg SC	29301	**800-772-7286**	864-587-4000
Greenville Technical College *Greer* 2522 Locust Hill Rd	Taylors SC	29687	**800-723-0673**	864-250-8000
North Greenville University 7801 N Tigerville Rd PO Box 1892	Tigerville SC	29688	**800-468-6642**	864-977-7000
University of South Carolina *Union* 401 E Main St	Union SC	29379	**800-768-5566**	864-429-8728

South Dakota

			Toll-Free	Phone
Mitchell Technical Institute 821 N Capital St	Mitchell SD	57301	**800-684-1969**	
Lake Area Technical Institute 1201 Arrow Ave PO Box 730	Watertown SD	57201	**800-657-4344**	605-882-5284

Tennessee

			Toll-Free	Phone
Chattanooga State Technical Community College 4501 Amnicola Hwy	Chattanooga TN	37406	**866-547-3733**	423-697-4400
Cleveland State Community College 3535 Adkisson Dr	Cleveland TN	37312	**800-604-2722**	423-472-7141
Columbia State Community College *Clifton* 795 Main St	Clifton TN	38425	**888-346-6581**	931-676-6966
Columbia State Community College 1665 Hampshire Pk	Columbia TN	38401	**800-848-0298**	931-540-2722
Volunteer State Community College 1480 Nashville Pk	Gallatin TN	37066	**888-335-8722**	615-452-8600
Roane State Community College 276 Patton Ln	Harriman TN	37748	**800-343-9104**	865-354-3000
Motlow State Community College PO Box 8500	Lynchburg TN	37352	**800-654-4877**	931-393-1544
Hiwassee College 225 Hiwassee College Dr	Madisonville TN	37354	**800-356-2187**	423-442-2001
Southwest Tennessee Community College 5983 Macon Cove PO Box 780	Memphis TN	38134	**877-717-7822**	901-333-5000
Walters State Community College 500 S Davy Crockett Pkwy	Morristown TN	37813	**800-225-4770**	423-585-2600

Texas

			Toll-Free	Phone
Texas State Technical College (TSTC) *Abilene* 650 E Hwy 80	Abilene TX	79601	**800-852-8784**	325-672-7091
Amarillo College 2201 S Washington St	Amarillo TX	79109	**800-227-8784**	806-371-5000
Smith System Driver Improvement Institute Inc 2301 E Lamar Blvd Ste 250	Arlington TX	76006	**800-777-7648**	817-652-6969
Austin Community College (ACC) 5930 Middle Fiskville Rd	Austin TX	78752	**877-442-3522**	512-223-7000
Austin Community College *Eastview* 3401 Webberville Rd	Austin TX	78702	**888-626-1697**	512-223-5100
Austin Community College *Northridge* 11928 Stonehollow Dr	Austin TX	78758	**888-626-1697**	512-223-4000
Austin Community College *Pinnacle* 7748 Hwy 290 W	Austin TX	78736	**888-626-1697**	512-223-8001
Austin Community College *Rio Grande* 1212 Rio Grande	Austin TX	78701	**888-626-1697**	512-223-3000
Austin Community College *Riverside* 1020 Grove Blvd	Austin TX	78741	**888-626-1697**	512-223-6000
Lee College 200 Lee Dr PO Box 818	Baytown TX	77520	**800-621-8724**	281-427-5611
Coastal Bend College *Beeville* 3800 Charco Rd	Beeville TX	78102	**866-722-2838**	361-358-2838
Howard College 1001 Birdwell Ln	Big Spring TX	79720	**877-898-3833**	432-264-5000
Panola College 1109 W Panola St	Carthage TX	75633	**800-252-9152**	903-693-2000
Clarendon College 1122 College Dr PO Box 968	Clarendon TX	79226	**800-687-9737**	806-874-3571
Del Mar College *East* 101 Baldwin Blvd	Corpus Christi TX	78404	**800-652-3357**	361-698-1200
Navarro College 3200 W Seventh Ave	Corsicana TX	75110	**800-628-2776**	903-874-6501
El Paso Community College *Valle Verde* 919 Hunter Dr	El Paso TX	79915	**800-531-8292**	404-679-4500
Galveston College 4015 Ave Q	Galveston TX	77550	**866-483-4242**	409-944-4242
Texas State Technical College *Harlingen* 1902 N Loop 499	Harlingen TX	78550	**800-852-8784**	956-364-4000
Central Texas College PO Box 1800	Killeen TX	76540	**800-792-3348**	254-526-7161
Kingwood College 20000 Kingwood Dr	Kingwood TX	77339	**800-883-7939**	281-312-1600
Brazosport College 500 College Dr	Lake Jackson TX	77566	**877-717-7873**	979-230-3000
Midland College 3600 N Garfield St	Midland TX	79705	**800-474-7164**	432-685-4500
Northeast Texas Community College 1735 Chapel Hill Rd	Mount Pleasant TX	75455	**800-870-0142**	903-572-1911
Lamar State College *Orange* 410 Front St	Orange TX	77630	**877-673-6839**	409-883-7750
Trinity Valley Community College *Palestine* PO Box 2530	Palestine TX	75802	**866-882-2937**	903-729-0256
Paris Junior College 2400 Clarksville St	Paris TX	75460	**800-232-5804**	903-785-7661
Lamar State College *Port Arthur* PO Box 310	Port Arthur TX	77641	**800-477-5872**	409-983-4921
Western Texas College 6200 College Ave	Snyder TX	79549	**888-468-6982**	325-573-8511
Wharton County Junior College *Sugar Land* 14004 University Blvd	Sugar Land TX	77479	**800-561-9252**	281-243-8447
Texas State Technical College *Sweetwater* 300 Homer K Taylor Dr	Sweetwater TX	79556	**877-450-3595**	325-235-7300

	Toll-Free	Phone
Temple College		
2600 S First St ....Temple TX 76504	800-460-4636*	254-298-8300
*Admissions		
Texarkana College		
2500 North Robison Rd ....Texarkana TX 75599	877-275-4377	903-838-4541
College of the Mainland		
1200 N Amburn Rd ....Texas City TX 77591	888-258-8859	409-938-1211
Tyler Junior College		
PO Box 9020 ....Tyler TX 75711	800-687-5680	903-510-2523
Vernon College		
4400 College Dr ....Vernon TX 76384	866-336-9371	940-552-6291
Victoria College		
2200 E Red River St ....Victoria TX 77901	877-843-4369	361-573-3291
Weatherford College		
225 College Pk Dr ....Weatherford TX 76086	800-287-5471	817-594-5471
Wharton County Junior College		
911 Boling Hwy ....Wharton TX 77488	800-561-9252	979-532-4560

Utah

	Toll-Free	Phone
College of Eastern Utah		
San Juan 639 W 100 S ....Blanding UT 84511	800-395-2969	435-678-2201
Snow College		
150 College Ave PO Box 1037 ....Ephraim UT 84627	800-848-3399	435-283-7000
Stevens Henager College		
1890 S 1350 W ....Ogden UT 84401	800-622-2640	
Utah Valley State College		
800 West University Pkwy ....Orem UT 84058	800-952-8220	801-863-8000
College of Eastern Utah		
451 E 400 N ....Price UT 84501	800-336-2381	435-613-5000

Vermont

	Toll-Free	Phone
Community College of Vermont		
Bennington 324 Main St ....Bennington VT 05201	800-431-0025	802-447-2361
Community College of Vermont		
Brattleboro		
70 Landmark Hill Ste 101 ....Brattleboro VT 05301	800-431-0025	802-254-6370
Community College of Vermont		
Middlebury		
10 Merchants Row Ste 223..................Middlebury VT 05753	800-431-0025	802-388-3032
Community College of Vermont		
Montpelier PO Box 489 ....Montpelier VT 05602	800-228-6686	802-828-4060
Community College of Vermont		
Morrisville		
197 Harrell St Ste 2 ....Morrisville VT 05661	800-431-0025	802-888-4258
Community College of Vermont		
Newport 100 Main St Ste 150..................Newport VT 05855	800-431-0025	802-334-3387
Community College of Vermont		
Upper Valley		
145 Billings Farm Rd ....White River Junction VT 05001	800-431-0025	802-295-8822

Virginia

	Toll-Free	Phone
Southside Virginia Community College		
109 Campus Dr ....Alberta VA 23821	888-220-7822	434-949-1000
Northern Virginia Community College		
Alexandria		
5000 Dawes Ave ....Alexandria VA 22311	855-259-1019	703-845-6200
Northern Virginia Community College		
Annandale		
8333 Little River Tpke ....Annandale VA 22003	877-408-2028	703-323-3000
Mountain Empire Community College		
3441 Mtn Empire Rd ....Big Stone Gap VA 24219	800-981-0600	276-523-2400
Southwest Virginia Community College		
724 Community College Rd ....Cedar Bluff VA 24609	855-877-3944	276-964-2555
Tidewater Community College		
Chesapeake 1428 Cedar Rd ....Chesapeake VA 23322	800-371-0898	757-822-5100
John Tyler Community College		
13101 Jefferson Davis Hwy ....Chester VA 23831	800-552-3490	804-796-4000
Danville Community College		
1008 S Main St ....Danville VA 24541	800-560-4291	434-797-2222
New River Community College		
5251 College Dr ....Dublin VA 24084	866-462-6722	540-674-3600
Paul D Camp Community College		
100 N College Dr PO Box 737 ....Franklin VA 23851	855-877-3918	757-569-6700
Rappahannock Community College		
Glenns 12745 College Dr ....Glenns VA 23149	800-836-9381	804-758-6700
Northern Virginia Community College		
Manassas 6901 Sudley Rd ....Manassas VA 20109	855-259-1019	703-257-6620
Patrick Henry Community College		
645 Patriot Ave ....Martinsville VA 24112	855-874-6692	276-638-8777
Lord Fairfax Community College		
Middletown		
173 Skirmisher Ln ....Middletown VA 22645	800-906-5322	540-868-7000
Tidewater Community College		
Norfolk 121 College Pl ....Norfolk VA 23510	800-371-0898	757-822-1110
Tidewater Community College		
Portsmouth		
7000 College Dr ....Portsmouth VA 23703	800-371-0898	757-822-2124
J Sargeant Reynolds Community College		
PO Box 85622 ....Richmond VA 23285	800-922-3420	804-371-3000
Virginia Western Community College		
3094 Colonial Ave ....Roanoke VA 24015	855-874-6690	540-857-8922
Paul D Camp Community College		
Hobbs Suffolk 271 Kenyon Rd ....Suffolk VA 23434	855-877-3918	757-925-6300
Tidewater Community College		
Virginia Beach		
1700 College Crescent ....Virginia Beach VA 23453	800-371-0898	757-822-7100
Rappahannock Community College		
Warsaw 52 Campus Dr ....Warsaw VA 22572	800-836-9381	804-333-6700
Blue Ridge Community College		
1 College Ln PO Box 80 ....Weyers Cave VA 24486	888-750-2722	540-234-9261

Washington

	Toll-Free	Phone
Grays Harbor College		
1620 Edward P Smith Dr ....Aberdeen WA 98520	800-562-4830	360-532-9020
Northwest Indian College		
2522 Kwina Rd ....Bellingham WA 98226	866-676-2772	360-676-2772
Olympic College		
1600 Chester Ave ....Bremerton WA 98337	800-259-6718	360-792-6050
Everett Community College		
2000 Tower St ....Everett WA 98201	866-575-9027	425-388-9100
Lower Columbia College		
1600 Maple St PO Box 3010 ....Longview WA 98632	866-900-2311	360-442-2301
Edmonds Community College		
20000 68th Ave W ....Lynnwood WA 98036	866-886-4854	425-640-1500
Big Bend Community College		
7662 Chanute St ....Moses Lake WA 98837	877-745-1212	509-793-2222
Skagit Valley College		
2405 E College Way ....Mount Vernon WA 98273	877-385-5360	360-416-7600
Pierce College		
Puyallup 1601 39th Ave SE ....Puyallup WA 98374	877-353-6763	253-840-8400
North Seattle Community College		
9600 College Way North ....Seattle WA 98103	866-427-4747	206-527-3600
Olympic College		
Shelton 937 W Alpine Way ....Shelton WA 98584	800-259-6718	360-427-2119
Shoreline Community College		
16101 Greenwood Ave N ....Shoreline WA 98133	866-427-4747	206-546-4101
Spokane Community College		
1810 N Greene St ....Spokane WA 99217	800-248-5644	509-533-7000
Spokane Falls Community College		
3410 W Ft George Wright Dr ....Spokane WA 99224	888-509-7944	509-533-3500
Walla Walla Community College		
500 Tausick Way ....Walla Walla WA 99362	877-992-9922	509-522-2500
Wenatchee Valley College		
1300 Fifth St ....Wenatchee WA 98801	877-982-4968	509-682-6800
Perry Technical Institute		
2011 W Washington Ave ....Yakima WA 98903	888-528-8586	509-453-0374

West Virginia

	Toll-Free	Phone
Potomac State College		
101 Ft Ave ....Keyser WV 26726	800-262-7332	304-788-6800
Eastern West Virginia Community & Technical College		
316 Eastern Dr ....Moorefield WV 26836	877-982-2322	304-434-8000
West Virginia University		
PO Box 6009 ....Morgantown WV 26506	800-344-9881	304-293-2121
West Virginia University		
Parkersburg		
300 Campus Dr ....Parkersburg WV 26104	800-982-9887	304-424-8000

Wisconsin

	Toll-Free	Phone
Lac Courte Oreilles Ojibwa Community College		
13466 W Trepania Rd ....Hayward WI 54843	888-526-6221	715-634-4790
College of Menominee Nation		
PO Box 1179 ....Keshena WI 54135	800-567-2344	715-799-5600
University of Wisconsin		
Richland		
1200 Hwy 14 W ....Richland Center WI 53581	800-947-3529	608-647-6186
University of Wisconsin		
Sheboygan 1 University Dr ....Sheboygan WI 53081	800-442-6459*	920-459-6600
*Help Line		
University of Wisconsin		
Marathon County		
518 S Seventh Ave ....Wausau WI 54401	888-367-8962	715-261-6100
University of Wisconsin		
Washington County		
400 S University Dr ....West Bend WI 53095	800-240-0276	262-335-5200

Wyoming

	Toll-Free	Phone
Casper College		
125 College Dr ....Casper WY 82601	800-442-2963	307-268-2100
Laramie County Community College		
1400 E College Dr ....Cheyenne WY 82007	800-522-2993	307-778-5222
Sheridan College		
Gillette 300 West Sinclair ....Gillette WY 82718	800-913-9139	307-686-0254
Laramie County Community College		
Albany County		
1125 Boulder Dr ....Laramie WY 82070	800-522-2993	307-721-5138
Northwest College		
231 W Sixth St ....Powell WY 82435	800-560-4692	307-754-6000
Central Wyoming College		
2660 Peck Ave ....Riverton WY 82501	800-735-8418	307-855-2000
Western Wyoming Community College		
2500 College Dr ....Rock Springs WY 82901	800-226-1181	307-382-1600
Sheridan College		
3059 Coffeen Ave PO Box 1500 ....Sheridan WY 82801	800-913-9139	307-674-6446
Eastern Wyoming College		
3200 W 'C' St ....Torrington WY 82240	800-658-3195	307-532-8200

163   COLLEGES - CULINARY ARTS

	Toll-Free	Phone
Arizona Culinary Institute		
10585 N 114th St Ste 401 ....Scottsdale AZ 85259	866-294-2433	480-603-1066
Baltimore International College		
17 Commerce St ....Baltimore MD 21202	800-624-9926	410-752-4710
Capital Culinary Institute of Keiser College		
Melbourne		
900 S Babcock St ....Melbourne FL 32901	877-636-3618	321-409-4800

	Toll-Free	Phone

Cooking & Hospitality Institute of Chicago
361 W Chestnut St ....Chicago IL 60610 **877-828-7772*** 312-944-0882
*Admissions

Culinary Institute Alain & Marie LeNotre
7070 Allensby ....Houston TX 77022 **888-536-6873** 713-692-0077

Culinary Institute of America
1946 Campus Dr ....Hyde Park NY 12538 **800-285-4627*** 845-452-9600
*Admissions

Culinary Institute of Charleston
7000 Rivers Ave ....Charleston SC 29406 **877-349-7184** 843-574-6111

French Culinary Institute
462 Broadway ....New York NY 10013 **888-324-2433**

Institute of Culinary Education
50 W 23rd St ....New York NY 10010 **800-522-4610** 212-847-0700

Kendall College
900 N Branch St ....Chicago IL 60642 **888-905-3632** 312-752-2024

Kitchen Academy
6370 W Sunset Blvd ....Hollywood CA 90028 **866-548-2223**

Lincoln Educational Services
200 Executive Dr ....West Orange NJ 07052 **800-254-0547** 973-736-9340
NASDAQ: LINC
Suffield 8 Progress Dr ....Shelton CT 06484 **844-215-1513** 203-929-0592

Louisiana Culinary Institute
10550 Airline Hwy ....Baton Rouge LA 70816 **877-533-3198**

New England Culinary Institute
56 College St ....Montpelier VT 05602 **877-223-6324** 802-223-6324

Robert Morris University Institute of Culinary Arts
401 S State St ....Chicago IL 60605 **800-762-5960** 312-935-5460

Stratford University School of Culinary Arts
7777 Leesburg Pk ....Falls Church VA 22043 **800-444-0804** 703-821-8570

164 COLLEGES - FINE ARTS

SEE ALSO Colleges & Universities - Four-Year ; Vocational & Technical Schools

	Toll-Free	Phone

American Academy of Art
332 S Michigan Ave ....Chicago IL 60604 **888-461-0600** 312-461-0600

American Academy of Dramatic Arts
120 Madison Ave ....New York NY 10016 **800-463-8990**

Antonelli Institute
300 Montgomery Ave ....Erdenheim PA 19038 **800-722-7871** 215-836-2222

Art Academy of Cincinnati
1212 Jackson St ....Cincinnati OH 45202 **800-323-5692** 513-562-6262

Art Institute of Atlanta
6600 Peachtree Dunwoody Rd NE
100 Embassy Row ....Atlanta GA 30328 **800-275-4242** 770-394-8300

Art Institute of California
Inland Empire
674 E Brier Dr ....San Bernardino CA 92408 **800-353-0812** 909-915-2100
Los Angeles
2900 31st St ....Santa Monica CA 90405 **888-646-4610** 855-784-1269
Orange County
3601 W Sunflower Ave ....Santa Ana CA 92704 **855-784-1269**
San Diego
7650 Mission Valley Rd ....San Diego CA 92108 **866-275-2422** 858-598-1200
San Francisco
10 United Nations Plz ....San Francisco CA 94102 **888-493-3261** 415-865-0198

Art Institute of Charlotte
3 Lake Pointe Plz
2110 Water Ridge Pkwy ....Charlotte NC 28217 **800-872-4417** 704-357-8020

Art Institute of Colorado
1200 Lincoln St ....Denver CO 80203 **800-275-2420** 303-837-0825

Art Institute of Dallas
8080 Pk Ln Ste 100 ....Dallas TX 75231 **800-275-4243** 214-692-8080

Art Institute of Fort Lauderdale
1799 SE 17th St ....Fort Lauderdale FL 33316 **800-275-7603** 954-463-3000

Art Institute of Houston
1900 Yorktown St ....Houston TX 77056 **800-275-4244** 855-784-1269

Art Institute of Indianapolis
3500 Depauw Blvd ....Indianapolis IN 46268 **866-441-9031** 855-784-1269

Art Institute of Las Vegas
2350 Corporate Cir ....Henderson NV 89074 **800-833-2678** 702-369-9944

Art Institute of New York City
218-232 W 40th St ....New York NY 10018 **855-784-1269**

Art Institute of Ohio
Cincinnati
8845 Governor's Hill Dr Ste 100 ....Cincinnati OH 45249 **866-613-5184** 855-784-1269

Art Institute of Philadelphia
1622 Chestnut St ....Philadelphia PA 19103 **800-275-2474** 855-784-1269

Art Institute of Pittsburgh
420 Blvd of the Allies ....Pittsburgh PA 15219 **800-275-2470** 855-784-1269

Art Institute of Portland
1122 NW Davis St ....Portland OR 97209 **888-228-6528** 855-784-1269

Art Institute of Seattle
2323 Elliott Ave ....Seattle WA 98121 **800-275-2471** 206-448-0900

Art Institute of Tampa
4401 N Himes Ave Ste 150 ....Tampa FL 33614 **866-703-3277** 855-784-1269

Art Institute of Washington
1820 N Ft Myer Dr ....Arlington VA 22209 **877-303-3771** 703-358-9550

Art Institutes International Minnesota, The
15 S Ninth St ....Minneapolis MN 55402 **800-777-3643** 855-784-1269

Art Institutes, The
1400 Penn Ave ....Pittsburgh PA 15222 **800-275-2470** 855-784-1269

California College of the Arts
Oakland 5212 Broadway ....Oakland CA 94618 **800-447-1278** 510-594-3600

California Institute of the Arts
24700 McBean Pkwy ....Valencia CA 91355 **800-545-2787** 661-255-1050

Cleveland Institute of Art
11141 E Blvd ....Cleveland OH 44106 **800-223-4700**

Columbus College of Art & Design
60 Cleveland Ave ....Columbus OH 43215 **877-997-2223** 614-224-9101

Cornish College of the Arts
1000 Lenora St ....Seattle WA 98121 **800-726-2787** 206-726-5141

	Toll-Free	Phone

Fashion Institute of Design & Merchandising
Los Angeles
919 S Grand Ave ....Los Angeles CA 90015 **800-624-1200*** 213-624-1200
*Admissions
Orange County
17590 Gillette Ave ....Irvine CA 92614 **888-974-3436** 949-851-6200
San Diego 350 Tenth Ave ....San Diego CA 92101 **800-243-3436** 619-235-2049
San Francisco
55 Stockton St ....San Francisco CA 94108 **800-422-3436** 415-675-5200

Illinois Institute of Art
Chicago
350 N Orleans St Ste 136-L ....Chicago IL 60654 **800-351-3450** 312-280-3500
Schaumburg
1000 N Plaza Dr ....Schaumburg IL 60173 **800-314-3450** 847-619-3450

Institute of American Indian Arts (IAIA)
83 Avan Nu Po Rd ....Santa Fe NM 87508 **800-804-6422** 505-424-2300

International Academy of Design & Technology
Las Vegas
2495 Village View Dr ....Henderson NV 89074 **866-400-4238** 702-990-0150

Kansas City Art Institute
4415 Warwick Blvd ....Kansas City MO 64111 **800-522-5224** 816-474-5224

Maine College of Art
522 Congress St ....Portland ME 04101 **800-639-4808** 207-775-3052

Memphis College of Art
1930 Poplar Ave ....Memphis TN 38104 **800-727-1088** 901-272-5100

Miami International University of Art & Design
1501 Biscayne Blvd ....Miami FL 33132 **800-225-9023** 305-428-5700

Minneapolis College of Art & Design
2501 Stevens Ave ....Minneapolis MN 55404 **800-874-6223** 612-874-3760

Moore College of Art & Design
20th St & the Pkwy ....Philadelphia PA 19103 **800-523-2025** 215-965-4000

New Hampshire Institute of Art
148 Concord St ....Manchester NH 03104 **866-241-4918** 603-623-0313

Otis College of Art & Design
9045 Lincoln Blvd ....Los Angeles CA 90045 **800-527-6847** 310-665-6820

Pennsylvania College of Art & Design
204 N Prince St ....Lancaster PA 17603 **800-689-0379** 717-396-7833

Rhode Island School of Design
2 College St ....Providence RI 02903 **800-364-7473** 401-454-6100

Ringling College of Art & Design
2700 N Tamiami Trl ....Sarasota FL 34234 **800-255-7695** 941-351-5100

Savannah College of Art & Design
342 Bull St ....Savannah GA 31402 **800-869-7223** 912-525-5100

Savannah College of Art & Design
Atlanta
1600 Peachtree St PO Box 77300 ....Atlanta GA 30357 **877-722-3285** 404-253-2700

School of Visual Arts
209 E 23rd St ....New York NY 10010 **800-436-4204** 212-592-2000

University of the Arts
320 S Broad St ....Philadelphia PA 19102 **800-616-2787** 215-717-6049

Virginia Marti College of Art & Design
11724 Detroit Ave ....Lakewood OH 44107 **800-473-4350**

Watkins College of Art & Design
2298 Rose Parks Blvd ....Nashville TN 37228 **866-887-6395** 615-383-4848

165 COLLEGES - TRIBAL

SEE ALSO Colleges - Community & Junior
Tribal Colleges generally serve geographically isolated American Indian populations that have no other means of accessing education beyond the high school level. They are unique institutions that combine personal attention with cultural relevance.

	Toll-Free	Phone

Anaheim University
1240 S State College Blvd Rm 110 ....Anaheim CA 92806 **800-955-6040** 714-772-3330

Baker University
618 E Eighth St ....Baldwin City KS 66006 **800-873-4282** 785-594-6451

Bay Mills Community College
12214 West Lakeshore Dr ....Brimley MI 49715 **800-844-2622** 906-248-3354

Cankdeska Cikana Community College
PO Box 269 ....Fort Totten ND 58335 **888-783-1463** 701-766-4415

College of Menominee Nation
PO Box 1179 ....Keshena WI 54135 **800-567-2344** 715-799-5600

College of Registered Nurses of Manitoba
890 Pembina Hwy ....Winnipeg MB R3M2M8 **800-665-2027** 204-774-3477

Fanshawe College
1001 Fanshawe College Blvd ....London ON N5Y5R6 **800-717-4412** 519-452-4430

Fond du Lac Tribal & Community College
2101 14th St ....Cloquet MN 55720 **800-657-3712** 218-879-0800

Grande Prairie Regional College
10726 106 Ave ....Grande Prairie AB T8V4C4 **888-539-4772** 780-539-2911

Institute of American Indian Arts (IAIA)
83 Avan Nu Po Rd ....Santa Fe NM 87508 **800-804-6422** 505-424-2300

La Cite 801 Aviation Dr ....Ottawa ON K1K4R3 **800-267-2483** 613-742-2483

Lac Courte Oreilles Ojibwa Community College
13466 W Trepania Rd ....Hayward WI 54843 **888-526-6221** 715-634-4790

Nebraska Indian Community College
PO Box 428 ....Macy NE 68039 **844-440-6422** 402-837-5078

Northwest Indian College
2522 Kwina Rd ....Bellingham WA 98226 **866-676-2772** 360-676-2772

O s u Center for Health Sciences
1111 W 17th St ....Tulsa OK 74107 **800-677-1972** 918-582-1972

Royal College of Dental Surgeons of Ontario
6 Crescent Rd ....Toronto ON M4W1T1 **800-565-4591** 416-961-6555

Saginaw Chippewa Tribal College
2274 Enterprise Dr ....Mount Pleasant MI 48858 **800-225-8172** 989-775-4123

Salish Kootenai College
PO Box 70 ....Pablo MT 59855 **877-752-6553** 406-275-4800

Turtle Mountain Community College
10145 BIA Rd 7 ....Belcourt ND 58316 **800-827-1100** 701-477-7862

	Toll-Free	Phone

166   COLLEGES & UNIVERSITIES - FOUR-YEAR

SEE ALSO Military Service Academies ; Universities - Canadian ; Colleges - Community & Junior ; Colleges & Universities - Historically Black ; Vocational & Technical Schools ; Colleges - Fine Arts ; Colleges & Universities - Graduate & Professional Schools

Alabama

					Toll-Free	Phone
Alabama Agricultural & Mechanical University						
4900 Meridian St N PO Box 908	Normal	AL	35762		800-553-0816	256-372-5000
Alabama State University						
915 S Jackson St	Montgomery	AL	36104		800-253-5037*	334-229-4100
Admissions						
Amridge University						
1200 Taylor Rd	Montgomery	AL	36117		888-790-8080	334-387-3877
Auburn University						
202 Mary Martin Hall	Auburn University	AL	36849		866-389-6770*	334-844-6425
Admissions						
Montgomery 7430 East Dr	Montgomery	AL	36117		800-227-2649	334-244-3000
Birmingham-Southern College						
900 Arkadelphia Rd	Birmingham	AL	35254		800-523-5793	205-226-4600
Faulkner University						
5345 Atlanta Hwy	Montgomery	AL	36109		800-879-9816	334-272-5820
Huntingdon College						
1500 E Fairview Ave	Montgomery	AL	36106		800-763-0313*	334-833-4497
Admissions						
Jacksonville State University						
700 Pelham Rd N	Jacksonville	AL	36265		800-231-5291	256-782-5781
Judson College 302 Bibb St	Marion	AL	36756		800-447-9472*	334-683-5110
Admissions						
Miles College						
5500 Myron Massey Blvd	Fairfield	AL	35064		800-445-0708*	205-929-1000
Admissions						
Samford University						
800 Lakeshore Dr	Birmingham	AL	35229		800-888-7218*	205-726-3673
Admissions						
South University						
Montgomery						
5355 Vaughn Rd	Montgomery	AL	36116		866-629-2962	334-395-8800
Spring Hill College						
4000 Dauphin St	Mobile	AL	36608		800-742-6704*	251-380-4000
Admissions						
Stillman College						
3601 Stillman Blvd	Tuscaloosa	AL	35401		800-841-5722	205-349-4240
Talladega College						
627 W Battle St	Talladega	AL	35160		866-540-3956	256-761-6100
Troy University						
600 University Ave	Troy	AL	36082		800-551-9716	334-670-3100
Montgomery						
231 Montgomery St PO Box 4419	Montgomery	AL	36104		888-357-8843	
Tuskegee University						
1200 W Montgomery Rd	Tuskegee	AL	36088		800-622-6531*	334-727-8011
Admissions						
United States Sports Academy, The						
1 Academy Dr	Daphne	AL	36526		800-223-2668	251-626-3303
University of Alabama						
PO Box 870132	Tuscaloosa	AL	35487		800-933-2262*	205-348-6010
Admissions						
Birmingham						
1720 second Ave S	Birmingham	AL	35294		800-421-8743	205-934-4011
Huntsville						
301 Sparkman Dr	Huntsville	AL	35899		800-824-2255	256-824-1000
University of Mobile						
5735 College Pkwy	Mobile	AL	36613		800-946-7267	251-675-5990
University of North Alabama						
1 Harrison Plz	Florence	AL	35632		800-825-5862	256-765-4608
University of South Alabama						
2500 Meisler Hall	Mobile	AL	36688		800-872-5247	251-460-6141
University of West Alabama						
100 US 11	Livingston	AL	35470		888-636-8800*	
Admissions						

Alaska

					Toll-Free	Phone
Alaska Pacific University						
4101 University Dr	Anchorage	AK	99508		800-252-7528	907-564-8248
University of Alaska Anchorage						
3211 Providence Dr	Anchorage	AK	99508		888-822-8973	907-786-1800
University of Alaska Fairbanks						
Signers' Hall 2nd Fl PO Box 757480	Fairbanks	AK	99775		800-478-1823	907-474-7500
Bristol Bay						
527 Seward St PO Box 1070	Dillingham	AK	99576		800-478-5109	907-842-5109
University of Alaska Southeast						
11066 Auke Lake Way	Juneau	AK	99801		877-465-4827	907-796-6000
Wayland Baptist University Anchorage						
7801 E 32 Ave	Anchorage	AK	99504		800-588-1928	907-333-2277

Arizona

					Toll-Free	Phone
West PO Box 37100	Phoenix	AZ	85069		855-278-5080	602-543-5500
Embry-Riddle Aeronautical University Prescott						
3700 Willow Creek Rd	Prescott	AZ	86301		800-888-3728	928-777-3728
Grand Canyon University						
3300 W Camelback Rd	Phoenix	AZ	85017		800-800-9776	602-639-7500
Indian Bible College						
2237 E Cedar Ave	Flagstaff	AZ	86004		866-503-7789	928-774-3890
Northern Arizona University						
PO Box 4084	Flagstaff	AZ	86011		888-628-2968*	928-523-5511
Ottawa University Phoenix						
10020 N 25th Ave	Phoenix	AZ	85021		800-235-9586	602-371-1188

				Toll-Free	Phone
Prescott College					
220 Grove Ave	Prescott	AZ	86301	877-350-2100	

Arkansas

					Toll-Free	Phone
Arkansas State University						
PO Box 1630	State University	AR	72467		800-382-3030	870-972-3024
Central Baptist College						
1501 College Ave	Conway	AR	72034		800-205-6872	501-329-6872
Harding University						
915 E Market Ave	Searcy	AR	72149		800-477-4407	501-279-4000
Henderson State University						
1100 Henderson St	Arkadelphia	AR	71999		800-228-7333	870-230-5000
Hendrix College						
1600 Washington Ave	Conway	AR	72032		800-277-9017	501-329-6811
John Brown University						
2000 W University St	Siloam Springs	AR	72761		877-528-4636*	479-524-9500
Lyon College						
2300 Highland Rd	Batesville	AR	72501		800-423-2542	870-793-9813
Ouachita Baptist University						
410 Ouachita St	Arkadelphia	AR	71998		800-342-5628*	870-245-5000
Admissions						
Philander Smith College						
900 Daisy Bates Dr	Little Rock	AR	72202		800-446-6772	501-370-5221
Southern Arkansas University						
100 E University St	Magnolia	AR	71753		800-332-7286	870-235-4000
University of Arkansas						
232 Silas Hunt Hall	Fayetteville	AR	72701		800-377-8632*	479-575-5346
Admissions						
Little Rock						
2801 S University Ave	Little Rock	AR	72204		800-482-8892	501-569-3000
Monticello PO Box 3600	Monticello	AR	71656		800-844-1826	870-460-1026
Pine Bluff						
1200 N University Dr	Pine Bluff	AR	71601		800-264-6585*	870-575-8000
Admissions						
University of the Ozarks						
415 N College Ave	Clarksville	AR	72830		800-264-8636*	479-979-1227
Admissions						
Williams Baptist College						
60 W Fulbright St	Walnut Ridge	AR	72476		800-722-4434	870-886-6741

British Columbia

					Toll-Free	Phone
North Island College						
2300 Ryan Rd	Courtenay	BC	V9N8N6		800-715-0914	250-334-5000
Selkirk College						
301 Frank Beinder Way	Castlegar	BC	V1N4L3		888-953-1133	250-365-7292

California

					Toll-Free	Phone
Academy of Art University						
79 New Montgomery St	San Francisco	CA	94105		800-544-2787	415-274-2200
Alliant International University						
10455 Pomerado Rd	San Diego	CA	92131		866-825-5426	858-635-4772
American Career College Inc						
151 Innovation Dr	Irvine	CA	92617		877-832-0790	
Azusa Pacific University						
901 E Alosta Ave PO Box 7000	Azusa	CA	91702		800-825-5278	626-969-3434
Biola University						
13800 Biola Ave	La Mirada	CA	90639		800-652-4652*	562-903-6000
Admissions						
California Baptist University						
8432 Magnolia Ave	Riverside	CA	92504		877-228-8866	951-689-5771
California Lutheran University						
60 W Olsen Rd	Thousand Oaks	CA	91360		877-258-3678	805-493-3135
California Maritime Academy						
200 Maritime Academy Dr	Vallejo	CA	94590		800-561-1945	707-654-1330
California State University						
401 Golden Shore	Long Beach	CA	90802		800-325-4000	562-951-4000
Chico 400 West First St	Chico	CA	95929		800-542-4426*	530-898-6321
Admissions						
Dominguez Hills						
1000 E Victoria St	Carson	CA	90747		888-545-6512	310-243-3696
East Bay						
25800 Carlos Bee Blvd	Hayward	CA	94542		800-884-1684	510-885-3000
Fresno 5241 N Maple Ave	Fresno	CA	93740		800-700-2320	559-278-4240
Fullerton						
800 N State College Blvd	Fullerton	CA	92834		888-433-9406	657-278-2011
Long Beach						
1250 Bellflower Blvd	Long Beach	CA	90840		800-663-1144	562-985-4111
Northridge						
18111 Nordhoff St	Northridge	CA	91330		800-399-4529	818-677-1200
Sacramento 6000 J St	Sacramento	CA	95819		800-667-7531	916-278-3901
San Marcos						
333 S Twin Oaks Valley Rd	San Marcos	CA	92096		888-225-5427	760-750-4000
Stanislaus 1 University Cir	Turlock	CA	95382		800-235-9292	209-667-3152
Chapman University						
1 University Dr	Orange	CA	92866		888-282-7759	714-997-6815
Cogswell Polytechnical College						
1175 Bordeaux Dr	Sunnyvale	CA	94089		800-264-7955	408-541-0100
Columbia College Hollywood						
18618 Oxnard St	Tarzana	CA	91356		800-785-0585	818-345-8414
Concordia University Irvine						
1530 Concordia W	Irvine	CA	92612		800-229-1200	949-854-8002
Continuing Education of The Bar Suite 410						
300 Frank H Ogawa Plz Ste 410	Oakland	CA	94612		800-232-3444	510-302-2000
Design Institute of San Diego						
8555 Commerce Ave	San Diego	CA	92121		800-619-4337	858-566-1200
Dominican University of California						
50 Acacia Ave	San Rafael	CA	94901		888-323-6763*	415-457-4440
Admissions						
Harvey Mudd College						
301 Platt Blvd	Claremont	CA	91711		877-827-5462	909-621-8000

	City	State	Zip	Toll-Free	Phone
Hebrew Union College Los Angeles					
3077 University Ave	Los Angeles	CA	90007	**800-899-0925**	213-749-3424
Holy Names University					
3500 Mountain Blvd	Oakland	CA	94619	**800-430-1321**	510-436-1000
Hope International University					
2500 E Nutwood Ave	Fullerton	CA	92831	**866-722-4673**	714-879-3901
Humboldt State University					
1 Harpst St	Arcata	CA	95521	**866-850-9556**	707-826-3011
John F Kennedy University					
100 Ellinwood Way	Pleasant Hill	CA	94523	**800-696-5358**	925-969-3300
La Sierra University					
4500 Riverwalk Pkwy	Riverside	CA	92515	**800-874-5587**	951-785-2000
Laguna College of Art & Design					
2222 Laguna Canyon Rd	Laguna Beach	CA	92651	**800-255-0762**	949-376-6000
Lincoln University					
401 15th St	Oakland	CA	94612	**888-810-9998**	510-628-8010
Loma Linda University					
11234 Anderson St	Loma Linda	CA	92354	**800-872-1212**	909-558-1000
Loyola Marymount University					
1 LMU Dr	Los Angeles	CA	90045	**800-568-4636**	310-338-2700
Master's College					
21726 Placerita Canyon Rd	Santa Clarita	CA	91321	**800-568-6248**	661-259-3540
Menlo College					
1000 El Camino Real	Atherton	CA	94027	**800-556-3656**	650-543-3753
Mills College					
5000 MacArthur Blvd	Oakland	CA	94613	**877-746-4557***	510-430-2135
*Admissions					
National Hispanic University					
14271 Story Rd	San Jose	CA	95127	**877-762-9801**	408-254-6900
National University					
11255 N Torrey Pines Rd	La Jolla	CA	92037	**800-628-8648**	858-642-8000
Northwestern Polytechnic University					
47671 Westinghouse Dr	Fremont	CA	94539	**877-878-8883**	510-592-9688
Notre Dame de Namur University					
1500 Ralston Ave	Belmont	CA	94002	**800-263-0545**	650-508-3600
Occidental College					
1600 Campus Rd	Los Angeles	CA	90041	**800-825-5262***	323-259-2700
*Admissions					
Pacific College Oriental Med Inc					
7445 Mission Valley Rd Ste 105	San Diego	CA	92108	**800-729-0941**	619-574-6909
Pacific Oaks College					
55 W Eureka St	Pasadena	CA	91103	**877-314-2380**	
Pacific Union College					
1 Angwin Ave	Angwin	CA	94508	**800-862-7080**	707-965-6336
Patten University					
2100 Franklin St Ste 350	Oakland	CA	94612	**866-841-1986**	
Pepperdine University					
24255 Pacific Coast Hwy	Malibu	CA	90263	**800-413-0848**	310-506-4000
Pitzer College					
1050 N Mills Ave PO Box A-202	Claremont	CA	91711	**800-748-9371**	909-621-8129
Point Loma Nazarene University					
3900 Lomaland Dr	San Diego	CA	92106	**800-733-7770***	619-849-2200
*Admissions					
Ryokan College					
11965 Venice Blvd Ste 304	Los Angeles	CA	90066	**866-796-5261**	310-390-7560
Saint Mary's College of California					
1928 St Mary's Rd	Moraga	CA	94556	**800-800-4762***	925-631-4000
*Admissions					
Samuel Merritt College					
370 Hawthorne Ave	Oakland	CA	94609	**800-607-6377***	510-869-6576
*Admissions					
San Diego Christian College					
200 Riverview Pkwy	Santee	CA	92071	**800-676-2242**	619-201-8700
San Francisco Conservatory of Music					
50 Oak St	San Francisco	CA	94102	**800-999-8219**	415-864-7326
Scripps College					
1030 Columbia Ave	Claremont	CA	91711	**800-770-1333**	909-621-8149
Simpson University					
2211 College View Dr	Redding	CA	96003	**888-974-6776**	530-224-5600
South Baylo University					
1126 N Brookhurst St	Anaheim	CA	92801	**888-642-2956**	714-533-1495
Southern California Seminary					
2075 E Madison Ave	El Cajon	CA	92019	**888-389-7244**	
Stanford University					
450 Serra Mall	Stanford	CA	94305	**877-407-9529**	650-723-2091
Thomas Aquinas College					
10000 Ojai Rd	Santa Paula	CA	93060	**800-634-9797**	805-525-4417
University of California (UCLA)					
Berkeley					
110 Sproul Hall MC Ste 5800	Berkeley	CA	94720	**866-740-1260**	510-642-6000
Davis 1 Shields Ave	Davis	CA	95616	**800-242-4723**	530-752-1011
Riverside					
900 University Ave	Riverside	CA	92521	**800-426-2586**	951-827-3411
San Diego 9500 Gilman Dr	La Jolla	CA	92093	**800-207-1710**	858-534-2230
Santa Barbara					
1210 Cheadle Hall	Santa Barbara	CA	93106	**888-488-8272**	805-893-8000
Santa Cruz 1156 High St	Santa Cruz	CA	95064	**800-933-7584**	831-459-2131
University of Judaism					
15600 Mulholland Dr	Los Angeles	CA	90077	**888-853-6763**	310-476-9777
University of La Verne					
1950 Third St	La Verne	CA	91750	**800-876-4858***	909-593-3511
*Admissions					
University of Redlands					
1200 E Colton Ave PO Box 3080	Redlands	CA	92373	**800-455-5064**	909-793-2121
University of San Diego					
5998 Alcala Pk	San Diego	CA	92110	**800-248-4873**	619-260-4600
University of San Francisco					
2130 Fulton St	San Francisco	CA	94117	**800-854-1385***	415-422-5555
*Admissions					
University of the Pacific					
3601 Pacific Ave	Stockton	CA	95211	**800-959-2867**	209-946-2211
Vanguard University of Southern California					
55 Fair Dr	Costa Mesa	CA	92626	**800-722-6279***	714-556-3610
*Admissions					
Westmont College					
955 La Paz Rd	Santa Barbara	CA	93108	**800-777-9011***	805-565-6000
*Admissions					
Whittier College					
13406 E Philadelphia St	Whittier	CA	90602	**800-299-4898**	562-907-4200
William Jessup University					
2121 University Ave	Rocklin	CA	95765	**800-355-7522**	916-577-2200
Woodbury University					
7500 Glenoaks Blvd	Burbank	CA	91510	**800-784-9663**	818-767-0888

Colorado

	City	State	Zip	Toll-Free	Phone
Adams State College					
208 Edgemont Blvd	Alamosa	CO	81102	**800-824-6494**	719-587-7712
Beth-El College of Nursing & Health Sciences					
1420 Austin Bluffs Pkwy	Colorado Springs	CO	80918	**800-990-8227**	719-255-8227
Colorado Christian University					
8787 W Alameda Ave	Lakewood	CO	80226	**800-443-2484**	303-963-3000
Colorado College					
14 E Cache La Poudre St	Colorado Springs	CO	80903	**800-542-7214**	719-389-6344
Colorado School of Mines					
1600 Maple St	Golden	CO	80401	**800-446-9488**	303-273-3000
Colorado State University					
200 West Lake St	Fort Collins	CO	80523	**800-491-4366**	970-491-1101
Colorado Technical University					
4435 N Chestnut St	Colorado Springs	CO	80907	**855-230-0555**	719-598-0200
Fort Lewis College					
1000 Rim Dr	Durango	CO	81301	**877-352-2656**	970-247-7010
Johnson & Wales University Denver					
7150 E Montview Blvd	Denver	CO	80220	**877-598-3368**	303-256-9300
Mesa State College					
1100 N Ave	Grand Junction	CO	81501	**800-982-6372**	970-248-1020
Naropa University					
2130 Arapahoe Ave	Boulder	CO	80302	**800-772-6951**	303-444-0202
National American University Colorado Springs					
1915 Jamboree Dr Ste 185	Colorado Springs	CO	80920	**855-448-2318**	316-448-5400
National American University Denver					
1325 S Colorado Blvd Ste 100	Denver	CO	80222	**855-448-2318**	303-758-6700
Regis University					
3333 Regis Blvd	Denver	CO	80221	**800-388-2366***	303-458-4100
*Admissions					
Colorado Springs					
7450 Campus Dr Ste 100	Colorado Springs	CO	80920	**800-568-8932**	
University of Colorado					
Colorado Springs					
PO Box 7150	Colorado Springs	CO	80933	**800-990-8227**	719-262-3000
University of Denver					
2199 S University Blvd	Denver	CO	80208	**800-525-9495**	303-871-2036
University of Northern Colorado					
501 20th St CB 92	Greeley	CO	80639	**888-700-4862***	970-351-2881
*Admissions					
US Air Force Academy (USAFA)					
2304 Cadet Dr Ste 3100	Air Force Academy	CO	80840	**800-443-9266**	719-333-1110
Western State College of Colorado					
600 N Adams St	Gunnison	CO	81231	**800-876-5309***	970-943-2119
*Admissions					

Connecticut

	City	State	Zip	Toll-Free	Phone
Albertus Magnus College					
700 Prospect St	New Haven	CT	06511	**800-578-9160***	203-773-8550
*Admissions					
Briarwood College					
2279 Mt Vernon Rd	Southington	CT	06489	**800-952-2444**	860-628-4751
Charter Oak State College					
55 Paul J Manafort Dr	New Britain	CT	06053	**800-235-6559**	860-832-3800
Connecticut College					
270 Mohegan Ave	New London	CT	06320	**800-892-3363**	860-439-2000
Eastern Connecticut State University					
83 Windham St	Willimantic	CT	06226	**877-353-3278***	860-465-5000
*Admissions					
Fairfield University					
1073 N Benson Rd	Fairfield	CT	06824	**800-822-8428**	203-254-4000
Hartford Seminary					
77 Sherman St	Hartford	CT	06105	**877-860-2255**	860-509-9500
Mitchell College					
437 Pequot Ave	New London	CT	06320	**800-443-2811***	860-701-5000
*Admitting					
Post University					
800 Country Club Rd	Waterbury	CT	06723	**800-345-2562**	203-596-4500
Quinnipiac University					
275 Mt Carmel Ave	Hamden	CT	06518	**800-462-1944***	203-582-8600
*Admissions					
Southern Connecticut State University					
501 Crescent St	New Haven	CT	06515	**888-500-7278**	203-392-5200
St Vincent's College					
2800 Main St	Bridgeport	CT	06606	**800-873-1013**	
University of Bridgeport					
126 Park Ave	Bridgeport	CT	06604	**800-392-3582**	203-576-4000
University of Hartford					
200 Bloomfield Ave	West Hartford	CT	06117	**800-947-4303**	860-768-4296
University of New Haven					
300 Boston Post Rd	West Haven	CT	06516	**800-342-5864**	203-932-7319
US Coast Guard Academy					
15 Mohegan Ave	New London	CT	06320	**800-883-8724**	860-444-8444
Wesleyan University					
70 Wyllys Ave	Middletown	CT	06459	**800-288-2020**	860-685-2000

Delaware

	City	State	Zip	Toll-Free	Phone
Delaware State University					
1200 N DuPont Hwy	Dover	DE	19901	**800-845-2544***	302-857-6351
*Admissions					
Goldey Beacom College					
4701 Limestone Rd	Wilmington	DE	19808	**800-833-4877**	302-998-8814
University of Delaware					
210 S College Ave	Newark	DE	19716	**844-237-1338**	302-831-2792
Wilmington University					
320 N DuPont Hwy	New Castle	DE	19720	**877-967-5464***	
*Admissions					

Classified Section

District of Columbia

				Toll-Free	Phone
Catholic University of America					
620 Michigan Ave NE	Washington	DC	20064	800-673-2772	202-319-5000
Gallaudet University					
800 Florida Ave NE	Washington	DC	20002	800-995-0550	202-651-5000
George Washington University					
2121 'I' St NW	Washington	DC	20052	866-498-3382	202-994-1000
Howard University					
2400 Sixth St NW	Washington	DC	20059	800-822-6363	202-806-6100
Trinity University					
125 Michigan Ave NE	Washington	DC	20017	800-492-6882*	202-884-9000
*Admissions					

Florida

				Toll-Free	Phone
Ave Maria University					
5050 Ave Maria Blvd	Naples	FL	34119	877-283-8648	239-280-2500
Baptist College of Florida					
5400 College Dr	Graceville	FL	32440	800-328-2660	850-263-3261
Barry University					
11300 NE Second Ave	Miami Shores	FL	33161	800-756-6000	305-899-3000
Orlando					
1650 Sandlake Rd Ste 390	Orlando	FL	32809	800-756-6000	407-438-4150
Tallahassee Community College					
444 Appleyard Dr Bldg A	Tallahassee	FL	32304	800-756-6000	850-201-8650
Bethune-Cookman College					
640 Dr Mary McLeod Bethune Blvd					
	Daytona Beach	FL	32114	800-448-0228*	386-481-2900
*Admissions					
Columbia College Orlando					
2600 Technology Dr Ste 100	Orlando	FL	32804	800-231-2391	407-293-9911
Eckerd College					
4200 54th Ave S	Saint Petersburg	FL	33711	800-456-9009*	727-867-1166
*Admissions					
Embry-Riddle Aeronautical University					
Daytona Beach					
600 S Clyde Morris Blvd	Daytona Beach	FL	32114	800-862-2416	386-226-6000
Flagler College					
74 King St	Saint Augustine	FL	32084	800-304-4208*	904-829-6481
*Admissions					
Florida A & M University					
1700 Lee Hall Dr	Tallahassee	FL	32307	866-642-1198	850-599-3000
Florida Atlantic University (FAU)					
777 Glades Rd	Boca Raton	FL	33431	800-299-4328*	561-297-3000
*Admissions					
Davie 3200 College Ave	Davie	FL	33314	800-764-2222	954-236-1000
Treasure Coast					
777 Glades Rd PO Box 3091	Boca Raton	FL	33431	800-552-4723	772-873-3300
Florida College					
119 N Glen Arven Ave	Temple Terrace	FL	33617	800-326-7655	813-988-5131
Florida Institute of Technology					
150 W University Blvd	Melbourne	FL	32901	800-888-4348	321-674-8000
Florida Memorial University					
15800 NW 42nd Ave	Miami Gardens	FL	33054	800-822-1362	305-626-3600
Florida Southern College					
111 Lake Hollingsworth Dr	Lakeland	FL	33801	800-274-4131*	863-680-4131
*Admissions					
Hodges University					
2655 Northbrooke Dr	Naples	FL	34119	800-466-8017	239-513-1122
Fort Myers					
4501 Colonial Blvd	Fort Myers	FL	33966	800-466-0019	239-938-7701
Jacksonville University					
2800 University Blvd N	Jacksonville	FL	32211	800-225-2027	904-256-8000
Johnson & Wales University North Miami					
1701 NE 127th St	North Miami	FL	33181	866-598-3567	800-342-5598
Logos Christian College					
6620 Southpoint Dr S Ste 115	Jacksonville	FL	32216	800-776-0127	904-329-1723
Lynn University					
3601 N Military Trl	Boca Raton	FL	33431	800-888-5966*	561-237-7900
*Admissions					
Northwood University Florida					
2600 N Military Trl	West Palm Beach	FL	33409	800-458-8325*	561-478-5500
*Admissions					
Nova Southeastern University					
3301 College Ave	Fort Lauderdale	FL	33314	800-541-6682	954-262-8000
Palm Beach Atlantic University					
PO Box 24708	West Palm Beach	FL	33416	888-468-6722	561-803-2000
Pensacola Christian College					
250 Brent Ln	Pensacola	FL	32503	800-722-4636	850-478-8496
Rollins College					
1000 Holt Ave	Winter Park	FL	32789	800-799-2586	407-646-2000
Saint Leo University					
33701 State Rd 52	Saint Leo	FL	33574	800-334-5532	352-588-8200
Palatka Ctr					
33701 State Rd 52 PO Box 6665	Saint Leo	FL	33574	800-334-5532	352-588-8200
Saint Thomas University					
16401 NW 37th Ave	Miami Gardens	FL	33054	800-367-9010	305-628-6546
South University West Palm Beach					
9801 Belvedere Rd					
University Ctr	West Palm Beach	FL	33411	800-688-0932	561-273-6500
Southeastern University					
1000 Longfellow Blvd	Lakeland	FL	33801	800-500-8760	863-667-5000
Stetson University					
421 N Woodland Blvd Unit 8378	DeLand	FL	32723	800-688-0101*	386-822-7100
*Admissions					
Trinity International University South Florida					
8190 W SR 84	Davie	FL	33324	800-822-3225	954-382-6400
University of Central Florida					
4000 Central Florida Blvd	Orlando	FL	32816	800-272-7252	407-823-2000
University of Florida					
219 Grinter Hall PO Box 115500	Gainesville	FL	32611	866-876-4472	352-392-3261
University of North Florida					
4567 St Johns Bluff Rd S	Jacksonville	FL	32224	866-697-7150	904-620-1000

				Toll-Free	Phone
University of South Florida					
Sarasota-Manatee					
8350 N Tamiami Trl	Sarasota	FL	34243	866-974-1222	941-359-4200
Warner Southern College					
13895 Hwy 27	Lake Wales	FL	33859	800-309-9563	
Webber International University					
1201 N Scenic Hwy	Babson Park	FL	33827	800-741-1844	

Georgia

				Toll-Free	Phone
Agnes Scott College					
141 E College Ave	Decatur	GA	30030	800-868-8602	404-471-6000
Atlanta					
6600 Peachtree Dunwoody Rd					
500 Embassy Row NE	Atlanta	GA	30328	800-491-0182	404-965-6500
Dunwoody					
6600 Peachtree-Dunwoody Rd					
500 Embassy Row	Atlanta	GA	30328	855-377-1888	404-965-6500
Armstrong Atlantic State University					
11935 Abercorn St	Savannah	GA	31419	800-633-2349	
Berry College					
2277 Martha Berry Hwy NW	Mount Berry	GA	30149	800-237-7942	706-232-5374
Brenau University					
500 Washington St	Gainesville	GA	30501	800-252-5119	770-534-6299
Brewton-Parker College					
201 David-Eliza Fountain Cir Hwy 280					
PO Box 197	Mount Vernon	GA	30445	800-342-1087	912-583-2241
Clark Atlanta University					
223 James P Brawley Dr SW	Atlanta	GA	30314	800-688-3228*	404-880-8000
*Admissions					
Columbus State University					
4225 University Ave	Columbus	GA	31907	866-264-2035	706-507-8800
Covenant College					
14049 Scenic Hwy	Lookout Mountain	GA	30750	888-451-2683	706-820-1560
Dalton State College					
650 N College Dr	Dalton	GA	30720	800-829-4436	706-272-4436
Emmanuel College					
181 Spring St	Franklin Springs	GA	30639	800-860-8800	706-245-7226
Emory University					
201 Dowman Dr	Atlanta	GA	30322	800-727-6036*	404-727-6036
*Admissions					
Fort Valley State University					
1005 State University Dr	Fort Valley	GA	31030	877-462-3878	478-825-6211
Georgia College & State University					
231 W Hancock St	Milledgeville	GA	31061	800-342-0471	478-445-5004
Macon 433 Cherry St Ste B	Macon	GA	31206	800-342-0471	478-752-4278
Georgia Southwestern State University					
800 Gsw State University Dr	Americus	GA	31709	800-338-0082*	229-928-1273
*Admissions					
LaGrange College					
601 Broad St	LaGrange	GA	30240	800-593-2885*	706-880-8000
*Admissions					
Life University					
1269 Barclay Cir	Marietta	GA	30060	800-543-3203	770-426-2884
Luther Rice College & Seminary					
3038 Evans Mill Rd	Lithonia	GA	30038	800-442-1577	
Macon State College					
100 University Pkwy	Macon	GA	31206	800-272-7619	478-471-2700
Mercer University					
1400 Coleman Ave	Macon	GA	31207	800-637-2378	478-301-2650
Cecil B Day					
3001 Mercer University Dr	Atlanta	GA	30341	800-840-8577	678-547-6089
Oglethorpe University					
4484 Peachtree RdNE	Atlanta	GA	30319	800-428-4484	404-364-8307
Paine College 1235 15th St	Augusta	GA	30901	800-476-7703	706-821-8200
Piedmont College					
165 Central Ave	Demorest	GA	30535	800-277-7020	706-776-0103
Reinhardt College					
7300 Reinhardt College Cir	Waleska	GA	30183	877-346-4273	770-720-5526
Shorter University					
315 Shorter Ave	Rome	GA	30165	800-868-6980	706-233-7319
South University Savannah					
709 Mall Blvd	Savannah	GA	31406	800-688-0932	912-201-8000
Spelman College					
350 Spelman Ln SW	Atlanta	GA	30314	800-982-2411*	404-681-3643
*Admissions					
Thomas University					
1501 Millpond Rd	Thomasville	GA	31792	800-538-9784	229-226-1621
Truett-McConnell College					
100 Alumni Dr	Cleveland	GA	30528	800-226-8621	706-865-2134
Valdosta State University					
1500 N Patterson St	Valdosta	GA	31698	800-618-1878	229-333-5800
Wesleyan College					
4760 Forsyth Rd	Macon	GA	31210	800-447-6610	478-757-5219

Hawaii

				Toll-Free	Phone
Atlantic International University					
900 Ft St Mall	Honolulu	HI	96813	800-993-0066	808-924-9567
Chaminade University					
3140 Waialae Ave	Honolulu	HI	96816	800-735-3733	808-735-4711
Hawaii Pacific University					
1164 Bishop St Ste 200	Honolulu	HI	96813	866-225-5478	808-544-0200
University of Hawaii					
Hilo 200 W Kawili St	Hilo	HI	96720	800-897-4456*	808-974-7414
*Admissions					
Manoa 2600 Campus Rd Rm 001	Honolulu	HI	96822	800-823-9771*	808-956-8975
*Admissions					
West Oahu 96-129 Ala Ike	Pearl City	HI	96782	866-299-8656	808-454-4700

Idaho

				Toll-Free	Phone
Brigham Young University Idaho					
525 S Ctr	Rexburg	ID	83460	866-672-2984	

			Toll-Free	Phone
College of Idaho				
2112 Cleveland Blvd ....Caldwell ID	83605		**800-224-3246***	208-459-5011
*Admissions				
Lewis-Clark State College				
500 Eighth Ave ....Lewiston ID	83501		**800-933-5272**	208-792-5272
Northwest Nazarene University				
623 Holly St ....Nampa ID	83686		**877-668-4968***	208-467-8000
*Admissions				
University of Idaho				
875 Perimeter Dr ....Moscow ID	83844		**888-884-3246**	208-885-6111

Illinois

			Toll-Free	Phone
American Intercontinental University				
231 N Martingale Rd 6th Fl.............Schaumburg IL	60173		**877-221-5800**	877-701-3800
American InterContinental University Los Angeles				
231 N Martingale Rd 6th Fl.............Schaumburg IL	60173		**877-701-3800**	
Augustana College				
639 38th St ....Rock Island IL	61201		**800-798-8100**	309-794-7000
Aurora University				
347 S Gladstone Ave ....Aurora IL	60506		**800-742-5281**	630-844-5533
Benedictine University				
5700 College Rd ....Lisle IL	60532		**888-829-6363**	630-829-6300
Blackburn College				
700 College Ave ....Carlinville IL	62626		**800-233-3550**	
Bradley University				
1501 W Bradley Ave ....Peoria IL	61625		**800-447-6460***	309-676-7611
*Admissions				
Chicago State University				
9501 S King Dr ....Chicago IL	60628		**800-937-3898**	773-995-2513
Columbia College Chicago				
600 S Michigan Ave ....Chicago IL	60605		**866-705-0200**	312-663-1600
Concordia University Chicago				
7400 Augusta St ....River Forest IL	60305		**888-258-6773**	708-771-8300
Dominican University				
7900 W Div St ....River Forest IL	60305		**800-828-8475**	708-366-2490
Eastern Illinois University				
600 Lincoln Ave ....Charleston IL	61920		**800-252-5711***	217-581-2223
*Admissions				
Elmhurst College				
190 Prospect Ave ....Elmhurst IL	60126		**800-697-1871**	630-617-3400
Eureka College				
300 E College Ave ....Eureka IL	61530		**888-438-7352***	309-467-6350
*Admissions				
Governors State University				
1 University Pkwy ....University Park IL	60484		**800-478-8478**	708-534-5000
Greenville College				
315 E College Ave ....Greenville IL	62246		**800-345-4440**	618-664-7100
Illinois College				
1101 W College Ave ....Jacksonville IL	62650		**866-464-5265***	217-245-3030
*Admissions				
Illinois Institute of Technology				
10 W 33rd St ....Chicago IL	60616		**800-448-2329**	312-567-3025
Illinois State University				
100 N University St ....Normal IL	61761		**800-366-2478***	309-438-2111
*Admissions				
Illinois Wesleyan University				
1312 Park St ....Bloomington IL	61701		**800-332-2498***	309-556-3031
*Admissions				
Judson University				
1151 N State St ....Elgin IL	60123		**800-879-5376***	847-628-2500
*Admissions				
Lake Forest College				
555 N Sheridan Rd ....Lake Forest IL	60045		**800-828-4751**	847-234-3100
Lewis University				
1 University Pkwy ....Romeoville IL	60446		**800-897-9000**	815-838-0500
Loyola University Chicago				
Lake Shore				
6525 N Sheridan Rd ....Chicago IL	60626		**800-262-2373**	773-508-3075
Water Tower				
820 N Michigan Ave ....Chicago IL	60611		**800-262-2373***	312-915-6500
*Admissions				
MacMurray College				
447 E College Ave ....Jacksonville IL	62650		**800-252-7485**	217-479-7056
McKendree College				
701 College Rd ....Lebanon IL	62254		**800-232-7228**	618-537-4481
Millikin University				
1184 W Main St ....Decatur IL	62522		**800-373-7733**	217-424-6211
Monmouth College				
700 E Broadway ....Monmouth IL	61462		**888-827-8268**	309-457-2311
National University of Health Sciences				
200 E Roosevelt Rd ....Lombard IL	60148		**800-826-6285**	630-629-2000
National-Louis University				
1000 Capitol Dr ....Wheeling IL	60090		**800-443-5522**	847-947-5718
Chicago 122 S Michigan Ave ....Chicago IL	60603		**800-443-5522**	888-658-8632
North Central College				
30 N Brainard St ....Naperville IL	60540		**800-411-1861**	630-637-5800
North Park University				
3225 W Foster Ave ....Chicago IL	60625		**800-888-6728**	773-244-5500
Northern Illinois University				
1425 W Lincoln Hwy ....DeKalb IL	60115		**800-892-3050**	815-753-1000
Northwestern University				
1801 Hinman Ave ....Evanston IL	60208		**800-227-7368**	847-491-7271
Olivet Nazarene University				
1 University Ave ....Bourbonnais IL	60914		**800-648-1463**	815-939-5011
Robert Morris College				
Chicago 401 S State St ....Chicago IL	60605		**800-762-5960**	312-935-6800
DuPage 905 Meridian Lake Dr ....Aurora IL	60504		**800-762-5960***	630-375-8100
*Admissions				
Orland Park				
82 Orland Square Dr ....Orland Park IL	60462		**800-762-5960**	
Rockford College				
5050 E State St ....Rockford IL	61108		**800-892-2984**	815-226-4000
Roosevelt University				
430 S Michigan Ave ....Chicago IL	60605		**877-277-5978***	312-341-3500
*Admissions				

			Toll-Free	Phone
Albert A Robin				
1400 N Roosevelt Blvd ....Schaumburg IL	60173		**877-277-5978***	847-619-7300
*Admissions				
Saint Anthony College of Nursing Health Sciences Center				
5658 E State St ....Rockford IL	61108		**800-977-8449**	815-282-7900
Saint Xavier University				
3700 W 103rd St ....Chicago IL	60655		**800-462-9288**	773-298-3000
School of the Art Institute of Chicago				
36 S Wabash Ave ....Chicago IL	60603		**800-232-7242***	312-629-6100
*Admissions				
Southern Illinois University				
Edwardsville				
1 Hairpin Dr ....Edwardsville IL	62026		**888-328-5168**	618-650-5555
Trinity International University				
2065 Half Day Rd ....Deerfield IL	60015		**800-822-3225**	847-945-8800
University of Illinois				
Springfield				
1 University Plz MS UHB 1080.............Springfield IL	62703		**888-977-4847**	217-206-4847
University of St Francis				
500 Wilcox St ....Joliet IL	60435		**800-735-7500**	
Western Illinois University				
1 University Cir ....Macomb IL	61455		**877-742-5948***	309-298-1414
*Admissions				
Quad Cities 3300 River Dr ....Moline IL	61265		**877-742-5948**	309-762-9481
Wheaton College				
501 College Ave ....Wheaton IL	60187		**800-222-2419**	630-752-5000

Indiana

			Toll-Free	Phone
Anderson University				
1100 E Fifth St ....Anderson IN	46012		**800-428-6414***	
*Admissions				
Ball State University				
2000 W University Ave ....Muncie IN	47306		**800-382-8540**	765-289-1241
Bethel College				
1001 W McKinley Ave ....Mishawaka IN	46545		**800-422-4101***	574-807-7000
*Admissions				
Butler University				
4600 Sunset Ave ....Indianapolis IN	46208		**800-368-6852**	317-940-8100
Calumet College of Saint Joseph				
2400 New York Ave ....Whiting IN	46394		**877-700-9100**	219-473-4215
DePauw University				
204 E Seminary St ....Greencastle IN	46135		**800-447-2495**	765-658-4006
Earlham College				
801 National Rd W ....Richmond IN	47374		**800-327-5426**	765-983-1600
Franklin College				
101 Branigin Blvd ....Franklin IN	46131		**800-852-0232**	
Goshen College				
1700 S Main St ....Goshen IN	46526		**800-348-7422**	574-535-7000
Grace College				
200 Seminary Dr ....Winona Lake IN	46590		**800-544-7223**	574-372-5100
Hanover College 484 Ball Dr ....Hanover IN	47243		**800-213-2178**	812-866-7000
Huntington University				
2303 College Ave ....Huntington IN	46750		**800-642-6493***	260-356-6000
*Admissions				
Indiana State University				
200 N Seventh St ....Terre Haute IN	47809		**800-468-6478**	
Indiana Tech				
1600 E Washington Blvd ....Fort Wayne IN	46803		**800-937-2448**	260-422-5561
Indiana University				
East 2325 Chester Blvd ....Richmond IN	47374		**800-959-3278**	765-973-8208
Kokomo				
2300 S Washington St PO Box 9003 ....Kokomo IN	46904		**888-875-4485**	765-455-9217
Northwest 3400 Broadway ....Gary IN	46408		**888-968-7486**	219-980-6500
South Bend				
1700 Mishawaka Ave PO Box 7111 ....South Bend IN	46634		**877-462-4872**	574-520-4870
Southeast				
4201 Grant Line Rd ....New Albany IN	47150		**800-852-8835**	812-941-2212
Indiana University-Purdue University				
Fort Wayne				
2101 E Coliseum Blvd ....Fort Wayne IN	46805		**800-324-4739**	260-481-6100
Indiana Wesleyan University				
4201 S Washington St ....Marion IN	46953		**800-332-6901**	765-677-2138
Manchester College				
604 E College Ave ....North Manchester IN	46962		**800-852-3648***	260-982-5000
*Admissions				
Marian University				
3200 Cold Spring Rd ....Indianapolis IN	46222		**800-772-7264***	317-955-6038
*Admissions				
Oakland City University				
138 North Lucretia St ....Oakland City IN	47660		**800-737-5125**	812-749-4781
Purdue University				
Schleman Hall				
475 Stadium Mall Dr. ....West Lafayette IN	47907		**800-743-3333**	765-494-1776
Rose-Hulman Institute of Technology				
5500 Wabash Ave ....Terre Haute IN	47803		**800-248-7448***	812-877-1511
*Admissions				
Saint Mary's College				
Le Mans Hall ....Notre Dame IN	46556		**800-551-7621***	574-284-4587
*Admissions				
Saint Mary-of-the-Woods College				
3301 St Mary Rd ....Saint Mary Of The Woods IN	47876		**800-926-7692**	812-535-5106
Taylor University				
236 W Reade Ave ....Upland IN	46989		**800-882-3456**	765-998-2751
Fort Wayne				
915 W Rudisill Blvd ....Fort Wayne IN	46807		**800-882-3456***	260-744-8790
*General				
University of Evansville				
1800 Lincoln Ave ....Evansville IN	47722		**800-423-8633**	812-488-2000
University of Indianapolis				
1400 E Hanna Ave ....Indianapolis IN	46227		**800-232-8634**	317-788-3368
University of Southern Indiana				
8600 University Blvd ....Evansville IN	47712		**800-467-1965**	812-464-1765
Valparaiso University				
1700 Chapel Dr ....Valparaiso IN	46383		**888-468-2576**	219-464-5011
Wabash College				
410 W Wabash Ave PO Box 352 ....Crawfordsville IN	47933		**800-345-5385**	765-361-6326

Iowa

			Toll-Free	Phone
Ashford University				
400 N Bluff Blvd	Clinton IA	52732	**800-242-4153**	563-242-4023
Briar Cliff University				
3303 Rebecca St	Sioux City IA	51104	**800-662-3303**	712-279-5321
Buena Vista University				
610 W Fourth St	Storm Lake IA	50588	**800-383-9600**	712-749-2253
Central College				
812 University St	Pella IA	50219	**877-462-3687**	641-628-5285
Clarke College				
1550 Clarke Dr	Dubuque IA	52001	**888-825-2753**	563-588-6300
Coe College				
1220 First Ave NE	Cedar Rapids IA	52402	**877-225-5263**	319-399-8500
Cornell College				
600 First St SW	Mount Vernon IA	52314	**800-747-1112***	319-895-4215
*Admissions				
Divine Word College				
102 Jacoby Dr SW	Epworth IA	52045	**800-553-3321**	563-876-3353
Dordt College				
498 Fourth Ave NE	Sioux Center IA	51250	**800-343-6738**	712-722-6080
Drake University				
2507 University Ave	Des Moines IA	50311	**800-443-7253**	515-271-3181
Graceland University				
1 University Pl	Lamoni IA	50140	**800-859-1215**	641-784-5000
Grand View College				
1200 Grandview Ave	Des Moines IA	50316	**800-444-6083**	515-263-2800
Grinnell College				
1115 Eighth Ave	Grinnell IA	50112	**800-247-0113**	641-269-3600
Iowa Braille & Sight Saving School				
1002 G Ave	Vinton IA	52349	**800-645-4579**	319-472-5221
Iowa State University				
100 Alumni Hall	Ames IA	50011	**800-262-3810***	515-294-4111
*Admissions				
Iowa Wesleyan College				
601 N Main St	Mount Pleasant IA	52641	**800-582-2383**	
Loras College				
1450 Alta Vista St	Dubuque IA	52001	**800-245-6727**	563-588-7100
Luther College				
700 College Dr	Decorah IA	52101	**800-458-8437**	563-387-2000
Maharishi University of Management				
1000 N Fourth St	Fairfield IA	52557	**800-369-6480**	641-472-1110
Morningside College				
1501 Morningside Ave	Sioux City IA	51106	**800-831-0806**	712-274-5000
Mount Mercy College				
1330 Elmhurst Dr NE	Cedar Rapids IA	52402	**800-248-4504**	319-368-6460
Northwestern College				
101 Seventh St SW	Orange City IA	51041	**800-747-4757**	712-707-7000
Saint Ambrose University				
518 W Locust St	Davenport IA	52803	**800-383-2627***	563-333-6000
*Admissions				
Simpson College				
701 N 'C' St	Indianola IA	50125	**800-362-2454**	515-961-6251
University of Dubuque				
2000 University Ave	Dubuque IA	52001	**800-722-5583**	563-589-3000
University of Iowa				
107 Calvin Hall	Iowa City IA	52242	**800-553-4692**	319-335-3847
University of Northern Iowa				
1222 W 27th St	Cedar Falls IA	50614	**800-772-2037***	319-273-2311
*Admissions				
Upper Iowa University				
605 Washington St PO Box 1857	Fayette IA	52142	**800-553-4150***	563-425-5200
*Admissions				
Waldorf College				
106 S Sixth St	Forest City IA	50436	**800-292-1903**	641-585-2450
Wartburg College				
100 Wartburg Blvd	Waverly IA	50677	**800-772-2085**	319-352-8264
William Penn University				
201 Trueblood Ave	Oskaloosa IA	52577	**800-779-7366**	

Kansas

			Toll-Free	Phone
Benedictine College				
1020 N Second St	Atchison KS	66002	**800-467-5340**	913-367-5340
Bethany College				
335 E Swensson St	Lindsborg KS	67456	**800-826-2281***	785-227-3380
*Admissions				
Bethel College				
300 E 27th St	North Newton KS	67117	**800-522-1887**	316-283-2500
Central Christian College				
PO Box 1403	McPherson KS	67460	**800-835-0078**	620-241-0723
Emporia State University				
1200 Commercial St	Emporia KS	66801	**877-468-6378**	620-341-1200
Fort Hays State University				
600 Park St	Hays KS	67601	**800-628-3478***	785-628-4000
*Admissions				
Friends University				
2100 W University Ave	Wichita KS	67213	**800-794-6945**	316-295-5000
Kansas State University				
119 Anderson Hall	Manhattan KS	66506	**800-432-8270***	785-532-6250
*Admissions				
Kansas Wesleyan University				
100 E Claflin Ave	Salina KS	67401	**800-874-1154**	785-827-5541
McPherson College				
1600 E Euclid	McPherson KS	67460	**800-365-7402**	620-242-0400
MidAmerica Nazarene University				
2030 E College Way	Olathe KS	66062	**800-800-8887**	913-782-3750
Newman University				
3100 McCormick Ave	Wichita KS	67213	**877-639-6268**	316-942-4291
Ottawa University				
1001 S Cedar St	Ottawa KS	66067	**800-755-5200***	785-242-5200
*Admissions				
Pittsburg State University				
1701 S Broadway St	Pittsburg KS	66762	**800-854-7488**	620-235-4251
Southwestern College				
100 College St	Winfield KS	67156	**800-846-1543**	

			Toll-Free	Phone
Sterling College				
125 W Cooper	Sterling KS	67579	**800-346-1017**	620-278-2173
University of Saint Mary				
4100 S Fourth St	Leavenworth KS	66048	**800-752-7043**	913-682-5151
Washburn University				
1700 SW College Ave	Topeka KS	66621	**800-736-9060**	785-670-1010
Wichita State University				
1845 Fairmount St	Wichita KS	67260	**800-362-2594***	316-978-3456
*Admissions				

Kentucky

			Toll-Free	Phone
Alice Lloyd College				
100 Purpose Rd	Pippa Passes KY	41844	**888-280-4252***	606-368-6000
*Admissions				
Asbury University				
1 Macklem Dr	Wilmore KY	40390	**800-888-1818***	859-858-3511
*Admissions				
Bellarmine University				
2001 Newburg Rd	Louisville KY	40205	**800-274-4723**	502-272-8000
Berea College 101 Chestnut St	Berea KY	40403	**800-326-5948**	859-985-3500
Brescia University				
717 Frederica St	Owensboro KY	42301	**877-273-7242***	270-685-3131
*Admissions				
Campbellsville University				
1 University Dr	Campbellsville KY	42718	**800-264-6014***	270-789-5000
*Admissions				
Centre College				
600 W Walnut St	Danville KY	40422	**800-423-6236**	859-238-5350
Eastern Kentucky University				
521 Lancaster Ave	Richmond KY	40475	**800-465-9191**	859-622-2106
Georgetown College				
400 E College St	Georgetown KY	40324	**800-788-9985***	502-863-8000
*Admissions				
Kentucky Christian University				
100 Academic Pkwy	Grayson KY	41143	**800-522-3181***	
*Admissions				
Kentucky State University				
400 E Main St	Frankfort KY	40601	**800-325-1716***	502-597-6000
*Admissions				
Kentucky Wesleyan College				
3000 Frederica St	Owensboro KY	42301	**800-999-0592***	270-852-3120
*Admissions				
Lindsey Wilson College				
210 Lindsey Wilson St	Columbia KY	42728	**800-264-0138**	270-384-2126
Mid-Continent University				
99 Powell Rd E	Mayfield KY	42066	**888-628-4723**	270-247-8521
Midway College				
512 E Stephens St	Midway KY	40347	**800-952-4122**	
Morehead State University				
100 Admissions Ctr	Morehead KY	40351	**800-585-6781**	606-783-2000
Murray State University				
102 Curris Ctr	Murray KY	42071	**800-272-4678**	270-809-3741
Hopkinsville				
5305 Ft Campbell Blvd	Hopkinsville KY	42240	**800-669-7654**	270-707-1525
Northern Kentucky University				
Nunn Dr	Highland Heights KY	41099	**800-637-9948***	859-572-5220
*Admissions				
Pikeville College				
147 Sycamore St	Pikeville KY	41501	**866-232-7700**	606-218-5250
Spalding University				
851 S Fourth St	Louisville KY	40203	**800-896-8941**	502-585-9911
Sullivan University				
3101 BaRdstown Rd	Louisville KY	40205	**800-844-1354**	502-456-6505
Thomas More College				
333 Thomas More Pkwy	Crestview Hills KY	41017	**800-825-4557**	859-344-3332
Transylvania University				
300 N Broadway	Lexington KY	40508	**800-872-6798**	859-233-8242
Union College				
310 College St	Barbourville KY	40906	**800-489-8646**	606-546-4151
University of Kentucky				
800 Rose St	Lexington KY	40536	**866-900-4685**	859-257-9000
University of Louisville				
2301 S Third St	Louisville KY	40292	**800-334-8635**	502-852-5555
University of the Cumberlands				
6178 College Station Dr	Williamsburg KY	40769	**800-343-1609**	606-539-4201
Western Kentucky University				
1906 College Heights Blvd	Bowling Green KY	42101	**800-495-8463***	270-745-0111
*Admissions				

Louisiana

			Toll-Free	Phone
Centenary College of Louisiana				
2911 Centenary Blvd	Shreveport LA	71104	**800-234-4448***	318-869-5131
Franciscan Missionaries of Our Lady University				
Our Lady of the Lake College				
5414 Brittany Dr	Baton Rouge LA	70808	**877-242-3509***	225-768-1700
*Admissions				
Grambling State University				
403 Main St	Grambling LA	71245	**800-569-4714**	318-247-3811
Louisiana College				
1140 College Dr	Pineville LA	71359	**800-487-1906**	318-487-7011
Louisiana State University				
Alexandria				
8100 US Hwy 71 S	Alexandria LA	71302	**888-473-6417***	318-445-3672
*Admissions				
Baton Rouge				
110 Thomas Boyd Hall	Baton Rouge LA	70803	**888-846-6810**	225-578-3202
Loyola University				
New Orleans				
6363 St Charles Ave	New Orleans LA	70118	**800-456-9652***	504-865-3240
*Admissions				
McNeese State University				
4205 Ryan St	Lake Charles LA	70609	**800-622-3352**	
Northwestern State University				
175 Sam Sibley Dr	Natchitoches LA	71497	**800-767-8115**	318-357-4078

				Toll-Free	Phone

Southeastern Louisiana University
| 500 Western Ave | Hammond | LA | 70402 | 800-222-7358 | 985-549-2062 |

Southern University & A & M College
156 Elton C Harrison Dr
| PO Box 9757 | Baton Rouge | LA | 70813 | 800-256-1531* | 225-771-5180 |
*Admissions

Tulane University
| 6823 St Charles Ave | New Orleans | LA | 70118 | 800-873-9283* | 504-865-5000 |
*Admissions

University of Louisiana
| Lafayette 611 McKinley St | Lafayette | LA | 70504 | 800-752-6553 | 337-482-1000 |
| Monroe 700 University Ave | Monroe | LA | 71209 | 800-372-5127* | 318-342-5430 |

University of New Orleans
| 2000 Lakeshore Dr | New Orleans | LA | 70148 | 800-256-5866* | 504-280-6000 |
*Admissions

Maine

				Toll-Free	Phone

Bates College
| 2 Andrews Rd | Lewiston | ME | 04240 | 888-522-8371 | 207-786-6255 |

Colby College
| 4800 Mayflower Hill | Waterville | ME | 04901 | 800-723-3032* | 207-859-4800 |
*Admissions

College of the Atlantic
| 105 Eden St | Bar Harbor | ME | 04609 | 800-528-0025* | 207-288-5015 |
*Admissions

Husson College
| 1 College Cir | Bangor | ME | 04401 | 800-448-7766 | 207-941-7000 |

Maine Maritime Academy
| 66 Pleasant St | Castine | ME | 04420 | 800-464-6565* | 207-326-4311 |
*Admissions

Saint Joseph's College of Maine
| 278 Whites Bridge Rd | Standish | ME | 04084 | 800-338-7057* | 207-893-7746 |
*Admissions

Thomas College
| 180 W River Rd | Waterville | ME | 04901 | 800-339-7001* | 207-859-1111 |
*Admissions

Unity College
| 90 Quaker Hill Rd | Unity | ME | 04988 | 800-624-1024 | 207-948-3131 |

University of Maine
| 5713 Chadbourne Hall | Orono | ME | 04469 | 877-486-2364* | 207-581-1110 |
*Admissions
| Augusta 46 University Dr | Augusta | ME | 04330 | 877-862-1234 | 207-621-3000 |
| Farmington 111 S St | Farmington | ME | 04938 | 800-871-7741 | 207-778-7000 |
Fort Kent
| 23 University Dr | Fort Kent | ME | 04743 | 888-879-8635* | 207-834-7500 |
*Admissions
| Machias 116 O'Brien Ave | Machias | ME | 04654 | 888-468-6866* | 207-255-1200 |
*Admissions

University of New England
| 11 Hills Beach Rd | Biddeford | ME | 04005 | 800-477-4863* | 207-283-0171 |
*Admissions
Westbrook College
| 716 Stevens Ave | Portland | ME | 04103 | 800-477-4863* | 207-797-7261 |
*Admissions

University of Southern Maine
| 96 Falmouth St | Portland | ME | 04103 | 800-800-4876 | 207-780-4141 |
| Gorham 37 College Ave | Gorham | ME | 04038 | 800-800-4876 | 207-780-5670 |
Lewiston-Auburn College
| 51 Westminster St | Lewiston | ME | 04240 | 800-800-4876 | 207-753-6500 |

Maryland

				Toll-Free	Phone

Bowie State University
| 14000 Jericho Pk Rd | Bowie | MD | 20715 | 877-772-6943 | 301-860-4000 |

Capitol Technology University
| 11301 Springfield Rd | Laurel | MD | 20708 | 800-950-1992 | 301-369-2800 |

Coppin State University
| 2500 W N Ave | Baltimore | MD | 21216 | 800-635-3674* | 410-951-3600 |
*Admissions

Goucher College
| 1021 Dulaney Valley Rd | Towson | MD | 21204 | 800-468-2437 | 410-337-6000 |

Hood College
| 401 Rosemont Ave | Frederick | MD | 21701 | 800-922-1599 | 301-696-3400 |

Loyola College
| 4501 N Charles St | Baltimore | MD | 21210 | 800-221-9107 | 410-617-5012 |

McDaniel College
| 2 College Hill | Westminster | MD | 21157 | 800-638-5005* | 410-857-2230 |
*Admissions

Morgan State University
| 1700 E Cold Spring Ln | Baltimore | MD | 21251 | 800-319-4678 | 443-885-3333 |

Mount Saint Mary's University
| 16300 Old Emmitsburg Rd | Emmitsburg | MD | 21727 | 800-448-4347* | 301-447-5214 |
*Admissions

Peabody Institute of the Johns Hopkins University
Peabody Conservatory of Music
| 1 E Mt Vernon Pl | Baltimore | MD | 21202 | 800-368-2521 | 667-208-6500 |

Saint Mary's College of Maryland
| 47645 College Dr | Saint Marys City | MD | 20686 | 800-492-7181* | 240-895-2000 |
*Admissions

Salisbury University
| 1200 Camden Ave | Salisbury | MD | 21801 | 888-543-0148 | 410-543-6000 |

Strayer University
| 4710 Auth Pl Ste 100 | Suitland | MD | 20746 | 888-311-0355 | |

Towson University
| 8000 York Rd | Towson | MD | 21252 | 866-301-3375 | 410-704-2113 |

University of Maryland
| 7569 Baltimore Ave | College Park | MD | 20742 | 800-422-5867* | 301-405-1000 |
*Admissions
Baltimore County
| 1000 Hilltop Cir | Baltimore | MD | 21250 | 800-810-0271 | 410-455-1000 |

US Naval Academy
| 121 Blake Rd | Annapolis | MD | 21402 | 888-249-7707* | 410-293-1000 |
*Admissions

Villa Julie College
| 1525 Green Spring Valley Rd | Stevenson | MD | 21153 | 877-468-6852 | 410-486-7001 |

Washington Adventist University
| 7600 Flower Ave | Takoma Park | MD | 20912 | 800-835-4212 | 301-891-4000 |

Washington College
| 300 Washington Ave | Chestertown | MD | 21620 | 800-422-1782 | 410-778-2800 |

Massachusetts

				Toll-Free	Phone

American International College
| 1000 State St | Springfield | MA | 01109 | 800-242-3142* | 413-205-3201 |

Amherst College
| 220 S Pleasant St | Amherst | MA | 01002 | 866-542-4438 | 413-542-2000 |

Anna Maria College
| 50 Sunset Ln | Paxton | MA | 01612 | 800-344-4586 | |

Assumption College
| 500 Salisbury St | Worcester | MA | 01609 | 888-882-7786 | 508-767-7000 |

Atlantic Union College
| 338 Main St | South Lancaster | MA | 01561 | 800-282-2030 | 978-368-2000 |

Babson College
| 231 Forest St | Babson Park | MA | 02457 | 800-488-3696* | 781-235-1200 |
*Admissions

Bay Path College
| 588 Longmeadow St | Longmeadow | MA | 01106 | 800-782-7284 | |

Becker College
| 61 Sever St | Worcester | MA | 01609 | 877-523-2537 | 508-791-9241 |

Berklee College of Music
| 1140 Boylston St | Boston | MA | 02215 | 800-421-0084 | 617-747-2221 |

Boston College
| 140 Commonwealth Ave | Chestnut Hill | MA | 02467 | 800-360-2522 | 617-552-3100 |

Brandeis University
| 415 S St | Waltham | MA | 02454 | 800-622-0622 | 781-736-3500 |

Clark University
| 950 Main St | Worcester | MA | 01610 | 800-462-5275 | 508-793-7711 |

College of the Holy Cross
| 1 College St | Worcester | MA | 01610 | 800-442-2421 | 508-793-2011 |

Curry College
| 1071 Blue Hill Ave | Milton | MA | 02186 | 800-669-0686 | 617-333-2210 |

Eastern Nazarene College
| 23 E Elm Ave | Quincy | MA | 02170 | 800-883-6288 | 617-745-3000 |

ELMS College
| 291 Springfield St | Chicopee | MA | 01013 | 800-255-3567* | 413-592-3189 |
*Admissions

Endicott College
| 376 Hale St | Beverly | MA | 01915 | 800-325-1114* | 978-927-0585 |
*Admissions

Framingham State College
| 100 State St PO Box 9101 | Framingham | MA | 01701 | 866-361-8970 | 508-620-1220 |

Gordon College
| 255 Grapevine Rd | Wenham | MA | 01984 | 800-343-1379 | 978-927-2300 |

Lasell College
| 1844 Commonwealth Ave | Newton | MA | 02466 | 888-222-5229* | 617-243-2225 |
*Admissions

Lesley University
| 29 Everett St | Cambridge | MA | 02138 | 800-999-1959 | 617-868-9600 |

Massachusetts College of Art
| 621 Huntington Ave | Boston | MA | 02115 | 800-834-3242 | 617-879-7222 |

Massachusetts College of Pharmacy & Health Sciences
| 179 Longwood Ave | Boston | MA | 02115 | 800-225-5506 | 617-732-2850 |

Massachusetts Maritime Academy
| 101 Academy Dr | Buzzards Bay | MA | 02532 | 800-544-3411* | 508-830-5000 |

Montserrat College of Art
| 23 Essex St | Beverly | MA | 01915 | 800-836-0487 | 978-921-4242 |

Mount Holyoke College
| 50 College St | South Hadley | MA | 01075 | 800-642-4483 | 413-538-2000 |

National Graduate School of Quality Management Inc, The
| 186 Jones Rd | Falmouth | MA | 02540 | 800-838-2580 | |

New England Conservatory
| 290 Huntington Ave | Boston | MA | 02115 | 800-841-8371 | 617-585-1100 |

Nichols College
| 129 Center Rd | Dudley | MA | 01571 | 800-470-3379 | |

Northeastern University
| 360 Huntington Ave | Boston | MA | 02115 | 855-476-3391 | 617-373-2000 |

Pine Manor College
| 400 Heath St | Chestnut Hill | MA | 02467 | 800-762-1357 | 617-731-7104 |

Regis College
| 235 Wellesley St | Weston | MA | 02493 | 866-438-7344 | 781-768-7000 |

School of the Museum of Fine Arts
| 230 The Fenway | Boston | MA | 02115 | 800-643-6078* | 617-369-3626 |
*Admissions

Simmons College
| 300 The Fenway | Boston | MA | 02115 | 800-345-8468 | 617-521-2000 |

Smith College
| 7 College Ln | NortHampton | MA | 01063 | 800-383-3232 | 413-584-2700 |

Springfield College
| 263 Alden St | Springfield | MA | 01109 | 800-343-1257* | 413-748-3136 |
*Admissions

Stonehill College
| 320 Washington St | Easton | MA | 02357 | 888-694-4554 | 508-565-1373 |

Suffolk University
| 8 Ashburton Pl | Boston | MA | 02108 | 800-678-3365 | 617-573-8460 |

University of Massachusetts
Boston
| 100 Morrissey Blvd Campus Ctr | Boston | MA | 02125 | 800-767-1833 | 617-287-6100 |
| Lowell 1 University Ave | Lowell | MA | 01854 | 800-480-3190 | 978-934-4000 |

Wentworth Institute of Technology
| 550 Huntington Ave | Boston | MA | 02115 | 800-556-0610 | 617-989-4590 |

Western New England College
| 1215 Wilbraham Rd | Springfield | MA | 01119 | 800-782-6665 | 413-782-3111 |

Wheaton College
| 26 E Main St | Norton | MA | 02766 | 800-394-6003* | 508-286-8200 |
*Admissions

Wheelock College
| 200 The Riverway | Boston | MA | 02215 | 800-734-5212 | 617-879-2206 |

Williams College
| 880 Main St | Williamstown | MA | 01267 | 877-374-7526 | 413-597-3131 |

Michigan

				Toll-Free	Phone

Adrian College
| 110 S Madison St | Adrian | MI | 49221 | 800-877-2246* | 517-265-5161 |
*Admissions

Albion College
| 611 E Porter St | Albion | MI | 49224 | 800-858-6770 | 517-629-1000 |

				Toll-Free	Phone
Alma College 614 W Superior St	Alma	MI	48801	**800-321-2562**	989-463-7111
Andrews University 4355 International Ct	Berrien Springs	MI	49104	**800-253-2874**	269-471-7771
Baker College					
Auburn Hills 1500 University Dr	Auburn Hills	MI	48326	**888-429-0410**	248-340-0600
Cadillac 9600 E 13th St	Cadillac	MI	49601	**888-313-3463**	231-876-3100
Flint 1050 W Bristol Rd	Flint	MI	48507	**800-964-4299**	
Jackson 2800 Springport Rd	Jackson	MI	49202	**888-343-3683**	517-788-7800
Owosso 1020 S Washington St	Owosso	MI	48867	**800-879-3797**	989-729-3350
Port Huron 3403 Lapeer Rd	Port Huron	MI	48060	**888-262-2442**	810-985-7000
Calvin College 3201 Burton St SE	Grand Rapids	MI	49546	**800-688-0122**	616-526-6000
Central Michigan University 102 Warriner Hall *Admissions	Mount Pleasant	MI	48859	**888-292-5366***	989-774-4000
Cornerstone University 1001 E Beltline Ave NE *Admissions	Grand Rapids	MI	49525	**800-787-9778***	616-222-1426
Davenport University					
Dearborn 4801 Oakman Blvd	Dearborn	MI	48126	**800-585-1479**	313-581-4400
Flint 4318 Miller Rd Ste A	Flint	MI	48507	**800-727-1443**	810-732-9977
Lansing 220 E Kalamazoo St	Lansing	MI	48933	**800-686-1600**	517-484-2600
Lettinga Campus 6191 Kraft Ave SE	Grand Rapids	MI	49512	**866-925-3884**	616-698-7111
Saginaw 5300 Bay Rd	Saginaw	MI	48604	**800-968-8133**	989-799-7800
Warren 27650 Dequindre Rd	Warren	MI	48092	**800-724-7708**	586-558-8700
Eastern Michigan University 900 Oakwood St	Ypsilanti	MI	48197	**800-468-6368**	734-487-1849
Ferris State University 1201 S State St	Big Rapids	MI	49307	**800-433-7747**	231-591-2000
Traverse City 2200 Dendrinos Dr Ste 100	Traverse City	MI	49684	**866-857-1954**	231-995-1734
Finlandia University 601 Quincy St	Hancock	MI	49930	**800-682-7604**	906-482-5300
Grand Valley State University 1 Campus Dr	Allendale	MI	49401	**800-748-0246**	616-331-5000
Hillsdale College 33 E College St	Hillsdale	MI	49242	**888-886-1174**	517-437-7341
Hope College 69 E Tenth St PO Box 9000 *Admissions	Holland	MI	49422	**800-968-7850***	616-395-7850
Kalamazoo College 1200 Academy St *Admissions	Kalamazoo	MI	49006	**800-253-3602***	269-337-7166
Kendall College of Art & Design of Ferris State University 17 Fountain St NW	Grand Rapids	MI	49503	**800-676-2787**	
Kettering University 1700 University Ave	Flint	MI	48504	**800-955-4464**	810-762-9500
Lawrence Technological University 21000 W 10-Mile Rd	Southfield	MI	48075	**800-225-5588**	248-204-3160
Madonna University 36600 Schoolcraft Rd	Livonia	MI	48150	**800-852-4951**	734-432-5339
Michigan State University 250 Hannah Admin Bldg	East Lansing	MI	48824	**800-500-1554**	517-355-1855
Michigan Technological University 1400 Townsend Dr	Houghton	MI	49931	**888-688-1885**	906-487-2335
Northern Michigan University 1401 Presque Isle Ave	Marquette	MI	49855	**800-682-9797**	906-227-2650
Northwood University Michigan 4000 Whiting Dr	Midland	MI	48640	**800-622-9000**	989-837-4200
Oakland University 2200 Squirrel Rd *Admissions	Rochester	MI	48309	**800-625-8648***	248-370-2100
Olivet College 320 S Main St	Olivet	MI	49076	**800-456-7189**	269-749-7000
Rochester College 800 W Avon Rd	Rochester Hills	MI	48307	**800-521-6010**	248-218-2011
Saginaw Valley State University 7400 Bay Rd	University Center	MI	48710	**800-968-9500**	989-964-4200
Siena Heights University 1247 E Siena Heights Dr	Adrian	MI	49221	**800-521-0009**	517-263-0731
Spring Arbor University 106 E Main St *Admissions	Spring Arbor	MI	49283	**800-968-9103***	517-750-6504
University of Detroit Mercy 4001 W McNichols Rd *Admissions	Detroit	MI	48221	**800-635-5020***	313-993-1000
University of Michigan					
Flint 303 E Kearsley St	Flint	MI	48502	**800-942-5636**	734-764-1817
Wayne State University 42 W Warren	Detroit	MI	48202	**877-978-4636**	313-577-3577

Minnesota

				Toll-Free	Phone
Argosy University 1515 Central Pkwy	Eagan	MN	55121	**888-844-2004**	651-846-2882
Augsburg College 2211 Riverside Ave	Minneapolis	MN	55454	**800-788-5678**	612-330-1000
Bemidji State University 1500 Birchmont Dr NE *Admissions	Bemidji	MN	56601	**800-475-2001***	218-755-2001
Bethany Lutheran College 700 Luther Dr	Mankato	MN	56001	**800-944-3066**	507-344-7000
Bethel University 3900 Bethel Dr	Saint Paul	MN	55112	**800-255-8706**	651-638-6400
Carleton College 100 S College St *Admissions	Northfield	MN	55057	**800-995-2275***	507-646-4000
College of Saint Catherine 2004 Randolph Ave	Saint Paul	MN	55105	**800-945-4599**	651-690-6000
Minneapolis 601 25th Ave S	Minneapolis	MN	55454	**800-945-4599**	651-690-7700
College of Saint Scholastica 1200 Kenwood Ave	Duluth	MN	55811	**800-447-5444**	218-723-6046
Concordia College 901 Eigth St S	Moorhead	MN	56562	**800-699-9897**	218-299-4000
Gustavus Adolphus College 800 W College Ave	Saint Peter	MN	56082	**800-487-8288**	507-933-8000
Hamline University 1536 Hewitt Ave	Saint Paul	MN	55104	**800-753-9753**	651-523-2207
Macalester College 1600 Grand Ave *Admissions	Saint Paul	MN	55105	**800-231-7974***	651-696-6357
Metropolitan State University 700 E Seventh St	Saint Paul	MN	55106	**888-234-2690**	651-793-1300
Minnesota State University					
Mankato 122 Taylor Ctr *Admissions	Mankato	MN	56001	**800-722-0544***	507-389-1822
Moorhead 1104 Seventh Ave S	Moorhead	MN	56563	**800-593-7246**	218-477-2161
North Central University 910 Elliot Ave S *Admissions	Minneapolis	MN	55404	**800-289-6222***	612-343-4460
Northwestern College 3003 Snelling Ave N	Saint Paul	MN	55113	**800-692-4020**	651-631-5100
Rasmussen College Inc 4400 W 78th St 6th Fl	Bloomington	MN	55345	**800-852-0929**	952-545-2000
Southwest Minnesota State University 1501 State St	Marshall	MN	56258	**800-642-0684**	
University of Minnesota 200 Oak St SE Ste 500	Minneapolis	MN	55455	**800-775-2187**	612-624-3333
Crookston 2900 University Ave 170 Owen Hall	Crookston	MN	56716	**800-862-6466**	218-281-8569
Duluth 1049 University Dr	Duluth	MN	55812	**800-232-1339**	218-726-8000
Morris 600 E Fourth St	Morris	MN	56267	**800-992-8863**	888-866-3382
Twin Cities 3 Morrill Hall 100 Church St SE	Minneapolis	MN	55455	**800-752-1000**	612-625-2008
University of Saint Thomas 2115 Summit Ave	Saint Paul	MN	55105	**800-328-6819**	651-962-5000
Winona State University 175 W Mark St	Winona	MN	55987	**800-342-5978**	507-457-5000

Mississippi

				Toll-Free	Phone
Belhaven College 1500 Peachtree St PO Box 153	Jackson	MS	39202	**800-960-5940**	601-968-5940
Blue Mountain College PO Box 160	Blue Mountain	MS	38610	**800-235-0136**	662-685-4771
Delta State University 1003 W Sunflower Rd	Cleveland	MS	38733	**800-468-6378**	662-846-4020
Jackson State University 1400 John R Lynch St	Jackson	MS	39217	**800-848-6817**	601-979-2121
Millsaps College 1701 N State St *Admissions	Jackson	MS	39210	**800-352-1050***	601-974-1000
Mississippi College 200 S Capitol St	Clinton	MS	39056	**800-738-1236**	601-925-3000
Mississippi University for Women 1100 College St MUW-1613	Columbus	MS	39701	**877-462-8439**	662-329-4750
Mississippi Valley State University 14000 Hwy 82	Itta Bena	MS	38941	**800-844-6885**	662-254-9041
Rust College 150 Rust Ave	Holly Springs	MS	38635	**888-886-8492**	662-252-8000
Tougaloo College 500 W County Line Rd *Admissions	Tougaloo	MS	39174	**888-424-2566***	601-977-7700
University of Mississippi PO Box 1848	University	MS	38677	**800-891-4596**	662-915-7211
University of Southern Mississippi 118 College Dr	Hattiesburg	MS	39406	**800-446-0892**	601-266-1000
William Carey University 498 Tuscan Ave	Hattiesburg	MS	39401	**800-962-5991**	601-318-6051

Missouri

				Toll-Free	Phone
Avila University 11901 Wornall Rd	Kansas City	MO	64145	**866-943-5787**	816-501-2400
Central Methodist University 411 Central Methodist Sq	Fayette	MO	65248	**877-268-1854**	660-248-3391
Chamberlain College of Nursing 11830 Westline Industrial Ste 106	Saint Louis	MO	63146	**888-556-8226**	314-991-6200
College of the Ozarks 1 Industrial Dr PO Box 17 *Admissions	Point Lookout	MO	65726	**800-222-0525***	417-334-6411
Columbia College 1001 Rogers St	Columbia	MO	65216	**800-231-2391**	573-875-8700
Columbia College Jefferson City 3314 Emerald Ln	Jefferson City	MO	65109	**800-231-2391**	573-634-3250
Columbia College Lake of the Ozarks 900 College Blvd	Osage Beach	MO	65065	**800-231-2391**	573-348-6463
Drury University 900 N Benton Ave	Springfield	MO	65802	**800-922-2274**	417-873-7879
Evangel University 1111 N Glenstone Ave *Admissions	Springfield	MO	65802	**800-382-6435***	417-865-2815
Graceland University Independence 1401 W Truman Rd	Independence	MO	64050	**800-833-0524**	816-833-0524
Hannibal-LaGrange Univ 2800 Palmyra Rd *Admissions	Hannibal	MO	63401	**800-454-1119***	573-221-3675
Lincoln University 820 Chestnut St *Admissions	Jefferson City	MO	65101	**800-521-5052***	573-681-5000
Lindenwood University 209 S Kings Hwy	Saint Charles	MO	63301	**877-615-8212**	636-949-2000
Missouri Baptist University 1 College Pk Dr	Saint Louis	MO	63141	**877-434-1115**	314-434-1115
Troy/Wentzville Extension 1 College Park Dr	Saint Louis	MO	63141	**877-434-1115**	314-434-1115
Missouri Southern State University 3950 Newman Rd	Joplin	MO	64801	**866-818-6778**	417-625-9300

			Toll-Free	Phone
Missouri State University (MSU)				
901 S National Ave	Springfield MO	65897	**800-492-7900**	417-836-5000
Missouri University of Science & Technology				
Rolla 1870 Miner Cir	Rolla MO	65409	**800-522-0938**	573-341-4111
Missouri Valley College				
500 E College St	Marshall MO	65340	**800-999-8219**	660-831-4000
Missouri Western State University				
4525 Downs Dr	Saint Joseph MO	64507	**800-662-7041**	816-271-4266
National American University Independence				
3620 Arrowhead Ave	Independence MO	64057	**866-628-1288**	816-412-7700
Northwest Missouri State University				
800 University Dr	Maryville MO	64468	**800-633-1175**	660-562-1148
Park University				
8700 NW River Pk Dr	Parkville MO	64152	**800-745-7275**	816-741-2000
Principia College				
13201 Clayton Rd	St. Louis MO	63131	**800-277-4648**	618-374-2131
Rockhurst University				
1100 Rockhurst Rd	Kansas City MO	64110	**800-842-6776**	816-501-4000
Saint Louis College of Pharmacy				
4588 Parkview Pl	Saint Louis MO	63110	**800-278-5267**	314-367-8700
Saint Louis University				
221 N Grand Blvd	Saint Louis MO	63103	**800-758-3678**	314-977-7288
Southwest Baptist University				
1600 University Ave	Bolivar MO	65613	**800-526-5859**	
Stephens College				
1200 E Broadway	Columbia MO	65215	**800-876-7207**	573-442-2211
Truman State University				
100 E Normal St	Kirksville MO	63501	**800-892-7792**	660-785-4000
University of Missouri (UMSL)				
Columbia 104 Jesse Hall	Columbia MO	65211	**800-856-2181**	573-882-6333
Kansas City				
5100 Rockhill Rd	Kansas City MO	64110	**800-775-8652**	816-235-1000
Saint Louis				
1 University Blvd	Saint Louis MO	63121	**888-462-8675***	314-516-5000
*Admissions				
Washington University in Saint Louis				
1 Brookings Dr	Saint Louis MO	63130	**800-638-0700**	314-935-5000
Westminster College				
501 Westminster Ave	Fulton MO	65251	**800-475-3361***	573-592-5251
*Admissions				
William Jewell College				
500 College Hill WJC	Liberty MO	64068	**888-253-9355**	816-781-7700
William Woods University				
1 University Ave	Fulton MO	65251	**800-995-3159***	573-592-4221
*Admissions				

Montana

			Toll-Free	Phone
Carroll College				
1601 N Benton Ave	Helena MT	59625	**800-992-3648**	406-447-4300
Montana State University				
Billings				
1500 University Dr	Billings MT	59101	**800-565-6782**	406-657-2011
Bozeman				
1401 West Lincoln St	Bozeman MT	59717	**888-678-2287***	406-994-2452
*Admissions				
Northern PO Box 7751	Havre MT	59501	**800-662-6132**	406-994-2452
Montana Tech of the University of Montana				
1300 West Park St	Butte MT	59701	**800-445-8324***	406-496-4101
*Admissions				
Rocky Mountain College				
1511 Poly Dr	Billings MT	59102	**800-877-6259**	406-657-1000
University of Montana				
32 Campus Dr	Missoula MT	59812	**800-462-8636***	406-243-6266
*Admissions				
Western 710 S Atlantic St	Dillon MT	59725	**877-683-7331***	406-683-7011
*Admissions				
University of Providence				
1301 20th St S	Great Falls MT	59405	**800-856-9544***	
*Admissions				
Yellowstone Baptist College				
1515 S Shiloh Rd	Billings MT	59106	**800-487-9950**	406-656-9950

Nebraska

			Toll-Free	Phone
Bellevue University				
1000 Galvin Rd S	Bellevue NE	68005	**800-756-7920**	402-293-2000
Chadron State College				
1000 Main St	Chadron NE	69337	**800-242-3766**	308-432-6000
Clarkson College				
101 S 42nd St	Omaha NE	68131	**800-647-5500**	402-552-3100
College of Saint Mary				
7000 Mercy Rd	Omaha NE	68106	**800-926-5534**	402-399-2400
Concordia University Nebraska				
800 N Columbia Ave	Seward NE	68434	**800-535-5494**	402-643-3651
Creighton University				
2500 California Plz	Omaha NE	68178	**800-282-5835**	402-280-2700
Doane College				
1014 Boswell Ave	Crete NE	68333	**800-333-6263**	402-826-2161
Grand Island				
3180 W US Hwy 34	Grand Island NE	68801	**800-333-6263**	308-398-0800
Lincoln 303 N 52nd St	Lincoln NE	68504	**888-803-6263**	402-466-4774
Hastings College				
710 N Turner Ave	Hastings NE	68901	**800-532-7642**	402-463-2402
Nebraska Wesleyan University				
5000 St Paul Ave	Lincoln NE	68504	**800-541-3818**	
Peru State College				
600 Hoyt St PO Box 10	Peru NE	68421	**800-742-4412**	402-872-3815
Summit Christian College				
2025 21st St	Gering NE	69341	**888-305-8083**	308-632-6933
Union College				
3800 S 48th St	Lincoln NE	68506	**800-228-4600***	402-486-2504
*Admissions				
University of Nebraska				
Kearney 2504 Ninth Ave	Kearney NE	68849	**800-532-7639**	308-865-8441
Lincoln 1410 Q St	Lincoln NE	68588	**800-742-8800**	402-472-2023

			Toll-Free	Phone
Omaha 6001 Dodge St	Omaha NE	68182	**800-858-8648**	402-554-2800
Wayne State College				
1111 Main St	Wayne NE	68787	**800-228-9972**	402-375-7000
York College 1125 E Eigth St	York NE	68467	**800-950-9675**	402-363-5600

Nevada

			Toll-Free	Phone
Great Basin College				
1500 College Pkwy	Elko NV	89801	**888-590-6726**	775-738-8493
Sierra Nevada College				
999 Tahoe Blvd	Incline Village NV	89451	**866-412-4636**	775-831-1314
University of Nevada				
Las Vegas				
4505 S Maryland Pkwy	Las Vegas NV	89154	**800-331-3103**	702-895-3011
Reno 1664 N Virginia St	Reno NV	89557	**866-263-8232**	775-784-1110

New Hampshire

			Toll-Free	Phone
Colby-Sawyer College				
541 Main St	New London NH	03257	**800-272-1015***	603-526-3700
*Admissions				
Dartmouth College				
6016 McNutt Hall	Hanover NH	03755	**800-490-7010**	603-646-1110
Franklin Pierce University				
Keene 17 Bradco St	Keene NH	03431	**800-325-1090**	603-899-4000
Lebanon				
24 Airport Rd Ste 19.	West Lebanon NH	03784	**800-325-1090**	603-298-5549
Manchester				
670 N Commercial St	Manchester NH	03101	**800-437-0048***	603-626-4972
*Admissions				
Portsmouth				
73 Corporate Dr	Portsmouth NH	03801	**800-325-1090**	603-433-2000
Rindge 40 University Dr	Rindge NH	03461	**800-437-0048***	603-899-4000
Granite State College				
8 Old Suncook Rd	Concord NH	03301	**888-228-3000**	603-228-3000
Berlin 25 Hall St	Concord NH	03301	**855-472-4255**	800-735-2964
Keene State College				
229 Main St	Keene NH	03435	**800-572-1909**	603-352-1909
New England College				
98 Bridge St	Henniker NH	03242	**800-521-7642***	603-428-2223
*Admissions				
Plymouth State University				
17 High St	Plymouth NH	03264	**800-842-6900**	603-535-2237
Rivier College 420 S Main St	Nashua NH	03060	**800-447-4843**	603-888-1311
Saint Anselm College				
100 St Anselm Dr	Manchester NH	03102	**888-426-7356**	603-641-7000
Southern New Hampshire University				
2500 N River Rd	Manchester NH	03106	**800-668-1249**	603-668-2211
University of New Hampshire				
3 Garrison Ave	Durham NH	03824	**800-313-5327**	603-862-1234

New Jersey

			Toll-Free	Phone
Bloomfield College				
467 Franklin St	Bloomfield NJ	07003	**800-848-4555**	973-748-9000
Caldwell University				
120 Bloomfield Ave	Caldwell NJ	07006	**888-864-9516***	973-618-3500
*Admissions				
Centenary College				
400 Jefferson St	Hackettstown NJ	07840	**800-236-8679***	908-852-1400
*Admissions				
College of Saint Elizabeth				
2 Convent Rd	Morristown NJ	07960	**800-210-7900***	973-290-4700
Fairleigh Dickinson University				
285 Madison Ave	Madison NJ	07940	**800-338-8803**	973-443-8500
Metropolitan 1000 River Rd	Teaneck NJ	07666	**800-338-8803**	201-692-2000
Felician College 262 S Main St	Lodi NJ	07644	**888-442-4551**	201-559-6000
Rutherford				
223 Montross Ave	Rutherford NJ	07070	**888-442-4551**	201-559-6000
Georgian Court University				
900 Lakewood Ave	Lakewood NJ	08701	**800-458-8422**	
Kean University				
1000 Morris Ave Kean Hall	Union NJ	07083	**800-882-1037**	908-737-7100
Monmouth University				
400 Cedar Ave	West Long Branch NJ	07764	**800-543-9671**	732-571-3456
Montclair State University				
1 Normal Ave	Montclair NJ	07043	**800-331-9205***	973-655-4000
*Admissions				
New Jersey City University				
2039 JFK Blvd	Jersey City NJ	07305	**888-441-6528**	201-200-2000
Princeton University				
33 Washington Rd	Princeton NJ	08544	**877-609-2273**	609-258-3000
Rider University				
2083 Lawrenceville Rd	Lawrenceville NJ	08648	**800-257-9026**	609-896-5000
Westminster Choir College				
101 Walnut Ln	Princeton NJ	08540	**800-962-4647**	609-921-7100
Rowan University				
201 Mullica Hill Rd	Glassboro NJ	08028	**877-787-6926***	856-256-4200
Seton Hall University				
400 S Orange Ave	South Orange NJ	07079	**800-992-4723**	973-761-9332
Stevens Institute of Technology				
Castle Pt on the Hudson	Hoboken NJ	07030	**800-458-5323**	201-216-5194
Thomas Edison State College				
101 W State St	Trenton NJ	08608	**888-442-8372**	609-777-5680
William Paterson University				
300 Pompton Rd	Wayne NJ	07470	**877-978-3923**	973-720-2000

New Mexico

			Toll-Free	Phone
College of Santa Fe				
1600 St Michaels Dr	Santa Fe NM	87505	**800-862-7759**	877-732-5977

					Toll-Free	Phone

College of the Southwest
6610 N Lovington Hwy ....Hobbs NM 88240 **800-530-4400** 575-392-6561

Eastern New Mexico University
1500 S Ave K ....Portales NM 88130 **800-367-3668** 575-562-1011

Eastern New Mexico University-ruidoso
709 Mechem Dr ....Ruidoso NM 88345 **800-934-3668** 575-257-2120

New Mexico Highlands University
PO Box 9000 ....Las Vegas NM 87701 **877-850-9064** 505-425-7511

New Mexico Institute of Mining & Technology (NMT)
801 Leroy Pl ....Socorro NM 87801 **800-428-8324*** 505-835-5434

New Mexico State University (NMSU)
MSC-3A PO Box 30001 ....Las Cruces NM 88003 **800-662-6678*** 575-646-3121
*Admissions

Santa Fe University of Art & Design
1600 St Michaels Dr ....Santa Fe NM 87505 **800-456-2673**

University of New Mexico (UNM)
1 University of New Mexico ....Albuquerque NM 87131 **800-225-5866** 505-277-0111
Gallup 200 College Rd ....Gallup NM 87301 **800-225-5866** 505-863-7500

Western New Mexico University
1000 W College St PO Box 680 ....Silver City NM 88061 **800-872-9668***
*Admissions

New York

					Toll-Free	Phone

Adelphi University
1 South Ave PO Box 701 ....Garden City NY 11530 **800-233-5744** 516-877-3050

Albany College of Pharmacy (ACPHS)
106 New Scotland Ave ....Albany NY 12208 **888-203-8010*** 518-694-7221
*General

Bard College
PO Box 5000 ....Annandale-on-Hudson NY 12504 **800-872-7423** 845-758-7472

Binghamton University
4400 Vestal Pkwy E ....Binghamton NY 13902 **800-782-0289** 607-777-2000

Canisius College
2001 Main St ....Buffalo NY 14208 **800-843-1517** 716-888-2200

Cazenovia College
8 Sullivan St ....Cazenovia NY 13035 **800-654-3210** 315-655-7208

Clarkson University
10 Clarkson Ave ....Potsdam NY 13699 **800-527-6577*** 315-268-6480
*Admissions

College of Mount Saint Vincent
6301 Riverdale Ave ....Riverdale NY 10471 **800-722-4867** 718-405-3304

College of New Rochelle
29 Castle Pl ....New Rochelle NY 10805 **800-933-5923** 914-654-5000

College of Saint Rose
979 Madison Ave ....Albany NY 12203 **800-637-8556**

College of Staten Island
2800 Victory Blvd ....Staten Island NY 10314 **888-442-4551** 718-982-2000

Concordia College New York
171 White Plains Rd ....Bronxville NY 10708 **800-937-2655*** 914-337-9300
*Admissions

D'Youville College
320 Porter Ave ....Buffalo NY 14201 **800-777-3921** 716-829-7600

Daemen College 4380 Main St ....Amherst NY 14226 **800-462-7652** 716-839-8225

Dominican College
470 Western Hwy ....Orangeburg NY 10962 **866-432-4636** 845-359-7800

Dowling College
150 Idle Hour Blvd ....Oakdale NY 11769 **800-369-5464** 631-244-3000

Elmira College 1 Pk Pl ....Elmira NY 14901 **800-935-6472*** 607-735-1724
*Admissions

Excelsior College
7 Columbia Cir ....Albany NY 12203 **888-647-2388** 518-464-8500

Farmingdale State University of New York
2350 Broadhollow Rd ....Farmingdale NY 11735 **800-557-7392** 631-420-2482

Fordham University
441 E Fordham Rd ....Bronx NY 10458 **800-367-3426** 718-817-3240
College at Lincoln Ctr
113 W 60th St ....New York NY 10023 **800-367-3426** 212-636-6000
Westchester
400 Westchester Ave ....West Harrison NY 10604 **800-606-6090** 914-367-3426

Fredonia State University of New York
Fredonia 280 Central Ave ....Fredonia NY 14063 **800-642-4272** 716-673-3111

Hamilton College
198 College Hill Rd ....Clinton NY 13323 **800-843-2655*** 315-859-4421
*Admissions

Hartwick College
1 Hartwick Dr ....Oneonta NY 13820 **888-427-8942** 607-431-4150

Hilbert College
5200 S Park Ave ....Hamburg NY 14075 **800-649-8003** 716-649-7900

Hobart & William Smith Colleges
300 Pulteney St ....Geneva NY 14456 **800-852-2256*** 315-781-3000
*Admissions

Hofstra University
1000 Fulton Ave ....Hempstead NY 11549 **800-463-7872** 516-463-6600

Houghton College
1 Willard Ave PO Box 128 ....Houghton NY 14744 **800-777-2556** 585-567-9200

Iona College 715 N Ave ....New Rochelle NY 10801 **800-264-6350** 914-633-2502

Ithaca College 953 Danby Rd ....Ithaca NY 14850 **800-429-4274*** 607-274-3124
*Admissions

Laboratory Institute of Merchandising
12 E 53rd St ....New York NY 10022 **800-677-1323** 212-752-1530

Le Moyne College
1419 Salt Springs Rd ....Syracuse NY 13214 **800-333-4733*** 315-445-4100
*Admissions

Lehman College
250 Bedford Pk Blvd W ....Bronx NY 10468 **800-311-5656** 718-960-8000

Long Island University
Brooklyn 1 University Plz ....Brooklyn NY 11201 **800-548-7526** 718-488-1011

Manhattan College
4513 Manhattan College Pkwy ....Bronx NY 10471 **855-841-2843** 718-862-8000

Manhattanville College
2900 Purchase St ....Purchase NY 10577 **800-328-4553** 914-323-5464

Marist College
3399 N Rd ....Poughkeepsie NY 12601 **800-436-5483** 845-575-3000

Medaille College
18 Agassiz Cir ....Buffalo NY 14214 **800-292-1582** 716-880-2200

Mercy College
555 Broadway ....Dobbs Ferry NY 10522 **800-637-2969** 914-674-7600
White Plains
277 Martine Ave Ste 201 ....White Plains NY 10601 **888-464-6737** 914-948-3666
Yorktown Heights
2651 Strang Blvd ....Yorktown Heights NY 10598 **877-637-2946** 914-245-6100

Molloy College
1000 Hempstead Ave ....Rockville Centre NY 11571 **888-466-5569*** 516-678-5000
*Admissions

Morrisville State College
80 Eaton St PO Box 901 ....Morrisville NY 13408 **800-258-0111*** 315-684-6000
*Admissions

Mount Saint Mary College
330 Powell Ave ....Newburgh NY 12550 **888-937-6762** 845-569-3248

Nazareth College of Rochester
4245 E Ave ....Rochester NY 14618 **800-860-6942** 585-389-2525

New York City College of Technology
300 Jay St ....Brooklyn NY 11201 **855-492-3633** 718-260-5000

New York Institute of Technology
New York Institute of Technology Northern Blvd
PO Box 8000 ....Old Westbury NY 11568 **800-345-6948** 516-686-1000
Manhattan 1855 Broadway ....New York NY 10023 **800-345-6948** 212-261-1500

New York School of Interior Design
170 E 70th St ....New York NY 10021 **800-336-9743** 212-472-1500

New York University
22 Washington Sq N ....New York NY 10011 **888-243-2358** 212-998-4500

Niagara University
5795 Lewiston Rd
PO Box 2011 ....Niagara University NY 14109 **800-778-3450** 716-285-1212

Nyack College 1 S Blvd ....Nyack NY 10960 **800-336-9225*** 845-358-1710

Pace University 1 Pace Plz ....New York NY 10038 **866-722-3338** 212-346-1200
Pleasantville/Briarcliff
861 Bedford Rd ....Pleasantville NY 10570 **866-722-3338** 914-773-3200

Parsons New School for Design
65 Fifth Ave ....New York NY 10011 **800-252-0852*** 212-229-8989
*Admissions

Paul Smith's College
7833 New York 30 ....Paul Smiths NY 12970 **800-421-2605*** 518-327-6227
*Admissions

Polytechnic University
Long Island 105 Maxess Rd ....Melville NY 11747 **877-503-7659*** 631-755-4300
*Admissions

Purchase College
735 Anderson Hill Rd ....Purchase NY 10577 **800-553-8118** 914-251-6000

Queens College
65-30 Kissena Blvd ....Flushing NY 11367 **888-888-0606** 718-997-5000

Rensselaer Polytechnic Institute
110 Eighth St ....Troy NY 12180 **800-433-4723** 518-276-6000

Roberts Wesleyan College
2301 Westside Dr ....Rochester NY 14624 **800-777-4792*** 585-594-6000
*Admissions

Russell Sage College 651st St ....Troy NY 12180 **888-837-9724*** 518-244-2217
*Admissions

Sage College of Albany
140 New Scotland Ave ....Albany NY 12208 **888-837-9724*** 518-292-1730
*Admissions

Saint John's University
8000 Utopia Pkwy ....Queens NY 11439 **888-978-5646** 718-990-2000

Saint Lawrence University
23 Romoda Dr ....Canton NY 13617 **800-285-1856*** 315-229-5261
*Admissions

Saint Thomas Aquinas College
125 Rt 340 ....Sparkill NY 10976 **800-262-3257** 845-398-4000

Sarah Lawrence College
1 Mead Way ....Bronxville NY 10708 **800-888-2858** 914-337-0700

Skidmore College
815 N Broadway ....Saratoga Springs NY 12866 **800-867-6007** 518-580-5000

State University of New York
Brockport
350 New Campus Dr ....Brockport NY 14420 **888-800-0029** 585-395-2751
College of Agriculture & Technology at Cobleskill
106 Suffolk Dr ....Cobleskill NY 12043 **800-295-8988** 518-255-5525
College of Environmental Science & Forestry
1 Forestry Dr ....Syracuse NY 13210 **800-777-7373*** 315-470-6500
*Admissions
Empire State College
1 Union Ave ....Saratoga Springs NY 12866 **800-847-3000** 518-587-2100
Geneseo 1 College Cir ....Geneseo NY 14454 **866-245-5211*** 585-245-5571
*Admitting
Maritime College
6 Pennyfield Ave Fort Schuyler ....Bronx NY 10465 **888-800-0029** 718-409-7200
New Paltz 1 Hawk Dr ....New Paltz NY 12561 **877-696-7411** 845-257-3212
Plattsburgh
101 Broad St ....Plattsburgh NY 12901 **888-673-0012*** 518-564-2040
*Admissions
Potsdam 44 Pierrpont Ave ....Potsdam NY 13676 **877-768-7326*** 315-267-2180
*Admissions
University at Buffalo
12 Capen Hall ....Buffalo NY 14260 **888-822-3648** 716-645-2450

Syracuse University
900 S Crouse Ave ....Syracuse NY 13244 **800-782-5867** 315-443-3611

University at Albany
1400 Washington Ave ....Albany NY 12222 **800-293-7869** 518-442-3300

University of Rochester
252 Elmwood Ave ....Rochester NY 14627 **888-822-2256*** 585-275-2121
*Admissions

University of Saint Francis
180 Remsen St ....Brooklyn Heights NY 11201 **800-356-8329** 718-522-2300

US Merchant Marine Academy
300 Steamboat Rd ....Kings Point NY 11024 **866-546-4778** 516-726-5800

Utica College
1600 Burrstone Rd ....Utica NY 13502 **800-782-8884*** 315-792-3111

Vassar College
124 Raymond Ave ....Poughkeepsie NY 12604 **800-827-7270** 845-437-7000

Vaughn College of Aeronautics & Technology
86-01 23rd Ave ....East Elmhurst NY 11369 **866-682-8446** 718-429-6600

				Toll-Free	Phone
Wagner College					
1 Campus Rd	Staten Island NY	10301		**800-221-1010***	718-390-3400
*Admissions					
Webb Institute					
298 Crescent Beach Rd	Glen Cove NY	11542		**866-708-9322**	516-671-2213
Wells College 170 Main St	Aurora NY	13026		**800-952-9355***	315-364-3266
*Admissions					

North Carolina

				Toll-Free	Phone
Barton College PO Box 5000	Wilson NC	27893		**800-345-4973**	252-399-6300
Belmont Abbey College					
100 Belmont-Mt Holly Rd	Belmont NC	28012		**888-222-0110**	704-461-6700
Bennett College					
900 E Washington St	Greensboro NC	27401		**800-413-5323***	336-370-8624
*Admissions					
Brevard College					
1 Brevard College Dr	Brevard NC	28712		**800-527-9090***	828-883-8292
*Admissions					
Campbell University					
450 Leslie Campbell Ave					
PO Box 546	Buies Creek NC	27506		**800-334-4111**	910-893-1290
Catawba College					
2300 W Innes St	Salisbury NC	28144		**800-228-2922**	704-637-4772
Chowan University					
1 University Pl	Murfreesboro NC	27855		**888-424-6926***	252-398-6439
*Admissions					
Davidson College					
209 Ridge Rd PO Box 7156	Davidson NC	28035		**800-768-0380**	
Duke University					
2138 Campus Dr PO Box 90586	Durham NC	27708		**800-443-3853**	919-684-3214
East Carolina University					
E Fifth St	Greenville NC	27858		**800-328-0577**	252-328-6131
Elizabeth City State University					
1704 Weeksville Rd	Elizabeth City NC	27909		**800-347-3278***	252-335-3400
Elon University 100 Campus Dr	Elon NC	27244		**800-334-8448**	336-278-2000
Fayetteville State University					
1200 Murchison Rd	Fayetteville NC	28301		**800-222-2594***	910-672-1371
*Admissions					
Gardner-Webb University					
110 S Main St PO Box 997	Boiling Springs NC	28017		**800-253-6472**	704-406-4000
Greensboro College					
815 W Market St	Greensboro NC	27401		**800-346-8226**	336-272-7102
Guilford College					
5800 W Friendly Ave	Greensboro NC	27410		**800-992-7759***	336-316-2000
*Admissions					
Heritage Bible College					
1747 Bud Hawkins Rd PO Box 1628	Dunn NC	28334		**800-297-6351**	910-892-3178
High Point University					
833 Montlieu Ave	High Point NC	27262		**800-345-6993**	336-841-9216
Johnson & Wales University Charlotte					
801 W Trade St	Charlotte NC	28202		**866-598-2427**	980-598-1100
Johnson C Smith University					
100 Beatties Ford Rd	Charlotte NC	28216		**800-782-7303***	704-378-1000
*Admissions					
King's College Library					
322 Lamar Ave	Charlotte NC	28204		**800-768-2255**	704-372-0266
Lees-McRae College					
191 Main St W	Banner Elk NC	28604		**800-280-4562**	828-898-5241
Lenoir-Rhyne University					
625 Seventh Ave NE	Hickory NC	28601		**800-277-5721**	828-328-7300
Livingstone College					
701 W Monroe St	Salisbury NC	28144		**800-835-3435**	704-216-6000
Meredith College					
3800 Hillsborough St	Raleigh NC	27607		**800-637-3348***	919-760-8600
*All					
Methodist University					
5400 Ramsey St	Fayetteville NC	28311		**800-488-7110**	910-630-7000
Montreat College					
310 Gaither Cir PO Box 1267	Montreat NC	28757		**800-622-6968**	828-669-8012
Mount Olive College					
634 Henderson St	Mount Olive NC	28365		**800-653-0854**	919-658-2502
North Carolina A & T State University					
1601 E Market St	Greensboro NC	27411		**800-443-8964***	336-334-7946
*Admissions					
North Carolina Central University					
1801 Fayetteville St	Durham NC	27707		**877-667-7533***	919-530-6100
*Admissions					
North Carolina State University					
2200 Hillsborough St	Raleigh NC	27695		**800-662-7301**	919-515-2011
North Carolina Wesleyan College					
3400 N Wesleyan Blvd	Rocky Mount NC	27804		**800-488-6292***	252-985-5100
*Admissions					
Pfeiffer University					
48380 Hwy 52 N	Misenheimer NC	28109		**800-338-2060**	704-463-1360
Piedmont Baptist College					
420 S Broad St	Winston-Salem NC	27101		**800-937-5097***	336-725-8344
*Admissions					
Queens University of Charlotte					
1900 Selwyn Ave	Charlotte NC	28274		**800-849-0202**	704-337-2212
Saint Augustine's College					
1315 Oakwood Ave	Raleigh NC	27610		**800-948-1126***	919-516-4000
*Admissions					
Salem College					
601 S Church St	Winston-Salem NC	27101		**800-327-2536***	336-721-2600
*Admissions					
Shaw University 118 E S St	Raleigh NC	27601		**800-214-6683***	919-546-8275
*Admissions					
St Andrews University					
1700 Dogwood Mile	Laurinburg NC	28352		**800-763-0198**	910-277-5555
University of North Carolina					
Asheville					
1 University Hts	Asheville NC	28804		**800-531-9842**	828-251-6481
Chapel Hill					
Jackson Hall CB 2200	Chapel Hill NC	27599		**800-962-8519**	919-966-3621
Pembroke PO Box 1510	Pembroke NC	28372		**800-949-8627**	910-521-6000

				Toll-Free	Phone
Wilmington					
601 S College Rd	Wilmington NC	28403		**800-596-2880**	910-962-3000
Warren Wilson College					
701 Warren Wilson Rd	Swannanoa NC	28778		**800-934-3536***	
*Admissions					
Western Carolina University (WCU)					
1 University Dr	Cullowhee NC	28723		**877-928-4968**	828-227-7211
Wingate University					
220 N Camden Rd	Wingate NC	28174		**800-755-5550**	704-233-8000
Winston-Salem State University					
601 S ML King Jr Dr	Winston-Salem NC	27110		**800-257-4052***	336-750-2000
*Admissions					

North Dakota

				Toll-Free	Phone
Dickinson State University					
291 Campus Dr	Dickinson ND	58601		**800-279-4295**	701-483-2507
Jamestown College					
6000 College Ln	Jamestown ND	58405		**800-336-2554**	701-252-3467
Mayville State University					
330 Third St NE	Mayville ND	58257		**800-437-4104**	
Minot State University					
500 University Ave W	Minot ND	58707		**800-777-0750**	701-858-3000
North Dakota State University					
1301 12th Ave N	Fargo ND	58105		**800-488-6378**	701-231-8011
University of Mary					
7500 University Dr	Bismarck ND	58504		**800-288-6279***	701-255-7500
*Admissions					
University of North Dakota					
PO Box 8357	Grand Forks ND	58202		**800-225-5863**	701-777-3000
Valley City State University					
101 College St SW	Valley City ND	58072		**800-532-8641**	701-845-7990

Ohio

				Toll-Free	Phone
Ashland University					
401 College Ave	Ashland OH	44805		**800-882-1548**	419-289-4142
Baldwin-Wallace College					
275 Eastland Rd	Berea OH	44017		**877-292-7759**	440-826-2222
Bluffton University					
1 University Dr	Bluffton OH	45817		**800-488-3257**	419-358-3000
Bowling Green State University					
1001 E Wooster St	Bowling Green OH	43403		**866-246-6732**	419-372-2531
Capital University					
College & Main St	Columbus OH	43209		**866-544-6175**	614-236-6101
Case Western Reserve University					
10900 Euclid Ave	Cleveland OH	44106		**800-967-8898**	216-368-2000
Cedarville University					
251 N Main St	Cedarville OH	45314		**800-233-2784**	937-766-7700
Central State University					
1400 Brush Row Rd PO Box 1004	Wilberforce OH	45384		**800-388-2781**	937-376-6011
Cleveland Institute of Music					
11021 E Blvd	Cleveland OH	44106		**800-686-1141**	216-791-5000
Cleveland State University					
2121 Euclid Ave	Cleveland OH	44115		**888-278-6446**	216-687-2000
College of Mount Saint Joseph					
5701 Delhi Rd	Cincinnati OH	45233		**800-654-9314**	513-244-4200
College of Wooster					
1189 Beall Ave	Wooster OH	44691		**800-877-9905**	330-263-2000
Defiance College					
701 N Clinton St	Defiance OH	43512		**800-520-4632**	419-784-4010
Denison University					
100 W College St	Granville OH	43023		**877-336-8648**	740-587-6394
Franklin University					
201 S Grant Ave	Columbus OH	43215		**877-341-6300**	614-797-4700
Heidelberg University					
310 E Market St	Tiffin OH	44883		**800-434-3352**	419-448-2000
Hiram College PO Box 67	Hiram OH	44234		**800-362-5280***	330-569-5169
*Admissions					
Hondros College of Nursing					
4140 Executive Pkwy	Westerville OH	43081		**855-906-8773**	
John Carroll University					
20700 N Pk Blvd	Cleveland OH	44118		**888-335-6800**	216-397-1886
Kent State University					
800 E Summit St PO Box 5190	Kent OH	44242		**800-988-5368**	330-672-3000
Ashtabula 3300 Lake Rd W	Ashtabula OH	44004		**800-988-5368**	440-964-3322
Stark					
6000 Frank Ave NW	North Canton OH	44720		**800-988-5368**	330-499-9600
Trumbull Campus					
4314 Mahoning Ave NW	Warren OH	44483		**800-988-5368**	330-847-0571
Tuscarawas					
330 University Dr NE	New Philadelphia OH	44663		**800-988-5368**	330-339-3391
Kenyon College					
103 College Dr	Gambier OH	43022		**800-848-2468**	740-427-5000
Lake Erie College					
391 West Washington St	Painesville OH	44077		**800-533-4996**	440-375-7050
Lourdes College					
6832 Convent Blvd	Sylvania OH	43560		**800-878-3210**	419-885-5291
Malone College					
2600 Cleveland Ave NW	Canton OH	44709		**800-521-1146**	
Marietta College					
215 Fifth St	Marietta OH	45750		**800-331-7896***	740-376-4000
*Admissions					
Miami University					
501 E High St	Oxford OH	45056		**866-426-4643**	513-529-1809
Mount Union College					
1972 Clark Ave	Alliance OH	44601		**800-334-6682***	330-823-2590
*Admissions					
Mount Vernon Nazarene University					
800 Martinsburg Rd	Mount Vernon OH	43050		**800-766-8206***	740-392-6868
*Admissions					
Muskingum College					
163 Stormont St	New Concord OH	43762		**800-752-6082***	740-826-8211
*Admissions					
Notre Dame College					
4545 College Rd	South Euclid OH	44121		**877-632-6446**	

				Toll-Free	Phone
Oberlin College & Conservatory 38 E College St	Oberlin	OH	44074	800-622-6243	440-775-8411
Ohio Dominican University 1216 Sunbury Rd	Columbus	OH	43219	800-955-6446	614-251-4500
Ohio Northern University 525 S Main St *Admissions	Ada	OH	45810	888-408-4668*	419-772-2000
Ohio State University 154 W 12th Ave	Columbus	OH	43210	800-426-5046	614-292-3980
Newark 1179 University Dr	Newark	OH	43055	800-963-9275	740-366-3321
Ohio University 120 Chubb Hall	Athens	OH	45710	800-858-6843	740-593-1000
Chillicothe 101 University Dr	Chillicothe	OH	45601	877-462-6824	740-774-7200
Eastern 45425 National Rd	Saint Clairsville	OH	43950	800-648-3331	740-695-1720
Lancaster 1570 Granville Pk	Lancaster	OH	43130	800-444-2910	740-654-6711
Southern 1804 Liberty Ave	Ironton	OH	45638	800-626-0513	740-533-4600
Ohio Wesleyan University 61 S Sandusky St Slocum Hall	Delaware	OH	43015	800-922-8953	740-368-2000
Otterbein College 1 S Grove St *Admissions	Westerville	OH	43081	800-488-8144*	614-823-1500
Shawnee State University 940 Second St	Portsmouth	OH	45662	800-959-2778	740-351-3221
Tiffin University 155 Miami St	Tiffin	OH	44883	800-968-6446	419-447-6442
Union Institute & University 440 E McMillan St	Cincinnati	OH	45206	800-486-3116	513-861-6400
University of Akron 277 E Buchtel Ave *Admissions	Akron	OH	44325	800-655-4884*	330-972-7100
University of Cincinnati 2600 Clifton Ave PO Box 210091	Cincinnati	OH	45221	866-397-3382	513-556-1100
University of Dayton 300 College Pk	Dayton	OH	45469	800-837-7433	937-229-4411
University of Findlay 1000 N Main St	Findlay	OH	45840	800-472-9502	419-422-8313
University of Rio Grande 218 N College Ave	Rio Grande	OH	45674	800-282-7201	
University of Toledo 2801 W Bancroft	Toledo	OH	43606	800-586-5336	419-530-4636
Ursuline College 2550 Lander Rd	Pepper Pike	OH	44124	888-778-5463	440-449-4200
Walsh University 2020 E Maple St *Admissions	North Canton	OH	44720	800-362-9846*	330-499-7090
Wilmington College of Ohio 1870 Quaker Way	Wilmington	OH	45177	800-341-9318	937-382-6661
Wittenberg University 200 W Ward St	Springfield	OH	45504	800-677-7558	937-327-6314
Wright State University 3640 Colonel Glenn Hwy *Admissions	Dayton	OH	45435	800-247-1770*	937-775-5740
Xavier University 3800 Victory Pkwy	Cincinnati	OH	45207	800-344-4698	513-745-3000
Youngstown State University 1 University Plz *Admissions	Youngstown	OH	44555	877-468-6978*	330-941-3000

Oklahoma

				Toll-Free	Phone
Bacone College 2299 Old Bacone Rd *Admissions	Muskogee	OK	74403	888-682-5514*	918-683-4581
Cameron University 2800 W Gore Blvd *Admissions	Lawton	OK	73505	888-454-7600*	580-581-2289
Hillsdale Free Will Baptist College PO Box 7208	Moore	OK	73153	800-460-6328	405-912-9000
Langston University 2017 Langston University PO Box 1500	Langston	OK	73050	877-466-2231	
Mid-America Christian University 3500 SW 119th St	Oklahoma City	OK	73170	888-888-2341	405-691-3800
Northeastern State University Muskogee 2400 W Shawnee	Muskogee	OK	74401	800-722-9614	918-683-0040
Tahlequah 600 N Grand Ave	Tahlequah	OK	74464	800-722-9614	918-456-5511
Oklahoma Baptist University 500 W University St	Shawnee	OK	74804	800-654-3285	405-275-2850
Oklahoma Christian University PO Box 11000	Oklahoma City	OK	73136	800-877-5010	
Oklahoma City University 2501 N Blackwelder Ave *Admissions	Oklahoma City	OK	73106	800-633-7242*	405-208-5050
Oklahoma Panhandle State University 323 Eagle Blvd	Goodwell	OK	73939	800-664-6778	580-349-2611
Oklahoma State University 219 Student Union Bldg	Stillwater	OK	74078	800-852-1255	405-744-5000
Oral Roberts University 7777 S Lewis Ave	Tulsa	OK	74171	800-678-8876	918-495-6161
Rogers State University 1701 W Will Rogers Blvd	Claremore	OK	74017	800-256-7511	918-343-7546
Saint Gregory's University 1900 W MacArthur St	Shawnee	OK	74804	888-784-7347*	405-878-5100
Southeastern Oklahoma State University 1405 N Fourth St	Durant	OK	74701	800-435-1327	580-745-2000
Southern Nazarene University 6729 NW 39th Expy	Bethany	OK	73008	800-648-9899	405-789-6400
Southwestern Christian University 7210 NW 39th Expy PO Box 340	Bethany	OK	73008	888-418-9272	405-789-7661
University of Oklahoma 1000 Asp Ave	Norman	OK	73019	800-234-6868	405-325-0311
University of Sciences & Arts of Oklahoma 1727 W Alabama Ave	Chickasha	OK	73018	800-933-8726	405-224-3140

				Toll-Free	Phone
University of Tulsa 800 S Tucker Rd	Tulsa	OK	74104	800-331-3050	918-631-2307

Oregon

				Toll-Free	Phone
Concordia University Portland 2811 NE Holman St	Portland	OR	97211	800-321-9371	503-288-9371
Eastern Oregon University 1 University Blvd	La Grande	OR	97850	800-452-8639	541-962-3393
George Fox University 414 N Meridian St	Newberg	OR	97132	800-765-4369	503-538-8383
Lewis & Clark College 0615 SW Palatine Hill Rd *Admissions	Portland	OR	97219	800-444-4111*	503-768-7040
Linfield College 900 SE Baker St *Admissions	McMinnville	OR	97128	800-640-2287*	503-883-2213
Marylhurst University 17600 Pacific Hwy 43 PO Box 261	Marylhurst	OR	97036	800-634-9982	503-636-8141
Northwest Christian College 828 E 11th Ave	Eugene	OR	97401	877-463-6622	541-343-1641
Oregon College of Art & Craft 8245 SW Barnes Rd	Portland	OR	97225	800-390-0632	503-297-5544
Oregon Institute of Technology 3201 Campus Dr	Klamath Falls	OR	97601	800-422-2017	541-885-1000
Oregon State University 104 Kerr Admin Bldg	Corvallis	OR	97331	800-291-4192	541-737-4411
Pacific Northwest College of Art 511 NW Broadway	Portland	OR	97209	888-390-7499	503-226-4391
Pacific University 2043 College Way *Admissions	Forest Grove	OR	97116	800-677-6712*	503-352-2007
Portland State University 1825 SW Broadway PO Box 751	Portland	OR	97201	800-547-8887	503-725-3000
Reed College 3203 SE Woodstock Blvd *Admissions	Portland	OR	97202	800-547-4750*	503-777-7511
Southern Oregon University 1250 Siskiyou Blvd Britt Hall	Ashland	OR	97520	800-482-7672	541-552-6411
University of Oregon 1585 E 13th Ave *Admissions	Eugene	OR	97403	800-232-3825*	541-346-1000
University of Portland 5000 N Willamette Blvd	Portland	OR	97203	888-627-5601	503-943-7147
Warner Pacific College 2219 SE 68th Ave	Portland	OR	97215	800-804-1510	503-517-1020
Western Oregon University 345 Monmouth Ave N *Admissions	Monmouth	OR	97361	877-877-1593*	503-838-8000
Willamette University 900 State St	Salem	OR	97301	877-542-2787	503-370-6303

Pennsylvania

				Toll-Free	Phone
Albright College 1621 N 13th St	Reading	PA	19604	800-252-1856	610-921-2381
Allegheny College 520 N Main St	Meadville	PA	16335	800-521-5293	814-332-4351
Alvernia College 540 Upland Ave	Reading	PA	19611	888-258-3764	610-796-8200
Arcadia University 450 S Easton Rd	Glenside	PA	19038	877-272-2342	215-572-2900
Automotive Training Center-Exton Campus 114 Pickering Way	Exton	PA	19341	888-321-8992	
Bloomsburg University 400 E Second St	Bloomsburg	PA	17815	888-651-6117	570-389-3900
Cabrini College 610 King of Prussia Rd	Radnor	PA	19087	800-848-1003	610-902-8552
California University of Pennsylvania 250 University Ave	California	PA	15419	888-412-0479	724-938-4000
Carlow University 3333 Fifth Ave	Pittsburgh	PA	15213	800-333-2275	412-578-6000
Carnegie Mellon University 5000 Forbes Ave	Pittsburgh	PA	15213	844-625-4600	412-268-2000
Cedar Crest College 100 College Dr *Admissions	Allentown	PA	18104	800-360-1222*	610-437-4471
Chatham University 1 Woodland Rd	Pittsburgh	PA	15232	800-837-1290	412-365-1100
Chestnut Hill College 9601 Germantown Ave	Philadelphia	PA	19118	800-248-0052	215-248-7001
Cheyney University of Pennsylvania 1837 University Cir PO Box 200	Cheyney	PA	19319	800-243-9639	610-399-2275
Clarion University of Pennsylvania 840 Wood St	Clarion	PA	16214	800-672-7171	814-393-2306
Venango 1801 W First St	Oil City	PA	16301	800-672-7171	814-676-6591
Curtis Institute of Music 1726 Locust St	Philadelphia	PA	19103	800-640-4155	215-893-5252
Delaware Valley College 700 E Butler Ave	Doylestown	PA	18901	800-233-5825	215-489-2211
Dickinson College PO Box 1773	Carlisle	PA	17013	800-644-1773	717-243-5121
Drexel University 3141 Chestnut St *Admissions	Philadelphia	PA	19104	866-358-1010*	215-895-2000
Duquesne University 600 Forbes Ave	Pittsburgh	PA	15282	800-456-0590	412-396-6000
East Stroudsburg University 200 Prospect St	East Stroudsburg	PA	18301	877-230-5547*	570-422-3542
Eastern University 1300 Eagle Rd	Wayne	PA	19087	800-452-0996*	610-341-5800
Edinboro University of Pennsylvania 200 E Normal St	Edinboro	PA	16444	888-846-2676	814-732-2761

			Toll-Free	Phone
Franklin & Marshall College				
PO Box 3003	Lancaster PA	17604	**877-678-9111**	717-291-3951
Gannon University				
109 University Sq	Erie PA	16541	**800-426-6668***	814-871-7000
*Admissions				
Geneva College				
3200 College Ave	Beaver Falls PA	15010	**800-847-8255**	724-847-6500
Gettysburg College				
300 N Washington St	Gettysburg PA	17325	**800-431-0803**	717-337-6000
Gratz College				
7605 Old York Rd	Melrose Park PA	19027	**800-475-4635**	215-635-7300
Great Lakes Institute of Technology Toni & Guy Hair				
5100 Peach St	Erie PA	16509	**800-394-4548**	814-864-6666
Gwynedd-Mercy College				
1325 Sunneytown Pk PO Box 901	Gwynedd Valley PA	19437	**800-342-5462***	215-646-7300
*Admissions				
Holy Family University				
9801 Frankford Ave	Philadelphia PA	19114	**800-422-0010**	215-637-7700
Indiana University of Pennsylvania				
1011 South Dr	Indiana PA	15705	**800-442-6830**	724-357-2100
Juniata College				
1700 Moore St	Huntingdon PA	16652	**877-586-4282**	814-641-3000
Keystone College				
1 College Green	La Plume PA	18440	**800-824-2764**	570-945-5141
King's College				
133 N River St	Wilkes-Barre PA	18711	**800-955-5777**	570-208-5858
Kutztown University				
15200 Kutztown Rd	Kutztown PA	19530	**877-628-1915**	610-683-4000
La Roche College				
9000 Babcock Blvd	Pittsburgh PA	15237	**800-838-4572***	412-367-9300
*Admissions				
La Salle University				
1900 W Olney Ave	Philadelphia PA	19141	**800-328-1910**	215-951-1500
Lebanon Valley College				
101 N College Ave	Annville PA	17003	**866-582-4236**	717-867-6181
Lincoln University				
1570 Old Baltimore Pk				
PO Box 179	Lincoln University PA	19352	**800-790-0191***	484-365-8000
*Admissions				
Lycoming College				
700 College Pl	Williamsport PA	17701	**800-345-3920**	570-321-4000
Mansfield University				
Alumni Hall	Mansfield PA	16933	**800-577-6826***	570-662-4000
*Admissions				
Mercyhurst College				
501 E 38th St	Erie PA	16546	**800-825-1926**	814-824-2202
Messiah College				
PO Box 3005	Grantham PA	17027	**800-233-4220**	717-691-6000
Millersville University of Pennsylvania				
PO Box 1002	Millersville PA	17551	**800-682-3648**	717-872-3011
Misericordia University				
301 Lake St	Dallas PA	18612	**866-262-6363**	570-674-6400
Moravian College				
1200 Main St	Bethlehem PA	18018	**800-441-3191**	610-861-1300
Mount Aloysius College				
7373 Admiral Perry Hwy	Cresson PA	16630	**888-823-2220**	814-886-6383
Neumann College 1 Neumann Dr	Aston PA	19014	**800-963-8626**	610-459-0905
Peirce College				
1420 Pine St	Philadelphia PA	19102	**888-467-3472**	215-545-6400
Pennsylvania State University				
201 Shields Bldg	University Park PA	16802	**800-279-8495**	814-865-4700
Altoona 3000 Ivyside Pk	Altoona PA	16601	**800-848-9843**	814-949-5466
Harrisburg				
777 W Harrisburg Pk	Middletown PA	17057	**800-222-2056**	717-948-6000
Pennsylvania State University at Erie				
Behrend College				
4701 College Dr	Erie PA	16563	**866-374-3378**	814-898-6000
Philadelphia University				
4201 Henry Ave	Philadelphia PA	19144	**800-951-7287***	215-951-2800
Point Park University				
201 Wood St	Pittsburgh PA	15222	**800-321-0129***	412-391-4100
*Admissions				
Robert Morris University				
6001 University Blvd	Moon Township PA	15108	**800-762-0097**	
Rosemont College				
1400 Montgomery Ave	Rosemont PA	19010	**888-521-0983***	610-527-0200
*Admissions				
Saint Joseph's University				
5600 City Ave	Philadelphia PA	19131	**888-232-4295**	610-660-1000
Saint Vincent College				
300 Fraser Purchase Rd	Latrobe PA	15650	**800-782-5549**	724-532-6600
Seton Hill University				
1 Seton Hill Dr	Greensburg PA	15601	**800-826-6234**	724-838-4255
Shippensburg University				
1871 Old Main Dr	Shippensburg PA	17257	**800-822-8028**	717-477-1231
Slippery Rock University				
1 Morrow Way	Slippery Rock PA	16057	**800-929-4778**	724-738-9000
Susquehanna University				
514 University Ave	Selinsgrove PA	17870	**800-326-9672**	570-374-0101
Swarthmore College				
500 College Ave	Swarthmore PA	19081	**800-667-3110***	610-328-8300
*Admissions				
Thiel College				
75 College Ave	Greenville PA	16125	**800-248-4435**	724-589-2000
Thomas Jefferson University				
1020 Walnut St	Philadelphia PA	19107	**800-533-3669**	215-955-6000
University of Pennsylvania				
3451 Walnut St	Philadelphia PA	19104	**800-537-5487**	215-898-5000
University of Pittsburgh				
4227 Fifth Ave	Pittsburgh PA	15260	**877-999-3223**	412-624-4141
Bradford 300 Campus Dr	Bradford PA	16701	**800-872-1787**	814-362-7555
Greensburg 150 Finoli Dr	Greensburg PA	15601	**888-843-4563**	724-837-7040
Johnstown				
157 Blackington Hall	Johnstown PA	15904	**800-765-4875**	814-269-7050
University of Scranton				
800 Linden St St Thomas Hall	Scranton PA	18510	**888-727-2686**	570-941-7400
University of the Sciences in Philadelphia				
600 S 43rd St	Philadelphia PA	19104	**888-857-6264**	215-596-8800

			Toll-Free	Phone
Ursinus College				
601 E Main St PO Box 1000	Collegeville PA	19426	**877-448-3282**	610-409-3200
Valley Forge Christian College				
1401 Charlestown Rd	Phoenixville PA	19460	**800-432-8322**	610-935-0450
Washington & Jefferson College				
60 S Lincoln St	Washington PA	15301	**888-926-3529**	724-222-4400
Waynesburg College				
51 W College St	Waynesburg PA	15370	**800-225-7393***	724-627-8191
West Chester University				
700 S High St	West Chester PA	19383	**877-315-2165**	610-436-1000
Westminster College				
319 S Market St	New Wilmington PA	16172	**800-942-8033**	724-946-8761
Widener University				
1 University Pl	Chester PA	19013	**888-943-3637***	610-499-4000
*Admissions				
Wilkes University				
84 West South St	Wilkes-Barre PA	18766	**800-945-5378**	
Wilson College				
1015 Philadelphia Ave	Chambersburg PA	17201	**800-421-8402***	717-264-4141
*Admissions				

Rhode Island

			Toll-Free	Phone
Bryant University				
1150 Douglas Pk	Smithfield RI	02917	**800-622-7001***	401-232-6000
Johnson & Wales University				
Providence				
8 Abbott Pk Pl	Providence RI	02903	**800-342-5598**	401-598-1000
Providence College				
1 Cunningham Sq	Providence RI	02918	**800-721-6444***	401-865-1000
*Admissions				
Rhode Island College				
600 Mt Pleasant Ave	Providence RI	02908	**800-669-5760**	401-456-8000
Roger Williams University				
1 Old Ferry Rd	Bristol RI	02809	**800-458-7144**	401-254-3500

South Carolina

			Toll-Free	Phone
Allen University				
1530 Harden St	Columbia SC	29204	**877-625-5368**	803-376-5700
Benedict College				
1600 Harden St	Columbia SC	29204	**800-868-6598**	803-253-5000
Bob Jones University				
1700 Wade Hampton Blvd	Greenville SC	29614	**800-252-6363***	864-242-5100
Charleston Southern University				
9200 University Blvd	Charleston SC	29423	**800-947-7474**	843-863-7050
Citadel, The				
171 Moultrie St	Charleston SC	29409	**800-868-1842**	843-953-5230
Claflin University				
400 Magnolia St	Orangeburg SC	29115	**800-922-1276**	803-535-5000
Clemson University				
105 Sikes Hall	Clemson SC	29634	**800-640-2657**	864-656-3311
Coastal Carolina University				
PO Box 261954	Conway SC	29528	**800-277-7000**	843-349-2170
Coker College				
300 E College Ave	Hartsville SC	29550	**800-950-1908**	843-383-8000
Columbia College				
1301 Columbia College Dr	Columbia SC	29203	**800-277-1301**	
Converse College				
580 E Main St	Spartanburg SC	29302	**800-766-1125***	864-596-9000
*Admissions				
Erskine College				
2 Washington St	Due West SC	29639	**888-359-4358***	
*Admissions				
Francis Marion University				
PO Box 100547	Florence SC	29501	**800-368-7551**	843-661-1231
Lander University				
320 Stanley Ave	Greenwood SC	29649	**800-922-1117***	864-388-8307
*Admissions				
Limestone College				
1115 College Dr	Gaffney SC	29340	**800-795-7151**	864-489-7151
Morris College				
100 W College St	Sumter SC	29150	**866-853-1345***	803-934-3200
*Admissions				
Newberry College				
2100 College St	Newberry SC	29108	**800-845-4955**	803-276-5010
Presbyterian College				
503 S Broad St	Clinton SC	29325	**800-476-7272**	
South Carolina State University				
300 College St NE	Orangeburg SC	29117	**800-260-5956***	803-536-7000
South University Columbia				
9 Science Ct	Columbia SC	29203	**800-688-0932**	803-799-9082
Southern Wesleyan University				
907 Wesleyan Dr	Central SC	29630	**800-282-8798**	864-644-5000
University of South Carolina				
1601 Greene St	Columbia SC	29208	**800-868-5872**	803-777-7000
Aiken 471 University Pkwy	Aiken SC	29801	**866-254-2366**	803-648-6851
Beaufort 801 Carteret St	Beaufort SC	29902	**866-455-4753**	843-521-4100
Sumter 200 Miller Rd	Sumter SC	29150	**888-872-7868**	803-775-8727
Upstate				
800 University Way	Spartanburg SC	29303	**800-277-8727**	864-503-5246
Voorhees College				
213 Wiggins Dr PO Box 678	Denmark SC	29042	**866-685-9904**	803-780-1234

South Dakota

			Toll-Free	Phone
Augustana College				
2001 S Summit Ave	Sioux Falls SD	57197	**800-727-2844**	605-274-0770
Black Hills State University				
1200 University St Unit 9502	Spearfish SD	57799	**800-255-2478**	605-642-6343

				Toll-Free	Phone
Dakota State University 820 N Washington Ave	Madison	SD	57042	**888-378-9988**	605-256-5139
Dakota Wesleyan University 1200 W University Ave	Mitchell	SD	57301	**800-333-8506**	605-995-2600
Mount Marty College 1105 W Eigth St	Yankton	SD	57078	**800-658-4552***	605-668-1545
*Admissions					
National American University 5301 Mt Rushmore Rd	Rapid City	SD	57701	**800-843-8892**	605-394-4800
Sioux Falls 5801 S corporate Pl	Sioux Falls	SD	57108	**800-388-5430**	605-336-4600
Northern State University 1200 S Jay St	Aberdeen	SD	57401	**800-678-5330**	
Presentation College 1500 N Main St	Aberdeen	SD	57401	**800-437-6060**	605-225-1634
South Dakota School of Mines & Technology 501 E St Joseph St	Rapid City	SD	57701	**800-544-8162**	605-394-2414
South Dakota State University PO Box 2201	Brookings	SD	57007	**800-952-3541**	605-688-4121
University of Sioux Falls 1101 W 22nd St	Sioux Falls	SD	57105	**800-888-1047**	605-331-6600
University of South Dakota 414 E Clark St	Vermillion	SD	57069	**877-269-6837**	605-677-5341

Tennessee

				Toll-Free	Phone
Aquinas College 4210 HaRding Rd	Nashville	TN	37205	**800-649-9956***	615-297-7545
*Admissions					
Austin Peay State University 601 College St	Clarksville	TN	37044	**800-844-2778***	931-221-7661
*Admissions					
Belmont University 1900 Belmont Blvd	Nashville	TN	37212	**800-563-6765**	615-460-6000
Bryan College 140 Landes Way	Dayton	TN	37321	**800-277-9522**	423-775-2041
Carson-Newman College 1646 Russell Ave	Jefferson City	TN	37760	**800-678-9061**	865-471-2000
Christian Bros University 650 E Pkwy S	Memphis	TN	38104	**800-288-7576***	901-321-3000
*Admissions					
Cumberland University 1 Cumberland Sq	Lebanon	TN	37087	**800-467-0562**	615-444-2562
East Tennessee State University PO Box 70731	Johnson City	TN	37614	**800-462-3878**	423-439-4213
Fisk University 1000 17th Ave N	Nashville	TN	37208	**888-702-0022**	615-329-8500
Freed-Hardeman University 158 E Main St	Henderson	TN	38340	**800-348-3481**	731-989-6651
King College 1350 King College Rd	Bristol	TN	37620	**800-362-0014***	423-652-4861
*Admissions					
Lane College 545 Ln Ave	Jackson	TN	38301	**800-960-7533***	731-426-7500
*Admissions					
Lee University 1120 N Ocoee St	Cleveland	TN	37311	**800-533-9930**	423-614-8000
Lincoln Memorial University 6965 Cumberland Gap Pkwy	Harrogate	TN	37752	**800-325-0900**	423-869-3611
Lipscomb University 3901 Granny White Pk	Nashville	TN	37204	**800-333-4358**	615-966-1000
Martin Methodist College 433 W Madison St	Pulaski	TN	38478	**800-467-1273**	931-363-9804
Maryville College 502 E Lamar Alexander Pkwy	Maryville	TN	37804	**800-597-2687**	865-981-8000
Middle Tennessee State University 1301 E Main St	Murfreesboro	TN	37132	**800-533-6878***	615-898-2300
*Admissions					
Milligan College 130 Richardson Rd	Milligan College	TN	37682	**800-262-8337**	423-461-8730
Nossi College of Art 590 Cheron Rd	Madison	TN	37115	**888-986-2787**	615-514-2787
Oxford Graduate School Inc 500 Oxford Dr	Dayton	TN	37321	**800-933-6188**	423-775-6596
Rhodes College 2000 N Pkwy	Memphis	TN	38112	**800-844-5969**	901-843-3700
Southern Adventist University 4881 Taylor Cir	Collegedale	TN	37315	**800-768-8437**	423-236-2000
Tennessee State University 3500 John A Merritt Blvd PO Box 9609	Nashville	TN	37209	**888-463-6878***	615-963-5000
*Admissions					
Tennessee Technological University 1 William L Jones Dr	Cookeville	TN	38505	**800-255-8881**	931-372-3888
Tennessee Temple University 1815 Union Ave	Chattanooga	TN	37404	**800-553-4050**	423-493-4100
Tennessee Wesleyan College 204 E College St	Athens	TN	37303	**844-742-5898**	423-745-7504
Trevecca Nazarene University 333 Murfreesboro Rd	Nashville	TN	37210	**888-210-4868**	615-248-1200
Tusculum College 60 Shiloh Rd	Greeneville	TN	37743	**800-729-0256**	423-636-7300
Union University 1050 Union University Dr	Jackson	TN	38305	**800-338-6466**	731-661-5210
University of Tennessee					
Chattanooga 615 McCallie Ave	Chattanooga	TN	37403	**800-882-6627**	423-425-4111
Martin 554 University St	Martin	TN	38238	**800-829-8861**	731-881-7020
University of the South 735 University Ave	Sewanee	TN	37383	**800-522-2234**	931-598-1238
Vanderbilt University 2201 W End Ave	Nashville	TN	37240	**800-288-0432**	615-322-7311

Texas

				Toll-Free	Phone
Angelo State University 2601 W Ave N ASU Stn 11014	San Angelo	TX	76909	**800-946-8627**	325-942-2041
Arlington Baptist College 3001 W Div St	Arlington	TX	76012	**800-899-0012**	817-461-8741
Austin College 900 N Grand Ave	Sherman	TX	75090	**800-526-4276**	903-813-3000
Austin Graduate School of Theology 7640 Guadalupe St	Austin	TX	78752	**866-287-4723**	512-476-2772
Baylor University 1301 S University Parks Dr	Waco	TX	76798	**800-229-5678**	
Concordia University Texas 11400 Concordia University Dr	Austin	TX	78726	**800-865-4282**	512-313-3000
Criswell College 4010 Gaston Ave	Dallas	TX	75246	**800-899-0012**	214-821-5433
Dallas Baptist University 3000 Mtn Creek Pkwy	Dallas	TX	75211	**800-460-1328**	214-333-7100
East Texas Baptist University 1209 N Grove St	Marshall	TX	75670	**800-804-3828**	903-935-7963
Hardin-Simmons University 2200 Hickory St	Abilene	TX	79698	**877-464-7889**	325-670-1206
Houston Baptist University 7502 Fondren Rd	Houston	TX	77074	**800-969-3210***	281-649-3000
*Admissions					
Howard Payne University 1000 Fisk St	Brownwood	TX	76801	**800-950-8465**	325-646-2502
Huston-Tillotson University 900 Chicon St	Austin	TX	78702	**800-343-3822**	512-505-3000
LeTourneau University 2100 S Mobberly Ave	Longview	TX	75602	**800-759-8811**	903-233-3000
Lubbock Christian University 5601 19th St	Lubbock	TX	79407	**800-933-7601**	806-720-7151
McMurry University 1400 Sayles Blvd	Abilene	TX	79697	**800-460-2392**	325-793-3800
Midwestern State University 3410 Taft Blvd	Wichita Falls	TX	76308	**800-842-1922***	940-397-4000
*Admissions					
Northwood University *Texas* 1114 W FM 1382	Cedar Hill	TX	75104	**800-927-9663**	800-622-9000
Our Lady of the Lake University 411 SW 24th St	San Antonio	TX	78207	**800-436-6558**	210-434-6711
Prairie View A & M University 700 University Dr PO Box 519	Prairie View	TX	77446	**877-241-1752**	936-261-3311
Rice University 6100 Main St	Houston	TX	77005	**866-294-4633**	713-348-0000
Saint Mary's University 1 Camino Santa Maria	San Antonio	TX	78228	**800-367-7868***	210-436-3126
*Admissions					
Sam Houston State University 1903 University Ave	Huntsville	TX	77340	**866-232-7528**	936-294-1111
Schreiner University 2100 Memorial Blvd	Kerrville	TX	78028	**800-343-4919**	830-792-7217
Southern Methodist University 6425 Boaz Ln	Dallas	TX	75205	**800-323-0672**	214-768-2000
Southwestern Adventist University 100 W Hillcrest Dr	Keene	TX	76059	**800-433-2240***	817-645-3921
*Admissions					
Southwestern Assemblies of God University 1200 Sycamore St	Waxahachie	TX	75165	**888-937-7248**	972-937-4010
Southwestern Christian College PO Box 10	Terrell	TX	75160	**800-925-9357**	972-524-3341
Southwestern University PO Box 770	Georgetown	TX	78627	**800-252-3166**	512-863-1200
Stephen F Austin State University 1936 N St PO Box 13051	Nacogdoches	TX	75962	**800-257-9558**	936-468-2504
Sul Ross State University E Hwy 90	Alpine	TX	79832	**888-722-7778**	432-837-8011
Tarleton State University PO Box T-0030	Stephenville	TX	76402	**800-687-8236**	254-968-9125
Texas A & M University Rudder Tower Ste 205	College Station	TX	77843	**888-890-5667**	979-845-8901
Galveston 200 Seawolf Pkwy	Galveston	TX	77554	**877-322-4443**	409-740-4428
Kingsville 700 University Blvd MSC 128	Kingsville	TX	78363	**800-726-8192**	361-593-2111
Texarkana 7101 University Ave	Texarkana	TX	75503	**866-791-9120**	903-223-3000
Texas Christian University TCU PO Box 297043	Fort Worth	TX	76129	**800-828-3764**	817-257-7490
Texas College 2404 N Grand Ave	Tyler	TX	75702	**800-306-6299**	903-593-8311
Texas Lutheran University 1000 W Ct St	Seguin	TX	78155	**800-771-8521**	830-372-8050
Texas State University *San Marcos* 601 University Dr	San Marcos	TX	78666	**866-294-0987***	512-245-2340
*Admissions					
Texas Tech University PO Box 45005	Lubbock	TX	79409	**888-270-3369**	806-742-1480
Texas Wesleyan University 1201 Wesleyan St	Fort Worth	TX	76105	**800-580-8980**	817-531-4444
Texas Woman's University 304 Admin Dr PO Box 425589	Denton	TX	76204	**866-809-6130**	940-898-3188
Trinity University 1 Trinity Pl	San Antonio	TX	78212	**800-874-6489**	210-999-7011
University of Dallas 1845 E Northgate Dr	Irving	TX	75062	**800-628-6999***	972-721-5266
*Admissions					
University of Houston *Victoria* 3007 N Ben Wilson St	Victoria	TX	77901	**877-970-4848**	361-570-4848
University of Mary Hardin-Baylor 900 College St	Belton	TX	76513	**800-727-8642**	254-295-8642
University of North Texas PO Box 311277	Denton	TX	76203	**800-868-8211**	940-565-2681
University of Saint Thomas 3800 Montrose Blvd	Houston	TX	77006	**800-856-8565**	713-522-7911
University of Texas					
Dallas International Ctr 800 W Campbell Rd SSB34	Richardson	TX	75080	**800-889-2443**	972-883-4189
Permian Basin 4901 E University Blvd	Odessa	TX	79762	**866-552-8872***	432-552-2020
*Admissions					

				Toll-Free	Phone
San Antonio					
6900 N Loop 1604 W	San Antonio	TX	78249	**800-669-0919**	210-458-4011
Tyler 3900 University Blvd	Tyler	TX	75799	**800-888-9537**	903-566-7000
University of the Incarnate Word					
4301 Broadway St Ste 285	San Antonio	TX	78209	**800-749-9673***	210-829-6000
*Admissions					
Wayland Baptist University					
1900 W Seventh St	Plainview	TX	79072	**800-588-1928**	806-291-1000
West Texas A & M University					
2501 Fourth Ave	Canyon	TX	79016	**877-656-2065**	806-651-2020
Wiley College					
711 Wiley Ave	Marshall	TX	75670	**800-658-6889***	903-927-3300
*Admissions					

Utah

				Toll-Free	Phone
Dixie State University					
225 S 700 E	Saint George	UT	84770	**855-628-8140**	435-652-7500
Utah State University					
1600 Old Main Hill	Logan	UT	84322	**800-488-8108**	435-797-1000
Weber State University					
3848 Harrison Blvd	Ogden	UT	84408	**800-848-7770**	801-626-6000
Davis					
2750 University Park Blvd	Layton	UT	84041	**800-848-7770**	801-395-3555
Westminster College					
1840 South 1300 East	Salt Lake City	UT	84105	**800-748-4753**	801-832-2200

Vermont

				Toll-Free	Phone
Bennington College					
1 College Dr	Bennington	VT	05201	**800-833-6845**	802-440-4325
Castleton State College					
86 Seminary St	Castleton	VT	05735	**800-639-8521**	802-468-5611
Champlain College					
163 S Willard St	Burlington	VT	05401	**800-570-5858**	802-860-2700
College of Saint Joseph in Vermont					
71 Clement Rd	Rutland	VT	05701	**877-270-9998***	802-773-5900
*Admissions					
Goddard College					
123 Pitkin Rd	Plainfield	VT	05667	**800-468-4888**	802-454-8311
Green Mountain College					
1 Brennan Cir	Poultney	VT	05764	**800-776-6675***	802-287-8000
*Admissions					
Johnson State College					
337 College Hill	Johnson	VT	05656	**800-635-2356**	802-635-2356
Lyndon State College					
1001 College Rd PO Box 919	Lyndonville	VT	05851	**800-225-1998**	802-626-6413
Marlboro College					
2582 S Rd PO Box A	Marlboro	VT	05344	**800-343-0049**	802-257-4333
Marlboro College Graduate Ctr					
PO Box A	Marlboro	VT	05344	**800-343-0049**	802-258-9200
Middlebury College					
131 S Main St	Middlebury	VT	05753	**877-214-3330**	802-443-3000
Norwich University					
158 Harmon Dr	Northfield	VT	05663	**800-468-6679**	802-485-2001
Saint Michael's College					
1 Winooski Pk	Colchester	VT	05439	**800-762-8000**	802-654-2000
Southern Vermont College					
982 Mansion Dr	Bennington	VT	05201	**800-378-2782**	802-442-5427
University of Vermont					
85 S Prospect St	Burlington	VT	05405	**800-499-0113**	802-656-3131

Virginia

				Toll-Free	Phone
Bluefield College					
3000 College Ave	Bluefield	VA	24605	**800-872-0175**	276-326-3682
Bridgewater College					
402 E College St	Bridgewater	VA	22812	**800-759-8328**	540-828-5375
Christendom College					
134 Christendom Dr	Front Royal	VA	22630	**800-877-5456**	540-636-2900
Christopher Newport University					
1 University Pl	Newport News	VA	23606	**800-333-4268***	757-594-7015
*Admissions					
Eastern Mennonite University					
1200 Pk Rd	Harrisonburg	VA	22802	**800-368-2665***	540-432-4118
*Admissions					
Emory & Henry College					
PO Box 10	Emory	VA	24327	**800-848-5493***	276-944-4121
*Admissions					
Ferrum College					
215 Ferrum Mtn Rd	Ferrum	VA	24088	**800-868-9797**	540-365-2121
George Mason University					
4400 University Dr	Fairfax	VA	22030	**888-627-6612**	703-993-1000
Hampden-Sydney College					
PO Box 667	Hampden Sydney	VA	23943	**800-755-0733***	434-223-6120
*Admissions					
Hampton University					
100 E Queen St	Hampton	VA	23668	**800-624-3341**	757-727-5000
Hollins University					
7916 Williamson Rd	Roanoke	VA	24020	**800-456-9595***	540-362-6401
*Admissions					
Liberty University					
1971 University Blvd	Lynchburg	VA	24502	**800-543-5317**	434-582-2000
Longwood University					
201 High St	Farmville	VA	23909	**800-281-4677**	434-395-2060
Lynchburg College					
1501 Lakeside Dr	Lynchburg	VA	24501	**800-426-8101**	434-544-8100
Mary Baldwin College					
318 Prospect St	Staunton	VA	24401	**800-468-2262***	540-887-7019
*Admissions					
Marymount University					
2807 N Glebe Rd	Arlington	VA	22207	**800-548-7638**	703-522-5600
Norfolk State University					
700 Park Ave	Norfolk	VA	23504	**800-274-1821**	757-823-8600
Old Dominion University					
Rollins Hall	Norfolk	VA	23529	**800-348-7926**	757-683-3685
Radford University					
801 E Main St	Radford	VA	24142	**800-890-4265***	540-831-5371
*Admissions					
Randolph College					
2500 Rivermont Ave	Lynchburg	VA	24503	**800-745-7692***	434-947-8000
*Admissions					
Randolph-Macon College					
PO Box 5005	Ashland	VA	23005	**800-888-1762**	804-752-7200
Roanoke College					
221 College Ln	Salem	VA	24153	**800-388-2276***	540-375-2270
*Admissions					
Shenandoah University					
1460 University Dr	Winchester	VA	22601	**800-432-2266**	540-665-4581
Southern Virginia University					
1 University Hill Dr	Buena Vista	VA	24416	**800-229-8420**	540-261-8400
Strayer University Alexandria					
2730 Eisenhower Ave	Alexandria	VA	22314	**888-311-0355**	
Strayer University Arlington					
2121 15th St N	Arlington	VA	22201	**888-478-7293**	703-892-5100
Strayer University Fredericksburg					
150 Riverside Pkwy Ste 100	Fredericksburg	VA	22406	**888-311-0355**	540-374-4300
Sweet Briar College					
134 Chappel Rd	Sweet Briar	VA	24595	**800-381-6142***	434-381-6100
*Admissions					
University of Mary Washington					
1301 College Ave	Fredericksburg	VA	22401	**800-468-5614***	540-654-2000
*Admissions					
University of Richmond					
28 Westhampton Way	Richmond	VA	23173	**800-700-1662**	804-289-8000
Westhampton College					
28 Westhampton Way	University Of Richmond	VA	23173	**800-700-1662**	804-289-8000
University of Virginia's College at Wise					
1 College Ave	Wise	VA	24293	**888-282-9324***	276-328-0102
*Admissions					
Virginia Commonwealth University					
910 W Franklin St	Richmond	VA	23284	**800-841-3638**	804-828-0100
Virginia Military Institute					
319 Letcher Ave	Lexington	VA	24450	**800-767-4207**	540-464-7211
Virginia State University					
1 Hayden Dr	Petersburg	VA	23806	**800-871-7611***	804-524-5000
*Admissions					
Virginia Union University					
1500 N Lombardy St	Richmond	VA	23220	**800-368-3227**	804-342-3570
Virginia Wesleyan College					
1584 Wesleyan Dr	Norfolk	VA	23502	**800-737-8684**	757-455-3200
Washington & Lee University					
204 W Washington St	Lexington	VA	24450	**800-221-3943**	540-458-8710

Washington

				Toll-Free	Phone
Central Washington University					
400 E University Way	Ellensburg	WA	98926	**866-298-4968***	509-963-1111
*Admissions					
City University					
521 Wall St Ste100	Seattle	WA	98121	**800-426-5596***	888-422-4898
*Admissions					
Digipen Institute of Technology					
9931 Willows Rd NE	Redmond	WA	98052	**866-478-5236**	425-558-0299
Eastern Washington University					
102 Sutton Hall	Cheney	WA	99004	**800-280-1256**	509-359-6200
Evergreen State College, The					
2700 Evergreen Pkwy	Olympia	WA	98505	**888-492-9480**	360-867-6000
Gonzaga University					
502 E Boone Ave	Spokane	WA	99258	**800-986-9585**	509-313-6572
Heritage University					
3240 Ft Rd	Toppenish	WA	98948	**888-272-6190**	509-865-8500
Northwest University					
5520 108th Ave NE	Kirkland	WA	98033	**800-669-3781***	425-822-8266
*Admissions					
Pacific Lutheran University					
1010 122nd St S	Tacoma	WA	98444	**800-274-6758**	253-531-6900
Saint Martin's University					
5300 Pacific Ave SE	Lacey	WA	98503	**800-368-8803***	360-438-4311
*Admissions					
Seattle Pacific University					
3307 Third Ave W	Seattle	WA	98119	**800-366-3344**	206-281-2000
Seattle University					
901 12th Ave	Seattle	WA	98122	**800-426-7123**	206-296-6000
University of Puget Sound					
1500 N Warner St	Tacoma	WA	98416	**800-396-7191**	253-879-3100
Walla Walla University					
204 S College Ave	College Place	WA	99324	**800-541-8900**	509-527-2327
Washington State University					
PO Box 641040	Pullman	WA	99164	**888-468-6978**	509-335-3564
Spokane					
310 N Riverpoint Blvd PO Box 1495	Spokane	WA	99210	**866-766-0767**	509-358-7978
Western Washington University					
516 High St	Bellingham	WA	98225	**800-261-7331**	360-650-3000
Whitman College					
345 Boyer Ave	Walla Walla	WA	99362	**877-462-9448***	509-527-5111
*Admissions					
Whitworth College					
300 W Hawthorne Rd	Spokane	WA	99251	**800-533-4668***	509-777-1000
*Admissions					

West Virginia

				Toll-Free	Phone
Alderson-Broaddus College					
101 College Hill Rd	Philippi	WV	26416	**800-263-1549***	304-457-1700
*Admissions					
Bethany College					
31 E Campus Dr	Bethany	WV	26032	**800-922-7611**	304-829-7000
Bluefield State College					
219 Rock St	Bluefield	WV	24701	**800-654-7798**	304-327-4000

	Toll-Free	Phone

Concord University
PO Box 1000 .... Athens WV 24712 **800-344-6679** 304-384-3115
Davis & Elkins College
100 Campus Dr .... Elkins WV 26241 **800-624-3157** 304-637-1900
Fairmont State University
1201 Locust Ave .... Fairmont WV 26554 **800-641-5678*** 304-367-4892
*Admissions
Glenville State College
200 High St .... Glenville WV 26351 **800-924-2010*** 304-462-7361
*Admissions
Marshall University
1 John Marshall Dr .... Huntington WV 25755 **800-642-3463** 304-696-3170
Salem International University
223 West Main St .... Salem WV 26426 **800-283-4562** 304-326-1109
Shepherd University
301 N King St .... Shepherdstown WV 25443 **800-344-5231** 304-876-5000
University of Charleston
2300 MacCorkle Ave SE .... Charleston WV 25304 **800-995-4682*** 304-357-4800
*Admissions
West Virginia State University
117 Ferrell Hall PO Box 368.......... Institute WV 25112 **800-987-2112** 304-766-3000
West Virginia University
PO Box 6009 .... Morgantown WV 26506 **800-344-9881** 304-293-2121
Institute of Technology
405 Fayette Pk .... Montgomery WV 25136 **888-554-8324** 304-442-1000
West Virginia Wesleyan College
59 College Ave .... Buckhannon WV 26201 **800-722-9933*** 304-473-8000
*Admitting
Wheeling Jesuit University
316 Washington Ave .... Wheeling WV 26003 **800-624-6992** 304-243-2000

Wisconsin

	Toll-Free	Phone

Alverno College
PO Box 343922 .... Milwaukee WI 53234 **800-933-3401** 414-382-6100
Bellin College of Nursing
3201 Eaton Rd .... Green Bay WI 54311 **800-236-8707** 920-433-6699
Beloit College
700 College St .... Beloit WI 53511 **800-331-4943*** 608-363-2500
*Admissions
Cardinal Stritch University
6801 N Yates Rd .... Milwaukee WI 53217 **800-347-8822** 414-410-4000
Carroll University
100 NE Ave .... Waukesha WI 53186 **800-227-7655** 262-547-1211
Carthage College
2001 Alford Pk Dr .... Kenosha WI 53140 **800-351-4058*** 262-551-8500
*Admissions
Columbia College of Nursing (CCON)
4425 N Port Washington Rd .... Glendale WI 53212 **800-221-5573** 414-326-2330
Concordia University Wisconsin
12800 N Lake Shore Dr .... Mequon WI 53097 **888-628-9472*** 262-243-5700
*Admissions
Edgewood College
1000 Edgewood College Dr .... Madison WI 53711 **800-444-4861** 608-663-2294
Lakeland College
PO Box 359 .... Sheboygan WI 53082 **800-569-2166** 920-565-2111
Lawrence University
115 S Drew St .... Appleton WI 54911 **800-432-5427** 920-832-7000
Maranatha Baptist Bible College
745 W Main St .... Watertown WI 53094 **800-622-2947** 920-206-2330
Marian University
45 S National Ave .... Fond du Lac WI 54935 **800-262-7426**
Marquette University
1217 W Wisconsin Ave .... Milwaukee WI 53233 **800-222-6544*** 414-288-7302
*Admissions
Milwaukee Institute of Art & Design
273 E Erie St .... Milwaukee WI 53202 **888-749-6423** 414-276-7889
Milwaukee School of Engineering
1025 N Broadway .... Milwaukee WI 53202 **800-332-6763** 414-277-7300
Mount Mary College
2900 N Menomonee River Pkwy ..... Milwaukee WI 53222 **800-321-6265*** 414-256-1219
*Admissions
Northland College
1411 Ellis Ave .... Ashland WI 54806 **800-753-1840** 715-682-1224
Ripon College
300 Seward St PO Box 248.............. Ripon WI 54971 **800-947-4766***
*Admissions
Saint Norbert College
100 Grant St .... De Pere WI 54115 **800-236-4878*** 920-403-3005
*Admissions
Silver Lake College
2406 S Alverno Rd .... Manitowoc WI 54220 **800-236-4752** 920-686-6175
University of Wisconsin (UWEC)
Eau Claire
Schofield Hall 111 105 Garfield Ave
.... Eau Claire WI 54701 **800-949-8932** 715-836-5415
La Crosse 328 Front St .... La Crosse WI 54601 **800-382-2150** 608-785-8000
Madison
702 W Johnson St Ste 1101.......... Madison WI 53715 **800-442-6459** 608-262-3961
Milwaukee PO Box 413 .... Milwaukee WI 53201 **800-442-6459** 414-229-1122
Parkside 900 Wood Rd .... Kenosha WI 53141 **800-742-2858** 262-595-2345
Platteville
1 University Plz .... Platteville WI 53818 **800-362-5515** 608-342-1125
Stout 802 S Broadway .... Menomonie WI 54751 **800-447-8688*** 715-232-1232
*Admissions
Viterbo University
900 Viterbo Dr .... La Crosse WI 54601 **800-848-3726** 608-796-3000

Wyoming

	Toll-Free	Phone

University of Wyoming
1000 E University Ave .... Laramie WY 82071 **800-342-5996*** 307-766-1121
*Admissions

	Toll-Free	Phone

167	COLLEGES & UNIVERSITIES - GRADUATE & PROFESSIONAL SCHOOLS

	Toll-Free	Phone

Algoma University
1520 Queen St E .... Sault Sainte Marie ON P6A2G4 **888-254-6628** 705-949-2301
Cegep De Matane
616 Ave Holy Redeemer .... Matane QC G4W1L1 **800-463-4299** 418-562-1240

167-1 Law Schools

Law schools listed here are approved by the American Bar Association.

	Toll-Free	Phone

Albany Law School of Union University (ALS)
80 New Scotland Ave .... Albany NY 12208 **800-448-3500** 518-445-2311
Appalachian School of Law
1169 Edgewater Dr .... Grundy VA 24614 **800-895-7411** 276-935-4349
Sandra Day O'Connor College of Law
PO Box 877906 .... Tempe AZ 85287 **855-278-5080** 480-727-8856
Barry University Dwayne O Andreas School of Law
6441 E Colonial Dr .... Orlando FL 32807 **800-756-6000** 321-206-5600
Baylor University
1301 S University Parks Dr .... Waco TX 76798 **800-229-5678**
Title IX Office
Clifton Robinson Tower Ste 285....... Waco TX 76798 **800-229-5678** 254-710-3821
Boston College Law School
885 Centre St .... Newton MA 02459 **800-321-2211** 617-552-8550
Boston University School of Law
765 Commonwealth Ave .... Boston MA 02215 **800-321-2211** 617-353-3100
California Western School of Law
225 Cedar St .... San Diego CA 92101 **800-255-4252** 619-239-0391
Campbell University Norman Adrian Wiggins School of Law
225 Hillsborough St .... Raleigh NC 27603 **800-334-4111** 919-865-4650
Case Western Reserve University School of Law
11075 E Blvd .... Cleveland OH 44106 **800-756-0036** 216-368-3600
Cleveland State University Cleveland-Marshall College of Law
1801 Euclid Ave LB 138 .... Cleveland OH 44115 **866-687-2304** 216-687-2344
Drake University Law School
2507 University Ave .... Des Moines IA 50311 **800-443-7253** 515-271-2824
Duke Law
210 Science Dr PO Box 90362........ Durham NC 27708 **888-529-2586** 919-613-7006
Florida Coastal School of Law
8787 Bay Pine Rd .... Jacksonville FL 32256 **877-210-2591** 904-680-7700
Golden Gate University School of Law
536 Mission St .... San Francisco CA 94105 **800-448-4968** 415-442-6600
Gonzaga University School of Law
721 N Cincinnati St PO Box 3528....... Spokane WA 99220 **800-793-1710*** 509-313-3700
*Admissions
Nova Southeastern University Shepard Broad Law Ctr
3305 College Ave .... Fort Lauderdale FL 33314 **800-986-6529** 954-262-6100
Ohio Northern University Claude W Pettit College of Law
525 S Main St .... Ada OH 45810 **877-452-9668** 419-772-2211
Quinnipiac University School of Law
275 Mt Carmel Ave .... Hamden CT 06518 **800-462-1944** 203-582-3400
Roger Williams University Ralph R Papitto School of Law
10 Metacom Ave .... Bristol RI 02809 **800-633-2727** 401-254-4500
Rutgers the State University of New Jersey
School of Law Camden
217 N Fifth St .... Camden NJ 08102 **800-466-7561** 856-225-6375
Saint Louis University School of Law
3700 Lindell Blvd .... Saint Louis MO 63108 **800-758-3678** 314-977-2766
Saint Thomas University School of Law
16401 NW 37th Ave .... Miami Gardens FL 33054 **800-245-4569** 305-623-2310
Samford University Cumberland School of Law
800 Lakeshore Dr .... Birmingham AL 35229 **800-888-7213** 205-726-2011
Southern Illinois University School of Law
1209 W Chautauqua Rd .... Carbondale IL 62901 **800-739-9187** 618-453-8858
Southern Methodist University Dedman School of Law
3300 University Blvd Ste 331 .... Dallas TX 75205 **888-768-5291** 214-768-2550
Southern University Law Ctr
2 Roosevelt Steptoe Dr .... Baton Rouge LA 70813 **800-537-1135** 225-771-6297
Texas Wesleyan University School of Law
1515 Commerce St .... Fort Worth TX 76102 **800-733-9529** 817-212-4000
Thomas Jefferson School of Law
1155 Island Ave .... San Diego CA 92101 **877-318-6901** 619-297-9700
Thomas M Cooley Law School
300 S Capitol Ave .... Lansing MI 48933 **800-243-2586** 517-371-5140
University of Akron School of Law
150 University Ave .... Akron OH 44325 **800-655-4884** 330-972-7331
University of Alabama
PO Box 870132 .... Tuscaloosa AL 35487 **800-933-2262*** 205-348-6010
*Admissions
University of Florida Levin College of Law
309 Village Dr PO Box 117620.......... Gainesville FL 32611 **877-429-1297** 352-273-0804
University of Houston Law Ctr
4604 Calhoun Rd .... Houston TX 77204 **800-252-9690** 713-743-2100
University of Idaho College of Law
709 Deakin St Rm 117 .... Moscow ID 83844 **888-884-3246** 208-885-6111
University of Iowa College of Law
130 Byington Rd .... Iowa City IA 52242 **800-553-4692** 319-335-3500
University of Kansas School of Law
1535 W 15th St .... Lawrence KS 66045 **866-220-3654** 785-864-4550
University of Memphis Cecil C Humphreys School of Law
3715 Central Ave .... Memphis TN 38152 **800-872-3728** 901-678-2421
University of Saint Thomas School of Law
1000 LaSalle Ave .... Minneapolis MN 55403 **800-328-6819** 651-962-4892
University of San Diego School of Law
5998 Alcala Pk .... San Diego CA 92110 **800-248-4873** 619-260-4528
University of South Dakota School of Law
414 E Clark St .... Vermillion SD 57069 **877-269-6837** 605-677-5443
University of Virginia School of Law
580 Massie Rd .... Charlottesville VA 22903 **877-307-0158** 434-924-7354
University of Washington School of Law
William H Gates Hall PO Box 353020.......... Seattle WA 98195 **866-866-0158** 206-543-4078

			Toll-Free	Phone

University of Wisconsin Law School
975 Bascom Mall .... Madison WI 53706   **866-301-1753**   608-262-2240
Valparaiso University Law
656 S Greenwich St .... Valparaiso IN 46383   **888-825-7652**   219-465-7829
Vermont Law School
168 Chelsea St PO Box 96 .... South Royalton VT 05068   **800-227-1395**   802-831-1239
Willamette University College of Law
245 Winter St SE .... Salem OR 97301   **844-232-7228**   503-370-6282
William Mitchell College of Law
875 Summit Ave .... Saint Paul MN 55105   **888-962-5529**   651-227-9171

167-2 Medical Schools

Medical schools listed here are accredited, MD-granting members of the Association of American Medical Colleges. Accredited Canadian schools that do not offer classes in English are not included among these listings.

			Toll-Free	Phone

Brody School of Medicine at East Carolina University
600 Moye Blvd .... Greenville NC 27834   **800-722-3281**   252-744-1020
Cincinnati Children's Hospital Medical Ctr
3333 Burnet Ave .... Cincinnati OH 45229   **800-344-2462**   513-636-4200
George Washington University School of Medicine & Health Sciences
2300 Eye St NW Ross Hall .... Washington DC 20037   **866-846-1107**   202-994-3506
Harvard Medical School
25 Shattuck St .... Boston MA 02115   **866-606-0573**   617-432-1550
Jefferson Medical College of Thomas Jefferson University
1015 Walnut St .... Philadelphia PA 19107   **800-533-3669**   215-955-6983
Joan C Edwards School of Medicine at Marshall University
1600 Medical Ctr Dr .... Huntington WV 25701   **877-691-1600**   304-691-1700
Loma Linda University School of Medicine
11175 Campus St .... Loma Linda CA 92350   **800-422-4558**   909-558-4467
Northeast Ohio Medical University
4209 St Rt 44 PO Box 95 .... Rootstown OH 44272   **800-686-2511**
NYU School of Medicine
560 First Ave .... New York NY 10016   **855-698-2220**   212-263-7300
Oregon Health & Science University (OHSU)
Bone Marrow Transplant Clinic
3181 SW Sam Jackson Pk Rd CB569 .... Portland OR 97239   **800-452-1369**   503-494-8500
School of Medicine
3181 SW Sam Jackson Pk Rd L-109 .... Portland OR 97239   **800-775-5460**   503-494-7800
Saint Louis University School of Medicine
1 N Grand .... Saint Louis MO 63103   **800-758-3678**
SIU School of Medicine
PO Box 19620 .... Springfield IL 62794   **800-342-5748**   217-545-8000
State University of New York Upstate Medical University
766 Irving Ave .... Syracuse NY 13210   **800-736-2171**   315-464-4570
Tulane University School of Medicine
1430 Tulane Ave .... New Orleans LA 70112   **800-588-5800**   504-988-5462
University of California Davis School of Medicine
4610 X St .... Sacramento CA 95817   **800-282-3284**   916-734-7131
University of Iowa Roy J & Lucille A Carver College of Medicine
200 CMAB .... Iowa City IA 52242   **800-725-8460**   319-335-6707
University of Louisville School of Medicine
323 E Chestnut St .... Louisville KY 40292   **800-334-8635**   502-852-5193
University of Mississippi School of Medicine
2500 N State St .... Jackson MS 39216   **888-815-2005**   601-984-1080
University of Missouri-Kansas City School of Medicine
2411 Holmes St .... Kansas City MO 64108   **800-735-2466**   816-235-1111
University of Nebraska School of Medicine
985527 Nebraska Medical Ctr .... Omaha NE 68198   **800-626-8431**   402-559-2259
University of North Dakota School of Medicine & Health Sciences
1301 N Columbia Rd Stop 9037 .... Grand Forks ND 58202   **800-225-5863**   701-777-5046
University of Ottawa Faculty of Medicine
451 Smyth Rd .... Ottawa ON K1H8M5   **877-868-8292**   613-562-5700
University of Rochester School of Medicine & Dentistry
601 Elmwood Ave .... Rochester NY 14642   **888-661-6162**   585-275-0017
University of Texas Medical Branch
301 University Blvd .... Galveston TX 77555   **800-228-1841**   409-772-2618
University of Texas Southwestern Medical Ctr Dallas
Hematopoietic Cell Transplant Program
5323 Harry Hines Blvd .... Dallas TX 75390   **866-645-6455**   214-648-3111
Southwestern Medical School
5323 Harry Hines Blvd .... Dallas TX 75390   **866-648-2455**   214-648-3111
University of Utah School of Medicine
30 N 1900 E .... Salt Lake City UT 84132   **844-988-7284**   801-581-7201
University of Vermont College of Medicine
89 Beaumont Ave E-126 Given Bldg .... Burlington VT 05405   **800-571-0668**   802-656-2156
Vanderbilt University School of Medicine
2215 Garland Ave .... Nashville TN 37232   **866-263-8263**   615-322-6109
Virginia Commonwealth University School of Medicine
1101 E Marshall St PO Box 980565 .... Richmond VA 23298   **800-332-8813**   804-828-9629
West Virginia University School of Medicine
1 Medical Center Dr PO Box 9100 .... Morgantown WV 26506   **800-543-5650**   304-293-0111

167-3 Theological Schools

Theological schools listed here are members of the Association of Theological Schools (ATS), an organization of graduate schools in the U.S. and Canada that conduct post-baccalaureate professional and academic degree programs to educate persons for the practice of ministry and for teaching and research in the theological disciplines. Listings include ATS accredited member schools, candidates for accredited membership, and associate member schools.

			Toll-Free	Phone

Acadia Divinity College
38 Highland Ave .... Wolfville NS B4P2R6   **866-875-8975**   902-585-2210
AMBS 3003 Benham Ave .... Elkhart IN 46517   **800-964-2627**   574-295-3726
Anderson University
1100 E Fifth St .... Anderson IN 46012   **800-428-6414***
*Admissions
Andover Newton Theological School
210 Herrick Rd .... Newton Center MA 02459   **800-964-2687**   617-964-1100

Andrews University Seventh-day Adventist Theological Seminary
4145 E Campus Cir Dr
Andrews University .... Berrien Springs MI 49104   **800-253-2874**   269-471-3537
Aquinas Institute of Theology
23 S Spring Ave .... Saint Louis MO 63108   **800-977-3869**   314-256-8800
Assemblies of God Theological Seminary
1435 N Glenstone Ave .... Springfield MO 65802   **800-467-2487**   417-268-1000
Azusa Pacific University
901 E Alosta Ave PO Box 7000 .... Azusa CA 91702   **800-825-5278**   626-969-3434
Bangor Theological Seminary
159 State St .... Portland ME 04101   **800-287-6781**   207-942-6781
Baptist Missionary Assn Theological Seminary
1530 E Pine St .... Jacksonville TX 75766   **800-259-5673**   903-586-2501
Barry University
11300 NE Second Ave .... Miami Shores FL 33161   **800-756-6000**   305-899-3000
Bethany Theological Seminary
615 National Rd W .... Richmond IN 47374   **800-287-8822**   765-983-1800
Bethel Seminary
3949 Bethel Dr .... Saint Paul MN 55112   **800-255-8706**   651-638-6400
Bexley Hall Seminary
1407 E 60th St .... Chicago IL 60637   **800-275-8235**   773-380-6780
Biblical Theological Seminary
200 N Main St .... Hatfield PA 19440   **800-235-4021**   215-368-5000
Biola University
13800 Biola Ave .... La Mirada CA 90639   **800-652-4652***   562-903-6000
*Admissions
Calvin Theological Seminary
3233 Burton St SE .... Grand Rapids MI 49546   **800-388-6034**   616-957-6036
Campbell University
450 Leslie Campbell Ave
PO Box 546 .... Buies Creek NC 27506   **800-334-4111**   910-893-1290
Canadian Southern Baptist Seminary
200 Seminary View .... Cochrane AB T4C2G1   **877-922-2727**   403-932-6622
Carey Theological College
5920 Iona Dr .... Vancouver BC V6T1J6   **844-862-2739**   604-224-4308
Catholic University of America
620 Michigan Ave NE .... Washington DC 20064   **800-673-2772**   202-319-5000
Cincinnati Christian University
2700 Glenway Ave .... Cincinnati OH 45204   **800-949-4228**   513-244-8100
Colgate Rochester Crozer Divinity School
1100 S Goodman St .... Rochester NY 14620   **888-937-3732**   585-271-1320
Columbia International University
7435 Monticello Rd .... Columbia SC 29203   **800-777-2227**   803-754-4100
Columbia Theological Seminary
701 S Columbia Dr .... Decatur GA 30030   **888-601-8916**   404-378-8821
Concordia Seminary
801 Seminary Pl .... Saint Louis MO 63105   **800-822-9545**   314-505-7000
Concordia Theological Seminary
6600 N Clinton St .... Fort Wayne IN 46825   **800-481-2155**   260-452-2100
Cornerstone University
1001 E Beltline Ave NE .... Grand Rapids MI 49525   **800-787-9778***   616-222-1426
*Admissions
Dallas Theological Seminary
3909 Swiss Ave .... Dallas TX 75204   **800-992-0998**   800-387-9673
Denver Seminary
6399 S Santa Fe Dr .... Littleton CO 80120   **800-922-3040**   303-761-2482
Dominican School of Philosophy & Theology
2301 Vine St .... Berkeley CA 94708   **888-450-3778**   510-849-2030
Duke University Divinity School
407 Chapel Dr PO Box 90968 .... Durham NC 27708   **800-367-3853**   919-660-3400
Earlham School of Religion
228 College Ave .... Richmond IN 47374   **800-432-1377**   765-983-1423
Eastern Mennonite University
1200 Pk Rd .... Harrisonburg VA 22802   **800-368-2665***   540-432-4118
*Admissions
Eden Theological Seminary
475 E Lockwood Ave .... Saint Louis MO 63119   **877-627-5652**   314-961-3627
Erskine Theological Seminary
2 Washington St PO Box 338 .... Due West SC 29639   **888-359-4358**   864-379-6571
Evangelical School of Theology
121 S College St .... Myerstown PA 17067   **800-532-5775**   717-866-5775
Franciscan School of Theology
1712 Euclid Ave .... Berkeley CA 94709   **855-355-1550**   760-547-1800
Fuller Theological Seminary
135 N Oakland Ave .... Pasadena CA 91182   **800-235-2222**   626-584-5200
General Theological Seminary
440 W 21st St .... New York NY 10011   **888-487-5649**   212-243-5150
George Fox Evangelical Seminary
12753 SW 68th Ave .... Portland OR 97223   **800-493-4937**   503-554-6150
Gordon-Conwell Theological Seminary
130 Essex St .... South Hamilton MA 01982   **800-428-7329**   978-468-7111
Grace College & Theological Seminary
200 Seminary Dr .... Winona Lake IN 46590   **800-544-7223**   574-372-5100
Graduate Theological Union
2400 Ridge Rd .... Berkeley CA 94709   **800-826-4488**   510-649-2400
Harding University
915 E Market Ave .... Searcy AR 72149   **800-477-4407***   501-279-4000
*Admissions
Hartford Seminary
77 Sherman St .... Hartford CT 06105   **877-860-2255**   860-509-9500
Howard University School of Divinity
2400 Sixth St NW .... Washington DC 20059   **800-822-6363**   202-806-6100
Iliff School of Theology
2201 S University Blvd .... Denver CO 80210   **800-678-3360**   303-744-1287
Jesuit School of Theology at Berkeley
1735 LeRoy Ave .... Berkeley CA 94709   **800-824-0122**   510-549-5000
La Sierra University
4500 Riverwalk Pkwy .... Riverside CA 92515   **800-874-5587**   951-785-2000
Lancaster Theological Seminary
555 W James St .... Lancaster PA 17603   **800-393-0654**   717-393-0654
Lexington Theological Seminary
230 Lexington Green Cir Ste 300 .... Lexington KY 40503   **866-296-6087**   859-252-0361
Lincoln Christian College Seminary
100 Campus View Dr .... Lincoln IL 62656   **888-522-5228**   217-732-3168
Lipscomb University
3901 Granny White Pk .... Nashville TN 37204   **800-333-4358**   615-966-1000
Louisville Presbyterian Theological Seminary
1044 Alta Vista Rd .... Louisville KY 40205   **800-264-1839**   502-895-3411

Classified Section

	Toll-Free	Phone

Luther Seminary
2481 Como Ave ....Saint Paul MN 55108 — 800-588-4373 — 651-641-3456

Lutheran School of Theology at Chicago
1100 E 55th St ....Chicago IL 60615 — 800-635-1116 — 773-256-0700

McCormick Theological Seminary
5460 S University Ave ....Chicago IL 60615 — 800-228-4687 — 773-947-6300

Meadville Lombard Theological School (MLTS)
610 S Michigan Ave ....Chicago IL 60605 — 800-848-0979 — 773-256-3000

Mennonite Brethren Biblical Seminary
4824 E Butler Ave ....Fresno CA 93727 — 800-251-6227 — 559-453-2000

Methodist Theological School in Ohio
3081 Columbus Pk ....Delaware OH 43015 — 800-333-6876 — 740-363-1146

Michigan Theological Seminary
41550 E Ann Arbor Trl ....Plymouth MI 48170 — 800-356-6639 — 734-207-9581

Mid-America Reformed Seminary
229 Seminary Dr ....Dyer IN 46311 — 888-440-6277 — 219-864-2400

Midwestern Baptist Theological Seminary
5001 N Oak Trafficway ....Kansas City MO 64118 — 800-944-6287 — 816-414-3700

Moravian Theological Seminary
1200 Main St ....Bethlehem PA 18018 — 800-843-6541 — 610-861-1516

Mount Angel Seminary
1 Abbey Dr ....Saint Benedict OR 97373 — 800-845-8272 — 503-845-3951

Mount Saint Mary's University
16300 Old Emmitsburg Rd ....Emmitsburg MD 21727 — 800-448-4347* — 301-447-5214
*Admissions

Multnomah University
8435 NE Glisan St ....Portland OR 97220 — 800-275-4672 — 503-255-0332

Nazarene Theological Seminary
1700 E Meyer Blvd ....Kansas City MO 64131 — 800-831-3011 — 816-268-5400

New Orleans Baptist Theological Seminary
3939 Gentilly Blvd ....New Orleans LA 70126 — 800-662-8701 — 504-282-4455

Newman Theological College (NTC)
10012-84 St ....Edmonton AB T6A0B2 — 844-392-2450 — 780-392-2450

North Park Theological Seminary
3225 W Foster Ave ....Chicago IL 60625 — 800-964-0101 — 773-244-6229

NYACK 350 N Highland Ave ....Nyack NY 10960 — 800-541-6891 — 845-353-2020

Oakland City University
138 North Lucretia St ....Oakland City IN 47660 — 800-737-5125 — 812-749-4781

Oral Roberts University
7777 S Lewis Ave ....Tulsa OK 74171 — 800-678-8876 — 918-495-6161

Pacific Lutheran Theological Seminary
2770 Marin Ave ....Berkeley CA 94708 — 800-235-7587

Pacific School of Religion
1798 Scenic Ave ....Berkeley CA 94709 — 800-999-0528 — 510-848-0528

Palmer Theological Seminary
588 N Gulph Rd ....King Of Prussia PA 19406 — 800-220-3287 — 610-896-5000

Payne Theological Seminary
1230 Wilberforce Clifton Rd ....Wilberforce OH 45384 — 888-816-8933 — 937-376-2946

Pentecostal Theological Seminary
900 Walker St NE ....Cleveland TN 37311 — 800-228-9126 — 423-478-1131

Phillips Theological Seminary
901 N Mingo Rd ....Tulsa OK 74116 — 800-843-4675 — 918-610-8303

Phoenix Seminary
4222 E Thomas Rd Ste 400 ....Phoenix AZ 85018 — 888-443-1020 — 602-850-8000

Pittsburgh Theological Seminary
616 N Highland Ave ....Pittsburgh PA 15206 — 800-451-4194 — 412-362-5610

Pontifical College Josephinum
7625 N High St ....Columbus OH 43235 — 888-252-5812 — 614-885-5585

Protestant Episcopal Theological Seminary in Virginia
3737 Seminary Rd ....Alexandria VA 22304 — 800-941-0083 — 703-370-6600

Providence College & Seminary
10 College Crescent ....Otterburne MB R0A1G0 — 800-668-7768 — 204-433-7488

Queen's College Faculty of Theology
210 Prince Philip Dr ....Saint John's NL A1B3R6 — 877-753-0116 — 709-753-0116

Reformed Theological Seminary
5422 Clinton Blvd ....Jackson MS 39209 — 800-543-2703 — 601-923-1600

Regent College
5800 University Blvd ....Vancouver BC V6T2E4 — 800-663-8664 — 604-224-3245

Roberts Wesleyan College
2301 Westside Dr ....Rochester NY 14624 — 800-777-4792* — 585-594-6000
*Admissions

Saint Peter's Seminary
1040 Waterloo St N ....London ON N6A3Y1 — 800-548-9649 — 519-432-1824

Samford University
800 Lakeshore Dr ....Birmingham AL 35229 — 800-888-7218* — 205-726-3673
*Admissions

San Francisco Theological Seminary
105 Seminary Rd ....San Anselmo CA 94960 — 800-447-8820 — 415-451-2800

Seminary of the southwest (SSW)
501 E 32nd PO Box 2247....................Austin TX 78705 — 800-252-5400 — 512-472-4133

Shaw University 118 E S St..............Raleigh NC 27601 — 800-214-6683* — 919-546-8275
*Admissions

Sioux Falls Seminary
2100 S Summit ....Sioux Falls SD 57105 — 800-440-6227 — 605-336-6588

Southeastern Baptist Theological Seminary
120 S Wingate St ....Wake Forest NC 27587 — 800-284-6317 — 919-556-3101

Southern Baptist Theological Seminary
2825 Lexington Rd ....Louisville KY 40280 — 800-626-5525

Southwestern Baptist Theological Seminary
PO Box 22740 ....Fort Worth TX 76122 — 877-467-9287 — 817-923-1921

Taylor University College & Seminary
11525 23rd Ave ....Edmonton AB T6J4T3 — 800-567-4988 — 780-431-5200

Trinity Episcopal School for Ministry
311 Eleventh St ....Ambridge PA 15003 — 800-874-8754 — 724-266-3838

Trinity International University
2065 Half Day Rd ....Deerfield IL 60015 — 800-822-3225 — 847-945-8800

Trinity Lutheran Seminary
2199 E Main St ....Columbus OH 43209 — 866-610-8571 — 614-235-4136

Trinity Western University
7600 Glover Rd ....Langley BC V2Y1Y1 — 888-468-6898 — 604-888-7511

Union Theological Seminary & Presbyterian School of Christian Education
3401 Brook Rd ....Richmond VA 23227 — 800-229-2990 — 804-355-0671

United Lutheran Seminary Gatteysburg
61 Seminary Rdg ....Gettysburg PA 17325 — 800-658-8437 — 717-334-6286

United Lutheran Seminary Philadelphia
7301 Germantown Ave ....Philadelphia PA 19119 — 800-286-4616 — 215-248-4616

University of Saint Thomas
2115 Summit Ave ....Saint Paul MN 55105 — 800-328-6819 — 651-962-5000

	Toll-Free	Phone

University of Saskatchewan
1121 College Dr ....Saskatoon SK S7N0W3 — 877-653-8501 — 306-966-8970

University of the South
735 University Ave ....Sewanee TN 37383 — 800-522-2234 — 931-598-1238

Vancouver School of Theology
The University of British Columbia
6015 Walter Gage Rd ....Vancouver BC V6T1Z1 — 866-822-9031 — 604-822-9031

Virginia Union University
1500 N Lombardy St ....Richmond VA 23220 — 800-368-3227 — 804-342-3570

Wartburg Theological Seminary
333 Wartburg Pl ....Dubuque IA 52003 — 800-225-5987 — 563-589-0200

Western Seminary
5511 SE Hawthorne Blvd ....Portland OR 97215 — 877-517-1800 — 503-517-1800

Western Theological Seminary
101 E 13th St ....Holland MI 49423 — 800-392-8554 — 616-392-8555

Westminster Theological Seminary
2960 Church Rd ....Glenside PA 19038 — 800-373-0119 — 215-887-5511

Westminster Theological Seminary in California
1725 Bear Vly Pkwy ....Escondido CA 92027 — 888-480-8474 — 760-480-8474

Winebrenner Theological Seminary
950 N Main St ....Findlay OH 45840 — 800-992-4987 — 419-434-4200

Yale Divinity School Admissions Office
409 Prospect St ....New Haven CT 06511 — 877-725-3334 — 203-432-5360

168   COLLEGES & UNIVERSITIES - HISTORICALLY BLACK

Historically Black Colleges & Universities (HBCUs) are colleges or universities that were established before 1964 with the intention of serving the African-American community. (Prior to 1964, African-Americans were almost always excluded from higher education opportunities at the predominantly white colleges and universities.)

	Toll-Free	Phone

Allen University
1530 Harden St ....Columbia SC 29204 — 877-625-5368 — 803-376-5700

Benedict College
1600 Harden St ....Columbia SC 29204 — 800-868-6598 — 803-253-5000

Bennett College
900 E Washington St ....Greensboro NC 27401 — 800-413-5323* — 336-370-8624
*Admissions

Bethune-Cookman College
640 Dr Mary McLeod Bethune Blvd
........................Daytona Beach FL 32114 — 800-448-0228* — 386-481-2900
*Admissions

Bishop State Community College
351 N Broad St ....Mobile AL 36603 — 800-523-7000 — 251-405-7000

Bluefield State College
219 Rock St ....Bluefield WV 24701 — 800-654-7798 — 304-327-4000

Bowie State University
14000 Jericho Pk Rd ....Bowie MD 20715 — 877-772-6943 — 301-860-4000

Central State University
1400 Brush Row Rd PO Box 1004 ....Wilberforce OH 45384 — 800-388-2781 — 937-376-6011

Cheyney University of Pennsylvania
1837 University Cir PO Box 200...............Cheyney PA 19319 — 800-243-9639 — 610-399-2275

Claflin University
400 Magnolia St ....Orangeburg SC 29115 — 800-922-1276 — 803-535-5000

Clark Atlanta University
223 James P Brawley Dr SW ....Atlanta GA 30314 — 800-688-3228* — 404-880-8000
*Admissions

Coppin State University
2500 W N Ave ....Baltimore MD 21216 — 800-635-3674* — 410-951-3600
*Admissions

Delaware State University
1200 N DuPont Hwy ....Dover DE 19901 — 800-845-2544* — 302-857-6351
*Admissions

Elizabeth City State University
1704 Weeksville Rd ....Elizabeth City NC 27909 — 800-347-3278* — 252-335-3400
*Admissions

Fayetteville State University
1200 Murchison Rd ....Fayetteville NC 28301 — 800-222-2594* — 910-672-1371
*Admissions

Fisk University
1000 17th Ave N ....Nashville TN 37208 — 888-702-0022 — 615-329-8500

Florida A & M University
1700 Lee Hall Dr ....Tallahassee FL 32307 — 866-642-1198 — 850-599-3000

Florida Memorial University
15800 NW 42nd Ave ....Miami Gardens FL 33054 — 800-822-1362 — 305-626-3600

Fort Valley State University
1005 State University Dr ....Fort Valley GA 31030 — 877-462-3878 — 478-825-6211

Grambling State University
403 Main St ....Grambling LA 71245 — 800-569-4714 — 318-247-3811

Hampton University
100 E Queen St ....Hampton VA 23668 — 800-624-3341 — 757-727-5000

Hinds Community College
501 E Main St PO Box 1100...................Raymond MS 39154 — 800-446-3722 — 601-857-3212

Howard University
2400 Sixth St NW ....Washington DC 20059 — 800-822-6363 — 202-806-6100

Huston-Tillotson University
900 Chicon St ....Austin TX 78702 — 800-343-3822 — 512-505-3000

Jackson State University
1400 John R Lynch St ....Jackson MS 39217 — 800-848-6817 — 601-979-2121

Johnson C Smith University
100 Beatties Ford Rd ....Charlotte NC 28216 — 800-782-7303* — 704-378-1000
*Admissions

Kentucky State University
400 E Main St ....Frankfort KY 40601 — 800-325-1716* — 502-597-6000
*Admissions

Lane College 545 Ln Ave ....Jackson TN 38301 — 800-960-7533* — 731-426-7500
*Admissions

Langston University
2017 Langston University PO Box 1500..........Langston OK 73050 — 877-466-2231

Lincoln University
820 Chestnut St ....Jefferson City MO 65101 — 800-521-5052* — 573-681-5000
*Admissions

Lincoln University
1570 Old Baltimore Pk
PO Box 179.........................Lincoln University PA 19352 — 800-790-0191* — 484-365-8000
*Admissions

				Toll-Free	Phone

Livingstone College
701 W Monroe St . . . . Salisbury NC 28144 **800-835-3435** 704-216-6000

Miles College
5500 Myron Massey Blvd . . . . Fairfield AL 35064 **800-445-0708*** 205-929-1000
*Admissions

Mississippi Valley State University
14000 Hwy 82 . . . . Itta Bena MS 38941 **800-844-6885** 662-254-9041

Morgan State University
1700 E Cold Spring Ln . . . . Baltimore MD 21251 **800-319-4678** 443-885-3333

Morris College
100 W College St . . . . Sumter SC 29150 **866-853-1345*** 803-934-3200
*Admissions

Norfolk State University
700 Park Ave . . . . Norfolk VA 23504 **800-274-1821** 757-823-8600

North Carolina A & T State University
1601 E Market St . . . . Greensboro NC 27411 **800-443-8964*** 336-334-7946
*Admissions

North Carolina Central University
1801 Fayetteville St . . . . Durham NC 27707 **877-667-7533*** 919-530-6100
*Admissions

Paine College 1235 15th St . . . . Augusta GA 30901 **800-476-7703** 706-821-8200

Prairie View A & M University
700 University Dr PO Box 519 . . . . Prairie View TX 77446 **877-241-1752** 936-261-3311

Rust College
150 Rust Ave . . . . Holly Springs MS 38635 **888-886-8492** 662-252-8000

Saint Augustine's College
1315 Oakwood Ave . . . . Raleigh NC 27610 **800-948-1126*** 919-516-4000
*Admissions

Shaw University 118 E S St . . . . Raleigh NC 27601 **800-214-6683*** 919-546-8275
*Admissions

Shelton State
Community College
9500 Old Greensboro Rd . . . . Tuscaloosa AL 35405 **877-838-2778** 205-391-2211

South Carolina State University
300 College St NE . . . . Orangeburg SC 29117 **800-260-5956*** 803-536-7000
*Admissions

Southern University & A & M College
156 Elton C Harrison Dr
PO Box 9757 . . . . Baton Rouge LA 70813 **800-256-1531*** 225-771-5180
*Admissions

Southwestern Christian College
PO Box 10 . . . . Terrell TX 75160 **800-925-9357** 972-524-3341

Spelman College
350 Spelman Ln SW . . . . Atlanta GA 30314 **800-982-2411*** 404-681-3643
*Admissions

Stillman College
3601 Stillman Blvd . . . . Tuscaloosa AL 35401 **800-841-5722** 205-349-4240

Tennessee State University
3500 John A Merritt Blvd
PO Box 9609 . . . . Nashville TN 37209 **888-463-6878*** 615-963-5000
*Admissions

Texas College
2404 N Grand Ave . . . . Tyler TX 75702 **800-306-6299** 903-593-8311

Tougaloo College
500 W County Line Rd . . . . Tougaloo MS 39174 **888-424-2566*** 601-977-7700

Tuskegee University
1200 W Montgomery Rd . . . . Tuskegee AL 36088 **800-622-6531*** 334-727-8011
*Admissions

Virginia State University
1 Hayden Dr . . . . Petersburg VA 23806 **800-871-7611*** 804-524-5000
*Admissions

Virginia Union University
1500 N Lombardy St . . . . Richmond VA 23220 **800-368-3227** 804-342-3570

Voorhees College
213 Wiggins Dr PO Box 678 . . . . Denmark SC 29042 **866-685-9904** 803-780-1234

West Virginia State University
117 Ferrell Hall PO Box 368 . . . . Institute WV 25112 **800-987-2112** 304-766-3000

Wiley College
711 Wiley Ave . . . . Marshall TX 75670 **800-658-6889*** 903-927-3300
*Admissions

Winston-Salem State University
601 S ML King Jr Dr . . . . Winston-Salem NC 27110 **800-257-4052*** 336-750-2000
*Admissions

169 COMMODITY CONTRACTS BROKERS & DEALERS

SEE ALSO Securities Brokers & Dealers ; Investment Advice & Management

				Toll-Free	Phone

Keeley Investment Corp
401 S La Salle St Ste 1201 . . . . Chicago IL 60605 **800-533-5344** 312-786-5000

OptionsXpress Inc
311 W Monroe Ste 1000 . . . . Chicago IL 60606 **888-280-8020** 312-630-3300

Zaner Group LLC
150 S Wacker Dr Ste 2350 . . . . Chicago IL 60606 **800-621-1414** 312-930-2703

170 COMMUNICATIONS TOWER OPERATORS

SEE ALSO Communications Lines & Towers Construction
Listed here are companies that own, operate, lease, maintain, and/or manage towers used by telecommunications services and radio broadcast companies, including free-standing towers as well as antenna systems mounted on monopoles or rooftops. Many of these companies also build their communications towers, but companies that only do the building are classified as heavy construction contractors.

				Toll-Free	Phone

American Tower Corp
116 Huntington Ave 11th Fl . . . . Boston MA 02116 **877-282-7483** 617-375-7500
NYSE: AMT

Crown Castle International Corp
1220 Augusta Dr Ste 500 . . . . Houston TX 77057 **877-486-9377** 713-570-3000
NYSE: CCI

LTS Wireless Inc
311 S LHS Dr . . . . Lumberton TX 77657 **800-255-5471** 409-755-4038

				Toll-Free	Phone

SBA Communications Corp
5900 Broken Sound Pkwy NW . . . . Boca Raton FL 33487 **800-487-7483** 561-995-7670
NASDAQ: SBAC

Tower Innovations
3266 Tower Dr . . . . Newburgh IN 47630 **800-664-8222** 812-853-0595

171 COMMUNITIES - ONLINE

SEE ALSO Internet Service Providers (ISPs)

				Toll-Free	Phone

Beliefnet
999 Waterside Dr Ste 1900 . . . . Norfolk VA 23510 **800-311-2458**

Lawyerscom
121 Chanlon Rd Ste 110 . . . . New Providence NJ 07974 **800-526-4902** 908-464-6800

Sensitech Ino
800 Cummings Ctr Ste 258x . . . . Beverly MA 01915 **800-843-8367** 978-927-7033

SHRM Global Forum
1800 Duke St . . . . Alexandria VA 22314 **800-283-7476** 703-548-3440

COMPRESSORS - AIR CONDITIONING & REFRIGERATION

SEE Air Conditioning & Heating Equipment - Commercial/Industrial

172 COMPRESSORS - AIR & GAS

				Toll-Free	Phone

Brabazon Pumps & Compressor
2484 Century Rd . . . . Green Bay WI 54303 **800-825-3222** 920-498-6020

Compressed Air Systems Inc
9303 Stannum St . . . . Tampa FL 33619 **800-626-8177** 813-626-8177

Compressor Engineering Corp (CECO)
5440 Alder Dr . . . . Houston TX 77081 **800-879-2326** 713-664-7333

Corken Inc
3805 NW 36th St . . . . Oklahoma City OK 73112 **800-631-4929** 405-946-5576

Curtis-Toledo Inc
1905 Kienlen Ave . . . . Saint Louis MO 63133 **800-925-5431** 314-383-1300

Dearing Compressor & Pump Co
3974 Simon Rd PO Box 6044 . . . . Youngstown OH 44501 **800-850-3440** 330-599-5720

Elliott Group
901 N Fourth St . . . . Jeannette PA 15644 **888-352-7278** 724-527-2811

Federal Equipment Co
5298 River Rd . . . . Cincinnati OH 45233 **877-435-4723** 513-621-5260

Fountainhead Group Inc
23 Garden St . . . . New York Mills NY 13417 **800-311-9903** 315-736-0037

Gardner Denver Water Jetting Systems Inc
785 Greens Pkwy Ste 225 . . . . Houston TX 77067 **800-580-5388**

Gas Technology Energy Concepts LLC
401 William L Gaiter Pkwy Ste 4 . . . . Buffalo NY 14215 **800-451-8294**

Guardair Corp
47 Veterans Dr . . . . Chicopee MA 01022 **800-482-7324** 413-594-4400

Mattson Spray Equipment
230 W Coleman St . . . . Rice Lake WI 54868 **800-877-4857** 715-234-1617

McGee Company Inc
1140 S Jason St . . . . Denver CO 80223 **800-525-8888**

Norwalk Compressor Co
1650 Stratford Ave . . . . Stratford CT 06615 **800-556-5001**

Pristech Products Inc
6952 Fairgrounds Pkwy Ste 107 . . . . San Antonio TX 78238 **800-432-8722** 210-520-8051

Puma Industries Inc
1992 Airways Blvd . . . . Memphis TN 38114 **888-848-1668** 901-744-7979

Rogers Machinery Company Inc
14650 SW 72nd Ave PO Box 230429 . . . . Portland OR 97224 **800-394-6151** 503-639-0808

Saylor Beall Mfg Company Inc
400 N Kibbee St PO Box 40 . . . . Saint Johns MI 48879 **800-248-9001** 989-224-2371

Scales Air Compressor Corp
110 Voice Rd . . . . Carle Place NY 11514 **877-798-0454** 516-248-9096

Spencer Turbine Co
600 Day Hill Rd . . . . Windsor CT 06095 **800-232-4321** 860-688-8361

Sullivan-Palatek Inc
1201 W US Hwy 20 . . . . Michigan City IN 46360 **800-438-6203** 219-874-2497

Thermionics Laboratory
1842 Sabre St . . . . Hayward CA 94545 **800-962-2310** 510-732-1755

Tuthill Vacuum Systems
4840 W Kearney St . . . . Springfield MO 65803 **800-634-2695** 417-865-8715

Wagner Spray Tech Corp
1770 Fernbrook Ln . . . . Plymouth MN 55447 **800-328-8251** 763-553-7000

Zeks Compressed Air Solutions
1302 Goshen Pkwy . . . . West Chester PA 19380 **800-888-2323** 610-692-9100

173 COMPUTER EQUIPMENT

SEE ALSO Flash Memory Devices ; Point-of-Sale (POS) & Point-of-Information (POI) Systems ; Calculators - Electronic ; Automatic Teller Machines (ATMs) ; Computer Networking Products & Systems ; Business Machines - Mfr ; Modems

173-1 Computer Input Devices

				Toll-Free	Phone

3M Touch Systems
501 Griffin Brook Dr . . . . Methuen MA 01844 **866-407-6666** 978-659-9000

Cirque Corp
2463 South 3850 West . . . . Salt Lake City UT 84120 **800-454-3375** 801-467-1100

Elo TouchSystems Inc
301 Constitution Dr . . . . Menlo Park CA 94025 **800-557-1458** 650-361-4700

Esterline Interface Technologies
600 W Wilbur Ave . . . . Coeur d'Alene ID 83815 **800-444-5923** 208-765-8000

Gyration Inc
3601-B Calle Tecate . . . . Camarillo CA 93012 **888-340-0033**

Kensington Computer Products Group
333 Twin Dolphin Dr 6th Fl . . . . Redwood Shores CA 94065 **800-535-4242** 855-692-0054

Kinesis Corp
22030 20th Ave SE Ste 102 . . . . Bothell WA 98021 **800-454-6374** 425-402-8100

				Toll-Free	Phone
Logitech Inc 6505 Kaiser Dr	Fremont	CA	94555	**800-231-7717***	510-795-8500
*Sales					
Numonics Corp					
101 Commerce Dr PO Box 1005	Montgomeryville	PA	18936	**800-523-6716**	215-362-2766
PolyVision Corp					
10700 Abbotts Bridge Rd Ste 100	Johns Creek	GA	30097	**888-325-6351**	678-542-3100
SMART Modular Technologies Inc					
39870 Eureka Dr	Newark	CA	94560	**800-956-7627**	510-623-1231
NASDAQ: SMOD					
SMART Technologies Inc					
3636 Research Rd NW	Calgary	AB	T2L1Y1	**888-427-6278**	403-245-0333
TSX: SMA					
TouchSystems Corp					
2222 W Rundberg Ln Ste 200	Austin	TX	78758	**800-320-5944**	512-846-2424
Wacom Technology Corp					
1311 SE Cardinal Ct	Vancouver	WA	98683	**800-922-6613**	360-896-9833

173-2 Computers

				Toll-Free	Phone
Aberdeen LLC					
9130 Norwalk Blvd	Santa Fe Springs	CA	90670	**800-500-9526**	562-699-6998
Acer America Corp					
333 W San Carlos St Ste 1500	San Jose	CA	95110	**866-695-2237**	408-533-7700
ACMA Computers Inc					
1565 Reliance Way	Fremont	CA	94539	**800-786-6888***	510-683-9090
*Sales					
Amax Engineering Corp					
1565 Reliance Way	Fremont	CA	94539	**800-889-2629***	510-651-8886
*Cust Svc					
Apple Inc 1 Infinite Loop	Cupertino	CA	95014	**800-275-2273***	408-996-1010
NASDAQ: AAPL ■ *Cust Svc					
Bytespeed LLC					
3131 24th Ave S	Moorhead	MN	56560	**877-553-0777**	218-227-0445
Chem USA Corp					
38507 Cherry St	Newark	CA	94560	**800-866-2436**	510-608-8818
Comark Corp 93 W St	Medfield	MA	02052	**800-280-8522**	508-359-8161
CSP Inc 43 Manning Rd	Billerica	MA	01821	**800-325-3110**	978-663-7598
NASDAQ: CSPI					
Datalux Corp					
155 Aviation Dr	Winchester	VA	22602	**800-328-2589**	540-662-1500
Dedicated Computing					
N26 W23880 Commerce Cir	Waukesha	WI	53188	**877-333-4848**	262-951-7200
Dell Inc 1 Dell Way	Round Rock	TX	78682	**800-879-3355**	512-338-4400
NASDAQ: DELL					
Drive Thru Technology Inc					
1755 N Main St	Los Angeles	CA	90031	**800-933-8388**	866-388-7877
Ectaco Inc					
31-21 31st St	Long Island	NY	11106	**800-710-7920**	718-728-6110
Equus Computer Systems Inc					
7725 Washington Ave S	Edina	MN	55439	**866-378-8727**	800-641-1475
Fujitsu America Inc					
1250 E Arques Ave	Sunnyvale	CA	94085	**800-538-8460**	408-746-6200
Gateway Inc					
7565 Irvine Ctr Dr	Irvine	CA	92618	**800-846-2000**	949-471-7040
Hewlett Packard Enterprise (Canada) Co (HP)					
5150 Spectrum Way	Mississauga	ON	L4W5G1	**888-447-4636**	905-206-4725
Hewlett-Packard Co					
3000 Hanover St	Palo Alto	CA	94304	**800-752-0900***	650-857-1501
NYSE: HPQ ■ *Sales					
International Business Machines Corp (IBM)					
1 New OrchaRd Rd	Armonk	NY	10504	**800-426-4968**	914-499-1900
NYSE: IBM					
Kontron S&T AG					
7631 Anagram Dr	Eden Prairie	MN	55344	**888-343-5396**	952-974-7000
LXE Inc					
125 Technology Pkwy	Norcross	GA	30092	**800-664-4593**	770-447-4224
MaxVision Corp					
495 Production Ave	Madison	AL	35758	**800-533-5805**	256-772-3058
Micro Express Inc					
8 Hammond Dr Ste 105	Irvine	CA	92618	**800-989-9900**	
Quantum3D Inc					
1759 McCarthy Blvd	Milpitas	CA	95035	**888-747-1020**	408-600-2500
Sharp Electronics Corp					
1 Sharp Plz	Mahwah	NJ	07430	**800-237-4277**	201-529-8200
Sony Electronics Inc					
1 Sony Dr	Park Ridge	NJ	07656	**800-222-7669***	201-930-1000
*Cust Svc					
Superchips Inc					
1790 E Airport Blvd	Sanford	FL	32773	**888-227-2447**	407-585-7000
Systemax Inc					
11 Harbor Pk Dr	Port Washington	NY	11050	**800-344-6783**	516-608-7000
NYSE: SYX					
Tangent Inc					
191 Airport Blvd	Burlingame	CA	94010	**800-342-9388**	650-342-9388
Toshiba America Inc					
1251 Ave of the Americas 41st Fl	New York	NY	10020	**800-457-7777**	212-596-0600
Toshiba America Information Systems Inc					
9740 Irvine Blvd	Irvine	CA	92618	**800-457-7777***	949-583-3000
*Cust Svc					
Transource Computers Corp					
2405 W Utopia Rd	Phoenix	AZ	85027	**800-486-3715**	623-879-8882
Twinhead Corp					
48303 Fremont Blvd	Fremont	CA	94538	**800-995-8946***	
*Sales					
Versalogic Corp					
4211 W 11th Ave	Eugene	OR	97402	**800-824-3163**	541-485-8575
WYSE Technology Inc					
3471 N First St	San Jose	CA	95134	**800-800-9973**	408-473-1200

173-3 Modems

				Toll-Free	Phone
ActionTec Electronics Inc					
760 N Mary Ave	Sunnyvale	CA	94085	**888-436-0657***	408-752-7700
*Tech Supp					

				Toll-Free	Phone
Biscom Inc					
321 Billerica Rd	Chelmsford	MA	01824	**800-477-2472**	978-250-1800
Canoga Perkins Corp					
20600 Prairie St	Chatsworth	CA	91311	**800-360-6642***	818-718-6300
*Tech Supp					
Cermetek Microelectronics Inc					
374 Turquoise St	Milpitas	CA	95035	**800-882-6271**	408-752-5000
Copia International Ltd					
1220 Iroquois Dr Ste 180	Naperville	IL	60187	**800-689-8898***	630-778-8898
*Sales					
Dataforth Corp					
3331 E Hemisphere Loop	Tucson	AZ	85706	**800-444-7644**	520-741-1404
FreeWave Technologies Inc					
5395 Pearl Pkwy	Boulder	CO	80301	**866-923-6168***	303-381-9200
*Cust Svc					
GRE America Inc					
425 Harbor Blvd	Belmont	CA	94002	**800-233-5973**	650-591-1400
Multi-Tech Systems					
2205 Woodale Dr	Mounds View	MN	55112	**800-328-9717***	763-785-3500
*Cust Svc					
Unlimited Systems Corp Inc					
9530 Padgett St	San Diego	CA	92126	**800-275-6354**	858-537-5010
US Robotics Corp					
1300 E Woodfield Dr Ste 506	Schaumburg	IL	60173	**877-710-0884**	847-874-2000
Western Telematic Inc					
5 Sterling	Irvine	CA	92618	**800-854-7226**	949-586-9950
Works Computing Inc					
1801 American Blvd E Ste 12	Bloomington	MN	55425	**866-222-4077**	952-746-1580
ZyXEL Communications Inc					
1130 N Miller St	Anaheim	CA	92806	**800-255-4101**	714-632-0882

173-4 Monitors & Displays

				Toll-Free	Phone
Barco Electronic Systems Pvt Ltd					
11101 Trade Ctr Dr	Rancho Cordova	CA	95670	**888-414-7226**	916-859-2500
Daktronics Inc					
201 Daktronics Dr	Brookings	SD	57006	**800-325-8766**	605-692-0200
NASDAQ: DAKT					
Dotronix Inc					
160 First St SE	New Brighton	MN	55112	**800-720-7218**	651-633-1742
Eizo Nanao Technologies Inc					
5710 Warland Dr	Cypress	CA	90630	**800-800-5202**	562-431-5011
General Digital Corp					
8 Nutmeg Rd S	South Windsor	CT	06074	**800-952-2535**	860-282-2900
Hantronix Inc					
10080 Bubb Rd	Cupertino	CA	95014	**800-525-0811**	408-252-1100
LG Electronics USA Inc					
1000 Sylvan Ave	Englewood Cliffs	NJ	07632	**800-243-0000***	201-816-2000
*Tech Supp					
NEC Display Solutions of America Inc					
500 Pk Blvd Ste 1100	Itasca	IL	60143	**800-632-4662***	630-467-3000
*Cust Svc					
Pioneer Electronics (USA) Inc					
1925 E Dominguez St	Long Beach	CA	90810	**800-421-1404**	310-952-2000
Planar Systems Inc					
1195 NW Compton Dr	Beaverton	OR	97006	**866-475-2627**	503-748-1100
NASDAQ: PLNR					
Sharp Electronics Corp					
1 Sharp Plz	Mahwah	NJ	07430	**800-237-4277**	201-529-8200
Sony Electronics Inc					
1 Sony Dr	Park Ridge	NJ	07656	**800-222-7669***	201-930-1000
*Cust Svc					
Tatung Company of America Inc					
2850 El Presidio St	Long Beach	CA	90810	**800-827-2850**	310-637-2105
TOTAL Marketing LLC					
1751 River Run Ste 200	Ft Worth	TX	76107	**800-998-5269**	817-560-3970
Trans-Lux Corp 26 Pearl St	Norwalk	CT	06850	**800-243-5544**	203-853-4321
OTC: TNLX					
Trans-Lux Fair-Play Inc					
1700 Delaware Ave	Des Moines	IA	50317	**800-247-0265**	515-265-5305
Video Display Corp					
1868 Tucker Industrial Rd	Tucker	GA	30084	**800-241-5005***	770-938-2080
OTC: VIDE ■ *Cust Svc					
Wells-Gardner Electronics Corp					
9500 W 55th St Ste A	McCook	IL	60525	**800-336-6630**	708-290-2100
NYSE: WGA					

173-5 Multimedia Equipment & Supplies

				Toll-Free	Phone
CORSAIR 46221 Landing Pkwy	Fremont	CA	94538	**888-222-4346**	510-657-8747
Kinyo Company Inc					
14235 Lomitas Ave	La Puente	CA	91746	**800-735-4696**	626-333-3711
Matrox Electronic Systems Ltd					
1055 St Regis Blvd	Dorval	QC	H9P2T4	**800-361-1408**	514-822-6000
SpeakerCraft Inc					
940 Columbia Ave	Riverside	CA	92507	**800-448-0976**	951-781-3030

173-6 Printers

				Toll-Free	Phone
AMT Datasouth Corp					
803 Camarillo Springs Rd Ste D	Camarillo	CA	93012	**800-215-9192**	805-388-5799
Citizen Systems America Corp					
363 Van Ness Way Ste 404	Torrance	CA	90501	**800-421-6516**	310-781-1460
Digital Design Inc					
67 Sand Pk Rd	Cedar Grove	NJ	07009	**800-967-7746**	973-857-9500
Epson America Inc					
3840 Kilroy Airport Way	Long Beach	CA	90806	**800-463-7766**	
Hewlett Packard Enterprise (Canada) Co (HP)					
5150 Spectrum Way	Mississauga	ON	L4W5G1	**888-447-4636**	905-206-4725
Hewlett-Packard Co					
3000 Hanover St	Palo Alto	CA	94304	**800-752-0900***	650-857-1501
NYSE: HPQ ■ *Sales					

				Toll-Free	Phone
International Business Machines Corp (IBM)					
1 New OrchaRd Rd	Armonk	NY	10504	**800-426-4968**	914-499-1900
NYSE: IBM					
Kroy LLC 3830 Kelley Ave	Cleveland	OH	44114	**888-888-5769***	216-426-5600
*Cust Svc					
Lexmark International Inc					
740 W New Cir Rd	Lexington	KY	40550	**800-539-6275***	859-232-2000
*NYSE: LXK ■ *Cust Svc*					
Mutoh America Inc					
2602 S 47th St Ste 102	Phoenix	AZ	85034	**800-996-8864**	480-968-7772
Oce-USA Inc					
5450 N Cumberland Ave	Chicago	IL	60656	**800-877-6232**	773-714-8500
Oki Data Americas Inc					
2000 Bishops Gate Blvd	Mount Laurel	NJ	08054	**800-654-3282***	856-235-2600
*Cust Svc					
Pentax Imaging Co					
633 17th St Ste 2600	Denver	CO	80202	**800-877-0155**	303-799-8000
Plastic Card Systems Inc					
31 Pierce St	Northborough	MA	01532	**800-742-2273**	508-351-6210
Primera Technology Inc					
2 Carlson Pkwy N	Plymouth	MN	55447	**800-797-2772**	763-475-6676
Printek Inc					
1517 Townline Rd	Benton Harbor	MI	49022	**800-368-4636**	269-925-3200
Printronix Inc					
6440 Oak Canyon Ste 200	Irvine	CA	92618	**800-665-6210**	714-368-2300
RISO Inc					
800 District Ave Ste 390	Burlington	MA	01803	**800-942-7476***	978-777-7377
*General					
Roland DGA Corp					
15363 Barranca Pkwy	Irvine	CA	92618	**800-542-2307**	949-727-2100
Sato America Inc					
10350A Nations Ford Rd	Charlotte	NC	28273	**888-871-8741**	704-644-1650
Seiko Instruments USA Inc (SII)					
21221 S Western Ave Ste 250	Torrance	CA	90501	**800-688-0817**	310-517-7700
Seiko Instruments USA Inc					
21221 S Western Ave Ste 250	Torrance	CA	90501	**800-688-0817***	310-517-7700
*Sales					
Sharp Electronics Corp					
1 Sharp Plz	Mahwah	NJ	07430	**800-237-4277**	201-529-8200
Star Micronics America Inc					
1150 King George's Post Rd	Edison	NJ	08837	**800-782-7636**	732-623-5500
Stratix					
4920 Avalon Ridge Pkwy	Norcross	GA	30071	**800-883-8300**	770-326-7580
Telpar Inc					
121 Broadway Ste 201	Dover	NH	03820	**800-872-4886**	603-750-7237
Toshiba America Inc					
1251 Ave of the Americas 41st Fl	New York	NY	10020	**800-457-7777**	212-596-0600
TransAct Technologies Inc					
1 Hamden Ctr 2319 Whitney Ave Ste 3B	Hamden	CT	06518	**800-243-8941**	
NASDAQ: TACT					
Unimark Products					
2016 Unimark 9818 Pflumm Rd	Lenexa	KS	66215	**800-255-6356***	913-649-2424
*Cust Svc					
Xante Corp					
2800 Dauphin St Ste 100	Mobile	AL	36606	**800-926-8839**	251-473-6502
Xerox Corp 201 Merritt 7	Norwalk	CT	06856	**800-327-9753**	888-242-9098
NYSE: XRX					
Zebra Technologies Corp					
475 Half Day Rd Ste 500	Lincolnshire	IL	60069	**800-423-0422**	847-634-6700
NASDAQ: ZBRA					

173-7 Scanning Equipment

				Toll-Free	Phone
Accu-Sort Systems Inc					
511 School House Rd	Telford	PA	18969	**800-227-2633**	215-723-0981
Bell + Howell					
3791 S Alston Ave	Durham	NC	27713	**800-961-7282**	847-675-7600
BenQ America Corp					
15375 Barranca Ste A205	Irvine	CA	92618	**866-600-2367**	949-255-9500
CardScan Inc					
25 First St Ste 107	Cambridge	MA	02141	**800-942-6739**	617-492-4200
Computerwise Inc					
302 N Winchester Ln	Olathe	KS	66062	**800-255-3739**	913-829-0600
Datalogic Scanning					
959 Terry St	Eugene	OR	97402	**800-695-5700**	541-683-5700
Hewlett-Packard Co					
3000 Hanover St	Palo Alto	CA	94304	**800-752-0900***	650-857-1501
*NYSE: HPQ ■ *Sales*					
iCAD Inc					
98 Spit Brook Rd Ste 100	Nashua	NH	03062	**866-280-2239**	603-882-5200
NASDAQ: ICAD					
InPath Devices					
3610 Dodge St Ste 200	Omaha	NE	68131	**800-988-1914**	402-345-9200
Oce-USA Inc					
5450 N Cumberland Ave	Chicago	IL	60656	**800-877-6232**	773-714-8500
Peripheral Dynamics Inc					
5150 Campus Dr	Plymouth Meeting	PA	19462	**800-523-0253**	610-825-7090
Roland DGA Corp					
15363 Barranca Pkwy	Irvine	CA	92618	**800-542-2307**	949-727-2100
Scan-Optics Inc					
169 Progress Dr	Manchester	CT	06042	**800-543-8681**	860-645-7878
Scantron Corp 34 Parker	Irvine	CA	92618	**800-722-6876**	949-639-7500
Stratix					
4920 Avalon Ridge Pkwy	Norcross	GA	30071	**800-883-8300**	770-326-7580
Wizcom Technologies Inc					
33 Boston Post Rd W Ste 320	Marlborough	MA	01752	**888-777-0552**	508-251-5388
ZBA Inc					
94 Old Camplain Rd	Hillsborough	NJ	08844	**800-750-4239**	908-359-2070

173-8 Storage Devices

				Toll-Free	Phone
Ampex Data Systems Corp					
500 Broadway	Redwood City	CA	94063	**800-752-7590**	650-367-2011
Apricorn Inc 12191 Kirkham Rd	Poway	CA	92064	**800-458-5448**	858-513-2000

				Toll-Free	Phone
Avere Systems					
910 River Ave	Pittsburgh	PA	15212	**888-882-8373**	412-894-2570
BridgeSTOR LLC					
18060 Old Coach Dr	Poway	CA	92064	**800-280-8204**	858-375-7076
Cirrascale Corp					
12140 Community Rd	Poway	CA	92064	**888-942-3800**	858-874-3800
CMS Peripherals Inc					
12 Mauchly Unit E	Irvine	CA	92618	**800-327-5773**	714-424-5520
CRU Acquisitions Group LLC					
1000 SE Tech Ctr Dr Ste 160	Vancouver	WA	98683	**800-260-9800**	360-816-1800
DataDirect Networks					
9351 Deering Ave	Chatsworth	CA	91311	**800-837-2298**	818-700-7600
Datalink Corp					
10050 Crosstown Cir Ste 500	Eden Prairie	MN	55344	**800-448-6314**	952-944-3462
Digital Peripheral Solutions Inc					
8015 E Crystal Dr	Anaheim	CA	92807	**877-998-3440**	
Disc Makers					
7905 N Rt 130	Pennsauken	NJ	08110	**800-468-9353**	
Dynamic Network Factory Inc					
21353 Cabot Blvd	Hayward	CA	94545	**800-947-4742**	510-265-1122
Edge Electronics Inc					
75 Orville Dr	Bohemia	NY	11716	**800-647-3343**	
Fujitsu Computer Products of America Inc					
1255 E Arques Ave	Sunnyvale	CA	94085	**800-626-4686**	408-746-7000
Hewlett Packard Enterprise (Canada) Co (HP)					
5150 Spectrum Way	Mississauga	ON	L4W5G1	**888-447-4636**	905-206-4725
Hewlett-Packard Co					
3000 Hanover St	Palo Alto	CA	94304	**800-752-0900***	650-857-1501
*NYSE: HPQ ■ *Sales*					
Hitachi America Ltd Computer Div					
2000 Sierra Pt Pkwy	Brisbane	CA	94005	**800-448-2244**	
International Business Machines Corp (IBM)					
1 New OrchaRd Rd	Armonk	NY	10504	**800-426-4968**	914-499-1900
NYSE: IBM					
Kanguru Solutions					
1360 Main St	Millis	MA	02054	**888-526-4878***	508-376-4245
*Sales					
LG Electronics USA Inc					
1000 Sylvan Ave	Englewood Cliffs	NJ	07632	**800-243-0000***	201-816-2000
*Tech Supp					
Luminex Software Inc					
871 Marlborough Ave	Riverside	CA	92507	**888-586-4639***	951 781 4100
*Sales					
Microboards Technology LLC					
8150 Mallory Ct	Chanhassen	MN	55317	**800-646-8881**	952-556-1600
Pioneer Electronics (USA) Inc					
1925 E Dominguez St	Long Beach	CA	90810	**800-421-1404**	310-952-2000
PURE Storage Inc					
650 Castro St Ste 400	Mountain View	CA	94041	**800-379-7873**	650-290-6088
Qualstar Corp					
3990-B Heritage Oak Ct	Simi Valley	CA	93063	**800-468-0680**	805-583-7744
NASDAQ: QBAK					
Quantum Corp					
224 Airport Pkwy Ste 300	San Jose	CA	95110	**800-677-6268***	408-944-4000
*NYSE: QTM ■ *Tech Supp*					
Quantum/ATL					
141 Innovation Dr	Irvine	CA	92617	**800-677-6268**	949-856-7800
Shaffstall Corp					
8531 Bash St	Indianapolis	IN	46250	**800-357-6250**	317-842-2077
Sony Electronics Inc					
1 Sony Dr	Park Ridge	NJ	07656	**800-222-7669***	201-930-1000
*Cust Svc					
Tandberg Data					
10225 Westmoor Dr Ste 125	Westminster	CO	80021	**800-392-2983**	303-442-4400
Think Cp Technologies					
16812 Hale Ave	Irvine	CA	92606	**800-726-2477**	949-833-3222
Tintri Inc					
2570 W El Camino Real	Mountain View	CA	94040	**855-484-6874**	650-209-3900
Toshiba America Inc					
1251 Ave of the Americas 41st Fl	New York	NY	10020	**800-457-7777**	212-596-0600
Unitrends Software Corp					
200 Wheeler Rd 2nd fl	Burlington	MA	01803	**866-359-5411**	803-454-0300
Western Digital Corp					
3355 Michelson Dr Ste 100	Irvine	CA	92612	**800-832-4778**	949-672-7000
NASDAQ: WDC					

174   COMPUTER EQUIPMENT & SOFTWARE - WHOL

SEE ALSO Business Machines - Whol ; Electrical & Electronic Equipment & Parts - Whol

				Toll-Free	Phone
Access Specialties International LLC					
15230 Carrousel Way	Rosemount	MN	55068	**800-332-1013**	651-453-1283
Ahearn & Soper Inc					
100 Woodbine Downs Blvd	Rexdale	ON	M9W5S6	**800-263-4258**	416-675-3999
Alexander Open Systems Inc					
12851 Foster St	Overland Park	KS	66213	**800-473-1110**	913-307-2300
Allied Group Inc, The					
25 Amflex Dr	Cranston	RI	02921	**800-556-6310**	401-946-6100
Altametrics					
3191 Red Hill Ave Ste 100	Costa Mesa	CA	92626	**800-676-1281**	
APCON Inc					
9255 SW Pioneer Ct	Wilsonville	OR	97070	**800-624-6808**	503-682-4050
ASA Tire Master Software					
651 S Stratford Dr	Meridian	ID	83642	**800-241-8472**	208-855-0781
ASI Corp 48289 Fremont Blvd	Fremont	CA	94538	**800-200-0274**	510-226-8000
Autostar Solutions Inc					
1300 Summit Ave Ste 800	Fort Worth	TX	76102	**800-682-2215**	
AVAD Canada Ltd					
205 Courtneypark Dr W Ste 103	Mississauga	ON	L5W0A5	**866-523-2823**	
Avnet Inc 2211 S 47th St	Phoenix	AZ	85034	**888-822-8638**	480-643-2000
NASDAQ: AVT					
Avnet Technology Solutions					
8700 S Price Rd	Tempe	AZ	85284	**800-409-1483**	480-794-6500
Axiom Memory Solutions LLC					
15 Chrysler	Irvine	CA	92618	**888-658-3326**	949-581-1450

			Toll-Free	Phone

Bay Technical Assoc Inc
5239 Ave A ....Long Beach Industrial Park MS 39560 **800-523-2702** 228-563-7334

Burstek
12801 Westlinks Dr Ste 101...................Fort Myers FL 33913 **800-709-2551** 239-495-5900

Butler Technologies Inc
231 W Wayne St ....Butler PA 16001 **800-494-6656** 724-283-6656

CAD/CAM Consulting Services Inc (CCCS)
1525 Rancho Conejo Blvd Ste 103.........Newbury Park CA 91320 **888-375-7676** 805-375-7676

CFP inc (CFP)
4560 L B Mcleod Rd ....Orlando FL 32811 **800-683-0693** 407-843-5811

Champion Solutions Group
791 Pk of Commerce Blvd Ste 200............Boca Raton FL 33487 **800-771-7000** 561-997-2900

Colorfx Inc
10776 Aurora Ave ....Des Moines IA 50322 **800-348-9044**

Column Technologies Inc
10 E 22nd St Ste 300......................Lombard IL 60148 **866-265-8665** 630-515-6660

Comprehensive Traffic Systems Inc
4300 Harlan St ....Wheat Ridge CO 80033 **888-353-9002**

Computer Aided Technology Inc
165 N Arlington Heights Rd
Ste 101..................................Buffalo Grove IL 60089 **888-308-2284**

Computer Dynamics Inc
3030 Whitehall Pk Dr......................Charlotte NC 28273 **866-599-6512**

Comstor Inc
520 White Plains Rd ....Tarrytown NY 10591 **800-955-9590** 914-829-7000

D & H Distributing Company Inc
2525 N Seventh St ....Harrisburg PA 17110 **800-340-1001**

Data Impressions
17418 Studebaker Rd ....Cerritos CA 90703 **800-777-6488** 562-207-9050

Data Sales Company Inc
3450 W Burnsville Pkwy....................Burnsville MN 55337 **800-328-2730** 952-890-8838

De Marque inc
400 Boul Jean-Lesage Bureau 540 ....Quebec QC G1K8W1 **888-458-9143** 418-658-9143

Decision Academic Inc
1705 Tech Ave Ste 1.....................Mississauga ON L4W0A2 **888-661-1933**

Desire2Learn Corp
151 Charles St W Ste 400..................Kitchener ON N2G1H6 **888-772-0325** 519-772-0325

Digital Storage Inc
7611 Green Meadows Dr...................Lewis Center OH 43035 **800-232-3475** 740-548-7179

Dirxion LLC
1859 Bowles Ave Ste 100..................Fenton MO 63026 **888-391-0202** 636-717-2300

Dlt Solutions
13861 Sunrise Valley Dr Ste 400 ....Herndon VA 20171 **800-262-4358** 703-709-7172

Dynamic Computer Corp
23400 Industrial Pk Ct ....Farmington Hills MI 48335 **866-257-2111** 248-473-2200

Electronic Environments Corp
410 Forest St ....Marlborough MA 01752 **800-342-5332** 508-229-1400

Eleven 315 SW 11th Ave ....Portland OR 97205 **866-435-3836** 503-222-4321

Elk River Systems Inc
22 S Central Ave PO Box 6934 ....Harlowton MT 59036 **888-771-0809**

ESRI Canada Ltd
12 Concorde Pl Ste 900 ....Toronto ON M3C3R8 **866-625-4577** 416-441-6035

General Data Co Inc
4354 Ferguson Dr ....Cincinnati OH 45245 **800-733-5252** 513-752-7978

Good Printers Inc
213 Dry River Rd ....Bridgewater VA 22812 **800-296-3731** 540-828-4663

Graphic Products Inc
PO Box 4030 ....Beaverton OR 97076 **888-326-9244** 503-644-5572

GTSI Corp
2553 Dulles View Dr Ste 100 ....Herndon VA 20171 **800-999-4874** 703-502-2000
NASDAQ: GTSI

Helmel Engineering Products Inc
6520 Lockport Rd ....Niagara Falls NY 14305 **800-237-8266** 716-297-8644

Home Automated Living Inc
14401 Sweitzer Ln Ste 600.................Laurel MD 20707 **800-935-5313** 301-498-7000

Integrated Services Inc
15115 SW Sequoia Pkwy Ste 110.........Portland OR 97224 **800-922-3099**

Intelligent Computer Solutions Inc
9350 Eton Ave ....Chatsworth CA 91311 **888-994-4678** 818-998-5805

JourneyEdcom Inc
80 E McDermott Dr ....Allen TX 75002 **800-876-3507** 972-481-2000

Juniper Payments
200 N Broadway Ste 700 ....Wichita KS 67202 **800-453-9400** 316-267-3200

Laser Pros International
1 International Ln ....Rhinelander WI 54501 **888-558-5277** 715-369-5995

Leadman Electronic USA Inc
382 Laurelwood Dr ....Santa Clara CA 95054 **877-532-3626** 408-738-1751

Legacy Electronics Inc
1220 N Dakota St PO Box 348 ....Canton SD 57013 **888-466-3853** 949-498-9600

Lindsey & Company Inc
2302 Llama Dr ....Searcy AR 72143 **800-890-7058** 501-268-5324

Long View Systems Corp
250-2 St SW Ste 2100 ....Calgary AB T2P0C1 **866-515-6900** 403-515-6900

M & A Technology Inc
2045 Chenault Dr ....Carrollton TX 75006 **800-225-1452** 972-490-5803

MacPractice Inc
233 N Eighth St Ste 300 ....Lincoln NE 68508 **877-220-8418** 402-420-2430

MasterGraphics Inc
2979 Triverton Pike Dr....................Madison WI 53711 **800-873-7238** 608-256-4884

Mimaki USA Inc
150 Satellite Blvd NE Ste A................Suwanee GA 30024 **888-530-3988**

Mythics Inc
4525 Main St Ste 1500....................Virginia Beach VA 23462 **866-698-4427** 757-412-4362

Ncs Global
32 Innovation Dr ....Rochester NH 03867 **800-711-6010** 603-926-4300

Open Storage Solutions Inc
2 Castleview Dr ....Toronto ON L6T5S9 **800-387-3419** 905-790-0660

Open Systems of Cleveland Inc
22999 Forbes Rd Ste A.....................Cleveland OH 44146 **888-881-6660** 440-439-2332

Paragon Development Systems Inc (PDS)
13400 Bishops Ln Ste 190................Brookfield WI 53005 **800-966-6090** 262-569-5300

Peak Technologies Inc
10330 Old Columbia Rd ....Columbia MD 21046 **800-926-9212**

PerfectForms Inc
2035 Corte Del Nogal Ste 165 ....Carlsbad CA 92011 **866-900-8588**

Programmer's Paradise Inc
1157 Shrewsbury Ave ....Shrewsbury NJ 07702 **800-599-4388** 732-389-8950

			Toll-Free	Phone

Promark Technology Inc
10900 Pump House Rd Ste B ....Annapolis Junction MD 20701 **800-634-0255** 240-280-8030

Prostar Computer Inc
837 Lawson St ....City of Industry CA 91748 **888-576-4742** 626-839-6472

Provantage Corp
7249 Whipple Ave NW ....North Canton OH 44720 **800-336-1166** 330-494-8715

Rpl Supplies Inc
141 Lanza Ave Bldg 3A......................Garfield NJ 07026 **800-524-0914** 973-767-0880

ScanSource Inc
6 Logue Ct ....Greenville SC 29615 **800-944-2432** 864-288-2432
NASDAQ: SCSC

Scivantage Inc
499 Washington Blvd 11th Fl ....Jersey City NJ 07310 **866-724-8268** 646-452-0050

Set Solutions Inc
1800 W Loop S Ste 700 ....Houston TX 77027 **888-353-0574** 713-956-6600

Software House International (SHI)
290 Davidson Ave ....Somerset NJ 08873 **888-764-8888**

Spruce 9 Cornell Rd Latham ....New York NY 12110 **800-777-8231**

Static Control Components Inc
3010 Lee Ave PO Box 152 ....Sanford NC 27331 **800-488-2426** 919-774-3808

Symco Group
5012 Bristol Industrial Way ....Buford GA 30518 **800-878-8002** 770-451-8002

Synergy Resources Inc
3500 Sunrise Hwy Bldg 100 Ste 201 .....Great River NY 11739 **866-896-6347** 631-665-2050

SYNNEX Canada
200 Ronson Dr ....Etobicoke ON M9W5Z9 **800-268-1220** 416-240-7012

Synex Corp 44201 Nobel Dr ....Fremont CA 94538 **800-756-1888*** 510-656-3333
*NYSE: SNX ■ *Cust Svc*

Syntelli Solutions Inc
13925 Ballantyne Corporate Pl
Ste 260.................................Charlotte NC 28277 **877-796-8355**

Tanner Research Inc
825 S Myrtle Ave ....Monrovia CA 91016 **877-325-2223** 626-471-9700

Tech Data Corp
5350 Tech Data Dr ....Clearwater FL 33760 **800-237-8931** 727-539-7429
NASDAQ: TECD

Tekla Inc
1075 Big Shanty Rd NW Ste 175 ....Kennesaw GA 30144 **877-835-5265** 770-426-5105

Telecorp Products Inc
2000 E Oakley Park Rd Ste 101 ....Walled Lake MI 48390 **800-634-1012** 248-960-1000

Teracai
217 Lawrence Rd E ....North Syracuse NY 13212 **800-913-9459** 315-883-3500

Tharo Systems Inc
2866 Nationwide Pkwy ....Brunswick OH 44212 **800-878-6833** 330-273-4408

TigerDirect Inc
7795 W Flagler St Ste 35 ....Miami FL 33144 **800-800-8300**

Transoft Solutions Inc
13575 Commerce Pkwy Ste 250...........Richmond BC V6V2L1 **888-244-8387** 604-244-8387

Unified Systems Group Inc
1235 64th Ave SE Ste 4a ....Calgary AB T2H2J7 **866-892-8988** 403-686-8088

Us Micro Corp
7000 Highlnds Pkwy SE ....Smyrna GA 30082 **888-876-4276** 770-437-0706

Vartek Services Inc
4770 Hempstead Station Dr ....Dayton OH 45459 **800-954-2524**

Virtucom Inc
5060 Avalon Ridge Pkwy Ste 300.........Norcross GA 30071 **800-890-2611** 770-908-8100

VLN Partners LLC
661 Andersen Dr ....Pittsburgh PA 15220 **877-856-3311** 412-381-0183

WDL Systems
220 Chatham Business Dr ....Pittsboro NC 27312 **800-548-2319*** 919-545-2500
Sales

West-Com Nurse Call Systems Inc
2200 Cordelia Rd ....Fairfield CA 94534 **800-761-1180** 707-428-5900

Westcon Comstor
520 White Plains Rd ....Tarrytown NY 10591 **877-642-7750** 914-829-7000

Westcon Group Inc
520 White Plains Rd ....Tarrytown NY 10591 **800-527-9516** 914-829-7000

Worth Higgins & Assoc Inc
8770 Park Central Dr ....Richmond VA 23227 **800-883-7768** 804-264-2304

Zuercher Technologies LLC
4509 W 58th St ....Sioux Falls SD 57108 **877-229-2205** 605-274-6061

COMPUTER & INTERNET TRAINING PROGRAMS

SEE Training & Certification Programs - Computer & Internet

175   ## COMPUTER MAINTENANCE & REPAIR

			Toll-Free	Phone

24hourtek LLC
268 Bush St ....San Francisco CA 94104 **855-378-0787** 415-294-4449

Accram Inc
2901 W Clarendon Ave ....Phoenix AZ 85017 **800-786-0288**

Acropolis Technology Group
300 Hunter Ave Ste 103 ....Clayton MO 62095 **800-742-6316** 314-890-2208

Advantech Corp
380 Fairview Way ....Milpitas CA 95035 **888-576-9668** 408-519-3898

Aixtek 890 Cowan Rd Ste C...............Burlingame CA 94010 **800-342-4525** 415-282-1188

Ariel Technologies
1980 E Lohman Ave ....Las Cruces NM 88001 **877-524-6860**

Bde Computer Services LLC
399 Lakeview Ave ....Clifton NJ 07011 **877-233-4877** 973-772-8507

BigByte Corp
47400 Seabridge Dr ....Fremont CA 94538 **800-536-6425** 510-249-1100

Brains II
165 Konrad Crescent ....Markham ON L3R9T9 **888-272-4672**

Brentech Inc
9340 Carmel Mtn Rd Ste C...............San Diego CA 92129 **800-709-0440** 858-484-7314

C&W Technologies
2522 SE Federal Hwy ....Stuart FL 34994 **844-241-6442** 772-287-5215

Cascade Computer Maintenance Inc
750 Front St NE ....Salem OR 97302 **800-421-7934** 503-581-0081

Computer Troubleshooters USA
7100 E Pleasant Valley Rd
Ste 300...............................Independence OH 44131 **877-704-1702** 216-674-0645

Computer Networking Products & Systems **551**

			Toll-Free	Phone

ComputerPlus Sales & Service Inc
5 Northway Ct — Greer SC 29651 — **800-849-4426** — 864-801-9003

Comware Technical Services Inc
17922 Sky Park Cir Ste E — Irvine CA 92614 — **800-460-1970** — 949-851-9600

Data Exchange Corp
3600 Via Pescador — Camarillo CA 93012 — **800-237-7911** — 805-388-1711

Data Vista Inc
5198 US-130 Ste A — Mansfield NJ 08016 — **800-797-3527** — 609-702-9300

Dataserv Corp 8625 F St — Omaha NE 68127 — **888-901-8700** — 402-339-8700

DBK Concepts Inc
12905 SW 129 Ave — Miami FL 33186 — **800-725-7226** — 305-596-7226

DecisionOne Corp
426 W Lancaster Ave — Devon PA 19333 — **800-767-2876** — 610-296-6000

Desktop Consulting Services
43311 Joy Rd — Canton MI 48187 — **888-600-2731**

Electrosonics
17150 15 Mile Rd — Fraser MI 48026 — **800-858-8448** — 586-415-5555

Emf Inc 60 Foundry St — Keene NH 03431 — **800-992-3003** — 603-352-8400

Essential Technologies Inc
1107 Hazeltine Blvd Ste 477 — Chaska MN 55318 — **844-375-7219** — 952-368-9001

Expert Laser Service
62 Pleasant St PO Box 744 — Southbridge MA 01550 — **800-622-3535**

Insight Computing LLC
448 Ignacio Blvd Ste 490 — Novato CA 94949 — **800-380-8985**

Integranetics
325 Park Plaza Dr 2b — Owensboro KY 42301 — **800-291-9307** — 270-685-6016

Integration Technologies Group Inc
2745 Hartland Rd Ste 200 — Falls Church VA 22043 — **800-835-7823** — 703-698-8282

Intratek Computer Inc
5431 Industrial Dr — Huntington Beach CA 92649 — **800-892-8282** — 714-892-0892

Matthijssen Inc
14 Rt 10 — East Hanover NJ 07936 — **800-845-2200**

Mike Collins & Associates Inc
6048 Century Oaks Dr — Chattanooga TN 37416 — **800-347-6950** — 423-892-8899

POSitive Software Co
604 W Kennewick Ave — Kennewick WA 99336 — **800-735-6860** — 509-371-0600

Pro-data Computer Services Inc
2809 S 160th St Ste 401 — Omaha NE 68130 — **800-228-6318** — 402-697-7575

Ptc Select LLC
2450 N Knoxville Ave — Peoria IL 61604 — **800-225-2320** — 309-685-8400

Reboot Computer Services Inc
70-11 Austin St Ste 3L — Forest Hills NY 11375 — **866-228-6286**

Rescuecom Corp
2560 Burnet Ave — Syracuse NY 13206 — **800-737-2837**

Sentinel Technologies Inc
2550 Warrenville Rd — Downers Grove IL 60515 — **800-769-4343** — 630-769-4300

Service Express Inc
3854 Broadmoor Ave SE — Grand Rapids MI 49512 — **800-940-4484** — 800-940-5585

Smartware Computer Services
2821 S Bay St Ste B — Eustis FL 32726 — **800-796-5000** — 352-483-4350

Tecinfo Communication LLC
601 N Deer Creek Dr E — Leland MS 38756 — **800-863-5415** — 662-686-9009

Teksouth Corp
1420 Northbrook Dr Ste 220 — Gardendale AL 35071 — **800-842-1470** — 205-631-1500

Wolf Technology Group Inc
1 Chick Springs Rd Ste 112 — Greenville SC 29609 — **833-482-6435**

176 COMPUTER NETWORKING PRODUCTS & SYSTEMS

SEE ALSO Telecommunications Equipment & Systems ; Modems ; Systems & Utilities Software

			Toll-Free	Phone

Allied Telesyn International Corp
19800 N Creek Pkwy Ste 100 — Bothell WA 98011 — **800-424-4284** — 425-481-3895

American Megatrends Inc (AMI)
5555 Oakbrook Pkwy Bldg 200 — Norcross GA 30093 — **800-828-9264** — 770-246-8600

ASA Computers Inc
645 National Ave — Mountain View CA 94043 — **800-732-5727** — 650-230-8000

Avaya Inc
211 Mt Airy Rd — Basking Ridge NJ 07920 — **866-462-8292** — 908-953-6000

Axis Communications Inc (ACI)
100 Apollo Dr — Chelmsford MA 01824 — **800-444-2947** — 978-614-2000

Black Box Corp 1000 Pk Dr — Lawrence PA 15055 — **877-877-2269**
NASDAQ: BBOX

Cambex Corp
337 Tpke Rd — Southborough MA 01772 — **800-325-5565** — 508-281-0209
OTC: CBEX

Chatsworth Products Inc
31425 Agoura Rd — Westlake Village CA 91361 — **800-834-4969** — 818-735-6100

CIENA Corp 7035 Ridge Rd — Hanover MD 21076 — **800-207-3714** — 410-694-5700

Cisco Systems Inc
170 W Tasman Dr — San Jose CA 95134 — **800-553-6387** — 408-526-4000
NASDAQ: CSCO

CompuCom Systems Inc
7171 Forest Ln — Dallas TX 75230 — **800-597-0555*** — 972-856-3600
*Cust Svc

Comtrol
100 Fifth Ave NW — Maple Grove MN 55112 — **800-926-6876** — 763-957-6000

Continental Resources Inc
175 Middlesex Tpke — Bedford MA 01730 — **800-937-4688** — 781-275-0850

Crystal Group Inc
850 Kacena Rd — Hiawatha IA 52233 — **877-279-7863** — 319-378-1636

Cubix Corp
2800 Lockheed Way — Carson City NV 89706 — **800-829-0550*** — 775-888-1000
*Sales

Cyberdata Corp 3 Justin Ct — Monterey CA 93940 — **800-363-8010** — 831-373-2601

D-Link Systems Inc
17595 Mt Herrmann St — Fountain Valley CA 92708 — **800-326-1688**

Daly Computers Inc
22521 Gateway Ctr Dr — Clarksburg MD 20871 — **800-955-3259** — 301-670-0381

Dell Inc 1 Dell Way — Round Rock TX 78682 — **800-879-3355** — 512-338-4400
NASDAQ: DELL

Digi International Inc
11001 Bren Rd E — Minnetonka MN 55343 — **877-912-3444** — 952-912-3444
NASDAQ: DGII

Dot Hill Systems Corp
1351 S Sunset St — Longmont CO 80501 — **800-872-2783** — 303-845-3200
NASDAQ: HILL

Echelon Corp
550 Meridian Ave — San Jose CA 95126 — **888-324-3566** — 408-938-5200
NASDAQ: ELON

Egenera Inc
80 Central St — Boxborough MA 01719 — **866-301-3117** — 978-206-6300

Extreme Networks Inc
3585 Monroe St — Santa Clara CA 95051 — **888-257-3000** — 408-579-2800
NASDAQ: EXTR

Ezenia! Inc
14 Celina Ave Ste 17 — Nashua NH 03063 — **800-966-2301** — 253-509-7850

F5 Networks Inc
401 Elliott Ave W — Seattle WA 98119 — **888-882-4447** — 206-272-5555
NASDAQ: FFIV

Fujitsu Computer Systems Corp
1250 E Arques Ave — Sunnyvale CA 94085 — **800-538-8460** — 408-746-6000

Futurex Inc
864 Old Boerne Rd — Bulverde TX 78163 — **800-251-5112** — 830-980-9782

iGo Inc
17800 N Perimeter Dr Ste 200 — Scottsdale AZ 85255 — **888-205-0093** — 480-596-0061
NASDAQ: IGOI

iLinc Communications Inc
2999 N 44th St Ste 650 — Phoenix AZ 85018 — **800-767-9054** — 602-952-1200

IMC Networks Corp
19772 Pauling — Foothill Ranch CA 92610 — **800-624-1070** — 949-465-3000

Juniper Networks Inc
1194 N Mathilda Ave — Sunnyvale CA 94089 — **888-586-4737** — 408-745-2000
NYSE: JNPR

Netplanner Systems Inc
3145 Northwoods Pkwy Ste 800 — Norcross GA 30071 — **800-795-1975** — 770-662-5482

Network Appliance Inc
495 E Java Dr — Sunnyvale CA 94089 — **800-443-4537*** — 408-822-6000
NASDAQ: NTAP ■ *Sales

Network Dynamics Inc
700 Brooker Creek Blvd Ste 1000 — Oldsmar FL 34677 — **877-818-8597** — 813-818-8597

Polycom Inc
4750 Willow Rd — Pleasanton CA 94588 — **800-765-9266**

PrimeArray Systems Inc
127 Riverneck Rd — Chelmsford MA 01824 — **800-433-5133** — 978-054-0250

Ringdale Inc
101 Halmar Cove — Georgetown TX 78628 — **888-288-9080** — 512-288-9080

Safari Circuits Inc
411 Washington St — Otsego MI 49078 — **888-694-7230** — 269-694-9471

Server Technology Inc
1040 Sandhill Dr — Reno NV 89521 — **800-835-1515** — 775-284-2000

SonicWALL Inc
2001 Logic Dr — San Jose CA 95124 — **888-557-6642** — 408-745-9600

SteelCloud Inc
20110 Ashbrook Pl Ste 270 — Ashburn VA 20147 — **800-296-3866** — 703-674-5500
OTC: SCLD

Storage Engine Inc
1 Sheila Dr — Tinton Falls NJ 07724 — **866-734-8899** — 732-747-6995

Strictly Business Computer Systems Inc
848 Fourth Ave Ste 200 — Huntington WV 25701 — **888-529-0401**

Systech Corp
16510 Via Esprillo — San Diego CA 92127 — **800-800-8970** — 858-674-6500

Systemax Inc
11 Harbor Pk Dr — Port Washington NY 11050 — **800-344-6783** — 516-608-7000
NYSE: SYX

TalkPoint Holdings LLC
100 William St Ste 100 — New York NY 10038 — **866-323-8660**

Technology Integration Group (TIG)
7810 Trade St — San Diego CA 92121 — **800-858-0549**

Tekworks Inc
13000 Gregg St Ste B — Poway CA 92064 — **877-835-9675** — 858-668-1705

Tel-e Technologies
7 Kodiak Crescent — Toronto ON M3J3E5 — **800-661-2340** — 416-631-1300

Telebyte Inc
355 Marcus Blvd — Hauppauge NY 11788 — **800-835-3298** — 631-423-3232

Telkonet Inc
10200 W Innovation Dr Ste 300 — Milwaukee WI 53226 — **888-703-9398*** — 414-223-0473
OTC: TKOI ■ *Sales

Transition Networks Inc
10900 Red Cir Dr — Minnetonka MN 55343 — **800-526-9267** — 952-941-7600

Transource Computers Corp
2405 W Utopia Rd — Phoenix AZ 85027 — **800-486-3715** — 623-879-8882

Trendware International Inc
20675 Manhattan Pl — Torrance CA 90501 — **888-326-6061** — 310-961-5500

UNICOM
565 Brea Canyon Rd Ste A — Walnut CA 91789 — **800-346-6668** — 626-964-7873

Unimark Products
2016 Unimark 9818 Pflumm Rd — Lenexa KS 66215 — **800-255-6356*** — 913-649-2424
*Cust Svc

US Robotics Corp
1300 E Woodfield Dr Ste 506 — Schaumburg IL 60173 — **877-710-0884** — 847-874-2000

Virtela Technology Services Inc
5680 Greenwood Plz Blvd — Greenwood Village CO 80111 — **877-803-9629** — 720-475-4000

Visara International Inc
2700 Gateway Centre Blvd Ste 600 — Morrisville NC 27560 — **888-334-4380** — 919-882-0200

WatchGuard Technologies Inc
505 Fifth Ave S Ste 500 — Seattle WA 98104 — **800-734-9905*** — 206-613-6600
*Sales

WAV Inc 2380 Prospect Dr — Aurora IL 60502 — **800-678-2419** — 630-818-1000

WideBand Corp
401 W Grand St — Gallatin MO 64640 — **888-663-3050** — 660-663-3000

Winchester Systems Inc
101 Billerica Ave Bldg 5 — Billerica MA 01862 — **800-325-3700*** — 781-265-0200
*Cust Svc

Works Computing Inc
1801 American Blvd E Ste 12 — Bloomington MN 55425 — **866-222-4077** — 952-746-1580

World Data Products Inc
1105 Xenium Ln N Ste 200 — Plymouth MN 55441 — **888-210-7636**

Classified Section

		Toll-Free	Phone

177 COMPUTER PROGRAMMING SERVICES - CUSTOM

SEE ALSO Computer Systems Design Services ; Computer Software

4th Source Inc
2502 N Rocky Point Dr Ste 960 ...... Tampa FL 33607 **855-875-4700**
AcademyOne Inc
101 Lindenwood Dr Ste 220 ...... Malvern PA 19355 **888-434-2150**
Access Innovations Inc
4725 Indian School Rd NE Ste 100 ...... Albuquerque NM 87110 **800-926-8328** 505-265-3591
AccuCode Inc
6886 S Yosemite St Ste 100 ...... Centennial CO 80112 **866-705-9879** 303-639-6111
Accumedic Computer Systems Inc
11 Grace Ave Ste 401 ...... Great Neck NY 11021 **800-765-9300** 516-466-6800
Accuzip
3216 El Camino Real ...... Atascadero CA 93422 **800-233-0555** 805-461-7300
Actsoft Inc
10006 N Dale Mabry Hwy Ste 100 ...... Tampa FL 33618 **888-732-6638** 813-936-2331
Advanced Chemistry Development Inc
110 Yonge St 14th Fl ...... Toronto ON M5C1T4 **800-304-3988** 416-368-3435
Advanced Computing Solutions Group Inc
19125 Northcreek Pkwy ...... Bothell WA 98011 **800-550-8007** 425-609-3165
Advanced Digital Data Inc
6 Laurel Dr ...... Flanders NJ 07836 **800-922-0972** 973-584-4026
AdvanTech Inc
2661 Riva Rd Ste 1050 ...... Annapolis MD 21401 **888-266-2841** 410-266-8000
Aeon Nexus Corp
174 Glen St ...... Glens Falls NY 12801 **866-252-1251** 518-338-1551
agencyQ
1825 K St NW Ste 500 ...... Washington DC 20006 **866-734-7932** 202-776-9090
AgileAssets Inc
3001 Bee Caves Rd Ste 200 ...... Austin TX 78746 **800-877-8734** 512-327-4200
Agilysys NV LLC
1000 Windward Concourse Ste 250 ...... Alpharetta GA 30005 **800-241-8768** 770-810-7800
Ahead Hum Resources
2209 Heather Ln ...... Louisville KY 40218 **888-749-1000** 502-485-1000
Alebra Technologies Inc
3810 Pheasant Ridge Dr NE Ste 100 ...... Minneapolis MN 55449 **888-340-2727** 651-366-6140
Alphinat Inc
2000 Peel Ste 680 ...... Montreal QC H3A2W5 **877-773-9799** 514-398-9799
Alta Via Consulting LLC
525 Tanasi Cir ...... Loudon TN 37774 **877-258-2842**
Altech Services Inc
695 US Rt 46W Ste 301B ...... Fairfield NJ 07004 **888-725-8324**
Altep Inc 7450 Remcon Cir ...... El Paso TX 79912 **800-263-0940** 915-533-8722
AMSNET Inc
502 Commerce Way ...... Livermore CA 94551 **800-893-3660**
Analytical Graphics Inc
220 Vly Creek Blvd ...... Exton PA 19341 **800-220-4785** 610-981-8000
Applied Business Software Inc
2847 Gundry Ave ...... Long Beach CA 90755 **800-833-3343**
Applied Software Inc
3915 National Dr Ste 200 ...... Burtonsville MD 20866 **888-624-8439**
AppTech Corp
2011 Palomar Airport Rd Ste 102 ...... Carlsbad CA 92011 **877-720-0022*** 760-707-5959
*Support
Apriva Inc
8501 N Scottsdale Rd Ste 110 ...... Scottsdale AZ 85253 **877-277-0728** 480-421-1210
Archive-cd LLC
910 Beverly Way ...... Jacksonville OR 97530 **800-323-1868** 541-899-5704
Aristatek Inc
710 E Garfield St Ste 220 ...... Laramie WY 82070 **877-912-2200** 307-721-2126
Aruba Networks Inc
1344 Crossman Ave ...... Sunnyvale CA 94089 **800-943-4526** 408-227-4500
Assist Cornerstone Technologies Inc
150 W Civic Ctr Dr Ste 601 ...... Sandy UT 84070 **800-732-0136**
Atlas Systems Inc
5712 Cleveland St Ste 200 ...... Virginia Beach VA 23462 **800-567-7401** 757-467-7872
Avidian Technologies Inc
2053 152nd Ave NE ...... Redmond WA 98052 **800-860-5534** 800-399-8980
Avtech Software Inc
16 Cutler St Cutler Mill ...... Warren RI 02885 **888-220-6700**
Axcient Inc
1161 San Antonio Rd ...... Mountain View CA 94043 **800-715-2339**
Axiom Software Ltd
115 Stevens Ave Ste 320 ...... Valhalla NY 10595 **800-588-8805** 914-769-8800
Axxiem Web Solutions
276 Fifth Ave Ste 704 ...... New York NY 10001 **877-429-9436*** 914-478-7600
*General
Barcontrol Systems & Services Inc
113 Edinburgh Ct ...... Greenville SC 29607 **800-947-4362** 864-421-0050
Basis Technology Corp
1 Alewife Ctr ...... Cambridge MA 02140 **800-697-2062** 617-386-2000
Bedrock Prime
1309 N Wilson Rd Ste A ...... Radcliff KY 40160 **866-334-5914** 270-351-8043
Benefit Express Services LLC
1700 E Golf Rd Ste 1000 ...... Schaumburg IL 60173 **877-369-2153**
Benelogic LLC
9475 Deereco Rd Ste 310 ...... Timonium MD 21093 **877-716-6615**
BeQuick Software Inc
601 Heritage Dr Ste 442 ...... Jupiter FL 33458 **866-267-5105** 561-721-9600
Berkeley Varitronics Systems Inc
255 Liberty St Liberty Corporate Pk ...... Metuchen NJ 08840 **888-737-4287** 732-548-3737
Billpro Management Systems Inc
30575 Euclid Ave ...... Wickliffe OH 44092 **800-736-0587** 440-516-3776
Blue Chip Computer Systems
2554 Lincoln Blvd Ste 232 ...... Venice CA 90291 **800-325-9868** 310-410-0126
Blue Mountain Quality Resources Inc
475 Rolling Ridge Dr Ste 200 ...... State College PA 16801 **800-982-2388** 814-234-2417
Boingo Wireless Inc
10960 Wilshire Blvd Ste 800 ...... Los Angeles CA 90024 **800-880-4117** 310-586-5180
Bradford Technologies Inc
302 Piercy Rd ...... San Jose CA 95138 **866-445-8367** 408-360-8520
BrainX 45 Rincon Dr ...... Camarillo CA 93012 **844-927-2469**
BTM Solutions Inc
572 Yorkville Rd E ...... Columbus MS 39702 **800-909-9381** 662-328-2400

BuildASigncom
11525B Stonehollow Dr Ste 100 ...... Austin TX 78758 **800-330-9622** 512-374-9850
Bullhorn Inc
33-41 Farnsworth St 5th Fl ...... Boston MA 02210 **800-206-7934** 617-478-9100
Buscomm Inc
11696 Lilburn Park Rd ...... Saint Louis MO 63146 **800-283-7755** 314-567-7755
CareWatch Inc
3483 Satellite Blvd Ste 211 S ...... Duluth GA 30096 **800-901-2454** 770-409-0244
Carina Technology Inc
2366 Whitesburg Dr ...... Huntsville AL 35801 **866-915-5464** 256-704-0422
Carnegie Learning Inc
501 Grant St Ste 1075 ...... Pittsburgh PA 15219 **888-851-7094**
Cherryroad Technologies Inc
301 Gibraltar Dr Ste 2C ...... Morris Plains NJ 07950 **877-402-7804** 973-402-7802
Cistera Networks Inc
5045 Lorimar Dr Ste 180 ...... Plano TX 75024 **866-965-8646** 972-381-4699
Citizant Inc
15000 Conference Center Dr Ste 500 ...... Chantilly VA 20151 **877-248-4926** 703-667-9420
Clients First Business Solutions LLC
670 N Beers St Bldg 4 ...... Holmdel NJ 07733 **866-677-6290**
CMA Consulting Services Inc
700 Troy Schenectady Rd ...... Latham NY 12110 **800-276-6101** 518-783-9003
Coaxis Inc
1515 SE Water Ave Ste 300 ...... Portland OR 97214 **800-333-3197**
CollabNet Inc
8000 Marina Blvd Ste 600 ...... Brisbane CA 94005 **888-532-6823** 650-228-2500
College Health Services LLC
112 Turnpike Rd Ste 304 ...... Westborough MA 01581 **866-636-8336**
Commercial Programming Systems Inc
4400 Coldwater Canyon Ave ...... Studio City CA 91604 **888-277-4562** 323-851-2681
Communications Resource Inc
8280 Greensboro Dr Ste 500 ...... Mc Lean VA 22102 **888-900-9757** 703-245-4120
COMPanion Corp
1831 Ft Union Blvd ...... Salt Lake City UT 84121 **800-347-6439** 801-943-7277
Complete Innovations Inc
WaterPark Pl 88 Queens Quay W Ste 200 ...... Toronto ON M5J0B8 **800-220-0779** 905-944-0863
Compli 711 SW Alder Ste 200 ...... Portland OR 97205 **877-522-4276*** 800-481-8309
*Support
Compusearch Software Systems Inc
21251 Ridgetop Cir ...... Dulles VA 20166 **855-817-2720** 571-449-4000
Computer Arts Inc
320 SW Fifth Ave ...... Meridian ID 83642 **800-365-9335** 208-385-9335
Computer Solutions
814 Arion Pkwy Ste 101 ...... San Antonio TX 78216 **800-326-4304** 210-369-0300
Computer Team Inc
1049 State St ...... Bettendorf IA 52722 **800-355-0450** 563-355-0426
ComputerLogic Inc
4951 Forsyth Rd ...... Macon GA 31210 **800-933-6564** 478-474-5593
Computerworks of Chicago Inc
5153 N Clark St ...... Chicago IL 60640 **800-977-8212** 773-275-4437
Computrition Inc
8521 Fallbrook Ave Ste 100 ...... West Hills CA 91304 **800-222-4488**
CoNetrix LLC
5214 68th St Ste 200 ...... Lubbock TX 79424 **800-356-6568** 806-687-8600
Construx Software
11820 Northup Way Ste E-200 ...... Bellevue WA 98005 **866-296-6300** 425-636-0100
Consult Usa Inc
634 Alpha Dr ...... Pittsburgh PA 15238 **866-963-8621** 412-963-8621
Corning Data Services Inc
139 Wardell St ...... Corning NY 14830 **800-455-5996** 607-936-4241
Corptax LLC
1751 Lake Cook Rd Ste 100 ...... Deerfield IL 60015 **800-966-1639**
Crescendo Systems Corp
1600 Montgolfier ...... Laval QC H7T0A2 **800-724-2930** 450-973-8029
Culinary Software Services Inc
1900 Folsom St Ste 210 ...... Boulder CO 80302 **800-447-1466** 303-447-3334
Customer Service Delivery Platform (CSDP)
15615 Alton Pkwy Ste 310 ...... Irvine CA 92618 **888-741-2737**
Cutting Edge Networked Storage
435 W Bradley Ave Ste C ...... El Cajon CA 92020 **800-257-1666** 619-258-7800
Cyber-Ark Software Inc
60 Wells Ave ...... Newton MA 02459 **888-808-9005** 617-965-1544
D-Ta Systems Inc
2500 Lancaster Rd ...... Ottawa ON K1B4S5 **877-382-3222** 613-745-8713
Data Financial Inc
1100 Glen Oaks Ln ...... Mequon WI 53092 **800-334-8334** 262-243-5511
Data Select Systems Inc
2829 Townsgate Rd Ste 300 ...... Westlake Village CA 91361 **800-535-9978** 805-446-2090
Data Ventures Inc
6101 Carnegie Blvd Ste 520 ...... Charlotte NC 28209 **888-431-2676** 704-887-1012
Dataclarity Corp
7200 Falls of Neuse Rd Ste 202 ...... Raleigh NC 27615 **800-963-5508** 919-256-6700
Datafirst Corp
2700 Sumner Blvd ...... Raleigh NC 27616 **800-634-8504** 919-876-6650
DataWorks Plus LLC
728 N Pleasantburg Dr ...... Greenville SC 29607 **866-632-2780** 864-672-2780
DecisionPoint Systems Inc
19655 Descartes ...... Foothill Ranch CA 92610 **800-336-3670** 949-465-0065
OTC: DPSI
Delta Data
1500 Sixth Ave Ste 1 ...... Columbus GA 31901 **800-723-8274** 706-324-0855
Denim Group Ltd
1354 N Loop 1604 E Ste 110 ...... San Antonio TX 78232 **844-572-4400**
Desco Dental Systems LLC
5005 W Loomis Rd Ste 100 ...... Greenfield WI 53220 **800-392-7610** 414-281-9192
Dh Web Inc
11377 Robinwood Dr Ste D ...... Hagerstown MD 21742 **877-567-6599** 301-733-7672
Digital ChoreoGraphics
PO Box 8268 ...... Newport Beach CA 92658 **800-548-1969** 949-548-1969
Digital I-Ollc
1424 30th St ...... San Diego CA 92154 **866-423-4433** 619-423-4433
Digital Intelligence Systems Corp (DISYS)
8270 Greensboro Dr Ste 1000 ...... McLean VA 22102 **855-765-8553** 703-752-7900
Dino Software Corp
PO Box 7105 ...... Alexandria VA 22307 **800-480-3466** 703-768-2610
Donatech Corp
2094 185th St Ste 110 ...... Fairfield IA 52556 **800-328-2133** 641-472-7474

				Toll-Free	Phone
DoubleCheck LLC 101 Gilbraltar Dr	Morris Plains	NJ	07950	**888-299-3980**	973-984-2229
Eagle Technology Inc 11019 N Towne Sq Rd	Mequon	WI	53092	**800-388-3268**	262-241-3845
Echo Group Inc, The 15 Washington St	Conway	NH	03818	**800-635-8209**	603-447-8600
Edge Systems LLC 3S721 W Ave Ste 200 *Tech Supp	Warrenville	IL	60555	**800-352-3343***	630-810-9669
Edgenet 2948 Sidco Dr	Nashville	TN	37204	**877-334-3638**	
EdgeWave Inc 15333 Ave of Science	San Diego	CA	92128	**800-782-3762**	858-676-2277
Education Management Systems Inc 4110 Shipyard Blvd	Wilmington	NC	28403	**800-541-8999**	910-799-0121
Electrocon International Inc 405 Little Lake Dr	Ann Arbor	MI	48103	**888-240-4044**	734-761-8612
Ellie Mae Inc 4155 Hopyard Rd Ste 200	Pleasanton	CA	94588	**800-848-4904**	925-227-7000
Energent Inc 22 Frederick St Ste 1114	Kitchener	ON	N2H6M6	**866-441-1143**	
Entero Corp 1040 Seventh Ave SW Ste 500	Calgary	AB	T2P3G9	**877-261-1820**	403-261-1820
Eoriginal Inc 351 W Camden St Ste 800	Baltimore	MD	21201	**866-935-1776**	
Epac Software Technologies Inc 42 Ladd St	East Greenwich	RI	02818	**888-336-3722**	
Eric A King 301 Grant St Ste 4300	Pittsburgh	PA	15219	**888-742-2454**	281-667-4200
Execu/Tech Systems Inc 537 Harrison Ave *Sales	Panama City	FL	32401	**800-232-1626***	850-747-0581
Execusys Inc 6767 N Wickham Rd	Melbourne	FL	32940	**800-454-3081**	321-253-0077
Extensis 1800 SW First Ave Ste 500	Portland	OR	97201	**800-796-9798**	503-274-2020
Externetworks 10 Corporate Pl S	Piscataway	NJ	08854	**800-238-6360**	732-465-0001
Eyefinity Inc 10875 International Dr Ste 200	Rancho Cordova	CA	95670	**877-448-0707**	
FieldWorker Products Ltd 88 Queens Quay W Ste 200	Toronto	ON	M5J0B8	**800-220-0779**	905-944-0863
FileCatalyst Inc 1725 St Laurent Blvd Ste 205	Ottawa	ON	K1G3V4	**877-327-9387**	613-667-2439
FileTrail Inc 1990 The Alameda	San Jose	CA	95126	**800-310-0299**	408-289-1300
First Insight Corp 6723 NE Bennett St Ste 200	Hillsboro	OR	97124	**800-920-1940**	
Freedom Scientific Inc 11800 31st Ct N	St. Petersburg	FL	33716	**800-444-4443**	727-803-8000
FusionStorm 2 Bryant St Ste 150	San Francisco	CA	94105	**800-228-8324**	
GeBBS Healthcare Solutions Inc 600 Corporate Pointe Ste 1250	Culver City	CA	90230	**888-539-4282**	
Gene Codes Corp 775 Technology Dr	Ann Arbor	MI	48108	**800-497-4939**	734-769-7249
Gevity Consulting Inc 375 Water St Ste 350	Vancouver	BC	V6B5C6	**800-785-3303**	604-608-1779
Global Nest LLC 281 State Rt 79 N Ste 208	Morganville	NJ	07751	**866-850-5872**	732-333-5848
Global Reach Internet Productions LLC 2321 N Loop Dr Ste 101	Ames	IA	50010	**877-254-9828**	515-996-0996
Go 2 Group 138 N Hickory Ave	Bel Air	MD	21014	**877-442-4669**	
GST Inc 12881 166th St	Cerritos	CA	90703	**800-833-0128**	562-345-8700
Gwynn Group 600 E Las Colinas Blvd Ste 520	Irving	TX	75039	**877-941-7075**	214-941-7075
H & W Computer Systems Inc 6154 N Meeker Pl Ste 100	Boise	ID	83713	**800-338-6692**	208-377-0336
Hanson Information System 2433 W White Oaks Dr	Springfield	IL	62704	**888-245-8468**	217-726-2400
Harvey Software Inc 7050 Winkler Rd Ste 104	Fort Myers	FL	33919	**800-231-0296**	
Hawk Ridge Systems 4 Orinda Way Bldg B Ste 100	Orinda	CA	94563	**877-266-4469**	
Health Care Software (HCS) 1599 Rt 34 S Ste 2	Wall Township	NJ	07727	**800-524-1038**	
Healthco Information Systems 7657 SW Mohawk St	Tualatin	OR	97062	**888-740-7734**	
Horizon Software International LLC 2850 Premier Pkwy Ste 100	Duluth	GA	30097	**800-741-7100**	770-554-6353
Human Factors International Inc 410 W Lowe Ave	Fairfield	IA	52556	**800-242-1480**	641-472-4480
Idea Works Inc, The 100 W Briarwood Ln	Columbia	MO	65203	**888-444-5772**	573-445-4554
Ideal Software Systems Inc 4909 29th Ave	Meridian	MS	39305	**800-964-3325**	601-693-1673
Ignify Inc 200 Pine Ave 4th Fl	Long Beach	CA	90802	**888-599-4332**	562-219-2000
iLookabout Corp 383 Richmond St Ste 408	London	ON	N6A3C4	**866-963-2015**	519-963-2015
Imaginet Resources Corp 233 Portage Ave	Winnipeg	MB	R3B2A7	**800-989-6022**	204-989-6022
Implementation & Consulting Services Inc (ICS) 500 Office Center Dr Ste 400	Washington	PA	19034	**844-432-8326**	
Infinite Campus Inc 4321 109th Ave NE	Blaine	MN	55449	**800-850-2335**	651-631-0000
Informant Technologies Inc 19 Jenkins Ave Ste 200	Lansdale	PA	19446	**877-503-4636**	215-412-9165
Infosilem 99 Emilien-marcoux Ste 201	Blainville	QC	J7C0B4	**866-420-5585**	450-420-5585
Infosource Inc 1300 City View Ctr	Oviedo	FL	32765	**800-393-4636**	407-796-5200
Ingenuity Systems Inc 1700 Seaport Blvd Ste 3	Redwood City	CA	94063	**866-464-3684**	
Inmedius Inc 2247 Babcock Blvd	Pittsburgh	PA	15237	**800-697-7110**	
Innovative Data Management Systems LLC 4006 W Azeele St	Tampa	FL	33609	**866-706-4588**	813-207-2025
Innovative Systems Group Inc 799 Roosevelt Rd	Glen Ellyn	IL	60137	**800-739-2400**	630-858-8500
Integrity Systems & Solutions LLC 1247 Highland Ave Ste 202	Cheshire	CT	06410	**866-446-8797**	
iRise 2301 Rosecrans Ave Ste 4100	El Segundo	CA	90245	**800-556-0399**	
Isc Sales Inc 4421 Tradition Trl	Plano	TX	75093	**800-836-7472**	972-964-2700
IV Most Consulting Inc 33 Park Dr	Mt Kisco	NY	10549	**800-448-6678**	914-864-2781
Ivenuecom 9925 Painter Ave Ste A	Whittier	CA	90605	**800-683-8314**	
Jolera Inc 365 Bloor St E 2nd Fl	Toronto	ON	M4W3L4	**800-292-4078**	416-410-1011
Keycentrix LLC 2420 N Woodlawn Bldg 500	Wichita	KS	67220	**800-444-8486**	
KEYW Corp 7740 Milestone Pkwy Ste 400	Hanover	MD	21076	**800-340-1001**	443-733-1600
KUBRA Data Transfer Ltd 5050 Tomken Rd	Mississauga	ON	L4W5B1	**800-766-6616**	905-624-2220
LanXpert Corp 605 Market St Ste 410	San Francisco	CA	94105	**888-499-1703**	415-543-1033
Lead Technologies Inc 1927 S Tryon St Ste 200	Charlotte	NC	28203	**800-637-4699**	704-332-5532
LifeWIRE Corp 129 Blantyre Ave Ste 200	Toronto	ON	M1N2R6	**888-738-4260**	
Logical Images Inc 3445 Winton Pl Ste 240	Rochester	NY	14623	**800-357-7611**	585-427-2790
Lynx Media Inc 12501 Chandler Blvd Ste 202	Valley Village	CA	91607	**800-451-5969**	818-761-5859
Marathon Digital Services 901 N Eighth st	Kansas City	KS	64108	**877-568-1121**	816-221-7881
McKissock LP 218 Liberty St	Warren	PA	16365	**800-328-2008**	814-723-6979
Meridian Technology Group Inc 12909 SW 68th Pkwy Ste 100	Portland	OR	97223	**800-755-1038**	503-697-1600
Mi-Corporation 4601 Creekstone Dr Ste 180	Durham	NC	27703	**888-621-6230**	919-485-4819
Micro Strategies Inc 1140 Parsippany Blvd	Parsippany	NJ	07054	**888-467-6588**	
MicroPact 12901 Worldgate Dr Ste 800	Herndon	VA	20170	**866-346-9492**	703-709-6110
Mimic Technologies Inc 811 First Ave 408	Seattle	WA	98104	**800-918-1670**	206-923-3337
Minuteman Group Inc 35 Bedford St 2	Lexington	MA	02420	**800-861-7493**	781-861-7493
MMIC Group 7701 France Ave S Ste 500	Minneapolis	MN	55435	**800-328-5532**	
Modulant Inc 15305 Dallas Pkwy Ste 300	Dallas	TX	75001	**800-470-3575**	972-378-6677
Money Tree Software Ltd 2430 NW Professional Dr	Corvallis	OR	97330	**877-421-9815**	541-754-3701
Mortgageflex Systems Inc 25 N Market St *General	Jacksonville	FL	32202	**800-326-3539***	904-356-2490
MRS Systems Inc 19000 33rd Ave W Ste 130	Seattle	WA	98036	**800-253-4827**	
Multisoft Corp 1723 SE 47th Terr	Cape Coral	FL	33904	**888-415-0554**	239-945-6433
Mutual Mobile Inc 206 E Ninth St Ste 1400	Austin	TX	78701	**800-208-3563**	
Netcellent System Inc 4030 Valley Blvd	Walnut	CA	91789	**888-595-3818**	909-598-9019
NetGain Technology LLC 720 W St Germain St	Saint Cloud	MN	56301	**877-797-4700**	
Network Data Security Experts Inc (NDSE) 521 Branchway Rd	North Chesterfield	VA	23236	**877-440-6373**	
Network Dynamics Inc 700 Brooker Creek Blvd Ste 1000	Oldsmar	FL	34677	**877-818-8597**	813-818-8597
Neudesic LLC 8105 Irvine Ctr Dr	Irvine	CA	92618	**800-805-1805**	949-754-4500
Nims & Assoc 1445 Technology Ln Ste A8	Petaluma	CA	94954	**877-454-3200**	707-781-6300
Noldus Information Technology Inc 1503 Edwards Ferry Rd NE Ste 201	Leesburg	VA	20176	**800-355-9541**	703-771-0440
Northwest Data Solutions LLC 2627 C St	Anchorage	AK	99503	**800-544-0786**	907-227-1676
Nova Libra Inc 8609 W Bryn Mawr Ave Ste 208	Chicago	IL	60631	**866-724-1807**	773-714-1441
Novex Software Developments Inc 8743 Commercial St	New Minas	NS	B4N3C4	**888-542-1813**	
NowDocs International Inc 1985 Lookout Dr	North Mankato	MN	56003	**888-669-3627**	
Oeconnection LLC 4205 Highlander Pkwy	Richfield	OH	44286	**888-776-5792**	330-523-1830
ONRAD Inc 1770 Iowa Ave Ste 280	Riverside	CA	92507	**800-848-5876**	
Open Dental Software 3995 Fairview Industrial Dr SE Ste 110	Salem	OR	97302	**866-239-0469**	503-363-5432
Optimum Solutions Corp 170 Earle Ave	Lynbrook	NY	11563	**800-227-0672**	516-247-5300
Orchard Software Corp 701 Congressional Blvd Ste 360	Carmel	IN	46032	**800-856-1948**	317-573-2633
OriginLab Corp 1 Roundhouse Plz Ste 303	Northampton	MA	01060	**800-969-7720**	413-586-2013
Ortho Computer Systems Inc 1107 Buckeye Ave	Ames	IA	50010	**800-678-4644**	515-233-1026
Overland Rentals Inc 1901 N State Hwy 360 Ste 340 *Sales	Grand Prairie	TX	75050	**844-943-7368***	800-944-7368
Pace Computer Solutions Inc 10500 Little Patuxent Pkwy Ste 310	Columbia	MD	21044	**888-225-7223**	443-539-0290
Paladin Data Systems Corp 19362 Powder Hill Pl NE	Poulsbo	WA	98370	**800-532-8448**	360-779-2400
Palmetto GBA LLC 17 Technology Cir AG-905	Columbia	SC	29203	**800-833-4455**	803-735-1034
PaperWise Inc 3171 E Sunshine	Springfield	MO	65804	**888-828-7505**	417-886-7505

					Toll-Free	Phone

PAR Excellence Systems Inc
11500 Northlake Dr . . . . Cincinnati OH 45249 **800-888-7279** 513-936-9744

Park Place Technologies Inc
5910 Landerbrook Dr . . . . Cleveland OH 44124 **877-778-8707**

Patriot Technologies Inc
5108 Pegasus Ct Ste F . . . . Frederick MD 21704 **888-417-9899** 301-695-7500

Pattern Insight Inc
465 Fairchild Dr Ste 209 . . . . Mountain View CA 94043 **866-582-2655**

Petz Enterprises LLC
7575 W Linne Rd . . . . Tracy CA 95304 **800-345-4337*** 209-835-2720
*Sales

Phunware Inc
7800 Shoal Creek Blvd . . . . Austin TX 78757 **855-521-8485**

PIC Business Systems Inc
5119 Beckwith Blvd Ste 106 . . . . San Antonio TX 78249 **800-742-7378**

Pipkins Inc
14515 N Outer 40 Rd Ste 130 . . . . Chesterfield MO 63017 **800-469-6106** 314-469-6106

Plan B Technologies Inc
185 Admiral Cochrane Dr Ste 150 . . . . Annapolis MD 21401 **888-925-1602** 301-860-1006

Portable Technology Solutions LLC
221 David Ct . . . . Calverton NY 11933 **877-640-4152**

Practice Technology Inc
1312 E Robinson St . . . . Orlando FL 32801 **866-974-3946** 407-228-4400

Preferred Medical Marketing Corp
15720 Brixham Hill Ave Ste 460 . . . . Charlotte NC 28277 **800-543-8176** 704-543-8103

Preferred Strategies LLC
2425 Porter St Ste 20 . . . . Soquel CA 95073 **888-232-7337**

Prelude Systems Inc
5095 Ritter Rd Ste 112 . . . . Mechanicsburg PA 17055 **800-579-1047**

Pro-cad Software Ltd
12 Elbow River Rd . . . . Calgary AB T3Z2V2 **888-477-6223** 403-216-3375

Promiles Software Development
1900 Texas Ave . . . . Bridge City TX 77611 **800-324-8588**

Property Panorama Inc
9475 Pinecone Dr . . . . Mentor OH 44060 **877-299-6306** 440-290-2200

Protech Systems Group
3350 Players Club Pkwy . . . . Memphis TN 38125 **800-459-5100** 901-767-7550

Providge Consulting
2207 Concord Pk Ste 537 . . . . Wilimington DE 19803 **888-927-6583**

Proxibid Inc 4411 S 96 St . . . . Omaha NE 68127 **877-505-7770** 402-505-7770

Proximo Consulting Services Inc
2500 Plaza Five . . . . Jersey City NJ 07311 **800-236-9250**

Ps Websolutions Inc
906 Carriage Path SE Ste 106 . . . . Smyrna GA 30082 **877-571-7829**

Psychology Software Tools Inc
Sharpsburg Business Park 311 23rd St Ext
Ste 200 . . . . Sharpsburg PA 15215 **888-540-9664** 412-449-0078

QHR Technologies Inc
1620 Dickson Ave Ste 300 . . . . Kelowna BC V1Y9Y2 **855-550-5004**

Quadramed Inc
12110 Sunset Hills Rd Ste 600 . . . . Reston VA 20190 **800-393-0278** 703-709-2300

Quantros Inc
691 S Milpitas Blvd Ste 100 . . . . Milpitas CA 95035 **877-782-6876**

Questionmark Corp
5 Hillandale Ave . . . . Stamford CT 06902 **800-863-3950** 203-358-3950

QuickStart
5910 Courtyard Dr Ste 170 . . . . Austin TX 78731 **866-991-3924**

Rapid Insight Inc
53 Technology Ln Ste 112 . . . . Conway NH 03818 **888-585-6511**

Rave Mobile Safety
492 Old Connecticut Path 2nd Fl . . . . Framingham MA 01701 **888-605-7164** 508-848-2484

RBB Innovations
2-258 Queen St E . . . . Sault Sainte Marie ON P6A1Y7 **800-796-7864** 705-942-9053

RDA Corp
303 International Cir Ste 340 . . . . Hunt Valley MD 21030 **888-441-1278** 410-308-9300

Rediker Software Inc
2 Wilbraham Rd . . . . Hampden MA 01036 **800-213-9860** 413-566-3463

Redspin A Division of CynergisTek
11410 Jollyville Rd Ste 2201 . . . . Austin TX 78759 **800-721-9177**

Referentia Systems Inc
155 Kapalulu Pl Ste 200 . . . . Honolulu HI 96819 **800-569-6255** 808-840-8500

RenoWorks Software Inc
2816 21 St NE . . . . Calgary AB T2E6Z2 **877-980-3880** 403-296-3880

Reporting Systems Inc
2200 Rimland Dr Ste 305 . . . . Bellingham WA 98226 **844-752-6066**

Resort Data Processing Inc
211 Eagle Rd . . . . Avon CO 81620 **877-779-3717** 970-845-1140

Resource & Financial Management Systems Inc
3073 Palisades Ct . . . . Tuscaloosa AL 35405 **800-701-7367**

RP Design Web Services
17 Meriden Ave Ste 2A . . . . Southington CT 06489 **800-847-3475** 203-271-7991

Sage Microsystems Inc
18 N Village Ave . . . . Exton PA 19341 **800-724-7400** 610-524-1300

Satmetrix Systems Inc
1100 Park Pl Ste 210 . . . . San Mateo CA 94403 **866-943-3760**

Saturn Systems Inc
314 W Superior St Ste 1015 . . . . Duluth MN 55802 **888-638-4335** 218-623-7200

Scala Inc
7 Great Valley Pkwy Ste 300 . . . . Malvern PA 19355 **888-722-5296** 610-363-3350

Scalar Decisions Inc
1 Toronto St 3rd Fl . . . . Toronto ON M5C2V6 **866-364-5588** 416-202-0020

School Webmasters
2846 E Nora St . . . . Mesa AZ 85213 **888-750-4556** 602-750-4556

SchoolCity Inc
2900 Lakeside Dr Ste 270 . . . . Santa Clara CA 95054 **800-343-6572**

SEDONA Corp
1003 W Ninth Ave 2nd Fl . . . . King Of Prussia PA 19406 **800-815-3307** 610-337-8400

Selbysoft Inc
8326 Woodland Ave E . . . . Puyallup WA 98371 **800-454-4434**

Service Objects Inc
27 E Cota St Ste 500 . . . . Santa Barbara CA 93101 **800-694-6269**

shared logic group inc, The
6904 Spring Vly Dr Ste 305 . . . . Holland OH 43528 **877-865-0083** 419-865-0083

Shelby Systems Inc
7345 Goodlett Farms Pkwy . . . . Cordova TN 38016 **800-877-0222** 901-757-2372

Sherrill-Lubinski Corp
240 Tamal Vista Blvd . . . . Corte Madera CA 94925 **800-548-6881** 415-927-8400

Signifi Solutions Inc
2100 Matheson Blvd E Ste 100 . . . . Mississauga ON L4W5E1 **877-744-6434** 905-602-7707

Sirsi Corp
3300 N Ashton Blvd Ste 500 . . . . Lehi UT 84043 **800-288-8020**

Smartronix Inc
44150 Smartronix Way . . . . Hollywood MD 20636 **866-442-7767** 301-373-6000

Soft Science
2101 CityWest Blvd . . . . Houston TX 77042 **888-507-6387** 281-861-0832

Softchalk LLC
22 S Auburn Ave . . . . Richmond VA 23221 **877-638-2425**

Softeq Development Corp
1155 Dairy Ashford Ste 125 . . . . Houston TX 77079 **888-552-5001** 281-552-5000

Softerware Inc
132 Welsh Rd Ste 140 . . . . Horsham PA 19044 **800-220-8111** 215-628-0400

Softplan Systems Inc
8118 Isabella Ln . . . . Brentwood TN 37027 **800-248-0164** 615-370-1121

Soliant Consulting Inc
14 N Peoria St 2H . . . . Chicago IL 60607 **800-582-0170** 312-850-3830

Southdata Inc
201 Technology Ln . . . . Mt Airy NC 27030 **800-549-4722**

Sparta Systems Inc
2000 Waterview Dr Ste 300 . . . . Holmdel NJ 08691 **888-261-5948** 609-807-5100

Spartan Technology
125 Venture Blvd . . . . Spartanburg SC 29306 **877-727-8260**

Stenograph LLC
1500 Bishop Ct . . . . Mount Prospect IL 60056 **800-323-4247** 847-803-1400

Sudjam LLC
520 E Broadway Ste 202 . . . . Glendale CA 91205 **800-555-1234** 818-206-1145

Survey & Ballot Systems Inc
7653 Anagram Dr . . . . Eden Prairie MN 55344 **800-974-8099** 952-974-2300

Synerion North America Inc
7420 Airport Rd Ste 101 . . . . Mississauga ON L4T4E5 **877-816-8463**

System Concepts Inc
15900 N 78th St . . . . Scottsdale AZ 85260 **800-553-2438** 480-951-8011

Systems Engineering Technologies Corp
6121 Lincolnia Rd Ste 200 . . . . Alexandria VA 22312 **800-385-8977** 703-941-7887

Systemtec Inc
246 Stoneridge Dr Ste 301 . . . . Columbia SC 29210 **888-900-1655** 803-806-8100

Tallan Inc
175 Capital Blvd Ste 401 . . . . Rocky Hill CT 06067 **800-677-3693** 860-633-3693

Tech Friends inc
PO Box 16480 . . . . Jonesboro AR 72403 **866-933-6386** 870-933-6386

Technical Toolboxes Ltd
3801 Kirby Dr Ste 520 . . . . Houston TX 77098 **866-866-6766** 713-630-0505

Tecplot Inc
3535 Factoria Blvd SE Ste 550 . . . . Bellevue WA 98006 **800-763-7005** 425-653-1200

Telosa Software Inc
610 Cowper St . . . . Palo Alto CA 94301 **800-676-5831**

Terra Dotta LLC
501 W Franklin St Ste 105 . . . . Chapel Hill NC 27516 **877-368-8277**

Terracor Business Solutions
677 St Mary's Rd . . . . Winnipeg MB R2M3M6 **877-942-0005** 204-477-5342

Tetrad Computer Applications Ltd
1465 Slater Rd PO Box 5007 . . . . Vancouver BC V6G2T3 **800-663-1334** 604-685-2295

Tier1 Inc
2403 Sidney St Ste 225 . . . . Pittsburgh PA 15203 **888-284-0202** 412-381-9201

Time Trak Systems Inc
933 Pine Grove . . . . Port Huron MI 48060 **888-484-6387** 810-984-1313

Timeware Inc
9329 Ravenna Rd Ste D . . . . Twinsburg OH 44087 **866-936-2420** 330-963-2700

Tips Inc
2402 Williams Dr . . . . Georgetown TX 78628 **800-242-8477** 512-863-3653

Tizbi Inc
800 Saint Mary's St Ste 402 . . . . Raleigh NC 27605 **888-729-0951**

Today's Business Computers
213 E Black Horse Pk . . . . Pleasantville NJ 08232 **800-371-5132** 609-645-5132

Tone Software Inc
1735 S Brookhurst St . . . . Anaheim CA 92804 **800-833-8663** 714-991-9460

Total Solutions Inc
1626 County Line Rd . . . . Madison AL 35756 **866-413-4111** 256-721-3987

Trade Manage Capital Inc
PO Box 295 . . . . Waldwick NJ 07463 **800-221-5676** 201-587-2424

Transpara Corp
4715 W Culpepper Dr . . . . Phoenix AZ 85087 **866-994-5747** 925-218-6983

TriZetto Corp
3300 Rider Trail S . . . . Earth City MO 63045 **800-969-3666** 314-802-6700

Truckers Helper LLC, The
630 S Wickham Rd . . . . Melbourne FL 32904 **800-875-7435** 321-956-7331

Twin Oaks Software Development Inc
1463 Berlin Tpke . . . . Berlin CT 06037 **866-278-6750** 860-829-6000

Unimax 121 S Eighth St . . . . Minneapolis MN 55402 **800-886-0390**

Unique Business Systems Corp
2901 Ocean Park Blvd # 215 . . . . Santa Monica CA 90405 **800-669-4827** 310-396-3929

United Systems & Software Inc
300 Colonial Center Pkwy Ste 150 . . . . Lake Mary FL 32746 **800-522-8774** 407-875-2120

Utilant LLC
475 Ellicott St Ste 5 . . . . Buffalo NY 14203 **888-884-5268**

V2Soft Inc
300 Enterprise Ct Ste 100 . . . . Bloomfield Hills MI 48302 **866-982-7638** 248-904-1700

Valid8 com Inc
500 W Cummings Pk Ste 6550 . . . . Woburn MA 01801 **855-482-5438** 781-938-1221

ValuSource LLC
4575 Galley Rd Ste 200E . . . . Colorado Springs CO 80915 **800-825-8763** 719-548-4900

Vector Planning & Services Inc
591 Camino De La Reina Ste 300 . . . . San Diego CA 92108 **888-522-5491** 619-297-5656

Verican Inc 227 E Florida Ave . . . . Hemet CA 92543 **800-888-0470** 415-296-7300

Verisurf Software Inc
4907 E Landon Dr . . . . Anaheim CA 92807 **888-713-7201** 714-970-1683

Veros Real Estate Solutions LLC
2333 N Broadway Ste 350 . . . . Santa Ana CA 92706 **866-458-3767** 714-415-6300

Vertical Management Systems Inc
15440 Laguna Canyon Rd Ste 160 . . . . Irvine CA 92618 **800-867-4357**

VideoMining Corp
403 S Allen St Ste 101 . . . . State College PA 16801 **800-898-9950**

Virtual Training Company Inc
5395 Main St . . . . Stephens City VA 22655 **888-316-5374** 540-869-8686

Vision Technologies Inc
530 McCormick Dr Ste G . . . . Glen Burnie MD 21061 **866-746-1122** 410-424-2183

		Toll-Free	Phone

Visual Learning Systems Inc
PO Box 8226 .... Missoula MT 59807 — **866-968-7857**

Visualware Inc
937 Sierra Dr PO Box 668 .... Turlock CA 95380 — **866-847-9273** — 209-262-3491

Vocera Communications Inc
525 RACE St Ste 150 .... San Jose CA 95126 — **800-473-3971**

W a m s Inc
1800 E Lambert Ave Ste 155 .... Brea CA 92821 — **800-421-7151**

Web Advanced
36 Discovery Ste 150 .... Irvine CA 92618 — **888-261-7414**

Weidenhammer Systems Corp
935 Berkshire Blvd .... Reading PA 19610 — **866-497-2227** — 610-378-1149

Welligent Inc
5005 Colley Ave .... Norfolk VA 23508 — **888-317-5960**

Workshare
208 Utah St Ste 350 .... San Francisco CA 94103 — **888-404-4246** — 415-590-7700

XSYS Inc 653 Steele Dr .... Valparaiso IN 46385 — **888-810-9797**

Youngsoft Inc
49197 Wixom Tech Dr .... Wixom MI 48393 — **888-470-4553** — 248-675-1200

Z-Law Software Inc
80 Upton Ave PO Box 40602 .... Providence RI 02940 — **800-526-5588** — 401-331-3002

Zasio Enterprises Inc
401 W Front St Ste 305 .... Boise ID 83702 — **800-513-1000**

Zenoss Inc
11305 Four Points Dr Bldg 1 Ste 300 .... Austin TX 78726 — **888-936-6770**

Zephyr-Tec Corp
9651 Business Ctr Dr Ste C .... Rancho Cucamonga CA 91730 — **877-493-7497** — 909-481-9991

COMPUTER RESELLERS

SEE Computer Equipment & Software - Whol

178   COMPUTER SOFTWARE

SEE ALSO Computer Networking Products & Systems ; Computer Equipment & Software - Whol ; Computer Stores ; Computer Programming Services - Custom ; Application Service Providers (ASPs) ; Computer Systems Design Services ; Educational Materials & Supplies

	Toll-Free	Phone

Williamson Law Book Co
790 Canning Pkwy .... Victor NY 14564 — **800-733-9522** — 585-924-3400

178-1 Business Software (General)

Companies listed here make general-purpose software products that are designed for use by all types of businesses, professionals, and, to some extent, personal users.

	Toll-Free	Phone

1MAGE Software Inc
7200 S Alton Way A206 .... Centennial CO 80112 — **800-844-1468**

4D Inc
3031 Tisch Way Ste 900 .... San Jose CA 95128 — **800-785-3303** — 408-557-4600

ACI Worldwide Inc
3520 Kraft Rd Ste 300 .... Naples FL 34105 — **877-276-5554** — 402-390-7600

ACOM Solutions Inc
2850 E 29th St .... Long Beach CA 90806 — **800-347-3638** — 562-424-7899

Adobe Systems Inc
345 Park Ave .... San Jose CA 95110 — **800-833-6687** — 408-536-6000
NASDAQ: ADBE

Advent Software Inc
600 Townsend St 5th Fl Ste 500 .... San Francisco CA 94103 — **800-727-0605** — 415-543-7696
NASDAQ: ADVS

AgilQuest Corp
9407 Hull St Rd .... Richmond VA 23236 — **888-745-7455** — 804-745-0467

American Business Systems Inc
315 Littleton Rd .... Chelmsford MA 01824 — **800-356-4034**

American Software Inc
470 E Paces Ferry Rd .... Atlanta GA 30305 — **800-726-2946** — 404-261-4381
NASDAQ: AMSWA

APPX Software Inc
11363 San Jose Blvd Ste 301 .... Jacksonville FL 32223 — **800-879-2779** — 904-880-5560

Astea International Inc
240 Gibraltar Rd .... Horsham PA 19044 — **800-878-4657** — 215-682-2500
NASDAQ: ATEA

athenahealth Inc
311 Arsenal St .... Watertown MA 02472 — **800-981-5084** — 617-402-1000
NASDAQ: ATHN

Attunity Inc
70 BlanchaRd Rd .... Burlington MA 01803 — **866-288-8648** — 781-730-4070

Baudville Inc
5380 52nd St SE .... Grand Rapids MI 49512 — **800-728-0888*** — 616-698-0889
*Orders

Blackbaud Inc
2000 Daniel Island Dr .... Charleston SC 29492 — **800-468-8996** — 843-216-6200
NASDAQ: BLKB

BMC Software Inc
2101 City W Blvd .... Houston TX 77042 — **800-841-2031** — 713-918-8800

Bottomline Technologies
325 Corporate Dr .... Portsmouth NH 03801 — **800-243-2528** — 603-436-0700
NASDAQ: EPAY

Bradmark Technologies Inc
4265 San Felipe St Ste 700 .... Houston TX 77027 — **800-621-2808** — 713-621-2808

Brady Identification Solutions
6555 W Good Hope Rd .... Milwaukee WI 53223 — **800-537-8791*** — 888-250-3082
*Cust Svc

Brainworks Software Inc
100 S Main St .... Sayville NY 11782 — **800-755-1111** — 631-563-5000

CA Inc 1 CA Plz .... Islandia NY 11749 — **800-225-5224**
NASDAQ: CA

Cicero Inc
8000 Regency Pkwy Ste 542 .... Cary NC 2/518 — **866-538-3588** — 919-380-5000

Cincom Systems Inc
55 Merchant St .... Cincinnati OH 45246 — **800-224-6266** — 513-612-2300

Cortera
901 Yamato Rd Ste 210 E .... Boca Raton FL 33431 — **877-569-7376**

		Toll-Free	Phone

Current Analysis Inc
21335 Signal Hill Plz Ste 200 .... Sterling VA 20164 — **877-787-8947** — 703-404-9200

Cyma Systems Inc
2330 W University Dr Ste 4 .... Tempe AZ 85281 — **800-292-2962**

D&B Sales & Marketing Solutions
103 JFK Pkwy .... Short Hills NJ 07078 — **866-473-3932** — 973-921-5500

Data Pro Acctg Software Inc
111 Second Ave NE Ste 1200 .... Saint Petersburg FL 33701 — **800-237-6377** — 727-803-1500

Datamatics Management Services Inc
330 New Brunswick Ave .... Fords NJ 08863 — **800-673-0366** — 732-738-9600

DELLEMC
6801 Koll Ctr Pkwy .... Pleasanton CA 94566 — **866-438-3622**

Drake Software
235 E Palmer St .... Franklin NC 28734 — **800-890-9500**

Edge Technologies
12110 Sunset Hills Rd Ste 600 .... Reston VA 22030 — **888-771-3343** — 703-691-7900

eSignal 3955 Pt Eden Way .... Hayward CA 94545 — **800-815-8256** — 510-266-6000

FileMaker Inc
5201 Patrick Henry Dr .... Santa Clara CA 95054 — **800-325-2747*** — 408-987-7000
*Cust Svc

Fischer International Systems Corp
9045 Strada Stell Ct Ste 201 .... Naples FL 34109 — **800-776-7258*** — 239-643-1500
*Tech Supp

FlexiInternational Software Inc
2 Enterprise Dr .... Shelton CT 06484 — **800-353-9492** — 203-925-3040
OTC: FLXI

Global Shop Solutions Inc
975 Evergreen Cir .... The Woodlands TX 77380 — **800-364-5958*** — 281-681-1959
*Sales

Global Software Inc
3201 Beechleaf Ct Ste 170 .... Raleigh NC 27604 — **800-326-3444** — 919-872-7800

Grandite Inc PO Box 47133 .... Quebec QC G1S4X1 — **866-808-3932** — 581-318-2018

GSE Systems Inc
1332 Londontown Blvd Ste 200 .... Sykesville MD 21784 — **800-638-7912*** — 410-970-7800
*NASDAQ: GVP ■ *Cust Svc*

HarrisData
13555 Bishops Ct Ste 300 .... Brookfield WI 53005 — **800-225-0585** — 262-784-9099

HighJump Software
5600 W 83rd St Ste 600 .... Minneapolis MN 55437 — **800-328-3271** — 952-947-4088

iCIMS Inc
90 Matawan Rd Pkwy 120 5th Fl. .... Matawan NJ 07747 — **800-889-4422** — 732-847-1941

IFS North America Inc
300 Pk Blvd Ste 555 .... Chicago IL 60143 — **888-437-4968**

Information & Computing Services Inc (ICS)
1650 Prudential Dr Ste 300 .... Jacksonville FL 32207 — **800-676-4427** — 904-399-8500

InfoVista Corp
12950 Worldgate Dr Ste 250 .... Herndon VA 20170 — **866-921-9219** — 703-435-2435

Innovative Systems Inc
790 Holiday Dr .... Pittsburgh PA 15220 — **800-622-6390** — 412-937-9300

Inova Solutions Inc
110 Avon St .... Charlottesville VA 22902 — **800-637-1077** — 434-817-8000

Inspiration Software Inc
6443 SW Beaverton Hillsdale Hwy
Ste 370 .... Portland OR 97221 — **800-877-4292** — 503-297-3004

Integrated Business Systems & Services Inc
1601 Shop Rd Ste E .... Columbia SC 29201 — **800-553-1038** — 803-736-5595

International Business Machines Corp (IBM)
1 New OrchaRd Rd .... Armonk NY 10504 — **800-426-4968** — 914-499-1900
NYSE: IBM

InterraTech Corp
PO Box 4 .... Mount Ephraim NJ 08059 — **888-589-4889** — 856-854-5100

InterSystems Corp
1 Memorial Dr .... Cambridge MA 02142 — **800-753-2571** — 617-621-0600

ISGN Corp (ISGN)
1333 Gateway Dr Ste 1000 .... Melbourne FL 32901 — **800-462-5545** — 860-656-7550

K-Systems Inc
2104 Aspen Dr .... Mechanicsburg PA 17055 — **800-221-0204** — 717-795-7711

Logility Inc
470 E Paces Ferry Rd .... Atlanta GA 30305 — **800-762-5207** — 404-261-9777

Longview Solutions
65 Allstate Pkwy Ste 200 .... Markham ON L3R9X1 — **888-454-2549** — 905-940-1510

M2 Technology Inc
21702 Hardy Oak Ste 100 .... San Antonio TX 78258 — **800-267-1760** — 210-566-3773

Malvern Systems Inc
81 Lancaster Ave Ste 219 .... Malvern PA 19355 — **800-296-9642**

Maverick Technologies
265 Admiral Trost Dr .... Columbia IL 62236 — **888-917-9109** — 618-281-9100

Mediagrif Interactive Technologies Inc
1111 St-Charles St W
E Tower Ste 255 .... Longueuil QC J4K5G4 — **877-677-9088** — 450-449-0102
TSE: MDF

MicroBiz Corp
655 Oak Grove Ave Ste 493 .... Menlo Park CA 94026 — **800-937-2289** — 702-749-5353

Microlink Enterprise Inc
20955 Pathfinder Rd Ste 100 .... Diamond Bar CA 91765 — **800-829-3688** — 562-205-1888

Microsoft Corp
1 Microsoft Way .... Redmond WA 98052 — **800-642-7676** — 425-882-8080
NASDAQ: MSFT

NetMotion Inc
701 N 34th St Ste 250 .... Seattle WA 98103 — **877-818-7626** — 206-691-5500

NewlineNoosh Inc
625 Ellis St Ste 300 .... Mountain View CA 94043 — **888-286-6674** — 650-637-6000

Objectivity Inc
3099 N First St Ste 200 .... San Jose CA 95134 — **800-767-6259** — 408-992-7100

OMD Corp
3705 Missouri Blvd .... Jefferson City MO 65109 — **866-440-8664** — 573-893-8930

OneSCM
6805 Capital of Texas Hwy Ste 370 .... Austin TX 78731 — **800-324-5143** — 512-231-8191

Open Systems Inc
4301 Dean Lakes Blvd .... Shakopee MN 55379 — **800-328-2276***
*Sales

Oracle Corp
500 Oracle Pkwy .... Redwood Shores CA 94065 — **800-392-2999*** — 800-633-0738
*NYSE: ORCL ■ *Sales*

Oracle Information Rights Management
500 Oracle Pkwy .... Redwood Shores CA 94065 — **800-633-0738**

Palisade Corp
130 E Seneca St Ste 505 .... Ithaca NY 14850 — **800-432-7475** — 607-277-8000

			Toll-Free	Phone

Paperclip Software Inc
1 University Plz . . . . Hackensack NJ 07601 **800-929-3503** 201-525-1221
Passport Corp 16 West St . . . . Warwick NY 10990 **800-926-6736**
Payspan Inc
7751 Belfort Pkwy Ste 200 . . . . Jacksonville FL 32256 **877-331-7154**
Pentagon 2000 Software Inc
15 West 34 St 5th Fl . . . . New York NY 10001 **800-643-1806** 212-629-7521
PeopleStrategy Inc
5883 Glenridge Dr Ste 200 . . . . Atlanta GA 30328 **855-488-4100**
Percussion Software Inc
600 Unicorn Pk Dr . . . . Woburn MA 01801 **800-283-0800** 781-438-9900
Personnel Data Systems Inc (PDS)
470 Norriltown Rd . . . . Blue Bell PA 19422 **800-243-8737** 610-238-4600
Pitney Bowes Group 1 Software
4200 Parliament Pl Ste 600 . . . . Lanham MD 20706 **800-367-6950** 301-731-2300
Planview Inc
12301 Research Blvd Research Park Plz
Ste 101 . . . . Austin TX 78759 **800-856-8600** 512-346-8600
Platform Computing Inc
3760 14th Ave . . . . Markham ON L3R3T7 **877-528-3676** 905-948-8448
Print-O-Stat Inc
1011 W Market St . . . . York PA 17404 **800-711-8014** 717-854-7821
Progress Software Corp
14 Oak Pk . . . . Bedford MA 01730 **800-477-6473** 781-280-4000
NASDAQ: PRGS
Quest Software Inc
5 Polairis Way . . . . Aliso Viejo CA 92656 **800-306-9329** 949-754-8000
Realtime Software Corp
24 Deane Rd . . . . Bernardston MA 01337 **800-323-1143** 847-803-1100
Red Wing Software Inc
491 Hwy 19 . . . . Red Wing MN 55066 **800-732-9464** 651-388-1106
Sage 271 17th St NW . . . . Atlanta GA 30363 **800-368-2405** 866-996-7243
SAS Institute Inc
100 SAS Campus Dr . . . . Cary NC 27513 **800-727-0025** 919-677-8000
Sciforma Corp
4880 Stevens Creek Blvd Ste 102 . . . . San Jose CA 95129 **800-533-9876*** 408-354-0144
*Sales
SDL 2550 N First St Ste 301 . . . . San Jose CA 95131 **800-933-6910** 408-743-3600
Silvon Software Inc
900 Oakmont Ln Ste 400 . . . . Westmont IL 60559 **800-874-5866** 630-655-3313
Software AG USA
11700 Plaza America Dr Ste 700 . . . . Reston VA 20190 **877-724-4965** 703-860-5050
Sophos Inc
3 Van de Graaff Dr 2nd Fl . . . . Burlington MA 01803 **866-866-2802**
Source Technologies
4205B Westinghouse Commons Dr . . . . Charlotte NC 28273 **800-922-8501** 704-969-7500
Stampscom Inc
1990 E Grand Ave . . . . El Segundo CA 90245 **855-889-7867**
NASDAQ: STMP
Superior Software Inc
16055 Ventura Blvd Ste 650 . . . . Encino CA 91436 **800-421-3264** 818-990-1135
SYSPRO
959 S Coast Dr Ste 100 . . . . Costa Mesa CA 92626 **800-369-8649** 714-437-1000
TECSYS Inc
1 Place Alexis Nihon Ste 800 . . . . Montreal QC H3Z3B8 **800-922-8649** 514-866-0001
Thomson Reuters
7322 Newman Blvd . . . . Dexter MI 48130 **800-968-8900***
*Cust Svc
Tribridge
4830 W Kennedy Blvd Ste 890 . . . . Tampa FL 33609 **877-744-1360**
Trintech Inc
15851 Dallas Pkwy Ste 900 . . . . Addison TX 75001 **800-416-0075** 972-701-9802
Ultimate Software Group Inc
2000 Ultimate Way . . . . Weston FL 33326 **800-432-1729** 954-331-7000
NASDAQ: ULTI
Validar Inc
800 Maynard Ave S Ste 401 . . . . Seattle WA 98134 **888-784-2929** 206-264-9151
Vertex Inc
1041 Old Cassatt Rd . . . . Berwyn PA 19312 **800-355-3500** 610-640-4200
Vignette Corp
1301 S Mopac Expy Ste 100 . . . . Austin TX 78746 **800-540-7292** 512-741-4300
Visible Systems Corp
201 Spring St . . . . Lexington MA 02421 **888-850-9911*** 781-778-0200
*Sales
Worden Bros Inc
4905 Pine Cone Dr . . . . Durham NC 27707 **800-776-4940** 919-408-0542

178-2 Computer Languages & Development Tools

			Toll-Free	Phone

BMC Software
2202 NW Shore Blvd Ste 650 . . . . Tampa FL 33607 **855-834-7487**
BSQUARE Corp
110 110th Ave NE Ste 300 . . . . Bellevue WA 98004 **888-820-4500** 425-519-5900
NASDAQ: BSQR
Data Access Corp
14000 SW 119th Ave . . . . Miami FL 33186 **800-451-3539** 305-238-0012
Empress Software Inc
11785 Beltsville Dr . . . . Beltsville MD 20705 **866-626-8888** 301-572-1600
FMS Inc
8150 Leesburg Pk Ste 600 . . . . Vienna VA 22182 **866-367-7801** 703-356-4700
Forth Inc
6080 Ctr Dr Ste 600 . . . . Los Angeles CA 90045 **800-553-6784** 310-999-6784
Green Hills Software Inc
30 W Sola St . . . . Santa Barbara CA 93101 **800-765-4733** 805-965-6044
Instantiations Inc
Officers Row Ste 1325B . . . . Vancouver WA 98661 **855-476-2558** 503-649-3836
LANSA Inc
2001 Butterfield Rd Ste 102 . . . . Downers Grove IL 60515 **800-457-4083** 630-874-7000
Mix Software Inc
1203 Berkeley Dr . . . . Richardson TX 75081 **800-333-0330** 972-231-0949
Prolifics
24025 Park Sorrento Ste 405 . . . . Calabasas CA 91302 **800-458-3313**
Revelation Software
99 Kinderkamack Rd . . . . Westwood NJ 07675 **800-262-4747** 201-594-1422
Rogue Wave Software Inc
5500 Flatiron Pkwy . . . . Boulder CO 80301 **800-487-3217** 303-473-9118

SlickEdit Inc
3000 Aerial Ctr Pkwy Ste 120 . . . . Morrisville NC 27560 **800-934-3348** 919-473-0070
Thoroughbred Software International Inc
285 Davidson Ave Ste 302 . . . . Somerset NJ 08873 **800-524-0430** 732-560-1377
Zortec International
25 Century Blvd Ste 103 . . . . Nashville TN 37214 **800-361-7005** 615-361-7000

178-3 Educational & Reference Software

			Toll-Free	Phone

Blackboard Inc
1899 L St NW 5th Fl . . . . Washington DC 20036 **800-424-9299** 202-463-4860
CompassLearning Inc
203 Colorado St . . . . Austin TX 78701 **800-232-9556** 512-478-9600
Fuel Education LLC
2300 Corporate Park Dr . . . . Herndon VA 20171 **866-912-8588**
Individual Software Inc
4255 HopyaRd Rd Ste 2 . . . . Pleasanton CA 94588 **800-822-3522** 925-734-6767
Inspiration Software Inc
6443 SW Beaverton Hillsdale Hwy
Ste 370 . . . . Portland OR 97221 **800-877-4292** 503-297-3004
Language Engineering Co
135 Beaver St Ste 204 . . . . Waltham MA 02452 **888-366-4532** 781-642-8900
LDP Inc
75 Kiwanis Blvd PO Box O . . . . West Hazleton PA 18201 **800-522-8413**
MindPlay Educational Software
4400 E Broadway Blvd Ste 400 . . . . Tucson AZ 85711 **800-221-7911** 520-888-1800
Queue Inc 703 Post Rd . . . . Fairfield CT 06824 **800-232-2224**
Saba Software Inc
2400 Bridge Pkwy . . . . Redwood Shores CA 94065 **877-722-2101** 650-581-2500
TSX: SABA
Scientific Learning Corp
300 Frank H Ogawa Plz Ste 600 . . . . Oakland CA 94612 **888-665-9707** 510-444-3500
OTC: SCIL
Transparent Language Inc
12 Murphy Dr . . . . Nashua NH 03062 **800-538-8867**

178-4 Electronic Purchasing & Procurement Software

			Toll-Free	Phone

Ariba Inc 807 11th Ave . . . . Sunnyvale CA 94089 **866-772-7422**
NYSE: SAP
CA Inc 1 CA Plz . . . . Islandia NY 11749 **800-225-5224**
NASDAQ: CA
Elavon
2 Concourse Pkwy Ste 800 . . . . Atlanta GA 30328 **800-725-1243** 678-731-5000
GXS Inc
9711 Washingtonian Blvd . . . . Gaithersburg MD 20878 **800-560-4347** 301-340-4000
International Business Machines Corp (IBM)
1 New OrchaRd Rd . . . . Armonk NY 10504 **800-426-4968** 914-499-1900
NYSE: IBM

178-5 Engineering Software

			Toll-Free	Phone

Accelrys Inc
10188 Telesis Ct Ste 100 . . . . San Diego CA 92121 **888-249-2284** 858-799-5000
Altium Inc
4225 Executive Sq Level 7 . . . . La Jolla CA 92037 **800-544-4186*** 858-864-1500
*Sales
ANSYS Inc
275 Technology Dr . . . . Canonsburg PA 15317 **800-937-3321** 724-820-4367
NASDAQ: ANSS
Applied Flow Technology Corp
2955 Professional Pl Ste 301 . . . . Colorado Springs CO 80904 **800-589-4943** 719-686-1000
Ashlar Inc
9600 Great Hills Trl Ste 150W-1625 . . . . Austin TX 78759 **800-877-2745** 512-250-2186
Aspen Technology Inc
200 Wheeler Rd . . . . Burlington MA 01803 **888-996-7100** 855-882-7736
NASDAQ: AZPN
Autodesk Inc
111 McInnis Pkwy . . . . San Rafael CA 94903 **800-964-6432*** 415-507-5000
*NASDAQ: ADSK ■ *Tech Supp*
Bentley Systems Inc
685 Stockton Dr . . . . Exton PA 19341 **800-236-8539** 610-458-5000
Bohannan Huston Inc
7500 Jefferson St NE . . . . Albuquerque NM 87109 **800-877-5332** 505-823-1000
Cadence Design Systems Inc
2655 Seely Ave . . . . San Jose CA 95134 **800-746-6223*** 408-943-1234
*NASDAQ: CDNS ■ *Cust Svc*
CambridgeSoft Corp
100 CambridgePark Dr . . . . Cambridge MA 02140 **800-315-7300** 617-588-9100
Direct Source Inc
8176 Mallory Ct . . . . Chanhassen MN 55317 **800-934-8055** 952-934-8000
DP Technology Corp
1150 Avenida Acaso . . . . Camarillo CA 93012 **800-627-8479** 805-388-6000
Evolution Computing
7000 N 16th St Ste 120 514 . . . . Phoenix AZ 85020 **800-874-4028**
Geocomp Corp
1145 Massachusetts Ave . . . . Boxborough MA 01719 **800-822-2669*** 978-635-0012
*Cust Svc
Infinite Graphics Inc
4611 E Lake St . . . . Minneapolis MN 55406 **800-679-0676** 612-721-6283
OTC: INFG
Intergraph Corp
19 Interpro Rd . . . . Madison AL 35758 **800-345-4856** 256-730-2000
Kubotek USA
2 Mt Royal Ave Ste 500 . . . . Marlborough MA 01752 **800-372-3872** 508-229-2020
LINDO Systems Inc
1415 N Dayton St . . . . Chicago IL 60622 **800-441-2378*** 312-988-7422
*Sales
Mentor Graphics Corp
8005 SW Boeckman Rd . . . . Wilsonville OR 97070 **800-592-2210** 503-685-7000
NASDAQ: MENT

			Toll-Free	Phone

National Instruments Corp
11500 N Mopac Expy .... Austin TX 78759   **800-433-3488***   512-683-0100
*NASDAQ: NATI ■ *Cust Svc*

Parametric Technology Corp (PTC)
140 Kendrick St .... Needham MA 02494   **800-613-7535**   781-370-5000
NASDAQ: PTC

Planit Solutions Inc
3800 Palisades Dr .... Tuscaloosa AL 35405   **800-280-6932**   205-556-9199

PMS Systems Corp
26707 Agoura Rd Ste 201. .... Calabasas CA 91302   **800-755-3968**   310-450-2566

Science Application International Corp Inc (SAIC Inc)
1710 SAIC Dr .... McLean VA 22102   **866-400-7242**   866-955-7242

Sesame Software
5201 Great America Pkwy Ste 320 .... Santa Clara CA 94160   **866-474-7575**   408-550-7999

Zuken USA
238 Littleton Rd Ste 100. .... Westford MA 01886   **800-447-7332**   978-692-4900

178-6   Games & Entertainment Software

			Toll-Free	Phone

Activision Inc
3100 Ocean Pk Blvd .... Santa Monica CA 90405   **800-509-5586**   310-255-2000

Disney Consumer Products
500 S Buena Vista St .... Burbank CA 91521   **855-553-4763***   818-560-1000
PR

Her Interactive Inc
1150 114th Ave SE Ste 200 .... Bellevue WA 98004   **800-461-8787***   425-460-8787
Orders

MakeMusic! Inc
7615 Golden Triangle Dr Ste M .... Eden Prairie MN 55344   **800-843-2066**   952-937-9611
NASDAQ: MMUS

Nintendo of America Inc
4820 150th Ave NE .... Redmond WA 98052   **800-255-3700***   425-882-2040
Cust Svc

178-7   Internet & Communications Software

			Toll-Free	Phone

@Comm Corp 150 Dow St .... Manchester NH 03101   **800-641-5400**   603-624-4424

Adaptive Micro Systems Inc
7840 N 86th St .... Milwaukee WI 53224   **800-558-4187**   414-357-2020

Akamai Technologies Inc
150 Broadway .... Cambridge MA 02142   **877-425-2624**   617-444-3000
NASDAQ: AKAM

Alhambra
8 Governor Wentworth Hwy .... Wolfeboro NH 03894   **800-329-9099**   603-569-0600

Amcom Software Inc
10400 Yellow Cir Dr .... Eden Prairie MN 55343   **800-852-8935**   952-230-5200

AnyDoc Software Inc
5404 Cypress Ctr Dr Ste 140 .... Tampa FL 33609   **888-495-2638**

Ariba Inc 807 11th Ave .... Sunnyvale CA 94089   **866-772-7422**
NYSE: SAP

Asure Software
110 Wild Basin Rd .... Austin TX 78746   **888-323-8835**   512-437-2700
NASDAQ: ASUR

AuthorizeNet Corp
PO Box 8999 .... San Francisco CA 94128   **877-447-3938**   801-492-6450

Avanquest Software USA
1333 W 120th Ave .... Westminster CO 80234   **800-011-2312**

Callware Technologies Inc
9100 S 500 W .... Sandy UT 84070   **800-888-4226**   801-988-6800

ClickSoftware Inc
35 Corporate Dr Ste 400. .... Burlington MA 01803   **888-438-3308**   781-272-5903

Cothern Computer Systems Inc
1640 Lelia Dr Ste 200. .... Jackson MS 39216   **800-844-1155**

Cykic Software Inc
PO Box 3098 .... San Diego CA 92163   **800-438-7325**   619-459-8799

DataMotion Inc
35 Airport Rd Ste 120. .... Morristown NJ 07960   **800-672-7233**   973-455-1245

DealerTrack Holdings Inc
1111 Marcus Ave Ste M04 .... Lake Success NY 11042   **877-357-8725**   516-734-3600
NASDAQ: TRAK

eAcceleration Corp
1050 NE Hostmark St Ste 100-B. .... Poulsbo WA 98370   **800-803-4588***   360-779-6301
Sales

Education Management Solutions Inc
436 Creamery Way Ste 300 .... Exton PA 19341   **877-367-5050**   610-701-7002

EXTOL International Inc
529 Terry Reiley Way .... Pottsville PA 17901   **800-542-7284**   570-628-5500

FutureSoft Inc
1660 Townhurst Dr Ste E .... Houston TX 77043   **800-989-8908**   281-496-9400

GeoTrust Inc
350 Ellis St Bldg J .... Mountain View CA 94043   **866-511-4141**   650-426-5010

Hilgraeve Inc
1287 N Telegraph Rd .... Monroe MI 48162   **800-826-2760***   734-243-0576
Sales

Hyland Software Inc
28500 Clemens Rd .... Westlake OH 44145   **888-495-2638**   440-788-5000

Information Builders Inc
2 Penn Plz .... New York NY 10121   **800-969-4636**   212-736-4433

Ion Networks Inc
120 Corporate Blvd Ste A .... South Plainfield NJ 07080   **800-722-8986**   908-546-3900

LassoSoft LLC PO Box 33 .... Manchester WA 98353   **888-286-7753**   954-302-3526

Moai Technologies Inc
100 First Ave 9th Fl .... Pittsburgh PA 15222   **800-814-1548**   412-454-5550

NetScout Systems Inc
310 Littleton Rd .... Westford MA 01886   **800-357-7666**   978-614-4000
NASDAQ: NTCT

Nuance Communications Inc
1 Wayside Rd .... Burlington MA 01803   **800-654-1187**   781-565-5000
NASDAQ: NUAN

Open Text Corp
275 Frank Tompa Dr .... Waterloo ON N2L0A1   **800-499-6544***   519-888-7111
*NASDAQ: OTEX ■ *General*

Open Text Corp (USA)
100 Tri-State International Pkwy
3rd Fl .... Lincolnshire IL 60069   **800-499-6544***   847-267-9330
*NASDAQ: OTEX ■ *Sales*

PCTEL Inc
471 Brighton Dr .... Bloomingdale IL 60108   **800-323-9122**   630-372-6800
NASDAQ: PCTI

Powersteering Software Inc
401 Congress Ave Ste 1850 .... Austin TX 78701   **866-390-9088**   617-492-0707

QSA ToolWorks LLC
3100 47th Ave .... Long Island NY 11101   **800-784-7018**   516-935-9151

Supportcom Inc
1200 Crossman Ave Ste 210-240 .... Sunnyvale CA 94089   **877-493-2778**   650-556-9440
NASDAQ: SPRT

Surety LLC
12020 Sunrise Vly Dr Ste 250 .... Reston VA 20191   **800-298-3115**   703-476-6030

Symantec Corp
350 Ellis St .... Mountain View CA 94043   **800-441-7234**   650-527-8000
NASDAQ: SYMC

Tangoe
169 Lackawanna Ave .... Parsippany NJ 07054   **844-484-5041**

UmeVoice Inc
1435 Technology Ln Ste B4 .... Petaluma CA 94954   **888-230-3300**   707-939-8607

Vendio Services Llc
1510 Fashion Island Blvd .... San Mateo CA 94403   **866-269-9549**

Vertical Communications Inc
3910 Freedom Cr Ste 103. .... Santa Clara CA 95054   **800-914-9985***   408-404-1600
*OTC: VRCC ■ *Sales*

Websense Inc
10240 Sorrento Valley Rd .... San Diego CA 92121   **800-723-1166**   858-320-8000
NASDAQ: WBSN

XAP Corp
3534 Hayden Ave .... Culver City CA 90232   **800-468-6927**   310-842-9800

Zone Alarm
800 Bridge Pkwy .... Redwood City CA 94065   **877-966-5221**   415-633-4500

178-8   Multimedia & Design Software

			Toll-Free	Phone

3D Systems Inc
333 Three D Systems Cir .... Rock Hill SC 29730   **800-793-3669**   803-326-3900

ACD Systems International Inc
129-1335 Bear Mtn Pkwy .... Victoria BC V9B6T9   **888-767-9888**   778-817-1168

Adobe Systems Inc
345 Park Ave .... San Jose CA 95110   **800-833-6687**   408-536-6000
NASDAQ: ADBE

Apple Inc 1 Infinite Loop .... Cupertino CA 95014   **800-275-2273***   408-996-1010
*NASDAQ: AAPL ■ *Cust Svc*

Auto FX Software
130 Inverness Plaz Ste 510. .... Birmingham AL 35242   **800-839-2008**   205-980-0056

Avid Technology Inc
65-75 Network Dri .... Burlington MA 01803   **800-949-2843**   978-640-6789
NASDAQ: AVID

Corel Corp 1600 Carling Ave .... Ottawa ON K1Z8R7   **800-772-6735***   613-728-8200
Orders

HydroCAD Software Solutions LLC
PO Box 477 .... Chocorua NH 03817   **800-927-7246**   603-323-8666

Image Labs International
PO Box 1545 .... Belgrade MT 59714   **800-785-5995**   406-585-7225

MicroVision Development Inc
5541 Fermi Ct Ste 120 .... Carlsbad CA 92008   **800-998-4555**   760-438-7781

Nemetschek North America
7150 Riverwood Dr .... Columbia MD 21046   **888-646-4223**   410-290-5114

NewTek Inc
5131 Beckwith Blvd .... San Antonio TX 78249   **800-862-7837***   210-370-8000
Cust Svc

PC/Nametag 124 Horizon Dr .... Verona WI 53593   **877-626-3824**   888-354-7868

Quark Inc 1800 Grant St .... Denver CO 80203   **800-676-4575***
Cust Svc

Scan-Optics Inc
169 Progress Dr .... Manchester CT 06042   **800-543-8681**   860-645-7878

Sigma Design
5521 Jackson St .... Alexandria LA 71303   **888-990-0900***   318-449-9900
Sales

SoftPress Systems Inc
3020 Bridgeway Ste 408. .... Sausalito CA 94965   **800-853-6454**   415-331-4820

TechSmith Corp
2405 Woodlake Dr .... Okemos MI 48864   **800-517-3001**   517-381-2300

Telestream Inc
848 Gold Flat Rd Ste 1 .... Nevada City CA 95959   **877-681-2088**   530-470-1300

Three D Graphics Inc
11340 W Olympic Blvd Ste 352 ...... Los Angeles CA 90064   **800-913-0008**   310-231-3330

Videotex Systems Inc
10255 Miller Rd .... Dallas TX 75238   **800-888-4336**   972-231-9200

Worldscom Inc 11 Royal Rd .... Brookline MA 02445   **800-315-2580**   617-725-8900

178-9   Personal Software

			Toll-Free	Phone

Avery Dennison Corp
207 Goode Ave .... Glendale CA 91203   **888-567-4387***   626-304-2000
*NYSE: AVY ■ *Cust Svc*

Corel Corp 1600 Carling Ave .... Ottawa ON K1Z8R7   **800-772-6735***   613-728-8200
Orders

Equis International
90 South 400 West Ste 620 .... Salt Lake City UT 84101   **800-882-3040***   801-265-9996
Sales

Intuit Inc
2632 Marine Way .... Mountain View CA 94043   **800-446-8848***   650-944-6000
*NASDAQ: INTU ■ *Cust Svc*

Microsoft Corp
1 Microsoft Way .... Redmond WA 98052   **800-642-7676**   425-882-8080
NASDAQ: MSFT

Nolocom 950 Parker St .... Berkeley CA 94710   **800-728-3555**

Sony Creative Software
8215 Greenway Blvd Ste 400 .... Middleton WI 53562   **800-577-6642**   608-203-7620

Classified Section

				Toll-Free	Phone

Stevens Creek Software
PO Box 2126 . . . . .Cupertino CA 95015   **800-823-4279**   408-725-0424

Symantec Corp
350 Ellis St . . . . .Mountain View CA 94043   **800-441-7234**   650-527-8000
NASDAQ: SYMC

178-10 Professional Software (Industry-Specific)

Companies listed here manufacture software designed for specific professions or business sectors (i.e., architecture, banking, investment, physical sciences, real estate, etc.).

				Toll-Free	Phone

AIMS Inc 235 Desiard St . . . . .Monroe LA 71201   **800-729-2467**   318-323-2467

Allot Communications
300 Tradecenter Ste 4680 . . . . .Woburn MA 01801   **877-255-6826**   781-939-9300

Allscripts Healthcare Solutions
222 Merchandise Mart Plz Ste 2024 . . . . .Chicago IL 60654   **800-654-0889**
NASDAQ: MDRX

Anchor Computer Inc
1900 New Hwy . . . . .Farmingdale NY 11735   **800-728-6262**   631-293-6100

ARI Network Services Inc
10850 W Pk Pl Ste 1200 . . . . .Milwaukee WI 53224   **877-805-0803**   414-973-4300

ASI DataMyte Inc
2800 Campus Dr Ste 60 . . . . .Plymouth MN 55441   **800-455-4359**   763-553-1040

Aspyra LLC
7400 Baymeadows Way Ste 101 . . . . .Jacksonville FL 32256   **800-437-9000**
OTC: APYI

Avantus
15 W Strong St Ste 20A . . . . .Pensacola FL 32501   **800-600-2510**   850-470-9336

Avaya Government Solutions Inc
12730 Fair Lakes Cir . . . . .Fairfax VA 22033   **800-492-6769**   703-653-8000

BenefitMall Inc
4851 LBJ Fwy Ste 1100 . . . . .Dallas TX 75244   **888-338-6293**   469-791-3300

CareCentric Inc
20 Church St 12th Fl .Hartford CT 06103   **800-808-1902**

CCH Small Firm Services
225 Chastain Meadows Ct NW Ste 200 . . . . .Kennesaw GA 30144   **866-345-4171***
*Sales

Cedara Software Corp
6303 Airport Rd Ste 500 . . . . .Mississauga ON L4V1R8   **800-724-5970**   905-364-8000

CliniComp International
9655 Towne Ctr Dr . . . . .San Diego CA 92121   **800-350-8202**   858-546-8202

Computers Unlimited
2407 Montana Ave .Billings MT 59101   **800-763-0308**   406-255-9500

Construction Systems Software Inc
PO Box 203184 . . . . .Austin TX 78720   **800-531-1035**

Datatel Inc
4375 Fair Lakes Ct . . . . .Fairfax VA 22033   **800-223-7036**

DealerTrack Holdings Inc
1111 Marcus Ave Ste M04 . . . . .Lake Success NY 11042   **877-357-8725**   516-734-3600
NASDAQ: TRAK

DIS Corp
1315 Cornwall Ave . . . . .Bellingham WA 98225   **800-426-8870***   360-733-7610
*Cust Svc

Eagle Point Software Corp
600 Star Brewery Dr Ste 200 . . . . .Dubuque IA 52001   **800-678-6565**

Ellucian 4375 Fair Lakes Ct . . . . .Fairfax VA 22033   **800-223-7036**   610-647-5930

Enghouse Systems Ltd
80 Tiverton Ct Ste 800 . . . . .Markham ON L3R0G4   **866-233-4606**   905-946-3200
TSX: ENGH

Environmental Systems Research Institute Inc
380 New York St .Redlands CA 92373   **800-447-9778***   909-793-2853
*Sales

Equis International
90 South 400 West Ste 620 . . . . .Salt Lake City UT 84101   **800-882-3040***   801-265-9996
*Sales

ERT
1818 Market St Ste 1000 . . . . .Philadelphia PA 19103   **800-704-9698**   215-972-0420
NASDAQ: ERT

Final Draft Inc
26707 W Agoura Rd Ste 205 . . . . .Calabasas CA 91302   **800-231-4055**   818-995-8995

Financial Engines Inc
1804 Embarcadero Rd . . . . .Palo Alto CA 94303   **888-443-8577**   408-498-6000
NASDAQ: FNGN

First DataBank Inc (FDB)
701 Gateway Blvd Ste 600 . . . . South San Francisco CA 94080   **800-633-3453***
*General

FXCM Inc 32 Old Slip . . . . .New York NY 10005   **888-503-6739**   212-897-7660
OTC: GLBR

GHG Corp
960 Clear Lake City Blvd . . . . .Webster TX 77598   **866-380-4146**   281-488-8806

Glimmerglass Networks Inc
26142 Eden Landing Rd . . . . .Hayward CA 94545   **877-723-1900**   510-723-1900

Global Turnkey Systems Inc
2001 US 46 . . . . .Parsippany NJ 07054   **800-221-1746**   973-331-1010

gomembers Inc
1155 Perimeter Ctr W . . . . .Atlanta GA 30338   **855-411-2783**

Infor Global Solutions
13560 Morris Rd Ste 4100 . . . . .Alpharetta GA 30004   **866-244-5479**   678-319-8000

Innovative Technologies Corp (ITC)
1020 Woodman Dr Ste 100 . . . . .Dayton OH 45432   **800-745-8050**   937-252-2145

Input 1 LLC
6200 Canoga Ave Ste 400 . . . . .Woodland Hills CA 91367   **888-882-2554**   818-713-2303

Intradiem
3650 Mansell Rd Ste 500 . . . . .Alpharetta GA 30022   **888-566-9457**   678-356-3500

Island Pacific Inc
17310 Red Hill Ave Ste 320 . . . . .Irvine CA 92614   **800-994-3847**   250-250-1000

iSqFt Inc
3825 Edwards Rd Ste 800 . . . . .Cincinnati OH 45209   **800-364-2059**   513-645-8004

iWay Software 2 Penn Plz . . . . .New York NY 10121   **800-736-6130***   212-736-4433
*Sales

Jenzabar Inc
101 Huntington Ave Ste 2200 . . . . .Boston MA 02199   **800-593-0028**   617-492-9099

Kinaxis 700 Silver Seven Rd . . . . .Ottawa ON K2V1C3   **877-546-2947***   613-592-5780
*General

Lumedx Corp
555 12th St Ste 2060 . . . . .Oakland CA 94607   **800-966-0699**   510-419-1000

Lynx Software Technologies Inc
855 Embedded Way . . . . .San Jose CA 95138   **800-255-5969**   408-979-3900

Management Information Control Systems Inc (MICS)
2025 Ninth St . . . . .Los Osos CA 93402   **800-838-6427**

Managing Editor Inc
610 York Rd # 250 . . . . .Jenkintown PA 19046   **800-638-1214**   215-886-5662

Manhattan Assoc Inc
2300 Windy Ridge Pkwy 10th Fl . . . . .Atlanta GA 30339   **877-756-7435**   770-955-7070
NASDAQ: MANH

Market Scan Information Systems Inc
811 Camarillo Springs Ste B . . . . .Camarillo CA 93012   **800-658-7226**

MDI Achieve
10900 Hampshire Ave S Ste 100 . . . . .Bloomington MN 55438   **800-869-1322**   952-995-9800

Media Cybernetics Inc
4340 E W Hwy Ste 400 . . . . .Bethesda MD 20814   **800-263-2088***   301-495-3305
*Sales

MedPlus Inc 4690 Pkwy Dr . . . . .Mason OH 45040   **800-444-6235**   513-229-5500

Minitab Inc
Quality Plz 1829 Pine Hall Rd . . . . .State College PA 16801   **800-448-3555**   814-238-3280

Mortgage Builder
24370 NW Hwy . . . . .Southfield MI 48075   **800-850-8060**

New England Computer Services Inc
322 E Main St 3rd Fl . . . . .Branford CT 06405   **800-766-6327***   475-221-8200
*Sales

NIC Inc
25501 W Valley Pkwy Ste 300 . . . . .Olathe KS 66061   **877-234-3468**
NASDAQ: EGOV

Olson Research Assoc Inc
10290 Old Columbia Rd . . . . .Columbia MD 21046   **888-657-6680**   410-290-6999

Opex Corp
305 Commerce Dr . . . . .Moorestown NJ 08057   **800-673-9288**   856-727-1100

Pason Systems Inc
6130 Third St SE . . . . .Calgary AB T2H1K4   **877-255-3158**   403-301-3400
TSX: PSI

Promodel Corp
3400 Bath Pk Ste 200 . . . . .Bethlehem PA 18017   **888-900-3090**   801-223-4600

QlikTech International AB
150 N Radnor Chester Rd Ste E220 . . . . .Radnor PA 19087   **888-828-9768**
NASDAQ: QLIK

Quality Systems Inc (QSI)
18111 Von Karman Ave Ste 700 . . . . .Irvine CA 92612   **800-888-7955***   949-255-2600
*NASDAQ: QSII ■ *Cust Svc*

QUMAS 66 York St . . . . .Jersey City NJ 07302   **800-577-1545***   973-805-8600
*Sales

Red Wing Software Inc
491 Hwy 19 . . . . .Red Wing MN 55066   **800-732-9464**   651-388-1106

RESUMate Inc
2500 Packard St Ste 200 . . . . .Ann Arbor MI 48104   **800-530-9310***   734-477-9402
*Cust Svc

Retail Pro International LLC
400 Plaza Dr Ste 200 . . . . .Folsom CA 95630   **800-738-2457**   916-605-7200
OTC: RTPRQ

Reynolds & Reynolds Co
1 Reynolds Way . . . . .Dayton OH 45430   **800-767-0080**   937-485-2000

RiskWatch (RWI)
1237 N Gulfstream Ave . . . . .Sarasota FL 34236   **800-360-1898**

Sapiens International Corp
4000 CentreGreen Way Ste 150 . . . . .Cary NC 27513   **888-281-1167**   919-405-1500
NASDAQ: SPNS

Scantron Corp 34 Parker . . . . .Irvine CA 92618   **800-722-6876**   949-639-7500

Siemens Product Lifecycle Management Software Inc
5800 Granite Pkwy Ste 600 . . . . .Plano TX 75024   **800-498-5351**   972-987-3000

Simulations Plus Inc
42505 Tenth St W . . . . .Lancaster CA 93534   **888-266-9294**   661-723-7723
NASDAQ: SLP

SolidWorks Corp
300 Baker Ave . . . . .Concord MA 01742   **800-693-9000**   978-371-5011

Synergex International Corp
2330 Gold Meadow Way . . . . .Gold River CA 95670   **800-366-3472**   916-635-7300

Synopsys Inc
700 E Middlefield Rd . . . . .Mountain View CA 94043   **800-541-7737**   500-501-1000
NASDAQ: SNPS

System Automation Corp
7110 Samuel Morse Dr . . . . .Columbia MD 21046   **800-839-4729**   301-837-8000

System Innovators Inc
10550 Deerwood Pk Blvd Ste 700 . . . . .Jacksonville FL 32256   **800-963-5000**

Thomson Elite
800 Corporate Pointe Ste 150 . . . . .Los Angeles CA 90230   **800-354-8337***   424-243-2100
*Cust Svc

TMW Systems Inc
21111 Chagrin Blvd . . . . .Beachwood OH 44122   **800-401-6682**   216-831-6606

TradeStation Group Inc
8050 SW Tenth St Ste 2000 . . . . .Plantation FL 33324   **800-871-3577**   954-652-7000

Transentric
1400 Douglas St Ste 0840 . . . . .Omaha NE 68179   **800-877-0328**   402-544-6000

TransWorks
2720 Dupont Commerce Crt Ste 230 . . . . .Fort Wayne IN 46825   **888-325-6510**

Tyler Technologies Inc
5949 Sherry Ln Ste 1400 . . . . .Dallas TX 75225   **800-431-5776**
NYSE: TYL

US Dataworks Inc
14090 SW Fwy Ste 300 . . . . .Sugar Land TX 77478   **888-254-8821**   281-504-8000
OTC: UDWK

US Digital Corp
1400 NE 136th Ave . . . . .Vancouver WA 98684   **800-736-0194**   360-260-2468

Vermont Systems Inc
12 Market Pl . . . . .Essex Junction VT 05452   **877-883-8757**   802-879-6993

Vertafore Inc
5 Waterside Crossing . . . . .Windsor CT 06095   **800-444-4813**

Vital Images Inc
5850 Opus Pkwy Ste 300 . . . . .Minnetonka MN 55343   **800-208-3005**   952-487-9500

VoltDelta Resources Inc
3750 Monroe Ave Ste 4B . . . . .Pittsford NY 14534   **866-436-1169**

Wolters Kluwer Financial Services Inc
100 S Fifth St Ste 700 . . . . .Minneapolis MN 55402   **800-552-9408**   612-656-7700

Wonderware Corp
26561 Rancho Pkwy S . . . . .Lake Forest CA 92630   **800-966-3371**   949-727-3200

Worksoft Inc
15851 Dallas Pkwy Ste 855 . . . . .Addison TX 75001   **866-836-1773**   214-239-0400

	Toll-Free	Phone

Xybernet Inc
10640 Scripps Ranch Blvd ....San Diego CA 92131 · **800-228-9026*** · 858-530-1900
*Cust Svc

178-11 Service Software

	Toll-Free	Phone

Alorica Inc
5 Park Plz Ste 1100 ....Irvine CA 92614 · **866-256-7422**
Amelicor 1525 W 820 N ....Provo UT 84601 · **800-992-1344**
Applied Systems Inc
200 Applied Pkwy ....University Park IL 60484 · **800-786-1362*** · 708-534-5575
*Sales
Aristotle Inc
205 Pennsylvania Ave SE ....Washington DC 20003 · **800-296-2747*** · 202-543-8345
*Sales
Cantata Health LLC
8383 158th Ave NE Ste 100 ....Redmond WA 98052 · **800-426-2675**
Datamann Inc
1994 Hartford Ave ....Wilder VT 05088 · **800-451-4263** · 802-295-6600
DPSI Inc
1801 Stanley Rd Ste 301 ....Greensboro NC 27407 · **800-897-7233** · 336-854-7700
Ebix Inc
5 Concourse Pkwy Ste 3200...........Atlanta GA 30328 · **800-755-2326** · 678-281-2020
NASDAQ: EBIX
Firstwave Technologies Inc
99 MedTech Dr ....Batavia NY 14020 · **877-784-0269**
Galaxy Hotel Systems LLC
5 Peters Canyon Ste 375 ....Irvine CA 92606 · **800-624-2953** · 714-258-5800
Insurance Data Processing Inc (IDP)
8101 Washington Ln ....Wyncote PA 19095 · **800-523-6745** · 215-885-2150
Jack Henry & Assoc Inc
663 W Hwy 60 PO Box 807 ....Monett MO 65708 · **800-299-4222** · 417-235-6652
NASDAQ: JKHY
Jobscope Corp
355 Woodruff Rd ....Greenville SC 29607 · **800-443-5794**
Kalibrate Technologies PLC
25B Hanover Rd ....Florham Park NJ 07932 · **800-727-6774*** · 973-549-1850
*Cust Svc
Key Information Systems Inc
30077 Agoura Ct 1st Fl. ....Agoura Hills CA 91301 · **877-442-3249** · 818-992-8950
Kronos Inc
297 Billerica Rd ....Chelmsford MA 01824 · **888-293-5549** · 978-250-9800
LexisNexis
5000 Sawgrass Village Cir ....Ponte Vedra Beach FL 32082 · **800-368-6955** · 904-273-5000
Manatron Inc
510 E Milham Ave ....Portage MI 49002 · **866-471-2900*** · 269-567-2900
*Cust Svc
Mediware Information Systems Inc
11711 W 79th St ....Lenexa KS 66214 · **800-255-0026** · 913-307-1000
Metafile Information Systems Inc
3428 Lakeridge Pl NW ....Rochester MN 55901 · **800-638-2445*** · 507-286-9232
*Sales
MicroStrategy
1850 Towers Crescent Plz ....Tysons Corner VA 22182 · **888-266-0321** · 703-848-8600
NASDAQ: MSTR
Netsmart Technologies Inc
3500 Sunrise Hwy Ste D-122 ....Great River NY 11739 · **800-421-7503** · 631-968-2000
Radware Inc
575 Corporate Dr Lobby 2 ....Mahwah NJ 07430 · **888-234-5763** · 400-920-2910
Sandata Technologies Inc
26 Harbor Park Dr ....Port Washington NY 11050 · **800-544-7263*** · 516-484-4400
*Sales
SS & C Technologies Inc
80 Lamberton Rd ....Windsor CT 06095 · **800-234-0556** · 860-298-4500
Strictly Business Computer Systems Inc
848 Fourth Ave Ste 200 ....Huntington WV 25701 · **888-529-0401**
TimeValue Software
22 Mauchly ....Irvine CA 92618 · **800-426-4741*** · 949-727-1800
*Sales
TMA Systems LLC
5100 E Skelly Dr Ste 900 ....Tulsa OK 74135 · **800-862-1130** · 918-858-6600
Voice & Data Networks Inc (VDN)
4218 Park Glen Rd ....St. Louis Park MN 55416 · **800-246-7999** · 952-946-5353
Xactware Solutions Inc
1100 W Traverse Pkwy ....Lehi UT 84043 · **800-424-9228*** · 801-764-5900
*Sales

178-12 Systems & Utilities Software

	Toll-Free	Phone

activePDF Inc
27405 Puerta Real Ste 100 ....Mission Viejo CA 92691 · **866-468-6733** · 949-582-9002
Allen Systems Group Inc (ASG)
1333 Third Ave S ....Naples FL 34102 · **800-932-5536** · 239-435-2200
Avatier Corp
2603 Camino Ramon Ste 110...........San Ramon CA 94583 · **800-609-8610** · 925-217-5170
Basis International Ltd
5901 Jefferson St NE ....Albuquerque NM 87109 · **800-423-1394*** · 505-345-5232
*Orders
Blue Lance Inc
410 Pierce St ....Houston TX 77002 · **800-856-2583** · 713-255-4800
BMC Software
2202 NW Shore Blvd Ste 650...........Tampa FL 33607 · **855-834-7487**
CA Inc 1 CA Plz ....Islandia NY 11749 · **800-225-5224**
NASDAQ: CA
CardLogix 16 Hughes Ste 100 ....Irvine CA 92618 · **866-392-8326** · 949-380-1312
Certicom Corp
4701 Tahoe Blvd Bldg A ....Mississauga ON L4W0B5 · **800-561-6100** · 905-507-4220
Check Point Software Technologies Ltd
800 Bridge Pkwy ....Redwood City CA 94065 · **800-429-4391** · 650-628-2000
NASDAQ: CHKP
Cincom Systems Inc
55 Merchant St ....Cincinnati OH 45246 · **800-224-6266** · 513-612-2300

Citrix Systems Inc
851 W Cypress Creek Rd ....Fort Lauderdale FL 33309 · **800-393-1888** · 954-267-3000
NASDAQ: CTXS
Columbia Data Products Inc
925 Sunshine Ln Ste 1080 ....Altamonte Springs FL 32714 · **800-613-6288*** · 407-869-6700
*Sales
CommuniGate Systems Inc
655 Redwood Hwy Ste 275. ....Mill Valley CA 94941 · **800-262-4722** · 415-383-7164
ComponentOne LLC
201 S Highland Ave 3rd Fl ....Pittsburgh PA 15206 · **800-858-2739** · 412-681-4343
Crossmatch
3950 RCA Blvd Ste 5001 ....Palm Beach Garden FL 33410 · **866-725-3926** · 561-622-1650
CSI International Inc
8120 State Rt 138 ....Williamsport OH 43164 · **800-795-4914** · 740-420-5400
CSP Inc 43 Manning Rd ....Billerica MA 01821 · **800-325-3110** · 978-663-7598
NASDAQ: CSPI
DataViz Inc
612 Wheelers Farms Rd ....Milford CT 06460 · **800-733-0030** · 203-874-0085
Datawatch Corp
271 Mill Rd ....Chelmsford MA 01824 · **800-445-3311** · 978-441-2200
NASDAQ: DWCH
DefendX Software
119 Drum Hill Rd Ste 383. ....Chelmsford MA 01824 · **800-390-6937** · 603-622-4400
Descartes Systems Group Inc
120 Randall Dr ....Waterloo ON N2V1C6 · **800-419-8495** · 519-746-8110
TSE: DSG
Digimarc Corp
9405 SW Gemini Dr ....Beaverton OR 97008 · **800-344-4627** · 503-469-4800
NASDAQ: DMRC
Entrust Datacard
5420 LBJ Fwy Ste 300 ....Dallas TX 75240 · **888-690-2424***
*Sales
Esker Inc
1212 Deming Way Ste 350. ....Madison WI 53717 · **800-368-5283** · 608-828-6000
Heroix Corp
165 Bay State Dr ....Braintree MA 02184 · **800-229-6500** · 781-848-1701
HID Global Corp
611 Center Ridge Dr ....Austin TX 78753 · **800-237-7769** · 512-776-9000
International Business Machines Corp (IBM)
1 New OrchaRd Rd ....Armonk NY 10504 · **800-426-4968** · 914-499-1900
NYSE: IBM
InterTrust Technologies Corp
920 Stewart Dr Ste 100. ....Sunnyvale CA 94085 · **800-393-2272** · 408-616-1600
Intrusion Inc
1101 E Arapaho Rd ....Richardson TX 75081 · **888-637-7770** · 972-234-6400
Ipswitch Inc
83 Hartwell Ave ....Lexington MA 02421 · **800-793-4825** · 781-676-5700
Kroll Ontrack Inc
9023 Columbine Rd ....Eden Prairie MN 55347 · **800-872-2599** · 952-937-5161
LapLink Software Inc
600 108th Ave NE Ste 610 ....Bellevue WA 98004 · **800-527-5465** · 425-952-6000
Luminex Software Inc
871 Marlborough Ave ....Riverside CA 92507 · **888-586-4639*** · 951-781-4100
*Sales
McAfee Inc
2821 Mission College Blvd ....Santa Clara CA 95054 · **888-847-8766*** · 408-988-3832
*Cust Svc
McCabe Software Inc
3300 N Ridge Rd ....Ellicott City MD 21043 · **800-638-6316** · 410-381-3710
Microsoft Corp
1 Microsoft Way ....Redmond WA 98052 · **800-642-7676** · 425-882-8080
NASDAQ: MSFT
Mindjet Corp
1160 Battery St E 4th Fl ....San Francisco CA 94111 · **877-646-3538** · 415-229-4200
Mitem Corp 640 Menlo Ave ....Menlo Park CA 94025 · **800-648-3660*** · 650-323-1500
*Sales
MTI Systems Inc
59 Interstate D ....West Springfield MA 01089 · **800-644-4318** · 413-733-1972
NetIQ Corp 1233 W Loop S ....Houston TX 77027 · **888-323-6768*** · 713-548-1700
*Sales
Network Appliance Inc
495 E Java Dr ....Sunnyvale CA 94089 · **800-443-4537*** · 408-822-6000
NASDAQ: NTAP ■ *Sales
Oracle Corp
500 Oracle Pkwy ....Redwood Shores CA 94065 · **800-392-2999*** · 800-633-0738
NYSE: ORCL ■ *Sales
Perceptics Corp
9737 Cogdill Rd Ste 200 ....Knoxville TN 37932 · **800-448-8544**
Phoenix Technologies Ltd
915 Murphy Ranch Rd ....Milpitas CA 95035 · **800-677-7305** · 408-570-1000
PKWare Inc
201 E Pittsburgh Ave Ste 400 ....Milwaukee WI 53204 · **866-583-1795** · 414-289-9788
Pragma Systems Inc
13809 Research Blvd Ste 675. ....Austin TX 78750 · **800-224-1675** · 512-219-7270
Process Software Corp
959 Concord St ....Framingham MA 01701 · **800-722-7770** · 508-879-6994
RadView Software Inc
991 Hwy 22 West Ste 200. ....Bridgewater NJ 08807 · **888-723-8439** · 908-526-7756
Raxco Software Inc
6 Montgomery Village Ave Ste 500. ....Gaithersburg MD 20879 · **800-546-9728*** · 301-527-0803
*Tech Supp
Red Hat Inc 1801 Varsity Dr ....Raleigh NC 27606 · **888-733-4281** · 919-754-3700
NYSE: RHT
Relais International
1690 Woodward Dr Ste 215 ....Ottawa ON K2C3R8 · **888-294-5244** · 613-226-5571
RSA Security Inc
174 Middlesex Tpke ....Bedford MA 01730 · **800-995-5095** · 781-515-5000
ScriptLogic Corp
6000 Broken Sound Pkwy NW ....Boca Raton FL 33487 · **800-306-9329** · 561-886-2400
Serengeti Systems Inc
1108 Lavaca St Ste 110 PMB 431 ....Austin TX 78701 · **800-634-3122** · 512-345-2211
Software Engineering of America Inc (SEA)
1230 Hempstead Tpke ....Franklin Square NY 11010 · **800-272-7322** · 516-328-7000
Software Pursuits Inc
1900 S Norfolk St ....San Mateo CA 94403 · **800-367-4823** · 650-372-0900
Stratus Technologies
111 Powdermill Rd ....Maynard MA 01754 · **800-787-2887** · 978-461-7000

				Toll-Free	Phone
Symantec Corp					
350 Ellis St	Mountain View	CA	94043	800-441-7234	650-527-8000
NASDAQ: SYMC					
Syncsort Inc					
50 Tice Blvd	Woodcliff Lake	NJ	07677	877-700-0970	
TeamQuest Corp					
1 TeamQuest Way	Clear Lake	IA	50428	800-551-8326	641-357-2700
TechSmith Corp					
2405 Woodlake Dr	Okemos	MI	48864	800-517-3001	517-381-2300
Thales e-Security Inc					
2200 N Commerce Pkwy Ste 200	Weston	FL	33326	888-744-4976	954-888-6200
TrendMicro Inc					
10101 N De Anza Blvd	Cupertino	CA	95014	800-228-5651	408-257-1500
Tripwire Inc					
101 SW Main St Ste 1500	Portland	OR	97204	800-874-7947*	503-276-7500
*General					
UltraBac Software					
15015 Main St Ste 200	Bellevue	WA	98007	866-554-8562	425-644-6000
VanDyke Software Inc					
4848 Tramway Ridge Dr NE Ste 101	Albuquerque	NM	87111	800-952-5210	505-332-5700
Vendant Inc					
4845 Pearl East Cir Ste 101	Bouler	CO	80301	800-714-4900	720-378-4420
Vision Solutions Inc					
15300 Barranca Pkwy	Irvine	CA	92618	800-683-4667	949-253-6500
Webroot Software Inc					
2560 55th St	Boulder	CO	80301	800-772-9383	303-442-3813
Wind River Systems Inc					
500 Wind River Way	Alameda	CA	94501	800-545-9463	510-748-4100
XIOtech Corp					
9950 Federal Dr Ste 100	Colorado Springs	CO	80921	866-472-6764	719-388-5500
Zix Corp					
2711 N Haskell Ave Ste 2300-LB	Dallas	TX	75204	888-771-4049	214-370-2000
NASDAQ: ZIXI					
Zone Alarm					
800 Bridge Pkwy	Redwood City	CA	94065	877-966-5221	415-633-4500

179   COMPUTER STORES

SEE ALSO Appliance & Home Electronics Stores

				Toll-Free	Phone
1 EDI Source Inc					
31875 Solon Rd	Solon	OH	44139	877-334-9650	
A Matter of Fax					
105 Harrison Ave	Harrison	NJ	07029	800-433-3329	973-482-3700
Aberdeen LLC					
9130 Norwalk Blvd	Santa Fe Springs	CA	90670	800-500-9526	562-699-6998
Accordant Company LLC					
365 S St Ste 100	Morristown	NJ	07960	800-363-1002	973-887-8900
Aim 2 Berkeley St Ste 403	Toronto	ON	M5A4J5	866-645-2224	416-594-9393
Aljex Software Inc					
50 Division St Ste 204	Somerville	NJ	08876	833-262-2314	
Arbutus Software Inc					
6450 Roberts St	Burnaby	BC	V5G4E1	877-333-6336	604-437-7873
Atiwa Computer Leasing Exchange					
6950 Portwest Dr Ste 100	Houston	TX	77024	800-428-2532	713-467-9390
Automated Medical Systems Inc					
2310 N Patterson St Bldg H	Valdosta	GA	31602	800-256-3240	229-253-9526
Azar Computer Software Services Inc					
1200 Regal Row	Austin	TX	78748	800-525-7844	
Balihoo					
404 S Eighth St Ste 300	Boise	ID	83702	866-446-9914	
Barcoding Inc					
2220 Boston St	Baltimore	MD	21231	888-412-7226	888-860-7226
Basic Software Systems					
905 N Kings Hwy	Texarkana	TX	75501	800-252-4476	903-792-4421
BCS Prosoft Inc					
2700 Lockhill Selma	San Antonio	TX	78230	800-882-6705	210-308-5505
Bizco Technologies Inc					
7950 "O" St	Lincoln	NE	68510	800-424-9677	
CDW Corp					
200 N Milwaukee Ave	Vernon Hills	IL	60061	800-800-4239	847-465-6000
Colligo Networks Inc					
400-1152 Mainland St	Vancouver	BC	V6B4X2	866-685-7962	604-685-7962
COMRES Inc					
424 SW 12th Ave	Deerfield Beach	FL	33442	877-379-9600	954-462-9600
Conference Group, The					
254 Chapman Rd Topkis Bldg Ste 200	Newark	DE	19702	877-716-8255	302-224-8255
ConnectWise Inc					
4110 George Rd Ste 200	Tampa	FL	33634	800-671-6898	813-463-4700
Crawford Technologies Inc					
45 St Clair Ave W Ste 102	Toronto	ON	M4V1K9	866-679-0864	416-923-0080
Dexter & Chaney Inc					
9700 Lake City Way NE	Seattle	WA	98115	800-875-1400	206-364-1400
DOVICO Software Inc					
236 St George St Ste 119	Moncton	NB	E1C1W1	800-618-8463	
ElectSolve Technology Solutions & Services Inc					
4300 Youree Dr Bldg 1	Shreveport	LA	71105	877-221-2055	318-221-2055
Employee Development Systems Inc					
7308 S Alton Way Ste 2J	Centennial	CO	80112	800-282-3374	
Envision Payment Solutions Inc					
PO Box 157	Suwanee	GA	30024	800-290-3957	770-709-3007
EWASTE+					
7318 Victor Mendon Rd	Victor	NY	14564	888-563-1340	
ExitCertified					
8950 Cal Center Dr Bldg 1 Ste 110	Sacramento	CA	95826	800-803-3948	916-669-3970
GameStop Corp					
625 Westport Pkwy	Grapevine	TX	76051	800-883-8895	817-424-2000
NYSE: GME					
Gateway Inc					
7565 Irvine Ctr Dr	Irvine	CA	92618	800-846-2000	949-471-7040
Gopher Electronics Company Inc					
222 Little Canada Rd	Saint Paul	MN	55117	800-592-9519	651-490-4900
Govconnection Inc					
7503 Standish Pl	Rockville	MD	20855	800-998-0009	
ICAM Technologies Corp					
21500 Nassr St	Sainte-anne-de-bellevue	QC	H9X4C1	800-827-4226	514-697-8033

				Toll-Free	Phone
Indigo Rose Corp					
123 Bannatyne Ave Ste 200	Winnipeg	MB	R3B0R3	800-665-9668	204-946-0263
Insight Enterprises Inc					
6820 S Harl Ave	Tempe	AZ	85283	800-467-4448	480-333-3000
NASDAQ: NSIT					
Instanet Solutions					
100 Wellington St Ste 201	London	ON	N6B2K6	800-668-8768	
Ipro Tech LLC					
1700 N Desert Dr Ste 101	Tempe	AZ	85281	877-324-4776	
Jive Communications Inc					
1275 W 1600 N Ste 100	Orem	UT	84057	866-768-5429	
Jonah Group Ltd, The					
461 King St W 3rd Fl	Toronto	ON	M5V1K4	888-594-6260	416-304-0860
KLJ Computer Solutions Inc					
PO Box 2040	Fall River	NS	B2T1K6	888-455-5669	902-425-7010
Knowledge Information Solutions Inc (KIS)					
2877 Guardian Ln Ste 201	Virginia Beach	VA	23452	877-547-7248	757-463-3232
Launch Pad 18130 Jorene Rd	Odessa	FL	33556	888-920-3450	
LD Systems LP					
407 Garden Oaks	Houston	TX	77018	800-416-9327	713-695-9400
Loki Systems Inc					
1258-13351 Commerce Pkwy	Richmond	BC	V6V2X7	800-378-5654	
London Computer Services					
9140 Waterstone Blvd	Cincinnati	OH	45249	800-669-0871	513-583-1482
Medflow Inc					
14045 Ballantyne Corporate Pl Ste 300	Charlotte	NC	28277	844-366-5129	704-750-5927
Medicat LLC					
303 Perimeter Ctr N Ste 320	Atlanta	GA	30346	866-633-4053	404-252-2295
Messaging Architects					
180 Peel St Ste 333	Montreal	QC	H3C2G7	866-497-0101	514-392-9220
Netgain Networks Inc					
8378 Attica Dr	Riverside	CA	92508	855-667-2364	951-656-0194
Newegg Inc					
16839 E Gale Ave	City of Industry	CA	91745	800-390-1119	626-271-9700
Oceanside Photo & Telescope (OPT)					
918 Mission Ave	Oceanside	CA	92054	800-483-6287	760-400-0164
Office Solutions Inc					
217 Mt Horeb Rd	Warren	NJ	07059	800-677-1778	
Omni-Medcom 160 Pope St	Cookshire	QC	J0B1M0	888-780-6081	
Omnivex Corp					
3300 Hwy 7 Ste 501	Concord	ON	L4K4M3	800-745-8223	905-761-6640
Open Automation Software					
5077 Bear Mtn Dr	Evergreen	CO	80439	800-533-4994	303-679-0898
Optiwave Systems Inc					
7 Capella Ct	Ottawa	ON	K2E7X1	866-576-6784	613-224-4700
Palomino Inc 545 King St W	Toronto	ON	M5V1M1	866-360-0360	416-964-7333
PC Connection Inc					
730 Milford Rd Rt 101A	Merrimack	NH	03054	888-213-0607	603-683-2000
NASDAQ: PCCC					
PC Connection Inc MacConnection Div					
730 Milford Rd	Merrimack	NH	03054	888-213-0260	
PC Mall Inc					
2555 W 190th St	Torrance	CA	90504	800-555-6255	310-354-5600
NASDAQ: PCMI					
Physmark Inc					
101 E Pk Blvd Ste 600	Plano	TX	75074	800-922-7060	972-231-8000
Pinnacle Corp, The					
201A E Abram St	Arlington	TX	76010	800-325-3535	817-795-5555
ProComp Software Consultants Inc					
4629 Aicholtz Rd	Cincinnati	OH	45244	800-783-1668	513-685-5245
Prolifiq Software Inc					
8585 SW Watson Ave Ste 200	Beaverton	OR	97008	800-840-7183	503-684-1415
Recursion Software Inc					
2591 Dallas Pkwy Ste 200	Frisco	TX	75034	800-727-8674	972-731-8800
RLM Communications Inc					
1027 E Manchester Rd	Spring Lake	NC	28390	877-223-1345	910-223-1350
Service Communications Inc (SCI)					
15223 NE 90th St	Redmond	WA	98052	800-488-0468	425-278-0300
Side Effects Software Inc					
123 Front St W Ste 1401	Toronto	ON	M5J2M2	888-504-9876	416-504-9876
Softechnologies Inc					
1504 W Northwest Blvd	Spokane	WA	99205	866-873-9799	
SPLICE Software Inc					
425 78 Ave SW	Calgary	AB	T2V5K5	855-677-5423	403-720-8326
Strata Health Solutions Inc					
933 - 17 Ave SW Ste 600	Calgary	BC	T2T5R6	866-556-5005	
Strategy Companion Corp					
3240 El Camino Real Ste 120	Irvine	CA	92602	800-905-6792	714-460-8398
TenAsys Corp					
1400 NW Compton Dr Ste 301	Hillsboro	OR	97006	877-277-9189	503-748-4720
TernPro					
320 Westlake Ave 4th Fl	Seattle	WA	98109	888-483-8779	
Tetrasoft Inc					
16647 Chesterfield Grove Rd Ste 120	Chesterfield	MO	63005	866-314-7557	636-530-7638
Top Producer Systems Inc					
10651 Shellbridge Way Ste 155	Richmond	BC	V6X2W8	800-821-3657	
Translationscom Inc					
3 Park Ave 39th Fl	New York	NY	10016	800-688-7205	212-689-1616
Tricerat Inc					
11500 Cronridge Dr Ste 100	Owings Mills	MD	21117	800-582-5167	410-715-4226
TVL Inc					
901 16th St W	North Vancouver	BC	V7P1R2	800-263-0000	
Valley Office Systems					
2050 First St	Idaho Falls	ID	83401	800-610-2865	208-529-2777
Vector Networks Inc					
541 Tenth St Unit 123	Atlanta	GA	30318	800-330-5035	770-622-2850
Vertex Systems Inc					
2550 Corporate Exchange Dr Ste 104	Columbus	OH	43231	866-981-2600	614-318-7100
VistaVu Solutions Inc					
30 Springborough Blvd SW Ste 214	Calgary	AB	T3H0N9	888-300-2727	403-263-2727
Vocantas Inc					
2934 Baseline Rd Ste 301	Ottawa	ON	K2H1B2	877-271-8853	613-271-8853

180   COMPUTER SYSTEMS DESIGN SERVICES

SEE ALSO Web Site Design Services
Companies that plan and design computer systems that integrate hardware, software, and communication technologies.

Name / Address	City	ST	Zip	Toll-Free	Phone
4Sight Group LLC 4023 Kennett Pk Ste 233	Wilmington	DE	19807	**800-490-2131**	
7strategy LLC 117 N Cooper St	Olathe	KS	66061	**888-231-3062**	
A Partner in Technology 105 Dresden Ave	Gardiner	ME	04345	**877-582-0888**	207-582-0888
AAJ Technologies 6301 NW Fifth Way Ste 1700	Fort Lauderdale	FL	33309	**800-443-5210**	954-689-3984
Aasys Group 11301 N US Hwy 301 Ste 106	Thonotosassa	FL	33592	**800-852-7091**	813-246-4757
Abacus Technology Corp 5404 Wisconsin Ave Ste 1100	Chevy Chase	MD	20815	**800-225-2135**	
Absolute Analysis Inc 2393 Teller Rd Ste 109	Newbury Park	CA	91320	**800-452-5174**	
ACB Solutions 551 W Dimond Blvd	Anchorage	AK	99515	**888-238-4225**	
Advanced Information Systems Group Inc 11315 Corporate Blvd Ste 210	Orlando	FL	32817	**800-593-8359**	407-581-2929
AETEA Information Technology Inc 1445 Research Blvd Ste 210	Rockville	MD	20850	**888-772-3832**	301-721-4200
AGSI 800 Battery Ave SE Ste 100	Atlanta	GA	30339	**800-768-2474**	404-816-7577
Algo Design Inc 6455 Doris Lussier Ste 300	Boisbriand	QC	J7H0E8	**800-267-2584**	450-681-2584
ALI's Database Consultants 1151 Williams Dr	Aiken	SC	29803	**866-257-8970**	803-648-5931
All Native Systems LLC 1 Mission Dr	Winnebago	NE	68071	**866-323-7636**	
All Systems Installation 8300 Tenth Ave N Ste A	Golden Valley	MN	55427	**800-403-4832**	763-593-1330
AlphaKOR Group Inc 7800 Twin Oaks Dr	Windsor	ON	N8N5B6	**877-944-6009**	519-944-6009
American Systems Corp 14151 Pk Meadow Dr Ste 500	Chantilly	VA	20151	**800-733-2721**	703-968-6300
Amgraf Inc 1501 Oak St	Kansas City	MO	64108	**800-304-4797**	816-474-4797
Antares Technology Solutions 8282 Goodwood Blvd Ste W-2	Baton Rouge	LA	70806	**800-366-8807**	225-922-7748
Applied Sciences Group Inc 2495 Main St Ste 407	Buffalo	NY	14214	**877-274-9811**	716-626-5100
APPNETCOM 7883 NC Hwy 105 S Ste C	Boone	NC	28607	**888-926-4584**	828-963-7286
Arlington Computer Products Inc 851 Commerce Ct *Orders	Buffalo Grove	IL	60089	**800-548-5105***	847-541-6333
Ashburn Consulting LLC 43848 Goshen Farm Ct	Leesburg	VA	20176	**866-576-9382**	703-652-9120
Asi Networks Inc 19331 E Walnut Dr N	City Of Industry	CA	91748	**800-251-1336**	
Asponte Technology Inc 11523 Palmbrush Trl Ste 137	Lakewood Ranch	FL	34202	**888-926-9434**	
AVS Installations LLC 400 Raritan Ctr Pkwy Ste D.	Edison	NJ	08837	**800-218-9177**	732-634-7903
Axyz Automation Inc 2844 E Kemper Rd	Cincinnati	OH	45241	**800-527-9670**	800-361-3408
Azure Horizons Inc 7115 W North Ave Ste 185	Oak Park	IL	60302	**877-494-6070**	708-838-7031
B Green Innovations Inc 750 Hwy 34	Matawan	NJ	07747	**877-996-9333**	
Bailiwick Services LLC 4260 Norex Dr	Chaska	MN	55318	**800-935-8840**	
Banetti Inc 55 NE 94th St	Miami	FL	33138	**855-855-7800**	
Bazon Cox & Associates Inc 1244 Executive Blvd	Chesapeake	VA	23320	**800-769-1763**	757-410-2128
Bell Techlogix 4400 W 96th St	Indianapolis	IN	46268	**866-782-2355**	317-333-7777
Binovia Corp 3021 N 204th St	Omaha	NE	68022	**877-331-0282**	402-331-0202
Blast Advanced Media 950 Reserve Dr Ste 150	Roseville	CA	95678	**888-252-7866**	916-724-6701
Blax Inc 9861 Colbert	Montreal	QC	H1J1Z9	**888-523-2529**	514-523-4600
Blough Tech Inc 119 S Broad St	Cairo	GA	39828	**800-957-0554**	229-377-8825
Blue Granite Inc 2750 Old Centre Rd Ste 150	Portage	MI	49024	**877-817-0736**	
Blue Tangerine Solutions Llc 1380 Sarno Rd Ste B	Melbourne	FL	32935	**800-870-4293**	321-309-6900
Bluelock LLC 6325 Morenci Trl	Indianapolis	IN	46268	**888-402-2583**	
Blytheco LLC 23161 Mill Creek Dr	Laguna Hills	CA	92653	**800-425-9843**	949-583-9500
Boxworks Technologies Inc 2065 Pkwy Blve	Salt Lake City	UT	84119	**877-495-2250**	801-214-6100
Bridgeline Digital 80 BlanchaRd Rd	Burlington	MA	01803	**800-603-9936**	781-376-5555
Broadleaf Services Inc 6 Fortune Dr	Billerica	MA	01821	**866-337-7733**	
CACI International Inc 1100 N Glebe Rd *NYSE: CACI*	Arlington	VA	22201	**866-606-3471**	703-841-7800
Cad Technology Center Inc 8101 Fourth Ave S Ste 100	Bloomington	MN	55425	**866-941-1181**	
Cadnet Services 100 Carl Dr Ste 12	Manchester	NH	03103	**866-522-3638**	
Cadnetics 400 Holiday Dri Ste 102	Pittsburgh	PA	15220	**855-494-0043**	412-642-2701
Cadre Computer Resources Co 201 E Fifth St Ste 1800	Cincinnati	OH	45202	**866-762-6700**	513-762-7350
Cal Net Technology Group 9420 Topanga Canyon Blvd Ste 100	Chatsworth	CA	91311	**866-999-2638**	
Calibre Systems Inc 6354 Walker Ln Ste 300	Alexandria	VA	22310	**888-225-4273**	703-797-8500
Camber Corp 670 Discovery Dr	Huntsville	AL	35806	**800-998-7988**	256-922-0200
Canweb Internet Services 1086 Modeland Rd	Sarnia	ON	N7S6L2	**877-422-6932**	519-332-6900
CARA Group Inc, The Drake Oak Brook Plz 2215 York Rd Ste 300	Oak Brook	IL	60523	**866-401-2272**	630-574-2272
Catapult Systems Inc 1221 S MoPac Expwy Ste 350	Austin	TX	78746	**800-528-6248**	512-328-8181
Cayman Technologies Inc 12954 Stonecreek Dr Ste E.	Pickerington	OH	43147	**877-370-9470**	614-759-9461
CBM of America Inc 1455 W Newport Ctr Dr	Deerfield Beach	FL	33442	**800-881-8202**	954-698-9104
Cbord Group Inc, The 950 Danby Rd Ste 100C	Ithaca	NY	14850	**844-462-2673**	
Cca Medical Inc 6 Southridge Ct	Greenville	SC	29607	**800-775-2556**	864-233-2700
CDMS Inc 550 Sherbrooke W West Tower Ste 250	Montreal	QC	H3A1B9	**866-337-2367**	514-286-2367
Cdo Technologies Inc 5200 Sprngfeld St Ste 320	Dayton	OH	45431	**866-307-6616**	937-258-0022
CGI Group Inc 1350 Ren,-l,vesque Blvd W 15th Fl *TSX: GIB/A*	Montreal	QC	H3G1T4	**800-828-8377**	514-841-3200
Chameleon Consulting Inc 89 Falmouth Rd W	Arlington	MA	02474	**866-903-7912**	781-646-2272
Chi Corp 5265 Naiman Pkwy	Cleveland	OH	44139	**800-828-0599**	440-498-2300
CIBER Inc 6363 S Fiddler's Green Cir Ste 1400 *NYSE: CBR*	Greenwood Village	CO	80111	**800-242-3799**	303-220-0100
Citadel Information Services Inc (CIS) 33 Wood Ave S Ste 720	Iselin	NJ	08830	**888-862-4823**	732-238-0072
Clarkston Consulting Research Triangle Park 2655 Meridian Pkwy.	Durham	NC	27713	**800-652-4274**	919-484-4400
Clever Devices Ltd 300 Crossways Pk Dr	Woodbury	NY	11797	**800-872-6129**	516-433-6100
Cognizant Technology Solutions Corp 500 Frank W Burr Blvd *NASDAQ: CTSH*	Teaneck	NJ	07666	**888-937-3277**	201-801-0233
Comm Source Data 200 Waler Way Bldg 1 Unit 1	Saint Augustine	FL	32086	**800-434-5750**	
Computer Power Solutions Inc 4644 Katella Ave	Los Alamitos	CA	90720	**800-444-1938**	562-493-4487
Computer Pundits Corp (CPC) 5001 American Blvd W Ste 310	Bloomington	MN	55437	**888-786-3487**	952-854-2422
Computer Task Group Inc (CTG) 800 Delaware Ave *OTC: CTG*	Buffalo	NY	14209	**800-992-5350**	716-882-8000
Comtech Network Systems Inc 1320 Lincoln Ave Ste 4.	Holbrook	NY	11741	**877-267-0750**	
Condortech Services Inc 6621-A Electronic Dr	Springfield	VA	22151	**800-842-9171**	703-916-9200
Connect Tech Inc 42 Arrow Rd	Guelph	ON	N1K1S6	**800-426-8979**	519-836-1291
Consult Dynamics Inc 1016 Delaware Ave	Wilmington	DE	19806	**800-784-4788**	302-654-1019
Convio Inc 11501 Domain Dr Ste 200	Austin	TX	78758	**888-528-9501**	512-652-2600
Creation Engine 425 North Whisman Rd Ste 300	Mountain View	CA	94043	**800-431-8713**	650-934-0176
Cronomagic Canada Inc 3333 boul Graham Ste 700.	Mont-Royal	QC	H3R3L5	**800-427-6012**	514-341-1579
Custom Computer Specialists Inc (CCS) 70 Suffolk Ct	Hauppauge	NY	11788	**800-598-8989**	
CWPS Inc 14120 A Sullyfield Cir	Chantilly	VA	20151	**877-297-7472**	703-263-9539
Cypress Networks 4125 Walker Ave	Greensboro	NC	27407	**866-625-3502**	336-841-3030
Cyquent Inc 5410 Edson Ln Ste 210C	Rockville	MD	20852	**866-509-0331**	240-292-0230
Data Consulting Group Inc 965 E Jefferson Ave	Detroit	MI	48207	**800-258-4343**	313-963-7771
Data Systems Analysts Inc (DSA) Eigth Neshaminy Interplex Ste 209	Trevose	PA	19053	**877-422-4372**	215-245-4800
DataComm Networks Inc 6801 N 54th St	Tampa	FL	33610	**800-544-4627**	
DataLink Interactive Inc 1120 Benfield Blvd Ste G	Millersville	MD	21108	**888-565-3279**	410-729-0440
Datapro Solutions Inc 6336 E Utah Ave	Spokane	WA	99212	**888-658-6881**	509-532-3530
Dataskill Inc 2190 Carmel Valley Rd Ste D	DelMar	CA	92014	**800-481-3282**	858-755-3800
Datatrend Technologies Inc 121 Cheshire Ln Ste 700	Minnetonka	MN	55305	**800-367-7472**	952-931-1203
Dcs Netlink 1800 Macauley Ave	Rice Lake	WI	54868	**877-327-6385**	715-236-7424
Delaney Computer Services Inc 575 Corporate Dr Ste 400.	Mahwah	NJ	07430	**844-832-4437**	201-669-4300
Delta Corporate Services Inc 129 Littleton Rd	Parsippany	NJ	07054	**800-335-8220**	973-334-6260
Denali Advance Integration (DAI) 17735 NE 65th St Ste 130	Redmond	WA	98052	**877-467-8008**	425-885-4000
Dental Systems Inc PO Box 7331	Baytown	TX	77522	**800-683-2501**	
Dialogic Inc 1504 Mccarthy Blvd	Milpitas	CA	95035	**800-755-4444**	408-750-9400
Digital Measures 301 N Broadway 4th Fl	Milwaukee	WI	53202	**866-348-5677**	
Dirks Group, The 3802 Hummingbird Rd	Wausau	WI	54401	**800-866-1486**	715-848-9865
DPE Systems Inc 120 Lakeside Ave Ste 230.	Seattle	WA	98122	**800-541-6566**	206-223-3737
Druide informatique Inc 1435 rue Saint-Alexandre Bureau 1040	Montreal	QC	H3A2G4	**800-537-8433**	514-484-4998

	City	State	ZIP	Toll-Free	Phone
Dyonyx LP 1235 N Loop W	Houston	TX	77008	855-749-6758*	713-485-7000
*General					
Echomountain Llc					
1483 Patriot Blvd	Glenview	IL	60026	877-311-1980	
eMagine 1082 Davol St	Fall River	MA	02720	877-530-7993	
Eos Systems Inc					
10 Kearney Rd Ste 102	Needham	MA	02494	855-453-2600	781-453-2600
Epoch Online					
324 W Pershing Blvd Ste 11	North Little Rock	AR	72114	877-312-7500	501-907-7500
eVerge Group Inc					
4965 Preston Pk Blvd Ste 700	Plano	TX	75093	888-548-1973	972-608-1803
FiberPlus Inc					
8240 Preston Ct Ste C	Jessup	MD	20794	800-394-3301	301-317-3300
Force 3 Inc					
2151 Priest Bridge Dr	Crofton	MD	21114	800-391-0204	
Fujitsu Consulting					
1250 E Arques Ave	Sunnyvale	CA	94085	800-831-3183	
Future Com Ltd					
3600 William D Tate Ave Ste 300	Grapevine	TX	76051	888-710-5250	817-510-1100
G2 Web Services LLC					
1750 112th Ave NE Ste C101	Bellevue	WA	98004	888-788-5353	
Garvin-Allen Solutions Ltd					
155 Chain Lake Dr Unit 12	Halifax	NS	B3S1B3	877-325-9062	902-453-3554
General Dynamics Information Technology					
3211 Jermantown Rd	Fairfax	VA	22030	800-242-0230	703-995-8700
Genesis 10					
950 Third Ave 2nd Fl	New York	NY	10022	800-261-1776	212-688-5522
GeoLogics Corp					
5285 Shawnee Rd Ste 300	Alexandria	VA	22312	800-684-3455	703-750-4000
Geoscape International Inc					
2100 W Flagler St	Miami	FL	33135	888-211-9353	
Global Consultants Inc					
25 Airport Rd	Morristown	NJ	07960	877-264-6424	973-889-5200
Global Help Desk Services Inc					
2080 Silas Deane Hwy	Rocky Hill	CT	06067	800-770-1075	
Global Technology Resources Inc					
990 S Broadway Ste 300	Denver	CO	80209	877-603-1984	303-455-8800
Globalspec Inc 350 Jordan Rd	Troy	NY	12180	800-261-2052	518-880-0200
Gold Key Technology Solutions					
4212 S Fifth St	Temple	TX	76501	866-321-1531	254-774-9035
GP Strategies Corp					
11000 Broken Land Pkwy Ste 200	Columbia	MD	21044	888-843-4784	443-367-9600
Grantek Systems Integration Inc					
4480 Harvester Rd	Burlington	ON	L7L4X2	866-936-9509	
Gray Matter Group					
88 Vilcom Ctr Dr Ste 180	Chapel Hill	NC	27514	877-970-4747	919-932-6150
Greenpages Inc					
33 Badgers Island W	Kittery	ME	03904	888-687-4876	207-439-7310
Henry A Bromelkamp & Co					
106 E 24th St	Minneapolis	MN	55404	877-767-6703	612-870-9087
Hixardt Technologies Inc					
119 W Intendencia St	Pensacola	FL	32502	866-985-3282	850-439-3282
House of Brick Technologies LLC					
9300 Underwood Ave Ste 300	Omaha	NE	68114	877-780-7038	402-445-0764
Howard Systems International					
2777 Summer St	Stamford	CT	06905	800-326-4860	
HubTech					
44 Norfolk Ave Ste 4	South Easton	MA	02375	877-482-8324	
Ibaset					
27442 Portola Pkwy	Foothill Ranch	CA	92610	877-422-7381	949-598-5200
Ice Technologies Inc					
411 SE Ninth St	Pella	IA	50219	877-754-8420	
IM. Systems Group Inc					
3206 Tower Oaks Blvd Ste 300	Rockville	MD	20852	866-368-9880	240-833-1889
iMakeNews Inc					
7400 Wilshire Place Dr	Houston	TX	77040	866-964-6397	937-485-8030
InCycle Software Inc					
1120 Avenue of The Americas 4th Fl	New York	NY	10036	800-565-0510	212-626-2608
Indigo Dynamic Networks Llc					
2413 W Algonquin Rd	Algonquin	IL	60102	888-464-6344	
Indtai Inc					
2095 Chain Bridge Rd Ste 300	Vienna	VA	22182	877-912-6672	
Inetsolution					
2075 W Big Beaver Rd Ste 222	Troy	MI	48084	855-728-5839	
Infolink Exp					
2880 Zanker Rd Ste 203	San Jose	CA	95134	800-280-7703	915-577-9466
Infosoft Group Inc					
1123 N Water St Ste 400	Milwaukee	WI	53202	800-984-3775	414-278-0700
Inovex Information Systems Inc					
7240 Pkwy Dr Ste 140	Hanover	MD	21076	800-469-9705	443-782-1452
Integral Solutions Group					
5700 N Blockstock Rd	Spartanburg	SC	29303	800-428-7280	
Intellicom Computer Consulting					
1702 Second Ave	Kearney	NE	68847	877-501-3375	308-237-0684
Intelligent Decisions Inc					
21445 Beaumeade Cir	Ashburn	VA	20147	800-929-8331	703-554-1600
IntelliSoft Group LLC					
61 Spit Brook Rd	Nashua	NH	03060	888-634-4464	
InterDev LLC					
2650 Holcomb Bridge Rd Ste 310	Alpharetta	GA	30022	877-841-8069	770-643-4400
InterVision Systems Technologies Inc					
2270 Martin Ave	Santa Clara	CA	95050	800-787-6707	408-980-8550
InterWorks Inc					
1425 S Sangre Rd	Stillwater	OK	74074	866-490-9643	405-624-3214
Intraprisetechknowlogies LLC					
3615 Harding Ave Ste 209	Honolulu	HI	96816	866-737-9991	
Intrepid Control Systems Inc					
31601 Research Park Dr	Madison Heights	MI	48071	800-859-6265	586-731-7950
IOActive Inc					
701 Fifth Ave Ste 6850	Seattle	WA	98104	866-760-0222	206-784-4313
Ip Convergence Inc					
PO Box 107	Argyle	TX	76226	800-813-5106	
IQware Inc					
5850 Coral Ridge Dr Ste 309	Coral Springs	FL	33076	877-698-5151	954-698-5151
IT Weapons					
7965 Goreway Dr Unit 1	Brampton	ON	L6T5T5	866-202-5298	905-494-1040
Iteck Solutions LLC					
4909 Morning Glory Ct Ste 250	Rockville	MD	20853	866-483-2544	301-929-1852

	City	State	ZIP	Toll-Free	Phone
Itergy					
2075 University Ste 700	Montreal	QC	H3A2L1	866-522-5881	514-845-5881
ITSource Technology Inc					
899 Northgate Dr Ste 304	San Rafael	CA	94903	866-548-4911	
J4 Systems Inc					
2521 Warren Dr Ste A	Rocklin	CA	95677	866-547-9783	916-303-7200
Jas Net Consulting Inc					
2053 Grant Rd Ste 321	Los Altos	CA	94024	888-527-6388	408-257-3279
Kanatek Technologies Inc					
359 Terry Fox Dr Ste 230	Kanata	ON	K2K2E7	800-526-2821	613-591-1482
Kerrington Group Inc					
24 S Fifth St	Fernandina Beach	FL	32034	800-582-0828	904-491-1411
KForce Government Soultions					
2750 Prosperity Ave Ste 300	Fairfax	VA	22031	800-200-7465	703-245-7350
Lighthouse Computer Services Inc					
6 Blackstone Valley Pl Ste 205	Lincoln	RI	02865	888-542-8030	401-334-0799
Link Medical Computing Inc					
1208 B VFW Pkwy Ste 203	Boston	MA	02132	888-893-0900	617-676-6165
Logicalis					
1 Penn Plz 51st Fl Ste 5130	New York	NY	10119	866-456-4422	
Logicease Solutions Inc					
1 Bay Plz Ste 520	Burlingame	CA	94010	866-212-3273	650-373-1111
Lynx Computer Technologies Inc					
7 Bristol Ct	Wyomissing	PA	19610	800-331-5969	610-678-8131
Maximizer Software Inc					
1090 W Pender St 10th Fl	Vancouver	BC	V6E2N7	800-804-6299	604-601-8000
Mdl Enterprise Inc					
9888 SW Fwy	Houston	TX	77074	800-879-0840	713-771-6350
MediaPro Inc					
20021 120th Ave NE Ste 102	Bothell	WA	98011	800-726-6951	425-483-4700
Microwest Software Systems Inc					
10981 San Diego Mson Rd Ste 210	San Diego	CA	92108	800-969-9699	619-280-0440
Miles Technologies Inc					
300 W Rt 38	Moorestown	NJ	08057	800-496-8001	856-439-0999
MSS Technologies Inc					
1555 E Orangewood Ave	Phoenix	AZ	85020	800-694-1302	602-387-2100
Muller Systems Corp					
926 Juliana Dr	Woodstock	ON	N4V1B9	800-668-6954	519-421-1800
Multiple Media Inc					
465 McGill St Office 1000	Montreal	QC	H2Y2H1	866-790-6626	514-276-7660
N'Ware Technologies Inc					
2885 81e Rue	Saint-georges	QC	G6A0C5	800-270-9420	418-227-4292
NAI solutions					
200 104th Ave Ste 324	Treasure Island	FL	33706	877-624-8311	
NCI Inc					
11730 Plaza America Dr	Reston	VA	20190	800-274-9694	703-707-6900
NASDAQ: NCIT					
Nerd Force Inc					
26500 W Agoura Rd	Calabasas	CA	91302	800-979-6373	
Netessentials Inc					
705 Eighth St Ste 1000	Wichita Falls	TX	76301	877-899-6387	940-767-6387
Netgain Information Systems Co					
128 W Columbus Ave	Bellefontaine	OH	43311	855-651-7001	937-593-7177
Netorian LLC					
210 Research Blvd Ste 160	Aberdeen	MD	21001	844-638-6742	
Network Performance Inc					
85 Green Mtn Dr	South Burlington	VT	05403	800-639-6091	802-859-0808
Networks of Florida					
25 W Avery St	Pensacola	FL	32501	800-368-2315	850-434-8600
NetXperts Inc					
1777 Botelho Dr Ste 102	Walnut Creek	CA	94596	888-271-9367	925-806-0800
NewAgeSys Inc					
231 Clarksville Rd Ste 200	Princeton Junction	NJ	08550	888-863-9243	609-919-9800
Novacoast Inc					
1505 Chapala St	Santa Barbara	CA	93101	800-949-9933	
NOVIPRO Inc					
2055 Peel St Ste 701	Montreal	QC	H3A1V4	866-726-5353	514-744-5353
Novo Solutions Inc					
516 S Independence Blvd	Virginia Beach	VA	23452	888-316-4559	757-687-6590
nQueue Inc					
7890 S Hardy Dr Ste 105	Tempe	AZ	85284	800-299-5933	
NTT DATA Inc 100 City Sq	Boston	MA	02129	800-745-3263	
Oar Net 1224 Kinnear Rd	Columbus	OH	43212	800-627-6420	614-292-9191
Official Payments Corp					
3550 Engineering Dr	Norcross	GA	30092	877-754-4413	770-325-3100
Omni Information Systems Inc					
PO Box 1429	Dacula	GA	30019	888-653-6664	678-377-5560
ONESPRING LLC					
980 Birmingham Rd Ste 501-165	Alpharetta	GA	30004	888-472-1840	
OnPath Business Solutions Inc					
1165 Kenaston St	Ottawa	ON	K1B3N9	855-420-3244	
P3 Inc 213 Hwy 35	Red Bank	NJ	07701	866-222-5169	
Pacific Software Publishing Inc					
1404 140th Pl NE	Bellevue	WA	98007	800-232-3989	
Pavliks Com 80 Bell Farm Rd	Barrie	ON	L4M5K5	877-728-5457	705-726-2966
PC Guardian Anti-Theft Products Inc					
2171 E Francisco Blvd Ste G	San Rafael	CA	94901	800-453-4195	415-259-3103
Pcm Networking					
2121 W First St	Fort Myers	FL	33901	866-726-6381	239-334-1615
PDX Inc					
101 Jim Wright Fwy S Ste 200	Fort Worth	TX	76108	800-433-5719	
Phoenix Integration Inc					
1715 Pratt Dr Ste 2000	Blacksburg	VA	24060	800-500-1936	540-961-7215
PIREL Inc					
1315 Rue Gay-Lussac	Boucherville	QC	J4B7K1	800-449-5199	450-449-5199
Planned Systems International Inc					
10632 Lttle Patuxent Pkwy	Columbia	MD	21044	800-275-7749	410-964-8000
Point Alliance Inc					
20 Adelaide St E Ste 500	Toronto	ON	M5C2T6	855-947-6468	
Pomeroy IT Solutions Inc					
1020 Petersburg Rd	Hebron	KY	41048	800-846-8727	859-586-0600
Practice Velocity LLC					
8777 Velocity Dr	Machesney Park	IL	61115	866-995-9863	
Presidio Networked Solutions Inc					
7601 Ora Glen Dr Ste 100	Greenbelt	MD	20770	800-452-6926	301-313-2000
Presteligence Inc					
8328 Cleveland Ave NW	Canton	OH	44720	888-438-6050	

				Toll-Free	Phone

Protocol Networks Inc
15 Shore Dr .... Johnston RI 02919 **877-676-0146**

PSI Services LLC
611 N Brand Blvd 1st Fl .... Glendale CA 91505 **800-367-1565**

Quadrant 4 System Corp
1501 E Woodfield Rd Ste 205 S .... Schaumburg IL 60173 **855-995-7367**

Qualex Consulting Services Inc
1111 Kane Concourse
Ste 320 .... Bay Harbor Islands FL 33154 **877-887-4727**

Radiant Networks
13000 Middletown Industrial Blvd
Ste D. .... Louisville KY 40223 **866-411-9526** 502-379-4800

Ranac
11650 Lantern Rd Ste 111 .... Fishers IN 46038 **888-335-0427**

RealSTEEL 1684 Medina Rd .... Medina OH 44256 **866-965-2688**

Redman Technologies Inc
10172-108 St .... Edmonton AB T5J1L3 **866-425-0022**

Relate Corp
5141 Verdugo Way Ste C .... Camarillo CA 93012 **800-428-3708**

Remote Operations Co
200 Pakerland Dr .... Green Bay WI 54303 **888-837-4466** 920-437-4466

Rex Black Consulting Services Inc
31520 Beck Rd .... Bulverde TX 78163 **866-438-4830** 830-438-4830

RiverPoint Group LLC
2200 E Devon Ave Ste 385 .... Des Plaines IL 60018 **800-297-5601** 847-233-9600

Rockport Technology Group Inc
5 Industrial Way Ste 2C .... Salem NH 03079 **800-399-7053** 603-681-0333

Rolta Tusc Inc
333 E Butterfield Rd Ste 900. .... Lombard IL 60148 **800-755-8872** 630-960-2909

Sabre Solution, The
200 E 31st St .... Savannah GA 31401 **888-494-7200** 912-355-7200

SAI Systems International Inc
5 Research Dr .... Shelton CT 06484 **877-724-4748** 203-929-0790

Sayers Group LLC
825 Corporate Woods Pkwy .... Vernon Hills IL 60061 **800-323-5357**

SCC Soft Computer Inc
5400 Tech Data Dr .... Clearwater FL 33760 **800-763-8352** 727-789-0100

Scorpion Design Inc
28480 Ave Stanford Ste 100 .... Valencia CA 91355 **866-622-5648**

Sda Consulting Inc
3011 183rd St # 377 .... Homewood IL 60430 **800-823-2990**

Securance Consulting
13904 Monroes Business Park .... Tampa FL 33635 **877-578-0215**

ShareSquared Inc
2155 Verdugo Blvd .... Montrose CA 91020 **800-445-1279**

Simacor LLC
10700 Hwy 55 Ste 170 .... Plymouth MN 55441 **888-284-4415** 763-544-4415

Skyweb Networks
2710 State St .... Saginaw MI 48602 **866-575-9932** 989-792-8681

SMS Data Products Group Inc
1751 Pinnacle Dr 12th Fl .... McLean VA 22102 **800-331-1767**

Softech & Associates Inc
1570 Corporate Dr Ste B. .... Costa Mesa CA 92626 **877-638-3241** 714-427-1122

Software Information Systems Inc (SIS)
165 Barr St .... Lexington KY 40507 **800-337-6914** 859-977-4747

Software Technology Group
555 S 300 E .... Salt Lake City UT 84111 **888-595-1001** 801-595-1000

Solid Border
1806 Turnmill St .... San Antonio TX 78248 **800-213-8175**

SolutionsIQ Inc
6801 185th Ave NE Ste 200 .... Redmond WA 98052 **800-235-4091** 425-451-2727

Sonos 614 Chapala St .... Santa Barbara CA 93101 **800-680-2345** 805-965-3001

Sparkhound Inc
11207 Proverbs Ave .... Baton Rouge LA 70816 **866-217-1500** 225-216-1500

Specific Impulse Inc
2601 Blanding Ave Ste 401 .... Alameda CA 94501 **800-470-0043** 510-251-2330

Sphere 3D Corp
240 Matheson Blvd E .... Mississauga ON L4Z1X1 **800-406-7325** 416-749-5999

Startech Computing Inc
1755 Old W Main St .... Red Wing MN 55066 **888-385-0607** 651-385-0607

Statera Inc
5619 DTC Pkwy Ste 900. .... Greenwood Village CO 80111 **866-697-0266**

Stefanini TechTeam Inc
27100 W Eleven-Mile Rd .... Southfield MI 48034 **800-522-4451**

Stg International Inc
4900 Seminary Rd Ste 1100 .... Alexandria VA 22311 **855-507-0660** 703-578-6030

Strata Information Group
3935 Harney St Ste 203 .... San Diego CA 92110 **800-776-0111**

Stratacache
2 Emmet St Ste 200 .... Dayton OH 45405 **800-244-8915** 937-224-0485

Sunquest Information Systems Inc
3300 E Sunrise Dr .... Tucson AZ 85718 **877-239-6337** 520-570-2000

Svam International Inc
233 E Shore Rd Ste 201 .... Great Neck NY 11023 **800-903-6716**

Swearingen Software Inc
PO Box 23018 .... Beaumont TX 77720 **800-992-1767**

Sykes Enterprises Inc
400 N Ashley Dr .... Tampa FL 33602 **800-867-9537**
NASDAQ: SYKE

Synergy Associates LLC
550 Clydesdale Trl .... Medina MN 55340 **888-763-9920**

Syscon Inc
94 McFarland Blvd .... Northport AL 35476 **888-797-2661** 205-758-2000

TAB Computer Systems Inc
29 Bissell St .... East Hartford CT 06118 **888-822-4435** 860-289-8850

Tangible Solutions Inc
1320 Matthews Township Pkwy Ste 201. .. Matthews NC 28105 **800-393-9886** 704-940-4200

Tango Management Consulting LLC
6225 N State Hwy 161 Ste 300. .... Irving TX 75038 **855-938-2646**

Tech Hero
200 E Robinson St Ste 425. .... Orlando FL 32801 **800-900-8324**

Techspeed Inc
280 SW Moonridge Pl .... Portland OR 97225 **800-750-4066** 503-291-0027

TECSys Development Inc
1600 Tenth St .... Plano TX 75074 **800-695-1258** 972-881-1553

Teksavers Inc
2120 Grand Ave Pkwy .... Austin TX 78728 **866-832-6188**

TeraMach Technologies Inc
1130 Morrison Dr Ste 105 .... Ottawa ON K2H9N6 **877-226-6549** 613-226-7775

Thomson Reuters DT Tax & Acctg
3333 Graham Blvd Ste 222 .... Montreal QC H3R3L5 **800-663-7829** 514-733-8355

TLX Inc
7944 E Beck Ln Ste 200 .... Scottsdale AZ 85260 **800-520-7493** 480-609-8888

TM Group Inc, The
27555 Executive Dr Ste 100 ...... Farmington Hills MI 48331 **888-482-2864** 248-489-0707

TOSS Corp
1253 Worcester Rd .... Framingham MA 01701 **888-884-8677** 508-820-2990

Tribridge
4830 W Kennedy Blvd Ste 890 .... Tampa FL 33609 **877-744-1360**

Tricolor Inc
1111 W Mockingbird Ln Ste 1500 .... Dallas TX 75247 **888-253-0423**

Turbotek Computer Corp
70 Zachary Rd Ste 3 .... Manchester NH 03109 **800-573-5393** 603-666-3062

Ungerboeck Systems International Inc
100 Ungerboeck Pk .... O'fallon MO 63368 **800-400-4052** 636-300-5606

US-Analytics
600 E Las Colinas Blvd Ste 2222 .... Irving TX 75039 **877-828-8727*** 214-630-0081
General

USDM Life Sciences
535 Chapala St .... Santa Barbara CA 93101 **888-231-0816**

USWired Inc
2107 N First St Ste 250 .... San Jose CA 95131 **877-879-4733** 408-432-1144

Vanguard Integrity Professionals Inc
6625 S Eastern Ave Ste 100 .... Las Vegas NV 89119 **877-794-0014** 702-794-0014

Vertisoft
990 Boul Pierre-roux E .... Victoriaville QC G6T0K9 **877-368-3241**

Victory Enterprises Inc
5200 30th St SW .... Davenport IA 52802 **800-670-5716** 563-884-4444

Visual Retail Plus
540 Hudson St .... Hackensack NJ 07601 **888-767-4004**

Voyager Systems Inc
360 Rt 101 .... Bedford NH 03110 **800-634-1966** 603-472-5172

WidePoint Corp
7926 Jones Branch Dr Ste 520. .... Mclean VA 22102 **877-919-5943*** 703-349-5644
Sales

Winning Technologies Great Lakes LLC
147 Triad Ctr W .... O Fallon MO 63366 **877-379-8279**

Working Machines Corp
2170 Dwight Way .... Berkeley CA 94704 **877-648-4800** 510-704-1100

Worx Group LLC, The
18 Waterbury Rd .... Prospect CT 06712 **800-732-8090** 203-758-3311

YouMail Inc
43 Corporate Pk Ste 200. .... Irvine CA 92606 **800-374-0013**

Zontec Inc
1389 Kemper Meadow Dr .... Cincinnati OH 45240 **866-955-0088** 513-648-9695
ZyQuest Inc 1385 W Main Ave .... De Pere WI 54115 **800-992-0533** 920-499-0533

181	CONCERT, SPORTS, OTHER LIVE EVENT PRODUCERS & PROMOTERS

				Toll-Free	Phone

Dallas Fan Fares Inc
5485 Beltline Rd Ste 270 .... Dallas TX 75254 **800-925-6979** 972-239-9969

Gilmore Entertainment Group
8901-A Business 17 N .... Myrtle Beach SC 29572 **800-843-6779** 843-913-4000

Harlem Globetrotters International Inc
400 E Van Buren St Ste 300 .... Phoenix AZ 85004 **800-641-4667** 208-568-6644

Top Rank Inc
3980 Howard Hughes Pkwy Ste 580. .... Las Vegas NV 89119 **800-943-0087**

182	CONCRETE - READY-MIXED

				Toll-Free	Phone

Bonded Concrete Inc
PO Box 189 .... Watervliet NY 12189 **800-252-8589** 518-273-5800

Boston Sand & Gravel Company Inc
100 N Washington St .... Boston MA 02114 **800-624-2724** 617-227-9000
OTC: BSND

Builders Redi-Mix Inc
30701 W 10 Mile Rd Ste 500
PO Box 2900. .... Farmington Hills MI 48333 **888-988-4400**

Building Products Corp
950 Freeburg Ave .... Belleville IL 62220 **800-233-1996** 618-233-4427

C J Horner Company Inc
105 W Grand Ave .... Hot Springs AR 71901 **800-426-4261** 501-321-9600

CalPortland
5975 E Marginal Way S .... Seattle WA 98134 **800-750-0123** 206-764-3000

Cemex USA
929 Gessner Rd Ste 1900. .... Houston TX 77024 **800-999-8529** 713-650-6200
NYSE: CX

Cemstone
2025 Centre Pt Blvd Ste 300. ...... Mendota Heights MN 55120 **800-642-3887** 651-688-9292

Central Builders Supply Company Inc
125 Bridge Ave PO Box 152 .... Sunbury PA 17801 **800-326-9361** 570-286-6461

Central Concrete Supply Company Inc
755 Stockton Ave .... San Jose CA 95126 **866-404-1000** 408-293-6272

Century Ready-Mix Corp
3250 Armand St PO Box 4420 .... Monroe LA 71211 **800-732-3969** 318-322-4444

Conproco Corp
17 Production Dr .... Dover NH 03820 **800-258-3500**

Eagle Materials Inc
3811 Turtle Creek Blvd Ste 1100 .... Dallas TX 75219 **800-759-7625** 214-432-2000
NYSE: EXP

Eastern Concrete Materials Inc
475 Market St .... Elmwood Park NJ 07407 **800-822-7242** 817-835-4105

Ernst Enterprises Inc
3361 Successful Way .... Dayton OH 45414 **800-353-1555** 937-233-5555

Hoover Inc
1205 Bridgestone Pkwy .... Lavergne TN 37086 **800-944-9200**

Janesville Sand & Gravel Co (JSG)
1110 Harding St PO Box 427 .... Janesville WI 53547 **800-955-7702** 608-754-7701

					Toll-Free	Phone
King's Material Inc						
650 12th Ave SW	Cedar Rapids	IA	52404		800-332-5298	319-363-0233
Knife River Corp						
3303 Rock Island Pl	Bismarck	ND	58504		800-982-5339	701-530-1380
Krehling Industries Inc						
1399 Hagy Way	Harrisburg	PA	17110		800-839-1654	717-232-7936
Kuhlman Corp						
1845 Indian Woods Cir	Maumee	OH	43537		800-669-3309	419-897-6000
L Suzio Concrete Company Inc						
975 Westfield Rd	Meriden	CT	06450		888-789-4626	203-237-8421
Lafarge North America Inc						
8700 W Bryn Mawr Ave Ste 300	Chicago	IL	60631		800-451-8346	773-372-1000
Lycon Inc						
1110 Harding St PO Box 427	Janesville	WI	53545		800-955-8758	608-754-7701
RiverStone Group Inc						
1701 Fifth Ave	Moline	IL	61265		800-906-2489	309-757-8250
Sequatchie Concrete Service Inc						
406 Cedar Ave	South Pittsburg	TN	37380		800-824-0824	423-837-7913
Shelby Materials						
157 E Rampart St PO Box 242	Shelbyville	IN	46176		800-548-9516	
Silvi Concrete Products Inc						
355 Newbold Rd	Fairless Hills	PA	19030		800-426-6273	215-295-0777
Speedway Redi Mix Inc						
1201 N Taylor Rd	Garrett	IN	46738		800-227-5649	260-357-6885
Tilcon Connecticut Inc						
PO Box 1357	New Britain	CT	06050		888-845-2666	860-224-6010
Titan America Inc						
1151 Azalea Garden Rd	Norfolk	VA	23502		800-468-7622	757-858-6500
United Companies						
2273 River Rd	Grand Junction	CO	81505		800-321-0807	970-243-4900
United Materials LLC						
3374 Walden Ave Ste 120	Depew	NY	14043		888-918-6483	716-213-5832

183   CONCRETE PRODUCTS - MFR

					Toll-Free	Phone
A Duchini Inc						
2550 McKinley Ave	Erie	PA	16503		800-937-7317	814-456-7027
Abresist Corp PO Box 38	Urbana	IN	46990		800-348-0717	260-774-3327
Accord Industries						
4001 Forsyth Rd	Winter Park	FL	32792		800-876-6989*	407-671-6989
*General						
Adams Products Co						
5701 McCrimmon Pkwy	Morrisville	NC	27560		800-672-3131	919-467-2218
Advanced Concrete Systems						
55 Advanced Ln	Middleburg	PA	17842		800-521-3788	
American Artstone Co						
2025 N Broadway St	New Ulm	MN	56073		800-967-2076	507-233-3700
Amvic Inc 501 McNicoll Ave	Toronto	ON	M2H2E2		877-470-9991	416-410-5674
ARDEX Inc						
400 Ardex Park Dr	Aliquippa	PA	15001		888-512-7339	724-203-5000
Basalite Concrete Products LLC						
605 Industrial Way	Dixon	CA	95620		800-776-6690	707-678-1901
Beavertown Block Company Inc						
3612 Paxtonville Rd	Middleburg	PA	17842		800-597-2565	570-837-1744
BNZ Materials Inc						
6901 S Pierce St Ste 260	Littleton	CO	80128		800-999-0890	303-978-1199
Burtco Inc						
185 Rt 123	Westminster Station	VT	05159		800-451-4401	802-722-3358
Carr Concrete Corp						
362 Waverly Rd	Williamstown	WV	26187		800-837-8918	304-464-4441
Cast-Crete Corp						
6324 County Rd 579	Seffner	FL	33584		800-999-4641	813-621-4641
Cement Industries Inc						
2925 Hanson St PO Box 823	Fort Myers	FL	33902		800-332-1440	239-332-1440
Century Group Inc, The						
1106 W Napoleon St PO Box 228	Sulphur	LA	70664		800-527-5232	337-527-5266
Chaney Enterprises						
12480 Mattawoman Dr PO Box 548	Waldorf	MD	20604		888-244-0411	301-932-5000
Clayton Block Co						
PO Box 3015	Lakewood	NJ	08701		800-662-3044	
Con Cast Pipe LP						
299 Brock Rd S	Puslinch	ON	N0B2J0		800-668-7473	519-763-8655
Con Forms						
777 Maritime Dr	Port Washington	WI	53074		800-223-3676	262-284-7800
Concrete Systems Inc						
9 Commercial St	Hudson	NH	03051		800-342-3374	603-889-4163
Construction Products Inc						
1631 Ashport Rd	Jackson	TN	38305		800-238-8226	731-668-7305
Dura-Stress Inc						
11325 County Rd 44	Leesburg	FL	34788		800-342-9239*	352-787-1422
*General						
E Dillon & Co						
2522 Swords Creek Rd PO Box 160	Swords Creek	VA	24649		800-234-8970	276-873-6816
Elderlee Inc						
729 Cross Rd	Oak Corners	NY	14518		800-344-5917	315-789-6670
EP Henry Corp 201 Park Ave	Woodbury	NJ	08096		800-444-3679	
Ernest Maier Inc						
4700 Annapolis Rd	Bladensburg	MD	20710		888-927-8303	301-927-8300
Fabcon Precast 6111 Hwy 13 W	Savage	MN	55378		800-727-4444	952-890-4444
Featherlite Bldg Products Corp						
508 McNeil St PO Box 425	Round Rock	TX	78681		800-792-1234	512-255-2573
Federal Block Corp						
247 Walsh Ave	New Windsor	NY	12553		800-724-1999	845-561-4108
Fibrebond Corp						
1300 Davenport Dr	Minden	LA	71055		800-824-2614	318-377-1030
Foltz Concrete Pipe Co LLC						
11875 N NC Hwy 150	Winston-Salem	NC	27127		800-229-8525	
Fritz Industries Inc						
180 Gordon Dr Ste 107	Exton	PA	19341		800-345-6202	
General Shale Products LLC						
3015 Bristol Hwy	Johnson City	TN	37601		800-414-4661	423-282-4661
Grand Blanc Cement Products						
10709 Ctr Rd	Grand Blanc	MI	48439		800-875-7500	810-694-7500
High Concrete Structures Inc						
125 Denver Rd	Denver	PA	17517		800-773-2278	717-336-9300

					Toll-Free	Phone
Hy-Grade Precast Concrete						
2411 First St	St Catharines	ON	L2R6P7		800-229-8568	905-684-8568
Isabel Bloom LLC						
736 Federal St Ste 2100	Davenport	IA	52803		800-273-5436	
Jensen Precast 521 Dunn Cir	Sparks	NV	89431		800-648-1134	855-468-5600
JW Peters Inc						
500 W Market St	Burlington	WI	53105		866-265-7888	262-763-2401
King's Material Inc						
650 12th Ave SW	Cedar Rapids	IA	52404		800-332-5298	319-363-0233
Kistner Concrete Products Inc						
8713 Read Rd	East Pembroke	NY	14056		800-809-2801	585-762-8216
L M Scofield Co						
6533 Bandini Blvd	Los Angeles	CA	90040		800-800-9900	323-720-3000
Lafarge North America Inc						
8700 W Bryn Mawr Ave Ste 300	Chicago	IL	60631		800-451-8346	773-372-1000
M-CON Products Inc						
2150 Richardson Side Rd	Carp	ON	K0A1L0		800-267-5515	613-831-1736
MantelsDirect						
217 N Seminary St	Florence	AL	35630		888-493-8898	256-765-2171
Metromont Corp						
PO Box 2486	Greenville	SC	29602		844-882-4015	
Midwest Tile & Concrete Products Inc						
4309 Webster Rd	Woodburn	IN	46797		800-359-4701	260-749-5173
Molin Concrete Products Co						
415 Lilac St	Lino Lakes	MN	55014		800-336-6546	651-786-7722
Montfort Bros Inc						
44 Elm St	Fishkill	NY	12524		800-724-1777	845-896-6225
Montfort Group, The						
44 Elm St	Fishkill	NY	12524		800-724-1777	845-896-6225
National Oilwell Varco (NOV)						
7909 Parkwood Cir Dr	Houston	TX	77036		888-262-8645	713-375-3700
NYSE: NOV						
New Milford Block & Supply						
574 Danbury Rd	New Milford	CT	06776		800-724-1888	860-355-1101
Norwalk Concrete Industries Inc						
80 Commerce Dr	Norwalk	OH	44857		800-733-3624	419-668-8167
Oldcastle Precast Inc						
7921 Southpark Plz Ste 200	Littleton	CO	80120		800-642-3755	303-209-8000
Preload Inc						
125 Kennedy Dr Ste 500	Hauppauge	NY	11788		888-773-5623	631-231-8100
Premier Concrete Products						
5102 Galveston Rd	Houston	TX	77017		800-575-7293	713-641-2727
QUIKRETE Cos						
3490 Piedmont Rd Ste 1300	Atlanta	GA	30305		800-282-5828	404-634-9100
RCP Block & Brick Inc						
8240 Broadway	Lemon Grove	CA	91945		800-794-4727	619-460-7250
Reading Precast Inc						
5494 Pottsville Pk	Leesport	PA	19533		800-724-4881	
Reading Rock Inc						
4600 Devitt Dr	Cincinnati	OH	45246		800-482-6466	513-874-2345
Rinker Materials Corp Concrete Pipe Div						
8311 W Carder Ct	Littleton	CO	80125		800-909-7763	303-791-1600
Rockwood Retaining Walls Inc						
7200 Hwy 63 N	Rochester	MN	55906		800-535-2375	888-288-4045
SD Ireland Co						
193 Industrial Ave	Williston	VT	05495		800-339-4565	802-863-6222
Selkirk Canada Corp						
375 Green Rd	Stoney Creek	ON	L8E4A5		800-263-9308	905-662-6600
Sequatchie Concrete Service Inc						
406 Cedar Ave	South Pittsburg	TN	37380		800-824-0824	423-837-7913
Stubbe's Precast						
30 Muir Line	Harley	ON	N0E1E0		866-355-2183	519-424-2183
Superlite Block Co Inc						
4150 W Turney Ave	Phoenix	AZ	85019		800-366-7877	602-352-3500
Terre Hill Silo Company Inc						
PO Box 10	Terre Hill	PA	17581		800-242-1509	717-445-3100
Tindall Corp						
2273 Hayne St	Spartanburg	SC	29301		800-849-4521	864-576-3230
Valley Blox Inc						
210 Stone Spring Rd	Harrisonburg	VA	22801		800-648-6725	540-434-6725
Wausau Tile Inc PO Box 1520	Wausau	WI	54402		800-388-8728	715-359-3121
Wells Concrete						
210 Inspiration Ln PO Box 656	Albany	MN	56307		800-658-7049	
Wieser Concrete Products Inc						
W3716 US Hwy 10	Maiden Rock	WI	54750		800-325-8456	715-647-2311
Wingra Stone Co						
2975 Kapec Rd PO Box 44284	Madison	WI	53744		800-249-6908	608-271-5555
York Bldg Products Co						
950 Smile Way	York	PA	17404		800-673-2408	717-848-2831

184   CONFERENCE & EVENTS COORDINATORS

					Toll-Free	Phone
ASD						
600 Corporate Pointe Ste 1000 10th Fl	Culver	CA	90230		800-421-4511	323-817-2200
Bixel & Co						
8721 Sunset Blvd Ste 101	Los Angeles	CA	90069		855-854-9830	310-854-3828
Can-do Promotions Inc						
6517 Wise Ave NW	North Canton	OH	44720		800-325-7981	
Conference & Travel						
5655 Coventry Ln	Fort Wayne	IN	46804		800-346-9807	260-434-6600
Convention Consultants Historic Savannah Foundation						
117 W Perry St	Savannah	GA	31401		800-559-6627	912-234-4088
Courtesy Assoc						
2025 M St NW Ste 800	Washington	DC	20036		800-647-4689	
Creative Impact Group Inc						
801 Skokie Blvd Ste 108	Northbrook	IL	60062		800-445-2171	
CSI Worldwide Inc						
40 Regency Plz	Glen Mills	PA	19342		800-523-7118	610-558-4500
Destination Services of Colorado Inc (DSC)						
PO Box 3660	Avon	CO	81620		855-866-5290	970-476-6565
Eagle Recognition						
2706 Mtn Industrial Blvd	Tucker	GA	30084		888-287-4240	770-985-0808
Exhibit Concepts Inc						
700 Crossroads Ct	Vandalia	OH	45377		800-324-5063	
Experient Inc						
2500 E Enterprise Pkwy	Twinsburg	OH	44087		800-935-8333	330-294-4194

				Toll-Free	Phone
Expo Group, The 5931 W Campus Cir Dr	Irving	TX	75063	**800-736-7775**	972-580-9000
ExpoMarketing LLC 2741 Dow Ave	Tustin	CA	92780	**800-867-3976**	
Freeman 1600 Viceroy Dr Ste 100	Dallas	TX	75235	**800-453-9228**	214-445-1000
Gavel International Corp 935 Lakeview Pkwy Ste 190	Vernon Hills	IL	60061	**800-544-2835**	
GES 7000 Lindell Rd	Las Vegas	NV	89118	**800-443-9767**	702-515-5500
Gls Group Inc 27850 Detroit Rd	Westlake	OH	44145	**800-955-9435**	440-899-7770
Graylyn International Conference Center Inc 1900 Reynolda Rd	Winston-Salem	NC	27106	**800-472-9596**	336-758-2600
Gtcbio 635 W Foothill Blvd	Monrovia	CA	91016	**800-422-8386**	626-256-6405
Idegy Inc 226 N Fifth St Ste 220	Columbus	OH	43215	**888-421-2288**	614-545-5000
International Meeting Managers Inc 4550 Post Oak Pl Ste 342	Houston	TX	77027	**800-423-7175**	713-965-0566
Management International Inc 1828 SE First Ave	Fort Lauderdale	FL	33316	**800-425-1995**	954-763-8003
Meeting Connection Inc, The 6373 Meadow Glen Dr N	Westerville	OH	43082	**800-398-2568**	614-898-9361
National Trade Productions Inc 313 S Patrick St	Alexandria	VA	22314	**800-687-7469**	703-683-8500
Paramount Convention Services Inc 5015 Fyler Ave	Saint Louis	MO	63139	**800-883-6578**	314-621-6677
Pittcon 300 Penn Ctr Blvd Ste 332	Pittsburgh	PA	15235	**800-825-3221**	412-825-3220
Prestige Accommodations International 1231 E Dyer Rd Ste 240	Santa Ana	CA	92705	**800-321-6338**	714-957-9100
Resource Connection Inc 161 S Main St	Middleton	MA	01949	**800-649-5228**	978-777-9333
Reverse Logistics Trends Inc 2300 Lakeview Pkwy Ste 700	Alpharetta	GA	30009	**866-801-6332**	801-331-8949
RX Worldwide Meetings Inc 3060 Communications Pkwy Ste 200	Plano	TX	75093	**800-562-1713**	214-291-2920
Splash!events Inc 210 Hillsdale Ave	San Jose	CA	95136	**866-204-6000**	408-287-8600
Steven Restivo Event Services LLC 805 Fourth St Ste 8	San Rafael	CA	94901	**800-310-6563**	415-456-6455
T3 Expo LLC 8 Lakeville Business Pk	Lakeville	MA	02347	**888-698-3397**	
Westbury National Show Systems Ltd 772 Warden Ave	Toronto	ON	M1L4T7	**855-752-1372**	416-752-1371

185 CONGLOMERATES

SEE ALSO Holding Companies

A business conglomerate is defined here as a corporation that consists of many business units in different industries.

				Toll-Free	Phone
3M Co 3M Ctr *NYSE: MMM*	Saint Paul	MN	55144	**800-364-3577**	651-733-1110
Alexander & Baldwin Inc 822 Bishop St *NYSE: ALEX*	Honolulu	HI	96813	**866-442-6551**	808-525-6611
Altria Group Inc 6601 W Broad St *NYSE: MO*	Richmond	VA	23230	**800-627-5200**	804-274-2200
Andersons Inc 1947 Briarfield Blvd PO Box 119 *NASDAQ: ANDE*	Maumee	OH	43537	**800-537-3370**	419-893-5050
APi Group Inc 1100 Old Hwy 8 NW	New Brighton	MN	55112	**800-223-4922**	
ARAMARK Corp 1101 Market St	Philadelphia	PA	19107	**800-388-3300**	215-238-3000
Ashland Inc 50 E River Ctr Blvd PO Box 391 *NYSE: ASH*	Covington	KY	41012	**877-546-2782**	859-815-3333
Berkshire Hathaway Inc 3555 Farnam St Ste 1440 *NYSE: BRK.A*	Omaha	NE	68131	**800-223-2064**	402-346-1400
Brown-Forman 850 Dixie Hwy *NYSE: BFA*	Louisville	KY	40210	**800-831-9146**	502-585-1100
Canadian Tire Corp Ltd 2180 Yonge St PO Box 770 Stn K *TSX: CTC.A*	Toronto	ON	M4P2V8	**800-387-8803**	416-480-3000
Chemed Corp 255 E Fifth St Ste 2600 *NYSE: CHE* ■ *General	Cincinnati	OH	45202	**800-224-3633***	513-762-6900
CSX Corp 500 Water St 15th Fl *NASDAQ: CSX*	Jacksonville	FL	32202	**800-737-1663**	904-359-3200
Deere & Co 1 John Deere Pl *NYSE: DE*	Moline	IL	61265	**800-765-9588**	309-765-8000
Delaware North Cos Inc 40 Fountain Plz	Buffalo	NY	14202	**800-828-7240**	716-858-5000
Empire Company Ltd 115 King St *TSE: EMP.A*	Stellarton	NS	B0K1S0	**800-387-0825**	902-755-4440
Fortune Brands Inc 520 Lake Cook Rd *NYSE: FBHS*	Deerfield	IL	60015	**800-225-2719**	847-484-4400
Griffon Corp 712 Fifth Ave 18th Fl *NYSE: GFF*	New York	NY	10019	**800-378-1475**	212-957-5000
Harris Teeter Inc PO Box 10100	Mathews	NC	28106	**800-432-6111**	
Harsco Corp 350 Poplar Church Rd *NYSE: HSC*	Camp Hill	PA	17011	**866-470-3900**	717-763-7064
Hitachi America Ltd 50 Prospect Ave	Tarrytown	NY	10591	**800-448-2244**	914-332-5800
Holiday Cos 4567 American Blvd W PO Box 1224	Bloomington	MN	55437	**800-745-7411**	952-830-8700
HT Hackney Co 502 S Gay St PO Box 238	Knoxville	TN	37901	**800-406-1291**	865-546-1291
iHeartMedia Inc 200 E Basse Rd	San Antonio	TX	78209	**800-829-6551**	210-822-2828
Kaman Corp 1332 Blue Hills Ave PO Box 1 *NYSE: KAMN*	Bloomfield	CT	06002	**866-450-3663**	860-243-7100
Kimball International Inc 1600 Royal St *NASDAQ: KBAL*	Jasper	IN	47549	**800-482-1616**	
Kohler Co Inc 444 Highland Dr	Kohler	WI	53044	**800-456-4537**	920-457-4441
MDU Resources Group Inc 1200 W Century Ave PO Box 5650 *NYSE: MDU*	Bismarck	ND	58506	**866-760-4852**	701-530-1000
NACCO Industries Inc 5875 Landerbrook Dr Ste 220 *NYSE: NC*	Cleveland	OH	44124	**877-756-5118**	440-229-5151
PepsiCo Inc 700 Anderson Hill Rd *NYSE: PEP* ■ *PR	Purchase	NY	10577	**800-433-2652***	914-253-2000
Procter & Gamble Co (PG) 1 Procter & Gamble Plz *NYSE: PG*	Cincinnati	OH	45202	**800-503-4611**	513-983-1100
Seaboard Corp 9000 W 67th St *NYSE: SEB*	Shawnee Mission	KS	66202	**866-676-8886**	913-676-8800
Siemens Corp 300 New Jersey Ave Ste 1000	Washington	DC	20001	**800-743-6367**	
SPX Corp 13515 Ballantyne Corporate Pl *NYSE: SPXC*	Charlotte	NC	28277	**877-247-3797**	704-752-4400
Time Warner Inc 1 Time Warner Ctr *NYSE: TWX*	New York	NY	10019	**866-463-6899**	212-484-8000
United Services Automobile Assn (USAA) 10750 McDermott Fwy	San Antonio	TX	78288	**800-531-8722**	
Weyerhaeuser Co 33663 Weyerhaeuser Way S *NYSE: WY*	Federal Way	WA	98003	**800-525-5440**	253-924-2345

186 CONSTRUCTION - BUILDING CONTRACTORS - NON-RESIDENTIAL

				Toll-Free	Phone
Adamo Construction Inc 11980 Woodside Ave Ste 5	Lakeside	CA	92040	**800-554-6364**	619-390-6706
Advanced Industrial Services Inc 3250 Susquehanna Trial	York	PA	17406	**800-544-5080**	717-764-9811
Allen Blasting & Coating Inc 1668 Old Hwy 61	Wever	IA	52658	**800-760-9186**	319-367-5500
Alten Construction 1141 Marina Way S	Richmond	CA	94804	**800-360-6397**	510-234-4200
Ameris Bank 24 Second Ave SE PO Box 3668	Moultrie	GA	31768	**866-616-6020**	
Anchor Tampa Inc 3907 W Osborne Ave	Tampa	FL	33614	**800-879-8685**	813-879-8685
Apex Homes Inc 7172 Rt 522	Middleburg	PA	17842	**800-326-9524**	570-837-2333
Auto Builders 5715 Corporate Way	West Palm Beach	FL	33407	**800-378-5946**	561-622-3515
Baron Sign Manufacturing 900 W 13th St	Riviera Beach	FL	33404	**800-531-9558**	
Becker Arena Products Inc 6611 W Hwy 13	Savage	MN	55378	**800-234-5522**	952-890-2690
Behlen Building Systems 4025 E 23rd St	Columbus	NE	68601	**800-228-0340**	
Brannan Paving Coltd 111 Elk Dr PO Box 3403	Victoria	TX	77903	**800-626-7064**	361-573-3130
Brasfield & Gorrie LLC 3021 Seventh Ave S	Birmingham	AL	35233	**800-239-8017**	205-328-4000
Budreck Truck Lines Inc 2642 Joseph Ct	University Park	IL	60484	**800-621-0013**	708-496-0522
Butler Brothers Supply Division Inc 2001 Lisbon St	Lewiston	ME	04240	**888-784-6875**	207-784-6875
Ca Lindman Inc 10401 Guilford Rd	Jessup	MD	20794	**877-737-8675**	301-470-4700
Carl Belt Inc 11521 Milnor Ave PO Box 1210	Cumberland	MD	21502	**888-729-1616**	301-729-8900
Cedar Grove Composting Inc 7343 E Marginal Way S	Seattle	WA	98108	**888-832-3008**	877-764-5748
CenTex House Leveling 1120 E 52nd St	Austin	TX	78723	**888-425-5438**	512-444-5438
Christman Co, The 2400 Sutherland Ave	Knoxville	TN	37919	**800-583-0148**	865-546-2440
Clark Construction Group LLC 7500 Old Georgetown Rd	Bethesda	MD	20814	**800-655-1330**	301-272-8100
Clark Transfer Inc 800A Paxton St	Harrisburg	PA	17104	**800-488-7585**	
Clarksdale Municipal School District 135 Washington Ave PO Box 1088	Clarksdale	MS	38614	**877-820-7831**	662-627-8500
Cleary Building Corp 190 Paoli St	Verona	WI	53593	**800-373-5550**	608-845-9700
Clinton Fences Company Inc 2630 Old Washington Rd	Waldorf	MD	20601	**800-323-6869**	301-645-8808
Conrad Schmitt Studios Inc 2405 S 162nd St	New Berlin	WI	53151	**800-969-3033**	262-786-3030
Cox Schepp Construction Inc 2410 Dunavant St	Charlotte	NC	28203	**800-954-0823**	704-716-2100
CSM Group Inc 600 E Michigan Ave Ste A	Kalamazoo	MI	49007	**877-386-8214**	
Danis Building Construction Co 3233 Newmark Dr	Dayton	OH	45342	**800-326-4701**	937-228-1225
Daryl Flood Inc 450 Airline Dr Ste 100	Coppell	TX	75019	**800-325-9340**	972-471-1496
Davenport Cos, The 20 N Main St	South Yarmouth	MA	02664	**800-822-3422**	508-398-2293

Company	City	ST	ZIP	Toll-Free	Phone
Daw Construction Group LLC 12552 South 125 West # 100	Draper	UT	84020	800-748-4778	801-553-9111
Deltec Homes Inc 69 Bingham Rd	Asheville	NC	28806	800-642-2508	
Diffenbaugh Inc 6865 Airport Dr	Riverside	CA	92504	800-394-5334	951-351-6865
Donahuefavret Contractors Inc 3030 E Causeway Approach	Mandeville	LA	70448	800-626-4431	985-626-4431
Duffield Aquatic 113 Metro Dr	Anderson	SC	29625	888-669-7551	864-226-5500
Duffield Assoc Inc 5400 Limestone Rd	Wilmington	DE	19808	877-732-9633	302-239-6634
El Group Inc, The 2101 Gateway Centre Blvd Ste 200	Morrisville	NC	27560	800-717-3472	919-657-7500
Ejh Construction Inc 30896 W 8 Mile Rd	Farmington Hills	MI	48336	800-854-4534	
Emery Air Charter Inc 1 Airport Cir	Rockford	IL	61109	800-435-8090	815-968-8287
Engelberth Construction Inc 463 Mtn View Dr Ste 200 Second Fl	Colchester	VT	05446	800-639-9011	802-655-0100
Engineering Economics Inc (EEI) 780 Simms St Ste 210	Golden	CO	80401	800-869-6902	
Environamics Inc 13935 S Point Blvd	Charlotte	NC	28273	800-262-3613	704-376-3613
Erdman 1 Erdman Pl	Madison	WI	53717	866-855-1001	
Evergreen Engineering Portland LLC 1740 Willow Creek Cir	Eugene	OR	97402	888-484-4771	
Fassberg Construction Co 17000 Ventura Blvd Ste 200	Encino	CA	91316	800-795-1747	818-386-1800
FBI Buildings Inc 3823 W 1800 S	Remington	IN	47977	800-552-2981	
Flintco LLC 1624 W 21st St	Tulsa	OK	74107	800-947-2828	918-587-8451
Fred Olivieri Construction Company Inc 6315 Promway Ave NW	North Canton	OH	44720	800-847-5085	330-494-1007
Frize Corp 16605 E Gale Ave	City of Industry	CA	91745	800-834-2127	
G&D Integrated 50 Commerce Dr	Morton	IL	61550	800-451-6680	
Galaxie Defense Marketing Services 5330 Napa St	San Diego	CA	92110	888-711-3427	619-299-9950
Gerald H Phipps 5995 Greenwood Florida Plaza Blvd Ste 100	Greenwood Village	CO	80111	877-574-4777	303-571-5377
Gerloff Company Inc 14955 Bulverde Rd	San Antonio	TX	78247	800-486-3621	210-490-2777
Gilbane Bldg Co New England Regional Office 7 Jackson Walkway	Providence	RI	02903	800-445-2263	401-456-5800
Gilbane Bldg Company Southwest Regional Office 1331 Lamar St Ste 1170	Houston	TX	77010	800-445-2263	713-209-1873
Gray Construction 10 Quality St	Lexington	KY	40507	800-814-8468	859-281-5000
Greystone Construction Co 500 S Marschall Rd Ste 300	Shakopee	MN	55379	888-742-6837	952-496-2227
Harkins Builders Inc 10490 Little Patuxent Pkwy Ste 400	Columbia	MD	21044	800-227-2345	410-750-2600
Haskell Co 111 Riverside Ave	Jacksonville	FL	32202	800-622-4326	904-791-4500
Hoffman Planning, Design, & Construction Inc 122 E College Ave Ste 1G	Appleton	WI	54911	800-236-2370	920-731-2322
Holloman Corp 333 N Sam Houston Pkwy E Ste 600	Houston	TX	77060	800-521-2461	281-878-2600
John E Jones Oil Co Inc 1016 S Cedar PO Box 546	Stockton	KS	67669	800-323-9821	785-425-6746
Kalamazoo Valley Plant Growers Cooperative Inc 8937 Krum Ave	Galesburg	MI	49053	800-253-4898	
Keller Inc N216 State Rd 55	Kaukauna	WI	54130	800-236-2534	920-766-5795
Kenny Construction Co 2215 Sanders Rd Ste 400	Northbrook	IL	60062	800-211-4226	831-724-1011
Kiwi Ii Construction Inc 28177 Keller Rd	Murrieta	CA	92563	877-465-4942	951-301-8975
Kustom US 265 Hunt Park Cv	Longwood	FL	32750	866-679-0699	
L Keeley Construction 500 S Ewing Ave Ste G	Saint Louis	MO	63103	866-553-3539	
Landis Construction LLC 8300 Earhart Blvd Ste 300 PO Box 4278	New Orleans	LA	70118	800-880-3290	504-833-6070
LeChase Construction Services LLC (LC) 205 Indigo Creek Dr	Rochester	NY	14626	888-953-2427	585-254-3510
Lightner Electronics Inc 1771 Beaver Dam Rd	Claysburg	PA	16625	866-239-3888	814-239-8323
Logan Trucking Inc 3224 Navarre Rd SW	Canton	OH	44706	800-683-0142	330-478-1404
Market Contractors 10250 NE Marx St	Portland	OR	97220	800-876-9133	503-255-0977
MDS Builders Inc 301 NW Crawford Blvd Ste 201	Boca Raton	FL	33432	844-637-2845	
Metal Masters Inc 3825 Crater Lake Hwy	Medford	OR	97504	800-866-9437	541-779-1049
Meyer & Najem Inc 11787 Lantern Rd Ste 100	Fishers	IN	46038	888-578-5131	317-577-0007
Mine & Mill Industrial Supply Company Inc 2500 S Combee Rd	Lakeland	FL	33801	800-282-8489	863-665-5601
Modular Connections LLC 1090 Industrial Blvd	Bessemer	AL	35022	877-903-6335	205-980-4565
Modular Genius Inc 1201 S Mountain Rd	Joppa	MD	21085	888-420-1113	410-676-3424
Moores Electrical & Mechanical PO Box 119	Altavista	VA	24517	888-722-2712	434-369-4374
Motor Service Inc 130 Byassee Dr	Hazelwood	MO	63042	800-966-5080	314-731-4111
Multigon Industries 525 Executive Blvd	Elmsford	NY	10523	800-289-6858	914-376-5200
National Fence Systems Inc 1033 Rt One	Avenel	NJ	07001	800-211-2444	
Near-Cal Corp 512 Chaney St	Lake Elsinore	CA	92530	800-969-3578	951-245-5400
Nujak Development Inc 714 N Massachusetts Ave	Lakeland	FL	33801	888-685-2526	863-686-1565
P A Landers Inc 351 Winter St	Hanover	MA	02339	800-660-6404	781-826-8818
Paragon Supply Co 160 Reaser Ct	Elyria	OH	44035	800-726-8041	440-365-8040
PDC Facilities Inc 700 Walnut Ridge Dr	Hartland	WI	53029	800-545-5998	262-367-7700
Peaklogix Inc 14409 Justice Rd	Midlothian	VA	23113	800-849-6332	
Perma-Seal Waterproofing 513 Rogers St	Downers Grove	IL	60515	800-421-7325	
Pioneer Construction Company Inc 550 Kirtland St SW	Grand Rapids	MI	49507	800-861-0874	616-247-6966
Plasteak Inc 3489 Sawmill Rd	Copley	OH	44321	800-320-1841	330-668-2587
PM Construction Co Inc PO Box 728	Saco	ME	04072	800-646-0068	207-282-7697
Porta-King Building Systems 4133 Shoreline Dr	Earth City	MO	63045	800-284-5346	
Portable Buildings Inc 3235 Bay Rd	Milford	DE	19963	800-205-5030	302-335-1300
R W Mercer Co 2322 Brooklyn Rd PO Box 180	Jackson	MI	49204	877-763-7237	517-787-2960
Ramtech Bldg Systems Inc 1400 Hwy 287 S	Mansfield	TX	76063	800-568-9376	817-473-9376
Ricks Barbecue 2347 US-43	Leoma	TN	38468	800-544-5864	931-852-2324
Roy Anderson Corp 11400 Reichold Rd	Gulfport	MS	39503	800-688-4003	228-896-4000
Rycon Construction Inc 2525 Liberty Ave	Pittsburgh	PA	15222	800-883-1901	412-392-2525
Scharine Group, The 4213 N Scharine Rd	Whitewater	WI	53190	800-472-2880	608-883-2880
Schmidt Bros Inc 420 N Hallett Ave	Swanton	OH	43558	800-200-7318	419-826-3671
Septagon Construction 113 E Third St	Sedalia	MO	65301	800-733-5999	660-827-2115
Signal Point Systems Inc 1270 Shiloh Rd Ste 100	Kennesaw	GA	30144	800-814-6502	770-499-0439
Stellar Group 2900 Hartley Rd	Jacksonville	FL	32257	800-488-2900	904-260-2900
Stidham Trucking Inc PO Box 308	Yreka	CA	96097	800-827-9500	530-842-4161
Sundt Construction Inc 2015 W River Rd Ste 101	Tucson	AZ	85704	800-467-5544	520-750-4600
Telecon Inc 7 450 rue du Mile-End	Montreal	QC	H2R2Z6	800-465-0349	514-644-2333
Trehel Corp 935 S Main St Ste 300 PO Box 6688	Greenville	SC	29601	800-319-7006	864-654-6582
Trotter & Morton Ltd 5711 1 St SE	Calgary	AB	T2H1H9	800-355-9401	403-255-7535
University Moving & Storage Co 23305 Commerce Dr	Farmington Hills	MI	48335	800-448-6683	248-615-7000
USM Inc 1700 Markley St Ste 100	Norristown	PA	19401	800-355-4000	
Virtexco Corp 977 Norfolk Sq	Norfolk	VA	23502	800-766-1082	757-466-1114
Walker Industries Holdings Ltd 2800 Thorold Townline Rd	Niagara Falls	ON	L2E6S4	866-694-9360	905-227-4142
Walsh Group Inc 929 W Adams St	Chicago	IL	60607	800-957-1842	312-563-5400
Wantman Group Inc 2035 Vista Pkwy Ste 100	West Palm Beach	FL	33411	866-909-2220	561-687-2220
Washington Local Schools 3505 W Lincolnshire Blvd	Toledo	OH	43606	800-462-3589	419-473-8251
Welch & Rushe Inc 391 Prince George's Blvd	Upper Marlboro	MD	20774	800-683-3852	301-430-6000
West Coast Construction 9021 Rancho Park Ct	Rancho Cucamonga	CA	91730	800-491-2032	
West Penn Power Co 800 Cabin Hill Dr	Greensburg	PA	15601	800-686-0021	
Windstar Lines Inc 1903 US Hwy 71 N	Carroll	IA	51401	888-494-6378	712-792-4221

187 CONSTRUCTION - BUILDING CONTRACTORS - RESIDENTIAL

Company	City	ST	ZIP	Toll-Free	Phone
Air Contact Transport Inc PO Box 570	Budd Lake	NJ	07828	800-765-2769	
Ball Homes LLC 3609 Walden Dr	Lexington	KY	40517	888-268-1101	865-556-0574
Bar None Auction Inc 4751 Power Inn Rd	Sacramento	CA	95826	866-372-1700	
Beals Martin 2596 Bay Rd	Redwood City	CA	94063	800-879-7730	650-364-8141
Dot-Line Transportation PO Box 8739	Fountain Valley	CA	92728	800-423-3780	323-780-9010
Drees Co 211 Grandview Dr	Fort Mitchell	KY	41017	866-265-2980	859-578-4200
Excel Homes Inc 10642 S Susquehanna Trl	Liverpool	PA	17045	844-875-9160	
Eyde Co 300 S Washington Sq Ste 400	Lansing	MI	48933	800-422-3933	517-351-2480
Fandor Homes 68 Romina Dr	Vaughan	ON	L4K4Z7	800-844-9936	905-669-5820
Harkins Builders Inc 10490 Little Patuxent Pkwy Ste 400	Columbia	MD	21044	800-227-2345	410-750-2600
Kopf Builders Inc 420 Avon Belden Rd	Avon Lake	OH	44012	888-933-5673	440-933-6908
LAS Enterprises Inc 2413 L & A Rd	Metairie	LA	70001	800-264-1527	504-887-1515
Mercy Housing Inc 1999 Broadway Ste 1000	Denver	CO	80202	866-338-0557	303-830-3300
Nordaas American Homes Company Inc 10091 State Hwy 22	Minnesota Lake	MN	56068	800-658-7076	507-462-3331
Sandlin Homes 5137 Davis Blvd	Fort Worth	TX	76180	800-821-4663	817-281-3509

	Toll-Free	Phone
Southern California Boiler Inc		
5331 Business Dr ....Huntington Beach CA 92649	**800-775-2645**	714-891-0701
Structural Component Systems Inc (SCS)		
1255 Front St ....Fremont NE 68026	**800-844-5622**	402-721-5622
TH Properties		
345 Main St Ste 112....................Harleysville PA 19438	**800-225-5847***	215-513-4270
*Sales		
United-Bilt Homes Inc		
8500 Line Ave ....Shreveport LA 71106	**800-551-8955**	318-861-4572
Vendini Inc		
660 Market St ....San Francisco CA 94104	**800-901-7173**	
Village Green Cos		
28411 Northwestern Hwy Ste 400................Southfield MI 48034	**866-396-1105**	
Walsh Group Inc		
929 W Adams St ....Chicago IL 60607	**800-957-1842**	312-563-5400
Weavertown Environmental Group		
2 Dorrington Rd ....Carnegie PA 15106	**800-746-4850**	

188   CONSTRUCTION - HEAVY CONSTRUCTION CONTRACTORS

	Toll-Free	Phone
Alta-Fab Structures Ltd		
1205-5th St ....Nisku AB T9E7L6	**800-252-7990**	780-955-7733
Bo-mac Contractors Ltd		
1020 Lindbergh Dr ....Beaumont TX 77707	**800-526-6221**	409-842-2125
Gulf Engineering LLC		
611 Hill St ....Jefferson LA 70121	**800-347-4749**	504-733-4868
Larkin Enterprises Inc		
317 W Broadway PO Box 405................Lincoln ME 04457	**800-990-5418**	207-794-8700
Lone Star Railroad Contractors Inc		
4201 S I-45 ....Ennis TX 75119	**800-838-7225**	972-878-9500
Oman Systems Inc		
3334 Powell Ave ....Nashville TN 37204	**800-541-0803**	615-385-2500
Power Grid Engineering LLC		
100 Colonial Ctr Pkwy Ste 400................Lake Mary FL 32746	**877-819-1171**	321-244-0170
R&R Contracting Inc		
5201 N Washington St ....Grand Forks ND 58203	**800-872-5975**	701-772-7667
Tecon Services Inc		
515 Garden Oaks Blvd ....Houston TX 77018	**800-245-1728**	713-691-2700
White Construction Inc		
3900 E White Ave ....Clinton IN 47842	**800-355-9401**	

188-1 Communications Lines & Towers Construction

	Toll-Free	Phone
MasTec Inc		
800 Douglas Rd 12th Fl................Coral Gables FL 33134	**800-531-5000**	305-599-1800
NYSE: MTZ		
Quanta Services Inc		
1360 Post Oak Blvd Ste 2100................Houston TX 77056	**800-872-0615**	713-629-7600
NYSE: PWR		

188-2 Foundation Drilling & Pile Driving

	Toll-Free	Phone
Case Foundation Co		
1325 West Lake St ....Roselle IL 60172	**800-999-4087**	630-529-2911
HJ Foundation Inc		
8275 N W 80 St ....Miami FL 33166	**866-751-4545**	305-592-8181
LG Barcus & Sons Inc		
1430 State Ave ....Kansas City KS 66102	**800-255-0180**	913-621-1100

188-3 Golf Course Construction

	Toll-Free	Phone
Harris Miniature Golf		
141 W Burk Ave ....Wildwood NJ 08260	**888-294-6530**	609-522-4200

188-4 Highway, Street, Bridge, Tunnel Construction

	Toll-Free	Phone
Allan A Myers Inc		
1805 Berks Rd PO Box 1340................Worcester PA 19490	**800-596-6118**	610-222-8800
ALLEN 525 Burbank St ....Broomfield CO 80020	**800-876-8600**	303-469-1857
Arrow Road Construction		
3401 S Busse Rd ....Mount Prospect IL 60056	**800-523-4417**	847-437-0700
Barriere Construction Co LLC		
1 Galleria Blvd Ste 1650................Metairie LA 70001	**800-234-5376**	504-581-7283
Boh Bros Construction Co LLC		
730 S Tonti St ....New Orleans LA 70119	**800-284-3377**	504-821-2400
Branch Highways Inc		
442 Rutherford Ave ....Roanoke VA 24016	**800-353-3747**	540-982-1678
Cianbro Corp		
101 Cianbro Sq ....Pittsfield ME 04967	**866-242-6276**	207-487-3311
Clark Construction Group LLC		
7500 Old Georgetown Rd ....Bethesda MD 20814	**800-655-1330**	301-272-8100
CRH Americas Inc		
900 Ashwood Pkwy Ste 700................Atlanta GA 30338	**800-241-7074**	770-522-5600
Crowder Constructors Inc		
6425 Brookshire Blvd ....Charlotte NC 28230	**800-849-2966**	704-372-3541
Cummins Construction Company Inc		
1420 W Chestnut Ave ....Enid OK 73702	**800-375-6001**	580-233-6000
Dean Word Company Ltd		
1245 River Rd ....New Braunfels TX 78130	**800-683-3926**	830-625-2365
Duininck Inc		
408 Sixth St PO Box 208 ....Prinsburg MN 56281	**800-328-8949***	
*General		
Elam Construction Inc		
556 Struthers Ave ....Grand Junction CO 81501	**800-675-4598**	970-242-5370
Evans & Assoc Construction Company Inc		
3320 N 14th St ....Ponca City OK 74601	**800-324-6693**	580-765-6693

	Toll-Free	Phone
Fred Weber Inc		
2320 Creve Coeur Mill Rd ....Maryland Heights MO 63043	**866-739-8855**	314-344-0070
Gallagher Asphalt Corp		
18100 S Indiana Ave ....Thornton IL 60476	**800-536-7160**	
Gilbert Southern Corp		
3555 Farnam St ....Omaha NE 68131	**800-901-1087**	402-342-2052
Glasgow Inc		
104 Willow Grove Ave ....Glenside PA 19038	**877-222-5514**	215-884-8800
Harper Industries Inc		
960 N H C Mathis Dr ....Paducah KY 42001	**800-669-0077**	270-442-2753
Hoover Construction Co		
302 S Hoover Rd PO Box 1007................Virginia MN 55792	**800-741-0970**	218-741-3280
HRI Inc		
1750 W College Ave ....State College PA 16801	**877-474-9999**	814-238-5071
Hutchens Construction Co		
1007 Main St ....Cassville MO 65625	**888-728-3482**	417-847-2489
Jack B Parson Cos		
2350 S 1900 W ....Ogden UT 84401	**888-672-7766**	801-731-1111
James D Morrissey Inc		
9119 Frankford Ave ....Philadelphia PA 19114	**877-536-6857**	215-708-8420
JF Shea Construction Inc		
655 Brea Canyon Rd ....Walnut CA 91789	**888-779-7333**	909-594-9500
JF White Contracting Co		
10 Burr St ....Framingham MA 01701	**866-539-4400**	508-879-4700
Kiewit Corp 3555 Farnam St ....Omaha NE 68131	**800-901-1087**	402-342-2052
Knife River Corp		
3303 Rock Island Pl ....Bismarck ND 58504	**800-982-5339**	701-530-1380
Kokosing Construction Company Inc		
17531 Waterford Rd PO Box 226................Fredericktown OH 43019	**800-800-6315**	740-694-6315
LC Whitford Company Inc		
164 N Main St ....Wellsville NY 14895	**800-321-3602**	585-593-3601
Lehigh Asphalt Paving & Construction Co Inc		
1314 E Broad St ....Tamaqua PA 18252	**877-222-5514**	570-668-4303
Manatt's Inc 1775 Old 6 Rd ....Brooklyn IA 52211	**800-532-1121**	641-522-9206
Matich Corp		
1596 Harry Sheppard Blvd ....San Bernardino CA 92408	**800-404-4975**	909-382-7400
Milestone Contractors LP		
3410 S 650 E ....Elizabethtown IN 47232	**800-377-7727**	812-579-5248
Palmer Paving Corp		
25 Blanchard St ....Palmer MA 01069	**800-244-8354**	413-283-8354
Pike Industries Inc		
3 Eastgate Pk Rd ....Belmont NH 03220	**800-283-0803**	603-527-5100
PJ Keating Co		
998 Reservoir Rd ....Lunenburg MA 01462	**800-441-4119**	978-582-5200
Ranger Construction Industries Inc		
101 Sansbury's Way ....West Palm Beach FL 33411	**800-969-9402**	561-793-9400
Reeves Construction Co Inc		
101 Sheraton Ct ....Macon GA 31210	**800-743-0593**	478-474-9092
Scott Construction Inc		
560 Munroe Ave ....Lake Delton WI 53940	**800-843-1556**	608-254-2555
Scruggs Company Inc		
PO Box 2065 ....Valdosta GA 31604	**800-230-7263**	229-242-2388
Shelly Co 80 Pk Dr ....Thornville OH 43076	**888-743-5590**	
Staker Parson Cos		
2350 S 1900 W ....Ogden UT 84401	**888-672-7766**	801-731-1111
Sukut Construction Inc		
4010 W Chandler Ave ....Santa Ana CA 92704	**888-785-8801**	
Sully-Miller Contracting Co Inc		
135 S State Collage Blvd Ste 400................Brea CA 92821	**800-300-4240**	714-578-9600
Sundt Construction Inc		
2015 W River Rd Ste 101................Tucson AZ 85704	**800-467-5544**	520-750-4600
Traylor Bros Inc		
835 N Congress Ave ....Evansville IN 47715	**866-895-1491**	812-477-1542
United Contractors Midwest Inc		
3151 Robbins Rd PO Box 13420 ....Springfield IL 62791	**800-381-5497**	217-546-6192
Vecellio & Grogan Inc		
PO Box 2438 ....Beckley WV 25802	**800-255-6575**	304-252-6575
Walsh Group Inc		
929 W Adams St ....Chicago IL 60607	**800-957-1842**	312-563-5400

188-5 Marine Construction

	Toll-Free	Phone
Andrie Inc		
561 E Western Ave ....Muskegon MI 49442	**800-722-2421**	231-728-2226
Bellingham Marine Industries Inc		
1001 C St ....Bellingham WA 98225	**800-733-5679**	360-676-2800
Dot-Line Transportation		
PO Box 8739 ....Fountain Valley CA 92728	**800-423-3780**	323-780-9010
Frontier-Kemper Constructors Inc		
1695 Allen Rd ....Evansville IN 47710	**877-554-8600**	812-426-2741
JR Filanc Construction Company Inc		
740 North Andreasen Dr ....Escondido CA 92029	**877-225-5428**	760-941-7130

188-6 Mining Construction

	Toll-Free	Phone
AME Inc		
2467 Coltharp Rd PO Box 909................Fort Mill SC 29716	**800-849-7766**	803-548-7766
Frontier-Kemper Constructors Inc		
1695 Allen Rd ....Evansville IN 47710	**877-554-8600**	812-426-2741
Sundt Construction Inc		
2015 W River Rd Ste 101................Tucson AZ 85704	**800-467-5544**	520-750-4600

188-7 Plant Construction

	Toll-Free	Phone
Brasfield & Gorrie LLC		
3021 Seventh Ave S ....Birmingham AL 35233	**800-239-8017**	205-328-4000
Cajun Constructors Inc		
15635 Airline Hwy ....Baton Rouge LA 70817	**800-944-5857**	225-753-5857
Cianbro Corp		
101 Cianbro Sq ....Pittsfield ME 04967	**866-242-6276**	207-487-3311

				Toll-Free	Phone
Clark Construction Group LLC					
7500 Old Georgetown Rd	Bethesda	MD	20814	**800-655-1330**	301-272-8100
Day & Zimmermann Group Inc					
1500 Spring Garden St	Philadelphia	PA	19130	**877-319-0270**	215-299-8000
Gilbane Bldg Co					
7 Jackson Walkway	Providence	RI	02903	**800-445-2263**	401-456-5800
Gray Construction					
10 Quality St	Lexington	KY	40507	**800-814-8468**	859-281-5000
Haskell Co					
111 Riverside Ave	Jacksonville	FL	32202	**800-622-4326**	904-791-4500
JF White Contracting Co					
10 Burr St	Framingham	MA	01701	**866-539-4400**	508-879-4700
Koch Specialty Plant Services					
12221 E Sam Houston Pkwy N	Houston	TX	77044	**800-765-9177**	713-427-7700
Northeast Remsco Construction Inc					
1433 Hwy 34 S Bldg B1	Farmingdale	NJ	07727	**800-879-8204**	732-557-6100
Turner Industries Group LLC					
8687 United Plaza Blvd	Baton Rouge	LA	70809	**800-288-6503**	225-922-5050
Walsh Group Inc					
929 W Adams St	Chicago	IL	60607	**800-957-1842**	312-563-5400

188-8 Railroad Construction

				Toll-Free	Phone
Acme Construction Company Inc					
7695 Bond St	Cleveland	OH	44139	**800-686-5077**	440-232-7474
WE Yoder Inc 41 S Maple St	Kutztown	PA	19530	**800-889-5149**	610-683-7383

188-9 Refinery (Petroleum or Oil) Construction

				Toll-Free	Phone
Turner Industries Group LLC					
8687 United Plaza Blvd	Baton Rouge	LA	70809	**800-288-6503**	225-922-5050
Underground Construction Company Inc					
5145 Industrial Way	Benicia	CA	94510	**800-227-2314**	707-746-8800

188-10 Water & Sewer Lines, Pipelines, Power Lines Construction

				Toll-Free	Phone
Bancker Construction Corp					
218 Blydenburgh Rd	Islandia	NY	11749	**800-767-7565**	631-582-8880
Cajun Constructors Inc					
15635 Airline Hwy	Baton Rouge	LA	70817	**800-944-5857**	225-753-5857
Cianbro Corp					
101 Cianbro Sq	Pittsfield	ME	04967	**866-242-6276**	207-487-3311
CRH Americas Inc					
900 Ashwood Pkwy Ste 700	Atlanta	GA	30338	**800-241-7074**	770-522-5600
Frontier-Kemper Constructors Inc					
1695 Allen Rd	Evansville	IN	47710	**877-554-8600**	812-426-2741
Garney Construction					
1333 NW Vivion Rd	Kansas City	MO	64118	**800-832-1517**	816-741-4600
Insituform Technologies Inc					
17988 Edison Ave	St. Louis	MO	63005	**800-234-2992***	636-530-8000
*Cust Svc					
JF Shea Construction Inc					
655 Brea Canyon Rd	Walnut	CA	91789	**888-779-7333**	909-594-9500
JF White Contracting Co					
10 Burr St	Framingham	MA	01701	**866-539-4400**	508-879-4700
JR Filanc Construction Company Inc					
740 North Andreasen Dr	Escondido	CA	92029	**877-225-5428**	760-941-7130
Koch Specialty Plant Services					
12221 E Sam Houston Pkwy N	Houston	TX	77044	**800-765-9177**	713-427-7700
Landmark Structures LP					
1665 Harmon Rd	Fort Worth	TX	76177	**800-888-6816**	817-439-8888
Layne 4520 N State Rd 37	Orleans	IN	47452	**855-529-6301***	812-865-3232
*All					
MasTec Inc					
800 Douglas Rd 12th Fl	Coral Gables	FL	33134	**800-531-5000**	305-599-1800
NYSE: MTZ					
McLean Contracting Co					
6700 McLean Way	Glen Burnie	MD	21060	**800-677-1997**	410-553-6700
Michels Corp					
817 W Main St	Brownsville	WI	53006	**877-297-8663**	920-583-3132
Miller Pipeline Corp					
8850 Crawfordsville Rd	Indianapolis	IN	46234	**800-428-3742**	317-293-0278
Northeast Remsco Construction Inc					
1433 Hwy 34 S Bldg B1	Farmingdale	NJ	07727	**800-879-8204**	732-557-6100
Penn Line Service Inc					
300 Scottdale Ave	Scottdale	PA	15683	**800-448-9110***	724-887-9110
*All					
Quanta Services Inc					
1360 Post Oak Blvd Ste 2100	Houston	TX	77056	**800-872-0615**	713-629-7600
NYSE: PWR					
RH White Construction Company Inc					
41 Central St PO Box 404	Auburn	MA	01501	**800-876-3837**	508-832-3295
Stuart C Irby Co					
815 Irby Dr	Jackson	MS	39201	**866-687-4729**	713-476-0788
Underground Construction Company Inc					
5145 Industrial Way	Benicia	CA	94510	**800-227-2314**	707-746-8800
West Valley Construction Company Inc					
580 McGlincey Ln	Campbell	CA	95008	**800-588-5510**	

189 CONSTRUCTION - SPECIAL TRADE CONTRACTORS

SEE ALSO Swimming Pools

189-1 Building Equipment Installation or Erection

				Toll-Free	Phone
Baltimore Rigging Company Inc, The					
6601 Tributary St	Baltimore	MD	21224	**800-626-2150**	443-696-4001
Bigge Crane & Rigging Co					
10700 Bigge Ave	San Leandro	CA	94577	**888-337-2444**	510-277-4747

				Toll-Free	Phone
Columbia Elevator Products Company Inc					
380 Horace St	Bridgeport	CT	06610	**888-858-1558**	
Elward Construction Co					
680 Harlan St	Lakewood	CO	80214	**800-933-5339**	303-239-6303
James Machine Works LLC					
1521 Adams St	Monroe	LA	71201	**800-259-6104**	318-322-6104
Schindler Elevator Corp					
20 Whippany Rd	Morristown	NJ	07960	**800-225-3123**	973-397-6500
W & H Systems Inc					
120 Asia Pl	Carlstadt	NJ	07072	**800-966-6993**	201-933-7840

189-2 Carpentry & Flooring Contractors

				Toll-Free	Phone
Archadeck					
2924 Emerywood Pkwy Ste 101	Richmond	VA	23294	**888-687-3325**	804-353-6999
Associated Floors					
32 Morris Ave	Springfield	NJ	07081	**800-800-4320**	
Carpenter Contractors of America Inc					
3900 Ave D NW	Winter Haven	FL	33880	**800-959-8806**	863-294-6449
Cincinnati Floor Company Inc					
5162 Broerman Ave	Cincinnati	OH	45217	**800-886-4501**	513-641-4500
Kalman Floor Company Inc					
1202 Bergen Pkwy Ste 110	Evergreen	CO	80439	**800-525-7840**	303-674-2290
Overhead Door Company of Sacramento Inc					
6756 Franklin Blvd	Sacramento	CA	95823	**800-929-3667**	916-421-3747
Sundt Construction					
2620 S 55th St	Tempe	AZ	85282	**800-280-3000**	480-293-3000

189-3 Concrete Contractors

				Toll-Free	Phone
Baker Concrete Construction Inc					
900 N Garver Rd	Monroe	OH	45050	**800-539-2224**	513-539-4000
Dywidag Systems International					
320 Marmon Dr	Bolingbrook	IL	60440	**800-457-7633**	630-739-1100
Harris Cos Inc					
909 Montreal Cir	Saint Paul	MN	55102	**800-466-3993**	651-602-6500
Kalman Floor Company Inc					
1202 Bergen Pkwy Ste 110	Evergreen	CO	80439	**800-525-7840**	303-674-2290
Larson Contracting Inc					
508 W Main St	Lake Mills	IA	50450	**800-765-1426**	641-592-5800
Oldcastle Precast Bldg Systems Div					
1401 Trimble Rd	Edgewood	MD	21040	**800-523-9144**	410-612-1213
Proshot Concrete Inc					
4158 Musgrove Dr	Florence	AL	35630	**800-633-3141**	256-263-0445
Suncoast Post-Tension LP					
509 N Sam Houston Pkwy E Ste 400	Houston	TX	77060	**800-847-8886**	281-668-1840
Weaver-Bailey Contractors Inc					
PO Box 60	El Paso	AR	72045	**800-253-3385**	501-796-2301

189-4 Electrical Contractors

				Toll-Free	Phone
AC Corp					
301 Creek Ridge Rd	Greensboro	NC	27406	**800-422-7378**	336-273-4472
Althoff Industries Inc					
8001 S Rt 31	Crystal Lake	IL	60014	**800-225-2443**	815-455-7000
Anixter Inc					
2301 Patriot Blvd	Glenview	IL	60026	**800-492-1212**	224-521-8000
Arrow Electric Company Inc					
317 Wabasso Ave	Louisville	KY	40209	**888-999-5591**	502-367-0141
Barth Electric Company Inc					
1934 N Illinois St	Indianapolis	IN	46202	**800-666-6226**	317-924-6226
Bruce & Merrilees Electric Co					
930 Cass St	New Castle	PA	16101	**800-652-5560**	724-652-5566
Cache Valley Electric Inc					
875 N 1000 W	Logan	UT	84321	**888-558-0600**	435-752-6405
Collins Electric Co Inc					
53 Second Ave	Chicopee	MA	01020	**877-553-2810**	413-592-9221
Custom Cable Industries Inc					
3221 Cherry Palm Dr	Tampa	FL	33619	**800-552-2232**	813-623-2232
EC Ernst Inc					
132 Log Canoe Cir	Stevensville	MD	21666	**800-683-7770**	301-350-7770
EcElectric					
2121 NW Thurman St	Portland	OR	97210	**800-659-3511**	503-224-3511
Edwin L Heim Co					
1918 Greenwood St	Harrisburg	PA	17104	**800-692-7316**	717-233-8711
Electronic Contracting Co					
6501 N 70th St	Lincoln	NE	68507	**800-366-5320**	402-466-8274
Elliot Companies, The					
673 Blue Sky Pkwy	Lexington	KY	40509	**888-768-2530**	859-263-5148
EMCOR Construction Services Inc					
1420 Spring Hill Rd Ste 500	McLean	VA	22102	**866-890-7794**	
EMCOR Group Inc					
301 Merritt 7 6th Fl	Norwalk	CT	06851	**866-890-7794**	203-849-7800
NYSE: EME					
Engineered Protection Systems Inc					
750 Front Ave NW	Grand Rapids	MI	49504	**800-966-9199**	616-459-0281
Gaylor Electric					
5750 Castle Creek Pkwy N Dr Ste 400	Indianapolis	IN	46250	**800-878-0577**	317-843-0577
GR Sponaugle & Sons Inc					
4391 Chambers Hill Rd	Harrisburg	PA	17111	**800-868-9353**	717-564-1515
Hooper Corp					
2030 Pennsylvania Ave	Madison	WI	53704	**877-630-7554**	608-249-0451
Industrial Contractors Inc					
701 Ch Dr	Bismarck	ND	58501	**800-467-3089**	701-258-9908
Industrial Power & Lighting Corp					
60 Depost St	Buffalo	NY	14206	**800-639-3702**	716-854-1811
Kirby Electric Inc					
415 Northgate D	Warrendale	PA	15086	**800-767-3263**	724-772-1800
Koontz-Wagner Electric Company Inc					
3801 Voorde Dr	South Bend	IN	46628	**800-345-2051**	574-232-2051

			Toll-Free	Phone
Lake Erie Electric				
25730 First St	Westlake OH	44145	**855-877-9393**	440-835-5565
Metropower 798 21st Ave	Albany GA	31701	**800-332-7345**	229-432-7345
Miller Electric Co				
2251 Rosselle St	Jacksonville FL	32204	**800-554-4761***	904-388-8000
*Sales				
MMR Group Inc				
15961 Airline Hwy	Baton Rouge LA	70817	**800-880-5090**	225-756-5090
Muska Electric Co				
1985 Oakcrest Ave	Roseville MN	55113	**800-694-0884**	651-636-5820
Muth Electric Inc				
1717 N Sanborn PO Box 1400	Mitchell SD	57301	**800-888-1597**	605-996-3983
MYR Group inc				
1701 W Golf Rd Ste 1012	Rolling Meadows IL	60008	**800-360-1321**	847-290-1891
Netsville Inc				
72 Cascade Dr	Rochester NY	14614	**888-638-7845**	585-232-5670
O'Connell Electric Co				
830 Phillips Rd	Victor NY	14564	**800-343-2176**	585-924-2176
Phillips Bros Electrical Contractors Inc				
235 Sweet Spring Rd	Glenmoore PA	19343	**800-220-5051**	
Rex Moore Electrical Contractors & Engineers				
6001 Outfall Cir	Sacramento CA	95828	**800-266-1922**	916-372-1300
SASCO Electric				
2750 Moore Ave	Fullerton CA	92833	**800-477-4422**	714-870-0217
Southern Air Inc				
2655 Lakeside Dr	Lynchburg VA	24501	**800-743-1214**	434-385-6200
Staley Inc				
8101 Fourche Rd	Little Rock AR	72209	**877-708-7532**	800-280-9675
Tri-City Electrical Contractors Inc				
430 W Dr	Altamonte Springs FL	32714	**800-768-2489**	407-788-3500
White Electrical Construction Co				
1730 Chattahoochee Ave	Atlanta GA	30318	**888-519-4483**	404-351-5740

189-5 Excavation Contractors

			Toll-Free	Phone
Andrews Excavating Inc				
5 W Willow Rd PO Box 249	Willow Street PA	17584	**800-730-6822**	717-464-3329
Case Foundation Co				
1325 West Lake St	Roselle IL	60172	**800 999 4087**	630 529 2011
CRH Americas Inc				
900 Ashwood Pkwy Ste 700	Atlanta GA	30338	**800-241-7074**	770-522-5600
Dywidag Systems International				
320 Marmon Dr	Bolingbrook IL	60440	**800-457-7633**	630-739-1100
Foundation Constructors Inc				
81 Big Break Rd	Oakley CA	94561	**800-841-8740**	925-754-6633
Geo-Solutions				
1250 Fifth Ave	New Kensington PA	15235	**800-544-6235**	412-856-7700
Hayward Baker Inc				
7550 Teague Rd Ste 300	Hanover MD	21076	**800-456-6548**	410-551-8200
J Fletcher Creamer & Son Inc				
101 E Broadway	Hackensack NJ	07601	**800-835-9801**	201-488-9800
Phillips & Jordan Inc				
10201 Parkside Dr Ste 300	Knoxville TN	37922	**800-955-0876**	865-688-8342
Raymond Excavating Co Inc				
800 Gratiot Blvd	Marysville MI	48040	**800-837-6770**	810-364-6881
Subsurface Constructors Inc				
110 Angelica St	Saint Louis MO	63147	**800-242-9425**	314-421-2460

189-6 Glass & Glazing Contractors

			Toll-Free	Phone
Enclos Corp				
2770 Blue Water Rd	Eagan MN	55121	**888-234-2966**	
Karas & Karas Glass Company Inc				
455 Dorchester Ave	Boston MA	02127	**800-888-1235**	617-268-8800
Lee & Cates Glass Inc				
5355 Shawland Rd	Jacksonville FL	32254	**888-844-1989**	904-358-8555
Sashco Inc				
720 S Rochester Ave Ste D	Ontario CA	91761	**800-600-3232**	909-937-8222

189-7 Masonry & Stone Contractors

			Toll-Free	Phone
Gallegos Corp PO Box 821	Vail CO	81658	**800-425-5346**	970-926-3737
International Chimney Corp				
55 S Long St	Williamsville NY	14221	**800-828-1446**	
Mid-Continental Restoration Company Inc				
401 E Hudson Rd PO Box 429	Fort Scott KS	66701	**800-835-3700**	620-223-3700
Ron Kendall Masonry Inc				
101 Benoist Farms Rd	West Palm Beach FL	33411	**866-844-1404**	561-793-5924

189-8 Painting & Paperhanging Contractors

			Toll-Free	Phone
Brock Group				
10343 Sam Houston Park Dr Ste 200	Houston TX	77064	**800-600-9675**	281-807-8200
CertaPro Painters Ltd				
150 Green Tree Rd Ste 1003	Oaks PA	19456	**800-689-7271**	
K2 Industrial Services				
3838 N Sam Houston Pkwy E Ste 285	Houston TX	77032	**800-347-4813**	
Long Painting Co				
21414 68th Ave S	Kent WA	98032	**800-687-5664**	253-234-8050
Midwest Pro Painting Inc				
12845 Farmington Rd	Livonia MI	48150	**800-860-6757**	734-427-1040
ML McDonald LLC				
50 Oakland St PO Box 315	Watertown MA	02471	**800-733-6243**	617-923-0900
National Services Group Inc				
1682 Langley Ave	Irvine CA	92614	**800-394-6000**	714-564-7900
TMI Coatings Inc				
3291 Terminal Dr	Saint Paul MN	55121	**800-328-0229**	651-452-6100

189-9 Plastering, Drywall, Acoustical, Insulation Contractors

			Toll-Free	Phone
Acousti Engineering Company of Florida Inc				
4656 34th St SW	Orlando FL	32811	**800-434-3467**	407-425-3467
Allied Construction Services & Color Inc				
2122 Fleur Dr PO Box 937	Des Moines IA	50304	**800-365-4855**	515-288-4855
API Construction Co				
1100 Old Hwy 8 NW	New Brighton MN	55112	**800-223-4922**	651-636-4320
Baker Triangle				
341 Hwy 80 E	Mesquite TX	75150	**800-458-3480**	972-289-5534
CE Thurston & Sons Inc				
3335 Croft St	Norfolk VA	23513	**800-444-7713**	757-855-7700
FL Crane & Sons Inc				
508 S Spring St PO Box 428	Fulton MS	38843	**800-748-9523**	662-862-2172
Henderson-Johnson Co Inc				
918 Canal St	Syracuse NY	13210	**800-492-3434**	315-479-5561
Irex Contracting Group				
120 N Lime St	Lancaster PA	17608	**800-487-7255**	
ML McDonald LLC				
50 Oakland St PO Box 315	Watertown MA	02471	**800-733-6243**	617-923-0900
Precision Walls Inc				
1230 NE MaynaRd Rd	Cary NC	27513	**800-849-9255**	919-832-0380
Western Partitions Inc				
26055 SW Canyon Creek Rd	Wilsonville OR	97070	**800-783-0315**	503-620-1600

189-10 Plumbing, Heating, Air Conditioning Contractors

			Toll-Free	Phone
AC Corp				
301 Creek Ridge Rd	Greensboro NC	27406	**800-422-7378**	336-273-4472
ACCO Engineered Systems				
6265 San Fernando Rd	Glendale CA	91201	**800-998-2226***	818-244-6571
*Cust Svc				
Air Comfort Corp				
2550 Braga Dr	Broadview IL	60155	**800-466-3779**	708-345-1900
Alaka'i Mechanical Corp				
2655 Waiwai Loop	Honolulu HI	96819	**800-600-1085**	808-834-1085
Alliod Firo Protootion LP				
PO Box 2842	Pearland TX	77588	**800-604-2600**	281-485-6803
Allied Mechanical Services Inc				
145 N Plains Industrial Rd	Wallingford CT	06492	**888-237-3017**	269-344-0191
Althoff Industries Inc				
8001 S Rt 31	Crystal Lake IL	60014	**800-225-2443**	815-455-7000
American Residential Services LLC				
9010 Maier Rd Ste 105	Laurel MD	20723	**866-399-2885**	901-271-9700
Anron Air Systems Inc				
440 Wyandanch Ave	West Babylon NY	11704	**800-421-0389**	631-643-3433
Armistead Mechanical Inc				
168 Hopper Ave	Waldwick NJ	07463	**800-587-5267**	201-447-6740
B-G Mechanical Service Inc				
12 Second Ave	Chicopee MA	01020	**800-992-7386**	413-888-1500
Baker Group				
4224 Hubbell Ave	Des Moines IA	50317	**855-262-4000**	515-262-4000
Butters-Fetting Company Inc				
1669 S First St	Milwaukee WI	53204	**800-361-6154**	414-645-1535
C & R Mechanical				
12825 Pennridge Dr	Bridgeton MO	63044	**800-524-3828**	314-739-1800
Central Mechanical Construction Company Inc				
631 Pecan Cir	Manhattan KS	66502	**800-631-6999**	785-537-2437
Climate Design Air ConditioningIn				
12530 47th Way N	Clearwater FL	33762	**888-572-7245**	
Coastal Mechanical Services LLC				
394 E Dr	Melbourne FL	32904	**866-584-9528**	321-725-3061
ColonialWebb Contractors Co				
2820 Ackley Ave	Richmond VA	23228	**877-208-3894**	804-916-1400
Comfort Systems USA Inc				
675 Bering Ste 400	Houston TX	77057	**800-723-8431**	713-830-9600
NYSE: FIX				
DeBra-Kuempel				
3976 Southern Ave	Cincinnati OH	45227	**800-395-5741**	513-271-6500
Dunbar Mechanical Inc				
2806 N Reynolds Rd	Toledo OH	43615	**800-719-2201**	419-537-1900
EMCOR Group Inc				
301 Merritt 7 6th Fl.	Norwalk CT	06851	**866-890-7794**	203-849-7800
NYSE: EME				
Fisher Container Corp				
1111 Busch Pkwy	Buffalo Grove IL	60089	**800-837-2247**	847-541-0000
Gold Mechanical Inc				
4735 W Division St	Springfield MO	65802	**877-873-9770**	417-873-9770
GR Sponaugle & Sons Inc				
4391 Chambers Hill Rd	Harrisburg PA	17111	**800-868-9353**	717-564-1515
Green Mechanical Construction Inc				
322 W Main St	Glasgow KY	42141	**800-264-6048**	
Grunau Company Inc				
1100 W Anderson Ct	Oak Creek WI	53154	**800-365-1920**	414-216-6900
Hardy Corp				
350 Industrial Dr	Birmingham AL	35211	**800-289-4822**	205-252-7191
Harold G Butzer Inc				
730 Wicker Ln	Jefferson City MO	65109	**800-769-1065**	573-636-4115
Harry Grodsky & Co Inc				
33 Shaws Ln PO Box 880	Springfield MA	01101	**800-843-4424**	413-785-1947
HE Neumann Inc				
100 Middle Creek Rd	Triadelphia WV	26059	**800-627-5312**	304-232-3040
Heerema Inc 200 Sixth Ave	Hawthorne NJ	07506	**800-346-4729**	973-423-0505
Heritage Mechanical Services Inc				
305 Suburban Ave	Deer Park NY	11729	**800-734-0384**	516-558-2000
Herman Goldner Inc				
7777 Brewster Ave	Philadelphia PA	19153	**800-355-5997**	215-365-5400
Hill Group, The				
11045 Gage Ave	Franklin Park IL	60131	**800-233-8990**	847-451-5000
Hooper Corp				
2030 Pennsylvania Ave	Madison WI	53704	**877-630-7554**	608-249-0451
Hubbard & Drake General Mechanical Contractors Inc				
PO Box 1867	Decatur AL	35602	**800-353-9245**	256-353-9244

Classified Section

Construction - Special Trade Contractors (Cont'd)

					Toll-Free	Phone
Hurckman Mechanical Industries Inc						
1450 Velp Ave	Green Bay	WI	54303		844-499-8771	920-499-8771
IMCOR-Interstate Mechanical Corp						
1841 E Washington St	Phoenix	AZ	85034		800-628-0211	602-257-1319
Industrial Contractors Inc						
701 Ch Dr	Bismarck	ND	58501		800-467-3089	701-258-9908
Jamar Co						
4701 Mike Colalillo Dr	Duluth	MN	55807		800-644-3624	218-628-1027
Janazzo Services Corp						
140 Norton St Rt 10 PO Box 469	Milldale	CT	06467		800-297-3931	860-621-7381
JF Ahern Co						
855 Morris St	Fond du Lac	WI	54935		800-532-0155	920-921-9020
John E Green						
220 Victor Ave	Highland Park	MI	48203		888-918-7002	313-868-2400
John W Danforth Co						
300 Colvin Woods Pkwy	Tonawanda	NY	14150		800-888-6119	716-832-1940
Lutz Frey Corp						
1195 Ivy Dr	Lancaster	PA	17601		800-280-6794	717-898-6808
MacDonald-Miller Facility Solutions Inc						
7717 Detroit Ave SE	Seattle	WA	98106		800-962-5979	206-763-9400
McClure Co						
4101 N Sixth St	Harrisburg	PA	17110		800-382-1319	717-232-9743
McCrea Equipment Company Inc						
4463 Beech Rd	Temple Hills	MD	20748		800-597-0091	
McKenney's Inc						
1056 Moreland Industrial Blvd SE	Atlanta	GA	30316		877-440-4204	404-622-5000
McKinstry Co						
5005 Third Ave S	Seattle	WA	98134		800-669-6223	206-762-3311
Midwest Mechanical Group						
801 Parkview Blvd	Lombard	IL	60148		800-214-3680	630-850-2300
Mr Rooter Corp						
1010 N University Parks Dr	Waco	TX	76707		855-982-2028	254-340-1321
MYR Group inc						
1701 W Golf Rd Ste 1012	Rolling Meadows	IL	60008		800-360-1321	847-290-1891
P1 Group Inc						
2151 Haskell Ave Bldg 1	Lawrence	KS	66046		800-376-2911	785-843-2910
Performance Contracting Group Inc						
16400 College Blvd	Lenexa	KS	66219		800-255-6886	913-888-8600
Poole & Kent Corp						
4530 Hollins Ferry Rd	Baltimore	MD	21227		800-468-0851	410-247-2200
Postler & Jaeckle Corp						
615 S Ave	Rochester	NY	14620		800-724-4252	585-546-7450
Pritchett Controls Inc						
6980 Muirkirk Meadows Dr	Beltsville	MD	20705		877-743-2363	301-470-7300
PSF Industries Inc						
65 S Horton St	Seattle	WA	98134		800-426-1204*	206-622-1252
*General						
Ray L Hellwig Plumbing & Heating Inc						
1301 Laurelwood Rd	Santa Clara	CA	95054		800-631-7013	408-727-5612
RK Mechanical Inc						
3800 Xanthia St	Denver	CO	80238		877-576-9696	303-355-9696
Rock Hill Mechanical Corp						
524 Clark Ave	Saint Louis	MO	63122		877-966-7792	314-966-0600
Southern Air Inc						
2655 Lakeside Dr	Lynchburg	VA	24501		800-743-1214	434-385-6200
Tatro Plumbing Company Inc						
1285 Acraway Ste 300	Garden City	KS	67846		888-828-7648	620-277-2167
Telgian Holdings Inc						
10230 S 50th Pl Ste 100	Phoenix	AZ	85044		877-835-4426	480-753-5444
William E Walter Inc						
1917 Howard Ave	Flint	MI	48503		800-681-3320	810-232-7459
Worth & Company Inc						
6263 Kellers Church Rd	Pipersville	PA	18947		800-220-5130	267-362-1100

189-11 Remodeling, Refinishing, Resurfacing Contractors

					Toll-Free	Phone
Bathcrest Inc						
3791 S 300 W	Salt Lake City	UT	84115		855-662-7220	
California Closet Co						
1716 Fourth St	Berkeley	CA	94710		888-336-9707*	510-763-2033
*General						
Closet Factory						
12800 S Broadway	Los Angeles	CA	90061		800-838-7995	310-516-7000
DreamMaker Bath & Kitchen by Worldwide						
510 N Valley Mills Dr Ste 304	Waco	TX	76710		800-583-2133	
Handyman Connection Inc						
11115 Kenwood Rd	Blue Ash	OH	45242		800-466-5530	513-771-3003
Kitchen Tune-Up 813 Cir Dr	Aberdeen	SD	57401		800-333-6385	605-225-4049
Miracle Method US Corp						
4310 Arrowswest Dr	Colorado Springs	CO	80907		800-444-8827	719-594-9196
Perma-Glaze Inc						
1638 Research Loop Rd Ste 160	Tucson	AZ	85710		800-332-7397	
Re-Bath LLC						
16879 N 75th Ave Ste 101	Peoria	AZ	85382		800-426-4573	

189-12 Roofing, Siding, Sheet Metal Contractors

					Toll-Free	Phone
Baker Roofing Co						
517 Mercury St	Raleigh	NC	27603		800-849-4096	919-813-6681
Beldon						
100 S Canyonwood Dr	Dripping Springs	TX	78620		855-971-6936	512-337-1820
Birdair Inc						
65 Lawrence Bell Dr Ste 100	Amherst	NY	14221		800-622-2246	716-633-9500
Bonland Industries Inc						
50 Newark-Pompton Tpke	Wayne	NJ	07470		800-232-6600	973-694-3211
Brazos Urethane Inc						
1031 Sixth St North	Texas City	TX	77590		866-527-2967	
Centimark Corp						
12 Grandview Cir	Canonsburg	PA	15317		800-558-4100	
Commercial Siding & Maintenance Co, The						
8059 Crile Rd	Painesville	OH	44077		800-229-4276	440-352-7800
DC Taylor Co						
312 29th St NE	Cedar Rapids	IA	52402		800-876-6346	319-363-2073

					Toll-Free	Phone
Dee Cramer Inc						
4221 E Baldwin Rd	Holly	MI	48442		888-342-6995	810-579-5000
Douglass Colony Group Inc						
5901 E 58th Ave	Commerce City	CO	80022		877-288-0650	303-288-2635
Heidler Roofing Services Inc						
2120 Alpha Dr	York	PA	17408		866-792-3549	717-792-3549
IG Inc 720 S Sara Rd	Mustang	OK	73064		800-654-8433	405-376-9393
Jamar Co						
4701 Mike Colalillo Dr	Duluth	MN	55807		800-644-3624	218-628-1027
Jottan Inc PO Box 166	Florence	NJ	08518		800-364-4234	609-447-6200
NIR Roof Care Inc						
12191 Regency Pkwy	Huntley	IL	60142		800-221-7663	847-669-3444
North American Roofing Services Inc						
41 Dogwood Rd	Asheville	NC	28806		800-551-5602	828-687-7767
Schust Engineering Inc						
701 North St	Auburn	IN	46706		800-686-9297	
Standard Roofing Co						
516 N McDonough St PO Box 1309	Montgomery	AL	36102		800-239-5705	334-265-1262

189-13 Sprinkler System Installation (Fire Sprinklers)

					Toll-Free	Phone
August Winter & Sons Inc						
2323 N Roemer Rd	Appleton	WI	54911		800-236-8882	920-739-8881
Cosco Fire Protection Inc						
1075 W Lambert Rd Bldg D	Brea	CA	92821		800-485-3795	714-989-1800
JF Ahern Co						
855 Morris St	Fond du Lac	WI	54935		800-532-0155	920-921-9020
John E Green						
220 Victor Ave	Highland Park	MI	48203		888-918-7002	313-868-2400
National Automatic Sprinkler Industries						
8000 Corporate Dr	Landover	MD	20785		800-638-2603	301-577-1700
SA Comunale Company Inc						
2900 Newpark Dr	Barberton	OH	44203		800-776-7181	330-706-3040

189-14 Structural Steel Erection

					Toll-Free	Phone
Advance Tank & Construction Co						
3700 E County Rd 64 PO Box 219	Wellington	CO	80549		800-422-3488	970-568-3444
Albany Steel Inc						
566 Broadway	Albany	NY	12204		800-342-9317	518-436-4851
Area Erectors Inc						
2323 Harrison Ave	Rockford	IL	61104		800-270-2732	815-398-6700
Central Maintenance & Welding Inc (CMW)						
2620 E Keysville Rd	Lithia	FL	33547		877-704-7411	813-737-1402
Century Steel Erectors Co						
210 Washington Ave	Dravosburg	PA	15034		888-601-8801	412-469-8800
LSE Crane & Transportation						
313 Westgate Rd	Lafayette	LA	70506		877-234-9435	337-234-9435
Waldinger Corp						
2601 Bell Ave	Des Moines	IA	50321		800-473-4934	515-284-1911
WO Grubb Steel Erection Inc						
5120 Jefferson Davis Hwy	Richmond	VA	23234		866-964-7822	804-271-9471

189-15 Water Well Drilling

					Toll-Free	Phone
Ohio Drilling Co						
2405 Bostic Blvd SW	Massillon	OH	44647		800-272-1711	330-832-1521
Raba-Kistner Consultants Inc						
12821 W Golden Ln	San Antonio	TX	78249		866-722-2547	210-699-9090
Rosencrantz-Bemis Water Well Co						
1105 Hwy 281 Bypass	Great Bend	KS	67530		800-466-2467	620-793-5512

189-16 Wrecking & Demolition Contractors

					Toll-Free	Phone
Bierlein Cos Inc						
2000 Bay City Rd	Midland	MI	48642		800-336-6626	989-496-0066
Cherry Demolition						
6131 Selinsky Rd	Houston	TX	77048		800-444-1123	713-987-0000
O'Rourke Wrecking Co						
660 Lunken Pk Dr	Cincinnati	OH	45226		800-354-9850	513-871-1400
Patuxent Cos						
2124 Priest Bridge Dr Ste 18	Crofton	MD	21114		800-628-4942	410-793-0181

190   CONSTRUCTION MACHINERY & EQUIPMENT

SEE ALSO Material Handling Equipment ; Industrial Machinery, Equipment, & Supplies

					Toll-Free	Phone
Acco Material Handling Solutions						
76 Acco Dr	York	PA	17402		800-967-7333	
Akkerman Inc						
58256 - 266th St	Brownsdale	MN	55918		800-533-0386	
Allen Engineering Corp (AEC)						
819 S Fifth St PO Box 819	Paragould	AR	72450		800-643-0095	870-236-7751
Allied Construction Products LLC						
3900 Kelley Ave	Cleveland	OH	44114		800-321-1046*	216-431-2600
*Cust Svc						
American Road Machinery Inc						
3026 Saratoga Ave	Canton	OH	44706		844-294-5862	
Ashland Industries Inc						
1115 Rail Dr	Ashland	WI	54806		877-634-4622	
Astec Industries Inc						
1725 Shepherd Rd	Chattanooga	TN	37421		800-272-7100	423-899-5898
NASDAQ: ASTE						
Atlantic Construction Fabrics Inc						
2831 CaRdwell Rd	Richmond	VA	23234		800-448-3636	

			Toll-Free	Phone
Bandit Industries Inc				
6750 W Millbrook Rd	Remus MI	49340	800-952-0178	989-561-2270
Bid-Well Corp PO Box 97	Canton SD	57013	800-843-9824	
Boart Longyear Co				
2640 W 1700 S	Salt Lake City UT	84104	800-453-8740	801-972-6430
Caron Compactor Co				
1204 Ullrey Ave	Escalon CA	95320	800-542-2766	209-838-2062
Central Mine Equipment Company Inc				
4215 Rider Trl N	Earth City MO	63045	800-325-8827	314-291-7700
Centurion Industries Inc				
1107 N Taylor Rd	Garrett IN	46738	888-832-4466	260-357-6665
Charles Machine Works Inc, The				
1959 W First Ave PO Box 1902	Perry OK	73077	844-572-1902	
Clm Equipment Company Inc				
3135 Hwy 90 E	Broussard LA	70518	800-256-0490	337-837-6693
CRC Evans Pipeline International Inc				
10700 E Independence St	Tulsa OK	74116	800-664-9224	918-438-2100
DENIS CIMAF Inc				
211 rue Notre-Dame	Roxton Falls QC	J0H1E0	877-279-2300	450-548-7007
ED Etnyre & Co				
1333 S Daysville Rd	Oregon IL	61061	800-995-2116	815-732-2116
Erie Strayer Co				
1851 Rudolph Ave PO Box 1031	Erie PA	16502	800-356-4848	814-456-7001
Esco Corp 2141 NW 25th Ave	Portland OR	97210	800-523-3795	503-228-2141
F&M Mafco Inc				
PO Box 11013	Cincinnati OH	45211	800-333-2151	513-367-2151
Gencor Industries Inc				
5201 N Orange Blossom Trl	Orlando FL	32810	888-887-1266*	407-290-6000
*NASDAQ: GENC ■ *General*				
GES Global Energy Services Inc				
3220 Cypress Creek Pkwy	Houston TX	77068	888-523-6797	
Gradall Industries Inc				
406 Mill Ave SW	New Philadelphia OH	44663	800-445-4752	330-339-2211
Guntert & Zimmerman Construction Div Inc				
222 E Fourth St	Ripon CA	95366	800-733-2912	209-599-0066
Gyrodata Inc				
23000 Northwest Lake Dr	Houston TX	77095	800-348-6063	281-213-6300
H & E Equipment Services Inc				
7500 Pecue Ln	Baton Rouge LA	70809	866-467-3682	225-298-5200
NASDAQ: HEES				
Hensley Industries Inc				
2100 Joe Field Rd	Dallas TX	75229	888 406 6262	972 241 2321
Hunter Heavy Equipment Inc				
2829 Texas Ave	Texas City TX	77590	800-562-7368	409-945-2382
Indco Inc				
4040 Earnings Way	New Albany IN	47150	800-942-4383	
Inquipco				
2730 N Nellis Blvd	Las Vegas NV	89115	800-598-3465	702-644-1700
JH Fletcher & Co Inc				
402 High St	Huntington WV	25705	800-327-6203	304-525-7811
Kor-it Inc				
1964 Auburn Blvd	Sacramento CA	95815	888-727-4560	
Lippmann-Milwaukee Inc				
3271 E Van Norman Ave	Cudahy WI	53110	800-648-0486	
Machine Maintenance Inc				
2300 Cassens Dr	Fenton MO	63026	800-325-3322	636-343-9970
McLellan Equipment Inc				
251 Shaw Rd	South San Francisco CA	94080	800-848-8449	
Midwestern Industries Inc				
915 Oberlin Rd SW	Massillon OH	44647	877-474-9464*	330-837-4203
*Cust Svc				
Mixer Systems Inc				
190 Simmons Ave	Pewaukee WI	53072	800-756-4937	262-691-3100
Mr Crane Inc				
647 N Hariton St	Orange CA	92868	800-598-3465	714-633-2100
Pengo Corp 500 E Hwy 10	Laurens IA	50554	800-599-0211*	712-845-2540
*Cust Svc				
Pierce Pacific Manufacturing Inc				
4424 NE 158th PO Box 30509	Portland OR	97294	800-760-3270	503-808-9110
Pro Tec Equipment Inc				
4837 W Grand River Ave	Charlotte MI	48813	800-292-1225	
Putzmeister America				
1733 90th St	Sturtevant WI	53177	800-553-3414	
Radwell International Ltd				
1 Millennium Dr	Willingboro NJ	08046	800-884-5500	609-288-9393
Ramsey Winch Company Inc				
1600 N Garnett Rd	Tulsa OK	74116	800-777-2760	918-438-2760
Reco Equipment Inc				
41245 Reco Rd	Belmont OH	41245	800-686-7326	740-782-1314
RKI Inc 2301 Central Pkwy	Houston TX	77092	800-346-8988	713-688-4414
Roadtec Inc				
800 Manufacturers Rd				
PO Box 180515	Chattanooga TN	37405	800-272-7100	423-265-0600
Rotochopper Inc				
217 West St PO Box 295	Saint Martin MN	56376	800-663-7574	320-548-3586
Shamokin Filler Company Inc				
PO Box 568	Shamokin PA	17872	800-577-8008	570-644-0437
Shimpo 1701 Glenlake Ave	Itasca IL	60143	800-842-1479	630-924-7138
Simco Drilling Equipment Inc				
PO Box 448	Osceola IA	50213	800-338-9925	641-342-2166
Stephens Manufacturing Co				
711 W Fourth St	Tompkinsville KY	42167	800-626-0200	270-487-6774
Superwinch Inc 359 Lake Rd	Dayville CT	06241	800-323-2031	
Swenson Spreader Co				
127 Walnut St	Lindenwood IL	61049	888-825-7323	815-393-4455
Test Mark Industries Inc				
995 North Market St	East Palestine OH	44413	800-783-3227	
Treeline Well Services Inc				
750 333 - 11th Ave SW	Calgary AB	T2R1L9	844-344-7447	403-266-2868
Varel International Energy Services Inc				
1625 W Crosby Dr Ste 124	Carrollton TX	75006	800-827-3526	972-242-1160
Virnig Manufacturing Inc				
101 Gateway Dr NE	Rice MN	56367	800-648-2408	
Wacker Neuson				
N 92 W 15000 Anthony Ave	Menomonee Falls WI	53051	800-770-0957	262-255-0500
Web Equipment				
464 Central Rd	Fredericksburg VA	22401	800-225-3858	540-657-5855

			Toll-Free	Phone
Werk-Brau Company Inc				
2800 Fostoria Ave	Findlay OH	45840	800-537-9561	
Wilco Marsh Buggies & Draglines Inc				
1304 Macarthur Ave	Harvey LA	70058	800-253-0869	504-341-3409
Young Corp 3231 Utah Ave S	Seattle WA	98134	800-321-9090	206-624-1071

191   CONSTRUCTION MATERIALS

SEE ALSO Home Improvement Centers

191-1 Brick, Stone, Related Materials

			Toll-Free	Phone
AHI Supply Inc				
PO Box 884	Friendswood TX	77549	800-873-5794	281-331-0088
Arley Wholesale				
700 N South Rd	Scranton PA	18504	800-233-4107	570-344-9874
Atlas Construction Supply Inc				
4640 Brinnell St	San Diego CA	92111	877-588-2100	858-277-2100
Bierschbach Equipment & Supply Co				
PO Box 1444	Sioux Falls SD	57101	800-843-3707	605-332-4466
Century Roof Tile				
23135 Saklan Rd	Hayward CA	94545	888-233-7548	510-780-9489
Consolidated Brick				
650 Bodwell St Ext	Avon MA	02322	800-321-0021	
Fay Block Materials Inc				
130 Builders Blvd	Fayetteville NC	28302	800-326-9198	
Foundation Technologies Inc				
1400 Progress Industrial Blvd	Lawrenceville GA	30043	800-773-2368	678-407-4640
Fullen Dock & Warehouse Inc				
382 Klinke Rd	Memphis TN	38127	800-467-7104	901-358-9544
Guaranteed Supply Co				
1211 Rotherwood Rd	Greensboro NC	27406	800-326-0810	336-273-3491
Henry Products Inc				
302 S 23rd Ave	Phoenix AZ	85009	800-525-5533	602-253-3191
In-O-Vate Technologies Inc				
810 Saturn St Ste 21	Jupiter FL	33477	888-443-7937	561-743-8696
Indital USA Ltd				
7947 Mesa Dr	Houston TX	77028	800-772-4706	
Jaeckle Wholesale Inc				
4101 Owl Creek Dr	Madison WI	53710	000-236-7225	600-030-5400
Lynx Brand Fence Products				
4330 76 Ave SE	Calgary AB	T2C2J2	800-665-5969	403-273-4821
Patene Building Supplies Ltd				
641 Speedvale Ave W	Guelph ON	N1K1E6	800-265-8319	519-824-4030
PRL Glass Systems Inc				
251 Mason Way	City Of Industry CA	91746	800-433-7044	626-961-5890
Quick Crete Products				
731 Parkridge Ave	Norco CA	92860	866-703-3434	
Rio Grande Co				
201 Santa Fe Dr	Denver CO	80223	800-935-8420	303-825-2211
Terrazzo & Marble Supply Company of Illinois				
77 Wheeling Rd	Wheeling IL	60090	800-762-7253	
Vimco Inc				
300 Hansen Access Rd	King Of Prussia PA	19406	800-468-4626*	610-768-0500
*Cust Svc				
Zeiser Wilbert Vault Inc				
750 Howard St	Elmira NY	14904	800-472-4335	607-733-0568

191-2 Construction Materials (Misc)

			Toll-Free	Phone
American Fence Inc				
2502 N 27th Ave	Phoenix AZ	85009	888-691-4565	602-272-2333
Arabel Inc				
16301 NW 49th Ave	Hialeah FL	33014	800-759-5959*	305-623-8302
*Sales				
Atlantic Forest Products LLC				
7000 Forest Dr	Sparrows Point MD	21219	800-551-2374	410-752-8092
Basic Components Inc				
1201 S Second Ave	Mansfield TX	76063	800-452-1780	817-473-7224
Chemung Supply Corp				
PO Box 527	Elmira NY	14903	800-733-5508	607-733-5506
CR Laurence Company Inc				
2503 E Vernon Ave PO Box 58923	Los Angeles CA	90058	800-421-6144	323-588-1281
DS Brown Co				
300 E Cherry St	North Baltimore OH	45872	800-848-1730	419-257-3561
Eastern Wholesale Fence Co Inc				
274 Middle Island Rd	Medford NY	11763	800-339-3362	631-698-0900
Empire Bldg Materials Inc				
PO Box 220	Bozeman MT	59771	800-548-8201	
Galloup 3838 Clay Ave SW	Wyoming MI	49548	888-755-3110	269-965-4005
Gossen /Corp				
2030 W Bender Rd	Milwaukee WI	53209	800-558-8984	414-228-9800
Kuriyama of America Inc				
360 E State Pkwy	Schaumburg IL	60173	800-800-0320	847-755-0360
Penrod Co				
272 Bendix Rd Ste 550	Virginia Beach VA	23452	800-537-3497	757-498-0186
Robert N Karpp Company Inc				
480 E First St	Boston MA	02127	800-244-5886	617-269-5880
Star Sales & Distributing Corp				
29 Commerce Way	Woburn MA	01801	800-222-8118	781-933-8830

191-3 Lumber & Building Supplies

			Toll-Free	Phone
84 Lumber Co				
1019 Rt 519	Eighty Four PA	15330	800-664-1984	724-228-8820
Alamo Lumber Co				
10800 Sentinel Dr	San Antonio TX	78217	855-828-9792	210-352-1300
Allied Bldg Products Corp				
15 E Union Ave	East Rutherford NJ	07073	800-541-2198	201-507-8400
Alpine Lumber Co				
10170 Church Ranch Way Ste 350	Westminster CO	80021	800-499-1634	303-451-8001

				Toll-Free	Phone

American International Forest Products LLC (AIFP)
5560 SW 107th Ave . . . . Beaverton OR 97005   **800-366-1611**   503-641-1611

Arnold Lumber Co
251 Fairgrounds Rd . . . . West Kingston RI 02892   **800-339-0116**   401-783-2266

Auburn Corp
10490 W 164th Pl . . . . Orland Park IL 60467   **800-393-1826**

Baille Lumber Co
4002 Legion Dr PO Box 6 . . . . Hamburg NY 14075   **800-950-2850**   716-649-2850

Big C Lumber Inc
50860 Princess Way PO Box 176 . . . . Granger IN 46530   **888-297-0010**   574-277-4550

Birmingham International Forest Products LLC
300 Riverhills Business Pk . . . . Birmingham AL 35242   **800-767-2437**   205-972-1500

Buckeye Pacific LLC
4386 SW Macadam Ave Ste 200 . . . . Portland OR 97207   **800-767-9191**   503-274-2284

Builders General Supply Co
15 Sycamore Ave . . . . Little Silver NJ 07739   **800-570-7227**

Chelsea Lumber Co
1 Old Barn Cir . . . . Chelsea MI 48118   **800-875-9126**   734-475-9126

Cleary Millwork Company Inc
235 Dividend Rd . . . . Rocky Hill CT 06067   **800-486-7600**   800-899-4533

Counter Pro Inc
210 Lincoln St . . . . Manchester NH 03103   **800-899-2444**   603-647-2444

Coventry Lumber Inc
2030 Nooseneck Hill Rd . . . . Coventry RI 02816   **800-390-0919**   401-821-2800

Creative Pultrusions Inc
214 Industrial Ln . . . . Alum Bank PA 15521   **888-274-7855**   814-839-4186

Doka USA Ltd
214 Gates Rd . . . . Little Ferry NJ 07643   **877-365-2872**   201-329-7839

Door Systems Inc
PO Box 511 . . . . Framingham MA 01704   **800-545-3667**   508-875-3508

Forest City Trading Group LLC
10250 SW Greenburg Rd Ste 300 . . . . Portland OR 97223   **800-767-3284**   503-246-8500

Foxworth-Galbraith Lumber Co
4965 Preston Pk Blvd Ste 400 . . . . Plano TX 75093   **800-688-8082**   972-665-2400

Frank Miller Lumber Company Inc
1690 Frank Miller Rd . . . . Union City IN 47390   **800-345-2643**   765-964-3196

Frank Paxton Lumber Co
7455 Dawson Rd . . . . Cincinnati OH 45243   **800-325-9800**   888-826-5580

Guardian Building Products (GBPD)
979 Batesville Rd . . . . Greer SC 29651   **800-569-4262**   864-297-6101

Hawaii Planing Mill Ltd (HPM)
16-166 Melekahiwa St . . . . Keaau HI 96749   **877-841-7633**   808-966-5693

Holt & Bugbee Co
1600 Shawsheen St . . . . Tewksbury MA 01876   **800-325-6010**

Huttig Bldg Products Inc (HBP)
555 Maryville University Dr
Ste 400 . . . . Saint Louis MO 63141   **800-325-4466**   314-216-2600
NASDAQ: HBP

Idaho Pacific Lumber Company Inc (IdaPac)
1770 Spanish Sun Way . . . . Meridian ID 83642   **800-231-2310**

Jewett-Cameron Trading Company Ltd
32275 NW Hillcrest PO Box 1010 . . . . . . North Plains OR 97133   **800-547-5877**   503-647-0110
NASDAQ: JCTCF

Magnolia Forest Products Inc
13252 I- 55 S PO Box 99 . . . . Terry MS 39170   **800-366-6374**

Matheus Lumber
15800 Woodinville-Redmond Rd NE . . . . Woodinville WA 98072   **800-284-7501**   425-489-3000

Mead Clark Lumber Co
2667 Dowd Dr PO Box 529 . . . . Santa Rosa CA 95407   **800-585-9663**   707-576-3333

MID-AM Bldg Supply Inc
1615 Omar Bradley Dr PO Box 645 . . . . Moberly MO 65270   **800-892-5850**

Millard Lumber Inc 12900 I St . . . . Omaha NE 68145   **800-228-9260**   402-896-2800

National Industrial Lumber Co
1 Chicago Ave . . . . Elizabeth PA 15037   **800-289-9352**

Ohio Valley Supply Co
3512 Spring Grove Ave . . . . Cincinnati OH 45223   **800-696-5608**   513-681-8300

Omega Products International
1681 California Ave . . . . Corona CA 92881   **800-600-6634**   951-737-7447

Pacific Source Inc
PO Box 2323 . . . . Woodinville WA 98072   **888-343-1515**

Palmer-Donavin Manufacturing Co
1200 Steelwood Rd . . . . Columbus OH 43212   **800-589-4412**   800-652-1234

Parksite Inc
1563 Hubbard Ave . . . . Batavia IL 60510   **800-338-3355**

Pyramid Interiors Distributors Inc
PO Box 181058 . . . . Memphis TN 38181   **800-456-0592**   901-375-4197

Quality Plywood Specialties Inc
13000 Automobile Blvd . . . . Clearwater FL 33762   **888-722-1181**   727-572-0500

Raymond Bldg Supply Corp
7751 Bayshore Rd . . . . North Fort Myers FL 33917   **877-731-7272**   239-731-8300

Reliable Wholesale Lumber Inc
7600 Redondo Cir . . . . Huntington Beach CA 92648   **877-795-4638**   714-848-8222

Richmond International Forest Products Inc
4050 Innslake Dr Ste 100 . . . . Glen Allen VA 23060   **800-767-0111**   804-747-0111

Riverhead Bldg Supply Corp
1093 Pulaski St . . . . Riverhead NY 11901   **800-378-3650**   631-727-3650

Riverside Forest Products Inc
2912 Professional Pkwy PO Box 211663 . . . . Augusta GA 30907   **888-855-8733**   706-855-5500

Russin Lumber Corp
21 Leonards Dr . . . . Montgomery NY 12549   **800-724-0010**   845-457-4000

Seaboard International Forest Products LLC
22F Cotton Rd . . . . Nashua NH 03063   **800-669-6800**   603-881-3700

Service Construction Supply Inc
PO Box 13405 . . . . Birmingham AL 35202   **866-729-4968**   205-252-3158

Solar Industries Inc
4940 S Alvernon Way PO Box 27337 . . . . Tucson AZ 85706   **800-449-2323**   520-519-8258

Spellman Hardwoods Inc
4645 N 43rd Ave . . . . Phoenix AZ 85031   **800-624-5401**   602-272-2313

Timber Products Co
305 S Fourth St PO Box 269 . . . . Springfield OR 97477   **800-954-4340**   541-995-0780

Tri-state Forest Products Inc
2105 Sheridan Ave . . . . Springfield OH 45505   **800-949-6325**   937-323-6325

Viking Forest Products LLC
7615 Smetana Ln . . . . Eden Prairie MN 55344   **800-733-3801**   952-941-6512

Wheeler Lumber LLC
9330 James Ave S . . . . Bloomington MN 55431   **800-328-3986**   952-929-7854

White Cap Industries Inc
1723 S Ritchie St . . . . Santa Ana CA 92705   **800-944-8322**   714-258-3300

				Toll-Free	Phone

Window Rama Enterprises Inc
71 Heartland Blvd . . . . Edgewood NY 11717   **800-897-7262**   631-667-8088

Zeeland Lumber & Supply Co
146 E Washington . . . . Zeeland MI 49464   **888-772-2119**   616-772-2119

191-4 Roofing, Siding, Insulation Materials

				Toll-Free	Phone

ABC Seamless
3001 Fiechtner Dr . . . . Fargo ND 58103   **800-732-6577**   701-293-5952

ABC Supply Company Inc
1 ABC Pkwy . . . . Beloit WI 53511   **888-492-1047**   608-362-7777

Beacon Roofing Supply Inc
1 Lakeland Pk Dr . . . . Peabody MA 01960   **877-645-7663**   978-535-7668
NASDAQ: BECN

Carlisle SynTec
1285 Ritner Hwy PO Box 7000 . . . . Carlisle PA 17013   **800-479-6832**

Crane Composites Inc
23525 W Eames St . . . . Channahon IL 60410   **800-435-0080**   815-467-8600

Frank Roberts & Sons Inc
1130 Robertsville Rd . . . . Punxsutawney PA 15767   **800-262-8955**   814-938-5000

General Insulation Company Inc
278 Mystic Ave Ste 209 . . . . Medford MA 02155   **800-229-9148**   781-391-2070

Harvey Industries Inc
1400 Main St . . . . Waltham MA 02451   **800-598-5400**

James Hardie Bldg Products
26300 La Alameda Ave Ste 400 . . . . Mission Viejo CA 92691   **888-542-7343**

MacArthur Co
2400 Wycliff St . . . . Saint Paul MN 55114   **800-777-7507**   651-646-2773

NCFI Polyurethanes
1515 Carter St . . . . Mount Airy NC 27030   **800-346-8229**   336-789-9161

Norandex Bldg Materials Distribution Inc
1 ABC Pkwy . . . . Beloit WI 53511   **800-528-0942**

Oberfields LLC
1165 Alum Creek Dr . . . . Columbus OH 43209   **800-845-7644**   614-252-0955

Olympia Tile International Inc
1000 Lawrence Ave W . . . . Toronto ON M6A1C6   **800-268-1613**   416-785-6666

Onduline North America Inc
4900 Ondura Dr . . . . Fredericksburg VA 22407   **800-777-7663**   540-898-7000

Philadelphia Reserve Supply Co
200 Mack Dr . . . . Croydon PA 19021   **800-347-7726**   215-785-3141

Plastatech Engineering Ltd
725 Morley Dr . . . . Saginaw MI 48601   **800-892-9358**   989-754-6500

SG Wholesale Roofing Supplies
1101 E Sixth St . . . . Santa Ana CA 92701   **800-464-2461***   714-568-1900
*Cust Svc

Shook & Fletcher Insulation Co
4625 Valleydale Rd . . . . Birmingham AL 35242   **888-829-2575**   205-991-7606

SPEC Building Materials Corp
2840 Roe Ln . . . . Kansas City KS 66103   **866-585-7785**   913-384-0804

Specialty Products & Insulation Co (SPI)
1650 Manheim Pk Ste 202 . . . . Lancaster PA 17601   **800-788-7764**   855-519-4044

Variform Inc
5020 Weston Pkwy Ste 400 . . . . Cary NC 27513   **800-800-2244**   888-975-9436

Wesco Cedar Inc PO Box 520 . . . . Creswell OR 97426   **800-547-2511**   541-688-5020

192   CONSULTING SERVICES - ENVIRONMENTAL

SEE ALSO Waste Management ; Recyclable Materials Recovery ; Remediation Services

				Toll-Free	Phone

A & A Maintenance Enterprise Inc
965 Midland Ave . . . . Yonkers NY 10704   **800-280-0601**

A&D Environmental Services Inc
PO Box 484 . . . . High Point NC 27261   **800-434-7750**

AirTek Indoor Air Solutions Inc
1241 Johnson Ave Ste 209 . . . . San Luis Obispo CA 93401   **877-858-6213**

Ameresco Inc
111 Speen St Ste 410 . . . . Framingham MA 01701   **866-263-7372**   508-661-2200

Aquatic Informatics Inc
1111 West Georgia St Ste 2400 . . . . Vancouver BC V6E4M3   **877-870-2782**   604-873-2782

Badger Express LLC
181 Quality Ct . . . . Fall River WI 53932   **800-972-0084**   920-484-5808

Blade Energy Partners Ltd
2600 Network Blvd Ste 550 . . . . Frisco TX 75034   **800-849-1545**   972-712-8407

Blue Pillar Inc
9025 N River Rd Ste 150 . . . . Indianapolis IN 46240   **888-234-3212**

Caravan Facilities Management LLC
1400 Weiss St . . . . Saginaw MI 48602   **855-211-7450**

Chicago Parking Meters LLC
205 N Michigan Ave Ste 1910 . . . . Chicago IL 60601   **877-242-7901**

Climate Registry, The
PO Box 811488 . . . . Los Angeles CA 90081   **866-523-0764**

Compaction Technologies Inc
8324 89th Ave N . . . . Brooklyn Park MN 55445   **877-860-6900**

Cramer Fish Sciences
7525 NE Ambassador Pl Ste C . . . . Portland OR 97220   **888-224-1221**   503-491-9577

Divisions Maintenance Group
1 RiverFrnt Pl Ste 510 . . . . Newport KY 41071   **877-448-9730**

Earth Networks Inc
12410 Milestone Ctr Dr Ste 300 . . . . Germantown MD 20876   **800-544-4429**   301-250-4000

Earth Systems Services Inc
720 Aerovista Pl Ste 102 . . . . San Luis Obispo CA 93401   **866-781-0112**   805-781-0112

Ehs-International Inc
1011 SW Klickitat Way Ste 104 . . . . Seattle WA 98134   **800-666-2959**   206-381-1128

Entact LLC
3129 Bass Pro Dr . . . . Grapevine TX 76051   **800-255-2771**

Environmental & Safety Designs Inc
5724 Summer Trees Dr . . . . Memphis TN 38134   **800-588-7962**   901-372-7962

Fauske & Assoc LLC
16w070 83rd St . . . . Burr Ridge IL 60527   **877-328-7531**   630-323-8750

FilterBoxx Water & Environmental Corp
200 Rivercrest Dr SE Ste 160 . . . . Calgary AB T2C2X5   **877-868-4747**   403-203-4747

G D G Environment Group Ltd
430 rue St-Laurent . . . . Trois-RiviŠres QC G8T6H3   **888-567-8567**

Company			Toll-Free	Phone

Gershman, Brickner & Bratton Inc
8550 Arlington Blvd Ste 304 .... Fairfax VA 22031 **800-573-5801** 703-573-5800
Gestion P R Maintenance Inc
639 King St W Ste 203 .... Kitchener ON N2G1C7 **800-719-2828** 905-304-8300
Giant Resource Recovery - Harleyville Inc (GRR)
654 Judge St PO Box 352 .... Harleyville SC 29448 **800-786-0477**
GLE Associates Inc
5405 Cypress Center Dr Ste 110 .... Tampa FL 33609 **888-453-4531** 813-241-8350
Groundwater & Environmental Services Inc (GES)
1599 Rte 34 Ste 1 .... Wall Township NJ 07727 **800-220-3068**
Heath Consultants Inc
9030 Monroe Rd .... Houston TX 77061 **800-432-8487** 713-844-1300
HKA Enterprises Inc
337 Spartangreen Blvd .... Duncan SC 29334 **800-825-5452** 864-661-5100
Inland Technologies Inc
14 Queen St PO Box 253 .... Truro NS B2N5C1 **877-633-5263** 902-895-6346
ISN Global Enterprises Inc
Po Box 1391 .... Claremont CA 91711 **877-376-4476** 909-670-0601
Keen Technical Solutions LLC
158 E Front St PO Box 2109 .... Traverse City MI 49685 **888-675-7772**
Kemron Environmental Services Inc
8521 Leesburg Pk Ste 175 .... Vienna VA 22182 **888-429-3516** 703-893-4106
KERAMIDA Inc
401 N College Ave .... Indianapolis IN 46202 **800-508-8034** 317-685-6600
Klean Industries Inc
700 W Georgia St .... Vancouver BC V7Y1K8 **866-302-5928** 604-637-9609
Logees Greenhouses Ltd
141 N St .... Danielson CT 06239 **888-330-8038** 860-774-8038
Los Alamos Technical Assoc Inc
6501 Americas Pkwy NE Ste 200 .... Albuquerque NM 87110 **800-952-5282** 505-884-3800
Medallion Laboratories
9000 Plymouth Ave N .... Minneapolis MN 55427 **800-245-5615** 763-764-4453
Mwh Global Inc
380 Interlocken Crescent Ste 200 .... Broomfield CO 80021 **866-257-5984** 303-533-1900
MyClean Inc
247 W 35th St Ste 9R .... New York NY 10001 **855-692-5326**
NAL
10416 Investment Cir .... Rancho Cordova CA 95670 **800-774-9555** 916-361-0555
Navarro Research & Engineering Inc
1020 Commerce Park Dr .... Oak Ridge TN 37830 **866-681-5265** 865-220-9650
Neo Corp 289 Silkwood Dr .... Canton NC 28716 **800-822-1247**
Omaha Public Power District (OPPD)
444 S 16th St Mall .... Omaha NE 68102 **800-331-5666** 402-536-4131
Ontario Clean Water Agency
1 Yonge St Ste 1700 .... Toronto ON M5E1E5 **800-667-6292** 416-775-0500
Osi Environmental Inc
300 Fayal Rd .... Eveleth MN 55734 **800-777-8542**
Partner Assessment Corp
2154 Torrance Blvd Ste 200 .... Torrance CA 90501 **800-419-4923**
Paul Davis Systems Canada Ltd
38 Crockford Blvd .... Toronto ON M1R3C2 **800-661-5975** 416-299-8890
PegEx Inc
2693 Research Park Dr Ste 201 .... Fitchburg WI 53711 **888-681-9616**
Perma-Fix Environmental Services Inc
8302 Dunwoody Pl Ste 250 .... Atlanta GA 30350 **800-365-6066** 770-587-9898
NASDAQ: PESI
PermaTreat Pest & Termite Control
501 Lafayette Blvd .... Fredericksburg VA 22401 **866-737-6287** 540-373-6655
PharmEcology Associates LLC
1001 Fannin .... Houston TX 77002 **877-247-7430**
Pinchin Group, The
2470 Milltower Ct .... Mississauga ON L5N7W5 **855-746-2446** 905-363-0678
Prestige Maintenance USA Ltd
1808 Tenth St Ste 300 .... Plano TX 75074 **800-321-4773** 972-578-9801
PSC 5151 San Felipe Ste 1100 .... Houston TX 77056 **800-726-1300**
R E I Consultants Inc
PO Box 286 .... Beaver WV 25813 **800-999-0105** 304-255-2500
Ran-Pro Farms Inc PO Box 300 .... Tyler TX 75710 **800-749-6266** 903-593-7381
RJN Group Inc
200 W Front St .... Wheaton IL 60187 **800-227-7838** 630-682-4700
S & ME Inc
3201 Spring Forest Rd .... Raleigh NC 27616 **800-849-2517*** 919-872-2660
*Cust Svc
Sabre Companies LLC, The
1891 New Scotland Rd .... Slingerlands NY 12159 **800-349-2799** 518-514-1572
Sanexen Environmental Services Inc
9935 rue de Ch√fteauneuf Entrance 1
Ste 200 .... Brossard QC J4Z3V4 **800-263-7870** 450-466-2123
SHIFT Energy Inc
1 Germain St 18th Fl. .... Saint John NB E2L4V1 **855-744-3860**
Source Intelligence LLC
1921 Palomar Oaks Way Ste 205 .... Carlsbad CA 92008 **877-916-6337**
SWCA Inc
3033 N Central Ave Ste 145 .... Phoenix AZ 85012 **800-828-8517** 602-274-3831
US. Facilities Inc
30 N 41 St Ste 400 .... Philadelphia PA 19104 **800-236-6241**
Utility Service Company Inc
535 Courtney Hodges Blvd .... Perry GA 31069 **855-526-4413** 478-987-0303
Vertex Companies Inc, The
400 Libbey Pkwy .... Weymouth MA 02189 **888-298-5162** 781-952-6000
Vivint Solar Inc
1800 W Ashton Blvd .... Lehi UT 84043 **877-404-4129** 801-216-3927
Western Technologies Inc
3737 E Broadway Rd .... Phoenix AZ 85040 **800-580-3737** 602-437-3737

193   CONSULTING SERVICES - HUMAN RESOURCES

SEE ALSO Professional Employer Organizations (PEOs)

		Toll-Free	Phone

ACRT Inc 1333 Home Ave .... Akron OH 44310 **800-622-2562**
Alliance For Employee Growth & Development Inc, The
80 Cottontail Ln Ste 320 .... Somerset NJ 08873 **800-323-3436**
Arthur J Gallagher & Co
2 Pierce Pl .... Itasca IL 60143 **888-285-5106** 630-773-3800
NYSE: AJG
Ashtead Technology Inc
19407 Pk Row Ste 170 .... Houston TX 77084 **800-242-3910** 281-398-9533

Atfocus
394 Old Orchard Grove .... Toronto ON M5M2E9 **866-349-2661** 416-485-4220
Atlantic Personnel Search Inc
9624 Pennsylvania Ave .... Upper Marlboro MD 20772 **877-229-5254** 301-599-2108
B E. Smith Inc
8801 Renner Ave .... Lenexa KS 66219 **855-296-6318**
Benz Communications LLC
209 Mississippi St .... San Francisco CA 94107 **888-550-5251**
Bessire & Associates Inc
7621 Little Ave Ste 106 .... Charlotte NC 28226 **800-797-7355** 704-341-1423
Challenger Gray & Christmas Inc
150 S Wacker Dr Ste 2800 .... Chicago IL 60606 **855-242-3424** 312-332-5790
Development Dimensions International
1225 Washington Pk .... Bridgeville PA 15017 **800-933-4463*** 412-257-0600
*Mktg
Dicentra 603-7 St Thomas St .... Toronto ON M5S2B7 **866-647-3279** 416-361-3400
Eda Staffing Inc
132 Central St Ste 206 .... Foxboro ME 02035 **800-886-9332** 508-543-0333
EDI Specialists Inc
31 Bellows Rd .... Raynham MA 02767 **800-821-4644**
Employer Plan Services Inc
2180 N Loop W Ste 400 .... Houston TX 77018 **800-447-6588** 713-351-3500
Employers Group
400 N Continental Blvd Ste 300 .... El Segundo CA 90245 **800-748-8484**
EnergX LLC
1000 B Clearview Ct .... Oak Ridge TN 37830 **866-932-1333**
Excel Staffing
2100 Osuna Rd NE Ste 100 .... Albuquerque NM 87113 **888-607-1695** 505-262-1871
Floyd Browne Group
3875 Embassy Pkwy .... Akron OH 44333 **800-362-2764*** 330-375-0800
*General
FPMI Solutions Inc
1033 N Fairfax St Ste 200 .... Alexandria VA 22314 **888-644-3764**
Gabriel Roeder Smith & Co (GRS)
1 Towne Sq Ste 800 .... Southfield MI 48076 **800-521-0498** 248-799-9000
Global Search Network Inc
118 S Fremont Ave .... Tampa FL 33606 **800-254-3398** 813-832-8300
Globe Consultants Inc
3112 Porter St Ste D .... Soquel CA 95073 **800-208-0663**
Goodwill Industries of Akron Ohio Inc, The
570 E Waterloo Rd .... Akron OH 44319 **800-989-8428** 330-724-6995
Hay Group Inc
1650 Arch St .... Philadelphia PA 19103 **800-716-4429** 215-861-2000
InfoMart Inc
1582 Terrell Mill Rd .... Marietta GA 30067 **800-800-3774** 770-984-2727
Insight 444 Scott Dr .... Bloomingdale IL 60108 **800-467-4448**
Insight Global Inc (IGI)
4170 Ashford Dunwoody Rd Ste 250 .... Atlanta GA 30319 **888-336-7463** 404-257-7900
ITR Group Inc
2520 Lexington Ave S Ste 500 .... Saint Paul MN 55120 **866-290-3423**
LifeCourse Associates Inc
9080 Eaton Park Rd .... Great Falls VA 22066 **866-537-4999**
Medicus Healthcare Solutions LLC
22 Roulston Rd Ste 5 .... Windham NH 03079 **855-301-0563**
Mission Search
2203 N Lois Ave Ste 1225 .... Tampa FL 33607 **877-479-1545**
Modern Management Inc
253 Commerce Dr Ste 105 .... Grayslake IL 60030 **800-323-1331** 847-945-7400
National Ctr for Retirement Benefits Inc
666 Dundee Rd Ste 1200 .... Northbrook IL 60062 **800-666-1000**
Onesmartworld Inc
79 Simcoe St .... Collingwood ON L9Y1H7 **800-387-6278** 705-444-1234
Riviera Advisors Inc
PO Box 41446 .... Long Beach CA 90853 **800-635-9063**
RLR Management Consulting Inc
77806 Flora Rd Ste D .... Palm Desert CA 92211 **888-757-7330** 760-200-4800
Roux Assoc Inc
209 Shafter St .... Islandia NY 11749 **800-322-7689** 631-232-2600
Runzheimer International
1 Runzheimer Pk .... Waterford WI 53185 **800-558-1702** 262-971-2200
Searchwide Inc
680 Commerce Dr Ste 220 .... Woodbury MN 55082 **888-386-6390** 651-275-1370
Selection Management Systems Inc
155 Tri County Pkwy Ste 150 .... Cincinnati OH 45246 **800-325-3609**
Senior Housing Companies
208 35th St Dr SE Ste 500 .... Cedar Rapids IA 52403 **800-366-6716**
Stanley Hunt DuPree & Rhine (SHDR)
7701 Airport Ctr Dr .... Greensboro NC 27409 **800-930-2441** 800-768-4873
Superior Environmental Corp
1128 Franklin Ct .... Marne MI 49435 **877-667-4142**
Tct Computing Group Inc
Po Box 402 .... Bel Air MD 21014 **866-828-6372** 410-893-5800
Tech Center Inc 265 S Main St .... Akron OH 44308 **800-990-8083** 330-762-6212
Thornmark Asset Management Inc
119 Spadina Ave Ste 701 .... Toronto ON M5V2L1 **877-204-6201** 416-204-6200
TRACOM Group, The
6675 S Kenton St Ste 118 .... Centennial CO 80111 **800-221-2321** 303-470-4900
ZE PowerGroup Inc
130 - 5920 No Two Rd .... Richmond BC V7C4R9 **866-944-1469** 604-244-1469

194   CONSULTING SERVICES - MANAGEMENT

SEE ALSO Management Services ; Association Management Companies

		Toll-Free	Phone

A C e International Company Inc
85 Independence Dr .... Taunton MA 02780 **800-223-4685**
Aa Temps Inc
7002 Little River Tpke .... Annandale VA 22003 **800-901-8367** 703-642-9050
Abba Technologies
5301 Beverly Hills Ave NE .... Albuquerque NM 87113 **888-222-2832** 505-889-3337
AC. Coy Co
395 Valley Brook Rd .... Canonsburg PA 15317 **800-784-5773** 724-820-1820
Achievement Incentives & Meetings
64 River Rd .... East Hanover NJ 07936 **800-454-1424** 973-386-9500
Advanced Energy Corp
909 Capability Dr Ste 2100 .... Raleigh NC 27606 **800-869-8001** 919-857-9000

Classified Section

				Toll-Free	Phone
Advantage Performance Group Inc					
700 Larkspur Landing Cir	Larkspur	CA	94939	**800-494-6646**	415-925-6832
AFC Industries Inc					
13-16 133rd Pl	College Point	NY	11356	**800-663-3412**	718-747-0237
Affinitas Corp					
1015 N 98th St Ste 100	Omaha	NE	68114	**800-369-6495**	402-505-5000
Affinity Wealth Management Inc					
1702 Lovering Ave	Wilmington	DE	19806	**800-825-8399**	302-652-6767
AFIMAC Inc 8160 Parkhill Dr	Milton	ON	L9T5V7	**800-554-4622**	
Agcall Inc					
251 Midpark Blvd SE	Calgary	AB	T2X1S3	**877-273-4333**	403-256-1229
Albert Moving					
4401 Barnett Rd	Wichita Falls	TX	76310	**800-460-9333**	940-696-7020
ALCO Sales & Service Co					
6851 High Grove Blvd	Burr Ridge	IL	60527	**800-323-4282**	630-655-1900
Aleut Management Services LLC					
5540 Tech Ctr Dr Ste 100	Colorado Springs	CO	80919	**800-377-7765**	719-531-9090
Allant Group Inc, The					
2655 Warrenville Rd Ste 200	Downers Grove	IL	60515	**800-367-7311**	
Allsup Inc 300 Allsup Pl	Belleville	IL	62223	**800-854-1418**	
Alpha & Omega Financial Management Consultants Inc					
8580 La Mesa Blvd Ste 100	La Mesa	CA	91942	**800-755-5060**	
Altair Engineering Inc					
1820 E Big Beaver Rd	Troy	MI	48083	**888-222-7822**	248-614-2400
Altman Weil Inc					
PO Box 625	Newtown Square	PA	19073	**866-886-3600**	610-359-9900
Amino Transport Inc					
223 NE Loop 820 Ste 101	Hurst	TX	76053	**800-304-3360**	
Anchor Benefit Consulting Inc					
2400 Maitland Ctr Pkwy Ste 111	Maitland	FL	32751	**800-845-7629**	407-667-8766
Andrews Logistics Inc					
2445 E Southlake Blvd	Southlake	TX	76092	**866-536-1234**	817-527-2770
Apollo Professional Svc					
29 Stiles Rd Ste 302	Salem	NH	03079	**866-277-3343**	
APPI Energy					
224 Phillip Morris Dr Ste 402	Salisbury	MD	21804	**800-520-6685**	
Aqua Finance Inc					
1 Corporate Dr Ste 300	Wausau	WI	54401	**800-234-3663**	
Associated Industries					
1206 N Lincoln Ste 200	Spokane	WA	99201	**800-720-4291**	509-326-6885
AssuredPartners NL					
2305 River Rd	Louisville	KY	40206	**888-499-8092**	502-894-2100
ASU Group, The					
2120 University Park Dr	Okemos	MI	48805	**800-968-0278**	517-349-2212
Atlas Brown Investment Advisors Inc					
333 E Main St - 400	Louisville	KY	40202	**866-871-0334**	502-271-2900
Audio Advisor					
3427 Kraft Ave SE	Grand Rapids	MI	49512	**800-942-0220**	
AXIOS HR					
528 Fourth St NW	Grand Rapids	MI	49504	**844-442-9467**	
Bay Dynamics					
595 Market St Ste 1300	San Francisco	CA	94105	**855-281-7362**	415-912-3130
BC One Call Ltd					
4259 Canada Way Ste 130	Burnaby	BC	V5G1H3	**800-474-6886**	604-257-1900
Beacon Financial Partners					
25800 Science Park Dr Ste 100	Beachwood	OH	44122	**866-568-3951**	216-910-1850
Benchmark Technologies International Inc (BTI)					
411 Hackensack Ave	Hackensack	NJ	07601	**800-265-8254**	201-996-0077
Benemax Inc 7 W Mill St	Medfield	MA	02052	**800-528-1530**	
Berkeley Communications Corp					
1321 67th St	Emeryville	CA	94608	**877-237-5266**	510-644-1599
Bernzott Capital Advisors					
888 W Ventura Blvd Ste B	Camarillo	CA	93010	**800-856-2646**	805-389-9445
Big Ceramic Store LLC					
543 Vista Blvd	Sparks	NV	89434	**888-513-5303**	
Blaine Tech Services Inc					
1680 Rogers Ave	San Jose	CA	95112	**800-545-7558**	408-573-0555
Blue Tent					
218 E Valley Rd	Carbondale	CO	81623	**877-716-9648**	970-704-3240
Bluepoint Leadership Development Ltd					
25 Whitney Dr	Milford	OH	45150	**888-221-8685**	513-683-4702
Boa Technology Inc					
1760 Platte St	Denver	CO	80202	**844-203-1297**	303-455-5126
Bonanza Trade & Supply					
6853 Lankershim Blvd	North Hollywood	CA	91605	**888-965-6577**	818-765-6577
Boomtown Internet Group Inc					
111 Rosemary Ln	Glenmoore	PA	19343	**888-454-3330**	
Booth					
4900 Nautilus Ct N Ste 220	Boulder	CO	80301	**800-332-6684**	303-581-1408
Booz Allen Hamilton Inc					
8283 Greensboro Dr	McLean	VA	22102	**866-390-3908**	703-902-5000
Brownlie & Braden LLC					
2820 Ross Tower 500 N Akard	Dallas	TX	75201	**888-339-4650**	214-219-4650
BTS USA Inc					
222 Kearny St Ste 1000	San Francisco	CA	94108	**800-445-7089**	415-362-4200
Bucher & Christian Consulting Inc					
9777 N College	Indianapolis	IN	46280	**866-363-1132**	
Building Performance Institute Inc					
107 Hermes Rd Ste 210	Malta	NY	12020	**877-274-1274**	518-899-2727
Burchfield Group Inc, The					
1295 Northland Dr Ste 350	St Paul	MN	55120	**800-778-1359**	651-389-5640
Business Resource Group (BRG)					
10440 N Central Expy Ste 1150	Dallas	TX	75231	**888-391-9166**	214-777-5100
Business Training Library Inc					
14500 S Outer Forty Ste 500	Town and Country	MO	63017	**888-432-3077**	
BusinessBroker Network LLC					
375 Northridge Rd Ste 475	Atlanta	GA	30350	**877-342-9786**	
C Myers Corp					
8222 S 48th St Ste 275	Phoenix	AZ	85044	**800-238-7475**	
Callahan Financial Planning Co					
3157 Farnam St Ste 7111	Omaha	NE	68131	**800-991-5195**	402-341-2000
Callisto Integration					
635 Fourth Line Ste 16	Oakville	ON	L6L5B3	**800-387-0467**	905-339-0059
Calnet Inc					
12359 Sunrise Vly Dr Ste 270	Reston	VA	20191	**877-322-5638***	703-547-6800
*General					
Capital Advisors Limited LLC					
20600 Chagrin Blvd	Shaker Heights	OH	44122	**888-295-7908**	216-295-7900

				Toll-Free	Phone
Capital Investment Advisors Inc					
200 Sandy Springs Pl NE Ste 300	Atlanta	GA	30328	**888-531-0018**	404-531-0018
Capitol Archives & Record Storage Inc					
133 Laurel St	Hartford	CT	06106	**800-381-2277**	860-951-8981
Carepro Health Services					
1014 Fifth Ave SE	Cedar Rapids	IA	52403	**800-575-8810**	
Carter Express Inc					
4020 W 73rd St	Anderson	IN	46011	**800-738-7705**	
Cascade Financial Management Inc					
950 17th St Ste 950	Denver	CO	80202	**800-353-0008**	
CastiaRx					
701 Emerson Rd Ste 301	Creve Coeur	MO	63141	**800-652-9550**	314-652-3121
CBI 600 Unicorn Park Dr	Woburn	MA	01801	**800-817-8601**	339-298-2100
Cenergistic Inc					
5950 Sherry Ln	Dallas	TX	75225	**855-798-7779**	
Center for Civic Education					
5145 Douglas Fir Rd	Calabasas	CA	91302	**800-350-4223**	818-591-9321
Center for Cultural Interchange					
746 N La Salle Dr	Chicago	IL	60654	**866-224-0061**	312-944-2544
Century Health Solutions Inc					
1500 SW Tenth Ave	Topeka	KS	66604	**800-227-0089**	785-270-4593
Certus International					
9 Cedarwood Dr Ste 8	Bedford	NH	03110	**800-969-3218**	603-627-1212
Champion College Services Inc					
7776 S Pointe Pkwy W Ste 250	Tempe	AZ	85044	**800-761-7376**	480-947-7375
CIMplify					
720 Cool Springs Blvd Ste 500	Franklin	TN	37067	**888-232-7026**	615-261-6700
Cipher Systems LLC					
185 Admiral Cochrane Dr Ste 210	Annapolis	MD	21401	**888-899-1523**	410-412-3326
Circadian Technologies Inc					
2 Main St Ste 310	Stoneham	MA	02180	**800-284-5001**	781-439-6300
Clarus Mktg Group LLC					
500 Enterprise Dr 2nd Fl	Rocky Hill	CT	06067	**855-226-7047**	860-358-9198
Cocciardi & Associates Inc					
4 Kacey Ct	Mechanicsburg	PA	17055	**800-377-3024**	717-766-4500
Communispond Inc					
12 Barns Ln	East Hampton	NY	11937	**800-529-5925**	631-907-8010
Community Care Inc					
1555 S Layton Blvd	Milwaukee	WI	53215	**866-992-6600**	414-385-6600
Compensation Resources Inc					
310 Rt 17 North	Upper Saddle River	NJ	07458	**877-934-0505**	201-934-0505
Comprehensive Financial Planning LLC					
530 Main Ave Ste A	Durango	CO	81301	**877-901-5227**	970-385-5227
Comprehensive Pharmacy Services Inc (CPS)					
6409 N Quail Hollow Rd	Memphis	TN	38120	**800-968-6962**	901-748-0470
Concensus Consulting LLC					
51 Dutilh Rd Ste 140	Cranberry Township	PA	16066	**888-349-1014**	
Condor Earth Technologies Inc					
21663 Brian Ln	Sonora	CA	95370	**800-800-0490**	209-532-0361
Contract Land Staff LLC					
2245 Texas Dr Ste 200	Sugar Land	TX	77479	**800-874-4519**	281-240-3370
CoreTech					
550 American Ave Ste 301	King of Prussia	PA	19406	**800-220-3337**	
Cornerstone Systems Inc					
3250 Players Club Pkwy	Memphis	TN	38125	**800-278-7677**	901-842-0660
Corporate Executive Board Co					
1919 N Lynn St	Arlington	VA	22209	**866-913-2632**	571-303-3000
NYSE: IT					
Corridor Group Inc, The					
6405 Metcalf Ste 108	Overland Park	KS	66202	**866-263-3795**	
Crandall Engineering Ltd					
1077 St George Blvd	Moncton	NB	E1E4C9	**866-857-2777**	506-857-2777
Creative Educational Concepts Inc					
501 Darby Creek Dr Unit 15	Lexington	KY	40509	**866-226-9650**	859-260-1717
Cso Insights					
36 Tamal Vista Blvd	Corte Madera	CA	94925	**877-506-2975**	
CU America Financial Services Inc					
200 W 22nd St Ste 280	Lombard	IL	60148	**800-351-0449**	630-620-5200
D Hilton Associates Inc					
9450 Grogans Mill Rd Ste 200	The Woodlands	TX	77380	**800-367-0433**	281-292-5088
Danville Signal Processing Inc					
38570 100th Ave	Cannon Falls	MN	55009	**877-230-5629**	507-263-5854
Data Partners					
12857 Banyan Creek Dr	Fort Myers	FL	33908	**866-423-1818**	
DELLEMC					
6801 Koll Ctr Pkwy	Pleasanton	CA	94566	**866-438-3622**	
Diversified Lenders Inc					
5607 S Ave Q	Lubbock	TX	79412	**800-288-3024**	806-795-7782
DM Transportation Management Services Inc					
740 Reading Ave	Boyertown	PA	19512	**888-399-0162**	610-367-0162
DME-Direct Inc					
28486 Westinghouse Pl Ste 120	Valencia	CA	91355	**877-721-7701**	
ECG Management Consultants					
1111 Third Ave Ste 2500	Seattle	WA	98101	**800-729-7635**	206-689-2200
Echo Global Logistics Inc					
600 W Chicago Ave Ste 725	Chicago	IL	60654	**800-354-7993**	
Effective Training Inc					
14143 Farmington Rd	Livonia	MI	48154	**800-886-0909**	
eHDL Inc 3106 Commerce Pkwy	Miramar	FL	33025	**800-338-1079**	
Ehlers & Assoc Inc					
3060 Centre Pointe Dr	Roseville	MN	55113	**800-552-1171**	651-697-8500
England Logistics Inc					
1325 South 4700 West	Salt Lake City	UT	84104	**800-848-7810**	801-656-4500
EP Wealth Advisors Inc					
21515 Hawthorne Blvd Ste 1200	Torrance	CA	90503	**800-272-2328**	310-543-4559
Eubel Brady & Suttman Asset Management Inc					
10100 Innovation Dr Ste 410	Dayton	OH	45342	**800-391-1223**	937-291-1223
Evensky & Katz LLC					
4000 Ponce de Leon Blvd Ste 850	Coral Gables	FL	33146	**800-448-5435**	305-448-8882
Extra Mile Mktg Inc					
12600 SE 38th St Ste 205	Bellevue	WA	98006	**866-907-1753**	425-746-1572
Faulk & Winkler LLC					
6811 Jefferson Hwy	Baton Rouge	LA	70806	**800-927-6811**	225-927-6811
First Command Financial Services Inc					
1 FirstComm Plz	Fort Worth	TX	76109	**800-443-2104**	817-731-8621
Fisher & Arnold Inc					
9180 Crestwyn Hills Dr	Memphis	TN	38125	**888-583-9724**	901-748-1811

Company / Address	City	State	Zip	Toll-Free	Phone
Flex-Pay Business Services Inc 723 Coliseum Dr Ste 200	Winston-Salem	NC	27106	**800-457-2143**	336-773-0128
Franchoice Inc 7500 Flying Cloud Dr Ste 600	Eden Prairie	MN	55344	**888-307-1371**	952-345-8400
Front Runner Consulting LLC 6850 O'Bannon Bluff	Loveland	OH	45140	**877-328-3360**	513-697-6850
Fusion Solutions Inc 16200 Addison Rd Ste 250	Addison	TX	75001	**888-817-1951**	972-764-1708
Geneva Capital LLC 522 Broadway St Ste 4	Alexandria	MN	56308	**800-408-9352**	
Genex Services Inc 440 E Swedesford Rd Ste 1000	Wayne	PA	19087	**888-464-3639**	610-964-5100
GEOSYS Inc 3030 Harbor Ln	Plymouth	MN	55447	**866-782-4661**	
Great Plains Tribal Chairmen's Health Board 1770 Rand Rd	Rapid City	SD	57702	**800-745-3466**	605-721-1922
Greater New York Dental Meeting 200 W 41st St Ste 800	New York	NY	10036	**844-797-7469**	212-398-6922
Greek Peak Mountain Resort 2000 NYS Rt 392	Cortland	NY	13045	**855-677-7927**	
Greenwich Assoc LLC 6 High Ridge Park	Stamford	CT	06905	**800-704-1027**	203-629-1200
GREYHAWK 2000 Midlantic Dr Ste 210	Mount Laurel	NJ	08054	**888-280-4295**	516-921-1900
Halo Group LLC 39475 13 Mile Rd Ste 201	Novi	MI	48377	**877-456-4256**	
Hay Group Inc 1650 Arch St	Philadelphia	PA	19103	**800-716-4429**	215-861-2000
Health Integrated 10008 N Dale Mabry Hwy	Tampa	FL	33618	**877-267-7577**	
Healthforce Partners Inc 18323 Bothell Everett Hwy	Bothell	WA	98012	**877-437-2497**	425-806-5700
Herbal Magic Inc 1867 Yonge St Ste 700	Toronto	ON	M4S1Y5	**866-514-0786**	
Horan Capital Management LLC 20 Wight Ave Ste 115	Hunt Valley	MD	21030	**800-592-7534**	410-494-4380
Human Resource Development Press Inc 22 Amherst Rd	Amherst	MA	01002	**800-822-2801**	
IBT Enterprises LLC 1770 Indian Trail Rd Ste 300	Norcross	GA	30093	**877-242-8428**	770-381-2023
Independents Service Co 2710 Market St	Hannibal	MO	63401	**800-325-3694**	573-221-4615
Innovative Resources Consultant Group Inc 1 Park Plz Ste 600	Irvine	CA	92614	**800-945-4724**	949-252-0590
Interaction Assoc 70 Fargo St Ste 908	Boston	MA	02210	**800-625-8049**	
Irvine Technology Corp 17900 Von Karman Ste 100	Irvine	CA	92614	**866-322-4482**	
iWay Software 2 Penn Plz	New York	NY	10121	**800-736-6130***	212-736-4433
*Sales					
John M Floyd & Associates Inc (JMFA) 125 N Burnett Dr	Baytown	TX	77520	**800-809-2307**	281-424-3800
Kepner-Tregoe Inc PO Box 704	Princeton	NJ	08542	**800-537-6378**	609-921-2806
Kline & Company Inc 35 Waterview Blvd Ste 305	Parsippany	NJ	07054	**800-290-5214**	973-435-6262
Knight Electronics Inc 10557 Metric Dr	Dallas	TX	75243	**800-323-2439**	214-340-0265
Knowledge Anywhere Inc 3015 112th Ave NE #210	Bellevue	WA	98004	**800-850-2025**	
Kroll Inc 600 Third Ave	New York	NY	10016	**800-675-3772**	212-593-1000
Lamont Engineers 548 Main St	Cobleskill	NY	12043	**800-882-9721**	518-234-4028
Larrabee Ventures Inc 15165 Ventura Blvd Ste 450	Sherman Oaks	CA	91403	**800-232-3584**	
LEK Consulting 28 State St 16th Fl	Boston	MA	02109	**800-929-4535**	617-951-9500
Leuthold Weeden Capital Management LLC 33 S Sixth St Ste 4600	Minneapolis	MN	55402	**800-273-6886**	612-332-9141
Lewin Group 3130 Fairview Pk Dr Ste 800	Falls Church	VA	22042	**877-227-5042**	703-269-5500
LexiCode 100 Executive Center Dr Ste 101	Columbia	SC	29210	**800-448-2633**	
LifeSafe Services LLC 5971 Powers Ave Ste 108	Jacksonville	FL	32217	**888-767-0050**	
Lyndacom Inc 6410 Via Real	Carpinteria	CA	93013	**888-335-9632**	805-477-3900
Manex Resource Group Inc 1100 - 1199 W Hastings St	Vancouver	BC	V6E3T5	**888-456-1112**	604-684-9384
Mariner Wealth Advisors 1 Giralda Farms Ste 130	Madison	NJ	07940	**800-364-2468**	
Marsh Berry & Company Inc 4420 Sherwin Rd	Willoughby	OH	44094	**800-426-2774**	440-354-3230
Marshall & Stevens Inc 601 S Figueroa St Ste 2301	Los Angeles	CA	90017	**800-950-9588**	213-612-8000
MBL International Corp 4 H Constitution Way	Woburn	MA	01801	**800-200-5459**	
McBee Assoc Inc 997 Old Eagle School Rd	Wayne	PA	19087	**800-767-6203**	610-964-9680
McDonald Partners LLC 1301 E Ninth St Ste 3700	Cleveland	OH	44114	**866-899-2997**	216-912-0567
MedExpert International Inc 1300 Hancock St	Redwood City	CA	94063	**800-999-1999**	650-326-6000
Medical Doctor Assoc 4775 Peachtree Industrial Blvd Ste 300	Norcross	GA	30092	**800-780-3500**	
Medlink Corp 10393 San Diego Mission Rd Ste 120	San Diego	CA	92108	**800-452-2400**	619-640-4660
MilesTek Corp 1506 I-35 W	Denton	TX	76207	**800-958-5173**	940-484-9400
Milliman USA 1301 Fifth Ave Ste 3800	Seattle	WA	98101	**866-767-1212**	206-624-7940
Mindlance 80 River St 4th Fl	Hoboken	NJ	07030	**877-965-2623**	
MMC Group LP 105 Decker Ct Ste 1100	Irving	TX	75062	**800-779-2505**	972-893-0100
Monroe Financial Partners Inc 100 N Riverside Plz Ste 1620	Chicago	IL	60606	**800-766-5560**	312-327-2530
Moulton Logistics Management 7850 Ruffner Ave	Van Nuys	CA	91406	**800-808-3304**	
MultiLingual Solutions Inc 22 W Jefferson St Ste 404	Rockville	MD	20850	**800-815-1964**	301-424-7444
Mx Group, The 7020 High Grove Blvd	Burr Ridge	IL	60527	**800-827-0170**	
Mzinga 10 Mall Rd	Burlington	MA	01803	**888-694-6428**	
Navitaire LLC 333 S Seventh St Ste 1700	Minneapolis	MN	55402	**877-216-6787**	612-317-7000
Netspeed Learning Solutions 6245 36th Ave NE	Seattle	WA	98115	**877-517-5271**	206-517-5271
Network Innovations Inc 4424 Manilla Rd SE	Calgary	AB	T2G4B7	**888-466-2772**	403-287-5000
New Benefits Ltd 14240 Proton Rd	Dallas	TX	75244	**800-800-8304**	972-404-8192
North Central Pennsylvania Regional Planning & Development Commission 651 Montmorenci Rd	Ridgway	PA	15853	**800-942-9467**	814-773-3162
O'Neill & Assoc LLC 617 646 1000 Thirty-One New Chardon St	Boston	MA	02114	**866-989-4321**	617-646-1000
Oakwood Capital Management LLC 12121 Wilshire Blvd Ste 1250	Los Angeles	CA	90025	**800-586-0600**	310-772-2600
Organizational Dynamics Inc 790 Boston Rd Ste 201	Billerica	MA	01821	**800-634-4636**	978-671-5454
Orion Development Group 177 Beach 116th St Ste 4	Rockaway Park	NY	11694	**800-510-2117**	718-474-4600
OZ Systems Inc 2201 E Lamar Blvd Ste 260	Arlington	TX	76006	**888-727-3366**	
Pacrim Hospitality Services Inc 30 Damascus Rd	Bedford	NS	B4A0C1	**800-561-7666**	
Paric Corp 77 Westport Plz Ste 250	St. Louis	MO	63146	**800-500-4320**	636-561-9500
Parsec Financial Management Inc 6 Wall St	Asheville	NC	28801	**888-877-1012**	828-255-0271
Patten & Patten Inc 520 Lookout St	Chattanooga	TN	37403	**800-757-3480**	423-756-3480
Penske Vehicle Services Inc 1225 E Maple Rd	Troy	MI	48083	**877-210-5290**	248-729-5400
Perry Johnson Registrars Inc 755 W Big Beaver Rd Ste 1340	Southfield	MI	48084	**800-800-7910**	248-358-3388
Philip Crosby Assoc 306 Dartmouth St	Boston	MA	02116	**877-276-7295**	
Pindler & Pindler Inc 11910 Poindexter Ave	Moorpark	CA	93021	**800-669-6002**	805-531-9090
Pinnacle Management Systems Inc 2140 East Southlake Blvd Ste L-803	Southlake	TX	76092	**888-975-1119**	703-382-9161
Plan Administrators Inc 1300 Enterprise Dr	De Pere	WI	54115	**800-236-7400**	
Presidio Group, The 6967 S River Gate Dr Ste 200	Salt Lake City	UT	84047	**800-924-1404**	801-924-1400
Press Ganey Associates Inc 404 Columbia Pl	South Bend	IN	46601	**800-232-8032**	
Pritchett LLC 8150 N Central Expy Ste 1350	Dallas	TX	75206	**800-992-5922**	214-239-9600
Professional Bank Services Inc 6200 Dutchmans Ln Ste 305	Louisville	KY	40205	**800-523-4778**	502-451-6633
Professional Research Consultants Inc 11326 P St	Omaha	NE	68137	**800-428-7455**	402-592-5656
Program Planning Professionals 1340 Eisenhower Pl	Ann Arbor	MI	48108	**877-728-2331**	734-741-7770
Progressive Mktg Products Inc 2620 Palisades Dr	Corona	CA	92882	**800-368-9700**	714-632-7100
Propel Tax PO Box 100350	San Antonio	TX	78201	**877-324-8445**	
Protected Investors of America Inc 235 Montgomery St Ste 1050	San Francisco	CA	94104	**800-786-2559**	
PsyMax Solutions LLC 25550 Chagrin Blvd Ste 100	Cleveland	OH	44122	**866-774-2273**	216-896-9991
Public Consulting Group Inc 148 State St	Boston	MA	02109	**800-210-6113**	
Quadel Consulting 1200 G St NW Ste 700	Washington	DC	20005	**866-640-1019**	202-789-2500
Quality Built LLC 401 SE 12th St Ste 200	Fort Lauderdale	FL	33316	**800-547-5125**	954-358-3500
Quality Group Inc, The 5825 Glenridge Dr NE Bldg 3 Ste 101	Atlanta	GA	30328	**800-772-3071**	404-843-9525
R W Rog & Company Inc 630 Johnson Ave Ste 103	Bohemia	NY	11716	**877-218-0085**	631-218-0077
Radio Communications Co 8035 Chapel Hill Rd	Cary	NC	27513	**800-508-7580**	919-467-2421
Reed Group 10355 Westmoor Dr Ste 210	Westminster	CO	80021	**800-347-7443**	
Reliability Center 501 Westover Ave	Hopewell	VA	23860	**800-457-0645**	804-458-0645
Robert E Nolan Company Inc 92 Hopmeadow St	Weatogue	CT	06089	**800-653-1941**	877-736-6526
Robson Forensic Inc 354 N Prince St	Lancaster	PA	17603	**800-813-6736**	717-293-9050
Roscoe Medical Inc 21973 Commerce Pkwy	Strongsville	OH	44149	**800-376-7263**	440-572-1962
Rose Displays Ltd 500 Narragansett Park Dr	Pawtucket	RI	02861	**888-452-9528**	
Sapient Corp 131 Dartmouth St	Boston	MA	02116	**866-796-6860**	617-621-0200
SeaMates International Inc 316 Main St PO Box 436	East Rutherford	NJ	07073	**800-541-4538**	201-896-8899
Secova Inc 3090 Bristol St Ste 200	Costa Mesa	CA	92626	**877-632-8122**	
Self Opportunity Inc 808 Office Park Cir	Lewisville	TX	75057	**800-594-7036**	214-222-1500
Sequent Energy Management 1200 Smith St	Houston	TX	77002	**866-581-8074**	832-397-1700
Sharkey Howes & Javer Inc 720 S Colorado Blvd Ste 600 S Twr	Denver	CO	80246	**800-557-9380**	303-639-5100
Sierra Group, The 588 N Gulph Rd # 110	King Of Prussia	PA	19406	**800-973-7687**	610-992-0288
Signature Inc 5115 Parkcenter Ave	Dublin	OH	43017	**800-398-0518**	614-766-5101
Simply Healthcare Plans Inc 1701 Ponce De Leon Blvd Ste 300	Coral Gables	FL	33134	**877-577-9042**	305-408-5890

				Toll-Free	Phone
Ssci 3065 Kent Ave	West Lafayette	IN	47906	**800-375-2179**	765-463-0112
Stertil-Koni USA Inc					
200 Log Canoe Cir	Stevensville	MD	21666	**800-336-6637**	410-643-9001
Tbm Consulting Group Inc					
4400 Ben Franklin Blvd	Durham	NC	27704	**800-438-5535**	919-471-5535
TheraTogs Inc					
305 Society Dr Ste 3-C	Telluride	CO	81435	**888-634-0495**	
Thyssen Krupp Hearn					
59 I- Dr	Wentzville	MO	63385	**877-854-7178**	636-332-1772
Tom McCall & Assoc Inc					
20180 Governors Hwy Ste 100	Olympia Fields	IL	60461	**800-715-5474**	708-747-5707
Tompkins International					
6870 Perry Creek Rd	Raleigh	NC	27616	**800-789-1257**	919-876-3667
Traffic Management Inc					
8862 W 35W Service Dr NE	Minneapolis	MN	55449	**888-726-9559**	763-544-3455
Travelclick					
7 Times Sq 38th Fl	New York	NY	10036	**866-674-4549**	212-817-4800
Valcom Consulting Group Inc					
85 Albert St	Ottawa	ON	K1P6A4	**866-561-5580**	613-594-5200
Vawter Financial Ltd					
1161 Bethel Rd Ste 304	Columbus	OH	43220	**800-955-1575**	614-451-1002
VerisVisalign					
920 S Broad St	Lansdale	PA	19446	**888-458-3747**	267-649-8001
Verity International Ltd					
200 King St W Ste 1301	Toronto	ON	M5H3T4	**877-623-2396**	416-862-8422
Watermark Capital Partners LLC					
150 North Riverside Plz Ste 4200	Chicago	IL	60606	**800-321-2211**	847-482-8600
Watermark Learning Inc					
7300 Metro Blvd Ste 207	Minneapolis	MN	55439	**800-646-9362**	952-921-0900
We Check Inc					
301 Moodie Dr Ste 320	Ottawa	ON	K2H9C4	**877-889-0602**	
Welocalize Inc					
241 E Fourth St Ste 207	Frederick	MD	21701	**800-370-9515**	301-668-0330
West Monroe Partners LLC					
222 W Adams St	Chicago	IL	60606	**800-828-6708**	312-602-4000
Westcare Management Inc					
3155 River Rd S Ste 100	Salem	OR	97302	**800-541-3732**	
White Oaks Wealth Advisors Inc					
80 S Eighth St IDS Ctr Ste 1725	Minneapolis	MN	55402	**800-596-3579**	612-455-6900
Wind River Financial Inc					
65 Buttonwood Ct	Madison	WI	53718	**866-356-0837**	

195   CONSULTING SERVICES - MARKETING

				Toll-Free	Phone
220 Group LLC, The					
3405 Kenyon St Ste 301	San Diego	CA	92110	**877-220-6584**	619-758-9696
360 Business Consulting					
1576 N Batavia Ave	Orange	CA	92867	**877-360-2492**	949-916-9120
7Summits LLC					
1110 Old World Third St Ste 500	Milwaukee	WI	53203	**866-705-6372**	877-803-9286
AcrobatAnt LLC 1336 E 15th St	Tulsa	OK	74120	**800-984-7239**	918-938-7901
Adams Direct & Media Services					
39 Faranella Dr	East Hanover	NJ	07936	**800-631-6245**	
Affirmative LLC					
11416 Hollister Dr	Austin	TX	78739	**866-966-9968**	
Advisors Excel LLC					
1300 SW Arrowhead Rd Ste 200	Topeka	KS	66604	**866-363-9595**	
AIS RealTime					
4440 Bowen Blvd SE	Grand Rapids	MI	49508	**877-314-1100**	
Apex Asset Management LLC					
2501 Oregon Pk Ste 201	Lancaster	PA	17601	**888-592-2149**	717-519-1770
Applied Marketing Research Inc					
420 W 98th St	Kansas City	MO	64114	**800-381-5599**	
Avideon Corp PO Box 4830	Baltimore	MD	21211	**888-368-1237**	
Bates Communications Inc					
40 Grove St Ste 310	Wellesley	MA	02482	**800-908-8239**	
Bayforce					
5100 W Kennedy Blvd Ste 425	Tampa	FL	33609	**877-642-4727**	
BCG Connect					
755 Middlesex Tpke	Billerica	MA	01821	**800-767-0067**	
BDS Marketing LLC 10 Holland	Irvine	CA	92618	**800-234-4237**	
Bellomy Research Inc					
175 Sunnynoll Ct	Winston-Salem	NC	27106	**800-443-7344**	
Beverage Marketing Corp					
850 Third Ave Ste 13C	New York	NY	10022	**800-275-4630**	212-688-7640
Birthday In A Box Inc					
7951 Cessna Ave	Gaithersburg	MD	20879	**800-237-6545**	
BMA Communications LLC					
15184 Hawk	St Fontana	CA	92336	**800-850-4262**	
Boost Rewards					
811 E Fourth St Ste B	Dayton	OH	45402	**800-324-9756**	
Brand Iron 821 22nd St	Denver	CO	80205	**800-343-6405**	303-534-1901
Brand Protection Agency LLC					
8750 N Central Expwy Ste 720	Dallas	TX	75231	**866-339-5657**	
Carey Color Inc					
6835 Ridge Rd	Wadsworth	OH	44281	**800-555-3142**	330-239-1835
Cargo Management Systems Llc					
827 E Main St	Richmond	KY	40475	**855-484-9235**	
Cdr Assessment Group Inc					
1644 S Denver Ave	Tulsa	OK	74119	**888-406-0100**	918-488-0722
Ceridian Benefits Services Inc					
3201 34th St S	St. Petersburg	FL	33711	**800-689-7893**	
Classical Marketing LLC					
2300 Cabot Dr Ste 390	Lisle	IL	60532	**800-613-3489**	847-969-1696
ComStar Networks LLC					
1820 NE Jensen Beach Blvd Ste 564	Jensen Beach	FL	34957	**800-516-1595**	
Concentrix Corp					
44201 Nobel Dr	Fremont	CA	94538	**800-747-0583**	
Cortac Group					
609 Deep Valley Dr Ste 200	Rolling Hills Estates	CA	90274	**877-216-1717**	
Creor Group					
952 School St Ste 310	Napa	CA	94559	**877-774-4312**	
Crossmark Inc 5100 Legacy Dr	Plano	TX	75024	**877-699-6275**	469-814-1000

				Toll-Free	Phone
d50 Media					
1330 Boylston St Ste 200	Chestnut Hill	MA	02461	**800-582-9606**	
Dane Media					
170 NE Second St Ste 394	Boca Raton	FL	33429	**888-233-2863**	
Data Banque Ltd					
4117 Liberty Ave	Pittsburgh	PA	15224	**877-860-2702**	
De Kadt Marketing & Research Inc					
162 Danbury Rd	Ridgefield	CT	06877	**800-243-2991**	203-431-1212
Do My Own Pest Control					
4260 Communications Dr	Norcross	GA	30093	**866-581-7378**	
Driveline Holdings Inc					
700 Freeport Pkwy Ste 100	Coppell	TX	75019	**888-824-7505**	
ebQuickstart					
3000 S IH 35 Ste 320	Austin	TX	78704	**800-566-3050**	512-637-9696
Eclipse Marketing Services Inc					
240 Cedar Knolls Rd Ste 100	Cedar Knolls	NJ	07927	**800-837-4648**	
Edufficient Inc					
6 Forest Ave 2nd Fl.	Paramus	NJ	07652	**888-648-1811**	201-881-0030
Egroup Inc					
482 Wando Park Blvd	Mount Pleasant	SC	29464	**877-347-6871**	
eGumBall Inc					
7525 Irvine Ctr Dr Ste 100	Irvine	CA	92618	**800-890-8940**	
Environics Analytics Group Ltd					
33 Bloor St E Ste 400	Toronto	ON	M4W3H1	**888-339-3304**	416-969-2733
EtQ Management Consultants Inc					
399 Conklin St Ste 208.	Farmingdale	NY	11735	**800-354-4476**	516-293-0949
Eze Castle Integration Inc					
260 Franklin St 12th Fl	Boston	MA	02110	**800-752-1382**	617-217-3000
FarmLink Marketing Solutions Inc					
93 Lombard Ave Ste 110	Winnipeg	MB	R3B3B1	**877-376-5465**	
Finity Inc					
1200 NW Natio Pkwy Ste 220	Portland	OR	97209	**800-509-1346**	503-808-9240
firstSTREET for Boomers & Beyond Inc					
1998 Ruffin Mill Rd	Colonial Heights	VA	23834	**800-958-8324**	804-524-9888
Flexi Display Marketing Inc					
24669 Halsted Rd	Farmington Hills	MI	48335	**800-875-1725**	248-987-6400
Frantz Group Inc, The					
1245 Cheyenne Ave	Grafton	WI	53024	**800-707-0064**	262-204-6000
FuelFX LLC 1811 Bering Dr	Houston	TX	77057	**855-472-7316**	
G3 Communications					
777 Terrace Ave Ste 202	Hasbrouck Heights	NJ	07604	**888-603-3626**	
GoalLine Solutions					
3115 Harvester Rd Ste 200	Burlington	ON	L7N3H8	**866-788-4625**	
Great Falls Marketing LLC					
121 Mill St	Auburn	ME	04210	**800-221-8895**	
Haley Marketing Group					
6028 Sheridan Dr PO Box 410	Williamsville	NY	14221	**888-696-2900**	
Hansa GCR LLC					
308 SW First Ave	Portland	OR	97204	**800-755-7683**	503-241-8036
HatchBeauty LLC					
10951 W Pico Blvd Ste 300	Los Angeles	CA	90064	**855-895-6980**	
Hcpro Inc					
75 Sylvan St Ste A-10.	Danvers	MA	01923	**800-650-6787**	
Hollis Marketing					
2130 Brenner St	Saginaw	MI	48602	**866-797-3301**	989-797-3300
Hunter Business Group LLC					
4650 N Port Washington Rd	Milwaukee	WI	53212	**800-423-4010**	
ICS Marketing Services Inc					
4225 Legacy Pkwy	Lansing	MI	48911	**888-394-1890**	517-394-1890
Inquiry Systems Inc					
1195 Goodale Blvd	Columbus	OH	43212	**800-508-1116**	614-464-3800
Integrity Marketing Solutions					
1311 Interquest Pkwy Ste 215	Colorado Springs	CO	80921	**877-352-2021**	
Invenio Marketing Solutions Inc					
2201 Donley Dr Ste 200	Austin	TX	78758	**800-926-1754**	
J Knipper & Company Inc					
1 Healthcare Way	Lakewood	NJ	08701	**888-564-7737**	
JHL Digital Direct					
3100 Borham Ave	Stevens Point	WI	54481	**800-236-0581**	715-341-0581
Kenneth Clark Company Inc					
10264 Baltimore National Pk	Ellicott City	MD	21042	**866-999-5116**	410-465-5116
Khong Guan Corp					
30068 Eigenbrodt Way	Union City	CA	94587	**877-889-8968**	510-487-7800
Kombi 5711 Ferrier St	Montreal	QC	H4P1N3	**800-203-0695**	514-341-4321
Kotler Marketing Group					
3509 Connecticut Ave Ste 1175	Washington	DC	20008	**800-331-9110**	202-331-0555
LandaJob					
222 W Gregory Blvd Ste 304	Kansas City	MO	64114	**800-931-8806**	816-523-1881
Lawgical Inc					
11693 San Vicente Blvd Ste 910.	Los Angeles	CA	90049	**800-811-4458**	
Legendary Marketing					
3729 S Lecanto Hwy	Lecanto	FL	34461	**800-827-1663**	352-527-3553
Lionshare Marketing Inc					
7830 Barton St	Overland Park	KS	66214	**800-928-0712**	913-631-8400
LOC Enterprises LLC					
7575 E Kemper Rd	Cincinnati	OH	45249	**888-963-6320**	
Magnets Usa					
817 Connecticut Ave NE	Roanoke	VA	24012	**800-869-7562**	
Mapping Analytics LLC					
120 Allens Creek Rd Ste 10	Rochester	NY	14618	**877-893-6490**	
MarketingProfs LLC					
419 N Larchmont Blvd #295	Los Angeles	CA	90004	**866-557-9625**	
Mcdaniels Marketing Communications					
11 Olt Ave	Pekin	IL	61554	**866-431-4230**	309-346-4230
Meridian One Corp					
5775 General Washington Dr	Alexandria	VA	22312	**800-636-2377**	
Missouri Enterprise					
900 Innovation Dr Ste 300	Rolla	MO	65401	**800-956-2682**	
Mpell Solutions LLC					
3142 Tiger Run Ct Ste 108	Carlsbad	CA	92010	**800-450-1575**	760-727-9600
Nelson Ink					
330 Second St N	Middle River	MN	56737	**800-644-9311**	218-222-3831
Netmarkcom					
3135 E 17th St Ste B.	Ammon	ID	83406	**800-935-5133**	208-522-1016
Netsertive Inc					
2400 Perimeter Park Dr Ste 100	Research Triangle Region	NC	27560	**800-940-4351**	

Company / Address	City	State	ZIP	Toll-Free	Phone
NexAge Technologies USA Inc 75 Lincoln Hwy Ste 101	Iselin	NJ	08830	866-866-5800	732-494-4944
NKP Medical Marketing Inc 8939 S Sepulveda Blvd Ste 320	Los Angeles	CA	90045	866-539-2201	
Notions Marketing Corp 1500 Buchanan Ave SW	Grand Rapids	MI	49507	800-748-0250	616-243-8424
NuGrowth Solutions 4181 ArlingGate Plz	Columbus	OH	43228	800-966-3051	
Oil Can Henry's 19150 SW 90th Ave	Tualatin	OR	97062	800-765-6244	503-783-3888
Opus Agency 9000 SW Nimbus Ave	Beaverton	OR	97008	888-887-8908	971-223-0777
OutboundEngine 98 San Jacinto Blvd Ste 1300	Austin	TX	78701	800-562-7315	
PDI 100 American Metro Blvd Ste 201	Hamilton	NJ	08619	800-242-7494	215-525-5207
Pedowitz Group, The 810 Mayfield Rd	Milton	GA	30009	855-738-6584	
PharmaCentra LLC 105 Industrial Dr	Americus	GA	31719	866-395-0088	
PharMethod Inc 1170 Wheeler Way	Langhorne	PA	19047	877-200-0736	215-354-1212
Piranha Marketing Inc 4440 S Rural Rd Bldg F	Tempe	AZ	85282	800-275-2643	480-858-0008
Premier Direct Marketing Inc 5051 Commerce Crossings Dr	Louisville	KY	40229	800-737-0205	502-367-6441
Prime Concepts Group Inc 1807 S Eisenhower St	Wichita	KS	67209	800-946-7804	316-942-1111
Printfection LLC 3700 Quebec St Unit 100-136	Denver	CO	80207	866-459-7990	
Pro-mail Associates Inc 22404 66th Ave S	Kent	WA	98032	855-867-5081	253-867-5081
Punchkick Interactive Inc 150 N Michigan Ave Ste 3900	Chicago	IL	60601	800-549-4104	
Quala-Tel Enterprises 9925 Business Park Ave Ste A	San Diego	CA	92131	800-442-1504	858-577-2900
Quintevents LLC 9300 Harris Corners Pkwy Ste 120	Charlotte	NC	28269	866-834-8663	
Ramapo Sales & Marketing Inc 4760 Goer Dr Ste F	North Charleston	SC	29406	800-866-9173	
Regalix Inc 1121 San Antonio Rd Ste B200	Palo Alto	CA	94303	888-683-4875	631-230-2629
Rely Services Inc 957 N Plum Grove Rd Ste B	Schaumburg	IL	60173	866-735-9328	847-310-8750
REVShare Corp 32836 Wolf Store Rd	Temecula	CA	92592	800-819-9945	
Rocket Media Inc 3335 E Baseline Rd	Gilbert	AZ	85234	800-339-7305	
Rymax Marketing Services Inc 19 Chapin Rd Bldg B PO Box 2024	Pine Brook	NJ	07058	866-796-2911	
Sales Readiness Group Inc 8015 SE 28th St Ste 200	Mercer Island	WA	98040	800-490-0715	206-905-8756
School Photo Marketing 200 D Campus Dr	Morganville	NJ	07751	877-543-9742	732-431-0440
Senior Marketing Specialist 801 Gray Oak Dr	Columbia	MO	65201	800-689-2800	
Signet Inc 1801 Shelby Oaks Dr Ste 12	Memphis	TN	38134	800-654-3889	
Skillpath Seminars 6900 Squibb Rd	Mission	KS	66202	800-873-7545	
Sky High Marketing 3550 E Post Rd	Las Vegas	NV	89120	800-246-7447	702-436-0867
Snipp Interactive Inc 530 Richmond St W Rear Lower Level	Toronto	ON	M5V1K4	888-997-6477	
Starmark International Inc 210 S Andrews Ave	Fort Lauderdale	FL	33301	888-280-9630	954-874-9000
Stevenson & Vestal 2347 W Hanford Rd	Burlington	NC	27215	800-535-3636	
Stone Coast Fund Services LLC 2 Portland Sq	Portland	ME	04101	888-699-2680	207-699-2680
Stoptech Ltd 365 Industrial Dr	Harrison	OH	45030	800-537-0102	513-202-5500
Strider 6-6150 Hwy 7 Ste 400	Woodbridge	ON	L4H0R6	800-314-8895	416-502-8895
Stuart Maue Mitchell & James Ltd 3840 McKelvey Rd	St. Louis	MO	63044	800-291-9940	
Suarez Corp Industries 7800 Whipple Ave NW	North Canton	OH	44720	800-764-0008	330-494-5504
Swiss Knife Shop 10 Northern Blvd Ste 8	Amherst	NH	03031	866-438-7947	603-732-0069
Symbolist 1090 Texan Trl	Grapevine	TX	76051	800-498-6885	
Synergy Direct Response 130 E Alton Ave	Santa Ana	CA	92707	888-902-6166	
Tactician Corp 305 N Main St	Andover	MA	01810	800-927-7666	978-475-4475
TASC Technical Services LLC 73 Newton Rd	Plaistow	NH	03865	877-304-8272	
Technical Communities Inc 1111 Bayhill Dr Ste 400	San Bruno	CA	94066	888-665-2765	650-624-0525
Transcosmos America Inc 879 W 190th St Ste 410	Gardena	CA	90248	844-630-2224	
Tvc Marketing 3200 W Wilshire Blvd	Oklahoma City	OK	73116	800-227-6459	405-843-2722
V-fluence Interactive 4579 Laclede Ave Ste 275	St. Louis	MO	63108	877-835-8362	
Venture Solutions Inc 1170 Grey Fox Rd	Arden Hills	MN	55112	800-728-2615	651-494-1740
W Ca Logistics LLC 643 Bodey Cir	Urbana	OH	43078	800-860-7838	937-653-6382
Wayne Reaves Software & Websites Inc 6211 Thomaston Rd	Macon	GA	31220	888-477-9707	
WebiMaxcom 2 Aquarium Loop Dr Ste 140	Camden	NJ	08103	888-932-4629	856-840-8301
Winn Technology Group Inc 523 Palm Harbor Blvd	Palm Harbor	FL	34683	800-444-5622	
WSI 20 Carlson Ct Ste 100	Mississauga	ON	M9W7K6	888-678-7588	905-678-7588
York Solutions 1 Westbrook Corporate Ctr Ste 910	Westchester	IL	60154	877-700-9675	708-531-8362
Zonic Design & Imaging Llc 875 Mahler Rd Ste 238	Burlingame	CA	94010	877-349-6642	415-643-3700

196 CONSULTING SERVICES - TELECOMMUNICATIONS

Company / Address	City	State	ZIP	Toll-Free	Phone
2020 Exhibits Inc 10550 S Sam Huston Pkwy W	Houston	TX	77071	800-856-6659	713-354-0900
360 Cloud Solutions LLC 1475 N Scottsdale Rd	Scottsdale	AZ	85257	800-360-8150	
A3 Communications Inc 1038 Kinley Rd Bldg B	Irmo	SC	29063	888-809-1473	
Aacom Inc 201 Stuyvesant Ave	Lyndhurst	NJ	07071	800-273-3719	201-438-2244
Acceles Inc 13771 N Fountain Hills Blvd Ste 114-115	Fountain Hills	AZ	85268	877-260-6725	
Accent Communication Services Inc 585 Sunbury Rd	Delaware	OH	43015	800-589-7379	740-548-7378
Adelphi Consulting Group Inc 8209 SW Cirrus Dr	Beaverton	OR	97008	800-698-1942	503-641-3501
Advance Communications & Consulting Inc 8803 Swigert Ct Unit A	Bakersfield	CA	93311	800-510-2148	661-664-0177
Aerial Innovations Inc 3703 W Azeele St	Tampa	FL	33609	800-223-1701	813-254-7339
Affinity Inc 10850 W Park Pl Ste 470	Milwaukee	WI	53224	877-399-2220	
Air Chek Inc 1936 Butler Bridge Rd	Mills River	NC	28759	800-247-2435	
Alidade Technology Inc 111 Knoll Dr	Collegeville	PA	19426	877-265-1581	
Amcest Nationwide Monitoring 1017 Walnut St	Roselle	NJ	07203	800-631-7370	
American Ecotech LLC 100 Elm St Factory D	Warren	RI	02885	877-247-0403	
Amplify Education Inc 55 Washington St Ste 800	Brooklyn	NY	11201	800-823-1969	212-213-8177
AMTEL 9707 Key West Ave Ste 202	Rockville	MD	20850	800-989-5566	301-721-3010
Ananke IT Solutions 20 Main St	East Greenwich	RI	02818	877-626-2653	401-331-2780
AppDetex 609 W Main St Ste 202	Boise	ID	83702	855-693-3839	
Arctic Wolf Networks Inc 111 West Evelyn Ave Ste 115	Sunnyvale	CA	94086	888-272-8429	
Astatech Inc 2525 Pearl Buck Rd	Bristol	PA	19007	800-387-2269	215-785-3197
Atlantic Prsnnel Tnant Scrning Inc 8895 N Military Trl Ste 301C	Palm Beach Gardens	FL	33410	877-747-2104	561-776-1804
Avantica Technologies 2680 Bayshore Pkwy Ste 416	Mountain View	CA	94043	877-372-1955	650-248-9678
AXIA Consulting LLC 1391 W Fifth Ave Ste 320	Columbus	OH	43212	866-937-5550	614-675-4050
Baka Communications Inc 630 The East Mall	Etobicoke	ON	M9B4B1	866-884-3329	416-641-2800
Benefitvision Inc 4522 RFD	Long Grove	IL	60047	800-810-2200	877-737-5526
Big Bang ERP Inc 105 De Louvain W	Montreal	QC	H2N1A3	844-361-4408	514-360-4408
Bluecube Information Technology 525 Milltown Rd Ste 301-B	North Brunswick	NJ	08902	888-380-6272	708-325-8328
Bradford & Galt Inc 11457 Olde Cabin Rd Ste 200	Saint Louis	MO	63141	800-997-4644	314-997-4644
Brazos Telecommunications Inc 109 N Ave D	Olney	TX	76374	800-687-3222	940-564-5659
BrightMove Inc 320 High Tide Dr # 201	Saint Augustine	FL	32080	877-482-8840	
BTI Group 4 N Second St Ste 560	San Jose	CA	95113	800-622-0192	408-246-1102
Bugcrowd 921 Front St 1st Fl	San Francisco	CA	94111	888-361-9734	
Canadian Professional Sales Association 310 Front St W Ste 800	Toronto	ON	M5V3B5	888-267-2772	416-408-2685
Canidium LLC 3801 Kirby Dr S456	Houston	TX	77024	877-651-1837	
Cardiff Park Advisors 2257 Vista La Nisa	Carlsbad	CA	92009	888-332-2238	760-635-7526
CareWorks Technologies Ltd 5555 Glendon Ct	Dublin	OH	43016	800-669-9623	
Carnegie East House For Seniors 1844 Second Ave	New York	NY	10128	888-410-0033	212-410-0033
Cash Flow Solutions Inc 5166 College Corner Pk	Oxford	OH	45056	800-736-5123	
Cask LLC 9350 Waxie Way Ste 210	San Diego	CA	92123	866-535-8915	
CCS Presentation Systems Inc 17350 N Hartford Dr	Scottsdale	AZ	85255	800-742-5036	480-348-0100
Celerity Consulting Group Inc 2 Gough St Ste 300	San Francisco	CA	94103	866-224-4333	415-986-8850
Chameleon Group LLC 951 Islington St	Portsmouth	NH	03801	800-773-9182	603-570-4300
Channel Solutions LLC 3145 E Chanl Blvd Ste 110	Phoenix	AZ	85048	866-501-9690	
Chase Enterprises Inc 6509 W Reno Ave	Oklahoma City	OK	73127	800-525-4970	405-495-1722
CHP International Inc 1040 N Blvd Ste 220	Oak Park	IL	60301	800-449-2614	708-848-9650
Cloud 9 Living 11101 W 120th Ave Ste 150	Broomfield	CO	80021	866-525-6839	
Coact Associates Ltd 2748 Centennial Rd	Toledo	OH	43617	866-646-4400	
Comnexia Corp 590 W Crssvlle Rd	Roswell	GA	30075	877-600-6550	
CompuOne Corp 9888 Carroll Centre Rd Ste 201	San Diego	CA	92126	888-226-6781	858-404-7000

	Toll-Free	Phone
Conde Group Inc		
4141 Jutland Dr Ste 130 . . . . San Diego CA 92117	800-838-0819	
ConSova Corp		
1536 Cole Blvd Ste 350 . . . . Lakewood CO 80401	866-529-9107	
Core Management Resources Group Inc		
515 Mulberry St . . . . Macon GA 31201	888-741-2673	478-741-3521
Core Vision IT Solutions		
1266 NW Hwy . . . . Palatine IL 60067	855-788-5835	
Corporate It Solutions Inc		
661 Pleasant St . . . . Norwood MA 02062	888-521-2487	
Cost Control Associates Inc		
310 Bay Rd . . . . Queensbury NY 12804	800-836-3787	518-798-4437
CRM Dynamics		
5800 Ambler Dr Unit 106 . . . . Mississauga ON L5W4J4	866-740-2424	
Crystal Communications Ltd		
1525 Lakeville Dr Ste 230 . . . . Kingwood TX 77339	888-949-6603	281-361-5199
Cycom Canada Corp		
31 Prince Andrew Pl . . . . North York ON M3C2H2	800-268-3171	416-494-5040
Cygnus Systems Inc		
24700 Northwestern Hwy Ste 600 . . . . Southfield MI 48075	800-388-2280	248-557-4600
Data Path 318 McHenry Ave . . . . Modesto CA 95354	888-693-2827	209-521-0055
Datascan LP		
2210 Hutton Dr Ste 100 . . . . Carrollton TX 75006	866-441-4848	
Datashield LLC		
455 E 200 S Ste 100 . . . . Salt Lake City UT 84111	866-428-4567	
Datatel Solutions Inc		
875 Laurel Dr . . . . Roseville CA 95678	888-224-8647	
David Horowitz Freedom Ctr		
PO Box 55089 . . . . Sherman Oaks CA 91499	800-752-6562	
DelaGet LLC		
5320 W 23rd St Ste 140 . . . . St Louis Park MN 55416	888-335-2438	
Delcom Group LP		
2525B E SH 121 Ste 400 . . . . Lewisville TX 75056	800-308-9228	214-389-5500
Delta Risk LLC		
106 S St Mary's St Ste 601 . . . . San Antonio TX 78205	888-763-3582	210-293-0707
Detechtion Technologies		
1100 Eighth Ave SW Ste 277 . . . . Calgary AB T2P3T8	800-780-9798	403-250-9220
Digitek Software Inc		
650 Radio Dr 43035 . . . . Lewis Center OH 43035	888-764-8845	
Dimension Consulting Inc		
501 W Broadway . . . . San Diego CA 92101	855-222-6444	703-636-0933
Directec Corp		
908 Lily Creek Rd Ste 101 . . . . Louisville KY 40243	800-588-7800	502-357-5000
Donnell Systems Inc		
130 S Main St Ste 375 . . . . South Bend IN 46601	800-232-3776	574-232-3784
Donriver Inc 701 Brazos St . . . . Austin TX 78701	866-733-1684	
Due North Consulting Inc		
3112 Blue Lake Dr Ste 110 . . . . Birmingham AL 35243	800-899-2676	205-989-9394
Dynamics Edge Inc		
2635 N First St Ste #148 . . . . San Jose CA 95134	800-453-5961	
EBI Consulting Inc		
21 B St . . . . Burlington MA 01803	800-786-2346	781-273-2500
ECS & R 3237 US Hwy 19 . . . . Cochranton PA 16314	866-815-0016	814-425-7773
ELi Inc		
2675 Paces Ferry Rd SE Ste 470 . . . . Atlanta GA 30339	800-497-7654	770-319-7999
Elk Environmental Services		
1420 Clarion St . . . . Reading PA 19601	800-851-7156	610-372-4760
Ellis		
1333 Corporate Dr Ste 266 . . . . Irving TX 75038	888-988-3767	972-256-3767
ePerformax Contact Centers & BPO		
100 Saddle Springs Blvd		
Ste 100 . . . . Thompsons Station TN 37179	888-384-7004	
Erick Nielsen Enterprises Inc		
4453 County Rd Mm # O . . . . Orland CA 95963	800-844-9409	530-865-9409
ESI Technologies		
1550 Metcalfe St Ste 1100 . . . . Montreal QC H3A1X6	800-260-3311	
Etera Consulting		
1100 17th St NW Ste 605 . . . . Washington DC 20036	800-674-3141	202-349-0177
Fdr & Cp Services Llc		
2503 Tabor Rd . . . . Bryan TX 77803	800-337-5325	
Fentress Inc		
945 Sunset Vly Dr . . . . Sykesville MD 21784	888-329-0040	
Fineline Technologies Inc		
3145 Medlock Bridge Rd . . . . Norcross GA 30071	800-500-8687	678-969-0835
Fortin Consulting Inc		
215 Hamel Rd . . . . Hamel MN 55340	844-273-3117	763-478-3606
Frank Lynn & Associates Inc		
500 Park Blvd Ste 785 . . . . Itasca IL 60143	800-245-5966	312-263-7888
FreshAddress Inc		
36 Crafts St . . . . Newton MA 02458	800-321-3009	
Geo-Comm Inc		
601 W St Germain St . . . . Saint Cloud MN 56301	888-436-2666	
Gift Card Systems Inc		
218 Cedar St . . . . Abilene TX 79601	888-745-4112	
Global Cloud		
30 W Third St Unit 2 . . . . Cincinnati OH 45202	866-244-0450	
Greenbusch Group Inc		
1900 W Nickerson St Ste 201 . . . . Seattle WA 98119	855-476-2874	206-378-0569
Greenview Data Inc		
8178 Jackson Rd . . . . Ann Arbor MI 48103	800-458-3348	734-426-7500
GreyCastle Security LLC		
500 Federal St Ste 540 . . . . Troy NY 12180	800-403-8350	518-274-7233
H3 Solutions Inc		
10432 Balls Ford Rd Ste 230 . . . . Manassas VA 20109	855-464-5914	
HBSC Strategic Services		
100 North Hill Dr Bldg 26 . . . . Brisbane CA 94005	800-970-7995	415-715-8767
HCI Group, The		
6440 Southpoint Pkwy Ste 300 . . . . Jacksonville FL 32216	866-793-2484	904-337-6300
Heritage Global Solutions Inc		
230 N Maryland Ave . . . . Glendale CA 91206	800-915-4474	818-547-4474
HR Focal Point LLC		
3948 Legacy Dr Ste 106 PO Box 369 . . . . Plano TX 75023	855-464-4737	
HRDQ		
827 Lincoln Ave Ste B-10 . . . . West Chester PA 19380	800-633-4533	610-279-2002
Ideal Consulting Services Inco		
521 American Legion Hwy . . . . Westport MA 02790	866-254-6136	508-636-6615
IeSmart Systems LLC		
15200 E Hardy Rd . . . . Houston TX 77032	866-437-6278	281-447-6278
Ifocus Consulting Inc		
100 39th St Ste 201 . . . . Astoria OR 97103	888-308-6192	503-338-7443
Imanami Corp		
2301 Armstrong St Ste 211 . . . . Livermore CA 94551	800-684-8515	925-371-3000
iMethods		
8787 Perimeter Park Blvd . . . . Jacksonville FL 32216	888-306-2261	
Improve Group Inc, The		
661 LaSalle St Ste 300 . . . . St Paul MN 55114	877-467-7847	651-315-8919
Impulse Technologies Ltd		
920 Gana Crt . . . . Mississauga ON L5S1Z4	800-667-5475	905-564-9266
Infotex Inc		
416 Main St Ste 3. . . . . Lafayette IN 47901	800-466-9939	
Integrated Document Technologies Inc (IDT)		
1009 W Hawthorn Dr . . . . Itasca IL 60143	877-722-6438	630-875-1100
Intelestream Inc		
27 North Wacker Dr Ste 370 . . . . Chicago IL 60606	800-391-4055	
Intrinium Inc		
609 N Argonne Rd . . . . Spokane Valley WA 99212	866-461-5099	
Iomosaic Corp 93 Stiles Rd . . . . Salem NH 03079	844-466-6724	603-893-7009
IPC Technologies Inc		
7200 Glen Forest Dr Ste 100 . . . . Richmond VA 23226	877-947-2835	
iStreet Solutions LLC		
1911 Douglas Blvd 85-200 . . . . Roseville CA 95661	866-976-3976	
iT Services 2		
2340 E Trinity Mills Rd Ste 300 . . . . Carrollton TX 75006	877-400-0293	
IT. Blueprint Solutions Consulting Inc		
170-422 Richards St . . . . Vancouver BC V6B2Z4	866-261-8981	
Janalent		
2341 Renaissance DR . . . . Las Vegas NV 89119	888-290-4870	
Jdk Consulting		
4924 Balboa Blvd Ste 487 . . . . Encino CA 91316	855-535-7877	818-705-8050
Jet Logistics Inc		
5400 Airport Dr . . . . Charlotte NC 28208	866-824-9394	
Kaseya Corp		
400 Totten Pond Rd Ste 200 . . . . Waltham MA 02451	877-926-0001	
Kinsbursky Brothers Inc		
125 E Commercial . . . . Anaheim CA 92801	800-548-8797	714-738-8516
Lakeview Professional Services Inc		
104 S Maple St . . . . Corona CA 92880	800-287-1371	951-371-3390
Laminar Consulting Services		
424 S Olive St . . . . Orange CA 92866	888-531-9995	
LAURUS Systems Inc		
3460 Ellicott Ctr Dr Ste 101 . . . . Ellicott City MD 21043	800-274-4212	410-465-5558
Lawrence Behr Assoc Inc		
3400 Tupper Dr . . . . Greenville NC 27834	800-522-4464	252-757-0279
LED Supply Co		
12340 W Cedar Dr . . . . Lakewood CO 80228	877-595-4769	
Liquid Networx Inc		
PO Box 780099 . . . . San Antonio TX 78278	866-547-8439	
Lucidview LLC		
80 Rolling Links Blvd . . . . Oak Ridge TN 37830	888-582-4384	865-220-8440
Luther Consulting LLC		
10435 Commerce Dr Ste 140 . . . . Carmel IN 46032	866-517-6570	317-636-0282
Management Network Group Inc (TMNG)		
7300 College Blvd Ste 302 . . . . Overland Park KS 66210	800-690-6903	913-345-9315
NASDAQ: CRTN		
Mar-Kee Group, The		
26248 Equity Dr . . . . Daphne AL 36526	888-300-4629	
Market Force Information Llc		
6025 The Corners Pkwy		
Ste 200 . . . . Peachtree Corners GA 30092	800-669-9939	770-441-5366
Marks Group P C		
45 E city ave Ste 342 . . . . Bala Cynwyd PA 19004	888-224-0649	
Marvin Huffaker Consulting Inc		
PO Box 72643 . . . . Chandler AZ 85050	888-690-0013	480-988-7215
Math Teachers Press Inc		
4850 Park Glen Rd . . . . St Louis Park MN 55416	800-852-2435	
Max Environmental Technologies Inc		
1815 Washington Rd . . . . Pittsburgh PA 15241	800-851-7845	412-343-4900
Max Technical Training		
4900 Pkwy Dr Ste 160 . . . . Mason OH 45040	866-595-6863	513-322-8888
mcaConnect LLC		
8055 E Tufts Ave Ste 1300 . . . . Denver CO 80237	866-662-0669	
MCM Services Group		
1300 Corporate Ctr Curve . . . . Eagan MN 55121	888-507-6262	
McVeigh Associates Ltd		
275 Dixon Ave . . . . Amityville NY 11701	800-726-5655	631-789-8833
MediRevv Inc		
2600 University Pkwy . . . . Coralville IA 52241	888-665-6310	
Medmart Inc		
10780 Reading Rd . . . . Cincinnati OH 45241	888-260-4430	513-733-8100
Michael Brandman Associates		
220 Commerce Ste 200 . . . . Irvine CA 92602	888-826-5814	714-508-4100
Michell Consulting Group		
8240 NW 52nd Terr Ste 410 . . . . Doral FL 33166	800-442-5011	305-592-5433
Midrange Solutions Inc		
20 Hillside Ave . . . . Springfield NJ 07081	800-882-4008	973-912-7050
MindSpark International Inc		
1205 Peachtree Pkwy Ste 1204 . . . . Cumming GA 30041	888-820-3616	
MOBI Wireless Management LLC		
6100 W 96th St Ste 150 . . . . Indianapolis IN 46278	855-259-6624	
Moran Technology Consulting Llc		
1215 Hamilton Ln Ste 200 . . . . Naperville IL 60540	888-699-4440	
MoreDirect Inc		
1001 Yamato Rd Ste 200 . . . . Boca Raton FL 33431	800-800-5555	561-237-3300
Morphix Business Consulting		
PO Box 5217 Stn A . . . . Calgary AB T2H1X3	866-680-2503	403-520-7710
Natl Elevator Industrial Educational Program		
11 Larsen Way . . . . Attleboro MA 02763	800-228-8220	508-699-2200
Nelrod Co		
3109 Lubbock Ave . . . . Fort Worth TX 76109	866-448-0961	817-922-9000
Neltner Billing & Consulting Services		
6463 Taylor Mill Rd . . . . Independence KY 41051	888-635-8637	
Netlink Software Group America Inc		
999 Tech Row . . . . Madison Heights MI 48071	800-485-4462	
Newdea Inc		
6400 So Fiddlers Green Cir		
Ste 1970 . . . . Greenwood Village CO 80111	877-412-4829	720-249-3030

	Toll-Free	Phone

Nfocus Consulting Inc
1594 Hubbard Dr . . . . Lancaster OH 43130 — **800-675-5809** — 740-654-5809

Nordisk Systems Inc
13475 SE Johnson Rd . . . . Milwaukie OR 97222 — **800-676-2777** — 503-353-7555

Northspan Group Inc, The
221 W First St . . . . Duluth MN 55802 — **800-232-0707** — 218-722-5545

Noxent Inc
6400 Boul Taschereau Bureau 220 . . . . Brossard QC J4W3J2 — **800-268-4364** — 450-926-0662

Nuvue Business Solutions
3061 Berks Way Ste 102. . . . . Raleigh NC 27614 — **800-688-8310** — 919-562-5599

Objectiva Software Solutions Inc
12770 El Camino Real Ste 300 . . . . San Diego CA 92130 — **800-878-6975** — 408-809-5950

Oceanus Partners
16540 Pointe Village Dr Ste 208. . . . . Lutz FL 33558 — **888-496-1117**

Omnia Group Inc, The
1501 W Cleveland St Ste 300. . . . . Tampa FL 33606 — **800-525-7117** — 813-254-9449

OmniVue Business Solutions LLC
1355 Windward Concourse Ste 200 . . . . Alpharetta GA 30005 — **866-900-6348** — 770-587-0095

Open Spatial Inc
5701 Lonetree Blvd Ste 211 . . . . Rocklin CA 95765 — **800-696-1238**

OPTIO LLC 390 Spaulding Ave SE . . . . Ada MI 49301 — **888-981-3282**

Palo Alto Networks Inc
4401 Great America Pkwy . . . . Santa Clara CA 95054 — **866-898-9087** — 408-753-4000

Parallax Press
2236 Sixth St . . . . Berkeley CA 94710 — **800-863-5290** — 510-540-6411

Pathway Health
11240 Stillwater Blvd N . . . . Lake Elmo MN 55042 — **877-777-5463**

PayneGroup Inc
1111 Third Ave Ste 2200 . . . . Seattle WA 98101 — **888-467-2963** — 206-344-8966

Pilat
460 US Hwy 22 W Ste 408 . . . . Whitehouse Station NJ 08889 — **800-338-9701**

Platinum Vault Inc
10554 Norwalk Blvd . . . . Santa Fe Springs CA 90670 — **888-671-2888** — 562-903-1494

PlusOne Solutions Inc
3501 Quadrangle Blvd Ste 120 . . . . Orlando FL 32817 — **877-943-0100** — 407-359-5929

PMOLink LLC
2001 Lakeshore Dr . . . . Mandeville LA 70448 — **800-401-5701** — 985-674-5968

Pollution Control Corp
500 W Country Club Rd . . . . Chickasha OK 73018 — **800-966-1265**

Portable Church Industries Inc
1923 Ring Dr . . . . Troy MI 48083 — **800-939-7722**

Proactive Management Consulting LLC
2700 Cumberland Pkwy SE . . . . Atlanta GA 30339 — **877-319-2198** — 770-319-7468

Product Safety Consulting Inc (PSC)
605 Country Club Dr Ste I & J . . . . Bensenville IL 60106 — **877-804-3066** — 630-238-0188

Profit Recovery Partners
2995 Red Hill Ave . . . . Costa Mesa CA 92626 — **877-484-7776**

Project Consulting Services Inc
3300 W Esplanade Ave S Ste 500. . . . . Metairie LA 70002 — **855-468-7473** — 504-833-5321

ProSource Solutions LLC
4199 Kinross Lakes Pkwy Ste 150 . . . . Richfield OH 44286 — **866-549-0279**

Quality Management Solutions LLC (QMS)
146 Lowell St Ste 300B . . . . Wakefield MA 01889 — **800-645-6430**

Quasius Investment Corp
4200 W Cypress St Ste 375 . . . . Tampa FL 33607 — **888-422-9786** — 813-249-2514

R2 Unified Technologies
980 N Federal Hwy Ste 410 . . . . Boca Raton FL 33432 — **866-464-7381** — 561-515-6800

Radiofrequency Safety International (RSI)
543 Main St . . . . Kiowa KS 67070 — **888-830-5648**

Rally Education
22 Railroad Ave . . . . Glen Head NY 11545 — **888-997-2559**

RDS Solutions LLC
99 Grayrock Rd . . . . Clinton NJ 08809 — **888-473-7435**

Redhawk Network Security LLC
62958 Layton Ave Ste One . . . . Bend OR 97701 — **866-605-6328**

RedLegg
319 1/2 State St Ste A. . . . . Geneva IL 60134 — **877-811-5040**

Research into Action Inc
3934 NE Mlking Jr Blvd Ste 300. . . . . Portland OR 97212 — **888-492-9100** — 503-287-9136

Revention Inc
1315 W Sam Houston Pkwy North Ste 100. . . . . Houston TX 77043 — **877-738-7444**

Ria Compliance Consultants Inc
11640 Arbor St Ste 100 . . . . Omaha NE 68144 — **877-345-4034**

Richard Carlton Consulting Inc
1941 Rollingwood Dr . . . . Fairfield CA 94534 — **800-325-2747** — 707-422-4053

Rimkus Consulting Group Inc
8 Greenway Plz Ste 500 . . . . Houston TX 77046 — **800-580-3228**

RISC Networks Inc
81 Broadway St Ste C. . . . . Asheville NC 28801 — **866-808-1227**

Roi Consulting LI Llc
176 Logan St Ste 22. . . . . Noblesville IN 46060 — **866-465-6470**

Rook Security
11350 N Meridian St Ste 600 . . . . Carmel IN 46032 — **888-712-9531**

Root Inc 5470 Main St . . . . Sylvania OH 43560 — **800-852-1315**

Safari Micro Inc
2185 W Pecos Rd . . . . Chandler AZ 85224 — **888-446-4770**

SATISFYD
47 E Chicago Ave Ste 360 . . . . Naperville IL 60540 — **800-562-9557**

Sererra Consulting Group LLC
4590 MacArthur Blvd Ste 500. . . . . Newport Beach CA 92660 — **877-276-3774**

Serti Informatique Inc
7555 Beclard St . . . . Montreal QC H1J2S5 — **800-361-6615** — 514-493-1909

Sign Biz Inc
24681 La Plz Ste 270 . . . . Dana Point CA 92629 — **800-633-5580** — 949-234-0408

Signal Securities Inc
700 Throckmorton St . . . . Fort Worth TX 76102 — **800-957-4256** — 817-877-4256

Signal-Tech
4985 Pittsburgh Ave . . . . Erie PA 16509 — **877-547-9900** — 814-835-3000

Simplicity Consulting Inc
6710 108th Ave NE Ste 354 . . . . Kirkland WA 98033 — **888-252-0385**

SinglePoint Solutions
210 Townepark Cir Ste 200. . . . . Louisville KY 40243 — **877-774-4840** — 502-212-4017

Sky I T Group LLC
330 Seventh Ave . . . . New York NY 10001 — **866-641-6017** — 212-868-7800

SmarTek21 LLC
12910 Totem Lake Blvd NE Ste 200 . . . . Kirkland WA 98034 — **888-221-9578**

Sonoma Technical Support Services
505-8840 210th St Ste 342 . . . . Langley BC V1M2Y2 — **866-898-3123**

Soundview Executive Book Summaries
511 School House Rd Ste 300 . . . . Kennett Square PA 19348 — **800-786-6279** — 484-730-1270

Source Data Products Inc
18350 Mt Langley St . . . . Fountain Valley CA 92708 — **800-333-2669** — 714-593-0387

Southland Safety LLC
1409 Kilgore Dr . . . . Henderson TX 75652 — **866-723-3719** — 903-657-8669

Sovereign Systems LLC
3930 E Jones Bridge Rd Ste 300 . . . . Norcross GA 30092 — **844-727-3622**

Spader Business Management
2101 W 41st St Ste 49 . . . . Sioux Falls SD 57105 — **800-772-3377**

Spire Consulting Group LLC
114 W Seventh St Ste 1300 . . . . Austin TX 78701 — **855-216-0812** — 512-637-0845

Spire Technologies Inc
2140 SW Jefferson St Ste 300 . . . . Portland OR 97201 — **800-481-7332** — 503-222-3086

Sri Quality Sys
300 Northpointe Cir #304 . . . . Seven Fields PA 16046 — **800-549-6709** — 724-934-9000

Starnet Data Design Inc
2659 Townsgate Rd Ste 227 . . . . Westlake Village CA 91361 — **800-779-0587** — 805-371-0585

Stria Inc
4300 Resnik Ct . . . . Bakersfield CA 93313 — **877-839-8952**

Surrex Solutions Corp
300 N Sepulveda Blvd Ste 1020 . . . . El Segundo CA 90245 — **866-308-2628** — 310-640-3000

Survival Strategies Inc
335 N Third St . . . . Burbank CA 91502 — **800-834-0357** — 818-276-1000

Systems Plus Computers Inc
12 Centerra Pkwy Ste 20. . . . . Lebanon NH 03766 — **800-388-8486** — 603-643-5800

Syvantis Technologies LLC
13822 Bluestem Ct . . . . Baxter MN 56425 — **800-450-8908**

Tallgrass Restoration LLC
2221 Hammond Dr . . . . Schaumburg IL 60173 — **877-699-8300** — 847-925-9830

Tango Consulting Group LLC
31 James Vincent Dr . . . . Clinton CT 06413 — **877-567-6045** — 860-669-9380

Tcs of America Enterprises Llc
PO Box 219 . . . . Brookline NH 03033 — **888-423-7820**

Te21 Inc
1184 Clements Ferry Rd Ste G . . . . Charleston SC 29492 — **866-982-8321** — 843-579-2520

Teachers' Curriculum Institute (TCI)
2440 W El Camino Real Ste 400. . . . . Mountain View CA 94040 — **800-497-6138**

Technical Assurance Inc
38112 Second St . . . . Willoughby OH 44094 — **866-953-3147** — 440-953-3147

Technolab International Corp
2020 NE 163 St . . . . Miami FL 33162 — **888-382-2851** — 305-433-2973

Technology Futures Inc (TFI)
13740 Research Blvd (N Hwy 183)
Ste C-1. . . . . Austin TX 78750 — **800-835-3887** — 512-258-8898

Technology Solutions Provider Inc (TSPI)
11490 Commerce Park Dr Ste 200 . . . . Reston VA 20191 — **877-455-8774**

TekScape inc
131 West 35th St 5th Fl . . . . New York NY 10001 — **855-835-7227**

Tel Tec Security Systems Inc
5020 Lisa Marie Ct . . . . Bakersfield CA 93313 — **800-292-9227** — 661-397-5511

Telephone Doctor Inc
30 Hollenberg Ct . . . . Bridgeton MO 63044 — **800-882-9911** — 314-291-1012

Tenzing Consulting LLC
2100 Georgetowne Dr Ste 302 . . . . Sewickley PA 15143 — **877-980-5300** — 724-940-4060

ThriveOn Inc 210 S 20th St . . . . New Ulm MN 56073 — **855-767-2571**

Tom Hopkins International
465 E Chilton Dr Ste 4 . . . . Chandler AZ 85255 — **800-528-0446** — 480-949-0786

Tradescape Inc
520 S El Camino Real Ste 640 . . . . San Mateo CA 94402 — **800-697-6068**

Training Modernization Group Inc
9737 Peppertree Rd . . . . Spotsylvania VA 22553 — **866-855-6449** — 540-295-9313

Tri-Basin Natural Resources District
1723 Burlington St . . . . Holdrege NE 68949 — **877-995-6688** — 308-995-6688

TrueCloud 2147 E Baseline Rd . . . . Tempe AZ 85283 — **866-990-8783**

Twin Technologies Inc
11 Computer Dr W . . . . Albany NY 12205 — **800-439-4821**

UpCurve Cloud
10801 National blvd 410 Ste 410 . . . . Los Angeles CA 90064 — **888-898-4787**

UpCurve Cloud
2815 Manor Rd Ste 201 . . . . Austin TX 78722 — **800-775-8378**

USC Consulting Group LLC
3000 Bayport Dr Ste 1010 . . . . Tampa FL 33607 — **800-888-8872**

Utilityone Inc PO Box 3027 . . . . York PA 17402 — **800-388-9088** — 717-840-4200

Venice Consulting Group
212 Marine St Ste 100 . . . . Santa Monica CA 90405 — **855-202-0824**

Vensai Technologies
2450 Atlanta Hwy Ste 1002. . . . . Cumming GA 30040 — **866-849-4057** — 770-888-4804

Verologix LLC
18100 Von Karman Ave Ste 850 . . . . Irvine CA 92612 — **800-403-8041**

West Side Telecommunications
1449 Fairmont Rd . . . . Morgantown WV 26501 — **800-296-9113** — 304-983-2211

Wilson Consulting Group
100 Old Schoolhouse Rd . . . . Mechanicsburg PA 17055 — **800-837-2265** — 717-591-3070

Wlh Consulting Inc
1417 Capri Ln . . . . Weston FL 33326 — **800-392-0745**

Woodbury Technologies Inc
1725 East 1450 South . . . . Clearfield UT 84015 — **800-408-8857** — 801-773-7157

YourAmigo Inc
4708 Del Valle Pkwy . . . . Pleasanton CA 94566 — **800-816-7054** — 510-813-1355

Youth Frontiers Inc
6009 Excelsior Blvd . . . . Minneapolis MN 55416 — **888-992-0222** — 952-922-0222

zedSuite
210 Water St Ste 400 . . . . St. John's NL A1C1A9 — **877-722-1177** — 709-722-7213

197 CONSUMER INFORMATION RESOURCES - GOVERNMENT

	Toll-Free	Phone

National Center for Immunization & Respiratory Disorders
1600 Clifton Rd NE MS E-05 . . . . Atlanta GA 30333 — **800-232-4636**
Travelers Health
1600 Clifton Rd NE . . . . Atlanta GA 30333 — **800-232-4636**

Consumer Product Safety Commission (CPSC)
4340 E W Hwy Ste 502. . . . . Bethesda MD 20814 — **800-638-2772** — 301-504-7923

Corp for National & Community Service
AmeriCorps USA
1201 New York Ave NW . . . . Washington DC 20525 — **800-833-3722** — 202-606-5000

				Toll-Free	Phone
Learn & Serve America					
1201 New York Ave NW	Washington	DC	20525	800-833-3722	202-606-5000
Department of Health & Human Services					
Office on Women's Health					
200 Independence Ave SW	Washington	DC	20201	800-994-9662	202-690-7650
Education Resource Information Ctr (ERIC)					
655 15th St NW Ste 500	Washington	DC	20005	800-538-3742	
Eldercare Locator					
1730 Rhode Island Ave NW Ste 1200	Washington	DC	20036	800-677-1116	
Energy Efficiency & Renewable Energy Information Ctr					
1000 Independence Ave SW	Washington	DC	20585	877-337-3463	202-586-4849
Foster Grandparent Program c/o Senior Corps					
1201 New York Ave NW	Washington	DC	20525	800-942-2677	202-606-5000
Grantsgov					
U.S. Department of Health & Human Services					
200 Independence Ave SW	Washington	DC	20201	877-696-6775	800-518-4726
Homeland Security Information Ctr					
National Technical Information Service					
5301 Shawnee Rd	Alexandria	VA	22312	800-553-6847	703-605-6000
National Clearinghouse for Alcohol & Drug Information					
5600 Fishers Ln	Rockville	MD	20857	800-729-6686	
National Institute for Literacy (NIFL)					
1775 'I' St NW Ste 730	Washington	DC	20006	800-228-8813	202-233-2025
National Institutes of Health (NIH)					
9000 Rockville Pk	Bethesda	MD	20892	800-411-1222	301-496-4000
National Mental Health Information Ctr					
PO Box 42557	Washington	DC	20015	800-487-4889	
National Technical Information Service (NTIS)					
5301 Shawnee Rd	Alexandria	VA	22312	800-363-2068	703-605-6060
Project Safe Neighborhoods (PSN)					
Office of Justice Programs					
810 Seventh St NW	Washington	DC	20531	888-744-6513	202-616-6500
PubMed					
US National Library of Medicine					
8600 Rockville Pike	Bethesda	MD	20894	888-346-3656	
Recreationgov					
1849 C St NW	Washington	DC	20240	877-444-6777	202-208-4743
US Dept of Labor Women's Bureau					
200 Constitution Ave NW Rm S-3002	Washington	DC	20210	800-827-5335	202-693-6710
US General Services Administration					
1800 F St NW	Washington	DC	20405	800-488-3111	

198   CONTAINERS - METAL (BARRELS, DRUMS, KEGS)

				Toll-Free	Phone
American Metal Crafters LLC					
695 High St	Middletown	CT	06457	800-840-9243	860-343-1960
C&C Fabrication Company Inc					
30 Fabrication Dr	Lacey's Spring	AL	35754	888-485-5130	256-881-7300
Chicago Steel Container Corp					
1846 S Kilbourn Ave	Chicago	IL	60623	800-633-4933	
Container Research Corp (CRC)					
2 New Rd	Aston	PA	19014	844-220-9574	
Csi Industries Inc					
6910 W Ridge Rd	Fairview	PA	16415	800-937-9033	814-474-9353
Gardner Manufacturing Inc					
1201 West Lake St	Horicon	WI	53032	800-558-8890	
Greif Inc 425 Winter Rd	Delaware	OH	43015	877-781-9797	
NYSE: GEF					
Imperial Industries Inc					
505 Industrial Park Ave	Rothschild	WI	54474	800-558-2945	715-359-0200
Industrial Container Services					
7152 First Ave S	Seattle	WA	98108	800-273-3786	206-763-2345
Innovative Fluid Handling Systems					
3300 E Rock Falls Rd	Rock Falls	IL	61071	800-435-7003	
Justrite Manufacturing Co					
2454 E Dempster St Ste 300	Des Plaines	IL	60016	800-798-9250	847-298-9250
McKey Perforating Company Inc					
3033 S 166th St	New Berlin	WI	53151	800-345-7373	262-786-2700
Myers Container Corp					
8435 NE Killingsworth	Portland	OR	97220	800-406-9377	503-501-5830
Packaging Specialties Inc					
300 Lake Rd	Medina	OH	44256	800-344-9271	330-723-6000
Quadra Tech Inc					
864 E Jenkins Ave	Columbus	OH	43207	800-443-2766	
Skolnik Industries Inc					
4900 S Kilbourn Ave	Chicago	IL	60632	800-441-8780	773-735-0700
Stackbin Corp					
29 Powderhill Rd	Lincoln	RI	02865	800-333-1603*	
*Sales					
USA Container Company Inc					
1776 S Second St	Piscataway	NJ	08854	888-752-7722	
Westmor Industries LLC					
3 Development Dr	Morris	MN	56267	800-992-8981	320-589-2100
Young Bros Stamp Works Inc					
1415 Howard Ave PO Box 75	Muscatine	IA	52761	800-553-8248	

199   CONTAINERS - PLASTICS (DRUMS, CANS, CRATES, BOXES)

				Toll-Free	Phone
Akro-Mils Inc 1293 S Main St	Akron	OH	44301	800-253-2467	
Beden-Baugh Products Inc					
105 Lisbon Rd	Laurens	SC	29360	866-598-5794	864-682-3136
Belco Mfg Company Inc					
2303 Taylors Valley Rd	Belton	TX	76513	800-251-8265	254-933-9000
Buckhorn Inc					
55 W Techne Ctr Dr	Milford	OH	45150	800-543-4454	
Case Design Corp					
333 School Ln	Telford	PA	18969	800-847-4176	215-703-0130
Chem-Tainer Industries Inc					
361 Neptune Ave	West Babylon	NY	11704	800-275-2436	631-661-8300
Comar Inc 1 Comar Pl	Buena	NJ	08310	800-962-6627	856-692-6100
Gatekeeper Systems Inc					
8 Studebaker	Irvine	CA	92618	888-808-9433	949-453-1940

				Toll-Free	Phone
Handley Industries Inc					
2101 Brooklyn Rd	Jackson	MI	49203	800-870-5088	517-787-8821
Hedwin Corp					
1600 Roland Heights Ave	Baltimore	MD	21211	800-638-1012	410-467-8209
HGI Skydyne					
100 River Rd	Port Jervis	NY	12771	800-428-2273	
Iroquois Products of Chicago					
2220 W 56th St	Chicago	IL	60636	800-453-3355	
Jewel Case Corp					
110 Dupont Dr	Providence	RI	02907	800-441-4447	401-943-1400
McConkey					
1615 Puyallup St PO Box 1690	Sumner	WA	98390	800-426-8124	253-863-8111
Menasha Corp					
1645 Bergstrom Rd	Neenah	WI	54956	800-558-5073	920-751-1000
Molded Fiber Glass Tray Co					
6175 US Hwy 6	Linesville	PA	16424	800-458-6050*	814-683-4500
*Sales					
ORBIS Corp					
1055 Corporate Center Dr	Oconomowoc	WI	53066	800-999-8683	800-890-7292
Pelican Products Inc					
147 N Main St	South Deerfield	MA	01373	800-542-7344	413-665-2163
Plas-Tanks Industries Inc					
39 Standen Dr	Hamilton	OH	45015	800-247-6709	513-942-3800
Plastic Forming Company Inc					
20 S Bradley Rd	Woodbridge	CT	06525	800-732-2060	203-397-1338
Rehrig Pacific Co					
4010 E 26th St	Los Angeles	CA	90058	800-421-6244	323-262-5145
River Bend Industries					
2421 16th Ave S	Moorhead	MN	56560	800-365-3070	
Rocket Jewelry Packaging & Displays					
375 Executive Blvd Ste W-4	Elmsford	NY	10523	800-762-5521	718-292-5370
Rotonics Manufacturing Inc					
6940 O St Ste 100	Lincoln	NE	68510	888-422-8683	402-467-5221
Schaefer Systems International Inc					
10021 Westlake Dr	Charlotte	NC	28241	800-876-6000	704-944-4500
Specialty Plastic Fabricators Inc					
9658 196th St	Mokena	IL	60448	800-747-9509	708-479-5501
Stack-On Products Co					
1360 N Old Rand Rd	Wauconda	IL	60084	800-323-9601	
Toter Inc PO Box 5338	Statesville	NC	28677	800-424-0422	
US Plastic Corp					
1390 Newbrecht Rd	Lima	OH	45801	800-537-9724	419-228-2242

200   CONTAINERS - WOOD

SEE ALSO Pallets & Skids

				Toll-Free	Phone
Abbot & Abbot Box Corp					
37-11 Tenth St	Long Island	NY	11101	888-525-7186	
BDL Supply					
15 Sprague Rd	South Charleston	OH	45368	888-728-9810	
Commercial Lumber & Pallet Co					
135 Long Ln	City Of Industry	CA	91746	800-252-4968	
Greif Inc 425 Winter Rd	Delaware	OH	43015	877-781-9797	
NYSE: GEF					
Liberty Bell Equipment Corp					
3201 S 76th St	Philadelphia	PA	19153	800-541-5827	215-492-6700
Maine Bucket Co					
21 Fireslate Pl	Lewiston	ME	04240	800-231-7072	207-784-6700
Mb Bark LLC					
100 Bark Mulch Dr	Auburn	ME	04210	800-866-4991	
Mele & Co 2007 Beechgrove Pl	Utica	NY	13501	800-635-6353	315-733-4600
Monte Package Company Inc					
3752 Riverside Rd	Riverside	MI	49084	800-653-2807	269-849-1722
Orange Fence & Supply					
205 Boston Post Rd	Orange	CT	06477	844-703-4267	203-904-2272
Pallet Services Inc					
201 E Fairhaven Ave	Burlington	WA	98233	800-769-2245	360-776-1130
Rochester Shoe Tree Company Inc					
1 Cedar Ln	Ashland	NH	03217	866-627-3800	
Texas Basket Co					
100 Myrtle Dr	Jacksonville	TX	75766	800-657-2200	903-586-8014
Wisconsin Box Company Inc					
929 Townline Rd	Wausau	WI	54402	800-876-6658	715-842-2248
Wolf Organization, The					
20 W Market St	York	PA	17401	800-388-9653	

201   CONTROLS - INDUSTRIAL PROCESS

				Toll-Free	Phone
Aalborg Instruments & Controls Inc					
20 Corporate Dr	Orangeburg	NY	10962	800-866-3837	845-770-3000
ADA-ES Inc					
640 Plz Dr Ste 270	Highlands Ranch	CO	80129	888-822-8617	720-598-3500
NASDAQ: ADES					
ADS Environmental Services					
4940 Research Dr	Huntsville	AL	35805	800-633-7246	256-430-3366
ALL-TEST Pro LLC					
123 Spencer Plain Rd	Old Saybrook	CT	06475	800-952-8776	860-399-4222
Alpha Technologies Services LLC					
3030 Gilchrist Rd	Akron	OH	44305	800-356-9886	330-745-1641
AMETEK Power Instruments					
255 North Union St	Rochester	NY	14605	800-950-6686	610-647-2121
AMETEKInc 1080 N Crooks	Clawson	MI	48017	800-635-0289	248-435-0700
Arcet Equipment Company Inc					
1700 Chamberlayne Ave	Richmond	VA	23222	800-388-0302	
ARi Industries Inc					
381 Ari Ct	Addison	IL	60101	800-237-6725	630-953-9100
Arzel Zoning Technology Inc					
4801 Commerce Pkwy	Cleveland	OH	44128	800-611-8312	
Athena Controls Inc					
5145 Campus Dr	Plymouth Meeting	PA	19462	800-782-6776	610-828-2490
Auburn Systems LLC					
8 Electronics Ave	Danvers	MA	01923	800-255-5008	978-777-2460

				Toll-Free	Phone
Automation Products Group Inc (APG)					
1025 W 1700 N	Logan	UT	84321	**888-525-7300**	435-753-7300
Automation Service					
13871 Parks Steed Dr	Earth City	MO	63045	**800-325-4808**	314-785-6600
Azonix Corp					
900 Middlesex Tpke Bldg 6	Billerica	MA	01821	**800-967-5558**	978-670-6300
Bacharach Inc					
621 Hunt Vly Cir	New Kensington	PA	15068	**800-736-4666**	724-334-5000
Barksdale Inc					
3211 Fruitland Ave	Los Angeles	CA	90058	**800-835-1060**	323-589-6181
Brookfield Engineering Lab Inc					
11 Commerce Blvd	Middleboro	MA	02346	**800-628-8139**	508-946-6200
Buhler Inc					
13105 12th Ave N	Plymouth	MN	55441	**800-722-7483**	763-847-9900
Campbell Scientific Inc					
815 W 1800 N	Logan	UT	84321	**844-454-2505**	
Canfield Connector Div					
8510 Foxwood Ct	Youngstown	OH	44514	**800-554-5071**	
Cec Controls Co Inc					
14555 Barber Ave	Warren	MI	48088	**877-924-0303**	586-779-0222
Chaney Instrument Co					
965 Wells St	Lake Geneva	WI	53147	**877-221-1252**	262-729-4852
Conax Buffalo Technologies LLC					
2300 Walden Ave	Buffalo	NY	14225	**800-223-2389**	716-684-4500
Cooper Atkins Corp					
33 Reeds Gap Rd	Middlefield	CT	06455	**800-835-5011***	860-349-3473
*Sales					
CUES Inc 3600 Rio Vista Ave	Orlando	FL	32805	**800-327-7791**	407-849-0190
Del Mar Scientific Acquisition Ltd					
4951 Airport Pkwy Ste 803	Addison	TX	75001	**800-722-4270**	972-661-5160
Dickson Co					
930 S Westwood Ave	Addison	IL	60101	**800-757-3747**	630-543-3747
Dwyer Instruments Inc					
102 Indiana Hwy 212 PO Box 373	Michigan City	IN	46360	**800-872-9141**	
Dynalco					
3690 NW 53rd St	Fort Lauderdale	FL	33309	**800-368-6666**	954-739-4300
Eldridge Products Inc					
465 Reservation Rd	Marina	CA	93933	**800-321-3569**	831-648-7777
Emerson 7070 Winchester Cir	Boulder	CO	80301	**800-522-6277**	303-530-8400
Encoder Products Co					
464276 Hwy 95 S PO Box 249	Sagle	ID	83860	**800-366-5412**	208-263-8541
Endress+Hauser Inc					
2350 Endress Pl	Greenwood	IN	46143	**888-363-7377**	317-535-7138
Enerac Inc 67 Bond St	Westbury	NY	11590	**800-695-3637**	516-997-2100 *
Fairchild Industrial Products Co					
3920 Westpoint Blvd	Winston-Salem	NC	27103	**800-334-8422**	336-659-3400
Fast Heat Inc					
776 Oaklawn Ave	Elmhurst	IL	60126	**877-747-8575**	630-359-6300
Fluid Components International					
1755 La Costa Meadows Dr	San Marcos	CA	92078	**800-863-8703**	760-744-6950
Forney Corp					
16479 N Dallas Pkwy Ste 600	Addison	TX	75001	**800-356-7740***	972-458-6100
*Cust Svc					
Galvanic Applied Sciences USA Inc					
41 Wellman St	Lowell	MA	01851	**866-252-8470**	978-848-2701
Gefran ISI Inc					
8 Lowell Ave	Winchester	MA	01890	**888-888-4474**	781-729-5249
Gems Sensors Inc					
1 Cowles Rd	Plainville	CT	06062	**800-378-1600**	855-877-9666
General Devices Company Inc					
1410 S Post Rd	Indianapolis	IN	46239	**800-821-3520**	317-897-7000
General Electric					
1100 Technology Pk Dr	Billerica	MA	01821	**800-833-9438**	978-437-1000
Geotech Environmental Equipment Inc					
2650 E 40th Ave	Denver	CO	80205	**800-833-7958**	303-320-4764
GfG Instrumentation Inc					
1194 Oak Vly Dr Ste 20	Ann Arbor	MI	48108	**800-959-0329**	734-769-0573
Harding Instruments					
7741 Wagner Rd NW	Edmonton	AB	T6E5B1	**888-792-1171**	780-462-7100
Healthspace USA Inc					
4860 Cox Rd Ste 200	Glen Allen	VA	23060	**866-860-4224**	804-935-8532
HO Trerice Co					
12950 W Eight-Mile Rd	Oak Park	MI	48237	**888-873-7423**	248-399-8000
HSQ Technology					
26227 Research Rd	Hayward	CA	94545	**800-486-6684**	510-259-1334
Industrial Scientific Corp					
7848 Steubenville Pk	Oakdale	PA	15071	**800-338-3287**	412-788-4353
ITT Industries Inc					
1133 Westchester Ave	White Plains	NY	10604	**800-254-2823**	914-641-2000
NYSE: ITT					
JMS Southeast Inc					
105 Temperature Ln	Statesville	NC	28677	**800-873-1835**	
Kistler-Morse Corp					
150 Venture Blvd	Spartanburg	SC	29306	**800-426-9010**	864-574-2763
Lake Shore Cryotronics					
575 McCorkle Blvd	Westerville	OH	43082	**877-969-0010**	614-891-2243
LaMotte Co					
802 Washington Ave	Chestertown	MD	21620	**800-344-3100**	410-778-3100
Linear Laboratories					
42025 Osgood Rd	Fremont	CA	94539	**800-536-0262**	510-226-0488
Magnetrol International Inc					
5300 Belmont Rd	Downers Grove	IL	60515	**800-624-8765**	630-969-4000
Malema Engineering Corp					
1060 S Rogers Cir	Boca Raton	FL	33487	**800-637-6418**	561-995-0595
MAMAC Systems Inc					
8189 Century Blvd	Minneapolis	MN	55317	**800-843-5116**	952-556-4900
Marsh Bellofram Corp					
8019 Ohio River Blvd	Newell	WV	26050	**800-727-5646**	304-387-1200
McCrometer Inc					
3255 W Stetson Ave	Hemet	CA	92545	**800-220-2279**	951-652-6811
MicroMod Automation Inc					
75 Town Centre Dr	Rochester	NY	14623	**800-480-1975**	585-321-9200
MKS Instruments Inc					
2 Tech Dr Ste 201	Andover	MA	01810	**800-428-9401**	978-645-5500
Moore Industries International Inc					
16650 Schoenborn St	North Hills	CA	91343	**800-999-2900**	818-894-7111
NDC Infrared Engineering					
5314 N Irwindale Ave	Irwindale	CA	91706	**800-866-4733**	626-960-3300

				Toll-Free	Phone
NRD LLC					
2937 Alt Blvd PO Box 310	Grand Island	NY	14072	**800-525-8076**	716-773-7634
Omega Engineering Inc					
1 Omega Dr PO Box 4047	Stamford	CT	06907	**800-826-6342**	203-359-1660
Onset Computer Corp					
PO Box 3450	Pocasset	MA	02559	**800-564-4377**	
OPW Fuel Management Systems					
6900 Santa Fe Dr	Hodgkins	IL	60525	**800-547-9393**	708-485-4200
Orange Research Inc					
140 Cascade Blvd	Milford	CT	06460	**800-989-5657**	203-877-5657
Orion Instruments LLC					
2105 Oak Villa Blvd	Baton Rouge	LA	70815	**866-556-7466**	225-906-2343
PakSense Inc					
6223 N Discovery Pl	Boise	ID	83713	**877-832-0720**	208-489-9010
Parker Hannifin Corp Veriflo Div					
250 Canal Blvd	Richmond	CA	94804	**800-272-7537**	510-235-9590
PdMA Corp					
5909-C Hampton Oaks Pkwy	Tampa	FL	33610	**800-476-6463**	813-621-6463
Pearpoint Inc					
72055 Corporate Way	Thousand Palms	CA	92276	**800-688-8094**	760-343-7350
Pentair 7433 Harwin Dr	Houston	TX	77036	**800-545-6258**	
PMC Engineering LLC					
11 Old Sugar Hollow Rd	Danbury	CT	06810	**800-869-5747**	203-792-8686
Portage Electric Products Inc					
7700 Freedom Ave NW	North Canton	OH	44720	**888-464-7374**	330-499-2727
Porter Instrument Company Inc					
245 Township Line Rd PO Box 907	Hatfield	PA	19440	**888-723-4001**	215-723-4000
Potter Electric Signal Company Inc					
5757 Phantom Dr Ste 125	Hazelwood	MO	63042	**800-325-3936**	314-878-4321
Pyromation Inc					
5211 Industrial Rd	Fort Wayne	IN	46825	**800-837-6805**	260-484-2580
RACO Mfg & Engineering Company Inc					
1400-62nd St	Emeryville	CA	94608	**800-722-6999**	
RAE Systems					
3775 North First St	San Jose	CA	95134	**877-723-2878**	408-952-8200
Raven Industries Inc					
205 E Sixth St	Sioux Falls	SD	57104	**800-243-5435**	605-336-2750
NASDAQ: RAVN					
Robertshaw Industrial Products					
1602 Mustang Dr	Maryville	TN	37801	**800-228-7429**	865-981-3100
Rochester Gauges Inc of Texas					
11616 Harry Hines Blvd	Dallas	TX	75229	**800-821-1829**	972-241-2161
Ronan Engineering Co					
21200 Oxnard St	Woodland Hills	CA	91367	**800-327-6626**	
Sable Systems International					
3840 N Commerce St	North Las Vegas	NV	89032	**866-217-6760**	800-330-0465
Scully Signal Co					
70 Industrial Way	Wilmington	MA	01887	**800-272-8559**	617-692-8600
See Water Inc					
22220 Opportunity Way Ste 101	Riverside	CA	92518	**888-733-9283**	951-487-8073
Sensidyne Inc					
16333 Bay Vista Dr	Clearwater	FL	33760	**800-451-9444**	727-530-3602
Sensus					
8601 Six Forks Rd Ste 700	Raleigh	NC	27615	**800-638-3748**	919-845-4000
Sierra Instruments Inc					
5 Harris Ct Bldg L	Monterey	CA	93940	**800-866-0200**	831-373-0200
SJE-Rhombus					
22650 County Hwy 6 PO Box 1708	Detroit Lakes	MN	56502	**800-746-6287**	218-847-1317
SOR Inc 14685 W 105th St	Lenexa	KS	66215	**800-676-6794**	913-888-2630
SpectraSensors Inc					
4333 W Sam Houston Pkwy N	Houston	TX	77043	**800-619-2861**	713-300-2700
Spectronics Corp					
956 Brush Hollow Rd	Westbury	NY	11590	**800-274-8888**	516-333-4840
Spirax Sarco Inc					
1150 Northpoint Blvd	Blythewood	SC	29016	**800-883-4411**	803-714-2000
Teledyne Advanced Pollution Instrumentation					
9480 Carroll Pk Dr	San Diego	CA	92121	**800-324-5190**	858-657-9800
Teledyne Monitor Labs Inc (TML)					
35 Inverness Dr E	Englewood	CO	80112	**800-422-1499**	303-792-3300
Tevet LLC 85 Spring St S	Mosheim	TN	37818	**866-886-8527**	678-905-1300
Titan Logix Corp					
4130 - 93 St	Edmonton	AB	T6E5P5	**877-462-4085**	780-462-4085
Transcat Inc					
35 Vantage Pt Dr	Rochester	NY	14624	**800-800-5001**	585-352-9460
NASDAQ: TRNS					
Troxler Electronic Laboratories Inc					
3008 E Cornwallis Rd					
PO Box 12057	Research Triangle Park	NC	27709	**877-876-9537**	919-549-8661
TSI Inc 500 CaRdigan Rd	Shoreview	MN	55126	**800-874-2811**	651-483-0900
Veeder-Root					
125 Powder Forest Dr	Simsbury	CT	06070	**888-262-7539**	860-651-2700
Wika Instrument Corp					
1000 Wiegand Blvd	Lawrenceville	GA	30043	**888-945-2872**	
Wilmington Instrument Company Inc					
332 N Fries Ave	Wilmington	CA	90744	**800-544-2843**	310-834-1133
Winland Electronics Inc					
1950 Excel Dr	Mankato	MN	56001	**800-635-4269**	
NYSE: WEX					
Yokogawa Corp of America					
12530 W Airport Blvd	Sugar Land	TX	77478	**800-888-6400**	281-340-3800
YSI Inc					
1700-1725 Brannum Ln	Yellow Springs	OH	45387	**800-765-4974***	937-767-7241
*Cust Svc					

202 CONTROLS - TEMPERATURE - RESIDENTIAL & COMMERCIAL

				Toll-Free	Phone
Azonix Corp					
900 Middlesex Tpke Bldg 6	Billerica	MA	01821	**800-967-5558**	978-670-6300
Cooper Atkins Corp					
33 Reeds Gap Rd	Middlefield	CT	06455	**800-835-5011***	860-349-3473
*Sales					
DeltaTRAK Inc PO Box 398	Pleasanton	CA	94566	**800-962-6776**	925-249-2250
Emerson Climate Technologies - Retail Solutions					
1065 Big Shanty Rd NW Ste 100	Kennesaw	GA	30144	**800-829-2724**	770-425-2724
Hansen Technologies Corp					
6827 High Grove Blvd	Burr Ridge	IL	60527	**800-426-7368**	630-325-1565

Classified Section

			Toll-Free	Phone
HSQ Technology				
26227 Research Rd	Hayward CA	94545	800-486-6684	510-259-1334
Johnson Controls Systems				
9410 Bunsen Pkwy Ste 100-B	Louisville KY	40220	800-765-7773	502-671-7300
Kidde-Fenwal Inc				
400 Main St	Ashland MA	01721	800-872-6527*	508-881-2000
*Hum Res				
KMC Controls Inc				
19476 Industrial Dr	New Paris IN	46553	877-444-5622	574-831-5250
Novar Controls Corp				
6060 Rockside Woods Blvd Ste 400	Cleveland OH	44131	800-348-1235	
Phoenix Controls				
75 Discovery Way	Acton MA	01720	800-340-0007	978-795-3400
Portage Electric Products Inc				
7700 Freedom Ave NW	North Canton OH	44720	888-464-7374	330-499-2727
Watlow Winona				
1241 Bundy Blvd	Winona MN	55987	800-928-5692	507-454-5300

203   CONTROLS & RELAYS - ELECTRICAL

			Toll-Free	Phone
Allied Controls Inc				
150 E Aurora St	Waterbury CT	06708	800-788-0955	203-757-4200
AMETEK National Controls Corp				
1725 Western Dr	West Chicago IL	60185	800-323-2593	630-231-5900
Anaheim Automation				
910 E Orangefair Ln	Anaheim CA	92801	800-345-9401*	714-992-6990
*Sales				
Artisan Controls Corp				
111 Canfield Ave Bldg B15-18	Randolph NJ	07869	800-457-4950	973-598-9400
Bright Image Corp				
2830 S18th Ave	Broadview IL	60155	888-449-5656	
Cleveland Motion Controls Inc				
7550 Hub Pkwy	Cleveland OH	44125	800-321-8072	216-524-8800
Contrex Inc				
8900 Zachary Ln N	Maple Grove MN	55369	800-342-4411	763-424-7800
DST Controls 651 Stone Rd	Benicia CA	94510	800-251-0773	
Ducommun Inc				
23301 Wilmington Ave	Carson CA	90745	800-522-6645	310-513-7280
NYSE: DCO				
Duct-O-Wire Co 345 Adams Cir	Corona CA	92882	800-752-6001	951-735-8220
Dynagraphics Corp				
4080 Norex Dr	Chaska MN	55318	800-959-0108	
Easter Owens Electric Co				
6692 Fig St	Arvada CO	80004	866-204-3707	303-431-0111
Electric Regulator Corp				
6189 El Camino Real	Carlsbad CA	92009	800-458-6566	760-438-7873
Electronic Theatre Controls Inc				
3031 Pleasantview Rd	Middleton WI	53562	800-688-4116	608-831-4116
Enercon Engineering Inc				
201 Altorfer Ln	East Peoria IL	61611	800-218-8831	309-694-1418
FSI Technologies Inc				
668 E Western Ave	Lombard IL	60148	800-468-6009	630-932-9380
FXC Corp 3410 S Susan St	Santa Ana CA	92704	800-845-8753	714-556-7400
Gentec Inc 2625 Dalton	Quebec QC	G1P3S9	800-463-4480	418-651-8000
GET Engineering Corp				
9350 Bond Ave	El Cajon CA	92021	877-494-1820	619-443-8295
Glendinning Marine Products				
740 Century Cir	Conway SC	29526	800-500-2380	843-399-6146
Globe Electronic Hardware Inc				
34-24 56th St	Woodside NY	11377	800-221-1505	718-457-0303
Guardian Electric Mfg Company Inc				
1425 Lake Ave	Woodstock IL	60098	800-762-0369	815-334-3600
HF scientific Inc				
3170 Metro Pkwy	Fort Myers FL	33916	888-203-7248	
Honeywell Sensing & Control				
11 W Spring St	Freeport IL	61032	800-537-6945*	815-235-5500
*Cust Svc				
Hydrolevel Co 83 Water St	New Haven CT	06511	800-654-0768	203-776-0473
Icm Controls Corp				
7313 William Barry Blvd	North Syracuse NY	13212	800-365-5525	315-233-5266
IDEC Corp 1175 Elko Dr	Sunnyvale CA	94089	800-262-4332	408-747-0550
Imperial Irrigation District (IID)				
PO Box 937	Imperial CA	92251	800-303-7756	760-482-9600
Inertia Dynamics Inc				
31 Industrial Park Rd	New Hartford CT	06057	800-800-6445	860-379-1252
Infitec Inc				
6500 Badgley Rd	East Syracuse NY	13057	800-334-0837	315-433-1150
Jennings Technology Co				
970 McLaughlin Ave	San Jose CA	95122	800-292-4025	408-292-4025
KB Electronics Inc				
12095 NW 39th St	Coral Springs FL	33065	800-221-6570	954-346-4900
Leach International Corp				
6900 Orangethorpe Ave	Buena Park CA	90622	800-232-7700	714-736-7598
Lutron Electronics Company Inc				
7200 Suter Rd	Coopersburg PA	18036	800-523-9466*	610-282-6280
*Tech Supp				
MagneTek Inc				
N49 W13650 Campbell Dr	Menomonee Falls WI	53051	800-288-8178	
NASDAQ: MAG				
Moog Inc Jamison Rd	East Aurora NY	14052	800-336-2112	716-652-2000
NYSE: MOG.A				
OMRON Corp 1 Commerce Dr	Schaumburg IL	60173	800-556-6766	847-843-7900
OMRON Scientific Technologies Inc				
6550 Dumbarton Cir	Fremont CA	94555	800-556-6766	510-608-3400
Ormec Systems Corp				
19 Linden Park	Rochester NY	14625	800-656-7632	585-385-3520
Parker Hannifin Corp Electromechanical Automation Div				
5500 Business Pk Dr	Rohnert Park CA	94928	800-358-9068	707-584-7558
Parker McCrory Manufacturing Co				
2000 Forest Ave	Kansas City MO	64108	800-662-1038	816-221-2000
Payne Engineering Co				
PO Box 70	Scott Depot WV	25560	800-331-1345*	304-757-7353
*Orders				
Polytron Corp				
4400 Wyland Dr	Elkhart IN	46516	888-228-0246	574-522-0246

			Toll-Free	Phone
PVA Tepla America Inc				
251 Corporate Terr	Corona CA	92879	800-527-5667*	951-371-2500
*Sales				
RCI Custom Products				
801 N East St Ste 2A	Frederick MD	21701	800-546-4724	301-620-9130
Relay Specialties Inc				
17 Raritan Rd	Oakland NJ	07436	800-526-5376	
Rockford Systems Inc				
4620 Hydraulic Rd	Rockford IL	61109	800-922-7533*	815-874-7891
*Cust Svc				
Sendec Corp				
72 Perinton Pkwy	Fairport NY	14450	800-295-8000	855-294-3800
Sequence Controls Inc				
150 Rosamond St	Carleton ON	K7C1V2	800-663-1833	613-257-7356
SOR Inc 14685 W 105th St	Lenexa KS	66215	800-676-6794	913-888-2630
Spectra Precision Inc				
10355 Westmoor Dr Ste 100	Westminster CO	80021	888-527-3771	
Sprecher + Schuh				
15910 International Plaza Dr	Houston TX	77032	877-721-5913	281-442-9000
State of The Art Inc				
2470 Fox Hill Rd	State College PA	16803	800-458-3401	
Sturdy Corp				
1822 Carolina Beach Rd	Wilmington NC	28401	800-721-3282	910-763-2500
Time Mark Corp				
11440 E Pine St	Tulsa OK	74116	800-862-2875	918-438-1220
Time-O-Matic Inc				
1015 Maple St	Danville IL	61832	800-637-2645	217-442-0611
Tornatech Inc				
7075 Place Robert-Joncas Ste 132	Saint-laurent QC	H4M2Z2	800-363-8448	514-334-0523
Wago Corp				
N120 W19129 Freistadt Rd	Germantown WI	53022	800-346-7245	262-255-6222
Yaskawa America Inc				
2121 Norman Dr S	Waukegan IL	60085	800-927-5292	847-887-7000

204   CONVENIENCE STORES

SEE ALSO Grocery Stores ; Gas Stations

			Toll-Free	Phone
7-Eleven Inc				
1722 Routh Ste 100	Dallas TX	75221	800-255-0711	
Cafepresscom Inc				
1850 Gateway Dr Ste 300	Foster City CA	94404	877-809-1659	502-822-7501
Fkg Oil Co 721 W Main	Belleville IL	62220	800-873-3546	618-233-6754
Holiday Stationstores				
4567 American Blvd W	Bloomington MN	55437	800-745-7411	952-830-8700
Kwik Trip Inc				
1626 Oak St PO Box 2107	La Crosse WI	54602	800-305-6666	608-781-8988
Loaf N' Jug Mini Mart				
442 Keeler Pkwy	Pueblo CO	81001	888-200-6211	
Love's Travel Stops				
10601 N Pennsylvania Ave	Oklahoma City OK	73120	800-655-6837	
Mac's Convenience Stores Inc				
305 Milner Ave Ste 400 4th Fl	Toronto ON	M1B3V4	800-268-5574	416-291-4441
Maverik Inc				
880 W Center St	North Salt Lake UT	84054	800-789-4455*	801-936-5573
*Cust Svc				
Quik Stop Markets Inc				
4567 Enterprise St	Fremont CA	94538	888-200-6211	510-657-8500
QuikTrip Corp				
4705 S 129th E Ave	Tulsa OK	74134	800-441-0253	918-615-7700
Sheetz Inc 5700 Sixth Ave	Altoona PA	16602	800-487-5444	814-941-5106
Speedway LLC 500 Speedway Dr	Enon OH	45323	800-643-1948*	937-864-3000
*Cust Svc				
Stripes Convenience Stores				
3200 Hackberry Rd	Irving TX	75063	800-255-0711	
NYSE: SUSS				
Wawa Inc 260 W Baltimore Pk	Media PA	19063	800-444-9292	610-358-8000

205   CONVENTION CENTERS

SEE ALSO Performing Arts Facilities ; Stadiums & Arenas
Listings are alphabetized by city names within state groupings.

Alaska

			Toll-Free	Phone
Centennial Hall Convention Ctr				
101 Egan Dr	Juneau AK	99801	800-478-4176	907-586-5283

Arizona

			Toll-Free	Phone
Yuma Civic Ctr				
1440 W Desert Hills Dr	Yuma AZ	85365	866-966-0220	928-373-5040

Arkansas

			Toll-Free	Phone
Hot Springs Convention Ctr (HSCVB)				
134 Convention Blvd PO Box 6000	Hot Springs AR	71902	800-625-7576	501-321-2277
Statehouse Convention Ctr				
101 S Spring St PO Box 3232	Little Rock AR	72201	800-844-4781	501-376-4781

British Columbia

			Toll-Free	Phone
Vancouver Convention & Exposition Centre (VCEC)				
1055 Canada Pl	Vancouver BC	V6C0C3	866-785-8232	604-689-8232

California

			Toll-Free	Phone
Monterey Conference Center				
1 Portola Plz	Monterey CA	93940	800-742-8091*	831-646-3388
*Sales				

			Toll-Free	Phone
Ontario Convention Ctr 2000 E Convention Ctr Way	Ontario CA	91764	800-455-5755	909-937-3000
San Jose Convention Ctr 408 Almaden Blvd	San Jose CA	95110	800-726-5673	408-792-4511
Santa Clara Convention Ctr 5001 Great America Pkwy	Santa Clara CA	95054	800-272-6822	408-748-7000
Santa Monica Civic Auditorium 1855 Main St	Santa Monica CA	90401	866-728-3229	310-458-8551
Visalia Convention Ctr 303 E Acequia Ave	Visalia CA	93291	800-640-4888	559-713-4000

Florida

			Toll-Free	Phone
Ocean Ctr 101 N Atlantic Ave	Daytona Beach FL	32118	800-858-6444	386-254-4500
Greater Fort Lauderdale-Broward County Convention Ctr 1950 Eisenhower Blvd	Fort Lauderdale FL	33316	800-327-1390	954-765-5900
Orange County Convention Ctr (OCCC) 9800 International Dr	Orlando FL	32819	800-345-9845	407-685-9800
Tampa Convention Ctr 333 S Franklin St	Tampa FL	33602	866-790-4111	813-274-8511

Georgia

			Toll-Free	Phone
AmericasMart 240 Peachtree St NW Ste 2200	Atlanta GA	30303	800-285-6278	
Northwest Georgia Trade & Convention Center 2211 Dug Gap Battle Rd	Dalton GA	30720	800-824-7469	706-272-7676

Hawaii

			Toll-Free	Phone
Hawaii Convention Ctr 1801 Kalakaua Ave	Honolulu HI	96815	800-295-6603	808-943-3500

Illinois

			Toll-Free	Phone
TheMART 222 Merchandise Mart Plz Ste 470	Chicago IL	60654	800-677-6278	
Gateway Ctr 1 Gateway Dr	Collinsville IL	62234	800-289-2388	618-345-8998
Oakley-Lindsay Ctr 300 Civic Ctr Plz	Quincy IL	62301	800-978-4748	217-223-1000

Indiana

			Toll-Free	Phone
Horizon Convention Ctr 401 S High St PO Box 842	Muncie IN	47305	888-288-8860	

Iowa

			Toll-Free	Phone
Sioux City Convention Ctr 801 Fourth St	Sioux City IA	51101	800-593-2228	712-279-4800

Kentucky

			Toll-Free	Phone
Kentucky International Convention Ctr 221 S Fourth St	Louisville KY	40202	800-701-5831	502-595-4381

Maryland

			Toll-Free	Phone
Baltimore Convention Ctr 1 W Pratt St	Baltimore MD	21201	800-327-4414	410-649-7000

Minnesota

			Toll-Free	Phone
Duluth Entertainment Convention Ctr 350 Harbor Dr	Duluth MN	55802	800-628-8385	218-722-5573
Minneapolis Convention Ctr 1301 Second Ave S	Minneapolis MN	55403	800-438-5547	612-335-6000
Mayo Civic Ctr 30 Civic Ctr Dr SE	Rochester MN	55904	800-422-2199	507-328-2220

Mississippi

			Toll-Free	Phone
Mississippi Coast Coliseum & Convention Ctr 2350 Beach Blvd	Biloxi MS	39531	800-726-2781	228-594-3700
Natchez Convention Ctr 211 Main St	Natchez MS	39120	888-475-9144	601-442-5880

Missouri

			Toll-Free	Phone
Kansas City Convention & Entertainment Centers 301 W 13th St	Kansas City MO	64105	800-767-7700	816-513-5000
Nrccua 3651 NE Ralph Powell Rd	Lees Summit MO	64064	800-876-1117	816-525-2201
America's Ctr Convention Ctr 701 Convention Plz Ste 300	Saint Louis MO	63101	800-325-7962	314-342-5036
Explore Saint Louis Executive Conference Ctr 701 Convention Plz	Saint Louis MO	63101	800-325-7962	314-421-1023

Montana

			Toll-Free	Phone
MetraPark 308 Sixth Ave N	Billings MT	59101	800-366-8538	406-256-2400

Nebraska

			Toll-Free	Phone
Lied Lodge & Conference Center 2700 Sylvan Rd	Nebraska City NE	68410	800-546-5433	402-873-8733

Nevada

			Toll-Free	Phone
Elko Convention & Visitors Authority 700 Moren Way	Elko NV	89801	800-248-3556	775-738-4091
City of Henderson Henderson Convention Ctr 200 S Water St	Henderson NV	89015	877-775-5252	702-267-2171
Sands Expo & Convention Ctr 201 Sands Ave	Las Vegas NV	89169	800-265-2235	702-733-5556
Reno-Sparks Convention Ctr 4590 S Virginia St	Reno NV	89502	800-367-7366	775-827-7600

New Jersey

			Toll-Free	Phone
Wildwoods Convention Ctr 4501 Boardwalk	Wildwood NJ	08260	800-992-9732	609-729-9000

New York

			Toll-Free	Phone
Office of General Services Corning Tower Empire State Plz 41st Fl Empire State Plz	Albany NY	12242	877-426-6006	518-474-3899
Buffalo Niagara Convention Ctr 153 Franklin St	Buffalo NY	14202	800-995-7570	716-855-5555
Oncenter Complex 800 S State St	Syracuse NY	13202	800-776-7548	315-435-8000

Ohio

			Toll-Free	Phone
John S Knight Ctr 77 E Mill St	Akron OH	44308	800-245-4254	330-374-8900
Greater Columbus Convention Ctr 400 N High St	Columbus OH	43215	800-626-0241	614-827-2500
Sharonville Convention Ctr 11355 Chester Rd	Sharonville OH	45246	800-294-3179	513-771-7744

Oklahoma

			Toll-Free	Phone
Tulsa Convention Ctr 100 Civic Ctr	Tulsa OK	74103	800-678-7177	918-894-4350

Ontario

			Toll-Free	Phone
Mckenna Distribution & Warehousing 1260 Lkshore Rd E	Mississauga ON	L5E3B8	800-561-4997	905-274-1234
Metro Toronto Convention Centre 255 Front St W	Toronto ON	M5V2W6	800-422-7969	416-585-8000

Oregon

			Toll-Free	Phone
City of Pendleton 500 SW Dorion Ave	Pendleton OR	97801	800-238-5355	541-966-0201
Oregon Convention Ctr 777 NE Martin Luther King Jr Blvd	Portland OR	97232	800-791-2250	503-235-7575
Salem Conference Ctr 200 Commercial St SE *Sales	Salem OR	97301	877-589-1700*	503-589-1700
Seaside Civic & Convention Ctr 415 First Ave	Seaside OR	97138	800-394-3303	503-738-8585

Pennsylvania

			Toll-Free	Phone
Pennsylvania Convention Ctr 1101 Arch St	Philadelphia PA	19107	800-428-9000	215-418-4700

Tennessee

			Toll-Free	Phone
Chattanooga Convention Ctr 1150 Carter St	Chattanooga TN	37402	800-962-5213	423-756-0001

Texas

			Toll-Free	Phone
Beaumont Civic Ctr Complex 701 Main St	Beaumont TX	77701	800-782-3081	409-838-3435
Dallas Convention Ctr 650 S Griffin St	Dallas TX	75202	877-850-2100	214-939-2750
El Paso Convention & Performing Arts Ctr 1 Civic Ctr Plz	El Paso TX	79901	800-351-6024	915-534-0600
Fort Worth Convention Ctr 200 Texas St	Fort Worth TX	76102	866-630-2588	800-433-5747
Moody Gardens Convention Ctr 7 Hope Blvd	Galveston TX	77554	888-388-8484	409-741-8484
Grapevine Convention Ctr, The 1209 S Main St	Grapevine TX	76051	866-782-7897	817-410-3459
George R Brown Convention Ctr 1001 Avenida de Las Americas	Houston TX	77010	800-427-4697	713-853-8000
Plano Centre 1520 K Ave	Plano TX	75074	800-613-3222	972-422-0296

Utah

	City	State	Zip	Toll-Free	Phone
Ogden Eccles Conference Ctr 2415 Washington Blvd	Ogden	UT	84401	**866-472-4627**	801-689-8600

Washington

	City	State	Zip	Toll-Free	Phone
Bell Harbor International Conference Ctr 2211 Alaskan Way Pier 66	Seattle	WA	98121	**888-772-4422**	206-441-6666
Yakima Convention Ctr 10 N Eigth St	Yakima	WA	98901	**800-221-0751**	509-575-6062

Wisconsin

	City	State	Zip	Toll-Free	Phone
Monona Terrace Community & Convention Ctr 1 John Nolen Dr	Madison	WI	53703	**800-947-3529**	608-261-4000

Wyoming

	City	State	Zip	Toll-Free	Phone
Casper Events Ctr 1 Events Dr	Casper	WY	82601	**800-442-2256**	307-235-8400

206 CONVENTION & VISITORS BUREAUS

SEE ALSO Travel & Tourism Information - Foreign Travel ; Travel & Tourism Information - Canadian

Listings are alphabetized by city names.

	City	State	Zip	Toll-Free	Phone
Aberdeen Convention & Visitors Bureau 10 Railroad Ave SW PO Box 78	Aberdeen	SD	57401	**800-645-3851**	605-225-2414
Abilene Convention & Visitors Bureau 1101 N First St	Abilene	TX	79601	**800-727-7704**	325-676-2556
Abilene Convention & Visitors Bureau 201 NW Second St	Abilene	KS	67410	**800-569-5915**	785-263-2231
Abingdon Convention & Visitors Bureau 335 Cummings St	Abingdon	VA	24210	**800-435-3440**	276-676-2282
Akron/Summit County Convention & Visitors Bureau 77 E Mill St	Akron	OH	44308	**800-245-4254**	330-374-8900
Albany County Convention & Visitors Bureau 25 Quackenbush Sq	Albany	NY	12207	**800-258-3582**	518-434-1217
Albany Visitors Association 110 Third Ave SE PO Box 965	Albany	OR	97321	**800-526-2256**	541-928-0911
Albuquerque Convention & Visitors Bureau 20 First Plz Ste 601	Albuquerque	NM	87102	**800-733-9918**	505-842-9918
Alexandria Convention & Visitors Assn 221 King St	Alexandria	VA	22314	**800-388-9119**	703-746-3301
Alexandria/Pineville Area Convention & Visitors Bureau (APACVB) 707 Main St PO Box 1070	Alexandria	LA	71301	**800-551-9546**	
Allegan County Tourist Council 3255 122nd Ave	Allegan	MI	49010	**888-425-5342**	269-686-9088
Alpena Area Convention & Visitors Bureau 235 W Chisholm St	Alpena	MI	49707	**800-425-7362**	989-354-4181
Alton Regional Convention & Visitors Bureau (ARCVB) 200 Piasa St	Alton	IL	62002	**800-258-6645**	618-465-6676
Amarillo Convention & Visitor Council 1000 S Polk St	Amarillo	TX	79101	**800-692-1338**	
Lorain County Visitors Bureau 8025 Leavitt Rd	Amherst	OH	44001	**800-334-1673**	440-984-5282
Anchorage Convention & Visitors Bureau 524 W Fourth Ave	Anchorage	AK	99501	**800-478-6657**	907-276-4118
Anderson/Madison County Visitors & Convention Bureau 6335 S Scatterfield Rd	Anderson	IN	46013	**800-533-6569**	765-643-5633
Steuben County Tourism Bureau 430 N Wayne St Ste 1B	Angola	IN	46703	**888-665-5668**	260-665-5386
Ann Arbor Area Convention & Visitors Bureau 120 W Huron St	Ann Arbor	MI	48104	**800-888-9487**	734-995-7281
Southernmost Illinois Tourism Bureau PO Box 378	Anna	IL	62906	**800-248-4373**	618-833-9928
Annapolis & Anne Arundel County Conference & Visitors Bureau (AAACCVB) 26 W St	Annapolis	MD	21401	**888-302-2852**	410-280-0445
Fox Cities Convention & Visitors Bureau 3433 W College Ave	Appleton	WI	54914	**800-236-6673**	920-734-3358
Arkansas City Convention & Visitors Bureau 106 S Summit St PO Box 795	Arkansas City	KS	67005	**800-794-4780**	620-442-0230
Arlington Convention & Visitors Bureau 1905 E Randol Mill Rd	Arlington	TX	76011	**800-433-5374**	
Aspen Chamber Resort Assn 590 N Mill St	Aspen	CO	81611	**800-670-0792**	970-925-1940
Athens Convention & Visitors Bureau 300 N Thomas St	Athens	GA	30601	**800-653-0603**	706-357-4430
Athens County Convention & Visitors Bureau 667 E State St	Athens	OH	45701	**800-878-9767**	740-592-1819
Cobb Travel & Tourism 1 Galleria Pkwy	Atlanta	GA	30339	**800-451-3480**	678-303-2622
Atlantic City Convention & Visitors Authority 2314 Pacific Ave	Atlantic City	NJ	08401	**888-228-4748**	609-348-7100
Auburn-Opelika Tourism Bureau 714 E Glenn Ave	Auburn	AL	36830	**866-880-8747**	334-887-8747
Augusta Metropolitan Convention & Visitors Bureau 1450 Greene St	Augusta	GA	30901	**800-726-0243**	706-823-6600
Aurora Area Convention & Visitors Bureau 43 W Galena Blvd	Aurora	IL	60506	**800-477-4369**	630-256-3190
Austin Convention & Visitors Bureau 535 E Fifth St	Austin	TX	78701	**800-926-2282**	512-474-5171
Greater Bakersfield Convention & Visitors Bureau 515 Truxtun Ave	Bakersfield	CA	93301	**866-425-7353**	661-852-7282
Baltimore Area Convention & Visitors Assn (BACVA) 100 Light St 12th Fl	Baltimore	MD	21202	**877-225-8466**	410-659-7300
Bandera County Convention & Visitors Bureau 126 State Hwy 16 S PO Box 171	Bandera	TX	78003	**800-364-3833**	830-796-3045
Clermont County Convention & Visitors Bureau (CCCVB) 410 E Main St PO Box 100	Batavia	OH	45103	**800-796-4282**	513-732-3600
Baton Rouge Convention & Visitors Bureau 359 Third St	Baton Rouge	LA	70801	**800-527-6843**	225-383-1825
Battle Creek/Calhoun County Convention & Visitors Bureau 1 Riverwalk Ctr 34 W Jackson St	Battle Creek	MI	49017	**800-397-2240**	
Beaumont Convention & Visitors Bureau 505 Willow St	Beaumont	TX	77701	**800-392-4401**	409-880-3749
Greene County Convention & Visitors Bureau 1221 Meadowbridge Dr	Beavercreek	OH	45434	**800-733-9109**	937-429-9100
Washington County Visitors Assn 12725 SW Millikan Way Ste 210	Beaverton	OR	97005	**800-537-3149**	503-644-5555
Southern West Virginia Convention & Visitors Bureau 1406 Harper Rd	Beckley	WV	25801	**800-847-4898**	304-252-2244
Bedford County Visitors Bureau 131 S Juliana St	Bedford	PA	15522	**800-765-3331**	814-623-1771
Southwestern Michigan Tourism Council 2300 Pipestone Rd	Benton Harbor	MI	49022	**800-764-2836**	269-925-6301
Big Spring 215 W Third St PO Box 3359	Big Spring	TX	79720	**866-222-7100**	432-264-6032
Flathead Convention & Visitors Bureau PO Box 2164	Bigfork	MT	59911	**800-543-3105**	406-756-9091
Billings Convention & Visitors Bureau 815 S 27th St PO Box 31177	Billings	MT	59107	**800-735-2635**	406-245-4111
Mississippi Gulf Coast Convention & Visitors Bureau 2350 Beach Blvd Ste A	Biloxi	MS	39531	**888-467-4853**	228-896-6699
Greater Birmingham Convention & Visitors Bureau 1819 Morris Ave	Birmingham	AL	35203	**800-458-8085**	205-458-8000
Bismarck-Mandan Convention & Visitors Bureau 1600 Burnt Boat Dr	Bismarck	ND	58503	**800-767-3555**	701-222-4308
Bloomington Convention & Visitors Bureau (BCVB) 7900 International Dr Ste 990	Bloomington	MN	55425	**800-346-4289**	952-858-8500
Bloomington-Normal Area Convention & Visitors Bureau 3201 CIRA Dr Ste 201	Bloomington	IL	61704	**800-433-8226**	309-665-0033
Bloomington/Monroe County Convention & Visitors Bureau 2855 N Walnut St	Bloomington	IN	47404	**800-800-0037**	812-334-8900
Columbia-Montour Visitors Bureau 121 Papermill Rd	Bloomsburg	PA	17815	**800-847-4810**	570-784-8279
Mercer County Convention & Visitors Bureau 621 Commerce St	Bluefield	WV	24701	**800-221-3206**	304-325-8438
Boise Convention & Visitors Bureau 250 S Fifth St Ste 300	Boise	ID	83702	**800-635-5240**	208-344-7777
North Carolina High Country Host 1700 Blowing Rock Rd	Boone	NC	28607	**800-438-7500**	828-264-1299
Greater Boston Convention & Visitors Bureau (GBCVB) 2 Copley Pl Ste 105	Boston	MA	02116	**888-733-2678**	617-536-4100
Boulder Convention & Visitors Bureau 2440 Pearl St	Boulder	CO	80302	**800-444-0447**	303-442-2911
Greater Bridgeport Conference & Vistors Ctr 164 W Main St	Bridgeport	WV	26330	**800-368-4324**	304-842-7272
Northwest Pennsylvania's Great Outdoors Visitors Bureau 2801 Maplevale Rd	Brookville	PA	15825	**800-348-9393**	814-849-5197
Brownsville Convention & Visitors Bureau 650 Ruben M Torres Sr Blvd	Brownsville	TX	78521	**800-626-2639**	956-546-3721
Buena Park Convention & Visitors Office 6601 Beach Blvd	Buena Park	CA	90621	**800-541-3953**	
Buffalo Niagara Convention & Visitors Bureau 403 Main St Ste 630	Buffalo	NY	14203	**800-283-3256**	716-852-2356
San Mateo County Convention & Visitors Bureau 111 Anza Blvd Ste 410	Burlingame	CA	94010	**800-288-4748**	650-348-7600
Burlington/Alamance County Convention & Visitors Bureau 200 S Main St PO Box 519	Burlington	NC	27216	**800-637-3804**	336-570-1444
Vermont Convention Bureau 60 Main St Ste 100	Burlington	VT	05401	**877-264-3503**	802-860-0606
Cadillac Area Visitors Bureau 201 N Mitchell St	Cadillac	MI	49601	**800-325-2525**	231-775-0657
Tourism Calgary 200 238 11th Ave SE	Calgary	AB	T2G0X8	**800-661-1678**	403-263-8510
Finger Lakes Visitors Connection 25 Gorham St	Canandaigua	NY	14424	**877-386-4669**	585-394-3915
Cape Girardeau Convention & Visitors Bureau 400 Broadway Ste 100	Cape Girardeau	MO	63701	**800-777-0068**	573-335-1631
Hamilton County Convention & Visitors Bureau Inc 37 E Main St	Carmel	IN	46032	**800-776-8687**	317-848-3181
Carrington Convention & Visitors Bureau 871 Main St	Carrington	ND	58421	**800-641-9668**	701-652-2524
Casper Area Convention & Visitors Bureau 139 W Second St Ste 1B	Casper	WY	82601	**800-852-1882**	307-234-5362
Cedar City-Brian Head Tourism & Convention Bureau 581 N Main St	Cedar City	UT	84721	**800-354-4849**	435-586-5124
Cedar Rapids Area Convention & Visitors Bureau 87 16th Ave Ste 200	Cedar Rapids	IA	52404	**800-735-5557**	319-398-5009
Chapel Hill/Orange County Visitors Bureau 501 W Franklin St	Chapel Hill	NC	27516	**888-968-2060**	
Charleston Area Convention & Visitors Bureau 423 King St	Charleston	SC	29403	**800-868-8118**	800-774-4444
Charlotte Convention & Visitors Bureau 500 S College St	Charlotte	NC	28202	**800-722-1994**	704-334-2282
Chattanooga Area Convention & Visitors Bureau 215 Broad St	Chattanooga	TN	37402	**800-322-3344**	423-756-8687
Chautauqua County Visitors Bureau Chautauqua Main Gate Rt 394 PO Box 1441	Chautauqua	NY	14722	**800-242-4569**	716-357-4569
Chesapeake Convention & Visitors Bureau 1224 Progressive Dr	Chesapeake	VA	23320	**888-889-5551**	757-382-6411
Cheyenne Area Convention & Visitors Bureau 121 W 15th St Ste 202	Cheyenne	WY	82001	**800-426-5009**	307-778-3133
Chicago Office of Tourism & Culture 78 E Washington St 4th Fl	Chicago	IL	60602	**888-871-5311**	312-744-2400
Greater Cincinnati Convention & Visitors Bureau 525 Vine St Ste 1200	Cincinnati	OH	45202	**800-543-2613**	513-621-2142
Clarksville/Montgomery County Tourist Commission 25 Jefferson St Ste 300	Clarksville	TN	37040	**800-530-2487**	931-647-2331
Clear Lake Convention & Visitors Bureau 205 Main Ave PO Box 188	Clear Lake	IA	50428	**800-285-5338**	641-357-2159
Visit St Petersburg Clearwater 13805 58th St N Ste 2-200	Clearwater	FL	33760	**877-352-3224**	727-464-7200

				Toll-Free	Phone

Park County Travel Council (PCTC)
836 Sheridan Ave PO Box 2454 ...... Cody WY 82414 — 800-393-2639 — 307-587-2297

Colby Convention & Visitors Bureau
350 S Range Ste 10 ...... Colby KS 67701 — 800-499-7928 — 785-460-7643

Experience Bryan College Station (BCSCVB)
715 University Dr E ...... College Station TX 77840 — 800-777-8292 — 979-260-9898

Colorado Springs Convention & Visitors Bureau
515 S Cascade Ave ...... Colorado Springs CO 80903 — 800-888-4748 — 719-635-7506

Experience Columbia SC
1101 Lincoln St ...... Columbia SC 29201 — 800-264-4884 — 803-545-0000

Columbus Area Visitors Ctr
506 Fifth St ...... Columbus IN 47201 — 800-468-6564 — 812-378-2622

Columbus Convention & Visitors Bureau
900 Front Ave ...... Columbus GA 31901 — 800-999-1613 — 706-322-1613

Columbus-Lowndes Convention & Visitors Bureau
117 Third St S PO Box 789 ...... Columbus MS 39703 — 800-327-2686 — 662-329-1191

Greater Columbus Convention & Visitors Bureau
277 W Nationwide Blvd Ste 125 ...... Columbus OH 43215 — 866-397-2657 — 614-221-6623

Polk County Travel & Tourism
20 E Mills St PO Box 308 ...... Columbus NC 28722 — 800-440-7848 — 828-894-2324

New Hampshire Div of Travel & Tourism Development
172 Pembroke Rd PO Box 1856 ...... Concord NH 03302 — 800-262-6660 — 603-271-2665

Coos Bay-North Bend Visitor & Convention Bureau
200 S Bayshore Dr ...... Coos Bay OR 97420 — 800-824-8486 — 541-269-0215

Iowa City/Coralville Area Convention & Visitors Bureau
900 First Ave/Hayden Fry Way ...... Coralville IA 52241 — 800-283-6592 — 319-337-6592

Iowa City/Coralville Area Convention & Visitors Bureau
900 First Ave Hayden Fry Way ...... Coralville IA 52241 — 800-283-6592 — 319-337-6592

Corpus Christi Convention & Visitors Bureau
101 N Shoreline Blvd Ste 430 ...... Corpus Christi TX 78401 — 800-678-6232 — 361-881-1888

Corvallis Tourism
420 NW Second St ...... Corvallis OR 97330 — 800-334-8118 — 541-757-1544

Northern Kentucky Convention & Visitors Bureau (NKYCVB)
50 E RiverCenter Blvd Ste 200 ...... Covington KY 41011 — 877-659-8474 — 859-261-4677

Montgomery County Visitors & Convention Bureau
218 E Pike St ...... Crawfordsville IN 47933 — 800-866-3973 — 765-362-5200

Dallas Convention & Visitors Bureau
325 N St Paul St Ste 700 ...... Dallas TX 75201 — 800-232-5527 — 214-571-1000

Central Florida Visitors & Convention Bureau
101 Adventure Ct ...... Davenport FL 33837 — 800-828-7655 — 863-420-2586

Tucker County Convention & Visitors Bureau
410 William Ave ...... Davis WV 26260 — 800-782-2775 — 304-259-5315

Dayton/Montgomery County Convention & Visitors Bureau
1 Chamber Plz Ste A ...... Dayton OH 45402 — 800-221-8235 — 937-226-8211

Decatur Area Convention & Visitors Bureau
202 E N St ...... Decatur IL 62523 — 800-331-4479 — 217-423-7000

Wicomico County Convention & Visitors Bureau
8480 Ocean Hwy ...... Delmar MD 21875 — 800-332-8687 — 410-548-4914

Denver Metro Convention & Visitors Bureau
1555 California St Ste 300 ...... Denver CO 80202 — 800-480-2010 — 303-892-1112

Greater Des Moines Convention & Visitors Bureau
400 Locust St Ste 265 ...... Des Moines IA 50309 — 800-451-2625 — 515-286-4960

Detroit Metropolitan Convention & Visitors Bureau
211 W Fort St Ste 1000 ...... Detroit MI 48226 — 877-424-5554 — 313-202-1800

Dickinson Convention & Visitors Bureau
72 E Museum Dr ...... Dickinson ND 58601 — 800-279-7391 — 701-483-4988

Visit Dothan Alabama
3311 Ross Clark Cir ...... Dothan AL 36303 — 888-449-0212 — 334-794-6622

DuQuoin Tourism Commission Inc
20 N Chestnut St PO Box 1037 ...... Du Quoin IL 62832 — 800-455-9570 — 618-542-8338

Dublin Convention & Visitors Bureau
9 S High St ...... Dublin OH 43017 — 800-245-8387 — 614-792-7666

Visit Duluth
21 W Superior St Ste 100 ...... Duluth MN 55802 — 800-438-5884 — 218-722-4011

Durango Area Tourism Office
828 Main Ave ...... Durango CO 81301 — 800-525-8855 — 970-247-3500

Durham Convention & Visitors Bureau
101 E Morgan St ...... Durham NC 27701 — 800-446-8604 — 919-687-0288

Eagan Convention & Visitors Bureau
1501 Central Pkwy ...... Eagan MN 55121 — 866-324-2620 — 651-675-5546

Talbot County Tourism Office
11 S Harrison St ...... Easton MD 21601 — 800-690-5080 — 410-770-8000

Effingham Convention & Visitors Bureau
201 E Jefferson Ave ...... Effingham IL 62401 — 800-772-0750 — 217-342-5305

Elgin Area Convention & Visitors Bureau
60 S Grove Ave ...... Elgin IL 60120 — 800-217-5362 — 847-695-7540

Elkhart County Convention & Visitors Bureau
219 Caravan Dr ...... Elkhart IN 46514 — 800-262-8161 — 574-262-8161

Howard County Tourism Council
3430 Court House Dr ...... Ellicott City MD 21043 — 866-313-6300 — 410-313-1900

Grays Harbor Tourism
PO Box 1229 ...... Elma WA 98541 — 800-621-9625 — 360-482-2651

VisitErie
208 E Bayfront Pkwy Ste 103 ...... Erie PA 16507 — 800-524-3743 — 814-454-1000

Eugene Cascades Coast
754 Olive St ...... Eugene OR 97440 — 800-547-5445 — 541-484-5307

Humboldt County Convention & Visitors Bureau
1034 Second St ...... Eureka CA 95501 — 800-346-3482 — 707-443-5097

Evansville Convention & Visitors Bureau
401 SE Riverside Dr ...... Evansville IN 47713 — 800-433-3025 — 812-421-2200

Iron Range Tourism Bureau
111 Station 44 Rd ...... Eveleth MN 55792 — 800-777-8497 — 218-749-8161

Fairbanks Convention & Visitors Bureau
101 Dunkel St Ste 111 ...... Fairbanks AK 99701 — 800-327-5774 — 907-456-5774

Fairfax County Convention & Visitors Bureau (FXVA)
3702 Pender Dr Ste 420 ...... Fairfax VA 22030 — 800-732-4732 — 703-790-0643

Fairmont Convention & Visitors Bureau
323 E Blue Earth Ave ...... Fairmont MN 56031 — 800-657-3280 — 507-235-8585

Fargo-Moorhead Convention & Visitors Bureau
2001 44th St S ...... Fargo ND 58103 — 800-235-7654 — 701-282-3653

Farmington Convention & Visitors Bureau
3041 E Main St ...... Farmington NM 87402 — 800-448-1240 — 505-326-7602

Fayetteville Area Convention & Visitors Bureau (FACVB)
245 Person St ...... Fayetteville NC 28301 — 800-255-8217 — 910-483-5311

Flagstaff Convention & Visitors Bureau
323 W Aspen Ave ...... Flagstaff AZ 86001 — 800-217-2367 — 928-779-7611

Florence Convention & Visitors Bureau
3290 W Radio Dr ...... Florence SC 29501 — 800-325-9005* — 843-664-0330
*General

Fond du Lac Convention & Visitors Bureau
171 S Pioneer Rd ...... Fond du Lac WI 54935 — 800-937-9123 — 920-923-3010

Fort Collins Convention & Visitors Bureau
19 Old Town Sq Ste 137 ...... Fort Collins CO 80524 — 800-274-3678 — 970-232-3840

Greater Fort Lauderdale Convention & Visitors Bureau
101 NE Third Ave Ste 100 ...... Fort Lauderdale FL 33301 — 800-227-8669 — 954-765-4466

Lee County Visitors & Convention Bureau
2201 Second St Ste 600 ...... Fort Myers FL 33901 — 800-237-6444 — 239-338-3500

Fort Smith Convention & Visitors Bureau
2 N 'B' ...... Fort Smith AR 72901 — 800-637-1477 — 479-783-8888

Fort Wayne/Allen County Convention & Visitors Bureau
927 S Harrison St ...... Fort Wayne IN 46802 — 800-767-7752 — 260-424-3700

Fort Worth Convention & Visitors Bureau
111 W Fourth St Ste 200 ...... Fort Worth TX 76102 — 800-433-5747 — 817-336-8791

Frankenmuth Convention & Visitors Bureau
635 S Main St ...... Frankenmuth MI 48734 — 800-386-8696 — 989-652-6106

Frankfort/Franklin County Tourist & Convention Commission
100 Capitol Ave ...... Frankfort KY 40601 — 800-960-7200 — 502-875-8687

Tourism Council of Frederick County Inc
151 S East St ...... Frederick MD 21701 — 800-999-3613 — 301-600-2888

Sandusky County Convention & Visitor's Bureau (SCCVB)
712 N St Ste 102 ...... Fremont OH 43420 — 800-255-8070 — 419-332-4470

Fresno & Clovis Convention & Visitors Bureau
1550 E Shaw Ave Ste 101 ...... Fresno CA 93710 — 800-788-0836 — 559-981-5500

Alachua County Visitors & Convention Bureau
30 E University Ave ...... Gainesville FL 32601 — 866-778-5002 — 352-374-5260

Galesburg Area Convention & Visitors Bureau
2163 E Main St ...... Galesburg IL 61401 — 800-916-3330 — 309-343-2485

Georgetown Convention & Visitors Bureau
1101 N College St ...... Georgetown TX 78626 — 800-436-8696 — 512-930-3545

Destination Gettysburg
571 W Middle St ...... Gettysburg PA 17325 — 800-337-5015

Greater Grand Forks Convention & Visitors Bureau
4251 Gateway Dr ...... Grand Forks ND 58203 — 800-866-4566 — 701-746-0444

Grand Junction Visitors & Convention Bureau
740 Horizon Dr ...... Grand Junction CO 81506 — 800-962-2547 — 970-244-1480

Grand Rapids/Kent County Convention & Visitors Bureau
171 Monroe Ave NW Ste 545 ...... Grand Rapids MI 49503 — 800-678-9859 — 616-258-7388

Grants Pass Visitors & Convention Bureau
1995 NW Vine St ...... Grants Pass OR 97526 — 800-547-5927 — 541-476-7574

Houma Area Convention & Visitors Bureau
114 Tourist Dr ...... Gray LA 70359 — 800-688-2732 — 985-868-2732

Greeley Chamber of Commerce
902 Seventh Ave ...... Greeley CO 80631 — 800-449-3866 — 970-352-3566

Greater Green Bay Convention & Visitors Bureau
1901 S Oneida St ...... Green Bay WI 54304 — 888-867-3342 — 920-494-9507

Greensboro Area Convention & Visitors Bureau
2200 Pinecroft Rd Ste 200 ...... Greensboro NC 27407 — 800-344-2282 — 336-274-2282

Greater Greenville Convention & Visitors Bureau
148 River St Ste 222 ...... Greenville SC 29601 — 800-351-7180 — 864-421-0000

Greenville-Pitt County Convention & Visitors Bureau (GPCCVB)
417 Cotanche St Ste 100 ...... Greenville NC 27858 — 800-537-5564 — 252-329-4200

Lake County Convention & Visitors Bureau
5465 W Grand Ave Ste 100 ...... Gurnee IL 60031 — 800-525-3669 — 847-662-2700

Hagerstown/Washington County Convention & Visitors Bureau
16 Public Sq ...... Hagerstown MD 21740 — 888-257-2600 — 301-791-3246

Hampton Conventions & Visitors Bureau
1919 Commerce Dr Ste 290 ...... Hampton VA 23666 — 800-487-8778 — 757-722-1222

Jefferson County Convention & Visitors Bureau
37 Washington Ct ...... Harpers Ferry WV 25425 — 866-435-5698

Hershey Harrisburg Region Visitors Bureau
3211 N Front St Ste 301-A ...... Harrisburg PA 17110 — 877-727-8573 — 717-231-7788

Long Island Convention & Visitors Bureau & Sports Commission
330 Motor Pkwy Ste 203 ...... Hauppauge NY 11788 — 877-386-6654 — 631-951-3900

Hays Convention & Visitors Bureau
2700 Vine St PO Box 490 ...... Hays KS 67601 — 800-569-4505 — 785-628-8202

Alpine Helen/White County Convention & Visitors Bureau
726 Bruckenstrasse PO Box 730 ...... Helen GA 30545 — 800-858-8027 — 706-878-2181

Henderson County Tourist Commission
101 N Water St Ste B ...... Henderson KY 42420 — 800-648-3128 — 270-826-3128

Huntingdon County Visitors Bureau
6993 Seven Pt Rd Ste 2 ...... Hesston PA 16647 — 888-729-7869 — 814-658-0060

Hickory Metro Convention & Visitors Bureau
1960 13th Ave Dr SE ...... Hickory NC 28602 — 800-509-2444 — 828-322-1335

High Point Convention & Visitors Bureau
1634 North Main St Ste 102 ...... High Point NC 27262 — 800-720-5255 — 336-884-5255

Hilton Head Island Visitors & Convention Bureau
1 Chamber of Commerce Dr
PO Box 5647 ...... Hilton Head Island SC 29938 — 800-523-3373 — 843-785-3673

Holland Area Convention & Visitors Bureau
76 E Eighth St ...... Holland MI 49423 — 800-506-1299 — 616-394-0000

Hawaii Visitors & Convention Bureau
2270 Kalakaua Ave Ste 801 ...... Honolulu HI 96815 — 800-464-2924

Hot Springs Convention & Visitors Bureau
134 Convention Blvd ...... Hot Springs AR 71901 — 800-543-2284 — 501-321-2277

Greater Houston Convention & Visitors Bureau
701 Avenida de las Americas Ste 200 ...... Houston TX 77010 — 800-446-8786

Cabell-Huntington Convention & Visitors Bureau
PO Box 347 ...... Huntington WV 25708 — 800-635-6329 — 304-525-7333

Huntington County Visitors & Convention Bureau
407 N Jefferson St ...... Huntington IN 46750 — 800-848-4282 — 260-359-8687

Huntington Beach Marketing & Visitors Bureau
301 Main St Ste 212 ...... Huntington Beach CA 92648 — 800-729-6232 — 714-969-3492

Huntsville/Madison County Convention & Visitor's Bureau
500 Church St NW Ste 1 ...... Huntsville AL 35801 — 800-843-0468 — 256-551-2230

Huron Chamber & Visitors Bureau
1725 Dakota Ave S ...... Huron SD 57350 — 800-487-6673 — 605-352-0000

Greater Hutchinson Convention & Visitors Bureau
117 N Walnut St PO Box 519 ...... Hutchinson KS 67504 — 800-691-4262 — 620-662-3391

Incline Village/Crystal Bay Visitors Bureau
969 Tahoe Blvd ...... Incline Village NV 89451 — 800-468-2463 — 775-832-1606

Indiana County Tourist Bureau
2334 Oakland Ave Ste 68 ...... Indiana PA 15701 — 877-746-3426 — 724-463-7505

Indianapolis Convention & Visitors Assn
200 S Capitol Ave Ste 300 ...... Indianapolis IN 46225 — 800-862-6912 — 317-262-3000

Organization	Address	City	State	ZIP	Toll-Free	Phone
Western Upper Peninsula Convention & Visitor Bureau	1200 E US 2	Ironwood	MI	49938	**800-522-5657**	906-932-4850
Irving Convention & Visitors Bureau	500 W Las Colinas Blvd	Irving	TX	75039	**800-247-8464**	972-252-7476
Ithaca/Tompkins County Convention & Visitors Bureau	904 E Shore Dr	Ithaca	NY	14850	**800-284-8422**	607-272-1313
Jackson County Convention & Visitors Bureau	141 S Jackson St	Jackson	MI	49201	**800-245-5282**	517-764-4440
Metro Jackson Convention & Visitors Bureau	111 E Capitol St Ste 102	Jackson	MS	39201	**800-354-7695**	601-960-1891
Jacksonville Convention & Visitors Bureau	310 E State St	Jacksonville	IL	62650	**800-593-5678**	217-243-5678
Onslow County Tourism	1099 Gum Branch Rd	Jacksonville	NC	28540	**800-932-2144**	
Visit Jacksonville	208 N Laura St Ste 1	Jacksonville	FL	32202	**800-733-2668**	904-798-9111
Discover Jamestown North Dakota	404 Louis L'Amour Ln	Jamestown	ND	58401	**800-222-4766**	701-251-9145
Jefferson City Convention & Visitors Bureau	700 E Capitol Ave	Jefferson City	MO	65101	**800-769-4183**	573-632-2820
Clark-Floyd Counties Convention & Tourism Bureau	315 Southern Indiana Ave	Jeffersonville	IN	47130	**800-552-3842**	812-282-6654
Greater Johnstown/Cambria County Convention & Visitors Bureau	111 Roosevelt Blvd Ste A	Johnstown	PA	15906	**800-237-8590**	814-536-7993
Heritage Corridor Convention & Visitors Bureau	339 W Jefferson St	Joliet	IL	60435	**800-926-2262**	815-727-2323
Joplin Convention & Visitors Bureau	602 S Main St	Joplin	MO	64801	**800-657-2534**	417-625-4789
Juneau Convention & Visitors Bureau	800 Glacier Ave Ste 201	Juneau	AK	99801	**888-581-2201**	907-586-1737
Kalamazoo County Convention & Visitors Bureau	141 E Michigan Ave Ste 100	Kalamazoo	MI	49007	**800-888-0509**	269-488-9000
Cabarrus County Convention & Visitors Bureau	3003 Dale Earnhardt Blvd	Kannapolis	NC	28083	**800-848-3740**	704-782-4340
Kansas City Convention & Visitors Assn	1321 Baltimore Ave	Kansas City	MO	64105	**800-767-7700**	816-691-3800
Kansas City Kansas Convention & Visitors Bureau Inc	PO Box 171517	Kansas City	KS	66117	**800-264-1563**	913-321-5800
Tri-Cities Visitor & Convention Bureau	7130 W Grandridge Blvd Ste B	Kennewick	WA	99336	**800-254-5824**	509-735-8486
Kenosha Area Convention & Visitors Bureau	812 56th St	Kenosha	WI	53140	**800-654-7309**	262-654-7307
Kerrville Convention & Visitors Bureau	2108 Sidney Baker St	Kerrville	TX	78028	**800-221-7958**	830-792-3535
Ketchikan Visitors Bureau	131 Front St	Ketchikan	AK	99901	**800-770-3300**	907-225-6166
Key West Visitors Ctr	510 Greene St 1st Fl *General	Key West	FL	33040	**800-533-5397***	305-294-2587
Monroe County Tourist Development Council	1201 White St Ste 102	Key West	FL	33040	**800-242-5229**	305-296-1552
Kingsport Convention & Visitors Bureau (KCVB)	400 Clinchfield St Ste 100	Kingsport	TN	37660	**800-743-5282**	423-392-8820
Armstrong County Tourist Bureau	125 Market St	Kittanning	PA	16201	**888-265-9954**	724-543-4003
Discover Klamath	205 Riverside Dr Ste B	Klamath Falls	OR	97601	**800-445-6728**	541-882-1501
Knoxville Tourism & Sports Corp	301 S Gay St	Knoxville	TN	37902	**800-727-8045**	865-523-7263
La Crosse Area Convention & Visitors Bureau	410 Veterans Memorial Dr	La Crosse	WI	54601	**800-658-9424**	608-782-2366
Lafayette Convention & Visitors Commission	1400 NW Evangeline Thwy	Lafayette	LA	70501	**800-346-1958**	337-232-3737
Lafayette-West Lafayette Convention & Visitors Bureau	301 Frontage Rd	Lafayette	IN	47905	**800-872-6648**	765-447-9999
Laguna Beach Visitors & Conference Bureau	381 Forest Ave	Laguna Beach	CA	92651	**800-877-1115**	949-497-9229
Southwest Louisiana Convention & Visitors Bureau	1205 N Lakeshore Dr	Lake Charles	LA	70601	**800-456-7952**	337-436-9588
Orlando North, Seminole County Tourism	1515 International Pkwy Ste 1013	Lake Mary	FL	32746	**800-800-7832**	407-665-2900
Chicago Southland CVB	2304 173rd St	Lansing	IL	60438	**888-895-8233**	708-895-8200
Greater Lansing Convention & Visitors Bureau	500 E Michigan Ave Ste 180	Lansing	MI	48912	**888-252-6746**	517-487-0077
Las Vegas Convention & Visitors Authority	3150 Paradise Rd	Las Vegas	NV	89109	**877-847-4858**	702-892-0711
Lexington Visitors Ctr	401 W Main St	Lexington	KY	40507	**800-845-3959**	859-233-7299
Laurel Highlands Visitors Bureau	120 E Main St	Ligonier	PA	15658	**800-333-5661**	724-238-5661
Lima/Allen County Convention & Visitors Bureau	144 S Main St Ste 101	Lima	OH	45801	**888-222-6075**	419-222-6075
Lincoln Convention & Visitors Bureau	3 Landmark Ctr 1128 Lincoln Mall Ste 100	Lincoln	NE	68508	**800-423-8212**	402-434-5335
Lincoln City Visitor & Convention Bureau	801 SW Hwy 101 Ste 401	Lincoln City	OR	97367	**800-452-2151**	541-996-1274
Lisle Convention & Visitors Bureau	925 Burlington Ave	Lisle	IL	60532	**800-733-9811**	630-769-1000
Lodi Conference & Visitors Bureau	115 S School St	Lodi	CA	95240	**800-798-1810**	209-365-1195
London/Laurel County Tourist Commission	140 Faith Assembly Church Rd	London	KY	40741	**800-348-0095**	606-878-6900
Long Beach Convention & Visitors Bureau	301 E Ocean Blvd	Long Beach	CA	90802	**800-452-7829**	562-436-3645
Louisville & Jefferson County Convention & Visitors Bureau	401 W Main St Ste 2300	Louisville	KY	40202	**800-626-5646**	502-584-2121
Lubbock Convention & Visitors Bureau	1500 Broadway St 6th Fl	Lubbock	TX	79401	**800-692-4035**	806-747-5232
Lumberton Area Visitors Bureau	3431 Lackey St	Lumberton	NC	28360	**800-359-6971**	910-739-9999
Mackinaw Area Visitors Bureau	10800 US 23	Mackinaw City	MI	49701	**800-666-0160**	231-436-5664
Greater Madison Convention & Visitors Bureau	22 E Mifflin Ave st Ste 200	Madison	WI	53703	**800-373-6376**	608-255-2537
Saint Tammany Parish Tourist & Convention Commission	68099 Hwy 59	Mandeville	LA	70471	**800-634-9443**	985-892-0520
Manhattan Convention & Visitors Bureau	501 Poyntz Ave	Manhattan	KS	66502	**800-759-0134**	785-776-8829
Greater Mankato Growth	1961 Premier Dr	Mankato	MN	56001	**800-697-0652**	507-385-6640
Outer Banks Visitors Bureau	1 Visitor Ctr Cir	Manteo	NC	27954	**877-629-4386**	252-473-2138
Marion-Grant County Convention & Visitors Bureau	1500 S Western Ave	Marion	IN	46953	**800-662-9474**	765-668-5435
Williamson County Tourism Bureau	1602 Sioux Dr *General	Marion	IL	62959	**800-433-7399***	618-997-3690
Marquette Country Convention & Visitors Bureau	117 West Washington St	Marquette	MI	49855	**800-544-4321**	906-228-7749
Marshall Area Convention & Visitors Bureau	317 W Main St	Marshall	MN	56258	**800-581-0081**	507-537-2271
Marshfield Convention & Visitors Bureau	700 S Central Ave PO Box 868	Marshfield	WI	54449	**800-422-4541**	715-384-3454
Mason City Convention & Visitors Bureau	2021 Fourth St SW Hwy 122 W	Mason City	IA	50401	**800-423-5724**	641-422-1663
Memphis Convention & Visitors Bureau	47 Union Ave	Memphis	TN	38103	**888-633-9099**	901-543-5300
Merced Conference & Visitors Bureau (MCVB)	710 W 16th St	Merced	CA	95340	**800-446-5353**	209-384-2791
Meridian/Lauderdale County Tourism Bureau	212 Constitution Ave	Meridian	MS	39301	**888-868-7720**	601-482-8001
Greater Miami Convention & Visitors Bureau	701 Brickell Ave Ste 2700	Miami	FL	33131	**800-933-8448**	305-539-3000
LaPorte County Convention & Visitors Bureau	4073 S Franklin St	Michigan City	IN	46360	**800-634-2650**	219-872-5055
Midland County Convention & Visitors Bureau	300 Rodd St Ste 101	Midland	MI	48640	**800-444-9979**	989-839-0340
The Milledgeville-Baldwin Convention & Visitors Bureau	200 W Hancock St	Milledgeville	GA	31061	**800-653-1804**	478-452-4687
Greater Milwaukee Convention & Visitors Bureau	648 N Plankinton Ave Ste 220	Milwaukee	WI	53203	**800-554-1448**	414-273-7222
Minot Convention & Visitors Bureau	1020 S Broadway	Minot	ND	58701	**800-264-2626**	701-857-8206
Modesto Convention & Visitors Bureau	1150 Ninth St Ste C	Modesto	CA	95354	**888-640-8467**	209-526-5588
Quad Cities Convention & Visitors Bureau	1601 River Dr Ste 110	Moline	IL	61265	**800-747-7800**	309-277-0937
Monterey County Convention & Visitors Bureau	PO Box 1770	Monterey	CA	93942	**888-221-1010**	
Montgomery Area Chamber of Commerce Convention & Visitor Bureau	300 Water St	Montgomery	AL	36104	**800-240-9452**	334-261-1100
Montrose Visitor Center	107 S Cascade Ave	Montrose	CO	81401	**855-497-8558**	970-249-5000
Greater Morgantown Convention & Visitors Bureau	341 Chaplin Rd First Fl	Morgantown	WV	26501	**800-458-7373**	304-292-5081
Knox County Convention & Visitors Bureau	107 S Main St	Mount Vernon	OH	43050	**800-837-5282**	740-392-6102
Muncie Visitors Bureau	3700 S Madison St	Muncie	IN	47302	**800-568-6862**	765-284-2700
Muskegon County Convention & Visitors Bureau	610 W Western Ave	Muskegon	MI	49440	**800-250-9283**	231-724-3100
Napa Valley Conference & Visitors Bureau	600 Main St	Napa	CA	94559	**855-847-6272**	707-251-5895
Greater Naples Marco Island Everglades Convention & Visitors Bureau	2800 Horseshoe Dr	Naples	FL	34104	**800-688-3600**	239-252-2384
Brown County Convention & Visitors Bureau	10 N Van Buren St PO Box 840	Nashville	IN	47448	**800-753-3255**	812-988-7303
Nashville Convention & Visitors Bureau (NCVB)	150 Fourth Ave N Ste G250	Nashville	TN	37219	**800-657-6910**	615-259-4730
Natchez Convention & Visitors Bureau	640 S Canal St	Natchez	MS	39120	**800-647-6724**	601-446-6345
Craven County Convention & Visitors Bureau	203 S Front St	New Bern	NC	28560	**800-437-5767**	252-637-9400
Greater New Braunfels Chamber of Commerce Inc, The	390 S Seguin Ave PO Box 311417	New Braunfels	TX	78130	**800-572-2626**	
Lawrence County Tourist Promotion Agency	229 S Jefferson St	New Castle	PA	16101	**888-284-7599**	724-654-8408
New Orleans Metropolitan Convention & Visitors Bureau	2020 St Charles Ave	New Orleans	LA	70130	**800-672-6124**	
Newberry Area Tourism Assn, The	PO Box 308	Newberry	MI	49868	**800-832-5216**	906-293-5562
Newport County Convention & Visitors Bureau	23 America's Cup Ave	Newport	RI	02840	**800-326-6030**	401-849-8048
Newport Beach Conference & Visitors Bureau	1200 Newport Ctr Dr Ste 120	Newport Beach	CA	92660	**800-216-1598**	949-719-6100
Newport News Tourism Development Office	702 Town Center Dr	Newport News	VA	23606	**888-493-7386**	757-926-1400
Newton Convention & Visitor Bureau	300 E 17th St S Ste 400	Newton	IA	50208	**800-798-0299**	641-792-0299
Niagara Tourism & Convention Corp	10 Rainbow Blvd	Niagara Falls	NY	14303	**877-325-5787**	716-282-8992
Norfolk Convention & Visitors Bureau	232 E Main St	Norfolk	VA	23510	**800-368-3097**	757-664-6620
Norman Convention & Visitors Bureau	309 E Main St	Norman	OK	73069	**800-767-7260**	405-366-8095
North Platte & Lincoln County Visitors Bureau	101 Halligan Dr	North Platte	NE	69101	**800-955-4528**	308-532-4729
North Ridgeville Visitors Bureau	34845 Lorain Rd	North Ridgeville	OH	44039	**800-334-5910**	440-327-3737
DuPage Convention & Visitors Bureau	915 Harger Rd Ste 240	Oak Brook	IL	60523	**800-232-0502**	630-575-8070
Oak Park Area Convention & Visitors Bureau	1118 Westgate	Oak Park	IL	60301	**888-625-7275**	708-524-7800
Yosemite Sierra Visitors Bureau	40637 Hwy 41	Oakhurst	CA	93644	**800-613-0709**	559-683-4636
Oakland Convention & Visitors Bureau	481 Water St	Oakland	CA	94607	**800-862-2543**	510-839-9000
Ogden/Weber Convention & Visitors Bureau	2438 Washington Blvd	Ogden	UT	84401	**800-255-8824**	801-778-6250
Oklahoma City Convention & Visitors Bureau	123 Park Ave	Oklahoma City	OK	73102	**800-225-5652**	405-297-8912
McDowell County Tourism Development Authority	91 S Catawba Ave	Old Fort	NC	28762	**888-233-6111**	828-668-4282

				Toll-Free	Phone
Olympia Lacey Tumwater Visitor & Convention Bureau 103 Sid Snyder Ave SW	Olympia	WA	98501	**877-704-7500**	360-704-7544
Greater Omaha Convention & Visitors Bureau 1001 Farnam St	Omaha	NE	68102	**866-937-6624**	402-444-4660
Ontario Area Chamber of Commerce 251 SW Ninth St	Ontario	OR	97914	**866-989-8012**	541-889-8012
Ontario Convention & Visitors Bureau 2000 E Convention Center Way	Ontario	CA	91764	**800-455-5755**	909-937-3000
Lake of the Ozarks Convention & Visitors Bureau 985 KK Dr	Osage Beach	MO	65065	**800-386-5253**	573-348-1599
Ottawa Tourism & Convention Authority 150 Elgin St Ste 1405	Ottawa	ON	K2P1L4	**800-363-4465**	613-237-5150
Overland Park Convention & Visitors Bureau 9001 W 110th St Ste 100	Overland Park	KS	66210	**800-262-7275**	913-491-0123
Owensboro Daviess County Convention & Visitors Bureau 215 E Second St	Owensboro	KY	42303	**800-489-1131**	270-926-1100
Oxford Convention & Visitors Bureau 102 Ed Perry Blvd	Oxford	MS	38655	**800-758-9177**	662-232-2367
Oxnard Convention & Visitors Bureau 2775 N Ventura Rd Ste 204	Oxnard	CA	93036	**800-269-6273**	805-385-7545
Park City Chamber of Commerce/Convention & Visitors Bureau 1850 Sidewinder Dr Ste 320	Park City	UT	84060	**800-453-1360**	435-649-6100
Greater Parkersburg Convention & Visitors Bureau 350 Seventh St	Parkersburg	WV	26101	**800-752-4982**	304-428-1130
Pasadena Convention & Visitors Bureau 300 E Green St	Pasadena	CA	91101	**800-307-7977**	626-795-9311
Pensacola Convention & Visitors Bureau 1401 E Gregory St	Pensacola	FL	32502	**800-874-1234**	850-434-1234
Peoria Area Convention & Visitors Bureau 456 Fulton St Ste 300	Peoria	IL	61602	**800-747-0302**	309-676-0303
Petoskey Area Visitors Bureau 401 E Mitchell St	Petoskey	MI	49770	**800-845-2828**	231-348-2755
Greater Phoenix Convention & Visitors Bureau 400 E Van Buren St Ste 600	Phoenix	AZ	85004	**877-225-5749**	602-254-6500
Pigeon Forge Dept of Tourism PO Box 1390	Pigeon Forge	TN	37868	**800-251-9100**	865-453-8574
Pine Bluff Convention & Visitors Bureau (PBCVB) 1 Convention Ctr Plz	Pine Bluff	AR	71601	**800-536-7660**	870-536-7600
Greater Pittsburgh Convention & Visitors Bureau 120 Fifth Ave 5th Ave Pl Ste 2800	Pittsburgh	PA	15222	**800-359-0758**	412-281-7711
Plano Convention & Visitors Bureau 2000 E Spring Creek Pkwy	Plano	TX	75074	**800-817-5266**	972-941-5840
Ponca City Tourism 420 E Grand Ave PO Box 1109	Ponca City	OK	74602	**866-763-8092**	580-765-4400
Port Arthur Convention & Visitors Bureau 3401 Cultural Ctr Dr	Port Arthur	TX	77642	**800-235-7822**	409-985-7822
Indiana Dunes the Casual Coast 1215 N State Rd 49	Porter	IN	46304	**800-283-8687**	219-926-2255
Travel Portland Pioneer Courthouse Sq 701 SW Sixth Ave	Portland	OR	97204	**877-678-5263**	503-275-9750
Providence Warwick Convention & Visitors Bureau 10 Memorial Blvd	Providence	RI	02903	**800-233-1636**	401-456-0200
Utah Valley Convention & Visitors Bureau 220 West Center St Ste 100	Provo	UT	84601	**800-222-8824**	801-851-2100
Plumas County Visitors Bureau 550 Crescent St	Quincy	CA	95971	**800-326-2247**	530-283-6345
Quincy Area Convention & Visitors Bureau (QACVB) 532 Gardner Expy	Quincy	IL	62301	**800-978-4748**	217-214-3700
Greater Raleigh Convention & Visitors Bureau 421 Fayetteville St Ste 1505	Raleigh	NC	27601	**800-849-8499**	919-834-5900
Palm Springs Desert Resorts Convention & Visitors Authority 70-100 Hwy 111	Rancho Mirage	CA	92270	**800-967-3767**	760-770-9000
Rapid City Convention & Visitors Bureau 444 Mt Rushmore Rd N	Rapid City	SD	57701	**800-487-3223**	605-718-8484
Rehoboth Beach Convention Ctr 229 Rehoboth Ave	Rehoboth Beach	DE	19971	**888-743-3628**	302-644-2288
Richardson Convention & Visitors Bureau 411 W Arapaho Rd Ste 105	Richardson	TX	75080	**888-690-7287**	972-744-4034
Richmond Metropolitan Convention & Visitors Bureau 401 N Third St	Richmond	VA	23219	**800-370-9004**	804-782-2777
Richmond/Wayne County Convention & Tourism Bureau 5701 National Rd E	Richmond	IN	47374	**800-828-8414**	765-935-8687
Ridgecrest Area Convention & Visitors Bureau (RACVB) 643 N China Lake Blvd Ste C	Ridgecrest	CA	93555	**800-847-4830**	760-375-8202
Riverside Convention & Visitors Bureau 3750 University Ave Ste 175	Riverside	CA	92501	**800-600-7080**	951-222-4700
Roanoke Valley Convention & Visitors Bureau 101 Shenandoah Ave NE	Roanoke	VA	24016	**800-635-5535**	540-342-6025
Rochester Convention & Visitors Bureau 30 Civic Ctr Dr SE Ste 200	Rochester	MN	55904	**800-634-8277**	507-288-4331
Visit Rochester 45 E Ave Ste 400	Rochester	NY	14604	**800-677-7282**	585-279-8300
Rockhill-York County Convention & Visitors Bureau 452 S Anderson Rd	Rock Hill	SC	29730	**888-702-1320**	803-329-5200
Rockford Area Convention & Visitors Bureau 102 N Main St	Rockford	IL	61101	**800-521-0849**	815-963-8111
Conference & Visitors Bureau of Montgomery County MD Inc 1801 Rockville Pk Ste 320	Rockville	MD	20852	**877-789-6904**	240-641-6750
Greater Rome Convention & Visitors Bureau 402 Civics Ctr Dr	Rome	GA	30161	**800-444-1834**	706-295-5576
Sacramento Convention & Visitors Bureau 1608 'I' St	Sacramento	CA	95814	**800-292-2334**	916-808-7777
Greater Saint Charles Convention & Visitors Bureau 230 S Main St	Saint Charles	MO	63301	**800-366-2427**	636-946-7776
Saint Cloud Area Convention & Visitors Bureau 1411 W St Germain St Ste 104	Saint Cloud	MN	56301	**800-264-2940**	320-251-4170
Saint Joseph Convention & Visitors Bureau 911 Frederick Ave	Saint Joseph	MO	64501	**800-785-0360**	816-233-6688
Auglaize & Mercer Counties Convention & Visitors Bureau 900 Edgewater Dr	Saint Marys	OH	45885	**800-860-4726**	419-394-1294
City Of Salem 101 S Broadway	Salem	IL	62881	**800-755-5000**	618-548-2222
Salem Convention & Visitors Assn 181 High St NE	Salem	OR	97301	**800-874-7012**	503-581-4325
Visit Salt Lake 90 SW Temple	Salt Lake City	UT	84101	**800-541-4955**	801-534-4900
San Angelo Chamber of Commerce 418 W Ave B	San Angelo	TX	76903	**800-252-1381**	325-655-4136
San Antonio Convention & Visitors Bureau 203 S St Marys St Ste 200	San Antonio	TX	78205	**800-447-3372**	210-207-6700
San Francisco Travel Assn 201 Third St Ste 900	San Francisco	CA	94103	**855-847-6272**	415-974-6900
San Jose Convention & Visitors Bureau 408 Almaden Blvd	San Jose	CA	95110	**800-726-5673**	
Puerto Rico Convention Center 500 Tanca Ste 402	San Juan	PR	00901	**800-875-4765**	787-725-2110
Marin Convention & Visitors Bureau 1 Mitchell Blvd Ste B	San Rafael	CA	94903	**866-925-2060**	415-925-2060
Santa Barbara Visitors Bureau & Film Commission 1601 Anacapa St	Santa Barbara	CA	93101	**800-676-1266**	805-966-9222
Santa Clara Convention/Visitors Bureau 1390 Madison St	Santa Clara	CA	95050	**800-272-6822**	408-244-8244
Santa Cruz County Conference & Visitors Council 303 Water St Ste 100	Santa Cruz	CA	95060	**800-833-3494**	831-425-1234
Santa Fe Convention Ctr 201 W Marcy St	Santa Fe	NM	87501	**800-777-2489**	505-955-6200
Santa Monica Convention & Visitors Bureau 1920 Main St Ste B	Santa Monica	CA	90405	**800-544-5319**	310-319-6263
Visit Sarasota County 1777 Main St Ste 302	Sarasota	FL	34236	**800-522-9799**	941-955-0991
Saratoga Convention & Tourism Bureau 60 Railroad Pl Ste 301	Saratoga Springs	NY	12866	**855-424-6073**	518-584-1531
Sault Sainte Marie Convention 225 E Portage Ave	Sault Sainte Marie	MI	49783	**800-647-2858**	906-632-3366
Savannah Area Convention & Visitors Bureau 101 E Bay St	Savannah	GA	31401	**877-728-2662**	912-644-6400
Greater Woodfield Convention & Visitors Bureau 1375 E Woodfield Rd Ste 120	Schaumburg	IL	60173	**800-847-4849**	847-490-1010
Scottsdale Convention & Visitors Bureau 4343 N Scottsdale Rd Ste 170	Scottsdale	AZ	85251	**800-782-1117**	480-421-1004
Seattle's Convention & Visitors Bureau 701 Pike St Ste 800	Seattle	WA	98101	**866-732-2695**	206-461-5800
Seward Convention & Visitors Bureau 2001 Seward Hwy	Seward	AK	99664	**800-257-7760**	907-224-8051
Shepherdsville-Bullitt County Tourist & Convention Commission 395 Paroquet Springs Dr	Shepherdsville	KY	40165	**800-526-2068**	502-543-8687
Shipshewana/LaGrange County Convention & Visitors Bureau 350 S Van Buren St Ste H	Shipshewana	IN	46565	**800-254-8090**	260-768-4008
Shreveport-Bossier Convention & Tourist Bureau 629 Spring St	Shreveport	LA	71101	**800-551-8682**	318-222-9391
Sioux Falls Convention & Visitors Bureau 200 N Phillips Ave Ste 102	Sioux Falls	SD	57104	**800-333-2072**	605-275-6060
Skagway Visitor Information 245 Broadway PO Box 1029	Skagway	AK	99840	**888-762-1898**	907-983-2854
Johnston County Visitors Bureau (JCVB) 234 Venture Dr	Smithfield	NC	27577	**800-441-7829**	919-989-8687
South Bend/Mishawaka Convention & Visitors Bureau 101 N Michigan St Ste 300	South Bend	IN	46601	**800-519-0577**	
Lake Tahoe Visitors Authority 3066 Lake Tahoe Blvd	South Lake Tahoe	CA	96150	**800-288-2463**	530-544-5050
South Padre Island Convention & Visitors Bureau 7355 Padre Blvd	South Padre Island	TX	78597	**800-767-2373**	956-761-6433
South Sioux City Convention & Visitors Bureau 4401 Dakota Ave	South Sioux City	NE	68776	**866-494-1307**	402-494-1307
Pinehurst Southern Pines Aberdeen Area 165 NE Broad St	Southern Pines	NC	28387	**800-346-5362**	910-692-6926
Spartanburg Convention & Visitors Bureau 298 Magnolia St	Spartanburg	SC	29306	**800-374-8326**	864-594-5050
Spokane Convention & Visitors Bureau Main Level River Park Sq 808 W Main Ave	Spokane	WA	99201	**800-662-0084**	509-624-1341
Greater Springfield Convention & Visitors Bureau 1441 Main St	Springfield	MA	01103	**800-723-1548**	413-787-1548
Greater Springfield Convention & Visitors Bureau 20 S Limestone St Ste 100	Springfield	OH	45502	**800-803-1553**	937-325-7621
Springfield Convention & Visitors Bureau 109 N Seventh St	Springfield	IL	62701	**800-545-7300**	217-789-2360
Springfield Missouri Convention & Visitors Bureau 815 E St Louis St Ste 100	Springfield	MO	65806	**800-678-8767**	417-881-5300
Brunswick & The Golden Isles of Georgia Visitors Bureau 529 Beachview Dr	St Simons Island	GA	31522	**800-933-2627**	912-638-9014
Centre County Convention & Visitors Bureau 800 E Park Ave	State College	PA	16803	**800-358-5466**	814-231-1400
Pocono Mountains Vacation Bureau 1004 W Main St	Stroudsburg	PA	18360	**800-722-9199**	570-421-5791
Racine County Convention & Visitors Bureau 14015 Washington Ave	Sturtevant	WI	53177	**800-272-2463**	262-884-6400
Central Oregon Visitors Assn 57100 Beaver Dr Bldg 6 Ste 130	Sunriver	OR	97707	**800-800-8334**	
Superior/Douglas County Convention & Visitors Bureau 305 Harborview Pkwy	Superior	WI	54880	**800-942-5313**	715-392-7151
Illinois South Tourism 4387 N Illinois St Ste 200	Swansea	IL	62226	**800-442-1488**	618-257-1488
Tacoma Regional Convention & Visitor Bureau 1516 Commerce St	Tacoma	WA	98402	**800-272-2662**	253-627-2836
North Lake Tahoe Resort Assn 100 N Lake Blvd	Tahoe City	CA	96145	**800-468-2463**	530-583-3494
North Lake Tahoe Visitors & Convention Bureau PO Box 1757	Tahoe City	CA	96145	**800-462-5196**	530-581-6900
Chambers of Commerce / Tourism 106 E Jefferson St	Tallahassee	FL	32301	**800-628-2866**	850-606-2305
Tampa Bay & Co 401 E Jackson St Ste 2100	Tampa	FL	33602	**877-230-0078**	813-223-1111
Tempe Tourism Office 222 S Mill Ave Ste 120	Tempe	AZ	85281	**866-914-1052**	480-894-8158
Three Lakes Information Bureau 1704 Superior St PO Box 268	Three Lakes	WI	54562	**800-972-6103**	715-546-3344
Destination toledo 401 Jefferson Ave	Toledo	OH	43604	**800-243-4667**	419-321-6404
Tomah Convention & Visitors Bureau 310 N Superior Ave PO Box 625	Tomah	WI	54660	**800-948-6624**	608-372-2166
Visit Topeka Inc 618 S Kansas Ave	Topeka	KS	66603	**800-235-1030**	785-234-1030
Toronto Convention & Visitors Assn 207 Queen's Quay W Ste 405 PO Box 126	Toronto	ON	M5J1A7	**800-499-2514**	416-203-2600

Name / Address	City	State	ZIP	Toll-Free	Phone
Smoky Mountain Visitors Bureau 7906 E Lamar Alexander Pkwy	Townsend	TN	37882	**800-525-6834**	865-448-6134
Traverse City Convention & Visitors Bureau 101 W Grandview Pkwy	Traverse City	MI	49684	**800-940-1120**	231-947-1120
DeKalb Convention & Visitors Bureau 1957 Lakeside Pkwy Ste 510	Tucker	GA	30084	**866-633-5252**	770-492-5000
Tulsa Convention & Visitors Bureau 1 W Third St Ste 100	Tulsa	OK	74103	**800-558-3311**	
Tunica MS 13625 Hwy 61 N	Tunica Resorts	MS	38664	**888-488-6422**	
Tyler Convention & Visitors Bureau (TCVB) 315 N Broadway Ave	Tyler	TX	75702	**800-235-5712**	903-592-1661
Oneida County Convention & Visitors Bureau PO Box 551	Utica	NY	13503	**800-426-3132**	315-724-7221
Mast General Store Inc Hwy 194	Valle Crucis	NC	28691	**866-367-6278**	828-963-6511
Vallejo Convention & Visitors Bureau 289 Mare Island Way *General	Vallejo	CA	94590	**866-921-9277***	707-642-3653
Greater Vancouver Convention & Visitors Bureau 200 Burrard St	Vancouver	BC	V6C3L6	**800-561-0123**	604-682-2222
Southwest Washington Convention & Visitors Bureau 1220 Main S Ste 220	Vancouver	WA	98660	**877-600-0800**	360-750-1553
Ventura Visitors & Convention Bureau 101 S California St	Ventura	CA	93001	**800-333-2989**	805-648-2075
Brevard County Tourism Development 2725 Judge Fran Jamieson Way	Viera	FL	32940	**800-955-8771**	321-633-2000
Virginia Beach Convention & Visitor Bureau (VBCVB) 2101 Parks Ave Ste 500	Virginia Beach	VA	23451	**800-700-7702**	757-385-4700
Visalia Convention & Visitors Bureau PO Box 2734	Visalia	CA	93279	**800-524-0303**	559-334-0141
Waco Convention & Visitors Bureau 100 Washington Ave	Waco	TX	76701	**800-321-9226**	254-750-5810
Kallman Worldwide Inc 4 N St Ste 800	Waldwick	NJ	07463	**877-492-7028**	201-251-2600
Warren County Visitors Bureau 22045 Rt 6	Warren	PA	16365	**800-624-7802**	814-726-1222
Washington DC Convention & Tourism Corp 901 Seventh St NW 4th Fl	Washington	DC	20001	**800-422-8644**	202-789-7000
Waterloo Convention & Visitor Bureau 500 Jefferson St	Waterloo	IA	50701	**800-728-8431**	319-233-8350
Wausau Central Wisconsin Convention & Visitors Bureau (CWCVB) 219 Jefferson St	Wausau	WI	54403	**888-948-4748**	715-355-8788
Tioga County Visitors Bureau 2053 Rt 660	Wellsboro	PA	16901	**888-846-4228**	570-724-0635
West Branch Area Chamber of Commerce 422 W Houghton Ave	West Branch	MI	48661	**800-755-9091**	989-345-2821
West Hollywood Marketing Corp 1017 N La Cienega Blvd Ste 400	West Hollywood	CA	90069	**800-368-6020**	310-289-2525
Monroe-West Monroe Convention & Visitors Bureau 601 Constitution Dr PO Box 1436	West Monroe	LA	71292	**800-843-1872**	318-387-5691
Discover The Palm Beaches 1555 Palm Beach Lakes Blvd Ste 800	West Palm Beach	FL	33401	**800-554-7256**	561-233-3000
Wheeling Convention & Visitors Bureau 1401 Main St	Wheeling	WV	26003	**800-828-3097**	304-233-7709
Westchester County Tourism & Film 148 Martine Ave Ste 104	White Plains	NY	10601	**800-833-9282**	914-995-8500
Wichita Convention & Visitors Bureau 515 Main St Ste 115	Wichita	KS	67202	**800-288-9424**	316-265-2800
Williamsburg Destination Marketing Committee 421 N Boundary St	Williamsburg	VA	23185	**800-368-6511**	757-229-6511
Martin County Travel & Tourism Authority 100 E Church St PO Box 382	Williamston	NC	27892	**800-776-8566**	252-792-6605
Greater Wilmington Convention & Visitors Bureau 100 W Tenth St Ste 20	Wilmington	DE	19801	**800-489-6664**	
Wilmington & Beaches CVB 505 Nutt St Unit A	Wilmington	NC	28401	**877-406-2356**	910-341-4030
Winnemucca Convention & Visitors Authority 50 W Winnemucca Blvd	Winnemucca	NV	89445	**800-962-2638**	775-623-5071
Winston-Salem Convention & Visitors Bureau 200 Brookstown Ave	Winston-Salem	NC	27101	**866-728-4200**	336-728-4200
Wisconsin Dells Visitors & Convention Bureau 701 Superior St PO Box 390	Wisconsin Dells	WI	53965	**800-223-3557**	608-254-8088
Wayne County Convention & Visitors Bureau 428 W Liberty St	Wooster	OH	44691	**800-362-6474**	
Mahoning County Convention & Visitors Bureau 21 W Boardman St	Youngstown	OH	44503	**800-447-8201**	330-740-2130
Yuma Convention & Visitors Bureau 201 N Fourth Ave	Yuma	AZ	85364	**800-293-0071**	928-783-0071

207 CONVEYORS & CONVEYING EQUIPMENT

SEE ALSO Material Handling Equipment

Name / Address	City	State	ZIP	Toll-Free	Phone
Airfloat LLC 2230 Brush College Rd	Decatur	IL	62526	**800-888-0018**	217-423-6001
Allor Manufacturing Inc 12534 Emerson Dr	Brighton	MI	48116	**888-382-6300**	248-486-4500
AMF Bakery Systems 2115 W Laburnum Ave	Richmond	VA	23227	**800-225-3771**	804-355-7961
Automatic Systems Inc 9230 E 47th St	Kansas City	MO	64133	**800-366-3488**	816-356-0660
Beltservice Corp 4143 Rider Trl N	Earth City	MO	63045	**800-727-2358**	314-344-8555
BW Container Systems 1305 Lakeview Dr	Romeoville	IL	60446	**800-527-0494**	630-759-6800
C & M Conveyor 4598 State Rd 37	Mitchell	IN	47446	**800-551-3195**	812-849-5647
Cambelt International Corp 2820 West 1100 South	Salt Lake City	UT	84104	**855-226-2358**	801-972-5511
Cambridge International 105 Goodwill Rd	Cambridge	MD	21613	**800-638-9560**	410-901-4979
Carrier Vibrating Equipment Inc 3400 Fern Valley Rd	Louisville	KY	40213	**800-547-7278**	502-969-3171
Christianson Systems Inc 20421 15th St SE PO Box 138	Blomkest	MN	56216	**800-328-8896**	320-995-6141
Conveyor Components Co 130 Seltzer Rd *Cust Svc	Croswell	MI	48422	**800-233-3233***	810-679-4211
Conveyors Inc 620 S Fourth Ave	Mansfield	TX	76063	**800-243-9327**	817-473-4645
Cyclonaire Corp 2922 N Division Ave	York	NE	68467	**800-445-0730**	402-362-2000
Dematic 507 Plymouth Ave NE *Cust Svc	Grand Rapids	MI	49505	**877-725-7500***	
Engineered Products Inc 500 Furman Hall Rd	Greenville	SC	29609	**888-301-1421**	864-234-4868
Essmueller Co 334 Ave A PO Box 1966	Laurel	MS	39440	**800-325-7175**	601-649-2400
Evana Automation 5825 Old Boonville Hwy	Evansville	IN	47715	**800-468-6774**	812-479-8246
Feeco International Inc 3913 Algoma Rd	Green Bay	WI	54311	**800-373-9347**	
Flexible Steel Lacing Co 2525 Wisconsin Ave	Downers Grove	IL	60515	**800-323-3444**	630-971-0150
Garvey Corp 208 S Rt 73	Blue Anchor	NJ	08037	**800-257-8581**	609-561-2450
Hansen Manufacturing Corp 5100 W 12th St	Sioux Falls	SD	57107	**800-328-1785**	605-332-3200
Hapman 6002 E N Ave	Kalamazoo	MI	49048	**800-427-6260**	269-343-1675
Hytrol Conveyor Company Inc 2020 Hytrol St	Jonesboro	AR	72401	**800-852-3233**	870-935-3700
Intelligrated Products 475 E High St PO Box 899	London	OH	43140	**866-936-7300**	740-490-0300
Jorgensen Conveyors Inc 10303 N Baehr Rd	Mequon	WI	53092	**800-325-7705**	262-242-3089
Kice Industries Inc 5500 N Mill Heights Dr	Wichita	KS	67219	**877-289-5423**	316-744-7151
KWS Mfg Company Ltd 3041 Conveyor Dr	Burleson	TX	76028	**800-543-6558**	817-295-2247
Laitram LLC 200 Laitram Ln	Harahan	LA	70123	**800-535-7631**	504-733-6000
Martin Engineering 1 Martin Pl	Neponset	IL	61345	**800-544-2947**	309-594-2384
Metzgar Conveyor Co Inc 901 Metzgar Dr NW	Comstock Park	MI	49321	**888-266-8390**	616-784-0930
Prab Inc 5944 E Kilgore Rd	Kalamazoo	MI	49048	**800-968-7722**	269-382-8200
Ralphs-pugh Company Inc 3931 Oregon St	Benicia	CA	94510	**800-486-0021**	707-745-6222
Rapat Corp 919 Odonnel St	Hawley	MN	56549	**800-325-6377**	218-483-3344
Rapid Industries 4003 Oaklawn Dr	Louisville	KY	40219	**800-727-4381**	502-968-3645
Renold Jeffrey 2307 Maden Dr	Morristown	TN	37813	**800-251-9012**	
Richards-Wilcox Inc 600 S Lake St	Aurora	IL	60506	**800-253-5668**	
Roll-A-Way Conveyor Inc 2335 Delaney Rd	Gurnee	IL	60031	**800-747-9024**	847-336-5033
Schroeder Industries LLC 580 W Pk Rd	Leetsdale	PA	15056	**800-722-4810**	724-318-1100
SencorpWhite 400 Kidds Hill Rd	Hyannis	MA	02601	**800-571-8822**	508-771-9400
Shick Tube Veyor Corp 4346 Clary Blvd	Kansas City	MO	64130	**877-744-2587**	816-861-7224
Shuttleworth Inc 10 Commercial Rd	Huntington	IN	46750	**800-444-7412**	260-356-8500
Stewart Systems 808 Stewart Ave	Plano	TX	75074	**800-966-5808**	972-422-5808
Superior Industries LLC 315 E State Hwy 28 PO Box 684	Morris	MN	56267	**800-321-1558**	320-589-2406
Sweet Mfg Company Inc 2000 E Leffel Ln *Cust Svc	Springfield	OH	45505	**800-334-7254***	937-325-1511
Swisslog 10825 E 47th Ave	Denver	CO	80239	**800-525-1841**	303-371-7770
Thomas Conveyor Co 555 N Burleson Blvd	Burleson	TX	76028	**800-433-2217**	817-295-7151
Transco Industries Inc 5534 NE 122nd Ave	Portland	OR	97230	**800-545-9991**	503-256-1955
Universal Industries Inc 5800 Nordic Dr	Cedar Falls	IA	50613	**800-553-4446**	319-277-7501
VAC-U-MAX 69 William St	Belleville	NJ	07109	**800-822-8629**	973-759-4600
W & H Systems Inc 120 Asia Pl	Carlstadt	NJ	07072	**800-966-6993**	201-933-7840
Webster Industries Inc 325 Hall St	Tiffin	OH	44883	**800-243-9327**	419-447-8232
Westfalia Technologies Inc 3655 Sandhurst Dr	York	PA	17406	**800-673-2522**	717-764-1115
Whirl Air Flow Corp 20055 177th St	Big Lake	MN	55309	**800-373-3461**	763-262-1200
White Conveyors Inc 10 Boright Ave	Kenilworth	NJ	07033	**800-524-0273**	908-686-5700
Wire Belt Company of America 154 Harvey Rd *Cust Svc	Londonderry	NH	03053	**800-922-2637***	603-644-2500
Young Industries Inc 16 Painter St	Muncy	PA	17756	**800-546-3165**	570-546-3165

208 CORD & TWINE

Name / Address	City	State	ZIP	Toll-Free	Phone
Ashaway Line & Twine Manufacturing Co 24 Laurel St	Ashaway	RI	02804	**800-556-7260**	401-377-2221
Atkins & Pearce Inc 1 Braid Way	Covington	KY	41017	**800-837-7477**	859-356-2001
Bridon Cordage LLC 909 E 16th St	Albert Lea	MN	56007	**800-533-6002**	507-377-1601
Carron Net Company Inc 1623 17th St PO Box 177	Two Rivers	WI	54241	**800-558-7768**	920-793-2217
Everson Cordage Works Inc 7180 Everson-Goshen Rd	Everson	WA	98247	**800-966-0203**	
I & I Sling Inc PO Box 2423	Aston	PA	19014	**800-874-3539**	610-485-8500

				Toll-Free	Phone
Pacific Fibre & Rope Company Inc					
903 Flint St	Wilmington	CA	90744	**800-825-7673**	310-834-4567
Pelican Rope Works Inc					
4001 W Carriage Dr	Santa Ana	CA	92704	**800-464-7673**	714-545-0116
PlymKraft Inc					
479 Export Cir	Newport News	VA	23601	**800-992-0854**	757-595-0364
Puget Sound Rope Corp					
1012 Second St	Anacortes	WA	98221	**888-525-8488**	360-293-8488
Rocky Mount Cord Co					
381 N Grace St	Rocky Mount	NC	27804	**800-342-9130***	252-977-9130
*Orders					
Samson Rope Technologies Inc					
2090 Thornton Rd	Ferndale	WA	98248	**800-227-7673***	360-384-4669
*Cust Svc					

209   CORK & CORK PRODUCTS

SEE ALSO Office & School Supplies

				Toll-Free	Phone
Expanko Resilient Flooring					
180 Gordon Dr Ste 107	Exton	PA	19341	**800-345-6202**	
Manton Industrial Cork Products Inc					
415 Oser Ave Unit U	Hauppauge	NY	11788	**800-663-1921**	
Maryland Cork Co Inc					
505 Blue Ball Rd Ste 190	Elkton	MD	21921	**800-662-2675**	410-398-2955

210   CORPORATE HOUSING

				Toll-Free	Phone
Churchill Corporate Services					
56 Utter Ave	Hawthorne	NJ	07506	**800-941-7458**	973-636-9400
Coast to Coast Corporate Housing					
10773 Los Alamitos Blvd	Los Alamitos	CA	90720	**800-451-9466**	
ExecSuite 702 3 Ave SW	Calgary	AB	T2P3B4	**800-667-4980**	403-294-5800
Klein & Company Corporate Housing Services Inc					
914 Washington Ave	Golden	CO	80401	**800-208-9826**	303-796-2100
Marriott International Inc					
10400 Fernwood Rd	Bethesda	MD	20817	**800-450-4442**	301-380-3000
NASDAQ: MAR					
Oakwood Crystal City					
400 15th St S	Arlington	VA	22202	**877-902-0832**	877-891-6844
Oakwood Worldwide					
2222 Corinth Ave	Los Angeles	CA	90064	**800-888-0808**	310-478-1021

211   CORRECTIONAL & DETENTION MANAGEMENT (PRIVATIZED)

SEE ALSO Correctional Facilities - Federal ; Correctional Facilities - State ; Juvenile Detention Facilities

				Toll-Free	Phone
Colorado Correctional Industries					
4999 Oakland St	Denver	CO	80239	**800-685-7891***	719-226-4206
*Cust Svc					
CoreCivic					
10 Burton Hills Blvd	Nashville	TN	37215	**800-624-2931**	615-263-3000
NYSE: CXW					

212   CORRECTIONAL FACILITIES - FEDERAL

SEE ALSO Correctional & Detention Management (Privatized) ; Correctional Facilities - State ; Juvenile Detention Facilities

				Toll-Free	Phone
Federal Correctional Institution (FCI)					
Bastrop					
1341 Hwy 95 N PO Box 730	Bastrop	TX	78602	**800-995-6429**	512-321-3903
Butner					
Old NC Hwy 75 PO Box 1000	Butner	NC	27509	**877-623-8426**	919-575-4541
Englewood					
9595 W Quincy Ave	Littleton	CO	80123	**877-623-8426**	303-763-4300
Fairton					
655 Fairton-Millville Rd PO Box 280	Fairton	NJ	08320	**877-623-8426**	856-453-1177
Forrest City					
1400 Dale Bumpers Rd	Forrest City	AR	72335	**877-623-8426**	870-630-6000
Loretto 772 St Joseph St	Loretto	PA	15940	**877-623-8426**	814-472-4140
Manchester					
805 Fox Hollow Rd	Manchester	KY	40962	**877-623-8426**	606-598-1900
MCKEAN FCI 6975 Rt 59	Lewis Run	PA	16738	**877-623-8426**	814-362-8900
Oxford PO Box 500	Oxford	WI	53952	**800-995-6423**	608-584-5511
Yazoo City					
2225 Haley Barbour Pkwy					
PO Box 5050	Yazoo City	MS	39194	**877-623-8426**	662-751-4800

213   CORRECTIONAL FACILITIES - STATE

SEE ALSO Correctional Facilities - Federal ; Correctional & Detention Management (Privatized) ; Juvenile Detention Facilities

Alaska

				Toll-Free	Phone
Fairbanks Correctional Ctr					
1931 Eagan Ave	Fairbanks	AK	99701	**844-934-2381**	907-458-6700

Arizona

				Toll-Free	Phone
Arizona State Prison Complex-Eyman					
4374 E Butte Ave	Florence	AZ	85132	**866-333-2039**	520-868-0201

Arkansas

				Toll-Free	Phone
Dept of Corrections Maximum Security Unit					
2501 State Farm Rd	Tucker	AR	72168	**866-801-3435**	501-842-3800

Delta Unit Arkansas Department of Corrections

				Toll-Free	Phone
880 E Gaines	Dermott	AR	71638	**800-482-1127**	870-538-2000

Colorado

				Toll-Free	Phone
Fremont Correctional Facility (FCF)					
E US Hwy 50 Evans Blvd PO Box 999	Canon City	CO	81215	**800-886-7683**	719-269-5002

Florida

				Toll-Free	Phone
Okeechobee Correctional Institution					
3420 NE 168th St	Okeechobee	FL	34972	**800-574-5729**	863-462-5400
South Bay Correctional Facility					
600 US Hwy 27 S	South Bay	FL	33493	**800-574-5729**	561-992-9505

Illinois

				Toll-Free	Phone
Centralia Correctional Ctr					
9330 Shattuc Rd PO Box 1266	Centralia	IL	62801	**844-258-9071**	
Danville Correctional Ctr					
3820 E Main St	Danville	IL	61834	**844-258-9071**	
Jacksonville Correctional Ctr					
2268 E Morton Ave	Jacksonville	IL	62650	**800-526-0844**	217-245-1481
Pontiac Correctional Ctr					
700 W Lincoln St	Pontiac	IL	61764	**800-275-7877**	815-842-2816
Stateville Correctional Ctr					
16830 S Broadway St PO Box 112	Joliet	IL	60434	**800-526-0844**	815-727-3607

Indiana

				Toll-Free	Phone
Miami Correctional Facility					
3038 W 850 S	Bunker Hill	IN	46914	**800-451-6028**	765-689-8920
Plainfield Correctional Facility					
727 Moon Rd	Plainfield	IN	46168	**800-451-6028**	317-839-2513
Rockville Correctional Facility					
811 W 50 N	Rockville	IN	47872	**800-451-6028**	765-569-3178
Wabash Valley Correctional Facility					
6908 S Old US Hwy 41 PO Box 500	Carlisle	IN	47838	**800-677-9800**	

Iowa

				Toll-Free	Phone
Iowa State Penitentiary					
Ave E & 1st St PO Box 409	Fort Madison	IA	52627	**800-382-0019**	319-372-1908

Kentucky

				Toll-Free	Phone
Blackburn Correctional Complex					
3111 Spurr Rd	Lexington	KY	40511	**800-808-1213**	859-246-2366
Correctional Institution for Women					
3000 Ash Ave	Pewee Valley	KY	40056	**877-687-6818**	502-241-8454
Luther Luckett Correctional Complex					
Dawkins Rd PO Box 6	LaGrange	KY	40031	**800-511-1670**	502-222-0363

Maryland

				Toll-Free	Phone
Jessup Correctional Institution					
PO Box 534	Jessup	MD	20794	**877-304-9755**	410-799-0100
Maryland Correctional Training Center					
18800 Roxbury Rd	Hagerstown	MD	21746	**877-692-8136**	240-420-1601
Roxbury Correctional Institution					
18701 Roxbury Rd	Hagerstown	MD	21746	**800-464-0764**	240-420-3000

Michigan

				Toll-Free	Phone
Baraga Correctional Facility					
13924 Wadaga Rd	Baraga	MI	49908	**800-326-4537**	906-353-7070
Hiawatha Correctional Facility					
4533 W Industrial Pk Dr	Kincheloe	MI	49786	**800-642-4838**	906-495-5661
Kinross Correctional Facility					
16770 S Watertower Dr	Kincheloe	MI	49788	**800-326-4537**	906-495-2282
Lakeland Correctional Facility					
141 First St	Coldwater	MI	49036	**800-326-4537**	517-278-6942

Missouri

				Toll-Free	Phone
Farmington Correctional Ctr					
1012 W Columbia St	Farmington	MO	63640	**800-844-6591**	573-218-7100
Western Missouri Correctional Ctr					
609 E Pence Rd	Cameron	MO	64429	**800-726-7390**	816-632-1390

Montana

				Toll-Free	Phone
Montana State Prison					
400 Conley Lake Rd	Deer Lodge	MT	59722	**888-739-9122**	406-846-1320

North Carolina

				Toll-Free	Phone
Sampson Correctional Institution					
700 NW Blvd Hwy 421N	Clinton	NC	28328	**800-368-1985**	910-592-2151
Wake Correctional Ctr					
1000 Rock Quarry Rd	Raleigh	NC	27610	**866-719-0108**	919-733-7988

Ohio

				Toll-Free	Phone
Lorain Correctional Institution					
2075 Avon Belden Rd	Grafton	OH	44044	**888-842-8464**	440-748-1049

		Toll-Free	Phone

Marion Correctional Institution
PO Box 57 . . . . Marion OH 43302 — 800-237-3454 — 740-382-5781

Richland Correctional Institution
1001 Olivesburg Rd . . . . Mansfield OH 44905 — 800-686-4208 — 419-526-2100

Southeastern Correctional Institution
5900 B I S Rd . . . . Lancaster OH 43130 — 800-237-3454 — 740-653-4324

Oklahoma

		Toll-Free	Phone

Davis Correctional Facility
6888 E 133rd Rd . . . . Holdenville OK 74848 — 877-834-1550 — 405-379-6400

South Carolina

		Toll-Free	Phone

Goodman Correctional Institution
4556 Broad River Rd . . . . Columbia SC 29210 — 866-230-7761 — 803-896-8565

Tennessee

		Toll-Free	Phone

Wayne County Boot Camp
PO Box 182 . . . . Clifton TN 38425 — 855-876-7283 — 931-676-3345

Vermont

		Toll-Free	Phone

Northern State Correctional Facility
2559 Glen Rd . . . . Newport VT 05855 — 800-347-0488 — 802-334-3364

Washington

		Toll-Free	Phone

Washington State Reformatory
16550 177th Ave SE PO Box 777 . . . . Monroe WA 98272 — 800-483-8314 — 360-794-2600

West Virginia

		Toll-Free	Phone

Northern Regional Correctional Facility
112 Northern Regional Correctional Dr
. . . . Moundsville WV 26041 — 866-984-8463 — 304-843-4067

214   COSMETICS, SKIN CARE, AND OTHER PERSONAL CARE PRODUCTS

SEE ALSO Perfumes

		Toll-Free	Phone

AHAVA North America
330 Seventh Ave . . . . New York NY 10001 — 800-366-7254

Aire-Master of America Inc
1821 N State Hwy CC . . . . Nixa MO 65714 — 800-525-0957 — 417-725-2691

Apothecary Products
11750 12th Ave S Burnsville . . . . Burnsville MN 55337 — 800-328-2742

At Last Naturals Inc
401 Columbus Ave . . . . Valhalla NY 10595 — 800-527-8123 — 914-747-3599

Aveda Corp
4000 Pheasant Ridge Dr . . . . Blaine MN 55449 — 800-644-4831

Bath & Body Works
7 Limited Pkwy E . . . . Reynoldsburg OH 43068 — 800-395-1001

Belcam Inc Delagar Div
27 Montgomery St . . . . Rouses Point NY 12979 — 800-328-3006 — 518-297-3366

Bronner Bros Inc
2141 Powers Ferry Rd . . . . Marietta GA 30067 — 800-241-6151 — 770-988-0015

CBI Laboratories
4201 Diplomacy Rd . . . . Fort Worth TX 76155 — 800-822-7546 — 972-241-7546

CCA Industries Inc
193 Conshohocken State Rd . . . . Penn Valley PA 19072 — 800-595-6230*
NYSE: CAW ■ *Cust Svc

Church & Dwight Company Inc
469 N Harrison St . . . . Princeton NJ 08543 — 800-617-4220
NYSE: CHD

Clinique Laboratories Inc
767 Fifth Ave . . . . New York NY 10153 — 800-419-4041 — 212-572-3983

Combe Inc
1101 Westchester Ave . . . . White Plains NY 10604 — 800-431-2610

Crabtree & Evelyn Ltd
102 Peake Brook Rd . . . . Woodstock CT 06281 — 800-272-2873 — 860-928-2761

DEB Inc
2815 Coliseum Centre Dr Ste 600 . . . . Charlotte NC 28217 — 800-248-7190 — 704-263-4240

Farouk Systems Inc
250 Pennbright Dr . . . . Houston TX 77090 — 800-237-9175 — 281-876-2000

Forever Living Products International Inc
7501 E McCormick Pkwy . . . . Scottsdale AZ 85258 — 888-440-2563 — 480-998-8888

GOJO Industries Inc
1 GOJO Plz Ste 500 . . . . Akron OH 44311 — 800-321-9647 — 330-255-6000

Guest Supply Inc
300 Davidson Ave . . . . Somerset NJ 08873 — 800-772-7676*
*Cust Svc — 732-868-2200

Gurwitch Products LLC
135 E 57th St . . . . New York NY 10022 — 888-637-2437 — 212-376-6300

Jan Marini Skin Research Inc
6951 Via Del Oro . . . . San Jose CA 95119 — 800-347-2223 — 408-362-0130

John Paul Mitchell Systems
1888 Century Park E Ste 1600 . . . . Los Angeles CA 90067 — 800-793-8790* — 800-027-4066
*Cust Svc

Johnson & Johnson Consumer Products Co
199 Grandview Rd . . . . Skillman NJ 08558 — 866-565-2229 — 908-874-1000

Johnson & Johnson Inc
890 Woodlawn Rd W` . . . . Guelph ON N1K1A5 — 877-223-9807

Key West Aloe
13095 N Telecom Pkwy . . . . Tampa FL 33637 — 800-445-2563

L'Oreal USA 575 Fifth Ave . . . . New York NY 10017 — 800-322-2036 — 212-818-1500

		Toll-Free	Phone

Luster Products Inc
1104 W 43rd St . . . . Chicago IL 60609 — 800-621-4255 — 773-579-1800

Mary Kay Inc PO Box 799045 . . . . Dallas TX 75379 — 800-627-9529* — 972-687-6300
*Cust Svc

Maybelline New York
575 Fifth Ave PO Box 1010. . . . . New York NY 10017 — 800-944-0730

Merle Norman Cosmetics Inc
9130 Bellanca Ave . . . . Los Angeles CA 90045 — 800-421-6648 — 310-641-3000

Neutrogena Corp
5760 W 96th St . . . . Los Angeles CA 90045 — 800-582-4048 — 310-642-1150

Obagi Medical Products Inc
3760 Kilroy Airport Way Ste 500 . . . . . . Long Beach CA 90806 — 800-636-7546 — 562-628-1007

Origins Natural Resources Inc
767 Fifth Ave . . . . New York NY 10153 — 800-674-4467*
*Cust Svc

Paramount Cosmetics Inc
93 Entin Rd Ste 4 . . . . Clifton NJ 07014 — 800-522-9880 — 973-472-2323

Person & Covey Inc
616 Allen Ave . . . . Glendale CA 91201 — 800-423-2341

Peter Thomas Roth Labs LLC
460 Park Ave 16th Fl . . . . New York NY 10022 — 800-787-7546 — 212-581-5800

Pfizer Inc 235 E 42nd St . . . . New York NY 10017 — 800-879-3477 — 212-733-2323
NYSE: PFE

Philosophy Inc
3809 E Watkins . . . . Phoenix AZ 85034 — 800-568-3151

Revlon Consumer Products Corp
1501 Williamsboro St . . . . Oxford NC 27565 — 800-473-8566 — 212-527-4000

Rozelle Cosmetics
4260 Loop Rd . . . . Westfield VT 05874 — 800-451-4216

Sephora USA Inc
525 Market St
1st Market Twr 32nd Fl . . . . San Francisco CA 94105 — 877-737-4672*
*Cust Svc

Sothys USA Inc
1500 NW 94th Ave . . . . Miami FL 33172 — 800-325-0503 — 305-594-4222

Star Nail Products Inc
29120 Ave Paine . . . . Valencia CA 91355 — 800-762-6245 — 661-257-7827

Tom's of Maine Inc
302 Lafayette Ctr . . . . Kennebunk ME 04043 — 800-367-8667

ULTA Beauty
1000 Remington Blvd Ste 120 . . . . Bolingbrook IL 60440 — 866-983-8582 — 630-410-4800

Urban Decay
833 W 16th St . . . . Newport Beach CA 92663 — 800-784-8722

Vi-Jon Labs Inc
8800 Page Ave . . . . Saint Louis MO 63114 — 800-227-1863 — 314-427-1000

Wahl Clipper Corp
2900 Locust St . . . . Sterling IL 61081 — 800-767-9245

Wella Corp
4500 Park Granada . . . . Calabasas CA 91302 — 800-422-2336

215   CREDIT CARD PROVIDERS & RELATED SERVICES

Companies listed here include those that issue credit cards as well as companies that provide services to these companies (i.e., rewards programs, theft prevention, etc.).

		Toll-Free	Phone

American Advisors Group
3800 W Chapman Ave 3rd Fl . . . . Orange CA 92868 — 866-948-0003

American Express Company Inc
World Financial Ctr 200 Vesey St . . . . New York NY 10285 — 800-528-4800 — 212-640-2000
NYSE: AXP

Applied Card Systems
50 Applied Card Way . . . . Glen Mills PA 19342 — 866-227-5627

Capital One Financial Corp
1680 Capital One Dr . . . . McLean VA 22102 — 800-655-2265 — 800-926-1000
NYSE: COF

Chevron Texaco Credit Card Ctr
PO Box P . . . . Concord CA 94524 — 800-243-8766

Diners Club International
8430 W Bryn Mawr Ave . . . . Chicago IL 60631 — 800-234-6377 — 773-380-5160

Green Dot Corp
3465 E Foothill Blvd . . . . Pasadena CA 91107 — 866-795-7597

Loan Science PO Box 81671 . . . . Austin TX 78708 — 866-311-9450

MasterCard Inc
2000 Purchase St . . . . Purchase NY 10577 — 800-100-1087 — 914-249-2000
NYSE: MA

Rewards Network
2 N Riverside Plz Ste 200 . . . . Chicago IL 60606 — 866-844-3753 — 866-559-3463

Transaction Network Services Inc
10740 Parkridge Blvd Ste 100 . . . . Reston VA 20191 — 866-523-0661 — 703-453-8300

Wright Express Corp
97 Darling Ave . . . . South Portland ME 04106 — 800-761-7181 — 207-773-8171
NYSE: WEX

216   CREDIT & FINANCING - COMMERCIAL

SEE ALSO Banks - Commercial & Savings ; Credit & Financing - Consumer

		Toll-Free	Phone

AFCO Credit Corp
14 Wall St . . . . New York NY 10005 — 800-288-6901 — 212-401-4400

American AgCredit (ACA)
PO Box 1120 . . . . Santa Rosa CA 95402 — 800-800-4865 — 707-545-1200

Arkansas Capital Corp Group
200 River Market Ave Ste 400 . . . . Little Rock AR 72201 — 800-216-7237 — 501-374-9247

ATEL Capital Group
600 California St 9th Fl . . . . San Francisco CA 94111 — 800-543-2835

Automotive Finance Corp (AFC)
13085 Hamilton Crossing Blvd . . . . Carmel IN 46032 — 888-335-6675 — 865-384-8250

Bank of America Business Capital
100 North Tryon St . . . . Charlotte NC 28255 — 800-521-3984

BMO Financial Corp
1 First Canadian Pl 21st Fl . . . . Toronto ON M5X1A1 — 800-553-0332 — 416-359-4440

Bombardier Capital Inc
1 Learjet Way Mailstop 1 . . . . Wichita KS 05446 — 800-949-5568 — 802-764-5232

Cascade Federal Credit Union
18020 80th Ave S . . . . Kent WA 98032 — 800-562-2853 — 425-251-8888

	City	State	ZIP	Toll-Free	Phone
CDC Small Business Finance Corp 2448 Historic Decatur Rd Ste 200	San Diego	CA	92106	**800-611-5170**	619-291-3594
Co-op Finance Assn Inc, The 10100 N Ambassador Dr Ste 315 PO Box 842702	Kansas City	MO	64153	**877-835-5232**	816-214-4200
Colonial Farm Credit Aca 7104 Mechanicsville Tpke	Mechanicsville	VA	23111	**800-777-8908**	804-746-1252
DLL 1111 Old Eagle School Rd	Wayne	PA	19087	**800-873-2474**	610-386-5000
Farm Credit Leasing (FCL) 600 Hwy 169 S Ste 300	Minneapolis	MN	55426	**800-444-2929**	952-417-7800
Farm Credit Of Central Florida Aca 115 S Missouri Ave Ste 400	Lakeland	FL	33815	**800-533-2773**	863-682-4117
Farm Credit Of Northwest Florida Aca 5052 Hwy 90	Marianna	FL	32446	**800-527-0647**	850-526-4910
FINANCIAL PACIFIC LEASING INC 3455 S 344th Way Ste 300	Federal Way	WA	98001	**800-447-7107**	253-568-6000
Ford Motor Credit Co 1 American Rd	Dearborn	MI	48126	**800-727-7000**	313-322-3000
Greenstone Farm Credit Services Aca 3515 West Rd	East Lansing	MI	48823	**800-444-3276**	800-968-0061
Imh Financial Corp 7001 N Scottsdale Rd Ste 2050	Scottsdale	AZ	85253	**800-510-6445**	480-840-8400
Jackson Purchase Ag Credit Assn PO Box 309	Mayfield	KY	42066	**877-422-4203**	270-247-5613
John Deere Credit Co 6400 NW 86th St	Johnston	IA	50131	**800-275-5322**	515-267-3000
Key Equipment Finance 1000 S McCaslin Blvd	Superior	CO	80027	**888-301-6238**	
Medallion Financial Corp 437 Madison Ave 38th Fl *NASDAQ: MFIN*	New York	NY	10022	**877-633-2554**	212-328-2100
New York Business Development Corp (NYBDC) 50 Beaver St Ste 500	Albany	NY	12207	**800-923-2504**	518-463-2268
Park Community Federal Credit Union PO Box 18630	Louisville	KY	40261	**800-626-2870**	502-968-3681
PDS Gaming Corp 6280 Annie Oakley Dr	Las Vegas	NV	89120	**800-479-3612**	702-736-0700
Phoenix American Inc 2401 Kerner Blvd	San Rafael	CA	94901	**866-895-5050**	
Phoenix Leasing Inc 2401 Kerner Blvd	San Rafael	CA	94901	**866-895-5050**	
Pinnacle Business Finance Inc 914 A St Ste 200	Tacoma	WA	98402	**800-566-1993**	253-284-5600
PMC Commercial Trust 17950 Preston Rd Ste 600 *NASDAQ: CMCT*	Dallas	TX	75252	**800-486-3223**	972-349-3200
Priority Capital Inc 174 Green St	Melrose	MA	02176	**800-761-2118**	781-321-8778
Puerto Rico Farm Credit Aca PO Box 363649	San Juan	PR	00936	**800-981-3323**	787-753-0579
Republic Financial Corp 5251 DTC Pkwy Ste 300	Greenwood Village	CO	80111	**800-596-3608**	303-751-3501
Schroder Investment Management North America Inc (SIMNA) 7 Bryant Pk	New York	NY	10018	**800-730-2932**	212-641-3800
Siemens Financial Services Inc 170 Wood Ave S	Iselin	NJ	08830	**800-327-4443**	732-590-6500
Snap-on Credit LLC 950 Technology Way Ste 301	Libertyville	IL	60048	**877-777-8455**	
Sta International 1400 Old Country Rd Ste 411	Westbury	NY	11590	**866-970-9882**	
Taycor LLC 6065 Bristol Pkwy	Culver City	CA	90230	**800-322-9738**	310-895-7704
Tyndall Federal Credit Union PO Box 59760	Panama City	FL	32412	**888-896-3255**	850-769-9999
Verizon Credit Inc 201 N Tampa St	Tampa	FL	33602	**800-483-7988**	202-789-1432
Wells Fargo 420 Montgomery St *NYSE: WFC*	San Francisco	CA	94104	**800-877-4833**	
Western Agcredit PO Box 95850	South Jordan	UT	84095	**800-824-9198**	801-571-9200
Xerox Financial Services Inc 800 Long Ridge Rd	Stamford	CT	06904	**800-275-9376**	888-242-9098

217 CREDIT & FINANCING - CONSUMER

SEE ALSO Banks - Commercial & Savings ; Credit Unions ; Credit & Financing - Commercial

	City	State	ZIP	Toll-Free	Phone
Budget Finance Co 1849 Sawtelle Blvd	Los Angeles	CA	90025	**800-225-6267**	310-696-4050
Credit Acceptance Corp 25505 W 12 Mile Rd	Southfield	MI	48034	**800-634-1506**	248-353-2700
Dastmalchi Enterprises Inc 4490 Von Karman Ave Ste 150	Newport Beach	CA	92660	**888-358-0331**	
DHI Mortgage Co Ltd 10700 Pecan Park Blvd Ste 450	Austin	TX	78750	**800-315-8434**	512-502-0545
Dollar Loan Ctr LLC 6122 W Sahara Ave	Las Vegas	NV	89146	**866-550-4352**	702-693-5626
Enerbank USA Inc 1245 E Brickyard Rd Ste 600	Salt Lake City	UT	84106	**888-390-1220**	
Farm Credit of The Virginias Aca 106 Sangers Ln	Staunton	VA	24401	**800-559-1016**	540-886-3435
Finance Factors Ltd 1164 Bishop St	Honolulu	HI	96813	**800-648-7136**	808-548-4940
First Insurance Funding Corp 450 Skokie Blvd Ste 1000	Northbrook	IL	60062	**800-837-3707**	
Ford Motor Credit Co 1 American Rd	Dearborn	MI	48126	**800-727-7000**	313-322-3000
Franklin Credit Management Corp 101 Hudson St	Jersey City	NJ	07302	**800-255-5897**	
Gateway Mortgage Group LLC 244 S Gateway Pl PO Box 974	Jenks	OK	74037	**877-764-9319**	877-406-8109
General Motors Acceptance Corp (GMAC) 200 Renaissance Ctr	Detroit	MI	48265	**877-320-2559**	
Guaranteed Rate Inc 3940 N Ravenswood	Chicago	IL	60613	**866-934-7283**	773-290-0505
Harley-Davidson Financial Services Inc PO Box 21489	Carson City	NV	89721	**888-691-4337**	
MCAP Financial Corp 1140 W Pender St	Vancouver	BC	V6E4G1	**800-977-5877**	604-681-8805
Mercedes-Benz Financial Services USA LLC PO Box 685	Roanoke	TX	76262	**800-654-6222**	
Merchant One Inc 524 Arthur Godfrey Rd 3rd Fl	Miami Beach	FL	33140	**800-910-8375**	800-610-4189
Nelnet Inc PO Box 8256 *NYSE: NNI*	Lincoln	NE	68501	**888-486-4722**	
Nicholas Financial Inc 2454 McMullen Booth Rd *NASDAQ: NICK*	Clearwater	FL	33759	**800-237-2721**	727-726-0763
Ontario Centres of Excellence Inc 156 Front St W Ste 200	Toronto	ON	M5J2L6	**866-759-6014**	416-861-1092
Prestige Financial Services Inc 351 W Opportunity Way	Draper	UT	84020	**888-822-7422**	
Prime Rate Premium Finance Corp 2141 Enterprise Dr PO Box 100507 *Cust Svc	Florence	SC	29501	**800-777-7458***	843-669-0937
Redwood Credit Union PO Box 6104	Santa Rosa	CA	95406	**800-479-7928**	707-545-4000
Regional Acceptance Corp 1424 E Fire Tower Rd	Greenville	NC	27858	**877-722-7299**	252-321-7700
Republic Finance 7031 Commerce Cir	Baton Rouge	LA	70809	**800-317-7662**	225-927-0005
Sallie Mae 12061 Bluemont Way *Cust Svc	Reston	VA	20190	**888-272-5543***	703-810-3000
Security Finance Corp 181 Security Pl	Spartanburg	SC	29304	**800-395-8195**	864-582-8193
Select Portfolio Servicing Inc PO Box 65250	Salt Lake City	UT	84165	**800-258-8602**	
SLM Corp 12061 Bluemont Way *NASDAQ: SLM* ■ *Cust Svc	Reston	VA	20190	**888-272-5543***	703-810-3000
Toyota Financial Services 19001 S Western Ave *Cust Svc	Torrance	CA	90501	**800-874-8822***	212-715-7386
Triad Financial Services Inc 4336 Pablo Oaks Ct	Jacksonville	FL	32224	**800-522-2013**	
Wallick & Volk Mortgage 222 E 18th St	Cheyenne	WY	82001	**800-280-8655**	307-634-5941
WebBank Corp 215 S State St Ste 1000	Salt Lake City	UT	84111	**888-881-3789**	801-456-8350
Wells Fargo Education Financial Services PO Box 5185	Sioux Falls	SD	57117	**800-658-3567**	

218 CREDIT REPORTING SERVICES

SEE ALSO

	City	State	ZIP	Toll-Free	Phone
Advantage Credit Inc 32065 Castle Ct Ste 300	Evergreen	CO	80439	**800-670-7993**	
Building Industry Credit Association 10601 Civic Center Dr	Rancho Cucamonga	CA	91730	**800-722-2422**	909-303-2300
CBCInnovis Inc 250 E Town St	Columbus	OH	43215	**877-284-8322**	
Coface Services North America Inc 50 Millstone Rd	East Windsor	NJ	08520	**877-626-3223**	609-469-0400
Constellation Technology Corp 7887 Bryan Dairy Rd Ste 100	Largo	FL	33777	**800-335-7355**	727-547-0600
Creditors Bureau Assoc 420 College St	Macon	GA	31201	**866-949-4213**	478-750-1111
Equifax Credit Marketing Services 1550 Peachtree St NW *NYSE: EFX* ■ *Sales	Atlanta	GA	30309	**800-660-5125***	404-885-8000
Equifax Inc 1550 Peachtree St NW *NYSE: EFX* ■ *Sales	Atlanta	GA	30309	**888-202-4025***	404-885-8000
Factual Data 5200 Hahns Peak Dr	Loveland	CO	80538	**800-929-3400**	
Fitch Ratings Inc 1 State St Plz	New York	NY	10004	**800-753-4824**	212-908-0500
Holloway Credit Solutions LLC 1286 Carmichael Way	Montgomery	AL	36106	**800-264-2700**	334-396-1200
Merchants Credit Bureau 955 Green St	Augusta	GA	30901	**800-426-5265**	706-823-6200
NACM Gulf States 10887 S Wilcrest Dr	Houston	TX	77099	**866-252-6226**	281-228-6100
Screeningone Inc 2233 W 190th St	Torrance	CA	90504	**888-327-6511**	
Strategic Information Resources Inc 155 Brookdale Dr	Springfield	MA	01104	**800-332-9479**	800-813-4381
Tele-Track 40 Pacifica Ste 900	Irvine	CA	92618	**800-729-6981**	949-214-1000
TransUnion LLC 555 W Adams St	Chicago	IL	60661	**866-922-2100**	
Trudiligence LLC 3190 S Wadsworth Blvd Ste 260	Lakewood	CO	80227	**800-580-0474**	303-692-8445

219 CREDIT UNIONS

	City	State	ZIP	Toll-Free	Phone
Affinity Federal Credit Union 73 Mountain View Blvd PO Box 621	Basking Ridge	NJ	07920	**800-325-0808**	
Air Force Federal Credit Union 1560 Cable Ranch Rd Ste 200	San Antonio	TX	78245	**800-227-5328**	210-673-5610
Alaska USA Federal Credit Union 4000 Credit Union Dr PO Box 196613	Anchorage	AK	99503	**800-525-9094**	907-563-4567
Allegacy Federal Credit Union 1691 Westbrook Plaza Dr	Winston-Salem	NC	27103	**800-782-4670**	336-774-3400
America First Credit Union 1344 W 4675 S	Ogden	UT	84405	**800-999-3961**	801-627-0900
American Airlines Employees Federal Credit Union 4151 Amon Carter Blvd	Fort Worth	TX	76155	**800-533-0035**	817-952-4500

Classified Section

Classified Section

Name / Address	City	ST	ZIP	Toll-Free	Phone
American Eagle Federal Credit Union 417 Main St	East Hartford	CT	06118	800-842-0145	860-568-2020
Americu Credit Union 1916 Black River Blvd	Rome	NY	13440	866-210-3876	
Amoco Federal Credit Union PO Box 889	Texas City	TX	77592	800-231-6053	409-948-8541
Andrews Federal Credit Union (AFCU) 5711 Allentown Rd	Suitland	MD	20746	800-487-5500	301-702-5500
ANG Federal Credit Union PO Box 170204	Birmingham	AL	35217	800-237-6211	205-841-4525
APCO Employees Credit Union 750 17th St North	Birmingham	AL	35203	800-249-2726	205-257-3601
Arizona Federal Credit Union PO Box 60070	Phoenix	AZ	85082	800-523-4603	602-683-1000
Ascend Federal Credit Union 520 Airpark Dr PO Box 1210	Tullahoma	TN	37388	800-342-3086	931-455-5441
Ascentra Credit Union 1710 Grant St	Bettendorf	IA	52722	800-426-5241	563-355-0152
Atlanta Postal Credit Union 501 Pulliam St SW Ste 350	Atlanta	GA	30312	800-849-8431	404-768-4126
Autotruck Federal Credit Union 3611 Newburg Rd	Louisville	KY	40218	800-459-2328	502-459-8981
Bank-Fund Staff Federal Credit Union PO Box 27755	Washington	DC	20038	800-923-7328	202-458-4300
Beacon Credit Union PO Box 627	Wabash	IN	46992	800-762-3136	260-563-7443
Bellco First Federal Credit Union 7600 E OrchaRd Rd Ste 400N	Greenwood Village	CO	80111	800-235-5261	303-689-7800
Bethpage Federal Credit Union 899 S Oyster Bay Rd	Bethpage	NY	11714	800-628-7070	
Campus Federal Credit Union PO Box 98036	Baton Rouge	LA	70898	888-769-8841	225-769-8841
Campus USA Credit Union PO Box 147029	Gainesville	FL	32614	800-367-6440	352-335-9090
CFCU Community Credit Union 1030 Craft Rd	Ithaca	NY	14850	800-428-8340	607-257-8500
Chartway Federal Credit Union 5700 Cleveland St	Virginia Beach	VA	23462	800-678-8765	757-552-1000
Citizens Equity First Credit Union 5401 W Dirksen Pkwy *Cust Svc	Peoria	IL	61607	800-633-7077*	309-633-7000
Class Act Federal Credit Union 3620 Fern Valley Rd	Louisville	KY	40219	800-292-2960	502-964-7575
Coast Central Credit Union Inc 2650 Harrison Ave	Eureka	CA	95501	800-974-9727	707-445-8801
Coastal Federal Credit Union 1000 St Albans Dr	Raleigh	NC	27609	800-868-4262	919-420-8000
Commonwealth Credit Union PO Box 978	Frankfort	KY	40602	800-228-6420	502-564-4775
Community America Credit Union (CACU) 9777 Ridge Dr	Lenexa	KS	66219	800-892-7957	913-905-7000
Community Resource Federal Credit Union 20 Wade Rd	Latham	NY	12110	888-783-2211	518-783-2211
Coosa Pines Federal Credit Union 17591 Plant Rd	Childersburg	AL	35044	800-237-9789	256-378-5559
Credit Human Federal Credit Union PO Box 1356	San Antonio	TX	78295	800-234-7228	210-258-1234
Credit Union Acceptance Company LLC 9601 Jones Rd Ste 108	Houston	TX	77065	866-970-2822	281-970-2822
Credit Union of Southern California PO Box 200	Whittier	CA	90608	866-287-6225	562-698-8326
Credit Union of Texas PO Box 517028	Dallas	TX	75251	800-314-3828	972-263-9497
Dearborn Federal Credit Union 400 Town Ctr Dr	Dearborn	MI	48126	888-336-2700	313-336-2700
Deer Valley Federal Credit Union 16215 N 28th Ave	Phoenix	AZ	85053	800-579-5051	602-375-7300
Delta Employees Credit Union 1025 Virginia Ave	Atlanta	GA	30354	800-544-3328	404-715-4725
Denver Fire Dept Federal Credit Union (DFDFCU) 12 Lakeside Ln	Denver	CO	80212	866-880-7770	303-228-5300
Desert Financial Credit Union 148 N 48th St	Phoenix	AZ	85034	800-456-9171	602-433-7000
Digital Employees' Federal Credit Union 220 Donald Lynch Blvd	Marlborough	MA	01752	800-328-8797	508-263-6700
Duca Financial Services Credit Union Ltd 5290 Yonge St	Toronto	ON	M2N5P9	866-900-3822	416-223-8502
Dupaco Community Credit Union 3999 Pennsylvania Ave	Dubuque	IA	52002	800-373-7600	563-557-7600
Educational Employees Credit Union PO Box 5242	Fresno	CA	93755	800-538-3328	559-437-7700
Educators Credit Union (ECU) 1400 N Newman Rd PO Box 081040	Racine	WI	53406	800-236-5898	262-886-5900
Eglin Federal Credit Union 838 Eglin Pkwy NE	Fort Walton Beach	FL	32547	800-367-6159	850-862-0111
Ent Federal Credit Union 7250 Campus Dr	Colorado Springs	CO	80920	800-525-9623	719-574-1100
Evansville Teachers Federal Credit Union PO Box 5129	Evansville	IN	47716	800-800-9271	812-477-9271
Faa Federal Credit Union 3920 Whitebrook Dr	Memphis	TN	38118	800-346-0069	901-366-0066
Fairwinds Federal Credit Union 3087 N Alafaya Trl	Orlando	FL	32826	800-443-6887	407-277-5045
Financial Partners Credit Union PO Box 7005	Downey	CA	90241	800-950-7328	562-923-0311
Firefighters Community Credit Union Inc 2300 St Clair Ave NE	Cleveland	OH	44114	800-621-4644	216-621-4644
First Community Credit Union (FCCU) 17151 Chesterfield Airport Rd	Chesterfield	MO	63005	800-767-8880	636-728-3333
Fort Knox Federal Credit Union PO Box 900	Radcliff	KY	40159	800-756-3678	502-942-0254
Fort Worth City Credit Union PO Box 100099	Fort Worth	TX	76185	888-732-3085	817-732-2803
Fort Worth Community Credit Union 1905 Forest Ridge Dr PO Box 210848	Bedford	TX	76021	800-817-8234	817-835-5000
Georgia Cu Affiliates 6705 Sugarloaf Pkwy Ste 200	Duluth	GA	30097	800-768-4282	770-476-9625
Georgia's Own Credit Union 1155 Peachtree St NE Ste 600	Atlanta	GA	30309	800-533-2062	
Greylock Federal Credit Union 150 W St	Pittsfield	MA	01201	800-207-5555	413-236-4000
Guadalupe Credit Union 3601 Mimbres Ln	Santa Fe	NM	87507	800-540-5382	505-982-8942
HarborOne Credit Union 770 Oak St PO Box 720	Brockton	MA	02301	800-244-7592	508-895-1000
Horizon Credit Union 13224 E Mansfield Ste 300	Spokane Valley	WA	99216	800-808-6402	
Hudson Valley Federal Credit Union 159 Barnegat Rd	Poughkeepsie	NY	12601	800-468-3011	845-463-3011
Hughes Federal Credit Union Inc PO Box 11900	Tucson	AZ	85734	866-760-3156	520-794-8341
Indiana Credit Union League 5975 Castle Creek Pkwy N Ste 300	Indianapolis	IN	46250	800-285-5300	317-594-5300
Indiana Members Credit Union (IMCU) 7110 W Tenth St	Indianapolis	IN	46214	800-556-9268	317-248-8556
Island Federal Credit Union 120 Motor Pkwy	Hauppauge	NY	11788	800-475-5263	631-851-1100
Keesler Federal Credit Union PO Box 7001	Biloxi	MS	39534	888-533-7537	228-385-5500
Kern Schools Federal Credit Union PO Box 9506	Bakersfield	CA	93389	800-221-3311	661-833-7900
KeyPoint Credit Union 2805 Bowers Ave	Santa Clara	CA	95051	888-255-3637	408-731-4100
Kinecta Federal Credit Union 1440 Rosecrans Ave PO Box 10003	Manhattan Beach	CA	90266	800-854-9846	310-643-5400
L & N Federal Credit Union 9265 Smyrna Pkwy	Louisville	KY	40229	800-443-2479	502-368-5858
La Capitol Federal Credit Union PO Box 3398	Baton Rouge	LA	70821	800-522-2748	225-342-5055
Lafayette Federal Credit Union (Inc) 3535 University Blvd W	Kensington	MD	20895	800-888-6560	301-929-7990
Landmark Credit Union 5445 S Westridge Dr PO Box 510910	New Berlin	WI	53151	800-801-1449	262-796-4500
Langley Federal Credit Union 1055 W Mercury Blvd	Hampton	VA	23666	800-826-7490	757-827-7200
Leominster Credit Union 20 Adams St	Leominster	MA	01453	800-649-4646	978-537-8021
Local Government Federal Credit Union 323 W Jones St Ste 600	Raleigh	NC	27603	888-732-8562	919-857-2150
Lockheed Federal Credit Union (LFCU) 2340 Hollywood Way	Burbank	CA	91505	800-328-5328	818-565-2020
Los Angeles Federal Credit Union PO Box 53032	Los Angeles	CA	90053	877-695-2328	818-242-8640
Los Angeles Police Federal Credit Union PO Box 10188	Van Nuys	CA	91410	877-695-2732	818-787-6520
Meriwest Credit Union PO Box 530953	San Jose	CA	95153	877-637-4937	
Midwest America Federal Credit Union 1104 Medical Pk Dr	Fort Wayne	IN	46825	800-348-4738	260-482-3334
Mission Federal Credit Union PO Box 919023	San Diego	CA	92191	800-500-6328	858-524-2850
Mountain America Credit Union PO Box 9001	West Jordan	UT	84084	800-748-4302	801-325-6228
Municipal Credit Union PO Box 3205	New York	NY	10007	866-512-6109	212-693-4900
Nassau Financial Federal Credit Union 1325 Franklin Ave Ste 500	Garden City	NY	11530	800-216-2328	516-742-4900
Neighbors Federal Credit Union PO Box 2831	Baton Rouge	LA	70821	866-819-2178	225-819-2178
New England Federal Credit Union PO Box 527	Williston	VT	05495	800-400-8790	802-879-8790
New Orleans Firemens Federal Credit Union PO Box 689	Metairie	LA	70004	800-647-1689	504-889-9090
North American Van Lines Inc 5001 US Hwy 30 W	Fort Wayne	IN	46818	800-348-2111	260-429-2511
North Country Federal Credit Union Inc 69 Swift St Ste 100	South Burlington	VT	05403	800-660-3258	802-657-6847
North Island Credit Union 5898 Copley Dr	San Diego	CA	92111	800-334-8788	
Oklahoma Federal Credit Union 517 NE 36th St	Oklahoma City	OK	73105	800-522-8510	405-524-6467
Orange County's Credit Union PO Box 11777	Santa Ana	CA	92711	888-354-6228	714-755-5900
Owensboro Federal Credit Union 717 Harvard Dr PO Box 1189	Owensboro	KY	42302	800-264-1054	270-683-1054
Pacific Marine Credit Union (PMCU) 1278 Rocky Point Dr	Oceanside	CA	92056	800-736-4500	760-631-8700
Pacific NW Federal Credit Union (PNWFCU) 12106 NE Marx St	Portland	OR	97220	866-692-8669	503-256-5858
Pacific Service Federal Credit Union PO Box 8191	Walnut Creek	CA	94596	888-858-6878	925-296-6200
Pearl Harbor Federal Credit Union (PHFCU) 94-449 Ukee St	Waipahu	HI	96797	800-987-5583	
Pennsylvania State Employees Credit Union 1 Innovation Way	Harrisburg	PA	17110	800-237-7328	717-255-1760
Pentagon Federal Credit Union 2930 Eisenhower Ave	Alexandria	VA	22314	800-247-5626	
Pine Bluff Cotton Belt Federal Credit Union 1703 River Pines Blvd	Pine Bluff	AR	71601	888-249-1904	870-535-6365
Police & Fire Federal Credit Union 901 Arch St	Philadelphia	PA	19107	800-228-8801	215-931-0300
Portland Teachers Credit Union PO Box 3750	Portland	OR	97208	800-527-3932	503-228-7077
Premier America Credit Union 19867 Prairie St PO Box 2178	Chatsworth	CA	91313	800-772-4000	818-772-4000
Premier Members Credit Union 5505 Arapahoe Ave	Boulder	CO	80303	800-468-0634	303-657-7000
Provident Central Credit Union 303 Twin Dolphin Dr	Redwood City	CA	94065	800-632-4600	650-508-0300
Randolph-Brooks Federal Credit Union PO Box 2097	Universal City	TX	78148	800-580-3300	210-945-3300
Redstone Federal Credit Union 220 Wynn Dr NW	Huntsville	AL	35893	800-234-1234	256-837-6110

				Toll-Free	Phone
Rhode Island State Employees Credit Union					
160 Francis St	Providence	RI	02903	855-322-7428	401-751-7440
Rockland Federal Credit Union					
241 Union St	Rockland	MA	02370	800-562-7328	781-878-0232
RTN Federal Credit Union					
600 Main St	Waltham	MA	02452	800-338-0221	781-736-9900
SAC Federal Credit Union (SAFCU)					
11515 S 39th St	Bellevue	NE	68123	800-228-0392	402-292-8000
SAFE Credit Union					
3720 Madison Ave	North Highlands	CA	95660	800-733-7233	916-979-7233
Safe Federal Credit Union					
201 N 12th St	West Columbia	SC	29169	800-763-8600	
Safeamerica Credit Union					
6001 Gibraltar Dr	Pleasanton	CA	94588	800-972-0999	925-734-4111
San Diego County Credit Union					
6545 Sequence Dr	San Diego	CA	92121	877-732-2848	
San Francisco Federal Credit Union					
770 Golden Gate Ave	San Francisco	CA	94102	800-852-7598	415-775-5377
Schools Financial Credit Union					
1485 Response Rd Ste 126.	Sacramento	CA	95815	800-962-0990	916-569-5400
Security Service Federal Credit Union					
16211 La Cantera Pkwy	San Antonio	TX	78256	800-527-7328	210-476-4000
Selco Community Credit Union					
299 E 11th Ave	Eugene	OR	97401	800-445-4483	541-686-8000
South Carolina Federal Credit Union					
PO Box 190012	North Charleston	SC	29419	800-845-0432	843-797-8300
Space Coast Credit Union					
8045 N Wickham Rd PO Box 419001	Melbourne	FL	32941	800-447-7228	321-752-2222
Stanford Federal Credit Union					
1860 Embarcadero Rd	Palo Alto	CA	94303	888-723-7328	650-723-2509
Star One Federal Credit Union					
PO Box 3643	Sunnyvale	CA	94088	866-543-5202	408-543-5202
State Employees Credit Union of Maryland Inc					
971 Corporate Blvd	Linthicum	MD	21090	800-879-7328	410-487-7328
State Employees Federal Credit Union					
700 Patroon Creek Blvd Patroon Creek Corporate Ctr.	Albany	NY	12206	800-727-3328	518-452-8234
State Employees' Credit Union (SECU)					
PO Box 29606	Raleigh	NC	27626	888-732-8562	919-857-2150
Sunstate Federal Credit Union (Inc)					
PO Box 1162	Gainesville	FL	32627	877-786-7828	352-381-5200
Teachers Credit Union (TCU)					
PO Box 1395	South Bend	IN	46624	800-552-4745	574-284-6247
Teachers Federal Credit Union (TFCU)					
2410 N Ocean Ave	Farmingville	NY	11738	800-341-4333	631-698-7000
Tech Credit Union					
10951 Broadway	Crown Point	IN	46307	800-276-8324	219-663-5120
Telcoe Federal Credit Union					
820 Lousiana St	Little Rock	AR	72201	800-482-9009	501-375-5321
Texans Credit Union					
777 E Campbell Rd	Richardson	TX	75081	800-843-5295	972-348-2000
Texas Dow Employees Credit Union (TDECU)					
1001 FM 2004	Lake Jackson	TX	77566	800-839-1154	979-297-1154
Tower Federal Credit Union					
7901 Sandy Spring Rd	Laurel	MD	20707	800-787-8328	301-497-7000
Travis Federal Credit Union					
1 Travis Way	Vacaville	CA	95687	800-877-8328	707-449-4000
Truity Credit Union					
PO Box 1358	Bartlesville	OK	74005	800-897-6991	877-744-2835
Truliant Federal Credit Union					
3200 Truliant Way	Winston-Salem	NC	27103	800-822-0382	336-659-1955
U S Employees O C Federal Credit Union					
PO Box 44000	Oklahoma City	OK	73144	800-227-6366	405-685-6200
Ukrainian National Federal Credit Union					
215 Second Ave	New York	NY	10003	866-859-5848	
United Nations Federal Credit Union (UNFCU)					
24-01 44th Rd Ct Sq Pl	Long Island	NY	11101	800-891-2471	347-686-6000
Unitus Community Credit Union					
PO Box 1937	Portland	OR	97207	800-452-0900	503-227-5571
University of Hawaii Federal Credit Union					
PO Box 22070	Honolulu	HI	96823	800-927-3397	808-983-5500
University of Hawaii Foundation, The					
2444 Dole St Bachman Hall 105	Honolulu	HI	96822	866-846-4262	808-956-8849
US Alliance Federal Credit Union					
411 Theodore Fremd Ave Ste 350.	Rye	NY	10580	800-431-2754	
Us Postal Service Federal Credit Union					
7905 Malcolm Rd Ste 311	Clinton	MD	20735	800-877-7328	301-856-5000
US. Eagle Federal Credit Union (USNMFCU)					
3939 Osuna Rd NE PO Box 129	Albuquerque	NM	87109	888-342-8766	505-342-8888
Valley First Credit Union					
PO Box 1411	Modesto	CA	95353	877-549-4567	209-549-8500
Vantage Credit Union (VCU)					
PO Box 4433	Bridgeton	MO	63044	800-522-6009	314-298-0055
Verity Credit Union					
PO Box 75974	Seattle	WA	98175	800-444-4589	206-440-9000
Virginia Credit Union					
7500 Boulders View Dr	Richmond	VA	23225	800-285-5051	804-323-6000
Visions Federal Credit Union (VFUC)					
24 McKinley Ave	Endicott	NY	13760	800-242-2120	607-754-7900
Vystar Credit Union					
1802 Kernan Blvd S	Jacksonville	FL	32246	800-445-6289	904-777-6000
Washington State Employees Credit Union					
330 Union Ave SE	Olympia	WA	98501	800-562-0999	360-943-7911
Wescom Credit Union					
123 S Marengo Ave PO Box 7058	Pasadena	CA	91101	888-493-7266	626-535-1000
Westerra Credit Union					
3700 E Alameda Ave	Denver	CO	80209	800-858-7212	303-321-4209
Wings Financial Credit Union					
14985 Glazier Ave Ste 100	Apple Valley	MN	55124	800-692-2274	
Workers' Credit Union					
815 Main St PO Box 900	Fitchburg	MA	01420	800-221-4020	978-345-1021
Wright-Patt Credit Union Inc					
2455 Executive Pk Blvd PO Box 286.	Fairborn	OH	45324	800-762-0047	937-912-7000
Y-12 Federal Credit Union					
501 Lafayette Dr	Oak Ridge	TN	37830	800-482-1043	865-482-1043
Yolo Federal Credit Union					
266 W Main St	Woodland	CA	95695	877-965-6328	530-668-2700

220 CRUISE LINES

SEE ALSO Cruises - Riverboat ; Ports & Port Authorities ; Travel Agencies ; Casinos

				Toll-Free	Phone
Baja Expeditions Inc					
3096 Palm St	San Diego	CA	92104	800-843-6967	858-581-3311
Blount Small Ship Adventures					
461 Water St	Warren	RI	02885	800-556-7450	401-247-0955
Bluewater Adventures Ltd					
252 E First St Ste 3.	North Vancouver	BC	V7L1B3	888-877-1770	604-980-3800
Carnival Cruise Lines					
3655 NW 87th Ave	Miami	FL	33178	800-764-7419	305-599-2600
China Ocean Shipping Co Americas Inc (COSCO)					
100 Lighting Way	Secaucus	NJ	07094	800-242-7354	201-422-0500
Costa Cruise Lines					
200 S Pk Rd Ste 200.	Hollywood	FL	33021	800-462-6782	954-266-5600
Cunard Line Ltd					
24303 Town Center Dr Ste 200.	Valencia	CA	91355	800-728-6273	661-753-1000
Great Lakes Cruise Co					
3270 Washtenaw Ave	Ann Arbor	MI	48104	888-891-0203	
Holland America Line					
450 Third Ave W	Seattle	WA	98119	800-426-0327	206-281-3535
Lindblad Expeditions					
96 Morton St 9th Fl	New York	NY	10014	800-397-3348	
Maine Windjammer Cruises					
PO Box 617	Camden	ME	04843	800-736-7981	207-236-2938
Oceania Cruises Inc					
8300 NW 33rd St Ste 308.	Miami	FL	33122	800-531-5619	305-514-2300
Princess Cruises					
24844 Rockefeller Ave	Santa Clarita	CA	91355	800-774-6237	661-753-0000
Royal Caribbean International					
1050 Caribbean Way	Miami	FL	33132	800-327-6700	305-539-6000
Sea Cloud Cruises Inc					
282 Grand Ave Ste 3.	Englewood	NJ	07631	888-732-2568	201-227-9404
SeaDream Yacht Club					
601 Brickell Key Dr Ste 1050	Miami	FL	33131	800-707-4911	305-631-6110
Windstar Cruises					
2101 Fourth Ave Ste 210	Seattle	WA	98121	800 268-7245*	206-733-2970
*Resv					

221 CRUISES - RIVERBOAT

SEE ALSO Cruise Lines ; Casinos

				Toll-Free	Phone
American Cruise Lines					
741 Boston Post Rd Ste 200.	Guilford	CT	06437	800-814-6880	203-453-8885
Englund Marine & Industrial Supply Co					
95 Hamburg Ave PO Box 296.	Astoria	OR	97103	800-228-7051	503-325-4341
French Country Waterways Ltd					
24 Bay Rd	Duxbury	MA	02332	800-222-1236	781-934-2454
Uniworld Boutique River Cruise Collection					
17323 Ventura Blvd	Encino	CA	91316	800-257-2407	818-382-7820
Victoria Cruises Inc					
57-08 39th Ave	Woodside	NY	11377	800-348-8084*	212-818-1680
*Cust Svc					
Viking River Cruises					
5700 Canoga Ave Ste 200.	Woodland Hills	CA	91367	877-668-4546*	818-227-1234
*Cust Svc					

222 CUTLERY

SEE ALSO Silverware

				Toll-Free	Phone
Atlanta Cutlery Corp					
2147 Gees Mill Rd	Conyers	GA	30013	800-883-0300	800-883-8838
Buck Knives Inc					
660 S Lochsa St	Post Falls	ID	83854	800-326-2825	208-262-0500
Crescent Manufacturing Co					
1310 Majestic Dr	Fremont	OH	43420	800-537-1330	419-332-6484
Dexter-Russell Inc					
44 River St	Southbridge	MA	01550	800-343-6042	508-765-0201
Fiskars Brands Inc					
7800 Discovery Dr	Middleton	WI	53562	866-348-5661	
Gerber Legendary Blades Inc					
14200 SW 72nd Ave	Portland	OR	97224	800-950-6161	
Ginsu Brands					
118 E Douglas Rd	Walnut Ridge	AR	72476	800-982-5233	
KA-BAR Knives Inc					
200 Homer St	Olean	NY	14760	800-282-0130	716-372-5952
Lamson & Goodnow Mfg Co					
45 Conway St	Shelburne Falls	MA	01370	800-872-6564	413-625-0201
Master Cutlery Inc					
700 Penhorn Ave	Secaucus	NJ	07094	888-271-7229	
Midwest Tool & Cutlery Co Inc					
1210 Progress St PO Box 160	Sturgis	MI	49091	800-782-4659	269-651-7964
Ontario Knife Co					
26 Empire St	Franklinville	NY	14737	800-222-5233	716-676-5527
Pacific Handy Cutter Inc					
17819 Gillette Ave	Irvine	CA	92614	800-229-2233*	714-662-1033
*Cust Svc					
Queen CutleryCom					
507 Chestnut St	Titusville	PA	16354	800-222-5233*	814-827-3673
*Sales					
Rada Manufacturing Co					
PO Box 838	Waverly	IA	50677	800-311-9691	319-352-5454
WR Case & Sons Cutlery Co					
50 Owens Way PO Box 4000	Bradford	PA	16701	800-523-6350	
Zippo Manufacturing Co					
33 Barbour St	Bradford	PA	16701	888-442-1932	814-368-2700

Classified Section

223 CYLINDERS & ACTUATORS - FLUID POWER

SEE ALSO Automotive Parts & Supplies - Mfr

				Toll-Free	Phone
Clippard Instrument Lab					
7390 Colerain Ave	Cincinnati	OH	45239	877-245-6247	513-521-4261
Control Line Equipment Inc					
14750 Industrial Pkwy	Cleveland	OH	44135	888-895-1440	216-433-7766
Cunningham Manufacturing Co					
318 S Webster St	Seattle	WA	98108	800-767-0038	206-767-3713
Eckel Mfg Company Inc					
8035 N County Rd W	Odessa	TX	79764	800-654-4779	432-362-4336
Hader/Seitz Inc					
15600 W Lincoln Ave	New Berlin	WI	53151	877-388-2101	
Hannon Hydraulics LLC					
625 N Loop 12	Irving	TX	75061	800-333-4266	972-438-2870
Helac Corp					
225 Battersby Ave	Enumclaw	WA	98022	800-327-2589	360-825-1601
Hol-Mac Corp PO Box 349	Bay Springs	MS	39422	800-844-3019	601-764-4121
Humphrey Products Co					
5070 E N Ave PO Box 2008	Kalamazoo	MI	49048	800-477-8707	
ITT Industries Inc Engineered Valves Div					
33 Centerville Rd	Lancaster	PA	17603	800-366-1111	717-509-2200
JARP Industries Inc					
1051 Pine St PO Box 923	Schofield	WI	54476	800-558-5950	715-359-4241
Micromatic LLC 525 Berne St	Berne	IN	46711	800-333-5752	260-589-2136
Norris Cylinder Co					
4818 W Loop 281	Longview	TX	75603	800-527-8418	903-757-7633
Ortman Fluid power					
1400 North 30th St Ste 20	Quincy	IL	62301	844-759-4922	217-277-0321
Parker Hannifin Corp Automation Actuator Div					
135 Quadral Dr	Wadsworth	OH	44281	800-272-7537	877-321-4736
Parker Hannifin Corp Cylinder Div					
500 S Wolf Rd	Des Plaines	IL	60016	800-272-7537	847-298-2400
Parker Instrumentation Group					
6035 Parkland Blvd	Cleveland	OH	44124	800-272-7537	216-896-3000
PHD Inc					
9009 Clubridge Dr	Fort Wayne	IN	46809	800-624-8511	260-747-6151
Sargent Controls & Aerospace					
5675 W Burlingame Rd	Tucson	AZ	85743	800-230-0359	520-744-1000
Southwestern Controls					
6720 Sands Point Dr Ste 100	Houston	TX	77074	800-444-9368	713-777-2626
Standex International Corp Custom Hoists Div					
771 County Rd 30A W	Ashland	OH	44805	800-837-4668	419-368-4721
Tol-O-Matic Inc					
3800 County Rd 116	Hamel	MN	55340	800-328-2174	763-478-8000

224 DATA COMMUNICATIONS SERVICES FOR WIRELESS DEVICES

Companies listed here deliver data such as customized news or stock information, other personalized content, and/or multimedia, audio, and video from the Internet to wireless devices (cellular phones, Personal Digital Assistants, pagers, laptop computers).

				Toll-Free	Phone
ADEX Corp					
1035 Windward Ridge Pkwy Ste 500	Alpharetta	GA	30005	800-451-9899	678-393-7900
Aldea Solutions Inc					
8550 Cote de Liesse Blvd Ste 200	Saint-Laurent	QC	H4T1H2	866-344-5432	514-344-5432
Alligato Inc					
1450-1055 W Hastings St	Vancouver	BC	V6E2E9	866-355-0187	
Altius Broadband Inc					
3314 Papermill Rd Ste 100	Phoenix	MD	21131	800-864-6546	410-667-1638
Ansatel Communications Inc					
940 Kingsway	Vancouver	BC	V5V3C4	866-872-6500	604-872-6500
Argon Technologies Inc					
4612 Wesley St	Greenville	TX	75401	888-651-1010	903-455-5036
Auto Data Direct Inc					
1379 Cross Creek Cir	Tallahassee	FL	32301	866-923-3123	850-877-8804
B2B2C Inc 2700 Rue Michelin	Laval	QC	H7L5Y1	800-965-9065	514-908-5420
Broadcast Microwave Services Inc (BMS)					
12305 Crosthwaite Cir	Poway	CA	92064	800-669-9667	858-391-3050
Buyatab Online Inc					
B1 - 788 Beatty St	Vancouver	BC	V6B2M1	888-267-0447	
CBOSS Inc					
827 Southwestern Run	Poland	OH	44514	866-726-0429	330-726-0429
Chatr Mobile					
333 Bloor St E 8th Fl	Toronto	ON	M4W1G9	800-485-9745	
Cirrus9 Inc 15 Market Sq	Saint John	NB	E2L1E8	855-643-6691	
Clevest Solutions Inc					
13911 Wireless Way Ste 100	Richmond	BC	V6V3B9	866-915-0088	604-214-9700
Cognify PO Box 69337	Oro Valley	AZ	85737	888-264-6439	
Cologix Inc					
2300 15th St Ste 300	Denver	CO	80202	800-638-6336	720-230-7000
Com-Net Services					
7786 S Commerce Ave	Baton Rouge	LA	70815	800-676-2137	225-928-1231
Commodity Systems Inc					
200 W Palmetto Park Rd Ste 200	Boca Raton	FL	33432	800-274-4727	561-392-8663
Condo Control Central					
2 Carlton St Ste 1000	Toronto	ON	M5B1J3	888-762-6636	416-961-7884
Cooptel					
5521 Valcourt Airport Rd	Valcourt	QC	J0E2L0	888-532-2667*	450-532-2667
*Consumer Assistance					
Data Conversion Laboratory Inc					
61-18 190th St Ste 205	Fresh Meadows	NY	11365	800-321-2816	718-357-8700
Dial800					
10940 Wilshire Blvd 17th Fl	Los Angeles	CA	90024	800-700-1987	
Discover Communications Inc					
30 Victoria Crescent	Brampton	ON	L6T1E4	888-456-8989	905-455-5600
Dissolve Inc 425 78 Ave SW	Calgary	AB	T2V5K5	800-518-6748	
Doublehorn Communications					
1601 Rio Grande St # 500	Austin	TX	78701	855-618-6423	512-637-5200
DRAIVER					
9393 W 110th St Ste 500	Overland Park	KS	66210	844-366-6837	

				Toll-Free	Phone
DXStormcom Inc					
824 Winston Churchill Blvd	Oakville	ON	L6J7X2	877-397-8676	905-842-8262
EDge Interactive Inc					
67 Mowat Ave Ste 533	Toronto	ON	M6K3E3	800-211-5577	416-494-3343
Fibernetics Corp					
605 Boxwood Dr	Cambridge	ON	N3E1A5	866-973-4237	519-489-6700
Fibre Noire Internet Inc					
550 Ave Beaumont Ste 320	Montreal	QC	H3N1V1	877-907-3002	
FONEX Data Systems Inc					
5400 Ch St-Francois	St-Laurent	QC	H4S1P6	800-363-6639	514-333-6639
Global Relay Communications Inc					
220 cambie St	Vancouver	BC	V6B2M9	866-484-6630	604-484-6630
Groupe Maskatel Lp					
770 Casavant Ouest Bd	Saint-Hyacinthe	QC	J2S7S3	877-627-5283	450-250-5050
Hotwire Communications LLC					
2100 W Cypress Creek Rd	Fort Lauderdale	FL	33309	800-355-5668	
Hover Networks Inc					
40 Gardenville Pkwy w	Buffalo	NY	14224	855-552-8900	
Huxley Communications Co-op					
102 N Main Ave	Huxley	IA	50124	800-231-4922	515-597-2212
iLeadscom					
567 San Nicolas Dr Ste 180	Newport Beach	CA	92660	877-245-3237	
Immediatek					
3301 Airport Fwy Ste 200	Bedford	TX	76021	888-661-6565	
InterStar Communications					
3900 North US 421 Hwy	Clinton	NC	28329	800-706-6538	910-564-4194
iTalkBB CA					
245 W Beaver Creek Rd Unit 9	Richmond Hill	ON	L4B1L1	877-482-5522	
Ituran USA Inc					
1700 NW 64th St Ste 100	Fort Lauderdale	FL	33309	866-543-5433	
Itx Corp					
1169 Pittsford Victor Rd Ste 100	Pittsford	NY	14534	800-600-7785	585-899-4888
Kin Communications Inc					
736 Granville St Ste 100	Vancouver	BC	V6Z1G3	866-684-6730	604-684-6730
Lemieux Bedard Communications Inc					
2665 King W Ste 315	Sherbrooke	QC	J1L2G5	800-823-0850	819-823-0850
LemonStand eCommerce Inc					
2416 Main St Ste 126	Vancouver	BC	V5T3E2	855-332-0555	604-398-4188
Link America Inc					
3002 Century Dr	Rowlett	TX	75088	800-318-4955	
Masergy 2740 N Dallas Pkwy	Plano	TX	75093	866-588-5885	
Metalink Technologies Inc					
417 Wayne Ave PO Box 1124	Defiance	OH	43512	888-999-8002	419-782-3472
Mojio Inc					
1080 Howe St 9th Fl	Vancouver	BC	V6Z2T1	855-556-6546	
Mornington Communications Co-operative Ltd					
16 Mill St E	Milverton	ON	N0K1M0	800-250-8750	519-595-8331
Netfast Communications					
989 Ave of the Americas 4th Fl	New York	NY	10018	888-678-6383	212-792-5200
Network Earth Inc					
2501 Alida St	Oakland	CA	94602	888-201-5160	
Nitel Inc					
1101 West Lake St 6th Fl	Chicago	IL	60607	888-450-2100	
NKTelco Inc					
301 W S St PO Box 219	New Knoxville	OH	45871	888-658-3526	419-753-5000
NTG Clarity Networks Inc					
2820 Fourteenth Ave Ste 202	Markham	ON	L3R0S9	800-838-7894	905-305-1325
NthGen Software Inc					
90 Sheppard Ave Ste 6	Toronto	ON	M2N3A1	888-260-4604	647-933-1169
Oil-Law Records Corp					
8 N W 65th St	Oklahoma City	OK	73116	888-464-5529	405-840-1631
Omnis Network LLC					
3655 Torrance Blvd Ste 180	Torrance	CA	90503	877-393-4678	310-316-9600
Outreach Communications					
2801 Glenda St	Haltom City	TX	76117	800-982-3760	817-288-7200
Powered By Search Inc					
505 Consumers Rd Ste 507	Toronto	ON	M2J4V8	866-611-5535	416-840-9044
PUC Inc					
500 Second Line E PO Box 9000	Sault Ste Marie	ON	P6B4K1	800-400-2255	705-759-6500
Recordtrak Inc					
651 Allendale Rd PO Box 61591	King Of Prussia	PA	19406	800-355-7400	
Rightway Gate Inc					
5858 Edison Pl	Carlsbad	CA	92008	888-398-4703	760-736-3700
RigNet Inc					
15115 Park Row Ste 300	Houston	TX	77084	800-638-8844	281-674-0100
Roam Mobility Holdings Inc					
60 James St 3rd fl	St. Catharines	ON	L2R7E7	800-282-1376	613-995-8210
Sandler Partners					
1200 Artesia Blvd Ste 305	Hermosa Beach	CA	90254	800-825-1055	310-796-1393
Satellite Management Services Inc					
4529 E Bwy Rd	Phoenix	AZ	85040	800-788-8388	602-386-4444
Skyway West					
3644 Beach Ave	Roberts Creek	BC	V0N2W2	877-771-1077	604-482-1228
Skyy Consulting Inc					
1335 Fourth St Ste 200	Santa Monica	CA	90401	877-897-3473	
Smart Cabling Solutions Inc					
1250 N Winchester St	Olathe	KS	66061	877-390-9501	913-390-9501
SPROUT Wellness Solutions Inc					
366 Adelaide St W Ste 301	Toronto	ON	M5V1R9	866-535-5027	
Superheat Fgh Services Inc					
313 Garnet Dr	New Lenox	IL	60451	888-508-3226	
Synchronoss Technologies Inc					
200 Crossing Blvd	Bridgewater	NJ	08807	866-620-3940	
OTC: SNCR					
TBayTel 1060 Lithium Dr	Thunder Bay	ON	P7B6G3	800-264-9501	807-623-4400
Telebyte Communications Inc					
6816 50 Ave	Red Deer	AB	T4N4E3	800-565-1849	403-346-9966
TeleCommunication Systems Inc					
275 W St Ste 400	Annapolis	MD	21401	800-810-0827	410-263-7616
NASDAQ: TSYS					
TeraGo Networks Inc					
55 Commerce Vly Dr W Ste 800	Thornhill	ON	L3T7V9	866-837-2461	866-837-2465
Threshold Communications					
16541 Redmond Way Ste 245C	Redmond	WA	98052	844-844-1382	206-812-6200
Totelcom Communications LLC					
6100 Hwy 16 S PO Box 290	De Leon	TX	76444	800-261-5911	254-893-1000
Trade Service Company LLC					
13280 Evening Creek Dr S Ste 200	San Diego	CA	92128	800-854-1527	

				Toll-Free	Phone

Transtelco Corp
500 W Overland Ave Ste 301 . . . . El Paso TX 79901 **877-918-3526**

Trojan Professional Services Inc
14410 Cerritos Ave . . . . Los Alamitos CA 90720 **800-451-9723**

Trulioo
1055 W Hastings Ste 1200 . . . . Vancouver BC V6B1L1 **888-773-0179**

Uniserve Communications
333 Terminal Ave Ste 330 . . . . Vancouver BC V6A4C1 **844-395-3900** 604-395-3900

UniteU Technologies Inc
12 Pine Cone Dr . . . . Pittsford NY 14534 **866-386-4838**

Used-Car-Partscom Inc
1980 Highland Pk . . . . Fort Wright KY 41017 **800-288-7415** 859-344-1925

Vitac Corp
8300 E Maplewood Ave
Ste 310 . . . . Greenwood Village CO 80111 **800-278-4822** 724-514-4111

Vitelity Communications
317 Inverness Way S Ste 140 . . . . Englewood CO 80112 **888-898-4835**

Westman Communications Group
1906 Park Ave . . . . Brandon MB R7B0R9 **800-665-3337** 204-725-4300

Wireless Analytics LLC
230 N St . . . . Danvers MA 01923 **888-588-5550** 978-762-0900

XipLink Inc
4200 St Laurent Blvd Ste 1010 . . . . Montreal QC H2W2R2 **855-408-2483** 514-848-9640

Zingle Inc
2270 Camino Vida Roble Ste K. . . . . Carlsbad CA 92011 **877-946-4536**

225   DATA PROCESSING & RELATED SERVICES

SEE ALSO Payroll Services ; Electronic Transaction Processing

				Toll-Free	Phone

1Cloud
25 Lowell St Ste 407. . . . . Manchester NH 03101 **855-256-8300**

Affinigent Inc
4 Kent Rd Ste 200. . . . . York PA 17402 **800-932-3380** 717-600-0033

AG Dealer Ltd
44 Byward Market Sq . . . . Ottawa ON K1N7A2 **800-665-1362** 613-596-8022

Altapacific Technology Group Inc
1525 E Shaw Ave Ste 201. . . . . Fresno CA 93710 **800-659-3655** 559-439-5700

AMSplus Inc
400 Washington St . . . . Braintree MA 02184 **888-239-9575**

Applied Imaging Inc
5555 Glenwood Hills Pkwy SE . . . . Grand Rapids MI 49512 **800-521-0983** 616-554-5200

Atlantech Online Inc
1010 Wayne Ave Ste 630 . . . . Silver Spring MD 20910 **800-256-1612** 301-589-3060

Automatic Data Processing Inc (ADP)
1 ADP Blvd . . . . Roseland NJ 07068 **800-225-5237**
NASDAQ: ADP

Avalign Technologies Inc
2275 Half Day R Ste 126. . . . . Bannockburn IL 60015 **855-282-5446**

Bankcard Central Llc
PO Box 12317 . . . . Kansas City MO 64116 **800-331-8882** 816-221-1133

Blizzard Internet Marketing Inc
1001 Grand Ave Ste 005. . . . . Glenwood Springs CO 81601 **888-840-5893** 970-928-7875

Blue Fountain Media Inc
102 Madison Ave 2nd Fl. . . . . New York NY 10016 **800-278-0816** 212-260-1978

Blue Rock Technologies
800 Kirts Blvd . . . . Troy MI 48084 **866-390-8200** 248-786-6100

BlueTie Inc
2480 Browncroft Blvd Ste 2b . . . . Rochester NY 14625 **800-258-3843** 585-586-2000

Cadence Group Inc
1095 Zonolite Rd Ste 105. . . . . Atlanta GA 30306 **888-346-8125**

Capax Global LLC
410 N Michigan Ave . . . . Chicago IL 60611 **866-780-0385**

Carahsoft Technology Corp
12369 Sunrise Vly Dr Ste D2 . . . . Reston VA 20191 **888-662-2724** 703-871-8500

Cass Information Systems Inc
13001 Hollenberg Dr . . . . Bridgeton MO 63044 **888-569-4707** 314-506-5500
NASDAQ: CASS

CCC Information Services Inc
222 Merchandise Mart Plz . . . . Chicago IL 60654 **800-621-8070**

CEI
801 NW St Mary Dr Ste 205. . . . . Blue Springs MO 64014 **800-473-1976** 816-228-2976

Central Service Assn
93 S Coley Rd . . . . Tupelo MS 38801 **877-842-5962** 662-842-5962

CitiusTech Inc
2 Research Way . . . . Princeton NJ 08540 **877-248-4871**

Claimsnetcom Inc
14860 Montfort Dr Ste 250. . . . . Dallas TX 75254 **800-356-1511** 972-458-1701

CNC Software Inc
671 Old Post Rd . . . . Tolland CT 06084 **800-228-2877** 860-875-5006

Cogeco Peer 1
413 Horner Ave . . . . Etobicoke ON M8W4W3 **877-720-2228** 877-504-0091

Colosseum Online Inc
800 Petrolia Rd . . . . Toronto ON M3J3K4 **877-739-7873** 416-739-7873

Communication Data Services
1901 Bell Ave . . . . Des Moines IA 50315 **866-897-7987** 515-246-6837

Computer Services Inc
3901 Technology Dr . . . . Paducah KY 42001 **800-545-4274** 270-442-7361
OTC: CSVI

Concord Document Services Inc
1321 W 12th St . . . . Los Angeles CA 90015 **800-246-7881** 213-745-3175

Continental Graphics Corp
4060 N Lakewood Blvd
Bldg 801 5th Fl. . . . . Long Beach CA 90808 **800-862-5691** 714-503-4200

CPT Group Inc
50 Corporate Park . . . . Irvine CA 92606 **800-542-0900** 877-705-5021

Critical Mention Inc
521 Fifth Ave . . . . New York NY 10175 **855-306-2626** 212-398-1141

Cst Data
10725 John Price Rd . . . . Charlotte NC 28273 **866-383-3282** 704-927-3282

CU*Answers
6000 28th St SE Ste 100. . . . . Grand Rapids MI 49546 **800-327-3478** 616-285-5711

Customer Paradigm Inc
5353 Manhattan Cir Ste 103. . . . . Boulder CO 80303 **888-772-0777** 303-499-9318

D K Global 420 Missouri Ct . . . . Redlands CA 92373 **866-375-2214** 909-747-0201

D Net Internet Service
189 E Palmer St . . . . Franklin NC 28734 **877-601-3638** 828-349-3638

Data Dash Inc
3928 Delor St . . . . Saint Louis MO 63116 **800-211-5988** 314-832-5788

Data Services Inc
31516 Winterplace Pkwy . . . . Salisbury MD 21804 **800-432-4066** 410-546-2206

Datamark Inc
123 W Mills Ave Ste 400 . . . . El Paso TX 79901 **800-477-1944**

Datex Billing Services Inc
5520 Explorer Dr Ste 202 . . . . Mississauga ON L4W5L1 **855-553-2839**

Destiny Solutions Inc
40 Holly St . . . . Toronto ON M4S3C3 **866-403-0500** 416-480-0500

Direct Online Marketing
4727 Jacob St . . . . Wheeling WV 26003 **800-979-3177** 304-214-4850

Directory One Inc
9135 Katy Fwy Ste 204 . . . . Houston TX 77024 **800-477-1324** 713-465-0051

DirectWest
355 Longman Crescent . . . . Regina SK S4W1A1 **800-667-8201** 306-777-0333

Doc 2 E-file Inc
4500 S Wayside Ste 102. . . . . Houston TX 77087 **888-649-2006** 713-649-2006

DOmedia LLC
274 Marconi Blvd One Marconi Pl
Ste 400 . . . . Columbus OH 43215 **866-939-3663**

DoxTek Inc 264 W Center St . . . . Orem UT 84057 **877-705-7226** 801-356-2230

DPF Data Services
1345 Campus Pkw Unit A8. . . . . Wall Township NJ 07753 **800-431-4416**

Dundee Internet Service Inc
168 Riley St . . . . Dundee MI 48131 **888-222-8485** 734-529-5331

DuVoice Corp
608 State St S . . . . Kirkland WA 98033 **800-888-1057** 425-889-9790

E Commerce Partners
59 Franklin St . . . . New York NY 10013 **866-431-6669** 212-334-3390

E-cubed Media Synthesis Ltd
3807 William St . . . . Burnaby BC V5C3J1 **800-294-1556** 604-294-1556

Ease Technologies Inc
10320 Little Patuxent Pkwy Ste 1104 . . . . Columbia MD 21044 **888-327-3911** 301-854-0010

EasyStreet
9705 SW Sunshine Ct . . . . Beaverton OR 97005 **800-207-0740*** 503-646-8400
*Support

Ebix BPO 151 N Lyon Ave . . . . Hemet CA 92543 **800-996-9964** 951-658-4000

Effective Data Inc
1515 E Wdfield Rd . . . . Schaumburg IL 60173 **877-825-5233** 847-969-9300

eGov Strategies LLC
101 W Ohio St Ste 2250 . . . . Indianapolis IN 46204 **877-634-3468**

Enhanced Software Products Inc
1811 N Hutchinson Rd . . . . Spokane WA 99212 **800-456-5750** 509-534-1514

Epic Cos
24955 Interstate 45 N . . . . The Woodlands TX 77380 **800-844-3742**

Equifax Inc
1550 Peachtree St NW . . . . Atlanta GA 30309 **888-202-4025*** 404-885-8000
NYSE: EFX ■ *Sales

Fair Isaac Corp
2665 Long Lake Rd Bldg C. . . . . Roseville MN 55113 **888-342-6336*** 612-758-5200
NYSE: FICO ■ *Cust Svc

Flightline Data Services Inc
138 Peachtree Ct . . . . Fayetteville GA 30215 **800-659-9859** 770-487-3482

Forte Data Systems Inc
3330 Paddock Pkwy . . . . Suwanee GA 30024 **800-571-8702** 678-208-0206

Gaggle Net
2205 E Empire St Ste B
PO Box 1352. . . . . Bloomington IL 61704 **800-288-7750** 309-665-0572

Genetec Inc
2280 Alfred-Nobel Blvd Ste 400 . . . . Montreal QC H4S2A4 **866-684-8006** 514-332-4000

GEOSPAN Corp
6901 E Fish Lake Rd Ste 156 . . . . Minneapolis MN 55369 **800-436-7726** 763-493-9320

Giact Systems Inc
700 Central Expy S . . . . Allen TX 75013 **866-918-2409**

Glance Networks Inc
1167 Massachusetts Ave . . . . Arlington MA 02476 **877-452-6236** 781-646-8505

Global Health Care Exchange LLC (GHX)
1315 W Century Dr . . . . Louisville CO 80027 **800-968-7449** 720-887-7000

Grant Street Group Inc
339 Sixth Ave Ste 1400 . . . . Pittsburgh PA 15222 **800-410-3445** 412-391-5555

GreenGeeks LLC
5739 Kanan Rd Ste 300 . . . . Agoura Hills CA 91301 **877-326-7483** 310-496-8946

Habanero Consulting Group Inc
510-1111 Melville St . . . . Vancouver BC V6E3V6 **866-841-6201** 604-709-6201

Health Management Systems Inc
401 Park Ave S . . . . New York NY 10016 **877-357-3268** 212-857-5000

Hivelocity Ventures Corp
8010 Woodland Ctr Blvd Ste 700 . . . . Tampa FL 33614 **888-869-4678** 813-471-0355

ICTV Brands Inc
489 Devon Park Dr Ste 315 . . . . Wayne PA 19087 **800-839-4906** 484-598-2300

Impatica Inc
2430 Don Reid Dr Ste 200 . . . . Ottawa ON K1H1E1 **800-548-3475** 613-736-9982

Inspired eLearning Inc
613 NW Loop 410 Ste 530 . . . . San Antonio TX 78216 **800-631-2078** 210-579-0224

Ivanti
8660 E Hartford Dr Ste 300. . . . . Scottsdale AZ 85255 **888-725-7828** 480-970-1025

iWeb Technologies Inc
20 Place du Commerce . . . . Montreal QC H3E1Z6 **800-100-3276**

Kelser Corp
43 Western Blvd . . . . Glastonbury CT 06033 **800-647-5316** 860-610-2200

Keystone Information Systems
1000 S Lenola Rd . . . . Maple Shade NJ 08052 **800-735-4862** 856-722-0700

Kirtley Technology Corp
8328 Lemont Rd . . . . Darien IL 60561 **888-757-0778** 630-512-0213

La Touraine Inc
110 W A St Ste 900 . . . . San Diego CA 92101 **800-893-8871** 619-237-5014

LoganBritton Inc
1700 Park St Ste 111 . . . . Naperville IL 60563 **800-362-4352**

Long Lines LLC
501 Fourth St PO Box 67 . . . . Sergeant Bluff IA 51054 **866-901-5664** 712-271-4000

Lowe-Martin Company Inc
400 Hunt Club Rd . . . . Ottawa ON K1V1C1 **866-521-9871** 613-741-0962

Marketware Inc
7070 Union Park Ctr Ste 300 . . . . Midvale UT 84047 **800-777-6368**

MCH Inc
601 E Marshall St . . . . Sweet Springs MO 65351 **800-776-6373**

			Toll-Free	Phone
MediConnect Global Inc				
10897 S Riverfront Pkwy Ste 500	South Jordan	UT 84095	800-489-8710	801-545-3700
MedPricer				
2346 Boston Post Rd Unit 2	Guilford	CT 06437	888-453-4554	203-453-4554
Metasense Inc				
403 Commerce Ln #5	West Berlin	NJ 08091	866-875-6382	856-873-9950
Mid America Computer Corp				
PO Box 700	Blair	NE 68008	800-622-2502	402-426-6222
Modern Earth				
449 Provencher Blvd	Winnipeg	MB R2J0B8	866-766-7640	204-885-2469
Mudiam Inc				
7100 regency Sq blvd	Houston	TX 77036	888-306-2062	713-484-7266
Musictoday LLC				
5391 Three Notch ƒ?Td Rd	Crozet	VA 22932	800-927-7821	434-244-7200
N-Dimension Solutions Inc				
9030 Leslie St Ste 300	Richmond Hill	ON L4B1G2	866-837-8884	
National Fulfillment Services				
105 Commerce Dr	Aston	PA 19014	800-637-1306	
Nexcessnet LLC				
21700 Melrose Ave	Southfield	MI 48075	866-639-2377	
Oly Penn Inc				
245 E Washington St	Sequim	WA 98382	800-303-8696	360-683-1456
One Technologies LLC				
8144 Walnut Hill Ln Ste 600	Dallas	TX 75231	888-550-8471	214-379-8216
Opal Soft				
1288 Kifer Rd # 201	Sunnyvale	CA 94086	800-632-2022	408-267-2211
Openface Inc 3445 Park Ave	Montreal	QC H2X2H6	800-865-8585	514-281-8585
Optimetra Inc				
1710 Chapel Hills Dr	Colorado Springs	CO 80920	800-758-9710	
Oristech Inc				
Po Box 310069	New Braunfels	TX 78131	800-929-9078	830-620-7422
P K W Associates Inc				
705 E Ordnance Rd Ste 108	Baltimore	MD 21226	888-358-3900	443-773-1000
PenTeleData				
540 Delaware Ave PO Box 197	Palmerton	PA 18071	800-281-3564	
Pinnacle Business Systems Inc				
3824 S Blvd St Ste 200	Edmond	OK 73013	800-311-0757	
PinnacleCart Inc				
3320 W Cheryl Dr Ste B200	Phoenix	AZ 85051	800-506-0398	
Pricon Inc				
1831 W Lincoln Ave	Anaheim	CA 92801	800-660-1831	714-758-8832
Printco Graphics Inc				
14112 Industrial Rd	Omaha	NE 68144	888-593-1080	402-593-1080
Printmail Systems Inc				
23 Friends Ln	Newtown	PA 18940	800-910-4844	215-860-4250
Prism Visual Software Inc				
1 Sagamore Hl Dr Ste 2B	Port Washington	NY 11050	800-260-2793	516-944-5920
Protogate Inc				
12225 World Trade Dr	San Diego	CA 92128	877-473-0190	858-451-0865
Pyramid Consulting Inc				
11100 Atlantis Pl	Alpharetta	GA 30022	877-248-0024	678-514-3500
Ramco Systems Corp				
3150 Brunswick Pk Ste 130	Lawrenceville	NJ 08648	800-472-6261	609-620-4800
Ramius Corp				
283 Blvd Alexandre Tach, Ste F2014	Gatineau	QC J9A1L8	888-932-2299	613-230-3808
Rangam Consultants Inc				
270 Davidson Ave Ste 103	Somerset	NJ 08873	877-388-1858	908-704-8843
Red Clay Interactive				
22 S Buford Village Way Ste 221	Buford	GA 30518	866-251-2800	770-297-2430
RedTail Solutions Inc				
69 Milk St Ste 100	Westborough	MA 01581	866-764-7601	508-983-1900
Right Systems Inc				
2600 Willamette Dr NE Ste C	Lacey	WA 98516	800-571-1717	360-956-0414
Ross Group Inc				
2730 Indian Ripple Rd	Dayton	OH 45440	800-734-9304	
Ryantech Cloud Services				
60 E Rio Salado Pkwy 9th Fl	Tempe	AZ 85281	866-804-9040	
Seagull Scientific Inc				
15325 SE 30th Pl Ste 100	Bellevue	WA 98007	800-758-2001	425-641-1408
Shop Floor Automations Inc				
5360 Jackson Dr	La Mesa	CA 91942	877-611-5825	619-461-4000
Sigma Solutions Inc				
607 E Sonterra Blvd Ste 250	San Antonio	TX 78258	800-567-5964	210-348-9876
Softlayer Technologies Inc				
4849 Alpha Rd	Dallas	TX 75244	866-398-7638*	214-442-0600
*Sales				
Southern Data Systems Inc				
1245 Land O Lakes Dr	Roswell	GA 30075	888-425-6151	770-993-7103
Spectrum Data Inc				
131 N Third St	Oregon	IL 61061	800-733-6567	
Storm Internet Services Inc				
1760 Courtwood Crescent	Ottawa	ON K2C2B5	866-257-8676	613-567-6585
Stratagem Inc				
10922 N Cedarburg Rd	Mequon	WI 53092	800-228-4422	262-532-2700
Synergon Solutions Inc				
1335 Gateway Dr	Melbourne	FL 32901	800-820-6103	321-728-2674
Systems House, The				
1033 Rte 46 E Ste A202	Clifton	NJ 07013	800-637-5556	973-777-8050
Taskstream LLC				
71 W 23rd St	New York	NY 10010	800-311-5656	212-868-2700
Tecnicard Inc				
3191 Coral Way Ste 800	Miami	FL 33145	800-317-6020	305-442-0018
Teradata Corp				
10000 Innovation Dr	Dayton	OH 45342	866-548-8348	
NYSE: TDC				
Townsend Security				
724 Columbia St Nw	Olympia	WA 98501	800-357-1019	360-359-4400
Trend				
660 American Ave Ste 203	King Of Prussia	PA 19406	877-330-9900	610-783-4650
Urban Web Design				
102-19 Dallas Rd	Victoria	BC V8V5A6	877-889-2573	250-380-1296
VEITS Group LLC				
7610 Olentangy River Rd Ste 200	Columbus	OH 43235	877-834-8702	614-467-5414
Versasuite				
10601 Pecan Park Blvd	Austin	TX 78750	800-903-8774	
Versatile Mobile Systems				
4900 Ritter Rd Ste 100	Mechanicsburg	PA 17055	800-262-1622	
NYSE: CVE				

			Toll-Free	Phone
WebLinc LLC				
22 S Third St 2nd Fl	Philadelphia	PA 19106	855-227-0511	
Williams Records Management				
1925 E Vernon Ave	Los Angeles	CA 90058	888-478-3453*	323-234-3453
*Cust Svc				
Wrightsoft Corp				
131 Hartwell Ave	Lexington	MA 02421	800-225-8697	
XEcom Inc				
1145 Nicholson Rd Ste 200	Newmarket	ON L3Y9C3	877-932-6640	416-214-5606
Xiologix				
8050 SW Warm Springs St Ste 100	Tualatin	OR 97062	888-492-6843	503-691-4364
Z57 Internet Solutions				
10045 Mesa Rim Rd	San Diego	CA 92121	800-899-8148	
ZirMed Inc				
888 W Market St	Louisvill	KY 40202	877-494-7633*	866-347-5653
*Support				

226 DATING SERVICES

			Toll-Free	Phone
American Homeowners Association (AHA)				
3001 Summer St	Stamford	CT 06905	800-470-2242	203-323-7715
Art Craft Display Inc				
500 Business Centre Dr	Lansing	MI 48917	800-878-0710	517-485-2221
Ashley Madison Agency, The				
2300 Yonge St	Toronto	ON M4P1E4	866-742-2218	
Balnea Spa				
319 chemin du Lac Gale	Bromont	QC J2L2S5	866-734-2110	450-534-0604
Caledon Laboratories Ltd				
40 Armstrong Ave	Georgetown	ON L7G4R9	877-225-3366	905-877-0101
Credit Plus Inc				
31550 WinterPl Pkwy	Salisbury	MD 21804	800-258-3287	410-742-9551
Digimap Data Services Inc				
40 Kodiak Cres Unit 13	Toronto	ON M3J3G5	877-344-4627	
Digiscribe International LLC				
150 Clearbrook Rd Ste 125	Elmsford	NY 10523	800-686-7577	
Forest Preserve Dist of Dupage County				
1717 31st St	Oak Brook	IL 60523	800-526-0857	630-616-8424
Friendfinder Network Inc				
6800 Broken Sound Pkwy Ste 200	Boca Raton	FL 33487	888-575-8383	561-912-7000
TSE: FFN				
iGov Technologies Inc				
9211 Palm River Rd Ste 110	Tampa	FL 33619	800-777-9375	813-612-9470
Omni Cubed Inc				
6125 Enterprise Dr Ste B155	Diamond Springs	CA 95619	877-311-1976	
Tarrytown House Estate & Conference Ctr				
49 E Sunnyside Ln	Tarrytown	NY 10591	800-553-8118	914-591-8200
Wedding Experience				
2307 Douglas Rd Ste 400	Coral Gables	FL 33145	866-223-9672	305-421-1260

227 DENTAL ASSOCIATIONS - STATE

SEE ALSO Health & Medical Professionals Associations

			Toll-Free	Phone
Alabama Dental Assn				
836 Washington Ave	Montgomery	AL 36104	800-489-2532	334-265-1684
Alaska Dental Society				
9170 Jewel Lake Rd Ste 203	Anchorage	AK 99502	800-478-4675	907-563-3003
Arizona Dental Assn				
3193 N Drinkwater Blvd	Scottsdale	AZ 85251	800-866-2732	480-344-5777
Arkansas State Dental Assn				
7480 Hwy 107	Sherwood	AR 72120	800-501-2732	501-834-7650
California Dental Assn				
1201 K St 14th Fl	Sacramento	CA 95814	800-736-7071	916-443-0505
Florida Dental Assn				
1111 E Tennessee St	Tallahassee	FL 32308	800-877-9922	850-681-3629
Georgia Dental Assn				
7000 Peachtree Dnwdy Rd NE Ste 200 Bldg 17	Atlanta	GA 30328	800-432-4357	404-636-7553
Hawaii Dental Assn				
1345 S Beretania St Ste 301	Honolulu	HI 96814	800-359-6725	808-593-7956
Illinois State Dental Society				
1010 S Second St	Springfield	IL 62704	888-286-2447	217-525-1406
Indiana Dental Assn				
1319 E Stop 10 Rd	Indianapolis	IN 46227	800-562-5646	317-634-2610
Iowa Dental Assn				
8797 NW 54th Ave Ste 100	Johnston	IA 50131	800-828-2181	515-331-2298
Louisiana Dental Assn				
7833 Office Pk Blvd	Baton Rouge	LA 70809	800-388-6642	225-926-1986
Maryland State Dental Assn				
8901 Herrmann Dr	Columbia	MD 21045	800-621-8099	410-964-2880
Massachusetts Dental Society				
2 Willow St	Southborough	MA 01745	800-342-8747	
Michigan Dental Assn				
3657 Okemos Rd Ste 200	Okemos	MI 48864	800-589-2632	517-372-9070
Minnesota Dental Assn				
1335 Industrial Blvd Ste 200	Minneapolis	MN 55413	800-950-3368	612-767-8400
Mississippi Dental Assn				
439 B katherine Dr	Flowood	MS 39232	800-562-2957	601-664-9691
Missouri Dental Assn				
3340 American Ave	Jefferson City	MO 65109	800-688-1907	573-634-3436
Montana Dental Assn				
17 1/2 S Last Chance Gulch PO Box 1154	Helena	MT 59624	800-257-4988	406-443-2061
Nevada Dental Assn				
8863 W Flamingo Rd Ste 102	Las Vegas	NV 89147	800-962-6710	702-255-4211
New Hampshire Dental Society				
23 S State St	Concord	NH 03301	800-244-5961	603-225-5961
New Mexico Dental Assn				
9201 Montgomery Blvd NE Ste 601	Albuquerque	NM 87111	888-787-1722	505-294-1368
New York State Dental Assn				
20 Corporate Woods Blvd #602	Albany	NY 12211	800-255-2100	518-465-0044
North Carolina Dental Society				
1600 Evans Rd	Cary	NC 27513	800-662-8754	919-677-1396
North Dakota Dental Assn				
1720 Burnt Boat Dr Ste 201	Bismarck	ND 58503	800-444-1330	701-223-8870

			Toll-Free	Phone

Oklahoma Dental Assn
317 NE 13th St .... Oklahoma City OK 73104 **800-876-8890** 405-848-8873
Oregon Dental Assn
PO Box 3710 .... Wilsonville OR 97070 **800-452-5628** 503-218-2010
South Carolina Dental Assn
120 Stonemark Ln .... Columbia SC 29210 **800-327-2598** 803-750-2277
South Dakota Dental Assn
804 N Euclid Ave Ste 103 .... Pierre SD 57501 **866-551-8023** 605-224-9133
Tennessee Dental Assn (TDA)
660 Bakers Bridge Ave Ste 300 .... Franklin TN 37067 **800-824-9722** 615-628-0208
Texas Dental Assn
1946 S IH-35 Ste 400 .... Austin TX 78704 **800-832-1145** 512-443-3675
Wisconsin Dental Assn
6737 W Washington St Ste 2360 .... West Allis WI 53214 **800-364-7646** 414-276-4520

228 DENTAL EQUIPMENT & SUPPLIES - MFR

			Toll-Free	Phone

3M Dental Products Div
3M Ctr .... Saint Paul MN 55144 **888-364-3577**
3M Unitek 2724 Peck Rd .... Monrovia CA 91016 **800-634-5300**
A-dec Inc 2601 Crestview Dr .... Newberg OR 97132 **800-547-1883*** 503-538-7478
*Cust Svc
Accutron Inc
1733 Parkside Ln .... Phoenix AZ 85027 **800-531-2221** 623-780-2020
ACTEON North America Inc
124 Gaither Dr Ste 140 .... Mount Laurel NJ 08054 **800-289-6367** 856-222-9988
Air Techniques Inc
1295 Walt Whitman Rd .... Melville NY 11747 **888-247-8481** 516-433-7676
Align Technology Inc
2560 Orchard Pkwy .... San Jose CA 95131 **800-577-8767** 408-470-1000
NASDAQ: ALGN
Alpha Pro Tech Ltd
60 Centurian Dr .... Markham ON L3R9R2 **800-749-1363** 905-479-0654
American Orthodontics Corp
1714 Cambridge Ave .... Sheboygan WI 53081 **800-558-7687** 920-457-5051
Aribex Inc 744 S 400 E .... Orem UT 84097 **866-340-5522** 801-226-5522
Barnhardt Mfg Co
1100 Hawthorne Ln .... Charlotte NC 28205 **800-277-0377**
Bicon LLC 501 Arborway .... Boston MA 02130 **800-882-4266** 617-524-4443
Brasseler USA
1 Brasseler Blvd .... Savannah GA 31419 **800 841-4522**
Buffalo Dental Manufacturing Company Inc
159 Lafayette Dr .... Syosset NY 11791 **800-828-0203** 516-496-7200
Coltene/Whaledent Inc
235 Ascot Pkwy .... Cuyahoga Falls OH 44223 **800-221-3046** 330-916-8800
Den-Mat Corp
2727 Skyway Dr .... Santa Maria CA 93455 **800-433-6628** 805-922-8491
DEN-TAL-EZ Group Inc
2 W Liberty Blvd Ste 160 .... Malvern PA 19355 **866-383-4636** 610-725-8004
DentalEZ Inc
2500 Hwy 31 S .... Bay Minette AL 36507 **866-383-4636** 251-937-6781
DenTek Oral Care Inc
307 Excellence Way .... Maryville TN 37801 **800-433-6835**
Dentsply International Inc Tulsa Dental Div
5100 E Skelly Dr Ste 300 .... Tulsa OK 74135 **800-662-1202** 918-493-6598
Dentsply Sirona
221 W Philadelphia St PO Box 872 .... York PA 17405 **800-877-0020** 717-845-7511
NASDAQ: XRAY
Dexta Corp 962 Kaiser Rd .... Napa CA 94558 **800-733-3982** 707-255-2454
G & H Wire Company Inc
2165 Earlywood Dr .... Franklin IN 46131 **800-526-1026** 317-346-6655
GC America Inc
3737 W 127th St .... Alsip IL 60803 **800-323-7063*** 708-597-0900
*Cust Svc
Great Lakes Orthodontic Laboratories Div
200 Cooper Ave .... Tonawanda NY 14150 **800-828-7626**
Hu-Friedy Mfg Company Inc
3232 N Rockwell St .... Chicago IL 60618 **800-483-7433** 773-975-6100
Hygenic Corp 1245 Home Ave .... Akron OH 44310 **800-321-2135** 330-633-8460
Isolite Systems
6868A Cortona Dr .... Santa Barbara CA 93117 **800-560-6066**
Keystone Dental Inc
144 Middlesex Tpke .... Burlington MA 01803 **866-902-9272** 781-328-3490
Kinetic Instrument Inc
17 Berkshire Blvd .... Bethel CT 06801 **800-233-2346** 203-743-0080
Kulzer LLC
4315 S Lafayette Blvd .... South Bend IN 46614 **800-431-1785**
Lancer Orthodontics Inc
1493 Poinsettia Ave Ste 143 .... Vista CA 92081 **800-854-2896*** 760-744-5585
NYSE: LANZ *Cust Svc
Lang Manufacturing Co
175 Messner Dr .... Wheeling IL 60090 **800-222-5264**
LifeCore Biomedical LLC
3515 Lyman Blvd .... Chaska MN 55318 **800-348-4368*** 952-368-4300
*Cust Svc
M & M Innovations
7424 Blythe Island Hwy .... Brunswick GA 31523 **800-688-3384** 912-265-7110
Metrex Research Corp
1717 West Collins Ave .... Orange CA 92867 **800-841-1428**
Midwest Dental Equipment Services & Supplies
2700 Commerce St .... Wichita Falls TX 76301 **800-766-2025**
Miltex Inc 589 Davies Dr .... York PA 17402 **866-854-8400** 717-840-9335
Myotronics-noromed Inc
5870 S 194th St .... Kent WA 98032 **800-426-0316** 206-243-4214
Nasseo Inc
13660 N 94th Dr D-7 .... Peoria AZ 85381 **866-207-8919**
NDX Stern Empire
1805 W 34th St .... Houston TX 77018 **800-229-0214** 713-688-1301
Nobel Biocare USA Inc
22715 Savi Ranch Pkwy .... Yorba Linda CA 92887 **800-993-8100** 714-282-4800
Novalab 2350 Power St .... Drummondville QC J2C7Z4 **800-474-6682** 819-474-2580
ORMCO Corp
1717 W Collins Ave .... Orange CA 92867 **800-854-1741*** 714-516-7400
*Cust Svc
Pentron Clinical Technologies LLC
1717 W Collins Ave .... Orange CA 92867 **800-551-0283** 714-516-7557

			Toll-Free	Phone

Practicon Inc
1112 Sugg Pkwy .... Greenville NC 27834 **800-959-9505** 252-752-5183
Premier Dental Products Co
1710 Romano Dr .... Plymouth Meeting PA 19462 **888-670-6100** 610-239-6000
Quantum Dental Technologies Inc
748 Briar Hill Ave .... Toronto ON M6B1L3 **866-993-9910**
Rocky Mountain Orthodontics Inc (RMO Inc)
650 W Colfax Ave .... Denver CO 80204 **800-525-6375** 303-592-8200
Sunstar Americas Inc
4635 W Foster Ave .... Chicago IL 60630 **888-777-3101**
Therapeutic Solutions International Inc
4093 Oceanside Blvd Ste B. .... Oceanside CA 92056 **877-468-4877**
TP Orthodontics Inc
100 Ctr Plz .... La Porte IN 46350 **800-348-8856** 219-785-2591
Water Pik Inc
1730 E Prospect Rd .... Fort Collins CO 80553 **800-525-2774**
Young Dental Manufacturing LLC
13705 Shoreline Ct E .... Earth City MO 63045 **800-325-1881**

229 DEPARTMENT STORES

			Toll-Free	Phone

Bon-Ton Stores Inc
2801 E Market St .... York PA 17405 **800-945-4438** 717-757-7660
NASDAQ: BONTQ
BootBarn Inc
620 Pan American Dr .... Livingston TX 77351 **888-440-2668**
CURTAIN & BATH OUTLET
1 Ann & Hope Way .... Cumberland RI 02864 **877-228-7824**
Dillard's Inc
1600 Cantrell Rd .... Little Rock AR 72201 **800-643-8274** 501-376-5200
NYSE: DDS
Fred's Inc
4300 New Getwell Rd .... Memphis TN 38118 **800-374-7417** 901-365-8880
NASDAQ: FRED
Gordman 12100 W Ctr Rd .... Omaha NE 68144 **800-743-8730**
Kohl's Corp
N 56 W 17000 Ridgewood Dr .... Menomonee Falls WI 53051 **855-564-5705** 262-703-7000
NYSE: KSS
Langstons Co
2034 NW Seventh St .... Oklahoma City OK 73106 **800-658-2831** 405-235-9536
Lord & Taylor
424 Fifth Ave .... New York NY 10018 **800-223-7440** 212-391-3344
Macy's Inc
7 W Seventh St .... Cincinnati OH 45202 **800-261-5385** 513-579-7000
NYSE: M
Proffitt & Goodson Inc
Old Kingston Pl 4800 Old Kingston Pk
Ste 200 .... Knoxville TN 37919 **866-776-3355** 865-584-1850
Sears Roebuck & Co
3333 Beverly Rd .... Hoffman Estates IL 60179 **800-349-4358** 847-286-2500
Shopko LLC
700 Pilgrim Way .... Green Bay WI 54304 **800-791-7333** 920-429-2211
Target Corp
1000 Nicollet Mall .... Minneapolis MN 55403 **800-440-0680*** 612-304-6073
NYSE: TGT ■ *Cust Svc
Tongass Trading Co
201 Dock St .... Ketchikan AK 99901 **800-235-5102** 907-225-5101
Von Maur Inc
6565 Brady St .... Davenport IA 52806 **877-866-6287** 563-388-2200
Wal-Mart Stores Inc
702 SW Eighth St .... Bentonville AR 72716 **800-925-6278*** 479-273-4000
NYSE: WMT ■ *Cust Svc
Walmartcom
1919 Davis St .... San Leandro CA 94577 **800-925-6278** 479-273-1329

230 DEVELOPMENTAL CENTERS

Residential facilities for the developmentally disabled.

			Toll-Free	Phone

Central Virginia Training Ctr
521 Colony Rd .... Madison Heights VA 24572 **866-897-6095** 434-947-6000
Sonoma Developmental Ctr
15000 Arnold Dr .... Eldridge CA 95431 **800-862-0007** 707-938-6000
Woodward Resource Ctr
1251 334th St .... Woodward IA 50276 **888-229-9223** 515-438-2600

231 DIAGNOSTIC PRODUCTS

SEE ALSO Medicinal Chemicals & Botanical Products ; Pharmaceutical Companies ; Pharmaceutical Companies - Generic Drugs ; Biotechnology Companies

			Toll-Free	Phone

Abaxis Inc
3240 Whipple Rd .... Union City CA 94587 **800-822-2947** 510-675-6500
NASDAQ: ABAX
Abbott Diagnostics
675 N Field Dr .... Lake Forest IL 60045 **800-387-8378** 224-667-6100
Accurate Chemical & Scientific Corp
300 Shames Dr .... Westbury NY 11590 **800-645-6264** 516-333-2221
Advanced Biotechnologies Inc (ABI)
1545 Progress Way .... Eldersburg MD 21784 **800-426-0764** 410-792-9779
Akorn Inc
1925 W Field Ct .... Lake Forest IL 60045 **800-932-5676** 847-279-6100
NASDAQ: AKRX
ALK 35-151 Brunel Rd .... Mississauga ON L4Z2H6 **800-663-0972** 905-290-9952
Aloha Medicinals Inc
2300 Arrowhead Dr .... Carson City NV 89706 **877-835-6091** 775-886-6300
AnaSpec Inc 34801 Campus Dr .... Fremont CA 94555 **800-452-5530** 510-791-9560
AntiCancer Inc
7917 Ostrow St .... San Diego CA 92111 **800-511-2555** 858-654-2555
Ascend Therapeutics Inc
607 Herndon Pkwy Ste 110 .... Herndon VA 20170 **888-412-5751** 703-471-4744

Company / Address	City	State	ZIP	Toll-Free	Phone
Athena Diagnostics Inc					
377 Plantation St 2nd Fl	Worcester	MA	01605	**800-394-4493**	508-756-2886
Bachem-Peninsula Laboratories Inc					
3132 Kashiwa St	Torrence	CA	90505	**888-422-2436**	310-539-4171
Baxter Corp					
7125 Mississauga Rd	Mississauga	ON	L5N0C2	**866-234-2345**	905-369-6000
Becton Dickinson & Co					
1 Becton Dr	Franklin Lakes	NJ	07417	**888-237-2762***	201-847-6800
NYSE: BDX ■ *Cust Svc					
Bee-alive Inc 151 N Rte 9 W	Congers	NY	10920	**800-543-2337**	
Bio-Rad Laboratories					
1000 Alfred Nobel Dr	Hercules	CA	94547	**800-424-6723**	510-724-7000
NYSE: BIO					
Biocell Laboratories Inc					
2001 University Dr	Rancho Dominguez	CA	90220	**800-222-8382**	310-537-3300
BioGenex Laboratories Inc					
4600 Norris Canyon Rd	San Ramon	CA	94583	**800-421-4149**	925-275-0550
Biohelix Corp					
500 Cummings Ste 5550	Beverly	MA	01915	**800-874-1517**	978-927-5056
Biomerica Inc					
1533 Monrovia Ave	Newport Beach	CA	92663	**800-854-3002***	949-645-2111
OTC: BMRA ■ *Cust Svc					
BioMerieux Inc					
595 Anglum Rd	Hazelwood	MO	63042	**800-634-7656**	314-731-8500
Bionostics Inc 7 Jackson Rd	Devens	MA	01434	**800-776-3856***	978-772-7070
*General					
Boiron 6 Campus Blvd	Newtown Square	PA	19073	**800-264-7661**	610-325-7464
Burlington Drug Company Inc					
91 Catamount Dr	Milton	VT	05468	**800-338-8703**	802-893-5105
Calmoseptine Inc					
16602 Burke Ln	Huntington Beach	CA	92647	**800-800-3405**	714-840-3405
Cancap Pharmaceutical Ltd					
13111 Vanier Pl Unit 180	Richmond	BC	V6V2J1	**877-998-2378**	604-278-2188
Cancer Genetics Inc					
Meadows Office Complex 201 Rt 17 N					
2nd Fl	Rutherford	NJ	07070	**888-334-4988**	201-528-9200
Cedarlane Laboratories Inc					
4410 Paletta Ct	Burlington	ON	L7L5R2	**800-268-5058**	905-878-8891
Centrix Pharmaceutical Inc					
951 Clint Moore Rd Ste A	Boca Raton	FL	33487	**866-991-9870**	205-991-9870
Chematics Inc					
PO Box 293	North Webster	IN	46555	**800-348-5174**	574-834-2406
Diamond Drugs Inc					
645 Kolter Dr	Indiana	PA	15701	**800-882-6337**	724-349-1111
DiaSorin Inc 1951 NW Ave	Stillwater	MN	55082	**855-677-0600**	651-439-9710
Digestive Care Inc					
1120 Win Dr	Bethlehem	PA	18017	**877-882-5950**	
DMS Pharmaceutical Group Inc					
810 Busse Hwy	Park Ridge	IL	60068	**877-788-1100**	847-518-1100
DuPont Qualicon					
Henry Clay Rd Bldg 400 Rt 141					
PO Box 80400	Wilmington	DE	19880	**800-863-6842**	302-695-5300
Eco Lips Inc					
329 Tenth Ave SE Ste 213	Cedar Rapids	IA	52401	**866-326-5477**	319-364-2477
Enzo Biochem Inc					
527 Madison Ave	New York	NY	10022	**800-522-5052**	212-583-0100
NYSE: ENZ					
Enzo Life Sciences Inc					
10 Executive Blvd	Farmingdale	NY	11735	**800-942-0430**	631-694-7070
Euro-Pharm International Canada Inc					
9400 Boul Langelier	Montreal	QC	H1P3H8	**888-929-0835**	514-323-8757
Face Stockholm Ltd					
324 Joslen Blvd	Hudson	NY	12534	**888-334-3223**	518-828-6600
Gen-Probe Inc					
10210 Genetic Center Dr	San Diego	CA	92121	**800-523-5001**	858-410-8000
GenBio					
15222 Ave of Science Ste A	San Diego	CA	92128	**800-288-4368***	858-592-9300
*Tech Supp					
Gibson Laboratories Inc					
1040 Manchester St	Lexington	KY	40508	**800-477-4763**	859-254-9500
Goodwin Biotechnology Inc					
1850 NW 69th Ave	Plantation	FL	33313	**800-814-8600**	954-327-9656
Guerbet LLC					
120 W Seventh St Ste 108	Bloomington	IN	47404	**877-729-6679**	812-333-0059
Healthy n Fit International Inc					
435 Yorktown Rd	Croton On Hudson	NY	10520	**800-338-5200**	914-271-6040
Helena Laboratories Inc					
1530 Lindbergh Dr	Beaumont	TX	77704	**800-231-5663**	409-842-3714
Hemagen Diagnostics Inc					
9033 Red Branch Rd	Columbia	MD	21045	**800-436-2436**	443-367-5500
OTC: HMGN					
Hitachi Chemical Diagnostics					
630 Clyde Ct	Mountain View	CA	94043	**800-233-6278**	650-961-5501
Honeys Place Inc					
640 Glenoaks Blvd	San Fernando	CA	91340	**800-910-3246**	
Hycor Biomedical Inc					
7272 Chapman Ave	Garden Grove	CA	92841	**800-382-2527***	714-933-3000
*Cust Svc					
IDEXX Laboratories Inc					
1 IDEXX Dr	Westbrook	ME	04092	**800-548-6733**	207-556-0300
NASDAQ: IDXX					
ImmucorGamma Inc					
3130 Gateway Dr PO Box 5625	Norcross	GA	30091	**800-829-2553***	770-441-2051
NASDAQ: BLUD ■ *Cust Svc					
ImmunoDiagnostics Inc					
1 Presidential Way Ste 104	Woburn	MA	01801	**800-573-1700**	781-938-6300
Immunovision Inc					
1820 Ford Ave	Springdale	AR	72764	**800-541-0960**	479-751-7005
IMMY (IMMY)					
2701 Corporate Centre Dr	Norman	OK	73069	**800-654-3639**	405-360-4669
Inova Diagnostics Inc					
9900 Old Grove Rd	San Diego	CA	92131	**800-545-9495**	858-586-9900
International Immunology Corp					
25549 Adams Ave	Murrieta	CA	92562	**800-843-2853**	951-677-5629
International Isotopes Inc					
4137 Commerce Cir	Idaho Falls	ID	83401	**800-699-3108**	208-524-5300
OTC: INIS					
InVitro International					
330 E Orangethorpe Ave Ste D	Placentia	CA	92870	**800-246-8487**	949-851-8356
Invivoscribe Technologies Inc					
6330 Nancy Ridge Dr Ste 106	San Diego	CA	92121	**866-623-8105**	858-224-6600
Iso-Tex Diagnostics Inc					
1511 County Rd 129	Pearland	TX	77511	**800-477-4839**	281-481-1232
Jackson ImmunoResearch Laboratories Inc					
872 W Baltimore Pk PO Box 9	West Grove	PA	19390	**800-367-5296**	
Kamiya Biomedical Co					
12779 Gateway Dr	Seattle	WA	98168	**800-526-4925**	206-575-8068
Kern Health Systems					
9700 Stockdale Hwy	Bakersfield	CA	93311	**888-466-2219**	661-664-5000
Kibow Biotech Inc					
4781 W Chester Pike Newtown Business Ctr					
	Newtown Square	PA	19073	**888-271-2560**	610-353-5130
KMI Diagnostics Inc					
8201 Central Ave NE Ste P	Minneapolis	MN	55432	**888-564-3424**	763-231-3313
Kohl & Frisch Ltd					
7622 Keele St	Concord	ON	L4K2R5	**800-265-2520**	
Lawton's Drug Stores Ltd					
236 Brownlow Ave Ste 270	Dartmouth	NS	B3B1V5	**866-990-1599**	902-468-1000
LifeScan Inc					
1000 Gibraltar Dr	Milpitas	CA	95035	**800-227-8862**	408-263-9789
Maine Biotechnology Services Inc					
1037 R Forest Ave	Portland	ME	04103	**800-925-9476**	207-797-5454
Marianna Industries Inc					
11222 "I" St	Omaha	NE	68137	**800-228-9060**	402-593-0211
MEDTOX Diagnostics Inc					
1238 Anthony Rd	Burlington	NC	27215	**800-334-1116**	336-226-6311
Meridian Bioscience Inc					
3471 River Hills Dr	Cincinnati	OH	45244	**800-543-1980***	513-271-3700
NASDAQ: VIVO ■ *Cust Svc					
Moss Inc PO Box 189	Pasadena	MD	21123	**800-932-6677**	410-768-3442
National Diagnostics Inc					
305 Patton Dr	Atlanta	GA	30336	**800-526-3867**	404-699-2121
Neci 334 Hecla St	Lake Linden	MI	49945	**888-648-7283**	906-296-1000
Neogen Corp 620 Lesher Pl	Lansing	MI	48912	**800-234-5333**	517-372-9200
NASDAQ: NEOG					
Odan Laboratories					
325 Stillview Ave	Pointe-Claire	QC	H9R2Y6	**888-252-6467**	514-428-1628
OraSure Technologies Inc					
220 E First St	Bethlehem	PA	18015	**800-869-3538**	610-882-1820
NASDAQ: OSUR					
Ortho-Clinical Diagnostics Inc					
1001 US Rt 202 N	Raritan	NJ	08869	**800-828-6316**	
Oxford Biomedical Research Inc					
2165 Avon Industrial Dr	Rochester Hills	MI	48309	**800-692-4633**	248-852-8815
Paramount Beauty Distributing Associates Inc					
41 Mercedes Way Unit 34	Edgewood	NY	11717	**800-755-7475**	631-242-3737
Parchem Trading Ltd					
415 Huguenot St	New Rochelle	NY	10801	**800-282-3982**	914-654-6800
PBA Health					
6300 Enterprise Rd	Kansas City	MO	64120	**800-333-8097**	816-245-5700
Peptides International Inc					
11621 Electron Dr	Louisville	KY	40299	**800-777-4779**	502-266-8787
PerkinElmer Inc					
940 Winter St	Waltham	MA	02451	**800-762-4000**	781-663-6050
NYSE: PKI					
Phadia US Inc					
4169 Commercial Ave	Portage	MI	49002	**800-346-4364**	269-492-1940
Pharmaceutical Assoc Inc					
1700 Perimeter Rd	Greenville	SC	29605	**888-233-2334**	864-277-7282
Pharmalucence Inc					
29 Dunham Rd	Billerica	MA	01821	**800-221-7554**	781-275-7120
Pharmasave Drugs (National) Ltd					
8411 - 200th St Ste 201	Langley	BC	V2Y0E7	**800-661-6106**	604-455-2400
Pharmascience Inc					
6111 Royalmount Ave Ste 100	Montreal	QC	H4P2T4	**866-853-1178**	514-340-9800
Pharmetics Inc					
3695 AutoRt Des Laurentides	Laval	QC	H7L3H7	**877-472-4433**	450-682-8580
Phoenix Pharmaceuticals Inc					
330 Beach Rd	Burlingame	CA	94010	**800-988-1205**	650-558-8898
Pointe Scientific Inc					
5449 Research Dr PO Box 87188	Canton	MI	48188	**800-445-9853**	734-487-8300
Polymedco Inc					
510 Furnace Dock Rd	Cortlandt Manor	NY	10567	**800-431-2123**	914-739-5400
PolyPeptide Laboratories Inc					
365 Maple Ave	Torrance	CA	90503	**800-338-4965**	310-782-3569
Polysciences Inc					
400 Valley Rd	Warrington	PA	18976	**800-523-2575***	215-343-6484
*Cust Svc					
Prasco LLC 6125 Commerce Ct	Mason	OH	45040	**866-525-0688**	513-618-3333
Promega Corp					
2800 Woods Hollow Rd	Madison	WI	53711	**800-356-9526**	608-274-4330
Prozyme Inc 3832 Bay Ctr Pl	Hayward	CA	94545	**800-457-9444**	510-638-6900
Purdue Pharma					
575 Granite Ct	Pickering	ON	L1W3W8	**800-387-5349**	905-420-6400
Qst Consultations Ltd					
11275 Edgewater Dr	Allendale	MI	49401	**866-757-4751**	
Quantimetrix Corp					
2005 Manhattan Beach Blvd	Redondo Beach	CA	90278	**800-624-8380**	310-536-0006
Quidel Corp					
10165 McKellar Ct	San Diego	CA	92121	**800-874-1517**	858-552-1100
NASDAQ: QDEL					
R & D Systems Inc					
614 McKinley Pl NE	Minneapolis	MN	55413	**800-343-7475**	612-379-2956
Research & Diagnostic Antibodies					
2645 W Cheyenne Ave	North Las Vegas	NV	89032	**800-858-7322**	702-638-7800
Roche Diagnostics Corp (RDC)					
9115 Hague Rd PO Box 50457	Indianapolis	IN	46250	**800-428-5076***	
*Cust Svc					
Rockland Immunochemicals Inc					
PO Box 326	Gilbertsville	PA	19525	**800-656-7625**	610-369-1008
SA Scientific Ltd					
4919 Golden Quail	San Antonio	TX	78240	**800-272-2710**	210-699-8800
Saskatchewan Health Research Foundation					
324-111 Research Dr	Saskatoon	SK	S7N3R2	**800-975-1699**	306-975-1680
Scantibodies Laboratory Inc					
9336 Abraham Way	Santee	CA	92071	**800-279-9181**	619-258-9300
SCIMEDX Corp 100 Ford Rd	Denville	NJ	07834	**800-221-5598**	973-625-8822

				Toll-Free	Phone

Sigma-Aldrich Corp
3050 Spruce St ....Saint Louis MO 63103 **800-325-3010** 314-771-5765
NASDAQ: SIAL
Southern Biotechnology Assoc Inc
160A Oxmoor Blvd ....Birmingham AL 35209 **800-722-2255** 205-945-1774
St Renatus LLC
1000 Centre Ave ....Fort Collins CO 80526 **888-686-2314** 970-282-0156
Streck Inc 7002 S 109th St ....Omaha NE 68128 **800-228-6090** 402-333-1982
Sunovion Pharmaceuticals Inc
84 Waterford Dr ....Marlborough MA 01752 **888-394-7377** 508-481-6700
Tec Laboratories Inc
7100 Tec Labs Way SW ....Albany OR 97321 **800-482-4464** 541-926-4577
Techne Corp
614 McKinley Pl NE ....Minneapolis MN 55413 **800-343-7475** 612-379-8854
NASDAQ: TECH
Teco Diagnostics
1268 N Lakeview Ave ....Anaheim CA 92807 **800-222-9880** 714-463-1111
Thermo Fisher Scientific
46360 Fremont Blvd ....Fremont CA 94538 **800-232-3342** 866-356-0354
Thermo Fisher Scientific
8365 Valley Pk ....Middletown VA 22645 **800-528-0494** 866-356-0354
Thermo Scientific
12076 Santa Fe Dr PO Box 14428 ....Lenexa KS 66215 **800-255-6730** 913-888-0939
Triad Isotopes Inc
4205 Vineland Rd Ste L1 ......Orlando FL 32811 **866-310-0086** 407-455-6700
Trinity Biotech PLC
5919 Farnsworth Ct ....Carlsbad CA 92008 **800-331-2291** 760-929-0500
NASDAQ: TRIB
Tyger Scientific Inc
324 Stokes Ave ....Ewing NJ 08638 **888-329-8990** 609-434-0143
Uman Pharma Inc
100 De L'Industrie Blvd ......Candiac QC J5R1J1 **877-444-9989** 450-444-9989
Utak Laboratories Inc
25020 Ave Tibbitts ....Valencia CA 91355 **800-235-3442** 661-294-3935
Valeo Pharma Inc
16667 Hymus Blvd Kirkland ....Kirkland QC H9H4R9 **888-694-0865** 514-694-0150
VistaPharm Inc
630 Central Ave ....New Providence NJ 07974 **877-437-8567**
Wako Chemicals USA Inc
1600 Bellwood Rd ....Richmond VA 23237 **800-992-9256** 804-271-7677
Worthington Biochemical Corp
730 Vassar Ave ....Lakewood NJ 08701 **800-445-9603** 732-942-1660
Xeris Pharmaceuticals Inc
180 N LaSalle St Ste 1810 ....Chicago IL 00601 **844-445-5704**
Zepto Metrix Corp
872 Main St ....Buffalo NY 14202 **800-274-5487*** 716-882-0920
*Cust Svc

---

232   DISPLAYS - EXHIBIT & TRADE SHOW

				Toll-Free	Phone

Downing Displays Inc
550 Techne Ctr Dr ....Milford OH 45150 **800-883-1800** 513-248-9800
Expon Exhibits
909 Fee Dr ....Sacramento CA 95815 **800-783-9766** 916-924-1600
Gilbert Displays Inc
110 Spagnoli Rd ....Melville NY 11747 **855-577-1100** 631-577-1100
Hadley Exhibits Inc
1700 Elmwood Ave ....Buffalo NY 14207 **800-962-8088** 716-874-3666
massAV 3 Radcliff Rd ....Tewksbury MA 01876 **800-423-7830**
Siegel Display Products
300 Sixth Ave N ....Minneapolis MN 55401 **800-626-0322** 612-340-1493
We Are Alexander
1227 Washington Ave ....Saint Louis MO 63103 **844-922-0002**

---

233   DISPLAYS - POINT-OF-PURCHASE

SEE ALSO Signs

				Toll-Free	Phone

Acrylic Design Assoc
6050 Nathan Ln N ....Plymouth MN 55442 **800-445-2167** 763-559-8395
AMD Industries Inc
4620 W 19th St ....Cicero IL 60804 **800-367-9999** 708-863-8900
Array Marketing
45 Progress Ave ....Toronto ON M1P2Y6 **800-295-4120** 416-299-4865
Art-Phyl Creations
16250 NW 48th Ave ....Hialeah FL 33014 **800-327-8318** 305-624-2333
Chicago Display Marketing Corp
2021 W St ....River Grove IL 60171 **800-681-4340** 708-842-0001
Colony Inc 2500 Galvin Dr ....Elgin IL 60123 **800-735-1300** 847-426-5300
Display Smart LLC
801 W 27th Terr ....Lawrence KS 66046 **888-843-1870** 785-843-1869
Display Technologies Inc
1111 Marcus Ave Ste M68 ....Lake Success NY 11042 **800-424-4220**
Frank Mayer & Assoc Inc
1975 Wisconsin Ave ....Grafton WI 53024 **855-294-2875**
Lingo Manufacturing Co
7400 Industrial Rd ....Florence KY 41042 **800-354-9771*** 859-371-2662
*Cust Svc
MDI Worldwide
38271 W 12-Mile Rd ....Farmington Hills MI 48331 **800-228-8925*** 248-553-1900
*Sales
Nashville Display
306 Hartmann Dr ....Lebanon TN 37087 **800-251-1150** 615-743-2900
New Dimensions Research Corp
260 Spagnoli Rd ....Melville NY 11747 **800-637-8870** 631-694-1356
Ovation Instore
57-13 49th Pl ....Maspeth NY 11378 **800-553-2202** 718-628-2600
Rapid Displays
4300 W 47th St ....Chicago IL 60632 **800-356-5775** 773-927-1091
United Displaycraft
333 E Touhy Ave ....Des Plaines IL 60018 **877-632-8767*** 847-375-3800
*General
Universal Display & Fixtures Co
726 E Hwy 121 ....Lewisville TX 75057 **800-235-0701** 972-221-5157

				Toll-Free	Phone

Visual Marketing Inc
154 W Erie St ....Chicago IL 60654 **800-662-8640** 312-664-9177
Vulcan Industries Inc
300 Display Dr ....Moody AL 35004 **888-444-4417** 205-640-2400

DOOR & WINDOW GLASS

SEE Glass - Flat, Plate, Tempered

---

234   DOORS & WINDOWS - METAL

SEE ALSO Shutters - Window (All Types)

				Toll-Free	Phone

AK Draft Seal Ltd
7470 Buller Ave ....Burnaby BC V5J4S5 **888-520-9009** 604-451-1080
Allmetal Inc
1 Pierce Pl Ste 295W ....Itasca IL 60143 **800-638-2599** 630-250-8090
Amsco Windows Inc
1880 S 1045 W ....Salt Lake City UT 84104 **800-748-4661** 801-972-6441
Anemostat
1220 Watsoncenter Rd PO Box 4938 ....Carson CA 90745 **877-423-7426** 310-835-7500
Asi Technologies Inc
5848 N 95th Ct ....Milwaukee WI 53225 **800-558-7068** 414-464-6200
ASSA ABLOY 110 Sargent Dr ....New Haven CT 06511 **800-377-3948**
Atrium Windows & Doors
3890 W NW Hwy Ste 500 ....Dallas TX 75220 **800-938-1000** 214-630-5757
Babcock-Davis
9300 73rd Ave N ....Brooklyn Park MN 55428 **888-412-3726**
Castle Impact Windows
7089 Hemstreet Pl ....West Palm Beach FL 33413 **800-643-6371** 561-683-4811
Clopay Bldg Products Inc
8585 Duke Blvd ....Mason OH 45040 **800-225-6729**
Columbia Mfg Corp
14400 S San Pedro St ....Gardena CA 90248 **800-729-3667** 310-327-9300
Cookson Co 2417 S 50th Ave ....Phoenix AZ 85043 **800-294-4358** 602-272-4244
Cornell Iron Works Inc
24 Elmwood Rd ....Mountain Top PA 18707 **800-233-8366**
Cornell Storefront Systems Inc
140 Maffet St ....Wilkes-Barre PA 18705 **800-882-6772** 570-706-2775
Deansteel Manufacturing Co
111 Merchant ....San Antonio TX 78204 **800-825-8271** 210-226-8271
Door Components Inc
7980 Redwood Ave ....Fontana CA 92336 **866-989-3667**
Dunbarton Corp PO Box 8577 ....Dothan AL 36304 **800-633-7553**
Dynaflair Corp
8147 Eagle Palm Dr ....Tampa FL 33605 **800-624-3667**
EFCO Corp 1000 County Rd ....Monett MO 65708 **800-221-4169** 417-235-3193
Electric Power Door
522 W 27th St ....Hibbing MN 55746 **800-346-5760** 218-263-8366
Elixir Industries Inc
24800 Chrisanta Dr Ste 210 ....Mission Viejo CA 92691 **800-421-1942** 949-860-5000
Fleming Door Products Ltd
101 Ashbridge Cir ....Woodbridge ON L4L3R5 **800-263-7515**
Futura Industries
11 Freeport Ctr Bldg H ......Clearfield UT 84016 **800-824-2049**
GlassCraft Door Co
2002 Brittmoore Rd ....Houston TX 77043 **800-766-2196** 713-690-8282
Graham Architectural Products Corp
1551 Mt Rose Ave ....York PA 17403 **800-755-6274** 717-849-8100
Hufcor Inc
2101 Kennedy Rd ....Janesville WI 53545 **800-356-6968** 608-756-1241
Hygrade Metal Moulding Manufacturing Corp
1990 Highland Ave ....Bethlehem PA 18020 **800-645-9475** 610-866-2441
International Revolving Door Co
2138 N Sixth Ave ....Evansville IN 47710 **800-745-4726** 812-425-3311
International Window Corp
5625 E Firestone Blvd ....South Gate CA 90280 **800-477-4032** 562-928-6411
Jamison Door Co
55 JV Jamison Dr ....Hagerstown MD 21740 **800-532-3667** 301-733-3100
Jantek Industries 230 Rt 70 ....Medford NJ 08055 **888-782-7937** 609-654-1030
Joyce Windows
1125 Berea Industrial Pkwy ....Berea OH 44017 **800-824-7988** 440-239-9100
Kane Manufacturing Corp
515 N Fraley St ....Kane PA 16735 **800-952-6399** 814-837-6464
Krieger Specialty Products Co
4880 Gregg Rd ....Pico Rivera CA 90660 **866-203-5060** 562-695-0645
LaForce Inc
1060 W Mason St ....Green Bay WI 54303 **800-236-8858**
Lapco Inc 12995 Rue Du Parc ....Mirabel QC J7J0W5 **800-433-1988** 450-971-0432
Lockheed Window Corp
925 S Main St PO Box 166 ....Pascoag RI 02859 **800-537-3061** 401-568-3061
Loxcreen Co Inc, The
1630 Old Dunbar Rd PO Box 4004 ....West Columbia SC 29172 **800-330-5699** 803-822-8200
M-D Bldg Products Inc
4041 N Santa Fe Ave ....Oklahoma City OK 73118 **800-654-8454***
*Cust Svc
McKeon Door Co
44 Sawgrass Dr ....Bellport NY 11713 **800-266-9392** 631-803-3000
MM Systems Corp
50 MM Way ....Pendergrass GA 30567 **800-241-3460** 706-824-7500
Moss Supply Company Inc
5001 N Graham St ....Charlotte NC 28269 **800-438-0770** 704-596-8717
Napoleon Spring Works
111 Weires Dr ....Archbold OH 43502 **800-338-5399** 419-445-1010
National Guard Products Inc
4985 E Raines Rd ....Memphis TN 38118 **800-647-7874**
Nystrom Inc
9300 73rd Ave N ....Minneapolis MN 55428 **800-547-2635** 763-488-9200
O'Keeffe's Inc
325 Newhall St ....San Francisco CA 94124 **888-653-3333** 415-822-4222
Overhead Door Corp
2501 S State Hwy 121 Bus Ste 200 ....Lewisville TX 75067 **800-275-3290** 469-549-7100
Overly Manufacturing Co
574 W Otterman St ....Greensburg PA 15601 **800-979-7300** 724-834-7300
Peelle Co
34 E Main St Ste 372 ....Smithtown NY 11787 **800-787-5020** 905-846-4545

Classified Section

				Toll-Free	Phone

Peerless Products Inc
2403 S Main St .... Fort Scott KS 66701 **866-420-4000** 620-223-4610
PGT 1070 Technology Dr .... Nokomis FL 34275 **800-282-6019** 941-480-1600
Phillips Manufacturing Co
4949 S 30th St .... Omaha NE 68107 **800-822-5055** 402-339-3800
Quaker Window Products Inc
504 S Hwy 63 S .... Freeburg MO 65035 **800-347-0438**
Raynor Garage Doors
1101 E River Rd .... Dixon IL 61021 **800-472-9667** 815-288-1431
Rebco Inc
1171-1225 Madison Ave .... Paterson NJ 07509 **800-777-0787** 973-684-0200
Reese Enterprises Inc
16350 Asher Ave .... Rosemount MN 55068 **800-328-0953** 651-423-1126
Richards-Wilcox Inc
600 S Lake St .... Aurora IL 60506 **800-253-5668**
Rytec Corp 1 Cedar Pkwy .... Jackson WI 53037 **800-628-1909** 262-677-9046
Seaway Manufacturing Corp
2250 E 33rd St .... Erie PA 16510 **800-458-2244** 814-898-2255
Southeastern Aluminum Products Inc
4925 Bulls Bay Hwy .... Jacksonville FL 32219 **800-243-8200***
*Sales
Southeastern Metals Mfg Company Inc
11801 Industry Dr .... Jacksonville FL 32218 **800-874-0335** 904-757-4200
Special-Lite Inc PO Box 6 .... Decatur MI 49045 **800-821-6531** 269-423-7068
Stanley Access Technologies
65 Scott Swamp Rd .... Farmington CT 06032 **800-722-2377** 860-677-2861
Structall Building Systems Inc
350 Burbank Rd .... Oldsmar FL 34677 **800-969-3706**
Super Sky Products Inc
10301 N Enterprise Dr .... Mequon WI 53092 **800-558-0467** 262-242-2000
Taylor Bldg Products
631 N First St .... West Branch MI 48661 **800-248-3600** 989-345-5110
Therma-Tru Corp
1750 Indian Wood Cir .... Maumee OH 43537 **800-537-8827** 419-891-7400
Thermo-Twin Industries Inc
1155 Allegheny Ave .... Oakmont PA 15139 **800-641-2211** 412-826-1000
TRACO
71 Progress Ave .... Cranberry Township PA 16066 **800-992-4444** 724-776-7000
Traditional Door Design & Millwork Ltd
261 Regina Rd .... Woodbridge ON L4L8M3 **877-226-9930** 416-747-1992
Tubelite Inc
4878 Mackinaw Trl .... Reed City MI 49677 **800-866-2227** 616-808-2505
United Steel Products Inc
33-40 127th Pl .... Flushing NY 11368 **888-683-2516**
Wayne-Dalton Corp
1 Door Dr PO Box 67 .... Mount Hope OH 44660 **800-827-3667** 330-674-7015
West Window Corp
226 Industrial Pk Dr .... Martinsville VA 24112 **800-446-4167** 276-638-2394
Western Window Systems
2200 E Riverview Dr .... Phoenix AZ 85034 **877-268-1300**
Willo Products Company Inc
714 Willo Industrial Dr SE .... Decatur AL 35601 **800-633-3276** 256-353-7161
Won-Door Corp
1865 South 3480 West .... Salt Lake City UT 84104 **800-453-8494** 801-973-7500

235 DOORS & WINDOWS - VINYL

				Toll-Free	Phone

American Exteriors LLC
7100 E Belleview Ave Ste 210 .... Littleton CO 80111 **800-794-6369** 208-424-7757
Associated Materials Inc Alside Div
PO Box 2010 .... Akron OH 44309 **800-922-6009***
*Cust Svc
CertainTeed Corp
750 E Swedesford Rd .... Valley Forge PA 19482 **800-782-8777*** 610-341-7000
*Prod Info
Champion Window Mfg Inc
12121 Champion Way .... Cincinnati OH 45241 **877-424-2674** 513-346-4600
Chelsea Bldg Products
565 Cedar Way .... Oakmont PA 15139 **800-424-3573**
Harry G Barr Co
6500 S Zero St .... Fort Smith AR 72903 **800-829-2277** 479-646-7891
Larson Manufacturing Co
2333 Eastbrook Dr .... Brookings SD 57006 **888-483-3768*** 605-692-6115
*Cust Svc
Moss Supply Company Inc
5001 N Graham St .... Charlotte NC 28269 **800-438-0770** 704-596-8717
Newmar Window Manufacturing Inc
7630 Airport Rd .... Mississauga ON L4T4G6 **800-263-5634** 905-672-1233
PGT 1070 Technology Dr .... Nokomis FL 34275 **800-282-6019** 941-480-1600
Provia Door Inc
2150 SR- 39 .... Sugarcreek OH 44681 **800-669-4711*** 403-555-5555
*General
Quanex Building Products Corp
1900 W Loop S Ste 1500 .... Houston TX 77027 **888-475-0633*** 713-961-4600
*Cust Svc
Rehau Inc
1501 EdwaRds Ferry Rd NE .... Leesburg VA 20176 **800-247-9445** 703-777-5255
Royal Group, The
71 Royal Group Crescent .... Woodbridge ON L4H1X9 **800-263-2353** 905-264-0701
RubbAir Door Div Eckel Industries Inc
100 Groton Shirley Rd .... Ayer MA 01432 **800-966-7822** 978-772-0480
Soft-Lite LLC
10250 Philipp Pkwy .... Streetsboro OH 44241 **800-551-1953** 330-528-3400
Thermal Windows & Doors
3700 Haney C .... Murrysville PA 15668 **800-245-1540** 724-325-6100
Veka Inc 100 Veka Dr .... Fombell PA 16123 **800-654-5589** 724-452-1000
Weather Shield Manufacturing Inc
1 Weather Shield Plz PO Box 309 .... Medford WI 54451 **800-222-2995** 715-748-2100
West Window Corp
226 Industrial Pk Dr .... Martinsville VA 24112 **800-446-4167** 276-638-2394
Windsor Windows & Doors
900 S 19th St .... West Des Moines IA 50265 **800-218-6186** 515-223-6660

236 DOORS & WINDOWS - WOOD

SEE ALSO Millwork ; Shutters - Window (All Types)

				Toll-Free	Phone

Allmar Inc
287 Riverton Ave .... Winnipeg MB R2L0N2 **800-230-5516** 204-668-1000
Andersen Corp
100 Fourth Ave N .... Bayport MN 55003 **888-888-7020** 651-264-5150
Construction Metals LLC
13169 B Slover Ave .... Fontana CA 92337 **800-576-9810** 909-390-9880
Endura Products Inc
8817 W Market St .... Colfax NC 27235 **800-334-2006**
Great Day Improvements LLC
700 E Highland Rd .... Macedonia OH 44056 **800-230-8301** 330-468-0700
Haley Bros Inc
6291 Orangethorpe Ave .... Buena Park CA 90620 **800-854-5951** 714-670-2112
Industrial Door Company Inc
360 Coon Rapids Blvd .... Minneapolis MN 55433 **888-798-0199** 763-786-4730
Jenkins Mfg Company Inc
1608 Frank Akers Rd .... Anniston AL 36207 **800-633-2323** 256-831-7000
Larson Manufacturing Co
2333 Eastbrook Dr .... Brookings SD 57006 **888-483-3768*** 605-692-6115
*Cust Svc
Lincoln Wood Products Inc
1400 W Taylor St PO Box 375 .... Merrill WI 54452 **800-967-2461** 715-536-2461
Marvin Windows & Doors
PO Box 100 .... Warroad MN 56763 **888-537-7828** 218-386-1430
Masonite International Corp
201 N Franklin St Ste 300 .... Tampa FL 33602 **800-895-2723** 813-877-2726
Mathews Bros Co
22 Perkins Rd .... Belfast ME 04915 **800-615-2004** 207-338-6490
Pella Corp 102 Main St .... Pella IA 50219 **877-473-5527*** 641-621-1000
*Cust Svc
Quaker Window Products Inc
504 S Hwy 63 S .... Freeburg MO 65035 **800-347-0438**
Semling-Menke Company Inc
PO Box 378 .... Merrill WI 54452 **800-333-2206** 715-536-9411
Trustile 1780 E 66th Ave .... Denver CO 80229 **888-286-3931**
Vancouver Door Company Inc
203 Fifth St NW .... Puyallup WA 98371 **800-999-3667** 253-845-9581
ViWinTech Windows & Door
2400 Irvin Cobb Dr .... Paducah KY 42003 **800-788-1050**
Weather Shield Manufacturing Inc
1 Weather Shield Plz PO Box 309 .... Medford WI 54451 **800-222-2995** 715-748-2100
Windsor Windows & Doors
900 S 19th St .... West Des Moines IA 50265 **800-218-6186** 515-223-6660

237 DRUG STORES

SEE ALSO Health Food Stores

				Toll-Free	Phone

Allergychoices Inc
2800 National Dr Ste 100 .... Onalaska WI 54650 **866-793-1680** 608-793-1580
Apple Valley Medical Clinic Ltd
14655 Galaxie Ave .... Apple Valley MN 55124 **800-233-8504** 952-432-6161
Aquatrol Inc
600 E North St PO Box 8012 .... Elburn IL 60119 **800-323-0688** 630-365-5400
Arbor Centers for Eyecare
2640 W 183rd St .... Homewood IL 60430 **866-798-6633** 708-798-6633
ARJ Infusion Services Inc
10049 Lakeview Ave .... Lenexa KS 66219 **866-451-8804**
Berr Pet Supply Inc
929 N Market Blvd .... Sacramento CA 95834 **888-237-7738** 916-921-0145
Carepoint Inc
215 E Bay St Ste 304 .... Charleston SC 29401 **800-296-1825** 843-853-6999
Community Pharmacies
16 Commerce Dr Ste 1 PO Box 528 .... Augusta ME 04332 **800-730-4840**
CVS Corp 1 CVS Dr .... Woonsocket RI 02895 **888-607-4287*** 401-765-1500
*Cust Svc
Discount Drug Mart Inc
211 Commerce Dr .... Medina OH 44256 **800-833-6278** 330-725-2340
Eye Center Surgeons & Associates Ll
401 Meridian St N Ste 200 .... Huntsville AL 35801 **800-233-9083** 256-705-3937
Fruth Pharmacy Inc
4016 Ohio River Rd .... Point Pleasant WV 25550 **800-438-5390** 304-675-1612
Gemmel Pharmacy Group Inc
143 N Euclid Ave .... Ontario CA 91762 **888-302-0229** 909-988-0591
General Hearing Corp
175 Brookhollow Esplanade .... Harahan LA 70123 **800-824-3021** 504-733-3767
Geneva Woods Pharmacy Inc
501 W International Airport Rd
Ste 1A .... Anchorage AK 99518 **800-478-0005** 907-565-6100
Grandview Pharmacy
474 Southpoint Cir .... Brownsburg IN 46112 **866-827-7575**
Harmon Stores Inc
650 Liberty Ave .... Union NJ 07083 **866-427-6661** 908-688-7023
Interstate Optical Co
680 Lindaire Ln .... Mansfield OH 44901 **800-472-5790**
Liberty Drug & Surgical Inc
195 Main St .... Chatham NJ 07928 **877-816-0111** 973-635-6200
Majestic Drug Company Inc
4996 Main St Rt 42 .... South Fallsburg NY 12779 **800-238-0220** 845-436-0011
Medical Center Pharmacy
2401 N Ocoee St .... Cleveland TN 37311 **877-753-9555** 423-476-5548
Mehron Inc
100 Red Schoolhouse Rd Ste C2 .... Chestnut Ridge NY 10977 **800-332-9955** 845-426-1700
Navarro Discount Pharmacy
9400 NW 104 St .... Medley FL 33178 **866-628-2776** 786-245-8524
Nucara Pharmacy Inc
209 E San Marnan Dr .... Waterloo IA 50702 **800-359-2357** 319-236-8891
Oncology Plus Inc
1070 E Brandon Blvd .... Brandon FL 33511 **877-410-0779**
Pet Health Pharmacy
12012 N 111th Ave .... Youngtown AZ 85363 **800-742-0516**

				Toll-Free	Phone

Pharmacy Providers of OK (PPOK)
3000 E Memorial Rd .... Edmond OK 73013 **877-557-5707**
Premium Rx National LLC
15809 Crabbs Branch Way .... Rockville MD 20855 **877-862-7796** 301-230-0908
Pro-tech Security Sales
1313 W Bagley Rd .... Berea OH 44017 **800-888-4002** 440-239-0100
Revolution Eyewear Inc
2853 Eisenhower St Ste 100............ Carrollton TX 75007 **800-986-0010**
Rite Aid Corp
30 Hunter Ln .... Camp Hill PA 17011 **800-748-3243** 717-761-2633
NYSE: RAD
Rxcom
101 Jim Wright Fwy S Ste 200 .... Fort Worth TX 76108 **800-433-5719** 817-246-6760
Rxusa Inc
81 Seaview Blvd .... Port Washington NY 11050 **800-764-3648** 516-467-2500
Safeguard Products Inc
2710 Division Hwy .... New Holland PA 17557 **800-433-1819** 717-354-4586
Smart Eye Care Ctr
255 Western Ave .... Augusta ME 04330 **800-459-5800** 207-622-5800
Symons Capital Management Inc
650 Washington Rd Ste 800.............. Pittsburgh PA 15228 **888-344-7740** 412-344-7690
Thrifty White Stores
6055 Nathan Lane N Ste 200 .... Plymouth MN 55442 **800-642-3275** 763-513-4300
Transcript Pharmacy Inc
2506 Lakeland Dr Ste 201 .... Jackson MS 39232 **866-420-4041**
Upstate Pharmacy Ltd
1900 N America Dr .... West Seneca NY 14224 **800-314-4655** 716-675-3784
Vision Source LP
23824 Hwy 59 N Ste 101 .... Kingwood TX 77339 **888-558-2020** 281-312-1111
Vitacostcom Inc
5400 Broken Sound Blvd NW Ste 500 ..... Boca Raton FL 33487 **800-381-0759**
Vitamin Shoppe Inc
2101 91st St .... North Bergen NJ 07047 **800-223-1216** 201-868-5959
NYSE: VSI
Walgreen Co 200 Wilmot Rd .... Deerfield IL 60015 **800-925-4733*** 847-940-2500
*Cust Svc

DRUGS - MFR

SEE Medicinal Chemicals & Botanical Products ; Pharmaceutical Companies ; Pharmaceutical Companies - Generic Drugs ; Vitamins & Nutritional Supplements ; Diagnostic Products ; Biotechnology Companies

238   DRUGS & PERSONAL CARE PRODUCTS - WHOL

Companies listed here distribute pharmaceuticals, over-the-counter (OTC) drugs, and/or personal care products typically found in drug stores.

				Toll-Free	Phone

Amerisource Bergen
1300 Morris Dr Ste 100 .... Chesterbrook PA 19087 **800-829-3132** 610-727-7000
NYSE: ABC
Bedford Road Pharmacy Inc
11306 Bedford Rd NE .... Cumberland MD 21502 **800-788-6693** 301-777-1771
Buffalo Supply Inc
1650A Coal Creek Dr .... Lafayette CO 80026 **800-366-1812** 303-666-6333
Cardinal Health Distribution
7000 Cardinal Pl .... Dublin OH 43017 **800-926-0834** 614-757-5000
Cardinal Health Nuclear Pharmacy Services
7000 Cardinal Pl .... Dublin OH 43017 **800-326-6457** 614-757-5000
Correct Rx Pharmacy Services Inc
1352-C Charwood Rd .... Hanover MD 21076 **800-636-0501**
Dakota Drug Inc 28 Main St N .... Minot ND 58703 **800-437-2018** 701-852-2141
DRAXIMAGE Inc
16751 Transcanada Hwy .... Kirkland QC H9H4J4 **888-633-5343** 514-630-7080
Familiprix Inc
6000 Rue Armand-Viau .... Quebec QC G2C2C5 **800-463-5160** 418-847-3311
Familymeds Inc
312 Farmington Ave .... Farmington CT 06032 **888-787-2800**
Ferring Pharmaceuticals Inc
100 Interpace Pkwy .... Parsippany NJ 07054 **888-337-7464** 973-796-1600
Forever Spring
2629 E Craig Rd Ste E .... Las Vegas NV 89030 **800-523-4334** 702-633-4283
Health Coalition Inc
8320 NW 30th Terr .... Doral FL 33122 **800-456-7283** 305-662-2988
Iredale Mineral Cosmetics Ltd
50 Church St .... Great Barrington MA 01230 **877-869-9420**
J&B Medical Supply Co Inc
50496 W Pontiac Trl .... Wixom MI 48393 **800-980-0047** 800-737-0045
Kinray Inc
152-35 Tenth Ave .... Whitestone NY 11357 **800-854-6729** 718-767-1234
Lil' Drug Store Products Inc
1201 Continental Pl NE .... Cedar Rapids IA 52402 **800-553-5022**
London Drugs Ltd
12251 Horseshoe Way .... Richmond BC V7A4X5 **888-991-2299**
Mechanical Servants Inc
2755 Thomas St .... Melrose Park IL 60160 **800-351-2000**
Methapharm Inc
11772 W Sample Rd .... Coral Springs FL 33065 **800-287-7686** 954-341-0795
Miami-Luken Inc
265 S Pioneer Blvd .... Springboro OH 45066 **800-856-0217**
Morris & Dickson Co Ltd
410 Kay Ln .... Shreveport LA 71115 **800-388-3833** 318-797-7900
Neil Medical Group Inc
2545 Jetport Rd .... Kinston NC 28504 **800-735-9111**
North Carolina Mutual Wholesale Drug Co
816 Ellis Rd .... Durham NC 27703 **800-800-8551** 919-596-2151
Omegachem
480 rue Perreault .... St-romuald QC G6W7V6 **800-661-6342** 418-837-4444
Parmed Pharmaceuticals Inc
4220 Hyde Pk Blvd .... Niagara Falls NY 14305 **800-727-6331**
Pharmacommunications Group Inc
100 Renfrew Dr .... Markham ON L3R9R6 **800-267-5409** 905-477-3100
Reese Pharmaceutical Co
10617 Frank Ave .... Cleveland OH 44106 **800-321-7178**
RG Shakour Inc
254 Tpke Rd .... Westborough MA 01581 **800-661-2030**

				Toll-Free	Phone

Sothys USA Inc
1500 NW 94th Ave .... Miami FL 33172 **800-325-0503** 305-594-4222
Sprout Pharmaceuticals Inc
4208 Six Forks Rd .... Raleigh NC 27609 **844-746-5745** 919-882-0850
Sterling Stores
1305 First Ave SW .... Austin MN 55912 **800-803-1503** 507-433-4586
US WorldMeds LLC
4010 Dupont Cir Ste L-07 .... Louisville KY 40207 **888-900-8796** 502-815-8000
Value Drug Co
195 Theater Dr .... Duncansville PA 16635 **800-252-3786**
Value Drug Mart Assoc Ltd
16504 - 121A Ave .... Edmonton AB T5V1J9 **888-554-8258** 780-453-1701

239   DUDE RANCHES

SEE ALSO Resorts & Resort Companies

				Toll-Free	Phone

320 Guest Ranch Inc
205 Buffalo Horn Creek Rd .... Gallatin Gateway MT 59730 **800-243-0320** 406-995-4283
63 Ranch PO Box 979 .... Livingston MT 59047 **888-395-5151**
7 D Ranch 7D Ranch PO Box 100........... Cody WY 82414 **888-587-9885** 307-587-9885
Air Ivanhoe Ltd
George and Jeanne Theriault PO Box 99. ... Foleyet ON P0M1T0 **800-955-2951** 705-899-2155
Bar Lazy J Guest Ranch
447 County Rd 3 PO Box N .... Parshall CO 80468 **800-396-6279** 970-725-3437
Black Mountain Ranch
4000 Conger Mesa Rd .... McCoy CO 80463 **800-967-2401** 970-653-4226
Bonanza Creek Country Guest Ranch
523 Bonanza Creek Rd .... Martinsdale MT 59053 **800-476-6045** 406-572-3366
Brooks Lake Lodge & Guest Ranch
458 Brooks Lake Rd .... Dubois WY 82513 **866-213-4022**
C Lazy U Ranch
3640 Colorado Hwy 125 PO Box 379 ...... Granby CO 80446 **800-228-9792** 970-887-3344
Camp Lebanon 1205 Acorn Rd .... Burtrum MN 56318 **800-816-1502** 320-573-2125
Camp Simcha 430 White Rd .... Glen Spey NY 12737 **888-756-1432** 845-856-1432
Cheley Colorado Camps Inc
601 Steele St .... Denver CO 80206 **800-359-7200** 303-377-3616
Circle Z Ranch PO Box 194 .... Patagonia AZ 85624 **888-854-2525** 520-394-2525
CM Ranch
167 Fish Hatchery Rd PO Box 217 .... Dubois WY 82513 **800 455 0721** 307 455 2331
Colorado Trails Ranch
12161 County Rd 240 .... Durango CO 81301 **800-323-3833** 866-942-3472
Concordia Language Villages
8659 Thorsonveien Rd .... Bemidji MN 56601 **800-450-2214** 800-222-4750
Coulter Lake Guest Ranch
80 County Rd 273 .... Rifle CO 81650 **800-858-3046** 970-625-1473
Drowsy Water Ranch
PO Box 147 .... Granby CO 80446 **800-845-2292** 970-725-3456
Eagle's Nest Foundation
43 Hart Rd .... Pisgah Forest NC 28768 **800-951-7442** 828-877-4349
Eatons' Ranch
270 Eatons' Ranch Rd .... Wolf WY 82844 **800-210-1049** 307-655-9285
Elk Mountain Ranch
PO Box 910 .... Buena Vista CO 81211 **800-432-8812**
Flying E Ranch
2801 W Wickenburg Way .... Wickenburg AZ 85390 **888-684-2650** 928-684-2690
Fresh Air Fund
633 Third Ave 14th Fl .... New York NY 10017 **800-367-0003**
Greenhorn Creek Guest Ranch
2116 Greenhorn Ranch Rd .... Quincy CA 95971 **800-334-6939** 530-283-0930
Guided Discoveries
27282 Calle Arroyo .... San Juan Capistrano CA 92675 **800-645-1423**
Harbor Health Systems LLC
PO Box 11779 .... Newport Beach CA 92658 **888-626-1737** 949-273-7020
Hawley Mountain Guest Ranch
4188 Main Boulder Rd .... McLeod MT 59052 **877-496-7848** 406-932-5791
Hideout Lodge & Guest Ranch, The
PO Box 206 .... Shell WY 82441 **800-354-8637** 307-765-2080
Kay El Bar Guest Ranch
PO Box 2480 .... Wickenburg AZ 85358 **800-684-7583** 928-684-7593
Laramie River Dude Ranch
25777 County Rd 103 .... Jelm WY 82063 **800-551-5731** 970-435-5716
Lazy L & B Ranch
1072 E Fork Rd .... Dubois WY 82513 **800-453-9488*** 307-455-2839
*Cust Svc
Long Hollow Ranch
17105 Holmes Rd .... Sisters OR 97759 **877-923-1901** 541-923-1901
Lozier's Box R Ranch
552 Willow Creek Rd PO Box 100 .... Cora WY 82925 **800-822-8466** 307-367-4868
Mountain Sky Guest Ranch
PO Box 1219 .... Emigrant MT 59027 **800-548-3392** 406-333-4911
North Fork Ranch (NFR)
55395 Hwy 285 PO Box B .... Shawnee CO 80475 **800-843-7895** 303-838-9873
Pine Butte Guest Ranch
351 S Fork Rd .... Choteau MT 59422 **877-812-3698** 800-628-6860
Rainbow Trout Ranch (RTR)
1484 FDR 250 PO Box 458. .... Antonito CO 81120 **800-633-3397** 719-376-2440
Rawah Ranch
11447 N County Rd 103 .... Glendevey CO 82063 **800-510-7071**
Rich Ranch
939 Cottonwood Lakes Rd .... Seeley Lake MT 59868 **800-532-4350** 406-677-2317
Skyhawks Sports Academy Inc
9425 N Nevada Ste 210 .... Spokane WA 99218 **800-804-3509** 509-466-6590
Smith Fork Ranch
45362 Needle Rock Rd .... Crawford CO 81415 **855-539-1492** 970-921-3454
Star Island Corp, The
30 Middle St .... Portsmouth NH 03801 **800-441-4620** 603-430-6272
Sundance Trail Guest Ranch
17931 Red Feather Lakes Rd ..... Red Feather Lakes CO 80545 **800-357-4930** 970-224-1222
Tanque Verde Ranch
14301 E Speedway .... Tucson AZ 85748 **800-234-3833** 520-296-6275
Tarryall River Ranch
27035 County Rd 77 .... Lake George CO 80827 **800-408-8407**
Thousand Pines Christian Camp & Conference Center
359 Thousnd Pines Rd .... Crestline CA 92325 **888-423-2267** 909-338-2705

				Toll-Free	Phone
Three Bars Cattle & Guest Ranch					
9500 Wycliffe Perry Creek Rd	Cranbrook	BC	V1C7C7	877-426-5230	250-426-5230
Triangle C Dude Ranch					
3737 Hwy 26	Dubois	WY	82513	800-661-4928	307-455-2225
Triple J Wilderness Ranch					
91 Mortimer Rd PO Box 310	Augusta	MT	59410	800-826-1300	406-562-3653
Tumbling River Ranch					
3715 Pk County Rd 62 PO Box 30	Grant	CO	80448	800-654-8770	303-838-5981
Vee Bar Guest Ranch					
38 Vee Bar Ranch Rd	Laramie	WY	82070	800-483-3227	307-745-7036
Vista Verde Guest & Ski Ranch					
PO Box 770465	Steamboat Springs	CO	80477	800-526-7433	970-879-3858
White Stallion Ranch					
9251 W Twin Peaks Rd	Tucson	AZ	85743	888-977-2624	520-297-0252
Wind River Ranch					
PO Box 3410	Estes Park	CO	80517	800-523-4212	970-586-4212

240 DUPLICATION & REPLICATION SERVICES

				Toll-Free	Phone
Corporate Disk Co					
4610 Crime Pkwy	McHenry	IL	60050	800-634-3475	
Digital Video Services					
401 Hall ST SW Ste 489	Grand Rapids	MI	49503	800-747-8273	616-975-9911
Illinois Blueprint Corp					
800 SW Jefferson Ave	Peoria	IL	61605	800-747-7070	309-676-1300
Online Copy Corp					
48815 Kato Rd	Fremont	CA	94539	800-833-4460	
Standard Digital Imaging					
4426 S 108th St	Omaha	NE	68137	800-642-8062	402-592-1292
Thomas Reprographics					
600 N Central Expy	Richardson	TX	75080	800-877-3776	972-231-7227

241 DUTY-FREE SHOPS

SEE ALSO Gift Shops

				Toll-Free	Phone
Niagara Duty Free Shop					
5726 Falls Ave	Niagara Falls	ON	L2G7T5	877-642-4337	905-374-3700
Peace Bridge Duty Free Inc					
1 Peace Bridge Plz	Fort Erie	ON	L2A5N1	800-361-1302	
Starboard Cruise Services Inc					
8400 NW 36th St	Miami	FL	33166	800-540-4785	786-845-7300
Tunnel Duty Free Shop Inc					
465 Goyeau St	Windsor	ON	N9A1H1	800-669-2105	519-252-2713

EDUCATIONAL INSTITUTIONS

SEE Preparatory Schools - Boarding ; Preparatory Schools - Non-boarding ; Colleges - Tribal ; Colleges & Universities - Historically Black ; Children's Learning Centers

242 EDUCATIONAL INSTITUTION OPERATORS & MANAGERS

				Toll-Free	Phone
Apollo Education Group Inc					
4025 S Riverpoint Pkwy	Phoenix	AZ	85040	800-990-2765	
Aqua Data Inc 95 Fifth Ave	Pincourt	QC	J7W5K8	800-567-9003	514-425-1010
Aqua Rehab Inc					
2145 rue Michelin	Laval	QC	H7L5B8	800-661-3472	450-687-3472
Axonify Inc					
450 Phillip St Ste 300	Waterloo	ON	N2L5J2	855-296-6439	519-585-1200
Bridgepoint Education					
13500 Evening Creek Dr N Ste 600	San Diego	CA	92123	866-475-0317	858-668-2586
NYSE: BPI					
Capella Education Co					
225 S Sixth St 9th Fl	Minneapolis	MN	55402	888-227-3552*	612-339-8650
NASDAQ: CPLA ■ *Cust Svc*					
Carney, Sandoe & Associates, LP					
44 Bromfield St	Boston	MA	02108	800-225-7986	617-542-0260
Center of Vocational Alternative For Men					
3770 N High St	Columbus	OH	43214	877-521-2682	614-294-7117
Early Learning Coalition of Miami Dade & Monroe					
2555 Ponce De Leon Blvd Ste 500	Coral Gables	FL	33134	800-962-2873	305-646-7220
eCornell 950 Danby Rd Ste 150	Ithaca	NY	14850	866-326-7635	607-330-3200
Education Management Corp (EDMC)					
210 Sixth Ave 33rd Fl	Pittsburgh	PA	15222	800-275-2440	412-562-0900
NASDAQ: EDMC					
Elenco Electronics Inc					
150 Carpenter Ave	Wheeling	IL	60090	800-533-2441	847-541-3800
Krm Information Services Inc					
200 Spring St	Eau Claire	WI	54703	800-775-7654	
Laureate Education Inc					
650 S Exeter St	Baltimore	MD	21202	866-452-8732	410-843-6100
LifeLearn Inc					
367 Woodlawn Rd W Unit 9	Guelph	ON	N1H7K9	888-770-2218	519-767-5043
Lincoln Educational Services					
200 Executive Dr	West Orange	NJ	07052	800-254-0547	973-736-9340
NASDAQ: LINC					
N R S I 179 Lafayette Dr	Syosset	NY	11791	800-331-3117	516-921-5500
National Heritage Academies					
3850 Broadmoor Ave SE Ste 201	Grand Rapids	MI	49512	877-223-6402*	
General					
Ohio Restaurant Assn					
1525 Bethel Rd Ste 201	Columbus	OH	43220	800-282-9049	614-442-3535
Pacific Resources for Education & Learning					
1136 Union Mall 9th Fl	Honolulu	HI	96813	800-377-4773	808-441-1300
Princeton Review Inc, The					
Cochituate Pl 24 Prime Pkwy Ste 201	Natick	MA	01760	800-273-8439	508-663-5050
Safe & Civil Schools					
2451 Willamette St	Eugene	OR	97405	800-323-8819	541-345-1442
Sylvan Learning Centers					
4 N Park Dr Ste 500	Hunt Valley	MD	21030	888-338-2283	800-627-4276

				Toll-Free	Phone
Symposia Medicus					
399 Taylor Blvd Ste 201	Pleasant Hill	CA	94523	800-327-3161	925-969-1789
Vertical Alliance Group Inc					
1730 Galleria Oaks	Texarkana	TX	75503	877-792-3866	903-792-3866

243 EDUCATIONAL MATERIALS & SUPPLIES

SEE ALSO Office & School Supplies ; Educational & Reference Software

				Toll-Free	Phone
3D Internet					
633 W Fifth St US Bank Twr					
28th Fl	Los Angeles	CA	90071	800-442-5299	
American Educational Products Inc					
401 Hickory St PO Box 2121	Fort Collins	CO	80522	800-289-9299	970-484-7445
Carolina Biological Supply Co					
2700 York Rd	Burlington	NC	27215	800-334-5551	336-584-0381
Carson-Dellosa Publishing Company Inc					
7027 Albert Pick Rd	Greensboro	NC	27409	800-321-0943	336-632-0084
Center Enterprises Inc					
30 Shield St	West Hartford	CT	06110	800-542-2214*	860-953-4423
*Orders					
Claridge Products & Equipment Inc					
601 Hwy 62 65 PO Box 910	Harrison	AR	72602	800-434-4610	870-743-2200
Creative Teaching Press Inc					
6262 Katella Ave	Cypress	CA	90630	800-444-4287	714-895-5047
Delta Education LLC					
80 NW Blvd	Nashua	NH	03063	800-258-1302	603-889-8899
Didax Inc 395 Main St	Rowley	MA	01969	800-458-0024	
Education Ctr Inc					
3515 W Market St Ste 200	Greensboro	NC	27403	800-714-7991	336-854-0309
Educational Insights Inc					
380 N Fairway Dr	Vernon Hills	IL	60061	800-995-4436	847-968-3722
Educators Resource Inc					
2575 Schillingers Rd	Semmes	AL	36575	800-868-2368*	
*Cust Svc					
Evan-Moor Educational Publishers Inc					
18 Lower Ragsdale Dr	Monterey	CA	93940	800-777-4362	831-649-5901
Fisher Science Education					
4500 Turnberry Dr	Hanover Park	IL	60133	800-955-1177	800-766-7000
Frog Street Press Inc					
800 Industrial Blvd Ste 100	Grapevine	TX	76051	800-884-3764	
Ghent Manufacturing Inc					
2999 Henkle Dr	Lebanon	OH	45036	800-543-0550	513-932-3445
Great Source Education Group					
181 Ballardvale St	Wilmington	MA	01887	800-289-4490	
Guidecraft USA					
55508 Hwy 19 W	Winthrop	MN	55396	800-524-3555	507-647-5030
Hayes School Publishing Co Inc					
321 Pennwood Ave	Pittsburgh	PA	15221	800-926-0704	412-371-2373
Incentive Publications Inc					
2400 Crestmoor Dr	Nashville	TN	37215	800-967-5325*	615-385-2934
*Mktg					
Kaplan Early Learning Co					
1310 Lewisville-Clemmons Rd	Lewisville	NC	27023	800-334-2014	336-766-7374
Learning Resources					
380 N Fairway Dr	Vernon Hills	IL	60061	800-222-3909	847-573-8400
Learning Wrap-Ups Inc					
1660 W Gordon Ave Ste 4	Layton	UT	84041	800-992-4966	801-497-0050
McDonald Publishing					
567 Hanley Industrial Ct	Saint Louis	MO	63144	800-722-8080	
McGraw-Hill Education					
8787 Orion Pl	Columbus	OH	43240	800-334-7344	
National School Products					
1523 Old Niles Ferry Rd	Maryville	TN	37803	800-627-9393	865-984-3960
Questar Assessment Inc					
5550 Upper 147th St W	Apple Valley	MN	55124	800-800-2598*	952-997-2700
OTC: QUSA ■ *Cust Svc*					
Rock 'N Learn Inc					
105 Commercial Cir	Conroe	TX	77304	800-348-8445	936-539-2731
Roylco Inc					
3251 Abbeville Hwy PO Box 13409	Anderson	SC	29624	800-362-8656	864-296-0043
School Specialty Inc					
PO Box 1579	Appleton	WI	54912	888-388-3224	419-589-1600
OTC: SCOO					
Teacher Created Resources					
6421 Industry Way	Westminster	CA	92683	888-343-4335	
TREND Enterprises Inc					
300 Ninth Ave SW	New Brighton	MN	55112	800-860-6762*	651-631-2850
*Cust Svc					
World*Class Learning Materials					
PO Box 639	Candler	NC	28715	800-638-6470	

244 EDUCATIONAL TESTING SERVICES - ASSESSMENT & PREPARATION

				Toll-Free	Phone
Alpine Testing Inc					
51 W Ctr St Ste 514	Orem	UT	84057	844-625-7463	
Applied Measurement Professionals Inc (AMP)					
18000 W 105th St	Olathe	KS	66061	800-345-6559	913-895-4600
Barron's Educational Series Inc					
250 Wireless Blvd	Hauppauge	NY	11788	800-645-3476	631-434-3311
Castle Worldwide Inc					
6001 Hospitality Ct Ste 100	Morrisville	NC	27560	800-655-4845	919-572-6880
College Board					
45 Columbus Ave	New York	NY	10023	800-927-4302	212-713-8000
Edcomm Inc					
1300 Virginia Dr Ste 220	Fort Washington	PA	19034	888-433-2666	215-542-6900
Fresh Air Educators Inc					
203-1568 Carling Ave	Ottawa	ON	K1Z7M4	866-495-4868	
General Educational Development Testing Service					
American Council on Education					
1 Dupont Cir NW	Washington	DC	20036	866-205-6267	202-939-9300
H & H Publishing Company Inc					
1231 Kapp Dr	Clearwater	FL	33765	800-366-4079	727-442-7760

		Toll-Free	Phone

Prometric
1501 S Clinton St . . . . Baltimore MD 21224 **866-776-6387** 443-455-8000
Silver Strong & Associates
3 Tice Rd . . . . Franklin Lakes NJ 07417 **800-962-4432**

245   ELECTRIC COMPANIES - COOPERATIVES (RURAL)

SEE ALSO Utility Companies

Companies listed here are members of the National Rural Electric Cooperative Association; most are consumer-owned, but some are public power districts. In addition, the companies listed are electricity distribution cooperatives. Companies that generate and/or transmit electricity, but do not distribute it, are not included.

Alabama

			Toll-Free	Phone

Baldwin EMC
19600 State Hwy 59 PO Box 220 . . . . Summerdale AL 36580 **800-837-3374** 251-989-6247
Central Alabama Electric Co-op
1802 Hwy 31 N . . . . Prattville AL 36067 **800-545-5735** 334-365-6762
Cherokee Electric Cooperative
1550 Clarence Chestnut Bypass PO Box O. . . . . Centre AL 35960 **800-952-2667** 256-927-5524
Covington Electric Co-op Inc
18836 US Hwy 84 . . . . Andalusia AL 36421 **800-239-4121** 334-222-4121
Cullman Electric Cooperative
1749 Eva Rd NE . . . . Cullman AL 35055 **800-242-1806** 256-737-3201
Dixie Electric Co-op
9100 Atlanta Hwy . . . . Montgomery AL 36117 **888-349-4332** 334-288-1163
North Alabama Electric Co-op
41103 US Hwy 72 . . . . Stevenson AL 35772 **800-572-2900** 256-437-2281
Pea River Electric Co-op
1311 W Roy Parker Rd PO Box 969 . . . . Ozark AL 36361 **800-264-7732** 334-774-2545
Pioneer Electric Co-op
300 Herbert St . . . . Greenville AL 36037 **800-239-3092** 334-382-6636
Sand Mountain Electric Co-op
402 Main St W . . . . Rainsville AL 35986 **877-843-2512** 256-638-2153
South Alabama Electric Co-op (SAEC)
PO Box 449 . . . . Troy AL 36081 **800-556-2060** 334-566-2060
Tallapoosa River Electric Co-op
15163 US Hwy 431 S PO Box 675 . . . . Lafayette AL 36862 **800-332-8732** 334-864-9331
Tombigbee Electric Co-op
7686 Hwy 43 . . . . Guin AL 35563 **800-621-8069** 205-468-3325

Alaska

			Toll-Free	Phone

Chugach Electric Assn Inc
5601 Electron Dr . . . . Anchorage AK 99518 **800-478-7494** 907-563-7494
Copper Valley Electric Assn Inc (CVEA)
Mile 187 Glenn Hwy PO Box 45 . . . . Glennallen AK 99588 **866-835-2832** 907-822-3211
Golden Valley Electrical Assn Inc
758 Illinois St . . . . Fairbanks AK 99701 **800-770-4832** 907-452-1151
Homer Electric Assn Inc
3977 Lake St . . . . Homer AK 99603 **800-478-8551** 907-235-8551
Nushagak Electric & Telephone Co-op Inc
557 Kenny Wren Rd . . . . Dillingham AK 99576 **800-478-5296** 907-842-5295

Arizona

			Toll-Free	Phone

Duncan Valley Electric Co-op Inc
PO Box 440 . . . . Duncan AZ 85534 **800-669-2503** 928-359-2503
Graham County Electric Inc
9 W Center St . . . . Pima AZ 85543 **800-577-9266** 928-485-2451
Navopache Electric Co-op Inc
1878 W White Mtn Blvd . . . . Lakeside AZ 85929 **800-543-6324** 928-368-5118

Arkansas

			Toll-Free	Phone

Arkansas Valley Electric Co-op Corp
1811 W Commercial St PO Box 47 . . . . Ozark AR 72949 **800-468-2176** 479-667-2176
Ashley-Chicot Electric Co-op Inc
307 E Jefferson St . . . . Hamburg AR 71646 **800-281-5212** 870-853-5212
Carroll Electric Co-op Corp
920 Hwy 62 Spur . . . . Berryville AR 72616 **800-432-9720** 870-423-2161
Clay County Electric Co-op Corp
3111 US-67 . . . . Corning AR 72422 **800-521-2450** 870-857-3521
Craighead Electric Co-op Corp
4314 Stadium Blvd PO Box 7503 . . . . Jonesboro AR 72403 **800-794-5012** 870-932-8301
First Electric Co-op Corp
1000 S JP Wright Loop Rd . . . . Jacksonville AR 72076 **800-489-7405** 501-982-4545
Mississippi County Electric Co-op
510 N Broadway St . . . . Blytheville AR 72315 **800-439-4563** 870-763-4563
Ouachita Electric Co-op Corp
700 Bradley Ferry Rd PO Box 877 . . . . Camden AR 71711 **877-252-4538** 870-836-5791
Ozarks Electric Co-op Corp
3641 W Wedington Dr . . . . Fayetteville AR 72704 **800-521-6144** 479-521-2900
Petit Jean Electric Co-op
270 Quality Dr PO Box 37 . . . . Clinton AR 72031 **800-786-7618** 501-745-2493
Rich Mountain Electric Co-op Inc
515 Janssen PO Box 897 . . . . Mena AR 71953 **877-828-4074** 479-394-4140
South Central Arkansas Electric Co-op
4818 Hwy 8 W PO Box 476 . . . . Arkadelphia AR 71923 **800-814-2931** 870-246-6701
Woodruff Electric Co-op
PO Box 1619 . . . . Forrest City AR 72336 **888-559-6400** 870-633-2262

California

			Toll-Free	Phone

Anza ElectricCo-op Inc
58470 Hwy 371 PO Box 391909 . . . . Anza CA 92539 **844-311-7201** 951-763-4333
Plumas-Sierra Rural Electric Co-op
73233 State Rt 70 . . . . Portola CA 96122 **800-555-2207** 530-832-4261

Surprise Valley Electrification Corp (SVEC)
516 US Hwy 395 E . . . . Alturas CA 96101 **866-843-2667** 530-233-3511

Colorado

			Toll-Free	Phone

Delta-Montrose Electric Assn
11925 6300 Rd . . . . Montrose CO 81401 **877-687-3632**
Empire Electric Assn Inc
801 N Broadway . . . . Cortez CO 81321 **800-709-3726** 970-565-4444
Grand Valley Rural Power Lines Inc
845 22 Rd PO Box 190 . . . . Grand Junction CO 81505 **877-760-7435** 970-242-0040
Gunnison County Electric Assn Inc
37250 W Hwy 50 PO Box 180 . . . . Gunnison CO 81230 **800-726-3523** 970-641-3520
Highline Electric Assn
1300 S Interocean Ave . . . . Holyoke CO 80734 **800-816-2236** 970-854-2236
Holy Cross Energy
PO Box 2150 . . . . Glenwood Springs CO 81602 **877-833-2555** 970-945-5491
Intermountain Rural Electric Assn
5496 Hwy 85 . . . . Sedalia CO 80135 **800-332-9540** 303-688-3100
KC Electric Assn 422 Third Ave . . . . Hugo CO 80821 **800-700-3123** 719-743-2431
La Plata Electric Assn Inc
45 Stewart St . . . . Durango CO 81303 **888-839-5732** 970-247-5786
Morgan County Rural Electric Assn
20169 US Hwy 34 . . . . Fort Morgan CO 80701 **877-495-6487** 970-867-5688
Mountain Parks Electric Inc
321 W Agate Ave . . . . Granby CO 80446 **877-887-3378** 970-887-3378
Mountain View Electric Assn Inc
1655 Fifth St PO Box 1600 . . . . Limon CO 80828 **800-388-9881** 719-775-2861
Poudre Valley Rural Electric Assn Inc
7649 Rea Pkwy . . . . Fort Collins CO 80528 **800-432-1012** 970-226-1234
San Isabel Electric inc
781 E Industrial Blvd . . . . Pueblo West CO 81007 **800-279-7432** 719-547-2160
San Luis Valley Rural Electric Co-op
3625 US Hwy 160 W . . . . Monte Vista CO 81144 **800-332-7634** 719-852-3538
San Miguel Power Assn Inc
170 W Tenth Ave . . . . Nucla CO 81424 **800-864-7256** 970-864-7311
Southeast Colorado Power Assn (SECPA)
27850 Harris Rd . . . . La Junta CO 81050 **800-332-8634** 719-384-2551
United Power Inc
500 Co-op Way . . . . Brighton CO 80603 **800-468-8809** 303-659-0551
White River Electric Assn (WREA)
PO Box 958 . . . . Meeker CO 81641 **800-922-1987** 970-878-5041
Y-W Electric Assn Inc
250 Main Ave PO Box Y . . . . Akron CO 80720 **800-660-2291** 970-345-2291
Yampa Valley Electric Assn Inc
2211 Elk River Rd . . . . Steamboat Springs CO 81626 **888-873-9832** 970-879-1160

Delaware

			Toll-Free	Phone

Delaware Electric Co-op Inc
14198 Sussex Hwy . . . . Greenwood DE 19950 **800-282-8595** 302-349-3147

Florida

			Toll-Free	Phone

Central Florida Electric Cooperative Inc
11491 NW 50th Ave . . . . Chiefland FL 32626 **800-227-1302** 352-493-2511
Choctawhatchee Electric Co-op Inc
1350 W Baldwin Ave . . . . DeFuniak Springs FL 32435 **800-342-0990** 850-892-2111
Clay Electric Co-operative Inc
10 Citrus Dr PO Box 308 . . . . Keystone Heights FL 32656 **800-224-4917** 352-473-4917
Escambia River Electric Co-op Inc
3425 Florida 4 . . . . Jay FL 32565 **800-235-3848** 850-675-4521
Florida Keys Electric Co-op Assn
91630 Overseas Hwy . . . . Tavernier FL 33070 **800-858-8845** 305-852-2431
Gulf Coast Electric Co-op Inc
722 W Hwy 22 PO Box 220 . . . . Wewahitchka FL 32465 **800-333-9392** 850-639-2216
LCEC
4980 Bayline Dr . . . . North Fort Myers FL 33917 **800-282-1643** 239-995-2121
Peace River Electric Cooperative Inc
210 Metheny Rd PO Box 1310 . . . . Wauchula FL 33873 **866-201-1814** 800-282-3824
West Florida Electric Co-op
5282 Peanut Rd . . . . Graceville FL 32440 **800-342-7400** 850-263-3231

Georgia

			Toll-Free	Phone

Altamaha Electric Membership Corp
611 W Liberty Ave PO Box 346 . . . . Lyons GA 30436 **800-822-4563** 912-526-8181
Amicalola Electric Membership Corp
544 Hwy 515 S . . . . Jasper GA 30143 **800-282-7411** 706-253-5200
Canoochee Electric Membership Corp
342 E Brazell St . . . . Reidsville GA 30453 **800-342-0134**
Carroll Electric Membership Corp (EMC)
155 N Hwy 113 . . . . Carrollton GA 30117 **800-282-7411** 770-832-3552
Central Georgia Electric Membership Corp
923 S Mulberry St . . . . Jackson GA 30233 **800-222-4877** 770-775-7857
Coastal Electric Co-op
1265 S Coastal Hwy . . . . Midway GA 31320 **800-421-2343** 912-884-3311
Coweta-Fayette Electric Membership Corp
807 Collinsworth Rd . . . . Palmetto GA 30268 **877-746-4362** 770-502-0226
Diverse Power Inc
1400 S Davis Rd . . . . LaGrange GA 30241 **800-845-8362** 706-845-2000
Flint Energies
3 S Macon St . . . . Reynolds GA 31076 **800-342-3616** 478-847-3415
Grady Electric Membership Corp (EMC)
1499 US Hwy 84 W . . . . Cairo GA 39828 **877-757-6060** 229-377-4182
Habersham Electric Membership Corp
6135 Georgia 115 . . . . Clarkesville GA 30523 **800-640-6812** 706-754-2114
Hart Electric Membership Corp
1071 Elberton Hwy . . . . Hartwell GA 30643 **800-241-4109** 706-376-4714
Irwin Electric Membership Corp
915 W Fourth St . . . . Ocilla GA 31774 **800-237-3745** 229-468-7415
Jackson Electric Membership Corp
850 Commerce Rd . . . . Jefferson GA 30549 **800-462-3691** 706-367-5281

Company	City ST Zip	Toll-Free	Phone
Jefferson Energy Co-op 3077 Hwy 17 N PO Box 457	North Wrens GA 30833	877-533-3377	706-547-2167
Little Ocmulgee Electric Membership Corp 26 W Railroad Ave	Alamo GA 30411	800-342-1290	912-568-7171
Middle Georgia Electric Membership Corp 600 Tippettville Rd	Vienna GA 31092	800-342-0144	229-268-2671
Mitchell Electric Membership Corp 475 Cairo Rd	Camilla GA 31730	800-479-6034	229-336-5221
Ocmulgee Electric Membership Corp 5722 Eastman St	Eastman GA 31023	800-342-5509	478-374-7001
Oconee Electric Membership Corp 3445 US Hwy 80 W	Dudley GA 31022	800-522-2930	478-676-3191
Okefenoke Rural Electric Membership Corp (REMC) 14384 Cleveland St PO Box 602	Nahunta GA 31553	800-262-5131	912-462-5131
Sawnee Electric Membership Corp 543 Atlantic Hwy	Cumming GA 30028	800-635-9131	770-887-2363
Sumter Electric Membership Corp 1120 Felder St	Americus GA 31709	800-342-6978	229-924-8041
Three Notch Electric Membership Corp PO Box 295	Donalsonville GA 39845	800-239-5377	229-524-5377
Tri-County Electric Membership Corp PO Box 487	Gray GA 31032	866-254-8100	478-986-8100
Tri-State Electric Membership Corp (TSEMC) 2310 Blue Ridge Dr	Blue Ridge GA 30513	800-351-1111	706-492-3251
Washington Electric Membership Corp 258 N Harris St	Sandersville GA 31082	800-552-2577	478-552-2577

Idaho

Company	City ST Zip	Toll-Free	Phone
Clearwater Power Co 4230 Hatwai Rd PO Box 997	Lewiston ID 83501	888-743-1501	208-743-1501
Fall River Rural Electric Co-op Inc 1150 N 3400 E	Ashton ID 83420	800-632-5726	208-652-7431
Idaho County Light & Power Co-op 1065 Hwy 13	Grangeville ID 83530	877-212-0424	208-983-1610
Kootenai Electric Co-op Inc 2451 West Dakota Ave	Hayden ID 83835	800-240-0459	208-765-1200
Northern Lights Inc 421 Cherry St PO Box 269	Sagle ID 83860	800-326-9594	208-263-5141
Raft River Rural Electric Co-op Inc 155 N Main St PO Box 617	Malta ID 83342	800-342-7732	208-645-2211
Salmon River Electric Co-op Inc 1130 Main St PO Box 384	Challis ID 83226	877-806-2283	208-879-2283

Illinois

Company	City ST Zip	Toll-Free	Phone
Adams Electric Co-op PO Box 247	Camp Point IL 62320	800-232-4797	217-593-7701
Clinton County Electric Co-op Inc 475 N Main St PO Box 40	Breese IL 62230	800-526-7282	618-526-7282
Corn Belt Energy Corp 1 Energy Way	Bloomington IL 61705	800-879-0339	309-662-5330
Eastern Illini Electric Co-op 330 W Ottawa PO Box 96	Paxton IL 60957	800-824-5102	217-379-2131
Egyptian Electric Co-op Assn PO Box 38	Steeleville IL 62288	800-606-1505	
Illinois Rural Electric Co-op 2 S Main St	Winchester IL 62694	800-468-4732	217-742-3128
Jo-Carroll Energy 793 US Hwy 20 W	Elizabeth IL 61028	800-858-5522	
Menard Electric Co-op 14300 State Hwy 97 PO Box 200	Petersburg IL 62675	800-872-1203	217-632-7746
MJM Electric Co-op Inc (MJMEC) 264 NE St PO Box 80	Carlinville IL 62626	800-648-4729	217-707-6156
Rural Electric Convenience Co-op Co 3973 W State Rt 104 PO Box 19	Auburn IL 62615	800-245-7322	217-438-6197
Shelby Electric Co-op (SEC) 1355 IL-128 state PO Box 560	Shelbyville IL 62565	800-677-2612	217-774-3986
SouthEastern Illinois Electric Cooperative Inc (SIPC) 100 Cooperative Way PO Box 1001	Carrier Mills IL 62917	800-833-2611	618-273-2611
Southern Illinois Electric Co-op 7420 US Hwy 51 S	Dongola IL 62926	800-762-1400	618-827-3555
Southwestern Electric Cooperative Inc 525 US Rt 40	Greenville IL 62246	800-637-8667	
Spoon River Electric Co-op Inc (SREC) 930 S Fifth Ave PO Box 340	Canton IL 61520	877-404-2572	309-647-2700
Tri-County Electric Co-op Inc 3906 Broadway St	Mount Vernon IL 62864	800-244-5151	618-244-5151
Wayne-White Counties Electric Co-op 1501 W Main St	Fairfield IL 62837	888-871-7695	618-842-2196
Western Illinois Electrical Co-op 524 N Madison St PO Box 338	Carthage IL 62321	800-576-3125	217-357-3125

Indiana

Company	City ST Zip	Toll-Free	Phone
Bartholomew County Rural Electric Membership Corp 1697 W Deaver Rd	Columbus IN 47201	800-927-5672	812-372-2546
Boone County Rural Electric Membership Corp 1207 Indianapolis Ave	Lebanon IN 46052	800-897-7362	765-482-2390
Clark County REMC 7810 State Rd 60 PO Box 411	Sellersburg IN 47172	800-462-6988	812-246-3316
Daviess-Martin County REMC 12628 E 75 N PO Box 430	Loogootee IN 47553	800-762-7362	812-295-4200
Decatur County Rural Electric Membership Corp 1430 W Main St PO Box 46	Greensburg IN 47240	800-844-7362	812-663-3391
Hendricks Power Co-op 86 N County Rd 500 E	Avon IN 46123	800-876-5473	317-745-5473
Jackson County Rural Electric Membership Corp 274 E Base Rd	Brownstown IN 47220	800-288-4458	812-358-4458
Jasper County Rural Electric Membership Corp 280 E 400 S	Rensselaer IN 47978	888-866-7362	219-866-4601
Jay County Rural Electric Membership Corp 484 S 200 W PO Box 904	Portland IN 47371	800-835-7362	260-726-7121
Johnson County Rural Electric Membership Corp 750 International Dr	Franklin IN 46131	800-382-5544	317-736-6174
Kosciusko Rural Electric Membership Corp (REMC) 370 S 250 E	Warsaw IN 46582	800-790-7362	574-267-6331
LaGrange County Rural Electric Membership Corp 1995 E US Hwy 20	LaGrange IN 46761	877-463-7165	260-463-7165
Miami-Cass County Rural Electric Membership Corp 3086 W 100 N PO Box 168	Peru IN 46970	800-844-6668* *General	765-473-6668
Noble REMC 300 Weber Rd PO Box 137	Albion IN 46701	800-933-7362	
Orange County Rural Electric Membership Corp 7133 N State Rd 337 PO Box 208	Orleans IN 47452	888-337-5900	812-865-2229
Parke County Rural Electric Membership Corp 119 W High St	Rockville IN 47872	800-537-3913	765-569-3133
Rush Shelby Energy Inc 2777 S 840 W PO Box 55	Manilla IN 46150	800-706-7362* *General	765-544-2600
South Central Indiana Rural Electric Membership Corp 300 Morton Ave	Martinsville IN 46151	800-264-7362	765-342-3344
Southeastern Indiana Rural Electric Membership Corp 712 S Buckeye St	Osgood IN 47037	800-737-4111	812-689-4111
Southern Indiana Rural Electric Co-op Inc 1776 Tenth St PO Box 219	Tell City IN 47586	800-323-2316	812-547-2316
Steuben County Rural Electric Membership Corp 1212 S Wayne St	Angola IN 46703	888-233-9088	260-665-3563
Tipmont REMC 403 S Main St	Linden IN 47955	800-726-3953	
Warren County Rural Electric Membership Corp 15 Midway St PO Box 37	Williamsport IN 47993	800-872-7319	765-762-6114
White County Rural Electric Membership Corp 302 N Sixth St	Monticello IN 47960	800-844-7161	574-583-7161
Whitewater Valley Rural Electric Membership Corp 101 Brownsville Ave	Liberty IN 47353	800-529-5557	765-458-5171
WIN Energy Rural Electric Membership Corp 3981 S US Hwy 41	Vincennes IN 47591	800-882-5140	812-882-5140

Iowa

Company	City ST Zip	Toll-Free	Phone
Access Energy Co-op 1800 W Washington St	Mount Pleasant IA 52641	866-242-4232	319-385-1577
Allamakee-Clayton Electric Co-op (ACEC) 229 Hwy 51 PO Box 715	Postville IA 52162	888-788-1551	563-864-7611
Butler County REC 521 N Main PO Box 98	Allison IA 50602	888-267-2726	319-267-2726
Calhoun County Electric Co-op Assn 1015 Tonawanda St PO Box 312	Rockwell City IA 50579	800-821-4879	712-297-7112
Chariton Valley Electric Co-op 2090 Hwy 5 PO Box 486	Albia IA 52531	800-475-1702	641-932-7126
Consumers Energy 2074 242nd St	Marshalltown IA 50158	800-696-6552	641-752-1593
East-Central Iowa Rural Electric Co-op 2400 Bing Miller Ln	Urbana IA 52345	877-850-4343	319-443-4343
Eastern Iowa Light & Power Co-op 600 E Fifth St PO Box 3003	Wilton IA 52778	800-728-1242	563-732-2211
Franklin Rural Electric Co-op 1560 Hwy 65 PO Box 437	Hampton IA 50441	800-750-3557	641-456-2557
Grundy County Rural Electric Co-op 303 N Park Ave PO Box 39	Grundy Center IA 50638	800-390-7605	319-824-5251
Heartland Power Co-op 216 Jackson St PO Box 65	Thompson IA 50478	888-584-9732	641-584-2251
Lyon Rural Electric Co-op 116 S Marshall St	Rock Rapids IA 51246	800-658-3976	712-472-2506
Maquoketa Valley Rural Electric Co-op 109 N Huber St	Anamosa IA 52205	800-927-6068	319-462-3542
Midland Power Co-op 1005 E Lincolnway PO Box 420	Jefferson IA 50129	800-833-8876	515-386-4111
Nishnabotna Valley Rural Electric Co-op 1317 Chatburn Ave	Harlan IA 51537	800-234-5122	712-755-2166
Osceola Electric Co-op Inc 1102 Egret Dr PO Box 127	Sibley IA 51249	888-754-2519	712-754-2519
Pella Co-op Electric Assn 2615 Washington St	Pella IA 50219	800-619-1040	641-628-1040
Raccoon Valley Electric Co-op 28725 Hwy 30 PO Box 486	Glidden IA 51443	800-253-6211	712-659-3649
Southern Iowa Electric Co-op Inc 22458 Hwy 2 PO Box 70	Bloomfield IA 52537	800-607-2027	641-664-2277
Southwest Iowa Rural Electric Co-op 1801 Grove Ave	Corning IA 50841	888-220-4869	641-322-3165
TIP Rural Electric Co-op 612 W Des Moines St PO Box 534	Brooklyn IA 52211	800-934-7976	641-522-9221
Western Iowa Power Co-op 809 Iowa 39	Denison IA 51442	800-253-5189	712-263-2943
Woodbury County Rural Electric Co-op Assn 1495 Humboldt Ave	Moville IA 51039	800-469-3125	712-873-3125

Kansas

Company	City ST Zip	Toll-Free	Phone
Ark Valley Electric Co-op Assn 10 E Tenth St	South Hutchinson KS 67504	888-297-9212	620-662-6661
Bluestem Electric Co-op Inc 614 E Hwy 24 PO Box 5	Wamego KS 66547	800-558-1580	785-456-2212
Butler Rural Electric Co-op Assn Inc 216 S Vine St PO Box 1242	El Dorado KS 67042	800-464-0060	316-321-9600
Caney Valley Electric Co-op Assn Inc, The 401 Lawrence St PO Box 308	Cedar Vale KS 67024	800-310-8911	620-758-2262
CMS Electric Co-op Inc 509 E Carthage St	Meade KS 67864	800-794-2353	620-873-2184
Doniphan Electric Co-op Assn Inc 530 W Jones St PO Box 699	Troy KS 66087	800-699-0810	785-985-3523
DS&O Electric Cooperative Inc 129 W Main St PO Box 286	Solomon KS 67480	800-376-3533	785-655-2011
Heartland Rural Electric Co-op 110 N Enterprise St	Girard KS 66743	888-835-9585	800-835-9586
Leavenworth-Jefferson Electric Co-op Inc 507 N Union St	McLouth KS 66054	888-796-6111	
Midwest Energy Inc 1330 Canterbury Dr	Hays KS 67601	800-222-3121	

Name / Address	City	State	Zip	Toll-Free	Phone
Prairie Land Electric Co-op Inc 14935 US Hwy 36	Norton	KS	67654	800-577-3323	785-877-3323
Radiant Electric Co-op Inc PO Box 390	Fredonia	KS	66736	800-821-0956	620-378-2161
Rolling Hills Electric Co-op Inc 3075B US Hwy 24 PO Box 339	Beloit	KS	67420	800-530-5572	785-534-1601
Sumner-Cowley Electric Co-op Inc 2223 N A St PO Box 220	Wellington	KS	67152	888-326-3356	620-326-3356
Victory Electric Co-op Assn Inc 3230 N 14th Ave	Dodge City	KS	67801	800-279-7915	620-227-2139
Western Co-op Electric Assn Inc 635 S 13th St	WaKeeney	KS	67672	800-456-6720	785-743-5561
Wheatland Electric Co-op Inc 101 S Main St	Scott City	KS	67871	800-762-0436	620-872-5885

Kentucky

Name / Address	City	State	Zip	Toll-Free	Phone
Big Sandy Rural Electric Cooperative Corp 504 11th St	Paintsville	KY	41240	888-789-7322	606-789-4095
Blue Grass Energy Co-op Corp 1201 Lexington Rd	Nicholasville	KY	40356	888-546-4243	859-885-4191
Cumberland Valley Electric Inc 6219 N US Hwy 25 E	Gray	KY	40734	800-513-2677	
Farmers Rural Electric Co-op Corp 504 S Broadway St	Glasgow	KY	42141	800-253-2191	270-651-2191
Fleming Mason Energy Co-op 1449 Elizaville Rd PO Box 328	Flemingsburg	KY	41041	800-464-3144	606-845-2661
Grayson Rural Electric Co-op Corp 109 Bagby Pk	Grayson	KY	41143	800-562-3532	606-474-5136
Inter-County Energy Co-op 1009 Hustonville Rd	Danville	KY	40422	888-266-7322	859-236-4561
Jackson Energy Co-op 115 Jackson Energy Ln	McKee	KY	40447	800-262-7480	606-364-1000
Jackson Purchase Energy Corp 2900 Irvin Cobb Dr	Paducah	KY	42002	800-633-4044	270-442-7321
Kenergy Corp 6402 Old Corydon Rd	Henderson	KY	42419	800-844-4832	270-826-3991
Licking Valley Rural Electric Co-op Corp 271 Main St	West Liberty	KY	41472	800-596-6530	606-743-3179
Nolin Rural Electric Co-op Corp 411 Ring Rd	Elizabethtown	KY	42701	888-637-4247	270-765-6153
Owen Electric Co-op Inc 8205 Hwy 127 N PO Box 400	Owenton	KY	40359	800-372-7612	502-484-3471
Pennyrile Rural Electric Co-op Corp 2000 Harrison St PO Box 2900 *Cust Svc	Hopkinsville	KY	42241	800-297-4710*	270-886-2555
Salt River Electric Co-op Corp 111 W Brashear Ave	Bardstown	KY	40004	800-221-7465	502-348-3931
Shelby Energy Co-op Inc 620 Old Finchville Rd	Shelbyville	KY	40065	800-292-6585	502-633-4420
South Kentucky Rural Electrical Co-op 925 N Main St PO Box 910	Somerset	KY	42502	800-264-5112	606-678-4121
Taylor County RECC 625 W Main St PO Box 100	Campbellsville	KY	42719	800-931-4551	270-465-4101
Warren Rural Electric Co-op Corp 951 Fairview Ave	Bowling Green	KY	42101	866-319-3234	270-842-6541
West Kentucky Rural Electric Co-op Corp PO Box 589	Mayfield	KY	42066	877-495-7322	270-247-1321

Louisiana

Name / Address	City	State	Zip	Toll-Free	Phone
Beauregard Electric Co-op Inc 1010 E First St	DeRidder	LA	70634	800-367-0275	337-463-6221
Concordia Electric Co-op Inc 1865 Hwy 84 W PO Box 337	Jonesville	LA	71343	800-617-6282	318-339-7969
Dixie Electric Membership Corp (DEMCO) PO Box 15659	Baton Rouge	LA	70895	800-262-0221	225-261-1221
Jefferson Davis Electric Co-op 906 N Lake Arthur Ave PO Box 1229	Jennings	LA	70546	800-256-5332	337-824-4330
Pointe Coupee Electric Membership Corp 2506 False River Dr PO Box 160	New Roads	LA	70760	800-738-7232	225-638-3751
Southwest Louisiana Electric Membership Corp 3420 NE Evangeline Thwy	Lafayette	LA	70509	888-275-3626	337-896-5384
Washington-Saint Tammany Electric Co-op 950 Pearl St PO Box 697	Franklinton	LA	70438	866-672-9773	985-839-3562

Maine

Name / Address	City	State	Zip	Toll-Free	Phone
Eastern Maine Electric Co-op Inc 21 Union St	Calais	ME	04619	800-696-7444	207-454-7555

Maryland

Name / Address	City	State	Zip	Toll-Free	Phone
Choptank Electric Co-op Inc 24820 Meeting House Rd PO Box 430	Denton	MD	21629	877-892-0001	

Michigan

Name / Address	City	State	Zip	Toll-Free	Phone
Cherryland Electric Co-op 5930 US 31 S PO Box 298	Grawn	MI	49637	800-442-8616	231-486-9200
Great Lakes Energy Co-op 1323 Boyne Ave	Boyne City	MI	49712	888-485-2537	231-582-6521
Midwest Energy & Communications 60590 Decatur Rd	Cassopolis	MI	49031	800-492-5989	
Presque Isle Electric & Gas Co-op PO Box 308	Onaway	MI	49765	800-423-6634	989-733-8515

Minnesota

Name / Address	City	State	Zip	Toll-Free	Phone
Agralite Electric Co-op 320 Hwy 12 SE	Benson	MN	56215	800-950-8375	320-843-4150
Arrowhead Electric Co-op Inc 5401 West Hwy 61 PO Box 39	Lutsen	MN	55612	800-864-3744	218-663-7239
Beltrami Electric Co-op Inc 4111 Technology Dr NW	Bemidji	MN	56601	800-955-6083	218-444-2540
Benco Electric Co-op 20946 549 Ave PO Box 8	Mankato	MN	56002	888-792-3626	507-387-7963
Brown County Rural Electric Assn 24386 State Hwy 4 PO Box 529	Sleepy Eye	MN	56085	800-658-2368	507-794-3331
Crow Wing Co-op Power & Light Co Hwy 371 N PO Box 507	Brainerd	MN	56401	800-648-9401	218-829-2827
Dakota Electric Assn 4300 220th St W	Farmington	MN	55024	800-874-3409	651-463-6144
East Central Energy PO Box 39	Braham	MN	55006	800-254-7944	
Federated Rural Electric Assn 77100 US Hwy 71 PO Box 69	Jackson	MN	56143	800-321-3520	507-847-3520
Freeborn-Mower Co-op Services 2501 E Main St	Albert Lea	MN	56007	800-734-6421	507-373-6421
Goodhue County Co-op Electric Assn 1410 Northstar Dr	Zumbrota	MN	55992	800-927-6864	507-732-5117
Itasca-Mantrap Co-op Electrical Assn 16930 County Rd 6	Park Rapids	MN	56470	888-713-3377	218-732-3377
Lake Country Power 2810 Elida Dr	Grand Rapids	MN	55744	800-421-9959	
Lake Region Co-op Electrical Assn 1401 S Broadway PO Box 643	Pelican Rapids	MN	56572	800-552-7658	218-863-1171
McLeod Co-op Power Assn 1231 Ford Ave N	Glencoe	MN	55336	800-494-6272	320-864-3148
Mille Lacs Electric Co-op PO Box 230	Aitkin	MN	56431	800-450-2191	218-927-2191
Minnesota Valley Co-op Light & Power Assn 501 S First St	Montevideo	MN	56265	800-247-5051	320-269-2163
Minnesota Valley Electric Co-op 125 Minnesota Vly Electric Dr PO Box 77024	Jordan	MN	55352	800-282-6832	952-492-2313
Nobles Co-op Electric 22636 US Hwy 59 PO Box 788	Worthington	MN	56187	800-776-0517	507-372-7331
North Itasca Electric Co-op Inc 301 Main Ave PO Box 227	Bigfork	MN	56628	800-762-4048	218-743-3131
North Star Electric Co-op 441 State Hwy 172 NW PO Box 719	Baudette	MN	56623	888-634-2202	218-634-2202
People's Energy Co-op 1775 Lake Shady Ave S	Oronoco	MN	55960	800-214-2694	507-367-7000
PKM Electric Co-op Inc 406 N Minnesota St	Warren	MN	56762	800-552-7366	218-745-4711
Red Lake Electric Co-op Inc 412 International Dr PO Box 430	Red Lake Falls	MN	56750	800-245-6068	218-253-2168
Red River Valley Co-op Power Assn 109 Second Ave E	Halstad	MN	56548	800-788-7784	218-456-2139
Renville-Sibley Co-op Power Assn 103 Oak St PO Box 68	Danube	MN	56230	800-826-2593	320-826-2593
Roseau Electric Co-op Inc 1107 Third St NE	Roseau	MN	56751	888-847-8840	218-463-1543
South Central Electric Assn 71176 Tiell Dr PO Box 150	Saint James	MN	56081	888-805-7232	507-375-3164
Stearns ElectricAssn 900 E Kraft Dr	Melrose	MN	56352	800-962-0655	320-256-4241
Steele-Waseca Co-op Electric (SWCE) 2411 W Bridge St PO Box 485	Owatonna	MN	55060	800-526-3514	507-451-7340
Todd-Wadena Electric Co-op 550 Ash Ave NE PO Box 431	Wadena	MN	56482	800-321-8932	218-631-3120
Traverse Electric Co-op Inc 1618 Broadway PO Box 66	Wheaton	MN	56296	800-927-5443	320-563-8616
Wild Rice Electric Co-op Inc 502 N Main PO Box 438	Mahnomen	MN	56557	800-244-5709	218-935-2517
Wright-Hennepin Co-op Electric Assn 6800 Electric Dr PO Box 330	Rockford	MN	55373	800-943-2667	763-477-3000

Mississippi

Name / Address	City	State	Zip	Toll-Free	Phone
Alcorn County Electric Power Association Inc 1909 S Tate St	Corinth	MS	38834	844-741-7071	662-287-4402
Coast Electric Power Assn 18020 Hwy Ste 603 *Cust Svc	Kiln	MS	39556	877-769-2372*	228-363-7000
Dixie Electric Power Assn 1863 US-184 PO Box 88	Laurel	MS	39443	888-465-9209	601-425-2535
Monroe County Electric Power Assn 601 N Main St	Amory	MS	38821	866-656-2962	662-256-2962
Pearl River Valley Electric Power Assn 1422 Hwy 13 N PO Box 1217	Columbia	MS	39429	855-277-8372	601-736-2666
Southern Pine Electric Power Assn 110 Risher St PO Box 60	Taylorsville	MS	39168	800-231-5240	601-785-6511
Southwest Mississippi Electric Power Assn 18671 Hwy 61 PO Box 5	Lorman	MS	39096	800-287-8564	
Yazoo Valley Electric Power Assn 2255 Gordon Ave	Yazoo City	MS	39194	800-281-5098	662-746-4251

Missouri

Name / Address	City	State	Zip	Toll-Free	Phone
Atchison-Holt Electric Co-op 18585 Industrial Rd PO Box 160	Rock Port	MO	64482	888-744-5366	660-744-5344
Barry Electric Co-op 4015 Main St PO Box 307	Cassville	MO	65625	866-847-2333	
Barton County Electric Co-op 91 US-160	Lamar	MO	64759	800-286-5636	417-682-5636
Black River Electric Co-op 2600 Hwy 67 PO Box 31	Fredericktown	MO	63645	800-392-4711	573-783-3381
Boone Electric Co-op 1413 Rangeline St	Columbia	MO	65201	800-225-8143	573-449-4181
Callaway Electric Co-op 1313 Co-op Dr PO Box 250	Fulton	MO	65251	888-642-4840	573-642-3326
Central Missouri ElectricCo-op Inc 22702 Hwy 65 PO Box 939	Sedalia	MO	65302	855-875-7165	660-826-2900

	City	State	ZIP	Toll-Free	Phone
Co-Mo Electric Co-op Inc 29868 Hwy 5 PO Box 220	Tipton	MO	65081	**800-781-0157**	660-433-5521
Consolidated Electric Co-op 3940 E Liberty St	Mexico	MO	65265	**800-621-0091**	573-581-3630
Crawford Electric Co-op Inc 10301 N Service Rd PO Box 10	Bourbon	MO	65441	**800-677-2667**	573-732-4415
Cuivre River Electric Co-op 1112 E Cherry St	Troy	MO	63379	**800-392-3709**	636-528-8261
Farmers' Electric Co-op 201 W Business 36 PO Box 680	Chillicothe	MO	64601	**800-279-0496**	660-646-4281
Gascosage Electric Co-op 803 S Hwy 28 PO Box G	Dixon	MO	65459	**866-568-8243**	573-759-7146
Grundy Electric Co-op Inc 4100 Oklahoma Ave	Trenton	MO	64683	**800-279-2249**	660-359-3941
Howell-Oregon Electric Co-op Inc 6327 N US Hwy 63 PO Box 649	West Plains	MO	65775	**855-385-9903**	417-256-2131
Intercounty Electric Co-op 102 Maple Ave	Licking	MO	65542	**866-621-3679**	573-674-2211
Laclede Electric Co-op 1400 E Rt 66	Lebanon	MO	65536	**800-299-3164**	417-532-3164
Lewis County Rural Electric Co-op 18256 Hwy 16 PO Box 68	Lewistown	MO	63452	**888-454-4485**	573-215-4000
Macon Electric Co-op 31571 Bus Hwy 36 E PO Box 157	Macon	MO	63552	**800-553-6901**	660-385-3157
Ozark Border Electric Co-op 3281 S Westwood	Poplar Bluff	MO	63901	**800-392-0567**	573-785-4631
Pemiscot-Dunklin Electric Co-op Hwy 412 W PO Box 509	Hayti	MO	63851	**800-558-6641**	573-757-6641
Ralls County Electric Co-op 17594 Hwy 19 PO Box 157	New London	MO	63459	**877-985-8711**	573-985-8711
Sac Osage Electric Co-op Inc 4815 E Hwy 54 PO Box 111	El Dorado Springs	MO	64744	**800-876-2701**	417-876-2721
Three Rivers Electric Co-op 1324 E Main St PO Box 918	Linn	MO	65051	**800-892-2251**	573-644-9000
Tri-County Electric Co-op PO Box 159	Lancaster	MO	63548	**888-457-3734**	660-457-3733
Webster Electric Co-op 1240 Spur Dr	Marshfield	MO	65706	**800-643-4305**	417-859-2216
White River Valley Electric Co-op Inc 2449 State Hwy 76 E	Branson	MO	65616	**800-879-4056**	417-335-9335

Montana

	City	State	ZIP	Toll-Free	Phone
Beartooth Electric Co-op Inc 1306 N Broadway St PO Box 1110	Red Lodge	MT	59068	**800-472-9821**	406-446-2310
Big Flat Electric Co-op Inc 333 S Seventh St	Malta	MT	59538	**800-242-2040**	406-654-2040
Flathead Electric Co-op Inc 2510 US Hwy 2 E	Kalispell	MT	59901	**800-735-8489**	406-751-4483
Glacier Electric Co-op Inc 410 E Main St	Cut Bank	MT	59427	**844-834-4457**	406-873-5566
Hill County Electric Co-op Inc PO Box 2330	Havre	MT	59501	**877-394-7804**	
Lincoln Electric Co-op Inc (LEC) 500 Osloski Rd PO Box 628	Eureka	MT	59917	**800-442-2994**	406-889-3301
Lower Yellowstone Rural Electric Assn Inc 3200 W Holly St PO Box 1047	Sidney	MT	59270	**844-441-5627**	406-488-1602
McCone Electric Co-op Inc 110 Main St	Circle	MT	59215	**800-684-3605**	406-485-3430
Missoula Electric Co-op Inc 1700 West Broadway	Missoula	MT	59808	**800-352-5200**	406-541-4433
Park Electric Co-op Inc 5706 US Hwy 89 S PO Box 1119	Livingston	MT	59047	**888-298-0657**	406-222-3100
Southeast Electric Co-op Inc (SECO) 110 S Main St	Ekalaka	MT	59324	**888-485-8762**	406-775-8762
Sun River Electric Co-op Inc 310 First Ave S PO Box 309	Fairfield	MT	59436	**800-452-7516**	406-467-2527
Vigilante Electric Co-op Inc 225 E Bannack St	Dillon	MT	59725	**800-221-8271**	
Yellowstone Valley Electric Co-op 150 Co-op Way	Huntley	MT	59037	**800-736-5323**	406-348-3411

Nebraska

	City	State	ZIP	Toll-Free	Phone
Burt County Public Power District 613 N 13th St	Tekamah	NE	68061	**888-835-1620**	402-374-2631
Butler Public Power District 1331 N Fourth St	David City	NE	68632	**800-230-0569**	402-367-3081
Chimney Rock Public Power District 128 Eighth St PO Box 608	Bayard	NE	69334	**877-773-6300**	308-586-1824
Cornhusker Public Power District 23169 235th Ave PO Box 9	Columbus	NE	68602	**800-955-2773**	402-564-2821
Cuming County Public Power District 500 S Main St	West Point	NE	68788	**877-572-2463**	402-372-2463
Custer Public Power District 625 E South St PO Box 10	Broken Bow	NE	68822	**888-749-2453**	308-872-2451
Dawson Public Power District 75191 Rd 433	Lexington	NE	68850	**800-752-8305**	308-324-2386
Elkhorn Rural Public Power District 206 N Fourth St	Battle Creek	NE	68715	**800-675-2185**	402-675-2185
Howard Greeley Rural Power 422 Howard Ave PO Box 105	Saint Paul	NE	68873	**800-280-4962**	308-754-4457
Loup Public Power District (LPPD) 2404 15th St PO Box 988	Columbus	NE	68602	**866-869-2087**	402-564-3171
McCook Public Power District 1510 N Hwy 83	McCook	NE	69001	**800-658-4285**	308-345-2500
Midwest Electric Co-op Corp 104 Washington Ave	Grant	NE	69140	**800-451-3691**	308-352-4356
Nebraska Public Power District 1414 15th St PO Box 499	Columbus	NE	68602	**877-275-6773**	402-564-8561
Norris Public Power District 606 Irving St PO Box 399	Beatrice	NE	68310	**800-858-4707**	402-223-4038
North Central Public Power District 1409 Main St PO Box 90	Creighton	NE	68729	**800-578-1060**	402-358-5112
Northwest Rural Public Power District 5613 State Hwy 87 PO Box 249	Hay Springs	NE	69347	**800-847-0492**	308-638-4445
Perennial Public Power District 2122 S Lincoln Ave	York	NE	68467	**800-289-0288**	402-362-3355
Polk County Rural Public Power District 115 W Third St PO Box 465	Stromsburg	NE	68666	**888-242-5265**	402-764-4381
South Central Public Power District (SCPPD) 275 S Main St PO Box 406	Nelson	NE	68961	**800-557-5254**	402-225-2351
Southern Public Power District (SPPD) 4550 W Husker Hwy PO Box 1687	Grand Island	NE	68803	**800-652-2013**	308-384-2350
Southwest Public Power District 221 S Main St PO Box 289	Palisade	NE	69040	**800-379-7977**	308-285-3295
Stanton County Public Power District 807 Douglas St	Stanton	NE	68779	**877-439-2300**	402-439-2228
Twin Valleys Public Power District PO Box 160	Cambridge	NE	69022	**800-658-4266**	
Wheat Belt Public Power District 11306 Rd 32 PO Box 177	Sidney	NE	69162	**800-261-7114**	308-254-5871

Nevada

	City	State	ZIP	Toll-Free	Phone
Valley Electric Assn Inc 800 E Hwy 372 PO Box 237	Pahrump	NV	89048	**800-742-3330**	775-727-5312

New Hampshire

	City	State	ZIP	Toll-Free	Phone
New Hampshire Electric Co-op 579 Tenney Mtn Hwy	Plymouth	NH	03264	**800-698-2007**	603-536-1800

New Jersey

	City	State	ZIP	Toll-Free	Phone
Sussex Rural Electric Co-op 64 County Rt 639 PO Box 346	Sussex	NJ	07461	**877-504-6463**	973-875-5101

New Mexico

	City	State	ZIP	Toll-Free	Phone
Columbus Electric Co-op Inc 900 N Gold St PO Box 631	Deming	NM	88031	**800-950-2667**	575-546-8838
Farmers Electric Co-op Inc 3701 Thornton PO Box 550	Clovis	NM	88101	**800-445-8541**	575-762-4466
Jemez Mountains Electric Co-op PO Box 128	Espanola	NM	87532	**888-755-2105**	505-753-2105
Mora-San Miguel Electric Co-op Hwy 518 Main St	Mora	NM	87732	**800-421-6773**	575-387-2205
Otero County Electric Cooperative Inc 404 Burro Ave PO Box 227	Cloudcroft	NM	88317	**800-548-4660**	575-682-2521
Socorro Electric Co-op Inc 215 Manzanares Ave PO Box H	Socorro	NM	87801	**800-351-7575**	575-835-0560
Springer Electric Co-op Inc 408 Maxwell Ave PO Box 698	Springer	NM	87747	**800-288-1353**	575-483-2421

New York

	City	State	ZIP	Toll-Free	Phone
Delaware County Electric Co-op (DCEC) 39 Elm St PO Box 471	Delhi	NY	13753	**866-436-1223**	607-746-2341
Otsego Electric Co-op Inc (OEC) PO Box 128	Hartwick	NY	13348	**844-843-6842**	607-293-6622
Steuben Rural Electric Co-op Inc 9 Wilson Ave	Bath	NY	14810	**800-843-3414**	607-776-4161

North Carolina

	City	State	ZIP	Toll-Free	Phone
Albemarle Electric Membership Corp PO Box 69	Hertford	NC	27944	**800-215-9915**	252-426-5735
Blue Ridge Electric Membership Corp 1216 Blowing Rock Blvd	Lenoir	NC	28645	**800-451-5474**	828-758-2383
Brunswick Electric Membership Corp 795 Ocean Hwy PO Box 826	Shallotte	NC	28459	**800-842-5871**	910-754-4391
Cape Hatteras Electric Co-op 47109 Light Plant Rd PO Box 9	Buxton	NC	27920	**800-454-5616**	252-995-5616
Carteret-Craven Electric Co-op (CCEC) 1300 Hwy 24 W PO Box 1490	Newport	NC	28570	**800-682-2217**	252-247-3107
Central Electric Membership Corp 128 Wilson Rd	Sanford	NC	27331	**800-446-7752**	919-774-4900
Edgecombe-Martin County Electric Membership Corp PO Box 188	Tarboro	NC	27886	**800-445-6486**	
EnergyUnited Electric Membership Corp PO Box 1831	Statesville	NC	28687	**800-522-3793**	704-873-5241
Four County Electric Membership Corp 1822 NC Hwy 53 W PO Box 667	Burgaw	NC	28425	**888-368-7289**	910-259-2171
French Broad Electric Membership Corp 3043 Nc 213 Hwy	Marshall	NC	28753	**800-222-6190**	828-649-2051
Halifax Electric Membership Corp 208 Whitfield St	Enfield	NC	27823	**800-690-0522**	252-445-5111
Haywood Electric Membership Corp 376 Grindstone Rd	Waynesville	NC	28785	**800-951-6088**	828-452-2281
Jones-Onslow Electric Membership Corp 259 Western Blvd	Jacksonville	NC	28546	**800-682-1515**	910-353-1940
Lumbee River Electric Membership Corp PO Box 830	Red Springs	NC	28377	**800-683-5571**	910-843-4131
Pee Dee Electric Membership Corp (PDEMC) 575 US Hwy 52 S	Wadesboro	NC	28170	**800-992-1626**	704-694-2114
Piedmont Electric Membership Corp 2500 Nc 86 PO Box 1179	Hillsborough	NC	27278	**800-222-3107**	919-732-2123
Randolph Electric Membership Corp 879 McDowell Rd PO Box 40	Asheboro	NC	27204	**800-672-8212**	336-625-5177
Roanoke Electric Co-op 518 NC 561 W	Aulander	NC	27805	**800-433-2236**	
Rutherford Electric Membership Corp 186 Hudlow Rd PO Box 1569	Forest City	NC	28043	**800-521-0920**	828-245-1621
South River Electric Membership Corp 17494 US 421 S PO Box 931	Dunn	NC	28335	**800-338-5530**	910-892-8071

			Toll-Free	Phone
Surry-Yadkin Electric Membership Corp				
510 S Main St	Dobson NC	27017	**800-682-5903**	336-356-8241
Tideland Electric Membership Corp				
25831 Hwy 264 E	Pantego NC	27860	**800-637-1079**	252-943-3046
Union Power Co-op				
1525 N Rocky River Rd	Monroe NC	28110	**800-922-6840**	704-289-3145
Wake Electric				
100 S Franklin St PO Box 1229	Wake Forest NC	27588	**800-474-6300**	

North Dakota

			Toll-Free	Phone
Capital Electric Co-op Inc				
4111 State St	Bismarck ND	58503	**888-223-1513**	701-223-1513
Cass County Electric Co-op Inc				
4100 32nd Ave SW	Fargo ND	58104	**800-248-3292**	701-356-4400
Dakota Valley Electric Co-op				
7296 Hwy 281	Edgeley ND	58433	**800-342-4671**	701-493-2281
KEM Electric Co-op Inc				
107 S Broadway	Linton ND	58552	**800-472-2673**	701-254-4666
McKenzie Electric Co-op Inc				
PO Box 649	Watford City ND	58854	**800-584-9239**	701-444-9288
McLean Electric Co-op Inc				
4031 Hwy 37 Bypass NW	Garrison ND	58540	**800-263-4922**	701-463-2291
Mor-Gran-Sou Electric Co-op Inc				
202 Sixth Ave W	Flasher ND	58535	**800-750-8212**	701-597-3301
Mountrail-Williams Electric Co-op				
218 58th St W PO Box 1346	Williston ND	58802	**800-279-2667**	701-577-3765
Nodak Electric Co-op Inc				
4000 32nd Ave S	Grand Forks ND	58201	**800-732-4373**	701-746-4461
North Central Electric Co-op Inc				
538 11th St W	Bottineau ND	58318	**800-247-1197**	701-228-2202
Northern Plains Electric Co-op				
1515 W Main St	Carrington ND	58421	**800-882-2500**	
Slope Electric Co-op Inc				
116 E 12th St PO Box 338	New England ND	58647	**800-559-4191**	701-579-4191
Verendrye Electric Co-op Inc				
615 Hwy 52	Velva ND	58790	**800-472-2141**	701-338-2855

Ohio

			Toll-Free	Phone
Adams Rural Electric Co-op Inc				
4800 SR 125	West Union OH	45693	**800-283-1846**	937-544-2305
Buckeye Rural Electric Co-op				
4848 State Rt 325 PO Box 200	Patriot OH	45658	**800-231-2732**	740-379-2025
Butler Rural Electric Co-op Inc (BREC)				
3888 Still-Beckett Rd	Oxford OH	45056	**800-255-2732**	513-867-4400
Carroll Electric Co-op Inc				
350 Canton Rd NW	Carrollton OH	44615	**800-232-7697**	330-627-2116
Denier Electric Co Inc				
10891 SR- 128	Harrison OH	45030	**800-676-3282**	513-738-2641
Firelands Electric Co-op Inc				
1 Energy Pl PO Box 32	New London OH	44851	**800-533-8658**	419-929-1571
Frontier Power Co				
770 S Second St PO Box 280	Coshocton OH	43812	**800-624-8050**	740-622-6755
Guernsey-Muskingum Electric Co-op				
17 S Liberty St	New Concord OH	43762	**800-521-9879**	740-826-7661
Hancock-Wood Electric Co-op Inc (HWEC)				
1399 Business Pk Dr S				
PO Box 190.	North Baltimore OH	45872	**800-445-4840**	
Holmes-Wayne Electric Co-op Inc				
6060 Ohio 83	Millersburg OH	44654	**866-674-1055**	330-674-1055
Lorain-Medina Rural Electric Co-op Inc				
22898 W Rd	Wellington OH	44090	**800-222-5673**	440-647-2133
Mid Ohio Energy Co-op Inc				
555 W Franklin St	Kenton OH	43326	**888-382-6732**	419-673-7289
North Central Electric Co-op Inc				
13978 E County Rd 56	Attica OH	44807	**800-426-3072**	419-426-3072
North Western Electric Co-op Inc				
04125 State Rt 576 PO Box 391	Bryan OH	43506	**800-647-6932**	419-636-5051
Paulding-Putman Electric Co-op				
910 N Williams St	Paulding OH	45879	**800-686-2357**	419-399-5015
Pioneer Electric Co-op				
344 W US Rt 36	Piqua OH	45356	**800-762-0997**	937-773-2523
South Central Power Company Inc				
2780 Coon Path Rd	Lancaster OH	43130	**800-282-5064**	740-653-4422
Union Rural Electric Co-op Inc				
15461 US 36E	Marysville OH	43040	**800-642-1826**	937-642-1826
Washington Electric Cooperative Inc				
440 Highland Ridge Rd	Marietta OH	45750	**877-594-9324**	740-373-2141

Oklahoma

			Toll-Free	Phone
Alfalfa Electric Co-op Inc				
121 E Main St	Cherokee OK	73728	**888-736-3837**	580-596-3333
Canadian Valley Electric Co-op				
11277 S 356 PO Box 751	Seminole OK	74868	**877-382-3680**	405-382-3680
Central Rural Electric Co-op				
3304 S Boomer Rd PO Box 1809	Stillwater OK	74076	**800-375-2884**	405-372-2884
Cimarron Electric Co-op				
PO Box 299	Kingfisher OK	73750	**800-375-4121**	405-375-4121
Cookson Hills Electric Cooperative Inc				
1002 E Main St	Stigler OK	74462	**800-328-2368**	
Harmon Electric Assn Inc (HEA)				
114 N First St PO Box 393	Hollis OK	73550	**800-643-7769**	580-688-3342
Indian Electric Co-op Inc				
2506 E Hwy 64	Cleveland OK	74020	**800-482-2750**	918-295-9500
Kay Electric Co-op (KEC)				
300 W Doolin Ave	Blackwell OK	74631	**800-535-1079**	580-363-1260
Kiamichi Electric Co-op Inc (KEC)				
966 SW Hwy 2 PO Box 340	Wilburton OK	74578	**800-888-2731**	918-465-2338
Kiwash Electric Co-op Inc				
120 W First St PO Box 100	Cordell OK	73632	**888-832-3362**	580-832-3361
Lake Region Electric Co-op Inc				
516 S Lake Region Rd	Hulbert OK	74441	**800-364-5732**	918-772-2526

			Toll-Free	Phone
Northeast Oklahoma Electric Co-op Inc				
443857 E Hwy 60 PO Box 948	Vinita OK	74301	**800-256-6405**	918-256-6405
Northwestern Electric Cooperative				
2925 William Ave PO Box 2707	Woodward OK	73801	**800-375-7423**	580-256-7425
Oklahoma Electric Co-op				
242 24th Ave NW	Norman OK	73069	**800-522-6543**	405-321-2024
Rural Electric Co-op (REC)				
13942 Hwy 76 PO Box 609	Lindsay OK	73052	**800-259-3504**	405-756-3104
Southeastern Electric Co-op Inc				
1514 E Hwy 70 PO Box 1370	Durant OK	74702	**866-924-1315**	580-924-2170
Southwest Rural Electric Assn				
700 N Broadway PO Box 310	Tipton OK	73570	**800-256-7973**	580-667-5281
Tri-County Electric				
995 Mile 46 Rd PO Box 880	Hooker OK	73945	**800-522-3315**	580-652-2418
Verdigris Valley Electric Co-op				
8901 E 146th St N	Collinsville OK	74021	**800-870-5948**	918-371-2584

Oregon

			Toll-Free	Phone
Blachly-Lane Inc				
PO Box 70	Junction City OR	97448	**800-446-8418**	541-688-8711
Consumers Power Inc (CPI)				
6990 W Hills Rd	Philomath OR	97370	**800-872-9036**	541-929-3124
Midstate Electric Co-op Inc				
16755 Finley Butte Rd	La Pine OR	97739	**800-722-7219**	541-536-2126
Tillamook People's Utility District				
1115 Pacific Ave	Tillamook OR	97141	**800-422-2535**	503-842-2535
Wasco Electric Co-op Inc				
PO Box 1700	The Dalles OR	97058	**800-341-8580**	541-296-2740
West Oregon Electric Co-op Inc				
652 Rose Ave PO Box 69	Vernonia OR	97064	**800-777-1276**	503-429-3021

Pennsylvania

			Toll-Free	Phone
Adams Electric Co-op Inc				
1338 Biglerville Rd PO Box 1055	Gettysburg PA	17325	**888-232-6732**	717-334-2171
Bedford Rural Electric Co-op Inc				
8846 Lincoln Hwy	Bedford PA	15522	**800-808-2732**	814-623-5101
Citizens' Electric Co				
1775 Industrial Blvd PO Box 551	Lewisburg PA	17837	**877-487-9384**	570-524-2231
Claverack Rural Electric Co-op Inc				
32750 W US 6	Wysox PA	18854	**800-326-9799**	570-265-2167
New Enterprise Rural Electric Co-op Inc				
3596 Brumbaugh Rd	New Enterprise PA	16664	**800-270-3177**	814-766-3221
REA Energy Co-op Inc				
75 Airport Rd	Indiana PA	15701	**800-211-5667**	724-349-4800
Somerset Rural Electric Co-op				
223 Industrial Pk Rd	Somerset PA	15501	**800-443-4255**	814-445-4106
Sullivan County Rural Electric Co-op Inc (SCREC)				
5675 Rt 87 PO Box 65	Forksville PA	18616	**800-570-5081**	570-924-3381
Tri-County Rural Electric Co-op Inc				
22 N Main St PO Box 526.	Mansfield PA	16933	**800-343-2559**	570-662-2175
Valley Rural Electric Co-op Inc				
10700 Fairgrounds Rd PO Box 477	Huntingdon PA	16652	**800-432-0680**	814-643-2650
Warren Electric Co-op Inc (WEC)				
320 E Main St PO Box 208	Youngsville PA	16371	**800-364-8640**	814-563-7548

South Carolina

			Toll-Free	Phone
Aiken Electric Co-op Inc				
2790 Wagener Rd	Aiken SC	29802	**877-264-5368***	803-649-6245
*Tech Supp				
Black River Electric Cooperative Inc				
1121 N Pike Rd W	Sumter SC	29153	**866-731-2732**	803-469-8060
Broad River Electric Co-op Inc				
811 Hamrick St	Gaffney SC	29342	**866-687-2667**	864-489-5737
Edisto Electric Co-op Inc				
896 Calhoun St	Bamberg SC	29003	**800-433-3292**	803-245-5141
Horry Electric Cooperative Inc				
2774 Cultra Rd	Conway SC	29526	**800-877-8339**	843-369-2211
Little River Electric Cooperative Inc (LRECI)				
300 Cambridge St	Abbeville SC	29620	**800-459-2141**	864-366-2141
Lynches River Electric Co-op Inc				
1104 W McGregor St	Pageland SC	29728	**800-922-3486**	843-672-6111
Mid-Carolina Electric Co-op Inc				
PO Box 669	Lexington SC	29071	**888-813-8000***	803-749-6555
*Cust Svc				
Newberry Electric Co-op Inc				
882 Wilson Rd	Newberry SC	29108	**800-479-8838**	803-276-1121
Pee Dee Electric Co-op Inc				
PO Box 491	Darlington SC	29540	**866-747-0060**	843-665-4070
Santee Electric Co-op Inc				
424 Sumter Hwy	Kingstree SC	29556	**800-922-1604**	843-355-6187
Tri-County Electric Co-op				
6473 Old State Rd	Saint Matthews SC	29135	**877-874-1215**	803-874-1215
York Electric Cooperative Inc				
1385 E Alexander Love Hwy PO Box 150	York SC	29745	**800-582-8810**	803-684-4248

South Dakota

			Toll-Free	Phone
Black Hills Electric Co-op				
25191 Co-op Way PO Box 792	Custer SD	57730	**800-742-0085**	605-673-4461
Bon Homme Yankton Electric Assn				
134 S Lidice St	Tabor SD	57063	**800-925-2929**	605-463-2507
Butte Electric Co-op				
109 Dartmouth Ave	Newell SD	57760	**800-928-8839**	605-456-2494
Cam-Wal Electric Co-op Inc				
PO Box 135	Selby SD	57472	**800-269-7676**	605-649-7676
Charles Mix Electric Assn Inc				
440 Lake St	Lake Andes SD	57356	**800-208-8587**	605-487-7321
Cherry-Todd Electric Co-op Inc				
625 W Second St	Mission SD	57555	**800-856-4417**	605-856-4416
Clay-Union Electric Corp				
1410 E Cherry St PO Box 317.	Vermillion SD	57069	**800-696-2832**	605-624-2673

		Toll-Free	Phone

Codington-Clark Electric Co-op
3520 Ninth Ave SW PO Box 880............ Watertown SD 57201 **800-463-8938** 605-886-5848
Dakota Energy Cooperative Inc
PO Box 830 .... Huron SD 57350 **800-353-8591** 605-352-8591
FEM Electric Assn Inc
PO Box 468 .... Ipswich SD 57451 **800-587-5880** 605-426-6891
Grand Electric Co-op Inc
801 Coleman Ave PO Box 39 .... Bison SD 57620 **800-592-1803** 605-244-5211
H-D Electric Co-op Inc
423 Third Ave S .... Clear Lake SD 57226 **800-781-7474** 605-874-2171
Lake Region Electric Assn Inc
1212 Main St .... Webster SD 57274 **800-657-5869** 605-345-3379
Oahe Electric Co-op Inc
102 S Cranford St PO Box 216............. Blunt SD 57522 **800-640-6243** 605-962-6243
Rosebud Electric Co-op Inc
512 Rosebud Ave PO Box 439 .... Gregory SD 57533 **888-464-9304** 605-835-9624
Sioux Valley-Southwestern Electric Co-op Inc
47092 SD Hwy 34 PO Box 216............. Colman SD 57017 **800-234-1960** 605-534-3535
Union County Electric Co-op Inc
122 W Main St .... Elk Point SD 57025 **888-356-3395** 605-356-3395
West Central Electric Co-op Inc
204 Main St PO Box 17 .... Murdo SD 57559 **800-242-9232** 605-669-2472
West River Electric Assn Inc
1200 W Fourth Ave PO Box 412............. Wall SD 57790 **888-279-2135**
Whetstone Valley Electric Co-op
1101 E Fourth Ave .... Milbank SD 57252 **800-568-6631** 605-432-5331

Tennessee

		Toll-Free	Phone

Caney Fork Electric Co-op Inc
920 Smithville Hwy PO Box 272............ McMinnville TN 37110 **888-505-3030** 931-473-3116
Cumberland Electric Membership Corp
1940 Madison St .... Clarksville TN 37043 **800-987-2362**
Fayetteville Public Utilities
408 W College St .... Fayetteville TN 37334 **800-379-2534** 931-433-1522
Forked Deer Electric Co-op
PO Box 67 .... Halls TN 38040 **844-333-2729** 731-836-7508
Gibson Electric Membership Corp
1207 S College St PO Box 47............. Trenton TN 38382 **800-977-4076** 731-855-4740
Greeneville Light & Power System
PO Box 1690 .... Greeneville TN 37744 **866-466-1438** 423-636-6200
La Follette Utilities Board
302 N Tennessee Ave PO Box 1411 ....La Follette TN 37766 **800-352-1340** 423-562-3316
Middle Tennessee Electric Membership Corp
555 New Salem Hwy .... Murfreesboro TN 37129 **877-777-9020**
Mountain Electric Co-op Inc
PO Box 180 .... Mountain City TN 37683 **800-638-3788*** 423-727-1800
*Cust Svc
Pickwick Electric Co-op
672 HWY 142 .... Selmer TN 38375 **800-372-8258** 731-645-3411
Sequachee Valley Electric Co-op
512 Cedar Ave PO Box 31 .... South Pittsburg TN 37380 **800-923-2203** 423-837-8605
Southwest Tennessee Electric Membership Corp
1009 E Main St .... Brownsville TN 38012 **800-772-0472** 731-772-1322
Tennessee Valley Electric Co-op
590 Florence Rd .... Savannah TN 38372 **866-925-4916** 731-925-4916
Tri-County Electric Membership Corp
405 College St .... Lafayette TN 37083 **800-369-2111** 615-666-2111
Upper Cumberland Electric Membership Corp
138 Gordonsville Hwy .... South Carthage TN 37030 **800-261-2940** 615-735-2940

Texas

		Toll-Free	Phone

Bandera Electric Co-op Inc
3172 State Hwy 16 N .... Bandera TX 78003 **866-226-3372**
Big Country Electric Co-op Inc
1010 W S First St PO Box 518 .... Roby TX 79543 **888-662-2232** 325-776-2244
Bowie-Cass Electric Co-op Inc
117 N St .... Douglassville TX 75560 **800-794-2919** 903-846-2311
Central Texas Electric Co-op Inc (CTEC)
386 Friendship Ln PO Box 553..........Fredericksburg TX 78624 **800-900-2832*** 830-997-2126
*General
Coleman County Electric Co-op Inc
3300 N Hwy 84 PO Box 860............. Coleman TX 76834 **800-560-2128** 325-625-2128
Comanche Electric Co-op Assn
201 W Wrights Ave .... Comanche TX 76442 **800-915-2533** 325-356-2533
Cooke County Electric Co-op
11799 W US Hwy 82 PO Box 530........ Muenster TX 76252 **800-962-0296** 940-759-2211
CoServ Electric
7701 S Stemmons Fwy .... Corinth TX 76210 **800-274-4014** 940-321-7800
Deep East Texas Electric Co-op Inc
880 Texas Hwy 21 E PO Box 736 ..... San Augustine TX 75972 **800-392-5986** 936-275-2314
Farmers Electric Co-op Inc
2000 E I-30 .... Greenville TX 75402 **800-541-2662** 903-455-1715
Fayette Electric Co-op Inc
357 N Washington St .... La Grange TX 78945 **800-874-8290** 979-968-3181
Grayson-Collin Electric Cooperative (GCEC)
14568 FM 121 PO Box 548 .... Van Alstyne TX 75495 **800-967-5235** 903-482-7100
Greenbelt Electric Co-op Inc
PO Box 948 .... Wellington TX 79095 **800-527-3082** 806-447-2536
Guadalupe Valley Electric Co-op Inc
825 E Sarah Dewitt Dr .... Gonzales TX 78629 **800-223-4832** 830-857-1200
Hamilton County Electric Co-op Assn
420 N Rice St PO Box 753 .... Hamilton TX 76531 **800-595-3401** 254-386-3123
Heart of Texas Electric Co-op
1111 Johnson Dr PO Box 357 .... McGregor TX 76657 **800-840-2957** 254-840-2871
Hilco Electric Co-op Inc
115 E Main PO Box 127 .... Itasca TX 76055 **800-338-6425** 254-687-2331
Karnes Electric Co-op Inc
1007 N Hwy 123 .... Karnes City TX 78118 **888-807-3952** 830-780-3952
Lyntegar Electric Co-op Inc
PO Box 970 .... Tahoka TX 79373 **877-218-2308** 806-561-4588
Magic Valley Electric Co-op Inc
1 3/4 Mile W Hwy 83 .... Mercedes TX 78570 **866-225-5683**
Medina Electric Co-op Inc
PO Box 370 .... Hondo TX 78861 **866-632-3532**

		Toll-Free	Phone

Navarro County Electric Co-op Inc
3800 Texas 22 PO Box 616............. Corsicana TX 75110 **800-771-9095** 903-874-7411
Navasota Valley Electric Co-op Inc
2281 E US Hwy 79 PO Box 848 .... Franklin TX 77856 **800-443-9462** 979-828-3232
North Plains Electric Co-op Inc
14585 Hwy 83 N PO Box 1008............ Perryton TX 79070 **800-272-5482** 806-435-5482
Nueces Electric Co-op Inc (NEC)
14353 Cooperative Ave .... Corpus Christi TX 78380 **800-632-9288** 361-387-2581
Panola-Harrison Electric Co-op
410 E Houston St .... Marshall TX 75670 **800-972-1093** 903-935-7936
Pedernales Electric Co-op Inc
PO Box 1 .... Johnson City TX 78636 **888-554-4732** 830-868-7155
Rio Grande Electric Cooperative Inc
778 E US Hwy 90 PO Box 1509 .... Brackettville TX 78832 **800-749-1509** 830-563-2444
Sam Houston Electric Co-op Inc
1157 E Church St .... Livingston TX 77351 **800-458-0381** 936-327-5711
San Bernard Electric Co-op Inc
309 W Main St .... Bellville TX 77418 **800-364-3171** 979-865-3171
San Patricio Electric Co-op Inc
402 E Sinton St .... Sinton TX 78387 **888-740-2220** 361-364-2220
South Plains Electric Co-op Inc
PO Box 1830 .... Lubbock TX 79408 **800-658-2655** 806-775-7766
Southwest Texas Electric Co-op Inc
101 E Gillis St PO Box 677............ Eldorado TX 76936 **800-643-3980** 325-853-2544
Swisher Electric Co-op Inc
401 SW Second St PO Box 67 .... Tulia TX 79088 **800-530-4344** 806-995-3567
Texas Electric Co-ops Inc
1122 Colorado St 24th Fl .... Austin TX 78701 **800-301-2860** 512-454-0311
Tri-County Electric Co-op Inc
600 NW Pkwy .... Azle TX 76020 **800-367-8232** 817-444-3201
Trinity Valley Electric Co-op Inc (TVEC)
1800 E HWY 243 .... Kaufman TX 75142 **800-766-9576** 972-932-2214
United Cooperative Services
3309 N Main St PO Box 16............ Cleburne TX 76033 **800-342-6239** 817-556-4000
Wharton County Electric Co-op Inc (WCEC)
1815 E Jackson St .... El Campo TX 77437 **800-460-6271** 979-543-6271
Wise Electric Co-op Inc
1900 N Trinity St .... Decatur TX 76234 **888-627-9326** 940-627-2167
Wood County Electric Co-op Inc
501 S Main St .... Quitman TX 75783 **800-762-2203** 903-763-2203

Utah

		Toll-Free	Phone

Dixie Power 71 E Hwy 56 .... Beryl UT 84714 **800-874-0904** 435-439-5311
Garkane Energy Co-op
120 W 300 S PO Box 465................. Loa UT 84747 **800-747-5403**

Vermont

		Toll-Free	Phone

Vermont Electric Co-op Inc
42 Wescom Rd .... Johnson VT 05656 **800-832-2667** 802-635-2331
Washington Electric Co-op
40 Church St .... East Montpelier VT 05651 **800-932-5245** 802-223-5245

Virginia

		Toll-Free	Phone

BARC Electric Co-op
84 High St PO Box 264............... Millboro VA 24460 **800-846-2272**
Central Virginia Electric Co-op
800 Co-op Way PO Box 247............. Lovingston VA 22949 **800-367-2832** 434-263-8336
Community Electric Co-op
52 W Windsor Blvd .... Windsor VA 23487 **855-700-2667** 757-242-6181
Craig-Botetourt Electric Cooperative
26198 Craigs Creek Rd PO Box 265.... New Castle VA 24127 **800-760-2232** 540-864-5121
Mecklenburg Electric Co-op
11633 Hwy Ninety Two .... Chase City VA 23924 **800-989-4161** 434-372-6100
Northern Neck Electric Co-op Inc
85 St Johns St PO Box 288 .... Warsaw VA 22572 **800-243-2860** 804-333-3621
Northern Virginia Electric Co-op
PO Box 2710 .... Manassas VA 20108 **888-335-0500** 703-335-0500
Southside Electric Co-op Inc
2000 W Virgina Ave .... Crewe VA 23930 **800-552-2118** 434-645-7721

Washington

		Toll-Free	Phone

Benton Rural Electric Assn (BREA)
402 Seventh St PO Box 1150 .... Prosser WA 99350 **800-221-6987** 509-786-2913
Big Bend Electric Co-op
1373 N Hwy 261 .... Ritzville WA 99169 **866-844-2363** 509-659-1700
Columbia Rural Electric Assn Inc
115 E Main St .... Dayton WA 99328 **800-642-1231** 509-382-2578
Elmhurst Mutual Power & Light Co
120 132nd St S .... Tacoma WA 98444 **855-841-2178** 253-531-4646
Inland Power & Light Company Inc
10110 W Hallett Rd .... Spokane WA 99224 **800-747-7151** 509-747-7151
Peninsula Light Co
13315 Goodnough Dr NW .... Gig Harbor WA 98332 **888-809-8021** 253-857-5950
Tanner Electric Co
45710 SE North Bend Way .... North Bend WA 98045 **800-472-0208** 425-888-0623

Wisconsin

		Toll-Free	Phone

Adams-Columbia Electric Co-op
401 E Lake St .... Friendship WI 53934 **800-831-8629**
Barron Electric Co-op
1434 State Hwy 25 N .... Barron WI 54812 **800-322-1008** 715-537-3171
Bayfield Electric Co-op Inc
68460 District St .... Iron River WI 54847 **800-278-0166** 715-372-4287
Chippewa Valley Electric Co-op
317 S Eigth St .... Cornell WI 54732 **800-300-6800** 715-239-6800
Clark Electric Co-op
124 N Main St PO Box 190........... Greenwood WI 54437 **800-272-6188** 800-927-5707

				Toll-Free	Phone

Dunn Energy Co-op
PO Box 220 . . . . Menomonie WI 54751 **800-924-0630** 715-232-6240

Jackson Electric Co-op
N6868 County Rd F
PO Box 546. . . . . Black River Falls WI 54615 **800-370-4607** 715-284-5385

Jump River Electric Co-op
PO Box 99 . . . . Ladysmith WI 54848 **866-273-5111** 715-532-5524

Oakdale Electric Co-op
PO Box 128 . . . . Oakdale WI 54649 **800-241-2468** 608-372-4131

Oconto Electric Co-op
PO Box 168 . . . . Oconto Falls WI 54154 **800-472-8410** 920-846-2816

Pierce Pepin Co-op Services
W7725 US Hwy 10 PO Box 420 . . . . Ellsworth WI 54011 **800-924-2133** 715-273-4355

Polk-Burnett Electric Co-op (PBEC)
1001 State Rd 35 . . . . Centuria WI 54824 **800-421-0283** 715-646-2191

Price Electric Co-op
508 N Lake Ave PO Box 110. . . . . Phillips WI 54555 **800-884-0881** 715-339-2155

Riverland Energy Co-op
N28988 State Rd 93 PO Box 277 . . . . Arcadia WI 54612 **800-411-9115** 608-323-3381

Saint Croix Electric Cooperative
1925 Ridgeway St PO Box 160 . . . . Hammond WI 54015 **800-924-3407** 715-796-7000

Scenic Rivers Energy Co-op
231 N Sheridan St . . . . Lancaster WI 53813 **800-236-2141** 608-723-2121

Taylor Electric Co-op
N1831 State Hwy 13 . . . . Medford WI 54451 **800-862-2407** 715-678-2411

Vernon Electric Co-op
110 Saugstad Rd . . . . Westby WI 54667 **800-447-5051** 608-634-3121

Wyoming

				Toll-Free	Phone

Big Horn Rural Electric Co-op
208 S Fifth St PO Box 270 . . . . Basin WY 82410 **800-564-2419** 307-568-2419

Bridger Valley Extreme Access
40014 Business Loop 1-80
PO Box 399. . . . . Mountain View WY 82939 **800-276-3481** 307-786-2800

Carbon Power & Light Inc
100 E Willow Ave PO Box 579 . . . . Saratoga WY 82331 **800-359-0249** 307-326-5206

High Plains Power Inc
1775 E Monroe PO Box 713. . . . . Riverton WY 82501 **800-445-0613** 307-856-9426

High West Energy Inc (HWE)
6270 County Rd 212 . . . . Pine Bluffs WY 82082 **888-834-1657** 307-245-3261

Lower Valley Energy
236 N Washington PO Box 188 . . . . Afton WY 83110 **800-882-5875** 307-885-3175

Powder River Energy Corp (PRE)
221 Main St PO Box 930 . . . . Sundance WY 82729 **800-442-3630**

Wheatland Rural Electric Assn
2154 S St PO Box 1209 . . . . Wheatland WY 82201 **800-344-3351** 307-322-2125

Wyrulec Co
3978 US Hwy 26/85 . . . . Torrington WY 82240 **800-628-5266** 307-837-2225

246 ELECTRICAL & ELECTRONIC EQUIPMENT & PARTS - WHOL

				Toll-Free	Phone

ACF Components & Fasteners Inc
31012 Huntwood Ave . . . . Hayward CA 94544 **800-227-2901*** 510-487-2100
*Cust Svc

Actify LLC
7635 Interactive Way Ste 200 . . . . Indianapolis IN 46278 **800-467-0830**

Adi American Distributors Inc
2 Emery Ave . . . . Randolph NJ 07869 **800-877-0510** 973-328-1181

Advanced MP Technology
1010 Calle Sombra . . . . San Clemente CA 92673 **800-492-3113** 949-492-3113

AE Petsche Company Inc
1501 Nolan Ryan Expy . . . . Arlington TX 76011 **844-237-7600**

Aesco Electronics Inc
2230 Picton Pkwy . . . . Akron OH 44312 **877-442-6987** 330-245-2630

Algo Communication Products Ltd
4500 Beedie St . . . . Burnaby BC V5J5L2 **800-226-7722** 604-438-3333

Allied Electronics Inc
7151 Jack Newell Blvd S . . . . Fort Worth TX 76118 **866-433-5722** 817-595-3500

Allstar Magnetics LLC
6205 NE 63rd St . . . . Vancouver WA 98661 **800-356-5977** 360-693-0213

America II Electronics Inc
2600 118th Ave N . . . . Saint Petersburg FL 33716 **800-767-2637** 727-573-0900

Argo International Corp
71 Veronica Ave Unit 1 . . . . Somerset NJ 08873 **866-289-2746** 732-979-2996

Audio-technica Us Inc
1221 Commerce Dr . . . . Stow OH 44224 **800-667-3745** 330-686-2600

Avnet Inc 2211 S 47th St . . . . Phoenix AZ 85034 **888-822-8638** 480-643-2000
NASDAQ: AVT

B&D Industries Inc
9720 Bell Ave SE . . . . Albuquerque NM 87123 **866-315-8349** 505-299-4464

Bearcom Inc
4009 Distribution Dr Ste 200 . . . . Garland TX 75041 **800-527-1670***
*Sales

Becker Electric Supply Inc
1341 E Fourth St . . . . Dayton OH 45402 **800-762-9515** 937-226-1341

Beyond Components
5 Carl Thompson Rd . . . . Westford MA 01886 **800-971-4242**

Billows Electric Supply
9100 State Rd . . . . Philadelphia PA 19136 **866-398-1162** 215-332-9700

Bisco Industries Inc
1500 N Lakeview Ave . . . . Anaheim CA 92807 **800-323-1232**

Border States Electric Supply
105 25th St N . . . . Fargo ND 58102 **800-800-0199** 701-293-5834

Broadfield Distributing Inc
67A Glen Cove Ave . . . . Glen Cove NY 11542 **800-634-5178** 516-676-2378

Buckles-Smith
801 Savaker Ave . . . . San Jose CA 95126 **800-833-7362**

Butler Supply Inc
965 Horan Dr . . . . St.Louis MO 63026 **800-850-9949** 636-349-9000

Cadex Electronics Inc
22000 Fraserwood Way . . . . Richmond BC V6W1J6 **800-565-5228** 604-231-7777

California Eastern Laboratories Inc (CEL)
4590 Patrick Henry Dr . . . . Santa Clara CA 95054 **800-390-3232** 408-919-2500

				Toll-Free	Phone

Carlton Bates Co
3600 W 69th St . . . . Little Rock AR 72209 **866-600-6040** 501-562-9100

Cell-Tel Government Systems Inc
8226-B Phillips Hwy Ste 290 . . . . Jacksonville FL 32256 **800-737-7545** 904-363-1111

Century Fasteners Corp
50-20 Ireland St . . . . Elmhurst NY 11373 **800-221-0769** 718-446-5000

Cms Communications Inc
722 Goddard Ave . . . . Chesterfield MO 63005 **800-755-9169**

Codale Electric Supply Inc
5225 West 2400 South
PO Box 702070. . . . . Salt Lake City UT 84120 **800-300-6634** 801-975-7300

Comtel Inc
39810 Grand River Ave Ste 180 . . . . Novi MI 48375 **800-335-2505** 248-888-4730

Corporate Telephone Services
184 W Second St . . . . Boston MA 02127 **800-274-1211** 617-625-1200

Cortelco Inc 1703 Sawyer Rd . . . . Corinth MS 38834 **800-288-3132** 662-287-5281

Crum Electric Supply Co
1165 W English Ave . . . . Casper WY 82601 **800-726-2239** 307-266-1278

Dakota Supply Group (DSG)
2601 Third Ave N . . . . Fargo ND 58102 **800-437-4702** 701-237-9440

Dee Electronics Inc
2500 16th Ave SW . . . . Cedar Rapids IA 52404 **800-747-3331** 319-365-7551

Digi-Key Corp
701 Brooks Ave S . . . . Thief River Falls MN 56701 **800-344-4539** 218-681-6674

Diversified Electronics Co Inc
PO Box 566 . . . . Forest Park GA 30298 **800-646-7278** 404-361-4840

Dominion Electric Supply Company Inc
5053 Lee Hwy . . . . Arlington VA 22207 **800-525-5006** 703-536-4400

Dow Electronics Inc
8603 E Adamo Dr . . . . Tampa FL 33619 **800-627-2900** 813-626-5195

E Sam Jones Distributor Inc
4898 S Atlanta Rd . . . . Atlanta GA 30339 **800-624-9849** 404-351-3250

Electric Supply & Equipment Co
1812 E Wendover Ave . . . . Greensboro NC 27405 **800-632-0268** 336-272-4123

Electric Supply Inc
4407 N Manhattan Ave . . . . Tampa FL 33614 **800-678-1894** 813-872-1894

Electro Brand Inc
1127 S Mannheim Rd Ste 305 . . . . Westchester IL 60154 **800-982-3954**

Electro-Matic Products Inc
23409 Industrial Pk Ct . . . . Farmington Hills MI 48335 **888-879-1088** 248-478-1182

ElectroTech Inc
7101 Madison Ave W . . . . Minneapolis MN 55427 **800-544-4288**

Elliott Electric Supply Co
2526 N Stallings Dr PO Box 630610 . . . . Nacogdoches TX 75963 **877-777-0242** 936-569-1184

Evans Enterprises Inc
1536 S Western Ave . . . . Oklahoma City OK 73109 **800-423-8267** 405-631-1344

Ewing-Foley Inc
10061 Bubb Rd Ste 1000 . . . . Cupertino CA 95014 **800-399-3319** 408-342-1200

Facility Solutions Group (FSG)
4401 Westgate Blvd Ste 310 . . . . Austin TX 78745 **800-854-6465** 512-440-7985

FD Lawrence Electric Co
3450 Beekman St . . . . Cincinnati OH 45223 **800-582-4490*** 513-542-1100
*Cust Svc

Fiber Instruments Sales Inc
161 Clear Rd . . . . Oriskany NY 13424 **800-500-0347*** 315-736-2206
*Sales

Fiber Optic Center New Trust
23 Centre St . . . . New Bedford MA 02740 **800-473-4237** 508-992-6464

Fidelitone Inc
1260 Karl Ct . . . . Wauconda IL 60084 **800-475-0917**

Flame Enterprises Inc
21500 Gledhill St . . . . Chatsworth CA 91311 **800-854-2255** 818-700-2905

Friedman Electric
1321 Wyoming Ave . . . . Exeter PA 18643 **800-545-5517** 570-654-3371

Fromm Electric Supply
2101 Centre Ave PO Box 15147 . . . . Reading PA 19605 **800-360-4441** 610-374-4441

FSG Lighting
4401 Westgate Blvd Ste 310 . . . . Austin TX 78745 **800-854-6465** 512-440-7985

Future Electronics
237 Hymus Blvd . . . . Pointe-Claire QC H9R5C7 **800-675-1619*** 514-694-7710
*Cust Svc

Futurecom Systems Group Inc
3277 Langstaff Rd . . . . Concord ON L4K5P8 **800-701-9180** 905-660-5548

Galco Industrial Electronics Inc
26010 Pinehurst Dr . . . . Madison Heights MI 48071 **888-783-4611** 248-542-9090

GBH Communications Inc
1309 S Myrtle Ave . . . . Monrovia CA 91016 **800-222-5424**

George R Peters Assoc Inc
PO Box 850 . . . . Troy MI 48099 **800-929-5972** 248-524-2211

Graybar Co Inc
34 N Meramec Ave . . . . Saint Louis MO 63105 **800-472-9227** 314-573-9200

Hammond Electronics Inc
1230 W Central Blvd . . . . Orlando FL 32805 **800-929-3672*** 407-849-6060
*Sales

Hartford Electric Supply Co (HESCO)
30 Inwood Rd Ste 1 . . . . Rocky Hill CT 06067 **800-969-5444** 860-236-6363

Headsets Direct Inc
1454 W Gurley St Ste A . . . . Prescott AZ 86305 **800-914-7996** 928-777-9100

Heartland Label Printers Inc
1700 Stephen St . . . . Little Chute WI 54140 **800-236-7914***
*General

Heilind Electronics Inc
58 Jonspin Rd . . . . Wilmington MA 01887 **800-400-7041** 978-657-4870

Hite Co 3101 Beale Ave . . . . Altoona PA 16601 **800-252-3598** 814-944-6121

HITEC Group Ltd
1743 Quincy Ave Unit #155 . . . . Naperville IL 60540 **800-288-8303**

HL Dalis Inc
35-35 24th St . . . . Long Island NY 11106 **800-453-2547** 718-361-1100

Honeywell International Inc
115 Tabor Rd . . . . Morris Plains NJ 07950 **877-841-2840** 480-353-3020

Hotan Corp
751 N Canyons Pkwy . . . . Livermore CA 94551 **800-656-1888** 925-290-1000

Houston Wire & Cable Co (HWC)
10201 N Loop E . . . . Houston TX 77029 **800-468-9473** 713-609-2100

Hutton Communications Inc
2520 Marsh Ln . . . . Carrollton TX 75006 **800-725-5264** 972-417-0100

IBS Electronics Inc
Lake Center Dr . . . . Santa Ana CA 92704 **800-527-2888** 714-751-6633

Company / Address	City	State	ZIP	Toll-Free	Phone
Industrial Electric Wire & Cable Inc (IEWC) 5001 S Towne Dr	New Berlin	WI	53151	**800-344-2323**	877-613-4392
Insulectro 20362 Windrow Dr	Lake Forest	CA	92630	**800-279-7686**	949-587-3200
Interstate Connecting Components Inc 120 Mt Holly By Pass	Lumberton	NJ	08048	**800-422-3911**	
Interstate Electrical Supply Inc 2300 Second Ave	Columbus	GA	31901	**800-903-4409**	706-324-1000
Jaco Electronics Inc 415 Oser Ave *OTC: JACO*	Hauppauge	NY	11788	**877-373-5226**	
Jasco Products Co 10 E Memorial Rd, Bldg B	Oklahoma City	OK	73114	**800-654-8483**	405-752-0710
Joliet Avionics Inc 43w730 US Hwy 30	Sugar Grove	IL	60554	**800-323-5966**	630-584-3200
Kehoe Component Sales Inc 34 Foley Dr	Sodus	NY	14551	**800-228-7223**	
Kendall Electric Inc 131 Grand Trunk Ave	Battle Creek	MI	49037	**800-632-5422**	269-965-6897
Kiddesigns LLC 1299 Main St	Rahway	NJ	07065	**800-777-5206**	732-382-1760
Kikusui America Inc 1633 Bayshore Hwy Ste 331	Burlingame	CA	94010	**877-876-2807**	650-259-5900
Kirby Risk Corp 1815 Sagamore Pkwy N PO Box 5089	Lafayette	IN	47904	**877-641-0929**	765-448-4567
KJB Security Products Inc 841-B Fessiers Pkwy	Nashville	TN	37210	**800-590-4272**	615-620-1370
Leff Electric 4700 Spring Rd	Cleveland	OH	44131	**800-686-5333**	216-432-3000
Lester Sales Co Inc 4312 W Minnesota St	Indianapolis	IN	46241	**888-963-6270**	317-244-7811
Lewis Electric Supply Company Inc 1306 Second St PO Box 2237	Muscle Shoals	AL	35662	**800-239-0681**	256-383-0681
Lowe Electric Supply Co 1525 Forsyth St PO Box 4767	Macon	GA	31208	**800-868-8661**	
Loyd's Electric Supply Inc (LES) 838 Stonetree Dr	Branson	MO	65616	**800-492-4030**	417-334-2171
Macnica Americas Inc 380 Stevens Ave Ste 206	Solana Beach	CA	92075	**888-399-4937**	858-771-0846
Maltby Electric Supply Company Inc 336 Seventh St	San Francisco	CA	94103	**800-339-0668**	415-863-5000
Marsh Electronics Inc 1563 S 101st St *Cust Svc	Milwaukee	WI	53214	**800-926-2774***	414-475-6000
Maurice Electrical Supply Co 6500A Seriff Rd	Landover	MD	20785	**866-913-0922**	301-333-5990
Mayer Electric Supply Co 3405 Fourth Ave S	Birmingham	AL	35222	**866-637-1255**	205-583-3500
Metro Wire & Cable Co 6636 Metropolitan Pkwy	Sterling Heights	MI	48312	**800-633-1432**	586-264-3050
MicroRam Electronics Inc 222 Dunbar Ct	Oldsmar	FL	34677	**800-642-7671**	813-854-5500
Mobile Communication of Gwinnett Inc 2241 Tucker Industrial Rd	Tucker	GA	30084	**800-749-7170**	770-963-3748
Mouser Electronics Corp 1000 N Main St	Mansfield	TX	76063	**800-346-6873**	817-804-3888
Murdock Industrial Supply 1111 E 1st	Wichita	KS	67214	**800-876-6867**	316-262-4476
Music People Inc 154 Woodlawn Rd Ste C	Berlin	CT	06037	**800-289-8889**	
NAC Group Inc 1790 Commerce Ave N	St Petersburg	FL	33716	**866-651-2901**	727-828-0187
NACB Group Corp 10 Starwood Dr	Hampstead	NH	03841	**800-370-2737**	603-329-4551
Nedco Electronics 594 American Way	Payson	UT	84651	**800-605-2323**	801-465-1790
Nelson Electric Supply Co Inc 926 State St	Racine	WI	53404	**800-806-3576**	262-635-5050
NEP Electronics Inc 805 Mittel Dr	Wood Dale	IL	60191	**800-284-7470**	630-595-8500
Nora Lighting Inc 6505 Gayhart St	Commerce	CA	90040	**800-686-6672**	323-767-2600
Northern 3625 Cincinnati Ave	Rocklin	CA	95765	**855-388-7422**	916-543-4000
Nu Horizons Electronics Corp 70 Maxess Rd	Melville	NY	11747	**855-326-4757**	631-396-5000
Nu-Lite Electrical Wholesalers 850 Edwards Ave	Harahan	LA	70123	**800-256-1603**	504-733-3300
Omni Cable Corp 2 Hagerty Blvd	West Chester	PA	19382	**888-292-6664**	610-701-0100
One Link Wireless 7321 Broadway Ext	Oklahoma City	OK	73116	**800-259-2929**	405-840-2345
Paige Electric Company LP 1160 Springfield Rd	Union	NJ	07083	**800-327-2443**	908-687-2722
Peerless Electronics Inc 700 Hicksville Rd	Bethpage	NY	11714	**800-285-2121**	516-594-3500
PEI-Genesis 2180 Hornig Rd	Philadelphia	PA	19116	**800-675-1214**	215-673-0400
PFT Alexander Inc 3250 E Grant St	Signal Hill	CA	90755	**800-696-1331**	562-595-1741
Platt Electric Supply 10605 SW Allen Blvd	Beaverton	OR	97005	**800-257-5288**	503-641-6121
Powell Electronics Inc 200 Commodore Dr	Swedesboro	NJ	08085	**800-235-7880**	856-241-8000
Power & Telephone Supply Company Inc 2673 Yale Ave *Cust Svc	Memphis	TN	38112	**800-238-7514***	901-866-3300
Priority Wire & Cable Inc PO Box 398 *General	North Little Rock	AR	72115	**800-945-5542***	501-372-5444
Professional Electric Products Co (PEPCO) 33210 Lakeland Blvd	Eastlake	OH	44095	**800-872-7000**	440-946-3790
Projections Unlimited Inc 15311 Varrenca Pkwy *Cust Svc	Irvine	CA	92618	**800-551-4405***	714-544-2700
QED Inc 1661 W Third Ave	Denver	CO	80223	**800-700-5011**	303-825-5011
Radar Inc 22214 20TH Ave SE Ste 101	Bothell	WA	98021	**800-282-2524**	

Company / Address	City	State	ZIP	Toll-Free	Phone
Radiophone Engineering Inc 534 W Walnut St	Springfield	MO	65806	**800-369-2929**	417-862-6653
Ralph Pill Electrical Supply Co 50 Von Hillern St	Boston	MA	02125	**800-897-1769**	617-265-8800
Rawson Inc 2010 McAllister	Houston	TX	77092	**800-779-1414**	
Reagan Wireless Corp 720 S Powerline Rd Ste D	Deerfield Beach	FL	33442	**877-724-3266**	954-596-2355
Regency Lighting Co 9261 Jordan Ave	Chatsworth	CA	91311	**800-284-2024**	
Renco Electronics Inc 595 International Pl	Rockledge	FL	32955	**800-645-5828**	321-637-1000
Rexel Inc 14951 Dallas Pkwy PO Box 9085	Dallas	TX	75254	**888-739-3577**	972-387-3600
Richardson Electronics Ltd 40 W 267 Keslinger Rd PO Box 393 *NASDAQ: RELL* ■ *Sales	LaFox	IL	60147	**800-348-5580***	630-208-2200
RS Electronics Inc 34443 Schoolcraft Rd	Livonia	MI	48150	**866-600-6040**	734-525-1155
Rumsey Electric Co 15 Colwell Ln	Conshohocken	PA	19428	**800-462-2402**	610-832-9000
S K C Communication Products Inc 8320 Hedge Ln Terr	Shawnee Mission	KS	66227	**800-882-7779**	913-422-4222
Sager Electronics Inc 19 Lorena Dr	Middleboro	MA	02346	**800-724-3780**	508-947-8888
Sandusky Electric Inc 1513 Sycamore Line	Sandusky	OH	44870	**800-356-1243**	419-625-4915
Schuster Electronics Inc 11320 Grooms Rd	Cincinnati	OH	45242	**800-521-1358**	
Scott Electric 1000 S Main St PO Box S	Greensburg	PA	15601	**800-442-8045**	724-834-4321
Sennheiser Electronics Corp 1 Enterprise Dr	Old Lyme	CT	06371	**877-736-6434**	860-434-9190
Service Electric Supply Inc 15424 Oakwood Dr	Romulus	MI	48174	**800-426-7575**	734-229-9100
Shepherd Electric Supply 7401 Pulaski Hwy *Sales	Baltimore	MD	21237	**800-253-1777***	410-866-6000
Sierra Electronics 690 E Glendale Ave Ste 9B PO Box 1545	Sparks	NV	89432	**800-874-7515**	775-359-1121
Singing Machine Company Inc, The 6601 Lyons Rd Bldg A-7 *OTC: SMDM*	Coconut Creek	FL	33073	**866-670-6888**	954-596-1000
Skywalker AV Supply 1760 West Terra Ln	O'Fallon	MO	63366	**800-844-9555**	636-272-8025
Smith 5306 Hollister Rd	Houston	TX	77040	**800-468-7866**	713-430-3000
Sommer Electric Corp 818 Third St NE	Canton	OH	44704	**800-766-6373**	
South Western Communications Inc 4871 Rosebud Ln	Newburgh	IN	47630	**800-903-8432**	812-477-6495
Southern Controls Inc 3511 Wetumpka Hwy	Montgomery	AL	36110	**800-392-5770**	
Spectra Integrated Systems Inc 8100 Arrowridge Blvd	Charlotte	NC	28273	**800-443-7561**	704-525-7099
Spectra Merchandising International Inc 4230 N Normandy Ave	Chicago	IL	60634	**800-777-5331**	773-202-8408
Springfield Electric Supply Co 700 N Ninth St	Springfield	IL	62702	**800-747-2101**	217-788-2100
Standard Electric Supply Co 222 N Emmber Ln PO Box 651	Milwaukee	WI	53233	**800-776-8222**	414-272-8100
Stanion Wholesale Electric Co 812 S Main St PO Box F	Pratt	KS	67124	**866-782-6466**	620-672-5678
State Electric Supply Company Inc 2010 Second Ave *Cust Svc	Huntington	WV	25703	**800-624-3417***	304-523-7491
Steiner Electric Co 1250 Touhy Ave	Elk Grove Village	IL	60007	**800-783-4637**	847-228-0400
Steven Engineering Inc 230 Ryan Way	South San Francisco	CA	94080	**800-258-9200**	650-588-9200
Storage Battery Systems Inc (SBS) N56 W16665 Ridgewood Dr	Menomonee Falls	WI	53051	**800-554-2243**	262-703-5800
Summit Electric Supply Co 2900 Stanford NE	Albuquerque	NM	87107	**800-824-4400**	505-346-9000
SVT 7699 Lochlin Dr	Brighton	MI	48116	**888-697-8832**	800-521-4188
Tacoma Electric Supply Inc 1311 S Tacoma Way	Tacoma	WA	98409	**800-422-0540**	253-475-0540
Taitron Components Inc 28040 W Harrison Pkwy *NASDAQ: TAIT*	Valencia	CA	91355	**800-247-2232**	661-257-6060
TeL Systems 7235 Jackson Rd	Ann Arbor	MI	48103	**800-686-7235**	734-761-4506
Telcobuy com L L C 60 Weldon Pkwy	St. Louis	MO	63043	**877-350-0191**	
Telesource Services LLC 1450 Highwood E	Pontiac	MI	48340	**800-525-4300**	248-335-3000
Terry-Durin Co 409 Seventh Ave SE	Cedar Rapids	IA	52401	**800-332-8114**	319-364-4106
TESSCO Technologies Inc 11126 McCormick Rd *NASDAQ: TESS*	Hunt Valley	MD	21031	**800-472-7373**	410-229-1000
Toa Canada Corp 6150 Kennedy Rd Unit 3	Mississauga	ON	L5T2J4	**800-263-7639**	905-564-3570
Tri-Ed Distribution Inc 135 Crossways Pk Dr W	Woodbury	NY	11797	**888-874-3336**	516-941-2800
Tri-State Armature & Electrical Works Inc 330 GE Patterson Ave	Memphis	TN	38126	**800-238-7654**	901-527-8412
Tri-State Utility Products Inc 1030 Atlanta Industrial Dr	Marietta	GA	30066	**800-282-7985**	770-427-3119
TTI Inc 2441 NE Pkwy *Sales	Fort Worth	TX	76106	**800-225-5884***	817-740-9000
Unique Communications Inc 3650 Coral Ridge Dr	Coral Springs	FL	33065	**800-881-8182**	954-735-4002
United Electrical Sales Ltd 4496 SW 36th St	Orlando	FL	32811	**800-432-5126**	407-246-1992
Universal Remote Control Inc 500 Mamaroneck Ave	Harrison	NY	10528	**800-901-0800**	
Valley Electric Supply Corp 1361 N State Rd PO Box 724	Vincennes	IN	47591	**800-825-7877**	812-882-7860

				Toll-Free	Phone
Van Meter Industrial Inc 850 32nd Ave SW	Cedar Rapids	IA	52404	**800-247-1410**	
Venkel Ltd 5900 Shepherd Mountain Cove	Austin	TX	78730	**800-950-8365**	512-794-0081
Viking Electric Supply Inc 451 Industrial Blvd W	Minneapolis	MN	55413	**800-435-3345**	612-627-1300
Virginia West Electric Supply Co (WVES) 250 12-th St W	Huntington	WV	25704	**800-624-3433**	304-525-0361
Voss Lighting PO Box 22159	Lincoln	NE	68542	**866-292-0529**	402-328-2281
Vsa Inc 6929 Seward Ave	Lincoln	NE	68507	**800-888-2140**	402-467-3668
Vyrian Inc 4660 Sweetwater Blvd Ste 200	Sugar Land	TX	77479	**866-874-0598**	
Wabash Electric Supply Inc 1400 S Wabash St	Wabash	IN	46992	**800-552-7777**	260-563-4146
Walters Wholesale Electric Co 2825 Temple Ave *Support	Signal Hill	CA	90755	**833-993-3266***	562-988-3100
Werner Electric Supply Co 2341 Industrial Dr	Neenah	WI	54956	**800-236-5026**	920-729-4500
Wes-Garde Components Group Inc 100 Shield St	West Hartford	CT	06110	**800-554-8866**	860-527-7705
West-Lite Supply Company Inc 12951 166th St	Cerritos	CA	90703	**800-660-6678**	562-802-0224
Whitlock Group 12820 W Creekk Pkwy	Richmond	VA	23238	**800-726-9843**	804-273-9100
Wieland Electric Inc (WEI) 49 International Rd	Burgaw	NC	28425	**800-943-5263**	910-259-5050
Williams Supply Inc 210 Seventh St	Roanoke	VA	24016	**800-533-6969**	540-343-9333
Wiremasters Inc 1788 N Pt Rd	Columbia	TN	38401	**800-635-5342**	615-791-0281
World Micro Components Inc 205 Hembree Park Dr Ste 105	Roswell	GA	30076	**800-400-5026**	770-698-1900
WW Grainger Inc 100 Grainger Pkwy NYSE: GWW	Lake Forest	IL	60045	**888-361-8649**	847-535-1000
XP Power 990 Benicia Ave	Sunnyvale	CA	94085	**800-253-0490**	408-732-7777
Yucca Telecom 201 W Second St	Portales	NM	88130	**866-239-6858**	575-226-2255
Zack Electronics Inc 1075 Hamilton Rd	Duarte	CA	91010	**800-466-0449**	626-303-0655

247 ELECTRICAL EQUIPMENT FOR INTERNAL COMBUSTION ENGINES

SEE ALSO Motors (Electric) & Generators ; Automotive Parts & Supplies - Mfr

				Toll-Free	Phone
Allied Toyotalift 1640 Island Home Ave	Knoxville	TN	37920	**866-538-0667**	865-573-0995
American Electronic Components 1101 Lafayette St	Elkhart	IN	46516	**888-847-6552**	574-295-6330
Camco Manufacturing Inc 121 Landmark Dr	Greensboro	NC	27409	**800-334-2004**	
CE Niehoff & Co 2021 Lee St *Tech Supp	Evanston	IL	60202	**800-643-4633***	847-866-6030
Champion Technologies Inc 845 Mckinley St	Eugene	OR	97402	**800-547-6180**	
Diesel Injection Service Company Inc 4710 Allmond Ave	Louisville	KY	40209	**877-361-2531**	
Edge Products 1080 S Depot Dr	Ogden	UT	84404	**888-360-3343**	801-476-3343
ETCO Inc Automotive Products Div 3004 62nd Ave E	Bradenton	FL	34203	**800-689-3826**	941-756-8426
Flight Systems Inc 505 Fishing Creek Rd	Lewisberry	PA	17339	**800-403-3728**	717-932-9900
Gits Manufacturing Co 4601 121st St	Urbandale	IA	50323	**800-323-3238**	
Goodall Manufacturing Co 7558 Washington Ave S	Eden Prairie	MN	55344	**800-328-7730**	952-941-6666
Ignition Systems & Controls LP 6300 W Hwy 80	Midland	TX	79706	**800-777-5559**	432-697-6472
Kelly Aerospace 1404 E S Blvd	Montgomery	AL	36116	**888-461-6077**	334-286-8551
Motorcar Parts & Accessories 2929 California St	Torrance	CA	90503	**800-890-9988**	310-212-7910
NGK Spark Plugs Inc 46929 Magellan	Wixom	MI	48393	**877-473-6767**	248-926-6900
NVT Phybridge 3495 Laird Rd Ste 12	Mississauga	ON	L5L5S5	**888-901-3633**	905-901-3633
Precision Parts & Remanufacturing Co 4411 SW 19th St	Oklahoma City	OK	73108	**800-654-3846**	405-681-2592
Prestolite Wire Corp 200 Galleria Officentre Ste 212	Southfield	MI	48034	**800-498-3132**	248-355-4422
Reviva Inc 5130 Main St NE	Fridley	MN	55421	**877-357-7634**	763-535-8900
Standard Motor Products Inc 37-18 Northern Blvd NYSE: SMP	Long Island	NY	11101	**800-895-1085**	718-392-0200
Transpo Electronics Inc 2150 Brengle Ave	Orlando	FL	32808	**800-327-6903**	
United Equipment Accessories Inc 2103 E Bremer Ave Hwy	Waverly	IA	50677	**800-394-9986**	
Van Bergen & Greener Inc 1818 Madison St	Maywood	IL	60153	**800-621-3889**	708-343-4700

248 ELECTRICAL SIGNALS MEASURING & TESTING INSTRUMENTS

				Toll-Free	Phone
3M Telecommunications Div 6801 River Place Blvd	Austin	TX	78726	**800-426-8688**	
Analog Devices Inc 3 Technology Way NASDAQ: ADI	Norwood	MA	02062	**800-262-5643**	781-329-4700
Anritsu Co 490 Jarvis Dr	Morgan Hill	CA	95037	**800-267-4878**	408-778-2000
Associated Equipment Corp 5043 Farlan Ave	Saint Louis	MO	63115	**800-949-1472**	314-385-5178

				Toll-Free	Phone
Bird Electronic Corp 30303 Aurora Rd	Solon	OH	44139	**866-695-4569**	440-248-1200
Bird Technologies Group Inc 30303 Aurora Rd	Solon	OH	44139	**866-695-4569**	440-248-1200
Communications Manufacturing Co (CMC) 2234 Colby Ave *Orders	Los Angeles	CA	90064	**800-462-5532***	310-828-3200
Curtis Instruments Inc 200 Kisco Ave	Mount Kisco	NY	10549	**800-777-3433**	914-666-2971
CyberOptics Corp 5900 Golden Hills Dr NASDAQ: CYBE ■ *Cust Svc	Minneapolis	MN	55416	**800-746-6315***	763-542-5000
DIT-MCO International Corp 5612 Brighton Terr	Kansas City	MO	64130	**800-821-3487**	816-444-9700
Doble Engineering Co Inc 85 Walnut St	Watertown	MA	02472	**888-443-6253**	617-926-4900
Dranetz-BMI 1000 New Durham Rd	Edison	NJ	08818	**800-372-6832**	732-287-3680
EXFO Inc 400 Godin Ave NASDAQ: EXFO	Quebec	QC	G1M2K2	**800-663-3936**	418-683-0211
Fluke Biomedical 6920 Seaway Blvd	Everett	WA	98203	**800-443-5853**	425-446-6945
Fluke Corp 6920 Seaway Blvd	Everett	WA	98203	**877-355-3225**	425-446-6100
Fluke Networks Inc 6920 Seaway Blvd	Everett	WA	98203	**800-283-5853**	425-446-4519
Giga-Tronics Inc 4650 Norris Canyon Rd OTC: GIGA	San Ramon	CA	94583	**800-726-4442**	925-328-4650
Greenlee Textron 1390 Aspen Way	Vista	CA	92081	**800-642-2155**	760-598-8900
Hickok Inc 10514 Dupont Ave OTC: HICKA	Cleveland	OH	44108	**800-342-5080**	216-541-8060
Hughes Corp Weschler Instruments Div 16900 Foltz Pkwy	Cleveland	OH	44149	**800-557-0064**	440-238-2550
ILX Lightwave Corp 31950 E Frontage Rd	Bozeman	MT	59715	**800-459-9459**	
Itron Inc 2111 N Molter Rd NASDAQ: ITRI	Liberty Lake	WA	99019	**800-635-5461**	509-924-9900
Ixia 26601 W Agoura Rd NASDAQ: XXIA	Calabasas	CA	91302	**877-367-4942**	818-871-1800
KLA-Tencor Corp 1 Technology Dr NASDAQ: KLAC	Milpitas	CA	95035	**800-600-2829**	408-875-3000
Knopp Inc 1307 66th St	Emeryville	CA	94608	**800-227-1848**	510-653-1661
Landis Gyr Inc 2800 Duncan Rd	Lafayette	IN	47904	**888-390-5733**	765-742-1001
LeCroy Corp 700 Chestnut Ridge Rd NASDAQ: LCRY	Chestnut Ridge	NY	10977	**800-553-2769**	845-425-2000
Megger 4271 Bronze Way	Dallas	TX	75237	**800-723-2861**	214-333-3201
Micro Control Co 7956 Main St NE	Minneapolis	MN	55432	**800-328-9923**	763-786-8750
Monroe Electronics Inc 100 Housel Ave	Lyndonville	NY	14098	**800-821-6001**	585-765-2254
National Instruments Corp 11500 N Mopac Expy NASDAQ: NATI ■ *Cust Svc	Austin	TX	78759	**800-433-3488***	512-683-0100
Newport Electronics Inc 2229 S Yale St *Cust Svc	Santa Ana	CA	92704	**800-639-7678***	203-968-7315
PerkinElmer Inc 940 Winter St NYSE: PKI	Waltham	MA	02451	**800-762-4000**	781-663-6050
Radiodetection Corp 154 Portland Rd	Bridgton	ME	04009	**877-247-3797**	207-647-9495
TEGAM Inc 10 Tegam Way	Geneva	OH	44041	**800-666-1010**	440-466-6100
Teradyne Inc Assembly Test Div 600 Riverpark Dr	North Reading	MA	01864	**800-837-2396**	978-370-2700
Trek Inc 11601 Maple Ridge Rd	Medina	NY	14103	**800-367-8735**	585-798-3140
Trilithic Inc 9710 Pk Davis Dr	Indianapolis	IN	46235	**800-344-2412**	317-895-3600
Wilcoxon Research Inc 20511 Seneca Meadows Pkwy	Germantown	MD	20876	**800-945-2696**	301-330-8811
Yokogawa Corp of America 12530 W Airport Blvd	Sugar Land	TX	77478	**800-888-6400**	281-340-3800
Zetec Inc 8226 Bracken Pl SE Ste 100	Snoqualmie	WA	98065	**800-643-1771**	425-974-2700

249 ELECTRICAL SUPPLIES - PORCELAIN

				Toll-Free	Phone
CeramTec North America Corp Technology Pl	Laurens	SC	29360	**800-752-7325**	864-682-3215
CoorsTek Inc 600 Ninth St	Golden	CO	80401	**800-821-6110**	303-278-4000
Fair-Rite Products Corp 1 Commerical Row PO Box J	Wallkill	NY	12589	**888-324-7748**	845-895-2055
International Ceramic Engineering 235 Brooks St	Worcester	MA	01606	**800-779-3321**	508-853-4700
Kyocera Industrial Ceramics Corp 5713 E Fourth Plain Rd	Vancouver	WA	98661	**888-955-0800**	360-696-8950
Medler Eelectric Company Inc 2155 Redman Dr	Alma	MI	48801	**800-229-5740**	
Search Results Saint-Gobain High-Performance Refractories 4702 Rt 982	Latrobe	PA	15650	**800-438-7237**	724-539-6000
Sunbelt Transformer Ltd 1922 S Martin Luther King Jr Dr	Temple	TX	76504	**800-433-3128**	254-771-3777

250 ELECTROMEDICAL & ELECTROTHERAPEUTIC EQUIPMENT

SEE ALSO Medical Instruments & Apparatus - Mfr

				Toll-Free	Phone
ABIOMED Inc 22 Cherry Hill Dr NASDAQ: ABMD	Danvers	MA	01923	**800-422-8666**	978-646-1400

				Toll-Free	Phone
Affymetrix Inc					
3420 Central Expy	Santa Clara	CA	95051	888-362-2447	866-356-0354
NASDAQ: AFFX					
Amedica Corp					
1885 West 2100 South	Salt Lake City	UT	84119	855-839-3500	
Artel 25 Bradley Dr	Westbrook	ME	04092	888-406-3463	207-854-0860
Avancen MOD Corp					
1156 Bowman Rd Ste 200	Mount Pleasant	SC	29464	800-607-1230	
Axiobionics					
6111 Jackson Rd Ste 200	Ann Arbor	MI	48103	800-552-3539	734-327-2946
Beacon Medaes					
1059 Paragon Way	Rock Hill	SC	29730	888-463-3427	803-817-5600
Bio Medical Innovations					
814 Airport Way	Sandpoint	ID	83864	800-201-3958	
Bovie Medical Corp					
5115 Ulmerton Rd	Clearwater	FL	33760	800-537-2790	
NYSE: BVX					
Cardiac Science Corp					
3303 Monte Villa Pkwy	Bothell	WA	98021	800-426-0337*	
*Cust Svc					
CAS Medical Systems Inc					
44 E Industrial Rd	Branford	CT	06405	800-227-4414	203-488-6056
NASDAQ: CASM					
Conmed Corp 525 French Rd	Utica	NY	13502	800-448-6506	315-797-8375
NASDAQ: CNMD					
CVAC Systems Inc					
26820 Hobie Cir Ste B	Murrieta	CA	92562	866-753-2822	951-699-2086
Draeger Medical Inc					
3135 Quarry Rd	Telford	PA	18969	800-437-2437	
Dynatronics Corp					
7030 Pk Centre Dr	Salt Lake City	UT	84121	800-874-6251	
NASDAQ: DYNT					
Eigen					
13366 Grass Vly Ave	Grass Valley	CA	95945	888-924-2020	530-274-1240
Fisher & Paykel Healthcare Inc					
173 Technology Dr Ste 100	Irvine	CA	92618	800-446-3908	949-453-4000
GE Healthcare					
8200 W Tower Ave	Milwaukee	WI	53223	800-558-5102	414-355-5000
GN Hearing					
8001 E Bloomington Fwy	Bloomington	MN	55420	888-735-4327	
HealthTronics Inc					
9825 Spectrum Dr Bldg 3	Austin	TX	78717	888-252-6575	512-328-2892
Inovio Pharmaceuticals Inc					
660 W Germantown Pk Ste 110	Plymouth	PA	19462	877-446-6846	267-440-4200
NASDAQ: INO					
IVY Biomedical Systems Inc					
11 Business Pk Dr	Branford	CT	06405	800-247-4614	203-481-4183
Kelyniam Global Inc					
97 River Rd	Canton	CT	06019	800-280-8192	
LiteCure LLC					
250 Corporate Blvd Ste B	Newark	DE	19702	877-627-3858	
Masimo Corp 40 Parker	Irvine	CA	92618	800-326-4890	949-297-7000
Medical Education Technologies Inc (METI)					
6300 Edgelake Dr	Sarasota	FL	34240	866-462-7920	941-377-5562
Medical Graphics Corp					
350 Oak Grove Pkwy	Saint Paul	MN	55127	800-950-5597	651-484-4874
NASDAQ: ANGN					
Medtronic					
710 Medtronic Pky	Minneapolis	MN	55432	800-633-8766	763-514-4000
Medtronic Inc					
710 Medtronic Pkwy NE	Minneapolis	MN	55432	800-328-2518*	763-514-4000
*NYSE: MDT ■ *Cust Svc*					
Medtronic of Canada Ltd					
99 Hereford St	Brampton	ON	L6Y0R3	800-268-5346	905-826-6020
Meridian Medical Technologies Inc					
6350 Stevens Forest Rd Ste 301	Columbia	MD	21046	800-638-8093	443-259-7800
Misonix Inc					
1938 NEW Hwy	Farmingdale	NY	11735	800-694-9612	631-694-9555
Mortara Instrument Inc					
7865 N 86th St	Milwaukee	WI	53224	800-231-7437	414-354-1600
Natus Medical Inc					
1501 Industrial Rd	San Carlos	CA	94070	800-255-3901	650-802-0400
NASDAQ: BABY					
NeuroMetrix 62 Fourth Ave	Waltham	MA	02451	888-786-7287	781-890-9989
NASDAQ: NURO					
Neuromonics Inc					
PO Box 351886	Westminster	CO	80035	866-606-3876	
Newport Medical Instruments Inc					
1620 Sunflower Ave	Costa Mesa	CA	92626	800-255-6774	714-427-5811
O-two Medical Technologies Inc					
7575 Kimbel St	Mississauga	ON	L5S1C8	800-387-3405	905-677-9410
Oscor Inc					
3816 DeSoto Blvd	Palm Harbor	FL	34683	800-726-7267*	727-937-2511
*Cust Svc					
OSI Systems Inc					
12525 Chadron Ave	Hawthorne	CA	90250	800-579-1639	310-978-0516
NASDAQ: OSIS					
Physio-Control Inc					
11811 Willows Rd NE	Redmond	WA	98052	800-442-1142	425-867-4000
PP Systems International Inc					
110 Haverhill Rd Ste 301	Amesbury	MA	01913	866-211-9346	978-834-0505
Respironics Novametrix LLC					
5 Technology Dr	Wallingford	CT	06492	800-345-6443	724-387-4000
Richard Wolf Medical Instruments Corp					
353 Corporate Woods Pkwy	Vernon Hills	IL	60061	800-323-9653	
Rockwell Medical Inc					
30142 Wixom Rd	Wixom	MI	48393	800-449-3353	248-960-9009
NASDAQ: RMTI					
SensorMedics Corp					
22745 Savi Ranch Pkwy	Yorba Linda	CA	92887	800-231-2466	714-283-2228
Solta Medical Inc					
25881 Industrial Blvd	Hayward	CA	94545	877-782-2286	
SonarMed Inc					
12220 N Meridian St Ste 150	Carmel	IN	46032	866-853-3684	317-489-3161
Spacelabs Health Care					
35301 SE Center St	Snoqualmie	WA	98065	800-522-7025	425-396-3300
Starkey Hearing Trechnologies					
2476 Argentia Rd Ste 301	Mississauga	ON	L5N6M1	888-282-1086	

				Toll-Free	Phone
Thoratec Corp					
6035 Stoneridge Dr	Pleasanton	CA	94588	800-528-2577	925-847-8600
Vasomedical Inc					
180 Linden Ave	Westbury	NY	11590	800-455-3327	516-997-4600
OTC: VASO					
VitaSound Audio Inc					
2880 Zanker Rd Ste 203	San Jose	CA	95134	888-667-7205	
Welch Allyn Inc					
4341 State St Rd	Skaneateles Falls	NY	13153	800-535-6663	
Welch Allyn Monitoring Inc					
8500 SW Creekside Pl	Beaverton	OR	97008	800-289-2500*	503-530-7500
*Cust Svc					
ZOLL Medical Corp					
269 Mill Rd	Chelmsford	MA	01824	800-348-9011	978-421-9655

251   ELECTRONIC BILL PRESENTMENT & PAYMENT SERVICES

SEE ALSO Application Service Providers (ASPs)

				Toll-Free	Phone
Capital Merchant Solutions Inc					
3005 Gill St	Bloomington	IL	61704	877-495-2419	
Corban Onesource					
235 Third St S Ste 300	St Petersburg	FL	33701	844-267-2261	
FIX Flyer LLC					
525 Seventh Ave Ste 812	New York	NY	10018	888-349-3593	
Ifrah Financial Services Inc					
17300 Chenal Pkwy Ste 150	Little Rock	AR	72223	800-954-3724	501-821-7733
Landmark Financial Group LLC					
181 Old Post Rd	Southport	CT	06890	800-437-4214	203-254-8422
Lear Capital Inc					
1990 S Bundy Dr Ste 600	Los Angeles	CA	90025	800-576-9355	
Money Movers Inc					
PO Box 241	Sebastopol	CA	95473	800-861-5029	707-829-5577
RTR Financial Services Inc					
2 Teleport Dr Ste 302	Staten Island	NY	10311	855-399-4787	718-668-2881
Simpay 1210 Northbrook Dr	Trevose	PA	19006	866-253-2227	
US. Bankcard Services Inc					
17171 E Gale Ave Ste 110	City Of Industry	CA	91745	888-888-8872	
USA Technologies Inc					
100 Deerfield Ln Ste 140	Malvern	PA	19355	800-633-0340	
Value Payment Systems LLC					
2207 Crestmoor Rd Ste 200	Nashville	TN	37215	888-877-0450	
Xetus Corp					
1325 Howard Ave Ste 527	Burlingame	CA	94010	877-469-3887	650-237-1225

252   ELECTRONIC COMMUNICATIONS NETWORKS (ECNS)

SEE ALSO Securities Brokers & Dealers ; Securities & Commodities Exchanges

ECNs are computerized trade-matching systems that unite best bid and offer prices and provide anonymity to investors.

				Toll-Free	Phone
Comm-Works Holdings LLC					
1405 Xenium Ln N Ste 120.	Minneapolis	MN	55441	800-853-8090	763-258-5800
Layer 3 Communications LLC					
109 Park of Commerce Dr Ste 1	Savannah	GA	31405	844-352-9373	770-225-5279

253   ELECTRONIC COMPONENTS & ACCESSORIES - MFR

SEE ALSO Printed Circuit Boards ; Semiconductors & Related Devices

				Toll-Free	Phone
3M Electronic Handling & Protection Div					
6801 River Place Blvd	Austin	TX	78726	800-328-1368	
3M Interconnect Solutions Div					
6801 River Place Blvd	Austin	TX	78726	800-225-5373	512-984-1800
Advanced Bionics LLC					
28515 Westinghouse Pl	Valencia	CA	91355	877-829-0026	661-362-1400
Alpha Group, The					
3767 Alpha Way	Bellingham	WA	98226	800-322-5742	360-647-2360
American International Inc					
1040 Avendia Acaso	Camarillo	CA	93012	800-336-6500	805-388-6800
American Power Conversion Corp (APC)					
132 Fairgrounds Rd	West Kingston	RI	02892	800-788-2208*	401-789-5735
*Cust Svc					
Ametek HDR Power Systems Inc					
3563 Interchange Rd	Columbus	OH	43204	888-797-2685	614-308-5500
AMETEK Solidstate Controls					
875 Dearborn Dr	Columbus	OH	43085	800-635-7300	614-846-7500
AMETEKInc 1080 N Crooks	Clawson	MI	48017	800-635-0289	248-435-0700
Amphenol Aerospace					
40-60 Delaware Ave	Sidney	NY	13838	800-678-0141	607-563-5011
Amphenol RF					
4 Old Newtown Rd	Danbury	CT	06810	800-627-7100	203-743-9272
Amphenol Sine Systems					
44724 Morley Dr	Clinton Township	MI	48036	800-394-7732	
Amphenol Spectra-Strip					
720 Sherman Ave	Hamden	CT	06514	800-846-6400	203-281-3200
AmRad Engineering Inc					
32 Hargrove Grade	Palm Coast	FL	32137	800-445-6033	386-445-6000
Anaren Microwave Inc					
6635 Kirkville Rd	East Syracuse	NY	13057	800-544-2414	315-432-8909
NASDAQ: ANEN					
Antec Inc					
47900 Fremont Blvd	Fremont	CA	94538	800-222-6832	510-770-1200
Arradiance Inc					
142 N Rd Ste F-150	Sudbury	MA	01776	800-659-2970	
AudioQuest Inc 2621 White Rd	Irvine	CA	92614	800-747-2770	949-585-0111
AVG Automation					
4140 Utica St	Bettendorf	IA	52722	877-774-3279	
Avionic Instruments Inc					
1414 Randolph Ave	Avenel	NJ	07001	800-468-3571	732-388-3500
Banner Engineering Corp					
9714 Tenth Ave N	Minneapolis	MN	55441	888-373-6767	763-544-3164

				Toll-Free	Phone
BEI Technologies Inc Industrial Encoder Div					
7230 Hollister Ave	Goleta	CA	93117	**800-350-2727***	805-968-0782
*Sales					
Bel Stewart Connector					
11118 Susquehanna Trl S	Glen Rock	PA	17327	**800-323-9612**	717-235-7512
Bergquist Co					
18930 W 78th St	Chanhassen	MN	55317	**800-347-4572**	952-835-2322
C & D Technologies Inc					
1400 Union Meeting Rd PO Box 3053	Blue Bell	PA	19422	**800-543-8630**	215-619-2700
Califone International Inc					
9135 Alabama Ave Ste B	Chatsworth	CA	91311	**800-722-0500**	818-407-2400
Camesa Inc 1615 Spur 529	Rosenberg	TX	77471	**800-866-0001**	281-342-4494
Campbell & George Co					
1100 Industrial Rd Ste 12	San Carlos	CA	94070	**800-682-4224**	650-654-5000
Celestica Inc					
844 Don Mills Rd	Toronto	ON	M3C1V7	**888-899-9998**	416-448-5800
NYSE: CLS					
CENTROSOLAR America Inc					
14350 N 87th St Ste 105	Scottsdale	AZ	85260	**877-348-2555**	
Clary Corp					
150 E Huntington Dr	Monrovia	CA	91016	**800-551-6111**	626-359-4486
Clinton Electronics Corp					
6701 Clinton Rd	Loves Park	IL	61111	**800-549-6393**	815-633-1444
Coilcraft Inc					
1102 Silver Lake Rd	Cary	IL	60013	**800-322-2645**	847-639-2361
Comdel Inc					
11 Kondelin Rd	Gloucester	MA	01930	**800-468-3144**	978-282-0620
Communications & Power Industries LLC					
607 Hansen Way	Palo Alto	CA	94303	**800-231-4818**	650-846-2900
Concepts Av Integration					
4610 S 133rd St Ste 106	Omaha	NE	68137	**877-422-3933**	402-298-5011
Cooper Industries					
600 Travis St Ste 5400	Houston	TX	77002	**866-853-4293**	713-209-8400
NYSE: ETN					
Cornucopia Tool & Plastics Inc					
448 Sherwood Rd PO Box 1915	Paso Robles	CA	93447	**800-235-4144**	805-369-0030
Crystek Crystals Corp					
12730 Commonwealth Dr	Fort Myers	FL	33913	**800-237-3061**	239-561-3311
Cyber Power Systems Inc					
4241 12th Ave E Ste 400	Shakopee	MN	55379	**877-297-6937**	952-403-9500
Cyberex 5900 Eastport Blvd	Richmond	VA	23231	**800-238-5000**	804-236-3300
Data Device Corp					
105 Wilbur Pl	Bohemia	NY	11716	**800-332-5757***	631-567-5600
*Cust Svc					
Digital Power Corp					
41324 Christy St	Fremont	CA	94538	**866-344-7697**	510-353-4023
Dow-Key Microwave Corp					
4822 McGrath St	Ventura	CA	93003	**800-266-3695**	805-650-0260
Eby Co 4300 H St	Philadelphia	PA	19124	**800-329-3430**	215-537-4700
Electrex Inc					
6 N Walnut St	Hutchinson	KS	67501	**800-319-3676**	
Electrocube Inc					
3366 Pomona Blvd	Pomona	CA	91768	**800-515-1112**	909-595-4037
Electroswitch Corp					
180 King Ave	Weymouth	MA	02188	**800-572-0479**	781-335-5200
Emerson Network Power Connectivity Solutions					
1050 Dearborn Dr	Columbus	OH	43085	**800-275-3500**	614-888-0246
EMF Corp 505 Pokagon Trl	Angola	IN	46703	**800-847-2818**	260-665-9541
Eoff Electric Company Inc					
3241 NW Industrial St	Portland	OR	97210	**800-285-3633**	503-222-9411
EPCOS Inc					
485-B Rt 1 S Ste 200	Iselin	NJ	08830	**800-689-3717**	732-906-4304
eSilicon Corp					
501 Macara Ave	Sunnyvale	CA	94085	**877-769-2447**	408-616-4600
Forbes Snyder Tristate Cash					
54 Northampton St	Easthampton	MA	01027	**800-222-4064**	413-529-2950
Franklin Empire					
8421 Darnley Rd	Montreal	QC	H4T2B2	**800-361-5044**	514-341-3720
Full Swing Golf Inc					
10890 Thornmint Rd	San Diego	CA	92127	**800-798-9094**	858-675-1100
GoMotion Inc					
10 Kendrick Rd Unit 3	Wareham	MA	02571	**866-446-1069**	508-322-7695
Greenlee Textron					
1390 Aspen Way	Vista	CA	92081	**800-642-2155**	760-598-8900
GW Lisk Company Inc					
2 S St	Clifton Springs	NY	14432	**800-776-9528**	315-462-2611
Honeywell Electronic Materials					
1349 Moffett Pk Dr	Sunnyvale	CA	94089	**877-841-2840**	
Hubbell Power Systems Inc					
210 N Allen St	Centralia	MO	65240	**800-346-3062**	573-682-5521
Integrated Magnetics Inc					
11248 Playa Ct	Culver City	CA	90230	**800-421-6692**	310-391-7213
InVue Security Products Inc					
10715 Sikes Pl Ste 200	Charlotte	NC	28277	**888-257-4272**	704-206-7849
ITT Industries Inc					
1133 Westchester Ave	White Plains	NY	10604	**800-254-2823**	914-641-2000
NYSE: ITT					
JAE Electronics Inc					
142 Technology Dr Ste 100	Irvine	CA	92618	**800-523-7278**	949-753-2600
Jenkins Electric Inc					
5933 Brookshire Blvd	Charlotte	NC	28216	**800-438-3003**	
Jewell Instruments LLC					
850 Perimeter Rd	Manchester	NH	03103	**800-227-5955**	603-669-6400
Johanson Mfg Corp					
301 Rockaway Valley Rd	Boonton	NJ	07005	**800-477-1272**	973-334-2676
Kepco Inc					
131-38 Sanford Ave	Flushing	NY	11355	**800-526-2324**	718-461-7000
La Marche Mfg Co					
106 Bradrock Dr	Des Plaines	IL	60018	**888-232-9562**	847-299-1188
Larco 210 NE Tenth Ave	Brainerd	MN	56401	**800-523-6996***	218-829-9797
*Cust Svc					
Lynn Electronics Corp					
154 Railroad Dr	Ivyland	PA	18974	**800-624-2220**	215-355-8200
MagneTek Inc					
N49 W13650 Campbell Dr	Menomonee Falls	WI	53051	**800-288-8178**	
NASDAQ: MAG					
Magtech Industries Corp					
5625 Arville St Ste A	Las Vegas	NV	89118	**888-954-4481**	702-364-9998
Marlow Industries Inc					
10451 Vista Pk Rd	Dallas	TX	75238	**877-627-5691**	
Maxwell Technologies Inc					
5271 Viewridge Ct Ste 100	San Diego	CA	92123	**877-511-4324**	858-503-3300
NASDAQ: MXWL					
Methode Electronics Inc					
7401 W Wilson Ave	Chicago	IL	60706	**877-316-7700**	708-867-6777
NYSE: MEI					
Microwave Filter Company Inc					
6743 Kinne St	East Syracuse	NY	13057	**800-448-1666**	315-438-4700
Molex Inc 2222 Wellington Ct	Lisle	IL	60532	**800-786-6539***	630-353-1314
*Cust Svc					
MtronPTI 1703 E Hwy 50	Yankton	SD	57078	**800-762-8800**	605-665-9321
Murata Electronics North America Inc					
2200 Lake Pk Dr	Smyrna	GA	30080	**800-704-6079**	770-436-1300
NewComLink Inc					
3900 N Capital Of Texas Hwy Ste 150	Austin	TX	78746	**888-988-0603**	
Newport Corp 1791 Deere Ave	Irvine	CA	92606	**800-222-6440***	949-863-3144
NASDAQ: NEWP ■ *Sales					
Niles Audio Corp					
1969 Kellog Ave	Carlsbad	CA	92008	**800-289-4434**	760-710-0992
Nortech Systems Inc					
7550 Meridian Cir N Ste 150	Maple Grove	MN	55369	**800-237-9576**	952-345-2244
NASDAQ: NSYS					
Nortek Security & Control LLC					
1950 Camino Vida Roble Ste 150	Carlsbad	CA	92008	**800-421-1587***	760-438-7000
*Cust Svc					
NWL Transformers Inc					
312 Rising Sun Rd	Bordentown	NJ	08505	**800-742-5695**	609-298-7300
Ohmite Manufacturing Co					
1600 Golf Rd Ste 850	Rolling Meadows	IL	60008	**866-964-6483**	
OSI Systems Inc					
12525 Chadron Ave	Hawthorne	CA	90250	**800-579-1639**	310-978-0516
NASDAQ: OSIS					
Panamax Inc					
1690 Corporate Cir	Petaluma	CA	94954	**800-472-5555**	707-283-5900
Para Systems Inc					
Minuteman UPS					
1455 LeMay Dr	Carrollton	TX	75007	**800-238-7272**	972-446-7363
PCB Group Inc 3425 Walden Ave	Depew	NY	14043	**800-828-8840**	716-684-0001
PerkinElmer Inc					
940 Winter St	Waltham	MA	02451	**800-762-4000**	781-663-6050
NYSE: PKI					
PG Life Link Inc					
167 Gap Way	Erlanger	KY	41018	**800-287-4123**	859-283-5900
Piller Inc 45 Turner Rd	Middletown	NY	10941	**800-597-6937**	
Plastronics Socket Co Inc					
2601 Texas Dr	Irving	TX	75062	**800-582-5822***	972-258-2580
*Cust Svc					
Positronic Industries Inc					
423 N Campbell Ave PO Box 8247	Springfield	MO	65801	**800-641-4054**	417-866-2322
Post Glover Resistors Inc					
1369 Cox Rd	Erlanger	KY	41018	**800-537-6144***	859-283-0778
*Cust Svc					
Pran Systems					
399 Jacquard St Ste 100	Quebec	QC	G1N4J6	**866-688-7726**	418-688-7726
Precision Devices Inc					
8840 N Greenview Dr	Middleton	WI	53562	**800-274-9825**	
Progressive Dynamics Inc					
507 Industrial Rd	Marshall	MI	49068	**800-848-0558**	269-781-4241
Quartzdyne Inc					
4334 West Links Dr	Salt Lake City	UT	84120	**800-222-3611**	801-839-1000
Raritan Computer Inc					
400 Cottontail Ln	Somerset	NJ	08873	**800-724-8090**	732-764-8886
Record					
4324 Phil Hargett Ct PO Box 3099	Monroe	NC	28111	**800-438-1937***	704-289-9212
*Sales					
RF Industries					
7610 Miramar Rd	San Diego	CA	92126	**800-233-1728**	858-549-6340
NASDAQ: RFIL					
Samtec Inc					
520 Park E Blvd PO Box 1147	New Albany	IN	47151	**800-726-8329**	812-944-6733
Schumacher Electric Corp					
801 E Business Ctr Dr	Mount Prospect	IL	60056	**800-621-5485**	
Scosche Industries Inc					
PO Box 2901	Oxnard	CA	93034	**800-363-4490**	
Seiko Instruments USA Inc					
21221 S Western Ave Ste 250	Torrance	CA	90501	**800-688-0817***	310-517-7700
*Sales					
Sendec Corp					
72 Perinton Pkwy	Fairport	NY	14450	**800-295-8000**	855-294-3800
Sigma Electronics Inc					
1027 Commercial Ave	East Petersburg	PA	17520	**866-569-2681**	717-569-2926
Signal Transformer Company Inc					
500 Bayview Ave	Inwood	NY	11096	**866-239-5777**	516-239-5777
Simplex Inc					
5300 Rising Moon Rd	Springfield	IL	62711	**800-637-8603**	
SL Power Electronics Inc					
6050 King Dr Bldg A	Ventura	CA	93003	**800-235-5929**	805-486-4565
Smart Power Systems Inc					
1760 Stebbins Dr	Houston	TX	77043	**800-882-8285**	713-464-8000
SNC Mfg Company Inc					
101 West Waukau Ave	Oshkosh	WI	54902	**800-558-3325**	920-231-7370
Spectrum Control Inc					
8031 Avonia Rd	Fairview	PA	16415	**855-294-3800**	
Standex Electronics Inc					
4538 Camberwell Rd	Cincinnati	OH	45209	**866-782-6339**	513-871-3777
Stevens Water Monitoring Systems					
12067 NE Glenn Widing Dr Ste 106	Portland	OR	97220	**800-452-5272**	503-445-8000
Sypris Electronics LLC					
10421 University Center Dr	Tampa	FL	33612	**800-937-9220**	813-972-6000
Sypris Solutions Inc					
101 Bullitt Ln Ste 450	Louisville	KY	40222	**800-588-9119**	502-329-2000
NASDAQ: SYPR					
System Sensor					
3825 Ohio Ave	Saint Charles	IL	60174	**800-736-7672***	630-377-6580
*Tech Supp					
Taiyo Yuden (USA) Inc					
10 N Martingale Rd Ste 575	Schaumburg	IL	60173	**800-348-2496**	630-237-2405

Company / Address	City	State	ZIP	Toll-Free	Phone
Times Microwave Systems Inc PO Box 5039	Wallingford	CT	06492	**800-867-2629**	203-949-8400
Tornado Spectral Systems 555 Richmond St W Ste 402	Toronto	ON	M5V3B1	**800-227-9770**	416-361-3444
Toshiba America Inc 1251 Ave of the Americas 41st Fl	New York	NY	10020	**800-457-7777**	212-596-0600
Total Technologies Ltd 9710 Research Dr	Irvine	CA	92618	**800-669-4885**	949-465-0200
TRAK Microwave Corp 4726 Eisenhower Blvd	Tampa	FL	33634	**888-283-8444**	813-901-7200
Triton Systems Inc 21405 B St	Long Beach	MS	39560	**866-787-4866**	228-575-3100
TSI Power Corp 1103 W Pierce Ave	Antigo	WI	54409	**800-874-3160**	715-623-0636
United Chemi-Con Inc 9801 W Higgins Rd	Rosemont	IL	60018	**800-344-4539**	847-696-2000
Viatran Corp 3829 Forest Pkwy Ste 500	Wheatfield	NY	14120	**800-688-0030**	716-629-3800
Viconics Technologies Inc 7262 Marconi 3rd fl	Montreal	QC	H2R2Z5	**800-563-5660**	514-321-5660
Vishay Intertechnology Inc 63 Lancaster Ave *NYSE: VSH*	Malvern	PA	19355	**800-567-6098**	610-644-1300
World Electronics Sales & Service Inc 3000 Kutztown Rd	Reading	PA	19605	**800-523-0427**	610-939-9800
Xantrex Technology Inc 3700 Gilmore Way	Burnaby	BC	V5G4M1	**800-670-0707**	604-422-8595
Z Communications Inc 14118 Stowe Dr Ste B	Poway	CA	92064	**877-808-1226**	858-621-2700
Zentech Manufacturing Inc 6980 Tudsbury Rd	Baltimore	MD	21244	**800-871-7838**	443-348-4500

254 ELECTRONIC ENCLOSURES

Company / Address	City	State	ZIP	Toll-Free	Phone
Buckeye ShapeForm 555 Marion Rd	Columbus	OH	43207	**800-728-0776**	614-445-8433
Equipto Electronics Corp 351 Woodlawn Ave	Aurora	IL	60506	**800-204-7225**	630-897-4691
Optima Stantron 1775 MacLeod Dr	Lawrenceville	GA	30043	**800-821-0019**	770-496-4000
TRI MAP International Inc 119 Val Dervin Pkwy Ste 5	Stockton	CA	95206	**888-687-4627**	209-234-0100
Zero Manufacturing Inc 500 W 200 N	North Salt Lake	UT	84054	**800-959-5050**	801-298-5900

255 ELECTRONIC TRANSACTION PROCESSING

Company / Address	City	State	ZIP	Toll-Free	Phone
Avid Payment Solutions 950 S Old Woodward Ste 220	Birmingham	MI	48009	**888-855-8644**	
Chase Paymentech Solutions LLC 14221 Dallas Pkwy *Cust Svc	Dallas	TX	75254	**800-708-3740***	
Elavon 2 Concourse Pkwy Ste 800	Atlanta	GA	30328	**800-725-1243**	678-731-5000
Global Payments Inc 3550 Lenox Rd Ste 3000 *NYSE: GPN*	Atlanta	GA	30326	**800-560-2960**	770-829-8000

256 ELEVATORS, ESCALATORS, MOVING WALKWAYS

Company / Address	City	State	ZIP	Toll-Free	Phone
Able Services 868 Folsom St	San Francisco	CA	94107	**800-461-9577**	415-546-6534
Abx Engineering 880 Hinckley Rd	Burlingame	CA	94010	**800-366-4588**	650-552-2322
Aegis Sciences Corp 515 Great Cir Rd	Nashville	TN	37228	**800-533-7052**	
Aerospec Inc 505 E Alamo Dr	Chandler	AZ	85225	**888-854-2376**	480-892-7195
Alabama Graphics & Engineering Supply Inc 2801 Fifth Ave S	Birmingham	AL	35233	**800-292-3806**	205-252-8505
Allana Buick & Bers Inc 990 Commercial St	Palo Alto	CA	94303	**800-378-3405**	650-543-5600
Allied Corrosion Industries Inc 1550 Cobb Industrial Dr	Marietta	GA	30066	**800-241-0809**	770-425-1355
American Aerospace Controls Inc 570 Smith St	Farmingdale	NY	11735	**888-873-8559**	631-694-5100
Archibald Gray & McKay Ltd 3514 White Oak Rd	London	ON	N6E2Z9	**800-336-9708**	519-685-5300
ARIZON COMPANIES 11880 Dorsett Rd	St. Louis	MO	63043	**800-325-1303**	314-739-0037
Arnold & Assoc 14275 Midway Rd Ste 170	Addison	TX	75001	**800-535-6329**	972-991-1144
Astrodyne Corp 375 Forbes Blvd	Mansfield	MA	02048	**800-823-8082**	508-964-6300
B M Ross & Assoc Ltd 62 N St	Goderich	ON	N7A2T4	**888-524-2641**	519-524-2641
Bagby Elevator Company Inc 3608 Messer Airport Hwy	Birmingham	AL	35222	**800-228-7544**	
Building & Earth Sciences Inc 5545 Derby Dr	Birmingham	AL	35210	**800-775-2468**	
Burns Engineering Inc 10201 Bren Rd E	Minnetonka	MN	55343	**800-328-3871**	952-935-4400
Cam Services Inc 5664 Selmaraine Dr	Culver City	CA	90230	**800-576-3050**	310-390-3552
Chisholm Fleming & Assoc 317 Renfrew Dr Ste 301	Markham	ON	L3R9S8	**888-241-4149**	905-474-1458
City of Clarksville 199 Tenth St	Clarksville	TN	37040	**800-342-1003**	931-645-7464
City of Vacaville Inc, The 650 Merchant St	Vacaville	CA	95688	**800-759-7159**	707-449-5100
Clarity Innovations Inc 1001 SE Water Ave Ste 400	Portland	OR	97214	**877-683-3187**	503-248-4300
Controlled Contamination Services LLC 6150 Lusk Blvd Ste B205	San Diego	CA	92121	**888-979-9608**	
Corradino Group 200 s Fifth st	Louisville	KY	40202	**800-880-8241**	502-587-7221
DBA Engineering Ltd 401 Hanlan Rd	Vaughan	ON	L4L3T1	**800-819-8833**	905-851-0090
Degree Controls Inc 18 Meadowbrook Dr	Milford	NH	03055	**877-334-7332**	603-672-8900
DJ & A PC 3203 S Russell St	Missoula	MT	59801	**800-398-3522**	406-721-4320
Elevator Equipment Corp 4035 Goodwin Ave	Los Angeles	CA	90039	**888-577-3326**	323-245-0147
Ems-tech Inc 699 Dundas St W	Belleville	ON	K8N4Z2	**844-450-8324**	613-966-6611
Engineering Data Design Corp 105 Daventry Ln Ste 100	Louisville	KY	40223	**888-678-0683**	502-412-4000
Environmental Health & Engineering Inc 117 Fourth Ave	Needham	MA	02494	**800-825-5343**	781-247-4300
ESE Inc 3600 DownWind Dr	Marshfield	WI	54449	**800-236-4778**	
Falcon Crest Aviation Supply Inc 8318 Braniff	Houston	TX	77061	**800-833-8229**	713-644-2290
FUTEK Advanced Sensor Technology Inc 10 Thomas	Irvine	CA	92618	**800-233-8835**	949-465-0900
Geotek Engineering & Testing Services Inc 909 E 50th St N	Sioux Falls	SD	57104	**800-354-5512**	605-335-5512
Giles Engineering Assoc Inc N8 W22350 Johnson Dr	Waukesha	WI	53186	**800-782-0610**	262-544-0118
Globex Corp 3620 Stutz Dr	Canfield	OH	44406	**800-533-8610**	330-533-0030
GMI Building Services Inc 8001 Vickers St	San Diego	CA	92111	**866-803-4464**	
Greenlancer 615 Griswold St Ste 300	Detroit	MI	48226	**866-436-1440**	
Gryphon International Engineering Services Inc 80 King St Ste 404	Saint Catharines	ON	L2R7G1	**800-268-9242**	905-984-8383
H&S Constructors Inc 1616 Valero Way	Corpus Christi	TX	78469	**800-727-8602**	361-289-5272
HH Angus & Assoc Ltd 1127 Leslie St	Toronto	ON	M3C2J6	**866-955-8201**	416-443-8200
Hunt Guillot & Assoc LLC 603 Reynolds Dr	Ruston	LA	71270	**866-255-6825**	318-255-6825
IEA 6325 Digital Way Ste 460	Indianapolis	IN	46278	**800-688-3775**	
INCERTEC LLC 160 83rd Ave NE	Fridley	MN	55432	**800-638-2573**	763-717-7016
Infratech Corp 2036 Baker Ct	Kennesaw	GA	30144	**800-574-6372**	
Interlink Network Systems Inc 495 Cranbury Rd	East Brunswick	NJ	08816	**877-872-6947**	732-846-2226
Jedson Engineering 705 Central Ave	Cincinnati	OH	45202	**866-729-3945**	513-965-5999
Kelly's Janitorial Service Inc 228 Hazel Ave	Trenton	NJ	08638	**800-227-0366**	609-771-0365
Kussmaul Electronics Company Inc 170 Cherry Ave	West Sayville	NY	11796	**800-346-0857**	631-567-0314
LARON Inc 4255 Santa Fe Dr	Kingman	AZ	86401	**800-248-3430**	928-757-8424
MadgeTech Inc 6 Warner Rd	Warner	NH	03278	**877-671-2885**	603-456-2011
ManTech Advanced Systems International Inc 12015 Lee Jackson Hwy	Fairfax	VA	22033	**800-800-4857**	703-218-6000
Matot Inc 2501 Van Buren St	Bellwood	IL	60104	**800-369-1070**	708-547-1888
Matrix Energy Services Inc 3221 Ramos Cir	Sacramento	CA	95827	**800-556-2123**	916-363-9283
McQ Inc 1551 Forbes St	Fredericksburg	VA	22405	**866-373-2374**	540-373-2374
Moffitt Corp Inc 1351 13th Ave S Ste 130	Jacksonville Beach	FL	32250	**800-474-3267**	904-241-9944
Motion Control Engineering Inc 11380 White Rock Rd	Rancho Cordova	CA	95742	**800-444-7442**	916-463-9200
NuVision Engineering Inc River Park Commons 2403 Sidney St Ste 700	Pittsburgh	PA	15203	**888-748-8232**	412-586-1810
Omicron Architecture Engineering Construction Ltd 595 Burrard St Three Bentall Centre Fifth Fl PO Box 49369	Vancouver	BC	V7X1L4	**877-632-3350**	604-632-3350
Radiant Technologies Inc 2835 Pan American Fwy NE	Albuquerque	NM	87107	**800-289-7176**	505-842-8007
Ricon Corp 7900 Nelson Rd	Panorama City	CA	91402	**800-322-2884**	818-267-3000
Schindler Elevator Corp 20 Whippany Rd	Morristown	NJ	07960	**800-225-3123**	973-397-6500
Schumacher Elevator Co 1 Schumacher Way	Denver	IA	50622	**800-779-5438**	319-984-5676
Technical Systems Integration Inc 816 Greenbrier Cir Ste 208	Chesapeake	VA	23320	**800-566-8744**	757-424-5793
Tulloch Engineering Inc 200 Main St	Thessalon	ON	P0R1L0	**800-797-2997**	705-842-3372
United Consulting Group Ltd 625 Holcomb Bridge Rd	Norcross	GA	30071	**800-266-0990**	770-209-0029
Waupaca Elevator Co Inc 1726 N Ballard Rd Ste 1	Appleton	WI	54911	**800-238-8739**	
Williams Engineering Canada Inc 10065 Jasper Ave Ste 200	Edmonton	AB	T5J3B1	**800-263-2393**	780-409-5300
York Building Services Inc 99 Grand St Ste 3	Moonachie	NJ	07074	**855-443-9675**	

257 EMBASSIES & CONSULATES - FOREIGN, IN THE US

SEE ALSO Travel & Tourism Information - Foreign Travel

Foreign embassies in the U.S. generally include consular services among their functions. These embassy-based consulates are listed here only if their address differs from the embassy's.

Company / Address	City	State	ZIP	Toll-Free	Phone
Antigua & Barbuda *Embassy* 3216 New Mexico Ave NW	Washington	DC	20016	**866-978-7299**	202-362-5122

		Toll-Free	Phone

Austria
Consulate General
11859 Wilshire Blvd Ste 501 .... Los Angeles CA 90025 **800-255-2414** 310-444-9310
Embassy
3524 International Ct NW .... Washington DC 20008 **800-255-2414** 202-895-6700
Canada
885 Second Ave 14th Fl .... New York NY 10017 **800-267-8376** 212-848-1100
Consulate General
500 N Akard St Ste 2900 .... Dallas TX 75201 **800-267-8376** 214-922-9806
Consulate General
1251 Ave of the Americas
Concourse Level .... New York NY 10020 **800-267-8376** 212-596-1628
Consulate General Of Italy
Consulate General
150 S Independence Mall W
1026 Public Ledger Bldg .... Philadelphia PA 19106 **800-531-0840** 215-592-7329
Fiji Embassy
1707 L St NW Ste 200 .... Washington DC 20036 **800-932-3454** 202-466-8320
France
Consulate General
3475 Piedmont Rd NE Ste 1840 .... Atlanta GA 30305 **888-937-2623** 404-495-1660
Consulate General
1395 Brickell Ave Ste 1050 .... Miami FL 33131 **877-624-8737** 305-403-4185
Consulate General
205 N Michigan Ave Ste 3700 .... Chicago IL 60601 **866-858-4430** 312-327-5200
Consulate General
777 Post Oak Blvd Ste 600 .... Houston TX 77056 **888-902-5322** 713-572-2799
Consulate General
540 Bush St .... San Francisco CA 94108 **800-553-4133** 415-397-4330
Embassy
4101 Reservoir Rd NW .... Washington DC 20007 **800-622-6232** 202-944-6000
Consulate General
100 Pine St Ste 3350 .... San Francisco CA 94111 **800-777-0133** 415-392-4214
Ireland
Embassy
2234 Massachusetts Ave NW .... Washington DC 20008 **866-560-1050** 202-462-3939
Kingdom of Morocco, The
Consulate General
10 E 40th St .... New York NY 10016 **800-787-8806** 212-758-2625
Consulate General
4506 Carolinas St .... Houston TX 77004 **877-639-4835** 713-271-6800
Micronesia
300 E 42nd St Ste 1600 .... New York NY 10017 **800-469-4828** 212-697-8370
Consulate 1725 N St NW .... Washington DC 20036 **877-730-9753** 202-223-4383
Netherlands
Embassy
4200 Linnean Ave NW .... Washington DC 20008 **877-388-2443**
New Zealand
Embassy
37 Observatory Cir NW .... Washington DC 20008 **866-639-9325** 202-328-4800
Nicaragua
Embassy
1627 New Hampshire Ave NW .... Washington DC 20009 **800-333-4636** 202-939-6570
Peru
Consulate General
3450 Wilshire Blvd .... Los Angeles CA 90010 **855-303-7378** 213-252-5910
Philippines
Consulate General
30 N Michigan Ave Ste 2100 .... Chicago IL 60602 **888-259-7838** 312-332-6458
Consulate General
556 Fifth Ave .... New York NY 10036 **866-589-1878** 212-764-1330
Turkey
Consulate General
1990 Post Oak Blvd Ste 1300 .... Houston TX 77056 **888-566-7656** 713-622-5849

---

258 **EMBROIDERY & OTHER DECORATIVE STITCHING**

		Toll-Free	Phone

Clothworks
6301 W Marginal Way SW .... Seattle WA 98106 **800-874-0541** 206-762-7886
EmbroidMe Inc
2121 Vista Pkwy .... West Palm Beach FL 33411 **877-877-0234** 561-640-7367
Fabri-Quilt Inc
901 E 14th Ave .... North Kansas City MO 64116 **800-279-0622** 816-421-2000
FlagZone LLC
105A Industrial Dr .... Gilbertsville PA 19525 **800-976-4201**
Herrschners Inc
2800 Hoover Rd .... Stevens Point WI 54481 **800-713-1239** 800-441-0838
Lion Bros Company Inc
300 Red Brook Blvd .... Owings Mills MD 21117 **800-365-6543*** 410-363-1000
*Cust Svc
Luv N' Care Ltd
3030 Aurora Ave .... Monroe LA 71201 **800-588-6227**
Monarch Textile Rental Services Inc
2810 Foundation Dr .... South Bend IN 46628 **800-589-9434** 574-233-9433
Moritz Embroidery Works Inc, The
Pocono Mountain Business Park 405 Industrial Park
PO Box 187 .... Mount Pocono PA 18344 **800-533-4183** 570-839-9600
National Emblem Inc
3925 E Vernon St PO Box 15680 .... Long Beach CA 90815 **800-877-6185** 310-515-5055
Osgood Textile Company Inc
333 Park St .... West Springfield MA 01089 **888-674-6638** 413-737-6488
Penn Emblem Co
10909 Dutton Rd .... Philadelphia PA 19154 **800-793-7366**
Schweizer Emblem Co
1022 Busse Hwy .... Park Ridge IL 60068 **800-942-5215*** 847-292-1022
*Cust Svc
SK Textile Inc
1 Knollcrest Dr .... Cincinnati OH 45237 **800-888-9112**

---

259 **EMPLOYMENT OFFICES - GOVERNMENT**

		Toll-Free	Phone

Employment & Training Administration
200 Constitution Ave NW .... Washington DC 20210 **866-487-2365**

		Toll-Free	Phone

Alaska
Arts Council
161 Klevin St Ste 102 .... Anchorage AK 99508 **888-278-7424** 907-269-6610
Employment Security Div
PO Box 115509 .... Juneau AK 99811 **888-448-3527** 907-465-2757
Judicial Council of California
455 Golden Gate Ave .... San Francisco CA 94102 **800-900-5980** 415-865-4200
Labor & Employment Dept
633 17th St Ste 201 .... Denver CO 80202 **800-388-5515** 303-318-9000
Delaware Employment & Training Div
4425 N Market St .... Wilmington DE 19802 **800-794-3032** 302-761-8085
Idaho Labor Dept
317 W Main St .... Boise ID 83735 **800-554-5627** 208-332-3570
Indiana
Agriculture Dept
101 W Washington St .... Indianapolis IN 46204 **800-677-9800**
Workforce Development Dept
402 W Washington St Rm W160 ...... Indianapolis IN 46204 **800-891-6499** 317-232-7670
Iowa
Adult Children & Family Services Div
1305 E Walnut St .... Des Moines IA 50319 **800-735-2942** 515-281-8977
Workforce Development
1000 E Grand Ave .... Des Moines IA 50319 **866-239-0843**
Louisiana
Agriculture & Forestry Dept
5825 Florida Blvd .... Baton Rouge LA 70806 **866-927-2476** 225-922-1234
Employment Services Bureau
55 State House Stn .... Augusta ME 04330 **888-457-8883** 207-623-7981
Career Education & Workforce Programs
201 N Washington Sq
Victor Office Center .... Lansing MI 48913 **888-253-6855** 517-335-5858
Employment Security Commission
1235 Echelon Pkwy PO Box 1699 .... Jackson MS 39215 **888-844-3577** 601-321-6000
Employment Security
32 S Main St .... Concord NH 03301 **800-852-3400** 603-224-3311
New York
Aging Office
2 Empire State Plz .... Albany NY 12223 **800-342-9871**
Labor Dept
WA Harriman Campus Bldg 12 .... Albany NY 12240 **888-469-7365** 518-457-9000
Workforce Developement Office
4020 F Fifth Ave PO Box 1618 .... Columbus OH 43219 **888-296-7541**
Oregon Employment Dept
875 Union St NE .... Salem OR 97311 **877-345-3484** 503-451-2400
Tennessee
Administrative Office of the Cts
511 Union St Ste 600 .... Nashville TN 37219 **800-448-7970** 615-741-2687
Labor & Workforce Development Dept
220 French Landing Dr .... Nashville TN 37243 **844-224-5818**
Texas
Aging & Disability Services
701 W 51st St .... Austin TX 78751 **888-388-6332** 512-438-3011
Aging & Rehabilitative Services Dept
8004 Franklin Farms Dr .... Richmond VA 23229 **800-552-5019** 804-662-7000
Employment Commission
703 E Main St .... Richmond VA 23219 **866-832-2363**
Employment Security Dept
212 Maple Park Ave SE .... Olympia WA 98501 **800-318-6022** 360-902-9500

---

260 **EMPLOYMENT SERVICES - ONLINE**

		Toll-Free	Phone

A-Check America Inc
1501 Research Park Dr .... Riverside CA 92507 **877-345-2021** 951-750-1501
A1 Staffing & Recruiting Agency Inc
7407 NW 23rd St .... Bethany OK 73008 **800-233-1261** 405-787-7600
Advantage RN LLC
9021 Meridian Way .... West Chester OH 45069 **866-301-4045**
agriCAREERS Inc 613 Main St .... Massena IA 50853 **800-633-8387** 712-779-3300
All-Star Recruiting LLC
6119 Lyons Rd .... Coconut Creek FL 33073 **800-928-0229**
Allegiant International LLC
450 E 96th St Ste 500 .... Indianapolis IN 46240 **866-841-3671**
Alpha Rae Personnel Inc
347 West Berry St 7th Fl .... Fort Wayne IN 46802 **800-837-8940** 260-426-8227
Apple & Assoc PO Box 996 .... Chapin SC 29036 **800-326-8490** 803-932-2000
Arc San Joaquin Inc
41 W Yokuts Ave .... Stockton CA 95207 **800-847-3030** 209-955-1625
Arctern Inc
1133 Ave of the Americas 15th Fl .... New York NY 10036 **800-231-4973**
Avjobs Inc
9609 S University Blvd Unit 630830 .... Littleton CO 80163 **888-624-8691** 303-683-2322
Backtrack Inc
8850 Tyler Blvd .... Mentor OH 44060 **800-991-9694**
Baltimore Teachers Union
Seton Business Park 5800 Metro Dr
2nd Fl .... Baltimore MD 21215 **800-332-6347** 410-358-6600
Barrett Group LLC, The
100 Jefferson Blvd Ste 310 .... Warwick RI 02888 **800-304-4473**
Bayside Solutions Inc
3000 Executive Pkwy Ste 510 .... San Ramon CA 94583 **800-220-0074**
Bcg Attorney Search
175 S Lake Ave Unit 200 .... Pasadena CA 91101 **800-298-6440**
BlueAlly
8609 Westwood Center Dr Ste 100 .... Vienna VA 22182 **888-768-2060**
CareerSource Flagler Volusia
359 Bill France Blvd .... Daytona Beach FL 32114 **800-476-7574** 386-323-7001
CASCO International Inc
4205 E Dixon Blvd .... Shelby NC 28152 **800-535-5690**
Chicago Nannies Inc
101 N Marion St Ste 300 .... Oak Park IL 60301 **866-900-9605** 708-524-2101
Children First Home Healthcare Service
4448 Edgewater Dr .... Orlando FL 32804 **800-207-0802** 407-513-3000
Choctaw Management Services Enterprise
2101 W Arkansas St .... Durant OK 74701 **866-326-1000**
Clearbridge Technology Group
6 Fortune Dr .... Billerica MA 01821 **877-808-2284** 781-916-2284

Classified Section

			Toll-Free	Phone
Coastal Administrative Services (CAS)				
PO Box 3070	Bellingham WA	98227	800-870-1831	
ComputerJobscom Inc				
1995 N Pk Pl SE	Atlanta GA	30339	800-850-0045	770-850-0045
Condustrial Inc				
514 East N St	Greenville SC	29601	888-794-7798	864-235-3619
CoWorx Staffing Services LLC				
1375 Plainfield Ave	Watchung NJ	07069	800-754-7000	908-757-5300
CPI Group Inc, The				
112 Fifth St N PO Box 828	Columbus MS	39703	888-566-8303	662-328-1042
CSS International Inc				
115 River Landing Dr Daniel Is	Charleston SC	29492	800-814-7705	
Dice Inc				
4101 NW Urbandale Dr	Urbandale IA	50322	877-386-3323	515-280-1144
Eliassen Group LLC				
55 Walkers Brook Dr 6th Fl.	Reading MA	01867	800-354-2773	
EmpireWorks Inc				
1940 Olivera Rd	Concord CA	94520	888-278-8200	
Employment Guide LLC, The				
4460 Corporation Ln Ste 317	Virginia Beach VA	23462	877-876-4039	
EverStaff LLC				
6150 oak Tree Blvd Ste 175	Cleveland OH	44131	877-392-6151	216-369-2566
ExecUNet Inc				
295 Westport Ave	Norwalk CT	06851	800-637-3126	
Expert Recruiters				
883 Helmcken St	Vancouver BC	V6Z1B1	888-407-7799	604-689-3600
Federal Staffing Resources LLC				
2200 Somerville Rd Ste 300	Annapolis MD	21401	866-886-2300	410-990-0795
Filter LLC				
1425 Fourth Ave Ste 1000	Seattle WA	98101	800-336-0809	
First Rate Staffing				
1920 W Camelback Rd Ste 102	Phoenix AZ	85015	800-357-6242	602-442-5277
Future Force Inc				
15800 NW 57th Ave	Miami Lakes FL	33014	800-683-0681	305-557-4900
Galaxy Software Solutions Inc				
5820 N Lilley Rd Ste 8	Canton MI	48187	877-269-4774	
Global HR Research LLC				
24201 Walden Ctr Dr Ste 206	Bonita Springs FL	34134	800-790-1205	239-274-0048
Greene Resources				
6601 Six Forks Rd	Raleigh NC	27615	800-784-9619	919-862-8602
Grimes Legal				
8264 Louisville Rd	Bowling Green KY	42101	800-875-3820	270-782-3820
Gurucom				
5001 Baum Blvd Ste 760	Pittsburgh PA	15213	888-678-0136	
Haskel Thompson & Associates LLC				
12734 Kenwood Ln Ste 74	Fort Myers FL	33907	800-470-4226	239-437-4600
HealthCareSource Inc				
100 Sylvan Rd Ste 100	Woburn MA	01801	800-869-5200	
HealthForce Ontario Marketing & Recruitment Agency				
163 Queen St E	Toronto ON	M5A1S1	800-596-4046	416-862-2200
Heart of the House Hospitality				
2346 S Lynhurst Dr Ste A-201	Indianapolis IN	46241	888-365-1440	
HighPoint Technology Solutions Inc				
2332 Galiano St 2nd Fl.	Coral Gables FL	33134	800-767-0893	
Hire Quest LLC				
4560 Great Oak Dr	North Charleston SC	29418	800-835-6755	843-723-7400
Hospital Employee Labor Pool				
765 The City Dr S Ste 405	Orange CA	92868	888-435-7689	
Howard E Nyhart Company Inc, The				
8415 Allison Pointe Blvd Ste 300	Indianapolis IN	46250	800-428-7106	317-845-3500
HR Advisors Inc				
25411 Cabot Rd Ste 212.	Laguna Hills CA	92653	877-344-8324	
HR Works Inc				
200 WillowBrook Ofc Pk	Fairport NY	14450	877-219-9062	585-381-8340
HRO Partners LLC				
855 Willow Tree Cir Ste 100	Cordova TN	38018	866-822-0123	
Impact Group				
12977 N Outer 40 Dr Ste 300	St. Louis MO	63141	800-420-2420	314-453-9002
Industry Specific Solutions LLC				
24901 Northwestern Hwy Ste 400.	Southfield MI	48075	877-356-3450	
Intellect Resources Inc				
3824 N Elm St Ste 102	Greensboro NC	27455	877-554-8911	
International Foundation of Employee Benefit Plans (IFEBP)				
18700 W Bluemound Rd	Brookfield WI	53045	888-334-3327	262-786-6700
Its Technologies Inc				
7060 Spring Meadows Dr W Ste D	Holland OH	43528	800-432-6607	
Jet Aviation				
114 Charles A Lindbergh Dr Teterboro Airport				
	Teterboro NJ	07608	800-441-6016	
JobMonkey Inc				
1409 Post Alley	Seattle WA	98101	800-230-1095	
Kavaliro Staffing Services				
12001 Research Pkwy Ste 344	Orlando FL	32826	800-562-1470	407-243-6006
Kendall & Davis Company Inc				
3668 S Geyer Rd Ste 100	St. Louis MO	63127	866-675-3755	
Kovasys Inc				
2550 Argentia Rd Ste 220.	Mississauga ON	L5N5R1	888-568-2747	416-800-4286
Legal Resources Inc				
2877 Guardian Ln Ste 101	Virginia Beach VA	23452	800-728-5768	757-498-1220
LI Roberts Group				
7475 Skillman St Ste 102c	Dallas TX	75231	877-878-6463	214-221-6463
Maven Group LLC, The				
320 N Salem St Ste 204	Apex NC	27502	800-343-6612	919-386-1010
Maxsys 173 Dalhousie St	Ottawa ON	K1N7C7	800-429-5177	613-562-9943
MDT Labor LLC				
2325 Paxton Church Rd Ste B	Harrisburg PA	17110	888-454-9202	
Meador Staffing Services Inc				
722A Fairmont Pkwy	Pasadena TX	77504	800-332-3310	713-941-0616
Medix				
222 S Riverside Plz Ste 2120	Chicago IL	60606	866-446-3349	
Mike Ferry Organization, The				
7220 S Cimarron Rd Ste 300	Las Vegas NV	89113	800-448-0647	702-982-6260
Mind Your Business Inc (myb)				
305 Eighth Ave E	Hendersonville NC	28792	888-869-2462	
Morgan Hunter Companies				
7600 W 110th St	Overland Park KS	66210	800-917-6447	913-491-3434
MyOpenJobs LLC				
203 Main St Ste 100.	Lake Dallas TX	75065	800-396-4822	

			Toll-Free	Phone
NationJob Inc				
920 Morgan St Ste T.	Des Moines IA	50309	800-292-7731	
Net-Temps Inc				
55 Middlesex St Ste 220.	North Chelmsford MA	01863	800-307-0062	978-251-7272
Nine Star Enterprises Inc				
730 I St	Anchorage AK	99501	800-478-7587	907-279-7827
NSTAR Global Services Inc				
120 Partlo St	Garner NC	27529	877-678-2766	
Olesky Associates Inc				
865 Washington St Ste 3	Newton MA	02460	800-486-4330	781-235-4330
On Time Staffing				
535 Rte 38 E Ste 412	Cherry Hill NJ	08002	855-866-2910	866-333-3007
Partnersolve Llc				
30 Southville Rd	Southborough MA	01772	855-445-2837	
People Plus Industrial Inc				
1095 Nebo Rd	Madisonville KY	42431	888-825-1500	270-825-8939
Perfect Fit Placement Inc				
1253 Berlin Tpke	Berlin CT	06037	800-290-2168	860-828-3127
Placement Strategies Inc				
6965 El Camino Real Ste 105-200	Carlsbad CA	92009	866-445-0710	909-597-0668
Planet Forward LLC				
800 Hillgrove Ave Ste 201	Western Springs IL	60558	888-845-2539	
Platinum Personnel				
1475 Ellis St	Kelowna BC	V1Y2A3	800-652-1511	250-979-7200
Priority Business Services Inc				
19712 MacArthur Blvd Ste 110.	Irvine CA	92612	800-710-8775	949-222-1122
PRN Health Services Inc				
4321 W College Ave Ste 200	Appleton WI	54914	888-830-8811	
Procel Temporary Services				
2447 Pacific Coast Hwy Ste 207	Hermosa Beach CA	90254	800-338-9905	310-372-0560
Quik Travel Staffing Inc				
175 E Olive Ave Ste 101	Burbank CA	91502	800-554-7501	800-554-2230
Recruitmilitary Inc				
422 W Loveland Ave	Loveland OH	45140	800-226-0841	513-683-5020
Renoir Staffing Services Inc				
1301 Marina Vlg Pkwy Ste 350.	Alameda CA	94501	866-672-3709	
Run Consultants LLC				
925 North Point Pkwy Ste 160	Alpharetta GA	30005	866-457-2193	
Salus Group Benefits Inc				
37525 Mound Rd	Sterling Heights MI	48310	866-991-9907	
Select Technical Staffing Inc				
1025 S 108th St	West Allis WI	53214	888-476-9331	414-476-9331
Set & Service Resources LLC				
5400 Glenwood Ave Ste 310.	Raleigh NC	27615	866-867-5571	
Sharf Woodward & Associates Inc				
5900 Sepulveda Blvd	Van Nuys CA	91411	877-482-6687	818-989-2200
Skillforce Inc				
405 Williams Ct Ste 106.	Baltimore MD	21220	866-581-8989	
SmartIT Staffing Inc				
6500 Technology Ctr Dr Ste 300.	Indianapolis IN	46278	800-336-4466	317-634-0211
Social Work pr.n. Inc				
10680 Barkley Ste 100	Overland Park KS	66212	800-595-9648	913-648-2984
Source2				
1245 W Fairbanks Ave	Winter Park FL	32789	800-557-6704	407-893-3711
Southern Healthcare Agency Inc				
PO Box 320999	Flowood MS	39232	800-880-2772	601-933-0037
Staffing Resource Group Inc, The				
405 Reo St Ste 255.	Tampa FL	33609	877-774-7742	
StartWire				
10 Water St Ste 150	Lebanon NH	03766	800-572-9470	
TalentLens Inc				
19500 Bulverde Rd	San Antonio TX	78259	888-298-6227	
Targeted Job Fairs Inc				
4441 Glenway Ave	Cincinnati OH	45205	800-695-1939	
Taylor & Hill Inc				
9941 Rowlett Rd	Houston TX	77075	800-318-0231	713-941-2671
Teach Away Inc				
147 Liberty St	Toronto ON	M6K3G3	855-483-2242	416-628-1386
Teachers on Reserve LLC				
604 Sonora Ave	Glendale CA	91201	800-457-1899	
Temps Plus Inc				
268 N Lincoln Ave Ste 12	Corona CA	92882	888-288-0808	
Unique Employment Services Inc				
4646 Corona Dr Ste 100.	Corpus Christi TX	78411	800-824-8367	361-852-6392
United Personnel Services Inc				
289 Bridge St	Springfield MA	01103	800-363-8200	413-736-0800
United Staffing Solutions (USS)				
111 Broadway 3rd Fl.	New York NY	10006	800-972-9725	
USAFact Inc				
6240 Box Springs Blvd	Riverside CA	92507	800-547-0263	951-656-7800
VetJobs Inc PO Box 71445	Marietta GA	30007	877-838-5627	770-993-5117
Waterstone Group Inc, The				
1145 W Main Ave Ste 209	De Pere WI	54115	800-291-3836	920-964-0333
WCG 915 Fort St 5th Fl	Victoria BC	V8V3K3	888-562-9283	250-389-0699
Wellness Coaches				
725 Skippack Pk Ste 300	Blue Bell PA	19422	866-894-1300	
Workforce Alliance Inc				
1951 N Military Trl Ste D	West Palm Beach FL	33409	800-204-2418	561-340-1060
Workincom Inc				
2255 Green Vista Dr Ste 402	Sparks NV	89431	800-774-8671	775-336-3366
Xcel HR				
7361 Calhoun Pl Ste 600	Rockville MD	20855	800-776-0076	

261   ENGINEERING & DESIGN

SEE ALSO Surveying, Mapping, Related Services

			Toll-Free	Phone
AGRA Industries Inc				
1211 W Water St	Merrill WI	54452	800-842-8033	715-536-9584
AKRF Inc 440 Park Ave S	New York NY	10016	800-899-2573	212-696-0670
Albert Kahn Assoc Inc				
3011 W Grand Blvd Ste 1800	Detroit MI	48202	800-833-0062	313-202-7000
American Engineering Testing Inc				
550 Cleveland Ave N	Saint Paul MN	55114	800-972-6364	651-659-9001
Amset Technical Consulting Inc				
1864 S Elmhurst Rd	Mount Prospect IL	60056	888-982-6783	847-229-1155

		Toll-Free	Phone

Applied Technology & Management Inc
411 Pablo Ave ....Jacksonville Beach FL 32250 **800-275-6488** 904-249-8009

ASG Renaissance
22226 Garrison St .... Dearborn MI 48124 **800-238-0890** 313-565-4700

Barnett Engineering Ltd
7710 5 St SE Ste 215 ....Calgary AB T2H2L9 **800-268-2646** 403-255-9544

Barr Engineering Co
4700 W 77th St ....Minneapolis MN 55435 **800-632-2277** 952-832-2600

Bartlett & West Engineers Inc
1200 SW Executive Dr ....Topeka KS 66615 **888-200-6464** 785-272-2252

Barton & Loguidice DPC
443 Electronics Pkwy ....Liverpool NY 13088 **800-724-1070** 315-457-5200

Belcan Corp
10200 Anderson Way ....Cincinnati OH 45242 **800-423-5226** 513-891-0972

Belstar Inc
8408 Arlington Blvd Ste 200..........................Fairfax VA 22031 **800-548-5921** 703-645-0280

Bergmann Assoc Inc
280 E Broad St Ste 200..........................Rochester NY 14614 **800-724-1168**

BESTECH
1040 Lorne St Unit 3 ....Sudbury ON P3C4R9 **877-675-7720** 705-675-7720

Beyer Blinder Belle
120 Broadway 20th Fl..........................New York NY 10271 **800-777-7892** 212-777-7800

Bionetics Corp, The
101 Production Dr Ste 100..........................Yorktown VA 23693 **800-868-0330** 757-873-0900

BL Co 355 Research Pkwy ....Meriden CT 06450 **800-301-3077** 203-630-1406

Braun Intertec Corp
11001 Hampshire Ave S ....Minneapolis MN 55438 **800-279-6100** 952-995-2000

Brinjac Engineering Inc
114 N Second St ....Harrisburg PA 17101 **877-274-6526** 717-233-4502

Brock Solutions Inc
86 Ardelt Ave ....Kitchener ON N2C2C9 **877-702-7625** 519-571-1522

C2AE
106 W Allegan St Ste 500..........................Lansing MI 48933 **866-454-3923**

Caribou Road Services Ltd
5110 52nd Ave ....Pouce Coupe BC V0C2C0 **800-667-2322** 250-786-5440

Carollo Engineers
2700 Ygnacio Valley Rd Ste 300..........................Walnut Creek CA 94598 **800-523-5826** 925-932-1710

CDI Corp
1735 Market St Ste 200..........................Philadelphia PA 19103 **866-472-2203** 215-282-8300

Century Engineering Inc
10710 Gilroy Rd ....Hunt Valley MD 21031 **800-318-6867** 443-589-2400

CEP Forensic inc
1345 Boul Louis-xiv Blvd ....Quebec QC G2L1M4 **855-622-4480** 418-622-4480

Civil & Environmental Consultants Inc
333 Baldwin Rd ....Pittsburgh PA 15205 **800-365-2324** 412-429-2324

Coneco Engineers & Scientists Inc
4 First St ....Bridgewater MA 02324 **800-548-3355** 508-697-3191

Cook Coggin Engineers Inc
703 Crossover Rd PO Box 1526. ....Tupelo MS 38802 **877-807-4667** 662-842-7381

Corrpro Cos Inc
1055 W Smith Rd ....Medina OH 44256 **800-443-3516** 330-723-5082

CPH Engineers
500 W Fulton St ....Sanford FL 32771 **866-609-0688**

Crawford Consulting Services Inc
239 Highland Ave ....East Pittsburgh PA 15112 **800-365-9010** 412-823-0400

CSS
10301 Democracy Ln Ste 300..........................Fairfax VA 22030 **800-888-4612** 703-691-4612

CT Consultants Inc
8150 Sterling Ct ....Mentor OH 44060 **800-925-0988** 440-951-9000

Dataline LLC
6703 Albunda Dr PO Box 50816..........................Knoxville TN 37950 **888-588-7740** 865-588-7740

David Evans & Assoc Inc (DEA)
2100 SW River Pkwy ....Portland OR 97201 **800-721-1916** 503-223-6663

Deighton Associates Ltd
223 Brock St N Unit 7. ....Whitby ON L1N4H6 **888-219-6605** 905-665-6605

DGT Associates
1071 Worcester Rd ....Framingham MA 01701 **800-696-2874** 508-879-0030

Doerfer Engineering Corp
PO Box 816 ....Waverly IA 50677 **877-483-4700**

Dubois & King Inc
28 N Main St ....Randolph VT 05060 **866-783-7101** 802-728-3376

Dyer Riddle Mills & Precourt Inc (DRMP)
941 Lake Baldwin Ln ....Orlando FL 32814 **800-375-3767** 407-896-0594

E3 Consulting Inc
3333 S Bannock St Ste 500 ....Englewood CO 80110 **877-788-6676** 303-762-7060

EADS Group 1126 Eigth Ave ....Altoona PA 16602 **800-626-0904** 814-944-5035

EarthRes Group Inc
6912 Old Easton Rd PO Box 468 ....Pipersville PA 18947 **800-264-4553** 215-766-1211

EMCOR Services Betlem
704 Clinton Ave S ....Rochester NY 14620 **800-423-8536**

Emprise Corp
3900 Kennesaw 75 Pkwy N W Ste 125 ....Kennesaw GA 30144 **800-278-2119** 770-425-1420

Engineering & Environmental Consultants Inc
4625 E Ft Lowell Rd ....Tucson AZ 85712 **800-887-2103** 520-321-4625

ENSCO Inc
3110 Fairview Pk Dr Ste 300 ....Falls Church VA 22042 **800-367-2682** 703-321-9000

ES. Fox Ltd
9127 Montrose Rd ....Niagara Falls ON L2E7J9 **866-233-8933** 905-354-3700

Fakouri Electrical Engineering Inc
30001 Comercio ....Rancho Santa Margarita CA 92688 **800-669-8862**

Farwest Corrosion Control Co
1480 W Artesia Blvd ....Gardena CA 90248 **888-532-7937** 310-532-9524

Flint Surveying & Engineering Company Inc
5370 Miller Rd ....Swartz Creek MI 48473 **800-624-6089** 810-230-1333

FOX Engineering Associates Inc
414 S 17th St Ste 107..........................Ames IA 50010 **800-433-3469** 515-233-0000

Freyssinet Inc
44880 Falcon Pl Ste 100 ....Sterling VA 20166 **800-423-6587** 703-378-2500

Fuss & O'Neill Consulting Engineers Inc
146 Hartford Rd ....Manchester CT 06040 **800-286-2469** 860-646-2469

Gannett Fleming Inc
207 Senate Ave ....Camp Hill PA 17011 **800-233-1055** 717-763-7211

George Reed Inc
140 Empire Ave ....Modesto CA 95354 **877-823-2305**

George, Miles & Buhr LLC
206 W Main St ....Salisbury MD 21801 **800-789-4462** 410-742-3115

GeoSyntec Consultants Inc
900 Broken Sound Pkwy NW Ste 200..........................Boca Raton FL 33487 **866-676-1101** 561-995-0900

Ghafari Assoc Inc
17101 Michigan Ave ....Dearborn MI 48126 **800-289-7822** 313-441-3000

Giffels-Webster Engineers Inc
28 W Adams Ste 1200 ....Detroit MI 48226 **866-271-9663**

Gillespie, Prudhon & Associates Inc
16111 SE 106th Ave Ste 100 ....Clackamas OR 97015 **800-595-2145** 503-657-0424

Gravitec Systems Inc
21291 Urdahl Rd NW ....Poulsbo WA 98370 **800-755-8455** 206-780-2898

Greeley & Hansen
100 S Wacker Dr Ste 1400 ....Chicago IL 60606 **800-837-9779** 312-558-9000

Guido Perla & Associates
701 Fifth Ave Ste 1200 ....Seattle WA 98104 **800-252-5232** 206-768-1515

Gulf Interstate Engineering
16010 Barkers Pt Ln Ste 600 ....Houston TX 77079 **800-521-8879** 713-850-3400

Haag Engineering Co
4949 W Royal Ln ....Irving TX 75063 **800-527-0168** 214-614-6500

Hammel Green & Abrahamson Inc
701 Washington Ave N ....Minneapolis MN 55401 **888-442-8255** 612-758-4000

Hazen & Sawyer PC
498 Seventh Ave 11th Fl..........................New York NY 10018 **888-514-2936** 212-539-7000

HDR Engineering Inc
8404 Indian Hills Dr ....Omaha NE 68114 **800-366-4411** 402-399-1000

HL Turner Group Inc, The
27 Locke Rd ....Concord NH 03301 **800-305-2289** 603-228-1122

HMC Archtiect
3546 Councours St ....Ontario CA 91764 **800-350-9979** 909-989-9979

Hn Burns Engineering Corp
3275 Progress Dr Ste A ....Orlando FL 32826 **800-728-6506** 407-273-3770

HRP Associates Inc
197 Scott Swamp Rd ....Farmington CT 06032 **800-246-9021**

I E T Inc 3539 Glendale Ave ....Toledo OH 43614 **800-278-1031** 419-385-1233

INTERA Inc
1812 Centre Creek Dr Ste 300 ....Austin TX 78754 **800-856-0217**

Intrinsix Corp
100 Campus Dr ....Marlborough MA 01752 **800-783-0330** 508-658-7600

Istech Inc 4691 Raycom Rd ....Dover PA 17315 **800-555-4880** 717-764-5565

James Machine Works LLC
1521 Adams St ....Monroe LA 71201 **800-259-6104** 318-322-6104

John A Martin & Association Inc
950 S Grand Ave 4th Fl. ....Los Angeles CA 90015 **800-776-2368** 213-483-6490

John M Campbell & Co
1215 Crossroads Blvd ....Norman OK 73072 **800-821-5933** 405-321-1383

Johnson Mirmiran & Thompson (JMT)
72 Loveton Cir ....Sparks MD 21152 **800-472-2310** 410-329-3100

Kanata Energy Group Ltd
1900 112 - Fourth Ave SW
Sun Life Plz III - East Twr ....Calgary AB T2P0H3 **844-526-2822** 587-774-7000

KCI Technologies Inc
936 Ridgebrook Rd ....Sparks MD 21152 **800-572-7496** 410-316-7800

KSA Engineers Inc
140 E Tyler St Ste 600 ....Longview TX 75601 **877-572-3647** 903-236-7700

Kta-Tator Inc
115 Technology Dr ....Pittsburgh PA 15275 **800-582-4243** 412-788-1300

Larson Design Group Inc
1000 Commerce Park Dr
2nd Fl Ste 201 ....Williamsport PA 17701 **877-323-6603**

LBA Group Inc
3400 Tupper Dr ....Greenville NC 27834 **800-522-4464** 252-757-0279

Lerch Bates Inc
8089 S Lincoln St Ste 300 ....Littleton CO 80122 **800-409-5471** 303-795-7956

LJB Inc 2500 Newmark Dr ....Miamisburg OH 45342 **866-552-3536** 937-259-5000

Lochsa Engineering Inc
6345 S Jones Blvd Ste 100. ....Las Vegas NV 89118 **866-606-9784** 702-365-9312

Lumos & Assoc Inc
800 E College Pkwy ....Carson City NV 89706 **800-621-7155** 775-883-7077

Macaulay-Brown Inc
4021 Executive Dr ....Dayton OH 45430 **800-432-3421** 937-426-3421

MAINTSTAR 28 Hammond Unit D. ....Irvine CA 92618 **800-255-5675** 949-458-7560

Mannik & Smith Group Inc
1800 Indian Wood Cir ....Maumee OH 43537 **888-891-6321** 419-891-2222

Maren Engineering Inc
111 W Taft Dr ....South Holland IL 60473 **800-875-1038** 708-333-6250

Martronic Engineering Inc (MEI)
874 Patriot Dr Unit D ....Moorpark CA 93021 **800-960-0808** 805-583-0808

MBS Assoc Inc
7800 E Kemper Rd Ste 160. ....Cincinnati OH 45249 **888-469-9301** 513-645-1600

McDonough Bolyard Peck Inc (MBP)
3040 Williams Dr Williams Plz 1
Ste 300. ....Fairfax VA 22031 **800-898-9088** 703-641-9088

McLaughlin Research Corp
132 Johnnycake Hill Rd ....Middletown RI 02842 **800-556-7154** 401-849-4010

Mecanica Solutions Inc
10000 Blvd Henri-Bourassa Ouest ....Montreal QC H4S1R5 **800-567-4223** 514-340-1818

Meier Enterprises Inc
12 W Kennewick Ave ....Kennewick WA 99336 **800-239-7589** 509-735-1589

Merrick & Co
2450 S Peoria St ....Aurora CO 80014 **800-544-1714** 303-751-0741

Microlynx Systems Ltd
1925 18 Ave NE Ste 107. ....Calgary AB T2E7T8 **866-835-4332** 403-275-7346

Mikros Engineering Inc
8755 Wyoming Ave N ....Brooklyn Park MN 55445 **800-394-5499** 763-424-4642

Miller Engineers & Scientists
5308 S 12th St ....Sheboygan WI 53081 **800-969-7013** 920-458-6164

Modjeski & Masters Inc
100 Sterling Pkwy Ste 302 ....Mechanicsburg PA 17050 **888-663-5375** 717-790-9565

Moffatt & Nichol Engineers
3780 Kilroy Airport Way # 750 ....Long Beach CA 90806 **888-399-6609** 562-590-6500

Morrison Hershfield Group Inc
125 Commerce Valley Dr W Ste 300. ....Markham ON L3T7W4 **888-649-4730** 416-499-3110

MSA Professional Services Inc
1230 South Blvd ....Baraboo WI 53913 **800-362-4505** 608-356-2771

New Holland Engineering
43 E Front St ....New Holland OH 43145 **800-734-8155** 740-495-5200

Nova Pole International Inc
2579 188 St ....Surrey BC V3Z2A1 **866-874-8889** 604-881-0090

NV5
2525 Natomas Pk Dr Ste 300 ....Sacramento CA 95833 **877-311-4180** 916-641-9100

			Toll-Free	Phone

Omnni Associates Inc
1 Systems Dr . . . . Appleton WI 54914 **800-571-6677** 920-735-6900

Ontario Society of Professional Engineers
4950 Yonge St Ste 502 . . . . North York ON M2N6K1 **866-763-1654** 416-223-9961

Orchard Hiltz & McCliment Inc (OHM)
34000 Plymouth Rd . . . . Livonia MI 48150 **888-522-6711** 734-522-6711

Packer Engineering Inc
420 N Main St . . . . Montgomery IL 60538 **866-264-4126** 630-701-7703

Parametrix Inc
1002 15th St SW . . . . Auburn WA 98001 **888-863-5128**

Parkhill Smith & Cooper Inc
4222 85th St . . . . Lubbock TX 79423 **800-400-6646** 806-473-2200

Passero Assoc
242 West Main St Ste 100 . . . . Rochester NY 14614 **800-836-0365** 585-325-1000

Patti Engineering Inc
2110 E Walton Blvd Ste A . . . . Auburn Hills MI 48326 **800-852-0994** 248-364-3200

PCA Engineering Inc
57 Cannonball Rd PO Box 196 . . . . . . Pompton Lakes NJ 07442 **800-666-7221** 973-616-4501

Pearson Engineering Associates Inc
8825 N 23rd Ave Ste 11 . . . . Phoenix AZ 85021 **866-747-9754** 602-264-0807

Picco Engineering
8611 Jane St Ste 200 . . . . Concord ON L4K2M6 **888-772-0773** 905-760-9688

Porter Consulting Engineers PC
552 State St . . . . Meadville PA 16335 **800-541-5941** 814-337-4447

Power Engineering Corp
PO Box 766 . . . . Wilkes-Barre PA 18703 **800-626-0903** 570-823-8822

Prima-Temp Inc
2820 Wilderness Pl Ste C . . . . Boulder CO 80301 **866-398-1032**

Proctor Engineering Group Ltd
418 Mission Ave . . . . San Rafael CA 94901 **888-455-5742** 415-451-2480

Professional Service Industries Inc (PSI)
1901 S Meyers Rd Ste 400 . . . . Oakbrook Terrace IL 60181 **800-548-7901** 630-691-1490

Prolitec Inc
1235 W Canal St . . . . Milwaukee WI 53233 **844-247-7599**

Propak Systems Ltd
440 East Lake Rd NE . . . . Airdrie AB T4A2J8 **800-408-4434** 403-912-7000

QCA Systems Ltd
#101-6951 72nd St . . . . Delta BC V4G0A2 **877-940-0868** 604-940-0868

Quantum Marine Stabilizers
3790 SW 30th Ave . . . . Fort Lauderdale FL 33312 **800-807-8360** 954-587-4205

R-S-H Engineering Inc
909 N 18th St Ste 200 . . . . Monroe LA 71201 **888-340-4884** 318-323-4009

Ready Technologies Inc
101 Capitol Way N Ste 301 . . . . Olympia WA 98501 **877-892-9104** 360-413-9800

Reigstad & Associates Inc
192 W Ninth St . . . . Saint Paul MN 55102 **800-355-8414** 651-292-1123

Rettew Assoc Inc
3020 Columbia Ave . . . . Lancaster PA 17603 **800-738-8395** 717-394-3721

Reynolds Smith & Hills Inc
10748 Deerwood Pk Blvd . . . . Jacksonville FL 32256 **800-741-2014** 904-256-2500

RMA Group Inc
12130 Santa Margarita Ct . . . . . . Rancho Cucamonga CA 91730 **800-480-4808** 909-989-1751

RMF Engineering Inc
5520 Research Pk Dr Ste 300 . . . . Baltimore MD 21228 **800-938-5760** 410-576-0505

Sabre Industries Inc
8653 E Hwy 67 . . . . Alvarado TX 76009 **866-254-3707** 817-852-1700

Scheeser Buckley Mayfield Inc
1540 Corporate Woods Pkwy . . . . Uniontown OH 44685 **800-451-0221** 330-896-4664

Schneider Corp
8901 Otis Ave . . . . Indianapolis IN 46216 **866-973-7100**

SCS Engineers
3900 Kilroy Airport Way Ste 100 . . . . . . Long Beach CA 90806 **800-326-9544** 562-426-9544

Shield Engineering Inc
4301 Taggart Creek Rd . . . . Charlotte NC 28208 **800-395-5220** 704-394-6913

Shive-Hattery Inc (SH)
316 Second St SE Ste 500
PO Box 1599 . . . . Cedar Rapids IA 52406 **800-798-0227** 319-362-0313

Short-Elliott-Hendrickson Inc
3535 Vadnais Ctr Dr . . . . Saint Paul MN 55110 **800-325-2055** 651-490-2000

Signa Engineering Corp
2 Northpoint Dr Ste 700 . . . . Houston TX 77060 **800-987-3331** 281-774-1000

Simmons Knife & Saw
400 Regency Dr . . . . Glendale Heights IL 60139 **800-252-3381** 630-912-2880

Simon & Assoc Inc
3200 Commerce St . . . . Blacksburg VA 24060 **800-763-4234** 540-951-4234

Simpson Gumpertz & Heger Inc
41 Seyon St Bldg 1 Ste 500 . . . . Waltham MA 02453 **800-729-7429** 781-907-9000

Skidmore Owings & Merrill LLP (SOM)
224 S Michigan Ave Ste 1000 . . . . Chicago IL 60604 **866-296-2688** 312-554-9090

Snowline Engineering
4261 Business Dr . . . . Cameron Park CA 95682 **800-361-6083** 530-677-2675

Sonalysts Inc
215 Hempstead Pkwy N . . . . Waterford CT 06385 **800-526-8091** 860-442-4355

Soutex Inc 357 Rue Jackson . . . . Quebec QC G1N4C4 **800-463-2839** 418-871-2455

Spec Ops Inc
319 Business Ln . . . . Ashland VA 23005 **800-774-3854** 804-752-4790

SPI/Mobile Pulley Works Inc
905 S Ann St . . . . Mobile AL 36605 **866-334-6325** 251-653-0606

Sponseller Group Inc
1600 Timberwolf Dr . . . . Holland OH 43528 **800-776-1625** 419-861-3000

Stanley Consultants Inc
225 Iowa Ave . . . . Muscatine IA 52761 **800-553-9694** 563-264-6600

Steven Schaefer Associates Inc
10411 Medallion Dr . . . . Cincinnati OH 45241 **800-542-3302** 513-542-3300

Stratasys Inc
7665 Commerce Way . . . . Eden Prairie MN 55344 **800-937-3010** 952-937-3000
NASDAQ: SSYS

Sunland Group Inc
1033 La Posada Dr Ste 370 . . . . Austin TX 78752 **866-732-8500** 512-494-0208

Support Systems Associates Inc (SSAI)
Marina Towers 709 S Harbor City Blvd
Ste 350 . . . . Melbourne FL 32901 **877-234-7724**

Syndesi Solutions
115 West Market St . . . . Athens AL 35611 **877-744-0568**

SYNEXXUS Inc
2425 Wilson Blvd Ste 400 . . . . Arlington VA 22201 **866-707-4594**

Systems & Processes Engineering Corp (SPEC)
4120 Commercial Ctr Dr Ste 500 . . . . Austin TX 78744 **800-789-7732** 512-479-7732

			Toll-Free	Phone

Taylor & Syfan Consulting Engineers Inc
684 Clarion Ct . . . . San Luis Obispo CA 93401 **800-579-3881** 805-547-2000

Tectonic Engineering & Surveying Consultants PC
70 Pleasant Hill Rd . . . . Mountainville NY 10953 **800-829-6531**

Teledyne Brown Engineering Inc
300 Sparkman Dr . . . . Huntsville AL 35805 **800-933-2091** 256-726-1000

Telics 3440 Lakemont Blvd . . . . Fort Mill SC 29708 **800-424-1454**

Terracon 18001 W 106th St . . . . Olathe KS 66061 **800-593-7777** 913-599-6886

Toledo Engineering Co Inc
3400 Executive Pkwy PO Box 2927 . . . . . . Toledo OH 43606 **800-654-4567** 419-537-9711

Tolunay-Wong Engineers Inc
10710 S Sam Houston Pkwy W . . . . Houston TX 77031 **888-887-9932**

TransCore
150 Fourth Ave N Ste 1200 . . . . Nashville TN 37219 **800-923-4824** 615-988-9993

Trayer Engineering Corp
898 Pennsylvania Ave . . . . San Francisco CA 94107 **800-377-1774** 415-285-7770

TriLeaf Corp
10845 Olive Blvd Ste 260 . . . . Saint Louis MO 63141 **800-652-5552** 314-997-6111

TrueNet Communications Corp
7666 Blanding Blvd . . . . Jacksonville FL 32244 **800-285-2028** 904-777-9052

Ulteig Engineers Inc
3350 38th Ave S . . . . Fargo ND 58104 **888-858-3441** 701-280-8500

Unified Industries Inc
6551 Loisdale Ct Ste 400 . . . . Springfield VA 22150 **800-666-1642** 703-922-9800

United States Steel Corp
600 Grant St . . . . Pittsburgh PA 15219 **866-433-4801** 412-433-1121
NYSE: X

Vanadium Group Corp
134 Three Degree Rd . . . . Pittsburgh PA 15237 **800-685-0354** 412-367-6060

Vanteon Corp
250 Cross Keys Office Pk Bldg 250 . . . . Fairport NY 14450 **888-506-5677** 585-419-9555

Veenstra & Kimm Inc
3000 Westown Pkwy . . . . West Des Moines IA 50266 **800-241-8000** 515-225-8000

VSE Corp
2550 Huntington Ave . . . . Alexandria VA 22303 **800-455-4873** 703-960-4600
NASDAQ: VSEC

Wade-Trim Group Inc
500 Griswold Ave Ste 2500 . . . . Detroit MI 48226 **800-482-2864** 313-961-3650

Walter P Moore
1301 Mckinney St Ste 1100 . . . . Houston TX 77010 **800-364-7300** 713-630-7300

Weston & Sampson Inc
5 Centennial Dr . . . . Peabody MA 01960 **800-726-7766** 978-532-1900

Wetland Studies & Solutions Inc
5300 Wellington Branch Dr . . . . Gainesville VA 20155 **800-247-1812** 703-679-5600

Whitney Bailey Cox & Magnani LLC
300 E Joppa Rd Ste 200 . . . . Baltimore MD 21286 **800-673-9312** 410-512-4500

Willdan
2401 E Katella Ave Ste 300 . . . . Anaheim CA 92806 **800-424-9144** 714-940-6300

Woodard & Curran
41 Hutchins Dr . . . . Portland ME 04102 **800-426-4262** 207-774-2112

Wright-Pierce
11 Bowdoin Mill Is Ste 140 . . . . Topsham ME 04086 **888-621-8156** 207-725-8721

262   ENGINES & TURBINES

SEE ALSO Motors (Electric) & Generators ; Automotive Parts & Supplies - Mfr ; Aircraft Engines & Engine Parts

			Toll-Free	Phone

Allied Power Group LLC
10131 Mills Rd . . . . Houston TX 77070 **888-830-3535** 281-444-3535

Arrow Engine Co
2301 E Independence St . . . . Tulsa OK 74110 **800-331-3662** 918-583-5711

Briggs & Stratton Corp
12301 W Wirth St . . . . Milwaukee WI 53222 **800-444-7774** 414-259-5333
NYSE: BGG

Brunswick Corp Mercury Marine Div
W 6250 Pioneer Rd . . . . Fond du Lac WI 54935 **866-408-6372** 920-929-5040

Capstone Turbine Corp
21211 Nordhoff St . . . . Chatsworth CA 91311 **866-422-7786** 818-734-5300
NASDAQ: CPST

Chromium Corp
14911 Quorum Dr Ste 600 . . . . Dallas TX 75254 **888-346-4747** 216-271-4910

Clayton Industries
17477 Hurley St . . . . City of Industry CA 91744 **800-423-4585** 626-435-1200

Cummins Inc
500 Jackson St PO Box 3005 . . . . Columbus IN 47201 **800-343-7357** 812-377-5000
NYSE: CMI

Delaware Mfg Industries Corp
3776 Commerce Ct . . . . Wheatfield NY 14120 **800-248-3642** 716-743-4360

Electro Steam Generator Corp
50 Indel Ave PO Box 438 . . . . Rancocas NJ 08073 **866-617-0764** 609-288-9071

EnPro Industries Inc Fairbanks Morse Engine
701 White Ave . . . . Beloit WI 53511 **800-356-6955**

Hatch & Kirk Inc
5111 Leary Ave NW . . . . Seattle WA 98107 **800-426-2818** 206-783-2766

JASPER Engines & Transmissions
815 Wernsing Rd PO Box 650 . . . . Jasper IN 47547 **800-827-7455** 812-482-1041

John Deere Power Systems
3801 W Ridgeway Ave . . . . Waterloo IA 50704 **800-533-6446**

Kohler Engines
444 Highland Dr . . . . Kohler WI 53044 **800-544-2444** 920-457-4441

Northern Lights Inc
4420 14th Ave NW . . . . Seattle WA 98107 **800-762-0165** 206-789-3880

NREC Power Systems
5222 Hwy 311 . . . . Houma LA 70360 **800-851-6732** 985-872-5480

Pratt & Whitney Canada Inc
1000 Marie-Victorin Blvd . . . . Longueuil QC J4G1A1 **800-268-8000** 450-677-9411

Springfield ReManufacturing Corp
4727 E Kearney . . . . Springfield MO 65803 **800-531-7134**

SRC Holdings Corp
531 S Union Ave . . . . Springfield MO 65802 **800-327-2253** 417-862-2337

Volvo Penta of the Americas Inc
1300 Volvo Penta Dr . . . . Chesapeake VA 23320 **800-522-1959** 757-436-2800

Westerbeke Corp
150 John Hancock Rd
Miles Standish Industrial Pk . . . . Taunton MA 02780 **800-582-7846** 508-823-7677

263 ENVELOPES

				Toll-Free	Phone
ADM Corp 100 Lincoln Blvd	Middlesex	NJ	08846	**800-327-0718**	732-469-0900
Alvah Bushnell Co 519 E Chelten Ave	Philadelphia	PA	19144	**800-255-7434**	800-814-7296
AmericanChurch Inc 100 Noll Plz	Huntington	IN	46750	**800-446-3035**	
Bowers Envelope Co 5331 N Tacoma Ave	Indianapolis	IN	46220	**800-333-4321**	317-253-4321
Craig Envelope Corp 12-01 44th Ave	Long Island City	NY	11101	**888-272-4436**	
Curtis 1000 Inc 1725 Breckinridge Pkwy Ste 500	Duluth	GA	30096	**877-287-8715**	678-380-9095
Heinrich Envelope Corp 925 Zane Ave N	Minneapolis	MN	55422	**800-346-7957**	763-544-3571
Love Envelopes Inc 10733 E Ute St	Tulsa	OK	74116	**800-532-9747**	918-836-3535
Mackay Envelope Co 2100 Elm St SE	Minneapolis	MN	55414	**800-622-5299**	
National Church Supply Co, The PO Box 269	Chester	WV	26034	**800-627-9900**	304-387-5200
Papercone Corp 3200 Fern Valley Rd	Louisville	KY	40213	**800-626-5308**	502-961-9493
Poly-Pak Industries Inc 125 Spagnoli Rd	Melville	NY	11747	**800-969-1993**	631-293-6767
Response Envelope Inc 1340 S Baker Ave	Ontario	CA	91761	**800-750-0046**	909-923-5855
Tension Envelope Corp 819 E 19th St	Kansas City	MO	64108	**800-388-5122**	
Top Flight Inc 1300 Central Ave	Chattanooga	TN	37408	**800-777-3740**	423-266-8171
United Envelope LLC 150 Industrial Park Dr	Mount Pocono	PA	18344	**800-752-4012**	570-839-1600
Western States Envelope & Label Co 4480 N 132nd St	Butler	WI	53007	**800-558-0514**	262-781-5540
Worcester Envelope Co 22 Millbury St	Auburn	MA	01501	**800-343-1398**	

264 EQUIPMENT RENTAL & LEASING

SEE ALSO Credit & Financing - Consumer ; Credit & Financing - Commercial ; Fleet Leasing & Management

264-1 Computer Equipment Leasing

				Toll-Free	Phone
Data Sales Company Inc 3450 W Burnsville Pkwy	Burnsville	MN	55337	**800-328-2730**	952-890-8838
Electro Rent Corp 6060 Sepulveda Blvd *NASDAQ: ELRC* ■ *Sales	Van Nuys	CA	91411	**800-688-1111***	818-787-2100
Hitachi Credit America Ltd 800 Connecticut Ave	Norwalk	CT	06854	**866-718-4222**	203-956-3000
Newport Leasing Inc 4750 Von Karman Ave *Cust Svc	Newport Beach	CA	92660	**800-274-0042***	949-476-8476
Rent-A-PC Inc 265 Oser Ave	Hauppauge	NY	11788	**800-888-8686**	631-273-8888
Summit Funding Group Inc 4680 Pkwy Dr Ste 300	Mason	OH	45040	**866-489-1222**	513-489-1222

264-2 Home & Office Equipment Rental (General)

				Toll-Free	Phone
Bestway Inc 12400 Coit Rd Ste 950	Dallas	TX	75251	**800-316-4567**	214-630-6655
Brook Furniture Rental Inc 100 N Field Dr Ste 220	Lake Forest	IL	60045	**877-285-7368**	
Buddy's Home Furnishings 4705 S Apopka Vineland Rd *Cust Svc	Orlando	FL	32819	**855-298-9325***	866-779-5058
Celtic Commercial Finance 4 Park Plz Ste 300	Irvine	CA	92614	**866-323-5842**	
Gordon Flesch Company Inc 2675 Research Pk Dr	Madison	WI	53711	**800-333-5905**	800-677-7877
LMG Inc 2350 Investors Row	Orlando	FL	32837	**888-226-3100**	407-850-0505
Marlin Business Services Inc 300 Fellowship Rd *NASDAQ: MRLN*	Mount Laurel	NJ	08054	**888-479-9111**	
Projection Presentation Technology 5803 Rolling Rd	Springfield	VA	22152	**800-377-7650**	703-912-1334
Rent-A-Center Inc 5501 Headquarters Dr *NASDAQ: RCII*	Plano	TX	75024	**800-422-8186**	
Rug Doctor LP 4701 Old Shepard Pl	Plano	TX	75093	**800-784-3628**	
Somerset Capital Group Ltd 612 Wheelers Farms Rd	Milford	CT	06461	**877-282-9922**	203-701-5100

264-3 Industrial & Heavy Equipment Rental

				Toll-Free	Phone
Aggreko 15600 John F Kennedy Blvd Ste 600	Houston	TX	77032	**833-507-6491**	
Ahern Rentals Inc 4241 Arville St	Las Vegas	NV	89103	**800-589-6797**	702-362-0623
Allied Steel Construction Co Inc 2211 NW First Terr	Oklahoma City	OK	73107	**800-522-4658**	405-232-7531
Buck & Knobby Equipment Co 6220 Sterns Rd	Ottawa Lake	MI	49267	**855-213-2825**	734-856-2811

				Toll-Free	Phone
Cloverdale Equipment Co 13133 Cloverdale St	Oak Park	MI	48237	**800-822-7999**	248-399-6600
Equipment Technology LLC 341 NW 122nd St	Oklahoma City	OK	73114	**888-748-3841**	
G & C Equipment Corp 1875 W Redondo Beach Blvd Ste 102	Gardena	CA	90247	**800-559-5529**	310-515-6715
H & E Equipment Services Inc 7500 Pecue Ln *NASDAQ: HEES*	Baton Rouge	LA	70809	**866-467-3682**	225-298-5200
Hawthorne Machinery Co 16945 Camino San Bernardo	San Diego	CA	92127	**800-437-4228**	858-674-7000
HB Rentals LC 5813 Hwy 90 E	Broussard	LA	70518	**800-262-6790**	337-839-1641
Klochko Equipment Rental Company Inc 2780 Corbin Ave	Melvindale	MI	48122	**800-783-7368**	313-386-7220
Marco Crane & Rigging Co 221 S 35th Ave	Phoenix	AZ	85009	**800-668-2671**	602-272-2671
Maxim Crane Works 1225 Washington Pk	Bridgeville	PA	15017	**877-629-5438**	412-504-0200
Medico Industries Inc 1500 Hwy 315	Wilkes-Barre	PA	18702	**800-633-0027**	570-825-7711
National Construction Rentals Inc 15319 Chatsworth St	Mission Hills	CA	91345	**800-352-5675**	
Raymond Handling Concepts Corp 41400 Boyce Rd	Fremont	CA	94538	**800-675-2500**	510-745-7500
Rush Enterprises Inc 555 IH 35 S Ste 500 *NASDAQ: RUSHA*	New Braunfels	TX	78130	**800-973-7874**	830-626-5200
Skyworks LLC 100 Thielman Dr	Buffalo	NY	14206	**877-601-5438**	716-822-5438
Star Rentals Inc 1919 Fourth Ave S	Seattle	WA	98134	**800-825-7880**	206-622-7880
Stephenson Equipment Inc (SEI) 7201 Paxton St	Harrisburg	PA	17111	**800-325-6455**	717-564-3434
Sunbelt Rentals Inc 2341 Deerfield Dr *General	Fort Mill	SC	29715	**800-667-9328***	704-348-2676
Tetra Corporate Services LLC 6995 Union Park Ctr Ste 360	Salt Lake City	UT	84047	**800-417-0548**	801-566-2600
Traffic Control Service Inc 2435 Lemon Ave	Signal Hill	CA	90755	**800-763-3999**	
Unitod Rontalc 3266 E Washington St	Phoenix	AZ	85233	**844-873-4948**	602-267-3898
United Rentals Inc 224 Selleck St *NYSE: URI*	Stamford	CT	06902	**800-877-3687**	203-622-3131
Western Oilfields Supply Co 3404 State Rd	Bakersfield	CA	93308	**800-742-7246**	661-399-9124

264-4 Medical Equipment Rental

				Toll-Free	Phone
American Shared Hospital Services 4 Embarcadero Ctr Ste 3700 *NYSE: AMS*	San Francisco	CA	94111	**800-735-0641**	415-788-5300
Dynasplint Systems Inc 770 Ritchie Hwy Ste W21	Severna Park	MD	21146	**800-638-6771**	410-544-9530
First Lease Inc 1 Walnut Grove Dr Ste 300	Horsham	PA	19044	**866-493-4778**	
Freedom Medical Inc 219 Welsh Pool Rd	Exton	PA	19341	**800-784-8849**	610-903-0200
Universal Hospital Services Inc 6625 W 78th St Ste 300	Minneapolis	MN	55439	**800-847-7368**	952-893-3200

264-5 Transport Equipment Rental

				Toll-Free	Phone
Flexi-Van Leasing Inc 251 Monroe Ave	Kenilworth	NJ	07033	**866-965-9288**	908-276-8000
Greenbrier Co 1 Centerpointe Dr Ste 200 *NYSE: GBX*	Lake Oswego	OR	97035	**800-343-7188**	503-684-7000
Railserve Inc 1691 Phoenix Blvd Ste 250	Atlanta	GA	30349	**800-345-7245**	770-996-6838
TTX Co 101 N Wacker Dr	Chicago	IL	60606	**800-889-4357**	312-853-3223

265 ETHICS COMMISSIONS

				Toll-Free	Phone
Federal Election Commission 999 E St NW	Washington	DC	20463	**800-424-9530**	202-694-1100
Alabama *Administrative Office of Alabama Courts* 300 Dexter Ave	Montgomery	AL	36104	**866-954-9411**	334-954-5000
Alaska *Arts Council* 161 Klevin St Ste 102	Anchorage	AK	99508	**888-278-7424**	907-269-6610
Arkansas *Administrative Office of the Courts* 625 Marshall St	Little Rock	AR	72201	**800-950-8221**	501-682-9400
Ethics Commission 501 Woodlane Ste 301n	Little Rock	AR	72203	**800-422-7773**	501-324-9600
Fair Political Practices Commission 428 J St Ste 620	Sacramento	CA	95814	**866-275-3772**	916-322-5660
Judicial Council of California 455 Golden Gate Ave	San Francisco	CA	94102	**800-900-5980**	415-865-4200
Transparency & Campaign Finance Commission 200 Piedmont Ave SE Ste 1416 W Tower	Atlanta	GA	30334	**866-589-7327**	404-463-1980
Indiana *Agriculture Dept* 101 W Washington St	Indianapolis	IN	46204	**800-677-9800**	
State Ethics Commission 315 W Ohio St Rm 104	Indianapolis	IN	46202	**866-805-8498**	800-677-9800

Classified Section

				Toll-Free	Phone

Iowa
Adult Children & Family Services Div
1305 E Walnut St .... Des Moines IA 50319 **800-735-2942** 515-281-8977
Louisiana
Agriculture & Forestry Dept
5825 Florida Blvd ....Baton Rouge LA 70806 **866-927-2476** 225-922-1234
Ethics Board
617 N Third St
LaSalle Bldg Ste 10-36.................Baton Rouge LA 70802 **800-842-6630** 225-219-5600
Ethics Commission
45 Calvert St .... Annapolis MD 21401 **877-669-6085** 410-260-7770
Minnesota
Aging Board 540 Cedar St ....Saint Paul MN 55155 **800-882-6262** 651-431-2500
Campaign Finance & Public Disclosure Board
190 Centennial Office Bldg 658 Cedar St
.... Saint Paul MN 55155 **800-657-3889** 651-539-1180
Montana
Arts Council PO Box 202201 ....Helena MT 59620 **800-282-3092** 406-444-6430
Ethical Standards Commission
28 W State St 8th Fl PO Box 082 ....Trenton NJ 08625 **888-223-1355** 609-292-1892
Ethics Administration
325 Don Gaspar St Ste 300 ....Santa Fe NM 87501 **800-477-3632** 505-827-3600
State Ethics Commission
Rm 309 Finance Bldg PO Box 11470 ......Harrisburg PA 17108 **800-932-0936** 717-783-1610
Texas
Aging & Disability Services
701 W 51st St ....Austin TX 78751 **888-388-6332** 512-438-3011
Public Disclosure Commission
711 Capitol Way Ste 206 PO Box 40908 ....Olympia WA 98504 **877-601-2828** 360-753-1111
Ethics Commission
210 Brooks St Ste 300 ....Charleston WV 25301 **866-558-0664** 304-558-0664
Ethics Board
212 E Washington Ave 3rd Fl..............Madison WI 53707 **866-868-3947** 608-266-8005

266   EXECUTIVE RECRUITING FIRMS

				Toll-Free	Phone

Battalia Winston International
555 Madison Ave .... New York NY 10022 **800-570-3118** 212-308-8080
Daniel & Yeager (D&Y)
6767 Old Madison Pk Ste 690 ....Huntsville AL 35806 **800-955-1919**
Diversified Search Cos
2005 Market St 33rd Fl..........Philadelphia PA 19103 **800-423-3932** 215-732-6666
Korn/Ferry International
1900 Ave of the Stars Ste 2600.....Los Angeles CA 90067 **877-345-3610** 310-552-1834
NYSE: KFY
Management Recruiters International Inc
1735 Market St Ste 200 ....Philadelphia PA 19103 **800-875-4000**
MSI International Inc
650 Park Ave ....King of Prussia PA 19406 **800-927-0919** 610-265-2000
Russell Reynolds Assoc Inc
277 Park Ave Ste 3800 ....New York NY 10166 **800-259-0470** 212-351-2000
Spencer Reed Group Inc
5700 W 112th St Ste 110 ....Overland Park KS 66211 **800-477-5035** 913-663-4400
Witt/Kieffer Ford Hadelman & Lloyd
2015 Spring Rd Ste 510 ....Oak Brook IL 60523 **888-281-1370** 630-990-1370

267   EXERCISE & FITNESS EQUIPMENT

SEE ALSO Sporting Goods

				Toll-Free	Phone

Body-Solid Inc
1900 Des Plaines Ave ....Forest Park IL 60130 **800-833-1227**
Cybex International Inc
10 Trotter Dr ....Medway MA 02053 **888-462-9239** 508-533-4300
Heartline Fitness Products Inc
8041 Cessna Ave Ste 200..........Gaithersburg MD 20879 **800-262-3348** 301-921-0661
Hoggan Scientific LLC
3653 W 1987 S ....Salt Lake City UT 84104 **800-678-7888** 801-572-6500
Hoist Fitness Systems Inc
9990 Empire St Ste 130 ....San Diego CA 92126 **800-548-5438** 858-578-7676
ICON Health & Fitness Inc
1500 S 1000 W ....Logan UT 84321 **800-999-3756** 435-750-5000
IronMaster LLC
14562 167th Ave SE ....Monroe WA 98272 **800-533-3339** 360-217-7780
Nautilus Inc
17750 SE Sixth Way ....Vancouver WA 98683 **800-628-8458**
NYSE: NLS
New York Barbells
160 Home St ....Elmira NY 14904 **800-446-1833**
Precor Inc
20031 142nd Ave NE ....Woodinville WA 98072 **800-786-8404** 425-486-9292
Pro Star Sports Inc
1133 Winchester Ave ....Kansas City MO 64126 **800-821-8482** 816-241-9737
Soloflex Inc
1281 NE 25th Ave Ste I..........Hillsboro OR 97124 **800-547-8802**
Spirit Manufacturing Inc
3000 Nestle Rd ....Jonesboro AR 72401 **800-258-4555** 870-935-1107
True Fitness Technology
865 Hoff Rd ....O'Fallon MO 63366 **800-426-6570** 888-491-2307
Vectra Fitness Inc
7901 S 190th St ....Kent WA 98032 **800-283-2872** 425-291-9550
Woodway USA
W229 N591 Foster Ct ....Waukesha WI 53186 **800-966-3929** 262-548-6235
York Barbell Co Inc
3300 BoaRd Rd ....York PA 17406 **800-358-9675*** 717-767-6481
*Cust Svc

268   EXPLOSIVES

				Toll-Free	Phone

Alliant Powder
2299 Snake River Ave ....Lewiston ID 83501 **800-276-9337** 800-379-1732

Austin Powder Co
25800 Science Pk Dr .... Cleveland OH 44122 **800-321-0752** 216-464-2400
Buckley Powder Co
42 Inverness Dr E ....Englewood CO 80112 **800-333-2266** 303-790-7007
Dyno Nobel Inc
2795 E Cottonwood Pkwy Ste 500 ....Salt Lake City UT 84121 **800-473-2675** 801-364-4800
Orica USA Inc
33101 E Quincy Ave .... Watkins CO 80137 **800-800-3855** 303-268-5000

269   EYE BANKS

SEE ALSO Organ & Tissue Banks ; Transplant Centers - Blood Stem Cell
Eye banks listed here are members of the Eye Bank Association of America (EBAA), an accrediting body for eye banks. The EBAA medical standards for member eye banks are endorsed by the American Academy of Ophthalmology.

				Toll-Free	Phone

Alabama Eye Bank
500 Robert Jemison Rd .... Birmingham AL 35209 **800-423-7811**
Alcon Laboratories Inc
6201 S Fwy .... Fort Worth TX 76134 **800-862-5266** 817-293-0450
Center for Organ Recovery & Education (CORE)
204 Sigma Dr RIDC Pk ....Pittsburgh PA 15238 **800-366-6777** 412-963-3550
Dakota Lions Sight & Health
4501 W 61st St N .... Sioux Falls SD 57107 **800-245-7846** 605-373-1008
Donor Network of Arizona
201 W Coolidge St .... Phoenix AZ 85013 **800-447-9477** 602-222-2200
Donor Network West
12667 Alcosta Blvd Ste 500 .... Oakland CA 94583 **888-570-9400**
Eye Bank for Sight Restoration Inc
120 Wall St 3rd Fl.................. New York NY 10005 **866-287-3937** 212-742-9000
Eye Bank of British Columbia
855 W 12th Ave JPPN - B205.......... Vancouver BC V5Z1M9 **800-667-2060** 604-875-4567
Heartland Lions Eye Bank
10100 N Ambassador Dr Ste 200 .... Kansas City MO 64153 **800-753-2265** 816-454-5454
Idaho Lions Eye Bank
1090 N Cole Rd .... Boise ID 83704 **800-546-6889** 208-338-5466
International Cornea Project
9246 Lightwave Ave Ste 120..................San Diego CA 92123 **800-393-2265** 858-694-0400
LABS Inc
6933 S Revere Pkwy .... Centennial CO 80112 **866-393-2244** 720-528-4750
Lions Eye Bank of Nebraska Inc
University of Nebraska Medical Ctr
985541 Nebraska Medical Ctr .... Omaha NE 68198 **800-225-7244** 402-559-4039
Lions Eye Bank of Wisconsin
2401 American Ln ....Madison WI 53704 **877-233-2354** 608-233-2354
Lions Foundation of Manitoba & Northwestern Ontario Inc
320 Sherbrook St .... Winnipeg MB R3B2W6 **800-552-6820** 204-772-1899
Lions Gift of Sight
1000 Westgate Dr Ste 260 ....Saint paul MN 55114 **866-887-4448*** 612-625-5159
*Cust Svc
Lions Medical Eye Bank & Research Ctr of Eastern Virginia
600 Gresham Dr .... Norfolk VA 23507 **800-453-6059**
Lone Star Lions Eye Bank
102 E Wheeler PO Box 347..................Manor TX 78653 **800-977-3937** 512-457-0638
National Disease Research Interchange (NDRI)
1628 John F Kennedy Blvd
8 Penn Ctr 8th Fl. ....Philadelphia PA 19103 **800-222-6374** 215-557-7361
New Mexico Lions Eye Bank
2501 Yale Blvd SE Ste 100 ....Albuquerque NM 87106 **888-616-3937** 505-266-3937
North Carolina Eye Bank Inc
3900 Westpoint Blvd Ste F ....Winston-Salem NC 27103 **800-552-9956**
Old Dominion Eye Bank (ODEF)
9200 Arboretum Pkwy Ste 104 ....Richmond VA 23236 **800-832-0728** 804-560-7540
Oregon Lions Sight & Hearing Foundation
1010 NW 22nd Ave Ste 144 ....Portland OR 97210 **800-635-4667** 503-413-7399
Rocky Mountain Lions Eye Bank (RMLEB)
1675 Viele Crst Ste El2049 PO Box 6026 ....Aurora CO 80045 **800-444-7479** 720-848-3937
San Diego Eye Bank (SDEB)
9246 Lightwave Ave Ste 120..................San Diego CA 92123 **800-393-2265** 858-694-0400
SightLife
221 Yale Ave N Ste 450 ....Seattle WA 98109 **800-847-5786** 206-682-8500
South Dakota Lions Eye Bank
4501 W 61st St N .... Sioux Falls SD 57107 **800-245-7846** 605-373-1008
Upstate New York Transplant Services Inc
110 Broadway ....Buffalo NY 14203 **800-227-4771** 716-853-6667

270   FABRIC STORES

SEE ALSO Patterns - Sewing

				Toll-Free	Phone

Everfast Inc
203 Gale Ln ....Kennett Square PA 19348 **800-213-6366*** 610-444-9700
*Cust Svc
Jo-Ann Fabrics & Crafts
5555 DARROW Rd ....Hudson OH 44236 **888-739-4120**
Jo-Ann Stores Inc (JAS)
5555 DARROW Rd ....Hudson OH 44236 **888-739-4120**
Mary Maxim Inc
2001 Holland Ave PO Box 5019 ....Port Huron MI 48061 **800-962-9504** 810-987-2000
RJR Fashion Fabrics
2610 Columbia St Ste B ....Torrance CA 90503 **800-422-5426** 310-222-8782
Tri-state Fabricators Inc
1146 Ferris Rd ....Amelia OH 45102 **888-523-1488** 513-752-5005
Vogue Fabrics
618 Hartrey Ave ....Evanston IL 60202 **800-433-4313**

271   FACILITIES MANAGEMENT SERVICES

SEE ALSO Correctional & Detention Management (Privatized)

				Toll-Free	Phone

ARAMARK Uniform & Career Apparel LLC
2860 Rudder Rd .... Memphis TN 38118 **800-272-6275**

			Toll-Free	Phone
Elite Corp 2878 Camino Del Rio S Ste 260	San Diego CA	92108	855-809-2047	619-574-1589
Financial & Realty Services LLC 1110 Bonifant St Ste 301	Silver Spring MD	20910	800-650-9714	301-650-9112
FLIK Conference Centers & Hotels 2 International Dr 2nd Fl	Rye Brook NY	10573	855-832-3545*	914-629-0542
*Resv				
Philotechnics Ltd 201 Renovare Blvd	Oak Ridge TN	37830	888-723-9278	865-483-1551
Phoenix Park 'n Swap 3801 E Washington St	Phoenix AZ	85034	800-772-0852	602-273-1250
Quality Solutions Inc 128 N First St	Colwich KS	67030	888-328-2454	316-721-3656
Viox Services Inc 15 W Voorhees St	Cincinnati OH	45215	888-846-9462	513-948-8469
Xanterra Parks & Resorts 6312 S Fiddlers Green Cir Ste 600-N	Greenwood Village CO	80111	800-236-7916	303-600-3400

272　　FACTORS

Factors are companies that buy accounts receivable (invoices) from other businesses at a discount.

			Toll-Free	Phone
Action Capital Corp 230 Peachtree St Ste 1910	Atlanta GA	30303	800-525-7767	404-524-3181
Advantage Funding Corp 1000 Parkwood Cir SE	Atlanta GA	30339	800-241-2274	770-955-2274
AmeriFactors 215 Celebration Pl Ste 340	Celebration FL	34747	800-884-3863	
Asta Funding Inc 210 Sylvan Ave	Englewood Cliffs NJ	07632	866-389-7627	201-567-5648
NASDAQ: ASFI				
Bibby Financial Services 600 TownPark Ln Ste 450	Kennesaw GA	30144	877-882-4229	
Crestmark Bank 5480 Corporate Dr Ste 350	Troy MI	48098	888-999-8050	
Diversified Funding Services Inc 125 Habersham Dr 2nd Fl	Fayetteville GA	30214	888-603-0055	770-603-0055
Goodman Factors 3010 LBJ Fwy Ste 140	Dallas TX	75234	877-446-6362	972-241-3297
Hamilton Group 100 Elwood Davis Rd	North Syracuse NY	13212	800-351-3066	315-413-0086
LSQ Funding Group LC 2600 Lucien Way Ste 100	Maitland FL	32751	800-474-7606	
Magnolia Financial Inc 187 W Broad St	Spartanburg SC	29306	866-573-0611	864-699-8178
Mazon Assoc Inc 800 W Airport Fwy Ste 900	Irving TX	75062	800-442-2740	972-554-6967
Merchant Factors Corp 1441 Broadway 22nd Fl	New York NY	10018	800-970-9997*	212-840-7575
*All				
Porter Capital Corp 2112 First Ave N	Birmingham AL	35203	800-737-7344	205-322-5442
Quantum Corporate Funding Ltd 1140 Ave of the Americas 16th Fl	New York NY	10036	800-352-2535	212-768-1200
Riviera Finance 220 Ave I	Redondo Beach CA	90277	800-872-7484	310-540-3993
RTS Financial Service 9300 Metcalf Ste 301	Overland Park KS	66212	877-242-4390	844-206-6123
Seven Oaks Capital Assoc LLC 7854 Anselmo Ln PO Box 82360	Baton Rouge LA	70810	800-511-4588	225-757-1919

273　　FARM MACHINERY & EQUIPMENT - MFR

SEE ALSO Lawn & Garden Equipment

			Toll-Free	Phone
AGCO Corp (AGCO) 4205 River Green Pkwy	Duluth GA	30096	877-525-4384	770-813-9200
NYSE: AGCO				
Alamo Group Inc 1627 E Walnut	Seguin TX	78155	800-788-6066*	830-379-1480
NYSE: ALG ■ *Cust Svc				
All-American Co-op PO Box 125	Stewartville MN	55976	888-354-4058	507-533-4222
Allied Systems Co 21433 SW Oregon St	Sherwood OR	97140	800-285-7000	503-625-2560
Amarillo Wind Machine Co 20513 Ave 256	Exeter CA	93221	800-311-4498	559-592-4256
Applegate Livestock Equipment Inc 902 S State Rd 32	Union City IN	47390	800-354-9502	765-964-4631
Arts-Way Mfg Co Inc 5556 Hwy 9 PO Box 288	Armstrong IA	50514	800-535-4517	712-864-3131
NASDAQ: ARTW				
Atom-Jet Industries Ltd 2110 Park Ave	Brandon MB	R7B0R9	800-573-5048	
B & H Manufacturing Inc 141 County Rd 34 E	Jackson MN	56143	800-240-3288	
Berg Equipment Co 2700 W Veterans Pkwy	Marshfield WI	54449	800-494-1738	715-384-2151
Bowie Industries Inc 1004 E Wise St	Bowie TX	76230	800-433-0934	940-872-1106
Brown Mfg Corp 6001 E Hwy 27	Ozark AL	36360	800-633-8909	
Broyhill Co 1 N Market Sq PO Box 475	Dakota City NE	68731	800-228-1003	402-987-3412
Bucklin Tractor & Implement Co 115 W Railroad PO Box 127	Bucklin KS	67834	800-334-4823	620-826-3271
Cal-Coast Dairy Systems Inc 424 S Tegner Rd	Turlock CA	95380	800-732-6826*	209-634-9026
*Cust Svc				
Chick Master Incubator Co 945 Lafayette Rd	Medina OH	44256	800-727-8726	330-722-5591
Conrad-American Inc 609 Main St	Houghton IA	52631	800-553-1791*	319-469-4141
*General				

			Toll-Free	Phone
CTB Inc 611 N Higbee St PO Box 2000	Milford IN	46542	800-261-8651	574-658-4191
Custom Products of Litchfield Inc 1715 S Sibley Ave	Litchfield MN	55355	800-222-5463	320-693-3221
Dig Corp 1210 Activity Dr	Vista CA	92081	800-322-9146	760-727-0914
DuraTech Industries International Inc PO Box 1940	Jamestown ND	58401	800-243-4601	701-252-4601
EZ Trail Inc 1050 E Columbia St PO Box 168	Arthur IL	61911	800-677-2802	217-543-3471
Fabrication JR Tardif Inc 62 Blvd Cartier	Rivi Re-Du-Loup QC	G5R6B2	877-962-7273	418-862-7273
Finn Corp 9281 Le St Dr	Fairfield OH	45014	800-543-7166	513-874-2818
Forsbergs Inc 1210 Pennington Ave PO Box 510	Thief River Falls MN	56701	800-654-1927*	218-681-1927
*Cust Svc				
Gandy Co 528 Gandrud Rd	Owatonna MN	55060	800-443-2476	507-451-5430
GMP Metal Products Inc 3883 Delor St	Saint Louis MO	63116	800-325-9808	314-481-0300
Hagie Manufacturing Co 721 Central Ave W	Clarion IA	50525	800-247-4885	515-532-2861
Hardi Inc 1500 W 76th St	Davenport IA	52806	866-770-7063	563-386-1730
Hastings Equity Mfg 1900 Summit Ave PO Box 1007	Hastings NE	68901	888-883-2189	402-462-2189
HCC Inc 1501 First Ave	Mendota IL	61342	800-548-6633	815-539-9371
HD Hudson Manufacturing Co 500 N Michigan Ave	Chicago IL	60611	800-977-7293	312-644-2830
Heartland Equipment Inc 2100 N Falls Blvd	Wynne AR	72396	800-530-7617	
Henderson Manufacturing Inc 1085 S Third St	Manchester IA	52057	800-359-4970	563-927-2828
Herschel-Adams Inc 1301 N 14th St	Indianola IA	50125	800-247-2167	
Hiniker Co 58766 240th St	Mankato MN	56002	800-433-5620	507-625-6621
Howse Implement Company Inc 2013 Hwy 184 E	Laurel MS	39443	888-358-3377	
Hutchinson/Mayrath/TerraTrack Industries 514 W Crawford St	Clay Center KS	67432	800-523-6993	785-632-2161
Jamesway Incubator Co Inc 30 High Ridge Ct	Cambridge ON	N1R7L3	800-438-8077	519-624-4646
KBH Corp, The 395 Anderson Blvd	Clarksdale MS	38614	800-843-5241	662-624-5471
Kelley Manufacturing Co 80 Vernon Dr PO Box 1467	Tifton GA	31793	800-444-5449	229-382-9393
Kelly Ryan Equipment Co 900 Kelly Ryan Dr	Blair NE	68008	800-640-6967	402-426-2151
KMW Ltd PO Box 327	Sterling KS	67579	800-445-7388	620-278-3641
Kubota Tractor Corp 3401 Del Amo Blvd	Torrance CA	90503	888-458-2682	310-370-3370
Lankota Inc 270 Westpark Ave	Huron SD	57350	866-526-5682	605-352-4550
Lindsay Corp 2222 N 111th St	Omaha NE	68164	800-829-5300	402-829-6800
NYSE: LNN				
Loftness Specialized Farm Equipment Inc 650 S Main St PO Box 337	Hector MN	55342	800-828-7624	320-848-6266
Mathews Co 500 Industrial Ave	Crystal Lake IL	60012	800-323-7045	815-459-2210
Miller Saint Nazianz Inc 511 E Main St	Saint Nazianz WI	54232	800-247-5557	920-773-2121
Modern Group Ltd 1655 Louisiana St	Beaumont TX	77701	800-231-8198*	409-833-2665
*Cust Svc				
Orthman Manufacturing Inc 75765 Rd 435 PO Box B	Lexington NE	68850	800-658-3270	308-324-4654
Osborne Industries Inc 120 N Industrial Ave	Osborne KS	67473	800-255-0316	785-346-2192
Peerless Manufacturing Co US Hwy 82 E	Shellman GA	39886	800-225-4617	229-679-5353
Precision Tank & Equipment Company Inc 3503 Conover Rd	Virginia IL	62691	800-258-4197	217-452-7228
Reinke Mfg Co Inc 5325 Reinke Rd	Deshler NE	68340	866-365-7381	402-365-7251
Root-Lowell Manufacturing Co 1000 Foreman Rd	Lowell MI	49331	800-748-0098	
Schlagel Inc 491 N Emerson	Cambridge MN	55008	800-328-8002	763-689-5991
Schuette Mfg & Steel Sales Inc 5028 Hwy 42	Manitowoc WI	54220	800-626-6409	920-758-2491
Scranton Mfg Company Inc 101 State St PO Box 336	Scranton IA	51462	800-831-1858	712-652-3396
Shivvers Inc 614 W English St	Corydon IA	50060	800-245-9093	641-872-1005
Simonsen Industries Inc 500 Iowa 31	Quimby IA	51049	800-831-4860	712-445-2211
Sioux Steel Co 196 1/2 E Sixth St	Sioux Falls SD	57104	800-557-4689	605-336-1750
Stock Equipment Co 16490 Chillicothe Rd	Chagrin Falls OH	44023	888-742-1249	440-543-6000
Sudenga Industries Inc 2002 Kingbird Ave	George IA	51237	888-783-3642	712-475-3301
Sukup Manufacturing Co 1555 255th St PO Box 677	Sheffield IA	50475	866-427-4422	641-892-4222
T-I Irrigation Co 151 E Hwy 6 AB Rd PO Box 1047	Hastings NE	68902	800-330-4264	402-462-4128
Top Air Sprayers 601 S Broad St	Kalida OH	45853	800-322-6301	419-532-3121
Toro Co Irrigation Div 5825 Jasmine St	Riverside CA	92504	800-654-1882	
Unverferth Mfg Company Inc 601 S Broad St	Kalida OH	45853	800-322-6301	419-532-3121
Vaderstad Industries Inc PO Box 123	Langbank SK	S0G2X0	800-667-4295	306-538-2221
Valmont Industries Inc 1 Valmont Plz	Omaha NE	68154	800-825-6668	402-963-1000
NYSE: VMI				
Westfield Industries Ltd 74 Hwy 205 E	Rosenort MB	R0G1W0	866-467-7207	204-746-2396
Wiese Industries 1501 Fifth St	Perry IA	50220	800-568-4391	515-465-9854

				Toll-Free	Phone
Woods Equipment Co 2606 S Illinois Rt 2 PO Box 1000	Oregon	IL	61061	**800-319-6637**	815-732-2141
Wylie Spray Center 702 E 40th St	Lubbock	TX	79404	**888-249-5162**	806-763-1335
Yetter Manufacturing Inc 109 S McDonough St PO Box 358	Colchester	IL	62326	**800-447-5777**	309-776-4111

274 FARM MACHINERY & EQUIPMENT - WHOL

				Toll-Free	Phone
Abilene Machine Inc PO Box 129	Abilene	KS	67410	**800-255-0337**	785-655-9455
Ag West Supply Inc 9055 Rickreall Rd	Rickreall	OR	97371	**800-842-2224**	503-363-2332
Agri-Service 300 Agri-Service Way	Kimberly	ID	83341	**800-388-3599**	208-734-7772
Arends & Sons Inc 715 S Sangamon Ave	Gibson City	IL	60936	**800-637-6052**	217-784-4241
Belarus Tractor International Inc 7842 N Faulkner Rd	Milwaukee	WI	53224	**800-356-2336**	
Blain Supply Inc 3507 E Racine St	Janesville	WI	53547	**800-210-2370**	608-754-2821
Blanchard Compact Equipment 1410 Ashville Hwy	Spartanburg	SC	29303	**888-799-3606**	864-582-1245
Burks Tractor Co Inc 3140 Kimberly Rd	Twin Falls	ID	83301	**800-247-7419**	208-733-5543
Carco International Inc 2721 Midland Blvd	Fort Smith	AR	72904	**800-824-3215**	479-441-3270
Carrico Implement Company Inc 3160 US 24 Hwy	Beloit	KS	67420	**877-542-4099**	785-738-5744
Farm Implement & Supply Company Inc 1200 S Washington Hwy 183	Plainville	KS	67663	**888-589-6029**	785-434-4824
Farmer Boy Ag 50 W Stoever Ave	Myerstown	PA	17067	**800-845-3374**	
Farmers Supply Sales Inc 1409 E Ave	Kalona	IA	52247	**800-493-4917**	319-656-2291
Gardner Inc 3641 Interchange Rd	Columbus	OH	43204	**800-848-8946**	614-456-4000
Glade & Grove Supply 305 CR 17A W	Avon Park	FL	33825	**800-433-4451**	877-513-8182
Greenline Equipment 14750 S Pony Express Rd	Bluffdale	UT	84065	**888-201-5500**	801-966-4231
Grossenburg Implement Inc 31341 US Hwy 18	Winner	SD	57580	**800-658-3440**	605-842-2040
Harcourt Equipment 313 Hwy 169 & 175 E	Harcourt	IA	50544	**800-445-5646**	515-354-5332
Hillsboro Equipment Inc E18898 Hwy 33	Hillsboro	WI	54634	**800-521-5133**	608-489-2275
HOLT Texas Ltd 3302 S WW White Rd	San Antonio	TX	78222	**800-275-4658**	210-648-1111
Honey Bee Manufacturing Ltd PO Box 120	Frontier	SK	S0N0W0	**855-330-2019**	306-296-2297
Hoober Inc 3452 Old Philadelphia Pk PO Box 518	Intercourse	PA	17534	**800-446-6237**	717-768-8231
Hurst Farm Supply Inc 105 Ave D	Abernathy	TX	79311	**800-535-8903**	806-298-2541
Implement Sales Company LLC 1574 Stone Ridge Dr	Stone Mountain	GA	30083	**800-955-9592**	770-908-9439
JD Equipment Inc 1660 US 42 NE	London	OH	43140	**800-659-5646**	614-879-6620
Jerry Pate Turf & Irrigation Inc 301 Schubert Dr	Pensacola	FL	32504	**800-700-7004**	850-479-4653
John Day Co 6263 Abbott Dr	Omaha	NE	68110	**800-767-2273**	402-455-8000
Larchmont Engineering & Irrigation Co 11 Larchmont Ln PO Box 66	Lexington	MA	02420	**877-862-2550**	781-862-2550
Littau Harvester Inc 855 Rogue Ave	Stayton	OR	97383	**866-262-2495**	503-769-5953
Luber Bros Inc 5224 Bear Creek Ct	Irving	TX	75061	**800-375-8237**	972-313-2020
Maine Potato Growers Inc 261 Main St	Presque Isle	ME	04769	**800-649-3358**	207-764-3131
Mid-State Equipment Inc W 1115 Bristol Rd	Columbus	WI	53925	**877-677-4020**	920-623-4020
Monroe Tractor & Implement Company Inc 1001 Lehigh Stn Rd	Henrietta	NY	14467	**866-683-5338**	585-334-3867
Peterson Tractor Co 955 Marina Blvd	San Leandro	CA	94577	**800-590-5945**	510-357-6200
Premier Equipment LLC 2025 US Hwy 14 W	Huron	SD	57350	**800-627-5469**	
Price Bros Equipment Co 619 S Washington St	Wichita	KS	67211	**877-957-9577**	
RDO Equipment Co 700 Seventh St S	Fargo	ND	58103	**800-247-4650**	877-444-7363
Revels Tractor Company Inc 2217 N Main St	Fuquay Varina	NC	27526	**800-849-5469**	919-552-5697
Roeder Implement Inc 2550 Rockdale Rd	Dubuque	IA	52003	**800-557-1184**	563-557-1184
Schmidt Machine Co 7013 Ohio 199	Upper Sandusky	OH	43351	**866-368-3814**	419-294-3814
SEMA Equipment Inc 11555 Hwy 60 Blvd	Wanamingo	MN	55983	**800-569-1377**	507-824-2256
Simpson Norton Corp 4144 S Bullard Ave	Goodyear	AZ	85338	**877-859-8676**	623-932-5116
Sioux Automation Ctr Inc 877 First Ave NW	Sioux Center	IA	51250	**866-722-1488**	712-722-1488
Sloan Implement Co 120 N Business 51	Assumption	IL	62510	**800-745-4020**	217-226-4411
South Plains Implement 1645 FM 403 PO Box 752	Brownfield	TX	79316	**800-725-5435**	806-637-3594
Spartan Distributors 487 W Div St	Sparta	MI	49345	**800-822-2216**	616-887-7301
Spike 1352 W Main	Tremonton	UT	84337	**800-821-4474**	
Teeter Irrigation Inc 2729 W Oklahoma	Ulysses	KS	67880	**800-524-5497**	620-353-1111
Tom Hassenfritz Equipment Co 1300 W Washington St	Mount Pleasant	IA	52641	**800-634-4885**	319-385-3114
Tractor Supply Co 5401 Virginia Way *NASDAQ: TSCO*	Brentwood	TN	37027	**877-718-6750**	615-440-4000
Western Implement Co Inc 2919 North Ave	Grand Junction	CO	81504	**800-338-6639**	970-242-7960
White's Inc 4614 Navigation Blvd PO Box 2344	Houston	TX	77011	**800-231-9559**	713-928-2632
Witmer's Construction Inc 39821 Salem Unity Rd	Salem	OH	44460	**888-427-2150**	330-427-2611
Wyatt-Quarles Seed Co 730 US Hwy 70 W	Garner	NC	27529	**800-662-7591**	919-772-4243

275 FARM PRODUCT RAW MATERIALS

				Toll-Free	Phone
Alliance Grain Co 1306 W Eigth St	Gibson City	IL	60936	**800-222-2451**	217-784-4284
Aurora Co-op Elevator Co 605 12th St PO Box 209	Aurora	NE	68818	**800-642-6795**	402-694-2106
Cargill Inc 15407 McGinty Rd W	Wayzata	MN	55391	**800-227-4455**	
Ceres Solutions LLP 2112 Indianapolis Rd PO Box 432 *General	Crawfordsville	IN	47933	**800-878-0952***	765-362-6700
Co-Alliance LLP 5250 E US Hwy 36 Bldg 1000	Avon	IN	46123	**800-525-0272**	317-745-4491
Co-op Elevator Co 7211 E Michigan Ave	Pigeon	MI	48755	**800-968-0601**	989-453-4500
Effingham Equity Inc 201 W Roadway Ave	Effingham	IL	62401	**800-223-1337**	217-342-4101
Federated Co-operatives Ltd 401 22nd St E PO Box 1050	Saskatoon	SK	S7K0H2	**800-848-6347**	306-244-3311
Frontier Co-op 211 S Lincoln PO Box 37	Brainard	NE	68626	**800-869-0379**	402-545-2811
Heartland Co-op 2829 Westown Pkwy Ste 350	West Des Moines	IA	50266	**800-513-3938**	515-225-1334
Italgrani USA Inc 7900 Van Buren St	Saint Louis	MO	63111	**800-274-1274**	314-638-1447
Joy Dog Food PO Box 305	Pinckneyville	IL	62274	**800-245-4125**	
MaxYield Co-op 313 Third Ave NE PO Box 49	West Bend	IA	50597	**800-383-0003**	515-887-7211
NEW Co-op Inc 2626 First Ave S	Fort Dodge	IA	50501	**800-362-2233**	515-955-2040
Northwest Grain Growers Inc 850 N Fourth Ave	Walla Walla	WA	99362	**800-994-4290**	509-525-6510
Parrish & Heimbecker Ltd (P&H) 201 Portage Ave Ste 1400	Winnipeg	MB	R3B3K6	**800-665-8937**	204-956-2030
Pendleton Grain Growers Inc 1000 SW Dorian St PO Box 1248	Pendleton	OR	97801	**800-422-7611**	541-278-5035
Plains Cotton Co-op Assn 3301 E 50th St PO Box 2827	Lubbock	TX	79408	**800-333-8011**	806-763-8011
Staplcotn Co-op Assn Inc 214 W Market St	Greenwood	MS	38930	**800-293-6231**	662-453-6231
Stratton Equity Co-op Co Inc 98 Colorado Ave PO Box 25	Stratton	CO	80836	**800-438-7070**	719-348-5326

276 FARM SUPPLIES

				Toll-Free	Phone
Agfinity 260 Factory Rd	Eaton	CO	80615	**800-433-4688**	970-454-4000
AgVantage FS Inc 1600 Eigth St SW	Waverly	IA	50677	**800-346-0058**	319-483-4900
Alforex Seeds 38001 County Rd 27	Woodland	CA	95695	**877-560-5181**	530-666-3331
BFG Supply Co LLC 14500 Kinsman Rd PO Box 479	Burton	OH	44021	**800-883-0234**	440-834-1883
Bleyhl Farm Service Inc 940 E Wine Country Rd *Cust Svc	Grandview	WA	98930	**800-862-6806***	509-882-2248
Bradley Caldwell Inc 200 Kiwanis Blvd *Cust Svc	Hazleton	PA	18202	**800-257-9100***	570-455-7511
CHS Inc 5500 Cenex Dr *NASDAQ: CHSCP*	Inver Grove Heights	MN	55077	**800-232-3639**	651-355-6000
Co-op Feed Dealers Inc 380 Broome Corporate Pkwy PO Box 670 *Cust Svc	Conklin	NY	13748	**800-333-0895***	607-651-9078
Countryside Co-op 514 E Main St	Durand	WI	54736	**800-236-7585**	715-672-8947
CropKing Inc 134 W Dr	Lodi	OH	44254	**800-321-5656**	330-302-4203
Crystal Valley Coop 721 W Humphrey PO Box 210	Lake Crystal	MN	56055	**800-622-2910**	507-726-6455
Edon Farmers Co-op Assn Inc 205 S Michigan St PO Box 308	Edon	OH	43518	**800-878-4093**	419-272-2121
Evergreen FS Inc 402 N Hershey Rd	Bloomington	IL	61704	**877-963-2392**	
Farm Service Co-op 2308 Pine St	Harlan	IA	51537	**800-452-4372**	712-755-3185
Federation Co-op 108 N Water St	Black River Falls	WI	54615	**800-944-1784**	715-284-5354
Fifield Land Co 4307 Fifield Rd	Brawley	CA	92227	**800-536-6395**	760-344-6391
Frenchman Valley Farmers Co-op Exchange 202 Broadway	Imperial	NE	69033	**800-538-2667**	308-882-3200
Gold Star FS Inc PO Box 135	Cambridge	IL	61238	**800-443-8497**	309-937-3369
Gowan Company LLC PO Box 5569	Yuma	AZ	85366	**800-883-1844**	928-783-8844
Grangetto's Farm & Garden Supply Co 1105 W Mission Ave	Escondido	CA	92025	**800-536-4671**	760-745-4671
Growth Products Ltd 80 Lafayette Ave	White Plains	NY	10603	**800-648-7626**	914-428-1316

				Toll-Free	Phone
Hummert International Inc 4500 Earth City Expy	Earth City	MO	63045	**800-325-3055**	
Hutchinson Co-Op PO Box 158	Hutchinson	MN	55350	**800-795-1299**	320-587-4647
Intermountain Farmers Assn 1147 West 2100 South	Salt Lake City	UT	84119	**800-748-4432**	801-972-2122
Kreamer Feed Inc PO Box 38	Kreamer	PA	17833	**800-767-4537**	570-374-8148
Kugler Co 209 W Third St PO Box 1748	McCook	NE	69001	**800-445-9116**	308-345-2280
Lakes Area Co-op 459 Third Ave SE PO Box 247	Perham	MN	56573	**866-346-5601**	218-346-6240
Legend Seeds Inc PO Box 241	De Smet	SD	57231	**800-678-3346**	605-854-3346
Martrex Inc 1107 Hazeltine Blvd Ste 535	Minnetonka	MN	55318	**800-328-3627**	952-933-5000
McFarlane Mfg Company Inc PO Box 100	Sauk City	WI	53583	**800-627-8569**	608-643-3321
Meherrin Agricultural & Chemical Co Inc 413 Main St	Severn	NC	27877	**800-775-0333**	252-585-1744
NEW Co-op Inc 2626 First Ave S	Fort Dodge	IA	50501	**800-362-2233**	515-955-2040
Northwest Wholesale Inc 1567 N Wenatchee Ave	Wenatchee	WA	98801	**800-874-6607**	509-662-2141
Nu Way Co-op Inc PO Box Q	Trimont	MN	56176	**800-445-4118**	
Orangeburg Pecan Company Inc 761 Russell St	Orangeburg	SC	29115	**800-845-6970**	
Orscheln Farm & Home LLC 1800 Overcenter Dr PO Box 698	Moberly	MO	65270	**800-498-5090**	800-577-2580
Panhandle Co-op Assn 401 S Beltline Hwy W *Cust Svc	Scottsbluff	NE	69361	**800-732-4546***	308-632-5301
Paris Farmers' Union PO Box D	South Paris	ME	04281	**800-639-3603**	207-743-8976
Quality Liquid Feeds Inc PO Box 240	Dodgeville	WI	53533	**800-236-2345**	608-935-2345
Red River Specialties Inc 1324 N Hearne Ave Ste 120	Shreveport	LA	71107	**800-256-3344**	318-425-5944
Reedsville Co-op Assn Inc PO Box 460	Reedsville	WI	54230	**800-236-4047**	920-754-4321
S R C Corp PO Box 30676	Salt Lake City	UT	84130	**800-888-4545**	801-268-4500
Slegers Seed Co 13031 Reflections Dr	Holland	MI	49424	**800-962-4999**	616-786-4999
Silver Edge Co-op 39999 Hilton Rd	Edgewood	IA	52042	**800-632-5953**	563-928-6419
Southern FS Inc 2002 E Main St PO Box 728	Marion	IL	62959	**800-492-7684**	618-993-2833
Southern States Co-op Inc 6606 W Broad St	Richmond	VA	23230	**866-372-8272**	804-281-1000
Southern States Frederick Co-op Inc 500 E South St	Frederick	MD	21701	**866-633-5747**	301-663-6164
Stanislaus Farm Supply Co 624 E Service Rd	Modesto	CA	95358	**800-323-0725**	209-538-7070
Tennessee Farmers Co-op 180 Old Nashville Hwy	La Vergne	TN	37086	**800-366-2667**	615-793-8011
United Suppliers Inc 30473 260th St PO Box 538	Eldora	IA	50627	**800-782-5123**	641-858-2341
Van Horn Inc PO Box 380	Cerro Gordo	IL	61818	**800-252-1615**	217-677-2131
Wabash Valley Service Company Inc 909 N Court St	Grayville	IL	62844	**888-869-8127**	618-375-2311
West-Con Co-op 520 Co Rd 9	Holloway	MN	56249	**800-368-3310**	320-394-2171
Wilco Farmers 200 Industrial Way	Mount Angel	OR	97362	**800-382-5339**	
Yankton Ag Service 114 Mulberry St	Yankton	SD	57078	**800-456-5528**	605-665-3691

277 FASHION DESIGN HOUSES

SEE ALSO Clothing & Accessories - Mfr

				Toll-Free	Phone
Carolina Herrera 501 Seventh Ave 17th Fl	New York	NY	10018	**866-254-7660**	
Diane Von Furstenberg 440 W 14th St	New York	NY	10014	**888-472-2383**	212-741-6607
Marc Jacobs International 72 Spring St	New York	NY	10012	**877-707-6272**	212-965-4000
Vivienne Tam 580 Eighth Ave 17th Fl	New York	NY	10018	**877-659-7994**	

278 FASTENERS & FASTENING SYSTEMS

SEE ALSO Hardware - Mfr ; Precision Machined Products

				Toll-Free	Phone
Atlas Bolt & Screw Co 1628 Troy Rd	Ashland	OH	44805	**800-321-6977**	419-289-6171
B & G Mfg Company Inc 3067 Unionville Pk	Hatfield	PA	19440	**800-366-3067**	215-822-1921
Captive Fastener Corp 19 Thornton Rd	Oakland	NJ	07436	**800-526-4430**	201-337-6800
E T & F Fastening Systems 29019 Solon Rd	Solon	OH	44139	**800-248-2376**	440-248-8655
Ford Fasteners Inc 110 S Newman St	Hackensack	NJ	07601	**800-272-3673**	201-487-3151
Hohmann & Barnard Inc 30 Rasons Ct	Hauppauge	NY	11788	**800-645-0616**	631-234-0600
ITW Brands 955 National Pkwy Ste 95500	Schaumburg	IL	60173	**877-489-2726**	847-944-2260
ITW Buildex 1349 W Bryn Mawr	Itasca	IL	60143	**800-848-5611**	
Mid-States Bolt & Screw Co 4126 Somers Dr	Burton	MI	48529	**800-482-0867**	
Mid-States Screw Corp 1817 18th Ave	Rockford	IL	61104	**888-354-6772**	815-397-2440
National Rivet & Manufacturing Co 21 E Jefferson St	Waupun	WI	53963	**888-324-5511**	920-324-5511
Ohio Nut & Bolt Co 5250 W 164th St	Brook Park	OH	44142	**800-437-1689**	
Pan American Screw Inc 630 Reese Dr SW *Cust Svc	Conover	NC	28613	**800-951-2222***	828-466-0060
PennEngineering & Manufacturing Corp 5190 Old Easton Rd	Danboro	PA	18916	**800-237-4736**	215-766-8853
Robertson Inc 1185 Corporate Dr Unit 1	Burlington	ON	L7L5V5	**800-268-5090**	905-332-7776
Scovill Fasteners Inc 1802 Scovill Dr *Cust Svc	Clarkesville	GA	30523	**888-726-8455***	706-754-1000
Stafast Products Inc 505 Lake Shore Blvd	Painesville	OH	44077	**800-782-3278**	440-357-5546

279 FENCES - MFR

SEE ALSO Recycled Plastics Products

				Toll-Free	Phone
Acorn Wire & Iron Works Inc 2035 S Racine Ave	Chicago	IL	60608	**800-552-2676**	773-585-0600
Conifex Timber Inc 980-700 W Georgia St PO Box 10070	Vancouver	BC	V7Y1B6	**866-301-2949**	604-216-2949
Dare Products Inc 860 Betterly Rd PO Box 157	Battle Creek	MI	49015	**800-922-3273**	269-965-2307
Epicurean Inc 257 B Main St	Superior	MN	54880	**866-678-3500**	218-740-3500
Master Halco Inc 3010 Lyndon B Johnson Fwy Ste 800	Dallas	TX	75234	**800-883-8384**	972-714-7300
Riverdale Mills Corp 130 Riverdale St	Northbridge	MA	01534	**800-762-6374**	508-234-8715
Taiga Building Products 800-4710 Kingsway	Burnaby	BC	V5H4M2	**800-663-1470**	604-438-1471
Tru-Link Fence Co 5009 West Lake St	Melrose Park	IL	60610	**800-568-9300**	847-568-9300
Walnut Hollow Farm Inc 1409 State Rd 23	Dodgeville	WI	53533	**800-395-5995**	608-935-2341
Western Bee Supplies Inc 5 Ninth Ave E	Polson	MT	59860	**800-548-8440**	406-883-2918

280 FERTILIZERS & PESTICIDES

SEE ALSO Farm Supplies

				Toll-Free	Phone
Abell LLC 2201 Old Sterlington Rd PO Box 4150	Monroe	LA	71211	**800-523-9871**	866-765-9957
Airgas Specialty Products 2530 Sever Rd Ste 300	Lawrenceville	GA	30043	**800-295-2225**	
Alabama Farmers Co-op Inc PO Box 2227	Decatur	AL	35609	**800-589-3206**	256-353-6843
California Ammonia Co (CALAMCO) 1776 W March Ln Ste 420	Stockton	CA	95207	**800-624-4200**	209-982-1000
Certis USA LLC 9145 Guilford Rd Ste 175	Columbia	MD	21046	**800-250-5024**	
CF Industries Inc 4 Pkwy N Ste 400	Deerfield	IL	60015	**800-462-8565**	847-405-2400
CFC Farm & Home Ctr 15172 Brandy Rd PO Box 2002	Culpeper	VA	22701	**800-284-2667**	540-825-2200
Coastal Agrobusiness Inc 112 Staton Rd	Greenville	NC	27834	**800-758-1828**	252-756-1126
Degesch America Inc PO Box 116	Weyers Cave	VA	24486	**800-330-2525**	540-234-9281
DuPont Crop Protection CRP 705/L1S11 PO Box 80705	Wilmington	DE	19880	**800-922-2368**	302-774-1000
Enforcer Products Inc PO Box 1060	Cartersville	GA	30120	**888-805-4357**	
FMC Corp 2929 Walnut St *NYSE: FMC*	Philadelphia	PA	19104	**888-548-4486**	215-299-6000
Frit Industries Inc 1792 Jodie Parker Rd	Ozark	AL	36360	**800-633-7685**	334-774-2515
Good Earth Inc PO Box 290	Lancaster	NY	14086	**800-877-0848**	716-684-8111
JR Simplot Co PO Box 27	Boise	ID	83707	**800-832-8893**	208-336-2110
Kellogg Garden Products 350 W Sepulveda Blvd	Carson	CA	90745	**800-232-2322**	
Kirby Agri Inc 500 Running Pump Rd PO Box 6277	Lancaster	PA	17607	**800-745-7524**	717-299-2541
Landec Ag LLC 201 N Michigan St	Oxford	IN	47971	**800-241-7252**	765-385-1000
Lebanon Seaboard Corp 1600 E Cumberland St	Lebanon	PA	17042	**800-233-0628**	717-273-1685
Miller Chemical & Fertilizer Corp 120 Radio Rd PO Box 333	Hanover	PA	17331	**800-233-2040**	717-632-8921
Na-Churs/Alpine Solutions 421 Leader St	Marion	OH	43302	**800-622-4877**	740-382-5701
PBI/Gordon Corp 1217 W 12th St	Kansas City	MO	64101	**800-821-7925**	816-421-4070
Safeguard Chemical Corp 411 Wales Ave	Bronx	NY	10454	**800-536-3170**	718-585-3170
Scotts Miracle-Gro Co 14111 Scottslawn Rd *NYSE: SMG* ■ *Cust Svc	Marysville	OH	43041	**800-543-8873***	937-644-0011
Share Corp 7821 N Faulkner Rd	Milwaukee	WI	53224	**800-776-7192**	
Southern States Chemical Co 1600 E President St	Savannah	GA	31404	**888-337-8922**	912-232-1101
Spectrum Brands 3001 Deming Way	Middleton	WI	53562	**800-566-7899**	608-275-3340
Stoller USA 4001 W Sam Houston Pkwy N Ste 100	Houston	TX	77043	**800-539-5283**	713-461-1493
Summit Chemical Co 235 S Kresson St	Baltimore	MD	21224	**800-227-8664**	410-522-0661
Tender Corp 106 Burndy Rd	Littleton	NH	03561	**800-258-4696**	603-444-5464
Van Diest Supply Co 1434 220th St PO Box 610	Webster City	IA	50595	**800-779-2424**	515-832-2366

			Toll-Free	Phone
Woodstream Corp				
69 N Locust St	Lititz PA	17543	800-800-1819*	717-626-2125
*All				
Y-Tex Corp 1825 Big Horn Ave	Cody WY	82414	800-443-6401	307-587-5515

281 FESTIVALS - BOOK

			Toll-Free	Phone
Boston Globe, The				
PO Box 55819	Boston MA	02205	888-694-5623	
Great Salt Lake Book Festival				
Utah Humanities Council				
202 W 300 N.	Salt Lake City UT	84103	877-786-7598	801-359-9670
Los Angeles Times Festival of Books				
Los Angeles Times 202 W First St	Los Angeles CA	90012	800-528-4637	213-237-5000
National Book Festival				
Library of Congress				
101 Independence Ave SE.	Washington DC	20540	888-714-4696	202-707-5000
Texas Book Festival				
610 Brazos St Ste 200	Austin TX	78701	800-222-8733	512-477-4055

282 FESTIVALS - FILM

			Toll-Free	Phone
AFI Fest				
2021 N Western Ave	Los Angeles CA	90027	866-234-3378	323-856-7600
Austin Film Festival				
1801 Salina St	Austin TX	78702	800-310-3378	512-478-4795
Outfest-Los Angeles Gay & Lesbian Film Festival				
3470 Wilshire Blvd Ste 935	Los Angeles CA	90010	800-726-7147	213-480-7088
Toronto International Film Festival Inc				
Reitman Sq 350 King St W	Toronto ON	M5V3X5	888-599-8433	

283 FIRE PROTECTION SYSTEMS

SEE ALSO *Personal Protective Equipment & Clothing ; Safety Equipment - Mfr ; Security Products & Services*

			Toll-Free	Phone
BRK Brands Inc				
3901 Liberty St Rd	Aurora IL	60504	800-323-9005	630-851-7330
Fike Corp				
704 SW Tenth St	Blue Springs MO	64015	877-342-3453	816-229-3405
Fire & Life Safety America				
3017 Vernon Rd	Richmond VA	23228	800-252-5069	804-222-1381
Fire Lite Alarms				
1 Fire-Lite Pl	Northford CT	06472	800-627-3473	203-484-7161
First Alert Inc				
3901 Liberty St Rd	Aurora IL	60504	800-323-9005	
Gamewell FCI				
12 Clintonville Rd	Northford CT	06472	800-606-1983	203-484-7161
Potter Electric Signal Company Inc				
5757 Phantom Dr Ste 125	Hazelwood MO	63042	800-325-3936	314-878-4321
Protek Cargo 1568 Airport Blvd	Napa CA	94558	800-439-1426	707-254-9627
Silent Knight				
7550 Meridian Cir Ste 100	Maple Grove MN	55369	800-328-0103	763-493-6400
Task Force Tips Inc				
3701 Innovation Way	Valparaiso IN	46383	800-348-2686	219-462-6161
Tyco SimplexGrinnell				
50 Technology Dr	Westminster MA	01441	800-746-7539	978-731-2500
Viking Corp				
210 N Industrial Pk Dr	Hastings MI	49058	800-968-9501	269-945-9501

284 FIREARMS & AMMUNITION (NON-MILITARY)

SEE ALSO *Weapons & Ordnance (Military) ; Sporting Goods*

			Toll-Free	Phone
Beretta USA Corp				
17601 Beretta Dr	Accokeek MD	20607	800-237-3882	301-283-2191
Crosman Corp				
7629 Rt 5 & 20	Bloomfield NY	14469	800-724-7486	
Defense Technology				
Safariland Group				
1855 S Loop Ave	Casper WY	82601	877-248-3835	307-235-2136
Federal Cartridge Co				
900 Ehlen Dr	Anoka MN	55303	800-379-1732	
Gun Parts Corp				
226 Williams Ln	Kingston NY	12401	866-686-7424	845-679-4867
H & R 1871				
60 Industrial Rowe	Gardner MA	01440	866-776-9292	
Hornady Manufacturing Co				
3625 W Old Potash Hwy	Grand Island NE	68803	800-338-3220	308-382-1390
Knight Rifles				
213 Dennis st Athens	Athens TN	37303	866-518-4181	
Lyman Products Corp				
475 Smith St	Middletown CT	06457	800-225-9626	860-632-2020
Marlin Firearms Co				
PO Box 1871	Madison NC	27025	800-544-8892*	
*Cust Svc				
OF Mossberg & Sons Inc				
7 Grasso Ave	North Haven CT	06473	800-363-3555	203-230-5300
Remington Arms Company Inc				
870 Remington Dr PO Box 700.	Madison NC	27025	800-243-9700	336-548-8700
Savage Arms Inc				
100 Springdale Rd	Westfield MA	01085	800-243-3220	413-568-7001
SIG SAUER Inc				
72 Pease Blvd	Newington NH	03801	866-345-6744	603-610-3000
Smith & Wesson Corp				
2100 Roosevelt Ave	Springfield MA	01104	800-331-0852*	413-781-8300
*Cust Svc				
Springfield Armory				
420 W Main St	Geneseo IL	61254	800-680-6866	309-944-5631

			Toll-Free	Phone
Taurus International Mfg Inc				
16175 NW 49th Ave	Miami Lakes FL	33014	800-327-3776	
Weatherby Inc				
1605 Commerce Way	Paso Robles CA	93446	800-227-2016	805-227-2600
Williams Gun Sight Co				
7389 Lapeer Rd	Davison MI	48423	800-530-9028	810-653-2131

285 FISHING - COMMERCIAL

			Toll-Free	Phone
Arctic Storm Management Group LLC				
2727 Alaskan Way Pier 69	Seattle WA	98121	800-929-0908	206-547-6557
Nova Fisheries				
2532 Yale Ave E	Seattle WA	98102	888-458-6682	206-781-2000
Ocean Beauty Seafoods Inc				
1100 W Ewing St	Seattle WA	98119	800-365-8950	206-285-6800

286 FIXTURES - OFFICE & STORE

SEE ALSO *Commercial & Industrial Furniture*

			Toll-Free	Phone
Angola Wire Products Inc				
803 Wohlert St	Angola IN	46703	800-800-7225	260-665-9447
Architectural Bronze Aluminum Corp				
655 Deerfield Rd Ste 100	Deerfield IL	60015	800-339-6581	
Bel-Mar Wire Products Inc				
2343 N Damen Ave	Chicago IL	60647	800-249-9450	773-342-3800
Benner-Nawman Inc				
3450 Sabin Brown Rd	Wickenburg AZ	85390	800-992-3833	928-684-2813
Best-Rite Mfg				
2885 Lorraine Ave	Temple TX	76501	800-749-2258	
Big Timberworks Inc				
1 Rabel Ln	Gallatin Gateway MT	59730	800-763-4639	406-763-4639
Borroughs Corp				
3002 N Burdick St	Kalamazoo MI	49004	800-748-0227	269-342-0161
Boston Group				
400 Riverside Ave	Medford MA	02155	800-225-1633	
Churchill Cabinet Co				
4616 W 19th St	Cicero IL	60804	800-379-9776*	708-780-0070
*Sales				
Cres-Cor 5925 Heisley Rd	Mentor OH	44060	877-273-7267	440-350-1100
Datum Filing Systems Inc				
89 Church Rd	Emigsville PA	17318	800-828-8018	717-764-6350
DeBourgh Manufacturing				
27505 Otero Ave	La Junta CO	81050	800-328-8829	
Dixie Store Fixtures & Sales Company Inc				
2425 First Ave N	Birmingham AL	35203	800-323-4943	205-322-2442
Durham Manufacturing Co				
201 Main St	Durham CT	06422	800-243-3774	860-349-3427
Econoco Corp				
300 Karin Ln	Hicksville NY	11801	800-645-7032	516-935-7700
EQUIPTO 225 Main St	Tatamy PA	18085	800-323-0801	610-253-2775
Ex-Cell Metal Products Inc				
11240 Melrose St	Franklin Park IL	60131	800-392-3557	847-451-0451
Frazier Industrial Co				
91 Fairview Ave	Long Valley NJ	07853	800-859-1342	908-876-3001
Hamilton Sorter Co Inc				
3158 Production Dr	Fairfield OH	45014	800-503-9966	513-870-4400
Handy Store Fixtures Inc				
337 Sherman Ave	Newark NJ	07114	800-631-4280	
Hoosier Co				
5421 W 86th St PO Box 681064.	Indianapolis IN	46268	800-521-4184	317-872-8125
Hufcor Inc				
2101 Kennedy Rd	Janesville WI	53545	800-356-6968	608-756-1241
InterMetro Industries Corp				
651 N Washington St	Wilkes-Barre PA	18705	800-992-1776*	570-825-2741
*Cust Svc				
International Visual Corp (IVC)				
11500 Blvd Armand Bombardier	Montreal QC	H1E2W9	866-643-0570	514-643-0570
Jaken Company Inc				
14420 My ford rf Ste 150	Irvine CA	92606	800-401-7225	714-522-1700
Jesco-Wipco Industries Inc				
950 Anderson Rd PO Box 388	Litchfield MI	49252	800-455-0019	517-542-2903
JL Industries Inc				
4450 W 78th St Cir	Bloomington MN	55435	800-554-6077	952-835-6850
John Boos & Co				
3601 S Banker St PO Box 609	Effingham IL	62401	888-431-2667	217-347-7701
Kardex Systems Inc				
114 Westview Ave	Marietta OH	45750	800-639-5805	740-374-9300
Killion Industries Inc				
1380 Poinsettia Ave	Vista CA	92081	800-421-5352	760-727-5102
Kwik-Wall Co				
1010 E Edwards St	Springfield IL	62703	800-280-5945	217-522-5553
LA Darling Co				
1401 Hwy 49B	Paragould AR	72450	800-682-5730	870-239-9564
Lista International Corp				
106 Lowland St	Holliston MA	01746	800-722-3020*	508-429-1350
*Cust Svc				
Lozier Corp				
6336 John J Pershing Dr	Omaha NE	68110	800-228-9882	402-457-8000
Lyon Work Space Products				
420 N Main St	Montgomery IL	60538	800-433-8488	630-892-8941
Modernfold Inc				
215 W New Rd	Greenfield IN	46140	800-869-9685	
National Partitions				
10300 Goldenfern Ln	Knoxville TN	37931	800-996-7266	865-670-2100
NNM Peterson Manufacturing Co				
24133 W 143rd St	Plainfield IL	60544	800-826-9086	815-436-9201
Pan-Osten Co				
6944 Louisville Rd	Bowling Green KY	42101	800-472-6678	270-783-3900
Panelfold Inc				
10700 NW 36th Ave	Miami FL	33167	800-433-3222	305-688-3501
Pentwater Wire Products Inc (PWP)				
474 Carroll St PO Box 947	Pentwater MI	49449	877-869-6911	231-869-6911

				Toll-Free	Phone
Plasticrest Products Inc					
4519 W Harrison St	Chicago	IL	60624	**800-828-2163**	773-826-2163
RC Smith Co					
14200 Southcross Dr W	Burnsville	MN	55306	**800-747-7648**	952-854-0711
Reeve Store Equipment Co					
9131 Bermudez St	Pico Rivera	CA	90660	**800-927-3383**	562-949-2535
Republic Storage Systems LLC					
1038 Belden Ave NE	Canton	OH	44705	**800-477-1255***	330-438-5800
*Sales					
Ridg-U-Rak Inc					
120 S Lake St	North East	PA	16428	**866-479-7225**	814-725-8751
Russ Bassett Co					
8189 Byron Rd	Whittier	CA	90606	**800-350-2445**	562-945-2445
Salsbury Industries Inc					
1010 E 62nd St	Los Angeles	CA	90001	**800-624-5299**	323-846-6700
Sandusky Lee Corp					
16125 Widmere Rd PO Box 517	Arvin	CA	93203	**800-886-8688***	661-854-5551
*Cust Svc					
Semasys Inc 4480 Blalock Rd	Houston	TX	77041	**800-231-1425***	
*Cust Svc					
Southern Imperial Inc					
1400 Eddy Ave	Rockford	IL	61103	**800-747-4665***	815-877-7041
*Cust Svc					
SpaceGuard Products Inc					
711 S Commerce Dr	Seymour	IN	47274	**800-841-0680**	812-523-3044
Spacesaver Corp					
1450 Janesville Ave	Fort Atkinson	WI	53538	**800-492-3434**	800-255-8170
Sparks Marketing Corp					
2828 Charter Rd	Philadelphia	PA	19154	**800-925-7727**	215-676-1100
Spectrum Industries Inc					
925 First Ave	Chippewa Falls	WI	54729	**800-235-1262**	715-723-6750
SPG International					
11230 Harland Dr	Covington	GA	30014	**877-503-4774**	770-787-9830
Stanley Vidmar Storage Technologies					
11 Grammes Rd	Allentown	PA	18103	**800-523-9462**	
Stevens Industries Inc					
704 W Main St	Teutopolis	IL	62467	**800-637-1609**	217-540-3100
Streater Inc					
411 S First Ave	Albert Lea	MN	56007	**800-527-4197**	
Structural Concepts Corp					
888 Porter Rd	Muskegon	MI	49441	**800-433-9489**	231-798-8888
Stylmark Inc					
6536 Main St NE	Fridley	MN	55432	**800-328-2495**	
Tesko Enterprises					
7350 W Montrose Ave	Norridge	IL	60706	**800-621-4514**	708-452-0045
Timely Inc 10241 Norris Ave	Pacoima	CA	91331	**800-247-6242**	818-492-3500
TJ Hale Co					
W 139 N 9499 Hwy 145	Menomonee Falls	WI	53051	**800-236-4253**	262-255-5555
Trendway Corp					
13467 Quincy St PO Box 9016	Holland	MI	49422	**800-968-5344**	616-399-3900
Trion Industries Inc					
297 Laird St	Wilkes-Barre	PA	18702	**800-444-4665**	
Unarco Material Handling Inc					
701 16th Ave E	Springfield	TN	37172	**800-862-7261**	
VIRA Insight LLC					
120 Dividend Dr Ste 100	Coppell	TX	75019	**800-305-8472**	
W/M Display Group					
1040 W 40th St	Chicago	IL	60609	**800-443-2000**	773-254-3700
Western Pacific Storage Systems Inc					
300 E Arrow Hwy	San Dimas	CA	91773	**800-732-9777**	

287 FLAGS, BANNERS, PENNANTS

				Toll-Free	Phone
Aaa Flag & Banner Manufacturing Co					
8937 National Blvd	Los Angeles	CA	90034	**855-836-3200**	310-836-3200
Olympus Flag & Banner					
9000 W Heather Ave	Milwaukee	WI	53224	**800-558-9620**	414-355-2010

288 FLASH MEMORY DEVICES

				Toll-Free	Phone
Advanced Micro Devices Inc (AMD)					
1 AMD PI PO Box 3453	Sunnyvale	CA	94088	**800-538-8450**	408-749-4000
NYSE: AMD					
Kingston Technology Co					
17600 Newhope St	Fountain Valley	CA	92708	**800-835-6575**	714-435-2600
Lexar Media Inc					
47300 Bayside Pkwy	Fremont	CA	94538	**877-747-4031**	408-933-1088
Micron Technology Inc					
8000 S Federal Way	Boise	ID	83707	**888-363-2589**	208-368-4000
NASDAQ: MU					
PNY Technologies Inc					
100 Jefferson Rd	Parsippany	NJ	07054	**800-769-0143**	973-515-9700
SanDisk Corp					
601 McCarthy Blvd	Milpitas	CA	95035	**866-726-3475**	408-801-1000
NASDAQ: SNDK					
Sony Electronics Inc					
1 Sony Dr	Park Ridge	NJ	07656	**800-222-7669***	201-930-1000
*Cust Svc					

289 FLEET LEASING & MANAGEMENT

				Toll-Free	Phone
Allstate Leasing Inc					
1 Olympic PI	Towson	MD	21204	**800-223-4885**	877-711-4211
Amerit Fleet Solutions					
1331 N California Blvd Ste 150	Walnut Creek	CA	94596	**877-512-6374**	
Donlen Corp					
2315 Sanders Rd	Northbrook	IL	60062	**800-323-1483**	847-714-1400
Emkay Inc					
805 W Thorndale Ave	Itasca	IL	60143	**800-621-2001**	630-250-7400
Executive Car Leasing Inc					
7807 Santa Monica Blvd	Los Angeles	CA	90046	**800-994-2277**	323-654-5000

				Toll-Free	Phone
Leasing Assoc Inc					
12600 N Featherwood Dr Ste 400	Houston	TX	77034	**800-449-4807**	832-300-1300
Lily Transportation Corp					
145 Rosemary St	Needham	MA	02494	**800-248-5459**	
Motorlease Corp					
1506 New Britain Ave	Farmington	CT	06032	**800-243-0182**	860-677-9711
RUAN Transportation Management Systems					
666 Grand Ave 3200 Ruan Ctr	Des Moines	IA	50309	**866-782-6669**	

FLOOR COVERINGS - MFR

SEE Carpets & Rugs ; Tile - Ceramic (Wall & Floor) ; Flooring - Resilient

290 FLOOR COVERINGS STORES

				Toll-Free	Phone
Action Floor Systems LLC					
4781 N US Hwy 51	Mercer	WI	54547	**800-746-3512**	715-476-3512
Boa-Franc					
1255-98th St	Saint-georges	QC	G5Y8J5	**800-463-1303**	418-227-1181
Carpet King Inc					
1815 W River Rd N	Minneapolis	MN	55411	**800-375-3608**	612-588-7600
Century Tile Supply Co					
747 E Roosevelt Rd	Lombard	IL	60148	**888-845-3968**	630-495-2300
Clark-Dunbar Flooring Superstore					
3232 Empire Dr	Alexandria	LA	71301	**800-256-1467**	318-445-0262
Eckards Home Improvement					
2402 N Belt Hwy	Saint Joseph	MO	64506	**800-264-2794**	816-279-4522
Elte 80 Ronald Ave	Toronto	ON	M6E5A2	**888-276-3583**	416-785-7885
Feizy Import & Export Co Ltd					
1949 Stemmons Fwy	Dallas	TX	75207	**800-779-0877**	214-747-6000
Floor Coverings International					
5250 Triangle Pwy Ste 100	Norcross	GA	30092	**800-955-4324***	770-874-7600
*Sales					
Flooring Sales Group					
1251 First Ave S	Seattle	WA	98134	**877-478-3577**	206-624-7800
Furniture Outlets USA Inc					
140 E Hinks Ln	Sioux Falls	SD	57104	**877-395-8998**	605-336-5000
Hagopian & Sons Inc					
14000 W 8 Mile Rd	Oak Park	MI	48237	**800-424-6742**	
Lumber Liquidators Inc					
1455 VFW Pkwy	West Roxbury	MA	02132	**800-227-0332**	617-327-1222
Quality Craft Ltd					
17750-65A Ave Ste 301	Surrey	BC	V3S5N4	**800-663-2252**	604-575-5550
Roysons Corp					
40 Vanderhoof Ave	Rockaway	NJ	07866	**888-769-7667**	973-625-5570
Teragren					
1920 S Proforma Ave	Ontario	CA	91761	**800-929-6333**	206-842-9477
Tom Duffy Co					
5200 Watt Ct Ste B	Fairfield	CA	94534	**800-479-5671**	

291 FLOORING - RESILIENT

SEE ALSO Recycled Plastics Products

				Toll-Free	Phone
American Floor Products Company Inc					
7977 Cessna Ave	Gaithersburg	MD	20879	**800-342-0424**	
Armstrong World Industries Inc					
2500 Columbia Ave	Lancaster	PA	17603	**800-233-3823***	717-397-0611
NYSE: AWI ■ *Cust Svc					
Congoleum Corp					
3500 Quakerridge Rd PO Box 3127	Mercerville	NJ	08619	**800-274-3266**	609-584-3601
Expanko Resilient Flooring					
180 Gordon Dr Ste 107	Exton	PA	19341	**800-345-6202**	
Forbo Flooring Systems					
8 Maplewood Dr					
Humboldt Industrial Pk.	Hazleton	PA	18202	**800-842-7839***	
*Cust Svc					
Formica Corp					
10155 Reading Rd	Cincinnati	OH	45241	**800-367-6422**	513-786-3400
Fryer-Knowles Inc					
205 S Dawson St	Seattle	WA	98108	**800-544-6052**	206-767-7710
Mannington Mills Inc					
75 Mannington Mills Rd	Salem	NJ	08079	**800-356-6787***	800-241-2262
*Cust Svc					
Pergo Inc					
3128 Highwoods Blvd Ste 100	Raleigh	NC	27604	**800-337-3746**	919-773-6000
Regupol America					
11 Ritter Way	Lebanon	PA	17042	**800-537-8737**	
Roppe Corp 1602 N Union St	Fostoria	OH	44830	**800-537-9527**	419-435-8546
Stonhard Inc					
1000 E Park Ave	Maple Shade	NJ	08052	**800-854-0310***	800-257-7953
*Cust Svc					
Superior Mfg Group					
5655 W 73rd St	Chicago	IL	60638	**800-621-2802**	708-458-4600
Tarkett Inc					
1001 Yamaska St E	Farnham	QC	J2N1J7	**800-363-9276**	450-293-3173

292 FLORISTS

SEE ALSO Garden Centers ; Flowers-by-Wire Services

				Toll-Free	Phone
1-800-Flowerscom Inc					
1 Old Country Rd Ste 110	Carle Place	NY	11514	**800-356-9377**	516-739-3083
NASDAQ: FLWS					
Arrow Florist & Park Avenue Greenhouses Inc					
757 Park Ave	Cranston	RI	02910	**800-556-7097**	401-785-1900
Ashland Addison Florist Co					
1640 W Fulton St	Chicago	IL	60612	**800-348-1157**	312-432-1800
Astoria-Pacific Inc					
15130 SE 82nd Dr	Clackamas	OR	97015	**800-536-3111**	503-657-3010
Bachman's Inc					
6010 Lyndale Ave S	Minneapolis	MN	55419	**888-222-4626**	612-861-7600

			Toll-Free	Phone
Baisch & Skinner Inc 2721 Lasalle St	Saint Louis MO	63104	**800-523-0013**	314-664-1212
Barry-owen Co Inc 5625 Smithway St	Los Angeles CA	90040	**800-682-6682**	323-724-4800
Birthday Direct 120 Commerce St	Muscle Shoals AL	35661	**888-491-9185**	256-381-0310
BloomNation LLC 8889 W Olympic Blvd	Beverly Hills CA	90211	**877-702-5666**	210-405-5050
Boite a Fleur De Laval Inc La 3266 Boul Sainte-Rose	Laval QC	H7P4K8	**800-784-3495**	450-622-0341
Burchell Nursery Inc, The 12000 Hwy 120	Oakdale CA	95361	**800-828-8733**	209-845-8733
Cactus Flower Florists 10822 N Scottsdale Rd	Scottsdale AZ	85254	**800-922-2887**	480-483-9200
Calendarscom LLC 6411 Burleson Rd	Austin TX	78744	**800-366-3645**	
Canada Flowers 4073 Longhurst Ave	Niagara Falls ON	L2E6G5	**888-705-9999**	905-354-2713
Continental Flowers Inc 8101 NW 21 St	Miami FL	33122	**800-327-2715**	
Country Lane Flower Shop 729 S Michigan Ave	Howell MI	48843	**800-764-7673**	517-546-1111
Danson Decor Inc 3425 Douglas B Floreani	St Laurent QC	H4S1Y6	**800-363-1865**	514-335-2435
Dr Delphinium Designs & Events 5806 W Lovers Ln & Tollway	Dallas TX	75225	**800-783-8790**	214-522-9911
Eastern Floral & Gift Shop 818 Butterworth St SW	Grand Rapids MI	49504	**800-494-2202**	616-949-2200
Felly's Flowers Inc 205 E Broadway	Madison WI	53716	**800-993-7673**	608-221-4200
FireKeepers Nottawaseppi Huron Band of the Potawatomi 11177 E Michigan Ave	Battle Creek MI	49014	**800-270-7117**	877-353-8777
Flower Patch Inc 4370 S 300 W *General	Murray UT	84107	**888-865-6858***	801-747-2824
Flower Pot Florists 2314 N Broadway St	Knoxville TN	37917	**800-824-7792**	865-523-5121
Flowerbudcom PO Box 761	Lake Oswego OR	97034	**877-524-5400**	
Flowers by Sleeman for All Seasons & Reasons Ltd 1201 Memorial Rd	Houghton MI	49931	**800-400-4023**	906-482-4023
Formaggio Kitchen on Line LLC 244 Huron Ave	Cambridge MA	02138	**888-212-3224**	617-354-4750
Freeman's Flowers & Event Consultants 2934 Duniven Cir	Amarillo TX	79109	**800-846-3104**	806-355-4451
Fruit Co, The 2900 Van Horn Dr	Hood River OR	97031	**800-387-3100**	541-387-3100
FTD Inc 3113 Woodcreek Dr *Cust Svc	Downers Grove IL	60515	**800-736-3383***	
Gift of Life Michigan 3861 Research Park Dr	Ann Arbor MI	48108	**866-500-5801**	
Gifts for You LLC 2425 Curtiss St	Downers Grove IL	60515	**866-443-8748**	
Golden Flowers 2600 NW 79th Ave	Doral FL	33122	**800-333-9929**	305-599-0193
Greeters of Hawaii Ltd 300 Rodgers Blvd Ste 266	Honolulu HI	96819	**800-366-8559**	808-836-0161
Grower Direct Fresh Cut Flowers 6303 Wagner Rd	Edmonton AB	T6E4N4	**877-277-4787**	780-436-7774
Higdon Florist 201 E 32nd St	Joplin MO	64804	**800-641-4726**	417-624-7171
Hillcrest Garden 95 W Century Rd	Paramus NJ	07652	**800-437-7000**	201-599-3030
Howard Bros Florists 8700 S Pennsylvania Ave	Oklahoma City OK	73159	**800-648-0524**	405-632-4747
John Wolf Florist 6228 Waters Ave	Savannah GA	31406	**800-944-6435**	912-352-9843
Johnston the Florist Inc 14179 Lincoln Way	North Huntingdon PA	15642	**800-356-9371**	412-751-2821
Jon's Nursery Inc 24546 Nursery Way	Eustis FL	32736	**800-322-4289**	352-357-4289
Ken's Flower Shop 140 W S Boundary St	Perrysburg OH	43551	**800-253-0100**	419-874-1333
Kuhn Flowers Inc 3802 Beach Blvd	Jacksonville FL	32207	**800-458-5846**	904-398-8601
Lion Ribbon 2015 W Front St	Berwick PA	18603	**800-551-5466**	
Lloyd's Florist 9216 Preston Hwy	Louisville KY	40229	**800-264-1825**	502-968-5428
Mayesh Wholesale Florist Inc 5401 W 104th St	Los Angeles CA	90045	**888-462-9374**	310-348-4921
Metropolitan Plant & Flower Exchange 2125 Fletcher Ave	Fort Lee NJ	07024	**800-638-7613**	201-944-1050
Nakase Bros Wholesale Nursery 9441 Krepp Dr	Huntington Beach CA	92646	**800-747-4388**	714-962-6604
Nanz & Kraft Florists Inc 141 Breckenridge Ln	Louisville KY	40207	**800-897-6551**	502-897-6551
National Floral Supply Inc 3825 LeonaRdtown Rd Ste 4.	Waldorf MD	20601	**800-932-2772**	301-932-7600
Niagara Helicopters Ltd 3731 Victoria Ave	Niagara Falls ON	L2E6V5	**800-281-8034**	905-357-5672
Norton's Flowers & Gifts 2900 Washtenaw Ave	Ypsilanti MI	48197	**800-682-8667**	734-434-2700
Phillip's Flower Shops Inc 524 N Cass Ave	Westmont IL	60559	**800-356-7257**	630-719-5200
Phoenix Flower Shops 5733 E Thomas Rd Ste 4	Scottsdale AZ	85251	**888-311-0404**	480-289-4000
Pope Scientific Inc 351 N Dekora Woods Blvd	Saukville WI	53080	**844-400-7673**	
Proflowerscom 4840 Eastgate Mall	San Diego CA	92121	**800-580-2913**	800-565-6609
Sawyer Nursery Inc 5401 Port Sheldon St	Hudsonville MI	49426	**888-378-7800**	
Schroeder's Flowerland Inc 1530 S Webster Ave	Green Bay WI	54301	**800-236-4769**	920-436-6363
Smith Southwestern Inc 1850 N Rosemont	Mesa AZ	85205	**800-783-3909**	480-854-9545
Strange's Florist Inc 3313 Mechanicsville Pk	Richmond VA	23223	**800-421-4070**	804-321-2200

			Toll-Free	Phone
Sunwest Silver Company Inc 324 Lomas Blvd NW	Albuquerque NM	87102	**800-771-3781**	505-243-3781
Thirstystone Resources Inc 1304 Corporate Dr	Gainesville TX	76240	**800-829-6888**	940-668-6793
Tipton & Hurst Inc 1801 N Grant St	Little Rock AR	72207	**800-666-3333**	501-666-3333
Valley Flowers Inc 3675 Foothill Rd	Carpinteria CA	93013	**800-549-5500**	805-684-6651
Veldkamp's Flowers 9501 W Colfax Ave	Lakewood CO	80215	**800-247-3730**	303-232-2673
Villere's Florist 750 Martin Behrman Ave	Metairie LA	70005	**800-845-5373**	504-833-3716
Viviano Flower Shop 32050 Harper Ave	Saint Clair Shores MI	48082	**800-848-4266**	586-293-0227
Vogue Flowers & Gifts Ltd 1114 N Blvd	Richmond VA	23230	**800-923-1010**	804-353-9600
Washington Floral Service Inc 2701 S 35th St	Tacoma WA	98409	**800-351-5515**	253-472-8343
Watanabe Floral Inc 1607 Hart St	Honolulu HI	96817	**888-832-9360**	808-832-9360
Winston Flowers 131 Newbury St	Boston MA	02116	**800-457-4901**	
Winward International Inc 3089 Whipple Rd	Union City CA	94587	**800-888-8898**	510-487-8686
Worrell Corp 305 S Post Rd	Indianapolis IN	46219	**800-297-9599**	

293 — FLOWERS & NURSERY STOCK - WHOL

SEE ALSO Horticultural Products Growers

			Toll-Free	Phone
Allstate Floral & Craft Inc 14038 Park Pl	Cerritos CA	90703	**800-433-4056**	562-926-2302
Arazoza Brothers Corp 15901 SW 242nd St	Homestead FL	33031	**800-238-1510**	305-246-3223
Ball Horticultural Co 622 Town Rd	West Chicago IL	60185	**800-879-2255**	630-231-3600
Central Garden & Pet Co 1340 Treat Blvd Ste 600 NASDAQ: CENT	Walnut Creek CA	94597	**800-356-2017**	925-948-4000
Cleveland Plant & Flower Co 12920 Corporate Dr	Cleveland OH	44130	**888-231-7569**	216-898-3500
Denver Wholesale Florists Co 4800 Dahlia St	Denver CO	80216	**800-829-8280**	303-399-0970
Distinctive Designs International Inc 120 Sibley Pl	Russellville AL	35654	**800-243-4787**	
DVFlora (DVWF) 520 Mantua Blvd N	Sewell NJ	08080	**800-676-1212**	856-468-7000
Esprit Miami 11475 NW 39th St	Miami FL	33178	**800-327-2320**	305-591-2244
Florist Distributing Inc 2403 Bell Ave	Des Moines IA	50321	**800-373-3741**	515-243-5228
Johnson Nursery Corp 985 Johnson Nursery Rd	Willard NC	28478	**800-624-8174**	910-285-7861
Karthauser & Sons Inc W 147 N 11100 Fond du Lac Ave	Germantown WI	53022	**800-338-8620**	262-255-7815
KENNICOTT BROTHERS CO 452 N Ashland Ave	Chicago IL	60622	**866-346-2826**	312-492-8200
L & L Nursery Supply Co Inc 2552 Shenandoah Way	San Bernardino CA	92407	**800-624-2517**	909-591-0461
Tapscott's 1403 E 18th St	Owensboro KY	42303	**800-626-1922**	270-684-2308
Teters Floral Products Inc 1425 S Lillian Ave	Bolivar MO	65613	**800-999-5996**	417-326-7654
Van Well Nursery 2821 Grant Rd	East Wenatchee WA	98802	**800-572-1553**	509-886-8189
Van Zyverden Inc 8079 Van Zyverden Rd	Meridian MS	39305	**800-332-2852**	601-679-8274
Zieger & Sons Inc 6215 Ardleigh St	Philadelphia PA	19138	**800-752-2003**	215-438-7060

294 — FLOWERS-BY-WIRE SERVICES

			Toll-Free	Phone
Teleflora Inc 11444 Olympic Blvd	Los Angeles CA	90064	**800-493-5610**	

295 — FOIL & LEAF - METAL

			Toll-Free	Phone
Air Cycle Corp 2200 Ogden Ave 100	Lisle IL	60532	**800-909-9709**	
Alamo Industrial Inc 1502 E Walnut St	Seguin TX	78155	**800-356-6286**	
American Ramp Sales Co 601 S Mckinley Ave	Joplin MO	64801	**800-949-2024**	417-206-6816
Astro Manufacturing & Design Corp 34459 Curtis Blvd	Eastlake OH	44095	**888-215-1746**	
Automated Precision Inc 15000 Johns Hopkins Dr	Rockville MD	20850	**800-537-2720**	
Automotive Resources Inc 12775 Randolph Ridge Ln	Manassas VA	20109	**800-562-3250**	
B&G Equipment Company Inc 135 Region S Dr	Jackson GA	30233	**800-544-8811**	678-688-5601
Begneaud Manufacturing Inc 306 E Amedee Dr	Lafayette LA	70583	**800-358-8970**	337-237-5069
Binder Metal Products Inc 14909 S Broadway	Gardena CA	90248	**800-233-0896**	323-321-4835
Bob's Barricades Inc 921 Shotgun Rd	Sunrise FL	33326	**800-432-5031**	954-423-2627
Buff & Shine Manufacturing 2139 E Del Amo Blvd	Rancho Dominguez CA	90220	**800-659-2833**	310-886-5111
Chem-pak Inc 242 Corning Way	Martinsburg WV	25405	**800-336-9828**	
Chemetal 39 O'Neil St	EastHampton MA	01027	**800-807-7341**	

				Toll-Free	Phone
Creamer Metal Products Inc					
77 S Madison Rd	London	OH	43140	800-362-1603	740-852-1752
Crown Roll Leaf Inc					
91 Illinois Ave	Paterson	NJ	07503	800-631-3831	973-742-4000
Diamond Z 11299 Bass Ln	Caldwell	ID	83605	800-949-2383	208-585-3031
FBN Metal Products					
5020 N Nathaniel Lyon St	Battlefield	MO	65619	800-538-2830	417-882-2830
Glendo Corp PO Box 1153	Emporia	KS	66801	800-835-3519	620-343-1084
Hodge Products Inc					
PO Box 1326	El Cajon	CA	92022	800-778-2217	
Ideal Shield 2525 Clark St	Detroit	MI	48209	866-825-8659	313-842-7290
Johnson Screens Inc					
1950 Old Hwy 8 NW	New Brighton	MN	55112	800-833-9473	651-636-3900
JW Winco Inc					
2815 S Calhoun Rd	New Berlin	WI	53151	800-877-8351	262-786-8227
Mid-State Machine & Fabricating Corp					
2730 Mine and Mill Rd	Lakeland	FL	33801	844-785-4180	
October Company Inc					
51 Ferry St	EastHampton	MA	01027	800-628-9346	413-527-9380
Pauli Systems Inc					
1820 Walters Ct	Fairfield	CA	94533	800-370-1115	707-429-2434
Precision Hose					
2200 Centre Park Ct	Stone Mountain	GA	30087	877-850-2662	770-413-5680
Shade Systems Inc					
4150 SW 19th St	Ocala	FL	34474	800-609-6066	352-237-0135
SUHM Spring Works Inc					
14650 Heathrow Forest Pkwy	Houston	TX	77032	800-338-6903	713-224-9293
Superior Metal Technologies LLC					
9850 E 30th St	Indianapolis	IN	46229	800-654-9850	317-897-9850
Tricor Metals Inc					
3225 W Old Lincoln Way	Wooster	OH	44691	800-421-5141	330-264-3299
Trulock Tool Co					
113 Drayton St	Whigham	GA	39897	800-293-9402	229-762-4678
Turbotec Products Inc					
651 Day Hill Rd	Windsor	CT	06095	800-394-1633	860-731-4200
Vooner Flogard Corp					
4729 Stockholm Ct	Charlotte	NC	28273	800-345-7879	704-552-9314
Wagman Metal Products Inc					
400 S Albemarle St	York	PA	17403	800-233-9461	717-854-2120
Warren Co, The					
2201 Loveland Ave	Eric	PA	16506	800-562-0357	

296 FOOD PRODUCTS - MFR

SEE ALSO Meat Packing Plants ; Poultry Processing ; Pet Products ; Livestock & Poultry Feeds - Prepared ; Ice - Manufactured ; Salt ; Bakeries ; Agricultural Products ; Beverages - Mfr

				Toll-Free	Phone
Cantrell					
1400 S Bradford St	Gainesville	GA	30501	800-922-1232	770-536-3611
Contemar Silo Systems Inc					
30 Pennsylvania Ave Unit 8	Concord	ON	L4K4A5	800-567-2741	905-669-3604
Flatout Inc 1422 Woodland Dr	Saline	MI	48176	888-254-5480	
Koss Industrial Inc					
1943 Commercial Way	Green Bay	WI	54311	800-844-6261	920-469-5300
Microthermics Inc					
3216-B Wellington Ct	Raleigh	NC	27615	800-466-2369	919-878-8045
Nemco Food Equipment Ltd					
301 Meuse Argonne	Hicksville	OH	43526	800-782-6761	419-542-7751
Qualtech Inc					
1880 Leon-Harmel St	Quebec	QC	G1N4K3	888-339-3801	418-686-3802
Remco Products Corp					
4735 W 106th St	Zionsville	IN	46077	800-585-8619	317-876-9856
Revent Inc					
100 Ethel Rd W	Piscataway	NJ	08854	800-822-9642	732-777-9433
Thomsen Group LLC					
1303 43rd St	Kenosha	WI	53140	800-558-4018	
US Beverage Net Inc					
225 W Jefferson St	Syracuse	NY	13202	888-298-3641	
Wixon Inc					
1390 E Bolivar Ave	Saint Francis	WI	53235	800-841-5304	414-769-3000

296-1 Bakery Products - Fresh

				Toll-Free	Phone
Bays Corp PO Box 1455	Chicago	IL	60690	800-367-2297	312-346-5757
Bimbo Bakeries USA					
PO Box 976	Horsham	PA	19044	800-984-0989	
Calise & Sons Bakery Inc					
2 Quality Dr	Lincoln	RI	02865	800-225-4737	401-334-3444
Carolina Foods Inc					
1807 S Tryon St	Charlotte	NC	28203	800-234-0441	704-333-9812
Dakota Brands International Inc					
2121 13th St NE	Jamestown	ND	58401	800-844-5073	701-252-5073
De Wafelbakkers LLC					
10000 Crystal Hill Rd	North Little Rock	AR	72113	800-924-3391	501-791-3320
Dinkel's Bakery					
3329 N Lincoln Ave	Chicago	IL	60657	800-822-8817*	773-281-7300
*Orders					
Ellison Bakery					
4108 W Ferguson Rd	Fort Wayne	IN	46809	800-711-8091	
Fantini Baking Company Inc					
375 Washington St	Haverhill	MA	01832	800-223-9037	
Grecian Delight Foods					
1201 Tonne Rd	Elk Grove Village	IL	60007	800-621-4387	
Greyston Bakery Inc					
104 Alexander St	Yonkers	NY	10701	800-289-2253	914-375-1510
H & S Bakery Inc					
601 S Caroline St	Baltimore	MD	21231	800-959-7655	410-276-7254
Heiners Bakery Inc					
1300 Adams Ave	Huntington	WV	25704	800-776-8411	304-523-8411
Herman Seekamp Inc					
1120 W Fullerton Ave	Addison	IL	60101	888-874-6814	

				Toll-Free	Phone
Klosterman Baking Company Inc					
4760 Paddock Rd	Cincinnati	OH	45229	877-301-1004	513-242-1004
Leidenheimer Baking Co					
1501 Simon Bolivar Ave	New Orleans	LA	70113	800-259-9099	504-525-1575
Martin's Famous Pastry Shoppe Inc					
1000 Potato Roll Ln	Chambersburg	PA	17202	800-548-1200*	717-263-9580
*Cust Svc					
McKee Foods Corp					
PO Box 750	Collegedale	TN	37315	800-522-4499*	423-238-7111
*Cust Svc					
Morabito Baking Company Inc					
757 Kohn St	Norristown	PA	19401	800-525-7747	610-275-5419
Orlando Baking Company Inc					
7777 Grand Ave	Cleveland	OH	44104	800-362-5504	216-361-1872
Pan-O-Gold Baking Co					
444 E St Germain	Saint Cloud	MN	56304	800-444-7005	320-251-9361
Pepperidge Farm Inc					
595 Westport Ave	Norwalk	CT	06851	888-737-7374*	
*PR					
Piantedosi Baking Company Inc					
240 Commercial St	Malden	MA	02148	800-339-0080	781-321-3400
Rothbury Farms					
PO Box 202	Grand Rapids	MI	49501	877-684-2879	
Schwebel Baking Co					
PO Box 6018	Youngstown	OH	44501	800-860-2867	330-783-2860
Signature Breads Inc					
100 Justin Dr	Chelsea	MA	02150	888-602-6533	
Sokol & Co					
5315 Dansher Rd	Countryside	IL	60525	800-328-7656*	
*Cust Svc					
Tasty Baking Co					
4300 S 26th St	Philadelphia	PA	19112	800-248-2789	215-221-8500
Wenner Bread Products Inc					
33 Rajon Rd	Bayport	NY	11705	800-869-6262	631-563-6262
Wolferman's					
2500 S Pacific Hwy PO Box 9100	Medford	OR	97501	800-999-0169	

296-2 Bakery Products - Frozen

				Toll-Free	Phone
Bridgford Foods Corp					
1308 N Patt St	Anaheim	CA	92801	800-854-3255	714-526-5533
NASDAQ: BRID					
Dessert Innovations Inc					
25-B Enterprise Blvd	Atlanta	GA	30336	800-359-7351	404-691-5000
Eli's Cheesecake Co					
6701 W Forest Preserve Dr	Chicago	IL	60634	800-999-8300	773-736-3417
Guttenplans Frozen Dough					
100 Hwy 36	Middletown	NJ	07748	888-422-4357*	732-495-9480
*General					
Main Street Gourmet Inc					
170 Muffin Ln	Cuyahoga Falls	OH	44223	800-678-6246	330-929-0000
Maplehurst Inc					
50 Maplehurst Dr	Brownsburg	IN	46112	800-428-3200	317-858-9000
Vie de France Yamazaki Inc					
2070 Chain Bridge Rd Ste 500	Vienna	VA	22182	800-446-4404*	703-442-9205
*General					

296-3 Butter (Creamery)

				Toll-Free	Phone
AMPI 315 N Broadway	New Ulm	MN	56073	800-533-3580	507-354-8295
Challenge Dairy Products Inc					
PO Box 2369	Dublin	CA	94568	800-733-2479	
Grassland Dairy Products Company Inc					
N 8790 Fairgrounds Ave	Greenwood	WI	54437	800-428-8837	
O-AT-KA Milk Products Co-op Inc					
700 Ellicott St	Batavia	NY	14020	800-828-8152	585-343-0536
Plainview Milk Products Co-Op					
130 Second St SW	Plainview	MN	55964	800-356-5606	507-534-3872

296-4 Cereals (Breakfast)

				Toll-Free	Phone
Big G Cereals					
PO Box 9452	Minneapolis	MN	55440	800-248-7310	
Bob's Red Mill Natural Foods Inc					
13521 SE Pheasant Ct	Milwaukie	OR	97222	800-553-2258	503-654-3215
Homestead Mills					
221 N River St PO Box 1115	Cook	MN	55723	800-652-5233	218-666-5233
Honeyville Grain Inc					
11600 Dayton Dr	Rancho Cucamonga	CA	91730	888-810-3212	909-980-9500
Kellogg Co					
1 Kellogg Sq PO Box 3599	Battle Creek	MI	49016	800-962-1413*	269-961-2000
*NYSE: K ■ *Cust Svc*					
New England Natural Bakers					
74 Fairview St E	Greenfield	MA	01301	800-910-2884	413-772-2239
Quaker Oats Co					
555 W Monroe St	Chicago	IL	60661	800-367-6287	312-821-1000
Weetabix Co Inc					
300 Nickerson Rd	Marlborough	MA	01752	800-343-0590	

296-5 Cheeses - Natural, Processed, Imitation

				Toll-Free	Phone
AMPI 315 N Broadway	New Ulm	MN	56073	800-533-3580	507-354-8295
Bel Brands USA Inc					
30 S Wacker Dr Ste 3000	Chicago	IL	60606	800-831-3724	920-788-3524
Berner Foods Inc					
2034 E Factory Rd	Dakota	IL	61018	800-819-8199	815-563-4222
Burnett Dairy Co-op					
11631 SR- 70	Grantsburg	WI	54840	800-854-2716	715-689-2468

					Toll-Free	Phone

Cacique Inc
14923 Procter Ave ... La Puente CA 91746 **800-521-6987** 626-961-3399
Dairiconcepts LP
3253 E Chestnut Expy ... Springfield MO 65802 **877-596-4374** 417-829-3400
Dairy Farmers of America Inc
10220 N Ambassador Dr ... Kansas City MO 64153 **888-332-6455** 816-801-6455
F & A Dairy Products Inc
Hwy 35 ... Dresser WI 54009 **800-826-5558** 715-755-3485
Farmdale Creamery Inc
1049 W Baseline St ... San Bernardino CA 92411 **800-346-7306** 909-889-3002
Galaxy Nutritional Foods Inc
66 Whitecap Dr ... North Kingstown RI 02852 **800-441-9419** 401-667-5000
Gossner Foods Inc
1051 N 1000 W ... Logan UT 84321 **800-944-0454** 435-227-2500
Grande Cheese Co
301 E Main St ... Lomira WI 53048 **800-772-3210**
Hilmar Cheese Company Inc
PO Box 910 ... Hilmar CA 95324 **800-577-5772** 209-667-6076
Jerome Cheese Co
547 W Nez Perce ... Jerome ID 83338 **800-757-7611** 208-324-8806
Kraft Heinz Co
200 E Randolph St ... Chicago IL 60601 **800-543-5335**
NASDAQ: KHC
Sargento Foods Inc
1 Persnickety Pl ... Plymouth WI 53073 **800-243-3737** 920-893-8484
Sartori
107 Pleasant View Rd ... Plymouth WI 53073 **800-558-5888***
*Cust Svc
Tillamook County Creamery Assn Inc
4185 Hwy 101 N ... Tillamook OR 97141 **800-542-7290** 503-815-1300
Tropical Cheese Industries Inc
450 Fayette St PO Box 1357 ... Perth Amboy NJ 08861 **888-874-4928** 732-442-4898

296-6 Chewing Gum

					Toll-Free	Phone

Concord Confections Ltd
345 Courtland Ave ... Concord ON L4K5A6 **800-267-0037** 905-660-8989
Topps Company Inc
1 Whitehall St ... New York NY 10004 **800-489-9149** 212-376-0300

296-7 Coffee - Roasted (Ground, Instant, Freeze-Dried)

					Toll-Free	Phone

Allegro Coffee Co
12799 Claude Ct ... Thornton CO 80241 **800-530-3995** 303-444-4844
ARCO Coffee Co
2206 Winter St ... Superior WI 54880 **800-283-2726** 715-392-4771
Boyd Coffee Co
19730 NE Sandy Blvd ... Portland OR 97230 **800-545-4077*** 503-666-4545
*Cust Svc
Cadillac Coffee Co
194 E Maple Rd ... Troy MI 48083 **800-438-6900** 248-545-2266
Coffee Holding Company Inc
3475 Victory Blvd ... Staten Island NY 10314 **800-458-2233** 718-832-0800
NASDAQ: JVA
Community Coffee Co
3332 Partridge Ln Bldg A ... Baton Rouge LA 70809 **800-688-0990** 800-884-5282
DeCoty Coffee Company Inc
1920 Austin St ... San Angelo TX 76903 **800-588-8001**
Excellent Coffee Co
259 E Ave ... Pawtucket RI 02860 **800-345-2007**
Farmer Bros Co
20333 S Normandie Ave ... Torrance CA 90502 **800-726-3870** 010-707-5200
NASDAQ: FARM
Frontier Natural Products Co-op
3021 78th St PO Box 299 ... Norway IA 52318 **800-669-3275** 319-227-7996
Hawaiian Isles Kona Coffee Co
2839 Mokumoa St ... Honolulu HI 96819 **800-657-7716***
*Orders
Melitta Canada Inc
50 Ronson Dr Unit 150 ... Toronto ON M9W1B3 **800-565-4882**
New England Coffee Co
100 Charles St ... Malden MA 02148 **800-225-3537**
Old Mansion Foods
3811 Corporate Rd PO Box 1838 ... Petersburg VA 23805 **800-476-1877** 804-862-9889
Paramount Coffee Co
5133 W Grand River Ave ... Lansing MI 48906 **800-968-1222**
Paul deLima Co Inc
7546 Morgan Rd ... Liverpool NY 13090 **800-962-8864** 315-457-3725
Red Diamond Inc 400 Park Ave ... Moody AL 35004 **800-292-4651** 205-577-4000
Reily Foods Co
400 Poydras St 10th Fl ... New Orleans LA 70130 **800-535-1961**
S & D Coffee Inc
300 Concord Pkwy ... Concord NC 28027 **800-933-2210***
*Cust Svc
Texas Coffee Co Inc
3297 S M L King Jr Pkwy ... Beaumont TX 77705 **800-259-3400** 409-835-3434
Torke Coffee Roasting Company Inc
3455 Paine Ave ... Sheboygan WI 53081 **800-242-7671**
White Coffee Corp
18-35 Steinway Pl ... Astoria NY 11105 **800-221-0140** 718-204-7900

296-8 Confectionery Products

					Toll-Free	Phone

Anthony-Thomas Candy Co
1777 Arlingate Ln ... Columbus OH 43228 **877-226-3921** 614-274-8405
Archer Daniels Midland Co
77 W Wacker Dr ... Chicago IL 60601 **800-637-5843** 217-424-5200
Asher's Chocolates
80 Wambold Rd ... Souderton PA 18964 **800-223-4420** 215-721-3000
Barry Callebaut USA LLC
400 Industrial Pk Rd ... Saint Albans VT 05478 **866-443-0460** 802-524-9711

BestCo Inc
288 Mazeppa Rd ... Mooresville NC 28115 **888-211-5530** 704-664-4300
Blommer Chocolate Co
600 W Kinzie St ... Chicago IL 60610 **800-621-1606** 312-226-7700
Brown & Haley PO Box 1596 ... Tacoma WA 98401 **800-426-8400**
Charms Co 7401 S Cicero Ave ... Chicago IL 60629 **800-267-0037** 773-838-3400
Cherrydale Farms Fundraising
707 N Vly Forge Rd ... Lansdale PA 19446 **877-619-4822**
Chocolates a la Carte
24836 Ave Rockefeller ... Valencia CA 91355 **800-818-2462***
*Cust Svc
Elmer Candy Corp
401 N Fifth St ... Ponchatoula LA 70454 **800-843-9537** 985-386-6166
Esther Price Candies Inc
1709 Wayne Ave ... Dayton OH 45410 **800-782-0326** 937-253-2121
Ferrero USA Inc
600 Cottontail Ln ... Somerset NJ 08873 **800-688-3552** 732-764-9300
Fowler's Chocolate Co
100 River Rock Dr Ste 102 ... Buffalo NY 14207 **800-824-2263** 716-877-9983
Gertrude Hawk Chocolates Inc
9 Keystone Pk ... Dunmore PA 18512 **866-932-4295** 800-822-2032
Ghirardelli Chocolate Co
1111 139th Ave ... San Leandro CA 94578 **800-877-9338**
Goetze's Candy Company Inc
3900 E Monument St ... Baltimore MD 21205 **800-295-8058*** 410-342-2010
*Orders
Guittard Chocolate Co
10 GuittaRd Rd ... Burlingame CA 94010 **800-468-2462** 650-697-4427
Harry London Candies Inc
5353 Lauby Rd ... North Canton OH 44720 **800-333-3629*** 330-494-0833
*Cust Svc
Hershey Co 100 Crystal A Dr ... Hershey PA 17033 **800-468-1714***
*NYSE: HSY ■ *Cust Svc*
Hillside Candy Co
35 Hillside Ave ... Hillside NJ 07205 **800-524-1304** 973-926-2300
James Candy Co
1519 Boardwalk ... Atlantic City NJ 08401 **800-441-1404*** 609-344-1519
*Orders
Jelly Belly Candy Co
1 Jelly Belly Ln ... Fairfield CA 94533 **800-323-9380** 707-428-2838
Just Born Inc
1300 Stefko Blvd ... Bethlehem PA 18017 **800-445-5787** 610-867-7568
Katharine Beecher
1250 Slate Hill Rd ... Camp Hill PA 17011 **800-233-7082**
Koeze Co PO Box 9470 ... Grand Rapids MI 49509 **800-555-9688**
Lammes Candies Since 1885 Inc
PO Box 1885 ... Austin TX 78767 **800-252-1885** 512-310-2223
Lindt & Sprungli USA
1 Fine Chocolate Pl ... Stratham NH 03885 **877-695-4638**
Lucks Co, The 3003 S Pine St ... Tacoma WA 98409 **800-426-9778** 253-383-4815
Madelaine Chocolate Novelties Inc
9603 Beach Ch Dr ... Rockaway Beach NY 11693 **800-322-1505** 718-945-1500
Malleys Chocolates
13400 Brookpark Rd ... Cleveland OH 44135 **800-275-6255** 216-362-8700
Morley Candy Makers Inc
23770 Hall Rd ... Clinton Township MI 48036 **800-651-7263**
Munson's Candy Kitchen Inc
174 Hop River Rd ... Bolton CT 06043 **888-686-7667** 860-649-4332
Paradise Inc
1200 W MLK Jr Blvd ... Plant City FL 33563 **800-330-8952**
OTC: PARF
Pearson's Candy Co
2140 W Seventh St ... Saint Paul MN 55116 **800-328-6507*** 651-698-0356
*Cust Svc
Pennsylvania Dutch Candies
1250 Slate Hill Rd ... Camp Hill PA 17011 **800-233-7082**
Russell Stover Candies Inc
4900 Oak St ... Kansas City MO 64112 **800-477-8683** 800-777-4004
See's Candies Inc
210 El Camino Real ... South San Francisco CA 94080 **800-877-7337*** 650-761-2490
*Cust Svc
Spangler Candy Co
400 N Portland St PO Box 71 ... Bryan OH 43506 **888-636-4221*** 419-636-4221
*Sales
Sweet Candy Co Inc
3780 W Directors Row ... Salt Lake City UT 84104 **800-669-8669** 801-886-1444
T R Toppers Inc
320 Fairchild ... Pueblo CO 81001 **800-748-4635** 719-948-4902
Tootsie Roll Industries Inc
7401 S Cicero Ave ... Chicago IL 60629 **866-972-6879** 773-838-3400
NYSE: TR
Vitasoy USA Inc
57 Russell St ... Woburn MA 01801 **800-848-2769**
Waymouth Farms Inc
5300 Boone Ave ... New Hope MN 55428 **800-527-0094** 763-533-5300
Wolfgang Candy Co
50 E Fourth Ave ... York PA 17404 **800-248-4273** 717-843-5536
World's Finest Chocolate Inc
4801 S Lawndale ... Chicago IL 60632 **888-821-8452**
Zachary Confections Inc
2130 IN-28 ... Frankfort IN 46041 **800-445-4222***
*Cust Svc

296-9 Cookies & Crackers

					Toll-Free	Phone

Benzel's Pretzel Bakery Inc
5200 Sixth Ave ... Altoona PA 16602 **800-344-4438** 814-942-5062
Bremner Biscuit Co
4600 Joliet St ... Denver CO 80239 **800-668-3273*** 855-972-0535
*Prod Info
Christie Cookie Co
1205 Third Ave N ... Nashville TN 37208 **800-458-2447** 615-242-3817
Delyse Inc 505 Reactor Way ... Reno NV 89502 **800-441-6887** 775-857-1811
Ellison Bakery
4108 W Ferguson Rd ... Fort Wayne IN 46809 **800-711-8091**

					Toll-Free	Phone

J & J Snack Foods Corp
6000 Central Hwy ....Pennsauken NJ 08109 **800-486-9533** 856-665-9533
NASDAQ: JJSF
Joy Cone Co 3435 Lamor Rd ....Hermitage PA 16148 **800-242-2663** 724-962-5747
Keystone Pretzels
124 W Airport Rd ....Lititz PA 17543 **888-572-4500**
Pretzels Inc
123 Harvest Rd PO Box 503 ....Bluffton IN 46714 **800-456-4838** 260-824-4838
Rudolph Foods Company Inc
6575 Bellefontaine Rd ....Lima OH 45804 **800-241-7675** 419-648-3611
Snyder's of Hanover
1250 York St PO Box 6917 ....Hanover PA 17331 **800-233-7125** 717-632-4477
Tom Sturgis Pretzels Inc
2267 Lancaster Pk ....Reading PA 19607 **800-817-3834** 610-775-0335
Wege Pretzel Co PO Box 334 ....Hanover PA 17331 **800-888-4646**

296-10 Dairy Products - Dry, Condensed, Evaporated

					Toll-Free	Phone

AMPI 315 N Broadway ....New Ulm MN 56073 **800-533-3580** 507-354-8295
Dairy Farmers of America Inc
10220 N Ambassador Dr ....Kansas City MO 64153 **888-332-6455** 816-801-6455
Davisco International Inc
719 N Main St ....Le Sueur MN 56058 **800-757-7611** 507-665-8811
Foremost Farms USA
E10889A Penny Ln ....Baraboo WI 53913 **800-362-9196** 608-355-8700
Gehl Foods
N116 W15970 Main St PO Box 1004 ....Germantown WI 53022 **800-521-2873** 262-251-8572
Instantwhip Foods Inc
2200 Cardigan Ave ....Columbus OH 43215 **800-544-9447*** 614-488-2536
*Cust Svc
Maple Island Inc
2497 Seventh Ave E Ste 105. ....St Paul MN 55109 **800-369-1022** 651-773-1000
Mead Johnson Nutritionals
2701 Patriot Blvd 4th Fl ....Glenview IL 60026 **800-231-5469** 847-832-2420
Meyenberg PO Box 934 ....Turlock CA 95381 **800-891-4628**
Milk Products LLC
PO Box 150 ....Chilton WI 53014 **800-657-0793** 920-849-2348
O-AT-KA Milk Products Co-op Inc
700 Ellicott St ....Batavia NY 14020 **800 828-8152** 585-343-0536
Volpi Foods
5263 Northrup Ave ....St Louis MO 63110 **800-288-3439** 314-772-8550

296-11 Diet & Health Foods

					Toll-Free	Phone

Eden Foods Inc
701 Tecumseh Rd ....Clinton MI 49236 **800-248-0320*** 517-456-7424
*Cust Svc
Isagenix International LLC
2225 S Price Rd ....Chandler AZ 85286 **877-877-8111** 480-889-5747
Medifast Inc
11445 Cronhill Dr ....Owings Mills MD 21117 **800-209-0878**
NYSE: MED
RC Fine Foods PO Box 236 ....Belle Mead NJ 08502 **800-526-3953** 908-359-5500
Tahitian Noni International
333 W Riverpark Dr ....Provo UT 84604 **800-445-2969*** 801-234-1000
*Cust Svc
Vitaminerals Inc
1815 Flower St ....Glendale CA 91201 **800-432-1856** 818-500-8718

296-12 Fats & Oils - Animal or Marine

					Toll-Free	Phone

Darling International Inc
251 O'Connor Ridge Blvd Ste 300 ....Irving TX 75038 **800-800-4841** 972-717-0300
NYSE: DAR
GA Wintzer & Son Co
204 W Auglaize St ....Wapakoneta OH 45895 **800-331-1801** 419-739-4900
Omega Protein Corp
2105 City W Blvd Ste 500. ....Houston TX 77042 **866-421-0831** 713-623-0060
Werner G Smith Inc
1730 Train Ave ....Cleveland OH 44113 **800-535-8343*** 216-861-3676
*General

296-13 Fish & Seafood - Canned

					Toll-Free	Phone

Beaver Street Fisheries Inc
1741 W Beaver St ....Jacksonville FL 32209 **800-874-6426** 904-354-8533
Bumble Bee Seafoods Inc
PO Box 85362 ....San Diego CA 92186 **800-800-8572** 858-715-4000
Los Angeles Smoking & Curing Co (LASCCO)
1100 W Ewing St ....Seattle WA 98119 **800-365-8950** 206-285-6800
Pacific Choice Seafoods Co
16797 SE 130th Ave ....Clackamas OR 97015 **800-882-0212** 707-442-2981
Petersburg Fisheries
PO Box 1147 ....Petersburg AK 99833 **877-772-4294** 907-772-4294
Vita Food Products Inc
2222 West Lake St ....Chicago IL 60612 **800-989-8482** 312-738-4500

296-14 Fish & Seafood - Fresh or Frozen

					Toll-Free	Phone

Blount Seafood Corp
630 Currant Rd ....Fall River MA 02720 **800-274-2526*** 774-888-1300
*Hotline
Consolidated Catfish Cos LLC
299 S St PO Box 271 ....Isola MS 38754 **800-228-3474** 662-962-3101
Crocker & Winsor Seafoods Inc
PO Box 51905 ....Boston MA 02205 **800-225-1597** 617-269-3100

Gorton's Inc
128 Rogers St ....Gloucester MA 01930 **800-222-6846** 978-283-3000
King & Prince Seafood Corp
1 King & Prince Blvd ....Brunswick GA 31520 **888-391-5223**
Morey's Seafood International LLC
1218 Hwy 10 S ....Motley MN 56466 **800-808-3474** 218-352-6345
Ocean Beauty Seafoods Inc
1100 W Ewing St ....Seattle WA 98119 **800-365-8950** 206-285-6800
Riverside Foods Inc
2520 Wilson St ....Two Rivers WI 54241 **800-678-4511** 920-793-4511
Stoller Fisheries
1301 18th St PO Box B. ....Spirit Lake IA 51360 **800-831-5174** 712-336-1750
Tampa Bay Fisheries Inc
3060 Gallagher Rd ....Dover FL 33527 **800-732-3663** 813-752-8883
UniSea Inc 15400 NE 90th St ....Redmond WA 98073 **800-535-8509** 425-881-8181

296-15 Flavoring Extracts & Syrups

					Toll-Free	Phone

DD Williamson & Company Inc
100 S Spring St ....Louisville KY 40206 **800-227-2635** 502-895-2438
Emerald Kalama Chemical LLC
1296 Third St NW ....Kalama WA 98625 **877-300-9545** 360-673-2550
Frutarom Corp
9500 Railroad Ave ....North Bergen NJ 07047 **866-229-7198** 201-861-9500
I Rice & Company Inc
11500 Roosevelt Blvd Bldg D ....Philadelphia PA 19116 **800-232-6022** 215-673-7423
Jel Sert Co
501 Conde St ....West Chicago IL 60185 **800-323-2592** 630-876-4838
Kalsec Inc 3713 W Main St ....Kalamazoo MI 49006 **800-323-9320** 269-349-9711
Limpert Bros Inc
202 NW Blvd ....Vineland NJ 08362 **800-691-1353** 856-691-1353
Lyons Magnus Inc
3158 E Hamilton Ave ....Fresno CA 93702 **800-344-7130**
Mother Murphy's Labs Inc
2826 S Elm St PO Box 16846. ......Greensboro NC 27416 **800-849-1277** 336-273-1737
Phillips Syrup Corp
28025 Ranney Pkwy ....Westlake OH 44145 **800-350-8443** 440-835-8001
Sea Breeze Inc 441 Rt 202 ....Towaco NJ 07082 **800-732-2733**
Sensient Technologies Corp
777 E Wisconsin Ave ....Milwaukee WI 53202 **800-558-9892** 414-271-6755
NYSE: SXT
Sethness Products Co
3422 W Touhy Ave ....Lincolnwood IL 60712 **888-772-1880** 847-329-2080
Western Syrup Co
13766 Milroy Pl ....Santa Fe Springs CA 90670 **800-521-3888** 562-921-4485
Wild Flavors Inc
1261 Pacific Ave ....Erlanger KY 41018 **800-263-5286** 859-342-3600

296-16 Flour Mixes & Doughs

					Toll-Free	Phone

Abitec Corp Inc PO Box 569 ....Columbus OH 43215 **800-555-1255*** 614-429-6464
*Sales
Bake'n Joy Foods Inc
351 Willow St S ....North Andover MA 01845 **800-666-4937** 978-683-1414
Dawn Food Products Inc
3333 Sargent Rd ....Jackson MI 49201 **800-292-1362*** 517-789-4400
*Cust Svc
Rhodes International Inc
PO Box 25487 ....Salt Lake City UT 84125 **800-876-7333*** 801-972-0122
*Cust Svc
Subco Foods Inc
4350 S Taylor Dr ....Sheboygan WI 53081 **800-473-0757** 920-457-7761
Watson Foods Company Inc
301 Heffernan Dr ....West Haven CT 06516 **800-388-3481** 203-932-3000

296-17 Food Emulsifiers

					Toll-Free	Phone

ADM Specialty Food Ingredients Div
4666 E Faries Pkwy ....Decatur IL 62526 **800-637-5843** 217-424-5200
American Lecithin Company Inc
115 Hurley Rd Unit 2B ....Oxford CT 06478 **800-364-4416** 203-262-7100
Crest Foods Company Inc
905 Main St ....Ashton IL 61006 **877-273-7893** 800-435-6972
Frutarom Corp
9500 Railroad Ave ....North Bergen NJ 07047 **866-229-7198** 201-861-9500

296-18 Fruits & Vegetables - Dried or Dehydrated

					Toll-Free	Phone

Basic American Foods
2185 N California Blvd Ste 215 ....Walnut Creek CA 94596 **800-227-4050**
Bernard Food Industries Inc
1125 Hartrey Ave ....Evanston IL 60204 **800-323-3663** 847-869-5222
Custom Culinary
2505 S Finley Rd ....Lombard IL 60148 **800-621-8827**
Del Monte Foods Co
1 Maritime Plz ....San Francisco CA 94111 **800-543-3090*** 415-247-3000
*Cust Svc
Freskeeto Frozen Foods Inc
8019 Rt 209 ....Ellenville NY 12428 **800-356-3663** 845-647-5111
Garry Packing Inc
11272 E Central Ave ....Del Rey CA 93616 **800-248-2126** 559-888-2126
Graceland Fruit Inc
1123 Main St ....Frankfort MI 49635 **800-352-7181** 231-352-7181
Idaho-Pacific Corp
4723 E 100 N PO Box 478 ....Ririe ID 83443 **800-238-5503*** 208-538-6971
*Sales
Larsen Farms 2650 N 2375 E ......Hamer ID 83425 **800-767-6104*** 208-662-5501
*Sales
Oregon Potato Co PO Box 3110 ......Pasco WA 99302 **800-336-6311** 509-545-4545

	Toll-Free	Phone
Small Planet Foods Inc		
106 Woodworth St ....Sedro Woolley WA 98284	800-624-4123	360-855-0100
Stapleton-Spence Packing Co		
1530 The Alameda Ste 320..................San Jose CA 95126	800-297-8815	408-297-8815
Sunsweet Growers Inc		
901 N Walton Ave ....Yuba City CA 95993	800-417-2253	530-674-5010

296-19 Fruits & Vegetables - Pickled

	Toll-Free	Phone
B & G Foods Inc		
4 Gatehall Dr Ste 110 ....Parsippany NJ 07054	800-811-8975	
NYSE: BGS		
Beaverton Foods Inc		
7100 NW Century Blvd ....Hillsboro OR 97124	800-223-8076	503-646-8138
Best Maid Products Inc		
PO Box 1809 ....Fort Worth TX 76101	800-447-3581	817-335-5494
Conway Import Co Inc		
11051 W Addison St ....Franklin Park IL 60131	800-323-8801	847-455-5600
Eastern Foods Inc		
1000 Naturally Fresh Blvd ....Atlanta GA 30349	800-765-1950	800-236-1119
Gold Pure Food Products Inc		
1 Brooklyn Rd ....Hempstead NY 11550	800-422-4681	
HV Food Products Co		
1221 Broadway ....Oakland CA 94612	877-853-7262	
Ken's Foods Inc		
1 D'Angelo Dr ....Marlborough MA 01752	800-633-5800	
Lee Kum Kee Inc		
14841 Don Julian Rd ....City of Industry CA 91746	800-654-5082*	626-709-1888
*Orders		
Litehouse Inc		
1109 N Ella Ave ....Sandpoint ID 83864	800-669-3169	
MA Gedney Co		
2100 Stoughton Ave ....Chaska MN 55318	888-244-0653	952-448-2612
Maurice's Gourmet Barbeque		
PO Box 6847 ....West Columbia SC 29171	800-628-7423	803-791-5887
McIlhenny Co Hwy 329 ....Avery Island LA 70513	800-634-9599*	
*Orders		
Moody Dunbar Inc		
PO Box 6048 ....Johnson City TN 37602	800-251-8202	423-952-0100
NewStar Fresh Foods LLC		
850 Work St Ste 101........................Salinas CA 93901	888-782-7220	805-487-3406
Olds Products Co		
10700 88th Ave ....Pleasant Prairie WI 53158	800-233-8064	262-947-3500
Spring Glen Fresh Foods Inc		
314 Spring Glen Dr ....Ephrata PA 17522	800-641-2853	717-733-2201
T Marzetti Co		
380 Polaris Pkwy Ste 400.....................Westerville OH 43082	800-999-1835	
Walden Farms		
1209 W St Georges Ave ....Linden NJ 07036	800-229-1706	

296-20 Fruits, Vegetables, Juices - Canned or Preserved

	Toll-Free	Phone
American Spoon Foods Inc		
1668 Clarion Ave ....Petoskey MI 49770	800-222-5886	888-735-6700
Apple & Eve Inc		
2 Seaview Blvd ....Port Washington NY 11050	800-969-8018	516-621-1122
B & G Foods Inc		
4 Gatehall Dr Ste 110 ....Parsippany NJ 07054	800-811-8975	
NYSE: BGS		
Braswell Food Co		
226 N Zetterower Ave ....Statesboro GA 30458	800-673-9388	912-764-6191
Bruce Foods Corp		
221 Southpark Plz PO Box 1030..............Lafayette LA 70508	800-299-9082	337-365-8101
Campbell Soup Co		
1 Campbell Pl ....Camden NJ 08103	800-257-8443	856-342-4800
NYSE: CPB		
Cincinnati Preserving Company Inc		
3015 E Kemper Rd ....Sharonville OH 45241	800-222-9966*	
*Cust Svc		
Cornelius Seed Corn Co		
14760 317th Ave ....Bellevue IA 52031	800-218-1862	
Del Monte Foods Co		
1 Maritime Plz ....San Francisco CA 94111	800-543-3090*	415-247-3000
*Cust Svc		
Del Monte Fresh		
PO Box 149222 ....Coral Gables FL 33114	800-950-3683*	305-520-8400
*Cust Svc		
Dole Packaged Foods Co		
1 Dole Dr ....Westlake Village CA 91362	800-356-3111	
Don Pepino Sales Co		
123 Railroad Ave ....Williamstown NJ 08094	888-281-6400	856-629-7429
Escalon Premier Brands		
1905 McHenry Ave ....Escalon CA 95320	800-255-5750	209-838-7341
Furmano Foods Inc		
770 Cannery Rd ....Northumberland PA 17857	877-877-6032	570-473-3516
Giorgio Foods Inc PO Box 96 ....Temple PA 19560	800-220-2139	610-926-2139
Hanover Foods Corp		
1550 York St PO Box 334......................Hanover PA 17331	800-888-4646	717-632-6000
OTC: HNFSA		
Hirzel Canning Company & Farms		
411 Lemoyne Rd ....Northwood OH 43619	800-837-1631	419-693-0531
House Foods America Corp		
7351 Orangewood Ave ....Garden Grove CA 92841	877-333-7077	714-901-4350
Ingomar Packing Co		
9950 S Ingomar Grade PO Box 1448 ......Los Banos CA 93635	800-328-0026	209-826-9494
Jasper Wyman & Son		
PO Box 100 ....Milbridge ME 04658	800-341-1758*	
*Sales		
JM. Smucker Co, The		
1 Strawberry Ln ....Orrville OH 44667	888-550-9555	
Lakeside Foods Inc		
808 Hamilton St ....Manitowoc WI 54220	800-466-3834	920-684-3356
Leelanau Fruit Co		
2900 SW Bay Shore Dr ....Suttons Bay MI 49682	800-431-0718	231-271-3514

	Toll-Free	Phone
Lyons Magnus Inc		
3158 E Hamilton Ave ....Fresno CA 93702	800-344-7130	
Mayer Bros Apple Products Inc		
3300 Transit Rd ....West Seneca NY 14224	800-696-2928	716-668-1787
Moody Dunbar Inc		
PO Box 6048 ....Johnson City TN 37602	800-251-8202	423-952-0100
Morgan Foods Inc		
90 W Morgan St ....Austin IN 47102	888-430-1780	812-794-1170
Mott's LLP PO Box 869077 ....Plano TX 75086	800-426-4891*	
*Consumer Info		
Mrs Clark's Foods		
740 SE Dalbey Dr ....Ankeny IA 50021	800-736-5674	515-299-6400
Muir Glen Organic		
PO Box 9452 ....Minneapolis MN 55440	800-832-6345	
National Fruit Product Co Inc		
701 Fairmont Ave ....Winchester VA 22601	800-655-4022	540-662-3401
Ocean Spray Cranberries Inc		
1 Ocean Spray Dr ....Lakeville-Middleboro MA 02349	800-662-3263	508-946-1000
Odwalla Inc 1 COCA-COLA Plz ....Atlanta GA 30313	800-639-2552	
Pacific Coast Producers		
631 N Cluff Ave ....Lodi CA 95240	877-618-4776	209-367-8800
Pastorelli Food Products Inc		
162 N Sangamon St ....Chicago IL 60607	800-767-2829	312-666-2041
Red Gold Inc 120 E Oak St ....Orestes IN 46063	800-772-5726	765-754-7527
Seneca Foods Corp		
3736 S Main St ....Marion NY 14505	800-622-6757	315-926-8100
NASDAQ: SENEA		
Simply Orange Juice Co		
2659 Orange Ave ....Apopka FL 32703	800-871-2653	
Stanislaus Food Products Co		
1202 D St ....Modesto CA 95354	800-327-7201	
Stapleton-Spence Packing Co		
1530 The Alameda Ste 320.....................San Jose CA 95126	800-297-8815	408-297-8815
Sun Orchard Inc		
1198 W Fairmont Dr ....Tempe AZ 85282	800-505-8423	
Talk O'Texas Brands Inc		
1610 Roosevelt St ....San Angelo TX 76905	800-749-6572	325-655-6077
Tip Top Canning Co		
505 S Second St PO Box 126..................Tipp City OH 45371	800-352-2635	937-667-3713
Truitt Bros Inc		
1105 Front St NE ....Salem OR 97301	800-547-8712	
Vegetable Juices Inc		
7400 S Narragansett ....Bedford Park IL 60638	888-776-9752*	708-924-9500
*General		
Vita-Pakt Citrus Products		
203 E Badillo St ....Covina CA 91723	888-684-8272	626-332-1101
Zeigler Beverages LLC		
1513 N Broad St ....Lansdale PA 19446	800-854-6123*	215-855-5161
*Sales		

296-21 Fruits, Vegetables, Juices - Frozen

	Toll-Free	Phone
Apio Inc PO Box 727 ....Guadalupe CA 93434	800-454-1355*	
*Sales		
Bernatello's PO Box 729 ....Maple Lake MN 55358	800-666-9455	952-831-6622
Capitol City Produce		
16550 Commercial Ave ....Baton Rouge LA 70816	800-349-1583	225-272-8153
Coloma Frozen Foods Inc		
4145 Coloma Rd ....Coloma MI 49038	800-642-2723	269-849-0500
Dole Food Company Inc		
1 Dole Dr ....Westlake Village CA 91362	800-232-8888	818-879-6600
NYSE: DOLE		
Giorgio Foods Inc PO Box 96 ....Temple PA 19560	800-220-2139	610-926-2139
Graceland Fruit Inc		
1123 Main St ....Frankfort MI 49635	800-352-7181	231-352-7181
HPC Foods Ltd 288 Libby St ....Honolulu HI 96819	877-370-0919	808-848-2431
JR Simplot Co PO Box 27 ....Boise ID 83707	800-832-8893	208-336-2110
Lakeside Foods Inc		
808 Hamilton St ....Manitowoc WI 54220	800-466-3834	920-684-3356
Leelanau Fruit Co		
2900 SW Bay Shore Dr ....Suttons Bay MI 49682	800-431-0718	231-271-3514
McCain Foods Ltd		
181 Bay St Ste 3600...........................Toronto ON M5J2T3	800-938-7799	416-955-1700
McCain Foods USA Inc		
2275 Cabot Dr ....Lisle IL 60532	800-938-7799	630-955-0400
Mrs Clark's Foods		
740 SE Dalbey Dr ....Ankeny IA 50021	800-736-5674	515-299-6400
NORPAC Foods Inc		
930 W Washington St ....Stayton OR 97383	800-733-9311	503-769-6361
Penobscot McCrum LLC		
28 Pierce St ....Belfast ME 04915	800-435-4456	207-338-4360
Seneca Foods Corp		
3736 S Main St ....Marion NY 14505	800-622-6757	315-926-8100
NASDAQ: SENEA		
Townsend Farms Inc		
23400 NE Townsend Way ....Fairview OR 97024	800-875-5291	503-666-1780
Vita-Pakt Citrus Products		
203 E Badillo St ....Covina CA 91723	888-684-8272	626-332-1101

296-22 Gelatin

	Toll-Free	Phone
Gelita USA Inc		
2445 Port Neal Industrial Rd ....Sergeant Bluff IA 51054	800-223-9244	712-943-5516
Subco Foods Inc		
4350 S Taylor Dr ....Sheboygan WI 53081	800-473-0757	920-457-7761

296-23 Grain Mill Products

	Toll-Free	Phone
ADM Milling Co (ADM)		
8000 W 110th St ....Overland Park KS 66210	800-422-1688	913-491-9400

Company / Address	City	State	Zip	Toll-Free	Phone
Ag Processing Inc 12700 W Dodge Rd PO Box 2047	Omaha	NE	68103	**800-247-1345**	402-496-7809
Bartlett & Co 4900 Main St Ste 12	Kansas City	MO	64112	**800-888-6300**	816-753-6300
Bay State Milling Co 100 Congress St	Quincy	MA	02169	**800-553-5687**	
Chelsea Milling Co 201 W N St PO Box 460	Chelsea	MI	48118	**800-727-2460**	734-475-1361
Farmers Rice Co-op PO Box 15223	Sacramento	CA	95851	**800-326-2799**	916-923-5100
Gold Medal PO Box 9452	Minneapolis	MN	55440	**800-248-7310**	
House-Autry Mills Inc 7000 US Hwy 301 S	Four Oaks	NC	27524	**800-849-0802**	
Indian Harvest Specialtifoods Inc 1012 Paul Bunyan Dr SE *Orders	Bemidji	MN	56601	**800-346-7032***	
Knappen Milling Co 110 S Water St	Augusta	MI	49012	**800-562-7736**	269-731-4141
Mallet & Company Inc 51 Arch St Ext	Carnegie	PA	15106	**800-245-2757**	412-276-9000
Manildra Group USA 4210 Shawnee Mission Pkwy Ste 312A	Shawnee Mission	KS	66205	**800-323-8435**	913-362-0777
Mennel Milling Co 128 W Crocker St	Fostoria	OH	44830	**800-688-8151**	
MGP Ingredients Inc 100 Commercial St PO Box 130 *NASDAQ: MGPI*	Atchison	KS	66002	**800-255-0302**	913-367-1480
Morrison Milling Co 319 E Prairie St	Denton	TX	76201	**800-531-7912**	940-387-6111
North Dakota Mill & Elevator 1823 Mill Rd	Grand Forks	ND	58203	**800-538-7721**	701-795-7000
Pacific Grain Products International Inc 351 Hanson Way PO Box 2060 *Cust Svc	Woodland	CA	95776	**800-333-0110***	530-631-5786
Pacific International Rice Mills Inc 845 Kentucky Ave	Woodland	CA	95695	**800-747-4764**	530-661-6028
Producers Rice Mill Inc PO Box 1248	Stuttgart	AR	72160	**800-369-7675**	870-673-4444
RiceTec Inc 1925 FM 2917 PO Box 1305	Alvin	TX	77511	**877-580-7423**	281-393-3532
Shawnee Milling Company Inc 201 S Broadway PO Box 1567	Shawnee	OK	74802	**800-654-2600**	405-273-7000
Siemer Milling Co 111 W Main St	Teutopolis	IL	62467	**800-826-1065**	217-857-3131
Wilkins-Rogers Inc 27 Frederick Rd *Cust Svc	Ellicott City	MD	21043	**877-438-4338***	410-465-5800

296-24 Honey

Company / Address	City	State	Zip	Toll-Free	Phone
Barkman Honey 120 Santa Fe St	Hillsboro	KS	67063	**800-364-6623**	
Dutch Gold Honey Inc 2220 Dutch Gold Dr	Lancaster	PA	17601	**800-846-2753**	717-393-1716
Glorybee Foods Inc 29548 B Airport Rd	Eugene	OR	97402	**800-456-7923**	541-689-0913
Honey Acres 1557 Hwy 67 N	Ashippun	WI	53003	**800-558-7745**	
Honeytree Inc 8570 M 50	Onsted	MI	49265	**800-968-1889**	517-467-2482
Pure Sweet Honey Farm Inc 514 Commerce Pkwy	Verona	WI	53593	**800-355-9601**	

296-25 Ice Cream & Frozen Desserts

Company / Address	City	State	Zip	Toll-Free	Phone
Anderson Erickson Dairy Co 2420 E University Ave	Des Moines	IA	50317	**800-234-6455**	515-265-2521
Baldwin Richardson Foods Co 1 Tower Ln Ste 2390 *Cust Svc	Oakbrook Terrace	IL	60181	**866-644-2732***	630-607-1780
Borden Dairy Co 8750 N Central Expy Ste 400	Dallas	TX	75231	**800-778-7879**	
Broughton Foods 1701 Green St	Marietta	OH	45750	**800-303-3400**	740-373-4121
Cedar Crest Specialties Inc 7269 Hwy 60 PO Box 260 *Hotline	Cedarburg	WI	53012	**800-877-8341***	262-377-7252
Coleman Dairy Inc 6901 I-30	Little Rock	AR	72209	**800-365-1551**	501-748-1700
Farr's Ice Cream - SLC 2575 South 300 West	South Salt Lake City	UT	84115	**877-553-2777**	801-484-8724
Galliker Dairy Company Inc 143 Donald Ln	Johnstown	PA	15907	**800-477-6455**	814-266-8702
Graeter's Inc 2145 Reading Rd	Cincinnati	OH	45202	**800-721-3323**	513-721-3323
Hershey Creamery Co 301 S Cameron St	Harrisburg	PA	17101	**888-240-1905**	717-238-8134
Hiland Dairy Co PO Box 2270	Springfield	MO	65801	**800-641-4022**	417-862-9311
J & J Snack Foods Corp 6000 Central Hwy *NASDAQ: JJSF*	Pennsauken	NJ	08109	**800-486-9533**	856-665-9533
Perry's Ice Cream Company Inc 1 Ice Cream Plz	Akron	NY	14001	**800-873-7797**	716-542-5492
Schwan's Co 115 W College Dr	Marshall	MN	56258	**800-533-5290**	507-532-3274
Sugar Creek Foods International 301 N El Paso St	Russellville	AR	72801	**800-445-2715**	
Turkey Hill Dairy Inc 2601 River Rd	Conestoga	PA	17516	**800-693-2479**	717-872-5461
Turner Dairy Farms Inc 1049 Jefferson Rd	Pittsburgh	PA	15235	**800-892-1039**	412-372-2211
Umpqua Dairy Products Co 1686 SE N St PO Box 1306	Grants Pass	OR	97526	**800-222-6455**	541-672-2638
Wells Enterprises Inc 1 Blue Bunny Dr *All	Le Mars	IA	51031	**800-942-3800***	712-546-4000

296-26 Meat Products - Prepared

Company / Address	City	State	Zip	Toll-Free	Phone
Aidells Sausage Co 1625 Alvarado St	San Leandro	CA	94577	**855-600-7697**	
Alderfer Inc 382 Main St PO Box 2 *Sales	Harleysville	PA	19438	**800-222-2319***	
Aliments Asta Inc 767 Rte 289	St Alexandre-De-Kamouraska	QC	G0L2G0	**800-463-1355**	418-495-2728
American Foods Group Inc 544 Acme St	Green Bay	WI	54302	**800-345-0293**	920-437-6330
Ballard's Farm Sausage Inc 7275 Right Fork Wilson Creek *General	Wayne	WV	25570	**800-346-7675***	304-272-5147
Berks Packing Company Inc 307-323 Bingaman St PO Box 5919	Reading	PA	19610	**800-882-3757**	
Best Provision Company Inc 144 Avon Ave	Newark	NJ	07108	**800-631-4466**	973-242-5000
Bridgford Foods Corp 1308 N Patt St *NASDAQ: BRID*	Anaheim	CA	92801	**800-854-3255**	714-526-5533
Burger's Ozark Country Cured Hams Inc 32819 Hwy 87	California	MO	65018	**800-203-4424**	573-796-3134
Caribbean Products Ltd 3624 Falls Rd	Baltimore	MD	21211	**888-689-5068**	
Carl Buddig & Co 950 175th St	Homewood	IL	60430	**888-633-5684**	708-798-0900
Carlton Foods Corp 880 Texas 46	New Braunfels	TX	78130	**800-628-9849**	830-625-7583
Cattaneo Bros Inc 769 Caudill St	San Luis Obispo	CA	93401	**800-243-8537**	
Cher-Make Sausage Co 2915 Calumet Ave	Manitowoc	WI	54220	**800-242-7679**	
Chicago Meat Authority Inc (CMA) 1120 W 47th Pl	Chicago	IL	60609	**800-383-3811**	773-254-3811
Chicopee Provision Co Inc 19 Sitarz St	Chicopee	MA	01013	**800-924-6328**	413-594-4765
Citterio USA Corp 2008 SR- 940	Freeland	PA	18224	**800-435-8888**	570-636-3171
Cloverdale Foods Co 3015 34th St NW	Mandan	ND	58554	**800-669-9511**	
Cook's Ham Inc 200 S Second St	Lincoln	NE	68508	**800-332-8400**	402-475-6700
D'Artagnan Inc 280 Wilson Ave Ste 1	Newark	NJ	07105	**800-327-8246**	973-344-0565
Daniele Inc PO Box 106	Pascoag	RI	02859	**800-451-2535**	401-568-6228
Dewied International Inc 5010 IH- 10 E	San Antonio	TX	78219	**800-992-5600**	210-661-6161
Dietz & Watson Inc 5701 Tacony St	Philadelphia	PA	19135	**800-333-1974**	215-831-9000
Fred Usinger Inc 1030 N Old World Third St	Milwaukee	WI	53203	**800-558-9998**	414-276-9100
Gallo Salame 2411 Baumann Ave	San Lorenzo	CA	94580	**800-988-6464**	
Hatfield Quality Meats Inc 2700 Clemens Rd	Hatfield	PA	19440	**800-743-1191**	215-368-2500
Hazle Park Packing Co 260 Washington Ave Hazle Pk	Hazletownship	PA	18202	**800-238-4331**	570-455-7571
Hormel Foods Corp 1 Hormel Pl *NYSE: HRL*	Austin	MN	55912	**800-523-4635**	507-437-5838
John Morrell & Co 805 E Kemper Rd	Cincinnati	OH	45246	**800-722-1127**	513-346-3540
Johnsonville Sausage LLC PO Box 906	Sheboygan Falls	WI	53085	**888-556-2728**	
Jones Dairy Farm 800 Jones Ave	Fort Atkinson	WI	53538	**800-635-6637**	
Kayem Foods Inc 75 Arlington St	Chelsea	MA	02150	**800-426-6100**	617-889-1600
Kent Quality Foods Inc 703 Leonard St NW	Grand Rapids	MI	49504	**800-748-0141**	
Kiolbassa Provision Co 1325 S Brazos St	San Antonio	TX	78207	**800-456-5465**	
Koegel Meats Inc 3400 W Bristol Rd	Flint	MI	48507	**800-678-1962**	810-238-3685
Kronos Products Inc 1 Kronos Dr	Glendale Heights	IL	60139	**800-621-0099**	224-353-5353
Maid-Rite Steak Company Inc 105 Keystone Industrial Pk	Dunmore	PA	18512	**800-233-4259**	570-343-4748
Makowski's Real Sausage 2710 S Poplar Ave	Chicago	IL	60608	**800-746-9554**	312-842-5330
Maple Leaf Foods Inc PO Box 61016 *TSE: MFI*	Winnipeg	MB	R3M3X8	**800-268-3708**	
Marathon Enterprises Inc 9 Smith St	Englewood	NJ	07631	**800-722-7388**	201-935-3330
Martin Rosol Inc 45 Grove St	New Britain	CT	06053	**800-937-2682**	860-223-2707
Miller Packing Co PO Box 1390	Lodi	CA	95241	**800-624-2328**	209-339-2310
Oberto Sausage Co 7060 S 238th St	Kent	WA	98032	**877-453-7591**	
Old Wisconsin Sausage Co 4036 Weeden Creek Rd	Sheboygan	WI	53083	**877-451-7988**	920-458-4304
Palmyra Bologna Company Inc 230 N College St	Palmyra	PA	17078	**800-282-6336**	717-838-6336
Park 100 Foods Inc 326 E Adams St	Tipton	IN	46072	**800-854-6504**	765-675-3480
Peer Foods Group Inc 1200 W 35th St	Chicago	IL	60609	**800-365-5644**	773-475-2375
Plumrose USA Inc 1901 Butterfield Rd Ste 305	Downers Grove	IL	60515	**800-526-4909**	732-624-4040

Classified Section

				Toll-Free	Phone
Premio Foods Inc					
50 Utter Ave	Hawthorne	NJ	07506	**800-864-7622**	
Randolph Packing Co					
275 Roma Jean Pkwy	Streamwood	IL	60107	**800-451-1607**	630-830-3100
Reser's Fine Foods Inc					
15570 SW Jenkins Rd	Beaverton	OR	97006	**800-333-6431**	503-643-6431
Sahlen Packing Company Inc					
318 Howard St	Buffalo	NY	14206	**800-466-8165**	716-852-8677
Silver Star Meats Inc					
1720 Middletown Rd	McKees Rocks	PA	15136	**800-548-1321**	412-777-4460
Specialty Foods Group Inc					
6 Dublin Ln	Owensboro	KY	42301	**800-238-0020**	270-926-2324
Stampede Meat Inc					
7351 S 78th Ave	Bridgeview	IL	60455	**800-353-0933**	
Standard Meat Company LP					
5105 Investment Dr	Dallas	TX	75236	**866-859-6313**	214-561-0561
Stock Yards Packing Co Inc					
2500 S Pacific Hwy PO Box 9100	Medford	OR	97501	**888-842-6111**	
Sugar Creek Packing Co					
2101 Kenskill Ave	Washington Court House	OH	43160	**800-848-8205**	740-335-7440
Tyson Prepared Foods Inc					
2200 Don Tyson Pkwy	Springdale	AR	72762	**800-233-6332**	479-290-4000
US Premium Beef LLC (USPB)					
12200 N Ambassador Dr					
PO Box 20103	Kansas City	MO	64163	**866-877-2525**	816-713-8800
Vienna Sausage Manufacturing Co					
2501 N Damen Ave	Chicago	IL	60647	**800-366-3647**	773-278-7800
Vista International Packaging LLC					
1126 88th Pl	Kenosha	WI	53143	**800-558-4058**	
Vollwerth & Co					
200 Hancock St PO Box 239	Hancock	MI	49930	**800-562-7620**	906-482-1550
Wimmer's Meat Products Inc					
126 W Grant St	West Point	NE	68788	**800-762-9865***	402-372-2437
*Cust Svc					

296-27 Milk & Cream Products

				Toll-Free	Phone
Agri-Mark Inc PO Box 5800	Lawrence	MA	01842	**800-225-0532**	978-689-4442
Alta Dena Dairy					
17851 E Railrd	City of Industry	CA	91748	**800-535-1369***	
*Orders					
AMPI 315 N Broadway	New Ulm	MN	56073	**800-533-3580**	507-354-8295
Anderson Erickson Dairy Co					
2420 E University Ave	Des Moines	IA	50317	**800-234-6455**	515-265-2521
Broughton Foods					
1701 Green St	Marietta	OH	45750	**800-303-3400**	740-373-4121
Clover Farms Dairy					
PO Box 14627	Reading	PA	19612	**800-323-0123**	610-921-9111
Cloverland Green Spring Dairy Inc					
2701 Loch Raven Rd	Baltimore	MD	21218	**800-492-0094***	410-235-4477
*Orders					
Coleman Dairy Inc					
6901 I-30	Little Rock	AR	72209	**800-365-1551**	501-748-1700
Dean Foods Co					
2711 N Haskell Ave Ste 3400	Dallas	TX	75204	**800-395-7004**	214-303-3400
NYSE: DF					
Eagle Family Foods Group LLC					
1 Strawberry Ln	Orrville	OH	44667	**888-550-9555**	
Farmland Dairies LLC					
520 Main Ave	Wallington	NJ	07057	**866-648-5252**	
Guida-Seibert Dairy Co					
433 Park St	New Britain	CT	06051	**800-832-8929**	
Harrisburg Dairies Inc					
2001 Herr St	Harrisburg	PA	17105	**800-692-7429**	
Hiland Dairy Co					
PO Box 2270	Springfield	MO	65801	**800-641-4022**	417-862-9311
Kemps LLC 1270 Energy Ln	Saint Paul	MN	55108	**800-322-9566**	
Land O'Lakes Inc Dairyman's Div					
400 S 'M' St	Tulare	CA	93274	**800-328-4155**	559-687-8287
Milkco Inc					
220 Deaverview Rd	Asheville	NC	28806	**800-842-8021**	828-254-9560
Oakhurst Dairy					
364 Forest Ave	Portland	ME	04101	**800-482-0718**	207-772-7468
Parmalat Canada Ltd					
405 the W Mall 10th Fl	Toronto	ON	M9C5J1	**800-563-1515**	
Prairie Farms Dairy Inc					
1100 N Broadway St	Carlinville	IL	62626	**800-654-2547**	217-854-2547
Royal Crest Dairy Inc					
350 S Pearl St	Denver	CO	80209	**888-226-6455**	303-777-2227
Shamrock Foods					
3900 E Camelback Rd Ste 300	Phoenix	AZ	85018	**800-289-3663**	602-477-2500
Southeast Milk Inc					
PO Box 3790	Belleview	FL	34420	**800-598-7866**	
Stremicks Heritage Foods					
4002 Westminster Ave	Santa Ana	CA	92703	**800-321-5960***	714-775-5000
*Orders					
Superior Dairy Inc					
4719 Navarre Rd SW	Canton	OH	44706	**800-597-5460**	330-477-4515
T Marzetti Company Allen Milk Div					
1709 Frank Rd	Columbus	OH	43223	**800-999-1835**	
Umpqua Dairy Products Co					
1686 SE N St PO Box 1306	Grants Pass	OR	97526	**800-222-6455**	541-672-2638
United Dairy Farmers					
3955 Montgomery Rd	Cincinnati	OH	45212	**866-837-4833***	513-396-8700
*General					
United Dairy Inc					
300 N Fifth St	Martins Ferry	OH	43935	**800-252-1542**	740-633-1451
WhiteWave Foods Co					
12002 Airport Way	Broomfield	CO	80021	**888-820-9283**	303-635-4000

296-28 Nuts - Edible

				Toll-Free	Phone
Azar Nut Co 1800 NW Dr	El Paso	TX	79912	**800-351-8178**	915-877-4079

				Toll-Free	Phone
Kar's Nuts					
1200 E 14 Mile Rd	Madison Heights	MI	48071	**800-527-6887**	
King Nut Co 31900 Solon Rd	Solon	OH	44139	**800-860-5464**	440-248-8484
Priester Pecan Company Inc					
208 Old Fort Rod E	Fort Deposit	AL	36032	**800-277-3226**	334-227-4301
Superior Nut Co Inc					
225 Monsignor O'Brien Hwy	Cambridge	MA	02141	**800-295-4093**	617-876-3808
Trophy Nut Company Inc					
320 N Second St	Tipp City	OH	45371	**800-729-6887**	937-667-8478

296-29 Oil Mills - Cottonseed, Soybean, Other Vegetable Oils

				Toll-Free	Phone
Abitec Corp Inc PO Box 569	Columbus	OH	43215	**800-555-1255***	614-429-6464
*Sales					
Ag Processing Inc					
12700 W Dodge Rd PO Box 2047	Omaha	NE	68103	**800-247-1345**	402-496-7809
American Lecithin Company Inc					
115 Hurley Rd Unit 2B	Oxford	CT	06478	**800-364-4416**	203-262-7100
Cargill Inc					
15407 McGinty Rd W	Wayzata	MN	55391	**800-227-4455**	
Owensboro Grain Co					
822 E Second St	Owensboro	KY	42303	**800-874-0305**	270-926-2032
Planters Cotton Oil Mill Inc					
2901 Planters Dr	Pine Bluff	AR	71601	**800-264-7070**	870-534-3631

296-30 Oils - Edible (Margarine, Shortening, Table Oils, etc)

				Toll-Free	Phone
Par-Way Tryson Co					
107 Bolte Ln	Saint Clair	MO	63077	**800-844-4554**	636-629-4545
Ventura Foods LLC 40 Pointe Dr	Brea	CA	92821	**800-421-6257**	714-257-3700

296-31 Pasta

				Toll-Free	Phone
Dakota Growers Pasta Company Inc					
1 Pasta Ave	Carrington	ND	58421	**866-569-4411**	701-652-2855
Monterey Pasta Co					
2315 Moore Ave	Fullerton	CA	92833	**800-588-7782**	
OB Macaroni Co					
3066 S E Loop 820	Fort Worth	TX	76140	**800-553-4336***	817-335-4629
*Orders					
Peking Noodle Co Inc					
1514 N San Fernando Rd	Los Angeles	CA	90065	**877-735-4648**	323-223-2023

296-32 Peanut Butter

				Toll-Free	Phone
Producers Peanut Company Inc					
PO Box 250	Suffolk	VA	23434	**800-847-5491**	757-539-7496

296-33 Salads - Prepared

				Toll-Free	Phone
D'Arrigo Bros Company of California Inc					
PO Box 850	Salinas	CA	93902	**800-995-5939***	831-455-4500
*Cust Svc					
Earth Island					
9201 Owensmouth Ave	Chatsworth	CA	91311	**888-394-3949**	818-725-2820
Kayem Foods Inc					
75 Arlington St	Chelsea	MA	02150	**800-426-6100**	617-889-1600
Ready Pac Produce Inc					
4401 Foxdale Ave	Irwindale	CA	91706	**800-800-7822**	
Reser's Fine Foods Inc					
15570 SW Jenkins Rd	Beaverton	OR	97006	**800-333-6431**	503-643-6431
Sandridge Food Corp (SFC)					
133 Commerce Dr	Medina	OH	44256	**800-627-2523**	330-725-2348
Suter Company Inc					
258 May St	Sycamore	IL	60178	**800-435-6942**	815-895-9186

296-34 Sandwiches - Prepared

				Toll-Free	Phone
Bridgford Foods Corp					
1308 N Patt St	Anaheim	CA	92801	**800-854-3255**	714-526-5533
NASDAQ: BRID					
Cloverdale Foods Co					
3015 34th St NW	Mandan	ND	58554	**800-669-9511**	
Hormel Foods Corp					
1 Hormel Pl	Austin	MN	55912	**800-523-4635**	507-437-5838
NYSE: HRL					
Konop Cos					
1725 Industrial Dr	Green Bay	WI	54302	**800-770-0477**	920-468-8517

296-35 Snack Foods

				Toll-Free	Phone
Better Made Snack Foods Inc					
10148 Gratiot Ave	Detroit	MI	48213	**800-332-2394**	313-925-4774
Bickel's Snack Foods					
1120 Zinns Quarry Rd	York	PA	17404	**800-233-1933**	717-843-0738
Cape Cod Potato Chip Co					
100 Breed's Hill Rd	Hyannis	MA	02601	**888-881-2447**	
Evans Food Group Ltd					
4118 S Halsted St	Chicago	IL	60609	**888-643-8267**	773-254-7400
Frito-Lay North America					
7701 Legacy Dr	Plano	TX	75024	**800-352-4477**	

			Toll-Free	Phone
Golden Flake Snack Foods Inc 1 Golden Flake Dr	Birmingham AL	35205	800-239-2447	205-323-6161
Herr Foods Inc 20 Herr Dr PO Box 300	Nottingham PA	19362	800-344-3777	610-932-9330
Martin's Potato Chips Inc 5847 Lincoln Hwy W PO Box 28	Thomasville PA	17364	800-272-4477	717-792-3565
Mike-Sell's Potato Chip Co 333 Leo St PO Box 115	Dayton OH	45404	800-257-4742	937-228-9400
Mission Foods 1159 Cottonwood Ln Ste 200	Irving TX	75038	800-443-7994	214-208-7010
Snyder of Berlin 1313 Stadium Dr	Berlin PA	15530	888-257-8042	
Uncle Ray's LLC 14245 Birwood St	Detroit MI	48238	800-800-3286	313-834-0800
UTZ Quality Foods Co 900 High St	Hanover PA	17331	800-367-7629	717-637-6644
Wise Foods Inc 228 Rasely St Ste 75 *Cust Svc	Berwick PA	18603	888-759-4401*	570-759-4000

296-36 Specialty Foods

			Toll-Free	Phone
Armanino Foods of Distinction Inc 30588 San Antonio St OTC: AMNF	Hayward CA	94544	800-255-5855	510-441-9300
Avanti Foods 109 Depot St	Walnut IL	61376	800-243-3739	815-379-2155
Beech-Nut Nutrition Corp 1 Nutritious Pl	Amsterdam NY	12010	800-233-2468	
Bruce Foods Corp 221 Southpark Plz PO Box 1030	Lafayette LA	70508	800-299-9082	337-365-8101
Campbell Soup Co 1 Campbell Pl NYSE: CPB	Camden NJ	08103	800-257-8443	856-342-4800
Cromers Pnuts LLC 3030 North Main St	Columbia SC	29201	800-322-7688	
Cuisine Solutions Corporate USA 22445 Sous Vide Ln Unit 100 OTC: CUSI	Sterling VA	20166	888-285-4679	703-270-2900
D & D Foods Inc 9425 N 48th St	Omaha NE	68152	800-208-0364	402-571-4113
Del Monte Foods Co 1 Maritime Plz *Cust Svc	San Francisco CA	94111	800-543-3090*	415-247-3000
Deli Express 16101 W 78th St	Eden Prairie MN	55344	800-328-8184	
Eden Foods Inc 701 Tecumseh Rd *Cust Svc	Clinton MI	49236	800-248-0320*	517-456-7424
El Encanto Inc 2001 Fourth St SW PO Box 293	Albuquerque NM	87103	800-888-7336	505-243-2722
Ener-G Foods Inc 5960 First Ave S PO Box 84487	Seattle WA	98124	800-331-5222	206-767-3928
Gerber Products Co 445 State St	Fremont MI	49413	800-284-9488	
Hain Celestial Group Inc 4600 Sleepytime Dr NASDAQ: HAIN	Boulder CO	80301	877-612-4246	
Hanover Foods Corp 1550 York St PO Box 334 OTC: HNFSA	Hanover PA	17331	800-888-4646	717-632-6000
Home Market Foods Inc 140 Morgan Dr	Norwood MA	02062	800-367-8325	781-948-1500
Hormel Foods Corp 1 Hormel Pl NYSE: HRL	Austin MN	55912	800-523-4635	507-437-5838
Juanita's Foods Inc PO Box 847	Wilmington CA	90748	800-303-2965	
Kahiki Foods Inc 1100 Morrison Rd	Gahanna OH	43230	855-524-4540	
La Reina Inc 316 N Ford Blvd	Los Angeles CA	90022	800-367-7522	323-268-2791
Leon's Texas Cuisine Co 2100 Redbud Blvd	McKinney TX	75069	800-527-1243	972-529-5050
Mancini Foods PO Box 157	Zolfo Springs FL	33890	800-741-1778	
McCain Foods Ltd 181 Bay St Ste 3600	Toronto ON	M5J2T3	800-938-7799	416-955-1700
McCain Foods USA Inc 2275 Cabot Dr	Lisle IL	60532	800-938-7799	630-955-0400
Michael Angelo's Gourmet Foods Inc 200 Michael Angelo Way	Austin TX	78728	877-482-5426	512-218-3500
Morgan Foods Inc 90 W Morgan St	Austin IN	47102	888-430-1780	812-794-1170
Mott's LLP PO Box 869077 *Consumer Info	Plano TX	75086	800-426-4891*	
Nardone Bros Baking Company Inc 420 New Commerce Blvd	Wilkes-Barre PA	18706	800-822-5320	570-823-0141
Overhill Farms Inc 2727 E Vernon Ave NYSE: OFI	Vernon CA	90058	800-859-6406	323-582-9977
Pastorelli Food Products Inc 162 N Sangamon St	Chicago IL	60607	800-767-2829	312-666-2041
Preferred Meal Systems Inc 5240 St Charles Rd *Cust Svc	Berkeley IL	60163	800-886-6325*	
Quaker Oats Co 555 W Monroe St	Chicago IL	60661	800-367-6287	312-821-1000
Ruiz Foods Inc PO Box 37	Dinuba CA	93618	800-477-6474	
Schwan's Co 115 W College Dr	Marshall MN	56258	800-533-5290	507-532-3274
Small Planet Foods Inc 106 Woodworth St	Sedro Woolley WA	98284	800-624-4123	360-855-0100
Suter Company Inc 258 May St	Sycamore IL	60178	800-435-6942	815-895-9186
Winter Gardens Quality Foods Inc 304 Commerce St PO Box 339	New Oxford PA	17350	800-242-7637	717-624-4911

296-37 Spices, Seasonings, Herbs

			Toll-Free	Phone
Abco Laboratories Inc 2450 S Watney Way	Fairfield CA	94533	800-678-2226	707-432-2200
American Outdoor Products Inc 6350 Gunpark Dr	Boulder CO	80301	800-641-0500	
Basic American Foods 2185 N California Blvd Ste 215	Walnut Creek CA	94596	800-227-4050	
Benson's Gourmet Seasonings PO Box 638	Azusa CA	91702	800-325-5619	626-969-4443
Frontier Natural Products Co-op 3021 78th St PO Box 299	Norway IA	52318	800-669-3275	319-227-7996
Fuchs North America 3800 Hampstead Mexico Rd	Hampstead MD	21074	800-365-3229	410-363-1700
Johnny's Fine Foods Inc 319 E 25th St *General	Tacoma WA	98421	800-962-1462*	253-383-4597
McCormick & Company Inc McCormick Flavor Div 226 Schilling Cir	Hunt Valley MD	21031	800-322-7742	
McCormick & Company Inc US Consumer Products Div 211 Schilling Cir	Hunt Valley MD	21031	800-632-5847	
McCormick Ingredients 18 Loveton Cir	Sparks MD	21152	800-632-5847	410-771-7301
Newly Weds Foods Inc 4140 W Fullerton Ave	Chicago IL	60639	800-621-7521	773-489-7000
Pepsi Bottling Ventures LLC 4141 Parklake Ave Ste 600	Raleigh NC	27612	800-662-8792	919-865-2300
Precision Foods Inc 11457 Olde Cabin Rd Ste 100	Saint Louis MO	63141	800-442-5242	314-567-7400
Sabra Dipping Co LLC 2420 49th St	Astoria NY	11103	888-957-2272	
SensoryEffects Flavor Co 231 Rock Industrial Park Dr	Bridgeton MO	63044	800-422-5444	314-291-5444
Spice Hunter Inc 2000 W Broad St	Richmond VA	23220	800-444-3061	
Spice World Inc 8101 Presidents Dr	Orlando FL	32809	800-433-4979	407-851-9432
World Spice Inc 223 E Highland Pkwy	Roselle NJ	07203	800-234-1060	

296-38 Sugar & Sweeteners

			Toll-Free	Phone
C & H Sugar Co 2300 Contra Costa Blvd Ste 600	Pleasant Hill CA	94523	800-773-1803	925-688-1731
Western Sugar Co-op 7555 E Hampden Ave Ste 520	Denver CO	80231	800-523-7497	303-830-3939

296-39 Syrup - Maple

			Toll-Free	Phone
Maple Grove Farms of Vermont 1052 Portland St	Saint Johnsbury VT	05819	800-525-2540	802-748-5141
Richards Maple Products Inc 545 Water St	Chardon OH	44024	800-352-4052	
Sea Breeze Inc 441 Rt 202	Towaco NJ	07082	800-732-2733	

296-40 Tea

			Toll-Free	Phone
Bigelow Tea 201 Black Rock Tpke	Fairfield CT	06825	888-244-3569	
Celestial Seasonings Inc 4600 Sleepytime Dr	Boulder CO	80301	800-351-8175	
Redco Foods Inc 1 Hansen Is	Little Falls NY	13365	800-556-6674	315-823-1300
S & D Coffee Inc 300 Concord Pkwy *Cust Svc	Concord NC	28027	800-933-2210*	

296-41 Vinegar & Cider

			Toll-Free	Phone
Boyajian Inc 144 Will Dr *General	Canton MA	02021	800-965-0665*	781-828-9966
Gold Pure Food Products Inc 1 Brooklyn Rd	Hempstead NY	11550	800-422-4681	
Heintz & Weber Co Inc 150 Reading Ave	Buffalo NY	14220	800-438-6878	716-852-7171
MA Gedney Co 2100 Stoughton Ave	Chaska MN	55318	888-244-0653	952-448-2612
Mizkan Americas Inc 1661 Feehanville Dr Ste 300	Mount Prospect IL	60056	800-323-4358	847-590-0059
National Fruit Product Co Inc 701 Fairmont Ave	Winchester VA	22601	800-655-4022	540-662-3401
Pastorelli Food Products Inc 162 N Sangamon St	Chicago IL	60607	800-767-2829	312-666-2041

296-42 Yeast

			Toll-Free	Phone
Brolite Products Inc 1900 S Park Ave	Streamwood IL	60107	888-276-5483	630-830-0340
DSM Food Specialties Inc 45 Waterview Blvd	Parsippany NJ	07054	800-526-0189	
Lesaffre Yeast Corp 7475 W Main St *Cust Svc	Milwaukee WI	53214	800-770-2714*	414-615-3300

				Toll-Free	Phone
Minn-Dak Yeast Company Inc					
18175 Red River Rd W	Wahpeton	ND	58075	**800-348-0991**	701-642-3300
Ohly Americas					
1115 Tiffany St	Boyceville	WI	54725	**800-321-2689**	320-587-2481

297   FOOD PRODUCTS - WHOL

SEE ALSO Beverages - Whol

				Toll-Free	Phone
Quantum Inc PO Box 2791	Eugene	OR	97402	**800-448-1448**	541-345-5556

297-1   Baked Goods - Whol

				Toll-Free	Phone
Wheat Montana Farms Inc					
10778 US Hwy 287	Three Forks	MT	59752	**800-535-2798**	406-285-3614

297-2   Coffee & Tea - Whol

				Toll-Free	Phone
Barrie House Coffee Company Inc					
4 Warehouse In	Elmsford	NY	10523	**800-876-2233**	
Becharas Brothers Coffee Co Inc					
14501 Hamilton Ave	Highland Park	MI	48203	**800-944-9675**	313-869-4700
Capricorn Coffees Inc					
353 Tenth St	San Francisco	CA	94103	**800-541-0758**	415-621-8500
Coffee Bean International					
9120 NE Alderwood Rd	Portland	OR	97220	**800-877-0474**	
Coffee Masters Inc					
7606 Industrial Ct	Spring Grove	IL	60081	**800-334-6485**	815-675-0088
Red Diamond Inc 400 Park Ave	Moody	AL	35004	**800-292-4651**	205-577-4000

297-3   Confectionery & Snack Foods - Whol

				Toll-Free	Phone
AMCON Distributing Co					
7405 Irvington Rd	Omaha	NE	68122	**888-201-5997**	402-331-3727
NYSE: DIT					
Brown & Haley PO Box 1596	Tacoma	WA	98401	**800-426-8400**	
Burklund Distributors Inc					
2500 N Main St Ste 3	East Peoria	IL	61611	**800-322-2876**	309-694-1900
Continental Concession Supplies Inc					
575 Jericho Tpke Ste 300	Jericho	NY	11753	**800-516-0090**	516-739-8777
Eby-Brown Co					
1415 W Diehl Rd Ste 300N	Naperville	IL	60563	**800-553-8249**	630-778-2800
Frito-Lay North America					
7701 Legacy Dr	Plano	TX	75024	**800-352-4477**	
Harold Levinson Assoc (HLA)					
21 Banfi Plz	Farmingdale	NY	11735	**800-325-2512**	631-962-2400
Keilson-Dayton Co					
107 Commerce Park Dr	Dayton	OH	45404	**800-759-3174**	937-236-1070
McDonald Wholesale Co					
2350 W Broadway St	Eugene	OR	97402	**877-722-5503**	541-345-8421
Sultana Distribution Services Inc					
600 Food Ctr Dr	Bronx	NY	10474	**877-617-5500**	718-617-5500
Superior Nut Co Inc					
225 Monsignor O'Brien Hwy	Cambridge	MA	02141	**800-295-4093**	617-876-3808
Trophy Nut Company Inc					
320 N Second St	Tipp City	OH	45371	**800-729-6887**	937-667-8478

297-4   Dairy Products - Whol

				Toll-Free	Phone
Ambriola Company Inc					
7 Patton Dr	West Caldwell	NJ	07006	**800-962-8224**	
AMPI 315 N Broadway	New Ulm	MN	56073	**800-533-3580**	507-354-8295
Broughton Foods					
1701 Green St	Marietta	OH	45750	**800-303-3400**	740-373-4121
Clofine Dairy Products Inc					
1407 New Rd	Linwood	NJ	08221	**800-441-1001**	609-653-1000
Clover-Stornetta Farms Inc					
PO Box 750369	Petaluma	CA	94975	**800-237-3315**	
Cream-O-Land Dairy Inc					
529 Cedar Ln	Florence	NJ	08518	**800-220-6455**	609-499-3601
Luberski Inc					
310 N Harbor Blvd Ste 205	Fullerton	CA	92832	**800-326-3220**	714-680-3447
Maryland & Virginia Milk Producers Co-op Assn Inc					
1985 Isaac Newton Sq W	Reston	VA	20190	**800-552-1976**	703-742-6800
Masters Gallery Foods Inc					
328 County Hwy PP PO Box 170	Plymouth	WI	53073	**800-236-8431***	920-893-8431
*General					
Plains Dairy Products					
300 N Taylor St	Amarillo	TX	79107	**800-365-5608**	806-374-0385
Prairie Farms Dairy Inc					
1100 N Broadway St	Carlinville	IL	62626	**800-654-2547**	217-854-2547
Roberts Dairy Co					
2901 Cuming St	Omaha	NE	68131	**800-779-4321**	402-344-4321
Rockview Dairies Inc					
7011 Stewart & Gray Rd	Downey	CA	90241	**800-423-2479**	562-927-5511
Sure Winner Foods Inc					
2 Lehner Rd	Saco	ME	04072	**800-640-6447**	207-282-1258
Umpqua Dairy Products Co					
1686 SE N St PO Box 1306	Grants Pass	OR	97526	**800-222-6455**	541-672-2638

297-5   Fish & Seafood - Whol

				Toll-Free	Phone
Beaver Street Fisheries Inc					
1741 W Beaver St	Jacksonville	FL	32209	**800-874-6426**	904-354-8533

				Toll-Free	Phone
Blount Seafood Corp					
630 Currant Rd	Fall River	MA	02720	**800-274-2526***	774-888-1300
*Hotline					
ConAgra Foods Foodservice Co					
5 ConAgra Dr	Omaha	NE	68102	**800-357-6543**	800-722-1344
Golden-Tech International Inc					
13555 SE 36th St Ste 330	Bellevue	WA	98006	**800-311-8090**	425-869-1461
Inland Seafood Corp					
1651 Montreal Cir	Tucker	GA	30084	**800-883-3474**	404-350-5850
Ipswich Shellfish Group					
8 Hayward St	Ipswich	MA	01938	**800-477-9424**	978-356-4371
Maine Lobster Direct					
48 Union Wharf	Portland	ME	04101	**800-556-2783**	
Metropolitan Poultry & Seafood Co					
1920 Stanford Ct	Landover	MD	20785	**800-522-0060**	301-772-0060
Morey's Seafood International LLC					
1218 Hwy 10 S	Motley	MN	56466	**800-808-3474**	218-352-6345
Quirch Foods Co					
7600 NW 82nd Pl	Miami	FL	33166	**800-458-5252**	305-691-3535
Sager's Seafood Plus Inc					
4802 Bridal Wreath Dr	Richmond	TX	77406	**800-929-3474**	
Slade Gorton Company Inc					
225 Southampton St	Boston	MA	02118	**800-225-1573**	617-442-5800
Southern Foods Inc					
3500 Old Battleground Rd	Greensboro	NC	27410	**800-642-3768**	
Stavis Seafoods Inc					
212 Northern Ave Ste 305	Boston	MA	02210	**800-390-5103**	617-897-1200
Troyer Foods Inc					
17141 State Rd 4	Goshen	IN	46528	**800-876-9377**	574-533-0302
Val's Distributing Co					
6124 E 30th St N	Tulsa	OK	74115	**800-274-9987**	918-835-9987

297-6   Frozen Foods (Packaged) - Whol

				Toll-Free	Phone
ConAgra Foods Foodservice Co					
5 ConAgra Dr	Omaha	NE	68102	**800-357-6543**	800-722-1344
Dot Foods Inc					
1 Dot Way PO Box 192	Mount Sterling	IL	62353	**800-366-3687**	217-773-4411

297-7   Fruits & Vegetables - Fresh - Whol

				Toll-Free	Phone
Albert's Organics Inc					
3268 E Vernon Ave	Vernon	CA	90058	**800-899-5944**	
Alpine Fresh Inc					
9300 NW 58th St Ste 201	Miami	FL	33178	**800-292-8777**	305-594-9117
Bix Produce Co					
1415 L'Orient St	Saint Paul	MN	55117	**800-642-9514**	651-487-8000
Bland Farms Inc					
1126 Raymond Bland Rd	Glennville	GA	30427	**800-440-9543**	
Calavo Growers Inc					
1141-A Cummings Rd	Santa Paula	CA	93060	**800-654-8758**	805-525-1245
NASDAQ: CVGW					
Caro Foods Inc					
2324 Bayou Blue Rd	Houma	LA	70364	**800-395-2276**	985-872-1483
Chico Produce Inc					
70 Pepsi Way PO Box 1069	Durham	CA	95938	**888-232-0908**	530-893-0596
Costa Fruit & Produce					
18 Bunker Hill Industrial Pk	Boston	MA	02129	**800-322-1374**	617-241-8007
Crosset Company Inc					
10295 Toebben Dr	Independence	KY	41051	**800-347-4902**	859-283-5830
Del Monte Fresh					
PO Box 149222	Coral Gables	FL	33114	**800-950-3683***	305-520-8400
*Cust Svc					
Dole Food Company Hawaii					
802 Mapunapuna St	Honolulu	HI	96819	**800-697-9100**	808-861-8015
Egan Bernard & Co					
1900 Old Dixie Hwy	Fort Pierce	FL	34946	**800-327-6676**	
FreshPoint Inc					
1390 Enclave Pkwy	Houston	TX	77077	**800-367-5690**	
General Produce Co					
1330 N 'B' St	Sacramento	CA	95811	**800-366-4991**	916-441-6431
H Smith Packing Corp					
99 Ft Fairfield Rd	Presque Isle	ME	04769	**800-393-9898**	207-764-4540
Hollar & Greene Produce Co Inc					
230 Cabbage Rd PO Box 3500	Boone	NC	28607	**800-222-1077**	828-264-2177
Indianapolis Fruit Company Inc					
4501 Massachusetts Ave	Indianapolis	IN	46218	**800-377-2425**	317-546-2425
Kegel's Produce Inc					
2851 Old Tree Dr	Lancaster	PA	17603	**800-535-3435**	717-392-6612
Melissa's/World Variety Produce Inc					
5325 S Soto St	Vernon	CA	90058	**800-588-0151**	
Muir Enterprises Inc					
3575 West 900 South					
PO Box 26775	Salt Lake City	UT	84104	**877-268-2002**	801-363-7695
North Bay Produce Inc					
PO Box 549	Traverse City	MI	49685	**800-678-1941**	
Organic Valley Family of Farms					
1 Organic Way	LaFarge	WI	54639	**888-444-6455**	
Pacific Coast Fruit Co					
201 NE Second Ave	Portland	OR	97232	**800-423-4945**	503-234-6411
Produce Source Partners					
13167 Telcourt Rd	Ashland	VA	23005	**800-344-4728**	804-262-8300
Progressive Produce Co					
5790 Peachtree St	Los Angeles	CA	90040	**800-900-0757**	323-890-8100
Sambazon					
209 Avenida Fabricante Ste 200	San Clemente	CA	92672	**877-726-2296**	
Sandridge Food Corp (SFC)					
133 Commerce Dr	Medina	OH	44256	**800-627-2523**	330-725-2348
Taylor Farms Inc					
150 Main St	Salinas	CA	93901	**877-323-7374**	
W R. Vernon Produce Co					
1035 N Cherry St PO Box 4054	Winston-Salem	NC	27101	**800-222-6406**	336-725-9741

297-8 Groceries - General Line

Company / Address	City	State	ZIP	Toll-Free	Phone
ACE Bakery 1 Hafis Rd	Toronto	ON	M6M2V6	**800-443-7929**	416-241-8433
Acme Food Sales Inc 5940 First Ave S	Seattle	WA	98108	**800-777-2263**	206-762-5150
Affiliated Foods Inc 1401 W Farmers Ave	Amarillo	TX	79118	**800-234-3661**	806-372-3851
Albert Guarnieri Co 1133 E Market St	Warren	OH	44483	**800-686-2639**	330-394-5636
AMCON Distributing Co 7405 Irvington Rd *NYSE: DIT*	Omaha	NE	68122	**888-201-5997**	402-331-3727
Amster-Kirtz Co 2830 Cleveland Ave NW	Canton	OH	44709	**800-257-9338**	330-535-6021
Apetito Canada Ltd 12 Indell Ln	Brampton	ON	L6T3Y3	**800-268-8199**	905-799-1022
Associated Food Stores Inc 1850 West 2100 South *Cust Svc	Salt Lake City	UT	84119	**888-574-7100***	801-973-4400
Associated Grocers Inc 8600 Anselmo Ln	Baton Rouge	LA	70810	**800-637-2021**	225-444-1000
Associated Grocers of New England Inc 11 Co-op Way	Pembroke	NH	03275	**800-242-2248**	603-223-6710
Associated Grocers of the South 3600 Vanderbilt Rd	Birmingham	AL	35217	**800-695-6051**	205-841-6781
Associated Wholesalers Inc PO Box 67	Robesonia	PA	19551	**800-927-7771**	610-693-3161
Bill & Ralphs Inc 118 B & R Dr	Sarepta	LA	71071	**800-406-3045**	
Bozzuto's Inc 275 School House Rd *OTC: BOZZ*	Cheshire	CT	06410	**800-458-5114**	203-272-3511
Bragg Live Food Products Inc PO Box 7	Santa Barbara	CA	93102	**800-446-1990**	
Brenham Wholesale Grocery Co 602 W First St	Brenham	TX	77833	**800-392-4869**	979-836-7925
Camp Olympia 723 Olympia Dr	Trinity	TX	75862	**800-735-6190**	936-594-2541
Cash-Wa Distributing Co 401 W Fourth St	Kearney	NE	68845	**800-652-0010**	308-237-3151
Chef's Requested Foods Inc 2600 Exchange Ave	Oklahoma City	OK	73108	**800-256-0259**	
Clean Foods Inc 4561 Market St Ste B	Ventura	CA	93003	**800-526-8328**	
Coastal Pacific Food Distributors Inc (CPFD) 1015 Performance Dr	Stockton	CA	95206	**800-500-2611**	209-983-2454
DiCarlo Distributors Inc 1630 N Ocean Ave	Holtsville	NY	11742	**800-342-2756**	631-758-6000
Dutch Valley Bulk Food Distributors Inc 7615 Lancaster Ave	Myerstown	PA	17067	**800-733-4191**	717-933-4191
F Mcconnell & Sons Inc 11102 Lincoln Hwy E	New Haven	IN	46774	**800-552-0835**	260-493-6607
Farner-Bocken Co 1751 US Hwy 30 E PO Box 368	Carroll	IA	51401	**800-274-8692**	712-792-3503
Feesers Inc 5561 Grayson Rd	Harrisburg	PA	17111	**800-326-2828**	717-564-4636
Field Trip Factory 2211 N Elston Ave Ste 304	Chicago	IL	60614	**800-987-6409**	
Flavor Dynamics Inc 640 Montrose Ave	South Plainfield	NJ	07080	**888-271-8424**	908-822-8855
Food Services of America Inc 16100 N 71st St Ste 400	Scottsdale	AZ	85254	**800-528-9346**	480-927-4000
Fuji Chemical Industries USA 3 Terri Ln Unit 12	Burlington	NJ	08016	**877-385-4777**	609-386-3030
G r Manufacturing Inc 4800 Commerce Dr	Trussville	AL	35173	**800-841-8001**	205-655-8001
George E DeLallo Co Inc 6390 Rt 30	Jeannette	PA	15644	**877-335-2556**	724-523-6577
Gold Coast Ingredients Inc 2429 Yates Ave	Commerce	CA	90040	**800-352-8673**	323-724-8935
Grocery People Ltd, The (TGP) 14505 Yellowhead Trl	Edmonton	AB	T5L3C4	**800-461-9401**	780-447-5700
Grocery Supply Co 130 Hillcrest Dr	Sulphur Springs	TX	75482	**800-231-1938**	903-885-7621
Hannaford Bros Co LLC 145 Pleasant Hill Rd	Scarborough	ME	04074	**800-213-9040**	
Harry's 17711 NE Riverside Pkwy	Portland	OR	97230	**800-307-7687**	503-257-7687
Honor Foods 1801 N Fifth St	Philadelphia	PA	19122	**800-462-2890**	215-236-1700
Imperial Trading Co Inc 701 Edwards Ave *Cust Svc	Elmwood	LA	70123	**800-775-4504***	504-733-1400
Jace Holdings Ltd 6649 Butler Crescent	Saanichton	BC	V8M1Z7	**800-667-8280**	250-544-1234
JM Swank LLC 395 Herky St	North Liberty	IA	52317	**800-593-6375**	319-626-3683
Johnson Bros Bakery Supply Inc 10731 I H 35 N	San Antonio	TX	78233	**800-590-2575**	
Jonathan Lord Corp 87 Carlough Rd	Bohemia	NY	11716	**800-814-7517**	631-517-1271
Jordano's Inc 550 S Patterson Ave	Santa Barbara	CA	93111	**800-325-2278**	805-964-0611
JTM Provisions Company Inc 200 Sales Dr	Harrison	OH	45030	**800-626-2308**	
Kings Super Markets Inc 700 Lanidex Plz	Parsippany	NJ	07054	**800-325-4647**	
La Petite Bretonne Inc 1210 Boul Mich Le-Bohec	Blainville	QC	J7C5S4	**800-361-3381**	450-435-3381
Larue Coffee 2631 S 156th Cir	Omaha	NE	68130	**800-658-4498**	402-333-9099
Laurel Grocery Co Inc 129 Barbourville Rd	London	KY	40744	**800-467-6601**	
Longos a fresh tradition 8800 Huntington Rd	Vaughan	ON	L4H3M6	**800-956-6467**	
Magnetic Springs Water Co 1917 Joyce Ave	Columbus	OH	43219	**800-572-2990**	614-421-1780
Maines Paper & Food Service Co 101 Broome Corporate Pkwy	Conklin	NY	13748	**800-366-3669**	607-779-1200
Marquez Bros International Inc 5801 Rue Ferrari	San Jose	CA	95138	**800-858-1119**	408-960-2700
McLane Company Inc 4747 McLane Pkwy	Temple	TX	76504	**800-299-1401**	254-771-7500
McLane Foodservice Inc 2085 Midway Rd	Carrollton	TX	75006	**800-299-1401**	972-364-2000
Merchants Co 1100 Edwards St PO Box 1351	Hattiesburg	MS	39401	**800-844-3663**	601-583-4351
Mineral Resources International 2720 Wadman Dr	Ogden	UT	84401	**800-731-7866**	801-731-7040
Monin Inc 2100 Range Rd	Clearwater	FL	33765	**855-352-8671**	
National Flavors Inc 3680 Stadium Park Way	Kalamazoo	MI	49009	**800-525-2431**	
Nuherbs co 14722 Wicks Blvd	San Leandro	CA	94577	**800-233-4307**	510-534-4372
Olean Wholesale Grocery Co-op Inc 1587 Haskell Rd PO Box 1070	Olean	NY	14760	**888-835-3026**	716-372-2020
Oppenheimer Cos Inc 877 W Main Ste 700	Boise	ID	83702	**800-727-9939**	208-343-4883
P J Noyes Company Inc 89 Bridge St	Lancaster	NH	03584	**800-522-2469**	
Paris Gourmet of New York Inc 145 Grand St	Carlstadt	NJ	07072	**800-727-8791**	
Peter's Choice Nutrition Center 4879 Fountain Ave	Los Angeles	CA	90029	**888-324-9904**	
Piggly Wiggly Carolina Company Inc 176 Croghan Spur Rd Ste 301	Charleston	SC	29407	**800-243-9880**	843-554-9880
Purity Wholesale Grocers Inc 5300 Broken Sound Blvd NW	Boca Raton	FL	33487	**800-323-6838**	561-994-9360
Rishi Tea LLC 185 S 33rd Ct	Milwaukee	WI	53208	**866-747-4483**	414-747-4001
Roman Meal Company Inc PO Box 2781	Fargo	ND	58108	**866-245-8921**	
Rutan Poly Industries Inc 39 Siding Pl	Mahwah	NJ	07430	**800-872-1474**	201-529-1474
S Abraham & Sons Inc (SAS) 4001 3 Mile Rd NW PO Box 1768 *General	Grand Rapids	MI	49534	**800-477-5455***	616-453-6358
Safeway Foods Inc MS 10501 PO Box 29093	Phoenix	AZ	85038	**877-723-3929**	
Shamrock Foods 3900 E Camelback Rd Ste 300	Phoenix	AZ	85018	**800-289-3663**	602-477-2500
Shanks Extracts Inc 350 Richardson Dr	Lancaster	PA	17603	**800-346-3135**	717-393-4441
Southco Distributing Co 2201 S John St	Goldsboro	NC	27530	**800-969-3172**	919-735-8012
Sukhi's Gourmet Indian Foods 25823 Clawiter Rd	Hayward	CA	94545	**888-478-5447**	
Super Store Industries 16888 McKinley Ave PO Box 549	Lathrop	CA	95330	**888-292-8004**	209-858-2010
SUPERVALU Inc 11840 Valley View Rd *NYSE: SVU* ■ *Cust Svc	Eden Prairie	MN	55344	**877-322-8228***	952-828-4000
SYGMA Network Inc 5550 Blazer Pkwy Ste 300	Dublin	OH	43017	**877-441-1144**	
Sysco Central Ohio Inc 2400 Harrison Rd	Columbus	OH	43204	**800-735-3341**	614-771-3801
Sysco Corp 5710 Pan Am Ave	Boise	ID	83716	**800-747-9726**	208-345-9500
Sysco Grand Rapids 3700 Sysco Ct SE	Grand Rapids	MI	49512	**800-669-6967**	616-949-3700
Thoms Proestler Co 8001 TPC Rd	Rock Island	IL	61204	**800-747-1234**	309-787-1234
Topco Assoc LLC 7711 Gross Pt Rd	Skokie	IL	60077	**888-423-0139**	847-745-2396
Unified Grocers Inc 5200 Sheila St	Commerce	CA	90040	**800-724-7762**	323-264-5200
Vistar Corp 12650 E Arapahoe Rd	Centennial	CO	80112	**800-880-9900**	303-662-7100
W L Halsey Grocery Company Inc PO Box 6485	Huntsville	AL	35824	**800-621-0240**	256-772-9691
Wakefern Food Corp 600 York St	Elizabeth	NJ	07207	**800-746-7748**	908-527-3300
Winkler Inc 535 E Medcalf St	Dale	IN	47523	**800-621-3843**	812-937-4421
Woeber Mustard Manufacturing Co 1966 Commerce Cir PO Box 388	Springfield	OH	45501	**800-548-2929**	
Wood-Fruitticher Grocery Company Inc 2900 Alton Rd	Birmingham	AL	35210	**800-328-0026**	205-836-9663
World Nutrition Inc 9449 N 90th St Ste 116	Scottsdale	AZ	85258	**800-548-2710**	

297-9 Meats & Meat Products - Whol

Company / Address	City	State	ZIP	Toll-Free	Phone
Bruss Co 3548 N Kostner Ave	Chicago	IL	60641	**800-621-3882**	
Calumet Diversified Meats Inc 10000 80th Ave	Pleasant Prairie	WI	53158	**800-752-7427**	262-947-7200
Cambridge Packing Company Inc 41-43 Foodmart Rd	Boston	MA	02118	**800-722-6726**	617-269-6700
Cardinal Meat Specialists Ltd 155 Hedgedale Rd	Brampton	ON	L6T5P3	**800-363-1439**	905-459-4436
ConAgra Foods Foodservice Co 5 ConAgra Dr	Omaha	NE	68102	**800-357-6543**	800-722-1344
Cusack Wholesale Meat Inc 301 SW 12th St	Oklahoma City	OK	73109	**800-241-6328**	405-232-2114
Day-Lee Foods Inc 13055 Molette St	Santa Fe Springs	CA	90670	**800-329-5331**	562-903-3020
Deen Meats PO Box 4155	Fort Worth	TX	76164	**800-333-3953**	817-335-2257
Heartland Meat Company Inc 3461 Main St	Chula Vista	CA	91911	**888-407-3668**	619-407-3668
Manda Fine Meats 2445 Sorrel Ave	Baton Rouge	LA	70802	**800-343-2642**	225-344-7636
Michael's Finer Meats & Seafoods 3775 Zane Trace Dr	Columbus	OH	43228	**800-282-0518**	614-527-4900
Midamar Corp PO Box 218	Cedar Rapids	IA	52406	**800-362-3711**	319-362-3711

				Toll-Free	Phone

Paper Pak Industries (PPI)
1941 N White Ave .... La Verne CA 91750 **888-293-6529** 909-392-1750
Quality Meats & Seafoods
700 Center St .... West Fargo ND 58078 **800-342-4250** 701-282-0202
Quirch Foods Co
7600 NW 82nd Pl .... Miami FL 33166 **800-458-5252** 305-691-3535
Sampco Inc
651 W Washington Blvd Ste 300 .... Chicago IL 60661 **800-767-0689** 312-346-1506
Southern Foods Inc
3500 Old Battleground Rd .... Greensboro NC 27410 **800-642-3768**
Thumann Inc 670 Dell Rd .... Carlstadt NJ 07072 **800-358-0761** 201-935-3636
Troyer Foods Inc
17141 State Rd 4 .... Goshen IN 46528 **800-876-9377** 574-533-0302
U W Provision Company Inc
PO Box 620038 .... Middleton WI 53562 **800-832-0517** 608-836-7421
Williams Sausage Company Inc
5132 Old Troy Hickman Rd .... Union City TN 38261 **800-844-4242** 731-885-5841

297-10 Poultry, Eggs, Poultry Products - Whol

				Toll-Free	Phone

Butts Foods Inc
2596 Bransford Ave .... Nashville TN 37204 **800-962-8570** 615-674-2030
Chino Valley Ranchers
331 W Citrus St .... Colton CA 92324 **800-354-4503** 626-652-0890
Dutt & Wagner of Virginia Inc
1142 W Main St .... Abingdon VA 24210 **800-688-2116** 276-628-2116
Metropolitan Poultry & Seafood Co
1920 Stanford Ct .... Landover MD 20785 **800-522-0060** 301-772-0060
Norbest Inc PO Box 890 .... Moroni UT 84646 **800-453-5327**
Nulaid Foods Inc
200 W Fifth St .... Ripon CA 95366 **800-788-8871** 209-599-2121
Quirch Foods Co
7600 NW 82nd Pl .... Miami FL 33166 **800-458-5252** 305-691-3535
RW Sauder Inc
570 Furnace Hills Pk .... Lititz PA 17543 **800-233-0413** 717-626-2074
Troyer Foods Inc
17141 State Rd 4 .... Goshen IN 46528 **800-876-9377** 574-533-0302
Zacky Farms
13200 Crossroads Pkwy N
Ste 250 .... City of Industry CA 91746 **800-888-0235** 562-641-2020

297-11 Specialty Foods - Whol

				Toll-Free	Phone

Charles C Parks Co
388 N Belvedere Dr .... Gallatin TN 37066 **800-873-2406** 615-452-2406
ConAgra Foods Foodservice Co
5 ConAgra Dr .... Omaha NE 68102 **800-357-6543** 800-722-1344
Conway Import Co Inc
11051 W Addison St .... Franklin Park IL 60131 **800-323-8801** 847-455-5600
CRS Onesource
2803 Tamarack Rd PO Box 1984 .... Owensboro KY 42302 **800-264-0710** 270-684-1469
Ellis Coffee Co
2835 Bridge St .... Philadelphia PA 19137 **800-822-3984**
Essex Food Ingredients
9 Lee Blvd .... Frazer PA 19355 **800-441-1017**
Hain Celestial Group Inc
4600 Sleepytime Dr .... Boulder CO 80301 **877-612-4246**
NASDAQ: HAIN
Industrial Commodities Inc
PO Box 4380 .... Glen Allen VA 23060 **800-523-7902**
Joffrey's Coffee & Tea Co
3803 Corporex Pk Dr .... Tampa FL 33619 **800-458-5282** 813-250-0404
John E Koerner & Company Inc
4820 Jefferson Hwy .... New Orleans LA 70121 **800-333-1913**
Love & Quiches Desserts
178 Hanse Ave .... Freeport NY 11520 **800-525-5251** 516-623-8800
Otto Brehm Inc PO Box 249 .... Yonkers NY 10710 **800-272-6886** 914-968-6100
Producers Rice Mill Inc
PO Box 1248 .... Stuttgart AR 72160 **800-369-7675** 870-673-4444
ReNew Life Formulas Inc
2076 Sunnydale Blvd .... Clearwater FL 33765 **800-830-1800**
Schreiber Foods International Inc
600 E Crescent Ave Ste 103 .... Upper Saddle River NJ 07458 **800-631-7070** 201-327-3535
Silver Springs Bottled Water Company Inc
PO Box 926 .... Silver Springs FL 34489 **800-556-0334**
Sturm Foods Inc PO Box 287 .... Manawa WI 54949 **800-347-8876** 920-596-2511
Sugar Foods Corp
950 Third Ave Ste 21 .... New York NY 10022 **800-732-8963** 212-753-6900
Sunsweet Growers Inc
901 N Walton Ave .... Yuba City CA 95993 **800-417-2253** 530-674-5010
United Sugars Corp
7803 Glenroy Rd Ste 300 .... Bloomington MN 55439 **800-984-3585** 952-896-0131

298 FOOD PRODUCTS MACHINERY

SEE ALSO Food Service Equipment & Supplies

				Toll-Free	Phone

Alto-Shaam Inc
W 164 N 9221 Water St
PO Box 450 .... Menomonee Falls WI 53052 **800-329-8744** 262-251-3800
American Permanent Ware Inc
729 Third Ave .... Dallas TX 75226 **800-527-2100** 214-421-7366
Anderson International Corp
4545 Boyce Pkwy .... Stow OH 44224 **800-336-4730** 216-641-1112
Atlas Metal Industries
1135 NW 159th Dr .... Miami FL 33169 **800-762-7565*** 305-625-2451
*Cust Svc
Atlas Pacific Engineering Co
1 Atlas Ave .... Pueblo CO 81001 **800-588-5438** 719-948-3040
Baader-Johnson
2955 Fairfax Trafficway .... Kansas City KS 66115 **800-288-3434** 913-621-3366

Belshaw Adamatic Bakery
814 44th St NW Ste 103 .... Auburn WA 98001 **800-578-2547** 206-322-5474
Belshaw Bros Inc
1750 22nd Ave S .... Seattle WA 98144 **800-578-2547** 206-322-5474
Bettcher Industries Inc
PO Box 336 .... Vermilion OH 44089 **800-321-8763** 440-965-4422
Brewmatic Co
20333 S Normandie Ave PO Box 2959 ... Torrance CA 90509 **800-421-6860** 310-787-5444
C Cretors & Co
3243 N California Ave .... Chicago IL 60618 **800-228-1885** 773-588-1690
Casa Herrerra Inc
2655 N Pine St .... Pomona CA 91767 **800-624-3916** 909-392-3930
Chester-Jensen Company Inc
PO Box 908 .... Chester PA 19016 **800-685-3750** 610-876-6276
Cleveland Range Co
1333 E 179th St .... Cleveland OH 44110 **800-338-2204** 216-481-4900
Colborne Foodbotics LLC
28495 N Ballard Dr .... Lake Forest IL 60045 **800-626-9501** 847-371-0101
CPM Wolverine Proctor LLC
251 Gibraltar Rd .... Horsham PA 19044 **800-428-0846** 215-443-5200
Delfield Co
980 S Isabella Rd .... Mount Pleasant MI 48858 **800-733-8821** 989-773-7981
Duke Manufacturing Co
2305 N Broadway .... Saint Louis MO 63102 **800-735-3853** 314-231-1130
Edlund Company Inc
159 Industrial Pkwy .... Burlington VT 05401 **800-772-2126** 802-862-9661
Feldmeier Equipment Inc
6800 Townline Rd .... Syracuse NY 13211 **800-258-0118** 315-454-8608
Fish Oven & Equipment Corp
120 W Kent Ave PO Box 875 .... Wauconda IL 60084 **877-526-8720** 847-526-8686
Food Warming Equipment Company Inc
1540 Carlemont Dr Ste A .... Crystal Lake IL 60014 **800-222-4393*** 815-459-7500
*Sales
Frymaster LLC
8700 Line Ave .... Shreveport LA 71106 **800-221-4583*** 318-865-1711
*Cust Svc
Garland Commercial Industries
185 S St .... Freeland PA 18224 **800-424-2411** 570-636-1000
Globe Food Equipment Co
2153 Dryden Rd .... Dayton OH 45439 **800-347-5423** 937-299-5493
Great Western Mfg Co Inc
2017 S Fourth St PO Box 149 .... Leavenworth KS 66048 **800-682-3121** 913-682-2291
Grindmaster-Cecilware Inc
4003 Collins Ln .... Louisville KY 40245 **800-695-4500** 502-425-4776
GS Blodgett Corp
44 Lakeside Ave .... Burlington VT 05401 **800-331-5842** 802-658-6600
Hayes & Stolz Industrial Manufacturing Co
3521 Hemphill St PO Box 11217 .... Fort Worth TX 76110 **800-725-7272** 817-926-3391
Heat & Control Inc
21121 Cabot Blvd .... Hayward CA 94545 **800-227-5980** 510-259-0500
Henny Penny Corp
1219 US 35 W PO Box 60 .... Eaton OH 45320 **800-417-8417** 937-456-8400
Hobart Corp 701 S Ridge Ave .... Troy OH 45374 **800-333-7447*** 937-332-3000
*Cust Svc
Insinger Machine Co
6245 State Rd .... Philadelphia PA 19135 **800-344-4802** 215-624-4800
Kwik Lok Corp PO Box 9548 .... Yakima WA 98909 **800-688-5945** 509-248-4770
Lawrence Equipment Inc
2034 Peck Rd .... El Monte CA 91733 **800-423-4500** 626-442-2894
LMC PO Box 428 .... Donalsonville GA 39845 **800-332-8232** 229-524-2197
Lucks Co, The 3003 S Pine St .... Tacoma WA 98409 **800-426-9778** 253-383-4815
Market Forge Industries Inc
35 Garvey St .... Everett MA 02149 **866-698-3188** 617-387-4100
Marlen International Inc
4780 NW 41st St Ste 100 .... Riverside MO 64150 **800-862-7536**
Merco-Savory Inc
1111 N Hadley Rd .... Fort Wayne IN 46804 **800-547-2513*** 260-459-8200
*Cust Svc
Microfluidics International Corp
90 Glacier Dr Ste 1000 .... Westwood MA 02090 **800-370-5452** 617-969-5452
Middleby Corp
1400 Toastmaster Dr .... Elgin IL 60120 **800-331-5842** 847-741-3300
NASDAQ: MIDD
Myers Engineering Inc
8376 Salt Lake Ave .... Bell CA 90201 **877-652-4767** 323-560-4723
Nitta Casings Inc
141 Southside Ave .... Bridgewater NJ 08807 **800-526-3970*** 908-218-4400
*Cust Svc
Oliver Products Co
445 Sixth St NW .... Grand Rapids MI 49504 **800-253-3893** 616-456-7711
Peerless Food Equipment
500 S Vandenmark Rd .... Sidney OH 45365 **877-795-7377** 937-492-4158
Piper Products Inc
300 S 84th Ave .... Wausau WI 54401 **800-544-3057** 715-842-2724
Prince Castle Inc
355 E Kehoe Blvd .... Carol Stream IL 60188 **800-722-7853** 630-462-8800
Resina West Inc
27455 Bostik Ct .... Temecula CA 92590 **800-207-4804** 951-296-6585
Ross Industries Inc
5321 Midland Rd .... Midland VA 22728 **800-336-6010** 540-439-3271
SaniServ Inc
451 E County Line Rd .... Mooresville IN 46158 **800-733-8073** 317-831-7030
Schlueter Co
320 N Main St .... Janesville WI 53545 **800-359-1700** 608-755-5444
Server Products Inc
3601 Pleasant Hill Rd PO Box 98 ..... Richfield WI 53076 **800-558-8722** 262-628-5100
Southbend Inc
1100 Old Honeycutt Rd .... Fuquay Varina NC 27526 **800-755-4777** 919-762-1000
Stoelting LLC 502 Hwy 67 .... Kiel WI 53042 **800-558-5807** 920-894-2293
Taylor 750 N Blackhawk Blvd .... Rockton IL 61072 **800-255-0626**
Town Food Service Equipment Co
72 Beadel St .... Brooklyn NY 11222 **800-221-5032** 718-388-5650
Ultrafryer Systems Inc
302 Spencer Ln .... San Antonio TX 78201 **800-545-9189**
Union Standard Equipment Co
801 E 141st St .... Bronx NY 10454 **877-282-7333** 718-585-0200
United Bakery Equipment Co Inc
15815 W 110th St .... Lenexa KS 66219 **888-823-2253** 913-541-8700

			Toll-Free	Phone

Univex Corp
3 Old Rockingham Rd . . . . Salem NH 03079 **800-258-6358** 603-893-6191

Van Doren Sales Inc
10 NE Cascade Ave . . . . East Wenatchee WA 98802 **866-886-1837** 509-886-1837

Vendome Copper & Brass Works Inc
729 Franklin St . . . . Louisville KY 40202 **888-384-5161** 502-587-1930

Viking Range Corp
111 Front St . . . . Greenwood MS 38930 **888-845-4641** 662-455-1200

Volckening 6700 Third Ave . . . . Brooklyn NY 11220 **800-221-0876** 718-836-4000

Wells Bloomfield Industries
10 Sunnen Dr . . . . Saint Louis MO 63143 **888-356-5362**

Wilbur Curtis Company Inc
6913 Acco St . . . . Montebello CA 90640 **800-421-6150** 323-837-2300

Winston Industries LLC
2345 Carton Dr . . . . Louisville KY 40299 **800-234-5286** 502-495-5400

299   FOOD SERVICE

SEE ALSO Restaurant Companies

			Toll-Free	Phone

Advance Food Company Inc
9987 Carver Rd Ste 500 . . . . Cincinnati OH 45242 **800-969-2747**

Bon Appetit Management Co
100 Hamilton Ave Ste 400 . . . . Palo Alto CA 94301 **800-765-9419** 650-798-8000

Canteen Service Co
712 Industrial Dr . . . . Owensboro KY 42301 **800-467-2471** 270-683-2471

Canteen Vending Services
Compass Group
2400 Yorkmont Rd . . . . Charlotte NC 28217 **800-357-0012** 704-328-4000

Cara Operations Ltd
199 Four Valley Dr . . . . Vaughan ON L4K0B8 **800-860-4082** 905-760-2244

Centerplate
2187 Atlantic St . . . . Stamford CT 06902 **800-698-6992** 203-975-5900

Compass Group North American Div (CGNAD)
2400 Yorkmont Rd . . . . Charlotte NC 28217 **800-357-0012** 704-328-4000

Foodbank of Southeastern Virginia & the Eastern Shore
800 Tidewater Dr . . . . Norfolk VA 23504 **877-486-4379** 757-627-6599

General Mills Inc
1 General Mills Blvd . . . . Minneapolis MN 55426 **800-248-7310**
NYSE: GIS

Guest Services Inc
3055 Prosperity Ave . . . . Fairfax VA 22031 **800-345-7534** 703-849-9300

Institutional Wholesale Co
535 Dry Valley Rd . . . . Cookeville TN 38506 **800-239-9588** 931-537-4000

Island Oasis Frozen Cocktail
141 Norfolk St . . . . Walpole MA 02081 **800-777-4752** 508-660-1176

Love & Quiches Desserts
178 Hanse Ave . . . . Freeport NY 11520 **800-525-5251** 516-623-8800

Signature Services Corp
2705 Hawes Ave . . . . Dallas TX 75235 **800-929-5519** 214-353-2661

Sodexho
9801 Washingtonian Blvd . . . . Gaithersburg MD 20878 **888-763-3967** 301-987-4000

Sportservice Corp
40 Fountain Plz . . . . Buffalo NY 14202 **800-828-7240** 716-858-5000

Summit Food Service Distributors Inc
580 Industrial Rd . . . . London ON N5V1V1 **800-265-9267** 519-453-3410

300   FOOD SERVICE EQUIPMENT & SUPPLIES

SEE ALSO Food Products Machinery

			Toll-Free	Phone

Adams-Burch Inc
1901 Stanford Ct . . . . Landover MD 20785 **800-347-8093*** 301-276-2000
*Cust Svc

Advance Tabco
200 Heartland Blvd . . . . Edgewood NY 11717 **800-645-3166** 631-242-8270

Atlanta Fixture & Sales Co
3185 NE Expy . . . . Atlanta GA 30341 **800-282-1977**

Bargreen Ellingson Inc
2925 70th Ave E . . . . Fife WA 98424 **866-722-2665** 253-722-2600

Boelter Cos Inc
N22W23685 Ridgeview Pkwy W . . . . West Waukesha WI 53188 **800-263-5837** 262-523-6200

Bolton & Hay Inc
2701 Delaware Ave . . . . Des Moines IA 50317 **800-362-1861** 515-265-2554

Browne & Co
505 Apple Creek Blvd Unit 2 . . . . Markham ON L3R5B1 **866-306-3672** 905-475-6104

Browne Foodservice
1122 US Rt 22 Ste 203 . . . . Mountainside NJ 07092 **888-289-1005** 973-232-1065

Cambro Manufacturing Co
5801 Skylab Rd . . . . Huntington Beach CA 92647 **800-833-3003** 714-848-1555

Carlisle FoodService Products Inc
4711 E Hefner Rd . . . . Oklahoma City OK 73131 **800-654-8210** 405-475-5600

Eagle Group Inc
100 Industrial Blvd . . . . Clayton DE 19938 **800-441-8440**

Edward Don & Co
9801 Adam Don Pkw . . . . Woodridge IL 60517 **800-777-4366***
*Cust Svc

Fit & Fresh Inc
295 Promenade St . . . . Providence RI 02908 **800-858-8840**

Genpak Carthage
505 E Cotton St . . . . Carthage TX 75633 **800-626-6695** 903-693-7151

Hotel & Restaurant Supply Inc
5020 Arundel Rd PO Box 6 . . . . Meridian MS 39302 **800-782-6651** 601-482-7127

Intedge Manufacturing
1875 Chumley Rd PO Box 969 . . . . Woodruff SC 29388 **866-969-9605** 864-969-9605

InterMetro Industries Corp
651 N Washington St . . . . Wilkes-Barre PA 18705 **800-992-1776*** 570-825-2741
*Cust Svc

Kittredge Equipment Co Inc
100 Bowles Rd . . . . Agawam MA 01001 **800-423-7082** 413-304-4100

Lakeside Manufacturing Inc
4900 W Electric Ave . . . . West Milwaukee WI 53219 **800-558-8565** 414-902-6400

Lancaster Commercial Products Inc
2353 Westbrooke Dr . . . . Columbus OH 43228 **844-324-1444** 614-263-2850

			Toll-Free	Phone

Maines Paper & Food Service Co
101 Broome Corporate Pkwy . . . . Conklin NY 13748 **800-366-3669** 607-779-1200

McLane Foodservice Inc
2085 Midway Rd . . . . Carrollton TX 75006 **800-299-1401** 972-364-2000

N Wasserstrom & Sons Inc
2300 Lockbourne Rd . . . . Columbus OH 43207 **800-444-4697** 614-228-5550

Natures Best 6 Pt Dr Ste 300 . . . . Brea CA 92821 **800-800-7799** 714-255-4600

PBI Market Equipment Inc
2667 Gundry Ave . . . . Signal Hill CA 90755 **800-421-3753** 562-595-4785

RAPIDS Wholesale Equipment Co
6201 S Gateway Dr . . . . Marion IA 52302 **800-472-7431** 319-447-1670

Regal Ware Inc
1675 Reigle Dr . . . . Kewaskum WI 53040 **800-800-2850** 262-626-2121

Restaurant & Stores Equipment Co
230 West 700 South . . . . Salt Lake City UT 84101 **800-877-0087** 801-364-1981

Restaurant Technologies Inc
2250 Pilot Knob Rd Ste 100 . . . . Mendota Heights MN 55120 **888-796-4997** 651-796-1600

Service Ideas Inc
2354 Ventura Dr . . . . Woodbury MN 55125 **800-328-4493** 651-730-8800

Smith & Greene Co
19015 66th Ave S . . . . Kent WA 98032 **800-232-8050**

Southern Foods Inc
3500 Old Battleground Rd . . . . Greensboro NC 27410 **800-642-3768**

TriMark USA Inc
505 Collins St . . . . South Attleboro MA 02703 **800-755-5580** 508-399-2400

Vollrath Co LLC, The
1236 N 18th St . . . . Sheboygan WI 53081 **800-624-2051** 920-457-4851

Wasserstrom Co
477 S Front St . . . . Columbus OH 43215 **866-634-8927** 614-228-6525

Western Pioneer Sales Co
6631 Calle Eva Miranda . . . . Glendale CA 91702 **800-640-4535** 818-244-1466

301   FOOTWEAR

			Toll-Free	Phone

Acor Orthopaedic Inc
18530 S Miles Pkwy . . . . Cleveland OH 44128 **800-237-2267** 216-662-4500

Acushnet holdings Corp
333 Bridge St . . . . Fairhaven MA 02719 **800-225-8500** 508-979-2000

Aerosoles Inc 201 Meadow Rd . . . . Edison NJ 08817 **800-798-9478** 732-985-6900

Aldo Shoes
2300 Emile Belanger . . . . Montreal QC H4R3J4 **888-818-2536** 514-747-2536

Allen-Edmonds Shoe Corp
201 E Seven Hills Rd . . . . Port Washington WI 53074 **800-235-2348*** 262-235-9261
*Cust Svc

Asics America Corp
29 Parker Ste 100 . . . . Irvine CA 92618 **800-333-8404** 949-453-8888

Badorf Shoe Co Inc
1958 Auction Rd . . . . Manheim PA 17545 **800-325-1545** 717-653-0155

Barbour Welting Company Div Barbour Corp
1001 N Montello St . . . . Brockton MA 02301 **800-955-9649** 508-583-8200

Brooks Sports Inc
19910 N Creek Pkwy Ste 200 . . . . Bothell WA 98011 **800-227-6657**

C & J Clark America Inc
156 Oak St . . . . Newton Upper Falls MA 02464 **800-211-5461***
*Cust Svc

Capezio 1 Campus Rd . . . . Totowa NJ 07512 **888-227-3946*** 973-595-9000
*Acctg

Chinese Laundry Shoes
3485 S La Cienega Blvd . . . . Los Angeles CA 90016 **888-935-8825** 310-838-2103

Cole-Haan
8701 Keystone Crossing . . . . Indianapolis IN 46240 **800-695-8945**

Consolidated Shoe Company Inc
22290 Timberlake Rd . . . . Lynchburg VA 24502 **800-368-7463** 434-239-0391

Cowtown Boots
11401 Gateway Blvd W . . . . El Paso TX 79936 **800-580-2698** 915-593-2929

Crocs Inc 6328 Monarch Pk Pl . . . . Niwot CO 80503 **866-306-3179** 303-848-7000
NASDAQ: CROX

Danner Shoe Manufacturing Co
17634 NE Airport . . . . Portland OR 97230 **800-345-0430*** 503-262-0103
*Cust Svc

Drew Shoe Corp
252 Quarry Rd . . . . Lancaster OH 43130 **800-837-3739** 740-653-4271

East Lion Corp
318 Brea Canyon Rd . . . . City of Industry CA 91789 **877-939-1818** 626-912-1818

Eastland Shoe Mfg Corp
4 Meeting House Rd . . . . Freeport ME 04032 **888-988-1998** 207-865-6314

ES Originals Inc
440 Ninth Ave 7th Fl . . . . New York NY 10001 **800-677-6577*** 212-736-8124
*General

Famous Footwear
247 Junction Rd . . . . Madison WI 53717 **800-888-7198*** 608-833-3340
*Cust Svc

Finish Line Inc, The
3308 N Mitthoeffer Rd . . . . Indianapolis IN 46235 **888-777-3949** 317-899-1022
NASDAQ: FINL

Florsheim Inc
333 W Estabrook Blvd . . . . Glendale WI 53212 **866-454-0449**

Foot Locker Inc
112 W 34th St . . . . New York NY 10120 **800-952-5210** 212-720-3700
NYSE: FL

Foot Solutions
4101 Roswell Rd . . . . Marietta GA 30062 **866-338-2597**

Footlockercom Inc
112 W 34th St . . . . New York NY 10120 **800-863-8932** 715-261-9719

Georgia Boot Inc
39 E Canal St . . . . Nelsonville OH 45764 **877-795-2410** 866-442-4908

Hush Puppies Co
9341 Courtland Dr NE . . . . Rockford MI 49351 **866-699-7365** 616-866-5500

IMPO PO Box 639 . . . . Santa Maria CA 93456 **800-367-4676**

Johnston & Murphy Inc
1415 Murfreesboro Rd . . . . Nashville TN 37217 **800-424-2854** 615-367-7168

Justin Boot Inc
610 W Daggett Ave . . . . Fort Worth TX 76104 **800-548-1021*** 817-332-4385
*Cust Svc

Kaepa USA Inc
9050 Autobahn Dr Ste 500 . . . . Dallas TX 75237 **800-880-9200**

				Toll-Free	Phone

Keds Corp
1400 Industries Rd ....Richmond IN 47374 **800-680-0966**

Kenneth Cole Productions Inc
603 W 50th St ....New York NY 10019 **800-536-2653**
NYSE: KCP

LaCrosse Footwear Inc
17634 NE Airport ....Portland OR 97230 **800-323-2668***
Cust Svc

Lake Catherine Footwear
3770 Malvern Rd PO Box 6048 ....Hot Springs AR 71901 **800-819-1901**

Lamey-Wellehan Inc
940 Turner St ....Auburn ME 04210 **800-370-6900** 207-784-6595

Lucchese Boot Co
20 ZANE GREY ....El Paso TX 79906 **800-637-6888** 888-582-1883

Merrell Footwear
9341 Courtland Dr NE ....Rockford MI 49351 **800-288-3124*** 616-866-5500
*Cust Svc

Mizuno USA
4925 Avalon Ridge Pkwy ....Norcross GA 30071 **800-966-1211** 770-441-5553

Munro & Co Inc
3770 Malvern Rd 71901 PO Box 6048 ....Hot Springs AR 71902 **800-819-1901** 501-262-6000

New Balance Athletic Shoe Inc
20 Guest St Brighton Landing..............Brighton MA 02135 **800-595-9138** 617-783-4000

Nike Inc 1 Bowerman Dr ....Beaverton OR 97005 **800-344-6453*** 503-671-6453
*NYSE: NKE ■ *Cust Svc*

Novus Inc
655 Calle Cubitas ....Guaynabo PR 00969 **888-530-4546** 787-272-4546

Nunn-Bush Shoe Co Inc
333 W Estabrook Blvd ....Glendale WI 53212 **866-484-3718**

Otomix Inc
747 Glasgow Ave ....Inglewood CA 90301 **800-701-7867** 310-215-6100

Payless ShoeSource Inc
3231 SE Sixth Ave ....Topeka KS 66607 **877-474-6379**

Phoenix Footwear Group Inc
5937 Darwin Ct Ste 109 ....Carlsbad CA 92008 **877-282-1168*** 760-602-9688
*OTC: PXFG ■ *Investor Rel*

Propet USA Inc
2415 W Valley Hwy N ....Auburn WA 98001 **800-877-6738** 253-854-7600

Puma 10 Lyberty Way ....Westford MA 01886 **888-565-7862*** 978-698-1000
*General

PW Minor & Son Inc
3 Tread Easy Ave ....Batavia NY 14020 **800-333-4067**

Red Wing Shoe Company Inc
314 Main St ....Red Wing MN 55066 **800-733-9464*** 844-314-6246
*Cust Svc

Reebok International Ltd
1895 JW Foster Blvd ....Canton MA 02021 **866-870-1743** 781-401-5000

Reyers 40 S Water Ave ....Sharon PA 16146 **800-245-1550*** 724-981-2200
*Cust Svc

Rockport Company Inc
1220 Washington St ....Newton MA 02465 **800-828-0545** 781-401-5000

Rocky Brands Inc
39 E Canal St ....Nelsonville OH 45764 **877-795-2410** 740-753-3130
NASDAQ: RCKY

SAS Shoemakers
1717 SAS Dr ....San Antonio TX 78224 **877-782-7463**

Saucony Inc 191 Spring St ....Lexington MA 02420 **800-282-6575**

Saxon Shoes
11800 W Broad St Ste 2750 ....Richmond VA 23233 **800-686-5616*** 804-285-3473
*General

Sebago USA LLC
9341 Courtland Dr ....Rockford MI 49351 **866-699-7367**

Shoe Carnival Inc
7500 E Columbia St ....Evansville IN 47715 **800-430-7463*** 812-867-6471
*NASDAQ: SCVL ■ *Cust Svc*

Shoe Sensation Inc
253 America Pl ....Jeffersonville IN 47130 **844-891-3070**

Shoe Show of Rocky Mountain Inc
2201 Trinity Church Rd ....Concord NC 28027 **888-557-4637*** 704-782-4143
*Cust Svc

Skechers USA Inc
228 Manhattan Beach Blvd ....Manhattan Beach CA 90266 **800-746-3411*** 310-318-3100
*NYSE: SKX ■ *Cust Svc*

Spalding PO Box 90015 ....Bowling Green KY 42103 **855-253-4533**

Stride Rite Corp
191 Spring St ....Lexington MA 02421 **800-299-6575*** 617-824-6000
*Cust Svc

Super Shoe Stores Inc
601 Dual Hwy ....Hagerstown MD 21740 **866-842-7510** 301-739-2130

Teva 123 N Leroux St ....Flagstaff AZ 86001 **800-367-8382*** 928-779-5938
*General

Timberland Co, The
200 Domain Dr ....Stratham NH 03885 **888-802-9947**
NYSE: VFC

Trimfoot Co LLC
115 Trimfoot Terr ....Farmington MO 63640 **800-325-6116**

Vans Inc
15700 Shoemaker Ave ....Santa Fe Springs CA 90670 **855-909-8267**

Weinbrenner Shoe Co Inc
108 S Polk St ....Merrill WI 54452 **800-569-6817*** 715-536-5521
*General

West Coast Shoe Co
52828 NW Shoe Factory Ln PO Box 607 ....Scappoose OR 97056 **800-326-2711** 503-543-7114

Weyco Group Inc
333 W Estabrook Blvd ....Glendale WI 53212 **866-454-0449** 414-908-1880
NASDAQ: WEYS

302   FORESTRY SERVICES

SEE ALSO Timber Tracts

				Toll-Free	Phone

Bioforest Technologies Inc
59 Industrial Park Crescent
Unit 1 ....Sault Sainte Marie ON P6B5P3 **888-236-7378** 705-942-5824

Continental Design & Engineering Inc
1524 Jackson St ....Anderson IN 46016 **800-875-4557** 765-778-9999

Resource Management Service LLC
31 Inverness Ctr Pkwy Ste 360..............Birmingham AL 35242 **800-995-9516**

Vestra Resources Inc
5300 Aviation Dr ....Redding CA 96002 **877-983-7872** 530-223-2585

303   FOUNDATIONS - COMMUNITY

SEE ALSO Charitable & Humanitarian Organizations

				Toll-Free	Phone

Arizona Community Foundation
2201 E Camelback Rd Ste 405B ....Phoenix AZ 85016 **800-222-8221** 602-381-1400

Cleveland Foundation
1422 Euclid Ave Ste 1300..................Cleveland OH 44115 **877-554-5054** 216-861-3810

Colorado Trust
1600 Sherman St ....Denver CO 80203 **888-847-9140** 303-837-1200

Community Foundation for Greater New Haven
70 Audubon St ....New Haven CT 06510 **877-829-5500** 203-777-2386

Dayton Foundation
40 N Main St Ste 500 ....Dayton OH 45423 **877-222-0410** 937-222-0410

Foundation for the Carolinas
217 S Tryon St ....Charlotte NC 28202 **800-973-7244** 704-973-4500

Gill Foundation Inc
1550 Wewatta St ....Denver CO 80202 **888-530-4455** 303-292-4455

Greater Cincinnati Foundation
200 W Fourth St ....Cincinnati OH 45202 **800-742-6253** 513-241-2880

Hawaii Community Foundation
65-1279 Kawaihae Rd ....Kamuela HI 96743 **888-731-3863** 808-537-6333

Minneapolis Foundation
80 S Eigth St 800 IDS Ctr ....Minneapolis MN 55402 **866-305-0543** 612-672-3878

Omaha Community Foundation (OCF)
302 S 36th St Ste 100.........................Omaha NE 68131 **800-794-3458** 402-342-3458

Pittsburgh Foundation, The
5 PPG Pl Ste 250 ....Pittsburgh PA 15222 **800-392-6900** 412-391-5122

Saint Paul Foundation, The
101 Fifth St E Ste 2400.....................Saint Paul MN 55101 **800-875-6167** 651-224-5463

304   FOUNDATIONS - CORPORATE

SEE ALSO Charitable & Humanitarian Organizations

				Toll-Free	Phone

Cargill Foundation
15407 McGinty Rd W Ste 46 ....Wayzata MN 55391 **800-227-4455** 877-765-8867

CIGNA Foundation
900 Cottage Grove Rd ....Bloomfield CT 06002 **866-438-2446**
NYSE: CI

Coca-Cola Foundation Inc
PO Box 1734 ....Atlanta GA 30301 **800-438-2653**

Dow Chemical Co
2030 Dow Ctr ....Midland MI 48674 **800-331-6451** 989-636-1000

General Mills Foundation
PO Box 9452 ....Minneapolis MN 55440 **800-248-7310**

General Motors Foundation Inc
PO Box 33170 ....Detroit MI 48232 **800-222-1020**

Hallmark Corp Foundation
2501 McGee St ....Kansas City MO 64108 **800-425-5627**

Infaith Community Foundation
625 Fourth Ave S Ste 1500.................Minneapolis MN 55415 **800-365-4172** 612-844-4110

MetLife Foundation
27-01 Queens Plz N ....Long Island NY 11101 **800-638-5433**

Principal Financial Services Inc
711 High St ....Des Moines IA 50392 **800-986-3343**

Revlon Foundation Inc
237 Park Ave ....New York NY 10017 **800-473-8566***
*Cust Svc

Whirlpool Foundation
2000 N M-63 ....Benton Harbor MI 49022 **800-952-9245** 269-923-5000

Xerox Foundation
45 Glover Ave ....Norwalk CT 06856 **800-275-9376**

305   FOUNDATIONS - PRIVATE

SEE ALSO Charitable & Humanitarian Organizations

				Toll-Free	Phone

Alfred P Sloan Foundation
630 Fifth Ave Ste 2550 ....New York NY 10111 **800-401-8004** 212-649-1649

Annie E Casey Foundation
701 St Paul St ....Baltimore MD 21202 **800-222-1099** 410-547-6600

Art Gallery of Ontario
317 Dundas St W ....Toronto ON M5T1G4 **877-225-4246** 416-979-6660

Bill & Melinda Gates Foundation
PO Box 23350 ....Seattle WA 98102 **800-728-3843** 206-709-3100

Careers The Next Generation Foundation
10470 176 St NW ....Edmonton AB T5S1L3 **888-757-7172** 780-426-3414

Colonial Williamsburg Foundation
PO Box 1776 ....Williamsburg VA 23187 **800-447-8679** 757-229-1000

Colorado School of Mines Foundation
1812 Illinois St ....Golden CO 80401 **800-446-9488** 303-273-3275

Corporation for Public Broadcasting (CPB)
401 Ninth St NW ....Washington DC 20004 **800-272-2190** 202-879-9600

Dave Thomas Foundation for Adoption
716 Mt Airyshire Blvd Ste 100 ....Columbus OH 43235 **800-275-3832**

Food & Water Watch
1616 P St NW Ste 300 ....Washington DC 20036 **855-340-8083** 202-683-2500

Free Methodist Foundation, The
8050 Spring Arbor Rd ....Spring Arbor MI 49283 **800-325-8975** 517-750-2727

Gates Family Foundation
1390 Lawrence St ....Denver CO 80204 **866-590-4377** 303-722-1881

Name / Address	City	ST	ZIP	Toll-Free	Phone
Georgia Northwestern Technical College Foundation Inc 1 Maurice Culberson Dr SW	Rome	GA	30161	**866-983-4682**	706-295-6842
Gleaner's Food Bank of Indianapolis 3737 Waldemere Ave	Indianapolis	IN	46241	**800-944-9166**	317-925-0191
Granite State Independent Living Foundation 21 Chenell Dr	Concord	NH	03301	**800-826-3700**	603-228-9680
Hearst Foundation, The 300 W 57th St 26th Fl.	New York	NY	10019	**800-841-7048**	212-649-3750
Idaho Community Foundation Inc 210 W State St	Boise	ID	83702	**800-657-5357**	208-342-3535
IU School of Medicine - Office of Gift Development 1110 W Michigan St Lo 506	Indianapolis	IN	46202	**800-643-6975**	317-274-3270
John Simon Guggenheim Memorial Foundation 90 Park Ave	New York	NY	10016	**800-232-0960**	212-687-4470
Kansas Health Foundation 309 E Douglas	Wichita	KS	67202	**800-373-7681**	316-262-7676
Kate B Reynolds Charitable Trust 128 Reynolda Vlg	Winston-Salem	NC	27106	**800-485-9080**	336-397-5500
Kidango Inc 44000 Old Warm Springs Blvd	Fremont	CA	94538	**800-262-4252**	408-258-3710
Kiwanis International Foundation 3636 Woodview Trace	Indianapolis	IN	46268	**800-549-2647**	317-875-8755
Liberty Fund Inc 8335 Allison Pt Trial Ste 300	Indianapolis	IN	46250	**800-955-8335**	317-842-0880
Lumina Foundation for Education 30 S Meridian St Ste 700	Indianapolis	IN	46204	**800-834-5756**	317-951-5300
Meadows Foundation Inc 3003 Swiss Ave	Dallas	TX	75204	**800-826-9431**	214-826-9431
Michael J Fox Foundation for Parkinson's Research Grand Central Stn PO Box 4777	New York	NY	10163	**800-708-7644**	
Mitchell Institute, The 75 Washington Ave Ste 2E	Portland	ME	04101	**888-220-7209**	207-773-7700
Moody Foundation 2302 Post Office St Ste 704	Galveston	TX	77550	**866-742-1133**	409-797-1500
National Foundation for Cancer Research (NFCR) 4600 E W Hwy Ste 525	Bethesda	MD	20814	**800-321-2873**	
National PTA 1250 N Pitt St	Alexandria	VA	22314	**800-307-4782**	703-518-1200
Nellie Mae Education Foundation 1250 Hancock St Ste 205N	Quincy	MA	02169	**877-635-5436**	781-348-4200
O & P Edge, The 11154 Huron St Ste 104	Northglenn	CO	80234	**866-613-0257**	303-255-0843
Ottawa Regional Cancer Foundation The 1500 Alta Vista Dr	Ottawa	ON	K1G3Y9	**855-247-3527**	613-247-3527
Patient Advocate Foundation Inc 700 Thimble Shoals Blvd Ste 200	Newport News	VA	23606	**800-532-5274**	
Phi Kappa Phi Foundation 7576 Goodwood Blvd	Baton Rouge	LA	70806	**800-804-9880**	225-388-4917
Public Interest Network 1543 Wazee St Ste 400	Denver	CO	80202	**800-401-6511**	303-573-5995
Public Welfare Foundation 1200 U St NW	Washington	DC	20009	**800-275-7934**	202-965-1800
Robert Wood Johnson Foundation PO Box 2316	Princeton	NJ	08543	**877-843-7953**	
SalesforceCom Foundation The Landmark @ One Market Ste 300	San Francisco	CA	94105	**800-667-6389**	
Seva Foundation 1786 Fifth St	Berkeley	CA	94710	**877-764-7382**	510-845-7382
Step Up For Students PO Box 54429	Jacksonville	FL	32245	**877-735-7837**	
Student Agencies Foundation Inc 409 College Ave	Ithaca	NY	14850	**800-631-8405**	607-272-2000
Student Veterans of America PO Box 77673	Washington	DC	20013	**866-320-3826**	202-223-4710
Surdna Foundation 330 Madison Ave 25th Fl	New York	NY	10016	**800-421-9512**	212-557-0010
Texas Methodist Foundation 11709 Boulder Ln Ste 100	Austin	TX	78726	**800-933-5502**	512-331-9971
Tides Canada Foundation 400-163 W Hastings St	Vancouver	BC	V6B1H5	**866-843-3722**	604-647-6611
Universitas Foundation of Canada 1035 Wilfrid-Pelletier Ave Ste 500	Quebec	QC	G1W0C5	**877-710-7377**	418-651-8975
Utility Notification Center of Colorado 16361 Table Mtn Pkwy	Golden	CO	80403	**800-922-1987**	303-232-1991
Way to Happiness Foundation International, The 201 E Broadway	Glendale	CA	91205	**800-255-7906**	818-254-0600

306 FOUNDRIES - INVESTMENT

Name / Address	City	ST	ZIP	Toll-Free	Phone
Waltek Inc 14310 Sunfish Lake Blvd	Ramsey	MN	55303	**800-937-9496**	763-427-3181

307 FOUNDRIES - IRON & STEEL

SEE ALSO Foundries - Nonferrous (Castings)

Name / Address	City	ST	ZIP	Toll-Free	Phone
Allegheny Technologies Inc 1000 Six PPG Pl *NYSE: ATI ■ *Sales*	Pittsburgh	PA	15222	**800-258-3586***	412-394-2800
Alloy Engineering & Casting Co 1700 W Washington St	Champaign	IL	61821	**800-348-2880**	217-398-3200
American Cast Iron Pipe Co (ACIPCO) 1501 31st Ave N	Birmingham	AL	35207	**800-442-2347**	205-325-7701
Bremen Castings Inc 500 N Baltimore Ave	Bremen	IN	46506	**800-837-2411**	
Castalloy Inc 1701 Industrial Ln PO Box 827	Waukesha	WI	53189	**800-211-0900**	262-547-0070
Columbia Steel Casting Co Inc 10425 N Bloss Ave	Portland	OR	97203	**800-547-9471**	503-286-0685
Complex Steel & Wire Corp 36254 Annapolis St	Wayne	MI	48184	**800-521-0666**	734-326-1600
Delta Centrifugal Corp PO Box 1043 *Sales*	Temple	TX	76503	**888-433-3100***	254-773-9055
EJ Group Inc 301 Spring St	East Jordan	MI	49727	**800-874-4100**	231-536-2261
Farrar Corp 142 W Burns St	Norwich	KS	67118	**800-536-2215**	620-478-2212
Frog Switch & Mfg Co 600 E High St	Carlisle	PA	17013	**800-233-7194**	717-243-2454
Harrison Steel Castings Co Inc 900 S Mound St	Attica	IN	47918	**800-659-4722**	765-762-2481
Hensley Industries Inc 2108 Joe Field Rd	Dallas	TX	75229	**888-406-6262**	972-241-2321
Hitachi Metals America Ltd 2 Manhattanville Rd Ste 301	Purchase	NY	10577	**800-777-5757**	914-694-9200
Howco Metals Management 9611 Telge Rd	Houston	TX	77095	**800-392-7720**	281-649-8800
McWane Inc 2900 Hwy 280 Ste 300	Birmingham	AL	35223	**800-634-4746**	205-414-3100
Neenah Foundry Co 2121 Brooks Ave	Neenah	WI	54956	**800-558-5075**	920-725-7000
Sentinel Bldg Systems Inc 237 S Fourth St PO Box 348	Albion	NE	68620	**800-327-0790**	402-395-5076
Sioux City Foundry Co 801 Div St	Sioux City	IA	51102	**800-831-0874**	712-252-4181
Standard Alloys & Mfg PO Box 969	Port Arthur	TX	77640	**800-231-8240**	409-983-3201
Steel Service Corp 2260 Flowood Dr PO Box 321425	Jackson	MS	39232	**800-844-9222**	601-939-9222
Talladega Castings & Machine Co Inc 228 N Ct St	Talladega	AL	35160	**800-766-6708**	256-362-5550
Talladega Machinery & Supply Co Inc 301 N Johnson Ave PO Box 736 *Cust Svc*	Talladega	AL	35161	**800-289-8672***	256-362-4124
Tyler Pipe Co 11910 CR 492	Tyler	TX	75706	**800-527-8478**	903-882-5511
US Pipe & Foundry Co 2 Chase Corporate Dr Ste 200	Birmingham	AL	35244	**866-347-7473**	
Waukesha Foundry Company Inc 1300 Lincoln Ave	Waukesha	WI	53186	**800-727-0741**	262-542-0741
Waupaca Foundry Inc 1955 Brunner Dr PO Box 249	Waupaca	WI	54901	**800-869-6820**	715-258-6611

308 FOUNDRIES - NONFERROUS (CASTINGS)

SEE ALSO Foundries - Iron & Steel

Name / Address	City	ST	ZIP	Toll-Free	Phone
Bunting Bearings Corp 1001 Holland Pk Blvd	Holland	OH	43528	**888-286-8464**	419-866-7000
Consolidated Metco Inc 5701 SE Columbia Way *Sales*	Vancouver	WA	98661	**800-547-9473***	
Deco Products Co 506 Sanford St	Decorah	IA	52101	**800-327-9751**	563-382-4264
Electric Materials Co 50 S Washington St	North East	PA	16428	**800-356-2211**	814-725-9621
Halex Co 23901 Aurora Rd	Bedford Heights	OH	44146	**800-749-3261**	
Lee Brass Co 1800 Golden Springs Rd *General*	Anniston	AL	36207	**800-876-1811***	
Littlestown Foundry Inc 150 Charles St PO Box 69	Littlestown	PA	17340	**800-471-0844**	717-359-4141
Madison-Kipp Corp 201 Waubesa St	Madison	WI	53704	**800-356-6148**	
Magnolia Metal Corp 10675 Bedford Ave Ste 200	Omaha	NE	68134	**800-228-4043**	402-455-8760
NGK Metals Corp 917 Hwy 11 S	Sweetwater	TN	37874	**800-523-8268**	423-337-5500
Piad Precision Casting Corp 112 Industrial Pk Rd	Greensburg	PA	15601	**800-441-9858**	724-838-5500
Premier Die Casting Co 1177 Rahway Ave	Avenel	NJ	07001	**800-394-3006**	732-634-3000
Stahl Specialty Co 111 E Pacific	Kingsville	MO	64061	**800-821-7852**	816-597-3322
Talladega Castings & Machine Co Inc 228 N Ct St	Talladega	AL	35160	**800-766-6708**	256-362-5550
Techni-Cast Corp 11220 Garfield Ave	South Gate	CA	90280	**800-923-4585**	562-923-4585
United Titanium Inc 3450 Old Airport Rd	Wooster	OH	44691	**800-321-4938**	330-264-2111
Ward Aluminum Casting Co 642 Growth Ave	Fort Wayne	IN	46808	**800-648-9918**	260-426-8700

309 FRAMES & MOULDINGS

Name / Address	City	ST	ZIP	Toll-Free	Phone
Alexandria Moulding 20352 Powerdam Rd	Alexandria	ON	K0C1A0	**866-377-2539**	613-525-2784
Groovfold Inc 1050 W State St	Newcomerstown	OH	43832	**800-367-1133**	740-498-8363
Larson-Juhl 3900 Steve Reynolds Blvd	Norcross	GA	30093	**800-221-4123**	770-279-5200
Quanex Building Products 2270 Woodale Dr	Mounds View	MN	55112	**800-233-4383**	763-231-4000
Royal Mouldings Ltd 135 Bearcreek Rd PO Box 610	Marion	VA	24354	**800-368-3117**	276-783-8161
Woodgrain Distribution 80 Shelby St	Montevallo	AL	35115	**800-756-0199**	205-665-2546

FRAMES & MOULDINGS - METAL

SEE Doors & Windows - Metal

Classified Section

				Toll-Free	Phone

310   FRANCHISES

SEE ALSO Remodeling, Refinishing, Resurfacing Contractors; Printing Companies - Commercial Printers; Candles; Travel Agency Networks; Convenience Stores; Ice Cream & Dairy Stores; Bakeries; Health Food Stores; Auto Supply Stores; Restaurant Companies; Optical Goods Stores; Real Estate Agents & Brokers; Hotels & Hotel Companies; Laundry & Drycleaning Services; Beauty Salons; Weight Loss Centers & Services; Pest Control Services; Cleaning Services; Staffing Services; Business Service Centers; Home Inspection Services; Car Rental Agencies; Children's Learning Centers; Automotive Services
Please see the category on Hotel & Resort Operation & Management for listings of hotel franchises.

Company	City	ST	ZIP	Toll-Free	Phone
1-800-Got-Junk 887 Great Northern Way	Vancouver	BC	V5T4T5	800-468-5865	
1-800-Water Damage 1167 Mercer St	Seattle	WA	98109	800-928-3732	206-381-3041
ABC Seamless 3001 Fiechtner Dr	Fargo	ND	58103	800-732-6577	701-293-5952
ActionCOACH 5781 S Ft Apache Rd	Las Vegas	NV	89148	888-483-2828	702-795-3188
Aire-Master of America Inc 1821 N State Hwy CC	Nixa	MO	65714	800-525-0957	417-725-2691
AmeriSpec Inc 3839 Forest Hill Irene Rd	Memphis	TN	38125	877-769-5217	
Archadeck 2924 Emerywood Pkwy Ste 101	Richmond	VA	23294	888-687-3325	804-353-6999
Baskin-Robbins Inc 130 Royall St	Canton	MA	02021	800-859-5339	781-737-3000
Beef O'Bradys Inc 5660 W Cypress St Ste A	Tampa	FL	33607	800-728-8878	813-226-2333
Benjamin Franklin Plumbing 12 Greenway Plz Ste 250	Houston	TX	77046	800-471-0809	713-877-3500
Big Apple Bagels 500 Lake Cook Rd Ste 475	Deerfield	IL	60015	800-251-6101	847-948-7520
Bojangles' Restaurants Inc 9432 Southern Pine Blvd	Charlotte	NC	28273	800-366-9921	704-335-1804
Boston Pizza Restaurants LP 14850 Quorum Dr Ste 201	Dallas	TX	75234	866-277-8721	972-484-9022
BrickKicker 849 N Ellsworth St	Naperville	IL	60563	800-821-1820	
Candy Bouquet International Inc 510 Mclean St	Little Rock	AR	72202	877-226-3901	501-375-9990
Captain D's LLC 624 Grassmere Park Dr Ste 30	Nashville	TN	37211	800-314-4819	615-391-5461
CardSmart Retail Corp 11 Executive Ave	Edison	NJ	08817	888-782-7050	800-654-6960
Carlson Wagonlit Travel Inc 701 Carlson Pkwy	Minnetonka	MN	55305	800-213-7295	
Carvel Express 200 Glenridge Pt Pkwy Ste 200	Atlanta	GA	30342	800-322-4848	
CertaPro Painters Ltd 150 Green Tree Rd Ste 1003	Oaks	PA	19456	800-689-7271	
Certified Restoration DryCleaning Network LLC 2060 Coolidge Hwy	Berkley	MI	48072	800-963-2736	
Charleys Philly Steaks 2500 Farmers Dr Ste 140	Columbus	OH	43235	800-437-8325	614-923-4700
Checkers Drive-In Restaurants Inc 4300 W Cypress St Ste 600	Tampa	FL	33607	800-800-8072	813-283-7000
Cleaning Authority 7230 Lee DeForest Dr	Columbia	MD	21046	888-658-0659	443-602-9154
Closet Factory 12800 S Broadway	Los Angeles	CA	90061	800-838-7995	310-516-7000
Coffee Beanery Ltd, The 3429 Pierson Pl	Flushing	MI	48433	800-441-2255	810-733-1020
Cold Stone Creamery Inc 9311 E Via De Ventura *Cust Svc	Scottsdale	AZ	85258	866-452-4252*	480-362-4800
ComForcare Senior Services Inc 2520 Telegraph Rd Ste 100	Bloomfield Hills	MI	48302	800-886-4044	248-745-9700
Computer Explorers 12715 Telge Rd	Cypress	TX	77429	800-531-5053	
Computer Troubleshooters USA 7100 E Pleasant Valley Rd Ste 300	Independence	OH	44131	877-704-1702	216-674-0645
Cookies By Design Inc 1865 Summit Ave Ste 605	Plano	TX	75074	800-945-2665	972-398-9536
Coverall Cleaning Concepts 5201 Congress Ave Ste 275	Boca Raton	FL	33487	800-537-3371	866-296-8944
Craters & Freighters 331 Corporate Cir Ste J	Golden	CO	80401	800-736-3335	
Creative Colors International Inc 19015 S Jodi Rd Ste E	Mokena	IL	60448	800-933-2656	708-478-1437
Crestcom International Ltd 6900 E Belleview Ave	Greenwood Village	CO	80111	800-333-7680	303-267-8200
CruiseOne Inc 1201 W Cypress Creek Rd Ste 100	Fort Lauderdale	FL	33309	800-278-4731	
D'Angelo Sandwich Shops 600 Providence Hwy	Dedham	MA	02026	800-727-2446	
Dairy Queen 7505 Metro Blvd	Minneapolis	MN	55439	800-883-4279	952-830-0200
DirectBuy Inc 8450 Broadway	Merrillville	IN	46410	800-320-3462	219-736-1100
Domino's Pizza Inc 30 Frank Lloyd Wright Dr NYSE: DPZ	Ann Arbor	MI	48106	800-253-8182	734-930-3030
Dr Vinyl & Assoc Ltd 1350 SE Hamblen Rd *General	Lees Summit	MO	64081	800-531-6600*	816-525-6060
DreamMaker Bath & Kitchen by Worldwide 510 N Valley Mills Dr Ste 304	Waco	TX	76710	800-583-2133	
Dunkin' Donuts 130 Royall St *Cust Svc	Canton	MA	02021	800-859-5339*	781-737-3000
Duraclean International Inc 220 Campus Dr	Arlington Heights	IL	60004	800-251-7070	
Edible Arrangements LLC 95 Barnes Rd *Cust Svc	Wallingford	CT	06492	877-363-7848*	304-894-8901
EmbroidMe Inc 2121 Vista Pkwy	West Palm Beach	FL	33411	877-877-0234	561-640-7367
Express Employment Professionals 9701 Boardwalk Blvd	Oklahoma City	OK	73162	800-222-4057	405-840-5000
Express Oil Change & Tire Engineers 1880 S Pk Dr	Hoover	AL	35244	888-945-1771	205-940-2226
Famous Dave's of America Inc 12701 Whitewater Dr Ste 200 NASDAQ: DAVE	Minnetonka	MN	55343	800-929-4040	952-294-1300
Fast-Fix Jewelry & Watch Repairs 451 Altamonte Ave	Altamonte Springs	FL	32701	800-359-0407	407-261-1595
FasTracKids International Ltd 6900 E Belleview Ave Ste 100	Greenwood Village	CO	80111	888-576-6888	303-224-0200
Figaro's Italian Pizza Inc 1500 Liberty St SE Ste 160	Salem	OR	97302	888-344-2767	503-371-9318
Fish Window Cleaning Services Inc 200 Enchanted Pkwy	Manchester	MO	63021	877-707-3474	636-779-1500
Floor Coverings International 5250 Triangle Pwy Ste 100 *Sales	Norcross	GA	30092	800-955-4324*	770-874-7600
Foot Solutions 4101 Roswell Rd	Marietta	GA	30062	866-338-2597	
Furniture Medic 3839 S Forest Hill Irene Rd	Memphis	TN	38125	888-611-7320	901-597-8727
GNC Inc 300 Sixth Ave NYSE: GNC	Pittsburgh	PA	15222	877-462-4700	412-228-4600
Goddard Systems Inc 1016 West Ninth Ave	King of Prussia	PA	19406	800-463-3273	877-256-7046
Grease Monkey International 5575 DTC Pkwy Ste 100	Greenwood Village	CO	80111	800-822-7706	303-308-1660
Great American Cookie Company Inc 3300 Chambers Rd	Horseheads	NY	14845	877-639-2361	
Great Clips Inc 4400 W 78th St Ste 700	Minneapolis	MN	55435	800-999-5959	952-893-9088
Great Harvest Bread Co 28 S Montana St	Dillon	MT	59725	800-442-0424	406-683-6842
Great Steak & Potato Co 9311 E Via de Ventura	Scottsdale	AZ	85258	866-452-4252	480-362-4800
Griswold Home Care 717 Bethlehem Pk Ste 300	Erdenheim	PA	19038	800-474-7965	
Growth Coach, The 10700 Montgomery Rd	Montgomery	OH	45242	855-300-2622	
Gymboree Corp 500 Howard St NASDAQ: GYMB	San Francisco	CA	94105	877-449-6932	
Hayes Handpiece Franchises Inc 5375 Avenida Encinas Ste C	Carlsbad	CA	92008	800-228-0521	
Homes & Land Magazine Affiliates LLC 1830 E Park Ave	Tallahassee	FL	32301	800-277-7800	850-701-2300
HomeTeam Inspection Service Inc 575 Chamber Dr	Milford	OH	45150	800-598-5297	
HomeVestors of America Inc 6500 Greenville Ave Ste 400	Dallas	TX	75206	866-200-6475	972-761-0046
HouseMaster 92 E Main St Ste 301	Somerville	NJ	08876	800-526-3939	732-469-6565
Ident-A-Kid Services of America 1780 102nd Ave N Ste 100	Saint Petersburg	FL	33716	800-890-1000	727-577-4646
IHOP Corp 450 N Brand Blvd	Glendale	CA	91203	866-444-5144	818-240-6055
Instant Imprints 6615 Flanders Dr Ste B	San Diego	CA	92121	800-542-3437	858-642-4848
Interim HealthCare Inc 1601 Sawgrass Corporate Pkwy	Sunrise	FL	33323	800-338-7786	954-858-6000
Jackson Hewitt Inc 3 Sylvan Way Ste 301 OTC: JHTXQ	Parsippany	NJ	07054	800-234-1040	973-630-1040
Jazzercise Inc 2460 Impala Dr *Cust Svc	Carlsbad	CA	92010	800-348-4748*	760-476-1750
Kinderdance International Inc 5238 Valleypointe Pkwy	Roanoke	VA	24019	800-554-2334	540-904-2595
Kitchen Tune-Up 813 Cir Dr	Aberdeen	SD	57401	800-333-6385	605-225-4049
Lawn Doctor Inc 142 SR 34	Holmdel	NJ	07733	800-845-0580	
Learning Express Inc 29 Buena Vista St	Devens	MA	01434	888-725-8697	978-889-1000
Liberty Tax Service Inc 1716 Corporate Landing Pkwy *Cust Svc	Virginia Beach	VA	23454	800-790-3863*	757-493-8855
Little Caesars Inc 2211 Woodward Ave	Detroit	MI	48201	800-722-3727	313-983-6000
Little Gym International Inc 7500 N Dobson Rd Ste 220 *General	Paradise Valley	AZ	85256	888-228-2878*	
Living Assistance Services Inc 937 Haverford Rd Ste 200	Bryn Mawr	PA	19010	800-365-4189	
Mad Science Group 8360 Bougainville St Ste 201	Montreal	QC	H4P2G1	800-586-5231	514-344-4181
Maid Brigade USA/Minimaid Canada 4 Concourse Pkwy Ste 200	Atlanta	GA	30328	866-800-7470	800-722-6243
Mathnasium LLC 5120 W Goldleaf Cir Ste 300	Los Angeles	CA	90056	877-601-6284	323-421-8000
McDonald's Corp 1 McDonald's Plz NYSE: MCD	Oak Brook	IL	60523	800-244-6227	630-623-3000
Merle Norman Cosmetics Inc 9130 Bellanca Ave	Los Angeles	CA	90045	800-421-6648	310-641-3000
Merlin 3815 E Main St Ste D	Saint Charles	IL	60174	800-652-9900	630-513-8200
Midas International Corp 823 Donald Ross Rd	Juno Beach	FL	33408	800-621-8545	630-438-3000
Minuteman Press International Inc 61 Executive Blvd	Farmingdale	NY	11735	800-645-3006	631-249-1370

	Toll-Free	Phone
Money Mailer LLC		
12131 Western Ave .... Garden Grove CA 92841	**800-468-5865**	714-889-3800
Mr Appliance Corp		
304 E Church Ave .... Killeen TX 76541	**888-998-2011**	
Mr Handyman International LLC		
3948 Ranchero Dr .... Ann Arbor MI 48108	**855-632-2126***	
*Cust Svc		
Mr Hero Restaurants		
7010 Engle Rd Ste 100 .... Middleburg Heights OH 44130	**888-860-5082**	440-625-3080
National Property Inspections Inc (NPI)		
9375 Burt St Ste 201 .... Omaha NE 68114	**800-333-9807**	402-333-9807
Navis Pack & Ship Centers		
12742 E Caley Ave Ste 2 A .... Centennial CO 80111	**800-344-3528**	
OpenWorks		
4742 N 24th St Ste 450 .... Phoenix AZ 85016	**800-777-6736**	602-224-0440
Orange Julius of America		
7505 Metro Blvd .... Minneapolis MN 55439	**866-793-7582**	952-830-0200
Padgett Business Services		
160 Hawthorne Pk .... Athens GA 30606	**800-723-4388**	
Pak Mail Centers of America Inc		
8601 W Cross Dr Ste F5 .... Littleton CO 80123	**800-778-6665***	303-971-0088
*Cust Svc		
Papa John's International Inc		
2002 Papa John's Blvd .... Louisville KY 40299	**877-547-7272**	502-261-7272
NASDAQ: PZZA		
Papa Murphy's International Inc		
8000 NE Pkwy Dr Ste 350. .... Vancouver WA 98662	**877-777-5062**	
Party City Corp		
25 Green Pond Rd Ste 1 .... Rockaway NJ 07866	**800-727-8924**	973-453-8600
Perma-Glaze Inc		
1638 Research Loop Rd Ste 160. .... Tucson AZ 85710	**800-332-7397**	
Petland Inc		
250 Riverside St .... Chillicothe OH 45601	**800-221-5935**	740-775-2464
Physicians Weight Loss Centers of America Inc		
395 Springside Dr .... Akron OH 44333	**800-205-7887**	
Pizza Inn Inc		
3551 Plano Pkwy .... The Colony TX 75056	**877-574-9924**	
NASDAQ: RAVE		
Pizza Ranch Inc		
204 19th St SE .... Orange City IA 51041	**800-321-3401**	
Postal Connections of America		
6136 Frisco Sq Blvd Ste 400 .... Frisco TX 75034	**800-767-8257**	
PostalAnnex+ Inc		
7580 Metropolitan Dr Ste 200 .... San Diego CA 92108	**800-456-1525**	619-563-4800
PostNet International Franchise Corp		
1819 Wazee St .... Denver CO 80202	**800-841-7171**	303-771-7100
Precision Auto Care Inc		
748 Miller Dr SE .... Leesburg VA 20175	**866-944-8863**	
OTC: PACI		
Pressed4Time Inc 50 Mendon St .... Upton MA 01568	**800-423-8711**	508-879-5966
Primrose School Franchising Co		
3660 Cedarcrest Rd .... Acworth GA 30101	**800-745-0677**	770-529-4100
Priority Management Systems Inc		
1595 Cliveden Ave Unit 7. .... Delta BC V3M6M2	**800-437-1032**	604-214-7772
ProForma		
8800 E Pleasant Valley Rd .... Independence OH 44131	**800-825-1525**	216-520-8400
Property Damage Appraisers Inc (PDA)		
6100 SW Blvd Ste 200 .... Fort Worth TX 76109	**800-749-7324**	
Rainbow International		
1010 N University Park Dr .... Waco TX 76707	**855-724-6269**	254-756-5463
Re-Bath LLC		
16879 N 75th Ave Ste 101 .... Peoria AZ 85382	**800-426-4573**	
RE/MAX International Inc		
5075 S Syracuse St .... Denver CO 80237	**800-525-7452***	303-770-5531
*Cust Svc		
Real Living Real Estate LLC		
77 E Nationwide Blvd .... Columbus OH 43215	**800-274-7653**	949-794-7900
Realty Executives International Inc		
645 E Missouri Ave Ste 210 .... Phoenix AZ 85020	**800-252-3366**	480-239-2038
Rescuecom Corp		
2560 Burnet Ave .... Syracuse NY 13206	**800-737-2837**	
Right at Home Inc		
6464 Center St Ste 150. .... Omaha NE 68106	**877-697-7537**	402-697-7537
RSVP Publications		
6730 W Linebaugh Ave Ste 201 .... Tampa FL 33625	**800-360-7787**	813-960-7787
Sea Tow Services International Inc		
1560 Youngs Ave PO Box 1178 .... Southold NY 11971	**800-473-2869**	877-568-1672
Second Cup Ltd		
6303 Airport Rd .... Mississauga ON L4V1R8	**877-212-1818**	
Signs by Tomorrow USA Inc		
8681 Robert Fulton Dr .... Columbia MD 21046	**800-765-7446**	410-312-3600
Sir Speedy Inc		
26722 Plaza Dr .... Mission Viejo CA 92691	**800-854-8297**	949-348-5000
Snap-on Inc 2801 80th St .... Kenosha WI 53143	**877-762-7664**	262-656-5200
NYSE: SNA		
Spring-Green Lawn Care Corp		
11909 Spaulding School Dr .... Plainfield IL 60585	**800-435-4051**	815-436-8777
Stork News of America Inc		
1305 Hope Mills Rd Ste A .... Fayetteville NC 28304	**800-633-6395**	910-426-1357
Stretch-N-Grow PO Box 7599 .... Seminole FL 33775	**800-348-0166**	
Successories Inc		
1040 Holland Dr .... Boca Raton FL 33487	**800-535-2773**	
Supercuts		
7201 Metro Blvd .... Minneapolis MN 55439	**877-857-2070**	
SuperShuttle International Inc		
14500 N Northsight Blvd Ste 329. .... Scottsdale AZ 85260	**800-258-3826**	480-609-3000
Terminix International Company LP		
860 Ridge Lake Blvd .... Memphis TN 38120	**877-837-6464**	
Truly Nolen of America Inc		
3636 E Speedway Blvd .... Tucson AZ 85716	**800-468-7859**	855-534-9139
Tuffy Assoc Corp		
7150 Granite Cir .... Toledo OH 43617	**800-228-8339**	419-865-6900
United Financial Services Group Inc		
325 Chestnut St Ste 3000. .... Philadelphia PA 19106	**800-626-0787**	215-238-0300
UPS Store, The		
6060 Cornerstone Ct W .... San Diego CA 92121	**800-789-4623**	858-455-8800
WIN Home Inspection		
3326 Aspen Grove Dr .... Franklin TN 37067	**800-309-6753**	

	Toll-Free	Phone
Wingstop Restaurants Inc		
908 Audelia Rd Ste 600 .... Richardson TX 75081	**877-411-9464**	
Wireless Zone LLC		
795 Brook St .... Rocky Hill CT 06067	**888-881-2622**	800-411-2355
Woodcraft Supply LLC		
1177 Rosemar Rd .... Parkersburg WV 26105	**800-535-4482**	
Worldwide Express		
2323 Victory Ave Ste 1600 .... Dallas TX 75219	**800-758-7447**	
WSI		
20 Carlson Ct Ste 100 .... Mississauga ON M9W7K6	**888-678-7588**	905-678-7588
Ziebart International Corp		
1290 E Maple Rd .... Troy MI 48083	**800-877-1312**	248-588-4100

311   FREIGHT FORWARDERS

SEE ALSO Logistics Services (Transportation & Warehousing)

	Toll-Free	Phone
Advance Transportation Systems Inc		
10558 Taconic Ter .... Cincinnati OH 45215	**800-878-4849**	513-771-4848
Airways Freight Corp		
3849 W Wedington Dr .... Fayetteville AR 72704	**800-643-3525**	479-442-6301
Allen Lund Company Inc		
4529 Angeles Crest Hwy .... La Canada CA 91011	**800-811-0083**	800-777-6142
Arrow Freight Management Inc		
1001 Berryville st .... El Paso TX 79928	**888-598-9891**	
Autobahn Freight Lines Ltd		
27 Automatic Rd .... Brampton ON L6S5N8	**877-989-9994**	416-741-5454
Axsun Group		
4900 Armand Frappier .... Saint-Hubert QC J3Z1G5	**888-992-9786**	450-445-3003
Blue-Grace Logistics LLC		
2846 S Falkenburg Rd .... Riverview FL 33578	**800-697-4477**	
CDS Logistics Management Inc		
1225 Bengies Rd Ste A .... Baltimore MD 21220	**866-649-9559**	410-314-8000
Coldiron Companies Inc		
200 N Sooner Rd .... Edmond OK 73034	**800-293-4369**	405-562-2910
ColdStar Solutions Inc		
1015 Henry Eng Pl .... Victoria BC V9B6B2	**800-201-1277**	250-381-3399
Combined Express Inc		
3685 Marshall Ln .... Bensalem PA 19020	**800-777-0458**	
ContainerWorld Forwarding Services Inc		
16133 Blundell Rd .... Richmond BC V6W0A3	**877-030-0080**	604-276-1300
Continental Traffic Service Inc (CTSI)		
5100 Poplar Ave 15th Fl .... Memphis TN 38137	**888-836-5135**	901-766-1500
DHL Global Forwarding		
6200 Edwards Blvd .... Mississauga ON L5T2V7	**855-345-7447**	289-562-6500
Evans Delivery Company Inc		
PO Box 268 .... Pottsville PA 17901	**800-666-7885**	570-385-9048
FESCO Agencies NA Inc		
1000 Second Ave Ste 1310. .... Seattle WA 98104	**800-275-3372**	206-583-0860
Fetch Logistics Inc		
25 Northpointe Pkwy Ste 200 .... Amherst NY 14228	**800-964-4940**	716-689-4556
Fleetgistics Holdings Inc		
2251 Lynx Ln Ste 7. .... Orlando FL 32804	**800-280-9097**	407-843-6505
Freight Logistics Inc		
PO Box 1712 .... Medford OR 97501	**800-866-7882**	541-734-5617
Frontier Logistics LP		
1806 S 16th St .... La Porte TX 77571	**800-610-6808**	
Gateway Logistics Group Inc, The		
18201 Viscount Rd .... Houston TX 77032	**800-338-8017**	281-443-7447
GTO 2000 Inc		
PO Box 2819 .... Gainesville GA 30503	**800-966-0801**	770-287-9233
HA Logistics Inc		
5175 Johnson Dr .... Pleasanton CA 94588	**800-449-5778**	925-251-9300
Hubtrucker Inc		
315 Freeport St Ste B .... Houston TX 77015	**866-913-6553**	713-547-5482
J & A Freight Systems Inc		
4704 Irving Park Rd Ste 8. .... Chicago IL 60641	**877-668-3378**	773-205-7720
Johanson Transportation Service Inc		
5583 E Olive Ave .... Fresno CA 93727	**800-742-2053**	559-458-2200
K&L Freight Management Inc		
745 S Rohlwing Rd .... Addison IL 60101	**800-770-9007**	630-607-1500
Knichel Logistics Inc		
5347 William Flynn Hwy 2nd Fl .... Gibsonia PA 15044	**888-386-7450**	724-449-3300
L H. P. Transportation Services Inc		
2032 E Kearney Ste 213 .... Springfield MO 65803	**800-642-1035**	417-865-7577
Logistics Plus Inc		
1406 Peach St .... Erie PA 16501	**866-564-7587**	814-461-7600
Longhorn Imports Inc		
2202 E Union Bower .... Irving TX 75061	**800-641-8348**	972-721-9102
Lynden Inc		
18000 International Blvd Ste 800 .... Seattle WA 98188	**888-596-3361**	206-241-8778
Maritime Company For Navigation, The		
249 Shipyard Blvd .... Wilmington NC 28412	**800-626-4777**	910-343-8900
Metro Express Transportation Services Inc		
875 Fee Fee Rd .... St. Louis MO 63043	**800-805-0073**	314-993-1511
NVC Logistics Group Inc		
1 Pond Rd .... Rockleigh NJ 07647	**800-526-0207**	
Oceanex		
630 boul Rene-Levesque W Ste 2550. .... Montreal QC H3B1S6	**888-875-9595**	514-875-9595
OIA Global Logistics Inc		
2100 SW River Pkwy .... Portland OR 97201	**800-938-3109**	503-736-5900
Ontario Northland Transportation Commission		
555 Oak St E .... North Bay ON P1B8L3	**800-363-7512**	705-472-4500
Phoenix International Freight Services Ltd		
1996-2018 CH Robinson Worldwide .... Eden Prairie MN 55347	**855-229-6128**	855-350-0014
Pioneer Transfer LLC		
2034 S St Aubin St PO Box 2567 .... Sioux City IA 51106	**800-325-4650**	712-274-2946
Priefert Manufacturing		
2630 S Jefferson Ave		
PO box 1540. .... Mount Pleasant TX 75455	**800-527-8616**	903-572-1741
Primary Freight Services Inc		
6545 Caballero Blvd .... Buena Park CA 90620	**800-635-0013**	310-635-3000
Quality Customs Broker Inc		
4464 S Whitnall Ave .... Saint Francis WI 53235	**888-813-4647**	414-482-9447
Quality Transportation		
36-40 37th St Ste 201 .... Long Island NY 11101	**800-677-2838**	212-308-6333

				Toll-Free	Phone
R & D Transportation Services Inc					
4036 Adolfo Rd	Camarillo	CA	93012	**800-966-7114**	805-529-7511
Recon Logistics LLC					
384 Inverness Pkwy Ste 270	Englewood	CO	80112	**866-424-7153**	
Rmx Global Logistics					
141 Union Blvd Ste 450	Evergreen	CO	80439	**888-824-7365**	
Rock-It Cargo USA Inc					
5343 W Imperial Hwy Ste 900	Los Angeles	CA	90045	**800-973-1727**	310-410-0935
Romar Transportation Systems Inc					
3500 S Kedzie Ave	Chicago	IL	60632	**800-621-5416**	773-376-8800
Satellite Logistics Group Inc					
12621 Featherwood Ste 390	Houston	TX	77034	**877-795-7540**	281-902-5500
Schenker Inc					
150 Albany Ave	Freeport	NY	11520	**800-843-1687**	516-377-3000
Schenker of Canada Ltd					
5935 Airport Rd 10th Fl	Mississauga	ON	L4V1W5	**800-461-3686**	905-676-0676
Scott Logistics Corp					
PO Box 391	Rome	GA	30162	**800-893-6689**	706-234-1184
Senvoy LLC					
18055 NE San Rafael St	Portland	OR	97230	**866-373-6869**	503-234-7722
Sho-Air International					
5401 Argosy Ave	Huntington Beach	CA	92649	**800-227-9111**	949-476-9111
Smith Systems Transportation Inc (SST)					
PO Box 2455	Scottsbluff	NE	69361	**800-897-5571**	
Sotech Nitram Inc					
1695 Boul Laval	Laval	QC	H7S2M2	**877-664-8726**	450-975-2100
Sunset Transportation Inc					
11325 Concord Village Ave	St Louis	MO	63123	**800-849-6540**	
Superior Freight Services Inc					
1230 Trapp Rd	Saint Paul	MN	55121	**800-298-4305**	952-854-5053
Tech Transport Inc					
PO Box 431	Milford	NH	03055	**800-641-5300**	
Terminal Corp, The					
1657 A S Highland Ave	Baltimore	MD	21224	**800-560-7207**	
Time Definite Services Inc					
1360 Madeline Ln Ste 300	Elgin	IL	60124	**800-466-8040**	
Total Quality Logistics Inc (TQL)					
4289 Ivy Pointe Blvd	Cincinnati	OH	45245	**800-580-3101**	513-831-2600
Trademark Transportation Inc					
739 Vandalia St	Saint Paul	MN	55114	**800-646-2550**	651-646-2500
Trans-Border Global Freight Systems Inc					
2103 Rt 9	Round Lake	NY	12151	**800-493-9444**	518-785-6000
Transaver LLC					
108 Washington St	Manlius	NY	13104	**800-698-8629**	315-399-1200
TransCore Link Logistics Corp					
6660 Kennedy Rd Ste 205	Mississauga	ON	L5T2M9	**800-263-6149**	
TransGuardian Inc					
St Vincent Jewelry Ctr 650 S Hill St Ste 519	Los Angeles	CA	90014	**877-570-7447**	213-622-5877
TRANSInternational System Inc					
130 E Wilson Bridge Rd Ste 150	Worthington	OH	43085	**800-340-7540**	614-891-4942
Transit Systems Inc					
999 Old Eagle School Rd Ste 114	Wayne	PA	19087	**800-626-1257**	
Transportation Management Assoc Inc					
344 Oak Grove Church Rd	Mocksville	NC	27028	**800-745-8292**	
TransPro Freight Systems Ltd					
8600 Escarpment Way	Milton	ON	L9T0M1	**800-268-6857**	905-693-0699
TransX Group of Cos					
2595 Inkster Blvd	Winnipeg	MB	R3C2E6	**877-558-9444**	204-632-6694
Travelers Transportation Services Inc					
195 Heart Lake Rd S	Brampton	ON	L6W3N6	**800-265-8789**	905-457-8789
Triple B Forwarders Inc					
1511 Glen Curtis St	Carson	CA	90746	**800-228-8465**	310-604-5840
Tucker Company Worldwide Inc					
900 Dudley Ave	Cherry Hill	NJ	08002	**800-229-7780**	856-317-9600
UTXL Inc					
10771 NW Ambassador Dr	Kansas City	MO	64153	**800-351-2821**	816-891-7770
Valley Express Llc					
6003 State Rd 76	Oshkosh	WI	54904	**800-594-4744**	920-231-1677

312   FREIGHT TRANSPORT - DEEP SEA (DOMESTIC PORTS)

				Toll-Free	Phone
Alaska Marine Lines Inc					
5615 W Marginal Way SW	Seattle	WA	98106	**800-326-8346***	206-763-4244
*Cust Svc					
Coastal Transportation Inc					
4025 13th Ave W	Seattle	WA	98119	**800-544-2580**	206-282-9979
Crowley Maritime Corp					
9487 Regency Square Blvd	Jacksonville	FL	32225	**800-276-9539**	904-727-2200
Freightquote					
901 W Carondelet Dr	Kansas City	MO	64114	**800-323-5441**	
Hapag-Lloyd America Inc					
401 E Jackson St	Tampa	FL	33602	**800-282-8977**	813-276-4600
Matson Navigation Co					
555 12th St	Oakland	CA	94607	**800-462-8766***	510-628-4000
*Cust Svc					
Northland Services Inc					
6700 W Marginal Way SW	Seattle	WA	98106	**800-426-3113**	206-763-3000
Overseas Shipholding Group Inc					
302 Knights Run Ave Ste 1200	Tampa	FL	33602	**800-851-9677**	813-209-0600
Seaboard Marine					
8001 NW 79th Ave	Miami	FL	33166	**866-676-8886**	305-863-4444
Totem Ocean Trailer Express Inc					
32001 32nd Ave S Ste 200	Federal Way	WA	98001	**800-426-0074**	253-449-8100
Trailer Bridge Inc					
10405 New Berlin Rd E	Jacksonville	FL	32226	**800-554-1589**	904-751-7100
OTC: TRBRQ					
US Shipping Corp					
399 Thornall St 8th Fl	Edison	NJ	08837	**866-942-6592**	732-635-1500
Western Pioneer Inc					
4601 Shilshole Ave NW	Seattle	WA	98107	**800-426-6783**	206-789-1930

313   FREIGHT TRANSPORT - DEEP SEA (FOREIGN PORTS)

				Toll-Free	Phone
Antillean Marine Shipping Corp					
3038 NW N River Dr	Miami	FL	33142	**888-633-6361**	305-633-6361
Artemus Group					
317 Office Square Ln Ste 202B	Virginia Beach	VA	23462	**866-744-7101**	
Fednav Ltd					
1000 Rue de la GauchetiFre O Bureau 3500	Montreal	QC	H3B4W5	**800-678-4842***	514-878-6500
*General					
Groupe Desgagnes Inc					
21 March-Champlain St	Quebec	QC	G1K8Z8	**800-463-0680**	418-692-1000
Hamburg Sud North America Inc					
465 S St	Morristown	NJ	07960	**888-228-8241**	973-775-5300
Hapag-Lloyd America Inc					
401 E Jackson St	Tampa	FL	33602	**800-282-8977**	813-276-4600
Interlog USA Inc					
9380 Central Ave NE Ste 350	Minneapolis	MN	55434	**800-603-6030**	
K Line America Inc					
4860 Cox Rd Ste 300	Glen Allen	VA	23060	**800-609-3221**	804-560-3600
Mckeil Marine Ltd					
208 Hillyard St	Hamilton	ON	L8L6B6	**800-454-4780**	905-528-4780
Overseas Shipholding Group Inc					
302 Knights Run Ave Ste 1200	Tampa	FL	33602	**800-851-9677**	813-209-0600
Seaboard Marine					
8001 NW 79th Ave	Miami	FL	33166	**866-676-8886**	305-863-4444
Tidewater Inc					
6002 Rogerdale Rd Ste 600	Houston	TX	77072	**800-678-8433**	713-470-5300
NYSE: TDW					

314   FREIGHT TRANSPORT - INLAND WATERWAYS

				Toll-Free	Phone
A & B Freight Line Inc					
4805 Sandy Hollow Rd	Rockford	IL	61109	**800-231-2235**	815-874-4700
American Commercial Barge Lines Inc					
1701 E Market St	Jeffersonville	IN	47130	**800-457-6377**	
AMJ Campbell International					
1445 Courtneypark Dr E	Mississauga	ON	L5T2E3	**800-363-6683**	905-670-6683
Andrie Inc					
561 E Western Ave	Muskegon	MI	49442	**800-722-2421**	231-728-2226
BBE 100 McMillan St	Yellowknife	NT	X1A3T2	**866-746-4223**	867-766-8666
Best Way Logistics					
14004 Century Ln	Grandview	MO	64030	**877-923-7892**	816-767-8008
Big Apple Car Inc					
169 Bay 17th St	Brooklyn	NY	11214	**800-251-5001**	718-630-0040
Calyx Transportation Group Inc					
National Fast Freight					
107 Alfred Kuehne Blvd	Brampton	ON	L6T4K3	**800-563-2223**	905-494-4808
Crowley Maritime Corp					
9487 Regency Square Blvd	Jacksonville	FL	32225	**800-276-9539**	904-727-2200
Custom Global Logistics LLC					
317 West Lake St	Northlake	IL	60164	**800-446-8336**	
Falcon Express Transportation Inc					
12200 Indian Creek Ct	Beltsville	MD	20705	**800-296-9696**	240-264-1215
Fednav Ltd					
1000 Rue de la GauchetiFre O Bureau 3500	Montreal	QC	H3B4W5	**800-678-4842***	514-878-6500
*General					
Focus Logistics Inc					
1311 Howard Dr	West Chicago	IL	60185	**877-924-3600**	630-231-8200
Frontline Logistics Inc					
10315 Grand River Ste 300	Brighton	MI	48116	**800-245-6632**	734-449-9474
Hackbarth Delivery Service Inc					
3504 Brookdale Dr N	Mobile	AL	36618	**800-277-3322**	251-478-1401
J S Logistics					
4550 Gustine Ave	Saint Louis	MO	63116	**800-814-2634**	314-832-6008
Keltic Transportation Inc					
90 MacNaughton Ave Caledonia Industrial Pk	Moncton	NB	E1H3L9	**888-854-1233**	506-854-1233
Kreative Carriers Transportation & Logistic Services					
61 Bluewater Rd	Bedford	NS	B4B1G8	**888-274-2444**	
Logistic Dynamics Inc					
155 Pineview Dr	Amherst	NY	14228	**800-554-3734**	716-250-3477
LTI Trucking Services Inc					
411 N Tenth St Ste 500	St. Louis	MO	63101	**800-642-7222**	
Lynnco Supply Chain Solutions Inc					
2448 E 81st St Ste 2600	Tulsa	OK	74137	**866-872-3264**	918-664-5540
Mackie Group 933 Bloor St W	Oshawa	ON	L1J5Y7	**800-565-4646**	905-728-2400
Marquette Transportation Company LLC					
150 Ballard Cir	Paducah	KY	42001	**800-456-9404**	270-443-9404
Milgram & Company Ltd					
400 - 645 Wellington	Montreal	QC	H3C0L1	**800-879-6144**	514-288-2161
OATS Inc					
2501 Maguire Blvd Ste 101	Columbia	MO	65201	**800-831-9219**	573-443-4516
RBS Bulk Systems Inc					
9910 -48 St SE	Calgary	AB	T2C2R2	**800-882-5930**	403-248-1530
Rowland Transportation Inc					
40824 Messick Rd	Dade City	FL	33525	**800-338-1146**	352-567-2002
Roy Miller Freight Lines LLC					
3165 E Coronado St	Anaheim	CA	92806	**800-336-5673**	714-632-5511
SCI 180 Attwell Dr Ste 600	Toronto	ON	M9W6A9	**866-773-7735**	416-401-3011
Stone Belt Freight Lines Inc					
101 W Dillman Rd	Bloomington	IN	47403	**800-264-2340**	812-824-6741
Tidewater Barge Lines Inc					
6305 NW Old Lower River Rd	Vancouver	WA	98660	**800-562-1607**	360-693-1491
Van-Kam Freightways Ltd					
10155 Grace Rd	Surrey	BC	V3V3V7	**800-663-2161**	604-582-7451
Vedder Transportation Group					
400 Riverside Rd	Abbotsford	BC	V2S4P4	**866-857-1375**	
VersaCold Logistics Services					
3371 No 6 Rd	Richmond	BC	V6V1P6	**877-207-1950**	604-258-0350

315   FRUIT GROWERS

SEE ALSO Crop Preparation Services ; Wines - Mfr

315-1 Berry Growers

			Toll-Free	Phone
Driscoll Strawberry Assoc Inc				
PO Box 50045	Watsonville CA	95077	800-871-3333	
Jasper Wyman & Son				
PO Box 100	Milbridge ME	04658	800-341-1758*	
*Sales				

315-2 Citrus Growers

			Toll-Free	Phone
ECA Edinburg Citrus Association				
PO Box 428	Edinburg TX	78540	877-381-1322	956-383-2743
Egan Bernard & Co				
1900 Old Dixie Hwy	Fort Pierce FL	34946	800-327-6676	

315-3 Deciduous Tree Fruit Growers

			Toll-Free	Phone
Blue Bird Inc				
10135 Mill Rd	Peshastin WA	98847	800-828-4106	509-548-1700
Capital Agricultural Property Services Inc				
801 Warrenville Rd Ste 150	Lisle IL	60532	800-243-2060	630-434-9150
Hudson River Fruit Distributors				
65 Old Indian Rd	Milton NY	12547	800-640-2774	
National Fruit Product Co Inc				
701 Fairmont Ave	Winchester VA	22601	800-655-4022	540-662-3401
Oregon Cherry Growers Inc				
1520 Woodrow NE	Salem OR	97301	800-367-2536	503-364-8421
Rice Fruit Co				
2760 Carlisle Rd	Gardners PA	17324	800-627-3359	717-677-8131

315-4 Fruit Growers (Misc)

			Toll-Free	Phone
Brooks Tropicals Inc				
18400 SW 256th St	Homestead FL	33090	800-327-4833	305-247-3544
Calavo Growers Inc				
1141-A Cummings Rd	Santa Paula CA	93060	800-654-8758	805-525-1245
NASDAQ: CVGW				
Del Monte Fresh				
PO Box 149222	Coral Gables FL	33114	800-950-3683*	305-520-8400
*Cust Svc				
Dole Food Company Inc				
1 Dole Dr	Westlake Village CA	91362	800-232-8888	818-879-6600
NYSE: DOLE				

315-5 Grape Vineyards

			Toll-Free	Phone
Spring Mountain Vineyards				
2805 Spring Mtn Rd	Saint Helena CA	94574	877-769-4637	707-967-4188
Windsor Vineyards				
205 Concourse Blvd	Santa Rosa CA	95403	800-289-9463	

316   FUEL DEALERS

			Toll-Free	Phone
AC & T Company Inc				
11535 Hopewell Rd	Hagerstown MD	21740	800-458-3835	301-582-2700
Alvin Hollis & Co				
1 Hollis St	South Weymouth MA	02190	800-649-5090	781-335-2100
AmeriGas Partners LP				
460 N Gulph Rd	King of Prussia PA	19406	800-427-4968	610-337-7000
NYSE: APU				
Apollo Oil LLC				
1175 Early Dr	Winchester KY	40391	800-473-5823	
Arguindegui Oil Companies				
4506 State 359 and Loop 20	Laredo TX	78042	800-722-5251	956-286-8330
Baytec Service LLC				
4761 Hwy 146 200	Bacliff TX	77518	800-560-2334	
Blossman Gas Inc				
4601 Hanshaw Rd	Ocean Springs MS	39564	800-256-7762	228-872-8747
Bowden Oil Company Inc				
PO Box 145	Sylacauga AL	35150	800-280-0393	256-245-5611
Buckley Energy Group Ltd				
154 Admiral St	Bridgeport CT	06605	800-937-2682	
Burns & McBride Inc				
18 Boulden Cir Ste 30	New Castle DE	19720	800-756-5110	302-656-5110
Co-op Gas Inc PO Box 27	Pauline SC	29374	888-578-5752	864-583-6546
Columbia Utilities Heating Corp				
8751 18th Ave	Brooklyn NY	11214	877-726-5862	
Cota & Cota Inc				
56 Bridge St	Bellows Falls VT	05101	888-268-2645	
D F Richard Inc 124 Broadway	Dover NH	03821	800-649-6457	603-742-2020
Davis Oil Co 904 Jernigan St	Perry GA	31069	888-448-5657	
DDLC Energy 410 Bank St	New London CT	06320	888-225-5540	
Delta Western Inc				
420 L St Ste 101	Anchorage AK	99501	800-478-2688	907-276-2688
Ed Staub & Sons Petroleum Inc				
1301 Esplanade Ave	Klamath Falls OR	97601	800-435-3835	
Energy Petroleum Co				
2130 Kienlen Ave	St. Louis MO	63121	800-536-6828	314-383-3700

			Toll-Free	Phone
FC Haab Company Inc				
2314 Market St	Philadelphia PA	19103	800-486-5663	215-563-0800
Ferrellgas Partners LP				
1 Liberty Plz	Liberty MO	64068	888-337-7355	816-792-1600
NYSE: FGP				
Fred M Schildwachter & Sons Inc				
1400 Ferris Pl	Bronx NY	10461	800-642-3646	718-828-2500
Gateway Energy Services Corp				
400 Rella Blvd Ste 300	Montebello NY	10901	800-805-8586	
Glassmere Fuel Service Inc				
1967 Saxonburg Blvd	Tarentum PA	15084	800-235-9054	
Kolkhorst Petroleum Co				
1685 E Washington	Navasota TX	77868	800-548-6671	936-825-6868
Kosco 2926 Rt 32 N	Saugerties NY	12477	800-755-6726	845-247-2200
Lansing Ice & Fuel Co				
911 Ctr St	Lansing MI	48906	800-678-7230	517-372-3850
Lazzari Fuel Company LLC				
11 Industrial Way	Brisbane CA	94005	800-242-7265	415-467-2970
Lincoln Land Oil Co				
PO Box 4307	Springfield IL	62708	800-238-4912	217-523-5050
Martin Resource Management Corp (MRMC)				
PO Box 191	Kilgore TX	75663	888-334-7473	903-983-6200
Metro Energy Group				
1011 Hudson Ave	Ridgefield NJ	07657	800-951-2941	201-941-3470
Mirabito Fuel Group Inc				
49 Ct St PO Box 5306	Binghamton NY	13902	800-934-9480	607-352-2800
Mitchell Supreme Fuel Co				
532 Freeman St	Orange NJ	07050	800-832-7090	973-678-1800
Parman Energy Corp				
7101 Cockrill Bend Blvd	Nashville TN	37209	800-727-7920	615-350-7920
Petroleum Heat & Power Co Inc				
9 W Broad St 3rd Fl	Stamford CT	06902	800-645-4328	
Phelps Sungas Inc				
224 Cross Rd	Geneva NY	14456	800-458-1085	315-789-3285
Quick Fuel Fleet Services Inc				
11815 W Bradley Rd	Milwaukee WI	53224	800-522-6287	
Reinhardt Corp				
3919 State Hwy 23	West Oneonta NY	13861	800-421-2867	607-432-6633
Ricochet Fuel Distributors Inc				
1201 Royal Pkwy	Euless TX	76040	800-284-2540	
Riggins Inc 3938 S Main Rd	Vineland NJ	08360	800-642-9148	856-825-7600
River Bend Business Products				
304 Downtown Plz	Fairmont MN	56031	800-783-3877	507-235-3800
Sharp Energy Inc				
648 Ocean Hwy	Pocomoke City MD	21851	888-742-7740	
Shipley Energy 415 Norway St	York PA	17403	800-839-1849	717-848-4100
Star Group LP				
2187 Atlantic St	Stamford CT	06902	800-960-7546	203-328-7310
NYSE: SGU				
Stripes Convenience Stores				
3200 Hackberry Rd	Irving TX	75063	800-255-0711	
NYSE: SUSS				
Suburban Propane LP				
240 Rt 10 W PO Box 206	Whippany NJ	07981	800-776-7263	973-503-9252
Superior Plus Energy Services Inc				
1870 S Winton Rd Ste 200	Rochester NY	14618	855-804-3835	
United Propane Gas				
4200 Cairo Rd	Paducah KY	42001	800-782-7743	
William G Satterlee & Sons Inc				
12475 Rt 119 Hwy N	Rochester Mills PA	15771	800-942-2214	724-397-2400
Wilson of Wallingford Inc				
221 Rogers Ln	Wallingford PA	19086	888-607-2621	610-566-7600
Wo Stinson & Son Ltd				
4726 Bank St	Ottawa ON	K1T3W7	800-267-9714	613-822-7400
Woodford Oil Company Inc				
13th St PO Box 567	Elkins WV	26241	800-927-3688	304-636-2688
Woodruff Energy				
73 Water St PO Box 777	Bridgeton NJ	08302	800-557-1121	
Worley & Obetz Inc				
85 White Oak Rd PO Box 429	Manheim PA	17545	800-697-6891	717-665-6891

317   FUND-RAISING SERVICES

			Toll-Free	Phone
ACCU Translations				
3 Mays Crescent	Waterdown ON	L0R2H4	800-668-0831	
AccuConference				
5 Concourse Pkwy Ste 1600	Atlanta GA	30328	800-989-9239*	404-920-6600
*Cust Svc				
Ackroo Inc				
62 Steacie Dr Ste 201	Ottawa ON	K2K2A9	888-405-0066	613-599-2396
Amerilist Inc				
978 Rt 45 Ste L2	Pomona NY	10970	800-457-2899	845-362-6737
APC Integrated Services Inc				
770 Spirit of St Louis Blvd	Chesterfield MO	63005	888-294-7886	
Apelles LLC				
3700 Corporate Dr Ste 240	Columbus OH	43231	800-825-4425	614-899-7322
Barchartcom Inc				
209 W Jackson 2nd Fl	Chicago IL	60606	800-238-5814	312-554-8122
Barnet Associates LLC				
2 Round Lake Rd	Ridgefield CT	06877	888-827-7070	
Barrent Group, The				
3056 104th St	Urbandale IA	50322	866-318-4448	
Barton Cotton Inc				
3030 Waterview Ave	Baltimore MD	21230	800-638-4652	800-348-1102
BeenVerified Inc (BV)				
48 W 38th St 8th Fl	New York NY	10018	888-579-5910	
Bentz Whaley Flessner				
7251 Ohms Ln	Minneapolis MN	55439	800-921-0111	952-921-0111
Big Mountain Imaging				
4725 Copper Sage Ct	Las Vegas NV	89115	877-229-4030	
Brakeley Briscoe Inc				
322 W Bellevue Ave	San Mateo CA	94402	800-416-3086	650-344-8883
Britestar Business				
1305-B Governor Ct	Abingdon MD	21009	888-409-6227	410-679-0441
Central Ontario Healthcare Procurement Alliance				
95 Mural St	Richmond Hill ON	L4B3G2	866-897-8812	905-886-5319

			Toll-Free	Phone
Concord Servicing Corp				
4150 N Drinkwater Blvd	Scottsdale AZ	85251	866-493-6393	
Creative Sign Designs				
12801 Commodity Pl	Tampa FL	33626	800-804-4809	
Crosbie & Company Inc				
150 King St W Sun Life Financial Tower				
15th Fl	Toronto ON	M5H1J9	866-873-7002	416-362-7726
CSA Group 178 Rexdale Blvd	Toronto ON	M9W1R3	800-463-6727	416-747-4000
Delbridge Solutions				
7560 Airport Rd Unit 12	Mississauga ON	L4T4H4	888-815-2996	
Diversitec LLC				
14321 Sommerville Ct	Midlothian VA	23113	800-229-6772	804-379-6772
Eichelbergers Inc				
107 Texaco Rd	Mechanicsburg PA	17050	800-371-3313	717-766-4800
Extended Presence				
3570 E 12th Ave Ste 200	Denver CO	80206	800-398-8957	303-892-5881
Fam Funds				
384 N Grand St PO Box 310	Cobleskill NY	12043	800-721-5391	518-234-4393
Field Nation LLC				
901 Marquette Ave Ste 2300	Minneapolis MN	55402	877-573-4353	
Galveston Central Appraisal District				
9850 Emmett F Lowry Expy Ste A	Texas City TX	77591	866-277-4725	409-935-1980
Global Pacific Financial Services Ltd				
10430 144 St	Surrey BC	V3T4V5	800-561-1177	
Greater Giving Inc				
1920 N W Amberglen Pkwy Ste 140	Beaverton OR	97006	800-276-5992	
Grenzebach Glier & Assoc Inc				
401 N Michigan Ave Ste 2800	Chicago IL	60611	800-222-9233	312-372-4040
Ho-Chunk Inc 1 Mission Dr	Winnebago NE	68071	800-439-7008	402-878-2809
IFS Financial Services Inc				
250 Brownlow Ave Ste 1	Dartmouth NS	B3B1W9	800-565-1153	902-481-6106
Info Cubic LLC				
9250 E Costilla Ave Ste 525	Greenwood Village CO	80112	877-360-4636	303-220-0170
Intronix Technologies Inc				
26 McEwan Dr W Unit 15	Bolton ON	L7E1E6	800-819-9996	905-951-3361
ISK Biosciences Corp				
7474 Auburn Rd Ste A	Concord OH	44077	877-706-4640	440-357-4640
Issuer Direct Corp				
500 Perimeter Park Dr Ste D	Morrisville NC	27560	877-481-4014	919-481-4000
J M Field Marketing Inc				
3570 NW 53rd Ct	Fort Lauderdale FL	33309	844-523-1957	954-523-1957
Joseph C Sansone Co				
18040 Edison Ave	Chesterfield MO	63005	800-394-0140	636-537-2700
LearnSpectrum				
9912 Georgetown Pke Ste D203	Great Falls VA	22066	888-682-9485	703-757-8200
Manus Group, The				
5000-18 Hwy 17 S Ste 134	Fleming Island FL	32003	888-735-8311	
MCMC LLC				
300 Crown Colony Dr Ste 203	Quincy MA	02169	866-401-6262	
MyUSACorporationcom Inc				
1 Radisson Plz Ste 800	New Rochelle NY	10801	877-330-2677	
Nomadic Display Capitol Inc				
5617 Industrial Dr	Springfield VA	22151	800-336-5019	
Nova Express Millennium Inc				
105 - 14271 Knox Way	Richmond BC	V6V2Z4	877-566-6839	604-278-8044
Office Liquidators Inc				
11111 W Sixth Ave	Denver CO	80215	800-279-3375	303-759-3375
Omnilingua Worldwide LLC				
306 Sixth Ave SE	Cedar Rapids IA	52401	800-395-6664	
OnCorp Direct Inc				
1033 Bay St Ste 313	Toronto ON	M5S3A5	800-461-7772	416-964-2677
Parenty Reitmeier Inc				
605 Des Meurons St	Winnipeg MB	R2H2R1	877-445-3737	204-237-3737
Periodical Publishers' Service Bureau				
653 W Fallbrook Ave Ste 101	Fresno CA	93711	888-206-0350	
Phone Ware Inc				
8902 Activity Rd	San Diego CA	92126	800-243-8329	858-459-3000
Planit Measuring Co, The				
94 Lkshore Rd E Unit C	Mississauga ON	L5G1E3	800-933-5136	905-271-7010
Polymer Solutions Inc				
2903-C Commerce St	Blacksburg VA	24060	877-961-4341	
Practice Concepts				
2706 Harbor Blvd	Costa Mesa CA	92626	877-778-2020	714-545-5110
Provista				
250 E John Carpenter Fwy	Irving TX	75062	888-538-4662	
QCSS Inc				
21925 Field Pkwy Ste 210	Deer Park IL	60010	888-229-7046	847-229-7046
Redeye Distribution Inc				
449a Trollingwood Rd	Haw River NC	27258	877-733-3931	
Reed Brennan Media Associates (RBMA)				
628 Virginia Dr	Orlando FL	32803	800-708-7311	407-894-7300
RGIS LLC				
2000 E Taylor Rd	Auburn Hills MI	48326	800-551-9130	248-651-2511
Robbinex Inc 41 Stuart St	Hamilton ON	L8L1B5	888-762-2463	905-523-7510
Round Sky Inc				
848 N Rainbow Blvd Ste 326	Las Vegas NV	89107	855-826-6284	
Skystone Partner				
635 W Seventh St Ste 107	Cincinnati OH	45203	800-883-0801	513-241-6778
Synergent 2 Ledgeview Dr	Westbrook ME	04092	800-341-0180	207-773-5671
TeamBonding 298 Tosca Dr	Stoughton MA	02072	888-398-8326	
Telenet Marketing Solutions				
1915 New Jimmy Daniel Rd	Athens GA	30606	877-282-2345	706-353-1940
Thermosoft International Corp				
701 corporate Woods Pkwy	Vernon Hills IL	60061	800-308-8057	847-279-3800
Thetubestore Inc				
120 Lancing Dr	Hamilton ON	L8W3A1	877-570-0979	905-570-0979
Trademark Co, The				
344 Maple Ave W PO Box 151	Vienna VA	22180	800-906-8626	
Travelink Inc				
404 BNA Dr #650	Nashville TN	37217	800-821-4671	615-367-4900
Ultraex Inc				
2633 Barrington Ct	Hayward CA	94545	800-882-1000	510-723-3760
Vantage Sourcing LLC				
4930 W St Hwy 52	Taylor AL	36305	866-580-4562	
Zerion Group PO Box 940411	Maitland FL	32794	877-872-1726	

318 — FURNACES & OVENS - INDUSTRIAL PROCESS

			Toll-Free	Phone
AJAX Electric Co				
60 Tomlinson Rd	Huntingdon Valley PA	19006	**800-516-9916**	215-947-8500
Ajax Tocco Magnethermic Corp				
1745 Overland Ave NE	Warren OH	44483	**800-547-1527**	330-372-8511
Alabama Specialty Products Inc				
152 Metal Samples Rd PO Box 8	Munford AL	36268	**888-388-1006**	256-358-5200
Alpha 1 Induction Service Ctr Inc				
1525 Old Alum Creek Dr	Columbus OH	43209	**800-991-2599**	614-253-8900
Armor Group Inc, The				
4600 N Mason-Montgomery Rd	Mason OH	45040	**800-255-0393**	
AVS Inc 60 Fitchburg Rd	Ayer MA	01432	**800-772-0710**	978-772-0710
BriskHeat Corp				
1055 Gibbard Ave	Columbus OH	43201	**800-848-7673**	614-294-3376
Cambridge Engineering Inc				
PO Box 1010	Chesterfield MO	63006	**800-899-1989**	636-532-2233
CCI Thermal Technologies Inc				
5918 Roper Rd	Edmonton AB	T6B3E1	**800-661-8529***	780-466-3178
*Cust Svc				
CMI EFCO Inc 435 W Wilson St	Salem OH	44460	**877-225-2674**	330-332-4661
Despatch Industries Inc				
8860 207th St W	Lakeville MN	55044	**800-726-0110**	952-469-5424
Detroit Radiant Product Co				
21400 Hoover Rd	Warren MI	48089	**800-222-1100**	586-756-0950
Detroit Stoker Co				
1510 E First St	Monroe MI	48161	**800-786-5374**	734-241-9500
Eclipse Inc				
1665 Elmwood Rd	Rockford IL	61103	**888-826-3473**	815-877-3031
Fast Heat Inc				
776 Oaklawn Ave	Elmhurst IL	60126	**877-747-8575**	630-359-6300
Gas-Fired Products Inc				
305 Doggett St	Charlotte NC	28203	**800-830-3983**	704-372-3485
Glenro Inc 39 McBride Ave	Paterson NJ	07501	**888-453-6761**	973-279-5900
Glo-Quartz Electric Heater Company Inc				
7084 Maple St	Mentor OH	44060	**800-321-3574***	440-255-9701
*Sales				
Heatrex Inc PO Box 515	Meadville PA	16335	**800-394-6589**	814-724-1800
Inductoheat Inc				
32251 N Avis Dr	Madison Heights MI	48071	**800-624-6297**	248-585-9393
Inductotherm Group				
10 Indel Ave PO Box 157	Rancocas NJ	08073	**800-257-9527**	609-267-9000
Industronics Service Co				
489 Sullivan Ave	South Windsor CT	06074	**800-878-1551**	860-289-1551
Ipsen Inc PO Box 6266	Rockford IL	61125	**800-727-7625**	815-332-4941
John Zink Hamworthy Combustion				
11920 E Apache St	Tulsa OK	74116	**800-421-9242**	918-234-1800
Johnson Gas Appliance Co				
520 E Ave NW	Cedar Rapids IA	52405	**800-553-5422**	319-365-5267
Lepel Corp				
W227 N937 Westmound Dr	Waukesha WI	53186	**800-548-8520**	631-586-3300
Novatec Inc				
222 Thomas Ave	Baltimore MD	21225	**800-237-8379**	410-789-4811
Paragon Industries Inc				
2011 S Town E Blvd	Mesquite TX	75149	**800-876-4328**	972-288-7557
Pillar Induction Co				
21905 Gateway Rd	Brookfield WI	53045	**800-558-7733**	262-317-5300
Pyronics Inc				
17700 Miles Rd	Cleveland OH	44128	**800-883-9218**	216-662-8800
Radyne Corp				
211 W Boden St	Milwaukee WI	53207	**800-236-8360**	414-481-8360
Rapid Engineering Inc				
1100 7-Mile Rd NW	Comstock Park MI	49321	**800-536-3461**	616-784-0500
Selas Heat Technology Company LLC				
130 Keystone Dr	Montgomeryville PA	18936	**800-523-6500**	215-646-6600
Steelman Industries Inc				
2800 Hwy 135 North	Kilgore TX	75662	**800-287-6633**	903-984-3061
Surface Combustion Inc				
1700 Indian Wood Cir	Maumee OH	43537	**800-537-8980**	419-891-7150
Tempco Electric Heater Corp				
607 N Central Ave	Wood Dale IL	60191	**888-268-6396**	630-350-2252
Thermal Circuits Inc				
1 Technology Way	Salem MA	01970	**800-808-4328**	978-745-1162
Thermal Engineering Corp				
2741 The Blvd	Columbia SC	29209	**800-331-0097**	803-783-0750
Thermal Equipment Corp				
2030 E University Dr	Rancho Dominguez CA	90220	**800-548-4422**	310-328-6600
Thermal Product Solutions				
3827 Riverside Rd	Riverside MI	49084	**800-873-4468**	269-849-2700
Truheat Inc 700 Grand St	Allegan MI	49010	**800-879-6199**	

319 — FURNITURE - MFR

SEE ALSO Cabinets - Wood ; Mattresses & Adjustable Beds ; Fixtures - Office & Store ; Recycled Plastics Products ; Baby Products

319-1 Commercial & Industrial Furniture

			Toll-Free	Phone
Adelphia Steel Equipment Co				
7372 State Rd	Philadelphia PA	19136	**800-865-8211**	215-333-6300
Allied Plastics Company Inc				
2001 Walnut St	Jacksonville FL	32206	**800-999-0386***	
*Cust Svc				
Allsteel Inc				
2210 Second Ave	Muscatine IA	52761	**888-255-7833***	563-272-4800
*Cust Svc				
Anthro Corp				
10450 SW Manhasset Dr	Tualatin OR	97062	**800-325-3841**	503-691-2556
Bernhardt Furniture Co				
1839 Morganton Blvd	Lenoir NC	28645	**800-638-2772**	
Bestar Inc				
4220 Villeneuve St	Lac-Megantic QC	G6B2C3	**888-823-7827**	819-583-1017

Company / Address	City	State	ZIP	Toll-Free	Phone
Bevco Precision Manufacturing Co 21320 Doral Rd	Waukesha	WI	53186	**800-864-2991**	262-798-9200
BGD Cos Inc 5323 Lakeland Ave N	Minneapolis	MN	55429	**800-699-3537**	612-338-6804
Biofit Engineered Products 15500 Biofit Way	Bowling Green	OH	43402	**800-597-0246**	419-823-1089
Borroughs Corp 3002 N Burdick St	Kalamazoo	MI	49004	**800-748-0227**	269-342-0161
Bright Chair Co 51 Railroad Ave	Middletown	NY	10940	**888-524-5997**	845-343-2196
Carolina Business Furniture LLC 535 Archdale Blvd	Archdale	NC	27263	**800-763-0212**	336-431-9400
Cramer Inc 1523 Grand Blvd	Kansas City	MO	64108	**800-366-6700**	
Danver 1 Grand St	Wallingford	CT	06492	**888-441-0537**	203-269-2300
Dar-Ran Furniture Industries 2402 Shore St	High Point	NC	27263	**800-334-7891**	336-861-2400
Dauphin North America 300 Myrtle Ave *Cust Svc	Boonton	NJ	07005	**800-631-1186***	973-263-1100
Emeco 805 W Elm Ave	Hanover	PA	17331	**800-366-5951**	717-637-5951
Ergotron Inc 1181 Trapp Rd *Sales	Saint Paul	MN	55121	**800-888-8458***	651-681-7600
First Office 1204 E Sixth St	Huntingburg	IN	47542	**800-983-4415**	
Flex-Y-Plan Industries Inc 6960 W Ridge Rd *Cust Svc	Fairview	PA	16415	**800-458-0552***	814-474-1565
Geiger International Inc 6095 Fulton Industrial Blvd SW	Atlanta	GA	30336	**800-456-6452**	404-344-1100
Global Industries Inc 17 W Stow Rd	Marlton	NJ	08053	**800-220-1900**	856-596-3390
Groupe Lacasse LLC 99 St-Pierre St	Sainte-Pie	QC	J0H1W0	**888-522-2773**	450-772-2495
Gunlocke Company LLC 1 Gunlocke Dr *Cust Svc	Wayland	NY	14572	**800-828-6300***	585-728-5111
Hausmann Industries Inc 130 Union St	Northvale	NJ	07647	**888-428-7626**	201-767-0255
Haworth Inc 1 Haworth Ctr	Holland	MI	49423	**800-344-2600**	616-393-3000
Herman Miller Inc 855 E Main Ave *NASDAQ: MLHR*	Zeeland	MI	49464	**800-443-4357**	616-654-3000
High Point Furniture Industries Inc 1104 Bedford St PO Box 2063	High Point	NC	27261	**800-447-3462**	336-434-5141
Hirsh Industries Inc 3636 Westown Pkwy Ste 100	West Des Moines	IA	50266	**800-383-7414**	515-299-3200
HON Co 200 Oak St	Muscatine	IA	52761	**800-553-8230**	563-272-7100
Huot Manufacturing Co 550 Wheeler St N	Saint Paul	MN	55104	**800-832-3838**	651-646-1869
IAC Industries 895 Beacon St	Brea	CA	92821	**800-989-1422**	714-990-8997
Indiana Furniture 1224 Mill St	Jasper	IN	47546	**800-422-5727**	812-482-5727
Invincible Office Furniture Co 842 S 26th St PO Box 1117	Manitowoc	WI	54220	**877-682-4601**	920-682-4601
Izzydesign 17237 Van Wagoner Rd	Spring Lake	MI	49456	**800-543-5449**	616-916-9369
Jasper Desk Co 415 E Sixth St *Cust Svc	Jasper	IN	47546	**800-365-7994***	812-482-4132
Jasper Seating Company Inc *Jasper Group* 225 Clay St	Jasper	IN	47546	**800-622-5661**	812-482-3204
Khoury Inc 1129 Webster Ave PO Box 1746	Waco	TX	76703	**800-725-6765**	254-754-5481
KI 1330 Bellevue St	Green Bay	WI	54302	**800-424-2432**	920-468-8100
Kimball Hospitality 1180 E 16th St	Jasper	IN	47549	**800-634-9510**	276-666-8933
Kimball Office Furniture Co 1600 Royal St	Jasper	IN	47549	**800-482-1818**	
Knoll Inc 1235 Water St *NYSE: KNL* ■ *Cust Svc	East Greenville	PA	18041	**800-343-5665***	
Lakeside Manufacturing Inc 4900 W Electric Ave	West Milwaukee	WI	53219	**800-558-8565**	414-902-6400
LB Furniture Industries LLC 99 S Third St	Hudson	NY	12534	**800-221-8752**	518-828-1501
Luxour 2245 Delany Rd	Waukegan	IL	60087	**800-323-4656**	847-244-1800
Magna Design Inc 12020 NE 26th PL	Bellevue	WA	98005	**800-426-1202**	206-852-5282
Martin Furniture 2345 Britannia Blvd *Cust Svc	San Diego	CA	92154	**800-268-5669***	
Marvel Group Inc 3843 W 43rd St *Cust Svc	Chicago	IL	60632	**800-621-8846***	773-523-4804
Maxon Furniture Inc 200 Oak St	Muscatine	IA	52761	**800-876-4274**	
Mayline Group 619 N Commerce St PO Box 728	Sheboygan	WI	53082	**800-822-8037**	920-457-5537
MLP Seating Corp 950 Pratt Blvd	Elk Grove Village	IL	60007	**800-723-3030**	847-956-1700
Montisa 323 Acorn St *Cust Svc	Plainwell	MI	49080	**800-875-6836***	269-924-0730
MTS Seating Inc 7100 Industrial Dr	Temperance	MI	48182	**800-329-0687**	734-847-3875
National Office Furniture 1205 Kimball Blvd	Jasper	IN	47549	**800-482-1717**	
Neutral Posture Inc 3904 N Texas Ave	Bryan	TX	77803	**800-446-3746**	979-778-0502
Nomanco Inc 501 Nmc Dr	Zebulon	NC	27597	**800-345-7279**	919-269-6500
Nova Solutions Inc 421 Industrial Ave	Effingham	IL	62401	**800-730-6682**	217-342-7070
Office Chairs Inc 14815 Radburn Ave	Santa Fe Springs	CA	90670	**866-624-4968**	562-802-0464
Omni International Inc 435 12th St SW	Vernon	AL	35592	**800-844-6664**	205-695-9173
Paoli Inc 201 E Martin St	Orleans	IN	47452	**800-472-8669**	
Penco Products Inc 1820 Stonehenge Dr	Greenville	NC	27858	**800-562-1000**	
Plymold 615 Centennial Dr	Kenyon	MN	55946	**800-759-6653**	
Reconditioned Systems Inc (RSI) 235 S 56th St	Chandler	AZ	85226	**800-280-5000**	
Robertson Furniture Company Inc 890 Elberton St	Toccoa	GA	30577	**800-241-0713**	706-886-1494
Safco Products Co 9300 West Research Center Rd *Cust Svc	New Hope	MN	55428	**800-328-3020***	888-971-6225
Shure Manufacturing Corp 1901 W Main St	Washington	MO	63090	**800-227-4873**	636-390-7100
Spectrum Industries Inc 925 First Ave	Chippewa Falls	WI	54729	**800-235-1262**	715-723-6750
Steelcase Inc 901 44th St SE *NYSE: SCS*	Grand Rapids	MI	49508	**888-783-3522**	800-333-9939
Stevens Industries Inc 704 W Main St	Teutopolis	IL	62467	**800-637-1609**	217-540-3100
Stylex PO Box 5038	Delanco	NJ	08075	**800-257-5742**	
TAB Products Co 605 Fourth St	Mayville	WI	53050	**888-466-8228**	
Tennsco Corp 201 Tennsco Dr PO Box 1888 *Cust Svc	Dickson	TN	37056	**866-446-8686***	
Trendway Corp 13467 Quincy St PO Box 9016	Holland	MI	49422	**800-968-5344**	616-399-3900
Tuohy Furniture Corp 42 St Albans Pl *Cust Svc	Chatfield	MN	55923	**800-533-1696***	507-867-4280
Viking Acoustical Corp 21480 Heath Ave	Lakeville	MN	55044	**800-328-8385**	952-469-3405
Vitro Seating Products Inc 201 Madison St *Cust Svc	Saint Louis	MO	63102	**800-325-7093***	314-241-2265
West Coast Industries Inc 10 Jackson St	San Francisco	CA	94111	**800-243-3150**	415-621-6656
Workplace Systems Inc 562 Mammoth Rd	Londonderry	NH	03053	**800-258-9700**	603-622-3727
Wright Line LLC 160 Gold Star Blvd	Worcester	MA	01606	**800-225-7348**	508-852-4300

319-2 Household Furniture

Company / Address	City	State	ZIP	Toll-Free	Phone
Ameriwood Home 410 E S First St *General	Wright City	MO	63390	**800-489-3351***	636-745-3351
Ashley Furniture Industries Inc 1 Ashley Way	Arcadia	WI	54612	**800-477-2222**	608-323-3377
Bassett Furniture Industries Inc 3525 Fairystone Pk Hwy PO Box 626 *NASDAQ: BSET*	Bassett	VA	24055	**877-525-7070**	276-629-6000
Broyhill Furniture Industries Inc 3483 Hickory Blvd *Cust Svc	Hudson	NC	28638	**800-225-0265***	
Brueton Industries Inc 146 Hanse Ave *Cust Svc	Freeport	NY	11520	**800-221-6783***	516-379-3400
Bush Industries Inc 1 Mason Dr	Jamestown	NY	14701	**800-950-4782**	716-665-2000
Century Furniture LLC 401 11th St NW	Hickory	NC	28601	**800-852-5552**	828-328-1851
DeFehr Furniture Ltd 125 Furniture Pk	Winnipeg	MB	R2G1B9	**877-333-3471**	204-988-5630
Dutailier Group Inc 299 Rue Chaput	Sainte-Pie	QC	J0H1W0	**800-363-9817**	450-772-2403
El Ran Furniture Ltd 2751 Transcanada Hwy	Pointe-Claire	QC	H9R1B4	**800-361-6546**	514-630-5656
Ethan Allen Interiors Inc Ethan Allen Dr *NYSE: ETH*	Danbury	CT	06811	**888-324-3571**	
Evenflo Company Inc 1801 Commerce Dr	Piqua	OH	45356	**800-233-5921**	
Fairfield Chair Co PO Box 1710	Lenoir	NC	28645	**800-841-6279**	828-758-5571
Finnleo Sauna 575 Cokato St E	Cokato	MN	55321	**800-346-6536**	
Hooker Furniture Corp 440 E Commonwealth Blvd *NASDAQ: HOFT* ■ *Cust Svc	Martinsville	VA	24112	**800-422-1511***	276-632-0459
Human Touch 3030 Walnut Ave	Long Beach	CA	90807	**800-742-5493**	562-426-8700
La-Z-Boy Inc 1284 N Telegraph Rd *NYSE: LZB*	Monroe	MI	48162	**800-375-6890**	734-242-1444
Lamont Ltd 1530 Bluff Rd	Burlington	IA	52601	**800-553-5621**	319-753-5131
Leathercraft PO Box 639	Conover	NC	28613	**800-627-1561**	
Lexington Home Brands 1300 National Hwy	Thomasville	NC	27360	**800-333-4300**	336-474-5300
Little Tikes Co, The 2180 Barlow Rd *Cust Svc	Hudson	OH	44236	**800-321-0183***	
Mantua Mfg Co 7900 Northfield Rd *Orders	Walton Hills	OH	44146	**800-333-8333***	
McGuire Furniture Co 1201 Bryant St	San Francisco	CA	94103	**800-662-4847**	415-626-1414
Mitchell Gold & Bob Williams Co (MGBW) 135 One Comfortable Pl	Taylorsville	NC	28681	**800-789-5401**	828-632-9200
Robern Inc 701 N Wilson Ave	Bristol	PA	19007	**800-877-2376**	215-826-9800
Room & Board Inc 4600 Olson Memorial Hwy	Golden Valley	MN	55422	**800-301-9720**	763-521-4431
Rumble Tuff Inc 865 N 1430 W	Orem	UT	84057	**855-228-8388**	801-609-8168
Sauder Woodworking Co 502 Middle St *Cust Svc	Archbold	OH	43502	**800-523-3987***	419-446-2711

				Toll-Free	Phone
Schnadig International Corp					
4200 Tudor Ln	Greensboro	NC	27410	800-468-8730	
Shermag Inc					
3035 Boul Industriel	Sherbrooke	QC	J1L2T9	800-567-3419	819-566-1515
SICO America Inc					
7525 Cahill Rd	Minneapolis	MN	55439	800-328-6138	952-941-1700
Standard Furniture Mfg Company Inc					
801 Hwy 31 S	Bay Minette	AL	36507	877-788-1899*	251-937-6741
*General					
Stork Craft Manufacturing Inc					
12033 Riverside Way Ste 200	Richmond	BC	V6W1G3	877-274-0277	604-274-5121
Suncast Corp 701 N Kirk Rd	Batavia	IL	60510	800-444-3310	800-846-2345
Vanguard Furniture Co Inc					
109 Simpson St	Conover	NC	28613	800-968-1702	828-328-5631
Whittier Wood Products					
3787 W First Ave PO Box 2827	Eugene	OR	97402	800-653-3336	541-687-0213
Zenith Products Corp					
400 Lukens Dr	New Castle	DE	19720	800-892-3986	

319-3 Institutional & Other Public Buildings Furniture

				Toll-Free	Phone
American Seating Co					
401 American Seating Ctr NW	Grand Rapids	MI	49504	800-748-0268*	616-732-6600
*Cust Svc					
Artco-Bell Corp					
1302 Industrial Blvd	Temple	TX	76504	877-778-1811	254-778-1811
Bretford Manufacturing Inc					
11000 Seymour Ave	Franklin Park	IL	60131	800-521-9614	847-678-2545
ENOCHS Examining Room Furniture					
14701 Cumberland Rd Ste 107	Noblesville	IN	46060	800-428-2305*	
*Cust Svc					
ErgoGenesis Workplace Solutions LLC					
1 BodyBilt Pl	Navasota	TX	77868	800-364-5299	936-825-1700
Fleetwood Group Inc					
11832 James St	Holland	MI	49424	800-257-6390	
Fordham Plastics					
1204 Village Market Pl Ste 262	Morrisville	NC	27560	866-467-0708	919-467-0708
Gaylord Bros					
7282 William Barry Blvd	Syracuse	NY	13212	800-345-5330	800-448-6160
Gunlocke Company LLC					
1 Gunlocke Dr	Wayland	NY	14572	800-828-6300*	585-728-5111
*Cust Svc					
Hard Mfg Company Inc					
230 Grider St	Buffalo	NY	14215	800-873-4273	
Hill-Rom Services Inc					
1069 SR 46 E	Batesville	IN	47006	800-267-2337	812-934-7777
Hussey Seating Co					
38 Dyer St Ext	North Berwick	ME	03906	800-341-0401	207-676-2271
Imperial Woodworks Inc					
PO Box 7835	Waco	TX	76714	800-234-6624	
Irwin Seating Company Inc					
3251 Fruit Ridge NW	Grand Rapids	MI	49544	866-464-7946	616-574-7400
Kimball Hospitality					
1180 E 16th St	Jasper	IN	47549	800-634-9510	276-666-8933
LB Furniture Industries LLC					
99 S Third St	Hudson	NY	12534	800-221-8752	518-828-1501
List Industries Inc					
401 Jim Moran Blvd	Deerfield Beach	FL	33442	800-776-1342	954-429-9155
Luxour 2245 Delany Rd	Waukegan	IL	60087	800-323-4656	847-244-1800
Meadows Office Interiors					
885 Third Ave 29th Fl	New York	NY	10022	800-337-6671	212-741-0333
Midwest Folding Products Inc					
1414 S Western Ave	Chicago	IL	60608	800-621-4716	312-666-3366
Mitchell Furniture Systems Inc					
1700 W St Paul Ave	Milwaukee	WI	53233	800-290-5960	
Mity-Lite Inc 1301 W 400 N	Orem	UT	84057	800-909-8034	801-224-0589
MLP Seating Corp					
950 Pratt Blvd	Elk Grove Village	IL	60007	800-723-3030	847-956-1700
Monroe Table Co					
316 N Walnut St	Salamanca	NY	14779	844-822-5370	716-945-7700
Nemschoff Inc					
909 N Eigth St	Sheboygan	WI	53081	800-203-8916*	
*Cust Svc					
New Holland Church Furniture					
313 Prospect St PO Box 217	New Holland	PA	17557	800-648-9663	
Omni International Inc					
435 12th St SW	Vernon	AL	35592	800-844-6664	205-695-9173
Shelby Williams Industries Inc					
810 West Hwy 25/70	Newport	TN	37821	800-873-3252*	423-623-0031
*General					
SICO America Inc					
7525 Cahill Rd	Minneapolis	MN	55439	800-328-6138	952-941-1700
Spectrum Industries Inc					
925 First Ave	Chippewa Falls	WI	54729	800-235-1262	715-723-6750
Sturdisteel Co PO Box 2655	Waco	TX	76702	800-433-3116	
Tesco Industries LP					
1035 E Hacienda	Bellville	TX	77418	800-699-5824	
TMI Systems Design Corp					
50 S Third Ave W	Dickinson	ND	58601	800-456-6716	701-456-6716
UMF Medical					
1316 Eisenhower Blvd	Johnstown	PA	15904	800-638-5322	814-266-8726
Virco Manufacturing Corp					
2027 Harpers Way	Torrance	CA	90501	800-448-4726*	310-533-0474
NASDAQ: VIRC ■ *Cust Svc					
Wieland 10785 Rose Ave	New Haven	IN	46774	888-943-5263	260-627-3686
Winco Inc 5516 SW First Ln	Ocala	FL	34474	800-237-3377	352-854-2929
Worden Company Inc					
199 E 17th St	Holland	MI	49423	800-748-0561	616-392-1848

319-4 Outdoor Furniture

				Toll-Free	Phone
Belson Outdoors Inc					
111 N River Rd	North Aurora	IL	60542	800-323-5664	

				Toll-Free	Phone
Bemis Manufacturing Co					
300 Mill St	Sheboygan Falls	WI	53085	800-558-7651	920-467-4621
Brown Jordan Co					
9860 Gidley St	El Monte	CA	91731	800-743-4252	626-279-5537
Cox Industries Inc					
860 Cannon Bridge Rd PO Box 1124	Orangeburg	SC	29116	800-476-4401	803-534-7467
DuMor Inc PO Box 142	Mifflintown	PA	17059	800-598-4018	717-436-2106
Gardenside Ltd					
808 Anthony St	Berkeley	CA	94710	888-999-8325	415-455-4500
Hatteras Hammocks Inc					
305 Industrial Blvd	Greenville	NC	27834	800-643-3522	252-758-0641
J Robert Scott Inc					
500 N Oak St	Inglewood	CA	90302	877-207-5130	310-680-4300
Kay Park Recreation Corp					
1301 Pine St	Janesville	IA	50647	800-553-2476*	877-529-7275
*Cust Svc					
Mallin Casual Furniture					
1 Minson Way	Montebello	CA	90640	800-251-6537	
Minson Corp 1 Minson Way	Montebello	CA	90640	800-251-6537	323-513-1041
OW Lee Company Inc					
1822 E Francis St	Ontario	CA	91761	800-776-9533	
RJ Thomas Mfg Company Inc					
PO Box 946	Cherokee	IA	51012	800-762-5002	712-225-5115
Twin Oaks Hammocks					
138 Twin Oaks Rd	Louisa	VA	23093	800-688-8946	540-894-5125
Wabash Valley Manufacturing Inc					
505 E Main St	Silver Lake	IN	46982	800-253-8619	260-352-2102
Walpole Woodworkers Inc					
767 E St	Walpole	MA	02081	800-343-6948*	508-668-2800
*Cust Svc					

320 FURNITURE - WHOL

				Toll-Free	Phone
A Lava & Son Co					
4800 S Kilbourn Ave	Chicago	IL	60632	800-777-5282	773-254-2800
ATD-American Co					
135 Greenwood Ave	Wyncote	PA	19095	866-283-9327	215-576-1380
Berco Inc 111 Winnebago	Saint Louis	MO	63118	888-772-4788	314-772-4700
Brondell Inc					
1159 Howard St	San Francisco	CA	94103	888-542-3355	
Business Furniture Corp					
8421 Bearing Dr Ste 200	Indianapolis	IN	46278	800-774-5544	317-216-1600
California Office Furniture					
3480 Industrial Blvd Ste 100	West Sacramento	CA	95691	877-442-6959	916-442-6959
Carithers Wallace Courtenay Co					
4343 NE Expy	Atlanta	GA	30340	800-292-8220	770-493-8200
Carroll Seating Company Inc					
10 Lincoln St	Kansas City	KS	66103	800-972-3779	816-471-2929
Champion Industries Inc					
PO Box 2968	Huntington	WV	25728	800-624-3431	304-528-2791
OTC: CHMP					
COECO Office Systems Co					
2521 N Church St	Rocky Mount	NC	27804	800-682-6844	252-977-1121
Conklin Office Furniture					
56 N Canal St	Holyoke	MA	01040	800-817-1187	413-315-6777
Evergreen Enterprises Inc					
5915 Midlothian Tpke	Richmond	VA	23225	800-774-3837	
EVS Ltd 3702 W Sample St	South Bend	IN	46619	800-364-3218	574-233-5707
Fournitures De Bureau Denis Inc					
2990 boul Le Corbusier	Laval	QC	H7L3M2	800-338-5567	
Heritage Office Furnishings					
1588 Rand Ave	Vancouver	BC	V6P3G2	888-775-4555	604-688-2381
J L Business Interiors Inc					
515 Schoenhaar Dr PO Box 303	West Bend	WI	53090	866-338-5524	262-338-2221
Kentwood Office Furniture Inc					
3063 Breton Rd SE	Grand Rapids	MI	49512	877-698-6250	616-957-2320
Magnussen Home Furnishings Ltd					
66 Hincks St	New Hamburg	ON	N3A2A3	877-552-5670	
Najarian Furniture Company Inc					
265 North Euclid Ave	Pasadena	CA	91101	888-781-3088	626-839-8700
National Business Furniture Inc					
735 N Water St Ste 440	Milwaukee	WI	53202	800-558-1010*	
*Sales					
Nevers Industries Inc					
14125 21st Ave N	Minneapolis	MN	55447	800-258-5591	763-210-4206
North Country Business Products Inc					
1112 S Railroad St SE	Bemidji	MN	56601	800-937-4140	
Office Environments Inc					
11407 Granite St	Charlotte	NC	28273	888-861-2525	704-714-7200
Office Star Products					
1901 S Archibald PO Box 3520	Ontario	CA	91761	800-950-7262	909-930-2000
Paragon Furniture Management Inc					
2224 E Randol Mill Rd	Arlington	TX	76011	800-451-8546	817-633-3242
Peabody Office Furniture Corp					
234 Congress St	Boston	MA	02110	800-263-2387	617-542-1902
Quality Enclosures Inc					
2025 Porter Lake Dr	Sarasota	FL	34240	800-881-0051	941-378-0051
R & M Office Furniture					
9615 Oates Dr	Sacramento	CA	95827	800-660-1756	916-362-1756
Red Thread					
300 E River Dr	East Hartford	CT	06108	800-635-4874	860-528-9981
Trade Products Corp					
12124 Popes Head Rd	Fairfax	VA	22030	888-352-3580	703-502-9000
Wasserstrom Co					
477 S Front St	Columbus	OH	43215	866-634-8927	614-228-6525
Wholesale Interiors Inc					
971 Supreme Dr	Bensenville	IL	60106	800-517-0717	

321 FURNITURE STORES

SEE ALSO Department Stores

				Toll-Free	Phone
Activeforevercom					
10799 N 90th St	Scottsdale	AZ	85260	800-377-8033	

Company	Address	City	State	Zip	Toll-Free	Phone
Addison House	5201 NW 77th Ave Ste 400	Doral	FL	33166	**800-426-2988**	305-640-2400
All Makes Office Equipment Co	2558 Farnam St	Omaha	NE	68131	**800-341-2413**	402-341-2413
American Freight Ohio Inc	2770 Lexington Ave	Mansfield	OH	44904	**800-420-2337**	419-884-2224
American Furniture Warehouse Co	8501 Grant St	Thornton	CO	80229	**888-615-9415**	303-289-3300
American Home Furnishings	3535 Menaul Blvd NE	Albuquerque	NM	87107	**800-854-6755**	505-883-2211
Ameublements Tanguay Inc	7200 Armand-Viau St	Quebec	QC	G2C2A7	**800-826-4829**	418-847-4411
Andreas Furniture Company Inc	114 Dover Rd NE	Sugarcreek	OH	44681	**800-846-7448**	330-852-2494
Arizona Leather Company Inc	4235 Schaefer Ave	Chino	CA	91710	**888-669-5328**	909-993-5101
August Inc	354 Congress Park Dr	Centerville	OH	45459	**800-318-5242**	937-434-2520
Baileys Furniture Outlet Inc	350 W Intl Airport Rd Ste 100	Anchorage	AK	99518	**888-563-4083**	
Bar Productscom Inc	1990 Lake Ave SE	Largo	FL	33771	**800-256-6396**	727-584-2093
Bay View Plaza Furniture Inc	2181 E Pass Rd	Gulfport	MS	39507	**800-748-9852**	228-896-4400
Beaufurn LLC	5269 US Hwy 158	Advance	NC	27006	**888-766-7706**	336-941-3446
Blackledge Furniture	233 SW Second St	Corvallis	OR	97333	**800-782-4851**	541-753-4851
Blacklion International Inc	10635 Park Rd	Charlotte	NC	28210	**866-466-5466**	
Boss Chair Inc	5353 Jillson St	Commerce	CA	90040	**800-593-1888**	323-262-1919
Business Interiors	1111 Valley View Ln	Irving	TX	75061	**800-568-9281**	
Casa Linda Furniture Inc	4815 Whittier Blvd	Los Angeles	CA	90022	**888-783-0631**	323-263-3851
Casual Designs Furniture Inc	36523 Lighthouse Rd	Selbyville	DE	19975	**888-629-1717**	302-436-8224
Charlotte Appliances Inc	3200 Lake Ave	Rochester	NY	14612	**800-244-0405**	585-663-5050
City Furniture Inc	6701 N Hiatus Rd	Tamarac	FL	33321	**866-930-4233**	954-597-2200
Cumberland Furniture	321 Terminal St SW	Grand Rapids	MI	49548	**800-401-7877**	
Dates Weiser Furniture Corp	1700 Broadway St	Buffalo	NY	14212	**800-466-7037**	716-891-1700
Dearden's Furniture Co	700 S Main St	Los Angeles	CA	90014	**800-545-5509**	213-362-9600
El Dorado Furniture Corp	4200 NW 167th St	Miami	FL	33054	**888-451-7800**	305-624-2400
Epoch Design	17617 NE 65th St Ste 2	Redmond	WA	98052	**800-589-7990**	
Ethan Allen Interiors Inc	Ethan Allen Dr *NYSE: ETH*	Danbury	CT	06811	**888-324-3571**	
Fast Fastfurnishings	340 S Lemon Ave Ste 6043	Walnut	CA	91789	**866-720-0126**	443-371-3278
FCC Commercial Furniture Inc	8452 Old Hwy 99 N	Roseburg	OR	97470	**800-322-7328**	
GCI Outdoor Inc	66 Killingworth Rd	Higganum	CT	06441	**800-956-7328**	860-345-9595
Gibraltar Steel Furniture Inc	9976 Westwanda Dr	Beverly Hills	CA	90210	**800-416-3635**	310-276-8889
Gressco Ltd	328 Moravian Valley Rd	Waunakee	WI	53597	**800-345-3480**	608-849-6300
Haverty Furniture Cos Inc	780 Johnson Ferry Rd NE Ste 800 *NYSE: HVT*	Atlanta	GA	30342	**888-428-3789**	
Healthy Back Store LLC	10300 Southard Dr	Beltsville	MD	20705	**800-469-2225**	
Heliodyne Corp	4910 Seaport Ave	Richmond	CA	94804	**888-878-8750**	510-237-9614
Hill Country Furniture Partners Ltd	1431 Fm 1101	New Braunfels	TX	78130	**877-314-8457**	
Hurwitz-Mintz Furniture Co	1751 Airline Dr	Metairie	LA	70001	**888-957-9555**	504-378-1000
IcwUSACom Inc	1487 Kingsley Dr	Medford	OR	97504	**800-558-4435**	541-608-2824
IKEA	420 Alan Wood Rd	Conshohocken	PA	19428	**800-434-4532**	809-567-4532
Innovative Mattress Solutions LLC	1721 Jaggie Fox Way	Lexington	KY	40511	**800-766-4163**	
International Contract Furnishings Inc (ICF)	19 Ohio Ave	Norwich	CT	06360	**800-237-1625**	860-886-1700
Inviting Homecom	4700 SW 51st St Unit 219	Davie	FL	33314	**866-751-6606**	781-444-8001
Jayson Home & Garden	1885 N Clybourn Ave	Chicago	IL	60614	**800-472-1885**	773-248-8180
Jerome's Furniture Warehouse	16960 Mesamint St	San Diego	CA	92127	**866-633-4094**	
Lacks Valley Stores Ltd	1300 San Patricia St	Pharr	TX	78577	**800-870-6999**	956-702-3361
Living Spaces Furniture LLC	14501 Artesia Blvd	La Mirada	CA	90638	**877-266-7300**	
Logo Inc	117 SE Pkwy	Franklin	TN	37064	**844-564-6432**	
London Luxury Bedding Inc	295 Fifth Ave Ste 817	New Rochelle	NY	10016	**877-636-2100**	914-636-2100
MacKenzie-Childs LLC	3260 SR-90	Aurora	NY	13026	**888-665-1999**	315-364-7123
Mathis Bros Furniture Inc	6611 S 101st East Ave *Cust Svc	Tulsa	OK	74133	**800-329-3434***	855-294-3434
Miskelly Furniture	101 Airport Rd	Jackson	MS	39208	**888-939-6288**	601-939-6288
Moser Corp	601 N 13th St	Rogers	AR	72756	**800-632-4564**	479-636-3481
N Tepperman Ltd	2595 Ouellette Ave	Windsor	ON	N8X4V8	**800-265-5062**	519-969-9700
Nashville Office Interiors	1621 Church St	Nashville	TN	37203	**877-342-0294**	615-329-1811
Near North Business Machines	86 W Rd	Huntsville	ON	P1H1M1	**800-522-3836**	705-787-0517
Nebraska Furniture Mart Inc	700 S 72nd St	Omaha	NE	68114	**800-336-9136**	402-397-6100
Nickerson Business Supplies	876A Lebanon St	Monroe	OH	45050	**888-385-9922**	513-539-6600
Norco Products Furniture Mfrs	4985 Blue Mtn Rd	Missoula	MT	59804	**800-662-2300**	406-251-3800
Northland Furniture Co	681 SE Glenwood	Bend	OR	97702	**800-497-7591**	
Nucraft Furniture Co	5151 W River Dr	Comstock Park	MI	49321	**877-682-7238**	616-784-6016
Olum's of Binghamton Inc	3701 Vestal Pkwy E *Cust Svc	Vestal	NY	13850	**855-264-8674***	607-729-5775
Osborne Wood Products Inc	4618 Hwy 123	Toccoa	GA	30577	**800-849-8876**	
Otterbine Barebo Inc	3840 Main Rd E	Emmaus	PA	18049	**800-237-8837**	610-965-6018
Parker Furniture	10375 SW Beaverton-Hillsdale Hwy	Beaverton	OR	97005	**866-515-9673**	503-644-0155
Patioshoppers Inc	41188 Sandalwood Cir	Murrieta	CA	92562	**800-940-6123**	951-696-1700
Pier 1 Kids	100 Pier 1 Pl	Fort Worth	TX	76102	**800-433-4035**	817-252-8000
Preservation Technologies LP	111 Thomson Park Dr	Cranberry Township	PA	16066	**800-416-2665**	724-779-2111
Raymour & Flanigan Furniture	PO Box 220 *Consumer Assistance	Liverpool	NY	13088	**866-383-4484***	315-453-2500
Reborn Cabinets	2981 E La Palma Ave	Anaheim	CA	92806	**888-273-2676**	714-630-2220
Regency Seating Inc	2375 Romig Rd	Akron	OH	44320	**866-816-9822**	330-848-3700
Reimagine Office Furnishings	1212 N 39th St Ste 200	Tampa	FL	33605	**877-763-4400**	
Rocky Top Furniture Inc	8957 Lexington Rd	Lancaster	KY	40444	**800-332-1143**	859-548-2828
Rothman Furniture Stores Inc	2101 E Terra Ln	O'Fallon	MO	63366	**877-704-0002**	
Sam Clar Office Furniture Inc	1221 Diamond Way	Concord	CA	94520	**800-726-2527**	
Schmidt-Goodman Office Products	1920 N Broadway	Rochester	MN	55906	**800-247-0663**	507-282-3870
Sit 'n Sleep	14300 S Main St	Gardena	CA	90248	**877-262-4006**	310-604-8903
Smart Furniture Inc	430 Market St	Chattanooga	TN	37402	**888-467-6278**	423-267-7007
Smith Village Home Furnishings	34 N Main St	Jacobus	PA	17407	**800-242-1921**	717-428-1921
Stacy Furniture & Design	1900 S Main St	Grapevine	TX	76051	**800-403-6077**	817-424-8800
Stageright Corp	495 Pioneer Pkwy	Clare	MI	48617	**800-438-4499**	989-386-7393
Star Furniture Company Inc	16666 Barker Springs Rd	Houston	TX	77084	**800-364-6661**	281-492-6661
Steinhafels	W 231 N 1013 County Hwy F *Cust Svc	Waukesha	WI	53186	**866-351-4600***	262-436-4600
Sunnyland Outdoor & Casual Furniture	7879 Spring Valley Rd Ste 125	Dallas	TX	75254	**877-239-3716**	972-239-3716
Swartz Kitchens & Baths	5550 Allentown Blvd (Rt 22)	Harrisburg	PA	17112	**800-652-0111**	717-652-7111
trade associates group Ltd	900 W Bliss St	Chicago	IL	60642	**800-621-8350**	773-871-1300
Tri-boro Shelving & Partition Corp	300 Dominion Dr	Farmville	VA	23901	**800-633-3070**	434-315-5600
Trinity Business Furniture	6089 Kennedy Rd	Trinity	NC	27370	**855-311-6660**	336-472-6660
Tupelo Furniture Market	1879 N Coley Rd	Tupelo	MS	38801	**800-844-0841**	662-842-4442
Urban Barn Ltd	4085 Marine Way Ste 1	Burnaby	BC	V5J5E2	**844-456-2200**	604-456-2200
US. Quality Furniture Services Inc	8920 Winkler Dr	Houston	TX	77017	**800-774-8700**	
USA Baby	793 Springer Dr	Lombard	IL	60148	**800-767-9464**	630-652-0600
Victory Furniture	2512 Santa Monica Blvd	Santa Monica	CA	90404	**800-953-2000**	310-264-1046
Walker's Furniture Inc	3808 N Sullivan Rd Bldg 22-C	Spokane Valley	WA	99216	**866-667-6655**	509-535-1995
Warehouse Home Furnishings Distributors Inc	1851 Telfair St PO Box 1140	Dublin	GA	31021	**800-456-0424**	
Wayneco Inc	800 Hanover Rd	York	PA	17408	**800-233-9313**	717-225-4413
Wayside Furniture Inc	1367 Canton Rd	Akron	OH	44312	**877-499-3968**	330-733-6221
WB Mason Company Inc	59 Centre St	Brockton	MA	02303	**888-926-2766**	
Weekends Only Inc	349 Marshall Ave 3rd Fl	Saint Louis	MO	63119	**855-803-5888**	314-447-1500
WG&R Furniture Co	900 Challenger Dr	Green Bay	WI	54311	**888-947-7782**	920-469-4880
Workplace Resource LLC	4400 NE Loop 410 Ste 130	San Antonio	TX	78218	**800-580-3000**	512-472-7300
WS Badcock Corp (WSBC)	PO Box 497	Mulberry	FL	33860	**800-223-2625**	
Yamada Enterprises	16552 Burke Ln	Huntington Beach	CA	92647	**800-444-4594**	

322 GAMES & GAMING

SEE ALSO Toys, Games, Hobbies ; Casino Companies ; Casinos ; Lotteries, Games, Sweepstakes

Company	Address	City	State	Zip	Toll-Free	Phone
American Gaming & Electronics	556 W Taylor Rd	Romeoville	IL	60446	**800-727-6807**	815-886-1447

				Toll-Free	Phone
Amtote International Inc					
11200 Pepper Rd	Hunt Valley	MD	21031	800-345-1566	410-771-8700
Arachnid Inc					
6212 Material Ave	Loves Park	IL	61111	800-435-8319	815-654-0212
Aristocrat Technologies					
7230 Amigo St	Las Vegas	NV	89119	800-748-4156	702-270-1000
Douglas Press Inc					
2810 Madison St	Bellwood	IL	60104	800-323-0705	708-547-8400
Gaming Partners International Inc					
3945 W Cheyenne Ave Ste 208	Las Vegas	NV	89032	800-728-5766	702-384-2425
NASDAQ: GPIC					
Mohegan Gaming & Entertainment (MGE)					
1 Mohegan Sun Blvd	Uncasville	CT	06382	888-777-7922*	888-226-7711
*Resv					
Smart Industries Corp					
1626 Delaware Ave	Des Moines	IA	50317	800-553-2442	515-265-9900
Video King Gaming Systems (VKGS LLC)					
2717 N 118 Cir Ste 210	Omaha	NE	68164	800-635-9912	402-951-2970

323   GARDEN CENTERS

SEE ALSO Horticultural Products Growers ; Seed Companies

				Toll-Free	Phone
Breck's PO Box 65	Guilford	IN	47022	800-644-5505	513-354-1511
Earl May Seed & Nursery					
208 N Elm St	Shenandoah	IA	51603	800-843-9608	712-246-1020
Flowerwood Garden Center Inc					
7625 US Hwy 14	Crystal Lake	IL	60012	800-643-5443	815-459-6200
Greenbrier Farms Inc					
225 Sign Pine Rd	Chesapeake	VA	23322	800-829-2141	757-421-2141
Home Depot Inc					
2455 Paces Ferry Rd NW	Atlanta	GA	30339	800-553-3199*	770-433-8211
NYSE: HD ■ *Cust Svc					
Johnson's Garden Centers					
2707 W 13th St	Wichita	KS	67203	888-542-8463	316-942-1443
JW Jung Seed Co					
335 S High St	Randolph	WI	53956	800-297-3123	920-326-3121
Lowe's Cos Inc					
1000 Lowe's Blvd	Mooresville	NC	28117	800-445-6937	704-758-1000
NYSE: LOW					
McKay Nursery Company Inc					
750 S Monroe St PO Box 185	Waterloo	WI	53594	800-236-4242	920-478-2121
Milaeger's Inc					
4838 Douglas Ave	Racine	WI	53402	800-669-1229	262-639-2040
Panhandle Co-op Assn					
401 S Beltline Hwy W	Scottsbluff	NE	69361	800-732-4546*	308-632-5301
*Cust Svc					
Plants of the Southwest					
3095 Agua Fria Rd	Santa Fe	NM	87507	800-788-7333	505-438-8888
Pleasant View Gardens Inc					
7316 Pleasant St	Loudon	NH	03307	866-862-2974	603-435-8361
Por La Mar Nursery					
905 S Patterson Ave	Santa Barbara	CA	93111	800-733-5286	805-699-4500
Round Butte Seed Growers Inc					
505 C St	Culver	OR	97734	866-385-7001	541-546-5222
Treeland Garden Center & Nursery					
1000 Huntington Tpke	Bridgeport	CT	06610	800-243-0232	203-372-3511
Village Nurseries					
1589 N Main St	Orange	CA	92867	800-542-0209	
Wal-Mart Stores Inc					
702 SW Eighth St	Bentonville	AR	72716	800-925-6278*	479-273-4000
NYSE: WMT ■ *Cust Svc					
Weingartz Supply Co					
46061 Van Dyke Ave	Utica	MI	48317	855-669-7278	586-731-7240
White Flower Farm Inc					
30 Irene St	Torrington	CT	06790	800-411-6159*	860-496-9624
*Cust Svc					

324   GAS STATIONS

SEE ALSO Convenience Stores

				Toll-Free	Phone
Alpena Oil Co Inc					
235 Water St	Alpena	MI	49707	800-968-1098	989-356-1098
AMBEST Inc					
5115 Maryland Way	Brentwood	TN	37027	800-910-7220	615-371-5187
B&t Service Station Contractors					
630 S Frontage Rd	Nipomo	CA	93444	888-862-2552	805-929-8944
Chevron Corp					
6001 Bollinger Canyon Rd	San Ramon	CA	94583	800-368-8357*	925-842-1000
NYSE: CVX ■ *Cust Svc					
Colonial Group Inc					
101 N Lathrop Ave	Savannah	GA	31415	800-944-3835	
Dunlap Oil Company Inc					
759 S Haskell Ave	Willcox	AZ	85643	800-854-1646	520-384-2248
Englefield Oil Co					
447 James Pkwy	Heath	OH	43056	800-837-4458*	740-928-8215
*Cust Svc					
Exxon Mobil Corp					
5959 Las Colinas Blvd	Irving	TX	75039	800-252-1800	972-444-1000
NYSE: XOM					
Forward Corp					
219 N Front St	Standish	MI	48658	800-664-4501	989-846-4501
GasAmerica Services Inc					
2700 W Main St	Greenfield	IN	46140	800-643-1948	866-920-5550
Gate Petroleum Co					
9540 San Jose Blvd PO Box 23627	Jacksonville	FL	32241	866-571-1982	904-737-7220
Houston Food Bank, The					
535 Portwall St	Houston	TX	77029	866-384-4277	713-223-3700
Hunt & Sons Inc					
5750 S Watt Ave	Sacramento	CA	95829	800-734-2999	916-383-4868
Imperial Oil Resources Ltd					
237 Fourth Ave SW PO Box 2480 Stn M	Calgary	AB	T2P3M9	800-567-3776	
Jubitz Corp					
33 NE Middlefield Rd	Portland	OR	97211	800-523-0600	503-283-1111

				Toll-Free	Phone
Monroe Oil Co					
519 E Franklin St	Monroe	NC	28112	800-452-2717*	704-289-5438
*General					
Native Pride 11359 Rt 20	Irving	NY	14081	800-619-8618	716-934-5130
Ney Oil Company Inc					
145 S Water St	Ney	OH	43549	800-962-9839	419-658-2324
O'Connell Oil Assoc Inc					
545 Merrill Rd	Pittsfield	MA	01201	800-464-4894	413-499-4800
Pilot Travel Centers LLC					
5508 Lonas Dr	Knoxville	TN	37939	800-562-6210	865-938-1140
Ports Petroleum Company Inc					
1337 Blachleyville Rd PO Box 1046	Wooster	OH	44691	800-562-0373	330-264-1885
RaceTrac Petroleum Inc					
3225 Cumberland Blvd Ste 100	Atlanta	GA	30339	888-636-5589	770-431-7600
Riiser Energy 709 S 20th Ave	Wausau	WI	54401	800-570-8024	715-845-7272
Rip Griffin Truck Travel Ctr Inc					
4710 Fourth St	Lubbock	TX	79416	800-333-9330	806-795-8785
Sampson-Bladen Oil Co Inc					
510 Commerce St PO Box 469	Clinton	NC	28329	800-849-4177	910-592-4177
Sapp Bros Truck Stops Inc					
9915 S 148th St	Omaha	NE	68138	800-233-4059	402-895-7038
Shirtcliff Oil Co					
PO Box 6003	Myrtle Creek	OR	97457	800-422-0536	541-863-5268
Speedway LLC 500 Speedway Dr	Enon	OH	45323	800-643-1948*	937-864-3000
*Cust Svc					
Spencer Cos Inc					
2600 Memorial Pkwy S	Huntsville	AL	35801	800-633-2910	256-533-1150
Town Pump Inc 600 S Main St	Butte	MT	59701	800-823-4931	406-497-6700
TravelCenters of America					
24601 Ctr Ridge Rd Ste 200	Westlake	OH	44145	800-632-9240	440-808-9100
True North Energy LLC					
5565 Airport Hwy	Toledo	OH	43615	888-245-9336	419-868-6800
UPI Energy LP					
105 Silvercreek Pkwy N Ste 200	Guelph	ON	N1H8M1	800-396-2667	519-821-2667
Van De Pol Enterprises Inc					
4895 S Airport Way	Stockton	CA	95206	800-379-0306	209-465-3421
Vermont Gas Systems Inc					
85 Swift St	South Burlington	VT	05403	800-639-8081	802-863-4511
W & H Co-op Oil Co					
407 13th St N	Humboldt	IA	50548	800-392-3816	515-332-2782
Wallis Companies					
106 E Washington St	Cuba	MO	65453	800-467-6652	573-885-2277

325   GAS TRANSMISSION - NATURAL GAS

Companies that transmit or store natural gas but do not distribute it.

				Toll-Free	Phone
ANR Pipeline Co					
717 Texas St	Houston	TX	77002	800-827-5267	888-427-2875
Boardwalk Pipeline Partners LP					
3800 Frederica St	Owensboro	KY	42301	866-913-2122	270-686-3620
NYSE: BWP					
Enterprise Products Partners LP					
1100 Louisiana St 10th Fl	Houston	TX	77002	866-230-0745	713-381-6500
NYSE: EPD					
Gas Transmission-Northwest					
1400 SW Fifth Ave Ste 900	Portland	OR	97201	888-750-6275	
Iroquois Gas Transmission System LP					
1 Corporate Dr Ste 600	Shelton	CT	06484	800-888-3982	203-925-7200
Kern River Gas Transmission Co					
2755 E Cottonwood Pkwy Ste 300	Salt Lake City	UT	84121	800-420-7500	801-937-6000
Kinder Morgan					
1001 Louisiana St Ste 1000	Houston	TX	77002	800-247-4122	713-369-9000
NYSE: KMI					
Northern Natural Gas Co					
1111 S 103rd St	Omaha	NE	68124	877-654-0646	402-398-7000
Spark Energy Gas LP					
2105 Citywest Blvd	Houston	TX	77042	877-547-7275	
TransCanada Pipelines Ltd					
450 First St SW	Calgary	AB	T2P5H1	800-661-3805	403-920-2000
Tri-Gas & Oil Company Inc					
3941 Federalsburg Hwy PO Box 465	Federalsburg	MD	21632	800-638-7802	410-754-8184
WBI Energy					
1250 W Century Ave	Bismarck	ND	58503	877-924-4677	701-530-1095
WBI Holdings Inc					
1250 W Century Ave	Bismarck	ND	58503	877-924-4677*	
*General					
Williams Partners LP					
1 Williams Ctr	Tulsa	OK	74172	800-600-3782	918-573-2000
NYSE: WPZ					

326   GASKETS, PACKING, SEALING DEVICES

SEE ALSO Automotive Parts & Supplies - Mfr

				Toll-Free	Phone
American Casting & Manufacturing Corp					
51 Commercial St	Plainview	NY	11803	800-342-0333	516-349-7010
American Packing & Gasket Co (APG)					
6039 Armour Dr PO Box 213	Houston	TX	77020	800-888-5223	713-675-5271
APM Hexseal Corp					
44 Honeck St	Englewood	NJ	07631	800-498-9034	201-569-5700
Apple Rubber Products Inc					
310 Erie St	Lancaster	NY	14086	800-828-7745*	716-684-6560
*Cust Svc					
Atlantic Gasket Corp					
3908 Frankford Ave	Philadelphia	PA	19124	800-229-8881	215-533-6400
Auburn Manufacturing Co					
29 Stack Rd	Middletown	CT	06457	800-427-5387	860-346-6677
Bal Seal Engineering Company Inc					
19650 Pauling	Foothill Ranch	CA	92610	800-366-1006	949-460-2100
California Gasket & Rubber Corp					
533 W Collins Ave	Orange	CA	92867	800-635-7084	714-202-8500
Calpico Inc					
1387 San Mateo Ave	South San Francisco	CA	94080	800-998-9115	650-588-2241

				Toll-Free	Phone

CGR Products Inc
4655 US Hwy 29 N . . . . .Greensboro NC 27405 **877-313-6785** 336-621-4568
Chicago Gasket Co
1285 W N Ave . . . . .Chicago IL 60642 **800-833-5666** 773-486-3060
Chicago Wilcox Mfg Co Inc
16928 State St . . . . South Holland IL 60473 **800-323-5282** 708-339-5000
Cometic Gasket Inc
8090 Auburn Rd . . . . .Concord OH 44077 **800-752-9850** 440-354-0777
Corpus Christi Gasket & Fastener Inc
PO Box 4074 . . . . Corpus Christi TX 78469 **800-460-6366** 361-884-6366
Ct Gasket & Polymer Company Inc
12308 Cutten Rd . . . . .Houston TX 77066 **800-299-1685**
Flow Dry Technology Inc
379 Albert Rd PO Box 190 . . . . .Brookville OH 45309 **800-533-0077** 937-833-2161
Flowserve Corp
5215 N O'Connor Blvd Ste 2300. . . . . .Irving TX 75039 **800-543-3927** 972-443-6500
NYSE: FLS
Gasket Manufacturing Co
18001 Main St . . . . .Gardena CA 90248 **800-442-7538** 310-217-5600
Gaskets Inc 301 W Hwy 16 . . . . .Rio WI 53960 **800-558-1833** 920-992-3137
Houston Mfg Specialty Company Inc
9909 Wallisville Rd . . . . .Houston TX 77013 **800-231-6030** 713-675-7400
IG Inc 720 S Sara Rd . . . . .Mustang OK 73064 **800-654-8433** 405-376-9393
Ilene Industries Inc
301 Stanley Blvd . . . . .Shelbyville TN 37160 **800-251-1602** 931-684-8731
Industrial Custom Products Inc
2801 37th Ave NE . . . . Minneapolis MN 55421 **800-654-0886** 612-781-2255
Industrial Gasket & Shim Company Inc (IGS)
200 Country Club Rd . . . . .Meadow Lands PA 15347 **800-229-1447** 724-222-5800
Intek Plastic Inc
1000 Spiral Blvd .Hastings MN 55033 **888-468-3531**
Interface Solutions Inc
216 Wohlsen Way . . . . Lancaster PA 17603 **800-942-7538**
Jade Engineered Plastic Inc
121 Broadcommon Rd . . . . .Bristol RI 02809 **800-557-9155** 401-253-4440
Lamons Gasket Co
7300 Airport Blvd .Houston TX 77061 **800-231-6906** 713-222-0284
Marco Rubber
35 Woodworkers Way . . . . .Seabrook NH 03874 **800-775-6525** 603-468-3600
Netherland Rubber Co
2931 Exon Ave .Cincinnati OH 45241 **800-582-1877**
Novagard Solutions Inc
5109 Hamilton Ave . . . . .Cleveland OH 44114 **800-380-0138** 216-881-8111
Ohio Gasket & Shim Company Inc
976 Evans Ave . . . . .Akron OH 44305 **800-321-2438**
Omega Shielding Products Inc
1384 Pompton Ave . . . . .Cedar Grove NJ 07009 **800-828-5784** 973-366-0080
Pacific States Felt & Mfg Company Inc
23850 Clawiter Rd . . . . .Hayward CA 94545 **800-566-8866** 510-783-0277
Pemko Mfg Company Inc
4226 Transport St .Ventura CA 93003 **800-283-9988** 805-642-2600
PPC Mechanical Seals
2769 Mission Dr . . . . .Baton Rouge LA 70805 **800-731-7325** 225-356-4333
Press-Seal Gasket Corp
2424 W State Blvd . . . . Fort Wayne IN 46808 **800-348-7325** 260-436-0521
Presscut Industries Inc
1730 Briercroft Ct . . . . .Carrollton TX 75006 **800-442-4924** 972-389-0615
Rotor Clip Company Inc
187 Davidson Ave . . . . .Somerset NJ 08873 **800-557-6867*** 732-469-7333
*Cust Svc
Schlegel Systems Inc
1555 Jefferson Rd . . . . .Rochester NY 14623 **888-924-7694** 585-427-7200
Seal Methods Inc
11915 Shoemaker Ave . . . . .Santa Fe Springs CA 90670 **800-423-4777** 562-944-0291
Sealing Devices Inc
4400 Walden Ave . . . . .Lancaster NY 14086 **800-727-3257*** 716-684-7600
*Cust Svc
Sealing Equipment Products Co Inc
123 Airpark Industrial Rd . . . . .Alabaster AL 35007 **800-633-4770**
Sorbothane Inc
2144 State Rt 59 . . . . .Kent OH 44240 **800-838-3906** 330-678-9444
Southern Rubber Company Inc
2209 Patterson St . . . . .Greensboro NC 27407 **800-333-7325** 336-299-2456
Specification Rubber Products Inc
1568 First St N . . . . .Alabaster AL 35007 **800-633-3415** 205-663-2521
Stic-adhesive Products Company Inc
3950 Medford St . . . . .Los Angeles CA 90063 **800-854-6813** 323-268-2956
T & E Industries Inc
215 Watchung Ave . . . . .Orange NJ 07050 **800-245-7080*** 973-672-5454
*Sales
Thermoseal 2350 Campbell Rd . . . . .Sidney OH 45365 **800-990-7325** 937-498-2222
UTEX Industries Inc
10810 Katy Fwy Ste 100. . . . . .Houston TX 77043 **800-359-9230** 713-467-1000
Vellumoid Inc
54 Rockdale St . . . . .Worcester MA 01606 **800-609-5558** 508-853-2500
William H Harvey
4334 S 67th St . . . . .Omaha NE 68117 **800-321-9532** 402-331-1175
Zero International Inc
415 Concord Ave . . . . .Bronx NY 10455 **800-635-5335** 718-585-3230

327 **GIFT SHOPS**

SEE ALSO Home Furnishings Stores ; Card Shops ; Duty-Free Shops

				Toll-Free	Phone

Atlantic Center For The Arts Inc
1414 Art Ctr Ave . . . . .New Smyrna Beach FL 32168 **800-393-6975** 386-427-6975
Brookstone Inc
1 Innovation Way . . . . .Merrimack NH 03054 **800-846-3000***
*Cust Svc
CM Paula Co 6049 Hi-Tek Ct . . . . .Mason OH 45040 **800-543-4464**
Disney Consumer Products
500 S Buena Vista St . . . . .Burbank CA 91521 **855-553-4763*** 818-560-1000
*PR
GiftCertificatescom
11510 Blondo St . . . . .Omaha NE 68164 **800-773-7368** 402-445-2300
Historical Research Ctr Inc
2107 Corporate Dr . . . . .Boynton Beach FL 33426 **800-985-9956**

Mole Hollow Candles Ltd
208 Charlton Rd Rt 20 PO Box 223 . . . . .Sturbridge MA 01566 **800-445-6653***
*Cust Svc
Olympia Promotions & Distribution
226 E Jericho Tpke . . . . .Mineola NY 11501 **800-846-7874** 516-775-4500
San Francisco Music Box Co
5370 W 95th St . . . . .Prairie Village KS 66207 **800-227-2190**
Silver Towne LP
120 E Union City Pk PO Box 424 . . . . .Winchester IN 47394 **800-788-7481** 765-584-7481
Tuesday Morning Corp
6250 LBJ Fwy . . . . .Dallas TX 75240 **800-457-0099** 972-387-3562
NASDAQ: TUES
Wendell August Forge Inc
2074 Leesburg-Grove City Rd . . . . .Mercer PA 16137 **866-354-5192** 724-748-9501
Yankee Candle Company Inc
PO Box 110 . . . . .South Deerfield MA 01373 **877-803-6890** 413-665-8306

328 **GIFTS & NOVELTIES - WHOL**

				Toll-Free	Phone

Archie Mcphee
10915 47th Ave W . . . . .Mukilteo WA 98275 **800-886-2221** 425-349-3838
Blair Cedar & Novelty Works Inc
680 W US Hwy 54 . . . . .Camdenton MO 65020 **800-325-3943** 573-346-2235
Drysdales Inc
3220 S Memorial Dr . . . . .Tulsa OK 74145 **800-444-6481** 918-664-6481
Fridgedoorcom 21 Dixwell Ave . . . . .Quincy MA 02169 **800-955-3741** 617-770-7913
Hayes Specialties Corp
1761 E Genesee .Saginaw MI 48601 **800-248-3603** 989-755-6541
Hornung's Golf Products Inc
815 Morris St . . . . .Fond du Lac WI 54935 **800-323-3569** 920-922-2640
Trends International LLC
5188 W 74th St . . . . .Indianapolis IN 46268 **866-406-7771** 317-388-1212
Unique Industries Inc
4750 League Island Blvd . . . . .Philadelphia PA 19112 **800-888-0559** 215-336-4300
Variety Distributors Inc
609 Seventh St . . . . .Harlan IA 51537 **800-274-1095** 712-755-2184
WinCraft Inc
960 E Mark St PO Box 888 . . . . .Winona MN 55987 **800-533-8006** 507-454-5510

329 **GLASS - FLAT, PLATE, TEMPERED**

				Toll-Free	Phone

Anthony International
12391 Montera Ave .Sylmar CA 91342 **800-772-0900** 818-365-9451
Apogee Enterprises Inc
4400 W 78th St Ste 520 . . . . .Minneapolis MN 55435 **877-752-3432** 952-835-1874
NASDAQ: APOG
Basco Shower Enclosures
7201 Snider Rd . . . . .Mason OH 45040 **800-543-1938** 513-573-1900
Binswanger Glass
965 Ridge Lake Blvd Ste 305 . . . . .Memphis TN 38120 **800-365-9922**
Bullseye Glass Co
3722 SE 21st Ave . . . . .Portland OR 97202 **888-220-3002** 503-232-8887
D & W Inc 941 Oak St . . . . .Elkhart IN 46514 **800-255-0829** 574-264-9674
Glassfab Tempering Services Inc
1448 Mariani Ct . . . . .Tracy CA 95376 **800-535-2133** 209-229-1060
Glaz-Tech Industries Inc
2207 E Elvira Rd .Tucson AZ 85756 **800-755-8062** 520-629-0268
Gray Glass Co
217-44 98th Ave . . . . .Queens Village NY 11429 **800-523-3320** 718-217-2943
Guardian Industries Corp
2300 Harmon Rd . . . . .Auburn Hills MI 48326 **800-822-5599** 248-340-1800
Hartung Glass Industries
17830 W Valley Hwy . . . . .Tukwila WA 98188 **800-552-2227**
Hartung Glass Industries
10450 SW Ridder Rd . . . . .Wilsonville OR 97070 **800-552-2227** 503-682-3846
Kokomo Opalescent Glass Co
1310 S Market St .Kokomo IN 46902 **877-475-6329** 765-457-8136
Northwestern Industries Inc
2500 W Jameson St . . . . .Seattle WA 98199 **800-426-2771** 206-285-3140
ODL Inc 215 E Roosevelt Ave . . . . .Zeeland MI 49464 **800-253-3900** 616-772-9111
Oldcastle BuildingEnvelope
5005 Lyndon B Johnson Fwy Ste 1050. . . . . .Dallas TX 75244 **866-653-2278**
Prelco Inc
94 Blvd Cartier . . . . .Rivišre-du-Loup QC G5R2M9 **800-463-1325** 418-862-2274
Spectrum Glass Co
PO Box 646 . . . . .Woodinville WA 98072 **800-426-3120** 425-483-6699
Thermoseal Glass Corp
400 Water St . . . . .Gloucester City NJ 08030 **800-456-7788** 856-456-3109
Tru Vue 9400 W 55th St . . . . .McCook IL 60525 **800-621-8339** 708-485-5080
Viracon Inc 800 Pk Dr . . . . .Owatonna MN 55060 **800-533-2080** 507-451-9555
Virginia Mirror Co Inc
300 Moss St S .Martinsville VA 24112 **800-368-3011** 276-632-9816
Wasco Products Inc
85 Spencer Dr Unit A PO Box 559 . . . . .Wells ME 04090 **800-388-0293**

330 **GLASS FIBERS**

				Toll-Free	Phone

Capitol Aluminum & Glass Corp
1276 W Main St . . . . .Bellevue OH 44811 **800-331-8268**
Fiberoptics Technology Inc
1 Quassett Rd . . . . .Pomfret CT 06258 **800-433-5248*** 860-928-0443
*Cust Svc
Gordon Glass Co
5116 Warrensville Center Rd . . . . .Maple Heights OH 44137 **888-663-9830**
Mesko Glass & Mirror Company Inc
801 Wyoming Ave . . . . .Scranton PA 18509 **800-982-4055** 570-346-0777
Moderne Glass Company Inc
1000 Industrial Blvd . . . . .Aliquippa PA 15001 **800-645-5131** 724-857-5700
Novatech Group Inc
1401 Nobel St .Sainte-julie QC J3E1Z4 **844-986-8001**

Classified Section

				Toll-Free	Phone
Sentinel Process Systems					
3265 Sunset Ln	Hatboro	PA	19040	**800-345-3569**	
Shaw Glass Company Inc					
55 Bristol Dr	South Easton	MA	02375	**800-225-0430**	

331   GLASS PRODUCTS - INDUSTRIAL (CUSTOM)

				Toll-Free	Phone
Abrisa Technologies					
200 S Hallock Dr	Santa Paula	CA	93060	**877-622-7472**	
Fredericks Co, The					
2400 Philmont Ave	Huntingdon Valley	PA	19006	**800-367-2919**	215-947-2500
Henderson Glass Inc					
715 S Blvd E	Rochester Hills	MI	48307	**800-694-0672**	
Lenoir Mirror Company Inc					
401 Kincaid St	Lenoir	NC	28645	**800-438-8204**	828-728-3271
North American Specialty Glass					
2175 Kumry Rd PO Box 70	Trumbauersville	PA	18970	**888-785-5962**	215-536-0333
Precision Electronic Glass Inc					
1013 Hendee Rd	Vineland	NJ	08360	**800-982-4734**	856-691-2234
Swift Glass Company Inc					
131 W 22nd St	Elmira Heights	NY	14903	**800-537-9438**	607-733-7166

332   GLASSWARE - LABORATORY & SCIENTIFIC

				Toll-Free	Phone
Ace Glass Inc					
1430 NW Blvd PO Box 688	Vineland	NJ	08360	**800-223-4524**	856-692-3333
Bellco Glass Inc					
340 Edrudo Rd	Vineland	NJ	08360	**800-257-7043**	856-691-1075
Eden Labs LLC					
309 S Cloverdale St	Seattle	WA	98108	**888-626-3271**	
Industrial Container & Supply Company Inc					
1845 South 5200 West	Salt Lake City	UT	84104	**800-748-4250**	801-972-1561
Quadrex Corp PO Box 3881	Woodbridge	CT	06525	**800-275-7033***	203-393-3112
*Sales					
Wale Apparatus Co Inc					
400 Front St	Hellertown	PA	18055	**800-334-9253**	610-838-7047
WB Bottle Supply Company Inc					
3400 S Clement Ave	Milwaukee	WI	53207	**800-738-3931**	414-482-4300

333   GLASSWARE & POTTERY - HOUSEHOLD

SEE ALSO Table & Kitchen Supplies - China & Earthenware

				Toll-Free	Phone
Anchor Hocking Co					
519 Pierce Ave	Lancaster	OH	43130	**800-562-7511**	740-681-6900
Berney-Karp Inc					
3350 E 26th St	Vernon	CA	90058	**800-237-6395**	323-260-7122
Blenko Glass Co PO Box 67	Milton	WV	25541	**877-425-3656**	304-743-9081
Ceramo Company Inc					
681 Kasten Dr	Jackson	MO	63755	**800-325-8303**	573-243-3138
Enesco LLC 225 Windsor Dr	Itasca	IL	60143	**800-436-3726**	630-875-5300
Fenton Art Glass Co					
700 Elizabeth St	Williamstown	WV	26187	**800-933-6766***	304-375-6122
*Cust Svc					
Friedman Bros Decorative Arts					
9015 NW 105th Way	Medley	FL	33178	**800-327-1065**	305-887-3170
Gardner Glass Products Inc					
301 Elkin Hwy PO Box 1570	North Wilkesboro	NC	28659	**800-334-7267**	
Haggerty Enterprises Inc					
370 Kimberly Dr	Carol Stream	IL	60188	**800-336-5282**	630-315-3300
Libbey Inc					
300 Madison Ave PO Box 10060	Toledo	OH	43699	**888-794-8469**	419-325-2100
NYSE: LBY					
Pfaltzgraff Co PO Box 21769	York	PA	17402	**800-999-2811**	
Swarovski North America Ltd					
1 Kenney Dr	Cranston	RI	02920	**800-289-4900**	401-463-6400
Tricorbraun Winepak					
2280 Cordelia Rd	Fairfield	CA	94534	**800-374-6594**	
Waterford Wedgwood USA Inc					
1330 Campus Pkwy	Wall	NJ	07753	**877-720-3486**	

334   GLOBAL DISTRIBUTION SYSTEMS (GDSS)

A global distribution system (GDS) is a computer reservations system that includes reservations databases of air travel suppliers in many countries. GDSs typically are owned jointly by airlines operating in different countries.

				Toll-Free	Phone
Amadeus North America Inc					
3470 NW 82nd Ave Ste 1000	Miami	FL	33122	**888-262-3387**	305-499-6000
Pegasus Solutions Co					
14000 N Pima Rd Ste 200	Scottsdale	AZ	85260	**800-843-4343**	480-624-6000

335   GOURMET SPECIALTY SHOPS

				Toll-Free	Phone
Graber Olive House Inc					
315 E Fourth St	Ontario	CA	91764	**800-996-5483**	
Harry & David Holdings Inc					
2500 S Pacific Hwy	Medford	OR	97501	**877-322-1200***	
*Cust Svc					
Hickory Farms Inc					
811 Madison Ave	Toledo	OH	43604	**800-753-8558**	
M&M Meat Shops Ltd					
2240 Argentia Rd Ste 100	Mississauga	ON	L5N2K7	**800-461-0171**	905-465-6325

336   GOVERNMENT - CITY

				Toll-Free	Phone
Alexandria City Hall					
301 King St	Alexandria	VA	22314	**800-543-8911**	703-838-4000
Atlanta City Hall					
55 Trinity Ave SW	Atlanta	GA	30303	**800-897-1910**	404-330-6004
Aurora City Hall					
15151 E Alameda Pkwy	Aurora	CO	80012	**800-895-4999**	303-739-7000
Bar Harbor Town Hall					
93 Cottage St	Bar Harbor	ME	04609	**800-232-4733**	207-288-4098
Boise City Hall					
150 N Capitol Blvd	Boise	ID	83702	**800-377-3529**	208-384-4422
Bridgeport City Hall					
999 Broad St	Bridgeport	CT	06604	**800-978-2828**	203-576-7201
Buffalo City Hall					
65 Niagara Sq	Buffalo	NY	14202	**800-541-2437**	716-851-4200
Charlotte City Hall					
Charlotte-Mecklenburg Government Ctr					
600 E 4th St	Charlotte	NC	28202	**800-418-2065**	704-336-2241
Chattanooga City Hall					
101 E 11th St Rm 100	Chattanooga	TN	37402	**866-894-5026**	423-643-6311
Cheyenne City Hall					
2101 O'Neil Ave	Cheyenne	WY	82001	**855-491-1859**	307-637-6200
Chicago City Hall					
121 N La Salle St	Chicago	IL	60602	**800-832-6352**	312-744-4958
City of Portland, Oregon					
1221 SW Fourth Ave Rm 110	Portland	OR	97204	**800-729-8807**	503-823-4000
Cleveland City Hall					
601 Lakeside Ave	Cleveland	OH	44114	**800-589-3101**	216-664-2000
Fremont City Hall					
PO Box 5006	Fremont	CA	94537	**800-462-3271**	510-284-4000
Gettysburg Borough Hall					
59 E High St	Gettysburg	PA	17325	**800-433-7317**	717-334-1160
Glendale (AZ) City Hall					
5850 W Glendale Ave	Glendale	AZ	85301	**800-367-8939**	623-930-2000
Grand Rapids City Hall					
300 Monroe Ave NW	Grand Rapids	MI	49503	**800-860-8610**	616-456-3010
Greenville City Hall					
206 S Main St	Greenville	SC	29601	**800-829-4477**	864-232-2273
Gulfport City Hall					
2309 15th St	Gulfport	MS	39501	**800-901-7072**	228-868-5700
Kansas City (KS) City Hall					
701 N Seventh St	Kansas City	KS	66101	**800-432-2484**	913-573-5000
Key West City Hall					
3132 Flagler Ave	Key West	FL	33040	**800-955-8770**	305-809-3700
Mesa City Hall PO Box 1466	Mesa	AZ	85211	**866-406-9659**	480-644-2221
Minneapolis City Hall					
350 S Fifth St	Minneapolis	MN	55415	**800-766-3777**	612-673-2244
Mobile City Hall					
205 Government St	Mobile	AL	36602	**800-957-3676**	251-208-7411
New Orleans City Hall					
1300 Perdido St	New Orleans	LA	70112	**800-256-2748**	504-658-4000
Oakland City Hall					
1 Frank H Ogawa Plz	Oakland	CA	94612	**800-834-3773**	510-615-5566
Ocean City City Hall					
301 Baltimore Ave	Ocean City	MD	21842	**800-626-2326**	410-289-8931
Olympia City Hall					
PO Box 1967	Olympia	WA	98507	**800-451-7985**	360-753-8447
Ottawa City Hall					
110 Laurier Ave W	Ottawa	ON	K1P1J1	**866-261-9799**	613-580-2400
Pittsburgh City Hall					
414 Grant St City-County Bldg	Pittsburgh	PA	15219	**800-932-0313**	412-255-2883
Plano City Hall 1520 K Ave	Plano	TX	75074	**800-832-5452**	972-941-7000
Rochester Mayor's					
201 Fourth St SE	Rochester	MN	55904	**800-657-3858**	507-328-2700
Saint Paul City Hall					
15 W Kellogg Blvd	Saint Paul	MN	55102	**800-895-1999**	651-266-8989
San Diego City Hall					
202 C St	San Diego	CA	92101	**866-470-1308**	619-533-4000
Stamford City Hall					
888 Washington Blvd 10th Fl	Stamford	CT	06901	**800-864-2742**	203-977-4150
Trenton City Hall					
319 E State St	Trenton	NJ	08608	**800-221-0051**	609-989-3000
Tulsa City Hall					
175 E Second St Ste 690	Tulsa	OK	74103	**800-522-6543**	918-596-2100

337   GOVERNMENT - COUNTY

				Toll-Free	Phone
Adams County					
110 W Main St	West Union	OH	45693	**800-840-5711**	937-544-2011
Aiken County					
420 Hampton Ave NE	Aiken	SC	29801	**866-876-7074**	803-642-2012
Alameda County					
1221 Oak St Ste 555	Oakland	CA	94612	**800-878-1313**	510-272-6984
Aleutians East Borough					
3380 C St Ste 205	Anchorage	AK	99503	**888-383-2699**	907-274-7555
Allamakee County					
110 Allamakee St	Waukon	IA	52172	**800-728-0131**	563-864-7454
Allen County 1 N Washington St	Iola	KS	66749	**866-444-1407**	620-365-1407
Allen Parish 8904 Hwy 165	Oberlin	LA	70655	**888-639-4868**	337-639-4868
Alpena County					
720 W Chisholm St	Alpena	MI	49707	**800-999-4487**	989-354-9500
Amador County 810 Ct St	Jackson	CA	95642	**800-775-9772**	209-223-6470
Anderson County					
PO Box 8002	Anderson	SC	29622	**800-447-5375**	864-260-4000
Arenac County PO Box 747	Standish	MI	48658	**800-232-5216**	989-846-4626
Armstrong County					
450 E Market St	Kittanning	PA	16201	**800-368-1066**	724-543-2500
Ashe County Chamber of Commerce					
1 N Jefferson Ave Ste C					
PO Box 31	West Jefferson	NC	28694	**888-343-2743**	336-846-9550

				Toll-Free	Phone
Atchison County 405 S Main St PO Box 243	Rock Port	MO	64482	**800-989-4115**	660-744-6562
Baldwin County 322 Courthouse Sq	Bay Minette	AL	36507	**800-403-4872**	251-937-9561
Baltimore County 401 Bosley Ave	Towson	MD	21204	**800-332-6347**	410-887-2139
Barnes County 230 Fourth St NW Rm 202	Valley City	ND	58072	**800-352-0867**	701-845-8500
Barry County 220 W State St	Hastings	MI	49058	**888-876-0993**	269-945-1290
Bartow County 135 W Cherokee Ave	Cartersville	GA	30120	**800-715-4225**	770-387-5030
Bath County PO Box 309	Warm Springs	VA	24484	**888-823-1710**	540-839-7221
Bay County 515 Center Ave	Bay City	MI	48708	**877-229-9960**	989-895-4280
Bayfield County PO Box 878	Washburn	WI	54891	**800-447-4094**	715-373-6100
Baylor County 301 N Washington	Seymour	TX	76380	**800-633-0852**	940-889-3148
Bell County 101 E Central Ave PO Box 768	Belton	TX	76513	**800-460-2355**	254-939-3521
Benewah County 701 College Ave	Saint Maries	ID	83861	**800-983-0937**	208-245-3212
Benzie County 448 Ct Pl	Beulah	MI	49617	**800-315-3593**	231-882-9671
Big Horn County 420 W C St	Basin	WY	82410	**800-500-2324**	307-568-2357
Blaine County 145 Lincoln Ave	Brewster	NE	68821	**800-657-2113**	308-547-2222
Blaine County 420 Ohio St	Chinook	MT	59523	**800-666-6124**	406-442-9830
Bland County 612 Main St Ste 104	Bland	VA	24315	**800-519-3468**	276-688-4622
Boone County 222 S Fourth St	Albion	NE	68620	**800-330-0755**	402-395-2055
Boone County 801 E Walnut St Rm 333	Columbia	MO	65201	**800-552-7583**	573-886-4270
Box Elder County 1 S Main St	Brigham City	UT	84302	**877-390-2326**	435-734-3300
Bradley County 101 E Cedar St	Warren	AR	71671	**877-531-3282**	
Brown County 305 E Walnut PO Box 23600	Green Bay	WI	54301	**800-362-9082**	920-448-4016
Brunswick County 30 Government Center Dr NE	Bolivia	NC	28422	**800-442-7033**	910-253-2657
Buckingham County 13360 W James Anderson Hwy	Buckingham	VA	23921	**800-440-6116**	434-969-4242
Bucks County 55 E Ct St	Doylestown	PA	18901	**888-942-8257**	215-348-6000
Burleigh County 514 E Thayer Ave PO Box 1055	Bismarck	ND	58502	**877-222-6682**	701-222-6690
Burnett County 7410 County Rd K	Siren	WI	54872	**800-788-3164**	715-349-2181
Butler County 205 W Central Ave	El Dorado	KS	67042	**800-822-6104**	316-322-4300
Butler County 315 High St	Hamilton	OH	45011	**800-582-4267**	513-887-3278
Calvert County 175 Main St	Prince Frederick	MD	20678	**800-492-7122**	410-535-1600
Camden County 520 Market St Ste 306	Camden	NJ	08102	**866-226-3362**	856-225-5300
Cameron Parish Police Jury 148 Smith Cir PO Box 1280	Cameron	LA	70631	**844-503-7283**	337-775-5718
Campbell County 1635 Reata Dr	Gillette	WY	82718	**800-457-9312**	307-682-0552
Cape May County 7 N Main St PO Box 5000	Cape May Court House	NJ	08210	**800-621-5388**	609-465-1010
Carbon County 2 Hazard Sq PO Box 129	Jim Thorpe	PA	18229	**800-441-1315**	570-325-3611
Carbon County PO Box 1017	Rawlins	WY	82301	**800-228-3547**	
Caribou County 159 S Main	Soda Springs	ID	83276	**800-972-7660**	208-547-4324
Carroll County 114 E Main St Ste C PO Box 175	Delphi	IN	46923	**866-374-6813**	765-564-6757
Carroll County 8215 Black Oak Rd	Mount Carroll	IL	61053	**800-485-0145**	815-244-2035
Carroll County Sheriff's Office 95 Water Village Rd PO Box 190	Ossipee	NH	03864	**800-552-8960**	603-539-2284
Carter County 101 First Ave SW	Ardmore	OK	73401	**800-231-8668**	580-223-8162
Cass County 346 Main St	Plattsmouth	NE	68048	**855-658-5736**	402-296-1028
Cayuga County 160 Genesee St 1st Fl	Auburn	NY	13021	**800-771-7755**	315-253-1271
Cedar County 400 Cedar St	Tipton	IA	52772	**800-735-3942**	563-886-2101
Charleston County 4045 Bridge View Dr	North Charleston	SC	29405	**800-735-2905**	843-958-4030
Charlevoix County 203 Antrim St	Charlevoix	MI	49720	**800-548-9157**	231-547-7200
Charlton County 68 Kingsland Ste B	Folkston	GA	31537	**800-436-7442**	
Chattooga County PO Box 211	Summerville	GA	30747	**800-436-7442**	
Chautauqua County 3 N Erie St	Mayville	NY	14757	**800-252-8748**	716-753-4211
Chester County 313 W Market St Ste 6202 PO Box 2748	West Chester	PA	19380	**800-692-1100**	610-344-6100
Chisago County 313 N Main St	Center City	MN	55012	**888-234-1246**	651-257-1300
Clallam County 223 E Fourth St	Port Angeles	WA	98362	**800-424-5555**	360-417-2318
Clay County PO Box 519	Fort Gaines	GA	39851	**800-436-7442**	
Clinton County 1900 N Third St PO Box 2957	Clinton	IA	52733	**866-227-9040**	563-243-6210
Cloud County Community college 2221 Campus Dr	Concordia	KS	66901	**800-729-5101**	
Coconino County 219 E Cherry Ave	Flagstaff	AZ	86001	**800-559-9289**	928-774-5011
Coffee County 101 S Peterson Ave Ste A-15	Douglas	GA	31533	**800-436-7442**	912-384-4895
Collin County 2300 Bloomdale Rd Ste 2106	McKinney	TX	75071	**800-974-2437**	972-548-4185
Columbia County 135 NE Hernando Ave # 203	Lake City	FL	32055	**800-342-8170**	386-755-4100
Columbus County PO Box 1587	Whiteville	NC	28472	**800-553-9759**	910-641-3000
Comal County 199 Main Plz	New Braunfels	TX	78130	**877-724-9475**	830-221-1100
Converse County 107 North Fifth St	Douglas	WY	82633	**800-460-5657**	307-358-2244
Coos County 250 N Baxter St	Coquille	OR	97423	**800-452-6010**	541-396-3121
Cottonwood County 900 Third Ave	Windom	MN	56101	**800-967-1763**	507-831-1905
County of Greene 93 E High St	Waynesburg	PA	15370	**888-852-5399**	724-852-5210
Cowley County 311 E Ninth Ave	Winfield	KS	67156	**800-876-3469**	620-221-5400
Craven County 406 Craven St	New Bern	NC	28560	**800-437-5767**	252-636-6600
Crawford County 903 Diamond Sq	Meadville	PA	16335	**800-585-3737**	814-333-7465
Crawford County 225 N Beaumont Rd	Prairie du Chien	WI	53821	**877-794-2372**	608-326-0200
Crawford County 302 Main St PO Box AS	Steelville	MO	65565	**866-566-8267**	573-775-2376
Crook County 300 NE Third St Crook County Courthouse Rm 23	Prineville	OR	97754	**800-735-2900**	541-447-6553
Crow Wing County 326 Laurel St	Brainerd	MN	56401	**888-829-6680**	218-824-1067
Daggett County 95 N First W	Manila	UT	84046	**800-764-0844**	435-784-3154
Dauphin County 2 S Second St 3rd Fl	Harrisburg	PA	17101	**800-328-0058**	717-780-6130
Decatur County 22 W Main St PO Box 488	Decaturville	TN	38329	**800-525-6834**	731-852-2131
Decatur County 150 Courthouse Sq Ste 244	Greensburg	IN	47240	**800-622-4941**	812-663-8223
Defiance County 500 Ct St	Defiance	OH	43512	**800-675-3953**	419-782-4761
Delaware County 101 N Sandusky St	Delaware	OH	43015	**800-277-2177**	740-833-2100
Delaware County 301 E Main St	Manchester	IA	52057	**800-839-5005**	
Denton County 1450 E McKinney	Denton	TX	76209	**800-388-8477**	940-349-2012
Deuel County 408 Fourth St W	Clear Lake	SD	57226	**800-872-6190**	605-874-2312
Dodge County 435 N Pk	Fremont	NE	68025	**800-331-5666**	402-727-2767
Dona Ana County 845 N Motel Blvd	Las Cruces	NM	88007	**800-477-3632**	575-647-7200
Doniphan County PO Box 278	Troy	KS	66087	**800-232-0170**	785-985-3513
Donley County 300 S Sully St 2nd Fl-Courthouse PO Box 909	Clarendon	TX	79226	**800-388-8075**	806-874-3625
Dorchester County Council 501 Court Ln	Cambridge	MD	21613	**800-272-9829**	410-228-1700
Dubuque County 720 Central Ave	Dubuque	IA	52001	**800-637-0128**	563-589-4432
Dukes County PO Box 190	Edgartown	MA	02539	**800-244-4630**	508-696-3840
Duplin County 112 Duplin St	Kenansville	NC	28349	**800-685-8916**	910-296-2150
Eagle County 500 Broadway - PO Box 850	Eagle	CO	81631	**800-225-6136**	970-328-8600
Early County PO Box 693	Blakely	GA	39823	**800-436-7442**	
Edmonson County PO Box 830	Brownsville	KY	42210	**800-368-8683**	270-597-2624
Edwards County 721 Marsh Ave PO Box 161	Kinsley	KS	67547	**877-464-3929**	620-659-2711
Effingham County 601 N Laurel St	Springfield	GA	31329	**800-338-6745**	912-754-2123
Elk County PO Box 606	Howard	KS	67349	**877-504-2490**	620-374-2490
Emmet County 200 Div St Ste 130	Petoskey	MI	49770	**866-731-1204**	231-348-1702
Esmeralda County PO Box 547	Goldfield	NV	89013	**800-884-4072**	775-485-6309
Essex County 305 Prince St	Tappahannock	VA	22560	**800-552-9745**	804-443-4611
Fairbanks North Star Borough 809 Pioneer Rd	Fairbanks	AK	99701	**800-331-6158**	907-459-1000
Fairfield County 210 E Main St	Lancaster	OH	43130	**800-450-8845**	740-652-7075
Florence County 180 N Irby St	Florence	SC	29501	**800-523-3577**	843-665-3035
Fluvanna County 132 Main St	Palmyra	VA	22963	**800-814-5339**	434-591-1910
Fountain County 301 Fourth St	Covington	IN	47932	**800-800-5556**	765-793-2411
Franklin County 355 W Main St	Malone	NY	12953	**800-397-8686**	518-481-1681
Franklin County 1016 N Fourth Ave	Pasco	WA	99301	**800-647-7706**	509-545-3535
Fremont County 450 N Second St	Lander	WY	82520	**800-967-2297**	307-332-2405
Fulton County 122 W Market St Ste 202	McConnellsburg	PA	17233	**800-328-0058**	717-485-6862
Garland County 501 Ouachita Ave	Hot Springs	AR	71901	**800-482-5964**	501-622-3610
Garvin County 201 W Grant St 2nd Fl	Pauls Valley	OK	73075	**800-231-8668**	405-238-2772
Gates County 200 Court St	Gatesville	NC	27938	**800-272-9829**	252-357-2411
Georgetown County 129 Screven St PO Box 421270	Georgetown	SC	29442	**800-868-2284**	843-545-3063
Gila County 1400 E Ash St	Globe	AZ	85501	**800-304-4452**	928-425-3231
Gillespie County 101 W Main St	Fredericksburg	TX	78624	**800-272-9829**	830-997-6515
Graham County 34 Wall St Ste 407	Asheville	NC	28801	**866-962-6246**	828-255-0182
Grant County 301 W Main St	John Day	OR	97845	**800-769-5664**	541-575-0547
Grant County 35 C St NW PO Box 37	Ephrata	WA	98823	**800-572-0119**	509-754-2011
Grant County 1800 Bronson Blvd	Fennimore	WI	53809	**866-472-6894**	608-822-3501

				Toll-Free	Phone
Green County 1016 16th Ave	Monroe	WI	53566	**800-947-3529**	608-328-9430
Green Lake County 492 Hill St	Green Lake	WI	54941	**800-664-3588**	920-294-4005
Greenbrier County 200 W Washington St	Lewisburg	WV	24901	**800-833-2068**	304-647-6602
Greene County 411 Main St	Catskill	NY	12414	**800-355-2287**	518-719-3270
Greene County 1034 Silver Dr	Greensboro	GA	30642	**800-248-7689**	706-453-7716
Haines Borough 103 Third Ave S PO Box 1209	Haines	AK	99827	**800-572-8006**	907-766-2231
Hamilton County 625 Georgia Ave	Chattanooga	TN	37402	**800-342-1003**	423-209-6500
Hampton (Independent City) 22 Lincoln St	Hampton	VA	23669	**800-555-3930**	757-727-8311
Hancock County 300 S Main St	Findlay	OH	45840	**888-534-1432**	419-424-7037
Hancock County PO Box 367	New Cumberland	WV	26047	**800-642-9066**	304-564-3311
Hancock County 418 Harrison St PO Box 575	Sneedville	TN	37869	**800-332-0900**	423-733-2519
Hancock County 12630 Broad St	Sparta	GA	31087	**800-255-0135**	706-444-5746
Haralson County 70 Murphy Campus Blvd	Waco	GA	30182	**800-955-7766**	770-537-5594
Hardeman County 100 N Main St	Bolivar	TN	38008	**800-336-2036**	731-658-3541
Hardin County 495 Main St	Savannah	TN	38372	**800-552-3866**	731-925-3921
Harlan County 311 Main St	Alma	NE	68920	**800-762-5498**	
Harlan County 201 S Main St	Harlan	KY	40831	**800-988-4660**	606-573-4495
Harper County 201 N Jennings Ave	Anthony	KS	67003	**877-537-2110**	620-842-5555
Harris County 159 S College St PO Box 426	Hamilton	GA	31811	**888-478-0010**	706-628-0010
Harris County 1019 Congress St 1st Fl	Houston	TX	77002	**800-983-9933**	713-755-5000
Harrison County 301 W Main St	Clarksburg	WV	26301	**888-509-6568**	304-624-8500
Harrisonburg (Independent City) 345 S Main St	Harrisonburg	VA	22801	**800-272-9829**	540-432-7701
Haywood County 1 N Washington St	Brownsville	TN	38012	**800-273-8712**	731-772-1432
Henry County 140 Henry Pkwy	McDonough	GA	30253	**800-955-7766**	770-954-2400
Hernando County 16110 Aviation Loop Dr	Brooksville	FL	34604	**800-601-4580**	352-754-4000
Hidalgo County 100 N Closner	Edinburg	TX	78539	**888-318-2811**	956-318-2100
Highland County 119 Governor Foraker Pl	Hillsboro	OH	45133	**800-774-1202**	937-393-1911
Hinsdale County 311 N Henson St	Lake City	CO	81235	**877-944-7575**	970-944-2225
Hopewell (Independent City) 300 N Main St	Hopewell	VA	23860	**800-552-7096**	804-541-2243
Houston County 401 E Houston Ave PO Box 370	Crockett	TX	75835	**800-275-8777**	936-544-3255
Howard County 104 N Buckeye Rm 104B	Kokomo	IN	46901	**800-913-6050**	765-456-2204
Hudspeth County 109 Brown St	Sierra Blanca	TX	79851	**888-368-4689**	915-369-2331
Huntingdon County 223 Penn St	Huntingdon	PA	16652	**800-373-0209**	814-643-3091
Huron County 250 E Huron Ave Rm 305	Bad Axe	MI	48413	**800-358-4862**	989-269-6431
Indiana County 825 Philadelphia St 3rd Fl	Indiana	PA	15701	**888-559-6355**	724-465-3805
Ionia County 100 W Main St	Ionia	MI	48846	**800-649-3777**	616-527-5322
Itasca County 123 NE Fourth St	Grand Rapids	MN	55744	**800-422-0312**	218-327-7363
Jackson County 401 Grindstaff Cove Rd	Sylva	NC	28779	**800-962-1911**	828-586-4055
Jefferson County 155 Main St 2nd Fl	Brookville	PA	15825	**800-852-8036**	814-849-3696
Jefferson County 532 Patriot Dr PO Box 890	Dandridge	TN	37725	**877-237-3847**	865-397-9642
Jefferson County 729 Maple St	Hillsboro	MO	63050	**800-243-6060**	636-797-5466
Jefferson County 302 E Broad St PO Box 630	Louisville	GA	30434	**866-527-2642**	478-625-8134
Jefferson County 300 Jefferson St PO Box 458	Oskaloosa	KS	66066	**800-332-6633**	785-403-0000
Jenkins County 548 Cotton Ave	Millen	GA	30442	**800-262-0128**	478-982-5595
Johnson County 111 S Cherry St	Olathe	KS	66061	**800-766-3777**	913-715-5000
Jones County 500 W Main St	Anamosa	IA	52205	**800-622-3849**	319-462-2282
Kane County 78 S 100 E	Kanab	UT	84741	**800-733-5263**	435-644-5033
Kay County 201 S Main St	Newkirk	OK	74647	**800-255-9456**	580-362-2565
Kimball County 114 E Third St	Kimball	NE	69145	**800-369-2850**	308-235-2241
King County 401 Fifth Ave 3rd Fl	Seattle	WA	98104	**800-325-6165**	206-296-1586
Klamath County 305 Main St	Klamath Falls	OR	97601	**800-377-6094**	541-883-5134
Knox County 200 S Cherry St	Galesburg	IL	61401	**800-916-3330**	309-343-3121
Kootenai County 451 N Government Way	Coeur d'Alene	ID	83814	**800-325-7940**	208-446-1000
Kosciusko County 100 W Center St	Warsaw	IN	46580	**800-840-8757**	574-372-2331
La Porte County 813 Lincolnway	La Porte	IN	46350	**800-654-3441**	219-326-6808
Lafourche Parish 402 Green St PO Box 5548	Thibodaux	LA	70302	**800-834-8832**	985-446-8427
Lake County 105 Main St	Painesville	OH	44077	**800-899-5253**	
Lane County 125 E Eigth Ave	Eugene	OR	97401	**800-281-2800**	541-682-4203
LaSalle County 707 E Etna Rd	Ottawa	IL	61350	**800-247-5243**	815-433-3366
Lawrence County 216 Collins Ave	South Point	OH	45680	**800-408-1334**	740-377-4550
Lawrence County County Courthouse 430 Court St	New Castle	PA	16101	**855-564-6116**	724-658-2541
Lawrence County 315 W Main	Walnut Ridge	AR	72476	**800-621-4000**	870-886-2525
Lea County 100 N Main St Ste 11	Lovington	NM	88260	**800-658-9955**	575-396-8619
Leavenworth County 300 Walnut St	Leavenworth	KS	66048	**855-893-9533**	913-684-0421
Leelanau County 8527 E Government Ctr Dr	Suttons Bay	MI	49682	**866-256-9711**	231-256-9824
Lewis County 112 Second St PO Box 129	Vanceburg	KY	41179	**800-230-5740**	606-796-2722
Lincoln County PO Box 978	Brookhaven	MS	39602	**800-613-4667**	601-833-1411
Lincoln County WY 925 Sage Ave	Kemmerer	WY	83101	**800-442-9001**	307-877-9056
Lincoln County 111 W 'B' St Ste C	Shoshone	ID	83352	**800-221-3295**	208-886-7641
Lincoln County Courthouse PO Box 373	Hamlin	WV	25523	**800-859-7375**	304-824-7990
Logan County 116 S Main St	Russellville	KY	42276	**800-693-3299**	270-726-2206
Lorain County 225 Ct St	Elyria	OH	44035	**800-750-0750**	440-329-5536
Macon County 410 N Missouri St Ste D	Macon	MO	63552	**800-981-9409**	660-676-0578
Madera County 200 W Fourth St	Madera	CA	93637	**800-427-6897**	559-675-7703
Madison County 146 W Ctr St	Canton	MS	39046	**800-428-0584**	601-859-1177
Madison County 182 NW College Loop PO Box 817	Madison	FL	32341	**877-272-3642**	850-973-2788
Madison County 73 Jefferson St	Winterset	IA	50273	**800-298-6119**	515-462-1185
Mahoning County 120 Market St	Youngstown	OH	44503	**800-548-7175**	330-740-2104
Marathon County 500 Forest St	Wausau	WI	54403	**800-247-5645**	715-261-1500
Marion County 200 E Washington St Ste W122	Indianapolis	IN	46204	**800-913-6050**	317-327-4740
Marion County 200 S Third St Ste 104	Marion	KS	66861	**800-305-8851**	620-382-2185
Marion County 118 Cross Creek Blvd	Salem	IL	62881	**800-438-4318**	618-548-3878
Mariposa County 5100 Bullion St PO Box 784	Mariposa	CA	95338	**800-549-6741**	209-966-3222
Maui County 200 S High St	Wailuku	HI	96793	**800-272-0117**	808-270-7748
McCook County 130 W Essex PO Box 504	Salem	SD	57058	**800-231-8346**	605-425-2781
McIntosh County PO Box 584	Darien	GA	31305	**800-436-7442**	
McKean County 500 W Main St	Smethport	PA	16749	**800-482-1280**	814-887-5571
Meagher County 15 W Main St	White Sulphur Springs	MT	59645	**800-332-2272**	406-547-3612
Mercer County 220 W Livingston St Ste 1	Celina	OH	45822	**800-686-1093**	419-586-3289
Mercer County 621 Commerce St PO Box 4088	Bluefield	WV	24701	**800-221-3206**	304-325-8438
Mercer County PO Box 39	Stanton	ND	58571	**800-441-2649**	
Milam County 107 W Main St	Cameron	TX	76520	**800-299-2437**	254-697-7049
Miller County 400 Laurel St Ste 105	Texarkana	AR	71854	**800-482-8998**	870-774-1501
Milwaukee County 901 N Ninth St	Milwaukee	WI	53233	**877-652-6377**	414-278-4143
Miner County Park Ave & Main St 401 N Main St 2nd Fl PO Box 86	Howard	SD	57349	**800-383-8000**	605-772-4671
Mississippi County 200 W Walnut St	Blytheville	AR	72315	**800-455-5600**	870-763-3212
Mitchell County 26 N Ct St PO Box 187	Camilla	GA	31730	**800-427-2457**	229-336-2000
Monroe County 124 W Commerce St	Aberdeen	MS	39730	**800-457-5351**	662-369-6488
Monroe County 38 W Main St PO Box 189	Forsyth	GA	31029	**800-282-5852**	478-994-7000
Monroe County 106 E First St	Monroe	MI	48161	**800-401-6402**	734-240-7020
Monterey County 168 W Alisal St	Salinas	CA	93901	**800-994-9662**	831-755-5115
Montgomery County PO Box 311	Norristown	PA	19404	**800-932-4600**	610-278-3346
Montmorency County PO Box 789	Atlanta	MI	49709	**877-742-7576**	989-785-8022
Montour County 29 Mill St	Danville	PA	17821	**800-632-9063**	570-271-3010
Morgan County 180 S Main St	Martinsville	IN	46151	**800-382-9467**	765-342-1007
Morrison County 213 SE First Ave	Little Falls	MN	56345	**866-401-1111**	320-632-2941
Muskogee County 229 W Okmulgee Ave	Muskogee	OK	74401	**800-444-1187**	918-682-6602
Nassau County PO Box 870	Fernandina Beach	FL	32035	**888-615-4398**	904-491-7300
Nassau County 240 Old Country Rd	Mineola	NY	11501	**800-460-5657**	516-571-2664
Nelson County 210 B Ave W Ste 203	Lakota	ND	58344	**800-472-2286**	701-247-2462
Nelson County 84 Courthouse Sq PO Box 336	Lovingston	VA	22949	**888-662-9400**	434-263-7000
Nemaha County 607 Nemaha	Seneca	KS	66538	**800-259-2829**	785-336-2106
Newton County 201 N Third St	Kentland	IN	47951	**888-663-9866**	219-474-6081
Niagara County PO Box 461	Lockport	NY	14095	**800-460-5657**	716-439-7022
Nicholas County Commission 700 Main St Ste 1	Summersville	WV	26651	**800-327-5405**	304-872-7830
Noble County 101 N Orange St	Albion	IN	46701	**800-840-8757**	260-636-2736
Norfolk (Independent City) 999 Waterside Dr Ste 2430	Norfolk	VA	23510	**800-664-1080**	757-664-4242

Name / Address	City	State	Zip	Toll-Free	Phone
North Slope Borough PO Box 69	Barrow	AK	99723	**800-478-0267**	907-852-2611
Northumberland County 201 Market St 2nd Fl	Sunbury	PA	17801	**800-692-4332**	570-988-4167
Northwest Arctic Borough PO Box 1110	Kotzebue	AK	99752	**800-478-1110**	907-442-2500
Noxubee County 198 Washington St PO Box 308	Macon	MS	39341	**800-487-0165**	662-726-4456
Ocean County 118 Washington St	Toms River	NJ	08753	**800-722-0291**	732-929-2018
Ogle County 105 S Fifth St	Oregon	IL	61061	**800-242-7642**	815-732-3201
Onslow County 4024 Richland Hwy	Jacksonville	NC	28540	**800-932-2144**	910-347-4717
Ontario County 20 Ontario St	Canandaigua	NY	14424	**800-247-7273**	585-396-4200
Orange County 200 Dailey Dr	Orange	VA	22960	**866-803-8641**	540-661-4550
Osage County 900 S St Paul Ave	Pawhuska	OK	74056	**888-287-3150**	918-287-3535
Otero County 13 W Third St Rm 210	La Junta	CO	81050	**800-438-3752**	719-383-3020
Otter Tail County 520 Fir Ave W	Fergus Falls	MN	56537	**800-232-9077**	218-998-8000
Palo Pinto County PO Box 219	Palo Pinto	TX	76484	**844-769-4976**	940-659-1277
Park County 1002 Sheridan Ave	Cody	WY	82414	**800-786-2844**	307-527-8510
Pasco County 7530 Little Rd	New Port Richey	FL	34654	**800-368-2411**	727-847-2411
Pawnee County 715 Broadway	Larned	KS	67550	**800-211-4401**	620-285-3721
Peoria County 324 Main St Rm 101	Peoria	IL	61602	**800-843-6154**	309-672-6059
Perry County 333 Seventh St PO Box 721	Tell City	IN	47586	**888-343-6262**	812-547-7933
Perry County 25 W Main St PO Box 37	New Bloomfield	PA	17068	**800-852-2102**	717-582-2131
Perry County 105 N Main St PO Box 207	New Lexington	OH	43764	**800-282-6556**	740-342-3156
Pershing County 398 Main St PO Box 89	Lovelock	NV	89419	**877-368-7828**	775-273-2401
Pickett County 1 Courthouse Sq Ste 200	Byrdstown	TN	38549	**888-406-4704**	931-864-3798
Pike County 506 Broad St	Milford	PA	18337	**866-681-4947**	570-296-7613
Pine County 635 Northridge Dr NW	Pine City	MN	55063	**800-450-7463**	320-591-1400
Pinellas County 333 Chestnut St	Clearwater	FL	33756	**800-806-5154**	727-464-3485
Pocahontas County PO Box 275	Marlinton	WV	24954	**800-336-7009**	
Polk County 111 Court Ave Administration Bldg	Des Moines	IA	50309	**800-848-0869**	515-286-3000
Portage County 449 S Meridian St 1st Fl	Ravenna	OH	44266	**800-772-3799**	330-297-9422
Presidio County PO Box 879	Marfa	TX	79843	**888-368-4689**	
Price County 126 Cherry St	Phillips	WI	54555	**800-362-9472**	715-339-3325
Pulaski County 143 Third St NW Ste 1	Pulaski	VA	24301	**800-211-5540**	540-980-7705
Pulaski County 100 N Main St Ste 202	Somerset	KY	42501	**877-655-7154**	606-678-4853
Pulaski County 137 StRobert Bld Ste A	St. Robert	MO	65584	**877-858-8687**	573-336-6355
Putnam County 117 Putnam Dr Ste A	Eatonton	GA	31024	**800-253-1077**	706-485-5826
Putnam County 130 Orie Griffin Blvd	Palatka	FL	32177	**800-426-9975**	386-329-0808
Racine County 730 Wisconsin Ave 1st Fl North end	Racine	WI	53403	**800-242-4202**	262-636-3121
Raleigh County 215 Main St	Beckley	WV	25801	**800-509-6568**	304-255-9178
Ramsey County 15 W Kellogg Blvd	Saint Paul	MN	55102	**866-520-7225**	651-266-8000
Randolph County 1302 N Randolph Ave	Elkins	WV	26241	**800-422-3304**	304-636-2780
Randolph County 372 Hwy JJ	Huntsville	MO	65259	**844-277-6555**	
Roane Alliance 1209 N Kentucky St	Kingston	TN	37763	**800-386-4686**	865-376-2093
Roanoke (Independent City) 210 Reserve Ave SW	Roanoke	VA	24016	**800-956-4237**	540-853-2000
Robertson County 523 S Brown St	Springfield	TN	37172	**866-355-6134**	615-384-0202
Rock County 51 S Main St	Janesville	WI	53545	**800-924-3570**	608-757-5660
Rockbridge County 150 S Main St	Lexington	VA	24450	**800-420-1663**	540-463-4361
Rockland County 11 New Hempstead Rd	New City	NY	10956	**800-662-1220**	845-638-5100
Rutland Region Chamber of Commerce 50 Merchants Row	Rutland	VT	05701	**800-756-8880**	802-773-2747
Sabine County *Chamber Of Commerce* 1555 Worth St PO Box 717	Hemphill	TX	75948	**800-986-5336**	409-787-2732
Saline County 200 N Main St Ste 117	Benton	AR	72015	**800-438-6233**	501-303-5630
San Benito County 450 Fourth St	Hollister	CA	95023	**800-503-9230**	831-636-4029
San Bernardino County 777 E Rialto Ave	San Bernardino	CA	92415	**888-818-8988**	909-387-8306
San Juan County 350 Ct St 2nd Fl	Friday Harbor	WA	98250	**800-762-3716**	360-378-2163
San Luis Obispo County 1055 Monterey St	San Luis Obispo	CA	93408	**800-834-4636**	805-781-5000
Sargent County 355 Main St	Forman	ND	58032	**866-634-8387**	701-724-6241
Sawyer County 10610 Main St Ste 10	Hayward	WI	54843	**877-699-4110**	715-634-4866
Schenectady County *Newyork* 620 State St	Schenectady	NY	12305	**877-846-7369**	518-388-4220
Schoharie County 284 Main St PO Box 429	Schoharie	NY	12157	**800-227-3552**	518-295-8347
Scotland County PO Box 489	Laurinburg	NC	28353	**800-913-6109**	910-277-2406
Sebastian County 35 S Sixth St Rm 105	Fort Smith	AR	72901	**800-637-9314**	479-782-5065
Sedgwick County 525 N Main St	Wichita	KS	67203	**800-527-0709**	316-660-9222
Shasta County 1643 Market St	Redding	CA	96099	**800-735-2922**	530-225-5730
Shelby County 612 Ct St	Harlan	IA	51537	**800-735-3942**	712-755-3831
Shelby County Alabama 200 W College St	Columbiana	AL	35051	**800-272-4263**	205-670-6550
Sheridan County 224 S Main St Ste B-2	Sheridan	WY	82801	**800-565-4502**	307-674-2500
Shoshone County 700 Bank St	Wallace	ID	83873	**800-325-7940**	208-752-3331
Skamania County 240 NW Vancouver Ave PO Box 790	Stevenson	WA	98648	**800-375-5283**	509-427-3770
Snohomish County 3000 Rockefeller Ave	Everett	WA	98201	**800-584-3578**	425-388-3411
Somerset County 11440 Ocean Hwy PO Box 243	Princess Anne	MD	21853	**800-521-9189**	410-651-2968
Somerset County 20 Grove St PO Box 3000	Somerville	NJ	08876	**800-246-0527**	908-231-7000
Spokane County 1116 W Broadway Ave	Spokane	WA	99260	**800-562-6000**	509-477-2265
St Louis County 100 N Fifth Ave W	Duluth	MN	55802	**800-450-9278**	218-726-2450
Steele County PO Box 296	Finley	ND	58230	**800-584-7077**	701-524-2152
Stevens County 215 S Oak St	Colville	WA	99114	**800-833-6388**	509-684-3751
Sullivan County 245 Muncy St PO Box 157	Laporte	PA	18626	**800-369-3599**	570-946-5201
Sullivan County 100 N St	Monticello	NY	12701	**800-320-2617**	845-794-3000
Susquehanna County 75 Public Ave	Montrose	PA	18801	**800-932-0313**	570-278-4600
Sutter County 433 Second St	Yuba City	CA	95991	**800-371-3177**	530-822-7134
Talbot County 11 N Washington St County Courthouse	Easton	MD	21601	**800-339-3403**	410-822-2611
Talbot County Board of Commissioners 74 W Monroe St PO Box 155	Talbotton	GA	31827	**800-486-7642**	706-665-3220
Taylor County 224 S Second St	Medford	WI	54451	**800-362-4802**	715-748-1456
Telfair County 91 Telfair Ave	McRae	GA	31055	**800-829-4933**	800-436-7442
Tennessee State Government *Obion County* 1604B W Reelfoot Ave	Union City	TN	38261	**800-222-8754**	731-884-2133
Tensas Parish 201 Hancock St PO Box 78	Saint Joseph	LA	71366	**800-256-6660**	318-766-3921
Teton County PO Box 1727	Jackson	WY	83001	**800-368-8683**	307-733-4430
Tipton County 220 Hwy 51 N Ste 2	Covington	TN	38019	**800-342-1003**	901-476-0207
Tompkins County 320 N Tioga St	Ithaca	NY	14850	**800-268-7869**	
Towns County 1411 Jack Dayton Cir	Young Harris	GA	30582	**800-984-1543**	706-896-4966
Trego County 216 N Main St	WaKeeney	KS	67672	**877-962-7248**	785-743-5785
Trempealeau County 36245 Main St	Whitehall	WI	54773	**877-538-2311**	715-538-2311
Turner County PO Box 191	Ashburn	GA	31714	**800-436-7442**	
Twin Falls County 2469 Wright Ave	Twin Falls	ID	83301	**800-377-3529**	208-736-4004
Tyler County 100 Bluff St Rm 110	Woodville	TX	75979	**800-256-6848**	409-283-2281
Uintah County 204 East 100 North	Vernal	UT	84078	**800-966-4680**	435-781-0770
Ulster County 244 Fair St	Kingston	NY	12401	**800-342-5826**	
Union County 1103 S First St	Clayton	NM	88415	**800-390-7858**	575-374-9253
Union County 1106 K Ave	La Grande	OR	97850	**800-735-1232**	541-963-1001
Union County 210 W Main St	Union	SC	29379	**800-273-5066**	864-429-1600
Upton County Sheriff PO Box 27	Rankin	TX	79778	**800-680-9052**	432-693-2422
Vermillion County 255 S Main St	Newport	IN	47966	**800-340-8155**	765-492-5345
Volusia County 123 W Indiana Ave	DeLand	FL	32720	**800-955-8771**	386-736-5920
Wabash County 221 S Miami St	Wabash	IN	46992	**800-346-2110**	260-563-7171
Wahkiakum County 64 Main St PO Box 157	Cathlamet	WA	98612	**800-359-1506**	360-795-3558
Waldo County 137 Church St	Belfast	ME	04915	**800-244-5211**	207-338-1710
Walker County 101 S Duke St PO Box 445	La Fayette	GA	30728	**800-424-8666**	706-638-1437
Warren County 220 N Commerce Ave Ste 100	Front Royal	VA	22630	**800-248-6342**	540-636-4600
Warren County 406 Justice Dr	Lebanon	OH	45036	**800-282-0253**	513-695-1358
Warren County 125 N Monroe St Ste 11	Williamsport	IN	47993	**800-622-4941**	765-762-3510
Washburn County PO Box 639	Shell Lake	WI	54871	**800-469-6562**	800-367-3306
Washington County 280 N College Ave Ste 300	Fayetteville	AR	72701	**800-563-0012**	479-444-1711
Washington Parish 909 Pearl St	Franklinton	LA	70438	**800-375-7570**	985-839-7825
Washtenaw County PO Box 8645	Ann Arbor	MI	48107	**800-440-7548**	734-222-6850
Waukesha County 515 W Moreland Blvd Rm 120	Waukesha	WI	53188	**800-247-5645**	262-548-7010
Wayne County 925 Court St	Honesdale	PA	18431	**800-321-9973**	570-253-5970
Wayne County 26 Church St	Lyons	NY	14489	**800-527-6510**	315-946-5400
Weber County 2380 Washington Blvd Ste 350	Ogden	UT	84401	**800-407-2757**	801-399-8454
West Baton Rouge Parish PO Box 757	Port Allen	LA	70767	**800-654-9701**	225-383-4755
West Carroll Parish PO Box 1078	Oak Grove	LA	71263	**800-256-6660**	318-428-3281
White County 110 N Main St	Monticello	IN	47960	**800-272-9829**	574-583-7032
White Pine County 801 Clark St	Ely	NV	89301	**800-884-4072**	775-293-6509

				Toll-Free	Phone
Whiteside County					
200 E Knox St	Morrison	IL	61270	**800-460-5657**	815-772-5100
Wilcox County					
103 N Broad St	Abbeville	GA	31001	**866-694-5824**	229-467-2737
Williamsburg (Independent City)					
401 Lafayette St	Williamsburg	VA	23185	**800-275-2355**	757-220-6100
Wood County					
1 Courthouse Sq	Bowling Green	OH	43402	**866-860-4140**	419-354-9000
Wood County PO Box 1796	Quitman	TX	75783	**800-253-8014**	903-763-2711
Worcester County					
1 W Market St Rm 1103	Snow Hill	MD	21863	**800-852-0335**	410-632-1194
Wyoming County 143 N Main St	Warsaw	NY	14569	**800-527-1757**	585-786-8810
Yakima County					
128 N Second St Rm 323	Yakima	WA	98901	**800-572-7354**	509-574-1430
Yates County					
417 Liberty St	Penn Yan	NY	14527	**866-212-5160**	315-536-5120
Yavapai County					
1015 Fair St	Prescott	AZ	86305	**800-659-7149**	928-771-3200
Yazoo County PO Box 186	Yazoo City	MS	39194	**800-381-0662**	662-746-1815
Yellow Medicine County					
415 Ninth Ave	Granite Falls	MN	56241	**800-366-4812**	320-564-3325
Yolo County					
625 Ct St Rm B01	Woodland	CA	95695	**800-433-5060**	530-666-8150
Yuma County 198 S Main St	Yuma	AZ	85364	**800-253-0883**	928-373-1010

338   GOVERNMENT - STATE

SEE ALSO Employment Offices - Government ; Lotteries, Games, Sweepstakes ; Veterans Nursing Homes - State ; Student Assistance Programs ; Parks - State ; Legislation Hotlines ; Correctional Facilities - State ; Ethics Commissions ; Sports Commissions & Regulatory Agencies - State ; Governors - State

338-1 Alabama

				Toll-Free	Phone
Administrative Office of Alabama Courts					
300 Dexter Ave	Montgomery	AL	36104	**866-954-9411**	334-954-5000
Banking Dept					
401 Adams Ave Ste 680	Montgomery	AL	36104	**866-465-2279**	334-242-3452
Crime Victims Compensation Commission					
5845 Carmichael Rd	Montgomery	AL	36117	**800-541-9388**	334-290-4420
Highway Patrol Div					
301 S Ripley St	Montgomery	AL	36104	**800-272-7930**	334-517-2950
Housing Finance Authority					
7460 Halcyon Pointe Dr Ste 200	Montgomery	AL	36117	**800-325-2432**	334-244-9200
Mental Health & Mental Retardation Dept					
100 N Union St PO Box 301410	Montgomery	AL	36130	**800-367-0955**	334-242-3454
National Guard					
1720 Congressman William L Dickinson Dr					
PO Box 3711	Montgomery	AL	36109	**800-464-8273**	334-271-7200
Prepaid Affordable College Tuition (PACT)					
100 N Union Ste 660	Montgomery	AL	36104	**800-252-7228**	
Public Health Dept					
201 Monroe St	Montgomery	AL	36104	**800-252-1818**	334-206-5300
Public Service Commission					
100 N Union St RSA Union					
PO Box 304260	Montgomery	AL	36130	**800-392-8050**	334-242-5218
Rehabilitation Services Dept					
602 S Lawrence St	Montgomery	AL	36104	**800-441-7607**	334-293-7500
Securities Commission					
401 Adams Ave Ste 280	Montgomery	AL	36104	**800-222-1253**	334-242-2984
Senior Services Dept					
201 Monroe Ste 350	Montgomery	AL	36104	**877-425-2243**	334-242-5743
State Parks Div					
64 N Union St Rm 538	Montgomery	AL	36130	**800-252-7275**	
Tourism Department					
401 Adams Ave PO Box 4927	Montgomery	AL	36104	**800-252-2262**	334-242-4169

338-2 Alaska

				Toll-Free	Phone
Arts Council					
161 Klevin St Ste 102	Anchorage	AK	99508	**888-278-7424**	907-269-6610
Banking Securities & Corporations Div					
333 Willoughby Ave 9th Fl					
PO Box 110800	Juneau	AK	99801	**888-925-2521**	907-465-2521
Commission on Postsecondary Education					
PO Box 110510	Juneau	AK	99811	**800-770-8973**	907-465-6671
Employment Security Div					
PO Box 115509	Juneau	AK	99811	**888-448-3527**	907-465-2757
Enterprise Technology Services Div					
State Office Bldg 333 Willoughby Ave					
5th Fl	Juneau	AK	99801	**888-565-8680**	
Housing Finance Corp					
4300 Boniface Pkwy 99504	Anchorage	AK	99504	**800-478-2432**	907-338-6100
Postsecondary Education Commission					
3030 Vintage Blvd PO Box 110510	Juneau	AK	99811	**800-441-2962**	907-465-2962
Vocational Rehabilitation Div					
801 W Tenth St PO Box 115516	Juneau	AK	99801	**800-478-2815**	907-465-2814

338-3 Arizona

				Toll-Free	Phone
Agriculture Dept					
1688 W Adams St	Phoenix	AZ	85007	**800-294-0308**	602-542-4373
Department of Insurance					
100 N 15th Ave Ste 102	Phoenix	AZ	85007	**800-325-2548**	602-364-2499
Education Dept					
1535 W Jefferson St	Phoenix	AZ	85007	**800-352-4558**	602-542-5393
Financial Institutions					
2910 N 44th St Ste 310	Phoenix	AZ	85018	**800-544-0708**	602-771-2800

				Toll-Free	Phone
Legislature					
Arizona State Capitol Complex 1700 W Washington St					
1700 W Washington St	Phoenix	AZ	85007	**800-352-8404**	602-926-3559
Lottery					
4740 E University Dr	Phoenix	AZ	85034	**800-639-8783**	480-921-4400
Medical Board					
9545 Doubletree Ranch Rd	Scottsdale	AZ	85258	**877-255-2212**	480-551-2700
Rehabilitation Services Admin					
3321 N 16th St Ste 200	Phoenix	AZ	85016	**800-563-1221**	602-266-9206
Secretary of State					
1700 W Washington St 7th Fl	Phoenix	AZ	85007	**800-458-5842**	602-542-4285
Securities Div					
1300 W Washington St 3rd Fl	Phoenix	AZ	85007	**866-837-4399**	602-542-4242
Treasurer					
1700 W Washington St Ste 102	Phoenix	AZ	85007	**877-365-8310**	602-542-7800
Vital Records Office					
1818 W Adams St	Phoenix	AZ	85007	**888-816-5907**	602-364-1300

338-4 Arkansas

				Toll-Free	Phone
Administrative Office of the Courts					
625 Marshall St	Little Rock	AR	72201	**800-950-8221**	501-682-9400
Aging & Adult Services Div					
PO Box 1437 Slot S-530	Little Rock	AR	72203	**800-482-8049**	501-682-2441
Attorney General					
323 Ctr St Ste 200	Little Rock	AR	72201	**800-482-8982***	501-682-2007
*Consumer Info					
Consumer Protection Div					
323 Ctr St Ste 200	Little Rock	AR	72201	**800-482-8982**	501-682-2007
Crime Victims Reparations Board					
323 Ctr St Ste 200	Little Rock	AR	72201	**800-482-8982**	501-682-2007
Environmental Quality Dept					
5301 Northshore Dr	Little Rock	AR	72118	**888-233-0326**	501-682-0744
Ethics Commission					
501 Woodlane St Ste 301n	Little Rock	AR	72203	**800-422-7773**	501-324-9600
Game & Fish Commission					
2 Natural Resource Dr	Little Rock	AR	72205	**800-364-4263**	501-223-6300
Highway & Transportation Dept					
10324 I-30	Little Rock	AR	72209	**800-245-1672**	501-569-2000
Insurance Dept					
1200 W Third St	Little Rock	AR	72201	**800-282-9134**	501-371-2600
Parks & Tourism Dept					
1 Capitol Mall Ste 4A-900	Little Rock	AR	72201	**800-628-8725**	501-682-7777
Rehabilitation Services					
525 W Capitol Ave	Little Rock	AR	72201	**800-330-0632**	501-296-1600
Securities Dept					
201 E Markham St Ste 300	Little Rock	AR	72201	**800-981-4429**	501-324-9260
State Medical Board					
1401 West Capitol Ave Ste 340	Little Rock	AR	72201	**888-228-1233**	501-296-1802

338-5 California

				Toll-Free	Phone
Arts Council					
1300 'I' St Ste 930	Sacramento	CA	95814	**800-201-6201**	916-322-6555
Bureau of Real Estate					
1651 Exposition Blvd	Sacramento	CA	95815	**877-373-4542**	
Child Support Services Dept					
PO Box 419064	Sacramento	CA	95741	**866-901-3212**	916-464-5000
Consumer Affairs Dept					
1625 N Market Blvd Ste N 112	Sacramento	CA	95834	**800-952-5210**	916-445-1254
Corrections Dept					
PO Box 942883	Sacramento	CA	94283	**877-256-6877**	916-324-7308
Fair Political Practices Commission					
428 J St Ste 620	Sacramento	CA	95814	**866-275-3772**	916-322-5660
Health Care Services Dept					
PO Box 997413 MS 8502	Sacramento	CA	95899	**800-735-2929**	
Housing Finance Agency					
500 Capitol Mall Ste 1400	Sacramento	CA	95814	**877-922-5432**	
Judicial Council of California					
455 Golden Gate Ave	San Francisco	CA	94102	**800-900-5980**	415-865-4200
Medical Board					
2005 Evergreen St Ste 1200	Sacramento	CA	95815	**800-633-2322**	916-263-2382
Motor Vehicles Dept					
4700 Broadway	Sacramento	CA	95820	**800-777-0133**	916-657-6437
Public Utilities Commission					
505 Van Ness Ave	San Francisco	CA	94102	**800-848-5580**	415-703-2782
Rehabilitation Dept					
721 Capitol Mall	Sacramento	CA	95814	**800-952-5544**	916-324-1313
Veterans Affairs Dept					
1227 'O' St	Sacramento	CA	95814	**800-952-5626**	916-653-1402
Victim Compensation Board					
PO Box 3036	Sacramento	CA	95812	**800-777-9229**	

338-6 Colorado

				Toll-Free	Phone
Children Youth & Families Office					
1575 Sherman St	Denver	CO	80203	**800-799-5876**	
CollegeInvest					
1560 Broadway Ste 1700	Denver	CO	80202	**800-448-2424**	303-376-8800
Division Of Criminal Justice					
700 Kipling St Ste 1000	Denver	CO	80215	**888-282-1080**	303-239-4442
Emergency Management Office					
9195 E Mineral Ave	Centennial	CO	80112	**877-820-7831**	720-279-0026
Insurance Div					
1560 Broadway Ste 850	Denver	CO	80202	**800-930-3745**	303-894-7499
Labor & Employment Dept					
633 17th St Ste 201	Denver	CO	80202	**800-388-5515**	303-318-9000
Lottery 225 N Main St	Pueblo	CO	81003	**800-999-2959**	719-546-2400
Natural Resources Dept					
1313 Sherman St Rm 718	Denver	CO	80203	**800-536-5308**	303-866-3311

					Toll-Free	Phone

Parks and Wildlife
1313 Sherman St Rm 618 .... Denver CO 80203   **800-678-2267*** 303-866-3437
*Campground Resv
Public Utilities Commission
1560 Broadway Ste 250 .... Denver CO 80202   **800-888-0170** 303-894-2000
Regulatory Agencies Dept
1560 Broadway Ste 110 .... Denver CO 80202   **800-886-7675** 303-894-7855
State Court Administrator
1300 Broadway Ste 210 .... Denver CO 80203   **800-888-0001** 720-625-5000
Supreme Court
1300 Broadway Ste 500 .... Denver CO 80203   **877-888-1370** 303-457-5800

338-7 Connecticut

					Toll-Free	Phone

Aging Commission
210 Capitol Ave .... Hartford CT 06106   **866-218-6631** 860-424-5274
Banking Dept
260 Constitution Plz .... Hartford CT 06103   **800-831-7225** 860-240-8230
Chief Medical Examiner
11 Shuttle Rd .... Farmington CT 06032   **800-842-8820** 860-679-3980
Child Support Assistance
55 Farmington Ave .... Hartford CT 06106   **800-228-5437**
Consumer Protection Dept
450 Columbus Blvd Ste 901 .... Hartford CT 06106   **800-838-6554** 860-713-6100
Emergency Management and Homeland Security Div
25 Sigourney St 6th Fl .... Hartford CT 06106   **800-397-8876** 860-256-0800
Higher Education Dept
450 Columbus Blvd Ste 510 .... Hartford CT 06103   **800-842-0229** 860-947-1800
Insurance Dept
153 Market St .... Hartford CT 06103   **800-203-3447** 860-297-3800
Public Utility Control Dept
10 Franklin Sq .... New Britain CT 06051   **800-382-4586** 860-827-1553
Real Estate & Professional Trades Div
165 Capitol Ave .... Hartford CT 06106   **800-838-6554** 860-713-6100
Rehabilitation Services Bureau
55 Farmington Ave 1st Fl .... Hartford CT 06105   **800-537-2549** 860-424-4844
Treasurer 55 Elm St .... Hartford CT 06106   **800-618-3404** 860-702-3000
Veterans Affairs Dept
287 W St .... Rocky Hill CT 06067   **800-447-0961** 860-721-5891
Victim Services Office
225 Spring St 4th Fl .... Wethersfield CT 06109   **800-822-8428**
Weights & Measures Div
450 Columbus Blvd .... Hartford CT 06103   **800-838-6554** 860-713-6100
Workers' Compensation Commission
21 Oak St 4th Fl .... Hartford CT 06106   **800-223-9675** 860-493-1500

338-8 Delaware

					Toll-Free	Phone

Aging & Adults with Physical Disabilites Services
1901 N DuPont Hwy .... New Castle DE 19720   **800-223-9074**
Agriculture Dept
2320 S DuPont Hwy .... Dover DE 19901   **800-282-8685** 302-698-4500
Consumer Protection Unit
820 N French St 5th Fl .... Wilmington DE 19801   **800-220-5424** 302-577-8600
Emergency Management Agency
165 Brick Store Landing Rd .... Smyrna DE 19977   **877-729-3362** 302-659-3362
Housing Authority
18 The Green .... Dover DE 19901   **888-363-8808** 302-739-4263
Parks & Recreation Div
89 Kings Hwy .... Dover DE 19901   **877-987-2757*** 302-739-9220
*Campground Resv
Thoroughbred Racing Commission
2320 S DuPont Hwy .... Dover DE 19901   **800-282-8685** 302-698-4500
Tourism Office 99 Kings Hwy .... Dover DE 19901   **866-284-7483** 302-739-4271
Veterans Affairs Commission
802 Silverlake Blvd Ste 100 .... Dover DE 19904   **800-344-9900** 302-739-2792
Weights & Measures Office
2320 S DuPont Hwy .... Dover DE 19901   **800-282-8685** 302-698-4575

338-9 District of Columbia

					Toll-Free	Phone

Convention & Tourism Corp
901 Seventh St NW 4th Fl .... Washington DC 20001   **800-422-8644** 202-789-7000
Tuition Assistance Grant Program
810 First St NE .... Washington DC 20001   **877-485-6751** 202-727-2824

338-10 Florida

					Toll-Free	Phone

Attorney General
State Capitol PL-01 .... Tallahassee FL 32399   **866-966-7226** 850-245-0140
Business & Professional Regulation Dept
2601 Blair Stone Rd .... Tallahassee FL 32399   **866-532-1440** 850-487-1395
Chief Financial Officer
200 E Gaines St .... Tallahassee FL 32399   **877-693-5236** 850-413-3089
Colleges & Universities Div
325 W Gaines St Ste 1414 .... Tallahassee FL 32399   **888-224-6684** 850-245-3200
Consumer Services Div
2005 Apalachee Pkwy .... Tallahassee FL 32399   **800-435-7352**
Education Dept
325 W Gaines St Ste 1514 .... Tallahassee FL 32399   **800-445-6739** 850-245-0505
Financial Services Dept
200 E Gaines St .... Tallahassee FL 32399   **800-342-2762** 850-413-3149
Insurance Regulation Office
200 E Gaines St .... Tallahassee FL 32399   **800-342-2762** 850-413-3140
Prepaid College Board
PO Box 6567 .... Tallahassee FL 32314   **800-552-4723**
Public Service Commission
2540 Shumard Oak Blvd .... Tallahassee FL 32399   **800-342-3552** 850-413-6042

Recreation & Parks Div
3900 Commonwealth Blvd .... Tallahassee FL 32399   **800-326-3521*** 850-245-2157
*Campground Resv
Secretary of State
RA Gray Bldg 500 S Bronough St .... Tallahassee FL 32399   **800-955-8771** 850-245-6500
Vocational Rehabilitation Services Div
4070 Esplanade Way .... Tallahassee FL 32399   **800-451-4327** 850-245-3399

338-11 Georgia

					Toll-Free	Phone

Aging Services Div
2 Peachtree St NW 3rd Fl .... Atlanta GA 30303   **866-552-4464** 404-657-5258
Arts Council 260 14th St NW .... Atlanta GA 30318   **800-222-6006** 404-685-2400
Banking & Finance Dept
2990 Brandywine Rd Ste 200 .... Atlanta GA 30341   **888-986-1633** 770-986-1633
Community Affairs Dept
60 Executive Pk S NE .... Atlanta GA 30329   **800-359-4663** 404-679-4940
Composite Medical Board
2 Peachtree St NW 36th Fl .... Atlanta GA 30303   **800-436-7442** 404-656-3913
Corrections Dept
300 Patrol Rd Forsyth .... Atlanta GA 31029   **888-343-5627** 404-656-4661
Department of Behavioral Health & Developmental Di
2 Peachtree St NW 24th Fl .... Atlanta GA 30303   **800-436-7442** 404-657-2252
Division of Child Support Services
2 Peachtree St NW .... Atlanta GA 30303   **800-436-7442**
Economic Development Dept
75 Fifth St NW Ste 845 .... Atlanta GA 30308   **800-255-0056** 404-962-4005
Emergency Management Agency (GEMA)
935 E Confederate Ave SE PO Box 18055 .. Atlanta GA 30316   **800-879-4362** 404-635-7000
Environmental Protection Div
2 Martin Luther King Jr Dr
Ste 1456 E tower .... Atlanta GA 30334   **888-373-5947** 404-657-5947
Governor's Office of Consumer Protection
2 ML King Jr Dr Ste 356 .... Atlanta GA 30334   **800-869-1123**
Insurance Commissioner
2 Martin Luther King Jr Dr
W Tower Ste 704 .... Atlanta GA 30334   **800-656-2298** 404-656-2070
Natural Resources Dept
2 ML King Jr Dr SE Ste 1252E .... Atlanta GA 30334   **800-366-2661** 404-656-3500
Ports Authority 2 Main St .... Savannah GA 31402   **800-342-8012** 912-964-3811
Professional Licensing Boards Div
237 Coliseum Dr .... Macon GA 31217   **844-753-7825** 478-207-2440
Public Service Commission
244 Washington St SW .... Atlanta GA 30334   **800-282-5813** 404-656-4501
Revenue Dept
1800 Century Ctr Blvd NE .... Atlanta GA 30345   **877-423-6711** 404-417-6760
Secretary of State
214 State Capitol .... Atlanta GA 30334   **800-436-7442**
Securities & Business Regulation Div
2 Martin Luther King Jr Dr SE
W Tower Ste 820 .... Atlanta GA 30334   **844-753-7825**
Student Finance Commission
2082 E Exchange Pl .... Tucker GA 30084   **800-505-4732** 800-436-7442
Tourism Div
75 Fifth St NW Ste 1200 .... Atlanta GA 30308   **800-255-0056*** 404-962-4000
*Resv
Transparency & Campaign Finance Commission
200 Piedmont Ave SE Ste 1416 W Tower .... Atlanta GA 30334   **866-589-7327** 404-463-1980
Veterans Service Dept
Floyd Veterans Memorial Bldg Ste 970E .. Atlanta GA 30334   **800-436-7442** 404-656-2300
Vital Records Office
2600 Skyland Dr NE .... Atlanta GA 30319   **800-436-7442** 404-679-4702

338-12 Hawaii

					Toll-Free	Phone

Child Support Enforcement Agency
Kakuhihewa Bldg 601 Kamokila Blvd
Ste 251 .... Kapolei HI 96707   **888-317-9081** 808-692-8265
Consumer Protection Office
235 S Beretania St 9th fl .... Honolulu HI 96813   **800-394-1902** 808-586-2630
Taxation Dept
830 Punchbowl St Rm 221 .... Honolulu HI 96813   **800-222-3229** 808-587-4242
Vocational Rehabilitation Div
1901 Bachelot St .... Honolulu HI 96817   **800-316-8005** 808-586-9744

338-13 Idaho

					Toll-Free	Phone

Aging Commission (ICOA)
341 W Washington 3rd Fl .... Boise ID 83702   **877-471-2777** 208-334-3833
Arts Commission
2410 Old Penitentiary Rd .... Boise ID 83712   **800-278-3863** 208-334-2119
Crime Victims Compensation Program
PO Box 83720 .... Boise ID 83720   **800-950-2110** 208-334-6000
Department of Commerce
700 W State St PO Box 83720 .... Boise ID 83720   **800-842-5858** 208-334-2470
Finance Dept
800 Pk Blvd Ste 200 PO Box 83720 .... Boise ID 83712   **888-346-3378** 208-332-8000
Health & Welfare Dept
450 W State St 10th Fl PO Box 83720 .... Boise ID 83720   **877-456-1233**
Housing & Finance Assn
565 W Myrtle Ave .... Boise ID 83702   **800-526-7145** 208-331-4700
Lottery
1199 Shoreline Ln Ste 100 .... Boise ID 83702   **800-432-5688** 208-334-2600
Parks & Recreation Dept
5657 Warm Springs Ave .... Boise ID 83716   **855-514-2429** 208-334-4199
Public Utilities Commission
472 W Washington Boise PO Box 83720 .... Boise ID 83720   **800-432-0369** 208-334-0300
Tax Commission
800 E Pk Blvd Plz 4 .... Boise ID 83712   **800-972-7660** 208-334-7660

			Toll-Free	Phone
Tourism Development Div				
700 W State St PO Box 83720	Boise ID	83720	**800-847-4843***	208-334-2470
*General				

338-14 Illinois

			Toll-Free	Phone
Aging Dept				
1 Natural Resources Way Ste 100	Springfield IL	62701	**800-252-8966**	217-785-3356
Agriculture Dept				
StateFairgrounds? PO Box 19281	Springfield IL	62794	**866-287-2999**	217-782-2172
Banks & Real Estate Div				
320 W Washington St	Springfield IL	62786	**888-473-4858**	
Commerce & Economic Opportunity Dept				
620 E Adams St	Springfield IL	62701	**800-526-0844**	
Commerce Commission				
527 E Capitol Ave	Springfield IL	62701	**800-524-0795**	217-782-2024
Crime Victims Services Div				
100 W Randolf Rd 13th Fl	Chicago IL	60601	**800-228-3368**	312-814-2581
Emergency Management Agency				
2200 S Dirksen Pkwy	Springfield IL	62703	**800-782-7860**	217-782-2700
Environmental Protection Agency				
1021 N Grand Ave E	Springfield IL	62794	**800-782-7860**	217-782-3397
Human Services Dept				
100 S Grand Ave E	Springfield IL	62762	**800-843-6154**	217-557-1601
Lottery				
101 W Jefferson St	Springfield IL	62702	**800-252-1775**	217-524-6435
Mental Health Div				
100 W Randolf St Ste 3-400	Chicago IL	60601	**800-252-2923**	800-526-0844
Revenue Dept				
101 W Jefferson St	Springfield IL	62702	**800-732-8866**	217-782-3336
Secretary of State				
213 State Capitol	Springfield IL	62756	**800-252-8980**	217-782-2201
State Board of Education				
100 N First St	Springfield IL	62777	**866-262-6663**	217-782-4321
Student Assistance Commission				
1755 Lake Cook Rd	Deerfield IL	60015	**877-877-3724**	800-899-4722
Tourism Bureau				
100 W Randolph St Ste 3-400	Chicago IL	60601	**800-226-6632**	312-814-4732
Treasurer				
Capitol Bldg 219 Statehouse	Springfield IL	62706	**866-458-7327**	
Veterans Affairs Dept				
69 W Washington				
George Dunn County Bldg Ste 1620	Chicago IL	60602	**800-437-9824**	312-814-2460
Workers' Compensation Commission				
100 W Randolph St Ste 8-200	Chicago IL	60601	**866-352-3033**	312-814-6611

338-15 Indiana

			Toll-Free	Phone
State Government Information				
402 W Washington St Rm W160	Indianapolis IN	46204	**800-457-8283**	317-233-0800
Agriculture Dept				
101 W Washington St	Indianapolis IN	46204	**800-677-9800**	
Arts Commission				
302 W Washington St	Indianapolis IN	46204	**800-677-9800**	
Attorney General				
302 W Washington St Rm E114	Indianapolis IN	46204	**800-677-9800**	
Child Support Bureau				
302 W Washington St Rm E-205	Indianapolis IN	46204	**800-840-8757**	800-677-9800
Consumer Protection Div				
402 W Washington St Rm W-478	Indianapolis IN	46204	**800-382-5516**	317-232-3001
Correction Dept				
302 W Washington St	Indianapolis IN	46204	**800-677-9800**	
Disability Aging & Rehabilitative Services Div				
402 W Washington St Ste W453				
PO Box 7083	Indianapolis IN	46207	**800-545-7763**	317-232-1147
Economic Development Corp				
1 N Capitol Ave Ste 700	Indianapolis IN	46204	**800-463-8081**	317-232-8800
Environmental Management Dept				
100 N Senate Ave	Indianapolis IN	46204	**800-451-6027**	317-232-8603
Family & Social Services Admin				
402 W Washington St Rm W-392				
PO Box 7083	Indianapolis IN	46207	**800-403-0864**	800-677-9800
Fish & Wildlife Div				
402 W Washington St Rm W273	Indianapolis IN	46204	**800-677-9800**	
General Assembly				
State House 200 W Washington St	Indianapolis IN	46204	**800-382-9842**	317-232-9600
Health Dept				
2 N Meridian St	Indianapolis IN	46204	**800-382-9480**	317-233-1325
Historical Bureau				
302 W Washington St Rm E018	Indianapolis IN	46204	**800-677-9800**	
Homeland Security Dept				
302 West Washington St	Indianapolis IN	46204	**800-457-8283**	800-677-9800
Housing Finance Authority				
30 S Meridian St Ste 1000	Indianapolis IN	46204	**800-872-0371**	317-232-7777
Insurance Dept				
311 W Washington St Ste 300	Indianapolis IN	46204	**800-622-4461***	317-232-2385
*Cust Svc				
Lieutenant Governor				
302 W Washington St Rm E018	Indianapolis IN	46204	**800-677-9800**	
Natural Resources Dept				
315 West Ohio St	Indianapolis IN	46204	**877-463-6367**	800-677-9800
Parole Services Div				
302 West Washington St Rm E334	Indianapolis IN	46204	**800-677-9800**	
Port Commission				
150 W Market St Ste 100	Indianapolis IN	46204	**800-232-7678**	317-232-9200
Professional Licensing Agency				
302 West Washington St	Indianapolis IN	46204	**800-677-9800**	
Revenue Dept				
100 N Senate Ave Rm N105	Indianapolis IN	46204	**800-677-9800**	
Securities Div				
302 W Washington St 5th Fl	Indianapolis IN	46204	**800-382-5516**	317-232-6201
State Ethics Commission				
315 W Ohio St Rm 104	Indianapolis IN	46202	**866-805-8498**	800-677-9800

			Toll-Free	Phone
State Parks & Reservoirs Div				
402 W Washington St Rm W298	Indianapolis IN	46204	**800-622-4931**	317-232-4124
State Police				
100 N Senate Ave	Indianapolis IN	46204	**800-677-9800**	
Students Assistance Commission				
150 W Market St Rm 414	Indianapolis IN	46204	**888-528-4719**	317-232-2350
Technology Office				
100 N Senate Ave	Indianapolis IN	46204	**800-382-1095**	317-233-2072
Tourism Development Office				
1 N Capitol Ave Ste 600	Indianapolis IN	46204	**800-457-8283**	317-232-8860
Treasurer				
315 West Ohio St	Indianapolis IN	46204	**800-677-9800**	
Utility Regulatory Commission				
302 W Washington St Rm E306	Indianapolis IN	46204	**800-677-9800**	
Veterans' Affairs Dept				
302 W Washington St Rm E418	Indianapolis IN	46204	**800-400-4520**	317-232-3910
Victims Services Div				
101 W Washington St				
Ste 1170	East Tower Indianapolis IN	46204	**800-353-1484**	317-232-1233
Weights & Measures Div				
2525 Shadeland Ave C-3	Indianapolis IN	46219	**800-677-9800**	
Worker's Compensation Board				
402 W Washington St Rm W196	Indianapolis IN	46204	**800-677-9800**	
Workforce Development Dept				
402 W Washington St Rm W160	Indianapolis IN	46204	**800-891-6499**	317-232-7670

338-16 Iowa

			Toll-Free	Phone
Adult Children & Family Services Div				
1305 E Walnut St	Des Moines IA	50319	**800-735-2942**	515-281-8977
Child Support Recovery Unit				
PO Box 9125	Des Moines IA	50306	**888-229-9223**	
Consumer Protection Div				
1305 E Walnut St 2nd Fl	Des Moines IA	50319	**888-777-4590**	515-281-5926
Department on Aging				
510 E 12th St Ste 2	Des Moines IA	50319	**800-532-3213**	515-725-3333
Human Services Dept				
1305 E Walnut St 5th Fl SE	Des Moines IA	50319	**800-362-2178**	515-242-5880
Insurance Div				
601 Locust St 4th Fl	Des Moines IA	50309	**877-955-1212**	515-281-5705
Medical Examiners Board				
400 SW Eigth St Ste C	Des Moines IA	50309	**844-474-4321**	515-281-5171
Revenue & Finance Dept				
1305 E Walnut St				
Hoover State Office Bldg	Des Moines IA	50319	**800-367-3388**	515-281-3114
Utilities Board				
1375 E Ct Ave Rm 69	Des Moines IA	50319	**877-565-4450**	515-725-7300
Vital Records Bureau				
321 E 12th St				
Lucas State Office Bldg	Des Moines IA	50319	**866-834-9671**	515-281-7689
Workforce Development				
1000 E Grand Ave	Des Moines IA	50319	**866-239-0843**	

338-17 Kansas

			Toll-Free	Phone
Attorney General				
120 SW Tenth Ave 2nd Fl	Topeka KS	66612	**888-428-8436**	785-296-2215
Consumer Protection Div				
534 S Kansas Ave Ste 1210	Topeka KS	66603	**800-452-6727**	785-296-5059
Healing Arts Board				
800 SW Jackson Lower Level Ste A	Topeka KS	66612	**888-886-7205**	785-296-7413
Insurance Dept				
420 SW Ninth St	Topeka KS	66612	**800-432-2484**	785-296-3071
Lieutenant Governor				
300 SW Tenth Ave	Topeka KS	66612	**800-766-3777**	785-296-3232
Rehabilitation Services Div				
915 SW Harrison				
Docking State Office Bldg 9th Fl N	Topeka KS	66612	**866-213-9079**	785-368-7471
Workers' Compensation Div				
401 SW Topeka Blvd Ste 2	Topeka KS	66603	**800-332-0353**	785-296-4000

338-18 Kentucky

			Toll-Free	Phone
Child Support Div				
730 Schenkel Ln	Frankfort KY	40601	**800-248-1163**	
Consumer Protection Div				
1024 Capital Ctr Dr Ste 200	Frankfort KY	40601	**888-432-9257**	502-696-5389
Crime Victims Compensation Board				
130 Brighton Pk Blvd	Frankfort KY	40601	**800-469-2120**	502-573-2290
Emergency Management Div				
100 Minuteman Pkwy	Frankfort KY	40601	**800-255-2587**	
Fish & Wildlife Resources Dept				
#1 Sportsman's Ln	Frankfort KY	40601	**800-858-1549**	502-564-3400
General Assembly				
700 Capitol Ave	Frankfort KY	40601	**800-372-7181**	502-564-3449
Health & Family Services Cabinet				
275 E Main St	Frankfort KY	40621	**800-372-2973**	502-564-7042
Higher Education Assistance Authority				
PO Box 798	Frankfort KY	40602	**800-928-8926**	
Historical Society				
100 W Broadway	Frankfort KY	40601	**877-444-7867**	502-564-1792
Housing Corp				
1231 Louisville Rd	Frankfort KY	40601	**800-633-8896**	502-564-7630
Insurance Dept				
215 W Main St	Frankfort KY	40601	**800-595-6053**	502-564-3630
Lottery Corp				
1011 W Main St	Louisville KY	40202	**800-937-8946**	502-560-1500
Real Estate Commission (KREC)				
10200 Linn Stn Rd Ste 201	Louisville KY	40223	**888-373-3300***	502-429-7250
*General				

	Toll-Free	Phone
Travel and Tourism Dept		
100 Airport Rd 2nd fl ....Frankfort KY 40601	800-225-8747	502-564-4930
Veterans Affairs Dept (KDVA)		
1111B Louisville Rd ....Frankfort KY 40601	800-572-6245	502-564-9203
Vocational Rehabilitation Dept		
275 E Main St ....Frankfort KY 40601	800-372-7172	502-564-4440

338-19 Louisiana

	Toll-Free	Phone
Agriculture & Forestry Dept		
5825 Florida Blvd ....Baton Rouge LA 70806	866-927-2476	225-922-1234
Community Services Office		
627 N Fourth St ....Baton Rouge LA 70802	888-524-3578	
Consumer Protection Office		
1885 N Third St ....Baton Rouge LA 70804	800-351-4889	225-326-6465
Contractors Licensing Board		
2525 Quail Dr ....Baton Rouge LA 70808	800-256-1392	225-765-2301
Crime Victims Reparations Board		
PO Box 3133 ....Baton Rouge LA 70821	888-684-2846	225-342-1749
Education Dept		
PO Box 94064 ....Baton Rouge LA 70804	877-453-2721	
Environmental Quality Dept		
602 N Fifth St ....Baton Rouge LA 70802	866-896-5337	225-219-5337
Ethics Board		
617 N Third St		
LaSalle Bldg Ste 10-36. ....Baton Rouge LA 70802	800-842-6630	225-219-5600
Financial Institutions Office		
PO Box 94095 ....Baton Rouge LA 70804	888-525-9414	225-925-4660
Housing Finance Agency		
2415 Quail Dr ....Baton Rouge LA 70808	888-454-2001	225-763-8700
Insurance Dept		
1702 N Third Str ....Baton Rouge LA 70802	800-259-5300	225-342-5900
Legislature		
PO Box 94062 ....Baton Rouge LA 70804	800-256-3793	225-342-2456
Lottery Corp		
555 Laurel St ....Baton Rouge LA 70801	877-770-7867	225-297-2000
Office of Student Financial Assistance		
602 N Fifth St ....Baton Rouge LA 70802	800-259-5626	225-219-1012
Office of the Governor		
PO Box 94004 ....Baton Rouge LA 70804	866-366-1121	225-342-7015
Public Service Commission		
PO Box 91154 ....Baton Rouge LA 70821	800-256-2397	225-342-4999
Rehabilitation Services		
627 N Fourth St ....Baton Rouge LA 70802	888-524-3578	
Revenue Dept		
617 N Third St PO Box 201 ....Baton Rouge LA 70802	855-307-3893	
State Parks Office		
PO Box 44426 ....Baton Rouge LA 70804	877-226-7652	225-342-8111
Veterans Affairs Dept		
PO Box 94095 ....Baton Rouge LA 70804	877-432-8982	225-219-5000
Weights & Measures Div		
5825 Florida Blvd ....Baton Rouge LA 70806	866-927-2476	225-922-1234
Wildlife & Fisheries Dept		
2000 Quail Dr ....Baton Rouge LA 70898	800-256-2749	225-765-2800

338-20 Maine

	Toll-Free	Phone
State Government Information		
26 Edison Dr ....Augusta ME 04330	888-577-6690	207-624-9494
Bureau of Financial Institutions		
36 State House Sta ....Augusta ME 04333	800-965-5235	207-624-8570
Consumer Protection Unit		
85 Leighton Rd ....Augusta ME 04333	800-436-2131	207-287-2923
Elder Services Office		
41 Anthony Ave ....Augusta ME 04333	888-568-1112	207-287-9200
Employment Services Bureau		
55 State House Stn ....Augusta ME 04330	888-457-8883	207-623-7981
Environmental Protection Dept		
17 State House Stn ....Augusta ME 04333	800-452-1942	207-287-7688
Finance Authority of Maine		
5 Community Dr PO Box 949 ....Augusta ME 04332	800-228-3734	207-623-3263
Governor 1 State House Stn ....Augusta ME 04333	855-721-5203	207-287-3531
Housing Authority		
353 Water St ....Augusta ME 04330	800-452-4668	207-626-4600
Insurance Bureau		
34 State House Stn ....Augusta ME 04333	800-300-5000	207-624-8475
Public Utilities Commission		
18 State House Stn ....Augusta ME 04333	800-437-1220	207-287-3831
Rehabilitation Services Bureau		
150 State House Sta ....Augusta ME 04333	800-698-4440	
Securities Div		
76 Northern Ave ....Gardiner ME 04345	877-624-8551	207-624-8551
Tourism Office		
59 State House Sta ....Augusta ME 04333	888-624-6345	207-624-7483
Vital Records Office		
220 Capitol St ....Augusta ME 04333	888-664-9491	207-287-3181
Workers' Compensation Board		
442 Civic Ctr Dr 27 State House Stn		
Ste 100. ....Augusta ME 04333	888-801-9087	207-287-3751

338-21 Maryland

	Toll-Free	Phone
Aging Dept		
301 W Preston St Ste 1007. ....Baltimore MD 21201	800-243-3425	410-767-1100
Assessments & Taxation Dept		
301 W Preston St ....Baltimore MD 21201	888-246-5941	410-767-1184
Court of Appeals		
361 Rowe Blvd ....Annapolis MD 21401	800-926-2583	410-260-1500
Department of Budget & Management		
45 Calvert St ....Annapolis MD 21401	800-705-3493	
Dept of Legislative Services		
90 State Cir ....Annapolis MD 21401	800-492-7122	410-946-5400
Education Dept		
200 W Baltimore St ....Baltimore MD 21201	888-246-0016	410-767-0100
Emergency Management Agency		
5401 Rue St Lo Dr ....Reisterstown MD 21136	877-636-2872	410-517-3600
Environment Dept		
1800 Washington Blvd ....Baltimore MD 21230	800-633-6101	410-537-3000
Ethics Commission		
45 Calvert St ....Annapolis MD 21401	877-669-6085	410-260-7770
Financial Regulation Div		
500 N Calvert St Ste 402 ....Baltimore MD 21202	888-784-0136	410-230-6100
Fisheries Service		
580 Taylor Ave ....Annapolis MD 21401	877-634-6361	
Governor		
State House 100 State Cir. ....Annapolis MD 21401	800-811-8336	410-974-3901
Higher Education Commission		
839 Bestgate Rd Ste 400. ....Baltimore MD 21201	800-974-0203	410-260-4500
Housing & Community Development Dept		
7800 Harkins Rd ....Lanham MD 21032	800-756-0119	301-429-7400
Insurance Administration		
200 St Paul Pl Ste 2700 ....Baltimore MD 21202	800-492-6116	410-468-2000
Labor & Industry Div		
1100 N Eutaw St Rm 600 ....Baltimore MD 21201	888-257-6674	410-767-2241
Motor Vehicle Administration		
6601 Ritchie Hwy NE ....Glen Burnie MD 21062	800-950-1682	410-768-7000
Natural Resources Dept		
580 Taylor Ave ....Annapolis MD 21401	877-620-8367	
Physician Quality Assurance Board		
4201 Patterson Ave ....Baltimore MD 21215	800-492-6836	410-764-4777
Public Service Commission		
6 St Paul St 16th Fl. ....Baltimore MD 21202	800-492-0474	410-767-8000
Securities Div		
200 St Paul Pl ....Baltimore MD 21202	888-743-0023	410-576-6360
State Forest & Park Service		
580 Taylor Ave ....Annapolis MD 21401	877-620-8367	
State Lottery		
1800 Washington Blvd Ste 330 ....Baltimore MD 21230	800-201-0108	410-230-8800
State Police		
1201 Reisterstown Rd ....Pikesville MD 21208	800-525-5555	410-653-4200
Teacher Certification & Accreditation Div		
200 W Baltimore St ....Baltimore MD 21201	888-246-0016	410-767-0412
Tourism Development Office		
401 E Pratt Str 14th Fl ....Baltimore MD 21202	877-333-4455	410-767-3400
Treasurer		
80 Calvert St Rm 109 ....Annapolis MD 21401	800-974-0468	410-260-7533
Vital Records Div		
6764-B Reisterstown Rd ....Baltimore MD 21215	800-832-3277	410-764-3038
Workers' Compensation Commission		
10 E Baltimore St ....Baltimore MD 21202	800-492-0479	410-864-5100

338-22 Massachusetts

	Toll-Free	Phone
Banks Div		
1000 Washington St 1st Fl ....Boston MA 02118	800-495-2265	617-956-1500
Child Support Enforcement Div		
51 Sleeper St 4th Fl ....Boston MA 02205	800-332-2733	617-660-1234
Cultural Council		
10 St James Ave 3rd Fl. ....Boston MA 02116	800-232-0960	617-858-2700
Governor		
24 Beacon St State House Rm 280 ....Boston MA 02133	888-870-7770	617-725-4005
Housing Finance Agency		
1 Beacon St ....Boston MA 02108	800-882-1154	617-854-1000
Insurance Div		
1000 Washington St Ste 810 ....Boston MA 02118	877-563-4467	617-521-7794
Medical Examiner		
720 Albany St ....Boston MA 02118	800-962-7877	617-267-6767
Mental Health Dept		
25 Staniford St ....Boston MA 02114	800-221-0053	617-626-8000
Parole Board 12 Mercer Rd ....Natick MA 01760	888-298-6272	508-650-4500
Revenue Dept PO Box 7010 ....Boston MA 02204	800-392-6089	617-887-6367
Securities Div		
1 Ashburton Pl 17th Fl ....Boston MA 02108	800-269-5428	617-727-3548
Travel & Tourism Office		
136 Blackstone St 5th Fl. ....Boston MA 02109	800-227-6277	617-973-8500

338-23 Michigan

	Toll-Free	Phone
Attorney General		
525 W Ottawa St ....Lansing MI 48909	877-765-8388	517-373-1110
Career Education & Workforce Programs		
201 N Washington Sq		
Victor Office Center. ....Lansing MI 48913	888-253-6855	517-335-5858
Child Support Office		
235 S Grand Ave PO Box 30037 ....Lansing MI 48933	866-661-0005	
Civil Service Dept		
400 S Pine St Capitol Commons Ctr		
PO Box 30002. ....Lansing MI 48909	800-788-1766	517-373-3030
Consumer Protection Div		
PO Box 30213 ....Lansing MI 48909	877-765-8388	517-373-1140
Crime Victims Services Commission		
320 S Walnut St Garden Level		
Lewis Cass Bldg ....Lansing MI 48933	877-251-7373	517-373-7373
Economic Development Corp (MEDC)		
300 N Washington Sq ....Lansing MI 48913	888-522-0103	
Education Trust		
PO Box 30198 ....Lansing MI 48909	800-638-4543*	517-335-4767
*General		
eLibrary Information		
702 W Kalamazoo St PO Box 30007 ....Lansing MI 48909	877-479-0021	517-373-4331
Financial & Insurance Regulation		
530 W Allegan St ....Lansing MI 48909	877-999-6442	517-373-0220

			Toll-Free	Phone
State Housing Development Authority				
PO Box 30044	Lansing MI	48909	866-466-7328	
State Lottery				
101 E Hillsdale St PO Box 30023	Lansing MI	48909	844-887-6836	517-335-5756
Student Financial Services Bureau				
Austin Bldg 430 W Allegan	Lansing MI	48922	888-447-2687	
Travel Michigan				
300 N Washington Sq	Lansing MI	48913	888-784-7328	517-335-4590
Workers Compensation Agency				
2501 Woodlake Cir	Okemos MI	48864	888-396-5041	517-284-8902

338-24 Minnesota

			Toll-Free	Phone
Aging Board 540 Cedar St	Saint Paul MN	55155	800-882-6262	651-431-2500
Arts Board				
400 Sibley St Ste 200	Saint Paul MN	55101	800-866-2787	651-215-1600
Attorney General				
445 Minnesota St Ste 1400	Saint Paul MN	55101	800-657-3787	651-296-3353
Campaign Finance & Public Disclosure Board				
190 Centennial Office Bldg 658 Cedar St	Saint Paul MN	55155	800-657-3889	651-539-1180
Child Support Enforcement Div				
444 Lafayette Rd N	Saint Paul MN	55164	800-747-5484	651-431-2000
Commerce Dept				
85 Seventh Pl E Ste 500	Saint Paul MN	55101	800-657-3602	651-539-1500
Department of Public Safety				
444 Minnesota St	Saint Paul MN	55101	800-657-3787	651-201-7000
Employment & Economic Development Dept (DEED)				
332 Minnesota St Ste E200	Saint Paul MN	55101	800-657-3858	651-259-7114
Governor				
130 State Capitol				
75 Rev Dr Martin Luther King Jr Blvd	Saint Paul MN	55155	800-657-3717	651-201-3400
Health Dept				
625 Robert St N	Saint Paul MN	55164	888-345-0823	651-201-4545
Housing Finance Authority				
400 Sibley St Ste 300	Saint Paul MN	55101	800-657-3769	651-296-7608
Labor & Industry Dept				
443 Lafayette Rd N	Saint Paul MN	55155	800-342-5354	651-284-5005
Legislature				
211 State Capitol	Saint Paul MN	55155	888-234-1112	651-296-2314
Medical Practice Board				
2829 University Ave SE Ste 500	Minneapolis MN	55414	800-657-3709	612-617-2130
Natural Resources Dept				
500 Lafayette Rd	Saint Paul MN	55155	888-646-6367	651-259-5300
Office of Higher Education				
1450 Energy Pk Dr Ste 350	Saint Paul MN	55108	800-657-3866	651-642-0567
Parks & Recreation Div				
500 Lafayette Rd	Saint Paul MN	55155	888-646-6367	651-259-5300
Public Utilities Commission				
121 Seventh Pl E Ste 350	Saint Paul MN	55101	800-657-3782	651-296-7124
Revenue Dept				
600 N Roberts St	Saint Paul MN	55101	800-657-3666	651-556-3000
Transportation Dept				
395 John Ireland Blvd	Saint Paul MN	55155	800-657-3774	651-296-3000
Workers" Compensation Div				
443 Lafayette Rd	Saint Paul MN	55155	800-342-5354	651-284-5005

338-25 Mississippi

			Toll-Free	Phone
State Government Information				
200 S Lamar Ste 800	Jackson MS	39201	877-290-9487	601-351-5023
Banking & Consumer Finance Dept				
PO Box 12129	Jackson MS	39236	800-844-2499	601-321-6901
Contractors Board				
2679 Crane Ridge Dr Ste C	Jackson MS	39216	800-880-6161	601-354-6161
Dept of Human Service				
200 S Lamar St	Jackson MS	39201	800-345-6347	601-359-4500
Development Authority				
501 NW St	Jackson MS	39201	800-360-3323	601-359-3449
Emergency Management Agency				
1 Mema Dr PO Box 5644	Pearl MS	39288	800-222-6362	601-933-6362
Employment Security Commission				
1235 Echelon Pkwy PO Box 1699	Jackson MS	39215	888-844-3577	601-321-6000
Enviromental Quality Dept				
515 E Amite St	Jackson MS	39201	888-786-0661	601-961-5611
Insurance Dept				
1001 Woolfolk State Office Bldg 501 NW St				
501 N West St	Jackson MS	39201	800-562-2957	601-359-3569
Rehabilitation Services Dept				
1281 Hwy 51 PO Box 1698	Madison MS	39110	800-443-1000	
Weights & Measures Div				
121 N Jefferson St	Jackson MS	39201	800-551-1830	601-359-1100
Worker's Compensation Commission				
1428 Lakeland Dr	Jackson MS	39216	866-473-6922	601-987-4200

338-26 Missouri

			Toll-Free	Phone
Attorney General				
207 W High St PO Box 899	Jefferson City MO	65102	800-392-8222	573-751-3321
Child Support Enforcement Div				
205 Jefferson St 1st Fl	Jefferson City MO	65103	800-859-7999	573-522-8024
Consumer Protection Div				
207 W High St PO Box 899	Jefferson City MO	65102	800-392-8222	573-751-3321
Finance Div				
Truman State Office Bldg				
Rm 630	Jefferson City MO	65102	888-246-7225	573-751-3242
Higher Education Dept				
205 Jefferson St	Jefferson City MO	65109	800-473-6757	573-751-2361
Historical Preservation Office				
1101 Riverside Dr	Jefferson City MO	65101	800-361-4827	573-751-3443

			Toll-Free	Phone
Insurance Dept				
301 W High St Rm 530	Jefferson City MO	65101	800-726-7390	573-751-4126
Lottery				
1823 Southridge Dr PO Box 1603	Jefferson City MO	65109	888-238-7633	573-751-4050
Natural Resources Dept				
1101 Riverside Dr	Jefferson City MO	65102	800-361-4827*	573-751-3443
*Cust Svc				
Professional Registration Div				
3605 Missouri Blvd PO Box 1335	Jefferson City MO	65102	800-735-2466	573-751-0293
Public Service Commission				
200 Madison St PO Box 360	Jefferson City MO	65102	800-819-3180	573-751-3234
Real Estate Commission				
3605 Missouri Blvd PO Box 1339	Jefferson City MO	65102	800-735-2466	573-751-2628
Securities Div				
600 W Main St Rm 229				
PO Box 1276	Jefferson City MO	65102	800-721-7996	573-751-4136
State Parks Div				
PO Box 176	Jefferson City MO	65102	800-334-6946	573-751-2479
Supreme Court				
207 W High St	Jefferson City MO	65101	888-541-4894	573-751-4144
Tourism Div				
PO Box 1055	Jefferson City MO	65102	800-519-2100	573-751-4133
Transportation Dept				
105 W Capitol Ave PO Box 270	Jefferson City MO	65102	888-275-6636	573-751-2551
Veterans Commission				
205 Jefferson St				
12th Fl Jefferson Bldg PO Drawer 147	Jefferson City MO	65102	866-838-4636	573-751-3779
Vocational & Adult Education Div				
3024 Dupont Cir PO Box 480	Jefferson City MO	65109	877-222-8963	573-751-3251
Workers Compensation Div				
PO Box 58	Jefferson City MO	65102	800-775-2667	573-751-4231

338-27 Montana

			Toll-Free	Phone
Arts Council PO Box 202201	Helena MT	59620	800-282-3092	406-444-6430
Banking & Financial Institutions Div				
301 S Park Ste 316 PO Box 200546	Helena MT	59620	800-914-8423	406-841-2920
Child & Family Services Div				
PO Box 8005	Helena MT	59604	866-820-5437	406-841-2400
Consumer Protection Office				
555 Fulller Ave	Helena MT	59620	800-481-6896	406-444-4500
Higher Education Board of Regents				
2500 Broadway St PO Box 203201	Helena MT	59620	877-501-1722	406-444-6570
Information Technology Services Div				
125 N Roberts St PO Box 200113	Helena MT	59620	800-628-4917	406-444-2511
Office of Governor				
PO Box 200801	Helena MT	59620	855-318-1330	406-444-3111
Revenue Dept				
125 N Roberts PO Box 5805	Helena MT	59604	866-859-2254	406-444-6900
Securities Dept				
840 Helena Ave	Helena MT	59601	800-332-6148	406-444-2040
Victim Services Office				
555 Fuller Ave PO Box 201410	Helena MT	59601	800-498-6455	406-444-1907

338-28 Nebraska

			Toll-Free	Phone
Arts Council 1004 Farnam St	Omaha NE	68131	800-341-4067	402-595-2122
Attorney General				
2115 State Capitol	Lincoln NE	68509	800-727-6432	402-471-2683
Child Support Enforcement Div				
PO Box 94728	Lincoln NE	68509	877-631-9973	402-471-3121
Economic Development Dept				
301 Centennial Mall S	Lincoln NE	68509	800-426-6505	402-471-3111
Emergency Management Agency				
2433 NW 24th St	Lincoln NE	68524	877-297-2368	402-471-7421
Environmental Quality Dept				
1200 N St Ste 400	Lincoln NE	68508	877-253-2603	402-471-2186
Health & Human Services Dept				
301 Centennial Mall S	Lincoln NE	68508	800-430-3244	402-471-3121
Historical Society				
1500 R St	Lincoln NE	68508	800-833-6747	402-471-3270
Insurance Dept				
941 O St Ste 400	Lincoln NE	68508	877-564-7323	402-471-2201
Investment Finance Authority				
1230 'O' St Ste 200	Lincoln NE	68508	800-204-6432	402-434-3900
Lieutenant Governor				
PO Box 94848	Lincoln NE	68508	800-747-8177	
Public Accountancy Board				
1526 K St Ste 410	Lincoln NE	68508	800-564-6111	402-471-3595
Public Service Commission				
1200 N St Ste 300	Lincoln NE	68508	800-526-0017	402-471-3101
Revenue Dept				
301 Centennial Mall S PO Box 94818	Lincoln NE	68509	800-742-7474	402-471-5729
Travel & Tourism Div				
301 Centennial Mall S	Lincoln NE	68509	877-632-7275	402-471-3796

338-29 Nevada

			Toll-Free	Phone
Bill Status				
401 S Carson St	Carson City NV	89701	800-978-2878	775-684-6827
Child Support Enforcement Office				
300 E Second St Ste 1200	Reno NV	89501	800-992-0900	775-448-5150
Economic Development Commission				
808 W Nye Ln	Carson City NV	89703	800-336-1600	775-687-9900
Motor Vehicles Dept				
555 Wright Way	Carson City NV	89711	877-368-7828	775-684-4368
Tourism Commission				
401 N Carson St	Carson City NV	89701	800-638-2328	

338-30   New Hampshire

	Toll-Free	Phone
Banking Dept 95 Pleasant St .... Concord NH 03301	800-437-5991	603-271-3561
Child Support Services		
129 Pleasant St .... Concord NH 03301	800-852-3345	603-271-4427
Employment Security		
32 S Main St .... Concord NH 03301	800-852-3400	603-224-3311
Environmental Services Dept		
29 Hazen Dr PO Box 95 .... Concord NH 03301	866-429-9278	603-271-3503
Governor		
State House 107 N Main St .... Concord NH 03301	800-852-3456	603-271-2121
Housing Finance Authority		
32 Constitution Dr .... Bedford NH 03110	800-439-7247	603-472-8623
Lottery Commission		
14 Integra Dr .... Concord NH 03301	800-852-3324	603-271-3391
Public Utilities Commission		
21 S Fruit St Ste 10 .... Concord NH 03301	800-852-3793*	603-271-2431
*Consumer Assistance		
Teacher Credentialing Bureau		
101 Pleasant St .... Concord NH 03301	866-444-4211	603-271-3494
Treasury Dept		
25 Capitol St Rm 121 .... Concord NH 03301	800-791-0920	603-271-2621
Victims' Assistance Commission		
33 Capitol St .... Concord NH 03301	800-300-4500	603-271-1284
Vocational Rehabilitation Office		
21 S Fruit St Ste 20 .... Concord NH 03301	800-299-1647	603-271-3471

338-31   New Jersey

	Toll-Free	Phone
Banking & Insurance Dept		
20 W State St PO Box 325 .... Trenton NJ 08625	800-446-7467	609-292-7272
Bill Status		
State House Annex PO Box 068 .... Trenton NJ 08625	800-792-8630	609-292-4840
Board of Public Utilities		
44 S Clinton Ave .... Newark NJ 07102	800-624-0241	
Child Support Office		
175 S Broad St PO Box 8068 .... Trenton NJ 08650	877-655-4371	
Consumer Affairs Div		
124 Halsey St .... Newark NJ 07102	800-242-5846	973-504-6200
Education Dept PO Box 500 .... Trenton NJ 08625	877-900-6960	609-376-3500
Ethical Standards Commission		
28 W State St 8th Fl PO Box 082 ..... Trenton NJ 08625	888-223-1355	609-292-1892
Higher Education Student Assistance Authority		
4 Quakerbridge Plz PO Box 540 .... Trenton NJ 08625	800-792-8670	609-584-4480
Mental Health Services Div		
PO Box 272 .... Trenton NJ 08625	800-382-6717	609-777-0700
Military & Veterans' Affairs Dept		
101 Eggert Crossing Rd .... Lawrenceville NJ 08648	800-624-0508	609-530-4600
Parks & Forestry Div		
PO Box 404 .... Trenton NJ 08625	800-843-6420	609-984-0370
Securities Bureau		
153 Halsey St 6th Fl .... Newark NJ 07102	866-446-8378	973-504-3600
Travel & Tourism Div		
225 W State St PO Box 460 .... Trenton NJ 08625	800-847-4865	609-599-6540
Victims of Crime Compensation Board		
50 Pk Pl .... Newark NJ 07102	877-658-2221	973-648-2107

338-32   New Mexico

	Toll-Free	Phone
Aging Agency		
2550 Cerrillos Rd PO Box 27118 .... Santa Fe NM 87505	800-432-2080	505-476-4799
Arts Div		
407 Galisteo St Ste 270 .... Santa Fe NM 87501	800-879-4278	505-827-6490
Child Support Enforcement Div		
PO Box 25110 .... Santa Fe NM 87504	800-288-7207	505-476-7207
Children Youth & Families Dept		
PO Box 5160 .... Santa Fe NM 87502	800-610-7610	800-432-2075
Consumer Protection Div		
408 Galisteo St Villagra Bldg		
PO Box 1508 .... Santa Fe NM 87501	844-255-9210	505-827-6000
Crime Victims Reparation Commission		
6200 Uptown Blvd Ste 210 .... Albuquerque NM 87110	800-306-6262	505-841-9432
Economic Development Dept		
PO Box 20003 .... Santa Fe NM 87504	800-374-3061	505-827-0300
Environment Dept		
1190 St Francis Dr Ste N4050 .... Santa Fe NM 87505	800-219-6157	505-827-2855
Ethics Administration		
325 Don Gaspar St Ste 300 .... Santa Fe NM 87501	800-477-3632	505-827-3600
Higher Education Dept		
2048 Galisteo St .... Santa Fe NM 87505	800-279-9777	505-476-8400
Highway & Transportation Dept (NMDOT)		
1120 Cerrillos Rd PO Box 1149 .... Santa Fe NM 87504	800-432-4269*	505-827-5100
*General		
Human Services Dept (NMHSD)		
PO Box 2348 .... Santa Fe NM 87504	888-997-2583	505-827-3100
Lottery		
4511 Osuna Rd NE .... Albuquerque NM 87109	800-572-1142	505-342-7600
Mortgage Finance Authority		
344 Fourth St SW .... Albuquerque NM 87102	800-444-6880	505-843-6880
Secretary of State		
325 Don Gaspar Ste 300 .... Santa Fe NM 87503	800-477-3632	505-827-3600
State Parks Division		
1220 S St Francis Dr .... Santa Fe NM 87505	888-667-2757	505-476-3355
Vital Records & Health Statistics Bureau		
1105 S St Francis Dr .... Santa Fe NM 87502	866-534-0051	505-827-0121
Vocational Rehabilitation Div		
435 St Michaels Dr Bldg D .... Santa Fe NM 87505	800-224-7005	505-954-8500
Workers' Compensation Admin		
2410 Ctr Ave SE PO Box 27198 .... Albuquerque NM 87125	800-255-7965	505-841-6000

338-33   New York

	Toll-Free	Phone
Aging Office		
2 Empire State Plz .... Albany NY 12223	800-342-9871	
Athletic Commission		
123 William St 20th Fl .... New York NY 10038	866-269-3769	212-417-5700
Banking Dept 1 State St .... New York NY 10004	877-226-5697	800-342-3736
Bill Status		
202 Legislative Office Bldg .... Albany NY 12248	800-342-9860	518-455-4218
Court of Appeals 20 Eagle St ...... Albany NY 12207	800-268-7869	
Department of Environmental Conservation		
625 Broadway .... Albany NY 12233	800-678-6399	518-408-5850
Division of Consumer Protection		
5 Empire State Plz Ste 2101 .... Albany NY 12223	800-697-1220	518-474-8583
Empire State Development		
30 S Pearl St 7th Fl .... Albany NY 12245	800-782-8369	518-292-5100
Health Dept		
Empire State Plz Corning Tower .... Albany NY 12237	866-881-2809	
Higher Education Services Corp		
99 Washington Ave .... Albany NY 12255	888-697-4372	518-473-1574
Housing Finance Agency		
641 Lexington Ave .... New York NY 10022	866-275-3427	212-688-4000
Labor Dept		
WA Harriman Campus Bldg 12 .... Albany NY 12240	888-469-7365	518-457-9000
Mental Health Office		
44 Holland Ave .... Albany NY 12229	800-597-8481	
Office of Court Admin		
4 ESP Ste 2001 Empire State Plz ...... Albany NY 12223	800-430-8457	212-428-2100
Office of the Professions		
89 Washington Ave .... Albany NY 12234	800-442-8106	518-474-3817
Recreation and Historic Preservation		
625 Broadway .... Albany NY 12207	800-456-2267	518-474-0456
Temporary & Disability Assistance Office		
40 N Pearl St 16th Fl .... Albany NY 12243	800-342-3009	518-473-1090
Vital Records Office		
800 N Pearl St .... Menands NY 12204	800-541-2831	
Workers' Compensation Board		
PO Box 5205 .... Binghamton NY 13902	877-632-4996	518-402-6070

338-34   North Carolina

	Toll-Free	Phone
Agriculture Dept		
2 W Edenton St 1001 MSC .... Raleigh NC 27601	800-735-2962	919-733-7125
Department of Military and Veterans Affairs		
413 North Salisbury S .... Raleigh NC 27603	844-624-8387	
Housing Finance Agency		
3508 Bush St .... Raleigh NC 27609	800-393-0988	919-877-5700
Labor Dept		
1101 Mail Service Ctr .... Raleigh NC 27699	800-625-2267	919-807-2796
Marine Fisheries Div		
3441 Arendell St .... Morehead City NC 28557	800-682-2632	252-726-7021
Parks & Recreation Div		
121 W Jones St NRC Bldg 2nd Fl ...... Raleigh NC 27603	877-722-6762	919-707-9300
Securities Div PO Box 29622 .... Raleigh NC 27626	800-688-4507	919-814-5400
Transportation Dept		
1 S Wilmington St .... Raleigh NC 27611	877-368-4968	
Utilities Commission		
4325 Mail Service Ctr Dobbs Bldg ..... Raleigh NC 27699	866-380-9816	919-733-7328
Victims Compensation Services Div		
4232 Mail Service Ctr .... Raleigh NC 27699	800-826-6200	919-733-7974
Vocational Rehabilitation Services Div		
2801 MSC .... Raleigh NC 27699	800-689-9090	919-855-3500

338-35   North Dakota

	Toll-Free	Phone
Accountancy Board		
2701 S Columbia Rd Ste D .... Grand Forks ND 58201	800-532-5904	701-775-7100
Aging Services Div		
1237 W Divide Ave Ste 6 .... Bismarck ND 58501	855-462-5465	701-328-4649
Agriculture Dept		
600 E Blvd Ave Dept 602 .... Bismarck ND 58505	800-242-7535	701-328-2231
Attorney General		
600 E Blvd Ave Dept 125 .... Bismarck ND 58505	800-472-2600	701-328-2210
Child Support Enforcement Div		
1600 E Century Ave Ste 2 PO Box 2057 .... Bismarck ND 58502	800-231-4255	701-328-3582
Consumer Protection Div		
1050 E Interstate Ave Ste 200 ...... Bismarck ND 58503	800-472-2600	701-328-3404
Drivers License & Traffic Safety Div		
608 E Blvd Ave .... Bismarck ND 58505	855-637-6237	701-328-2500
Financial Institutions Dept		
2000 Schafer St Ste G .... Bismarck ND 58501	800-366-6888	701-328-9933
Governor 600 E Blvd Ave .... Bismarck ND 58505	888-328-2112	701-328-2200
Housing Finance Agency		
2624 Vermont Ave PO Box 1535 .... Bismarck ND 58502	800-292-8621	701-328-8080
Insurance Dept		
600 E Blvd Ave .... Bismarck ND 58505	800-247-0560	701-328-2440
Labor and Human Rights Dept		
600 E Blvd Ave Dept 406 .... Bismarck ND 58505	800-582-8032	701-328-2660
Parks & Recreation Dept		
1600 E Century Ave Ste 3 PO Box 5594 ... Bismarck ND 58506	800-366-6888	701-328-5357
Secretary of State		
600 E Blvd Ave Dept 108 .... Bismarck ND 58505	800-352-0867	701 328-2900
Securities Dept		
600 E Blvd Ave State Capitol 5th Fl ... Bismarck ND 58505	800-297-5124	701-328-2910
Tax Dept 600 E Blvd Ave .... Bismarck ND 58505	800-638-2901	701-328-3470
Testing & Safety Div		
600 E Blvd Ave Dept 408 .... Bismarck ND 58505	877-245-6685	701-328-2400
Tourism Div		
1600 E Century Ave Ste 2 .... Bismarck ND 58502	800-435-5663	701-328-2525

Classified Section

			Toll-Free	Phone
Transportation Dept				
608 E Blvd Ave	Bismarck ND	58505	855-637-6237	701-328-2500
Veterans Affairs Dept				
4201 38th St SW Ste 104 PO Box 9003	Fargo ND	58104	866-634-8387	701-239-7165
Vocational Rehabilitation Div				
1237 W Divide Ave Ste 2	Bismarck ND	58501	888-862-7342	701-328-8800
Workers Compensation				
1600 E Century Ave Ste 1	Bismarck ND	58503	800-777-5033	701-328-3800

338-36 Ohio

			Toll-Free	Phone
Aging Dept				
246 N High St 1st Fl	Columbus OH	43215	800-266-4346	614-466-5500
Agriculture Dept				
8995 E Main St	Reynoldsburg OH	43068	800-282-1955	614-728-6201
Consumer Protection Section				
30 E Broad St 14th Fl	Columbus OH	43215	800-282-0515	614-466-4986
Education Dept				
25 S Front St	Columbus OH	43215	877-644-6338	
Financial Institutions Div				
77 S High St 21st Fl	Columbus OH	43266	866-278-0003	614-728-8400
Historical Society				
800 E 17th Ave	Columbus OH	43211	800-686-6124	614-297-2300
Housing Finance Agency				
57 E Main St	Columbus OH	43215	888-362-6432	614-466-7970
Insurance Dept				
50 W Town St Ste 300 3rd Fl	Columbus OH	43215	800-686-1526	614-644-2658
Mental Health Dept				
30 E Broad St 8th Fl	Columbus OH	43215	877-275-6364	614-466-2596
Parks & Recreation Div				
2045 Morse Rd Bldg C-3	Columbus OH	43229	866-644-6727	614-265-6561
Parole Board				
770 W Broad St	Columbus OH	43222	888-344-1441	614-752-1200
Public Utilities Commission				
180 E Broad St	Columbus OH	43215	800-686-7826	614-466-3016
Taxation Dept PO Box 530	Columbus OH	43216	888-405-4089	614-466-2166
Travel & Tourism Div				
PO Box 1001	Columbus OH	43216	800-282-5393	614-466-8844
Treasurer				
30 E Broad St 9th Fl	Columbus OH	43215	800-228-1102	614-466-2160
Tuition Trust Authority				
35 E Chestnut St 8th Fl	Columbus OH	43215	800-233-6734*	614-752-9400
*Cust Svc				
Wildlife Div				
2045 Morse Rd Bldg G	Columbus OH	43229	800-945-3543	614-265-6300
Workers' Compensation Bureau				
30 W Spring St	Columbus OH	43215	800-644-6292	614-644-6292
Workforce Developement Office				
4020 E Fifth Ave PO Box 1618	Columbus OH	43219	888-296-7541	
Youth Services Dept				
30 W Spring St	Columbus OH	43215	855-577-7714	614-466-4314

338-37 Oklahoma

			Toll-Free	Phone
Commerce Dept				
900 N Stiles Ave	Oklahoma City OK	73104	800-879-6552	405-815-6552
Environmental Quality Dept				
707 N Robinson	Oklahoma City OK	73102	800-869-1400	405-702-0100
Housing Finance Agency				
100 NW 63rd St Ste 200	Oklahoma City OK	73116	800-256-1489	405-848-1144
Insurance Dept (OID)				
3625 NW 56th Ste 100	Oklahoma City OK	73112	800-522-0071	405-521-2828
Real Estate Commission				
1915 N Stiles Ave Ste 200	Oklahoma City OK	73105	866-521-3389	405-521-3387
Rehabilitative Services Dept				
3535 NW 58th St Ste 500	Oklahoma City OK	73112	800-845-8476	405-951-3400
Travel Promotion Div				
900 N Stiles Ave	Oklahoma City OK	73104	800-652-6552	
Vital Records Div				
1000 NE Tenth St	Oklahoma City OK	73117	800-522-0203	405-271-5600

338-38 Oregon

			Toll-Free	Phone
Crime Victims Service Div				
1162 Ct St NE	Salem OR	97301	877-877-9392	503-378-4400
Dept of Transportation				
355 Capitol St NE MS 11	Salem OR	97301	888-275-6368	503-986-4000
Energy Dept 550 Capitol St NE	Salem OR	97301	800-221-8035	503-378-4040
Environmental Quality Dept				
700 NE Multnomah St	Portland OR	97204	800-452-4011	503-229-5696
Finance & Corporate Securities Div				
350 Winter St NE Rm 410 PO Box 14480	Salem OR	97309	866-814-9710	503-378-4140
Financial Fraud/Consumer Protection Section				
1162 Ct St NE	Salem OR	97301	877-877-9392	503-378-4400
Fish & Wildlife Dept (ODFW)				
4034 Fairview Industrial Dr SE	Salem OR	97302	800-720-6339	503-947-6000
Insurance Div 3225 State St	Salem OR	97309	866-814-9710	503-378-4140
Legislative Assembly				
900 Ct St NE	Salem OR	97301	800-332-2313	
Military Dept				
1776 Militia Way SE PO Box 14350	Salem OR	97309	800-452-7500	503-584-3980
Parks & Recreation Dept (OPRD)				
725 Summer St NE Ste C	Salem OR	97301	800-551-6949	503-986-0707
Revenue Dept 955 Ctr St NE	Salem OR	97301	800-356-4222	503-378-4988
Student Assistance Commission				
1500 Valley River Dr Ste 100	Eugene OR	97401	800-452-8807	541-687-7400
Veterans' Affairs Dept				
700 Summer St NE	Salem OR	97301	800-828-8801	503-373-2000
Vocational Rehabilitation Services Office (OVRS)				
700 Summer St NE Ste 150	Salem OR	97310	800-692-9666	503-373-2085

338-39 Pennsylvania

			Toll-Free	Phone
Attorney General				
Strawberry Sq 16th Fl	Harrisburg PA	17120	800-385-1044	717-787-3391
Banking Dept				
17 N Second St Ste 1300	Harrisburg PA	17101	800-722-2657	717-783-4721
Community & Economic Development Dept				
400 N St 4th Fl	Harrisburg PA	17120	866-466-3972	
Consumer Advocate				
555 Walnut St 5th Fl Forum Pl	Harrisburg PA	17101	800-684-6560	717-783-5048
Driver & Vehicle Services Bureau				
1101 S Front St	Harrisburg PA	17104	800-932-4600	800-265-0921
Higher Education Assistance Agency				
1200 N Seventh St	Harrisburg PA	17102	800-213-9827	
Insurance Dept				
1326 Strawberry Sq	Harrisburg PA	17120	877-881-6388	717-787-2317
Public Utility Commission				
400 N St Keystone Bldg PO Box 3265	Harrisburg PA	17120	800-692-7380	717-783-1740
State Ethics Commission				
Rm 309 Finance Bldg PO Box 11470	Harrisburg PA	17108	800-932-0936	717-783-1610
State Parks				
Rachel Carson State Office Bldg 400 Market St PO Box 8551	Harrisburg PA	17105	888-727-2757	717-787-6640
Transportation Dept				
400 N St	Harrisburg PA	17120	800-932-4600	717-787-2838
Victims Compensation Assistance Program				
PO Box 1167	Harrisburg PA	17108	800-233-2339	717-783-5153
Vital Records Div				
PO Box 1528	New Castle PA	16103	844-228-3516	800-254-5164
Vocational Rehabilitation Office (OVR)				
1521 N Sixth St	Harrisburg PA	17102	800-442-6351	717-787-5244
Workers Compensation Bureau				
1171 S Cameron St Rm 324	Harrisburg PA	17104	800-482-2383	717-783-5421

338-40 Rhode Island

			Toll-Free	Phone
Child Support Services				
77 Dorrance St	Providence RI	02903	800-745-5555	401-458-4400
Children Youth & Families Dept				
101 Friendship St	Providence RI	02903	800-742-4453	401-528-3502
Housing & Mortgage Finance Corp				
44 Washington St	Providence RI	02903	800-427-5560	401-457-1234
Tourism Div				
315 Iron Horse Way Ste 101	Providence RI	02908	800-556-2484	401-278-9100

338-41 South Carolina

			Toll-Free	Phone
State Government Information				
1301 Gervais St Ste 710	Columbia SC	29201	866-340-7105	803-771-0131
Child Support Enforcement Office				
3150 Harden St Ext PO Box 1469	Columbia SC	29203	800-768-5858	803-898-9282
Commerce Dept				
1201 Main St Ste 1600	Columbia SC	29201	800-868-7232	803-737-0400
Education Lottery				
PO Box 11949	Columbia SC	29211	866-736-9819*	803-737-2002
*Help Line				
Social Services Dept				
1535 Confederate Ave	Columbia SC	29202	800-616-1309	803-898-7601
State Ports Authority				
176 Concord St	Charleston SC	29401	800-845-7106	843-723-8651
Vocational Rehabilitation Dept				
1410 Boston Ave PO Box 15	West Columbia SC	29171	800-832-7526	803-896-6500

338-42 South Dakota

			Toll-Free	Phone
Arts Council 711 E Wells Ave	Pierre SD	57501	800-952-3625	
Child Support Div				
700 Governors Dr	Pierre SD	57501	800-286-9145	605-773-3641
Consumer Protection Div				
1302 E Hwy 14 Ste 3	Pierre SD	57501	800-300-1986	605-773-4400
Department of Health				
600 E Capitol Ave Robert Hayes Bldg	Pierre SD	57501	800-738-2301	605-773-3361
Personnel Bureau				
500 E Capitol Ave	Pierre SD	57501	877-573-7347	605-773-3148
Rehabilitation Services Div				
500 E Capitol Ave	Pierre SD	57501	877-873-8500	605-773-3318
Social Services Dept				
700 Governors Dr	Pierre SD	57501	800-597-1603	605-773-3165
Tourism Office				
711 E Wells Ave	Pierre SD	57501	800-732-5682	605-773-3301

338-43 Tennessee

			Toll-Free	Phone
Administrative Office of the Cts				
511 Union St Ste 600	Nashville TN	37219	800-448-7970	615-741-2687
Child Support Services Div				
400 Deaderick St	Nashville TN	37243	800-838-6911	615-313-4880
Consumer Affairs Div				
500 James Robertson Pkwy	Nashville TN	37243	800-342-8385	615-741-4737
Department of Financial Institutions				
312 Rosa L Parks Ave 2nd Fl	Nashville TN	37243	800-231-7831	615-741-2236
Housing Development Agency				
502 Deaderick St Andrew Jackson Bldg 3rd Fl	Nashville TN	37243	800-228-8432	615-815-2200

				Toll-Free	Phone

Human Services Dept
400 Deaderick St .... Nashville TN 37248 **866-311-4287** 615-313-4700
Insurance Div
500 James Robertson Pkwy .... Nashville TN 37243 **800-342-4029** 615-741-2241
Labor & Workforce Development Dept
220 French Landing Dr .... Nashville TN 37243 **844-224-5818**
Lottery
1 Century Pl 26 Century Blvd Ste 200
PO Box 291869 .... Nashville TN 37214 **800-826-4311** 615-324-6500
Mental Health & Developmental Disabilities Dept
500 Deaderick St .... Nashville TN 37243 **800-560-5767**
Securities Div
500 James Robertson Pkwy 8th Fl .... Nashville TN 37243 **800-863-9117** 615-741-2947
Student Assistance Corp
404 James Robertson Pkwy Ste 1510 .... Nashville TN 37243 **800-342-1663** 615-741-1346
Supreme Court
511 Union St
Nashville City Ctr Ste 600 .... Nashville TN 37219 **800-448-7970** 615-741-2687
Vital Records Div
Andrew Johnson Twr 710 James Robertson Pkwy
1st Fl. .... Nashville TN 37243 **855-809-0072** 615-741-1763
Workers Compensation Div
220 French Landing Dr .... Nashville TN 37243 **844-224-5818** 615-741-6642

338-44 Texas

				Toll-Free	Phone

Aging & Disability Services
701 W 51st St .... Austin TX 78751 **888-388-6332** 512-438-3011
Agriculture Dept
PO Box 12847 .... Austin TX 78711 **800-835-5832*** 512-463-7476
*Cust Svc
Arts Commission
920 Colorado Ste 501 PO Box 13406 .... Austin TX 78701 **800-252-9415** 512-463-5535
Assistive & Rehabilitation Services Dept
4800 N Lamar Blvd 3rd Fl. .... Austin TX 78756 **800-252-7009** 512-377-0500
Banking Dept
2601 N Lamar Blvd .... Austin TX 78705 **877-276-5554** 512-475-1300
Comptroller of Public Accounts
111 E 17th St .... Austin TX 78774 **800-252-5555** 512-463-4444
Crime Victims Services Div
PO Box 12198 .... Austin TX 78711 **800-983-9933** 512-936-1200
General Land Office
1700 N Congress Ave Ste 935 .... Austin TX 78701 **800-998-4456** 512-463-5001
Governor PO Box 12428 .... Austin TX 78711 **800-843-5789** 512-463-2000
Information Resources Dept
300 W 15th St Ste 1300 .... Austin TX 78701 **855-275-3471** 512-475-4700
Insurance Dept
333 Guadalupe St PO Box 149104 .... Austin TX 78714 **800-578-4677**
Licensing & Regulation Dept
920 Colorado .... Austin TX 78701 **800-803-9202** 512-463-6599
Medical Board PO Box 2018 .... Austin TX 78768 **800-248-4062*** 512-305-7010
*Cust Svc
Motor Vehicle Div
4000 Jackson Ave .... Austin TX 78731 **888-368-4689**
Parks & Wildlife Dept
4200 Smith School Rd .... Austin TX 78744 **800-792-1112** 512-389-4800
Public Utility Commission
PO Box 13326 .... Austin TX 78711 **888-782-8477** 512-936-7000
Railroad Commission
1701 N Congress Ave PO Box 12967 .... Austin TX 78711 **877-228-5740** 512-463-7058
Vital Statistics Bureau
1100 W 49th St PO Box 12040 .... Austin TX 78756 **888-963-7111**
Workers Compensation Commission
7551 Metro Ctr Dr Ste 100 .... Austin TX 78744 **800-252-7031***
*Cust Svc

338-45 Utah

				Toll-Free	Phone

Aging & Adult Services Div
195 N 1950 W .... Salt Lake City UT 84116 **877-424-4640** 801-538-3910
Child & Family Services Div
195 N 1950 W .... Salt Lake City UT 84116 **855-323-3237** 801-538-4100
Community & Economic Development Dept
60 E S Temple 3rd Fl .... Salt Lake City UT 84111 **855-204-9046** 801-538-8680
Consumer Protection Div
160 E Broadway 2nd Fl
PO Box 146704 .... Salt Lake City UT 84111 **800-721-7233** 801-530-6601
Environmental Quality Dept
195 North 1950 West .... Salt Lake City UT 84116 **800-458-0145** 801-536-4400
Governor
350 N State St Ste 200
PO Box 142220 .... Salt Lake City UT 84114 **800-705-2464** 801-538-1000
Health Dept
PO Box 141010 .... Salt Lake City UT 84114 **888-222-2542** 801-538-6003
Higher Education Assistance Authority
PO Box 145110 .... Salt Lake City UT 84114 **877-336-7378** 801-321-7294
Higher Education System
60 S 400 W .... Salt Lake City UT 84101 **877-336-7378** 801-321-7294
Housing Corp
2479 S Lake Park Blvd .... West Valley City UT 84120 **800-284-6950** 801-902-8200
Labor Commission
PO Box 146600 .... Salt Lake City UT 84114 **800-530-5090** 801-530-6800
Lieutenant Governor
Utah State Capitol Complex Ste 220
PO Box 142325 .... Salt Lake City UT 84114 **800-995-8683** 801-538-1041
Motor Vehicle Div
PO Box 30412 .... Salt Lake City UT 84130 **800-368-8824** 801-297-7780
Occupational & Professional Licensing Div
PO Box 146741 .... Salt Lake City UT 84111 **866-275-3675** 801-530-6628
Office for Victims of Crime
350 E 500 S Ste 200 .... Salt Lake City UT 84111 **800-621-7444** 801-238-2360
Office of Tourism
300 N State St .... Salt Lake City UT 84114 **800-200-1160** 801-538-1900

Parks & Recreation Div
1594 W N Temple Ste 116 .... Salt Lake City UT 84116 **800-322-3770** 801-538-7220
Public Service Commission
160 E 300 S .... Salt Lake City UT 84111 **866-772-8824** 801-530-6716
Securities Div
160 E 300 S 2nd Fl. .... Salt Lake City UT 84111 **800-721-7233** 801-530-6600
Tax Commission
210 N 1950 W .... Salt Lake City UT 84134 **800-662-4335** 801-297-2200
Veterans' Affairs Office
550 Foothills Dr Ste 105. .... Salt Lake City UT 84113 **800-894-9497** 801-326-2372
Vital Records & Statistics Office
288 N 1460 W PO Box 141012 .... Salt Lake City UT 84114 **888-222-2542**
Workers' Compensation Fund
100 W Towne Ridge Pkwy .... Sandy UT 84070 **800-446-2667** 385-351-8000

338-46 Vermont

				Toll-Free	Phone

Aging & Disabilities Dept
280 State Dr HC2 South .... Waterbury VT 05671 **888-405-5005** 802-241-2401
Children & Families Dept
280 State Dr HC 1 N. .... Waterbury VT 05671 **800-786-3214** 802-241-2100
Consumer Assistance Program
146 University Pl .... Burlington VT 05405 **800-649-2424** 802-656-3183
Crime Victim Services Ctr
58 S Main St Ste 1 .... Waterbury VT 05676 **800-750-1213** 802-241-1250
Emergency Management Office
45 State Dr .... Waterbury VT 05671 **800-347-0488** 802-244-8721
Executive Office of Governor
109 State St .... Montpelier VT 05609 **800-649-6825** 802-828-3333
Motor Vehicles Dept
120 State St .... Montpelier VT 05603 **888-998-3766** 802-828-2000
Office of Veteran Affairs
118 State St .... Montpelier VT 05620 **888-666-9844** 802-828-3379
Vocational Rehabilitation Div
HC 2 S 280 State Dr .... Waterbury VT 05671 **866-879-6757** 802-447-2781

338-47 Virginia

				Toll-Free	Phone

Aging & Rehabilitative Services Dept
8004 Franklin Farms Dr .... Richmond VA 23229 **800-552-5019** 804-662-7000
Aging Dept
1610 Forest Ave Ste 100. .... Henrico VA 23229 **800-552-3402** 804-662-9333
Community College System
300 Arboretum Pl Ste 200 .... Richmond VA 23236 **844-897-9096**
Criminal Injuries Compensation Fund (CICF)
PO Box 26927 .... Richmond VA 23261 **800-552-4007**
Employment Commission
703 E Main St .... Richmond VA 23219 **866-832-2363**
Health Professions Dept
9960 Mayland Dr Ste 300. .... Henrico VA 23233 **800-533-1560** 804-367-4400
Housing Development Authority
601 S Belvidere St .... Richmond VA 23220 **877-843-2123**
Information Technologies Agency (VITA)
11751 Meadowville Ln .... Chester VA 23836 **866-637-8482**
Social Services Dept
801 E Main St .... Richmond VA 23219 **800-552-3431** 804-726-7000
State Corp Commission
1300 E Main St PO Box 1197 .... Richmond VA 23218 **800-552-7945** 804-371-9967
State Parks Div
600 E Main St 24th Fl. .... Richmond VA 23219 **800-933-7275*** 804-692-0403
*Resv
Vital Records Div
2001 Maywill St PO Box 1000 .... Richmond VA 23230 **877-572-6333** 804-662-6200
Workers Compensation Commission
333 E Franklin St .... Richmond VA 23219 **877-664-2566**

338-48 Washington

				Toll-Free	Phone

Aging & Disability Services Administration
4450 Tenth Ave SE .... Lacey WA 98503 **800-422-3263** 360-725-2300
Child Support Div
PO Box 11520 .... Tacoma WA 98411 **800-457-6202** 360-664-5321
Employment Security Dept
212 Maple Park Ave SE .... Olympia WA 98501 **800-318-6022** 360-902-9500
Financial Institutions Dept
PO Box 41200 .... Olympia WA 98504 **877-746-4334** 360-902-8703
Historical Society
1911 Pacific Ave .... Tacoma WA 98402 **888-238-4373** 253-272-3500
Housing Finance Commission
1000 Second Ave Ste 2700 .... Seattle WA 98104 **800-767-4663** 206-464-7139
Indeterminate Sentence Review Board
4317 Sixth Ave SE .... Olympia WA 98504 **866-948-9266** 360-407-2400
Natural Resources Dept
1111 Washington St SE PO Box 47000 .... Olympia WA 98504 **800-258-5990** 360-902-1000
Public Disclosure Commission
711 Capitol Way Ste 206 PO Box 40908 .... Olympia WA 98504 **877-601-2828** 360-753-1111
Revenue Dept PO Box 47478 .... Olympia WA 98504 **800-647-7706** 360-705-6714
Secretary of State
PO Box 40220 .... Olympia WA 98504 **800-822-1065** 360-902-4151
Securities Div PO Box 9033 .... Olympia WA 98507 **877-746-4334** 360-902-8760
Social & Health Services Dept
PO Box 45131 .... Olympia WA 98504 **800-737-0617** 360-902-8400
State Parks & Recreation Commission
1111 Israel Rd SW .... Tumwater WA 98501 **888-226-7688*** 360-725-9770
*Campground Resv
Utilities & Transportation Commission
1300 S Evergreen Pk Dr SW
PO Box 47250 .... Olympia WA 98504 **888-333-9882** 360-664-1160
Veterans Affairs Dept
1102 Quince St SE PO Box 41150 .... Olympia WA 98504 **800-562-0132** 360-725-2200

Vocational Rehabilitation Div

				Toll-Free	Phone
PO Box 45340	Olympia	WA	98504	800-637-5627	360-725-3636

338-49 West Virginia

				Toll-Free	Phone
State Government Information					
100 Dee Dr	Charleston	WV	25311	888-558-7002	304-558-7000
Children & Families Bureau					
350 Capitol St Rm 730	Charleston	WV	25301	800-352-6513	304-558-0628
Community Development Div					
1900 Kanawha Blvd E	Charleston	WV	25311	800-982-3386	304-558-2234
Consumer Protection Div					
812 Quarrier St 1st Fl PO Box 1789	Charleston	WV	25301	800-368-8808	304-558-8986
Crime Victims Compensation Fund					
1900 Kanawha Blvd E Rm W-334	Charleston	WV	25305	877-562-6878	304-347-4850
Department of veterans assistance					
1900 Kanawha Blvd E bldg 5 Rm 205	Charleston	WV	25305	888-838-2332	304-558-3661
Development Office					
1900 Kanawah Blvd E	Charleston	WV	25305	800-982-3386	304-558-2234
Ethics Commission					
210 Brooks St Ste 300	Charleston	WV	25301	866-558-0664	304-558-0664
Higher Education Policy Commission					
1018 Kanawha Blvd E Ste 700	Charleston	WV	25301	888-825-5707	304-558-2101
Housing Development Fund					
5710 MacCorkle Ave SE	Charleston	WV	25304	800-933-9843	304-391-8600
Insurance Commission					
900 Pennsylvania Ave	Charleston	WV	25302	888-879-9842	304-558-3354
Lottery					
900 Pennsylvania Ave PO Box 2067	Charleston	WV	25302	800-982-2274	304-558-0500
Motor Vehicles Div					
5707 MacCorkle Ave SE PO Box 17020	Charleston	WV	25317	800-642-9066	304-926-3802
Office of Technology					
1900 Kanawha Blvd ECapitol Complex					
Bldg 5 10th Fl	Charleston	WV	25304	877-558-9966	304-558-5472
Public Service Commission					
201 Brooke St PO Box 812	Charleston	WV	25301	800-344-5113	304-340-0300
Secretary of State					
1900 Kanawha Blvd E					
Bldg 1 Ste 157K	Charleston	WV	25305	866-767-8683	304-558-6000
Securities Div					
1900 Kanawha Blvd E					
Bldg 1 Rm W-100	Charleston	WV	25305	877-982-9148	304-558-2251
Tourism Div					
90 MacCorkle Ave SW	South Charleston	WV	25303	800-225-5982	304-558-2200
Treasurer					
1900 Kanawha Blvd E					
Bldg 1 Ste E-145.	Charleston	WV	25305	800-422-7498	304-558-5000

338-50 Wisconsin

				Toll-Free	Phone
Crime Victims Services Office					
17 W Main St PO Box 7857	Madison	WI	53703	800-446-6564	608-266-1221
Department of Safety & Professional Services					
1400 E Washington Ave Rm 112	Madison	WI	53703	877-617-1565	608-266-2112
Ethics Board					
212 E Washington Ave 3rd Fl	Madison	WI	53707	866-868-3947	608-266-8005
Historical Society					
816 State St	Madison	WI	53706	888-936-7463	
Housing & Economic Development Authority					
201 W Washington Ave Ste 700	Madison	WI	53703	800-334-6873	608-266-7884
Insurance Commission					
125 S Webster St	Madison	WI	53707	800-236-8517	608-266-3585
Legislature State Capitol	Madison	WI	53702	800-362-9472	608-266-9960
Natural Resources Dept					
101 S Webster St PO Box 7921	Madison	WI	53707	888-936-7463	608-266-2621
Public Instruction Dept					
125 S Webster St PO Box 7841	Madison	WI	53707	800-441-4563	608-266-3390
Public Service Commission					
4822 Madison Yards Way N Tower 6th Fl	Madison	WI	53705	888-816-3831	608-266-5481
State Patrol Div					
4802 Sheboygan Ave Rm 551 PO Box 7912	Madison	WI	53707	844-847-1234	
Teacher Education & Licensing Bureau					
125 S Webster St	Madison	WI	53703	800-441-4563	608-266-3390
Veterans Affairs Dept					
201 W Washington Ave PO Box 7843	Madison	WI	53707	800-947-8387	608-266-1311
Vital Records Office					
1 W Wilson St	Madison	WI	53703	800-947-3529	608-266-1865
Vocational Rehabilitation Div					
201 E Washington Ave PO Box 7852	Madison	WI	53707	800-442-3477	608-261-0050

338-51 Wyoming

				Toll-Free	Phone
Aging Div					
2300 Capitol Ave 4th Fl	Cheyenne	WY	82002	800-442-2766	307-777-7995
Business Council					
214 W 15th St	Cheyenne	WY	82002	800-262-3425	307-777-2800
Health Dept					
401 Hathaway Bldg	Cheyenne	WY	82002	866-571-0944	307-777-7656
Highway Patrol (WHP)					
5300 Bishop Blvd	Cheyenne	WY	82009	800-442-9090	307-777-4301
Insurance Dept					
106 E Sixth Ave	Cheyenne	WY	82001	800-438-5768	307-777-7401
Tourism Div					
5611 High Plains Rd	Cheyenne	WY	82007	800-225-5996	307-777-7777

339　　GOVERNMENT - US - EXECUTIVE BRANCH

SEE ALSO Parks - National - US ; Cemeteries - National ; Correctional Facilities - Federal ; Coast Guard Installations ; Military Bases

339-1 US Department of Agriculture

				Toll-Free	Phone
Department of Agriculture (USDA)					
1400 Independence Ave SW	Washington	DC	20250	844-433-2774	202-720-3631
Animal & Plant Health Inspection Service (APHIS)					
National Veterinary Services Laboratories					
4700 River Rd	Riverdale	MD	20737	844-820-2234	
Forest Service (USFS)					
1400 Independence Ave SW	Washington	DC	20050	800-832-1355	202-205-8333
Forest Service Regional Offices					
Region 8 (Southern Region)					
1720 Peachtree Rd NW	Atlanta	GA	30309	877-372-7248	414-297-3600
National Agricultural Library					
10301 Baltimore Ave	Beltsville	MD	20705	800-633-7701	301-504-5755
National Agricultural Statistics Service (NASS)					
1400 Independence Ave SW	Washington	DC	20250	800-727-9540	202-720-2707
Rural Development					
1400 Independence Ave SW	Washington	DC	20250	800-414-1226	202-720-9540
Secretary of Agriculture					
1400 Independence Ave SW	Washington	DC	20250	800-832-1355	202-720-3631
World Agricultural Outlook Board					
1400 Independence Ave SW	Washington	DC	20250	800-949-3964	202-720-6030

339-2 US Department of Commerce

				Toll-Free	Phone
Economic Development Administration Regional Office					
Atlanta					
401 W Peachtree St NW Ste 1820	Atlanta	GA	30308	800-518-4726	404-730-3002
Seattle					
915 Second Ave Rm 1890	Seattle	WA	98174	800-518-4726	206-220-7660
Minority Business Development Agency (MBDA)					
1401 Constitution Ave NW	Washington	DC	20230	888-324-1551	
San Francisco Region					
1401 Constitution Ave	Washington	DC	20230	888-889-0538	202-482-2000
Minority Business Development Agency Regional Offices					
Chicago Region					
105 W Adams St Ste 2300	Chicago	IL	60603	888-324-1551	312-353-0182
National Environmental Satellite Data & Information Service					
National Coastal Data Development Ctr					
Bldg 1100 Ste 101	Stennis Space Center	MS	39529	866-732-2382	228-688-2936
National Technical Information Service (NTIS)					
5285 Port Royal Rd	Springfield	VA	22161	800-553-6847*	703-605-6000
*Orders					
North American Industry Classification System (NAICS)					
US Census Bureau					
4600 Silver Hill Rd	Washington	DC	20233	800-923-8282	301-763-4636
United States Patent & Trademark Office					
PO Box 1450	Alexandria	VA	22313	800-786-9199	571-272-5600
US Census Bureau Regional Offices					
Atlanta					
101 Marietta St NW Ste 3200	Atlanta	GA	30303	800-424-6974	404-730-3832
Boston 4 Copley Pl Ste 301	Boston	MA	02117	800-562-5721	617-424-4501
Chicago					
1111 W 22nd St Ste 400	Oak Brook	IL	60523	800-865-6384	630-288-9200
Denver					
6950 W Jefferson Ave Ste 250	Lakewood	CO	80235	800-852-6159	303-264-0202
Los Angeles					
15350 Sherman Way Ste 400	Van Nuys	CA	91406	800-992-3530	818-267-1700
New York 32 Old Slip 9th Fl	New York	NY	10005	800-991-2520	212-584-3400
Philadelphia					
100 S Independence Mall W					
Ste 410	Philadelphia	PA	19106	800-262-4236	215-717-1800

339-3 US Department of Defense

				Toll-Free	Phone
Defense Commissary Agency					
1300 E Ave	Fort Lee	VA	23801	877-332-2471	804-734-8000
Defense Contract Audit Agency					
8725 John J Kingman Rd Ste 2135	Fort Belvoir	VA	22060	855-414-5892	703-767-3265
Defense Contract Management Agency					
6350 Walker Ln Ste 300	Alexandria	VA	22310	888-576-3262	
Defense Logistics Agency (DLA)					
8725 John J Kingman Rd	Fort Belvoir	VA	22060	877-352-2255	
Defense Technical Information Center (DTIC)					
8725 John J Kingman Rd Ste 0944	Fort Belvoir	VA	22060	800-225-3842	
Defense Threat Reduction Agency					
8725 John T Kingman Rd MS 6201	Fort Belvoir	VA	22060	800-701-5096	703-767-5870

339-4 US Department of Defense - Department of the Army

				Toll-Free	Phone
US Army War College					
122 Forbes Ave	Carlisle	PA	17013	800-453-0992	717-245-3131

339-5 US Department of Defense - Department of the Navy

				Toll-Free	Phone
Naval Sea Systems Command					
1333 Isaac Hull Ave SE					
Washington Navy Yard	Washington	DC	20376	800-356-8464	202-781-4123
Navy Personnel Command (NPC)					
5720 Integrity Dr	Millington	TN	38055	866-827-5672	

339-6 US Department of Defense - US Marine Corps

				Toll-Free	Phone
Marine PO Box 5185	Des Plaines	IL	60019	800-627-4637	

339-7 US Department of Education

				Toll-Free	Phone
Department of Education					
400 Maryland Ave SW	Washington	DC	20202	**800-872-5327**	202-401-2000
Inspector General's Fraud & Abuse Hotline					
400 Maryland Ave SW	Washington	DC	20202	**800-647-8733**	
U.S. Department of Education					
Region 6					
1999 Bryan St Ste 1510	Dallas	TX	75202	**877-521-2172**	214-661-9600
US. Department of Education					
Office of Career, Technical, and Adult Education					
550 12th St SW 11th Fl	Washington	DC	20202	**800-872-5327**	202-245-7700
National Institute for Literacy (NIFL)					
1775 'I' St NW Ste 730	Washington	DC	20006	**800-228-8813**	202-233-2025
Secretary of Education					
400 Maryland Ave SW	Washington	DC	20202	**800-872-5327**	202-401-3000

339-8 US Department of Energy

				Toll-Free	Phone
BPA					
Bonneville Power Administration					
905 NE 11th Ave	Portland	OR	97232	**800-282-3713**	503-230-3000
Federal Energy Regulatory Commission					
888 First St NE	Washington	DC	20426	**866-208-3372**	202-502-8200
Federal Energy Regulatory Commission Regional Offices					
New York					
19 W 34th St Ste 400	New York	NY	10001	**844-434-0053**	
San Francisco					
100 First St Ste 2300	San Francisco	CA	94105	**844-434-0053**	

339-9 US Department of Health & Human Services

				Toll-Free	Phone
Department of Health & Human Services (HHS)					
330 Independence Ave SW	Washington	DC	20201	**877-696-6775**	202-619-0150
Department of Health & Human Services Regional Offices					
Region 7 601 E 12th St	Kansas City	MO	64106	**800-447-8477**	816-426-2821
US Health & Human Services Department					
Region 9					
90 Seventh St Ste 4-100	San Francisco	CA	94103	**800-368-1019**	
Administration on Aging (AoA)					
1 Massachusetts Ave NW	Washington	DC	20001	**800-677-1116**	202-357-3584
Agency for Healthcare Research & Quality					
540 Gaither Rd	Rockville	MD	20850	**800-358-9295**	301-427-1364
Agency for Toxic Substances & Disease Registry					
4770 Buford Hwy NE	Atlanta	GA	30341	**800-232-4636**	
AIDSinfo PO Box 6303	Rockville	MD	20849	**800-448-0440**	301-315-2816
National Center for Chronic Disease Prevention					
4770 Buford Hwy NE	Atlanta	GA	30341	**800-232-4636**	
National Center for Emerging & Zoonotic Infectious					
1600 Clifton Rd	Atlanta	GA	30333	**800-232-4636**	404-639-3311
National Center for Environmental Health					
4770 Buford Hwy NE	Atlanta	GA	30341	**800-232-4636**	
National Center for Health Marketing					
1600 Clifton Rd NE	Atlanta	GA	30333	**800-311-3435**	404-639-3311
National Center for HIV/AIDS Viral Hepatitis STD					
1600 Clifton Rd	Atlanta	GA	30333	**800-232-4636**	
National Center for Immunization & Respiratory Disorders					
1600 Clifton Rd NE MS E-05	Atlanta	GA	30333	**800-232-4636**	
National Center for Injury Prevention & Control					
4770 Buford Hwy NE	Atlanta	GA	30341	**800-232-4636**	
National Center for Public Health Informatics					
1600 Clifton Rd NE	Atlanta	GA	30329	**888-232-6348**	800-232-4636
Centers for Disease Control & Prevention					
National Center on Birth Defects & Developmental Dept					
1600 Clifton Rd	Atlanta	GA	30329	**800-232-4636**	404-639-3311
National Institute for Occupational Safety & Health					
200 Independence Ave SW	Washington	DC	20201	**800-356-4674**	404-639-3286
National Office of Public Health Genomics					
1600 Clifton Rd MS K-89	Atlanta	GA	30329	**800-232-4636**	
Travelers Health					
1600 Clifton Rd NE	Atlanta	GA	30333	**800-232-4636**	
Centers for Medicare & Medicaid Services (CMS)					
7500 Security Blvd	Baltimore	MD	21244	**800-633-4227**	
Medicare.gov					
7500 Security Blvd	Baltimore	MD	21244	**800-633-4227**	
Child Welfare Information Gateway					
Children's Bureau/ACYF 330 C St SW	Washington	DC	20201	**800-394-3366**	703-385-7565
Department of Health & Human Services					
Office on Women's Health					
200 Independence Ave SW	Washington	DC	20201	**800-994-9662**	202-690-7650
Food & Drug Administration (FDA)					
5600 Fishers Ln	Rockville	MD	20857	**888-463-6332**	301-827-2410
Center for Devices & Radiological Health (CDRH)					
10903 New Hampshire Ave	Silver Spring	MD	20993	**800-638-2041**	301-796-7100
CFSAN					
5100 Paint Branch Pkwy	College Park	MD	20740	**888-723-3366**	
Health Resources & Services Administration (HRSA)					
5600 Fishers Ln	Rockville	MD	20857	**888-275-4772**	301-443-2216
National Clearinghouse for Alcohol & Drug Information					
5600 Fishers Ln	Rockville	MD	20857	**800-729-6686**	
National Hansen's Disease Program (NHDP)					
1770 Physicians Pk Dr	Baton Rouge	LA	70816	**800-221-9393**	
National Institutes of Health (NIH)					
9000 Rockville Pk	Bethesda	MD	20892	**800-411-1222**	301-496-4000
Center for Scientific Review					
6701 Rockledge Dr MSC 7950	Bethesda	MD	20892	**800-438-4380**	301-435-1115
National Cancer Institute					
9609 Medical Center Dr					
BG 9609 MSC 9760	Bethesda	MD	20892	**800-422-6237**	301-435-3848
National Institute of Arthritis & Musculoskeletal					
1 AMS Cir	Bethesda	MD	20892	**877-226-4267**	301-495-4484
National Institute of Mental Health					
6001 Executive Blvd Rm 6200 MSC 9663	Bethesda	MD	20892	**866-615-6464**	301-443-4513
National Institute of Neurological Disorders					
PO Box 5801	Bethesda	MD	20824	**800-352-9424**	301-496-5751
National Library of Medicine					
8600 Rockville Pk	Bethesda	MD	20894	**888-346-3656**	301-594-5983
Office of Rare Diseases					
6701 Democracy Blvd Ste 1001	Bethesda	MD	20892	**800-942-6825**	301-402-4336
The National Institute on Deafness and Other Communication Disorders					
31 Ctr Dr MSC 2320	Bethesda	MD	20892	**800-241-1044**	301-496-7243
National Mental Health Information Ctr					
PO Box 42557	Washington	DC	20015	**800-487-4889**	
NIH Osteoporosis & Related Bone Diseases-National Resource Ctr					
2 AMS Cir	Bethesda	MD	20892	**800-624-2663**	202-223-0344
Office of Public Health & Science					
200 Independence Ave SW Rm 716G	Washington	DC	20201	**877-696-6775**	202-690-7694
Office of Public Health & Science Regional Offices					
Region VII					
200 Independence Ave SW					
Rm 509F HHH Bldg	Washington	DC	20201	**877-696-6775**	
Secretary of Health & Human Services					
200 Independence Ave SW	Washington	DC	20201	**877-696-6775**	
Substance Abuse & Mental Health Services Administration (SAMHSA)					
1 Choke Cherry Rd	Rockville	MD	20857	**877-726-4727**	240-276-2000
Center for Mental Health Services					
1 Choke Cherry Ln	Rockville	MD	20857	**877-726-4727**	
Center for Substance Abuse Prevention					
1 Choke Cherry Rd	Rockville	MD	20857	**877-726-4727**	240-276-2420
Center for Substance Abuse Treatment					
5600 Fishers Ln PO Box 2345	Rockville	MD	20857	**877-726-4727**	240-276-2130
VA Oakland Regional Benefit Office					
1301 Clay St N Tower	Oakland	CA	94612	**877-696-6775**	

339-10 US Department of Homeland Security

				Toll-Free	Phone
Department of Homeland Security					
Ready Campaign					
500 C St SW	Washington	DC	20472	**800-462-7585**	800-621-3362
Federal Emergency Management Agency (FEMA)					
500 C St SW	Washington	DC	20472	**800-621-3362**	202-646-2500
FEMA for Kids					
500 C St SW	Washington	DC	20472	**800-621-3362**	
National Flood Insurance Program					
500 C St SW	Washington	DC	20472	**800-427-4661**	
Region 3					
1 Independence Mall					
615 Chestnut St 6th Fl	Philadelphia	PA	19106	**800-621-3362**	215-931-5500
US Fire Administration					
16825 S Seton Ave	Emmitsburg	MD	21727	**888-382-3827**	301-447-1000
Federal Emergency Management Agency Regional Office (FEMA)					
Region 1 99 High St	Boston	MA	02110	**877-336-2627**	877-336-2734
Region 5					
536 S Clark St 6th Fl	Chicago	IL	60605	**877-336-2627**	312-408-5500
Federal Emergency Management Agency Regional Offices					
Region 6 800 N Loop 288	Denton	TX	76209	**800-426-5460**	940-898-5399
Region 9					
1111 Broadway Ste 1200	Oakland	CA	94607	**877-336-2627**	510-627-7100
Federal Law Enforcement Training Ctr					
1131 Chapel Crossing Rd	Glynco	GA	31524	**800-743-5382**	912-267-2100
Transportation Security Administration					
Federal Air Marshal Service					
601 S 12th St	Arlington	VA	22202	**866-289-9673**	
US Citizenship & Immigration Services Regional Offices					
70 Kimball Ave	South Burlington	VT	05403	**800-767-1833**	
US Coast Guard					
Law Enforcement Office					
2100 Second St SW	Washington	DC	20593	**800-982-8813**	
National Maritime Ctr					
100 Forbes Dr	Martinsburg	WV	25404	**888-427-5662**	304-433-3400
US Coast Guard Academy					
15 Mohegan Ave	New London	CT	06320	**800-883-8724**	860-444-8444
US Customs & Border Protection					
1300 Pennsylvania Ave NW	Washington	DC	20229	**877-227-5511**	703-526-4200
US Immigration & Customs Enforcement (ICE)					
425 'I' St NW	Washington	DC	20536	**866-347-2423**	

339-11 US Department of Housing & Urban Development

				Toll-Free	Phone
Department of Housing & Urban Development (HUD)					
451 Seventh St SW	Washington	DC	20410	**800-569-4287**	202-708-0685
Department of Housing & Urban Development Regional Offices					
Boston Regional Office					
Thomas P O'Neill Jr Federal Bldg					
10 Causeway St 3rd Fl	Boston	MA	02222	**800-225-5342**	617-994-8200
Chicago Regional Office					
Ralph Metcalfe Federal Bldg					
77 W Jackson Blvd	Chicago	IL	60604	**800-955-2232**	312-353-6236
Mid-Atlantic Region					
100 Penn Sq E	Philadelphia	PA	19107	**800-225-5342**	215-656-0500
New York City Regional Office					
26 Federal Plz Ste 3541	New York	NY	10278	**800-496-4294**	212-264-8000
Rocky Mountain Region					
1670 Broadway 25th Fl	Denver	CO	80202	**800-955-2232**	303-672-5440
Government National Mortgage Assn					
451 Seventh St SW Rm B-133	Washington	DC	20410	**800-234-4662**	202-708-1535
HUD Office of Public & Indian Housing					
Real Estate Assessment Ctr					
550 12th St SW Ste 100	Washington	DC	20410	**888-245-4860**	202-708-1112

339-12 US Department of the Interior

				Toll-Free	Phone
Bureau of Indian Affairs Regional Offices (BIA)					
Alaska Region					
3601 C St Ste 1100	Anchorage	AK	99503	**800-645-8397**	907-271-4085

				Toll-Free	Phone

Eastern Oklahoma Region
3100 W Peak Blvd PO Box 8002 ....Muskogee OK 74402 **800-645-8397** 918-781-4600
Northwest Region
911 NE 11th Ave ....Portland OR 97232 **800-645-8397** 503-231-6702
Pacific Region
2800 Cottage Way ....Sacramento CA 95825 **800-645-8397** 916-978-6000
Rocky Mountain Region
316 N 26th St ....Billings MT 59101 **800-645-8397** 406-247-7943
Southern Plains Region
PO Box 368 ....Anadarko OK 73005 **800-645-8465** 405-247-6673
Bureau of Land Management
Wild Horse & Burro Program
1849 C St NW Rm 5665..................Washington DC 20240 **866-468-7826** 202-208-3801
Bureau of Land Management Regional Offices
Eastern States Office
7450 Boston Blvd ....Springfield VA 22153 **800-370-3936** 703-440-1600
National Interagency Fire Ctr
3833 S Development Ave ....Boise ID 83705 **877-471-2262** 208-387-5512
US Fish & Wildlife Service (USFWS)
1849 C St NW ....Washington DC 20240 **800-344-9453**
US Fish & Wildlife Service Regional Offices
Southeast Region
1875 Century Blvd 3rd Fl..................Atlanta GA 30345 **800-364-4263** 404-679-4000
US Geological Survey (USGS)
12201 Sunrise Valley Dr ....Reston VA 20192 **888-275-8747** 703-648-6723
Ask USGS
12201 Sunrise Valley Dr ....Reston VA 20192 **888-275-8747** 703-648-5953

339-13 US Department of Justice

				Toll-Free	Phone

Community Oriented Policing Services (COPS)
145 N St NE ....Washington DC 20530 **800-421-6770**
Drug Enforcement Administration Regional Offices
Dallas Div
10160 Technology Blvd E ....Dallas TX 75220 **800-882-9539** 214-366-6900
Washington DC Div
800 K St NW Ste 500 ....Washington DC 20001 **800-488-3111** 202-305-8500
Federal Bureau of Prisons
National Institute of Corrections
320 First St NW ....Washington DC 20534 **800-995-6423** 202-307-3106
National Institute of Corrections Information Ctr
11900 E Cornell Ave Unit C ....Aurora CO 80014 **800-877-1461**
Immigrant & Employee Rights Section-US. Department of Justice Civil Rights Division
950 Pennsylvania Ave NW Ste 4706........Washington DC 20530 **800-255-7688** 202-616-5594
National Criminal Justice Reference Service
PO Box 6000 ....Rockville MD 20849 **800-851-3420** 202-836-6998
Office of Justice Programs
Bureau of Justice Assistance
810 Seventh St NW ....Washington DC 20531 **888-744-6513** 202-616-6500
Office for Victims of Crime
810 Seventh St NW ....Washington DC 20531 **800-363-0441** 202-307-5983
Office of the Pardon Attorney
145 N St NE Rm 5E....................Washington DC 20530 **800-514-0301** 202-616-6070
US Marshals Service
401 Courthouse Sq ....Alexandria VA 22314 **800-336-0102*** 202-307-9100
*General
US Parole Commission
5550 Friendship Blvd Rm 420 ....Chevy Chase MD 20815 **888-585-9103** 202-346-7000

339-14 US Department of Labor

				Toll-Free	Phone

Department of Labor (DOL)
200 Constitution Ave NW ....Washington DC 20210 **866-487-2365**
Job Corps
200 Constitution Ave NW Ste N4463........Washington DC 20210 **800-733-5627** 202-693-3000
Department of Labor Regional Offices
Region 1 - Boston
JFK Federal Bldg Rm E-260 ....Boston MA 02203 **800-347-8029** 866-487-2365
Region 8 - Denver
1999 Broadway Ste 1620 ....Denver CO 80202 **800-827-5335** 303-844-1286
Employment & Training Administration
200 Constitution Ave NW ....Washington DC 20210 **866-487-2365**
Bureau of Labor Statistics
Southeast Information Office
61 Forsyth St SW Rm 7T25 ....Atlanta GA 30303 **800-347-3764** 404-893-4222
Employment Standards Administration
200 Constitution Ave NW Rm N-1301 ....Washington DC 20210 **866-487-2365**
Office of Labor-Management Standards (OLMS)
200 Constitution Ave NW ....Washington DC 20210 **866-487-2365**
Wage & Hour Div
200 Constitution Ave NW ....Washington DC 20210 **866-487-9243**
Labor Racketeering & Fraud Investigations Office
200 Constitution Ave NW Rm S-5506 ....Washington DC 20210 **800-347-3756** 202-693-6999
Mine Safety & Health Administration (MSHA)
1100 Wilson Blvd ....Arlington VA 22209 **800-746-1553** 202-693-9400
Occupational Safety & Health Administration (OSHA)
200 Constitution Ave NW ....Washington DC 20210 **800-321-6742** 202-693-1999
Occupational Safety & Health Administration Regional Offices
Region 1
JFK Federal Bldg Rm E-340 ....Boston MA 02203 **800-321-6742** 617-565-9860
Region 10
300 Fifth Ave Ste 1280.....................Seattle WA 98104 **800-321-6742*** 206-757-6700
*Help Line
Region 2
201 Varick St Rm 670......................New York NY 10014 **800-321-6742** 212-337-2378
Region 3
Curtis Ctr 170 S Independence Mall W
Ste 740W ....Philadelphia PA 19106 **800-321-6742** 215-861-4900
Region 4
61 Forsyth St SW Rm 6T50 ....Atlanta GA 30303 **800-321-6742** 678-237-0400
Office of Disability Employment Policy
200 Constitution Ave NW ....Washington DC 20210 **866-633-7365** 202-693-7880
Secretary of Labor
200 Constitution Ave NW ....Washington DC 20210 **866-487-2365** 202-693-6000

				Toll-Free	Phone

United States Department of Labor (DOL)
Office of Workers' Compensation Programs
200 Constitution Ave Ste S3524............Washington DC 20210 **866-487-2365**
Women's Bureau
200 Constitution Ave NW Rm S3002 ....Washington DC 20210 **800-827-5335** 202-693-6710
US Department of Labor
200 Constitution Ave NW Rm S-3002 ....Washington DC 20210 **800-827-5335** 202-693-6710
Women's Bureau Regional Offices
Region 1
JFK Federal Bldg Rm 525-A ....Boston MA 02203 **800-827-5335** 617-565-1988
Region 10
300 Fifth Ave Ste 1230 ....Seattle WA 98104 **800-827-5335** 206-757-6740
Region 2
201 Varick St Rm 602......................New York NY 10014 **800-827-5335** 646-264-3789
Region 3
The Curtis Ctr Ste 631 E West
170 S Independence Mall West ....Philadelphia PA 19106 **800-827-5335** 866-487-2365
Region 5
230 S Dearborn St Rm 1022................Chicago IL 60604 **800-827-5335** 312-353-6985
Region 7
2300 Main St Ste 1050.................Kansas City MO 64108 **800-827-5335** 816-285-7233
Region 8
1999 Broadway Ste 1620 PO Box 46550 ....Denver CO 80201 **800-827-5335** 303-844-1286
Region 9
90 Seventh St Ste 2650 ....San Francisco CA 94103 **800-827-5335** 866-487-2365

339-15 US Department of State

				Toll-Free	Phone

Bureau of Consular Affairs
2201 C St NW SA 17 9th Fl ....Washington DC 20522 **888-407-4747** 202-501-4444
Office of Children's Issues
2201 C St NW SA-17 9th Fl ....Washington DC 20522 **888-407-4747** 202-501-4444
Passport Services
600 19th St NW
1st Fl Sidewalk Level ....Washington DC 20006 **888-874-7793** 877-487-2778
Bureau of Diplomatic Security
DS Public Affairs
Bureau of Diplomatic Security US. Department of State Washington DC 20522 **866-217-2089** 571-345-3146
International Boundary & Water Commission - US & Mexico
2616 W Paisano Dr Ste C-100 ....El Paso TX 79922 **800-262-8857** 915-351-1030
Passport Services Regional Offices
Boston Agency
10 Cswy St
Tip O'Neill Federal Bldg Rm 247............Boston MA 02222 **877-487-2778**
Connecticut Agency
850 Canal St ....Stamford CT 06902 **877-487-2778**
Honolulu Agency
300 Ala Moana Blvd Ste I-330 ....Honolulu HI 96850 **877-487-2778**
Los Angeles Agency
11000 Wilshire Blvd Ste 1000 ....Los Angeles CA 90024 **877-487-2778**
New Orleans Agency
365 Canal St Ste 1300 ....New Orleans LA 70130 **877-487-2778**
New York Agency
376 Hudson St ....New York NY 10014 **877-487-2778**
Seattle Agency
300 Fifth Ave Ste 600......................Seattle WA 98104 **877-487-2778**
Washington (DC) Agency
600 19th St NW ....Washington DC 20006 **877-487-2778**
US Passports & International Travel
Chicago Passport Agency
101 W Congress Pkwy 9th Fl.................Chicago IL 60605 **877-487-2778**
San Francisco Passport Agency
450 Golden Gate Ave
3rd Fl Ste 3-2501......................San Francisco CA 94102 **877-487-2778**

339-16 US Department of Transportation

				Toll-Free	Phone

Federal Aviation Administration (FAA)
800 Independence Ave SW ....Washington DC 20591 **866-835-5322**
Flight Standards Service
800 Independence Ave SW ....Washington DC 20591 **866-835-5322** 202-267-8237
Safety Hotline
800 Independence Ave SW ....Washington DC 20591 **800-255-1111**
Federal Aviation Administration Northwest Mountain Region
1601 Lind Ave SW ....Renton WA 98057 **800-220-5715** 425-227-2001
Federal Highway Administration
National Highway Institute
4600 Fairfax Dr Ste 800 ....Arlington VA 22203 **877-558-6873** 703-235-0500
Federal Motor Carrier Safety Administration (FMCSA)
1200 New Jersey Ave SE ....Washington DC 20590 **800-832-5660**
Federal Railroad Administration Regional Offices (FRA)
Region 1
55 Broadway Rm 1077 ....Cambridge MA 02142 **800-724-5991** 202-366-4000
Region 2
Baldwin Tower 1510 Chester Pike ....Crum Lynne PA 19022 **800-724-5991** 202-366-4000
Region 3
61 Forsyth St SW Ste 16T20 ....Atlanta GA 30303 **800-724-5993** 202-366-4000
Region 4 200 W Adams St ....Chicago IL 60606 **800-724-5040** 202-366-4000
Region 6
901 Locust St Ste 464 ....Kansas City MO 64106 **800-724-5996** 202-366-4000
Region 8
703 Broadway St Ste 650 ....Vancouver WA 98660 **800-724-5998** 202-366-4000
Maritime Administration (MARAD)
1200 New Jersey Ave SE ....Washington DC 20590 **800-996-2723*** 202-366-5807
*Hotline
National Highway Traffic Safety Administration (NHTSA)
1200 New Jersey Ave SE ....Washington DC 20590 **888-327-4236** 202-366-9550
National Center for Statistics & Analysis
1200 New Jersey Ave SE ....Washington DC 20590 **800-934-8517** 202-366-1503
Vehicle Research & Test Ctr
10820 SR 347 PO Box B37 ....East Liberty OH 43319 **800-262-8309** 937-666-4511
National Highway Traffic Safety Administration Regional Offices
NHTSA Region 3
1200 New Jersey Ave SE West Bldg ....Washington DC 20590 **888-327-4236**

	City	State	Zip	Toll-Free	Phone
Pipeline & Hazardous Materials Safety Administration					
Office of Hazardous Materials Safety					
1200 New Jersey Ave SE	Washington	DC	20590	**800-467-4922**	202-366-4433
Research & Innovative Technology Administration (RITA)					
1200 New Jersey Ave SE	Washington	DC	20590	**800-853-1351**	202-366-7582
Bureau of Transportation Statistics					
1200 New Jersey Ave SE	Washington	DC	20590	**855-368-4200**	
Office of Research, Development & Technology Programs					
1200 New Jersey Ave SE	Washington	DC	20590	**800-853-1351**	
Saint Lawrence Seaway Development Corp					
1200 New Jersey Ave SE	Washington	DC	20590	**800-785-2779**	202-366-0091
Secretary of Transportation					
1200 New Jersey Ave SE	Washington	DC	20590	**855-368-4200**	

339-17 US Department of the Treasury

	City	State	Zip	Toll-Free	Phone
Department of the Treasury					
1500 Pennsylvania Ave NW	Washington	DC	20220	**800-359-3898**	202-622-2000
Alcohol & Tobacco Tax & Trade Bureau					
1310 G St NW PO Box 12	Washington	DC	20005	**877-882-3277**	202-453-2180
Bureau of Engraving & Printing					
14th & C Sts SW	Washington	DC	20228	**877-874-4114**	
Bureau of the Public Debt					
PO Box 7015	Parkersburg	WV	26106	**800-722-2678**	
TreasuryDirect					
PO Box 7015	Parkersburg	WV	26106	**844-284-2676**	
Comptroller of the Currency					
250 E St SW	Washington	DC	20219	**800-613-6743***	202-874-5000
*Cust Svc					
Internal Revenue Service					
Taxpayer Advocate Service					
77 K St NE Ste 1500	Washington	DC	20002	**877-777-4778**	202-803-9800
US Mint 801 Ninth St NW	Washington	DC	20220	**800-872-6468***	202-354-7462
*Cust Svc					
Denver 320 W Colfax Ave	Denver	CO	80204	**800-642-6116**	303-405-4761
San Francisco					
155 Hermann St	San Francisco	CA	94102	**800-872-6468**	415-575-8000
West Point (NY)					
1063 NY 218	West Point	NY	10996	**800-872-6468**	845-446-6200

339-18 US Department of Veterans Affairs

	City	State	Zip	Toll-Free	Phone
Department of Veterans Affairs (VA)					
810 Vermont Ave NW	Washington	DC	20420	**800-827-1000***	202-461-7600
*Cust Svc					
Public & Intergovernmental Affairs Office					
810 Vermont Ave NW	Washington	DC	20420	**800-273-8255**	
Secretary of Veterans Affairs					
810 Vermont Ave NW	Washington	DC	20420	**844-698-2311**	
Board of Veterans' Appeals					
810 Vermont Ave NW	Washington	DC	20420	**800-923-8387**	
Center for Women Veterans					
810 Vermont Ave NW	Washington	DC	20420	**800-827-1000**	
US Department of Veterans Affairs					
Office of Research & Development					
810 Vermont Ave NW	Washington	DC	20420	**844-698-2311**	800-827-1000
Veterans Benefits Administration					
810 Vermont Ave NW	Washington	DC	20420	**800-827-1000**	
Veterans Health Administration					
810 Vermont Ave NW	Washington	DC	20420	**844-698-2311**	
Gulf War Veterans Information					
810 Vermont Ave NW	Washington	DC	20420	**800-313-2232**	

339-19 US Independent Agencies Government Corporations & Quasi-Official Agencies

Included also among these listings are selected Federal Boards, Committees, and Commissions.

	City	State	Zip	Toll-Free	Phone
Federal Election Commission					
999 E St NW	Washington	DC	20463	**800-424-9530**	202-694-1100
Architectural & Transportation Barriers Compliance Board					
1331 F St NW Ste 1000	Washington	DC	20004	**800-872-2253**	202-272-0080
Commission on Presidential Scholars					
US Presidential Scholars Program					
400 Maryland Ave SW					
US. Department of Education	Washington	DC	20202	**800-872-5327**	202-401-0961
Commodity Futures Trading Commission					
1155 21 St NW	Washington	DC	20581	**866-366-2382**	202-418-5000
Commodity Futures Trading Commission Regional Offices					
Central Region					
525 W Monroe St	Chicago	IL	60661	**800-621-3570**	312-596-0700
Consumer Product Safety Commission (CPSC)					
4340 E W Hwy Ste 502	Bethesda	MD	20814	**800-638-2772**	301-504-7923
Corp for National & Community Service					
AmeriCorps USA					
1201 New York Ave NW	Washington	DC	20525	**800-833-3722**	202-606-5000
Learn & Serve America					
1201 New York Ave NW	Washington	DC	20525	**800-833-3722**	202-606-5000
Corporation for National & Community Service					
Senior Corps					
1201 New York Ave NW	Washington	DC	20525	**800-833-3722**	202-606-5000
Defense Nuclear Facilities Safety Board					
625 Indiana Ave NW Ste 700	Washington	DC	20004	**800-788-4016**	202-694-7000
Denali Commission					
510 L St Ste 410	Anchorage	AK	99501	**888-480-4321**	907-271-1414
Environmental Protection Agency (EPA)					
1200 Pennsylvania Ave NW	Washington	DC	20460	**888-372-8255**	202-564-4700
US National Response Team					
1200 Pennsylvania Ave NW	Washington	DC	20593	**800-424-9346**	202-267-2675
Environmental Protection Agency Regional Offices					
Region 1					
1 Congress St Ste 1100	Boston	MA	02114	**888-372-7341**	617-918-1111
Region 10					
1200 Sixth Ave Ste 900	Seattle	WA	98101	**800-424-4372**	206-553-1200
Region 2 290 Broadway	New York	NY	10007	**800-621-8431**	212-637-3000
Region 3 1650 Arch St	Philadelphia	PA	19103	**800-438-2474**	215-814-5000
Region 4					
Sam Nunn Atlanta Federal Ctr					
61 Forsyth St SW	Atlanta	GA	30303	**800-241-1754**	404-562-9900
Region 5 77 W Jackson Blvd	Chicago	IL	60604	**800-621-8431**	312-353-2000
Region 6					
1445 Ross Ave Ste 1200	Dallas	TX	75202	**800-887-6063**	214-665-2200
Region 7 901 N Fifth St	Kansas City	KS	66101	**800-223-0425**	913-551-7003
Region 8 1595 Wynkoop St	Denver	CO	80202	**800-227-8917**	303-312-6312
Region 9					
75 Hawthorne St	San Francisco	CA	94105	**866-372-9378**	415-947-8000
Equal Employment Opportunity Commission (EEOC)					
1801 L St NW	Washington	DC	20507	**800-669-4000**	202-663-4191
Equal Employment Opportunity Commission Regional Office					
Atlanta District					
100 Alabama St SW Ste 4R30	Atlanta	GA	30303	**800-669-6820**	
Birmingham District					
1130 22nd St S Ste 2000	Birmingham	AL	35205	**800-669-4000**	205-212-2100
Charlotte District					
129 W Trade St Ste 400	Charlotte	NC	28202	**800-669-4000**	704-344-6682
Chicago District					
500 W Madison St Ste 2000	Chicago	IL	60661	**800-669-4000**	312-869-8084
Dallas District					
207 S Houston St 3rd Fl	Dallas	TX	75202	**800-669-4000**	214-253-2700
Houston District					
1201 Louisiana St 6th Fl	Houston	TX	77002	**800-669-4000**	
Los Angeles District					
255 E Temple St 4th Fl	Los Angeles	CA	90012	**800-669-4000**	
New York District					
33 Whitehall St 5th Fl	New York	NY	10004	**866-408-8075**	212-336-3620
Philadelphia District					
801 Market St Ste 1300	Philadelphia	PA	19107	**800-669-4000**	
Saint Louis District					
1222 Spruce St Rm 8100	Saint Louis	MO	63103	**800-669-4000**	314-539-7800
San Francisco District					
450 Golden Gate Ave 5 W					
PO Box 36025	San Francisco	CA	94102	**800-669-4000**	
Export-Import Bank of the US					
811 Vermont Ave NW	Washington	DC	20571	**800-565-3946**	202-565-3946
Federal Communications Commission (FCC)					
445 12th St SW	Washington	DC	20554	**888-225-5322**	
Federal Deposit Insurance Corp					
550 17th St NW	Washington	DC	20429	**877-275-3342**	
Federal Deposit Insurance Corp Regional Offices					
Atlanta Regional Office					
10 Tenth St NW Ste 800	Atlanta	GA	30309	**800-765-3342**	678-916-2200
Boston Area Office					
15 Braintree Hill Office Pk Ste 300	Braintree	MA	02184	**866-728-9953**	781-794-5500
Chicago Area Office					
300 S Riverside Plz Ste 1700	Chicago	IL	60606	**800-944-5343**	312-382-6000
Dallas Area Office					
1601 Bryan St	Dallas	TX	75201	**800-568-9161**	214-754-0098
Kansas City Area Office					
2345 Grand Blvd Ste 1200	Kansas City	MO	64108	**800-209-7459**	816-234-8000
Memphis Area Office					
5100 Poplar Ave Ste 1900	Memphis	TN	38137	**800-210-6354**	901-685-1603
New York Area Office					
350 Fifth Ave Ste 1200	New York	NY	10118	**800-334-9593**	917-320-2500
San Francisco Area Office					
25 Jessie St at Ecker Sq					
Ste 2300	San Francisco	CA	94105	**800-756-3558**	415-546-0160
Federal Labor Relations Authority					
1400 K St NW	Washington	DC	20424	**800-331-3572**	202-357-6029
Federal Trade Commission (FTC)					
600 Pennsylvania Ave NW	Washington	DC	20580	**877-382-4357**	202-326-2222
National Do Not Call Registry					
600 Pennsylvania Ave NW	Washington	DC	20580	**888-382-1222**	
Federal Trade Commission Regional Offices					
East Central Region					
1111 Superior Ave Ste 200	Cleveland	OH	44114	**877-382-4357**	216-263-3455
Midwest Region					
55 W Monroe St Ste 1825	Chicago	IL	60603	**877-382-4357**	
NortheastRegion					
1 Bowling Green	New York	NY	10004	**877-382-4357**	212-607-2829
Northwest Region					
915 Second Ave Rm 2896	Seattle	WA	98174	**877-382-4357**	
Southeast Region					
225 Peachtree St NE	Atlanta	GA	30303	**877-382-4357**	
Southwest Region					
1999 Bryan St Ste 2150	Dallas	TX	75201	**877-382-4357**	214-979-9350
Western Region					
901 Market St Ste 570	San Francisco	CA	94103	**877-382-4357**	
General Services Administration					
Federal Citizen Information Center					
PO Box 100	Pueblo	CO	81009	**888-878-3256**	
General Services Administration Regional Offices					
Region 1 - New England					
10 Cswy St					
Thomas P O'Neill Federal Bldg Rm 900	Boston	MA	02222	**866-734-1727**	
Region 4 - Southeast Sunbelt					
1800 F St NW	Washington	DC	20405	**800-333-4636**	
Region 8 - Rocky Mountain					
Denver Federal Ctr Bldg 41	Denver	CO	80225	**888-999-4777**	303-236-7329
Indian Arts & Crafts Board					
1849 C St NW MS 2528-MIB	Washington	DC	20240	**888-278-3253**	202-208-3773
Merit Systems Protection Board (MSPB)					
1615 M St NW	Washington	DC	20419	**800-209-8960**	202-653-7200
Merit Systems Protection Board Regional Offices (MSPB)					
Atlanta Region					
401 W Peachtree St NW 10th Fl	Atlanta	GA	30308	**800-209-8960**	404-730-2751
Central Region					
230 S Dearborn St 31st Fl	Chicago	IL	60604	**800-424-9121**	312-353-2923

Classified Section

	City	State	ZIP	Toll-Free	Phone
Migratory Bird Conservation Commission					
5275 Leesburg Pk	Falls Church	VA	22041	**800-344-9453**	
National Archives & Records Administration (NARA)					
8601 Adelphi Rd	College Park	MD	20740	**866-272-6272**	
Archival Research Catalog					
8601 Adelphi Rd	College Park	MD	20740	**866-272-6272**	
Office of the Federal Register					
7 G St NW Ste A-734	Washington	DC	20401	**877-684-6448**	202-741-6000
National Archives & Records Administration Regional Offices					
Great Lakes Region					
7358 S Pulaski Rd	Chicago	IL	60629	**800-447-1830**	773-948-9001
Northeast Region					
380 Trapelo Rd	Waltham	MA	02452	**866-406-2379**	202-357-5946
Pacific Alaska Region					
6125 Sand Pt Way NE	Seattle	WA	98115	**866-325-7208**	206-336-5115
Pacific Region					
1000 Commodore Dr	San Bruno	CA	94066	**800-234-8861**	202-357-5946
Southeast Region					
5780 Jonesboro Rd	Morrow	GA	30260	**800-447-1830**	202-357-5946
National Credit Union Administration					
1775 Duke St	Alexandria	VA	22314	**800-827-9650***	703-518-6300
*Fraud Hotline					
National Credit Union Administration Regional Offices					
Region 1					
9 Washington Sq Washington Ave Ext	Albany	NY	12205	**800-755-1030**	518-862-7400
Region 3					
7000 Central Pkwy Ste 1600	Atlanta	GA	30328	**800-827-9650**	678-443-3000
Region 5					
1230 W Washington St Ste 301	Tempe	AZ	85281	**800-995-9064**	602-302-6000
National Endowment for the Humanities (NEH)					
400 Seventh St SW	Washington	DC	20506	**800-634-1121**	202-606-8400
National Labor Relations Board (NLRB)					
1099 14th St NW	Washington	DC	20570	**866-667-6572**	202-273-1991
Region 1					
10 Causeway St 6th Fl	Boston	MA	02222	**866-667-6572**	617-565-6700
National Labor Relations Board Regional Offices					
Region 10					
233 Peachtree St NE Ste 1000	Atlanta	GA	30303	**866-667-6572**	404-331-2896
Region 11					
4035 University Pkwy Ste 200	Winston-Salem	NC	27106	**866-667-6572**	336-631-5201
Region 12					
201 E Kennedy Blvd Ste 530	Tampa	FL	33602	**866-667-6572**	813-228-2641
Region 13 200 W Adams St	Chicago	IL	60606	**866-667-6572**	312-353-7570
Region 14					
1222 Spruce St Rm 8302	Saint Louis	MO	63103	**866-667-6572**	314-539-7770
Region 15					
1515 Poydras St Rm 610	New Orleans	LA	70112	**866-667-6572**	504-589-6361
Region 16					
819 Taylor St Rm 8A24	Fort Worth	TX	76102	**866-667-6572**	817-978-2921
Region 17					
8600 Farley St Ste 100	Overland Park	KS	66212	**866-667-6572**	913-967-3000
Region 18					
330 Second Ave S Ste 790	Minneapolis	MN	55401	**866-667-6572**	612-348-1757
Region 19					
915 Second Ave Rm 2948	Seattle	WA	98174	**844-762-6572**	206-220-6300
Region 2					
26 Federal Plz Rm 3614	New York	NY	10278	**866-667-6572**	212-264-0300
Region 20					
901 Market St Ste 400	San Francisco	CA	94103	**866-667-6572**	415-356-5130
Region 21					
888 S Figueroa St 9th Fl	Los Angeles	CA	90017	**866-667-6572**	213-894-5200
Region 22					
20 Washington Pl 5th Fl	Newark	NJ	07102	**866-667-6572**	973-645-2100
Region 24					
525 FD Roosevelt Ave Ste 1002	San Juan	PR	00918	**866-667-6572**	787-766-5347
Region 25					
575 N Pennsylvania St					
Minton-Capehart Federal Bldg Ste 238	Indianapolis	IN	46204	**866-667-6572**	317-226-7381
Region 26					
80 Monroe Ave Ste 350	Memphis	TN	38103	**866-667-6572**	901-544-0018
Region 27					
1961 Stout St Ste 13-103	Denver	CO	80294	**844-762-6572**	303-844-3551
Region 28					
2600 N Central Ave Ste 1800	Phoenix	AZ	85004	**866-667-6572**	602-640-2160
Region 29					
1 Metrotech Ctr 15th Fl	Brooklyn	NY	11201	**866-667-6572**	718-330-7713
Region 3					
Niagara Ctr Bldg					
130 S Elmwood Ave Ste 630	Buffalo	NY	14202	**866-667-6572**	716-551-4931
Region 30					
1015 Half St SE	Washington	DC	20570	**844-762-6572**	202-273-1000
Region 31					
11150 W Olympic Blvd Ste 700	Los Angeles	CA	90064	**866-667-6572**	310-235-7352
Region 32					
1301 Clay St Rm 300N	Oakland	CA	94612	**866-667-6572**	510-637-3300
Region 34 450 Main St	Hartford	CT	06103	**866-667-6572**	860-240-3522
Region 5					
103 S Gay St 8th Fl	Baltimore	MD	21202	**866-667-6572**	410-962-2822
Region 6					
1000 Liberty Ave Rm 904	Pittsburgh	PA	15222	**866-667-6572**	412-395-4400
Region 7					
477 Michigan Ave Rm 300	Detroit	MI	48226	**866-667-6572**	313-226-3200
Region 8					
1240 E Ninth St Rm 1695	Cleveland	OH	44199	**866-667-6572**	216-522-3715
Region 9					
550 Main St Rm 3003	Cincinnati	OH	45202	**866-667-6572**	513-684-3686
National Railroad Passenger Corp					
60 Massachusetts Ave NE	Washington	DC	20002	**800-872-7245**	202-906-3741
Nuclear Regulatory Commission Regional Offices					
Region 1					
2100 Renaissance Blvd	King of Prussia	PA	19406	**800-432-1156**	610-337-5000
Region 3					
2443 Warrenville Rd Ste 210	Lisle	IL	60532	**800-522-3025**	630-829-9500
Region 4					
1600 E Lamar Blvd	Arlington	TX	76011	**800-952-9677**	817-860-8100
US NRC Region II					
61 Forsyth St SW Ste 23T85	Atlanta	GA	30303	**800-577-8510**	404-562-4400
Occupational Safety & Health Review Commission Regional Offices					
Atlanta Region					
100 Alabama St SW Rm 2R90	Atlanta	GA	30303	**800-321-6742**	404-562-1640
Office of Special Counsel					
1730 M St NW Ste 218	Washington	DC	20036	**800-872-9855**	202-254-3600
OSC Headquarters					
1730 M St NW Ste 218	Washington	DC	20036	**800-872-9855**	202-254-3600
Overseas Private Investment Corp (OPIC)					
1100 New York Ave NW	Washington	DC	20527	**800-225-5722**	202-336-8400
Peace Corps					
1111 20th St NW	Washington	DC	20526	**800-424-8580**	202-692-1040
Peace Corps Regional Offices					
Atlanta Regional Office					
1111 20th St NW	Washington	DC	20526	**855-855-1961**	202-692-2250
Chicago Regional Office					
230 S Dearborn St Ste 2020	Chicago	IL	60604	**800-424-8580**	312-353-4990
Dallas Regional Office					
1100 Commerce St Ste 427	Dallas	TX	75242	**855-855-1961**	
Denver Regional Office					
1111 20th St NW	Washington	DC	20526	**855-855-1961**	
Los Angeles Regional Office					
2361 Rosecrans Ave Ste 155	El Segundo	CA	90245	**800-424-8580**	310-356-1100
Mid-Atlantic Regional Office					
1525 Wilson Blvd Ste 100	Arlington	VA	22209	**800-424-8580**	202-692-1040
New York Regional Office					
201 Varick St Ste 1025	New York	NY	10014	**800-424-8580**	212-352-5440
Northwest Regional Office					
1601 Fifth Ave Ste 605	Seattle	WA	98101	**800-424-8580**	206-553-5490
San Francisco Regional Office					
1301 Clay St Ste 620-N	Oakland	CA	94612	**800-424-8580**	510-452-8444
Pension Benefit Guaranty Corp					
1200 K St NW	Washington	DC	20005	**800-400-7242***	202-326-4000
*Cust Svc					
Railroad Retirement Board					
844 N Rush St	Chicago	IL	60611	**877-772-5772**	312-751-4300
Securities & Exchange Commission (SEC)					
100 F St NE	Washington	DC	20549	**800-732-0330**	202-942-8088
Securities & Exchange Commission Regional Offices					
Los Angeles Regional Office					
5670 Wilshire Blvd 11th Fl	Los Angeles	CA	90036	**800-732-0330**	323-965-3998
Selective Service System					
1515 Wilson Blvd	Arlington	VA	22209	**888-655-1825**	847-688-6888
Selective Service System Regional Offices					
Region 1 PO Box 94638	Palatine	IL	60094	**888-655-1825**	847-688-6888
Region 2 PO Box 94638	Palatine	IL	60094	**888-655-1825**	847-688-6888
Small Business Administration (SBA)					
409 Third St SW	Washington	DC	20416	**800-827-5722**	202-205-6600
Small Business Administration Regional Offices					
Region 6					
4300 Amon Carter Blvd Ste 108	Fort Worth	TX	76155	**800-274-2812**	817-684-5581
Social Security Administration (SSA)					
6401 Security Blvd	Baltimore	MD	21235	**800-772-1213**	410-965-8904
Social Security Administration Regional Offices					
Region 4					
61 Forsyth St SW Ste 23T29	Atlanta	GA	30303	**800-772-1213**	
US Commission on Civil Rights					
1331 Pennsylvania Ave NW Ste 1150	Washington	DC	20425	**800-552-6843**	202-376-7700
US Commission on Civil Rights Regional Offices					
Central Regional Office					
400 State Ave Ste 908	Kansas City	KS	66101	**800-552-6843**	913-551-1400
Eastern Regional Office					
624 Ninth St NW	Washington	DC	20425	**800-552-6843**	202-376-7700
Midwestern Regional Office					
55 W Monroe St Ste 410	Chicago	IL	60603	**800-552-6843**	312-353-8311
Southern Regional Office					
61 Forsyth St SW Ste 1840 T	Atlanta	GA	30303	**800-552-6843**	404-562-7000
US Election Assistance Commission					
1201 New York Ave NW Ste 300	Washington	DC	20005	**866-747-1471**	202-566-3100
US General Services Administration (GSA)					
1275 First St NW	Washington	DC	20405	**800-424-5210**	202-208-7642
US General Services Administration					
1800 F St NW	Washington	DC	20405	**800-488-3111**	
US Institute of Peace					
2301 Constitution Ave NW	Washington	DC	20037	**800-868-8064**	202-457-1700
US Postal Service (USPS)					
475 L'Enfant Plz W SW	Washington	DC	20260	**800-275-8777***	202-268-2000
*Cust Svc					

340 GOVERNMENT - US - JUDICIAL BRANCH

340-1 US Bankruptcy Courts

	City	State	ZIP	Toll-Free	Phone
US Bankruptcy Court					
Alaska					
605 W Fourth Ave Ste 138	Anchorage	AK	99501	**800-859-8059**	907-271-2655
Arizona					
230 N First Ave Ste 101	Phoenix	AZ	85003	**800-556-9230**	602-682-4000
Arkansas					
300 W Second St	Little Rock	AR	72201	**800-676-6856**	501-918-5500
California Southern					
325 W F St	San Diego	CA	92101	**800-676-6856**	619-557-5620
Connecticut					
450 Main St 7th Fl	Hartford	CT	06103	**800-676-6856**	860-240-3675
Eastern District of Washington					
904 W Riverside Ave Ste 304	Spokane	WA	99201	**800-519-2549**	509-458-5300
Florida Northern					
110 E Park Ave Ste 100	Tallahassee	FL	32301	**888-765-1752**	850-521-5001
Georgia Northern					
75 Spring St SW	Atlanta	GA	30303	**800-676-6856**	404-215-1000
Georgia Southern					
125 Bull St	Savannah	GA	31401	**800-676-6856**	912-650-4100
Louisiana Eastern					
500 Poydras St Ste B-601	New Orleans	LA	70130	**800-676-6856**	504-589-7878
Louisiana Western					
300 Fannin St Ste 2201	Shreveport	LA	71101	**866-721-2105**	318-676-4267

Classified Section

	City	State	Zip	Toll-Free	Phone
Michigan Eastern					
211 W Fort St Ste 1820	Detroit	MI	48226	**800-676-6856**	313-234-0065
Michigan Western					
1 Div Ave N Rm 200	Grand Rapids	MI	49503	**800-859-7375**	616-456-2693
Minnesota					
300 S Fourth St 301 US Courthouse	Minneapolis	MN	55415	**866-260-7337**	612-664-5260
Missouri Eastern					
111 S Tenth St 4th Fl	Saint Louis	MO	63102	**866-803-9517**	314-244-4500
Montana 400 N Main St	Butte	MT	59701	**888-888-2530**	406-497-1240
New York Eastern					
271 Cadman Plz E	Brooklyn	NY	11201	**800-676-6856**	347-394-1700
Northern District of Iowa					
111 Seventh Ave SE 6th Fl	Cedar Rapids	IA	52401	**866-222-8029**	319-286-2200
Oklahoma Western					
215 Dean A McGee Ave	Oklahoma City	OK	73102	**800-676-6856**	405-609-5700
Oregon					
1001 SW Fifth Ave Ste 700	Portland	OR	97204	**800-676-6856**	503-326-1500
Pennsylvania Middle					
197 S Main St	Wilkes-Barre	PA	18701	**877-298-2053**	570-831-2500
Pennsylvania Western					
5414 US Steel Tower 600 Grant St	Pittsburgh	PA	15219	**800-676-6856**	412-644-2700
Puerto Rico					
300 Recinto Sur St	San Juan	PR	00901	**866-222-8029**	787-977-6000
Tennessee Western					
200 Jefferson Ave Ste 413	Memphis	TN	38103	**800-406-0190**	901-328-3500
Texas Northern					
1100 Commerce St Rm 1254	Dallas	TX	75242	**800-442-6850**	214-753-2000
West Virginia Southern					
300 Virginia St E Rm 3200	Charleston	WV	25301	**800-685-1111**	304-347-3003
Wisconsin Eastern					
US Federal Courthouse					
517 E Wisconsin Ave Rm 126	Milwaukee	WI	53202	**877-781-7277**	414-297-3291
Wyoming					
2120 Capitol Ave Ste 6004	Cheyenne	WY	82001	**800-676-6856**	307-433-2200

340-2 US District Courts

	City	State	Zip	Toll-Free	Phone
United States District Court					
Western District of Michigan					
110 Michigan St NW					
399 Federal Bldg	Grand Rapids	MI	49503	**800-290-2742**	616-456-2381
United States District Court, Central District					
312 N Spring St	Los Angeles	CA	90012	**800-676-6856**	213-894-1565
US District Court Alabama Northern					
1729 Fifth Ave N	Birmingham	AL	35203	**800-676-6856**	205-278-1700
US District Court Colorado					
901 19th St	Denver	CO	80294	**800-359-8699**	303-844-3433
US District Court for the District of Alaska					
222 W Seventh Ave Ste 4	Anchorage	AK	99513	**866-243-3814**	907-677-6100
US District Court Georgia Northern					
75 Spring St SW	Atlanta	GA	30303	**800-827-2982**	404-215-1600
US District Court Mississippi Southern					
501 E Court St Ste 2500	Jackson	MS	39201	**866-517-7682**	601-965-4439
US District Court Missouri Western					
400 E Ninth St	Kansas City	MO	64106	**800-466-9302**	816-512-5000
US District Court Nebraska					
111 S 18th Plz Ste 1152	Omaha	NE	68102	**866-220-4381**	402-661-7350
US District Court Nevada					
333 Las Vegas Blvd S	Las Vegas	NV	89101	**800-676-6856**	702-464-5400
US District Court North Carolina Western					
401 W Trade St	Charlotte	NC	28202	**866-851-1605**	704-350-7400
US District Court Northern District Of Florida					
111 N Adams St	Tallahassee	FL	32301	**800-676-6856**	850-521-3501
US District Court Ohio Northern					
801 W Superior Ave	Cleveland	OH	44113	**800-355-8498**	216-357-7000
US District Court Oklahoma Northern					
333 W Fourth St	Tulsa	OK	74103	**866-213-1957**	918-699-4700
US District Court Oklahoma Western					
200 NW Fourth St Rm 1210	Oklahoma City	OK	73102	**888-609-6953**	405-609-5000
US District Court Vermont					
11 Elmwood Ave Rm 506	Burlington	VT	05401	**800-837-8718**	802-951-6301

341 GOVERNMENT - US - LEGISLATIVE BRANCH

SEE ALSO Legislation Hotlines

	City	State	Zip	Toll-Free	Phone
Calgary Economic Development					
731 First St SE	Calgary	AB	T2G2G9	**888-222-5855**	403-221-7831
Library of Congress					
National Library Service for the Blind					
1291 Taylor St NW	Washington	DC	20542	**888-657-7323**	202-707-5100
US Copyright Office					
101 Independence Ave SE	Washington	DC	20559	**877-476-0778**	202-707-3000
Tourism Abbotsford Society					
34561 Delair Rd	Abbotsford	BC	V2S2E1	**888-332-2229**	604-859-1721
US Government Printing Office Bookstore (GPO)					
732 N Capitol St NW	Washington	DC	20401	**866-512-1800**	202-512-1800

341-1 US Senators, Representatives, Delegates

The circled letter S denotes that a listing is for a senator.

District of Columbia

	City	State	Zip	Toll-Free	Phone
Levin Sander (Rep D - MI)					
1236 Longworth House Office Bldg	Washington	DC	20515	**888-810-3880**	
Bacon Don (Rep R - NE)					
1516 Longworth House Office Bldg	Washington	DC	20515	**888-221-7452**	202-225-4155
Sablan Gregorio (Rep D - MP)					
2411 Rayburn House Office Bldg	Washington	DC	20515	**877-446-3465**	202-225-2646
Latta Robert E (Rep R - OH)					
2448 Rayburn House Office Bldg	Washington	DC	20515	**800-541-6446**	202-225-6405
Barletta Lou (Rep R - PA)					
2049 Rayburn House Office Bldg	Washington	DC	20515	**855-241-5144**	202-225-6511
Casey Robert P Jr. (Sen D - PA)					
393 Russell Senate Office Bldg	Washington	DC	20510	**866-802-2833**	202-224-6324
Scott Tim (Sen R - SC)					
717 Hart Senate Office Bldg	Washington	DC	20510	**855-425-6324**	202-224-6121
Rounds Mike (Sen R - SD)					
502 Hart Senate Office Bldg	Washington	DC	20510	**844-875-5268**	202-224-5842
Thune John (Sen R - SD)					
511 Dirksen Senate Office Bldg	Washington	DC	20510	**866-850-3855**	202-224-2321
Arrington Jodey (Rep R - TX)					
1029 Longworth House Office Bldg	Washington	DC	20515	**888-217-0281**	202-225-4005
Gohmert Louie (Rep R - TX)					
2243 Rayburn House Office Bldg	Washington	DC	20515	**866-535-6302**	202-225-3035
Poe Ted (Rep R - TX)					
2132 Rayburn Bldg	Washington	DC	20515	**866-425-6565**	202-225-6565
Murray Patty (Sen D - WA)					
154 Russell Senate Office Bldg	Washington	DC	20510	**866-481-9186**	202-224-2621
Duffy Sean P (Rep R - WI)					
2330 Rayburn House office Bldg	Washington	DC	20515	**855-584-4251**	202-225-3365
Barrasso John (Sen R - WY)					
307 Dirksen Senate Office Bldg	Washington	DC	20510	**866-235-9553**	202-224-6441
Enzi Michael B (Sen R - WY)					
379A Russell Senate Office Bldg	Washington	DC	20510	**888-250-1879**	202-224-3424

342 GOVERNORS - STATE

Listings for governors are organized by state names.

	City	State	Zip	Toll-Free	Phone
Colyer Jeff (R)					
State Capitol					
300 SW Tenth Ave Ste 241S	Topeka	KS	66612	**877-579-6757**	785-296-3232
Edwards John Bel (D)					
PO Box 94004	Baton Rouge	LA	70804	**866-366-1121**	225-342-7015
Hogan Larry (R)					
100 State Cir	Annapolis	MD	21401	**800-811-8336**	410-974-3901
Baker Charlie (R)					
State House 24 Beacon St					
Office of the Governor Rm 280	Boston	MA	02133	**888-870-7770**	617-725-4005
Dayton Mark (D)					
130 State Capitol					
75 Rev Dr Martin Luther King Jr Blvd	St. Paul	MN	55155	**800-657-3717**	651-201-3400
Bullock Steve (D)					
State Capitol PO Box 200801	Helena	MT	59620	**855-318-1330**	406-444-3111
Abbott Greg (R)					
State Insurance Bldg 1100 San Jacinto					
PO Box 12428	Austin	TX	78701	**800-843-5789**	512-463-2000
Herbert Gary Richard (R)					
Utah State Capitol Complex 350 N State St Ste 200					
PO Box 142220	Salt Lake City	UT	84114	**800-705-2464**	801-538-1000
Scott Phil (R)					
109 State St Pavilion Office Bldg	Montpelier	VT	05609	**800-649-6825**	802-828-3333
Justice Jim (R)					
State Capitol 1900 Kanawha Blvd E	Charleston	WV	25305	**888-438-2731**	304-558-2000

343 GRAPHIC DESIGN

SEE ALSO Typesetting & Related Services

	City	State	Zip	Toll-Free	Phone
Adcolor Inc					
230 Charlois Blvd	Winston-Salem	NC	27103	**800-688-0629**	
Adrenalin Inc 54 W 11th Ave	Denver	CO	80204	**888-757-5646**	303-454-8888
Armada Group, The					
325 Soquel Ave	Santa Cruz	CA	95062	**800-408-2120**	
Austin Graphics Inc					
1198 Second Ave E	Owen Sound	ON	N4K2J1	**800-265-6964**	519-376-2116
B&B Image Group					
1712 Marshall St NE	Minneapolis	MN	55413	**888-788-9461**	612-788-9461
Bendsen Signs & Graphics Inc					
1506 E McBride Ave	Decatur	IL	62526	**866-275-6407**	217-877-2345
BrandEquity International					
7 Great Meadow Rd	Newton	MA	02462	**800-969-3150**	
Cactus Punch Inc					
1224 Heil Quaker Blvd	LaVergne	TN	37086	**800-446-2333**	
Capstone Production Group					
1638 S Saunders St	Raleigh	NC	27603	**800-951-4005**	919-838-8030
CottonimagesCom Inc					
10481 NW 28th St	Miami	FL	33172	**888-642-7999**	305-251-2560
David Berman Developments					
340 Selby Ave	Ottawa	ON	K2A3X6	**800-665-1809**	613-728-6777
Democrat Printing & Lithographing Company Inc					
6401 Lindsey Rd	Little Rock	AR	72206	**800-622-2216**	
Direct Edge Media					
2900 E White Star Ave	Anaheim	CA	92806	**800-556-5576**	714-221-8686
Firstbase Services Ltd					
34609 Delair Rd	Abbotsford	BC	V2S2E1	**800-758-2922**	604-850-5334
H&H Group, The					
854 N Prince St	Lancaster	PA	17603	**866-338-7569**	717-393-3941
Hotcards Com Inc					
2400 Superior Ave	Cleveland	OH	44114	**800-787-4831**	216-241-4040
Hudson Printing & Graphic Design					
611 S Mobberly Ave	Longview	TX	75602	**800-530-4888**	903-758-1773
Kane Graphical Corp					
2255 W Logan Blvd	Chicago	IL	60647	**800-992-2921**	
Metro Creative Graphics Inc					
519 Eigth Ave	New York	NY	10018	**800-223-1600**	212-947-5100
Mike Davis & Associates Inc					
15505 Long Vista Dr # 200	Austin	TX	78728	**888-836-8442**	512-836-8442
Newhall Klein Inc					
6109 W Kl Ave	Kalamazoo	MI	49009	**866-639-4255**	269-544-0844
Oden & Associates Inc					
119 S Main St Ste 300	Memphis	TN	38103	**800-371-6233**	901-578-8055
Offwhite 521 Ft St	Marietta	OH	45750	**800-606-1610**	740-373-9010
Plastic Package Inc					
4600 Beloit Dr	Sacramento	CA	95838	**800-356-6900**	916-921-3399

				Toll-Free	Phone
Printing House Ltd, The 1403 Bathurst St	Toronto	ON	M5R3H8	800-874-0870	416-536-6113
Rocket Communications Inc 81 Langton St Ste 12	San Francisco	CA	94103	844-897-6253	415-863-0101
Signature Graphics Inc 1000 Signature Dr	Porter	IN	46304	800-356-3235	219-926-4994
Spire Inc 65 Bay St	Boston	MA	02125	877-350-8837	617-350-8837
Store Decor Co, The 5050 Boyd Blvd	Rowlett	TX	75088	800-831-3267	972-475-4404
Terrapin Systems LLC 9841 Washingtonian Blvd Ste 200	Gaithersburg	MD	20878	866-837-7797	301-530-9106
Theprinterscom 3500 E College Ave	State College	PA	16801	800-359-2097	
Vango Graphics Inc 1371 S Inca St	Denver	CO	80223	877-722-6168	303-722-6109
West Canadian Digital Imaging Inc 200 - 1601 Ninth Ave SE	Calgary	AB	T2G0H4	800-267-2555	403-245-2555
William Fox Munroe Inc (WFM) 3 E Lancaster Ave	Shillington	PA	19607	800-344-2402	610-775-4521
Xplane Corp 811 SW Sixth Ave Ste 500	Portland	OR	97204	855-548-4343	

344 GROCERY STORES

SEE ALSO Wholesale Clubs ; Convenience Stores ; Ice Cream & Dairy Stores ; Bakeries ; Health Food Stores ; Gourmet Specialty Shops

				Toll-Free	Phone
A-Pac Manufacturing Company Inc 2719 Courier NW	Grand Rapids	MI	49534	800-272-2634	
Acme Markets Inc 75 Valley Stream Pkwy	Malvern	PA	19355	877-932-7948	610-889-4000
Advanced Orthomolecular Research Inc 3900 - 12 St NE	Calgary	AB	T2E8H9	800-387-0177	403-250-9997
AG. Ferrari Foods 2000 N Loop Rd	Alameda	CA	94502	877-878-2783	510-351-5520
Alaska Commercial Co 125 Main St	Aniak	AK	99557	800-563-0002	
Arkansas Poly Inc 1248 S 28th St	Van Buren	AR	72956	800-364-5036	479-474-5036
Autry Greer & Sons Inc 2850 W Main St	Mobile	AL	36612	800-999-7750	251-457-8655
Banner Wholesale Grocers Inc 3000 S Ashland	Chicago	IL	60608	844-421-2650	312-421-2650
Bashas Inc 22402 S Bashas Rd	Chandler	AZ	85248	800-755-7292	480-895-5369
Big Y Foods Inc 2145 Roosevelt Ave *Cust Svc	Springfield	MA	01102	800-828-2688*	413-784-0600
Buehler Food Markets Inc 1401 Old Mansfield Rd	Wooster	OH	44691	800-998-4438	330-264-4355
Byrd Cookie Company Inc 6700 Waters Ave	Savannah	GA	31406	800-291-2973	912-355-1716
Downs Food Group 418 Benzel Ave SW	Madelia	MN	56062	800-967-2474	507-642-3203
EuroPharma Inc 955 Challenger Dr	Green Bay	WI	54311	866-598-5487	920-406-6500
Field Fresh Foods Inc 14805 S San Pedro St	Gardena	CA	90248	800-411-0588	
Food City 1005 N Arizona Ave	Chandler	AZ	85224	800-755-7292	480-857-2198
FreshDirect Inc 23-30 Borden Ave	Long Island	NY	11101	866-511-1240	718-928-1000
Fry's Food Stores of Arizona Inc 500 S 99th Ave	Tolleson	AZ	85353	866-221-4141	
G & J Land & Marine Food Distributors 506 Front St	Morgan City	LA	70380	800-256-9187	985-385-2620
GermanDelicom 601 Westport Pkwy Ste 100	Grapevine	TX	76051	877-437-6269	817-410-9955
Giant Eagle Inc 101 Kappa Dr *Cust Svc	Pittsburgh	PA	15238	800-553-2324*	412-963-6200
Giant Food Inc 8301 Professional Pl Ste 115	Landover	MD	20785	888-469-4426	
Giant Food Stores LLC 1149 Harrisburg Pk	Carlisle	PA	17013	888-814-4268	717-249-4000
Golub Corp 461 Nott St	Schenectady	NY	12308	800-666-7667	
Haggen Inc 2900 Woburn St	Bellingham	WA	98226	800-995-1902	360-676-5300
Hancock County Co-op Oil Assn 245 State St	Garner	IA	50438	800-924-2667	641-923-2635
Heinen's Inc 4540 Richmond Rd	Cleveland	OH	44128	855-475-2300	
Honey Baked Ham Company LLC, The 1081 E Long Lake Rd	Troy	MI	48098	800-367-7720	248-689-4890
IGA Inc 8745 W Higgins Rd Ste 350	Chicago	IL	60631	800-321-5442	773-693-4520
Ingles Markets Inc 2913 US Hwy 70 W *NASDAQ: IMKTA*	Black Mountain	NC	28711	800-635-5066	828-669-2941
International Gourmet Foods Inc 7520 Fullerton Rd	Springfield	VA	22153	800-522-0377	703-569-4520
International Plastics Inc 185 Commerce Ctr	Greenville	SC	29615	800-820-4722	864-297-8000
InVite Health Inc 1 Garden State Plz	Paramus	NJ	07652	800-349-0929	201-587-2222
Jamac Frozen Foods 570 Grand St	Jersey City	NJ	07302	800-631-0440	201-333-6200
K-VA-T Food Stores Inc PO Box 1158	Abingdon	VA	24212	800-826-8451	276-623-5100
Kajun Kettle Foods 405 Alpha Dr	Destrehan	LA	70047	800-331-9612	504-733-8800
Klass Ingredients Inc 3885 N Buffalo St	Orchard Park	NY	14127	800-662-6577	716-662-6665
Krist Oil Co 303 Selden Rd	Iron River	MI	49935	800-722-6691	906-265-6144
Kroger Co 1014 Vine St *NYSE: KR*	Cincinnati	OH	45202	800-576-4377	513-762-4000
Kuukpik Corp PO Box 89187	Nuiqsut	AK	99789	866-480-6220	907-480-6220
Lake Erie Frozen Foods Co 1830 Orange Rd	Ashland	OH	44805	800-766-8501	419-289-9204
LIFEFORCE USA 495 Raleigh Ave	El Cajon	CA	92020	800-531-4877	858-218-3200
Loblaw Cos Ltd 1 President's Choice Cir	Brampton	ON	L6Y5S5	888-495-5111	905-459-2500
Lorann Oils 4518 Aurelius Rd	Lansing	MI	48910	800-862-8620	517-882-0215
Lowes Food Stores Inc 1381 Old Mill Cir Ste 200	Winston-Salem	NC	27103	800-669-5693	336-659-0180
Martin & Bayley Inc 1311 A W Main	Carmi	IL	62821	800-876-2511	618-382-2334
McClancy Seasoning Co 1 Spice Rd	Fort Mill	SC	29707	800-843-1968	803-548-2366
McFarling Foods Inc 333 West 14th St	Indianapolis	IN	46202	800-622-9003	
Meijer Inc 2929 Walker Ave NW	Grand Rapids	MI	49544	800-543-3704	616-453-6711
Merchants Grocery Co 800 Maddox Dr PO Box 1268	Culpeper	VA	22701	877-897-9893	540-825-0786
Metabolic Maintenance 601 N Larch St PO Box 940	Sisters	OR	97759	800-772-7873	
Milford Markets Inc PO Box 7812	Edison	NJ	08818	800-746-7748	
Mother's Market & Kitchen 1890 Newport Blvd	Costa Mesa	CA	92627	800-595-6667	949-631-4741
Natural Healthy Concepts 310 N Westhill Blvd	Appleton	WI	54914	866-505-7501	920-968-2350
Pick N Save 6950 W State St	Wauwatosa	WI	53213	800-576-4377	414-475-7181
Piggly Wiggly Carolina Company Inc 176 Croghan Spur Rd Ste 301	Charleston	SC	29407	800-243-9880	843-554-9880
Pittsburg Wholesale Groceries Inc 727 Kennedy St	Oakland	CA	94606	800-200-4244	
Pressed Juicery LLC 1550 17th St	Santa Monica	CA	90404	855-755-8423	
Publix Super Markets Inc 3300 Publix Corporate Pkwy *PR	Lakeland	FL	33811	800-242-1227*	863-688-1188
Quality Food Centers 10116 NE 8th	Bellevue	WA	98004	800-576-4377	425-455-0870
Rainbow Grocery Co-op Inc 1745 Folsom St	San Francisco	CA	94103	877-720-2667	415-863-0620
Raley's 500 W Capitol Ave	Sacramento	CA	95605	800-925-9989	916-373-3333
Ralphs Grocery Co 1014 Vine St *Cust Svc	Cincinnati	OH	45202	800-576-4377*	
Roasterie Inc, The 1204 W 27th St	Kansas City	MO	64108	800-376-0245	816-931-4000
Schnuck Markets Inc 11420 Lackland Rd	Saint Louis	MO	63146	800-264-4400	314-994-4400
Shop 'n Save 10461 Manchester Rd	Kirkwood	MO	63122	800-428-6974	314-984-0322
ShopRite PO Box 7812	Edison	NJ	08818	800-746-7748	
Smart & Final Inc 600 Citadel Dr	Commerce	CA	90040	800-894-0511	323-869-7500
Sobeys Inc 115 King St	Stellarton	NS	B0K1S0	800-723-3929	902-752-8371
Starco Impex 2710 S 11th St	Beaumont	TX	77701	866-740-9601	
Stop & Shop Supermarket Co 1385 Hancock St	Quincy	MA	02169	800-767-7772	781-397-0006
Super H Mart Inc 2550 Pleasant Hill Rd	Duluth	GA	30096	877-427-7386	678-543-4000
Supermercado Mi Tierra LLC 9520 International Blvd	Oakland	CA	94603	800-225-9902	510-567-8617
SUPERVALU Inc 11840 Valley View Rd *NYSE: SVU* ■ *Cust Svc	Eden Prairie	MN	55344	877-322-8228*	952-828-4000
Tadych's Econofoods 1600 Stephenson	Iron Mountain	MI	49801	877-295-4558	906-774-1911
Total Wine & More 6600 Rockledge Dr	Bethesda	MD	20817	855-328-9463	
United Coop N7160 Raceway Rd	Beaver Dam	WI	53916	800-924-2991	920-887-1756
VitaDigestcom 20687-2 Amar Rd Ste 258	Walnut	CA	91789	877-848-2168	
Vyse Gelatin Co 5010 Rose St	Schiller Park	IL	60176	800-533-2152	847-678-4780
Wegmans Food Markets Inc 1500 Brooks Ave PO Box 30844	Rochester	NY	14603	800-934-6267	585-328-2550
Weis Markets 1000 S Second St PO Box 471 *NYSE: WMK*	Sunbury	PA	17801	866-999-9347	
Western Bagel Baking Corp 7814 Sepulveda Blvd	Van Nuys	CA	91405	800-555-0882	818-786-5847
WinCo Foods Inc 8200 W Fairview Ave	Boise	ID	83704	888-674-6854	208-377-9840
Wing Hing Foods Inc 2539 E Philadelphia St	Ontario	CA	91761	855-734-2742	909-627-7312
ZeaVision LLC 716-I Crown Industrial Ct	Chesterfield	MO	63005	866-833-2800	314-628-1000

345 GYM & PLAYGROUND EQUIPMENT

				Toll-Free	Phone
American Athletic Inc (AAI) 200 American Ave	Jefferson	IA	50129	800-247-3978	
American Playground Corp 2328 Jefferson St	Anderson	IN	46016	800-541-1602	765-642-0288
BCI Burke Company Inc 660 Van Dyne Rd	Fond du Lac	WI	54937	800-356-2070	920-921-9220
Columbia Cascade Co 1300 SW Sixth Ave Ste 310	Portland	OR	97201	800-547-1940	503-223-1157

			Toll-Free	Phone

Grounds For Play Inc
1050 Columbia Dr . . . . Carrollton GA 30117 **800-552-7529**
Jaypro Sports Inc
976 Hartford Tpke . . . . Waterford CT 06385 **800-243-0533***
*Cust Svc
Landscape Structures Inc
601 Seventh St S . . . . Delano MN 55328 **800-328-0035** 763-972-3391
Miracle Recreation Equipment Co
878 Hwy 60 . . . . Monett MO 65708 **800-523-4202** 417-235-6917
PlayCore Inc
544 Chestnut St . . . . Chattanooga TN 37402 **877-762-7563**
Playworld Systems Inc
1000 Buffalo Rd . . . . Lewisburg PA 17837 **800-233-8404** 570-522-9800
School-Tech Inc
745 State Cir . . . . Ann Arbor MI 48108 **800-521-2832**
SportsPlay Equipment Inc
5642 Natural Bridge Ave . . . . Saint Louis MO 63120 **800-727-8180** 314-389-4140

346   GYPSUM PRODUCTS

			Toll-Free	Phone

American Gypsum
3811 Turtle Creek Blvd Ste 1200 . . . . Dallas TX 75219 **866-439-5800** 214-530-5500
CertainTeed Gypsum
2424 Lakeshore Rd W . . . . Mississauga ON L5J1K4 **800-233-8990** 905-823-9881
Eagle Materials Inc
3811 Turtle Creek Blvd Ste 1100 . . . . Dallas TX 75219 **800-759-7625** 214-432-2000
NYSE: EXP
KCG Inc
15720 W 108th St Ste 100 . . . . Lenexa KS 66219 **855-858-3344**
Lafarge North America Inc
8700 W Bryn Mawr Ave Ste 300 . . . . Chicago IL 60631 **800-451-8346** 773-372-1000
National Gypsum Co
2001 Rexford Rd . . . . Charlotte NC 28211 **800-628-4662** 704-365-7300
PABCO Gypsum 37851 Cherry St . . . . Newark CA 94560 **877-449-7786** 510-792-9555
USG Corp 550 W Adams St . . . . Chicago IL 60661 **800-874-4968** 312-436-4000
NYSE: USG

347   HAIRPIECES, WIGS, TOUPEES

			Toll-Free	Phone

Aderans Hair Goods Inc
9135 Independence Ave . . . . Chatsworth CA 91311 **877-413-5225***
*Sales
Alkinco PO Box 278 . . . . New York NY 10116 **800-424-7118** 212-719-3070
Headstart Hair For Men Inc
3395 Cypress Gardens Rd . . . . Winter Haven FL 33884 **800-645-6525** 863-324-5559
Henry Margu Inc
540 Commerce St . . . . Yeadon PA 19050 **800-345-8284** 610-622-0515
HPH Corp
1529 SE 47th Terr . . . . Cape Coral FL 33904 **800-654-9884** 239-540-0085
Jacquelyn Wigs
15 W 37th St 4th Fl . . . . New York NY 10018 **800-272-2424** 212-302-2266
Jean Paree Weegs Inc
4041 South 700 East Ste 2 . . . . Salt Lake City UT 84107 **800-422-9447***
*Orders
Jon Renau Collection
2510 Island View Way . . . . Vista CA 92081 **800-462-9447** 760-598-0067
Louis Ferre Inc
302 Fifth Ave . . . . New York NY 10001 **800-695-1061**
National Fiber Technology LLC
15 Union St . . . . Lawrence MA 01840 **800-842-2751*** 978-686-2964
*Cust Svc
Rene Of Paris
9135 Independence Ave . . . . Chatsworth CA 91311 **800-353-7363***
*Sales
Wig America Co
27317 Industrial Blvd . . . . Hayward CA 94545 **800-338-7600** 510-887-9579
YK International Co
3246 W Montrose Ave . . . . Chicago IL 60618 **800-266-5254** 773-583-5270

348   HANDBAGS, TOTES, BACKPACKS

SEE ALSO Tarps, Tents, Covers ; Luggage, Bags, Cases ; Leather Goods - Personal ; Sporting Goods

			Toll-Free	Phone

Dow Cover Co Inc
373 Lexington Ave . . . . New Haven CT 06513 **800-735-8877** 203-469-5394
Kate Spade 135 Fifth Ave . . . . New York NY 10010 **866-999-5283**
Vera Bradley Designs
2208 Production Rd . . . . Fort Wayne IN 46808 **800-975-8372** 260-482-4673

349   HARDWARE - MFR

			Toll-Free	Phone

Aceco 4419 Federal Way . . . . Boise ID 83716 **800-359-7012** 208-343-7712
Acorn Manufacturing Company Inc
457 School St . . . . Mansfield MA 02048 **800-835-0121** 508-339-2977
Acryline USA Inc
2015 Becancour . . . . Lyster QC G0S1V0 **800-567-0920**
AGM Container Controls Inc
3526 E Ft Lowell Rd . . . . Tucson AZ 85716 **800-995-5590** 520-881-2130
Albion Industries Inc
800 N Clark St . . . . Albion MI 49224 **800-835-8911** 517-629-9441
Allied Fastener & Tool Inc
1130 Ng St . . . . Lake Worth FL 33460 **877-353-3731** 561-585-2113
American Bolt & Screw Manufacturing Corp
14650 Miller Ave Ste 200 . . . . Fontana CA 92336 **800-325-0844** 909-390-0522
Architectural Builders Hardware Manufacturing
1222 Ardmore Ave Apt W . . . . Itasca IL 60143 **800-932-9224** 630-875-9900
Arrow Lock Co
100 Arrow Dr . . . . New Haven CT 06511 **800-839-3157**

			Toll-Free	Phone

Assa Abloy of Canada Ltd
160 Four Vly Dr . . . . Vaughan ON L4K4T9 **800-461-3007** 905-738-2466
ASSA Inc 110 Sargent Dr . . . . New Haven CT 06511 **800-235-7482** 203-624-5225
Attwood Corp
1016 N Monroe St . . . . Lowell MI 49331 **844-808-5704** 616-897-9241
Automotive Racing Products Inc
1863 Eastman Ave . . . . Ventura CA 93003 **800-826-3045** 805-339-2200
Bad Dog Tools
24 Broadcommon Rd . . . . Bristol RI 02809 **800-252-1330** 401-253-1330
Baier Marine Company Inc
2920 Airway Ave . . . . Costa Mesa CA 92626 **800-455-3917**
Baldwin Hardware Corp
841 E Wyomissing Blvd . . . . Reading PA 19611 **800-566-1986** 610-777-7811
Band-It-IDEX Inc
4799 Dahlia St . . . . Denver CO 80216 **800-525-0758**
Barnhill Bolt Company Inc
2500 Princeton Dr NE . . . . Albuquerque NM 87107 **800-472-3900** 505-884-1808
Baron Mfg Company LLC
730 Baker St . . . . Itasca IL 60143 **800-368-8585** 630-628-9110
Belwith International Ltd
3100 Broadway Ave . . . . Grandville MI 49418 **800-235-9484**
Berenson Corp 2495 Main St . . . . Buffalo NY 14214 **800-333-0578** 716-833-3100
Best Access Systems
6161 E 75th St . . . . Indianapolis IN 46250 **855-365-2407** 317-849-2250
Bete Fog Nozzle Inc
50 Greenfield St . . . . Greenfield MA 01301 **800-235-0049** 413-772-0846
Blum Inc 7733 Old Plank Rd . . . . Stanley NC 28164 **800-438-6788** 704-827-1345
Bommer Industries Inc
PO Box 187 . . . . Landrum SC 29356 **800-334-1654** 864-457-3301
Bronze Craft Corp 37 Will St . . . . Nashua NH 03060 **800-488-7747**
Cal-Royal Products Inc
6605 Flotilla St . . . . City Of Commerce CA 90040 **800-876-9258** 323-888-6601
Charles Leonard Inc
145 Kennedy Dr . . . . Hauppauge NY 11788 **800-999-7202** 631-273-6700
Chicago Nut & Bolt Inc
150 Covington Dr . . . . Bloomingdale IL 60108 **888-529-8600** 630-529-8600
Chief Manufacturing
301 Mcintosh Pkwy . . . . Thomaston GA 30286 **800-722-2061**
Circle Bolt & Nut Company Inc
158 Pringle St . . . . Kingston PA 18704 **800-548-2658** 570-718-6001
Circor Aerospace Inc
2301 Wardlow Cir . . . . Corona CA 92880 **800-344-8724** 951-270-6200
Classic Brass Inc
2051 Stoneman Cir . . . . Lakewood NY 14750 **800-869-3173** 716-763-1400
Cloud-rider Designs Ltd
1260 Eighth Ave . . . . Regina SK S4R1C9 **800-632-1255** 306-761-2119
Colonial Bronze Co
511 Winsted Rd . . . . Torrington CT 06790 **800-355-7903***
*All   860-489-9233
Columbia River Knife & Tool Inc
18348 SW 126th Pl . . . . Tualatin OR 97062 **800-891-3100** 503-685-5015
Component Hardware Group Inc
1890 Swarthmore Ave . . . . Lakewood NJ 08701 **800-526-3694** 732-363-4700
Craft Inc
1929 County St PO Box 3049 . . . . South Attleboro MA 02703 **800-827-2388** 508-761-7917
Dayton Superior Corp
1125 Byers Rd . . . . Miamisburg OH 45342 **800-745-3700** 937-866-0711
DESTACO
15 Corporate Dr . . . . Auburn Hills MI 48326 **888-337-8226** 248-836-6700
Dixie Industries
3510 N Orchard Knob Ave . . . . Chattanooga TN 37406 **800-933-4943** 423-698-3323
Dize Company Inc, The
1512 S Main St . . . . Winston-Salem NC 27127 **800-583-8243** 336-722-5181
Door Engineering & Mfg LLC
400 Cherry St . . . . Kasota MN 56050 **800-959-1352** 507-931-6910
DORMA Group North America
Dorma Dr . . . . Reamstown PA 17567 **800-523-8483** 717-336-3881
Dortronics Systems Inc
1668 Sag Harbor Tpke . . . . Sag Harbor NY 11963 **800-906-0137**
Drivekore Inc
101 Wesley Dr . . . . Mechanicsburg PA 17055 **800-382-1311** 717-766-7636
Dynamation Research Inc
2301 Pontius Ave . . . . Los Angeles CA 90064 **800-726-7997** 310-477-1224
East Teak Trading Group Inc
1106 Drake Rd . . . . Donalds SC 29638 **800-338-5636** 864-379-2111
Eastern Co, The
112 Bridge St PO Box 460 . . . . Naugatuck CT 06770 **800-221-0982** 203-729-2255
NASDAQ: EML
Eberhard Hardware Manufacturing Ltd
1523 Bellmill Rd . . . . Tillsonburg ON N4G0C9 **800-567-3344** 519-688-3443
Eberhard Mfg Co
21944 Drake Rd . . . . Strongsville OH 44149 **800-334-6706** 440-238-9720
Emtek Products Inc
15250 Stafford St . . . . City of Industry CA 91744 **800-356-2741** 626-961-0413
Engineered Products Co (EPCO)
601 Kelso St PO Box 108 . . . . Flint MI 48506 **888-414-3726** 810-767-2050
ER Wagner Mfg Company Inc
W130 N8691 Old Orchard Rd . . . . Menomonee Falls WI 53051 **800-558-5596**
ESPE Mfg Company Inc
9220 Ivanhoe St . . . . Schiller Park IL 60176 **800-367-3773*** 847-678-8950
*Cust Svc
Fastbolt Corp
200 Louis St . . . . South Hackensack NJ 07606 **800-631-1980** 201-440-9100
Freud America Inc
218 Feld Ave . . . . High Point NC 27263 **800-334-4107** 336-434-3171
Fulton Corp 303 Eighth Ave . . . . Fulton IL 61252 **800-252-0002**
G G Schmitt & Sons Inc
2821 Old Tree Dr . . . . Lancaster PA 17603 **866-724-6488** 717-394-3701
Genie Co
1 Door Dr PO Box 67 . . . . Mount Hope OH 44660 **800-354-3643**
Granite Security Products Inc
4801 Esco Dr . . . . Fort Worth TX 76140 **877-948-6723** 469-735-4901
Grass America Inc
1202 NC Hwy 66 S . . . . Kernersville NC 27284 **800-334-3512**
H & C Tool Supply Corp
235 Mt Read Blvd . . . . Rochester NY 14611 **800-323-4624** 585-235-5700
H & L Advantage Inc
3500 Busch Dr SW . . . . Grandville MI 49418 **800-581-2343** 616-532-1012

				Toll-Free	Phone

HA Guden Company Inc
99 Raynor Ave .... Ronkonkoma NY 11779 **800-344-6437** 631-737-2900

Hager Co 139 Victor St .... Saint Louis MO 63104 **800-325-9995** 314-772-4400

Hampton Products International Corp
50 Icon .... Foothill Ranch CA 92610 **800-562-5625** 949-472-4256

Hi Tech Seals Inc
9211-41 Ave .... Edmonton AB T6E6R5 **800-661-6055** 780-438-6055

Hindley Mfg Company Inc
9 Havens St .... Cumberland RI 02864 **800-323-9031** 401-722-2550

Hudson Lock Inc 81 Apsley St .... Hudson MA 01749 **800-434-8960**

Inpower LLC 3555 Africa Rd .... Galena OH 43021 **866-548-0965** 740-548-0965

Inventory Sales Co
9777 Reavis Rd .... St Louis MO 63123 **866-417-3801**

Jacknob Corp 290 Oser Ave ...... Hauppauge NY 11788 **888-231-9333** 631-231-9400

Jacob Holtz Co
10 Industrial Hwy MS-6
Airport Business Complex B .... Lester PA 19029 **800-445-4337** 215-423-2800

Jarvis Caster Co
203 Kerth St .... St Joseph MI 49085 **800-253-0868**

Kaba Ilco Corp
400 Jeffreys Rd .... Rocky Mount NC 27804 **800-334-1381** 252-446-3321

Kanebridge Corp
153 Bauer Dr .... Oakland NJ 07436 **888-222-9221** 201-337-2300

Kason Industries Inc
57 Amlajack Blvd .... Newnan GA 30265 **800-935-3550** 770-304-3000

Keystone Electronics Corp
31-07 20th Rd .... Astoria NY 11105 **800-221-5510** 718-956-8900

Knape & Vogt Manufacturing Co
2700 Oak Industrial Dr NE ...... Grand Rapids MI 49505 **800-253-1561**

KW Automotive North America Inc
300 W Pontiac Way .... Clovis CA 93612 **800-445-3767**

LE Johnson Products Inc
2100 Sterling Ave .... Elkhart IN 46516 **800-837-5664** 574-293-5664

Liberty Hardware Manufacturing Corp
140 Business Pk Dr ...... Winston-Salem NC 27107 **800-652-7277** 336-769-4077

Liberty Hardware Mfg Corp
140 Business Pk Dr ...... Winston-Salem NC 27107 **800-542-3789** 336-769-4077

Lockmasters Security Institute
2101 John C Watts Dr ...... Nicholasville KY 40356 **800-654-0637** 859-885-6041

Magnus Mobility Systems Inc
2805 Barranca Pkwy .... Irvine CA 92606 **800-858-7801** 714-771-2630

Master Lock Company LLC
6744 S Howell Ave PO Box 927 ...... Oak Creek WI 53154 **800-464-2088**

Medeco Security Locks Inc
3625 Alleghany Dr .... Salem VA 24153 **800-839-3157** 540-380-5000

Nagel Chase Inc
2323 Delaney Rd .... Gurnee IL 60031 **800-323-4552**

Nik-O-Lok Co
3130 N Mitthoeffer Rd ...... Indianapolis IN 46235 **800-428-4348** 317-899-6955

Norshield Corp
3232 Mobile Hwy .... Montgomery AL 36108 **855-859-3716** 334-551-0650

P M Industrial Supply Co
9613 Canoga Ave .... Chatsworth CA 91311 **800-382-3684** 818-341-9180

Payson Casters Inc
2323 N Delaney Rd .... Gurnee IL 60031 **800-323-4552** 847-336-6200

PDQ Manufacturing
2754 Creek Hill Rd .... Leola PA 17540 **800-441-9692** 717-656-4281

Purdy Corp
101 Prospect Ave .... Cleveland OH 44115 **800-547-0780**

Qual-Craft Industries
PO Box 559 .... Stoughton MA 02072 **800-231-5647**

Renovator's Supply Inc
Renovators Old ML .... Millers Falls MA 01349 **800-659-2211** 413-423-3300

Rockford Process Control Inc
2020 Seventh St .... Rockford IL 61104 **800-228-3779** 815-966-2000

Rocky Mountain Hardware Inc
1020 Airport Way .... Hailey ID 83333 **888-788-2013** 208-788-2013

Rousseau Metal Inc
105 Ave De Gasp Ouest ...... St Jean-Port-Joli QC G0R3G0 **866-463-4270** 418-598-3381

Rutherford Controls Int'l Corp
210 Shearson Crescent .... Cambridge ON N1T1J6 **800-265-6630** 519-621-7651

RWM Casters Co PO Box 668 ...... Gastonia NC 28053 **800-634-7704**

S Parker Hardware Manufacturing Corp
PO Box 9882 .... Englewood NJ 07631 **800-772-7537** 201-569-1600

Salice America Inc
2123 Crown Centre Dr .... Charlotte NC 28227 **800-222-9652** 704-841-7810

Sargent & Greenleaf Inc
1 Security Dr .... Nicholasville KY 40356 **800-826-7652** 859-885-9411

Sargent Manufacturing Co
100 Sargent Dr .... New Haven CT 06511 **800-727-5477**

Saturn Fasteners Inc
425 S Varney St .... Burbank CA 91502 **800-947-9414** 818-846-7145

Savant Manufacturing Inc
2930 Hwy 383 PO Box 520 .... Kinder LA 70648 **800-326-6880** 337-738-5896

Seastrom Mfg Company Inc
456 Seastrom St .... Twin Falls ID 83301 **800-634-2356** 208-737-4300

Sebewaing Tool & Engineering Co
415 Union St .... Sebewaing MI 48759 **800-453-2207** 989-883-2000

Securitron Magnalock Corp
10027 S 51st St Ste 102 .... Phoenix AZ 85044 **800-624-5625***
*Sales

Security Door Controls Inc
801 Avenida Acaso .... Camarillo CA 93012 **800-413-8783** 805-494-0622

Shepherd Caster
203 Kerth St .... Saint Joseph MI 49085 **800-253-0868** 269-983-7351

Sherwood Windows Ltd
37 Iron St .... Toronto ON M9W5E3 **800-770-5256** 416-675-3262

Signature Hardware
2700 Crescent Spring Pk .... Erlanger KY 41017 **866-855-2284**

Simpson Strong-Tie Company Inc
5956 W Las Positas Blvd .... Pleasanton CA 94588 **800-925-5099** 925-560-9000

Southco
210 N Brinton Lake Rd .... Concordville PA 19331 **877-821-0666** 610-459-4000

Spalding Hardware Ltd
1616 10 Ave SW .... Calgary AB T3C0J5 **800-837-0850**

Spokane Hardware Supply Inc
2001 E Trent Ave .... Spokane WA 99202 **800-888-1663** 509-535-1663

				Toll-Free	Phone

Starborn Industries Inc
45 Mayfield Ave .... Edison NJ 08837 **800-596-7747**

Tiffin Metal Products Co
450 Wall St .... Tiffin OH 44883 **800-537-0983**

Tompkins Industries Inc
1912 E 123rd .... Olathe KS 66061 **800-255-1008** 913-764-8088

Trimark Corp PO Box 350 ...... New Hampton IA 50659 **800-447-0343** 641-394-3188

Trimco/Builders Brass Works
3528 Emery St .... Los Angeles CA 90023 **800-637-8746** 323-262-4191

Truth Hardware Inc
700 W Bridge St .... Owatonna MN 55060 **800-866-7884***
*Cust Svc

TS Distributors Inc
4404 Windfern Rd .... Houston TX 77041 **800-392-3655**

Unicorp 291 Cleveland St ...... Orange NJ 07050 **800-526-1389** 973-674-1700

Urania Engineering Company Inc
198 S Poplar St .... Hazleton PA 18201 **800-533-1985** 570-455-7531

Weber-Knapp Co
441 Chandler St .... Jamestown NY 14701 **800-828-9254** 716-484-9135

Weiser 19701 Da Vinci ...... Lake Forest CA 92610 **800-677-5625**

Wright Tool Co
1 Wright Dr PO Box 512 ...... Barberton OH 44203 **800-321-2902** 330-848-0600

Yale Residential Security Products Inc
100 Yale Ave .... Lenoir City TN 37771 **800-438-1951**

Yale Security Inc
1902 Airport Rd .... Monroe NC 28110 **800-438-1951**

Yardley Products Corp
10 W College Ave .... Yardley PA 19067 **800-457-0154** 215-493-2700

350   HARDWARE - WHOL

				Toll-Free	Phone

Aarch Caster & Equipment
314 Axminister Dr .... Fenton MO 63026 **888-349-0220** 866-206-8792

Aero-Space Southwest Inc
21450 N Third Ave .... Phoenix AZ 85027 **800-289-2779** 623-582-2779

All State Fastener Corp
15460 E 12 Mile Rd .... Roseville MI 48066 **800-755-8959** 586-773-5400

All-Pro Fasteners Inc
1916 Peyco Dr N .... Arlington TX 76001 **800-361-6627** 817-467-5700

Associated Steel Corp
18200 Miles Rd .... Cleveland OH 44128 **800-321-9300**

Baer Supply Co
909 Forest Edge Dr ...... Vernon Hills IL 60061 **800-944-2237** 800-289-2237

Bargain Supply Co
844 E Jefferson St .... Louisville KY 40206 **800-322-5226** 502-562-5000

Blish-Mize Co
223 S Fifth St .... Atchison KS 66002 **800-995-0525** 913-367-1250

Bolt Products Inc
16725 E Johnson Dr ...... City Of Industry CA 91745 **800-423-6503** 626-961-4401

Bostwick-Braun Co
7349 Crossleigh Ct .... Toledo OH 43617 **800-777-9640**

Builders Hardware & Supply Company Inc
1516 15th Ave W .... Seattle WA 98119 **800-828-1437** 206-281-3700

Cascade Wholesale Hardware Inc
5650 NW .... Hillsboro OR 97124 **800-877-9987***
*General

Caster Technology Corp
11552 Markon Dr .... Garden Grove CA 92841 **866-547-8090** 714-893-6886

Charter Industries
3900 S Greenbrooke Dr SE ...... Kentwood MI 49512 **800-538-9088**

Compatico Inc
5005 Kraft Ave SE Ste A ...... Grand Rapids MI 49512 **800-336-1772** 616-940-1772

Conveyer & Caster Corp
3501 Detroit Ave .... Cleveland OH 44113 **800-777-0600** 216-631-4448

DAKE 724 Robbins Rd ...... Grand Haven MI 49417 **800-846-3253** 800-937-3253

Denver Wire Rope & Supply Inc
4100 Dahlia St .... Denver CO 80216 **800-873-3697** 303-377-5166

Desoto Sales Inc
20945 Osborne St .... Canoga Park CA 91304 **800-826-9779** 818-998-0853

Digi-Trax
650 Heathrow Dr .... Lincolnshire IL 60069 **800-356-6126** 847-613-2100

Dixie Construction Products Inc
970 Huff Rd NW .... Atlanta GA 30318 **800-992-1180** 404-351-1100

EB Bradley Co
5080 S Alameda St .... Los Angeles CA 90058 **800-533-3030** 323-585-9201

Fastec Industrial
112 Sherlake Rd .... Knoxville TN 37922 **800-837-2505**

Fastenal Co
2001 Theurer Blvd .... Winona MN 55987 **877-507-7555** 507-454-5374
NASDAQ: FAST

General Fasteners Co
37584 Amrhein Rd .... Livonia MI 48150 **800-945-2658**

Hans Johnsen Co
8901 Chancellor Row .... Dallas TX 75247 **800-879-1515*** 214-879-1550
*Sales

Harbor Freight Tools
3491 Mission Oaks Blvd ...... Camarillo CA 93011 **800-444-3353** 805-445-4791

Hardware Distribution Warehouses Inc (HDW)
6900 Woolworth Rd .... Shreveport LA 71129 **800-256-8527*** 318-686-8527
*Cust Svc

Hardware Suppliers of America Inc (HSI)
1400 E Fire Tower Rd .... Greenville NC 27858 **800-334-5625**

Hillman Group Inc
10590 Hamilton Ave ...... Cincinnati OH 45231 **800-800-4900** 513-851-4900

Hodell-natco Industries Inc
7825 Hub Pkwy .... Cleveland OH 44125 **800-321-4862** 216-447-0165

House-Hasson Hardware Inc
3125 Water Plant Rd .... Knoxville TN 37914 **800-333-0520**

Industrial Hardware & Specialties Inc
17-B Kentucky Ave .... Paterson NJ 07503 **800-684-4010** 973-684-4010

J & E Supply & Fastner Company Inc
1903 SE 59th St .... Oklahoma City OK 73129 **800-677-7922** 405-670-1234

Jay Cee Sales & Rivet Inc
32861 Chesley Dr .... Farmington MI 48336 **800-521-6777** 248-478-2150

			Toll-Free	Phone
Jensen Distribution Services				
PO Box 3708 .... Spokane WA		99220	800-234-1321*	
*General				
Karl W Richter Ltd				
350 Middlefield Rd .... Scarborough ON		M1S5B1	877-597-8665	416-757-8951
Max Tool Inc				
119b Citation Ct .... Birmingham AL		35209	800-783-6298	205-942-2466
MaxTool				
5798 Ontario Mills Pkwy .... Ontario CA		91764	800-629-3325	909-568-2800
Monroe Hardware Co				
101 N Sutherland Ave .... Monroe NC		28110	800-222-1974	704-289-3121
Onity Inc				
4001 Fairview Industrial Dr SE .... Salem OR		97302	800-424-1433	
Orgill Inc 3742 Tyndale Dr .... Memphis TN		38125	800-347-2860	901-754-8850
Portland Bolt & Manufacturing Company Inc				
3441 NW Guam St .... Portland OR		97210	800-547-6758	503-227-5488
Regitar USA Inc				
2575 Container Dr .... Montgomery AL		36109	877-734-4827	334-244-1885
Repaircliniccom Inc				
48600 Michigan Ave .... Canton MI		48188	800-269-2609	734-495-3079
Ryobi Technologies Inc				
1428 Pearman Dairy Rd .... Anderson SC		29625	800-525-2579	
Signal Industrial Products Corp				
1601 Cowart St .... Chattanooga TN		37408	800-728-1326	423-756-4980
Silicone Specialties Inc				
430 S Rockford Ave .... Tulsa OK		74120	888-243-0672	918-587-5567
Specialty Bolt & Screw Inc				
235 Bowles Rd .... Agawam MA		01001	800-322-7878	413-789-6700
Supply Technologies LLC				
6065 Parkland Blvd .... Cleveland OH		44124	800-695-8650	440-947-2100
Techni-Tool Inc				
1547 N Trooper Rd PO Box 1117 .... Worcester PA		19490	800-832-4866*	
*Cust Svc				
Triangle Fastener Corp				
1925 Preble Ave .... Pittsburgh PA		15233	800-486-1832*	412-321-5000
*General				
Wallace Hardware Company Inc				
5050 S Davy Crockett Pkwy				
PO Box 6004 .... Morristown TN		37815	800-776-0976	
Wurth Revcar Fasteners Inc				
3845 Thirlane Rd .... Roanoke VA		24019	800-542-5762	
WW Grainger Inc				
100 Grainger Pkwy .... Lake Forest IL		60045	888-361-8649	847-535-1000
NYSE: GWW				

351   HEALTH CARE PROVIDERS - ANCILLARY

SEE ALSO Hospices ; Home Health Services ; Vision Correction Centers

			Toll-Free	Phone
Amedisys Inc				
5959 S Sherwood Forest Blvd .... Baton Rouge LA		70816	800-464-0020	225-292-2031
NASDAQ: AMED				
American Family Care				
3700 Cahaba Beach Rd .... Birmingham AL		35242	833-361-4643	800-258-7535
American Red Cross In Greater New York (Inc)				
520 W 49th St .... New York NY		10019	877-733-2767	
AmeriHealth Mercy Health Plan				
8040 Carlson Rd Ste 500 .... Harrisburg PA		17112	888-991-7200	717-651-3540
AmSurg Corp				
1A Burton Hills Blvd .... Nashville TN		37215	800-945-2301	615-665-1283
NASDAQ: AMSG				
CareSource 230 N Main St .... Dayton OH		45402	800-488-0134	937-224-3300
Children's Bureau of Southern California				
1910 Magnolia Ave .... Los Angeles CA		90004	800-730-3933	213-342-0100
DaVita Inc 1551 Wewatta St .... Denver CO		80202	800-310-4872	303-405-2100
NYSE: DVA				
Encompass Health				
3660 Grandview Pkwy Ste 200 .... Birmingham AL		35243	800-765-4772	205-967-7116
NYSE: EHC				
Fresenius Medical Care North America				
920 Winter St .... Waltham MA		02451	800-662-1237	781-699-9000
Hanger Orthopedic Group Inc				
10910 Domain Dr Ste 300 .... Austin TX		78758	877-442-6437	512-777-3800
HealthDrive Corp				
888 Worcester St .... Wellesley MA		02482	888-964-6681	
Healthways Inc				
701 Cool Springs Blvd .... Franklin TN		37067	800-327-3822	
NASDAQ: HWAY				
Hudson River Healthcare Inc				
1037 Main St .... Peekskill NY		10566	844-474-2273	
Miracle-Ear Inc				
5000 Cheshire Pkwy N .... Minneapolis MN		55446	800-464-8002	
SCAN Health Plan				
3800 Kilroy Airport Way Ste 100 .... Long Beach CA		90806	800-247-5091	562-989-5100
US Physical Therapy				
1300 W Sam Houston Pkwy S Ste 300 .... Houston TX		77042	800-580-6285	713-297-7000
NYSE: USPH				

352   HEALTH CARE SYSTEMS

SEE ALSO General Hospitals - US

Health Care Systems are one or more hospitals owned, leased, sponsored, or managed by a central organization. Single-hospital systems are not included here; however, some large hospital networks or alliances may be listed.

			Toll-Free	Phone
Adventist Health				
2100 Douglas Blvd .... Roseville CA		95661	877-336-3566	916-781-2000
Albert Einstein Healthcare Network				
5501 Old York Rd .... Philadelphia PA		19141	800-346-7834	215-456-7890
Alexian Bros Health System				
3040 Salt Creek Ln .... Arlington Heights IL		60005	800-432-5005	847-385-7100
Allina Health System				
710 E 24th St .... Minneapolis MN		55404	800-233-8504	612-813-3600
American Kidney Stone Management Ltd (AKSM)				
797 Thomas Ln .... Columbus OH		43214	800-637-5188	614-447-0281

			Toll-Free	Phone
American Renal Assoc Inc				
500 Cummings Ctr Ste 6550 .... Beverly MA		01915	877-997-3625	978-922-3080
Amery Hospital & Clinic				
265 Griffin St E .... Amery WI		54001	800-424-5273	715-268-8000
ApolloMD				
5665 New Northside Dr Ste 200 .... Atlanta GA		30328	866-827-6556	770-874-5400
Appalachian Regional Healthcare Service (ARH)				
80 Hospital Dr PO Box 8086 .... Barbourville KY		40906	888-654-0015	859-226-2440
Baptist Memorial Health Care Corp				
350 N Humphreys Blvd .... Memphis TN		38120	800-422-7847	901-227-5920
Benedictine Health System				
503 E Third St Ste 400 .... Duluth MN		55805	800-833-7208	218-786-2370
Catholic Healthcare West				
185 Berry St Ste 300 .... San Francisco CA		94107	844-274-8497	
Centra Health Inc				
1920 Atherholt Rd .... Lynchburg VA		24501	800-947-5442	434-200-3000
Chase Brexton Health Services Inc				
1111 N Charles St .... Baltimore MD		21201	866-392-4483	410-837-2050
Christiana Care Health System				
501 W 14th St .... Wilmington DE		19801	855-250-9594	302-366-1929
Community Health Systems Inc				
4000 Meridian Blvd .... Franklin TN		37067	888-373-9600	615-465-7000
NYSE: CYH				
Community Services Group (CSG)				
320 Highland Dr PO Box 597 .... Mountville PA		17554	877-907-7970	717-285-7121
Crozer-Keystone Health System (CKHS)				
190 W Sproul Rd .... Springfield PA		19064	800-254-3258	610-328-8700
DCH Health System				
809 University Blvd E .... Tuscaloosa AL		35401	800-266-4324	205-759-7111
Eastern Maine Healthcare Systems (EMHS)				
797 Wilson St Ste 4 .... Brewer ME		04412	877-366-3662	207-973-5578
Fairview Health Services				
2450 Riverside Ave .... Minneapolis MN		55454	800-824-1953	612-672-2020
Great Plains Health Alliance Inc				
625 Third St .... Phillipsburg KS		67661	800-432-2779	785-543-2111
Guthrie Healthcare System				
1011 North Elmer Ave .... Sayre PA		18840	888-448-8474	570-887-4401
HCA Midwest Health System				
903 E 104th St Ste 500 .... Kansas City MO		64131	800-386-9355	816-508-4000
Health Net Of Arizona Inc				
1230 W Washington St .... Tempe AZ		85281	800-291-6911	602-794-1400
Henry Ford Health System				
1 Ford Pl .... Detroit MI		48202	800-436-7936	
ICG Link Inc				
7003 Chadwick Dr Ste 111 .... Brentwood TN		37027	877-397-7605	615-370-1530
Inova Health System				
8110 Gatehouse Rd .... Falls Church VA		22042	855-694-6682	
INTEGRIS Health Inc				
3300 NW Expy .... Oklahoma City OK		73112	888-951-2277	405-951-2277
Intermountain HealthCare				
36 S State St .... Salt Lake City UT		84111	800-843-7820*	801-442-2000
*Hum Res				
Island Peer Review Organization Inc (IPRO)				
1979 Marcus Ave .... Lake Success NY		11042	888-880-9976	516-326-7767
Jarrard Phillips Cate & Hancock Inc				
219 Ward Cir .... Brentwood TN		37027	888-844-6274	312-419-0575
Kindred Healthcare Inc				
680 S Fourth Ave .... Louisville KY		40202	800-545-0749	502-596-7300
NYSE: KND				
Lifespring Inc				
460 Spring St .... Jeffersonville IN		47130	800-456-2117	812-280-2080
MedStar Health				
10980 Grantchester Way .... Columbia MD		21044	877-772-6505	410-772-6500
Memorial Hermann Healthcare System				
7600 Beechnut St .... Houston TX		77074	800-777-6330	713-456-4280
MemorialCare Medical Group				
17762 Beach Blvd .... Huntington Beach CA		92647	866-276-3627	714-848-0080
Methodist Health Care System				
6565 Fannin St .... Houston TX		77030	877-726-9362	713-790-3311
Methodist Healthcare Ministries of South Texas Inc				
4507 Medical Dr .... San Antonio TX		78229	800-959-6673	210-692-0234
Methodist Hospitals of Dallas				
1441 N Beckley Ave .... Dallas TX		75203	800-725-9664	214-947-8181
Northwestern Counseling & Support Services Inc				
107 Fisher Pond Rd .... Saint Albans VT		05478	800-834-7793	802-524-6554
OSF Healthcare System				
800 NE Glen Oak Ave .... Peoria IL		61603	877-574-5678	
Palomar Pomerado Health				
15615 Pomerado Rd .... Poway CA		92064	800-628-2880	858-613-4000
Planned Parenthood of Indiana & Kentucky				
200 S Meridian St PO Box 397 .... Indianapolis IN		46206	800-230-7526	
Premier Inc				
12255 El Camino Real .... San Diego CA		92130	877-777-1552	858-481-2727
Riverside Health System				
701 Town Ctr Dr Ste 1000 .... Newport News VA		23606	800-759-1001	757-534-7000
Riverside-San Bernardino County Indian Health Inc (RSBCIH)				
11555 1/2 Potrero Rd .... Banning CA		92220	800-732-8805	951-849-4761
Schumacher Clinical Partners				
200 Corporate Blvd .... Lafayette LA		70508	800-893-9698	
Scripps Health				
4275 Campus Pt Ct .... San Diego CA		92121	800-727-4777	
Sea Mar Community Health Ctr				
1040 S Henderson St .... Seattle WA		98108	855-289-4503	206-763-5277
Senior Whole Health LLC (SWH)				
58 Charles St .... Cambridge MA		02141	888-794-7268	617-494-5353
Sharp Healthcare				
8695 Spectrum Ctr Blvd .... San Diego CA		92123	800-827-4277	858-499-4000
Shriners Hospitals for Children				
2900 N Rocky Pt Dr .... Tampa FL		33607	800-237-5055	813-281-0300
Southern Illinois Healthcare				
1239 E Main St .... Carbondale IL		62902	866-744-2468	618-457-5200
SSM Health				
1000 N Lee PO Box 205 .... Oklahoma City OK		73102	866-203-5846	405-272-7279
St Elizabeth's Medical Ctr				
736 Cambridge St .... Brighton MA		02135	800-488-5959	617-789-3000
Sutter Health				
2200 River Plz .... Sacramento CA		95833	888-888-6044	916-733-8800

	Toll-Free	Phone

Tenet Healthcare Corp
1445 Ross Ave ....Dallas TX 75202 **800-743-6333** 469-893-2000
NYSE: THC

Texas Health Resources
612 E Lamar Blvd ....Arlington TX 76011 **877-847-9355**

TheraCare
116 W 32nd St 8th Fl ....New York NY 10001 **800-505-7000** 212-564-2350

Truman Medical Ctr
2301 Holmes St ....Kansas City MO 64108 **800-318-2596** 816-404-1000

University of Maryland Medical System
22 S Greene St ....Baltimore MD 21201 **800-492-5538** 410-328-8667

Vantage Health Plan Inc
130 Desiard St Ste 300.........................Monroe LA 71201 **888-823-1910** 318-361-0900

Veterans Health Administration
810 Vermont Ave NW ....Washington DC 20420 **844-698-2311**

Virtua Health
303 Lippincott Dr 4th Fl ....Marlton NJ 08053 **888-847-8823** 609-914-6000

West Penn Allegheny Health System
4800 Friendship Ave ....Pittsburgh PA 15224 **800-994-6610**

Wheaton Franciscan Healthcare
3801 Spring St ....Racine WI 53405 **877-304-6332** 262-687-4011

Wingate Healthcare
63 Kendrick St ....Needham MA 02494 **800-946-4283**

353   HEALTH & FITNESS CENTERS

SEE ALSO Spas - Health & Fitness ; Weight Loss Centers & Services

	Toll-Free	Phone

Anytime Fitness Inc
12181 Margo Ave S ....Hastings MN 55033 **888-827-9262**

Brick Bodies Fitness Services Inc
212 W Padonia Rd ....Timonium MD 21093 **866-952-7425** 410-252-8058

Dumbell Man Fitness Equipment, The
655 Hawaii Ave ....Torrance CA 90503 **800-432-6266** 310-381-2900

Fitness Depot
1808 Lower Roswell Rd ....Marietta GA 30068 **800-974-6828**

Flex Hr
10700 Medlock Bridge Rd Ste 206.........................Johns Creek GA 30097 **877-735-3947** 770-814-4225

G & G Fitness Equipment Inc
7350 Transit Rd ....Williamsville NY 14221 **800-537-0516** 716-633-2527

Healthtrax Fitness & Wellness
100 Simsbury Rd ....Avon CT 06001 **800-505-5000** 860-284-1190

In-Shape Health Clubs
6 S El Dorado St Ste 600.........................Stockton CA 95210 **877-446-7427** 209-472-2450

Jersey Strong
762 SR- 18 ....East Brunswick NJ 08816 **888-564-6969** 732-390-7390

Jonas Fitness Inc
16969 N Texas Ave ....Webster TX 77598 **800-324-9800**

Jordan Essentials
1520 N Commercial Rd ....Nixa MO 65714 **877-662-8669**

Kinderdance International Inc
5238 Valleypointe Pkwy ....Roanoke VA 24019 **800-554-2334** 540-904-2595

Landings Club Inc
71 Green Island Rd ....Savannah GA 31411 **800-841-7011** 912-598-8050

Les Entreprises Energie Cardio
1040 Blvd Michele-Bohec Ste 120.........................Blainville QC J7C5E2 **877-363-7443** 450-979-3613

Little Gym International Inc
7500 N Dobson Rd Ste 220 ....Paradise Valley AZ 85256 **888-228-2878***
General

Mdr Fitness Corp
14101 NW Fourth St ....Sunrise FL 33325 **800-637-8227** 954-845-9500

Mountainside Fitness
9745 W Happy Valley Rd ....Peoria AZ 85383 **866-686-3488**

Peoplefit Health & Fitness Center
237 Lexington St ....Woburn MA 01801 **855-784-4663** 781-932-9332

Rivers Club Inc
301 Grant St ....Pittsburgh PA 15219 **800-433-5079**

skoah Inc
4800 Kingsway Ave Ste 309.........................Burnaby BC V5H4J2 **888-697-5624** 604-901-4780

TuffStuff Fitness Equipment Inc
13971 Norton Ave ....Chino CA 91710 **888-884-8275** 909-629-1600

World Health
7222 Edgemont Blvd NW ....Calgary AB T3A2X7 **866-278-4131** 403-239-4048

354   HEALTH FOOD STORES

	Toll-Free	Phone

Christopher Enterprises
155 W 2050 N ....Spanish Fork UT 84660 **800-453-1406**

Ginsberg's Foods Inc
29 Ginsberg Ln PO Box 17.........................Hudson NY 12534 **800-999-6006** 518-828-4004

GNC Inc 300 Sixth Ave ....Pittsburgh PA 15222 **877-462-4700** 412-228-4600
NYSE: GNC

Netrition Inc
25 Corporate Cir Ste 118 ....Albany NY 12203 **888-817-2411** 518-464-0765

Vincit Group, The
412 Georgia Ave Ste 300 ....Chattanooga TN 37403 **888-484-6248**

Whole Foods Market Inc
550 Bowie St ....Austin TX 78703 **888-992-6227** 512-477-4455

355   HEALTH & MEDICAL INFORMATION - ONLINE

	Toll-Free	Phone

At Health LLC
2733 E Battlefield Ste 266.........................Springfield MO 65804 **888-284-3258**

BabyCenter LLC
163 Freelon St ....San Francisco CA 94107 **866-732-8243** 415-537-0900

Cheshire Center Pediatric Comm
2500 N Church St ....Greensboro NC 27405 **800-360-1099** 336-375-2240

Dannemiller Inc
5711 NW Pkwy ....San Antonio TX 78249 **800-328-2308**

MedlinePlus
US National Library of Medicine
8600 Rockville Pk.........................Bethesda MD 20894 **888-346-3656**

	Toll-Free	Phone

PubMed
US National Library of Medicine
8600 Rockville Pike ....Bethesda MD 20894 **888-346-3656**

HEATING EQUIPMENT - ELECTRIC

SEE Air Conditioning & Heating Equipment - Residential

356   HEATING EQUIPMENT - GAS, OIL, COAL

SEE ALSO Boiler Shops ; Furnaces & Ovens - Industrial Process ; Air Conditioning & Heating Equipment - Commercial/Industrial ; Air Conditioning & Heating Equipment - Residential

	Toll-Free	Phone

Aerco International Inc
159 Paris Ave ....Northvale NJ 07647 **800-526-0288** 201-768-2400

Aquatherm Industries Inc
1940 Rutgers University Blvd ....Lakewood NJ 08701 **800-535-6307**

Bosch Thermotechnology
340 Mad River Pk ....Waitsfield VT 05673 **800-283-3787**

Electro-Flex Heat Inc
5 Northwood Rd ....Bloomfield CT 06002 **800-585-4213** 860-242-6287

Freeman Gas Inc
113 Peake Rd ....Roebuck SC 29376 **800-277-5730** 864-582-5475

Hearth & Home Technologies Inc
7571 215th St W ....Lakeville MN 55044 **888-427-3973** 952-985-6000

John Zink Hamworthy Combustion
11920 E Apache St ....Tulsa OK 74116 **800-421-9242** 918-234-1800

LB White Company Inc
W 6636 LB White Rd ....Onalaska WI 54650 **800-345-7200** 608-783-5691

Meeder Equipment Co
12323 Sixth St ....Rancho Cucamonga CA 91739 **800-423-3711** 909-463-0600

Powrmatic Inc PO Box 439 ....Finksburg MD 21048 **800-966-9100** 410-833-9100

Raypak Inc 2151 Eastman Ave ....Oxnard CA 93030 **800-438-4328** 805-278-5300

Reimers Electra Steam Inc
4407 Martinsburg Pk ....Clear Brook VA 22624 **800-872-7562** 540-662-3811

Roberts-Gordon Inc
1250 William St PO Box 44 ....Buffalo NY 14240 **800-828-7450** 716-852-4400

RW Beckett Corp PO Box 1289 ....Elyria OH 44036 **800-645-2876** 440-327-1060

Schwank Infrared Radiant Heaters
2 Schwank Way at Hwy 56N ....Waynesboro GA 30830 **877-446-3727**

Spectrolab Inc
12500 Gladstone Ave ....Sylmar CA 91342 **800-936-4888** 818-365-4611

Taco Inc 1160 Cranston St ....Cranston RI 02920 **888-778-2733** 401-942-8000

Utica Boilers Inc PO Box 4729 ....Utica NY 13504 **800-325-5479** 866-847-6656

Water Furnace International Inc
9000 Conservation Way ....Fort Wayne IN 46809 **800-222-5667** 260-478-5667

Wayne Combustion Systems
801 Glasgow Ave ....Fort Wayne IN 46803 **855-929-6327** 260-425-9200

Williams Comfort Products
250 W Laurel St ....Colton CA 92324 **866-677-8444** 909-825-0993

357   HEAVY EQUIPMENT DISTRIBUTORS

SEE ALSO Farm Machinery & Equipment - Whol ; Industrial Equipment & Supplies (Misc) - Whol

	Toll-Free	Phone

Absolute Machine Tools Inc
7420 Industrial Pkwy ....Lorain OH 44053 **800-852-7825** 440-960-6911

Action Lift Inc 1 Memco Dr ....Pittston PA 18640 **800-294-5438** 570-655-2100

Adams Air & Hydraulics Inc
7209 E Adamo Dr ....Tampa FL 33619 **800-282-4165** 813-626-4128

Adept Corp
4601 N Susquehanna Trial ....York PA 17406 **800-451-2254** 717-266-3606

Admar Supply Co Inc
1950 Brighton Henriett ....Rochester NY 14623 **800-836-2367** 585-272-9390

Air Center Inc
1201 E Whitcomb Ave ....Madison Heights MI 48071 **800-247-2959**

Ajacs Die Sales Corp
4625 Clay Ave SW ....Grand Rapids MI 49548 **800-968-6868** 616-452-1469

Alban Tractor Co
8531 Pulaski Hwy ....Baltimore MD 21237 **800-492-6994** 410-686-7777

Alta Equipment Co
28775 Beck Rd ....Wixom MI 48393 **800-261-9642**

Anderson Equipment Co
1000 Washington Pk ....Bridgeville PA 15017 **800-414-4554** 412-343-2300

Andrews & Hamilton Company Inc
3829 S Miami Blvd ....Durham NC 27703 **800-443-6866** 919-787-4100

Apex Packing & Rubber Co Inc
1855 New Hwy Ste D ....Farmingdale NY 11735 **800-645-9110** 631-420-8150

Argo Sales inc
717-7th Ave SW Ste 1300 ....Calgary AB T2P0Z3 **866-930-6633** 403-265-6633

Attica Hydraulic Exchange Inc
48175 Gratiot Ave ....Chesterfield MI 48051 **800-422-4279** 586-949-4240

Bacon-Universal Company Inc
918 Ahua St ....Honolulu HI 96819 **800-352-3508** 808-839-7202

Bailey Company Inc, The
501 Cowan St ....Nashville TN 37207 **800-342-1665**

Balzer Pacific Equipment Co
2136 SE Eigth Ave ....Portland OR 97214 **800-442-0966** 503-232-5141

Baron Oilfield Supply Ltd
9515-108 St ....Grande Prairie AB T8V5R7 **888-532-5661** 780-532-5661

Bertelkamp Automation Inc
4716 Middle Creek Ln ....Knoxville TN 37921 **800-251-9134** 865-588-7691

Bevco Sales International Inc
9354 194 St ....Surrey BC V4N4E9 **800-663-0090** 604-888-1455

Blue Giant Equipment Corp
85 Heart Lake Rd S ....Brampton ON L6W3K2 **800-668-7078** 905-457-3900

Branom Instrument Co
5500 Fourth Ave So ....Seattle WA 98108 **800-767-6051** 206-762-6050

Brenner-Fiedler & Associates Inc
4059 Flat Rock Dr ....Riverside CA 92505 **800-843-5558**

Burns Controls Co
13735 Beta Rd ....Dallas TX 75244 **800-442-2010** 972-233-6712

Company / Address	City	State	ZIP	Toll-Free	Phone
C M S North America 4095 Korona Ct SE	Caledonia	MI	49316	**800-931-6083**	616-698-9970
Cameron Instruments Inc 173 Woolwich St	Guelph	ON	N1H3V4	**888-863-8010**	519-824-7111
Caster Concepts Inc 16000 E Michigan Ave	Albion	MI	49224	**800-800-0036**	517-629-8838
Cherry's Industrial Equipment 600 Morse Ave	Elk Grove Village	IL	60007	**800-350-0011**	847-364-0200
Cisco Air Systems Inc 214 27th St	Sacramento	CA	95816	**800-813-6763**	916-444-2525
Clarke Power Services Inc 3133 E Kemper Rd	Cincinnati	OH	45241	**800-513-9591**	513-771-2200
Clausing Industrial Inc 3963 Emerald Dr	Kalamazoo	MI	49001	**800-323-0972**	
Cleveland Bros Equipment Company Inc 5300 Paxton St	Harrisburg	PA	17111	**866-551-4602**	717-564-2121
Coair Industrial Air Compressor & Sandblasting 5405 Sarosto St	Levis	QC	G6V5B6	**888-835-0141**	418-835-0141
Colby Equipment Company Inc 3048 Ridgeview Dr	Indianapolis	IN	46226	**800-443-2981**	317-545-4221
Coleman Instrument Co 11575 Goldcoast Dr	Cincinnati	OH	45249	**800-899-5745**	513-489-5745
Colorid LLC 20480 Chartwls Ctr Dr	Cornelius	NC	28031	**888-682-6567**	704-987-2238
Conveyor Handling Company Inc 6715 Santa Barbara Ct	Elkridge	MD	21075	**877-553-2296**	
Delta t Systems Inc 2171 HWY 175	Richfield	WI	53076	**800-733-4204**	262-628-0331
Diamond Equipment Inc 1060 E Diamond Ave	Evansville	IN	47711	**800-258-4428**	812-425-4428
Doverco Inc 2111 32e Ave	Lachine	QC	H8T3J1	**800-363-0697**	514-420-6060
Durkin Equipment Company Inc 2383 Chaffee Dr	Saint Louis	MO	63146	**800-264-3875**	314-432-2040
Elliott & Frantz Inc 450 E Church Rd	King Of Prussia	PA	19406	**800-220-3025**	610-279-5200
Ellison Educational Equipment Inc 25862 Commercentre Dr	Lake Forest	CA	92630	**800-253-2240**	949-598-8822
Empire Southwest Co 1725 S Country Club Dr	Mesa	AZ	85210	**800-367-4731**	480-633-4000
Erb Equipment Co Inc 200 Erb Industrial Dr	Fenton	MO	63026	**800-634-9661**	636-349-0200
Estes Equipment Company Inc 2007 Polk St	Chattanooga	TN	37408	**800-933-7837**	423-756-0090
Exact Metrology 11575 Goldcoast Dr	Cincinnati	OH	45249	**866-722-2600**	513-831-6620
Falcon Executive Aviation Inc 4766 E Falcon Dr	Mesa	AZ	85215	**800-237-2359**	480-832-0704
Flint Machine Tools Inc 3710 Hewatt Ct	Snellville	GA	30039	**800-984-2620**	770-985-2626
Florida Handling Systems Inc 2651 State Rd 60 W	Bartow	FL	33830	**800-664-3380**	863-534-1212
Foley Equipment 1550 SW St	Wichita	KS	67213	**877-761-9027**	
FORCE America Inc 501 E Cliff Rd	Burnsville	MN	55337	**800-328-2732**	952-707-1300
Fordia Inc 2745 de Miniac Ville Saint Laurent	Saint Laurent	QC	H4S1E5	**800-768-7274**	514-336-9211
Foxx Equipment Co 421 SW Blvd	Kansas City	MO	64108	**800-821-2254**	816-421-3600
Franks Supply Company Inc 3311 Stanford Dr NE	Albuquerque	NM	87107	**800-432-5254**	505-884-0000
Garden State Engine & Equipment 3509 Rt 22 E	Somerville	NJ	08876	**800-479-3857**	908-534-5444
General Equipment & Supplies Inc 4300 Main Ave	Fargo	ND	58103	**800-437-2924**	701-282-2662
Gill Services Inc 650 Aldine Bender Rd	Houston	TX	77060	**800-375-7881**	281-820-5400
Glauber Equipment Corp 1600 Commerce Pkwy	Lancaster	NY	14086	**888-452-8237**	716-681-1234
Green Line Hose & Fittings (BC.) Ltd 1477 Derwent Way	Delta	BC	V3M6N3	**800-665-5444**	604-525-6700
Grimstad S84w18887 Enterprise Dr	Muskego	WI	53150	**877-474-6782**	414-422-2300
Groupe Canimex 285 Saint-Georges St	Drummondville	QC	J2C4H3	**855-777-1335**	819-477-1335
H Gr Industrial Surplus 20001 Euclid Ave	Euclid	OH	44117	**866-447-7117**	216-486-4567
H&R Construction Parts & Equipment Inc 20 Milburn St	Buffalo	NY	14212	**800-333-0650**	716-891-4311
Handi-Ramp 510 N Ave	Libertyville	IL	60048	**800-876-7267**	847-680-7700
Heavy Machines Inc 3926 E Rains Rd	Memphis	TN	38118	**888-366-9028**	901-260-2200
Hei-Tek Automation 2102 West Quail Ave Ste 4	Phoenix	AZ	85027	**800-926-2099**	
Henderson Sewing Machine Company Inc Waits Dr Industrial Pk	Andalusia	AL	36420	**800-824-5113**	334-222-2451
Heritage Equipment Co 9000 Heritage Dr	Plain City	OH	43064	**800-282-7961**	614-873-3941
Hooper Handling Inc 5590 Camp Rd	Hamburg	NY	14075	**800-649-5590**	716-649-5590
Hydraulic Controls Inc 4700 San Pablo Ave	Emeryville	CA	94608	**800-847-6900**	510-658-8300
Identity Automation LP 8833 N Sam Houston Pkwy W	Houston	TX	77064	**877-221-8401**	
Idesco Corp 37 W 26th St	New York	NY	10010	**800-336-1383**	212-889-2530
Improved Construction Methods 1040 N Redmond Rd	Jacksonville	AR	72076	**877-494-5793**	
Innovent Air Handling Equipment 60 28th Ave N	Minneapolis	MN	55411	**877-218-4129**	612-877-4800
Janell Inc 6130 Cornell Rd	Cincinnati	OH	45242	**888-489-9111**	513-489-9111
JL. Souser & Associates Inc 3495 Industrial Dr	York	PA	17402	**800-757-0181**	717-505-3800
Jobe & Company Inc 9004 Yellow Brick Rd Ste F	Rosedale	MD	21237	**855-805-2599**	410-288-0560
John Fabick Tractor Co 1 Fabick Dr *Cust Svc	Fenton	MO	63026	**800-845-9188***	636-343-5900

Company / Address	City	State	ZIP	Toll-Free	Phone
Kibble Equipment 1150 S Victory Dr	Mankato	MN	56001	**800-624-8983**	507-387-8201
Kropp Equipment Inc 1020 Kennedy Ave	Schererville	IN	46375	**866-402-2222**	
Leavitt Machinery & Rentals Inc 24389 Fraser Hwy	Langley	BC	V2Z2L3	**877-850-6499**	604-607-4450
Lift Technologies Inc 7040 S Hwy 11	Westminster	SC	29693	**888-946-3330**	
Liftow 3150 American Dr	Toronto	ON	L4V1B4	**866-465-4386**	
M R L Equipment Company Inc PO Box 31154	Billings	MT	59107	**877-788-2907**	406-869-9900
MacAllister Machinery Company Inc 7515 E 30th St	Indianapolis	IN	46219	**800-382-1896**	317-545-2151
Machinery & Equipment Company Inc 3401 Bayshore Blvd	Brisbane	CA	94005	**800-227-4544**	415-467-3400
Magnus Equipment 4500 Beidler Rd	Willoughby	OH	44094	**800-456-6423**	440-942-8488
Maltz Sales Company Inc 67 Green St	Foxboro	MA	02035	**800-370-0439**	508-203-2400
Markem-Imaje Inc 100 Chastain Center Blvd Ste 165	Mississauga	ON	L4W2T7	**800-267-5108**	
Mckinney Petroleum Equipment Inc 3926 Halls Mill Rd	Mobile	AL	36693	**800-476-7867**	251-661-8800
Methods Machine Tools Inc 65 Union Ave	Sudbury	MA	01776	**877-668-4262**	978-443-5388
MG. Newell Corp 301 Citation Ct	Greensboro	NC	27409	**800-334-0231**	336-393-0100
MH. Equipment Co 2001 E Hartman Rd	Chillicothe	IL	61523	**877-884-8465**	309-579-8020
Milton CAT 30 Industrial Dr	Londonderry	NH	03053	**800-473-5298**	603-665-4500
Mississippi Valley Equipment Company Inc 1198 Pershall Rd	Saint Louis	MO	63137	**800-325-8001**	314-869-8600
Mister Safety Shoes Inc 2300 Finch Ave W Unit 6	North York	ON	M9M2Y3	**800-707-0051**	416-746-3001
Mobile Parts Inc 2472 Evans Rd PO Box 327	Val Caron	ON	P3N1P5	**800-461-4055**	705-897-4955
Modern Automation Inc 134 Tennsco Dr	Dickson	TN	37055	**800-921-9705**	615-446-1990
Monroe Tractor & Implement Company Inc 1001 Lehigh Stn Rd	Henrietta	NY	14467	**866-683-5338**	585-334-3867
Multi-shifter Inc 11110 Park Charlotte Blvd	Charlotte	NC	28278	**800-457-4472**	704-588-9611
Mustang Tractor & Equipment Co 12800 NW Fwy	Houston	TX	77040	**800-256-1001**	832-500-3674
O'keefe Elevator Company Inc 1402 Jones St	Omaha	NE	68102	**800-369-6317**	402-345-4056
Ohio Machinery Co 3993 E Royalton Rd	Broadview Heights	OH	44147	**800-837-6200**	440-526-6200
Optimal Engineering Systems 6901 Woodley Ave	Van Nuys	CA	91406	**888-777-1826**	818-222-9200
Owen Equipment Co 13101 NE Whitaker Way	Portland	OR	97230	**800-992-3656**	503-255-9055
Oxford Alloys Inc 2632 Tee Dr	Baton Rouge	LA	70814	**800-562-3355**	225-273-4800
Parlec Inc 101 Perinton Pkwy	Fairport	NY	14450	**800-866-5872**	585-425-4400
Patten Industries Inc 635 West Lake St	Elmhurst	IL	60126	**877-688-6812**	630-279-4400
PCE Pacific Inc 22011 26th Ave SE	Bothell	WA	98021	**800-321-4723**	425-487-9600
Petersen Inc 1527 North 2000 West	Ogden	UT	84404	**800-410-6789**	801-732-2000
Pneumatic & Hydraulic Systems Company Inc 1338 Petroleum Pkwy	Broussard	LA	70518	**877-836-1999**	337-839-1999
Power Motive Corp 5000 Vasquez Blvd	Denver	CO	80216	**800-627-0087**	303-355-5900
Profile Food Ingredients LLC 1151 Timber Dr	Elgin	IL	60123	**877-632-1700**	847-622-1700
Quest Engineering Inc 2300 Edgewood Ave S	Minneapolis	MN	55426	**800-328-4853**	952-546-4441
R R Floody Co 5065 27th Ave	Rockford	IL	61109	**800-678-6639**	815-399-1931
R&M Materials Handling Inc 4501 Gateway Blvd	Springfield	OH	45502	**800-955-9967**	937-328-5100
Rasmussen Equipment Co 3333 West 2100 South	Salt Lake City	UT	84119	**800-453-8032**	801-972-5588
RBI Corp 10201 Cedar Ridge Dr	Ashland	VA	23005	**800-444-7370**	804-550-2210
RDO Equipment Co 700 Seventh St S	Fargo	ND	58103	**800-247-4650**	877-444-7363
Rego-fix Tool Corp 7752 Moller Rd	Indianapolis	IN	46268	**800-999-7346**	317-870-5959
Rencor Controls Inc 21 Sullivan Pkwy	Fort Edward	NY	12828	**866-472-7030**	518-747-4171
Ri-go Lift Truck Ltd 175 Courtland Ave	Concord	ON	L4K4T2	**855-211-9673**	647-846-8475
RJM Sales Inc 454 Park Ave	Scotch Plains	NJ	07076	**800-752-9055**	908-322-7880
Road Machinery Co 926 S Seventh St	Phoenix	AZ	85034	**800-989-7121**	
Roland Machinery Co 816 N Dirksen Pkwy	Springfield	IL	62702	**800-252-2926**	217-789-7711
Rowlands Sales Company Inc Butler Industrial Pk	Hazleton	PA	18201	**800-582-6388**	570-455-5813
Rudd Equipment Co 4344 Poplar Level Rd	Louisville	KY	40213	**800-527-2282**	502-456-4050
Ryder Material Handling 210 Annagem Blvd	Mississauga	ON	L5T2V5	**800-268-2125**	
S & s Industrial Equipment & Supply Company Inc 7 Chelten Way	Trenton	NJ	08638	**800-282-3506**	609-695-3800
SDT North America Inc 1532 Ontario St	Cobourg	ON	K9A4R5	**800-667-5325**	905-377-1313
Sidel Systems Usa Inc 12500 El Camino Real	Atascadero	CA	93422	**800-668-5003**	805-462-1250
Simark Controls Ltd 10509 46 St SE	Calgary	AB	T2C5C2	**800-565-7431**	403-236-0580

Company	City	State	Zip	Toll-Free	Phone
Single Source Technologies Inc 2600 Superior Ct	Auburn Hills	MI	48326	800-336-7283	248-232-6232
Southeastern Equipment Company Inc 10874 E Pike Rd	Cambridge	OH	43725	800-798-5438	740-432-6303
Southwest Materials Handling Company Inc 4719 Almond St	Dallas	TX	75247	866-674-6067	214-630-1375
Speco Inc 3946 Willow Rd	Schiller Park	IL	60176	800-541-5415	847-678-4240
Stan Houston Equipment Co 501 S Marion Rd	Sioux Falls	SD	57106	800-952-3033	605-336-3727
Stoffel Equipment Company Inc 7764 N 81st St	Milwaukee	WI	53223	800-354-7502	414-354-7500
Sugino Corp 1380 Hamilton Pkwy	Itasca	IL	60143	888-784-4661	630-250-8585
Sun Packaging Technologies Inc 2200 NW 32nd St Ste 1700	Pompano Beach	FL	33069	800-866-0322	954-978-3080
Systec Conveyor Corp 10010 Conveyor Dr	Indianapolis	IN	46235	800-578-1755	
Texas Gauge & Control Inc 7575 Dillon St	Houston	TX	77061	800-914-0009	713-641-2282
Tipco Punch Inc 1 Coventry Rd	Brampton	ON	L6T4B1	800-544-8444	905-791-9811
Toll Gas & Welding Supply 3005 Niagara Ln N	Plymouth	MN	55447	877-865-5427	763-551-5300
Tool Technology Distributors Inc 3110 Osgood Ct	Fremont	CA	94539	800-335-8437	510-656-8220
Triflo International Inc 1000 FM 830	Willis	TX	77318	800-332-0993	936-856-8551
Trio Pac Inc 386 Mcarthur	Saint-Laurent	QC	H4T1X8	888-565-6722	514-733-7793
Tyler Equipment Corp 251 Shaker Rd	East Longmeadow	MA	01028	800-292-6351	413-525-6351
Valin Corp 555 E California Ave	Sunnyvale	CA	94086	800-774-5630	408-730-9850
Valley Litho Supply Inc 1047 Haugen Ave	Rice Lake	WI	54868	800-826-6781	
VARGO 3709 Pkwy Ln	Hilliard	OH	43026	877-876-6384	614-876-1163
Victor L Phillips Co 4100 Gardner Ave	Kansas City	MO	64120	800-878-9290	816-241-9290
Vinson Process Controls Company LP 2747 Highpoint Oaks Dr	Lewisville	TX	75067	800-420-6571	972-459-8200
Wallace Cranes 71 N Bacton Hill Rd	Malvern	PA	19355	800-553-5438	610-647-1400
Westbrook Engineering 23501 Mound Rd	Warren	MI	48091	800-899-8182	586-759-3100
White's Farm Supply Inc 4154 State Rt 31	Canastota	NY	13032	800-633-4443	315-697-2214
Winchester Equipment Co 121 Indian Hollow Rd	Winchester	VA	22603	800-323-3581	
Wisconsin Lift Truck Corp 3125 Intertech Dr	Brookfield	WI	53045	800-634-9010	262-781-8010
Wojanis Inc 1001 Montour W Ind Pk	Coraopolis	PA	15108	800-345-9024	724-695-1415
WOODCO USA 773 McCarty Dr	Houston	TX	77029	800-496-6326	713-672-9491

358   HELICOPTER TRANSPORT SERVICES

SEE ALSO Ambulance Services ; Air Charter Services

Company	City	State	Zip	Toll-Free	Phone
Accel Aviation Accessories LLC 11900 Lacy Ln	Fort Myers	FL	33966	888-686-4880	239-275-8202
Air Logistics Inc 4605 Industrial Dr	New Iberia	LA	70560	800-365-6771	337-365-6771
Coastal Helicopters Inc 8995 Yandukin Dr	Juneau	AK	99801	800-789-5610	907-789-5600
Corporate Helicopters of San Diego 3753 John J Montgomery Dr Ste 2	San Diego	CA	92123	800-345-6737	858-505-5650
Eagle Copters Ltd 823 Mctavish Rd NE	Calgary	AB	T2E7G9	800-564-6469	403-250-7370
Island Express Helicopter Service 1175 Queens Hwy S *Cust Svc	Long Beach	CA	90802	800-228-2566*	310-510-2525
Midwest Helicopter Airways Inc 525 Executive Dr	Willowbrook	IL	60527	800-323-7609	630-325-7860
PHI Inc 2001 SE Evangeline Thwy PO Box 90808 *NASDAQ: PHII*	Lafayette	LA	70508	866-815-7101	337-235-2452
VIH Aviation Group 1962 Canso Rd	North Saanich	BC	V8L5V5	866-844-4354	250-656-3987
VIH Logging Ltd 1962 Canso Rd	North Saanich	BC	V8L5V5	866-844-4354	250-656-3987
Yellowhead Helicopters Ltd 3010 Selwyn Rd	Valemount	BC	V0E2Z0	888-566-4401	

359   HOLDING COMPANIES

SEE ALSO Conglomerates
A holding company is a company that owns enough voting stock in another firm to control management and operations by influencing or electing its board of directors.

359-1 Airlines Holding Companies

Company	City	State	Zip	Toll-Free	Phone
Alaska Air Group Inc 19300 International Blvd *NYSE: ALK*	Seattle	WA	98188	800-654-5669	206-433-3200
AMR Corp 4333 Amon Carter Blvd PO Box 619616 *OTC: AAL*	Fort Worth	TX	76155	800-535-5225	817-963-1234
Frontier Airlines Inc 7001 Tower Rd	Denver	CO	80249	800-265-5505	720-374-4200
JetBlue Airways Corp 118-29 Queens Blvd *NASDAQ: JBLU*	Forest Hills	NY	11375	800-538-2583	718-286-7900

359-2 Bank Holding Companies

Company	City	State	Zip	Toll-Free	Phone
Access National Corp 1800 Robert Fulton Dr Ste 310 *NASDAQ: ANCX*	Reston	VA	20191	800-931-0370	703-871-2100
Accuristix 2844 Bristol Cir	Oakville	ON	L6H6G4	866-356-6830	905-829-9927
Alpine Bank of Colorado 2200 Grand Ave	Glenwood Springs	CO	81601	888-425-7463	970-945-2424
AMB Financial Corp 8230 Hohman Ave *OTC: AMFC*	Munster	IN	46321	800-436-5113	219-836-5870
Amboy Bancorp 3590 US Hwy 9 S	Old Bridge	NJ	08857	800-942-6269	732-591-8700
American National Bank 628 Main St *NASDAQ: AMNB*	Danville	VA	24541	800-240-8190	434-792-5111
American River Bankshares 3100 Zinfandel Dr Ste 450 *NASDAQ: AMRB*	Rancho Cordova	CA	95670	800-544-0545	
American State Bank 1401 Ave Q	Lubbock	TX	79401	800-531-1401	806-767-7000
Andrus Transportation Services LLC 3185 East Deseret Dr North	Saint George	UT	84790	800-888-5838	435-673-1566
Annapolis Bancorp Inc 1000 Bestgate Rd *NASDAQ: ANNB*	Annapolis	MD	21401	800-555-5455	410-224-4455
Arrow Financial Corp 250 Glen St *NASDAQ: AROW*	Glens Falls	NY	12801	888-444-0058	518-415-4307
Associated Banc-Corp 1305 Main St *NYSE: ASB ■ *PR*	Stevens Point	WI	54481	800-236-8866*	715-341-0400
Atlantic Coast Bank (ACFC) 505 Haines Ave *NASDAQ: ACFC*	Waycross	GA	31501	800-342-2824	912-283-4711
BancorpSouth Inc 2910 W Jackson St *NYSE: BXS*	Tupelo	MS	38801	888-797-7711	662-680-2000
Bank Independent 710 S Montgomery Ave	Sheffield	AL	35660	877-865-5050	256-386-5000
Bank Mutual Corp 4949 W Brown Deer Rd *NASDAQ: BKMU*	Milwaukee	WI	53223	844-256-8684	414-354-1500
Bank of Commerce Holdings 1901 Churn Creek Rd *NASDAQ: BOCH*	Redding	CA	96002	800-421-2575	530-224-3333
Bank of Greene County, The PO Box 470 *NASDAQ: GCBC*	Catskill	NY	12414	888-439-4272	518-943-2600
Bank of Hawaii Corp 130 Merchant St 16th Fl *NYSE: BOH*	Honolulu	HI	96813	888-643-3888	
Bank of South Carolina Corp 256 Meeting St *NASDAQ: BKSC*	Charleston	SC	29401	800-523-4175	843-724-1500
Bank of the Ozarks Inc PO Box 8811 *NASDAQ: OZK*	Little Rock	AR	72231	800-274-4482	501-978-2265
Bar Harbor Bankshares 82 Main St PO Box 400 *NYSE: BHB*	Bar Harbor	ME	04609	888-853-7100	207-288-3314
Barnes Transportation Services Inc 2309 Whitley Rd	Wilson	NC	27895	800-898-5897	
BB & T Corp 200 W Second St *NYSE: BBT*	Winston-Salem	NC	27101	800-226-5228	
Benny Whitehead Inc 3576 S Eufaula Ave	Eufaula	AL	36027	800-633-7617	334-687-8055
Berkshire Bancorp Inc 24 North St PO Box 1308 *NYSE: BHLB*	Pittsfield	MA	01202	800-773-5601	
Bmo Bankcorp Inc 111 W Monroe St	Chicago	IL	60603	888-340-2265	
Brannen Banks of Florida Inc PO Box 1929	Inverness	FL	34451	866-546-8273	352-726-1221
Bridge Bank 55 Almaden Blvd Ste 200 *NASDAQ: BDGE ■ *General*	San Jose	CA	95113	866-273-4265*	408-423-8500
Broadway Financial Corp 5055 Wilshire Blvd Ste 100 *NASDAQ: BYFC*	Los Angeles	CA	90036	888-988-2265	
Brookline Bank 131 Clarendon St PO Box 470469 *Cust Svc	Brookline	MA	02116	877-668-2265*	617-425-4600
C & F Financial Co 1313 E Main St Ste 400 *NASDAQ: CFFI*	Richmond	VA	23219	855-602-2001	
Camden National Corp 2 Elm St *NASDAQ: CAC*	Camden	ME	04843	800-860-8821	207-236-8821
Capital City Bank Group Inc PO Box 900 *NASDAQ: CCBG*	Tallahassee	FL	32302	888-671-0400	850-402-7500
Capitol Federal Financial 700 Kansas Ave *NASDAQ: CFFN*	Topeka	KS	66603	888-822-7333	785-235-1341
Cathay General Bancorp Inc 777 N Broadway *NASDAQ: CATY*	Los Angeles	CA	90012	800-922-8429	213-625-4700
Central Pacific Financial Corp PO Box 3590 *NYSE: CPF*	Honolulu	HI	96811	800-342-8422	808-544-0500

					Toll-Free	Phone

Central Valley Community Bancorp
7100 N Financial Dr Ste 101 .... Fresno CA 93720 **866-294-9588** 559-298-1775
NASDAQ: CVCY

Century Bancorp Inc
400 Mystic Ave .... Medford MA 02155 **866-823-6887** 781-393-4160
NASDAQ: CNBKA

CFBank 7000 N High St .... Worthington OH 43085 **866-668-4606** 614-334-7979
NASDAQ: CFBK

Chemical Bank 333 E Main St .... Midland MI 48640 **800-867-9757** 989-839-5350
NASDAQ: CHFC

Citizens Financial Group Inc
1 Citizens Dr .... Riverside RI 02915 **800-922-9999** 401-456-7000

City Holding Co
25 Gatewater Rd .... Charleston WV 25313 **800-528-2273** 304-769-1100
NASDAQ: CHCO

Clifton Savings Bancorp Inc
1433 Van Houten Ave .... Clifton NJ 07013 **888-562-6727** 973-473-2200
NASDAQ: CSBK

CNB Financial Corp
1 S Second St PO Box 42 .... Clearfield PA 16830 **800-492-3221** 814-765-9621
NASDAQ: CCNE

Colorado Business Bank
821 17th St .... Denver CO 80202 **800-574-4714** 303-293-2265

Columbia Bank
1301 A St Ste 800 .... Tacoma WA 98402 **800-305-1905** 253-305-1900
NASDAQ: COLB

Commercial National Financial Corp
900 Ligonier St .... Latrobe PA 15650 **800-803-2265** 724-539-3501
OTC: CNAF

Community Bank System Inc
5790 Widewaters Pkwy .... Syracuse NY 13214 **866-764-8638** 315-445-2282
NYSE: CBU

Community Investors Bancorp Inc
119 S Sandusky Ave .... Bucyrus OH 44820 **800-222-4955** 419-562-7055
OTC: CIBN

Community Shores Bank Corp
1030 W Norton Ave .... Muskegon MI 49441 **888-853-6633** 231-780-1800
NASDAQ: CSHB

Compass Bancshares Inc
15 S 20th St .... Birmingham AL 35233 **800-266-7277** 205-297-1986

ConnectOne Bank
301 Sylvan Ave .... Englewood Cliffs NJ 07632 **844-266-2548**
NASDAQ: CNOB

Crazy Woman Creek Bancorp Inc
PO Box 1020 .... Buffalo WY 82834 **877-684-2766** 307-684-5591

Cullen/Frost Bankers Inc
100 W Houston St .... San Antonio TX 78205 **800-562-6732** 210-220-4011
NYSE: CFR

CVB Financial Corp
701 N Haven Ave PO Box 51000 .... Ontario CA 91764 **888-222-5432** 909-980-4030
NASDAQ: CVBF

Dime Community Bancshares Inc
209 Havemeyer St .... Brooklyn NY 11211 **800-321-3463** 718-782-6200
NASDAQ: DCOM

Eagle Bancorp Inc
7815 Woodmont Ave .... Bethesda MD 20814 **800-364-8313** 301-986-1800
NASDAQ: EGBN

East West Bank
135 N Los Robles Ave 7th Fl .... Pasadena CA 91101 **888-895-5650** 626-768-6000
NASDAQ: EWBC

Eastern Bank Corp
265 Franklin St .... Boston MA 02110 **800-327-8376*** 800-333-7234
*Cust Svc

Enterprise Financial Services Corp
150 N Meramec Ave .... Clayton MO 63105 **800-396-8141** 314-725-5500
NASDAQ: EFSG

Evans Bancorp Inc
1 Grimsby Dr .... Hamburg NY 14075 **866-310-0763** 716-926-2000
NYSE: EVBN

Fauquier Bankshares Inc
10 Courthouse Sq .... Warrenton VA 20186 **800-638-3798** 540-347-2700
NASDAQ: FBSS

Fidelity Federal Bancorp
18 NW Fourth St .... Evansville IN 47708 **800-280-8280** 812-424-0921
OTC: FDLB

Financial Institutions Inc
220 Liberty St .... Warsaw NY 14569 **866-296-3743** 585-786-1100
NASDAQ: FISI

First American Bank
1650 Louis Ave PO Box 0794 .... Elk Grove Village IL 60009 **866-449-1150** 847-952-3700

First BanCorp PO Box 9146 .... San Juan PR 00908 **866-695-2511** 787-725-2511
NYSE: FBP

First Bancorp 341 N Main St .... Troy NC 27371 **800-548-9377** 910-576-6171
NASDAQ: FBNC

First Busey Corp
100 West University Ave .... Champaign IL 61820 **800-672-8739** 217-365-4516
NASDAQ: BUSE

First Citizens Bank
350 S Beverly D Ste 150 .... Beverly Hills CA 90212 **888-323-4732** 310-552-1776

First Citizens National Bank Charitable Foundation
PO Box 1708 .... Mason City IA 50402 **800-423-1602** 641-423-1600

First Commonwealth Financial Corp
601 Philadelphia St .... Indiana PA 15701 **800-711-2265** 724-463-8555
NYSE: FCF

First Defiance Financial Corp
601 Clinton St .... Defiance OH 43512 **800-472-6292** 419-782-5015
NASDAQ: FDEF

First Federal Savings Bank of Frankfort
216 W Main St PO Box 535 .... Frankfort KY 40602 **888-818-3372** 502-223-1638

First Financial Bancorp (FFB)
255 E Fifth St Ste 700 .... Cincinnati OH 45202 **877-322-9530**
NASDAQ: FFBC

First Financial Bankshares Inc
400 Pine St PO Box 701 .... Abilene TX 79601 **855-660-5862** 325-627-7155
NASDAQ: FFIN

First Financial Corp
1 First Financial Plz .... Terre Haute IN 47807 **800-511-0045** 812-238-6000
NASDAQ: THFF

First Horizon National Corp
165 Madison .... Memphis TN 38103 **800-489-4040** 901-523-4444
NYSE: FHN

First Interstate Bancsystem Inc
401 N 31st St .... Billings MT 59101 **888-752-3341** 406-255-5000
NASDAQ: FIBK

First Merchants Corp
200 E Jackson St .... Muncie IN 47305 **800-205-3464**
NASDAQ: FRME

First Midwest Bancorp Inc
1 Pierce Pl Ste 1500 .... Itasca IL 60143 **800-322-3623** 630-875-7450
NASDAQ: FMBI

First National Bank
4220 William Penn Hwy .... Monroeville PA 15146 **800-555-5455**

First National of Nebraska Inc
PO Box 2490 .... Omaha NE 68103 **800-688-7070** 402-341-0500

First Southern Bank
301 S Ct St .... Florence AL 35630 **800-625-7131*** 256-718-4200
*General

First State Bank
730 Harry Sauner Rd .... Hillsboro OH 45133 **800-987-2566*** 937-393-9170
*General

First Trinity Financial Corp
7633 E 63rd Pl Ste 230 .... Tulsa OK 74133 **888-883-1499**

First United Bank & Trust
19 S Second St .... Oakland MD 21550 **888-692-2654**
NASDAQ: FUNC

FirstFed Bancorp Inc
1630 Fourth Ave N PO Box 340 .... Bessemer AL 35020 **800-436-5112** 205-428-8472

Flushing Financial Corp
1979 Marcus Ave .... New Hyde Park NY 11042 **800-581-2889** 718-961-5400
NASDAQ: FFIC

German American Bancorp
711 Main St .... Jasper IN 47546 **800-482-1314** 812-482-1314
NASDAQ: GABC

Glacier Bancorp Inc
PO Box 27 .... Kalispell MT 59903 **800-735-4371** 406-756-4200
NASDAQ: GBCI

Greenwood Racing Inc
3001 St Rd .... Bensalem PA 19020 **888-238-2946** 215-639-9000

Guaranty Bancshares Inc
100 W Arkansas St PO Box 1158 .... Mount Pleasant TX 75455 **888-572-9881** 903-572-9881

Honmi Bank
3660 Wilshire Blvd PH-A .... Los Angeles CA 90010 **877-808-4266** 213-382-2200

Harleysville Bank
271 Main St .... Harleysville PA 19438 **888-256-8828** 215-256-8828
NASDAQ: HARL

Heritage Bank
101 N Main St .... Jonesboro GA 30236 **866-971-0106** 770-478-8881

Heritage Bank
201 Fifth Ave SW .... Olympia WA 98501 **800-455-6126** 360-943-1500

HMN Financial Inc
1016 Civic Ctr Dr NW .... Rochester MN 55901 **888-257-2000** 507-535-1309
NASDAQ: HMNF

Home City Financial Corp
2454 N Limestone St .... Springfield OH 45503 **866-421-2331** 937-390-0470
OTC: HCFL

Home Federal Bank
1602 Cumberland Ave .... Middlesboro KY 40965 **800-354-0182** 606-248-1095
OTC: HFBA

Huntington Bancshares Inc
7 Easton Oval .... Columbus OH 43219 **800-480-2265**
NASDAQ: HBAN

IBERIABANK Corp
200 W Congress St .... Lafayette LA 70501 **800-968-0801**
NASDAQ: IBKC

Independent Bank Corp
230 W Main St .... Ionia MI 48846 **888-300-3193** 616-527-2400
NASDAQ: IBCP

Jeffersonville Bancorp
4866 State Rt 52 PO Box 398 .... Jeffersonville NY 12748 **800-472-3272** 845-482-4000
OTC: JFBC

Johnson Financial Group Inc
555 Main St Ste 400 .... Racine WI 53403 **888-769-3796**

Keweenaw Financial Corp
235 Quincy St .... Hancock MI 49930 **866-482-0404** 906-482-0404

KeyCorp 127 Public Sq .... Cleveland OH 44114 **800-539-9055** 216-689-8481
NYSE: KEY

Lakeland Bancorp Inc
250 Oak Ridge Rd .... Oak Ridge NJ 07438 **866-224-1379** 973-697-2000
NASDAQ: LBAI

Lakeland Financial Corp
202 E Ctr St .... Warsaw IN 46580 **800-827-4522** 574-267-6144
NASDAQ: LKFN

Macatawa Bank Corp
10753 Macatawa Dr PO Box 3119 .... Holland MI 49424 **877-820-2265** 616-820-1444
NASDAQ: MCBC

MB Financial Inc
6111 N River Rd .... Rosemont IL 60018 **888-422-6562**
NASDAQ: MBFI

MBT Financial Corp
102 E Front St .... Monroe MI 48161 **800-321-0032** 734-241-3431
NASDAQ: MBTF

Mercantil Commercebank Holding Corp
PO Box 226555 .... Miami FL 33222 **888-629-0810** 305-629-1212

Mercantile Bank
200 N 33rd St PO Box 3455 .... Quincy IL 62305 **800-405-6372** 217-223-7300
NASDAQ: MBWM

Mesa Systems Inc
2275 South 900 West .... Salt Lake City UT 84119 **800-523-4656**

MidSouth Bancorp Inc
102 Versailles Blvd .... Lafayette LA 70501 **800-213-2265** 337-237-8343
NYSE: MSL

MutualFirst Financial Inc
110 E Charles St .... Muncie IN 47305 **800-382-8031** 765-747-2800
NASDAQ: MFSF

NASB Financial Inc
12520 S 71 Hwy .... Grandview MO 64030 **800-677-6272** 816-765-2200
NASDAQ: NASB

Classified Section

				Toll-Free	Phone
National Bankshares Inc					
101 Hubbard St	Blacksburg	VA	24060	**800-552-4123**	540-951-6300
NASDAQ: NKSH					
NBT Bancorp Inc					
52 S Broad St	Norwich	NY	13815	**800-628-2265**	607-337-2265
NASDAQ: NBTB					
North State Bank Inc					
6204 Falls of Neuse Rd	Raleigh	NC	27609	**877-357-2265**	919-787-9696
Northbridge Financial Corp					
105 Adelaide St W Ste 700	Toronto	ON	M5H1P9	**855-620-6262**	416-350-4400
Northeast Bancorp					
500 Canal St	Lewiston	ME	04240	**800-284-5989**	207-786-3245
NASDAQ: NBN					
Northern States Financial Corp					
1601 N Lewis Ave	Waukegan	IL	60085	**800-339-4432**	847-244-6000
OTC: NSFC					
Northwest Bank PO Box 128	Warren	PA	16365	**800-859-1000**	814-728-7263
Ocwen Financial Corp					
1661 Worthington Rd Ste 100	West Palm Beach	FL	33409	**800-746-2936**	561-682-8000
NYSE: OCN					
Ohio Valley Banc Corp					
420 Third Ave	Gallipolis	OH	45631	**800-468-6682**	740-446-2631
NASDAQ: OVBC					
Old Point Financial Corp					
1 W Mellen St PO Box 3392	Hampton	VA	23663	**800-952-0051**	757-728-1200
NASDAQ: OPOF					
Old Second Bancorp Inc					
37 S River St	Aurora	IL	60506	**877-866-0202**	630-892-0202
NASDAQ: OSBC					
Opus Bank					
19900 MacArthur Blvd 12th Fl	Irvine	CA	92612	**855-678-7226**	949-250-9800
Owen Community Bank					
279 E Morgan St	Spencer	IN	47460	**800-690-2095**	812-829-2095
Park National Bank					
50 N Third St PO Box 3500	Newark	OH	43058	**888-791-8633**	740-349-8451
NYSE: PRK					
Pathfinder Bancorp Inc					
214 W First St	Oswego	NY	13126	**800-811-5620**	315-343-0057
NASDAQ: PBHC					
Patriot National Bancorp Inc					
900 Bedford St	Stamford	CT	06901	**888-728-7468**	
NASDAQ: PNBK					
Peapack-Gladstone Bank					
500 Hills Dr Ste 300 PO Box 700	Bedminster	NJ	07921	**800-742-7595**	908-234-0700
NASDAQ: PGC					
Peoples Bancorp Inc					
138 Putnam St	Marietta	OH	45750	**800-374-6123**	740-373-3155
NASDAQ: PEBO					
Peoples Bancorp of North Carolina Inc					
518 W 'C' St	Newton	NC	28658	**800-948-7195**	828-464-5620
NASDAQ: PEBK					
PlainsCapital Bank					
325 N Saint Paul St Ste 800	Dallas	TX	75201	**866-762-8392**	
Prosperity Bank					
1301 N Mechanic	El Campo	TX	77437	**800-531-1401***	
NYSE: PB ■ *Cust Svc					
Provident Bank					
3756 Central Ave	Riverside	CA	92506	**800-442-5201**	951-686-6060
NASDAQ: PROV					
Quad City Bank & Trust					
3551 Seventh St	Moline	IL	61265	**866-676-0551**	309-736-3580
NASDAQ: QCRH					
Regions Financial Corp					
1900 Fifth Ave N	Birmingham	AL	35203	**866-688-0658**	
NYSE: RF					
Renasant Corp 209 Troy St	Tupelo	MS	38804	**800-680-1601***	
NASDAQ: RNST ■ *Cust Svc					
Republic Bancorp Inc					
601 W Market St	Louisville	KY	40202	**888-540-5363**	502-584-3600
NASDAQ: RBCAA					
Republic First Bancorp Inc					
50 S 16th St Ste 2400	Philadelphia	PA	19102	**888-875-2265**	
NASDAQ: FRBK					
Richline Group Inc					
6701 Nob Hill Rd	Tamarac	FL	33321	**800-327-1808**	954-718-3200
S&T Bancorp Inc					
800 Philadelphia St	Indiana	PA	15701	**800-325-2265**	724-349-1800
NASDAQ: STBA					
Salisbury Bancorp Inc					
5 Bissell St PO Box 1868	Lakeville	CT	06039	**800-222-9801**	860-435-9801
NASDAQ: SAL					
Sandy Spring Bancorp Inc					
17801 Georgia Ave	Olney	MD	20832	**800-399-5919**	301-774-6400
NASDAQ: SASR					
SB One Bank					
100 Enterprise Dr Ste 700	Rockaway	NJ	07866	**800-511-9900**	973-383-2211
NASDAQ: SBBX					
Seacoast Banking Corp of Florida					
PO Box 9012	Stuart	FL	34995	**800-706-9991***	772-287-4000
NASDAQ: SBCF ■ *All					
Sierra Bancorp					
86 N Main St PO Box 1930	Porterville	CA	93257	**888-454-2265**	559-782-4900
NASDAQ: BSRR					
Southern Missouri Bancorp Inc					
531 Vine St	Poplar Bluff	MO	63901	**855-452-7272**	573-778-1800
NASDAQ: SMBC					
SouthFirst Bancshares Inc					
126 N Norton Ave PO Box 167	Sylacauga	AL	35150	**800-239-1492**	256-245-4365
OTC: SZBI					
Southside Bancshares Inc					
1201 S Beckham Ave	Tyler	TX	75701	**877-639-3511**	903-531-7111
NASDAQ: SBSI					
Southwest Georgia Financial Corp					
201 First St SE	Moultrie	GA	31768	**888-683-2265**	229-985-1120
NYSE: SGB					
SSMB Pacific Holding Company Inc					
1755 Adams Ave	San Leandro	CA	94577	**866-572-2525**	510-836-6100
Stock Yards					
1040 E Main St	Louisville	KY	40206	**800-625-9066**	502-625-1790
NASDAQ: SYBT					

				Toll-Free	Phone
SunTrust Banks Inc					
303 Peachtree St NE	Atlanta	GA	30308	**800-786-8787**	404-588-7711
NYSE: STI					
Synovus Financial Corp					
1111 Bay Ave Ste 400	Columbus	GA	31901	**888-796-6887**	706-649-2311
NYSE: SNV					
Timberland Bancorp Inc					
624 Simpson Ave	Hoquiam	WA	98550	**800-562-8761**	360-533-4747
NASDAQ: TSBK					
Titonka Bancshares Inc					
PO Box 309	Titonka	IA	50480	**866-985-3247**	515-928-2142
TriCo Bancshares					
63 Constitution Dr	Chico	CA	95973	**800-922-8742**	530-898-0300
NASDAQ: TCBK					
Trustco Bank Corp NY					
PO Box 1082	Schenectady	NY	12301	**800-670-3110**	518-377-3311
NASDAQ: TRST					
Trustmark National Bank					
248 E Capitol St PO Box 291	Jackson	MS	39201	**800-243-2524***	601-208-5111
NASDAQ: TRMK ■ *Cust Svc					
Umpqua Investments Inc					
1 SW Columbia St Ste 300	Portland	OR	97258	**866-486-7782**	800-452-1929
NASDAQ: UMPQ					
Union Bank Co, The					
105 Progressive Dr	Columbus Grove	OH	45830	**800-837-8111**	419-659-2141
NASDAQ: UBOH					
Union Bankshares Inc					
20 Lower Main St	Morrisville	VT	05661	**866-862-1891**	802-888-6600
NASDAQ: UNB					
United Bancorp Inc					
201 S Fourth St	Martins Ferry	OH	43935	**888-275-5566**	740-633-0445
NASDAQ: UBCP					
United Security Bancshares Inc					
PO Box 249	Thomasville	AL	36784	**866-546-8273**	334-636-5424
Unity Bancorp Inc					
64 Old Hwy 22	Clinton	NJ	08809	**800-618-2265**	908-730-7630
NASDAQ: UNTY					
Universal Enterprises Inc					
8625 SW Cascade Ave	Beaverton	OR	97008	**800-547-5740**	503-644-8723
Univest Corp of Pennsylvania					
14 N Main St PO Box 64197	Souderton	PA	18964	**877-723-5571**	
NASDAQ: UVSP					
US Bancorp					
800 Nicollet Mall	Minneapolis	MN	55402	**800-872-2657**	651-466-3000
NYSE: USB					
Valley National Bancorp					
1455 Valley Rd	Wayne	NJ	07470	**800-522-4100**	973-305-8800
NYSE: VLY					
Veteran's Truck Line Inc					
800 Black Hawk Dr	Burlington	WI	53105	**800-456-9476**	262-539-3400
VIST Financial Corp					
1240 Broadcasting Rd	Wyomissing	PA	19610	**888-238-3330**	610-208-0966
NASDAQ: VIST					
Washington Federal Inc					
425 Pike St	Seattle	WA	98101	**800-324-9375**	206-624-7930
NASDAQ: WAFD					
Washington Trust Bancorp Inc					
23 Broad St	Westerly	RI	02891	**800-475-2265**	
NASDAQ: WASH					
Wayne Savings Bancshares Inc					
1908 Cleveland Rd	Wooster	OH	44691	**800-414-1103**	330-264-5767
NASDAQ: WAYN					
Webster City Federal Bancorp					
820 Des Moines St	Webster City	IA	50595	**866-519-4004**	515-832-3071
NASDAQ: WCFB					
Webster Financial Corp					
PO Box 10305	Waterbury	CT	06726	**800-325-2424**	
NYSE: WBS					
West Bancorp Inc					
PO Box 65020	West Des Moines	IA	50265	**800-810-2301**	515-222-2300
NASDAQ: WTBA					
Westfield Financial Inc					
141 Elm St	Westfield	MA	01085	**800-995-5734**	413-568-1911
NASDAQ: WNEB					
Winona National Bank					
204 Main St PO Box 499	Winona	MN	55987	**800-546-4392**	507-454-8800
WSFS Financial Corp					
500 Delaware Ave	Wilmington	DE	19801	**888-973-7226**	302-792-6000
NASDAQ: WSFS					
WTB Financial Corp					
PO Box 2127	Spokane	WA	99210	**800-788-4578**	

359-3 Holding Companies (General)

				Toll-Free	Phone
Agri-Fab Inc					
809 S Hamilton St	Sullivan	IL	61951	**800-448-9282**	
Alutiiq LLC					
3909 Arctic Blvd Ste 500	Anchorage	AK	99503	**800-829-8547**	907-222-9500
American Standard Cos Inc					
1 Centennial Ave	Piscataway	NJ	08855	**800-442-1902**	
Atlas Concrete Products					
65 Burritt St	New Britain	CT	06053	**800-774-1112**	860-224-2244
Atlas Copco North America LLC					
7 Campus Dr Ste 200	Parsippany	NJ	07054	**800-732-6762**	973-397-3400
Atlas World Group Inc					
1212 St George Rd	Evansville	IN	47711	**800-252-8885**	812-424-2222
BT Conferencing Inc					
30 Braintree Hill Office Pk Ste 301	Braintree	MA	02184	**866-766-8777**	617-801-6700
Cardinal Health Inc					
7000 Cardinal Pl	Dublin	OH	43017	**800-926-0834**	614-757-5000
NYSE: CAH					
Clayton Holdings LLC					
1500 Market St	Philadelphia	PA	19102	**877-291-5301**	215-231-1563
Comcast Corp					
1701 JFK Blvd	Philadelphia	PA	19103	**800-266-2278**	215-665-1700
NASDAQ: CMCSA					

	Toll-Free	Phone
Conagra Brands Inc 1 ConAgra Dr .... Omaha NE 68102 *NYSE: CAG*	877-266-2472	402-240-4000
CONSOL Energy Inc 1000 Consol Energy Dr ...... Canonsburg PA 15317 *NYSE: CNX*	800-544-8024	724-485-4000
CUI Global Inc 20050 SW 112th Ave ...... Tualatin OR 97062 *NASDAQ: CUI*	800-275-4899	503-612-2300
Deluxe Corp 3680 Victoria St N ...... Shoreview MN 55126 *NYSE: DLX ■ *Cust Svc*	800-328-0304*	651-483-7111
Dicke Safety Products 1201 Warren Ave ...... Downers Grove IL 60515	877-891-0050	630-969-0050
Elvis Presley Enterprises Inc 3734 Elvis Presley Blvd PO Box 16508 .... Memphis TN 38116	800-238-2000	901-332-3322
Esmark Steel Group 2500 Euclid Ave ...... Chicago Heights IL 60411	800-323-0340	708-756-0400
Eyak Corp, The 360 W Benson Blvd Ste 210 ...... Anchorage AK 99503	800-478-7161	907-334-6971
FedEx Corp 3610 Hacks Cross Rd ...... Memphis TN 38125 *NYSE: FDX*	800-463-3339	901-369-3600
Hitch Enterprises Inc 309 Northridge Cir PO Box 1308 ...... Guymon OK 73942	800-951-2533	580-338-8575
Icahn Enterprises LP 767 Fifth Ave 47th Fl ...... New York NY 10153 *NASDAQ: IEP*	800-255-2737	212-702-4300
InstaMed Communications LLC 1880 John F Kennedy Blvd 12th Fl ...... Philadelphia PA 19103	800-507-3800	215-789-3680
Joseph Cory Holdings LLC 150 Meadowlands Pkwy 4th Fl ...... Secaucus NJ 07094	877-267-9001	
Kyocera International Inc 8611 Balboa Ave ...... San Diego CA 92123	877-248-4237	858-576-2600
Liberty Diversified International Inc 5600 Hwy 169 N ...... New Hope MN 55428	800-421-1270	763-536-6600
Marsh & McLennan Cos Inc 1166 Ave of the Americas ...... New York NY 10036 *NYSE: MMC*	866-374-2662	212-345-5000
MDC Holdings Inc 4350 S Monaco St Sto 500 ...... Denver CO 80237 *NYSE: MDC*	888-500-7060	303-773-1100
NewMarket Corp 330 S Fourth St ...... Richmond VA 23219 *NYSE: NEU*	800-625-5191	804-788-5000
NuStar GP Holdings LLC 19003 I-10 W ...... San Antonio TX 78257 *NYSE: NSH*	800-866-9060	210-918-2000
OKI Developments Inc 1416 112th Ave NE ...... Bellevue WA 98004	877-465-3654	425-454-2800
Otc Global Holdings 5151 San Felipe Ste 2200 ...... Houston TX 77056	877-737-8511	713-358-5450
Otter Tail Corp 4334 18th Ave SW PO Box 9156 ...... Fargo ND 58106 *NASDAQ: OTTR*	866-410-8780	701-232-6414
Pacific Food Importers Inc 18620 80th Ct S Bldg F ...... Kent WA 98032	800-225-4029	206-682-2740
Pearson Inc 1330 Ave of the Americas 7th Fl ...... New York NY 10019	877-311-0948	
Pro-Dex Inc 2361 McGaw Ave ...... Irvine CA 92614 *NASDAQ: PDEX*	800-562-6204	
Revlon Inc 237 Park Ave ...... New York NY 10017 *NYSE: REV*	800-473-8566	212-527-4000
Rosen's Diversified Inc 1120 Lake Ave PO Box 933 ...... Fairmont MN 56031	800-345-0293	507-238-6001
Sbeeg Holdings Licensing LLC 5900 Wilshire Blvd 30th Fl ...... Los Angeles CA 90036	800-411-0305	323-655-8000
SGS North America Inc 201 State Rt 17 N ...... Rutherford NJ 07070	800-645-5227	201-508-3000
Shenandoah Telecommunications Co 500 Shentel Way ...... Edinburg VA 22824 *NASDAQ: SHEN*	800-743-6835	540-984-5224
Strata Products Worldwide LLC 8995 Roswell Rd Ste 200 ...... Sandy Springs GA 30350	800-691-6601	770-321-2500
Sumitomo Corp of America 300 Madison Ave ...... New York NY 10017	877-980-3283	212-207-0700
Superior Group Inc 250 International Dr ...... Williamsville NY 14221	800-568-8310	
Telephone & Data Systems Inc 30 N La Salle St Ste 4000 ...... Chicago IL 60602 *NYSE: TDS*	877-337-1575	312-630-1900
ThyssenKrupp Elevator 9280 Crestwyn Hills Dr ...... Memphis TN 38125	877-230-0303	901-261-1800
Tredegar Corp 1100 Boulders Pkwy ...... North Chesterfield VA 23225 *NYSE: TG*	800-411-7441	804-330-1000
Union Pacific Corp 1400 Douglas St ...... Omaha NE 68179 *NYSE: UNP*	888-870-8777	402-544-5000
VENSURE Employer Services Inc 4140 E Baseline Rd Ste 201 ...... Mesa AZ 85206	800-409-8958	
Warren Equities Inc 27 Warren Way ...... Providence RI 02905	866-867-4075	401-781-9900
Williams Companies Inc 1 Williams Ctr ...... Tulsa OK 74172 *NYSE: WMB*	800-945-5426	918-573-2000
Worthington Direct Holdings LLC 6301 Gaston Ave Ste 670 ...... Dallas TX 75214	800-599-6636	
YRC Worldwide Inc 10990 Roe Ave ...... Overland Park KS 66211 *NASDAQ: YRCW*	800-846-4300	913-696-6100

359-4 Insurance Holding Companies

	Toll-Free	Phone
AFLAC Inc 1932 Wynnton Rd ...... Columbus GA 31999 *NYSE: AFL*	800-992-3522	706-323-3431

	Toll-Free	Phone
AIG SunAmerica Inc 21650 Oxnard St ...... Woodland Hills CA 91367	800-445-7862	
AMBAC Financial Group Inc 1 State St Plz ...... New York NY 10004 *NASDAQ: AMBC*	800-221-1854	212-668-0340
American Fidelity Assurance Co PO Box 268886 ...... Oklahoma City OK 73126	800-662-1113	
AmeriTrust Group Inc 26255 American Dr ...... Southfield MI 48034 *NYSE: MIG*	800-482-2726	248-358-1100
Anthem Inc 120 Monument Cir 200 ...... Indianapolis IN 46204	800-331-1476	317-488-6000
Aon Corp 200 E Randolph St ...... Chicago IL 60601	877-384-4276	312-381-1000
Assurant Group 11222 Quail Roost Dr ...... Miami FL 33157	800-852-2244	305-253-2244
Assurant Inc 1 Chase Manhattan Plz ...... New York NY 10005 *NYSE: AIZ*	800-852-2244	
Cincinnati Financial Corp 6200 S Gilmore Rd ...... Fairfield OH 45014 *NASDAQ: CINF*	800-364-3400	513-870-2000
Citizens Financial Corp 12910 Shelbyville Rd Ste 300 ...... Louisville KY 40243 *OTC: CFIN*	800-843-7752	502-244-2420
CNA Financial Corp 333 S Wabash Ave ...... Chicago IL 60604 *NYSE: CNA*	800-262-4357	312-822-5000
Conseco Inc 11825 N Pennsylvania St ...... Carmel IN 46032 *NYSE: CNO*	866-595-2255	
CUNA Mutual Group 5910 Mineral Point Rd ...... Madison WI 53705	800-356-2644	608-238-5851
Donegal Group Inc 1195 River Rd ...... Marietta PA 17547 *NASDAQ: DGICA*	800-877-0600	717-426-1931
EMC Insurance Group Inc 717 Mulberry St ...... Des Moines IA 50309 *NASDAQ: EMCI*	800-447-2295	515-280-2511
Everest Re Group Ltd 477 Martinsville Rd PO Box 830 .... Liberty Corner NJ 07938	800-269-6660	908-604-3000
Federated Insurance Cos 121 E Pk Sq PO Box 328 ...... Owatonna MN 55060	800-533-0472	507-455-5200
Hartford Financial Services Group Inc 690 Asylum Ave ...... Hartford CT 06115 *NYSE: HIG*	866-553-5663	860-547-5000
HealthMarkets Inc 9151 Blvd 26 ...... North Richland Hills TX 76180	800-827-9990	
Horace Mann Educators Corp 1 Horace Mann Plz ...... Springfield IL 62715 *NYSE: HMN*	800-999-1030	217-789-2500
Investors Title Co 121 N Columbia St ...... Chapel Hill NC 27514 *NASDAQ: ITIC*	800-326-4842	919-968-2200
Kansas City Life Insurance Co 3520 Broadway ...... Kansas City MO 64111 *OTC: KCLI*	800-821-6164	816-753-7000
Kingsway America Inc (KAI) 150 NW Pt Blvd ...... Elk Grove Village IL 60007	800-232-0631	847-700-9100
Legal & General America Inc 1701 Research Blvd ...... Rockville MD 20850	800-638-8428	301-279-4800
Lincoln National Corp (LNC) 150 N Radnor-Chester Rd ...... Radnor PA 19087 *NYSE: LNC*	877-275-5462	866-533-3410
Markel Corp 4521 Highwoods Pkwy ...... Glen Allen VA 23060 *NYSE: MKL*	800-446-6671	
Mutual of Omaha Co 3300 Mutual of Omaha Plz ...... Omaha NE 68175	800-775-6000	866-688-7957
Navigators Group Inc 1 Penn Plz 32nd Fl ...... New York NY 10119 *NASDAQ: NAVG*	866-408-1922	212-244-2333
Pacific Mutual Holding Co 700 Newport Ctr Dr ...... Newport Beach CA 92660	800-347-7787	949-219-3011
PICO Holdings Inc 7979 Ivanhoe Ave Ste 300 ...... La Jolla CA 92037 *NASDAQ: PICO*	888-389-3222	858-456-6022
PMI Mortgage Insurance Co 3003 Oak Rd ...... Walnut Creek CA 94597 *OTC: PMI*	800-288-1970	
ProAssurance Corp 100 Brookwood Pl ...... Birmingham AL 35209 *NYSE: PRA*	800-282-6242	205-877-4400
Protective Life Corp 2801 Hwy 280 S ...... Birmingham AL 35223 *NYSE: PL*	800-866-9933	844-733-5433
Reinsurance Group of America Inc 16600 Swingley Ridge Rd ...... Chesterfield MO 63017 *NYSE: RGA*	800-985-4326	636-736-7000
RLI Corp 9025 N Lindbergh Dr ...... Peoria IL 61615 *NYSE: RLI ■ *Cust Svc*	800-331-4929*	309-692-1000
Security Benefit Group of Cos 1 Security Benefit Pl ...... Topeka KS 66636	800-888-2461	785-438-3000
Selective Insurance Group Inc 40 Wantage Ave ...... Branchville NJ 07890 *NASDAQ: SIGI*	800-777-9656	973-948-3000
Summit Holding Southeast Inc PO Box 600 ...... Gainesville GA 30503	800-971-2667	678-450-5825
Sun Life Financial Inc 150 King St W ...... Toronto ON M5H1J9 *TSX: SLF*	877-786-5433	416-979-9966
Torchmark Corp 3700 S Stonebridge Dr ...... McKinney TX 75070 *NYSE: TMK*	877-577-3899	972-569-4000
Travelers Cos Inc 385 Washington St ...... Saint Paul MN 55102 *NYSE: TRV*	800-328-2189	651-310-7911
ULLICO Inc 1625 Eye St NW ...... Washington DC 20006	800-431-5425	
UnumProvident Corp 1 Fountain Sq ...... Chattanooga TN 37402	800-262-0018	423-294-1011

	Toll-Free	Phone
Western & Southern Financial Group 400 Broadway ....Cincinnati OH 45202	877-367-9734	
White Mountains Insurance Group Ltd 80 S Main St ....Hanover NH 03755	866-295-3762	603-640-2200
WR Berkley Corp 475 Steamboat Rd ....Greenwich CT 06830 *NYSE: WRB*	800-238-6225	203-629-3000

359-5 Utilities Holding Companies

	Toll-Free	Phone
ALLETE Inc 30 W Superior St ....Duluth MN 55802 *NYSE: ALE*	800-228-4966	218-279-5000
Ameren Corp 1901 Chouteau Ave ....Saint Louis MO 63103 *NYSE: AEE*	800-552-7583	314-621-3222
American Electric Power Company Inc 1 Riverside Plz ....Columbus OH 43215 *NYSE: AEP ■ *Cust Svc*	800-277-2177*	614-716-1000
American States Water Co 630 E Foothill Blvd ....San Dimas CA 91773 *NYSE: AWR*	800-999-4033	909-394-3600
American Water Works Co Inc 1025 Laurel Oak Rd ....Voorhees NJ 08043 *NYSE: AWK*	888-282-6816	856-346-8200
Artesian Resources Corp 664 Churchmans Rd ....Newark DE 19702 *NASDAQ: ARTNA*	800-332-5114	302-453-6900
Atmos Energy Corp PO Box 650205 ....Dallas TX 75265 *NYSE: ATO*	888-286-6700	972-934-9227
Black Hills Corp 625 Ninth St ....Rapid City SD 57701 *NYSE: BKH*	866-264-8003	605-721-1700
CenterPoint Energy Inc 1111 Louisiana St ....Houston TX 77002 *NYSE: CNP ■ *Cust Svc*	800-495-9880*	713-207-1111
CH Energy Group Inc 284 S Ave ....Poughkeepsie NY 12601 *NYSE: CHG*	800-527-2714	845-452-2000
CMS Energy Corp 1 Energy Plz ....Jackson MI 49201 *NYSE: CMS*	800-477-5050	517-788-0550
Connecticut Water Service Inc 93 W Main St ....Clinton CT 06413 *NASDAQ: CTWS*	800-286-5700	
Consolidated Edison Inc 4 Irving Pl ....New York NY 10003 *NYSE: ED*	800-752-6633	212-460-4600
Dominion Resources Inc 120 Tredegar St ....Richmond VA 23219 *NYSE: D*	800-552-4034	804-819-2000
DPL Inc 1065 Woodman Dr ....Dayton OH 45432 *NYSE: AES*	800-433-8500	800-736-3001
DTE Energy Co 1 Energy Plz ....Detroit MI 48226 *NYSE: DTE*	800-477-4747	313-235-4000
Duquesne Light Holdings Inc 411 Seventh Ave ....Pittsburgh PA 15219	888-393-7000	412-393-7000
Edison International 2244 Walnut Grove Ave ....Rosemead CA 91770 *NYSE: EIX ■ *Cust Svc*	800-655-4555*	626-302-1212
Energen Corp 605 Richard Arrington Blvd N ....Birmingham AL 35203 *NYSE: EGN*	800-654-3206	205-326-2700
Eversource 800 Boylston St ....Boston MA 02199 *NYSE: NST*	800-592-2000	
FirstEnergy Corp 76 S Main St ....Akron OH 44308 *NYSE: FE*	800-633-4766	
FPL Group Inc NextEra Energy Inc 700 Universe Blvd ....Juno Beach FL 33408 *NYSE: NEE*	888-218-4392	561-694-4000
Holly Energy Partners LP 100 Crescent Ct Ste 1600 ....Dallas TX 75201	800-642-1687	214-871-3555
IDACORP Inc 1221 W Idaho St ....Boise ID 83702 *NYSE: IDA*	800-242-0681	208-388-2200
MidAmerican Energy Holdings Co 500 E Court Ave PO Box 657 ....Des Moines IA 50303	888-427-5632	
National Fuel Gas Co 6363 Main St ....Williamsville NY 14221 *NYSE: NFG ■ *Cust Svc*	800-365-3234*	716-857-7000
National Grid USA Service Company Inc 25 Research Dr ....Westborough MA 01582	800-548-8000	508-389-2000
OGE Energy Corp 321 N Harvey St ....Oklahoma City OK 73102 *NYSE: OGE*	800-272-9741	405-553-3000
PG & E Corp 77 Beale St 24th Fl ....San Francisco CA 94105 *NYSE: PCG*	800-743-5000	415-267-7000
Pinnacle West Capital Corp 400 N Fifth St ....Phoenix AZ 85004 *NYSE: PNW*	800-457-2983	602-250-1000
PNM Resources Inc Alvarado Sq ....Albuquerque NM 87158 *NYSE: PNM*	888-342-5766	505-241-2700
Public Service Enterprise Group Inc 80 Park Plz ....Newark NJ 07102 *NYSE: PEG ■ *Cust Svc*	800-436-7734*	973-430-7000
Puget Energy 10885 NE Fourth St ....Bellevue WA 98004	888-225-5773	
SCANA Corp 220 Operation Way ....Cayce SC 29033 *NYSE: SCG*	800-251-7234	803-217-9000
Sempra Energy Corp 101 Ash St ....San Diego CA 92101 *NYSE: SRE*	800-411-7343	619-696-2000
Unitil Corp 6 Liberty Ln W ....Hampton NH 03842 *NYSE: UTL*	800-852-3339	603-772-0775

	Toll-Free	Phone
Vectren Corp 211 NW Riverside Dr ....Evansville IN 47708 *NYSE: VVC*	800-227-1376	812-491-4000
Westar Energy Inc 818 S Kansas Ave ....Topeka KS 66612 *NYSE: WR*	800-383-1183	
WGL Holdings Inc 101 Constitution Ave NW ....Washington DC 20080 *NYSE: WGL*	800-645-3751	703-750-2000

360   HOME FURNISHINGS - WHOL

	Toll-Free	Phone
AA Importing Co Inc 7700 Hall St ....Saint Louis MO 63147 *Cust Svc*	800-325-0602*	314-383-8800
Adleta Co 1645 Diplomat Dr ....Carrollton TX 75006	800-423-5382	972-620-5600
Alchemy of England 3516 Roberts Cut Off Rd ....Fort Worth TX 76114	800-578-1065	817-236-3141
Architex International 3333 Commercial Ave ....Northbrook IL 60062	800-621-0827	
Bettendorf-Stanford 1370 W Main St ....Salem IL 62881	800-548-2253	618-548-3555
Bishop Distributing Co 5200 36th St SE ....Grand Rapids MI 49512 *Cust Svc*	800-748-0363*	
Bisque Imports 1 Belmont Ave ....Belmont NC 28012	888-568-5991	704-829-9290
BR Funsten & Co 5200 Watt Ct Ste B ....Fairfield CA 94534	888-261-2871	209-825-5375
C & F Enterprises Inc 819 Bluecrab Rd ....Newport News VA 23606	888-889-9868	757-873-5688
Cambridge Silversmith Ltd 116 Lehigh St ....Fairfield NJ 07004	800-890-3366	973-227-4400
Carlton Group Inc 120 Landmark Dr ....Greensboro NC 27409	800-722-7824	336-668-7677
Carnations Home Fashions Inc 53 Jeanne Dr ....Newburgh NY 12550	800-866-8949	212-679-6017
CCA Global Partners 4301 Earth City Expy ....Earth City MO 63045	800-466-6984	314-506-0000
CDC Distributors 10511 Medallion Dr ....Cincinnati OH 45241	800-678-2321	513-771-3100
Christopher Guy 8900 Beverly Blvd ....West Hollywood CA 90048	800-476-9505	323-509-4034
Cookshack 2304 N Ash St ....Ponca City OK 74601	800-423-0698	580-765-3669
Cool Gear International LLC 10 Cordage Park Cir ....Plymouth MA 02360	855-393-2665	
Decorative Crafts Inc 50 Chestnut St ....Greenwich CT 06830	800-431-4455	203-531-1500
Derr Flooring Company Inc 525 Davisville Rd PO Box 912 ....Willow Grove PA 19090	800-523-3457	215-657-6300
Down Under Bedding & Mattresses 5170 Dixie Rd Unit 3 ....Mississauga ON L4W1E3	888-624-6484	905-624-5854
Erickson's Flooring & Supply Company Inc 1013 Orchard St ....Ferndale MI 48220	866-541-9663	
Fabricut Inc 9303 E 46th St ....Tulsa OK 74145	800-999-8200	918-622-7700
Farrey's Wholesale Hardware Company Inc 1850 NE 146th St ....North Miami FL 33181	888-854-5483	305-947-5451
Finial Co, The 4030 La Reunion Pkwy ....Dallas TX 75212	800-392-4341	214-678-0805
Gourmet Settings 245 W Beaver Creek Rd Ste 10 ....Richmond Hill ON L4B1L1	800-551-2649	
Halstead International Inc 15 Oakwood Ave ....Norwalk CT 06850	866-843-8453	
Home Design Outlet Ctr 400 County Ave ....Secaucus NJ 07094	800-701-0388	
Home Essentials & Beyond Inc 200 Theodore Conrad Dr ....Jersey City NJ 07305	800-417-6218	732-590-3600
Horizons Window Fashions Inc 1705 Waukegan Rd ....Waukegan IL 60085	800-858-2352	
Jackson George N Ltd 1139 Mcdermot Ave ....Winnipeg MB R3E0V2	800-665-8978	204-786-3821
JJ Haines & Company Inc 6950 Aviation Blvd ....Glen Burnie MD 21061	800-922-9248	
Johnson Window Films Inc 20655 Annalee Ave ....Carson CA 90746	800-448-8468	310-631-6672
Kanawha Scales & Systems Inc Rock Branch Industrial Pk 303 Jacobson Dr ....Poca WV 25159	800-955-8321	304-755-8321
Kashmir Fabrics + Furnishings 3191 Commonwealth Dr ....Dallas TX 75247	800-527-4630	214-631-8040
Kiefer Specialty Flooring Inc 2910 Falling Waters Blvd ....Lindenhurst IL 60046	800-322-5448	847-245-8450
Klaff's 28 Washington St ....South Norwalk CT 06854	800-552-3371	203-866-1603
Kozy Heat Fireplace 204 Industrial Park Dr ....Lakefield MN 56150	844-395-0405	
Lanz Cabinet Shop Inc 3025 W Seventh Pl ....Eugene OR 97402	800-788-6332	541-485-4050
Legendary Whitetails 820 Enterprise Dr ....Slinger WI 53086	800-875-9453	
Longust Distributing Inc 2432 W Birchwood Ave ....Mesa AZ 85202	800-352-0521	480-820-6244
Lonseal Inc 928 E 238th St ....Carson CA 90745	800-832-7111	310-830-7111
M Block & Sons Inc 5020 W 73rd St ....Bedford Park IL 60638	800-621-8845	708-728-8400
Maxtex Inc 3620 Francis Cir ....Alpharetta GA 30004	800-241-1836	770-772-6757
Midwest Designer Supply Inc N30 W22377 Green Rd Ste C ....Waukesha WI 53186	888-523-2611	
More Space Place Inc 5040 140th Ave N ....Clearwater FL 33760	888-731-3051	
National Credit Adjusters LLC 327 N Fourth Ave PO Box 3023 ....Hutchinson KS 67504	888-768-0674	
Northern States Metals Co 3207 Innovation Pl ....Youngstown OH 44509	800-689-0666	

	Toll-Free	Phone

Omega Moulding Company Ltd
1 Saw Grass Dr .... Bellport NY 11713 **800-289-6634**

OneCoast Network LLC
230 Spring St Ste 1800 .... Atlanta GA 30303 **866-592-5514**

Phoenix AMD International Inc
41 Butler Ct .... Bowmanville ON L1C4P8 **800-661-7313**

Pompanoosuc Mills
3184 Rte 5 S .... East Thetford VT 05043 **800-841-6671**

Regent Products Corp
8999 Palmer St .... River Grove IL 60171 **800-583-1002** 708-583-1000

Reliable Factory Supply Co
PO Box 340 .... Thomaston CT 06787 **800-288-8464**

Revman International Inc
350 Fifth Ave 70th Fl .... New York NY 10118 **800-237-0658**

Selective Enterprises Inc
10701 Texland Blvd .... Charlotte NC 28273 **800-334-1207** 704-588-3310

Sobel Westex Inc
2670 Western Ave .... Las Vegas NV 89109 **855-697-6235**

SOG Specialty Knives & Tools LLC
6521 212th St SW .... Lynnwood WA 98036 **888-405-6433** 425-771-6230

Springs Window Fashions LP
7549 Graber Rd .... Middleton WI 53562 **877-792-0002** 608-836-1011

Stephen Miller Gallery
800 Santa Cruz Ave .... Menlo Park CA 94025 **888-566-8833** 650-327-5040

Sterling Cut Glass Company Inc
5020 Olympic Blvd .... Erlanger KY 41018 **800-543-1317** 859-283-2333

T & A Supply Company Inc
6821 S 216th St Bldg A PO Box 927 ..... Kent WA 98032 **800-562-2857** 253-872-3682

Tailored Living LLC
19000 MacArthur Blvd Ste 100 .... Irvine CA 92612 **866-675-8819**

Thompson Olde Inc
3250 Camino Del Sol .... Oxnard CA 93030 **800-827-1565** 805-983-0388

Three Hands Corp
13259 Ralston Ave .... Sylmar CA 91342 **800-443-5443** 818-833-1200

Wanke Cascade Co
6330 N Cutter Cir .... Portland OR 97217 **800-365-5053** 503-289-8609

Weightech
1649 Country Elite Dr .... Waldron AR 72958 **800-457-3720** 479-637-4182

WMF Americas Inc
2121 Frden Rd .... Millville NJ 08332 **800-966-3009** 704-882-3898

World Kitchen LLC
1200 S Antrim Way .... Greencastle PA 17225 **800-999-3436**

Zodax Inc
14040 Arminta St .... Panorama City CA 91402 **800-800-3443** 818-785-5626

361 HOME FURNISHINGS STORES

SEE ALSO Department Stores ; Furniture Stores

	Toll-Free	Phone

Altmeyer Home Stores Inc
6515 Rt 22 .... Delmont PA 15626 **800-394-6628** 724-468-3434

Art Material Services Inc
625 Joyce Kilmer Ave .... New Brunswick NJ 08901 **888-522-5526** 732-545-8888

Bath + Beyond, The
77 Connecticut St .... San Francisco CA 94107 **800-696-6662** 415-689-6338

Bauerware LLC
3886 17th St .... San Francisco CA 94114 **877-864-5662** 415-864-3886

Beacon Products LLC
2041 58th Ave Cir E .... Bradenton FL 34203 **800-345-4928**

Bed Bath & Beyond Inc
650 Liberty Ave .... Union NJ 07083 **800-462-3966** 908-688-0888
NASDAQ: BBBY

Bitterman Scales LLC
413 Radcliff Rd .... Willow Street PA 17584 **877-464-3009** 717-464-3009

Blanco America Inc
110 Mt Holly By-Pass .... Lumberton NJ 08048 **800-451-5782**

Bristol Aluminum
5514 Bristol Emilie Rd .... Levittown PA 19057 **800-338-5532** 215-946-3160

Burlington Coat Factory
1830 Rt 130 N .... Burlington NJ 08016 **855-355-2875** 609-387-7800

Container Store, The
500 Freeport Pkwy .... Coppell TX 75019 **800-733-3532** 972-538-6000

Cost Plus Inc 200 Fourth St .... Oakland CA 94607 **877-967-5362** 510-893-7300
NASDAQ: CPWM

Cutlery & More LLC
135 Prairie Lake Rd .... East Dundee IL 60118 **800-650-9866**

Delfin Design & Manufacturing Inc
23301 Antonio Pkwy .... Rancho Santa Margarita CA 92688 **800-354-7919** 949-888-4644

Design Within Reach Inc
711 Canal St 3rd Fl .... Stamford CT 06902 **800-944-2233** 203-614-0600
NASDAQ: DWRI

DirectBuy Inc
8450 Broadway .... Merrillville IN 46410 **800-320-3462** 219-736-1100

Edward Joy Electric
905 Canal St .... Syracuse NY 13210 **800-724-0664** 315-474-3361

Elite Lighting Company Inc
412 S Cypress St .... Mullins SC 29574 **800-343-0764**

Force Flow Inc
2430 Stanwell Dr .... Concord CA 94520 **800-893-6723**

GEARYS Beverly Hills
351 N Beverly Dr .... Beverly Hills CA 90210 **800-793-6670**

Gracious Home
1220 Third Ave .... New York NY 10021 **800-338-7809** 212-517-6300

Grand Rapids Scale Company Inc
4215 Stafford Ave SW .... Grand Rapids MI 49548 **800-348-5701**

Granite City Electric Supply Co
19 Quincy Ave .... Quincy MA 02169 **800-850-9400** 617-472-6500

Gump's 135 Post St .... San Francisco CA 94108 **800-766-7628** 415-982-1616

Habitat Housewares
800 E Dimond Blvd Ste 3-207 .... Anchorage AK 99515 **800-770-1856** 907-561-1856

Hammacher Schlemmer & Co
9307 N Milwaukee Ave .... Niles IL 60714 **800-321-1484**

Hussong Manufacturing Company Inc
204 Industrial Park Rd .... Lakefield MN 56150 **800-253-4904** 507-662-6641

Hy Cite Enterprises LLC
333 Holtzman Rd .... Madison WI 53713 **877-494-2289**

	Toll-Free	Phone

Kirkland's Inc
5310 Maryland Way .... Brentwood TN 37027 **877-541-4855**
NASDAQ: KIRK

Kitchen Collection Inc
71 E Water St .... Chillicothe OH 45601 **888-548-2651*** 740-773-9150
*General

Kitchen Craft Cookware
4129 United Ave .... Mount Dora FL 32757 **800-800-2850** 352-483-7600

Kwik-Covers LLC
811 Ridge Rd .... Webster NY 14580 **866-586-9620** 585-787-9620

Lamps Plus Inc
20250 Plummer St .... Chatsworth CA 91311 **800-782-1967**

Lindamar Industries Inc
1603 Commerce Way .... Paso Robles CA 93446 **800-235-1811** 805-237-1910

Litelab Corp 251 Elm St .... Buffalo NY 14203 **800-238-4120** 716-856-4491

Luxury Bath Technologies
1800 Industrial Dr .... Libertyville IL 60048 **800-263-9882**

Lynx Grills Inc
5895 Rickenbacker Rd .... Commerce CA 90040 **888-289-5969** 323-838-1770

Mason Structural Steel Inc
7500 Northfield Rd .... Walton Hills OH 44146 **800-686-1223** 440-439-1040

Mattress Firm Inc
5815 Gulf Fwy .... Houston TX 77023 **800-821-6621** 713-923-1090

Moline Machinery LLC
114 S Central Ave .... Duluth MN 55807 **800-767-5734**

Panaram International
126 Greylock Ave .... Belleville NJ 07109 **800-872-8695** 973-751-1100

Perdue Inc
5 W Forsyth St Ste 100 .... Jacksonville FL 32202 **800-732-5857** 904-737-5858

Pier 1 Imports Inc
100 Pier 1 Pl .... Fort Worth TX 76102 **800-245-4595** 817-252-8000
NYSE: PIR

Real Floors Inc
1791 Williams Dr .... Marietta GA 30066 **800-728-2690** 770-590-7334

Restoration Hardware Inc
2900 N MacArthur Dr Ste 100 .... Tracy CA 95376 **800-910-9836**

Seattle Lighting Fixture Co
222 Second Ave Ext S .... Seattle WA 98104 **800-689-1000*** 206-622-4736
*Cust Svc

Sentran LLC 4355 Lowell St .... Ontario CA 91761 **888-545-8988** 909-605-1544

Smoky Mountain Knife Works Inc
2320 Winfield Dunn Pkwy
PO Box 4430 .... Sevierville TN 37876 **800-251-9306**

Sur La Table PO Box 840 .... Brownsburg IN 46112 **800-243-0852**

Timberlane Inc
150 Domorah Dr .... Montgomeryville PA 18936 **800-250-2221** 215-616-0600

TJX Cos Inc
770 Cochituate Rd .... Framingham MA 01701 **800-926-6299** 508-390-1000
NYSE: TJX

Totalcomp Scales & Components
99 Reagent Ln .... Fair Lawn NJ 07410 **800-631-0347** 201-797-2718

Transducer Techniques Inc
42480 Rio Nedo .... Temecula CA 92590 **800-344-3965** 951-719-3965

Villeroy & Boch USA Inc
3A S Middlesex Ave .... Monroe Township NJ 08331 **800-536-2284**

Waterford Wedgwood USA Inc
1330 Campus Pkwy .... Wall NJ 07753 **877-720-3486**

Williams-Sonoma Inc
3250 Van Ness Ave .... San Francisco CA 94109 **800-838-2589** 415-421-7900
NYSE: WSM

World Class Lighting
14350 60th St N .... Clearwater FL 33760 **877-499-6753** 727-524-7661

Z Gallerie Inc
1855 W 139th St .... Gardena CA 90249 **800-358-8288** 310-630-1200

362 HOME HEALTH SERVICES

SEE ALSO Hospices

	Toll-Free	Phone

Abbi Home Care Inc
6453 SW Blvd .... Benbrook TX 76132 **877-383-2224** 817-377-0889

Advantage Home Health Care Inc
4008 N Wheeling Ave .... Muncie IN 47304 **800-884-5088** 765-284-1211

Alacare Home Health & Hospice
2400 John Hawkins Pkwy .... Birmingham AL 35244 **800-852-4724** 205-981-8000

Alaska Native Tribal Health Consortium Inc
4000 Ambassador Dr .... Anchorage AK 99508 **800-655-4837** 907-729-1900

AllCare Health
740 SE Seventh St .... Grants Pass OR 97526 **888-460-0185** 541-471-4106

Almost Family Inc
9510 Ormsby Stn Rd Ste 300 .... Louisville KY 40223 **800-828-9769** 502-891-1000
NASDAQ: AFAM

Altamed Health Services Corp
4650 W Sunset Blvd M/S 76 .... Los Angeles CA 90027 **877-462-2582** 323-669-2113

Amedisys Inc
5959 S Sherwood Forest Blvd .... Baton Rouge LA 70816 **800-464-0020** 225-292-2031
NASDAQ: AMED

American HomePatient Inc
5200 Maryland Way Ste 400 .... Brentwood TN 37027 **800-890-7271** 615-221-8884

Amerita Inc
7307 S Revere Pky Ste 200 .... Centennial CO 80112 **800-360-4755** 303-355-4745

Anthelio Healthcare Solutions Inc
5400 LBJ Fwy Ste 200 .... Dallas TX 75240 **855-268-4354** 214-257-7000

Apria Healthcare Group Inc
26220 Enterprise Ct .... Lake Forest CA 92630 **800-277-4288** 949-639-2000

ARK Diagnostics Inc
48089 Fremont Blvd .... Fremont CA 94538 **877-869-2320**

Aroostook Home Health Services
658 Main St A .... Caribou ME 04736 **877-688-9977** 207-492-8290

BAYADA Home Health Care
1 W Main St .... Moorestown NJ 08057 **877-591-1527** 856-231-1000

Bios Corp 309 E Dewey Ave .... Sapulpa OK 74066 **888-920-3600**

Calea Ltd
2785 Skymark Ave Unit 2 .... Mississauga ON L4W4Y3 **888-909-3299** 905-238-1234

Care Partners
68 Sweeten Creek Rd .... Asheville NC 28803 **800-627-1533** 828-252-2255

Classified Section

				Toll-Free	Phone

Carter Healthcare
3105 S Meridian Ave .... Oklahoma City OK 73119 — **888-951-1112** 405-947-7700

Central Vermont Home Health & Hospice
600 Granger Rd .... Barre VT 05641 — **800-286-1219** 802-223-1878

Christian Horizons
200 N Postville Dr .... Lincoln IL 62656 — **800-535-8717** 217-732-9651

ComForcare Senior Services Inc
2520 Telegraph Rd Ste 100 .... Bloomfield Hills MI 48302 — **800-886-4044** 248-745-9700

Commonwealth Health Corporation Inc
800 Park St .... Bowling Green KY 42101 — **800-786-1581** 270-745-1500

Comprehensive Health Service
8600 Astronaut Blvd .... Cape Canaveral FL 32920 — **800-638-8083** 321-783-2720

Coram Healthcare Corp
555 17th St Ste 1500 .... Denver CO 80202 — **800-267-2642**

Delaware Hospice Inc
1786 Wilmington-W Chester Pk
Ste 200 A .... Glen Mills DE 19342 — **800-838-9800** 302-478-5707

Fletcher's Medical Supplies Inc
6851 S Distribution Ave .... Jacksonville FL 32256 — **855-541-7809** 904-387-4481

General Healthcare Resources Inc
2250 Hickory Rd Ste 240 .... Plymouth Meeting PA 19462 — **800-879-4471** 610-834-1122

Genesis Home Care Inc
116 E Heritage Dr .... Tyler TX 75703 — **800-947-0273** 903-509-3374

Griswold Home Care
717 Bethlehem Pk Ste 300 .... Erdenheim PA 19038 — **800-474-7965**

Hamacher Resource Group Inc
W 229 N 2510 Duplainville Rd .... Waukesha WI 53186 — **800-888-0889**

Help At Home Inc
1 N State St Ste 800 .... Chicago IL 60602 — **800-404-3191** 312-762-0900

Home Bound Healthcare Inc
14216 McCarthy Rd .... Lemont IL 60439 — **800-444-7028** 708-798-0800

Home Care Network Inc
190A E Spring Valley Rd .... Centerville OH 45458 — **800-417-0291** 937-435-1142

Home Healthcare, Hospice & Community Services Inc
312 Marlboro St .... Keene NH 03431 — **800-541-4145** 603-352-2253

Home Instead Inc
13323 California St .... Omaha NE 68154 — **888-484-5759** 402-498-4466

Home Staff Health Services
40 Millbrook St .... Worcester MA 01606 — **800-779-3312**

Home Staff Inc
5509 N Cumberland Ave Ste 514 .... Chicago IL 60656 — **888-806-6924** 773-467-6002

Homecare of Mid Missouri Inc
102 W Reed St .... Moberly MO 65270 — **800-246-6400** 660-263-1517

Homewatch CareGivers
7100 E Belleview Ave
Ste 101 .... Greenwood Village CO 80111 — **800-777-9770**

Interim HealthCare Inc
1601 Sawgrass Corporate Pkwy .... Sunrise FL 33323 — **800-338-7786** 954-858-6000

Kelly Home Care Services Inc
999 W Big Beaver Rd .... Troy MI 48084 — **800-755-8636** 248-362-4444

Lakewood Health System
49725 County 83 .... Staples MN 56479 — **800-525-1033** 218-894-1515

LHC Group Inc
901 Hugh Wallis Rd S .... Lafayette LA 70508 — **866-542-4768** 337-289-8188
NASDAQ: LHCG

Lifelink Foundation Inc
9661 Delaney Creek Blvd .... Tampa FL 33619 — **800-262-5775** 813-253-2640

Lincare Holdings Inc
19387 US 19 N .... Clearwater FL 33764 — **800-284-2006**
NASDAQ: LNCR

Living Assistance Services Inc
937 Haverford Rd Ste 200 .... Bryn Mawr PA 19010 — **800-365-4189**

Mains'l Services Inc
7000 78th Ave N .... Brooklyn Park MN 55445 — **800-441-6525**

MDX Medical Inc
160 Chubb Ave Ste 301 .... Lyndhurst NJ 07071 — **866-325-8972** 201-842-0760

Med Team Home Health Care
131 S Beckham Ave .... Tyler TX 75702 — **800-825-2873** 903-592-9747

MEDCURE 1811 NE Sandy Blvd .... Portland OR 97230 — **866-560-2525** 503-257-9100

Medical Cost Management Corp
105 W Adams St Ste 2200 .... Chicago IL 60603 — **800-367-9938** 312-236-2694

Medical Services of America Inc (MSA)
171 Monroe Ln .... Lexington SC 29072 — **800-845-5850** 803-957-0500

Mena Regional Health System
311 Morrow St N .... Mena AR 71953 — **800-394-6185** 479-394-6100

Meridian Health System
1967 Hwy 34 Bldg C Ste 104 .... Wall NJ 07719 — **800-560-9990**

Metro Pavia Health System
MaraMar Plaza Bldg Avenida San Patricio
Ste 960 .... Guaynabo PR 00968 — **888-882-0882** 787-620-9770

Miracle Healthcare
4322 N Hamilton Rd .... Gahanna OH 43230 — **844-560-7775** 614-237-7702

New Choices Inc
2501 18th St Ste 201 .... Bettendorf IA 52722 — **888-355-5502** 563-355-5502

Nizhoni Health Systems LLC
5 Middlesex Ave .... Somerville MA 02145 — **800-915-3211**

North Los Angel County Regional Ctr
9200 Oakdale Ave Ste 100 .... Chatsworth CA 91311 — **800-430-4263** 818-778-1900

Nurse On Call Inc
111 Westwood Pl Ste 400 .... Brentwood TN 37027 — **855-350-3800**

Nurses Unlimited
511 N Lincoln PO Box 4534 .... Odessa TX 79761 — **888-245-1061*** 432-580-2085
*Compliance

Ohel Children's Home & Family Services Inc
4510 16th Ave .... Brooklyn NY 11204 — **800-603-6435** 718-851-6300

Optimae LifeServices Inc
301 W Burlington Ave .... Fairfield IA 52556 — **800-735-2942** 641-472-1684

Outreach Healthcare Inc
269 W Renner Pkwy .... Richardson TX 75080 — **800-793-0081**

Passport Program-western
925 Euclid Ave Ste 600 .... Cleveland OH 44115 — **800-626-7277** 216-621-0303

Pathways Home Health Hospice
585 N Mary Ave .... Sunnyvale CA 94085 — **888-755-7855**

Pediatric Home Respiratory Services Inc
2800 Cleveland Ave N .... Roseville MN 55113 — **800-225-7477** 651-642-1825

Personal-Touch Home Care Inc
186-18 Hillside Ave .... Jamaica NY 11432 — **888-275-4147** 718-468-2500

Phoenix Home Care Inc
3033 S Kansas Expy .... Springfield MO 65807 — **855-881-7442** 417-881-7442

Pioneers Medical Ctr
100 Pioneers Medical Center Dr .... Meeker CO 81641 — **800-332-1168** 970-878-5047

PreCheck Inc
2500 E T C Jester Blvd .... Houston TX 77008 — **800-999-9861**

Preferred Homecare Infusion LLC
4601 E Hilton Ave Ste 100 .... Phoenix AZ 85034 — **800-636-2123** 480-446-9010

Princeton HealthCare System
905 Herrontown Rd .... Princeton NJ 08540 — **866-460-4776** 609-497-3300

Promera Health
61 Accord Park Dr .... Norwell MA 02061 — **888-878-9058**

PSA healthcare
400 Interstate N Pkwy SE Ste 1600 .... Atlanta GA 30339 — **800-408-4442** 770-441-1580

Qualchoice of Arkansas Inc
12615 Chenal Pkwy Ste 300 .... Little Rock AR 72211 — **800-235-7111**

Right at Home Inc
6464 Center St Ste 150 .... Omaha NE 68106 — **877-697-7537** 402-697-7537

Selfhelp Community Services
520 Eigth Ave 5th Fl .... New York NY 10018 — **866-735-1234** 212-971-7600

Society's Assets Inc
5200 Washington Ave Ste 225 .... Racine WI 53406 — **800-378-9128** 262-637-9128

Solano Coalition for Better Health
744 Empire St Ste 210 .... Fairfield CA 94533 — **800-978-7547**

Star Multi Care Services Inc
115 Broad Hollow Rd Ste 275 .... Melville NY 11747 — **877-920-0600** 631-424-7827

Sunrise Home Health Services
3200 Broadway Blvd Ste 260 .... Garland TX 75043 — **800-296-7823** 972-278-1414

Visiting Nurse Assn of Morris County (Inc)
175 South St .... Morristown NJ 07960 — **800-938-4748** 973-539-1216

363 HOME IMPROVEMENT CENTERS

SEE ALSO Construction Materials

				Toll-Free	Phone

Ace Hardware Corp
2200 Kensington Ct .... Oak Brook IL 60523 — **866-290-5334**

Alaska Industrial Hardware Inc
2192 Viking Dr .... Anchorage AK 99501 — **800-478-7201** 907-276-7201

Arlington Coal & Lumber Company Inc
41 Park Ave .... Arlington MA 02476 — **800-649-8101** 781-643-8100

Atlanta Hardwood Corp
5596 Riverview Rd SE .... Mableton GA 30126 — **800-476-5393** 404-792-2290

Belknap White Group, The
111 Plymouth St .... Mansfield MA 02048 — **866-298-0708** 800-283-7500

Carlisle Wide Plank Floors Inc
1676 Rt 9 .... Stoddard NH 03464 — **800-595-9663** 603-446-3937

Future Home Technology Inc
33 Ralph St .... Port Jervis NY 12771 — **800-342-8650**

H2O Concepts International Inc
22405 N 19th Ave .... Phoenix AZ 85027 — **888-275-4261** 623-582-5222

Hitachi Systems Security Inc
955 Michele-Bohec Blvd Ste 244 .... Blainville QC J7C5J6 — **866-430-8166** 450-430-8166

Home Depot Inc
2455 Paces Ferry Rd NW .... Atlanta GA 30339 — **800-553-3199*** 770-433-8211
NYSE: HD ■ **Cust Svc*

Len-Co Lumber Corp
1445 Seneca St .... Buffalo NY 14210 — **800-258-4585** 716-822-0243

Linen Chest Inc
4455 AutoRt Des Laurentides .... Laval QC H7L5X8 — **800-363-3832** 514-341-7077

Lowe's Cos Inc
1000 Lowe's Blvd .... Mooresville NC 28117 — **800-445-6937** 704-758-1000
NYSE: LOW

Lowe's Home Centers Inc
PO Box 1111 .... North Wilkesboro NC 28656 — **800-445-6937**

MarJam Supply Co Inc
20 Rewe St .... Brooklyn NY 11211 — **800-848-8407*** 718-388-6465
*All

Martin Door Manufacturing Inc
2828 South 900 West .... Salt Lake City UT 84119 — **800-388-9310** 801-973-9310

Northern Tool & Equipment Co
2800 Southcross Dr W .... Burnsville MN 55306 — **800-222-5381*** 952-894-9510
*Cust Svc

Orchard Supply Hardware
6450 Via del Oro .... San Jose CA 95119 — **800-952-5210** 408-281-3500

Pandel Inc 21 River Dr .... Cartersville GA 30120 — **800-537-3868** 770-382-1034

Paramount Builders Inc
501 Central Dr .... Virginia Beach VA 23454 — **888-340-9002** 757-340-9000

Pilgrim Home & Hearth Alliance LLC
5600 Imhoff Dr Ste G .... Concord CA 94520 — **800-227-1044**

Preverco Inc
285 Rue De Rotterdam
.... Saint-augustin-de-desmaures QC G3A2E5 — **877-667-2725** 418-878-8930

Simonson Properties Co
535 First St NE .... Saint Cloud MN 56304 — **888-843-8789** 320-252-9385

Solutioninc Technologies Ltd
5692 Bloomfield St .... Halifax NS B3K1T2 — **888-496-2221** 902-420-0077

Star Lumber & Supply
325 S W St .... Wichita KS 67213 — **800-797-9556** 316-942-2221

Sutherland Lumber Co
4000 Main St .... Kansas City MO 64111 — **800-821-2252** 816-756-3000

True Value Co
8600 W Bryn Mawr Ave .... Chicago IL 60631 — **800-897-3112** 773-695-5000

WE Aubuchon Company Inc
95 Aubuchon Dr .... Westminster MA 01473 — **800-431-2712** 978-874-0521

364 HOME INSPECTION SERVICES

				Toll-Free	Phone

A2Z Field Services LLC
7450 Industrial Pkwy Ste 105 .... Plain City OH 43064 — **800-713-2001** 614-873-0211

AmeriSpec Inc
3839 Forest Hill Irene Rd .... Memphis TN 38125 — **877-769-5217**

BrickKicker
849 N Ellsworth St .... Naperville IL 60563 — **800-821-1820**

			Toll-Free	Phone
HomeTeam Inspection Service Inc				
575 Chamber Dr	Milford OH	45150	800-598-5297	
HouseMaster				
92 E Main St Ste 301	Somerville NJ	08876	800-526-3939	732-469-6565
Insparisk LLC				
18-10 Whitestone Expy 3rd Fl	Whitestone NY	11357	888-464-6772	
Inspection Depot Inc				
3131 Saint Johns Bluff Rd	Jacksonville FL	32246	888-589-2112	
iv3 Solutions Corp				
50 Minthorn Blvd Ste 301	Markham ON	L3T7X8	877-995-2651	
National Property Inspections Inc (NPI)				
9375 Burt St Ste 201	Omaha NE	68114	800-333-9807	402-333-9807
Remote Access Technology Inc				
61 Atlantic St	Dartmouth NS	B2Y4P4	877-356-2728	902-434-4405
WIN Home Inspection				
3326 Aspen Grove Dr	Franklin TN	37067	800-309-6753	

365   HOME SALES & OTHER DIRECT SELLING

			Toll-Free	Phone
4Life Research 9850 S 300 W	Sandy UT	84070	888-454-3374*	801-256-3102
*Sales				
Amway Corp 7575 Fulton St E	Ada MI	49355	800-253-6500	616-787-4000
Cargo Control USA Inc				
PO Box 2806	Sanford NC	27331	888-775-5059	919-775-5059
Color Me Beautiful				
7000 Infantry Ridge Rd Ste 200	Manassas VA	20109	800-265-6763	
Colorado Prime Foods				
500 Bi-County Blvd Ste 400	Farmingdale NY	11735	800-365-2404	631-694-1111
Conklin Company Inc				
551 Valley Pk Dr	Shakopee MN	55379	800-888-8838	952-445-6010
Delaney Educational Enterprises Inc				
1455 W Morena Blvd	San Diego CA	92110	800-788-5557	
Digital Air Strike Co				
6991 E Camelback Rd Ste B111	Scottsdale AZ	85251	888-713-8958	
Email Co, The				
15 Kainona Ave	Toronto ON	M3H3H4	877-933-6245	
Farrar Pump & Machinery Company Inc				
1701 S Big Bend Blvd	Saint Louis MO	63117	800-752-1050	314-644-1050
Getconnect				
14114 Dallas Pkwy Ste 430	Dallas TX	75254	888-200-1831	
Golden Neo-Life Diamite International				
3500 Gateway Blvd	Fremont CA	94538	800-432-5842	
Insight 6820 S Harl Ave	Tempe AZ	85283	800-467-4448	
Kaeser & Blair Inc				
4236 Grissom Dr	Batavia OH	45103	800-642-0790	
KMA One				
6815 Meadowridge Ct	Alpharetta GA	30005	888-500-2536	770-886-4000
Kwik Kafe Company Inc				
204 Furnace St	Bluefield VA	24605	800-533-4066	276-322-4691
Magnetscom				
51 Pacific Ave Ste 4	Jersey City NJ	07304	866-229-8237	
Mail Shark				
4125 New Holland Rd	Mohnton PA	19540	888-457-4275	610-621-2994
Mary Kay Inc PO Box 799045	Dallas TX	75379	800-627-9529*	972-687-6300
*Cust Svc				
Melaleuca Inc				
3910 S Yellowstone Hwy	Idaho Falls ID	83402	800-282-3000*	208-522-0700
*Sales				
Mt Shasta Spring Water Company Inc				
1878 Twin View Blvd	Redding CA	96003	800-922-6227	530-246-8800
Noevir USA Inc 1095 Main St	Irvine CA	92614	800-872-8817	949-660-1111
Ozarka Water Co				
729 SW Third St	Oklahoma City OK	73109	800-310-8474	405-235-8474
Pampered Chef Ltd				
1 Pampered Chef Ln	Addison IL	60101	888-687-2433	
Partylite Gifts Inc				
59 Armstrong Rd	Plymouth MA	02360	888-999-5706	508-830-3100
Poly Expert Inc 850 ave Munck	Laval QC	H7S1B1	877-384-5060	
PostcardMania				
2145 Sunnydale Blvd Bldg 101	Clearwater FL	33765	800-628-1804	
Princess House Inc				
470 Miles Standish Blvd	Taunton MA	02780	800-622-0039*	508-823-0711
*Sales				
Redi-Direct Marketing Inc				
107 Little Falls Rd	Fairfield NJ	07004	800-635-5833	973-808-4500
Reliv International Inc				
136 Chesterfield Industrial Blvd	Chesterfield MO	63005	800-735-4887	636-537-9715
NASDAQ: RELV				
Rena Ware International Inc				
15885 NE 28th St	Bellevue WA	98008	800-721-5156	425-881-6171
Saladmaster Inc				
4300 Amon Carter Blvd Ste 100	Arlington TX	76018	800-765-5795	817-633-3555
Select Publishing Inc				
6417 Normandy Ln	Madison WI	53719	800-278-5670	608-277-5787
Shaklee Corp				
4747 Willow Rd	Pleasanton CA	94588	800-742-5533	925-924-2000
SK Food Group Inc				
4600 37th Ave SW	Seattle WA	98126	800-722-6290	206-935-8100
Smartpak Equine LLC				
40 Grissom Rd Ste 500	Plymouth MA	02360	888-752-5171	774-773-1000
Stampin Up 12907 S 3600 W	Riverton UT	84065	800-782-6787*	
*Cust Svc				
Success Motivation International Inc				
4567 Lakeshore Dr	Waco TX	76710	800-876-2389*	254-776-7551
*Sales				
Sunrider International				
1625 Abalone Ave	Torrance CA	90501	888-278-6743*	310-781-3808
*Orders				
Thirty-One Gifts				
3425 Morse Crossing	Columbus OH	43219	866-443-8731	
Vorwerk USA Company LP				
3255 E Thousand Oaks Blvd				
Unit B	Thousand Oaks CA	91362	888-867-9375	

			Toll-Free	Phone
WEBCARGO Inc				
800 Pl Victoria				
Ste 2603 Tour de la bourse CP 329	Montreal QC	H4Z1G8	866-905-0123	514-905-5223
WebEyeCare Inc				
10 Canal St Ste 302	Bristol PA	19007	888-536-7480	
YourAreaCode LLC				
6242 28th St Ste B	Grand Rapids MI	49546	888-244-7751	616-622-2000

366   HOME WARRANTY SERVICES

			Toll-Free	Phone
American Home Shield				
150 Peabody Pl	Memphis TN	38102	888-682-1043	901-537-8000
Asset				
15050 Ave of Science	San Diego CA	92128	888-303-8755	
Blue Ribbon Home Warranty Inc				
95 S Wadsworth Blvd	Lakewood CO	80226	800-571-0475	303-986-3900
Cross Country Home Services				
1625 NW 136th Ave Ste 200	Sunrise FL	33323	800-778-8000*	954-845-2468
*Cust Svc				
Cypress Care Inc				
2736 Meadow Church Rd Ste 300	Duluth GA	30097	800-419-7191	
Home Security of America Inc				
310 N Midvale Blvd	Madison WI	53705	800-367-1448	
Warrantech Corp Inc				
2200 Hwy 121	Bedford TX	76021	800-833-8801	817-785-6601

367   HORSE BREEDERS

SEE ALSO Livestock Improvement Services

			Toll-Free	Phone
Darby Dan Farm				
3225 Old Frankfort Pk	Lexington KY	40510	888-321-0424	859-254-0424
Glencrest Farm				
1576 Moores Mill Rd PO Box 4468	Midway KY	40347	800-903-0136	859-233-7032

368   HORTICULTURAL PRODUCTS GROWERS

SEE ALSO Seed Companies ; Garden Centers

			Toll-Free	Phone
Aris Horticulture Inc				
115 Third St SE	Barberton OH	44203	800-232-9557	
Battlefield Farms Inc				
23190 Clarks Mtn Rd	Rapidan VA	22733	800-722-0744	
Bay City Flower Company Inc				
2265 Cabrillo Hwy S	Half Moon Bay CA	94019	800-399-5858*	650-726-5535
*Sales				
CD Ford & Sons Inc				
PO Box 300	Geneseo IL	61254	800-383-4661	309-944-4661
Color Spot Nurseries Inc				
2575 Olive Hill Rd	Fallbrook CA	92028	800-554-4065	760-695-1480
Costa Nursery Farms Inc				
21800 SW 162nd Ave	Miami FL	33170	800-327-7074	
Cuthbert Greenhouses Inc				
4900 Hendron Rd	Groveport OH	43125	800-321-1939	614-836-3866
Dallas Johnson Greenhouse Inc				
2802 Twin City Dr	Council Bluffs IA	51501	800-445-4794	712-366-0407
Dan Schantz Farm & Greenhouses LLC				
8025 Spinnerstown Rd	Zionsville PA	18092	800-451-3064	610-967-2181
DeLeon's Bromeliads Co				
13745 SW 216th St	Miami FL	33170	800-448-8649	305-238-6028
Dramm & Echter Inc				
1150 Quail Gardens Dr	Encinitas CA	92024	800-854-7021	760-436-0188
Ever-Bloom Inc				
4701 Foothill Rd	Carpinteria CA	93013	800-388-8112	805-684-5566
Farmers West				
5300 Foothill Rd	Carpinteria CA	93013	800-549-0085	805-684-5531
Garden State Growers				
99 Locust Grove Rd	Pittstown NJ	08867	800-288-8484	908-730-8888
Green Circle Growers Inc				
51051 US Hwy 20	Oberlin OH	44074	800-368-4759	440-775-1411
Greenleaf Nursery Co				
28406 Hwy 82	Park Hill OK	74451	800-331-2982	918-457-5172
Kerry's Nursery Inc				
21840 SW 258th St	Homestead FL	33031	800-331-9127	
Knox Nursery Inc				
940 Avalon Rd	Winter Garden FL	34787	800-441-5669	
Matsui Nursery Inc				
1645 Old Stage Rd	Salinas CA	93908	800-793-6433	831-422-6433
McLellan Botanicals				
2352 San Juan Rd	Aromas CA	95004	800-467-2443	
Metrolina Greenhouses Inc				
16400 Huntersville-Concord Rd	Huntersville NC	28078	800-543-3915	704-875-1371
Nurserymen's Exchange				
2651 N Cabrillo Hwy	Half Moon Bay CA	94019	800-227-5229*	650-726-6361
*General				
Panzer Nursery Inc				
17980 W Baseline Rd	Beaverton OR	97006	888-212-5327	503-645-1185
Parks Bros Farm Inc				
6733 Parks Rd	Van Buren AR	72956	800-334-5770	479-410-2217
Rockwell Farms				
332 Rockwell Farms Rd	Rockwell NC	28138	800-635-6576	
Smith Gardens Inc				
4164 Meridian St Ste 400	Bellingham WA	98226	800-755-6256	360-733-4671
Speedling Inc				
4447 Old 41 Hwy S	Ruskin FL	33570	800-881-4769*	
*Cust Svc				
Sun Valley Floral Farms Inc				
3160 Upper Bay Rd	Arcata CA	95521	800-747-0396	
Woodburn Nursery & Azaleas				
13009 McKee School Rd NE	Woodburn OR	97071	888-634-2232*	503-634-2231
*Sales				
Young's Plant Farm				
863 Airport Rd	Auburn AL	36830	800-304-8609	

Classified Section

369 — HOSE & BELTING - RUBBER OR PLASTICS

SEE ALSO Automotive Parts & Supplies - Mfr

			Toll-Free	Phone
ABC Industrie PO Box 77 ....Warsaw IN		46581	**800-426-0921**	574-267-5166
Aero Rubber Company Inc				
8100 W 185th St ....Tinley Park IL		60487	**800-662-1009**	
American Hose & Rubber Co Inc				
3645 E 44th St ....Tucson AZ		85713	**800-272-7537**	520-514-1666
Ammeraal Beltech USA				
7501 N St Louis Ave ....Skokie IL		60076	**800-323-4170***	847-673-6720
*Cust Svc				
Apache Hose & Belting Co Inc				
4805 Bowling St SW ....Cedar Rapids IA		52404	**800-553-5455***	319-365-0471
*Sales				
Atco Rubber Products Inc				
7101 Atco Dr ....Fort Worth TX		76118	**800-877-3828**	817-595-2894
Belting Industries Group				
1090 Lousons Rd ....Union NJ		07083	**800-843-2358**	908-272-8591
Carlstar Group LLC, The				
725 Cool Springs Blvd Ste 500 ....Franklin TN		37067	**800-889-7367**	615-503-0220
Chemprene Inc				
483 Fishkill Ave ....Beacon NY		12508	**800-431-9981**	845-831-2800
Cobon Plastics Corp 90 S St ....Newark NJ		07114	**800-360-1324**	973-344-6330
Cooper Tire & Rubber Co				
701 Lima Ave ....Findlay OH		45840	**800-854-6288**	419-423-1321
NYSE: CTB				
Dormont Manufacturing Co				
6015 Enterprise Dr ....Export PA		15632	**800-367-6668**	
Fenner Drives				
311 W Stiegel St ....Manheim PA		17545	**800-243-3374***	717-665-2421
*Sales				
Flexaust Co				
1510 Armstrong Rd ....Warsaw IN		46580	**800-343-0428**	574-267-7909
Flexfab LLC				
1699 W M-43 Hwy ....Hastings MI		49058	**800-331-0003**	
Freelin-Wade Co				
1730 NE Miller St ....McMinnville OR		97128	**888-373-9233**	503-434-5561
Gates Corp 1551 Wewatta St ....Denver CO		80202	**800-709-6001**	303-744-1911
Habasit ABT Inc				
150 Industrial Pk Rd ....Middletown CT		06457	**800-522-2358**	860-632-2211
Habasit Belting Inc				
1400 Clinton St ....Buffalo NY		14206	**800-325-1585**	716-824-8484
HBD/Thermoid Inc				
1301 W Sandusky Ave ....Bellefontaine OH		43311	**800-543-8070**	937-593-5010
Industrial Rubber Works				
1700 Nicholas Blvd ....Elk Grove Village IL		60007	**800-852-1855**	847-952-1800
Key Fire Hose Corp (KFH)				
PO Box 7107 ....Dothan AL		36302	**800-447-5666**	334-671-5532
Legg Company Inc				
325 E Tenth St ....Halstead KS		67056	**800-835-1003***	
*Sales				
Lockwood Products Inc				
5615 Willow Ln ....Lake Oswego OR		97035	**800-423-1625**	
Mattracks Inc				
202 Cleveland Ave E ....Karlstad MN		56732	**877-436-7800**	218-436-7000
Mulhern Belting Inc				
148 Bauer St ....Oakland NJ		07436	**800-253-6300**	201-337-5700
NewAge Industries Inc				
145 James Way ....SouthHampton PA		18966	**800-506-3924**	215-526-2300
Parker Fluid Connectors Group				
6035 Parkland Blvd ....Cleveland OH		44124	**800-272-7537***	216-896-3000
*General				
Ro-Lab American Rubber Co Inc				
8830 W Linne Rd ....Tracy CA		95304	**800-298-2066**	209-836-0965
Salem-Republic Rubber Co				
475 W California Ave ....Sebring OH		44672	**800-686-4199**	877-425-5079
Sparks Belting Co				
3800 Stahl Dr SE ....Grand Rapids MI		49546	**800-451-4537**	616-949-2750
Swan Products LLC				
1201 Delaware Ave ....Marion OH		43302	**800-800-4673**	
Titeflex Corp				
603 Hendee St ....Springfield MA		01139	**800-765-2525**	413-739-5631
US Rubber Corp				
211 E Loop 336 ....Conroe TX		77301	**800-872-3587**	

370 — HOSPICES

SEE ALSO Specialty Hospitals

Alabama

			Toll-Free	Phone
HomeCare of East Alabama Medical Ctr				
665 Opelika Rd ....Auburn AL		36830	**866-542-4768**	334-826-3131
Hospice of Cullman County				
1912 Alabama Hwy 157 ....Cullman AL		35058	**877-271-4176**	256-737-2502
Hospice of Marshall County				
408 Martling Rd ....Albertville AL		35951	**888-334-9336**	256-891-7724
Hospice of the Valley				
240 Johnston St SE PO Box 2745 ....Decatur AL		35602	**877-260-3657**	256-350-5585
Hospice of West Alabama				
3851 Loop Rd ....Tuscaloosa AL		35404	**877-362-7522**	205-523-0101

Arkansas

			Toll-Free	Phone
Arkansas Hospice				
14 Parkstone Cir ....North Little Rock AR		72116	**877-257-3400**	501-748-3333
AseraCare Hospice				
1000 Fianna Way ....Fort Smith AR		72919	**888-868-1957**	

California

			Toll-Free	Phone
Community Hospice Inc				
4368 Spyres Way ....Modesto CA		95356	**866-645-4567**	209-578-6300

			Toll-Free	Phone
Elizabeth Hospice				
500 La Terraza Blvd Ste 130 ....Escondido CA		92025	**800-797-2050**	760-737-2050
Hospice of Redlands Community Hospital				
350 Terracina Blvd ....Redlands CA		92373	**888-397-4999**	909-335-5643
Livingston Memorial Visiting Nurse Assn Hospice				
1996 Eastman Ave Ste 101 ....Ventura CA		93003	**800-830-8881**	805-642-1608
Torrance Memorial Home Health & Hospice				
3330 Lomita Blvd ....Torrance CA		90505	**800-906-9909**	310-784-3739
VITAS Healthcare Corp of California				
9655 Granite Ridge Dr Ste 300 ....San Diego CA		92123	**866-418-4827**	858-499-8901
VITAS Healthcare Corp of San Gabriel Cities				
1343 N Grand Ave ....Covina CA		91724	**866-418-4827**	
VNA & Hospice of Northern California				
1900 Powell St Ste 300 ....Emeryville CA		94608	**800-698-1273**	510-450-8596
VNA & Hospice of Southern California				
150 W First St Ste 270 ....Claremont CA		91711	**888-357-3574**	909-624-3574

Colorado

			Toll-Free	Phone
Hospice & Palliative Care of Western Colorado				
2754 Compass Dr Ste 377 ....Grand Junction CO		81506	**866-310-8900**	970-241-2212
Hospice of Boulder County				
2594 Trlridge Dr E ....Lafayette CO		80026	**877-986-4766**	303-449-7740
Hospice of Northern Colorado (HNC)				
2726 W 11th St Rd ....Greeley CO		80634	**800-564-5563**	970-352-8487

Connecticut

			Toll-Free	Phone
Hospice of Southeastern Connecticut Inc				
227 Dunham St ....Norwich CT		06360	**877-654-4035**	860-848-5699

Florida

			Toll-Free	Phone
Bigbend Hospice				
1723 Mahan Ctr Blvd ....Tallahassee FL		32308	**800-772-5862**	850-878-5310
Community Hospice of Northeast Florida				
4266 Sunbeam Rd ....Jacksonville FL		32257	**800-274-6614**	904-268-5200
Cornerstone Hospice & Palliative Care				
2445 Ln Pk Rd ....Tavares FL		32778	**866-742-6655**	
Covenant Hospice				
5041 N 12th Ave ....Pensacola FL		32504	**800-541-3072**	850-433-2155
Gulfside Hospice Inc				
6224 Lafayette St ....New Port Richey FL		34652	**800-561-4883**	727-845-5707
Hope Hospice				
9470 HealthPark Cir ....Fort Myers FL		33908	**800-835-1673**	239-482-4673
Hospice of Marion County				
3231 SW 34th Ave ....Ocala FL		34474	**888-482-5018**	352-873-7400
Hospice of Northeast Florida				
4266 Sunbeam Rd ....Jacksonville FL		32257	**866-253-6681**	904-268-5200
Hospice of Saint Francis Inc				
1250 Grumman Pl Ste B ....Titusville FL		32780	**866-269-4240**	321-269-4240
Lifepath Hospice				
3010 W Azeele St ....Tampa FL		33609	**800-209-2200**	813-877-2200
Tidewell Hospice				
5955 Rand Blvd ....Sarasota FL		34238	**800-959-4291**	941-552-7500
Treasure Health				
1201 SE Indian St ....Stuart FL		34997	**800-299-4677**	772-403-4500
Visiting Nurse Assn of the Treasure Coast				
1110 35th Ln ....Vero Beach FL		32960	**800-749-5760**	772-567-5551
VITAS Healthcare Corp				
201 S Biscayne Blvd Ste 400 ....Miami FL		33131	**800-873-5198**	305-374-4143

Georgia

			Toll-Free	Phone
Heyman HospiceCare				
420 E Second Ave ....Rome GA		30161	**800-324-1078**	706-509-3200
Hospice of NE Georgia Medical Ctr				
2150 Limestone Pkwy Ste 222 ....Gainesville GA		30501	**888-572-3900**	770-533-8888
Hospice of Southwest Georgia				
114 A Mimosa Dr ....Thomasville GA		31792	**800-290-6567**	229-584-5500
Pine Pointe Hospice & Palliative Care				
6261 Peak Rd ....Macon GA		31210	**800-211-1084**	478-633-5660

Illinois

			Toll-Free	Phone
Advocate Hospice				
1441 Branding Ave Ste 200 ....Downers Grove IL		60515	**800-564-2025**	630-963-6800
Carle Hospice 611 W Park St ....Urbana IL		61801	**800-239-3620**	217-383-3311
Covenant Care Home				
5700 Old Orchard Rd ....Skokie IL		60077	**877-708-7689**	
Harbor Light Hospice				
1 N 131 County Farm Rd ....Winfield IL		60190	**800-419-0542**	630-682-3871
Hospice of Kankakee Valley Inc				
482 Main St NW ....Bourbonnais IL		60914	**855-871-4695**	815-939-4141
Hospice of Lincolnland				
1000 Health Center Dr ....Mattoon IL		61938	**800-454-4055**	217-258-2525
Hospice of Southern Illinois				
305 S Illinois St ....Belleville IL		62220	**800-233-1708**	618-235-1703
Joliet Area Community Hospice				
250 Water Stone Cir ....Joliet IL		60431	**800-360-1817**	815-740-4104
OSF Hospice				
2265 W Altorfer Dr ....Peoria IL		61615	**800-673-5288**	
Unity Hospice				
700 S Clinton St Ste 210 ....Chicago IL		60607	**888-949-1188**	312-427-6000

Indiana

			Toll-Free	Phone
Center for Hospice Care Inc				
111 Sunnybrook Ct ....South Bend IN		46637	**800-413-9083**	574-243-3100

Iowa

	Toll-Free	Phone
Cedar Valley Hospice 2101 Kimball Ave Ste 401 ....Waterloo IA 50702	800-617-1972	319-272-2002
Hospice of Siouxland 4300 Hamilton Blvd ....Sioux City IA 51104	800-383-4545	712-233-4144
Mercy Medical Center North Iowa 1000 Fourth St SW ....Mason City IA 50401	800-297-4719	641-428-7000

Kansas

	Toll-Free	Phone
Harry Hynes Memorial Hospice 313 S Market St ....Wichita KS 67202	800-767-4965	316-265-9441
Midland Hospice Care 200 SW Frazier Cir ....Topeka KS 66606	800-491-3691	785-232-2044

Kentucky

	Toll-Free	Phone
Bluegrass Care Navigators 2312 Alexandria Dr ....Lexington KY 40504	855-492-0812	
Community Hospice 1480 Carter Ave ....Ashland KY 41101	800-926-6184	606-329-1890
Heritage Hospice Inc 120 Enterprise Dr PO Box 1213 ....Danville KY 40423	800-203-6633	859-236-2425
Hospice of Lake Cumberland 100 Pkwy Dr ....Somerset KY 42503	800-937-9596	606-679-4389
Saint Anthony's Hospice 2410 S Green St ....Henderson KY 42420	866-380-2326	270-826-2326

Louisiana

	Toll-Free	Phone
CommCare Corp 601 Poydras St 2755 Pan American Life Ctr ....New Orleans LA 70130	877-792-5434	504-324-8950

Maryland

	Toll-Free	Phone
Carroll Hospice 292 Stoner Ave ....Westminster MD 21157	800-966-3877	410-871-8000
Coastal Hospice & Palliative Care 2604 Old Ocean City Rd PO Box 1733 ....Salisbury MD 21804	800-780-7886	410-742-8732
Gilchrist Center Baltimore 11311 McCormick Rd Ste 350 ....Hunt Valley MD 21301	888-823-8880	
Hospice of the Chesapeake John & Cathy Belcher Campus 90 Ritchie Hwy ....Pasadena MD 21122 *General	877-462-1101*	410-987-2003

Massachusetts

	Toll-Free	Phone
Baystate Visiting Nurse Association & Hospice 50 Maple St ....Springfield MA 01199	800-249-8298	413-794-6411
Community VNA 10 Emory St ....Attleboro MA 02703	800-220-0110	508-222-0118
Hospice & Palliative Care of Cape Cod Inc 765 Attucks Ln ....Hyannis MA 02601	800-642-2423	508-957-0200
Hospice of the North Shore 75 Sylvan St Ste B-102 ....Danvers MA 01923	888-283-1722	978-774-7566
Merrimack Valley Hospice 360 Merrimack St Bldg 9 ....Lawrence MA 01843	800-933-5593	
Old Colony Hospice 1 Credit Union Way ....Randolph MA 02368	800-370-1322	781-341-4145

Michigan

	Toll-Free	Phone
Angela Hospice Home Care 14100 Newburgh Rd ....Livonia MI 48154 *General	866-464-7810*	734-464-7810
Arbor Hospice & Home Care 2366 Oak Vly Dr ....Ann Arbor MI 48103	888-992-2273	734-662-5999
Henry Ford Health System 1 Ford Pl ....Detroit MI 48202	800-436-7936	
Department of Food and Nutrition Services 2799 W Grand Blvd ....Detroit MI 48202	800-436-7936	313-916-1071
Hospice at Home 4025 Health Pk Ln ....Saint Joseph MI 49085	800-717-3811	269-429-7100
Hospice of Holland Inc 270 Hoover Blvd ....Holland MI 49423	800-255-3522	616-396-2972
Hospice of Michigan 400 Mack Ave ....Detroit MI 48201	888-247-5701	313-578-6259
MidMichigan Home Care 3007 N Saginaw Rd ....Midland MI 48640	800-852-9350	989-633-1400
Munson Healthcare 1105 Sixth St ....Traverse City MI 49684	800-468-6766	231-935-5000

Minnesota

	Toll-Free	Phone
Fairview Hospice 2450 26th Ave S ....Minneapolis MN 55406	800-285-5647	612-728-2455
Health Partners 8170 33rd Ave S ....Minneapolis MN 55425	800-247-7015	952-883-6877

Mississippi

	Toll-Free	Phone
Hospice Ministries 450 Towne Center Blvd ....Ridgeland MS 39157	800-273-7724	601-898-1053
Mid-Delta Health Systems Inc 405 N Hayden St ....Belzoni MS 39038	800-543-9055	662-247-2418

Missouri

	Toll-Free	Phone
Heartland Hands-Hope Hospice 137 N Belt Hwy ....Saint Joseph MO 64506	800-443-1143	816-271-7190
Odyssey Healthcare of Kansas City 4911 S Arrowhead Dr ....Independence MO 64055	800-944-4357	816-795-1333
Saint Luke's Home Care & Hospice 3100 Broadway St Ste 1000 ....Kansas City MO 64111	888-303-7576	816-756-1160
Visiting Nurse Assocation of Greater St Louis *Hospice Care* 2029 Woodland Pkwy Ste 105 ....Maryland Heights MO 63146	800-392-4740	314-918-7171
VNA Hospice Care (VNA) 2029 Woodland Pkwy Ste 105 ....Maryland Heights MO 63146	800-392-4740	314-918-7171

Nebraska

	Toll-Free	Phone
Visiting Nurse Assn 12565 W Ctr Rd Ste 100 ....Omaha NE 68144	800-456-8869	402-342-5566

New Hampshire

	Toll-Free	Phone
Concord Regional Visiting Nurse Assoc Hospice Program 30 Pillsbury St ....Concord NH 03301	800-924-8620	603-224-4093
Home Health & Hospice Care 7 Executive Park Dr ....Merrimack NH 03054	800-887-5973	603-882-2941

New Jersey

	Toll-Free	Phone
Karen Ann Quinlan Hospice 99 Sparta Ave ....Newton NJ 07860	800-882-1117	973-383-0115
Lighthouse Hospice 1040 Kings Hwy N Ste 100 ....Cherry Hill NJ 08034 *General	888-467-7423*	856-414-1155
Samaritan Hospice 5 Eves Dr Ste 300 ....Marlton NJ 08053	800-229-8183	856-596-1600
South Jersey Healthcare HospiceCare 2848 S Delsea Dr Bldg 1 ....Vineland NJ 08360	800-770-7547	
VNA of Central Jersey (VNACJ) 176 Riverside Ave ....Red Bank NJ 07701	800-862-3330	

New York

	Toll-Free	Phone
HomeCare & Hospice 1225 W State St ....Olean NY 14760	800-339-7011	716-372-5735
Hospice Care Inc 4277 Middle Settlement Rd ....New Hartford NY 13413	800-317-5661	315-735-6484
Hospice Care Network 99 Sunnyside Blvd ....Woodbury NY 11797	800-405-6731	516-832-7100
Hospice Family Care 550 E Main St ....Batavia NY 14020	800-719-7129	585-343-7596
Hospice of Orange & Sullivan Counties 800 Stony Brook Ct ....Newburgh NY 12550	800-924-0157	845-561-6111
Hospice of Westchester 1025 Westchester Ave Ste 200 ....White Plains NY 10604	800-860-9808	914-682-1484

North Carolina

	Toll-Free	Phone
CarePartners Mountain Area Hospice PO Box 5779 ....Asheville NC 28813	800-627-1533	828-255-0231
Four Seasons Hospice & Palliative Care 571 S Allen Rd ....Flat Rock NC 28731	866-466-9734	828-692-6178
Hospice & Palliative Care Center of Alamance-Caswell 914 Chapel Hill Rd ....Burlington NC 27215	800-588-8879	336-532-0100
Hospice & Palliative CareCenter 101 Hospice Ln ....Winston-Salem NC 27103	888-876-3663	336-768-3972
Hospice at Charlotte 1420 E Seventh St ....Charlotte NC 28204	800-835-5306	704-375-0100
Hospice of Stanly County 960 N First St ....Albemarle NC 28001	800-230-4236	704-983-4216
Hospice of the Carolina Foothills 374 Hudlow Rd PO Box 336 ....Forest City NC 28043	800-218-2273	828-245-0095
Hospice of Wake County Inc 250 Hospice Cir ....Raleigh NC 27607	888-900-3959	919-828-0890
Kitty Askins Hospice Ctr 107 Handley Pk Ct ....Goldsboro NC 27534	800-692-4442	919-735-2145
Lower Cape Fear Hospice & Life Care 1414 Physicians Dr ....Wilmington NC 28401	800-733-1476	910-796-7900

North Dakota

	Toll-Free	Phone
Hospice of the Red River Valley 1701 38th ST S Ste 101 ....Fargo ND 58103	800-237-4629	

Ohio

	Toll-Free	Phone
Bridge Home Health & Hospice 15100 Birchaven Ln ....Findlay OH 45840	800-982-3306	419-423-5351
FairHope Hospice & Palliative Care Inc 282 Sells Rd ....Lancaster OH 43130	800-994-7077	740-654-7077
Heartland Hospice Services 333 N Summit St ....Toledo OH 43604	800-366-1232	419-252-5500
Hospice of Central Ohio 2269 Cherry Valley Rd ....Newark OH 43055	800-804-2505	740-788-1400
Hospice of Dayton 324 Wilmington Ave ....Dayton OH 45420	800-653-4490	937-256-4490
Hospice of Medina County 5075 Windfall Rd ....Medina OH 44256	800-700-4771	330-722-4771

				Toll-Free	Phone
Hospice of North Central Ohio 1050 Dauch Dr	Ashland	OH	44805	**800-952-2207**	419-281-7107
Hospice of Northwest Ohio 30000 E River Rd	Perrysburg	OH	43551	**866-661-4001**	419-661-4001
Hospice of the Cleveland Clinic 6801 Brecksville Rd	Independence	OH	44131	**866-223-8100**	800-223-2273
Hospice of the Western Reserve 300 E 185th St	Cleveland	OH	44119	**800-707-8922**	216-383-2222
Hospice of Visiting Nurse Service 3358 Ridgewood Rd	Akron	OH	44333	**800-335-1455**	330-665-1455
Quaker Heights Nursing Home Inc 514 High St	Waynesville	OH	45068	**800-319-1317**	513-897-6050
State of the Heart Hospice 1350 N Broadway	Greenville	OH	45331	**800-417-7535**	937-548-2999
Stein Hospice 1200 Sycamore Line	Sandusky	OH	44870	**800-625-5269**	419-625-5269
Valley Hospice Inc 380 Summit Ave	Steubenville	OH	43952	**877-467-7423**	740-859-5660
Visiting Nurse Assn of Ohio 2500 E 22nd St	Cleveland	OH	44115	**877-698-6264**	216-931-1300

Oklahoma

				Toll-Free	Phone
Grace Hospice 6400 S Lewis Ave Ste 1000	Tulsa	OK	74136	**800-659-0307**	918-744-7223

Oregon

				Toll-Free	Phone
Willamette Valley Hospice 1015 Third St NW	Salem	OR	97304	**800-555-2431**	503-588-3600

Pennsylvania

				Toll-Free	Phone
Berks VNA 1170 Berkshire Blvd	Wyomissing	PA	19610	**855-843-8627**	
Celtic Healthcare 150 Scharberry Ln	Mars	PA	16046	**800-355-8894**	
Chandler Hall Hospice 99 Barclay St	Newtown	PA	18940	**888-603-1973**	215-860-4000
Compassionate Care Hospice 3331 St Rd Ste 410	Bensalem	PA	19020	**800-584-8165**	215-245-3525
Family Hospice & Palliative Care 50 Moffett St	Pittsburgh	PA	15243	**800-513-2148**	412-572-8800
Forbes Hospice 4800 Friendship Ave	Pittsburgh	PA	15224	**800-381-8080**	412-578-5000
Holy Redeemer Home Care & Hospice 12265 Townsend Rd Ste 400	Philadelphia	PA	19154	**888-678-8678**	
Hospice of Central Pennsylvania 1320 Linglestown Rd	Harrisburg	PA	17110	**866-779-7374**	717-732-1000
Hospice of Lancaster County 685 Good Dr PO Box 4125	Lancaster	PA	17604	**888-236-9563**	717-295-3900
Lehigh Valley Hospice (LVHN) 3080 Hamilton Blvd Ste 250	Allentown	PA	18103	**888-402-5846**	
St John Diakon Hospice 1201 N Church St	Hazleton	PA	18202	**877-666-5784**	
VNA 154 Hindman Rd	Butler	PA	16001	**877-862-6659**	724-282-6806
VNA Hospice & Home Health of Lackawanna County 301 Delaware Ave	Olyphant	PA	18447	**800-936-7671**	570-383-5180

South Carolina

				Toll-Free	Phone
Hospice Community Care PO Box 993	Rock Hill	SC	29731	**800-895-2273**	803-329-1500
McLeod Hospice 1203 E Cheves St	Florence	SC	29506	**800-768-4556**	843-777-2564
Open Arms Hospice 1836 W Georgia Rd	Simpsonville	SC	29680	**866-473-6276**	864-688-1700
Palmetto Health 1400 Pickens St	Columbia	SC	29202	**800-238-1884**	803-296-3100

Tennessee

				Toll-Free	Phone
Alive Hospice Inc 1718 Patterson St	Nashville	TN	37203	**800-327-1085**	615-327-1085
Amedisys 209 Tenth Ave S Ste 512	Nashville	TN	37203	**800-464-0020**	423-587-9484
Hospice of Chattanooga 4411 Oakwood Dr	Chattanooga	TN	37416	**800-267-6828**	423-892-4289
Methodist Alliance Hospice 6400 Shelby View Dr Ste 101	Memphis	TN	38134	**800-541-8277**	901-516-1999

Texas

				Toll-Free	Phone
Community Hospice of Texas 6100 Western Pl Ste 105	Fort Worth	TX	76107	**800-226-0373**	
Daybreak Venture LLC 401 N Elm St	Denton	TX	76201	**800-345-5603**	940-387-4388
Hendrick Hospice Care 1682 Hickory St	Abilene	TX	79601	**800-622-8516**	325-677-8516
Home Hospice of Grayson County 505 W Ctr St	Sherman	TX	75090	**888-233-7455**	903-868-9315
Hope Hospice 611 N Walnut Ave	New Braunfels	TX	78130	**800-499-7501**	830-625-7500
Hospice Austin 4107 Spicewood Springs Rd Ste 100	Austin	TX	78759	**800-445-3261**	512-342-4700
Hospice Brazos Valley 502 W 26th St	Bryan	TX	77803	**800-824-2326**	979-821-2266
Hospice of East Texas 4111 University Blvd	Tyler	TX	75701	**800-777-9860**	903-266-3400
Hospice of San Angelo 36 E Twohig St PO Box 471	San Angelo	TX	76903	**800-499-6524**	325-658-6524

				Toll-Free	Phone
Hospice of South Texas 605 E Locust Ave	Victoria	TX	77901	**800-874-6908**	361-572-4300
Hospice of Wichita Falls 4909 Johnson Rd	Wichita Falls	TX	76310	**800-378-2822**	940-691-0982
Lubbock Regional Mental Health Mental Retardation Center 1602 Tenth St PO Box 2828	Lubbock	TX	79408	**800-687-7581**	806-766-0310

Virginia

				Toll-Free	Phone
Capital Hospice Inc 2900 Telestar Ct	Falls Church	VA	22042	**855-571-5700**	703-538-2065
Hospice of the Piedmont 675 Peter Jefferson Pkwy Ste 300	Charlottesville	VA	22911	**800-975-5501**	434-817-6900
Mary Washington Hospice 5012 Southpoint Pkwy	Fredericksburg	VA	22407	**800-257-1667**	540-741-1667

Washington

				Toll-Free	Phone
Harbors Home Health & Hospice 201 Seventh St	Hoquiam	WA	98550	**800-772-1319**	360-532-5454
Providence Hospice of Seattle 2811 S 102nd St Ste 200	Tukwila	WA	98168	**888-782-4445**	206-320-4000
Providence Sound Home Care & Hospice 4200 Sixth Ave SE Ste 201	Lacey	WA	98503	**800-869-7062**	

West Virginia

				Toll-Free	Phone
Hospice of Huntington 1101 Sixth Ave	Huntington	WV	25701	**800-788-5480**	304-529-4217
Hospice of the Panhandle 330 Hospice Ln	Kearneysville	WV	25430	**800-345-6538**	304-264-0406
Kanawha Hospice Care 1606 Kanawha Blvd W	Charleston	WV	25387	**800-560-8523**	304-768-8523

Wisconsin

				Toll-Free	Phone
Beloit Regional Hospice 655 Third St Ste 200	Beloit	WI	53511	**877-363-7421**	608-363-7421
Gundersen Lutheran at Home HomeCare & Hospice 914 Green Bay St *General	La Crosse	WI	54601	**800-362-9567***	608-775-8435
Hospice Alliance 10220 Prairie Ridge Blvd	Pleasant Prairie	WI	53158	**800-830-8344**	262-652-4400
HospiceCare 5395 E Cheryl Pkwy	Madison	WI	53711	**800-553-4289**	608-276-4660
Theda Care at Home 3000 E College Ave	Appleton	WI	54915	**800-984-5554**	920-969-0919
Unity Hospice 2366 Oak Ridge Cir	De Pere	WI	54115	**800-990-9249**	920-338-1111
VITAS Healthcare Corp of California 2675 N Mayfair Rd Ste 500	Wauwatosa	WI	53226	**866-418-4827**	414-257-2600

371   HOSPITAL HOSPITALITY HOUSES

				Toll-Free	Phone
American Cancer Society Hope Lodge of Buffalo 250 Williams St NW	Atlanta	GA	30303	**800-227-2345**	
American Cancer Society Hope Lodge of Charleston 269 Calhoun St	Charleston	SC	29401	**800-227-2345**	843-958-0930
American Cancer Society Joe Lee Griffin Hope Lodge 1104 Ireland Way	Birmingham	AL	35205	**800-227-2345**	205-558-7860
American Cancer Society Winn-Dixie Hope Lodge 250 Williams St NW	Atlanta	GA	30303	**800-227-2345**	404-327-9200
Bannister Family House 406 Dickinson St	San Diego	CA	92103	**800-926-8273**	619-543-7977
Beacon House 1301 N Third St	Marquette	MI	49855	**800-562-9753**	906-225-7100
Casa Esperanza 1005 Yale NE	Albuquerque	NM	87106	**866-654-1338**	505-246-2700
Conine Clubhouse 1005 Joe DiMaggio Dr	Hollywood	FL	33021	**866-532-4362**	954-265-5324
Cynthia C & William E. Perry Pavilion 9400 Turkey Lake Rd	Orlando	FL	32819	**800-447-1435**	321-842-8844
Gift of Life Transplant House 705 Second St SW	Rochester	MN	55902	**800-479-7824**	507-288-7470
Inn at Virginia Mason 1006 Spring St	Seattle	WA	98104	**800-283-6453**	
Mario Pastega Guest House 3505 NW Samaritan Dr	Corvallis	OR	97330	**800-863-5241**	541-768-4650
Nebraska House 983285 Nebraska Medical Ctr	Omaha	NE	68198	**800-401-4444**	402-559-5000
Rosenbaum Family House 30 Family House Dr PO Box 8228	Morgantown	WV	26506	**855-988-2273**	304-598-6094
Zachary & Elizabeth Fisher House 111 Rockville Pk Ste 420	Rockville	MD	20850	**888-294-8560**	

372   HOSPITAL HOSPITALITY HOUSES - RONALD MCDONALD HOUSE

				Toll-Free	Phone
Ronald McDonald House *Akron* 245 Locust St	Akron	OH	44302	**800-262-0333**	330-253-5400
Albany 139 S Lake Ave	Albany	NY	12208	**866-244-8464**	518-438-2655
Albuquerque 1011 Yale Ave NE	Albuquerque	NM	87106	**877-842-8960**	505-842-8960
Ann Arbor 1600 Washington Hts	Ann Arbor	MI	48104	**800-544-8684**	734-994-4442
Las Vegas 2323 Potosi St	Las Vegas	NV	89146	**888-248-1561**	702-252-4663
Phoenix 501 E Roanoke Ave	Phoenix	AZ	85004	**877-333-2978**	602-264-2654
Seattle 5130 40th Ave NE	Seattle	WA	98105	**866-987-9330**	206-838-0600

Classified Section

			Toll-Free	Phone

Wilmington
1901 Rockland Rd ....Wilmington DE 19803 **888-656-4847** 302-656-4847
Winston-Salem
419 S Hawthorne Rd ....Winston-Salem NC 27103 **855-227-7435** 336-723-0228
Ronald McDonald House Charities?
110 N Carpenter St ....Chicago IL 60607 **888-236-6167** 630-623-7048

373   HOSPITALS

SEE ALSO Veterans Nursing Homes - State ; Health Care Systems ; Hospices ; Health Care Providers - Ancillary

	Toll-Free	Phone

HOSPITALS - DEVELOPMENTAL DISABILITIES

373-1 Children's Hospitals

			Toll-Free	Phone

Children's Healthcare of Atlanta at Egleston
1405 Clifton Rd NE ....Atlanta GA 30322 **888-785-7778** 404-785-6000
Children's Healthcare of Atlanta at Scottish Rite
1001 Johnson Ferry Rd NE ....Atlanta GA 30342 **888-785-7778** 404-785-5252
Children's Hospital
200 Henry Clay Ave ....New Orleans LA 70118 **800-299-9511** 504-899-9511
Children's Hospital Boston
300 Longwood Ave ....Boston MA 02115 **800-355-7944** 617-355-6000
Children's Hospital Medical Ctr of Akron
1 Perkins Sq ....Akron OH 44308 **800-262-0333** 330-543-1000
Children's Hospital of Alabama
1600 Seventh Ave S ....Birmingham AL 35233 **800-504-9768** 205-939-9100
Children's Hospital of the King's Daughters
601 Children's Ln ....Norfolk VA 23507 **800-395-2453** 757-668-7000
Children's Hospital of Wisconsin
9000 W Wisconsin Ave ....Milwaukee WI 53226 **800-266-0366** 414-266-2000
Children's Hospitals & Clinics Minneapolis
2525 Chicago Ave ....Minneapolis MN 55404 **866-225-3251** 612-813-6000
Children's Institute of Pittsburgh
1405 Shady Ave ....Pittsburgh PA 15217 **877-433-1109** 412-420-2400
Children's Medical Ctr
1 Children's Plz ....Dayton OH 45404 **800-228-4055** 937-641-3000
Children's Mercy Hospital & Clinics
2401 Gillham Rd ....Kansas City MO 64108 **866-512-2168** 816-234-3000
Children's National Medical Ctr (CNMC)
111 Michigan Ave NW ....Washington DC 20010 **800-884-5433** 202-476-5000
Children's Specialized Hospital
150 New Providence Rd ....Mountainside NJ 07092 **888-244-5373**
Cincinnati Children's Hospital Medical Ctr
3333 Burnet Ave ....Cincinnati OH 45229 **800-344-2462** 513-636-4200
Copper Hills Youth Ctr
5899 Rivendell Dr ....West Jordan UT 84081 **800-776-7116**
CS Mott Children's Hospital
1500 E Medical Ctr Dr ....Ann Arbor MI 48109 **800-211-8181** 734-936-4000
Devereux
1291 Stanley Rd NW PO Box 1688..........Kennesaw GA 30156 **800-342-3357** 678-303-5233
Devereux Advanced Behavioral Health
8000 Devereux Dr ....Viera FL 32940 **800-338-3738** 321-242-9100
Devereux Cleo Wallace
8405 Church Ranch Blvd ....Westminster CO 80021 **800-456-2536** 303-466-7391
Driscoll Children's Hospital
3533 S Alameda St ....Corpus Christi TX 78411 **800-324-5683** 361-694-5000
Gillette Children's Specialty Healthcare
200 E University Ave ....Saint Paul MN 55101 **800-719-4040** 651-291-2848
Gulf Coast Treatment Ctr
1015 Mar-Walt Dr ....Fort Walton Beach FL 32547 **800-537-5433** 850-863-4160
HSC Pediatric Ctr
1731 Bunker Hill Rd NE ....Washington DC 20017 **800-226-4444** 202-832-4400
JD McCarty Ctr for Children with Developmental Disabilities
2002 E Robinson St ....Norman OK 73071 **800-777-1272** 405-307-2800
Kennedy Krieger Institute
707 N Broadway ....Baltimore MD 21205 **800-873-3377** 443-923-9200
KidsPeace Orchard Hills Campus
5300 Kids Peace Dr ....Orefield PA 18069 **800-257-3223**
Lucile Packard Children's Hospital (LPCH)
725 Welch Rd ....Palo Alto CA 94304 **800-995-5724** 650-497-8000
Mary Bridge Children's Hospital & Health Ctr
317 Martin Luther King Jr Way ....Tacoma WA 98405 **800-552-1419** 253-403-1400
Miami Children's Hospital
3100 SW 62nd Ave ....Miami FL 33155 **800-432-6837** 305-666-6511
New York City Children's Ctr-Queens Campus (NYCCC)
74-03 Commonwealth Blvd ....Bellerose NY 11426 **800-597-8481** 718-264-4500
Phoenix Children's Hospital
1919 E Thomas Rd ....Phoenix AZ 85016 **888-908-5437** 602-546-1000
Rady Children's Hospital (RCH)
3020 Children's Way 3rd Fl. ....San Diego CA 92123 **800-788-9029** 858-576-1700
Saint Louis Children's Hospital
1 Children's Pl ....Saint Louis MO 63110 **800-427-4626** 314-454-6000
Seattle Children's Hospital
4800 Sand Pt Way NE ....Seattle WA 98105 **866-987-2000** 206-987-2000
Shriners Hospitals for Children
2900 N Rocky Point Dr ....Tampa FL 33607 **800-361-7256** 514-842-4464
Shriners Hospitals for Children Boston
51 Blossom St ....Boston MA 02114 **800-255-1916** 617-722-3000
Shriners Hospitals for Children Erie
1645 W Eigth St ....Erie PA 16505 **800-873-5437** 814-875-8700
Shriners Hospitals for Children Galveston
2900 Rocky Pt Dr ....Tampa FL 33607 **844-739-0849** 813-281-0300
Shriners Hospitals for Children Greenville
950 W Faris Rd ....Greenville SC 29605 **800-361-7256** 864-271-3444
Shriners Hospitals for Children Lexington
1900 Richmond Rd ....Lexington KY 40502 **800-668-4634** 859-266-2101
Shriners Hospitals for Children Los Angeles
3160 Geneva St ....Los Angeles CA 90020 **888-486-5437** 864-240-8155
Shriners Hospitals for Children Philadelphia
3551 N Broad St ....Philadelphia PA 19140 **800-281-4050** 215-430-4000

			Toll-Free	Phone

Shriners Hospitals for Children Salt Lake City
Fairfax Rd & Virginia St ....Salt Lake City UT 84103 **800-313-3745** 801-536-3500
Shriners Hospitals for Children Tampa
12502 N Pine Dr ....Tampa FL 33612 **800-237-5055** 813-972-2250
Streamwood Behavioral Health Ctr
1400 E Irving Pk Rd ....Streamwood IL 60107 **800-272-7790** 630-837-9000
Texas Children's Hospital
6621 Fannin St ....Houston TX 77030 **800-364-5437** 832-824-1000
Texas Scottish Rite Hospital for Children
2222 Welborn St ....Dallas TX 75219 **800-421-1121** 214-559-5000
Women's & Children's Hospital of Buffalo
219 Bryant St ....Buffalo NY 14222 **800-462-7653** 716-878-7000
Youth Villages Inner Harbour
4685 Dorsett Shoals Rd ....Douglasville GA 30135 **800-255-8657** 770-852-6300

373-2 General Hospitals - Canada

			Toll-Free	Phone

Belleville General Hospital
265 Dundas St E ....Belleville ON K8N5A9 **800-483-2811** 613-969-7400
British Columbia's Women's Hospital & Health Centre
4500 Oak St ....Vancouver BC V6H3N1 **888-300-3088** 604-875-2424
Brockville General Hospital
75 Charles St ....Brockville ON K6V1S8 **800-567-7415** 613-345-5645
Children's Hospital of Eastern Ontario
401 Smyth Rd ....Ottawa ON K1H8L1 **866-797-0007** 613-737-7600
CHU Sainte-Justine
3175 Ch de la Cote-Sainte-Catherine .....Montreal QC H3T1C5 **888-235-3667** 514-345-4931
Concordia Hospital
1095 Concordia Ave ....Winnipeg MB R2K3S8 **888-315-9257** 204-667-1560
Cornwall Community Hospital
840 McConnell Ave ....Cornwall ON K6H5S5 **866-263-1560** 613-938-4240
Eagle Ridge Hospital & Health Care Ctr
475 Guildford Way ....Port Moody BC V3H3W9 **800-465-4911** 604-461-2022
Foothills Medical Centre (FMC)
1403 29th St NW ....Calgary AB T2N2T9 **888-342-2471** 780-342-2000
Hamilton Health Sciences
1200 Main St W ....Hamilton ON L8N3Z5 **800-680-9868** 905-522-3863
High River Hospital
560 Ninth Ave W ....High River AB T1V1B3 **800-332-1414** 403-652-2200
Hotel Dieu Hospital
166 Brock St ....Kingston ON K/L5G2 **855-544-3400** 613-544-3310
Jeffrey Hale Saint Brigid's
1250 ch Sainte-Foy ....Quebec QC G1S2M6 **888-984-5333** 418-684-5333
Joseph Brant Memorial Hospital (JBMH)
1230 N Shore Blvd ....Burlington ON L7S1W7 **800-810-0000** 905-632-3737
Kelowna General Hospital (KGH)
2268 Pandosy St ....Kelowna BC V1Y1T2 **888-877-4442** 250-862-4000
Lacombe Hospital & Care Ctr
5430 47th Ave ....Lacombe AB T4L1G8 **800-291-2782** 403-782-3336
Lakeridge Health Oshawa
1 Hospital Ct ....Oshawa ON L1G2B9 **866-338-1778** 905-576-8711
Montfort Hospital
713 Montreal Rd ....Ottawa ON K1K0T2 **866-670-4621** 613-746-4621
Montreal Heart Institute
5000 Belanger St E ....Montreal QC H1T1C8 **855-922-6387** 514-376-3330
Pembroke Regional Hospital
705 MacKay St ....Pembroke ON K8A1G8 **866-996-0991** 613-732-2811
Peter Lougheed Ctr
3500 26th Ave NE ....Calgary AB T1Y6J4 **800-282-9911** 403-943-4555
Powell River General Hospital
5000 Joyce Ave ....Powell River BC V8A5R3 **800-567-8911** 604-485-3211
Quebec 41 Boul Comtois ....Louiseville QC J5V2H8 **888-693-3506** 819-228-2731
Ross Memorial Hospital (RMH)
10 Angeline St N ....Lindsay ON K9V4M8 **800-510-7365** 705-324-6111
Rouge Valley Ajax & Pickering
580 Harwood Ave S ....Ajax ON L1S2J4 **866-752-6989** 905-683-2320
Royal Alexandra Hospital
10240 Kingsway Ave ....Edmonton AB T5H3V9 **800-332-1414** 780-735-4111
Royal University Hospital
103 Hospital Dr ....Saskatoon SK S7N0W8 **800-458-1179** 306-655-1000
Saguenay-Lac-Saint-Jean Integrated Health & Social Services Ctr
930 Jacques-Cartier St E ....Chicoutimi QC G7H7K9 **800-370-4980** 418-545-4980
Saint Joseph's Healthcare Hamilton
50 Charlton Ave E ....Hamilton ON L8N4A6 **800-461-2156** 905-522-1155
Saint Joseph's Lifecare Ctr
99 Wayne Gretzky Pkwy ....Brantford ON N3S6T6 **888-699-7817** 519-751-7096
Saint Michael's Hospital
30 Bond St ....Toronto ON M5B1W8 **866-797-0000** 416-360-4000
Saskatoon City Hospital
701 Queen St ....Saskatoon SK S7K0M7 **855-655-7612** 306-655-8000
Southlake Regional Health Ctr
596 Davis Dr ....Newmarket ON L3Y2P9 **800-445-1822** 905-895-4521
Stratford General Hospital
46 General Hospital Dr ....Stratford ON N5A2Y6 **888-275-1102** 519-272-8210
Thunder Bay Regional Health Sciences Centre
980 Olvier Rd ....Thunder Bay ON P7B6V4 **800-465-5003** 807-684-6000
Timmins & District Hospital
700 Ross Ave E ....Timmins ON P4N8P2 **888-340-3003** 705-267-2131
Vernon Jubilee Hospital
2101 32nd St ....Vernon BC V1T5L2 **800-224-9376** 250-545-2211
West Coast General Hospital
3949 Port Alberni Hwy ....Port Alberni BC V9Y4S1 **800-317-7878** 250-731-1370
Yarmouth Regional Hospital (YRH)
60 Vancouver St ....Yarmouth NS B5A2P5 **800-460-2110** 902-742-3541

373-3 General Hospitals - US

Alabama

			Toll-Free	Phone

Baptist Medical Ctr South
2105 E S Blvd ....Montgomery AL 36116 **800-356-9596** 334-288-2100
Bryan W Whitfield Memorial Hospital
105 Hwy 80 E PO Box 890 ....Demopolis AL 36732 **800-453-2395** 334-289-4000

Classified Section

				Toll-Free	Phone

DCH Regional Medical Ctr
809 University Blvd E .... Tuscaloosa AL 35401 **800-356-9596** 205-759-7111
Northport Medical Ctr
2700 Hospital Dr .... Northport AL 35476 **866-840-0750** 205-333-4500
Quality of Life Health Services Inc
1411 Piedmont Cutoff .... Gadsden AL 35903 **888-490-0131** 256-492-0131
Saint Vincent's Hospital
810 St Vincent's Dr .... Birmingham AL 35205 **800-965-7231** 205-939-7000
Thomas Hospital
750 Morphy Ave .... Fairhope AL 36532 **800-422-2027** 251-928-2375

Alaska

				Toll-Free	Phone

Alaska Native Medical Ctr (ANMC)
4315 Diplomacy Dr .... Anchorage AK 99508 **800-478-6661*** 907-563-2662
*Admitting

Arizona

				Toll-Free	Phone

Banner Del E Webb Memorial Hospital
14502 W Meeker Blvd .... Sun City West AZ 85375 **800-254-4357** 623-214-4000
HonorHealth John C Lincoln Medical Center
250 E Dunlap Ave .... Phoenix AZ 85020 **800-223-3131** 623-580-5800
Kingman Regional Medical Ctr (KRMC)
3269 Stockton Hill Rd .... Kingman AZ 86409 **877-757-2101** 928-757-2101
Maricopa Medical Ctr
2601 E Roosevelt St .... Phoenix AZ 85008 **866-749-2876** 602-344-5011
Mayo Clinic Hospital
5777 E Mayo Blvd .... Phoenix AZ 85054 **888-266-0440** 480-342-2000
Saint Luke's Medical Ctr
1800 E Van Buren St .... Phoenix AZ 85006 **800-446-2279** 602-251-8100
Steward Health Care (TSLH)
Tempe Saint Luke's Hospital
1500 S Mill Ave .... Tempe AZ 85281 **877-351-9355** 480-784-5500
Tucson Medical Ctr
5301 E Grant Rd .... Tucson AZ 85712 **800-526-5353** 520-327-5461
Yavapai Regional Medical Ctr
1003 Willow Creek Rd .... Prescott AZ 86301 **877-843-9762** 928-445-2700

Arkansas

				Toll-Free	Phone

Medical Ctr of South Arkansas
700 W Grove St .... El Dorado AR 71730 **800-285-1131** 870-863-2000
Northwest Medical Ctr
609 W Maple Ave .... Springdale AR 72764 **800-734-2024** 479-751-5711
Ouachita County Medical Ctr (OCMC)
PO Box 797 .... Camden AR 71711 **877-836-2472** 870-836-1000
Sparks Regional Medical Ctr (SRMC)
1001 Towson Ave .... Fort Smith AR 72901 **800-285-1131** 479-441-4000
UAMS Medical Ctr
4301 W Markham St .... Little Rock AR 72205 **877-467-6560** 501-686-7000

California

				Toll-Free	Phone

Adventist Health Lodi Memorial
975 S Fairmont Ave .... Lodi CA 95240 **800-323-3360** 209-334-3411
Alvarado Hospital Medical Ctr
6655 Alvarado Rd .... San Diego CA 92120 **800-258-2723** 619-287-3270
Arrowhead Regional Medical Ctr
400 N Pepper Ave .... Colton CA 92324 **855-422-8029** 909-580-1000
Beverly Hospital
309 W Beverly Blvd .... Montebello CA 90640 **800-618-6664** 323-726-1222
Cedars-Sinai Medical Ctr (CSMC)
8700 Beverly Blvd .... Los Angeles CA 90048 **800-233-2771** 310-423-3277
CHA Hollywood Presbyterian Medical Center
1300 N Vermont Ave .... Los Angeles CA 90027 **800-465-3203** 213-413-3000
Community Hospital of the Monterey Peninsula (CHOMP)
23625 Holman Hwy .... Monterey CA 93940 **888-452-4667** 831-624-5311
Community Regional Medical Ctr
2823 Fresno St .... Fresno CA 93721 **800-994-6610** 559-459-6000
Contra Costa Health Services
2500 Alhambra Ave .... Martinez CA 94553 **877-661-6230** 925-370-5000
Dominican Hospital (DH)
1555 Soquel Dr .... Santa Cruz CA 95065 **866-466-1401** 831-462-7700
Downey Regional Medical Ctr
11500 Brookshire Ave .... Downey CA 90241 **800-954-8000** 562-904-5000
Enloe Medical Ctr
1531 Esplanade .... Chico CA 95926 **800-822-8102** 530-332-7300
Fountain Valley Regional Hospital & Medical Ctr
17100 Euclid St .... Fountain Valley CA 92708 **866-904-6871** 714-966-7200
Good Samaritan Hospital
2425 Samaritan Dr .... San Jose CA 95124 **800-307-7631** 408-559-2011
Hoag Hospital Irvine (HHI)
16200 Sand Canyon Ave .... Irvine CA 92618 **800-309-9729** 949-764-4624
John Muir Medical Ctr (JMMC)
1601 Ygnacio Valley Rd .... Walnut Creek CA 94598 **844-398-5376** 925-939-3000
Kaiser Permanente
6041 Cadillac Ave .... Los Angeles CA 90034 **800-954-8000**
Kaiser Permanente Bellflower Medical Offices
9400 E Rosecrans Ave .... Bellflower CA 90706 **800-823-4040**
Kaiser Permanente Harbor City Medical Ctr
25825 S Vermont Ave .... Harbor City CA 90710 **800-464-4000** 310-325-5111
Kaiser Permanente Hospital
441 N Lakeview Ave .... Anaheim CA 92807 **800-464-4000** 714-279-4000
Kaiser Permanente Medical Center-South Sacramento
6600 Bruceville Rd .... Sacramento CA 95823 **800-464-4000** 916-688-2000
Kaiser Permanente Medical Ctr
710 Lawrence Expy .... Santa Clara CA 95051 **800-464-4000** 408-851-1000
Kaiser Permanente Medical Ctr
1200 El Camino Real .... South San Francisco CA 94080 **800-464-4000** 650-742-2000
Kaiser Permanente Medical Ctr San Francisco
2425 Geary Blvd .... San Francisco CA 94115 **800-464-4000** 415-833-2000

Kaiser Permanente Riverside Medical Ctr
10800 Magnolia Ave .... Riverside CA 92505 **800-464-4000*** 951-353-2000
*Cust Svc
Kaiser Permanente Walnut Creek Medical Ctr
1425 S Main St .... Walnut Creek CA 94596 **800-464-4000** 925-295-4000
Loma Linda University Medical Ctr
11234 Anderson St .... Loma Linda CA 92354 **877-558-6248** 909-558-4000
Marin General Hospital
250 Bon Air Rd .... Greenbrae CA 94904 **888-996-9644** 415-925-7000
Marina Del Rey Hospital
4650 Lincoln Blvd .... Marina del Rey CA 90292 **888-600-5600** 310-823-8911
Memorial Medical Ctr (MMC)
1700 Coffee Rd .... Modesto CA 95355 **800-477-2258** 209-526-4500
Mercy San Juan Medical Ctr
6501 Coyle Ave .... Carmichael CA 95608 **855-409-5280** 916-537-5000
Methodist Hospital of Sacramento
7500 Hospital Dr .... Sacramento CA 95823 **855-361-4103** 916-423-3000
Methodist Hospital of Southern California
300 W Huntington Dr .... Arcadia CA 91007 **888-388-2838** 626-898-8000
Northeast Valley Health Corp
1172 N Maclay Ave .... San Fernando CA 91340 **800-313-4942** 818-898-1388
Orange Coast Memorial Medical Ctr (OCMMC)
9920 Talbert Ave .... Fountain Valley CA 92708 **877-597-4777** 714-378-7000
Peninsula Hospital
1501 Trousdale Dr .... Burlingame CA 94010 **800-559-9960** 650-696-5400
Providence Saint Joseph Medical Ctr
501 S Buena Vista St .... Burbank CA 91505 **800-750-7703** 818-843-5111
Redlands Community Hospital Foundation
PO Box 3391 .... Redlands CA 92373 **888-397-4999** 909-335-5500
Regional Medical Ctr of San Jose (RMCSJ)
225 N Jackson Ave .... San Jose CA 95116 **800-307-7135** 408-259-5000
Rideout Memorial Hospital
726 Fourth St .... Marysville CA 95901 **888-923-3800** 530-749-4300
Roseville Medical Ctr
1 Medical Plz .... Roseville CA 95661 **800-866-7724** 916-781-1000
Saddleback Memorial Medical Ctr
24451 Health Ctr Dr .... Laguna Hills CA 92653 **800-553-6537** 949-837-4500
Saint Jude Medical Ctr
101 E Valencia Mesa Dr .... Fullerton CA 92835 **800-378-4189** 714-871-3280
San Gabriel Valley Medical Ctr
438 W Las Tunas Dr .... San Gabriel CA 91776 **888-214-3874** 626-289-5454
Santa Clara Valley Medical Ctr
751 S Bascom Ave .... San Jose CA 95128 **800-814-4351** 408-885-5000
Scripps Green Hospital
9898 Genesee Ave .... La Jolla CA 92037 **800-727-4777** 858-554-9100
Scripps Memorial Hospital-La Jolla
9888 Genesee Ave .... La Jolla CA 92037 **800-727-4777**
Scripps Mercy Hospital
4077 Fifth Ave .... San Diego CA 92103 **800-727-4777** 619-294-8111
Seton Medical Ctr
1900 Sullivan Ave .... Daly City CA 94015 **833-427-7436** 650-992-4000
Sonora Regional Medical Ctr (SRMC)
1000 Greenly Rd .... Sonora CA 95370 **877-336-3566*** 209-536-5000
*Compliance
Summit Medical Ctr
350 Hawthorne Ave .... Oakland CA 94609 **800-478-8837** 510-655-4000
Sutter Auburn Faith Community Hospital (SAFH)
11815 Education St .... Auburn CA 95602 **800-478-8837** 530-888-4500
Sutter General Hospital
2801 L St .... Sacramento CA 95816 **800-478-8837** 916-454-2222
Sutter Medical Ctr of Santa Rosa
3325 Chanate Rd .... Santa Rosa CA 95404 **800-651-5111** 707-576-4006
Sutter Memorial Hospital
5151 F St .... Sacramento CA 95819 **800-478-8837** 916-454-3333
Sutter Solano Medical Ctr (SSMC)
300 Hospital Dr .... Vallejo CA 94589 **800-866-7724** 707-554-4444
Torrance Memorial Medical Ctr
3330 Lomita Blvd .... Torrance CA 90505 **800-551-1300** 310-325-9110
UC Irvine Healthcare
101 the City Dr S .... Orange CA 92868 **877-824-3627** 714-456-7890
Ventura County Medical Ctr
3291 Loma Vista Rd .... Ventura CA 93003 **888-285-5012** 805-652-6000
White Memorial Medical Ctr
1720 Cesar E Chavez Ave .... Los Angeles CA 90033 **800-806-0993** 323-268-5000
Whittier Hospital Medical Ctr
9080 Colima Rd .... Whittier CA 90605 **800-613-4291** 562-945-3561
Woodland Healthcare
1325 Cottonwood St .... Woodland CA 95695 **844-274-8497**

Colorado

				Toll-Free	Phone

Littleton Adventist Hospital
7700 S Broadway .... Littleton CO 80122 **800-390-4166** 303-730-8900
Mercy Regional Medical Center
1010 Third Springs Blvd .... Durango CO 81301 **800-345-2516** 970-247-4311
North Suburban Medical Ctr (NSMC)
9191 Grant St .... Thornton CO 80229 **877-647-7440** 303-451-7800
Parkview Medical Ctr
400 W 16th St .... Pueblo CO 81003 **800-543-4046** 719-584-4000
Penrose Hospital
2222 N Nevada Ave .... Colorado Springs CO 80907 **800-398-2045** 719-776-5000
Rose Medical Ctr
4567 E Ninth Ave .... Denver CO 80220 **877-647-7440** 303-320-2121
Saint Mary-Corwin Medical Ctr
1008 Minnequa Ave .... Pueblo CO 81004 **800-228-4039** 719-557-4000
Swedish Medical Ctr
501 E Hampden Ave .... Englewood CO 80113 **866-779-3347** 303-788-5000

Connecticut

				Toll-Free	Phone

Bridgeport Hospital
267 Grant St .... Bridgeport CT 06610 **800-688-4954** 203-384-3000
Danbury Hospital (DH)
24 Hospital Ave .... Danbury CT 06810 **800-516-3658** 203-739-7000
Greenwich Hospital
5 Perryridge Rd .... Greenwich CT 06830 **800-657-8355** 203-863-3000

				Toll-Free	Phone
Hartford Hospital					
80 Seymour St	Hartford	CT	06102	**800-545-7664**	860-545-5000
Hospital of Saint Raphael					
1450 Chapel St	New Haven	CT	06511	**888-700-6543**	203-789-3000
Lawrence & Memorial Hospital					
365 Montauk Ave	New London	CT	06320	**800-579-3341**	860-442-0711
Middlesex Hospital					
28 Crescent St	Middletown	CT	06457	**800-548-2394**	860-358-6000
Saint Francis Hospital & Medical Ctr					
114 Woodland St	Hartford	CT	06105	**800-993-4312**	860-714-4000
Saint Vincent's Medical Ctr					
2800 Main St	Bridgeport	CT	06606	**877-255-7847**	203-576-6000
University of Connecticut Health Ctr					
John Dempsey Hospital					
263 Farmington Ave	Farmington	CT	06030	**800-535-6232**	860-679-2000

Delaware

				Toll-Free	Phone
Bayhealth Medical Ctr					
21 W Clarke Ave	Milford	DE	19963	**877-453-7107**	302-422-3311
Kent General Hospital					
640 S State St	Dover	DE	19901	**888-761-8300**	302-674-4700

District of Columbia

				Toll-Free	Phone
George Washington University Hospital					
900 23rd St NW	Washington	DC	20037	**888-449-3627**	202-715-4000
Washington Hospital Ctr					
110 Irving St NW	Washington	DC	20010	**855-546-1686**	202-877-7000

Florida

				Toll-Free	Phone
Aventura Hospital					
20900 Biscayne Blvd	Aventura	FL	33180	**800-523-5772**	305-682-7000
Blake Medical Ctr					
2020 59th St W	Bradenton	FL	34209	**800-523-5827**	941-792-6611
Brandon Regional Hospital					
119 Oakfield Dr	Brandon	FL	33511	**800 733-0429**	813-681-5551
Citrus Memorial Hospital					
502 W Highland Blvd	Inverness	FL	34452	**800-437-2672**	352-726-1551
Coral Gables Hospital Inc (CGH)					
3100 Douglas Rd	Coral Gables	FL	33134	**866-728-3677**	305-445-8461
Florida Hospital Heartland Medical Ctr					
4200 Sun 'n Lake Blvd	Sebring	FL	33871	**800-756-4447**	863-314-4466
Florida Hospital North Pinellas					
1395 S Pinellas Ave	Tarpon Springs	FL	34689	**800-558-6365**	727-942-5000
Florida Hospital Oceanside					
264 S Atlantic Ave	Ormond Beach	FL	32176	**800-558-6365**	386-672-4161
Florida Hospital Zephyrhills					
7050 Gall Blvd	Zephyrhills	FL	33541	**800-558-6365**	813-788-0411
Gulf Coast Medical Ctr					
449 W 23rd St	Panama City	FL	32405	**800-296-2611**	850-769-8341
Holmes Regional Medical Ctr					
1350 Hickory St	Melbourne	FL	32901	**800-716-7737**	321-434-7000
Holy Cross Hospital					
4725 N Federal Hwy	Fort Lauderdale	FL	33308	**888-419-3456**	954-771-8000
Lower Keys Medical Ctr					
5900 College Rd	Key West	FL	33040	**800-355-2470**	305-294-5531
Martin Health System (MMHS)					
200 SE Hospital Ave PO Box 9010	Stuart	FL	34994	**844-630-4968**	772-287-5200
Morton Plant Hospital					
300 Pinellas St	Clearwater	FL	33756	**800-229-2273**	727-462-7000
North Shore Medical Ctr					
1100 NW 95th St	Miami	FL	33150	**800-984-3434**	305-835-6000
Oakhill Hospital					
11375 Cortez Blvd	Brooksville	FL	34613	**877-442-2362**	352-596-6632
Orlando Regional Medical Ctr (ORMC)					
1414 Kuhl Ave	Orlando	FL	32806	**800-424-6998**	321-841-5111
Palms West Hospital (PWH)					
13001 Southern Blvd	Loxahatchee	FL	33470	**877-549-9337**	561-798-3300
Parrish Medical Ctr					
951 N Washington Ave	Titusville	FL	32796	**800-227-9954**	321-268-6111
Raulerson Hospital					
1796 Hwy 441 N	Okeechobee	FL	34972	**877-549-9337**	863-763-2151
Sacred Heart Hospital of Pensacola					
5151 N Ninth Ave	Pensacola	FL	32504	**800-874-1026**	850-416-7000
Saint Lucie Medical Ctr					
1800 SE Tiffany Ave	Port Saint Lucie	FL	34952	**800-382-3522**	772-335-4000
Sarasota Memorial Hospital					
1700 S Tamiami Trl	Sarasota	FL	34239	**800-764-8255**	941-917-9000
Shands Hospital at the University of Florida					
1600 SW Archer Rd	Gainesville	FL	32608	**855-483-7546**	352-265-0111
South Bay Hospital					
4016 Sun City Ctr Blvd	Sun City Center	FL	33573	**888-499-1293**	813-634-3301
South Miami Hospital					
6200 SW 73rd St	Miami	FL	33143	**800-228-6557**	786-662-4000
St Petersburg General Hospital					
6500 38th Ave N	Saint Petersburg	FL	33710	**800-733-0610**	727-384-1414
Town & Country Hospital					
6001 Webb Rd	Tampa	FL	33615	**866-463-7449**	813-888-7060
Westside Regional Medical Ctr					
8201 W Broward Blvd	Plantation	FL	33324	**800-523-5658**	954-473-6600

Georgia

				Toll-Free	Phone
Candler Hospital					
5353 Reynolds St	Savannah	GA	31405	**800-622-6877**	912-819-6000
Coffee Regional Medical Ctr (CRMC)					
1101 Ocilla Rd	Douglas	GA	31533	**800-555-4444**	912-384-1900
Colquitt Regional Medical Ctr (CRMC)					
3131 S Main St PO Box 40	Moultrie	GA	31768	**888-262-2762**	229-985-3420
East Georgia Regional Medical Ctr (EGRMC)					
1499 Fair Rd	Statesboro	GA	30458	**844-455-8708**	912-486-1000
Floyd Medical Ctr					
304 Turner McCall Blvd	Rome	GA	30165	**866-874-2772**	706-509-5000
John D Archbold Memorial Hospital					
915 Gordon Ave	Thomasville	GA	31792	**800-341-1009**	229-228-2000
Meadows Regional Medical Ctr (MRMC)					
1 Meadows Pkwy	Vidalia	GA	30474	**800-382-4023**	912-535-5555
Phoebe Putney Memorial Hospital					
417 W Third Ave	Albany	GA	31701	**866-514-0015**	229-312-1000
Saint Mary's Health Care System					
1230 Baxter St	Athens	GA	30606	**800-233-7864**	706-389-3000
Tift Regional Medical Ctr					
1641 Madison Ave	Tifton	GA	31794	**800-648-1935**	229-382-7120
University Health Care System					
1350 Walton Way	Augusta	GA	30901	**866-591-2502**	706-722-9011
Wellstar Douglas Hospital					
8954 Hospital Dr	Douglasville	GA	30134	**888-800-5094**	770-949-1500
Wellstar Kennestone Hospital					
677 Church St	Marietta	GA	30060	**888-800-5094**	770-793-5000

Hawaii

				Toll-Free	Phone
Wilcox Memorial Hospital (WMH)					
3-3420 Kuhio Hwy	Lihue	HI	96766	**877-709-9355**	808-245-1100

Idaho

				Toll-Free	Phone
Saint Alphonsus Regional Medical Ctr					
1055 N Curtis Rd	Boise	ID	83706	**877-401-3627**	208-367-2121
Saint Joseph Regional Medical Ctr					
415 Sixth St	Lewiston	ID	83501	**800-678-2511**	208-743-2511
West Valley Medical Ctr					
1717 Arlington Ave	Caldwell	ID	83605	**866-270-2311**	208-459-4641

Illinois

				Toll-Free	Phone
Advocate Christ Medical Ctr					
4440 W 95th St	Oak Lawn	IL	60453	**800-323-8622**	708-684-8000
Advocate Good Shepherd Hospital (AGSH)					
450 W Hwy 22	Barrington	IL	60010	**800-775-4784**	847-381-9600
Advocate Sherman Hospital					
1425 N Randall Rd	Elgin	IL	60123	**800-397-9000**	847-742-9800
Alexian Bros Medical Ctr					
800 Biesterfield Rd	Elk Grove Village	IL	60007	**800-432-5005**	847-437-5500
Blessing Health System					
Broadway at 11th St	Quincy	IL	62301	**866-460-3933**	217-223-8400
Centegra Memorial Medical Ctr					
3701 Doty Rd	Woodstock	IL	60098	**877-236-8347**	815-338-2500
CGH Medical Ctr (CGHMC)					
100 E LeFevre Rd	Sterling	IL	61081	**800-625-4790**	815-625-0400
Decatur Memorial Hospital					
2300 N Edward St	Decatur	IL	62526	**866-364-3600**	217-876-8121
Evanston Hospital					
2650 Ridge Ave	Evanston	IL	60201	**888-364-6400**	847-570-2000
FHN Memorial Hospital					
1045 W Stephenson St	Freeport	IL	61032	**800-747-4131**	815-599-6000
Genesis Medical Ctr Illini Campus					
801 Illini Dr	Silvis	IL	61282	**800-250-6020**	309-281-4000
GlenOaks Hospital					
701 Winthrop Ave	Glendale Heights	IL	60139	**866-751-7127**	630-545-8000
Gottlieb Memorial Hospital					
701 W N Ave	Melrose Park	IL	60160	**800-424-4840**	708-681-3200
Louis A Weiss Memorial Hospital					
4646 N Marine Dr	Chicago	IL	60640	**800-503-1234**	773-878-8700
Loyola University Medical Ctr					
2160 S First Ave	Maywood	IL	60153	**888-584-7888**	
MacNeal Hospital					
3249 S Oak Park Ave	Berwyn	IL	60402	**888-622-6325**	708-783-9100
Memorial Hospital of Carbondale					
405 W Jackson St	Carbondale	IL	62902	**800-457-1393**	618-549-0721
Mount Sinai Hospital Medical Ctr of Chicago					
California Ave 15th St	Chicago	IL	60608	**877-448-7848**	773-542-2000
Northwestern Medicine Kishwaukee Hospital					
1 Kish Hospital Dr	DeKalb	IL	60115	**800-397-1521**	815-756-1521
Norwegian-American Hospital					
1044 N Francisco Ave	Chicago	IL	60622	**877-624-9333**	773-292-8200
OSF Saint Anthony Medical Ctr					
5666 E State St	Rockford	IL	61108	**800-343-3185**	815-226-2000
OSF Saint Francis Medical Ctr					
530 NE Glen Oak Ave	Peoria	IL	61637	**888-627-5673**	309-655-2000
OSF Saint Mary Medical Ctr					
3333 N Seminary St	Galesburg	IL	61401	**877-795-0416**	309-344-3161
Rockford Memorial Hospital					
2400 N Rockton Ave	Rockford	IL	61103	**800-756-4147**	815-971-5000
Rush-Copley Medical Ctr (RCMC)					
2000 Ogden Ave	Aurora	IL	60504	**866-426-7539**	630-978-6200
Saint John's Hospital					
800 E Carpenter St	Springfield	IL	62769	**855-228-4438**	217-544-6464
Sarah Bush Lincoln Health Ctr (SBLHC)					
1000 Health Ctr Dr PO Box 372	Mattoon	IL	61938	**800-345-3191**	217-258-2525
SwedishAmerican Hospital					
1401 E State St	Rockford	IL	61104	**800-322-4724**	779-696-4400
University of Chicago Medical Ctr					
5841 S Maryland Ave	Chicago	IL	60637	**888-824-0200**	773-702-1000
Vista Medical Ctr					
1324 N Sheridan Rd	Waukegan	IL	60085	**800-843-2464**	847-360-3000
West Suburban Hospital Medical Ctr					
3 Erie Ct	Oak Park	IL	60302	**866-938-7256**	708-383-6200
Westlake Hospital					
1225 West Lake St	Melrose Park	IL	60160	**800-570-8809**	708-681-3000

Indiana

				Toll-Free	Phone
Beacon Health System					
615 N Michigan St	South Bend	IN	46601	**800-850-7913**	574-647-1000

				Toll-Free	Phone
Columbus Regional Hospital					
2400 E 17th St	Columbus	IN	47201	800-841-4938	812-379-4441
Community Hospital Anderson (CHA)					
1515 N Madison Ave	Anderson	IN	46011	800-777-7775	765-298-4242
Deaconess Hospital					
600 Mary St	Evansville	IN	47747	800-677-3422	812-450-5000
Franciscan Health Inc					
1501 Hartford St	Lafayette	IN	47904	800-371-6011	765-423-6011
Indiana University Hospital					
550 N University Blvd	Indianapolis	IN	46202	800-248-1199	317-274-5000
Lutheran Hospital of Indiana					
7950 W Jefferson Blvd	Fort Wayne	IN	46804	800-444-2001	260-435-7001
Margaret Mary Community Hospital Inc					
321 Mitchell Ave PO Box 226	Batesville	IN	47006	800-562-5698	812-934-6624
Memorial Hospital & Health Care Ctr					
800 W Ninth St	Jasper	IN	47546	800-852-7279	812-996-2345
Methodist Hospital					
1701 N Senate Blvd PO Box 1367	Indianapolis	IN	46202	800-899-8448	317-962-2000
Parkview Hospital					
2200 Randallia Dr	Fort Wayne	IN	46805	888-737-9311	260-373-4000
Riverview Hospital					
395 Westfield Rd	Noblesville	IN	46060	800-523-6001	317-773-0760
Saint Joseph Hospital					
700 Broadway	Fort Wayne	IN	46802	800-258-0974	260-425-3000
Saint Joseph Regional Medical Ctr Mishawaka					
5215 Holy Cross Pkwy	Mishawaka	IN	46545	800-274-1314	574-335-5000
Schneck Medical Ctr					
411 W Tipton St	Seymour	IN	47274	800-234-9222	812-522-2349
Terre Haute Regional Hospital (THRH)					
3901 S Seventh St	Terre Haute	IN	47802	866-270-2311	812-232-0021
Union Hospital					
1606 N Seventh St	Terre Haute	IN	47804	800-355-2470	812-238-7000

Iowa

				Toll-Free	Phone
Allen Memorial Hospital					
1825 Logan Ave	Waterloo	IA	50703	888-343-4165	319-235-3941
Buena Vista Regional Medical Ctr					
PO Box 309	Storm Lake	IA	50588	877-401-8030	712-732-4030
Finley Hospital					
350 N Grandview Ave	Dubuque	IA	52001	800-582-1891	563-582-1881
Jennie Edmundson Hospital					
933 E Pierce St	Council Bluffs	IA	51503	800-958-6498	712-396-6000
Mercy Iowa City					
500 E Market St	Iowa City	IA	52245	800-637-2942	319-339-0300
Mercy Medical Ctr (MMC)					
801 Fifth St	Sioux City	IA	51102	800-352-3559	712-279-2010
Mercy Medical Ctr					
1111 Sixth Ave	Des Moines	IA	50314	800-637-2993	515-247-3121
Mercy Medical Ctr North Iowa					
1000 Fourth St SW	Mason City	IA	50401	800-433-3883	641-428-7000
Orange City Area Health System					
1000 Lincoln Cir SE	Orange City	IA	51041	800-808-6264	712-737-4984
Ottumwa Regional Health Ctr					
1001 Pennsylvania Ave	Ottumwa	IA	52501	800-933-6742	641-684-2300
Saint Luke's Regional Medical Ctr					
2720 Stone Park Blvd	Sioux City	IA	51104	800-352-4660	712-279-3500
University of Iowa Hospitals & Clinics					
200 Hawkins Dr	Iowa City	IA	52242	800-777-8442	

Kansas

				Toll-Free	Phone
Coffeyville Regional Medical Ctr					
1400 W Fourth St	Coffeyville	KS	67337	800-540-2762	620-251-1200
Hays Medical Ctr (HMC)					
2220 Canterbury Dr	Hays	KS	67601	800-248-0073	785-650-2759
Hutchinson Regional Healthcare System					
1701 E 23rd St	Hutchinson	KS	67502	800-267-6891	620-665-2000
Lawrence Memorial Hospital (LMH)					
325 Maine St	Lawrence	KS	66044	800-749-4144	785-505-5000
Menorah Medical Ctr					
5721 W 119th St	Overland Park	KS	66209	800-766-3777	913-498-6000
Mercy Health Ctr Fort Scott					
401 Woodland Hills Blvd	Fort Scott	KS	66701	800-464-7942	620-223-2200
Overland Park Regional Medical Ctr					
10500 Quivira Rd	Overland Park	KS	66215	800-849-0829	913-541-5000
Providence Medical Ctr					
8929 Parallel Pkwy	Kansas City	KS	66112	800-281-7777	913-596-4000
Robert J Dole VA Medical Center					
5500 E Kellogg St	Wichita	KS	67218	888-878-6881	316-685-2221
Stormont-Vail Regional Health Ctr					
1500 SW Tenth Ave	Topeka	KS	66604	800-432-2951	785-354-6000
University of Kansas Health system					
3901 Rainbow Blvd	Kansas City	KS	66160	844-323-1227	913-588-1227
University of Kansas Health System St Francis Campus					
1700 SW Seventh St	Topeka	KS	66606	855-578-3726	785-295-8000
Wesley Medical Ctr					
550 N Hillside St	Wichita	KS	67214	800-362-0288	316-962-2000

Kentucky

				Toll-Free	Phone
Baptist Health					
1 Trillium Way	Corbin	KY	40701	800-395-4435	606-528-1212
Frankfort Regional Medical Ctr					
299 King's Daughters Dr	Frankfort	KY	40601	888-696-4505	502-875-5240
Greenview Regional Hospital					
1801 Ashley Cir	Bowling Green	KY	42104	800-605-1466	270-793-1000
Hardin Memorial Hospital					
913 W Dixie Ave	Elizabethtown	KY	42701	800-955-9455	270-706-1212
Harlan ARH Hospital					
81 Ballpark Rd	Harlan	KY	40831	800-274-9375	606-573-8100
Highlands Regional Medical Ctr (HRMC)					
5000 KY Rt 321	Prestonsburg	KY	41653	800-533-4762	606-886-8511
Jennie Stuart Medical Ctr					
320 W 18th St PO Box 2400	Hopkinsville	KY	42241	800-887-5762	270-887-0100

				Toll-Free	Phone
Kindred Hospital Louisville					
1313 St Anthony Pl	Louisville	KY	40204	800-648-6057	502-587-7001
King's Daughters Medical Ctr					
2201 Lexington Ave	Ashland	KY	41101	888-377-5362	606-408-8999
Methodist Hospital					
1305 N Elm St	Henderson	KY	42420	800-241-8322	270-827-7700
Owensboro Health (OMHS)					
811 E Parish Ave PO Box 20007	Owensboro	KY	42303	877-888-6647	270-691-8040
TJ Samson Community Hospital					
1301 N Race St	Glasgow	KY	42141	800-651-5635	270-651-4444
University of Louisville Hospital					
530 S Jackson St	Louisville	KY	40202	800-891-0947	502-562-3000
Williamson ARH Hospital					
260 Hospital Dr	South Williamson	KY	41503	888-654-0015*	606-237-1700
*General					

Louisiana

				Toll-Free	Phone
CHRISTUS Shreveport-Bossier Health System					
1453 E Bert Kouns	Shreveport	LA	71105	888-681-4138	318-681-4500
East Jefferson General Hospital (EJGH)					
4200 Houma Blvd	Metairie	LA	70006	866-280-7737	504-454-4000
Lake Charles Memorial Health System (LCMH)					
1701 Oak Pk Blvd	Lake Charles	LA	70601	800-494-5264	337-494-3000
Lakeview Regional Medical Ctr					
95 Judge Tanner Blvd	Covington	LA	70433	866-452-5384	985-867-3800
Natchitoches Regional Medical Center					
501 Keyser Ave	Natchitoches	LA	71457	888-728-8383	318-214-4200
Ochsner					
1514 Jefferson Hwy	New Orleans	LA	70121	800-343-0269	504-842-3000
Ochsner Medical Ctr Baton Rouge					
17000 Medical Ctr Dr	Baton Rouge	LA	70816	800-231-5257	225-752-2470
Ochsner Medical Ctr West Bank					
2500 Belle Chasse Hwy	Gretna	LA	70056	800-231-5257	504-391-5454
River Oaks Hospital					
1525 River Oaks Rd W	New Orleans	LA	70123	800-366-1740	
River Parishes Hospital					
500 Rue De Sante	Laplace	LA	70068	800-231-5275	985-652-7000
Terrebonne General Medical Ctr (TGMC)					
8166 Main St	Houma	LA	70360	888-850-6270	985-873-4141
Thibodaux Regional Medical Ctr (TRMC)					
602 N Acadia Rd	Thibodaux	LA	70301	800-822-8442	985-447-5500
Tulane Medical Ctr (TMC)					
1415 Tulane Ave	New Orleans	LA	70112	800-588-5800	504-988-5263

Maine

				Toll-Free	Phone
Franklin Community Health Network					
111 Franklin Health Commons	Farmington	ME	04938	800-398-6031	207-778-6031
Maine Medical Ctr (MMC)					
22 Bramhall St	Portland	ME	04102	877-339-3107	207-662-0111
MaineGeneral Medical Center (MGMC)					
Augusta 361 Old Belgrade Rd	Augusta	ME	04330	855-464-4463	207-621-6100
Mercy Hospital					
144 State St	Portland	ME	04101	800-293-6583	207-879-3000

Maryland

				Toll-Free	Phone
Braddock Hospital					
12500 Willowbrook Rd	Cumberland	MD	21502	888-369-1122	240-964-7000
Franklin Square Hospital Ctr					
9000 Franklin Sq Dr	Baltimore	MD	21237	888-404-3549	443-777-7000
Good Samaritan Hospital of Maryland					
5601 Loch Raven Blvd	Baltimore	MD	21239	855-633-5655	410-532-8000
Harbor Hospital Ctr					
3001 S Hanover St	Baltimore	MD	21225	800-280-9006	410-350-3200
Howard County General Hospital					
5755 Cedar Ln	Columbia	MD	21044	866-323-4615	410-740-7890
Mercy Medical Ctr (MMC)					
345 St Paul Pl	Baltimore	MD	21202	800-636-3729	410-332-9000
Northwest Hospital Ctr					
5401 Old Ct Rd	Randallstown	MD	21133	800-876-1175	410-521-2200
Peninsula Regional Medical Ctr					
100 E Carroll St	Salisbury	MD	21801	800-543-7780	410-546-6400
Prince George's Hospital Ctr					
3001 Hospital Dr	Cheverly	MD	20785	800-463-6295	301-618-2000
Saint Agnes HealthCare					
900 S Caton Ave	Baltimore	MD	21229	800-875-8750	410-368-6000
Sinai Hospital of Baltimore					
2401 W Belvedere Ave	Baltimore	MD	21215	800-876-1175	410-601-9000
Suburban Hospital					
8600 Old Georgetown Rd	Bethesda	MD	20814	800-456-4543	301-896-3100

Massachusetts

				Toll-Free	Phone
Beth Israel Deaconess Hospital-Milton					
199 Reedsdale Rd	Milton	MA	02186	800-462-5540	617-696-4600
Beth Israel Deaconess Medical Ctr (BIDMC)					
330 Brookline Ave	Boston	MA	02215	800-667-5356	617-667-7000
Boston Medical Ctr					
1 Boston Medical Ctr Pl	Boston	MA	02118	800-249-2007	617-638-8000
Cape Cod Hospital					
27 Park St	Hyannis	MA	02601	800-545-5014	508-771-1800
Charlton Memorial Hospital					
363 Highland Ave	Fall River	MA	02720	800-276-0103	508-679-3131
Good Samaritan Medical Ctr					
235 N Pearl St	Brockton	MA	02301	800-488-5959	508-427-3000
Harrington Hospital (HMH)					
100 South St	Southbridge	MA	01550	800-416-6072	508-765-9771
HealthAlliance Leominster Hospital					
60 Hospital Rd	Leominster	MA	01453	800-462-5540	978-466-2000
Jordan Hospital					
275 Sandwich St	Plymouth	MA	02360	800-256-7326	508-746-2000

				Toll-Free	Phone
Lahey Clinic Foundation Inc 41 Mall Rd	Burlington	MA	01805	800-524-3955	781-744-8000
Lawrence Memorial Hospital of Medford 170 Governors Ave	Medford	MA	02155	800-540-9191	781-306-6000
Lowell General Hospital (LGH) 295 Varnum Ave	Lowell	MA	01854	800-544-2424	978-937-6000
MetroWest Medical Ctr 115 Lincoln St	Framingham	MA	01702	800-872-5473	508-383-1000
Leonard Morse Campus 67 Union St	Natick	MA	01760	800-872-5473	508-650-7000
New England Baptist Hospital 125 Parker Hill Ave	Boston	MA	02120	855-370-6324	617-754-5000
Saint Anne's Hospital 795 Middle St	Fall River	MA	02721	800-488-5959	508-674-5600
Saint Luke's Hospital of New Bedford 101 Page St	New Bedford	MA	02740	800-497-1727	508-997-1515
Saint Vincent Hospital-Worcester Medical Ctr 123 Summer St	Worcester	MA	01608	877-633-2368	508-363-5000
Tufts Medical Ctr (TMC) 800 Washington St	Boston	MA	02111	866-220-3699	617-636-5000
UMass Memorial Medical Care *Bone Marrow Transplant* 55 Lake Ave N	Worcester	MA	01655	855-862-7763	508-334-1000
UMass Memorial Medical Ctr *Memorial Campus* 119 Belmont St	Worcester	MA	01605	800-225-8885	508-334-1000
University Campus 55 Lake Ave N	Worcester	MA	01655	800-225-8885	508-334-1000

Michigan

				Toll-Free	Phone
Allegiance Health 205 NE Ave	Jackson	MI	49201	800-872-6480	517-788-4800
Bay Regional Medical Ctr (BRMC) 1900 Columbus Ave	Bay City	MI	48708	800-656-3950	989-894-3000
DMC Sinai-Grace Hospital 6071 W Outer Dr	Detroit	MI	48235	888-362-2500	313-966-3300
Henry Ford Hospital 2799 W Grand Blvd	Detroit	MI	48202	800-999-4340	313-916-2600
Hurley Medical Ctr 1 Hurley Plz	Flint	MI	48503	800-336-8999	810-262-9000
Ingham Regional Medical Ctr 401 W Greenlawn Ave	Lansing	MI	48910	800-261-8018	517-975-6000
Lakeland Medical Center-Niles 31 N St Joseph Ave	Niles	MI	49120	800-968-0115	269-683-5510
Memorial Healthcare Ctr 826 W King St	Owosso	MI	48867	800-206-8706	
Mercy Health *Muskegon Campus* 1500 E Sherman Blvd	Muskegon	MI	49444	800-368-4125	231-672-2000
Metro Health Hospital 5900 Byron Ctr Ave	Wyoming	MI	49519	800-968-0051	616-252-7200
Oakwood Heritage Hospital 10000 Telegraph Rd	Taylor	MI	48180	800-543-9355	313-295-5000
Oakwood Southshore Medical Ctr 5450 Fort St	Trenton	MI	48183	800-543-9355	734-671-3800
Saint Joseph Mercy Ann Arbor 5301 McAuley Dr	Ypsilanti	MI	48197	866-522-8268	734-712-3456
Saint Joseph Mercy Oakland 44405 Woodward Ave	Pontiac	MI	48341	800-396-1313	248-858-3000
Saint Mary Mercy Hospital 36475 Five-Mile Rd	Livonia	MI	48154	800-464-7492	734-655-4800
Sparrow Health System 1215 E Michigan Ave	Lansing	MI	48912	800-772-7769	517-364-1000
Spectrum Health Blodgett Campus 100 Michigan St NE	Grand Rapids	MI	49503	866-989-7999	616-774-7444
St John Providence 28000 Dequindre	Warren	MI	48092	866-501-3627	586-573-5000
St John Providence Health System 28000 Dequindre	Warren	MI	48092	866-501-3627	
St Mary's of Michigan (STMH) 800 S Washington Ave	Saginaw	MI	48601	877-738-6672	989-907-8115

Minnesota

				Toll-Free	Phone
Abbott Northwestern Hospital 800 E 28th St	Minneapolis	MN	55407	800-582-5175	612-863-4000
Affiliated Community Medical Centers (ACMC) 101 Willmar Ave SW	Willmar	MN	56201	888-225-6580	320-231-5000
Cambridge Medical Ctr (CMC) 701 S Dellwood St	Cambridge	MN	55008	800-252-4133	763-689-7700
Essentia Health 502 E Second St	Duluth	MN	55805	855-469-6532	218-786-8376
Fairview University Medical Ctr Mesabi 750 E 34th St	Hibbing	MN	55746	888-870-8626	218-262-4881
Glacial Ridge Hospital Foundation Inc 10 Fourth Ave SE	Glenwood	MN	56334	866-667-4747	320-634-4521
Lake Region Hospital 712 S Cascade St	Fergus Falls	MN	56537	800-439-6424	218-736-8000
Mayo Clinic Health System Austin 1000 First Dr NW	Austin	MN	55912	888-609-4065	507-433-7351
Mayo Clinic Health System Southwest Minnesota 1025 Marsh St	Mankato	MN	56001	800-327-3721	507-625-4031
Mille Lacs Health System 200 Elm St N	Onamia	MN	56359	877-535-3154	320-532-3154
Rice Memorial Hospital 301 Becker Ave SW	Willmar	MN	56201	800-543-7709	320-235-4543
Ridgeview Medical Ctr (RMC) 500 S Maple St	Waconia	MN	55387	800-967-4620	952-442-2191
United Hospital 333 N Smith Ave	Saint Paul	MN	55102	800-869-1320	651-241-8000
University of Minnesota Medical Ctr Fairview - University Campus 500 Harvard St	Minneapolis	MN	55455	800-688-5252	612-273-3000

Mississippi

				Toll-Free	Phone
Baptist Medical Ctr 1225 N State St	Jackson	MS	39202	800-948-6262	601-968-1000
Baptist Memorial Hospital Golden Triangle 2520 Fifth St N	Columbus	MS	39705	800-422-7847	662-244-1000
Forrest General Hospital 6051 US Hwy 49	Hattiesburg	MS	39402	800-503-5980	601-288-7000
Northwest Mississippi Regional Medical Ctr 1970 Hospital Dr	Clarksdale	MS	38614	800-582-2233	662-627-3211

Missouri

				Toll-Free	Phone
Barnes-Jewish Saint Peters Hospital 4901 Forest Park Ave	St. Louis	MO	63108	800-536-2653	314-747-9322
Bothwell Regional Health Ctr 601 E 14th St	Sedalia	MO	65301	800-635-9194	660-826-8833
Cox Hospital North 1423 N Jefferson Ave	Springfield	MO	65802	800-711-9455	417-269-3000
Cox Medical Center South 3801 S National Ave	Springfield	MO	65807	800-711-9455	417-269-6000
Freeman Health System 1102 W 32nd St	Joplin	MO	64804	800-297-3337	417-347-1111
Hannibal Regional Hospital 6500 Hospital Dr	Hannibal	MO	63401	888-426-6425	573-248-1300
Jefferson Regional Medical Ctr 1400 Hwy 61 S	Festus	MO	63028	800-318-2596	636-933-1000
Liberty Hospital 2525 Glenn Hendren Dr	Liberty	MO	64068	800-344-3829	816-781-7200
Mercy 1235 E Cherokee	Springfield	MO	65804	800-909-8326	417-820-2000
Mercy 615 S New Ballas Rd	Saint Louis	MO	63141	800-318-2596	314-251-6000
Missouri Baptist Hospital of Sullivan 751 Sappington Bridge Rd	Sullivan	MO	63080	800-939-2273	573-468-4186
Missouri Baptist Medical Ctr 3015 N Ballas Rd	Saint Louis	MO	63131	800-392-0936	314-996-5000
Ozarks Medical Ctr 1100 N Kentucky Ave	West Plains	MO	65775	800-356-5395	417-256-9111
Parkland Health Ctr 1101 W Liberty St	Farmington	MO	63640	800-734-3944	573-756-6451
Poplar Bluff Regional Medical Ctr 2620 N Westwood Blvd	Poplar Bluff	MO	63901	855-444-7276	573-785-7721
Saint Alexius Hospital *Broadway Campus* 3933 S Broadway	Saint Louis	MO	63118	800-245-1431	314-865-7000
Saint Anthony's Medical Ctr 10010 Kennerly Rd	Saint Louis	MO	63128	800-554-9550	314-525-1000
Saint Francis Medical Ctr 211 Saint Francis Dr	Cape Girardeau	MO	63703	888-216-3293	573-331-3000
Saint Luke's Hospital & Regional Trauma Ctr 4401 Wornall Rd	Kansas City	MO	64111	866-261-5915	816-932-2000
Southeast Missouri Hospital (SMH) 1701 Lacey St	Cape Girardeau	MO	63701	800-800-5123	573-334-4822
St Luke's Des Peres Hospital 2345 Dougherty Ferry Rd	Saint Louis	MO	63122	888-457-5203	314-966-9100
Truman Medical Ctr Hospital Hill 2301 Holmes St	Kansas City	MO	64108	800-318-2596	816-404-1000

Montana

				Toll-Free	Phone
Billings Clinic 2800 Tenth Ave N	Billings	MT	59101	800-332-7156	406-238-2501
Holy Rosary Healthcare 2600 Wilson St	Miles City	MT	59301	800-843-3820	406-233-2600
Kalispell Regional Medical Ctr 310 Sunnyview Ln	Kalispell	MT	59901	800-228-1574	406-752-5111

Nebraska

				Toll-Free	Phone
Bryan Health 1600 S 48th St	Lincoln	NE	68506	800-742-7844	402-481-7333
CHI Health Good Samaritan 10 E 31st St	Kearney	NE	68847	800-277-4306	308-865-7100
Creighton University Medical Ctr 601 N 30th St	Omaha	NE	68131	800-368-5097	402-280-2700
Immanuel Medical Ctr 6901 N 72nd St	Omaha	NE	68122	800-253-4368	402-572-2121
Mary Lanning Memorial Hospital 715 N St Joseph Ave	Hastings	NE	68901	800-269-0473	402-463-4521
Nebraska Medical Ctr, The 4350 Dewey Ave	Omaha	NE	68105	800-922-0000	402-552-2000

New Hampshire

				Toll-Free	Phone
Catholic Medical Ctr (CMC) 100 McGregor St	Manchester	NH	03102	800-437-9666	603-668-3545
Dartmouth-Hitchcock Medical Ctr 1 Medical Ctr Dr	Lebanon	NH	03756	800-543-1624	603-650-5000
Elliot Hospital 1 Elliot Way Ste 100	Manchester	NH	03103	800-922-4999	603-627-1669
Portsmouth Regional Hospital 333 Borthwick Ave	Portsmouth	NH	03801	800-685-8282	603-436-5110
Wentworth-Douglass Hospital 789 Central Ave	Dover	NH	03820	877-201-7100	603-742-5252

New Jersey

				Toll-Free	Phone
Atlantic Health System 475 South St	Morristown	NJ	07960	800-247-9580	973-971-5000
Clara Maass Medical Ctr 1 Clara Maass Dr	Belleville	NJ	07109	800-300-0628	973-450-2000

Classified Section

		Toll-Free	Phone
Community Medical Ctr (CMC)			
99 Hwy 37 W ....Toms River NJ 08755		888-724-7123	732-557-8000
Cooper University Hospital			
3 Cooper Plz ....Camden NJ 08103		800-826-6737	856-342-2000
Jersey Shore University Medical Ctr			
1945 Rt 33 ....Neptune NJ 07753		800-560-9990	732-775-5500
Kennedy Health System-Cherry Hill			
2201 Chapel Ave W ....Cherry Hill NJ 08002		866-224-0264	856-488-6500
Lifeline Medical Assoc LLC			
99 Cherry Hill Rd Ste 220...Parsippany NJ 07054		800-845-2785	
Memorial Hospital of Salem County			
310 Woodstown Rd ....Salem NJ 08079		800-753-3779	856-935-1000
Monmouth Medical Ctr			
300 Second Ave ....Long Branch NJ 07740		888-724-7123	732-222-5200
Morristown Medical Ctr			
100 Madison Ave ....Morristown NJ 07960		877-310-7226	973-971-5000
Muhlenberg Regional Medical Ctr (MRMC)			
Park Ave & Randolph Rd ......Plainfield NJ 07060		877-271-4176	908-668-2000
Newark Beth Israel Medical Ctr			
201 Lyons Ave ....Newark NJ 07112		800-780-1140	973-926-7000
Ocean Medical Ctr (OMC)			
425 Jack Martin Blvd ....Brick NJ 08724		800-560-9990	732-840-2200
Our Lady of Lourdes Medical Ctr			
1600 Haddon Ave ....Camden NJ 08103		888-568-7337	856-757-3500
Overlook Medical Ctr			
99 Beauvoir Ave ....Summit NJ 07902		800-619-4024	908-522-2000
Raritan Bay Medical Ctr			
530 New Brunswick Ave ......Perth Amboy NJ 08861		800-701-0710	732-442-3700
Robert Wood Johnson University Hospital			
1 Robert Wood Johnson Pl ...New Brunswick NJ 08901		888-637-9584	732-828-3000
Robert Wood Johnson University Hospital at Rahway (RWJUHR)			
865 Stone St ....Rahway NJ 07065		800-443-4605	732-381-4200
Saint Barnabas Medical Ctr			
94 Old Short Hills Rd ......West Orange NJ 07052		888-724-7123	973-322-5000
SJH Regional Medical Ctr (SJHRMC)			
1505 W Sheman Ave ....Vineland NJ 08360		800-770-7547	856-641-8000
University Medical Ctr at Princeton (UMCP)			
253 Witherspoon St ....Princeton NJ 08540		877-932-8935	609-497-4304
Valley Health System			
223 N Van Dien Ave ....Ridgewood NJ 07450		800-825-5391	201-447-8000
Warren Hospital			
185 Roseberry St ....Phillipsburg NJ 08865		800-220-8116	908-859-6700

New Mexico

		Toll-Free	Phone
Lea Regional Medical Ctr			
5419 N Lovington Hwy ....Hobbs NM 88240		877-492-8001	575-492-5000
Lovelace Medical Ctr			
5400 Gibson Blvd SE ......Albuquerque NM 87108		888-281-6531	505-727-8000
Plains Regional Medical Ctr			
2100 N ML King Blvd ....Clovis NM 88101		800-923-6980	505-769-2141
Presbyterian Hospital			
1100 Central Ave SE ......Albuquerque NM 87106		888-977-2333	505-841-1234
Presbyterian Kaseman Hospital			
8300 Constitution Ave NE ...Albuquerque NM 87110		800-356-2219	505-291-2000

New York

		Toll-Free	Phone
Albany Medical Center			
43 New Scotland Ave ....Albany NY 12208		866-262-7476	518-262-3125
Arnot Ogden Medical Ctr			
600 Roe Ave ....Elmira NY 14905		800-952-2662	607-737-4100
Bassett Healthcare Network			
1 Atwell Rd ....Cooperstown NY 13326		800-227-7388	607-547-3456
BronxCare Family Wellness Center			
1276 Fulton Ave ....Bronx NY 10456		877-451-9361	718-590-1800
Buffalo General Hospital			
100 High St ....Buffalo NY 14203		800-506-6480	716-859-5600
Columbia Memorial Hospital			
71 Prospect Ave ....Hudson NY 12534		866-539-1370	518-828-7601
Corning Hospital			
176 Denison Pkwy E ....Corning NY 14830		877-750-2042	607-937-7200
De Graff Memorial Hospital			
445 Tremont St ......North Tonawanda NY 14120		800-506-6480	716-694-4500
Highland Hospital of Rochester			
1000 S Ave ....Rochester NY 14620		800-499-9298	585-473-2200
Long Island College Hospital (LICH)			
339 Hicks St ....Brooklyn NY 11201		800-227-8922	718-780-1000
Mount Sinai Medical Ctr, The			
1 Gustave L Levy Pl ....New York NY 10029		800-637-4624	212-241-6500
Mount Sinai Queens			
25-10 30th Ave ....Astoria NY 11102		800-968-7637	718-932-1000
New York Presbyterian Hospital			
525 E 68th St ....New York NY 10021		888-694-5700	212-746-5454
North Central Bronx Hospital			
3424 Kossuth Ave ....Bronx NY 10467		877-207-2134	718-519-5000
North Shore University Hospital			
300 Community Dr ....Manhasset NY 11030		888-214-4065	516-562-0100
Northern Westchester Hospital			
400 E Main St ....Mount Kisco NY 10549		877-469-4362	914-666-1200
Orange Regional Medical Ctr			
707 E Main St ....Middletown NY 10940		888-321-6762	845-343-2424
Queens Hospital Ctr			
82-68 164th St ....Jamaica NY 11432		888-692-6116	718-883-3000
Richmond University Medical Ctr			
355 Bard Ave ....Staten Island NY 10310		800-422-8798	718-818-1234
Rochester Regional Health (RGHS)			
1425 Portland Ave ....Rochester NY 14621		877-922-5465	585-922-4000
Saint James Mercy Hospital			
411 Canisteo St ....Hornell NY 14843		800-346-2211	607-324-8000
Saint Joseph's Hospital			
555 E Market St ....Elmira NY 14901		800-952-2662	607-733-6541
Saint Joseph's Hospital Health Ctr			
301 Prospect Ave ....Syracuse NY 13203		888-785-6371	315-448-5111
Saint Peter's Health Care Services			
315 S Manning Blvd ....Albany NY 12208		800-432-7876	518-525-1550

		Toll-Free	Phone
Samaritan Medical Ctr			
830 Washington St ....Watertown NY 13601		877-888-6138	315-785-4000
Sisters of Charity Hospital of Buffalo			
2157 Main St ....Buffalo NY 14214		800-698-4543	716-862-1000
Sisters of Charity Hospital, St Joseph Campus			
2605 Harlem Rd ....Cheektowaga NY 14225		800-698-4543	716-891-2400
Strong Memorial Hospital			
Stem Cell Transplantation Ctr			
601 Elmwood Ave ....Rochester NY 14642		888-661-6162	585-275-2100
University of Rochester Medical Ctr			
601 Elmwood Ave ....Rochester NY 14642		800-999-6673	585-275-2100
University Hospital SUNY Upstate Medical University			
750 E Adams St ....Syracuse NY 13210		877-464-5540	315-464-5540

North Carolina

		Toll-Free	Phone
Annie Penn Hospital			
618 S Main St ....Reidsville NC 27320		866-391-2734	336-951-4000
Carolinas Medical Center-NorthEast			
920 Church St N ....Concord NC 28025		800-575-1275	704-403-1275
Carolinas Medical Center-University			
8800 N Tryon St ....Charlotte NC 28262		800-821-1535	704-863-6000
Carolinas Medical Ctr Mercy			
2001 Vail Ave ....Charlotte NC 28207		800-821-1535	
Central Carolina Hospital			
1135 Carthage St ....Sanford NC 27330		800-292-2262	919-774-2100
Grace Hospital			
2201 S Sterling St ....Morganton NC 28655		800-624-3004	828-580-5000
High Point Regional Health System (HPRHS)			
601 N Elm St PO Box HP-5 ......High Point NC 27262		877-878-7644	336-878-6000
Moore Regional Hospital			
155 Memorial Dr PO Box 3000...Pinehurst NC 28374		866-415-2778	910-715-1000
Morehead Memorial Hospital			
117 E King's Hwy ....Eden NC 27288		800-291-4020	336-623-9711
Moses H Cone Memorial Hospital			
1200 N Elm St ....Greensboro NC 27401		866-391-2734	336-832-7000
New Hanover Regional Medical Ctr			
2131 S 17th St ....Wilmington NC 28401		877-228-8135	910-343-7000
Pender Memorial Hospital			
507 E Fremont St ....Burgaw NC 28425		888-815-5188	910-259-5451
Rex Healthcare			
4420 Lake Boone Trl ....Raleigh NC 27607		800-624-3004	919-784-3100
Rowan Regional Medical Ctr (RRMC)			
612 Mocksville Ave ....Salisbury NC 28144		888-844-0080	704-210-5000
Rutherford Regional Health System			
288 S Ridgecrest Ave ......Rutherfordton NC 28139		800-542-4225	828-286-5000
Sampson Regional Medical Ctr			
607 Beaman St ....Clinton NC 28328		800-827-5312	910-592-8511
Scotland Memorial Hospital			
500 Lauchwood Dr ....Laurinburg NC 28352		800-557-9249	910-291-7000
Thomasville Medical Ctr			
207 Old Lexington Rd ....Thomasville NC 27360		888-844-0080	336-472-2000

North Dakota

		Toll-Free	Phone
Altru Hospital			
1200 S Columbia Rd ....Grand Forks ND 58201		800-732-4277	701-780-5000
CHI St Alexius Health Bismarck			
900 E Broadway Ave ....Bismarck ND 58501		877-530-5550	701-530-7000
Trinity Health			
1 Burdick Expy W PO Box 5020 ...Minot ND 58702		800-862-0005	701-857-5000
Trinity Hospital Saint Joseph's			
1 W Burdick Expy ....Minot ND 58701		800-247-1316	701-857-5000

Ohio

		Toll-Free	Phone
Adena Regional Medical Ctr			
272 Hospital Rd ....Chillicothe OH 45601		800-582-7277	740-779-7500
Akron General Medical Ctr			
400 Wabash Ave ....Akron OH 44307		800-221-4601	330-344-6000
Ashtabula County Medical Ctr (ACMC)			
2420 Lake Ave ....Ashtabula OH 44004		800-722-3330	440-997-2262
Atrium Medical Ctr			
1 Medical Ctr Dr ....Middletown OH 45005		800-338-4057	513-424-2111
Bethesda Hospital			
2951 Maple Ave ....Zanesville OH 43701		800-322-4762	740-454-4000
Clinton Memorial Hospital (CMH)			
610 W Main St ....Wilmington OH 45177		800-803-9648	937-382-6611
Doctors Hospital			
5100 W Broad St ....Columbus OH 43228		800-432-3309	614-544-1000
Euclid Hospital			
18901 Lake Shore Blvd ....Euclid OH 44119		800-223-2273	
Fairfield Medical Ctr (FMC)			
401 N Ewing St ....Lancaster OH 43130		800-548-2627	740-687-8000
Fairview Hospital			
18101 Lorain Ave ....Cleveland OH 44111		800-801-2273	216-444-0261
Firelands Regional Medical Ctr			
1111 Hayes Ave ....Sandusky OH 44870		800-342-1177	419-557-7400
Fisher-Titus Medical Ctr (FTMC)			
272 Benedict Ave ....Norwalk OH 44857		800-589-3862	419-668-8101
Hillcrest Hospital			
6780 Mayfield Rd ......Mayfield Heights OH 44124		800-707-8922	440-312-4500
Lakewood Hospital			
14519 Detroit Ave ....Lakewood OH 44107		866-588-2264	216-521-4200
Lima Memorial Hospital			
1001 Bellefontaine Ave ....Lima OH 45804		877-362-5672	419-228-3335
Marietta Memorial Hospital			
401 Matthew St ....Marietta OH 45750		800-523-3977	740-374-1400
Marymount Hospital			
12300 McCracken Rd ......Garfield Heights OH 44125		800-801-2273	216-581-0500
Mercer County Joint Township Community Hospital			
800 W Main St ....Coldwater OH 45828		888-844-2341	419-678-2341
Mercy Medical Ctr			
1320 Mercy Dr NW ....Canton OH 44708		800-223-8662	330-489-1000

Name / Address	Location	ST	ZIP	Toll-Free	Phone
Miami Valley Hospital 1 Wyoming St	Dayton	OH	45409	800-544-0630*	937-208-8000
*All					
Mount Carmel West Hospital 793 W State St	Columbus	OH	43222	800-346-1009	614-234-5000
ProMedica 2142 N Cove Blvd	Toledo	OH	43606	866-865-4677	419-291-5437
Riverside Methodist Hospital 3535 Olentangy River Rd	Columbus	OH	43214	800-837-7555	614-566-4378
Saint Thomas Hospital 444 N Main St	Akron	OH	44310	800-237-8662	330-375-3000
Summa Barberton Hospital 155 Fifth St NE	Barberton	OH	44203	888-905-6071	330-615-3000
Union Hospital 659 Blvd	Dover	OH	44622	800-541-6664	330-343-3311
University Hospitals of Cleveland 11100 Euclid Ave	Cleveland	OH	44106	866-844-2273	216-844-1000
University of Toledo Medical Center, The (PCGH) 7007 Powers Blvd	Parma	OH	44129	855-292-4292	440-743-3000
University of Toledo Medical Center, The 3000 Arlington Ave	Toledo	OH	43614	800-586-5336	419-383-4000
Upper Valley Medical Ctr (UVMC) 3130 N County Rd 25-A	Troy	OH	45373	866-608-3463	937-440-4000
Wood County Hospital 950 W Wooster St	Bowling Green	OH	43402	800-288-4470	419-354-8900

Oklahoma

Name / Address	Location	ST	ZIP	Toll-Free	Phone
Grady Memorial Hospital 2220 Iowa Ave	Chickasha	OK	73018	800-299-9665	405-224-2300
INTEGRIS Baptist Regional Health Ctr 200 Second Ave SW	Miami	OK	74355	888-951-2277	918-542-6611
INTEGRIS Bass Baptist Health Ctr 600 S Monroe	Enid	OK	73701	888-951-2277	580-233-2300
INTEGRIS Southwest Medical Ctr 4401 S Western St	Oklahoma City	OK	73109	888-949-3816	405-636-7000
Jackson County Memorial Hospital 1200 E Pecan St	Altus	OK	73521	800-595-0455	580-379-5000
SSM Health St Anthony 1000 N Lee St	Oklahoma City	OK	73101	800-227-6964	405-272-7000

Oregon

Name / Address	Location	ST	ZIP	Toll-Free	Phone
Bay Area Hospital 1775 Thompson Rd	Coos Bay	OR	97420	800-798-0799	541-269-8111
Good Samaritan Regional Medical Ctr 3600 NW Samaritan Dr	Corvallis	OR	97330	800-640-5339	541-768-5111
Legacy Emanuel Hospital & Health Ctr 2801 N Gantenbein Ave	Portland	OR	97227	888-598-4232	503-413-2200
Legacy Good Samaritan Hospital 1015 NW 22nd Ave	Portland	OR	97210	800-733-9959	503-335-3500
Legacy Meridian Park Hospital 19300 SW 65th Ave	Tualatin	OR	97062	800-944-4773	503-692-1212
Providence Health & Services 9205 SW Barnes Rd	Portland	OR	97225	800-562-8964	503-216-1234
Providence Medford Medical Ctr 1111 Crater Lake Ave	Medford	OR	97504	877-541-0588	541-732-5000
Providence Portland Medical Ctr 4805 NE Glisan St	Portland	OR	97213	800-833-8899	503-215-1111
Sacred Heart Medical Ctr 1255 Hilyard St	Eugene	OR	97401	800-288-7444	541-686-7300
Salem Hospital 665 Winter St SE	Salem	OR	97301	800-876-1718	

Pennsylvania

Name / Address	Location	ST	ZIP	Toll-Free	Phone
Albert Einstein Medical Ctr 5501 Old York Rd	Philadelphia	PA	19141	800-346-7834	
Altoona Regional Health System Altoona Hospital 620 Howard Ave	Altoona	PA	16601	877-855-8152	814-889-2011
Aria Health Bucks County Campus 380 N Oxford Valley Rd	Langhorne	PA	19047	877-808-2742	
Berwick Hospital Ctr, The 701 E 16th St	Berwick	PA	18603	800-654-5988	570-759-5000
Brandywine Hospital 201 Reeceville Rd	Coatesville	PA	19320	800-430-3762	610-383-8000
Clarion Hospital (CH) 1 Hospital Dr	Clarion	PA	16214	800-522-0505	814-226-9500
Clearfield Hospital 809 Tpke Ave PO Box 992	Clearfield	PA	16830	800-281-8000	814-765-5341
Delaware County Memorial Hospital 501 N Lansdowne Ave	Drexel Hill	PA	19026	877-884-1564	610-284-8100
Divine Providence Hospital 1100 Grampian Blvd	Williamsport	PA	17701	800-433-0816	570-326-8000
DuBois Regional Medical Ctr 100 Hospital Ave	Du Bois	PA	15801	800-254-5164	814-371-2200
Easton Hospital 250 S 21st St	Easton	PA	18042	866-800-3880	610-250-4000
Frick Hospital 508 S Church St	Mount Pleasant	PA	15666	877-771-1234	724-547-1500
Geisinger Health System (CMC) 1800 Mulberry St	Scranton	PA	18510	800-230-4565	570-703-8000
Geisinger South Wilkes-Barre (GSWB) 25 Church St	Wilkes-Barre	PA	18765	800-230-4565	570-808-3100
Geisinger Wyoming Valley Medical Ctr 1000 E Mountain Dr	Danville	PA	17822	800-230-4565	570-271-8600
Hanover Hospital 300 Highland Ave	Hanover	PA	17331	800-673-2426	717-637-3711
Harrisburg Hospital 111 S Front St	Harrisburg	PA	17101	888-782-5678	717-782-3131
Heritage Valley Health System 1000 Dutch Ridge Rd	Beaver	PA	15009	877-771-4847	724-728-7000
Holy Redeemer Hospital & Medical Ctr 1648 Huntingdon Pk	Meadowbrook	PA	19046	800-818-4747	215-947-3000
Meadville Medical Ctr (MMC) 751 Liberty St	Meadville	PA	16335	800-254-5164	814-333-5000

Name / Address	Location	ST	ZIP	Toll-Free	Phone
Memorial Medical Ctr 1086 Franklin St	Johnstown	PA	15905	800-441-2555	814-534-9000
Mount Nittany Medical Ctr 1800 E Park Ave	State College	PA	16803	866-686-6171	814-231-7000
Penn State Milton S Hershey Medical Ctr 500 University Dr	Hershey	PA	17033	800-731-3032	717-531-6955
Pinnacle Health Hospital at Community General 4300 Londonderry Rd	Harrisburg	PA	17109	888-782-5678	717-652-3000
Regional Hospital of Scranton 746 Jefferson Ave	Scranton	PA	18510	800-654-5988	570-770-3000
Riddle Memorial Hospital 1068 W Baltimore Pk	Media	PA	19063	866-225-5654	484-227-9400
Robert Packer Hospital 1 Guthrie Sq	Sayre	PA	18840	888-448-8474	570-888-6666
Saint Joseph Medical Ctr 2500 Bernville Rd	Reading	PA	19605	800-969-5007	610-378-2000
Sewickley Valley Hospital 720 Blackburn Rd	Sewickley	PA	15143	800-400-6180	877-771-4847
Taylor Hospital 175 E Chester Pk	Ridley Park	PA	19078	800-254-3258	610-595-6000
Thomas Jefferson University Hospital 111 S 11th St	Philadelphia	PA	19107	800-533-3669	215-955-6000
University of Pittsburgh Medical Ctr (UPMC) *Horizon* 110 N Main St	Greenville	PA	16125	888-447-1122	724-588-2100
Passavant 9100 Babcock Blvd	Pittsburgh	PA	15237	800-533-8762	412-367-6700
Shadyside 5230 Centre Ave	Pittsburgh	PA	15232	800-533-8762	412-623-2121
South Side 2000 Mary St	Pittsburgh	PA	15203	800-533-8762	412-488-5550
UPMC Pinnacle Lancaster 250 College Ave	Lancaster	PA	17603	877-456-9617	717-291-8211
UPMC Pinnacle Memorial 325 S Belmont St	York	PA	17405	800-436-4326	717-843-8623
UPMC Presbyterian 200 Lothrop St	Pittsburgh	PA	15213	877-986-9862	412-647-8762
Warren General Hospital 2 Crescent Pk W	Warren	PA	16365	800-777-9441	814-723-3300

Rhode Island

Name / Address	Location	ST	ZIP	Toll-Free	Phone
Kent Hospital 455 Toll Gate Rd	Warwick	RI	02886	800-892-9291	401-737-7000
Memorial Hospital of Rhode Island (MHRI) 111 Brewster St	Pawtucket	RI	02860	800-647-4362	401-729-2000
Westerly Hospital 25 Wells St	Westerly	RI	02891	800-933-5960	401-596-6000

South Carolina

Name / Address	Location	ST	ZIP	Toll-Free	Phone
Aiken Regional Medical Centers 302 University Pkwy	Aiken	SC	29801	800-245-3679	803-641-5000
Beaufort Memorial Hospital 955 Ribaut Rd	Beaufort	SC	29902	877-532-6472	843-522-5200
Bon Secours Saint Francis Hospital 2095 Henry Tecklenburg Dr	Charleston	SC	29414	800-863-2273	843-402-1000
Colleton Medical Ctr (CMC) 501 Robertson Blvd	Walterboro	SC	29488	866-492-9083	843-782-2000
Piedmont Medical Ctr 222 S Herlong Ave	Rock Hill	SC	29732	800-222-4218	803-329-1234
Regional Medical Ctr, The 3000 St Matthews Rd	Orangeburg	SC	29118	800-476-3377	803-395-2200
Spartanburg Regional Medical Ctr (SRMC) 101 E Wood St	Spartanburg	SC	29303	800-318-2596	864-560-6000
Trident Medical Ctr 9330 Medical Plaza Dr	Charleston	SC	29406	866-492-9085	843-797-7000

South Dakota

Name / Address	Location	ST	ZIP	Toll-Free	Phone
Avera Saint Luke's Hospital 305 S State St	Aberdeen	SD	57401	800-658-3535	605-622-5000
Huron Regional Medical Ctr (HRMC) 172 Fourth St SE	Huron	SD	57350	800-529-0115	605-353-6200
Prairie Lakes Hospital & Care Ctr 401 Ninth Ave NW	Watertown	SD	57201	877-917-7547	605-882-7000

Tennessee

Name / Address	Location	ST	ZIP	Toll-Free	Phone
Athens Regional Medical Ctr 1114 W Madison Ave	Athens	TN	37303	800-855-2880	423-745-1411
Baptist Memorial Hospital Union City 1201 Bishop St	Union City	TN	38261	800-344-2470	731-885-2410
Blount Memorial Hospital 907 E Lamar Alexander Pkwy	Maryville	TN	37804	800-448-0219	865-983-7211
Cookeville Regional Medical Ctr (CRMC) 1 Medical Ctr Blvd	Cookeville	TN	38501	800-897-1898	931-528-2541
Delta Medical Center (DMC) 3000 Getwell Rd	Memphis	TN	38118	877-627-4395	
Erlanger Health System 975 E Third St	Chattanooga	TN	37403	877-849-8338	423-778-7000
Laughlin Memorial Hospital 1420 Tusculom Blvd	Greeneville	TN	37745	800-852-7157	423-787-5000
Nashville General Hospital 1818 Albion St	Nashville	TN	37208	800-318-2596	615-341-4000
Parkridge East Hospital 941 Spring Creek Rd	Chattanooga	TN	37412	800-605-1527	423-894-7870
Saint Thomas Hospital 4220 Harding Rd	Nashville	TN	37205	800-400-5800	615-222-2111
Skyline Hospital 3441 Dickerson Pk	Nashville	TN	37207	800-242-5662	615-769-2000
Tristar Southern Hills Medical Ctr 391 Wallace Rd	Nashville	TN	37211	800-242-5662	615-781-4000
Vanderbilt University Medical Ctr 1215 21st Ave S	Nashville	TN	37232	877-936-8422	615-322-5000

Texas

			Toll-Free	Phone
Abilene Regional Medical Ctr 6250 S Hwy 83-84	Abilene	TX 79606	800-888-2504	325-428-1000
Baptist Medical Ctr 111 Dallas St	San Antonio	TX 78205	866-309-2873	210-297-7000
Baylor Scott & White Health 1650 W College St	Grapevine	TX 76051	800-422-9567	817-481-1588
Central Texas Medical Ctr (CTMC) 1301 Wonder World Dr	San Marcos	TX 78666	800-927-9004	512-353-8979
CHRISTUS Southeast Texas Health System 2830 Calder St	Beaumont	TX 77702	866-683-3627	409-892-7171
CHRISTUS Southeast Texas Health System 3600 Gates Blvd PO Box 3696	Port Arthur	TX 77642	866-683-3627	409-985-7431
Conroe Regional Medical Ctr 504 Medical Ctr Blvd	Conroe	TX 77304	888-633-2687	936-539-1111
Del Sol Medical Ctr 10301 Gateway W	El Paso	TX 79925	800-322-0712	915-595-9000
Doctors Hospital of Laredo 10700 McPherson Rd	Laredo	TX 78045	844-244-4874	956-523-2000
East Houston Regional Medical Ctr 13111 E Fwy	Houston	TX 77015	800-979-3627	713-393-2000
Memorial Hermann Memorial City Hospital 921 Gessner Rd	Houston	TX 77024	800-526-2121	713-242-3000
Methodist Hospital 8109 Fredericksburg Rd	San Antonio	TX 78229	800-333-7333	210-575-0355
Metroplex Hospital 2201 S Clear Creek Rd	Killeen	TX 76549	800-926-7664	254-526-7523
Metropolitan Methodist Hospital 1310 McCullough Ave	San Antonio	TX 78212	800-553-6321	210-757-2200
Midland Memorial Hospital 400 Rosalind Redfern Grover Pkwy	Midland	TX 79701	800-833-2916	432-685-1111
Nacogdoches Medical Ctr 4920 NE Stallings Dr	Nacogdoches	TX 75965	866-898-8446	936-569-9481
Northeast Baptist Hospital 8811 Village Dr	San Antonio	TX 78217	800-201-9353	210-297-2000
Northeast Methodist Hospital 12412 Judson Rd	San Antonio	TX 78233	800-333-7333	210-757-7000
Northwest Texas Hospital 1501 S Coulter	Amarillo	TX 79106	800-887-1114	806-354-1000
Scott & White Medical Center 2401 S 31st St	Temple	TX 76508	800-792-3710	254-724-2111
Southwest General Hospital (SGH) 7400 Barlite Blvd	San Antonio	TX 78224	877-898-6080	210-921-2000
Texas Healthcare PLLC 2821 Lackland Rd Ste 300	Fort Worth	TX 76116	877-238-6200	817-378-3640
Texoma Medical Ctr 5016 S US Hwy 75	Denison	TX 75020	800-256-0943	903-416-4000
University of Texas Medical Branch Hospitals 301 University Blvd	Galveston	TX 77555	800-201-0527	409-772-1011

Utah

			Toll-Free	Phone
Davis Hospital & Medical Ctr (DHMC) 1600 W Antelope Dr	Layton	UT 84041	877-898-6080	801-807-1000
Intermountain Healthcare Logan Regional Hospital 500 E 1400 N	Logan	UT 84341	800-442-4845	435-716-1000
LDS Hospital 8th Ave & C St	Salt Lake City	UT 84143	888-301-3880	801-408-1100
Mountain View Hospital 1000 East 100 North	Payson	UT 84651	877-865-9738	801-465-7000
Ogden Regional Medical Ctr 5475 Adams Ave Pkwy	Ogden	UT 84405	877-870-3745	801-479-2111
Saint Mark's Hospital 1200 East 3900 South	Salt Lake City	UT 84124	800-370-1983	801-268-7111

Vermont

			Toll-Free	Phone
Brattleboro Memorial Hospital Inc 17 Belmont Ave	Brattleboro	VT 05301	866-972-5266	802-257-0341
Copley Hospital System 528 Washington Hwy	Morrisville	VT 05661	800-564-1612	802-888-8888
University of Vermont Medical Center, The (FAHC) 111 Colchester Ave	Burlington	VT 05401	800-358-1144	802-847-0000

Virginia

			Toll-Free	Phone
Alleghany Regional Hospital 1 ARH Ln	Low Moor	VA 24457	866-393-0026	540-862-6011
Augusta Medical Ctr (AMC) 78 Medical Ctr Dr PO Box 1000	Fishersville	VA 22939	800-932-0262	540-932-4000
Carilion Roanoke Community Hospital (CRCH) 101 Elm Ave SE	Roanoke	VA 24013	800-422-8482	540-985-8000
Carilion Roanoke Memorial Hospital 1906 Belleview Ave	Roanoke	VA 24014	800-422-8482	540-981-7000
Chesapeake Regional Medical Ctr 736 Battlefield Blvd N	Chesapeake	VA 23320	800-456-8121	757-312-8121
CJW Medical Ctr 7101 Jahnke Rd	Richmond	VA 23225	800-468-6620	804-320-3911
Danville Regional Medical Ctr 142 S Main St	Danville	VA 24541	800-688-3762	434-799-2100
Inova Alexandria Hospital 4320 Seminary Rd	Alexandria	VA 22304	800-526-7101	703-504-3000
Inova Fairfax Hospital 3300 Gallows Rd	Falls Church	VA 22042	800-838-8238	703-776-4001
Lewis-Gale Medical Ctr 1900 Electric Rd	Salem	VA 24153	800-541-9992	540-776-4000
Mary Washington Hospital 1001 Sam Perry Blvd	Fredericksburg	VA 22401	800-395-2455	540-741-1100
Prince William Hospital 8700 Sudly Rd	Manassas	VA 20110	800-526-7101	703-369-8000
Reston Hospital Ctr 1850 Town Ctr Pkwy *General	Reston	VA 20190	888-327-8882*	703-689-9000
Sentara Careplex Hospital 3000 Colliseum Dr	Hampton	VA 23666	800-736-8272	757-736-1000
Sentara Leigh Hospital 830 Kempsville Rd	Norfolk	VA 23502	800-237-4822	757-261-6000
Sentara Martha Jefferson Hospital (MJH) 500 Martha Jefferson Dr	Charlottesville	VA 22911	888-652-6663	434-654-7000
Sentara Virginia Beach General Hospital 1060 First Colonial Rd	Virginia Beach	VA 23454	800-736-8272	757-395-8000
Shore Memorial Hospital 20480 Market St PO Box 430	Onancock	VA 23417	800-834-7035	757-302-2100
Twin County Regional Hospital 200 Hospital Dr	Galax	VA 24333	800-295-3342	276-236-8181
University of Virginia Health System 1215 Lee St	Charlottesville	VA 22908	800-251-3627	434-924-0211
UVA Health System 501 Sunset Ln	Culpeper	VA 22701	866-608-4749	540-829-4100
Virginia Baptist Hospital 3300 Rivermont Ave	Lynchburg	VA 24503	866-749-4455	434-200-3000

Washington

			Toll-Free	Phone
Auburn Regional Medical Ctr 202 N Div St	Auburn	WA 98001	866-268-7223	253-833-7711
Capital Medical Ctr 3900 Capital Mall Dr SW	Olympia	WA 98502	888-677-9757	360-754-5858
Good Samaritan Hospital (GSH) 407 14th Ave SE	Puyallup	WA 98372	800-776-4048	253-697-4000
Kadlec Regional Medical Ctr 888 Swift Blvd	Richland	WA 99352	800-780-6067	509-946-4611
Legacy Salmon Creek Hospital 2211 NE 139th St	Vancouver	WA 98686	877-270-5566	360-487-1000
Northwest Hospital & Medical Ctr 1550 N 115th St	Seattle	WA 98133	877-694-4677	206-364-0500
Olympic Medical Ctr 939 Caroline St	Port Angeles	WA 98362	888-362-6260	360-417-7000
PeaceHealth St Joseph Medical Ctr 2901 Squalicum Pkwy	Bellingham	WA 98225	800-541-7209	360-734-5400
Providence Centralia Hospital 914 S Scheuber Rd *Help Line	Centralia	WA 98531	877-736-2803*	360-736-2803
Providence Sacred Heart Medical Ctr 101 W Eigth Ave	Spokane	WA 99204	800-442-8534	888-294-8455
Providence St Mary Medical Ctr 401 W Poplar St	Walla Walla	WA 99362	877-215-7833	509-525-3320
Qualis Health PO Box 33400	Seattle	WA 98133	800-949-7536	206-364-9700
Tacoma General Hospital 315 MLK Jr Way	Tacoma	WA 98405	800-552-1419	253-403-1000
UW Medicine Eastside Hospital & Specialty 3100 Northup Way	Bellevue	WA 98004	877-520-5000	

West Virginia

			Toll-Free	Phone
Logan Regional Medical Ctr 20 Hospital Dr	Logan	WV 25601	888-982-9144	304-831-1101
Stonewall Jackson Memorial Hospital (SJMH) 230 Hospital Plz	Weston	WV 26452	866-637-0471	304-269-8000
United Hospital Ctr 327 Medical pk Dr	Bridgeport	WV 26330	800-607-8888	681-342-1000
Wheeling Hospital 1 Medical Pk	Wheeling	WV 26003	800-626-0023	304-243-3000

Wisconsin

			Toll-Free	Phone
Appleton Medical Ctr 1818 N Meade St	Appleton	WI 54911	800-236-4101	920-731-4101
Aspirus Wausau Hospital 333 Pine Ridge Blvd	Wausau	WI 54401	800-283-2881	715-847-2121
Aurora Sinai Medical Ctr 945 N 12th St	Milwaukee	WI 53201	888-863-5502	414-219-2000
Bay Area Medical Ctr (BAMC) 3100 Shore Dr	Marinette	WI 54143	888-788-2070	715-735-4200
Beloit Health System 1969 W Hart Rd	Beloit	WI 53511	800-637-2641	608-363-5724
Columbia Saint Mary's Hospital Ozaukee 13111 N Port Washington Rd	Mequon	WI 53097	800-457-6004	262-243-7300
Fort Atkinson Memorial Hospital 611 Sherman Ave E	Fort Atkinson	WI 53538	800-844-5575	920-568-5000
Franciscan Skemp Health Care 700 W Ave S	La Crosse	WI 54601	800-362-5454	608-785-0940
Gundersen Lutheran Medical Ctr 1836 S Ave	La Crosse	WI 54601	800-362-9567	608-782-7300
HSHS St Joseph's Hospital 2661 County Hwy I	Chippewa Falls	WI 54729	877-723-1811	715-723-1811
HSHS St Vincent Hospital 835 S Van Buren St	Green Bay	WI 54301	800-211-2209	
Memorial Medical Ctr 1615 Maple Ln	Ashland	WI 54806	888-868-9292	715-685-5500
Mercy Hospital & Trauma Ctr 1000 Mineral Point Ave	Janesville	WI 53548	800-756-4147	608-756-6000
Mercy Medical Ctr (MMC) 500 S Oakwood Rd	Oshkosh	WI 54904	800-894-9327	920-223-2000
Monroe Clinic Hospital 515 22nd Ave	Monroe	WI 53566	800-338-0568	608-324-2000
Oconomowoc Memorial Hospital 791 Summit Ave	Oconomowoc	WI 53066	800-242-0313	262-569-9400
Richland Hospital Inc, The 333 E Second St	Richland Center	WI 53581	888-467-7485	608-647-6321
Sacred Heart Hospital 900 W Clairemont Ave	Eau Claire	WI 54701	888-445-4554	715-717-4121
Saint Elizabeth Hospital 1506 S Oneida St	Appleton	WI 54915	800-223-7332	920-738-2000

				Toll-Free	Phone
Saint Mary's Hospital					
2251 N Shore Dr	Rhinelander	WI	54501	800-578-0840*	715-361-2000
*Cust Svc					
Saint Michael's Hospital					
900 Illinois Ave	Stevens Point	WI	54481	800-420-2622	715-346-5000
St Agnes Hospital					
430 E Div St	Fond du Lac	WI	54935	800-922-3400	920-929-2300
Theda Clark Medical Ctr					
130 Second St	Neenah	WI	54956	800-236-3122	920-729-3100
University of Wisconsin Hospital & Clinics					
600 Highland Ave	Madison	WI	53792	800-323-8942	608-263-6400
Waukesha Memorial Hospital					
725 American Ave	Waukesha	WI	53188	800-326-2011	262-928-1000
Wheaton Franciscan - Saint Joseph					
5000 W Chambers St	Milwaukee	WI	53210	800-914-6601	414-447-2000
Wheaton Franciscan Healthcare					
3801 Spring St	Racine	WI	53405	877-304-6332	262-687-4011
All Saints 3801 Spring St	Racine	WI	53405	877-304-6332	262-687-4011

Wyoming

				Toll-Free	Phone
Memorial Hospital of Sweetwater County					
1200 College Dr	Rock Springs	WY	82901	866-571-0944*	307-362-3711
*General					
Meredith & Jeannie Ray Cancer Ctr					
255 N 30th St	Laramie	WY	82072	800-854-1115	307-742-7586
Wyoming Medical Ctr					
1233 E Second St	Casper	WY	82601	800-822-7201	307-577-7201

373-4 Military Hospitals

				Toll-Free	Phone
Brooke Army Medical Center (BAMC)					
3551 Roger Brooke Dr	Fort Sam Houston	TX	78234	800-443-2262	
Keller Army Community Hospital					
900 Washington Rd	West Point	NY	10996	800-552-2907	845-938-7992
Lyster Army Health Clinic					
Andrews Ave	Fort Rucker	AL	36362	800-261-7193	
Naval Hospital Bremerton					
1 Bo1 Rd	Bremerton	WA	98312	800-422-1383	360-475-4000

373-5 Psychiatric Hospitals

Listings here include state psychiatric facilities as well as private psychiatric hospitals.

				Toll-Free	Phone
Appalachian Behavioral Healthcare					
100 Hospital Dr	Athens	OH	45701	800-372-8862	740-594-5000
Arizona State Hospital					
2500 E Van Buren St	Phoenix	AZ	85008	877-588-5163	602-244-1331
Atascadero State Hospital					
10333 S Camino Real	Atascadero	CA	93422	844-210-6207	805-468-2000
Aurora Las Encinas Hospital					
2900 E Del Mar Blvd	Pasadena	CA	91107	800-792-2345	626-795-9901
Austin State Hospital					
4110 Guadalupe St	Austin	TX	78751	866-407-3773	512-452-0381
Banner Behavioral Health Hospital					
7575 E Earll Dr	Scottsdale	AZ	85251	800-254-4357	480-941-7500
Belmont Ctr for Comprehensive Treatment					
4200 Monument Rd	Philadelphia	PA	19131	800-220-4357	
Brentwood Hospital					
1006 Highland Ave	Shreveport	LA	71101	877-678-7500	318-678-7500
Bronx Psychiatric Ctr					
1500 Waters Pl	Bronx	NY	10461	800-597-8481	718-931-0600
BryLin Hospitals					
1263 Delaware Ave	Buffalo	NY	14209	800-727-9546	716-886-8200
Buffalo Psychiatric Ctr					
400 Forest Ave	Buffalo	NY	14213	800-597-8481	716-885-2261
Carrier Clinic					
252 County Rd 601	Belle Mead	NJ	08502	800-933-3579	
Catawba Hospital					
5525 Catawba Hospital Dr	Catawba	VA	24070	800-451-5544	540-375-4200
Cedar Springs Behavioral Health System					
2135 Southgate Rd	Colorado Springs	CO	80906	800-888-1088	719-633-4114
Central Louisiana State Hospital					
242 W Shamrock St	Pineville	LA	71360	888-342-6207	318-484-6200
Central Washington Hospital					
1201 S Miller St	Wenatchee	WA	98801	800-365-6428	509-662-1511
Chester Mental Health Ctr					
1315 Lehman Dr	Chester	IL	62233	800-843-6154	618-826-4571
Chicago Lakeshore Hospital					
4840 N Marine Dr	Chicago	IL	60640	800-888-0560*	773-878-9700
*Cust Svc					
Chicago-Read Mental Health Ctr					
4200 N Oak Park Ave	Chicago	IL	60634	800-322-7143	773-794-4000
Clifton T Perkins Hospital Ctr (CTPHC)					
1 Renaissance Blvd	Oakbrook	IL	60181	800-994-6610	
Coastal Harbor Treatment Ctr					
1150 Cornell Ave	Savannah	GA	31406	844-657-2638	912-354-3911
College Hospital					
10802 College Pl	Cerritos	CA	90703	800-352-3301	562-924-9581
College Hospital Costa Mesa					
301 Victoria St	Costa Mesa	CA	92627	800-773-8001	949-642-2734
Creedmoor Psychiatric Ctr					
79-25 Winchester Blvd	Queens Village	NY	11427	800-597-8481	718-464-7500
Del Amo Hospital					
23700 Camino Del Sol	Torrance	CA	90505	800-533-5266	310-530-1151
Delaware Psychiatric Ctr					
1901 N Dupont Hwy	New Castle	DE	19720	800-652-2929	302-255-2700
Elmira Psychiatric Ctr					
100 Washington St	Elmira	NY	14901	800-597-8481	607-737-4711
Fairmount Behavioral Health System					
561 Fairthorne Ave	Philadelphia	PA	19128	800-235-0200	215-487-4000
Fort Lauderdale Behavioral Health Center					
5757 N Dixie Hwy	Oakland Park	FL	33334	800-585-7527	954-734-2000

				Toll-Free	Phone
Four Winds Hospital					
800 Cross River Rd	Katonah	NY	10536	800-528-6624	914-763-8151
Friends Hospital					
4641 Roosevelt Blvd	Philadelphia	PA	19124	800-889-0548	215-831-4600
Georgia Regional Hospital at Atlanta					
3073 Panthersville Rd	Atlanta	GA	30034	800-436-7442	404-243-2100
Georgia Regional Hospital at Savannah					
1915 Eisenhower Dr	Savannah	GA	31406	800-436-7442	912-356-2011
Green Oaks Hospital					
7808 Clodus Fields Dr	Dallas	TX	75251	800-866-6554	972-991-9504
Griffin Memorial Hospital					
900 E Main St	Norman	OK	73071	800-955-3468*	405-321-4880
*General					
Hamilton Ctr Inc					
620 Eighth Ave	Terre Haute	IN	47804	800-742-0787	
Havenwyck Hospital					
1525 University Dr	Auburn Hills	MI	48326	800-401-2727	248-373-9200
Hill Crest Behavioral Health Services					
6869 Fifth Ave S	Birmingham	AL	35212	800-292-8553	205-833-9000
Holly Hill Hospital					
3019 Falstaff Rd	Raleigh	NC	27610	800-447-1800	919-250-7000
Horsham Clinic					
722 E Butler Pk	Ambler	PA	19002	800-237-4447	215-643-7800
Kalamazoo Psychiatric Hospital					
1312 Oakland Dr	Kalamazoo	MI	49008	888-509-7007	269-337-3000
Kerrville State Hospital					
721 Thompson Dr	Kerrville	TX	78028	888-963-7111	830-896-2211
Kingsboro Psychiatric Ctr					
681 Clarkson Ave	Brooklyn	NY	11203	800-597-8481	
Lakeside Behavioral Health System					
2911 Brunswick Rd	Memphis	TN	38133	800-232-5253	901-377-4700
McLean Hospital 115 Mill St	Belmont	MA	02478	800-333-0338	
Meadows Psychiatric Ctr					
132 The Meadows Dr	Centre Hall	PA	16828	800-641-7529	814-364-2161
Memorial Hermann Prevention & Recovery Ctr (MHPARC)					
3043 Gessner	Houston	TX	77080	877-464-7272	713-939-7272
Mendota Mental Health Institute					
301 Troy Dr	Madison	WI	53704	800-323-8942	608-301-1000
Menninger Clinic					
12301 Main St	Houston	TX	77035	800-351-9058	713-275-5000
Moccasin Bend Mental Health Institute					
100 Moccasin Bend Rd	Chattanooga	TN	37405	800-560-5767	423-265-2271
Mohawk Valley Psychiatric Ctr					
1400 Noyes St	Utica	NY	13502	800-597-0481	315-738-3800
Napa State Hospital					
2100 Napa-Vallejo Hwy	Napa	CA	94558	866-327-4762	707-253-5000
New Hampshire Hospital					
36 Clinton St	Concord	NH	03301	800-735-2964	603-271-5200
New Mexico Behavioral Health Institute					
3695 Hot Springs Blvd	Las Vegas	NM	87701	800-446-5970	505-454-2100
North Dakota State Hospital					
2605 Cir Dr	Jamestown	ND	58401	888-862-7342	701-253-3650
Oklahoma Forensic Ctr					
24800 S 4420 Rd	Vinita	OK	74301	800-752-9475	918-256-7841
State Hospital 2600 Ctr St NE	Salem	OR	97301	800-544-7078	503-945-2800
Pembroke Hospital					
199 Oak St	Pembroke	MA	02359	800-222-2237	781-829-7000
Pilgrim Psychiatric Ctr					
998 Crooked Hill Rd	West Brentwood	NY	11717	800-597-8481	631-761-3500
Pine Rest Christian Mental Health Services					
300 68th St SE PO Box 165	Grand Rapids	MI	49501	800-678-5500	616-455-5000
Poplar Springs Hospital					
350 Poplar Dr	Petersburg	VA	23805	866-546-2229	804-733-6874
Psychiatric Institute of Washington					
4228 Wisconsin Ave NW	Washington	DC	20016	800-369-2273	202-885-5600
Richard H Hutchings Psychiatric Ctr					
620 Madison St	Syracuse	NY	13210	800-597-8481	315-426-3600
Ridge Behavioral Health System					
3050 Rio Dosa Dr	Lexington	KY	40509	800-753-4673	859-269-2325
River Park Hospital					
1230 Sixth Ave	Huntington	WV	25701	800-621-2673	304-526-9111
Riverview Psychiatric Ctr					
250 Arsenal St 11 State House Stn	Augusta	ME	04332	888-261-6684	207-624-4600
Rochester Psychiatric Ctr					
1111 Elmwood Ave	Rochester	NY	14620	800-310-1160	585-454-1490
Rogers Memorial Hospital Inc					
34700 Valley Rd	Oconomowoc	WI	53066	800-767-4411	262-646-4411
Sheppard Pratt Health System (SPHS)					
6501 N Charles St	Baltimore	MD	21285	800-627-0330	410-938-3000
Spring Harbor Hospital					
123 Andover Rd	Westbrook	ME	04092	888-524-0080	207-761-2200
Springfield Hospital Ctr					
6655 Sykesville Rd	Sykesville	MD	21784	800-333-7564	410-970-7000
Summit Behavioral Healthcare					
1101 Summit Rd	Cincinnati	OH	45237	800-372-8862	513-948-3600
Timberlawn Mental Health System					
4600 Samuell Blvd	Dallas	TX	75228	800-426-4944	214-381-7181
Trenton Psychiatric Hospital					
PO Box 7500	West Trenton	NJ	08628	800-382-6717	609-633-1500
University Behavioral Ctr					
2500 Discovery Dr	Orlando	FL	32826	800-999-0807	407-281-7000
Warren State Hospital					
33 Main Dr	North Warren	PA	16365	800-932-0313	
Western State Hospital					
9601 Steilacoom Blvd SW	Tacoma	WA	98498	877-501-2233	253-582-8900
Westwood Lodge Hospital					
45 Clapboardtree St	Westwood	MA	02090	800-222-2237	781-762-7764

373-6 Rehabilitation Hospitals

				Toll-Free	Phone
Allied Services Rehabilitation Hospital					
100 Abington Executive Pk	Clarks Summit	PA	18508	888-734-2272	570-348-1300
Bryn Mawr Rehab Hospital					
414 Paoli Pk	Malvern	PA	19355	866-225-5654	484-596-5400
Burke Rehabilitation Hospital					
785 Mamaroneck Ave	White Plains	NY	10605	888-992-8753	914-597-2500

Classified Section

				Toll-Free	Phone
Charlotte Institute of Rehabilitation					
1100 Blythe Blvd ....Charlotte	NC	28203		800-634-2256	704-355-4300
Craig Hospital					
3425 S Clarkson St ....Englewood	CO	80113		800-247-0257	303-789-8000
Crotched Mountain Foundation					
1 Verney Dr ....Greenfield	NH	03047		800-433-2900	603-547-3311
Daniel Drake Center					
151 W Galbraith Rd ....Cincinnati	OH	45216		800-948-0003	513-418-2500
Edwin Shaw Rehab					
1621 Flickinger Rd ....Akron	OH	44312		800-221-4601	330-784-1271
Encompass Health Corp					
3660 Grandview Pkwy Ste 200.................Birmingham	AL	35243		800-310-4919	205-967-7116
Encompass Health Corp					
107 Governors Dr ....Huntsville	AL	35801		800-467-3422	256-535-2300
Encompass Health Corp					
1212 W Lancaster ....Fort Worth	TX	76102		800-870-2336	817-870-2336
Encompass Health Corp					
6701 Oakmont Blvd ....Fort Worth	TX	76132		800-325-3591	817-370-4700
Encompass Health Rehabilitation Hospital of Austin					
330 W Ben White Blvd ....Austin	TX	78704		800-765-4772	512-730-4800
Frazier Rehabilitation Institute					
220 Abraham Flexner Way ....Louisville	KY	40202		800-333-2230	502-582-7400
Gaylord Hospital					
Gaylord Farms Rd PO Box 400.................Wallingford	CT	06492		866-429-5673	203-284-2800
HealthSouth MountainView Regional Rehabilitation Hospital					
1160 Van Voorhis Rd ....Morgantown	WV	26505		800-388-2451	304-598-1100
HealthSouth Nittany Valley Rehabilitation Hospital					
550 W College Ave ....Pleasant Gap	PA	16823		800-842-6026	814-359-3421
HealthSouth Rehabilitation Hospital of Altoona					
2005 Vly View Blvd ....Altoona	PA	16602		800-873-4220	814-944-3535
HealthSouth Rehabilitation Hospital of Fayetteville					
153 E Monte Painter ....Fayetteville	AR	72703		800-749-2257	479-444-2200
HealthSouth Rehabilitation Hospital of Kingsport					
113 Cassel Dr ....Kingsport	TN	37660		800-454-7422	423-246-7240
Madonna Rehabilitation Hospital					
5401 S St ....Lincoln	NE	68506		800-676-5448	402-489-7102
Marianjoy Rehabilitation Hospital					
26 W 171 Roosevelt Rd ....Wheaton	IL	60187		800-462-2366	630-462-4000
Mary Free Bed Rehabilitation Hospital					
235 Wealthy St SE ....Grand Rapids	MI	49503		800-528-8989	616-840-8000
Methodist Rehabilitation Ctr					
1350 E Woodrow Wilson Dr ....Jackson	MS	39216		800-223-6672	601-981-2611
Rancho Los Amigos National Rehabilitation Ctr					
7601 E Imperial Hwy ....Downey	CA	90242		877-726-2461	562-385-7111
Rehabilitation Hospital of Indiana					
4141 Shore Dr ....Indianapolis	IN	46254		866-510-2273	317-329-2000
Southern Indiana Rehabilitation Hospital					
3104 Blackiston Blvd ....New Albany	IN	47150		800-737-7090	812-941-8300
Southern Kentucky Rehabilitation Hospital					
1300 Campbell Ln ....Bowling Green	KY	42104		800-989-5775	270-782-6900
Spalding Rehabilitation Hospital					
900 Potomac St ....Aurora	CO	80011		800-367-3309	303-367-1166
Spaulding Rehabilitation Hospital					
125 Nashua St ....Boston	MA	02114		888-774-0055	617-573-7000
TIRR Memorial Hermann Hospital					
1333 Moursund St ....Houston	TX	77030		800-447-3422	713-799-5000

373-7 Specialty Hospitals

				Toll-Free	Phone
Barbara Ann Karmanos Cancer Institute					
4100 John R St ....Detroit	MI	48201		800-527-6266	
Bascom Palmer Eye Institute					
900 NW 17th St ....Miami	FL	33136		800-329-7000	305-326-6000
Dana-Farber Cancer Institute					
44 Binney St ....Boston	MA	02115		866-408-3324	617-632-3000
Dermatology Assoc of Atlanta PC					
5555 Peachtree Dunwoody Rd NE Ste 190 ....Atlanta	GA	30342		800-233-0706	404-256-4457
Eleanor Slater Hospital					
14 Harrington Rd ....Cranston	RI	02920		800-438-8477	401-462-2339
Fox Chase Cancer Ctr					
333 Cottman Ave ....Philadelphia	PA	19111		888-369-2427	215-728-6900
Georgia Cancer Specialists PC (GCS)					
1835 Savoy Dr ....Atlanta	GA	30341		800-491-5991	770-496-9400
Hughston Orthopedic Hospital					
100 Frist Ct ....Columbus	GA	31908		855-795-3609	706-494-2100
James, The 460 W Tenth Ave ....Columbus	OH	43210		800-293-5066	
Kindred Healthcare Inc					
7710 Rialto Blvd Ste 150 ....Austin	TX	78735		866-546-3733	512-288-0859
Kindred Hospital Fort Worth Southwest					
7800 Oakmont Blvd ....Fort Worth	TX	76132		800-359-7412	817-346-0094
Kindred Hospital Northland					
500 NW 68th St ....Kansas City	MO	64118		800-545-0749	816-420-6300
Leahi Hospital					
3675 Kilauea Ave ....Honolulu	HI	96816		800-845-6733	808-733-8000
Massachusetts Eye & Ear					
243 Charles St ....Boston	MA	02114		800-841-2900	617-523-7900
MD Anderson Cancer Ctr					
1515 Holcombe Blvd ....Houston	TX	77030		800-889-2094	713-792-2121
Memorial Sloan-Kettering Cancer Ctr					
1275 York Ave ....New York	NY	10065		800-525-2225	212-639-2000
Midwestern Regional Medical Ctr (MRMC)					
2520 Elisha Ave ....Zion	IL	60099		800-615-3055	847-872-4561
Moffitt Cancer Center University of S Florida					
12902 Magnolia Dr. ....Tampa	FL	33612		800-456-3434	888-663-3488
National Jewish Medical & Research Ctr					
1400 Jackson St ....Denver	CO	80206		877-225-5654	303-388-4461
New York Eye & Ear Infirmary					
310 E 14th St ....New York	NY	10003		800-522-4582	212-979-4000
Odessa Regional Medical Ctr					
520 E Sixth St ....Odessa	TX	79761		877-898-6080	432-582-8000
Roswell Park Cancer Institute					
Elm and Carlton St ....Buffalo	NY	14263		877-275-7724	716-845-2300
Saint Vincent Women's Hospital					
8111 Township Line Rd ....Indianapolis	IN	46260		800-582-8258	317-415-8111

				Toll-Free	Phone
Siteman Cancer Ctr					
4921 Parkview Pl ....Saint Louis	MO	63110		800-600-3606	314-362-5196
Texas Ctr for Infectious Diseases					
2303 SE Military Dr ....San Antonio	TX	78223		800-839-5864	210-534-8857
Texas Orthopedic Hospital					
7401 Main St ....Houston	TX	77030		866-783-4549	713-799-8600
UC Davis Cancer Ctr					
2315 Stockton Blvd ....Sacramento	CA	95817		800-362-5566	530-752-1011
Woman's Hospital					
100 Woman's Wy ....Baton Rouge	LA	70815		800-620-8474	225-927-1300
Women & Infants Hospital of Rhode Island					
101 Dudley St ....Providence	RI	02905		800-711-7011	401-274-1100
Women's & Children's Hospital (WCH)					
4600 Ambassador Caffery Pkwy ....Lafayette	LA	70508		888-569-8331	337-521-9100

373-8 Veterans Hospitals

Listings for veterans hospitals are organized by states, and then by city names within those groupings.

				Toll-Free	Phone
Tuscaloosa VA Medical Ctr					
3701 Loop Rd E ....Tuscaloosa	AL	35404		888-269-3045	205-554-2000
VA Medical Ctr					
2400 Hospital Rd ....Tuskegee	AL	36083		800-214-8387	334-727-0550
Northern Arizona VA Health Care System					
500 Hwy 89 N ....Prescott	AZ	86313		800-949-1005	928-445-4860
Southern Arizona Veterans Healthcare System					
3601 S Sixth Ave ....Tucson	AZ	85723		800-470-8262	520-792-1450
Veterans Health Care System of the Ozarks					
1100 N College Ave ....Fayetteville	AR	72703		800-691-8387	479-443-4301
VA Greater Los Angeles Healthcare System					
11301 Wilshire Blvd ....Los Angeles	CA	90073		800-952-4852	310-478-3711
VA San Diego Healthcare System					
3350 La Jolla Village Dr ....San Diego	CA	92161		800-331-8387	858-552-8585
San Francisco VA Medical Ctr					
4150 Clement St ....San Francisco	CA	94121		877-487-2838	415-221-4810
Denver Veterans Affairs Medical Ctr					
1055 Clermont St ....Denver	CO	80220		888-336-8262	303-399-8020
Veterans Affairs Medical Ctr					
1601 Kirkwood Hwy ....Wilmington	DE	19805		800-450-8262	302-994-2511
Veterans Affairs Medical Ctr					
10000 Bay Pines Blvd ....Bay Pines	FL	33744		888-820-0230	727-398-6661
Malcom Randall VAMC NF/SGVHS					
1601 SW Archer Rd ....Gainesville	FL	32608		800-324-8387	352-376-1611
Veterans Affairs Medical Ctr					
1201 NW 16th St ....Miami	FL	33125		888-276-1785	305-324-4455
Veterans Affairs Medical Ctr					
13000 Bruce B Downs Blvd ....Tampa	FL	33612		888-716-7787	813-972-2000
Carl Vinson Veterans Affairs Medical Ctr					
1826 Veterans Blvd ....Dublin	GA	31021		800-595-5229	478-272-1210
Boise VA Medical Center					
500 W Fort St ....Boise	ID	83702		866-437-5093	208-422-1000
Veterans Affairs Medical Ctr					
820 S Damen Ave ....Chicago	IL	60612		888-569-5282	312-569-8387
Veterans Affairs Medical Ctr					
2121 Lake Ave ....Fort Wayne	IN	46805		800-360-8387	260-426-5431
Richard L Roudebush VA Medical Ctr					
1481 W Tenth St ....Indianapolis	IN	46202		888-878-6889	317-554-0000
VA Central Iowa Health Care System					
3600 30th St ....Des Moines	IA	50310		800-294-8387	515-699-5999
Veterans Affairs Medical Ctr					
601 Hwy 6 W ....Iowa City	IA	52246		866-687-7382	319-338-0581
Dwight D Eisenhower V A Medical Ctr					
4101 S Fourth St ....Leavenworth	KS	66048		800-952-8387	913-682-2000
Colmery-O'Neil Veterans Affairs Medical Ctr					
2200 SW Gage Blvd ....Topeka	KS	66622		800-574-8387	785-350-3111
Alexandria Veterans Affairs Medical Ctr					
2495 Shreveport Hwy 71 N ....Pineville	LA	71360		800-375-8387	318-473-0010
Overton Brooks Veterans Affairs Medical Ctr					
510 E Stoner Ave ....Shreveport	LA	71101		800-863-7441	318-221-8411
Veterans Affairs Medical Ctr					
10 N Greene St ....Baltimore	MD	21201		800-463-6295	410-605-7000
Veterans Affairs Medical Ctr					
940 Belmont St ....Brockton	MA	02301		800-865-3384	508-583-4500
Veterans Affairs Medical Ctr					
150 S Huntington Ave ....Jamaica Plain	MA	02130		800-273-8255	
Veterans Affairs Medical Ctr					
2215 Fuller Rd ....Ann Arbor	MI	48105		800-361-8387	734-769-7100
US. Department of Veterans Affairs					
325 E 'H' St ....Iron Mountain	MI	49801		800-215-8262	906-774-3300
Veterans Affairs Medical Ctr					
1500 Weiss St ....Saginaw	MI	48602		877-222-8387	989-497-2500
Veterans Affairs Health Care System					
1 Veterans Dr ....Minneapolis	MN	55417		866-414-5058	612-725-2000
John J Pershing Veterans Affairs Medical Ctr					
1500 N Westwood Blvd ....Poplar Bluff	MO	63901		888-557-8262	573-686-4151
VA Nebraska-Western Iowa Health Care System					
600 S 70th St ....Lincoln	NE	68510		866-851-6052	402-489-3802
Veterans Affairs Medical Ctr					
4101 Woolworth Ave ....Omaha	NE	68105		800-451-5796	402-346-8800
VA Sierra Nevada Health Care System					
975 Kirman Ave ....Reno	NV	89502		888-838-6256	775-786-7200
Veterans Affairs Medical Ctr					
718 Smyth Rd ....Manchester	NH	03104		800-892-8384	603-624-4366
East Orange Campus of the VA New Jersey Health Care System (NJHCS)					
385 Tremont Ave ....East Orange	NJ	07018		844-872-4681*	
*General					
Stratton Veterans Affairs Medical Ctr					
113 Holland Ave ....Albany	NY	12208		800-223-4810	518-626-5000
Bath Veterans Affairs Medical Ctr					
76 Veterans Ave ....Bath	NY	14810		877-845-3247	607-664-4000
Veterans Affairs Medical Ctr					
3495 Bailey Ave ....Buffalo	NY	14215		800-532-8387	716-834-9200
VA Hudson Valley Health Care System					
Montrose Campus					
2094 Albany Post Rd ....Montrose	NY	10548		800-269-8749	914-737-4400

					Toll-Free	Phone
Veterans Affairs Medical Ctr	79 Middleville Rd	Northport	NY	11768	**800-877-6976**	631-261-4400
Veterans Affairs Medical Ctr	800 Irving Ave	Syracuse	NY	13210	**800-792-4334**	315-425-4400
Veterans Affairs Medical Ctr	1100 Tunnel Rd	Asheville	NC	28805	**800-932-6408**	828-298-7911
Veterans Affairs Medical Ctr	508 Fulton St	Durham	NC	27705	**888-878-6890**	919-286-0411
WG Bill Hefner Veterans Affairs Medical Ctr	1601 Brenner Ave	Salisbury	NC	28144	**800-469-8262**	704-638-9000
Louis Stokes Cleveland Veterans Affairs Medical Ctr	10701 E Blvd	Cleveland	OH	44106	**888-838-6446**	216-791-3800
Dayton Va Medical Ctr	4100 W Third St	Dayton	OH	45428	**800-368-8262**	937-268-6511
Veterans Affairs Medical Ctr	921 NE 13th St	Oklahoma City	OK	73104	**866-835-5273**	405-456-1000
Altoona VA Medical Ctr	2907 Pleasant Vly Blvd	Altoona	PA	16602	**877-626-2500**	
Erie VA Medical Ctr	135 E 38th St	Erie	PA	16504	**800-274-8387**	814-868-8661
Veterans Affairs Medical Ctr	1700 S Lincoln Ave	Lebanon	PA	17042	**800-409-8771**	
Veterans Affairs Medical Ctr	830 Chalkstone Ave	Providence	RI	02908	**866-590-2976**	401-273-7100
Ralph H Johnson VA Medical Center	109 Bee St	Charleston	SC	29401	**888-878-6884**	843-577-5011
Veterans Affairs Medical Ctr	6439 Garners Ferry Rd	Columbia	SC	29209	**888-651-2683**	803-776-4000
Veterans Affairs Medical Ctr	1030 Jefferson Ave	Memphis	TN	38104	**800-636-8262**	901-523-8990
James H Quillen Veterans Affairs Medical Ctr	Corner of Lamont & Veterans Way	Mountain Home	TN	37684	**877-573-3529**	423-926-1171
Veterans Affairs Medical Ctr	1310 24th Ave S	Nashville	TN	37212	**800-228-4973**	615-327-4751
Thomas E Creek Veterans Affairs Medical Ctr	6010 Amarillo Blvd W	Amarillo	TX	79106	**800-687-8262**	806-355-9703
VA Medical Ctr	4500 S Lancaster Rd	Dallas	TX	75216	**800-849-3597**	214-742-8387
Veterans Affairs Medical Ctr	2002 Holcombe Blvd	Houston	TX	77030	**800-553-2278**	713-791-1414
South Texas Veterans Health Care System	7400 Merton Minter St	San Antonio	TX	78229	**800-209-7377**	210-617-5300
Central Texas Veterans Health Care System	1901 Veterans Memorial Dr	Temple	TX	76504	**800-423-2111**	254-778-4811
Veterans Affairs Medical Ctr	500 Foothill Dr	Salt Lake City	UT	84148	**800-613-4012**	801-582-1565
White River Junction Veterans Affairs Medical Ctr	215 N Main St	White River Junction	VT	05009	**866-687-8387**	802-295-9363
Veterans Affairs Medical Ctr	100 Emancipation Dr	Hampton	VA	23667	**800-488-8244**	757-722-9961
Salem Veterans Affairs Medical Ctr	1970 Roanoke Blvd	Salem	VA	24153	**888-982-2463**	540-982-2463
Veterans Affairs Puget Sound Medical Ctr	1660 S Columbian Way	Seattle	WA	98108	**800-329-8387**	206-762-1010
Louis A Johnson Veterans Affairs Medical Ctr	1 Medical Ctr Dr	Clarksburg	WV	26301	**800-733-0512**	304-623-3461
Huntington Veterans Affairs Medical Ctr	1540 Spring Valley Dr	Huntington	WV	25704	**800-827-8244**	304-429-6741
Veterans Affairs Medical Ctr	2500 Overlook Terr	Madison	WI	53705	**888-478-8321**	608-256-1901
Tomah Veterans Affairs Medical Ctr	500 E Veterans St	Tomah	WI	54660	**800-872-8662**	608-372-3971

374 HOT TUBS, SPAS, WHIRLPOOL BATHS

					Toll-Free	Phone
Alaglass Swimming Pools	165 Sweet Bay Rd	Saint Matthews	SC	29135	**877-655-7179**	
Atlantic Spas & Billiards	8721 Glenwood Ave	Raleigh	NC	27617	**800-849-8827**	919-783-7447
Best Bath Systems	723 Garber St	Caldwell	ID	83605	**866-333-8657**	208-342-6823
Cal Spas Inc	1462 E Ninth St	Pomona	CA	91766	**800-225-7727**	909-623-8781
Jason International Inc	8328 MacArthur Dr	North Little Rock	AR	72118	**800-255-5766**	501-771-4477
Kallista Inc	1227 N Eigth St Ste 2 *Cust Svc	Sheboygan	WI	53081	**888-452-5547***	920-457-4441
Koral Industries Inc	1504 S Kaufman St	Ennis	TX	75119	**800-627-2441**	972-875-6555
Marquis Spas Corp	596 Hoffman Rd	Independence	OR	97351	**800-275-0888**	503-838-0888
Master Spas Inc	6927 Lincoln Pkwy	Fort Wayne	IN	46804	**800-860-7727**	260-436-9100
Plastic Development Co Inc	75 Palmer Industrial Rd PO Box 4007	Williamsport	PA	17701	**800-451-1420**	
Royal Manufacturing	14635 Chrisman Rd	Houston	TX	77039	**800-826-0074**	281-442-3400
Spa Manufacturers	6060 Ulmerton Rd	Clearwater	FL	33760	**877-530-9493**	727-530-9493
ThermoSpas Hot Tubs	10 Research Pkwy Ste 300	Wallingford	CT	06492	**800-876-0158**	
Watertech Whirlpool Bath & Spa	2507 Plymouth Rd	Johnson City	TN	37601	**800-289-8827**	
Watkins Mfg Corp	1280 Pk Ctr Dr	Vista	CA	92081	**800-999-4688**	

375 HOTEL RESERVATIONS SERVICES

					Toll-Free	Phone
AC Central Reservations Inc	201 Tilton Rd London Sq Mall Ste 17B	Northfield	NJ	08225	**888-227-6667**	609-383-8880
Alexandria & Arlington Bed & Breakfast Networks (AABBN)	4938 Hampden Ln Ste 164	Bethesda	MD	20814	**888-549-3415**	703-549-3415
B & B Agency of Boston	47 Commercial Wharf Apt 3	Boston	MA	02110	**800-248-9262**	617-720-3540
Branson's Best Reservations	2875 Green Mtn Dr	Branson	MO	65616	**800-335-2555**	417-339-2204
Capitol Reservations	1730 Rhode Island Ave NW	Washington	DC	20036	**800-847-4832**	202-452-1270
Greater New Orleans Hotel & Lodging Assn	2020 St Charles Ave 5th Fl	New Orleans	LA	70130	**866-366-1121**	504-525-2264
Hawaii's Best Bed & Breakfasts	571 Pauku St	Kailua	HI	96734	**800-262-9912**	808-263-3100
Hot Rooms	444 N Michigan Ave Ste 1200	Chicago	IL	60611	**800-468-3500**	773-468-7666
Jackson Hole Central Reservations (JHCR)	140 E Broadway Ste 24 PO Box 2618	Jackson	WY	83001	**888-838-6606**	307-733-4005
Key West Key	726 Passover Ln	Key West	FL	33040	**800-881-7321**	
Know Before You Go Reservations	8000 International Dr	Orlando	FL	32819	**800-749-1993**	
Lasvegasticketscom	5030 Paradise Rd Ste B108	Las Vegas	NV	89119	**800-597-7469**	702-597-1588
Leading Hotels of the World	485 Lexington Ave Ste 401	New York	NY	10017	**800-745-8883**	212-515-5600
Long & Foster Vacation Rentals	41 Maryland Ave	Annapolis	MD	21401	**800-981-8234**	410-263-3262
Nantucket Accommodations	1 Macys Ln	Nantucket	MA	02554	**866-743-3330**	508-228-9559
Ocean City Hotel-Motel-Restaurant Assn	PO Box 340	Ocean City	MD	21843	**800-626-2326**	410-289-6733
Quikbook	381 Park Ave S	New York	NY	10016	**800-789-9887**	212-779-7666
San Diego Concierge	4422 Glacier Ave E	San Diego	CA	92120	**800-979-9091**	619-280-4121
Stay Aspen Snowmass	255 Gold Rivers Ct Ste 300	Basalt	CO	81621	**888-649-5982**	970-429-5037
Washington DC Accommodations	2201 Wisconsin Ave NW Ste C-120	Washington	DC	20007	**800-503-3330**	202-289-2220
Winter Park Resort	85 Parsenn Rd *Resv	Winter Park	CO	80482	**800-903-7275***	970-726-5514
Xanterra South Rim LLC	10 Albright St PO Box 699	Grand Canyon	AZ	86023	**800-843-8723**	928-638-2631

376 HOTELS - CONFERENCE CENTER

					Toll-Free	Phone
Acoma Business Enterprise	PO Box 310	Acoma	NM	87034	**888-759-2489**	
Airlie Conference Ctr	6809 Airlie Rd	Warrenton	VA	20187	**800-288-9573**	540-347-1300
Alexandra Hotel	77 Ryerson Ave	Toronto	ON	M5T2V4	**800-567-1893**	416-504-2121
Banff Centre for Arts & Creativity	107 Tunnel Mtn Dr PO Box 1020	Banff	AB	T1L1H5	**800-884-7574**	403-762-6100
Chaminade Resort & Spa	1 Chaminade Ln	Santa Cruz	CA	95065	**800-283-6569**	831-475-5600
Chattanoogan, The	1201 Broad St	Chattanooga	TN	37402	**877-756-1684**	423-756-3400
Cheyenne Mountain Conference Resort	3225 Broadmoor Valley Rd	Colorado Springs	CO	80906	**800-428-8886**	719-538-4000
Coconut Mallory Resort & Marina	1445 S Roosevelt Blvd	Key West	FL	33040	**866-316-1843**	
College Park Marriott Hotel & Conference Center	3501 University Blvd E	Hyattsville	MD	20783	**800-721-7033**	301-985-7300
Conference Ctr at NorthPointe	100 Green Meadows Dr S	Lewis Center	OH	43035	**844-475-5045**	614-880-4300
Cook Hotel & Conference Ctr	3848 West Lakeshore Dr	Baton Rouge	LA	70808	**866-610-2665**	225-383-2665
Country Springs Hotel & Conference Ctr	2810 Golf Rd	Pewaukee	WI	53072	**800-247-6640**	262-547-0201
Crystal Mountain Resort	12500 Crystal Mtn Dr	Thompsonville	MI	49683	**800-968-7686**	231-378-2000
Dellisart Lodging LLC	10800 Alpharetta Hwy Ste 208-776	Roswell	GA	30076	**877-606-0591**	847-306-0954
Delta Hotels	2685 Rue King O	Sherbrooke	QC	J1L1C1	**800-268-1133**	819-822-1989
DNC Parks & Resorts at KSC Inc	250 Delaware Ave	Buffalo	NY	14202	**855-433-4210**	
Dolce Hayes Mansion	200 Edenvale Ave	San Jose	CA	95136	**866-981-3300**	408-226-3200
Dolce Hotels & Resorts	201 Aberdeen Pkwy	Peachtree City	GA	30269	**800-983-6523**	770-487-2666
Doral Arrowwood Conference Resort	975 Anderson Hill Rd	Rye Brook	NY	10573	**844-211-0512**	844-214-5500
Emory Conference Ctr Hotel	1615 Clifton Rd	Atlanta	GA	30329	**800-933-6679**	404-712-6000
Evergreen Marriott Conference Resort	4021 Lakeview Dr	Stone Mountain	GA	30083	**800-983-4240**	
Founders Inn	5641 Indian River Rd	Virginia Beach	VA	23464	**800-926-4466**	757-424-5511
Glen Cove Mansion Hotel & Conference Ctr	200 Dosoris Ln	Glen Cove	NY	11542	**877-782-9426**	516-671-6400
Grandover Resort & Conference Ctr	1000 Club Rd	Greensboro	NC	27407	**800-472-6301**	336-294-1800
Hamilton Park Hotel & Conference Ctr	175 Park Ave	Florham Park	NJ	07932	**877-999-3223**	973-377-2424
Hickory Ridge Marriott Conference Hotel	10400 Fernwood Rd	Bethesda	MD	20817	**800-334-0344**	301-380-3000
Hidden Valley Resort & Conference Ctr	1 Craighead Dr PO Box 4420	Hidden Valley	PA	15502	**800-452-2223**	814 443-8000
Hotel at Auburn University & Dixon Conference Ctr, The	241 S College St	Auburn	AL	36830	**800-228-2876**	334-821-8200
Hotel Roanoke & Conference Ctr	110 Shenandoah Ave	Roanoke	VA	24016	**866-594-4722**	540-985-5900
Hotels Etc Inc	910 Athens Hwy Ste K-214	Loganville	GA	30052	**877-967-7283**	

Classified Section

					Toll-Free	Phone
Inn at Virginia Tech & Skelton Conference Ctr						
901 Prices Fork Rd	Blacksburg	VA	24061		877-200-3360	540-231-8000
Islander Resort						
82100 Overseas Hwy PO Box 766	Islamorada	FL	33036		800-753-6002	305-664-2031
Ivey Spencer Leadership Ctr						
551 Windermere Rd	London	ON	N5X2T1		800-407-9832	519-679-4546
James L Allen Ctr						
2211 Campus Dr	Evanston	IL	60208		877-755-2227	847-467-7000
Kingbridge Centre, The						
12750 Jane St	King City	ON	L7B1A3		800-827-7221	905-833-3086
Kingsmill Resort & Spa						
1010 Kingsmill Rd	Williamsburg	VA	23185		800-832-5665	757-253-1703
Lakeview Golf Resort & Spa						
1 Lakeview Dr	Morgantown	WV	26508		800-624-8300	304-594-1111
Lansdowne Resort						
44050 Woodridge Pkwy	Leesburg	VA	20176		877-513-8400	703-729-8400
Lodge At Breckenridge, The						
112 Overlook Dr	Breckenridge	CO	80424		800-736-1607	970-453-9300
Marietta Conference Ctr & Resort						
500 Powder Springs St	Marietta	GA	30064		888-685-2500	770-427-2500
Marriott Montgomery Prattville at Capitol Hill						
2500 Legends Cir	Prattville	AL	36066		800-593-6429*	334-290-1235
*Resv						
Mena Tours & Travel						
5209 N Clark St	Chicago	IL	60640		800-937-6362	773-275-2125
Millennium Broadway Hotel New York						
145 W 44th St	New York	NY	10036		800-622-5569	212-768-4400
National Center for Employee Development (NCED)						
2701 E Imhoff Rd	Norman	OK	73071		866-438-6233	405-366-4420
NAV Canada Training & Conference Ctr						
1950 Montreal Rd	Cornwall	ON	K6H6L2		877-832-6416	613-936-5800
Penn Stater Conference Ctr Hotel						
215 Innovation Blvd	State College	PA	16803		800-233-7505	814-863-5000
PNK (River City) LLC						
777 River City Casino Blvd	Saint Louis	MO	63125		888-578-7289	
Quintess Collection LLC						
11101 W 120th Ave Ste 200	Broomfield	CO	80021		800-895-4301	
Resort at Squaw Creek						
400 Squaw Creek Rd PO Box 3333	Olympic Valley	CA	96146		800-327-3353	530-583-6300
Rodd Hotels & Resorts						
PO Box 432	Charlottetown	PE	C1A7K7		800-565-7633	902-892-7448
Saratoga Hilton						
534 Broadway	Saratoga Springs	NY	12866		800-445-8667	518-584-4000
Sheraton Old San Juan Hotel						
100 Brumbaugh St	San Juan	PR	00901		888-627-8185	787-289-1914
Skamania Lodge						
1131 SW Skamania Lodge Way	Stevenson	WA	98648		800-221-7117	509-314-4177
Snowbird Ski & Summer Resort						
Hwy 210 PO Box 929000	Snowbird	UT	84092		800-453-3000	801-742-2222
Stoweflake Mountain Resort & Spa						
1746 Mountain Rd PO Box 369	Stowe	VT	05672		800-253-2232	802-253-7355
Vdara Hotel & Spa						
2600 W Harmon Ave	Las Vegas	NV	89158		866-745-7111	702-590-2111
White Oaks Resort & Spa						
253 Taylor Rd SS4	Niagara-on-the-Lake	ON	L0S1J0		800-263-5766*	905-688-2550
*Resv						
Windemere Hotel & Conference Center						
2047 S Hwy 92	Sierra Vista	AZ	85635		800-825-4656	520-459-5900
Woodlands Resort & Conference Ctr, The						
2301 N Millbend Dr	The Woodlands	TX	77380		800-433-2624*	281-367-1100
*Resv						

377   HOTELS - FREQUENT STAY PROGRAMS

					Toll-Free	Phone
Aava Whistler Hotel Ltd						
4005 Whistler Way	Whistler	BC	V0N1B4		800-663-5644	604-932-2522
Apple Farm Bakery						
2015 Monterey St	San Luis Obispo	CA	93401		800-255-2040	805-544-2040
Bay Landing Hotel						
1550 Bayshore Hwy	Burlingame	CA	94010		866-783-9612	650-259-9000
Beach Terrace Motor Inn						
3400 Atlantic Ave	Wildwood	NJ	08260		800-841-8416	609-522-8100
Bear Creek Mountain Resort						
101 Doe Mtn Ln	Macungie	PA	18062		866-754-2822	610-641-7101
Best Western InnTowner, The						
2424 University Ave	Madison	WI	53726		800-258-8321	608-233-8778
Beverly Hills Plaza Hotel						
10300 Wilshire Blvd	Los Angeles	CA	90024		800-800-1234	310-275-5575
Boston Common Hotel						
40 Trinity Pl	Boston	MA	02116		800-580-0194	
Buena Vista Motor Inn						
1599 Lombard St	San Francisco	CA	94123		800-835-4980	415-923-9600
Caneel Bay Resort						
PO Box 720	St. John	VI	00831		855-226-3358	212-845-0581
Chestnut Mountain Resort						
8700 W Chestnut Mountain Rd	Galena	IL	61036		800-397-1320	
Christie Lodge PO Box 1196	Avon	CO	81620		888-325-6343	970-845-4504
Chukchansi Gold Resort & Casino						
711 Lucky Ln	Coarsegold	CA	93614		866-794-6946	
Comfort Inn & Suites						
2485 Hotel Circle Pl	San Diego	CA	92108		888-221-6039	
Country Hearth Inn Inc						
50 Glenlake Pkwy NE Ste 350	Atlanta	GA	30328		888-443-2784	770-393-2662
Crowne Plaza Niagara Falls - Fallsview						
5685 Falls Ave	Niagara Falls	ON	L2E6W7		800-263-7135	905-374-4447
Danfords Hotel & Marina						
25 E Broadway	Port Jefferson	NY	11777		800-332-6367	
Days Inn Hinton-Jasper Hotel						
358 Smith St	Hinton	AB	T7V2A1		800-259-4827	780-817-1960
Eastover Estate & Eco-Village						
430 East St PO Box 2282	Lenox	MA	01240		866-264-5139	
Fairmont San Francisco Hotel, The						
950 Mason St	San Francisco	CA	94108		800-257-7544	415-772-5000
Fort William Henry Corp, The						
48 Canada St	Lake George	NY	12845		800-234-0267	518-668-3081

					Toll-Free	Phone
Fountain Grove Inn, The						
101 Fountaingrove Pkwy	Santa Rosa	CA	95403		800-222-6101	707-578-6101
Gainey Suites Hotel						
7300 E Gainey	Scottsdale	AZ	85258		800-970-4666	480-922-6969
GrandLife Hotels						
310 W Broadway	New York	NY	10013		800-965-3000	212-965-3000
Great Wolf Lodge of Sandusky LLC						
4600 Milan Rd US 250	Sandusky	OH	44870		800-641-9653	
Hanover Marriott						
1401 Rt 10 E	Whippany	NJ	07981		800-983-4240	
Harrah's Las Vegas						
3475 Las Vegas Blvd S	Las Vegas	NV	89109		800-214-9110	
Hilton Savannah Desoto						
15 E Liberty St	Savannah	GA	31401		844-279-5094	
Holiday Inn Baltimore Inner Harbor Hotel						
301 W Lombard St	Baltimore	MD	21201		877-834-3613	410-685-3500
Holiday Inn By the Bay						
88 Spring St	Portland	ME	04101		800-345-5050	207-775-2311
Horseshoe Valley Resort Ltd						
1101 Horseshoe Valley Rd - Comp 10 RR 1	Barrie	ON	L4M4Y8		800-461-5627	705-835-2790
Hotel Blue						
717 Central Ave NW	Albuquerque	NM	87102		877-878-4868	505-924-2400
Inn at Mamas Fish House						
799 Poho Pl	Paia	HI	96779		800-860-4852	808-579-8488
Intercontinental San Francisco						
888 Howard St	San Francisco	CA	94103		888-811-4273	
Kontiki Beach Resort						
2290 N Fulton Beach Rd	Rockport	TX	78382		800-388-0649	361-729-2318
Lahaina Shores Beach Resort						
475 Front St	Lahaina	HI	96761		866-934-9176	
Lakeview Hotels & Resorts						
Lakeview Inns & Suites - Hinton						
185 Carlton St Ste 600	Winnipeg	MB	R3C3J1		877-355-3500	780-865-2575
Lancaster Group Inc, The						
3411 Richmond Ave Ste 460	Houston	TX	77046		888-365-7829	713-224-6000
Lodge at Tiburon, The						
1651 Tiburon Blvd	Tiburon	CA	94920		800-762-7770	415-435-3133
London West Hollywood Hotel						
1020 N San Vicente Blvd	West Hollywood	CA	90069		866-282-4560	
Marin Suites Hotel LLC						
45 Tamal Vista Blvd	Corte Madera	CA	94925		800-362-3372	415-924-3608
Meadowmere Resort						
74 Main St	Ogunquit	ME	03907		800-633-8718	207-646-9661
Melrose Hotel Washington DC, The						
2430 Pennsylvania Ave NW	Washington	DC	20037		800-635-7673	202-955-6400
Menominee Hotel						
N277 Hwy 47/55 PO Box 760	Keshena	WI	54135		800-343-7778	
Midamerica Hotels Corp						
105 S Mt Auburn Rd	Cape Girardeau	MO	63703		888-866-4326	573-334-0546
Oak Plantation Resort & Suites Condominium Assn						
4090 Enchanted Oaks Cir	Kissimmee	FL	34741		888-411-4141	
Oceana Resorts LLC						
1000 Second Ave S Ste 110	North Myrtle Beach	SC	29582		866-469-7853	
Oceano Hotel & Spa Half Moon Bay Harbor						
280 Capistrano Rd	Half Moon Bay	CA	94019		888-623-2661	650-726-5400
Old Edwards Inn & Spa						
445 Main St	Highlands	NC	28741		866-526-8008	
Omni Hotels Select Guest Loyalty Program						
11819 Miami St 3rd Fl	Omaha	NE	68164		800-843-6664*	
*Cust Svc						
Pearl Hotel Waikiki						
415 Nahua St	Honolulu	HI	96815		855-518-3455	808-922-1616
Perry Group International						
1 Market Plz Ste 3600	San Francisco	CA	94105		800-580-3950	
Plaza Hotel, The						
5th Ave at Central Park S	New York	NY	10019		866-940-9361	212-759-3000
Prince Preferred Guest Program						
100 Holomoana St	Honolulu	HI	96815		800-774-6234	
Pueblo Bonito Golf & Spa Resorts						
4350 La Jolla Village Dr	San Diego	CA	92122		800-990-8250	858-642-2050
Radisson Hotel & Suites						
100 W Michigan	Kalamazoo	MI	49007		888-288-8889	
Ramada Inn Airport						
2275 Marina Mile Blvd STATE Rd 84	Fort Lauderdale	FL	33312		800-509-9854	954-584-4000
Saskatoon Inn Hotel & Conference Centre						
2002 Airport Dr	Saskatoon	SK	S7L6M4		800-667-8789	306-242-1440
Sheraton Oklahoma City Hotel						
1 N Broadway	Oklahoma City	OK	73102		888-627-8416	405-235-2780
Silver Lake Resort Ltd						
7751 Black Lake Rd	Kissimmee	FL	34747		800-226-6090*	407-397-2828
*General						
Spectra Co 2510 Supply St	Pomona	CA	91767		800-375-1771	
Sunstream Hotels & Resorts						
6231 Estero Blvd	Fort Myers Beach	FL	33931		844-652-3696	239-765-4111
Tahoe Biltmore Lodge & Casino						
5 NV-28	Crystal Bay	NV	89402		800-245-8667	
Terranea Resort & Spa						
100 Terranea Way	Rancho Palos Verdes	CA	90275		866-547-3066	310-265-2800
Twin Pine Casino						
22223 Hwy 29 PO Box 789	Middletown	CA	95461		800-564-4872	707-987-0197
Vacationer RV Resort						
1581 E Main St	El Cajon	CA	92021		877-626-4409	
Virgin River Casino Corp						
100 Pioneer Blvd	Mesquite	NV	89027		877-438-2929	
W New York- Union Square						
201 Park Ave S	New York	NY	10003		877-822-0000	212-253-9119
Washington Jefferson LLC						
318 W 51st St	New York	NY	10019		888-567-7550	212-246-7550
Westin Atlanta Perimeter North, The						
7 Concourse Pkwy NE	Atlanta	GA	30328		888-627-8407	770-395-3900
Westin Michigan Avenue Hotel						
909 N Michigan Ave	Chicago	IL	60611		888-627-8385	312-943-7200
Westin Reston Heights, The						
11750 Sunrise Vly Dr	Reston	VA	20191		888-627-8344	703-391-9000

378 HOTELS & HOTEL COMPANIES

SEE ALSO Hotels - Frequent Stay Programs ; Resorts & Resort Companies ; Hotels - Conference Center ; Hotel Reservations Services ; Corporate Housing ; Casino Companies

Name	Address	City	State	Zip	Toll-Free	Phone
1886 Crescent Hotel & Spa	75 Prospect Ave	Eureka Springs	AR	72632	**877-342-9766**	855-725-5720
Academy Hotel Colorado Springs, The	8110 N Academy Blvd	Colorado Springs	CO	80920	**800-766-8524**	719-598-5770
Acadia Inn	98 Eden St	Bar Harbor	ME	04609	**800-638-3636**	207-288-3500
Accent Inns Vancouver Airport	10551 St Edwards Dr	Richmond	BC	V6X3L8	**800-663-0298**	604-273-3311
Accent Inns Vancouver-Burnaby	3777 Henning Dr	Burnaby	BC	V5C6N5	**800-663-0298**	604-473-5000
Acqua Hotel	555 Redwood Hwy	Mill Valley	CA	94941	**888-662-9555**	415-380-0400
Acqualina	17875 Collins Ave	Sunny Isles Beach	FL	33160	**877-312-9742**	305-918-8000
Adams Oceanfront Resort	4 Read St	Dewey Beach	DE	19971	**800-448-8080**	302-227-3030
Admiral Fell Inn	888 S Broadway	Baltimore	MD	21231	**866-583-4162**	410-522-7377
Admiral on Baltimore	2 Baltimore Ave	Rehoboth Beach	DE	19971	**888-882-4188**	302-227-1300
Adventureland Inn	305 34th Ave NW	Altoona	IA	50009	**800-910-5382**	515-265-7321
Affina Dumont	150 E 34th St	New York	NY	10016	**866-233-4642**	212-481-7600
Affinia 50	155 E 50th St	New York	NY	10022	**866-246-2203**	212-751-5710
Affinia Manhattan	371 Seventh Ave	New York	NY	10001	**866-246-2203**	212-563-1800
Airtel Plaza Hotel	7277 Valjean Ave	Van Nuys	CA	91406	**877-939-9268**	818-997-7676
Ala Moana Hotel	410 Atkinson Dr	Honolulu	HI	96814	**800-367-6025**	808-955-4811
Albert at Bay Suite Hotel	435 Albert St	Ottawa	ON	K1R7X4	**800-267-6644**	613-238-8858
Albion Hotel	1650 James Ave *General	Miami Beach	FL	33139	**877-782-3557***	305-913-1000
Alexis Hotel	1007 First Ave	Seattle	WA	98104	**866-356-8894**	206-624-4844
Alise Boston - A Staypineapple Hotel, The	54 Berkeley St	Boston	MA	02116	**800-842-3450**	617-585-5625
Alohilani Resort	2490 Kalakaua Ave	Honolulu	HI	96815	**800-367-6060**	808-922-1233
Alpenhof Lodge	3255 W Village Dr	Teton Village	WY	83025	**800-732-3244**	307-733-3242
Ambrosia House Tropical Lodging	622 Fleming St	Key West	FL	33040	**800-535-9838**	305-296-9838
AmericInn International LLC	250 Lake Dr E *Resv	Chanhassen	MN	55317	**800-634-3444***	952-294-5000
Ameristar Casino Hotel Council Bluffs	2200 River Rd	Council Bluffs	IA	51501	**866-667-3386**	712-328-8888
Amway Grand Plaza Hotel	187 Monroe Ave NW	Grand Rapids	MI	49503	**800-253-3590**	616-774-2000
Anaheim Hotel, The	1700 S Harbor Blvd	Anaheim	CA	92802	**800-631-4144**	714-772-5900
Andrews Hotel	624 Post St	San Francisco	CA	94109	**800-926-3739**	415-563-6877
Antler Inn	43 W Pearl St PO Box 575	Jackson	WY	83001	**800-483-8667**	307-733-2535
Apple Tree Inn	9508 N Div St	Spokane	WA	99218	**800-323-5796**	509-466-3020
Applewood Manor Inn	62 Cumberland Cir	Asheville	NC	28801	**800-442-2197**	828-254-2244
Aqua Bamboo Waikiki	2425 Kuhio Ave	Honolulu	HI	96815	**855-747-0754**	808-922-7777
ARC the Hotel Ottawa	140 Slater St	Ottawa	ON	K1P5H6	**800-699-2516**	613-238-2888
Argonaut Hotel	495 Jefferson St	San Francisco	CA	94109	**866-415-0704**	415-563-0800
Arizona Charlie's Boulder Casino & Hotel	4575 Boulder Hwy	Las Vegas	NV	89121	**888-236-9066**	702-951-5800
Asticou Inn	15 Peabody Dr	Northeast Harbor	ME	04662	**800-258-3373**	207-276-3344
Aston Hotels & Resorts	2155 Kalakaua Ave Ste 500	Honolulu	HI	96815	**800-775-4228**	808-931-1400
Astor Crowne Plaza	739 Canal St	New Orleans	LA	70130	**877-408-9661**	504-962-0500
Astor Hotel, The	924 E Juneau Ave	Milwaukee	WI	53202	**800-558-0200**	414-271-4220
Atheneum Suite Hotel & Conference Ctr	1000 Brush Ave	Detroit	MI	48226	**800-772-2323**	313-962-2323
Atlantic Eyrie Lodge	6 Norman Rd	Bar Harbor	ME	04609	**800-422-2883**	
Atlantic Sands Hotel	1 Baltimore Ave	Rehoboth Beach	DE	19971	**800-422-0600**	302-227-2511
Atrium Hotel	18700 MacArthur Blvd	Irvine	CA	92612	**800-854-3012**	949-833-2770
Auberge du Soleil	180 Rutherford Hill Rd	Rutherford	CA	94573	**800-348-5406**	707-963-1211
Auberge du Vieux-Port	97 Rue de la Commune E	Montreal	QC	H2Y1J1	**888-660-7678**	514-876-0081
Auberge Saint-Antoine	8 rue Saint-Antoine	Quebec	QC	G1K4C9	**888-692-2211**	418-692-2211
Avalon Corporate Furnished Apartments	1553 Empire Blvd	Webster	NY	14580	**800-934-9763**	585-671-4421
Avenue Inn & Spa	33 Wilmington Ave	Rehoboth Beach	DE	19971	**800-433-5870**	
Avenue Plaza Resort	2111 St Charles Ave	New Orleans	LA	70130	**800-614-8685**	504-566-1212
Ayres Hotel Anaheim	2550 E Katella Ave	Anaheim	CA	92806	**800-595-5692**	714-634-2106
Bahama House	2001 S Atlantic Ave	Daytona Beach Shores	FL	32118	**800-571-2001**	
Balance Rock Inn	21 Albert Meadow	Bar Harbor	ME	04609	**800-753-0494**	207-288-2610
Balmoral Inn	120 Balmoral Ave	Biloxi	MS	39531	**800-393-9131**	228-388-6776
Bar Harbor Hotel-Bluenose Inn	90 Eden St	Bar Harbor	ME	04609	**800-445-4077**	207-288-3348
Barnstead Inn	349 Bonnet St	Manchester Center	VT	05255	**800-331-1619**	802-362-1619
Barrington Hotel & Suites	263 Shepherd of the Hills Expy	Branson	MO	65616	**800-760-8866**	417-334-8866
Bay Club Hotel & Marina	2131 Shelter Island Dr	San Diego	CA	92106	**800-672-0800**	619-224-8888
Bay Park Hotel	1425 Munras Ave *Resv	Monterey	CA	93940	**800-338-3564***	831-649-1020
Beacher's Lodge	6970 A1A S	Saint Augustine	FL	32080	**800-527-8849**	904-471-8849
Beacon Hotel	720 Ocean Dr	Miami Beach	FL	33139	**877-674-8200**	305-674-8200
Beaver Creek Lodge	26 Avon Dale Ln	Beaver Creek	CO	81620	**800-525-7280**	970-845-9800
Beechwood Hotel	363 Plantation St	Worcester	MA	01605	**800-344-2589**	508-754-5789
Bell Tower Hotel	300 S Thayer St	Ann Arbor	MI	48104	**800-562-3559**	734-769-3010
Bell Tower Inn	1235 Second St SW	Rochester	MN	55902	**800-448-7583**	507-289-2233
Bellasera Hotel	221 Ninth St S	Naples	FL	34102	**844-898-4184**	239-649-7333
Bellevue Club Hotel	11200 SE Sixth St	Bellevue	WA	98004	**800-579-1110**	
Bellmoor, The	6 Christian St	Rehoboth Beach	DE	19971	**800-425-2355**	302-227-5800
Benjamin, The	125 E 50th St	New York	NY	10022	**866-222-2365**	212-715-2500
Benson, The	309 SW Broadway	Portland	OR	97205	**800-663-1144**	503-228-2000
Berkeley Hotel, The	1200 E Cary St	Richmond	VA	23219	**888-780-4422**	804-780-1300
Bernards Inn	27 Mine Brook Rd	Bernardsville	NJ	07924	**888-766-0002**	908-766-0002
Bernardus Lodge	415 Carmel Valley Rd	Carmel Valley	CA	93924	**800-223-2533**	831-658-3400
Best Western Chincoteague Island	7105 Maddox Blvd	Chincoteague Island	VA	23336	**800-780-7234**	757-336-6557
Best Western International Inc	6201 N 24th Pkwy	Phoenix	AZ	85016	**800-528-1234**	602-957-4200
Best Western Victorian Inn	487 Foam St	Monterey	CA	93940	**800-232-4141**	831-373-8000
Betsy Hotel	1440 Ocean Dr	Miami Beach	FL	33139	**866-792-3879**	305-531-6100
Beverly Hills Hotel	9641 Sunset Blvd	Beverly Hills	CA	90210	**800-650-1842**	310-276-2251
Beverly Hilton	9876 Wilshire Blvd	Beverly Hills	CA	90210	**800-605-8896**	310-274-7777
Beverly Wilshire - A Four Seasons Hotel	9500 Wilshire Blvd	Beverly Hills	CA	90212	**800-545-4000**	310-275-5200
Bienville House Hotel	320 Decatur St	New Orleans	LA	70130	**800-535-7836**	504-529-2345
Biltmore Greensboro Hotel	111 W Washington St *General	Greensboro	NC	27401	**800-332-0303***	336-272-3474
Biltmore Suites	205 W Madison St	Baltimore	MD	21201	**800-868-5064**	410-728-6550
Bismarck Expressway Suites	180 E Bismarck Expy	Bismarck	ND	58504	**888-774-5566**	701-222-3311
Blackfoot Inn	5940 Blackfoot Trl SE	Calgary	AB	T2H2B5	**800-661-1151**	403-252-2253
Blackwell, The	2110 Tuttle Pk Pl	Columbus	OH	43210	**866-247-4003**	614-247-4000
Blakely New York	136 W 55th St	New York	NY	10019	**800-735-0710**	212-245-1800
Blantyre	16 Blantyre Rd PO Box 995	Lenox	MA	01240	**844-881-0104**	413-637-3556
Blue Horizon Hotel	1225 Robson St	Vancouver	BC	V6E1C3	**800-663-1333**	604-688-1411
Blue Moon Hotel	944 Collins Ave	Miami Beach	FL	33139	**800-553-7739**	305-673-2262
Bluenose Inn & Suites	636 Bedford Hwy	Halifax	NS	B3M2L8	**800-553-5339**	800-565-2301
Boardwalk Plaza Hotel	2 Olive Ave	Rehoboth Beach	DE	19971	**800-332-3224**	302-227-7169
Bodega Bay Lodge	103 Coast Hwy 1 *Resv	Bodega Bay	CA	94923	**888-875-2250***	707-875-3525
Bohemian Hotel Celebration	700 Bloom St	Celebration	FL	34747	**888-249-4007**	407-566-6000
Bond Place Hotel	65 Dundas St E	Toronto	ON	M5B2G8	**800-268-9390**	416-362-6061
Boone Tavern Hotel of Berea College	100 S Main St	Berea	KY	40404	**800-366-9358**	859-985-3700
Boston Harbor Hotel	70 Rowes Wharf	Boston	MA	02110	**800-752-7077**	617-439-7000
Boston Park Plaza Hotel & Towers	50 Park Plz	Boston	MA	02116	**800-225-2008**	617-426-2000
Boulder Station Hotel & Casino	4111 Boulder Hwy	Las Vegas	NV	89121	**800-683-7777**	702-432-7777
Bourbon Orleans - A Wyndham Historic Hotel	717 Orleans St	New Orleans	LA	70116	**866-513-9744**	504-523-2222
Brazilian Court, The	301 Australian Ave	Palm Beach	FL	33480	**800-552-0335**	561-655-7740
Breakers at Waikiki, The	250 Beach Walk	Honolulu	HI	96815	**800-426-0494**	808-923-3181
Breakers Hotel & Suites	105 Second St	Rehoboth Beach	DE	19971	**800-441-8009**	302-227-6688

				Toll-Free	Phone
Brent House Hotel 1512 Jefferson Hwy	New Orleans	LA	70121	800-535-3986	504-842-4140
Bridgewater Hotel 212 Wedgewood Dr	Fairbanks	AK	99701	800-528-4916	
Bristol Hotel 1055 First Ave	San Diego	CA	92101	800-662-4477	619-232-6141
Brookshire Suites 120 E Lombard St	Baltimore	MD	21202	855-345-5033	410-625-1300
Brookstown Inn 200 Brookstown Ave	Winston-Salem	NC	27101	800-845-4262	336-725-1120
Brown County Inn 51 State Rd 46	Nashville	IN	47448	800-772-5249	812-988-2291
Brown Palace Hotel 321 17th St	Denver	CO	80202	800-321-2599	303-297-3111
Brown's Wharf Inn 121 Atlantic Ave	Boothbay Harbor	ME	04538	800-334-8110	207-633-5440
Bryant Park Hotel 40 W 40th St	New York	NY	10018	877-640-9300	212-869-0100
Budget Host International 2307 Roosevelt Dr	Arlington	TX	76016	800-283-4678	817-861-6088
Business Inn 180 MacLaren St	Ottawa	ON	K2P0L3	800-363-1777	613-232-1121
C'mon Inn Grand Forks 3051 32nd Ave S	Grand Forks	ND	58201	800-255-2323	701-775-3320
Caesars License Company LLC 3655 Las Vegas Blvd S	Las Vegas	NV	89109	877-796-2096	702-946-7000
California Hotel & Casino 12 E Ogden Ave	Las Vegas	NV	89101	800-634-6505	702-385-1222
Cambridge Suites Hotel Halifax 1583 Brunswick St	Halifax	NS	B3J3P5	800-565-1263	902-420-0555
Cambridge Suites Hotel Toronto 15 Richmond St E	Toronto	ON	M5C1N2	800-463-1990	416-368-1990
Canad Inns - Club Regent Casino Hotel 1415 Regent Ave W	Winnipeg	MB	R2C3B2	888-332-2623	204-667-5560
Canad Inns Fort Garry 1824 Pembina Hwy	Winnipeg	MB	R3T2G2	888-332-2623	204-261-7450
Canad Inns Garden City 2100 McPhillips St	Winnipeg	MB	R2V3T9	888-332-2623	204-633-0024
Canad Inns Polo Park 1405 St Matthews Ave	Winnipeg	MB	R3G0K5	888-332-2623	204-775-8791
Canal Park Lodge 250 Canal Pk Dr	Duluth	MN	55802	800-777-8560	218-279-6000
Canandaigua Inn on the Lake 770 S Main St	Canandaigua	NY	14424	800-228-2801	585-394-7800
Canary Hotel 31 W Carrillo	Santa Barbara	CA	93101	866-999-5401	805-884-0300
Cannery Casino & Hotel, The Cannery Casino Resorts LLC 2121 E Craig Rd	North Las Vegas	NV	89030	866-999-4899	702-507-5700
Capital Hill Hotel & Suites 88 Albert St	Ottawa	ON	K1P5E9	800-463-7705	613-235-1413
Capital Hotel 111 W Markham St	Little Rock	AR	72201	877-637-0037	501-374-7474
Capitol Hill Hotel 200 C St SE	Washington	DC	20003	800-491-2505	202-543-6000
Capitol Plaza Hotel & Conference Ctr 100 State St	Montpelier	VT	05602	800-274-5252	802-223-5252
Capitol Plaza Hotel Jefferson City 415 W McCarty St	Jefferson City	MO	65101	800-338-8088	573-635-1234
Caribe Royale 8101 World Ctr Dr *Resv	Orlando	FL	32821	800-823-8000*	407-238-8000
Caribe Royale Orlando All-Suites Hotel & Convention Ctr 8101 World Ctr Dr *Resv	Orlando	FL	32821	800-823-8300*	407-238-8000
Carlyle Hotel, The 1731 New Hampshire Ave NW	Washington	DC	20009	877-301-0019	202-234-3200
Carmel River Inn 26600 Oliver Rd	Carmel	CA	93923	800-882-8142	831-624-1575
Carnegie Hotel 1216 W State of Franklin Rd	Johnson City	TN	37604	866-757-8277	423-979-6400
Carolina Inn 211 Pittsboro St	Chapel Hill	NC	27516	800-962-8519	919-933-2001
Carousel Beachfront Hotel & Suites 11700 Coastal Hwy	Ocean City	MD	21842	800-641-1000	410-524-1000
Carousel Inn & Suites 1530 S Harbor Blvd	Anaheim	CA	92802	800-854-6767	714-758-0444
Cartier Place Suite Hotel 180 Cooper St	Ottawa	ON	K2P2L5	800-236-8399	613-236-5000
Casa Madrona Hotel 801 Bridgeway *General	Sausalito	CA	94965	800-288-0502*	415-332-0502
Casa Monica Hotel 95 Cordova St *Help Line	Saint Augustine	FL	32084	800-648-1888*	904-827-1888
Casa Munras Hotel 700 Munras Ave	Monterey	CA	93940	800-222-2446	831-375-2411
Casino Royale Hotel 3411 Las Vegas Blvd S	Las Vegas	NV	89109	800-854-7666	702-737-3500
Castle in the Sand Hotel 3701 Atlantic Ave	Ocean City	MD	21842	800-552-7263	410-289-6846
Century Plaza Hotel & Spa 1015 Burrard St	Vancouver	BC	V6Z1Y5	800-663-1818	604-687-0575
Century Suites Hotel 300 SR-446	Bloomington	IN	47401	800-766-5446	812-336-7777
Chamberlain West Hollywood 1000 Westmount Dr	West Hollywood	CA	90069	877-686-2082	310-657-7400
Chancellor Hotel on Union Square 433 Powell St	San Francisco	CA	94102	800-428-4748	415-362-2004
Charles Hotel Harvard Square 1 Bennett St	Cambridge	MA	02138	800-882-1818	617-864-1200
Charleston Place 205 Meeting St	Charleston	SC	29401	888-635-2350	843-722-4900
Chateau Lacombe Hotel 10111 Bellamy Hill	Edmonton	AB	T5J1N7	800-661-8801	780-428-6611
Chateau Louis Hotel & Conference Ctr 11727 Kingsway	Edmonton	AB	T5G3A1	800-661-9843	780-452-7770
Chateau on the Lake 415 N State Hwy 265	Branson	MO	65616	888-333-5253	417-334-1161
Chŷteau Vaudreuil Hotel & Suites 21700 Rt Transcanada Hwy	Vaudreuil-Dorion	QC	J7V8P3	800-363-7896	450-455-0955
Chateau Versailles 1659 Sherbrooke St W	Montreal	QC	H3H1E3	888-933-8111	514-933-3611
Chelsea Savoy Hotel 204 W 23rd St	New York	NY	10011	866-929-9353	212-929-9353
Chestnut Hill Hotel 8229 Germantown Ave	Philadelphia	PA	19118	800-628-9744	215-242-5905
Chiltern Inn 11 Cromwell Harbor Rd	Bar Harbor	ME	04609	800-709-0114	207-288-3371
Choice Hotels International Inc 1 Choice Hotels Cir Ste 400 NYSE: CHH	Rockville	MD	20850	800-424-6423	301-592-5000
Chrysalis Inn & Spa 804 Tenth St	Bellingham	WA	98225	888-808-0005	360-756-1005
Churchill Hotel 1914 Connecticut Ave NW	Washington	DC	20009	800-424-2464	202-797-2000
Cincinnatian Hotel 601 Vine St	Cincinnati	OH	45202	800-942-9000	513-381-3000
Circus Circus Hotel & Casino Reno 500 N Sierra St	Reno	NV	89503	800-648-5010	775-329-0711
Circus Circus Hotel Casino & Theme Park Las Vegas 2880 Las Vegas Blvd S *Resv	Las Vegas	NV	89109	800-634-3450*	702-734-0410
Cliff House at Pikes Peak 306 Canyon Ave	Manitou Springs	CO	80829	888-212-7000	719-785-1000
Clinton Inn Hotel 145 Dean Dr	Tenafly	NJ	07670	800-275-4411	201-871-3200
Coast Edmonton House Suite Hotel 1090 W Georgia S Ste 900	Vancouver	BC	V6E3V7	800-716-6199	604-682-7982
Coastal Inn Concorde 379 Windmill Rd	Dartmouth	NS	B3A1J6	800-565-1565	
Coastal Inns Inc 111 Warwick St PO Box 280	Digby	NS	B0V1A0	800-401-1155	
Coastal Palms Hotel 120th St Coastal Hwy	Ocean City	MD	21842	800-641-0011	
Cocca's Inn & Suites 42 Wolf Rd	Albany	NY	12205	888-426-2227	518-459-5670
Colby Hill Inn 33 The Oaks PO Box 779	Henniker	NH	03242	800-531-0330	603-428-3281
Colonnade Hotel 120 Huntington Ave	Boston	MA	02116	800-962-3030	617-424-7000
Colony Hotel & Cabana Club 525 E Atlantic Ave	Delray Beach	FL	33483	800-552-2363	561-276-4123
Colorado Belle Hotel & Casino 2100 S Casino Dr *Resv	Laughlin	NV	89029	877-460-0777*	702-298-4000
Columns, The 3811 St Charles Ave	New Orleans	LA	70115	800-445-9308	504-899-9308
Comfort Inn & Suites Milwaukee 916 E State St	Milwaukee	WI	53202	888-221-6039	
Commander Hotel 1401 Atlantic Ave	Ocean City	MD	21842	888-289-6166	
Commonwealth Park Suites Hotel 901 Bank St	Richmond	VA	23219	888-343-7301	804-343-7300
Conch House Heritage Inn 625 Truman Ave	Key West	FL	33040	800-207-5806	305-293-0020
Conch House Marina Resort 57 Comares Ave	Saint Augustine	FL	32080	800-940-6256	904-829-8646
Contactpointe of Pittsburgh 2593 Wexford Bayne Rd Ste 200	Sewickley	PA	15143	877-255-4916	412-788-0680
Copley Square Hotel 47 Huntington Ave	Boston	MA	02116	800-225-7062	617-536-9000
Cornhusker Hotel, The 333 S 13th St	Lincoln	NE	68508	866-706-7706	402-474-7474
Cosmopolitan Hotel Toronto 8 Colborne St	Toronto	ON	M5E1E1	800-958-3488	416-350-2000
Country Inn at the Mall 936 Stillwater Ave *Resv	Bangor	ME	04401	800-244-3961*	207-941-0200
Courtyard Fort Lauderdale Beach 440 Seabreeze Blvd	Fort Lauderdale	FL	33316	888-236-2427	954-524-8733
Cove Inn 900 Broad Ave S	Naples	FL	34102	800-255-4365	239-262-7161
Cowboy Village Resort 120 S Flat Creek Dr PO Box 38	Jackson	WY	83001	800-962-4988	307-733-3121
Creekside Inn 3400 El Camino Real	Palo Alto	CA	94306	800-492-7335	650-493-2411
Cross Creek Resort 3815 Pennsylvania 8	Titusville	PA	16354	800-461-3173	814-827-9611
Crown American Hotels Co Pasquerilla Plz	Johnstown	PA	15907	800-245-9295	814-533-4600
Crown Reef Resort 2913 S Ocean Blvd	Myrtle Beach	SC	29577	800-291-6598	843-626-8077
Crowne Plaza Syracuse 701 E Genesee St	Syracuse	NY	13210	866-305-4134	315-479-7000
Crystal Beach Suites & Health Club 6985 Collins Ave	Miami Beach	FL	33141	888-643-4630	305-865-9555
Crystal Inn 185 S State St Ste 1300 *General	Salt Lake City	UT	84111	800-662-2525*	801-320-7200
Crystal Inn Salt Lake City Downtown 230 W 500 S	Salt Lake City	UT	84101	800-662-2525	801-328-4466
Curtis, The 1405 Curtis St	Denver	CO	80202	800-525-6651	303-571-0300
Dan'l Webster Inn 149 Main St	Sandwich	MA	02563	800-444-3566	508-888-3622
Dauphine Orleans Hotel 415 Dauphine St	New Orleans	LA	70112	800-521-7111	504-586-1800
Days Inns Worldwide Inc 215 W 94th St Broadway	New York	NY	10025	800-225-3297	212-866-6400
Daytona Beach Resort & Conference Ctr 2700 N Atlantic Ave	Daytona Beach	FL	32118	800-654-6216	386-672-3770
Daytona Inn Beach Resort 219 S Atlantic Ave *General	Daytona Beach	FL	32118	800-874-1822*	386-252-3626
Deerfoot Inn & Casino 1000 11500 35th St SE	Calgary	AB	T2Z3W4	877-236-5225	403-236-7529
Del Monte Lodge Renaissance Rochester Hotel & Spa, The 41 N Main St	Pittsford	NY	14534	866-237-5979	800-983-4240

Name / Address	City	State	ZIP	Toll-Free	Phone
Delta King Riverboat Hotel 1000 Front St	Sacramento	CA	95814	**800-825-5464**	916-444-5464
Destination Hotels & Resorts Inc 10333 E Dry Creek Rd Ste 450	Englewood	CO	80112	**855-893-1011**	303-799-3830
Dinah's Garden Hotel 4261 El Camino Real	Palo Alto	CA	94306	**800-227-8220**	650-493-2844
Dolphin Beach Resort 4900 Gulf Blvd	Saint Pete Beach	FL	33706	**800-237-8916**	727-360-7011
Donatello, The 501 Post St	San Francisco	CA	94102	**800-258-2366**	415-441-7100
DoubleTree by Hilton Hotel Downtown Wilmington - Legal District 700 N King St	Wilmington	DE	19801	**855-610-8733**	302-655-0400
Downtown Erie Hotel 18 W 18th St	Erie	PA	16501	**800-832-9101**	814-456-2961
Drake Hotel, The 140 E Walton Pl	Chicago	IL	60611	**800-553-7253**	312-787-2200
Driftwood Hotel 435 Willoughby Ave	Juneau	AK	99801	**800-544-2239**	907-586-2280
Driftwood Shores Resort 88416 First Ave	Florence	OR	97439	**800-422-5091**	541-997-8263
Drury Hotels Company LLC 721 Emerson Rd Ste 400	Saint Louis	MO	63141	**800-378-7946**	314-429-2255
Duke's 8th Avenue Hotel 630 W Eigth Ave	Anchorage	AK	99501	**800-478-4837**	907-274-6213
Dunes Manor Hotel 2800 Baltimore Ave	Ocean City	MD	21842	**800-523-2888**	410-289-1100
Dunhill Hotel 237 N Tryon St	Charlotte	NC	28202	**800-354-4141**	704-332-4141
Dynasty Suites 1235 W Colton Ave *General	Redlands	CA	92374	**800-874-8958***	909-793-6648
Eagle Mountain House 179 Carter Notch Rd PO Box 804	Jackson	NH	03846	**800-966-5779**	603-383-9111
Eden House 1015 Fleming St	Key West	FL	33040	**800-533-5397**	305-296-6868
Edgewater Beach Hotel 1901 Gulf Shore Blvd N	Naples	FL	34102	**866-624-1695**	239-403-2000
Edgewater Hotel 2411 Alaskan Way	Seattle	WA	98121	**800-624-0670**	206-728-7000
Edgewater Resort 200 Edgewater Cir	Hot Springs	AR	71913	**800-234-3687**	501-767-3311
Edgewater Resort & Waterpark 2400 London Rd	Duluth	MN	55812	**800-777-7925**	218-728-3601
El Cortez Hotel & Casino 600 E Fremont St	Las Vegas	NV	89101	**800-634-6703**	702-385-5200
El Tovar Hotel 1 El Tovar Rd	Grand Canyon	AZ	86023	**888-297-2757**	928-638-2631
Elan Hotel 8435 Beverly Blvd	Los Angeles	CA	90048	**866-203-2212**	323-658-6663
Eldorado Hotel 309 W San Francisco St	Santa Fe	NM	87501	**800-955-4455**	505-988-4455
Eldorado Hotel Casino 345 N Virginia St *Resv	Reno	NV	89501	**800-879-8879***	775-786-5700
Eldridge Hotel 701 Massachusetts St	Lawrence	KS	66044	**800-527-0909**	785-749-5011
Eliot Hotel, The 370 Commonwealth Ave	Boston	MA	02215	**800-443-5468**	617-267-1607
Elk Country Inn 480 W Pearl St PO Box 1255	Jackson	WY	83001	**800-483-8667**	307-733-2364
Embassy Hotel & Suites 25 Cartier St	Ottawa	ON	K2P1J2	**800-661-5495**	613-237-2111
Emerald Queen Hotel & Casino 5700 Pacific Hwy E *Resv	Fife	WA	98424	**888-831-7655***	253-594-7777
Enclave Suites of Orlando 6165 Carrier Dr	Orlando	FL	32819	**800-457-0077**	407-351-1155
Ethan Allen Hotel 21 Lake Ave Ext	Danbury	CT	06811	**800-742-1776**	203-744-1776
Euro-Suites Hotel University Centre 501 Chestnut Ridge Rd	Morgantown	WV	26505	**800-678-4837**	
Evergreen Lodge 250 S Frontage Rd W	Vail	CO	81657	**800-284-8245**	970-476-7810
Excalibur Hotel & Casino 3850 S Las Vegas Blvd	Las Vegas	NV	89109	**877-750-5464**	702-597-7777
Executive Hotel Vintage Court 650 Bush St	San Francisco	CA	94108	**888-388-3932**	415-392-4666
Executive Inn Group Corp *Executive Hotels & Resorts* 1080 Howe St 8th Fl	Vancouver	BC	V6Z2T1	**866-642-6888**	604-642-5250
Executive Pacific Plaza Hotel 400 Spring St	Seattle	WA	98104	**888-388-3932**	206-623-3900
Expressway Hotels 4303 17th Ave S	Fargo	ND	58103	**877-239-4303**	701-239-4303
Extended Stay America 11525 N Community House Rd Ste 100	Charlotte	NC	28277	**800-804-3724**	980-345-1600
Crossland Economy Studios 11525 N Community House Rd Ste 100	Charlotte	NC	28277	**877-398-3633**	980-345-1600
Extended Stay Hotels 530 Woods Lake Rd	Greenville	SC	29607	**800-804-3724**	
Fairbanks Princess Riverside Lodge 4477 Pikes Landing Rd	Fairbanks	AK	99709	**800-426-0500**	907-455-4477
Fairmount Hotel, The 401 S Alamo St	San Antonio	TX	78205	**877-229-8808**	210-224-8800
Fargo C'mon Inn Hotel 4338 20th Ave SW	Fargo	ND	58103	**800-334-1570**	701-277-9944
Fearrington House 2000 Fearrington Village Ctr	Pittsboro	NC	27312	**800-277-0130**	919-542-2121
Fiesta Henderson 777 West Lake Mead Pkwy	Henderson	NV	89015	**888-899-7770**	702-558-7000
Findlay Inn & Conference Ctr 200 E Main Cross St *Cust Svc	Findlay	OH	45840	**800-825-1455***	419-422-5682
Fireside Inn & Suites 25 Airport Rd	West Lebanon	NH	03784	**877-258-5900**	603-298-5900
First Gold Hotel 270 Main St	Deadwood	SD	57732	**800-274-1876**	605-578-9777

Name / Address	City	State	ZIP	Toll-Free	Phone
Fitzpatrick Manhattan Hotel 687 Lexington Ave	New York	NY	10022	**800-367-7701**	212-355-0100
Flagship All Suites Resort 60 N Maine Ave	Atlantic City	NJ	08401	**800-647-7890**	609-343-7447
Foley House Inn 14 West Hull St	Savannah	GA	31401	**800-647-3708**	
Foot of the Mountain Motel 200 W Arapahoe Ave	Boulder	CO	80302	**866-773-5489**	303-442-5688
Foothills Inn 1625 N La Crosse St	Rapid City	SD	57701	**877-428-5666**	605-348-5640
Fort Garry, The 222 Broadway	Winnipeg	MB	R3C0R3	**800-665-8088**	204-942-8251
Four Points by Sheraton Charlotte 315 E Woodlawn Rd	Charlotte	NC	28217	**800-368-7764**	704-522-0852
Four Points by Sheraton French Quarter 541 Bourbon St	New Orleans	LA	70130	**866-716-8133**	504-524-7611
Four Queens Hotel & Casino 202 Fremont St	Las Vegas	NV	89101	**800-634-6045**	702-385-4011
Four Sails Resort Hotel 3301 Atlantic Ave	Virginia Beach	VA	23451	**800-227-4213**	757-491-8100
Four Seasons Hotels Inc 1165 Leslie St	Toronto	ON	M3C2K8	**800-332-3442**	416-449-1750
Francis Marion Hotel, The 387 King St	Charleston	SC	29403	**877-756-2121**	843-722-0600
Franklin, The 164 E 87th St	New York	NY	10128	**800-607-4009**	212-369-1000
Fremont Hotel & Casino 200 Fremont St	Las Vegas	NV	89101	**800-634-6460**	702-385-3232
French Quarter Suites Hotel 1119 N Rampart St	New Orleans	LA	70116	**800-457-2253**	504-524-7725
G6 Hospitality LLC *Motel 6* 4001 International Pkwy	Carrollton	TX	75007	**800-466-8356**	972-360-9000
Galt House Hotel 140 N Fourth St	Louisville	KY	40202	**800-843-4258**	502-589-5200
Garden City Hotel 45 Seventh St	Garden City	NY	11530	**877-549-0400**	516-747-3000
Garden Court Hotel 520 Cowper St	Palo Alto	CA	94301	**800-824-9028**	650-322-9000
Gardens Hotel 526 Angela St	Key West	FL	33040	**800-526-2664**	305-294-2661
Garland, The 4222 Vineland Ave	North Hollywood	CA	91602	**800-238-3759**	818-980-8000
Garrett's Desert Inn 311 Old Santa Fe Trl	Santa Fe	NM	87501	**800-888-2145**	505-982-1851
Gastonian, The 220 E Gaston St	Savannah	GA	31401	**800-322-6603**	912-232-2869
Gaylord Opryland Hotel & Convention Ctr 2800 Opryland Dr	Nashville	TN	37214	**888-236-2427**	615-889-1000
Georgian Court Hotel 773 Beatty St	Vancouver	BC	V6B2M4	**800-663-1155**	604-682-5555
Georgian Hotel, The 1415 Ocean Ave	Santa Monica	CA	90401	**800-538-8147**	
Georgian Resort 384 Canada St	Lake George	NY	12845	**800-525-3436**	518-668-5401
Georgian Terrace Hotel 659 Peachtree St NE	Atlanta	GA	30308	**800-651-2316**	404-897-1991
Gideon Putnam Resort & Spa 24 Gideon Putnam Rd	Saratoga Springs	NY	12866	**800-452-7275**	518-584-3000
Glass House Inn 3202 W 26th St	Erie	PA	16506	**800-956-7222**	814-833-7751
Glen Grove Suites 2837 Yonge St	Toronto	ON	M4N2J6	**800-565-3024**	416-489-8441
Glendorn 1000 Glendorn Dr	Bradford	PA	16701	**800-843-8568**	814-362-6511
Glenerin Inn, The 1695 The Collegeway	Mississauga	ON	L5L3S7	**877-991-9971**	905-828-6103
Glenmore Inn 1000 Glenmore Court SE	Calgary	AB	T2C2E6	**800-661-3163**	403-279-8611
Glidden House 1901 Ford Dr	Cleveland	OH	44106	**866-812-4537**	216-231-8900
Glorietta Bay Inn 1630 Glorietta Blvd	Coronado	CA	92118	**800-283-9383**	619-435-3101
Gold Coast Hotel & Casino 4000 W Flamingo Rd	Las Vegas	NV	89103	**800-331-5334**	702-367-7111
Goldbelt Hotel Juneau 3025 Clinton Dr	Juneau	AK	99801	**800-770-5866**	907-790-4990
Golden Eagle Resort 511 Mountain Rd	Stowe	VT	05672	**866-970-0786**	802-253-4811
Golden Hotel, The 800 Eleventh St	Golden	CO	80401	**800-233-7214**	303-279-0100
Goldener Hirsch Inn 7570 Royal St E *Cust Svc	Park City	UT	84060	**800-252-3373***	435-649-7770
Good Hotel *Good Hotel* 112 Seventh St	San Francisco	CA	94103	**800-444-5819**	415-621-7001
Good-Nite Inn Fremont 4135 Cushing Pkwy	Fremont	CA	94538	**800-648-3466**	510-656-9307
Gouverneur Hotel Montreal (Place-Dupuis) 1000 Sherbrooke St W Ste 2300	Montreal	QC	H3A3R3	**888-910-1111**	
Governor Calvert House 58 State Cir	Annapolis	MD	21401	**800-847-8882**	410-263-2641
Governor's Inn 700 W Sioux Ave *General	Pierre	SD	57501	**877-523-0080***	605-224-4200
Governor's Inn 210 Richards Blvd	Sacramento	CA	95811	**800-999-6689**	916-448-7224
Grace Mayflower Inn & Spa 118 Woodbury Rd Rte 47	Washington	CT	06793	**800-550-8095**	860-868-9466
Grafton on Sunset 8462 West Sunset Blvd	West Hollywood	CA	90069	**800-821-3660**	
Gramercy Park Hotel 2 Lexington Ave	New York	NY	10010	**866-784-1300**	212-920-3300
Grand America Hotel 555 S Main St	Salt Lake City	UT	84111	**800-304-8696**	801-258-6000
Grand Country Inn Grand Country Sq 1945 W 76 Country Blvd	Branson	MO	65616	**888-505-4096**	

	Toll-Free	Phone
Grand Del Mar		
5300 Grand Del Mar Ct ....San Diego CA 92130	855-314-2030	858-314-2000
Grand Gateway Hotel		
1721 N LaCrosse St ....Rapid City SD 57701	866-742-1300	
Grand Hotel Minneapolis, The		
615 Second Ave S ....Minneapolis MN 55402	866-843-4726	612-288-8888
Grand Hotel of Cape May		
Beach Ave ....Cape May NJ 08204	800-257-8550	609-884-5611
Grand Hotel, The		
149 State Rt 64 ....Grand Canyon AZ 86023	888-634-7263	928-638-3333
Grand Oaks Hotel		
2315 Green Mountain Dr ....Branson MO 65616	800-553-6423	
Grand Summit Hotel		
570 Springfield Ave ....Summit NJ 07901	800-346-0773	908-273-3000
GRAND TIMES HOTEL		
6515 Wilfrid-Hamel Blvd ....Quebec QC G2E5W3	888-902-4444	418-877-7788
Grande Colonial		
910 Prospect St ....La Jolla CA 92037	888-828-5498	
Grant Plaza Hotel		
465 Grant Ave ....San Francisco CA 94108	800-472-6899	415-434-3883
Granville Island Hotel		
1253 Johnston St ....Vancouver BC V6H3R9	800-663-1840*	604-683-7373
*Resv		
Green Valley Ranch Resort Casino & Spa		
2300 Paseo Verde Pkwy ....Henderson NV 89052	866-782-9487*	702-617-7777
*Resv		
Greyfield Inn		
4 N Second St Ste 300 ....Fernandina Beach FL 32034	866-401-8581	904-261-6408
Habana Inn		
2200 NW 40th St ....Oklahoma City OK 73112	800-988-2221	405-528-2221
Habitat Suites		
500 E Highland Mall Blvd ....Austin TX 78752	800-535-4663	512-467-6000
Hacienda The at Hotel Santa Fe		
1501 Paseo del Peralta ....Santa Fe NM 87501	855-825-9876	505-955-7805
Halekulani Hotel		
2199 Kalia Rd ....Honolulu HI 96815	800-367-2343	808-923-2311
Half Moon Bay Lodge & Conference Ctr		
2400 S Cabrillo Hwy ....Half Moon Bay CA 94019	800-710-0778	650-726-9000
Halifax Marriott Harborfront Hotel		
1919 Upper Water St ....Halifax NS B3J3J5	800-450-4442	902-421-1700
Halliburton House Inn		
5184 Morris St ....Halifax NS B3J1B3	888-512-3344	902-420-0658
Hallmark Inns & Resorts		
1400 S Hemlock St ....Cannon Beach OR 97110	888-448-4449	503-436-1566
Hanover Inn Dartmouth		
2 E Wheelock St ....Hanover NH 03755	800-443-7024	603-643-4300
Harbor View Hotel		
131 N Water St Martha's Vineyard		
PO Box 7 ....Edgartown MA 02539	800-225-6005	508-627-7000
Harborside Inn		
1 Christie's Landing ....Newport RI 02840	800-427-9444	401-846-6600
Hard Rock Hotel & Casino Biloxi		
777 Beach Blvd ....Biloxi MS 39530	877-877-6256	228-374-7625
Hard Rock Hotel San Diego		
207 Fifth Ave ....San Diego CA 92101	866-751-7625	619-702-3000
Harrah's Council Bluffs		
1 Harrahs Blvd ....Council Bluffs IA 51501	800-342-7724	712-329-6000
Harraseeket Inn		
162 Main St ....Freeport ME 04032	800-342-6423	207-865-9377
Harvard Square Hotel		
110 Mt Auburn St Harvard Sq ....Cambridge MA 02138	800-458-5886	617-864-5200
Harvest Inn 1 Main St ....Saint Helena CA 94574	800-950-8466	707-963-9463
Hassayampa Inn		
122 E Gurley St ....Prescott AZ 86301	800-322-1927*	928-778-9434
*Cust Svc		
Hastings House Country House Hotel		
160 Upper Ganges Rd ....Salt Spring Island BC V8K2S2	800-661-9255	
Hawaiian Inn		
2301 S Atlantic Ave ....Daytona Beach Shores FL 32118	800-922-3023	386-255-5411
Hawthorne Inn & Conference Ctr		
420 High St ....Winston-Salem NC 27101	877-777-3099	336-777-3000
Hay-Adams Hotel		
800 16th St NE ....Washington DC 20006	800-853-6807	202-638-6600
Heartland Inns 87-2nd St ....Coralville IA 52241	800-334-3277*	319-351-8132
*Resv		
Henley Park Hotel		
926 Massachusetts Ave NW ....Washington DC 20001	800-222-8474	202-638-5200
Henlopen Hotel		
511 N Boardwalk ....Rehoboth Beach DE 19971	800-441-8450	302-227-2551
Heritage Hotels & Resorts Inc		
201 Third St NW Ste 1150 ....Albuquerque NM 87102	877-901-7666	505-836-6700
Hermitage Hotel		
231 Sixth Ave N ....Nashville TN 37219	888-888-9414	615-244-3121
Hermosa Inn		
5532 N Palo Cristi Rd ....Paradise Valley AZ 85253	800-241-1210	602-955-8614
Hershey Lodge		
325 University Dr ....Hershey PA 17033	844-330-1802	717-533-3311
Hilgard House Hotel & Suites		
927 Hilgard Ave ....Los Angeles CA 90024	800-826-3934	310-208-3945
Hilltop Inn of Vermont		
3472 Airport Rd ....Montpelier VT 05602	877-609-0003	802-229-5766
Hilton Worldwide		
7930 Jones Branch Dr ....McLean VA 22102	800-445-8667	703-883-1000
Historic Bullock Hotel		
633 Main St ....Deadwood SD 57732	800-336-1876	605-578-1745
Historic French Market Inn		
509 Decatur St ....New Orleans LA 70130	800-366-2743	504-561-5621
Historic Inns of Annapolis		
58 State Cir ....Annapolis MD 21401	800-847-8882	410-263-2641
Holiday Inn		
301 Government St ....Mobile AL 36602	888-465-4329	251-694-0100
Holiday Inn Express DFW North		
4550 W John Carpenter Fwy ....Irving TX 75063	800-465-4329	972-929-4499
Holiday Inn Resort Daytona Beach Oceanfront		
1615 S Atlantic Ave ....Daytona Beach FL 32118	877-834-3613	386-255-0921
Horton Grand Hotel		
311 Island Ave ....San Diego CA 92101	800-542-1886	619-544-1886
Hospitality International Inc		
1726 Montreal Cir ....Tucker GA 30084	800-251-1962	
Master Hosts Inns & Resorts		
1726 Montreal Cir Ste 110 ....Tucker GA 30084	800-892-8405	770-270-1180
Passport Inn		
1726 Montreal Cir Ste 110 ....Tucker GA 30084	800-892-8405	770-270-1180
Red Carpet Inn		
1726 Montreal Cir ....Tucker GA 30084	800-247-4677	
Scottish Inns		
1726 Montreal Cir ....Tucker GA 30084	800-251-1962	
Hospitality Suites Resort		
409 N Scottsdale Rd ....Scottsdale AZ 85257	800-445-5115	480-949-5115
Hotel & Suites Normandin		
4700 Pierre-Bertrand Blvd ....Quebec QC G2J1A4	800-463-6721	418-622-1611
Hotel 43 981 Grove St ....Boise ID 83702	800-243-4622	208-342-4622
Hotel 71 71 St Pierre St ....Quebec QC G1K4A4	888-692-1171	418-692-1171
Hotel Allegro Chicago		
171 W Randolph St ....Chicago IL 60601	800-643-1500	312-236-0123
Hotel Ambassadeur		
3401 Blvd Ste-Anne ....Quebec QC G1E3L4	800-363-4619	
Hotel Andra 2000 Fourth Ave ....Seattle WA 98121	877-448-8600	206-448-8600
Hotel at Old Town Wichita		
830 E First St ....Wichita KS 67202	877-265-3869	316-267-4800
Hotel Beacon 2130 Broadway ....New York NY 10023	800-572-4969	212-787-1100
Hotel Boulderado		
2115 13th St ....Boulder CO 80302	800-433-4344	303-442-4344
Hotel Captain Cook		
939 W Fifth Ave ....Anchorage AK 99501	800-843-1950	907-276-6000
Hotel Chateau Bellevue		
16 Rue de la Porte ....Quebec QC G1R4M9	877-849-1877	418-692-2573
Hotel Chateau Laurier		
1220 Pl George-V Ouest ....Quebec QC G1R5B8	877-522-8108	418-522-8108
Hotel Classique		
2815 Laurier Blvd ....Quebec QC G1V4H3	800-463-1885	
Hotel Colorado		
526 Pine St ....Glenwood Springs CO 81601	800-544-3998	970-945-6511
Hotel Congress		
311 E Congress St ....Tucson AZ 85701	800-722-8848	520-622-8848
Hotel Contessa		
306 W Market St ....San Antonio TX 78205	866-435-0900	210-229-9222
Hotel de Anza		
233 W Santa Clara St ....San Jose CA 95113	800-843-3700	408-286-1000
Hotel Deca		
4507 Brooklyn Ave NE ....Seattle WA 98105	800-899-0251	206-634-2000
Hotel Del Sol		
3100 Webster St ....San Francisco CA 94123	877-433-5765	415-921-5520
Hotel Derek 2525 W Loop S ....Houston TX 77027	866-292-4100	713-961-3000
Hotel Drisco		
2901 Pacific Ave ....San Francisco CA 94115	800-634-7277	415-346-2880
Hotel du Pont		
11th & Market Sts ....Wilmington DE 19801	800-441-9019	302-594-3100
Hotel Edison 228 W 47th St ....New York NY 10036	800-637-7070	212-840-5000
Hotel Encanto de Las Cruces		
705 S Telshor Blvd ....Las Cruces NM 88011	866-383-0443	575-522-4300
Hotel Galvez - A Wyndham Historic Hotel		
2024 Seawall Blvd ....Galveston TX 77550	800-996-3426	409-765-7721
Hotel George 15 E St NW ....Washington DC 20001	800-576-8331*	202-347-4200
*General		
Hotel Grand Pacific		
463 Belleville St ....Victoria BC V8V1X3	800-663-7550	250-386-0450
Hotel Granduca		
1080 Uptown Pk Blvd ....Houston TX 77056	888-472-6382	713-418-1000
Hotel Griffon		
155 Steuart St ....San Francisco CA 94105	800-321-2201	415-495-2100
Hotel Jerome 330 E Main St ....Aspen CO 81611	855-331-7213	
Hotel La Rose		
308 Wilson St ....Santa Rosa CA 95401	800-527-6738	707-579-3200
Hotel Le Bleu		
370 Fourth Ave ....Brooklyn NY 11215	866-427-6073	718-625-1500
Hotel Le Cantlie Suites		
1110 Sherbrooke St W ....Montreal QC H3A1G9	800-567-1110	514-842-2000
Hotel Le Capitole		
972 Rue St-Jean ....Quebec QC G1R1R5	800-261-9903	418-694-4444
Hotel Le Clos Saint-Louis		
69 St Louis St ....Quebec QC G1R3Z2	800-461-1311	418-694-1311
Hotel Le Marais		
717 Conti St ....New Orleans LA 70130	800-935-8740	504-525-2300
Hotel le Priori		
15 Sault-au-Matelot St ....Quebec QC G1K3Y7	800-351-3992	418-692-3992
Hotel Le Soleil		
567 Hornby St ....Vancouver BC V6C2E8	877-632-3030	604-632-3000
Hotel Le St-James		
355 St Jacques St ....Montreal QC H2Y1N9	866-841-3111	514-841-3111
Hotel Lombardy		
2019 Pennsylvania Ave NW ....Washington DC 20006	800-424-5486	202-828-2600
Hotel Lord-Berri		
1199 Berri St ....Montreal QC H2L4C6	888-363-0363	514-845-9236
Hotel Lucia		
400 SW Broadway ....Portland OR 97205	877-225-1717	503-225-1717
Hotel Manoir Victoria		
44 Cote du Palais ....Quebec QC G1R4H8	800-463-6283	418-692-1030
Hotel Marlowe Cambridge		
25 Edwind H Land Blvd ....Cambridge MA 02141	800-825-7140	617-868-8000
Hotel Max 620 Stewart St ....Seattle WA 98101	866-833-6299	206-728-6299
Hotel Mead		
451 E Grand Ave ....Wisconsin Rapids WI 54494	800-843-6323	
Hotel Mela 120 W 44th St ....New York NY 10036	877-452-6352	212-710-7000
Hotel Metro		
411 E Mason St ....Milwaukee WI 53202	877-638-7620	414-272-1937
Hotel Monaco Chicago		
225 N Wabash Ave ....Chicago IL 60601	866-610-0081	312-960-8500
Hotel Monaco Denver		
1717 Champa St ....Denver CO 80202	800-990-1303	303-296-1717
Hotel Monaco Portland		
506 SW Washington at Fifth Ave ....Portland OR 97204	866-861-9514	503-222-0001
Hotel Monaco Salt Lake City		
15 West 200 South ....Salt Lake City UT 84101	800-805-1801*	801-595-0000
*Resv		

Name / Address	City	ST	Zip	Toll-Free	Phone
Hotel Monaco Seattle 1101 Fourth Ave	Seattle	WA	98101	**800-715-6513**	206-621-1770
Hotel Monte Vista 100 N San Francisco St	Flagstaff	AZ	86001	**800-545-3068**	928-779-6971
Hotel Monteleone 214 Royal St	New Orleans	LA	70130	**866-338-4684**	504-523-3341
Hotel Nikko San Francisco 222 Mason St	San Francisco	CA	94102	**866-636-4556**	415-394-1111
Hotel Northampton 36 King St	NorthHampton	MA	01060	**800-547-3529**	413-584-3100
Hotel Oceana *Santa Barbara* 202 W Cabrillo Blvd	Santa Barbara	CA	93101	**800-965-9776**	805-965-4577
Hotel Omni Mont-Royal 1050 Sherbrooke St W	Montreal	QC	H3A2R6	**800-843-6664**	514-284-1110
Hotel Orrington 1710 Orrington Ave	Evanston	IL	60201	**888-677-4648**	847-866-8700
Hotel Phillips 106 W 12th St	Kansas City	MO	64105	**877-704-5341**	816-221-7000
Hotel Plaza Athenee 37 E 64th St	New York	NY	10065	**800-447-8800**	212-734-9100
Hotel Plaza Quebec 3031 Laurier Blvd	Qu,bec	QC	G1V2M2	**800-567-5276**	418-658-2727
Hotel Plaza Real 125 Washington Ave	Santa Fe	NM	87501	**855-752-9273**	505-988-4900
Hotel Provincial 1024 Rue Chartres	New Orleans	LA	70116	**800-535-7922**	504-581-4995
Hotel Rex San Francisco 562 Sutter St *Resv	San Francisco	CA	94102	**800-433-4434***	415-433-4434
Hotel Rodney 142 Second St	Lewes	DE	19958	**800-824-8754**	302-645-6466
Hotel Roger Williams 131 Madison Ave *Resv	New York	NY	10016	**888-448-7788***	212-448-7000
Hotel Rouge 1315 16th St NW	Washington	DC	20036	**800-738-1202**	202-232-8000
Hotel Ruby Foo's 7655 Decarie Blvd	Montreal	QC	H4P2H2	**800-361-5419**	514-731-7701
Hotel Saint Francis 210 Don Gaspar Ave	Santa Fe	NM	87501	**800-529-5700**	505-983-5700
Hotel Saint Regis Detroit 3071 W Grand Blvd *Resv	Detroit	MI	48202	**855-400-7738***	313-873-3000
Hotel San Carlos 202 N Central Ave	Phoenix	AZ	85004	**866-253-4121**	602-253-4121
Hotel Santa Barbara 533 State St	Santa Barbara	CA	93101	**800-549-9869**	805-957-9300
Hotel Santa Fe 1501 Paseo de Peralta	Santa Fe	NM	87501	**855-825-9876**	505-982-1200
Hotel Sepia 3135 Ch St-Louis	Sainte-Foy	QC	G1W1R9	**888-301-6837**	418-653-4941
Hotel Shelley 844 Collins Ave	Miami Beach	FL	33139	**877-762-3477**	305-531-3341
Hotel Spero 405 Taylor St	San Francisco	CA	94102	**866-575-9941**	415-885-2500
Hotel Strasburg, The 213 S Holliday St	Strasburg	VA	22657	**800-348-8327**	540-465-9191
Hotel Teatro 1100 Fourteenth St	Denver	CO	80202	**888-727-1200**	303-228-1100
Hotel Triton 342 Grant Ave	San Francisco	CA	94108	**800-800-1299**	415-394-0500
Hotel Universel 2300 Ch St-Foy	Quebec	QC	G1V1S5	**800-463-4495**	
Hotel Valley Ho 6850 E Main St	Scottsdale	AZ	85251	**866-882-4484**	480-376-2600
Hotel Viking 1 Bellevue Ave	Newport	RI	02840	**800-556-7126**	401-847-3300
Hotel Vintage Park 1100 Fifth Ave	Seattle	WA	98101	**800-853-3914**	206-624-8000
Hotel Wales 1295 Madison Ave	New York	NY	10128	**866-925-3746**	212-876-6000
Hotel ZaZa Dallas 2332 Leonard St	Dallas	TX	75201	**800-597-8399**	214-468-8399
Hotel ZaZa Houston 5701 Main St *Resv	Houston	TX	77005	**888-880-3244***	713-526-1991
Humphrey's Half Moon Inn & Suites 2303 Shelter Island Dr	San Diego	CA	92106	**800-542-7400**	619-224-3411
Hyannis Holiday Motel 131 Ocean St	Hyannis	MA	02601	**800-423-1551**	508-775-1639
Hyannis Travel Inn 18 N St	Hyannis	MA	02601	**800-352-7190**	508-775-8200
Hyatt Corp *Hyatt Regency Hotels* 396 Alhambra Cir Ste 788 *Resv	Coral Gables	FL	33134	**800-233-1234***	312-750-1234
Hyatt Hotels Corp 71 S Wacker Dr *NYSE: H*	Chicago	IL	60606	**888-591-1234**	312-750-1234
Hyatt Place Hotels 150 N Riverside Plz	Chicago	IL	60606	**888-492-8847**	312-750-1234
Hyatt Place Waikiki Beach 175 Paoakalani Ave	Honolulu	HI	96815	**877-367-1912**	808-922-3861
Ilikai Hotel & Suites 1777 Ala Moana Blvd	Honolulu	HI	96815	**866-536-7973**	808-949-3811
Imperial of Waikiki 205 Lewers St	Honolulu	HI	96815	**800-347-2582**	808-923-1827
Ingleside Inn 200 W Ramon Rd	Palm Springs	CA	92264	**800-772-6655**	760-325-0045
Inlet Tower Hotel & Suites 1020 W 12th Ave	Anchorage	AK	99501	**800-544-0786**	907-276-0110
Inn & Spa at Loretto 211 Old Santa Fe Trl	Santa Fe	NM	87501	**800-727-5531**	505-988-5531
Inn Above Tide, The 30 El Portal	Sausalito	CA	94965	**800-893-8433**	415-332-9535
Inn at Camachee Harbor 201 Yacht Club Dr	Saint Augustine	FL	32084	**800-688-5379**	904-825-0003
Inn at Gig Harbor 3211 56th St NW	Gig Harbor	WA	98335	**800-795-9980**	253-858-1111
Inn at Morro Bay 60 State Pk Rd	Morro Bay	CA	93442	**800-321-9566**	805-772-5651
Inn at Mystic 3 Williams Ave PO Box 526	Mystic	CT	06355	**800-237-2415**	860-536-9604
Inn at Otter Crest 301 Otter Crest Loop	Otter Rock	OR	97369	**800-452-2101**	541-765-2111
Inn at Pelican Bay 800 Vanderbilt Beach Rd	Naples	FL	34108	**800-597-8770**	239-597-8777
Inn at Perry Cabin 308 Watkins Ln	Saint Michaels	MD	21663	**800-722-2949**	410-745-2200
Inn at Saint John 939 Congress St	Portland	ME	04102	**800-636-9127**	207-773-6481
Inn at Spanish Head 4009 SW Hwy 101	Lincoln City	OR	97367	**800-452-8127**	541-996-2161
Inn at the Market 86 Pine St	Seattle	WA	98101	**800-446-4484**	206-443-3600
Inn At The Quay 900 Quayside Dr	New Westminster	BC	V3M6G1	**800-663-2001**	604-520-1776
Inn at Union Square 440 Post St	San Francisco	CA	94102	**800-288-4346**	415-397-3510
Inn at, The Tides, The 800 Coast Hwy 1	Bodega Bay	CA	94923	**800-541-7788**	707-875-2751
Inn of Long Beach 185 Atlantic Ave	Long Beach	CA	90802	**800-230-7500**	562-435-3791
Inn of the Anasazi 113 Washington Ave	Santa Fe	NM	87501	**888-767-3966**	505-988-3030
Inn of the Governors 101 W Alameda St	Santa Fe	NM	87501	**800-234-4534**	505-982-4333
Inn on Biltmore Estate 1 Antler Hill Rd	Asheville	NC	28803	**800-411-3812**	828-225-1600
Inn on Fifth 699 Fifth Ave S	Naples	FL	34102	**888-403-8778**	239-403-8777
Inn on Gitche Gumee 8517 Congdon Blvd	Duluth	MN	55804	**800-317-4979**	218-525-4979
Inn on Lake Superior 350 Canal Pk Dr	Duluth	MN	55802	**888-668-4352**	218-726-1111
Inn on the Alameda 303 E Alameda St	Santa Fe	NM	87501	**888-984-2121**	
Inn on the Paseo 630 Paseo de Peralta	Santa Fe	NM	87501	**855-984-8200**	505-984-8200
InnSuites Hospitality Trust InnSuites Hotels & Suites 475 N Granada Ave	Tucson	AZ	85701	**800-842-4242**	520-622-0923
InnSuites Hotel Tempe/Phoenix Airport 1651 W Baseline Rd	Tempe	AZ	85283	**800-842-4242**	480-897-7900
InterContinental Hotels Group (IHG) 3 Ravinia Dr Ste 100	Atlanta	GA	30346	**866-803-2143**	770-604-2000
Crowne Plaza Atlanta Perimeter 4355 Ashford Dunwoody Rd	Atlanta	GA	30346	**800-621-0555**	770-395-7700
International Hotel of Calgary 220 Fourth Ave SW	Calgary	AB	T2P0H5	**800-661-8627**	403-265-9600
Iroquois New York 49 W 44th St	New York City	NY	10036	**800-332-7220**	212-840-3080
Island Hotel, The 690 Newport Ctr Dr	Newport Beach	CA	92660	**866-554-4620**	949-759-0808
Jackson Hole Lodge 420 W Broadway PO Box 1805	Jackson	WY	83001	**800-604-9404**	307-733-2992
James Chicago, The 55 E Ontario	Chicago	IL	60611	**888-526-3778**	312-337-1000
James Gettys Hotel 27 Chambersburg St	Gettysburg	PA	17325	**888-900-5275**	717-337-1334
James New York - NoMad, The 88 Madison Ave *Resv	New York	NY	10016	**800-601-8500***	212-532-4100
Jefferson Hotel 101 W Franklin St	Richmond	VA	23220	**800-424-8014**	804-649-4750
Joie de Vivre Hospitality Inc 650 California St 7th Fl.	San Francisco	CA	94108	**800-738-7477**	
Jolly Hotel Madison Towers 22 E 38th St *Resv	New York	NY	10016	**888-726-0528***	212-802-0600
Jolly Roger Inn 640 W Katella Ave	Anaheim	CA	92802	**888-296-5986**	714-782-7500
Kahala Mandarin Oriental Hotel Hawaii Resort 5000 Kahala Ave	Honolulu	HI	96816	**800-367-2525**	808-739-8888
Kawada Hotel 200 S Hill St	Los Angeles	CA	90012	**800-752-9232**	213-621-4455
Kellogg Hotel & Conference Ctr Michigan State University 219 S Harrison Rd	East Lansing	MI	48824	**800-875-5090**	517-432-4000
Kensington Hotel, The 3500 S State St *Orders	Ann Arbor	MI	48108	**800-344-7829***	734-761-7800
Kensington Park Hotel 450 Post St	San Francisco	CA	94102	**800-553-1900**	
Kensington Riverside Inn 1126 Memorial Dr NW	Calgary	AB	T2N3E3	**877-313-3733**	403-228-4442
Key Lime Inn 725 Truman Ave	Key West	FL	33040	**800-549-4430**	305-294-5229
Keystone Lodge & Spa PO Box 38	Keystone	CO	80435	**877-625-1556**	970-496-4000
Killington Grand Resort Hotel & Conference Ctr 4763 Killington Rd	Killington	VT	05751	**800-621-6867**	802-422-3333
Kimball Terrace Inn 10 Huntington Rd	Northeast Harbor	ME	04662	**800-454-6225**	207-276-3383
Kimberly Hotel 145 E 50th St	New York	NY	10022	**800-683-0400**	212-755-0400
Kimpton Hotel & Restaurant Group 422 SW Broadway	Portland	OR	97205	**800-263-2305**	503-228-1212
Kimpton Hotel & Restaurant Group LLC 1733 N St NW	Washington	DC	20036	**800-775-1202**	202-393-3000
Kimpton Hotel & Restaurant Group LLC 222 Kearny St Ste 200	San Francisco	CA	94108	**800-546-7866**	415-397-5572
King Kamehameha's Kona Beach Hotel 75-5660 Palani Rd	Kailua-Kona	HI	96740	**800-367-2111**	808-329-2911
King Pacific Lodge 4850 Cowley Crescen	Richmond	BC	V7E0B5	**855-825-9378**	604-503-5474
Kitano New York 66 Park Ave E 38th St	New York	NY	10016	**800-548-2666**	212-885-7000

				Toll-Free	Phone
Knob Hill Inn					
960 N Main St PO Box 1327	Ketchum	ID	83340	**800-526-8010**	208-726-8010
Kona Kai Resort					
1551 Shelter Island Dr	San Diego	CA	92106	**800-566-2524**	619-221-8000
L' Appartement Hotel					
455 Sherbrooke W	Montreal	QC	H3A1B7	**800-363-3010**	514-284-3634
L'Ermitage Beverly Hills Hotel					
9291 Burton Way	Beverly Hills	CA	90210	**877-235-7582**	310-278-3344
L'Hotel du Vieux-Quebec					
1190 St Jean St	Quebec	QC	G1R1S6	**800-361-7787**	418-692-1850
L'Hotel Quebec					
3115 des Hotels Ave	Quebec	QC	G1W3Z6	**800-567-5276**	418-658-5120
La Fonda					
100 E San Francisco St	Santa Fe	NM	87501	**800-523-5002**	505-982-5511
La Pensione Hotel					
606 W Date St	San Diego	CA	92101	**800-232-4683**	619-236-8000
La Posada Hotel & Suites					
1000 Zaragoza St	Laredo	TX	78040	**800-444-2099***	956-722-1701
*Resv					
La Quinta Inn & Suites Boise Towne Square					
7965 W Emerald St	Boise	ID	83704	**800-600-6001**	208-378-7000
La Quinta Inn & Suites Pocatello					
1440 Bench Rd	Pocatello	ID	83201	**800-600-6001**	208-234-7500
La Quinta Inn & Suites Secaucus Meadowlands					
350 Lighting Way	Secaucus	NJ	07094	**800-753-3757***	201-863-8700
*General					
Lafayette Hotel					
101 Front St	Marietta	OH	45750	**800-331-9336**	740-373-5522
Lafayette Park Hotel					
3287 Mt Diablo Blvd	Lafayette	CA	94549	**855-382-8632**	800-394-3112
Lake Louise Inn					
210 Village Rd PO Box 209	Lake Louise	AB	T0L1E0	**800-661-9237**	403-522-3791
Lake Lure Inn & Spa, The					
2771 Memorial Hwy	Lake Lure	NC	28746	**888-434-4970**	
Lake Placid Lodge					
144 Lodge Way	Lake Placid	NY	12946	**877-523-2700**	518-523-2700
Lakeside Inn					
100 N Alexander St	Mount Dora	FL	32757	**800-556-5016**	352-383-4101
Lamothe House Hotel					
621 Esplanade Ave	New Orleans	LA	70116	**800-535-7815**	
Lancaster Hotel					
701 Texas St	Houston	TX	77002	**800-231-0336**	713-228-9500
Landmark Inn					
230 N Front St	Marquette	MI	49855	**888-752-6362***	906-228-2580
*General					
Langdon Hall Country House Hotel & Spa					
1 Langdon Dr	Cambridge	ON	N3H4R8	**800-268-1898**	519-740-2100
Langham Boston, The					
250 Franklin St	Boston	MA	02110	**800-791-7781**	617-451-1900
Lantern Lodge Motor Inn					
411 N College St	Myerstown	PA	17067	**800-262-5564**	717-866-6536
Laurel Inn, The					
444 Presidio Ave	San Francisco	CA	94115	**800-552-8735**	415-567-8467
Le Chamois					
4557 Blackcomb Way	Whistler	BC	V0N1B4	**888-621-1177**	604-932-8700
Le Meridian 20 Sidney St	Cambridge	MA	02139	**800-543-4300**	617-577-0200
Le Meridien Chambers Minneapolis					
901 Hennepin Ave	Minneapolis	MN	55403	**877-782-0116***	612-767-6900
*General					
Le M,ridien Delfina Santa Monica					
530 W Pico Blvd	Santa Monica	CA	90405	**888-627-8532**	310-399-9344
Le Montrose Suite Hotel					
900 Hammond St	West Hollywood	CA	90069	**800-776-0666**	310-855-1115
Le Nouvel Montreal Hotel & Spa					
1740 Rene-Levesque Blvd W	Montreal	QC	H3H1R3	**800-363-6063**	514-931-8841
Le Port-Royal Hotel & Suites					
144 St Pierre St	Quebec	QC	G1K8N8	**866-417-2777**	418-692-2777
Le Richelieu Hotel					
1234 Chartres St	New Orleans	LA	70116	**800-535-9653**	504-529-2492
Le Saint Sulpice					
414 Rue St Sulpice	Montreal	QC	H2Y2V5	**877-785-7423***	514-288-1000
*General					
Lenox Hotel 61 Exeter St	Boston	MA	02116	**800-225-7676**	617-536-5300
Leola Village Inn & Suites					
38 Deborah Dr	Leola	PA	17540	**877-669-5094**	717-656-7002
Les Suites Hotel Ottawa					
130 Besserer St	Ottawa	ON	K1N9M9	**866-682-0879**	613-232-2000
LHotel Montreal					
262 St Jacques St W	Old Montreal	QC	H2Y1N1	**877-553-0019**	514-985-0019
Lighthouse Club Hotel					
201 60th St	Ocean City	MD	21842	**888-371-5400**	410-524-5400
Lighthouse Lodge & Cottages					
1150 Lighthouse Ave	Pacific Grove	CA	93950	**800-858-1249**	831-655-2111
Linden Row Inn					
100 E Franklin St	Richmond	VA	23219	**800-348-7424**	804-783-7000
Listel Hotel, The					
1300 Robson St	Vancouver	BC	V6E1C5	**800-663-5491**	604-684-8461
Little America Hotel & Resort Cheyenne					
2800 W Lincolnway	Cheyenne	WY	82009	**800-445-6945**	307-775-8400
Little America Hotel & Towers Salt Lake City					
555 S Main St	Salt Lake City	UT	84101	**800-453-9450**	801-258-6568
Little America Hotel Flagstaff					
2515 E Butler Ave	Flagstaff	AZ	86004	**800-352-4386**	928-779-7900
Little America Hotels & Resorts					
500 S Main St	Salt Lake City	UT	84101	**800-281-7899**	801-596-5700
Little Nell, The					
675 E Durant Ave	Aspen	CO	81611	**888-843-6355**	970-920-4600
Lodge At Breckenridge, The					
112 Overlook Dr	Breckenridge	CO	80424	**800-736-1607**	970-453-9300
Lodge at the Mountain Village					
1850 Sidewinder Dr Ste 320	Park City	UT	84060	**800-453-1360**	
Loews Hotel 1000					
1000 First Ave	Seattle	WA	98104	**877-315-1088**	206-957-1000
Loews Hotels & Co					
667 Madison Ave	New York	NY	10065	**800-235-6397**	
Lone Oak Lodge					
2221 N Fremont St	Monterey	CA	93940	**800-283-5663***	831-372-4924
*General					
Long House Alaskan Hotel					
4335 Wisconsin St	Anchorage	AK	99517	**888-243-2133**	907-243-2133
Lonsdale Quay Hotel					
123 Carrie Cates Ct	North Vancouver	BC	V7M3K7	**800-836-6111**	604-986-6111
Lord Elgin Hotel					
100 Elgin St	Ottawa	ON	K1P5K8	**800-267-4298**	613-235-3333
Lord Nelson Hotel & Suites					
1515 S Park St	Halifax	NS	B3J2L2	**800-565-2020**	902-423-6331
Lord Stanley Suites on the Park					
1889 Alberni St	Vancouver	BC	V6G3G7	**888-767-7829**	604-688-9299
Los Angeles Athletic Club					
431 W Seventh St	Los Angeles	CA	90014	**800-421-8777**	213-625-2211
LQ Management LLC					
909 Hidden Rdg Ste 600	Irving	TX	75038	**800-753-3757**	214-492-6600
La Quinta Inn & Suites					
909 Hidden Rdg Ste 600	Irving	TX	75038	**800-753-3757**	214-492-6600
Lumen, The					
6101 Hillcrest Ave	Dallas	TX	75205	**800-908-1140**	214-219-2400
Luxe Hotel Sunset Blvd					
11461 Sunset Blvd	Los Angeles	CA	90049	**800-468-3541**	310-476-6571
Luxor Hotel & Casino					
3900 Las Vegas Blvd S	Las Vegas	NV	89119	**800-288-1000***	702-262-4000
*Resv					
MacArthur Place					
29 E MacArthur St	Sonoma	CA	95476	**800-722-1866**	707-938-2929
Madison Concourse Hotel & Governors Club					
1 W Dayton St	Madison	WI	53703	**800-356-8293**	608-257-6000
Madison Hotel, The					
1 Convent Rd	Morristown	NJ	07960	**800-526-0729**	973-285-1800
Magnolia Hotel & Spa, The					
623 Courtney St	Victoria	BC	V8W1B8	**877-624-6654**	250-381-0999
Magnolia Hotel Dallas					
1401 Commerce St	Dallas	TX	75201	**888-915-1110**	214-915-6500
Magnolia Hotel Denver					
818 17th St	Denver	CO	80202	**888-915-1110**	303-607-9000
Magnolia Hotel Houston					
1100 Texas Ave	Houston	TX	77002	**888-915-1110**	713-221-0011
Main Street Station Hotel & Casino					
200 N Main St	Las Vegas	NV	89101	**800-713-8933**	702-387-1896
Maison Dupuy Hotel					
1001 Toulouse St	New Orleans	LA	70112	**800-535-9177**	504-586-8000
Majestic Hotel, The					
528 W Brompton	Chicago	IL	60657	**800-727-5108**	773-404-3499
Malaga Inn 359 Church St	Mobile	AL	36602	**800-235-1586**	251-438-4701
Malibu Beach Inn					
22878 Pacific Coast Hwy	Malibu	CA	90265	**800-462-5428**	
Mandarin Oriental Hotel Group (USA)					
345 California St Ste 1250	San Francisco	CA	94104	**800-526-6566**	415-772-8800
Mandarin Oriental Miami					
500 Brickell Key Dr	Miami	FL	33131	**800-526-6566**	305-913-8288
Mandarin Oriental New York					
80 Columbus Cir	New York	NY	10023	**866-801-8880**	212-805-8800
Mandarin Oriental Washington DC					
1330 Maryland Ave SW	Washington	DC	20024	**888-888-1778**	202-554-8588
Manor House Inn					
106 West St	Bar Harbor	ME	04609	**800-437-0088**	
Mansfield Hotel, The					
12 W 44th St	New York	NY	10036	**844-591-5565***	212-277-8700
*Admissions					
Mansion on Forsyth Park					
700 Drayton St	Savannah	GA	31401	**888-213-3671**	912-238-5158
Mansion View Inn & Suites					
529 S Fourth St	Springfield	IL	62701	**800-252-1083**	217-544-7411
Maple Hill Farm Bed & Breakfast Inn					
11 Inn Rd	Hallowell	ME	04347	**800-622-2708**	207-622-2708
Marina Inn at Grande Dunes					
8121 Amalfi Pl	Myrtle Beach	SC	29572	**877-913-1333***	843-913-1333
*Resv					
Mark Spencer Hotel					
409 SW 11th Ave	Portland	OR	97205	**800-548-3934**	503-224-3293
Mark Twain Hotel					
225 NE Adams St	Peoria	IL	61602	**866-325-6351**	309-676-3600
Market Pavilion Hotel					
225 E Bay St	Charleston	SC	29401	**877-440-2250**	843-723-0500
Marquesa Hotel					
600 Fleming St	Key West	FL	33040	**800-869-4631**	305-292-1919
Marriott Charleston Hotel					
170 Lockwood Blvd	Charleston	SC	29403	**888-236-2427**	843-723-3000
Marriott Columbus					
800 Front Ave	Columbus	GA	31901	**800-455-9261**	706-324-1800
Marriott International Inc					
10400 Fernwood Rd	Bethesda	MD	20817	**800-450-4442**	301-380-3000
NASDAQ: MAR					
Maryland Inn 58 State Cir	Annapolis	MD	21401	**800-847-8882**	410-263-2641
Matrix Hotel 10640-100 Ave	Edmonton	AB	T5J3N8	**866-465-8150**	780-429-2861
Maumee Bay Lodge & Conference Ctr					
1750 Pk Rd Ste 2	Oregon	OH	43616	**800-282-7275**	419-836-1466
Mayfair Hotel & Spa					
3000 Florida Ave	Coconut Grove	FL	33133	**800-433-4555**	305-441-0000
Mayflower Park Hotel					
405 Olive Way	Seattle	WA	98101	**800-426-5100**	206-623-8700
Mayo Clinic					
4500 San Pablo Rd	Jacksonville	FL	32224	**888-255-4458**	904-992-9992
McCamly Plaza Hotel					
50 Capital Ave SW	Battle Creek	MI	49017	**800-337-0300**	269-963-7050
MCM Elegante Suites					
4250 Ridgemont Dr	Abilene	TX	79606	**888-897-9644**	325-698-1234
Meeting Street Inn					
173 Meeting St	Charleston	SC	29401	**800-842-8022**	843-723-1882
Menger Hotel					
204 Alamo Plz	San Antonio	TX	78205	**800-345-9285**	210-223-4361
Mercer Hotel 147 Mercer St	New York	NY	10012	**888-918-6060**	212-966-6060
Meridian Plaza Resort					
2310 N Ocean Blvd	Myrtle Beach	SC	29577	**888-590-0801**	843-626-4734
Metropolitan Hotel Vancouver					
645 Howe St	Vancouver	BC	V6C2Y9	**800-667-2300**	604-687-1122
Metterra Hotel on Whyte					
10454 82nd Ave	Edmonton	AB	T6E4Z7	**866-465-8150**	780-465-8150

				Toll-Free	Phone

Miami International Airport Hotel
NW 20th St & Le Jeune Rd .... Miami FL 33122 **800-327-1276** 305-871-4100

Midtown Hotel
220 Huntington Ave .... Boston MA 02115 **800-343-1177** 617-262-1000

Mill Falls
312 Daniel Webster Hwy .... Meredith NH 03253 **844-745-2931**

Mill Street Inn 75 Mill St .... Newport RI 02840 **800-392-1316** 401-849-9500

Mill Valley Inn
165 Throckmorton Ave .... Mill Valley CA 94941 **855-334-7946** 415-389-6608

Minto Rentals In Ottawa
185 Lyons St N .... Ottawa ON K1R7Y4 **800-267-3377** 613-232-2200

Mira Monte Inn & Suites
69 Mt Desert St .... Bar Harbor ME 04609 **800-553-5109**

Mirbeau Inn & Spa
851 W Genesee St .... Skaneateles NY 13152 **877-647-2328** 315-685-5006

Mission Inn
3649 Mission Inn Ave .... Riverside CA 92501 **800-843-7755** 951-784-0300

Misty Harbor & Barefoot Beach Resort
118 Weirs Rd .... Gilford NH 03249 **800-336-4789** 603-293-4500

Miyako Hotel Los Angeles
328 E First St .... Los Angeles CA 90012 **800-228-6596** 213-617-2000

MODA Hotel 900 Seymour St .... Vancouver BC V6B3L9 **877-683-5522** 604-683-4251

Mojave A Desert Resort
73721 Shadow Mtn Dr .... Palm Desert CA 92260 **800-391-1104*** 760-346-6121
*Resv

Monarch Hotel & Conference Ctr
12566 SE 93rd Ave .... Clackamas OR 97015 **800-492-8700** 503-652-1515

Mondrian Hotel
8440 Sunset Blvd .... West Hollywood CA 90069 **800-525-8029** 323-650-8999

Monmouth Historic Inn & Gardens
1358 John A Quitman Blvd .... Natchez MS 39120 **800-828-4531** 601-442-5852

Monte Carlo Inn-Airport Suites
7035 Edwards Blvd .... Mississauga ON L5T2H8 **800-363-6400** 905-564-8500

Monterey Bay Inn
242 Cannery Row .... Monterey CA 93940 **800-424-6242** 831-373-6242

Monterey Plaza Hotel & Spa
400 Cannery Row .... Monterey CA 93940 **877-862-7552**

Morgans Hotel Group
1685 Collins Ave .... South Beach FL 33139 **800-606-6090** 305-672-2000
NASDAQ: MHGC

Mosser Hotel
54 Fourth St .... San Francisco CA 94103 **800-227-3804** 415-986-4400

Motel 6 Wichita
8302 E Kellogg Dr .... Wichita KS 67207 **800-466-8356** 800-899-9841

Mount View Hotel & Spa
1457 Lincoln Ave .... Calistoga CA 94515 **800-816-6877** 707-942-6877

Mountain Haus 292 E Meadow Dr .... Vail CO 81657 **800-237-0922** 970-476-2434

Mountain Villas
9525 W Skyline Pkwy .... Duluth MN 55810 **866-688-4552**

Muse, The 130 W 46th St .... New York NY 10036 **877-692-6873** 212-485-2400

Mutiny Hotel
2951 S Bayshore Dr .... Miami FL 33133 **888-868-8469** 305-441-2100

Napa River Inn 500 Main St .... Napa CA 94559 **877-251-8500** 707-251-8500

National Hotel
1677 Collins Ave .... Miami Beach FL 33139 **800-327-8370** 305-532-2311

Nativo Lodge Hotel
6000 Pan American Fwy NE ...... Albuquerque NM 87109 **888-628-4861** 505-798-4300

New Haven Hotel
229 George St .... New Haven CT 06510 **800-644-6835** 203-498-3100

New Otani Kaimana Beach Hotel
2863 Kalakaua Ave .... Honolulu HI 96815 **800-356-8264** 808-923-1555

New York Palace Hotel
455 Madison Ave 50th St .... New York NY 10022 **800-697-2522** 212-888-7000

New York's Hotel Pennsylvania
401 Seventh Ave .... New York NY 10001 **800-223-8585** 212-736-5000

Newport Beach Hotel & Suites
1 Wave Ave .... Middletown RI 02842 **800-655-1778** 401-846-0310

Newport Harbor Hotel & Marina
49 America's Cup Ave .... Newport RI 02840 **800-955-2558** 401-847-9000

Nine Zero Hotel
90 Tremont St .... Boston MA 02108 **866-906-9090** 617-772-5800

Nittany Lion Inn
200 W Park Ave .... State College PA 16803 **800-233-7505** 814-865-8500

Norwood Hotel
112 Marion St .... Winnipeg MB R2H0T1 **888-888-1878** 204-233-4475

O Henry Hotel
624 Green Valley Rd .... Greensboro NC 27408 **800-965-8259** 336-854-2000

Ocean Forest Plaza
201 74th Ave N .... Myrtle Beach SC 29572 **800-726-3783***
*General

Ocean Key Resort
424 Atlantic Ave .... Virginia Beach VA 23451 **800-955-9700** 757-425-2200

Ocean Pointe Suites at Key Largo
500 Burton Dr .... Tavernier FL 33070 **800-882-9464** 305-853-3000

Ocean Sky Hotel & Resort
4060 Galt Ocean Dr .... Fort Lauderdale FL 33308 **800-678-9022** 954-565-6611

OHANA Waikiki Beachcomber Hotel
2300 Kalakaua Ave .... Honolulu HI 96815 **866-956-4262**

Old Mill Toronto
21 Old Mill Rd .... Toronto ON M8X1G5 **866-653-6455** 416-236-2641

Omni Hotels 4001 Maple Ave .... Dallas TX 75219 **800-843-6664** 402-952-6664

Onyx Hotel 155 Portland St .... Boston MA 02114 **866-660-6699** 617-557-9955

Opus Hotel 322 Davie St .... Vancouver BC V6B5Z6 **866-642-6787**

Orchards Inn of Sedona
254 Hwy N 89 A .... Sedona AZ 86336 **855-474-7719**

Orleans Las Vegas Hotel & Casino
4500 W Tropicana Ave .... Las Vegas NV 89103 **800-675-3267** 702-365-7111

Outrigger Enterprises Group
2375 Kuhio Ave .... Honolulu HI 96815 **866-956-4262**

Outrigger Hotels Hawaii
Outrigger Hotels & Resorts
2375 Kuhio Ave .... Honolulu HI 96815 **800-688-7444** 866-956-4262

Outrigger Waikiki on the Beach
2335 Kalakaua Ave .... Honolulu HI 96815 **800-688-7444** 808-923-0711

Oxford Hotel 1600 17th St .... Denver CO 80202 **800-228-5838** 303-628-5400

Oxford Suites Boise
1426 S Entertainment Ave .... Boise ID 83709 **888-322-8001*** 208-322-8000
*General

Oxford Suites Spokane Valley
15015 E Indiana Ave .... Spokane Valley WA 99216 **866-668-7848** 509-847-1000

Oyster Point Hotel, The
146 Bodman Pl .... Red Bank NJ 07701 **800-345-3484** 732-530-8200

Pacific Inn
600 Marina Dr .... Seal Beach CA 90740 **866-466-0300** 562-493-7501

Pacific Inn Resort & Conference Centre
1160 King George Hwy .... Surrey BC V4A4Z2 **800-667-2248** 604-535-1432

Pacific Terrace Hotel
610 Diamond St .... San Diego CA 92109 **800-344-3370** 858-581-3500

Palace Casino 158 Howard Ave .... Biloxi MS 39530 **800-725-2239** 228-386-2315

Palace Hotel
2 New Montgomery St .... San Francisco CA 94105 **866-716-8136** 415-512-1111

Palace Station Hotel & Casino
2411 W Sahara Ave .... Las Vegas NV 89102 **800-634-3101*** 702-367-2411
*Resv

Palmer Inn, The
3499 Rt One S .... Princeton NJ 08540 **800-688-0500** 609-452-2500

Pan Pacific Hotel Vancouver
999 Canada Pl Ste 300 .... Vancouver BC V6C3B5 **800-937-1515** 604-662-8111

Pan Pacific Seattle
2125 Terry Ave .... Seattle WA 98121 **877-324-4856** 206-264-8111

Pantages Hotel
200 Victoria St .... Toronto ON M5B1V8 **855-852-1777** 416-362-1777

Par-A-Dice Hotel
21 Blackjack Blvd .... East Peoria IL 61611 **800-727-2342** 309-699-7711

Paramount Hotel
808 SW Taylor St .... Portland OR 97205 **855-215-0160** 503-223-9900

Park Shore Waikiki Hotel
2586 Kalakaua Ave .... Honolulu HI 96815 **866-536-7975** 808-954-7426

Park Vista Resort Hotel
705 Cherokee OrchaRd Rd PO Box 30 .... Gatlinburg TN 37738 **800-227-5622*** 865-436-9211
*Sales

Parkway Inn
125 N Jackson St PO Box 494 .... Jackson WY 83001 **800-247-8390**

Paso Robles Inn
1103 Spring St .... Paso Robles CA 93446 **800-676-1713** 805-238-2660

Peabody Memphis, The
149 Union Ave .... Memphis TN 38103 **800-732-2639** 901-529-4000

Peery Hotel
110 West 300 South .... Salt Lake City UT 84101 **800-331-0073** 801-521-4300

Pegasus International Hotel
501 Southard St .... Key West FL 33040 **800-397-8148** 305-294-9323

Pelican Grand Beach Resort
2000 N Ocean Blvd .... Fort Lauderdale FL 33305 **800-525-6232** 954-568-9431

Peninsula Beverly Hills
9882 S Santa Monica Blvd .... Beverly Hills CA 90212 **800-462-7899** 310-551-2888

Peninsula Chicago
108 E Superior St .... Chicago IL 60611 **866-288-8889** 312-337-2888

Peninsula New York
700 Fifth Ave .... New York NY 10019 **800-262-9467** 212-956-2888

Penn's View Hotel
14 N Front St .... Philadelphia PA 19106 **800-331-7634** 215-922-7600

Peppermill Hotel & Casino
2707 S Virginia St .... Reno NV 89502 **800-648-6992** 775-826-2121

Pfister Hotel
424 E Wisconsin Ave .... Milwaukee WI 53202 **800-558-8222** 414-273-8222

Phoenix Grand Hotel Salem
201 Liberty St SE .... Salem OR 97301 **877-540-7800** 503-540-7800

Phoenix Park Hotel
520 N Capitol St .... Washington DC 20001 **800-824-5419** 202-638-6900

Pier 5 Hotel
711 Eastern Ave .... Baltimore MD 21202 **866-583-4162** 410-539-2000

Pine Crest Inn
85 Pine Crest Ln .... Tryon NC 28782 **800-633-3001** 828-859-9135

Planters Inn
112 N Market St .... Charleston SC 29401 **800-845-7082** 843-722-2345

Platinum Hotel
211 E Flamingo Rd .... Las Vegas NV 89169 **877-211-9211*** 702-365-5000
*General

Plaza Hotel & Casino
1 Main St .... Las Vegas NV 89101 **800-634-6575** 702-386-2110

Plaza Resort Club 121 W St .... Reno NV 89501 **800-628-5974** 775-786-2200

Plaza Suites Silicon Valley
3100 Lakeside Dr .... Santa Clara CA 95054 **800-345-1554** 408-748-9800

Plump Jack's Squaw Valley Inn
1920 Squaw Valley Rd
PO Box 2407 .... Olympic Valley CA 96146 **800-323-7666** 530-583-1576

Point Plaza Suites & Conference Hotel
950 J Clyde Morris Blvd .... Newport News VA 23601 **800-841-1112** 757-599-4460

Pontchartrain
2031 St Charles Ave .... New Orleans LA 70130 **800-708-6652**

Port-O-Call Hotel
1510 Boardwalk .... Ocean City NJ 08226 **800-334-4546** 609-399-8812

Portland Harbor Hotel
468 Fore St .... Portland ME 04101 **888-798-9090** 207-775-9090

Portland Regency Hotel
20 Milk St .... Portland ME 04101 **800-727-3436** 207-774-4200

Portofino Hotel & Yacht Club
260 Portofino Way .... Redondo Beach CA 90277 **800-468-4292** 310-379-8481

Portofino Inn & Suites Anaheim
1831 S Harbor Blvd .... Anaheim CA 92802 **800-398-3963*** 714-782-7600
*Resv

Portola Plaza Hotel
2 Portola Plz .... Monterey CA 93940 **888-222-5851** 831-649-4511

Post Hotel, The
200 Pipestone Rd PO Box 69 .... Lake Louise AB T0L1E0 **800-661-1586** 403-522-3989

Prairie Band Casino & Resort
12305 150th Rd .... Mayetta KS 66509 **888-727-4946** 785-966-7777

Preferred Hotel Group
Preferred Hotels & Resorts Worldwide Inc
311 S Wacker Dr Ste 1900 .... Chicago IL 60606 **800-650-1281** 312-913-0400

Prestige Harbourfront Resort & Convention Centre
251 Harbourfront Dr NE .... Salmon Arm BC V1E2W7 **877-737-8443** 250-833-5800

Prince George Hotel, The
1725 Market St .... Halifax NS B3J3N9 **800-565-1567** 902-425-1986

	City	State	ZIP	Toll-Free	Phone
Princess Bayside Beach Hotel & Golf Ctr					
4801 Coastal Hwy	Ocean City	MD	21842	**888-622-9743***	410-723-2900
*General					
Publick House Historic Resort					
277 Main St Rt 131	Sturbridge	MA	01566	**800-782-5425***	508-347-3313
*Cust Svc					
Puffin Inn					
4400 SpenaRd Rd	Anchorage	AK	99517	**800-478-3346**	907-243-4044
Quality Hotel-airport					
7228 Wminster Hwy	Richmond	BC	V6X1A1	**877-244-3051**	604-244-3051
Quality Inn & Suites Plano East - Richardson					
1600 N Central Expy	Plano	TX	75074	**877-386-4383**	972-578-8555
Quality Inn Halifax Airport					
60 Sky Blvd	Goffs	NS	B2T1K3	**800-667-3333**	902-873-3000
Quebec Inn					
7175 Blvd Hamel Ouest	Quebec	QC	G2G1B6	**800-567-5276**	418-872-9831
Queen Anne Hotel					
1590 Sutter St	San Francisco	CA	94109	**800-227-3970**	415-441-2828
Quimby House Inn					
109 Cottage St	Bar Harbor	ME	04609	**800-344-5811**	207-288-5811
Rabbit Hill Inn					
48 Lower Waterford Rd					
PO Box 55	Lower Waterford	VT	05848	**800-626-3215**	802-748-5168
Radisson Chicago-O'Hare Hotel					
1450 E Touhy Ave	Des Plaines	IL	60018	**888-201-1718**	888-288-8889
Radisson Hotel Bloomington Mall of America					
1700 American Blvd E	Bloomington	MN	55425	**800-967-9033***	952-854-8700
*Resv					
Radisson Hotel Gateway Seattle-Tacoma Airport					
18118 International Blvd	Seattle	WA	98188	**888-288-8889**	
Railroad Pass Hotel & Casino					
2800 S Boulder Hwy	Henderson	NV	89002	**800-654-0877**	702-294-5000
Ranch at Steamboat					
1800 Ranch Rd	Steamboat Springs	CO	80487	**888-686-8075**	970-879-3000
Ranch Inn 45 E Pearl St	Jackson	WY	83001	**800-348-5599**	307-733-6363
Raphael Kansas City					
325 Ward Pkwy	Kansas City	MO	64112	**800-821-5343**	816-756-3800
Red Lion Hotels Corp					
201 W N River Dr Ste 100	Spokane	WA	99201	**800-733-5466***	
NYSE: RLH ■ *Resv					
Red Rock Resort Spa & Casino					
11011 W Charleston Blvd	Las Vegas	NV	89135	**866-767-7773**	702-797-7777
Regency Fairbanks Hotel					
95 Tenth Ave	Fairbanks	AK	99701	**800-478-1320**	907-459-2700
Regency Suites Calgary					
610 Fourth Ave SW	Calgary	AB	T2P0K1	**800-468-4044**	403-231-1000
Regency Suites Hotel Midtown Atlanta					
975 W Peachtree St	Atlanta	GA	30309	**800-642-3629**	404-876-5003
Residence & Conference Centre - Toronto					
1760 Finch Ave E	Toronto	ON	M2J5G3	**877-225-8664**	416-491-8811
Rittenhouse Hotel					
210 W Rittenhouse Sq	Philadelphia	PA	19103	**800-635-1042**	215-546-9000
Ritz-Carlton Dallas					
2121 McKinney Ave	Dallas	TX	75201	**800-960-7082***	214-922-0200
*Resv					
River's Edge Resort Cottages					
4200 Boat St	Fairbanks	AK	99709	**800-770-3343**	907-474-0286
Riveredge Resort Hotel					
17 Holland St	Alexandria Bay	NY	13607	**800-365-6987**	315-482-9917
Riverstone Billings Inn					
880 N 29th St	Billings	MT	59101	**800-231-7782**	406-252-6800
Riverview Plaza Hotel					
64 S Water St	Mobile	AL	36602	**800-321-2211**	251-438-4000
Riviera Hotel					
1431 Robson St	Vancouver	BC	V6G1C1	**888-699-5222**	604-685-1301
Robert Treat Hotel 50 Pk Pl	Newark	NJ	07102	**800-569-2300**	973-622-1000
Rock View Resort					
1049 Parkview Dr	Hollister	MO	65672	**800-375-9530**	417-334-4678
Rocklin Park Hotel					
5450 China Garden Rd	Rocklin	CA	95677	**888-630-9400**	916-630-9400
Roger Smith Hotel					
501 Lexington Ave	New York	NY	10017	**800-445-0277**	212-755-1400
Roosevelt Hotel					
45 E 45th St	New York	NY	10017	**877-322-8228**	212-661-9600
Rose Hotel 807 Main St	Pleasanton	CA	94566	**800-843-9540**	925-846-8802
Rosedale on Robson Suite Hotel					
838 Hamilton St	Vancouver	BC	V6B6A2	**800-661-8870**	604-689-8033
Rosellen Suites at Stanley Park					
2030 Barclay St	Vancouver	BC	V6G1L5	**888-317-6648**	604-689-4807
Rosen Centre Hotel					
9840 International Dr	Orlando	FL	32819	**800-204-7234**	407-996-9840
Rosen Hotels & Resorts Inc					
9840 International Dr	Orlando	FL	32819	**800-204-7234**	407-996-9840
Rosen Plaza Hotel					
9700 International Dr	Orlando	FL	32819	**800-366-9700**	407-996-9700
Rosen Shingle Creek					
9939 Universal Blvd	Orlando	FL	32819	**866-996-9939**	407-996-9939
Rosewood Hotels & Resorts					
500 Crescent Ct Ste 300	Dallas	TX	75201	**888-767-3966**	214-880-4200
Royal Garden at Waikiki Hotel					
440 Olohana St	Honolulu	HI	96815	**800-428-1932**	855-421-4785
Royal Holiday Beach Resort					
1988 Beach Blvd	Biloxi	MS	39531	**800-874-0402***	228-388-7553
*Resv					
Royal Park Hotel-brookshire & The Commons					
600 E University Dr	Rochester	MI	48307	**800-339-2761**	248-652-2600
Royal Sonesta Hotel Boston					
40 Edwin H Land Blvd	Cambridge	MA	02142	**800-766-3782**	617-806-4200
Royal Sonesta Hotel New Orleans					
300 Bourbon St	New Orleans	LA	70130	**800-766-3782**	504-586-0300
Royal Sonesta Hotel New Orleans					
300 Bourbon St	New Orleans	LA	70130	**800-766-3782**	504-586-0300
Royalton Hotel					
44 W 44th St	New York	NY	10036	**800-606-6090**	212-869-4400
Rushmore View Inn					
522 Hwy 16A	Keystone	SD	57751	**800-888-2603**	
Saint Michaels Harbour Inn & Marina					
101 N Harbor Rd	Saint Michaels	MD	21663	**800-955-9001**	410-745-9001
Saint Paul Hotel					
350 Market St	Saint Paul	MN	55102	**800-292-9292**	651-292-9292
Saint Regis Hotel					
602 Dunsmuir St	Vancouver	BC	V6B1Y6	**800-770-7929**	604-681-1135
Salvatore's Hospitality					
6461 Transit Rd	Buffalo	NY	14043	**877-456-4097**	716-635-9000
Sam's Town Hotel & Gambling Hall					
5111 Boulder Hwy	Las Vegas	NV	89122	**800-897-8696**	702-456-7777
San Carlos Hotel					
150 E 50th St	New York	NY	10022	**800-722-2012**	212-755-1800
Sands Casino Resort Bethlehem					
77 Sands Blvd	Bethlehem	PA	18015	**877-726-3777**	
Sands Ocean Club Resort					
9550 Shore Dr	Myrtle Beach	SC	29572	**888-999-8485***	
*General					
Sands Regency Casino Hotel					
345 N Arlington Ave	Reno	NV	89501	**800-233-4939***	775-348-2200
*Resv					
Sanibel Inn 937 E Gulf Dr	Sanibel	FL	33957	**866-565-5480**	239-472-3181
Santa Barbara Inn					
901 E Cabrillo Blvd	Santa Barbara	CA	93103	**800-231-0431**	805-966-2285
Santa Maria Inn					
801 S Broadway	Santa Maria	CA	93454	**800-462-4276**	805-928-7777
Saratoga Hilton					
534 Broadway	Saratoga Springs	NY	12866	**800-445-8667**	518-584-4000
Satellite Hotel					
411 Lakewood Cir	Colorado Springs	CO	80910	**800-423-8409**	719-596-6800
Scotsman Inn West					
5922 W Kellogg St	Wichita	KS	67209	**800-950-7268**	316-943-3800
Sea Ranch Lodge					
60 Sea Walk Dr PO Box 44	The Sea Ranch	CA	95497	**800-732-7262**	707-785-2371
Sea View Hotel					
9909 Collins Ave	Bal Harbour	FL	33154	**800-447-1010**	305-866-4441
Seaport Hotel & World Trade Ctr					
1 Seaport Ln	Boston	MA	02210	**877-732-7678**	617-385-4000
Seaside Inn					
541 E Gulf Dr	Sanibel Island	FL	33957	**866-717-2323**	
Sedona Rouge Hotel & Spa					
2250 W SR- 89A	Sedona	AZ	86336	**866-312-4111**	928-203-4111
Seelbach Hilton Louisville					
500 S Fourth St	Louisville	KY	40202	**800-333-3399**	502-585-3200
Sentinel Hotel					
614 SW 11th Ave	Portland	OR	97205	**888-246-5631**	503-224-3400
Setai, The					
2001 Collins Ave	Miami Beach	FL	33139	**888-625-7500**	305-520-6000
Shades of Green on Walt Disney World Resort					
1950 W Magnolia Palm Dr	Lake Buena Vista	FL	32830	**888-593-2242**	407-824-3400
Sheraton Colonial Hotel & Golf Club Boston North					
1 Audubon Rd	Wakefield	MA	01880	**866-716-8133**	781-245-9300
Sheraton Gateway Hotel Los Angeles					
6101 W Century Blvd	Los Angeles	CA	90045	**888-627-7104**	310-642-1111
Sheraton Suites Calgary Eau Claire					
255 Barclay Parade SW	Calgary	AB	T2P5C2	**866-716-8134**	403-266-7200
Sherry-Netherland Hotel					
781 Fifth Ave	New York	NY	10022	**877-743-7710**	212-355-2800
Shilo Inn Suites Salem					
3304 Market St	Salem	OR	97301	**800-222-2244**	503-581-4001
Shutters on the Beach					
1 Pico Blvd	Santa Monica	CA	90405	**866-527-6612**	310-458-0030
Siena Hotel					
1505 E Franklin St	Chapel Hill	NC	27514	**800-223-7379**	919-929-4000
Silver Cloud Hotel Seattle Broadway					
1100 Broadway	Seattle	WA	98122	**800-590-1801**	206-325-1400
Silver Cloud Inn Seattle-Lake Union					
1150 Fairview Ave N	Seattle	WA	98109	**800-330-5812***	206-447-9500
*General					
Silver Cloud Inn University District					
5036 25th Ave NE	Seattle	WA	98105	**800-205-6940**	206-526-5200
Silver King Hotel					
1485 Empire Ave	Park City	UT	84060	**888-667-2775**	435-649-5500
Silver Smith Hotel & Suites					
10 S Wabash Ave	Chicago	IL	60603	**800-979-0084**	312-372-7696
SilverBirch Hotels & Resorts					
1640 - 1188 W Georgia St	Vancouver	BC	V6E4A2	**800-431-0070**	604-646-2447
Silverdale Beach Hotel					
3073 NW Bucklin Hill Rd	Silverdale	WA	98383	**800-544-9799**	360-698-1000
Simonton Court Historic Inn & Cottages					
320 Simonton St	Key West	FL	33040	**800-944-2687**	
Sir Francis Drake Hotel					
450 Powell St	San Francisco	CA	94102	**800-795-7129**	415-392-7755
Ski Bromont 150 Champlain	Bromont	QC	J2L1A2	**866-276-6668**	450-534-2200
Snowbird Mountain Lodge					
4633 Santeetlah Rd	Robbinsville	NC	28771	**800-941-9290**	828-479-3433
Snowy Owl Inn					
41 Village Rd	Waterville Valley	NH	03215	**800-766-9969**	603-236-8383
Sofia Hotel					
150 W Broadway	San Diego	CA	92101	**800-826-0009**	619-234-9200
SoHo Metropolitan Hotel					
318 Wellington St W	Toronto	ON	M5V3T4	**866-764-6638**	416-599-8800
Somerset Inn					
2601 W Big Beaver Rd	Troy	MI	48084	**800-228-8769**	248-643-7800
Sonesta Hotel & Suites Coconut Grove					
2889 McFarlane Rd	Miami	FL	33133	**800-766-3782**	305-529-2828
Soniat House					
1133 Chartres St	New Orleans	LA	70116	**800-544-8808**	504-522-0570
Sophie Station Suites					
1717 University Ave	Fairbanks	AK	99709	**800-528-4916**	
South Beach Marina Inn & Vacation Rentals					
232 S Sea Pines Dr	Hilton Head Island	SC	29928	**800-367-3909**	843-671-6498
South Pier Inn on the Canal					
701 Lake Ave S	Duluth	MN	55802	**800-430-7437**	218-786-9007
South Point Hotel & Casino					
9777 Las Vegas Blvd S	Las Vegas	NV	89183	**866-796-7111**	866-791-7626
Southampton Inn					
91 Hill St	SoutHampton	NY	11968	**800-832-6500**	631-283-6500
Spindrift Inn					
652 Cannery Row	Monterey	CA	93940	**800-841-1879**	831-646-8900

		Toll-Free	Phone

Spring Creek Ranch
1600 N East Butte Rd PO Box 4780 . . . . Jackson WY 83001 **800-443-6139** 307-733-8833
St James Hotel 406 Main St . . . . Red Wing MN 55066 **800-252-1875**
St Julien Hotel & Spa
900 Walnut St . . . . Boulder CO 80302 **877-303-0900** 720-406-9696
Stamford Suites
720 Bedford St . . . . Stamford CT 06901 **866-394-4365** 203-359-7300
Stanley Hotel
333 Wonderview Ave . . . . Estes Park CO 80517 **800-976-1377** 970-577-4000
Star Island Resort
5000 Ave of the Stars . . . . Kissimmee FL 34746 **800-513-2820** 407-997-8000
Starwood Hotels & Resorts Worldwide Inc
Westin Hotels & Resorts
1111 Westchester Ave . . . . White Plains NY 10604 **888-625-5144** 914-640-8100
State Plaza Hotel
2117 E St NW . . . . Washington DC 20037 **866-868-7774** 202-861-8200
Sterling Hotel 1300 H St . . . . Sacramento CA 95814 **800-365-7660** 916-448-1300
Stockyards Hotel
109 E Exchange Ave . . . . Fort Worth TX 76164 **800-423-8471** 817-625-6427
Stone Castle Hotel & Conference Ctr, The
3050 Green Mtn Dr . . . . Branson MO 65616 **800-677-6906** 417-335-4700
Stonewall Jackson Hotel & Conference Ctr
24 S Market St . . . . Staunton VA 24401 **866-880-0024** 540-885-4848
Stoney Creek Inn
101 Mariner's Way . . . . East Peoria IL 61611 **800-659-2220** 309-694-1300
Strater Hotel 699 Main Ave . . . . Durango CO 81301 **800-247-4431** 970-247-4431
Strathcona Hotel 60 York St . . . . Toronto ON M5J1S8 **800-268-8304** 416-363-3321
Strathcona Hotel, The
919 Douglas St . . . . Victoria BC V8W2C2 **800-663-7476** 250-383-7137
Stratosphere Tower Hotel & Casino
2000 S Las Vegas Blvd . . . . Las Vegas NV 89104 **800-998-6937** 702-380-7777
Sturbridge Host Hotel & Conference Ctr
366 Main St . . . . Sturbridge MA 01566 **800-582-3232** 508-347-7393
Suites at Fisherman's Wharf
2655 Hyde St . . . . San Francisco CA 94109 **800-227-3608** 415-771-0200
Suites Hotel in Canal Park, The
325 Lake Ave S . . . . Duluth MN 55802 **800-794-1716** 218-727-4663
Summit Lodge & Spa
4359 Main St . . . . Whistler BC V0N1B4 **888-913-8811** 604-932-2778
Sun Viking Lodge
2411 S Atlantic Ave . . . . Daytona Beach Shores FL 32118 **800-874-4469** 386-252-6252
Suncoast Hotel & Casino
9090 Alta Dr . . . . Las Vegas NV 89145 **877-677-7111** 702-636-7111
Sundial Boutique Hotel
4340 Sundial Crescent . . . . Whistler BC V0N1B4 **800-661-2321** 604-932-2321
Sunset Inn Travel Apartments
1111 Burnaby St . . . . Vancouver BC V6E1P4 **800-786-1997** 604-688-2474
Sunset Marquis Hotel & Villas
1200 N Alta Loma Rd . . . . West Hollywood CA 90069 **800-858-9758** 310-657-1333
Sunset Station Hotel & Casino
1301 W Sunset Rd . . . . Henderson NV 89014 **888-786-7389** 702-547-7777
Surf & Sand Resort
1555 S Coast Hwy . . . . Laguna Beach CA 92651 **877-741-5908** 888-579-8544
Surfsand Resort
148 W Gower Rd . . . . Cannon Beach OR 97110 **800-547-6100** 503-436-2274
Swag, The 2300 Swag Rd . . . . Waynesville NC 28785 **800-789-7672** 828-926-0430
Taj Boston 15 Arlington St . . . . Boston MA 02116 **866-969-1825** 617-536-5700
Taj Campton Place
340 Stockton St . . . . San Francisco CA 94108 **866-969-1825** 415-781-5555
Teton Mountain Lodge & Spa
3385 Cody Ln . . . . Teton Village WY 83025 **800-631-6271** 307-201-6066
Thayer Hotel
674 Thayer Rd . . . . West Point NY 10996 **800-247-5047** 845-446-4731
Tickle Pink Inn at Carmel Highlands
155 Highland Dr . . . . Carmel CA 93923 **800-635-4774** 831-624-1244
Tidewater Inn & Conference Ctr
101 E Dover St . . . . Easton MD 21601 **800-237-8775** 410-822-1300
Time Hotels 224 W 49th St . . . . New York NY 10019 **877-846-3692** 212-246-5252
Tivoli Lodge
386 Hanson Ranch Rd . . . . Vail CO 81657 **800-451-4756** 970-476-5615
Towers at the Kahler Grand, The
20 Second Ave SW . . . . Rochester MN 55902 **800-940-6811** 507-208-1409
Town & Country Inn
20 State RT 2 . . . . Shelburne NH 03581 **800-325-4386*** 603-466-3315
*General
Town & Country Inn & Conference Ctr
2008 Savannah Hwy . . . . Charleston SC 29407 **800-334-6660** 843-571-1000
Town Inn Suites
620 Church St . . . . Toronto ON M4Y2G2 **800-387-2755** 416-964-3311
Tremont Chicago
100 E Chestnut St . . . . Chicago IL 60611 **888-627-8281** 312-751-1900
Trianon Old Naples
955 Seventh Ave S . . . . Naples FL 34102 **877-482-5228** 239-435-9600
Tropical Winds Oceanfront Hotel
1398 N Atlantic Ave . . . . Daytona Beach FL 32118 **800-245-6099** 386-258-1016
Tropicana Inn & Suites
1540 S Harbor Blvd . . . . Anaheim CA 92802 **800-828-4898** 714-635-4082
Trump International Hotel & Tower
725 Fifth Ave . . . . New York NY 10022 **888-448-7867** 312-588-8000
Tugboat Inn
80 Commercial St PO Box 267 . . . . Boothbay Harbor ME 04538 **800-248-2628** 207-633-4434
Tuscany Suites & Casino
255 E Flamingo Rd . . . . Las Vegas NV 89169 **877-887-2261*** 702-893-8933
*Resv
UMass Hotel at the Campus Ctr
1 Campus Ctr Way . . . . Amherst MA 01003 **877-822-2110** 413-549-6000
Umstead Hotel & Spa
100 Woodland Pond . . . . Cary NC 27513 **866-877-4141** 919-447-4000
University Inn Seattle
4140 Roosevelt Way NE . . . . Seattle WA 98105 **800-733-3855** 206-632-5055
University Place
310 SW Lincoln St . . . . Portland OR 97201 **866-845-4647** 503-725-4926
US Grant, The
326 Broadway . . . . San Diego CA 92101 **866-716-8136** 619-232-3121
Valley River Inn
1000 Vly River Way . . . . Eugene OR 97401 **800-543-8266** 541-743-1000
Vanderbilt Grace 41 Mary St . . . . Newport RI 02840 **888-826-4255** 401-846-6200

Varscona Hotel
8208 106th St . . . . Edmonton AB T6E6R9 **866-465-8150** 780-434-6111
Viceroy Santa Monica
1819 Ocean Ave . . . . Santa Monica CA 90401 **888-622-4567** 310-260-7500
Victoria Inn Winnipeg
1808 Wellington Ave . . . . Winnipeg MB R3H0G3 **877-842-4667** 204-786-4801
Victoria Regent Hotel, The
1234 Wharf St . . . . Victoria BC V8W3H9 **800-663-7472** 250-386-2211
Village Latch Inn
101 Hill St PO Box 3000. . . . . SouthHampton NY 11968 **800-545-2824** 631-283-2160
Villagio Inn & Spa
6481 Washington St . . . . Yountville CA 94599 **800-351-1133** 707-944-8877
Vintage House
6541 Washington St . . . . Yountville CA 94599 **800-351-1133***
*Cust Svc
Vintners Inn
4350 Barnes Rd . . . . Santa Rosa CA 95403 **800-421-2584** 707-575-7350
Virginian Lodge
750 W Broadway PO Box 1052. . . . . Jackson Hole WY 83001 **800-262-4999** 307-733-2792
Virginian Suites
1500 Arlington Blvd . . . . Arlington VA 22209 **866-371-1446** 703-522-9600
Viscount Gort Hotel
1670 Portage Ave . . . . Winnipeg MB R3J0C9 **800-665-1122** 204-775-0451
Viscount Suite Hotel
4855 E Broadway Blvd . . . . Tucson AZ 85711 **800-527-9666*** 520-745-6500
*Resv
Waikiki Parc Hotel
2233 Helumoa Rd . . . . Honolulu HI 96815 **800-422-0450** 808-921-7272
Waikiki Resort Hotel
2460 Koa Ave . . . . Honolulu HI 96815 **800-367-5116** 808-922-4911
Warwick Denver Hotel
1776 Grant St . . . . Denver CO 80203 **800-203-3232** 303-861-2000
Warwick Melrose Hotel
3015 Oak Lawn Ave . . . . Dallas TX 75219 **800-521-7172** 214-521-5151
Warwick New York Hotel
65 W 54th St . . . . New York NY 10019 **800-203-3232** 212-247-2700
Warwick Seattle Hotel
401 Lenora St . . . . Seattle WA 98121 **800-426-9280** 206-443-4300
Washington Court Hotel
525 New Jersey Ave NW . . . . Washington DC 20001 **800-321-3010** 202-628-2100
Washington Duke Inn & Golf Club
3001 Cameron Blvd . . . . Durham NC 27705 **800-443-3853** 919-490-0999
Washington Plaza Hotel
10 Thomas Cir NW . . . . Washington DC 20005 **800-424-1140** 202-842-1300
Washington Square Hotel
103 Waverly Pl . . . . New York NY 10011 **800-222-0418** 212-777-9515
Waterford Retirement Residence
2431 Bank St . . . . Ottawa ON K1V8R9 **877-688-4929** 613-737-0811
Waterfront Hotel
10 Washington St . . . . Oakland CA 94607 **888-842-5333** 510-836-3800
Weber's Inn
3050 Jackson Rd . . . . Ann Arbor MI 48103 **800-443-3050*** 734-769-2500
*Resv
Wedgewood Hotel
845 Hornby St . . . . Vancouver BC V6Z1V1 **800-663-0666** 604-689-7777
Wedgewood Resort Hotel
212 Wedgewood Dr . . . . Fairbanks AK 99701 **800-528-4916**
Wellington Hotel
871 Seventh Ave . . . . New York NY 10019 **800-652-1212** 212-247-3900
Wellington Resort
551 Thames St . . . . Newport RI 02840 **800-228-2968** 401-849-1770
Westgate Branson Woods
2201 Roark Valley Rd . . . . Branson MO 65616 **877-253-8572** 417-334-2324
Westgate Painted Mountain Country Club
6302 E McKellips Rd . . . . Mesa AZ 85215 **888-433-3707** 480-654-3611
Westmark Hotels Inc
300 Elliott Ave W . . . . Seattle WA 98119 **800-544-0970**
White Elephant Inn & Cottages
50 Easton St . . . . Nantucket MA 02554 **800-475-2637** 508-228-2500
Whitehall Hotel
105 E Delaware Pl . . . . Chicago IL 60611 **800-948-4255** 312-944-6300
Whitney Hotel, The
610 Poydras St . . . . New Orleans LA 70130 **844-581-4222** 504-581-4222
Wickaninnish Inn
500 Osprey Ln PO Box 250 . . . . Tofino BC V0R2Z0 **800-333-4604** 250-725-3100
Willows Historic Palm Springs Inn
412 W Tahquitz Canyon Way . . . . Palm Springs CA 92262 **800-966-9597** 760-320-0771
Willows Lodge
14580 NE 145th St . . . . Woodinville WA 98072 **877-424-3930** 425-424-3900
Windsor Arms Hotel
18 St Thomas St . . . . Toronto ON M5S3E7 **877-999-2767** 416-971-9666
Windsor Court Hotel
300 Gravier St . . . . New Orleans LA 70130 **888-596-0955** 504-523-6000
Wonder View Inn & Suites
50 Eden St PO Box 25 . . . . Bar Harbor ME 04609 **888-439-8439** 207-288-3358
Woodloch Pines Inc
731 Welcome Lake Rd . . . . Hawley PA 18428 **800-966-3562** 570-685-8000
WOODMARK HOTEL
1200 Carillon Pt . . . . Kirkland WA 98033 **800-822-3700** 425-822-3700
Wort Hotel 50 N Glenwood . . . . Jackson WY 83001 **800-322-2727*** 307-733-2190
*Cust Svc
Wyndham Hotel Group
Travelodge
1910 Eigth Ave NE . . . . Aberdeen SD 57041 **800-525-4055*** 605-229-8058
*Resv
Wyndham Vacation Resorts
6277 Sea Harbor Dr . . . . Orlando FL 32821 **800-251-8736**
Wyndham Lake Buena Vista
1850 Hotel Plaza Blvd . . . . Lake Buena Vista FL 32830 **800-624-4109** 407-828-4444
Yankee Inn
461 Pittsfield Lenox Rd . . . . Lenox MA 01240 **800-835-2364** 413-499-3700
Yarmouth Resort
343 Main St Rt 28 . . . . West Yarmouth MA 02673 **877-838-3524** 508-775-5155
Yogo Inn 211 E Main St . . . . Lewistown MT 59457 **800-860-9646** 406-535-8721

379   ICE - MANUFACTURED

				Toll-Free	Phone
Hanover Foods Corp					
1550 York St PO Box 334	Hanover	PA	17331	**800-888-4646**	717-632-6000
OTC: HNFSA					
House of Flavors Inc					
110 N William St	Ludington	MI	49431	**800-930-7740**	231-845-7369
Reddy Ice Holdings Inc					
8750 N Central Expy Ste 1800	Dallas	TX	75231	**800-683-4423**	214-526-6740
OTC: RDDYQ					

380   ICE CREAM & DAIRY STORES

				Toll-Free	Phone
Baskin-Robbins Inc					
130 Royall St	Canton	MA	02021	**800-859-5339**	781-737-3000
Carvel Express					
200 Glenridge Pt Pkwy Ste 200	Atlanta	GA	30342	**800-322-4848**	
Cloverland Green Spring Dairy Inc					
2701 Loch Raven Rd	Baltimore	MD	21218	**800-492-0094***	410-235-4477
*Orders					
Cold Stone Creamery Inc					
9311 E Via De Ventura	Scottsdale	AZ	85258	**866-452-4252***	480-362-4800
*Cust Svc					
Dairy Queen					
7505 Metro Blvd	Minneapolis	MN	55439	**800-883-4279**	952-830-0200
Kilwins Quality Confections Inc (KQC)					
1050 Bay View Rd	Petoskey	MI	49770	**888-454-5946**	
Royal Crest Dairy Inc					
350 S Pearl St	Denver	CO	80209	**888-226-6455**	303-777-2227

381   IMAGING EQUIPMENT & SYSTEMS - MEDICAL

SEE ALSO Medical Instruments & Apparatus - Mfr

				Toll-Free	Phone
Agfa Corp 611 River Dr	Elmwood Park	NJ	07407	**888-274-8626**	201-440-2500
Alpine Solutions Inc					
3222 Corte Malpaso Ste 203-206	Camarillo	CA	93012	**855-388-1883**	805-388-1699
BrainLAB Inc					
5 Westbrook Corporate Ctr	Westchester	IL	60154	**800-784-7700**	708-409-1343
CIVCO Medical Solutions					
102 First St	Kalona	IA	52247	**877-329-2482**	319-248-6757
Dentsply Sirona					
221 W Philadelphia St PO Box 872	York	PA	17405	**800-877-0020**	717-845-7511
NASDAQ: XRAY					
Digirad Corp					
13100 Gregg St Ste A	Poway	CA	92064	**800-947-6134**	858-726-1600
NASDAQ: DRAD					
Hitachi Medical Systems America Inc					
1959 Summit Commerce Pk	Twinsburg	OH	44087	**800-800-3106**	330-425-1313
Hologic Inc 35 Crosby Dr	Bedford	MA	01730	**800-523-5001**	781-999-7300
NASDAQ: HOLX					
iCAD Inc					
98 Spit Brook Rd Ste 100	Nashua	NH	03062	**866-280-2239**	603-882-5200
NASDAQ: ICAD					
ImageWorks					
250 Clearbrook Rd	Elmsford	NY	10523	**800-592-6666**	914-592-6100
Merge Healthcare					
350 N Orleans St 1st Fl	Chicago	IL	60654	**877-446-3743**	312-565-6868
One Call Medical Inc (OCM)					
20 Waterview Blvd PO Box 614	Parsippany	NJ	07054	**800-872-2875**	973-257-1000
PerkinElmer Inc					
940 Winter St	Waltham	MA	02451	**800-762-4000**	781-663-6050
NYSE: PKI					
Philips Medical Systems					
3000 Minuteman Rd	Andover	MA	01810	**800-934-7372**	978-687-1501
Precision Optics Corp Inc					
22 E Broadway	Gardner	MA	01440	**800-447-2812**	978-630-1800
OTC: PEYE					
S & S Technology					
10625 Telge Rd	Houston	TX	77095	**800-231-1747**	281-815-1300
Shimadzu Medical Systems					
20101 S Vermont Ave	Torrance	CA	90502	**800-477-1227***	310-217-8855
*General					
SonoSite Inc					
21919 30th Dr SE	Bothell	WA	98021	**888-482-9449**	425-951-1200
NASDAQ: SONO					
Stereotaxis Inc					
4320 Forest Park Ave	Saint Louis	MO	63108	**866-646-2346**	314-678-6100
NASDAQ: STXS					
Topcon Medical Systems Inc					
111 Bauer Dr	Oakland	NJ	07436	**800-223-1130**	201-599-5100
Toshiba America Inc					
1251 Ave of the Americas 41st Fl	New York	NY	10020	**800-457-7777**	212-596-0600
Varian Medical Systems Inc					
3100 Hansen Way	Palo Alto	CA	94304	**800-544-4636**	650-493-4000
NYSE: VAR					
Wolf X-Ray Corp					
100 W Industry Ct	Deer Park	NY	11729	**800-356-9729***	631-242-9729
*Cust Svc					

382   IMAGING SERVICES - DIAGNOSTIC

				Toll-Free	Phone
Alliance Imaging Inc					
100 Bayview Cir Ste 400	Newport Beach	CA	92660	**800-544-3215**	949-242-5300
Center for Diagnostic Imaging					
5775 Wayzata Blvd Ste 190	Saint Louis Park	MN	55416	**800-537-0005**	952-541-1840
Johns Dental Laboratory Inc					
423 S 13th St	Terre Haute	IN	47807	**800-457-0504**	812-232-6026

				Toll-Free	Phone
MNAP Medical Solutions Inc					
9908 E Roosevelt Blvd	Philadelphia	PA	19115	**888-674-4381**	215-464-3300

383   INCENTIVE PROGRAM MANAGEMENT SERVICES

SEE ALSO Conference & Events Coordinators

Many of the companies listed here provide travel as a reward for employees or corporate customers in order to boost sales or employee performance. Most of these companies are members of the Society of Incentive & Travel Executives. Some of the companies listed offer merchandise or other types of incentives as well.

				Toll-Free	Phone
ITAGroup					
4600 Westown Pkwy	West Des Moines	IA	50266	**800-257-1985**	
Marketing Innovators International Inc					
9701 W Higgins Rd	Rosemont	IL	60018	**800-543-7373**	
Motivation Through Incentives Inc					
10400 W 103 St Ste 10	Overland Park	KS	66214	**800-826-3464**	913-438-2600
Provident Travel					
11309 Montgomery Rd	Cincinnati	OH	45249	**800-354-8108**	513-247-1100
Student Advantage LLC					
280 Summer St	Boston	MA	02210	**800-333-2920**	
Viktor Incentives & Meetings					
4020 Copper View Ste 130	Traverse City	MI	49684	**800-748-0478**	231-947-0882

384   INDUSTRIAL EQUIPMENT & SUPPLIES (MISC) - WHOL

				Toll-Free	Phone
AaronEquipment Company Inc					
735 E Green St	Bensenville	IL	60106	**800-492-2766**	630-350-2200
Abatix Corp					
2400 Skyline Dr Ste 400	Mesquite	TX	75149	**800-426-3983**	214-381-0322
Adco Manufacturing Inc					
2170 Academy Ave	Sanger	CA	93657	**888-608-5946**	559-875-5563
AIM Supply Co					
7337 Bryan Dairy Rd	Largo	FL	33777	**800-999-0125**	727-544-6652
Aimco 10000 SE Pine St	Portland	OR	97216	**800-852-1368**	
Airgas Inc					
259 N Radnor-Chester Rd Ste 100	Radnor	PA	19087	**800-255-2165**	610-687-5253
NYSE: ARG					
AIV LP					
7140 W Sam Houston Pkwy N Ste 100	Houston	TX	77040	**800-447-4230**	713-462-4181
Alamo Iron Works Inc					
943 AT&T Ctr Pkwy	San Antonio	TX	78219	**800-292-7817**	210-223-6161
AMI Bearings Inc					
570 N Wheeling Rd	Mount Prospect	IL	60056	**800-882-8642**	847-759-0620
Atlantic Lift Truck Inc					
2945 Whittington Ave	Baltimore	MD	21230	**800-638-4566**	410-644-7777
Austin Pump & Supply Co					
PO Box 17037	Austin	TX	78760	**800-252-9692**	512-442-2348
Barco Products					
24 N Washington Ave	Batavia	IL	60510	**800-338-2697**	
Barnes Distribution					
1301 E Ninth St Ste 700	Cleveland	OH	44114	**800-726-9626**	216-416-7200
Bearing Distributors Inc					
8000 Hub Pkwy	Cleveland	OH	44125	**888-423-4872**	216-642-9100
Berendsen Fluid Power					
401 S Boston Ave Ste 1200	Tulsa	OK	74103	**800-360-2327**	918-592-3781
Bolttech Mannings					
501 Mosside Blvd	North Versailles	PA	15137	**888-846-8827**	724-872-4873
Brake Supply Company Inc					
5501 Foundation Blvd	Evansville	IN	47725	**800-457-5788**	812-467-1000
Brauer Material Handling Systems Inc					
226 Molly Walton Dr	Hendersonville	TN	37075	**800-645-6083**	
Briggs Equipment					
10540 N Stemmons Fwy	Dallas	TX	75220	**800-606-1833**	214-630-0808
Briggs Industrial Equipment					
10550 N Stemmons Fwy	Dallas	TX	75220	**800-516-9206**	214-630-0808
Brinker Brown Fastener & Supply Inc					
12290 Crystal Commerce Loop	Fort Myers	FL	33966	**800-527-5530**	239-939-3535
Canadian Bearings Ltd					
1600 Drew Rd	Mississauga	ON	L5S1S5	**800-229-2327**	905-670-6700
Carolina Material Handling Services Inc					
PO Box 6	Columbia	SC	29202	**800-922-6709**	803-695-0149
Cascade Machinery & Electric Inc					
4600 E Marginal Way S	Seattle	WA	98134	**800-289-0500**	206-762-0500
Central Power Systems & Services					
9200 W Liberty Dr	Liberty	MO	64068	**800-444-0442**	816-781-8070
Cisco-Eagle					
2120 Valley View Ln	Dallas	TX	75234	**888-877-3861**	972-406-9330
CMC Construction Services					
9103 E Almeda Rd	Houston	TX	77054	**877-297-9111**	713-799-1150
Conveyco Technologies Inc					
PO Box 1000	Bristol	CT	06011	**800-229-8215**	860-589-8215
Cross Co					
4400 Piedmont Pkwy	Greensboro	NC	27410	**800-858-1737**	336-856-6000
Detroit Pump & Mfg Co					
450 Fair St Bldg D	Ferndale	MI	48220	**800-686-1662**	248-544-4242
DXP Enterprises Inc					
7272 Pinemont Dr	Houston	TX	77040	**800-830-3973**	713-996-4700
NASDAQ: DXPE					
Eastern Lift Truck Company Inc					
549 E Linwood Ave	Maple Shade	NJ	08052	**866-980-7175**	856-779-8880
Endries International Inc					
714 W Ryan St PO Box 69	Brillion	WI	54110	**800-852-5821**	920-756-5381
Engman-Taylor Company Inc (ETCO)					
W142 N9351 Fountain Blvd	Menomonee Falls	WI	53051	**800-236-1975**	262-255-9300
Enpro Inc 121 S LombaRd Rd	Addison	IL	60101	**800-323-2416**	
ErieTec Inc 1432 E 12th St	Erie	PA	16503	**800-777-6871**	814-453-6871
Fairmont Supply Co					
437 Jefferson Ave	Washington	PA	15301	**800-245-9900**	
FCx Performance					
3000 E 14th Ave	Columbus	OH	43219	**800-253-6223**	
Forklifts of Minnesota Inc					
2201 W 94th St	Bloomington	MN	55431	**800-752-4300**	952-887-5400

Company	Address	City	State	ZIP	Toll-Free	Phone
FUJIFILM Graphic System USA Inc	45 Crosby Dr	Bedford	MA	01730	**800-755-3854**	781-271-4400
FW Webb Co	160 Middlesex Tpke	Bedford	MA	01730	**800-343-7555**	781-272-6600
Ganesh Machinery	20869 Plummer St	Chatsworth	CA	91311	**888-542-6374**	818-349-9166
Gas Equipment Company Inc	11616 Harry Hines Blvd	Dallas	TX	75229	**800-821-1829**	972-241-2333
General Tool & Supply Co Inc	2705 NW Nicolai St	Portland	OR	97210	**800-526-9328**	503-226-3411
Gosiger Inc	108 McDonough St	Dayton	OH	45402	**877-288-1538**	937-228-5174
H G Makelim Co	219 Shaw Rd	South San Francisco	CA	94080	**800-471-0590**	650-873-4757
Hagemeyer North America Inc	1460 Tobias Gadson Blvd	Charleston	SC	29407	**877-462-7070**	843-745-2400
Haggard & Stocking Assoc	5318 Victory Dr	Indianapolis	IN	46203	**800-622-4824**	317-788-4661
Hahn Systems LLC	8416 Zionsville Rd	Indianapolis	IN	46268	**800-201-4246**	317-243-3796
Harrington Industrial Plastics LLC	14480 Yorba Ave	Chino	CA	91710	**800-213-4528**	909-597-8641
Herc-U-Lift Inc	5655 Hwy 12 W	Maple Plain	MN	55359	**800-362-3500**	763-479-2501
Hull Lift Truck Inc	28747 Old US 33 W	Elkhart	IN	46516	**888-284-0364**	574-293-8651
IBT Inc	9400 W 55th St	Merriam	KS	66203	**800-332-2114**	913-677-3151
IKO International Inc	91 Walsh Dr Fox Hill Industrial Pk	Parsippany	NJ	07054	**800-922-0337**	973-402-0254
Indeck Power Equipment Co	1111 Willis Ave	Wheeling	IL	60090	**800-446-3325**	847-541-8300
Indoff Inc	11816 Lackland Rd	Saint Louis	MO	63146	**800-486-7867**	314-997-1122
Industrial Controls Distributors Inc (ICD)	1776 Bloomsbury Ave; *Sales	Wanamassa	NJ	07712	**800-281-4788***	732-918-9000
Industrial Diesel Inc	8705 Harmon Rd	Fort Worth	TX	76177	**800-323-3659**	817-232-1071
Industrial Supply Solutions Inc	520 Elizabeth St	Charleston	WV	25311	**800-346-5341**	304-346-5341
Integra Services Technologies Inc	5000 E 2nd Unit E	Benicia	CA	95410	**800-779-2658**	707-751-0685
J H. Bennett & Company Inc	PO Box 8028; *General	Novi	MI	48376	**800-837-5426***	248-596-5100
Jabo Supply Corp	5164 County Rd 64/66	Huntington	WV	25705	**800-334-5226**	304-736-8333
Jefferds Corp	2070 Winfield Rd	Saint Albans	WV	25177	**888-848-6216**	304-755-8111
Kaplan Industries Inc	6255 Kilby Rd	Harrison	OH	45030	**800-257-8299**	856-779-8181
Kennametal	1662 MacMillan Park Dr; *NYSE: KMT* ■ *Cust Svc	Fort Mill	SC	29707	**800-446-7738***	
Kimball Midwest	4800 Robert Rd	Columbus	OH	43228	**800-233-1294**	800-214-9440
Lawson Products Inc	1666 E Touhy Ave	Des Plaines	IL	60018	**800-323-5922**	847-827-9666
Lipten Company LLC	28054 Ctr Oaks Ct	Wixom	MI	48393	**800-860-0790**	248-374-8910
Logan Corp	555 Seventh Ave	Huntington	WV	25701	**888-853-4751**	304-526-4700
M & L Industries Inc	1210 St Charles St; *General	Houma	LA	70360	**800-969-0068***	985-876-2280
Mac-Gray Corp	404 Wyman St Ste 400; *NYSE: TUC*	Waltham	MA	02451	**888-622-4729**	781-487-7600
Machinery Sales Co	17253 Chestnut St	City of Industry	CA	91748	**800-588-8111**	626-581-9211
Mahar Tool Supply Co Inc	112 Williams St PO Box 1747	Saginaw	MI	48602	**800-456-2427**	989-799-5530
McCall Handling Co	8801 Wise Ave	Dundalk	MD	21222	**888-870-0685**	410-388-2600
McGill Hose & Coupling Inc	41 Benton Dr PO Box 408	East Longmeadow	MA	01028	**800-669-1467**	413-525-3977
McKinley Equipment Corp	17611 Armstrong Ave	Irvine	CA	92614	**800-770-6094**	949-261-9222
Minnesota Supply Company Inc	6470 Flying Cloud Dr	Eden Prairie	MN	55344	**800-869-1028**	952-828-7300
Modern Group Ltd	2501 Durham Rd	Bristol	PA	19007	**800-223-3827**	215-943-9100
Motion Industries Inc	1605 Alton Rd	Birmingham	AL	35210	**800-526-9328**	205-956-1122
MSC Industrial Direct Co	75 Maxess Rd; *NYSE: MSM*	Melville	NY	11747	**800-645-7270**	516-812-2000
Multiquip Inc	18910 Wilmington Ave	Carson	CA	90746	**800-421-1244**	310-537-3700
NC Machinery Co	17025 W Valley Hwy	Tukwila	WA	98188	**800-562-4735**	
Nebraska Machinery Co Inc	3501 S Jeffers St	North Platte	NE	69101	**800-494-9560**	308-532-3100
Nelson-Jameson Inc	2400 E Fifth St PO Box 647	Marshfield	WI	54449	**800-826-8302**	715-387-1151
Nu-Life Environmental Inc	PO Box 1527	Easley	SC	29641	**800-654-1752**	864-855-5155
O Berk Co	3 Milltown Ct	Union	NJ	07083	**800-631-7392**	
Piping & Equipment Inc	9100 Canniff St	Houston	TX	77017	**888-889-9683**	713-947-9393
Production Tool Supply	8655 E Eight Mile Rd	Warren	MI	48089	**800-366-3600**	
Remstar International Inc	41 Eisenhower Dr	Westbrook	ME	04092	**800-639-5805**	
Rex Supply Co	3715 Harrisburg Blvd	Houston	TX	77003	**800-369-0669**	
Riekes Equipment Co	6703 L St	Omaha	NE	68117	**800-856-0931**	402-593-1181

Company	Address	City	State	ZIP	Toll-Free	Phone
Robert Dietrick Co Inc	PO Box 605	Fishers	IN	46038	**866-767-1888**	317-842-1991
Royal Bearing Inc	17719 NE Sandy Blvd	Portland	OR	97230	**800-279-0992**	503-231-0992
RS Hughes Company Inc	1162 Sonora Ct	Sunnyvale	CA	94086	**877-774-8443**	408-739-3211
Ryan Herco Products Corp	3010 N San Fernando Blvd	Burbank	CA	91504	**800-848-1141**	818-841-1141
Shively Bros Inc	2919 S Grand Travers St PO Box 1520	Flint	MI	48501	**800-530-9352**	810-232-7401
SKS Bottle & Packaging Inc	2600 Seventh Ave Bldg 60 W	Watervliet	NY	12189	**800-880-6990**	518-880-6980
SLC Meter LLC	595 Bradford St	Pontiac	MI	48340	**800-433-4332**	248-625-0667
Smith Power Products Inc	3065 W California Ave	Salt Lake City	UT	84104	**800-658-5352**	801-415-5000
So Cal. Sandbags Inc	12620 Bosley Ln	Corona	CA	92883	**800-834-8682**	951-277-3404
Sooner Pipe LLC	1331 Lamar St Ste 970	Houston	TX	77010	**800-888-9161**	713-759-1200
Southern Pump & Tank Co	4800 N Graham St; *Cust Svc	Charlotte	NC	28269	**800-477-2826***	704-596-4373
Strategic Distribution Inc	1414 Radcliffe St Ste 300	Bristol	PA	19007	**800-322-2644**	215-633-1900
Tech 24	410 E Washington St	Greenville	SC	29601	**888-774-4950**	
Teeco Products Inc	16881 Armstrong Ave	Irvine	CA	92606	**800-854-3463**	949-261-6295
Tencarva Machinery Company Inc	12200 Wilfong Ct	Midlothian	VA	23112	**800-849-5764**	804-639-4646
Texas Process Equipment Co	5215 Ted St	Houston	TX	77040	**800-828-4114**	713-460-5555
TF Hudgins Inc	4405 Directors Row	Houston	TX	77092	**800-582-3834**	713-682-3651
Timco Rubber	125 Blaze Industrial Pkwy PO Box 35135	Berea	OH	44017	**800-969-6242**	216-267-6242
Total Filtration Services Inc	2725 Commerce Pkwy	Auburn Hills	MI	48326	**800-331-3118**	248-377-4004
Travers Tool Company Inc	128-15 26th Ave; *Cust Svc	Flushing	NY	11354	**800-221-0270***	718-886-7200
Valtra Inc	8750 Pioneer Blvd	Santa Fe Springs	CA	90670	**800-989-5244**	562-949-8625
Vellano Bros Inc	7 Hemlock St	Latham	NY	12110	**800-342-9855**	518-785-5537
Voto Manufacturers Sales Co	500 N Third St PO Box 1299	Steubenville	OH	43952	**800-848-4010**	740-282-3621
Werres Corp	807 E South St	Frederick	MD	21701	**800-638-6563**	
Windsor Factory Supply Ltd	730 N Service Rd	Windsor	ON	N8X3J3	**800-387-2659**	519-966-2202
Yamazen Inc	735 E Remington Rd	Schaumburg	IL	60173	**800-882-8558**	

385 INDUSTRIAL MACHINERY, EQUIPMENT, & SUPPLIES

SEE ALSO Conveyors & Conveying Equipment ; Material Handling Equipment ; Rolling Mill Machinery ; Textile Machinery ; Woodworking Machinery ; Paper Industries Machinery ; Printing & Publishing Equipment & Systems ; Food Products Machinery ; Packaging Machinery & Equipment ; Furnaces & Ovens - Industrial Process ; Machine Shops

Company	Address	City	State	ZIP	Toll-Free	Phone
Acme Electric	N56 W13385 Silver Spring Dr	Menomonee Falls	WI	53051	**800-334-5214**	
Acorn Gencon Plastics Inc	15125 Proctor Ave	City of Industry	CA	91746	**800-782-7706**	626-968-6681
Aeroglide Corp	100 Aeroglide Dr	Cary	NC	27511	**800-722-7483**	919-851-2000
Alemite LLC	1057-521 Corporate Ctr Dr Ste 100	Fort Mill	SC	29715	**800-267-8022**	803-802-0001
Allentown Equipment	1733 90th St	Sturtevant	WI	53177	**800-553-3414**	
American Baler Co	800 E Centre St	Bellevue	OH	44811	**800-843-7512**	419-483-5790
AO Smith Water Products Co	500 Tennessee Waltz Pkwy	Ashland City	TN	37015	**800-527-1953**	866-362-9898
Apache Stainless Equipment Corp	200 W Industrial Dr PO Box 538	Beaver Dam	WI	53916	**800-444-0398**	920-356-9900
Azon USA Inc	643 W Crosstown Pkwy	Kalamazoo	MI	49008	**800-788-5942**	269-385-5942
Besser Co	801 Johnson St	Alpena	MI	49707	**800-530-9980**	800-968-0444
Blower Application Company Inc	N 114 W 19125 Clinton Dr	Germantown	WI	53022	**800-959-0880**	262-255-5580
Burke E Porter Machinery Co	730 Plymouth Ave NE	Grand Rapids	MI	49505	**800-562-9133**	616-234-1200
Charles Ross & Son Co	710 Old Willets Path	Hauppauge	NY	11788	**800-243-7677**	631-234-0500
Chemineer Inc	5870 Poe Ave	Dayton	OH	45414	**800-643-0641**	937-454-3200
Chief Automotive Systems Inc	1924 E Fourth St	Grand Island	NE	68802	**800-445-9262**	308-384-9747
Clean Diesel Technologies Inc	4567 Telephone Rd Ste 206; *NASDAQ: CDTI*	Ventura	CA	93003	**800-661-9963**	805-639-9458
CMA Dishmachines	12700 Knott St	Garden Grove	CA	92841	**800-854-6417**	714-898-8781
Corotec Corp	145 Hyde Rd	Farmington	CT	06032	**800-423-0348**	860-678-0038
CUNO Inc	400 Research Pkwy	Meriden	CT	06450	**800-243-6894**	203-237-5541
Davis-Ulmer Sprinkler Company Inc	1 Commerce Dr	Amherst	NY	14228	**877-691-3200**	716-691-3200
Despatch Industries Inc	8860 207th St W	Lakeville	MN	55044	**800-726-0110**	952-469-5424
Dings Co	4740 W Electric Ave	Milwaukee	WI	53219	**800-494-1918**	414-672-7830

	Toll-Free	Phone

Ecodyne Ltd
4475 Corporate Dr .... Burlington ON L7L5T9 · 888-326-3963 · 905-332-1404

Enerflex Systems Ltd
1331 Macleod Trail SE Ste 904 .... Calgary AB T2G0K3 · 800-242-3178 · 403-387-6377
TSX: EFX

Engis Corp 105 W Hintz Rd .... Wheeling IL 60090 · 800-993-6447 · 847-808-9400

Equipment Manufacturing Corp (EMC)
14930 Marquardt Ave .... Santa Fe Springs CA 90670 · 888-833-9000 · 562-623-9394

FANUC America Corp
3900 W Hamlin Rd .... Rochester Hills MI 48309 · 800-477-6268 · 248-377-7000

Farrel Corp 25 Main St .... Ansonia CT 06401 · 800-800-7290 · 203-736-5500

Fluid Management Inc
1023 S Wheeling Rd .... Wheeling IL 60090 · 800-462-2466 · 847-537-0880

Forward Technology Inc
260 Jenks Ave .... Cokato MN 55321 · 800-307-6040* · 320-286-2578
*Cust Svc

Fusion Inc
4658 E 355th St .... Willoughby OH 44094 · 800-626-9501 · 440-946-3300

Gamajet Cleaning Systems Inc
604 Jeffers Cir .... Exton PA 19341 · 877-426-2538* · 610-408-9940
*Sales

General Equipment Co
620 Alexander Dr SW PO Box 334 .... Owatonna MN 55060 · 800-533-0524* · 507-451-5510
*Cust Svc

George Koch Sons LLC
10 S 11th Ave .... Evansville IN 47712 · 888-873-5624 · 812-465-9600

Glastender Inc
5400 N Michigan Rd .... Saginaw MI 48604 · 800-748-0423 · 989-752-4275

Gougler Industries Inc
711 Lake St .... Kent OH 44240 · 800-527-2282 · 330-673-5826

Graham Corp 20 Florence Ave .... Batavia NY 14020 · 800-828-8150* · 585-343-2216
NYSE: GHM ■ *Orders

Gregory Poole Equipment Co
4807 Beryl Rd PO Box 469 .... Raleigh NC 27606 · 800-451-7278 · 919-828-0641

Guzzler Manufacturing Inc
1621 S Illinois St .... Streator IL 61364 · 800-627-3171 · 815-672-3171

Hamon Research-Cottrell Inc
58 E Main St PO Box 1500 .... Somerville NJ 08876 · 800-445-6578 · 908-333-2000

Harrington Hoists Inc
401 W End Ave .... Manheim PA 17545 · 800-233-3010 · 717-665-2000

Hosokawa Polymer Systems
63 Fuller Way .... Berlin CT 06037 · 800-233-6112 · 860-828-0541

Husky Injection Molding Systems Ltd
500 Queen St S .... Bolton ON L7E5S5 · 800-465-4875 · 905-951-5000

Hydro-Thermal Corp
400 Pilot Ct .... Waukesha WI 53188 · 800-952-0121 · 262-548-8900

Jesco-Wipco Industries Inc
950 Anderson Rd PO Box 388 .... Litchfield MI 49252 · 800-455-0019 · 517-542-2903

Kobelco Stewart Bolling Inc (KSBI)
1600 Terex Rd .... Hudson OH 44236 · 800-464-0064 · 330-655-3111

Koch Membrane Systems Inc
850 Main St .... Wilmington MA 01887 · 888-677-5624 · 978-657-4250

Kois Bros Equipment Company Inc
5200 Colorado Blvd .... Commerce CO 80022 · 800-672-6010 · 303-298-7370

Komline-Sanderson Engineering Corp
12 Holland Ave .... Peapack NJ 07977 · 800-225-5457 · 908-234-1000

Lawton Industries Inc
4353 Pacific St .... Rocklin CA 95677 · 800-692-2600 · 916-624-7894

Lesman Instrument Co
135 Bernice Dr .... Bensenville IL 60106 · 800-953-7626 · 630-595-8400

Leviathan Corp
55 Washington St Ste 457 .... Brooklyn NY 11201 · 855-687-8721

Lincoln Industrial Corp
5148 N Hanley Rd .... Saint Louis MO 63134 · 800-424-5359 · 314-679-4200

Marathon Equipment Co
PO Box 1798 .... Vernon AL 35592 · 800-633-8974 · 205-695-9105

Maruka USA Inc
1210 NE Douglas St .... Lee's Summit MO 64086 · 800-262-7852

Materials Transportation Co (MTC)
1408 S Commerce PO Box 1358 .... Temple TX 76503 · 800-433-3110 · 254-298-2900

McNeil & NRM Inc
96 E Crosier St .... Akron OH 44311 · 800-669-2525 · 330-253-2525

Michigan Fluid Power Inc
4556 Spartan Industrial Dr SW .... Grandville MI 49418 · 800-635-0289 · 616-538-5700

Michigan Wheel Corp
1501 Buchanan Ave SW .... Grand Rapids MI 49507 · 800-369-4335 · 616-452-6941

Mico Inc
1911 Lee Blvd .... North Mankato MN 56003 · 800-477-6426 · 507-625-6426

Micro-Poise Measurment Systems LLC
555 Mondial Pkwy .... Streetsboro OH 44241 · 800-428-3812 · 330-541-9100

Minuteman International Inc
14N845 US Rte 20 .... Pingree Grove IL 60140 · 800-323-9420 · 847-264-5400

Monroe Environmental Corp
810 W Front St .... Monroe MI 48161 · 800-992-7707 · 734-242-7654

Moody-Price LLC
18320 Petroleum Dr .... Baton Rouge LA 70809 · 800-272-9832

MP Global Products
2500 Old Hadar Rd PO Box 2283 .... Norfolk NE 68702 · 888-379-9695

Mueller Steam Specialty
1491 NC Hwy 20 W .... Saint Pauls NC 28384 · 800-334-6259 · 910-865-8241

National Super Service Company Inc
3115 Frenchman Rd .... Toledo OH 43607 · 800-677-1663* · 419-531-2121
*Cust Svc

Neumayer Equipment Company Inc
5060 Arsenal St .... Saint Louis MO 63139 · 800-843-4563 · 314-772-4501

Nexen Group Inc
560 Oak Grove Pkwy .... Vadnais Heights MN 55127 · 800-843-7445 · 651-484-5900

Nordson Corp
28601 Clemens Rd .... Westlake OH 44145 · 800-321-2881 · 440-892-1580
NASDAQ: NDSN

North Light Color
5008 Hillsboro Ave N .... New Hope MN 55428 · 866-922-4700 · 763-531-8222

Northern Industrial Sales Ltd
3526 Opie Cres .... Prince George BC V2N2P9 · 800-668-3317 · 250-562-4435

Oil & Gas Equipment Corp
8 Rd 350 .... Flora Vista NM 87415 · 800-868-9624 · 505-333-2300

Oscar Wilson Engines & Parts Inc
826 Lone Star Dr .... O Fallon MO 63366 · 800-873-6722 · 636-978-1313

Pall Corp
2200 Northern Blvd .... East Hills NY 11548 · 800-645-6532 · 516-484-5400
NYSE: PLL

Parkson Corp
1401 W Cyperess Creek Rd .... Fort Lauderdale FL 33309 · 888-727-5766

Paul Mueller Co
1600 W Phelps St .... Springfield MO 65802 · 800-683-5537 · 417-575-9000
OTC: MUEL

PDQ Manufacturing Inc
1698 Scheuring Rd .... De Pere WI 54115 · 800-227-3373 · 920-983-8333

Permadur Industries Inc
186 Rt 206 S .... Hillsborough NJ 08844 · 800-392-0146 · 908-359-9767

Peterson Machine Tool Inc
1100 N Union St .... Council Grove KS 66846 · 800-835-3528 · 620-767-6721

Phillips Machine Service Inc
367 George St .... Beckley WV 25801 · 800-733-1521 · 304-255-0537

Pioneer/Eclipse Corp
1 Eclipse Rd .... Sparta NC 28675 · 800-367-3550* · 336-372-8080
*Cust Svc

Pipe & Tube Supply Inc
1407 N Cypress .... North Little Rock AR 72114 · 800-770-8823 · 501-372-6556

Premier Safety & Service Inc
2 Industrial Pk Dr .... Oakdale PA 15071 · 800-828-1080 · 724-693-8699

PSB Industries Inc PO Box 1318 .... Erie PA 16512 · 800-829-1119 · 814-453-3651

PTI Technologies Inc
501 Del Norte Blvd .... Oxnard CA 93030 · 800-331-2701 · 805-604-3700

R&R Products Inc
3334 E Milber St .... Tucson AZ 85714 · 800-528-3446 · 520-889-3593

SAES Pure Gas Inc
4175 Santa Fe Rd .... San Luis Obispo CA 93401 · 800-934-3628 · 805-541-9299

Salem Tools Inc
1602 Midland Rd .... Salem VA 24153 · 800-390-4348

Shop-Vac Corp
2323 Reach Rd PO Box 3307 .... Williamsport PA 17701 · 844-807-7711 · 570-326-0502

Shuert Technologies LLC
6600 Dobry Rd .... Sterling Heights MI 48314 · 877-748-3781 · 586-254-4590

SJF Material Handling Equipment
211 Baker Ave .... Winsted MN 55395 · 800-598-5532 · 320-485-2824

STI Electronics Inc
261 Palmer Rd .... Madison AL 35758 · 888-650-3006 · 256-461-9191

Super Products LLC
17000 W Cleveland Ave .... New Berlin WI 53151 · 800-837-9711 · 262-784-7100

Swiss Precision Instruments Inc
11450 Markon Dr .... Garden Grove CA 92841 · 888-774-8200 · 714-799-1555

Synventive Molding Solutions Inc
10 Centennial Dr .... Peabody MA 01960 · 800-367-5662 · 978-750-8065

Tennant Co
701 N Lilac Dr .... Minneapolis MN 55422 · 800-553-8033* · 763-540-1200
NYSE: TNC ■ *Cust Svc

Thermotron Industries Co
291 Kollen Pk Dr .... Holland MI 49423 · 800-409-3449 · 616-393-4580

Thomas Engineering Inc
575 W Central Rd .... Hoffman Estates IL 60192 · 800-634-9910 · 847-358-5800

Timesavers Inc
11123 89th Ave N .... Maple Grove MN 55369 · 800-537-3611 · 763-488-6600

Tool Smith Company Inc
1300 Fourth Ave S .... Birmingham AL 35233 · 800-317-8665 · 205-323-2576

Unified Brands
1055 Mendell Davis Dr .... Jackson MS 39272 · 888-994-7636

Universal Machine & Engineering Corp
645 Old Reading Pk .... Stowe PA 19464 · 800-879-2477 · 610-323-1810

Vacudyne Inc
375 E Joe Orr Rd .... Chicago Heights IL 60411 · 800-459-9591 · 708-757-5200

Van Air Systems Inc
2950 Mechanic St .... Lake City PA 16423 · 800-840-9906 · 814-774-2631

Vermeer Midsouth Inc
1200 Vermeer Cv .... Cordova TN 38018 · 800-264-4123

Videojet Technologies Inc
1500 Mittel Blvd .... Wood Dale IL 60191 · 800-843-3610* · 630-860-7300
*Cust Svc

W M Sprinkman Corp
404 Pilot Ct .... Waukesha WI 53188 · 800-816-1610

Western Hydro Corp
3449 Enterprise Ave .... Hayward CA 94545 · 800-972-5945 · 510-783-9166

WH Bagshaw Company Inc
1 Pine St Ext .... Nashua NH 03060 · 800-343-7467 · 603-883-7758

Windsor K„rcher Group
1351 W Stanford Ave .... Englewood CO 80110 · 800-444-7654 · 303-762-1800

386   INFORMATION RETRIEVAL SERVICES (GENERAL)

SEE ALSO Investigative Services

	Toll-Free	Phone

247Sports
12 Cadillac Dr Ste 230 .... Brentwood TN 37027 · 888-508-3055

411 Local Search Corp
1500 Don Mills Rd Ste 600 N York .... Toronto ON M3B3K4 · 866-411-4411 · 647-723-9929

Acquizitionbiz Inc
1100 Rene-Levesque Blvd W 24th Fl .... Montreal QC H3B4X9 · 866-499-0334 · 514-499-0334

AdMobilize LLC
1680 Michigan Ave Ste 918 .... Miami Beach FL 33139 · 888-628-7494

Advantix Solutions Group
1202 Richardson Dr Ste 200 .... Richardson TX 75080 · 866-238-2684

Airespring Inc
6060 Sepulveda Blvd Ste 220 .... Van Nuys CA 91411 · 888-389-2899 · 818-786-8990

airG
1133 Melville St Ste 710 .... Vancouver BC V6E4E5 · 866-874-8136 · 604-408-2228

All Property Management
PO Box 1013 Ste 325 .... Winthrop WA 98862 · 877-234-9723

All Web Leads Inc
7300 FM 2222 Bldg 2 Ste 100 .... Austin TX 78730 · 888-522-7355

Amernet
315 Montgomery St .... San Francisco CA 94104 · 877-616-5100

Amigos Library Services
14400 Midway Rd .... Dallas TX 75244 · 800-843-8482 · 972-851-8000

Annex Cloud
5301 Beethoven St Ste 260 .... Los Angeles CA 90066 · 866-802-8806

	Toll-Free	Phone

AOAExcel Inc
243 N Lindbergh Blvd 1st Fl................St. Louis MO 63141 **800-365-2219**

Apmetrix Inc
2815 Forbs Ave Ste 107-40...............Hoffman Estates IL 60192 **800-490-3184** 312-416-0950

Apptopia Inc
132 Lincoln St 3rd Fl.......................Boston MA 02111 **855-277-8674**

Arkadin Inc
5 Concourse Pkwy Ste 1600..............Atlanta GA 30328 **866-551-1432**

AroundWireCom LLC
9455 De Soto Ave........................Chatsworth CA 91311 **888-382-3793**

Audio Authority Corp
2048 Mercer Rd...........................Lexington KY 40511 **800-322-8346** 859-233-4599

Axiom Education LLC
4 Research Dr.............................Shelton CT 06484 **888-801-8183**

Axon Sports 505 S 24th Ave.............Wausau WI 54401 **877-399-2966**

Best Telecom Inc
278 E End Ave............................Beaver PA 15009 **888-365-2273**

Binary Group Inc
4250 N Fairfax Dr Ste 600................Arlington VA 22203 **855-424-6279** 571-480-4444

Bliss Direct Media
641 15th Ave NE.......................Saint Joseph MN 56374 **800-578-7947** 320-271-1600

BloomNet Inc
1 Old Country Rd Ste 500...............Carle Place NY 11514 **866-256-6663**

Bocada LLC
5555 Lakeview Dr Ste 201................Kirkland WA 98033 **866-262-2321** 425-898-2400

BoeFly LLC
50 W 72nd St Ste C4.....................New York NY 10023 **800-277-3158**

Branding Brand
2313 E Carson St.......................Pittsburgh PA 15203 **888-979-5018**

Broadband Dynamics LLC
8757 E Via De Commercio..............Scottsdale AZ 85258 **888-801-1034**

BroadVoice Inc
9221 Corbin Ave Ste 155...............Northridge CA 91324 **866-247-3194*** 888-325-5875
*Sales

BurrellesLuce
30 B Vreeland Rd PO Box 674.........Florham Park NJ 07932 **800-631-1160** 973-992-6600

C Spire
1018 Highland Colony Pkwy Ste 300.....Ridgeland MS 39157 **855-277-4735**

Camperoo Inc
599 Third St Ste 309....................San Francisco CA 94109 **888-538-8809**

Care Zono Inc
1463 E Republican St Ste 198............Seattle WA 98112 **888-407-7785**

Carrillo Business Technologies Inc
750 The City Dr S Ste 225................Orange CA 92868 **888-241-7585**

CatholicMatch LLC
PO Box 154.............................Zelienople PA 16063 **888-605-3977**

CCI Network Services
155 North 400 West Ste 100.........Salt Lake City UT 84103 **877-592-8049** 801-994-4100

CharityUSAcom LLC
600 University St
Ste 1000 One Union Square...............Seattle WA 98101 **888-811-5271** 206-268-5400

Chemical Abstracts Service (CAS)
2540 Olentangy River Rd................Columbus OH 43202 **800-848-6538** 614-447-3600

Citation Communications Inc
1855 Indian Rd Ste 207............West Palm Beach FL 33409 **800-286-5109** 561-688-0330

Cityfone PO Box 19372..................Burnaby BC V5H4J8 **888-499-7566**

CloudCheckr Inc
342 N Goodman St.....................Rochester NY 14607 **833-253-2425**

CloudSway LLC
711 Pacific Ave.........................Tacoma WA 98402 **855-212-5683**

Comwave Networks Inc
61 Wildcat Rd.........................Toronto ON M3J2P5 **877-474-6638** 416-663-9700

ConceptShare Inc
130 Slater St.............................Ottawa ON K1P6E2 **844-227-7848** 613-903-4431

Crosslake Communications
35910 County Rd 66 PO Box 70..........Crosslake MN 56442 **800-992-8220** 218-692-2777

Curatel LLC
1605 W Olympic Blvd Ste 800..........Los Angeles CA 90015 **866-287-2366**

Custom Toll Free
10940 Wilshire Blvd 17th Fl..............Los Angeles CA 90024 **800-287-8664**

Cybereason Inc
200 Clarendon St 5th Fl...................Boston MA 02116 **855-695-8200**

CypherWorX Inc
130 Andrews St........................Rochester NY 14604 **888-685-4440**

Data Transmission Network Corp
9110 W Dodge Rd Ste 200.................Omaha NE 68114 **800-485-4000** 402-390-2328

DataTrail Corp
7056B Farrell Rd SE.......................Calgary AB T2H0T2 **877-885-6254** 403-253-3651

DebtFolio Inc
35 Braintree Hill Office Pk Ste 107.........Braintree MA 02184 **866-876-3654**

Declara Inc
977 Commercial St.......................Palo Alto CA 94303 **877-216-0604**

Deliverycom LLC
235 Park Ave S 5th Fl.....................New York NY 10038 **800-709-7191**

DFT Communications
38 Temple St...........................Fredonia NY 14063 **877-653-3100** 716-673-3000

Dialink Corp
1660 S Amphlett Blvd Ste 340..........San Mateo CA 94402 **800-896-3425**

doggyloot LLC
213 N Racine Ave.......................Chicago IL 60607 **800-398-6081***
*Cust Svc

DPL Wireless 53 Clark Rd.............Rothesay NB E2E2K9 **800-561-8880** 506-847-2347

DrivingSales LLC
8871 S Sandy Pkwy Ste 250...............Sandy UT 84070 **866-943-8371**

Druva
150 Mathilda Pl Ste 450................Sunnyvale CA 94086 **844-303-7882** 650-241-3501

DSG Tag Systems Inc
5455 152nd St Ste 214....................Surrey BC V3S5A5 **877-589-8806**

EatStreet Inc
316 Washington Ave Ste 725.............Madison WI 53703 **866-654-8777**

EBSCO Information Services
PO Box 1943..........................Birmingham AL 35201 **800-758-5995** 205-991-6600

Edison Carrier Solutions
2 Innovation Way 1st Fl..................Pomona CA 91768 **800-634-7999**

Edufii Inc
130 Buena Vista Ave...................Mill Valley CA 94941 **888-414-7276**

Ekahau
1925 Isaac Newton Sq E Ste 200...........Reston VA 20190 **866-435-2428**

	Toll-Free	Phone

ELM Resources
12950 Race Track Rd Ste 201..............Tampa FL 33626 **866-524-8198**

Enprecis Inc
60 Courtneypark Dr W Unit 3.........Mississauga ON L5W0B3 **877-476-9274** 905-565-5777

Environmental Data Resources Inc (EDR)
6 Armstrong Rd 4th Fl.....................Shelton CT 06484 **800-352-0050** 203-783-0300

eScreen Inc
7500 W 110th St Ste 500..............Overland Park KS 66210 **800-881-0722** 913-327-5915

Everlaw 2036 Bancroft Way............Berkeley CA 94704 **844-383-7529**

EverTrue LLC
330 Congress St 2nd Fl...................Boston MA 02210 **855-387-8783**

Everwise Corp
1178 Broadway 4th Fl....................New York NY 10001 **888-734-0011**

Experis Data Centers Inc
7811 Montrose Rd Ste 360..............Potomac MD 20854 **877-689-3282**

ezCater Inc
101 Arch St Ste 1510.....................Boston MA 02110 **800-488-1803**

FamilySearch
35 N W Temple St....................Salt Lake City UT 84150 **866-406-1830**

FirstGiving Inc
100 Cambridge Park Dr...............Cambridge MA 02240 **800-687-8505**

Flowroute Inc
1218 Third Ave 600th Fl...................Seattle WA 98101 **855-356-9768**

Fluidware 12 York St 2nd Fl...............Ottawa ON K1N5S6 **866-218-5127**

FocusVision Worldwide Inc
1266 E Main St..........................Stamford CT 06902 **800-433-8128** 203-961-1715

FOI Services Inc
704 Quince OrchaRd Rd Ste 275......Gaithersburg MD 20878 **800-654-1147** 301-975-9400

FOIA Group Inc (FGI)
1250 Connecticut Ave NW Ste 200.......Washington DC 20036 **888-461-7951** 716-608-0800

Forex Newscom
55 Water St 50th Fl.....................New York NY 10041 **888-503-6739**

ForSaleByOwnercom Llc
701 Griswold...........................Detroit MI 48226 **888-367-7253**

Franchise Information Services Inc
4075 Wilson Blvd Ste 410................Arlington VA 22203 **800-485-9570**

Frontier Networks Inc
530 Kipling Ave........................Toronto ON M8Z5E3 **866-833-2323** 416-847-5240

FTJ FundChoice LLC
2300 Litton Ln Ste 102....................Hebron KY 41048 **800-379-2513**

Geotab Inc
1081 S Service Rd W......................Oakville ON L6L6K3 **877-436-8221** 416-434-4309

Get It LLC
128 N Pitt St Ste 2.....................Alexandria VA 22314 **877-285-7861**

GigMasterscom Inc
33 S Main St...........................Norwalk CT 06854 **866-342-9794**

GitHub
88 Colin P Kelly Junior St.............San Francisco CA 94107 **877-448-4820**

GlobaFone Inc
1950 Lafayette Rd Ste 207..............Portsmouth NH 03801 **800-826-6152** 603-433-7232

Helixstorm Inc
27238 Via Industria......................Temecula CA 92590 **888-434-3549**

Helpjuice Inc
211 E Seventh St..........................Austin TX 78701 **888-230-3420**

Hireology
303 E Wacker Dr Ste 400..................Chicago IL 60601 **844-383-2633** 312-253-7870

Host Department LLC
45277 Fremont Blvd Ste 11................Fremont CA 94538 **866-887-4678**

I Am Athlete LLC
6701 Center Dr Ste 700.................Los Angeles CA 90045 **877-462-7979**

IBISWorld Inc
11755 Wilshire blvd 11th fl..............Los Angeles CA 90025 **800-330-3772**

IdeaTek 111 Old Mill St....................Buhler KS 67522 **855-433-2835**

iLearning Gateway Inc
2650 Vly View Ln Bldg 1 Ste 200...........Dallas TX 75234 **888-464-2672**

IMVU Inc
PO Box 390012.....................Mountain View CA 94039 **866-761-0975** 650-321-8334

InComm Conferencing Inc
208 Harristown Rd Ste 202...............Glen Rock NJ 07452 **877-804-2062** 201-612-9696

infoUSA Inc 5711 S 86th Cir.................Omaha NE 68127 **800-321-0869** 800-835-5856

Innovative Telecom Solutions Inc
9 Vela Way..............................Edgewater NJ 07020 **800-510-3000**

Intelletrace Inc
936 B Seventh St........................Novato CA 94945 **800-618-5877** 415-493-2200

International Automotive Technicians' Network Inc
PO Box 1599...............................Brea CA 92822 **800-272-7467** 714-257-1335

Iowa Communications Network Inc
Grimes State Office Bldg 400 E 14th St
....Des Moines IA 50319 **800-532-1290** 515-725-4692

ISLC Inc 14 Savannah Hwy...............Beaufort SC 29906 **888-828-4752** 843-770-1000

Junction Networks Inc
55 Broad St 20th Fl......................New York NY 10004 **800-801-3381**

Kahuna Inc
811 Hamilton St......................Redwood City CA 94063 **844-465-2486**

Landel Telecom
142 Martinvale Ln.......................San Jose CA 95119 **855-624-5284**

Lexicon International Corp
1400A Adams Rd........................Bensalem PA 19020 **800-448-8201** 215-639-8220

Lingo Inc
7901 Jones Branch Dr Ste 900............Mclean VA 22102 **888-546-4699**

LINQ Services
1200 Steuart St Unit C3.................Baltimore MD 21230 **800-421-5467**

Logical Net Corp
1462 Erie Blvd.......................Schenectady NY 12305 **800-600-0638** 518-292-4500

Martindale-Hubbell
121 Chanlon Rd Ste 110.............New Providence NJ 07974 **800-526-4902**

MemberPlanet
23224 Crenshaw Blvd...................Torrance CA 90505 **800-952-5210** 916-445-1254

MENTIS
3 Columbus Cir 15th Fl..................New York NY 10019 **800-267-0858** 212-203-4365

MERX Networks Inc
6 Antares Dr Phase II Unit 103...........Ottawa ON K2E8A9 **800-964-6379** 613-727-4900

MessageBank LLC
250 W 57th St Ste 1100.................New York NY 10107 **800-989-8001** 212-333-9300

MobileIQ Inc
4800 Baseline Rd Ste E104-247............Boulder CO 80303 **866-261-8600**

MOGL Loyalty Services Inc
9645 Scranton Rd Ste 110...............San Diego CA 92121 **888-664-5669**

Name / Address	City	State	Zip	Toll-Free	Phone
Moseo Corp 2722 Elake Ave E	Seattle	WA	98102	**800-741-0926**	
Mountain Telephone Co 405 Main St	West Liberty	KY	41472	**800-939-3121**	606-743-3121
MVS Group 1086 Goffle Rd	Hawthorne	NJ	07506	**800-619-9989**	201-447-1505
MyCorporation Business Services Inc 26025 Mureau Rd Ste 120	Calabasas	CA	91302	**877-692-6772**	
NADAguidescom 3186 K Airway Ave	Costa Mesa	CA	92626	**800-966-6232**	
National Technical Information Service (NTIS) 5285 Port Royal Rd *Orders	Springfield	VA	22161	**800-553-6847***	703-605-6000
New Pros Data Inc 155 Hidden Ravines Dr	Powell	OH	43065	**800-837-5478**	740-201-0410
NewCloud Networks 160 Inverness Dr W	Englewood	CO	80112	**855-255-5001**	
Newsbank Inc 5801 Pelican Bay Blvd Ste 600	Naples	FL	34108	**800-243-7694**	800-762-8182
Nexogy 2121 Ponce de leon Blvd Ste 200	Coral Gables	FL	33134	**866-639-6492**	
Next Net Media LLC 4801 Gulf Blvd Ste 334	St Pete Beach	FL	33706	**800-737-5820**	
Nextiva 8800 E Chaparral Rd Ste 300	Scottsdale	AZ	85250	**800-799-0600**	800-983-4289
nexVortex Inc 510 Spring St Ste 250	Herndon	VA	20170	**855-639-8888**	
Nexxtworks Inc 30798 US Hwy 19 N	Palm Harbor	FL	34684	**888-533-8353**	
Niche Directories LLC 909 N Sepulveda Blvd 11th Fl	El Segundo	CA	90026	**877-242-9330**	
Northeast Florida Telephone Company Inc 130 N Fourth St	Macclenny	FL	32063	**800-416-6707**	904-259-2261
Northwest Communications Coop 111 Railroad Ave PO Box 38	Ray	ND	58849	**800-245-5884**	701-568-3331
Oklahoma Telephone & Telegraph Inc 26 N Otis Ave	Dustin	OK	74839	**800-869-1989**	
OneMorePallet 9891 Montgomery Rd Ste 122	Cincinnati	OH	45242	**855-438-1667**	
Orbitel Communications LLC 21116 N John Wayne Pkwy Ste B-9	Maricopa	AZ	85239	**800-998-8084**	520-568-8890
Ovid Technologies Inc 333 Seventh Ave 20th Fl	New York	NY	10001	**800-950-2035**	646-674-6300
PackLatecom Inc 100 Four Falls Corporate Ctr Ste 104	West Conshohocken	PA	19428	**877-472-2552**	
Pageplus Cellular 9700 NW 112th Ave	Miami	FL	33178	**800-550-2436**	
Peerless Network Inc 222 S Riverside Plz Ste 2730	Chicago	IL	60606	**888-380-2721**	312-506-0920
Pineland Telephone Cooperative Inc 30 S Rountree St	Metter	GA	30439	**800-247-1266**	912-685-2121
Pinnacle Communications Corp 19821 Executive Park Cir	Germantown	MD	20874	**800-644-9101**	301-601-0777
PK4 Media 2250 E Maple Ave	El Segundo	CA	90245	**888-320-6281**	
PriceWaiter LLC 426 Market St	Chattanooga	TN	37421	**855-671-9889**	
Pure Auto LLC 164 Market St Ste 250	Charleston	SC	29401	**877-860-7873**	
Purple Communications Inc 595 Menlo Dr	Rocklin	CA	95765	**800-900-9478**	
Qualaroo Inc 122 E Houston St	San Antonio	TX	78205	**888-449-3364**	
Rallyorgorg 995 Market St 2nd Fl	San Francisco	CA	94105	**888-648-2220**	
Ready Set Work LLC (RSW) 1487 Dunwoody Dr Ste 200	West Chester	PA	19380	**877-507-3706**	
RefWorks LLC 7200 Wisconsin Ave Ste 601	Bethesda	MD	20814	**800-843-7751**	301-961-6700
Reliance Connects 61 W Mesquite Blvd	Mesquite	NV	89027	**866-894-4657**	702-346-5211
Rentals Inc 3585 Engineering Dr	Norcross	GA	30092	**888-501-7368**	
Reputation Rhino LLC 300 Park Ave 12th Fl	New York	NY	10022	**888-975-3331**	
Revestor 505 Montgomery St 11th Fl	San Francisco	CA	94111	**800-569-2674**	
Rise Broadband 61 Inverness Dr E Ste 250	Englewood	CO	80112	**844-411-7473**	
RivalHealth LLC 1121 Situs Ct Ste 190	Raleigh	NC	27606	**888-949-1001**	919-803-6709
Riviera Telephone Co 103 S 8th PO Box 997	Riviera	TX	78379	**877-296-3232**	361-296-3232
RTT Mobile Interpretation 901 Woodland St	Nashville	TN	37206	**855-894-4788**	
SchoolDocs LLC 5944 Luther Ln Ste 600	Dallas	TX	75225	**866-311-2293**	
Scott Enterprises Inc 2225 Downs Dr 6th Fl Exce stes	Erie	PA	16509	**877-866-3445**	814-868-9500
Seize The Deal LLC 1851 N Greenville Ave Ste 100	Richardson	TX	75081	**866-210-0881**	
Sell My Timeshare Now LLC 383 Central Ave Ste 260	Dover	NH	03820	**877-815-4227**	603-516-0200
Setel 1165 s Sixth st	Macclenny	FL	32063	**800-662-0716**	904-259-1300
Smart Choice Communications LLC 16 W 45th St	New York	NY	10036	**800-217-3096**	212-660-7300
Social Strategy1 5000 Sawgrass Village Cir Ste 30	Ponte Vedra Beach	FL	32082	**877-771-3366**	
Sogetel Inc 111 rue du 12-Novembre	Nicolet	QC	J3T1S3	**866-764-3835**	819-293-6125
SpinGo Solutions Inc 14193 S Minuteman Dr Ste 100	Draper	UT	84020	**877-377-4646**	
Spira Data Corp 707 Seventh Ave SW Ste 1000	Calgary	AB	T2P3H6	**855-666-6353**	403-263-6475
SportsEngine 807 Broadway St NE Ste 300 *Sales	Minneapolis	MN	55413	**888-379-1035***	
SpotOn Inc 300 California St 4th Fl	San Francisco	CA	94104	**877-814-4102**	
Spreedly Inc 733 Foster St	Durham	NC	27701	**888-727-7750**	
Sqrrl Data Inc 125 Cambridgepark Dr Ste 401	Cambridge	MA	02140	**800-395-9683**	617-902-0784
Stickkcom LLC 109 S Fifth St	New York	NY	11249	**866-578-4255**	347-394-4964
Telco IQ 4300 Forbes Blvd Ste 210	Lanham	MD	20706	**877-835-2647**	202-595-1500
Tele Atlas North America Inc 11 Lafayette St	Lebanon	NH	03766	**844-394-2020**	
Telephone Electronics Corp (TEC) 700 W St	Jackson	MS	39201	**800-832-2515**	601-353-9118
TelSpan Inc 101 W Washington St E Tower Ste 1200	Indianapolis	IN	46204	**800-800-1729**	
Thomson Reuters 22 Thomson Pl	Boston	MA	02210	**888-216-1929**	617-856-2000
TicketBiscuit LLC 5120 Cyrus Cir Ste 101	Birmingham	AL	35242	**866-757-8330**	205-757-8330
TouchLogic Corp 30 Kinnear Ct Ste 202	Richmond Hill	ON	L4B1K8	**877-355-4774**	
Touchstorm LLC 450 Lexington Ave 4th Fl	New York	NY	10017	**877-794-6101**	
Townes Tele-Communications Inc 120 E First St	Lewisville	AR	71845	**800-255-1975**	870-921-4224
TransWorld Network Corp 255 Pine Ave N	Oldsmar	FL	34677	**800-253-0665**	813-891-4700
TruMarx Data Partners Inc 30 S Wacker Dr Ste 2200	Chicago	IL	60606	**844-878-6279**	
US Farm Data Inc 10824 Old Mill Rd Ste 8	Omaha	NE	68154	**800-960-6267**	
US News University Connection LLC 9417 Princess Palm Ave	Tampa	FL	33619	**866-442-6587**	
USA Communications Inc 920 E 56th St Ste B	Kearney	NE	68847	**877-234-0102**	
uShip Inc 205 E Riverside Dr	Austin	TX	78704	**800-698-7447**	
Vanguard Systems Inc 2901 Dutton Mill Rd Ste 220	Aston	PA	19014	**800-445-1418**	
Vanilla Forums Inc 388 Rue Saint-Jacques Ste 800	Montreal	QC	H2Y1S1	**866-845-0815**	
Vectus Inc 18685 Main St 101 PMB 360	Huntington Beach	CA	92648	**866-483-2887**	
Vessel Metrics LLC Soveral Harbor 2401 PGA Blvd Ste 155	Palm Beach Gardens	FL	33410	**888-214-1710**	
Vetstreet 780 Township Line Rd	Yardley	PA	19067	**888-799-8387**	215-493-0621
VirtualPBXcom Inc 111 N Market St Ste 402	San Jose	CA	95113	**888-825-0800**	408-414-7646
VoIP Innovations Inc 8 Penn Ctr W Ste 101	Pittsburgh	PA	15276	**877-478-6471**	
Weblocom Inc 2075 Blvd Robert-Bourassa	Montreal	QC	H3A2L1	**866-381-3395**	514-364-3636
WellAware 3424 Paesanos Pkwy Ste 200	San Antonio	TX	78231	**855-935-5292**	210-816-4600
West Coast Green Institute 760 Market St Ste 1028	San Francisco	CA	94102	**800-724-4880**	415-955-1935
West Group 610 Opperman Dr *Cust Svc	Eagan	MN	55123	**800-328-4880***	651-687-7000
WhoKnows 585 Broadway St	Redwood City	CA	94063	**800-348-5031**	
WyzAnt Inc 1714 N Damen Ave Ste 3N	Chicago	IL	60647	**877-999-2681**	
Xtel Communications Inc 401 Rt 73 n	Marlton	NJ	08053	**800-438-9835**	856-596-4000
XTRAC LLC 245 Summer St	Boston	MA	02210	**855-975-3569**	
Yesware Inc 75 Kneeland St 1st Fl	Boston	MA	02111	**855-937-9273**	
YouVisit 20533 Biscayne Blvd Ste 1322	Aventura	FL	33180	**866-585-7158**	

387 INK

Name / Address	City	State	Zip	Toll-Free	Phone
Braden Sutphin Ink Co 3650 E 93rd St	Cleveland	OH	44105	**800-289-6872**	216-271-2300
Central Ink Corp 1100 Harvester Rd	West Chicago	IL	60185	**800-345-2541**	630-231-6500
Engage Technologies Corp 7041 Boone Ave N	Brooklyn Park	MN	55428	**800-877-5658**	
Gans Ink & Supply Company Inc 1441 Boyd St	Los Angeles	CA	90033	**800-421-6167**	
Independent Ink Inc 13700 Gramercy Pl	Gardena	CA	90249	**800-446-5538**	310-523-4657
International Coatings Co 13929 166th St	Cerritos	CA	90703	**800-423-4103**	562-926-1010
Matsui International Company Inc 1501 W 178th St	Gardena	CA	90248	**800-359-5679**	310-767-7812
Nazdar 8501 Hedge Ln Terr	Shawnee	KS	66227	**800-767-9942**	913-422-1888
Nor-Cote International Inc 506 Lafayette Ave	Crawfordsville	IN	47933	**800-488-9180**	765-362-9180
Reaxis Inc 941 Robinson Hwy	Mcdonald	PA	15057	**800-426-7273**	
Sensient Technologies Corp 777 E Wisconsin Ave *NYSE: SXT*	Milwaukee	WI	53202	**800-558-9892**	414-271-6755
Siegwerk USA Co 3535 SW 56th St	Des Moines	IA	50321	**800-728-8200**	515-471-2100
Spectrachem 10 Dell Glen Ave	Lodi	NJ	07644	**800-524-2806**	973-253-3553
Sun Chemical Corp 35 Waterview Blvd	Parsippany	NJ	07054	**800-543-2323**	973-404-6000
Tonertype of Florida LLC 5313 Johns Rd Ste 210	Tampa	FL	33634	**888-916-1300**	813-915-1300
Toyo Ink America LLC 1225 N Michael Dr *General	Wood Dale	IL	60191	**866-969-8696***	630-930-5100

	City	State	Zip	Toll-Free	Phone
U-mark Inc 102 Iowa Ave	Belleville	IL	62220	**866-383-6275**	618-235-7500

388 INSULATION & ACOUSTICAL PRODUCTS

	City	State	Zip	Toll-Free	Phone
Applegate Insulation Manufacturing Inc 1000 Highview Dr	Webberville	MI	48892	**800-627-7536**	517-521-3545
CertainTeed Corp 750 E Swedesford Rd *Prod Info	Valley Forge	PA	19482	**800-782-8777***	610-341-7000
Claremont Sales Corp 35 Winsome Dr PO Box 430	Durham	CT	06422	**800-222-4448**	860-349-4499
Dryvit Systems Inc 1 Energy Way	West Warwick	RI	02893	**800-556-7752**	401-822-4100
Isolatek International Inc 41 Furnace St	Stanhope	NJ	07874	**800-631-9600**	973-347-1200
ITW Insulation Systems 1370 E 40th St Ste 1 Bldg 7	Houston	TX	77022	**800-231-1024**	713-691-7002
Johns Manville Corp 717 17th St PO Box 5108 *Prod Info	Denver	CO	80217	**800-654-3103***	303-978-2000
Knauf Insulation 1 Knauf Dr	Shelbyville	IN	46176	**800-825-4434**	317-398-4434
Nu-Wool Company Inc 2472 Port Sheldon Rd	Jenison	MI	49428	**800-748-0128**	616-669-0100
Rock Wool Manufacturing Co 8610 Spruiell St PO Box 506	Leeds	AL	35094	**800-874-7625**	205-699-6121
Scott Industries Inc 1573 Hwy 136 W PO Box 7	Henderson	KY	42419	**800-951-9276**	270-831-2037
Soundcoat Co 1 Burt Dr	Deer Park	NY	11729	**800-394-8913**	631-242-2200
Thermafiber Inc 3711 W Mill St	Wabash	IN	46992	**888-834-2371**	260-563-2111
Thermwell Products Co 420 Rt 17 S	Mahwah	NJ	07430	**800-526-5265**	201-684-4400

389 INSURANCE AGENTS, BROKERS, SERVICES

	City	State	Zip	Toll-Free	Phone
A Plus Benefits Inc 395 W 600 N	Lindon	UT	84042	**800-748-5102**	801-443-1090
Actuarial Systems Corp 15840 Monte St Ste 108	Sylmar	CA	91342	**800-950-2082**	
Affinion Group Inc 6 High Ridge Pk	Stamford	CT	06905	**800-252-2148**	203-956-1000
Agency Software Inc 215 W Commerce Dr	Hayden Lake	ID	83835	**800-342-7327**	208-762-7188
Alliance Worldwide Investigative Group Inc 4 Executive Park Dr	Clifton Park	NY	12065	**800-579-2911**	518-514-2944
Allied Solutions LLC 350 Veterans Way	Carmel	IN	46032	**800-826-9384**	
Allstate 2775 Sanders Rd	Northbrook	IL	60062	**800-255-7828**	847-402-5000
Amfed Cos LLC 576 Highland Colony Pkwy	Ridgeland	MS	39157	**800-264-8085**	601-853-4949
ANCO Insurance 1111 Briarcrest Dr PO Box 3889	Bryan	TX	77802	**800-749-1733**	979-776-2626
Andreini & Co 220 W 20th Ave	San Mateo	CA	94403	**800-969-2522**	650-573-1111
Andrew G Gordon Inc 306 Washington St	Norwell	MA	02061	**866-243-2259**	781-659-2262
Aon Risk Services Inc 200 E Randolph St	Chicago	IL	60601	**877-384-4276**	312-381-1000
Argenia LLC 11524 Fairview Rd	Little Rock	AR	72212	**800-482-5968**	501-227-9670
Arthur J Gallagher & Co 2 Pierce Pl *NYSE: AJG*	Itasca	IL	60143	**888-285-5106**	630-773-3800
Arthur J Glatfelter Agency Inc PO Box 2726	York	PA	17405	**800-233-1957**	717-741-0911
Assurity Life Insurance Co 2000 Q St	Lincoln	NE	68503	**800-869-0355**	402-476 6500
Benefit & Risk Management Services Inc (BRMS) 80 Iron Point Cir Ste 200 PO Box 2140	Folsom	CA	95763	**888-326-2555**	
Benefit Communications Inc (BCI) 2977 Sidco Dr	Nashville	TN	37204	**800-489-3786**	
Berkley Risk Administrators Company LLC 222 S Ninth St Ste 2700	Minneapolis	MN	55402	**800-449-7707**	612-766-3000
Bilbrey Insurance Services Inc 5701 Greendale Rd	Johnston	IA	50131	**800-383-0116**	
Bischoff Insurance Agency Inc 1300 Oakridge Dr Ste 100	Fort Collins	CO	80525	**888-229-5558**	970-223-9400
Bolton & Co 3475 E Foothill Blvd Ste 100	Pasadena	CA	91107	**800-439-9337**	626-799-7000
Burnham & Flower Group Inc 315 S Kalamazoo Mall	Kalamazoo	MI	49007	**888-748-7966**	269-381-1173
C P H & Assoc 711 S Dearborn St Unit 205	Chicago	IL	60605	**800-875-1911**	312-987-9823
Cailor Fleming & Associates Inc 4610 Market St	Youngstown	OH	44512	**800-796-8495**	330-782-8068
Callbright Corp 6700 Hollister	Houston	TX	77040	**877-462-2552**	855-225-5274
CalSurance 681 S Parker St Ste 300	Orange	CA	92868	**800-762-7800**	714-939-0800
Carl Nelson Insurance Agency I 1519 N 11th Ave	Hanford	CA	93230	**800-582-4264**	559-584-4495
Casswood Insurance Agency Ltd 5 Executive Pk Dr	Clifton Park	NY	12065	**800-972-2242**	518-373-8700
Charles L Crane Agency Co 100 N Broadway Ste 900	Saint Louis	MO	63102	**800-264-8722**	314-241-8700
Clifford & Rano Associates Inc 57 Cedar St	Worcester	MA	01609	**800-660-8284**	508-752-8284
CNA National Warranty Corp 4150 N Drinkwater Blvd Ste 400	Scottsdale	AZ	85251	**800-345-0191**	
Collier Insurance 606 S Mendenhall Rd Ste 200 *General	Memphis	TN	38117	**866-600-2655***	901-529-2900
Combined Specialities International Inc 205 San Marin Dr Ste 5	Novato	CA	94945	**866-893-9510**	415-209-0012
Common Census Inc 90 Bridge St Ste 105	Westbrook	ME	04092	**800-552-7373**	207-854-5454
Corporate Claims Management Inc 782 Spirit 40 Pk	Chesterfield	MO	63005	**800-449-2264**	
Cross Financial Corp 74 Gilman Rd PO Box 1388	Bangor	ME	04401	**800-999-7345**	207-947-7345
Cumbre Insurance Services LLC 3333 Concours Ste 5100	Ontario	CA	91764	**800-998-7986**	909-484-2456
Dale Barton Agency 1100 East 6600 South	Salt Lake City	UT	84121	**866-288-1666**	801-288-1600
Daniel & Henry Co 1001 Highlands Plaza Dr W Ste 500	Saint Louis	MO	63110	**800-256-3462**	314-421-1525
Dawson Insurance Agency Inc 721 First Ave N	Fargo	ND	58107	**800-220-4514**	701-237-3311
Direct Response Insurance Administrative Services (DRIASI) 7930 Century Blvd	Chanhassen	MN	55317	**800-688-0760**	
Distinguished Programs Group LLC, The 1180 Ave Of The Americas 16th Fl	New York	NY	10036	**888-355-4626**	212-297-3100
Dyatech 381 Highland Colony Pky	Ridgeland	MS	39157	**866-651-4222**	601-914-0533
Eagan Insurance Agency Inc 2629 N Cswy Blvd	Metairie	LA	70002	**888-882-9600**	504-836-9600
Elant Inc 46 Harriman Dr	Goshen	NY	10924	**800-501-3936**	
Emery & Webb Inc 989 Main St	Fishkill	NY	12524	**800-942-5818**	845-896-6727
Employers Insurance Company of Nevada 9790 Gateway Dr Ste 100	Reno	NV	89521	**888-682-6671**	
Encon Group Inc 500-1400 Blair Pl	Ottawa	ON	K1J9B8	**800-267-6684**	613-786-2000
EOI Service Company Inc 1820 E First St Ste 400	Santa Ana	CA	92705	**800-229-4364**	714-935-0503
FairMarket Life Settlements Corp 435 Ford Rd Ste 120	St Louis Park	MN	55426	**866-326-3757**	
Faribo Insurance Agency Inc 1404 Seventh St NW	Faribault	MN	55021	**888-923-0430**	507-334-3929
Farmers Fire Insurance Co 2875 Eastern Blvd	York	PA	17402	**800-537-0928**	717-751-4435
Farris Evans Insurance Agency Inc 1568 Union Ave	Memphis	TN	38104	**800-395-8207**	901-274-5424
FDI Group 39500 High Pointe Blvd Ste 400	Novi	MI	48375	**800-828-0759**	
First American Home Buyers Protection 1 First American Way	Santa Ana	CA	92707	**800-854-3643**	714-250-3000
Flood & Peterson 2000 S Colorado Blvd Twr 1 4000	Denver	CO	80222	**800-356-2295**	970-356-0123
Fortun Insurance Agency Inc 365 Palermo Ave	Coral Gables	FL	33134	**877-643-2055**	305-445-3535
Fred Loya Insurance 1800 Lee Trevino Ste 201	El Paso	TX	79936	**800-554-0595**	915-590-5692
Fringe Benefits Management Co 3101 Sessions Rd	Tallahassee	FL	32303	**800-872-0345**	850-425-6200
Frontier Adjusters of America Inc 4745 N Seventh St Ste 320	Phoenix	AZ	85014	**800-426-7228**	
GCube Insurance Services Inc 3101 Wcoast Hwy Ste 100	Newport Beach	CA	92663	**877-903-4777**	949-515-9981
Gebco Insurance Assoc 8600 LaSalle Rd Ste 338	Towson	MD	21286	**800-464-3226**	410-668-3100
Gerald J Sullivan & Assoc Inc 800 W Sixth St Ste 1800	Los Angeles	CA	90017	**800-421-8969**	213-626-1000
Graham Co, The 1 Penn Sq W 25th Fl	Philadelphia	PA	19102	**888-472-4262**	215-567-6300
Haas & Wilkerson Inc 4300 Shawnee Mission Pkwy	Fairway	KS	66205	**800-821-7703**	913-432-4400
Healy Group Inc, The 17535 Generations Dr	South Bend	IN	46635	**800-667-4613**	574-271-6000
Herbert H Landy Insurance Agency Inc 75 Second Ave Ste 410	Needham	MA	02494	**800-336-5422**	
Hibbs Hallmark & Co 501 Shelley Dr	Tyler	TX	75701	**800-765-6767**	
Hinkle Insurance Agency Inc 600 Olde Hickory Rd Ste 200	Lancaster	PA	17601	**877-408-1418**	717-560-9733
Holmes Murphy & Assoc Inc 3001 Westown Pkwy	West Des Moines	IA	50266	**800-247-7756**	515-223-6800
Hometown Quotes LLC 304 Inverness Pkwy S Ste 395	Englewood	CO	80112	**800-820-2981**	
Horton Group, The 10320 Orland Pkwy	Orland Park	IL	60467	**800-383-8283**	708-845-3000
Housing Authority Risk Retention Group Inc PO Box 189	Cheshire	CT	06410	**800-873-0242**	
HUB International Insurance Services 333 W El Camino Real Ste 330	Sunnyvale	CA	94087	**877-530-8897**	650-964-8000
Hub International Ltd 1065 Ave of the Americas	New York	NY	10018	**800-456-5293**	212-338-2000
Hunt Insurance Agency Inc 12000 S Harlem Ave	Palos Heights	IL	60463	**800-772-6484**	708-361-5300
Hylant Group 811 Madison Ave	Toledo	OH	43604	**800-249-5268**	419-255-1020
ICI Mutual Insurance Co 1401 H St NW Ste 1000	Washington	DC	20005	**800-643-4246**	
Independant Insurance Services In 3956 N Pine St	Davenport	IA	52806	**800-373-1562**	563-383-5555
Insurance Services Office Inc (ISO) 545 Washington Blvd	Jersey City	NJ	07310	**800-888-4476**	201-469-2000
InterWest Insurance Services Inc 8950 Cal Ctr Dr Bldg 3 Ste 200	Sacramento	CA	95826	**800-444-4134**	916-488-3100
J C Taylor Antique Automobile Agency Inc 320 S 69th St	Upper Darby	PA	19082	**800-345-8290**	
J Smith Lanier & Co 300 W Tenth St	West Point	GA	31833	**800-226-4522**	706-645-2211
Jake A Parrott Insurance Agency Inc 2508 N Herritage St	Kinston	NC	28501	**800-727-7688**	252-523-1041
James Greene & Assoc Inc 275 W Kiehl Ave	Sherwood	AR	72120	**800-422-3384**	501-834-4001
Johns Eastern Co Inc PO Box 110259 *General	Lakewood Ranch	FL	34211	**877-326-5326***	941-907-3100

Classified Section

				Toll-Free	Phone

KAFL Inc
85 Allen St Ste 300 . . . . Rochester NY 14608 **800-272-6488** 585-271-6400

Keenan & Assoc PO Box 4328 . . . . Torrance CA 90510 **800-654-8102** 310-212-3344

Lawley Service Insurance
361 Delaware Ave . . . . Buffalo NY 14202 **800-860-5741*** 716-849-8618
  *Cust Svc

Le Mars Insurance Co
PO Box 1608 . . . . Le Mars IA 51031 **800-545-6480**

Leap/Carpenter/Kemps Insurance Agency
3187 Collins Dr . . . . Merced CA 95348 **800-221-0864** 209-384-0727

leavitt group Enterprises
216 S 200 W . . . . Cedar City UT 84720 **800-264-8085** 435-586-6553

Lewer Agency Inc
4534 Wornall Rd . . . . Kansas City MO 64111 **800-821-7715**

Lincoln General Insurance Co
3501 Concord Rd . . . . York PA 17402 **800-876-3350** 717-757-0000

LISI Inc
1600 W Hillsdale Blvd . . . . San Mateo CA 94402 **800-930-5190** 650-348-4131

Loesel Schaaf Insurance Agency Inc
3537 W 12th St . . . . Erie PA 16505 **877-718-9935** 814-833-5433

Lovitt & Touche Inc
7202 E Rosewood St Ste 200
PO Box 32702 . . . . Tucson AZ 85710 **800-426-2756** 520-722-3000

Managed Care of America Inc
1910 Cochran Rd Ste 605 . . . . Pittsburgh PA 15220 **800-922-4966** 412-922-2803

Managed HealthCare Northwest Inc
422 E Burnside St Ste 215
PO Box 4629 . . . . Portland OR 97208 **800-648-6356** 503-413-5800

Marsh & Mclennan Agency
250 Pehle Ave . . . . Saddle Brook NJ 07663 **800-669-6330** 800-642-0106

Marshall & Sterling Inc
110 Main St . . . . Poughkeepsie NY 12601 **800-333-3766** 845-454-0800

Matson & Cuprill
100 E-Business Way Ste 160 . . . . Cincinnati OH 45249 **800-944-8596** 513-563-7526

McGriff Seibels & Williams Inc
2211 Seventh Ave S . . . . Birmingham AL 35233 **800-476-2211** 205-252-9871

MedCost Benefit Services LLC
165 Kimel Park Dr . . . . Winston-Salem NC 27114 **800-433-9178** 800-795-1023

Medical Eye Services Inc
345 Baker St E . . . . Costa Mesa CA 92626 **800-877-6372** 714-619-4660

Medical Risk Managers Inc
1170 Ellington Rd . . . . South Windsor CT 06074 **800-732-3248**

Mesirow Financial Insurance Services Div
353 N Clark St . . . . Chicago IL 60654 **800-453-0600** 312-595-6200

MGM Industries Inc
287 Freehill Rd . . . . Hendersonville TN 37075 **800-476-5584** 615-824-6572

Michigan Insurance Co
1700 E Beltline NE Ste 100
PO Box 152120 . . . . Grand Rapids MI 49515 **888-606-6426**

Minnesota Lawyers Mutual Insurance Co
333 S Seventh St Ste 2200 . . . . Minneapolis MN 55402 **800-422-1370** 877-880-1335

MMG Insurance Co
44 Maysville St PO Box 729 . . . . Presque Isle ME 04769 **800-343-0533**

Moloney Securities
13537 Barrett Pkwy Dr Ste 300 . . . . Manchester MO 63021 **800-628-6002** 314-909-0600

MSI Benefits Group Inc
245 Townpark Dr Ste 100 . . . . Kennesaw GA 30144 **800-580-1629** 770-425-1231

National Electronic Attachment Inc (NEA)
100 Ashford Ctr N Ste 300 . . . . Dunwoody GA 30338 **800-782-5150**

National Farm Life Insurance Co
6001 Bridge St . . . . Fort Worth TX 76112 **800-772-7557** 817-451-9550

NCCI Holdings Inc
901 Peninsula Corporate Cir . . . . Boca Raton FL 33487 **800-622-4123*** 561-893-1000
  *Cust Svc

Norfolk & Dedham Group
222 Ames St . . . . Dedham MA 02027 **800-688-1825**

Noridian Healthcare Solutions LLC
900 42th St S PO Box 6055 . . . . Fargo ND 58103 **800-633-4227**

North Star Resource Group Inc
2701 University Ave SE N Star Professional Ctr
. . . . Minneapolis MN 55414 **800-820-4205** 612-617-6000

Northwest Administrators Inc
2323 Eastlake Ave E . . . . Seattle WA 98102 **877-304-6702** 206-329-4900

Ogren Insurance
6929 Hohman Ave . . . . Hammond IN 46324 **800-936-4736**

Omni Life Assocates Inc
375 N Broadway Ste 203 . . . . Jericho NY 11753 **800-966-6583** 516-938-2465

Oswald Companies
1100 Superior Ave Ste 1500 . . . . Cleveland OH 44114 **855-467-9253** 216-367-8787

Otis-Magie Insurance Agency Inc
332 W Superior St Ste 700 . . . . Duluth MN 55802 **800-241-2425** 218-722-7753

Pacesetter Claims Service Inc
2871 N Hwy 167 . . . . Catoosa OK 74015 **888-218-4880** 918-665-8887

Parker Smith & Feek Inc
2233 112th Ave NE . . . . Bellevue WA 98004 **800-457-0220***
  *Cust Svc

Parkville Insurances Services Inc
15242 E Whittier Blvd PO Box 1275 . . . . Whittier CA 90603 **800-350-2702** 562-945-2702

Piedmont Community Health Plan Inc
2512 Langhorne Rd . . . . Lynchburg VA 24501 **800-400-7247** 434-947-4463

Planned Administrators Inc
PO Box 6927 . . . . Columbia SC 29260 **800-768-4375** 803-462-0151

Policemen's Annuity & Benefit Fund of Chicago
221 North LaSalle St Ste 1626 . . . . Chicago IL 60601 **800-656-6606** 312-744-3891

POMCO 2425 James St . . . . Syracuse NY 13206 **855-247-0353** 315-432-9171

Purves & Assoc Insurance
500 Fourth St . . . . Davis CA 95616 **800-681-2025** 530-756-5561

Rain & Hail LLC
9200 Northpark Dr Ste 100 . . . . Johnston IA 50131 **800-776-4045** 515-559-1200

Rampart Brokerage Corp
1983 Marcus Ave Ste C130 . . . . New Hyde Park NY 11042 **800-772-6727** 516-538-7000

Reid Jones McRorie & Williams Inc (RJMW)
2200 Executive St PO Box 669248 . . . . Charlotte NC 28208 **800-785-2604**

Renaissance Group
981 Worcester St . . . . Wellesley MA 02482 **800-514-2667**

RF Ougheltree & Associates LLC
300 Executive Dr Ste 350 . . . . West Orange NJ 07052 **800-388-0215**

Robert Moreno Insurance Services
2260 Savi Ranch Pkwy PO Box 87023 . . . . Yorba Linda CA 92887 **800-815-7647** 714-738-1383

RSI Insurance Brokers Inc
4000 Westerly Pl Ste 110 . . . . Newport Beach CA 92660 **800-828-5273** 714-546-6616

Sahouri Insurance
8200 Grnsburg Dr Ste 1550 . . . . Mclean VA 22102 **855-242-6660** 703-883-0500

Scott Danahy Naylon Company Inc (SDN)
300 Spindrift Dr . . . . Williamsville NY 14221 **800-728-6362** 716-633-3400

Selectpath Benefits & Financial Inc
310-700 Richmond St . . . . London ON N6A5C7 **888-327-5777** 519-675-1177

Selectquote Insurance Services
595 Market St 10th Fl . . . . San Francisco CA 94105 **800-670-3213**

Senior Market Sales Inc (SMS)
8420 W Dodge Rd Ste 510 . . . . Omaha NE 68114 **800-786-5566** 402-397-3311

SilverStone Group
11516 Miracle Hills Dr Ste 100 . . . . Omaha NE 68154 **800-288-5501** 402-964-5400

Stallings Crop Insurance Corp
PO Box 6100 . . . . Lakeland FL 33807 **800-721-7099** 863-647-2747

Star Casualty Insurance Company Inc
PO Box 451037 . . . . Miami FL 33134 **877-782-7210**

Starkweather & Shepley Inc
60 Catamore Blvd . . . . East Providence RI 02914 **800-854-4625** 401-435-3600

Sullivan Curtis Monroe
1920 Main St . . . . Irvine CA 92614 **800-427-3253** 949-250-7172

Swan & Sons-Morss Company Inc
309 E Water St PO Box 179 . . . . Elmira NY 14901 **877-407-1657** 607-734-6283

Tetrault Insurance Agency Inc
4317 Acushnet Ave . . . . New Bedford MA 02745 **800-696-9991** 508-995-8365

Thomas George Associates Ltd
10 Larkfield Rd . . . . East Northport NY 11731 **800-443-8338** 631-261-8800

TPM Life Insurance Co
1850 William Penn Way Ste 202 . . . . Lancaster PA 17601 **800-555-3122** 717-394-7156

TRICOR Insurance Inc
230 W Cherry St . . . . Lancaster WI 53813 **877-468-7426** 608-723-6441

U S Risk Insurance Group Inc
10210 N Central Expy . . . . Dallas TX 75231 **800-926-9155** 214-265-7090

United Underwriters Inc
PO Box 971000 . . . . Orem UT 84097 **866-686-4833** 801-226-2662

Van Dyk Group Inc, The
12800 Long Beach Blvd . . . . Beach Haven NJ 08008 **800-222-0131** 609-492-1511

VIVA Health Inc
1222 14th Ave S . . . . Birmingham AL 35205 **800-633-1542** 205-939-1718

Wallace Welch & Willingham
300 First Ave S 4th Fl . . . . Saint Petersburg FL 33701 **800-783-5085** 727-522-7777

Weber Insurance Corp
505 Corporate Dr W . . . . Langhorne PA 19047 **888-860-0400** 215-860-0400

WellCare of Georgia Inc
8725 Henderson Rd . . . . Tampa FL 33634 **800-919-8807**

West Point Underwriters LLC
7785 66th St . . . . Pinellas Park FL 33781 **800-688-6213** 727-507-7565

Wharton Group
101 S Livingston Ave . . . . Livingston NJ 07039 **800-521-2725** 973-992-5775

William Penn Assn
709 Brighton Rd . . . . Pittsburgh PA 15233 **800-848-7366** 412-231-2979

Willis Group Holdings Ltd
200 Liberty St 3rd Fl . . . . New York NY 10281 **800-234-8596** 212-915-8888
  NASDAQ: WSH

Wolverine Mutual Insurance Co
1 Wolverine Way . . . . Dowagiac MI 49047 **800-733-3320** 269-782-3451

390 INSURANCE COMPANIES

SEE ALSO Viatical Settlement Companies ; Home Warranty Services

390-1 Animal Insurance

				Toll-Free	Phone

Crum & Forster Pet Insurance Group
305 Madison Ave . . . . Morristown NJ 07962 **844-592-4879**

Henry Equestrian Insurance Brokers Ltd
53 Prospect St . . . . Newmarket ON L3Y3T1 **800-565-4321** 905-727-1144

Veterinary Pet Insurance Inc
PO Box 2344 . . . . Brea CA 92822 **800-872-7387**

390-2 Life & Accident Insurance

				Toll-Free	Phone

Advance Insurance Company of Kansas
1133 SW Topeka Blvd . . . . Topeka KS 66629 **800-530-5989** 785-273-9804

Aetna Inc
151 Farmington Ave . . . . Hartford CT 06156 **800-872-3862** 860-273-0123
  NYSE: AET

Allianz Life Insurance Company of North America
PO Box 1344 . . . . Minneapolis MN 55416 **800-950-5872**

Allstate Life Insurance Co
3100 Sanders Rd . . . . Northbrook IL 60062 **800-366-1411*** 847-402-5000
  *Cust Svc

Amalgamated Life
333 Westchester Ave . . . . White Plains NY 10604 **866-975-4089** 914-367-5000

American Amicable Life Insurance Co
PO Box 2549 . . . . Waco TX 76702 **800-736-7311** 254-297-2777

American Equity Investment Life Insurance Co
6000 Westown Pkwy . . . . West Des Moines IA 50266 **888-221-1234** 515-221-0002

American Family Insurance
6000 American Pkwy . . . . Madison WI 53783 **800-692-6326**

American Family Life Assurance Company of Columbus (AFLAC)
1932 Wynnton Rd . . . . Columbus GA 31999 **800-992-3522*** 706-323-3431
  *Cust Svc

American Family Mutual Insurance Co
6000 American Pkwy . . . . Madison WI 53783 **800-374-0008*** 800-692-6326
  *Cust Svc

American Income Life Insurance Co (AIL)
1200 Wooded Acres . . . . Waco TX 76710 **800-433-3405** 254-761-6400

American Standard Insurance Company of Wisconsin
6000 American Pkwy . . . . Madison WI 53783 **800-692-6326** 608-249-2111

	City	State	Zip	Toll-Free	Phone
American Trust Administrators Inc					
7223 W 95th St Ste 301	Overland Park	KS	66212	**800-842-4121**	913-378-9938
American United Life Insurance Co					
1 American Sq PO Box 368	Indianapolis	IN	46206	**800-537-6442**	317-285-1877
Americo Financial Life & Annuity Insurance Co					
PO Box 410288	Kansas City	MO	64141	**800-231-0801**	
Americo Financial Life & Annuity Insurance Co					
PO Box 410288	Kansas City	MO	64141	**800-231-0801**	
Ameritas Direct 5900 'O' St	Lincoln	NE	68510	**800-555-4655**	
Ameritas Life Insurance Corp					
5900 'O' St	Lincoln	NE	68510	**800-745-1112**	402-467-1122
Anthem Life Insurance Co					
6740 N High St Ste 200	Worthington	OH	43085	**800-551-7265**	614-436-0688
Arch Insurance Group Inc					
1 Liberty Plz 53rd Fl	New York	NY	10006	**866-993-9978**	212-651-6500
Assurant Employee Benefits					
2323 Grand Blvd	Kansas City	MO	64108	**800-733-7879**	816-474-2345
Aurora National Life Assurance Co					
PO Box 4490	Hartford	CT	06147	**800-265-2652**	
Baltimore Life Cos					
10075 Red Run Blvd	Owings Mills	MD	21117	**800-628-5433**	410-581-6600
Bankers Fidelity Life Insurance Co					
4370 Peachtree Rd NE	Atlanta	GA	30319	**866-458-7504**	800-241-1439
NASDAQ: AAME					
Banner Life Insurance Co					
1701 Research Blvd	Rockville	MD	20850	**800-638-8428**	301-279-4800
Beneficial Financial Group					
55 N 300 W	Salt Lake City	UT	84145	**800-233-7979**	801-933-1100
Best Life & Health Insurance Co					
2505 McCabe Way	Irvine	CA	92614	**800-433-0088**	949-253-4080
Bristol West Insurance Group					
900 S Pine Island Rd Ste 600	Plantation	FL	33324	**888-888-0080**	
Catholic Order of Foresters					
355 Shuman Blvd PO Box 3012	Naperville	IL	60566	**800-552-0145**	630-983-4900
Central States Health & Life Company of Omaha					
1212 N 96th St	Omaha	NE	68114	**800-826-6587**	
CIGNA 900 Cottage Grove Rd	Hartford	CT	06002	**800-244-6224**	860-226-6000
Citizens Insurance Company of America					
400 E Anderson Ln	Austin	TX	78752	**800-880-5044**	512-837-7100
Citizens Security Life Insurance Co					
12910 Shelbyville Rd Ste 300	Louisville	KY	40243	**800-843-7752**	502-244-2420
Colonial Life & Accident Insurance Co					
1200 Colonial Life Blvd	Columbia	SC	29210	**800-325-4368**	803-213-7250
Colonial Penn Life Insurance Co					
399 Market St	Philadelphia	PA	19181	**800-523-9100**	877-877-8052
Columbus Life Insurance Co					
400 E Fourth St	Cincinnati	OH	45202	**800-677-9595**	
Companion Life Insurance Co					
7909 Parklane Rd Ste 200	Columbia	SC	29223	**800-753-0404**	803-735-1251
Concord Group Insurance Cos					
4 Bouton St	Concord	NH	03301	**800-852-3380**	
Conseco Senior Health Insurance Co					
11825 N Pennsylvania St	Carmel	IN	46032	**866-595-2255**	
COUNTRY Insurance & Financial Services					
1705 Towanda Ave	Bloomington	IL	61701	**888-211-2555**	866-268-6879
Creative Mktg International Corp					
11460 Tomahawk Creek Pkwy	Leawood	KS	66211	**800-992-2642**	913-814-0510
ELCO Mutual Life & Annuity					
916 Sherwood Dr	Lake Bluff	IL	60044	**888-872-7954**	800-321-3526
Epic Life Insurance Co					
1717 W Broadway	Madison	WI	53713	**800-520-5750***	
*Sales					
Equitable Life & Casualty Insurance Co					
3 Triad Ctr	Salt Lake City	UT	84180	**877-358-4060***	
*Cust Svc					
Erie Family Life Insurance Co					
100 Erie Insurance Pl	Erie	PA	16530	**800-458-0811**	814-870-2000
Farm Bureau Life Insurance Co					
5400 University Ave	West Des Moines	IA	50266	**800-247-4170**	515-225-5400
Farm Family Life Insurance Co					
PO Box 656	Albany	NY	12201	**800-948-3276**	518-431-5000
Farmers New World Life Insurance					
3003 77th Ave SE	Mercer Island	WA	98040	**800-493-4917**	
Federal Life Insurance Co Mutual					
3750 W Deerfield Rd	Riverwoods	IL	60015	**800-233-3750**	847-520-1900
Federated Life Insurance Co					
121 E Pk Sq PO Box 328	Owatonna	MN	55060	**800-533-0472**	507-455-5200
Federated Mutual Insurance Co					
121 E Pk Sq PO Box 328	Owatonna	MN	55060	**800-533-0472**	507-455-5200
First UNUM Life Insurance Co					
2211 Congress St	Portland	ME	04122	**800-633-7491**	207-575-2211
FirstCare					
1901 W Loop 289 Ste #9	Lubbock	TX	79407	**800-884-4901**	806-784-4300
Gerber Life Insurance Co					
1311 Mamaroneck Ave	White Plains	NY	10605	**800-704-2180**	914-272-4000
Grange Insurance					
671 S High St	Columbus	OH	43206	**800-422-0550**	
Great American Life Insurance Co					
Great American Financial Resources Inc					
301 E Fourth St	Cincinnati	OH	45202	**800-545-4269**	513-369-5000
Great-West Life & Annuity Insurance Co					
8515 E OrchaRd Rd	Greenwood Village	CO	80111	**800-537-2033**	303-737-3000
Greek Catholic Union of the USA					
5400 Tuscarawas Rd	Beaver	PA	15009	**800-722-4428**	724-495-3400
Guarantee Trust Life Insurance Co					
1275 Milwaukee Ave	Glenview	IL	60025	**800-338-7452**	847-699-0600
Guardian Life Insurance Company of America					
7 Hanover Sq	New York	NY	10004	**888-600-4667**	888-482-7342
GuideOne Mutual Insurance Co					
1111 Ashworth Rd	West Des Moines	IA	50265	**877-448-4331**	844-948-4968
Hartford Life & Accident Insurance Co					
1 Hartford Plz	Hartford	CT	06155	**877-896-9320**	860-547-5000
Harvey Watt & Co					
475 N Central Ave	Atlanta	GA	30354	**800-241-6103**	404-767-7501
Horace Mann Life Insurance Co					
1 Horace Mann Plz	Springfield	IL	62715	**800-999-1030**	217-789-2500
Humana Inc 500 W Main St	Louisville	KY	40202	**800-486-2620**	502-580-1000
NYSE: HUM					

	City	State	Zip	Toll-Free	Phone
Illinois Mutual Life Insurance Co					
300 SW Adams St	Peoria	IL	61634	**800-380-6688**	309-674-8255
Indiana Farm Bureau Insurance Co					
225 SE St PO Box 1250	Indianapolis	IN	46206	**800-723-3276**	317-692-7200
Industrial Alliance Insurance & Financial Services Inc					
1080 Grande Allee W					
PO Box 1907 Sta Therminus	Quebec	QC	G1K7M3	**888-266-2224**	418-684-5405
Insurance Marketing Agencies Inc					
306 Main St	Worcester	MA	01608	**800-891-1226**	508-753-7233
Investors Heritage Life Insurance Co (IHLIC)					
200 Capital Ave PO Box 717	Frankfort	KY	40602	**800-422-2011**	
Jackson National Life Insurance Co					
1 Corporate Way	Lansing	MI	48951	**800-644-4565**	517-381-5500
John Hancock Life Insurance Co					
601 Congress St	Boston	MA	02210	**800-248-6110**	866-888-7803
John Hancock New York					
100 Summit Lake Dr 2nd Fl	Valhalla	NY	10595	**800-732-5543**	866-888-7803
Lafayette Life Insurance Co					
400 Broadway	Cincinnati	OH	45202	**800-443-8793**	
Life Insurance Co of Alabama					
302 Broad St	Gadsden	AL	35901	**800-226-2371**	256-543-2022
Lincoln Heritage Life Insurance Co					
4343 E Camelback Rd Ste 400	Phoenix	AZ	85018	**800-438-7180**	800-433-8181
Lincoln National Life Insurance Co					
1300 S Clinton St	Fort Wayne	IN	46802	**800-454-6265**	
London Life Insurance Co					
255 Dufferin Ave	London	ON	N6A4K1	**800-990-6654**	519-432-5281
Madison National Life Insurance Company Inc					
PO Box 5008	Madison	WI	53705	**800-356-9601**	608-830-2000
Massachusetts Mutual Life Insurance Co					
100 Bright Meadow Blvd	Enfield	CT	06082	**800-272-2216**	
Medico					
1010 North 102nd St Ste 201	Omaha	NE	68114	**800-547-2401**	
Medico Group 1515 S 75th St	Omaha	NE	68124	**800-228-6080**	402-391-6900
MetLife Inc 200 Park Ave	New York	NY	10166	**800-638-5433**	212-578-2211
NYSE: MET					
Midland National Life Insurance Co					
1 Sammons Plz	Sioux Falls	SD	57193	**800-923-3223**	605-335-5700
Modern Woodmen of America					
1701 First Ave	Rock Island	IL	61201	**800-447-9811**	
Motorists Insurance Group					
471 E Broad St	Columbus	OH	43215	**800-876-6642**	614-225-8211
Mutual Insurance Company of Arizona					
PO Box 33180	Phoenix	AZ	85067	**800-352-0402**	602-956-5276
Mutual of America Life Insurance Co					
320 Park Ave	New York	NY	10022	**800-468-3785**	212-224-1600
Mutual Trust Life Insurance Co					
1200 Jorie Blvd	Oak Brook	IL	60522	**800-323-7320**	
National Guardian Life Insurance Co (NGL)					
2 E Gilman St	Madison	WI	53703	**800-548-2962**	
National Mutual Benefit					
6522 Grand Teton Plz	Madison	WI	53719	**800-779-1936**	608-833-1936
National Western Life Insurance Co					
850 E Anderson Ln	Austin	TX	78752	**800-531-5442**	512-836-1010
NASDAQ: NWLI					
Nationwide Life & Annuity Insurance Co					
1 Nationwide Pl	Columbus	OH	43215	**800-882-2822**	855-473-6410
Nationwide Mutual Insurance Co					
1 Nationwide Plz	Columbus	OH	43215	**877-669-6877**	
New York Life Insurance & Annuity Corp					
51 Madison Ave	New York	NY	10010	**800-598-2019**	212-576-7000
North Carolina Mutual Life Insurance Co					
411 W Chapel Hill St	Durham	NC	27701	**800-626-1899**	
Old American Insurance Co					
3520 Broadway	Kansas City	MO	64111	**800-733-6242**	816-753-7000
OneAmerica Financial Partners Inc (PML)					
PO Box 368	Indianapolis	IN	46206	**800-249-6269**	317-285-1877
Oxford Life Insurance Co					
2721 N Central Ave	Phoenix	AZ	85004	**800-308-2318***	602-263-6666
*Cust Svc					
Pacific Guardian Life Insurance Company Ltd					
1440 Kapiolani Blvd Ste 1700	Honolulu	HI	96814	**800-367-5354**	808-955-2236
Pacific Life Insurance Co					
700 Newport Ctr Dr	Newport Beach	CA	92660	**800-800-7646**	949-219-3011
Pan-American Life Insurance Co					
601 Poydras St	New Orleans	LA	70130	**877-939-4550***	
*Life Ins					
Pekin Life Insurance Co					
2505 Ct St	Pekin	IL	61558	**800-322-0160**	
OTC: PKIN					
Penn Mutual 600 Dresher Rd	Horsham	PA	19044	**800-523-0650***	215-956-8000
*Cust Svc					
Penn Mutual Life Insurance Co					
600 Dresher Rd	Horsham	PA	19044	**800-523-0650***	215-956-8000
*Cust Svc					
Penn Treaty Network America Insurance Co					
3440 Lehigh St	Allentown	PA	18103	**800-362-0700**	
Physicians Mutual Insurance Co					
2600 Dodge St	Omaha	NE	68131	**800-228-9100**	402-633-1000
Property-Owners Insurance Co					
PO Box 30660	Lansing	MI	48909	**800-288-8740**	517-323-1200
Prudential Financial Inc					
751 Broad St	Newark	NJ	07102	**800-843-7625**	973-802-6000
NYSE: PRU					
RBC Insurance Services					
PO Box 789	Greenville	SC	29602	**800-551-8354**	864-609-8111
Reliable Life Insurance Co					
100 King St W PO Box 557	Hamilton	ON	L8N3K9	**800-465-0661**	905-523-5587
Reliance Standard Life Insurance					
2001 Market St Ste 1500	Philadelphia	PA	19103	**800-351-7500**	267-256-3500
SABRE Strategic Partners					
5025 Orbitor Dr Bldg 3 Ste 300	Mississauga	ON	L4W4Y5	**800-314-3346**	905-206-0900
Security Life Insurance Co of America					
10901 Red Cir Dr	Minnetonka	MN	55343	**800-328-4667**	717-397-2751
Security Mutual Life Insurance Co of New York					
100 Court St PO Box 1625	Binghamton	NY	13901	**800-927-8846**	800-346-7171
Security National Financial Corp (SNFC)					
5300 South 360 West	Salt Lake City	UT	84123	**800-574-7117**	801-264-1060
NASDAQ: SNFCA					

Classified Section

	Toll-Free	Phone

Settlers Life Insurance Co
1969 Lee Hwy . . . . Bristol VA 24201 800-523-2650 276-645-4300

Shenandoah Life Insurance Co
2301 Brambleton Ave . . . . Roanoke VA 24015 800-848-5433 540-985-4400

Standard Security Life Insurance Co of New York
485 Madison Ave 14th Fl . . . . New York NY 10022 800-477-0087 212-355-4141

State Life Insurance Co
1 American Sq PO Box 368 . . . . Indianapolis IN 46206 800-537-6442* 317-285-1877
*Cust Svc

Sun Life Assurance Company of Canada
1 Sun Life Executive Pk
PO Box 9106 . . . . Wellesley Hills MA 02481 800-786-5433 781-237-6030

Symetra Life Insurance Co
777 108th Ave NE Ste 1200 . . . . Bellevue WA 98004 800-574-0233 425-256-8000

Texas Life Insurance Co
900 Washington PO Box 830 . . . . Waco TX 76703 800-283-9233 254-752-6521

The Savings Bank Mutual Life Insurance Company of Massachusetts (SBLI)
1 Linscott Rd . . . . Woburn MA 01801 888-630-5000

Thrivent Financial for Lutherans
4321 N BallaRd Rd . . . . Appleton WI 54919 800-847-4836

Transamerica Occidental Life Insurance Co
1150 S Olive St . . . . Los Angeles CA 90015 800-852-4678* 213-742-2111
*Cust Svc

Trustmark Insurance Co
400 Field Dr . . . . Lake Forest IL 60045 888-246-9949 847-615-1500

United American Insurance Co
PO Box 8080 . . . . McKinney TX 75070 800-755-2137

United Heritage Life Insurance Co
PO Box 7777 . . . . Meridian ID 83680 800-657-6351 208-493-6100

United Insurance Holdings Corp
360 Central Ave Ste 900 . . . . Saint Petersburg FL 33701 800-861-4370 800-295-8016
NASDAQ: UIHC

United of Omaha Life Insurance Co
Mutual of Omaha Plz . . . . Omaha NE 68175 866-688-7957

United World Life Insurance Co
3300 Mutual of Omaha Plz . . . . Omaha NE 68175 866-688-7957

USAA Life Insurance Co (USAA)
9800 Fredericksburg Rd . . . . San Antonio TX 78288 800-531-8000 210-531-8722

Utica National Insurance Group
180 Genesee St . . . . New Hartford NY 13413 800-274-1914 315-734-2000

Variable Annuity Life Insurance Co (VALIC)
2929 Allen Pkwy . . . . Houston TX 77019 800-448-2542

Washington National Insurance Co
11825 N Pennsylvania St . . . . Carmel IN 46032 866-595-2255

Western & Southern Life Insurance Co
400 Broadway . . . . Cincinnati OH 45202 800-926-1993

Western Fraternal Life Assn (WFLA)
1900 First Ave NE . . . . Cedar Rapids IA 52402 877-935-2467 319-363-2653

Western United Life Assurance Co
929 W Sprague Ave PO Box 2290 . . . . Spokane WA 99210 800-247-2045* 509-835-2500
*General

William Penn Life Insurance Co of New York
100 Quentin Roosevelt Blvd . . . . Garden City NY 11530 800-346-4773

Woman's Life Insurance Society
1338 Military St PO Box 5020 . . . . Port Huron MI 48061 800-521-9292 810-985-5191

390-3 Medical & Hospitalization Insurance

Companies listed here provide managed care and/or traditional hospital and medical service plans to individuals and/or groups. Managed care companies typically offer plans as Health Maintenance Organizations (HMOs), Preferred Provider Organizations (PPOs), Exclusive Provider Organizations (EPOs), and/or Point of Service (POS) plans. Other types of hospital and medical service plans offered by companies listed here include indemnity plans and medical savings accounts.

	Toll-Free	Phone

AARP Services Inc
PO Box 1017 . . . . Montgomeryville PA 18936 800-523-5800

Aetna Inc
151 Farmington Ave . . . . Hartford CT 06156 800-872-3862 860-273-0123
NYSE: AET

AF & L Insurance Co
580 Virginia Dr Ste 330 . . . . Ft. Washington PA 19034 800-659-9206 215-918-0515

Alberta Blue Cross
10009 108th St NW . . . . Edmonton AB T5J3C5 800-661-6995 780-498-8000

American Specialty Health Plans
10221 Wateridge Cir . . . . San Diego CA 92121 800-848-3555

AMERIGROUP Corp
4425 Corporation Ln . . . . Virginia Beach VA 23462 800-600-4441 757-490-6900
NYSE: AGP

Anthem Blue Cross & Blue Shield
2015 Staples Mill Rd . . . . Richmond VA 23230 800-451-1527 855-636-6136

Anthem Blue Cross & Blue Shield Maine
2 Gannett Dr . . . . South Portland ME 04106 800-482-0966* 855-636-6136
*Cust Svc

Anthem Blue Cross & Blue Shield of Connecticut
370 Bassett Rd . . . . North Haven CT 06473 855-636-6136

Anthem Blue Cross & Blue Shield of Nevada
9133 W Russell Rd . . . . Las Vegas NV 89148 855-636-6136

Anthem Blue Cross Blue Shield Colorado
700 Broadway . . . . Denver CO 80273 877-833-5742 303-831-2131

Arkansas Blue Cross Blue Shield
PO Box 2181 . . . . Little Rock AR 72203 800-238-8379

AvMed 4300 NW 89th Blvd . . . . Gainesville FL 32606 800-346-0231 352-372-8400

Benecaid Health Benefit Solutions Inc
185 The W Mall Ste 800 . . . . Toronto ON M9C5L5 877-797-7448 416-626-8786

Blue Care Network of Michigan
20500 Civic Ctr Dr . . . . Southfield MI 48076 800-662-6667

Blue Cross & Blue Shield of Alabama
450 Riverchase Pkwy E . . . . Birmingham AL 35244 800-292-8868 205-988-2200

Blue Cross & Blue Shield of Kansas City
2301 Main St . . . . Kansas City MO 64108 800-892-6048 816-395-2222

Blue Cross & Blue Shield of Michigan
600 Lafayette Blvd E . . . . Detroit MI 48226 855-237-3501 313-225-9000

Blue Cross & Blue Shield of Mississippi
PO Box 1043 . . . . Jackson MS 39215 800-222-8046 601-932-3704

Blue Cross & Blue Shield of Montana
560 N Park Ave PO Box 4309 . . . . Helena MT 59604 800-447-7828 406-437-5000

Blue Cross & Blue Shield of Nebraska
1919 Aksarben Dr PO Box 3248 . . . . Omaha NE 68180 800-422-2763 402-982-7000

Blue Cross & Blue Shield of New Mexico
PO Box 27630 . . . . Albuquerque NM 87125 800-835-8699 505-291-3500

Blue Cross & Blue Shield of North Carolina
1965 Ivory Creek Blvd PO Box 2291 . . . . Durham NC 27707 800-446-8053* 919-489-7431
*Cust Svc

Blue Cross & Blue Shield of Oklahoma
1215 S Boulder Ave . . . . Tulsa OK 74119 800-942-5837* 918-560-3500
*Cust Svc

Blue Cross & Blue Shield of Rhode Island
500 Exchange St . . . . Providence RI 02903 800-637-3718 401-459-1000

Blue Cross & Blue Shield of Texas Inc
1001 E Lookout Dr . . . . Richardson TX 75082 800-521-2227 972-766-6900

Blue Cross & Blue Shield of Vermont
445 Industrial Ln . . . . Montpelier VT 05602 800-247-2583* 802-223-6131
*Cust Svc

Blue Cross Blue Shield of Arizona
2444 W Las Palmaritas Dr . . . . Phoenix AZ 85021 800-232-2345 602-864-4400

Blue Cross Blue Shield of Delaware
PO Box 1991 . . . . Wilmington DE 19899 800-572-4400 800-876-7639

Blue Cross Blue Shield of Georgia
3350 Peachtree Rd NE . . . . Atlanta GA 30326 800-441-2273* 404-842-8000
*Cust Svc

Blue Cross Blue Shield of Illinois
300 E Randolph St . . . . Chicago IL 60601 800-972-8382 312-653-6000

Blue Cross Blue Shield of Kansas
1133 SW Topeka Blvd . . . . Topeka KS 66629 800-432-0216 785-291-7000

Blue Cross Blue Shield of Louisiana
5525 Reitz Ave . . . . Baton Rouge LA 70898 800-599-2583 800-495-2583

Blue Cross Blue Shield of Massachusetts
401 Pk Dr . . . . Boston MA 02215 800-262-2583 617-246-5000

Blue Cross Blue Shield of North Dakota
4510 13th Ave S . . . . Fargo ND 58121 800-342-4718 701-282-1864

Blue Cross Blue Shield of Wyoming
4000 House Ave . . . . Cheyenne WY 82001 800-851-9145 307-634-1393

Blue Cross of California
2 Gannett Dr . . . . South Portland ME 04106 800-999-3643 855-636-6136

Blue Cross of Idaho
3000 E Pine Ave . . . . Meridian ID 83642 800-274-4018 208-345-4550

BlueCross BlueShield of Western New York
257 W Genesee St . . . . Buffalo NY 14202 800-888-0757 716-887-6900

Capital District Physicians' Health Plan
500 Patroon Creek Blvd . . . . Albany NY 12206 888-258-0477 518-641-3000

Capital Health Plan
PO Box 15349 . . . . Tallahassee FL 32317 800-390-1434 850-383-3333

Cdspi 155 Lesmill Rd . . . . Toronto ON M3B2T8 800-561-9401 416-296-9401

Centene Corp
7700 Forsyth Blvd . . . . Saint Louis MO 63105 800-293-0056* 314-725-4477
NYSE: CNC ■ *General

Chiropractic Health Plan of California
PO Box 190 . . . . Clayton CA 94517 800-995-2442

CIGNA Healthcare of North Carolina Inc
701 Corporate Ctr Dr . . . . Raleigh NC 27607 800-942-1654 888-521-5869

Community Care 218 W Sixth St . . . . Tulsa OK 74119 800-278-7563 918-594-5200

CompBenefits Corp
100 Mansell Ct E Ste 400 . . . . Roswell GA 30076 800-633-1262 770-552-7101

Comprehensive Health Services Inc (CHSI)
10701 Parkridge Blvd Ste 200 . . . . Reston VA 20191 800-638-8083 703-760-0700

ConnectiCare Inc
175 Scott Swamp Rd . . . . Farmington CT 06032 800-251-7722* 860-674-5700
*Cust Svc

Coventry Health Care Inc
6730-B Rockledge Dr Ste 700 . . . . Bethesda MD 20817 800-348-2922 301-581-0600

Coventry Health Care of Delaware Inc
750 Prides Crossing Ste 200 . . . . Newark DE 19713 800-833-7423

Coventry Health Care of Georgia Inc
1100 Cir 75 Pkwy Ste 1400 . . . . Atlanta GA 30339 800-470-2004 678-202-2100

Coventry Health Care of Iowa Inc
4320 114th St . . . . Urbandale IA 50322 800-470-6352 515-225-1234

Coventry Health Care of Kansas Inc
8320 Ward Pkwy . . . . Kansas City MO 64114 800-969-3343

Dakotacare
2600 W 49th St PO Box 7406 . . . . Sioux Falls SD 57117 800-325-5598 605-334-4000

Davis Vision Inc
711 Troy-Schenectady Rd . . . . Latham NY 12110 800-999-5431

Dean Health Insurance Inc
1277 Deming Way . . . . Madison WI 53717 800-279-1301

Delta Dental Insurance Company of Alaska
PO Box 1809 . . . . Alpharetta GA 30023 800-521-2651

Delta Dental of Arizona
PO Box 43026 . . . . Phoenix AZ 85080 800-352-6132

Delta Dental of Arkansas
1513 Country Club Rd . . . . Sherwood AR 72120 800-462-5410 501-835-3400

Delta Dental of Colorado
4582 S Ulster St Ste 800 . . . . Denver CO 80237 800-233-0860 303-741-9300

Delta Dental of Idaho
555 E Parkcenter Blvd PO Box 2870 . . . . Boise ID 83706 800-356-7586 208-489-3580

Delta Dental of Indiana
PO Box 30416 . . . . Lansing MI 48909 800-524-0149

Delta Dental of Iowa
9000 Northpark Dr . . . . Johnston IA 50131 800-544-0718* 515-331-4594
*Cust Svc

Delta Dental of Kansas
1619 N Waterfront Pkwy PO Box 789769 . . . . Wichita KS 67278 800-234-3375 316-264-4511

Delta Dental of Kentucky
10100 Linn Station Rd . . . . Louisville KY 40223 800-955-2030*
*Cust Svc

Delta Dental of Louisiana
PO Box 1803 . . . . Alpharetta GA 30023 800-422-4234

Delta Dental of Massachusetts
465 Medford St . . . . Boston MA 02129 800-872-0500*
*Cust Svc

Delta Dental of Michigan
PO Box 30416 . . . . Lansing MI 48909 800-524-0149

Delta Dental of Minnesota
PO Box 330 . . . . Minneapolis MN 55440 800-553-9536 651-406-5900

			Toll-Free	Phone
Delta Dental of Missouri				
PO Box 8690	Saint Louis MO	63126	**800-335-8266**	314-656-3000
Delta Dental of Montana				
PO Box 1803	Alpharetta GA	30023	**800-422-4234**	
Delta Dental of New Jersey				
1639 State Rt 10	Parsippany NJ	07054	**800-624-2633**	973-285-4000
Delta Dental of New Mexico				
2500 Louisiana Blvd NE Ste 600	Albuquerque NM	87110	**800-999-0963**	505-883-4777
Delta Dental of New York Inc				
1 Delta Dr	Mechanicsburg PA	17055	**800-932-0783**	
Delta Dental of North Carolina				
4242 Six Forks Rd Ste 970	Raleigh NC	27609	**800-587-9514**	919-424-1046
Delta Dental of Ohio				
PO Box 30416	Lansing MI	48909	**800-524-0149**	
Delta Dental of Oklahoma				
16 NW 63rd St	Oklahoma City OK	73116	**800-522-0188**	405-607-2100
Delta Dental of Pennsylvania				
1 Delta Dr	Mechanicsburg PA	17055	**800-932-0783**	
Delta Dental of Pennsylvania & Alpha Dental Programs Inc				
PO Box 2105	Mechanicsburg PA	17055	**800-932-0783**	
Delta Dental of Rhode Island				
10 Charles St	Providence RI	02904	**800-598-6684**	401-752-6000
Delta Dental of South Dakota				
720 N Euclid Ave PO Box 1157	Pierre SD	57501	**800-627-3961**	605-224-7345
Delta Dental of Tennessee				
240 Venture Cir	Nashville TN	37228	**800-223-3104***	
*Cust Svc				
Delta Dental of Virginia				
4818 Starkey Rd	Roanoke VA	24018	**800-237-6060**	540-989-8000
Delta Dental of West Virginia				
PO Box 2105	Mechanicsburg PA	17055	**800-932-0783**	
Delta Dental of Wisconsin				
2801 Hoover Rd PO Box 828	Stevens Point WI	54481	**800-236-3713**	715-344-6087
Delta Dental of Wyoming				
6234 Yellowstone Rd PO Box 29	Cheyenne WY	82009	**800-735-3379**	307-632-3313
EmblemHealth Co				
55 Water St	New York NY	10041	**800-447-8255**	646-447-5000
Excellus BlueCross BlueShield				
PO Box 22999	Rochester NY	14692	**800-278-1247**	585-454-1700
Excellus BlueCross BlueShield of Central New York				
333 Butternut Dr	Syracuse NY	13214	**800-633-6066**	315-671-6400
EyeMed Vision Care				
4000 Luxottica Pl	Mason OH	45040	**866-939-3633**	513-765-4321
Fallon Community Health Plan Inc				
10 Chestnut St	Worcester MA	01608	**800-333-2535**	508-799-2100
First Choice Health Plan				
600 University St Ste 1400	Seattle WA	98101	**800-467-5281**	
Foster Thomas Inc				
1788 Forest Dr	Annapolis MD	21401	**800-372-3626**	
Geisinger Health Plan				
100 N Academy Ave	Danville PA	17822	**800-447-4000**	570-271-8760
Great American Supplemental Benefits				
PO Box 26580	Austin TX	78755	**866-459-4272**	
Hanover Insurance Co				
440 Lincoln St	Worcester MA	01653	**800-853-0456**	508-855-1000
Harvard Pilgrim Health Care Inc				
93 Worcester St	Wellesley MA	02481	**888-888-4742**	617-509-1000
Hawaii Dental Service				
700 Bishop St Ste 700	Honolulu HI	96813	**800-232-2533**	808-521-1431
Hawaii Medical Service Assn				
818 Keeaumoku St	Honolulu HI	96814	**800-776-4672**	808-948-6111
Health Alliance Plan				
2850 W Grand Blvd	Detroit MI	48202	**800-422-4641**	313-872-8100
Health Tradition Health Plan				
1808 E Main St	Onalaska WI	54650	**800-545-8499**	608-781-9692
HealthPartners Inc				
PO Box 1309	Minneapolis MN	55440	**800-883-2177**	952-883-5000
Healthplex Inc				
333 Earl Ovington Blvd	Uniondale NY	11553	**800-468-0608***	516-542-2200
*Cust Svc				
Heritage Summit HealthCare of Florida Inc				
PO Box 2928	Lakeland FL	33806	**800-282-7644**	863-665-6629
Highmark Inc				
120 Fifth Ave Pl	Pittsburgh PA	15222	**800-992-0246**	412-544-7000
Humana Inc 500 W Main St	Louisville KY	40202	**800-486-2620**	502-580-1000
NYSE: HUM				
Humana Military Healthcare Services				
500 W Main St	Louisville KY	40202	**800-444-5445***	
*General				
Independence Blue Cross				
1901 Market St	Philadelphia PA	19103	**800-275-2583**	
Independent Health				
511 Farber Lakes Dr	Buffalo NY	14221	**800-247-1466**	716-631-3001
IOA Re Inc				
190 W Germantown Pk Ste 200	East Norriton PA	19401	**800-462-2300**	610-940-9000
Kaiser Foundation Health Plan Inc				
1 Kaiser Plz	Oakland CA	94612	**800-464-4000**	408-972-3000
Kaiser Permanente				
3495 Piedmont Rd NE 9 Piedmont Center	Atlanta GA	30305	**800-611-1811**	404-364-7000
Kaiser Permanente				
3600 Broadway	Oakland CA	94611	**800-464-4000**	510-752-1000
Kaiser Permanente Hawaii				
1292 Waianuenue Ave	Hilo HI	96720	**800-966-5955**	808-334-4400
Kaiser Permanente Northwest				
500 NE Multnomah St Ste 100	Portland OR	97232	**800-813-2000**	503-813-2000
LA Care Health Plan				
555 W Fifth St 29th Fl	Los Angeles CA	90013	**888-839-9909**	213-694-1250
MEDICA 401 Carlson Pkwy	Minnetonka MN	55305	**800-952-3455***	866-317-1169
*Cust Svc				
Medical Benefits Mutual Life Insurance Co				
1975 Tamarack Rd	Newark OH	43058	**800-423-3151**	740-522-8425
Medical Mutual of Ohio				
2060 E Ninth St	Cleveland OH	44115	**800-700-2583**	216-687-7000
MetLife Inc 200 Park Ave	New York NY	10166	**800-638-5433**	212-578-2211
NYSE: MET				
Molina Healthcare Inc				
200 Oceangate Ste 100	Long Beach CA	90802	**888-562-5442**	562-435-3666
NYSE: MOH				

			Toll-Free	Phone
MVP Health Care				
625 State St	Schenectady NY	12305	**800-777-4793**	518-370-4793
ODS Cos 601 SW Second Ave	Portland OR	97204	**888-221-0802**	503-228-6554
Oxford Health Plans LLC				
48 Monroe Tpke	Trumbull CT	06611	**800-444-6222**	203-459-9100
Paramount Health Care				
1901 Indian Wood Cir	Maumee OH	43537	**800-462-3589**	419-887-2525
Physicians Plus Insurance Corp				
2650 Novation Pkwy	Madison WI	53713	**800-545-5015**	608-282-8900
Preferred CommunityChoice PPO				
218 W Sixth St	Tulsa OK	74119	**800-884-4776**	918-594-5200
Premera Blue Cross Blue				
7001 220th St SW Bldg 1	Mountlake Terrace WA	98043	**855-629-0987***	
*Cust Svc				
Priority Health				
1231 E Beltline NE	Grand Rapids MI	49525	**800-942-0954**	616-942-0954
Regence Blue Cross Blue Shield of Oregon				
PO Box 1071	Portland OR	97207	**888-734-3623**	888-675-6570
Regence BlueCross BlueShield of Utah				
2890 E Cottonwood Pkwy	Salt Lake City UT	84121	**800-624-6519***	888-367-2119
*Cust Svc				
Rocky Mountain Health Plans				
2775 Crossroads Blvd				
PO Box 10600	Grand Junction CO	81502	**800-843-0719**	
SafeGuard Health Enterprises Inc				
95 Enterprise Ste 100	Aliso Viejo CA	92656	**800-880-1800**	949-425-4300
Sagamore Health Network				
11555 N Meridian St Ste 600	Carmel IN	46032	**800-364-3469**	317-573-2886
Scott & White Health Plan				
2401 S 31st St	Temple TX	76508	**800-321-7947**	254-298-3000
Sharp Health Plan				
4305 University Ave Ste 200	San Diego CA	92105	**800-359-2002**	619-228-2300
Spectera Inc				
6220 Old Dobbin Ln Liberty 6 Ste 200	Columbia MD	21045	**800-638-3120**	
Trillium Community Health Plan Inc				
1800 Millrace Dr	Eugene OR	97403	**877-600-5472**	541-485-2155
Tufts Associated Health Plans				
705 Mt Auburn St	Watertown MA	02472	**800-462-0224**	617-972-9400
Union Pacific Railroad Employees' Health Systems				
1040 North 2200 West	Salt Lake City UT	84116	**800-547-0421**	801-595-4300
UnitedHealth Group Inc				
9900 Bren Rd E	Minnetonka MN	55343	**800-328-5979**	952-936-1300
NYSE: UNH				
Unity Health Insurance				
840 Carolina St	Sauk City WI	53583	**800-362-3308**	608-644-3430
Univera Healthcare				
205 Pk Club Ln	Buffalo NY	14221	**877-883-9577**	716-847-1480
Washington Dental Service				
9706 Fourth Ave NE	Seattle WA	98115	**800-367-4104**	206-522-1300
WellCare 8735 Henderson Rd	Tampa FL	33634	**800-960-2530**	813-290-6208
WellCare Health Plans Inc				
PO Box 31372	Tampa FL	33631	**866-530-9491**	

390-4 Property & Casualty Insurance

			Toll-Free	Phone
Accident Fund Co				
232 S Capitol Ave PO Box 40790	Lansing MI	48901	**888-276-0327***	517-342-4200
*Mktg				
Acuity Insurance				
2800 S Taylor Dr	Sheboygan WI	53081	**800-242-7666**	
Aegis Security Insurance Co				
4507 N Front St Ste 200	Harrisburg PA	17110	**800-233-2160**	
Agricultural Workers Mutual Auto Insurance Co				
PO Box 88	Fort Worth TX	76101	**800-772-7424**	817-831-9900
ALLIED Group Inc				
1100 Locust St	Des Moines IA	50391	**800-532-1436**	
Allied Insurance				
1100 Locust St	Des Moines IA	50391	**800-532-1436**	
American Commerce Insurance Co				
3590 Twin Creeks Dr	Columbus OH	43204	**800-848-2945**	614-308-3366
American Family Mutual Insurance Co				
6000 American Pkwy	Madison WI	53783	**800-374-0008***	800-692-6326
*Cust Svc				
American Modern Home Insurance Co				
PO Box 5323	Cincinnati OH	45201	**800-543-2644**	513-943-7200
American National Property & Casualty Co				
1949 E Sunshine St	Springfield MO	65899	**800-333-2860**	417-887-0220
American Southern Insurance Co				
3715 Northside Pkwy NW				
Bldg 400 Ste 800	Atlanta GA	30327	**800-241-1172**	404-266-9599
AMERISAFE Inc				
2301 Hwy 190 W	DeRidder LA	70634	**800-256-9052**	337-463-9052
NASDAQ: AMSF				
Amerisure Insurance Co				
26777 Halsted Rd	Farmington Hills MI	48331	**800-257-1900**	248-615-9000
Amica Mutual Insurance Co				
100 Amica Way	Lincoln RI	02865	**800-652-6422**	
Arbella Insuranc				
1100 Crown Colony Dr PO Box 699103	Quincy MA	02269	**800-972-5348**	617-328-2800
Armed Forces Insurance Exchange (AFI)				
550 Eisenhower Rd	Leavenworth KS	66048	**800-255-6792**	
Arrowpoint Capital				
3600 Arco Corporate Dr Ste 100	Charlotte NC	28273	**866-236-7750**	704-522-2000
Associated Industries Of Massachusetts Mutual Insurance Com				
PO Box 4070	Burlington MA	01803	**866-270-3354**	781-221-1600
AssuranceAmerica Corp				
5500 I- N Pkwy Ste 600	Atlanta GA	30328	**800-450-7857**	770-952-0200
Auto-Owners Insurance Co				
6101 Anacapri Blvd	Lansing MI	48917	**800-346-0346**	517-323-1200
Avemco Insurance Co				
8490 Progress Dr Ste 100	Frederick MD	21701	**888-241-7891**	
Baldwin & Lyons Inc				
111 Congressional Blvd Ste 500	Carmel IN	46032	**800-644-5501**	317-636-9800
NASDAQ: BWINB				
Berkshire Hathaway Homestates Cos (BHHC)				
PO Box 2048	Omaha NE	68103	**888-495-8949**	

	City	State	ZIP	Toll-Free	Phone
BITCO Insurance Cos					
3700 Market Square Cir	Davenport	IA	52807	**800-475-4477**	
Brotherhood Mutual Insurance Co (BMI)					
6400 Brotherhood Way	Fort Wayne	IN	46825	**800-333-3735***	
*Cust Svc					
Canada Life Assurance Co, The					
330 University Ave	Toronto	ON	M5G1R8	**888-252-1847**	416-597-1456
Capitol Indemnity Corp					
1600 Aspen Commons	Middleton	WI	53562	**800-475-4450**	608-829-4200
CAPSPECIALTY					
1600 Aspen Commons Ste 300	Middleton	WI	53562	**800-475-4450**	608-829-4200
Carolina Casualty Insurance Co					
5011 Gate Pkwy Ste 200	Jacksonville	FL	32256	**800-874-8053**	904-363-0900
Central Insurance Cos					
800 S Washington St	Van Wert	OH	45891	**800-736-7000**	419-238-1010
Century-National Insurance Co					
16650 Sherman Way	Van Nuys	CA	91406	**800-733-0880***	
*Cust Svc					
Chubb & Son					
15 Mountain View Rd	Warren	NJ	07059	**800-252-4670**	908-903-2000
Church Mutual Insurance Co					
3000 Schuster Ln	Merrill	WI	54452	**800-554-2642**	715-536-5577
Civil Service Employees Insurance Co					
2121 N California Blvd Ste 900	Walnut Creek	CA	94596	**800-282-6848**	
Colorado Farm Bureau Mutual Insurance Co					
PO Box 5647	Denver	CO	80217	**800-315-5998**	303-749-7500
Concord Group Insurance Cos					
4 Bouton St	Concord	NH	03301	**800-852-3380**	
Continental Casualty Co					
333 S Wabash Ave	Chicago	IL	60604	**800-262-2000**	312-822-5000
Continental Western Group					
11201 Douglas Ave	Urbandale	IA	50322	**800-235-2942**	515-473-3000
Cornhusker Casualty Co					
PO Box 2048	Omaha	NE	68103	**888-495-8949**	
Country Mutual Insurance Co					
1701 Towanda Ave	Bloomington	IL	61701	**888-211-2555***	866-268-6879
*Cust Svc					
Crum & Forster Insurance Inc					
305 Madison Ave PO Box 1973	Morristown	NJ	07962	**800-690-5520**	973-490-6600
Cumberland Insurance Group					
633 Shiloh Pk	Bridgeton	NJ	08302	**800-232-6992**	
Donegal Mutual Insurance Co					
1195 River Rd PO Box 302	Marietta	PA	17547	**800-877-0600**	
Economical Insurance					
111 Westmount Rd S PO Box 2000	Waterloo	ON	N2J4S4	**800-265-2180**	519-570-8200
Erie Indemnity Co					
Erie Insurance Group					
100 Erie Insurance Pl	Erie	PA	16530	**800-458-0811**	814-870-2000
NASDAQ: ERIE					
Erie Insurance Exchange					
100 Erie Insurance Pl	Erie	PA	16530	**800-458-0811**	814-870-2000
Erie Insurance Property & Casualty Co					
100 Erie Insurance Pl	Erie	PA	16530	**800-458-0811**	814-870-2000
Everest Reinsurance Co					
477 Martinsville Rd	Liberty Corner	NJ	07938	**800-269-6660**	908-604-3000
Farm Family Casualty Insurance Co					
PO Box 656	Albany	NY	12201	**800-843-3276**	518-431-5000
Farmers Alliance Mutual Insurance Co					
1122 N Main PO Box 1401	McPherson	KS	67460	**800-362-1075**	620-241-2200
Farmers Insurance Exchange					
6301 Owensmouth Ave	Woodland Hills	CA	91367	**855-808-6599**	800-493-4917
Farmers Mutual Hail Insurance Company of Iowa					
6785 Westown Pkwy	West Des Moines	IA	50266	**800-247-5248**	
Farmers Mutual Insurance Company of Nebraska					
501 S 13th St PO Box 81529	Lincoln	NE	68501	**800-742-7433**	402-434-8300
FCCI Insurance Group					
6300 University Pkwy	Sarasota	FL	34240	**800-226-3224**	941-907-3224
Federated Mutual Insurance Co					
121 E Pk Sq PO Box 328	Owatonna	MN	55060	**800-533-0472**	507-455-5200
First Insurance Company of Hawaii Ltd					
1100 Ward Ave PO Box 2866	Honolulu	HI	96803	**800-272-5202**	808-527-7777
Florida Family Insurance					
27599 Riverview Ctr Blvd Ste 100	Bonita Springs	FL	34134	**888-850-4663**	888-486-4663
Florida Farm Bureau Insurance Cos					
5700 SW 34th St	Gainesville	FL	32608	**866-275-7322**	352-378-1321
FM Global					
270 Central Ave PO Box 7500	Johnston	RI	02919	**800-343-7722**	401-275-3000
Foremost Insurance Co					
5600 Beech Tree Ln	Caledonia	MI	49316	**800-532-4221**	
Frankenmuth Insurance					
1 Mutual Ave	Frankenmuth	MI	48787	**800-234-4433**	989-652-6121
Franklin Mutual Insurance Co					
5 Broad St	Branchville	NJ	07826	**800-842-0551**	973-948-3120
General Star National Insurance Co					
120 Long Ridge Rd PO Box 10354	Stamford	CT	06902	**800-624-5237**	203-328-5000
Germania Farm Mutual Insurance Assn					
507 Hwy 290 E	Brenham	TX	77833	**800-392-2202**	979-836-5224
Golden Eagle Insurance					
9145 Miller Rd	Johnstown	OH	43031	**800-461-9224**	
Grain Dealers Mutual Insurance Co					
6201 Corporate Dr	Indianapolis	IN	46278	**800-428-7081**	317-388-4500
Grange Mutual Casualty Co					
671 S High St	Columbus	OH	43206	**800-422-0550**	
Great West Casualty Co					
1100 W 29th St PO Box 277	South Sioux City	NE	68776	**800-228-8602**	402-494-2411
Grinnell Mutual Reinsurance Co					
4215 Hwy 146 PO Box 790	Grinnell	IA	50112	**800-362-2041**	641-269-8000
GuideOne Mutual Insurance Co					
1111 Ashworth Rd	West Des Moines	IA	50265	**877-448-4331**	844-948-4968
Hagerty Insurance Agency LLC					
141 River's Edge Dr Ste 200 PO Box 1303	Traverse City	MI	49684	**877-922-9701**	800-922-4050
Hanover Insurance Co					
440 Lincoln St	Worcester	MA	01653	**800-853-0456**	508-855-1000
Hartford Casualty Insurance Co					
690 Asylum Ave	Hartford	CT	06155	**800-243-5860**	860-547-5000
Hingham Mutual Fire Insurance Co					
230 Beal St	Hingham	MA	02043	**800-341-8200**	781-749-0841
Hortica Insurance					
1 Horticultural Ln PO Box 428	Edwardsville	IL	62025	**800-851-7740**	618-656-4240
ICW Group					
11455 El Camino Real	San Diego	CA	92130	**800-877-1111**	858-350-2400
IMT Group, The					
PO Box 1336	Des Moines	IA	50266	**800-274-3531**	
Injured Workers Insurance Fund					
8722 Loch Raven Blvd	Towson	MD	21286	**800-264-4943**	410-494-2000
Insurance Company of the West					
11455 El Camino Real	San Diego	CA	92130	**800-877-1111**	858-350-2400
Lititz Mutual Insurance Co					
2 N Broad St PO Box 900	Lititz	PA	17543	**800-626-4751**	717-626-4751
Lumbermen's Underwriting Alliance (LUA)					
1905 NW Corporate Blvd Ste 110	Boca Raton	FL	33431	**800-327-0630**	561-994-1900
Main Street America Group, The					
4601 Touchton Rd E Ste 3400	Jacksonville	FL	32246	**800-258-5310**	877-425-2467
MAPFRE Insurance					
211 Main St	Webster	MA	01570	**800-221-1605**	508-943-9000
MAPFRE Insurance					
211 Main St	Webster	MA	01570	**800-922-8276**	
Markel Corp					
4521 Highwoods Pkwy	Glen Allen	VA	23060	**800-446-6671**	
Markel Specialty Commercial					
4600 Cox Rd	Glen Allen	VA	23060	**800-416-4364**	800-446-6671
Merchants Insurance Group					
250 Main St	Buffalo	NY	14202	**800-462-1077**	
Mercury Insurance Group					
4484 Wilshire Blvd	Los Angeles	CA	90010	**800-956-3728**	323-937-1060
NYSE: MCY					
Michigan Millers Mutual Insurance Co					
2425 E Grand River Ave PO Box 30060	Lansing	MI	48912	**800-888-1914**	
Mid-Continent Group					
1437 S Boulder Ave W PO Box 1409	Tulsa	OK	74119	**800-722-4994**	918-587-7221
Middlesex Mutual Assurance Co					
213 Ct St PO Box 891	Middletown	CT	06457	**800-622-3780**	
Midwest Employers Casualty Co					
14755 N Outer 40 Dr Ste 300	Chesterfield	MO	63017	**877-975-2667**	636-449-7000
Mutual of Enumclaw Insurance Co					
1460 Wells St	Enumclaw	WA	98022	**800-366-5551**	360-825-2591
National Fire & Marine Insurance Co					
3024 Harney St	Omaha	NE	68131	**866-720-7861**	402-916-3000
National Grange Mutual Insurance Co					
55 W St	Keene	NH	03431	**800-258-5310**	603-352-4000
National Indemnity Co					
1314 Douglas St Ste 1400	Omaha	NE	68102	**866-720-7861**	402-916-3000
National Interstate Corp					
3250 I- Dr	Richfield	OH	44286	**800-929-1500**	330-659-8900
NASDAQ: NATL					
Nationwide Mutual Fire Insurance Co					
1 Nationwide Plz	Columbus	OH	43215	**877-669-6877**	800-882-2822
Nautilus Insurance Group LLC					
7233 E Butherus Dr	Scottsdale	AZ	85260	**800-842-8972**	480-951-0905
New Mexico Mutual					
PO Box 27825	Albuquerque	NM	87125	**800-788-8851**	505-345-7260
New York Central Mutual Fire Insurance Co (NYCM)					
1899 Central Plz E	Edmeston	NY	13335	**800-234-6926**	
North American Specialty Insurance Co					
650 Elm St 6th Fl	Manchester	NH	03101	**800-542-9200**	603-644-6600
North Carolina Farm Bureau Mutual Insurance Co (NCFBMIC)					
PO Box 27427	Raleigh	NC	27611	**800-584-1143**	919-782-1705
Northern Security Insurance Co					
PO Box 188	Montpelier	VT	05601	**800-451-5000**	802-223-2341
Northland Insurance Co					
385 Washington St	Saint Paul	MN	55102	**800-237-9334**	
Northwestern Pacific Indemnity Co					
15 Mtn View Rd	Warren	NJ	07059	**800-252-4670***	908-903-2000
*Claims					
Odyssey Re Holdings Corp					
300 First Stamford Pl	Stamford	CT	06902	**866-745-4440**	203-977-8000
Ohio Casualty					
9450 SewaRd Rd	Fairfield	OH	45014	**800-843-6446**	
Ohio Indemnity Co					
250 E Broad St 7th Fl	Columbus	OH	43215	**800-628-8581**	
OneBeacon Insurance Group					
605 Hwy 169 N Ste 800	Plymouth	MN	55441	**800-662-0156**	781-332-7000
Oregon Mutual Insurance Co					
PO Box 808	McMinnville	OR	97128	**800-888-2141**	503-472-2141
Pacific Specialty Insurance Co					
3601 Haven Ave	Menlo Park	CA	94025	**800-962-1172**	
Pekin Insurance (FAIA)					
2505 Court St	Pekin	IL	61558	**800-322-0160**	309-346-1161
Penn National Insurance Co					
2 N Second St PO Box 2361	Harrisburg	PA	17101	**800-388-4764**	717-234-4941
Pennsylvania Manufacturers Assn Co					
380 Sentry Pkwy	Blue Bell	PA	19422	**800-222-2749**	
Pharmacists Mutual Insurance Co					
808 US Hwy 18 West PO Box 370	Algona	IA	50511	**800-247-5930***	
*General					
Philadelphia Consolidated Holding Corp					
231 Saint Asaph's Rd Ste 100	Bala Cynwyd	PA	19004	**888-647-8639**	610-617-7900
Philadelphia Contributionship Insurance Co					
212 S Fourth St	Philadelphia	PA	19106	**888-627-1752***	215-627-1752
*Cust Svc					
Pinnacol Assurance					
7501 E Lowry Blvd	Denver	CO	80230	**800-873-7242**	303-361-4000
Preferred Employers Insurance Co					
PO Box 85478	San Diego	CA	92186	**888-472-9001***	866-472-9602
*Cust Svc					
Preferred Mutual Insurance Co					
1 Preferred Way	New Berlin	NY	13411	**800-333-7642**	607-847-6161
Princeton Excess & Surplus Lines Insurance Co					
555 College Rd E	Princeton	NJ	08543	**800-544-2378**	609-243-4200
Princeton Insurance Co					
746 Alexander Rd PO Box 5322	Princeton	NJ	08540	**800-334-0588**	609-452-9404
Progressive Corp, The					
6300 Wilson Mills Rd PO Box W33	Mayfield Village	OH	44143	**888-806-9598**	440-461-5000
Providence Mutual Fire Insurance Co					
340 E Ave	Warwick	RI	02886	**877-763-1800**	401-827-1800

Company	Address	City	State	ZIP	Toll-Free	Phone
Prudential Financial Inc	751 Broad St	Newark	NJ	07102	**800-843-7625**	973-802-6000
	NYSE: PRU					
QBE Farmers Union Insurance	5619 DTC Pkwy Ste 300	Greenwood Village	CO	80111	**800-347-1961**	303-337-5500
QBE Holdings Inc	Wall St Plz 88 Pine St	New York	NY	10005	**800-362-5448**	212-422-1212
Quincy Mutual Fire Insurance Co	57 Washington St	Quincy	MA	02169	**800-899-1116**	
Republic Western Insurance Co	2721 N Central Ave	Phoenix	AZ	85004	**800-528-7134***	
	*Claims					
RLI Insurance Co	9025 N Lindbergh Dr	Peoria	IL	61615	**800-331-4929**	309-692-1000
Royal & SunAlliance Insurance Co of Canada (RSA)	18 York St Ste 800	Toronto	ON	M5J2T8	**800-268-8406**	416-366-7511
RTW Inc	PO Box 390327	Minneapolis	MN	55439	**800-789-2242***	952-893-0403
	*Sales					
Rural Mutual Insurance Company Inc	1241 John Q Hammons Dr	Madison	WI	53717	**800-362-7881**	608-836-5525
Safe Auto Insurance Co	4 Easton Oval PO Box 182109	Columbus	OH	43219	**800-723-3288**	614-231-0200
Safeway Insurance Group	790 Pasquinelli Dr	Westmont	IL	60559	**800-273-0300**	630-887-8300
Sagamore Insurance Co	111 Congressional Blvd Ste 500	Carmel	IN	46032	**800-317-9402**	
Savers Property & Casualty Insurance Co	11880 College Blvd Ste 500	Overland Park	KS	66210	**800-825-9489**	913-339-5000
Scott Insurance	1301 Old Graves Mill Rd	Lynchburg	VA	24502	**800-365-0101**	434-832-2100
Secura Insurance Cos	PO Box 819	Appleton	WI	54912	**800-558-3405**	920-739-3161
Sentry Insurance A Mutual Co	1800 N Point Dr PO Box 8032	Stevens Point	WI	54481	**800-473-6879**	
Sentry Insurance Co	2 Technology Park Dr	Westford	MA	01886	**800-373-6879**	978-392-7119
SS Nesbitt & Co Inc	3500 Blue Lake Dr	Birmingham	AL	35243	**800-422-3223**	205-262-2700
State Auto Property & Casualty Insurance Co	518 E Broad St	Columbus	OH	43215	**800-444-9950**	614-464-5000
State Compensation Insurance Fund	333 Bush St	San Francisco	CA	94104	**866-721-3498**	
State Farm Fire & Casualty Co	1 State Farm Plz	Bloomington	IL	61710	**800-782-8332**	
State Farm Insurance	333 First Commerce Dr	Aurora	ON	L4G8A4	**877-659-1570**	
Texas Mutual Insurance Co	6210 E Hwy 290	Austin	TX	78723	**888-532-5246**	512-224-3800
Tokio Marine America	1221 Ave Ste 1500	New York	NY	10020	**800-628-2796**	212-297-6600
Topa Insurance Corp	24025 Park Sorrento Ste 300	Calabasas	CA	91302	**877-353-8672**	310-201-0451
UFG	118 Second Ave SE PO Box 73909	Cedar Rapids	IA	52407	**800-895-6253**	319-399-5700
	NASDAQ: UFCS					
ULLICO Casualty Co	1625 I St NW	Washington	DC	20006	**800-431-5425**	
Unico American Corp	23251 Mulholland Dr	Woodland Hills	CA	91364	**800-669-9800**	
Union Standard Insurance Co	122 W Carpenter Fwy Ste 350	Irving	TX	75039	**800-444-0049**	972-719-2400
United Heartland Inc	PO Box 3026	Milwaukee	WI	53201	**866-206-5851**	
United National Group	3 Bala Plz E Ste 300	Bala Cynwyd	PA	19004	**800-333-0352**	610-664-1500
United National Insurance Co	3 Bala Plz E Ste 300	Bala Cynwyd	PA	19004	**800-333-0352**	610-664-1500
Universal Insurance Holding Inc (UIH)	1110 W Commerical Blvd Ste 100	Fort Lauderdale	FL	33309	**800-509-5586**	
	NYSE: UVE					
USA Workers Injury Network	1250 S Capital of Texas Hwy Bldg 3 Ste 500	Austin	TX	78746	**800-872-0020***	
	*Cust Svc					
USAA Property & Casualty Insurance Group	9800 Fredericksburg Rd	San Antonio	TX	78288	**800-531-8722**	210-531-8722
Utica First Insurance Co	5981 Airport Rd	Oriskany	NY	13424	**800-456-4556**	315-736-8211
Utica National Insurance Group	180 Genesee St	New Hartford	NY	13413	**800-274-1914**	315-734-2000
Vermont Mutual Insurance Co	89 State St PO Box 188	Montpelier	VT	05601	**800-451-5000**	802-223-2341
West Bend Mutual Insurance Co	1900 S 18th Ave	West Bend	WI	53095	**800-236-5010**	262-334-5571
Western National Mutual Insurance Co	5350 W 78th St	Edina	MN	55439	**800-862-6070**	952-835-5350
Western Reserve Group, The	1685 Cleveland Rd PO Box 36	Wooster	OH	44691	**800-362-0426**	
Wisconsin Reinsurance Corp	2810 City View Dr	Madison	WI	53707	**800-939-9473**	608-242-4500
Zenith Insurance Co	PO Box 9055	Van Nuys	CA	91409	**800-440-5020**	818-713-1000

390-5 Surety Insurance

Company	Address	City	State	ZIP	Toll-Free	Phone
AMBAC Assurance Corp	1 State St Plz	New York	NY	10004	**800-221-1854**	212-658-7470
American Public Life Insurance Co	2305 Lakeland Dr PO Box 925	Jackson	MS	39205	**800-256-8606**	601-936-6600
Bond Pro LLC	302 Knights Run Ave Ste 1160	Tampa	FL	33602	**888-789-4985**	813-413-7576
Catholic Mutual Group	10843 Old Mill Rd	Omaha	NE	68154	**800-228-6108**	402-551-8765
Central Insurance Cos	800 S Washington St	Van Wert	OH	45891	**800-736-7000**	419-238-1010
Century Insurance Group	550 Polaris Pkwy Ste 300	Westerville	OH	43082	**877-855-8462**	614-895-2000
Chubb Specialty Insurance	82 Hopmeadow St	Simsbury	CT	06070	**800-252-4670**	860-408-2000
Connecticut Medical Insurance Co (CMIC)	80 Glastonbury Blvd 3rd Fl	Glastonbury	CT	06033	**800-228-0287**	860-633-7788
Copic Insurance Co	7351 Lowry Blvd	Denver	CO	80230	**800-421-1834**	720-858-6000
Dentists Insurance Co, The	1201 K St 17th Fl	Sacramento	CA	95814	**800-733-0633**	
Doctors' Co, The	185 Greenwood Rd	Napa	CA	94558	**800-421-2368**	
Euler Hermes ACI	800 Red Brook Blvd	Baltimore	MD	21117	**877-883-3224**	410-753-0753
Everest Reinsurance Co	477 Martinsville Rd	Liberty Corner	NJ	07938	**800-269-6660**	908-604-3000
Federated Mutual Insurance Co	121 E Pk Sq PO Box 328	Owatonna	MN	55060	**800-533-0472**	507-455-5200
Financial Guaranty Insurance Co	463 Seventh Ave	New York	NY	10018	**800-352-0001**	212-312-3000
First Insurance Company of Hawaii Ltd	1100 Ward Ave PO Box 2866	Honolulu	HI	96803	**800-272-5202**	808-527-7777
Illinois State Medical Inter-Insurance Exchange (ISMIE)	20 N Michigan Ave Ste 700	Chicago	IL	60602	**800-782-4767**	312-782-2749
Insurance Company of the West	11455 El Camino Real	San Diego	CA	92130	**800-877-1111**	858-350-2400
International Fidelity Insurance Co (IFIC)	1 Newark Ctr 1111 Raymond Blvd 20th Fl	Newark	NJ	07102	**800-333-4167**	
KAMMCO (KAMMCO)	623 SW Tenth Ave	Topeka	KS	66612	**800-232-2259**	785-232-2224
Life of the South Insurance Co	10151 Deerwood Pk Blvd Bldg 100	Jacksonville	FL	32256	**800-888-2738**	904-350-9660
Louisiana Medical Mutual Insurance Co	1 Galleria Blvd Ste 700	Metairie	LA	70001	**800-452-2120**	
Media/Professional Insurance Inc	1201 Walnut Ste 1800	Kansas City	MO	64106	**866-282-0565**	816-471-6118
Medical Assurance Inc	100 Brookwood Pl Ste 300	Birmingham	AL	35209	**800-282-6242***	205-877-4400
	*Cust Svc					
Medical Mutual Group	700 Spring Forest Rd	Raleigh	NC	27609	**800-662-7917**	919-872-7117
Medical Mutual Insurance Company of Maine	1 City Ctr PO Box 15275	Portland	ME	04112	**800-942-2791**	207-775-2791
Medical Mutual Liability Insurance Society of Maryland	225 International Cir PO Box 8016	Hunt Valley	MD	21030	**800-492-0193**	410-785-0050
Medical Protective Co	5814 Reed Rd	Fort Wayne	IN	46835	**800-463-3776**	260-485-9622
Mortgage Guaranty Insurance Corp	270 E Kilbourn Ave	Milwaukee	WI	53202	**800-558-9900**	414-347-6480
NCMIC Insurance Co	14001 University Ave	Clive	IA	50325	**800-769-2000**	800-247-8043
Norcal Mutual Insurance Company Inc	575 Market St Ste 1000	San Francisco	CA	94105	**800-652-1051**	855-882-3412
Old Republic Insured Automotive Services Inc	8282 S Memorial Dr	Tulsa	OK	74133	**800-331-3780**	
Old Republic Surety	445 S Moorlands Rd Ste 200	Brookfield	WI	53005	**800-217-1792**	262-797-2640
Pekin Life Insurance Co	2505 Ct St	Pekin	IL	61558	**800-322-0160**	
	OTC: PKIN					
Penn National Insurance Co	2 N Second St PO Box 2361	Harrisburg	PA	17101	**800-388-4764**	717-234-4941
Pennsylvania Medical Society (PAMED)	777 E Park Dr PO Box 8820	Harrisburg	PA	17105	**800-228-7823**	717-558-7750
Podiatry Insurance Company of America	3000 Meridian Blvd Ste 400	Franklin	TN	37067	**800-251-5727**	615-984-2005
Princeton Insurance Co	746 Alexander Rd PO Box 5322	Princeton	NJ	08540	**800-334-0588**	609-452-9404
Protective Insurance Co	111 Congressional Blvd Ste 500	Carmel	IN	46032	**800-644-5501**	
Radian Group Inc	1500 Market St	Philadelphia	PA	19102	**800-523-1988**	
Republic Mortgage Insurance Co	101 N Cherry St Ste 101	Winston-Salem	NC	27101	**800-999-7642**	
RLI Insurance Co	9025 N Lindbergh Dr	Peoria	IL	61615	**800-331-4929**	309-692-1000
State Volunteer Mutual Insurance Co (SVMIC)	101 W Pk Dr Ste 300	Brentwood	TN	37027	**800-342-2239**	615-377-1999
Surety Group Inc	12890 Lebanon Rd	Mt. Juliet	TN	37122	**800-486-8211**	844-432-6637
Texas Hospital Insurance Exchange	8310 N Capital of Texas Hwy Ste 250	Austin	TX	78731	**800-792-0060**	512-451-5775
Texas Lawyers Insurance Exchange (TLIE)	1801 S MoPac Ste 300	Austin	TX	78746	**800-252-9332**	512-480-9074
Transamerica	4333 Edgewood Rd NE	Cedar Rapids	IA	52499	**800-852-4678**	319-355-8511
Triad Guaranty Insurance Corp	101 S Stratford Rd	Winston-Salem	NC	27104	**888-691-8074***	336-723-1282
	*Cust Svc					
ULLICO Casualty Co	1625 I St NW	Washington	DC	20006	**800-431-5425**	
United Guaranty Corp (UGC)	230 N Elm St	Greensboro	NC	27401	**877-642-4642**	
United National Group	3 Bala Plz E Ste 300	Bala Cynwyd	PA	19004	**800-333-0352**	610-664-1500
Utica National Insurance Group	180 Genesee St	New Hartford	NY	13413	**800-274-1914**	315-734-2000
Vision Financial Corp	PO Box 506	Keene	NH	03431	**800-793-0223**	
Warranty Group Inc, The	175 W Jackson 11th Fl	Chicago	IL	60604	**800-621-2130**	312-356-3000
Zurich American Insurance Co	1299 Zurich Way	Schaumburg	IL	60196	**800-382-2150**	

		Toll-Free	Phone

390-6 Title Insurance

Most title insurance companies also provide other real estate services such as escrow, flood certification, appraisals, etc.

			Toll-Free	Phone
Attorney's Title Insurance Fund Inc				
6545 Corporate Ctr Blvd	Orlando FL	32822	800-336-3863	407-240-3863
Chicago Title & Trust Co				
171 N Clark St	Chicago IL	60601	800-621-1919	312-223-2000
Commonwealth Land Title Insurance Co				
601 Riverside Ave	Jacksonville FL	32204	888-866-3684	
Entitle Direct Group Inc				
200 Marshall Dr	Pittsburgh PA	15108	877-936-8485	
Fidelity National Title Group Inc				
601 Riverside Ave	Jacksonville FL	32204	888-866-3684	904-854-8100
Fidelity National Title Insurance Co				
601 Riverside Ave	Jacksonville FL	32204	888-866-3684	
First American Corp				
1 First American Way	Santa Ana CA	92707	800-854-3643	714-250-3000
NYSE: FAF				
Hanover Insurance Co				
440 Lincoln St	Worcester MA	01653	800-853-0456	508-855-1000
Meridian Title Corp				
202 S Michigan St	South Bend IN	46601	800-777-1574	
Mississippi Valley Title Services Co				
1022 Highland Colony Pkwy Ste 200	Ridgeland MS	39157	800-647-2124	601-969-0222
Monroe Title Insurance Corp				
47 W Main St	Rochester NY	14614	800-966-6763	585-232-4950
Old Republic National Title Insurance Co (ORTIG)				
400 Second Ave S	Minneapolis MN	55401	800-328-4441	612-371-1111
Placer Title Co				
189 Fulweiler Ave	Auburn CA	95603	800-317-8407	530-887-2410
Stewart Information Services Corp				
1980 Post Oak Blvd Ste 800	Houston TX	77056	800-729-1900	713-625-8100
NYSE: STC				
Stewart REI Data Inc				
1980 Post Oak Blvd Ste 800	Houston TX	77056	800-729-1900	212-922-0050
Stewart Title Guaranty Co				
1980 Post Oak Blvd Ste 800	Houston TX	77056	800-729-1900	713-625-8100
Title Guaranty of Hawaii Inc				
235 Queen St	Honolulu HI	96813	800-222-3229	808-533-6261
Title Resources Guaranty Co (TRGC)				
8111 LBJ Fwy Ste 1200	Dallas TX	75251	800-526-8018	
USHEALTH Group Inc				
300 Burnett St Ste 200	Fort Worth TX	76102	800-387-9027	

390-7 Travel Insurance

Most of the companies listed here are insurance agencies and brokerages that specialize in selling travel insurance policies, rather than the insurers who underwrite the policies.

			Toll-Free	Phone
Access America				
2805 N Parham Rd	Richmond VA	23294	800-284-8300	
All Aboard Benefits				
6162 E Mockingird Ln Ste 104	Dallas TX	75214	800-462-2322	214-821-6677
Highway To Health Inc				
1 Radnor Corporate Ctr Ste 100	Radnor PA	19087	888-243-2358	
Insurance Consultants International				
1840 Deer Creek Rd Ste 200	Monument CO	80132	800-576-2674	719-573-9080
International SOS				
3600 Horizon Blvd Ste 300	Trevose PA	19053	800-523-6586	215-942-8000
Pan-American Life Insurance Co				
601 Poydras St	New Orleans LA	70130	877-939-4550*	
*Life Ins				
Travel Insured International				
855 Winding Brook Dr PO Box 6503	Glastonbury CT	06033	800-243-3174	
Wallach & Company Inc				
107 W Federal St	Middleburg VA	20118	800-237-6615	540-687-3166

391 INTERCOM EQUIPMENT & SYSTEMS

			Toll-Free	Phone
Anacom General Corp				
1240 S Claudina St	Anaheim CA	92805	800-955-9540	714-774-8484
Clear-Com USA				
850 Marina Village Pkwy	Alameda CA	94501	800-462-4357	510-337-6600
Clever Devices Ltd				
300 Crossways Pk Dr	Woodbury NY	11797	800-872-6129	516-433-6100
Crest Healthcare Supply				
195 Third St	Dassel MN	55325	800-328-8908	
David Clark Co				
360 Franklin St	Worcester MA	01604	800-298-6235*	508-751-5800
*Cust Svc				
Lee Dan Communications Inc				
155 Adams Ave	Hauppauge NY	11788	800-231-1414	631-231-1414

392 INTERIOR DESIGN

			Toll-Free	Phone
24 Asset Management Corp				
13155 SW 42nd St Ste 200	Miami FL	33175	855-414-2424	
Academy Fire Protection Inc				
42 Broadway 2nd Fl	Lynbrook NY	11563	800-773-4736	
Accent 7171 Mercy Rd Ste 100	Omaha NE	68106	800-397-7243	402-397-9920
AdHub LLC, The				
146 Alexander St	Rochester NY	14607	866-712-2986	585-442-2585
Advance Group, The				
185 Price Pkwy	Farmingdale NY	11735	877-273-6481	
Aetna Integrated Services				
646 Parsons Ave	Columbus OH	43206	866-238-6201	

		Toll-Free	Phone

			Toll-Free	Phone
Aftermath Claim Science Inc				
4580 Weaver Pkwy Ste 200	Warrenville IL	60555	800-962-6831	630-922-1900
AM Technical Solutions Inc				
2213 RR 620 N Ste 105	Austin TX	78734	888-729-1548	
Angus Systems Group Ltd				
1125 Leslie St	Toronto ON	M3C2J6	877-442-6487	416-385-8550
AnswerLive LLC				
1101 Cherryville	Shelby NC	28150	800-472-4495	704-333-8880
Apollo Retail Specialists LLC				
4450 E Adamo Dr	Tampa FL	33605	866-872-0666	813-712-2525
Aram A Kaz Co, The				
365 Silas Deane Hwy	Wethersfield CT	06109	800-969-2251	860-529-6900
Ark TeleServices				
2 E Merrick Rd	Valley Stream NY	11580	800-898-5367	
ArroHealth				
49 Wireless Blvd Ste 140	Hauppauge NY	11788	866-449-8844	631-780-5000
ARS National Services Inc				
201 W Grand Ave	Escondido CA	92025	800-456-5053	
ATIS Elevator Inspections LLC				
1976 Innerbelt Business Ctr	St. Louis MO	63114	855-755-2847	
AtoZdatabases com				
PO Box 27757	Omaha NE	68127	877-428-0101	
BA Exhibits inc				
2191 Mendenhall Dr Ste 101	North Las Vegas NV	89081	800-579-3888	
BestPass Inc				
828 Washington Ave	Albany NY	12203	888-410-9696	518-458-1579
BizQuest				
101 California St 43rd Fl	San Francisco CA	94111	844-495-3091*	888-280-3815
*Advertising				
C m Buck & Associates Inc				
6850 Guion Rd	Indianapolis IN	46268	800-382-3961	317-293-5704
Canada Media Fund				
50 Wellington St E Ste 202	Toronto ON	M5E1C8	877-975-0766	416-214-4400
CardTrak LLC				
4055 Tamiami Trl	Port Charlotte FL	33952	800-344-7714	
Carenet Healthcare Services				
11845 Interstate 10 W Ste 400	San Antonio TX	78230	800-809-7000	
Cascade365				
1670 Corporate Cir Ste 202	Petaluma CA	94954	888-417-1531	707-981-4002
Cathedral Village				
600 E Cathedral Rd	Philadelphia PA	19128	800-382-1385	215-487-1300
CBE Companies Inc				
1309 Technology Pkwy	Cedar Falls IA	50613	800-925-6686	
Cedar Graphics Inc				
311 Parsons Dr	Hiawatha IA	52233	800-393-2399	319-395-6900
Center Stage Productions Inc				
20-10 Maple Ave	Fair Lawn NJ	07410	800-955-1663	973-423-5000
Central Credit Services LLC				
9550 Regency Sq Blvd Ste 500A	Jacksonville FL	32225	888-904-1800	
Ci Radar LLC				
40 Technology Pkwy S				
Ste 150	Peachtree Corners GA	30092	888-421-0617	678-680-2103
CISCO Inc 1702 Townhurst	Houston TX	77043	800-231-3686	713-461-9407
Classic Hostess Inc				
2 Skillman St Ste 313	Brooklyn NY	11205	888-280-6539	718-534-0690
Clover Wireless				
2700 W Higgins Rd Ste 100	Hoffman Estates IL	60169	866-734-6548	
CMS Mid-Atlantic Inc				
295 Totowa Rd	Totowa NJ	07512	800-267-1981	
CO-OP Financial Services Inc				
9692 Haven Ave	Rancho Cucamonga CA	91730	800-782-9042	
CoinLab Inc				
71 Columbia St Ste 300	Seattle WA	98104	855-522-2646	
Corix Utilities (US) Inc				
11020 West Plank Crt Ste 100	Milwaukee WI	53226	877-678-3842	414-203-8700
Custom Exhibits Corp				
1830 N Indianwood Ave	Broken Arrow OK	74012	800-664-0309	918-250-2121
D P Brown of Saginaw Inc				
2845 Universal Dr	Saginaw MI	48603	877-799-9400	989-799-9400
Dallas Data Center Inc				
110 S Main St Ste 600	Wichita KS	67202	800-326-6059	316-462-4001
Dinova LLC				
6455 E Johns Crossing Ste 220	Johns Creek GA	30097	888-346-6828	
Drummac Inc				
251 Levy Rd	Atlantic Beach FL	32233	800-780-0111	904-241-4999
EchoData Services Inc				
121 N Shirk Rd	New Holland PA	17557	800-511-3870	
eCollect PO Box 241548	Mayfield OH	44124	888-569-6001	
EV Connect Inc				
615 North Nash St Ste 203	El Segundo CA	90245	866-790-3155	
Exhibit Source Inc, The				
145 Wells Ave	Newton Center MA	02459	866-949-6113	781-449-1600
Farm First Dairy Co-op				
4001 Nakoosa Trl Ste 100	Madison WI	53714	800-525-7704	608-244-3373
FCI Lender Services Inc				
8180 E Kaiser Blvd	Anaheim Hills CA	92808	800-931-2424	714-282-2424
Fisher Group Inc				
4517 W 1730 S	Salt Lake City UT	84104	800-365-8920	801-262-6451
Gallun Snow				
1920 Market St Ste 201	Denver CO	80202	866-846-7514	303-433-9500
Gehring LP & Gehring Diato LP				
24800 Drake Rd	Farmington Hills MI	48335	888-923-9760	248-427-3901
Global Building Services Inc				
25129 The Old Rd Ste 102	Stevenson Ranch CA	91381	800-675-6643	
Global Contact Services LLC				
118 S Main St	Salisbury NC	28144	844-324-5427	704-647-9621
Global Linguist Solutions LLC				
1155 Herndon Pkwy Ste 100	Falls ChurchHerndon VA	20170	800-349-9142	
Goldec Hamm's Manufacturing Ltd				
6760 65 Ave	Red Deer AB	T4P1A5	800-661-1665	403-343-6607
Good Leads 224 Main St Unit 2B	Salem NH	03079	866-894-5323	603-894-5323
Grid One Solutions Inc				
700 Turner Way Ste 205	Aston PA	19014	800-606-7981	
H & P Leasing Inc				
1849 Flowood Dr	Flowood MS	39232	877-377-7052	601-939-2200
Imagine Advertising & Publishing Inc				
3100 Medlock Bridge Rd				
Ste 370	Peachtree Corners GA	30071	866-832-3214	770-734-0966

			Toll-Free	Phone

InfoSend Inc
4240 E La Palma Ave . . . . Anaheim CA 92807 **800-955-9330** 714-993-2690

Infospan Inc
31878 Del Obispo St
Ste 118 . . . . San Juan Capistrano CA 92675 **866-611-8611** 949-260-9990

Inovar Inc 1073 W 1700 N . . . . Logan UT 84321 **866-898-4949** 435-792-4949

InsideUp Inc
9245 Activity Rd Ste 210 . . . . .San Diego CA 92126 **800-889-6178** 858-397-5733

InstaGift LLC
1500 First Ave N Ste 65 . . . . Birmingham AL 35203 **877-870-3463**

Intland GmbH
968 Inverness Way .Sunnyvale CA 94087 **866-468-5210**

Invisible Hand Networks Inc
670 Broadway Ste 302 . . . . New York NY 10012 **866-637-5286** 212-400-7416

ISPN Network Services
14303 W 95th St . . . . Lenexa KS 66215 **866-584-4776**

JobDiva
116 John St Ste 1406. . . . . New York NY 10038 **866-562-3482**

Jomax Recovery Services
9242 W Union Hills Dr Ste 102 . . . . .Peoria AZ 85382 **888-866-0721**

Kinark Child
500 Hood Rd Ste 200 . . . . Markham ON L3R9Z3 **800-230-8533** 905-474-9595

Language Scientific
101 Station Landing Ste 500 . . . . Medford MA 02155 **800-240-0246** 617-621-0940

LeaseQ Inc
1 Burlington Woods Dr Ste 200 . . . . Burlington MA 01803 **888-688-4519**

Lehman Hardware & Appliances Inc
4779 Kidron Rd . . . . .Dalton OH 44618 **888-438-5346** 800-438-5346

LeTip International Inc
4838 E Baseline Rd Ste 123 . . . . .Mesa AZ 85206 **800-255-3847** 480-264-4600

M & W Transportation Company Inc
1110 Pumping Sta Rd . . . . Nashville TN 37210 **800-251-4209** 615-256-5755

Matrix Companies, The
7162 Reading Rd Ste 250. . . . . Cincinnati OH 45237 **877-550-7973** 513-351-1222

Meta5 Inc 122 W Main St . . . . Babylon NY 11702 **866-638-2555** 631-587-6800

Milestone Technologies Inc
3101 Skyway Ct . . . . Fremont CA 94539 **877-651-2454**

MMS Education
1 Summit Sq 1717 Langhorne-Newtown Rd
Ste 301 . . . . .Newtown PA 19047 **866-395-3193**

Mo-Tires Ltd
2830 5 Ave N . . . . Lethbridge AB T1H0P1 **800-774-3888** 403-329-4533

Monterey Financial Services Inc
4095 Avenida De La Plata . . . . .Oceanside CA 92056 **800-456-2225** 760-639-3500

MTI America
1350 S Powerline Rd Ste 200 . . . Pompano Beach FL 33069 **800-553-2155**

myFreightWorld LLC
7133 W 95th St Ste 205 . . . . .Overland Park KS 66212 **877-549-9438**

NEI Global Relocation Inc
2707 N 118th St . . . . Omaha NE 68164 **800-533-7353** 402-397-8486

NetworkOmni
4353 Park Ter Dr . . . . .Westlake Village CA 91361 **800-543-4244** 818-706-7890

Networld Media Group LLC
13100 Eastpoint Park Blvd Ste 100. . . . . Louisville KY 40223 **877-441-7545** 502-241-7545

Nitelines USA Inc
2180 Satellite Blvd Ste 400. . . . . Duluth GA 30097 **844-661-9120**

Noritsu Technical Services
6900 Noritsu Ave . . . . .Buena Park CA 90620 **888-435-7448** 714-521-9040

Orion Food Systems LLC
2930 W Maple . . . . Sioux Falls SD 57107 **800-648-6227** 800-336-1320

Paragon International Inc
2885 N Berkeley Lake Rd Ste 17. . . . . Duluth GA 30096 **800-526-1095**

Phyle Inventory Control Specialists Inc
4150 Grange Hall Rd . . . . .Holly MI 48442 **888-303-8482**

Pioneer Magnetics
1745 Berkeley St . . . . Santa Monica CA 90404 **800-269-6426** 310-829-6751

Plantscape Inc
3101 Liberty Ave .Pittsburgh PA 15201 **800-303-1380** 412-281-6352

Polygon Network PO Box 4806 . . . . Dillon CO 80435 **800-221-4435**

Press-A-Print International LLC
1463 Commerce Way . . . . .Idaho Falls ID 83401 **888-880-0004**

Primeritus Financial Services Inc
440 Metroplex Dr .Nashville TN 37211 **888-833-4238**

QualiTest Ltd
1 Post Rd 3rd Fl . . . . Fairfield CT 06824 **877-882-9540**

R H K Hydraulic Cylinder Services Inc
13111 159th St . . . . Edmonton AB T5V1H6 **800-406-3111** 780-452-2876

RealtyBid International Inc
3225 Rainbow Dr Ste 248. . . . . Rainbow City AL 35906 **877-518-5600**

Records Consultants Inc (RCI)
12829 Wetmore Rd . . . . San Antonio TX 78247 **877-363-4127** 210-366-4127

Renbor Sales Solutions Inc
256 Thornway Ave . . . . .Thornhill ON L4J7X8 **855-257-2537** 416-671-3555

RJE Business Interiors Inc
623 Broadway St .Cincinnati OH 45202 **800-236-8232** 513-641-3700

Rockford Mercantile Agency Inc
2502 S Alpine Rd . . . . Rockford IL 61108 **800-369-6116** 815-229-3328

Sacor Financial Inc
1911 Douglas Blvd 85-126 . . . . Roseville CA 95661 **866-556-0231**

Scribendi Inc
405 Riverview Dr Ste 304. . . . . .Chatham ON N7M0N3 **877-351-1626** 519-351-1626

Sea Pearl Seafood Company Inc
14120 Shell Belt Rd . . . . Bayou La Batre AL 36509 **800-872-8804** 251-824-2129

Seaborn Health Care
8918 78th Ave . . . . Seminole FL 33777 **800-335-6176** 727-398-1710

Service Companies Inc, The
14750 NW 77th Ct Ste 100. . . . . .Miami Lakes FL 33016 **800-385-8800** 305-681-8800

Setina Manufacturing Company Inc
2926 Yelm Hwy SE . . . . Olympia WA 98501 **800-426-2627** 360-491-6197

Simple Verity Inc
1218 Third Ave . . . . Seattle WA 98101 **855-583-7489** 617-905-7467

Skyline 3355 Discovery Rd . . . . St Paul MN 55121 **800-328-2725** 651-234-6592

Smart Care Equipment Solutions
370 Wabasha St N .St. Paul MN 55102 **800-822-2302** 651-250-5555

sortimat Technology
5655 Meadowbrook Industrial Ct
. . . . Rolling Meadows IL 60008 **800-385-6805** 847-925-1234

Springboard Nonprofit Consumer Credit Management
4351 Latham St . . . . Riverside CA 92501 **888-425-3453**

Star 6688 93rd Ave N . . . . Minneapolis MN 55445 **800-419-7827** 763-561-4655

StreamSend 78 York St . . . . Sacramento CA 95814 **877-439-4078** 916-326-5407

Summit Account Resolution
12201 Champlin Dr . . . . Champlin MN 55316 **888-822-7509** 888-222-0793

Sunset Farm Foods Inc
1201 Madison Hwy . . . . .Valdosta GA 31601 **800-882-1121** 229-242-3389

Superior Vision
939 Elkridge Landing Rd Ste 200 . . . . Linthicum MD 21090 **800-243-1401** 410-752-0121

Tektronix Component Solutions Inc
2905 SW Hocken Ave . . . . Beaverton OR 97005 **800-833-9200**

ThinkDirect Marketing Group Inc
8285 Bryan Dairy Rd Ste 150 . . . . Largo FL 33773 **800-325-3155** 727-369-2700

TrueAccord Corp
303 Second St S Ste 750 . . . . .San Francisco CA 94107 **866-611-2731**

Uhl Company Inc
9065 Zachary Ln N . . . . .Maple grove MN 55369 **800-815-3820** 763-425-7226

Up Communications Services LLC
103 SE Atlantic St . . . . Tullahoma TN 37388 **877-667-0968**

Viking Client Services Inc
7500 Office Ridge Cir Ste 100 . . . . Eden Prairie MN 55344 **800-767-7895** 952-944-7575

Villa Lighting Supply Inc
2929 Chouteau Ave . . . . Saint Louis MO 63103 **800-325-0963**

VIPdesk Connect Inc
908 King St Ste 400W . . . . Alexandria VA 22314 **844-874-3472**

Wachs Water Services
801 Asbury Dr . . . . Buffalo Grove IL 60089 **800-525-5821**

Walls 360 5054 Bond St . . . . Las Vegas NV 89118 **888-244-9969**

Warranty Life Services Inc
4152 Meridian St Ste 105-29 . . . . .Bellingham WA 98226 **888-927-7269**

WorkersCompensationcom LLC
PO Box 2432 . . . . Sarasota FL 34230 **866-927-2667** 941-366-3791

WorldPantrycom Inc
790 Tennessee St . . . . .San Francisco CA 94107 **866-972-6879**

Worldwide Court Reporters
3000 Weslayan St Ste 235 . . . . Houston TX 77027 **800-745-1101**

Wyse Meter Solutions Inc
RPO Newmarket Ct PO Box 95530 . . . . Newmarket ON L3Y8J8 **866-681-9465**

393   INTERNET BACKBONE PROVIDERS

Companies that are, in effect, Internet service providers for Internet Service Providers (ISPs).

			Toll-Free	Phone

Cogent Communications Group Inc
1015 31st St NW . . . . Washington DC 20007 **877-875-4432** 202-295-4200
NASDAQ: CCOI

iPass Inc
3800 Bridge Pkwy . . . . Redwood Shores CA 94065 **877-236-3807** 650-232-4100
NASDAQ: IPAS

SunGard Availability Services
680 E Swedesford Rd . . . . Wayne PA 19087 **800-468-7483** 484-582-2000

Verizon Business
1 Verizon Way . . . . Basking Ridge NJ 07920 **877-297-7816*** 202-789-1432
*Cust Svc

XO Communications Inc
13865 Sunrise Vly Dr . . . . Herndon VA 20171 **866-349-0134** 703-547-2000

394   INTERNET BROADCASTING

			Toll-Free	Phone

Audible Inc 1 Washington Pk . . . . .Newark NJ 07102 **888-283-5051** 973-820-0400

BankCard Services
21281 S Western Ave . . . . Torrance CA 90501 **888-339-0100** 213-365-1122

Compugen Inc
100 Via Renzo Dr . . . . Richmond Hill ON L4S0B8 **800-387-5045** 905-707-2000

Eventure Interactive Inc
3420 Bristol St 6th Fl . . . . Costa Mesa CA 92626 **855-986-5669**

MedAltus
944 College Park Rd Ste B . . . . .Summerville SC 29486 **800-393-3848**

Media Temple
6060 Center Dr 5th Fl. . . . . Los Angeles CA 90045 **877-578-4000**

MediaBrains Inc
9015 Strada Stell Ct Ste 203. . . . . Naples FL 34109 **866-627-2467** 239-594-3200

Ning Interactive Inc
1906 El Camino Real . . . . .Menlo Park CA 94027 **855-233-6436**

Time 4 Learning
6300 NE First Ave Ste 203 . . . . Fort Lauderdale FL 33334 **888-771-0914**

win-OMT Software Inc
280 - 1630 Ness Ave . . . . Winnipeg MB R3J3X1 **888-665-0501** 204-786-3994

Yodle Inc
330 W 34th St 18th Fl. . . . . New York NY 10001 **877-276-5104**

395   INTERNET DOMAIN NAME REGISTRARS

			Toll-Free	Phone

Acumenex Com
2201 Brant St . . . . Burlington ON L7P3N8 **877-788-5028** 905-319-2468

AITDomainscom
421 Maiden Ln . . . . Fayetteville NC 28301 **877-549-2881**

AT-NET Services Inc
3401 St Vardell Ln Ste D . . . . Charlotte NC 29217 **866-708-0886** 704-831-2500

Bankers Data Services Inc
521 W 11th St . . . . Alma GA 31510 **888-458-8652** 912-632-2060

Best Registration Services Inc
1418 S Third St . . . . Louisville KY 40208 **800-977-3475** 502-637 4528

Bradford Scott Data Corp
1001 Chestnut Hills Pkwy Ste 1 . . . . .Fort Wayne IN 46814 **800-430-5120** 260-625-5107

Checkbox Survey Inc
44 Pleasant St . . . . .Watertown MA 02472 **866-430-8274** 617-231-8890

Cloudwerx Data Solutions Inc
1440 28th St NE Ste 2 . . . . .Calgary AB T2A7W6 **855-550-5004** 403-538-6659

				Toll-Free	Phone
Cvikota Company Inc					
2031 32nd St S	La Crosse	WI	54601	800-657-5175	608-788-8103
Document Imaging Systems Corp (DISC)					
1523 Fenpark Dr	Fenton	MO	63026	800-710-3472	
Domain-It!					
9891 Montgomery Rd	Cincinnati	OH	45242	866-269-2355*	513-351-4222
*General					
DomainPeople Inc					
550 Burrard St Ste 200 Bentall 5	Vancouver	BC	V6C2B5	877-734-3667	604-639-1680
Dotster					
8100 NE Pkwy Dr Ste 300					
PO Box 821066	Vancouver	WA	98682	800-401-5250	360-449-5800
Dynadot LLC PO Box 345	San Mateo	CA	94401	866-652-2039*	650-585-1961
*Cust Svc					
easyDNS Technologies Inc					
219 Dufferin St Ste 300A	Toronto	ON	M6K3J1	855-321-3279	416-535-8672
Etera Solutions Llc					
354 TurnPark St Ste 203	Canton	MA	02021	888-536-6515	
Indros Group					
210 Richardson St	Brooklyn	NY	11222	866-463-7671	
Intrada Technologies					
31 Ashler Manor Dr	Muncy	PA	17756	800-858-5745	
Jsa Technologies					
201 Main St Ste 1320	Fort Worth	TX	76102	877-572-8324	
Livecareer					
1 Hallidie Plz Ste 600	San Francisco	CA	94102	800-652-8430	
MINDBODY Inc					
4051 Broad St Ste 220	Sn Luis Obisp	CA	93401	877-755-4279	
Netfronts Web Hosting					
459 N 300 W Ste 16	Kaysville	UT	84037	800-675-4622	801-497-0878
Network Solutions LLC					
13861 Sunrise Valley Dr Ste 300	Herndon	VA	20171	800-361-5712	703-668-4600
Nexonia Inc					
2 St Clair Ave E Ste 750	Toronto	ON	M4T2T5	800-291-4829*	416-480-0688
*Sales					
Nexternal Solutions Inc					
785 Grand Ave Ste 216	Carlsbad	CA	92008	800-914-6161	760-730-9015
Omedix Inc					
7114 E Stetson Dr Ste 360	Scottsdale	AZ	85251	877-866-3349	
Registercom Inc					
575 Eigth Ave 8th Fl	New York	NY	10018	888-734-4783	
ScaleGrid					
2225 E Bayshore Rd	Palo Alto	CA	94303	866-449-2478	
SI Holdings					
3267 Bee Caves Rd Ste 107	Austin	TX	78746	866-551-4646	
Silex Technology America Inc					
167 W 7065 S Ste 330	Midvale	UT	84047	866-765-8761	801-748-1199
SolutionStream 249 N 1200 E	Lehi	UT	84043	800-314-3451	
STARTEL 16 Goodyear B-125	Irvine	CA	92618	800-782-7835	
Studio Desgraff					
2831 rue King Ouest	Sherbrooke	QC	J1L1C6	800-292-5110	819-823-8024
T3 Software Builders Inc					
1708 Chester Mill Rd	Silver Spring	MD	20906	800-281-4879	301-260-9504
Terraine Inc					
310 S Harrington St	Raleigh	NC	27603	800-531-1242	
Whitecap Canada Inc					
200 Yorkland Blvd Ste 920	Toronto	ON	M2J5C1	855-393-9977	
Zibiz Corp					
50 Alexander Ct	Ronkonkoma	NY	11779	888-263-6005	

396   INTERNET SEARCH ENGINES, PORTALS, DIRECTORIES

				Toll-Free	Phone
Ancestrycom 360 W 4800 N	Provo	UT	84604	800-262-3787*	801-705-7000
*Cust Svc					
BioSpace Inc					
10506 Justin Dr	Urbandale	IA	50322	888-246-7722	877-277-7585
FindLaw 610 Opperman Dr	Eagan	MN	55123	800-392-6206	651-687-6393
Genealogycom 360 W 4800 N	Provo	UT	84604	800-262-3787	
HomeAdvisor					
14023 Denver W Pkwy Ste 200	Golden	CO	80401	800-474-1596	303-963-7200
Hotelroomscom Inc					
108-18 Queens Blvd	Forest Hills	NY	11375	800-486-7000	718-730-6000
Law Engine					
7660-H Fay Ave Ste 342	La Jolla	CA	92037	800-894-2889	858-456-1234
Nabet 700-M Unifor					
100 Lombard St Ste 203	Toronto	ON	M5C1M3	800-889-9487	416-536-4827
Nursing Ctr					
323 Norristown Rd Ste 200	Ambler	PA	19002	800-346-7844	800-787-8985
Tucows Inc 96 Mowat Ave	Toronto	ON	M6K3M1	800-371-6992	416-535-0123
NASDAQ: TC					
USGS Education					
USGS National Ctr 12201 Sunrise Vly Dr	Reston	VA	20192	800-228-0975	703-648-5953
Wired News					
Wired 520 Third St Ste 305	San Francisco	CA	94107	800-769-4733	
YELLOWPAGEScom LLC					
208 S Akard	Dallas	TX	75202	866-329-7118	

397   INTERNET SERVICE PROVIDERS (ISPS)

				Toll-Free	Phone
ABT Internet Inc					
175 E Shore Rd	Great Neck	NY	11023	800-367-3414	516-829-5484
Access US					
712 N Second St Ste 300	Saint Louis	MO	63102	800-638-6373	314-655-7700
Aplus 3680 Victoria St N	Shoreview	MN	55126	877-532-0132	651-481-4598
AT & T Inc					
175 E Houston St PO Box 2933	San Antonio	TX	78299	800-351-7221	210-821-4105
NYSE: AT&T					
Cable One Inc					
210 E Earll Dr	Phoenix	AZ	85012	877-692-2253	602-364-6000
ClearSail Communications LLC					
3950 Braxton	Houston	TX	77063	888-905-0888	713-230-2800
DSL extreme					
9221 Corbin Ave Ste 260	Northridge	CA	91324	866-243-8638	

				Toll-Free	Phone
EarthLink Inc					
1170 Peachtree St Ste 900	Atlanta	GA	30309	866-383-3080	
NASDAQ: ELNK					
Expedient Communications					
810 Parish St	Pittsburgh	PA	15220	877-570-7827	
Frontline Communications					
PO Box 98	Orangeburg	NY	10962	888-376-6854	
HughesNet					
11717 Exploration Ln	Germantown	MD	20876	866-347-3292	301-428-5500
iSelect Internet Inc					
1420 W Kettleman Ln Ste E	Lodi	CA	95242	877-837-1427	209-334-0496
Net Access Corp					
2300 15th St Ste 300	Denver	CO	80202	800-638-6336	973-590-5000
NetZero Inc					
21301 Burbank Blvd	Woodland Hills	CA	91367	800-638-9376	818-287-3000
New Edge Networks					
3000 Columbia House Blvd Ste 106	Vancouver	WA	98661	877-725-3343	360-693-9009
TOASTnet					
4841 Monroe St Ste 307	Toledo	OH	43623	888-862-7863	419-292-2200
Verizon Business					
1 Verizon Way	Basking Ridge	NJ	07920	877-297-7816*	202-789-1432
*Cust Svc					

398   INVENTORY SERVICES

				Toll-Free	Phone
Douglas-Guardian Services Corp					
14800 St Mary's Ln	Houston	TX	77079	800-255-0552	281-531-0500
MSI Inventory Service Corp					
PO Box 320129	Flowood	MS	39232	800-820-1460	601-939-0130
WIS International					
9265 Sky Park Ct Ste 100	San Diego	CA	92123	800-268-6848	858-565-8111

399   INVESTIGATIVE SERVICES

SEE ALSO Public Records Search Services ; Information Retrieval Services (General) ; Security & Protective Services

				Toll-Free	Phone
Accurate Biometrics Inc					
4849 N Milwaukee Ave Ste 101	Chicago	IL	60630	866-361-9944	773-685-5699
American Guard Services Inc					
1299 E Artesia Blvd	Carson	CA	90746	800-662-7372	310-645-6200
ASK Services Inc					
42180 Ford Rd Ste 101	Canton	MI	48187	888-416-1313	734-983-9040
Bombet Cashio & Assoc					
11220 N Harrells Ferry Rd	Baton Rouge	LA	70816	800-256-5333	225-275-0796
Camping Investigations					
4427 N 27th Ave	Phoenix	AZ	85017	800-862-8458	602-864-7860
CareerBuilder Employment Screening LLC					
Atrium Corporate Ctr 3800 Golf Rd					
Ste 120	Rolling Meadows	IL	60008	866-255-1852	
Claims Verification Inc					
6700 N Andrews Ave Ste 200	Ft. Lauderdale	FL	33309	888-284-2000	
Donan Engineering LLC					
12450 Lk Sta Pl	Louisville	KY	40299	800-482-5611	
Frasco Investigative Services					
215 W Alameda Ave	Burbank	CA	91502	877-372-7261	
Gregg Investigations Inc					
500 E Milwaukee St	Janesville	WI	53545	800-866-1976	
Hettrick Cyr & Associates (HC&A)					
59 Sycamore St	Glastonbury	CT	06033	888-805-0300	860-652-9997
Inquiries Inc 129 N W St	Easton	MD	21601	866-987-3767	
International Investigators Inc					
3216 N Pennsylvania St	Indianapolis	IN	46205	800-403-8111	317-925-1496
Kessler International					
45 Rockefeller Plz Ste 2000	New York	NY	10111	800-932-2221	212-286-9100
Michael Ramey & Assoc Inc					
PO Box 744	Danville	CA	94526	800-321-0505	
North Winds Investigations Inc					
119 S Second St PO Box 1654	Rogers	AR	72756	800-530-4514	479-925-1612
Owens & Assoc Investigations					
8765 Aero Dr Ste 306	San Diego	CA	92123	800-297-1343	
Palmer Investigative Services					
624 W Gurley St Ste A	Prescott	AZ	86304	800-280-2951	928-778-2951
Private Eyes Inc					
2700 Ygnacio Valley Rd Ste 100	Walnut Creek	CA	94598	877-292-3331	925-927-3333
Research Assoc Inc					
27999 Clemens Rd	Cleveland	OH	44145	800-255-9693	440-892-9439
Rick Johnson & Associates of Colorado					
1649 Downing St	Denver	CO	80218	800-530-2300	303-296-2200
Southern Research Company Inc					
2850 Centenary Blvd	Shreveport	LA	71104	888-772-6952	318-227-9700
Starside Security & Investigation Inc					
1930 S Brea Canyon Rd Ste 220	Diamond Bar	CA	91765	888-478-2774	909-396-9999
Thillens Inc					
4242 N Elston Ave	Chicago	IL	60618	888-539-4446	773-539-4444
Vericon Resources Inc					
3295 River Exchange Dr Ste 405	Norcross	GA	30092	800-795-3784	770-457-9922
VTS Investigations LLC					
7 S State St	Elgin	IL	60123	800-538-4464	
Wood & Tait LLC					
64-5249 Kauakea Rd PO Box 6180	Kamuela	HI	96743	800-774-8585	808-885-5090

400   INVESTMENT ADVICE & MANAGEMENT

SEE ALSO Securities Brokers & Dealers ; Mutual Funds ; Commodity Contracts Brokers & Dealers ; Investment Guides - Online

				Toll-Free	Phone
Acumen Capital Finance Partners Ltd					
404 Sixth Ave SW Ste 700	Calgary	AB	T2P0R9	888-422-8636	403-571-0300
Advent Capital Management LLC					
888 Seventh Ave 31st Fl	New York	NY	10019	888-523-8368	212-482-1600

				Toll-Free	Phone
AGF Management Ltd 66 Wellington St W 31st Fl	Toronto	ON	M5K1E9	**800-268-8583**	905-214-8203
AllianceBernstein Holding LP (AB) 1345 Ave of the Americas *NYSE: AB* ■ *Cust Svc	New York	NY	10105	**800-221-5672***	212-486-5800
Allianz Global Investors of America LP 600 West Broadway San Diego	Newport Beach	CA	92101	**800-656-6226**	
American Capital Partners LLC 205 Oser Ave	Hauppauge	NY	11788	**800-393-0493**	631-851-0918
American Century Investments Inc PO Box 419200	Kansas City	MO	64141	**800-345-2021**	816-531-5575
Ameriprise Financial Inc 834 Ameriprise Financial Ctr *NYSE: AMP*	Minneapolis	MN	55474	**866-673-3673**	612-671-3131
Amivest Capital Management 703 Market St 18th Fl	San Francisco	CA	94103	**800-541-7774**	
Analytic Investors LLC 555 W Fifth St 50th Fl	Los Angeles	CA	90013	**800-618-1872**	213-688-3015
Appleton Group LLC, The 100 W Lawrence St Ste 306	Wisconsin	WI	54911	**866-993-7727**	920-993-7727
Appleton Partners Inc 1 Post Office Sq 6th Fl	Boston	MA	02109	**800-338-0745**	617-338-0700
ARGI Investment Services LLC (ARGI) 2110 High Wickham Pl	Louisville	KY	40223	**866-568-9719**	502-753-0609
Aristotle Capital Management LLC 11100 Santa Monica Blvd Ste 1700	Los Angeles	CA	90025	**877-478-4722**	310-478-4005
Ashfield Capital Partners LLC 801 Montgomery St Ste 200	San Francisco	CA	94133	**877-391-4747**	415-391-4747
Assante Financial Management Ltd 199 Bay St Ste 2700	Toronto	ON	M5L1E2	**888-348-9994**	416-348-9994
Asset Strategy Consultants LLC 6 N Park Dr Ste 208	Hunt Valley	MD	21030	**866-344-8282**	410-528-8282
AssetMark Inc 1655 Grant St 10th Fl	Concord	CA	94520	**800-664-5345**	
Atlantic Trust 100 International Dr 23rd Fl	Baltimore	MD	21202	**866-644-4144**	202-783-4144
Badgley Phelps & Bell Inc 1420 Fifth Ave Ste 3200	Seattle	WA	98101	**800-869-7173**	206-623-6172
Bahl & Gaynor Investment Counsel 255 East Fifth St Ste 2700	Cincinnati	OH	45202	**800-341-1810**	513-287-6100
Bailard 950 Tower Ln Ste 1900	Foster City	CA	94404	**800-224-5273**	650-571-5800
BAM Advisor Services 8182 Maryland Ave Ste 500	St Louis	MO	63105	**800-711-2027**	
Bankers Financial Products Corp 201 N Main St Ste 4	Fort Atkinson	WI	53538	**800-348-1831**	
Barrow Hanley Mewhinney & Strauss LLC 2200 Ross Ave 31st Fl	Dallas	TX	75201	**800-543-0407**	214-665-1900
Bartlett & Co 600 Vine St Ste 2100	Cincinnati	OH	45202	**800-800-4612**	513-621-4612
Beacon Trust Co 163 Madison Ave Ste 600	Morristown	NJ	07960	**866-377-8090**	973-377-8090
Bell Investment Advisors 1111 Broadway Ste 1630	Oakland	CA	94607	**800-700-0089**	510-433-1066
Berkshire Advisors Inc 2240 Ridgewood Rd	Wyomissing	PA	19610	**800-566-4325**	610-376-6970
Bernicke Wealth Management 1565 Bluestem Blvd	Altoona	WI	54720	**866-832-1173**	715-832-1173
Bessemer Trust Co 630 Fifth Ave	New York	NY	10111	**866-271-7403**	212-708-9100
Birch Hill Investment Advisors LLC 24 Federal St 10th Fl	Boston	MA	02110	**800-441-3453**	617-502-8300
Boenning & Scattergood Inc 200 Barr Harbor Dr Four Tower Bridge Ste 300	West Conshohocken	PA	19428	**800-883-1212**	610-832-1212
Boston Advisors Inc 1 Liberty Sq 10th Fl	Boston	MA	02109	**800-523-5903**	617-348-3100
Boston Family Office LLC, The 88 Broad St 2nd Fl	Boston	MA	02110	**800-900-4401**	617-624-0800
Brandes Investment Partners LP 11988 El Camino Real Ste 600	San Diego	CA	92191	**800-237-7119**	858-755-0239
Brandywine Capital Associates Inc 100 S Church St	West Chester	PA	19382	**888-344-2920**	610-344-2910
Brandywine Global Investment Management LLC 2929 Arch St 8th Fl	Philadelphia	PA	19104	**800-348-2499**	215-609-3500
Brown Investment Advisory & Trust Co 901 S Bond St Ste 400	Baltimore	MD	21231	**800-645-3923**	410-537-5400
BTS Asset Management Inc 420 Bedford St Ste 340	Lexington	MA	02420	**800-343-3040**	
Buckman Buckman & Reid Inc 174 Patterson Ave	Shrewsbury	NJ	07702	**800-531-0303**	732-530-0303
Calamos Asset Management Inc 2020 Calamos Ct *NASDAQ: CLMS*	Naperville	IL	60563	**800-582-6959**	630-245-7200
Caldwell Trust Co 1400 Ctr Rd	Venice	FL	34292	**800-338-9476**	941-493-3600
Callan Associates Inc 600 Montgomery St Ste 800	San Francisco	CA	94111	**800-227-3288**	516-150-2772
Cambiar Investors Inc 2401 E Second Ave Ste 500	Denver	CO	80206	**888-673-9950**	
Cambria Capital LLC 488 E Winchester St Ste 200	Salt Lake City	UT	84107	**877-226-0477**	801-320-9606
CapFinancial Partners LLC 4208 Six Forks Rd Ste 1700	Raleigh	NC	27609	**800-216-0645**	919-870-6822
Capital Growth Management LP 1 International Pl	Boston	MA	02110	**800-345-4048**	617-737-3225
Capital Institutional Services Inc 1700 Pacific Ave Ste 1100	Dallas	TX	75201	**800-247-6729**	214-720-0055
Capital Premium Financing Inc 12235 South 800 East	Draper	UT	84020	**877-730-1906**	800-767-0705
CAPTRUST 4208 Six Forks Rd Ste 1700	Raleigh	NC	27609	**800-216-0645**	
Carolinas Investment Consulting LLC 5605 Carnegie Blvd Ste 400	Charlotte	NC	28209	**800-255-2904**	704-643-2455
Casey Research LLC 55 NE Fifth Ave	Delray Beach	FL	33483	**888-512-2739**	602-445-2736
Century Wealth Management LLC 1770 Kirby Pkwy Ste 117	Memphis	TN	38138	**855-850-5532**	901-850-5532
Churchill Corporate Services 56 Utter Ave	Hawthorne	NJ	07506	**800-941-7458**	973-636-9400
Clark Capital Management Group Inc (CCMG) 1650 Market St 1 Liberty Pl 53rd Fl	Philadelphia	PA	19103	**800-766-2264**	215-569-2224
Cohen & Steers Inc 280 Park Ave 10th Fl *NYSE: CNS*	New York	NY	10017	**800-330-7348**	
Columbia Threadneedle Investments PO Box 8081	Boston	MA	02266	**800-426-3750**	
Commonwealth Financial Network 29 Sawyer Rd	Waltham	MA	02453	**800-237-0081**	781-736-0700
Compak Asset Management 1801 Dove St	Newport Beach	CA	92660	**800-388-9700**	
Conestoga Capital Advisors LLC` CrossPoint at Valley Forge 550 E Swedesford Rd Ste 120	Radnor	PA	19087	**800-320-7790**	484-654-1380
Connors Investor Services Inc 1210 Broadcasting Rd Ste 200	Wyomissing	PA	19610	**877-376-7418**	610-376-7418
Cornerstone Advisors Asset Management Inc 74 W Broad St Ste 340	Bethlehem	PA	18018	**800-923-0900**	610-694-0900
Creative Financial Group (CFG) 16 Campus Blvd	Newtown Square	PA	19073	**800-893-4824**	610-325-6100
Crestwood Advisors LLC 50 Federal St Ste 810	Boston	MA	02110	**877-273-7896**	617-523-8880
Crown Financial Ministries 601 Broad St SE	Gainesville	GA	30501	**800-722-1976**	770-534-1000
Cullinan Associates Inc 295 N Hubbards Ln 2nd Fl	Louisville	KY	40207	**800-611-4841**	502-893-0300
Cumberland Private Wealth Management Inc 99 Yorkville Ave Ste 300	Toronto	ON	M5R3K5	**800-929-8296**	416-929-1090
Curran Investment Management 30 S Pearl St Omni Plz 9th Fl	Albany	NY	12207	**866-432-1246**	518-391-4200
Dalton Greiner Hartman Maher & Company LLC 565 Fifth Ave Ste 2101	New York	NY	10017	**800-653-2839**	212-557-2445
Design ProfessionalXL Group 2959 Salinas Hwy	Monterey	CA	93940	**800-227-4284**	831-649-5522
Desjardins Securities Inc 1170 Peel St Ste 300	Montreal	QC	H3B0A9	**866-985-7585**	514-985-7585
Dodge & Cox 555 California St 40th Fl	San Francisco	CA	94104	**800-621-3979**	415-981-1710
Driehaus Capital Management Inc 25 E Erie St	Chicago	IL	60611	**800-688-8819**	312-587-3800
Duff & Phelps Investment Management Co 200 S Wacker Dr Ste 500	Chicago	IL	60606	**800-338-0214**	312-263-2610
Eagle Asset Management 880 Carillon Pkwy	Saint Petersburg	FL	33716	**800-237-3101**	
Earnest Partners LLC 1180 Peachtree St Ste 2300	Atlanta	GA	30309	**800-322-0068**	404-815-8772
Edgar Lomax Co 6564 Loisdale Ct Ste 310	Springfield	VA	22150	**866-205-0524**	703-719-0026
Elan Financial Services Commerce Ct 4 Stn Sq Ste 620	Pittsburgh	PA	15219	**800-343-7064**	
Eliot Rose Asset Management LLC 1000 Chapel View Blvd Ste 240	Cranston	RI	02920	**866-585-5100**	401-588-5100
Envision Capital Management Inc 2301 Rosecrans Ave Ste 4180	El Segundo	CA	90245	**800-400-0989**	310-445-3252
Estrada Hinojosa & Company Inc 1717 Main St LB47	Dallas	TX	75201	**800-676-5352**	214-658-1670
Federated Investors 1001 Liberty Ave Federated Investors Twr *NYSE: FII*	Pittsburgh	PA	15222	**800-245-0242**	412-288-1900
Fidelity Investments Institutional Services Co Inc 82 Devonshire St	Boston	MA	02109	**800-343-3548**	617-563-9840
Fiduciary Management Inc of Milwaukee 100 E Wisconsin Ave Ste 2200	Milwaukee	WI	53202	**800-264-7684**	414-226-4545
Financial Resource Group LLC 12900 Preston Rd Ste 100 LB-104	Dallas	TX	75230	**866-473-7132**	972-960-7790
First Fidelity Capital Markets Inc 10463 Stonebridge Blvd	Boca Raton	FL	33498	**800-485-3670**	561-558-0730
First Pacific Advisors Inc 11601 Wilshire Blvd Ste 1200	Los Angeles	CA	90025	**800-982-4372**	310-473-0225
Fisher Investments 13100 Skyline Blvd	Woodside	CA	94062	**800-550-1071**	
Flexible Plan Investments Ltd 3883 Telegraph Rd Ste 100	Bloomfield Hills	MI	48302	**800-347-3539**	248-642-6640
FMR Corp 82 Devonshire St	Boston	MA	02109	**800-343-3548**	
Foothills Asset Management Ltd 8767 E Via de Ventura Ste 175	Scottsdale	AZ	85258	**800-663-9870**	480-777-9870
Ford Equity Research Inc 11722 Sorrento Valley Rd Ste I	San Diego	CA	92121	**800-842-0207**	858-755-1327
Fort Washington Investment Advisors Inc 303 Broadway Ste 1200	Cincinnati	OH	45202	**888-244-8167**	513-361-7600
Franklin Resources Inc 1 Franklin Pkwy Bdge 970 1st Fl *NYSE: BEN*	San Mateo	CA	94403	**800-632-2301**	650-312-2000
Gannett Welsh & Kotler LLC 222 Berkeley St	Boston	MA	02116	**800-225-4236**	617-236-8900
Gemini Companies, The 80 Arkay Dr Ste 110	Hauppauge	NY	11788	**855-891-0092**	
Global Cash Card 7 Corporate Pk Ste 130	Irvine	CA	92606	**888-220-4477**	949-751-0360
Goldman Sachs Asset Management (GSAM) 200 W St	New York	NY	10282	**800-526-7384**	212-902-1000
Greystone Managed Investments Inc 300 Park Centre 1230 Blackfoot Dr	Regina	SK	S4S7G4	**800-213-4286**	306-779-6400
Hamilton Capital Management 5025 Arlington Centre Blvd	Columbus	OH	43220	**888-833-5951**	614-273-1000
Harbour Investments Inc 575 D'Onofrio Dr Ste 300	Madison	WI	53719	**888-855-6960**	608-662-6100
Harrington Investments Inc 1001 Second St Ste 325	Napa	CA	94559	**800-788-0154**	
Haywood Securities Inc Waterfront Centre 200 Burrard St Ste 700	Vancouver	BC	V6C3L6	**800-663-9499**	604-697-7100
HD Vest Financial Services 6333 N State Hwy 161 4th Fl	Irving	TX	75038	**866-218-8206**	972-870-6000

	Toll-Free	Phone

Hengehold Capital Management LLC
6116 Harrison Ave ....Cincinnati OH 45247 — **877-598-5120** — 513-598-5120

Herndon Plant Oakley Ltd
800 N Shoreline Blvd
Ste 2200 South........................Corpus Christi TX 78401 — **800-888-4894** — 361-888-7611

HSBC Bank USA
452 Fifth Ave ....New York NY 10018 — **800-975-4722**

ICM Asset Management Inc
601 W Main Ave ....Spokane WA 99201 — **800-488-4075** — 509-455-3588

ICON Advisers Inc
5299 DTC Blvd Ste 1200 ....Greenwood Village CO 80111 — **800-828-4881** — 303-790-1600

Imperial Capital LLC
10100 Santa Monica Blvd Ste 2400 ....Los Angeles CA 90067 — **800-929-2299** — 310-246-3700

Integra Capital Ltd
2020 Winston Park Dr Ste 200 ....Oakville ON L6H6X7 — **800-363-2480** — 905-829-1131

International Risk Management Institute Inc (IRMI)
12222 Merit Dr Ste 1600 ....Dallas TX 75251 — **800-827-4242** — 972-960-7693

Investment Scorecard Inc
601 Grassmere Park Dr Ste 1 ....Nashville TN 37211 — **800-555-6035** — 615-301-1975

Investors Group Inc
447 Portage Ave ....Winnipeg MB R3B3H5 — **888-746-6344**
TSE: IGM

Jacuzzi Brands LLC
13925 City Ctr Dr Ste 200 ....Chino Hills CA 91709 — **866-234-7727**

James Investment Research Inc
1349 Fairgrounds Rd ....Xenia OH 45385 — **800-995-2637** — 937-426-7640

Jeffrey Matthews Financial Group LLC, The
30B Vreeland Rd Ste 210 ....Florham Park NJ 07932 — **888-467-3636** — 973-805-6222

John G Ullman & Associates Inc
51 E Market St ....Corning NY 14830 — **800-936-3785** — 607-936-3785

Johnson Investment Counsel Inc
3777 W Fork Rd ....Cincinnati OH 45247 — **800-541-0170** — 513-661-3100

JPMorgan Fleming Asset Management
PO Box 8528 ....Boston MA 02266 — **800-480-4111**

Jra Financial Advisors
7373 Kirkwood Ct Ste 300 ....Maple Grove MN 55369 — **800-278-5988** — 763-315-8000

Kayne Anderson Capital Advisors LP
1800 Ave of the Stars 3rd Fl ....Los Angeles CA 90067 — **800-638-1496** — 310-282-7900

KCM Investment Advisors LLC
750 Lindaro St Ste 350......................San Rafael CA 94901 — **888-287-5555** — 415-461-7788

Keats, Connelly & Associates LLC
3336 N 32nd St Ste 100........................Phoenix AZ 85018 — **800-678-5007** — 602-955-5007

Kirr Marbach & Co Investment Management
621 Washington St..........................Columbus IN 47201 — **800-808-9444** — 812-376-9444

Koonce Securities Inc
6550 Rock Spring Dr Ste 600............Bethesda MD 20817 — **800-368-2806** — 301-897-9700

Kootenay Savings Credit Union
1199 Cedar Ave ....Trail BC V1R4B8 — **800-665-5728**

Laird Norton Tyee
801 Second Ave Ste 1600.......................Seattle WA 98104 — **800-426-5105**

Landaas & Co
411 E Wisconsin Ave 20th Fl ....Milwaukee WI 53202 — **800-236-1096** — 414-223-1099

Laurentian Bank Securities Inc
1981 McGill College Ave Ste 100............Montreal QC H3A3K3 — **888-350-8577** — 514-350-2800

Leconte Wealth Management LLC
703 William Blount Dr ....Maryville TN 37801 — **888-236-6630** — 865-379-8200

Leerink Swann & Co
1 Federal St 37th Fl ....Boston MA 02110 — **800-808-7525**

Linscomb & Williams Inc
1400 Post Oak Blvd Ste 1000................Houston TX 77056 — **800-960-1200** — 713-840-1000

Litman Gregory Research Inc
100 Larkspur Landing Cir Ste 204 ....Larkspur CA 94939 — **800-960-0188** — 925-254-8999

Logan Capital Management Inc
6 Coulter Ave Ste 2000.......................Ardmore PA 19003 — **800-215-1100**

Loomis Sayles & Company Inc LP
1 Financial Ctr ....Boston MA 02111 — **800-343-2029** — 800-633-3330

Lord Abbett & Co
90 Hudson St ....Jersey City NJ 07302 — **888-522-2388**

Mackenzie Financial Corp
180 Queen St W ....Toronto ON M5V3K1 — **888-653-7070** — 416-922-5322

Madison Investment Advisors Inc
550 Science Dr ....Madison WI 53711 — **800-767-0300** — 608-274-0300

Manarin Investment Counsel Ltd
505 N 210th St ....Omaha NE 68022 — **800-397-1167** — 402-676-8717

Marketocracy Inc
1208 W Magnolia Ste 236 ....Fort Worth TX 76104 — **877-462-4180**

Marquette Asset Management
33 S Sixth St Ste 4540...................Minneapolis MN 55402 — **866-661-3770** — 612-661-3770

Marshall & Sullivan Inc
1109 First Ave Ste 200.........................Seattle WA 98101 — **800-735-7290** — 206-621-9014

Maxim Group LLC
405 Lexington Ave ....New York NY 10174 — **800-724-0761** — 212-895-3500

Mengis Capital Management Inc
1 SW Columbia St Ste 780...................Portland OR 97258 — **877-916-0780** — 503-916-0776

MFS Investment Management
111 Huntington Ave ....Boston MA 02199 — **800-637-8255** — 617-954-5000

Mission Wealth
1123 Chapala St 3rd Fl......................Santa Barbara CA 93101 — **888-642-7221** — 805-882-2360

Morley Financial Services Inc
1300 SW Fifth Ave Ste 3300..................Portland OR 97201 — **800-548-4806** — 503-484-9300

Morningstar Inc
22 W Washington St ....Chicago IL 60602 — **800-735-0700*** — 312-696-6000
NASDAQ: MORN ■ *Orders

Navellier Securities Corp
1 E Liberty St Ste 504...........................Reno NV 89501 — **800-887-8671** — 775-785-2300

Neiman Funds Management LLC
6631 Main St ....Williamsville NY 14221 — **877-385-2720**

Neuberger Berman LLC
605 Third Ave ....New York NY 10158 — **800-223-6448**

NorthCoast Asset Management LLC
1 Greenwich Office Pk ....Greenwich CT 06831 — **800-274-5448** — 203-532-7000

Northern Trust Company of Connecticut
300 Atlantic St Ste 400.......................Stamford CT 06901 — **866-876-9944** — 312-630-0779

Northland Securities Inc
150 S Fifth St Ste 3300....................Minneapolis MN 55402 — **800-851-2920** — 612-851-5900

Northwestern Mutual Investment Services LLC
611 E Wisconsin Ave Ste 300................Milwaukee WI 53202 — **866-664-7737**

Odlum Brown Ltd
250 Howe St Ste 1100 ....Vancouver BC V6C3S9 — **866-636-8222** — 604-669-1600

Osborne Partners Capital Management LLC
580 California St Ste 1900 ....San Francisco CA 94104 — **800-362-7734** — 415-362-5637

Oxford Financial Group Ltd
11711 N Meridian St Ste 600 ....Carmel IN 46032 — **800-722-2289** — 317-843-5678

Pacific Investment Management Company LLC
840 Newport Ctr Dr ....Newport Beach CA 92660 — **800-387-4626** — 949-720-6000

Parsons Capital Management Inc
10 Weybosset St Ste 1000 ....Providence RI 02903 — **888-521-2440** — 401-521-2440

Payden & Rygel
333 S Grand Ave ....Los Angeles CA 90071 — **800-572-9336** — 213-625-1900

Peak Financial Management Inc
The Wellesley Office Park 20 William St
Ste 135.....................................Wellesley MA 02481 — **877-567-9500** — 781-487-9500

Peninsula Asset Management Inc
1111 Third Ave W Ste 340 ....Bradenton FL 34205 — **800-269-6417**

Perkins Investment Management LLC
311 S Wacker Dr Ste 6000 ....Chicago IL 60606 — **866-922-0355**

Personal Capital Corp
1 Circle Star Way 1st Fl ....San Carlos CA 94070 — **855-855-8005**

Pittenger & Anderson Inc
5533 S 27th St Ste 201.........................Lincoln NE 68512 — **800-897-1588** — 402-328-8800

Producers Financial
5350 Tomah Dr Ste 3800 ....Colorado Springs CO 80918 — **800-985-5549** — 719-535-0739

Prudential Financial Inc
751 Broad St ....Newark NJ 07102 — **800-843-7625** — 973-802-6000
NYSE: PRU

Putnam Investments
30 Dan Rd PO Box 8383........................Canton MA 02021 — **888-478-8626** — 617-292-1000

PVG Asset Management Corp
24918 Genesee Trl Rd ....Golden CO 80401 — **800-777-0818**

QCI Asset Management
40A Grove St ....Pittsford NY 14534 — **800-836-3960** — 585-218-2060

Quaker Funds
1180 W Swedesford Rd Ste 150 ....Berwyn PA 19312 — **800-220-8888** — 610-455-2200

R N Croft Financial Group Inc
218 Steeles Ave E ....Thornhill ON L3T1A6 — **877-249-2884** — 905-695-7777

Radnor Financial Advisors Inc
485 Devon Park Dr Ste 119 ....Wayne PA 19087 — **888-271-9922** — 610-975-0280

Raymond James Ltd
2200-925 W Georgia St Cathedral Pl ....Vancouver BC V6C3L2 — **888-545-6624** — 604-659-8000

Rising Results Inc
201 Edward Curry Ave Ste 202........Staten Island NY 10314 — **800-837-4648** — 718-370-8300

RNC Genter Capital Management
11601 Wilshire Blvd 25th Fl...............Los Angeles CA 90025 — **800-877-7624** — 310-477-6543

Roffman Miller Assoc Inc
1835 Market St Ste 500 ....Philadelphia PA 19103 — **800-995-1030** — 215-981-1030

Ronald Blue & Company LLC
300 Colonial Center Pkwy Ste 300............Roswell GA 30076 — **800-841-0362** — 770-280-6000

Royce & Assoc LLC
745 Fifth Ave ....New York NY 10151 — **800-221-4268**

Ruane Cunniff & Goldfarb Inc
9 W 57th St Ste 5000 ....New York NY 10019 — **800-686-6884**

Russell Investments
1301 Second Ave 18th Fl ....Seattle WA 98101 — **800-426-7969** — 206-505-7877

Saturna Capital Corp
1300 N State St ....Bellingham WA 98225 — **888-732-6262** — 360-734-9900

Schultz Collins Lawson Chambers Inc
455 Market St Ste 1250 ....San Francisco CA 94105 — **877-291-2205** — 415-291-3000

Segall Bryant & Hamill
540 W Madison St Ste 1900....................Chicago IL 60661 — **800-836-4265** — 312-474-1222

Select Portfolio Management Inc
120 Vantis ....Aliso Viejo CA 92656 — **800-445-9822** — 949-975-7900

Sheaff Brock Investment Advisors LLC
8801 River Crossing Blvd Ste 100 ....Indianapolis IN 46240 — **866-575-5700** — 317-705-5700

Signator Investors Inc
197 Clarendon St C-8 ....Boston MA 02116 — **800-543-6611**

Signature Estate & Investment Advisors LLC (SEIA)
2121 Ave Of The Stars Ste 1600..............Los Angeles CA 90067 — **800-723-5115** — 310-712-2323

Smith Graham & Co
600 Travis St
6900 JPMorgan Chase Tower...................Houston TX 77002 — **800-739-4470** — 713-227-1100

Sound Shore Management Inc
8 Sound Shore Dr Ste 180 ....Greenwich CT 06830 — **800-551-1980** — 203-629-1980

South Texas Money Management Ltd
700 N Saint Mary's Ste 100 ....San Antonio TX 78205 — **800-805-1385** — 210-824-8916

Southeastern Asset Management Inc
6410 Poplar Ave Ste 900 ....Memphis TN 38119 — **800-445-9469** — 901-761-2474

Spire Investment Partners LLC
7901 Jones Branch Dr ....Mclean VA 22102 — **888-737-8907** — 703-748-5800

Stansberry & Assoc Investment Research LLC
1217 Saint Paul St ....Baltimore MD 21202 — **888-261-2693**

State Universities Retirement System of Illinois
1901 Fox Dr ....Champaign IL 61820 — **800-275-7877** — 217-378-8800

Sterling Mutuals Inc
1090 University Ave 2nd Fl....................Windsor ON N9A5S4 — **800-354-4956**

Stoever Glass & Company Inc
30 Wall St ....New York NY 10005 — **800-223-3881** — 212-952-1910

Strategic Financial Alliance Inc, The
2200 Century Pkwy Ste 500 ....Atlanta GA 30345 — **888-447-2444** — 678-954-4000

T Rowe Price Assoc Inc
100 E Pratt St ....Baltimore MD 21202 — **800-638-7890** — 410-345-2000

Tamarac Inc
701 Fifth Ave 14th Fl ....Seattle WA 98104 — **866-525-8811**

Technomart RGA Inc
401 Washington Ave Ste 1101 ....Baltimore MD 21204 — **800-877-6555** — 410-828-6555

Thompson Siegel & Walmsley Inc
6806 Paragon Pl Ste 300 ....Richmond VA 23230 — **800-697-1056** — 804-353-4500

Titlemax of South Carolina Inc
15 Bull St ....Savannah GA 31401 — **888-485-3629**

Tom Johnson Investment Management Inc
201 Robert S Kerr Ave ....Oklahoma City OK 73102 — **888-404-8546** — 405-236-2111

Treflie Capital Management
35 Ezekills Holw ....Sag Harbor NY 11963 — **866-236-3363** — 631-725-2500

Turner Investment Partners Inc
1205 Westlakes Dr Ste 100....................Berwyn PA 19312 — **800-224-6312** — 484-329-2300

			Toll-Free	Phone

TYGH Capital Management Inc
1211 S W Fifth Ave Ste 2100 . . . . Portland OR 97204 **800-972-0150** 503-972-0150
Univers Workplace Benefits Inc
897 12th St . . . . Hammonton NJ 08037 **800-343-0240**
US Global Investors Inc
7900 Callaghan Rd . . . . San Antonio TX 78229 **800-873-8637** 210-308-1234
NASDAQ: GROW
USAA Investment Management
9800 Fredericksburg Rd
PO Box 659453 . . . . San Antonio TX 78288 **800-531-8722**
Value Line Asset Management
551 Fifth Ave 3rd Fl . . . . New York NY 10176 **800-634-3583** 212-907-1500
Vanguard Group
455 Devon Pk Dr . . . . Wayne PA 19087 **877-662-7447** 610-669-1000
VCI Emergency Vehicle
43 Jefferson Ave . . . . Berlin NJ 08009 **800-394-2162** 856-768-2162
VectorVest Inc
20472 Chartwell Ctr Dr Ste D . . . . Cornelius NC 28031 **800-130-1519** 888-658-7638
Virtus Investment Partners Inc
100 Pearl St 9th Fl . . . . Hartford CT 06103 **800-243-1574** 413-775-6091
Waddell & Reed Financial Inc
6300 Lamar Ave . . . . Overland Park KS 66201 **888-923-3355** 913-236-2000
NYSE: WDR
Wealth Conservancy Inc, The
1525 Spruce St Ste 300 . . . . Boulder CO 80302 **888-440-1919** 303-444-1919
Wealthfront Inc
541 Cowper St . . . . Palo Alto CA 94301 **844-995-8437**
Webb Financial Group
8120 Penn Ave S Ste 177 . . . . Bloomington MN 55431 **800-927-9322** 952-837-3200
Weil Co, The
11236 El Camino Real Ste 200 . . . . San Diego CA 92130 **800-355-9345** 858-724-6040
Wilshire Assoc Inc
1299 Ocean Ave Ste 700 . . . . Santa Monica CA 90401 **855-626-8281** 310-451-3051
Woodmont Investment Counsel LLC
401 Commerce St Ste 5400 . . . . Nashville TN 37219 **800-278-8003** 615-297-6144
Workplace Answers LLC
3701 Executive Ctr Dr Ste 201 . . . . Austin TX 78731 **866-861-4410**
Wright Investors' Service
440 Wheelers Farms Rd . . . . Milford CT 06461 **800-232-0013**
Yacktman Asset Management Co
6300 Bridgepoint Pkwy Bldg 1 Ste 320 . . . . Austin TX 78730 **800-835-3879** 512-767-6700

401	INVESTMENT COMPANIES - SMALL BUSINESS

The companies listed here conform to the Small Business Administration's standards for investing.

			Toll-Free	Phone

Galliard Capital Management Inc
800 La Salle Ave Ste 1100 . . . . Minneapolis MN 55402 **800-717-1617** 612-667-3220
GamePlan Financial Marketing LLC
300 ParkBrooke Pl Ste 200 . . . . Woodstock GA 30189 **800-886-4757*** 678-238-0601
*Cust Svc
Hornor Townsend & Kent Inc (HTK)
600 Dresher Rd Ste C1C . . . . Horsham PA 19044 **800-289-9999**
Impact Seven Inc
147 Lake Almena Dr . . . . Almena WI 54805 **800-685-9353** 715-357-3334

402	INVESTMENT COMPANIES - SPECIALIZED SMALL BUSINESS

Companies listed here conform to the Small Business Administration's requirements for investment in minority companies.

			Toll-Free	Phone

Al Copeland Investments Inc
1001 Harimaw Ct S . . . . Metairie LA 70001 **800-401-0401** 504-830-1000
ALCO Inc 6925 - 104 St . . . . Edmonton AB T6H2L5 **800-563-1498** 780-435-3502
Burney Co
1800 Alexander Bell Dr Ste 510 . . . . Reston VA 20191 **866-928-7639**
Canadian Home Income Plan Corp
1881 Yonge St Ste 300 . . . . Toronto ON M4S3C4 **866-758-2447** 416-925-4757
Du Quebec
1400 Blvd Guillaume-Couture . . . . Levis QC G6W8K7 **800-749-3646** 418-838-5602
Portland Investment Counsel Inc
1375 Kerns Rd . . . . Burlington ON L7P4V7 **888-710-4242** 905-331-4242
RD Legal Funding LLC
45 Legion Dr . . . . Cresskill NJ 07626 **800-565-5177**
Security Credit Services LLC
2653 W Oxford Loop Ste 108 . . . . Oxford MS 38655 **866-699-7889**
Smith Affiliated Capital (SAC)
800 Third Ave 12th Fl . . . . New York NY 10022 **888-387-3298** 212-644-9440

403	INVESTMENT GUIDES - ONLINE

SEE ALSO Buyer's Guides - Online

			Toll-Free	Phone

Briefingcom Inc
401 N Michigan Ste 2910 . . . . Chicago IL 60611 **800-752-3013*** 312-670-4463
*General
eSignal 3955 Pt Eden Way . . . . Hayward CA 94545 **800-815-8256** 510-266-6000
FactSet Research Systems Inc
601 Merritt 7 . . . . Norwalk CT 06851 **877-322-8738** 203-810-1000
NYSE: FDS
Harris myCFO Inc
2200 Geng Rd Ste 100 . . . . Palo Alto CA 94303 **866-966-1130** 650-210-5000
Hoover's Inc
5800 Airport Blvd . . . . Austin TX 78752 **800-486-8666** 512-374-4500
InvestorPlacecom
2420A Gehman Ln . . . . Lancaster PA 17602 **800-219-8592**
Motley Fool Inc
2000 Duke St 4th Fl . . . . Alexandria VA 22314 **800-292-7677** 703-838-3665
Stockwatch
700 W Georgia St PO Box 10371 . . . . Vancouver BC V7Y1J6 **800-268-6397** 604-687-1500

TheStreetcom Inc
14 Wall St 15th Fl . . . . New York NY 10005 **800-562-9571** 212-321-5000
NASDAQ: TST

404	INVESTMENT (MISC)

SEE ALSO Investment Newsletters ; Banks - Commercial & Savings ; Mortgage Lenders & Loan Brokers ; Securities Brokers & Dealers ; Mutual Funds ; Commodity Contracts Brokers & Dealers ; Franchises ; Real Estate Investment Trusts (REITs) ; Venture Capital Firms ; Royalty Trusts ; Investment Guides - Online

			Toll-Free	Phone

Adams Funds
500 E Pratt St Ste 1300 . . . . Baltimore MD 21202 **800-638-2479** 410-752-5900
NYSE: ADX
Fidelity Investments Charitable Gift Fund
PO Box 770001 . . . . Cincinnati OH 45277 **800-262-6039**
Haverford Trust Co, The
3 Radnor Corp Ctr 100 Matsonford Rd
Ste 450 . . . . Radnor PA 19087 **888-995-1979** 610-995-8700
HomeVestors of America Inc
6500 Greenville Ave Ste 400 . . . . Dallas TX 75206 **866-200-6475** 972-761-0046
Main Street Capital Corp
1300 Post Oak Blvd . . . . Houston TX 77056 **800-966-1559** 713-350-6000
NYSE: MAIN
Moors & Cabot Inc
111 Devonshire St . . . . Boston MA 02109 **800-426-0501**
Pembina Pipeline Corp
585 Eighth Ave SW . . . . Calgary AB T2P1G1 **888-428-3222** 403-231-7500
TSE: PPL
Superior Plus Income Fund
1400 840-7 Ave SW . . . . Calgary AB T2P3G2 **866-490-7587** 403-218-2951
Thomas H Lee Partners LP
100 Federal St . . . . Boston MA 02110 **877-456-3427** 617-227-1050

405	JANITORIAL & CLEANING SUPPLIES - WHOL

			Toll-Free	Phone

Accutemp Products Inc
8415 N Clinton Pk . . . . Fort Wayne IN 46825 **800-210-5907**
Advanced Vacuum Company Inc
1215 Business Pkwy N . . . . Westminster MD 21157 **800-272-2525** 410-876-8200
Brady Industries Inc
7055 Lindell Rd . . . . Las Vegas NV 89118 **800-293-4698** 702-876-3990
C&T Design & Equipment Company Inc
2750 Tobey Dr . . . . Indianapolis IN 46219 **800-966-3374**
Culinary Depot Inc
2 Melnick Dr . . . . Monsey NY 10952 **888-845-8200**
Fitch Co 2201 Russell St . . . . Baltimore MD 21230 **800-933-4824** 410-539-1953
Industrial Soap Co
722 S Vandeventer Ave . . . . Saint Louis MO 63110 **800-405-7627** 314-241-6363
J Ennis Fabrics Ltd
12122 - 68 St . . . . Edmonton AB T5B1R1 **800-663-6647**
Kenway Distributors Inc
6320 Strawberry Ln . . . . Louisville KY 40214 **800-292-9478** 502-367-2201
Mobile Fixture & Equipment Company Inc
1155 Montlimar Dr . . . . Mobile AL 36609 **800-345-6458** 251-342-0455
Mortech Manufacturing Inc
411 N Aerojet Ave . . . . Azusa CA 91702 **800-410-0100** 626-334-1471
Rose Products & Services Inc
545 Stimmel Rd . . . . Columbus OH 43223 **800-264-1568** 614-443-7647
Taylor Freezers of California
221 Harris Ct . . . . South San Francisco CA 94080 **877-978-4800**

406	JEWELERS' FINDINGS & MATERIALS

			Toll-Free	Phone

Best Priced Products Inc
PO Box 1174 . . . . White Plains NY 10602 **800-824-2939** 914-345-3800
Brooks Instrument LLC
407 West Vine St . . . . Hatfield PA 19440 **888-554-3569**
Chauvin Arnoux Inc
15 Faraday Dr . . . . Dover NH 03820 **800-343-1391** 603-749-6434
Comark Instruments Inc
PO Box 500 . . . . Beaverton OR 97077 **800-555-6658** 503-643-5204
Cransmart Systems Inc
4908 97 St NW . . . . Edmonton AB T6E5S1 **888-562-3222** 780-437-2986
Cyber-Rain Inc
5535 Balboa Blvd Ste 115 . . . . Encino CA 91316 **877-888-1452**
David H Fell & Company Inc
6009 Bandini Blvd . . . . Commerce CA 90040 **800-822-1996** 323-722-9992
Delta M Corp
1003 Larsen Dr . . . . Oak Ridge TN 37830 **800-922-0083** 865-483-1569
DTNIQ Inc
9110 W Dodge Rd Ste 200 . . . . Omaha NE 68114 **800-475-4755** 402-390-2328
Emme E2MS LLC PO Box 2251 . . . . Bristol CT 06011 **800-396-0523**
Environmental Systems Products Inc
7 Kripes Rd . . . . East Granby CT 06026 **800-446-4708** 860-392-2100
Findings Inc 160 Water St . . . . Keene NH 03431 **800-225-2706** 603-352-3717
FoodChek Systems Inc
1414 8 St SW Ste 450 . . . . Calgary AB T2R1J6 **877-298-0208** 403-269-9424
Fugro-Roadware Inc
2505 Meadowvale Blvd . . . . Mississauga ON L5N5S2 **800-828-2726** 905-567-2870
Guardian Interlock Systems
228 Church St . . . . Marietta GA 30060 **800-499-0994**
Humboldt Manufacturing Co
875 Tollgate Rd . . . . Elgin IL 60123 **800-544-7220**
HydroPoint Data Systems Inc
1720 Corporate Cir . . . . Petaluma CA 94954 **800-362-8774**
Intoximeters Inc
2081 Craig Rd . . . . Saint Louis MO 63146 **800-451-8639** 314-429-4000
JASCO Inc 28600 Mary's Ct . . . . Easton MD 21601 **800-333-5272** 410-822-1220

				Toll-Free	Phone
Kejr Inc 1835 Wall St	Salina	KS	67401	800-436-7762	785-825-1842
Krohn Industries Inc PO Box 98	Carlstadt	NJ	07072	800-526-6299	201-933-9696
Lee's Morvillo Group 160 Niantic Ave	Providence	RI	02907	800-821-1700	401-353-1740
Lifeloc Technologies Inc 12441 W 49th Ave	Wheat Ridge	CO	80033	800-722-4817	303-431-9500
Modern Machine & Tool Company Inc 11844 Jefferson Ave	Newport News	VA	23606	800-482-1835	757-873-1212
MTI Instruments Inc 325 Washington Ave Ext	Albany	NY	12205	800-342-2203	518-218-2550
Northern Digital Inc 103 Randall Dr	Waterloo	ON	N2V1C5	877-634-6340	519-884-5142
OmniMetrix LLC 5225 Belle Wood Ct	Buford	GA	30518	800-854-7342	770-209-0012
Paul H Gesswein & Co 255 Hancock Ave	Bridgeport	CT	06605	800-544-2043	203-366-5400
Precision Specialties Co 1201 E Pecan St	Sherman	TX	75090	800-527-3295	
Precision Time Systems Inc 5433 Main St	Shallotte	NC	28470	877-416-6660	910-253-9850
Rad-Comm Systems Corp 2931 Portland Dr	Oakville	ON	L6H5S4	800-588-5229	905-829-8290
Rainwise Inc 18 River Field Rd	Trenton	ME	04605	800-762-5723	207-288-5169
Romanoff International Supply Corp 9 Deforest St *Cust Svc	Amityville	NY	11701	800-221-7448*	
Romet Ltd 1080 Matheson Blvd E	Mississauga	ON	L4W2V2	800-387-3201	905-624-1591
Santa Barbara Control Systems 5375 Overpass Rd	Santa Barbara	CA	93111	800-621-2279	805-683-8833
Senet Inc 100 Market St Ste 302	Portsmouth	NH	03801	877-807-5755	
Signalisation Ver-Mac Inc 1781 Bresse	Quebec	QC	G2G2V2	888-488-7446	418-654-1303
SIX Safety Systems Inc 250031 Mountain View Trl	Calgary	AB	T3Z3S3	888-918-9440	403-288-9440
Space Optics Research Labs LLC 7 Stuart Rd	Chelmsford	MA	01824	800-552-7675	978-250-8640
Stuller Settings Inc PO Box 87777	Lafayette	LA	70598	800-877-7777	
Tavis Corp 3636 State Hwy 49 S	Mariposa	CA	95338	800-842-6102	209-966-2027
Veris Industries Inc 16640 SW 72nd Ave	Portland	OR	97224	800-354-8556	503-598-4564
Victor Settings Inc 25 Brook Ave	Maywood	NJ	07607	800-322-9008	201-845-4433
Zepp Labs Inc 75 E Santa Clara St 6th Fl	San Jose	CA	95113	866-400-9377	

407   JEWELRY - COSTUME

				Toll-Free	Phone
1928 Jewelry Co 3000 West Empire Blvd	Burbank	CA	91504	800-227-1928	818-841-1928
A & Z Hayward Co 655 Waterman Ave	East Providence	RI	02914	800-556-7462	401-438-0550
Speidel 34 Branch Ave	Providence	RI	02904	800-441-2200	401-519-2000

408   JEWELRY - PRECIOUS METAL

				Toll-Free	Phone
American Achievement Corp 7211 Cir S Rd	Austin	TX	78745	800-531-5055	512-444-0571
Balfour 7211 Cir S Rd	Austin	TX	78745	800-225-3687	
Byard F Brogan Inc PO Box 0369	Glenside	PA	19038	800-232-7642	215-885-3550
David Yurman Designs Inc 24 Vestry St	New York	NY	10013	888-398-7626	
Hammerman Bros Inc 50 W 57th 12th Fl	New York	NY	10019	800-223-6436	212-956-2800
Harry Klitzner Inc 530 Wellington Ave Ste 11	Cranston	RI	02910	800-621-0161	
Harry Winston Inc 718 Fifth Ave	New York	NY	10019	800-988-4110	212-399-1000
Ira Green Inc 177 Georgia Ave *General	Providence	RI	02905	800-663-7487*	
James Avery Craftsman Inc 145 Avery Rd N	Kerrville	TX	78029	800-283-1770	830-895-6800
Jostens Inc 3601 Minnesota Ave Ste 400	Minneapolis	MN	55435	800-235-4774	952-830-3300
Kinsley & Sons Inc 24 S Church St Ste A *General	Union	MO	63084	800-468-4428*	
Maui Divers of Hawaii 1520 Liona St	Honolulu	HI	96814	800-462-4454	808-946-7979
Mtm Recognition Corp 3201 SE 29th St	Oklahoma City	OK	73115	877-686-7464	405-670-4545
Novell Design Studio 2100 Felver Ct	Rahway	NJ	07065	888-668-3551	732-428-8300
OC Tanner Co 1930 S State St	Salt Lake City	UT	84115	800-453-7490	
OROCAL GOLD NUGGET CO 1720 Bird St	Oroville	CA	95965	800-367-6225	530-533-5065
Ostbye & Anderson Inc 10055 51st Ave N	Minneapolis	MN	55442	866-553-1515	
Relios Inc 6815 Academy Pkwy W NE	Albuquerque	NM	87109	800-827-6543	505-345-5304
Stanley Creations Inc 1414 Willow Ave	Melrose Park	PA	19027	800-220-1414	215-635-6207
Sunshine Minting Inc 7600 Mineral Dr Ste 700	Coeur d'Alene	ID	83815	800-274-5837	208-772-9592

				Toll-Free	Phone
Terryberry Co 2033 Oak Industrial Dr NE	Grand Rapids	MI	49505	800-253-0882	616-458-1391
Tiffany & Co 727 Fifth Ave *NYSE: TIF ■ *Orders	New York	NY	10022	800-526-0649*	212-755-8000
Wheeler Mfg Co Inc 107 Main Ave PO Box 629	Lemmon	SD	57638	800-843-1937	
Wright & Lato 2100 Felver Ct	Rahway	NJ	07065	800-724-1855	973-674-8700

409   JEWELRY STORES

				Toll-Free	Phone
Aucoin-Hart 1525 Metairie Rd	Metairie	LA	70005	800-992-8743	504-834-9999
Ben Bridge Jeweler Inc PO Box 1908 *Cust Svc	Seattle	WA	98111	888-917-9171*	888-448-1912
Birks 1240 du Sq-Phillips St	Montreal	QC	H3B3H4	800-758-2511	
Blue Nile Inc 705 Fifth Ave S Ste 900 *NASDAQ: NILE	Seattle	WA	98104	800-242-2728	206-336-6700
Borsheim's Inc 120 Regency Pkwy	Omaha	NE	68114	800-642-4438	402-391-0400
Brian Gavin Diamonds 7322 SW Frwy Ste 1810 - Arena One	Houston	TX	77074	866-611-4465	
Coleman E Adler & Sons Inc 722 Canal St	New Orleans	LA	70130	800-925-7912	504-523-5292
Color Merchants 6 E 45th St Rm 1704	New York	NY	10017	800-356-3851	212-682-4788
Dunkin's Diamonds Inc 897 Hebron Rd	Heath	OH	43056	877-343-4883	740-522-1468
Fantasy Diamond Corp 1550 W Carrol Ave	Chicago	IL	60607	800-621-4445	312-583-3200
Freeman Marcus Jewelers 76 Merchants Row	Rutland	VT	05701	800-451-4167	802-773-2792
Garfield Refining Co 810 E Cayuga St	Philadelphia	PA	19124	800-523-0968	
GN Diamond LLC 800 Chestnut St	Philadelphia	PA	19107	800-724-8810	215-925-5111
H E. Murdock Co Inc 88 Main St	Waterville	ME	04901	888-974-1805	800-439-3297
H Stern Jewelers Inc 645 Fifth Ave	New York	NY	10022	800-747-8376	212-688-0300
Harry Ritchie's Jewelers Inc 956 Willamette St *Cust Svc	Eugene	OR	97401	800-935-2850*	541-686-1787
Harry Winston Inc 718 Fifth Ave	New York	NY	10019	800-988-4110	212-399-1000
Helzberg Diamonds 1825 Swift Ave	North Kansas City	MO	64116	800-435-9237	816-842-7780
Jay Roberts Jewelers 515 Rt 73 S	Marlton	NJ	08053	888-828-8463	856-596-8600
JewelryWebcom Inc 98 Cuttermill Rd Ste 464	Great Neck	NY	11021	800-955-9245	516-482-3982
Kay Jewelers 375 Ghent Rd	Akron	OH	44333	800-527-8029	
King's Jewelry & Loan 800 S Vermont Ave	Los Angeles	CA	90005	800-378-1111	213-383-5555
Lori Bonn Jewelery 114 Linden St	Oakland	CA	94607	877-507-4206	510-286-8181
Lux Bond & Green Inc 46 Lasalle Rd	West Hartford	CT	06107	800-524-7336	
Mann's Jewelers Inc 2945 Monroe Ave	Rochester	NY	14618	800-828-6234	585-271-4000
Mervis Diamond Importers 1900 Mervis Way	Tysons	VA	22182	800-437-5683	703-448-9000
Morgan & Co 1131 Glendon Ave	Los Angeles	CA	90024	800-458-4367	310-208-3377
Park Lane Jewelry 100 E Commerce Dr	Schaumburg	IL	60173	800-621-0088	
Reeds Jewelers Inc PO Box 2229 *Orders	Wilmington	NC	28402	877-406-3266*	
Republic Metals Corp 12900 NW 38th Ave	Miami	FL	33054	888-685-8505	305-685-8505
Ross Simons Jewelers Inc 9 Ross Simons Dr	Cranston	RI	02920	800-835-0919	
Samuels Diamonds 9607 Research Blvd Ste 100 Bldg F	Austin	TX	78759	877-388-1836	
Shane Co 9790 E Arapahoe Rd	Greenwood Village	CO	80112	866-467-4263	303-799-4700
Sol Jewelry Designs Inc 550 S Hill St Ste 1020	Los Angeles	CA	90013	888-323-7772	213-622-7772
Tiffany & Co 727 Fifth Ave *NYSE: TIF ■ *Orders	New York	NY	10022	800-526-0649*	212-755-8000
Trabert & Hoeffer 111 E Oak St	Chicago	IL	60611	800-539-3573	312-787-1654
Van Cleef & Arpels Inc 744 Fifth Ave	New York	NY	10019	877-826-2533	212-896-9284
Wilkerson 222 S Main St	Stuttgart	AR	72160	800-631-1999	
Zale Corp *Zales Jewelers Div* 901 W Walnut Hill Ln *Cust Svc	Irving	TX	75038	800-311-5393*	972-580-4000

410   JEWELRY, WATCHES, GEMS - WHOL

				Toll-Free	Phone
Bennett Brothers Inc 30 E Adams St	Chicago	IL	60603	800-621-2626	312-263-4800
Broco Products Inc 18624 Syracuse Ave	Cleveland	OH	44110	800-321-0837	216-531-0880
Charles & Colvard Ltd 170 Southport Dr *NASDAQ: CTHR	Morrisville	NC	27560	800-210-4367	919-468-0399

Classified Section

	Toll-Free	Phone
Continental Coin & Jewlery Co 5627 Sepulveda Blvd .... Van Nuys CA 91411	800-552-6467	818-781-4232
EH Ashley & Company Inc 1 White Squadron Rd .... Riverside RI 02915	800-735-7424	401-431-0950
Empire Diamond Corp 350 Fifth Ave Ste 4000 .... New York NY 10118	800-728-3425	212-564-4777
FAF 26 Lark Industrial Pkwy .... Greenville RI 02828	800-949-3311	
Fire Mountain Gems Inc 1 Fire Mountain Way .... Grants Pass OR 97526	800-355-2137	
Frederick Goldman Inc 154 W 14th St .... New York NY 10011	800-221-3232	
Gemex Systems Inc 6040 W Executive Dr Ste A .... Mequon WI 53092	866-694-3639	262-242-1111
Gerson Co 1450 S Lone Elm Rd .... Olathe KS 66061	800-444-8172	913-262-7400
Identification Plates Inc 1555 High Point Dr .... Mesquite TX 75149	800-395-2570	972-216-1616
Imerys Filtration Minerals Inc 130 Castilian Dr .... Goleta CA 93117	800-893-4445	805-562-0200
Jewel-Craft Inc 4122 Olympic Blvd .... Erlanger KY 41018	800-525-5482	859-282-2400
Joseph Blank Inc 62 W 47th St Ste 808 .... New York NY 10036	800-223-7666	212-575-9050
Kabana Inc 616 Indian School Rd NW .... Albuquerque NM 87102	800-521-5986	
Kendra Scott LLC 1400 S Congress Ave Ste A-170 .... Austin TX 78704	866-677-7023	
Lashbrook Designs 131 E 13065 S .... Draper UT 84020	888-252-7388	
Leo Wolleman Inc 31 S St Ste 4-N-3 .... Mt Vernon NY 10550	800-223-5667	212-840-1881
Metal Marketplace International (MMI) 718 Sansom St .... Philadelphia PA 19106	800-523-9191	215-592-8777
Mikimoto (America) Company Ltd 730 Fifth Ave .... New York NY 10019	844-341-0579	
Quality Gold Inc 500 Quality Blvd .... Fairfield OH 45014	800-354-9833	
Seno Jewelry LLC 259 W 30th St 10th Fl. .... New York NY 10001	888-660-2910	212-619-4552
Tara Pearls 10 W 46th Ste 600 .... New York NY 10036	888-575-8272	

411   JUVENILE DETENTION FACILITIES

SEE ALSO Correctional Facilities - Federal ; Correctional & Detention Management (Privatized) ; Correctional Facilities - State
Listings are organized alphabetically by states.

	Toll-Free	Phone

LABELS - FABRIC

SEE Narrow Fabric Mills

	Toll-Free	Phone
Johnson Youth Ctr 3252 Hospital Dr .... Juneau AK 99801	800-780-9972	907-586-9433
McLaughlin Youth Ctr 2600 Providence Dr .... Anchorage AK 99508	800-478-2221	907-261-4399
Nome Youth Facility 804 E Fourth St .... Nome AK 99762	800-770-5650	907-443-5434
Ventura Youth Correctional Facility 3100 Wright Rd .... Camarillo CA 93010	866-232-5627	805-485-7951
Marvin W Foote Youth Services Ctr 13500 E Fremont Pl .... Englewood CO 80112	800-970-3468	303-768-7501
Spring Creek Youth Services Ctr 3190 E Las Vegas St .... Colorado Springs CO 80906	800-388-5515	719-390-2700
Zebulon Pike Youth Services Ctr 1427 W Rio Grande .... Colorado Springs CO 80906	800-970-3468	719-633-8713
Ferris School 959 Centre Rd .... Wilmington DE 19805	800-292-9582	302-993-3800
New Castle County Detention Ctr 963 Centre Rd .... Wilmington DE 19805	800-969-4357	302-633-3100
Bay Regional Juvenile Detention Ctr 450 E 11th St .... Panama City FL 32401	800-355-2280	850-872-4706
Hillsborough Regional Juvenile Detention Ctr West 3948 ML King Jr Blvd .... Tampa FL 33614	800-355-2280	813-871-7650
Logansport Juvenile Correctional Facility 1118 S St Rd 25 .... Logansport IN 46947	800-800-5556	800-677-9800
Plainfield Re-Entry Educational Facility 501 W Main St .... Plainfield IN 46168	800-677-9800	
State Training School 3211 Edgington Ave .... Eldora IA 50627	800-362-2178	641-858-5402
Cuyahoga Hills Juvenile Correctional Facility 4321 Green Rd .... Highland Hills OH 44128	800-872-3132	216-464-8200
Camp Florence 4859 S Jetty Rd .... Florence OR 97439	800-588-9003	541-997-2076
STAR Academy 12279 Brady Dr .... Custer SD 57730	800-265-9684	605-673-2521

412   LABELS - OTHER THAN FABRIC

	Toll-Free	Phone
Accurate Dial & Nameplate Inc 329 Mira Loma Ave .... Glendale CA 91204	800-400-4455	323-245-9181
Acro Labels Inc 2530 Wyandotte Rd .... Willow Grove PA 19090	800-355-2235	215-657-5366
Alcop Adhesive Label Co 826 Perkins Ln .... Beverly NJ 08010	888-313-3017	609-871-4400
AME Label Corp 25155 W Ave Stanford .... Valencia CA 91355	866-278-9268	661-257-2200
American Law Label Inc 1677 S Research Loop .... Tucson AZ 85710	888-529-5223	
Arch Crown Tags Inc 460 Hillside Ave .... Hillside NJ 07205	800-526-8353	973-731-6300
Avery Dennison Corp 207 Goode Ave .... Glendale CA 91203 *NYSE: AVY* ■ *Cust Svc*	888-567-4387*	626-304-2000

	Toll-Free	Phone
Blue Ribbon Tag & Label Corp 4035 N 29th Ave .... Hollywood FL 33020	800-433-4974	954-922-9292
Brady Corp 6555 W Good Hope Rd .... Milwaukee WI 53223 *NYSE: BRC* ■ *Cust Svc*	800-541-1686*	414-358-6600
Brady Identification Solutions 6555 W Good Hope Rd .... Milwaukee WI 53223 *Cust Svc*	800-537-8791*	888-250-3082
Cellotape Inc 47623 Fremont Blvd .... Fremont CA 94538	800-231-0608	510-651-5551
Chase Corp 26 Summer St .... Bridgewater MA 02324 *NYSE: CCF*	800-323-4182	781-332-0700
Clamp Swing Pricing Company Inc 8386 Capwell Dr .... Oakland CA 94621	800-227-7615	510-567-1600
Commercial Mailing Accessories Inc 28220 Playmor Beach Rd .... Rocky Mount MO 65072	800-325-7303	
Data Label Inc 1000 Spruce St .... Terre Haute IN 47807	800-457-0676	812-232-0408
Discount Labels Inc 4115 Profit Ct .... New Albany IN 47150	800-995-9500	
East West Label Co 1000 E Hector St .... Conshohocken PA 19428	800-441-7333	610-825-0410
General Data Co Inc 4354 Ferguson Dr .... Cincinnati OH 45245	800-733-5252	513-752-7978
Gilbreth Packaging Systems 3001 State Rd .... Croydon PA 19021	800-630-2413	
Grand Rapids Label Co 2351 Oak Industrial Dr NE .... Grand Rapids MI 49505	800-552-5215	616-459-8134
Green Bay Packaging Inc 1700 Webster Ct .... Green Bay WI 54302	800-236-8400	920-433-5111
Harris Industries Inc 5181 Argosy Ave .... Huntington Beach CA 92649	800-222-6866	714-898-8048
Impact Label Corp 8875 Krum Ave .... Galesburg MI 49053	800-820-0362	
International Label & Printing Company Inc 2550 United Ln .... Elk Grove Village IL 60007	800-244-1442	
Labelmaster Co 5724 N Pulaski Rd .... Chicago IL 60646	800-621-5808	773-478-0900
Labeltape Inc 5100 Beltway Dr SE .... Caledonia MI 49316	800-928-4537	616-698-1830
Lancer Label 301 S 74th St .... Omaha NE 68114 *Cust Svc*	800-228-7074*	402-390-9119
LGInternational 6700 SW Bradbury Ct .... Portland OR 97224	800-345-0534	503-620-0520
McCourt Label Co 20 Egbert Ln .... Lewis Run PA 16738	800-458-2390	814-362-3851
MPI Label Systems Inc 450 Courtney Rd .... Sebring OH 44672	800-423-0442	330-938-2134
National Printing Converters Inc 18 S Murphy Ave .... Brazil IN 47834	800-877-6724	
Phifer Inc 4400 Kauloosa Ave PO Box 1700 ...... Tuscaloosa AL 35401	800-633-5955	205-345-2120
Print-O-Tape Inc 755 Tower Rd .... Mundelein IL 60060	800-346-6311	847-362-1476
Printed Systems 1265 Gillingham Rd .... Neenah WI 54956 *Sales	800-352-2332*	
Quikstik Labels 220 Broadway .... Everett MA 02149	800-225-3496	617-389-7570
Reidler Decal Corp 264 Industrial Pk Rd PO Box 8 .... Saint Clair PA 17970	800-628-7770	
Shamrock Scientific Specialty Systems Inc 34 Davis Dr .... Bellwood IL 60104	800-323-0249	
Smyth Cos Inc 1085 Snelling Ave N .... Saint Paul MN 55108	800-473-3464	651-646-4544
Spinnaker Coating Inc 518 E Water St .... Troy OH 45373	800-543-9452	937-332-6500
Tape & Label Converters Inc 8231 Allport Ave .... Santa Fe Springs CA 90670	888-285-2462	562-945-3486
Tapecon Inc 10 Latta Rd .... Rochester NY 14612	800-333-2407	585-621-8400
TAPEMARK Co 1685 Marthaler Ln .... St Paul MN 55118	800-535-1998	651-455-1611
Whitlam Label Company Inc 24800 Sherwood Ave .... Center Line MI 48015	800-755-2235	586-757-5100
Wright Global Graphics 5115 Prospect St .... Thomasville NC 27360	800-678-9019	336-472-4200
WS Packaging Group Inc 2571 S Hemlock Rd .... Green Bay WI 54229	800-236-3424	800-818-5481

413   LABOR UNIONS

	Toll-Free	Phone
Actors' Equity Assn 1560 Broadway .... New York NY 10036	866-270-4232	212-869-8530
AFT Healthcare 555 New Jersey Ave NW .... Washington DC 20001	800-238-1133	202-879-4400
Air Line Pilots Assn 535 Herndon Pkwy .... Herndon VA 20170	877-331-1223	703-689-2270
Alberta Union of Prov Employees 10451 170 St NW .... Edmonton AB T5P4S7	800-232-7284	780-930-3300
Allied Pilots Association 14600 Trinity Blvd O'Connell Bldg Ste 500 .... Fort Worth TX 76155	800-272-7456	817-302-2272
Amalgamated Transit Union (ATU) 10000 New Hampshire Ave .... Silver Spring MD 20903	888-240-1196	202-537-1645
American Federation of Government Employees 80 F St NW .... Washington DC 20001	888-844-2343	202-737-8700
American Federation of Musicians of the US & Canada (AFM) 1501 Broadway Ste 600 .... New York NY 10036	800-762-3444	212-869-1330
American Federation of Television & Radio Artists (AFTRA) 260 Madison Ave 7th Fl .... New York NY 10016	800-638-6796	212-532-0800
Aqtis 1001 De Maisonneuve East Blvd Ste 900 .... Montreal QC H2L4P9	888-647-0681	514-844-2113
Association of Flight Attendants 501 Third St NW .... Washington DC 20001	800-424-2401	202-434-1300

Classified Section

	City	State	Zip	Toll-Free	Phone
BC. Government & Service Employees' Union					
4911 Canada Way	Burnaby	BC	V5G3W3	**800-663-1674**	604-291-9611
Directors Guild of America					
7920 W Sunset Blvd	Los Angeles	CA	90046	**800-421-4173**	310-289-2000
Freelancers Union					
408 Jay St 2nd Fl	Brooklyn	NY	11201	**888-447-9883**	718-532-1515
International Alliance of Theatrical Stage Employee (IATSE)					
1430 Broadway 20th Fl	New York	NY	10018	**800-456-3863**	212-730-1770
International Assn of Bridge Structural Ornamental & Reinforcing Iron Workers					
1750 New York Ave NW Ste 400	Washington	DC	20006	**800-368-0105**	202-383-4800
International Longshore & Warehouse Union					
1188 Franklin St 4th Fl	San Francisco	CA	94109	**866-266-0013**	415-775-0533
International Organization of Masters Mates & Pilots					
700 Maritime Blvd	Linthicum Heights	MD	21090	**877-667-5522**	410-850-8700
International Union of Bricklayers & Allied Craftworkers (BAC)					
1776 eye St NW	Washington	DC	20006	**888-880-8222**	202-783-3788
International Union of Painters & Allied Trades (IUPAT)					
7234 Pkwy Dr	Hanover	MD	21076	**800-554-2479**	410-564-5900
International Union of Police Assn					
1549 Ringling Blvd Ste 600	Sarasota	FL	34236	**800-247-4872**	941-487-2560
International Union Security Police & Fire Professionals of America (SPFPA)					
25510 Kelly Rd	Roseville	MI	48066	**800-228-7492**	586-772-7250
Laborers' International Union of North America					
905 16th St NW	Washington	DC	20006	**800-548-6242**	202-737-8320
Llorens Pharmaceuticals International Div					
7080 NW 37th Ct	Miami	FL	33147	**866-595-5598**	305-716-0595
National Air Traffic Controllers Assn (NATCA)					
1325 Massachusetts Ave NW	Washington	DC	20005	**800-266-0895**	202-628-5451
National Alliance of Postal & Federal Employees					
1628 11th St NW	Washington	DC	20001	**800-222-8733**	202-939-6325
National Association of Letter Carriers (NALC)					
100 Indiana Ave NW	Washington	DC	20001	**800-424-5186**	202-393-4695
National Basketball Players Assn (NBPA)					
1133 Avenue of Americas	New York	NY	10036	**800-955-6272**	212-655-0880
Ocsea-Afscme Local					
390 Worthington Rd Ste A	Westerville	OH	43082	**800-969-4702**	614-865-4700
Ontario Nurses Association					
85 Grenville St Ste 400	Toronto	ON	M5S3A2	**800-387-5580**	416-964-8833
Plumbing Industry Board Trade Education Committee					
3711 47th Ave	Long Island	NY	11101	**800-638-7442**	718-752-9630
Power Worker's Union, The					
244 Eglinton Ave E	Toronto	ON	M4P1K2	**800-958-8798**	416-481-4491
RWDSU 30 E 29th St	New York	NY	10016	**866-781-4430**	212-684-5300
Screen Actors Guild (SAG)					
5757 Wilshire Blvd	Los Angeles	CA	90036	**800-724-0767**	323-954-1600
Seafarers International Union					
5201 Auth Way	Camp Springs	MD	20746	**800-252-4674**	301-899-0675
Seiu Local 503					
488 E 11th Ave Ste B100	Eugene	OR	97401	**800-452-2146**	541-342-1055
Service Employees International Union					
1800 Massachusetts Ave NW	Washington	DC	20036	**800-424-8592**	202-730-7000
Shopper Local					
2327 Englert Dr	Durham	NC	27713	**877-251-4592**	
Smart Union (SMWIA)					
1750 New York Ave NW 6th Fl	Washington	DC	20006	**800-457-7694**	202-662-0800
Unifor 301 Laurier Ave W	Ottawa	ON	K1P6M6	**877-230-5201**	613-230-5200
Union of American Physicians & Dentists					
180 Grand Ave Ste 1380	Oakland	CA	94612	**800-622-0909**	510-839-0193
UNITE HERE 275 Seventh Ave	New York	NY	10001	**800-452-4155**	212-265-7000
United Brotherhood of Carpenters & Joiners of America					
101 Constitution Ave NW	Washington	DC	20001	**800-530-5090**	202-546-6206
United Food & Commercial Workers International Union (UFCW)					
1775 K St NW	Washington	DC	20006	**800-551-4010**	202-223-3111
United Food & Commercial Workers Union Local 555					
7095 SW Sandburg St	Tigard	OR	97281	**800-452-8329**	503-684-2822

414 LABORATORIES - DENTAL

SEE ALSO Laboratories - Medical

	City	State	Zip	Toll-Free	Phone
1 Biotechnology PO Box 758	Oneco	FL	34264	**800-951-4246**	941-355-8451
A & M Dental Laboratories Inc					
425 S Santa Fe St	Santa Ana	CA	92705	**800-487-8051**	714-547-8051
Accu Reference Medical Lab					
1901 E Linden Ave Unit 4	Linden	NJ	07036	**877-733-4522**	
Affiliated Medical Services Laboratory Inc					
2916 E Central Ave	Wichita	KS	67214	**800-876-0243**	316-265-4533
Alcopro Inc					
2547 Sutherland Ave	Knoxville	TN	37919	**800-227-9890**	865-525-4900
American Health Assoc					
671 Ohio Pk Ste K	Cincinnati	OH	45245	**800-522-7556**	
Applied Diagnostics Inc					
1140 Business Center Dr Ste 370	Houston	TX	77043	**855-239-8378**	713-271-4133
Boos Dental Laboratory					
1000 Boone Ave N Ste 660	Golden Valley	MN	55427	**800-333-2667**	763-544-1446
Calgary Laboratory Services					
3535 Research Rd NW	Calgary	AB	T2L2K8	**800-661-3450**	403-770-3500
Cleveland HeartLab Inc					
6701 Carnegie Ave Ste 500	Cleveland	OH	44103	**866-358-9828**	
Clinical Pathology Laboratories Inc					
9200 Wall St	Austin	TX	78754	**800-595-1275**	512-339-1275
Coast2Coast Diagnostics Inc					
600 N Tustin Ave Ste 110	Santa Ana	CA	92705	**800-730-9263**	
Dental Technologies Inc (DTI)					
5601 Arnold Rd	Dublin	CA	94568	**800-229-0936**	925-829-3611
Diagnostic Laboratory of Oklahoma LLC					
225 N East 97th St	Oklahoma City	OK	73114	**800-891-2917**	405-608-6100
Distinctive Dental Studio Ltd Inc					
1504 Wall St	Naperville	IL	60563	**800-552-7890**	
DynaLifeDX Diagnostic Laboratory Services					
10150 - 102 St Ste 200	Edmonton	AB	T5J5E2	**800-661-9876**	780-451-3702
Elisa Act Biotechnologies					
109 Carpenter Dr Ste 100	Sterling	VA	20164	**800-553-5472**	703-796-0400
First - Call Medical Inc					
574 Boston Rd Unit 11	Billerica	MA	01821	**800-274-5399**	
First Dental Health					
5771 Copley Dr Ste 101	San Diego	CA	92111	**800-334-7244**	
Foundation Laboratory					
1716 W Holt Ave	Pomona	CA	91768	**800-843-7190**	909-623-9301
Gamma Dynacare Medical Laboratories Inc					
115 Midair Ct	Brampton	ON	L6T5M3	**800-668-2714**	
Genetic Assays Inc					
4711 Trousdale Dr Ste 209	Nashville	TN	37220	**800-390-5280**	
Genetics Associates Inc					
1916 Patterson St Ste 400	Nashville	TN	37203	**800-331-4363**	615-327-4532
Imaging Healthcare Specialists Medical Group Inc					
6256 Greenwich Dr Ste 150	San Diego	CA	92122	**866-558-4320**	
Insight Medical Holdings Ltd					
200 Meadowlark Health Ctr 156 St and 89 Ave	Edmonton	AB	T5R5W9	**866-771-9446**	780-669-2222
Integrated Regional Laboratories					
5361 NW 33rd Ave	Ft. Lauderdale	FL	33309	**800-522-0232**	
Kaylor Dental Laboratory Inc					
619 N Florence St	Wichita	KS	67212	**800-657-2549**	316-943-3226
Kimball Genetics Inc					
8490 Upland Dr Ste 100	Englewood	CO	80112	**800-444-9111**	
Knight Dental Group					
3659 Tampa Rd	Oldsmar	FL	34677	**800-359-2043**	813-854-3333
Main Street Radiology					
136-25 37th Ave	Flushing	NY	11354	**888-930-4674**	718-428-1500
Mayo Collaborative Services Inc					
3050 Superior Dr NW	Rochester	MN	55901	**800-533-1710**	507-266-5700
Med Fusion					
2501 S State Hwy 121 Business Ste 1100	Lewisville	TX	75067	**855-500-8535**	972-966-7000
Medical Instrument Development Laboratories Inc					
557 McCormick St	San Leandro	CA	94577	**800-929-5227**	510-357-3952
Mo Bio Laboratories					
2746 Loker Ave W Ste A	Carlsbad	CA	92010	**800-362-7737**	
Modern Dental Laboratory USA					
500 Stephenson Hwy Ste 100	Troy	MI	48083	**877-711-8778**	
Molecular Imaging Services Inc					
10 Whitaker Ct	Bear	DE	19701	**866-937-8855**	
MRI Group					
2100 Harrisburg Pk	Lancaster	PA	17601	**888-674-1377**	717-291-1016
Nakanishi Dental Laboratory Inc					
2959 Northup Way	Bellevue	WA	98004	**800-735-7231**	425-822-2245
O'Brien Dental Lab Inc					
4311 SW Research Way	Corvallis	OR	97333	**800-445-5941**	541-754-1238
Orthodent Ltd 311 Viola Ave	Oshawa	ON	L1H3A7	**800-267-8463**	905-436-3133
Pathology & Cytology Laboratories Inc					
290 Big Run Rd	Lexington	KY	40503	**800-264-0514**	859-278-9513
Pathology Group of The Mid South					
7550 Wolf River Blvd Ste 200	Germantown	TN	38138	**877-608-2756**	901-542-6800
Pathology Laboratories Inc					
1946 N 13th St Ste 301	Toledo	OH	43604	**800-281-8804**	419-255-4600
PeaceHealth Laboratories					
123 International Way	Springfield	OR	97477	**800-826-3616**	541-341-8010
PersonalizeDx 2980 Scott St	Vista	CA	92081	**855-739-5669**	
Phenopath Laboratories PLLC					
551 North 34th St Ste 100	Seattle	WA	98103	**888-927-4366**	206-374-9000
Physicians Laboratory Services Inc					
4840 "F" St	Omaha	NE	68117	**800-642-1117**	402-731-4145
Posca Bros Dental Laboratory Inc					
641 W Willow St	Long Beach	CA	90806	**800-537-6722**	562-427-1811
Quality Bioresources Inc					
1015 N Austin St	Seguin	TX	78155	**888-674-7224**	830-372-4797
Roe Dental Laboratory Inc					
7165 E Pleasant Valley Rd	Independence	OH	44131	**800-228-6663**	216-663-2233
Shiel Medical Laboratory Inc					
292 63 Flushing Ave Brooklyn Navy Yard Bldg	Brooklyn	NY	11205	**800-553-0873**	718-552-1000
Simply Whispers					
50 Perry Ave	Attleboro	MA	02703	**800-451-5700**	508-455-0864
South Bay Expressway LP					
1129 La Media Rd	San Diego	CA	92154	**888-889-1515**	619-661-7070
Touchstone Medical Imaging LLC					
1431 Perrone Way	Franklin	TN	37069	**877-275-9077**	615-661-9200
TriCore Reference Laboratories					
1001 Woodward Pl NE	Albuquerque	NM	87102	**800-245-3296**	505-938-8888
Utah Imaging Associates Inc					
1433 N 1075 W Ste 104	Farmington	UT	84025	**800-475-3698**	
Warde Medical Laboratory (WML)					
300 W Textile Rd	Ann Arbor	MI	48108	**800-760-9969**	734-214-0300
Weland Clinical Laboratories PC					
1911 First Ave SE	Cedar Rapids	IA	52402	**800-728-1503**	319-366-1503

415 LABORATORIES - DRUG-TESTING

SEE ALSO Laboratories - Medical

	City	State	Zip	Toll-Free	Phone
ArcticDx Inc					
MaRs Ctr 661 University Ave Ste 455	Toronto	ON	M5G1M1	**866-964-5182**	
Bio-Reference Laboratories Inc					
481 Edward H Ross Dr	Elmwood Park	NJ	07407	**800-229-5227**	
DrugScan Inc					
200 Precision Rd Ste 200 PO Box 347	Horsham	PA	19044	**800-235-4890**	
LabOne Inc 10101 Renner Blvd	Lenexa	KS	66219	**800-646-7788**	913-888-1770
Onsite Health Diagnostics					
1199 S Beltline Rd Ste 120	Coppell	TX	75019	**877-366-7483**	
United States Drug Testing Laboratories (USDTL)					
1700 S Mt Prospect Rd	Des Plaines	IL	60018	**800-235-2367**	847-375-0770

416 LABORATORIES - GENETIC TESTING

SEE ALSO Laboratories - Medical

	City	State	Zip	Toll-Free	Phone
American National Red Cross					
Portland Platelet Donation Ctr					
3131 N Vancouver Ave	Portland	OR	97227	**800-733-2767**	

Name / Address	City	State	Zip	Toll-Free	Phone
Center for Genetic Testing at Saint Francis 6465 S Yale Ave	Tulsa	OK	74136	**877-789-6001**	918-502-1720
Commonwealth Biotechnologies Inc 601 Biotech Dr	Richmond	VA	23235	**800-735-9224**	804-648-3820
DNA Diagnostics Ctr (DDC) 1 DDC Way	Fairfield	OH	45014	**800-613-5768**	513-881-7800
GenQuest DNA Analysis Laboratory 133 Coney Island Dr	Sparks	NV	89431	**877-362-5227**	775-358-0652
Genzyme Genetics 3400 Computer Dr	Westborough	MA	01581	**800-255-7357**	508-898-9001
Identity Genetics Inc 1321 Sixth St	Brookings	SD	57006	**800-861-1054**	605-697-5300
Laboratory Corp of America Holdings 358 S Main St *NYSE: LH*	Burlington	NC	27215	**800-334-5161**	336-584-5171
LABS Inc 6933 S Revere Pkwy	Centennial	CO	80112	**866-393-2244**	720-528-4750
Maxxam 335 LaiRd Rd Unit 2	Guelph	ON	N1G4P7	**877-706-7678**	
Medical Genetics Consultants 819 DeSoto St	Ocean Springs	MS	39564	**800-362-4363**	
Memorial Blood Centers (MBC) 737 Pelham Blvd *Cust Svc	Saint Paul	MN	55114	**888-448-3253***	
Molecular Pathology Laboratory Network Inc 250 E Broadway	Maryville	TN	37804	**800-932-2943**	865-380-9746
NMS Labs 3701 Welsh Rd	Willow Grove	PA	19090	**800-522-6671**	215-657-4900
Paternity Testing Corp (PTC) 300 Portland St	Columbia	MO	65201	**888-837-8323**	573-442-9948
Rhode Island Blood Ctr 405 Promenade St	Providence	RI	02908	**800-283-8385**	401-453-8360
South Texas Blood & Tissue Ctr 6211 IH-10 W	San Antonio	TX	78201	**800-292-5534**	210-731-5555
State University of New York Upstate Medical University Tissue Typing Laboratory 750 E Adams St	Syracuse	NY	13210	**877-464-5540**	315-464-4775
University of North Texas Health Science Ctr 3500 Camp Bowie Blvd	Fort Worth	TX	76107	**800-687-7580**	817-735-2000

417 LABORATORIES - MEDICAL

SEE ALSO Laboratories - Dental ; Laboratories - Drug-Testing ; Laboratories - Genetic Testing ; Blood Centers ; Organ & Tissue Banks

Name / Address	City	State	Zip	Toll-Free	Phone
ABC American Bio-clinical 2730 N Main St	Los Angeles	CA	90031	**800-262-1688**	
Aurum Ceramic Dental Laboratories Ltd 115 17 Ave SW	Calgary	AB	T2S0A1	**800-665-8815**	403-228-5120
Bio-Reference Laboratories Inc 481 Edward H Ross Dr	Elmwood Park	NJ	07407	**800-229-5227**	
Bostwick Laboratories 4355 Innslake Dr	Glen Allen	VA	23060	**877-865-3262**	
Calvert Labs 1225 Crescent Green Ste 115	Cary	NC	27518	**800-300-8114**	919-854-4453
Cell Signaling Technology Inc 3 Trask Ln	Danvers	MA	01923	**877-678-8324**	978-867-2300
Cmi 6704 Guada Coma Dr	Schertz	TX	78154	**800-840-1070**	210-967-6169
DIANON Systems Inc 1 Forest Pkwy	Shelton	CT	06484	**800-328-2666**	203-926-7100
DiaSorin Molecular LLC 11331 Vly View St	Cypress	CA	90630	**800-838-4548**	562-240-6500
Equipoise Dental Laboratory Inc 85 Portland Ave	Bergenfield	NJ	07621	**800-999-4950**	201-385-4750
Genetrack Biolabs Inc 401-1508 Broadway W	Vancouver	BC	V6J1W8	**888-828-1899**	604-325-7282
Genova Diagnostics 63 Zillicoa St	Asheville	NC	28801	**800-522-4762**	828-253-0621
Global Neuro-Diagnostics LP 2670 Firewheel Dr Ste B	Flower Mound	TX	75028	**866-848-2522**	
Great Plains Laboratory Inc 11813 W 77th St	Lenexa	KS	66214	**800-288-0383**	913-341-8949
Harmony Dental Lab 758 W Duval St	Jacksonville	FL	32202	**888-354-3594**	
Health Network Laboratory 2024 Lehigh St	Allentown	PA	18103	**877-402-4221**	610-402-8170
Identigene LLC 2495 S West Temple	Salt Lake City	UT	84115	**888-404-4363**	
Igenex 795 San Antonio Rd	Palo Alto	CA	94303	**800-832-3200**	650-424-1191
Keller Laboratories Inc 160 Larkin Williams Industrial Ct	Fenton	MO	63026	**800-325-3056**	636-600-4200
LabOne Inc 10101 Renner Blvd	Lenexa	KS	66219	**800-646-7788**	913-888-1770
Laboratory Corp of America Holdings 358 S Main St *NYSE: LH*	Burlington	NC	27215	**800-334-5161**	336-584-5171
Machaon Diagnostics Inc 3023 Summit St	Oakland	CA	94609	**800-566-3462**	510-839-5600
Medical Diagnostic Laboratories LLC 2439 Kuser Rd	Hamilton	NJ	08690	**877-269-0090**	609-570-1000
National Genetics Institute 2440 S Blvd Ste 235	Los Angeles	CA	90064	**800-352-7788**	310-996-0036
NeuroScience Inc 373 280th St	Osceola	WI	54020	**888-342-7272**	715-294-2144
NMS Labs 3701 Welsh Rd	Willow Grove	PA	19090	**800-522-6671**	215-657-4900
Norgen Biotek Corp 3430 Schmon Pkwy	Thorold	ON	L2V4Y6	**866-667-4362**	
Opmedic Group Inc 1361 Beaumont Ave Ste 301	Mount-royal	QC	H3P2W3	**888-776-2732**	514-345-8535
Parkway Clinical Laboratories Inc 3494 Progress Dr	Bensalem	PA	19020	**800-327-2764**	215-245-5112
PathLogic 1166 National Dr Ste 80	Sacramento	CA	95834	**844-603-3071**	866-863-1496
Penta Laboratories (PL) 7868 Deering Ave	Canoga Park	CA	91304	**800-421-4219**	818-882-3872
Persante Health Care Inc 200 E Park Dr Ste 600	Mt Laurel	NJ	08054	**800-753-3779**	
Physician's Automated Laboratory Inc (PALLAB) 9830 Brimhall Rd	Bakersfield	CA	93312	**800-675-2271**	661-829-2260
Quest Diagnostics at Nichols Institute 33608 Ortega Hwy	San Juan Capistrano	CA	92675	**800-642-4657**	949-728-4000
Quest Diagnostics Inc 3 Giralda Farms *NYSE: DGX*	Madison	NJ	07940	**800-222-0446**	201-393-5000
South Bend Medical Foundation 530 N Lafayette Blvd	South Bend	IN	46601	**800-544-0925**	574-234-4176
Specialty Laboratories Inc 27027 Tourney Rd *Sales	Valencia	CA	91355	**800-421-7110***	661-799-6543
Strand Diagnostics LLC 5770 Decatur Blvd Ste A	Indianapolis	IN	46241	**888-924-6779**	317-455-2100
Sunrise Medical Laboratories Inc 250 Miller Pl *Cust Svc	Hicksville	NY	11801	**800-782-0282***	631-435-1515
Visalia Medical Lab 5400 W Hillsdale Ave	Visalia	CA	93291	**800-486-2362**	559-738-7500

418 LABORATORY ANALYTICAL INSTRUMENTS

SEE ALSO Glassware - Laboratory & Scientific ; Laboratory Apparatus & Furniture

Name / Address	City	State	Zip	Toll-Free	Phone
Abaxis Inc 3240 Whipple Rd *NASDAQ: ABAX*	Union City	CA	94587	**800-822-2947**	510-675-6500
American Biologics 1180 Walnut Ave	Chula Vista	CA	91911	**800-227-4473**	619-429-8200
BD Biosciences 2350 Qume Dr	San Jose	CA	95131	**800-223-8226**	877-232-8995
Bio/Data Corp PO Box 347	Horsham	PA	19044	**800-257-3282**	215-441-4000
Bioanalytical Systems Inc 2701 Kent Ave *NASDAQ: BASI*	West Lafayette	IN	47906	**800-845-4246**	765-463-4527
BioTek Instruments Inc 100 Tigan St PO Box 998	Winooski	VT	05404	**888-451-5171**	802-655-4040
Bruker Daltonics Inc 40 Manning Rd	Billerica	MA	01821	**800-672-7676**	978-663-3660
Buehler Ltd 41 Waukegan Rd *Sales	Lake Bluff	IL	60044	**800-283-4537***	847-295-6500
California Analytical Instruments Inc 1312 W Grove Ave	Orange	CA	92865	**800-959-0949**	714-974-5560
Caliper Life Sciences Inc 68 Elm St	Hopkinton	MA	01748	**800-762-4000**	781-663-6050
CAO Group Inc 4628 Skyhawk Dr	West Jordan	UT	84084	**877-877-9778**	801-256-9282
CDS Analytical Inc 465 Limestone Rd	Oxford	PA	19363	**800-541-6593**	610-932-3636
CEM Corp 3100 Smith Farm Rd	Matthews	NC	28104	**800-726-3331**	704-821-7015
Cepheid 904 E Caribbean Dr	Sunnyvale	CA	94089	**888-838-3222**	408-541-4191
Cetac Technologies Inc 14306 Industrial Rd	Omaha	NE	68144	**800-369-2822**	402-733-2829
CHEMetrics Inc 4295 Catlett Rd	Midland	VA	22728	**800-356-3072**	
Chrom Tech Inc PO Box 240248	Apple Valley	MN	55124	**800-822-5242**	952-431-6000
CMI Inc 316 E Ninth St	Owensboro	KY	42303	**866-835-0690**	
Corning Inc Life Sciences Div 836 N St Bldg 300 Ste 3401	Tewksbury	MA	01876	**800-492-1110**	607-974-9000
Eppendorf North America Inc 102 Motor Pkwy	Hauppage	NY	11788	**800-645-3050**	
FEI Co 5350 NE Dawson Creek Dr *NASDAQ: FEIC* ■ *Cust Svc	Hillsboro	OR	97124	**866-693-3426***	503-726-7500
FORNEY LLC 2050 Jackson's Pointe Ct	Zelienople	PA	16063	**800-367-6397**	724-346-7400
Gambro BCT 10811 W Collins Ave	Lakewood	CO	80215	**877-339-4228**	303-231-4357
Gatan Inc 5794 W Las Positas Blvd	Pleasanton	CA	94588	**888-887-3377**	925-463-0200
GrayWolf Sensing Solutions LLC 6 Research Dr	Shelton	CT	06484	**800-218-7997**	203-402-0477
Hach Co PO Box 389	Loveland	CO	80539	**800-227-4224**	970-669-3050
Hamilton Co 4970 Energy Way	Reno	NV	89502	**800-648-5950**	775-858-3000
Harvard Bioscience Inc 84 October Hill Rd Ste 10 *NASDAQ: HBIO*	Holliston	MA	01746	**800-272-2775**	508-893-8999
Helena Laboratories Inc 1530 Lindbergh Dr	Beaumont	TX	77704	**800-231-5663**	409-842-3714
Horiba Instruments Inc 17671 Armstrong Ave	Irvine	CA	92614	**800-446-7422**	949-250-4811
hygiena LLC 941 Avenida Acaso	Camarillo	CA	93012	**877-494-4364**	805-388-8007
Illumina Inc 9885 Towne Centre Dr *NASDAQ: ILMN*	San Diego	CA	92121	**800-809-4566**	858-202-4500
Instrumentation Laboratory Inc 180 Hartwell Rd *Sales	Bedford	MA	01730	**800-955-9525***	781-861-0710
Kurt J Lesker Co 1925 Rt 51	Jefferson Hills	PA	15025	**800-245-1656**	
Labcon North America Inc 3700 Lkeville Hwy	Petaluma	CA	94954	**800-227-1466**	707-766-2100
LaMotte Co 802 Washington Ave	Chestertown	MD	21620	**800-344-3100**	410-778-3100
Leco Corp 3000 Lakeview Ave	Saint Joseph	MI	49085	**800-292-6141**	269-985-5496
Li Cor Inc PO Box 4425	Lincoln	NE	68504	**800-447-3576**	402-467-3576
Luminex Corp 12212 Technology Blvd *NASDAQ: LMNX*	Austin	TX	78727	**888-219-8020**	512-219-8020
Mandel Scientific 2 Admiral Pl	Guelph	ON	N1G4N4	**888-883-3636**	519-763-9292

	Toll-Free	Phone
Med-Plus Medical Supplies		
PO Box 1242 ....Monsey NY 10942	888-433-2300	718-222-4416
Micromeritics Instrument Corp		
1 Micromeritics Dr ....Norcross GA 30093	800-229-5052	770-662-3620
Modal Shop Inc, The		
1776 Mentor Ave ....Cincinnati OH 45212	800-860-4867	513-351-9919
Molecular Devices Inc (MDI)		
1311 Orleans Dr ....Sunnyvale CA 94089	800-635-5577	408-747-1700
Monogram Biosciences Inc		
345 Oyster Pt Blvd .....South San Francisco CA 94080	800-777-0177	650-635-1100
MPD Inc 316 E Ninth St ....Owensboro KY 42303	866-225-5673	270-685-6200
New Objective Inc		
2 Constitution Way ....Woburn MA 01801	888-220-2998	781-933-9560
Nor-Cal Controls Inc		
1952 Concourse Dr ....San Jose CA 95131	800-233-2013	408-435-0400
Noran Instruments Inc		
5225 Verona Rd ....Madison WI 53711	800-532-4752	608-276-6100
Nova Biomedical Corp		
200 Prospect St ....Waltham MA 02454	800-458-5813*	781-894-0800
*Sales		
OI Corp		
151 Graham Rd PO Box 9010......College Station TX 77842	800-653-1711	979-690-1711
Olis Inc		
130 Conway Dr Ste A B & C.........Bogart GA 30622	800-852-3504	706-353-6547
Pall Life Sciences		
600 S Wagner Rd ....Ann Arbor MI 48103	800-521-1520	734-665-0651
Particle Measuring Systems Inc		
5475 Airport Blvd ....Boulder CO 80301	800-238-1801*	303-443-7100
*Cust Svc		
PerkinElmer Inc		
940 Winter St ....Waltham MA 02451	800-762-4000	781-663-6050
NYSE: PKI		
Sakura Finetek USA Inc		
1750 W 214th St ....Torrance CA 90501	800-725-8723	310-972-7800
Schroer Manufacturing Co		
511 Osage Ave ....Kansas City KS 66105	800-444-1579	913-281-1500
Scientific Industries Inc		
70 Orville Dr ....Bohemia NY 11716	888-850-6208	631-567-4700
SEER Technology Inc		
2681 Parleys Way Ste 201 .....Salt Lake City UT 84109	877-505-7337	801-746-7888
Shimadzu Scientific Instruments Inc		
7102 Riverwood Dr ....Columbia MD 21046	800-477-1227	410-381-1227
Siskiyou Corp		
110 SW Booth St ....Grants Pass OR 97526	877-313-6418	541-479-8697
Spectra Services Inc		
6359 Dean Pkwy ....Ontario NY 14519	800-955-7732	585-265-4320
Spectrum Laboratories Inc		
18617 Broadwick St ......Rancho Dominguez CA 90220	800-634-3300	310-885-4600
Spectrum Systems Inc		
3410 W Nine-Mile Rd ....Pensacola FL 32526	800-432-6119	850-944-3392
STARR Life Sciences Corp		
333 Alegheney Ave Ste 300 ....Oakmont PA 15139	866-978-2779	
Supelco Inc		
595 N Harrison Rd ....Bellefonte PA 16823	800-247-6628	814-359-2147
Tekran Instruments Corp		
230 Tech Ctr Dr ....Knoxville TN 37912	888-383-5726	865-688-0688
Temptronic Corp		
41 Hampden Rd ....Mansfield MA 02048	800-558-5080*	781-688-2300
*Tech Support		
Upchurch Scientific Inc		
619 Oak St ....Oak Harbor WA 98277	800-426-0191	360-679-2528
Vernier Software & Technology LLC		
13979 SW Millikan Way ....Beaverton OR 97005	800-387-2474	503-277-2299
Waters Corp 34 Maple St ....Milford MA 01757	800-252-4752	508-478-2000
NYSE: WAT		
ZAPS Technologies Inc		
4314 SW Research Way ....Corvallis OR 97333	866-390-9387	
ZTR Control Systems Inc		
8050 County Rd 101 E ....Minneapolis MN 55379	855-724-5987	

419 LABORATORY APPARATUS & FURNITURE

SEE ALSO Glassware - Laboratory & Scientific ; Scales & Balances ; Laboratory Analytical Instruments

	Toll-Free	Phone
Baker Company Inc		
175 Gatehouse Rd ....Sanford ME 04073	800-992-2537	207-324-8773
Bel-Art Products Inc		
661 Rte 23 S ....Wayne NJ 07440	800-423-5278	973-694-0500
Boekel Scientific		
855 Pennsylvania Blvd ....Feasterville PA 19053	800-336-6929	215-396-8200
Caliper Life Sciences Inc		
68 Elm St ....Hopkinton MA 01748	800-762-4000	781-663-6050
Cole-Parmer Instrument Co		
625 E Bunker Ct ....Vernon Hills IL 60061	800-323-4340	847-549-7600
Corning Inc Life Sciences Div		
836 N St Bldg 300 Ste 3401 ....Tewksbury MA 01876	800-492-1110	607-974-9000
Edstrom Industries Inc		
819 Bakke Ave ....Waterford WI 53185	800-558-5913	262-534-5181
Ika-Works Inc		
2635 Northchase Pkwy SE ......Wilmington NC 28405	800-733-3037	910-452-7059
Kewaunee Scientific Corp		
2700 W Front St PO Box 1842 .....Statesville NC 28687	800-824-6626	704-873-7202
NASDAQ: KEQU		
Labconco Corp		
8811 Prospect Ave ....Kansas City MO 64132	800-821-5525*	816-333-8811
*Cust Svc		
Omnicell Inc		
1201 Charleston Rd ....Mountain View CA 94043	800-850-6664	650-251-6100
NASDAQ: OMCL		
Pacific Combustion Engineering Co		
2107 Border Ave ....Torrance CA 90501	800-342-4442	310-212-6300
Parr Instrument Co		
211 53rd St ....Moline IL 61265	800-872-7720	309-762-7716
Parter Medical Products Inc		
17015 Kingsview Ave ....Carson CA 90746	800-666-8282	310-327-4417

	Toll-Free	Phone
Percival Scientific Inc		
505 Research Dr ....Perry IA 50220	800-695-2743	
Preston Industries Inc		
6600 W Touhy Ave ....Niles IL 60714	800-229-7569	847-647-0611
ThermoGenesis Corp		
2711 Citrus Rd ....Rancho Cordova CA 95742	800-783-8357	916-858-5100
NASDAQ: KOOL		
Thomas Scientific		
1654 High Hill Rd PO Box 99.......Swedesboro NJ 08085	800-345-2100	

420 LADDERS

	Toll-Free	Phone
ALACO Ladder Co 5167 G St ....Chino CA 91710	888-310-7040	909-591-7561
Ballymore Co		
501 Gunnard Carlson Dr ....Coatesville PA 19365	800-762-8327	610-593-5062
Cotterman Co		
130 Seltzer Rd ....Croswell MI 48422	800-552-3337	810-679-4400
Duo-Safety Ladder Corp		
513 W Ninth Ave ....Oshkosh WI 54902	877-386-5377	920-231-2740
Lynn Ladder & Scaffolding Company Inc		
20 Boston St ....Lynn MA 01904	800-225-2510	781-598-6010
Werner Co 93 Werner Rd ....Greenville PA 16125	888-523-3371	
Wing Enterprises Inc		
1198 N Spring Creek ....Springville UT 84663	866-872-5901	801-489-3684

421 LANDSCAPE DESIGN & RELATED SERVICES

	Toll-Free	Phone
Cagwin & Dorward Inc		
1565 S Novato Blvd Ste B..........Novato CA 94947	800-891-7710	415-892-7710
Environmental Earthscapes Inc		
5075 S Swan Rd ....Tucson AZ 85706	800-571-1575	520-571-1575
Landscape Concepts Management		
31745 Alleghany Rd ....Grayslake IL 60030	866-655-3800	847-223-3800
Lipinski Landscape & Irrigation Contractors Inc		
100 Sharp Rd ....Marlton NJ 08053	800-644-6035	
Mission Landscape Services Inc		
536 E Dyer Rd ....Santa Ana CA 92707	800-545-9963	
US Lawns Inc		
6700 Forum Dr Ste 150 ....Orlando FL 32821	800-875-2967	407-246-1630

422 LANGUAGE SCHOOLS

SEE ALSO Translation Services

	Toll-Free	Phone
All Languages Ltd		
306-421 Bloor St E ....Toronto ON M4W3T1	800-567-8100	416-975-5000
AmeriSpan		
1500 Walnut St ....Philadelphia PA 19102	800-879-6640	215-751-1100
Berlitz Languages Inc		
7 Roszel Rd ....Princeton NJ 08540	866-423-7548	
Colorado School of English		
331 14th St ....Denver CO 80202	877-234-0654	720-932-8900
Lado International College		
401 Ninth St NW Ste C100 ......Washington DC 20004	800-281-7710	202-223-0023
Lingua Language Center		
111 East Las Olas Blvd ....Fort Lauderdale FL 33301	888-654-6482	954-577-9955
POLY Languages Institute Inc (POLY)		
5757 Wilshire Blvd Ste 510 ......Los Angeles CA 90036	877-738-5787	323-933-9399
Tamwood International College		
300-909 Burrard St ....Vancouver BC V6Z2N2	866-533-0123	604-899-4480

423 LASER EQUIPMENT & SYSTEMS - MEDICAL

SEE ALSO Medical Instruments & Apparatus - Mfr

	Toll-Free	Phone
BioLase Inc 4 Cromwell ....Irvine CA 92618	888-424-6527	
Candela Corp		
530 Boston Post Rd ....Wayland MA 01778	800-733-8550	508-358-7400
Cynosure Inc 5 Carlisle Rd ....Westford MA 01886	800-886-2966	978-256-4200
NASDAQ: CYNO		
Iridex Corp		
1212 Terra Bella Ave ....Mountain View CA 94043	800-388-4747*	650-940-4700
NASDAQ: IRIX ■ *Cust Svc		
Laserscope 3070 Orchard Dr ....San Jose CA 95134	800-878-3399	408-943-0636
Lumenis Ltd		
2033 Gateway Pl Ste 200 ....San Jose CA 95110	877-586-3647	408-764-3000
Spectranetics Corp		
9965 Federal Dr ....Colorado Springs CO 80921	800-231-0978	719-447-2000
NASDAQ: SPNC		
Trimedyne Inc		
15091 Bake Pkwy ....Irvine CA 92618	800-733-5273	949-559-5300
OTC: TMED		

424 LASERS - INDUSTRIAL

	Toll-Free	Phone
Coherent Inc		
5100 Patrick Henry Dr ....Santa Clara CA 95054	800-527-3786*	408-764-4000
NASDAQ: COHR ■ *Sales		
Continuum		
3150 Central Expy ....Santa Clara CA 95051	888-532-1064	408-727-3240
Electro Scientific Industries Inc		
13900 NW Science Pk Dr ....Portland OR 97229	800-331-4708*	503-641-4141
NASDAQ: ESIO ■ *Cust Svc		
IPG Photonics Corp		
50 Old Webster Rd ....Oxford MA 01540	877-980-1550	508-373-1100
NASDAQ: IPGP		
Laser Excel		
N6323 Berlin Rd ....Green Lake WI 54941	800-285-6544	

		Toll-Free	Phone
TRUMPF Group 111 Hyde Rd ....Farmington CT 06032		800-306-1077	860-255-6000

425   LAUNDRY & DRYCLEANING SERVICES

SEE ALSO Linen & Uniform Supply

		Toll-Free	Phone
CSC ServiceWorks 303 Sunnyside Blvd Ste 70..................Plainview NY 11803		877-264-6622	516-349-8555
Dove Cleaners Inc 1560 Yonge St ....Toronto ON M4T2S9		866-999-3683	416-413-7900
Lapels Dry Cleaning 962 Washington St ....Hanover MA 02339		866-695-2735	781-829-9935
Nu-Yale Cleaners 6300 Hwy 62 ....Jeffersonville IN 47130		888-644-7400	812-285-7400
Pressed4Time Inc 50 Mendon St ....Upton MA 01568		800-423-8711	508-879-5966

LAUNDRY EQUIPMENT - HOUSEHOLD

SEE Appliances - Major - Mfr ; Appliances - Whol

426   LAUNDRY EQUIPMENT & SUPPLIES - COMMERCIAL & INDUSTRIAL

		Toll-Free	Phone
Autec Inc 2500 W Front St ....Statesville NC 28677		800-438-3028	704-871-9141
Colmac Industries Inc PO Box 72 ....Colville WA 99114		800-926-5622	509-684-4505
CSC ServiceWorks 303 Sunnyside Blvd Ste 70..................Plainview NY 11803		877-264-6622	516-349-8555
Eco Water Systems Inc 1890 Woodlane Dr ....Woodbury MN 55125		800-808-9899	
Ellis Corp 1400 W Bryn Mawr Ave ....Itasca IL 60143		800-611-6806	630-250-9222
GA Braun Inc 79 General Irwin Blvd ....Syracuse NY 13212		800-432-7286	315-475-3123
Kemco Systems Inc 11500 47th St N ....Clearwater FL 33762		800-633-7055	727-573-2323
Minnesota Chemical Co 2285 Hampden Ave ....St. Paul MN 55114		800-328-5689	651-646-7521
Thermal Engineering of Arizona Inc 2250 W Wetmore Rd ....Tucson AZ 85705		866-832-7278	520-888-4000
Vac-Con Inc 969 Hall Park Dr ....Green Cove Spgs FL 32043		888-920-2945	904-493-4969

427   LAW FIRMS

SEE ALSO Bar Associations - State ; Arbitration Services - Legal ; Litigation Support Services ; Legal Professionals Associations

		Toll-Free	Phone
Ahmad, Zavitsanos, Anaipakos, Alavi & Mensing PC 1 Houston Ctr 1221 McKinney St Ste 3460 ....Houston TX 77010		800-856-8153	713-655-1101
Alan b Harris Attorney at Law 409 N Texas Ave ....Odessa TX 79761		800-887-1676	432-580-3118
American LegalNet Inc 16501 Ventura Blvd Ste 615.................Encino CA 91436		800-293-2771	818-817-9225
Armentor Glenn Law Corp 300 Stewart St ....Lafayette LA 70501		800-960-5551	337-233-1471
Arnold & Itkin LLP 6009 Memorial Dr ....Houston TX 77007		888-493-1629	713-222-3800
Arthur, Chapman, Kettering, Smetak & Pikala PA 500 Young Quinlan Bldg 81 S Ninth St ....Minneapolis MN 55402		800-916-9262	612-339-3500
Asian Pacific American Legal Center of Southern California 1145 Wilshire Blvd 2nd Fl ....Los Angeles CA 90017		800-520-2356	213-977-7500
Atkinson Conway & Gagnon Inc 420 L St Ste 500....................Anchorage AK 99501		800-478-1900	907-276-1700
Attorney Aid Divorce & Bankruptcy Center Inc 3605 Long Beach Blvd Ste 300.........Long Beach CA 90807		877-905-5297	562-988-0885
Baker Donelson Bearman Caldwell & Berkowitz PC 165 Madison Ave 1st Tennessee Bldg Ste 2000 ....Memphis TN 38103		800-973-1177	901-526-2000
Barker Martin PS 719 Second Ave Ste 1200...................Seattle WA 98104		888-381-9806	360-756-9806
Barnes & Thornburg LLP 11 S Meridian St ....Indianapolis IN 46204		800-236-1352	317-236-1313
Barris, Sott, Denn & Driker PLLC 333 W Fort St Ste 1200 ....Detroit MI 48226		877-529-8750	313-965-9725
BCF LLP 25th Fl 1100 Rene-Levesque Blvd W ....Montreal QC H3B5C9		866-511-8501	514-397-8500
Beasley Allen Crow Methvin 218 Commerce St ....Montgomery AL 36104		800-898-2034	334-269-2343
Bennett Jones LLP 855 Second St S W 4500 Bankers Hall E ....Calgary AB T2P4K7		800-222-6479	403-298-3100
Berding & Weil LLP 2175 N California Blvd Ste 500 ....Walnut Creek CA 94596		800-838-2090	925-838-2090
Berger & Montague PC 1622 Locust St ....Philadelphia PA 19103		800-424-6690	215-875-3000
Best, Vanderlaan & Harrington 25 E Washington St Ste 800....................Chicago IL 60602		800-351-4316	312-819-1100
Blank Rome LLP 1 Logan Sq 130 N 18th St ....Philadelphia PA 19103		800-973-1177	215-569-5500
Blasingame, Burch, Garrard & Ashley PC 440 College Ave Ste 320 ....Athens GA 30601		866-354-3544	706-608-8212
Blitt & Gaines PC 661 Glenn Ave ....Wheeling IL 60090		888-920-0620	847-403-4900
Blue Williams LLP 3421 N Causeway Blvd Ste 900 ....Metairie LA 70002		800-326-4991	504-831-4091
Boren, Oliver & Coffey LLP 59 N Jefferson St ....Martinsville IN 46151		800-403-9971	765-342-0147

		Toll-Free	Phone
Brann & Isaacson 184 Main St ....Lewiston ME 04243		800-225-6964	207-786-3566
Brent Coon & Associates (BCA) 215 Orleans St ....Beaumont TX 77701		866-335-2666	409-835-2666
Brewer & Pritchard PC 800 Bering Dr Ste 201A ....Houston TX 77057		800-236-7468	
Brock & Scott PLLC 4550 country club Rd ....Winston-Salem NC 27104		844-856-6646	336-354-1797
Broyles Kight & Ricafort PC 8250 Haverstick Rd Ste 100 ....Indianapolis IN 46240		888-834-2692	317-571-3600
Burns Burns Walsh & Walsh PA 704 Topeka Ave ....Lyndon KS 66451		888-528-3186	785-828-4418
Cameron, Hodges, Coleman, LaPointe & Wright PA 111 N Magnolia Ave Ste 1350 ....Orlando FL 32801		888-841-5030	407-841-5030
Cannon & Dunphy Sc 595 N Barker Rd ....Brookfield WI 53045		855-570-2676	
Carter Mario Injury Lawyers 176 Wethersfield Ave ....Hartford CT 06114		844-634-5656	
Cavanagh Law Firm, The 1850 N Central Ave ....Phoenix AZ 85004		888-824-3476	602-322-4000
Cellino & Barnes PC 2500 Main Place Twr ....Buffalo NY 14202		800-888-8888	
Clark, Gagliardi & Miller PC 99 Court St ....White Plains NY 10601		800-734-5694	
Cochran Firm LLC 111 E Main St ....Dothan AL 36301		800-843-3476	334-793-1555
Cohen Highley LLP 255 Queens Ave ....London ON N6A5R8		800-563-1020	519-672-9330
Collins & Lacy PC 1330 Lady St 6th Fl ....Columbia SC 29201		888-648-0526	803-256-2660
Consumer Attorneys of California 770 L St Ste 1200....................Sacramento CA 95814		800-424-2725	916-442-6902
Cooper Legal Services Dwayne E Cooper Attorney at Law 718 S Washinton St ....Marion IN 46953		800-959-1825	765-573-3133
Copple, Rockey, Mckeever & Schlecht PC LLO 2425 Taylor Ave ....Norfolk NE 68701		888-860-2425	402-371-4300
Cory Watson Crowder & DeGaris 2131 Magnolia Ave ....Birmingham AL 35205		800-852-6299	205-328-2200
Cozen O'Connor 1900 Market St ....Philadelphia PA 19103		800-523-2900	215-665-2000
Dale Buchanan & Associates 1206 Pointe Ctr Dr Ste 110............Chattanooga TN 37421		800-945-4950	
Daniel & Stark Law Offices 100 W William Joel Bryan Pkwy ....Bryan TX 77803		800-474-1233	979-846-8686
Davies Pearson PC 920 Fawcett Ave ....Tacoma WA 98401		800-439-1112	253-620-1500
Davis Law Firm 10500 Heitage Blvd Ste 102 ....San Antonio TX 78216		800-770-0127	210-444-4444
Dinkes & Schwitzer 820 Second Ave 1st Fl ....New York NY 10017		800-933-1212	212-683-3800
Docken & Co 900-800 6 Ave SW ....Calgary AB T2P3G3		877-269-3612	403-269-3612
Domengeaux Wright Roy & Edwards LLC 556 Jefferson St Ste 500..................Lafayette LA 70501		800-375-6186	337-233-3033
Donohoe & Stapleton LLC 2781 Zelda Rd ....Montgomery AL 36106		800-365-6896	334-269-3355
eLawMarketing 25 Robert Pitt Dr Ste 209G ....Monsey NY 10952		866-833-6245	
Elliott, Ostrander & Preston PC Union Bank Tower 707 SW Washington St Ste 1500 ....Portland OR 97205		866-716-3410	503-224-7112
Emerson Thomson & Bennett LLC 1914 Akron Peninsula Rd ....Akron OH 44313		800-822-8113	330-434-9999
Evan K Thalenberg Law Offices 216 E Lexington St ....Baltimore MD 21202		800-778-1181	410-625-9100
Faegre & Benson LLP 90 S Seventh St 2200 Wells Fargo Bldg ....Minneapolis MN 55402		800-328-4393	612-766-7000
Fafinski Mark & Johnson PA 775 Prairie Center Dr Ste 400............Eden Prairie MN 55344		855-806-1525	952-995-9500
Farr, Farr, Emerich, Hackett & Carr PA 99 Nesbit St Earl D Farr Bldg ....Punta Gorda FL 33950		855-327-7529	941-639-1148
Ferrara Fiorenza Larrison Barrett & Reitz PC 5010 Campuswood Dr ....East Syracuse NY 13057		800-777-4742	315-437-7600
Fieger Law 19390 W 10-Mile Rd ....Southfield MI 48075		800-294-6637	248-558-2315
Field Law 10175 101 ST NW Ste 2500..................Edmonton AB T5J0H3		800-222-6479	780-423-3003
Foster Townsend LLP 150 Dufferin Ave ....London ON N6A5N6		888-354-0448	519-672-5272
Fox Rothschild LLP 2000 Market St 10th Fl ....Philadelphia PA 19103		800-580-9136	215-299-2000
Fraser Stryker PC LLO 500 Energy Plz 409 S 17th St ....Omaha NE 68102		800-544-6041	402-341-6000
Fredrickson, Mazeika & Grant LLP 5720 Oberlin Dr ....San Diego CA 92121		800-231-8440	858-642-2002
Gallagher, Gams, Pryor, Tallan & Littrell LLP 471 E Broad St 19th Fl ....Columbus OH 43215		866-378-1624	614-228-5151
Garan Lucow Miller PC 1000 Woodbridge St ....Detroit MI 48207		800-875-1530	313-446-1530
Garden City Group LLC 105 Maxess Rd ....Melville NY 11747		888-404-8013	631-470-5000
General Code 781 Elmgrove Rd ....Rochester NY 14624		800-836-8834	585-328-1810
Gentry Locke Rakes & Moore LLP 10 Franklin Rd S E Ste 900..................Roanoke VA 24011		866-983-0866	540-983-9300
Gibson Dunn & Crutcher LLP 333 S Grand Ave ....Los Angeles CA 90071		888-203-1112	213-229-7000
Gilman & Pastor LLP 63 Atlantic Ave Ste 3...................Boston MA 02110		877-428-7374	888-252-0048
Gislason & Hunter LLP 2700 S Broadway ....New Ulm MN 56073		800-469-0234	507-354-3111
Goehring, Rutter & Boehm 437 Grant St 14th fl ....Pittsburgh PA 15219		866-677-5970	412-281-0587
Goldberg Weisman Cairo 1 E Upper Wacker Dr Ste 3800 ....Chicago IL 60601		800-464-4772	312-273-6745
Goodell Devries Leech & Dann LLP 1 South St 20th Fl. ....Baltimore MD 21202		888-229-4354	410-783-4000

Firm / Address	City	State	Zip	Toll-Free	Phone
Goyette & Associates Inc 2366 Gold Meadow Way Ste 200	Gold River	CA	95670	**888-993-1600**	916-851-1900
Grant, Konvalinka & Harrison PC Republic Ctr 633 Chestnut St 9th Fl	Chattanooga	TN	37450	**888-463-8117**	423-933-2731
Gunster Yoakley & Stewart Pa 777 S Flagler Dr Ste 500 E	West Palm Beach	FL	33401	**800-749-1980**	561-655-1980
Gurstel Chargo LLP 6681 Country Club Dr	Golden Valley	MN	55427	**877-750-6335**	877-344-4002
Harman, Claytor, Corrigan & Wellman PC PO Box 70280	Richmond	VA	23255	**877-747-4229**	804-747-5200
Harrang Long Gary Rudnick PC 360 E Tenth Ave Ste 300	Eugene	OR	97401	**800-315-4172**	541-485-0220
Harris Wyatt & Amala Attorneys at Law 5778 Commercial St SE	Salem	OR	97306	**800-853-2144**	503-378-7744
Hartnett Law Firm, The 2920 N Pearl St	Dallas	TX	75201	**800-900-9702**	214-742-4655
Heard & Smith LLP 3737 Broadway Ste 310	San Antonio	TX	78209	**800-584-3700**	210-820-3737
Herman Herman Katz & Cotlar LLP 820 Okeefe Ave	New Orleans	LA	70113	**844-943-7626**	504-581-4892
Hertz Schram & Saretsky PC 1760 S Telegraph Rd Ste 300	Bloomfield Hills	MI	48302	**866-775-5987**	248-335-5000
Horowitt, Darryl J - Coleman & Horowitt LLP 499 W Shaw Ave Ste 116	Fresno	CA	93704	**800-891-8362**	559-248-4820
Iowa Legal Aid 1111 Ninth St Ste 230	Des Moines	IA	50314	**800-992-8161**	515-243-1193
Jacko Law Group PC 5920 Friars Rd Ste 208	San Diego	CA	92108	**866-497-2298**	619-298-2880
Jackson & Hertogs LLP 201 Mission St Ste 700	San Francisco	CA	94105	**800-780-2008**	415-986-4559
Jacksonville Area Legal Aid (JALA) 126 W Adams St	Jacksonville	FL	32202	**866-356-8371**	904-356-8371
James Hoyer PA 2801 W Busch Blvd Ste 200	Tampa	FL	33618	**800-651-2502**	813-375-3700
Javitch Block LLP 700 Walnut St Ste 302	Cincinnati	OH	45202	**800-837-0109**	513-744-9600
Jeansonne & Remondet LLC 200 W Congress St Ste 1100 PO Box 91530	Lafayette	LA	70509	**800-446-2745**	337-237-4370
Jeffrey P Scott & Associates LLC 2356 University Ave W Ste 400	St. Paul	MN	55114	**866-442-3092**	651-968-1457
Jenkins Fenstermaker PLLC 325 Eighth St	Huntington	WV	25701	**866-617-4736**	304-523-2100
John C Heath, Attorney at Law PLLC 360 N Cutler Dr PO Box 510290	North Salt Lake	UT	84054	**877-575-2317**	
Joseph, Greenwald & Laake PA 6404 Ivy Ln Ste 400	Rockville	MD	20770	**877-412-7429**	301-220-2200
Judicare Wisconsin Inc Attys 401 Fifth St Ste 200	Wausau	WI	54403	**800-472-1638**	715-842-1681
Justia Inc 1380 Pear Ave Unit 2b	Mountain View	CA	94043	**800-300-0001**	888-587-8421
K&L Gates LLP 210 Sixth Ave	Pittsburgh	PA	15222	**800-452-8260**	412-355-6500
Katz & Korin PC 334 N Senate Ave The Emelie Bldg	Indianapolis	IN	46204	**800-464-2427**	317-464-1100
Katz Law Office Ltd 2408 W Cermak Rd	Chicago	IL	60608	**866-352-3033**	773-847-8982
Keesal Young & Logan 400 Oceangate	Long Beach	CA	90802	**800-877-7049**	562-436-2000
Kelley & Ferraro LLP Ernst & Young Tower 950 Main Ave Ste 1300	Cleveland	OH	44113	**800-398-1795**	216-202-3450
Kimball, Tirey & St John LLP 7676 Hazard Center Dr	San Diego	CA	92108	**800-564-6611**	
King & Schickli PLLC 800 Corporate Dr Ste 200	Lexington	KY	40503	**888-364-5712**	859-274-4287
Kirkland & Ellis LLP 200 E Randolph Dr	Chicago	IL	60601	**800-647-7600**	312-861-2000
Kline & Specter PC 1525 Locust St	Philadelphia	PA	19102	**800-243-1100**	215-772-1000
Knox McLaughlin Gornall & Sennett PC 120 W Tenth St	Erie	PA	16501	**800-939-9886**	814-459-2800
Landrum & Shouse LLP 106 W Vine St Ste 800	Lexington	KY	40507	**888-322-2505**	859-554-4038
Larson King LLP 30 E Seventh St Ste 2800	Saint Paul	MN	55101	**877-373-5501**	651-312-6500
Lawton & Cates SC 10 E Doty St Ste 400	Madison	WI	53703	**800-900-4539**	608-282-6200
Legal Aid Society of Palm Beach County Inc 423 Fern St Ste 200	West Palm Beach	FL	33401	**800-403-9353**	561-655-8944
Lesperance & Martineau 1440 Ste-Catherine W Bureau 700	Montreal	QC	H3G1R8	**888-273-8387**	514-861-4831
Lewis Wagner LLP 501 Indiana Ave Ste 200	Indianapolis	IN	46202	**800-237-0505**	317-237-0500
Littler Mendelson PC 650 California St 20th Fl	San Francisco	CA	94108	**888-548-8537**	415-433-1940
Lloyd & McDaniel PLC 11405 Park Rd Ste 200	Louisville	KY	40223	**866-548-2486**	
Lloyd Gray Whitehead Monroe (LGWM) 880 Montclair Rd Ste 100	Birmingham	AL	35213	**800-967-7299**	205-967-8822
Lone Star Legal Aid 500 Jefferson St 17th Fl	Houston	TX	77002	**800-733-8394**	713-652-0077
Lopez Mchugh LLP 1123 Admiral Peary Way	Philadelphia	PA	19112	**877-703-7070**	215-952-6910
Lynch, Traub, Keefe & Errante A Professional Corp 52 Trumbull St	New Haven	CT	06510	**888-692-7403**	203-787-0275
Macera & Jarzyna LLP 1200-427 Laurier Ave W	Ottawa	ON	K1R7Y2	**800-379-6668**	613-238-8173
Maher, Guiley & Maher PA 271 West Canton Ave Ste 1 PO Box 2209	Winter Park	FL	32789	**855-338-0720**	
Mallilo & Grossman 16309 Northern Blvd	Flushing	NY	11358	**866-593-6274**	718-461-6633
Marshall Dennehey Warner Coleman & Goggin 1845 Walnut St	Philadelphia	PA	19103	**800-220-3308**	215-575-2600
Martin, Harding & Mazzotti LLP 1222 Troy-Schenectady Rd	Niskayuna	NY	12309	**800-529-1010**	518-862-1200

Firm / Address	City	State	Zip	Toll-Free	Phone
Maxwell Noll 600 S Lake Ave	Pasadena	CA	91106	**800-660-2466**	
May, Adam, Gerdes & Thompson LLP 503 S Pierre St	Pierre	SD	57501	**800-636-8803**	605-224-8803
McAfee & Taft A Professional Corp 211 N Robinson	Oklahoma City	OK	73102	**800-235-9621**	405-235-9621
Mccallum, Hoaglund, Cook & Irby LLP 905 Montgomery Hwy Ste 201	Vestavia	AL	35216	**866-974-8145**	205-824-7767
McCranie, Sistrunk, Anzelmo, Hardy, McDaniel & Welch LLC 909 Poydras St Ste 1000	New Orleans	LA	70112	**800-977-8810**	504-831-0946
McGuireWoods LLP Gateway Plz 800 E Canal St	Richmond	VA	23219	**877-712-8778**	804-775-1000
Mckenzie Lake Lawyers LLP 140 Fullarton St Ste 1800	London	ON	N6A5P2	**800-261-4844**	519-672-5666
McLennan Ross LLP 600 W Chambers 12220 Stony Plain Rd	Edmonton	AB	T5N3Y4	**800-567-9200**	780-482-9200
McManis Faulkner Fairmont Plz 50 W San Fernando St 10th Fl	San Jose	CA	95113	**800-767-3263**	408-279-8700
McTeague Higbee Case Cohen Whitney & Toker PA 4 Union Pk PO Box 5000	Topsham	ME	04086	**800-482-0958**	207-725-5581
Mike Kelly Law Group LLC 500 Taylor St Ste 400	Columbia	SC	29201	**866-692-0123**	803-726-0123
Miller & Luring Company LPa 314 W Main St	Troy	OH	45373	**800-381-9680**	937-339-2627
Morgan Lewis & Bockius LLP 1701 Market St	Philadelphia	PA	19103	**866-963-7137**	215-963-5000
Morrison & Foerster LLP 425 Market St	San Francisco	CA	94105	**800-952-5210**	415-268-7000
Morrison Scott Alan Law Offices of pa 141 W Patrick St Ste 300	Frederick	MD	21701	**866-220-5185**	301-694-6262
Nagle & Associates 380 Knollwood St Ste 320	Salem	NC	27103	**800-411-1583**	336-723-4500
Nahon, Saharovich & Trotz PLC 488 S Menhenhall Rd	Memphis	TN	38117	**800-529-4004**	901-683-7000
Nelson & Kennard 2180 Harvard St Ste 160	Sacramento	CA	95815	**866-920-2295**	916-920-2295
Nelson Mullins Riley & Scarborough LLP 1320 Main St 17th Fl	Columbia	SC	29201	**800-237-2000**	803-799-2000
Nevada Disability Advocacy & Law Center 2820 W Charleston Blvd Ste 11	Las Vegas	NV	89102	**888-349-3843**	702-257-8150
Niedner, Bodeux, Carmichael, Huff, Lenox & Pashos LLP 131 Jefferson St	Saint Charles	MO	63301	**888-572-2192**	636-949-9300
Ohio Legal Assistance Foundation 10 W Broad St Ste 950	Columbus	OH	43215	**800-877-9772**	614-715-8560
Orrick 666 Fifth Ave	New York	NY	10103	**866-342-5259**	212-506-5000
Pallett Valo LLP 77 City Ctr Dr Ste 300	Mississauga	ON	L5B1M5	**800-323-3781**	905-273-3300
Parr Richey Frandsen Patterson Kruse LLP Capital Ctr N 251 N Illinois St Ste 1800	Indianapolis	IN	46204	**888-337-7766**	317-269-2500
Pellettieri Rabstein & Altman 100 Nassau Pk Blvd	Princeton	NJ	08540	**800-432-5297**	609-520-0900
Perantinides & Nolan Company LPa 80 S Summit St Ste 300	Akron	OH	44308	**800-253-5452**	330-253-5454
Perkins Coie LLP 1201 Third Ave Ste 4900	Seattle	WA	98101	**888-720-8382**	206-359-8000
Peter J Jaensch Immigration 2198 Main St	Sarasota	FL	34237	**800-870-3676**	941-366-9841
Phelan Hallinan & Schmieg LLP 400 Fellowship Rd Ste 100	Mount Laurel	NJ	08054	**800-382-8746**	
Phillips & Webster Pllc Attys 17410 133rd Ave NE Ste 301	Woodinville	WA	98072	**800-708-6000**	425-482-1111
Pickrel Schaeffer & Ebeling 40 N Main St - Kettering Tower	Dayton	OH	45423	**800-908-4490**	937-223-1130
Pines Bach 122 W Washington Ave Ste 900	Madison	WI	53703	**866-443-8661**	608-807-0752
Portnoff Law Associates Ltd 2700 Horizon Dr Ste 100	King of Prussia	PA	19406	**866-211-9466**	
Proskauer Rose LLP 11 Times Sq	New York	NY	10036	**866-444-3272**	212-969-3000
Rainwater, Holt & Sexton PA 801 Technology Dr	Little Rock	AR	72223	**800-434-4800**	501-868-2500
Rajkowski Hansmeier Ltd 11 Seventh Ave N	Saint Cloud	MN	56303	**800-445-9617**	320-251-1055
Relin, Goldstein & Crane LLP 28 E Main St Ste 1800	Rochester	NY	14614	**888-984-2351**	
Reminger 101 W Prospect Ave Ste 1400	Cleveland	OH	44115	**800-486-1311**	216-687-1311
Rendigs, Fry, Kiely & Dennis LLP 600 Vine St Ste 2650	Cincinnati	OH	45202	**800-274-2330**	513-381-9200
Reynolds, Mirth, Richards & Farmer LLP Manulife Pl 10180-101 St Ste 3200	Edmonton	AB	T5J3W8	**800-661-7673**	780-425-9510
Rieders, Travis, Humphrey, Waters & Dohrmann 161 W Third St	Williamsport	PA	17701	**800-326-9259**	570-323-8711
Robbins Arroyo LLP 600 B St Ste 1900	San Diego	CA	92101	**800-350-6003**	
Rosenn, Jenkins & Greenwald LLP 15 S Franklin St	Wilkes-Barre	PA	18711	**800-888-4754**	570-826-5600
Ross & Matthews PC 3650 Lovell Ave	Fort Worth	TX	76107	**800-458-6982**	
Rowley Chapman & Barney Ltd 63 E Main St Ste 501	Mesa	AZ	85201	**888-476-8411**	480-833-1113
RW. Lynch Company Inc 2333 San Ramon Vly Blvd	San Ramon	CA	94583	**800-594-8940**	925-837-3877
Sachs Waldman PC 1000 Farmer St	Detroit	MI	48226	**800-638-6722**	313-965-3464
Sackett & Assoc 1055 Lincoln Ave	San Jose	CA	95125	**800-913-3000**	408-295-7755
Schlichter, Bogard & Denton 100 S Fourth St Ste 900	St. Louis	MO	63102	**800-873-5297**	314-621-6115
Schneiderman & Sherman 23938 Research Dr Ste 300	Farmington Hills	MI	48335	**866-867-7688**	248-539-7400
Searcy Denney Scarola Barnhart Po Box 3626	West Palm Beach	FL	33402	**800-780-8607**	561-686-6300
Settle & Pou PC 3333 Lee Pkwy 8th Fl	Dallas	TX	75219	**800-538-4661**	214-520-3300

			Toll-Free	Phone

Shermeta, Adams & Von Allmen PC
1030 Doris Rd Ste 200 . . . . .Auburn Hills MI 48326 **800-451-7992** 248-519-1700

Shernoff Bidart Darras & Echeverria LLP
600 S Indian Hill Blvd . . . . .Claremont CA 91711 **800-458-3386** 909-621-4935

Shook & Stone Attorneys at Law
710 S Fourth St . . . . .Las Vegas NV 89101 **888-662-2013** 702-385-2220

Shook Hardy & Bacon LLP
2555 Grand Blvd . . . . .Kansas City MO 64108 **855-380-7584** 816-474-6550

Sieben Polk PA
2600 Eagan Woods Dr Ste 50 . . . . .Eagan MN 55121 **800-620-1829** 651-304-6708

Sigman Janssen Stack Sewall & Pitz
303 S Memorial Dr . . . . .Appleton WI 54911 **800-775-1441** 920-731-5201

Silver & Archibald LLP
997 S Milledge Ave . . . . .Athens GA 30605 **877-526-6281** 706-548-8122

Silver Golub & Teitell LLP
184 Atlantic St . . . . .Stamford CT 06901 **866-248-8744** 203-325-4491

Sindel, Sindel & Noble PC
8000 Maryland Ave Ste 910 . . . . .Saint Louis MO 63105 **866-489-5504** 314-499-1282

Siskinds LLP
680 Waterloo St PO Box 2520 . . . . .London ON N6A3V8 **877-672-2121** 519-672-2121

Skoler, Abbott & Presser PC
1 Monarch Pl Ste 2000 . . . . .Springfield MA 01144 **800-274-6774** 413-737-4753

Slack & Davis LLP
2705 Bee Caves Rd Ste 220 . . . . .Austin TX 78746 **800-455-8686** 512-795-8686

Smith Hartvigsen PLLC
257 E 200 S Ste 500 . . . . .Salt Lake City UT 84111 **877-825-2064** 801-413-1600

Smith, Sovik, Kendrick & Sugnet PC
250 S Clinton St Ste 600 . . . . .Syracuse NY 13202 **800-675-0011** 315-474-2911

Snell & Wilmer LLP
1 Arizona Ctr 400 E Van Buren St
Ste 1900 . . . . .Phoenix AZ 85004 **800-322-0430** 602-382-6000

Spence Law Firm LLC
15 S Jackson St . . . . .Jackson WY 83001 **800-967-2117** 307-733-7290

Spilman Thomas & Battle PLLC
300 Kanawha Blvd E . . . . .Charleston WV 25301 **800-967-8251** 304-340-3800

Stark & Stark
993 Lenox Dr Bldg 2 . . . . .Lawrenceville NJ 08648 **800-535-3425** 609-896-9060

Steele Law Firm p C The
949 County Rt 53 . . . . .Oswego NY 13126 **877-496-2687** 315-216-4721

Stueve Siegel Hanson LLP
460 Nichols Rd Ste 200 . . . . .Kansas City MO 64112 **800-714-0360** 816-714-7100

Sweeney Law Firm
8109 Lima Rd . . . . .Fort Wayne IN 46818 **866-793-6339** 260-420-3137

Taylor Wellons Politz & Duhe Aplc
8550 United Plaza Blvd Ste 101 . . . . .Baton Rouge LA 70809 **877-850-1047** 225-387-9888

Taylor, Porter, Brooks & Phillips LLP
450 Laurel St Ste 800 . . . . .Baton Rouge LA 70801 **800-310-7029** 225-387-3221

Texas Legal Services Center Inc
2101 S IH 35 Frontage Rd . . . . .Austin TX 78741 **888-343-4414** 800-622-2520

Thompson Hine LLP
127 Public Sq 3900 Key Ctr . . . . .Cleveland OH 44114 **877-257-3382** 216-566-5500

Thorp Reed & Armstrong LLP
301 Grant St 14th Fl . . . . .Pittsburgh PA 15219 **800-949-3120** 412-394-7711

Thorsnes Bartolotta McGuire
2550 Fifth Ave 11th Fl . . . . .San Diego CA 92103 **800-577-2922** 619-236-9363

Walker, Morgan & Kinard
135 E Main St . . . . .Lexington SC 29072 **800-922-8411** 803-675-5942

Weston Hurd LLP
The Tower at Erieview 1301 E Ninth St
Ste 1900 . . . . .Cleveland OH 44114 **800-336-4952** 216-241-6602

White Buffalo Club
160 W Gill Ave . . . . .Jackson WY 83001 **888-256-8182** 307-734-4900

Williams, Turner & Holmes PC
744 Horizon Crt Ste 115 . . . . .Grand Junction CO 81506 **800-548-6528** 970-242-6262

Woods Rogers PLC
10 S Jefferson St Ste 1400 . . . . .Roanoke VA 24011 **800-552-4529** 540-983-7600

Youth Advocate Programs Inc (YAP)
2007 N Third St PO Box 950 . . . . .Harrisburg PA 17102 **800-324-5794** 717-232-7580

428   LAWN & GARDEN EQUIPMENT

SEE ALSO Farm Machinery & Equipment - Mfr

			Toll-Free	Phone

Ames True Temper Inc
465 Railroad Ave . . . . .Camp Hill PA 17011 **800-393-1846**

Ariens Co 655 W Ryan St . . . . .Brillion WI 54110 **800-678-5443** 920-756-2141

Armatron International Inc
15 Highland Ave . . . . .Malden MA 02148 **800-343-3280** 781-321-2300

Artcraft Company Inc, The
200 John L Dietsch Blvd . . . . .North Attleboro MA 02763 **800-659-4042** 508-695-4042

Brinly-Hardy Co
3230 Industrial Pkwy . . . . .Jeffersonville IN 47130 **877-728-8224** 812-218-7200

California Flexrake Corp
9620 Gidley St . . . . .Temple City CA 91780 **800-266-4200** 626-443-4026

Carswell Distributing Co
3750 N Liberty St . . . . .Winston-Salem NC 27105 **800-929-1948** 336-767-7700

CMD Products
1410 Flightline Dr Ste D . . . . .Lincoln CA 95648 **800-210-9949** 916-434-0228

Commerce Corp
7603 Energy Pkwy . . . . .Baltimore MD 21226 **800-883-0234** 410-255-3500

Corona Clipper Inc
22440 Tomasco Canyon Rd . . . . .Corona CA 92883 **800-234-2547** 951-737-6515

Dultmeier Sales LLC
13808 Industrial Rd . . . . .Omaha NE 68137 **888-677-5054** 402-333-1444

EarthWay Products Inc
1009 Maple St . . . . .Bristol IN 46507 **800-294-0671** 574-848-7491

Echo Inc 400 Oakwood Rd . . . . .Lake Zurich IL 60047 **800-673-1558** 855-706-1522

Encore Manufacturing Company Inc
2415 Ashland Ave . . . . .Beatrice NE 68310 **800-267-4255**

Gilmour 7800 Discovery Dr . . . . .Middleton WI 53562 **866-348-5661***
*Cust Svc

Grassland Equipment & Irrigation Corp
892-898 Troy Schenectady Rd . . . . .Latham NY 12110 **800-564-5587** 518-785-5841

Green Depot Inc
1 Ivy Hill Rd . . . . .Brooklyn NY 11211 **800-238-5008** 718-782-2991

Harnack Co
6016 Nordic Dr . . . . .Cedar Falls IA 50613 **800-772-2022*** 319-277-0660
*Cust Svc

Hutson 306 Andrus Dr . . . . .Murray KY 42071 **866-488-7662** 270-886-3994

Jacobsen 11108 Quality Dr . . . . .Charlotte NC 28273 **800-848-1636** 704-504-6600

Lawn Equipment Parts Co
1475 River Rd PO Box 466 . . . . .Marietta PA 17547 **800-365-3726** 717-426-5200

Lodi Pumb & Irrigation
1301 E Armstrong Rd . . . . .Lodi CA 95242 **800-634-7272**

MacKissic Inc
PO Box 111 . . . . .Parker Ford PA 19457 **800-348-1117** 610-495-7181

Melnor Inc 109 Tyson Dr . . . . .Winchester VA 22603 **877-283-0697** 540-722-5600

Midwest Bio-systems Inc
28933 35 E St . . . . .Tampico IL 61283 **877-649-2114** 815-438-7200

MTD Products Inc
5965 Grafton Rd . . . . .Valley City OH 44280 **800-800-7310** 330-225-2600

Oliver M Dean Inc
125 Brooks St . . . . .Worcester MA 01606 **800-648-3326** 508-856-9100

Precision Products Inc
316 Limit St . . . . .Lincoln IL 62656 **800-225-5891*** 217-735-1590
*Cust Svc

Rugg Manufacturing Corp
554 Willard St . . . . .Leominster MA 01453 **800-633-8772**

Simplicity Manufacturing Inc
PO Box 702 . . . . .Milwaukee WI 53201 **800-837-6836**

Stens Corp 2424 Cathy Ln . . . . .Jasper IN 47546 **800-457-7444** 812-482-2526

Stihl Inc
536 Viking Dr . . . . .Virginia Beach VA 23452 **800-467-8445*** 757-486-9100
*Cust Svc

Storr Tractor Co
3191 Rt 22 . . . . .Branchburg NJ 08876 **800-526-3802** 908-722-9830

Swisher Mower & Machine Company Inc
1602 Corporate Dr . . . . .Warrensburg MO 64093 **800-222-8183** 660-747-8183

Toro Co
8111 Lyndale Ave . . . . .Bloomington MN 55420 **888-384-9939**
NYSE: TTC

Toro Co Commercial Products Div
8111 Lyndale Ave . . . . .Bloomington MN 55420 **800-348-2424*** 952-888-8801
*Cust Svc

Tuff Torq Corp
5943 Commerce Blvd . . . . .Morristown TN 37814 **866-572-3441** 423-585-2000

Weathermatic
3301 W Kingsley Rd . . . . .Garland TX 75041 **888-484-3776** 972-278-6131

Wesspur Tree Equipment
2121 Iron St . . . . .Bellingham WA 98225 **800-268-2141** 360-734-5242

429   LEATHER GOODS - PERSONAL

SEE ALSO Handbags, Totes, Backpacks ; Footwear ; Luggage, Bags, Cases ; Leather Goods (Misc) ; Clothing & Accessories - Mfr

			Toll-Free	Phone

Bottega Veneta Inc
699 Fifth Ave . . . . .New York NY 10022 **800-845-6790**

Buxton Co
245 Cadwell Dr . . . . .Springfield MA 01104 **800-426-3638** 413-734-5900

Carroll Cos Inc
1640 Old Hwy 421 S . . . . .Boone NC 28607 **800-884-2521** 828-264-2521

Coach Inc 342 Madison Ave . . . . .New York NY 10173 **800-444-3611** 212-599-4777
NYSE: COH

Dooney & Bourke Inc
1 Regent St . . . . .East Norwalk CT 06855 **800-347-5000*** 203-853-7515
*Cust Svc

430   LEATHER GOODS (MISC)

			Toll-Free	Phone

Action Co
1425 N Tennessee St . . . . .McKinney TX 75069 **800-937-3700*** 972-542-8700
*Sales

Auburn Leather Co
125 N Caldwell St . . . . .Auburn KY 42206 **800-635-0617** 270-542-4116

Carroll Cos Inc
1640 Old Hwy 421 S . . . . .Boone NC 28607 **800-884-2521** 828-264-2521

Gould & Goodrich Leather Inc
709 E McNeil St . . . . .Lillington NC 27546 **800-277-0732** 910-893-2071

Hunter Co
3300 W 71st Ave . . . . .Westminster CO 80030 **800-676-4868** 303-427-4626

431   LEATHER TANNING & FINISHING

			Toll-Free	Phone

Hermann Oak Leather Co
4050 N First St . . . . .Saint Louis MO 63147 **800-325-7950** 314-421-1173

Leatherock International Inc
5285 Lovelock St . . . . .San Diego CA 92110 **800-466-6667** 619-299-7625

Seidel Tanning Corp
1306 E Meinecke Ave . . . . .Milwaukee WI 53212 **800-826-6379** 414-562-4030

SHOWA 579 Edison St .Menlo GA 30731 **800-241-0323**

432   LEGISLATION HOTLINES

			Toll-Free	Phone

Alabama
Administrative Office of Alabama Courts
300 Dexter Ave . . . . .Montgomery AL 36104 **866-954-9411** 334-954-5000

Indiana
Agriculture Dept
101 W Washington St . . . . .Indianapolis IN 46204 **800-677-9800**

Dept of Legislative Services
90 State Cir . . . . .Annapolis MD 21401 **800-492-7122** 410-946-5400

Minnesota
Aging Board 540 Cedar St . . . . .Saint Paul MN 55155 **800-882-6262** 651-431-2500

				Toll-Free	Phone
Montana					
Arts Council PO Box 202201	Helena	MT	59620	**800-282-3092**	406-444-6430
Nevada					
Bill Status 401 S Carson St	Carson City	NV	89701	**800-978-2878**	775-684-6827
Bill Status State House Annex PO Box 068	Trenton	NJ	08625	**800-792-8630**	609-292-4840
New York					
Aging Office 2 Empire State Plz	Albany	NY	12223	**800-342-9871**	
Bill Status 202 Legislative Office Bldg	Albany	NY	12248	**800-342-9860**	518-455-4218
Wyoming					
Aging Div 2300 Capitol Ave 4th Fl	Cheyenne	WY	82002	**800-442-2766**	307-777-7995

433 LIBRARIES

SEE ALSO Library Systems - Regional - Canadian

433-1 Medical Libraries

				Toll-Free	Phone
Leon S McGoogan Library of Medicine University of Nebraska Medical Ctr 42nd and Emile	Omaha	NE	68198	**866-800-5209**	402-559-4000
Moody Medical Library 914 Market st	Galveston	TX	77555	**866-235-5223**	409-772-2372
National Institutes of Health (NIH) 9000 Rockville Pk	Bethesda	MD	20892	**800-411-1222**	301-496-4000
National Library of Medicine 8600 Rockville Pk	Bethesda	MD	20894	**888-346-3656**	301-594-5983
Oregon Health & Science University (OHSU) *Bone Marrow Transplant Clinic* 3181 SW Sam Jackson Pk Rd CB569	Portland	OR	97239	**800-452-1369**	503-494-8500
Raymon H Mulford Library 3000 Arlington Ave	Toledo	OH	43614	**800-321-8383**	419-383-4225
Robert B Greenblatt MD Library *Medical College of Georgia* 1439 Lny Walker Blvd	Augusta	GA	30912	**800-715-4225**	706-721-3441
Rosalind Franklin University of Medicine & Science Learning Resource Ctr 3333 Green Bay Rd	North Chicago	IL	60064	**800-244-1177**	847-578-3000
Rowland Medical Library University of Mississippi 2500 N State St	Jackson	MS	39216	**800-621-8099**	601-984-1231
Ruth Lilly Medical Library 975 W Walnut St IB 100	Indianapolis	IN	46202	**877-952-1988**	317-274-7182
Saint Louis University 221 N Grand Blvd	Saint Louis	MO	63103	**800-758-3678**	314-977-7288
Texas A & M University Rudder Tower Ste 205	College Station	TX	77843	**888-890-5667**	979-845-8901
University of California Irvine *Library* PO Box 19557	Irvine	CA	92623	**800-843-2763**	949-824-6836
University of Nebraska Medical Ctr McGoogan Library of Medicine 986705 Nebraska Medical Ctr	Omaha	NE	68198	**866-800-5209**	402-559-4006
University of Pennsylvania 3451 Walnut St	Philadelphia	PA	19104	**800-537-5487**	215-898-5000
University of Tennessee Health Science Ctr *Health Sciences Library & Biocommunications Ctr* 877 Madison Ave	Memphis	TN	38103	**877-747-0004**	901-448-5634
University of Texas Southwestern Medical Ctr at Dallas Library, The 5323 Harry Hines Blvd	Dallas	TX	75390	**866-645-6455**	214-648-2001
West Virginia University PO Box 6009	Morgantown	WV	26506	**800-344-9881**	304-293-2121

433-2 Presidential Libraries

				Toll-Free	Phone
Abraham Lincoln Presidential Library & Museum 112 N Sixth St	Springfield	IL	62701	**800-610-2094**	217-557-6250
Dwight D Eisenhower Presidential Library & Museum 200 SE Fourth St	Abilene	KS	67410	**877-746-4453**	785-263-6700
Franklin D Roosevelt Presidential Library & Museum 4079 Albany Post Rd	Hyde Park	NY	12538	**800-337-8474**	845-486-7770
Harry S Truman Presidential Library & Museum 500 W Hwy 24	Independence	MO	64050	**800-833-1225**	816-268-8200
John F Kennedy Presidential Library & Museum Columbia Point	Boston	MA	02125	**866-535-1960**	617-514-1600
LBJ Library & Museum 2313 Red River St	Austin	TX	78705	**800-874-6451**	512-721-0216
Ronald Reagan Presidential Library & Museum 40 Presidential Dr	Simi Valley	CA	93065	**800-410-8354**	805-522-2977
Rutherford B Hayes Presidential Ctr Spiegel Grove	Fremont	OH	43420	**800-998-7737**	419-332-2081

433-3 Public Libraries

Listings for public libraries are alphabetized by city name within each state grouping.

Alabama

				Toll-Free	Phone
Auburn Public Library 749 E Thach Ave	Auburn	AL	36830	**800-888-2726**	334-501-3190
Mobile Public Library 701 Government St	Mobile	AL	36602	**877-322-8228**	251-208-7073

Alaska

				Toll-Free	Phone
Homer Public Library 500 Hazel Ave	Homer	AK	99603	**800-478-4441**	907-235-3180
Juneau Public Libraries 292 Marine Way	Juneau	AK	99801	**800-478-4176**	907-586-5324

Arizona

				Toll-Free	Phone
Mohave Educational Services Cooperative Inc 625 E Beale St	Kingman	AZ	86401	**800-742-2437**	928-753-6945
Pima County Public Library 101 N Stone Ave	Tucson	AZ	85701	**877-705-5437**	520-791-4010

California

				Toll-Free	Phone
Placer County Library 350 Nevada St	Auburn	CA	95603	**800-488-4308**	530-886-4500
Berkeley Public Library 2090 Kittredge St	Berkeley	CA	94704	**800-870-3663**	510-981-6100
Beverly Hills Public Library 444 N Rexford Dr	Beverly Hills	CA	90210	**800-238-0172**	310-288-2220
Daly City Public Library 40 Wembley Dr	Daly City	CA	94015	**888-227-7669**	650-991-8025
Downey City Library (DCL) 11121 Brookshire Ave	Downey	CA	90241	**877-846-3452**	562-904-7360
El Centro Public Library 539 State St	El Centro	CA	92243	**877-482-5656**	760-337-4565
Alameda County Library 2450 Stevenson Blvd	Fremont	CA	94538	**888-663-0660**	510-745-1500
Fremont Main Library 2400 Stevenson Blvd	Fremont	CA	94538	**800-434-0222**	510-745-1400
Huntington Beach Public Library (HBPL) 7111 Talbert Ave	Huntington Beach	CA	92648	**800-565-0148**	714-842-4481
Santa Clara County Library 14600 Winchester Blvd	Los Gatos	CA	95032	**800-286-1991**	408-293-2326
Merced County Library 2100 O St	Merced	CA	95340	**866-249-0773**	209-385-7643
Monterey Public Library 580 Pacific St	Monterey	CA	93940	**800-338-0505**	831-646-3933
Napa County Library 580 Coombs St	Napa	CA	94559	**877-279-2987**	707-253-4241
City of Palm Springs 300 S Sunrise Way	Palm Springs	CA	92262	**800-611-1911**	760-322-7323
Contra Costa County Library 75 Santa Barbara Rd	Pleasant Hill	CA	94523	**800-984-4636**	
Shasta Public Library 1100 Parkview Ave	Redding	CA	96001	**800-735-2922**	530-245-7250
RICHMOND CITY HALL 450 Civic Ctr Plz	Richmond	CA	94804	**800-833-2900**	510-620-6555
Riverside City Public Library 3581 Mission Inn Ave	Riverside	CA	92501	**888-225-7377**	951-826-5201
Roseville Public Library 225 Taylor St	Roseville	CA	95678	**800-984-4636**	916-774-5221
Sacramento Public Library 828 'I' St	Sacramento	CA	95814	**800-561-4636**	916-264-2700
San Diego Public Library 820 E St	San Diego	CA	92101	**866-470-1308**	619-236-5800
San Jose Public Library 150 E San Fernando St	San Jose	CA	95113	**800-735-2929**	408-808-2000
Santa Barbara Public Library 40 E Anapamu St	Santa Barbara	CA	93101	**800-354-9660**	805-962-7653
Stockton-San Joaquin County Public Library (SSJCPL) 605 N El Dorado St	Stockton	CA	95202	**866-805-7323**	209-937-8416
Tulare County Library System 200 W Oak Ave	Visalia	CA	93291	**866-290-8681**	559-713-2700
Watsonville Public Library 275 Main St Ste 100	Watsonville	CA	95076	**800-281-7275**	831-768-3400
Woodland Public Library 250 First St	Woodland	CA	95695	**800-321-2752**	530-661-5980
Yolo County Library 226 Buckeye St	Woodland	CA	95695	**800-755-6864**	530-666-8005

Colorado

				Toll-Free	Phone
Farr Regional Library 1939 61st Ave	Greeley	CO	80634	**888-861-7323**	
Bemis Public Library 6014 S Datura St	Littleton	CO	80120	**800-895-1999**	303-795-3961
Westminster Public Library 7392 Irving St	Westminster	CO	80030	**800-424-1554**	303-430-2400

Connecticut

				Toll-Free	Phone
Bristol Public Library 5 High St	Bristol	CT	06010	**877-603-7323**	860-584-7787
Cheshire Public Library 104 Main St	Cheshire	CT	06410	**800-275-2273**	203-272-2245
Welles-Turner Memorial Library 2407 Main St	Glastonbury	CT	06033	**800-411-9671**	860-652-7719
Groton Public Library 52 Newtown Rd	Groton	CT	06340	**800-989-0900**	860-441-6750
New Fairfield Free Public Library 2 Brush Hill Rd	New Fairfield	CT	06812	**877-227-7487**	203-312-5679
Norwalk Public Library 1 Belden Ave	Norwalk	CT	06850	**800-382-9463**	203-899-2780

Delaware

				Toll-Free	Phone
Hockessin Library 1023 Valley Rd	Hockessin	DE	19707	**888-352-7722**	302-239-5160
New Castle Public Library 424 Delaware St	New Castle	DE	19720	**877-225-7351**	302-328-1995
New Castle County Library 750 Library Ave	Newark	DE	19711	**877-225-7351**	302-731-7550
Kirkwood Library 6000 Kirkwood Hwy	Wilmington	DE	19808	**888-352-7722**	302-995-7663

Florida

				Toll-Free	Phone
DeSoto County Library					
125 N Hillsboro Ave	Arcadia	FL	34266	800-843-5678	
Walton-De Funiak Library					
3 Cir Dr	DeFuniak Springs	FL	32435	800-342-0141	850-892-3624
Lee County Library					
2050 Central Ave	Fort Myers	FL	33901	800-854-8195	239-479-4636
Alachua County Library District					
401 E University Ave	Gainesville	FL	32601	866-341-2730	352-334-3900
Heartland Library Co-op					
319 W Center Ave	Sebring	FL	33870	800-843-5678	
Palm Beach County Public Library System					
3650 Summit Blvd	West Palm Beach	FL	33406	888-780-4962	561-233-2600

Georgia

				Toll-Free	Phone
Columbus Public Library					
3000 Macon Rd	Columbus	GA	31906	800-652-0782	706-243-2669

Illinois

				Toll-Free	Phone
Downers Grove Public Library					
1050 Curtiss St	Downers Grove	IL	60515	800-227-0625	630-960-1200
Elk Grove Village Public Library					
1001 Wellington Ave	Elk Grove Village	IL	60007	800-252-8980	847-439-0447
Evanston Public Library					
1703 Orrington Ave	Evanston	IL	60201	888-253-7003	847-448-8600
Grande Prairie Public Library					
3479 W 183rd St	Hazel Crest	IL	60429	800-321-9511	708-798-5563
Ela Area Public Library District					
275 Mohawk Trl	Lake Zurich	IL	60047	800-436-0709	847-438-3433

Indiana

				Toll-Free	Phone
Wells County Public Library					
200 W Washington St	Bluffton	IN	46714	800-824-6111	260-824-1612
Carmel Clay Public Library					
55 Fourth Ave SE	Carmel	IN	46032	800-908-4490	317-844-3361
Bartholomew County Public Library					
536 Fifth St	Columbus	IN	47201	800-685-0524	812-379-1255
Fayette County Public Library					
828 N Grand Ave	Connersville	IN	47331	844-829-3746	765-827-0883
Kokomo-Howard County Public Library					
220 N Union St	Kokomo	IN	46901	800-837-0971	765-457-3242
Tippecanoe County Public Library					
627 S St	Lafayette	IN	47901	800-542-7818	765-429-0100

Iowa

				Toll-Free	Phone
Mason City Public Library					
225 Second St SE	Mason City	IA	50401	800-532-1531	641-421-3668

Kansas

				Toll-Free	Phone
Dorothy Bramlage Public Library Junction City					
230 W Seventh St	Junction City	KS	66441	800-727-2785	785-238-4311
Leavenworth Public Library					
417 Spruce St	Leavenworth	KS	66048	800-829-3676	913-682-5666
Salina Public Library					
301 W Elm St	Salina	KS	67401	800-362-2642	785-825-4624

Kentucky

				Toll-Free	Phone
McCracken County Public Library					
555 Washington St	Paducah	KY	42003	866-829-7532	270-442-2510

Louisiana

				Toll-Free	Phone
Beauregard Parish Library					
205 S Washington Ave	Deridder	LA	70634	800-524-6239	337-463-6217

Maine

				Toll-Free	Phone
Portland Public Library					
5 Monument Sq	Portland	ME	04101	800-848-5800	207-871-1700

Maryland

				Toll-Free	Phone
Harford County Public Library					
1221-A Brass Mill Rd	Belcamp	MD	21017	800-944-7403	410-575-6761
Caroline County Public Library					
100 Market St	Denton	MD	21629	800-832-3277	410-479-1343

Massachusetts

				Toll-Free	Phone
Brookline Public Library					
361 Washington St	Brookline	MA	02445	800-447-8844	617-730-2370
Burlington Public Library					
22 Sears St	Burlington	MA	01803	800-422-2462	781-270-1690
Cambridge Public Library					
449 Broadway	Cambridge	MA	02138	800-327-5050	617-349-4040
Fall River Public Library					
104 N Main St	Fall River	MA	02720	800-331-3764	508-946-8600

				Toll-Free	Phone
Marlborough Public Library					
35 W Main St	Marlborough	MA	01752	800-592-2000	508-624-6900
Medford Public Library					
111 High St	Medford	MA	02155	800-447-8844	781-395-7950
Sharon Public Library					
90 S Main St	Sharon	MA	02067	800-825-3260	781-784-1578
Springfield City Library					
220 State St	Springfield	MA	01103	800-852-3133	413-263-6828
Wayland Free Public Library					
41 Cochituate Rd	Wayland	MA	01778	800-592-2000	508-358-2311
Tufts Library 46 Broad St	Weymouth	MA	02188	888-283-3757	781-337-1402

Michigan

				Toll-Free	Phone
Alpena County George N Fletcher Public Library					
211 N First Ave	Alpena	MI	49707	877-737-4106	989-356-6188
Bloomfield Township Public Library					
1099 Lone Pine Rd	Bloomfield Hills	MI	48302	800-318-2596	248-642-5800
Canton Public Library					
1200 S Canton Ctr Rd	Canton	MI	48188	888-988-6300	734-397-0999
Kent District Library					
814 W River Ctr Dr NE	Comstock Park	MI	49321	877-243-2466	616-784-2007
Genesee District Library					
Flint Township-McCarty Library					
2071 Graham Rd	Flint	MI	48532	866-732-1120	810-732-9150
Capital Area District Libraries					
401 S Capitol Ave	Lansing	MI	48933	866-561-2500	517-367-6300
Peter White Public Library					
217 N Front St	Marquette	MI	49855	800-992-9012	906-228-9510
Grace A Dow Memorial Library					
1710 W St Andrews Rd	Midland	MI	48640	800-422-5245	989-837-3430
Monroe County Library System					
3700 S Custer Rd	Monroe	MI	48161	800-462-2050	734-241-5277
Muskegon Area District Library					
4845 Airline Rd	Muskegon	MI	49444	877-569-4801	231-737-6248
Saint Clair County Library System					
210 McMorran Blvd	Port Huron	MI	48060	877-987-7323	810-987-7323
Troy Public Library					
510 W Big Beaver Rd	Troy	MI	48084	800-649-7377	248-524-3538
Waterford Township Public Library					
5168 Civic Ctr Dr	Waterford	MI	48329	800-773-2587	248-674-4831

Minnesota

				Toll-Free	Phone
Buckham Memorial Library					
11 Div St E	Faribault	MN	55021	800-658-2354	507-334-2089
Lake Agassiz Regional Library (LARL)					
118 Fifth St S PO Box 900	Moorhead	MN	56560	800-247-0449	218-233-3757
Owatonna Public Library					
105 N Elm St	Owatonna	MN	55060	800-657-3864	507-444-2460
Scott County Library System					
1615 Weston Ct	Shakopee	MN	55379	877-772-8346	952-707-1770
Washington County Library					
8595 Central Pk Pl	Woodbury	MN	55125	800-657-3750	651-275-8500

Missouri

				Toll-Free	Phone
Daniel Boone Regional Library					
100 W Broadway	Columbia	MO	65203	800-324-4806	573-443-3161
Linda Hall Library					
5109 Cherry St	Kansas City	MO	64110	800-662-1545	816-363-4600
Saint Louis Public Library (SLPL)					
1301 Olive St	Saint Louis	MO	63103	800-916-8938	314-241-2288
Saint Louis County Library (SLCL)					
1640 S Lindbergh Blvd	St. Louis	MO	63131	800-473-0060	314-994-3300

Montana

				Toll-Free	Phone
Lewis & Clark Library					
120 S Last Chance Gulch	Helena	MT	59601	800-733-2767	406-447-1690

New Jersey

				Toll-Free	Phone
Jersey City Free Public Library					
472 Jersey Ave	Jersey City	NJ	07302	800-443-0315	201-547-4501
Atlantic County Library-Mays Landing					
40 Farragut Ave	Mays Landing	NJ	08330	800-852-7899	609-345-6700
Mount Laurel Library					
100 Walt Whitman Ave	Mount Laurel	NJ	08054	888-576-5529	856-234-7319
Teaneck Public Library					
840 Teaneck Rd	Teaneck	NJ	07666	800-245-1377	201-837-4171
Camden County Library					
203 Laurel Rd	Voorhees	NJ	08043	877-222-3737	856-772-1636

New York

				Toll-Free	Phone
Baldwinsville Public Library					
33 E Genesee St	Baldwinsville	NY	13027	800-388-2000	315-635-5631
Bronx Library Ctr					
310 E Kings Bridge Rd	Bronx	NY	10458	800-342-3688	718-579-4244
Finger Lakes Library System					
1300 Dryden Rd	Ithaca	NY	14850	800-909-3557	607-273-4074
Tompkins County Public Library					
101 E Green St	Ithaca	NY	14850	800-772-7267	607-272-4557
Northern New York Library Network					
6721 US Hwy 11	Potsdam	NY	13676	877-833-1674	315-265-1119
West Islip Public Library					
3 Higbie Ln	West Islip	NY	11795	866-833-1122	631-661-7080

North Carolina

		Toll-Free	Phone
Forsyth County Public Library 201 North Chestnut St ....Winston-Salem NC 27101		866-345-1884	336-703-2665

North Dakota

		Toll-Free	Phone
Minot Public Library 516 Second Ave SW ....Minot ND 58701		800-843-9948	701-852-1045

Ohio

		Toll-Free	Phone
Pickaway County District Public Library 1160 North Court St ....Circleville OH 43113		800-733-2767	740-477-1644
Cleveland Public Library 325 Superior Ave ....Cleveland OH 44114		800-362-1262	216-623-2800
Portage County District Library 10482 S St..................................Garrettsville OH 44231		800-500-5179	330-527-4378
Mansfield-Richland County Public Library 43 W Third St ....Mansfield OH 44902		877-795-2111	419-521-3100
Cuyahoga County Public Library 2111 Snow Rd ....Parma OH 44134		800-749-5560	216-398-1800
Troy-Miami County Public Library 419 W Main St ....Troy OH 45373		866-657-8556	937-339-0502
Westerville Public Library 126 S State St ....Westerville OH 43081		800-816-0662	614-882-7277

Oklahoma

		Toll-Free	Phone
Lawton Public Library 110 SW Fourth St ....Lawton OK 73501		855-895-8064	580-581-3450
Southeastern Public Library System of Oklahoma (SEPLSO) 401 N Second St ....McAlester OK 74501		800-562-9520	918-426-0456
Eastern Oklahoma District Library System 801 W Okmulgee Ave ....Muskogee OK 74401		888-291-8152	918-682-6657
Stillwater Public Library 1107 S Duck St ....Stillwater OK 74074		800-829-3676	405-372-3633

Oregon

		Toll-Free	Phone
Ledding Library 10660 SE 21st Ave ....Milwaukie OR 97222		800-701-8560	503-786-7580

Pennsylvania

		Toll-Free	Phone
Erie County Library System 160 E Front St ....Erie PA 16507		800-352-0026	814-451-6900
Adams County Public Library 140 Baltimore St ....Gettysburg PA 17325		800-548-3240	717-334-5716
Osterhout Free Library 71 S Franklin St ....Wilkes-Barre PA 18701		800-732-0999	570-823-0156

Rhode Island

		Toll-Free	Phone
Pawtucket Public Library 13 Summer St ....Pawtucket RI 02860		800-359-3090	401-725-3714

South Carolina

		Toll-Free	Phone
Charleston County Public Library 68 Calhoun St ....Charleston SC 29401		800-768-3676	843-805-6930
Orangeburg County Library (OCL) 510 Louis St ....Orangeburg SC 29115		800-922-2594	803-531-4636

Tennessee

		Toll-Free	Phone
Clarksville Montgomery County Public Library 350 Pageant Ln ....Clarksville TN 37040		877-239-6635	931-648-8826
Blue Grass Regional Library 104 E Sixth St ....Columbia TN 38401		888-345-5575	931-388-9282
Fayette County Library 216 W Market St ....Somerville TN 38068		866-465-3591	901-465-5248

Texas

		Toll-Free	Phone
Carrollton Public Library 4220 N Josey Ln ....Carrollton TX 75010		888-727-2978	972-466-4800
Corsicana Public Library 100 N 12th St ....Corsicana TX 75110		877-648-2836	903-874-4731
DeSoto Public Library 211 E Pleasant Run Rd ....Desoto TX 75115		800-886-9008	972-230-9656
Fort Worth Public Library 200 Texas St ....Fort Worth TX 76102		800-433-5747	
Hood County Public Library 222 N Travis St ....Granbury TX 76048		800-452-9292	817-573-3569
Hurst Public Library 901 Precinct Line Rd ....Hurst TX 76053		800-344-8377	817-788-7300
New Braunfels Public Library 700 E Common St ....New Braunfels TX 78130		800-434-8013	830-221-4300
Plano Public Library System 5024 Custer Rd ....Plano TX 75023		800-473-5707	972-769-4200
Richardson Public Library 900 Civic Ctr Dr ....Richardson TX 75080		800-735-2989	972-744-4350
Marcive Inc PO Box 47508 Ste 160 ....San Antonio TX 78265		800-531-7678	

		Toll-Free	Phone
San Benito Public Library 401 North Sam Houston Blvd ....San Benito TX 78586		800-444-1187	956-361-3860
Wharton County Library 1920 N Fulton St ....Wharton TX 77488		800-244-5492	979-532-8080

Utah

		Toll-Free	Phone
Weber County Library 2464 Jefferson Ave ....Ogden UT 84401		866-678-5342	801-337-2632
Provo City Library 550 N University Ave ....Provo UT 84601		800-914-8931	801-852-6650

Virginia

		Toll-Free	Phone
Jefferson-Madison Regional Library 201 E Market St ....Charlottesville VA 22902		866-979-1555	434-979-7151
Hampton Public Library 4207 Victoria Blvd ....Hampton VA 23669		800-552-7096	757-727-1154
York County Public Library 8500 George Washington Memorial Hwy ....Yorktown VA 23692		800-552-7945	757-890-3377

Washington

		Toll-Free	Phone
Kitsap Regional Library 1301 Sylvan Way ....Bremerton WA 98310		877-883-9900	360-405-9100
Puyallup Public Library 333 S Meridian ....Puyallup WA 98371		844-821-8911	253-841-4321
Seattle Public Library 1000 Fourth Ave ....Seattle WA 98104		800-829-3676	206-386-4636
Pierce County Library System 3005 112th St E ....Tacoma WA 98446		800-346-0995	253-548-3300
Timberland Regional Library 415 Tumwater Blvd SW ....Tumwater WA 98501		877-284-6237	360-943-5001

West Virginia

		Toll-Free	Phone
Fayette County Public Library 531 Summit St ....Oak Hill WV 25901		855-275-5737	304-465-0121
Mary H Weirton Public Library 3442 Main St ....Weirton WV 26062		800-774-2429	304-797-8510

Wisconsin

		Toll-Free	Phone
Northern Waters Library Service 3200 E Lakeshore Dr ....Ashland WI 54806		800-228-5684	715-682-2365
Indianhead Federated Library System 1538 Truax Blvd ....Eau Claire WI 54703		800-321-5427	715-839-5082
South Central Library System 4610 S Biltmore Ln ....Madison WI 53718		855-516-7257	608-246-7970
Milwaukee Public Library 814 W Wisconsin Ave ....Milwaukee WI 53233		866-947-7363	414-286-3000
Oshkosh Public Library 106 Washington Ave ....Oshkosh WI 54901		800-236-0850	920-236-5205
Mead Public Library 710 N Eigth St ....Sheboygan WI 53081		800-441-4563	920-459-3400
Watertown Public Library 100 S Water St ....Watertown WI 53094		800-829-3676	920-262-4090

433-4 Special Collections Libraries

		Toll-Free	Phone
AIDS Library 1233 Locust St 2nd Fl ....Philadelphia PA 19107		877-613-4533	215-985-4851
Bentley Historical Library 1150 Beal Ave ....Ann Arbor MI 48109		866-233-6661	734-764-3482

433-5 State Libraries

		Toll-Free	Phone
California State Library 900 N St ....Sacramento CA 95814		800-952-5666	916-654-0261
Connecticut State Library 231 Capitol Ave ....Hartford CT 06106		866-886-4478	860-757-6510
Idaho Commission for Libraries (ICFL) 325 W State St ....Boise ID 83702		800-458-3271	208-334-2150
Illinois State Library 300 S Second St ....Springfield IL 62701		800-665-5576	217-782-2994
Indiana State Library (ISL) 115 W Washington St Ste 960S ....Indianapolis IN 46204		800-451-6028	800-677-9800
Iowa State Library 1007 E Grand Ave Capitol Bldg Second Fl..................Des Moines IA 50319		800-248-4483	515-281-4105
Kentucky Dept for Libraries & Archives 300 Coffee Tree Rd ....Frankfort KY 40602		800-372-2968	502-564-8300
Library of Michigan, The 702 W Kalamazoo St PO Box 30007..........Lansing MI 48909		800-726-7323	517-373-1300
Maine State Library 64 State House Stn ....Augusta ME 04333		800-427-8336	207-287-5600
Massachusetts Board of Library Commissioners 98 N Washington St ....Boston MA 02114		800-952-7403	617-725-1860
Nebraska Library Commission 1200 N St Ste 120 ....Lincoln NE 68508		800-307-2665	402-471-2045
Nevada State Library & Archives (NSLA) 100 N Stewart St ....Carson City NV 89701		800-922-2880	775-684-3360
New Hampshire State Library 20 Park St ....Concord NH 03301		800-639-5290	603-271-2144
North Dakota State Library (NDSL) 604 E Blvd Ave ....Bismarck ND 58505		800-472-2104	701-328-4622
Oklahoma Dept of Libraries 200 NE 18th St ....Oklahoma City OK 73105		800-522-8116	405-521-2502

	City	State	Zip	Toll-Free	Phone
South Carolina State Library					
1500 Senate St	Columbia	SC	29201	**888-221-4643**	803-734-8666
South Dakota State Library					
800 Governors Dr	Pierre	SD	57501	**800-423-6665**	605-773-3131
State Library of Ohio					
274 E First Ave Ste 100	Columbus	OH	43201	**800-686-1532**	614-644-7061
Utah State Library					
250 N 1950 W Ste A	Salt Lake City	UT	84116	**800-662-9150**	801-715-6777
Washington State Library					
PO Box 40220	Olympia	WA	98504	**800-822-1065**	360-902-4151
West Virginia Library Commission					
1900 Kanawha Blvd E	Charleston	WV	25305	**800-642-9021**	304-558-2041

433-6 University Libraries

Listings for university libraries are arranged by states.

	City	State	Zip	Toll-Free	Phone
Auburn University					
202 Mary Martin Hall	Auburn University	AL	36849	**866-389-6770***	334-844-6425
*Admissions					
University of Alabama					
PO Box 870132	Tuscaloosa	AL	35487	**800-933-2262***	205-348-6010
*Admissions					
University of Alaska Fairbanks					
Signers' Hall 2nd Fl PO Box 757480	Fairbanks	AK	99775	**800-478-1823**	907-474-7500
Arizona State University					
Hayden Library					
300 E Orange Mall	Tempe	AZ	85281	**800-728-0209**	480-965-3417
University of Arkansas					
232 Silas Hunt Hall	Fayetteville	AR	72701	**800-377-8632***	479-575-5346
*Admissions					
California Lutheran University Pearson Library					
60 W Olsen Rd	Thousand Oaks	CA	91360	**877-258-3678**	805-493-3250
Stanford University Green Library					
557 Escondido Mall	Stanford	CA	94305	**800-521-0600**	650-723-1493
University of California Irvine					
Library PO Box 19557	Irvine	CA	92623	**800-843-2763**	949-824-6836
University of Southern California					
Doheny Memorial Library					
3550 Trousdale Pkwy					
University Pk Campus	Los Angeles	CA	90089	**800-775-7330**	213-740-4039
Colorado State University					
200 West Lake St	Fort Collins	CO	80523	**800-491-4366**	970-491-1101
University of Colorado at Colorado Springs					
Kraemer Family Library					
1420 Austin Bluffs Pkwy					
PO Box 7150	Colorado Springs	CO	80918	**800-990-8227**	719-255-3295
Eastern Connecticut State University Smith Library					
83 Windham St	Willimantic	CT	06226	**800-578-1449**	860-465-4506
University of Connecticut					
Babbidge Library					
369 Fairfield Rd	Storrs	CT	06269	**888-603-9635**	860-486-2219
Wesleyan University Olin Library					
252 Church St	Middletown	CT	06459	**800-421-1561**	860-685-2660
Gallaudet University Library					
800 Florida Ave NE	Washington	DC	20002	**800-995-0550**	202-651-5217
George Washington University					
2121 'I' St NW	Washington	DC	20052	**866-498-3382**	202-994-1000
Barry University					
11300 NE Second Ave	Miami Shores	FL	33161	**800-756-6000**	305-899-3000
Florida A & M University					
1700 Lee Hall Dr	Tallahassee	FL	32307	**866-642-1198**	850-599-3000
Florida Atlantic University (FAU)					
777 Glades Rd	Boca Raton	FL	33431	**800-299-4328***	561-297-3000
*Admissions					
SH. Coleman Library					
FAMU Libraries					
1500 S Martin Luther King Blvd	Tallahassee	FL	32307	**800-540-6754**	850-599-3370
Stetson University DuPont-Ball Library					
421 N Woodland Blvd	DeLand	FL	32723	**800-688-0101**	386-822-7183
University of Florida Libraries					
PO Box 117001	Gainesville	FL	32611	**877-351-2377**	352-392-0342
Georgia Institute of Technology Library					
266 Fourth St NW	Atlanta	GA	30332	**888-225-7804**	404-894-4500
Mercer University					
1400 Coleman Ave	Macon	GA	31207	**800-637-2378**	478-301-2650
University of Georgia Library					
320 S Jackson St	Athens	GA	30602	**877-314-5560**	706-542-0621
Hawaii Pacific University					
1164 Bishop St Ste 200	Honolulu	HI	96813	**866-225-5478**	808-544-0200
University of Idaho					
875 Perimeter Dr	Moscow	ID	83844	**888-884-3246**	208-885-6111
Illinois Institute of Technology					
10 W 33rd St	Chicago	IL	60616	**800-448-2329**	312-567-3025
Illinois State University Milner Library					
201 N School St	Normal	IL	61790	**800-366-2478**	309-438-3451
Northern Illinois University University Libraries					
1425 W Lincoln Hwy	DeKalb	IL	60115	**800-892-3050**	815-753-1000
Southern Illinois University Edwardsville					
Lovejoy Library					
30 Hairpin Dr Campus Box 1063	Edwardsville	IL	62026	**888-328-5168**	618-650-4636
Western Illinois University					
1 University Cir	Macomb	IL	61455	**877-742-5948***	309-298-1414
*Admissions					
Malpass Library					
1 University Cir	Macomb	IL	61455	**800-413-6544**	309-298-2762
Cunningham Memorial Library					
510 N 6 1/2 St	Terre Haute	IN	47809	**800-851-4279**	812-237-2580
DePauw University West Library					
11 E Larabee St	Greencastle	IN	46135	**800-447-2495**	765-658-4420
Indiana University-Purdue University Indianapolis					
Library					
755 W Michigan St	Indianapolis	IN	46202	**888-422-0499**	317-274-0462
Purdue University					
Schleman Hall					
475 Stadium Mall Dr.	West Lafayette	IN	47907	**800-743-3333**	765-494-1776
Grinnell College Burling Library					
6th Ave High St	Grinnell	IA	50112	**800-247-0113**	641-269-3371
Northwestern State University Watson Memorial Library					
913 University Pkwy	Natchitoches	LA	71497	**888-540-9657**	318-357-4477
University of Maine					
5713 Chadbourne Hall	Orono	ME	04469	**877-486-2364***	207-581-1110
*Admissions					
Salisbury University Blackwell Library					
1101 Camden Ave	Salisbury	MD	21801	**888-543-0148**	410-543-6130
University of Maryland					
7569 Baltimore Ave	College Park	MD	20742	**800-422-5867***	301-405-1000
*Admissions					
College of the Holy Cross Dinand Library					
1 College St	Worcester	MA	01610	**877-433-1843**	508-793-2642
Simmons College Beatley Library					
300 The Fenway	Boston	MA	02115	**800-831-4284**	617-521-2780
Andrews University James White Library					
4190 Admin Dr	Berrien Springs	MI	49104	**800-253-2874**	269-471-3264
Eastern Michigan University Halle Library					
955 W Cir Dr	Ypsilanti	MI	48197	**888-888-3465**	734-487-0020
Ferris State University					
1201 S State St	Big Rapids	MI	49307	**800-433-7747**	231-591-2000
FLITE Library					
1010 Campus Dr	Big Rapids	MI	49307	**800-433-7747**	231-591-3602
Grand Valley State University Zumberge Library					
1 Campus Dr	Allendale	MI	49401	**800-879-0581**	616-331-3252
Hope College Van Wylen Library					
53 Graves Pl	Holland	MI	49423	**800-968-7850**	616-395-7790
Michigan State University Library					
366 W Circle Dr	East Lansing	MI	48824	**800-500-1554**	517-353-8700
Saginaw Valley State University Zahnow Library					
7400 Bay Rd	University Center	MI	48710	**800-968-9500**	989-964-4240
University of Michigan Dearborn					
Mardigian Library					
4901 Evergreen Rd	Dearborn	MI	48128	**877-619-6650**	313-593-5000
Minnesota State University Mankato					
Memorial Library					
601 Maywood Ave PO Box 8419	Mankato	MN	56002	**800-722-0544**	507-389-5952
Saint John's University Alcuin Library					
2835 Abbey Plz	Collegeville	MN	56321	**800-544-1489**	320-363-2122
University of Minnesota Crookston					
UMC Library					
2900 University Ave	Crookston	MN	56716	**800-862-6466**	218-281-8399
University of Minnesota Duluth					
Kathryn A. Martin Library					
416 Library Dr	Duluth	MN	55812	**866-999-6995**	218-726-8102
University of Saint Thomas O'Shaughnessy-Frey Library					
2115 Summit Ave	Saint Paul	MN	55105	**800-328-6819**	651-962-5494
University of Mississippi					
PO Box 1848	University	MS	38677	**800-891-4596**	662-915-7211
Williams Library					
1 Library Loop	University	MS	38677	**800-891-4596**	662-915-7091
University of Missouri Kansas City					
Nichols Library					
800 E 51st St	Kansas City	MO	64110	**800-775-8652**	816-235-1000
Montana State University					
Billings					
1500 University Dr	Billings	MT	59101	**800-565-6782**	406-657-2011
University of Montana Missoula					
Mansfield Library					
32 Campus Dr	Missoula	MT	59812	**800-240-4939**	406-243-2053
Peru State College Library					
600 Hoyt St PO Box 10	Peru	NE	68421	**800-742-4412**	402-872-3815
University of New Hampshire					
3 Garrison Ave	Durham	NH	03824	**800-313-5327**	603-862-1234
New Mexico State University (NMSU)					
MSC-3A PO Box 30001	Las Cruces	NM	88003	**800-662-6678***	575-646-3121
*Admissions					
Fordham University					
441 E Fordham Rd	Bronx	NY	10458	**800-367-3426**	718-817-3240
Pace University 1 Pace Plz	New York	NY	10038	**866-722-3338**	212-346-1200
Birnbaum Library					
1 Pace Plz	New York	NY	10038	**800-498-2071**	212-346-1332
Appalachian State University					
Belk Library					
218 College St PO Box 32026	Boone	NC	28608	**877-423-0086**	828-262-2300
North Carolina State University Libraries					
CB 7111	Raleigh	NC	27695	**877-601-0590**	919-515-2843
Ashland University Library					
401 College Ave	Ashland	OH	44805	**866-434-5222**	419-289-5400
Kent State University					
800 E Summit St PO Box 5190	Kent	OH	44242	**800-988-5368**	330-672-3000
Ohio Northern University Heterick Memorial Library					
525 S Main St	Ada	OH	45810	**866-943-5787**	419-772-2181
Ohio State University					
154 W 12th Ave	Columbus	OH	43210	**800-426-5046**	614-292-3980
Ohio State University, The					
University Libraries					
1858 Neil Ave Mall	Columbus	OH	43210	**800-555-1212**	614-292-6785
Ohio University					
120 Chubb Hall	Athens	OH	45710	**800-858-6843**	740-593-1000
University of Cincinnati Langsam Library					
PO Box 210033	Cincinnati	OH	45221	**866-397-3382**	513-556-1515
University of Library					
302 Buchtel Common	Akron	OH	44325	**800-425-7668**	330-972-5355
University of Toledo Carlson Library					
2801 W Bancroft MS 507	Toledo	OH	43606	**800-586-5336**	419-530-2324
Xavier University Library					
3800 Victory Pkwy	Cincinnati	OH	45207	**888-468-4509**	513-745-3881
Oklahoma State University					
219 Student Union Bldg	Stillwater	OK	74078	**800-852-1255**	405-744-5000
Oral Roberts University Library					
7777 S Lewis Ave	Tulsa	OK	74171	**800-678-8876**	918-495-6723
Pacific University Library					
2043 College Way	Forest Grove	OR	97116	**800-677-6712**	503-352-1400
Western Oregon University Hamersly Library					
345 N Monmouth Ave	Monmouth	OR	97361	**877-877-1593**	503-838-8418
Dickinson College Waidner-Spahr Library					
PO Box 1773	Carlisle	PA	17013	**800-543-3809**	717-245-1397
Drexel University Hagerty Library					
3300 Market St	Philadelphia	PA	19104	**888-278-8825**	215-895-2767

				Toll-Free	Phone

East Stroudsburg University Kemp Library
200 Prospect St .... East Stroudsburg PA 18301 **877-422-1378** 570-422-3465
Edinboro University of Pennsylvania Baron-Forness Library (EUB)
200 Tartan Rd .... Edinboro PA 16444 **888-845-2890** 814-732-2273
Franklin & Marshall College Shadek-Fackenthal Library
450 College Ave .... Lancaster PA 17604 **866-366-7655** 717-358-4216
Indiana University of Pennsylvania Stapleton Library
1011 S Dr .... Indiana PA 15705 **888-342-2383** 724-357-2340
Pennsylvania State University
201 Shields Bldg .... University Park PA 16802 **800-279-8495** 814-865-4700
University of Pittsburgh
4227 Fifth Ave .... Pittsburgh PA 15260 **877-999-3223** 412-624-4141
Salve Regina University McKillop Library
100 Ochre Pt Ave .... Newport RI 02840 **800-388-6139** 401-341-2291
Francis Marion University Rogers Library
PO Box 100547 .... Florence SC 29502 **800-368-7551**
University of South Carolina
1601 Greene St .... Columbia SC 29208 **800-868-5872** 803-777-7000
South Dakota State University Briggs Library
1300 N Campus Dr .... Brookings SD 57007 **800-786-2038** 605-688-5106
Rhodes College Barret Library
2000 N Pkwy .... Memphis TN 38112 **800-844-5969** 901-843-3000
University of Memphis McWherter Library
126 Ned R McWherter Library ...... Memphis TN 38152 **866-670-6147** 901-678-2201
University of Tennessee Knoxville
Hodges Library
1015 Volunteer Blvd .... Knoxville TN 37996 **800-426-9119** 865-974-4351
Abilene Christian University Brown Library (ACU)
221 Brown Library .... Abilene TX 79699 **800-460-6228** 325-674-2316
Angelo State University Henderson Library
2025 S Johnson St .... San Angelo TX 76909 **800-946-8627** 325-942-2051
Sixth Floor Museum
411 Elm St .... Dallas TX 75202 **888-485-4854** 214-747-6660
Stephen F Austin State University Steen Library (SFASU)
1936 N St .... Nacogdoches TX 75962 **800-765-1534** 936-468-3401
Texas A & M University
Rudder Tower Ste 205. ...... College Station TX 77843 **888-890-5667** 979-845-8901
Texas Christian University Mary Couts Burnett Library
2800 S University Dr .... Fort Worth TX 76129 **866-321-7428** 817-257-7000
University Libraries
1155 Union Cir Ste 305190 .... Denton TX 76203 **877-872-0264** 940-565-2411
Weber State University
3848 Harrison Blvd .... Ogden UT 84408 **800-848-7770** 801-626-6000
Stewart Library
3921 Central Campus Dr Dept 2901. ..... Ogden UT 84408 **877-306-3140** 801-626-6403
George Mason University
4400 University Dr .... Fairfax VA 22030 **888-627-6612** 703-993-1000
Regent University
Library
1000 Regent University Dr ..... Virginia Beach VA 23464 **888-249-1822** 757-352-4916
University of Richmond
28 Westhampton Way .... Richmond VA 23173 **800-700-1662** 804-289-8000
Virginia Commonwealth University Cabell Library
901 Park Ave PO Box 842033. ...... Richmond VA 23284 **844-352-7399** 804-828-1111
William & Mary
400 Landrum Dr .... Williamsburg VA 23187 **800-462-3683** 757-221-3072
Central Washington University Brooks Library
400 E University Way .... Ellensburg WA 98926 **800-290-3327** 509-963-3682
Gonzaga University Foley Library
502 E Boone Ave .... Spokane WA 99258 **800-498-5941** 509-323-5931
Seattle University Lemieux Library
901 12th Ave .... Seattle WA 98122 **800-426-7123** 206-296-6210
Washington State University
PO Box 641040 .... Pullman WA 99164 **888-468-6978** 509-335-3564
West Virginia University
PO Box 6009 .... Morgantown WV 26506 **800-344-9881** 304-293-2121
Lawrence University Mudd Library
711 E Boldt Way .... Appleton WI 54911 **800-432-5427** 920-832-6750
Marquette University Raynor Memorial Library
1355 W Wisconsin Ave .... Milwaukee WI 53233 **800-876-1715** 414-288-7556
University of Wisconsin Eau Claire
McIntyre Library
105 Garfield Ave .... Eau Claire WI 54702 **877-267-1384** 715-836-3715
University of Wisconsin Oshkosh
Polk Library
801 Elmwood Ave .... Oshkosh WI 54901 **800-574-5041** 920-424-4333
University of Wyoming Libraries
1000 E University Ave Dept 3334 .... Laramie WY 82071 **800-442-6757** 307-766-3190

---

434 — LIBRARY ASSOCIATIONS - STATE & PROVINCE

				Toll-Free	Phone

Adriance Memorial Library
93 Market St .... Poughkeepsie NY 12601 **800-804-0092** 845-485-3445
Barrie Public Library
60 Worsley St .... Barrie ON L4M1L6 **800-222-8477** 705-728-1010
Castle Branch Inc
1844 Sir Tyler Dr .... Wilmington NC 28405 **888-723-4263**
Deerfield Public Library Inc
920 Waukegan Rd .... Deerfield IL 60015 **800-829-4059** 847-945-3311
Illinois Library Assn (ILA)
33 W Grand Ave Ste 401. .... Chicago IL 60654 **877-565-1896** 312-644-1896
Indiana Library Federation (ILF)
941 E 86th St Ste 260. .... Indianapolis IN 46240 **800-326-0013** 317-257-2040
Mishawaka-Penn-Harris Public Library Indiana
209 Lincoln Way E .... Mishawaka IN 46544 **800-622-4970** 574-259-5277
New York Library Assn (NYLA)
6021 State Farm Rd .... Guilderland NY 12084 **800-252-6952*** 518-432-6952
*General
North Carolina Library Assn (NCLA)
1811 Capital Blvd .... Raleigh NC 27604 **888-977-3143** 919-839-6252
Pennsylvania Library Assn (PaLA)
220 Cumberland Pkwy Ste 10. ...... Mechanicsburg PA 17055 **800-622-3308** 717-766-7663
Rolling Meadows Library
3110 Martin Ln .... Rolling Meadows IL 60008 **800-232-3798** 847-259-6050
Solano County Library
1150 Kentucky St .... Fairfield CA 94533 **866-572-7587**

				Toll-Free	Phone

State Education Resource Ctr
25 Industrial Park Rd .... Middletown CT 06457 **800-842-8678** 860-632-1485

435 — LIBRARY SYSTEMS - REGIONAL - CANADIAN

				Toll-Free	Phone

North Ontario Library Service
334 Regent St .... Sudbury ON P3C4E2 **800-461-6348** 705-675-6467

436 — LIGHT BULBS & TUBES

				Toll-Free	Phone

AETEK UV Systems
1229 Lakeview Ct .... Romeoville IL 60446 **800-333-2304** 630-226-4200
Bayco Products Inc
640 Sanden Blvd .... Wylie TX 75098 **800-233-2155** 469-326-9400
Eye Lighting International NA
9150 Hendricks Rd .... Mentor OH 44060 **888-665-2677*** 440-354-2938
*Cust Svc
Interlectric Corp
1401 Lexington Ave .... Warren PA 16365 **800-722-2184** 814-723-6061
LCD Lighting Inc
37 Robinson Blvd .... Orange CT 06477 **800-826-9465** 203-795-1520
Ledtronics Inc
23105 Kashiwa Ct .... Torrance CA 90505 **800-579-4875** 310-534-1505
Light Sources Inc
37 Robinson Rd .... Orange CT 06477 **800-826-9465** 203-799-7877
Litetronics International Inc
4101 W 123rd St .... Alsip IL 60803 **800-860-3392** 708-389-8000
PerkinElmer Inc
940 Winter St .... Waltham MA 02451 **800-762-4000** 781-663-6050
NYSE: PKI
Philips Lighting Co
200 Franklin Sq Dr .... Somerset NJ 08873 **800-555-0050**
Sun Ergoline Inc
1 Walter Kratz Dr .... Jonesboro AR 72401 **888-771-0996**
Technical Consumer Products Inc
325 Campus Dr .... Aurora OH 44202 **800-324-1496** 330-995-6111
Trojan Inc
198 Trojan St .... Mount Sterling KY 40353 **800-264-0526**
Ushio America Inc
5440 Cerritos Ave .... Cypress CA 90630 **800-326-1960** 714-236-8600
UVP Inc 2066 W 11th St .... Upland CA 91786 **800-452-6788*** 909-946-3197
*Cust Svc
Venture Lighting International Inc
32000 Aurora Rd .... Solon OH 44139 **800-451-2606** 440-248-3510

437 — LIGHTING EQUIPMENT - VEHICULAR

				Toll-Free	Phone

Able 2 Products Company Inc
PO Box 543 .... Cassville MO 65625 **800-641-4098** 417-847-4791
Avtec Inc 6 Industrial Pk .... Cahokia IL 62206 **800-552-8832** 618-337-7800
Federal Signal Corp Emergency Products Div
2645 Federal Signal Dr .... University Park IL 60466 **800-264-3578** 708-534-3400
JW Speaker Corp
N 120 W 19434 Freistadt Rd
PO Box 1011. .... Germantown WI 53022 **800-558-7288** 262-251-6660
Luminator 900 Klein Rd .... Plano TX 75074 **800-388-8205** 972-424-6511
Peterson Manufacturing Co
4200 E 135th St .... Grandview MO 64030 **800-821-3490** 816-765-2000
Teledyne Lighting & Display Products
5005 McConnell Ave .... Los Angeles CA 90066 **800-563-4020** 805-373-4545
Truck-Lite Company Inc
310 E Elmwood Ave .... Falconer NY 14733 **800-562-5012***
*Cust Svc
Vehicle Safety Mfg LLC
408 Central Ave .... Newark NJ 07107 **800-832-7233*** 973-643-3000
*General

438 — LIGHTING FIXTURES & EQUIPMENT

				Toll-Free	Phone

AFX Inc
2345 Ernie Krueger Cir .... Waukegan IL 60087 **800-873-2326** 847-249-5970
American Louver Co
7700 N Austin Ave .... Skokie IL 60077 **800-772-0355**
AmerillumBrands
3728 Maritime Way .... Oceanside CA 92056 **800-439-0549** 760-727-7675
Boyd Lighting Co
944 Folsom St .... San Francisco CA 94107 **800-224-2693*** 415-778-4300
*Cust Svc
Brinkmann Corp
4215 McEwen Rd .... Dallas TX 75244 **800-527-0717** 972-387-4939
Carlisle & Finch Co, The
4562 W Mitchell Ave .... Cincinnati OH 45232 **800-828-3186** 513-681-6080
Commercial Lighting Industries
81161 Indio Blvd .... Indio CA 92201 **800-755-0155**
Con-Tech Lighting
2783 Shermer Rd .... Northbrook IL 60062 **800-728-0312** 847-559-5500
Cooper Industries
600 Travis St Ste 5400 .... Houston TX 77002 **866-853-4293** 713-209-8400
NYSE: ETN
Corbett Lighting Inc
14508 Nelson Ave .... City of Industry CA 91744 **800-533-8769** 626-336-4511
Dazor Lighting Solutions
430 Industrial Dr .... Maryland Heights MO 63043 **800-345-9103** 314-652-2400
Dual-Lite Inc
701 Millennium Blvd .... Greenville SC 29607 **866-898-0131** 864-678-1000
Elk Lighting Inc
12 Willow Ln .... Nesquehoning PA 18240 **800-613-3261**

				Toll-Free	Phone
Energy Focus Inc					
32000 Aurora Rd	Solon	OH	44139	**800-327-7877**	440-715-1300
OTC: EFOI					
Fulton Industries Inc					
135 E Linfoot St	Wauseon	OH	43567	**800-537-5012**	419-335-3015
GE Lighting Systems Inc					
3010 Spartanburg Hwy	East Flat Rock	NC	28726	**888-694-3533**	828-693-2000
HE Williams Inc					
831 West Fairview Ave	Carthage	MO	64836	**866-358-4065**	417-358-4065
High End Systems Inc					
2105 Gracy Farms Ln	Austin	TX	78758	**800-890-8989**	512-836-2242
Hinkley Lighting					
12600 Berea Rd	Cleveland	OH	44111	**800-446-5539**	216-671-3300
Holophane					
3825 Columbus Rd					
Granville Business Park Bldg A	Granville	OH	43023	**866-759-1577**	
Hubbell Lighting Inc					
701 Millennium Blvd	Greenville	SC	29607	**800-345-4928**	864-678-1000
Hydrel 12881 Bradley Ave	Sylmar	CA	91342	**866-533-9901**	
Kenall Mfg 1020 Lakeside Dr	Gurnee	IL	60031	**800-453-6255**	262-891-9700
Koehler Lighting Products					
380 Stewart Rd	Hanover Township	PA	18706	**800-788-1696***	570-825-1900
*Cust Svc					
Kurtzon Lighting Inc					
1420 S Talman Ave	Chicago	IL	60608	**800-837-8937**	773-277-2121
Ledalite Architectural Products					
19750-92A Ave	Langley	BC	V1M3B2	**800-665-5332**	604-888-6811
Legion Lighting Company Inc					
221 Glenmore Ave	Brooklyn	NY	11207	**800-453-4466**	718-498-1770
Lithonia Lighting					
1 Lithonia Way	Conyers	GA	30012	**800-858-7763**	770-922-9000
LSI Industries Inc					
10000 Alliance Rd	Cincinnati	OH	45242	**800-436-7800**	513-793-3200
NASDAQ: LYTS					
Luxo Corp					
5 Westchester Plz	Elmsford	NY	10523	**800-222-5896**	914-345-0067
Mag Instrument Inc					
2001 S Hillman Ave	Ontario	CA	91761	**800-289-6241**	909-947-1006
Mercury Lighting Products Company Inc					
20 Audrey Pl	Fairfield	NJ	07004	**800-637-2584**	973-244-9444
Minka Group					
1151 W Bradford Ct	Corona	CA	92882	**800-221-7977**	951-735-9220
Mule Lighting Inc					
46 Baker St	Providence	RI	02905	**800-556-7690**	401-941-4446
Musco Sports Lighting LLC					
100 First Ave W PO Box 808	Oskaloosa	IA	52577	**800-825-6020**	641-673-0411
North Star Lighting Inc					
2150 Parkes Dr	Broadview	IL	60155	**800-229-4330**	708-681-4330
Norwell Manufacturing Inc					
82 Stevens St	East Taunton	MA	02718	**800-822-2831**	508-823-1751
Pacific Coast Lighting					
20238 Plummer St	Chatsworth	CA	91311	**800-709-9004**	818-886-9751
Paramount Industries Inc					
304 N Howard St	Croswell	MI	48422	**800-521-5405**	810-679-2551
Paul C Buff Inc					
2725 Bransford Ave	Nashville	TN	37204	**800-443-5542**	615-383-3982
Philips Luminaire					
776 S Green St	Tupelo	MS	38804	**800-234-1890**	
Prescolite Inc					
701 Millennium Blvd	Greenville	SC	29607	**888-777-4832**	864-678-1000
RAB Lighting					
170 Ludlow Ave	Northvale	NJ	07647	**888-722-1000**	201-784-8600
Rejuvenation Inc					
2550 NW Nicolai St	Portland	OR	97210	**888-401-1900**	503-238-1900
Renova Lighting Systems Inc					
36 Bellair Ave	Warwick	RI	02886	**800-635-6682**	401-737-6700
Sea Gull Lighting Products LLC A Generations Brands Co					
301 W Washington St	Riverside	NJ	08075	**800-347-5483**	800-519-4092
SIMKAR Corp					
700 Ramona Ave	Philadelphia	PA	19120	**800-523-3602**	215-831-7700
Spectrolab Inc					
12500 Gladstone Ave	Sylmar	CA	91342	**800-936-4888**	818-365-4611
Strand Lighting					
10911 Petal St	Dallas	TX	75238	**800-733-0564**	214-647-7880
Streamlight Inc					
30 Eagleville Rd	Eagleville	PA	19403	**800-523-7488**	610-631-0600
Super Sky Products Inc					
10301 N Enterprise Dr	Mequon	WI	53092	**800-558-0467**	262-242-2000
Tech Lighting LLC					
7400 Linda Ave	Skokie	IL	60077	**800-522-5315**	847-410-4400
Topaz Lighting Corp					
925 Waverly Ave	Holtsville	NY	11742	**800-666-2852**	
Tri-Lite Inc					
1642 N Besly Ct	Chicago	IL	60642	**800-322-5250**	773-384-7765
Troy-CSL Lighting Inc					
14508 Nelson Ave	City of Industry	CA	91744	**800-533-8769**	626-336-4511
Western Reflections					
261 Commerce Way	Gallatin	TN	37066	**800-507-8302***	615-451-9700
*Cust Svc					

439 LIME

				Toll-Free	Phone
Carmeuse North America					
11 Stanwix St 11th Fl	Pittsburgh	PA	15222	**866-243-0965**	412-995-5500
Graymont Ltd					
10991 Shellbridge Way Ste 200	Richmond	BC	V6X3C6	**866-207-4292**	604-276-9331
Texas Lime Co					
15865 Farm Rd 1434 PO Box 851	Cleburne	TX	76033	**800-772-8000**	817-641-4433

440 LIMOUSINE SERVICES

				Toll-Free	Phone
Alliance Limousine					
14553 Delano St Ste 210	Van Nuys	CA	91411	**800-954-5466**	

				Toll-Free	Phone
American Coach Limousine					
1100 Jorie Blvd Ste 314	Oak Brook	IL	60523	**888-709-5466**	630-629-0001
American Limousines Inc					
4401 E Fairmount Ave	Baltimore	MD	21224	**800-787-1690**	410-522-0400
Arizona Limousines Inc					
8900 N Central Ave Ste 101	Phoenix	AZ	85020	**800-678-0033**	602-267-7097
Bayview Limousine Service					
15701 Nelson Pl S	Seattle	WA	98188	**800-606-7880**	206-824-6200
Carey Executive Limousine					
245 University Ave	Atlanta	GA	30315	**800-241-3943**	404-223-2000
Carey International Inc					
4530 Wisconsin Ave NW	Washington	DC	20016	**800-336-4646**	301-698-3900
Classic Touch Limousine Inc					
908 N Walnut St	Bloomington	IN	47404	**800-319-0082**	812-339-7269
Company Car Chauffeured Transportation					
7138 Envoy Ct	Dallas	TX	75247	**888-559-0708**	214-824-0011
Elite Limousine Service Inc					
1059 12th Ave Ste E	Honolulu	HI	96816	**800-776-2098**	808-735-2431
Gateway Limousines					
1550 Gilbreth Rd	Burlingame	CA	94010	**800-486-7077**	650-697-5548
Grand Avenue Worldwide					
186 N First St	Nashville	TN	37213	**866-455-2823**	615-714-5466
International Chauffeured Service Worldwide					
53 E 34th St	New York	NY	10016	**800-266-5254**	212-213-0302
Mears Transportation Group					
324 W Gore St	Orlando	FL	32806	**800-759-5219**	407-422-4561
Pontarelli Limousine Service					
5584 N Northwest Hwy	Chicago	IL	60630	**800-322-5466**	312-494-6700
R & R Limousine					
4403 Kiln Ct	Louisville	KY	40218	**800-582-5576**	502-458-1862
Regency Limousine Inc					
331 Danbury Rd	Wilton	CT	06897	**800-243-5606**	203-762-7780
Royal Coachman Worldwide					
88 Ford Rd Ste 26	Denville	NJ	07834	**800-472-7433**	973-400-3200
Starlite Limousines LLC					
PO Box 13542	Scottsdale	AZ	85267	**877-474-4847**	480-422-3619
SuperShuttle International Inc					
14500 N Northsight Blvd Ste 329	Scottsdale	AZ	85260	**800-258-3826**	480-609-3000
US Coachways Inc					
100 St Mary's Ave Ste 2B	Staten Island	NY	10305	**800-359-5991**	718-477-4242
XYZ Two Way Radio Inc					
275 20th St	Brooklyn	NY	11215	**800-535-3377**	718-499-2007

441 LINEN & UNIFORM SUPPLY

				Toll-Free	Phone
Ace ImageWear					
4120 Truman Rd	Kansas City	MO	64127	**800-366-0564**	816-231-5737
Ace-Tex Enterprises					
7601 Central St	Detroit	MI	48210	**800-444-3800**	313-834-4000
Admiral Linen Service Inc					
2030 Kipling St	Houston	TX	77098	**800-321-1948**	713-529-2608
AmeriPride Services Inc					
10801 Wayzata Blvd	Minnetonka	MN	55305	**800-750-4628***	952-738-4200
*Cust Svc					
Apparelmaster					
123 Harrison Ave	Harrison	OH	45030	**877-543-1678**	513-202-1600
Arrow Uniform Rental Inc					
6400 Monroe Blvd	Taylor	MI	48180	**888-332-7769**	313-299-5000
Capitol Uniform & Linen Service					
195 Commerce Way	Dover	DE	19904	**800-822-7352**	302-674-1511
Cintas Corp					
PO Box 625737	Cincinnati	OH	45262	**800-786-4367**	513-573-4155
NASDAQ: CTAS					
Continental Linen Services					
4200 Manchester Rd	Kalamazoo	MI	49001	**800-878-4357**	
Iron City Workplace Services					
6640 Frankstown Ave	Pittsburgh	PA	15206	**800-532-2010**	412-661-2001
ITU AbsorbTech Inc					
2700 S 160th St	New Berlin	WI	53151	**888-729-4884**	
Mickey's Linen					
4601 W Addison St	Chicago	IL	60641	**800-545-7511**	
Model Coverall Service Inc					
100 28th St SE	Grand Rapids	MI	49548	**800-968-6491**	616-241-6491
Morgan Services Inc					
323 N Michigan Ave	Chicago	IL	60601	**888-966-7426**	312-346-3181
Prudential Overall Supply					
PO Box 11210	Santa Ana	CA	92711	**800-767-5536**	949-250-4855
Roscoe Co					
3535 W Harrison St	Chicago	IL	60624	**888-476-7263***	773-722-5000
*Cust Svc					
Sitex Corp					
1300 Commonwealth Dr	Henderson	KY	42420	**800-278-3537**	270-827-3537
Summit Golf Brands Inc					
8 W 40th St 2nd Fl	New York	NY	10018	**800-926-8010**	
Textile Care Services Inc					
225 Wood Lake Dr SE	Rochester	MN	55904	**800-422-0945**	
Unitech Services Group					
295 Parker St	Springfield	MA	01151	**800-344-3824**	413-543-6911
Valiant Products Corp					
2727 Fifth Ave W	Denver	CO	80204	**800-347-2727***	303-892-1234
*Cust Svc					

442 LIQUOR STORES

				Toll-Free	Phone
Flanigan's					
5059 NE 18th Ave	Fort Lauderdale	FL	33334	**800-833-5239**	954-377-1961
NYSE: BDL					
Fox Run Vineyards					
670 State Rt 14	Penn Yan	NY	14527	**800-636-9786**	315-536-4616
Gold Standard Enterprises Inc					
5100 W Dempster St	Skokie	IL	60077	**888-942-9463**	847-674-4200
Liquor Mart Inc					
1750 15th St	Boulder	CO	80302	**800-597-4440**	303-449-3374

					Toll-Free	Phone

Patz & Hall Wine Co
851 Napa Vly Corporate Way Ste A . . . . Napa CA 94558   877-265-6700   707-931-2440
Saratoga Liquor Company Inc
3215 James Day Ave . . . . Superior WI 54880   800-472-6923   715-394-4487
Spec's Wines Spirits & Finer Foods
2410 Smith St . . . . Houston TX 77006   888-526-8787   713-526-8787
Touring & Tasting
125 S Quarantina St . . . . Santa Barbara CA 93103   800-850-4370   805-965-2813
Wiederkehr Wine Cellars Inc
3324 Swiss Family Dr . . . . Wiederkehr Village AR 72821   800-622-9463   479-468-9463
Wine Club, The
1431 S Village Way . . . . Santa Ana CA 92705   800-966-5432   714-835-6485
Winecom Inc
222 Sutter St Ste 450 . . . . San Francisco CA 94108   800-592-5870
WineShop At Home
525 Airpark Rd . . . . Napa CA 94558   800-946-3746   707-253-0200
Zachys Wine & Liquor Inc
16 E Pkwy . . . . Scarsdale NY 10583   800-723-0241   914-874-8000

443   LITIGATION SUPPORT SERVICES

					Toll-Free	Phone

Al Betz & Associates Inc
PO Box 665 Ste 30 . . . . Westminster MD 21158   877-402-3376
Atkinson-Baker Inc (ABI)
500 N Brand Blvd 3rd Fl . . . . Glendale CA 91203   800-288-3376   818-551-7300
Axley 2 E Mifflin St Ste 200 . . . . Madison WI 53703   800-368-5661   608-257-5661
Benefit Recovery Group
6745 Lenox Center Ct Ste 100 . . . . Memphis TN 38115   866-384-4051
Boccardo Law Firm Inc, The
111 W Saint John St Ste 400 . . . . San Jose CA 95113   800-662-9807
Brown Hay & Stephens LLP
205 S fifth St Ste 700 . . . . Springfield IL 62701   888-666-8491
Burton Neil & Assoc
1060 Andrew Dr Ste 160 . . . . West Chester PA 19380   866-696-2120   610-696-2120
Carson Boxberger LLP
301 W Jefferson Blvd Ste 200 . . . . Fort Wayne IN 46802   800-900-4250   260-423-9411
Cochran, Kroll & Associates PC
15510 Farmington Rd . . . . Livonia MI 48154   800-322-5543
Collins Law Firm PC, The
1770 Park St Ste 200 . . . . Naperville IL 60563   866-480-8223   630-687-9838
Columbia Legal Services
600 Larson Bldg 6 S Second St . . . . Seattle WA 98901   800-631-1323   509-575-5593
Compex Legal Services Inc
325 S Maple Ave . . . . Torrance CA 90503   800-426-6739*
*Cust Svc
CourtCall
6383 Arizona Cir . . . . Los Angeles CA 90045   888-882-6878   310-342-0888
Courtroom Sciences Inc
4950 N O'Connor Rd . . . . Irving TX 75062   800-514-5879   972-717-1773
DecisionQuest
21535 Hawthorne Blvd Ste 310 . . . . Torrance CA 90503   800-887-5696   310-618-9600
Depobook Reporting Services
1600 G St Ste 101 . . . . Modesto CA 95354   800-830-8885   209-544-6466
DOAR Inc
1370 Broadway 15th Fl . . . . New York NY 10018   800-875-8705   212-235-2700
Eric Buchanan & Associates Pllc
414 Mccallie Ave . . . . Chattanooga TN 37402   877-634-2506
FTI Consulting
909 Commerce Rd . . . . Annapolis MD 21401   800-334-5701
NYSE: FCN
Goldberg & Osborne
4423 E Thomas Rd Ste 3 . . . . Phoenix AZ 85018   800-843-3245   602-808-6200
Hahn & Bowersock Corp
151 Kalmus Dr Ste L1 . . . . Costa Mesa CA 92626   800-660-3187
Hart King
4 Hutton Centre Dr Ste 900 . . . . Santa Ana CA 92707   866-718-7148   714-432-8700
Jane Rose Reporting
80 Fifth Ave . . . . New York NY 10011   800-825-3341   212-727-7773
Johnstone Adams Bailey Gordon & Harris L L C
1 St Louis St Ste 4000 . . . . Mobile AL 36602   844-682-7682   251-432-7682
Jury Research Institute
2617 Danville Blvd PO Box 100 . . . . Alamo CA 94507   800-233-5879   925-932-5663
Lawyers Group Advertising Inc
28 Thorndal Cir . . . . Darien CT 06820   800-948-1080
Legal Aid of West Virginia Inc
922 Quarrier St 4th Fl . . . . Charleston WV 25301   866-255-4370   304-343-4481
Legal Cost Control Inc (LCC)
8 Kings Hwy W Ste C . . . . Haddonfield NJ 08033   800-493-7345   856-216-0800
Martin Law Firm
2059 N Green Acres Rd . . . . Fayetteville AR 72702   800-633-2160   479-442-2244
Michael J O'Connor & Associates LLC
608 W Oak St . . . . Frackville PA 17931   800-518-4529   570-874-3300
New Mexico Legal Aid Inc
301 Gold Ave SW . . . . Albuquerque NM 87102   866-416-1922   505-243-7871
Newby Pridgen Sartip & Masel Llc
4593 Oleander Dr . . . . Myrtle Beach SC 29577   800-858-5592   843-449-9417
Norris Injury Lawyers
10 Old Montgomery Hwy . . . . Birmingham AL 35209   800-477-7510
Professional Shorthand Reporters Inc (PSR)
601 Poydras St Ste 1615 . . . . New Orleans LA 70130   800-536-5255   504-529-5255
R C Mc Lean & Assoc Inc
210 N Tustin Ave . . . . Santa Ana CA 92705   800-883-7243   714-347-1000
Ralph Rosenberg Court Reporters Inc
1001 Bishop St Ste 2460 . . . . Honolulu HI 96813   888-524-5888
Salon Marrow Dyckman Newman & Broudy LLP
292 Madison Ave . . . . New York NY 10017   888-317-8676
Schroeter Goldmark & Bender Ps
810 Third Ave . . . . Seattle WA 98104   800-809-2234   206-622-8000
Simmons Hanly Conroy LLC
230 W Monroe Ste 2221 . . . . Chicago IL 60606   877-438-6610
Stahancyk Kent & Hook
2400 SW Fourth Ave . . . . Portland OR 97201   877-673-7632   503-222-9115
Stubbs & Perdue PA
9208 Falls of Neuse Rd Ste 201 . . . . Raleigh NC 27615   800-348-9404
US Legal Support Inc
363 N Sam Houston Pkwy E Ste 1200 . . . . Houston TX 77060   800-567-8757   713-653-7100

					Toll-Free	Phone

Vantage Solutions Llc
1035 W Lake St Ste 205 . . . . Chicago IL 60607   877-816-4818   312-440-0602
Veritext LLC
290 W Mt Pleasant Ave Ste 3200 . . . . Livingston NJ 07039   800-567-8658
Wilkes & McHugh P A
1 N Dale Mabry Hwy Ste 800 . . . . Tampa FL 33609   800-255-5070
Wingfield J e & Associates PC
700 Fifth St NW Ste 300 . . . . Washington DC 20001   800-338-5954   202-789-8000

444   LIVESTOCK - WHOL

SEE ALSO Cattle Ranches, Farms, Feedlots (Beef Cattle) ; Hog Farms

					Toll-Free	Phone

All West Select Sires
PO Box 507 . . . . Burlington WA 98233   800-426-2697
Blue Grass Stockyard
1274 HWY 90 W PO Box 980 . . . . Albany KY 42602   800-621-3972   606-387-4681
Empire Livestock Marketing LLC
5001 Brittonfield Pkwy . . . . East Syracuse NY 13057   800-462-8802   315-433-9129
Equity Co-op Livestock Sales Assn
401 Commerce Ave . . . . Baraboo WI 53913   800-362-3989   608-356-8311
Keeneland Association Inc
4201 Versailles Rd . . . . Lexington KY 40510   800-456-3412   859-254-3412
Lewiston Sales Inc
21241 Dutchmans Crossing Rd . . . . Lewiston MN 55952   800-732-6334   507-523-2112
Lynch Livestock Co
331 Third St NW . . . . Waucoma IA 52171   800-468-3178   563-776-3311
National Commission Assn
2501 Exchange Ave Ste 102 . . . . Oklahoma City OK 73108   800-999-8998   405-232-3128
Producers Livestock Marketing Assn
4809 S 114th St . . . . Omaha NE 68137   800-257-4046   402-597-9189
Roswell Livestock Auction Sales Inc
900 N Garden PO Box 2041 . . . . Roswell NM 88202   800-748-1541   575-622-5580
Turner County Stockyard
1315 US Hwy 41 S . . . . Ashburn GA 31714   800-344-9808   229-567-3371
United Producers Inc
8351 N High St Ste 250 . . . . Columbus OH 43235   800-456-3276
Winner Livestock Auction Co
31690 Livestock Barn Rd . . . . Winner SD 57580   800-201-0451   605-842-0451

445   LIVESTOCK & POULTRY FEEDS - PREPARED

					Toll-Free	Phone

AC Nutrition 158 N Main St . . . . Winters TX 79567   800-588-3333   325-754-4546
AG Partners Inc
512 S Eigth St PO Box 467 . . . . Lake City MN 55041   800-772-2990   651-345-3328
Ag Processing Inc
12700 W Dodge Rd PO Box 2047 . . . . Omaha NE 68103   800-247-1345   402-496-7809
Agri-King Inc
18246 Waller Rd . . . . Fulton IL 61252   800-435-9560
Ahrberg Milling Co
200 S Depot PO Box 968 . . . . Cushing OK 74023   800-324-0267   918-225-0267
AL Gilbert Co
304 N Yosemite Ave . . . . Oakdale CA 95361   800-400-6377   209-847-1721
Alabama Farmers Co-op Inc
PO Box 2227 . . . . Decatur AL 35609   800-589-3206   256-353-6843
Albion Laboratories Inc
67 S Main St Ste 100 . . . . Layton UT 84041   800-453-2406   801-773-4631
Bagdad Roller Mills Inc
5740 Elmburg Rd . . . . Bagdad KY 40003   800-928-3333   502-747-8968
Belstra Milling Company Inc
424 15th St . . . . Demotte IN 46310   800-276-2789
BioZyme Inc
6010 Stockyards Expy . . . . Saint Joseph MO 64504   800-821-3070   816-238-3326
Blue Seal Feeds Inc
2905 US Hwy 61 N . . . . Muscatine IA 52761   866-647-1212*
*Cust Svc
Buckeye Nutrition
330 E Schultz Ave . . . . Dalton OH 44618   800-417-6460
D & D Commodities Ltd
PO Box 359 . . . . Stephen MN 56757   800-543-3308
Darling International Inc
251 O'Connor Ridge Blvd Ste 300 . . . . Irving TX 75038   800-800-4841   972-717-0300
NYSE: DAR
Diamond V
2525 60th Ave SW PO Box 74570 . . . . Cedar Rapids IA 52404   800-373-7234   319-366-0745
Eagle Roller Mill Co
1101 Airport Rd . . . . Shelby NC 28150   800-223-9108   704-487-5061
Effingham Equity Inc
201 W Roadway Ave . . . . Effingham IL 62401   800-223-1337   217-342-4101
First Co-op Assn (FCA)
960 Riverview Dr PO Box 60 . . . . Cherokee IA 51012   877-753-5400   712-225-5400
FL Emmert Co Inc
2007 Dunlap St . . . . Cincinnati OH 45214   800-441-3343   513-721-5808
Flint River Mills Inc
1100 Dothan Rd . . . . Bainbridge GA 39817   800-841-8502
FM Brown's Sons Inc
205 Woodrow Ave PO Box 2116 . . . . Sinking Spring PA 19608   800-334-8816
Form-A-Feed Inc (FAF)
740 Bowman St . . . . Stewart MN 55385   800-422-3649   320-562-2413
Friona Industries
500 S Taylor St Ste 601 . . . . Amarillo TX 79101   800-658-6014   806-374-1811
Furst-McNess Co
120 E Clark St . . . . Freeport IL 61032   800-435-5100   815-235-6151
Hubbard Feeds Inc
111 W Cherry St Ste 500 . . . . Mankato MN 56001   800-869-7219   507-388-9400
John A Van Den Bosch Co
4511 Holland Ave . . . . Holland MI 49424   800-968-6477
Kay Dee Feed Company Inc
1919 Grand Ave . . . . Sioux City IA 51106   800-831-4815*   712-277-2011
*Cust Svc
Kemin Industries Inc
2100 Maury St . . . . Des Moines IA 50317   800-777-8307   515-559-5100
Land O'Lakes Inc Western Feed Div
4001 Lexington Ave N . . . . Arden Hills MN 55126   800-328-9680

	City	State	ZIP	Toll-Free	Phone
Manna Pro Corp 707 Spirit 40 Pk Dr Ste 150	Chesterfield	MO	63005	**800-690-9908**	
Mark Hershey Farms Inc 479 Horseshoe Pk	Lebanon	PA	17042	**888-801-3301**	717-867-4624
Merrick's Inc 2415 Parview Rd PO Box 620307	Middleton	WI	53562	**800-637-7425**	608-831-3440
Milk Specialties Co 7500 Flying Cloud Dr Ste 500	Eden Prairie	MN	55344	**800-323-4274**	952-942-7310
Mountaire Corp PO Box 1320	Millsboro	DE	19966	**877-887-1490**	302-934-1100
Moyer & Son Inc 113 E Reliance Rd	Souderton	PA	18964	**866-669-3747**	215-799-2000
NRV Inc N8155 American St	Ixonia	WI	53036	**800-558-0002**	920-261-7000
Oberbeck Grain Co 700 Walnut St	Highland	IL	62249	**800-632-2012**	618-654-2387
Producers Co-op Assoc 300 E Buffalo St	Girard	KS	66743	**800-442-2809**	620-724-8241
Provimi North America Inc 10 Nutrition Way PO Box 69	Brookville	OH	45309	**800-257-3788**	
Quali Tech Inc 318 Lake Hazeltine Dr	Chaska	MN	55318	**800-328-5870**	952-448-5151
Ragland Mills Inc 14079 Hammer Rd	Neosho	MO	64850	**888-549-8014**	417-451-2510
Ralco Nutrition Inc 1600 Hahn Rd	Marshall	MN	56258	**800-533-5306**	
Rangen Inc 115 13th Ave S *Cust Svc	Buhl	ID	83316	**800-657-6446***	208-543-6421
Seminole Feed 335 NE Watula Ave PO Box 940	Ocala	FL	34470	**800-683-1881**	352-732-4143
Star Milling Co 24067 Water St	Perris	CA	92570	**800-733-6455**	951-657-3143
Triple Crown Nutrition Inc 315 Lake St E Ste 300	Wayzata	MN	55391	**800-451-9916**	
Trouw Nutrition 115 Executive Dr	Highland	IL	62249	**800-365-1357**	618-654-2070
United Animal Health 4310 State Rd 38 W	Sheridan	IN	46069	**800-382-9909**	317-758-4495
Valley Proteins Inc 151 Valpro Dr	Winchester	VA	22603	**800-871-3406**	540-877-2590
Vita Plus Corp 2514 Fish Hatchery Rd	Madison	WI	53713	**800-362-8334**	608-256-1988
Zeigler Bros Inc 400 GaRdner Stn Rd	Gardners	PA	17324	**800-841-8800**	717-677-6181

446 LOGGING

	City	State	ZIP	Toll-Free	Phone
Canal Wood LLC 2430 Main St	Conway	SC	29526	**866-587-1460**	843-488-9663
Cousineau Inc 3 Valley Rd PO Box 58	North Anson	ME	04958	**877-268-7463**	207-635-4445
Greif Inc 425 Winter Rd *NYSE: GEF*	Delaware	OH	43015	**877-781-9797**	
Midwest Walnut 1914 Tostevin	Council Bluffs	IA	51503	**800-592-5688**	712-325-9191
Morbark Inc 8507 S Winn Rd	Winn	MI	48896	**800-831-0042**	989-866-2381
Roseburg Forest Products Co PO Box 1088	Roseburg	OR	97470	**800-245-1115**	541-679-3311
Swanson Group Inc 2695 Glendale Valley Rd PO Box 250	Glendale	OR	97442	**800-331-0831**	541-832-1121

447 LOGISTICS SERVICES (TRANSPORTATION & WAREHOUSING)

SEE ALSO Rail Transport Services ; Trucking Companies ; Commercial Warehousing ; Marine Services ; Freight Forwarders

	City	State	ZIP	Toll-Free	Phone
A Duie Pyle Inc 650 Westtown Rd PO Box 564	West Chester	PA	19381	**800-523-5020**	610-696-5800
Access Business Group 7575 Fulton St E *Cust Svc	Ada	MI	49355	**800-879-2732***	
Acme Wire Products Co 7 Broadway Ave	Mystic	CT	06355	**800-723-7015**	860-572-0511
AN Deringer Inc 64 N Main St	Saint Albans	VT	05478	**800-448-8108**	802-524-8110
APL Logistics Inc 17600 N Perimeter Dr Ste 150	Scottsdale	AZ	85255	**844-479-9620**	602-457-4297
Associated Global Systems Inc 3333 New Hyde Pk Rd *Cust Svc	New Hyde Park	NY	11042	**800-645-8300***	516-627-8910
Atlantic Bulk Carrier Corp PO Box 112	Providence Forge	VA	23140	**800-966-0030**	804-966-5459
B-H Transfer Co 750 Sparta Rd PO Box 151	Sandersville	GA	31082	**800-342-6462**	478-552-5119
Bender Group 345 Parr Cir	Reno	NV	89512	**800-621-9402**	
Bulldog Hiway Express 3390 Buffalo Ave	Charleston	SC	29418	**800-331-9515**	843-744-1651
Caterpillar 501 S W Jefferson Ave	Peoria	IL	61630	**888-614-4328**	309-675-2337
Cdo Technologies Inc 5200 Sprngfeld St Ste 320	Dayton	OH	45431	**866-307-6616**	937-258-0022
Central Transportation Systems 4105 Rio Bravo Ste 100	El Paso	TX	79902	**855-636-9780**	
CH Robinson Worldwide Inc 14701 Charlson Rd *NASDAQ: CHRW* ■ *Cust Svc	Eden Prairie	MN	55347	**855-229-6128***	952-683-3950
Clean Air Technology Inc 41105 Capital Dr	Canton	MI	48187	**800-459-6320**	
Clipper Exxpress Inc 9014 Heritage Pkwy Ste 300	Woodridge	IL	60517	**800-678-2547**	630-739-0700
Conley Transport Ii Inc 2104 Eastline Rd	Searcy	AR	72143	**800-338-8700**	
Coyote Logistics LLC 2545 W Diversey Ave	Chicago	IL	60647	**877-626-9683**	
Crane Worldwide Logistics LLC 1500 Rankin Rd	Houston	TX	77073	**888-870-2726**	281-443-2777
Daniel F Young Inc 1235 Westlakes Dr Ste 255	Berwyn	PA	19312	**866-407-0083**	610-725-4000
Daniel Group Ltd, The 400 Clarice Ave Ste 200	Charlotte	NC	28204	**877-967-4242**	
Danny Herman Trucking Inc PO Box 55	Mountain City	TN	37683	**800-251-7500**	
Dennis K Burke Inc 284 Eastern Ave	Chelsea	MA	02150	**800-289-2875**	617-884-7800
Dependable Highway Express Inc 2440 S 48th Ave	Phoenix	AZ	85043	**800-472-2037**	602-278-4401
Dohrn Transfer Co 625 Third Ave	Rock Island	IL	61201	**888-364-7621**	309-794-0723
DSC Logistics 1750 S Wolf Rd	Des Plaines	IL	60018	**800-372-1960**	
FedEx Supply Chain Services Inc 5455 Darrow Rd	Hudson	OH	44236	**800-463-3339**	901-369-3600
Fremont Contract Carriers Inc (FCC) 865 S Bud Blvd	Fremont	NE	68025	**800-228-9842**	
Griffin Transport Services 5360 Capital Ct	Reno	NV	89502	**800-361-5028**	775-331-8010
Gypsum Express Ltd 8280 Sixty Rd PO Box 268	Baldwinsville	NY	13027	**800-621-7901**	315-638-2201
H E Whitlock Inc PO Box 8030	Pueblo	CO	81008	**866-933-0709**	719-544-9475
Hanson Logistics 2900 S State St	Saint Joseph	MI	49085	**888-772-1197**	269-982-1390
Higher Ed Growth LLC 1702 E McNair Dr	Tempe	AZ	85283	**866-433-8532**	
Horizon Air Freight Inc 152-15 Rockaway Blvd	Jamaica	NY	11434	**800-221-6028**	718-528-3800
Hub Group Inc 2000 Clearwater Dr *NASDAQ: HUBG*	Oak Brook	IL	60523	**800-377-5833**	630-271-3600
InterChez Logistics Systems Inc 600 Alpha Pkwy	Stow	OH	44224	**800-780-4707**	330-923-5080
JB Hunt Transport Services Inc 615 JB Hunt Corporate Dr *NASDAQ: JBHT*	Lowell	AR	72745	**800-643-3622**	479-820-0000
Kenco Group Inc 2001 Riverside Dr	Chattanooga	TN	37406	**800-758-3289**	
Kintetsu World Express USA Inc 1 Jericho Plz Ste 100	Jericho	NY	11753	**800-275-4045**	516-933-7100
L&B Transport LLC 708 US190 PO Box 74870	Port Allen	LA	70767	**800-545-9401**	225-387-0894
Landstar Logistics Inc 13410 Sutton Pk Dr S	Jacksonville	FL	32224	**800-072 9400**	904-398-9400
LeSaint Logistics 868 W Crossroads Pkwy	Romeoville	IL	60446	**877-566-9375**	630-243-5950
M & J Transportation 3536 Nicholson Ave	Kansas City	MO	64120	**866-298-3858**	816-231-6733
Matson Logistics Inc 555 12th St	Oakland	CA	94607	**800-762-8766**	510-628-4000
Midwest Specialized Transportation Inc 4515 Hwy 63 N PO Box 6418	Rochester	MN	55906	**800-927-8007**	507-424-4838
MIQ Logistics LLC 11501 Outlook St Ste 500	Overland Park	KS	66211	**877-246-4909**	913-696-7100
NFI Industries (NFI) 1515 Burnt Mill Rd	Cherry Hill	NJ	08003	**877-634-3777**	
Oakley Transport Inc 101 ABC Rd	Lake Wales	FL	33859	**800-969-8265**	863-638-1435
Omnitrans Inc 500 Merrick Rd	Lynbrook	NY	11563	**877-806-2541**	516-561-9300
Pegasus Logistics Group Inc 306 Airline Dr Ste 100	Coppell	TX	75019	**800-997-7226**	469-671-0300
Pierce Distribution Services Co PO Box 15600	Loves Park	IL	61132	**800-466-7397**	
RADIANT GLOBAL LOGISTICS 405 114th Ave SE 3rd Fl	Bellevue	WA	98004	**800-843-4784**	425-462-1094
Red Rock Distributing Co 1 NW 50th St	Oklahoma City	OK	73118	**800-323-7109**	405-677-3373
Red Star Oil 802 Purser Dr	Raleigh	NC	27603	**800-774-6033**	919-772-1944
Renodis Inc 476 Robert St N	Saint Paul	MN	55101	**866-200-8986**	651-556-1200
RIM Logistics Ltd 200 N Gary Ave	Roselle	IL	60172	**888-275-0937**	630-595-0610
Rural Health Resource Ctr 525 S Lake Ave Ste 320	Duluth	MN	55802	**800-997-6685**	218-727-9390
Ryder System Inc 11690 NW 105th St *NYSE: R*	Miami	FL	33178	**800-297-9337**	305-500-3726
S & H Express Inc 400 Mulberry St	York	PA	17403	**800-637-9782**	717-848-5015
Schneider National Inc 3101 S Packerland Dr PO Box 2545	Green Bay	WI	54306	**800-558-6767**	920-592-2000
Seko 1100 Arlington Heights Rd Ste 600	Itasca	IL	60143	**800-228-2711**	630-919-4800
Shaker Group Inc, The 862 Albany Shaker Rd	Latham	NY	12110	**800-267-0314**	518-786-9286
Slay Industries Inc 1441 Hampton Ave	Saint Louis	MO	63139	**800-852-7529**	314-647-7529
Store Opening Solutions (SOS) 800 Middle Tennessee Blvd	Murfreesboro	TN	37129	**877-388-9262**	
Survival Systems Training Ltd 40 Mt Hope Ave	Dartmouth	NS	B2Y4K9	**800-788-3888**	902-465-3888
Technical Transportation Inc 1701 W Northwest Hwy Ste 100	Grapevine	TX	76051	**800-852-8726**	
Thoroughbred Direct Intermodal Services 5165 Campus Dr Ste 400	Plymouth Meeting	PA	19462	**877-250-2902**	
Titan Global Distribution 11973 Westline Industrial Dr Ste 200	Saint Louis	MO	63143	**800-325-4074**	314-817-0051
UPS Supply Chain Solutions 12380 Morris Rd	Alpharetta	GA	30005	**800-742-5727**	913-693-6151
Vimich Traffic Logistics 12201 Tecumseh Rd	Tecumseh	ON	N8N1M3	**800-284-1045**	
Wallace & Carey 5445-8 St NE	Calgary	AB	T2K5R9	**800-661-1504**	403-275-7360
Weber Logistics 13530 Rosecrans Ave	Santa Fe Springs	CA	90670	**855-469-3237**	

				Toll-Free	Phone
Wilheit Packaging LLC 1527 May Dr	Gainesville	GA	30507	**800-727-4421**	770-532-4421
Willson International Ltd 2345 Argentia Rd Ste 201	Mississauga	ON	L5N8K4	**800-754-1918**	905-363-1133
Wise Consulting Associates Inc 54 Scott Adam Rd Ste 206	Hunt Valley	MD	21030	**800-654-4550**	410-628-0100
XPO Logistics Inc 6805 Perimeter Dr	Dublin	OH	43016	**800-837-7584**	614-923-1400

448 LONG-TERM CARE FACILITIES

SEE ALSO Retirement Communities ; Veterans Nursing Homes - State ; Long-Term Care Facilities Operators

Free-standing facilities accredited by the Joint Commission on Accreditation of Healthcare Organizations. Listings in this category are organized alphabetically by states.

				Toll-Free	Phone
Casa Colina Hospital & Centers for Healthcare 255 E Bonita Ave	Pomona	CA	91767	**866-724-4127**	
Extended Care Hospital Westminster 206 Hospital Cir	Westminster	CA	92683	**800-236-9747**	714-891-2769
Front Porch Communities & Services 800 N Brand Blvd 19th Fl	Glendale	CA	91203	**800-233-3709**	
La Jolla Nursing & Rehabilitation Ctr 2552 Torrey Pines Rd	La Jolla	CA	92037	**800-861-0086**	858-453-5810
Noble Horizons 17 Cobble Rd	Salisbury	CT	06068	**800-733-2767**	860-435-9851
Armed Forces Retirement Home - Washington 3700 N Capitol St NW	Washington	DC	20011	**800-422-9988***	
*Admissions					
Area Agency On Aging 9549 Koger Blvd Gadsden Bldg Ste 100	St Petersburg	FL	33702	**800-963-5337**	727-570-9696
Kula Hospital 100 Keokea Pl	Kula	HI	96790	**800-845-6733**	808-878-1221
Barton W Stone Christian Home 873 Grove St	Jacksonville	IL	62650	**800-397-1313**	217-479-3400
OSF HealthCare 800 NE Glen Oak Ave	Peoria	IL	61603	**888-627-5673**	877-574-5678
Heritage Ctr 1201 W Buena Vista Rd	Evansville	IN	47710	**800-704-0700**	812-429-0700
Pyramid Point Post-Acute Rehabilitation Ctr 8530 Township Line Rd	Indianapolis	IN	46260	**800-861-0086**	317-876-9955
StVincent Health 2001 W 86th St	Indianapolis	IN	46260	**866-338-2345**	317-338-2345
CareOne 57 Old Rd to Nine Acre Corner	Concord	MA	01742	**855-277-8550**	
Central Boston Elder Services Inc 2315 Washington St	Boston	MA	02119	**800-922-2275**	617-277-7416
Colonial Nursing & Rehabilitation Inc 125 Broad St	Weymouth	MA	02188	**800-245-8389**	781-337-3121
Worcester Skilled Care Ctr 59 Acton St	Worcester	MA	01604	**800-946-4283**	508-791-3147
Hope Network 3075 Orchard Vista Dr SE	Grand Rapids	MI	49546	**800-695-7273**	616-301-8000
ManorCare Health Services - Mountainside 1180 Rt 22 W	Mountainside	NJ	07092	**800-366-1232**	908-654-0020
Voorhees Pediatric Facility 1304 Laurel Oak Rd	Voorhees	NJ	08043	**888-873-5437**	856-346-3300
Willow Creek Rehabilitation & Care Ctr 1165 Easton Ave	Somerset	NJ	08873	**800-486-0027**	732-246-4100
Comprehensive Care Management Corp (CCM) 1250 Waters Pl Tower 1 Ste 602	Bronx	NY	10461	**877-226-8500**	
Jewish Home Lifecare 120 W 106th St	New York	NY	10025	**800-544-0304**	212-870-5000
St Mary's Healthcare System for Children 29-01 216th St	Bayside	NY	11360	**888-543-7697**	718-281-8800
Kindred Hospital Greensboro 2401 Southside Blvd	Greensboro	NC	27406	**877-836-2671**	336-271-2800
Wilmington Health 1202 Medical Center Dr	Wilmington	NC	28401	**800-334-3053**	910-341-3300
Area Agency On Aging 10b Inc 1550 Corporate Woods Pkwy	Uniontown	OH	44685	**800-421-7277**	330-896-9172
Oklahoma Veterans Ctr Norman 1776 E Robinson St	Norman	OK	73071	**800-782-5218**	405-360-5600
Kindred Hospice 190 Bilmar Dr Ste 200	Pittsburgh	PA	15205	**866-546-3733**	412-494-5500
Presbyterian SeniorCare-Westminster Place 1215 Hulton Rd	Oakmont	PA	15139	**877-772-6500**	412-828-5600
South Mountain Restoration Ctr 10058 S Mountain Rd	South Mountain	PA	17261	**800-932-0313**	
Golden LivingCenter - Western Reserve 2601 Network Blvd Ste 102	Frisco	TX	75034	**877-823-8375**	479-201-2000
Berkshire Health & Rehabilitation Ctr 705 Clearview Dr	Vinton	VA	24179	**800-321-1245**	540-982-6691
Riverside Regional Convalescent Ctr 1000 Old Denbigh Blvd	Newport News	VA	23602	**800-759-1001**	757-875-2000

449 LONG-TERM CARE FACILITIES OPERATORS

				Toll-Free	Phone
Active Day/Senior Care Inc 6 Neshaminy Interplex Ste 401	Trevose	PA	19053	**877-435-3372**	888-338-6898
Aegis Assisted Living 4585 W Lake Sammamish Pkwy NE	Redmond	WA	98052	**888-252-3447**	866-688-5829
American Religious Town Hall Meeting Inc PO Box 180118	Dallas	TX	75218	**800-783-9828**	214-328-9828
ElderWood Senior Care 5271 Main St	Williamsville	NY	14221	**888-826-9663**	716-565-9663
Five Star Quality Care Inc 400 Centre St	Newton	MA	02458	**866-230-1286**	617-796-8387
NYSE: FVE					
Genesis HealthCare Corp 101 E State St	Kennett Square	PA	19348	**800-944-7776**	610-444-6350
Kindred Healthcare Inc 680 S Fourth Ave	Louisville	KY	40202	**800-545-0749**	502-596-7300
NYSE: KND					
National HealthCare Corp 100 E Vine St PO Box 1398	Murfreesboro	TN	37133	**800-877-1600**	615-890-2020
NYSE: NHC					
Sunrise Senior Living LLC 7902 Westpark Dr	McLean	VA	22102	**888-434-4648**	703-273-7500
NYSE: SRZ					

450 LOTTERIES, GAMES, SWEEPSTAKES

SEE ALSO Games & Gaming

				Toll-Free	Phone
Alta Ski Lifts Co Alta Ski Area Hwy 210 Little Cottonwood Canyon	Alta	UT	84092	**800-453-8488**	801-359-1078
Lottery 4740 E University Dr	Phoenix	AZ	85034	**800-639-8783**	480-921-4400
Bay Mills Resort & Casinos 11386 West Lakeshore Dr	Brimley	MI	49715	**888-422-9645**	
Black Mesa Casino 25 Hagon Rd	Algodones	NM	87001	**877-529-2946**	505-867-6700
British Columbia Lottery Corp (BCLC) 74 W Seymour St	Kamloops	BC	V2C1E2	**866-815-0222**	250-828-5500
Catfish Bend Casinos II LLC 3001 Winegard Dr	Burlington	IA	52601	**866-792-9948**	
Chinook Winds Casino Resort 1777 NW 44th St	Lincoln City	OR	97367	**888-244-6665**	
Choctaw Casino Resorts 3735 Choctaw Rd	Durant	OK	74701	**888-652-4628**	580-920-0160
Chumash Casino Resort 3400 E Hwy 246	Santa Ynez	CA	93460	**800-248-6274**	805-686-0855
Lottery 225 N Main St	Pueblo	CO	81003	**800-999-2959**	719-546-2400
Cypress Bayou Casino 832 Martin Luther King Rd	Charenton	LA	70523	**800-284-4386**	
Fortune Bay Resort & Casino 1430 Bois Forte Rd	Tower	MN	55790	**800-992-7529**	218-753-6400
Georgia Lottery Corp 250 Williams St NW Ste 3000	Atlanta	GA	30303	**800-425-8259**	404-215-5000
Lottery 1199 Shoreline Ln Ste 100	Boise	ID	83702	**800-432-5688**	208-334-2600
Lottery 101 W Jefferson St	Springfield	IL	62702	**800-252-1775**	217-524-6435
Iowa					
Adult Children & Family Services Div 1305 E Walnut St	Des Moines	IA	50319	**800-735-2942**	515-281-8977
Lottery Corp 1011 W Main St	Louisville	KY	40202	**800-937-8946**	502-560-1500
Louisiana					
Agriculture & Forestry Dept 5825 Florida Blvd	Baton Rouge	LA	70806	**866-927-2476**	225-922-1234
Lottery Corp 555 Laurel St	Baton Rouge	LA	70801	**877-770-7867**	225-297-2000
State Lottery 1800 Washington Blvd Ste 330	Baltimore	MD	21230	**800-201-0108**	410-230-8800
State Lottery 101 E Hillsdale St PO Box 30023	Lansing	MI	48909	**844-887-6836**	517-335-5756
Minnesota					
Aging Board 540 Cedar St	Saint Paul	MN	55155	**800-882-6262**	651-431-2500
Lottery 1823 Southridge Dr PO Box 1603	Jefferson City	MO	65109	**888-238-7633**	573-751-4050
Mole Lake Casino Lodge & Conference Ctr 3084 State Hwy 55	Crandon	WI	54520	**800-236-9466**	715-478-3200
Nebraska Lottery 1800 "O" St PO Box 98901	Lincoln	NE	68509	**800-587-5200**	402-471-6100
Lottery Commission 14 Integra Dr	Concord	NH	03301	**800-852-3324**	603-271-3391
Lottery 4511 Osuna Rd NE	Albuquerque	NM	87109	**800-572-1142**	505-342-7600
Odawa Casino Resort, The 1760 Lears Rd	Petoskey	MI	49770	**877-442-6464**	
Ohio Lottery Commission 615 W Superior Ave	Cleveland	OH	44113	**800-686-4208**	216-787-3200
River Rock Entertainment Authority 3250 Hwy 128 E	Geyserville	CA	95441	**877-883-7777**	707-857-2777
Riverwalk Casino Hotel 1046 Warrenton Rd	Vicksburg	MS	39180	**866-615-9125**	601-634-0100
Shooting Star Casino 777 SE Casino Rd	Mahnomen	MN	56557	**800-453-7827**	
Soboba Casino 23333 Soboba Rd	San Jacinto	CA	92583	**866-476-2622**	951-665-1000
Education Lottery PO Box 11949	Columbia	SC	29211	**866-736-9819***	803-737-2002
*Help Line					
Spirit Lake Casino & Resort 7889 Hwy 57	Saint Michael	ND	58370	**800-946-8238**	701-766-4747
Stockman's Casino 1560 W Williams Ave	Fallon	NV	89406	**855-423-2117**	
Suquamish Clearwater Casino Resort 15347 Suquamish Way NE	Suquamish	WA	98392	**800-375-6073**	360-598-8700
Tennessee					
Administrative Office of the Cts 511 Union St Ste 600	Nashville	TN	37219	**800-448-7970**	615-741-2687
Lottery 1 Century Pl 26 Century Blvd Ste 200 PO Box 291869	Nashville	TN	37214	**800-826-4311**	615-324-6500
Vermont					
Aging & Disabilities Dept 280 State Dr HC2 South	Waterbury	VT	05671	**888-405-5005**	802-241-2401
Aging & Rehabilitative Services Dept 8004 Franklin Farms Dr	Richmond	VA	23229	**800-552-5019**	804-662-7000
Lottery 900 Pennsylvania Ave PO Box 2067	Charleston	WV	25302	**800-982-2274**	304-558-0500
Western Canada Lottery Corp 125 Garry St 10th Fl	Winnipeg	MB	R3C4J1	**800-665-3313**	

Classified Section

451   LUGGAGE, BAGS, CASES

SEE ALSO Handbags, Totes, Backpacks ; Leather Goods - Personal

	Toll-Free	Phone
Ameripack Inc		
107 N Gold Dr ...... Robbinsville NJ 08691	800-456-7963	609-259-7004
Anvil Cases		
15730 Salt Lake Ave ...... City of Industry CA 91745	800-359-2684	626-968-4100
Calzone Case Co		
225 Black Rock Ave ...... Bridgeport CT 06605	800-243-5152*	203-367-5766
*Cust Svc		
CH Ellis Co Inc		
2432 SE Ave ...... Indianapolis IN 46201	800-466-3351*	317-636-3351
*Sales		
Coach Inc 342 Madison Ave ...... New York NY 10173	800-444-3611	212-599-4777
NYSE: COH		
Delsey Luggage		
6735 Business Pkwy Ste A ...... Elkridge MD 21075	800-558-3344	410-796-5655
Platt Luggage Inc		
4051 W 51st St ...... Chicago IL 60632	800-222-1555	773-838-2000
SKB Corp 434 W Levers Pl ...... Orange CA 92867	800-410-2024*	714-637-1252
*Sales		
Targus Inc 1211 N Miller St ...... Anaheim CA 92806	877-482-7487	714-765-5555
Travelpro USA		
700 Banyan Trl ...... Boca Raton FL 33431	800-741-7471	561-998-2824
Zero Manufacturing Inc		
500 W 200 N ...... North Salt Lake UT 84054	800-959-5050	801-298-5900

452   MACHINE SHOPS

SEE ALSO Precision Machined Products

	Toll-Free	Phone
Acme Cryogenics Inc		
2801 Mitchell Ave ...... Allentown PA 18103	800-422-2790	610-966-4488
American Grinding & Machine Co		
2000 N Mango Ave ...... Chicago IL 60639	877-988-4343	773-889-4343
Archer Screw Products Inc		
11341 Melrose Ave ...... Franklin Park IL 60131	800-952-7897	
Boston Centerless Inc		
11 Presidential Way ...... Woburn MA 01801	800-343-4111	781-994-5000
Brandywine Machine Company Inc		
300 Creek Rd ...... Downingtown PA 19335	800-523-7128	
Burger & Brown Engineering Inc		
4500 E 142nd St ...... Grandview MO 64030	800-764-3518	816-878-6675
Cardo Systems Inc		
1204 Pkwy View Dr ...... Pittsburgh PA 15205	800-488-0363	412-788-4533
Chalmers & Kubeck Inc		
150 Commerce Dr ...... Aston PA 19014	800-242-5637	610-494-4300
Chapel Steel Co		
590 N Bethlehem Pk ...... Lower Gwynedd PA 19002	800-570-7674	215-793-0899
Cleveland Tool & Machine		
5240 Smith Rd ...... Brook Park OH 44142	800-253-4502	216-267-6010
CNC Industries Ltd		
9331 39 Ave ...... Edmonton AB T6E5T3	877-262-2343	780-469-2346
Custom Brackets		
32 Alpha Pk ...... Cleveland OH 44143	800-530-2289	440-446-0819
Digital Machining Systems LLC		
929 Ridge Rd ...... Duson LA 70529	800-530-8945	337-984-6013
Egge Machine Company Inc		
11707 Slauson Ave ...... Santa Fe Springs CA 90670	800-866-3443	562-945-3419
Empire Bakery Equipment		
171 Greenwich St ...... Hempstead NY 11550	800-878-4070	516-538-1210
Femco Machine Co		
754 S Main St Ext ...... Punxsutawney PA 15767	800-458-3445	814-938-9763
Festo Corp		
395 Moreland Dr ...... Hauppauge NY 11788	800-993-3786	
Fixtureworks LLC		
33792 Doreka ...... Fraser MI 48026	888-794-8687	586-294-1188
Granite State Manufacturing Co		
124 Joliette St ...... Manchester NH 03102	800-464-7646	
Haas Automation Inc		
2800 Sturgis Rd ...... Oxnard CA 93030	800-331-6746	805-278-1800
Highway Machine Company Inc (HMC)		
3010 S Old US Hwy 41 ...... Princeton IN 47670	866-990-9462	812-385-3639
Hughes Supply Company of Thomasville Inc		
175 Kanoy Rd PO Box 1003 ...... Thomasville NC 27360	800-747-8141	336-475-8146
Industrial Tool Inc		
9210 52nd Ave N ...... New Hope MN 55428	800-776-4455*	763-533-7244
*Sales		
Island Timberlands LP		
65 Front St 4th Fl ...... Nanaimo BC V9R5H9	800-663-5555	250-755-3500
J C Steele & Sons Inc		
710 S Mulberry St ...... Statesville NC 28677	800-278-3353	704-872-3681
Jewell Group		
130 Research Pkwy ...... Davenport IA 52806	800-831-8665	563-355-5010
Kamet Manufacturing Solutions		
171 Commercial St ...... Sunnyvale CA 94086	800-888-2089	408-522-8000
Kurt Manufacturing Co		
5280 Main St NE ...... Minneapolis MN 55421	800-458-7855	763-572-1500
Laser Excel		
N6323 Berlin Rd ...... Green Lake WI 54941	800-285-6544	
LaVezzi Precision Inc		
250 Madsen Dr ...... Bloomingdale IL 60108	800-323-1772	
Lemco Tool Corp		
1850 Metzger Ave ...... Cogan Station PA 17728	800-233-8713	570-494-0620
Lith-O-Roll Corp		
9521 Telstar Ave ...... El Monte CA 91731	800-423-4176	626-579-0340
Litton Engineering Laboratories		
200 Litton Dr Ste 200 ...... Grass Valley CA 95945	800-821-8866	530-273-6176
Marine Exhaust Systems of Alabama Inc		
757 Nichols Ave ...... Fairhope AL 36532	800-237-3160	251-928-1234
Marshall Screw Products Co		
3820 Chandler Dr NE ...... Minneapolis MN 55421	800-321-6727	

	Toll-Free	Phone
Micro Instrument Corp (MIC)		
1199 Emerson St PO Box 60619 ...... Rochester NY 14606	800-200-3150	585-458-3150
Mittler Corp		
10 Cooperative Way ...... Wright City MO 63390	800-467-2464	636-745-7757
OGS Industries 976 Evans Ave ...... Akron OH 44305	800-321-2438	
Peeco 7050 West Ridge Rd ...... Fairview PA 16415	800-235-9382	814-474-5561
Photofabrication Engineering Inc (PEI)		
500 Fortune Blvd ...... Milford MA 01757	800-253-8518	508-478-2025
Potomac Electric Corp		
1 Westinghouse Plz ...... Boston MA 02136	877-737-2662	
Quality Mfg Company Inc (QMI)		
PO Box 616 ...... Winchester KY 40392	866-460-6459	859-744-0420
Santinelli International Inc		
325 Oser Ave ...... Hauppauge NY 11788	800-644-3343	
Schmiede Corp		
1865 Riley Creek Rd PO Box 1630 ...... Tullahoma TN 37388	800-535-1851	931-455-4801
Sintel Inc		
18437 171st Ave ...... Spring Lake MI 49456	800-394-8276	616-842-6960
Solid Concepts Inc		
28309 Ave Crocker ...... Valencia CA 91355	888-311-1017	661-295-4400
Standard Locknut Inc		
1045 E 169th St ...... Westfield IN 46074	800-783-6887	317-867-0100
Stellar Technology Inc		
237 Commerce Dr ...... Amherst NY 14228	800-274-1846	716-250-1900
Stillwater Technologies Inc		
1040 S Dorset ...... Troy OH 45373	800-338-7561	937-440-2500
T R C Hydraulics Inc		
7 Mosher Dr ...... Dartmouth NS B3B1E5	800-668-9000	902-468-4605
Tacoma Screw Products Inc		
2001 Center St ...... Tacoma WA 98409	800-562-8192	253-572-3444
Tier One LLC 31 Pecks Ln ...... Newtown CT 06470	877-251-2228	
Twin City EDM		
7940 Rancher Rd NE ...... Fridley MN 55432	800-397-0338	763-783-7808
Unisource Manufacturing Inc		
8040 NE 33rd Dr ...... Portland OR 97211	800-234-2566	503-281-4673
Vescio Threading Co		
14002 Anson Ave ...... Santa Fe Springs CA 90670	800-361-4218	562-802-1868
Wahlco Inc		
2722 S Fairview St ...... Santa Ana CA 92704	800-423-5432	714-979-7300
Weldmac Manufacturing Co		
1451 N Johnson Ave ...... El Cajon CA 92020	800-252-1533	619-440-2300
Windham Manufacturing Company Inc		
8520 Forney Rd ...... Dallas TX 75227	888-965-0093	214-388-0511
Windings Inc		
208 N Valley St PO Box 566 ...... New Ulm MN 56073	800-795-8533	507-359-2034
Xtek Inc		
11451 Reading Rd ...... Cincinnati OH 45241	888-332-9835	513-733-7800

453   MACHINE TOOLS - METAL CUTTING TYPES

SEE ALSO Machine Tools - Metal Forming Types ; Metalworking Devices & Accessories

	Toll-Free	Phone
Abbco Inc 304 Meyer Rd ...... Bensenville IL 60106	866-986-6546	630-595-7115
Allied Tool Products		
9334 N 107th St ...... Milwaukee WI 53224	800-558-5147	414-355-8280
Barnes International Inc		
814 Chestnut St PO Box 1203 ...... Rockford IL 61105	800-435-4877	815-964-8661
Burr Oak Tool Inc		
405 W S St ...... Sturgis MI 49091	800-861-8864	269-651-9393
Continental Machines Inc		
5505 W 123rd St ...... Savage MN 55378	888-362-5572	952-890-3300
Crafts Technology		
91 Joey Dr ...... Elk Grove Village IL 60007	800-323-6802	847-758-3100
Darex		
210 E Hersey St PO Box 730 ...... Ashland OR 97520	800-597-6170	
Davenport Machine Inc		
167 Ames St ...... Rochester NY 14611	800-344-5748	585-235-4545
EH Wachs Co		
600 Knightsbridge Pkwy ...... Lincolnshire IL 60069	800-323-8185	847-537-8800
Extrude Hone LLC		
235 Industry Blvd ...... Irwin PA 15642	800-835-3668	724-863-5900
Flow International Corp		
23500 64th Ave S ...... Kent WA 98032	800-446-3569	253-850-3500
NASDAQ: FLOW		
GF Machining Solutions		
560 Bond St ...... Lincolnshire IL 60069	800-282-1336	847-913-5300
Grob Inc 1731 Tenth Ave ...... Grafton WI 53024	800-225-6481	262-377-1400
Hardinge Inc 1 Hardinge Dr ...... Elmira NY 14902	800-843-8801	607-734-2281
NASDAQ: HDNG		
Hause Machines		
809 S Pleasant St ...... Montpelier OH 43543	800-932-8665	419-485-3158
Huffman Corp		
1050 Huffman Way ...... Clover SC 29710	888-483-3626	803-222-4561
Hurco Cos Inc		
1 Technology Way ...... Indianapolis IN 46268	800-634-2416*	317-293-5309
NASDAQ: HURC ■ *Sales		
Hypertherm Inc		
21 Great Hollow Rd PO Box 5010 ...... Hanover NH 03755	800-643-0030	603-643-3441
Hypneumat Inc		
5900 W Franklin Dr ...... Franklin WI 53132	800-228-9949	414-423-7400
Kaufman Mfg Co		
547 S 29th St PO Box 1056 ...... Manitowoc WI 54221	800-420-6641	920-684-6641
Kennametal		
1662 McMillan Park Dr ...... Fort Mill SC 29707	800-446-7738*	
NYSE: KMT ■ *Cust Svc		
Klingelhofer Corp		
165 Mill Ln ...... Mountainside NJ 07092	800-879-5546	908-232-7200
Koike Aronson Inc		
635 W Main St PO Box 307 ...... Arcade NY 14009	800-252-5232	585-492-2400
Kyocera Tycom Corp		
3565 Cadillac ...... Costa Mesa CA 92626	800-823-7284	714-428-3600
Lucas Precision LP		
13020 St Clair Ave ...... Cleveland OH 44108	800-336-1262	216-451-5588
Makino 7680 Innovation Way ...... Mason OH 45040	888-625-4661	513-573-7200

Machine Tools - Metal Cutting Types (Cont'd)

	Toll-Free	Phone
McLean Inc		
3409 E Miraloma Ave ....Anaheim CA 92806	800-451-2424*	714-996-5451
*Cust Svc		
Metal Cutting Corp		
89 Commerce Rd ....Cedar Grove NJ 07009	800-783-6382	973-239-1100
Monarch Lathes		
615 N Oaks Ave PO Box 4609 ....Sidney OH 45365	800-543-7666	937-492-4111
NNT Corp 1320 Norwood Ave ....Itasca IL 60143	800-556-9999	630-875-9600
North American Products Corp		
1180 Wernsing Rd ....Jasper IN 47546	800-457-7468*	812-482-2000
*Cust Svc		
Oliver of Adrian Inc		
1111 E Beecher St PO Box 189..................Adrian MI 49221	877-668-0885	517-263-2132
Parker Majestic Inc		
300 N Pike Rd ....Sarver PA 16055	866-572-7537	724-352-1551
Peddinghaus Corp		
300 N Washington Ave ....Bradley IL 60915	800-786-2448	815-937-3800
Pioneer Broach Co		
6434 Telegraph Rd ....Los Angeles CA 90040	800-621-1945	323-728-1263
RF Cook Manufacturing Co		
4585 Allen Rd ....Stow OH 44224	800-430-7536	330-923-9797
Rothenberger USA		
7130 Clinton Rd ....Loves Park IL 61111	800-545-7698	815-397-0260
Rottler Mfg 8029 S 200th St ....Kent WA 98032	800-452-0534	253-872-7050
S & M Machine Service Inc		
109 E Highland Dr ....Oconto Falls WI 54154	800-323-1579	920-846-8130
Servo Products Co		
34940 Lakeland Blvd ....Eastlake OH 44095	800-521-7359	440-942-9999
Setco Sales Co		
5880 Hillside Ave ....Cincinnati OH 45233	800-543-0470	513-941-5110
Southwestern Industries Inc		
2615 Homestead Pl ....Rancho Dominguez CA 90220	800-421-6875	310-608-4422
Sunnen Products Co		
7910 Manchester Ave ....Saint Louis MO 63143	800-325-3670	314-781-2100
Technidrill Systems Inc		
429 Portage Blvd ....Kent OH 44240	844-313-7012	330-678-9980
Thermal Dynamics		
82 Benning St ....West Lebanon NH 03784	800-752-7621	603-298-5711
Tool-Flo Mfg Inc		
7803 Hansen Rd ....Houston TX 77061	800-345-2815	713-941-1080
Toyoda Machinery USA Inc		
316 W University Dr ....Arlington Heights IL 60004	800-257-2985	847-253-0340
TRU TECH Systems Inc		
24550 N River Rd PO Box 46965 ......Mount Clemens MI 48043	877-878-8324	586-469-2700
US Tool Grinding Inc		
2000 Progress Dr ....Farmington MO 63640	800-222-1771	573-431-3856
Vernon Tool Company Ltd		
1170 Trademark Dr Ste 101 ....Reno NV 89521	866-571-1066	775-673-2200
WF Meyers Co 1008 13th St ....Bedford IN 47421	800-457-4055	812-275-4485
Whitney Tool Company Inc		
906 R St ....Bedford IN 47421	800-536-1971	812-275-4491
Wisconsin Machine Tool Corp		
3225 Gateway Rd Ste 100..................Brookfield WI 53045	800-243-3078	262-317-3048

454   MACHINE TOOLS - METAL FORMING TYPES

SEE ALSO Machine Tools - Metal Cutting Types ; Tool & Die Shops ; Metal-working Devices & Accessories ; Rolling Mill Machinery

	Toll-Free	Phone
Advanced Hydraulics Inc		
13568 Vintage Pl ....Chino CA 91710	888-581-8079	909-590-7644
Amada America Inc		
7025 Firestone Blvd ....Buena Park CA 90621	800-626-6612	714-739-2111
Badge A Minit Ltd		
345 N Lewis Ave ....Oglesby IL 61348	800-223-4103	
Bliss Clearing Niagara (BCN)		
1004 E State St ....Hastings MI 49058	800-642-5477	269-948-3300
DR Sperry & Co		
623 Rathbone Ave ....Aurora IL 60506	888-997-9297	630-892-4361
Edwards Manufacturing Co		
1107 Sykes St ....Albert Lea MN 56007	800-373-8206	507-373-8206
Emery Corp PO Box 1104 ....Morganton NC 28680	800-255-0537	828-433-1536
GEMCOR Corp		
1750 Union Rd ....West Seneca NY 14224	800-325-1596	716-674-9300
Grant Assembly Technologies		
90 Silliman Ave ....Bridgeport CT 06605	800-227-2150	203-366-4557
Greenerd Press & Machine Company Inc		
41 Crown St PO Box 886 ....Nashua NH 03061	800-877-9110	603-889-4101
Heim LP 6360 W 73rd St ....Chicago IL 60638	800-927-9393	708-496-7450
Mate Precision Tooling Inc		
1295 Lund Blvd ....Anoka MN 55303	800-328-4492	763-421-0230
MegaFab PO Box 457 ....Hutchinson KS 67504	800-338-5471	620-663-1127
Murata Machinery USA Inc		
2120 Queen City Dr ....Charlotte NC 28208	800-428-8469	
Pacific Press Technologies		
714 Walnut St ....Mount Carmel IL 62863	800-851-3586	618-262-8666
Reed 28 Sword St ....Auburn MA 01501	800-343-6068	508-753-6530
Schleuniger Inc		
87 Colin Dr ....Manchester NH 03103	877-902-1470*	603-668-8117
*Tech Supp		
Strippit Inc/LVD		
12975 Clarence Ctr Rd ....Akron NY 14001	800-828-1527	716-542-4511
Tools for Bending Inc		
194 W Dakota Ave ....Denver CO 80223	800-873-3305*	303-777-7170
*Cust Svc		
Williams White & Co		
600 River Dr ....Moline IL 61265	877-797-7650	
Wysong Inc 4820 US 29 N ....Greensboro NC 27405	800-299-7664	336-621-3960

455   MAGAZINES & JOURNALS

SEE ALSO Periodicals Publishers

	Toll-Free	Phone
Texas Fish & Game Magazine		
247 Airtex Dr ....Houston TX 77090	800-725-1134	281-227-3001

455-1 Agriculture & Farming Magazines

	Toll-Free	Phone
Alfa Corp 2108 E S Blvd ....Montgomery AL 36116	800-964-2532	
American Agriculturist		
5227-B Baltimore Pk ....Littlestown PA 17340	800-441-1410	717-359-0150
Beef Magazine		
7900 International Dr Ste 300..................Minneapolis MN 55425	800-722-5334*	952-851-9329
*Cust Svc		
Farm Industry News		
7900 International Dr Ste 300..................Minneapolis MN 55425	800-722-5334*	630-524-4749
*Cust Svc		
Farm Journal		
30 S 15th Ste 900..................Philadelphia PA 19102	800-331-9310	215-557-8757
Farm Show Magazine		
20088 Kenwood Trial ....Lakeville MN 55044	800-834-9665	
Floridagriculture Magazine		
PO Box 147030 ....Gainesville FL 32614	866-275-7322	
Georgia Farm Bureau News		
1620 Bass Rd ....Macon GA 31210	800-342-1192	478-474-8411
Hoard's Dairyman Magazine		
28 Milwaukee Ave W PO Box 801 ......Fort Atkinson WI 53538	800-245-8222	920-563-5551
Iowa Farm Bureau Spokesman Magazine		
5400 University Ave ....West Des Moines IA 50266	866-598-3693	515-225-5413
Kansas Living Magazine		
2627 KFB Plz ....Manhattan KS 66503	800-406-3053	785-587-6000
Pork checkoff		
1776 NW 114th St ....Des Moines IA 50325	800-456-7675	515-223-2600
Soybean Digest		
7900 International Dr Ste 300..................Minneapolis MN 55425	800-722-5334*	952-851-4667
*Cust Svc		
Texas Farm Bureau PO Box 2689 ....Waco TX 76702	800-488-7872	254-772-3030

455-2 Art & Architecture Magazines

	Toll-Free	Phone
Airbrush Action Inc		
PO Box 438 ....Allenwood NJ 08720	800-876-2472	732-223-7878
Architectural Digest		
1 World Trade Ctr ....New York NY 10007	800-365-8032	
Art in America Magazine		
110 Greene St 2nd Fl ....New York NY 10012	800-925-8059*	212-398-1690
*Cust Svc		
Artforum International Magazine		
350 Seventh Ave ....New York NY 10001	800-966-2783	212-475-4000
Artist's Magazine, The		
4700 E Galbraith Rd ....Cincinnati OH 45236	800-422-2550	513-531-2222
ARTnews Magazine		
110 Greene St 2nd Fl ....New York NY 10012	800-284-4625	212-398-1690
HOW Design Magazine		
4700 E Galbraith Rd ....Cincinnati OH 45236	800-333-1115*	513-531-2690
*Cust Svc		
Pastel Journal		
4700 E Galbraith Rd ....Cincinnati OH 45236	800-422-2550	513-531-2222
Southwest Art Magazine		
10901 W 120th Ave Ste 340 ....Broomfield CO 80021	877-212-1938	303-442-0427
Sunshine Artist Magazine		
4075 LB McLeod Rd Ste E ....Orlando FL 32811	800-597-2573	800-331-0038

455-3 Automotive Magazines

	Toll-Free	Phone
American Iron Magazine		
1010 Summer St ....Stamford CT 06905	877-693-3572*	203-425-8777
*Cust Svc		
AutoWeek Magazine		
1155 Gratiot Ave ....Detroit MI 48207	888-288-6954*	313-446-6000
*Circ		
Easyriders Magazine		
28210 Dorothy Dr ....Agoura Hills CA 91301	800-323-3484	818-889-8740
Grassroots Motorsports Magazine		
915 Ridgewood Ave ....Holly Hill FL 32117	800-520-8292	386-239-0523
Hemmings Motor News		
222 Main St ....Bennington VT 05201	800-227-4373	802-442-3101
Hot Rod Magazine		
6420 Wilshire Blvd ....Los Angeles CA 90048	800-800-4681*	323-782-2000
*Orders		
Lowrider Magazine		
1821 E Dyer Rd PO Box 420235..................Santa Ana CA 92705	800-283-2013	
Motor Trend Magazine		
6420 Wilshire Blvd 7th Fl ....Los Angeles CA 90048	800-800-6848	323-782-2000
Motorcycle Consumer News Magazine		
3 Burroughs ....Irvine CA 92618	888-333-0354	
Speed Sport		
142 F S Cardigan Way ....Mooresville NC 28117	866-455-2531	704-790-0136

455-4 Boating Magazines

	Toll-Free	Phone
Blue Water Sailing Magazine		
747 Aquidneck Ave Ste 201 ....Middletown RI 02842	888-800-7245	401-847-7612
Power & Motoryacht Magazine		
10 Bokum Rd ....Essex CT 06426	800-284-8036	860-767-3200
SAIL Magazine 10 Bokum Rd ....Essex CT 06426	800-745-7245	860-767-3200
Sea Magazine		
17782 Cowan St Ste C ....Irvine CA 92614	800-873-7327	949-660-6150
Yachting Magazine		
460 N Orlando Ave ....Winter Park FL 32789	800-999-0869	

455-5 Business & Finance Magazines

			Toll-Free	Phone
Advisor Today				
2901 Telestar Ct	Falls Church VA	22042	**877-866-2432**	703-770-8267
Alaska Business Monthly				
501 W Northern Lights Blvd Ste 100	Anchorage AK	99503	**800-770-4373**	907-276-4373
American Banker Magazine				
1 State St Plz 27th Fl	New York NY	10004	**800-221-1809**	212-803-8200
Appraisal Journal				
200 W Madison Ste 1500	Chicago IL	60606	**888-756-4624**	
Area Development Magazine				
400 Post Ave	Westbury NY	11590	**800-735-2732**	516-338-0900
Arkansas Business LP				
114 Scott St	Little Rock AR	72201	**888-322-6397**	501-372-1443
Association Management Magazine				
1575 'I' St NW	Washington DC	20005	**888-950-2723**	202-371-0940
Best's Review Ambest Rd	Oldwick NJ	08858	**800-424-2378**	908-439-2200
Black Enterprise Magazine				
130 Fifth Ave	New York NY	10011	**800-727-7777***	212-242-8000
*Cust Svc				
British Standards Institution, The				
12110 Sunset Hills Rd Ste 200	Reston VA	20190	**800-862-4977**	345-086-9001
Business Facilities Magazine				
44 Apple St Ste 3	Tinton Falls NJ	07724	**800-524-0337**	732-842-7433
Business Insurance Magazine				
711 Third Ave	New York NY	10017	**877-812-1587**	212-210-0100
Business Journal, The				
25 E Boardman St	Youngstown OH	44501	**800-837-6397**	330-744-5023
California Real Estate Magazine				
525 S Virgil Ave	Los Angeles CA	90020	**888-811-5281**	213-739-8200
Central New York Business Journal, The				
269 W Jefferson St	Syracuse NY	13202	**800-836-3539**	315-579-3919
Columbus Business First				
303 W Nationwide Blvd	Columbus OH	43215	**800-486-3289**	614-461-4040
Communications News				
PO Box 866	Osprey FL	34229	**800-827-9715**	941-539-7579
Contract Design Magazine				
100 Broadway 14th fl	New York NY	10005	**800-697-8859**	
Crain's Chicago Business Magazine				
150 N Michigan Ave 16th Fl	Chicago IL	60001	**877-812-1590**	312-649-5200
Crain's Cleveland Business Magazine				
700 W St Clair Ave Ste 310	Cleveland OH	44113	**888-909-9111**	216-522-1383
Crain's Detroit Business Magazine				
1155 Gratiot Ave	Detroit MI	48207	**888-909-9111**	313-446-6000
Crain's New York Business Magazine				
685 Third Ave	New York NY	10017	**877-824-9379**	212-210-0100
Des Moines 100 Fourth St	Des Moines IA	50309	**800-673-4763**	515-288-3336
Drug Topics Magazine				
25115 Country Club Blvd Millennium Pl E	North Olmsted OH	44070	**877-922-2022***	440-891-2792
*Cust Svc				
E-Commerce Times (ECT)				
16133 Ventura Blvd Ste 700	Encino CA	91436	**877-328-5500**	818-461-9700
Editor & Publisher Magazine				
17782 Cowan St C	Irvine CA	92614	**855-896-7433**	949-660-6150
Expansion Management Magazine				
1300 E Ninth St	Cleveland OH	44114	**866-505-7173**	216-696-7000
Fast Company Magazine				
7 World Trade Ctr	New York NY	10007	**800-542-6029**	800-501-9571
Finance & Commerce				
730 Second Ave S				
US Trust Bldg Ste 100	Minneapolis MN	55402	**800-451-9998**	617-249-2600
Forbes Magazine				
60 Fifth Ave	New York NY	10011	**800-295-0893**	
Harvard Business Review				
60 Harvard Way	Boston MA	02163	**800-274-3214**	617-783-7500
HRMagazine 1800 Duke St	Alexandria VA	22314	**800-283-7476**	703-548-3440
Inc Magazine				
7 World Trade Ctr	New York NY	10007	**800-234-0999**	212-389-5377
Indianapolis Business Journal (IBJ)				
41 E Washington St Ste 200	Indianapolis IN	46204	**800-428-7081**	317-634-6200
Journal of Accountancy				
220 Leigh Farm Rd	Durham NC	27707	**888-777-7077**	
Journal of Financial Planning Assn				
7535 E Hampden Ave Ste 600	Denver CO	80231	**800-322-4237**	303-759-4900
Journal of Property Management				
430 N Michigan Ave	Chicago IL	60611	**800-837-0706**	
Law Enforcement Technology Magazine				
1233 Janesville Ave	Fort Atkinson WI	53538	**800-547-7377**	
Leadership Journal				
465 Gundersen Dr	Carol Stream IL	60188	**800-777-3136**	630-260-6200
Marketing News				
311 S Wacker Dr Ste 5800	Chicago IL	60606	**800-262-1150**	312-542-9000
National Assn of Credit Management				
8840 Columbia 100 Pkwy	Columbia MD	21045	**800-955-8815**	410-740-5560
National Association of Housing & Redevelopment Officials				
630 'I' St NW	Washington DC	20001	**877-866-2476**	202-289-3500
Palm Beach Daily Business Review				
324 Datura St Ste 140	West Palm Beach FL	33401	**800-777-7300**	561-820-2060
Print Magazine				
10151 Carver Rd Ste 200	Blue Ash OH	45242	**877-860-9145**	513-531-2690
Purchasing Magazine				
225 Wyman St	Waltham MA	02451	**888-393-5000**	
Realtor Magazine				
430 N Michigan Ave	Chicago IL	60611	**800-874-6500**	
Rough Notes Company Inc, The				
11690 Technology Dr	Carmel IN	46032	**800-428-4384**	317-582-1600
Self-Employed America Magazine				
PO Box 241	Annapolis Junction MD	20701	**800-649-6273**	
Selling Power Magazine				
1140 International Pkwy	Fredericksburg VA	22406	**800-752-7355**	540-752-7000
Signal Magazine				
4400 Fair Lakes Ct	Fairfax VA	22033	**800-336-4583**	703-631-6100
Sloan Management Review				
77 Massachusetts Ave E60-100	Cambridge MA	02139	**800-876-5764**	617-253-7170

			Toll-Free	Phone
Strategic Finance Magazine				
10 Paragon Dr Ste 1	Montvale NJ	07645	**800-638-4427**	201-573-9000
Training Magazine				
27020 Noble Rd	Excelsior MN	55331	**877-865-9361**	847-559-7596
Utah Business Magazine				
90 South 400 West Ste 650	Salt Lake City UT	84101	**888-414-5566**	801-568-0114
Your Church Magazine				
465 Gundersen Dr	Carol Stream IL	60188	**877-247-4787**	630-260-6200

455-6 Children's & Youth Magazines

			Toll-Free	Phone
Creative Kids Magazine				
PO Box 8813	Waco TX	76714	**800-998-2208**	254-756-3337
Cricket Media Inc				
1751 Pinnacle Dr Ste 600	McLean VA	22102	**800-821-0115**	
Girls' Life Acqusition Co				
3 S Frederick St Ste 806	Baltimore MD	21202	**800-931-2237**	410-426-9600
New Moon Magazine				
PO Box 161287	Duluth MN	55816	**800-381-4743**	218-878-9673
Owl Magazine				
10 Lower Spadina Ave Ste 400	Toronto ON	M5V2Z2	**800-551-6957**	416-340-2700
Turtle Magazine				
1100 Waterway Blvd	Indianapolis IN	46202	**800-558-2376**	317-634-1100
Wild Animal Baby Magazine				
11100 Wildlife Ctr Dr	Reston VA	20190	**800-822-9919**	
Your Big Backyard Magazine				
11100 Wildlife Ctr Dr	Reston VA	20190	**800-822-9919**	

455-7 Computer & Internet Magazines

			Toll-Free	Phone
Computer Magazine				
10662 Los Vaqueros Cir	Los Alamitos CA	90720	**800-272-6657***	714-821-8380
*Orders				
Computers in Libraries Magazine				
143 Old Marlton Pk	Medford NJ	08055	**800-300-9868**	609-654-6266
Computerworld Magazine				
1 Speen St	Framingham MA	01701	**800-343-6474**	508-879-0700
eContent Magazine				
143 Old Marlton Pk	Medford NJ	08055	**800-300-9868**	609-654-6266
Federal Computer Week Magazine				
3141 Fairview Pk Dr Ste 777	Falls Church VA	22042	**877-534-2208**	703-876-5100
IEEE Computer Graphics & Applications Magazine				
10662 Los Vaqueros Cir				
PO Box 3014	Los Alamitos CA	90720	**800-272-6657**	714-821-8380
IEEE Micro Magazine				
10662 Los Vaqueros Cir				
PO Box 3014	Los Alamitos CA	90720	**800-272-6657**	714-821-8380
Macworld Magazine				
501 Second St Ste 600	San Francisco CA	94107	**800-288-6848***	415-243-0505
*Cust Svc				
MultiMedia Schools Magazine				
143 Old Marlton Pk	Medford NJ	08055	**800-300-9868**	609-654-6266
Oracle Magazine				
500 Oracle Pkwy	Redwood Shores CA	94065	**800-392-2999**	650-506-7000
Searcher: The Magazine for Database Professionals				
143 Old Marlton Pk	Medford NJ	08055	**800-300-9868**	609-654-6266
Ziff Davis LLC				
28 E 28th St	New York NY	10016	**800-289-0429**	212-503-3500

455-8 Education Magazines & Journals

			Toll-Free	Phone
Academe Magazine				
1133 Nineteenth St NW Ste 200	Washington DC	20036	**800-424-2973**	202-737-5900
AEA Advocate Magazine				
345 E Palm Ln	Phoenix AZ	85004	**800-352-5411**	602-264-1774
Alabama School Journal				
422 Dexter Ave	Montgomery AL	36104	**800-392-5839**	334-834-9790
American Educator Magazine				
555 New Jersey Ave NW	Washington DC	20001	**800-238-1133**	202-879-4400
Arkansas Educator Magazine				
1500 W Fourth St	Little Rock AR	72201	**800-632-0624**	501-375-4611
Chronicle of Higher Education, The				
1255 23rd St NW Ste 700	Washington DC	20037	**800-728-2803**	202-466-1000
Education Ctr Inc				
3515 W Market St Ste 200	Greensboro NC	27403	**800-714-7991**	336-854-0309
Education Week Magazine				
6935 Arlington Rd	Bethesda MD	20814	**800-346-1834**	301-280-3100
Educational Leadership Magazine				
1703 N Beauregard St	Alexandria VA	22311	**800-933-2723**	703-578-9600
ISTA Advocate Magazine				
150 W Market St Ste 900	Indianapolis IN	46204	**800-382-4037**	317-263-3400
KEA News 401 Capital Ave	Frankfort KY	40601	**800-231-4532**	502-875-2889
Library Journal				
160 Varick St 11th Fl	New York NY	10013	**800-588-1030**	646-380-0700
Louisiana Association of Educators				
8322 One Kalais Ave	Baton Rouge LA	70809	**800-256-4523**	225-343-9243
MAA FOCUS				
1529 18th St NW	Washington DC	20036	**800-741-9415**	202-387-5200
Maine Educator Magazine				
35 Community Dr	Augusta ME	04330	**800-332-8529**	207-622-5866
MEA Voice Magazine				
1216 Kendale Blvd PO Box 2573	East Lansing MI	48826	**800-292-1934**	
Minnesota Educator Magazine				
41 Sherburne Ave	Saint Paul MN	55103	**800-652-9073**	651-227-9541
Missouri State Teachers Assn				
407 S Sixth St	Columbia MO	65201	**800-392-0532***	573-442-3127
*General				
MTA Today Magazine				
20 Ashburton Pl	Boston MA	02108	**800-392-6175**	617-878-8000
NCAE News Bulletin				
PO Box 27347	Raleigh NC	27611	**800-662-7924**	919-832-3000

		Toll-Free	Phone
NCTM News Bulletin			
1906 Assn Dr	Reston VA 20191	800-235-7566	703-620-9840
New Hampshire Educator Magazine			
9 S Spring St	Concord NH 03301	866-556-3264	603-224-7751
New York Teacher Magazine			
800 Troy-Schenectady Rd	Latham NY 12110	800-342-9810	518-213-6000
NSEA Voice Magazine			
605 S 14th St Ste 200	Lincoln NE 68508	800-742-0047	402-475-7611
Ohio Education Assn (OEA)			
225 E Broad St	Columbus OH 43215	800-282-1500	614-228-4526
Oklahoma Education Association			
323 E Madison PO Box 18485	Oklahoma City OK 73154	800-522-8091	405-528-7785
Oregon Education Magazine (OEA)			
6900 SW Atlanta St Bldg 1	Portland OR 97223	800-858-5505	503-684-3300
Scholastic Coach & Athletic Director Magazine			
557 Broadway	New York NY 10012	800-724-6527*	212-343-6100
*General			
Teacher Magazine			
6935 Arlington Rd Ste 100	Bethesda MD 20814	800-346-1834	301-280-3100
TSTA Advocate Magazine			
316 W 12th St	Austin TX 78701	877-275-8782	512-476-5355
Vermont NEA Today Magazine			
10 Wheelock St	Montpelier VT 05602	800-649-6375	802-223-6375
Virginia Journal of Education			
116 S Third St	Richmond VA 23219	800-552-9554	804-648-5801
West Virginia School Journal			
1558 Quarrier St	Charleston WV 25311	800-642-8261	304-346-5315
Young Children Magazine			
1313 L St NW Ste 500 PO Box 97156	Washington DC 20005	800-424-2460	202-232-8777

455-9 Entertainment & Music Magazines

		Toll-Free	Phone
American Cinematographer Magazine			
1782 N Orange Dr	Los Angeles CA 90028	800-448-0145	323-969-4333
Dance Magazine			
333 Seventh Ave 11th Fl	New York NY 10001	800-331-1750	212-979-4800
Entertainment Weekly Magazine			
225 Liberty St	New York NY 10281	800-828-6882	
Film Society of Lincoln Center			
70 Lincoln Center Plz	New York NY 10023	888-313-6085	212-875-5610
Grammy Magazine			
3030 Olympic Blvd	Santa Monica CA 90404	800-423-2017	310-392-3777
Guitar Player Magazine			
28 E 28th St 12th Fl	New York NY 10016	800-289-9839*	212-378-0400
*Cust Svc			
Hollywood Reporter			
5055 Wilshire Blvd Ste 500	Los Angeles CA 90036	866-525-2150	323-525-2000
Keyboard Magazine			
28 E 28th St 12th Fl	New York NY 10016	800-483-2433*	212-378-0400
*Cust Svc			
Multichannel News			
28 E 28th St 12th Fl	New York NY 10016	888-343-5563*	
*Cust Svc			
Pollstar			
4697 W Jacquelyn Ave	Fresno CA 93722	800-344-7383	559-271-7900
Videomaker Magazine			
1350 E Ninth St PO Box 4591	Chico CA 95927	800-284-3226	530-891-8410

455-10 Fraternal & Special Interest Magazines

		Toll-Free	Phone
AARP the Magazine			
601 E St NW	Washington DC 20049	888-687-2277	202-434-3525
AAUW Outlook Magazine			
1111 16th St NW	Washington DC 20036	800-326-2289	202-785-7700
Adoptive Families Magazine			
108 W 39th St Ste 805	New York NY 10018	800-372-3300	646-366-0830
American Spirit			
1776 D St NW	Washington DC 20006	800-449-1776	202-628-1776
Columbia Magazine			
1 Columbus Plz	New Haven CT 06510	800-380-9995	203-752-4000
Elks Magazine			
2750 N Lakeview Ave	Chicago IL 60614	800-892-8384	773-755-4700
Lion Magazine			
300 W 22nd St	Oak Brook IL 60523	800-710-7822*	630-571-5466
*Circ			
Moose Magazine			
155 S International Dr	Mooseheart IL 60539	800-544-4407	630-859-2000
Royal Neighbor Magazine			
230 16th St	Rock Island IL 61201	800-627-4762	309-788-4561
Scouting Magazine			
1325 W Walnut Hill Ln PO Box 152079	Irving TX 75015	800-323-0732	972-580-2000
United Commercial Travellers			
1801 Watermark Dr Ste 100	Columbus OH 43215	800-848-0123	614-228-3276
Woodmen Life 1700 Farnam St	Omaha NE 68102	800-225-3108	402-342-1890

455-11 General Interest Magazines

		Toll-Free	Phone
Atlantic Monthly Magazine			
600 New Hampshire Ave NW	Washington DC 20037	800-234-2411*	202-266-6000
*Cust Svc			
Black Enterprise Magazine			
130 Fifth Ave	New York NY 10011	800-727-7777*	212-242-8000
*Cust Svc			
Bridal Guide Magazine			
228 E 45th St 11th Fl	New York NY 10017	800-472-7744	212-838-7733
Christianity Today			
465 Gundersen Dr	Carol Stream IL 60188	800-222-1840*	630-260-6200
College Outlook & Career Opportunities Magazine			
20 E Gregory Blvd	Kansas City MO 64114	800-274-8867	816-361-0616

		Toll-Free	Phone
Consumer Reports Magazine			
101 Truman Ave	Yonkers NY 10703	800-333-0663*	914-378-2000
*Orders			
Cook's Illustrated Magazine			
PO Box 470739	Brookline MA 02447	800-526-8442*	617-232-1000
*Circ			
Cuisine Magazine			
2200 Grand Ave	Des Moines IA 50312	800-311-3995	
Essence Magazine			
241 37th St 4th Fl	Brooklyn NY 11232	800-274-9398	
Family Cir Magazine			
375 Lexington Ave 9th Fl	New York NY 10017	800-627-4444	
Food & Wine Magazine			
1120 Sixth Ave Ste 9	New York NY 10036	800-333-6569	813-979-6625
Franchise Handbook			
5555 N Port Washington Rd Ste 305	Milwaukee WI 53217	800-272-0246	414-882-2878
Harper's Magazine			
666 Broadway 11th Fl	New York NY 10012	800-444-4653	212-420-5720
Interview Magazine			
575 Broadway Ste 5	New York NY 10012	800-925-9574	212-941-2900
Marie Claire Magazine			
300 W 57th St 34th Fl	New York NY 10019	800-777-3287	515-282-1607
Martha Stewart Living Magazine			
601 W 26th St 9th Fl	New York NY 10001	800-999-6518	
Ms Magazine			
1600 Wilson Blvd Ste 801	Arlington VA 22209	866-672-6363	703-522-4201
New York Review of Books			
435 Hudson St 3rd Fl	New York NY 10014	800-354-0050	212-757-8070
People Magazine			
Time & Life Bldg 1271 Avenue of the Americas 28th Fl	New York NY 10020	800-541-9000	212-522-3347
Psychology Today			
115 E 23 St 9th Fl	New York NY 10010	800-931-2237	212-260-7210
Saturday Evening Post, The			
1100 Waterway Blvd	Indianapolis IN 46202	800-829-5576	317-634-1100
Smithsonian Magazine			
600 Maryland Ave Ste 6001	Washington DC 20024	800-766-2149	202-633-6090
Sun Magazine			
8815 Conroy Windermere Rd Ste 130	Orlando FL 32835	888-218-9968	407-477-2815
Utne Reader Magazine			
1503 SW 42nd St	Topeka KS 66609	800-736-8863*	612-338-5040
*Cust Svc			
Vanity Fair Magazine			
1 World Trade Ctr	New York NY 10007	800-365-0635	
Western Living Magazine (WL)			
2608 Granville St Ste 560	Vancouver BC V6H3V3	800-363-3272	604-877-7732
Wilson Quarterly Magazine			
1300 Pennsylvania Ave NW	Washington DC 20004	888-947-9018*	202-691-4122
*Orders			
Women's Wear Daily Magazine			
475 Fifth Ave 3rd Fl	New York NY 10017	866-401-7801	212-213-1900

455-12 Government & Military Magazines

		Toll-Free	Phone
Air Force Magazine			
1501 Lee Hwy	Arlington VA 22209	800-727-3337	703-247-5800
ARMY Magazine			
2425 Wilson Blvd	Arlington VA 22201	800-336-4570	703-841-4300
FRA Today 125 NW St	Alexandria VA 22314	800-372-1924	703-683-1400
Governing Magazine			
1100 Connecticut Ave NW Ste 1300	Washington DC 20036	800-940-6039	202-862-8802
Military Engineer Magazine			
607 Prince St	Alexandria VA 22314	800-336-3097*	703-549-3800
*Cust Svc			
Public Employee Magazine			
1625 L St NW	Washington DC 20036	800-792-0045	855-237-2631

455-13 Health & Fitness Magazines

		Toll-Free	Phone
American Fitness Magazine			
1750 E Northrop Blvd Ste 200	Chandler AZ 85286	800-446-2322	
Cooking Light Magazine			
2100 Lakeshore Dr	Birmingham AL 35209	800-366-4712	205-445-6000
Diabetes Forecast Magazine			
1701 N Beauregard St	Alexandria VA 22311	800-676-4065	703-549-1500
FITNESSRX FOR MEN			
60 Rt 25A Ste 1	Setauket NY 11733	800-653-1151	631-751-9696
Heart & Soul Magazine			
15480 Annapolis Rd Ste 202-225	Bowie MD 20715	800-834-8813	
Men's Health Magazine			
400 S Tenth St	Emmaus PA 18098	800-666-2303	
Muscle & Fitness Hers Magazine			
21100 Erwin St	Woodland Hills CA 91367	800-340-8954	
Prevention Magazine			
733 Third Ave	Emmaus PA 10017	800-813-8070	

455-14 Hobby & Personal Interests Magazines

		Toll-Free	Phone
Antique Trader 700 E State St	Iola WI 54990	800-258-0929	503-319-0799
AOPA Pilot Magazine			
421 Aviation Way	Frederick MD 21701	800-872-2672	301-695-2000
Arabian Horse World			
1316 Tamson Dr Ste 101	Cambria CA 93428	800-955-9423	805-771-2300
Better Homes & Gardens Wood Magazine			
1716 Locust St	Des Moines IA 50309	800-374-9663	
Bicycling Magazine			
400 S Tenth St	Emmaus PA 18098	800-666-2806	
Birds & Blooms			
5400 S 60th St	Greendale WI 53129	888-860-8040	
BirdWatching Magazine			
25 Braintree Hill Office Pk Ste 404	Braintree MA 02184	877-252-8141	

				Toll-Free	Phone
Blood-Horse Magazine					
PO Box 911088	Lexington	KY	40591	**800-866-2361**	859-278-2361
Classic Trains Magazine					
21027 Crossroads Cir PO Box 1612	Waukesha	WI	53187	**800-533-6644**	262-796-8776
COINage Magazine					
3585 Maple St Ste 232	Ventura	CA	93003	**800-764-6278**	
CRAFT Ideas					
911 S Vandemark Rd	Sidney	OH	45365	**800-253-4555**	937-498-2111
Creating Keepsakes Magazine					
14850 Pony Express Rd	Bluffdale	UT	84065	**888-247-5282**	801-816-8300
Daily Racing Form					
100 Broadway 7th Fl	New York	NY	10005	**800-306-3676***	212-366-7600
*Cust Svc					
Digital Photographer Magazine					
12121 Wilshire Blvd 12th Fl	Los Angeles	CA	90025	**800-537-4619**	310-820-1500
Equus Magazine					
656 Quince OrchaRd Rd Ste 600	Gaithersburg	MD	20878	**800-829-5910**	301-977-3900
Family Handyman Magazine					
2915 Commers Dr Ste 700	Eagan	MN	55121	**800-285-4961**	
Family Tree Magazine					
4700 E Galbraith Rd	Cincinnati	OH	45236	**855-278-0408**	
Fine Woodworking Magazine					
63 S Main St PO Box 5506	Newtown	CT	06470	**800-283-7252**	203-426-8171
Flying Magazine					
460 N Orlando Ave Ste 200	Winter Park	FL	32789	**800-678-0797***	407-628-4802
*Cust Svc					
Horse Illustrated					
4101 Tates Creek Centre Dr					
Ste 150-324	Lexington	KY	40517	**844-330-6373**	
McCall Patterns Magazine					
120 Broadway	New York	NY	10271	**800-782-0323**	
McCall's Quilting					
741 Corporate Cir Ste A	Golden	CO	80401	**800-944-0736**	303-215-5600
Nuts & Volts Magazine					
430 Princeland Ct	Corona	CA	92879	**800-783-4624***	951-371-8497
*Orders					
Outdoor Photographer Magazine					
25 Braintree Hill Office Pk Ste 404	Braintree	MA	02184	**800-283-4410***	617-706-9110
*Cust Svc					
Outside Magazine					
400 Market St	Santa Fe	NM	87501	**888-909-2382***	505-989-7100
*General					
Popular Mechanics Magazine					
300 W 57th St	New York	NY	10019	**800-333-4948**	
Practical Horseman Magazine					
656 Quince OrchaRd Rd Ste 600	Gaithersburg	MD	20878	**800-365-5548**	
QST Magazine 225 Main St	Newington	CT	06111	**888-277-5289**	860-594-0200
Quilter's Newsletter Magazine					
741 Corporate Cir Ste A	Golden	CO	80401	**800-477-6089**	303-215-5600
Quiltmaker Magazine					
741 Corporate Cir Ste A	Golden	CO	80401	**800-388-7023**	800-881-6634
Rock & Gem Magazine					
290 Maple Ct Ste 232	Ventura	CA	93003	**866-377-4666**	805-644-3824
Scale Auto Magazine					
21027 Crossroads Cir	Waukesha	WI	53186	**800-533-6644***	262-796-8776
*Cust Svc					
Smoke Magazine 26 Broadway	New York	NY	10004	**800-766-2633**	
US Chess Federation					
PO Box 3967	Crossville	TN	38557	**800-903-8723***	931-787-1234
*Sales					
Western Horseman Magazine					
2112 Montgomery St	Fort Worth	TX	76107	**800-877-5278**	817-737-6397
Wine Spectator Magazine					
825 Eighth Ave	New York	NY	10019	**800-752-7799***	212-684-4224
*Orders					
Woodshop News 10 Bokum Rd	Essex	CT	06426	**800-444-7686**	860-767-8227
Woodsmith Magazine					
2200 Grand Ave	Des Moines	IA	50312	**800-333-5075***	
*Cust Svc					

455-15 Law Magazines & Journals

				Toll-Free	Phone
Alabama Lawyer Magazine					
415 Dexter Ave	Montgomery	AL	36104	**800-354-6154**	334-269-1515
Arizona Attorney Magazine					
4201 N 24th St Ste 200	Phoenix	AZ	85016	**866-482-9227**	602-252-4804
Arkansas Lawyer Magazine					
2224 Cottondale Ln	Little Rock	AR	72202	**800-609-5668**	501-375-4606
Colorado Lawyer Magazine					
1900 Grant St 9th Fl	Denver	CO	80203	**800-332-6736**	303-860-1115
Georgia Bar Journal					
104 Marietta St NW Ste 100	Atlanta	GA	30303	**866-773-2782**	404-527-8700
Harvard Law Review					
1511 Massachusetts Ave					
Gannett House	Cambridge	MA	02138	**800-828-7571**	617-495-4650
Hawaii Bar Journal					
1100 Alakea St Ste 1000	Honolulu	HI	96813	**888-586-1056**	808-537-1868
Journal of the Kansas Bar Assn					
1200 SW Harrison St	Topeka	KS	66612	**800-928-3111**	785-234-5696
Maryland Bar Journal					
520 W Fayette St	Baltimore	MD	21201	**800-492-1964**	410-685-7878
Michigan Bar Journal					
306 Townsend St	Lansing	MI	48933	**888-726-3678**	517-346-6300
Mississippi Lawyer Magazine					
643 N State St	Jackson	MS	39202	**800-682-6423**	601-948-4471
Montana Lawyer Magazine					
7 W Sixth Ave Ste 2B	Helena	MT	59601	**877-880-1335**	
New York Law Journal					
120 Broadway 5th Fl	New York	NY	10271	**877-256-2472**	
New York State Bar News					
1 Elk St	Albany	NY	12207	**800-442-3863**	518-463-3200
Oregon State Bar Bulletin, The					
16037 SW Upper Boones Ferry Rd					
PO Box 231935	Tigard	OR	97281	**800-452-8260**	503-620-0222
Texas Bar Journal					
1414 Colorado St	Austin	TX	78701	**800-204-2222**	512-463-1463

				Toll-Free	Phone
Washington Lawyer Magazine					
1101 K St NW Ste 200	Washington	DC	20005	**877-333-2227**	202-737-4700
Washington State Bar News					
1325 Fourth Ave Ste 600	Seattle	WA	98101	**800-945-9722**	

455-16 Medical Magazines & Journals

				Toll-Free	Phone
Access Magazine					
444 N Michigan Ave Ste 3400	Chicago	IL	60611	**800-243-2342**	312-440-8900
American Diabetes Association Inc					
2451 Crystal Dr Ste 900	Arlington	VA	22202	**800-342-2383**	800-806-7801
American Journal of Psychiatry					
1000 Wilson Blvd Ste 1825	Arlington	VA	22209	**800-368-5777**	703-907-7300
Annals of Internal Medicine Magazine					
190 N Independence Mall West	Philadelphia	PA	19106	**800-523-1546**	215-351-2400
Dental Economics Magazine					
1421 S Sheridan Rd	Tulsa	OK	74112	**800-331-4463**	
Family Practice Management					
11400 Tomahawk Creek Pkwy	Leawood	KS	66211	**800-274-2237**	913-906-6000
Infection Control Today Magazine					
3300 N Central Ave Ste 300	Phoenix	AZ	85012	**800-581-1811**	480-990-1101
Internal Medicine News					
5635 Fishers Ln Ste 6000	Rockville	MD	20852	**877-524-9336**	240-221-2400
Journal of the American Dietetic Assn					
1600 John F Kennedy Blvd	Philadelphia	PA	19103	**800-654-2452**	
Journal of the American Medical Assn (JAMA)					
PO Box 10946	Chicago	IL	60654	**800-262-2350**	312-670-7827
Journal of the Louisiana State Medical Society					
6767 Perkins Rd Ste 100	Baton Rouge	LA	70808	**800-375-9508**	225-763-8500
Journal of the Medical Assn of Georgia					
1849 The Exchange Ste 200	Atlanta	GA	30339	**800-282-0224**	678-303-9290
Mayo Clinic Proceedings Magazine					
Siebens Bldg 770	Rochester	MN	55905	**800-654-2452***	507-284-2094
*Cust Svc					
Missouri Medicine Magazine					
PO Box 1028	Jefferson City	MO	65102	**800-869-6762**	573-636-5151
NASW News					
750 First St NE Ste 700	Washington	DC	20002	**800-227-3590**	202-408-8600
New England Journal of Medicine					
10 Shattuck St	Boston	MA	02115	**800-843-6356**	617-734-9800
Nursecom					
1721 Moon Lake Blvd Ste 540	Hoffman Estates	IL	60109	**800-866-0919**	
Ohio State Medical Association, The					
5115 Parkcenter Ave Ste 200	Dublin	OH	43017	**800-766-6762**	
Psychotherapy Networker					
5135 MacArthur Blvd NW	Washington	DC	20016	**888-851-9498**	
US Pharmacist Magazine					
160 Chubb Ave Ste 304	Lyndhurst	NJ	07071	**800-825-4696**	
Virginia Medical News					
2924 Emerywood Pkwy Ste 300	Richmond	VA	23294	**800-746-6768**	
West Virginia State Medical Assn					
4307 MacCorkle Ave SE	Charleston	WV	25364	**800-257-4747**	304-925-0342

455-17 Political & Current Events Magazines

				Toll-Free	Phone
American Spectator Magazine					
933 N Kenmore St Ste 405	Arlington	VA	22201	**800-524-3469**	703-807-2011
Foreign Affairs					
58 E 68th St	New York	NY	10065	**800-829-5539***	212-434-9527
*Cust Svc					
Freeman, The					
30 S Broadway	Irvington-on-Hudson	NY	10533	**800-960-4333***	914-591-7230
*Sales					
Maclean's					
1 Mount Pleasant Rd 11th Fl	Toronto	ON	M4Y2Y5	**800-268-9119**	416-764-1300
Mother Jones Magazine					
222 Sutter St Ste 600	San Francisco	CA	94108	**800-438-6656**	415-321-1700
Nation Magazine					
33 Irving Pl	New York	NY	10003	**800-333-8536***	212-209-5400
*Cust Svc					
National Journal					
600 New Hampshire Ave NW	Washington	DC	20037	**800-613-6701**	202-739-8400
New Republic, The					
1620 L St NW Ste 300C	Washington	DC	20036	**800-827-1289**	202-508-4444
Newsweek Magazine					
7 Hanover Sq	New York	NY	10004	**800-631-1040***	
*Cust Svc					
Reason Magazine					
3415 S Sepulveda Blvd Ste 400	Los Angeles	CA	90034	**888-732-7668***	310-391-2245
*Cust Svc					
US News & World Report					
1050 Thomas Jefferson St NW	Washington	DC	20007	**800-836-6397**	202-955-2000

455-18 Religious & Spiritual Magazines

				Toll-Free	Phone
B'Nai B'Rith Magazine					
2020 K St NW 7th Fl	Washington	DC	20006	**888-388-4224**	202-857-6600
Biblical Archaeology Review					
4710 41st St NW	Washington	DC	20016	**800-221-4644**	202-364-3300
Catholic Digest					
PO Box 6015	New London	CT	06320	**800-678-2836**	
Charisma Magazine					
600 Rinehart Rd	Lake Mary	FL	32746	**800-749-6500**	407-333-0600
Christianity Today Magazine					
465 Gundersen Dr	Carol Stream	IL	60188	**800-999-1704**	630-260-6200
Episcopal Life Magazine					
815 Second Ave Episcopal Church Ctr	New York	NY	10017	**800-334-7626**	212-716-6000
Lutheran Magazine					
8765 W Higgins Rd	Chicago	IL	60631	**800-638-3522**	
Moment Magazine					
4115 Wisconsin Ave NW Ste 10	Washington	DC	20016	**800-777-1005**	202-363-6422

Classified Section

				Toll-Free	Phone
Presbyterians Today Magazine					
100 Witherspoon St	Louisville	KY	40202	800-728-7228	800-872-3283
Today's Christian Woman Magazine					
465 Gundersen Dr	Carol Stream	IL	60188	877-247-4787*	630-260-6200
*Orders					
US Catholic Magazine					
205 W Monroe	Chicago	IL	60606	800-328-6515*	312-236-7782
*Cust Svc					

455-19 Science & Nature Magazines

				Toll-Free	Phone
American Scientist Magazine					
3106 E NC Hwy 54					
PO Box 13975	Research Triangle Park	NC	27709	800-243-6534	919-549-4691
Archaeology Magazine					
36-36 33rd St	Long Island	NY	11106	877-275-9782	718-472-3050
Audubon Magazine					
225 Varick St 7th Fl	New York	NY	10014	800-274-4201*	212-979-3000
*Cust Svc					
Aviation Week & Space Technology Magazine					
1200 G St NW	Washington	DC	20005	800-525-5003	
Friends of the Earth Magazine					
1100 15th St NW	Washington	DC	20005	877-843-8687	202-783-7400
National Parks Magazine					
777 Sixth St NW Ste 700	Washington	DC	20001	800-628-7275*	202-223-6722
*General					
Nature					
529 14th St NW					
968 National Press Bldg	Washington	DC	20045	800-524-0384	202-737-2355
Orion Magazine					
187 Main St	Great Barrington	MA	01230	888-909-6568	413-528-4422
Science Magazine					
1200 New York Ave NW	Washington	DC	20005	866-434-2227	202-326-6500
Science News					
1719 North St NW	Washington	DC	20036	800-552-4412*	202-785-2255
*Cust Svc					
Scientist, The					
478 Bay St Ste A213	Midland	ON	L4R1K9	888-781-0328	705-528-6888
Sierra Magazine					
85 Second St 2nd Fl	San Francisco	CA	94105	866-338-1015	415-977-5500
Sky & Telescope Magazine					
90 Sherman St	Cambridge	MA	02140	800-253-0245	617-864-7360
Smithsonian Air & Space Magazine					
PO Box 37012	Washington	DC	20013	800-766-2149*	202-633-6070
*Cust Svc					

455-20 Sports Magazines

				Toll-Free	Phone
American Rifleman Magazine					
11250 Waples Mill Rd	Fairfax	VA	22030	800-672-3888	
Baseball America Magazine					
4319 S Alston Ave Ste 103	Durham	NC	27713	800-845-2726	
Bassmaster					
3500 Blue Lake Dr Ste 330	Birmingham	FL	35243	877-227-7872	
Climbing Magazine					
5720 Flatiron Pkwy	Boulder	CO	80301	800-829-5895	303-253-6412
Competitor Magazine					
9477 Waples St Ste 150	San Diego	CA	92121	800-311-1255	
Ducks Unlimited Magazine					
1 Waterfowl Way	Memphis	TN	38120	800-453-8257	901-758-3825
Salt Water Sportsman Magazine					
460 N Orlando Ave Ste 200	Winter Park	FL	32789	800-759-2127	407-628-4802
Snow Goer Magazine					
10405 Sixth Ave N Ste 210	Plymouth	MN	55441	800-710-5249	763-383-4400
Sport Fishing Magazine					
460 N Orlando Ave Ste 200	Winter Park	FL	32789	800-879-0496	
Sports Afield Magazine					
15621 Chemical Ln	Huntington Beach	CA	92649	800-451-4788	714-373-4910
Sports Business Daily					
120 W Morehead St Ste 310	Charlotte	NC	28202	800-829-9839	704-973-1410
Sports Spectrum Magazine					
640 Plaza Dr Ste 110	Highlands Ranch	CO	80129	866-821-2971	704-821-2971
Travel + Leisure Magazine					
225 Liberty St	New York	NY	10281	800-888-8728	

455-21 Trade & Industry Magazines

				Toll-Free	Phone
AAPG Explorer Magazine					
1444 S Boulder Ave	Tulsa	OK	74119	800-364-2274	918-584-2555
Aerospace America Magazine					
1801 Alexander Bell Dr Ste 500	Reston	VA	20191	800-639-2422	703-264-7500
Air Conditioning Heating & Refrigeration News					
2401 W Big Beaver Rd Ste 700	Troy	MI	48084	800-837-8337	248-362-3700
American Society of Civil Engineers (ASCE)					
1801 Alexander Bell Dr	Reston	VA	20191	800-548-2723	703-295-6300
Automotive News Magazine					
1155 Gratiot Ave	Detroit	MI	48207	877-812-1584	313-446-0450
Builder Magazine					
1 Thomas Cir NW Ste 600	Washington	DC	20005	800-325-6180	202-452-0800
Chemical Processing Magazine					
1501 E Woodfield Rd Ste 400N	Schaumburg	IL	60173	800-343-4048	630-467-1300
Chemical Week					
140 E 45th St					
2 Grand Central Tower 40th Fl	New York	NY	10017	866-501-7540*	212-884-9528
*Cust Svc					
Civil Engineering Magazine					
1801 Alexander Bell Dr	Reston	VA	20191	800-548-2723	703-295-6300
DaySpa Magazine					
7628 Densmore Ave	Van Nuys	CA	91406	800-442-5667	818-782-7328
Design News 225 Wyman St	Waltham	MA	02451	800-869-6882	763-746-2792
Engineering News-Record (ENR)					
350 fifth Ave Ste 6000	New York	NY	10118	877-876-8208	646-849-7100

				Toll-Free	Phone
EPRI Journal					
3420 Hillview Ave	Palo Alto	CA	94304	800-313-3774	650-855-2121
Fine Homebuilding Magazine					
63 S Main St PO Box 5506	Newtown	CT	06470	800-309-8955*	203-426-8171
*Edit					
Institute of Scrap Recycling Industries Magazine					
1250 H St NW Ste 400	Washington	DC	20005	800-767-7236	202-662-8500
Journal of Petroleum Technology					
222 Palisades Creek Dr	Richardson	TX	75080	800-456-6863	972-952-9393
Journal of Protective Coatings & Linings					
2100 Wharton St Ste 310	Pittsburgh	PA	15203	800-837-8303	412-431-8300
Land Line Magazine					
1 NW Oodia Dr PO Box 1000	Grain Valley	MO	64029	800-444-5791	816-229-5791
Modern Machine Shop Magazine					
6915 Valley Ave	Cincinnati	OH	45244	800-950-8020	513-527-8800
Nailpro Magazine					
7628 Densmore Ave	Van Nuys	CA	91406	800-442-5667	818-782-7328
National Fisherman Magazine					
121 Free St	Portland	ME	04101	800-959-5073	207-842-5608
National Fitness Trade Journal					
PO Box 2490	White City	OR	97503	877-867-7835	541-830-0400
Oil & Gas Journal					
1455 W Loop S	Houston	TX	77027	800-633-1656	918-831-9423
Proceedings of the IEEE Magazine					
445 Hoes Ln	Piscataway	NJ	08855	800-678-4333	732-562-5478
Product Design & Development Magazine					
199 E Badger Rd Ste 201	Madison	WI	53713	800-869-6882	973-920-7000
Quality Progress					
ASQ					
600 N Plankinton Ave PO Box 3005	Milwaukee	WI	53201	800-248-1946*	414-272-8575
*Cust Svc					
Travel Weekly Crossroads Magazine					
100 Lighting Way	Secaucus	NJ	07094	800-635-1666	201-902-2000
Von Rabenau Media Corp					
332 S Michigan Ave 9th fl	Chicago	IL	60654	800-229-1967	312-849-2220
Women's Wear Daily Magazine					
475 Fifth Ave 3rd Fl	New York	NY	10017	866-401-7801	212-213-1900
Writer's Digest					
4700 E Galbraith Rd	Cincinnati	OH	45236	800-283-0963*	513-531-2690
*Cust Svc					

455-22 Travel & Regional Interest Magazines

				Toll-Free	Phone
Alaska Magazine					
301 Arctic Slope Ave Ste 300	Anchorage	AK	99518	800-288-5892	386-246-0444
Arizona Highways Magazine					
2039 W Lewis Ave	Phoenix	AZ	85009	800-543-5432	
Atlanta Magazine					
260 Peachtree St Ste 300	Atlanta	GA	30303	800-930-3019	404-527-5500
Baltimore Magazine					
1000 Lancaster St Ste 400	Baltimore	MD	21202	800-935-0838*	443-873-3900
*Cust Svc					
Buffalo Spree Magazine					
100 Corporate Pkwy Ste 220	Buffalo	NY	14226	855-697-7733	716-783-9119
Cape Cod Life Magazine					
13 Steeple St Ste 204 PO Box 1439	Mashpee	MA	02649	800-698-1717	508-419-7381
Chesapeake Bay Magazine					
601 Sixth St Ste 180	Annapolis	MD	21403	877-804-8624	410-263-2662
Chicago Magazine					
435 N Michigan Ave Ste 1100	Chicago	IL	60611	800-999-0879	312-222-8999
Cleveland Magazine					
1422 Euclid Ave Ste 730	Cleveland	OH	44115	800-210-7293	216-771-2833
Connecticut Magazine					
100 Gando Dr	New Haven	CT	06513	877-396-8937	203-789-5300
Down East					
680 Commercial St	Rockport	ME	04856	800-766-1670	207-594-9544
Family Motor Coaching Magazine					
8291 Clough Pk	Cincinnati	OH	45244	800-543-3622	513-474-3622
Honolulu Magazine					
1000 Bishop St Ste 405	Honolulu	HI	96813	800-788-4230	808-534-7546
Houston LifeStyle Magazine					
10707 Corporate Dr Ste 170	Stafford	TX	77477	866-505-4456	281-240-2445
Indianapolis Monthly Magazine					
40 Monument Cir Ste 100	Indianapolis	IN	46204	888-403-9005*	317-237-9288
*Circ					
Jacksonville Magazine					
1261 King St	Jacksonville	FL	32204	800-962-0214	904-389-3622
Los Angeles Magazine					
5900 Wilshire Blvd 10th Fl	Los Angeles	CA	90036	800-876-5222*	323-801-0100
*Cust Svc					
Louisville Magazine					
137 W Muhammad Ali Blvd Ste 101	Louisville	KY	40202	866-832-0011	502-625-0100
Michigan United Conservation Clubs					
2101 Wood St	Lansing	MI	48912	800-777-6720	517-371-1041
Milwaukee Magazine					
126 N Jefferson St	Milwaukee	WI	53202	800-662-4818	414-273-1101
Minneapolis-Saint Paul Magazine					
220 S Sixth St Ste 500	Minneapolis	MN	55402	800-999-5589	612-339-7571
MotorHome Magazine					
2750 Park View Ct Ste 240	Oxnard	CA	93036	800-678-1201*	805-667-4100
*Cust Svc					
National Geographic Traveler Magazine					
1145 17th St NW	Washington	DC	20036	800-647-5463	202-857-7000
Nevada Magazine					
401 N Carson St	Carson City	NV	89701	855-729-7117	775-687-5416
New Jersey Monthly Magazine					
55 Pk Pl PO Box 920	Morristown	NJ	07963	888-419-0419	973-539-8230
New Mexico Magazine					
PO Box 12002	Santa Fe	NM	87504	800-898-6639	
New Orleans Magazine					
110 Veterans Blvd Ste 123	Metairie	LA	70005	877-221-3512*	504-828-1380
*Edit					
New York Magazine					
75 Varick St	New York	NY	10013	800-678-0900	212-508-0700
Ohio Magazine					
1422 Euclid Ave Ste 730	Cleveland	OH	44115	800-210-7293	216-771-2833

				Toll-Free	Phone
Orange Coast Magazine					
3701 Birch St Ste 100	Newport Beach	CA	92660	**800-397-8179**	949-862-1133
Oregon Coast Magazine					
88906 Hwy 101 N Ste 2	Florence	OR	97439	**800-348-8401**	541-997-8401
Palm Beach Illustrated Magazine					
1000 N Dixie Hwy Ste C	West Palm Beach	FL	33401	**800-308-7346**	561-659-6160
Palm Springs Life Magazine					
303 N Indian Canyon	Palm Springs	CA	92262	**800-775-7256**	760-325-2333
Phoenix Magazine					
15169 N Scottsdale Ste 310	Scottsdale	AZ	85254	**866-481-6970**	480-664-3960
San Francisco Magazine					
243 Vallejo St	San Francisco	CA	94111	**866-736-2499**	404-443-1180
Southern Living Magazine					
2100 Lakeshore Dr	Birmingham	AL	35209	**877-262-5866**	205-445-6000
Southern Living Magazine					
2100 Lakeshore Dr	Birmingham	AL	35209	**800-366-4712**	866-772-7083
Travel Agent Magazine					
757 Third Ave	New York	NY	10017	**855-424-6247**	212-895-8200
Travelhost Magazine					
10701 N Stemmons Fwy	Dallas	TX	75220	**800-527-1782**	972-556-0541
Western Outdoors Magazine					
185 Avenida La Pata	San Clemente	CA	92673	**800-290-2929**	949-366-0030
Where Chicago Magazine					
1165 N Clark St Ste 302	Chicago	IL	60610	**800-680-4035**	312-642-1896
Yankee Magazine					
1121 Main St PO Box 520	Dublin	NH	03444	**800-288-4284**	603-563-8111

456　MAGNETS - PERMANENT

				Toll-Free	Phone
Electron Energy Corp					
924 Links Ave	Landisville	PA	17538	**800-824-2735**	717-898-2294
Eneflux Armtek Magnetics Inc					
700 Hicksville Rd Ste 110	Bethpage	NY	11714	**877-363-3589**	516-576-3434
Flexmag Industries Inc					
107 Industry Rd	Marietta	OH	45750	**800-543-4426**	740-374-8024
Magnetic Component Engineering Inc					
2830 Lomita Blvd	Torrance	CA	90505	**800-989-5656**	310-784-3100
Magnum Magnetics Corp					
801 Masonic Pk Rd	Marietta	OH	45750	**800-258-0991**	740-373-7770
Mohr Corp PO Box 1600	Brighton	MI	48114	**800-223-6647**	010 225-9494

457　MAIL ORDER HOUSES

SEE ALSO Seed Companies ; Checks - Personal & Business ; Computer Stores ; Book, Music, Video Clubs ; Art Supply Stores

				Toll-Free	Phone
2 Checkoutcom Inc					
1785 O'Brien Rd	Columbus	OH	43228	**877-294-0273**	614-921-2450
Advanced Image Direct					
1415 S Acacia Ave	Fullerton	CA	92831	**800-540-3848**	714-502-3900
Aeromedixcom LLC					
Po Box 14730	Jackson	WY	83002	**888-362-7123**	307-732-2642
Avanzado LLC					
25330 Interchange Ct	Farmington Hills	MI	48335	**800-913-1058**	
Backcountrycom					
2607 S 3200 W Ste A	West Valley City	UT	84119	**800-409-4502***	
*Orders					
Blueport Commerce					
500 Harrison Ave Ste 3R	Boston	MA	02118	**855-277-0614**	
Brokers Worldwide					
701C Ashland Ave	Folcroft	PA	19032	**800-624-5287**	610-461-3661
Budco Inc PO Box 3065	Tulsa	OK	74101	**800-747-7307**	
Certif-a-gift Company the					
1625 E Algonquin Rd	Arlington Heights	IL	60005	**800-545-5156**	
Chadwick's of Boston					
75 Aircraft Rd	Southington	CT	06489	**877-330-3393**	
Cinmar LLC					
5566 W Chester Rd	West Chester	OH	45069	**888-263-9850**	
Crutchfield Corp					
1 Crutchfield Pk	Charlottesville	VA	22911	**888-955-6000***	434-817-1000
*Sales					
Current USA Inc					
1005 E Woodmen Rd	Colorado Springs	CO	80920	**800-848-2848***	
*Cust Svc					
Design Toscano Inc					
1400 Morse Ave	Elk Grove Village	IL	60007	**800-525-5141**	
Digi-Key Corp					
701 Brooks Ave S	Thief River Falls	MN	56701	**800-344-4539**	218-681-6674
E-filliate Inc					
11321 White Rock Rd	Rancho Cordova	CA	95742	**800-592-7031**	916-858-1000
EVINE Live Inc					
6740 Shady Oak Rd	Eden Prairie	MN	55344	**800-676-5523**	
Fingerhut					
6250 Ridgewood Dr	St. Cloud	MN	56303	**800-208-2500**	
Forestry Suppliers Inc					
205 W Rankin St	Jackson	MS	39201	**800-752-8460***	601-354-3565
*Cust Svc					
Gaiam Inc					
833 W S Boulder Rd Bldg G	Louisville	CO	80027	**877-989-6321**	303-222-3600
NASDAQ: GAIA					
Hammacher Schlemmer & Co					
9307 N Milwaukee Ave	Niles	IL	60714	**800-321-1484**	
Hanna Andersson Corp					
1010 NW Flanders St	Portland	OR	97209	**800-222-0544***	
*Cust Svc					
Harry & David Holdings Inc					
2500 S Pacific Hwy	Medford	OR	97501	**877-322-1200***	
*Cust Svc					
Hello Direct Inc 77 NE Blvd	Nashua	NH	03062	**800-435-5634**	
J Crew Group Inc					
770 Broadway	New York	NY	10003	**800-562-0258**	212-209-2500
Jackson & Perkins					
2 Floral Ave	Hodges	SC	29653	**800-292-4769***	
*Cust Svc					

				Toll-Free	Phone
JC Whitney					
761 Progress Pkwy	La Salle	IL	61301	**866-529-5530**	312-431-6098
JDR Microdevices Inc					
229 Polaris Ave Ste 17	Mountain View	CA	94043	**800-538-5000**	650-625-1400
Lands' End Inc					
1 Lands' End Ln	Dodgeville	WI	53595	**800-963-4816***	
*Orders					
Levenger					
420 S Congress Ave	Delray Beach	FL	33445	**800-544-0880***	561-276-2436
*Cust Svc					
LL Bean Inc 15 Casco St	Freeport	ME	04033	**800-341-4341**	207-552-3080
Mary Maxim Inc					
2001 Holland Ave PO Box 5019	Port Huron	MI	48061	**800-962-9504**	810-987-2000
Miles Kimball Co					
250 City Ctr Bldg	Oshkosh	WI	54906	**855-202-7394***	
*Cust Svc					
Mystic Stamp Co 9700 Mill St	Camden	NY	13316	**866-660-7147**	315-245-2690
NASCO International Inc					
901 Janesville Ave	Fort Atkinson	WI	53538	**800-558-9595***	920-563-2446
*Orders					
National Wholesale Company Inc					
400 National Blvd	Lexington	NC	27294	**800-480-4673**	
Norm Thompson Outfitters Inc					
3188 NW Aloclek Dr	Hillsboro	OR	97124	**800-547-1160**	877-718-7899
Now Courier Inc					
PO Box 6066	Indianapolis	IN	46206	**800-543-6066**	
NRC Sports Inc					
206 Worcester Rd Ste 36-38	Princeton	MA	01541	**800-243-5033**	978-464-2433
Oriental Trading Company Inc					
5455 S 90th St	Omaha	NE	68127	**800-875-8480**	402-596-1200
Patagonia					
259 W Santa Clara St	Ventura	CA	93001	**800-638-6464***	805-643-8616
*Cust Svc					
Roaman's 2300 SE Ave	Indianapolis	IN	46201	**800-840-6214**	317-266-3300
RSVP Direct Inc					
550 Northgate Pkwy	Wheeling	IL	60090	**866-507-5182**	847-215-9054
S & S Worldwide Inc					
75 Mill St	Colchester	CT	06415	**800-243-9232***	860-537-3451
*Orders					
Southern Fulfillment Services LLC					
1650 90th Ave	Vero Beach	FL	32966	**800-891-2120**	772-226-3500
StubHub					
199 Fremont St 4th Fl.	San Francisco	CA	94105	**866-788-2482**	
Sunnyland Farms Inc					
PO Box 8200	Albany	GA	31706	**800-999-2488**	
Tech4Learning Inc					
10981 San Diego Mission Rd Ste 120	San Diego	CA	92108	**877-834-5453**	619-563-5348
Tog Shop Inc 30 Tozer Rd	Beverly	MA	01915	**800-767-6666**	
TravelSmith Outfitters					
75 Aircraft RD	Southington	CT	06489	**800-770-3387**	
Unicover Corp					
1 Unicover Ctr	Cheyenne	WY	82008	**800-443-4225***	307-771-3000
*Cust Svc					
Unistar-Sparco Computers Inc					
7089 Ryburn Dr	Millington	TN	38053	**800-840-8400**	901-872-2272
Van Dyke Supply Co					
39771 Sd Hwy 34	Woonsocket	SD	57385	**800-279-7985**	704-279-7985
Victorian Trading Co					
15600 W 99th St	Lenexa	KS	66219	**800-700-2035***	913-438-3995
*Cust Svc					
Wild Wings LLC					
2101 S Hwy 61	Lake City	MN	55041	**800-445-4833**	
Williams-Sonoma Inc					
3250 Van Ness Ave	San Francisco	CA	94109	**800-838-2589**	415-421-7900
NYSE: WSM					
Wintersilks LLC PO Box 196	Jessup	PA	18434	**800-648-7455**	800-718-3687
Women's International Pharmacy Inc					
PO Box 6468	Madison	WI	53716	**800-279-5708**	
Woodcraft Supply LLC					
1177 Rosemar Rd	Parkersburg	WV	26105	**800-535-4482**	
Zapposcom					
400 E Stewart Ave	Las Vegas	NV	89101	**800-927-7671**	

458　MALLS - SHOPPING

				Toll-Free	Phone
Antique Mall					
1251 S Virginia St	Reno	NV	89502	**888-316-6255**	775-324-4141
Arizona Mills					
5000 Arizona Mills Cir	Tempe	AZ	85282	**877-746-6642**	317-636-1600
Boulder Arts & Crafts					
1421 Pearl St Mall	Boulder	CO	80302	**866-656-2667**	303-443-3683
Bronx Council on the Arts					
1738 Hone Ave	Bronx	NY	10461	**866-564-5226**	718-931-9500
Burlington Mall					
75 Middlesex Tpke	Burlington	MA	01803	**877-746-6642**	781-272-8667
Complexe Les Ailes					
705 rue Sainte-Catherine Ouest	Montreal	QC	H3B4G5	**800-998-6844**	514-288-3708
Copley Place					
100 Huntington Ave Ste 100	Boston	MA	02116	**877-746-6642**	617-262-6600
Del Amo Fashion Ctr					
3525 Carson St	Torrance	CA	90503	**877-746-6642**	310-542-8525
Fairlane Town Ctr					
18900 Michigan Ave	Dearborn	MI	48126	**800-992-9500**	
Fashion Island Shopping Ctr					
401 Newport Ctr Dr	Newport Beach	CA	92660	**855-658-8527**	949-721-2000
Festival Flea Market Mall					
2900 W Sample Rd	Pompano Beach	FL	33073	**800-353-2627**	954-979-4555
Franklin Mills					
1455 Franklin Mills Cir	Philadelphia	PA	19154	**877-746-6642***	317-636-1600
*General					
Gardner Village					
1100 W 7800 S	West Jordan	UT	84088	**800-662-4335**	801-566-8903
Genesee Valley Ctr					
3341 S Linden Rd	Flint	MI	48507	**866-236-1128**	810-732-4000
Great Lakes Mall					
7850 Mentor Ave	Mentor	OH	44060	**877-746-6642**	317-636-1600

				Toll-Free	Phone
Greenwood Park Mall					
1251 US Hwy 31 N	Greenwood	IN	46142	877-746-6642	317-881-6758
Haywood Mall					
700 Haywood Rd	Greenville	SC	29607	800-331-5479	864-288-0511
Ingram Park Mall					
6301 NW Loop 410	San Antonio	TX	78238	877-746-6642	210-684-9570
King of Prussia Mall					
160 N Gulph Rd	King of Prussia	PA	19406	877-746-6642	610-265-5727
Lenox Square Mall					
3393 Peachtree Rd NE	Atlanta	GA	30326	800-266-2278	404-233-6767
Liberty Tree Mall					
100 Independence Way	Danvers	MA	01923	877-746-6642	978-777-0794
Mill Creek Mall					
654 Millcreek Mall	Erie	PA	16565	800-615-3535	814-868-9000
North East Mall					
1101 Melbourne St Ste 1000	Hurst	TX	76053	877-746-6642	817-284-3427
North Star Mall					
7400 San Pedro Ave	San Antonio	TX	78216	800-866-6511	210-340-6627
Orland Square					
288 Orland Sq	Orland Park	IL	60462	877-746-6642	708-349-1646
Outlets at Anthem					
4250 W Anthem Way	Phoenix	AZ	85086	888-482-5834	623-465-9500
Oxford Valley Mall					
225 W Washington St	Indianapolis	IN	46204	800-461-3439	317-636-1600
Potomac Mills					
2700 Potomac Mills Cir	Woodbridge	VA	22192	877-746-6642	317-636-1600
Puente Hills Mall					
1600 Azusa Ave	City of Industry	CA	91748	800-743-3463	626-912-8777
River Oaks Ctr					
96 River Oaks Ctr Dr	Calumet City	IL	60409	877-746-6642	317-636-1600
Rolling Oaks Mall					
6909 N Loop 1604 E	San Antonio	TX	78247	877-746-6642	317-636-1600
Roosevelt Field Mall					
630 Old Country Rd	Garden City	NY	11530	877-746-6642	516-742-8001
Security Square Mall					
6901 Security Blvd	Baltimore	MD	21244	800-977-2769	410-265-6000
Shop at North Bridge, The					
520 N Michigan Ave	Chicago	IL	60611	800-977-6255	312-327-2300
Shoppes at Bel Air, The					
3299 Bel Air Mall	Mobile	AL	36606	800-275-8777	251-478-1893
Shops at Woodlake					
725 Woodlake Rd	Kohler	WI	53044	855-444-2838	920-459-1713
Solomon Pond Mall					
601 Donald Lynch Blvd	Marlborough	MA	01752	877-746-6642	508-303-6255
South Coast Plaza					
3333 Bristol St	Costa Mesa	CA	92626	800-782-8888	
South Shore Plaza					
250 Granite St	Braintree	MA	02184	877-746-6642	781-843-8200
Southdale Ctr					
10 Southdale Ctr	Edina	MN	55435	877-746-6642	952-925-7874
Southern Park Mall					
7401 Market St	Youngstown	OH	44512	877-746-6642	317-636-1600
SouthPark Mall					
4400 Sharon Rd	Charlotte	NC	28211	888-726-5930	704-364-4411
Spring Hill Mall					
1072 Spring Hill Mall	West Dundee	IL	60118	800-718-8788	847-428-2200
Square One Mall					
1201 Broadway	Saugus	MA	01906	877-746-6642	781-233-8787
Stanford Shopping Ctr					
660 Stanford Shopping Ctr	Palo Alto	CA	94304	800-284-8273	650-617-8200
Stoneridge Shopping Ctr					
1 Stoneridge Mall	Pleasanton	CA	94588	877-746-6642	317-636-1600
Tacoma Mall 4502 S Steele St	Tacoma	WA	98409	877-746-6642	253-475-4566
Tanger Outlet Ctr San Marcos					
4015 S IH-35 Ste 319	San Marcos	TX	78666	800-408-8424	512-396-7446
Tri-County Mall					
11700 Princeton Pk	Cincinnati	OH	45246	866-905-4675	513-671-0120
University Park Mall					
6501 N Grape Rd	Mishawaka	IN	46545	877-746-6642	574-277-2223
Vaughan Mills					
1 Bass Pro Mills Dr	Vaughan	ON	L4K5W4	800-998-6844	905-879-2110
Viejas Outlet Ctr					
5005 Willows	Alpine	CA	91901	877-303-2695	619-659-2070
Walden Galleria					
1 Walden Galleria	Buffalo	NY	14225	800-297-5009	716-681-7600
Washington Square Mall					
10202 E Washington St	Indianapolis	IN	46229	800-283-9490	317-636-1600
Westchester, The					
125 Westchester Ave	White Plains	NY	10601	877-746-6642	914-421-1333
Westfield Shoppingtown Annapolis					
2002 Annapolis Mall	Annapolis	MD	21401	800-805-2339	410-266-5432

459   MALTING PRODUCTS

SEE ALSO Breweries

				Toll-Free	Phone
Briess Malting Co					
625 S Irish Rd	Chilton	WI	53014	800-657-0806	920-849-7711
Premier Malt Products Inc					
88 Market St	Saddle Brook	NJ	07663	800-521-1057*	586-443-3355
*Cust Svc					

460   MANAGED CARE - BEHAVIORAL HEALTH

				Toll-Free	Phone
American Behavioral Benefits Managers					
2204 Lakeshore Dr Ste 135	Birmingham	AL	35209	800-925-5327	205-871-7814
Associated Behavioral Health					
4700 42nd Ave SW Ste 470	Seattle	WA	98116	800-858-6702	206-935-1282
CIGNA Behavioral Health Inc					
11095 Viking Dr Ste 350	Eden Prairie	MN	55344	800-753-0540	800-433-5768
ComPsych Corp					
455 N City Front Plaza Dr 13th Fl	Chicago	IL	60611	800-851-1714	312-595-4000
COPE Inc					
1120 G St NW Ste 550	Washington	DC	20005	800-247-3054	202-628-5100

				Toll-Free	Phone
CorpCare Associates Inc					
7000 Peachtree Dunwoody Rd					
Bldg 4 Ste 300	Atlanta	GA	30328	800-728-9444	770-200-8085
EAP Systems					
500 W Cummings Pk	Woburn	MA	01801	800-535-4841	781-935-8850
FEI Behavioral Health					
648 N Plankinton Ave Ste 425	Milwaukee	WI	53203	800-987-4368	
Frontier Health PO Box 9054	Gray	TN	37615	877-928-9062	423-467-3600
Gilsbar					
2100 Covington Ctr	Covington	LA	70433	800-445-7227	985-892-3520
Holman Group					
9451 Corbin Ave	Northridge	CA	91324	800-321-2843	818-704-1444
Interface EAP Inc (IEAP)					
10370 Richmond Ave Ste 1100					
PO Box 421879	Houston	TX	77042	800-324-4327	713-781-3364
Magellan Health Services Inc					
55 Nod Rd	Avon	CT	06001	800-424-4399	860-237-4161
NASDAQ: MGLN					
Managed Health Network Inc					
1600 Los Gamos Dr Ste 300	San Rafael	CA	94903	800-327-2133	
MENTOR Network, The					
313 Congress St 5th Fl	Boston	MA	02210	800-388-5150	617-790-4800
MHNet Behavioral Health					
9606 N MoPac Exwy Ste 600	Austin	TX	78759	888-646-6889	
Mohawk Shared Services					
5295 John Lucas Dr Unit 5	Burlington	ON	L7L6A8	888-521-8300	289-337-5000
National Employee Assistance Services Inc					
N 17 W 24100 Riverwood Dr Ste 300	Waukesha	WI	53188	800-634-6433	262-574-2500
New Directions Behavioral Health LLC					
PO Box 6729	Leawood	KS	66206	800-624-5544	
Perspectives Ltd					
20 N Clark St Ste 2650	Chicago	IL	60602	800-866-7556	
Preferred Mental Health Management Inc					
7309 E 21st St N Ste 110	Wichita	KS	67206	800-819-9571	316-262-0444
United Behavioral Health Inc					
425 Market St 27th Fl	San Francisco	CA	94105	800-888-2998	415-547-5000

461   MANAGEMENT SERVICES

SEE ALSO Investment Advice & Management ; Hotels & Hotel Companies ; Educational Institution Operators & Managers ; Association Management Companies ; Incentive Program Management Services ; Pharmacy Benefits Management Services ; Facilities Management Services

				Toll-Free	Phone
2 Places At 1 Time Inc					
1000 NW 57th Crt Ste 590	Miami	FL	33126	877-275-2237	
360 Technologies Inc					
15401 Debba Dr	Austin	TX	78734	888-883-0360	512-266-7360
ABELSoft Inc					
3310 S Service Rd	Burlington	ON	L7M4K8	800-267-2235	905-333-3200
Acc Technical Services Inc					
106 Dwight Park Cir	Syracuse	NY	13209	855-484-4500	315-484-4500
Accent Computer Solutions Inc					
8438 Red Oak St	Rancho Cucamonga	CA	91730	800-481-4369	909-204-4801
Accompass 1052 Yonge St	Toronto	ON	M4W2L1	866-969-8588	416-969-8588
Ace Product Management Group Inc					
12801 W Silver Spring Rd	Butler	WI	53007	800-294-9007	262-754-8490
Acoustic Sounds Inc					
1500 S Ninth St	Salina	KS	67401	888-926-2564	785-825-8609
Acranet 521 W Maxwell Ave	Spokane	WA	99201	800-304-1249	
Act2 Retirement Consulting LLC					
100 Painters Mill Rd	Owings Mills	MD	21117	866-992-9256	443-379-0375
Advantech Manufacturing Inc					
2450 S Commerce Dr	New Berlin	WI	53151	800-511-2096	262-786-1600
AIB International Inc					
1213 Bakers Way PO Box 3999	Manhattan	KS	66505	800-633-5137	785-537-4750
Aks Infotech					
2088 US 130 N Ste 203	Monmouth Junction	NJ	08852	800-771-7000	609-301-4607
Alaris Group Inc					
4108 N 79th Ave W	Duluth	MN	55810	888-425-2747	
Alcazar Networks Inc					
419 State Ave Ste 3	Emmaus	PA	18049	800-349-6192	484-664-2800
AllMed Healthcare Management Inc					
111 SW Fifth Ave Ste 1400	Portland	OR	97204	800-400-9916	
Amarillo Economic Development Corp					
801 S Fillmore Ste 205	Amarillo	TX	79101	800-333-7892	806-379-6411
American Dental Partners Inc					
401 Edgewater Pl Ste 430	Wakefield	MA	01880	800-838-6563	781-213-6500
American Utility Management Inc					
2211 S York Rd Ste 320	Oak Brook	IL	60523	866-520-1245	
AMFM Inc					
240 Capitol St Ste 500	Charleston	WV	25301	800-348-1623	304-344-1623
Archway Marketing Services Inc					
19850 S Diamond Lake Rd	Rogers	MN	55374	866-779-9855	763-428-3300
Arcweb Technologies LLC					
234 Market St 5th Fl	Philadelphia	PA	19106	800-846-7980	
Aurora Systems Consulting Inc					
2510 W 237th St Ste 202	Torrance	CA	90505	888-282-0696	
Authenticity Consulting Inc					
4008 Lake Dr Ave N	Minneapolis	MN	55422	800-971-2250	763-971-8890
Author Services Inc					
7051 Hollywood Blvd	Hollywood	CA	90028	800-624-6504	323-466-3310
Auto Profit Masters					
250 E Dry Creek Rd	Littleton	CO	80122	866-826-7911	303-795-5838
Avatar Management Services Inc					
8157 Bavaria Dr E	Macedonia	OH	44056	800-728-2827	330-963-3900
B3 Solutions LLC					
901 North Pitt St Ste 300	Alexandria	VA	22314	877-872-9839	571-384-1400
Baker Foodservice Design Inc					
2220 E Paris Ave SE	Grand Rapids	MI	49546	800-968-4011	616-942-4011
Baker Krizner Financial Planning					
2230 N Limestone St	Springfield	OH	45503	888-390-8753	937-390-8750
Bankruptcy Management Solutions Inc					
5 Peters Canyon Rd Ste 200	Irvine	CA	92606	800-634-7734	
Banyan Water Inc					
11002-B Metric Blvd	Austin	TX	78758	800-276-1507	

	Toll-Free	Phone

BCN Services Inc
3650 W Liberty Rd ....Ann Arbor MI 48103 — **800-891-9911** — 734-994-4100

Benefact Consulting Group
6285 Northam Dr Ste 200..................Mississauga ON L4V1X5 — **855-829-2225**

Benefit Advantage Inc
3431 Commodity Ln ....Green Bay WI 54304 — **800-686-6829** — 920-339-0351

Benetrends Inc
1180 Welsh Rd ....North Wales PA 19454 — **866-423-6387** — 267-498-0059

Birner Dental Management Services Inc
1777 S Harrison St Ste 1400 ....Denver CO 80210 — **877-898-1083** — 303-691-0680

BIZDOC Capital Group
5024 Night Hawk Dr NE ....Rio Rancho NM 87144 — **844-249-3621**

BlessingWhite
200 Clocktower Dr ....Hamilton NJ 08690 — **800-222-1349** — 609-528-3535

BMM Testlabs
815 Pilot Rd Ste G ....Las Vegas NV 89119 — **800-791-6536** — 702-407-2420

Brillio
5201 Great America Pkwy ....Santa Clara CA 95054 — **800-317-0575**

BSC America Inc
803 Bel Air Rd ....Bel Air MD 21014 — **800-764-7400**

Business Valuation Center LLC
1717 Pennsylvania Ave NW Ste 1025..........Washington DC 20006 — **800-856-6780** — 703-787-0012

BusinessPlans Inc
432 E Pearl St ....Miamisburg OH 45342 — **800-865-4485**

Cannon Cochran Management Services Inc
2 E Main St Towne Centre Bldg
Ste 208 ....Danville IL 61832 — **800-252-5059** — 217-446-1089

Capital Realty Advisors Inc
600 Sandtree Dr Ste 109...........Palm Beach Gardens FL 33403 — **800-940-1088** — 561-624-5888

Capital Review Group (CRG)
2415 E Camelback Rd Ste 700 ....Phoenix AZ 85016 — **877-666-5539**

CapSouth Partners Inc
2216 W Main St ....Dothan AL 36301 — **800-929-1001** — 334-673-8600

Carolina Advanced Digital Inc
133 Triangle Trade Dr ....Cary NC 27513 — **800-435-2212** — 919-460-1313

Carpedia International Ltd
75 Navy St ....Oakville ON L6J2Z1 — **877-445-8288**

CBR-Technology Corp
15581 Sunburst Ln ....Huntington Beach CA 92647 — **800-227-0700** — 714-901-5740

CE Resource Inc
PO Box 997581 ....Sacramento CA 95899 — **800-707-5644**

Chartis Group LLC
220 W Kinzie St 3rd Fl ....Chicago IL 60654 — **877-667-4700**

Cirro Energy
2745 Dallas Pkwy Ste 200 ....Plano TX 75093 — **800-692-4776**

Cleantech Open, The
425 Broadway ....Redwood City CA 94063 — **888-989-6736**

Coalition of Health Services Inc
301 S Polk St Ste 740.....................Amarillo TX 79101 — **800-442-7893** — 806-337-1700

Coker Consulting
2400 Lakeview Pkwy Ste 400 ....Alpharetta GA 30009 — **800-345-5829**

Community Eldercare Services LLC (CES)
PO Box 3667 ....Tupelo MS 38803 — **877-461-1062**

Compmanagement Inc
PO Box 884 ....Dublin OH 43017 — **800-825-6755** — 614-376-5300

Concentra Inc
5080 Spectrum Dr Ste 1200 W..............Addison TX 75001 — **866-944-6046**

Concord Marketing Solutions Inc
195 Exchange Blvd ....Glendale Heights IL 60139 — **800-648-8588** — 630-893-6453

Conger & Elsea Inc
9870 Hwy 92 ....Woodstock GA 30188 — **800-875-8709** — 770-926-1131

Conway Management Co
547 Amherst St Ste 106 ....Nashua NH 03063 — **800-359-0099** — 603-889-1130

Corizon
105 Westpark Dr Ste 200 ....Brentwood TN 37027 — **800-729-0069**

Cortex Consultants Inc
1027 Pandora Ave ....Victoria BC V8V3P6 — **866-931-1192** — 250-360-1492

Corum Group Ltd
19805 N Creek Pkwy Ste 300 ....Bothell WA 98011 — **800-228-8281** — 425-455-8281

CorVel Corp
2010 Main St Ste 600.....................Irvine CA 92614 — **888-726-7835** — 949-851-1473
NASDAQ: CRVL

Corvirtus
4360 Montebello Dr Ste 400...........Colorado Springs CO 80918 — **800-322-5329**

Courtemanche & Assoc
4475 Morris Park Dr Ste B ....Charlotte NC 28227 — **800-356-2501** — 704-573-4535

Coyle Hospitality Group
244 Madison Ave #369 ....New York NY 10016 — **800-891-9292** — 212-629-2083

CRAssoc Inc (CRA)
8580 Cinderbed Rd Ste 2400 ....Newington VA 22122 — **877-272-8960**

Critical Business Analysis Inc (CBA)
133 W Second St ....Perrysburg OH 43551 — **800-874-8080**

Customer Group, The
641 W Lake St Ste 304 ....Chicago IL 60661 — **844-802-7867**

D&S Communications Inc
1355 N Mclean Blvd ....Elgin IL 60123 — **800-227-8403**

Data Records Management Services Llc
1400 Husband Rd ....Paducah KY 42003 — **800-443-1610** — 270-443-1255

Davis Demographics & Planning Inc
11850 Pierce St Ste 200...................Riverside CA 92505 — **888-337-4471** — 951-270-5211

DealNet Capital Corp
325 Milner Ave Ste 300 ....Toronto ON M1B5N1 — **855-912-3444**

Deep East Texas Council of Governments
274 E Lamar St ....Jasper TX 75951 — **800-256-6848** — 409-384-5704

Defence Construction Canada
Constitution Sq 350 Albert St 19th Fl..........Ottawa ON K1A0K3 — **800-514-3555** — 613-998-9548

DevFacto Technologies Inc
2250 Scotia Place Tower 1 10060 Jasper Ave
.....................................Edmonton AB T5J3R8 — **877-323-3832**

Digital Street Inc
69550 Hwy 111 Ste 201 ....Rancho Mirage CA 92270 — **866-464-5100**

Dresser & Associates Inc
243 US Rt 1 ....Scarborough ME 04074 — **866-885-7212** — 207-885-0809

Eagle's Flight, Creative Training Excellence Inc
489 Clair Rd W ....Guelph ON N1L0H7 — **800-567-8079** — 519-767-1747

EASI 7301 Pkwy Dr ....Hanover MI 21076 — **888-963-7740** — 410-567-8061

Eisenbach Consulting LLC
5759 Eagles Nest Blvd Ste 1................Tyler TX 75703 — **800-977-4020**

	Toll-Free	Phone

Elitexpo Cargo Systems
845 Commerce Dr ....South Elgin IL 60177 — **800-543-5484**

Ensave Energy Performance Inc
65 Millet St Ste 105 ....Richmond VT 05477 — **800-732-1399**

Entelechy Enterprises Inc
889 E Shore Dr ....Silver Lake NH 03875 — **800-376-8368** — 603-424-1237

Envirologic Technologies Inc
2960 Interstate Pkwy ....Kalamazoo MI 49048 — **800-272-7802** — 269-342-1100

Ephor Group LLC
24 E Greenway Plz Ste 440 ....Houston TX 77046 — **800-379-9330**

Equias Alliance LLC
8000 Ctrview Pkwy Ste 525 ....Cordova TN 38018 — **844-553-7872**

Ethos Risk Services Inc
300 First Ave S Ste 300 ....St. Petersburg FL 33701 — **866-783-0525**

Expense Reduction Analysts Inc
16415 Addison Rd Ste 410................Addison TX 75001 — **877-299-7801** — 469-310-2970

Family Business Institute Inc, The
4050 Wake Forest Rd Ste 110................Raleigh NC 27609 — **877-326-2493**

Family Circle Tennis Ctr
161 Seven Farms Dr ....Daniel Island SC 29492 — **800-677-2293** — 843-856-7900

Ferrilli
41 S Haddon Ave Ste 7...................Haddonfield NJ 08033 — **888-864-3282**

Firm Consulting Group
2107 W Cass St Ste B.....................Tampa FL 33606 — **877-636-9525**

First Health Group Corp
Coventry
3200 Highland Ave ....Downers Grove IL 60515 — **800-247-2898** — 630-737-7900

First Sun EAP
2700 Middleburg Dr Ste 208 ....Columbia SC 29204 — **800-968-8143** — 803-376-2668

First Western Advisors
6440 Millrock Dr ....Salt Lake City UT 84121 — **800-937-3500** — 801-930-6500

Flippen Group, The
1199 Haywood Dr ....College Station TX 77845 — **800-316-4311** — 979-693-7660

FocusCFO
1010 Jackson Hole Dr Ste 202...............Columbus OH 43004 — **855-236-0600**

Foley Carrier Services LLC
140 Huyshope Ave ....Hartford CT 06106 — **800-253-5506**

Fortune Practice Management
1265 El Camino Real Ste 205...............Santa Clara CA 95050 — **800-628-1052**

Franchise Co, The (TFC)
14502 N Dale Mabry Ste 200 ....Tampa FL 33618 — **800-294-5591**

Freight Transportation Research Associates Inc
1720 N Kinser Pk ....Bloomington IN 47404 — **888-988-1699** — 812-988-1699

Geo-instruments Inc
24 Celestial Dr ....Narragansett RI 02882 — **800-477-2506**

Global Quality Assurance Inc
6900 Tavistock Lakes Blvd Ste 400...........Orlando FL 32827 — **888-322-3330**

Gottlieb Martin & Associates Inc
4932 Sunbeam Rd ....Jacksonville FL 32257 — **800-833-9986** — 904-346-3088

Group Management Services Inc
3296 Columbia Rd Ste 101................Richfield OH 44286 — **888-823-2084** — 330-659-0100

Hall Hodges & Associates Inc
700 N Brand Blvd Ste 650 ....Glendale CA 91203 — **800-490-1447** — 818-244-8930

Handel Group Llc
247 Limestone Rd ....Ridgefield CT 06877 — **800-617-7040** — 917-670-8782

Harkcon
1390 Chain Bridge Rd 570 ....Mclean VA 22101 — **800-499-6456**

Health Decisions Inc
2510 Meridian Pkwy ....Durham NC 27713 — **888-779-3771** — 919-967-2399

HealthAxis Inc
7301 N State Hwy 161 ....Irving TX 75039 — **888-974-2947** — 972-443-5000

Healthlinx Transitional Leadership Inc
1404 Goodale Blvd Ste 400 ....Columbus OH 43212 — **800-980-4820**

Helix Design Inc
175 Lincoln St Ste 201 ....Manchester NH 03103 — **800-511-5593**

Hexavest Inc
1250 Ren, L,vesque Blvd W Ste 4200..........Montreal QC H3B4W8 — **800-225-6265** — 514-390-8484

Hg Solutions
3701 S Lawrence St ....Tacoma WA 98409 — **866-988-2626** — 253-588-2626

Hill Physicians Medical Group Inc
2409 Camino Ramon PO Box 5080 ....San Ramon CA 94583 — **800-445-5747** — 925-820-8300

Holt Marketing Services Inc
3075 Boardwalk Ste 2....................Saginaw MI 48603 — **800-698-2449** — 989-791-2475

HowGood Inc
93 Commercial St ....Brooklyn NY 11222 — **888-601-3015**

Hru Inc Technical Resources
3451 Dunckel Rd ....Lansing MI 48911 — **888-205-3446** — 517-272-5888

Hygieneering Inc
7575 Plaza Ct ....Willowbrook IL 60527 — **800-444-7154** — 630-654-2550

IHL Group
1650 Murfreesboro Rd Ste 206..............Franklin TN 37067 — **888-445-6777** — 615-591-2955

In Touch Business Consultants
11370 66th St 132 ....Largo FL 33773 — **877-676-5492**

INFOCUS Marketing Inc
4245 Sigler Rd ....Warrenton VA 20187 — **800-708-5478**

Innovatia Inc
1 Germain St ....Saint John NB E2L4V1 — **800-363-3358** — 506-640-4000

Inovo LLC
213 S Ashley St Ste 300...................Ann Arbor MI 48104 — **888-464-6686**

Insperity Inc
19001 Crescent Springs Dr ....Kingwood TX 77339 — **800-237-3170** — 866-715-3552

Integra Group
16 Triangle Park Dr Ste 1600 ....Cincinnati OH 45246 — **800-424-8384** — 513-326-5600

Interact Performance Systems Inc
180 N Rverview Dr Ste 165.................Anaheim CA 92808 — **800-944-7553** — 714-283-8288

ipCapital Group Inc
426 Industrial Ave Ste 150 ....Williston VT 05495 — **888-853-2212** — 802-859-7800

IQ Technology Solutions
5595 Equity Ave Ste 300..................Reno NV 89502 — **866-842-4748** — 775-352-2301

Irc Building Sciences Group
2121 Argentia Rd Ste 401.................Mississauga ON L5N2X4 — **888-607-5245** — 905-607-7244

Jamsan Hotel Management Inc
440 Bedford St ....Lexington MA 02420 — **800-523-5549** — 781-863-8500

JobsOhio
41 S High St Ste 1500 ....Columbus OH 43215 — **855-874-2530** — 614-224-6446

Jolt Consulting Group
112 Spring St Ste 301 ....Saratoga Springs NY 12866 — **877-249-6262**

Company / Address	City	State	ZIP	Toll-Free	Phone
Justice Solutions of America Inc					
2750 Taylor Ave Ste A-56	Orlando	FL	32806	**888-577-4766**	
Keating Technologies Inc					
25 Royal Crest Ct Ste 120	Markham	ON	L3R9X4	**877-532-8464**	905-479-0230
Keller Fay Group					
65 Church St	New Brunswick	NJ	08901	**800-273-8439**	732-846-6800
Klemmer & Associates Leaders					
1340 Commerce St	Petaluma	CA	94954	**800-577-5447**	707-559-7722
Kotter International					
5 Bennett St	Cambridge	MA	02138	**855-400-4712**	617-600-6787
Latitude Consulting Group Inc					
100 E Michigan Ave Ste 200	Saline	MI	48176	**888-577-2797**	
Lawrence Merchandising					
1405 Xenium Ln N Ste 250	Plymouth	MN	55441	**800-328-3967**	763-383-5700
Learning Unlimited					
4137 S Harvard Ave Ste A	Tulsa	OK	74135	**888-622-4203**	918-622-3292
Legal Club of America Corp					
7771 W Oakland Park Blvd Ste 217	Sunrise	FL	33351	**800-316-5387**	954-377-0222
Level II Inc					
555 Andover Park W Ste 110	Tukwila	WA	98188	**888-232-9609**	206-575-7682
Lifewings					
9198 Crestwyn Hills Dr	Memphis	TN	38125	**800-290-9314**	
Lost Recovery Network Lrni					
406 Dixon St	Vidalia	GA	30474	**877-693-1456**	912-537-3901
Loyalty Methods Inc					
80 Yesler Way Ste 310	Seattle	WA	98104	**800-693-2040**	206-257-2111
M2 Logistics Inc					
2701 Executive Dr	Green Bay	WI	54304	**800-391-5121**	920-569-8800
Macadamian Technologies Inc					
165 Rue Wellington	Gatineau	QC	J8X2J3	**877-779-6336**	819-772-0300
MaguireZay					
17194 Preston Rd Ste 102-143	Dallas	TX	75248	**888-400-6929**	214-692-5002
Marketri LLC					
1700 Market St Ste 1005	Philadelphia	PA	19103	**800-695-1356**	
Masters Advisors Inc					
480 New Holland Ave Ste 7201	Lancaster	PA	17602	**800-571-1323**	717-581-1323
Mattersight Corp					
200 W Madison St Ste 3100	Chicago	IL	60606	**877-235-6925**	
MavenWire LLC					
630 Freedom Business Ctr					
3rd Fl	King Of Prussia	PA	19406	**866-343-4870**	
Medexcel USA Inc					
484 Temple Hill Rd	New Windsor	NY	12553	**800-563-6384**	845-565-3700
Medium Blue Search Engine Marketing					
3365 Piedmont Rd NE St 1400 2nd Fl	Atlanta	GA	30305	**866-436-2583**	678-536-8336
Medusind Solutions Inc					
31103 Rancho Viejo Rd					
Ste 2150	San Juan Capistrano	CA	92675	**877-741-4573**	
Metasystems Inc					
13700 State Rd Ste 1	North Royalton	OH	44133	**800-788-5253**	440-526-1454
MHM Services Inc					
1593 Spring Hill Rd Ste 600	Vienna	VA	22182	**800-416-3649**	703-749-4600
Mitchell Selling Dynamics					
1360 Puritan Ave	Birmingham	MI	48009	**800-328-9696**	248-644-8092
Modis Inc 10 Bay St 7th Fl	Toronto	ON	M5J2R8	**800-842-5907**	904-360-2300
Montana Manufacturing Extension Center					
2310 University Way Bldg 2	Bozeman	MT	59715	**800-637-4634**	406-994-3812
Mortgage Banking Solutions					
Frost Bank Tower 401 Congress Ave					
Ste 1540	Austin	TX	78701	**800-476-0853**	512-977-9900
Mpa Media					
5406 Bolsa Ave	Huntington Beach	CA	92649	**800-324-7758**	
MyLLCcom Inc					
1910 Thomes Ave	Cheyenne	WY	82001	**888-886-9552**	
Navigate Power					
2211 N Elston Ste 208	Chicago	IL	60614	**888-601-1789**	
Navin, Haffty & Associates LLC					
1900 West Park Dr Ste 180	Westborough	MA	01581	**888-837-1300**	781-871-6770
Navtech Seminars & Gps Supply					
5501 Backlick Rd Ste 230	Springfield	VA	22151	**800-628-0885**	703-256-8900
Netcracker Technology Corp					
95 Sawyer Rd University Ofc Pk III	Waltham	MA	02453	**800-477-5785**	781-419-3300
Network Medical Management Inc					
1668 S Garfield Ave 2nd Fl	Alhambra	CA	91801	**877-282-8272**	626-282-0288
NextServices Inc					
500 E Eisenhower Pkwy Ste 130	Ann Arbor	MI	48108	**866-362-6398**	734-677-7700
Noninvasive Medical Technologies Inc					
6412 S Arville St	Las Vegas	NV	89118	**888-466-8552**	702-614-3360
North Channel Capital Management Group					
5550 S 59th St Ste 26	Lincoln	NE	68516	**877-421-6501**	402-421-6500
Ohm Systems Inc					
10250 Chester Rd	Cincinnati	OH	45215	**800-878-0646**	513-771-0008
Ologie LLC 447 E Main St	Columbus	OH	43215	**800-962-1107**	614-221-1107
Olympique Expert Building Care					
26232 Enterprise Ct	Lake Forest	CA	92630	**866-659-6747**	949-455-0796
On-line Taxes Inc					
724 Jules St	Saint Joseph	MO	64501	**800-829-1040**	
Organo Gold International Inc					
5505 Hovander Rd	Ferndale	WA	98248	**877-674-2661**	
Orion Registrar Inc					
7850 Vance Dr	Arvada	CO	80003	**800-446-0674**	303-456-6010
Oyster Consulting LLC					
4128 Innslake Dr	Glen Allen	VA	23060	**888-965-5401**	804-965-5400
Path-2 Ventures LLC					
223 E Blvd	Charlotte	NC	28203	**888-692-1057**	
Pediatrix Medical Group Inc					
1301 Concord Terr	Sunrise	FL	33323	**800-243-3839**	954-384-0175
PFSweb Inc					
505 Millennium Dr Ste 500	Allen	TX	75013	**888-330-5504**	972-881-2900
NASDAQ: PFSW					
Pinpoint Technologies					
17802 Irvine Blvd Ste 215	Tustin	CA	92780	**866-603-7770**	714-505-7600
Pinyon Environmental Inc					
3222 S Vance St Unit 200	Lakewood	CO	80227	**888-641-7337**	303-980-5200
Pitney Bowes inc					
3001 Summer St	Stamford	CT	06926	**844-256-6444**	203-356-5000
Planners Network Inc, The					
43418 Business Park Dr	Temecula	CA	92590	**866-676-6288**	
Playback Now Inc					
3139 Campus Dr Ste 700	Norcross	GA	30071	**800-241-7785**	770-447-0616
Pln & Associates Inc					
15400 Jennings Ln Ste 300	Bowie	MD	20721	**800-699-0299**	301-390-4635
Portico Healthnet					
1600 University Ave W Ste 211	Saint Paul	MN	55104	**866-489-4899**	651-489-2273
Power Wellness					
851 Oak Creek Dr	Lombard	IL	60148	**877-888-2988**	630-570-2600
PreferredOne Administrative Services Inc					
6105 Golden Hills Dr	Golden Valley	MN	55416	**800-451-9597**	763-847-4000
Proenergy Services LLC					
2001 ProEnergy Blvd	Sedalia	MO	65301	**844-367-4948**	
Prospect Medical Holdings Inc					
3415 S Sepulveda Blvd 9th Fl	Los Angeles	CA	90034	**800-708-3230**	310-943-4500
Protocol Driven Healthcare Inc					
40 Morristown Rd Ste 2D	Bernardsville	NJ	07924	**888-816-4006**	515-277-1376
Provell Inc					
855 Village Center Dr Ste 116	North Oaks	MN	55127	**800-624-2946**	952-258-2000
PuroClean					
6001 Hiatus Rd Ste 13	Tamarac	FL	33321	**800-775-7876**	
PVA Consulting Group Inc					
20865 Ch de la Cote Nord Ste 200	Boisbriand	QC	J7E4H5	**877-970-1970**	450-970-1970
Quality Administration LLC					
610 Indian Trail Ct	Smithville	MO	64089	**866-902-2090**	816-532-2090
Quality Media Resources Inc					
10929 SE 23rd St	Bellevue	WA	98004	**800-800-5129**	
RBN Energy LLC					
2323 S Shepherd Dr Ste 1010	Houston	TX	77019	**888-400-9838**	
ReachForce Inc					
2711 W Anderson Ln Ste 200	Austin	TX	78757	**844-254-5405**	
Real Story Group, The					
3470 Olney-Laytonsville Rd Ste 131	Olney	MD	20832	**800-325-6190**	617-340-6464
Realstreet Staffing					
2500 Wallington Way Ste 208	Marriottsville	MD	21104	**877-480-8002**	410-480-8002
Red Spot Interactive					
1001 Jupiter Park Dr	Jupiter	FL	33458	**800-401-7931**	
Redmonk 95 High St Ste 206	Portland	ME	04101	**866-733-6665**	
Retirement Advantage Inc, The					
47 Park Pl Ste 850	Appleton	WI	54914	**888-872-2364**	
RHA Health Services Inc					
17 Church St	Asheville	NC	28801	**866-742-2428**	828-232-6844
Rideau Inc 473 Deslauriers	Montreal	QC	H4N1W2	**800-363-6464**	
River West Meeting Associates Inc					
3616 N Lincoln Ave	Chicago	IL	60613	**888-534-5292**	773-755-3000
Roco Rescue					
7077 Exchequer Dr	Baton Rouge	LA	70809	**800-647-7626**	225-755-7626
Royale Management Services Inc					
2319 N Andrews Ave	Fort Lauderdale	FL	33311	**800-382-1040**	954-563-1269
RTM Consulting Inc (RTMC)					
4335 Ferguson Dr Ste 210	Cincinnati	OH	45245	**855-786-2555**	
Ruggie Wealth Management					
2100 Lake Eustis Dr	Tavares	FL	32778	**888-343-2711**	352-343-2700
Sales Concepts Inc					
610 Hembree Pkwy	Roswell	GA	30076	**800-229-2328**	678-624-9229
Schneider Electric					
10350 Ormsby Pk Pl Ste 400	Louisville	KY	40223	**866-907-8664**	502-429-3800
School Innovations & Advocacy Inc					
5200 Golden Foothill Pkwy	El Dorado Hills	CA	95762	**877-954-4357**	800-487-9234
Scott Sheldon LLC					
1375 S Main St Ste 203	North Canton	OH	44720	**844-835-2527**	234-347-0689
SEA Ltd					
7349 Worthington-Galena Rd	Columbus	OH	43085	**800-782-6851**	
Select Medical Corp					
4714 Gettysburg Rd	Mechanicsburg	PA	17055	**888-735-6332**	717-972-1100
Seton Hotel 144 E 40th St	New York	NY	10016	**866-697-3866**	212-889-5301
Shaker International					
3201 Entp Pkwy Ste 360	Cleveland	OH	44122	**888-485-7633**	
Sheridan Healthcare Inc					
1613 NW 136th Ave Ste 200	Sunrise	FL	33323	**800-437-2672**	
Sigma Breakthrough Technologies Inc					
123 N Edward Gary 2nd Fl	San Marcos	TX	78666	**888-752-7070**	512-353-7489
Signum Group LLC					
1200 Stephenson Hwy	Troy	MI	48083	**844-854-3282**	
Silliman Associates Inc Thomas					
425 N Lee St	Alexandria	VA	22314	**800-454-5554**	703-548-4100
Simunition Ltd					
65 Sandscreen Rd	Avon	CT	06001	**800-465-8255**	860-404-0162
Site Tech Systems					
2513 N Oak St Ste 305	Myrtle Beach	SC	29577	**800-470-2895**	843-808-9716
Solutions 21					
152 Wabash St	Pittsburgh	PA	15220	**866-765-2121**	
Solutions AE Inc					
236 Auburn Ave	Atlanta	GA	30303	**888-562-4441**	
Sparus					
3175 Corners N Ct	Peachtree Corners	GA	30071	**800-241-5057**	
Spectrum Healthcare Resources Inc					
12647 Olive Blvd Ste 600	Saint Louis	MO	63141	**800-325-3982**	
Speed Consulting LLC					
500 Cantrell St	Waxahachie	TX	75165	**800-256-7140**	
SSA Consultants Inc					
9331 Bluebonnet Blvd	Baton Rouge	LA	70810	**800-634-2758**	225-769-2676
Steering Group Inc, The					
1078 Dixie Belle Ct	Lawrenceville	GA	30045	**866-290-8123**	800-405-3068
Stock & Option Solutions Inc					
6399 San Ignacio Ave Ste 100	San Jose	CA	95119	**888-767-0199**	408-979-8700
Surge Resources					
920 Candia Rd	Manchester	NH	03109	**800-787-4387**	603-623-0007
Szarka Financial Management					
29691 Lorain Rd	North Olmsted	OH	44070	**800-859-8095**	440-779-1430
Talent Curve					
14 Bridle Path	Pittsboro	NC	27312	**866-494-0248**	
TalentMap					
245 Menten Pl Ste 301	Ottawa	ON	K2H9E8	**888-641-1113**	613-248-3417
Taos Mountain					
121 Daggett Dr	San Jose	CA	95134	**888-826-7686**	408-588-1200
TaxMatrix 1011 Mumma Rd	Lemoyne	PA	17043	**855-788-3375**	
Team Quality Services Inc					
4483 County Rd 19 Ste B	Auburn	IN	46706	**866-568-8326**	260-572-0060

	Toll-Free	Phone
Tekmasters Llc		
4437 brookfield corporate Dr Ste 201A................Chantilly VA 20151	855-856-7877	703-349-1110
TeleProviders Inc		
23461 S Pointe Dr Ste 185.............Laguna Hills CA 92653	888-999-4244	
TenStep Inc		
181 Waterman St ....Marietta GA 30060	877-536-8434	770-795-9097
Three Rivers Planning & Development District Inc		
75 S Main St PO Box 690...................Pontotoc MS 38863	877-489-6911	662-489-2415
Total Contentz		
540 Millers Run Rd Ste 200 ....Morgan PA 15064	888-722-5688	805-522-5900
Traffic Group Inc, The		
9900 Franklin Sq Dr ....Baltimore MD 21236	800-583-8411	410-931-6600
Trainertainment LLC		
PO Box 2168 ....Keller TX 76248	800-860-8474	817-886-4840
Treeline Associates Inc		
5300 Lakewood Rd ....Whitehall MI 49461	888-231-8039	248-814-7151
Trisoft Technologies Inc		
14429 Independence Dr ....Plainfield IL 60544	866-364-7031	
Trissential LLC		
1905 E Wayzata Blvd Ste 333 ....Wayzata MN 55391	888-595-7970	
Trusted Advisor Associates Llc		
193 Zeppi Ln ....West Orange NJ 07052	855-878-7801	
TTG Consultants		
4727 Wilshire Blvd ....Los Angeles CA 90010	800-736-8840	323-936-6600
Turpin Sales & Marketing Inc		
330 Cold Spring Ave ....West Springfield MA 01089	877-377-7573	
Unisource NTC		
1336 Moorpark Rd Ste 159.............Thousand Oaks CA 91360	800-736-8470	747-226-0978
US-Reports Inc		
5802 Wright Dr ....Loveland CO 80538	800-223-2310	
USA Risk Group Inc		
2418 Airport Rd Ste 2A.......................Barre VT 05641	800-872-7475	
Valtim Inc 1095 Venture Dr ....Forest VA 24551	800-230-2857	434-525-3004
Vanir Construction Management Inc		
4540 Duckhorn Dr Ste 300................Sacramento CA 95834	888-912-1201	916-575-8888
Vendors Exchange International Inc		
8700 Brookpark Rd ....Cleveland OH 44129	800-321-2311	216-432-1800
Veri-Tax		
30 Executive Pk Ste 200 ....Irvine CA 92614	800-969-5100	
Verisk Analytics		
545 Washington Blvd ....Jersey City NJ 07310	800-888-4476	201-469-3000
NASDAQ: VRSK		
Verity Professionals		
8000 Avalon Blvd Ste 100 ....Alpharetta GA 30009	888-367-3110	404-920-6400
Vermont Energy Investment Corp		
128 Lakeside Ave Ste 401..................Burlington VT 05401	800-639-6069	802-658-6060
Vertigraph Inc		
12959 Jupiter Rd Ste 252.....................Dallas TX 75238	800-989-4243	214-340-9436
VetStrategy		
30 Whitmore Rd ....Woodbridge ON L4L7Z4	866-901-6471	
Vetter Senior Living		
20220 Harney St ....Elkhorn NE 68022	800-388-4264	402-895-3932
Volt VIEWtech Inc		
4761 E Hunter Ave ....Anaheim CA 92807	888-396-9927	714-695-3377
Waypoint Consulting		
1450 E Boot Rd ....West Chester PA 19380	866-826-7075	
Wicklander Zulawski & Associates Inc		
4932 Main St ....Downers Grove IL 60515	800-222-7789	
Winfree Business Growth Advisors		
10808 Ward Ave ....Louisville KY 40223	800-616-9260	502-253-0700
Worklife Balance com		
7742 Spalding Dr Ste 356 ....Atlanta GA 30092	877-644-0064	770-997-7881
Zero Technologies LLC		
7 Neshaminy Interplex Ste 116..............Trevose PA 19053	800-503-2939	

462   MANNEQUINS & DISPLAY FORMS

	Toll-Free	Phone
Silvestri Studio Inc		
8125 Beach St ....Los Angeles CA 90001	800-647-8874	323-277-4420

463   MARINE SERVICES

SEE ALSO Logistics Services (Transportation & Warehousing) ; Freight Transport - Deep Sea (Foreign Ports) ; Freight Transport - Deep Sea (Domestic Ports) ; Freight Transport - Inland Waterways

	Toll-Free	Phone
Andrie Inc		
561 E Western Ave ....Muskegon MI 49442	800-722-2421	231-728-2226
Bay Houston Towing Co		
2243 Milford St ....Houston TX 77253	800-324-3755	713-529-3755
Crowley Maritime Corp		
9487 Regency Square Blvd ....Jacksonville FL 32225	800-276-9539	904-727-2200
Edison Chouest Offshore		
16201 E Main St ....Galliano LA 70354	866-925-5161	985-601-4444
Express Cargo USA LLC		
1790 Yardley-Langhorne Rd Carriage House 202 ....Yardley PA 19067	888-505-7361	201-603-9155
Foss Maritime Co		
1151 Fairview Ave N ....Seattle WA 98109	800-426-2885	206-281-3800
Great Lakes Towing Co		
4500 Div Ave ....Cleveland OH 44102	800-321-3663	216-621-4854
Hopkins-Carter Company Inc		
3300 NW 21st St ....Miami FL 33142	800-595-9656	305-635-7377
Hornbeck Offshore Services Inc		
103 Northpark Blvd Ste 300................Covington LA 70433	800-642-9816	985-727-2000
NYSE: HOS		
Kinder Morgan Bulk Terminals Inc		
7116 Hwy 23 ....Sorrento LA 70778	800-232-1627	225-675-5387
McAllister Towing & Transportation Co Inc		
17 Battery Pl Ste 1200 ....New York NY 10004	888-764-5980	212-269-3200
New York State Canal Corp		
200 Southern Blvd PO Box 189 ....Albany NY 12201	800-422-6254	518-449-6000

	Toll-Free	Phone
Sause Bros		
3710 NW Front Ave ....Portland OR 97210	800-488-4167	503-222-1811
Sea Tow Services International Inc		
1560 Youngs Ave PO Box 1178 ....Southold NY 11971	800-473-2869	877-568-1672
SSA Marine		
1131 SW Klickitat Way ....Seattle WA 98134	800-422-3505	206-623-0304
Tidewater Inc		
6002 Rogerdale Rd Ste 600 ....Houston TX 77072	800-678-8433	713-470-5300
NYSE: TDW		
Virginia International Terminals Inc		
7737 Hampton Blvd ....Norfolk VA 23505	800-541-2431*	757-440-7000
*General		

464   MARKET RESEARCH FIRMS

SEE ALSO

	Toll-Free	Phone
1STWEST Background Due Diligence LLC		
1536 Cole Blvd Ste 335 ....Lakewood CO 80401	866-670-3443	
Aberdeen Group Inc		
60 Hickory Dr 5th Fl ....Waltham MA 02451	800-577-7891	617-854-5200
Ameresco Canada Inc		
90 Sheppard Ave E ....North York ON M2N3A1	888-483-7267	416-512-7700
Arbitron Inc		
9705 Patuxent Woods Dr ....Columbia MD 21046	800-543-7300	410-312-8000
NYSE: ARB		
Artafact LLC 43165 Sabercat ....Fremont CA 94539	800-618-3228	510-651-9178
AVMetrics LLC		
90 W Cochran St Ste C....................Simi Valley CA 93065	800-240-1049	805-421-5056
Clear Seas Research		
2401 W Big Beaver Rd ....Troy MI 48084	800-811-6640	248-786-1683
Collective[i]		
130 Madison Ave ....New York NY 10016	888-890-0020	
comScore Inc		
11950 Democracy Dr # 600 ....Reston VA 20190	866-276-6972	703-438-2000
Connected Nation		
191 W Professional Park Ct b ....Bowling Green KY 42104	877-846-7710	270-781-4320
Datassential		
1762 Westwood Blvd Ste 250.............Los Angeles CA 90024	888-556-3687	312-655-0622
Demand Metric 463 King St..................London ON N6B1S8	866-947-7744	519-495-9619
Digital Traffic Systems Inc		
8401 Jefferson St NE Ste A...............Albuquerque NM 87113	855-328-2487	505-881-4470
Gallup Inc 1001 Gallup Dr ....Omaha NE 68102	800-500-8282	402-951-2003
Gartner Inc		
56 Top Gallant Rd ....Stamford CT 06902	866-471-2526	203-964-0096
NYSE: IT		
GRFI Ltd		
400 E Randolph St Ste 700..................Chicago IL 60601	888-856-5161	
HRA - Healthcare Research & Analytics LLC		
400 Lanidex Plz ....Parsippany NJ 07054	800-929-5400	973-240-1200
IDC (IDC) 5 Speen St ....Framingham MA 01701	800-343-4952	508-872-8200
Information Resources Inc		
150 N Clinton St ....Chicago IL 60661	866-262-5973	312-726-1221
Investorideascom		
1385 Gulf Rd Ste 102.................Point Roberts WA 98281	800-665-0411	
JD Power & Assoc		
2625 Townsgate Rd Ste 100.........Westlake Village CA 91361	800-274-5372	805-418-8000
KIKO 2722 Fulton Dr NW ....Canton OH 44718	800-533-5456	330-453-9187
Luth Research Inc		
1365 Fourth Ave ....San Diego CA 92101	800-465-5884	619-234-5884
M/A/R/C Research		
1660 Westridge Cir ....Irving TX 75038	800-884-6272	972-983-0400
m2M Strategies LLC		
33 Buford Village Way Ste 329 ....Buford GA 30518	800-345-1070	678-835-9080
MaritzCX Research LLC		
1355 N Hwy Dr ....Fenton MO 63099	877-462-7489	385-695-2940
Market Decisions Research		
75 Washington Ave Ste 2C ....Portland ME 04101	800-293-1538	207-767-6440
Market Strategies Inc		
17430 College Pkwy ....Livonia MI 48152	800-420-9366	734-542-7600
MarketVision Research Inc		
5151 Pfeiffer Rd Ste 300.................Cincinnati OH 45242	800-232-4250	513-791-3100
National Research Corp		
1245 Q St ....Lincoln NE 68508	800-388-4264	402-475-2525
NASDAQ: NRCI		
NPD Group Inc		
900 W Shore Rd ....Port Washington NY 11050	866-444-1411	516-625-0700
OnCard Marketing Inc		
132 West 31st St Ste 702 ....New York NY 10001	866-996-8729	
Open Minds 163 York St ....Gettysburg PA 17325	877-350-6463	717-334-1329
Opinion Research Corp (ORC)		
902 Carnegie Ctr Ste 220 ....Princeton NJ 08540	800-444-4672	
PayNet Inc		
5750 Old Orchard Rd Ste 250.................Skokie IL 60077	866-825-3400	
Protelus		
11000 NE 33rd Pl Ste 320 ....Bellevue WA 98004	800-585-0207	
RateHubca		
411 Richmond St E Ste 208 ....Toronto ON M5A3S5	800-679-9622	
RealityCheck Inc		
2033 N Geyer Rd ....Saint Louis MO 63131	866-751-2094	314-909-9095
Reis Inc		
530 Fifth Ave 5th Fl ....New York NY 10036	800-366-7347	
NASDAQ: REIS		
Relevancy Group, The		
505 Congress St Ste 602 ....Boston MA 02210	877-972-6886	
RRC Assoc		
4770 Baseline Rd Ste 360..................Boulder CO 80303	888-449-4772	303-449-6558
Ruf Strategic Solutions		
1533 E Spruce St ....Olathe KS 66061	800-829-8544	
Seneca Consulting Group Inc		
111 Smithtown Byp Ste 112 ....Hauppauge NY 11788	866-487-4157	631-577-4092
Service 800		
2190 W Wayzata Blvd ....Minneapolis MN 55356	800-475-3747	952-475-3747
Sharetracker PO Box 20 ....Ashland MO 65010	888-628-3088	
Standards Council of Canada		
270 Albert St Ste 200 ....Ottawa ON K1P6N7	800-844-6790	613-238-3222

				Toll-Free	Phone

Strategy Institute
401 Richmond St W Ste 401 . . . . Toronto ON M5V3A8 **866-298-9343**
Survey Service Inc
1911 Sheridan Dr . . . . Buffalo NY 14223 **800-507-7969** 716-876-6450
TRC
1300 Virginia Dr Ste 200 . . . . Fort Washington PA 19034 **800-275-2827** 215-641-2200
Trinity Green Services LLC
751 Hebron Pkwy Ste 225 . . . . Lewisville TX 75057 **888-243-3605** 214-446-9500
Unmetric Inc
2001 Victoria Rd . . . . Mundelein IL 60060 **855-558-5588**
Valient Market Research Inc
PO Box 335 . . . . Exton PA 19341 **844-332-7082**
Walker Information Inc
301 Pennsylvania Pkwy . . . . Indianapolis IN 46280 **800-334-3939** 317-843-3939
XtremeEDA Corp
200-25 Holland Ave . . . . Ottawa ON K1Y4R9 **800-586-0280**

465 MARKING DEVICES

American Marking Systems Inc
1015 Paulison Ave PO Box 1677 . . . . Clifton NJ 07011 **800-782-6766** 973-478-5600
Cable Markers Company Inc
13805-C Alton Pkwy . . . . Irvine CA 92618 **800-746-7655**
Carco Inc
10333 Shoemaker PO Box 13859 . . . . Detroit MI 48213 **800-255-3924** 313-925-9000
CH Hanson Co
2000 N Aurora Rd . . . . Naperville IL 60563 **800-827-3398** 630-848-2000
Cosco Industries Inc
7220 W Wilson Ave . . . . Harwood Heights IL 60706 **800-296-8970**
Diagraph
2538 Wisconsin Ave . . . . Downers Grove IL 60515 **800-626-3464** 630-968-0646
Excelsior Marking Products
888 W Waterloo Rd . . . . Akron OH 44314 **800-433-3615** 330-745-2300
Hitt Marking Devices Inc
3231 W MacArthur Blvd . . . . Santa Ana CA 92704 **800-969-6699** 714-979-1405
Huntington Park Rubber Stamp Co
2761 E Slauson Ave PO Box 519 . . . . Huntington Park CA 90255 **800-882-0129** 323-582-6461
Infosight Corp
PO Box 5000 . . . . Chillicothe OH 45601 **800-401-0716** 740-642-3600
Jackson Marking Products Co
9105 N Rainbow Ln . . . . Mount Vernon IL 62864 **800-782-6722** 618-242-1334
La-Co/Markal Co
1201 Pratt Blvd . . . . Elk Grove Village IL 60007 **800-621-4025** 847-956-7600
Matthews International Corp Marking Products Div
6515 Penn Ave . . . . Pittsburgh PA 15206 **800-775-7775** 412-665-2500
Menke Marking Devices
13253 Alondra Blvd . . . . Santa Fe Springs CA 90670 **800-231-6023** 562-921-1380
New Method Steel Stamps Inc
31313 Kendall Ave . . . . Fraser MI 48026 **800-582-0199** 586-293-0200
Schwaab Inc
11415 W Burleigh St . . . . Milwaukee WI 53222 **800-935-9877** 414-771-4150
Schwerdtle Stamp Co
166 Elm St . . . . Bridgeport CT 06604 **800-535-0004** 203-330-2750
Signet Marking Devices
3121 Red Hill Ave . . . . Costa Mesa CA 92626 **800-421-5150**
Stamprite 154 S Larch St . . . . Lansing MI 48912 **800-328-1988** 517-487-5071
Tacoma Rubber Stamp & Sign
919 Market St . . . . Tacoma WA 98402 **800-544-7281** 253-383-5433
Wendell's Inc
6601 Bunker Lake Blvd NW . . . . Ramsey MN 55303 **800-936-3355** 763-576-8200

466 MASS TRANSPORTATION (LOCAL & SUBURBAN)

SEE ALSO Bus Services - Intercity & Rural

Alameda-Contra Costa Transit District
1600 Franklin St 10th Fl . . . . Oakland CA 94612 **877-878-8883** 510-891-4777
Alaska Marine Highway System
6858 Glacier Hwy PO Box 112505 . . . . Juneau AK 99811 **800-642-0066** 907-465-3941
Altamont Commuter Express (ACE)
949 E Ch St . . . . Stockton CA 95202 **800-411-7245**
Ann Arbor Transportation Authority
2700 S Industrial Hwy . . . . Ann Arbor MI 48104 **800-835-4603** 734-973-6500
Caledonia Haulers LLC
420 West Lincoln St PO Box 31 . . . . Caledonia MN 55921 **800-325-4728** 507-725-9000
Cape Cod Regional Transit Authority (CCRTA)
215 Iyannough Rd PO Box 1988. . . . . Hyannis MA 02601 **800-352-7155** 508-775-8504
Catalina Express Berth 95 . . . . San Pedro CA 90731 **800-481-3470** 310-519-1212
Central Puget Sound Regional Transit Authority
401 S Jackson St . . . . Seattle WA 98104 **800-201-4900** 206-398-5000
Cliff Viessman Inc
215 First Ave PO Box 175 . . . . Gary SD 57237 **800-328-2408** 605-272-5241
Delaware Transit Corp
119 Lower Beach St . . . . Wilmington DE 19805 **800-652-3278**
GO Transit 20 Bay St Ste 600 . . . . Toronto ON M5J2W3 **888-438-6646** 416-869-3200
Horizon Freight System Inc
6600 Bessemer Ave . . . . Cleveland OH 44127 **800-480-6829** 216-341-7410
Los Angeles County Metropolitan Transportation Authority
1 Gateway Plz . . . . Los Angeles CA 90012 **866-827-8646** 213-922-6000
Mission Petroleum Carriers Inc
8450 Mosley . . . . Houston TX 77075 **800-737-9911** 713-943-8250
Monterey-Salinas Transit (MST)
19 Upper Ragsdale Dr Ste 200 . . . . Monterey CA 93940 **888-678-2871**
Norfolk Southern Corp
3 Commercial Pl . . . . Norfolk VA 23510 **800-635-5768*** 855-667-3655
*NYSE: NSC ■ *Cust Svc*
Northern Indiana Commuter Transportation District
33 E US Hwy 12 . . . . Chesterton IN 46304 **800-743-3333** 219-926-5744
Orange County Transportation Authority
550 S Main St PO Box 14184 . . . . Orange CA 92863 **800-600-9191** 714-560-6282
Packard Transport Inc
24021 S Municipal Dr PO Box 380 . . . . Channahon IL 60410 **800-467-9260** 815-467-9260
Pierce Transit
3701 96th St SW PO Box 99070 . . . . Lakewood WA 98499 **800-562-8109** 253-581-8000

Regional Transportation Authority
175 W Jackson Blvd Ste 1550 . . . . Chicago IL 60604 **800-232-0502** 312-913-3200
Regional Transportation Commission of Southern Nevada (RTC)
600 S Grand Central Pkwy Ste 350 . . . . . . Las Vegas NV 89106 **800-228-3911** 702-676-1500
Regional Transportation District (RTD)
1961 Stout St . . . . Denver CO 80202 **800-366-7433** 303-628-9000
Reliable Carriers Inc
41555 Koppernick Rd . . . . Canton MI 48187 **800-521-6393** 734-453-6677
Riverside Transit Agency (RTA)
1825 Third St PO Box 59968 . . . . Riverside CA 92517 **800-800-7821** 951-565-5000
San Mateo County Transit District
1250 San Carlos Ave PO Box 3006 . . . . . . San Carlos CA 94070 **800-660-4287** 650-508-6200
Santa Clara Valley Transportation Authority (VTA)
3331 N First St . . . . San Jose CA 95134 **800-894-9908** 408-321-2300
Sonoma County Transit
355 W Robles Ave . . . . Santa Rosa CA 95407 **800-345-7433** 707-576-7433
Southern California Regional Rail Authority
700 S Flower St Ste 2600 . . . . Los Angeles CA 90017 **800-371-5465** 213-452-0200
Suburban Mobility Authority for Regional Transportation (SMART)
535 Griswold St Ste 600 . . . . Detroit MI 48226 **866-962-5515** 313-223-2100
Toronto Transit Commission (TTC)
1900 Yonge St . . . . Toronto ON M4S1Z2 **800-223-6192** 416-393-4000
Tri-Rail
800 NW 33rd St . . . . Pompano Beach FL 33064 **800-874-7245** 954-783-6030
Utah Transit Authority (UTA)
PO Box 30810 . . . . Salt Lake City UT 84130 **888-743-3882** 801-262-5626
VIA Metropolitan Transit
800 W Myrtle St . . . . San Antonio TX 78212 **866-362-4200** 210-362-2000
Washington Metropolitan Area Transit Authority
600 Fifth St NW . . . . Washington DC 20001 **800-523-7009** 202-637-7000
York County Transportation Authority
1230 Roosevelt Ave . . . . York PA 17404 **800-632-9063** 717-846-5562

467 MATCHES & MATCHBOOKS

DD Bean & Sons Co
207 Peterborough St . . . . Jaffrey NH 03452 **800-326-8311** 603-532-8311
Maryland Match Corp
605 Alluvion St . . . . Baltimore MD 21230 **800-423-0013** 410-752-8164

468 MATERIAL HANDLING EQUIPMENT

SEE ALSO Conveyors & Conveying Equipment

Advance Lifts Inc
701 Kirk Rd . . . . Saint Charles IL 60174 **800-843-3625** 630-584-9881
Air Technical Industries
7501 Clover Ave . . . . Mentor OH 44060 **800-321-9680** 440-951-5191
American Crane & Equipment Corp
531 Old Swede Rd . . . . Douglassville PA 19518 **877-877-6778** 610-385-6061
American Power Pull Corp
550 W Linfoot St PO Box 109 . . . . Wauseon OH 43567 **800-808-5922** 419-335-7050
ATAP Inc 130 Industry way . . . . Eastaboga AL 36260 **800-362-2827** 256-362-2221
Autoquip Corp
1058 W Industrial Rd . . . . Guthrie OK 73044 **888-811-9876** 405-282-5200
Bayhead Products Corp
173 Crosby Rd . . . . Dover NH 03820 **800-229-4323** 603-742-3000
Berns 1250 W 17th St . . . . Long Beach CA 90813 **800-421-3773** 562-437-0471
Breeze-Eastern Corp
35 Melanie Ln . . . . Whippany NJ 07981 **800-929-1919** 973-602-1001
Busse/SJI Corp
124 N Columbus St . . . . Randolph WI 53956 **800-882-4995**
Cascade Corp
2201 NE 201st Ave . . . . Fairview OR 97024 **800-227-2233** 503-669-6300
NYSE: CASC
Charnstrom 5391 12th Ave E . . . . Shakopee MN 55379 **800-328-2962***
Cust Svc
Clark Material Handling Co
700 Enterprise Dr . . . . Lexington KY 40510 **866-252-5275** 859-422-6400
Columbus McKinnon Corp
140 John James Audubon Pkwy . . . . Amherst NY 14228 **800-888-0985** 716-689-5400
NASDAQ: CMCO
Craneveyor Corp
1524 Potrero Ave . . . . South El Monte CA 91733 **888-501-0050**
Crosby Group, The
2801 Dawson Rd . . . . Tulsa OK 74110 **800-772-1500** 918-834-4611
Crysteel Mfg Inc
52182 Ember Rd . . . . Lake Crystal MN 56055 **800-533-0494*** 507-726-2728
Orders
Dematic
507 Plymouth Ave NE . . . . Grand Rapids MI 49505 **877-725-7500***
Cust Svc
Detroit Hoist Co
6650 Sterling Dr N . . . . Sterling Heights MI 48312 **800-521-9126** 586-268-2600
Downs Crane & Hoist Company Inc
8827 Juniper St . . . . Los Angeles CA 90002 **800-748-5994** 323-589-6061
Drake-Scruggs Equipment Inc
2000 S Dirksen Pkwy . . . . Springfield IL 62703 **877-799-0398** 217-753-3871
Escalera Inc
708 S Industrial Dr PO Box 1359 . . . . Yuba City CA 95993 **800-622-1359** 530-673-6318
Excellon Automation Inc
20001 S Rancho Way . . . . Rancho Dominguez CA 90220 **800-392-3556** 310-668-7700
FL Smidth Inc 2040 Ave C . . . . Bethlehem PA 18017 **800-523-9482** 610-264-6011
Genie Industries Inc
18340 NE 76th St . . . . Redmond WA 98052 **800-536-1800** 425-881-1800
Gunnebo-Johnson Corp
1240 N Harvard Ave . . . . Tulsa OK 74115 **800-331-5460*** 918-832-8933
Sales
Harlan Global Manufacturing LLC
27 Stanley Rd . . . . Kansas City KS 66115 **800-255-4262** 913-342-5650
Harper Trucks Inc
PO Box 12330 . . . . Wichita KS 67277 **800-835-4099** 316-942-1381
Hilman Inc 12 Timber Ln . . . . Marlboro NJ 07746 **888-276-5548*** 732-462-6277
Cust Svc

				Toll-Free	Phone
Indusco Group 1200 West Hamburg St	Baltimore	MD	21230	**800-727-0665**	
Iowa Mold Tooling Co Inc (IMT) 500 W US Hwy 18	Garner	IA	50438	**800-247-5958**	641-923-3711
Kelly Systems Inc 422 N Western Ave	Chicago	IL	60612	**800-258-8237**	312-733-3224
Ken Garner Manufacturing - Rho Inc 1201 E 28th St # B	Chattanooga	TN	37404	**888-454-7207**	423-698-6200
Konecranes America 7300 Chippewa Blvd	Houston	TX	77086	**800-231-0241**	281-445-2225
Kornylak Corp 400 Heaton St	Hamilton	OH	45011	**800-837-5676**	513-863-1277
Landoll Corp 1900 North St *Cust Svc	Marysville	KS	66508	**800-446-5175***	785-562-5381
Leebaw Mfg Company Inc PO Box 553	Canfield	OH	44406	**800-841-8083**	
Lift-All Company Inc 1909 McFarland Dr	Landisville	PA	17538	**800-909-1964**	717-898-6615
Liftone 440 E Westinghouse Blvd	Charlotte	NC	28273	**855-543-8663**	
Lovegreen Industrial Services Inc 2280 Sibley Ct	Eagan	MN	55122	**800-262-8284**	651-890-1166
Magline Inc 1205 W Cedar St	Standish	MI	48658	**800-624-5463**	
Manitex Inc 3000 S Austin Ave	Georgetown	TX	78626	**877-314-3390**	512-942-3000
Matot Inc 2501 Van Buren St	Bellwood	IL	60104	**800-369-1070**	708-547-1888
Maxon Industries Inc 11921 Slauson Ave	Santa Fe Springs	CA	90670	**800-227-4116**	562-464-0099
Mazzella Lifting Technologies 21000 Aerospace Pkwy	Cleveland	OH	44142	**800-362-4601**	440-239-7000
McGuire W194 N11481 McCormick Dr PO Box 309	Germantown	WI	53022	**800-624-8473**	518-828-7652
Morris Material Handling Inc 315 W Forest Hill Ave	Oak Creek	WI	53154	**800-933-3001**	414-764-6200
NMC-Wollard Inc 2021 Truax Blvd	Eau Claire	WI	54703	**800-656-6867**	715-835-3151
North American Industries Inc 80 Holton St	Woburn	MA	01801	**800-847-8470**	781-897-4100
Nutting 450 Pheasant Ridge Dr	Watertown	SD	57201	**800-533-0337**	800-967-7333
Ohio Magnetics Inc 5400 Dunham Rd	Maple Heights	OH	44137	**800-486-6446**	216-662-8484
Pettibone Michigan 1100 Superior Ave	Baraga	MI	49908	**800-467-3884**	906-353-4800
Positech Corp 191 N Rush Lake Rd	Laurens	IA	50554	**800-831-6026**	712-841-4548
Process Equipment Inc 2770 Welborn St PO Box 1607	Pelham	AL	35124	**888-663-2028**	205-663-5330
Production Equipment Co 401 Liberty St	Meriden	CT	06450	**800-758-5697**	203-235-5795
Proserv Anchor Crane Group 455 Aldine Bender Rd	Houston	TX	77060	**800-835-2223**	281-405-9048
PTR Baler & Compactor Co 2207 E Ontario St	Philadelphia	PA	19134	**800-523-3654**	
Pucel Enterprises Inc 1440 E 36th St	Cleveland	OH	44114	**800-336-4986**	216-881-4604
Raymond Corp 22 S Canal St *General	Greene	NY	13778	**800-235-7200***	607-656-2311
RKI Inc 2301 Central Pkwy	Houston	TX	77092	**800-346-8988**	713-688-4414
Scott Industrial Systems Inc 4433 Interpoint Blvd	Dayton	OH	45424	**800-416-6023**	937-233-8146
Sherman & Reilly Inc 400 W 33rd St *Sales	Chattanooga	TN	37410	**800-251-7780***	423-756-5300
Snorkel 2009 Roseport Rd	Elwood	KS	66024	**800-255-0317**	785-989-3000
Southeast Industrial Equipment Inc 12200 Steele Creek Rd	Charlotte	NC	28273	**866-696-9125**	704-399-9700
Southworth Products Corp PO Box 1380	Portland	ME	04104	**800-743-1000**	207-878-0700
Steel King Industries Inc 2700 Chamber St	Stevens Point	WI	54481	**800-826-0203**	715-341-3120
Streator Dependable Manufacturing Co 1705 N Shabbona St	Streator	IL	61364	**800-795-0551**	815-672-0551
Taylor-Dunn Manufacturing Co 2114 W Ball Rd	Anaheim	CA	92804	**800-688-8680**	
Terex Corp Crane Div 202 Raleigh St	Wilmington	NC	28412	**877-794-5284**	910-395-8500
Terex-Telelect Inc 500 Oakwood Rd PO Box 1150	Watertown	SD	57201	**800-982-8975**	605-882-4000
Thern Inc 5712 Industrial Pk Rd PO Box 347	Winona	MN	55987	**800-843-7648**	507-454-2996
Triple/S Dynamics Inc 1031 S Haskell Ave PO Box 151027	Dallas	TX	75315	**800-527-2116**	214-828-8600
Vibra Screw Inc 755 Union Blvd	Totowa	NJ	07512	**800-243-7677**	973-256-7410
Waldon Mfg LLC 201 W Oklahoma Ave	Fairview	OK	73737	**866-283-2759**	580-227-3711
Western Hoist Inc 1839 Cleveland Ave	National City	CA	91950	**888-994-6478**	619-474-3361
Whiting Corp 26000 Whiting Way	Monee	IL	60449	**800-861-5744**	
WinHolt Equipment Group 141 Eileen Way	Syosset	NY	11791	**800-444-3595**	516-222-0335

469 MATTRESSES & ADJUSTABLE BEDS

SEE ALSO Household Furniture

				Toll-Free	Phone
Bechik Products Inc 860 Blue Gentian Rd Ste 140	Eagan	MN	55121	**800-328-6569**	
Bergad Inc 747 Eljer Way	Ford City	PA	16226	**888-476-8664**	724-763-2883
Bowles Mattress Co Inc 1220 Watt St	Jeffersonville	IN	47130	**800-223-7509**	812-288-8614
Classic Brands LLC 8214 Wellmoor Ct	Jessup	MD	20794	**877-707-7533**	410-904-0006
Comfortex Inc 1680 Wilkie Dr	Winona	MN	55987	**800-445-4007**	507-454-6579
Corsicana Bedding Inc PO Box 1050	Corsicana	TX	75151	**800-323-4349**	903-872-2591
Cotton Belt Inc 401 E Sater St	Pinetops	NC	27864	**800-849-4192**	252-827-4192
Englander International 1308 Teasley Ln Ste 183	Denton	TX	76205	**800-489-9994**	888-909-0551
Imperial Bedding Co 720 11th St PO Box 5347	Huntington	WV	25703	**800-529-3321**	304-529-3321
Jackson Mattress Company Inc 3154 Camden Rd	Fayetteville	NC	28306	**800-763-7378**	910-425-0131
Jamison Bedding Inc PO Box 681948 *Cust Svc	Franklin	TN	37068	**800-255-1883***	615-794-1883
King Koil Licensing Company Inc 7501 S Quincy St	Willowbrook	IL	60527	**800-525-8331**	
Kingsdown Inc 126 W Holt St *Cust Svc	Mebane	NC	27302	**800-354-5464***	919-563-3531
Kolcraft Enterprises Inc 10832 NC Hwy 211 E *Cust Svc	Aberdeen	NC	28315	**800-453-7673***	910-944-9345
Leggett & Platt Inc 1 Leggett Rd PO Box 757 *NYSE: LEG*	Carthage	MO	64836	**800-888-4569**	417-358-8131
Palliser Furniture Upholstery Ltd 70 Lexington Pk	Winnipeg	MB	R2G4H2	**866-444-0777**	
Restonic Mattress Corp 737 Main St	Buffalo	NY	14203	**800-898-6075**	
Riverside Mattress Co 225 Dunn Rd	Fayetteville	NC	28312	**888-288-5195**	910-483-0461
Serta Mattress 3 Golf Ctr Ste 392	Hoffman Estates	IL	60169	**888-557-3782**	888-708-1466
Tempur-Pedic North America LLC 1000 Tempur Way	Lexington	KY	40511	**800-821-6621**	
Therapedic International 103 College Rd E 2nd Fl	Princeton	NJ	08540	**800-314-4433**	609-720-0700

470 MEASURING, TESTING, CONTROLLING INSTRUMENTS

SEE ALSO Electrical Signals Measuring & Testing Instruments

				Toll-Free	Phone
All Weather Inc 1165 National Dr	Sacramento	CA	95834	**800-824-5873**	916-928-1000
AMETEK Inc Test & Calibration Instruments Div 8600 Somerset Dr	Largo	FL	33773	**800-733-5427**	727-538-6132
Beta LaserMike Inc 8001 Technology Blvd	Dayton	OH	45424	**800-886-9935**	937-233-9935
Canberra Industries Inc 800 Research Pkwy *Sales	Meriden	CT	06450	**800-243-3955***	203-238-2351
Clayton Industries 17477 Hurley St	City of Industry	CA	91744	**800-423-4585**	626-435-1200
Crane Nuclear Inc 2825 Cobb International Blvd	Kennesaw	GA	30152	**800-795-8013**	770-429-4600
Davis Instrument Corp 3465 Diablo Ave	Hayward	CA	94545	**800-678-3669**	510-732-9229
Delta Cooling Towers Inc PO Box 315	Rockaway	NJ	07866	**800-289-3358**	973-586-2201
Dynisco LLC 38 Forge Pkwy *General	Franklin	MA	02038	**800-396-4726***	508-541-9400
Endevco Corp 30700 Rancho Viejo Rd	San Juan Capistrano	CA	92675	**800-982-6732**	949-493-8181
Enidine Inc 7 Centre Dr	Orchard Park	NY	14127	**800-852-8508**	716-662-1900
Entest Inc 15020 Beltway Dr	Addison	TX	75001	**800-955-0077**	972-980-9876
Fairfield Industries Inc 1111 Gillingham Ln	Sugar Land	TX	77478	**800-231-9809**	281-275-7500
Fiber Instruments Sales Inc 161 Clear Rd *Sales	Oriskany	NY	13424	**800-500-0347***	315-736-2206
Fisher Research Laboratory Inc 1120 Alza Dr	El Paso	TX	79907	**800-685-5050**	915-225-0333
Garrett Metal Detectors 1881 W State St	Garland	TX	75042	**800-234-6151**	972-494-6151
George Risk Industries Inc 802 S Elm St *OTC: RSKIA* ■ *Sales	Kimball	NE	69145	**800-523-1227***	308-235-4645
Herman H Sticht Company Inc 45 Main St Ste 701	Brooklyn	NY	11201	**800-221-3203**	718-852-7602
Interface Inc 7401 E Butherus Dr	Scottsdale	AZ	85260	**800-947-5598**	480-948-5555
L-3 Avionics Systems 5353 52nd St SE	Grand Rapids	MI	49512	**800-253-9525**	616-949-6600
Ludlum Measurements Inc 501 Oak St	Sweetwater	TX	79556	**800-622-0828**	325-235-5494
Magnetic Analysis Corp 103 Fairview Park Dr	Elmsford	NY	10523	**800-463-8622**	914-530-2000
Marposs Corp 3300 Cross Creek Pkwy	Auburn Hills	MI	48326	**888-627-7677**	248-370-0404
Metrix Instrument Co 8824 Fallbrook Dr	Houston	TX	77064	**800-638-7494**	281-940-1802
MTS Systems Corp 14000 Technology Dr *NASDAQ: MTSC* ■ *Cust Svc	Eden Prairie	MN	55344	**800-328-2255***	952-937-4000
Mustang Dynamometer 2300 Pinnacle Pkwy	Twinsburg	OH	44087	**888-468-7826**	330-963-5400
Ohmart/VEGA Corp 4241 Allendorf Dr	Cincinnati	OH	45209	**800-367-5383**	513-272-0131
Preco Electronics Inc 10335 W Emerald St	Boise	ID	83704	**866-977-7326**	208-323-1000
Rochester Gauges Inc of Texas 11616 Harry Hines Blvd	Dallas	TX	75229	**800-821-1829**	972-241-2161
Rudolph Technologies Inc 16 Jonspin Rd *NASDAQ: RTEC*	Wilmington	MA	01887	**877-467-8365**	973-691-1300

Classified Section

				Toll-Free	Phone
Setra Systems Inc					
159 Swanson Rd	Boxborough	MA	01719	800-257-3872	978-263-1400
Sierra Monitor Corp					
1991 Tarob Ct	Milpitas	CA	95035	888-509-1970	408-262-6611
OTC: SRMC					
Smiths Detection					
2202 Lakeside Blvd	Edgewood	MD	21040	800-297-0955	410-510-9100
Sorrento Electronics Inc					
4949 Greencraig Ln	San Diego	CA	92123	800-252-1180	858-522-8300
SuperFlow Technologies Group					
4747 Centennial Blvd	Colorado Springs	CO	80919	800-471-7701	719-471-1746
Taber Industries					
455 Bryant St	North Tonawanda	NY	14120	800-333-5300	716-694-4000
Testing Machines Inc					
40 McCullough Dr	New Castle	DE	19720	800-678-3221*	302-613-5600
*General					
Unilux Inc					
59 N Fifth St	Saddle Brook	NJ	07663	800-522-0801	201-712-1266
Vaisala Inc 10-D Gill St	Woburn	MA	01801	888-824-7252	781-933-4500
Vivax-Metrotech Corp					
3251 Olcott St	Santa Clara	CA	95054	800-446-3392	408-734-1400
White's Electronics Inc					
1011 Pleasant Valley Rd	Sweet Home	OR	97386	800-547-6911*	541-367-6121
*Sales					

471   MEAT PACKING PLANTS

SEE ALSO Poultry Processing

				Toll-Free	Phone
Abbyland Foods Inc					
502 E Linden St PO Box 69	Abbotsford	WI	54405	800-732-5483	715-223-6386
Allen Bros Inc					
3737 S Halsted St	Chicago	IL	60609	800-548-7777	773-890-5100
Alpine Meats					
9850 Lowr Sacramento Rd	Stockton	CA	95210	800-399-6328	209-477-2691
American Foods Group Inc					
544 Acme St	Green Bay	WI	54302	800-345-0293	920-437-6330
Carolina Packers Inc					
2999 S Bright Leaf Blvd	Smithfield	NC	27577	800-682-7675	919-934-2181
Central Nebraska Packing Inc					
2800 E Eigth St PO Box 550	North Platte	NE	69103	800-445-2881*	308-532-1250
*Cust Svc					
Chisesi Bros Meat Packing Co					
5221 Jefferson Hwy	New Orleans	LA	70123	800-966-3550	504-822-3550
Clougherty Packing Co					
3049 E Vernon Ave	Los Angeles	CA	90058	800-846-7635*	
*Sales					
Cougle Commission Co					
345 N Aberdeen St	Chicago	IL	60607	800-568-2240	312-666-7861
Cudahy Patrick Inc					
1 Sweet Apple-Wood Ln	Cudahy	WI	53110	800-486-6900	414-744-2000
Curtis Packing Co					
2416 Randolph Ave	Greensboro	NC	27406	800-852-7890	336-275-7684
Eddy Packing Company Inc					
404 Airport Dr	Yoakum	TX	77995	800-292-2361	361-293-2361
Esskay Inc					
111 Commerce St	Smithfield	VA	23430	855-411-7675	
Farm Boy Meats					
2761 N Kentucky Ave	Evansville	IN	47711	800-852-3976	812-425-5231
Food Consulting Co, The					
13724 Recuerdo Dr	Del Mar	CA	92014	800-793-2844	858-793-4658
Greater Omaha Packing Company Inc					
3001 L St	Omaha	NE	68107	800-747-5400	402-731-1700
Harris Ranch Beef Co					
16277 S McCall Ave PO Box 220	Selma	CA	93662	800-742-1955	
Hatfield Quality Meats Inc					
2700 Clemens Rd	Hatfield	PA	19440	800-743-1191	215-368-2500
J Freirich Foods Inc					
815 W Kerr St PO Box 1529	Salisbury	NC	28144	800-554-4788	800-221-1315
JH Routh Packing Company Inc					
4413 W Bogart Rd	Sandusky	OH	44870	800-446-6759	419-626-2251
John Morrell & Co					
805 E Kemper Rd	Cincinnati	OH	45246	800-722-1127	513-346-3540
Morrilton Packing Company Inc					
51 Blue Diamond Dr	Morrilton	AR	72110	800-264-2475	501-354-2474
National Beef Packing Co LLC					
12200 Ambassador Dr Ste 500					
PO Box 20046	Kansas City	MO	64163	800-449-2333	
Pearl Meat Packing Company Inc					
27 York Ave	Randolph	MA	02368	800-462-3022	781-228-5100
Plumrose USA Inc					
1901 Butterfield Rd Ste 305	Downers Grove	IL	60515	800-526-4909	732-624-4040
Quality Meats & Seafoods					
700 Center St	West Fargo	ND	58078	800-342-4250	701-282-0202
Quincy Street Inc					
13350 Quincy St	Holland	MI	49424	800-784-6290	616-399-3330
Rose Packing Company Inc					
65 S Barrington Rd	South Barrington	IL	60010	800-323-7363	847-381-5700
Sam Hausman Meat Packer Inc					
4261 Beacon	Corpus Christi	TX	78403	800-364-5521	361-883-5521
Sioux-Preme Packing Co					
4241 US 75th Ave	Sioux Center	IA	51250	800-735-7675*	
*General					
Travisco					
7210 Clinton Hwy PO Box 670	Powell	TN	37849	800-247-7606	
Tyson Pet Products Inc					
812 Third St NW	Independence	IA	50644	877-303-9247	

472   MEDICAL ASSOCIATIONS - STATE

SEE ALSO Health & Medical Professionals Associations

				Toll-Free	Phone
Alabama Medical Assn					
19 S Jackson St	Montgomery	AL	36104	800-239-6272	
Arizona Medical Assn, The (ArMA)					
810 W Bethany Home Rd	Phoenix	AZ	85013	800-482-3480	602-246-8901
Asah 2125 Hwy 33	Trenton	NJ	08690	800-955-2321	609-890-1400
California Medical Assn					
1201 J St Ste 200	Sacramento	CA	95814	800-300-1506	916-444-5532
Colorado Medical Society					
7351 Lowry Blvd	Denver	CO	80230	800-654-5653	720-859-1001
Hawaii Medical Assn					
1360 S Beretania St	Honolulu	HI	96816	888-536-2792	808-536-7702
Illinois State Medical Society					
20 N Michigan Ave Ste 700	Chicago	IL	60602	800-782-4767	312-782-1654
Indiana State Medical Assn					
322 Canal Walk	Indianapolis	IN	46202	800-257-4762	317-261-2060
Iowa Medical Society					
515 E Locust St Ste 400	Des Moines	IA	50309	800-747-3070	515-223-1401
Kansas Medical Society					
623 SW Tenth Ave	Topeka	KS	66612	800-332-0156	785-235-2383
Louisiana State Medical Society					
6767 Perkins Rd Ste 100	Baton Rouge	LA	70808	800-375-9508	225-763-8500
Maryland State Medical Society					
1211 Cathedral St	Baltimore	MD	21201	800-492-1056	410-539-0872
Massachusetts Medical Society (MMS)					
860 Winter St	Waltham	MA	02451	800-322-2303	781-893-4610
Medical Assn of Georgia (MAG)					
1849 The Exchange Ste 200	Atlanta	GA	30339	800-282-0224	678-303-9290
Medical Society of Virginia					
2924 Emerywood Pkwy Ste 300	Richmond	VA	23294	800-746-6768	
Michigan State Medical Society					
120 W Saginaw St	East Lansing	MI	48823	800-482-4881	517-337-1351
Missouri State Medical Assn					
113 Madison St	Jefferson City	MO	65101	800-869-6762	573-636-5151
Montana Medical Assn					
2021 11th Ave Ste 1	Helena	MT	59601	877-443-4000	406-443-4000
New Hampshire Medical Society					
7 N State St	Concord	NH	03301	800-564-1909	
New Jersey Medical Society					
2 Princess Rd	Lawrenceville	NJ	08648	800-706-7893	609-896-1766
New Mexico Medical Society (NMMS)					
316 Osuna Rd NE Ste 501	Albuquerque	NM	87107	800-748-1596	505-828-0237
New York State Medical Assn					
865 Merrick Ave PO Box 5404	Westbury	NY	11590	800-523-4405	516-488-6100
North Carolina Medical Society					
222 N Person St	Raleigh	NC	27601	800-722-1350	919-833-3836
Ohio State Medical Assn					
3401 Mill Run Dr	Hilliard	OH	43026	800-766-6762	
Oregon Medical Assn (OMA)					
11740 SW 68th Pkwy Ste 100	Portland	OR	97223	877-605-3229	503-619-8000
Ovarian Cancer Research Fund Alliance					
1101 14th St NW Ste 850	Washington	DC	20005	866-399-6262	202-331-1332
Penna State Education Assn Harrisburg (PSEA)					
400 N Third St PO Box 1724	Harrisburg	PA	17105	800-944-7732	717-255-7000
Pennsylvania Medical Society					
777 E Pk Dr	Harrisburg	PA	17111	800-228-7823	855-726-3348
South Carolina Medical Assn					
132 Westpark Blvd	Columbia	SC	29210	800-327-1021	803-798-6207
Texas Medical Assn					
401 W 15th St	Austin	TX	78701	800-880-1300	512-370-1300
Vermont Medical Society					
134 Main St	Montpelier	VT	05601	800-640-8767	802-223-7898
Washington State Medical Assn					
2001 Sixth Ave Ste 2700	Seattle	WA	98121	800-552-0612	206-441-9762
Wisconsin State Medical Society					
330 E Lakeside St PO Box 1109	Madison	WI	53701	866-442-3800	

473   MEDICAL & DENTAL EQUIPMENT & SUPPLIES - WHOL

				Toll-Free	Phone
A Plus International Inc					
5138 Eucalyptus Ave	Chino	CA	91710	800-762-1123	909-591-5168
ABC Home Medical Supply Inc					
397 Eagleview Blvd	Exton	PA	19341	866-897-8588	
Ace Medical Inc					
94-910 Moloalo St	Waipahu	HI	96797	866-678-3601	808-678-3600
Adventure Medical Kits					
7700 Edgewater Dr Ste 526					
PO Box 43309.	Oakland	CA	94624	800-324-3517	
Aeroflow Inc					
3165 Sweeten Creek Rd	Asheville	NC	28803	888-345-1780	
Aethon Inc					
200 Business Ctr Dr	Pittsburgh	PA	15205	888-201-9522	412-322-2975
Aktina Medical Physics Corp					
360 N Rt 9W	Congers	NY	10920	888-433-3380	845-268-0101
Allegro Industries					
1360 Shiloh Church Rd	Piedmont	SC	29673	800-622-3530	864-846-8740
Alma Lasers Inc					
485 Half Day Rd Ste 100	Buffalo Grove	IL	60089	866-414-2562	
Alpha Imaging Inc					
4455 Glenbrook Rd	Willoughby	OH	44094	800-331-7327	440-953-3800
Alpha Source Inc					
6619 W Calumet Rd	Milwaukee	WI	53223	800-654-9845	414-760-2222
Amendia Inc					
1755 W Oak Pkwy	Marietta	GA	30062	877-755-3329	
American Medical ID					
949 Wakefield Ste 100	Houston	TX	77018	800-363-5985	
Ampronix Inc 15 Whatney	Irvine	CA	92618	800-400-7972	949-273-8000
Andrew Technologies LLC					
1421 Edinger Ave Ste D	Tustin	CA	92780	888-959-7674	
Andromed Inc					
5003 Levy St	Saint Laurent	QC	H4R2N9	888-336-0043	514-336-0043
Anesthesia Service Inc					
1821 N Classen Blvd	Oklahoma City	OK	73106	800-336-3356	405-525-3588
Ansar Group Inc, The					
242 S Eighth St Ste 1 1st Fl	Philadelphia	PA	19107	888-883-7804	877-228-6863
Applied Medical Technology Inc					
8000 Katherine Blvd	Brecksville	OH	44141	800-869-7382	440-717-4000
Aqueduct Medical Inc					
665 Third St Ste 20.	San Francisco	CA	94107	877-365-4325	

Company / Address	City	State	Zip	Toll-Free	Phone
Arcamed Inc 5101 Decatur Blvd Ste A	Indianapolis	IN	46241	**877-545-6622**	317-822-7799
Avalign Technologies Inc 272 E Deerpath Rd Ste 208	Lake Forest	IL	60045	**855-282-5446**	
Banyan International Corp 11629 49th Pl W	Mukilteo	WA	98275	**888-782-8548**	
Bisco Dental Products (Canada) Inc 2571 Smith St	Richmond	BC	V6X2J1	**800-667-8811**	604-276-8662
Block Scientific Inc 22 Sawgrass Dr	Bellport	NY	11713	**866-203-5777**	631-589-1118
Blue Ridge X-Ray Company Inc 120 Vista Blvd	Arden	NC	28704	**800-727-7290**	
Burkhart Dental Supply Co 2502 S 78th St *Cust Svc	Tacoma	WA	98409	**800-562-8176***	253-474-7761
Burlington Medical Supplies Inc 3 Elmhurst St	Newport News	VA	23603	**800-221-3466**	
Byram Healthcare Centers Inc 120 Bloomingdale Rd	White Plains	NY	10605	**800-354-4054**	877-902-9726
CAN-med Healthcare 99 Susie Lake Crescent	Halifax	NS	B3S1C3	**800-565-7553**	902-455-4649
Canadian Hospital Specialties ULC 2810 Coventry Rd	Oakville	ON	L6H6R1	**800-461-1423**	905-825-9300
CardioMed Supplies Inc 199 Saint David St	Lindsay	ON	K9V5K7	**800-387-9757**	705-328-2518
CAREstream Medical Ltd 20133 102 Ave Units 1	Langley	BC	V1M4B4	**888-310-2186**	
Carolina Apothecary Inc 726 S Scales St	Reidsville	NC	27320	**800-633-1447**	336-342-0071
Cascade Orthopedic Supply Inc 2638 Aztec Dr	Chico	CA	95928	**800-888-0865**	
CCS Medical Inc 1505 LBJ Fwy Ste 600	Farmers Branch	TX	75234	**800-726-9811**	800-260-8193
CERAGEM Co Inc 3699 Wilshire Blvd Ste 930	Los Angeles	CA	90010	**800-903-9333**	213-480-7070
Charter Medical Ltd 3948-A Westpoint Blvd	Winston-Salem	NC	27103	**866-458-3116**	
Dectro International Inc 1000 Blvd du Parc-Technologique	Quebec	QC	G1P4S3	**800-463-5566**	418-650-0303
Dedicated Distribution Inc 640 Miami Ave	Kansas City	KS	66105	**800-325-8367**	
Delta Medical Systems Inc 3280 Gateway Rd Ste 200	Brookfield	WI	53045	**800-798-7574**	
Derma Sciences 311 Enterprise Dr	Plainsboro	NJ	08536	**800-825-4325**	609-514-4744
DogLeggs LLC 1155 Elm St	York	PA	17403	**800-313-1218**	
Dr Fresh Inc 6645 Caballero Blvd	Buena Park	CA	90620	**866-373-7371**	
Dukal Corp 2 Fleetwood Ct	Ronkonkoma	NY	11779	**800-243-0741**	631-656-3800
Electromek Diagnostic Systems Inc 412 W US Hwy 40	Troy	IL	62294	**800-466-6761**	618-667-6761
EndoShape Inc 5425 Airport Blvd Ste 101	Boulder	CO	80301	**844-870-5070**	303-951-6898
Enthermics Inc W164 N9221 Water St	Menomonee Falls	WI	53051	**800-862-9276**	262-251-8356
Erchonia Corp 650 Atlantis Rd	Melbourne	FL	32904	**888-242-0571**	321-473-1251
Expeditor Systems Inc 4090 Nine McFarland Dr	Alpharetta	GA	30004	**800-843-9651**	
Fresenius Medical Care 920 Winter St	Waltham	MA	02451	**800-662-1237**	781-699-9000
GE Walker Inc 4420 E Adamo Dr Ste 206	Tampa	FL	33605	**800-749-2483**	
Global Medical Imaging LLC 222 Rampart St	Charlotte	NC	28203	**800-958-9986**	
Goetze Dental 3939 NE 33 Terr	Kansas City	MO	64117	**800-692-0804**	816-413-1200
Golden Technologies Inc 401 Bridge St	Old Forge	PA	18518	**800-624-6374**	
Griswold Machine & Engineering Inc 8530 M 60	Union City	MI	49094	**800-248-2054**	517-741-4300
Grogans Health Care Supply Inc 1016 S Broadway St	Lexington	KY	40504	**800-365-1020**	859-254-6661
Hanson Medical Systems Inc 1954 Howell Branch Rd	Winter Park	FL	32792	**877-671-3883**	407-671-3883
Healthcom 1600 W Jackson St	Sullivan	IL	61951	**800-525-6237**	
HealthSmart International 1931 Norman Dr	Waukegan	IL	60085	**800-526-4753**	
HemaSource Inc 4158 Nike Dr	West Jordan	UT	84088	**888-844-4362**	
Henry Schein Inc 135 Duryea Rd *NASDAQ: HSIC*	Melville	NY	11747	**800-582-2702**	631-843-5500
Integra LifeSciences Corp 311 Enterprise Dr	Plainsboro	NJ	08536	**800-654-2873**	609-275-0500
Jorgensen Laboratories Inc 1450 Van Buren Ave	Loveland	CO	80538	**800-525-5614**	970-669-2500
Karl Storz Endoscopy-america Inc 600 Corporate Pt	Culver City	CA	90230	**800-321-1304**	310-338-8100
KCI Medical Canada Inc 75 Courtneypark Dr W Unit 2	Mississauga	ON	L5W0E3	**800-668-5403**	905-565-7187
Keir Surgical Ltd 126-408 E Kent Ave S	Vancouver	BC	V5X2X7	**800-663-4525**	604-261-9596
Kentec Medical Inc 17871 Fitch	Irvine	CA	92614	**800-825-5996**	949-863-0810
Keystone Industries 480 S Democrat Rd	Gibbstown	NJ	08027	**800-333-3131**	856-663-4700
Laerdal Medical Corp 167 Myers Corners Rd PO Box 1840	Wappingers Falls	NY	12590	**800-227-1143**	845-297-7770
Leeches USA Ltd 300 Shames Dr	Westbury	NY	11590	**800-645-3569**	516-333-2570
LENSAR Inc 2800 Discovery Dr	Orlando	FL	32826	**888-536-7271**	
Les Wilkins & Assoc Inc 6850 35th Ave NE	Seattle	WA	98115	**800-426-6634**	206-522-0908
Life-Assist Inc 11277 Sunrise Park Dr	Rancho Cordova	CA	95742	**800-824-6016**	
Mada Medical Products Inc 625 Washington Ave	Carlstadt	NJ	07072	**800-526-6370**	201-460-0454
Magnaserv Enterprises Inc 2862 SE Monroe St	Stuart	FL	34997	**866-283-4288**	
Marketlab Inc 6850 Southbelt Dr	Caledonia	MI	49316	**866-237-3722**	616-656-2484
MCI Optonix LLC 2020 Contractors Rd Ste 8	Sedona	AZ	86336	**800-678-6649**	
McKesson Medical Group Extended Care 8121 Tenth Ave N	Golden Valley	MN	55427	**800-328-8111**	
McKesson Medical-Surgical 8741 Landmark Rd	Richmond	VA	23228	**800-446-3008**	415-983-8300
Medcare Products Inc 151 E Cliff Rd	Burnsville	MN	55337	**800-695-4479**	952-894-7076
MedSupply 5850 E Shields Ave Ste 105	Fresno	CA	93727	**800-889-9081**	559-292-1540
Mergenet Solutions Inc 1701 W Hillsboro Blvd Ste 303	Deerfield Beach	FL	33442	**888-956-2526**	561-208-3770
Merry X-Ray Corp 4909 Murphy Canyon Rd Ste 120	San Diego	CA	92123	**800-635-9729**	
Mesa Laboratories Inc 12100 W Sixth Ave *NASDAQ: MLAB* ■ *Sales	Lakewood	CO	80228	**800-992-6372***	303-987-8000
MinXray Inc 3611 Commercial Ave	Northbrook	IL	60062	**800-221-2245**	847-564-0323
Mizuho OSI Inc 30031 Ahern Ave	Union City	CA	94587	**800-777-4674**	510-429-1500
Mmar Medical Group Inc 9619 Yupondale Dr	Houston	TX	77080	**800-662-7633**	713-465-2003
Mobile Medical International Corp 2176 Portland St PO Box 672	St. Johnsbury	VT	05819	**800-692-5205**	802-748-2322
Modo 20325 NW von Neumann Dr	Beaverton	OR	97006	**800-685-8784**	
Moore Medical Corp 389 John Downey Dr *Sales	New Britain	CT	06050	**800-234-1464***	860-826-3600
Nationwide Medical Equipment Inc 1510 Stuart Rd NE Ste 109	Cleveland	TN	37312	**888-826-6245**	423-478-7433
Nbn Infusions 2 Pin Oak Ln Ste 250	Cherry Hill	NJ	08003	**800-253-9111**	856-669-0217
Nota Scientific Inc 4206 Sylon Blvd	Hainesport	NJ	08036	**800-343-6015**	609-265-8210
Neuro-Tec Inc 975 Cobb Pl Blvd Ste 301	Kennesaw	GA	30144	**800-554-3407**	
NeuroPace Inc 455 N Bernardo Ave	Mountain View	CA	94043	**866-726-3876**	
Nidek Inc 47651 Westinghouse Dr	Fremont	CA	94539	**800-223-9044**	510-226-5700
Nihon Kohden America Inc 90 Icon	Foothill Ranch	CA	92610	**800-325-0283**	949-580-1555
Noraxon US.A. Inc 15770 N Greenway-Hayden Loop Ste 100	Scottsdale	AZ	85260	**800-364-8985**	480-443-3413
North American Rescue LLC 35 Tedwall Ct	Greer	SC	29650	**888-689-6277**	
NOVA Medical Products 1470 Beachey Pl	Carson	CA	90746	**800-557-6682**	
Numotion 126 Airport Rd	Scott City	MO	63780	**877-856-9154**	573-334-0600
Nurse Assist Inc 3400 Northern Cross Blvd	Fort Worth	TX	76137	**800-649-6800**	817-231-1300
NXC Imaging 2118 Fourth Ave S	Minneapolis	MN	55404	**800-328-5016**	
Oakworks Inc 923 E Wellspring Rd	New Freedom	PA	17349	**800-558-8850**	717-235-6807
OEC Medical Systems Inc 384 Wright Brothers Dr	Salt Lake City	UT	84116	**800-874-7378**	
Omega Medical Health Systems Inc 1200 E High St Ste 106	Pottstown	PA	19464	**866-716-6342**	
Omron Healthcare Inc 1925 W Field Ct	Lake Forest	IL	60045	**877-216-1333**	847-680-6200
Onyx Medical Corp 1800 N Shelby Oaks Dr	Memphis	TN	38134	**800-238-6981**	
Orthopedic Designs North America Inc 5912 Breckenridge Pkwy Ste F	Tampa	FL	33610	**888-635-8535**	
Ottobock North America 11501 Alterra Pky Ste 600	Austin	TX	78758	**800-328-4058**	
Owens & Minor Inc 9120 Lockwood Blvd *NYSE: OMI*	Mechanicsville	VA	23116	**800-488-8850**	804-723-7000
Paragon Medical Inc 8 Matchett Industrial Park Dr	Pierceton	IN	46562	**800-225-6975**	574-594-2140
Patterson Dental Supply Inc 1031 Mendota Heights Rd *NASDAQ: PDCO*	Saint Paul	MN	55120	**800-328-5536**	
Pearson Dental Supplies Inc 13161 Telfair Ave	Sylmar	CA	91342	**800-535-4535**	818-362-2600
Perio Sciences LLC 11700 Preston Rd Ste 660	Dallas	TX	75230	**800-915-8110**	
Permobil Inc 300 Duke Dr	Lebanon	TN	37090	**800-736-0925**	615-547-1889
PerSys Medical Co 5310 Elm St	Houston	TX	77081	**888-737-7978**	
Philips Healthcare 22100 Bothell Everett Hwy	Bothell	WA	98021	**888-744-5477**	
PickPoint 3149 Skyway Ct Ste 101	Fremont	CA	94539	**800-636-1288**	925-924-1700
Precision BioLogic Inc 140 Eileen Stubbs Ave	Dartmouth	NS	B3B0A9	**800-267-2796**	902-468-6422
Prestige Medical Corporation International 8600 Wilbur Ave	Northridge	CA	91324	**800-762-3333**	818-993-3030
Proa Medical Inc 2512 Artesia Blvd Ste 305-C	Redondo Beach	CA	90278	**800-899-3385**	
ProMed Molded Products Inc 15600 Medina Rd	Plymouth	MN	55447	**855-331-3800**	763-331-3800
Radiancy Inc 40 Ramland Rd S Ste 200	Orangeburg	NY	10962	**888-661-2220**	845-398-1647

				Toll-Free	Phone
RedRick Technologies Inc					
21624 Adelaide Rd	Mount Brydges	ON	N0L1W0	**800-340-9511**	
Reshape Medical					
100 Calle Iglesia	San Clemente	CA	92672	**844-937-7374**	
Rgh Enterprises Inc					
1810 Summit Commerce Pk	Twinsburg	OH	44087	**800-307-5930**	330-963-6998
Saebo Inc					
2709 Water Ridge Pkwy					
Ste 100 Six LakePointe Plz	Charlotte	NC	28217	**888-284-5433**	
SciCan Ltd					
701 Technology Dr	Canonsburg	PA	15317	**800-572-1211**	724-820-1600
Shared Service Systems Inc					
1725 S 20th St	Omaha	NE	68108	**800-228-9976**	402-536-5300
SLMP LLC					
407 Interchange St	Mckinney	TX	75071	**800-442-3573**	972-436-1010
SmartScrubs LLC					
3400 E Mcdowell Rd	Phoenix	AZ	85008	**800-800-5788**	
Somagen Diagnostics Inc					
9220 25th Ave	Edmonton	AB	T6N1E1	**800-661-9993**	780-702-9500
Specialty Surgical Products Inc					
1131 US Hwy 93 N	Victor	MT	59875	**888-878-0811**	406-961-0102
SST Group Inc					
309 Laurelwood Rd Ste 20	Santa Clara	CA	95054	**800-944-6281**	408-350-3450
Synovis Micro Companies Alliance Inc					
439 Industrial Ln	Birmingham	AL	35211	**800-510-3318**	205-941-0111
Sysmex America Inc					
577 Aptakisic Rd	Lincolnshire	IL	60069	**800-379-7639**	800-462-1262
Tech West Vacuum Inc					
2625 N Argyle Ave	Fresno	CA	93727	**800-428-7139**	559-291-1650
Technical Instrument San Francisco					
1826 Rollins Rd	Burlingame	CA	94010	**866-800-9797**	650-651-3000
Tetra Medical Supply Corp					
6364 W Gross Pt Rd	Niles	IL	60714	**800-621-4041***	847-647-0590
*Cust Svc					
Therapy Support Inc					
2803 N Oak Grove Ave	Springfield	MO	65803	**877-885-4325**	417-447-0987
Thermedx LLC					
31200 Solon Rd Unit 1	Solon	OH	44139	**888-542-9276**	440-542-0883
Ti Ba Enterprises Inc					
25 Hytec Cir	Rochester	NY	14606	**800-836-8422**	585-247-1212
Tosoh Bioscience Inc					
6000 Shoreline Ct Ste 101	South San Francisco	CA	94080	**800-248-6764**	650-615-4970
TPC Advance Technology Inc					
18525 Gale Ave	City Of Industry	CA	91748	**800-560-8222**	626-810-4337
Tri State Distribution Inc					
600 Vista Dr	Sparta	TN	38583	**800-392-9824**	
Tri-State Surgical Supply & Equipment Ltd					
409 Hoyt St	Brooklyn	NY	11231	**800-899-8741**	718-624-1000
Triangle X-ray Co					
4900 Thornton Rd Ste 117	Raleigh	NC	27616	**866-763-9729**	919-876-6156
Trudell Medical Group Ltd					
758 Third St	London	ON	N5V5J7	**800-757-4881**	519-685-8800
Turn-key Medical Inc					
365 SW Fifth Ave	Meridian	ID	83642	**877-484-9549**	
USDiagnostics Inc					
2 Parade St	Huntsville	AL	35806	**888-669-4337**	256-534-4881
Valeritas Inc					
750 Rt 202 S Ste 600	Bridgewater	NJ	08807	**855-384-8848**	908-927-9920
VasoHealthcare					
Revolution Mill Studios 1150 Revolution Mill Dr St	Greensboro	NC	27405	**877-900-8276**	336-398-8276
Ventec Life Systems					
19021 120th Ave NE Ste E101	Bothell	WA	98011	**844-640-4357**	844-698-6276
VWR International					
100 Matsonford Rd Bldg 1 Ste 200	Radnorpa	PA	19087	**800-932-5000**	610-431-1700
Water-Jel Technologies LLC					
50 Broad St	Carlstadt	NJ	07072	**800-693-1171**	201-806-3040
Western Drug					
3604 San Fernando Rd	Glendale	CA	91204	**800-891-3661**	818-956-6691
William V MacGill & Co					
1000 N Lombard Rd	Lombard	IL	60148	**800-323-2841**	630-889-0500
Z-Medica Corp					
4 Fairfield Blvd	Wallingford	CT	06492	**800-343-8656**	203-294-0000
Zee Medical Inc					
22 Corporate Pk	Irvine	CA	92606	**800-435-7763**	

MEDICAL FACILITIES

SEE Substance Abuse Treatment Centers ; Hospices ; Developmental Centers ; Imaging Services - Diagnostic ; Health Care Providers - Ancillary ; Hospitals

474   MEDICAL INSTRUMENTS & APPARATUS - MFR

SEE ALSO Medical Supplies - Mfr ; Imaging Equipment & Systems - Medical

				Toll-Free	Phone
Accurate Surgical & Scientific Instruments Corp					
300 Shames Dr	Westbury	NY	11590	**800-645-3569**	516-333-2570
AccuTech LLC					
2641 La Mirada Dr	Vista	CA	92081	**800-749-9910**	760-599-6555
ACIST Medical Systems Inc					
7905 Fuller Rd	Eden Prairie	MN	55344	**888-667-6648**	952-941-3507
Acme United Corp					
55 Walls Dr Ste 201	Fairfield	CT	06824	**800-835-2263**	
NYSE: ACU					
Ad-tech Medical Instrument Corp					
400 W Oakview Pky	Oak Creek	WI	53154	**800-776-1555**	262-634-1555
AESCULAP Inc					
3773 Corporate Pkwy	Center Valley	PA	18034	**800-282-9000**	
AirClean Systems Inc					
3248 Lake Woodard Dr	Raleigh	NC	27604	**800-849-0472**	919-255-3220
Alfa Wassermann Inc					
4 Henderson Dr	West Caldwell	NJ	07006	**800-220-4488**	973-882-8630
Allied Healthcare Products Inc					
1720 Sublette Ave	Saint Louis	MO	63110	**800-444-3954**	314-771-2400
NASDAQ: AHPI					

				Toll-Free	Phone
Altimate Medical Inc					
262 West First St	Morton	MN	56270	**800-342-8968**	507-697-6393
Andover Healthcare Inc					
9 Fanaras Dr	Salisbury	MA	01952	**800-432-6686**	978-465-0044
Artisan Laboratories Inc					
2532 SE Hawthorne Blvd	Portland	OR	97214	**800-222-6721**	503-238-6006
Aspen Medical Products					
6481 Oak Cyn	Irvine	CA	92618	**800-295-2776**	
Atrium Medical Corp					
5 Wentworth Dr	Hudson	NH	03051	**800-528-7486**	603-880-1433
B Braun Medical Inc					
824 12th Ave	Bethlehem	PA	18018	**800-523-9676**	610-691-5400
Bard Inc Peripheral Vascular					
1625 W Third St	Tempe	AZ	85281	**800-321-4254**	480-894-9515
Baxter International Inc					
1 Baxter Pkwy	Deerfield	IL	60015	**800-422-9837**	847-948-2000
NYSE: BAX					
BD Medical 9450 S State St	Sandy	UT	84070	**888-237-2762**	801-565-2300
Becton Dickinson & Co					
1 Becton Dr	Franklin Lakes	NJ	07417	**888-237-2762***	201-847-6800
NYSE: BDX ■ *Cust Svc					
Beekley Corp 1 Prestige Ln	Bristol	CT	06010	**800-233-5539**	860-583-4700
Best Theratronics Ltd					
413 March Rd	Ottawa	ON	K2K0E4	**866-792-8598**	613-591-2100
Best Vascular					
4350 International Blvd Ste A	Norcross	GA	30093	**800-668-6783**	770-717-0904
Bio Compression Systems Inc					
120 W Commercial Ave	Moonachie	NJ	07074	**800-888-0908**	201-939-0716
BioCardia Inc					
125 Shoreway Rd Ste B	San Carlos	CA	94070	**800-624-1179**	650-226-0120
Biodex Medical Systems Inc					
20 Ramsay Rd	Shirley	NY	11967	**800-224-6339**	631-924-9000
BioFlex Laser Therapy					
411 Horner Ave	Etobicoke	ON	M8W4W3	**888-557-4004**	416-251-1055
BioMerieux Inc					
595 Anglum Rd	Hazelwood	MO	63042	**800-634-7656**	314-731-8500
Biomet Microfixation Inc					
1520 Tradeport Dr	Jacksonville	FL	32218	**800-874-7711**	904-741-4400
Bioseal					
167 W Orangethorpe Ave	Placentia	CA	92870	**800-441-7325**	714-528-4695
Biosense Webster Inc					
3333 S Diamond Canyon Rd	Diamond Bar	CA	91765	**800-729-9010**	909-839-8500
Blackburn's Physicians Pharmacy Inc					
301 Corbet St	Tarentum	PA	15084	**800-472-2440**	724-224-9100
Boston Scientific Corp					
300 Boston Scientific Way	Marlborough	MA	01752	**800-876-9960**	508-683-4000
NYSE: BSX					
Braff Group, The					
1665 Washington Rd Ste 3	Pittsburgh	PA	15228	**888-922-5169**	412-833-5733
Bunnell Inc					
436 Lawndale Dr	Salt Lake City	UT	84115	**800-800-4358**	801-467-0800
Cadwell Laboratories Inc					
909 N Kellogg St	Kennewick	WA	99336	**800-245-3001**	509-735-6481
Cantel Medical Corp					
150 Clove Rd 9th Fl	Little Falls	NJ	07424	**800-714-4152**	973-890-7220
NYSE: CMN					
CardiacAssist Inc					
240 Alpha Dr	Pittsburgh	PA	15238	**800-373-1607**	412-963-7770
Cardiovascular Systems Inc					
1225 Old H 8 NW	St Paul	MN	55112	**877-274-0360**	651-259-1600
Carestream Health					
150 Verona St	Rochester	NY	14608	**888-777-2072**	585-627-1800
CAS Medical Systems Inc					
44 E Industrial Rd	Branford	CT	06405	**800-227-4414**	203-488-6056
NASDAQ: CASM					
Certified Safety Manufacturing Inc					
1400 Chestnut Ave	Kansas City	MO	64127	**800-854-7474**	
Conmed Corp 525 French Rd	Utica	NY	13502	**800-448-6506**	315-797-8375
NASDAQ: CNMD					
CONMED Linvatec					
11311 Concept Blvd	Largo	FL	33773	**800-448-6506***	727-392-6464
*Cust Svc					
Cook Inc PO Box 4195	Bloomington	IN	47402	**800-457-4500**	812-339-2235
Cook Medical Inc					
PO Box 4195	Bloomington	IN	47402	**800-457-4500**	812-339-2235
Cook Urological Inc					
PO Box 4195	Bloomington	IN	47402	**800-457-4500**	812-339-2235
Cooper Cos Inc					
6140 Stoneridge Mall Rd Ste 590	Pleasanton	CA	94588	**888-822-2660**	925-460-3600
NYSE: COO					
CooperSurgical Inc					
95 Corporate Dr	Trumbull	CT	06611	**800-645-3760**	203-929-6321
Cordis Corp					
14201 NW 60th Ave	Miami Lakes	FL	33014	**800-327-7714**	786-313-2000
CP Medical Inc					
1775 Corporate Dr Ste 150	Norcross	GA	30093	**800-950-2763**	678-710-2016
CR Bard Inc Urological Div					
8195 Industrial Blvd	Covington	GA	30014	**800-526-4455**	770-784-6100
Cutera Inc					
3240 Bayshore Blvd	Brisbane	CA	94005	**888-428-8372**	415-657-5500
NASDAQ: CUTR					
Cutting Edge Products LLC					
350 Turk Hill Pk	Fairport	NY	14450	**800-889-4184**	
Dale Medical Products Inc					
PO Box 1556	Plainville	MA	02762	**800-343-3980**	
Davol Inc					
100 Crossings Blvd	Warwick	RI	02886	**800-556-6756***	
*Cust Svc					
Defibtech LLC					
741 Boston Post Rd Ste 201	Guilford	CT	06437	**866-333-4248**	203-453-4507
Dymedix Diagnostics					
5985 Rice Creek Pkwy	Shoreview	MN	55126	**888-212-1100**	763-789-8280
Encision Inc					
6797 Winchester Cir	Boulder	CO	80301	**800-998-0986**	303-444-2600
OTC: ECIA					
Endologix Inc 11 Studebaker	Irvine	CA	92618	**800-983-2284**	949-457-9546
NASDAQ: ELGX					
Eternity Healthcare Inc					
8755 Ash St	Vancouver	BC	V6P6T3	**855-324-1110**	604-324-1113

	Toll-Free	Phone
Gaymar Industries Inc		
10 Centre Dr .... Orchard Park NY 14127	**800-828-7341**	800-327-0770
GEM Edwards Inc		
5640 Hudson Industrial Pkwy PO Box 429 .... Hudson OH 44236	**800-733-7976**	
GF Health Products Inc		
2935 NE Pkwy .... Atlanta GA 30360	**800-347-5678**	770-447-1609
Gyrus ACMI		
6655 Wedgwood Rd Ste 160 .... Maple Grove MN 55311	**800-387-0437**	763-416-3000
Haemonetics Corp		
400 Wood Rd .... Braintree MA 02184	**800-225-5242**	781-848-7100
NYSE: HAE		
Hartwell Medical Corp		
6354 Corte del Abeto Ste F .... Carlsbad CA 92011	**800-633-5900**	760-438-5500
Henry Troemner LLC		
201 Wolf Dr .... Thorofare NJ 08086	**800-352-7705**	856-686-1600
Hill-Rom Services Inc		
1069 SR 46 E .... Batesville IN 47006	**800-267-2337**	812-934-7777
Hoggan Scientific LLC		
3653 W 1987 S .... Salt Lake City UT 84104	**800-678-7888**	801-572-6500
Hospital Marketing Services Company Inc		
162 Great Hill Rd .... Naugatuck CT 06770	**800-786-5094**	203-723-1466
InfraReDx Inc		
34 Third Ave .... Burlington MA 01803	**888-680-7339**	781-221-0053
Inovise Medical Inc		
8770 SW Nimbus Ave Ste D .... Beaverton OR 97008	**877-466-8473**	503-431-3800
Inrad Inc		
4375 Donker Ct SE .... Kentwood MI 49512	**800-558-4647**	616-301-7800
Insulet Corp 9 Oak Park Dr .... Bedford MA 01730	**800-591-3455**	781-457-5000
Intuitive Surgical Inc		
1266 Kifer Rd Bldg 101 .... Sunnyvale CA 94086	**888-868-4647**	408-523-2100
NASDAQ: ISRG		
Johnson Matthey Medical Products		
1401 King Rd .... West Chester PA 19380	**800-442-1405**	610-648-8000
Katalyst Surgical LLC		
754 Goddard Ave .... Chesterfield MO 63005	**888-452-8259**	
Kinamed Inc 820 Flynn Rd .... Camarillo CA 93012	**800-827-5775**	805-384-2748
Kirwan Surgical Products Inc		
180 Enterprise Dr .... Marshfield MA 02050	**888-547-9267**	781-834-9500
Knit Rite Inc		
120 Osage Ave .... Kansas City KS 66105	**800-821-3094**	913-281-4600
Landice Inc		
111 Canfield Ave .... Randolph NJ 07869	**800-526-3423**	973-927-9010
Lifescan Canada Ltd		
210-4321 Still Creek Dr .... Burnaby BC V5C6S7	**800-663-5521**	604-293-2266
Maxtec		
2305 South 1070 West .... Salt Lake City UT 84119	**800-748-5355**	801-266-5300
Medegen Medical Products LLC		
360 Motor Pkwy Ste 800 .... Hauppauge NY 11788	**800-511-6298**	
Medi-Nuclear Corp Inc		
4610 Littlejohn St .... Baldwin Park CA 91706	**800-321-5981**	626-960-9822
Medica Corp 5 Oak Park Dr ...... Bedford MA 01730	**800-777-5983**	781-275-4892
Medicatech USA Inc		
50 Maxwell Ave .... Irvine CA 92618	**800-817-5030**	949-679-2881
Medin Corp 11 Jackson Rd ...... Totowa NJ 07512	**800-922-0476**	973-779-2400
MedRx Inc		
1200 Starkey Rd Ste 105 .... Largo FL 33771	**888-392-1234**	727-584-9600
Medtronic		
710 Medtronic Pky .... Minneapolis MN 55432	**800-633-8766**	763-514-4000
Medtronic Inc		
710 Medtronic Pkwy NE .... Minneapolis MN 55432	**800-328-2518***	763-514-4000
NYSE: MDT ■ *Cust Svc*		
Medtronic Neurosurgery		
125 Cremona Dr .... Goleta CA 93117	**800-468-9710***	800-633-8766
Cust Svc		
Mercury Medical		
11300 49th St N .... Clearwater FL 33762	**800-237-6418**	727-573-0088
Meridian Medical Technologies Inc		
6350 Stevens Forest Rd Ste 301 .... Columbia MD 21046	**800-638-8093**	443-259-7800
Merit Medical Systems Inc		
1600 W Merit Pkwy .... South Jordan UT 84095	**800-356-3748**	801-253-1600
NASDAQ: MMSI		
MicroAire Surgical Instruments Inc		
3590 Grand Forks Blvd .... Charlottesville VA 22911	**800-722-0822**	
Microflex Corp 2301 Robb Dr .... Reno NV 89523	**800-876-6866**	775-746-6600
Microlife USA Inc		
1617 Gulf to Bay Blvd Second Fl		
Ste B .... Clearwater FL 33755	**888-314-2599**	727-451-0484
MicroLumen Inc		
1 Microlumen Way .... Oldsmar FL 34677	**800-968-9014**	813-886-1200
Midmark Corp 60 Vista Dr ...... Versailles OH 45380	**800-643-6275**	937-526-7975
MiMedx Group Inc		
1775 W Oak Commons Ct NE .... Marietta GA 30062	**888-543-1917**	
Minntech Corp		
14605 28th Ave N .... Minneapolis MN 55447	**800-328-3345**	763-553-3300
Monroe Wheelchair		
388 Old Niskayuna Rd .... Latham NY 12110	**888-546-8595**	518-783-1653
Morgan Scientific Inc		
151 Essex St .... Haverhill MA 01832	**800-525-5002**	978-521-4440
Mott Corp 84 Spring Ln ...... Farmington CT 06032	**800-289-6688**	860-747-6333
MPM Medical Inc		
2301 Crown Ct .... Irving TX 75038	**800-232-5512**	972-893-4090
Mui Scientific		
145 Traders Blvd E .... Mississauga ON L4Z3L3	**800-303-6611**	905-890-5525
Nasiff Associates		
841-1 County Rt 37 .... Central Square NY 13036	**866-627-4332**	315-676-2346
NormaTec 480 Pleasant St .... Watertown MA 02472	**800-335-0960**	
Novosci 2021 Airport Rd .... Conroe TX 77301	**800-854-0567**	281-363-4949
Nspire Health Inc		
1830 Lefthand Cir .... Longmont CO 80501	**800-574-7374**	303-666-5555
Nubenco Medical		
1 Kalisa Way .... Paramus NJ 07652	**800-633-1322**	201-967-9000
Nutech Medical Inc		
2641 Rocky Ridge Ln .... Birmingham AL 35216	**800-824-9194**	205-290-2158
NuVasive Inc		
7475 Lusk Blvd .... San Diego CA 92121	**800-475-9131**	858-909-1800
NASDAQ: NUVA		

	Toll-Free	Phone
NxStage Medical Inc		
350 Merrimack St .... Lawrence MA 01843	**866-697-8243**	978-687-4700
NASDAQ: NXTM		
Ortho-Clinical Diagnostics Inc		
1001 US Rt 202 N .... Raritan NJ 08869	**800-828-6316**	
Osteomed Corp		
3885 Arapaho Rd .... Addison TX 75001	**800-456-7779***	972-677-4600
Cust Svc		
Pace Tech Inc		
2040 Calumet St .... Clearwater FL 33765	**800-722-3024**	727-442-8118
PARI Respiratory Equipment Inc		
2412 PARI Way .... Midlothian VA 23112	**800-327-8632**	
Parker Laboratories Inc		
286 Eldridge Rd .... Fairfield NJ 07004	**800-631-8888**	973-276-9500
PatientKeeper Inc		
880 Winter St Ste 300 .... Waltham MA 02451	**888-994-2443**	781-373-6100
Pepin Manufacturing Inc		
1875 Hwy 61 S .... Lake City MN 55041	**800-291-6505**	651-345-5655
Pepose Vision Institute PC		
1815 Clarkson Rd .... Chesterfield MO 63017	**877-862-2020**	636-728-0111
Peregrine Surgical Ltd		
51 Britain Dr .... New Britain PA 18901	**877-348-0456**	215-348-0456
PerkinElmer Inc		
940 Winter St .... Waltham MA 02451	**800-762-4000**	781-663-6050
NYSE: PKI		
Perry Baromedical Corp		
3750 Prospect Ave .... Riviera Beach FL 33404	**800-741-4376**	561-840-0395
Pilling Surgical		
2917 Weck Dr .... Research Triangle Park NC 27709	**866-246-6990***	919-544-8000
Cust Svc		
PneumRx 530 Logue Ave ...... Mountain View CA 94043	**800-226-7625**	650-625-8910
Prism Medical Inc		
485 Millway Ave Unit 2 .... Concord ON L4K3V4	**877-304-5438**	416-260-2145
Prodigy Diabetes Care LLC		
2701-A Hutchison McDonald Rd		
PO Box 481928 .... Charlotte NC 28269	**800-366-5901**	
Pronk Technologies Inc		
8933 Lankershim Blvd .... Sun Valley CA 91352	**800-609-9802**	818-768-5600
Propper Mfg Company Inc		
36-04 Skillman Ave .... Long Island NY 11101	**800-832-4300***	718-392-6650
Cust Svc		
Pryor Products		
1819 Peacock Blvd .... Oceanside CA 92056	**800-854-2280**	760-724-8244
ResMed Inc		
9001 Spectrum Ctr Blvd .... San Diego CA 92123	**800-424-0737**	858-836-5000
NYSE: RMD		
Salter Labs 100 Sycamore Rd .... Arvin CA 93203	**800-421-0024**	661-854-3166
Sechrist Industries Inc		
4225 E La Palma Ave .... Anaheim CA 92807	**800-732-4747**	714-579-8400
Shofu Dental Corp		
1225 Stone Dr .... San Marcos CA 92078	**800-827-4638**	760-736-3277
Smith & Nephew Inc Endoscopy Div		
150 Minuteman Rd .... Andover MA 01810	**800-343-5717**	978-749-1000
Sorin Group USA Inc		
14401 W 65th Way .... Arvada CO 80004	**800-289-5759**	303-424-0129
Sound Imaging Inc		
7580 Trade St .... San Diego CA 92121	**866-530-7850**	
Starplex Scientific Inc		
50 A Steinway Blvd .... Etobicoke ON M9W6Y3	**800-665-0954**	416-674-7474
STERIS Corp 5960 Heisley Rd .... Mentor OH 44060	**800-548-4873**	440-354-2600
NYSE: STE		
Stryker Corp		
2825 Airview Blvd .... Kalamazoo MI 49002	**800-616-1406**	269-385-2600
NYSE: SYK		
Synemed Inc		
4562 E Second St Ste A .... Benicia CA 94510	**800-777-0650**	707-745-8386
Techno-Aide Inc		
7117 Centennial Blvd .... Nashville TN 37209	**800-251-2629**	615-350-7030
Teleflex Medical OEM		
50 Plantation Dr .... Jaffrey NH 03452	**800-548-6600**	603-532-7706
TERATECH Corp		
77 Terrace Hall Ave .... Burlington MA 01803	**866-837-2766**	781-270-4143
Terumo Cardiovascular Systems Corp		
6200 Jackson Rd .... Ann Arbor MI 48103	**800-262-3304**	734-663-4145
Terumo Medical Corp		
2101 Cottontail Ln .... Somerset NJ 08873	**800-283-7866**	732-302-4900
TheraTest Laboratories Inc		
1120 Dupage Ave .... Lombard IL 60148	**800-441-0771**	
Topcon Medical Systems Inc		
111 Bauer Dr .... Oakland NJ 07436	**800-223-1130**	201-599-5100
Trans1 Inc		
3804 Park Ave Ste C .... Wilmington NC 28403	**888-526-1879**	
Urologix Inc		
14405 21st Ave N .... Minneapolis MN 55447	**800-475-1403**	763-475-1400
Utah Medical Products Inc		
7043 S 300 W .... Midvale UT 84047	**866-754-9789**	801-566-1200
NASDAQ: UTMD		
Vasamed Inc		
7615 Golden Triangle Dr Ste A ...... Eden Prairie MN 55344	**800-695-2737**	
Vascular Solutions Inc		
6464 Sycamore Ct .... Minneapolis MN 55369	**877-979-4300**	763-656-4300
Ventana Medical Systems Inc		
1910 Innovation Pk Dr .... Tucson AZ 85755	**800-227-2155**	520-887-2155
Veridex LLC		
700 US Hwy Rt 202 S .... Raritan NJ 08869	**877-837-4339**	
VitalAire Canada Inc		
6990 Creditview Rd Unit 6 .... Mississauga ON L5N8R9	**888-629-0202**	
Vivosonic Inc		
5535 Eglinton Ave W Ste 222 .... Toronto ON M9C5K5	**877-255-7685**	416-231-9997
W A Baum Company Inc		
620 Oak St .... Copiague NY 11726	**888-281-6061**	631-226-3940
WalkMed Infusion LLC		
6555 S Kenton St Ste 304 .... Centennial CO 80111	**800-578-0555**	303-420-9569
Wells Johnson Co		
8000 S Kolb Rd .... Tucson AZ 85756	**800-528-1597**	520-298-6069

475 — MEDICAL SUPPLIES - MFR

SEE ALSO Personal Protective Equipment & Clothing

Company / Address	City	ST	ZIP	Toll-Free	Phone
A-M Systems Inc 131 Business Park Loop	Sequim	WA	98382	800-426-1306	360-683-8300
Adhesives Research Inc 400 Seaks Run Rd PO Box 100	Glen Rock	PA	17327	800-445-6240	717-235-7979
Adroit Medical Systems Inc 1146 CaRding Machine Rd	Loudon	TN	37774	800-267-6077	865-458-8600
Advanced Sterilization Products (ASP) 33 Technology Dr	Irvine	CA	92618	888-783-7723	
AESCULAP Inc 3773 Corporate Pkwy	Center Valley	PA	18034	800-282-9000	
Allied Healthcare Products Inc 1720 Sublette Ave *NASDAQ: AHPI*	Saint Louis	MO	63110	800-444-3954	314-771-2400
AMG Medical Inc 8505 Dalton	Montreal	QC	H4T1V5	800-363-2381	514-737-5251
Animas Corp 200 Lawrence Dr	West Chester	PA	19380	877-937-7867	
Armstrong Medical Industries Inc 575 Knightsbridge Pkwy *Cust Svc*	Lincolnshire	IL	60069	800-323-4220*	847-913-0101
Arthrex Inc 1370 Creekside Blvd	Naples	FL	34108	800-934-4404	239-643-5553
Aspen Surgical 6945 Southbelt Dr SE	Caledonia	MI	49316	888-364-7004	616-698-7100
Avery Dennison Corp 207 Goode Ave *NYSE: AVY ■ *Cust Svc*	Glendale	CA	91203	888-567-4387*	626-304-2000
Baxter International Inc 1 Baxter Pkwy *NYSE: BAX*	Deerfield	IL	60015	800-422-9837	847-948-2000
Baylis Medical Company Inc 5959 Trans-Canada Hwy	Montreal	QC	H4T1A1	800-850-9801	514-488-9801
Becton Dickinson & Co 1 Becton Dr *NYSE: BDX ■ *Cust Svc*	Franklin Lakes	NJ	07417	888-237-2762*	201-847-6800
Beltone Electronics Corp 2601 Patriot Blvd	Glenview	IL	60026	800-235-8663	847-832-3300
BioHorizons Inc 2300 Riverchase Ctr	Birmingham	AL	35244	888-246-8338	205-967-7880
Biomet Inc 56 E Bell Dr PO Box 587	Warsaw	IN	46582	800-348-9500	574-267-6639
BioPro Inc 2929 Lapeer Rd	Port Huron	MI	48060	800-252-7707	810-982-7777
Bristol-Myers Squibb Co 345 Park Ave *NYSE: BMY*	New York	NY	10154	800-332-2056	212-546-4000
BSN Medical Inc 5825 Carnegie Blvd	Charlotte	NC	28209	800-552-1157	704-554-9933
Burke Inc 1800 Merriam Ln *Sales*	Kansas City	KS	66106	800-255-4147*	
Capstone Therapeutics Corp 1275 W Washington St Ste 101 *OTC: CAPS*	Tempe	AZ	85281	800-937-5520	602-286-5520
Centurion Medical Products 100 Centurion Way	Williamston	MI	48895	800-248-4058	517-546-5400
Chattanooga Group 4717 Adams Rd	Hixson	TN	37343	800-592-7329	423-870-2281
Community Surgical Supply Inc 1390 Rt 37 W	Toms River	NJ	08755	800-349-2990	732-349-2990
Conventus Orthopaedics Inc 10200 73rd Ave N Ste 122	Maple Grove	MN	55369	855-418-6466	763-515-5000
Cramer Products Inc 153 W Warren St	Gardner	KS	66030	800-345-2231	
Cyberonics Inc 100 Cyberonics Blvd *NASDAQ: CYBX*	Houston	TX	77058	800-332-1375	281-228-7262
DeRoyal Industries Inc 200 DeBusk Ln	Powell	TN	37849	800-251-9864	865-938-7828
DJ Orthopedics Inc 1430 Decision St	Vista	CA	92081	800-321-9549	760-727-1280
Dynarex Corp 10 Glenshaw St	Orangeburg	NY	10962	888-335-7500	845-365-8201
Ehob Inc 250 N Belmont Ave	Indianapolis	IN	46222	800-899-5553	317-972-4600
Ergodyne Corp 1021 Bandana Blvd E Ste 220	Saint Paul	MN	55108	800-225-8238	651-642-9889
Exactech Inc 2320 NW 66th Ct *NASDAQ: EXAC*	Gainesville	FL	32653	800-392-2832	352-377-1140
Ferno-Washington Inc 70 Weil Way	Wilmington	OH	45177	800-733-3766	937-382-1451
Fillauer Inc PO Box 5189	Chattanooga	TN	37406	800-251-6398	423-624-0946
Flexible Lifeline Systems Inc 14325 W Hardy Rd	Houston	TX	77060	800-353-9425	
Freeman Manufacturing Co 900 W Chicago Rd	Sturgis	MI	49091	800-253-2091	269-651-2371
GF Health Products Inc 2935 NE Pkwy	Atlanta	GA	30360	800-347-5678	770-447-1609
Gyrus Medical Inc ENT Div 136 Turnpike Rd	Southborough	MA	01772	800-757-2942	508-804-2600
Hanger Inc 10910 Domain Dr Ste 300	Austin	TX	78758	877-442-6437	512-777-3800
Hanger Orthopedic Group Inc 10910 Domain Dr Ste 300	Austin	TX	78758	877-442-6437	512-777-3800
Hans Rudolph Inc 8325 Cole Pkwy	Shawnee	KS	66227	800-456-6695	913-422-7788
Hermell Products Inc 9 Britton Dr	Bloomfield	CT	06002	800-233-2342	860-242-6550
Hollister Inc 2000 Hollister Dr	Libertyville	IL	60048	800-323-4060	847-680-1000
Hoveround Corp 2151 Whitfield Industrial Way	Sarasota	FL	34243	800-542-7236	
Howard Leight Industries 7828 Waterville Rd	San Diego	CA	92154	800-430-5490	
Hy-Tape International PO Box 540	Patterson	NY	12563	800-248-0101	
ICU Medical Inc 951 Calle Amanecer *NASDAQ: ICUI*	San Clemente	CA	92673	800-824-7890	949-366-2183
Ideal Tape Co 1400 Middlesex St	Lowell	MA	01851	800-284-3325	
Invacare Corp 1 Invacare Way *NYSE: IVC*	Elyria	OH	44036	800-333-6900	440-329-6000
Johnson & Johnson Consumer Products Co 199 Grandview Rd	Skillman	NJ	08558	866-565-2229	908-874-1000
Johnson & Johnson Inc 890 Woodlawn Rd W	Guelph	ON	N1K1A5	877-223-9807	
K-Tube Technologies 13400 Kirkham Way	Poway	CA	92064	800-394-0058	858-513-9229
Langer Inc 2905 Veterans' Memorial Hwy	Ronkonkoma	NY	11779	800-645-5520	
LPS Industries Inc 10 Caesar Pl *Sales*	Moonachie	NJ	07074	800-275-6577*	201-438-3515
M & C Specialties Co 90 James Way	SouthHampton	PA	18966	800-441-6996*	215-322-1600
MAQUET Cardiovascular LLC 45 Barbour Pond Dr	Wayne	NJ	07470	888-627-8383	
Medical Action Industries Inc (MAI) 500 Expy Dr S	Brentwood	NY	11717	800-645-7042	631-231-4600
MedShape Inc 1575 Northside Dr NW Ste 440	Atlanta	GA	30318	877-343-7016	
Medtronic Inc 710 Medtronic Pkwy NE *NYSE: MDT ■ *Cust Svc*	Minneapolis	MN	55432	800-328-2518*	763-514-4000
Medtronic MiniMed Inc 18000 Devonshire St	Northridge	CA	91325	800-646-4633	
Medtronic Powered Surgical Solutions 4620 N Beach St	Fort Worth	TX	76137	800-643-2773	817-788-6400
Medtronic Surgical Technologies 6743 Southpoint Dr N	Jacksonville	FL	32216	800-874-5797	904-296-9600
Mentor Corp 201 Mentor Dr *NASDAQ: MENT*	Santa Barbara	CA	93111	800-525-0245	805-879-6000
Merits Health Products Inc 730 NE 19th Pl	Cape Coral	FL	33909	800-963-7487	239-772-0579
MicroVention Inc 1311 Valencia Ave	Tustin	CA	92780	800-990-8368	714-247-8000
Milestone Scientific Inc 220 S Orange Ave *OTC: MLSS*	Livingston	NJ	07039	800-862-1125	973-535-2717
Miracle-Ear Inc 5000 Cheshire Pkwy N	Minneapolis	MN	55446	800-464-8002	
Monaghan Medical Corp 5 Latour Ave Ste 1600	Plattsburgh	NY	12901	800-833-9653	
MP Biomedicals LLC 3 Hutton Ctr Dr Ste 100	Santa Ana	CA	92707	800-633-1352	949-833-2500
Nearly Me Technologies Po Box 21475	Waco	TX	76702	800-887-3370	254-662-1752
NELCO Inc 3 Gill St Unit D	Woburn	MA	01801	800-635-2613	781-933-1940
NorMed PO Box 3644	Seattle	WA	98124	800-288-8200	
Nu-Hope Laboratories Inc 12640 Branford St	Pacoima	CA	91331	800-899-5017	818-899-7711
Ortho Development Corp 12187 S Business Pk Dr	Draper	UT	84020	800-429-8339	801-553-9991
Orthofix Inc 1720 Bray Central Dr	McKinney	TX	75069	800-527-0404	469-742-2500
Osteomed Corp 3885 Arapaho Rd *Cust Svc*	Addison	TX	75001	800-456-7779*	972-677-4600
Pacific Medical Inc 1700 N Chrisman Rd	Tracy	CA	95304	800-726-9180	
Passy-Muir Inc 4521 Campus Dr Pmb 273	Irvine	CA	92612	800-634-5397	949-833-8255
PeelMaster Packaging Corp 6153 W Mulford St Unit C	Niles	IL	60714	855-966-6200	
Perma-Type Company Inc 83 NW Dr	Plainville	CT	06062	800-243-4234	860-747-9999
Phonic Ear Inc 2080 Lakeville Hwy	Petaluma	CA	94954	800-227-0735	707-769-1110
Phygen LLC 2301 Dupont Ave Ste 110	Irvine	CA	92612	800-939-7008	949-752-7885
Posey Co 5635 Peck Rd	Arcadia	CA	91006	800-447-6739	626-443-3143
Precision Dynamics Corp 27770 N Entertainment Dr Ste 200	Valencia	CA	91355	800-847-0670	661-257-0233
Pride Mobility Products Corp 182 Susquehanna Ave	Exeter	PA	18643	800-800-8586	
Pro Orthopedic Devices Inc 2884 E Ganley Rd	Tucson	AZ	85706	800-523-5611	520-294-4401
Prosthetic Design Inc 700 Harco Dr	Clayton	OH	45315	800-459-0177	
Retractable Technologies Inc 511 Lobo Ln *NYSE: RVP*	Little Elm	TX	75068	888-806-2626	972-294-1010
Rusch Inc 2917 Weck Dr PO Box 12600	Research Triangle Park	NC	27709	866-246-6990	919-544-8000
Sas Safety Corp 3031 Gardenia Ave	Long Beach	CA	90807	800-262-0200	562-427-2775
Smith & Nephew Inc 1450 E Brooks Rd *Cust Svc*	Memphis	TN	38116	800-238-7538*	901-396-2121
Smiths Medical Respiratory Support Products 5200 Upper Metro Pl Ste 200	Dublin	OH	43017	800-258-5361	214-618-0218
Sonic Innovations Inc 2501 Cottontail Ln	Somerset	NJ	08873	888-678-4327	888-423-7834
Southmedic Inc 50 Alliance Blvd	Barrie	ON	L4M5K3	800-463-7146	705-726-9383

				Toll-Free	Phone

Span-America Medical Systems Inc
70 Commerce Ctr .... Greenville SC 29615 **800-888-6752** 864-288-8877
NASDAQ: SPAN

Spenco Medical Corp
PO Box 2501 .... Waco TX 76702 **800-877-3626**

Standard Textile Company Inc
1 Knollcrest Dr .... Cincinnati OH 45237 **800-999-0400** 513-761-9255

Starkey Hearing Technologies
6700 Washington Ave S .... Eden Prairie MN 55344 **800-328-8602** 888-251-9340

STERIS Corp 5960 Heisley Rd .... Mentor OH 44060 **800-548-4873** 440-354-2600
NYSE: STE

Sunrise Medical Inc
2842 Business Park Ave .... Fresno CA 93727 **800-333-4000**

Synovis Life Technologies Inc
2575 University Ave W .... Saint Paul MN 55114 **800-255-4018** 651-796-7300
NASDAQ: SYNO

Tamarack Habilitation Technologies Inc
1670 94th Ln NE .... Blaine MN 55449 **866-795-0057** 763-795-0057

TIDI Products LLC
570 Enterprise Dr .... Neenah WI 54956 **800-521-1314**

TS03 Inc 2505 Dalton Ave .... Quebec QC G1P3S5 **866-715-0003** 418-651-0003

Utah Medical Products Inc
7043 S 300 W .... Midvale UT 84047 **866-754-9789** 801-566-1200
NASDAQ: UTMD

West Pharmaceutical Services Inc
101 Gordon Dr .... Lionville PA 19341 **800-345-9800** 610-594-2900
NYSE: WST

Wright Medical Group Inc
1023 Cherry Rd .... Memphis TN 38117 **800-238-7117** 901-867-9971
NASDAQ: WMGI

Wright Medical Technology Inc
5677 Airline Rd .... Arlington TN 38002 **800-238-7117** 901-867-9971

Zimmer Biomet
1800 W Ctr St PO Box 708 .... Warsaw IN 46580 **800-613-6131** 574-267-6131

476   MEDICAL TRANSCRIPTION SERVICES

Companies listed here have a national or regional clientele base.

				Toll-Free	Phone

ASL Distribution Services Ltd
2160 Buckingham Rd .... Oakville ON L6H6M7 **800-387-7995** 905-829-5141

FreightPros
3307 Northland Dr Ste 360 .... Austin TX 78731 **888-297-6968**

Multivans Inc
13289 Coleraine Dr .... Bolton ON L7E3B6 **800-698-9249** 905-857-3171

Southern Motor Carriers Rate Conference Inc
500 Westpark Dr .... Peachtree City GA 30269 **800-845-8090** 770-486-5800

Thomas Transcription Services Inc
PO Box 26613 .... Jacksonville FL 32226 **888-878-2889** 904-751-5058

Transport Jacques Auger Inc
860 Archimede St .... Levis QC G6V7M5 **800-387-3835** 418-835-9266

Warren Gibson Ltd
206 Church St S PO Box 100 .... Alliston ON L9R1T9 **800-461-4374** 705-435-4342

477   MEDICINAL CHEMICALS & BOTANICAL PRODUCTS

SEE ALSO Pharmaceutical Companies ; Pharmaceutical Companies - Generic Drugs ; Vitamins & Nutritional Supplements ; Diagnostic Products ; Biotechnology Companies
Companies listed here manufacture medicinal chemicals and botanical products in bulk for sale to pharmaceutical, vitamin, and nutritional product companies.

				Toll-Free	Phone

ACIC Pharmaceuticals Inc
81 St Claire Blvd .... Brantford ON N3S7X6 **800-265-6727** 519-751-3668

Anika Therapeutics Inc
32 Wiggins Ave .... Bedford MA 01730 **800-299-7089** 781-457-9000
NASDAQ: ANIK

Avanti Polar Lipids Inc
700 Industrial Pk Dr .... Alabaster AL 35007 **800-227-0651** 205-663-2494

Bachem Bioscience Inc
3132 Kashiwa St .... Torrance CA 90505 **888-422-2436** 310-539-4171

Balchem Corp
52 Sunrise Pk Rd PO Box 600 .... New Hampton NY 10958 **877-407-8289** 845-326-5613
NASDAQ: BCPC

Bio-Botanica Inc
75 Commerce Dr .... Hauppauge NY 11788 **800-645-5720** 631-231-5522

Cambrex Corp
1 Meadowlands Plz .... East Rutherford NJ 07073 **866-286-9133** 201-804-3000
NYSE: CBM

Charm Sciences Inc
659 Andover St .... Lawrence MA 01843 **800-343-2170** 978-687-9200

Cyanotech Corp
73-4460 Queen Kaahumanu Hwy
Ste 102 .... Kailua-Kona HI 96740 **800-453-1187*** 808-326-1353
NASDAQ: CYAN ■ *Sales*

Designing Health Inc
28410 Witherspoon Pkwy .... Valencia CA 91355 **800-774-7387** 661-257-1705

George Uhe Company Inc
219 River Dr .... Garfield NJ 07026 **800-850-4075** 201-843-4000

Greer Laboratories Inc
639 Nuway Cir NE PO Box 800 .... Lenoir NC 28645 **800-378-3906***
Cust Svc

ICC Industries Inc
460 Park Ave .... New York NY 10022 **800-422-1720** 212-521-1700

Interchem Corp 120 Rt 17 N .... Paramus NJ 07652 **800-261-7332** 201-261-7333

Lannett Company Inc (LCI)
13200 Townsend Rd .... Philadelphia PA 19154 **800-325-9994** 215-333-9000
NYSE: LCI

LycoRed 377 Crane St .... Orange NJ 07050 **877-592-6733**

NHK Laboratories Inc
12230 E Florence Ave .... Santa Fe Springs CA 90670 **866-645-5227** 562-944-5400

One Lambda
21001 Kittridge St .... Canoga Park CA 91303 **800-822-8824** 818-449-3230

PendoPharm Inc
6111 Royalmount Ave .... Montreal QC H4P2T4 **866-926-7653*** 514-340-5045
Cust Svc

Rainbow Light
125 McPherson St .... Santa Cruz CA 95060 **800-475-1890** 831-429-9089

Scientific Protein Laboratories Inc
700 E Main St .... Waunakee WI 53597 **800-334-4775** 608-849-5944

Siegfried USA LLC
33 Industrial Pk Rd .... Pennsville NJ 08070 **877-763-8630*** 856-678-3601
Cust Svc

Sigma-Aldrich Corp
3050 Spruce St .... Saint Louis MO 63103 **800-325-3010** 314-771-5765
NASDAQ: SIAL

Spectrum Laboratory Products Inc
14422 S San Pedro St .... Gardena CA 90248 **800-772-8786*** 310-516-8000
General

SPI Pharma
Rockwood Office Pk 503 Carr Rd
Ste 210 .... Wilmington DE 19809 **800-789-9755** 302-576-8567

Starwest Botanicals Inc
11253 Trade Ctr Dr .... Rancho Cordova CA 95742 **888-273-4372*** 916-638-8100
General

Terry Laboratories Inc
7005 Technology Dr .... Melbourne FL 32904 **800-367-2563** 321-259-1630

United-Guardian Inc (UGI)
230 Marcus Blvd PO Box 18050 .... Hauppauge NY 11788 **800-645-5566** 631-273-0900
NASDAQ: UG

478   METAL - STRUCTURAL (FABRICATED)

				Toll-Free	Phone

A J Sackett & Sons Co, The
1701 S Highland Ave .... Baltimore MD 21224 **800-274-4466** 410-276-4466

Aerospace America Inc
900 Harry Truman Pkwy .... Bay City MI 48706 **800-237-6414**

AmChel Communications Inc
1703 Martinez Ln .... Wylie TX 75098 **866-388-6959** 972-442-1030

Amerimax Home Products Inc
450 Richardson Dr .... Lancaster PA 17603 **800-347-2586**

Anchor Fabrication
1200 Lawson Rd .... Fort Worth TX 76131 **800-635-0386**

Apex Industries Inc
100 Millennium Blvd .... Moncton NB E1E2G8 **800-268-3331** 506-857-1620

Baker Tankhead Inc
10405 N Iwy .... Fort Worth TX 76177 **866-232-8030** 817-232-8030

Bamco Inc
30 Baekeland Ave .... Middlesex NJ 08846 **800-245-0210**

Baron Metal Industries Inc
101 Ashbridge Cir .... Woodbridge ON L4L3R5 **800-263-7515** 416-749-2111

Braden Mfg LLC
5199 N Mingo Rd .... Tulsa OK 74117 **800-272-3360**

Central Minnesota Fabricating Inc
2725 W Gorton Ave .... Willmar MN 56201 **800-839-8857** 320-235-4181

Central Steel Fabricators Inc
1843 S 54th Ave .... Cicero IL 60804 **855-652-7010** 708-652-2037

CENTRIA
1005 Beaver Grade Rd .... Moon Township PA 15108 **800-759-7474** 412-299-8000

Cessco Fabrication & Engineering Ltd
7310-99 St .... Edmonton AB T6E3R8 **800-272-9698** 780-433-9531

Chase Industries Inc
10021 Commerce Park Dr .... Cincinnati OH 45246 **800-543-4455** 513-860-5565

CMC Capitol City Steel
14501 S IH 35 .... Buda TX 78610 **888-682-7337** 512-282-8820

CMC Rebar Georgia
251 Hosea Rd .... Lawrenceville GA 30046 **888-682-7337** 770-963-6251

Craig Manufacturing Ltd
96 Mclean Ave .... Hartland NB E7P2K5 **800-565-5007**

Discount RampsCom LLC
760 S Indiana Ave .... West Bend WI 53095 **888-651-3431**

Don Young Co
8181 Ambassador Row .... Dallas TX 75247 **800-367-0390** 214-630-0934

Dropbox Inc 401 S Ninth St .... Ironton OH 45638 **888-388-7768**

Etobicoke Ironworks Ltd
141 Rivalda Rd .... Weston ON M9M2M6 **866-274-6971** 416-742-7111

Excel Bridge Manufacturing Co
12001 Shoemaker Ave .... Santa Fe Springs CA 90670 **800-548-0054** 562-944-0701

Fabral Inc
3449 Hempland Rd .... Lancaster PA 17601 **800-477-2741** 717-397-2741

FWT LLC 5750 E I-20 .... Fort Worth TX 76119 **800-433-1816** 817-255-3060

Garaga Inc 8500 25th Ave .... St Georges QC G6A1K5 **800-464-2724** 418-227-2828

GLM Industries LP
1508 - Eighth St .... Nisku AB T9E7S6 **800-661-9828** 780-955-2233

Grain Belt Supply Company Inc
PO Box 615 .... Salina KS 67402 **800-447-0522** 785-827-4491

Herber Aircraft Service Inc
1401 E Franklin Ave .... El Segundo CA 90245 **800-544-0050** 310-322-9575

Hurco Technologies Inc
409 Enterprise St .... Harrisburg SD 57032 **800-888-1436**

J C. Macelroy Company Inc
PO Box 850 .... Piscataway NJ 08855 **800-622-3576** 732-572-7100

Jesse Engineering Co
1840 Marine View Dr .... Tacoma WA 98422 **800-468-3595** 253-922-7433

JH Industries Inc
1981 E Aurora Rd .... Twinsburg OH 44087 **800-321-4968** 330-963-4105

Linetec 725 S 75th Ave .... Wausau WI 54401 **888-717-1472** 715-843-4100

Mason Corp
123 W Oxmoor Rd .... Birmingham AL 35209 **800-868-4100** 205-942-4100

McElroy Metal Inc
1500 Hamilton Rd .... Bossier City LA 71111 **800-562-3576** 318-747-8097

Merchant & Evans Inc
308 Connecticut Dr .... Burlington NJ 08016 **800-257-6215** 609-387-3033

Midwest Metal Products Co
2100 W Mt Pleasant Rd .... Muncie IN 47302 **888-741-1044**

Mobility Center Inc
6693 Dixie Hwy .... Bridgeport MI 48722 **866-361-7559** 989-777-0910

Nabco Entrances Inc
S82W18717 Gemini Dr .... Muskego WI 53150 **888-679-3319** 877-622-2694

			Toll-Free	Phone
Nello Corp				
1201 S Sheridan St PO Box 1960	South Bend IN	46619	800-806-3556	574-288-3632
Nucor Corp				
1915 Rexford Rd	Charlotte NC	28211	800-294-1322	704-366-7000
NYSE: NUE				
Nucor Corp Vulcraft Div				
1501 W Darlington St	Florence SC	29501	888-000-0000	
Owen Industries Inc				
501 Ave H	Carter Lake IA	51510	800-831-9252	712-347-5500
Paxton & Vierling Steel Co				
501 Ave H	Carter Lake IA	51510	800-831-9252	712-347-5500
Price Steel Ltd				
13500 156 St	Edmonton AB	T5V1L3	800-661-6789	780-447-9999
Processed Metals Innovators LLC				
600 21st Ave	Bloomer WI	54724	888-877-7277	715-568-1700
Qualico Steel Co Inc				
7797 E State Hwy 52	Webb AL	36376	866-234-5382	334-793-1290
Ralston Metal Products Ltd				
50 Watson Rd S	Guelph ON	N1L1E2	800-265-7611	
Ram Welding Company Inc				
93 Rado Dr	Naugatuck CT	06770	800-927-6485	203-729-2289
RSDC of Michigan LLC				
1775 Holloway Dr	Holt MI	48842	877-881-7732	
Schuff Steel Inc				
1920 Ledo Rd	Albany GA	31707	866-252-4628	229-883-4506
Sims Cab Depot				
200 Moulinette Rd	Long Sault ON	K0C1P0	800-225-7290	613-534-2289
SnowBear Ltd				
259 Third Concession rd	Princeton ON	N0J1V0	800-337-2327	
Southeast Fabricators Inc				
7301 University Blvd E	Cottondale AL	35453	800-932-3227	205-556-3227
Southland Steel Fabricators Inc				
251 Greensburg St	Greensburg LA	70441	800-738-7734	225-222-4141
Spectrum Products				
7100 Spectrum Ln	Missoula MT	59808	800-791-8056	
Steele Solutions Inc				
9909 S 57th St	Franklin WI	53132	888-542-5099	414-367-5099
Steffes Corp				
3050 Hwy 22 N	Dickinson ND	58601	888-783-3337	701-483-5400
Stupp Bros Inc				
3800 Weber Rd	Saint Louis MO	63125	800-535-9999	314-638-5000
T Bruce Sales Inc				
9 Carbaugh St	West Middlesex PA	16159	800-944-0738	724-528-9961
TFT Inc				
2991 N Osage Dr PO Box 445	Tulsa OK	74127	800-303-7982	918-834-2366
Tie Down Engineering Inc				
255 Villanova Dr SW	Atlanta GA	30336	800-241-1806	404-344-0000
Trulite Glass & Aluminum Solutions LLC				
800 Fairway Dr Ste 200	Deerfield Beach FL	33441	800-432-8132	
Union Metal Corp				
1432 Maple Ave NE PO Box 73028	Canton OH	44705	800-327-0097	330-456-7653
United Window & Door				
24-36 Fadem Rd	Springfield NJ	07081	800-848-4550	
USP Structural Connectors Inc				
703 Rogers Dr	Montgomery MN	56069	800-328-5934	
W & W Steel Co				
1730 W Reno Ave	Oklahoma City OK	73106	800-222-1868	405-235-3621
Watson Bowman Acme Corp				
95 Pineview Dr	Amherst NY	14228	800-677-4922	
WaUSAu Window & Wall Systems				
7800 International Dr	Wausau WI	54401	877-678-2983	715-845-2161
Wojan Window & Door Corp				
217 Stover Rd	Charlevoix MI	49720	800-632-9827	
WSF Industries Inc				
7 Hackett Dr	Tonawanda NY	14150	800-874-8265	716-692-4930
Zimmerman Metals Inc				
201 E 58th Ave	Denver CO	80216	800-247-4202	303-294-0180

479   METAL COATING, PLATING, ENGRAVING

			Toll-Free	Phone
A-Brite Plating Company Inc				
3000 W 121st St	Cleveland OH	44111	800-252-2995	
Alcoa Inc				
201 Isabella St	Pittsburgh PA	15212	800-388-4825	412-553-4545
NYSE: AA				
Alumicor Ltd				
290 Humberline Dr	Toronto ON	M9W5S2	877-258-6426	416-745-4222
American Nickeloid Co				
2900 Main St	Peru IL	61354	800-645-5643	815-223-0373
Bon Chef Inc 205 SR- 94	Lafayette NJ	07848	800-331-0177	
Charlotte Anodizing Products Inc				
591 E Packard Hwy	Charlotte MI	48813	800-818-6945	517-543-1911
Chem Processing Inc				
3910 Linden Oaks Dr	Rockford IL	61109	800-262-2119	
Chicago Metallic Corp				
4849 S Austin Ave	Chicago IL	60638	800-323-7164	
Continental Studwelding Ltd				
35 Devon Rd	Brampton ON	L6T5B6	800-848-9442	905-792-3650
Corrosion Monitoring Services Inc				
902 Equity Dr	Saint Charles IL	60174	800-637-6592	
CVD Diamond Corp				
2061 Piper Ln	London ON	N5V3S5	877-457-9903	519-457-9903
Deposition Sciences Inc				
3300 Coffey Ln	Santa Rosa CA	95403	866-433-7724	707-573-6700
East Side Plating Inc				
8400 SE 26th Pl	Portland OR	97202	800-394-8554	503-654-3774
Everlube Products				
100 Cooper Cir	Peachtree City GA	30269	800-428-7802	770-261-4800
FW Gartner Thermal Spraying Ltd				
25 Southbelt Industrial Dr	Houston TX	77047	888-439-4872	713-225-0010
Galvan Industries Inc				
7320 Millbrook Rd	Harrisburg NC	28075	800-277-5678*	704-455-5102
*General				
GM Nameplate Inc				
2040 15th Ave W	Seattle WA	98119	800-366-7668	206-284-2200

			Toll-Free	Phone
Hadronics Inc				
4570 Steel Pl	Cincinnati OH	45209	800-829-0826	513-321-9350
Ingot Metal Company Ltd				
111 Fenmar Dr	Weston ON	M9L1M3	800-567-7774	416-749-1372
J & M Plating Inc				
4500 Kishwaukee St	Rockford IL	61109	877-344-3044	815-964-4975
LB Foster Co				
415 Holiday Dr	Pittsburgh PA	15220	800-255-4500	
NASDAQ: FSTR				
Lorin Industries				
1960 S Roberts St	Muskegon MI	49443	800-654-1159	231-722-1631
Magnetic Metals Corp				
1900 Hayes Ave	Camden NJ	08105	800-257-8174	856-964-7842
Master Finish Co				
2020 Nelson SE	Grand Rapids MI	49510	877-590-5819	616-245-1228
Max Levy Autograph Inc				
2710 Commerce Way	Philadelphia PA	19154	800-798-3675	
Metal Cladding Inc				
230 S Niagara St	Lockport NY	14094	800-432-5513	
Meziere Enterprises Inc				
220 S Hale Ave	Escondido CA	92029	800-208-1755	760-746-3273
Nd Industries Inc				
1000 N Crooks Rd	Clawson MI	48017	800-471-5000	248-288-0000
Nor-Ell Inc				
851 Hubbard Ave	Saint Paul MN	55104	877-276-4075	651-487-1441
O E C Graphics Inc				
555 W Waukau Ave PO Box 2443	Oshkosh WI	54902	800-388-7770	920-235-7770
Pioneer Metal Finishing LLC				
486 Globe Ave	Green Bay WI	54304	877-721-1100	
Plasma Ruggedized Solutions Inc				
2284 Ringwood Ave Ste A	San Jose CA	95131	800-994-7527	408-954-8405
Premier Die Casting Co				
1177 Rahway Ave	Avenel NJ	07001	800-394-3006	732-634-3000
Roesch Inc 100 N 24th St	Belleville IL	62222	800-423-6243	
Towne Technologies Inc				
6-10 Bell Ave PO Box 460	Somerville NJ	08876	800-837-2515	908-722-9500
Ultra-tech Enterprises Inc				
4701 Taylor Rd	Punta Gorda FL	33950	800-293-2001	
US Chrome Corp				
175 Garfield Ave	Stratford CT	06615	800-637-9019	
Willington Nameplate				
11 Middle River Dr	Stafford Springs CT	06076	877-967-4743	

480   METAL FABRICATING - CUSTOM

			Toll-Free	Phone
Afco Industries Inc				
3400 Roy St	Alexandria LA	71302	800-551-6576	
Brakewell Steel Fabricator Inc				
55 Leone Ln	Chester NY	10918	888-914-9131	845-469-9131
Chicago Metal Fabricators Inc				
3724 S Rockwell St	Chicago IL	60632	877-400-5995	773-523-5755
Cross Bros Inc				
5255 Sheila St	Los Angeles CA	90040	866-939-1057	323-266-2000
CSM Metal Fabricating & Engineering Inc				
1800 S San Pedro St	Los Angeles CA	90015	800-272-4806	213-748-7321
Fabricated Components Inc				
PO Box 431	Stroudsburg PA	18360	800-233-8163	570-421-4110
International Extrusions Inc				
5800 Venoy Rd	Garden City MI	48135	800-242-8876	734-427-8700
Liquidmetal Technologies Inc (LQMT)				
30452 Esperanza	Rancho Santa Margarita CA	92688	888-203-1112	949-635-2100
OTC: LQMT				
MP Metal Products Inc				
W1250 Elmwood Ave	Ixonia WI	53036	800-824-6744	920-261-9650
Sommer Metalcraft Corp				
315 Poston Dr	Crawfordsville IN	47933	888-876-6637	
White River Distributors Inc				
720 Ramsey	Batesville AR	72501	800-548-7219	870-793-2374

481   METAL FORGINGS

			Toll-Free	Phone
A & A Global Industries Inc				
17 Stenersen Ln	Cockeysville MD	21030	800-638-6000	410-252-1020
Alcoa Wheel Products International				
1600 Harvard Ave	Cleveland OH	44105	800-242-9898	216-641-3600
Aluminum Precision Products Inc				
3333 W Warner St	Santa Ana CA	92704	800-411-8983	714-546-8125
Coulter Forge Technology Inc				
1494 67th St	Emeryville CA	94608	800-648-4884	510-420-3500
Ellwood City Forge				
800 Commercial Ave	Ellwood City PA	16117	800-843-0166	724-752-0055
Federal Flange				
4014 Pinemont St	Houston TX	77018	800-231-0150	713-681-0606
Ferguson Perforating & Wire Co				
130 Ernest St	Providence RI	02905	800-341-9800	401-941-8876
Fine Line Production				
2221 Regal Pkwy	Euless TX	76040	800-887-5625	817-267-6750
Forged Products Inc (FPI)				
6505 N Houston Rosslyn Rd	Houston TX	77091	800-876-3416	713-462-3416
Frontier Metal Stamping				
3764 Puritan Way	Frederick CO	80516	888-316-1266	877-549-5955
Green Bay Drop Forge				
1341 State St	Green Bay WI	54304	800-824-4896	920-432-6401
H & L Tooth Company Inc				
10055 E 56 St N	Tulsa OK	74117	800-458-6684	
Jorgensen Forge Corp				
8531 E Marginal Way S	Tukwila WA	98108	800-231-5382	206-762-1100
Kerkau Manufacturing Co				
1321 S Valley Ctr Dr	Bay City MI	48706	800-248-5060	989-686-0350
Liberty Forge Inc				
1507 Fort Worth St PO Box 1210	Liberty TX	77575	800-231-2377	936-336-5785
Machine Specialty & Manufacturing Inc				
215 Rousseau Rd	Youngsville LA	70592	800-256-1292	337-837-0020

				Toll-Free	Phone

Norforge & Machining Inc
195 N Dean St ....Bushnell IL 61422 **800-839-3706** 309-772-3124

Performance Stamping Company Inc
20 Lake Marian Rd ....Carpentersville IL 60110 **800-935-0393** 847-426-2233

Phoenix Forging Company Inc
800 Front St ....Catasauqua PA 18032 **800-444-3674** 610-264-2861

Randall Bearings Inc
1046 Greenlawn Ave PO Box 1258.................Lima OH 45802 **800-626-7071** 419-223-1075

Scot Forge Co
8001 Winn Rd PO Box 8.................Spring Grove IL 60081 **800-435-6621** 847-587-1000

St Croix Forge
5195 Scandia Trl ....Forest Lake MN 55025 **866-668-7642** 651-287-8289

Thoro'Bred Inc
5020 E La Palma Ave ....Anaheim CA 92807 **800-854-6059** 714-779-2581

Western Forge & Flange Co
687 County Rd 2201 ....Cleveland TX 77327 **800-352-6433** 281-727-7060

Wozniak Industries Inc Commercial Forged Products Div
5757 W 65th St ....Bedford Park IL 60638 **800-637-2695** 708-458-1220

Wrought Washer Manufacturing Inc
2100 S Bay St ....Milwaukee WI 53207 **800-558-5217** 414-744-0771

Young Manufacturing Inc
2331 N 42nd St ....Grand Forks ND 58203 **800-451-9884** 701-772-5541

482 METAL HEAT TREATING

				Toll-Free	Phone

Akron Steel Treating Co
336 Morgan Ave ....Akron OH 44311 **800-364-2782** 330-773-8211

Alfe Heat Treating Inc
6920 Pointe Inverness Way Ste 140 ....Fort Wayne IN 46804 **888-747-2533**

Bluewater Thermal Solutions
126 Millport Cir Ste 201.....................Greenville SC 29607 **877-990-0050** 864-990-0050

Curtiss-Wright Corp
10 Waterview Blvd 2nd Fl ....Parsippany NJ 07054 **855-449-0995** 973-541-3700
NYSE: CW

Euclid Heat Treating Co
1340 E 222nd St ....Euclid OH 44117 **800-962-2909** 216-481-8444

FPM LLC
1501 S Lively Blvd .... Elk Grove Village IL 60007 **877-437-6432** 847-228-2525

Gibraltar Industries Inc
3556 Lakeshore Rd ....Buffalo NY 14219 **800-247-8368** 716-826-6500
NASDAQ: ROCK

HI TecMetal Group Inc
1101 E 55th St ....Cleveland OH 44103 **877-484-2867** 216-881-8100

Industrial Steel Treating Inc
613 Carroll St ....Jackson MI 49202 **800-253-9534**

Miller Consolidated Industries Inc
2221 Arbor Blvd ....Dayton OH 45439 **800-589-4133** 937-294-2681

Nitrex Metal Inc
3474 Poirier Blvd ....Saint-Laurent QC H4R2J5 **877-335-7191** 514-335-7191

Opticote Inc
10455 Seymour ....Franklin Park IL 60131 **800-248-6784** 847-678-8900

Pacific Metallurgical Inc
925 Fifth Ave S ....Kent WA 98032 **800-428-9436**

Rex Heat Treat
951 W Eigth St PO Box 270 ....Lansdale PA 19446 **800-220-4739** 215-855-1131

Solar Atmospheres Inc
1969 Clearview Rd ....Souderton PA 18964 **800-347-3236** 215-721-1502

Stahl Specialty Co
111 E Pacific ....Kingsville MO 64061 **800-821-7852** 816-597-3322

Texas Heat Treating Inc
155 Texas Ave ....Round Rock TX 78664 **800-580-5884** 512-255-5884

Ward Aluminum Casting Co
642 Growth Ave ....Fort Wayne IN 46808 **800-648-9918** 260-426-8700

483 METAL INDUSTRIES (MISC)

SEE ALSO Steel - Mfr ; Wire & Cable ; Metal Tube & Pipe ; Foundries - Investment ; Foundries - Iron & Steel ; Foundries - Nonferrous (Castings) ; Metal Heat Treating

				Toll-Free	Phone

Alcoa Inc
201 Isabella St ....Pittsburgh PA 15212 **800-388-4825** 412-553-4545
NYSE: AA

Allegheny Technologies Inc
1000 Six PPG Pl ....Pittsburgh PA 15222 **800-258-3586*** 412-394-2800
*NYSE: ATI ▪ *Sales*

Altec Aluminum Technologies
Bldg 242 America Pl ....Jeffersonville IN 47130 **800-922-9692**

Ampco Metal Inc
1117 E Algonquin Rd ....Arlington Heights IL 60005 **800-844-6008** 847-437-6000

Anaheim Extrusion Company Inc
1330 N Kraemer Blvd PO Box 6380 ....Anaheim CA 92806 **800-660-3318** 714-630-3111

Arvinyl Metal Laminates Corp
233 N Sherman Ave ....Corona CA 92882 **800-278-4695**

Big River Zinc Corp
2401 Mississippi Ave ....Sauget IL 62201 **800-274-4002** 618-274-5000

Bonnell Aluminum
25 Bonnell St PO Box 428 ....Newnan GA 30263 **800-846-8885** 770-253-2020

Broco Inc
10868 Bell Ct ....Rancho Cucamonga CA 91730 **800-845-7259** 909-483-3222

Bunting Magnetics Co
500 S Spencer Ave ....Newton KS 67114 **800-835-2526** 316-284-2020

Cabot Supermetals
1095 Windward Ridge Pkwy Ste 200 ....Alpharetta GA 30005 **800-472-4889**

Cannon Muskegon Corp
2875 Lincoln St ....Muskegon MI 49441 **800-253-0371** 231-755-1681

Cardinal Aluminum Co
6910 Preston Hwy ....Louisville KY 40219 **800-398-7833*** 502-969-9302
**Cust Svc*

Chase Brass & Copper Co
14212 Selwyn Dr ....Montpelier OH 43543 **800-537-4291** 419-485-3193

Chicago Extruded Metals Co (CXM)
1601 S 54th Ave ....Cicero IL 60804 **800-323-8102***
**Cust Svc*

Croft LLC
107 Oliver Emmerich Dr ....McComb MS 39648 **800-222-3195** 601-684-6121

Curtis Steel Co (CSC)
6504 Hurst St ....Houston TX 77008 **800-749-4621** 713-861-4621

Custom Aluminum Products Inc
414 Div St ....South Elgin IL 60177 **800-745-6333**

Doe Run Co, The
1801 Pk 270 Dr Ste 300 ....Saint Louis MO 63146 **800-356-3786** 314-453-7100

Dynamet Inc
195 Museum Rd ....Washington PA 15301 **800-237-9655** 724-228-1000

Elmet Technologies Inc
1560 Lisbon St ....Lewiston ME 04240 **800-343-8008** 207-333-6100

Glines & Rhodes Inc
189 E St ....Attleboro MA 02703 **800-343-1196** 508-226-2000

H Kramer & Co
1345 W 21st St ....Chicago IL 60608 **800-621-2305** 312-226-6600

Haynes International Inc
1020 W Park Ave PO Box 9013 ....Kokomo IN 46904 **800-354-0806** 765-456-6000
NASDAQ: HAYN

Hoover & Strong Inc
10700 Trade Rd ....North Chesterfield VA 23236 **800-759-9997*** 804-794-3700
**Cust Svc*

Hussey Copper Ltd
100 Washington St ....Leetsdale PA 15056 **800-733-8866** 724-251-4200

Industrial Tectonics Inc
7222 Huron River Dr ....Dexter MI 48130 **866-816-8904** 734-426-4681

JW Aluminum
435 Old Mt Holly Rd ....Mount Holly SC 29445 **877-586-5314***
**Sales*

Kaiser Aluminum Corp
27422 Portola Pkwy Ste 200...............Foothill Ranch CA 92610 **800-873-2011*** 949-614-1740
**Sales*

Light Metals Corp
2740 Prairie St SW ....Wyoming MI 49519 **888-363-8257** 616-538-3030

Linemaster Switch Corp
29 Plaine Hill Rd ....Woodstock CT 06281 **800-974-3668** 860-974-1000

Loxcreen Co Inc, The
1630 Old Dunbar Rd PO Box 4004 ....West Columbia SC 29172 **800-330-5699** 803-822-8200

Lucas-Milhaupt Inc
5656 S Pennsylvania Ave ....Cudahy WI 53110 **800-558-3856** 414-769-6000

Luvata Appleton LLC
553 Carter Ct ....Kimberly WI 54136 **800-749-5510** 920-749-3820

Luvata Ohio Inc
1376 Pittsburgh Dr ....Delaware OH 43015 **800-749-5510** 740-363-1981

Magnetech Industrial Services Inc
800 Nave Rd SE ....Massillon OH 44646 **800-837-1614***
**General* 330-830-3500

Memry Corp 3 Berkshire Blvd ....Bethel CT 06801 **866-466-3679** 203-739-1100

Metglas Inc 440 Allied Dr ....Conway SC 29526 **800-581-7654** 843-349-7319

Micro Surface Engr Inc
1550 E Slauson Ave ....Los Angeles CA 90011 **800-322-5832** 323-582-7348

Midland Industries Inc
1424 N Halsted St ....Chicago IL 60642 **800-662-8228** 312-664-7300

Mueller Brass Co
2199 Lapeer Ave ....Port Huron MI 48060 **800-553-3336** 810-987-7770

Mueller Industries Inc
8285 Tournament Dr Ste 150 ....Memphis TN 38125 **800-348-8464** 901-753-3200
NYSE: MLI

NN Inc
2000 Waters Edge Dr ....Johnson City TN 37604 **877-888-0002** 423-434-8300
NASDAQ: NNBR

Patrick Industries Inc Patrick Metals Div
5020 Lincolnway E ....Mishawaka IN 46544 **800-922-9692** 574-255-9692

Penn Aluminum International Inc
1117 N Second St ....Murphysboro IL 62966 **800-445-7366*** 618-684-2146
**All*

Revere Copper Products Inc
1 Revere Pk ....Rome NY 13440 **800-448-1776**

Ross Metals Corp
54 W 47th St ....New York NY 10036 **800-334-7191**

Southwire Co
1 Southwire Dr ....Carrollton GA 30119 **800-444-1700** 770-832-4242

Special Metals Corp
4317 Middle Settlement Rd ....New Hartford NY 13413 **800-334-8351** 315-798-2900

Taber Extrusions LP
915 S Elmira Ave ....Russellville AR 72802 **800-563-6853** 479-968-1021

Tree Island Industries
3933 Boundary Rd ....Richmond BC V6V1T8 **800-663-0955** 604-524-3744

Valmont Industries Inc
1 Valmont Plz ....Omaha NE 68154 **800-825-6668** 402-963-1000
NYSE: VMI

Victory White Metal Co
3027 E 55th St ....Cleveland OH 44127 **800-635-5050** 216-271-1400

Wiley Sanders Truck Lines Inc
PO Box 707 ....Troy AL 36081 **800-392-8017**

Worthington Industries
200 Old Wilson Bridge Rd ....Columbus OH 43085 **800-944-2255** 614-438-3210
NYSE: WOR

Xyron Inc
15820 N 90th St Ste 6 ....Scottsdale AZ 85258 **800-793-3523**

484 METAL PRODUCTS - HOUSEHOLD

				Toll-Free	Phone

All-Clad Metalcrafters LLC
424 Morganza Rd ....Canonsburg PA 15317 **800-255-2523*** 724-745-8300
**Cust Svc*

Calphalon Corp PO Box 583 ....Toledo OH 43697 **800-809-7267**

Lifetime Brands Inc
1000 Steward Ave ....Garden City NY 11530 **800-252-3390** 516-683-6000
NASDAQ: LCUT

ME Heuck Co
1600 Beech St ....Terre Haute IN 47804 **866-634-3825*** 812-238-5000
**Cust Svc*

Meyer Corp 1 Meyer Pl ....Vallejo CA 94590 **800-888-3883*** 707-551-2800
**Cust Svc*

Nordic Ware 5005 Hwy 7 ....Minneapolis MN 55416 **877-466-7342** 952-920-2888

					Toll-Free	Phone
Regal Ware Inc						
1675 Reigle Dr	Kewaskum	WI	53040		800-800-2850	262-626-2121
Rena Ware International Inc						
15885 NE 28th St	Bellevue	WA	98008		800-721-5156	425-881-6171
Saladmaster Inc						
4300 Amon Carter Blvd Ste 100	Arlington	TX	76018		800-765-5795	817-633-3555
Whitesell Corp						
2703 Avalon Ave	Muscle Shoals	AL	35662		855-227-4515*	
*General						
Wilton Armetale Co						
903 Square St	Mount Joy	PA	17552		800-779-4586	717-653-4444
Wilton Industries Inc						
2240 W 75th St	Woodridge	IL	60517		800-794-5866	630-963-7100

485 METAL PRODUCTS (MISC)

					Toll-Free	Phone
Aluchem Inc 1 Landy Ln	Cincinnati	OH	45215		800-336-8519	513-733-8519
Aluminum Ladder Co						
1430 W Darlington St	Florence	SC	29501		800-752-2526	843-662-2595
Bead Industries Inc						
11 Cascade Blvd	Milford	CT	06460		800-297-4851	203-301-0270
Carolina Carports Inc						
187 Cardinal Ridge Trl	Dobson	NC	27017		800-670-4262	
General Magnaplate Corp						
1331 Us Rt 1	Linden	NJ	07036		800-441-6173	908-862-6200
Lechler Inc						
445 Kautz Rd	Saint Charles	IL	60174		800-777-2926*	630-377-6611
*Cust Svc						
Liberty Safe & Security Products Inc						
1199 W Utah Ave	Payson	UT	84651		800-247-5625	801-925-1000
Metalworking Group Inc						
9070 Pippin Rd	Cincinnati	OH	45251		800-476-9409	513-521-4114
Spraying Systems Co						
PO Box 7900	Wheaton	IL	60189		800-800-6509	630-665-5000
Viking Materials Inc						
3225 Como Ave SE	Minneapolis	MN	55414		800-682-3942*	612-617-5800
*General						

486 METAL STAMPINGS

SEE ALSO Metal Stampings - Automotive ; Closures - Metal or Plastics ; Electronic Enclosures

					Toll-Free	Phone
Accurate Perforating Co						
3636 S Kedzie Ave	Chicago	IL	60632		800-621-0273	773-254-3232
Admiral Craft Equipment Corp						
940 S Oyster Bay Rd	Hicksville	NY	11801		800-223-7750	516-433-3535
Alcoa Inc						
201 Isabella St	Pittsburgh	PA	15212		800-388-4825	412-553-4545
NYSE: AA						
All New Stamping Co						
10801 Lower Azusa Rd	El Monte	CA	91731		800-877-7775	
American Metalcraft Inc						
3708 N River Rd Ste 800	Franklin Park	IL	60131		800-333-9133	708-345-1177
American Products LLC						
597 Evergreen Rd	Strafford	MO	65757		855-736-2135	417-736-2135
Ametco Manufacturing Corp						
4326 Hamann Industrial Pky	Willoughby	OH	44094		800-321-7042	
Ataco Steel Products Corp						
PO Box 270	Cedarburg	WI	53012		800-536-4822	262-377-3000
Bazz Houston Co						
12700 Western Ave	Garden Grove	CA	92841		800-385-9608	714-898-2666
BTD Manufacturing						
1111 13th Ave SE	Detroit Lakes	MN	56501		866-562-3986	
Dayton Rogers Manufacturing Co						
8401 W 35 W Service Dr	Minneapolis	MN	55449		800-677-8881	763-784-7714
Delta Consolidated Industries Inc						
4800 Krueger Dr	Jonesboro	AR	72401		800-643-0084	870-935-3711
Diamond Manufacturing Co						
243 West Eighth St PO Box 4174	Wyoming	PA	18644		800-233-9601	
Diamond Perforated Metals Inc						
7300 W Sunnyview Ave	Visalia	CA	93291		800-642-4334	559-651-1889
DORMA Architectural Hardware						
DORMA Dr Drawer AC	Reamstown	PA	17567		800-523-8483	717-336-3881
Fulton Industries Inc						
135 E Linfoot St	Wauseon	OH	43567		800-537-5012	419-335-3015
GMP Metal Products Inc						
3883 Delor St	Saint Louis	MO	63116		800-325-9808	314-481-0300
Hendrick Manufacturing Co						
1 Seventh Ave	Carbondale	PA	18407		800-225-7373*	
*Cust Svc						
Heyco Products						
1800 Industrial Way N	Toms River	NJ	08755		800-526-4182	732-286-1800
Hobson & Motzer Inc						
30 Air Line Dr	Durham	CT	06422		800-476-5111	860-349-1756
HPL Stampings Inc						
425 Enterprise Pkwy	Lake Zurich	IL	60047		800-927-0397	847-540-1400
Innovative Stamping Corp						
2068 E Gladwick St	Compton	CA	90220		800-400-0047	310-537-6996
Jagemann Stamping Co						
5757 W Custer St	Manitowoc	WI	54220		888-337-7853	920-682-4633
Ken-Tron Manufacturing Inc						
PO Box 21250	Owensboro	KY	42304		800-872-9336	270-684-0431
Kennedy Manufacturing Co						
1260 Industrial Dr	Van Wert	OH	45891		800-413-8665	
Kickhaefer Mfg Co (KMC)						
1221 S Park St PO Box 348	Port Washington	WI	53074		800-822-6080	262-377-5030
Knaack Manufacturing Co						
420 E Terra Cotta Ave	Crystal Lake	IL	60014		800-456-7865	
Midwest Wire Products Inc						
PO Box 770	Sturgeon Bay	WI	54235		800-445-0225	920-743-6591
Penn United Technology Inc						
799 N Pike Rd	Cabot	PA	16023		866-572-7537	724-352-1507

					Toll-Free	Phone
Quality Perforating Inc (QPI)						
166 Dundaff St	Carbondale	PA	18407		800-872-7373	570-282-4344
Saunders Manufacturing Co						
65 Nickerson Hill Rd	Readfield	ME	04355		800-341-4674	207-512-2550
Stack-On Products Co						
1360 N Old Rand Rd	Wauconda	IL	60084		800-323-9601	
Steel City Corp						
190 N Meridian Rd	Youngstown	OH	44501		800-321-0350	330-792-7663
Stewart EFI LLC						
45 Old Waterbury Rd	Thomaston	CT	06787		800-393-5387	860-283-8213
Waterloo Industries Inc						
1500 Waterloo Dr	Sedalia	MO	65301		800-833-8851*	800-558-5528
*Cust Svc						

487 METAL STAMPINGS - AUTOMOTIVE

SEE ALSO Automotive Parts & Supplies - Mfr

					Toll-Free	Phone
Advance Engineering Co						
7505 Baron Dr	Canton	MI	48187		800-497-6388	313-537-3500
Lake Air						
7709 Winpark Dr	Minneapolis	MN	55427		888-785-2422	763-546-0994
Philippi-Hagenbuch Inc						
7424 W Plank Rd	Peoria	IL	61604		800-447-6464	309-697-9200
Polar ware 502 Hgwy 67	Kiel	WI	53402		800-237-3655	
Shiloh Industries Corp						
880 Steel Dr	Valley City	OH	44280		800-414-3627	330-558-2600
Spartanburg Steel Products Inc						
1290 New Cut Rd PO Box 6428	Spartanburg	SC	29304		888-974-7500	864-585-5211
Stewart EFI LLC						
45 Old Waterbury Rd	Thomaston	CT	06787		800-393-5387	860-283-8213
Syracuse Stamping Co						
1054 S Clinton St	Syracuse	NY	13202		800-581-5555	315-476-5306

488 METAL TUBE & PIPE

					Toll-Free	Phone
AK Tube LLC						
30400 E Broadway	Walbridge	OH	43465		800-955-8031	419-661-4150
American Cast Iron Pipe Co (ACIPCO)						
1501 31st Ave N	Birmingham	AL	35207		800-442-2347	205-325-7701
Atlas Tube 1855 E 122nd St	Chicago	IL	60633		800-733-5683	773-646-4500
Bull Moose Tube Co						
1819 Clarkson Rd Ste 100	Chesterfield	MO	63017		800-325-4467	636-537-2600
California Steel & Tube						
16049 Stephens St	City of Industry	CA	91745		800-338-8823	626-968-5511
Cerro Flow Products Inc						
PO Box 66800	Saint Louis	MO	63166		888-237-7611	618-337-6000
Charlotte Pipe & Foundry Co						
2109 Randolph Rd	Charlotte	NC	28207		800-438-6091	704-372-5030
Dixie Pipe Sales Inc						
2407 Broiler	Houston	TX	77054		800-733-3494	713-796-2021
Earle M Jorgensen Co						
10650 S Alameda St	Lynwood	CA	90262		800-336-5365*	323-567-1122
*Sales						
Energy Alloys LLC						
3 Waterway Square Pl Ste 600	The Woodlands	TX	77380		866-448-9831	832-601-5800
Felker Bros Corp						
22 N Chestnut Ave	Marshfield	WI	54449		800-826-2304	715-384-3121
Hanna Steel Corp						
3812 Commerce Ave PO Box 558	Fairfield	AL	35064		800-633-8252	205-780-1111
Industrial Tube & Steel Corp						
4658 Crystal Pkwy	Kent	OH	44240		800-662-9567	330-474-5530
International Metal Hose Co						
520 Goodrich Rd	Bellevue	OH	44811		800-458-6855	419-483-7690
Jackson Tube Service Inc						
8210 Industry Pk Dr	Piqua	OH	45356		800-543-8910	937-773-8550
Leavitt Tube						
1717 W 115th St	Chicago	IL	60643		800-532-8488	773-239-7700
LeFiell Manufacturing Co						
13700 Firestone Blvd	Santa Fe Springs	CA	90670		800-451-5971	
Lock Joint Tube Inc						
515 W Ireland Rd	South Bend	IN	46614		800-257-6859	574-299-5326
Morris Coupling Co						
2240 W 15th St	Erie	PA	16505		800-426-1579	814-459-1741
Northwest Pipe Co						
12005 N Burgard	Portland	OR	97203		800-989-9631	503-285-1400
NASDAQ: NWPX						
Plymouth Tube Co						
29W150 Warrenville Rd	Warrenville	IL	60555		800-323-9506*	630-393-3550
*Mktg						
PTC Alliance						
Copperleaf Corporate Ctr						
6051 Wallace Rd Ext Ste 200	Wexford	PA	15090		800-274-8823	412-299-7900
Quality Edge Inc						
2712 Walkent Dr NW	Walker	MI	49544		888-784-0878	
Southland Tube Inc						
3525 Richard Arrington Blvd N	Birmingham	AL	35234		800-543-9024	205-251-1884
Stupp Corp						
12555 Ronaldson Rd	Baton Rouge	LA	70807		800-535-9999	225-775-8800
Tex-Tube Co						
1503 N Post Oak Rd	Houston	TX	77055		800-839-7473	713-686-4351
Tube Methods Inc						
416 Depot St	Bridgeport	PA	19405		800-220-2123	610-279-7700
Valmont Industries Inc						
1 Valmont Plz	Omaha	NE	68154		800-825-6668	402-963-1000
NYSE: VMI						
Western Tube & Conduit Corp						
2001 E Dominguez St	Long Beach	CA	90810		800-310-8823	
Wheatland Tube Co						
700 S Dock St	Sharon	PA	16146		800-257-8182	
Yarde Metals Inc						
45 Newell St	Southington	CT	06489		800-444-9494	860-406-6061

489   METAL WORK - ARCHITECTURAL & ORNAMENTAL

			Toll-Free	Phone
Alabama Metal Industries Corp (AMICO) 3245 Fayette Ave	Birmingham AL	35208	800-366-2642	205-787-2611
Alvarado Mfg Company Inc 12660 Colony St	Chino CA	91710	800-423-4143	909-591-8431
American Stair Corp Inc 642 Forestwood Dr	Romeoville IL	60446	800-872-7824	
Ameristar Fence Products Inc 1555 N Mingo Rd	Tulsa OK	74116	888-333-3422	918-835-0898
ATAS International Inc 6612 Snowdrift Rd	Allentown PA	18106	800-468-1441	610-395-8445
Bil-Jax Inc 125 Taylor Pkwy	Archbold OH	43502	800-537-0540	419-445-8915
Brand Energy & Infrastructure Services Inc 1325 Cobb International Dr Ste A-1	Kennesaw GA	30152	855-746-4477	678-285-1400
Chicago Metallic Corp 4849 S Austin Ave	Chicago IL	60638	800-323-7164	
Construction Specialties Inc 3 Werner Way	Lebanon NJ	08833	800-972-7214	908-236-0800
Duvinage Corp 60 W Oak Ridge Dr	Hagerstown MD	21740	800-541-2645	301-733-8255
Fisher & Ludlow Nucor Grating Inc 2000 Corporate Dr PO Box 1238	Wexford PA	15090	800-334-2047	724-934-5320
Goldline International Inc 1601 Cloverfield Blvd 100 S Tower	Santa Monica CA	90404	877-376-2646	310-587-1423
Hafele America Company Inc 3901 Cheyenne Dr *Cust Svc	Archdale NC	27263	800-423-3531*	336-434-2322
Hapco Inc 26252 Hillman Hwy	Abingdon VA	24210	800-368-7171	276-628-7171
Irvine Access Floors Inc 9425 Washington Blvd	Laurel MD	20723	800-969-8870	301-617-9333
Jerith Mfg Company Inc 14400 McNulty Pl	Philadelphia PA	19154	800-344-2242	215-676-4068
King Architectural Metals Inc PO Box 271169	Dallas TX	75227	800-542-2379	
Lapmaster International LLC 501 W Algonquin Rd	Mount Prospect IL	60056	877-352-8637	
MiTek Canada Inc 100 Industrial Rd	Bradford ON	L3Z3G7	800-268-3434	
NSK America Corp 1800 Global Pkwy	Hoffman Estates IL	60192	800-585-4675	847-843-7664
Overly Manufacturing Co 574 W Otterman St	Greensburg PA	15601	800-979-7300	724-834-7300
Quickmill Inc 760 Rye St	Peterborough ON	K9J6W9	800-295-0509	705-745-2961
Spider Staging Corp 365 Upland Dr	Tukwila WA	98188	877-774-3370	206-575-6445
Steel Ceilings Inc 451 E Coshocton St	Johnstown OH	43031	800-848-0496	740-967-1063
Superior Aluminum Products Inc 555 E Main St PO Box 430	Russia OH	45363	800-548-8656	937-526-4065
T Tech Inc 510 Guthridge Ct	Norcross GA	30092	800-370-1530	770-455-0676
Tate Inc 7510 Montevideo Rd	Jessup MD	20794	800-231-7788	410-799-4200
VELUX America Inc 450 Old BrickyaRd Rd PO Box 5001	Greenwood SC	29648	800-888-3589	803-396-5700
Vicwest Corp 1296 S Service Rd W	Oakville ON	L6L5T7	800-265-6583	905-825-2252
Wolf Robotics LLC 4600 Innovation Dr	Fort Collins CO	80525	866-965-3911	970-225-7600
Wooster Products Inc 1000 Spruce St PO Box 6005	Wooster OH	44691	800-321-4936	330-264-2844

490   METALS SERVICE CENTERS

			Toll-Free	Phone
A & B Aluminum & Brass Foundry 11165 Denton Dr	Dallas TX	75229	800-743-4995	972-247-3579
A&B Process Systems Corp 201 S Wisconsin Ave	Stratford WI	54484	888-258-2789	715-687-4332
ABC Metals Inc 500 W Clinton St	Logansport IN	46947	800-238-8470	
ABT Inc 259 Murdock Rd	Troutman NC	28166	800-438-6057	
Accent Packaging 10131 FM 2920 Rd	Tomball TX	77375	800-383-8047	281-251-3700
Accurate Alloys Inc 5455 Irwindale Ave	Irwindale CA	91706	800-842-2222	626-338-4012
Acier Picard Inc 3000 Rue De L' Etchemin	Levis QC	G6W7X6	888-834-0646	418-834-8300
Advanced Support Products Inc 20820 FM 2854 Rd	Montgomery TX	77375	800-941-5737	936-597-4731
Aladdin Steel Inc PO Box 89	Gillespie IL	62033	800-637-4455	217-839-2121
Alaskan Copper & Brass Co 3223 Sixth Ave S	Seattle WA	98134	800-552-7661	206-623-5800
Alcoa Inc 201 Isabella St *NYSE: AA*	Pittsburgh PA	15212	800-388-4825	412-553-4545
Alfiniti Inc 1152 rue Manic	Chicoutimi QC	G7K1A2	800-334-8731	418-696-2545
All American Grating Inc 3001 Grand Ave	Pittsburgh PA	15225	800-962-9692	412-771-6970
All Foils Inc 16100 Imperial Pkwy	Strongsville OH	44149	800-521-0054	440-572-3645
All Metals Industries Inc 4 Higgins Dr	Belmont NH	03220	800-654-6043	603-267-7023
Alliance Corp 2395 Meadowpine Blvd	Mississauga ON	L5N7W6	888-821-4797	
Alro Steel Corp 3100 E High St	Jackson MI	49204	800-877-2576	517-787-5500

			Toll-Free	Phone
Aluminum & Stainless Inc PO Box 3484	Lafayette LA	70502	800-252-9074	337-837-4381
Aluminum Distributing 2930 SW Second Ave	Fort Lauderdale FL	33315	866-825-9271	954-523-6474
American Chrome Co 518 W Crossroads Pkwy	Bolingbrook IL	60440	800-562-4488	630-685-2200
American Douglas Metals Inc 783 Thorpe Rd	Orlando FL	32824	800-428-0023	407-855-6590
American Strip Steel Inc 901 Coopertown Rd	Delanco NJ	08075	800-526-1216	
American Wire Rope & Sling 3122 Engle Rd	Fort Wayne IN	46809	800-466-7520	866-578-4700
AMI Metals Inc 1738 General George Patton Dr	Brentwood TN	37027	800-727-1903	615-377-0400
Applied Laser Technologies 8404 Venture Cir	Schofield WI	54476	888-359-3002	715-359-3002
Art Iron Inc 860 Curtis St	Toledo OH	43609	800-472-1113	419-241-1261
ASA Alloys Inc 81 Steinway Blvd	Etobicoke ON	M9W6H6	800-387-9166	416-213-0000
Atlas Bronze 445 Bunting Ave	Trenton NJ	08611	800-478-0887	
Atlas Steel Products Co 7990 Bavaria Rd	Twinsburg OH	44087	800-444-1682	330-425-1600
Aviva Metals 2929 W 12th St	Houston TX	77008	800-231-0771	
B&L Pipeco Services 20465 SH 249 Ste 200	Houston TX	77070	800-927-4732	281-955-3500
Basic Metals Inc W180 Nn11819 River Ln	Germantown WI	53022	800-989-1996	262-255-9034
BC Wire Rope & Rigging 2720 E Regal Park Dr	Anaheim CA	92806	800-669-5919	
Berlin Metals LLC 3200 Sheffield Ave	Hammond IN	46327	800-754-8867	219-933-0111
BMG Metals Inc 950 Masonic Ln	Richmond VA	23231	800-552-1510	804-226-1024
Bobco Metals LLC 2000 S Alameda St	Los Angeles CA	90058	800-262-2605	
Bohler-Uddeholm North America 2505 Millenium Dr	Elgin IL	60124	800-638-2520	
Brown-Strauss Steel 2495 Uravan St *Sales	Aurora CO	80011	800-677-2778*	303-371-2200
Cambridge Street Metal Corp (CSM) 82 Stevens St	East Taunton MA	02718	800-254-7580	508-822-2278
Carpenter Technology Corporation - Latrobe Operations (PA) 2626 Ligonier St	Latrobe PA	15650	800-241-8527	724-537-7711
Certex USA Inc 1721 W Culver St	Phoenix AZ	85007	800-225-2103	602-271-9048
Chapin & Bangs Co, The 165 River St	Bridgeport CT	06604	800-972-9615	
Chatham Steel Corp 501 W Boundary St	Savannah GA	31401	800-800-1337	912-233-5751
Cherokee Steel Supply 196 Leroy Anderson Dr	Monroe GA	30655	800-729-0334	770-207-4621
Chicago Tube & Iron Co 1 Chicago Tube Dr *Cust Svc	Romeoville IL	60446	800-972-0217*	815-834-2500
City Pipe & Supply Corp PO Box 2112	Odessa TX	79760	844-307-4044	432-332-1541
Clayton Metals Inc 546 Clayton Ct	Wood Dale IL	60191	800-323-7628	
Coastal Corrosion Control Surveys LLC 10172 Mammoth Ave	Baton Rouge LA	70814	800-894-2120	225-275-6131
Columbia Pipe & Supply Co 1120 W Pershing Rd	Chicago IL	60609	888-429-4635	773-927-6600
Connect-Air International Inc 4240 'B' St NW	Auburn WA	98001	800-247-1978	253-813-5599
Consolidated Steel Services Inc 632 Glendale Vly Blvd	Fallentimber PA	16639	800-237-8783	814-944-5890
Consumers Pipe & Supply Co 13424 Arrow Blvd	Fontana CA	92335	800-338-7473	909-728-4828
Contractors Steel Co 36555 Amrhein Rd	Livonia MI	48150	800-521-3946	734-464-4000
Crestwood Tubulars Inc PO Box 6950	St. Louis MO	63123	800-238-7473	
Dakota Riggers & Tool Supply Inc 704 E Benson Rd	Sioux Falls SD	57104	800-888-1612	605-335-0041
Damascus Steel Casting Co Blockhouse Rd Run Extn	New Brighton PA	15066	800-920-2210	724-846-2770
Dameron Alloy Foundries Inc 6330 Gateway Dr Ste B	Cypress CA	90630	800-421-1985	714-820-6699
Delta Steel Inc 7355 Roundhouse Ln	Houston TX	77078	800-324-0220	713-635-1200
Domtech Inc 40 East Davis St	Trenton ON	K8V6S4	888-278-8258	613-394-4884
Eagle Stainless Tube & Fabrication Inc 10 Discovery Way	Franklin MA	02038	800-528-8650	508-528-8650
East Coast Metals 171 Ruth Rd	Harleysville PA	19438	800-355-2060	215-256-9550
Eaton Steel Corp 10221 Capital Ave	Oak Park MI	48237	800-527-3851	248-398-3434
Ed Fagan Inc 769 Susquehanna Ave	Franklin Lakes NJ	07417	800-335-6827	201-891-4003
Extrudex Aluminum Ltd 411 Chrislea Rd	Woodbridge ON	L4L8N4	800-668-7210	416-745-4444
Fox Valley Spring Company Inc N915 Craftsmen Dr	Greenville WI	54942	800-776-2645	920-757-7777
GB Tubulars Inc 950 Threadneedle St Ste 130	Houston TX	77079	888-245-3848	713-465-3585
General Steel Inc PO Box 1503	Macon GA	31202	800-476-2794	478-746-2794
Gibbs Wire & Steel Company Inc Metals Dr PO Box 520	Southington CT	06489	800-800-4422	860-621-0121
Golden Aluminum Inc 1405 14th St	Fort Lupton CO	80621	800-838-1004	
Hanna Steel Corp 3812 Commerce Ave PO Box 558	Fairfield AL	35064	800-633-8252	205-780-1111
Hansen Architectural Systems 5500 SE Alexander St	Hillsboro OR	97123	800-599-2965	

Company / Address	City	State	ZIP	Toll-Free	Phone
High Steel Service Center LLC					
400 Steel Way	Lancaster	PA	17601	**800-732-0346**	717-299-8989
Howard Precision Metals Inc					
PO Box 240127	Milwaukee	WI	53224	**800-444-0311**	414-355-9611
Hynes Industries					
3760 Oakwood	Youngstown	OH	44515	**800-321-9257**	
Ideal Manufacturing Inc					
2011 Harnish Blvd	Billings	MT	59101	**800-523-3888**	406-656-4360
Independence Tube Corp					
6226 W 74th St	Chicago	IL	60638	**800-376-6000**	
Industrial Material Corp					
7701 Harborside Dr	Galveston	TX	77554	**800-701-4462**	409-744-4538
Infra Metals Co					
4501 Curtis Ave	Baltimore	MD	21225	**800-235-3979**	
International Mold Steel Inc					
6796 Powerline Dr	Florence	KY	41042	**800-625-6653**	859-342-6000
Iowa Spring Manufacturing & Sales Co					
2112 Greene St	Adel	IA	50003	**800-622-2203**	515-993-4791
Ken-Mac Metals Inc					
17901 Englewood Dr	Cleveland	OH	44130	**800-831-9503**	440-234-7500
Key Bellevilles Inc					
100 Key Ln	Leechburg	PA	15656	**800-245-3600**	724-295-5111
Keystone Profiles Ltd					
220 Seventh Ave	Beaver Falls	PA	15010	**800-777-1533**	724-506-1500
KGS Steel Inc 3725 Pine Ln	Bessemer	AL	35022	**800-533-3846**	205-425-0800
Kivort Steel					
380 Hudson River Rd	Waterford	NY	12188	**800-462-2616**	518-590-7233
Klein Steel Service					
105 Vanguarden Pkwy	Rochester	NY	14606	**800-477-6789***	585-328-4000
*Cust Svc					
Kreher Steel Company LLC					
1550 N 25th Ave	Melrose Park	IL	60160	**800-323-0745**	
Kymera International					
901 Lehigh Ave	Union	NJ	07083	**800-232-3198**	908-851-4500
Laibe Corp					
1414 Bates St	Indianapolis	IN	46201	**800-942-3388**	317-231-2250
Lapham-Hickey Steel Corp					
5500 W 73rd St	Chicago	IL	60638	**800-323-8443**	708-496-6111
Lee Steel Holdings LLC					
27555 Executive Dr Ste 177	Farmington Hills	MI	48331	**855-533-7833**	313-925-2100
Lindquist Steels Inc					
1050 Woodend Rd	Stratford	CT	06615	**800-243-9637**	
Livingston Pipe & Tube Inc					
1612 Rt 4 N	Staunton	IL	62088	**800-548-7473**	618-635-8700
Majestic Steel USA					
5300 Majestic Pkwy	Cleveland	OH	44146	**800-321-5590**	440-786-2666
Mandel Metals Inc					
11400 W Addison Ave	Franklin Park	IL	60131	**800-962-9851**	847-455-6606
Manzi Metals Inc					
15293 Flight Path Dr	Brooksville	FL	34604	**800-799-8211**	352-799-8211
Marmon/Keystone Corp					
PO Box 992	Butler	PA	16003	**800-544-1748**	724-283-3000
Mazel & Company Inc					
4300 W Ferdinand St	Chicago	IL	60624	**800-525-4023**	773-533-1600
McNichols Co					
9401 Corporate Lake Dr	Tampa	FL	33634	**877-884-4653**	
Mead Metals Inc					
555 Cardigan Rd	St. Paul	MN	55126	**800-992-1484**	651-484-1400
Merfish Pipe & Supply Co					
PO Box 15879	Houston	TX	77220	**800-869-5731**	713-869-5731
Merit USA 620 Clark Ave	Pittsburg	CA	94565	**800-445-6374**	
Metal Supermarkets IP Inc					
520 Abilene Dr 2nd Fl	Mississauga	ON	L5T2H7	**866-867-9344**	905-362-8226
Metaltech Service Center Inc					
9915 Monroe	Houston	TX	77075	**800-644-1204**	713-991-5100
Mueller Metals LLC					
2152 Schwartz Rd	San Angelo	TX	76904	**866-651-6702**	
MultAlloy Inc					
8511 Monroe St	Houston	TX	77061	**800-568-9551**	
Napco Steel Inc					
1800 Arthur Dr	West Chicago	IL	60185	**800-292-8010**	630-293-1900
National Specialty Alloys LLC					
18250 Keith Harrow Blvd	Houston	TX	77084	**800-847-5653***	281-345-2115
*General					
National Tube Supply Co					
925 Central Ave	University Park	IL	60466	**800-229-6872**	
New Process Steel Corp					
1322 N Post Oak	Houston	TX	77055	**800-392-4989**	713-686-9631
North American Steel Co					
18300 Miles Ave	Cleveland	OH	44128	**800-321-9310**	216-475-7300
Nucor Steel Marion Inc					
912 Cheney Ave	Marion	OH	43302	**800-333-4011**	740-383-4011
O'neal Flat Rolled Metals					
1229 S Fulton Ave	Brighton	CO	80601	**800-336-3365**	303-654-0300
O'Neal Steel Inc					
744 41st St N	Birmingham	AL	35222	**800-861-8272**	205-599-8000
Ohio Steel Sheet & Plate Inc					
7845 Chestnut Ridge Rd	Hubbard	OH	44425	**800-827-2401**	
Ohio Valley Aluminum Company LLC					
1100 Brooks Industrial Rd	Shelbyville	KY	40065	**800-692-4145**	502-633-2783
OnlineMetalscom					
1848 Westlake Ave N Ste A	Seattle	WA	98109	**800-704-2157**	
Oshkosh Coil Spring Inc					
3575 N Main St	Oshkosh	WI	54901	**800-638-8360**	920-235-7620
Owen Industries Inc					
501 Ave H	Carter Lake	IA	51510	**800-831-9252**	712-347-5500
Pacesetter Steel Service Inc					
1045 Big Shanty Rd	Kennesaw	GA	30144	**800-749-6505**	770-919-8000
Pacific Steel & Recycling					
1401 Third St NW	Great Falls	MT	59404	**800-889-6264**	406-771-7222
Packaging Inc					
7200 93rd Ave N Ste 190	Brooklyn Park	MN	55445	**800-328-6650**	952-935-3421
Paco Steel & Engineering Corp					
19818 S Alameda St	Rancho Dominguez	CA	90221	**800-421-1473**	310-537-6375
Palmer Manufacturing					
18 N Bechtle Ave	Springfield	OH	45504	**800-457-5456**	937-323-6339
Paragon Steel Enterprises LLC					
4211 County Rd 61	Butler	IN	46721	**800-411-5677**	260-868-1100

Company / Address	City	State	ZIP	Toll-Free	Phone
Parker Steel Co					
1625 Indian Wood Cir	Maumee	OH	43537	**800-333-4140**	419-473-2481
Peerless Steel Corp					
2450 Austin	Troy	MI	48083	**800-482-3947**	248-528-3200
Pentz Design Pattern & Foundry					
14823 Main St NE	Duvall	WA	98019	**800-411-6555**	425-788-6490
Perforated Tubes Inc					
4850 Fulton St E	Ada	MI	49301	**888-869-5736**	616-942-4550
Peterson Steel Corp					
61 W Mountain St	Worcester	MA	01606	**800-325-3245**	508-853-3630
Phillips & Johnston Inc					
21w179 Hill Ave	Glen Ellyn	IL	60137	**877-411-8823**	630-469-8150
Phoenix Metals Co					
4685 Buford Hwy	Norcross	GA	30071	**800-241-2290**	770-447-4211
Phoenix Tube Company Inc					
1185 Win Dr	Bethlehem	PA	18017	**800-526-2124**	610-865-5337
Pioneer Steel Corp					
7447 Intervale St	Detroit	MI	48238	**800-999-9440**	313-933-9400
Posner Industries Inc					
8641 Edgeworth Dr	Capitol Heights	MD	20743	**888-767-6377**	301-350-1000
Precision Steel Warehouse Inc					
3500 Wolf Rd	Franklin Park	IL	60131	**800-323-0740**	847-455-7000
Premier Aluminum LLC					
3633 S Memorial Dr	Racine	WI	53403	**800-254-9261**	262-554-2100
PRL Aluminum					
14760 Don Julian Rd	City Of Industry	CA	91746	**877-775-2586**	
ProCo Sound Inc					
5278 Lovers Ln	Portage	MI	49002	**800-253-7360**	
Quality Metals Inc					
2575 Doswell Ave	St Paul	MN	55108	**800-328-4893**	651-645-5875
Rangers Die Casting Co					
10828 S Alameda St	Lynwood	CA	90262	**877-386-9969**	310-764-1800
Rayco Industries Inc					
1502 Valley Rd	Richmond	VA	23222	**800-505-7111**	804-321-7111
Rigidized Metals Corp					
658 Ohio St	Buffalo	NY	14203	**800-836-2580**	716-849-4760
Rockingham Steel Inc					
2565 John Wayland Hwy	Harrisonburg	VA	22803	**800-738-1742**	540-433-3000
Rolled Alloys Inc					
125 W Sterns Rd	Temperance	MI	48182	**800-521-0332**	734-847-0561
Rolled Steel Products Corp					
2187 Garfield Ave	Los Angeles	CA	90040	**800-400-7833**	323-723-8836
Roton Products Inc					
660 E Elliott Ave	Kirkwood	MO	63122	**800-467-6866**	314-821-4400
Russel Metals Inc					
6600 Financial Dr	Mississauga	ON	L5N7J6	**800-268-0750**	905-819-7777
TSE: RUS					
Saginaw Pipe Company Inc					
1980 Hwy 31 S PO Box 8	Saginaw	AL	35137	**800-433-1374**	205-664-3670
Salit Steel Ltd					
7771 Stanley Ave	Niagara Falls	ON	L2E6V6	**800-263-7110**	905-354-5691
Searing Industries Inc					
8901 Arrow Rt	Rancho Cucamonga	CA	91730	**800-874-4412**	909-948-3030
Service Steel Aerospace Corp					
4609 70th St E	Fife	WA	98424	**800-426-9794**	253-627-2910
Shamrock Steel Sales Inc					
238 W County Rd S	Odessa	TX	79763	**800-299-2317**	432-337-2317
Sheffield Metals International Inc					
5467 Evergreen Pkwy	Sheffield Village	OH	44054	**800-283-5262**	440-934-8500
Sim-Tex LP 20880 FM 362 Rd	Waller	TX	77484	**866-829-8939**	713-450-3940
Siskin Steel & Supply Co Inc					
1901 Riverfront Pkwy	Chattanooga	TN	37408	**800-756-3671**	423-756-3671
Solon Manufacturing Co					
425 Center St	Chardon	OH	44024	**800-323-9717**	440-286-7149
South st Paul Steel Supply Company Inc					
200 Hardman Ave N	South Saint Paul	MN	55075	**800-456-7777**	651-451-6666
Southern Copper & Supply Company Inc					
875 Yeager Pkwy	Pelham	AL	35124	**800-289-2728**	205-664-9440
Southern Wire					
8045 Metro Rd	Olive Branch	MS	38654	**800-238-0333**	
Special Metals Inc					
2009 S Broadway	Moore	OK	73160	**800-727-7177**	
Specialty Pipe & Tube Inc					
PO Box 516	Mineral Ridge	OH	44440	**800-842-5839**	330-505-8262
St Louis Pipe & Supply Inc					
17740 Edison Ave	Chesterfield	MO	63005	**800-737-7473**	636-391-2500
State Pipe & Supply Inc					
9615 S Norwalk Blvd	Santa Fe Springs	CA	90670	**800-733-6410**	562-695-5555
State Steel Supply Co					
208 Ct St	Sioux City	IA	51101	**800-831-0862**	712-277-4000
Steel Supply Co, The					
5101 Newport Dr	Rolling Meadows	IL	60008	**800-323-7571**	
Steel Unlimited Inc					
456 W Valley Blvd	Rialto	CA	92376	**800-544-6453**	909-873-1222
Steel Warehouse Company Inc					
2722 W Tucker Dr	South Bend	IN	46619	**800-348-2529**	574-236-5100
Sylvania Steel Corp					
4169 Holland Sylvania Rd	Toledo	OH	43623	**800-435-0986***	419-885-3838
*General					
Taco Metals Inc					
50 NE 179th St	Miami	FL	33162	**800-653-8568**	305-652-8566
TCI Aluminum/North Inc					
2353 Davis Ave	Hayward	CA	94545	**800-824-6197**	510-786-3750
Terra Nova Steel & Iron (Ontario) Inc					
3595 Hawkestone Rd	Mississauga	ON	L5C2V1	**877-427-0269**	905-273-3872
Texas Pipe & Supply Co Inc					
2330 Holmes Rd	Houston	TX	77051	**800-233-8736**	713-799-9235
Three D Metals Inc					
5462 Innovation Dr	Valley City	OH	44280	**800-362-9905**	330-220-0451
ThyssenKrupp Materials NA					
22355 W 11 Mile Rd	Southfield	MI	48033	**800-926-2600**	248-233-5600
Tioga Pipe Supply Company Inc					
2450 Wheatsheaf Ln	Philadelphia	PA	19137	**800-523-3678**	215-831-0700
Tomson Steel Co (Inc)					
PO Box 940	Middletown	OH	45042	**800-837-3001**	
Totten Tubes Inc					
500 Danlee St	Azusa	CA	91702	**800-882-3748**	

				Toll-Free	Phone

Tri Star Metals LLC
375 Village Dr .... Carol Stream IL 60188 **800-541-2294** 630-462-7600

Trident Steel Corp
12825 Flushing Meadows Dr Ste 110 .... St. Louis MO 63131 **800-777-9687** 314-822-0500

Triple-S Steel Supply LLC
6000 Jensen Dr .... Houston TX 77026 **800-231-1034** 713-697-7105

Tubular Steel Inc
1031 Executive Pkwy Dr .... Saint Louis MO 63141 **800-388-7491** 314-851-9200

Turret Steel Industries Inc
105 Pine St .... Imperial PA 15126 **800-245-4800** 724-218-1014

United Aluminum Corp
100 United Dr .... North Haven CT 06473 **800-243-2515** 203-239-5881

United States Brass & Copper
1401 Brook Dr .... Downers Grove IL 60515 **800-821-2854**

Universal Metals LLC
805 Chicago St .... Toledo OH 43611 **800-853-8890** 419-726-0850

Universal Steel America Houston Inc
1230 E Richey Rd .... Houston TX 77073 **866-988-3800** 281-821-7400

Valiant Steel & Equipment Inc
6455 Old Peachtree Rd .... Norcross GA 30071 **800-939-9905** 770-417-1235

Viking Materials Inc
3225 Como Ave SE .... Minneapolis MN 55414 **800-682-3942*** 612-617-5800
*General

Vista Metals Inc
65 Ballou Blvd .... Bristol RI 02809 **800-431-4113** 401-253-1772

West Central Steel Inc
110 19th St NW PO Box 1178 .... Willmar MN 56201 **800-992-8853**

Westfield Steel Inc
530 State Rd 32 W .... Westfield IN 46074 **800-622-4984**

White Aluminum Products LLC
2101 US Hwy 441 .... Leesburg FL 34748 **888-474-5884**

Willbanks Metals Inc
1155 NE 28th St .... Fort Worth TX 76106 **800-772-2352** 817-625-6161

Wire Rope Industries Ltd
5501 Trans-Canada Hwy .... Pointe-claire QC H9R1B7 **800-565-5501** 514-697-9711

Wiscolift Inc
W6396 Speciality Dr .... Greenville WI 54942 **800-242-3477** 920-757-8832

Wisconsin Steel & Tube Corp
1555 N Mayfair Rd .... Milwaukee WI 53226 **800-279-8335** 414-453-4441

Wrisco Industries Inc
355 Hiatt Dr Ste B .... Palm Beach Gardens FL 33418 **800-627-2646** 561-626-5700

491 — METALWORKING DEVICES & ACCESSORIES

SEE ALSO Machine Tools - Metal Cutting Types ; Machine Tools - Metal Forming Types ; Tool & Die Shops

				Toll-Free	Phone

Acme Industrial Co
441 Maple Ave .... Carpentersville IL 60110 **800-323-5582** 847-428-3911

Advanced Machine & Engineering Co
2500 Latham St .... Rockford IL 61103 **800-225-4263** 815-962-6076

Allied Machine & Engineering Corp
120 Deeds Dr .... Dover OH 44622 **800-321-5537** 330-343-4283

American Drill Bushings Co (ADB)
5740 Hunt Rd .... Valdosta GA 31606 **800-423-4425** 229-253-8928

ASKO Inc
501 W Seventh Ave .... Homestead PA 15120 **800-321-1310** 412-461-4110

Besly Cutting Tools Inc
520 Blackhawk Blvd Ste135 .... South Beloit IL 61080 **800-435-2965** 815-389-2231

Big Kaiser Precision Tooling Inc
641 Fargo Ave .... Elk Grove Village IL 60007 **888-866-5776** 847-228-7660

Buck Chuck Co
2155 Traversefield Dr .... Traverse City MI 49686 **800-228-2825**

Carbro Corp
15724 Condon Ave PO Box 278 .... Lawndale CA 90260 **888-738-4400** 310-643-8400

Carl Zeiss Industrial Metrology
6250 Sycamore Ln N .... Maple Grove MN 55369 **800-327-9735** 763-744-2400

CJT Koolcarb Inc
494 Mission St .... Carol Stream IL 60188 **800-323-2299** 630-690-5933

Cline Tool & Service Co
PO Box 866 .... Newton IA 50208 **866-561-3022**

Deltronic Corp
3900 W Segerstrom Ave .... Santa Ana CA 92704 **800-451-6922** 714-545-5800

Detroit Edge Tool Co
6570 E Nevada St .... Detroit MI 48234 **800-404-2038** 313-366-4120

Edmunds Gages
45 Spring Ln .... Farmington CT 06032 **800-878-1622** 860-677-2813

Forkardt
2155 Traverse Field Dr .... Traverse City MI 49686 **800-544-3823** 231-995-8300

Fullerton Tool Company Inc
121 Perry St .... Saginaw MI 48602 **855-722-7243** 989-799-4550

Garr Tool Co 7800 N Alger Rd .... Alma MI 48801 **800-248-9003** 989-463-6171

General Broach Co
307 Salisbury St .... Morenci MI 49256 **800-889-7555** 517-458-7555

Gilman USA
1230 Cheyenne Ave PO Box 5 .... Grafton WI 53024 **800-445-6267** 262-377-2434

Glastonbury Southern Gage
46 Industrial Pk Rd .... Erin TN 37061 **800-251-4243**

Guhring Inc
1445 Commerce Ave .... Brookfield WI 53045 **800-776-6170** 262-784-6730

Hannibal Carbide Tool Inc
5000 Paris Gravel Rd .... Hannibal MO 63401 **800-451-9436** 573-221-2775

Hardinge Inc 1 Hardinge Dr .... Elmira NY 14902 **800-843-8801** 607-734-2281
NASDAQ: HDNG

Hougen Manufacturing Inc
3001 Hougen Dr .... Swartz Creek MI 48473 **800-426-7818*** 810-635-7111
*Orders

Huron Machine Products Inc
228 SW 21st Terr .... Fort Lauderdale FL 33312 **800-327-8186** 954-587-4541

Husqvarna Construction Products
17400 W 119th St .... Olathe KS 66061 **800-288-5040** 913-928-1000

Industrial Tools Inc (ITI)
1111 S Rose Ave .... Oxnard CA 93033 **800-266-5561** 805-483-1111

Jergens Inc
15700 S Waterloo Rd .... Cleveland OH 44110 **800-537-4367** 877-486-1454

Kennametal
1662 MacMillan Park Dr .... Fort Mill SC 29707 **800-446-7738***
NYSE: KMT ■ *Cust Svc

KEO Cutters Inc
25040 Easy St .... Warren MI 48089 **888-390-2050** 586-771-2050

Lancaster Knives Inc
165 Ct St .... Lancaster NY 14086 **800-869-9666** 716-683-5050

Lovejoy Tool Company Inc
133 Main St .... Springfield VT 05156 **800-843-8376** 802-885-2194

Melin Tool Co
5565 Venture Dr Unit C .... Cleveland OH 44130 **800-521-1078** 216-362-4200

Micro 100 Tool Corp
1410 E Pine Ave .... Meridian ID 83642 **800-421-8065** 208-888-7310

NED Corp 31 Town Forest Rd .... Oxford MA 01540 **800-343-6086**

Niagara Cutter Inc
2805 Bellingham Dr .... Troy MI 48083 **800-832-8326** 248-528-5220

North American Tool Corp
215 Elmwood Ave .... South Beloit IL 61080 **800-872-8277** 815-389-2300

Onsrud Cutter LP
800 Liberty Dr .... Libertyville IL 60048 **800-234-1560** 847-362-1560

OSG Tap & Die Inc
676 E Fullerton Ave .... Glendale Heights IL 60139 **800-837-2223** 630-790-1400

Phillips Corp
7390 Coca Cola Dr .... Hanover MD 21076 **800-878-4242** 410-564-2929

Powers Fasteners Inc
2 Powers Ln .... Brewster NY 10509 **800-524-3244**

Products Engineering Corp
2645 Maricopa St .... Torrance CA 90503 **800-923-6255** 310-787-4500

Regal-Beloit Corp
200 State St .... Beloit WI 53511 **800-672-6495** 608-364-8800
NYSE: RBC

Reiff & Nestor Co
50 Reiff St .... Lykens PA 17048 **800-521-3422** 717-453-7113

S-T Industries Inc
301 Armstrong Blvd N PO Box 517 ...... Saint James MN 56081 **800-326-2039** 507-375-3211

Scotchman Industries Inc
180 E Hwy 14 .... Philip SD 57567 **800-843-8844** 605-859-2542

Seco Tools 2805 Bellingham Dr .... Troy MI 48083 **800-832-8326** 248-528-5200

Spiralock Corp
25235 Dequindre Rd .... Madison Heights MI 48071 **800-521-2688** 586-949-0440

Star Cutter Co
23461 Industrial Pk Dr .... Farmington MI 48335 **877-635-3488** 248-474-8200

Starrett Webber Gage Div
24500 Detroit Rd .... Cleveland OH 44145 **800-255-3924** 440-835-0001

Stilson Products
15935 Sturgeon St .... Roseville MI 48066 **888-400-5978** 586-778-1100

Tapmatic Corp
802 S Clearwater Loop .... Post Falls ID 83854 **800-854-6019*** 208-773-8048
*General

Thread Check Inc
390 Oser Ave .... Hauppauge NY 11788 **800-767-7633** 631-231-1515

TM Smith Tool International Corp
360 Hubbard Ave .... Mount Clemens MI 48043 **800-521-4894** 586-468-1465

United Drill Bushing Corp
12200 Woodruff Ave .... Downey CA 90241 **800-486-3466** 562-803-1521

Viking Drill & Tool Inc
355 State St .... Saint Paul MN 55107 **800-328-4655** 651-227-8911

Walker Magnetics Group Inc
20 Rockdale St .... Worcester MA 01606 **800-962-4638** 508-853-3232

Walter USA Inc
N22 W23855 Ridgeview Pkwy W .... Waukesha WI 53188 **800-945-5554**

Zenith Cutter Co
5200 Zenith Pkwy .... Loves Park IL 61111 **800-223-5202** 815-282-5200

492 — METALWORKING MACHINERY

SEE ALSO Rolling Mill Machinery

				Toll-Free	Phone

Armstrong Mfg Co
2700 SE Tacoma St .... Portland OR 97202 **800-426-6226** 503-228-8381

Bartell Machinery Systems LLC
6321 Elmer Hill Rd .... Rome NY 13440 **800-537-8473** 315-336-7600

Belvac Production Machinery Inc
237 Graves Mill Rd .... Lynchburg VA 24502 **800-423-5822** 434-239-0358

Eubanks Engineering Co
3022 Inland Empire Blvd .... Ontario CA 91764 **800-729-4208** 909-483-2456

Granutech-Saturn Systems Corp
201 E Shady Grove .... Grand Prairie TX 75050 **877-582-7800**

Pannier Corp
207 Sandusky St .... Pittsburgh PA 15212 **877-726-6437** 412-323-4900

Pines Technology
30505 Clemens Rd .... Westlake OH 44145 **800-207-2840** 440-835-5553

Red Bud Industries
200 B & E Industrial Dr .... Red Bud IL 62278 **800-851-4612*** 618-282-3801
*Cust Svc

Rowe Machinery & Automation Inc
76 Hinckley Rd .... Clinton ME 04927 **800-247-2645** 207-426-2351

Sweed Machinery Inc
653 Second Ave PO Box 228 .... Gold Hill OR 97525 **800-888-1352*** 541-855-1512
*Sales

493 — METERS & OTHER COUNTING DEVICES

				Toll-Free	Phone

AMETEK Inc Dixson Div
287 27 Rd .... Grand Junction CO 81503 **888-302-0639** 970-242-8863

AMETEK Sensor Technology Drexelbrook Div
205 Keith Valley Rd .... Horsham PA 19044 **800-553-9092*** 215-674-1234
*Cust Svc

Auto Meter Products Inc
413 W Elm St .... Sycamore IL 60178 **866-248-6356** 815-895-8141

Badger Meter Inc
4545 W Brown Deer Rd .... Milwaukee WI 53224 **800-876-3837** 414-355-0400
NYSE: BMI

				Toll-Free	Phone
Clark-Reliance Corp 16633 Foltz Pkwy	Strongsville	OH	44149	**800-238-4027**	440-572-1500
Duncan Solutions Inc 633 W Wisconsin Ave Ste 1600	Milwaukee	WI	53203	**888-993-8622**	
Electro-Sensors Inc 6111 Blue Circle Dr *NASDAQ: ELSE*	Minnetonka	MN	55343	**800-328-6170**	952-930-0100
Elster American Meter Co 2221 Industrial Rd	Nebraska City	NE	68410	**877-595-6254**	402-873-8200
Greenwald Industries 212 Middlesex Ave	Chester	CT	06412	**800-221-0982**	860-526-0800
Laser Technology Inc 7070 S Tucson Way	Englewood	CO	80112	**800-280-6113**	303-649-1000
Maxima Technologies Stewart Warner 1811 Rohrerstown Rd	Lancaster	PA	17601	**800-676-1837**	717-581-1000
PMP Corp 25 Security Dr *Cust Svc	Avon	CT	06001	**800-243-6628***	860-677-9656
POM Inc 200 S Elmira Ave	Russellville	AR	72802	**800-331-7275**	479-968-2880
Sparling Instruments Company Inc 4097 N Temple City Blvd *Sales	El Monte	CA	91731	**800-800-3569***	626-444-0571

494 MICROGRAPHICS PRODUCTS & SERVICES

				Toll-Free	Phone
BMI Imaging Systems 1115 E Arques Ave	Sunnyvale	CA	94085	**800-359-3456**	408-736-7444
Comstor Productivity Ctr Inc 441 W Sharp Ave	Spokane	WA	99201	**800-776-2451**	509-534-5080
DPF Data Services 1345 Campus Pkw Unit A8	Wall Township	NJ	07753	**800-431-4416**	
Eye Communication Systems Inc 455 E Industrial Dr	Hartland	WI	53029	**800-558-2153**	262-367-1360
HF Group Inc 203 W Artesia Blvd	Compton	CA	90220	**800-421-5000**	310-605-0755
Indus International Inc 340 S Oak St PO Box 890	West Salem	WI	54669	**800-843-9377**	608-786-0300

495 MILITARY BASES

SEE ALSO Coast Guard Installations

495-1 Air Force Bases

				Toll-Free	Phone
Eielson Air Force Base 354 Broadway St Unit 2B	Eielson AFB	AK	99702	**800-538-6647**	907-377-1110
Kirtland Air Force Base 2000 Wyoming Blvd SE Ste A-1	Kirtland AFB	NM	87117	**877-246-1453**	505-846-5991
Laughlin Air Force Base 561 Liberty Dr Ste 3	Laughlin AFB	TX	78843	**866-966-1020**	830-298-3511
Little Rock Air Force Base 1250 Thomas Ave	Little Rock AFB	AR	72099	**800-557-6815**	501-987-1110
Los Angeles Air Force Base 483 N Aviation Blvd Los Angeles AFB	El Segundo	CA	90245	**800-275-8777**	310-653-1110
Luke Air Force Base 14185 W Falcon St	Luke AFB	AZ	85309	**855-655-1004**	623-856-5853
Maxwell Air Force Base 55 Le May Plaza S	Maxwell AFB	AL	36112	**877-353-6807**	334-953-2014
Mountain Home Air Force Base 366 Gunfighter Ave Ste 498	Mountain Home AFB	ID	83648	**855-366-0140**	208-828-6800
Seymour Johnson Air Force Base 1510 Wright Bros Ave	Seymour Johnson AFB	NC	27531	**800-525-0102**	919-722-0027
Shaw Air Force Base 20 FW/SEF 517 Lance Ave Ste 215	Shaw AFB	SC	29152	**800-235-7776**	803-895-1971
Sheppard Air Force Base 419 G Ave Ste 1	Sheppard AFB	TX	76311	**877-676-1847**	940-676-2511
Tyndall Air Force Base 555 Suwannee Rd Rm 140-A-1	Tyndall AFB	FL	32403	**800-356-5273**	850-283-1110
Vance Air Force Base 246 Brown Pkwy Ste 102	Enid	OK	73703	**866-966-1020**	580-213-7522
Wright-Patterson Air Force Base 5030 Patterson Pkwy	Wright-Patterson AFB	OH	45433	**800-225-5288**	937-257-1110

495-2 Army Bases

				Toll-Free	Phone
Fort Detrick 810 Schreider St	Frederick	MD	21702	**800-256-7621**	301-619-7613

495-3 Marine Corps Bases

				Toll-Free	Phone
Marine Corps Base Quantico 3250 Catlin Ave	Quantico	VA	22134	**800-268-3710**	703-432-0303

495-4 Naval Installations

				Toll-Free	Phone
Naval Air Station Jacksonville 6801 Roosevelt Blvd	Jacksonville	FL	32212	**800-849-6024**	904-542-2338
Naval Air Station Joint Reserve Base New Orleans 301 Russell Ave	New Orleans	LA	70143	**800-729-7327**	504-678-3260
Naval Air Station Patuxent River 22268 Cedar Point Road Bldg 409	Patuxent River	MD	20670	**877-995-5247**	301-342-3000
Naval Station Great Lakes 2601E Paul Jones St	Great Lakes	IL	60088	**800-393-0865**	847-688-3500
Navy Lodge Pensacola Naval Air Station Bldg 3875	Pensacola	FL	32508	**800-628-9466**	850-456-8676
US. Fleet Forces Command 1562 Mitscher Ave Ste 250	Norfolk	VA	23551	**800-473-3549**	757-836-3630

496 MILITARY SERVICE ACADEMIES

				Toll-Free	Phone
US Air Force Academy (USAFA) 2304 Cadet Dr Ste 3100	Air Force Academy	CO	80840	**800-443-9266**	719-333-1110
US Naval Academy 121 Blake Rd *Admissions	Annapolis	MD	21402	**888-249-7707***	410-293-1000

497 MILLWORK

SEE ALSO Doors & Windows - Wood ; Shutters - Window (All Types) ; Lumber & Building Supplies ; Home Improvement Centers

				Toll-Free	Phone
Anlin Industries 1665 Tollhouse Rd	Clovis	CA	93611	**800-287-7996**	559-322-1531
Arcways Inc 1076 Ehlers Rd	Neenah	WI	54956	**800-558-5096**	
Boiseries Raymond Inc 11880 56e Ave	Montreal	QC	H1E2L6	**800-361-6577**	514-494-1141
Buffelen Woodworking Co 1901 Taylor Way	Tacoma	WA	98421	**800-423-8810**	253-627-1191
Canamould Extrusions Inc 101a Roytec Rd	Woodbridge	ON	L4L8A9	**866-874-6762**	905-264-4436
Carter-Lee ProBuild 1717 W Washington St	Indianapolis	IN	46222	**800-344-9242**	317-639-5431
Cascade Wood Products Inc PO Box 2429	White City	OR	97503	**800-423-3311**	541-826-2911
Centennial Windows Ltd 687 Sovereign Rd	London	ON	N5V4K8	**800-265-1995**	519-451-0508
Central Woodwork Inc 870 Keough Rd	Collierville	TN	38017	**800-788-3775**	901-363-4141
Colonial Millwork Ltd PO Box 436	Beverly	WV	26253	**800-833-7612**	
Commercial & Architectural Products Inc PO Box 250	Dover	OH	44622	**800-377-1221**	330-343-6621
Contact Industries Inc 9200 SE Sunnybrook Blvd Ste 200	Clackamas	OR	97015	**800-547-1038**	503-228-7361
Cox Interior Inc 1751 Old Columbia Rd	Campbellsville	KY	42718	**800-733-1751**	
Crown Column & Millwork Co LLC 3810 Pleasant Valley Rd	Attalla	AL	35954	**888-862-0880**	
Dac Products Inc 625 Montroyal Rd	Rural Hall	NC	27045	**800-431-1982**	
Dashwood Industries Ltd 69323 Richmond St	Centralia	ON	N0M1K0	**800-265-4284**	519-228-6624
Delden Manufacturing Company Inc 3530 N Kimball Dr	Kansas City	MO	64161	**800-821-3708**	816-413-1600
Dorris Lumber & Moulding Co, The 2601 Redding Ave	Sacramento	CA	95820	**800-827-5823**	916-452-7531
Graves Lumber Co 1315 S Cleveland-Massillon Rd	Copley	OH	44321	**877-500-5515**	330-666-1115
HB&G Inc PO Box 589	Troy	AL	36081	**800-264-4424**	334-566-5000
Horner Millwork Corp 1255 Grand Army Hwy	Somerset	MA	02726	**800-543-5403**	508-679-6479
Huttig Bldg Products Inc (HBP) 555 Maryville University Dr Ste 400 *NASDAQ: HBP*	Saint Louis	MO	63141	**800-325-4466**	314-216-2600
Inline Fibreglass Ltd 30 Constellation Ct	Toronto	ON	M9W1K1	**866-566-5656**	416-679-1171
Jeld-Wen Inc PO Box 1329	Klamath Falls	OR	97601	**800-535-3936**	
Lafayette Wood-Works Inc 3004 Cameron St	Lafayette	LA	70506	**800-960-3311**	337-233-5250
Laflamme Doors & Windows 39 Industrielle St	St Apollinaire	QC	G0S2E0	**800-463-1922**	
Louisiana-Pacific Corp 414 Union St Ste 2000 *NYSE: LPX*	Nashville	TN	37219	**888-820-0325**	615-986-5600
Mann & Parker Lumber Company Inc, The 335 N Constitution Ave	New Freedom	PA	17349	**800-632-9098**	717-235-4834
MCD Innovations 3303 N MCDonald St	Mckinney	TX	75071	**800-804-1757**	972-548-1850
Menzner Lumber & Supply Co PO Box 217	Marathon	WI	54448	**800-257-1284**	
Michbi Doors Inc 75 Emjay Blvd	Brentwood	NY	11717	**800-854-4541**	631-231-9050
Nana Wall Systems Inc 707 Redwood Hwy	Mill Valley	CA	94941	**800-873-5673**	415-383-3148
New England Garage Door 15 Campanelli Cir	Canton	MA	02021	**800-676-7734**	781-821-2737
Nickell Moulding Company Inc 3015 Mobile Dr	Elkhart	IN	46515	**800-838-2151**	574-264-3129
North Atlantic Corp 1255 Grand Army Hwy	Somerset	MA	02726	**800-543-5403**	
Ornamental Moulding & Millwork 3804 Comanche Rd	Archdale	NC	27263	**800-779-1135**	
Paltech Enterprises Inc 2560 Bing Miller Ln	Urbana	IA	52345	**800-949-1006**	319-443-2700
Quanex Building Products 2270 Woodale Dr	Mounds View	MN	55112	**800-233-4383**	763-231-4000
Randall Bros Inc 665 Marietta St NW *Cust Svc	Atlanta	GA	30313	**800-476-4539***	404-892-6666
Raynor Garage Doors 1101 E River Rd	Dixon	IL	61021	**800-472-9667**	815-288-1431
Reeb Millwork Corp 7475 Henry Clay Blvd	Liverpool	NY	13088	**800-862-8622**	315-451-6699
Shanahan's LP 13139 80th Ave	Surrey	BC	V3W3B1	**888-591-5999**	604-591-5111

				Toll-Free	Phone
Shaw/Stewart Lumber Co 645 Johnson St NE	Minneapolis	MN	55413	800-233-0101	612-378-1520
Shuster's Bldg Components 2920 Clay Pk	Irwin	PA	15642	800-676-0640	724-446-7000
Somerset Door & Column Co 174 Sagamore St	Somerset	PA	15501	800-242-7916	814-444-9427
Sundt Construction 2620 S 55th St	Tempe	AZ	85282	800-280-3000	480-293-3000
Sunrise Mfg Inc 2665 Mercantile Dr	Rancho Cordova	CA	95742	800-748-6529	916-635-6262
Tru Tech Corp 20 Vaughan Vly Blvd	Vaughan	ON	L4H0B1	888-760-0099	905-856-0096
Weaber Inc 1231 Mt Wilson Rd	Lebanon	PA	17042	800-745-9663	717-867-2212
Werzalit of America Inc 40 Holly Ave	Bradford	PA	16701	800-999-3730	814-362-3881
Window & Door Factory, The 5595 Magnatron Ste C	San Diego	CA	92111	855-230-6558	
Woodgrain Millworks Inc 300 NW 16th St	Fruitland	ID	83619	888-783-5485	208-452-3801
Young Mfg Company Inc 521 S Main St PO Box 167	Beaver Dam	KY	42320	800-545-6595	270-274-3306

498   MINERAL PRODUCTS - NONMETALLIC

SEE ALSO Insulation & Acoustical Products

				Toll-Free	Phone
Burgess Pigment Company Inc 525 Beck Blvd PO Box 349	Sandersville	GA	31082	800-841-8999	478-552-2544
Dicalite Management Group Inc 1 Bala Ave Ste 310	Bala Cynwyd	PA	19004	866-728-3303	610-660-8808
Eagle-Picher Minerals Inc 9785 Gateway Dr *Cust Svc	Reno	NV	89521	800-228-3865*	775-824-7600
Graphel Corp 6115 Centre Pk Dr	West Chester	OH	45069	800-255-1104	513-779-6166
Graphite Sales Inc 16710 W Pk Cir Dr	Chagrin Falls	OH	44023	800-321-4147	440-543-8221
Hill & Griffith Co 1085 Summer St	Cincinnati	OH	45204	800-543-0425	513-921-1075
La Habra Products Inc 4125 E La Palma Ave Ste 250	Anaheim	CA	92807	866-516-0061	714-778-2266
Miller & Co LLC 9700 W Higgins Rd Ste 1000	Rosemont	IL	60018	800-727-9847	847-696-2400
Miller Studio 734 Fair Ave NW	New Philadelphia	OH	44663	800-332-0050	330-339-1100
Multicoat Corp 23331 Antonio Pkwy	Rancho Santa Margarita	CA	92688	877-685-8426	
Oil-Dri Corp of America 410 N Michigan Ave Ste 400 *NYSE: ODC*	Chicago	IL	60611	800-645-3747	312-321-1515
Silbrico Corp 6300 River Rd	Hodgkins	IL	60525	800-323-4287	708-354-3350
US Diamond Wheel Co 101 Kendall Pt Dr	Oswego	IL	60543	800-223-0457	800-851-1095
USG Corp 550 W Adams St *NYSE: USG*	Chicago	IL	60661	800-874-4968	312-436-4000
Von Roll Isola USA 200 Von Roll Dr	Schenectady	NY	12306	800-654-7652	518-344-7100
Ziegler Chemical & Mineral Corp 600 Prospect Ave	Piscataway	NJ	08854	888-213-7500	732-752-4111

499   MINING - COAL

				Toll-Free	Phone
Alpha Natural Resources Inc 636 Shelby St 3rd Fl *OTC: ANR*	Bristol	TN	37620	866-322-5742	423-574-5100
Cloud Peak Energy Inc 505 S Gillette Ave PO Box 3009	Gillette	WY	82717	866-470-4300	307-687-6000
East Fairfield Coal Co (EFCC) 10900 S Ave PO Box 217	North Lima	OH	44452	800-241-7074	330-549-2165
James River Coal Co 901 E Byrd St Ste 1600 *NASDAQ: JRVR*	Richmond	VA	23219	877-283-6545	804-780-3000
Natural Resource Partners LP 1201 Louisiana St Ste 3400 *NYSE: NRP*	Houston	TX	77002	888-334-7102	713-751-7507
Westmoreland Coal Co 9540 S Maroon Cir Ste 300 *NASDAQ: WLBA*	Englewood	CO	80112	855-922-6463	303-922-6463

500   MINING - METALS

				Toll-Free	Phone
Agnico-Eagle Mines Ltd 145 King St E Ste 500 *NYSE: AEM*	Toronto	ON	M5C2Y7	888-822-6714	416-947-1212
Alamos Gold Inc 181 Bay St Ste 3910 *NYSE: AGI*	Toronto	ON	M5J2T3	866-788-8801	416-368-9932
B2 Gold Corp 595 Burrard St Ste 3100 PO Box 49143	Vancouver	BC	V7X1J1	800-316-8855	604-681-8371
Badger Mining Corp 409 S Church St CA Chier Resource Ctr	Berlin	WI	54923	800-932-7263	920-361-2388
Barrick Gold Corp TD Canada Trust Tower 161 Bay St PO Box 212 *NYSE: ABX*	Toronto	ON	M5J2S1	800-720-7415	416-861-9911
Barrick Gold Corp 161 Bay St 3700	Toronto	ON	M5J2S1	800-720-7415	416-861-9911
BCM Resources Corp 1040 W Georgia St	Vancouver	BC	V6E4H1	888-646-0144	604-646-0144

				Toll-Free	Phone
Crystallex International Corp 8 King St E Ste 1201	Toronto	ON	M5C1B5	800-738-1577	416-203-2448
Eldorado Gold Corp 550 Burrard St *NYSE: ELD*	Vanouver	BC	V6C2B5	888-353-8166	604-687-4018
First Quantum Minerals Ltd 543 Granville St 14th Fl *TSX: FM*	Vancouver	BC	V6C1X8	888-688-6577	604-688-6577
Gold Reserve Inc 926 W Sprague Ave Ste 200 *OTC: GDRZF*	Spokane	WA	99201	800-625-9550	509-623-1500
Goldcorp Inc 666 Burrard St Ste 3400 *NYSE: GG*	Vancouver	BC	V6C2X8	800-567-6223	604-696-3000
IAMGOLD Corp 401 Bay St Ste 3200 PO Box 153 *TSE: IMG*	Toronto	ON	M5H2Y4	888-464-9999	416-360-4710
IBC Advanced Alloys Corp 401 Arvin Rd	Franklin	IN	46131	800-423-5612	317-738-2558
Kinross Gold Corp 25 York St 17th Fl	Toronto	ON	M5J2V5	866-561-3636	416-365-5123
Materion Corp 6070 Parkland Blvd *NYSE: MTRN*	Mayfield Heights	OH	44124	800-321-2076	216-486-4200
North American Palladium Ltd 1 University Ave Ste 402 *TSX: PDL*	Toronto	ON	M5J2P1	888-360-7590	416-360-7590
NovaGold Resources Inc 789 W Pender St Ste 720 *NYSE: NG*	Vancouver	BC	V6C1H2	866-669-6277	604-669-6227
Rubicon Minerals Corp 21 King St W Ste 830 *OTC: RBYCF*	Toronto	ON	M5H3T9	844-818-1776	416-766-2804
Sherritt International Corp 1133 Yonge St *TSE: S*	Toronto	ON	M4T2Y7	800-704-6698	416-924-4551
SSR Mining Inc 999 W Hastings St Ste 1180 *NASDAQ: SSRM*	Vancouver	BC	V6C2W2	888-338-0046	604-689-3846
Teck Resources Ltd 501 N Riverpoint Blvd Ste 300	Spokane	WA	99202	866-225-0198	800-432-3206
US Energy Corp 877 N Eigth W *NASDAQ: USEG*	Riverton	WY	82501	800-776-9271	307-856-9271
Western Copper Corp 1040 W Georgia St 1st Fl	Vancouver	BC	V6E4H1	888-966-9995	604-684-9497
Wharf Resources USA Inc 10928 Wharf Rd	Lead	SD	57754	800-567-6223	605-584-1441

501   MINING - MINERALS

501-1   Chemical & Fertilizer Minerals Mining

				Toll-Free	Phone
American Borate Corp 5700 Cleveland St Ste 350	Virginia Beach	VA	23462	800-486-1072	757-490-2242
New Riverside Ochre Co 75 Old River Rd SE *Orders*	Cartersville	GA	30120	800-248-0176*	770-382-4568
Searles Valley Minerals 9401 Indian Creek Pkwy Ste 1000	Overland Park	KS	66210	800-637-2775	913-344-9500
United Salt Corp 4800 San Felipe St	Houston	TX	77056	800-554-8658	713-877-2600

501-2   Clay, Ceramic, Refractory Minerals Mining

				Toll-Free	Phone
Black Hills Bentonite PO Box 9 *Orders*	Mills	WY	82644	800-700-8666*	307-265-3740
I-Minerals Inc 880 - 580 Hornby St	Vancouver	BC	V6C3B6	877-303-6573	604-303-6573
Milwhite Inc 5487 S Padre Island Hwy	Brownsville	TX	78521	800-442-0082	956-547-1970
RT Vanderbilt Company Inc 30 Winfield St *Cust Svc*	Norwalk	CT	06855	800-243-6064*	203-853-1400
US Silica Co 8490 Progress Dr Ste 300	Frederick	MD	21701	800-243-7500	304-258-2500
Wyo-Ben Inc 1345 Discovery Dr *Cust Svc*	Billings	MT	59102	800-548-7055*	406-652-6351

501-3   Minerals Mining (Misc)

				Toll-Free	Phone
ILC Resources 3301 106th Cir	Urbandale	IA	50322	800-247-2133	515-243-8106
RT Vanderbilt Company Inc 30 Winfield St *Cust Svc*	Norwalk	CT	06855	800-243-6064*	203-853-1400
Stornoway Diamond Corp 1111 St-Charles Ouest Tour Ouest Ste 400 *TSX: SWY*	Longueuil	QC	J4K5G4	877-331-2232	450-616-5555
Vanderbilt Minerals Corp 30 Winfield St	Norwalk	CT	06855	800-243-6064	203-853-1400

501-4   Sand & Gravel Pits

				Toll-Free	Phone
Edward C Levy Co 9300 Dix Ave	Dearborn	MI	48120	877-938-0007	313-843-7200

Classified Section

				Toll-Free	Phone
Fisher Sand & Gravel Co					
3020 Energy Dr PO Box 1034	Dickinson	ND	58602	**800-932-8740**	701-456-9184
Janesville Sand & Gravel Co (JSG)					
1110 Harding St PO Box 427	Janesville	WI	53547	**800-955-7702**	608-754-7701
Lafarge North America Inc					
8700 W Bryn Mawr Ave Ste 300	Chicago	IL	60631	**800-451-8346**	773-372-1000
LG Everist Inc					
300 S Phillips Ave Ste 200	Sioux Falls	SD	57117	**800-843-7992**	605-334-5000
Mark Sand & Gravel Co					
525 Kennedy Pk Rd PO Box 458	Fergus Falls	MN	56537	**800-427-8316**	218-736-7523
Pike Industries Inc					
3 Eastgate Pk Rd	Belmont	NH	03220	**800-283-0803**	603-527-5100
Pounding Mill Quarry Corp					
171 St Clair S Crossing	Bluefield	VA	24605	**888-661-7625**	276-326-1145
US Silica Co					
8490 Progress Dr Ste 300	Frederick	MD	21701	**800-243-7500**	304-258-2500

501-5 Stone Quarries - Crushed & Broken Stone

				Toll-Free	Phone
Edward C Levy Co					
9300 Dix Ave	Dearborn	MI	48120	**877-938-0007**	313-843-7200
Harney Rock & Paving Co					
457 S Date Ave	Burns	OR	97720	**888-298-2681**	541-573-7855
HB Mellot Estate Inc					
100 Mellott Dr	Warfordsburg	PA	17267	**800-634-5634**	301-678-2050
Hunt Midwest Enterprises Inc					
8300 NE Underground Dr	Kansas City	MO	64161	**800-551-6877**	816-455-2500
Hunt Midwest Mining Inc					
8300 NE Underground Dr	Kansas City	MO	64161	**800-551-6877**	816-455-2500
JF Shea Co Inc					
655 Brea Canyon Rd	Walnut	CA	91789	**800-685-6494**	909-594-9500
Lafarge North America Inc					
8700 W Bryn Mawr Ave Ste 300	Chicago	IL	60631	**800-451-8346**	773-372-1000
LG Everist Inc					
300 S Phillips Ave Ste 200	Sioux Falls	SD	57117	**800-843-7992**	605-334-5000
Pike Industries Inc					
3 Eastgate Pk Rd	Belmont	NH	03220	**800-283-0803**	603-527-5100
Pounding Mill Quarry Corp					
171 St Clair S Crossing	Bluefield	VA	24605	**888-661-7625**	276-326-1145
Texas Crushed Stone Co					
5300 S IH-35 PO Box 1000	Georgetown	TX	78627	**800-772-8272**	512-930-0106
Tilcon NY Inc					
162 Old Mill Rd	West Nyack	NY	10994	**800-872-7762**	845-358-4500
Vulcan Materials Co					
1200 Urban Ctr Dr PO Box 385014	Birmingham	AL	35238	**800-615-4331**	205-298-3000
NYSE: VMC					
Vulcan Materials Company Western Div					
1200 Urban Center Dr	Birmingham	AL	35242	**800-615-4331**	205-298-3000
NYSE: VMC					

501-6 Stone Quarries - Dimension Stone

				Toll-Free	Phone
American Clay Enterprises LLC					
2418 Second St SW	Albuquerque	NM	87102	**866-404-1634**	505-243-5300
CRH Americas Inc					
900 Ashwood Pkwy Ste 700	Atlanta	GA	30338	**800-241-7074**	770-522-5600
Eden Stone Company Inc					
W4520 Lime Rd	Eden	WI	53019	**800-472-2521**	920-477-2521
Pounding Mill Quarry Corp					
171 St Clair S Crossing	Bluefield	VA	24605	**888-661-7625**	276-326-1145

502 MISSILES, SPACE VEHICLES, PARTS

SEE ALSO Weapons & Ordnance (Military)

				Toll-Free	Phone
Aerojet PO Box 13222	Sacramento	CA	95813	**800-637-7200**	916-355-4000
Esterline Mason					
13955 Balboa Blvd	Sylmar	CA	91342	**800-232-7700**	818-361-3366
HITCO Carbon Composites Inc					
1600 W 135th St	Gardena	CA	90249	**800-421-5444**	310-527-0700
International Launch Services (ILS)					
1875 Explorer St Ste 700	Reston	VA	20190	**800-852-4980**	571-633-7400
Lockheed Martin Corp					
6801 Rockledge Dr	Bethesda	MD	20817	**866-562-2363**	301-897-6000
NYSE: LMT					
Lockheed Martin Space Systems Co Michoud Operations					
13800 Old Gentilly Rd	New Orleans	LA	70129	**866-562-2363**	504-257-3311

503 MOBILE HOMES & BUILDINGS

				Toll-Free	Phone
Cavalier Homes Alabama					
32 Wilson Blvd 100 PO Box 300	Addison	AL	35540	**800-465-7923**	
Cavco Industries Inc					
1001 N Central Ave 8th Fl	Phoenix	AZ	85004	**800-790-9111**	602-256-6263
NASDAQ: CVCO					
Destiny Industries LLC					
250 R W Bryant Rd	Moultrie	GA	31788	**866-782-6600**	
Fleetwood Homes of Idaho Inc					
2611 E Comstock Ave	Nampa	ID	83687	**800-334-8958**	877-413-9849
Fleetwood Homes of Virginia Inc					
90 Weaver St	Rocky Mount	VA	24151	**866-890-6206**	540-483-5171
Franklin Homes Inc					
10655 Hwy 43	Russellville	AL	35653	**800-332-4511**	
Homark Company Inc					
100 Third St PO Box 309	Red Lake Falls	MN	56750	**800-382-1154**	218-253-2777
Jacobsen Homes					
600 Packard Ct	Safety Harbor	FL	34695	**800-843-1559**	727-726-1138
Luxury Retreats					
5530 St Patrick St Ste 2210	Montreal	QC	H4E1A8	**877-993-0100**	
Manufactured Housing Enterprises Inc					
09302 St Rt 6 Rt 6	Bryan	OH	43506	**800-821-0220**	419-636-4511
Nashua Homes of Idaho Inc					
PO Box 170008	Boise	ID	83717	**855-766-0222**	208-345-0222
Nobility Homes Inc					
3741 SW Seventh St	Ocala	FL	34474	**800-476-6624**	352-732-5157
OTC: NOBH					
R-Anell Custom Homes Inc					
235 Anthony Grave Rd	Crouse	NC	28033	**800-951-5511***	574-533-7100
*Cust Svc					
Ritz-Craft Corp of Pennsylvania Inc					
15 Industrial Pk Rd	Mifflinburg	PA	17844	**800-326-9836**	570-966-1053
Satellite Industries Inc					
2530 Xenium Ln N	Minneapolis	MN	55441	**800-328-3332**	
Skyline Corp					
2520 By-Pass Rd	Elkhart	IN	46514	**800-348-7469**	574-294-6521
NYSE: SKY					
Spartan Showcase Inc					
c/o Prock Operations Inc					
321 E Hardy St	St James	MO	65559	**800-325-0775**	
Wick Buildings					
405 Walter Rd	Mazomanie	WI	53560	**855-438-9425**	

504 MODELING AGENCIES

SEE ALSO Modeling Schools

				Toll-Free	Phone
Jancyn Inc					
1100 Lincoln Ave Ste 367	San Jose	CA	95125	**800-339-2861**	

505 MODELING SCHOOLS

				Toll-Free	Phone
Barbizon International LLC					
4950 W Kennedy Blvd Ste 200	Tampa	FL	33615	**800-330-8361**	
Cpr Savers & First Aid Supply					
7904 E Chaparral Rd Ste A110-242	Scottsdale	AZ	85250	**800-480-1277**	
Frederick Taylor University					
2050 W Chapman Ave Ste 108	Orange	CA	92868	**888-370-7589**	714-949-2304
Pima Medical Institute					
3350 E Grant Rd Ste 200	Tucson	AZ	85716	**888-556-7334**	520-326-1600
Rhino Medical Staffing					
2000 E Lamar Blvd Ste 250	Arlington	TX	76006	**866-267-4466**	817-795-2295
St Luke's College					
2800 Pierce St Ste 410	Sioux City	IA	51104	**800-352-4660**	712-279-3149

506 MOPS, SPONGES, WIPING CLOTHS

SEE ALSO Cleaning Products ; Brushes & Brooms

				Toll-Free	Phone
A&B Wiper Supply Inc					
11350 Norcom Rd	Philadelphia	PA	19154	**800-333-7247**	215-482-6100
Abco Cleaning Products					
6800 NW 36th Ave	Miami	FL	33147	**888-694-2226**	305-694-2226
Bro-Tex Inc					
800 Hampden Ave	Saint Paul	MN	55114	**800-328-2282**	651-645-5721
Continental Commercial Products (CCP)					
11840 Westline Industrial Dr	St. Louis	MO	63146	**800-325-1051**	
Ettore Products Co					
2100 N Loop Rd	Alameda	CA	94502	**800-438-8673**	510-748-4130
Golden Star Inc					
4770 N Belleview Ave Ste 209	Kansas City	MO	64116	**800-821-2792**	816-842-0233
United Textile Company Inc					
14275 Catalina St	San Leandro	CA	94577	**800-233-0077***	510-276-2288
*General					
Wipe-Tex International Corp					
110 E 153rd St	Bronx	NY	10451	**800-643-9607**	718-665-0013

507 MORTGAGE LENDERS & LOAN BROKERS

SEE ALSO Banks - Commercial & Savings

				Toll-Free	Phone
21st Mortgage Corp					
620 Market St Ste 100	Knoxville	TN	37902	**800-955-0021**	865-523-2120
Ascentium Capital LLC					
23970 Hwy 59 N	Kingwood	TX	77339	**866-722-8500**	
BRT Apartments Corp					
60 Cutter Mill Rd Ste 303	Great Neck	NY	11021	**800-450-5816**	516-466-3100
NYSE: BRT					
Canada Deposit Insurance Corp					
50 O'Connor St 17th Fl	Ottawa	ON	K1P6L2	**800-461-2342**	613-996-2081
CitiMortgage Inc					
1000 Technology Dr	O'Fallon	MO	63368	**800-283-7918***	
*Cust Svc					
Dominion Lending Centres Inc					
2215 Coquitlam Ave	Port Coquitlam	BC	V3B1J6	**866-928-6810**	
EverHome Mortgage Co					
301 W Bay St	Jacksonville	FL	32202	**888-882-3837***	
*Cust Svc					
Extraco Technology PO Box 2299	Waco	TX	76703	**866-428-9070**	
Fannie Mae					
3900 Wisconsin Ave NW	Washington	DC	20016	**800-732-6643**	800-232-6643
OTC: FNMA					
First Equity Mortgage Bankers					
9300 S Dadeland Blvd Ste 500	Miami	FL	33156	**800-973-3654**	305-666-3333
Freddie Mac					
8200 Jones Branch Dr	McLean	VA	22102	**800-424-5401**	703-903-2000
North Central Region					
333 W Wacker Dr Ste 2500	Chicago	IL	60606	**800-373-3343**	312-407-7400
Northeast Region					
8200 Jones Branch Dr	McLean	VA	22102	**800-373-3343**	703-903-2000
Southeast/Southwest Region					
2300 Windy Ridge Pkwy Ste 200N	Atlanta	GA	30339	**800-373-3343**	770-857-8800

Classified Section

	Toll-Free	Phone
George Mason Mortgage Corp		
4100 Monu Crnr Dr Ste 100............Fairfax VA 22030	**800-867-6859**	703-273-2600
Government National Mortgage Assn		
451 Seventh St SW Rm B-133............Washington DC 20410	**800-234-4662**	202-708-1535
Guild Mortgage Co		
5898 Copley Dr 4th & 5th Fl............San Diego CA 92111	**800-365-4441**	
HomeSteps 500 Plano Pkwy............Carrollton TX 75010	**800-972-7555**	
HSBC Bank USA 2929 Walden Ave............Depew NY 14043	**800-975-4722**	866-379-5621
Huntington Mortgage Co		
7575 Huntington Pk Dr............Columbus OH 43235	**800-323-4695**	614-480-6505
Inland Mortgage Corp		
2901 Butterfield Rd............Oak Brook IL 60523	**800-826-8228**	630-218-8000
Lion Inc 320 E Main St............Lake Zurich IL 60047	**800-867-6320**	872-228-5466
loanDepot		
26642 Towne Centre Dr............Foothill Ranch CA 92610	**888-337-6888**	
Merix Financial		
56 Temperance St Ste 400............Toronto ON M5H3V5	**877-637-4911**	
Midland Mortgage Co		
999 NW Grand Blvd Ste 100............Oklahoma City OK 73118	**800-654-4566**	
MMA Capital Management LLC (MuniMae)		
3600 O'Donnell St Ste 600............Baltimore MD 21224	**855-650-6932**	443-263-2900
OTC: MMAC		
Mortgage Investors Group		
8320 E Walker Springs Ln............Knoxville TN 37923	**800-489-8910**	865-691-8910
National Rural Utilities Co-op Finance Corp		
2201 Co-op Way............Herndon VA 20171	**800-424-2954**	703-709-6700
Payscape Advisors		
729 Lambert Dr NE............Atlanta GA 30324	**888-351-6565**	
PHH Mortgage Corp		
3000 Leadenhall Rd............Mount Laurel NJ 08054	**800-210-8849**	
Plaza Home Mortgage Inc		
4820 Eastgate Mall Ste 100............San Diego CA 92121	**866-260-2529**	858-346-1208
Redwood Trust Inc		
1 Belvedere Pl Ste 300............Mill Valley CA 94941	**866-269-4976**	415-389-7373
NYSE: RWT		
Regions Mortgage Inc		
215 Forrest St............Hattiesburg MS 39401	**800-986-2462**	
Residential Mortgage LLC		
100 Calais Dr............Anchorage AK 99503	**888-357-2707**	907-222-8800
Safeguard Properties Inc		
7887 Safeguard Cir............Valley View OH 44125	**800-852-8306**	216-520-1334
Stanley Jay s & Assoc		
5313 Mcclanahan Dr Ste G5............North Little Rock AR 72116	**888-758-4728**	501-758-8029
SunTrust Mortgage Inc		
1001 Semmes Ave............Richmond VA 23224	**800-634-7928**	
Truwest Credit Union		
PO Box 3489............Scottsdale AZ 85271	**855-878-9378**	480-441-5900
Universal Lending Corp (ULC)		
6775 E Evans Ave............Denver CO 80224	**800-758-4063**	
Vanderbilt Mortgage & Finance Inc		
500 Alcoa Trl............Maryville TN 37804	**800-970-7250**	
Wells Fargo Home Mortgage		
2840 Ingersoll Ave............Des Moines IA 50312	**800-401-1957**	515-237-5196

508 MORTUARY, CREMATORY, CEMETERY PRODUCTS & SERVICES

	Toll-Free	Phone
AJ Desmond & Sons Funeral Directors		
2600 Crooks Rd............Troy MI 48084	**800-210-7135**	248-362-2500
Baue Funeral Homes		
620 Jefferson St............Saint Charles MO 63301	**888-724-0073**	636-940-1000
Carriage Services Inc		
3040 Post Oak Blvd Ste 300............Houston TX 77056	**866-332-8400**	713-332-8400
NYSE: CSV		
Church & Chapel Metal Arts Inc		
2616 W Grand Ave............Chicago IL 60612	**800-992-1234**	
EVERGREEN MORTUARY & CEMETERY		
3015 N Oracle Rd............Tucson AZ 85705	**800-852-0269**	520-257-4831
Forest Lawn Memorial-Parks & Mortuaries		
1712 S Glendale Ave............Glendale CA 91205	**800-204-3131**	323-254-3131
Mount Sinai Memorial Park		
5950 Forest Lawn Dr............Los Angeles CA 90068	**800-600-0076**	323-469-6000
Service Corp International		
1929 Allen Pkwy............Houston TX 77019	**800-758-5804**	713-522-5141
NYSE: SCI		
Spring Grove Cemetery		
4521 Spring Grove Ave............Cincinnati OH 45232	**888-853-2230**	513-681-7526
Stewart Enterprises Inc		
1333 S Clearview Pkwy............New Orleans LA 70121	**877-239-3264**	713-522-5141
NASDAQ: STEI		
Woodlawn Cemetery Inc, The		
Webster Ave & E 233rd St............Bronx NY 10470	**877-496-6352**	718-920-0500

509 MOTION PICTURE DISTRIBUTION & RELATED SERVICES

	Toll-Free	Phone
Baker & Taylor Inc		
2550 W Tyvola Rd Ste 300............Charlotte NC 28217	**800-775-1800**	
Bridgestone Multimedia Group Inc		
300 N Mckemy Ave............Chandler AZ 85226	**866-774-3774**	
Extreme Reach Inc		
75 Second Ave Ste 720............Needham MA 02494	**877-769-9382**	781-577-2016
Facets Multimedia Inc		
1517 W Fullerton Ave............Chicago IL 60614	**800-331-6197***	773-281-9075
*Cust Svc		
First Run Features		
630 Ninth Ave Ste 1213............New York NY 10036	**800-229-8575**	212-243-0600
Ingram Entertainment Inc		
2 Ingram Blvd............La Vergne TN 37089	**800-621-1333**	615-287-4000
Kultur International Films Ltd		
PO Box 755............Forked River NJ 08731	**888-329-2580**	
MPI Media Group		
16101 108th Ave............Orland Park IL 60467	**800-323-0442**	
Paramount Pictures Corp		
5555 Melrose Ave............Los Angeles CA 90038	**844-392-9033**	

510 MOTION PICTURE PRODUCTION - SPECIAL INTEREST

SEE ALSO Motion Picture & Television Production ; Animation Companies

	Toll-Free	Phone
Active Parenting Publishers		
1955 Vaughn Rd Ste 108............Kennesaw GA 30144	**800-825-0060**	770-429-0565
American Educational Products Inc		
401 Hickory St PO Box 2121............Fort Collins CO 80522	**800-289-9299**	970-484-7445
Coastal Training Technologies Corp		
500 Studio Dr............Virginia Beach VA 23452	**866-333-6888**	757-498-9014
CRM Learning		
11400 SE Eighth St Ste 210............Bellevue WA 92004	**800-421-0833**	760-431-9800
Hammond Communications Group Inc		
173 Trade St............Lexington KY 40511	**888-424-1878**	859-254-1878
Intaglio LLC		
3 Mile Rd NW Ste 3106............Grand Rapids MI 49534	**800-632-9153**	616-243-3300
Keystone Learning Systems LLC		
6030 Daybreak Cir Ste A150 116............Clarksville MD 21029	**800-949-5590**	410-800-4000
Kultur International Films Ltd		
PO Box 755............Forked River NJ 08731	**888-329-2580**	
Medcom Trainex		
6060 Phyllis Dr............Cypress CA 90630	**800-877-1443***	
*Cust Svc		
National Film Board of Canada		
Stn Centre-Ville PO Box 6100............Montreal QC H3C3H5	**800-267-7710**	514-283-9000
Nightingale-Conant Corp		
6245 W Howard St............Niles IL 60714	**800-557-1660***	
*Cust Svc		
PADI Americas		
30151 Tomas St............Rancho Santa Margarita CA 92688	**800-527-8378**	949-858-7234

511 MOTION PICTURE & TELEVISION PRODUCTION

SEE ALSO Motion Picture Production - Special Interest ; Animation Companies

	Toll-Free	Phone
Audio General Inc (AGI)		
1680 Republic Rd............Huntingdon Valley PA 19006	**866-866-2600**	267-288-0300
Aurora Pictures Inc		
5249 Chicago Ave............Minneapolis MN 55417	**800-346-9487**	612-821-6490
Bioquant Image Analysis Corp		
5611 Ohio Ave............Nashville TN 37209	**800-221-0549**	615-350-7866
Bullfrog Films Inc		
372 Dautrich Rd............Reading PA 19606	**800-543-3764**	610-779-8226
Cev Multimedia Ltd		
1020 SE Loop 289............Lubbock TX 79404	**877-610-5017**	
Cintrex Audio Visual		
656 Axminister Dr............Fenton MO 63026	**800-325-9541**	636-343-0178
Communica 31 N Erie St............Toledo OH 43604	**800-800-7890**	
FDC Graphics Films Inc		
3820 William Richardson Dr............South Bend IN 46628	**800-634-7523**	574-273-4400
Kantola Productions LLC		
55 Sunnyside Ave............Mill Valley CA 94941	**800-280-1180**	415-381-9363
McHenry Creative Services Inc		
345 Main St............Harleysville PA 19438	**877-627-0345**	
Pacific Title Archives		
10717 Vanowen St............North Hollywood CA 91605	**800-968-9111**	818-760-4223
Paramount Pictures Corp		
5555 Melrose Ave............Los Angeles CA 90038	**844-392-9033**	
Pot O' Gold Cinema Advertising		
11555 Central Pkwy............Jacksonville FL 32224	**800-446-5330**	904-744-7478
Reaction Audio Visual LLC		
30400 Esperanza............Rancho Santa Margarita CA 92618	**877-273-6887**	
Rodgers & Hammerstein Organization, The		
229 W 28th St 11th Fl.............New York NY 10001	**800-400-8160**	212-541-6600
Samson Technologies Inc		
45 Gilpin Ave............Hauppauge NY 11788	**800-372-6766**	631-784-2200
Smp Communications Corp		
7626 E Greenway Rd Ste 100............Scottsdale AZ 85260	**888-796-3342**	480-905-4100
Sundance Institute		
1825 Three Kings Dr............Park City UT 84060	**888-285-7790**	801-328-3456
Swank Motion Pictures Inc		
10795 Watson Rd............St Louis MO 63127	**888-389-3622**	314-984-6000
Video Symphony Entertraining Inc		
266 E Magnolia Blvd............Burbank CA 91502	**888-370-7589**	818-557-6500
Vista Electronics Inc		
27525 Newhall Ranch Rd............Valencia CA 91355	**800-847-8299**	661-294-9820
Visual Communications Group Inc		
1548 Cliff Rd E............Burnsville MN 55337	**800-566-4162**	
Warner Bros Television Production Inc		
4000 Warner Blvd............Burbank CA 91522	**800-462-8855**	818-954-1853
Worktank Enterprises LLC		
400 E Pine St Ste 301.............Seattle WA 98122	**877-975-8265**	

MOTION PICTURE THEATERS

SEE Theaters - Motion Picture

512 MOTOR SPEEDWAYS

	Toll-Free	Phone
Atlanta Motor Speedway		
PO Box 500............Hampton GA 30228	**877-926-7849**	770-946-4211
Auto Club Speedway		
9300 Cherry Ave............Fontana CA 92335	**800-944-7223**	909-429-5000
Brainerd International Raceway		
5523 Birchdale Rd............Brainerd MN 56401	**866-444-4455**	218-824-7223
Bristol Motor Speedway		
151 Speedway Blvd............Bristol TN 37620	**866-415-4158**	423-989-6933
Carolina Dragway		
302 Dragstrip Rd............Aiken SC 29803	**877-471-7223**	803-471-2285

	City	State	Zip	Toll-Free	Phone
Chicagoland Speedway 500 Speedway Blvd	Joliet	IL	60433	**888-629-7223**	815-722-5500
Darlington Raceway 1301 Harry Bird Hwy	Darlington	SC	29532	**866-459-7223**	
Hamilton County Speedway 1200 Bluff St	Webster City	IA	50595	**800-873-1507**	515-832-6000
Heartland Park Topeka 7530 SW Topeka Blvd	Topeka	KS	66619	**844-200-6472**	785-862-4781
Hickory Motor Speedway 3130 Hwy 70 SE	Newton	NC	28658	**800-843-8725**	828-324-4535
Kentucky Speedway 1 Speedway Blvd *Resv	Sparta	KY	41086	**888-652-7223***	859-578-2300
Las Vegas Motor Speedway 7000 Las Vegas Blvd N	Las Vegas	NV	89115	**800-644-4444**	702-644-4444
Lime Rock Park 60 White Hollow Rd	Lakeville	CT	06039	**800-722-3577**	860-435-5000
Martinsville Speedway PO Box 3311	Martinsville	VA	24115	**877-722-3849**	276-666-7200
Michigan International Speedway 12626 US 12	Brooklyn	MI	49230	**800-354-1010**	517-592-6666
Pocono Raceway Long Pond Rd PO Box 500	Long Pond	PA	18334	**800-722-3929**	570-646-2300
Road America N 7390 Hwy 67	Elkhart Lake	WI	53020	**800-365-7223**	920-892-4576
Road Atlanta Raceway 5300 Winder Hwy	Braselton	GA	30517	**800-849-7223**	770-967-6143
Sebring International Raceway 113 Midway Dr	Sebring	FL	33870	**800-626-7223**	863-655-1442
Sonoma Raceway 29355 Arnold Dr Hwy 37 & 121	Sonoma	CA	95476	**800-870-7223**	707-938-8448
South Boston Speedway 1188 James D Hagood Hwy PO Box 1066	South Boston	VA	24592	**877-440-1540**	434-572-4947
Summit Motorsports Park 1300 Ohio 18	Norwalk	OH	44857	**800-729-6455**	800-230-3030
Texas Motorplex 7500 W Hwy 287	Ennis	TX	75119	**800-668-6775**	972-878-2641

513 MOTOR VEHICLES - COMMERCIAL & SPECIAL PURPOSE

SEE ALSO Weapons & Ordnance (Military) ; Automobiles - Mfr ; Motorcycles & Motorcycle Parts & Accessories ; Campers, Travel Trailers, Motor Homes ; Snowmobiles ; All-Terrain Vehicles

	City	State	Zip	Toll-Free	Phone
Allied Body Works Inc 625 S 96th St *General	Seattle	WA	98108	**800-733-7450***	206-763-7811
Auto Truck Inc 1420 Brewster Creek Blvd	Bartlett	IL	60103	**877-284-4440**	630-860-5600
Bianchi Honda 8430 Peach St	Erie	PA	16509	**866-979-8132**	814-864-5809
Champion Bus Inc 331 Graham Rd	Imlay City	MI	48444	**800-776-4943**	810-724-6474
Coach & Equipment Manufacturing Corp 130 Horizon Pk Dr PO Box 36	Penn Yan	NY	14527	**800-724-8464**	315-536-2321
Curtis Industries LLC 70 Hartwell St	West Boylston	MA	01583	**800-343-7676**	508-853-2200
Dealers Truck Equipment Co 2460 Midway St	Shreveport	LA	71108	**800-259-7569**	318-635-7567
Diamond Coach Corp 2300 W Fourth St	Oswego	KS	67356	**800-442-4645**	620-795-2191
Dick Gores Rv World 14590 Duval Pl W	Jacksonville	FL	32218	**800-635-7008**	904-741-5100
Douglass Truck Bodies Inc 231 21st St	Bakersfield	CA	93301	**800-635-7641**	661-327-0258
E-Z-GO 1451 Marvin Griffin Rd	Augusta	GA	30906	**800-241-5855**	
Ebus Inc 9250 Washburn Rd	Downey	CA	90242	**888-925-4263**	562-904-3474
Elliott Machine Works Inc 1351 Freese Works Pl	Galion	OH	44833	**800-299-0412**	419-468-4709
Erie Vehicle Co 60 E 51st St	Chicago	IL	60615	**888-550-3743**	773-536-6300
Fleet Engineers Inc 1800 E Keating Ave *Cust Svc	Muskegon	MI	49442	**800-333-7890***	231-777-2537
Fleet Equipment Corp 567 Commerce St	Franklin Lakes	NJ	07417	**800-631-0873**	201-337-3294
Fontaine Modification 9827 Mt Holly Rd	Charlotte	NC	28214	**800-366-8246**	704-391-1355
Fontaine Truck Equipment Co 7574 Commerce Cir	Trussville	AL	35173	**800-874-9780**	205-661-4900
Ford of Ocala Inc 2816 NW Pine Ave	Ocala	FL	34475	**888-255-1788**	352-732-4800
General Motors Corp (GMC) 100 Renaissance Ctr *NYSE: GM*	Detroit	MI	48265	**800-462-8782**	313-556-5000
General Truck Body 7110 Jensen Dr	Houston	TX	77093	**800-395-8585**	713-692-5177
Gillig Corp 25800 Clawiter Rd	Hayward	CA	94545	**800-735-1500**	510-785-1500
Gowans-Knight Co Inc 49 Knight St	Watertown	CT	06795	**800-352-4871**	860-274-8801
Hackney 911 W Fifth St PO Box 880	Washington	NC	27889	**800-763-0700**	252-946-6521
Heil Environmental Ltd 2030 Hamilton Pl Blvd Ste 200	Chattanooga	TN	37421	**866-367-4345**	423-899-9100
Hercules Manufacturing Co 800 Bob Posey St	Henderson	KY	42420	**800-633-3031**	270-826-9501
HME Inc 1950 Byron Ctr Ave SW	Wyoming	MI	49519	**800-269-7335**	616-534-1463
Johnson Refrigerated Truck Bodies 215 E Allen St *Sales	Rice Lake	WI	54868	**800-922-8360***	715-234-7071
Joyce Koons Buick Gmc 10660 Automotive Dr	Manassas	VA	20109	**866-755-0072**	703-368-9100
Labrie Enviroquip Group 175-B Rte Marie-Victorin	Levis	QC	G7A2T3	**800-463-6638**	418-831-8250
Laird Noller Ford Inc 2245 SW Topeka Blvd	Topeka	KS	66611	**877-803-1859**	785-235-9211
Leson Chevrolet Co Inc 1501 Westbank Express	Harvey	LA	70058	**877-496-2420**	504-366-4381
Liberty Toyota Scion 4397 Rt 130 S	Burlington	NJ	08016	**888-809-7798**	609-386-6300
Libertyville Chevrolet Inc 1001 S Milwaukee Ave *Sales	Libertyville	IL	60048	**877-520-1807***	847-362-1400
Lodal Inc 620 N Hooper St PO Box 2315	Kingsford	MI	49802	**800-435-3500**	906-779-1700
Lumberton Honda Mitsubishi Inc 301 Wintergreen Dr	Lumberton	NC	28358	**855-712-9438**	910-739-9871
LZ Truck Equipment Inc 1881 Rice St	Saint Paul	MN	55113	**800-247-1082**	651-488-2571
Matt Castrucci Auto Mall of Dayton 3013 Mall Pk Dr	Dayton	OH	45459	**855-204-5293**	
Mc-Coy-Mills 700 W Commonwealth *Sales	Fullerton	CA	92832	**888-434-3145***	
McDaniel Motor Co 1111 Mt Vernon Ave	Marion	OH	43302	**877-362-0288**	740-389-2355
McGuire Cadillac Inc 910 Rt 1 N	Woodbridge	NJ	07095	**866-552-4208**	
McNeilus Truck & Manufacturing Inc 524 E Hwy St PO Box 70	Dodge Center	MN	55927	**888-686-7278**	507-374-6321
Mel Rapton Inc 3630 Fulton Ave	Sacramento	CA	95821	**800-529-3053**	916-482-5400
MH EBY 1194 Main St PO Box 127	Blue Ball	PA	17506	**800-292-4752**	717-354-4971
Mickey Truck Bodies Inc 1305 Trinity Ave	High Point	NC	27261	**800-334-9061**	336-882-6806
Miller Industries Inc 8503 Hilltop Dr *NYSE: MLR*	Ooltewah	TN	37363	**800-292-0330**	423-238-4171
Momentum Bmw Ltd 10002 SW Fwy	Houston	TX	77074	**800-731-8114**	855-645-6452
Monroe Truck Equipment Inc 1051 W Seventh St	Monroe	WI	53566	**800-356-8134**	608-328-8127
Morgan Corp 111 Morgan Way PO Box 588	Morgantown	PA	19543	**800-666-7426**	
Morgan Olson 1801 S Nottawa Rd	Sturgis	MI	49091	**800-624-9005**	
Morse Operations Inc 3790 W Blue Heron Blvd	Riviera Beach	FL	33404	**800-755-2593**	866-590-0873
Murrays Ford Inc 3007 Blinker Pkwy	Du Bois	PA	15801	**800-371-6601**	
Nacarato Volvo Truck 519 New Paul Rd	La Vergne	TN	37086	**888-392-8486**	
North Florida Lincoln Mercury 4620 Southside Blvd	Jacksonville	FL	32216	**888-457-1949**	877-941-1435
Obs Inc 1324 WTuscarawas St PO Box 6210	Canton	OH	44706	**800-362-9592**	330-453-3725
Oshkosh Truck Corp 2307 Oregon St	Oshkosh	WI	54903	**800-392-9921**	920-235-9150
Parkway Chevrolet Inc 25500 Tomball Pkwy	Tomball	TX	77375	**888-929-4556**	
Pierce Mfg Inc 2600 American Dr PO Box 2017 *Cust Svc	Appleton	WI	54912	**888-974-3723***	920-832-3000
Porter Truck Sales LP 135 McCarty St	Houston	TX	77029	**800-956-2408**	713-672-2400
Prevost Car Inc 35 boul Gagnon	Sainte-Claire	QC	G0R2V0	**877-773-8678**	418-883-3391
Quad-City Peterbilt Inc 8100 N Fairmount St	Davenport	IA	52806	**888-774-1618**	
R & S/Godwin Truck Body Co LLC 5168 US Hyw 23 S PO Box 420	Ivel	KY	41642	**800-826-7413**	606-874-2151
Rdk Truck Sales Inc 3214 Adamo Dr	Tampa	FL	33605	**877-735-4636**	813-241-0711
Reading Truck Body Inc 201 Hancock Blvd *All	Reading	PA	19611	**800-458-2226***	
Rihm Kenworth (RK) 425 Concord St S	South St.Paul	MN	55075	**800-988-8235**	651-646-7833
RKI Inc 2301 Central Pkwy	Houston	TX	77092	**800-346-8988**	713-688-4414
Rush Truck Ctr - Lubbock 4515 Ave A	Lubbock	TX	79404	**888-987-2458**	806-686-3600
Rydell Chevrolet Inc 18600 Devonshire St	Northridge	CA	91324	**866-697-5167**	
Saf-T-Cab Inc PO Box 2587	Fresno	CA	93745	**800-344-7491**	559-268-5541
Sanders Ford Inc 1135 Lejeune Blvd *General	Jacksonville	NC	28540	**888-897-8527***	910-455-1911
Scania USA Inc 121 Interpark Blvd Ste 601	San Antonio	TX	78216	**800-272-2642**	210-403-0007
Scelzi Equipment Inc 1030 W Gladstone St	Azusa	CA	91702	**800-858-2883**	626-334-0573
Schetky Northwest Sales Inc 8430 NE Killingsworth St	Portland	OR	97220	**800-255-8341**	503-607-3137
Segway Inc 14 Technology Dr	Bedford	NH	03110	**866-473-4929**	603-222-6000
Shealy's Truck Ctr Inc 1340 Bluff Rd	Columbia	SC	29201	**800-951-8580**	803-771-0176
Snethkamp Chrysler Dodge Jeep Ram 11600 Telegraph Rd	Redford	MI	48239	**888-455-6146**	313-429-0013
Somerset Welding & Steel Inc 10558 Somerset Pk	Somerset	PA	15501	**800-777-2671**	814-444-3400
STAHL/A Scott Fetzer Co 3201 W Old Lincoln Way	Wooster	OH	44691	**800-277-8245**	330-264-7441
Steve Hopkins Inc 2499 Auto Mall Pkwy	Fairfield	CA	94533	**877-873-3913**	707-427-1000
Steve Landers Toyota 10825 Colonel Glenn Rd	Little Rock	AR	72204	**866-584-3844**	
Sunbury Motor Co 943 N Fourth St	Sunbury	PA	17801	**866-440-7854**	570-286-7746

			Toll-Free	Phone
Superior Auto Sales Inc				
5201 Camp Rd	Hamburg NY	14075	**866-439-9637**	716-649-6695
Superior Motors Inc				
282 John C Calhoun Dr	Orangeburg SC	29115	**877-375-4759**	
Superior Trailer Sales Co				
501 Hwy 80	Sunnyvale TX	75182	**800-637-0324**	972-226-3893
Supreme Corp				
2581 E Kercher Rd	Goshen IN	46528	**800-642-4889***	
*All				
Sutphen Corp PO Box 158	Amlin OH	43002	**800-726-7030**	614-889-1005
Svi Inc 440 Mark Leany Dr	Henderson NV	89011	**800-784-8726**	
Sweeney Buick				
7997 Market St	Youngstown OH	44512	**866-560-9470**	
Ten-8 Fire Equipment Inc				
2904 59th Ave Dr E	Bradenton FL	34203	**877-989-7660**	941-756-7779
Thomson-Macconnell Cadillac Inc				
2820 Gilbert Ave	Cincinnati OH	45206	**877-472-0738**	888-838-1071
Trailercraft Inc				
222 W 92nd Ave	Anchorage AK	99515	**800-478-3238**	907-563-3238
Truck Utilities Inc				
2370 English St	Saint Paul MN	55109	**800-869-1075**	651-484-3305
Tymco Inc				
225 E Industrial Blvd PO Box 2368	Waco TX	76703	**800-258-9626**	254-799-5546
Unicell Body Co				
571 Howard St	Buffalo NY	14206	**800-628-8914***	716-853-8628
*Cust Svc				
United Ford Parts & Distribtion Ctr Inc				
12007 E 61st St	Broken Arrow OK	74012	**800-800-9001**	918-317-6800
Valley Chevrolet Inc				
601 Kidder St	Wilkes-Barre PA	18702	**877-207-9214**	570-821-2772
Wheeled Coach Industries Inc				
2737 Forsyth Rd	Winter Park FL	32792	**800-932-7077**	407-677-7777
Wichita Kenworth Inc				
5115 N Broadway	Wichita KS	67219	**800-825-5558**	316-838-0867
Yark Automotive Group Inc				
6019 W Central Ave	Toledo OH	43615	**866-390-8894**	

514 MOTORCYCLES & MOTORCYCLE PARTS & ACCESSORIES

			Toll-Free	Phone
American Honda Motor Company Inc				
1919 Torrance Blvd	Torrance CA	90501	**800-999-1009**	310-783-3170
Compositech Inc				
5315 Walt Pl	Indianapolis IN	46254	**800-447-8372**	317-481-1120
Corbin				
2360 Technology Pkwy	Hollister CA	95023	**800-538-7035**	
Edelbrock Corp				
2700 California St	Torrance CA	90503	**800-739-3737**	310-781-2222
ElliptiGO Inc				
722 Genevieve St Ste O	Solana Beach CA	92075	**888-796-8227**	858-876-8677
Harley-Davidson Inc				
3700 W Juneau Ave	Milwaukee WI	53208	**800-424-9393**	414-342-4680
NYSE: HOG				
Hed Cycling Products				
1735 TERRACE Dr	Roseville MN	55113	**888-246-3639**	
Lehman Trikes Inc				
125 Industrial Dr	Spearfish SD	57783	**888-394-3357**	605-642-2111
National Cycle Inc				
2200 S Maywood Dr PO Box 158	Maywood IL	60153	**877-972-7336**	708-343-0400
Persons Majestic Mfg Co				
PO Box 370	Huron OH	44839	**800-772-2453**	419-433-9057
Rivco Products Inc				
440 S Pine St	Burlington WI	53105	**888-801-8222**	262-763-8222
Rolf Prima Wheel Systems				
940 Wilson St	Eugene OR	97402	**888-308-7700**	541-868-1715
Yamaha Motor Corp USA				
6555 Katella Ave	Cypress CA	90630	**800-962-7926***	
*Cust Svc				

515 MOTORS (ELECTRIC) & GENERATORS

SEE ALSO Automotive Parts & Supplies - Mfr

			Toll-Free	Phone
ADS/Transicoil				
9 Iron Bridge Dr	Collegeville PA	19426	**800-323-7115**	484-902-1100
Advantage Manufacturing Inc				
616 S Santa Fe St	Santa Ana CA	92705	**800-636-8866**	
AO Smith Electrical Products Co				
531 N Fourth St	Tipp City OH	45371	**800-543-9450**	937-667-2431
Arco Electric Products Corp				
2325 E Michigan Rd	Shelbyville IN	46176	**800-428-4370**	317-398-9713
Aura Systems Inc				
1310 E Grand Ave	El Segundo CA	90245	**800-909-2872**	
OTC: AUSI				
Autotrol Corp				
365 E Prairie St	Crystal Lake IL	60014	**800-228-6207**	815-459-3080
Bluffton Motor Works LLC				
410 E Spring St	Bluffton IN	46714	**800-579-8527**	260-827-2200
Bodine Electric Co				
201 Northfield Rd	Northfield IL	60093	**800-726-3463**	773-478-3515
CALEX Manufacturing Co				
2401 Stanwell Dr	Concord CA	94520	**800-542-3355**	925-687-4411
Continental Electric Motors Inc				
23 Sebago St	Clifton NJ	07013	**800-335-6718**	
Dumore Corp				
1030 Veterans St	Mauston WI	53948	**888-467-8288**	608-847-6420
eCycle LLC				
4105 Leap Rd Ste 250	Hilliard OH	43026	**877-215-5255**	
Electric Motors & Specialties Inc				
701 W King St PO Box 180	Garrett IN	46738	**800-474-0520**	260-357-4141
Elwood Corp High Performance Motors Group				
2701 N Green Bay Rd	Racine WI	53404	**800-558-9489**	262-637-6591
Engine Power Source Inc				
348 Bryant Blvd	Rock Hill SC	29732	**800-374-7522**	704-944-1999

			Toll-Free	Phone
Five Star Electric of Houston Inc				
19424 Pk Row Dr Ste 100	Houston TX	77084	**888-492-7090**	281-492-7090
FLANDERS Inc				
8101 Baumgart Rd	Evansville IN	47725	**855-875-5888**	812-867-7421
Franklin Electric Co Inc				
9255 Coverdale Rd	Fort Wayne IN	46809	**800-962-3787**	260-824-2900
NASDAQ: FELE				
Generac Power Systems Inc				
PO Box 8	Waukesha WI	53187	**888-436-3722**	262-544-4811
Gillette Generators Inc				
1340 Wade Dr	Elkhart IN	46514	**800-777-9639**	574-264-9639
Hansen Corp				
901 S First St	Princeton IN	47670	**800-328-8996**	812-385-3415
Himoinsa Power Systems Inc				
16002 W 110th St	Lenexa KS	66219	**866-710-2988**	913-495-5557
Joliet Equipment Corp				
1 Doris Ave	Joliet IL	60433	**800-435-9350**	815-727-6606
Kencoil Inc				
2805 Engineers Rd	Belle Chasse LA	70037	**800-221-8577**	504-394-4010
Kraft Power Corp				
199 Wildwood Ave	Woburn MA	01801	**800-969-6121**	781-938-9100
Kurz industrial Solutions				
1325 McMahon Dr	Neenah WI	54956	**800-776-3629**	920-886-8200
Marathon Electric Inc				
100 E Randolf St PO Box 8003	Wausau WI	54402	**800-616-7077**	715-675-3311
Martindale Electric Co				
1375 Hird Ave	Cleveland OH	44107	**800-344-9191**	216-521-8567
Molon Motor & Coil Corp				
300 N Ridge Ave	Arlington Heights IL	60005	**800-526-6867**	847-253-6000
Morrill Motors Inc				
229 S Main Ave	Erwin TN	37650	**888-743-7001**	
Motor Appliance Corp				
601 International Ave	Washington DC	20004	**800-622-3406**	636-231-6100
Motor Products Owosso Corp				
201 S Delaney Rd	Owosso MI	48867	**800-248-3841**	
MTU Onsite Energy Corp				
100 Power Dr	Mankato MN	56001	**800-325-5450**	507-625-7973
Nidec Motor Corp				
8050 W Florissant Ave	Saint Louis MO	63136	**888-637-7333**	
Peerless Electric				
1401 W Market St	Warren OH	44485	**800-676-3651**	330-399-3651
PennEngineering & Manufacturing Corp				
5190 Olrf Faston Rd	Danboro PA	18916	**800-237-4736**	215-766-8853
Piller Inc 45 Turner Rd	Middletown NY	10941	**800-597-6937**	
Polyspede Electronics Company Inc				
6770 Twin Hills Ave	Dallas TX	75231	**888-476-5944**	214-363-7245
RAE Corp 4615 Prime Pkwy	McHenry IL	60050	**800-323-7049**	815-385-3500
Reuland Electric Co				
17969 E Railroad St	Industry CA	91748	**888-964-6411**	
Sacramento Computer Power Inc				
829 W Stadium Ln	Sacramento CA	95834	**800-441-1412**	
Specialty Motors Inc				
25060 Ave Tibbitts	Valencia CA	91355	**800-232-2612**	661-257-7388
Sterling Electric Inc				
7997 Allison Ave	Indianapolis IN	46268	**800-654-6220***	317-872-0471
*Cust Svc				
Stimple & Ward Co				
3400 Babcock Blvd	Pittsburgh PA	15237	**800-792-6457**	412-364-5200
Swiger Coils Systems Inc				
4677 Mfg Rd	Cleveland OH	44135	**800-321-3310**	216-362-7500
Tampa Armature Works Inc (TAW)				
6312 78th St	Riverview FL	33578	**800-333-9449**	813-621-5661
Toshiba International Corp				
13131 W Little York Rd	Houston TX	77041	**800-231-1412**	713-466-0277
Unitron LP				
10925 Miller Rd PO Box 38902	Dallas TX	75238	**800-527-1279**	214-340-8600
Wolverine Power Systems Inc				
3229 80th Ave	Zeeland MI	49464	**800-485-8068**	616-879-0040
Yamaha Motor Corp USA				
6555 Katella Ave	Cypress CA	90630	**800-962-7926***	
*Cust Svc				
Yaskawa America Inc				
2121 Norman Dr S	Waukegan IL	60085	**800-927-5292**	847-887-7000

516 MOVING COMPANIES

SEE ALSO Trucking Companies
Companies that have the moving of household belongings as their primary business.

			Toll-Free	Phone
A Colonial Moving & Storage Co				
17 Mercer St	Hackensack NJ	07601	**877-549-7783**	201-343-5777
Ace World Wide Moving				
1900 E College Ave	Cudahy WI	53110	**800-558-3980**	414-764-1000
Air Van				
2340 130th Ave NE Ste 201	Bellevue WA	98005	**800-989-8905**	425-629-4101
Allied International NA Inc				
700 Oakmont Ln	Westmont IL	60559	**800-444-6787**	630-570-3500
American Red Ball Transit Company Inc				
PO Box 1127	Indianapolis IN	46206	**800-733-8139**	
Arnoff Moving & Storage Inc				
1282 Dutchess Tpke	Poughkeepsie NY	12603	**800-633-6683**	888-430-9542
Atlantic Relocation Systems Inc				
1314 Chattahoochee Ave NW	Atlanta GA	30318	**800-241-1140***	404-351-5311
*Cust Svc				
Atlas Van Lines Inc				
1212 St George Rd	Evansville IN	47711	**800-638-9797**	812-424-2222
Bekins Van Lines LLC				
8010 Castleton Rd	Indianapolis IN	46250	**800-456-8092**	
Berger Transfer & Storage Inc				
2950 Long Lake Rd	Saint Paul MN	55113	**877-268-2101**	
Beverly Hills Transfer & Storage Co				
15500 S Main St	Gardena CA	90248	**800-999-7114**	310-532-1121
Bohrens Moving & Storage Inc				
3 Applegate Dr	Robbinsville NJ	08691	**800-326-4736**	609-208-1470
Buehler Companies				
16456 E Airport Cir Ste 100	Aurora CO	80011	**800-234-6683**	303-388-4000

Moving Companies (Cont'd)

Company	City	State	ZIP	Toll-Free	Phone
Callan & Woodworth Moving & Storage 900 Hwy 212	Michigan City	IN	46360	800-584-0551	219-874-3274
Cartwright Cos, The 11901 Cartwright Ave	Grandview	MO	64030	800-821-2334	
Castine Moving & Storage 1235 Chestnut St	Athol	MA	01331	800-225-8068	978-249-9105
Coast to Coast Moving & Storage Co 136 41st Ave	Brooklyn	NY	11232	800-872-6683	718-443-5800
Cook Moving Systems Inc 1845 Dale Rd	Buffalo	NY	14225	800-828-7144	
Corrigan Moving Systems 23923 Research Dr	Farmington Hills	MI	48335	800-267-7442	
East Side Moving & Storage 4836 SE Powell Blvd	Portland	OR	97206	800-547-4600	503-777-4181
Hilford Moving & Storage 1595 Arundell Ave	Ventura	CA	93003	800-739-6683	805-210-8252
I-Go Van & Storage 9820 S 142nd St	Omaha	NE	68138	800-228-9276	402-891-1222
Johnson Storage & Moving Co 221 Broadway	Denver	CO	80202	800-289-6683	
King Relocation Services 13535 Larwin Cir	Santa Fe Springs	CA	90670	800-854-3679	
Mayflower Transit LLC 1 Mayflower Dr	Fenton	MO	63026	800-325-9970	636-305-4000
McCollister's Transportation Group Inc 1800 Rt 130 N	Burlington	NJ	08016	800-257-9595	609-386-0600
National Van Lines Inc 2800 W Roosevelt Rd	Broadview	IL	60155	877-590-2810	708-450-2900
Nationwide Van Lines Inc 1421 NW 65th Ave	Plantation	FL	33313	800-310-0056	954-585-3945
Nelson Westerberg Inc 1500 Arthur Ave	Elk Grove Village	IL	60007	800-245-2080	847-437-2080
NorthStar Moving Corp 9120 Mason Ave	Chatsworth	CA	91311	800-275-7767	818-727-0128
Palmer Moving & Storage 24660 Dequindre Rd	Warren	MI	48091	800-521-3954	586-834-3400
Paxton Van Lines Inc 5300 Port Royal Rd	Springfield	VA	22151	800-336-4536	703-321-7600
Pickens-Kane Moving Co 410 N Milwaukee Ave	Chicago	IL	60610	888-871-9998	312-942-0330
S & M Moving Systems Inc 12128 Burke St	Santa Fe Springs	CA	90670	800-528-4561	562-567-2100
Smith Dray Line 320 Frontage Rd	Greenville	SC	29611	877-203-7048	
Starving Students Moving & Storage Co 1850 Sawtelle Blvd Ste 300	Los Angeles	CA	90025	888-931-6683	
Stevens Worldwide Van Lines 527 W Morley Dr	Saginaw	MI	48601	877-490-0713	800-678-3836
Suddath Cos 815 S Main St	Jacksonville	FL	32207	800-395-7100	904-352-2577
Truckin Movers Corp 1031 Harvest St	Durham	NC	27704	800-334-1651	919-682-2300
Two Guys Relocation Systems Inc 3571 Pacific Hwy	San Diego	CA	92101	800-896-4897	619-296-7995
Two Men & A Truck International Inc 3400 Belle Chase Way	Lansing	MI	48911	800-345-1070	517-394-7210
United Van Lines Inc 1 United Dr	St. Louis	MO	63026	877-740-3040	636-343-3900
Von Paris Enterprises Inc 8691 Larkin Rd	Savage	MD	20763	800-866-6355	410-888-8500
Wheaton Van Lines Inc 8010 Castleton Rd	Indianapolis	IN	46250	800-932-7799	800-248-7962

517   MUSEUMS

SEE ALSO Museums - Children's ; Museums & Halls of Fame - Sports
Listings for museums are organized alphabetically within state and province groupings.
(Canadian provinces are interfiled among the US states, in alphabetical order.)

MOTORS - FLUID POWER

SEE Pumps & Motors - Fluid Power

Alabama

	City	State	ZIP	Toll-Free	Phone
Alabama Constitution Village 109 Gates Ave	Huntsville	AL	35801	800-678-1819	256-564-8100
Birmingham Civil Rights Institute 1720 University Blvd	Birmingham	AL	35203	866-328-9696	205-328-9696
Huntsville Museum of Art 300 Church St SW	Huntsville	AL	35801	800-786-9095	256-535-4350

Alaska

	City	State	ZIP	Toll-Free	Phone
Alaska Native Heritage Ctr 8800 Heritage Ctr Dr	Anchorage	AK	99504	800-315-6608	907-330-8000
Fraternal Order of Alaska State Troopers Museum 245 W Fifth Ave	Anchorage	AK	99501	800-770-5050	907-279-5050
University of Alaska Museum of the North 907 Yukon Dr	Fairbanks	AK	99775	866-478-2721	907-474-7505

Alberta

	City	State	ZIP	Toll-Free	Phone
Reynolds-Alberta Museum 6426 40 Ave PO Box 6360	Wetaskiwin	AB	T9A2G1	800-661-4726	780-312-2065
Royal Tyrrell Museum PO Box 7500	Drumheller	AB	T0J0Y0	888-440-4240	403-823-7707

Arizona

	City	State	ZIP	Toll-Free	Phone
Arizona State Capitol Museum 1700 W Washington St	Phoenix	AZ	85007	800-228-4710	602-542-4675
Center for Creative Photography 1030 N Olive Rd	Tucson	AZ	85721	888-472-4732	520-621-7968
DeGrazia Gallery in the Sun 6300 N Swan Rd	Tucson	AZ	85718	800-545-2185	520-299-9191
Meteor Crater & Museum of Astrogeology Exit 233 off I-40	Winslow	AZ	86047	800-289-5898	

Arkansas

	City	State	ZIP	Toll-Free	Phone
Arkansas State University Museum PO Box 490	State University	AR	72467	800-342-2923	870-972-2074

British Columbia

	City	State	ZIP	Toll-Free	Phone
Royal British Columbia Museum (RBCM) 675 Belleville St	Victoria	BC	V8W9W2	888-447-7977	250-356-7226

California

	City	State	ZIP	Toll-Free	Phone
Ardenwood Historic Farm 34600 Ardenwood Blvd	Fremont	CA	94555	888-327-2757	510-544-2797
California State Archives 1020 'O' St	Sacramento	CA	95814	800-633-5155	916-653-7715
de Saisset Museum at Santa Clara University 500 El Camino Real	Santa Clara	CA	95053	866-554-6800	408-554-4528
Death Valley Museum Death Vly National Pk PO Box 579	Death Valley	CA	92328	800-544-0551	760-786-3200
Heritage Square Museum 3800 Homer St	Los Angeles	CA	90031	800-375-1771	323-225-2700
Hiller Aviation Museum 601 Skyway Rd	San Carlos	CA	94070	888-500-1555	650-654-0200
Intel Museum 2200 Mission College Blvd	Santa Clara	CA	95052	800-628-8686	408-765-5050
Japanese American National Museum 369 E First St	Los Angeles	CA	90012	800-461-5266	213-625-0414
Jensen-Alvarado Historic Ranch & Museum 4307 Briggs St	Riverside	CA	92509	800-234-7275	951-369-6055
Museum of History & Art 1100 Orange Ave	Coronado	CA	92118	866-599-7242	619-435-7242
Museum of Tolerance 1399 S Roxbury Dr	Los Angeles	CA	90035	800-900-9036	310-553-8403
Oakland Museum of California 1000 Oak St	Oakland	CA	94607	888-625-6873* *General	510-238-2200
Randall Museum 199 Museum Way	San Francisco	CA	94114	866-807-7148	415-554-9600
Ronald Reagan Presidential Library & Museum 40 Presidential Dr	Simi Valley	CA	93065	800-410-8354	805-522-2977
San Diego Natural History Museum 1788 El Prado PO Box 121390	San Diego	CA	92101	877-946-7797	619-232-3821
Tech Museum of Innovation 201 S Market St	San Jose	CA	95113	800-411-7245	408-294-8324
Turtle Bay Exploration Park 840 Auditorium Dr	Redding	CA	96001	800-887-8532	530-243-8850
University Art Museum 1250 N Bellflower Blvd	Long Beach	CA	90840	800-437-2934	562-985-5761

Colorado

	City	State	ZIP	Toll-Free	Phone
Byers-Evans House Museum 1310 Bannock St	Denver	CO	80204	800-824-0150	303-620-4933
Colorado Railroad Museum 17155 W 44th Ave	Golden	CO	80403	800-365-6263	303-279-4591
Leanin' Tree Museum of Western Art 6055 Longbow Dr	Boulder	CO	80301	800-525-0656	
Manitou Cliff Dwellings Museum 10 Cliff Rd	Manitou Springs	CO	80829	800-354-9971	719-685-5242
Miramont Castle Museum 9 Capitol Hill Ave	Manitou Springs	CO	80829	888-685-1011	719-685-1011
Western Museum of Mining & Industry 225 N Gate Blvd	Colorado Springs	CO	80921	800-752-6558	719-488-0880

Connecticut

	City	State	ZIP	Toll-Free	Phone
Mystic Seaport -- The Museum of America & the Sea 75 Greenmanville Ave PO Box 6000	Mystic	CT	06355	888-973-2767	860-572-0711

Delaware

	City	State	ZIP	Toll-Free	Phone
Delaware Art Museum 2301 Kentmere Pkwy	Wilmington	DE	19806	866-232-3714	302-571-9590
Indian River Lifesaving Station Museum 25039 Costal Hwy	Rehoboth Beach	DE	19971	877-987-2757	302-227-6991
Taylor & Messick Inc 325 Walt Messick Rd	Harrington	DE	19952	800-237-1272	302-398-3729
Winterthur Museum & Country Estate 5105 Kennett Pk	Winterthur	DE	19735	800-448-3883	302-888-4600

District of Columbia

	City	State	ZIP	Toll-Free	Phone
African-American Civil War Memorial & Museum 1925 Vermont Ave NW	Washington	DC	20001	800-753-9222	202-667-2667
National Gallery of Art 6th St & Constitution Ave NW	Washington	DC	20565	800-697-9350	202-737-4215
National Geographic Society Explorers Hall 1145 17th St NW	Washington	DC	20036	800-647-5463	
National Museum of Natural History (Smithsonian Institution) 10th St & Constitution Ave NW	Washington	DC	20560	866-868-7774	202-633-1000
National Museum of Women in the Arts 1250 New York Ave NW	Washington	DC	20005	866-875-4627	202-783-5000

Florida

			Toll-Free	Phone
Bailey Matthews Shell Museum				
3075 Sanibel-Captiva Rd PO Box 1580	Sanibel FL	33957	**888-679-6450**	239-395-2233
Boca Raton Museum of Art				
501 Plaza Real Mizner Pk	Boca Raton FL	33432	**866-481-1689**	561-392-2500
Broward County Historical Commission				
151 SW Second St	Fort Lauderdale FL	33301	**866-682-2258**	954-765-4670
Colonial Quarter				
33 St George St	Saint Augustine FL	32084	**888-991-0933**	
Florida Museum of Natural History				
3215 Hull Rd	Gainesville FL	32611	**800-595-7760**	352-392-1721
Gillespie Museum of Minerals				
421 N Woodland Blvd Unit 8403	DeLand FL	32723	**800-688-0101**	386-822-7330
Halifax Historical Museum				
252 S Beach St	Daytona Beach FL	32114	**800-677-6884**	386-255-6976
Indian Temple Mound Museum				
107 Miracle Strip Pkwy SW	Fort Walton Beach FL	32548	**866-847-1301**	850-833-9500
Kingsley Plantation				
11676 Palmetto Ave	Jacksonville FL	32226	**877-874-2478**	904-251-3537
Museum of Arts & Sciences				
352 S Nova Rd	Daytona Beach FL	32114	**866-439-4769**	386-255-0285
Museum of Science & History of Jacksonville				
1025 Museum Cir	Jacksonville FL	32207	**800-581-7245**	904-396-6674
Museum of Science & Industry				
4801 E Fowler Ave	Tampa FL	33617	**800-995-6674**	813-987-6000
Naples Museum of Art				
5833 Pelican Bay Blvd	Naples FL	34108	**800-597-1900**	239-597-1111
National Museum of Naval Aviation				
1750 Radford Blvd Ste C	Pensacola FL	32508	**800-247-6289***	850-452-3604
*General				
Old Florida Museum				
259 San Marco Ave	Saint Augustine FL	32084	**800-813-3208**	904-824-8874
Orange County Regional History Ctr				
65 E Central Blvd	Orlando FL	32801	**800-965-2030**	407-836-8500
Ripley's Believe It or Not! Museum				
19 San Marco Ave	Saint Augustine FL	32084	**800-226-6545**	904-824-1606
Tallahassee Museum of History & Natural Science				
3945 Museum Dr	Tallahassee FL	32310	**800-628-2866**	850-575-8684
Tampa Museum of Art				
120 W Gasparilla Plz	Tampa FL	33602	**866-790-4111**	813-274-8211

Georgia

			Toll-Free	Phone
World of Coca-Cola Atlanta				
121 Baker St NW	Atlanta GA	30313	**888-855-5701**	404-676-5151

Hawaii

			Toll-Free	Phone
Polynesian Cultural Ctr				
55-370 Kamehameha Hwy	Laie HI	96762	**800-367-7060**	808-293-3005

Idaho

			Toll-Free	Phone
Museum of North Idaho				
115 NW Blvd PO Box 812	Coeur d'Alene ID	83816	**800-344-4867**	208-664-3448

Illinois

			Toll-Free	Phone
Abraham Lincoln Presidential Library & Museum				
112 N Sixth St	Springfield IL	62701	**800-610-2094**	217-557-6250
Clarke House Museum				
1827 S Indiana Ave	Chicago IL	60616	**800-798-0988**	312-744-4958
Field Museum				
1400 S Lake Shore Dr	Chicago IL	60605	**800-438-9644**	312-922-9410
Illinois State Military Museum				
1301 N MacArthur Blvd	Springfield IL	62702	**800-732-8868**	217-761-3910
Museum of Science & Industry				
5700 S Lake Shore Dr	Chicago IL	60637	**800-468-6674**	773-684-1414
Oriental Institute Museum				
1155 E 58th St University of Chicago	Chicago IL	60637	**800-791-9354**	773-702-9514
Rockford Art Museum				
711 N Main St	Rockford IL	61103	**800-521-0849**	815-968-2787

Indiana

			Toll-Free	Phone
Children's Museum of Indianapolis				
3000 N Meridian St	Indianapolis IN	46208	**800-820-6214**	317-334-3322
Conner Prairie Living History Museum				
13400 Allisonville Rd	Fishers IN	46038	**800-966-1836**	317-776-6000
Firefighters' Museum				
226 W Washington Blvd	Fort Wayne IN	46802	**800-767-7752**	260-426-0051
Indiana State Museum				
650 W Washington St	Indianapolis IN	46204	**800-382-9842**	317-232-1637
Studebaker National Museum				
201 Chapin St	South Bend IN	46601	**888-391-5600**	574-235-9714

Iowa

			Toll-Free	Phone
Iowa Gold Star Military Museum				
7105 NW 70th Ave	Johnston IA	50131	**800-294-6607**	515-252-4531
John Wayne Birthplace & Museum				
205 S John Wayne Dr	Winterset IA	50273	**877-462-1044**	515-462-1044
National Mississippi River Museum & Aquarium				
350 E Third St	Dubuque IA	52001	**800-226-3369**	563-557-9545

Kansas

			Toll-Free	Phone
Dwight D Eisenhower Presidential Library & Museum				
200 SE Fourth St	Abilene KS	67410	**877-746-4453**	785-263-6700
Kansas Cosmosphere				
1100 N Plum St	Hutchinson KS	67501	**800-397-0330**	620-662-2305
Kansas Museum of History				
6425 SW Sixth St	Topeka KS	66615	**800-279-3730**	785-272-8681
Museum of World Treasures				
835 E First St	Wichita KS	67202	**888-700-1311**	316-263-1311

Kentucky

			Toll-Free	Phone
American Saddlebred Museum				
4083 Iron Works Pkwy	Lexington KY	40511	**800-829-4438**	859-259-2746
Filson Historical Society				
1310 S Third St	Louisville KY	40208	**800-928-7000**	502-635-5083
International Museum of the Horse				
4089 Iron Works Pkwy	Lexington KY	40511	**800-678-8813**	859-259-4232
Kentucky Derby Museum				
704 Central Ave	Louisville KY	40208	**800-593-3729**	502-637-1111
Louisville Science Ctr				
727 W Main St	Louisville KY	40202	**800-591-2203**	502-561-6100
National Corvette Museum				
350 Corvette Dr	Bowling Green KY	42101	**800-538-3883**	270-781-7973
Shaker Village of Pleasant Hill				
3501 Lexington Rd	Harrodsburg KY	40330	**800-734-5611**	859-734-5411

Louisiana

			Toll-Free	Phone
Historic New Orleans Collection				
533 Royal St	New Orleans LA	70130	**800-535-9595**	504-523-4662
Lafayette Museum				
1400 NW Evangeline Trwy	Lafayette LA	70501	**800-346-1958**	337-234-2208
Longue Vue House & Gardens				
7 Bamboo Rd	New Orleans LA	70124	**800-476-9137**	504-488-5488
Louisiana State Museum				
751 Chartres St	New Orleans LA	70116	**800-568-6968**	504-568-6968
Meadows Museum of Art at Centenary College				
2911 Centenary Blvd	Shreveport LA	71104	**800-234-4448**	318-869-5169
Nottoway Plantation				
31025 Louisiana Hwy 1	White Castle LA	70788	**866-527-6884**	225-545-2730
Plaquemine Lock State Historic Site				
57730 Main St	Plaquemine LA	70764	**877-987-7158**	225-687-7158
Sci-Port Discovery Ctr				
820 Clyde Fant Pkwy	Shreveport LA	71101	**877-724-7678**	318-424-3466
Southern University Museum of Art (SUSLA)				
3050 Martin Luther King Jr Dr	Shreveport LA	71107	**800-458-1472**	318-670-6000
West Baton Rouge Museum				
845 N Jefferson Ave	Port Allen LA	70767	**888-881-6811**	225-336-2422

Maine

			Toll-Free	Phone
Penobscot Marine Museum				
5 Church St PO Box 498	Searsport ME	04974	**800-268-8030**	207-548-2529

Manitoba

			Toll-Free	Phone
Ivan Franko Museum				
200 McGregor St	Winnipeg MB	R2W2K4	**866-747-9323**	204-589-4397

Maryland

			Toll-Free	Phone
Accokeek Foundation				
3400 Bryan Pt Rd	Accokeek MD	20607	**800-217-4273**	301-283-2113
B & O Railroad Museum				
901 W Pratt St	Baltimore MD	21223	**866-468-7630**	410-752-2490
Fort McHenry National Monument & Historic Shrine				
2400 E Fort Ave	Baltimore MD	21230	**866-945-7920**	410-962-4290
Jewish Museum of Maryland				
15 Lloyd St	Baltimore MD	21202	**800-235-4045***	410-732-6400
*All				

Massachusetts

			Toll-Free	Phone
Childrens Discovery Museum, The				
177 Main St	Acton MA	01720	**800-544-6666**	978-264-4200
Fuller Craft Museum				
455 Oak St	Brockton MA	02301	**800-639-4808**	508-588-6000
John F Kennedy Presidential Library & Museum				
Columbia Point	Boston MA	02125	**866-535-1960**	617-514-1600
MIT Museum				
265 Massachusetts Ave	Cambridge MA	02139	**800-228-9000**	617-253-4444
New Bedford Whaling Museum				
18 Johnny Cake Hill	New Bedford MA	02740	**800-453-5040**	508-997-0046
Peabody Essex Museum				
161 Essex St East India Sq	Salem MA	01970	**866-745-1876**	978-745-9500
Salem Witch Museum				
19 1/2 Washington Sq N	Salem MA	01970	**800-392-6100**	978-744-1692
Springfield Museums				
21 Edwards St	Springfield MA	01103	**800-625-7738**	413-263-6800

Michigan

			Toll-Free	Phone
Air Zoo, The				
6151 Portage Rd	Portage MI	49002	**866-524-7966**	269-382-6555
Flint Institute of Arts				
1120 E Kearsley St	Flint MI	48503	**800-222-7270**	810-234-1695
Gallerie 454				
15105 Kercheval Ave	Grosse Pointe Park MI	48230	**800-914-3538**	313-822-4454
Gerald R Ford Museum				
303 Pearl St NW	Grand Rapids MI	49504	**800-888-9487**	616-254-0400
Grand Rapids Art Museum				
101 Monroe Center St NW	Grand Rapids MI	49503	**800-272-8258**	616-831-1000

				Toll-Free	Phone
Greenfield Village					
20900 Oakwood Blvd	Dearborn	MI	48124	800-835-5237	313-271-1620
Henry Ford Museum					
20900 Oakwood Blvd	Dearborn	MI	48124	800-835-5237	313-271-1620
Kelsey Museum of Archaeology					
434 S State St					
University of Michigan	Ann Arbor	MI	48109	800-562-3559	734-763-3559
Midland Ctr for the Arts Inc					
1801 W St Andrews Rd	Midland	MI	48640	800-523-7649	989-631-5930

Minnesota

				Toll-Free	Phone
Mill City Museum					
704 S Second St	Minneapolis	MN	55401	800-657-3773	612-341-7555
Minneapolis Institute of Arts					
2400 Third Ave S	Minneapolis	MN	55404	888-642-2787	612-870-3000
Minnesota Discovery Ctr					
1005 Discovery Dr	Chisholm	MN	55719	800-372-6437	218-254-7959
Minnesota Historical Society History Ctr Museum					
345 Kellogg Blvd W	Saint Paul	MN	55102	800-657-3773	651-259-3001
Minnesota State University Moorhead Regional Science Ctr					
1104 Seventh Ave S	Moorhead	MN	56563	800-593-7246	218-477-2920
Science Museum of Minnesota					
120 W Kellogg Blvd	Saint Paul	MN	55102	800-221-9444	651-221-9444
Tweed Museum of Art					
1201 ordean Ct	Duluth	MN	55812	866-999-6995	218-726-8222

Mississippi

				Toll-Free	Phone
Mississippi Agriculture & Forestry Museum/National Agricultural Aviation Museum					
1150 Lakeland Dr	Jackson	MS	39216	800-844-8687	601-359-1100
Mississippi Museum of Art					
380 S Lamar St	Jackson	MS	39201	866-843-9278	601-960-1515
Mississippi Museum of Natural Science					
2148 Riverside Dr	Jackson	MS	39202	800-467-2757	601-576-6000

Missouri

				Toll-Free	Phone
Harry S Truman Presidential Library & Museum					
500 W Hwy 24	Independence	MO	64050	800-833-1225	816-268-8200
Hollywood Wax Museum					
3030 W Hwy 76	Branson	MO	65616	800-214-3661	417-337-8277
Laura Ingalls Wilder Museum & Home					
3068 Hwy A	Mansfield	MO	65704	877-924-7126	
Missouri History Museum					
5700 Lindell Blvd PO Box 11940	Saint Louis	MO	63112	800-610-2094	314-746-4599
Museum of Art & Archaeology					
1 Pickard Hall	Columbia	MO	65211	866-447-9821	573-882-3591
Pony Express National Museum					
914 Penn St	Saint Joseph	MO	64503	800-530-5930	816-279-5059
Saint Louis Science Ctr					
5050 Oakland Ave	Saint Louis	MO	63110	800-456-7572	314-289-4400
State Historical Society of Missouri, The					
1020 Lowry St	Columbia	MO	65201	800-747-6366	573-882-1187

Montana

				Toll-Free	Phone
Montana Historical Society Museum					
225 N Roberts St	Helena	MT	59620	800-243-9900	406-444-2694

Nebraska

				Toll-Free	Phone
Joslyn Art Museum					
2200 Dodge St	Omaha	NE	68102	800-965-2030	402-342-3300
Museum of Nebraska History					
15th & P St PO Box 82554	Lincoln	NE	68508	800-833-6747	402-471-4754
Sheldon Museum of Art					
PO Box 880300	Lincoln	NE	68588	800-833-6747	402-472-2461
University of Nebraska-Lincoln					
1400 R St	Lincoln	NE	68588	800-242-3766	402-472-7211

Nevada

				Toll-Free	Phone
Lost City Museum of Archeology					
721 S Moapa Valley Blvd	Overton	NV	89040	800-326-6868	775-687-4810
Marjorie Barrick Museum					
4505 S Maryland Pkwy	Las Vegas	NV	89154	877-895-0334	702-895-3381

New Brunswick

				Toll-Free	Phone
New Brunswick Museum					
1 Market Sq	Saint John	NB	E2L4Z6	888-268-9595	506-643-2300
University of Moncton					
18 Ave Antonine-Maillet	Moncton	NB	E1A3E9	800-331-9283	506-858-4088

New Hampshire

				Toll-Free	Phone
New Hampshire Institute of Art					
148 Concord St	Manchester	NH	03104	866-241-4918	603-623-0313

New Jersey

				Toll-Free	Phone
Aljira Ctr for Contemporary Arts					
591 Broad St	Newark	NJ	07102	800-852-7699	973-622-1600
Creative Glass Center of America					
1501 Glasstown Rd	Millville	NJ	08332	800-998-4552	856-825-6800
Mid Atlantic Center for The Arts					
1048 Washington St	Cape May	NJ	08204	800-275-4278	609-884-5404

				Toll-Free	Phone
Newark Museum					
49 Washington St	Newark	NJ	07102	888-370-6765	973-596-6550

New Mexico

				Toll-Free	Phone
Historical Lawmen Museum					
845 Motel Blvd	Las Cruces	NM	88007	877-827-7200	575-647-7200
Indian Pueblo Cultural Ctr					
2401 12th St NW	Albuquerque	NM	87104	866-855-7902	505-843-7270
New Mexico Museum of Art					
107 W Palace Ave	Santa Fe	NM	87501	877-567-7380	505-476-5072
New Mexico Museum of Space History					
Top of Hwy 2001	Alamogordo	NM	88311	877-333-6589	575-437-2840
Wheelwright Museum of the American Indian					
704 Camino Lejo	Santa Fe	NM	87505	800-607-4636	505-982-4636

New York

				Toll-Free	Phone
Buffalo Museum of Science					
1020 Humboldt Pkwy	Buffalo	NY	14211	866-291-6660	716-896-5200
Cloisters Museum					
Fort Tryon Pk	New York	NY	10040	800-662-3397	212-923-3700
Corning Museum of Glass					
1 Museum Way	Corning	NY	14830	800-732-6845*	607-937-5371
*Cust Svc					
Franklin D Roosevelt Presidential Library & Museum					
4079 Albany Post Rd	Hyde Park	NY	12538	800-337-8474	845-486-7770
Intrepid Sea-Air-Space Museum					
W 46th St & 12th Ave Pier 86	New York	NY	10036	877-957-7447	212-245-0072
Madame Tussauds New York Inc					
234 W 42nd St Times Sq	New York	NY	10036	800-434-7894	212-512-9600
Metropolitan Museum of Art					
1000 Fifth Ave	New York	NY	10028	800-468-7386	212-535-7710
National Museum of the American Indian (Smithsonian Institution)					
1 Bowling Green	New York	NY	10004	800-242-6624	212-514-3700
Roberson Museum & Science Ctr					
30 Front St	Binghamton	NY	13905	888-269-5325	607-772-0660
Solomon R Guggenheim Museum					
1071 Fifth Ave	New York	NY	10128	800-329-6109	212-423-3500
Whitney Museum of American Art					
945 Madison Ave	New York	NY	10021	800-944-8639	212-570-3600
Yager Museum of Art & Culture, The					
Hartwick College PO Box 4022	Oneonta	NY	13820	888-427-8942	607-431-4000

North Carolina

				Toll-Free	Phone
Charlotte Hawkins Brown Museum					
PO Box B	Sedalia	NC	27342	800-767-1560	336-449-4846
EnergyExplorium					
13339 Hagers Ferry Rd	Huntersville	NC	28078	800-777-9898	980-875-5600
Folk Art Ctr PO Box 9545	Asheville	NC	28815	888-672-7717	828-298-7928
International Civil Rights Ctr & Museum					
134 S Elm St	Greensboro	NC	27401	800-748-7116	336-274-9199
Museum of Anthropology					
Wake Forest University	Winston-Salem	NC	27109	888-925-3622	336-758-5000
Old Salem					
600 S Main St	Winston-Salem	NC	27101	800-441-5305	336-721-7300
Reynolda House Museum of American Art					
2250 Reynolda Rd	Winston-Salem	NC	27106	888-663-1149	336-758-5150

Nova Scotia

				Toll-Free	Phone
Fisheries Museum of the Atlantic					
68 Bluenose Dr PO Box 1363	Lunenburg	NS	B0J2C0	866-579-4909	902-634-4794

Ohio

				Toll-Free	Phone
Cincinnati Art Museum					
953 Eden Pk Dr	Cincinnati	OH	45202	877-472-4226	513-721-2787
Cincinnati History Museum					
1301 Western Ave					
Cincinnati Museum Ctr.	Cincinnati	OH	45203	800-733-2077	513-287-7000
Cleveland Museum of Art, The					
11150 E Blvd	Cleveland	OH	44106	877-262-4748*	216-421-7350
*Sales					
Cleveland Museum of Natural History					
1 Wade Oval Dr	Cleveland	OH	44106	800-317-9155	216-231-4600
COSI Columbus					
333 W Broad St	Columbus	OH	43215	888-819-2674	614-228-2674
COSI Toledo 1 Discovery Way	Toledo	OH	43604	800-590-9755	419-244-2674
Dayton Art Institute					
456 Belmonte Pk N	Dayton	OH	45405	800-272-8258	937-223-5277
Hale Farm & Village					
2686 Oakhill Rd PO Box 296	Bath	OH	44210	877-425-3327	330-666-3711
International Women's Air & Space Museum					
1501 N Marginal Rd					
Burke Lakefront Airport	Cleveland	OH	44114	877-287-4752	216-623-1111
Invent Now Inc					
3701 Highland Park NW	North Canton	OH	44720	800-968-4332	
Museum of Natural History & Science					
1301 Western Ave					
Cincinnati Museum Ctr.	Cincinnati	OH	45203	800-733-2077	513-287-7000
National Afro-American Museum & Cultural Ctr					
1350 Brush Row Rd PO Box 578	Wilberforce	OH	45384	800-752-2603	937-376-4944
National Inventors Hall of Fame					
3701 Highland Park NW	North Canton	OH	44720	800-968-4332	
Ohio Historical Society					
1982 Velma Ave	Columbus	OH	43211	800-686-6124	614-297-2300
Roscoe Village					
600 N Whitewoman St	Coshocton	OH	43812	800-877-1830	740-622-7644
Sauder Village 22611 SR 2	Archbold	OH	43502	800-590-9755	419-446-2541

				Toll-Free	Phone
Stan Hywet Hall & Gardens 714 N Portage Path	Akron	OH	44303	**888-836-5533**	330-836-5533
Toledo Museum of Art 2445 Monroe St	Toledo	OH	43620	**800-644-6862**	419-255-8000

Oklahoma

				Toll-Free	Phone
Cherokee Heritage Ctr & National Museum 21192 S Keeler Dr	Park Hill	OK	74451	**888-999-6007**	918-456-6007
Gilcrease Museum 1400 N Gilcrease Museum Rd	Tulsa	OK	74127	**888-655-2278**	918-596-2700
Oklahoma City Museum of Art 415 Couch Dr	Oklahoma City	OK	73102	**800-579-9278**	405-236-3100
Will Rogers Memorial Museum 1720 W Will Rogers Blvd	Claremore	OK	74017	**800-324-9455**	918-341-0719
Woolaroc Ranch Museum & Wildlife Preserve 1925 Woolaroc Ranch Rd	Bartlesville	OK	74003	**888-966-5276**	918-336-0307

Ontario

				Toll-Free	Phone
Canada Agriculture & Food Museum 901 Prince of Wales Dr	Ottawa	ON	K2C3K1	**866-442-4416**	613-991-3044
Canada Science & Technology Museum 2421 Lancaster Rd	Ottawa	ON	K1G5A3	**866-442-4416**	613-991-3044
Canadian Museum of Nature 240 McLeod St	Ottawa	ON	K2P2R1	**800-263-4433**	613-566-4700
Fort Henry National Historic Site PO Box 213 *Cust Svc	Kingston	ON	K7L4V8	**800-437-2233***	613-542-7388
Mackenzie House Museum 82 Bond St	Toronto	ON	M5B1X2	**800-668-2437**	416-392-6915
Ontario Science Ctr 770 Don Mills Rd	Toronto	ON	M3C1T3	**888-696-1110**	416-696-1000
Royal Canadian Military Institute 426 University Ave	Toronto	ON	M5G1S9	**800-585-1072**	416-597-0286

Oregon

				Toll-Free	Phone
Hallie Ford Museum of Art 700 State St	Salem	OR	97301	**844-232-7228**	503-370-6855
Oregon Museum of Science & Industry 1945 SE Water Ave	Portland	OR	97214	**800-955-6674**	503-797-4000

Pennsylvania

				Toll-Free	Phone
Polish American Cultural Ctr Museum 308 Walnut St	Philadelphia	PA	19106	**800-422-1275**	215-922-1700
State Museum of Pennsylvania, The 300 N St	Harrisburg	PA	17120	**800-654-5984**	717-787-4980

Quebec

				Toll-Free	Phone
Canadian Museum of Civilization 100 Laurier St	Gatineau	QC	K1A0M8	**800-555-5621**	819-776-7000

Saskatchewan

				Toll-Free	Phone
RCMP Heritage Ctr 5907 Dewdney Ave	Regina	SK	S4T0P4	**866-567-7267**	306-522-7333

South Carolina

				Toll-Free	Phone
Ripley's Believe It or Not! Museum 901 N Ocean Blvd	Myrtle Beach	SC	29577	**800-905-4228**	843-448-2331

South Dakota

				Toll-Free	Phone
Adams Museum 54 Sherman St	Deadwood	SD	57732	**800-335-0275**	605-578-1714
Center for Western Studies 2101 S Summit Ave Augustana College	Sioux Falls	SD	57197	**800-727-2844**	605-274-4007
Museum of Geology South Dakota School of Mines & Technology 501 E St Joseph St	Rapid City	SD	57701	**800-544-8162**	605-394-2467
Washington Pavilion 301 S Main	Sioux Falls	SD	57104	**877-927-4728**	605-367-6000

Tennessee

				Toll-Free	Phone
Belle Meade Plantation 5025 Harding Pk	Nashville	TN	37205	**800-270-3991**	615-356-0501
Country Music Hall of Fame & Museum 222 Fifth Ave S	Nashville	TN	37203	**800-852-6437**	615-416-2001
East Tennessee Historical Society 601 S Gay St PO Box 1629	Knoxville	TN	37901	**800-407-4324**	865-215-8824
Graceland (Elvis Presley Mansion) 3734 Elvis Presley Blvd	Memphis	TN	38116	**800-238-2000**	901-332-3322
Mississippi River Museum 125 N Front St	Memphis	TN	38103	**800-507-6507**	901-576-7241
Reece Museum 363 Stout Dr	Johnson City	TN	37614	**855-590-3878**	423-439-4392
Rocky Mount Museum 200 Hyder Hill Rd PO Box 160	Piney Flats	TN	37686	**888-538-1791**	423-538-7396
Tennessee State Museum 505 Deaderick St	Nashville	TN	37243	**800-407-4324**	615-741-2692
Upper Room Chapel & Museum 1908 Grand Ave	Nashville	TN	37212	**800-972-0433**	615-340-7200

Texas

				Toll-Free	Phone
Amon Carter Museum 3501 Camp Bowie Blvd	Fort Worth	TX	76107	**800-573-1933**	817-738-1933
Contemporary Arts Museum Houston 5216 Montrose Blvd	Houston	TX	77006	**800-982-2787**	713-284-8250
Elisabet Ney Museum 304 E 44th St	Austin	TX	78751	**800-680-7289**	512-458-2255
Fort Worth Museum of Science & History 1600 Gendy St	Fort Worth	TX	76107	**888-255-9300**	817-255-9300
Frontiers of Flight Museum 6911 Lemon Ave	Dallas	TX	75209	**800-568-8924**	214-350-1651
John E Conner Museum 905 W Santa Gertrudis Ave 700 University Blvd	Kingsville	TX	78363	**800-726-8192**	361-593-2810
LBJ Library & Museum 2313 Red River St	Austin	TX	78705	**800-874-6451**	512-721-0216
Lone Star Flight Museum 11551 Aerospace Ave	Houston	TX	77034	**888-359-5736**	346-708-2517
Modern Art Museum of Fort Worth 3200 Darnell St	Fort Worth	TX	76107	**866-824-5566**	817-738-9215
National Border Patrol Museum 4315 Woodrow Bean TransMtn Rd	El Paso	TX	79924	**877-276-8738**	915-759-6060
Sixth Floor Museum 411 Elm St	Dallas	TX	75202	**888-485-4854**	214-747-6660
Texas Memorial Museum 2400 Trinity St	Austin	TX	78705	**800-687-4132**	512-471-1604
USS Lexington Museum on the Bay 2914 N Shoreline Blvd	Corpus Christi	TX	78402	**800-523-9539**	361-888-4873

Utah

				Toll-Free	Phone
Springville Museum of Art 126 E 400 S	Springville	UT	84663	**800-833-6667**	801-489-2727

Vermont

				Toll-Free	Phone
Bennington Museum 75 Main St	Bennington	VT	05201	**800-205-8033**	802-442-2494

Virginia

				Toll-Free	Phone
Anderson Gallery 325 N Harrison St	Richmond	VA	23284	**866-534-3201**	804-828-0100
Carlyle House Historic Park 121 N Fairfax St	Alexandria	VA	22314	**800-877-0954**	703-549-2997
DeWitt Wallace Decorative Arts Museum 326 Francis St W	Williamsburg	VA	23185	**800-447-8679**	
Mariners' Museum 100 Museum Dr	Newport News	VA	23606	**800-581-7245**	757-596-2222
NAUTICUS the National Maritime Ctr 1 Waterside Dr	Norfolk	VA	23510	**800-664-1080**	757-664-1000
Richmond National Battlefield Park 3215 E Broad St	Richmond	VA	23223	**866-733-7768**	804-226-1981
Virginia Aquarium & Marine Science Center 717 General Booth Blvd	Virginia Beach	VA	23451	**800-822-3224**	757-385-3474
Virginia Historical Society Museum of Virginia History 428 N Blvd	Richmond	VA	23220	**800-473-0060**	804-340-1800
Virginia Museum of Transportation 303 Norfolk Ave	Roanoke	VA	24016	**800-578-4111**	540-342-5670

Washington

				Toll-Free	Phone
Bellevue Arts Museum 510 Bellevue Way NE	Bellevue	WA	98004	**800-367-2648**	425-519-0770
Burke Museum of Natural History & Culture 17th Ave NE & NE 45th St	Seattle	WA	98195	**800-411-9671**	206-543-5590
Fireworks 3307 Utah Ave S	Seattle	WA	98134	**800-505-8882**	206-682-8707
Jundt Art Museum 502 E Boone Ave	Spokane	WA	99258	**800-986-9585**	509-313-6611
Museum of Flight, The 9404 E Marginal Way S	Seattle	WA	98108	**800-833-6384**	206-764-5700
Port Townsend Marine Science Ctr 532 Battery Way	Port Townsend	WA	98368	**800-566-3932**	360-385-5582
Washington State Capital Museum 211 21st Ave SW	Olympia	WA	98501	**888-238-4373**	
Wing Luke Asian Museum 719 S King St	Seattle	WA	98104	**800-961-6119**	206-623-5124

West Virginia

				Toll-Free	Phone
Challenger Learning Ctr (CLC) 316 Washington Ave Wheeling Jesuit University	Wheeling	WV	26003	**800-624-6992**	304-243-2279
Kruger Street Toy & Train Museum 144 Kruger St	Wheeling	WV	26003	**877-242-8133**	304-242-8133
Museums of Oglebay Institute 1330 National Rd	Wheeling	WV	26003	**800-624-6988**	304-242-7272
West Virginia State Museum 1900 Kanawha Blvd E	Charleston	WV	25305	**800-946-9471**	304-558-0220

Wisconsin

				Toll-Free	Phone
Circus World Museum 550 Water St	Baraboo	WI	53913	**866-693-1500**	608-356-8341
EAA AirVenture Museum 3000 Poberezny Rd	Oshkosh	WI	54902	**888-322-3229**	920-426-4800
Kenosha Public Museum 5500 First Ave	Kenosha	WI	53140	**888-258-9966**	262-653-4140

					Toll-Free	Phone
Milwaukee Art Museum						
700 N Art Museum Dr	Milwaukee	WI	53202		877-638-7620	414-224-3200
Neville Public Museum of Brown County						
210 Museum Pl	Green Bay	WI	54303		800-895-0071	920-448-4460
Wisconsin Historical Museum						
30 N Carroll St	Madison	WI	53703		888-999-1669	608-264-6555
Wisconsin Maritime Museum						
75 Maritime Dr	Manitowoc	WI	54220		866-724-2356	920-684-0218

Wyoming

				Toll-Free	Phone
Fort Caspar Museum					
4001 Fort Caspar Rd	Casper	WY	82604	800-877-7353	307-235-8400
Geological Museum					
1000 E University Ave	Laramie	WY	82071	800-842-2776	307-766-2646
Museum of the Mountain Man					
700 E Hennick St	Pinedale	WY	82941	877-686-6266	307-367-4101
National Museum of Wildlife Art					
2820 Rungius Rd PO Box 6825	Jackson	WY	83002	800-313-9553	307-733-5771

518 MUSEUMS - CHILDREN'S

Children's museums are organized alphabetically by states.

				Toll-Free	Phone
Discovery Ctr (TDC)					
1944 N Winery Ave	Fresno	CA	93703	800-946-3039	559-251-5533
EcoTarium					
222 Harrington Way	Worcester	MA	01604	800-625-7738	508-929-2700
Discovery Ctr of Springfield					
438 E St Louis St	Springfield	MO	65806	888-636-4395	417-862-9910
Discovery Place					
301 N Tryon St	Charlotte	NC	28202	800-935-0553	704-372-6261
Cinergy Children's Museum					
1301 Western Ave					
Cincinnati Museum Ctr.	Cincinnati	OH	45203	800-733-2077	513-287-7000
Children's Museum of Oak Ridge					
461 W Outer Dr	Oak Ridge	TN	37830	877-524-1223	865-482-1074

519 MUSEUMS & HALLS OF FAME - SPORTS

				Toll-Free	Phone
1932 & 1980 Lake Placid Winter Olympic Museum					
2634 Main St	Lake Placid	NY	12946	800-462-6236	518-523-1655
American Museum of Fly Fishing					
4104 Main Rd	Manchester	VT	05254	800-333-1550	802-362-3300
American Water Ski Hall of Fame & Museum					
1251 Holy Cow Rd	Polk City	FL	33868	800-533-2972	863-324-2472
Canadian Golf Hall of Fame & Museum					
1333 Dorval Dr Ste 1	Oakville	ON	L6M4X7	800-263-0009	905-849-9700
Cheap Joe's Art Stuff Inc					
374 Industrial Park Dr	Boone	NC	28607	800-227-2788	828-262-5459
Don Garlits Museums					
13700 SW 16th Ave	Ocala	FL	34473	877-271-3278	352-245-8661
Fox Cities Performing Arts Ctr					
400 W College Ave	Appleton	WI	54911	800-982-2787	800-216-7469
Greyhound Hall of Fame					
407 S Buckeye Ave	Abilene	KS	67410	800-932-7881	785-263-3000
Hendrick Motorsports Museum					
4400 Papa Joe Hendrick Blvd	Charlotte	NC	28262	877-467-4890	
Improv Asylum 216 Hanover St	Boston	MA	02113	888-396-6887	617-263-6887
International Bowling Museum & Hall of Fame					
621 Six Flags Dr	Arlington	TX	76011	800-514-2695	817-385-8215
Louisville Slugger Museum					
800 W Main St	Louisville	KY	40202	877-775-8443	
Mississippi Sports Hall of Fame & Museum					
1152 Lakeland Dr	Jackson	MS	39216	800-280-3263	601-982-8264
Missouri Sports Hall of Fame					
3861 E Stan Musial Dr	Springfield	MO	65809	800-498-5678	417-889-3100
Moncton Museum					
20 Mountain Rd	Moncton	NB	E1C2J8	800-363-4558	506-856-4383
Motorcycle Hall of Fame Museum					
13515 Yarmouth Dr	Pickerington	OH	43147	800-262-5646	614-856-2222
National Baseball Hall of Fame & Museum					
25 Main St	Cooperstown	NY	13326	888-425-5633	607-547-7200
National Museum of Racing & Hall of Fame					
191 Union Ave	Saratoga Springs	NY	12866	800-562-5394	518-584-0400
National Softball Hall of Fame & Museum					
2801 NE 50th St	Oklahoma City	OK	73111	800-654-8337	405-424-5266
National Sprint Car Hall of Fame & Museum					
1 Sprint Capital Pl	Knoxville	IA	50138	800-874-4488	641-842-6176
North Carolina Sports Hall of Fame					
5 E Edenton St NC Museum of History	Raleigh	NC	27601	877-627-6724	919-807-7900
Texas Sports Hall of Fame					
1108 S University Parks Dr	Waco	TX	76706	800-567-9561	254-756-1633
Us Art Company Inc					
66 Pacella Park Dr	Randolph	MA	02368	800-872-7826	
US. National Ski Hall of Fame					
610 Palms Ave	Ishpeming	MI	49849	800-648-0720	906-485-6323

520 MUSIC DISTRIBUTORS

				Toll-Free	Phone
A-r Editions Inc					
1600 Aspen Cmns Ste 100	Middleton	WI	53562	800-736-0070	608-836-9000
Baker & Taylor Inc					
2550 W Tyvola Rd Ste 300	Charlotte	NC	28217	800-775-1800	
Gotham Distributing Corp					
60 Portland Rd	Conshohocken	PA	19428	800-446-8426	610-649-7650
Malaco Music Group Inc					
3023 W Northside Dr	Jackson	MS	39213	800-272-7936*	601-982-4522
*Cust Svc					
Select-O-Hits Inc					
1981 Fletcher Creek Dr	Memphis	TN	38133	800-346-0723	901-388-1190

521 MUSIC STORES

SEE ALSO Book, Music, Video Clubs

				Toll-Free	Phone
Amazoncom Inc					
1200 12th Ave S Ste 1200	Seattle	WA	98144	800-201-7575*	206-266-1000
NASDAQ: AMZN ■ *Cust Svc					
Bay Pointe Technology					
2662 Brecksville Rd	Richfield	OH	44286	800-746-1420	
Best Buy Company Inc					
7601 Penn Ave S	Richfield	MN	55423	888-237-8289	612-291-1000
NYSE: BBY					
CD Universe					
101 N Plains Industrial Rd	Wallingford	CT	06492	800-231-7937	203-294-1648
Complia Health					
1827 Walden Office Sq Ste 104	Schaumburg	IL	60173	866-802-7704	
DSN Group Inc					
152 Lorraine Dr	Lake Zurich	IL	60047	888-445-2919	
FirstCom Music					
1325 Capital Pkwy Ste 109	Carrollton	TX	75006	800-858-8880*	972-389-2800
*Cust Svc					
Hansen Software Corp					
1855 Kirschner Rd Ste 380	Kelowna	BC	V1Y4N7	877-795-2274	
Ita Inc 2162 Dana Ave	Cincinnati	OH	45207	800-899-8877	
Med-Tech Resource Inc					
29485 Airport Rd	Eugene	OR	97402	888-627-7779	
Mississippi Music Inc					
222 N Main St	Hattiesburg	MS	39401	800-844-5821	
Paradigm Design Associates Inc					
4 Center Rd Unit 5	Old Saybrook	CT	06475	800-495-3295	
Retail Computer Group LLC, The					
8194 Traphagen St NW	Massillon	OH	44646	800-944-0917	
SEAS Education					
955 Wallace Knob Ste 1	Mountain Home	AR	72654	877-221-7327	
Signix Inc					
1110 Market St Ste 402	Chattanooga	TN	37402	877-890-5350	
Sperry Software Inc					
12443 San Jose Blvd Ste 503	Jacksonville	FL	32223	800-878-1645	
Test com Inc					
3558 Lee Rd	Shaker Heights	OH	44120	877-502-8600	
TriStar Inc					
3740 E La Salle St	Phoenix	AZ	85040	800-800-1714	
V-Technologies LLC					
675 W Johnson Ave	Cheshire	CT	06410	800-462-4016	
Workspace com Inc					
10451 Mill Run Cir Ste 400	Owings Mills	MD	21117	888-245-9168	

522 MUSICAL INSTRUMENT STORES

				Toll-Free	Phone
Alamo Music Ctr					
425 N Main Ave	San Antonio	TX	78205	800-822-5010	844-251-1922
American Musical Supply					
PO Box 152	Spicer	MN	56288	800-458-4076	320-796-2088
Amro Music Stores					
2918 Poplar Ave	Memphis	TN	38111	800-626-2676*	901-323-8888
*General					
Annex Pro Inc					
49 Dunlevy Ave Ste 220	Vancouver	BC	V6A3A3	800-682-6639	604-682-6639
Brook Mays Music Co					
8605 John Carpenter Fwy	Dallas	TX	75247	800-637-8966*	214-631-0928
*Cust Svc					
Buddy Rogers Music Inc					
6891 Simpson Ave	Cincinnati	OH	45239	800-536-2263	513-729-1950
Cascio Interstate Music					
13819 W National Ave	New Berlin	WI	53151	800-462-2263	262-789-7600
Cream City Music					
12505 W Bluemound Rd	Brookfield	WI	53005	800-800-0087	262-860-1800
Elderly Instruments					
1100 N Washington Ave	Lansing	MI	48906	888-473-5810	517-372-7890
First Act Inc					
745 Boylston St	Boston	MA	02116	888-551-1115	
Fletcher Music Centers Inc					
3966 Airway Cir	Clearwater	FL	33762	800-258-1088	727-571-1088
Foxes Music Co					
416 S Washington St	Falls Church	VA	22046	800-446-4414	703-533-7393
Front End Audio					
130 Hunter Village Dr Ste D	Irmo	SC	29063	888-228-4530	803-748-0914
Gigasonic 260 E Gish Rd	San Jose	CA	95112	888-246-4442	408-573-1400
Graves Piano & Organ Company Inc					
5798 Karl Rd	Columbus	OH	43229	800-686-4322	614-847-4322
Hermes Music 401 S Broadway	Pharr	TX	78501	800-994-9150	
International Violin Co Ltd					
1421 Clarkview Rd	Baltimore	MD	21209	800-542-3538	410-832-2525
JW Pepper & Son Inc					
2480 Industrial Blvd	Paoli	PA	19301	800-345-6296	610-648-0500
Lone Star Percussion					
10611 Control Pl	Dallas	TX	75238	866-792-0143	214-340-0835
M Steinert & Sons Co					
1 Columbus Ave	Boston	MA	02116	877-343-0662	617-426-1900
Marshall Music Co					
4555 Wilson Ave SW Ste 1	Grandville	MI	49418	800-242-4705	616-530-7700
Music & Arts Centers Inc					
4626 Wedgewood Blvd	Frederick	MD	21703	888-731-5396	301-620-4040
Musiciansbuycom Inc					
7830 Byron Dr Ste 1	West Palm Beach	FL	33404	877-778-7845	561-842-4246
Quantum Audio Designs Inc					
PO Box 130	Benton	MO	63736	888-545-4404	573-545-4404
Reverb Music LLC					
3316 N Lincoln Ave	Chicago	IL	60657	888-686-7872	773-525-7773
Sherman Clay & Company Inc					
1111 Bayhill Dr Ste 450	San Bruno	CA	94066	888-562-4069	
Stanton's Sheet Music					
330 S Fourth St	Columbus	OH	43215	800-426-8742	614-224-4257

		Toll-Free	Phone

Steve's Music
51 Rue Saint-antoine O St W ....Montreal QC H2Z1G9 **877-978-3837** 514-878-2216

Strait Music Co
2428 W Ben White Blvd ....Austin TX 78704 **800-725-8877** 512-476-6927

Sweetwater Sound Inc
5501 US Hwy 30 W ....Fort Wayne IN 46818 **800-222-4700** 260-432-8176

Tom Lee Music Ltd
929 Granville St ....Vancouver BC V6Z1L3 **888-886-6533** 604-685-8471

West Music Inc
1212 Fifth St ....Coralville IA 52241 **800-373-2000** 319-351-2000

World Music Supply
2414 W Seventh St ....Muncie IN 47302 **800-867-4611** 765-213-6085

523   MUSICAL INSTRUMENTS

		Toll-Free	Phone

Alembic Inc
3005 Wiljan Ct ....Santa Rosa CA 95407 **800-322-5893** 707-523-2611

Allen Organ Co
150 Locust St ....Macungie PA 18062 **800-582-4466** 610-966-2202

Avedis Zildjian Co
22 Longwater Dr ....Norwell MA 02061 **800-229-8672** 781-871-2200

Carvin Corp
12340 World Trade Dr ....San Diego CA 92128 **800-854-2235** 858-487-8700

CF Martin & Company Inc
510 Sycamore St PO Box 329..................Nazareth PA 18064 **888-433-9177** 610-759-2837

Chime Master Systems
PO Box 936 ....Lancaster OH 43130 **800-344-7464**

Conn-Selmer Inc
600 Industrial Pkwy ....Elkhart IN 46516 **800-348-7426** 574-522-1675

Daisy Rock Guitars
16320 Roscoe Blvd Ste 100 ....Van Nuys CA 91410 **877-693-2479** 855-417-8677

Deering Banjo Co
3733 Kenora Dr ....Spring Valley CA 91977 **800-845-7791** 619-464-8252

Edwards Instrument Co
530 S Hwy H ....Elkhorn WI 53121 **800-562-6838** 262-723-4221

Ernie Ball
151 Suburban Rd ....San Luis Obispo CA 93401 **866-823-2255** 800-543-2255

Fender Musical Instruments Corp
17600 N Perimeter Dr Ste 100 ....Scottsdale AZ 85255 **800-488-1818*** 480-596-9690
*Cust Svc

George Heinl & Co
201 Church St ....Toronto ON M5B1Y7 **800-387-7858** 416-363-0093

Getzen Company Inc
530 S Cty Hwy H PO Box 440...................Elkhorn WI 53121 **800-366-5584** 262-723-4221

GHS Corp
2813 Wilber Ave ....Battle Creek MI 49037 **800-388-4447**

Gibson 309 Plus Pk Blvd ....Nashville TN 37217 **800-444-2766** 615-871-4500

Gibson Guitar Corp
309 Plus Park Blvd ....Nashville TN 37217 **800-444-2766**

Hanser Music Group
9615 Inter-Ocean Dr ....Cincinnati OH 45246 **800-999-5558** 859-817-7100

Hohner Inc
12020 Volunteer Blvd ....Mt. Juliet TN 37122 **888-627-3987**

J D'Addario & Company Inc
595 Smith St ....Farmingdale NY 11735 **800-323-2746** 631-439-3300

JD Calato Mfg Company Inc
4501 Hyde Pk Blvd ....Niagara Falls NY 14305 **800-358-4590*** 716-285-3546
*Cust Svc

Lindeblad Piano Restoration
101 Us 46 ....Pine Brook NJ 07058 **888-587-4266**

Lowrey Organ Co
989 AEC Dr ....Wood Dale IL 60191 **800-451-5939**

Lyon & Healy Harps Inc
168 N Ogden Ave ....Chicago IL 60607 **800-621-3881** 312-786-1881

Maas-Rowe Carillons Inc
2255 Meyers Ave ....Escondido CA 92029 **800-854-2023**

Manhasset Specialty Co
3505 Fruitvale Blvd ....Yakima WA 98902 **800-795-0965** 509-248-3810

Marimba One Inc
901 O St Ste D ....Arcata CA 95521 **888-990-6663** 707-822-9570

Morley
100 High Grove Blvd ....Glendale Heights IL 60139 **800-284-5172** 847-639-4646

NATIVE INSTRUMENTS NORTH AMERICA INC
6725 Sunset Blvd 5th Fl ....Los Angeles CA 90028 **866-556-6487** 323-467-5260

Organ Supply Industries Inc
2320 W 50th St ....Erie PA 16506 **800-458-0289** 814-835-2244

Prestini Corp
351 E Patagonia Hwy Ste 4......................Nogales AZ 85621 **800-528-6569*** 520-287-4931
*General

Remo Inc 28101 Industry Dr ....Valencia CA 91355 **800-525-5134** 661-294-5600

Rhythm Tech
29 Beechwood Ave ....New Rochelle NY 10801 **800-726-2279** 914-636-6900

Sabian Ltd 219 Main St ....Meductic NB E6H2L5 **800-817-2242** 506-272-2019

Schaff Piano Supply Co
451 Oakwood Rd ....Lake Zurich IL 60047 **800-747-4266** 847-438-4556

Schecter Guitar Research Inc
10953 Pendleton St ....Sun Valley CA 91352 **800-660-6621** 818-846-2700

Schulmerich Carillons Inc
Carillon Hill ....Sellersville PA 18960 **800-772-3557** 215-257-2771

Steinway & Sons
1 Steinway Pl ....Long Island NY 11105 **800-783-4692** 718-721-2600

Suzuki Musical Instrument Corp
PO Box 710459 ....Santee CA 92072 **800-854-1594*** 619-258-1896
*Cust Svc

Ultimate Support Systems Inc
5836 Wright Dr ....Loveland CO 80538 **800-525-5628** 970-776-1920

Wenger Corp
555 Pk Dr PO Box 448 ....Owatonna MN 55060 **800-493-6437** 507-455-4100

Wicks Pipe Organ Co
416 Pine St ....Highland IL 62249 **877-654-2191*** 618-654-2191
*Cust Svc

524   MUTUAL FUNDS

		Toll-Free	Phone

ACG Advisory Services Inc
1640 Huguenot Rd ....Midlothian VA 23113 **800-231-6409** 804-323-1886

Agilith Capital Inc
20 Queen St W Ste 3311 PO Box 30..............Toronto ON M5H3R3 **866-345-1231** 416-915-0284

Alberta Enterprise Corp
10088 102 Ave ....Edmonton AB T5J2Z2 **877-336-3474** 587-402-6601

Alerus Retirement & Benefits
2 Pine Tree Dr Ste 400 ....Arden Hills MN 55112 **800-433-1685** 800-795-2697

Alger Family of Funds
PO Box 8480 ....Boston MA 02266 **800-992-3863**

Altavista Wealth Management Inc
4 Vanderbilt Park Dr Ste 310 ....Asheville NC 28803 **866-684-2600**

American Century Proprietary Holdings Inc
PO Box 419200 ....Kansas City MO 64141 **800-345-2021** 816-531-5575

Aquila Group of Funds
380 Madison Ave Ste 2300. ....New York NY 10017 **800-437-1020** 212-697-6666

Arizona State Retirement System
3300 N Central Ave ....Phoenix AZ 85012 **800-621-3778** 602-240-2000

Artisan Funds PO Box 8412 ....Boston MA 02266 **800-344-1770***
*Cust Svc

Asset Preservation Advisors Inc
3344 Peachtree Rd Ste 2050. ....Atlanta GA 30326 **800-833-8985** 404-261-1333

Baron Funds
767 Fifth Ave 49th Fl ....New York NY 10153 **800-992-2766** 212-583-2000

Bridges Investment Counsel Inc
256 Durham Plz 8401 W Dodge Rd Ste 256.........Omaha NE 68114 **866-934-4700**

Cabot Wealth Management Inc
216 Essex St ....Salem MA 01970 **800-888-6468** 978-745-9233

Calvert Investments Inc
4550 Montgomery Ave Ste 1000N ....Bethesda MD 20814 **800-368-2748** 800-368-2745

CGM Funds PO Box 8511 ....Boston MA 02266 **800-345-4048** 617-859-7714

Chandler Asset Management Inc
6225 Lusk Blvd ....San Diego CA 92121 **800-317-4747**

Claremont Companies Inc
1 Lakeshore Ctr ....Bridgewater MA 02324 **800-848-9077** 508-279-4300

Clipper Fund
2949 E Elvira Rd Ste 101 ....Tucson AZ 85756 **800-432-2504**

CornerCap Investment Counsel Inc
1355 Peachtree St NE The Peachtree
Ste 1700 ....Atlanta GA 30309 **800-728-0670** 4U4-870-0700

Cozad Asset Management Inc
2501 Galen Dr ....Champaign IL 61821 **800-437-1686** 217-356-8363

Davis Funds
2949 E Elvira Rd Ste 101 ....Tucson AZ 85756 **800-279-0279**

Delaney Capital Management Ltd
TD Bank Twr 4410-66 Wellington St W...........Toronto ON M5K1H1 **800-268-2733** 416-361-0688

Dodge & Cox Funds 50 Dan Rd ......Canton MA 02021 **800-621-3979**

Domini Social Investments
PO Box 9785 ....Providence RI 02940 **800-582-6757**

Eaton Vance Mutual Funds
2 International Pl ....Boston MA 02110 **800-225-6265** 800-836-2414

Equity Investment Corp
3007 Piedmont Rd Ste 200. ....Atlanta GA 30305 **877-342-0111** 404-239-0111

Essex Financial Services Inc
176 Westbrook Rd ....Essex CT 06426 **800-900-5972** 860-767-4300

Ferguson Wellman Capital Management Inc
888 S W Fifth Ave ....Portland OR 97204 **800-327-5765** 503-226-1444

Fidelity Advisor Funds
PO Box 770002 ....Cincinnati OH 45277 **800-522-7297**

Fidelity Investment Funds
PO Box 770001 ....Cincinnati OH 45277 **800-343-3548**

Fidelity Investments
483 Bay St Ste 200. ....Toronto ON M5G2N7 **800-263-4077** 416-307-5200

Fidelity Investments Institutional Operations Co Inc
PO Box 770002 ....Cincinnati OH 45277 **877-208-0098**

First American Funds
PO Box 701 ....Milwaukee WI 53201 **800-677-3863**

Fondaction
Bureau 501 125 boul Charest Est ....Montreal QC H2K4S3 **800-253-6665** 514-525-5505

Fonds de solidarite FTQ
545 Cremazie Blvd E Ofc 200 ....Montreal QC H2M2W4 **800-567-3663**

GAMCO Investors Inc
1 Corporate Ctr ....Rye NY 10580 **800-422-3554** 914-921-5100
NYSE: GBL

Glenmede Funds
1650 Market St Ste 1200 ....Philadelphia PA 19103 **800-966-3200** 215-419-6000

Goldman Sachs 200 W St ....New York NY 10282 **800-526-7384** 212-902-1000
NYSE: GS

Guild Investment Management Inc
12400 Wilshire Blvd Ste 1080 ....Los Angeles CA 90025 **800-645-4100** 310-826-8600

Hartford Funds
30 Dan Rd Ste 55022 ....Canton MA 02021 **888-843-7824**

Heartland Funds
789 N Water St Ste 500 ....Milwaukee WI 53202 **800-432-7856** 414-347-7777

Huron Valley Financial Inc
2395 Oak Vly Dr Ste 200 ....Ann Arbor MI 48103 **800-650-7441** 734-669-8000

ICMARC
777 N Capitol St NE Ste 600. ....Washington DC 20002 **800-669-7471*** 202-962-4600
*General

ING Funds
7337 E Doubletree Ranch Rd ....Scottsdale AZ 85258 **800-992-0180**

Invesco
11 Greenway Plz Ste 100 ....Houston TX 77046 **800-959-4246** 713-626-1919

Invesco Canada Ltd
5140 Yonge St Ste 800 ....Toronto ON M2N6X7 **800-874-6275** 416-590-9855

JAG Advisors
9841 Clayton Rd ....Saint Louis MO 63124 **800-966-4596** 314-997-1277

JMT Consulting Group Inc
2200-2202 Rt 22 ....Patterson NY 12563 **888-368-2463** 845-278-9262

John Hancock Funds
601 Congress St ....Boston MA 02210 **800-338-8080** 617-375-1500

Lincluden Investment Management
1275 N Service Rd W Ste 607. ....Oakville ON L6M3G4 **800-532-7071** 905-825-9000

				Toll-Free	Phone
Loomis Sayles Funds					
1 Financial Ctr	Boston MA	02111		800-633-3330	617-482-2450
Louisbourg Investments					
1000-770 Main St	Moncton NB	E1C1E7		888-608-7070	506-853-5410
Mairs & Power Inc					
332 Minnesota St W					
Ste 1520 First National Bank Bldg	Saint Paul MN	55101		800-304-7404	651-222-8478
MASTER Teacher Inc, The					
2600 Leadership Ln	Manhattan KS	66505		800-669-9633	
Mawer Investment Management Ltd					
517 - Tenth Ave S W Ste 600	Calgary AB	T2R0A8		800-889-6248	
MD Financial Management					
1870 Alta Vista Dr	Ottawa ON	K1G6R7		800-267-4022	613-731-4552
Missouri State Employees' Retirement System					
907 Wildwood Dr	Jefferson City MO	65109		800-827-1063	573-632-6100
Monetta Financial Services Inc					
1776A S Naperville Rd Ste 100	Wheaton IL	60189		800-241-9772	630-462-9800
Mutual Benefit Group					
409 Penn St PO Box 577	Huntingdon PA	16652		800-283-3531	814-643-3000
Neuberger Berman Funds					
PO Box 8403	Boston MA	02266		800-877-9700	212-476-8800
New Mexico Educational Retirement Board					
701 Camino de Los Marquez					
PO Box 26129	Santa Fe NM	87502		866-691-2345	505-827-8030
Northern Institutional Funds					
801 S Canal St C5S	Chicago IL	60607		800-637-1380	
Northstar Investment Advisors LLC					
700 17th St Ste 2350	Denver CO	80202		800-204-6199	303-832-2300
Novare Capital Management					
521 E Morehead St The Morehead Bldg					
Ste 510	Charlotte NC	28202		877-334-3698	704-334-3698
Oak Associates Funds					
c/o Ultimus Fund Solutions 225 Pictoria Dr					
PO Box 46707	Cincinnati OH	45246		888-462-5386	
Oakmark Family of Funds					
330 W nineth St	Kansas City MO	64105		800-625-6275	617-483-8327
Old Dominion Capital Management Inc					
815 E Jefferson St	Charlottesville VA	22902		800-446-2029	434-977-1550
OppenheimerFunds Inc					
225 Liberty St	New York NY	10281		800-525-7048	
Pax World Fund Family					
30 Penhallow St Ste 400	Portsmouth NH	03801		800-767-1729	603-431-8022
Phillips, Hager & North Investment Management Ltd					
200 Burrard St 20th Fl	Vancouver BC	V6C3N5		800-661-6141	
PIMCO Institutional Funds					
PO Box 219024	Kansas City MO	64121		800-927-4648	
Priviti Capital Corp					
850 444 Fifth Ave S W	Calgary AB	T2P2T8		855-333-9943	403-263-9943
Punch & Associates Inc					
7701 France Ave S Ste 300	Edina MN	55435		800-241-5552	952-224-4350
Putnam Family of Funds					
PO Box 41203	Providence RI	02940		800-225-1581	
Qwest Investment Management Corp					
750 West Pender St Ste 802	Vancouver BC	V6C2T8		866-602-1142	604-601-5804
Rydex Funds					
805 King Farm Blvd Ste 600	Rockville MD	20850		800-820-0888*	301-296-5100
*Cust Svc					
Sandstone Asset Management Inc					
101 6 St SW	Calgary AB	T2P5K7		866-318-6140	403-218-6125
School Employees Retirement System of Ohio					
300 E Broad St Ste 100	Columbus OH	43215		800-878-5853	614-222-5853
SEAMARK Asset Management Ltd					
810-1801 Hollis St	Halifax NS	B3J3N4		888-303-5055	902-423-9367
Security Funds					
1 Security Benefit Pl	Topeka KS	66636		800-888-2461	785-438-3000
SEI 1 Freedom Vly Dr	Oaks PA	19456		800-342-5734	610-676-1000
NASDAQ: SEIC					
Selected Funds PO Box 8243	Boston MA	02266		800-243-1575	
Sentry Investments Inc					
Commerce Court W 199 Bay St Ste 2700					
PO Box 108	Toronto ON	M5L1E2		888-246-6656	416-861-8729
Sequoia Fund Inc					
767 Fifth Ave Ste 4701	New York NY	10153		800-686-6884	
Sound Shore Fund					
3 Canal Plz	Portland ME	04101		800-754-8758	
Sprott Inc					
Royal Bank Plz South Twr 200 Bay St					
Ste 2600	Toronto ON	M5J2J1		855-943-8099	416-943-8099
SSgA Funds 1 Lincoln St	Boston MA	02111		800-997-7327	617-786-3000
State Farm Mutual Funds					
PO Box 219548	Kansas City MO	64121		800-447-4930	
State Teachers Retirement System of Ohio					
275 E Broad St	Columbus OH	43215		888-227-7877	
Steadyhand Investment Funds LP					
1747 W Third Ave	Vancouver BC	V6J1K7		888-888-3147	
Steele Capital Management Inc					
788 Main St #200	Dubuque IA	52001		800-397-2097	563-588-2097
Terracap Group					
100 Sheppard Ave E Ste 502	Toronto ON	M2N6N5		800-363-3207	416-222-9345
TFS Capital LLC					
10 N High St Ste 500	West Chester PA	19380		888-837-4446	
Thornburg Investment Management Funds					
2300 N Ridgetop Rd	Santa Fe NM	87506		800-533-9337	505-984-0200
Tillar-Wenstrup Advisors LLC					
1065 E Centerville Sta Rd	Centerville OH	45459		800-207-1143	937-428-9700
Torray Fund					
7501 Wisconsin Ave Ste 750 W	Bethesda MD	20814		800-443-3036	301-493-4600
Trez Capital LP					
1550 - 1185 W Georgia St	Vancouver BC	V6E4E6		877-689-0821	604-689-0821
Trillium Asset Management LLC					
2 Financial Ctr 60 S St Ste 1100	Boston MA	02111		800-548-5684	617-423-6655
Trinity Fiduciary Partners LLC					
325 S Mesquite St Ste 104	Arlington TX	76010		877-334-1283	
Vaughan Nelson Investment Management LP					
600 Travis St Ste 6300	Houston TX	77002		888-888-8676	713-224-2545
Vested Business Brokers Inc					
50 Karl Ave # 102	Smithtown NY	11787		877-735-5224	631-265-7300

				Toll-Free	Phone
Victory Funds					
4900 Tiedeman Rd 4th Fl	Brooklyn OH	43219		877-660-4400	216-898-2400
Vision Capital Management Inc					
1 SW Columbia Ste 915	Portland OR	97258		800-707-5335	
Wealthsimple Inc					
860 Richmond St W 3rd Fl	Toronto ON	M6J1C9		855-255-9038	
Welch Group LLC, The					
3940 Montclair Rd	Birmingham AL	35213		800-709-7100	205-879-5001
Wilshire Mutual Funds Inc					
PO Box 219512	Kansas City MO	64121		888-200-6796	

525   NAVIGATION & GUIDANCE INSTRUMENTS & SYSTEMS

				Toll-Free	Phone
AAI Corp					
124 Industry Ln	Hunt Valley MD	21030		800-655-2616	410-666-1400
Adducent Technology Inc					
PO Box 1057	Rohnert Park CA	94927		800-648-0656	
Alpine Electronics of America					
19145 Gramercy Pl	Torrance CA	90501		800-257-4631	310-326-8000
CMI Inc 316 E Ninth St	Owensboro KY	42303		866-835-0690	
FLIR Systems Inc					
27700-A SW Pkwy Ave	Wilsonville OR	97070		877-773-3547	503-498-3547
NASDAQ: FLIR					
Frontier Electronic Systems Corp					
4500 W Sixth Ave	Stillwater OK	74074		800-677-1769	405-624-1769
Garmin Ltd 1200 E 151st St	Olathe KS	66062		888-442-7646	913-397-8200
NASDAQ: GRMN					
General Dynamics Advanced Information Systems					
12450 Fair Lakes Cir	Fairfax VA	22033		877-449-0600	
Honeywell Aerospace					
1944 E Sky Harbor Cir	Phoenix AZ	85034		800-601-3099	
ITT Industries Inc					
1133 Westchester Ave	White Plains NY	10604		800-254-2823	914-641-2000
NYSE: ITT					
Jewell Instruments LLC					
850 Perimeter Rd	Manchester NH	03103		800-227-5955	603-669-6400
L-3 Avionics Systems					
5353 52nd St SE	Grand Rapids MI	49512		800-253-9525	616-949-6600
L-3 Communications Corp Randtron Antenna Systems Div					
130 Constitution Dr	Menlo Park CA	94025		866-900-7270*	650-326-9500
*Sales					
L3 Technologies Inc					
1 Federal St	Camden NJ	08103		800-339-6197	856-338-3000
Laitram LLC 200 Laitram Ln	Harahan LA	70123		800-535-7631	504-733-6000
Lockheed Martin Corp					
6801 Rockledge Dr	Bethesda MD	20817		866-562-2363	301-897-6000
NYSE: LMT					
Lowrance Electronics Inc					
12000 E Skelly Dr	Tulsa OK	74128		800-628-4487	918-437-6881
Lycoming Engines					
652 Oliver St	Williamsport PA	17701		800-258-3279	570-323-6181
Mackay Communications Inc					
3691 Trust Dr	Raleigh NC	27616		888-798-7979	281-478-6245
Oregon Aero Inc					
34020 Skyway Dr	Scappoose OR	97056		800-888-6910	503-543-7399
Raymarine Inc 9 Townsend W	Nashua NH	03063		800-539-5539	603-324-7900
Rockwell Collins Inc					
400 Collins Rd NE	Cedar Rapids IA	52498		888-721-3094	319-295-1000
NYSE: COL					
Rostra Precision Controls Inc					
2519 Dana Dr	Laurinburg NC	28352		800-782-3379*	910-276-4854
*Cust Svc					
SELEX LP					
11300 W 89th St	Overland Park KS	66214		800-765-0861	913-495-2600
Shadin LP					
6831 Oxford St	St Louis Park MN	55426		800-328-0584	952-927-6500
Solacom Technologies Inc					
84 Jean-Proulx	Gatineau QC	J8Z1W1		888-765-2266	
Superior Air Parts Inc					
621 S Royal Ln Ste 100	Coppell TX	75019		800-420-4727	
Systron Donner Inertial					
355 Lennon Ln	Walnut Creek CA	94598		866-234-4976	925-979-4400
Thales ATM 23501 W 84th St	Shawnee KS	66227		800-624-7497	913-422-2600
Trimble Navigation Ltd					
935 Stewart Dr	Sunnyvale CA	94085		800-538-7800	408-481-8000
NASDAQ: TRMB					
Whistler Group Inc					
13016 N Walton Blvd	Bentonville AR	72712		800-531-0004*	479-273-6012
*Cust Svc					
Wipaire Inc					
1700 Henry Ave	South St. Paul MN	55075		888-947-2473	651-451-1205
Zonar Systems LLC					
18200 Cascade Ave S	Seattle WA	98188		877-843-3847	206-878-2459

526   NEWS SYNDICATES, SERVICES, BUREAUS

				Toll-Free	Phone
AccuWeather Inc					
385 Science Pk Rd	State College PA	16803		800-566-6606*	814-235-8650
*Sales					
American Baptist News Service					
PO Box 851	Valley Forge PA	19482		800-222-3872	610-768-2000
American Chiropractor, The					
8619 NW 68th St	Miami FL	33166		888-369-1396	
Argus Interactive Agency Inc					
217 N Main St Ste 200	Santa Ana CA	92701		866-595-9597	
Business Wire					
101 California St 20th Fl	San Francisco CA	94111		800-227-0845	415-986-4422
California Newspaper Service Bureau					
915 E First St	Los Angeles CA	90012		800-788-7840	213-229-5500
eDirectory					
7004 Little River Tpke Ste O	Annandale VA	22003		800-630-4694	
Gateway Newstands					
240 Chrislea Rd	Woodbridge ON	L4L8V1		800-942-5351	905-851-9652

				Toll-Free	Phone
Inman					
75 N Woodward Ave Ste 80368	Tallahassee	FL	32313	**800-775-4662**	510-658-9252
Kagan					
981 Calle Amanecer	San Clemente	CA	92673	**800-933-2667**	949-369-6310
Kansas Press Assn Inc					
5423 SW Seventh St	Topeka	KS	66606	**855-572-1863**	785-271-5304
Kearney Hub					
13 E 22nd PO Box 1988	Kearney	NE	68847	**800-950-6113**	308-237-2152
King Features Syndicate Inc					
300 W 57th St	New York	NY	10019	**800-708-7311**	212-969-7550
Levy Home Entertainment LLC					
1420 Kensington Rd Ste 300	Oak Brook	IL	60523	**800-549-5389**	708-547-4400
Los Angeles Times-Washington Post News Service Inc					
1150 15th St NW	Washington	DC	20071	**800-627-1150**	202-334-6000
Market Wire Inc					
100 N Sepulveda Blvd Ste 325	El Segundo	CA	90245	**800-774-9473***	310-765-3200
*General					
New York Times News Service Div					
620 Eigth Ave	New York	NY	10018	**800-698-4637**	866-870-2095
NewRetirement LLC					
100 Pine St Ste 590	San Francisco	CA	94111	**866-441-0246**	415-738-2435
Sift Media (US) Inc					
120 E 23rd St 4th Fl	New York	NY	10010	**855-253-8392**	
Softomate LLC					
901 N Pitt St Ste 325	Alexandria	VA	22314	**877-243-8735**	
United Methodist News Service					
810 12th Ave S	Nashville	TN	37203	**800-251-8140**	615-742-5470
Website Magazine Inc					
999 E Touhy Ave	Des Plaines	IL	60018	**800-817-1518**	773-628-2779

527 NEWSLETTERS

527-1 Banking & Finance Newsletters

				Toll-Free	Phone
Electronic Commerce & Law Report					
1801 S Bell St	Arlington	VA	22202	**800-372-1033**	
Louisiana Banker					
PU Box 2871	Baton Rouge	LA	70821	**888-249-3050**	225-387-3282
New York Banker					
99 Park Ave 4th Fl	New York	NY	10016	**800-346-3860**	212 297-1600

527-2 Business & Professional Newsletters

				Toll-Free	Phone
Antitrust & Trade Regulation Daily					
1801 S Bell St	Arlington	VA	22202	**800-372-1033**	
CD Publications					
8204 Fenton St	Silver Spring	MD	20910	**800-666-6380**	301-588-6380
Corporate Writer & Editor					
111 E Wacker Dr Ste 500	Chicago	IL	60601	**800-878-5331**	312-960-4140
Customer Communicator, The (TCC)					
712 Main St Ste 187B	Boonton	NJ	07005	**800-232-4317**	973-265-2300
Daily Report for Executives					
1801 S Bell St	Arlington	VA	22202	**800-372-1033**	
Daily Tax Report					
1801 S Bell St	Arlington	VA	22202	**800-372-1033**	
Distribution Center Management (DCM)					
712 Main St Ste 187B	Boonton	NJ	07005	**800-232-4317**	973-265-2300
Government Employee Relations Report					
1801 S Bell St	Arlington	VA	22202	**800-372-1033**	
Law Officer's Bulletin					
610 Opperman Dr	Eagan	MN	55123	**800-344-5008**	651-687-7000
Manager's Intelligence Report (MIR)					
316 N Michigan Ave Ste 400	Chicago	IL	60601	**800-878-5331**	
Ragan Communications Inc					
316 N Michigan Ave Ste 400	Chicago	IL	60601	**800-878-5331**	312-960-4100
Teamwork Newsletter					
2222 Sedwick Dr	Durham	NC	27713	**800-223-8720**	

527-3 Computer & Internet Newsletters

				Toll-Free	Phone
Biotechnology Software					
140 Huguenot St 3rd Fl	New Rochelle	NY	10801	**800-654-3237**	914-740-2100
Lawrence Ragan Communications Inc					
316 N Michigan Ave Ste 400	Chicago	IL	60601	**800-878-5331**	312-960-4100
Microprocessor Report					
355 Chesley Ave	Mountain View	CA	94040	**800-413-2881**	408-270-3772
Washington Internet Daily					
2115 Ward Ct NW	Washington	DC	20037	**800-771-9202**	202-872-9200

527-4 Education Newsletters

				Toll-Free	Phone
Education Grants Alert					
360 Hiatt Dr	Palm Beach Gardens	FL	33418	**800-621-5463**	561-622-6520
Educational Research Newsletter					
PO Box 2347	South Portland	ME	04116	**800-321-7471**	207-632-1954
School Law News					
360 Hiatt Dr	Palm Beach Gardens	FL	33418	**800-341-7874**	

527-5 Energy & Environmental Newsletters

				Toll-Free	Phone
Clean Air Report					
1919 S Eads St Ste 201	Arlington	VA	22202	**800-424-9068**	703-416-8505
Daily Environment Report					
1801 S Bell St	Arlington	VA	22202	**800-372-1033**	
Environment Reporter					
1801 S Bell St	Arlington	VA	22202	**800-372-1033**	

				Toll-Free	Phone
Inside NRC					
2 Penn Plz 25th Fl	New York	NY	10121	**800-752-8878**	
Oil Price Information Service					
3349 Hwy 138 Bldg D Ste D	Wall	NJ	07719	**888-301-2645***	732-901-8800
*Cust Svc					
Solid Waste Assn of North America (SWANA)					
1100 Wayne Ave Ste 700	Silver Spring	MD	20910	**800-467-9262**	301-585-2898
Toxics Law Reporter					
1801 S Bell St	Arlington	VA	22202	**800-372-1033**	

527-6 General Interest Newsletters

				Toll-Free	Phone
NRTA/AARP Bulletin					
601 E St NW	Washington	DC	20049	**888-867-2277**	202-434-3525
Regent Group Inc					
4501 Forbes Blvd Ste 100	Lanham	MD	20706	**888-354-6309**	301-459-8020

527-7 Government & Law Newsletters

				Toll-Free	Phone
Alcoholic Beverage Control					
PO Box 27491	Richmond	VA	23261	**800-552-3200**	804-213-4565
Bloomberg BNA					
1801 S Bell St	Arlington	VA	22022	**800-960-1220**	703-341-5777
Class Action Litigation Report					
1801 S Bell St	Arlington	VA	22202	**800-372-1033**	
Community Development Digest					
8204 Fenton St	Silver Spring	MD	20910	**800-666-6380**	301-588-6380
Computer Technology Law Report					
1801 S Bell St	Arlington	VA	22202	**800-372-1033**	
Criminal Law Reporter					
1801 S Bell St	Arlington	VA	22202	**800-372-1033**	
Daily Labor Report					
1801 S Bell St	Arlington	VA	22202	**800-372-1033**	
Development Director's Letter					
8204 Fenton St	Silver Spring	MD	20910	**800-666-6380**	301-588-6380
Employment Discrimination Report					
1801 S Bell St	Arlington	VA	22202	**800-372-1033**	
Expert Evidence Report					
1801 S Bell St	Arlington	VA	22202	**800-372-1033**	
Federal Assistance Monitor					
8204 Fenton St	Silver Spring	MD	20910	**800-666-6380**	301-588-6300
Federal Contracts Report					
1801 S Bell St	Arlington	VA	22202	**800-372-1033**	
Health Law Reporter					
1801 S Bell St	Arlington	VA	22202	**800-372-1033**	
IRS Practice Adviser					
1801 S Bell St	Arlington	VA	22202	**800-372-1033**	
Medical Research Law & Policy Report					
1801 S Bell St	Arlington	VA	22202	**800-372-1033**	
Mergers & Acquisitions Law Report					
1801 S Bell St	Arlington	VA	22202	**800-372-1033**	
Money & Politics Report					
1801 S Bell St	Arlington	VA	22202	**800-372-1033**	
Patent Trademark & Copyright Law Daily					
1801 S Bell St	Arlington	VA	22202	**800-372-1033**	
Roll Call					
1625 Eye St NW Ste 200	Washington	DC	20006	**800-432-2250**	202-650-6500
Securities Law Daily					
1801 S Bell St	Arlington	VA	22202	**800-372-1033**	
Workplace Law Report					
1801 S Bell St	Arlington	VA	22202	**800-372-1033**	

527-8 Health & Social Issues Newsletters

				Toll-Free	Phone
Aging News Alert					
8204 Fenton St	Silver Spring	MD	20910	**800-666-6380**	301-588-6385
AICR Newsletter					
1759 R St NW	Washington	DC	20009	**800-843-8114**	202-328-7744
APCO Bulletin					
351 N Williamson Blvd	Daytona Beach	FL	32114	**888-272-6911**	386-322-2500
Children & Youth Funding Report					
8204 Fenton St	Silver Spring	MD	20910	**800-666-6380**	301-588-6380
Harvard Women's Health Watch					
PO Box 9308	Big Sandy	TX	75755	**877-649-9457**	
Health Care Daily Report					
1801 S Bell St	Arlington	VA	22202	**800-372-1033**	
International Medical Device Regulatory Monitor					
300 N Washington St Ste 200	Falls Church	VA	22046	**888-838-5578**	703-538-7600
Mayo Clinic Health Letter					
200 First St NW	Rochester	MN	55905	**800-291-1128**	
OSHA Up-to-Date Newsletter					
1121 Spring Lake Dr	Itasca	IL	60143	**800-621-7615***	630-285-1121
*Cust Svc					

527-9 Investment Newsletters

				Toll-Free	Phone
Cabot Wealth Network					
176 N St PO Box 2049	Salem	MA	01970	**800-326-8826***	
*Orders					
Chartist Newsletter					
PO Box 758	Seal Beach	CA	90740	**800-942-4278**	562-596-2385
Commodity Research Bureau					
330 S Wells St Ste 612	Chicago	IL	60606	**800-621-5271**	312-554-8456
Dow Theory Forecasts					
7412 Calumet Ave	Hammond	IN	46324	**800-233-5922**	
DRIP Investor					
7412 Calumet Ave	Hammond	IN	46324	**800-233-5922**	219-852-3220
Elliott Wave Theorist					
PO Box 1618	Gainesville	GA	30503	**800-336-1618**	770-536-0309

		Toll-Free	Phone
Gold Newsletter PO Box 84900	Phoenix AZ 85071	800-877-8847	
Investing Daily 7600A Leesburg Pk W Bldg Ste 300	Falls Church VA 22043	800-832-2330	703-394-4931
Investment Quality Trends (IQT) 2888 Loker Ave E Ste 116	Carlsbad CA 92010	866-927-5250	
InvestorPlace Media LLC 9201 Corporate Blvd Ste 200	Rockville MD 20850	800-219-8592	
Option Advisor 5151 Pfeiffer Rd Ste 250	Cincinnati OH 45242	800-448-2080	513-589-3800
Personal Finance Newsletter 7600A Leesburg Pk W Bldg Ste 300	Falls Church VA 22043	800-832-2330	703-394-4931
Peter Dag Portfolio Strategy & Management, The 65 Lake Front Dr	Akron OH 44319	800-833-2782	330-644-2782
Profitable Investing 9201 Corporate Blvd	Rockville MD 20850	800-211-8566	

527-10 Marketing & Sales Newsletters

		Toll-Free	Phone
Marketing Library Services 143 Old Marlton Pk	Medford NJ 08055	800-300-9868	609-654-6266
Sales Leader 2222 Sedwick Dr	Durham NC 27713	800-223-8720	

527-11 Media & Communications Newsletters

		Toll-Free	Phone
Communications Daily 2115 Ward Ct NW	Washington DC 20037	800-771-9202	202-872-9200
Jack O'Dwyer's PR Newsletter 271 Madison Ave Ste 600	New York NY 10016	866-395-7710	212-679-2471
Media Law Reporter 1801 S Bell St	Arlington VA 22202	800-372-1033	
Media Relations Report 316 N Michigan Ave Ste 400	Chicago IL 60601	800-878-5331	312-960-4100

527-12 Science & Technology Newsletters

		Toll-Free	Phone
Frost & Sullivan 7550 IH 10 W Ste 400	San Antonio TX 78229	877-463-7678	210-348-1000
Genetic Engineering News 140 Huguenot St 3rd Fl	New Rochelle NY 10801	888-211-4235	914-740-2100
Geophysical Research Letter 2000 Florida Ave NW	Washington DC 20009	800-966-2481	202-462-6900

527-13 Trade & Industry Newsletters

		Toll-Free	Phone
AviationWeek 1200 G St NW Ste 900	Washington DC 20005	800-525-5003	
Construction Claims Monthly 2222 Sedwick Rd	Durham NC 27713	800-223-8720	
Construction Labor Report 1801 S Bell St	Arlington VA 22202	800-372-1033	
DealersEdge PO Box 606	Barnegat Light NJ 08006	800-321-5312	609-879-4456
Funeral Service Insider 3349 Hwy 138 Bldg D Ste B	Wall NJ 07719	800-500-4585	
InfoMine Inc 580 Hornby St Ste 900	Vancouver BC V6C3B6	888-683-2037	604-683-2037
Kiplinger Agriculture Letter 1729 H St NW	Washington DC 20006	800-544-0155	202-887-6400
Metals Week 2 Penn Plz	New York NY 10121	800-752-8878	
National Farmers Union News (NFU) 20 F St NW Ste 300	Washington DC 20001	800-442-8277	202-554-1600
Pro Farmer 6612 Chancellor Dr Ste 300 *Cust Svc	Cedar Falls IA 50613	800-772-0023*	319-277-1278
Questex LLC 275 Grove St Ste 2-130	Newton MA 02466	888-552-4346	617-219-8300
Shopping Centers Today 1221 Ave of the Americas	New York NY 10020	888-427-2885	646-728-3800
Uniform Commercial Code Law Letter 610 Opperman Dr *Cust Svc	Eagan MN 55123	800-328-4880*	651-687-7000

528 NEWSPAPERS

SEE ALSO Newspaper Publishers

528-1 Daily Newspapers - Canada

		Toll-Free	Phone
Calgary Herald 215-16th St SE	Calgary AB T2E7P5	800-372-9219	403-235-7100
Chronicle Herald, The PO Box 610	Halifax NS B3J2T2	800-563-1187	902-426-2811
Edmonton Journal 10006 - 101 St	Edmonton AB T5J0S1	800-232-9486	780-429-5100
Edmonton Sun 10006 101 St	Edmonton AB T5J0S1	888-786-7821	780-468-0100
L'Acadie-Nouvelle 476 St-Pierre Blvd W PO Box 5536	Caraquet NB E1W1B7	800-561-2255	506-727-4444
Le Devoir 1265 Berri 8th Fl	Montreal QC H2L4X4	800-463-7559	514-985-3333
Le Quotidien & Progres Dimanche 1051 boul Talbot	Chicoutimi QC G7H5C1	800-866-3658	418-545-4664
London Free Press 369 York St PO Box 2280	London ON N6A4G1	866-541-6757	519-679-1111
Observer, The 140 S Front St	Sarnia ON N7T7M8	866-541-6757	519-344-3641
Ottawa Citizen 1101 Baxter Rd PO Box 5020	Ottawa ON K2C3M4	800-267-6100	613-829-9100
Ottawa Sun 1101 Baxter Rd	Ottawa ON K2C3M4	855-786-8812	613-829-9100
Record, The 160 King St E	Kitchener ON N2G4E5	800-265-8261	519-894-2231
Regina Leader Post 1964 Park St PO Box 2020	Regina SK S4P3G4	800-667-9999	306-781-5211
Spectator, The 44 Frid St	Hamilton ON L8N3G3	800-263-6902	905-526-3333
Telegraph-Journal 210 Crown St PO Box 2350	Saint John NB E2L3V8	888-295-8665	
Times Colonist 2621 Douglas St	Victoria BC V8T4M2	800-663-6384	250-380-5211
Times-Transcript 939 Main St	Moncton NB E1C8P3	800-561-7166	
Toronto Star 1 Yonge St	Toronto ON M5E1E6	800-268-9756	416-869-4949
Toronto Sun 333 King St E	Toronto ON M5A3X5	888-786-7821	416-947-2222
Vancouver Sun 200 Granville St Ste 1	Vancouver BC V6C3N3	866-372-3707	604-605-2000
Windsor Star, The 300 Ouellette Ave	Windsor ON N9A7B4	800-265-5647	888-394-9296
Winnipeg Free Press 1355 Mountain Ave	Winnipeg MB R2X3B6	800-542-8900	204-697-7000

528-2 Daily Newspapers - US

Listings here are organized by city names within state groupings. Most of the fax numbers given connect directly to the newsroom.

Alabama

		Toll-Free	Phone
Anniston Star 4305 McClellan Blvd PO Box 2285	Anniston AL 36206	866-814-9253	256-236-1551
Birmingham News 1731 First Ave N	Birmingham AL 35203	800-568-4123	205-325-4444
Decatur Daily 201 First Ave SE	Decatur AL 35601	888-353-4612	256-353-4612
Dothan Eagle PO Box 1968	Dothan AL 36302	800-811-1771	334-792-3141
Alabama Media Group 200 Westside Sq Ste 100	Huntsville AL 35801	800-239-5271	256-532-4000
Montgomery Advertiser 425 Molton St	Montgomery AL 36104	877-424-0007	334-262-1611
Daily Sentinel 701 Veterans Dr	Scottsboro AL 35768	877-985-9212	256-259-1020
Tuscaloosa News 315 28th Ave	Tuscaloosa AL 35401	800-888-8639	205-345-0505

Alaska

		Toll-Free	Phone
Anchorage Daily News 1001 Northway Dr	Anchorage AK 99508	800-478-4200	907-257-4200

Arizona

		Toll-Free	Phone
East Valley Tribune 120 W First Ave	Mesa AZ 85210	877-728-5414	480-898-6500
Arizona Republic 200 E Van Buren St	Phoenix AZ 85004	800-331-9303	602-444-8000
Arizona Daily Star 4850 S Park Ave	Tucson AZ 85714	800-695-4492	520-573-4343

Arkansas

		Toll-Free	Phone
Times Record 3600 Wheeler Ave	Fort Smith AR 72901	888-274-4051	479-785-7700
Jonesboro Sun 518 Carson St	Jonesboro AR 72401	800-237-5341	870-935-5525
Arkansas Democrat-Gazette 121 E Capital St *Cust Svc	Little Rock AR 72203	800-482-1121*	501-378-3400

California

		Toll-Free	Phone
Times-Standard 930 Sixth St	Eureka CA 95501	800-564-5630	707-441-0500
Fresno Bee 1626 E St	Fresno CA 93786	800-877-3400	559-441-6111
Sentinel, The 300 W Sixth St	Hanford CA 93230	888-606-0605	559-582-0471
Investor's Business Daily 12655 Beatrice St	Los Angeles CA 90066	800-831-2525	310-448-6000
Los Angeles Times 202 W First St	Los Angeles CA 90012	800-528-4637	213-237-5000
Modesto Bee 1325 H St	Modesto CA 95354	800-776-4233	209-578-2000
Monterey County Herald 2200 Garden Rd	Monterey CA 93940	800-688-1808	831-372-3311
Marin Independent Journal 150 Alameda Del Prado	Novato CA 94949	877-229-8655	415-883-8600
Desert Sun 750 N Gene Autry Trl	Palm Springs CA 92263	800-233-3741	760-322-8889
Antelope Valley Press 37404 Sierra Hwy	Palmdale CA 93550	888-874-2527	661-273-2700
Sacramento Bee PO Box 15779 *Cust Svc	Sacramento CA 95852	800-284-3233*	800-222-7463
San Diego Daily Transcript 2131 Third Ave	San Diego CA 92101	800-697-6397	619-232-4381
San Diego Union-Tribune 350 Camino De La Reina	San Diego CA 92108	800-244-6397	619-299-3131
San Francisco Chronicle 901 Mission St	San Francisco CA 94103	866-732-4766	415-777-1111
El Mexicano 5801 Rue Ferrari	San Jose CA 95138	800-858-1119	
San Mateo County Times 4 N Second St Ste 800	San Jose CA 95113	800-870-6397	408-920-5000
Tribune, The 3825 S Higuera St	San Luis Obispo CA 93401	800-477-8799	805-781-7800

			Toll-Free	Phone

Press Democrat
427 Mendocino Ave .... Santa Rosa CA 95401   **800-675-5056**   707-546-2020
Recordnetcom
530 E Market St .... Stockton CA 95202   **800-606-9741**   209-943-6568
Vallejo Times Herald
420 Virginia St Ste 2A .... Vallejo CA 94590   **800-600-1141**   707-644-1141

Colorado

			Toll-Free	Phone

Aspen Times, The
314 E Hyman Ave .... Aspen CO 81611   **800-525-6200**   970-925-3414
Durango Herald
1275 Main Ave .... Durango CO 81301   **800-530-8318**   970-247-3504
Coloradoan, The
1300 Riverside Ave .... Fort Collins CO 80524   **877-424-0063**   970-493-6397
Greeley Tribune
501 Eighth Ave .... Greeley CO 80631   **800-275-0321**   970-352-0211
Times-Call, The
350 Terry St .... Longmont CO 80501   **800-279-8537**   303-776-2244
Pueblo Chieftain
825 W Sixth St .... Pueblo CO 81003   **800-279-6397**   719-544-3520

Connecticut

			Toll-Free	Phone

Connecticut Post
410 State St .... Bridgeport CT 06604   **800-542-2517***   203-333-0161
*Edit
News-Times 333 Main St .... Danbury CT 06810   **877-542-6057**   203-744-5100
Hartford Courant
285 Broad St .... Hartford CT 06115   **800-524-4242**   860-241-6200
Journal Inquirer
306 Progress Dr PO Box 510 .... Manchester CT 06045   **800-237-3606**   860-646-0500
Record-Journal
500 South Broad St 2nd Fl .... Meriden CT 06450   **800-228-6915**   203-235-1661
New Haven Register
40 Sargent Dr .... New Haven CT 06511   **888-969-0949**   203-789-5200

Delaware

			Toll-Free	Phone

Delaware State News
110 Galaxy Dr .... Dover DE 19901   **800-282-8586**   302-674-3600
News Journal
950 W Basin Rd .... New Castle DE 19720   **800-235-9100**   302-324-2500

District of Columbia

			Toll-Free	Phone

Washington Post
1301 K St NW .... Washington DC 20071   **800-627-1150**   202-334-6100

Florida

			Toll-Free	Phone

El Nuevo Herald
3511 NW 91st Ave .... Doral FL 33172   **866-949-6722**   305-376-3535
South Florida Sun-Sentinel
200 E Las Olas Blvd .... Fort Lauderdale FL 33301   **800-548-6397***   954-356-4000
*Cust Svc
Florida Times-Union
1 Riverside Ave .... Jacksonville FL 32202   **800-472-6397**   904-359-4111
Ledger, The 300 W Lime St .... Lakeland FL 33815   **888-431-7323**   863-802-7000
Naples Daily News
1100 Immokalee Rd .... Naples FL 34110   **800-404-7343**   239-213-6000
Orlando Sentinel
633 N Orange Ave .... Orlando FL 32801   **800-974-7488**   407-420-5000
Sanford Herald, The
217 E First St .... Sanford FL 32771   **800-955-8770**   407-322-2611
Sarasota Herald-Tribune
1741 Main St .... Sarasota FL 34236   **866-284-7102**   941-953-7755
Palm Beach Post
2751 S Dixie Hwy .... West Palm Beach FL 33405   **800-432-7595**   561-820-4100

Georgia

			Toll-Free	Phone

Athens Banner-Herald
1 Press Pl .... Athens GA 30601   **800-533-4252**   706-549-0123
Atlanta Journal-Constitution
223 Perimeter Ctr Pkwy NE .... Atlanta GA 30346   **800-933-9771**   404-526-5151
Augusta Chronicle
725 Broad St .... Augusta GA 30901   **866-249-8223**   706-724-0851
Columbus Ledger-Enquirer
17 W 12th St .... Columbus GA 31901   **800-282-7859**   706-324-5526
Gainesville Times
345 Green St NW .... Gainesville GA 30501   **800-395-5005**   770-532-1234
Telegraph, The
1675 Montpelier Ave .... Macon GA 31201   **800-679-6397**   478-744-4200
Savannah Morning News
1375 Chatham Pkwy .... Savannah GA 31405   **800-533-1150**   912-236-9511
Valdosta Daily Times
PO Box 968 .... Valdosta GA 31603   **800-600-4838**   229-244-1880

Hawaii

			Toll-Free	Phone

Honolulu Advertiser
500 Ala Moana Blvd Ste 7-210 .... Honolulu HI 96813   **800-801-5999**   808-529-4747

Idaho

			Toll-Free	Phone

Idaho Statesman PO Box 40 .... Boise ID 83707   **800-635-8934**   208-377-6400
Post-Register
PO Box 1800 .... Idaho Falls ID 83403   **800-574-6397**   208-522-1800

Idaho State Journal
305 S Arthur Ave .... Pocatello ID 83204   **800-669-9777**   208-232-4161
Times-News PO Box 548 .... Twin Falls ID 83303   **800-658-3883**   208-733-0931

Illinois

			Toll-Free	Phone

Telegraph, The PO Box 278 .... Alton IL 62002   **866-299-9256**   618-463-2500
Daily Herald
155 E Algonquin Rd .... Arlington Heights IL 60005   **888-903-4070**   847-427-4300
Belleville News-Democrat
120 S Illinois St .... Belleville IL 62220   **800-642-3878**   618-234-1000
Pantagraph PO Box 2907 .... Bloomington IL 61702   **800-747-7323**   309-829-9000
Southern Illinoisan
710 N Illinois Ave .... Carbondale IL 62901   **800-228-0429**   618-529-5454
News-Gazette Inc, The
15 Main St .... Champaign IL 61820   **800-660-7323**   217-351-5252
Commercial-News 17 W N St .... Danville IL 61832   **877-732-8258**   217-446-1000
Telegraph 113 S Peoria Ave .... Dixon IL 61021   **800-798-4085**   815-284-2224
Journal-Standard
27 S State Ave .... Freeport IL 61032   **800-325-6397**   815-232-1171
Daily Journal
8 Dearborn Sq .... Kankakee IL 60901   **866-299-9256**   815-937-3300
NASDAQ: DJCO
News-Tribune 426 Second St .... La Salle IL 61301   **800-892-6452**   815-223-3200
Quincy Herald-Whig
130 S Fifth St .... Quincy IL 62301   **800-373-9444**   217-223-5100
Rock Island Argus
1724 Fourth Ave .... Rock Island IL 61201   **800-660-2472**   309-786-6441

Indiana

			Toll-Free	Phone

Herald Bulletin
1133 Jackson St .... Anderson IN 46016   **800-750-5049**   765-622-1212
Times-Mail 813 16th St .... Bedford IN 47421   **800-782-4405**   812-275-3355
Republic, The
2980 N National Rd Ste A .... Columbus IN 47201   **800-876-7811**   812-372-7811
Evansville Courier & Press
300 E Walnut St .... Evansville IN 47713   **844-900-7104**   812-464-7620
Journal Gazette
600 W Main St .... Fort Wayne IN 46802   **888-966-4532**   260-461-8773
News-Sentinel
600 W Main St .... Fort Wayne IN 46802   **800-324-0505**   260-461-8519
Daily Journal
777 Walnut St .... Franklin IN 46131   **888-736-7101**   317-736-2777
Goshen News
114 S Main St PO Box 569 .... Goshen IN 46527   **800-487-2151**   574-533-2151
Indianapolis Star
307 N Pennsylvania St .... Indianapolis IN 46204   **800-669-7827**   317-444-4000
Kokomo Tribune (KT)
300 N Union St PO Box 9014 .... Kokomo IN 46901   **800-382-0696**   765-459-3121
Journal & Courier
217 N Sixth St .... Lafayette IN 47901   **800-456-3223***   765-423-5511
*News Rm
Muncie Star-Press
345 S High St .... Muncie IN 47305   **800-783-7827**   765-213-5700
Times, The 601 W 45th Ave .... Munster IN 46321   **866-301-3331**   219-933-3200
South Bend Tribune
225 W Colfax Ave .... South Bend IN 46626   **800-220-7378**   574-235-6464
Tribune-Star PO Box 149 .... Terre Haute IN 47808   **800-783-8742**   812-231-4200

Iowa

			Toll-Free	Phone

Hawk Eye, The
800 S Main St PO Box 10 .... Burlington IA 52601   **800-397-1708**   319-754-8461
Gazette, The
501 Second Ave SE .... Cedar Rapids IA 52401   **800-397-8333**   319-398-8333
Daily Nonpareil
535 W Broadway Ste 300 .... Council Bluffs IA 51503   **800-283-1882**   712-328-1811
Quad-City Times
500 E Third St .... Davenport IA 52801   **800-437-4641**   563-383-2200
Des Moines Register
715 Locust St .... Des Moines IA 50309   **800-247-5346**   515-284-8000
Telegraph Herald
801 Bluff St .... Dubuque IA 52001   **800-553-4801**   563-588-5611
Messenger, The
713 Central Ave .... Fort Dodge IA 50501   **800-622-6613**   515-573-2141
Globe-Gazette
300 N Washington .... Mason City IA 50402   **800-421-0546**   641-421-0500
Ottumwa Courier
213 E Second St .... Ottumwa IA 52501   **800-532-1504**   641-684-4611
Sioux City Journal
515 Pavonia St .... Sioux City IA 51101   **800-397-3530**   712-293-4300
Pilot Tribune
PO Box 1187 .... Storm Lake IA 50588   **800-447-1985**   712-732-3130
Waterloo Cedar Falls Courier
PO Box 540 .... Waterloo IA 50701   **800-798-1730**   800-798-1717

Kansas

			Toll-Free	Phone

Hutchinson News
300 W Second St .... Hutchinson KS 67504   **800-766-3311**   620-694-5700
Salina Journal PO Box 740 .... Salina KS 67402   **800-827-6363**   785-823-6363
Topeka Capital-Journal
616 SE Jefferson St .... Topeka KS 66607   **800-777-7171**   785-295-1111
Wichita Eagle, The
825 E Douglas Ave .... Wichita KS 67202   **800-200-8906**   316-268-6000

Kentucky

			Toll-Free	Phone

Times-Tribune, The
201 N Kentucky Ave .... Corbin KY 40701   **877-629-9722**   606-528-2464

(Left column along the outer margin) Classified Section

				Toll-Free	Phone
Courier-Journal					
525 W Broadway PO Box 740031	Louisville	KY	40201	**800-765-4011**	502-582-4011
Messenger-Inquirer					
1401 Fredrica St	Owensboro	KY	42301	**800-633-2008**	270-926-0123

Louisiana

				Toll-Free	Phone
Alexandria Daily Town Talk					
PO Box 7558	Alexandria	LA	71306	**800-523-8391**	318-487-6397
Advocate, The					
7290 Blue Bonnet Blvd	Baton Rouge	LA	70810	**800-960-6397**	225-383-1111
Daily Advertiser, The					
1100 Bertrand Dr	Lafayette	LA	70506	**800-259-8852**	337-289-6300
Times-Picayune					
3800 Howard Ave	New Orleans	LA	70125	**800-925-0000**	504-826-3279
Times 401 Market St	Shreveport	LA	71101	**866-979-6397**	318-459-3200

Maine

				Toll-Free	Phone
Bangor Daily News					
491 Main St PO Box 1329	Bangor	ME	04402	**800-432-7964**	207-990-8000
Sun-Journal PO Box 4400	Lewiston	ME	04243	**800-482-0759**	207-784-5411

Maryland

				Toll-Free	Phone
Baltimore Sun					
501 N Calvert St	Baltimore	MD	21278	**800-829-8000**	410-332-6000
Frederick News Post					
351 Ballenger Ctr Dr	Frederick	MD	21703	**800-486-1177**	301-662-1177
Daily Times 618 Beam St	Salisbury	MD	21801	**877-335-6278**	410-749-7171

Massachusetts

				Toll-Free	Phone
Sun Chronicle PO Box 600	Attleboro	MA	02703	**800-323-4673**	508-222-7000
MetroWest Daily News					
33 New York Ave	Framingham	MA	01701	**800-624-7355**	508-626-4412
Cape Cod Times 319 Main St	Hyannis	MA	02601	**800-451-7887**	508-775-1200
Daily Item, The 110 Munroe St	Lynn	MA	01901	**800-876-7060**	781-593-7700
Haverhill Gazette					
100 Turnpike St	N Andover	MA	01845	**888-411-3245**	978-946-2000
Eagle-Tribune					
100 Tpke St	North Andover	MA	01845	**800-927-9200**	978-946-2000

Michigan

				Toll-Free	Phone
Huron Daily Tribune					
211 N Heisterman St	Bad Axe	MI	48413	**800-322-1184**	989-269-6461
Battle Creek Enquirer					
77 E Michigan Ave Ste 101.	Battle Creek	MI	49017	**800-333-4139**	269-964-7161
Detroit Free Press					
615 W Lafayette Blvd	Detroit	MI	48226	**800-395-3300**	313-222-6400
Detroit News					
615 W Lafayette Blvd	Detroit	MI	48226	**800-395-3300***	313-222-2300
*General					
Lansing State Journal					
120 E Lenawee St	Lansing	MI	48919	**800-234-1719**	517-377-1000
Midland Daily News					
124 McDonald St	Midland	MI	48640	**877-411-2762**	989-835-7171
Saginaw News					
203 S Washington Ave	Saginaw	MI	48607	**877-611-6397**	989-752-7171
Herald-Palladium					
3450 Hollywood Rd	Saint Joseph	MI	49085	**800-356-4262**	269-429-2400
Traverse City Record-Eagle					
120 W Front St	Traverse City	MI	49684	**800-968-8273**	231-946-2000

Minnesota

				Toll-Free	Phone
Duluth News-Tribune					
424 W First St	Duluth	MN	55802	**800-456-8080***	218-723-5281
*Circ					
Free Press 418 S Second St	Mankato	MN	56001	**800-657-4662**	507-625-4451
Saint Cloud Times					
3000 Seventh St N	Saint Cloud	MN	56303	**877-424-4921**	320-255-8700
West Central Tribune					
PO Box 839	Willmar	MN	56201	**800-450-1150**	320-235-1150

Mississippi

				Toll-Free	Phone
Hattiesburg American					
825 N Main St	Hattiesburg	MS	39401	**800-844-2637**	601-582-4321
Clarion-Ledger, The					
201 S Congress St	Jackson	MS	39201	**877-850-5343**	601-961-7000
Northeast Mississippi Daily Journal					
1242 S Green St	Tupelo	MS	38804	**800-264-6397**	662-842-2611

Missouri

				Toll-Free	Phone
Southeast Missourian					
301 Broadway St	Cape Girardeau	MO	63701	**800-879-1210**	573-335-6611
Columbia Daily Tribune					
101 N Fourth St	Columbia	MO	65201	**800-333-6799**	573-815-1700
Columbia Missourian					
221 S Eighth St	Columbia	MO	65201	**855-270-6572**	573-882-5700
Joplin Globe 117 E Fourth St	Joplin	MO	64801	**800-444-8514**	417-623-3480
Kansas City Star					
1729 Grand Ave	Kansas City	MO	64108	**877-962-7827**	
Daily Journal					
1513 St Joe Dr PO Box A	Park Hills	MO	63601	**800-660-8166**	573-431-2010

				Toll-Free	Phone
Daily American Republic					
208 Poplar St PO Box 7	Poplar Bluff	MO	63901	**888-276-2242**	573-785-1414

Montana

				Toll-Free	Phone
Billings Gazette					
401 N 28th St	Billings	MT	59101	**800-543-2505**	406-657-1200
Montana Standard					
25 W Granite St	Butte	MT	59701	**800-877-1074**	406-496-5500
Great Falls Tribune					
205 River Dr S	Great Falls	MT	59405	**800-438-6600**	406-791-1444
Independent Record					
PO Box 4249	Helena	MT	59604	**800-523-2272**	406-447-4000
Missoulian PO Box 8029	Missoula	MT	59807	**800-366-7102**	406-523-5200

Nebraska

				Toll-Free	Phone
Grand Island Independent					
422 W First St	Grand Island	NE	68801	**800-658-3160**	308-382-1000
Lincoln Journal-Star					
926 P St	Lincoln	NE	68508	**800-742-7315**	402-475-4200
Norfolk Daily News					
PO Box 977	Norfolk	NE	68702	**877-371-1020**	402-371-1020
Omaha World-Herald					
1314 Douglas St	Omaha	NE	68102	**800-284-6397**	402-444-1000

Nevada

				Toll-Free	Phone
Reno Gazette-Journal					
PO Box 22000	Reno	NV	89520	**800-970-7366**	775-788-6397

New Hampshire

				Toll-Free	Phone
Valley News					
24 Interchange Dr	West Lebanon	NH	03784	**800-874-2226**	603-298-8711

New Jersey

				Toll-Free	Phone
Courier-Post					
301 Cuthbert Blvd	Cherry Hill	NJ	08002	**800-677-6289**	856-663-6000
Asbury Park Press					
3601 Hwy 66 PO Box 1550.	Neptune	NJ	07754	**800-822-9770**	732-922-6000
Star-Ledger, The					
1 Star Ledger Plz	Newark	NJ	07102	**800-501-2100**	973-877-4141
New Jersey Herald					
2 Spring St	Newton	NJ	07860	**800-424-3725**	973-383-1500
Daily Journal 891 E Oak Rd	Vineland	NJ	08360	**800-222-0104**	856-691-5000
Gloucester County Times					
309 S Broad St	Woodbury	NJ	08096	**800-300-9321**	856-845-3300

New Mexico

				Toll-Free	Phone
Daily Times					
201 N Allen Ave	Farmington	NM	87401	**877-599-3331**	505-325-4545
Las Cruces Sun-News					
256 W Las Cruces Ave	Las Cruces	NM	88005	**877-827-7200**	575-541-5400

New York

				Toll-Free	Phone
Buffalo News					
1 News Plz PO Box 100	Buffalo	NY	14240	**800-777-8640**	716-849-4444
Evening Observer					
8-10 E Second St PO Box 391	Dunkirk	NY	14048	**800-836-0931**	716-366-3000
Star-Gazette					
310 E Church St PO Box 285	Elmira	NY	14902	**800-836-8970**	607-734-5151
Post-Star					
76 Lawrence St	Glens Falls	NY	12801	**800-724-2543**	518-792-3131
Register-Star 364 Warren St	Hudson	NY	12534	**800-836-4069**	518-828-1616
Ithaca Journal					
123 W State St	Ithaca	NY	14850	**866-254-3068**	607-272-2321
Post-Journal					
15 W Second St	Jamestown	NY	14701	**866-756-9600**	716-487-1111
Newsday Inc					
598 Broadhollow Rd	Melville	NY	11747	**888-280-4719**	631-843-4050
Times Herald-Record					
40 Mulberry St PO Box 2046	Middletown	NY	10940	**888-620-1700**	845-341-1100
New York Daily News					
450 W 33rd St	New York	NY	10001	**800-692-6397**	646-473-0100
New York Post					
1211 Ave of the Americas	New York	NY	10036	**800-552-7678**	212-930-8000
Olean Times-Herald					
639 Norton Dr	Olean	NY	14760	**800-722-8812**	716-372-3121
Daily Star 102 Chestnut St	Oneonta	NY	13820	**800-721-1000**	607-432-1000
Press-Republican					
170 Margaret St PO Box 459	Plattsburgh	NY	12901	**800-288-7323**	518-561-2300
Poughkeepsie Journal					
85 Civic Ctr Plz	Poughkeepsie	NY	12601	**800-765-1120**	845-437-4800
Daily Record 16 W Main St	Rochester	NY	14614	**800-451-9998**	585-232-6920
Democrat & Chronicle					
55 Exchange Blvd	Rochester	NY	14614	**800-790-9565**	585-232-7100
Daily Gazette Co, The					
2345 Maxon Rd Ext PO Box 1090.	Schenectady	NY	12301	**800-262-2211**	518-374-4141
Staten Island Advance					
950 W FingerboaRd Rd	Staten Island	NY	10305	**800-675-8645**	718-981-1234
Post-Standard					
220 S Warren St	Syracuse	NY	13202	**866-447-3787**	315-470-0011
Watertown Daily Times					
260 Washington St	Watertown	NY	13601	**800-642-6222**	315-782-1000

	Toll-Free	Phone

North Carolina

				Toll-Free	Phone
Courier-Tribune					
500 Sunset Ave	Asheboro	NC	27203	**800-488-0444**	336-625-2101
Asheville Citizen Times					
14 O'Henry Ave	Asheville	NC	28801	**800-672-2472**	828-252-5611
Charlotte Observer, The					
600 S Tryon St	Charlotte	NC	28202	**800-332-0686**	704-358-5000
Fayetteville Observer					
458 Whitfield St	Fayetteville	NC	28306	**800-345-9895**	910-323-4848
News & Record					
200 E Market St	Greensboro	NC	27401	**800-553-6880**	336-373-7000
Times-News					
PO Box 490	Hendersonville	NC	28793	**800-849-8050**	828-692-0505
News & Observer					
215 S McDowell St	Raleigh	NC	27602	**800-522-4205**	919-829-4500
Winston-Salem Journal					
418 N Marshall St	Winston-Salem	NC	27101	**800-642-0925**	336-727-7211

North Dakota

				Toll-Free	Phone
Bismarck Tribune					
707 E Front Ave	Bismarck	ND	58504	**866-476-5348**	701-223-2500
Forum, The 101 N Fifth St	Fargo	ND	58102	**800-274-5445**	701-235-7311
Minot Daily News					
301 Fourth St SE	Minot	ND	58702	**800-735-3119**	701-857-1900

Ohio

				Toll-Free	Phone
Star Beacon PO Box 2100	Ashtabula	OH	44005	**800-554-6768**	440-998-2323
Chillicothe Gazette					
50 W Main St	Chillicothe	OH	45601	**877-424-0215**	740-773-2111
Cincinnati Enquirer					
312 Elm St	Cincinnati	OH	45202	**800-876-4500**	513-721-2700
Dayton Daily News					
1611 S Main St	Dayton	OH	45409	**888-397-6397**	937-225-2000
Record-Courier 1050 W Main St	Kent	OH	44240	**800-560-9657**	330-541-9400
Lancaster Eagle-Gazette					
138 W Chestnut St	Lancaster	OH	43130	**877-513-7355**	740-654-1321
Lima News 3515 Elida Rd	Lima	OH	45807	**800-686-9924**	419-223-1010
Morning Journal					
1657 Broadway Ave	Lorain	OH	44052	**888-757-0727**	440-245-6901
News Journal					
70 W Fourth St	Mansfield	OH	44903	**877-424-0216**	419-522-3311
Marion Star, The					
163 E Center St	Marion	OH	43302	**877-987-2782**	740-387-0400
Gazette, The					
885 W Liberty St	Medina	OH	44256	**800-633-4623**	330-725-4299
Times Reporter					
629 Wabash Ave NW	New Philadelphia	OH	44663	**800-686-5577**	330-364-5577
Advocate, The 22 N First St	Newark	OH	43055	**877-424-0208**	740-345-4053
Portsmouth Daily Times					
637 Sixth St	Portsmouth	OH	45662	**800-582-7277**	740-353-3101
Springfield News-Sun					
202 N Limestone St	Springfield	OH	45503	**800-441-6397**	937-328-0300
Blade 541 N Superior St	Toledo	OH	43660	**800-245-3317**	419-724-6000
News-Herald					
7085 Mentor Ave	Willoughby	OH	44094	**800-947-2737**	440-951-0000
Daily Record					
212 E Liberty St PO Box 918	Wooster	OH	44691	**800-686-2958**	330-264-1125
Zanesville Times Recorder					
3871 Gorsky Dr Unit G1	Zanesville	OH	43701	**877-424-0214**	740-452-4561

Oklahoma

				Toll-Free	Phone
Enid News & Eagle					
227 W Broadway PO Box 1192	Enid	OK	73701	**800-299-6397**	580-548-8186
Journal Record Oklahoma City					
101 N Robinson St Ste 101	Oklahoma City	OK	73102	**800-451-9998**	405-235-3100
Oklahoman, The					
100 W Main St	Oklahoma City	OK	73102	**877-987-2737**	405-475-3311
Tulsa World 315 S Boulder Ave	Tulsa	OK	74103	**800-897-3557**	918-583-2161

Oregon

				Toll-Free	Phone
Bulletin, The					
1777 Chandler Ave	Bend	OR	97702	**800-503-3933**	541-382-1811
Register-Guard 3500 Chad Dr	Eugene	OR	97408	**800-377-7428**	541-485-1234
Daily Courier					
409 SE Seventh St	Grants Pass	OR	97526	**800-228-0457**	541-474-3700
Daily Journal of Commerce					
921 SW Washington St Ste 210	Portland	OR	97205	**800-451-9998**	503-226-1311
Oregonian 1320 SW Broadway	Portland	OR	97201	**800-723-3638***	503-221-8100
*News Rm					
Statesman Journal					
280 Church St NE	Salem	OR	97301	**800-874-7012**	503-399-6611

Pennsylvania

				Toll-Free	Phone
Morning Call PO Box 1260	Allentown	PA	18105	**800-666-5492**	610-820-6500
Altoona Mirror					
301 Cayuga Ave	Altoona	PA	16602	**800-222-1962**	814-946-7411
Butler Eagle					
114 W Diamond St	Butler	PA	16001	**800-842-8098**	724-282-8000
Sentinel, The 457 E N St	Carlisle	PA	17013	**800-829-5570**	717-243-2611
Public Opinion					
77 N Third St	Chambersburg	PA	17201	**800-782-0661**	717-264-6161
Erie Times-News 205 W 12th St	Erie	PA	16534	**800-352-0043**	814-870-1600

				Toll-Free	Phone
Evening Sun					
135 Baltimore St	Hanover	PA	17331	**888-256-0125**	717-755-4452
Hazleton Standard Speaker					
21 N Wyoming St	Hazleton	PA	18201	**800-843-6680***	570-455-3636
*Cust Svc					
Wayne Independent					
220 Eigth St	Honesdale	PA	18431	**800-598-5002**	570-253-3055
Tribune-Democrat					
425 Locust St	Johnstown	PA	15907	**855-255-5975**	814-532-5050
Lebanon Daily News					
718 Poplar St	Lebanon	PA	17042	**800-457-5929**	717-272-5611
Meadville Tribune					
947 Federal Ct	Meadville	PA	16335	**800-879-0006**	814-724-6370
Patriot-News					
2020 Technology Pkwy Ste 300	Mechanicsburg	PA	17050	**800-692-7207**	717-255-8100
Philadelphia Inquirer					
801 Market St Ste 300					
PO Box 8263	Philadelphia	PA	19107	**800-341-3413**	215-854-2000
Pittsburgh Tribune-Review					
503 Martindale St Ste 300	Pittsburgh	PA	15212	**800-909-8742**	412-321-6460
Scranton Times-Tribune					
149 Penn Ave	Scranton	PA	18503	**800-228-4637**	570-348-9100
Herald, The 52 S Dock St	Sharon	PA	16146	**800-981-1692**	724-981-6100
Centre Daily Times					
3400 E College Ave	State College	PA	16801	**800-327-5500**	814-238-5000
Pocono Record					
511 Lenox St	Stroudsburg	PA	18360	**800-530-6310**	570-421-3000
Delaware County Daily Times					
639 S Chester Rd	Swarthmore	PA	19081	**888-799-6299**	610-622-8800
Valley News Dispatch					
210 Fourth Ave	Tarentum	PA	15084	**800-909-8742**	
Herald-Standard					
8 E Church St	Uniontown	PA	15401	**800-342-8254**	724-439-7500
Daily Local News					
250 N Bradford Ave	West Chester	PA	19382	**800-568-7355**	610-696-1775
Williamsport Sun-Gazette					
252 W Fourth St	Williamsport	PA	17701	**800-339-0289**	570-326-1551
York Daily Record (YDR)					
1891 Loucks Rd	York	PA	17408	**800-559-3520**	717-771-2000

Rhode Island

				Toll-Free	Phone
Providence Journal					
75 Fountain St	Providence	RI	02902	**888-697-7656**	401-277-7303

South Carolina

				Toll-Free	Phone
Island Packet, The					
10 Buck Island Rd	Bluffton	SC	29910	**877-706-8100**	
Greenville News					
305 S Main St	Greenville	SC	29601	**800-800-5116**	864-298-4100
Sun News					
914 Frontage Rd E	Myrtle Beach	SC	29578	**800-568-1800**	843-626-8555

South Dakota

				Toll-Free	Phone
Aberdeen American News					
124 S Second St	Aberdeen	SD	57402	**800-925-4100**	605-229-5555
Capital Journal					
333 W Dakota Ave	Pierre	SD	57501	**800-537-0025**	605-224-7301
Rapid City Journal					
507 Main St	Rapid City	SD	57701	**800-843-2300**	605-394-8300

Tennessee

				Toll-Free	Phone
Jackson Sun					
245 W LaFayette St	Jackson	TN	38301	**800-372-3922**	731-427-3333
Johnson City Press					
204 W Main St	Johnson City	TN	37604	**800-949-3111**	423-929-3111
Kingsport Times-News					
701 Lynn Garden Dr	Kingsport	TN	37660	**800-251-0328**	423-246-8121
Knoxville News-Sentinel					
2332 News Sentinel Dr	Knoxville	TN	37921	**800-237-5821**	865-521-8181
Commercial Appeal					
495 Union Ave	Memphis	TN	38103	**800-444-6397**	901-529-2345
Citizen Tribune					
1609 W First N St PO Box 625	Morristown	TN	37815	**800-624-0281**	423-581-5630
Tennessean 1100 Broadway	Nashville	TN	37203	**800-342-8237**	615-259-8000

Texas

				Toll-Free	Phone
Abilene Reporter-News					
101 Cypress St	Abilene	TX	79601	**866-604-2020**	325-673-4271
Amarillo Globe News					
PO Box 2091	Amarillo	TX	79166	**800-692-4052**	806-376-4488
Austin American-Statesman					
305 S Congress Ave	Austin	TX	78704	**800-445-9898**	512-445-4040
Brownsville Herald, The					
1135 E Van Buren St	Brownsville	TX	78520	**800-488-4301**	956-542-4301
Bryan-College Station Eagle					
1729 Briarcrest Dr	Bryan	TX	77802	**800-299-7355**	979-776-4444
Brazosport Facts					
720 S Main St	Clute	TX	77531	**800-864-8340**	979-265-7411
Caller-Times					
820 N Lower Broadway	Corpus Christi	TX	78401	**800-827-2011**	361-884-2011
Dallas Morning News					
508 Young St	Dallas	TX	75202	**800-925-1500**	214-977-8222
Denton Record-Chronicle					
314 E Hickory St	Denton	TX	76201	**800-275-1722**	940-387-3811
Galveston County Daily News					
8522 Teichman Rd PO Box 628	Galveston	TX	77553	**800-561-3611**	409-683-5200

Classified Section

					Toll-Free	Phone

Houston Chronicle
801 Texas Ave .... Houston TX 77002 — **800-735-3800** — 713-362-7171

Laredo Morning Times
111 Esperanza Dr .... Laredo TX 78041 — **800-232-7907** — 956-728-2500

Longview News-Journal
320 E Methvin St .... Longview TX 75601 — **800-825-9799** — 903-757-3311

Lubbock Avalanche-Journal
710 Ave J .... Lubbock TX 79401 — **800-692-4021** — 806-762-8844

Monitor, The
1400 E Nolana Loop .... Mcallen TX 78504 — **800-366-4343** — 956-683-4000

Midland Reporter-Telegram
PO Box 1650 .... Midland TX 79702 — **800-542-3952** — 432-682-5311

Odessa American PO Box 2952 .... Odessa TX 79760 — **800-592-4433** — 432-337-4661

Herald Democrat
603 S Sam Rayburn Fwy .... Sherman TX 75090 — **800-827-7183** — 903-893-8181

Victoria Advocate
PO Box 1518 .... Victoria TX 77902 — **800-234-8108** — 361-575-1451

Waco Tribune-Herald
900 Franklin Ave .... Waco TX 76701 — **800-678-8742** — 254-757-5757

Utah

	Toll-Free	Phone

Herald Journal 75 W 300 N .... Logan UT 84321 — **800-275-0423** — 435-752-2121

Standard-Examiner
332 Standard Way .... Ogden UT 84404 — **888-221-7070** — 801-625-4200

Daily Herald
1555 N Freedom Blvd .... Provo UT 84604 — **800-880-8075** — 801-373-5050

Deseret News
55 North 300 West Ste 500 .... Salt Lake City UT 84101 — **866-628-4677** — 801-204-6100

Vermont

	Toll-Free	Phone

Burlington Free Press
100 Bank St .... Burlington VT 05401 — **800-427-3124** — 802-660-1819

Rutland Herald PO Box 668 .... Rutland VT 05702 — **800-498-4296**

Virginia

	Toll-Free	Phone

Bristol Herald-Courier
320 Bob Morrison Blvd .... Bristol VA 24201 — **888-228-2098** — 276-669-2181

Free Lance Star
616 Amelia St .... Fredericksburg VA 22401 — **800-877-0500** — 540-374-5000

News & Advance
PO Box 10129 .... Lynchburg VA 24506 — **800-275-8830** — 434-385-5555

Martinsville Bulletin
PO Box 3711 .... Martinsville VA 24115 — **800-234-6575** — 276-638-8801

Roanoke Times
201 W Campbell Ave SW .... Roanoke VA 24011 — **800-346-1234** — 540-981-3340

News Leader
11 N Central Ave .... Staunton VA 24401 — **800-793-2459** — 540-885-7281

Washington

	Toll-Free	Phone

Tri-City Herald
333 W Canal Dr .... Kennewick WA 99336 — **800-874-0445** — 509-582-1500

Daily News
770 11th Ave PO Box 189 .... Longview WA 98632 — **800-341-4745** — 360-577-2500

Skagit Valley Herald
1000 E College Way .... Mount Vernon WA 98273 — **800-683-3300** — 360-424-3251

Olympian, The PO Box 407 .... Olympia WA 98507 — **800-905-0296** — 360-754-5400

Peninsula Daily News
305 W First St PO Box 1330 .... Port Angeles WA 98362 — **800-826-7714** — 360-452-2345

Seattle Post-Intelligencer
200 First Ave W Ste 230 .... Seattle WA 98119 — **800-542-0820** — 206-448-8030

Columbian
701 W Eigth St PO Box 180 .... Vancouver WA 98660 — **800-743-3391** — 360-694-3391

Wenatchee World
14 N Mission St .... Wenatchee WA 98801 — **800-572-4433** — 509-663-5161

Yakima Herald-Republic
PO Box 9668 .... Yakima WA 98909 — **800-343-2799** — 509-248-1251

West Virginia

	Toll-Free	Phone

Register-Herald
801 N Kanawha St .... Beckley WV 25801 — **800-950-0250** — 304-255-4400

Clarksburg Exponent Telegram
324 Hewes Ave .... Clarksburg WV 26301 — **800-982-6034** — 304-626-1400

Exponent Telegram
324 Hewes Ave .... Clarksburg WV 26301 — **800-982-6034**

Herald-Dispatch
946 Fifth Ave .... Huntington WV 25701 — **800-444-2446** — 304-526-4000

Journal, The
207 W King St .... Martinsburg WV 25402 — **800-448-1895** — 304-263-8931

Parkersburg News
519 Juliana St .... Parkersburg WV 26101 — **800-642-1997** — 304-485-1891

Wisconsin

	Toll-Free	Phone

Leader-Telegram
701 S Farwell St .... Eau Claire WI 54701 — **800-236-8808** — 715-833-9200

GazetteXtra
Janesville Gazette
1 S Parker Dr PO Box 5001 .... Janesville WI 53547 — **800-362-6712** — 608-755-8250

Kenosha News
5800 Seventh Ave .... Kenosha WI 53140 — **800-292-2700** — 262-657-1000

La Crosse Tribune
401 N Third St .... La Crosse WI 54601 — **800-262-0420** — 608-782-9710

Capital Times
1901 Fish Hatchery Rd .... Madison WI 53713 — **800-362-8333** — 608-252-6400

Wisconsin State Journal
1901 Fish Hatchery Rd .... Madison WI 53713 — **800-362-8333** — 608-252-6200

Herald Times Reporter
902 Franklin St .... Manitowoc WI 54220 — **800-783-7323** — 920-684-4433

Journal Times 212 Fourth St .... Racine WI 53403 — **888-460-8725**

Sheboygan Press
632 Center Ave .... Sheboygan WI 53081 — **800-686-3900** — 920-843-9656

Waukesha County Freeman
801 N Barstow St PO Box 7 .... Waukesha WI 53187 — **800-762-6219** — 262-542-2501

Wausau Daily Herald
800 Scott St .... Wausau WI 54403 — **800-477-4838** — 715-842-2101

Wyoming

	Toll-Free	Phone

Star-Tribune 170 Star Ln .... Casper WY 82604 — **866-981-6397** — 307-266-0500

Wyoming Tribune-Eagle
702 W Lincolnway .... Cheyenne WY 82001 — **800-561-6268** — 307-634-3361

528-3 National Newspapers

	Toll-Free	Phone

Alliance Publishing Company Inc
40 S Linden Ave .... Alliance OH 44601 — **800-778-0098** — 330-821-1200

Bedford Gazette
424 W Penn St .... Bedford PA 15522 — **800-242-4250** — 814-623-1151

Charleston Newspapers Ltd
1001 Virginia St E .... Charleston WV 25301 — **800-982-6397** — 304-348-4848

Circle Media Inc
5817 Old Leeds Rd .... Irondale AL 35210 — **800-356-9916**

Daily Item, The
200 Market St .... Sunbury PA 17801 — **800-326-9608** — 570-286-5671

Drummer Online & Wright County Journal Press
108 Central Ave PO Box 159 .... Buffalo MN 55313 — **800-880-5047** — 763-682-1221

Grant County Herald
35 Central Ave N .... Elbow Lake MN 56531 — **877-852-2796** — 218-685-5326

Havre Daily News
119 Second St .... Havre MT 59501 — **800-993-2459** — 406-265-6795

he Press & Sun-Bulletin
33 Lewis Rd Ste 9 .... Binghamton NY 13905 — **800-253-5343** — 607-798-1234

High Country News
119 Grand Ave .... Paonia CO 81428 — **800-311-5852** — 970-527-4898

Jewish Press Inc
4915 16th Ave .... Brooklyn NY 11204 — **800-992-1600** — 718-330-1100

Kentucky New Era
1618 E Ninth St .... Hopkinsville KY 42240 — **877-463-9372** — 270-886-4444

La Jolla Light Newspaper
565 Pearl St Ste 300 .... La Jolla CA 92037 — **800-691-0952** — 858-459-4201

Lafromboise Communications Inc
321 N Pearl St .... Centralia WA 98531 — **800-356-4404** — 360-736-3311

Lawyers Weekly Inc
10 Milk St Ste 1000 .... Boston MA 02108 — **800-444-5297** — 617-451-7300

Lewistown News-Argus, The
521 W Main St PO Box 900 .... Lewistown MT 59457 — **800-879-5627** — 406-535-3401

Mid Atlantic Printers Ltd
503 Third St .... Altavista VA 24517 — **888-231-3175** — 434-369-6633

Mobridge Tribune
1413 E Grand Xing .... Mobridge SD 57601 — **800-594-9418** — 605-845-3646

Morris Herald-News
1804 N Division St .... Morris IL 60450 — **800-397-9397** — 815-942-3221

New Century Press Inc
310 First Ave .... Rock Rapids IA 51246 — **800-621-0801** — 712-472-2525

News Examiner, The
847 Washington St .... Montpelier ID 83254 — **800-847-0465** — 208-847-0552

News-banner Publications Inc
125 N Johnson St .... Bluffton IN 46714 — **800-579-7476** — 260-824-0224

Payson Roundup Newspaper
708 N Beeline Hwy .... Payson AZ 85541 — **800-253-9405** — 928-474-5251

Santa Cruz Sentinel Inc
207 Church St .... Santa Cruz CA 95060 — **800-952-2335** — 831-423-4242

Sentinel Power Services Inc
7517 E Pine St .... Tulsa OK 74115 — **800-831-9550** — 918-359-0350

Sentinel Systems Corp
1620 Kipling St .... Lakewood CO 80215 — **800-456-9955** — 303-242-2000

Smart Business Network Inc
835 Sharon Dr Ste 200 .... Cleveland OH 44145 — **800-988-4726**

Swift Communications Inc
580 Mallory Way .... Carson City NV 89701 — **800-551-5691** — 775-283-5500

USA Today
7950 Jones Branch Dr .... McLean VA 22108 — **800-872-0001***
*Cust Svc — 703-854-3400

Wall Street Journal, The
1211 Ave of the Americas .... New York NY 10036 — **800-568-7625***
*General — 212-416-2000

Winneconne News
908 E Main St .... Winneconne WI 54986 — **800-545-5026** — 920-582-4541

528-4 Weekly Newspapers

Listings here are organized by city names within state groupings.

California

	Toll-Free	Phone

Independent, The
2250 First St .... Livermore CA 94550 — **877-952-3588** — 925-447-8700

Los Angeles Downtown News
1264 W First St .... Los Angeles CA 90026 — **877-338-1010** — 213-481-1448

Mammoth Times, The
PO Box 3929 .... Mammoth Lakes CA 93546 — **800-427-7623** — 760-934-3929

Almanac, The
3525 Alameda De Las Pulgas .... Menlo Park CA 94025 — **800-799-4811** — 650-854-2626

Milpitas Post
59 Marylinn Dr .... Milpitas CA 95035 — **800-870-6397** — 408-262-2454

Colorado

			Toll-Free	Phone
Sentinel 12100 E Iliff Ave Ste 102	Aurora CO	80014	855-269-4484	303-750-7555

Connecticut

			Toll-Free	Phone
Bridgeport News 1000 Bridgeport Ave *Advestisement	Shelton CT	06484	855-247-8573*	860-491-9988

Delaware

			Toll-Free	Phone
Dover Post 1196 S Little Creek Rd	Dover DE	19901	800-942-1616	302-678-3616

Florida

			Toll-Free	Phone
Clay Today 3513 US Hwy 17	Fleming Island FL	32003	888-434-9844	904-264-3200

Illinois

			Toll-Free	Phone
Chicago Tribune 160 N Stetson Ave	Chicago IL	60601	800-874-2863	312-222-3232
Des Plaines Journal 622 Graceland Ave	Des Plaines IL	60016	800-719-4881	847-299-5511
Galena Gazette 716 S Bench St	Galena IL	61036	800-373-6397	815-777-0019

Indiana

			Toll-Free	Phone
Hendricks County Flyer 8109 Kingston St Ste 500	Avon IN	46123	800-359-3747	317-272-5800

Louisiana

			Toll-Free	Phone
Times of Acadiana 1100 Bertrand Dr	Lafayette LA	70506	877-289-2216	337-289-6300

Michigan

			Toll-Free	Phone
Camden Publications 331 E Bell St	Camden MI	49232	800-222-6336	517-368-0365
Cedar Springs Post 36 E Maple PO Box 370	Cedar Springs MI	49319	888-937-4514	616-696-3655
Dearborn Times-Herald 13730 Michigan Ave	Dearborn MI	48126	866-468-7630	313-584-4000
Grand Valley Advance 2141 Port Sheldon St	Jenison MI	49428	800-878-1400	

Minnesota

			Toll-Free	Phone
Morrison County Record 216 SE First St	Little Falls MN	56345	888-637-2345	320-632-2345

Missouri

			Toll-Free	Phone
Farmington Press 218 N Washington St	Farmington MO	63640	800-455-0206	573-756-8927
Jefferson County Journal 1405 N Truman Blvd	Festus MO	63028	800-365-0820	636-937-9811
Washington Missourian 14 W Main St PO Box 336	Washington MO	63090	888-239-7701	636-239-7701

New Jersey

			Toll-Free	Phone
Hunterdon County Democrat 8 Minneakoning Rd	Flemington NJ	08822	888-782-7533	908-782-4747
Central Record PO Box 1027	Medford NJ	08055	800-825-7653	609-654-5000

North Dakota

			Toll-Free	Phone
Plains Reporter PO Box 1447	Williston ND	58802	800-950-2165	701-572-2165

Ohio

			Toll-Free	Phone
Record-Courier 1050 W Main St	Kent OH	44240	800-560-9657	330-541-9400
Suburban Press & Metro Press 1550 Woodville Rd	Millbury OH	43447	800-300-6158	419-836-2221

Oregon

			Toll-Free	Phone
Hillsboro Argus 1500 SW First Ave	Portland OR	97201	800-544-0505	503-648-1131

Pennsylvania

			Toll-Free	Phone
York Sunday News 1891 Loucks Rd	York PA	17408	888-629-4095	717-767-6397

Vermont

			Toll-Free	Phone
World, The 403 US Rt 302-Berlin	Barre VT	05641	800-639-9753	802-479-2582

Virginia

			Toll-Free	Phone
Mechanicsville Local 6400 Mechanicsville Tpke	Mechanicsville VA	23111	800-468-3382	804-746-1235

Washington

			Toll-Free	Phone
Tribune Newspapers of Snohomish County 127 Ave C Ste B PO Box 499	Snohomish WA	98291	877-894-4663	360-568-4121

528-5 Weekly Newspapers - Alternative

			Toll-Free	Phone
Chico News & Review 353 E Second St	Chico CA	95928	866-703-3873	530-894-2300
Dayton City Paper 126 N Main St Ste 240	Dayton OH	45402	888-228-3630	937-222-8855
Houston Press 1621 Milam St Ste 100	Houston TX	77002	877-926-8300	713-280-2400
LA Weekly 6715 Sunset Blvd	Los Angeles CA	90028	866-789-6188	
Long Island Press 575 Underhill Blvd Ste 210	Syosset NY	11791	800-545-6683	516-284-3300
Memphis Flyer 460 Tennessee St	Memphis TN	38103	877-292-3804	901-521-9000
Minneapolis/St Paul City Pages 401 N Third St Ste 550	Minneapolis MN	55401	844-387-6962	612-375-1015
OC Weekly 2975 Red Hill Ave Ste 150	Costa Mesa CA	92626	800-300-4345	714-550-5900
Pacific Northwest Inlander 1227 W Summit Pkwy	Spokane WA	99201	866-444-3066	509-325-0634

529   NURSES ASSOCIATIONS - STATE

SEE ALSO Health & Medical Professionals Associations

			Toll-Free	Phone
Alabama State Nurses Assn (ASNA) 360 N Hull St	Montgomery AL	36104	800-270-2762	334-262-8321
Alaska Municipal League Joint Insurance Assn 807 G St Ste 356	Anchorage AK	99501	800-337-3682	907-258-2625
Arizona Osteopathic Medical Assn 5150 N 16th St Ste A122	Phoenix AZ	85016	888-266-6699	602-266-6699
CAI-CLAC 1809 S St Ste 101-245	Sacramento CA	95811	888-909-7403	916-791-4750
Chester County Bar Association, The 15 W Gay St 2nd Fl	West Chester PA	19380	800-701-5161	610-692-1889
Delaware Nurses Assn (DNA) 4765 Ogletown-Stanton Rd Ste L10	Newark DE	19713	800-626-4081	302-733-5880
Federal Hearings & Appeals Services Inc 117 W Main St	Plymouth PA	18651	800-664-7177	570-779-5122
Georgia Municipal Association 201 Pryor St SW	Atlanta GA	30303	888-488-4462	404-688-0472
Georgia Nurses Assn (GNA) 3032 Briarcliff Rd NE	Atlanta GA	30329	800-324-0462	404-325-5536
Hawaii Nurses Assn (HNA) 949 Kapiolani Blvd Ste 107	Honolulu HI	96814	800-617-2677	808-531-1628
Ichp Building Company LLC 4055 N Perryville Rd	Loves Park IL	61111	800-363-8012	815-227-9292
Idaho Nurses Assn (INA) 1850 E Southern Ave Ste 1	Tempe AZ	85282	888-721-8904	
Illinois Health Care Association 1029 S Fourth St	Springfield IL	62703	800-252-8988	217-528-6455
Illinois Nurses Assn (INA) 105 W Adams St Ste 2101	Chicago IL	60603	800-262-2500	312-419-2900
International Association of Privacy Professionals (Iapp) 75 Rochester Ave Ste 4	Portsmouth NH	03801	800-266-6501	603-427-9200
Iowa Mortgage Association 8800 NW 62nd Ave	Johnston IA	50131	800-800-2353	515-286-4352
Kentucky Bankers Assn 600 W Main St Ste 400	Louisville KY	40202	800-392-4045	502-582-2453
Kentucky Hospital Assn 2501 Nelson Miller Pkwy	Louisville KY	40223	888-393-7353	502-426-6220
League of Kansas Municipalities, The 300 SW Eighth Ave Ste 100	Topeka KS	66603	800-445-5588	785-354-9565
Louisiana State Nurses Assn (LSNA) 543 Spanish Town Rd	Baton Rouge LA	70802	800-457-6378	225-201-0993
Maryland Municipal League 1212 W St	Annapolis MD	21401	800-492-7121	410-295-9100
Massachusetts Nurses Assn (MNA) 340 Tpke St	Canton MA	02021	800-882-2056	781-821-4625
Mha an Association of Montana Health Care Providers 2625 Winne Ave	Helena MT	59601	800-351-3551	406-442-1911
Minnesota Nurses Assn (MNA) 345 Randolph Ave Ste 200	Saint Paul MN	55102	800-536-4662	651-414-2800
Nebraska Nurses Assn (NNA) PO Box 3107	Kearney NE	68848	888-885-7025	
New Jersey State Nurses Assn (NJSNA) 1479 Pennington Rd	Trenton NJ	08618	800-662-0108	609-883-5335
New York County Lawyers Association 14 Vesey St	New York NY	10007	800-255-0569	212-267-6646
North Carolina Nurses Assn (NCNA) 103 Enterprise St PO Box 12025	Raleigh NC	27605	800-626-2153	919-821-4250
Ohio Nurses Assn (ONA) 4000 E Main St	Columbus OH	43213	800-735-0056	614-237-5414
Oregon Nurses Assn (ONA) 18765 SW Boones Ferry Rd	Tualatin OR	97062	800-634-3552	503-293-0011

Classified Section

	Toll-Free	Phone

Oregon Society of CPA's
10206 SW Laurel St . . . . Beaverton OR 97005 | 800-255-1470 | 503-641-7200

Pennsylvania Assn of Staff Nurses & Allied Professionals (PASNAP)
1 Fayette St Ste 475 . . . . Conshohocken PA 19428 | 800-500-7850 | 610-567-2907

Planetree Inc 130 Division St . . . . Derby CT 06418 | 800-222-2818 | 203-732-1365

Red Hat Society Store
431 S Acacia Ave . . . . Fullerton CA 92831 | 866-386-2850 | 714-738-0001

South Carolina Education Association, The
421 Zimalcrest Dr . . . . Columbia SC 29210 | 800-422-7232 | 803-772-6553

South Dakota Nurses Assn (SDNA)
PO Box 1015 . . . . Pierre SD 57501 | 888-425-3032 | 605-945-4265

Tennessee State Employees Association
627 Woodland St . . . . Nashville TN 37206 | 800-251-8732 | 615-256-4533

Vermont State Nurses Assn (VSNA)
4 Carmichael St Ste 111 Rm 215 . . . . Essex VT 05452 | 877-810-5972 |

Washington State Nurses Assn (WSNA)
575 Andover Pk W Ste 101 . . . . Seattle WA 98188 | 800-231-8482 | 206-575-7979

West Virginia Nurses Assn (WVNA)
PO Box 1946 . . . . Charleston WV 25327 | 800-400-1226 | 304-417-1497

Western Institutional Review Board Inc
1019 39th Ave SE Ste 120 . . . . Puyallup WA 98374 | 800-562-4789 | 360-252-2500

530   OFFICE & SCHOOL SUPPLIES

SEE ALSO Writing Paper ; Printing & Photocopying Supplies ; Pens, Pencils, Parts ; Office Supply Stores

	Toll-Free	Phone

Acroprint Time Recorder Co
5640 Departure Dr . . . . Raleigh NC 27616 | 800-334-7190 | 919-872-5800

American Product Distributors Inc (APD)
8350 Arrowridge Blvd . . . . Charlotte NC 28273 | 800-849-5842 | 704-522-9411

American Solutions for Business
31 E Minnesota Ave E . . . . Glenwood MN 56334 | 800-862-3690 |

Arlington Industries Inc
1616 Lakeside Dr . . . . Waukegan IL 60085 | 800-323-4147 | 847-689-2754

Aurora Corp of America
3500 Challenger St . . . . Torrance CA 90503 | 800-327-8508 | 310-793-5650

Avery Dennison Corp
207 Goode Ave . . . . Glendale CA 91203 | 888-567-4387* | 626-304-2000
*NYSE: AVY ■ *Cust Svc*

Avery Dennison Worldwide Office Products Div
207 Goode Ave . . . . Glendale CA 91203 | 800-462-8379 | 626-304-2000

Bartizan Corp
217 Riverdale Ave . . . . Yonkers NY 10705 | 800-899-2278 | 914-965-7977

Baumgarten's 144 Ottley Dr . . . . Atlanta GA 30324 | 800-247-5547 | 404-874-7675

C-Line Products Inc
1100 E Business Ctr Dr . . . . Mount Prospect IL 60056 | 800-323-6084 | 847-827-6661

Cardinal Office Products Inc
576 E Main St . . . . Frankfort KY 40601 | 800-589-5886 | 502-875-3300

Case Logic Inc
6303 Dry Creek Pkwy . . . . Longmont CO 80503 | 800-925-8111 | 303-652-1000

Champion Industries Inc
PO Box 2968 . . . . Huntington WV 25728 | 800-624-3431 | 304-528-2791
OTC: CHMP

Dahle North America Inc
49 Vose Farm Rd . . . . Peterborough NH 03458 | 800-243-8145 | 603-924-0003

Deflect-O Corp
7035 E 86th St . . . . Indianapolis IN 46250 | 800-428-4328 |

Douglas Stewart Co, The
2402 Advance Rd . . . . Madison WI 53718 | 800-279-2795 | 608-221-1155

Eaton Office Supply Company Inc
180 John Glenn Dr . . . . Buffalo NY 14228 | 800-365-3237 | 716-691-6100

GBS Corp
7233 Freedom Ave NW . . . . North Canton OH 44720 | 800-552-2427 | 330-494-5330

International Imaging Materials Inc
310 Commerce Dr . . . . Amherst NY 14228 | 888-464-4625 | 716-691-6333

Lakeshore Learning Materials
2695 E Dominguez St . . . . Carson CA 90895 | 800-778-4456 | 310-537-8600

Lee Products Co
800 E 80th St . . . . Bloomington MN 55420 | 800-989-3544 | 952-854-3544

Magna Visual Inc
9400 Watson Rd . . . . Sappington MO 63126 | 800-843-3399 |

Millennium Marking Company Inc
2600 Greenleaf Ave . . . . Elk Grove Village IL 60007 | 800-453-5362 |

PBS Supply Company Inc
7013 S 216th St . . . . Kent WA 98032 | 877-727-7515 | 253-395-5550

PerfectData Corp
1323 Conshohocken Rd . . . . Plymouth Meeting PA 19462 | 800-973-7332 |

Staples Business Advantage
500 Staples Dr . . . . Framingham MA 01702 | 877-826-7755 |

TAB Products Co
605 Fourth St . . . . Mayville WI 53050 | 888-466-8228 |

Van Ausdall & Farrar Inc
6430 E 75th St . . . . Indianapolis IN 46250 | 800-467-7474 | 317-634-2913

Weeks-Lerman Group
58-38 Page Pl . . . . Maspeth NY 11378 | 800-544-5959 | 718-803-5000

531   OFFICE SUPPLY STORES

	Toll-Free	Phone

Audit & Adjustment Company Inc
20700 44th Ave W Ste 100 . . . . Lynnwood WA 98036 | 800-526-1074 | 425-776-9797

BenefitHelp Solutions Inc
10505 SE 17th Ave . . . . Milwaukie OR 97222 | 888-398-8057 | 503-219-3679

Benjamin Office Supply & Services Inc
758 E Gude Dr . . . . Rockville MD 20850 | 877-439-2677 | 301-340-1384

C M School Supply Inc
940 N Central Ave . . . . Upland CA 91786 | 800-464-6681 | 909-982-9695

Create-a-card Inc
16 Brasswood Rd . . . . Saint James NY 11780 | 800-753-6867 | 631-584-2273

DBI Inc 912 E Michigan Ave . . . . Lansing MI 48912 | 800-968-1324 | 517-485-3200

Discover Group Inc
2741 W 23rd St . . . . Brooklyn NY 11224 | 866-456-6555 | 718-456-4500

Dynetics
1002 Explorer Blvd . . . . Huntsville AL 35806 | 800-964-4291 | 256-964-4000

	Toll-Free	Phone

Eakes Office Plus
617 W Third St . . . . Grand Island NE 68801 | 800-652-9396 | 308-382-8026

Econ-o-copy Inc
4437 Trenton St Ste A . . . . Metairie LA 70006 | 877-256-0310 | 504-457-0032

Egyptian Workspace Partner
129 W Main St . . . . Belleville IL 62220 | 800-642-3949* | 618-234-2323
**Cust Svc*

Envoy Plan Services Inc
901 Calle Amanecer Ste 200 . . . . San Clemente CA 92673 | 800-248-8858 | 949-366-5070

Friend's Professional Stationery Inc
1535 Lewis Ave . . . . Zion IL 60099 | 800-323-4394 |

Gobin's Inc
615 N Santa Fe Ave . . . . Pueblo CO 81003 | 800-425-2324 | 719-544-2324

Hurst Group 500 Buck Pl . . . . Lexington KY 40511 | 800-926-4423 | 859-255-4422

Kennedy Office Supply
4211-A Atlantic Ave . . . . Raleigh NC 27604 | 800-733-9401 | 919-878-5400

Koch Brothers
325 Grand Ave . . . . Des Moines IA 50306 | 800-944-5624 | 515-283-2451

Lamination Depot Inc
1601 Alton Pkwy Ste E . . . . Irvine CA 92606 | 800-925-0054 | 714-954-0632

Matik Inc 33 Brook St . . . . West Hartford CT 06110 | 800-245-1628 | 860-232-2323

Mg Scientific Inc
8500 107th St . . . . Pleasant Prairie WI 53158 | 800-343-8338 | 262-947-7000

Northern Business Products Inc
PO Box 16127 . . . . Duluth MN 55816 | 800-647-8775 | 218-726-0167

Novatech
4106 Charlotte Ave . . . . Nashville TN 37209 | 800-264-0637 | 615-577-7677

Office Depot Inc
2200 Old Germantown Rd . . . . Delray Beach FL 33445 | 800-937-3600 | 561-438-4800
NASDAQ: ODP

Opus Framing Ltd
3445 Cornett Rd . . . . Vancouver BC V5M2H3 | 800-663-6953 | 604-435-9991

Phillips Group
501 Fulling Mill Rd . . . . Middletown PA 17057 | 800-538-7500 | 717-944-0400

Polack Corp, The
1400 Keystone Ave . . . . Lansing MI 48911 | 800-392-8759 | 517-272-1400

Prestige Graphics Inc
9630 Ridgehaven Ct Ste B . . . . San Diego CA 92123 | 800-383-9361 | 858-560-8213

Printers & Stationers Inc
113 N Ct St . . . . Florence AL 35630 | 800-624-5334 | 256-764-8061

Smith & Butterfield Co Inc
2800 Lynch Rd . . . . Evansville IN 47711 | 800-321-6543 | 812-422-3261

Stationers Inc
100 Industrial Ln . . . . Huntington WV 25702 | 800-862-7200 | 304-528-2780

Techneal Inc
2100 S Reservoir St . . . . Pomona CA 91766 | 800-545-6325 | 909-465-6325

Total Merchant Concepts Inc
12300 NE Fourth Plain Rd A . . . . Vancouver WA 98682 | 888-249-9919 | 360-253-5934

Triplett Office Essentials Corp
3553 109th St . . . . Urbandale IA 50322 | 800-437-5034 | 515-270-9150

Variant Microsystems
4128 Business Ctr Dr . . . . Fremont CA 94538 | 800-827-4268 | 510-440-2870

Veritas Press
1805 Olde Homestead Ln . . . . Lancaster PA 17601 | 800-922-5082 | 717-519-1974

WALZ Label & Mailing Systems
624 High Point Ln . . . . East Peoria IL 61611 | 877-971-1500 | 309-698-1500

Wist Office Products Co
107 W Julie Dr . . . . Tempe AZ 85283 | 800-999-9478 | 480-921-2900

Zymo Research Corp
17062 Murphy Ave . . . . Irvine CA 92614 | 888-882-9682 | 949-679-1190

532   OIL & GAS EXTRACTION

	Toll-Free	Phone

A H Belo Corp
1954 Commerce St PO Box 224866 . . . . Dallas TX 75201 | 800-230-1074 | 214-977-8200
NYSE: AHC

Allied-Horizontal Wireline Services
3200 Wilcrest Dr Ste 170 . . . . Houston TX 77042 | 888-494-9580 | 713-343-7280

AMERIgreen Energy Inc
1650 Manheim Pk Ste 201 . . . . Lancaster PA 17601 | 888-423-8357 | 717-945-1392

Anadarko Petroleum Corp
1201 Lake Robbins Dr . . . . The Woodlands TX 77380 | 800-800-1101 | 832-636-1000
NYSE: APC

Apache Corp
2000 Post Oak Blvd Ste 100 . . . . Houston TX 77056 | 800-272-2434 | 713-296-6000
NYSE: APA

Applied LNG
5716 Corsa Ave Ste 200 . . . . Westlake Village CA 91362 | 800-609-1702 | 818-450-3650

Baytex Energy Corp
2800 520 - Third Ave SW . . . . Calgary AB T2P0R3 | 800-524-5521 | 587-952-3000

BHP Billiton Petroleum (Americas) Inc
1360 Post Oak Blvd Ste 150 . . . . Houston TX 77056 | 800-359-1692 | 713-961-8500

Cabot Oil & Gas Corp
840 Gessner Rd Ste 1400 . . . . Houston TX 77024 | 800-434-3985 | 281-848-2799
NYSE: COG

Callon Petroleum Co
200 N Canal St . . . . Natchez MS 39120 | 800-451-1294 | 601-442-1601
NYSE: CPE

Canadian Natural Resources Ltd (CNRL)
855 Second St SW Ste 2100 . . . . Calgary AB T2P4J8 | 888-878-3700 | 403-517-6700
NYSE: CNQ

Canyon Explorations Inc
675 W Clay Ave . . . . Flagstaff AZ 86001 | 800-654-0723 | 928-774-4559

Chevron Corp
6001 Bollinger Canyon Rd . . . . San Ramon CA 94583 | 800-368-8357* | 925-842-1000
*NYSE: CVX ■ *Cust Svc*

Cimmaron Field Services Inc
303 W Wall St Bank of America Tower
Ste 600 . . . . Midland TX 79701 | 877-944-2705 |

Citizens Gas Fuel Co
127 North Main St . . . . Adrian MI 49221 | 800-482-7171 | 517-265-2144

ClearStream Energy Services
311 - 6 Ave SW Ste 415 . . . . Calgary AB T2P3H2 | 855-410-9835 | 587-318-0997

Coastal Mountain Fuels
501 Industrial Park Pl . . . . Gold River BC V0P2G0 | 800-798-3835 |

				Toll-Free	Phone
Comstock Resources Inc 5300 Town & Country Blvd Ste 500 *NYSE: CRK*	Frisco	TX	75034	**800-929-4884**	972-668-8800
Corridor Resources Inc 5475 Spring Garden Rd	Halifax	NS	B3J3T2	**888-429-4511**	902-429-4511
Crown Energy Co 1117 NW 24th St	Oklahoma City	OK	73106	**877-228-0801**	405-526-0111
Delphi Energy Corp 333 - 7 Ave SW Ste 2300	Calgary	AB	T2P2Z1	**800-430-7207**	403-265-6171
Denbury Resources Inc 5320 Legacy Dr *NYSE: DNR* ■ *General	Plano	TX	75024	**800-348-9030***	972-673-2000
Devon Energy Corp 333 West Sheridan Ave *NYSE: DVN*	Oklahoma City	OK	73102	**800-361-3377**	405-235-3611
DFI 2404 51 Ave NW	Edmonton	AB	T6P0E4	**877-334-7453**	
Dorchester Minerals LP 3838 Oak Lawn Ave Ste 300 *NASDAQ: DMLP*	Dallas	TX	75219	**800-690-6903**	214-559-0300
Doyon Ltd 1 Doyon Pl Ste 300	Fairbanks	AK	99701	**888-478-4755**	907-459-2000
Eagle Energy Trust 500 4 Ave SW Ste 2710	Calgary	AB	T2P2V6	**855-531-1575**	403-531-1575
EnCana Corp 500 Ctr St SE Po Box 2850 *TSE: ECA*	Calgary	AB	T2G1A6	**888-568-6322**	403-645-2000
EQT Corp 625 Liberty Ave Ste 1700 *NYSE: EQT*	Pittsburgh	PA	15222	**800-242-1776**	412-553-5700
Extreme Plastics Plus 360 Epic Circle Dr	Fairmont	WV	26554	**866-408-2837**	
Exxon Mobil Corp 5959 Las Colinas Blvd *NYSE: XOM*	Irving	TX	75039	**800-252-1800**	972-444-1000
Gear Energy Ltd 240 - Fourth Ave SW Ste 2600	Calgary	AB	T2P2V6	**877-494-3430**	403-538-8435
Geoforce Inc 750 Canyon Dr Ste 140	Coppell	TX	75019	**888-574-3878**	972-546-3878
Husky Energy Inc 707 Eigth Ave SW PO Box 6525 Stn D *TSE: HSE*	Calgary	AB	T2P1H5	**877-262-2111**	403-298-6111
Loftin Equipment Company Inc 12 N 45th Ave	Phoenix	AZ	85043	**800-437-4376**	602-272-9466
Manitok Energy Inc 444 Seventh Ave SW Ste 700	Calgary	AB	T2P0X8	**877-503-5957**	403-984-1750
Mitsubishi Hitachi Power Systems Americas Inc (MHPS) 400 Colonial Ctr Pkwy	Lake Mary	FL	32746	**800-445-9723**	407-688-6100
Newfield Exploration Co 24 Waterway Ave Ste 900 *NYSE: NFX*	The Woodlands	TX	77380	**866-902-0562**	281-847-6000
Noble Energy Inc 100 Glenborough Dr Ste 100 *NYSE: NBL*	Houston	TX	77067	**800-220-5824**	281-872-3100
North Atlantic 29 Pippy Pl	St. John's	NL	A1B3X2	**877-635-3645**	709-463-8811
Ohio Gas Co PO Box 528	Bryan	OH	43506	**800-331-7396**	419-636-1117
OriginClear Inc 5645 W Adams Blvd	Los Angeles	CA	90016	**877-999-6645**	323-939-6645
Oryx Midstream Services LLC 4000 N Big Spring Ste 400	Midland	TX	79705	**844-394-0841**	432-684-4272
Parsley Energy Inc 303 Colorado St Ste 3000	Austin	TX	78701	**855-214-5200**	737-704-2300
Pemex Procurement International Inc 10344 Sam Houston Park Dr	Houston	TX	77064	**888-254-1487**	713-430-3100
Penn Virginia Corp 100 Matsonford Rd Ste 200 *NASDAQ: PVAC*	Radnor	PA	19087	**877-316-5288**	610-687-8900
Perpetual Energy Inc 605 5 Ave SW Ste 3200	Calgary	AB	T2P3H5	**800-811-5522**	403-269-4400
Petroleum Development Corp (PDC) 120 Genesis Blvd PO Box 26 *NASDAQ: PDCE*	Bridgeport	WV	26330	**800-624-3821**	303-860-5800
PHX Energy Services Corp 1400-250 2 St SW	Calgary	AB	T2P0C1	**800-909-9819**	403-543-4466
Pioneer Natural Resources Co 5205 N O'Connor Blvd Ste 200 *NYSE: PXD*	Irving	TX	75039	**888-234-6372**	972-444-9001
Reserve Petroleum Co 6801 Broadway Ext Ste 300	Oklahoma City	OK	73116	**800-690-6903**	405-848-7551
Rife Resources Ltd 400 144 - Fourth Ave SW	Calgary	AB	T2P3N4	**888-257-1873**	403-221-0800
Saguaro Resources Ltd 3000 500 - Fourth Ave SW	Calgary	AB	T2P2V6	**855-835-4434**	403-453-3040
Shell Canada Ltd 400 Fourth Ave SW	Calgary	AB	T2P0J4	**877-656-3111**	403-691-3111
Shell Oil Co 910 Louisanna St	Houston	TX	77002	**888-467-4355**	713-241-6161
Sinopec Daylight Energy Ltd 112-4th Ave SW Sun Life Plz E Tower Ste 2700	Calgary	AB	T2P0H3	**877-266-6901**	403-266-6900
Southwestern Energy Co 10000 Energy Dr *NYSE: SWN*	Spring	TX	77389	**866-322-0801**	832-796-1000
Spartan Energy Corp 850 - Second St SW Ste 500	Calgary	AB	T2P0R8	**866-567-3105**	403-355-8920
Steelhead LNG Corp 650 - 669 Howe St	Vancouver	BC	V6C0B4	**855-860-8744**	604-235-3800
Strata Oil & Gas Inc 10010 - 98 St PO Box 7770	Peace River	AB	T8S1T3	**877-237-5443**	403-237-5443
Suncor Energy Inc 150 - 6 Ave SW PO Box 2844 *NYSE: SU*	Calgary	AB	T2P3E3	**800-558-9071**	403-296-8000
Sunoco Inc 1735 Market St *NYSE: SUN*	Philadelphia	PA	19103	**800-786-6261**	
Tourmaline Oil Corp 250 Sixth Ave SW Ste 3700	Calgary	AB	T2P3H7	**877-504-4252**	403-266-5992
TTHE TERMO Co 3275 Cherry Ave	Long Beach	CA	90807	**888-260-4715**	562-595-7401
Unit Corp 7130 S Lewis Ave Ste 1000 *NYSE: UNT*	Tulsa	OK	74136	**800-722-3612**	918-493-7700
Value Creation Inc 1100 635 - Eighth Ave SW	Calgary	AB	T2P3M3	**855-908-8800**	403-539-4500
Wagner Oil Co 500 Commerce St Ste 600	Fort Worth	TX	76102	**800-457-5332**	817-335-2222
Warren Resources Inc 1114 Ave of the Americas 34th Fl *NASDAQ: WRES*	New York	NY	10036	**877-587-9494**	212-697-9660
Wayne Oil Company Inc 1301 Wayne Memorial Dr	Goldsboro	NC	27534	**800-641-2816**	919-735-2021
Western Land Services Inc 1100 Conrad Industrial Dr	Ludington	MI	49431	**800-968-4840**	
Whitecap Resources Inc 3800 525 - Eighth Ave SW	Calgary	AB	T2P1G1	**866-590-5289**	403-266-0767
Whiting Petroleum Corp 1700 Broadway Ste 2300 *NYSE: WLL*	Denver	CO	80290	**800-723-4608**	303-837-1661
Wilshire Enterprises Inc 100 Eagle Rock Ave Ste 100 *OTC: WLSE*	East Hanover	NJ	07936	**888-697-3962**	973-585-7770
XTO Energy Inc 810 Houston St	Fort Worth	TX	76102	**800-299-2800**	817-870-2800

533 OIL & GAS FIELD EQUIPMENT

				Toll-Free	Phone
Alberta Oil Tool 9530 60th Ave	Edmonton	AB	T6E0C1	**877-432-3404**	780-434-8566
Carbo Ceramics Inc 575 N Dairy Ashford Rd Ste 300 *NYSE: CRR*	Houston	TX	77079	**800-551-3247**	281-921-6400
Dril-Quip Inc 6401 N Eldridge Pkwy *NYSE: DRQ*	Houston	TX	77041	**877-316-2631**	713-939-7711
Drillers Service Inc 1792 Highland Ave NE	Hickory	NC	28601	**800-334-2308**	828-322-1100
GEFCO Inc (GEFCO) 2215 S Van Buren	Enid	OK	73703	**800-759-7441**	580-234-4141
Morris Industries Inc 777 Rt 23	Pompton Plains	NJ	07444	**800-835-0777**	973-835-6600
Morrison Bros Co 570 E Seventh St	Dubuque	IA	52001	**800-553-4840**	563 583-5701
Schramm Inc 800 E Virginia Ave	West Chester	PA	19380	**888-737-9438**	610-696-2500
Southern Company Inc 3101 Carrier St	Memphis	TN	38116	**800-264-7626**	901-345-2531
Southwest Oilfield Products Inc 10340 Wallisville Rd	Houston	TX	77013	**800-392-4600**	713-675-7541
Tam International Inc 4620 Southerland Rd	Houston	TX	77092	**800-462-7617**	713-462-7617
Weatherford International Inc 515 Post Oak Blvd Ste 600 *NYSE: WFT*	Houston	TX	77027	**866-398-0010**	713-693-4000
Winston/Royal Guard Corp 1604 Cherokee Trace	White Oak	TX	75693	**800-527-8465**	903-757-7341

534 OIL & GAS FIELD EXPLORATION SERVICES

				Toll-Free	Phone
Allied Oilfield Machine & Pump LLC 202 Hulon Moreland Rd	Levelland	TX	79336	**855-378-4787**	
Arctic Slope Regional Corp 1230 Agvik St PO Box 129	Barrow	AK	99723	**800-770-2772**	907-852-8633
Bankers Petroleum Ltd 3700 888 - Third St SW	Calgary	AB	T2P5C5	**888-797-7170**	403-513-2699
Belvedere Terminals Inc 111 NE Second Ave NE St	Petersburg	FL	33701	**800-716-8515**	
Cad Control Systems 1017 Frenchman Dr	Broussard	LA	70518	**800-543-1968**	337-369-3737
Dawson Geophysical Co 508 W Wall St Ste 800 *NASDAQ: DWSN*	Midland	TX	79701	**800-332-9766**	432-684-3000
Emera Energy Inc 1223 Lower Water St PO Box 910	Halifax	NS	B3J2W5	**866-474-7800**	902-474-7800
EOG Resources Inc 1111 Bagby Sky Lobby 2 *NYSE: EOG*	Houston	TX	77002	**877-363-3647**	713-651-7000
EXCO Resources Inc 12377 Merit Dr Ste 1700 *OTC: XCO*	Dallas	TX	75251	**888-788-9449**	214-368-2084
GulfMark Energy Inc 17 S Briar Hollow Ln Ste 100	Houston	TX	77027	**800-340-1495**	
Intercept Energy Services Inc 11464 - 149 St	Edmonton	AB	T5M1W7	**877-975-0558**	
Lavigne Oil Company LLC 11203 Proverbs Ave	Baton Rouge	LA	70816	**800-349-0170**	
LineStar Services Inc 5391 Bay Oaks Dr	Pasadena	TX	77505	**800-790-3758**	281-422-4989
Mustang Fuel Corp 9800 N Oklahoma Ave	Oklahoma City	OK	73114	**800-332-9400**	405-748-9400
Navigator Energy Services 2626 Cole Ave Ste 900	Dallas	TX	75204	**888-991-1162**	214-880-6000
Noble Royalties Inc (NRI) 15303 N Dallas Pkwy Ste 1350	Addison	TX	75001	**888-346-6253**	972-720-1888
Panhandle Royalty Co 5400 N Grand Blvd Grand Ctr Bldg Ste 300	Oklahoma City	OK	73112	**800-884-4225**	405-948-1560
Plains Midstream Canada 607 Eighth Ave SW Ste 1400	Calgary	AB	T2P0A7	**866-343-5182**	403-298-2100
Power Service Products Inc PO Box 1089	Weatherford	TX	76086	**800-643-9089**	817-599-9486
Purestream Services 2401 Foothill Dr	Salt Lake City	UT	84109	**855-778-7342**	801-869-4455

Company	Address	City	State	Zip	Toll-Free	Phone
Radius Professional HDD Tools	2525 Ranger Hwy PO Box 3106	Weatherford	TX	76088	**800-892-9114**	
Stratagraph Inc	125 Raggio Rd	Scott	LA	70583	**800-256-1147**	

535 OIL & GAS FIELD SERVICES

SEE ALSO Oil & Gas Field Exploration Services

Company	Address	City	State	Zip	Toll-Free	Phone
4Refuel Canada LP	9440 - 202 ST Ste 215	Langley	BC	V1M4A6	**888-473-3835**	
Allamon Tool Company Inc	18935 Freeport Dr	Montgomery	TX	77356	**877-449-5433**	
Argus Machine Company Ltd	5820 97th St NW	Edmonton	AB	T6E3J1	**888-434-9451**	780-434-9451
Atlanta Petroleum Equipment Co	4732 N Royal Atlanta Dr	Tucker	GA	30084	**800-562-4060**	770-491-6644
B & R Eckel's Transport Ltd	5514B - 50 Ave	Bonnyville	AB	T9N2K8	**800-661-3290**	780-826-3889
Badger Daylighting Corp	919 11th Ave SW 4th Fl	Calgary	AB	T2R-1P3	**877-322-3437**	403-264-8500
Blakely Construction Company Inc	2830 W I-20	Odessa	TX	79763	**800-604-9339**	432-381-3540
Calfrac Well Services Ltd	411 8 Ave SW	Calgary	AB	T2P1E3	**866-770-3722**	403-266-6000
Camex Equipment Sales & Rental Inc	1806 Second St	Nisku	AB	T9E0W8	**877-955-2770**	780-955-2770
Central Industries Inc	11438 Cronridge Dr Ste W	Owings Mills	MD	21117	**800-304-8484**	
Colloid Environmental Technologies Co (CETCO)	2870 Forbs Ave	Hoffman Estates	IL	60192	**800-527-9948**	847-851-1899
Construction Process Solutions Ltd	3950 Virginia Ave	Cincinnati	OH	45227	**877-295-9876**	513-271-9026
Cougar Drilling Solutions Inc	7319 - 17 St	Edmonton	AB	T6P1P1	**877-439-3376**	
Diamond Oil Well Drilling Company Inc	15415 Katy Fwy Ste 100	Houston	TX	77094	**800-848-1980**	281-492-5300
Diamond Services Corp	503 S DeGravelle Rd	Amelia	LA	70340	**800-879-1162**	985-631-2187
Dwfritz Automation Inc	12100 SW Tualatin Rd	Wilsonville	OR	97070	**800-763-4161**	503-598-9393
Eaton Oil Tools Inc	118 Rue DuPain	Broussard	LA	70518	**800-232-5317**	337-856-8820
ExPert E&P Consultants LLC	101 Ashland Way	Madisonville	LA	70447	**888-231-8639**	844-522-7900
Gulf Offshore Logistics LLC	120 White Rose Dr	Raceland	LA	70394	**866-532-1060**	
Helix Energy Solutions Inc	400 N Sam Houston Pkwy E Ste 400 *NYSE: HLX*	Houston	TX	77060	**888-345-2347**	281-618-0400
Hilliard Energy Inc	3001 W Loop 250 N Ste E103	Midland	TX	79705	**800-287-0014**	432-683-9100
Jones & Frank Corp	1330 St Mary's St Ste 210	Raleigh	NC	27605	**800-286-4133**	919-838-7555
Katalyst Data Management LLC	10311 Westpark Dr	Houston	TX	77042	**855-529-6444**	281-529-3200
Koch Specialty Plant Services	12221 E Sam Houston Pkwy N	Houston	TX	77044	**800-765-9177**	713-427-7700
LaBarge Coating LLC	211 N Broadway Ste 3050	Saint Louis	MO	63102	**866-992-4191**	314-646-3400
Leam Drilling Systems Inc	2027a Airport Rd	Conroe	TX	77301	**800-426-5349**	
Mansfield Oil Co	1025 Airport Pkwy SW	Gainesville	GA	30501	**800-695-6626**	
Matrix Service Co	5100 E Skelly Dr 74135 *NASDAQ: MTRX*	Tulsa	OK	74135	**866-367-6879**	
MGS Services LLC	18775 N Frederick Ave Ste 205	Gaithersburg	MD	20879	**877-647-4255**	301-330-9793
Milbar Hydro-Test Inc	651 Aero Dr	Shreveport	LA	71107	**800-259-8210**	318-227-8210
NANA Regional Corporation Inc	1001 E Benson Blvd	Kotzebue	AK	99752	**800-478-3301**	907-442-3301
Newpark Mats & Integrated Services LLC	2700 Research Forest Dr Ste 100	The Woodlands	TX	77381	**877-628-7623**	281-362-6800
Oceaneering International Inc	11911 FM 529 *NYSE: OII*	Houston	TX	77041	**844-381-9324**	713-329-4500
Offshore Energy Services Inc	5900 US Hwy 90 E	Broussard	LA	70518	**800-489-6202**	337-837-1024
Painted Pony Petroleum Ltd	736 Sixth Ave SW Ste 1800	Calgary	AB	T2P3T7	**866-975-0440**	403-475-0440
Platinum Control Technologies Corp	2822 W Fifth St	Fort Worth	TX	76107	**877-374-1115**	817-529-6485
Pride International Inc	5847 San Felipe St Ste 3300	Houston	TX	77057	**877-736-3772**	713-789-1400
Production Management Industries LLC	9761 Hwy 90 E	Morgan City	LA	70380	**888-229-3837**	985-631-3837
Questor Technology Inc	1121 940 - Sixth Ave SW	Calgary	AB	T2P3T1	**844-477-8669**	403-571-1530
Real Time Measurements Inc	4615 - 112th Ave SE Ste 125	Calgary	AB	T2C5J3	**866-720-3444**	403-720-3444
Rig-Chem Inc	132 Thompson Rd	Houma	LA	70363	**800-375-7208**	985-873-7208
SageRider Inc	12950 S Kirkwood Ste 160	Stafford	TX	77477	**877-219-4730**	
Schlumberger Wireline & Testing	210 Schlumberger Dr	Sugar Land	TX	77478	**800-272-7328**	281-285-4551
Spatial Insights Inc	4938 Hampden Ln	Bethesda	MD	20814	**800-347-5291**	
Sproule Associates Ltd	900 N Tower Sun Life Plz 140 Fourth Ave SW	Calgary	AB	T2P3N3	**877-777-6135**	403-294-5500
Stric-Lan Companies LLC	104 Sable St	Duson	LA	70529	**800-749-4586**	337-984-7850
Supreme Oil Co	2109 W Monte Vista Rd	Phoenix	AZ	85009	**800-752-7888**	
Team Inc	200 Hermann Dr *NYSE: TISI*	Alvin	TX	77511	**800-662-8326**	281-331-6154
Terroco Industries Ltd	27212 Twp Rd 391	Red Deer	AB	T4N5E1	**800-670-1100**	403-346-1171
TK Stanley Inc	6739 Hwy 184	Waynesboro	MS	39367	**800-477-2855**	
Valiant TMs	6555 Hawthorne Dr	Windsor	ON	N8T3G6	**888-497-5537**	519-974-5200

536 OIL & GAS WELL DRILLING

Company	Address	City	State	Zip	Toll-Free	Phone
Callon Petroleum Co	200 N Canal St *NYSE: CPE*	Natchez	MS	39120	**800-451-1294**	601-442-1601
Diamond Offshore Drilling Inc	15415 Katy Fwy *NYSE: DO*	Houston	TX	77094	**800-848-1980**	281-492-5300
Doyon Drilling Inc	11500 C St Ste 200	Anchorage	AK	99515	**800-478-9675**	907-563-5530
GEO Drilling Fluids Inc	1431 Union Ave	Bakersfield	CA	93305	**800-438-7436**	661-325-5919
Helmerich & Payne Inc	1437 S Boulder Ave *NYSE: HP*	Tulsa	OK	74119	**800-205-4913**	918-742-5531
High Arctic Energy Services Inc	700-2nd St SW Ste 500	Calgary	AB	T2P2T8	**800-668-7143**	403-508-7836
Iron Horse Energy Services Inc	1901 Dirkson Dr NE	Redcliff	AB	T0J2P0	**877-526-4666**	403-526-4600
Justiss Oil Company Inc	1120 E Oak St	Jena	LA	71342	**800-256-2501**	318-992-4111
McClelland Oilfield Rentals Ltd	8720-110 St	Grande Prairie	AB	T8V8K1	**866-539-3656**	780-539-3656
Nabors Industries Ltd	515 W Greens Rd Ste 1200	Houston	TX	77067	**800-422-2066**	281-874-0035
Noble Corp	13135 S Dairy Ashford Rd Ste 800 *NYSE: NE*	Sugar Land	TX	77478	**877-285-4162**	281-276-6100
ProPetro Services Inc	1706 S Midkiff Rd Bldg B PO Box 873	Midland	TX	79701	**800-221-1037**	432-688-0012
Roll'n Oilfield Industries Ltd	305 5208 ? 53 Ave	Red Deer	AB	T4N5K2	**800-662-7139**	403-343-1710
Total Energy Services Ltd	2550 300-5th Ave SW Ste 2550 *NYSE: TOT*	Calgary	AB	T2P3C4	**877-818-6825**	403-216-3939
Unit Corp	7130 S Lewis Ave Ste 1000 *NYSE: UNT*	Tulsa	OK	74136	**800-722-3612**	918-493-7700
US. Energy Development Corp	2350 N Forest Rd	Getzville	NY	14068	**800-636-7606**	716-636-0401

537 OILS & GREASES - LUBRICATING

SEE ALSO Chemicals - Specialty ; Petroleum Refineries

Company	Address	City	State	Zip	Toll-Free	Phone
American Lubrication Equipment Corp	11212A McCormick Rd PO Box 1350	Hunt Valley	MD	21030	**888-252-9300**	410-252-9300
Amsoil Inc	925 Tower Ave *Sales	Superior	WI	54880	**800-777-7094***	715-392-7101
BG Products Inc	740 S Wichita St	Wichita	KS	67213	**800-961-6228**	
BP Lubricants USA Inc	1500 Valley Rd	Wayne	NJ	07470	**800-333-3991**	973-633-2200
Canada Forgings Inc	130 Hagar St	Welland	ON	L3B5P8	**800-263-0440**	905-735-1220
Castrol Industrial North America Inc	150 W Warrenville Rd	Naperville	IL	60563	**877-641-1600**	
Chem-Trend LP	1445 McPherson Pk Dr	Howell	MI	48843	**800-727-7730**	517-546-4520
CRC Industries Inc	885 Louis Dr *Cust Svc	Warminster	PA	18974	**800-556-5074***	215-674-4300
D-A Lubricant Co	1340 W 29th St	Indianapolis	IN	46208	**800-645-5823**	317-923-5321
Elco Corp	1000 Belt Line St	Cleveland	OH	44109	**800-321-0467**	216-749-2605
Fiske Bros Refining Co	129 Lockwood St	Newark	NJ	07105	**800-733-4755**	973-589-9150
Hangsterfer's Laboratories Inc	175 Ogden Rd	Mantua	NJ	08051	**800-433-5823**	856-468-0216
Hercules Chemical Company Inc	111 S St	Passaic	NJ	07055	**800-221-9330**	
Houghton International Inc	945 Madison Ave PO Box 930	Valley Forge	PA	19482	**888-459-9844**	610-666-4000
Hydrotex Inc	12920 Senlac Dr	Farmers Branch	TX	75234	**800-527-9439**	
ITW Fluids North America	475 N Gary Ave	Carol Stream	IL	60188	**800-452-5823**	
Jackson Oil & Solvents Inc	1970 Kentucky Ave	Indianapolis	IN	46221	**800-221-4603**	317-636-4421
Jet-Lube Inc	4849 Homestead Rd Ste 232	Houston	TX	77226	**800-538-5823**	713-670-5700
Kl ber Lubrication NA LP	32 Industrial Dr	Londonderry	NH	03053	**800-447-2238**	603-647-4104
Leadership Performance Sustainability Laboratories	4647 Hugh Howell Rd	Tucker	GA	30084	**800-241-8334**	
Lubrication Engineers Inc	300 Bailey Ave	Fort Worth	TX	76107	**800-537-7683**	817-834-6321
Lubrication Technologies Inc	900 Mendelssohn Ave N	Golden Valley	MN	55427	**800-328-5573**	763-545-0707
Lubrizol Corp	29400 Lakeland Blvd *NYSE: LZ*	Wickliffe	OH	44092	**800-380-5397**	440-943-4200
Metalworking Lubricants Co	25 W Silverdome Industrial Park	Pontiac	MI	48342	**800-394-5494**	248-332-3500
Northtown Products Inc	5202 Argosy Ave	Huntington Beach	CA	92649	**800-972-7274**	714-897-0700

	Toll-Free	Phone
Oil Ctr Research LLC		
106 Montrose Ave ....Lafayette LA 70503	800-256-8977	337-993-3559
Orelube Corp, The		
20 Sawgrass Dr ....Bellport NY 11713	800-645-9124	631-205-9700
Perkins Oil Company Inc		
4707 Pflaum Rd ....Madison WI 53718	800-634-9937	608-221-4736
Primrose Oil Company Inc		
11444 Denton Dr ....Dallas TX 75229	800-275-2772	
Schaeffer Mfg Company Inc		
102 Barton St ....Saint Louis MO 63104	800-325-9962*	314-865-4100
*Cust Svc		
Schultz Lubricants Inc		
164 Shrewsbury St .... West Boylston MA 01583	800-262-3962	508-835-4446
Smitty's Supply Inc		
63399 Hwy 51 N PO Box 530 .... Roseland LA 70456	800-256-7575	985-748-3247
Southwestern Petroleum Corp		
PO Box 961005 ....Fort Worth TX 76161	800-877-9372	
Sun Drilling Products Corp		
503 Main St ....Belle Chasse LA 70037	800-962-6490	504-393-2778
Texas Refinery Corp		
840 N Main St ....Fort Worth TX 76164	800-827-0711	817-332-1161
Total Lubricants USA		
5 N Stiles St ....Linden NJ 07036	800-323-3198	908-862-9300
Universal Environmental Services LLC		
411 Dividend Dr .... Peachtree City GA 30269	800-988-7977	
Valvoline LLC		
100 Valvoline Way ....Lexington KY 40509	800-832-6825	859-357-7777
WD-40 Co 1061 Cudahy Pl ....San Diego CA 92110	800-448-9340	619-275-1400
NASDAQ: WDFC		

---

538   OPHTHALMIC GOODS

SEE ALSO Personal Protective Equipment & Clothing

	Toll-Free	Phone
Aearo Technologies LLC		
5457 W 79th St ....Indianapolis IN 46268	877-327-4332	
Art-Craft Optical Company Inc		
57 Goodway Dr S ....Rochester NY 14623	800-828-8288	585-546-6640
Bausch & Lomb Inc		
1400 N Goodman St ....Rochester NY 14609	800-553-5340	
Beitler-Mckee Optical Co		
160 S 22nd St ....Pittsburgh PA 15203	800-989-4700	412-481-4700
Conforma Laboratories Inc		
4705 Colley Ave ....Norfolk VA 23508	800-426-1700	757-321-0200
Cooper Cos Inc		
6140 Stoneridge Mall Rd Ste 590 .....Pleasanton CA 94588	888-822-2660	925-460-3600
NYSE: COO		
CooperVision Inc		
209 High Point Dr ....Victor NY 14564	800-538-7850	585-385-6810
Costa Del Mar		
2361 Mason Ave Ste 100 .... Daytona Beach FL 32117	800-447-3700	386-274-4000
DAC Technologies		
3630 W Miller Ste 350 ....Garland TX 75041	800-800-1550	972-677-2700
Essilor of America Inc		
13515 N Stemmons Fwy ....Dallas TX 75234	800-377-4567	
Eye-Kraft Optical Inc		
8 McLeland Rd ....Saint Cloud MN 56303	888-455-2022	
Gargoyles Inc		
500 George Washington Hwy ....Smithfield RI 02917	866-807-0195	401-231-3800
GENTEX Corp 324 Main St ....Simpson PA 18407	888-894-1755	570-282-3550
Homer Optical Company Inc		
2401 Linden Ln ....Silver Spring MD 20910	800-627-2710	301-585-9060
Icare Industries Inc		
4399 35th St N ....Saint Petersburg FL 33714	877-422-7352	727-526-0501
IcareLabs		
4399 35th St N ....Saint Petersburg FL 33714	877-422-7352	
Johnson & Johnson Vision Care Inc		
7500 Centurion Pkwy ....Jacksonville FL 32256	800-843-2020	800-874-5278
Maui Jim Inc 721 Wainee St ....Lahaina HI 96761	888-352-2001	808-661-8841
Night Optics USA Inc		
15182 Triton Ln Ste 101 ....Huntington Beach CA 92649	800-306-4448	
Oakley Inc 1 Icon ....Foothill Ranch CA 92610	800-403-7449*	949-672-6925
*Cust Svc		
Signature Eyewear Inc		
498 N Oak St ....Inglewood CA 90302	800-765-3937	310-330-2700
OTC: SEYE		
STAAR Surgical Co		
1911 Walker Ave ....Monrovia CA 91016	800-352-7842	626-303-7902
NASDAQ: STAA		
Transitions Optical Inc		
9251 Belcher Rd ....Pinellas Park FL 33782	800-533-2081	727-545-0400
US Vision Inc		
1 Harmon Dr Glen Oaks Industrial Pk.......Glendora NJ 08029	866-435-7111	856-228-1000
Vision-Ease Lens Inc		
7000 Sunwood Dr NW ....Ramsey MN 55303	800-328-3449*	320-251-8140
*Cust Svc		
X-Cel Optical Company Inc		
806 S Benton Dr ....Sauk Rapids MN 56379	800-747-9235*	320-251-8404
*General		
Younger Optics		
2925 California St ....Torrance CA 90503	800-366-5367	310-783-1533

---

539   OPTICAL GOODS STORES

	Toll-Free	Phone
Barnett & Ramel Optical Co		
7154 N 16th St ....Omaha NE 68112	800-228-9732	
BARSKA Optics		
1721 Wright Ave ....La Verne CA 91750	888-666-6769	
Binders		
284 S Sharon Amity Rd ....Charlotte NC 28211	888-472-6866	704-442-2608
Cliff Weil Inc		
8043 Industrial Pk Rd ....Mechanicsville VA 23116	800-446-9345	804-746-1321
Epic Labs		
95 Third St NE PO Box 7430 ....Waite Park MN 56387	877-374-2522	

	Toll-Free	Phone
Eye Glass World Inc		
2435 Commerce Ave Bldg 2200 ....Duluth GA 30096	800-637-3597	
Eye-Mart Express Inc		
13800 Senlac Dr Ste 200 .... Farmers Branch TX 75234	888-372-2763	972-488-2016
General Vision Services LLC		
520 Eigth Ave 9th Fl ....New York NY 10018	855-653-0586	
Hart Specialties Inc		
5000 New Horizons Blvd ....Amityville NY 11701	800-221-6966	631-226-5600
JAK Enterprises Inc		
8309 N Knoxville Ave ....Peoria IL 61615	800-752-3295	309-692-8222
JC Penney Optical Co		
821 N Central Expy ....Plano TX 75075	866-435-7111	
LensCrafters Inc		
4000 Luxottica Pl ....Mason OH 45040	877-753-6727	513-765-4321
Magnifying Ctr		
10086 W McNab Rd ....Tamarac FL 33321	800-364-1612	954-722-1580
Match Eyewear LLC		
1600 Shames Dr ....Westbury NY 11590	877-886-2824	
Medical Associates Healthcare		
911 Carter St NW ....Elkader IA 52043	800-648-6868	563-245-1717
Moscot 108 Orchard St ....New York NY 10002	866-667-2687	212-477-3796
National Vision Inc		
2435 Commerce Ave Bldg 2200 ....Duluth GA 30096	800-637-3597*	770-822-3600
*Cust Svc		
Native Eyewear Inc		
1114 Neon Forest Cir Unit 5.........Longmont CO 80504	888-776-2848	
Ophthalmic Consultants of Boston Inc		
50 Staniford St Ste 600.................Boston MA 02114	800-635-0489	617-367-4800
OptiCare PC		
87 Grandview Ave ....Waterbury CT 06708	800-225-5393	203-574-2020
Optovue Inc 2800 Bayview Dr ....Fremont CA 94538	866-344-8948	
Rockwell Laser Industries Inc		
7754 Camargo Rd ....Cincinnati OH 45243	800-945-2737	513-272-9900
Rx Optical 1700 S Park St ....Kalamazoo MI 49001	800-792-2737	269-342-0003
SPY Inc 2070 Las Palmas Dr ....Carlsbad CA 92011	800-779-3937	
SVS Vision		
140 Macomb Pl ....Mount Clemens MI 48043	800-787-4600	586-468-7612
Tryiton Eyewear LLC		
147 Post Rd E ....Westport CT 06880	888-896-3885	203-544-0770
Union Eyecare Centers		
4750 Beidler Rd ....Willoughby OH 44094	800-443-9699	216-986-9700
US Vision Inc		
1 Harmon Dr Glen Oaks Industrial Pk.......Glendora NJ 08029	866-435-7111	856-228-1000
Visionworks of America Inc		
175 E Houston St ....San Antonio TX 78205	800-669-1183	
Vistar Eye Center		
2802 Brandon Ave ....Roanoke VA 24015	866-615-5454	540-855-5100
Vogue Optical		
5 Brackley Pt Rd ....Charlottetown PE C1A6X8	866-594-3937	902-566-3326
Volk Optical Inc		
7893 Enterprise Dr ....Mentor OH 44060	800-345-8655	440-942-6161
Vuzix Corp		
2166 Brighton Henrietta Town Line Rd		
.................Rochester NY 14623	800-436-7838	585-359-5900
Wiley X Inc		
7800 Patterson Pass Rd ....Livermore CA 94550	800-776-7842	925-243-9810

---

540   OPTICAL INSTRUMENTS & LENSES

SEE ALSO Laboratory Analytical Instruments

	Toll-Free	Phone
Alcon Canada Inc		
2665 Meadowpine Blvd ....Mississauga ON L5N8C7	800-268-4574	905-826-6700
Allergan Inc 2525 Dupont Dr ....Irvine CA 92612	800-347-4500	714-246-4500
NYSE: AGN		
American Polarizers Inc		
141 S Seventh St ....Reading PA 19602	800-736-9031	610-373-5177
American Technology Network Corp		
1341 San Mateo Ave .... South San Francisco CA 94080	800-910-2862	650-989-5100
Applied Fiber Inc		
PO Box 1339 ....Leesburg GA 31763	800-226-5394	229-759-8301
B E Meyers & Co Inc		
9461 Willows Rd NE ....Redmond WA 98052	800-327-5648	425-881-6648
Burris Company Inc		
331 E Eighth St ....Greeley CO 80631	888-228-7747	970-356-1670
Bushnell Corp		
9200 Cody St ....Overland Park KS 66214	800-423-3537	913-752-3400
Carl Zeiss Inc 1 Zeiss Dr ....Thornwood NY 10594	800-233-2343	914-747-1800
ChromaGen Vision LLC		
326 W Cedar St Ste 1 ....Kennett Square PA 19348	855-473-2323	
Conoptics International Sales Corp		
19 Eagle Rd ....Danbury CT 06810	800-748-3349	203-743-3349
CST/Berger Corp		
255 W Fleming St ....Watseka IL 60970	800-435-1859	815-432-5237
Deltronic Corp		
3900 W Segerstrom Ave ....Santa Ana CA 92704	800-451-6922	714-545-5800
Edmund Optics Inc		
101 E Gloucester Pk ....Barrington NJ 08007	800-363-1992	
Epilog Corp		
16371 Table Mtn Pkwy ....Golden CO 80403	888-437-4564	303-277-1188
Eschenbach Optik of America Inc		
22 Shelter Rock Ln ....Danbury CT 06810	800-487-5389	
G-S Supplies		
1150 University Ave Ste 5.................Rochester NY 14607	800-295-3050	585-241-2370
Gould Technology LLC		
1121 Benfield Blvd Stes J-P ....Millersville MD 21108	800-544-6853	410-987-5600
Karl Storz Imaging Inc		
175 Cremona Dr ....Goleta CA 93117	800-796-8909	805-968-3568
LaserMax Corp		
3495 Winton Pl ....Rochester NY 14623	800-527-3703	585-272-5420
Latham & Phillips Ophthalmic Products Inc		
224 James St ....Bensenville IL 60106	800-729-1959	
Leica Camera AG		
1 Pearl Ct ....Allendale NJ 07401	800-222-0118	
Leupold & Stevens Inc		
14400 NW Greenbrier Pkwy ....Beaverton OR 97006	800-538-7653	

	City	State	ZIP	Toll-Free	Phone
Lyric Optical Company Wholsle 3533 Cardiff Ave	Cincinnati	OH	45209	**800-543-7376**	513-321-2456
Meade Instruments Corp 27 Hubble	Irvine	CA	92618	**800-626-3233**	949-451-1450
Mirrotek International LLC 90 Dayton Ave	Passaic	NJ	07055	**888-659-3030**	973-472-1400
Newport Corp 1791 Deere Ave *NASDAQ: NEWP* ■ *Sales	Irvine	CA	92606	**800-222-6440***	949-863-3144
Opti-Craft 17311 NE Halsey	Portland	OR	97230	**800-288-8048**	503-256-5330
Optical Dynamics Corp 1950 Production Ct	Louisville	KY	40299	**800-587-2743**	502-671-2020
Optical Gaging Products Inc 850 Hudson Ave	Rochester	NY	14621	**800-647-4243**	585-544-0450
Parker Hannifin Corp Daedal Div 1140 Sandy Hill Rd	Irwin	PA	15642	**800-245-6903**	724-861-8200
PerkinElmer Inc 940 Winter St *NYSE: PKI*	Waltham	MA	02451	**800-762-4000**	781-663-6050
Ross Optical Industries Inc 1410 Gail Borden Pl	El Paso	TX	79935	**800-880-5417**	915-595-5417
Seiler Instrument & Mfg Company Inc 3433 Tree Court Industrial Blvd	Saint Louis	MO	63122	**800-489-2282**	314-968-2282
Sorenson Media Inc 25 East Scenic Pointe Dr Ste 100	Draper	UT	84020	**888-767-3676**	801-501-8650
Stevens Water Monitoring Systems 12067 NE Glenn Widing Dr Ste 106	Portland	OR	97220	**800-452-5272**	503-445-8000
Veeco Instruments Inc 1 Terminal Dr *NASDAQ: VECO*	Plainview	NY	11803	**888-724-9511**	516-677-0200
Western Ophthalmics Corp 19019 36th Ave W Ste G	Lynnwood	WA	98036	**800-426-9938**	425-672-9332
Zygo Corp Laurel Brook Rd *NASDAQ: ZIGO*	Middlefield	CT	06455	**800-994-6669**	860-347-8506

541 ORGAN & TISSUE BANKS

SEE ALSO Eye Banks

	City	State	ZIP	Toll-Free	Phone
Aberhart Centre 11402 University Ave	Edmonton	AB	T6G2J3	**866-407-1970**	780-407-7510
Alamo Tissue Service Ltd 5844 Rocky Point Dr	San Antonio	TX	78249	**800-226-9091**	210-738-2663
AlloSource 6278 S Troy Cir	Centennial	CO	80111	**800-557-3587**	720-873-0213
Bio-Tissue 7000 SW 97th Ave Ste 211	Miami	FL	33173	**888-296-8858**	
Bone Bank Allografts 4808 Research Dr *Sales	San Antonio	TX	78240	**800-397-0088***	210-696-7616
California Cryobank Inc 11915 La Grange Ave	Los Angeles	CA	90025	**866-927-9622**	310-443-5244
California Cryobank Inc 950 Massachusetts Ave	Cambridge	MA	02139	**888-810-2796**	617-497-8646
Community Tissue Services 2900 College Dr	Kettering	OH	45420	**800-684-7783**	
Cryobiology Inc 4830D Knightsbridge Blvd	Columbus	OH	43214	**800-359-4375**	614-451-4375
Donor Alliance Inc 720 S Colorado Blvd Ste 800-N	Denver	CO	80246	**888-868-4747**	303-329-4747
Donor Network West 12667 Alcosta Blvd Ste 500	Oakland	CA	94583	**888-570-9400**	
Gift of Hope Organ & Tissue Donor Network 425 Spring Lake Dr	Itasca	IL	60143	**877-577-3747**	630-758-2600
Gift of Life Donor Program 401 N Third St	Philadelphia	PA	19123	**800-543-6391**	215-557-8090
Indiana Donor Network 3760 Guion Rd	Indianapolis	IN	46222	**888-275-4676**	
Kentucky Organ Donor Affiliates (KODA) 10160 Linn Station Rd	Louisville	KY	40223	**800-525-3456**	502-581-9511
LifeBanc 4775 Richmond Rd	Cleveland	OH	44128	**888-558-5433**	216-752-5433
Lifeline of Ohio 770 Kinnear Rd Ste 200	Columbus	OH	43212	**800-525-5667**	614-291-5667
LifeLink Tissue Bank 9661 Delaney Creek Blvd	Tampa	FL	33619	**800-683-2400**	813-886-8111
LifeNet 1864 Concert Dr	Virginia Beach	VA	23453	**800-847-7831**	
LifeNet Health Northwest 501 SW 39th St	Renton	WA	98057	**800-847-7831**	425-981-8900
LifeShare Transplant Donor Services of Oklahoma 4705 NW Expy	Oklahoma City	OK	73132	**888-580-5680**	405-840-5551
Lifesharing 7436 Mission Valley Rd	San Diego	CA	92108	**888-423-6667**	619-543-7225
Louisiana Organ Procurement Agency (LOPA) 3545 N I-10 Service Rd Ste 300	Metairie	LA	70002	**800-521-4483**	
Mid-America Transplant Services (MTS) 1110 Highlands Plaza Dr E Ste 100	Saint Louis	MO	63110	**888-376-4854**	314-735-8200
Musculoskeletal Transplant Foundation 125 May St Ste 300	Edison	NJ	08837	**800-946-9008**	732-661-0202
Nevada Donor Network Inc 2055 E Sahara Ave	Las Vegas	NV	89104	**855-683-6667**	702-796-9600
New England Donor Services 60 First Ave	Waltham	MA	02451	**800-446-6362**	
Nova Scotia Health Authority 5788 University Ave	Halifax	NS	B3H1V7	**888-429-8167**	902-429-8167
OneLegacy Transplant Donor Network 221 S Figueroa St Ste 500	Los Angeles	CA	90012	**800-786-4077**	213-229-5600
Rocky Mountain Tissue Bank 2993 S Peoria St Ste 390	Aurora	CO	80014	**800-424-5169**	303-337-3330
ScienceCare Inc 21410 N 19th Ave Ste 126	Phoenix	AZ	85027	**800-417-3747**	
Sierra Donor Services 3940 Industrial Blvd	West Sacramento	CA	95833	**877-401-2546**	
South Texas Blood & Tissue Ctr 6211 IH-10 W	San Antonio	TX	78201	**800-292-5534**	210-731-5555
Southeast Tissue Alliance (SETA) 6241 NW 23rd St Ste 400	Gainesville	FL	32653	**866-432-1164**	352-248-2114
Tennessee/DCI Donor Services 1600 Hayes St	Nashville	TN	37203	**877-401-2517**	
Wright Medical Technology Inc 5677 Airline Rd	Arlington	TN	38002	**800-238-7117**	901-867-9971

542 PACKAGE DELIVERY SERVICES

	City	State	ZIP	Toll-Free	Phone
Crosscountry Courier Inc PO Box 4030	Bismarck	ND	58502	**800-521-0287**	701-222-8498
Federal Express Europe Inc 3610 Hacks Cross Rd	Memphis	TN	38125	**800-463-3339**	901-369-3600
FedEx Custom Critical Inc 1475 Boettler Rd	Uniontown	OH	44685	**800-463-3339**	
Hot Shot Delivery Inc 335 Garden Oaks Blvd	Houston	TX	77018	**866-261-3184**	713-869-5525
Mass Bay Transportation Authority (MBTA) 10 Park Plz Ste 5610	Boston	MA	02116	**800-392-6100**	617-222-3200
Master Package Corp, The 200 Madson St	Owen	WI	54460	**800-396-8425**	715-229-2156
Network Global Logistics (NGL) 320 Interlocken Pkwy Ste 100	Broomfield	CO	80021	**866-938-1870**	
Newgistics Inc 7171 Southwest Pkwy Bldg 300 Ste 400	Austin	TX	78735	**877-860-5997**	512-225-6000
One Source Industries LLC 185 Technology Dr	Irvine	CA	92618	**800-899-4990**	
Priority Express Courier 5 Chelsea Pkwy	Boothwyn	PA	19061	**800-526-4646**	610-364-3300
Purolator Inc 5995 Avebury Rd	Mississauga	ON	L5R3T8	**888-744-7123**	905-712-8101
Unishippers Assn Inc 746 E Winchester Ste 200	Salt Lake City	UT	84107	**800-999-8721**	
United Parcel Service Inc (UPS) 55 Glenlake Pkwy NE *NYSE: UPS* ■ *Cust Svc	Atlanta	GA	30328	**800-742-5877***	404-828-6000
Washington Express Service LLC 12240 Indian Creek Ct Ste 100	Beltsville	MD	20705	**800-939-5463**	301-210-0899
Worldwide Express 2323 Victory Ave Ste 1600	Dallas	TX	75219	**800-758-7447**	
WPX Delivery Solutions 3320 W Valley Hwy N Ste 111	Auburn	WA	98001	**800-562-1091**	253-876-2760

543 PACKAGING MACHINERY & EQUIPMENT

	City	State	ZIP	Toll-Free	Phone
A-B-C Packaging Machine Corp 811 Live Oak St	Tarpon Springs	FL	34689	**800-237-5975**	727-937-5144
Accuplace 1800 NW 69th Ave	Plantation	FL	33313	**866-820-0434**	954-791-1500
All - Fill Inc 418 Creamery Way	Exton	PA	19341	**866-255-3455**	
AMS Filling Systems 2500 Chestnut Tree Rd	Honey Brook	PA	19344	**800-647-5390**	610-942-4200
Automated Packaging Systems Inc 10175 Phillip Pkwy *Sales	Streetsboro	OH	44241	**800-527-0733***	330-342-2000
B & H Manufacturing Co 3461 Roeding Rd	Ceres	CA	95307	**888-643-0444**	209-537-5785
Barry-Wehmiller Cos Inc Accraply Div 3580 Holly Ln N	Plymouth	MN	55447	**800-328-3997**	763-557-1313
Belco Packaging Systems Inc 910 S Mountain Ave	Monrovia	CA	91016	**800-833-1833**	626-357-9566
Brenton LLC 4750 County Rd 13 NE	Alexandria	MN	56308	**800-535-2730**	320-852-7705
Campbell Wrapper Corp 1415 Fortune Ave	De Pere	WI	54115	**800-727-4210**	920-983-7100
Data Technology Inc 14225 Dayton Cir Ste 4 *General	Omaha	NE	68137	**888-334-9300***	402-891-0711
Delkor Systems Inc 4300 Round Lake Rd W	St. Paul	MN	55112	**800-328-5558**	
E-pak Machinery Inc 1535 S State Rd 39	La Porte	IN	46350	**800-328-0466**	219-393-5541
Elmar Worldwide Inc 200 Gould Ave PO Box 245 *Cust Svc	Depew	NY	14043	**800-433-3562***	716-681-5650
Flexicon Corp 2400 Emrick Blvd	Bethlehem	PA	18020	**888-353-9426**	610-814-2400
Hartness International Inc 500 Hartness Dr PO Box 26509	Greenville	SC	29615	**800-845-8791**	864-297-1200
Heat Seal LLC 4580 E 71st St Ste 100	Cleveland	OH	44125	**800-342-6329**	216-341-2022
Heisler Industries Inc 224 Passaic Ave	Fairfield	NJ	07004	**800-496-7621**	973-227-6300
IDD Process & Packaging 5450 Tech Cir	Moorpark	CA	93021	**800-621-4144**	805-529-9890
Kliklok-Woodman 5224 Snapfinger Woods Dr	Decatur	GA	30035	**800-621-4170**	770-981-5200
Krones Inc 9600 S 58th St PO Box 321801	Franklin	WI	53132	**800-752-3787**	414-409-4000
Lantech Inc 11000 Bluegrass Pkwy	Louisville	KY	40299	**800-866-0322**	502-815-9109
Loveshaw Corp 2206 Easton Tpke *Cust Svc	South Canaan	PA	18459	**800-747-1586***	570-937-4921
Mooney General Paper Co 1451 Chestnut Ave PO Box 3800	Hillside	NJ	07205	**800-882-8846**	973-926-3800
Muller Martini 456 Wheeler Rd	Hauppauge	NY	11788	**888-268-5537**	631-582-4343
National Instrument LLC 4119 Fordleigh Rd	Baltimore	MD	21215	**866-258-1914**	410-764-0900
New Jersey Machine Inc 56 Etna Rd *Sales	Lebanon	NH	03766	**800-432-2990***	603-448-0300

Classified Section

	Toll-Free	Phone

Ossid Corp
4000 College Rd ....Battleboro NC 27809 **800-334-8369** 252-446-6177

Packaging Systems International Inc
4990 Acoma St ....Denver CO 80216 **800-525-6110** 303-296-4445

Pearson Packaging Systems
8120 W Sunset Hwy ....Spokane WA 99224 **800-732-7766**

Rollstock Inc
5720 Brighton Ave ....Kansas City MO 64130 **800-295-2949** 616-570-0430

Schneider Packaging Equipment Company Inc
5370 Guy Young Rd ....Brewerton NY 13029 **800-829-9266** 315-676-3035

Shibuya Hoppmann Corp
13129 Airpark Dr Ste 120 ....Elkwood VA 22718 **800-368-3582*** 540-829-2564
*Cust Svc

Standard Knapp Inc
63 Pickering St ....Portland CT 06480 **800-628-9565*** 860-342-1100
*Cust Svc

Taylor Products Company Inc
2205 Jothi Ave ....Parsons KS 67357 **888-882-9567** 620-421-5550

Thiele Technologies
315 27th Ave NE ....Minneapolis MN 55418 **800-932-3647** 612-782-1200

Triangle Package Machinery Co
6655 W Diversey Ave ....Chicago IL 60707 **800-621-4170** 773-889-0200

Universal Labeling Systems
3501 Eigth Ave S ....Saint Petersburg FL 33711 **877-236-0266** 727-327-2123

US Digital Media Inc
1929 W Lone Cactus Dr ....Phoenix AZ 85027 **877-992-3766** 623-587-4900

Wulftec International Inc
209 Wulftec St ....Ayer's Cliff QC J0B1C0 **877-985-3832** 819-838-4232

544 PACKAGING MATERIALS & PRODUCTS - PAPER OR PLASTICS

SEE ALSO Coated & Laminated Paper ; Bags - Plastics ; Bags - Paper ; Paper Converters ; Plastics Foam Products ; Blister Packaging

	Toll-Free	Phone

Adhesive Packaging Specialties Inc
103 Foster St ....Peabody MA 01960 **800-222-1117** 978-531-3300

Admiral Packaging Inc
10 Admiral St ....Providence RI 02908 **800-556-6454** 401-274-7000

Advance Bag & Packaging Technologies
5720 Williams Lake Rd ....Waterford MI 48329 **800-475-2247** 248-674-3126

Alliance Rubber Co
210 Carpenter Dam Rd ....Hot Springs AR 71901 **800-626-5940** 501-262-2700

American Packaging Corp
777 Driving Park Ave ....Rochester NY 14613 **800-551-8801** 585-254-9500

Apco Extruders Inc
180 National Rd ....Edison NJ 08817 **800-942-8725*** 732-287-3000
*Orders

Automated Packaging Systems Inc
10175 Phillip Pkwy ....Streetsboro OH 44241 **800-527-0733*** 330-342-2000
*Sales

BagcraftPapercon
3900 W 43rd St ....Chicago IL 60632 **800-621-8468** 773-254-8000

Bedford Industries Inc
1659 Rowe Ave ....Worthington MN 56187 **877-233-3673*** 507-376-4136
*Cust Svc

Bemis Company Inc
2301 Industrial Dr ....Neenah WI 54956 **800-544-4672** 920-527-5000
NYSE: BMS

BPM Inc 200 W Front St ....Peshtigo WI 54157 **800-826-0494** 715-582-4551

Bryce Corp
4505 Old Lamar Ave ....Memphis TN 38118 **800-238-7277** 901-369-4400

Burrows Paper Corp Packaging Group
2000 Commerce Ctr Dr ....Franklin OH 45005 **800-732-1933** 937-746-1933

Carton Service Inc
First Quality Dr PO Box 702 ....Shelby OH 44875 **800-533-7744*** 419-342-5010
*General

Charter Films Inc
1901 Winter St PO Box 277 ....Superior WI 54880 **877-411-3456** 715-395-8258

Command Plastic Corp
124 W Ave ....Tallmadge OH 44278 **800-321-8001** 330-434-3497

Consolidated Container Co (CCC)
3101 Towercreek Pkwy Ste 300 ....Atlanta GA 30339 **888-831-2184*** 678-742-4600
*Sales

Crawford Industries
1414 Crawford Dr ....Crawfordsville IN 47933 **800-428-0840**

Crown Packaging Corp
17854 Chesterfld Airport Rd ....Chesterfield MO 63005 **888-880-0852** 314-731-4927

Cryovac Food Packaging & Food Solutions
100 Rogers Bridge Rd ....Duncan SC 29334 **800-391-5645**

Custom Paper Tubes
15900 Industrial Pkwy PO Box 35140 ....Cleveland OH 44135 **800-343-8823** 216-362-2964

DuPont Packaging & Industrial Polymers
Barley Mill Plz 26-2122
PO Box 80026 ....Wilmington DE 19880 **800-438-7225** 703-305-7666

Fisher Container Corp
1111 Busch Pkwy ....Buffalo Grove IL 60089 **800-837-2247** 847-541-0000

Flextron Industries Inc
720 Mt Rd ....Aston PA 19014 **800-633-2181** 610-459-4600

Flower City Tissue Mills Inc
700 Driving Park Ave ....Rochester NY 14613 **800-595-2030** 585-458-9200

FPC Flexible Packaging Corp
1891 Eglinton Ave E ....Toronto ON M1L2L7 **888-288-7386** 416-288-3060

General Plastic Extrusions Inc
1238 Kasson Dr ....Prescott WI 54021 **800-532-3888** 715-262-3806

Genpak Corp
68 Warren St ....Glens Falls NY 12801 **800-626-6695**

Gift Wrap Co
338 Industrial Blvd ....Midway GA 31320 **800-443-4429***
*General

Green Bay Packaging Inc
1700 Webster Ct ....Green Bay WI 54302 **800-236-8400** 920-433-5111

Huhtamaki Inc North America
9201 Packaging Dr ....DeSoto KS 66018 **800-255-4243** 913-583-3025

Indiana Ribbon Inc
106 N Second St ....Wolcott IN 47995 **800-531-3100** 219-279-2112

Innovative Enterprises Inc
25 Town & Country Dr ....Washington MO 63090 **800-280-0300** 636-390-0300

	Toll-Free	Phone

International Paper Co
6400 Poplar Ave ....Memphis TN 38197 **800-223-1268*** 901-419-9000
*NYSE: IP ■ *Prod Info*

LallyPak Inc
1209 Central Ave ....Hillside NJ 07205 **800-523-8484** 908-351-4141

Laminations
3010 E Venture Dr ....Appleton WI 54911 **800-925-2626** 920-831-0596

Lewis Label Products
2300 Race St ....Ft Worth TX 76111 **800-772-7728**

LPS Industries Inc
10 Caesar Pl ....Moonachie NJ 07074 **800-275-6577*** 201-438-3515
*Sales

Novacel 21 Third St ....Palmer MA 01069 **877-668-2235** 413-283-3468

Oracle Packaging
220 E Polo Rd ....Winston-Salem NC 27105 **800-634-3645** 888-260-3947

Pactiv Corp
1900 W Field Ct ....Lake Forest IL 60045 **888-828-2850** 847-482-2000

Pak West Paper & Packaging
4042 W Garry Ave ....Santa Ana CA 92704 **800-927-7299** 714-557-7420

Pratt Industries USA
1800C Sarasota Pkwy ....Conyers GA 30013 **800-835-2088** 770-918-5678

Robinson Industries Inc
3051 W Curtis Rd ....Coleman MI 48618 **877-465-4055** 989-465-6111

Rx Systems Inc
121 Point West Blvd ....St. Charles MO 63301 **800-922-9142**

Sabert Corp
2288 Main St Ext ....Sayreville NJ 08872 **800-722-3781**

Sealed Air Corp Packaging Products Div
301 Mayhill St ....Saddle Brook NJ 07663 **800-648-9093** 201-712-7000

Silgan Holdings Inc
4 Landmark Sq Ste 400 ....Stamford CT 06901 **800-732-0330** 203-975-7110
NASDAQ: SLGN

UFP Technologies Inc
172 E Main St ....Georgetown MA 01833 **800-372-3172** 978-352-2200
NASDAQ: UFPT

Unger Co 12401 Berea Rd ....Cleveland OH 44111 **800-321-1418** 216-252-1400

Viskase Cos Inc
333 E Butterfield Rd Ste 40 ....Lombard IL 60148 **800-323-8562** 630-874-0700

Warp Bros Flex-O-Glass Inc
4647 W Augusta Blvd ....Chicago IL 60651 **800-621-3345** 773-261-5200

Weyerhaeuser Co
33663 Weyerhaeuser Way S ....Federal Way WA 98003 **800-525-5440** 253-924-2345
NYSE: WY

Winpak Ltd
100 Salteaux Crescent ....Winnipeg MB R3J3T3 **800-041 2600** 204-889-1015
TSE: WPK

WS Packaging Group Inc
2571 S Hemlock Rd ....Green Bay WI 54229 **800-236-3424** 800-818-5481

545 PACKING & CRATING

	Toll-Free	Phone

Allied Container Systems Inc
39 Ygnacio Valley Rd No 402 ....Walnut Creek CA 94596 **800-943-6510** 925-944-7600

Craters & Freighters
331 Corporate Cir Ste J ....Golden CO 80401 **800-736-3335**

Fapco Inc 216 Post Rd ....Buchanan MI 49107 **800-782-0167**

Navis Pack & Ship Centers
12742 E Caley Ave Ste 2 A ....Centennial CO 80111 **800-344-3528**

Packaging Services of Maryland Inc
16461 Elliott Pkwy ....Williamsport MD 21795 **800-223-6255** 301-223-6200

Rollins Moving & Storage Inc
1900 E Leffel Ln ....Springfield OH 45505 **800-826-8094** 937-325-2484

Southern States Packaging Co
PO Box 650 ....Spartanburg SC 29304 **800-621-2051**

Tech Packaging Inc
13241 Bartram Pk Blvd Ste 601 ....Jacksonville FL 32258 **866-453-8324** 904-288-6403

Unicep Packaging Inc
1702 Industrial Dr ....Sandpoint ID 83864 **800-354-9396** 208-265-9696

546 PAINTS, VARNISHES, RELATED PRODUCTS

	Toll-Free	Phone

Aervoe Industries Inc
1100 Mark Cir ....Gardnerville NV 89410 **800-227-0196** 775-783-3100

Aexcel Corp
7373 Production Dr ....Mentor OH 44060 **800-854-0782** 440-974-3800

Akron Paint & Varnish Inc
1390 Firestone Pkwy ....Akron OH 44301 **800-772-3452** 330-773-8911

American Safety Technologies Inc
565 Eagle Rock Ave ....Roseland NJ 07068 **800-631-7841**

Behr Process Corp
3400 W Segerstrom Ave ....Santa Ana CA 92704 **800-854-0133** 714-545-7101

Benjamin Moore & Co
101 Paragon Dr ....Montvale NJ 07645 **800-344-0400** 855-724-6802

BryCoat Inc 207 Vollmer Ave ....Oldsmar FL 34677 **800-989-8788** 727-490-1000

Carboline Co
350 Hanley Industrial Ct ....Saint Louis MO 63144 **800-848-4645** 314-644-1000

Coating & Adhesive Corp (CAC)
1901 Popular St PO Box 1080 ....Leland NC 28451 **800-410-2999** 910-371-3184

DAP Products Inc
2400 Boston St Ste 200 ....Baltimore MD 21224 **800-543-3840*** 888-327-8477
*Cust Svc

Davis Paint Company Inc
1311 Iron St ....North Kansas City MO 64116 **800-821-2029** 816-471-4447

Duckback 101 Prospect Ave ....Cleveland OH 44115 **800-825-5382**

Dunn-Edwards Corp
4885 E 52nd Pl ....Los Angeles CA 90058 **800-537-4098** 323-771-3330

DuPont Performance Coatings
1007 Market St ....Wilmington DE 19898 **800-441-7515** 302-774-1000

Farrell-Calhoun Inc
221 E Carolina Ave ....Memphis TN 38126 **888-832-7735** 901-526-2211

FinishMaster Inc
115 W Washington St 700 S ....Indianapolis IN 46204 **888-311-3678** 317-237-3678

Classified Section

	Toll-Free	Phone
Gemini Coatings Inc		
421 SE 27th St ...El Reno OK 73036	800-262-5710	405-262-5710
Harrison Paint Co		
1329 Harrison Ave SW ...Canton OH 44706	800-321-0680	330-455-5125
HB Fuller Co		
1200 Willow Lake Blvd PO Box 64683 ...St. Paul MN 55164	888-423-8553	651-236-5900
NYSE: FUL		
Hentzen Coatings Inc		
6937 W Mill Rd ...Milwaukee WI 53218	800-236-6589	414-353-4200
Hirshfield's Inc		
725 Second Ave N ...Minneapolis MN 55405	800-432-3701	612-377-3910
Hudson Color Concentrates Inc		
50 Francis St ...Leominster MA 01453	888-858-9065	978-537-3538
ICP Construction		
150 Dascomb Rd ...Andover MA 01810	800-225-1141	978-965-2122
Insl-X 101 Paragon Dr ...Montvale NJ 07645	855-724-6802	
Kelly-Moore Paint Company Inc		
987 Commercial St ...San Carlos CA 94070	800-874-4436	650-592-8337
Kop-Coat Inc		
3040 William Pitt Way ...Pittsburgh PA 15238	800-221-4466	412-227-2700
Lansco Colors		
1 Blue Hill Plz 11th Fl		
PO Box 1685. ...Pearl River NY 10965	800-526-2783	845-507-5942
Lumberjack Building Centers		
3470 Pointe Tremble Rd ...Algonac MI 48001	800-466-5164	810-794-4921
Mantros-Haeuser & Company Inc		
1175 Post Rd E ...Westport CT 06880	800-344-4229*	203-454-1800
*General		
Masterchem Industries LLC		
3135 Old Hwy M ...Imperial MO 63052	866-774-6371	
Michelman Inc		
9080 Shell Rd ...Cincinnati OH 45236	800-333-1723	513-793-7766
Minwax Co		
10 Mountainview Rd ...Upper Saddle River NJ 07458	800-523-9299	
Mobile Paint		
4775 Hamilton Blvd ...Theodore AL 36582	800-621-6952	251-443-6110
Neogard Div Jones-blair Co		
2728 Empire Central St ...Dallas TX 75235	800-492-9400	214-353-1600
O'Leary Paint		
300 E Oakland Ave ...Lansing MI 48906	800-477-2066	517-487-2066
Painters Supply & Equipment Co		
25195 Brest Rd ...Taylor MI 48180	800-589-8100	734-946-8119
Penn Color Inc		
400 Old Dublin Pk ...Doylestown PA 18901	866-617-7366	215-345-6550
Pioneer Mfg		
4529 Industrial Pkwy ...Cleveland OH 44135	800-877-1500	216-671-5500
PPG Industries Inc		
17451 Von Karman Ave ...Irvine CA 92614	800-544-3338	949-474-0400
Republic Powdered Metals Inc		
2628 Pearl Rd ...Medina OH 44256	800-382-1218	
Rodda Paint Co		
6107 N Marine Dr ...Portland OR 97203	800-452-2315	503-521-4300
RPM International Inc		
2628 Pearl Rd ...Medina OH 44256	800-776-4488	330-273-5090
NYSE: RPM		
Rust-Oleum Corp		
11 E Hawthorn Pkwy ...Vernon Hills IL 60061	800-323-3584	847-367-7700
Samuel Cabot Inc		
100 Hale St ...Newburyport MA 01950	800-877-8246	978-465-1900
Seymour of Sycamore Inc		
917 Crosby Ave ...Sycamore IL 60178	800-435-4482	815-895-9101
Sheboygan Paint Co (SPC)		
1439 N 25th St PO Box 417 ...Sheboygan WI 53081	800-773-7801	920-458-2157
Sherwin-Williams Automotive Finishes		
4440 Warrensville Ctr Rd		
...Warrensville Heights OH 44128	800-798-5872	
Sterling-Clark-Lurton Corp		
PO Box 130 ...Norwood MA 02062	800-225-9872	781-762-5400
Textured Coatings Of America		
2422 E 15th St ...Panama City FL 32405	800-454-0340	
Tnemec Company Inc		
6800 Corporate Dr ...Kansas City MO 64120	800-863-6321	816-483-3400
Whitmore Manufacturing Co		
930 Whitmore Dr ...Rockwall TX 75087	800-699-6318	972-771-1000
Willamette Valley Co		
1075 Arrowsmith St ...Eugene OR 97402	800-333-9826	541-484-9621
WM Barr & Company Inc		
PO Box 1879 ...Memphis TN 38101	800-238-2672	901-775-0100
Wolf Gordon Inc		
33-00 47th Ave ...Long Island NY 11101	800-347-0550	
Yenkin-Majestic Paint Corp		
1920 Leonard Ave ...Columbus OH 43219	800-848-1898	614-253-8511

547   PALLETS & SKIDS

	Toll-Free	Phone
Anderson Forest Products Inc		
1267 Old Edmonton Rd ...Tompkinsville KY 42167	800-489-6778	270-487-6778
CTC Packaging		
5264 Lake St PO Box 456. ...Sandy Lake PA 16145	800-241-0900*	724-376-7315
*General		
Hill Wood Products Inc		
9483 Ashawa Rd ...Cook MN 55723	800-788-9689	
Hunter Woodworks Inc		
21038 S Wilmington Ave PO Box 4937 ...Carson CA 90749	800-966-4751	323-775-2544
Litco International Inc		
1 Litco Dr PO Box 150 ...Vienna OH 44473	800-236-1903	330-539-5433
Pallet Consultants Corp		
810 NW 13th Ave ...Pompano Beach FL 33069	888-782-2909	954-946-2212
Pallet Masters Inc		
655 E Florence Ave ...Los Angeles CA 90001	800-675-2579	323-758-6559
PalletOne Inc		
1470 US Hwy 17 S ...Bartow FL 33830	800-771-1148	863-533-1147
Pasco		
2600 S Hanley Rd Ste 450 ...Saint Louis MO 63144	800-489-3300	314-781-2212

	Toll-Free	Phone
Potomac Supply Corp		
1398 Kinsale Rd ...Kinsale VA 22488	800-365-3900*	804-472-2527
*Sales		
Tasler Inc		
1804 Tasler Dr ...Webster City IA 50595	800-482-7537	515-832-5200

548   PAPER - MFR

SEE ALSO Packaging Materials & Products - Paper or Plastics

548-1 Coated & Laminated Paper

	Toll-Free	Phone
BPM Inc 200 W Front St ...Peshtigo WI 54157	800-826-0494	715-582-4551
Diversified Labeling Solutions		
1285 Hamilton Pkwy ...Itasca IL 60143	800-397-3013	630-625-1225
Fortifiber Building Systems Group		
300 Industrial Dr ...Fernley NV 89408	800-773-4777	775-333-6400
Lofton Label Inc		
6290 Claude Way ...Inver Grove Heights MN 55076	877-447-8118	651-552-6257
Nashua Corp		
11 Trafalgar Sq 2nd Fl ...Nashua NH 03063	800-430-7488	603-880-2323
National/AZON		
1148 Rochester Rd ...Troy MI 48083	800-325-5939	248-307-9308
Technicote Westfield Inc		
222 Mound Ave ...Miamisburg OH 45342	800-358-4448	
TST/Impreso Inc		
652 Southwestern Blvd ...Coppell TX 75019	800-527-2878	972-462-0100
Wcp Solutions		
6703 S 234th St Ste 120. ...Kent WA 98032	877-398-3030	

548-2 Writing Paper

	Toll-Free	Phone
Anna Griffin Inc		
99 Armour Dr ...Atlanta GA 30324	888-817-8170	404-817-8170
Crane & Co Inc 30 S St ...Dalton MA 01226	800-268-2281*	
*Cust Svc		
Geographics		
108 Main St 3rd Fl ...Norwalk CT 06851	800-436-4919	
Gordon Paper Company Inc		
PO Box 1806 ...Norfolk VA 23501	800-457-7366	757-464-3581
Louisiana Assn For, The Blind, The		
1750 Claiborne Ave ...Shreveport LA 71103	877-913-6471	318-635-6471
Mafcote Industries Inc		
108 Main St ...Norwalk CT 06851	800-526-4280*	203-847-8500
*Cust Svc		
Mohawk Fine Papers Inc		
465 Saratoga St ...Cohoes NY 12047	800-843-6455	518-237-1740
Performance Office Papers		
21565 Hamburg Ave ...Lakeville MN 55044	800-458-7189	
Specialty Loose Leaf Inc		
1 Cabot St ...Holyoke MA 01040	800-227-3623	413-532-0106
Top Flight Inc		
1300 Central Ave ...Chattanooga TN 37408	800-777-3740	423-266-8171

549   PAPER - WHOL

	Toll-Free	Phone
Anchor Paper Company Inc		
480 Broadway St ...Saint Paul MN 55101	800-652-9755	651-298-1311
Atlantic Packaging Co		
806 N 23rd St ...Wilmington NC 28405	800-722-5841	910-343-0624
Brawner Paper Company Inc		
5702 Armour Dr ...Houston TX 77020	800-962-9384	713-675-6584
Cole Papers Inc		
1300 N 38th St ...Fargo ND 58102	800-800-8090	701-282-5311
Com-Pac International Inc		
800 W Industrial Park Rd ...Carbondale IL 62901	800-824-0817	
Field Paper Co 3950 D St ...Omaha NE 68107	800-969-3435	
Gpa Specialty Printable Sbstrt		
8740 W 50th St ...McCook IL 60525	800-395-9000	773-650-2020
GreenLine Paper Company Inc		
631 S Pine St ...York PA 17403	800-641-1117	717-845-8697
Hearn Paper Co		
556 N Meridian Rd ...Youngstown OH 44509	800-225-2989	
Kelly Paper Co		
288 Brea Canyon Rd ...Walnut CA 91789	800-675-3559	
Lindenmeyr Munroe		
14 Research Pkwy ...Wallingford CT 06492	800-842-8480	
Lindenmeyr Munroe Central Central National-Gottesman Inc		
3 Manhattanville Rd ...Purchase NY 10577	800-221-3042	
Mac Papers		
3300 Phillips Hwy PO Box 5369. ...Jacksonville FL 32207	800-622-2968	904-348-3300
Midland Paper		
101 E Palatine Rd ...Wheeling IL 60090	800-323-8522	847-777-2700
Millcraft Paper Co		
6800 Grant Ave ...Cleveland OH 44105	800-860-2482	216-441-5500
Miller Supply Inc		
29902 Avenida de las Banderas		
...Rancho Santa Margarita CA 92688	888-240-9237	
Murnane Paper Corp		
345 W Fischer Farm Rd ...Elmhurst IL 60126	855-632-8191	630-530-8222
Newell Paper Co		
1212 Grand Ave ...Meridian MS 39301	800-844-8894	
PaperDirect Inc		
1005 E Woodmen Rd ...Colorado Springs CO 80920	800-272-7377	800-338-3346
Redd Paper Co 3851 Ctr Loop ...Orlando FL 32808	800-961-6656	407-299-6656
Roosevelt Paper Co		
1 Roosevelt Dr ...Mount Laurel NJ 08054	800-523-3470	856-303-4100
Spicers Paper Inc		
12310 Slauson Ave ...Santa Fe Springs CA 90670	800-774-2377	562-698-1199
White Paper Co 9990 River Way ...Delta BC V4G1M9	888-840-7300	604-951-3900

550 PAPER CONVERTERS

				Toll-Free	Phone
Ameri-Fax Corp					
6520 W 20th Ave Unit 2	Hialeah	FL	33016	**800-262-8214**	305-828-1701
BagcraftPapercon					
3900 W 43rd St	Chicago	IL	60632	**800-621-8468**	773-254-8000
C-P Flexible Packaging					
15 Grumbacher Rd	York	PA	17406	**800-815-0667**	717-764-1193
Caraustar Industries Inc					
5000 Austell-Powder Springs Rd Ste 300	Austell	GA	30106	**800-858-1438**	770-948-3100
Case Paper Company Inc					
500 Mamaroneck Ave	Harrison	NY	10528	**800-222-2922**	888-227-3178
Cindus Corp 515 Stn Ave	Cincinnati	OH	45215	**800-543-4691**	
Commercial Cutting & Graphics LLC					
208 Central Ave	Mansfield	OH	44905	**800-995-2251**	419-526-4800
Crusader Paper Company Inc					
350 Holt Rd	North Andover	MA	01845	**800-421-0007**	
Kanzaki Specialty Papers					
20 Cummings St	Ware	MA	01082	**888-526-9254**	413-967-6204
Lauterbach Group Inc					
W222 N5710 Miller Way	Sussex	WI	53089	**800-841-7301***	262-820-8130
*Sales					
Mafcote Industries Inc					
108 Main St	Norwalk	CT	06851	**800-526-4280***	203-847-8500
*Cust Svc					
Maritime Paper Products Ltd					
25 Borden Ave PO Box 668	Dartmouth	NS	B2Y3Y9	**800-565-5353**	902-468-5353
Max International Converters Inc					
2360 Dairy Rd	Lancaster	PA	17601	**800-233-0222**	
Pacon Corp					
2525 N Casaloma Dr	Appleton	WI	54912	**800-333-2545**	
Paper Systems Inc					
185 S Pioneer Blvd	Springboro	OH	45066	**888-564-6774**	937-746-6841
Protect-All Inc					
109 Badger Pkwy	Darion	WI	53114	**888-432-8526**	
Southeastern Paperboard Inc					
100 S Harris Rd	Piedmont	SC	29673	**800-229-7372**	864-277-7353
Spectra-Kote Corp					
301 E Water St	Gettysburg	PA	17325	**800-241-4626**	717-334-3177
Spinnaker Coating Inc					
518 E Water St	Troy	OH	45373	**800-543-9452**	937-332-6500
TimeMed Labeling Systems Inc					
144 Tower Dr	Burr Ridge	IL	60527	**800-323-4840***	630-986-1800
*Cust Svc					
Woodland Paper Inc					
50785 Pontiac Trl	Wixom	MI	48393	**800-979-9919**	248-926-5550

551 PAPER FINISHERS (EMBOSSING, COATING, GILDING, STAMPING)

				Toll-Free	Phone
Colad Group 801 Exchange St	Buffalo	NY	14210	**800-950-1755**	716-961-1776
Complemar Partners					
500 Lee Rd	Rochester	NY	14606	**800-388-7254**	585-647-5800
Loroco Industries Inc					
5000 Creek Rd	Cincinnati	OH	45242	**800-215-9474**	513-891-9544
MDC Inc 2547 Progress Rd	Madison	WI	53716	**800-395-9405**	608-221-3422
Walton Press (WP)					
402 Mayfield Dr	Monroe	GA	30655	**800-354-0235**	770-267-2596

552 PAPER INDUSTRIES MACHINERY

				Toll-Free	Phone
Baumfolder Corp					
1660 Campbell Rd	Sidney	OH	45365	**800-543-6107**	937-492-1281
BW Papersystems					
3333 Crocker Ave	Sheboygan	WI	53082	**888-310-1898**	920-458-2500
Cranston Machinery Company Inc					
2251 SE Oak Grove Blvd	Oak Grove	OR	97267	**800-547-1012**	503-654-7751
Entwistle Co Dietzco Div					
6 Bigelow St	Hudson	MA	01749	**800-445-8909**	508-481-4000

553 PAPER MILLS

SEE ALSO Pulp Mills ; Paperboard Mills

				Toll-Free	Phone
Advanced Poly Packaging Inc					
1331 Emmitt Rd	Akron	OH	44306	**800-754-4403**	330-785-4000
Appleton Coated LLC					
540 Prospect St	Combined Locks	WI	54113	**888-488-6742**	
Arjobex America Inc					
10901 Westlake Dr	Charlotte	NC	28273	**800-765-9278**	
Armor Protective Packaging					
951 Jones St	Howell	MI	48843	**800-365-1117**	517-546-1117
BPM Inc 200 W Front St	Peshtigo	WI	54157	**800-826-0494**	715-582-4551
Burrows Paper Corp					
501 W Main St	Little Falls	NY	13365	**800-272-7122**	315-823-2300
Cases By Source Inc					
215 Island Rd	Mahwah	NJ	07430	**888-515-5255**	
Cauthorne Paper Co					
12124 S Washington Hwy	Ashland	VA	23005	**800-552-3011**	804-798-6999
Conder Flag Co					
4705 Dwight Evans Rd	Charlotte	NC	28217	**855-344-1500**	704-529-1976
FiberMark North America Inc					
161 Wellington Rd	Brattleboro	VT	05302	**800-784-8558***	802-257-0365
*Cust Svc					

				Toll-Free	Phone
Finch Paper LLC					
1 Glen St	Glens Falls	NY	12801	**800-833-9983**	518-793-2541
Frankston Packaging					
699 N Frankston Hwy	Frankston	TX	75763	**800-881-1495**	903-876-2550
Green Field Paper Co					
7196 Clairemont Mesa Blvd	San Diego	CA	92111	**888-402-9979**	858-565-2585
Inland Empire Paper Co					
3320 N Argonne Rd	Millwood	WA	99212	**866-437-7711**	509-924-1911
International Paper Co					
6400 Poplar Ave	Memphis	TN	38197	**800-223-1268***	901-419-9000
NYSE: IP ■ *Prod Info					
K D M Enterprise LLC					
820 Commerce Pkwy	Carpentersville	IL	60110	**877-591-9768**	847-783-0333
Kimberly-Clark Corp					
351 Phelps Dr	Irving	TX	75038	**888-525-8388**	972-281-1200
NYSE: KMB					
LBP Manufacturing Inc					
1325 S Cicero Ave	Cicero	IL	60804	**800-545-6200**	708-652-5600
Marq Packaging Systems Inc					
3801 W Washington Ave	Yakima	WA	98903	**800-998-4301**	509-966-4300
Merchants Paper Co					
4625 SE 24th Ave	Portland	OR	97202	**800-605-6301**	503-235-2171
Monadnock Paper Mills Inc					
117 Antrim Rd	Bennington	NH	03442	**800-221-2159***	603-588-3311
*Orders					
Nelson Jit Packaging Supplies Inc					
4022 W Turney Ave Ste 3	Phoenix	AZ	85019	**800-939-3647**	623-939-3365
Oakland Packaging & Supply					
3200 Regatta Blvd Unit F	Richmond	CA	94804	**800-237-3103**	510-307-4242
Pratt Industries USA					
1800C Sarasota Pkwy	Conyers	GA	30013	**800-835-2088**	770-918-5678
Resolute Forest Products					
111 Robert-Bourassa Blvd Ste 5000	Montreal	QC	H3C2M1	**800-361-2888**	514-875-2160
Seaman Paper Co of Massachusetts					
51 Main St	Otter River	MA	01436	**800-784-7783**	978-632-1513
Sierra Converting Corp					
1400 Kleppe Ln	Sparks	NV	89431	**800-332-8221**	
Standard Bag Manufacturing Co					
1800 SW Merlo Dr	Beaverton	OR	97003	**800-654-1395**	
Verso Corp					
6775 Lenox Ctr Ct	Memphis	TN	38115	**877-837-7606**	
NYSE: VRS					
Xamax Industries Inc					
63 Silvermine Rd	Seymour	CT	06483	**888-926-2988**	203-888-7200

554 PAPER PRODUCTS - SANITARY

				Toll-Free	Phone
Hoffmaster 2920 N Main St	Oshkosh	WI	54901	**800-327-9774**	920-235-9330
Kimberly-Clark Corp					
351 Phelps Dr	Irving	TX	75038	**888-525-8388**	972-281-1200
NYSE: KMB					
Kleen Test Products Corp					
1611 Sunset Rd	Port Washington	WI	53074	**800-634-7328**	262-284-6600
Principle Business Enterprises Inc					
PO Box 129	Dunbridge	OH	43414	**800-467-3224**	419-352-1551
Solaris Paper Inc					
13415 Carmenita Rd	Santa Fe Springs	CA	90670	**888-998-4778**	

555 PAPER PRODUCTS - WHOL

				Toll-Free	Phone
American Hotel Register Co					
100 S Milwaukee Ave	Vernon Hills	IL	60061	**800-323-5686**	847-743-3000
American Paper & Twine Co					
7400 Cockrill Bend Blvd	Nashville	TN	37209	**800-251-2437**	615-350-9000
Atlantic Paper & Twine Co Inc					
85 York Ave	Pawtucket	RI	02860	**800-613-0950**	401-725-0950
Brame Specialty Company Inc					
PO Box 271	Durham	NC	27702	**800-672-0011**	919-598-1500
Butler-Dearden Paper Service Inc					
PO Box 1069	Boylston	MA	01505	**800-634-7070**	508-869-9000
Central Paper Products Co Inc					
350 Gay St John C Mongan Industrial Park	Manchester	NH	03103	**800-339-4065**	603-624-4065
Dacotah Paper Co					
3940 15th Ave N	Fargo	ND	58102	**800-270-6352**	701-281-1730
Ernest Paper Products					
5777 Smithway St	Commerce	CA	90040	**800-233-7788**	
Fleetwood-Signode					
3624 West Lake Ave	Glenview	IL	60026	**800-862-7997**	847-657-5111
Garland C Norris Co					
1101 Terry Rd	Apex	NC	27502	**800-331-8920**	919-387-1059
Gem State Paper & Supply Co					
1801 Highland Ave E	Twin Falls	ID	83303	**800-727-2737**	208-733-6081
H T. Berry Co Inc PO Box B	Canton	MA	02021	**800-736-2206**	781-828-6000
Harder Corp 7029 Raywood Rd	Monona	WI	53713	**800-261-3400**	608-271-5127
Heartland Paper Co					
808 W Cherokee St	Sioux Falls	SD	57104	**800-843-7922***	605-336-1190
*Cust Svc					
**Johnston	Food Service & Cleaning Solutions**					
2 Eagle Dr	Auburn	NY	13021	**800-800-7123**	315-253-8435
Landsberg Orora					
1640 S Greenwood Ave	Montebello	CA	90640	**888-526-3723***	323-832-2000
*Cust Svc					
Leonard Paper Co					
725 N Haven St	Baltimore	MD	21205	**800-327-5547***	
*Cust Svc					
M Conley Co					
1312 Fourth St SE	Canton	OH	44707	**800-362-6001**	330-456-8243
Mayfield Paper Co					
1115 S Hill St	San Angelo	TX	76903	**800-725-1441**	325-653-1444
National Paper & Sanitary Supply					
2511 S 156th Cir	Omaha	NE	68130	**800-647-2737**	402-330-5507
Nichols PO Box 291	Muskegon	MI	49443	**800-442-0213**	231-799-2120

				Toll-Free	Phone
Pacific Packaging Products Inc					
24 Industrial Way	Wilmington	MA	01887	800-777-0300	978-657-9100
Packaging Distribution Services Inc (PDS)					
2308 Sunset Rd	Des Moines	IA	50321	800-747-2699	515-243-3156
Paterson Pacific Parchment Co					
625 Greg St	Sparks	NV	89431	800-678-8104	775-353-3000
Phillips Distribution Inc					
3000 E Houston St	San Antonio	TX	78219	800-580-2397	210-227-2397
Pollock Paper & Packaging					
1 Pollock Pl	Grand Prairie	TX	75050	800-843-7320*	972-263-2126
*Cust Svc					
S Freedman & Sons Inc					
3322 Pennsy Dr	Landover	MD	20785	800-545-7277	301-322-5000
Saint Louis Paper & Box Co					
3843 Garfield Ave	Saint Louis	MO	63113	800-779-7901	314-531-7900
Schwarz					
8338 Austin Ave	Morton Grove	IL	60053	800-323-4903	
Shorr Packaging Inc					
800 N Commerce St	Aurora	IL	60504	888-885-0055	630-978-1000
Snyder Paper Corp					
250 26th St Dr SE PO Box 758	Hickory	NC	28603	800-222-8562	828-328-2501
TSN Inc 4001 Salazar Way	Frederick	CO	80504	888-997-5959*	303-530-0600
*General					

556 PAPERBOARD & CARDBOARD - DIE-CUT

				Toll-Free	Phone
Alvah Bushnell Co					
519 E Chelten Ave	Philadelphia	PA	19144	800-255-7434	800-814-7296
Blanks/USA Inc					
7700 68th Ave N #7	Minneapolis	MN	55428	800-328-7311	
Crescent Cardboard Company LLC					
100 W Willow Rd	Wheeling	IL	60090	888-293-3956	847-537-3400
Demco Inc					
4810 Forest Run Rd	Madison	WI	53704	800-356-1200*	608-241-1201
*Orders					
GBS Filing Solutions					
224 Morges Rd	Malvern	OH	44644	800-873-4427	330-494-5330
Tap Packaging Solutions					
2160 Superior Ave	Cleveland	OH	44114	800-827-5679	216-781-6000
Topps Company Inc					
1 Whitehall St	New York	NY	10004	800-489-9149	212-376-0300
University Products Inc					
517 Main St	Holyoke	MA	01040	800-628-1912	413-532-3372

557 PAPERBOARD MILLS

SEE ALSO Pulp Mills ; Paper Mills

				Toll-Free	Phone
Cascades Inc					
404 Marie-Victorin Blvd	Kingsey Falls	QC	J0A1B0	800-361-4070	819-363-5100
TSX: CAS					
FiberMark North America Inc					
161 Wellington Rd	Brattleboro	VT	05302	800-784-8558*	802-257-0365
*Cust Svc					
International Paper Co					
6400 Poplar Ave	Memphis	TN	38197	800-223-1268*	901-419-9000
NYSE: IP ■ *Prod Info					
Newman & Company Inc					
6101 Tacony St	Philadelphia	PA	19135	800-523-3256	215-333-8700
Packaging Corp of America					
1955 W Field Ct	Lake Forest	IL	60045	800-456-4725	
NYSE: PKG					
Pactiv Corp					
1900 W Field Ct	Lake Forest	IL	60045	888-828-2850	847-482-2000
Superior Packaging Solutions					
26858 Almond Ave	Redlands	CA	92374	844-792-2626	
WinterBell Co					
2018 Brevard Rd	High Point	NC	27263	800-685-2957	336-887-2651

558 PARKING SERVICE

				Toll-Free	Phone
Ace Parking Management Inc					
645 Ash St	San Diego	CA	92101	855-223-7275*	619-233-6624
*General					
Allpro Parking LLC					
465 Main St Lafayette Court Bldg					
Ste 105	Buffalo	NY	14203	877-849-7275	716-849-7275
Baltimore County Revenue Authority					
115 Towsontown Blvd E	Baltimore	MD	21286	888-246-5384	410-887-8216
Edison Properties LLC					
100 Washington St	Newark	NJ	07102	888-727-5327	973-643-0895
Park 'N Fly					
2060 Mt Paran Rd Ste 207	Atlanta	GA	30327	800-325-4863*	
*Cust Svc					
Park To Fly					
1900 Jetport Dr					
Exit 8 off S R 528 (Beachline)	Orlando	FL	32809	888-851-8875	407-851-8875
Parking Panda Corp					
3422 Fait Ave	Baltimore	MD	21224	800-232-6415	
Parking Solutions Inc					
353 W Nationwide Blvd	Columbus	OH	43215	888-469-7690	614-469-7000
PPS Parking & Transportation Inc					
1800 E Garry Ave Ste 107	Santa Ana	CA	92705	800-701-3763	949-223-8707
Standard Parking Corp					
200 E Randolph St Ste 7700	Chicago	IL	60611	888-700-7275	312-274-2000

PARKS - AMUSEMENT

SEE Amusement Parks ; Amusement Park Companies

559 PARKS - NATIONAL - CANADA

				Toll-Free	Phone
Parks Canada					
30 Victoria St	Gatineau	QC	J8X0B3	888-773-8888	819-420-9486
Banff National Park					
PO Box 900	Banff	AB	T1L1K2	877-737-3783	403-762-1550
Bois Blanc Island Lighthouse National Historic Site					
30 Victoria St	Lachine	QC	J8X0B3	888-773-8888	
Glacier National Park					
PO Box 350	Revelstoke	BC	V0E2S0	866-787-6221	250-837-7500
Kluane National Park & Reserve of Canada					
PO Box 5495	Haines Junction	YT	Y0B1L0	877-852-3100	867-634-7250
Mingan Archipelago National Park Reserve of Canada					
1340 de la Digue St	Havre-Saint-Pierre	QC	G0G1P0	877-737-3783	418-538-3331
Mount Revelstoke National Park of Canada					
PO Box 350	Revelstoke	BC	V0E2S0	866-787-6221	250-837-7500
Point Pelee National Park of Canada					
407 Monarch Ln RR 1	Leamington	ON	N8H3V4	888-773-8888	519-322-2365
Prince Albert National Park of Canada					
Northern Prairies Field Unit					
PO Box 100	Waskesiu Lake	SK	S0J2Y0	877-737-3783*	306-663-4522
*Campground Resv					
Prince Edward Island National Park of Canada					
2 Palmers Ln	Charlottetown	PE	C1A5V8	800-663-7192*	902-672-6350
*Campground Resv					
Riel House National Historic Site of Canada					
330 River Rd	Winnipeg	MB	R2M3Z8	888-773-8888	519-826-5391
Sirmilik National Park					
PO Box 300	Pond Inlet	NU	X0A0S0	888-773-8888	867-899-8092
St Andrews Blockhouse National Historic Site of Canada					
30 Victoria St	Gatineau	QC	J8X0B3	888-773-8888	819-420-9486
Wapusk National Park					
PO Box 127	Churchill	MB	R0B0E0	888-773-8888	204-675-8863

560 PARKS - NATIONAL - US

SEE ALSO Nature Centers, Parks, Other Natural Areas ; Parks - State ; Cemeteries - National

Alaska

				Toll-Free	Phone
Gates of the Arctic National Park & Preserve					
4175 Geist Rd	Fairbanks	AK	99709	866-869-6887	907-457-5752
Lake Clark National Park & Preserve					
240 W Fifth Ave Ste 236	Anchorage	AK	99501	800-365-2267	907-644-3626

Arizona

				Toll-Free	Phone
Casa Grande Ruins National Monument					
1100 W Ruins Dr	Coolidge	AZ	85128	877-642-4743	520-723-3172
Chiricahua National Monument					
12856 E Rhyolite Creek Rd	Willcox	AZ	85643	877-444-6777	520-824-3560

Arkansas

				Toll-Free	Phone
Buffalo National River					
402 N Walnut St Ste 136	Harrison	AR	72601	800-447-7538	870-439-2502
Hot Springs National Park					
101 Reserve St	Hot Springs	AR	71901	800-582-2244	501-620-6715

California

				Toll-Free	Phone
Cabrillo National Monument					
1800 Cabrillo Memorial Dr	San Diego	CA	92106	800-236-7916	619-557-5450
Eugene O'Neill National Historic Site					
1000 Kuss Rd	Danville	CA	94526	866-945-7920	925-838-0249
Lassen Volcanic National Park					
38050 Hwy 36 E PO Box 100	Mineral	CA	96063	800-427-7623	530-595-4480
Pinnacles National Monument					
5000 Hwy 146	Paicines	CA	95043	877-444-6777	831-389-4485
Point Reyes National Seashore					
1 Bear Valley Rd	Point Reyes Station	CA	94956	877-874-2478	415-464-5100
Santa Monica Mountains National Recreation Area					
401 W Hillcrest Dr	Thousand Oaks	CA	91360	888-275-8747	805-370-2300

Colorado

				Toll-Free	Phone
Colorado National Monument					
1750 Rim Rock Dr	Fruita	CO	81521	866-945-7920	970-858-3617

Florida

				Toll-Free	Phone
Dry Tortugas National Park					
PO Box 6208	Key West	FL	33041	800-788-0511	305-242-7700
Everglades National Park					
40001 SR-9336	Homestead	FL	33034	800-788-0511	305-242-7700
William J Rish Recreational Park					
6773 Cape San Blas Rd	Port St Joe	FL	32456	800-470-8101	

Georgia

				Toll-Free	Phone
Chattahoochee River National Recreation Area					
1978 Island Ford Pkwy	Atlanta	GA	30350	877-874-2478	678-538-1200
Cumberland Island National Seashore					
101 Wheeler St	Saint Marys	GA	31558	877-860-6787	912-882-4336

Idaho

	Toll-Free	Phone
Craters of the Moon National Monument & Preserve		
PO Box 29 .... Arco ID 83213	**800-562-3408**	208-527-1335
Nez Perce National Historical Park		
39063 US Hwy 95 .... Spalding ID 83540	**800-537-7962**	208-843-2261

Indiana

	Toll-Free	Phone
Lincoln Boyhood National Memorial		
2916 E S St PO Box 1816............. Lincoln City IN 47552	**800-445-9667**	812-937-4541

Louisiana

	Toll-Free	Phone
New Orleans Jazz National Historical Park		
419 Decatur St .... New Orleans LA 70130	**877-520-0677**	504-589-4806
Poverty Point National Monument		
c/o Poverty Point State Pk PO Box 276.............. Epps LA 71237	**888-926-5492**	318-926-5492

Maryland

	Toll-Free	Phone
Fort McHenry National Monument & Historic Shrine		
2400 E Fort Ave .... Baltimore MD 21230	**866-945-7920**	410-962-4290

Massachusetts

	Toll-Free	Phone
Boston Harbor Islands National Recreation Area		
408 Atlantic Ave Ste 228.................. Boston MA 02110	**877-874-2478**	617-223-8666

Minnesota

	Toll-Free	Phone
Voyageurs National Park		
360 Hwy 11 E .... International Falls MN 56649	**888-381-2873**	218-283-6600

Mississippi

	Toll-Free	Phone
Brice's Crossroads National Battlefield Site		
2680 Natchez Trace Pkwy .... Tupelo MS 38804	**800-305-7417**	662-680-4025
Natchez Trace National Scenic Trail		
2680 Natchez Trace Pkwy .... Tupelo MS 38804	**800-305-7417**	662-680-4025
Tupelo National Battlefield		
2680 Natchez Trace Pkwy .... Tupelo MS 38804	**800-305-7417**	662-680-4025

Missouri

	Toll-Free	Phone
Jefferson National Expansion Memorial		
11 N Fourth St .... Saint Louis MO 63102	**855-733-4522**	314-655-1700
Ozark National Scenic Riverways		
404 Watercress Dr PO Box 490 .... Van Buren MO 63965	**877-444-6777**	573-323-4236

New York

	Toll-Free	Phone
Eleanor Roosevelt National Historic Site		
4097 Albany Post Rd .... Hyde Park NY 12538	**800-337-8474**	845-229-9115

Ohio

	Toll-Free	Phone
Cuyahoga Valley National Park		
15610 Vaughn Rd .... Brecksville OH 44141	**800-445-9667**	216-524-1497

Oregon

	Toll-Free	Phone
Oregon Caves National Monument		
19000 Caves Hwy .... Cave Junction OR 97523	**877-245-9022**	541-592-2100

Pennsylvania

	Toll-Free	Phone
Delaware National Scenic River		
Delaware Water Gap National Recreation Area		
1978 River Rd.......................... Bushkill PA 18324	**800-543-4295**	570-426-2435
Independence National Historical Park		
143 S Third St .... Philadelphia PA 19106	**800-537-7676**	215-597-8787
Steamtown National Historic Site		
150 S Washington Ave .... Scranton PA 18503	**888-693-9391**	570-340-5200

Texas

	Toll-Free	Phone
Padre Island National Seashore		
PO Box 181300 .... Corpus Christi TX 78480	**800-343-2368**	361-949-8068
Rio Grande Wild & Scenic River		
PO Box 129 .... Big Bend National Park TX 79834	**800-839-7238**	432-477-2251
San Antonio Missions National Historical Park		
2202 Roosevelt Ave .... San Antonio TX 78210	**866-945-7920**	210-534-8833

Utah

	Toll-Free	Phone
Canyonlands National Park		
2282 SW Resource Blvd .... Moab UT 84532	**800-394-9978**	435-719-2313

Virginia

	Toll-Free	Phone
Colonial National Historical Park		
PO Box 210 .... Yorktown VA 23690	**866-945-7920**	757-898-3400
Red Hill Patrick Henry National Memorial		
1250 Red Hill Rd .... Brookneal VA 24528	**800-514-7463**	434-376-2044
Richmond National Battlefield Park		
3215 E Broad St .... Richmond VA 23223	**866-733-7768**	804-226-1981
Shenandoah National Park		
3655 US Hwy 211E .... Luray VA 22835	**800-732-0911**	540-999-3500

561 — PARKS - STATE

SEE ALSO Nature Centers, Parks, Other Natural Areas ; Parks - National - US ; Parks - National - Canada

	Toll-Free	Phone

Alabama

	Toll-Free	Phone
Blue Springs State Park		
2595 Alabama 10 .... Clio AL 36017	**800-252-7275**	
Cheaha Resort State Park		
19644 Hwy 281 .... Delta AL 36258	**800-610-5801**	256-488-5111
Lakepoint Resort State Park		
104 Lakepoint Dr .... Eufaula AL 36027	**800-544-5253**	334-687-8011

Alaska

	Toll-Free	Phone
Chugach State Park		
18620 Seward Hwy .... Anchorage AK 99516	**800-478-6196**	907-345-5014
Denali State Park		
7278 E Bogard Rd .... Wasilla AK 99654	**800-478-6196**	907-745-3975

Arizona

	Toll-Free	Phone
ARIZONA STATE PARKS		
Lyman Lake State Park		
PO Box 1428 .... Saint Johns AZ 85936	**877-697-2757**	928-337-4441

Arkansas

	Toll-Free	Phone
Arkansas Museum of Natural Resources		
3853 Smackover Hwy .... Smackover AR 71762	**888-287-2757**	870-725-2877
Bull Shoals-White River State Park		
153 Dam Overlook Ln .... Bull Shoals AR 72169	**877-879-2741**	
Cane Creek State Park		
50 State Pk Rd .... Star City AR 71667	**888-287-2757**	870-628-4714
Conway Cemetery State Park		
1 Capitol Mall 1 Capitol Mall .... Little Rock AR 72201	**888-287-2757**	
Cossatot River State Park-Natural Area		
1980 Hwy 278 W .... Wickes AR 71973	**877-665-6343**	870-385-2201
DeGray Lake Resort State Park		
2027 State Pk Entrance Rd .... Bismarck AR 71929	**800-737-8355**	501-865-5810
Jacksonport State Park		
205 Ave St .... Newport AR 72112	**877-879-2741**	870-523-2143
Lake Chicot State Park		
2542 Hwy 257 .... Lake Village AR 71653	**800-264-2430**	870-265-5480
Ozark Folk Ctr State Park		
1032 Park Ave .... Mountain View AR 72560	**800-264-3655**	870-269-3851
Queen Wilhelmina State Park		
3877 Arkansas 88 .... Mena AR 71953	**888-287-2757**	479-394-2863
South Arkansas Arboretum		
PO Box 7010 .... El Dorado AR 71731	**888-287-2757**	
State Parks of Arkansas		
Herman Davis State Park		
Corner of Ark 18 Baltimore St .... Manila AR 72442	**888-287-2757**	

California

	Toll-Free	Phone
Hearst San Simeon State Historical Monument		
750 Hearst Castle Rd .... San Simeon CA 93452	**800-444-4445**	805-927-2020
Morro Strand State Beach		
1416 Ninth St .... Sacramento CA 95814	**800-777-0369**	
Providence Mountains State Recreation Area		
1416 Ninth St .... Sacramento CA 95814	**800-777-0369**	
State of California		
Morro Bay State Park		
Morro Bay State Park Rd .... Morro Bay CA 93442	**800-777-0369**	805-772-2560
Torrey Pines State Natural Reserve		
9th St .... Sacramento CA 95814	**866-240-4655**	916-653-6995
Watts Towers of Simon Rodia State Historic Park		
1765 E 107th St .... Los Angeles CA 90002	**866-240-4655**	213-847-4646

Colorado

	Toll-Free	Phone
Cherry Creek State Park		
4201 S Parker Rd .... Aurora CO 80014	**866-265-6447**	303-690-1166

Florida

	Toll-Free	Phone
Big Shoals State Park		
11330 SE County Rd 135 .... White Springs FL 32096	**877-635-3655**	386-397-2733
Little Talbot Island State Park		
12157 Heckscher Dr .... Jacksonville FL 32226	**800-326-3521**	904-251-2320
Lovers Key State Park		
8700 Estero Blvd .... Fort Myers Beach FL 33931	**800-326-3521**	239-463-4588

				Toll-Free	Phone
Lower Wekiva River Preserve State Park					
1800 Wekiwa Cir	Apopka	FL	32712	**800-326-3521**	407-884-2008
Myakka River State Park					
13208 SR 72	Sarasota	FL	34241	**800-326-3521**	941-361-6511
Natural Bridge Battlefield Historic State Park					
7502 Natural Bridge Rd	Tallahassee	FL	32305	**800-326-3521**	850-922-6007
Oleta River State Park					
3400 NE 163rd St	North Miami Beach	FL	33160	**800-326-3521**	305-919-1846
Oscar Scherer State Park					
1843 S Tamiami Trl	Osprey	FL	34229	**800-326-3521**	941-483-5956
Ravine Gardens State Park					
1600 Twigg St	Palatka	FL	32177	**800-326-3521**	386-329-3721
Rock Springs Run State Reserve					
30601 CR 433	Sorrento	FL	32776	**800-326-3521**	407-884-2008

Georgia

				Toll-Free	Phone
Fort McAllister State Historic Park					
3894 Ft McAllister Rd	Richmond Hill	GA	31324	**800-864-7275**	912-727-2339
Fort Mountain State Park					
181 Ft Mtn Pk Rd	Chatsworth	GA	30705	**800-864-7275**	706-422-1932
George T Bagby State Park & Lodge					
330 Bagby Pkwy	Fort Gaines	GA	39851	**877-591-5575**	229-768-2571
Georgia department of natural resources					
Fort King George State Historic Site Darien					
302 McIntosh Rd SE	Darien	GA	31305	**800-864-7275**	912-437-4770
Little White House State Historic Site					
401 Little White House Rd	Warm Springs	GA	31830	**800-864-7275**	
Unicoi State Park & Lodge					
1788 Hwy 356 Rd	Helen	GA	30545	**800-573-9659**	
Wormsloe State Historic Site					
7601 Skidaway Rd	Savannah	GA	31406	**800-864-7275**	912-353-3023

Hawaii

				Toll-Free	Phone
Hawaii Information Consortium (HIC)					
201 Merchant St Ste 1805	Honolulu	HI	96813	**800-295-0089**	808-695-4620

Idaho

				Toll-Free	Phone
Dworshak State Park					
9934 Freeman Creek	Lenore	ID	83541	**888-922-6743**	208-476-5994
Harriman State Park					
3489 Green Canyon Rd	Island Park	ID	83429	**866-634-3246**	208-558-7368
Henrys Lake State Park					
3917 E 5100 N	Island Park	ID	83429	**888-922-6743**	208-558-7532
Heyburn State Park					
57 Chatcolet Rd	Plummer	ID	83851	**866-634-3246**	208-686-1308
Lake Cascade State Park					
970 Dam Rd	Cascade	ID	83611	**866-634-3246**	208-382-6544
Three Island Crossing State Park					
1083 S Three Island Park Dr	Glenns Ferry	ID	83623	**888-922-6743**	208-366-2394

Indiana

				Toll-Free	Phone
Harmonie State Park					
3451 Harmonie State Pk Rd	New Harmony	IN	47631	**866-622-6746**	812-682-4821
Lincoln State Park					
Hwy 162 PO Box 216	Lincoln City	IN	47552	**877-478-3657**	812-937-4710
Pokagon State Park					
450 Ln 100 Lake James	Angola	IN	46703	**800-677-9800**	
White River State Park					
302 W Washington St Rm E418	Indianapolis	IN	46204	**800-665-9056**	317-233-2434

Iowa

				Toll-Free	Phone
Lake Wapello State Park					
15248 Campground Rd	Drakesville	IA	52552	**866-495-4868**	641-722-3371
Twin Lakes State Park					
6685 Twin Lakes Rd	Rockwell City	IA	50579	**800-361-8072**	

Kentucky

				Toll-Free	Phone
Blue Licks Battlefield State Resort Park					
10299 Maysville Rd	Carlisle	KY	40311	**800-443-7008**	859-289-5507
Buckhorn Lake State Resort Park					
4441 Ky Hwy 1833	Buckhorn	KY	41721	**800-325-0058**	606-398-7510
Cumberland Falls State Resort Park					
7351 Hwy 90	Corbin	KY	40701	**800-325-0063**	
Kenlake State Resort Park					
542 Kenlake Rd	Hardin	KY	42048	**800-325-0143**	270-474-2211
Kentucky State Parks					
Jenny Wiley State Resort Park					
75 Theatre Ct	Prestonsburg	KY	41653	**800-325-0142**	606-889-1790
Lake Barkley State Resort Park					
3500 State Pk Rd	Cadiz	KY	42211	**800-325-1708**	
Natural Bridge State Resort Park					
2135 Natural Bridge Rd	Slade	KY	40376	**800-325-1710**	
Pennyrile Forest State Resort Park					
20781 Pennyrile Lodge Rd	Dawson Springs	KY	42408	**800-325-1711**	270-797-3421
Pine Mountain State Resort Park					
1050 State Pk Rd	Pineville	KY	40977	**800-325-1712**	
Rough River Dam State Resort Park					
450 Lodge Rd	Falls of Rough	KY	40119	**800-325-1713**	270-257-2311

Louisiana

				Toll-Free	Phone
Bayou Segnette State Park					
7777 Westbank Expy	Westwego	LA	70094	**888-677-2296**	504-736-7140

				Toll-Free	Phone
Centenary State Historic Site					
3522 College St	Jackson	LA	70748	**888-677-2364**	225-634-7925
Chemin-A-Haut State Park					
14656 State Pk Rd	Bastrop	LA	71220	**888-677-2436**	318-283-0812
Cypremort Point State Park					
306 Beach Ln	Cypremort Point	LA	70538	**888-867-4510**	337-867-4510
Fairview-Riverside State Park					
119 Fairview Dr	Madisonville	LA	70447	**888-677-3247**	985-845-3318
Fontainebleau State Park					
67825 US Hwy 190	Mandeville	LA	70448	**888-677-3668**	985-624-4443
Fort Jesup State Historic Site					
32 Geoghagan Rd	Many	LA	71449	**888-677-5378**	318-256-4117
Fort Saint Jean Baptiste State Historic Site					
155 Jefferson St	Natchitoches	LA	71457	**888-677-7853**	318-357-3101
Grand Isle State Park					
Admiral Craik Dr	Grand Isle	LA	70358	**888-787-2559**	985-787-2559
Jimmie Davis State Park					
1209 State Pk Rd	Chatham	LA	71226	**888-677-2263**	318-249-2595
Lake Bistineau State Park					
103 State Pk Rd	Doyline	LA	71023	**888-677-2478**	318-745-3503
Lake Bruin State Park					
201 State Pk Rd	Saint Joseph	LA	71366	**888-677-2784**	318-766-3530
Lake Claiborne State Park					
225 State Pk Rd	Homer	LA	71040	**888-677-2524**	318-927-2976
Lake D'Arbonne State Park					
3628 Evergreen Rd	Farmerville	LA	71241	**888-677-5200**	318-368-2086
Longfellow-Evangeline State Historic Site					
1200 N Main St	Saint Martinville	LA	70582	**888-677-2900**	337-394-3754
Los Adaes State Historic Site					
6354 Hwy 485	Robeline	LA	71469	**888-677-5378**	318-472-9449
Louisiana State Arboretum					
1300 Sudie Lawton Ln	Ville Platte	LA	70586	**888-677-6100**	337-363-6289
Mansfield State Historic Site					
15149 Hwy 175	Mansfield	LA	71052	**888-677-6267**	318-872-1474
Marksville State Historic Site					
837 ML King Dr	Marksville	LA	71351	**888-253-8954**	318-253-8954
North Toledo Bend State Park					
2907 N Toledo Pk Rd	Zwolle	LA	71486	**888-677-6400**	318-645-4715
Poverty Point Reservoir State Park					
1500 Poverty Pt Pkwy	Delhi	LA	71232	**800-474-0392**	318-878-7536
Poverty Point State Historic Site					
6859 Hwy 577	Pioneer	LA	71266	**888-926-5492**	318-926-5492
Rebel State Historic Site					
1260 Hwy 1221	Marthaville	LA	71450	**888-677-3600**	318-472-6255
Saint Bernard State Park					
501 St Bernard Pkwy	Braithwaite	LA	70040	**888-677-7823**	504-682-2101
Sam Houston Jones State Park					
107 Sutherland Rd	Lake Charles	LA	70611	**888-677-7264**	337-855-2665
South Toledo Bend State Park					
120 Bald Eaglel Rd	Anacoco	LA	71403	**888-398-4770**	337-286-9075
Tickfaw State Park					
27225 Patterson Rd	Springfield	LA	70462	**888-981-2020**	225-294-5020
Winter Quarters State Historic Site					
4929 Hwy 608	Newellton	LA	71357	**888-677-9468**	888-677-2784

Maine

				Toll-Free	Phone
Allagash Wilderness Waterway					
106 Hogan Rd Ste 7	Bangor	ME	04401	**800-332-1501**	207-941-4014
Fort Kent State Historic Site					
106 Hogan Rd	Bangor	ME	04401	**800-332-1501**	207-941-4014
John Paul Jones State Historic Site					
106 Hogan Rd Ste 7	Bangor	ME	04401	**800-452-1942**	207-941-4014
Mainegov					
Fort O'Brien State Historic Site					
c/o Cobscook Bay State Park 40 S Edmunds Rd					
	Edmunds Township	ME	04628	**800-332-1501**	207-726-4412
Shackford Head State Park					
106 Hogan Ave	Bangor	ME	04401	**800-400-6856**	207-941-4014

Maryland

				Toll-Free	Phone
Assateague State Park					
7307 Stephen Decatur Hwy	Berlin	MD	21811	**888-432-2267**	410-641-2120
Casselman River Bridge State Park					
580 Taylor Ave	Annapolis	MD	21401	**877-620-8367**	
Gambrill State Park					
8602 Gambrill Pk Rd	Frederick	MD	21702	**800-830-3974**	816-842-8600
Merkle Wildlife Sanctuary					
580 Taylor Ave	Annapolis	MD	21401	**877-620-8367**	
Morgan Run Natural Environment Area					
Benrose Ln	Westminster	MD	21157	**800-830-3974**	410-461-5005
New Germany State Park					
349 Headquarters Ln	Grantsville	MD	21536	**800-830-3974**	301-895-5453
Pocomoke State Forest					
580 Taylor Ave	Annapolis	MD	21401	**877-620-8367**	
Saint Mary's River State Park					
c/o Pt Lookout State Pk					
11175 Pt Lookout Rd	Scotland	MD	20687	**800-830-3974**	301-872-5688
Soldiers Delight Natural Environment Area					
5100 Deer Park Rd	Owings Mills	MD	21117	**800-830-3974**	410-461-5005
Somers Cove Marina					
715 Broadway	Crisfield	MD	21817	**800-967-3474**	410-968-0925
Youghiogheny Scenic & Wild River					
c/o Deep Creek Lake Recreation Area					
898 State Pk Rd	Swanton	MD	21561	**800-248-1893**	301-387-5563

Massachusetts

				Toll-Free	Phone
Moore State Park Mill St	Paxton	MA	01612	**800-437-5922**	508-792-3969

Michigan

	Toll-Free	Phone

				Toll-Free	Phone

Albert E Sleeper State Park
6573 State Pk Rd . . . . Caseville MI 48725 **888-784-7328**
State of Michigan
Island Lake Recreation Area
12950 E Grand River Ave . . . . Brighton MI 48116 **800-447-2757** 810-229-7067
North Higgins Lake State Park
11747 N Higgins Lake Dr . . . . Roscommon MI 48653 **800-447-2757** 989-821-6125

Minnesota

				Toll-Free	Phone

Big Stone Lake State Park
35889 Meadowbrook State Pk Rd . . . . Ortonville MN 56278 **888-646-6367** 320-839-3663
Blue Mounds State Park
1410 161st St . . . . Luverne MN 56156 **888-646-6367** 507-283-6050
Carley State Park
19041 Hwy 74 . . . . Altura MN 55910 **888-646-6367** 507-932-3007
Charles A Lindbergh State Park
1615 Lindbergh Dr S . . . . Little Falls MN 56345 **888-646-6367** 320-616-2525
Crow Wing State Park
3124 State Pk Rd . . . . Brainerd MN 56401 **888-646-6367** 218-825-3075
Father Hennepin State Park
41294 Father Hennepin Pk Rd PO Box 397 . . . . Isle MN 56342 **888-646-6367** 320-676-8763
Forestville/Mystery Cave State Park
21071 County 118 . . . . Preston MN 55965 **888-646-6367** 507-352-5111
Fort Ridgely State Park
72158 County Rd 30 . . . . Fairfax MN 55332 **888-646-6367** 507-426-7840
Fort Snelling State Park
101 Snelling Lake Rd . . . . Saint Paul MN 55111 **888-646-6367** 612-279-3550
Frontenac State Park
29223 County 28 Blvd . . . . Frontenac MN 55026 **888-646-6367** 651-345-3401
George H Crosby Manitou State Park
c/o Tettegouche State Pk
5702 Hwy 61 . . . . Silver Bay MN 55614 **888-646-6367** 218-353-8800
Glacial Lakes State Park
25022 County Rd 41 . . . . Starbuck MN 56381 **888-646-6367** 320-239-2860
Gooseberry Falls State Park
3206 Hwy 61 . . . . Two Harbors MN 55616 **888-646-6367** 218-595-7100
Grand Portage State Park
9393 E Hwy 61 . . . . Grand Portage MN 55605 **888-646-6367** 218-475-2360
Great River Bluffs State Park
43605 Kipp Dr . . . . Winona MN 55987 **888-646 6367** 507-643-6849
Myre-Big Island State Park
19499 780th Ave . . . . Albert Lea MN 56007 **888-646-6367** 507-668-7060
Saint Croix State Park
30065 St Croix Pk Rd . . . . Hinckley MN 55037 **888-646-6367** 320-384-6591
Sakatah Lake State Park
50499 Sakatah Lake State Pk Rd . . . . Waterville MN 56096 **888-646-6367** 507-698-7850
Savanna Portage State Park
55626 Lake Pl . . . . McGregor MN 55760 **888-646-6367** 218-426-3271
Sibley State Park
800 Sibley Pk Rd . . . . New London MN 56273 **888-646-6367** 320-354-2055
Soudan Underground Mine State Park
1302 McKinley Park Rd . . . . Soudan MN 55782 **888-646-6367** 218-300-7000
Split Rock Creek State Park
50th Ave . . . . Jasper MN 56144 **888-646-6367** 507-348-7908

Mississippi

				Toll-Free	Phone

LeFleur's Bluff State Park
2140 Riverside Dr . . . . Jackson MS 39202 **800-237-6278** 601-987-3923
Tombigbee State Park
264 Cabin Dr . . . . Tupelo MS 38804 **800-467-2757** 662-842-7669

Missouri

				Toll-Free	Phone

Hawn State Park
12096 Pk Dr . . . . Sainte Genevieve MO 63670 **877-422-6766** 573-883-3603
Onondaga Cave State Park
7556 Hwy H . . . . Leasburg MO 65535 **877-422-6766** 573-245-6576
Saint Joe State Park
2800 Pimville Rd . . . . Park Hills MO 63601 **877-422-6766** 573-431-1069

New Jersey

				Toll-Free	Phone

Long Pond Ironworks State Park
c/o Ringwood State Pk
1304 Sloatsburg Rd . . . . Ringwood NJ 07456 **800-852-7899** 973-962-7031
Norvin Green State Forest
c/o Ringwood State Pk
1304 Sloatsburg Rd . . . . Ringwood NJ 07456 **800-852-7899** 973-962-7031
Ringwood State Park
1304 Sloatsburg Rd . . . . Ringwood NJ 07456 **800-852-7899** 973-962-7031
Walt Whitman House State Historic Site
330 Mickle Blvd . . . . Camden NJ 08103 **800-843-6420**

New York

				Toll-Free	Phone

Bethpage State Park
Bethpage Pkwy . . . . Farmingdale NY 11735 **800-456-2267** 516-249-0701
Crown Point State Historic Site
21 Grandview Dr . . . . Crown Point NY 12928 **800-456-2267** 518-597-4666
Fair Haven Beach State Park
14985 State Park Rd . . . . Fair Haven NY 13156 **800-456-2267*** 315-947-5205
General
Fillmore Glen State Park
1686 St Rt 38 . . . . Moravia NY 13118 **800-456-2267** 315-497-0130
Hudson River Islands State Park
Schodack Island State Pk . . . . Schodack Landing NY 12156 **800-456-2267** 518-732-0187
John Boyd Thacher State Park
1 Hailes Cave Rd . . . . Voorheesville NY 12186 **800-456-2267** 518-872-1237
John Jay Homestead State Historic Site
PO Box 832 . . . . Katonah NY 10536 **800-456-2267** 914-232-5651

Schoharie Crossing State Historic Site
129 Schoharie St PO Box 140 . . . . Fort Hunter NY 12069 **800-456-2267** 518-829-7516
Schuyler Mansion State Historic Site
32 Catherine St . . . . Albany NY 12202 **800-456-2267** 518-434-0834
Senate House State Historic Site
296 Fair St . . . . Kingston NY 12401 **800-456-2267** 845-338-2786

North Carolina

				Toll-Free	Phone

Goose Creek State Park
2190 Camp Leach Rd . . . . Washington NC 27889 **877-722-6762** 919-707-9300
Gorges State Park
976 Grassy Ridge Rd . . . . Sapphire NC 28774 **800-277-9611** 828-966-9099
Jones Lake State Park
4117 NC 242 Hwy . . . . Elizabethtown NC 28337 **800-277-9611** 910-588-4550
Jordan Lake State Recreation Area
280 State Pk Rd . . . . Apex NC 27523 **877-722-6762** 919-362-0586
Lake Norman State Park
759 State Pk Rd . . . . Troutman NC 28166 **877-722-6762** 919-707-9300
Lumber River State Park
2819 Princess Ann Rd . . . . Orrum NC 28369 **800-277-9611** 910-628-4564
Stone Mountain State Park
3042 Frank Pkwy . . . . Roaring Gap NC 28668 **877-722-6762** 919-707-9300

North Dakota

				Toll-Free	Phone

Former Governors' Mansion State Historic Site
612 E Blvd Ave . . . . Bismarck ND 58505 **866-243-5352** 701-328-2666

Ohio

				Toll-Free	Phone

Deer Creek State Park
20635 State Pk Rd 20
PO Box 125. . . . . Mount Sterling OH 43143 **866-644-6727*** 740-869-3124
*Resv
Delaware State Park
5202 US Rt 23 N . . . . Delaware OH 43015 **866-644-6727** 740-363-4561
Geneva State Park
4499 Pandanarum Rd . . . . Geneva OH 44041 **866-644-6727** 440-466-8400
Jefferson Lake State Park
2045 Morse Rd Bdg G . . . . Richmond OH 43229 **800-945-3543**
Mary Jane Thurston State Park
1466 State Rt 65 . . . . McClure OH 43534 **866-644-6727** 419-832-7662
Mosquito Lake State Park
1439 State Rt 305 . . . . Cortland OH 44410 **866-644-6727** 330-637-2856
Mount Gilead State Park
4119 State Rte 95 . . . . Mount Gilead OH 43338 **866-644-6727**
Paint Creek State Park
280 Taylor Rd . . . . Bainbridge OH 45612 **866-644-6727** 937-981-7061
Scioto Trail State Park
144 Lake Rd . . . . Chillicothe OH 45601 **866-644-6727** 740-887-4818
Strouds Run State Park
2045 Morse Rd . . . . Columbus OH 43229 **800-945-3543** 740-592-2302
Van Buren State Park
12259 Township Rd 218 . . . . Van Buren OH 45889 **866-644-6727** 419-832-7662

Oklahoma

				Toll-Free	Phone

Beaver Dunes State Park
Hwy 270 N . . . . Beaver OK 73932 **800-654-8240** 580-625-3373
Beavers Bend Resort Park
PO Box 10 . . . . Broken Bow OK 74728 **800-435-5514** 580-494-6300
Cherokee State Park
N 4475 Rd . . . . Langley OK 74350 **866-602-4653** 918-435-8066
Disney/Little Blue State Park
Hwy 28 E . . . . Disney OK 74340 **800-622-6317** 918-435-8066
Dripping Springs State Park
16830 Dripping Springs Rd . . . . Okmulgee OK 74447 **800-622-6317** 918-756-5971
Fort Cobb Lake State Park
27022 Copperhead Rd . . . . Fort Cobb OK 73038 **800-622-6317** 405-643-2249
Great Plains State Park
22487 E 1566 Rd . . . . Mountain Park OK 73559 **800-622-6317** 580-569-2032
Honey Creek State Park
901 State Pk Rd . . . . Grove OK 74344 **800-622-6317** 918-786-9447
Keystone State Park
1926 S Hwy 151 . . . . Sand Springs OK 74063 **800-654-8240** 918-865-4991
Lake Murray State Park
900 N Stiles Ave . . . . Oklahoma City OK 73152 **800-652-6552**
Lake Wister State Park
25567 US Hwy 270 . . . . Wister OK 74966 **800-622-6317** 918-655-7212
Osage Hills State Park
2131 Osage Hills State Pk Rd . . . . Pawhuska OK 74056 **800-622-6317** 918-336-4141
Robbers Cave State Park
Hwy 2 N . . . . Wilburton OK 74578 **800-654-8240** 918-465-2565
Sequoyah Bay State Park
6237 E 100th St N . . . . Wagoner OK 74467 **800-622-6317** 918-683-0878
Snowdale State Park
501 S 439 . . . . Salina OK 74361 **800-622-6317** 918-434-2651
Twin Bridges State Park
14801 Hwy 137 S . . . . Fairland OK 74343 **800-622-6317** 918-540-2545

Oregon

				Toll-Free	Phone

Alfred A Loeb State Park
725 Summer St NE Ste C . . . . Salem OR 97301 **800-551-6949** 503-986-0707
Alsea Bay Historic Interpretive Ctr
725 Summer St NE Ste C . . . . Salem OR 97301 **800-551-6949**
Beverly Beach State Park
198 NE 123rd St . . . . Newport OR 97365 **800-551-6949**
Bonnie Lure State Recreation Area
11321 SW Terwilliger Blvd . . . . Portland OR 97219 **800-551-6949**

	Toll-Free	Phone

Bridal Veil Falls State Scenic Viewpoint
I-84 ....Bridal Veil OR 97010 **800-551-6949**

Cape Arago State Park
Cape Arago Hwy ....Coos Bay OR 97420 **800-551-6949**

Cape Lookout State Park
13000 Whiskey Creek Rd W ....Tillamook OR 97141 **800-551-6949**

Cline Falls State Scenic Viewpoint
7100 OR-126 ....Redmond OR 97756 **800-551-6949**

Coquille Myrtle Grove State Natural Site
Powers Hwy ....Myrtle Point OR 97458 **800-551-6949**

Cove Palisades State Park
7300 Jordan Rd ....Culver OR 97734 **800-551-6949**

Crissey Field State Recreation Site
1655 Hwy 101 N ....Brookings OR 97415 **800-551-6949** 541-469-2021

D River State Recreation Site
725 Summer St NE Ste C ....Salem OR 97301 **800-551-6949** 541-994-7341

Dabney State Recreation Area
725 Summer St NE Ste C ....Salem OR 97301 **800-551-6949** 503-695-2261

Darlingtonia State Natural Site
84505 Hwy 101 S ....Florence OR 97439 **800-551-6949** 541-997-3851

Del Rey Beach State Recreation Site
100 Peter Iredale Rd ....Hammond OR 97121 **800-551-6949**

Driftwood Beach State Recreation Site
5580 S Coast Hwy ....Newport OR 97366 **800-551-6949**

Ellmaker State Wayside
198 NE 123rd St ....Newport OR 97365 **800-551-6949**

Fall Creek State Recreation Area
84610 Peninsula Rd ....Fall Creek OR 97438 **800-551-6949**

Farewell Bend State Recreation Area
23751 Old Hwy 30 ....Huntington OR 97907 **800-551-6949**

Fogarty Creek State Recreation Area
US-101 ....Depoe Bay OR 97341 **800-452-5687** 800-551-6949

Fort Rock State Natural Area
725 Summer St NE Ste C ....Salem OR 97301 **800-551-6949**

Gleneden Beach State Recreation Site
198 NE 123rd St ....Newport OR 97365 **800-551-6949**

Golden & Silver Falls State Natural Area
Glenn Creek Rd ....Coos Bay OR 97420 **800-551-6949**

Government Island State Recreation Area
7005 NE Marine Dr ....Portland OR 97218 **800-551-6949** 503-281-0944

Governor Patterson Memorial State Recreation Site
1770 SW Pacific Coast Hwy ....Waldport OR 97394 **800-551-6949**

H B. Van Duzer Forest State Scenic Corridor
8300 Salmon River Hwy ....Otis OR 97368 **800-551-6949**

Heceta Head Lighthouse State Scenic Viewpoint
93111 Hwy 101 N ....Florence OR 97439 **800-551-6949**

Joseph H Stewart State Recreation Area
35251 Hwy 62 ....Trail OR 97541 **800-452-5687** 541-560-3334

Koberg Beach State Recreation Site
725 Summer St NE Ste C ....Salem OR 97301 **800-551-6949** 503-986-0707

Lake Owyhee State Park
725 Summer St NE Ste C ....Salem OR 97301 **800-551-6949** 503-986-0707

Lewis & Clark State Recreation Site
725 Summer St NE Ste C ....Salem OR 97301 **800-551-6949** 503-986-0707

Manhattan Beach State Recreation Site
Hwy 101 N ....Rockaway Beach OR 97136 **800-551-6949**

North Santiam State Recreation Area
PO Box 549 ....Detroit OR 97342 **800-551-6949**

OC&E Woods Line State Trail
46000 Hwy 97 N ....Chiloquin OR 97624 **800-551-6949** 541-883-5558

Oceanside Beach State Recreation Site
13000 Whiskey Creek Rd W ....Tillamook OR 97141 **800-551-6949**

Ona Beach State Park
5580 S Coast Hwy ....Newport OR 97366 **800-551-6949**

Ontario State Recreation Site
23751 Old Hwy 30 ....Huntington OR 97907 **800-551-6949**

Oregon Parks & Recreation Department
Depoe Bay Whale Watching Center
119 SW Hwy 101 ....Depoe Bay OR 97341 **800-551-6949** 541-765-3304

Oregon state Parks
Devil's Lake State Recreation Area
1452 NE Sixth Dr ....Lincoln City OR 97367 **800-551-6949** 541-994-2002

Paradise Point State Recreation Site
PO Box 1345 ....Port Orford OR 97465 **800-551-6949**

Seneca Fouts Memorial State Natural Area
Hood River ....Hood River OR 97031 **800-551-6949**

Shore Acres State Park
725 Summer St NE Ste C ....Salem OR 97301 **800-551-6949** 541-888-3732

South Beach State Park
5580 S Coast Hwy ....Newport OR 97366 **800-452-5687** 800-551-6949

Starvation Creek State Park
Historic Columbia River Hwy State Trl
...............................Cascade Locks OR 97014 **800-551-6949**

Stonefield Beach State Recreation Site
95330 US-101 ....Florence OR 97439 **800-551-6949**

Succor Creek State Natural Area
1298 Lake Owyhee Dam Rd ....Adrian OR 97901 **800-551-6949**

Tokatee Klootchman State Natural Site
93111 Hwy 101 N ....Florence OR 97439 **800-551-6949**

Touvelle State Recreation Site
Table Rock Rd ....Central Point OR 97502 **800-551-6949**

Tub Springs State Wayside
Tub Springs State Wayside ....Ashland OR 97520 **800-551-6949**

Umpqua Lighthouse State Park
Umpqua Lighthouse State Park ....Reedsport OR 97467 **800-551-6949** 541-271-4118

Unity Lake State Recreation Site
725 Summer St NE Ste C ....Salem OR 97301 **800-551-6949** 541-932-4453

Willamette Stone State Heritage Site
11321 SW Terwilliger Blvd ....Portland OR 97219 **800-551-6949**

William M Tugman State Park
72549 Hwy 101 ....Lakeside OR 97449 **800-551-6949**

Winchuck State Recreation Site
1655 Hwy 101 N ....Brookings OR 97415 **800-551-6949**

Yachats Ocean Road State Natural Site
5580 S Coast Hwy ....Newport OR 97366 **800-551-6949**

Pennsylvania

				Toll-Free	Phone

Pine Grove Furnace State Park
1100 Pine Grove Rd ....Gardners PA 17324 **888-727-2757** 717-486-7174

Presque Isle State Park
301 Peninsula Dr Ste 1................Erie PA 16505 **888-727-2757** 814-833-7424

Prompton State Park
c/o Lackawanna ......North Abington Township PA 18414 **888-727-2757** 570-945-3239

Salt Springs State Park
c/o Lackawanna ......North Abington Township PA 18414 **888-727-2757** 570-945-3239

South Carolina

	Toll-Free	Phone

Aiken State Natural Area
1145 State Pk Rd ....Windsor SC 29856 **866-345-7275** 803-649-2857

Edisto Beach State Park
8377 State Cabin Rd ....Edisto Island SC 29438 **866-345-7275** 843-869-2156

Hampton Plantation State Historic Site
1950 Rutledge Rd ....McClellanville SC 29458 **866-345-7275** 843-546-9361

Hickory Knob State Resort Park
1591 Resort Dr ....McCormick SC 29835 **800-491-1764** 864-391-2450

Huntington Beach State Park
16148 Ocean Hwy ....Murrells Inlet SC 29576 **800-491-1764** 843-237-4440

Lake Greenwood State Recreation Area
302 State Pk Rd ....Ninety Six SC 29666 **866-345-7275** 864-543-3535

Little Pee Dee State Park
1298 State Pk Rd ....Dillon SC 29536 **800-491-1764** 843-774-8872

South Dakota

	Toll-Free	Phone

Beaver Creek Nature Area
48351 264th St ....Valley Springs SD 57068 **800-710-2267** 605-594-3824

George S Mickelson Trail
11361 Nevada Gulch Rd ....Lead SD 57754 **800-888-1798** 605-584-3896

Indian Creek Recreation Area
12905 288th Ave ....Mobridge SD 57604 **800-710-2267*** 605-845-7112
*Resv

Lake Thompson Recreation Area
21176 Flood Club Rd ....Lake Preston SD 57249 **800-710-2267** 605-847-4893

State of South Dakota
Lake Cochrane Recreation Area
3454 Edgewater Dr ....Gary SD 57237 **800-710-2267** 605-882-5200

Tennessee

	Toll-Free	Phone

Big Ridge State Park
1015 Big Ridge Rd ....Maynardville TN 37807 **800-471-5305** 865-992-5523

Cove Lake State Park
110 Cove Lake Ln ....Caryville TN 37714 **800-250-8615** 423-566-9701

Edgar Evins State Park
1630 Edgar Evins State Pk Rd .....Silver Point TN 38582 **800-250-8619** 931-858-2114

Montgomery Bell State Resort Park
1020 Jackson Hill Rd ....Burns TN 37029 **800-250-8613** 615-797-9052

Pickett State Park
4605 Pickett Pk Hwy ....Jamestown TN 38556 **877-260-0010** 931-879-5821

Rock Island State Park
82 Beach Rd ....Rock Island TN 38581 **800-713-6065** 931-686-2471

Tims Ford State Park
570 Tims Ford Dr ....Winchester TN 37398 **800-471-5295** 931-962-1183

Texas

	Toll-Free	Phone

Hueco Tanks State Historic Site
6900 Hueco Tanks Rd Ste 1 ....El Paso TX 79938 **800-792-1112** 915-857-1135

Longhorn Cavern State Park
PO Box 732 ....Burnet TX 78611 **877-441-2883** 830-598-2283

Texas Parks & Wildlife Department
4200 Smith School Rd ....Austin TX 78744 **800-792-1112** 512-389-4800

Utah

	Toll-Free	Phone

Huntington State Park
PO Box 1343 ....Huntington UT 84528 **800-322-3770** 435-687-2491

Millsite State Park
Ferron Canyon Rd PO Box 1343........Huntington UT 84528 **800-322-3770** 435-384-2552

Red Fleet State Park
8750 North Hwy 191 ....Vernal UT 84078 **800-322-3770** 435-789-4432

Steinaker State Park
4335 N Hwy 191 ....Vernal UT 84078 **800-322-3770** 435-789-4432

Willard Bay State Park
900 W 650 N Ste A ....Willard UT 84340 **800-322-3770** 435-734-9494

Vermont

	Toll-Free	Phone

Alburg Dunes State Park
151 Coon Pt Rd ....Alburg VT 05440 **800-262-5226** 802-796-4170

Crystal Lake State Park
96 Bellwater Ave ....Barton VT 05822 **888-409-7579** 802-525-6205

Lake Carmi State Park
460 Marsh Farm Rd ....Enosburg Falls VT 05450 **888-409-7579*** 802-933-8383
*Resv

Seyon Lodge State Park
1 National Life Dr ....Vermont VT 05620 **888-409-7579** 802-584-3829

Stillwater State Park
44 Stillwater Rd ....Groton VT 05046 **888-409-7579** 802-584-3822

Waterbury Ctr State Park
177 Reservoir Rd ....Waterbury Center VT 05677 **800-837-4261** 802-244-1226

		Toll-Free	Phone

Virginia

False Cape State Park
4001 Sandpiper Rd . . . . Virginia Beach VA 23456 — 800-933-7275* — 757-426-7128
*General

Washington

Fort Casey State Park
1280 S Engle Rd . . . . Coupeville WA 98239 — 888-226-7688 — 360-678-4519
Lake Sammamish State Park
2000 NW Sammamish Rd . . . . Issaquah WA 98027 — 888-226-7688 — 425-649-4275
Pearrygin Lake State Park
561 Bear Creek Rd . . . . Winthrop WA 98862 — 888-226-7688 — 509-996-2370
Twin Harbors Beach State Park
3120 Hwy 105 . . . . Westport WA 98595 — 888-226-7688 — 360-268-9717

Wisconsin

Black River State Forest
W10325 Hwy 12 . . . . Black River WI 54615 — 888-936-7463
Heritage Hill State Historical Park
2640 S Webster Ave . . . . Green Bay WI 54301 — 800-721-5150 — 920-448-5150
Lake Kegonsa State Park
2405 Door Creek Rd . . . . Stoughton WI 53589 — 888-947-2757* — 608-873-9695
*General
Newport State Park
475 County Rd NP . . . . Ellison Bay WI 54210 — 800-847-8882 — 920-854-2500

562 — PARTY GOODS

		Toll-Free	Phone

Amscan Inc
80 Grasslands Rd . . . . Elmsford NY 10523 — 800-444-8887 — 914-345-2020
Balloons Everywhere Ino
16474 Greeno Rd . . . . Fairhope AL 36532 — 800-239-2000
Beistle Co
1 Beistle Plz . . . . Shippensburg PA 17257 — 800-445-2131 — 717-532-2131
Paper Store Inc 20 Main St . . . . Acton MA 01720 — 844-480-7100
Party City Corp
25 Green Pond Rd Ste 1 . . . . Rockaway NJ 07866 — 800-727-8924 — 973-453-8600

563 — PATTERNS - INDUSTRIAL

		Toll-Free	Phone

Adel Wiggins Group of Transdigm Inc
5000 Triggs St . . . . Los Angeles CA 90022 — 800-624-3576 — 323-269-9181
American Micro Products Inc
4288 Armstrong Blvd . . . . Batavia OH 45103 — 800-479-2193
Block & Co
1111 S Wheeling Rd . . . . Wheeling IL 60090 — 800-323-7556
Ceramic Technology Inc
606 Wardell Industrial Pk . . . . Cedar Bluff VA 24609 — 800-437-1142
Freeman Mfg & Supply Co
1101 Moore Rd . . . . Avon OH 44011 — 800-321-8511 — 440-934-1902
Gulf Manufacturing LLC
1221 Indiana St . . . . Humble TX 77396 — 800-333-4493 — 281-446-0093
Magnetic Products Inc
683 Town Center Dr . . . . Highland MI 48357 — 800-544-5930
Spx Flow 611 Sugar Creek Rd . . . . Delavan WI 53115 — 800-252-5200
Tubular Products Co
1400 Red Hollow Rd . . . . Birmingham AL 35215 — 800-456-8823 — 205-856-1300

564 — PATTERNS - SEWING

		Toll-Free	Phone

Bonfit America Inc
5741 Buckingham Pkwy Unit A. . . . . Culver City CA 90230 — 800-526-6348 — 310-204-7880

565 — PAWN SHOPS

		Toll-Free	Phone

CWB Maxium Financial
30 Vogell Rd Ste 1 . . . . Richmond Hill ON L4B3K6 — 800-379-5888 — 905-780-6150
EZCORP Inc 1901 Capital Pkwy . . . . Austin TX 78746 — 800-873-7296 — 855-241-1261
NASDAQ: EZPW
FirstCash Inc
1600 W Seventh St . . . . Fort Worth TX 76102 — 800-290-4598 — 817-335-1100
NASDAQ: FCFS
Go Apply Inc
27081 Aliso Creek Rd Ste 200 . . . . Aliso Viejo CA 92656 — 888-435-3239

566 — PAYROLL SERVICES

SEE ALSO Professional Employer Organizations (PEOs) ; Data Processing & Related Services

		Toll-Free	Phone

Automatic Data Processing Inc (ADP)
1 ADP Blvd . . . . Roseland NJ 07068 — 800-225-5237
NASDAQ: ADP
Corporate Business Solutions
1523 Johnson Ferry Rd Ste 200 . . . . Marietta GA 30062 — 800-239-8182 — 404-521-6030
Employers Resource Management Co
1301 S Vista Ave Ste 200 . . . . Boise ID 83705 — 800-574-4668 — 208-376-3000
Media Services
500 S Sepulveda Blvd 4th Fl. . . . . Los Angeles CA 90049 — 800-738-0409 — 310-440-9600

		Toll-Free	Phone

Patriot Staffing & Services Llc
47 Eggert Ave . . . . Metuchen NJ 08840 — 888-412-6999
SurePayroll
2350 Ravine Way Ste 100. . . . . Glenview IL 60025 — 877-954-7873 — 847-676-8420

567 — PENS, PENCILS, PARTS

SEE ALSO Art Materials & Supplies - Mfr ; Office & School Supplies

		Toll-Free	Phone

Alvin & Company Inc
1335 Blue Hills Ave . . . . Bloomfield CT 06002 — 800-444-2584 — 860-243-8991
Avery Dennison Corp
207 Goode Ave . . . . Glendale CA 91203 — 888-567-4387* — 626-304-2000
NYSE: AVY ■ *Cust Svc
Dixon Ticonderoga Co
195 International Pkwy . . . . Heathrow FL 32746 — 800-824-9430
Dri Mark Products Inc
999 S Oyster Bay Rd Ste 312 . . . . Bethpage NY 11714 — 800-645-9662 — 516-484-6200
Fisher Space Pen Co
711 Yucca St . . . . Boulder City NV 89005 — 800-102-7366 — 702-293-3011
Listo Pencil Corp
1925 Union St . . . . Alameda CA 94501 — 800-547-8648 — 510-522-2910
Musgrave Pencil Company Inc
701 W Ln St . . . . Shelbyville TN 37160 — 800-736-2450 — 931-684-3611
National Pen Corp (NPC)
12121 Scripps Summit Dr . . . . San Diego CA 92131 — 888-672-7370
Pentel of America Ltd
2715 Columbia St . . . . Torrance CA 90503 — 855-528-4101 — 760-200-0547

568 — PERFORMING ARTS FACILITIES

SEE ALSO Convention Centers ; Theaters - Broadway ; Theaters - Resident ; Stadiums & Arenas
Most of the fax numbers provided for these facilities are for the box office.

California

		Toll-Free	Phone

California Ctr for the Arts
340 N Escondido Blvd . . . . Escondido CA 92025 — 800-988-4253 — 760-839-4138
Cerritos Ctr for the Performing Arts
18000 Park Plaza Dr . . . . Cerritos CA 90703 — 800-300-4345 — 562-916-8501
Gary Soren Smith Ctr for the Fine & Performing Arts
Ohlone College
43600 Mission Blvd . . . . Fremont CA 94539 — 800-309-2131 — 510-659-6031
Good Company Players
928 E Olive Ave . . . . Fresno CA 93728 — 800-371-4747 — 559-266-0660
McCallum Theatre
73000 Fred Waring Dr . . . . Palm Desert CA 92260 — 866-889-2787 — 760-340-2787
Pantages Theatre
6233 Hollywood Blvd . . . . Los Angeles CA 90028 — 800-430-8903
Pasadena Convention Center
300 E Green St . . . . Pasadena CA 91101 — 800-307-7977 — 626-793-2122
San Jose Convention Ctr
408 Almaden Blvd . . . . San Jose CA 95110 — 800-726-5673 — 408-792-4511
San Jose Ctr for the Performing Arts
255 S Almaden Blvd . . . . San Jose CA 95113 — 800-726-5673 — 408-288-2800
Wiltern Theatre
3790 Wilshire Blvd . . . . Los Angeles CA 90010 — 800-348-8499 — 213-388-1400

Colorado

		Toll-Free	Phone

Denver Ctr for the Performing Arts
1101 13th St . . . . Denver CO 80204 — 800-641-1222 — 303-893-4000
Wheeler Opera House
320 E Hyman Ave . . . . Aspen CO 81611 — 866-449-0464 — 970-920-5770

Connecticut

		Toll-Free	Phone

Bushnell Ctr for the Performing Arts
166 Capitol Ave . . . . Hartford CT 06106 — 888-824-2874 — 860-987-6000
Long Wharf Theatre
222 Sargent Dr . . . . New Haven CT 06511 — 800-782-8497 — 203-787-4282
Westport Country Playhouse
25 Powers Ct . . . . Westport CT 06880 — 888-927-7529 — 203-227-4177

District of Columbia

		Toll-Free	Phone

DAR Constitution Hall
1776 D St NW . . . . Washington DC 20006 — 800-449-1776 — 202-628-1776

Florida

		Toll-Free	Phone

Barbara B Mann Performing Arts Hall
13350 FSW Pkwy . . . . Fort Myers FL 33919 — 800-440-7469 — 239-481-4849
Curtis M Phillips Ctr for the Performing Arts
3201 Hull Rd PO Box 112750. . . . . Gainesville FL 32611 — 800-905-2787 — 352-392-1900
David A Straz Jr Ctr for the Performing Arts
1010 N WC MacInnes Pl . . . . Tampa FL 33602 — 800-955-1045 — 813-222-1000
Florida Theatre
128 E Forsyth St Ste 300 . . . . Jacksonville FL 32202 — 800-734-4667 — 904-355-5661
Ocean Ctr
101 N Atlantic Ave . . . . Daytona Beach FL 32118 — 800-858-6444 — 386-254-4500
Philharmonic Ctr for the Arts
5833 Pelican Bay Blvd . . . . Naples FL 34108 — 800-597-1900 — 239-597-1111
Raymond F Kravis Ctr for the Performing Arts
701 Okeechobee Blvd . . . . West Palm Beach FL 33401 — 800-572-8471 — 561-832-7469
Ruth Eckerd Hall
1111 McMullen Booth Rd . . . . Clearwater FL 33759 — 800-875-8682 — 727-791-7060
University of West Florida Center for Fine & Performing Arts
11000 University Pkwy Bldg 82 . . . . Pensacola FL 32514 — 800-263-1074 — 850-474-2000

	Toll-Free	Phone
Van Wezel Performing Arts Ctr		
777 N Tamiami Trl ....Sarasota FL 34236	800-826-9303	941-953-3368

Georgia

	Toll-Free	Phone
Atlanta Civic Ctr		
395 Piedmont Ave NE ....Atlanta GA 30308	877-430-7596	404-523-6275
Fox Theatre		
660 Peachtree St NE ....Atlanta GA 30308	855-285-8499	404-881-2100
Savannah Civic Ctr		
301 W Oglethorp Ave ....Savannah GA 31401	800-337-1101	912-651-6550

Illinois

	Toll-Free	Phone
Auditorium Theatre		
50 E Congress Pkwy ....Chicago IL 60605	800-982-2787	312-341-2310
Broadway In Chicago		
24 W Randolph St ....Chicago IL 60601	800-359-2525	312-977-1700
Krannert Ctr for the Performing Arts		
500 S Goodwin Ave ....Urbana IL 61801	800-527-2849	217-333-6700
Parkland College Theatre		
2400 W Bradley Ave ....Champaign IL 61821	800-346-8089	217-351-2528
Symphony Ctr		
220 S Michigan Ave ....Chicago IL 60604	800-223-7114*	312-294-3000
*Cust Svc		

Indiana

	Toll-Free	Phone
Christel DeHaan Fine Arts Ctr		
1400 E Hanna Ave		
University of Indianapolis ....Indianapolis IN 46227	800-232-8634	317-788-3566
Morris Performing Arts Ctr		
211 N Michigan St ....South Bend IN 46601	800-537-6415	574-235-9190

Kentucky

	Toll-Free	Phone
Kentucky Ctr for, The Performing Arts, The		
501 W Main St ....Louisville KY 40202	800-775-7777	502-562-0100

Louisiana

	Toll-Free	Phone
Lake Charles Civic Ctr		
900 Lakeshore Dr ....Lake Charles LA 70601	888-620-1749	337-491-1256
Strand Theatre		
619 Louisiana Ave ....Shreveport LA 71101	800-313-6373	318-226-1481

Maryland

	Toll-Free	Phone
Joseph Meyerhoff Symphony Hall		
1212 Cathedral St ....Baltimore MD 21201	877-276-1444	410-783-8100
Maryland Hall for the Creative Arts		
801 Chase St ....Annapolis MD 21401	866-438-3808	410-263-5544
Merriweather Post Pavilion (MPP)		
10475 Little Patuxent Pkwy ....Columbia MD 21044	877-435-9849	410-715-5550

Massachusetts

	Toll-Free	Phone
Boston Symphony Hall		
301 Massachusetts Ave ....Boston MA 02115	888-266-1200	617-266-1492
South Shore Music Circus		
130 Sohier St ....Cohasset MA 02025	800-514-3849	781-383-9850
Wang Theatre 270 Tremont St ....Boston MA 02116	800-982-2787	

Michigan

	Toll-Free	Phone
Fisher Theatre		
3011 W Grand Blvd ....Detroit MI 48202	800-982-2787	313-872-1000
Midland Ctr for the Arts Inc		
1801 W St Andrews Rd ....Midland MI 48640	800-523-7649	989-631-5930
Wharton Ctr for the Performing Arts		
Michigan State University ....East Lansing MI 48824	800-942-7866	517-432-2000

Minnesota

	Toll-Free	Phone
Guthrie Theater		
818 S Second St ....Minneapolis MN 55415	877-447-8243*	612-377-2224
*Resv		
Orchestra Hall		
1111 Nicollet Mall ....Minneapolis MN 55403	800-292-4141	612-371-5600

Missouri

	Toll-Free	Phone
Fabulous Fox, The		
527 N Grand Blvd ....Saint Louis MO 63103	800-293-5949	314-534-1678
Juanita K Hammons Hall for the Performing Arts		
901 S National Ave ....Springfield MO 65897	888-476-7849	417-836-7678
Legends Theater		
1600 W Hwy 76 ....Branson MO 65616	800-374-7469	702-253-1333
Midland by AMC, The		
1228 Main St ....Kansas City MO 64105	800-653-8000	816-283-9900
Starlight Theatre		
4600 Starlight Rd ....Kansas City MO 64132	800-776-1730	816-363-7827

Montana

	Toll-Free	Phone
Alberta Bair Theater for the Performing Arts		
2722 Third Ave N Ste 200 PO Box 1556 ....Billings MT 59103	877-321-2074	406-256-8915

Nebraska

	Toll-Free	Phone
Lied Ctr for Performing Arts		
301 N 12th St ....Lincoln NE 68588	800-432-3231	402-472-4700
Omaha Community Playhouse		
6915 Cass St ....Omaha NE 68132	888-782-4338	402-553-0800
Orpheum Theatre 409 S 16th St ....Omaha NE 68102	866-434-8587	402-345-0202

New Hampshire

	Toll-Free	Phone
Hopkins Ctr for the Arts		
6041 Wilson Hall ....Hanover NH 03755	800-451-4067	603-646-2422

New Jersey

	Toll-Free	Phone
New Jersey Performing Arts Ctr		
1 Ctr St ....Newark NJ 07102	888-466-5722	973-642-8989
Patriots Theater		
Memorial Dr ....Trenton NJ 08608	866-847-7682	609-984-8484
PNC Bank Art Ctr		
Exit 116 Garden State Pkwy ....Holmdel NJ 07733	800-745-3000	
State Theatre		
15 Livingston Ave ....New Brunswick NJ 08901	800-432-9382	732-247-7200

New Mexico

	Toll-Free	Phone
Greer Garson Theatre Ctr		
1600 St Michael's Dr ....Santa Fe NM 87505	800-456-2673	505-473-6011

North Carolina

	Toll-Free	Phone
Flat Rock Playhouse		
2661 Greenville Hwy ....Flat Rock NC 28731	866-732-8008	828-693-0731

North Dakota

	Toll-Free	Phone
Chester Fritz Auditorium		
3475 University Ave ....Grand Forks ND 58202	800-375-4068	701-777-3076
Festival Concert Hall		
North Dakota State University		
12th Ave N ....Fargo ND 58105	800-726-1724	701-231-7932

Ohio

	Toll-Free	Phone
Cincinnati Playhouse in the Park		
962 Mt Adams Cir ....Cincinnati OH 45202	800-582-3208	513-345-2242
Fraze Pavilion		
695 Lincoln Pk Blvd ....Dayton OH 45429	800-514-3849	937-296-3300
Playhouse Square		
1501 Euclid Ave Ste 200 ....Cleveland OH 44115	866-546-1353	216-771-4444
Stambaugh Auditorium		
1000 Fifth Ave ....Youngstown OH 44504	866-516-2269	330-747-5175
Stranahan Theater		
4645 Heatherdowns Blvd ....Toledo OH 43614	866-381-7469	419-381-8851
Victoria Theatre		
138 N Main St ....Dayton OH 45402	888-228-3630	937-228-3630

Ontario

	Toll-Free	Phone
Centre in the Square		
101 Queen St N ....Kitchener ON N2H6P7	800-265-8977	519-578-1570

Oregon

	Toll-Free	Phone
Pentacle Theater		
324 52nd Ave NW ....Salem OR 97304	800-333-0774	503-364-7200

Pennsylvania

	Toll-Free	Phone
Erie Playhouse 13 W Tenth St ....Erie PA 16501	800-305-0669	814-454-2852
Heinz Hall for the Performing Arts		
600 Penn Ave ....Pittsburgh PA 15222	800-743-8560	412-392-4900
Liacouras Ctr		
1776 N Broad St ....Philadelphia PA 19121	800-298-4200	215-204-2400
Walnut Street Theatre		
825 Walnut St ....Philadelphia PA 19107	800-982-2787	215-574-3550

South Carolina

	Toll-Free	Phone
Alabama Theatre		
4750 Hwy 17 S ....North Myrtle Beach SC 29582	800-342-2262	843-272-1111
Arts Ctr of Coastal Carolina		
14 Shelter Cove Ln ....Hilton Head Island SC 29928	888-860-2787	843-686-3945
Carolina Opry		
8901 Hwy 17 N ....Myrtle Beach SC 29572	800-843-6779	

Tennessee

	Toll-Free	Phone
Grand Ole Opry		
2804 opryland Dr ....Nashville TN 37214	800-733-6779	615-871-6779
Knoxville Civic Auditorium/Coliseum		
500 Howard Baker Jr Ave ....Knoxville TN 37915	877-995-9961	865-215-8900

				Toll-Free	Phone
Ryman Auditorium					
116 Fifth Ave N	Nashville	TN	37219	800-733-6779	615-458-8700

Texas

				Toll-Free	Phone
Bass Performance Hall					
4th & Calhoun Sts	Fort Worth	TX	76102	877-212-4280	817-212-4300
CONVENTION & SPORTS FACILITIES					
900 E Market St	San Antonio	TX	78205	877-504-8895	210-207-8500
El Paso Convention & Performing Arts Ctr					
1 Civic Ctr Plz	El Paso	TX	79901	800-351-6024	915-534-0600
Grand 1894 Opera House					
2020 Postoffice St	Galveston	TX	77550	800-821-1894	409-765-1894
Wichita Falls CVB					
1000 Fifth St	Wichita Falls	TX	76301	800-799-6732	
Williams Performing Arts Ctr					
Abilene Christian University					
1600 Campus Ct	Abilene	TX	79601	800-460-6228	325-674-2199

Utah

				Toll-Free	Phone
Salt Lake Community College Grand Theatre					
1575 S State St	Salt Lake City	UT	84115	800-524-9400	801-957-3322

Virginia

				Toll-Free	Phone
Jefferson Ctr					
541 Luck Ave Ste 221	Roanoke	VA	24016	866-345-2550	540-343-2624
MetroStage					
1201 N Royal St	Alexandria	VA	22314	800-494-8497	703-548-9044
Wolf Trap Foundation for the Performing Arts					
1645 Trap Rd	Vienna	VA	22182	877-965-3872	703-255-1900

Wisconsin

				Toll-Free	Phone
Marcus Ctr for the Performing Arts					
929 N Water St	Milwaukee	WI	53202	888-612-3500	414-273-7206
Weidner Ctr for the Performing Arts					
2420 Nicolet Dr					
University of Wisconsin at Green Bay	Green Bay	WI	54311	800-895-0071	920-465-2726

569   PERFORMING ARTS ORGANIZATIONS

SEE ALSO Arts & Artists Organizations

569-1 Dance Companies

				Toll-Free	Phone
Aspen Santa Fe Ballet					
0245 Sage Way	Aspen	CO	81611	866-449-0464	970-925-7175
Ballet British Columbia					
677 Davie St	Vancouver	BC	V6B2G6	855-985-2787	604-732-5003
Buglisi Dance Theatre					
229 W 42nd St Ste 502	New York	NY	10036	800-754-0797	212-719-3301
Columbia City Ballet					
1545 Main St	Columbia	SC	29201	800-899-7408	803-799-7605
Dayton Contemporary Dance Co					
840 Germantown St	Dayton	OH	45402	888-228-3630	937-228-3232
Houston Ballet					
601 Preston St	Houston	TX	77002	800-828-2787	713-523-6300
Hubbard Street Dance Chicago					
1147 W Jackson Blvd	Chicago	IL	60607	800-982-2787	312-850-9744
Mark Morris Dance Group					
3 Lafayette Ave	Brooklyn	NY	11217	800-957-1046	718-624-8400
Miami City Ballet					
2200 Liberty Ave	Miami Beach	FL	33139	877-929-7010	305-929-7000
Minnesota Ballet					
301 W First St Ste 800	Duluth	MN	55802	800-627-3529	218-529-3742

569-2 Opera Companies

				Toll-Free	Phone
Florentine Opera Co					
700 N Water St Ste 950	Milwaukee	WI	53202	800-326-7372	414-291-5700
Florida Grand Opera					
8390 NW 25th St	Miami	FL	33122	800-741-1010	305-854-1643
Fort Worth Opera					
1300 Gendy St	Fort Worth	TX	76107	877-396-7372	817-731-0833
Hawaii Opera Theatre					
848 S Beretania St Ste 301	Honolulu	HI	96813	800-836-7372	808-596-7372
Houston Grand Opera					
510 Preston St	Houston	TX	77002	800-626-7372	713-546-0200
Opera Colorado					
695 S Colorado Blvd Ste 20	Denver	CO	80246	800-414-2251	303-778-1500
Opera San Jose					
2149 Paragon Dr	San Jose	CA	95131	877-707-7827	408-437-4450
Portland Opera					
211 SE Caruthers St	Portland	OR	97214	866-739-6737	503-241-1407
San Francisco Opera					
301 Van Ness Ave	San Francisco	CA	94102	800-308-2898	415-861-4008
Santa Fe Opera, The					
301 Opera Dr	Santa Fe	NM	87506	800-280-4654	505-986-5900
Sarasota Opera					
61 N Pineapple Ave	Sarasota	FL	34236	866-951-0111	941-366-8450
Seattle Opera 1020 John St	Seattle	WA	98109	800-426-1619*	206-389-7600
*Sales					
Toledo Opera					
425 Jefferson Ave Ste 601	Toledo	OH	43604	866-860-9048	419-255-7464
Tulsa Opera					
1610 S Boulder Ave	Tulsa	OK	74119	866-298-2530	918-582-4035

569-3 Orchestras

				Toll-Free	Phone
Austin Symphony Orchestra					
1101 Red River St	Austin	TX	78701	888-462-3787	512-476-6064
Baltimore Symphony Orchestra					
1212 Cathedral St	Baltimore	MD	21201	877-276-1444	410-783-8100
Bangor Symphony Orchestra					
PO Box 1441	Bangor	ME	04402	800-639-3221*	207-942-5555
*General					
Boston Pops					
301 Massachusetts Ave Symphony Hall	Boston	MA	02115	888-266-1200	617-266-1492
Boston Symphony Orchestra					
301 Massachusetts Ave Symphony Hall	Boston	MA	02115	888-266-1200	617-266-1492
Chicago Symphony Orchestra					
220 S Michigan Ave	Chicago	IL	60604	800-223-7114	312-294-3000
Cleveland Orchestra, The					
11001 Euclid Ave Severance Hall	Cleveland	OH	44106	800-686-1141	216-231-1111
Colorado Symphony Orchestra					
1245 Champa St	Denver	CO	80204	877-292-7979	303-292-5566
Columbus Symphony Orchestra					
55 E State St	Columbus	OH	43215	800-653-8000	614-228-9600
Dayton Philharmonic Orchestra					
126 N Main St Ste 210	Dayton	OH	45402	888-228-3630	937-224-3521
Detroit Symphony Orchestra					
3711 Woodward Ave	Detroit	MI	48201	800-434-6340	313-576-5111
Dubuque Symphony Orchestra					
2728 Asbury Rd Ste 900	Dubuque	IA	52001	866-803-9280	563-557-1677
Edmonton Symphony Orchestra					
9720 102nd Ave	Edmonton	AB	T5J4B2	800-563-5081	780-428-1108
Flagstaff Symphony Orchestra					
113 E Aspen Ave # A	Flagstaff	AZ	86001	888-520-7214	928-774-5107
Grand Rapids Symphony					
300 Ottawa Ave NW Ste 100	Grand Rapids	MI	49503	800-982-2787	616-454-9451
Illinois Symphony Orchestera					
524 E Capitol Ave	Springfield	IL	62701	800-401-7222	217-522-2838
Indianapolis Symphony Orchestra					
45 Monument Cir	Indianapolis	IN	46204	800-366-8457	317-262-1100
Kennedy Ctr Opera House Orchestra					
John F Kennedy Ctr for the Performing Arts					
2700 F St NW	Washington	DC	20566	800-444-1324	
Knoxville Symphony Orchestra					
100 S Gay St Ste 302	Knoxville	TN	37902	800-845-5665	865-291-3310
Lexington Philharmonic					
161 N Mill St	Lexington	KY	40507	888-494-4226	859-233-4226
Milwaukee Symphony Orchestra					
1101 N Market St Ste 100	Milwaukee	WI	53202	888-367-8101	414-291-7605
Minnesota Orchestra					
1111 Nicollet Mall Orchestra Hall	Minneapolis	MN	55403	800-292-4141	612-371-5600
Modesto Symphony Orchestra					
911 13th St	Modesto	CA	95354	877-488-3380	209-523-4156
Music of the Baroque					
111 N Wabash Ave Ste 810	Chicago	IL	60602	800-595-4849	312-551-1414
New Hampshire Music Festival Orchestra					
42 Main St	Plymouth	NH	03264	800-662-2739	603-238-9007
New World Symphony					
500 17th St	Miami Beach	FL	33139	800-597-3331	305-673-3330
Orchestra New England					
PO Box 200123	New Haven	CT	06520	800-595-4849	203-777-4690
Orchestre Symphonique de Montreal					
1600 Saint-Urbain St	Montreal	QC	H2X0S1	888-842-9951	514-842-9951
Oregon Symphony Orchestra					
921 SW Washington St Ste 200	Portland	OR	97205	800-228-7343	503-228-4294
Phoenix Symphony					
1 N First St Ste 200	Phoenix	AZ	85004	800-776-9080	602-495-1117
Pittsburgh Symphony Orchestra					
600 Penn Ave	Pittsburgh	PA	15222	800-743-8560	412-392-4900
River City Brass Band Inc					
500 Grant St Ste 2720	Pittsburgh	PA	15219	800-292-7222	412-434-7222
Saint Louis Symphony Orchestra					
718 N Grand Blvd	Saint Louis	MO	63103	800-232-1880	314-533-2500
Sarasota Orchestra					
709 N Tamiami Trl	Sarasota	FL	34236	866-508-0611	941-953-4252
Seattle Symphony					
200 University St	Seattle	WA	98101	866-833-4747	206-215-4700
South Bend Symphony Orchestra (SBSO)					
127 N Michigan St	South Bend	IN	46601	800-537-6415	574-232-6343
Spokane Symphony PO Box 365	Spokane	WA	99210	800-899-1482	509-624-1200
Symphony Nova Scotia					
6101 University Ave					
Dalhousie Arts Ctr.	Halifax	NS	B3H4R2	800-874-1669	902-494-3820
Symphony Silicon Valley					
345 S First St	San Jose	CA	95113	800-736-7401	408-286-2600
Tacoma Symphony					
901 Broadway Ste 600	Tacoma	WA	98402	800-291-7593	253-272-7264
Windsor Symphony Orchestra					
121 University Ave	West Windsor	ON	N9A5P4	888-327-8327	519-973-1238

569-4 Theater Companies

				Toll-Free	Phone
Actors Theatre of Louisville					
316 W Main St	Louisville	KY	40202	800-428-5849	502-584-1205
Alabama Shakespeare Festival					
1 Festival Dr	Montgomery	AL	36117	800-841-4273	
Arkansas Repertory Theatre					
601 Main St PO Box 110	Little Rock	AR	72203	866-684-3737	501-378-0405
Erie Playhouse 13 W Tenth St	Erie	PA	16501	800-305-0669	814-454-2852
Guthrie Theater					
818 S Second St	Minneapolis	MN	55415	877-447-8243*	612-377-2224
*Resv					
Lincoln Ctr Theater					
150 W 65th St	New York	NY	10023	800-432-7250	

			Toll-Free	Phone
Maltz Jupiter Theatre				
1001 E Indiantown Rd	Jupiter FL	33477	800-445-1666	561-743-2666
Nebraska Repertory Theatre				
PO Box 880201	Lincoln NE	68588	800-432-3231	402-472-7211
Omaha Community Playhouse				
6915 Cass St	Omaha NE	68132	888-782-4338	402-553-0800
Pacific Repertory Theater				
PO Box 222035	Carmel CA	93922	866-622-0709	831-622-0700
Seattle Repertory Theatre (SRT)				
155 Mercer St PO Box 900923	Seattle WA	98109	877-900-9285	206-443-2210
Shakespeare Theatre				
516 Eigth St SE	Washington DC	20003	877-487-8849	202-547-3230
Theatre For A New Audience				
154 Christopher St Ste 3D	New York NY	10014	866-811-4111	212-229-2819
Tihati Productions Ltd				
3615 Harding Ave Ste 507	Honolulu HI	96816	877-846-5554	808-735-0292

570   PERFUMES

SEE ALSO Cosmetics, Skin Care, and Other Personal Care Products

			Toll-Free	Phone
Chanel Inc 15 E 57th St	New York NY	10022	800-550-0005	212-355-5050
Crabtree & Evelyn Ltd				
102 Peake Brook Rd	Woodstock CT	06281	800-272-2873	860-928-2761
Eagle Marketing Inc Perfume Originals Products Div				
150 W First St	Cortland NE	68331	800-233-7424	
Elizabeth Arden Inc				
880 SW 145th Ave Ste 200	Pembroke Pines FL	33027	800-326-7337	954-364-6900
NASDAQ: RDEN				
Key West Aloe				
13095 N Telecom Pkwy	Tampa FL	33637	800-445-2563	
ULTA Beauty				
1000 Remington Blvd Ste 120	Bolingbrook IL	60440	866-983-8582	630-410-4800

571   PERSONAL EMERGENCY RESPONSE SYSTEMS

			Toll-Free	Phone
AlertOne Services Inc				
1000 Commerce Park Dr Ste 300	Williamsport PA	17701	866-581-4540*	
*Cust Svc				
Life Alert's Encino				
16027 Ventura blvd Ste 400	Encino CA	91436	800-920-3410	
LifeFone				
16 Yellowstone Ave	White Plains NY	10607	888-687-0451	

572   PERSONAL PROTECTIVE EQUIPMENT & CLOTHING

SEE ALSO Medical Supplies - Mfr ; Safety Equipment - Mfr ; Sporting Goods ; Safety Equipment - Whol

			Toll-Free	Phone
Aearo Technologies LLC				
5457 W 79th St	Indianapolis IN	46268	877-327-4332	
Allen-Vanguard Corp				
2400 St Laurent Blvd	Ottawa ON	K1G5B4	800-644-9078	613-739-9646
Bullard Co				
1898 Safety Way	Cynthiana KY	41031	800-227-0423	859-234-6611
David Clark Co				
360 Franklin St	Worcester MA	01604	800-298-6235*	508-751-5800
*Cust Svc				
Encon Safety Products Co				
6825 W Sam Houston Pkwy N PO Box 3826	Houston TX	77041	800-283-6266	713-466-1449
Fibre-Metal				
2000 Plainfield Pk	Cranston RI	02921	800-430-4110	
Fire-End & Croker Corp				
7 Westchester Plz	Elmsford NY	10523	800-759-3473	914-592-3640
Galls Inc 2680 Palumbo Dr	Lexington KY	40509	800-477-7766	859-266-7227
Globe Mfg Co				
37 Loudon Rd	Pittsfield NH	03263	800-232-8323	603-435-8323
Graham Medical Products				
2273 Larsen Rd	Green Bay WI	54303	800-558-6765*	
*Cust Svc				
Handgards Inc				
901 Hawkins Blvd	El Paso TX	79915	800-351-8161	
Honeywell Safety Products				
2000 Plainfield Pk	Cranston RI	02921	800-430-4110*	401-943-4400
*Cust Svc				
ILC Dover Inc				
1 Moonwalker Rd	Frederica DE	19946	800-631-9567	302-335-3911
Kappler Inc				
55 Grimes Dr PO Box 490	Guntersville AL	35976	800-600-4019	256-505-4005
Lakeland Industries Inc				
701-7 Koehler Ave	Ronkonkoma NY	11779	800-645-9291	631-981-9700
NASDAQ: LAKE				
Louis M Gerson Company Inc				
16 Commerce Blvd	Middleboro MA	02346	800-225-8623	508-947-4000
MCR Safety 5321 E Shelby Dr	Memphis TN	38118	800-955-6887	901-795-5810
Medline Industries Inc				
1 Medline Pl	Mundelein IL	60060	800-633-5463*	847-949-5500
*Cust Svc				
Moldex Metric Inc				
10111 W Jefferson Blvd	Culver City CA	90232	800-421-0668	310-837-6500
MTS Safety Products Inc (MTS)				
PO Box 204	Golden MS	38847	800-647-8168*	
*General				
National Safety Apparel Inc (NSA)				
15825 Industrial Pkwy	Cleveland OH	44135	800-553-0672	
Newtex Industries Inc				
8050 Victor Mendon Rd	Victor NY	14564	800-836-1001	585-924-9135
Plastic Safety Systems Inc				
2444 Baldwin Rd	Cleveland OH	44104	800-662-6338	
PolyConversions Inc				
505 Condit Dr	Rantoul IL	61866	888-893-3330	217-893-3330
Precept Medical Products Inc				
370 Airport Rd	Arden NC	28704	800-438-5827	828-681-0209

			Toll-Free	Phone
Saf-T-Gard International Inc				
205 Huehl Rd	Northbrook IL	60062	800-548-4273	847-291-1600
Safariland LLC				
13386 International Pkwy	Jacksonville FL	32218	800-347-1200	904-741-5400
Safe-T-Gard Corp				
4975 Miller St Unit B	Wheat Ridge CO	80033	800-356-9026*	303-763-8900
*Cust Svc				
Scott Health & Safety				
4320 Goldmine Rd PO Box 569	Monroe NC	28110	800-247-7257	704-291-8300
Seattle Manufacturing Corp				
6930 Salashan Pkwy	Ferndale WA	98248	800-426-6251	360-366-5534
Sellstrom Manufacturing Co				
2050 Hammond Dr	Schaumburg IL	60173	800-323-7402	847-358-2000
Standard Textile Company Inc				
1 Knollcrest Dr	Cincinnati OH	45237	800-999-0400	513-761-9255
Steel Grip Inc				
1501 E Voorhees St	Danville IL	61832	800-223-1595	217-442-6240
Steiner Industries				
5801 N Tripp Ave	Chicago IL	60646	800-621-4515	773-588-3444
Strong Enterprises Inc				
11236 Satellite Blvd	Orlando FL	32837	800-344-6319	407-859-9317
Tingley Rubber Corp				
1551 S Washington Ave Ste 403	Piscataway NJ	08854	800-631-5498*	
*Cust Svc				
United Pioneer Co				
2777 Summer St Ste 206	Stamford CT	06905	800-466-9823	
Uvex Safety Inc				
900 Douglas Pk	Smithfield RI	02917	800-682-0839*	
*General				
White Knight Engineered Products				
9525 Monroe Rd Ste 100	Charlotte NC	28270	888-743-4700	704-542-6876
Wolf X-Ray Corp				
100 W Industry Ct	Deer Park NY	11729	800-356-9729*	631-242-9729
*Cust Svc				

573   PEST CONTROL SERVICES

			Toll-Free	Phone
A 1 Termite & Pest Control Inc				
2686 Morganton Blvd SW	Lenoir NC	28645	800-532-7378	828-758-4312
Action Pest Control Inc				
2301 S Green River Rd	Evansville IN	47715	800-467-5530	812-477-5546
Antimite Associates Inc				
5867 Pine Ave	Chino Hills CA	91709	800-974-2847	909-606-2300
Arrow Environmental Services Inc				
6225 Tower Ln	Sarasota FL	34240	888-424-2324	941-377-0888
Bain Pest Control Service Inc				
1320 Middlesex St	Lowell MA	01851	800-272-3661	978-452-9621
Banks Pest Control Inc				
215 Golden State Ave	Bakersfield CA	93301	800-662-6300	661-323-7858
Bird Solutions International				
1338 N Melrose Dr Ste H	Vista CA	92083	800-210-9514	760-758-9747
Burns Pest Elimination Inc				
2620 Grovers Ave	Phoenix AZ	85053	877-971-4782	602-971-4782
Copesan Services Inc				
W175 N5711 Technology Dr	Menomonee Falls WI	53051	800-267-3726	
Dewey Services Inc				
939 E Union St	Pasadena CA	91106	877-339-3973	
Fischer Environmental Service Inc				
1980 Surgi Dr	Mandeville LA	70448	800-391-2565	
Gilbert Industries Inc				
5611 Krueger Dr	Jonesboro AR	72401	800-643-0400	870-932-6070
Green Lawn Fertilizing Inc				
1004 Saunders Ln	West Chester PA	19380	888-581-5296	
Home Paramount Pest Control Cos Inc				
PO Box 850	Forest Hill MD	21050	888-888-4663	410-510-0700
Horizon Termite & Pest Control Corp				
45 Cross Ave	Midland Park NJ	07432	888-612-2847	201-447-2530
Jp Mchale Pest Management Inc				
241 Bleakley Ave	Buchanan NY	10511	800-479-2284	
Knockout Pest Control Inc				
1009 Front St	Uniondale NY	11553	800-244-7378	
Lawn Doctor Inc 142 SR 34	Holmdel NJ	07733	800-845-0580	
Lloyd Pest Control Co Inc, The				
1331 Morena Blvd Ste 300	San Diego CA	92110	800-223-2847	
Massey Services Inc				
315 Groveland St E	Orlando FL	32804	888-262-7739	407-645-2500
McCall Service Inc				
2861 College St	Jacksonville FL	32205	800-342-6948	904-389-5561
NaturaLawn of America Inc				
1 E Church St	Frederick MD	21701	800-989-5444	
ORKIN LLC				
2170 Piedmont Rd NE	Atlanta GA	30324	877-250-1652	
PCO Services Corp				
5840 Falbourne St	Mississauga ON	L5R4B5	800-800-6754	905-502-9700
Pest Shield Pest Control Inc				
15329 Tradesman	San Antonio TX	78249	888-728-8237	210-525-8823
Plunkett's Pest Control				
40 NE 52nd Way	Fridley MN	55421	866-906-1780	
Presto-X Co				
10421 Portal Rd Ste 101	La Vista NE	68128	800-759-1942	
Railinc Corp				
7001 Weston Pkwy Ste 200	Cary NC	27513	877-724-5462	919-651-5000
Schendel Pest Services				
1035 SE Quincy St	Topeka KS	66612	800-591-7378	785-232-9357
Senske Services				
400 N Quay St	Kennewick WA	99336	877-944-4007	509-374-5000
Smithereen Pest Management Services				
7400 N Melvina Ave	Niles IL	60714	800-336-3500	847-647-0010
Sprague Pest Solutions				
2725 Pacific Ave Ste 200	Tacoma WA	98402	800-272-4988	253-272-4400
Spring-Green Lawn Care Corp				
11909 Spaulding School Dr	Plainfield IL	60585	800-435-4051	815-436-8777
Terminix International Company LP				
860 Ridge Lake Blvd	Memphis TN	38120	877-837-6464	
Terminix Service Inc				
3612 Fernandina Rd	Columbia SC	29210	877-855-4093	

			Toll-Free	Phone
TruGreen ChemLawn				
860 Ridge Lake Blvd	Memphis TN	38120	**866-369-9539**	
Truly Nolen of America Inc				
3636 E Speedway Blvd	Tucson AZ	85716	**800-468-7859**	855-534-9139
TruTech LLC PO Box 6849	Marietta GA	30065	**844-492-5974**	
Waltham Services Inc				
817 Moody St	Waltham MA	02453	**866-974-7378**	781-893-1810
Western Exterminator Co				
305 N Crescent Way	Anaheim CA	92801	**800-698-2440**	714-239-2800
Western Pest Services Inc				
800 Lanidex Plz	Parsippany NJ	07054	**877-250-3857**	

PESTICIDES

574   PET PRODUCTS

SEE ALSO Livestock & Poultry Feeds - Prepared ; Leather Goods - Personal

			Toll-Free	Phone
Ainsworth Pet Nutrition				
984 Water St	Meadville PA	16335	**800-323-7738**	814-724-7710
BioZyme Inc				
6010 Stockyards Expy	Saint Joseph MO	64504	**800-821-3070**	816-238-3326
Church & Dwight Company Inc				
469 N Harrison St	Princeton NJ	08543	**800-617-4220**	
NYSE: CHD				
Companion Pets Inc (CPI)				
2001 N Black Canyon Hwy	Phoenix AZ	85009	**800-646-3611**	602-255-0166
Doctors Foster & Smith Inc				
2253 Air Pk Rd PO Box 100	Rhinelander WI	54501	**800-826-7206**	800-381-7179
Efficas Inc				
7007 Winchester Cir Ste 120	Boulder CO	80301	**866-446-0388**	303-381-2070
FL Emmert Co Inc				
2007 Dunlap St	Cincinnati OH	45214	**800-441-3343**	513-721-5808
Hartz Mountain Corp, The				
400 Plaza Dr	Secaucus NJ	07094	**800-275-1414**	
Healthy Pet				
6960 Salashan Pkwy	Ferndale WA	98248	**800-242-2287**	360-734-7415
IAMS Co 3700 Ohio 65	Leipsic OH	45856	**800-675-3849***	419-943-4267
*Cust Svc				
Jeffers Inc				
310 W Saunders Rd PO Box 100	Dothan AL	36301	**800-533-3377**	334-793-6257
John A Van Den Bosch Co				
4511 Holland Ave	Holland MI	49424	**800-968-6477**	
Joy Dog Food				
PO Box 305	Pinckneyville IL	62274	**800-245-4125**	
Kaytee Products Inc				
521 Clay St	Chilton WI	53014	**800-529-8331**	920-849-2321
Manna Pro Corp				
707 Spirit 40 Pk Dr Ste 150	Chesterfield MO	63005	**800-690-9908**	
Mark Hershey Farms Inc				
479 Horseshoe Pk	Lebanon PA	17042	**888-801-3301**	717-867-4624
MIDWEST Homes for Pets				
3142 S Cowan Rd PO Box 1031	Muncie IN	47302	**800-428-8560**	765-289-3355
Moyer & Son Inc				
113 E Reliance Rd	Souderton PA	18964	**866-669-3747**	215-799-2000
Multipet International Inc				
265 W Commercial Ave	Moonachie NJ	07074	**800-900-6738**	201-438-6600
Nestle Purina PetCare Co				
801 Chouteau Ave	Saint Louis MO	63102	**800-778-7462**	314-982-1000
North States Industries Inc				
1507 92nd Ln NE	Blaine MN	55449	**800-848-8421**	763-486-1756
Pet Safe International				
10427 Electric Ave	Knoxville TN	37932	**800-732-2677***	865-777-5404
*Cust Svc				
Pet Supermarket Inc				
1100 International Pkwy	Sunrise FL	33323	**866-434-1990**	954-351-0834
Pet Valu Canada Inc				
225 Royal Crest Crt	Markham ON	L3R9X6	**800-845-4759**	905-946-1200
PETCO Animal Supplies Inc				
9125 Rehco Rd	San Diego CA	92121	**877-738-6742**	858-453-7845
Petland Inc				
250 Riverside St	Chillicothe OH	45601	**800-221-5935**	740-775-2464
Petmate				
2300 E Randol Mill Rd	Arlington TX	76011	**877-738-6283**	
PetMed Express Inc				
1441 SW 29th Ave	Pompano Beach FL	33069	**800-738-6337**	954-979-5995
NASDAQ: PETS				
PETsMART Inc				
19601 N 27th Ave	Phoenix AZ	85027	**800-738-1385***	623-580-6100
NASDAQ: PETM ■ *Cust Svc				
Prevue Pet Products Inc				
224 N Maplewood Ave	Chicago IL	60612	**800-243-3624**	312-243-3624
Prince Corp				
8351 County Rd H	Marshfield WI	54449	**800-777-2486**	
Ralco Nutrition Inc				
1600 Hahn Rd	Marshall MN	56258	**800-533-5306**	
Rolf C Hagen Corp				
305 Forbes Blvd	Mansfield MA	02048	**800-724-2436***	508-339-9531
*Cust Svc				
Star Milling Co				
24067 Water St	Perris CA	92570	**800-733-6455**	951-657-3143
Sunshine Mills Inc				
500 Sixth St SW	Red Bay AL	35582	**800-633-3349**	256-356-9541
TFP nutrition				
915 S Fredonia St	Nacogdoches TX	75964	**800-392-3110**	936-564-3711
Triumph Sunshine mills Inc				
500 Sixth St SW	Red Bay AL	35582	**800-705-2111**	256-356-9541
United Pacific Pet				
12060 Cabernet Dr	Fontana CA	92337	**800-979-3333**	951-360-8550
United Pharmacal Company of Missouri Inc				
3705 Pear St	Saint Joseph MO	64503	**800-254-8726**	816-233-8800

575   PETROLEUM & PETROLEUM PRODUCTS - WHOL

			Toll-Free	Phone
Allied Oil & Supply Inc				
2209 S 24th St	Omaha NE	68108	**800-333-3717**	402-267-1375
AmeriGas Propane Inc				
PO Box 965	Valley Forge PA	19482	**800-934-6802**	610-337-7000
Aos Thermal Compounds LLC				
22 Meridian Rd Ste 6	Eatontown NJ	07724	**888-662-7337**	732-389-5514
AR. Sandri Inc				
400 Chapman St	Greenfield MA	01301	**800-628-1900**	
Atlas Oil Co 24501 Ecorse Rd	Taylor MI	48180	**800-878-2000**	313-292-5500
Axeon Specialty Products LLC				
750 Washington Blvd Ste 600	Stamford CT	06901	**855-378-4958**	
Best Line Oil Co Inc				
219 N 20th St	Tampa FL	33605	**800-382-1811**	813-248-1044
Blueox Energy Products & Services				
38 N Canal St	Oxford NY	13830	**877-233-8176**	
Bowlin Travel Centers Inc				
150 Louisiana Blvd NE	Albuquerque NM	87108	**800-716-8413**	
OTC: BWTL				
Boyett Petroleum				
601 McHenry Ave	Modesto CA	95350	**800-545-9212**	209-577-6000
BP Lubricants USA Inc				
1500 Valley Rd	Wayne NJ	07470	**800-333-3991**	973-633-2200
Bradco Inc				
107-11th Ave PO Box 997	Holbrook AZ	86025	**800-442-4770**	928-524-3976
Bretthauer Oil Co				
453 SW Washington St	Hillsboro OR	97123	**800-359-3113**	503-648-2531
Burkett Oil Company Inc				
6788 Best Friend Rd	Norcross GA	30071	**800-228-1786**	770-447-8030
Byron Originals Fuel Sales				
119 E State Hwy 175 PO Box 279	Ida Grove IA	51445	**800-594-9421**	
Cardwell Distributing Inc				
8137 S State St	Midvale UT	84047	**800-561-0051**	801-561-4251
Cargill Energy				
PO Box 9300	Minneapolis MN	55440	**800-227-4455**	
Carson 3125 NW 35th Ave	Portland OR	97210	**800-998-7767**	503-224-8500
Champlain Oil Company Inc				
45 San Remo Dr	South Burlington VT	05403	**800-649-3229**	802-864-5380
Colonial Group Inc				
101 N Lathrop Ave	Savannah GA	31415	**800-944-3835**	
Condon Oil Co				
126 E Jackson St	Ripon WI	54971	**800-452-1212**	920-748-3186
Consolidated Energy Co				
910 Main St	Jesup IA	50648	**800-338-3021**	
Dickey Transport				
401 E Fourth St	Packwood IA	52580	**800-247-1081**	
Dominion Aviation Services Inc				
7511 Airfield Dr	Richmond VA	23237	**800-366-7793**	804-271-7793
Doss Aviation Inc				
3670 Rebecca Ln	Colorado Springs CO	80917	**888-803-4415**	719-570-9804
Duncan Oil Company Inc				
849 Factory Rd	Beavercreek OH	45434	**800-527-2559**	
Earhart Petroleum Inc				
PO Box 39	Troy OH	45373	**800-686-2928**	937-335-2928
East River Energy Inc				
401 Soundview Rd PO Box 388	Guilford CT	06437	**800-336-3762**	203-453-1200
EEL River Fuels Inc				
3371 N State St	Ukiah CA	95482	**800-343-8354**	707-462-5554
Englefield Oil Co				
447 James Pkwy	Heath OH	43056	**800-837-4458***	740-928-8215
*Cust Svc				
Farmers Ranchers Coop				
224 S Main St	Ainsworth NE	69210	**800-233-6627**	402-387-2811
Federated Co-ops Inc				
502 S Second St	Princeton MN	55371	**800-638-8228**	763-389-2582
Fleetwing Corp				
742 S Combee Rd	Lakeland FL	33801	**800-282-5678**	863-665-7557
Foster Blue Water Oil LLC				
36065 Water St	Richmond MI	48062	**800-426-3800**	586-727-3996
Foster Fuels Inc				
16720 Brookneal Hwy	Brookneal VA	24528	**800-344-6457**	434-376-2322
Gassco Inc PO Box 9866	Bakersfield CA	93389	**800-390-7837**	661-832-7406
Gate Petroleum Co				
9540 San Jose Blvd PO Box 23627	Jacksonville FL	32241	**866-571-1982**	904-737-7220
Glacial Lakes Energy LLC				
301 20th Ave SE PO Box 933	Watertown SD	57201	**866-934-2676**	605-882-8480
Global Partners LP				
800 South St Ste 500 PO Box 9161	Waltham MA	02454	**800-685-7222**	781-894-8800
NYSE: GLP				
Halron Lubricants Inc				
1618 State St	Green Bay WI	54304	**800-236-5845**	920-436-4000
Hasco Oil Company Inc				
2800 Temple Ave	Long Beach CA	90806	**800-456-8491**	562-595-8491
Heartland Petroleum LLC				
4001 E Fifth Ave	Columbus OH	43219	**800-889-7831**	614-441-4001
Heritage Petroleum LLC				
516 N Seventh Ave	Evansville IN	47710	**800-422-3645**	812-422-3251
Highlands Fuel Delivery LLC				
190 Commerce Way	Portsmouth NH	03801	**888-310-1924**	
Hill City Oil Company Inc				
1409 Dunn St	Houma LA	70360	**800-492-8377**	985-851-4000
HN. Funkhouser & Company Inc				
2150 S Loudoun St	Winchester VA	22601	**800-343-6556**	540-662-9000
Inter City Oil Company Inc (ICO)				
1921 S St	Duluth MN	55812	**800-642-5542**	218-728-3641
Isgett Distributors Inc				
51 Highland Ctr Blvd	Asheville NC	28806	**800-358-0080**	828-667-9846
JJ Powell Inc				
109 W Presqueisle St	Philipsburg PA	16866	**800-432-0866**	814-342-3190
Johnson Oil Co (JOC)				
1918 Church St	Gonzales TX	78629	**800-284-2432**	
Lanman Oil Co Inc				
PO Box 108	Charleston IL	61920	**800-677-2819**	

Classified Section

	Toll-Free	Phone
Leffler Energy Inc		
15 Mt Joy St .... Mount Joy PA 17552	800-984-1411	
Licking Valley Oil Inc		
PO Box 246 .... Butler KY 41006	800-899-9449	859-472-7111
Lyden Oil Company Inc		
30692 Tracy Rd .... Walbridge OH 43465	800-362-9410	419-666-1948
MacEwen Petroleum Inc		
18 Adelaide St PO Box 100 .... Maxville ON K0C1T0	800-267-7175	
Main-Care Energy		
1 Booth Ln PO Box 11029 .... Albany NY 12211	800-542-5552	
Maritime Energy Inc		
234 Park St PO Box 485 .... Rockland ME 04841	800-333-4489	
Martin Eagle Oil Company Inc		
2700 James St .... Denton TX 76205	800-316-6148	940-383-2351
Martin Midstream Partners LP		
4200 Stone Rd .... Kilgore TX 75662	800-256-6644	903-983-6200
NASDAQ: MMLP		
Mc Glaughlin Oil Co, The		
3750 E Livingston Ave .... Columbus OH 43227	800-839-6589	614-231-2518
McCall Oil & Chemical Corp		
5480 NW Front Ave .... Portland OR 97210	800-622-2558	503-221-6400
Merle Boes Inc		
11372 E Lakewood Blvd .... Holland MI 49424	800-545-0706	616-392-7036
MG Oil Inc 1180 Creek Dr .... Rapid City SD 57703	800-333-5173	605-342-0527
National Oil & Gas Inc		
409 N Main St .... Bluffton IN 46714	800-322-8454	260-824-2220
NOCO Energy Corp		
2440 Sheridan Dr .... Tonawanda NY 14150	800-500-6626	716-833-6626
Offen Petroleum Inc		
5100 E 78th Ave .... Commerce CO 80022	866-657-3835	303-297-3835
Orange Line Oil Company Inc		
404 E Commercial St .... Pomona CA 91767	800-492-6864	909-623-0533
Panef Inc		
5700 W Douglas Ave .... Milwaukee WI 53218	800-448-1247	414-464-7200
Papco Inc		
4920 Southern Blvd .... Virginia Beach VA 23462	800-899-0747	757-499-5977
PetroCard Systems Inc		
730 Central Ave S .... Kent WA 98032	800-950-3835	253-852-2777
Petroleum Traders Corp		
7120 Pointe Inverness Way .... Fort Wayne IN 46804	800-348-3705	
PetroLiance LLC		
739 N State St .... Elgin IL 60123	800-628-7231	877-738-7699
Pro Petroleum Inc		
4985 N Sloan Ln .... Las Vegas NV 89115	877-791-4900	
R K Allen Oil Inc		
36002 AL Hwy 21 .... Talladega AL 35161	800-445-5823	256-362-4261
R Kidd Fuels Corp		
1172 Twinney Dr .... Newmarket ON L3Y9E2	866-274-2315	
Ramos Oil Company Inc		
1515 S River Rd .... West Sacramento CA 95691	800-477-7266*	916-371-2570
*Cust Svc		
Reeder Distributors Inc		
5450 Wilbarger St .... Fort Worth TX 76119	800-722-3103	817-429-5957
Renkert Oil		
3817 Main St PO Box 246 .... Morgantown PA 19543	800-423-6457	610-286-8012
Retif Oil & Fuel Inc		
527 Destrehan Ave .... Harvey LA 70058	800-349-9000	
RKA Petroleum Companies Inc		
28340 Wick Rd .... Romulus MI 48174	866-509-3288	800-875-3835
Sapp Bros Petroleum Inc		
9915 S 148th St .... Omaha NE 68138	800-233-4059	402-895-2202
Senergy Petroleum LLC		
622 S 56th Ave .... Phoenix AZ 85043	800-964-0076	602-272-6795
Shoco Oil Inc		
5135 E 74th Ave .... Commerce CO 80037	800-854-5553	303-289-1677
Sierra Energy		
1020 Winding Creek Rd Ste #100 ...... Roseville CA 95678	800-576-2264	916-218-1600
Southern Maryland Oil Co Inc (SMO)		
109 N Maple Ave .... La Plata MD 20646	888-222-3720	
Spencer Cos Inc		
2600 Memorial Pkwy S .... Huntsville AL 35801	800-633-2910	256-533-1150
Sprague Energy		
185 International Dr Ste 200 .... Portsmouth NH 03801	800-225-1560	603-431-1000
Stern Oil Company Inc		
PO Box 218 .... Freeman SD 57029	800-477-2744	605-925-7999
Sun Coast Resources Inc		
6405 Cavalcade St Bldg 1 .... Houston TX 77028	800-677-3835	713-844-9600
Taylor Enterprises Inc (TEI)		
2586 Southport Rd .... Spartanburg SC 29302	800-922-3149	864-573-9518
Technical Gas Products Inc		
66 Leonardo Dr .... North Haven CT 06473	800-847-0745	
Texas Enterprises		
5005 E Seventh St .... Austin TX 78702	800-545-4412	512-385-2167
Titan Laboratories		
1380 Zuni St PO Box 40567 .... Denver CO 80204	800-848-4826	
Tri-Con Inc		
7076 W Port Arthur Rd PO Box 20555 ...... Beaumont TX 77705	800-876-7102	409-835-2237
Tropic Oil Company Inc		
10002 NW 89th Ave .... Miami FL 33178	866-645-3835	305-888-4611
Truman Arnold Cos		
701 S Robison Rd .... Texarkana TX 75501	800-235-5343	903-794-3835
Tulco Oils Inc 5240 E Pine .... Tulsa OK 74115	800-375-2347	918-838-3354
Turner Gas Company Inc		
2825 W 500 S .... Salt Lake City UT 84104	800-932-4277	
Ullman Oil Inc		
PO Box 23399 .... Chagrin Falls OH 44023	800-543-5195	440-543-5195
Valor Oil 1200 Alsop Ln .... Owensboro KY 42303	844-468-2567	
Vesco Oil Corp		
16055 W 12-Mile Rd .... Southfield MI 48076	800-527-5358	
Walthall Oil Company Inc		
2510 Allen St .... Macon GA 31216	800-633-5685	478-781-1234
Warren Oil Company Inc		
PO Box 1507 .... Dunn NC 28335	800-779-6456	910-892-6456
Western States Petroleum Inc		
450 S 15th Ave .... Phoenix AZ 85007	800-220-1353	602-252-4011
World Fuel Services Corp		
9800 NW 41st St Ste 400 .... Miami FL 33178	800-345-3818	305-428-8000
NYSE: INT		

	Toll-Free	Phone
Yorkston Oil Company Inc		
2801 Roeder Ave .... Bellingham WA 98225	800-401-2201	360-734-2201

576   PETROLEUM REFINERIES

	Toll-Free	Phone
A H Belo Corp		
1954 Commerce St PO Box 224866 .... Dallas TX 75201	800-230-1074	214-977-8200
NYSE: AHC		
Allegheny Petroleum Products Co		
999 Airbrake Ave .... Wilmerding PA 15148	800-600-2900	412-829-1990
Calumet Specialty Products Partners LP		
2780 Waterfront Pkwy E Dr		
Ste 200 .... Indianapolis IN 46214	800-437-3188	317-328-5660
NASDAQ: CLMT		
Chevron Canada Ltd		
1200 - 1050 W Pender St .... Vancouver BC V6E3T4	800-663-1650	604-668-5300
Chevron Corp		
6001 Bollinger Canyon Rd .... San Ramon CA 94583	800-368-8357*	925-842-1000
NYSE: CVX ■ *Cust Svc		
Chevron Global Marine Products LLC		
9401 Williamsburg Plz Ste 201 .... Louisville KY 40222	800-283-9582	914-285-7390
Cross Oil Refining & Marketing Inc		
484 E Sixth St .... Smackover AR 71762	800-725-3066	870-881-8700
Exxon Mobil Corp		
5959 Las Colinas Blvd .... Irving TX 75039	800-252-1800	972-444-1000
NYSE: XOM		
Harms Oil Co		
337 22nd Ave S .... Brookings SD 57006	800-376-8476	605-696-5000
Hart Petroleum		
323 Skidmores Rd .... Deer Park NY 11729	800-796-3342	631-667-3200
Hough Petroleum Corp		
340 Fourth St .... Ewing NJ 08638	800-400-7154	609-771-1022
Hutchens Petroleum Corp		
22 Performance Dr .... Stuart VA 24171	800-537-7433	276-694-7000
Imperial Oil Resources Ltd		
237 Fourth Ave SW PO Box 2480 Stn M .... Calgary AB T2P3M9	800-567-3776	
International Group Inc		
85 Old Eagle School Rd .... Wayne PA 19087	800-852-6537	610-687-9030
Lionetti Associates LLC		
450 S Front St .... Elizabeth NJ 07202	800-734-0910	
Lipton Energy 458 S St .... Pittsfield MA 01201	877-443-9191	413-443-9191
Millsap Fuel Distributors Ltd		
905 Ave P S .... Saskatoon SK S7M2X3	800-667-9767	306-244-7916
Montana Refining Co		
1900 Tenth St NE .... Great Falls MT 59404	800-437-3188	317-328-5660
Murphy Oil Corp		
200 Peach St .... El Dorado AR 71730	888-289-9314	870-862-6411
SEMCO ENERGY Gas Co		
1411 Third St Ste A .... Port Huron MI 48060	800-624-2019	
Source North America Corp		
510 S Westgate .... Addison IL 60101	800-621-5524	847-364-9000
Star-Seal		
6596 New Peachtree Rd .... Atlanta GA 30340	800-779-6066	770-455-6551
Sunoco Inc		
1735 Market St .... Philadelphia PA 19103	800-786-6261	
NYSE: SUN		
Supreme Petroleum Inc		
1200 Progress Rd PO Box 1246 .... Smithfield VA 23434	800-924-5823	757-934-0550

577   PETROLEUM STORAGE TERMINALS

	Toll-Free	Phone
Best-Wade Petroleum Inc		
201 Dodge Dr .... Ripley TN 38063	888-888-6457	731-635-9661
Blaylock Oil Company Inc		
724 S Flagler Ave .... Homestead FL 33030	877-944-4262	305-247-7249
Buckley Oil Company Inc		
1809 Rock Island St .... Dallas TX 75207	800-721-4147	214-421-4147
Busch Distributors Inc		
7603 State Rt 270 .... Pullman WA 99163	800-752-2295	509-339-6600
Cary Oil Company Inc		
110 Mackenan Dr .... Cary NC 27511	800-227-9645	919-462-1100
Central Crude Inc		
4187 Hwy 3059 PO Box 1863 .... Lake Charles LA 70602	800-245-8408	337-436-1000
Cross Petroleum Inc		
6920 Lockheed Dr .... Redding CA 96002	800-655-4427	530-221-2588
Don Small & Sons Oil Distributing Co Inc		
112 Third St NW PO Box 626 .... Auburn WA 98071	800-626-3213	253-833-0430
Dooley's Petroleum Inc		
304 Main Ave .... Murdock MN 56271	800-520-2466	320-875-2641
Douglass Distributing Co		
325 E Forest Ave .... Sherman TX 75090	800-736-4316	903-893-1181
E & V Energy		
5700 State Rt 34 .... Auburn NY 13021	800-455-6522	315-253-6522
Gresham Petroleum Co		
415 Pershing Ave PO Box 690 .... Indianola MS 38751	800-748-8934	662-884-5000
Hampel Oil Distributors Inc		
3727 S W St .... Wichita KS 67217	800-530-5848	
HOC Industries Inc		
3511 N Ohio .... Wichita KS 67219	800-999-9645	316-838-4663
Houston-Pasadena Apache Oil Company LP		
5136 Spencer Hwy .... Pasadena TX 77505	800-248-6388	
Jack Becker Distributors Inc		
6800 Suemac Pl .... Jacksonville FL 32254	800-488-8411	
Johnson Oil Co		
502 S Otsego Ave PO Box 629 .... Gaylord MI 49735	800-292-3941	989-732-2451
Link Energy Inc		
211 1500 14 St SW .... Calgary AB T3C1C9	855-444-5465	
Magellan Midstream Partners LP		
1 Williams Ctr .... Tulsa OK 74172	800-574-6671	918-574-7000
NYSE: MMP		
MFA Oil Co		
1 Ray Young Dr PO Box 519 .... Columbia MO 65201	800-366-0200	573-442-0171

	Toll-Free	Phone
RelaDyne LLC		
8280 Montgomery Rd Ste 101 ....Cincinnati OH 45236	**888-830-3156**	513-489-6000
Sweetwater Valley Oil Company Inc		
1236 New Hwy 68 ....Sweetwater TN 37874	**800-362-4519**	423-337-6671

578 PHARMACEUTICAL COMPANIES

SEE ALSO Medicinal Chemicals & Botanical Products ; Pharmaceutical Companies - Generic Drugs ; Vitamins & Nutritional Supplements ; Pharmaceutical & Diagnostic Products - Veterinary ; Diagnostic Products ; Biotechnology Companies

	Toll-Free	Phone
Allergan Inc 2525 Dupont Dr ....Irvine CA 92612	**800-347-4500**	714-246-4500
NYSE: AGN		
Alva-Amco Pharmacal Cos Inc		
7711 Merrimac Ave ....Niles IL 60714	**800-792-2582**	847-663-0700
Amphastar Pharmaceuticals Inc		
11570 Sixth St ....Rancho Cucamonga CA 91730	**800-423-4136**	909-980-9484
AstraZeneca Canada Inc		
1004 Middlegate Rd ....Mississauga ON L4Y1M4	**800-565-5877**	905-277-7111
AstraZeneca Pharmaceuticals LP		
1800 Concord Pk PO Box 15437 ....Wilmington DE 19850	**800-236-9933**	
Bausch & Lomb Inc		
1400 N Goodman St ....Rochester NY 14609	**800-553-5340**	
Bausch & Lomb Pharmaceuticals Inc		
8500 Hidden River Pkwy ....Tampa FL 33637	**800-323-0000***	800-553-5340
*Cust Svc		
Baxter International Inc		
1 Baxter Pkwy ....Deerfield IL 60015	**800-422-9837**	847-948-2000
NYSE: BAX		
Bayer Inc 77 Belfield Rd ....Toronto ON M9W1G6	**800-622-2937**	416-248-0771
Biocare Medical LLC		
60 Berry Dr ....Pacheco CA 94553	**800-799-9499**	925-603-8000
Blistex Inc 1800 Swift Dr ....Oak Brook IL 60523	**800-837-1800***	630-571-2870
*Cust Svc		
Boehringer Ingelheim Pharmaceuticals Inc		
900 Ridgebury Rd ....Ridgefield CT 06877	**800-243-0127**	203-798-9988
Bracco Diagnostics Inc		
259 Prospect Plns Rd ....Cranbury NJ 08512	**800-631-5245**	609-514-2200
Bristol-Myers Squibb Canada Inc		
2344 Alfred-Nobel Blvd Ste 300.........Montreal QC H4S0A4	**800-267-0005***	514-333-3200
*Cust Svc		
Bristol-Myers Squibb Co		
345 Park Ave ....New York NY 10154	**800-332-2056**	212-546-4000
NYSE: BMY		
Care-Tech Laboratories Inc		
3224 S KingsHwy Blvd ....Saint Louis MO 63139	**800-325-9681**	314-772-4610
Chembio Diagnostics Inc		
3661 Horseblock Rd ....Medford NY 11763	**844-243-6246**	631-924-1135
NASDAQ: CEMI		
Combe Inc		
1101 Westchester Ave ....White Plains NY 10604	**800-431-2610**	
Covalon Technologies Ltd		
405 Britannia Rd E Ste 106.........Mississauga ON L4Z3E6	**877-711-6055**	905-568-8400
Dickinson Brands Inc		
31 E High St ....East Hampton CT 06424	**888-860-2279**	860-267-2279
DPT Laboratories Ltd		
318 McCullough ....San Antonio TX 78215	**866-225-5378**	
Dynavax Technologies Corp		
2929 Seventh St Ste 100 ....Berkeley CA 94710	**877-848-5100**	510-848-5100
NASDAQ: DVAX		
Edwards Lifesciences Corp		
1 Edwards Way ....Irvine CA 92614	**800-424-3278**	949-250-2500
NYSE: EW		
Eisai Inc		
100 Tice Blvd ....Woodcliff Lake NJ 07677	**866-613-4724**	201-692-1100
Eli Lilly & Co		
Lilly Corporate Ctr ....Indianapolis IN 46285	**800-545-5979***	317-276-2000
*NYSE: LLY ■ *Prod Info*		
Eli Lilly Canada Inc		
3650 Danforth Ave ....Toronto ON M1N2E8	**888-545-5972**	416-694-3221
Endo Pharmaceuticals Inc		
1400 Atwater Dr ....Malvern PA 19355	**800-462-3636***	484-216-0000
*Cust Svc		
FFF Enterprises Inc		
41093 County Ctr Dr ....Temecula CA 92591	**800-843-7477**	951-296-2500
First Priority Inc		
1590 Todd Farm Dr ....Elgin IL 60123	**800-650-4899**	847-289-1600
G & W Laboratories Inc		
111 Coolidge St ....South Plainfield NJ 07080	**800-922-1038**	
Galderma Laboratories Inc		
14501 N Fwy ....Fort Worth TX 76177	**866-735-4137**	817-961-5000
Germiphene Corp		
1379 Colborne St E ....Brantford ON N3T5M1	**800-265-9931**	
GlaxoSmithKline Inc		
7333 Mississauga Rd N ....Mississauga ON L5N6L4	**800-387-7374**	905-819-3000
Halocarbon Products Corp		
6525 The Corners Pkwy Ste 200 ....Peachtree Corners GA 30092	**800-338-5803**	470-419-6364
Hope Pharmaceuticals Inc		
16416 N 92nd St Ste 125 ....Scottsdale AZ 85260	**800-755-9595**	480-607-1970
Humco Holding Group Inc		
201 W Fifth St ....Austin TX 78701	**800-662-3435**	855-925-4736
Immtech Pharmaceuticals		
1 N End Ave ....New York NY 10282	**877-898-8038**	212-791-2911
IQVIA		
16720 Trans-Canada Hwy ....Kirkland QC H9H5M3	**866-267-4479***	514-428-6000
*General		
Jaapharm Canada Inc		
510 Rowntree Dairy Rd Bldg B ....Woodbridge ON L4L8H2	**800-465-9587**	905-851-7885
Janssen Pharmaceutica Inc		
1125 Trenton-Harbourton Rd ....Titusville NJ 08560	**800-526-7736**	908-218-6095
Jazz Pharmaceuticals Inc		
3180 Porter Dr ....Palo Alto CA 94304	**866-997-3688**	650-496-3777
Juniper Pharmaceuticals Inc		
33 Arch St ....Boston MA 02110	**866-566-5636**	617-639-1500
NASDAQ: JNP		
Keryx Biopharmaceuticals Inc		
1 Marina Park Dr 20th Fl ....Boston MA 02210	**800-903-0247**	617-466-3500
NASDAQ: KERX		
King Bio 3 Westside Dr ....Asheville NC 28806	**800-237-4100**	855-739-7127
Konsyl Pharmaceuticals Inc		
8050 Industrial Park Rd ....Easton MD 21601	**800-356-6795**	410-822-5192
Major Pharmaceutical Co		
31778 Enterprise Dr ....Livonia MI 48150	**800-875-0123**	800-616-2471
Medical Products Laboratories Inc		
9990 Global Rd ....Philadelphia PA 19115	**800-523-0191**	215-677-2700
Medicis Pharmaceutical Corp		
7720 N Dobson Rd ....Scottsdale AZ 85256	**866-246-8245***	800-321-4576
*Cust Svc		
Melaleuca Inc		
3910 S Yellowstone Hwy ....Idaho Falls ID 83402	**800-282-3000***	208-522-0700
*Sales		
Mentholatum Company Inc		
707 Sterling Dr ....Orchard Park NY 14127	**800-688-7660**	716-677-2500
Merck & Company Inc		
2000 Galloping Hill Rd ....Kenilworth NJ 07033	**800-444-2080***	908-740-4000
*NYSE: MRK ■ *Cust Svc*		
Mission Pharmacal		
PO Box 786099 ....San Antonio TX 78278	**800-531-3333**	210-696-8400
Mylan 1000 Mylan Blvd ....Canonsburg PA 15317	**800-527-4278**	724-514-1800
Mylan Pharmaceuticals Inc		
781 Chestnut Ridge Rd ....Morgantown WV 26505	**800-796-9526**	304-599-2595
Myriad RBM 3300 Duval Rd ....Austin TX 78759	**866-726-6277**	512-835-8026
Neos Therapeutics		
2940 N Hwy 360 Ste 400 ....Grand Prairie TX 75050	**844-375-8324**	972-408-1300
Novartis Pharmaceuticals Canada Inc		
385 boul Bouchard ....Dorval QC H9S1A9	**800-465-2244**	514-631-6775
Novartis Pharmaceuticals Co		
25 Old Mill Rd ....Suffern NY 10901	**888-669-6682**	845-368-6000
Novo Nordisk of North America Inc		
100 College Rd W ....Princeton NJ 08540	**800-727-6500**	609-987-5800
Novo Nordisk Pharmaceuticals Inc		
800 Scudders Mill Rd ....Plainsboro NJ 08536	**800-727-6500***	609-987-5800
*Cust Svc		
Numark Brands LLC		
105 Fieldcrest Ave Ste 502A.........Edison NJ 08837	**800-338-8079**	800-214-2379
OMI Industries (OMI)		
1 Corporate Dr Ste 100.........Long Grove IL 60047	**800-662-6367**	
Otsuka America Pharmaceutical Inc		
2440 Research Blvd ....Rockville MD 20850	**800-562-3974**	301-424-9055
Particle Dynamics International LLC		
2629 S Hanley Rd ....Saint Louis MO 63144	**800-452-4682**	314-968-2376
Pfizer Animal Health		
5 Giralda Farms ....Madison NJ 07940	**888-963-8471**	
Pfizer Canada Inc		
17300 TransCanada Hwy ....Kirkland QC H9J2M5	**800-463-6001**	514-695-0500
Pfizer Inc 235 E 42nd St ....New York NY 10017	**800-879-3477**	212-733-2323
NYSE: PFE		
Prometheus Laboratories Inc		
9410 Carroll Pk Dr ....San Diego CA 92121	**888-892-8391**	
ProPhase Labs Inc		
621 Shady Retreat Rd ....Doylestown PA 18901	**800-505-2653**	215-345-0919
NASDAQ: PRPH		
Protide Pharmaceuticals Inc		
505 Oakwood Rd Ste 200 ....Lake Zurich IL 60047	**800-552-3569**	847-726-3100
Qualicaps Inc		
6505 Franz Warner Pkwy ....Whitsett NC 27377	**800-227-7853**	336-449-3900
Regis Technologies Inc		
8210 Austin Ave ....Morton Grove IL 60053	**800-323-8144**	847-967-6000
Salix Pharmaceuticals Inc		
8510 Colonnade Ctr Dr ....Raleigh NC 27615	**800-508-0024**	919-862-1000
SciClone Pharmaceuticals Inc		
950 Tower Ln Ste 900.........Foster City CA 94404	**800-724-2566**	650-358-3456
NASDAQ: SCLN		
Silipos Inc		
7049 Williams Rd ....Niagara Falls NY 14304	**800-229-4404**	716-283-0700
SISU Inc		
7635 N Fraser Way Ste 102 ....Burnaby BC V5J0B8	**800-663-4163**	604-420-6610
Sovereign Pharmaceuticals Ltd		
7590 Sand St ....Fort Worth TX 76118	**877-248-0228**	817-284-0429
SSS Co 71 University Ave ....Atlanta GA 30315	**800-237-3843**	404-521-0857
Standing Stone Inc		
49 Richmondville Ave ....Westport CT 06880	**800-648-9877**	
Taro Pharmaceutical Industries Ltd		
126 E Dr ....Brampton ON L6T1C1	**800-268-1975**	905-791-8276
UCB Pharma Inc		
1950 Lake Pk Dr ....Smyrna GA 30080	**800-477-7877**	770-970-7500
United Therapeutics Corp		
1040 Spring St ....Silver Spring MD 20910	**877-864-8437**	301-608-9292
NASDAQ: UTHR		
Upsher-Smith Laboratories Inc		
6701 Evenstad Dr ....Maple Grove MN 55369	**800-654-2299**	763-315-2000
Vivus Inc		
1172 Castro St ....Mountain View CA 94040	**800-607-0088**	650-934-5200
NASDAQ: VVUS		
WF Young Inc		
302 Benton Dr ....East Longmeadow MA 01028	**800-628-9653**	413-526-9999
Wright Group, The		
6428 Airport Rd ....Crowley LA 70526	**800-201-3096**	337-783-3096
ZLB Behring LLC		
1020 First Ave PO Box 61501 ....King of Prussia PA 19406	**800-683-1288**	610-878-4000
Zogenix Inc		
12400 High Bluff Dr Ste 650.........San Diego CA 92130	**866-964-3649**	858-259-1165

Classified Section

579 PHARMACEUTICAL COMPANIES - GENERIC DRUGS

SEE ALSO Medicinal Chemicals & Botanical Products ; Pharmaceutical Companies ; Vitamins & Nutritional Supplements ; Pharmaceutical & Diagnostic Products - Veterinary ; Diagnostic Products ; Biotechnology Companies

				Toll-Free	Phone
Apotex Corp					
2400 N Commerce Pkwy Ste 400	Weston	FL	33326	877-427-6839	
Glenwood LLC 111 Cedar Ln	Englewood	NJ	07631	800-542-0772	201-569-0050
Healthpoint					
3909 Hulen St	Fort Worth	TX	76107	800-441-8227*	817-900-4000
*Cust Svc					
Hikma					
246 Industrial Way W	Eatontown	NJ	07724	800-631-2174*	
*Cust Svc					
Impax Laboratories Inc					
30831 Hun2od Ave	Hayward	CA	94544	877-994-6729	510-240-6450
Letco Medical Inc					
1316 Commerce Dr NW	Decatur	AL	35601	800-239-5288	256-350-1297
Lts Lohmann Therapy Systems Corp					
21 Henderson Dr	West Caldwell	NJ	07006	800-587-1872	973-396-5345
Mericon Industries Inc					
8819 N Pioneer Rd	Peoria	IL	61615	800-242-6464	309-693-2150
Morton Grove Pharmaceuticals Inc					
6451 Main St	Morton Grove	IL	60053	800-346-6854	847-967-5600
Mylan Pharmaceuticals ULC					
85 Advance Rd	Etobicoke	ON	M8Z2S6	800-575-1379	416-236-2631
Nephron Pharmaceuticals Corp					
4500 12th St Ext	West Columbia	SC	29172	800-443-4313	803-569-2800
NuCare Pharmaceuticals Inc					
622 W Katella Ave	Orange	CA	92867	888-482-9545	
Osteohealth Co					
1 Luitpold Dr	Shirley	NY	11967	800-874-2334	631-924-4000
Par Pharmaceutical Cos Inc					
6 Ram Ridge Rd	Chestnut Ridge	NY	10977	800-828-9393	800-462-3636
NASDAQ: ENDP					
Perrigo Co 515 Eastern Ave	Allegan	MI	49010	800-719-9260	269-673-8451
NYSE: PRGO					
Pharmavite LLC					
8510 Balboa Blvd Ste 100	Northridge	CA	91325	800-423-2405	818-221-6200
Sentry BioPharma Services Inc					
4605 Decatur Blvd Ameriplex Pk	Indianapolis	IN	46241	866-757-7400	317-856-5889
Skilled Care Pharmacy Inc					
6175 Hi Tek Ct	Mason	OH	45040	800-334-1624	513-459-7455
Taro Pharmaceuticals USA Inc					
3 Skyline Dr	Hawthorne	NY	10532	800-544-1449	914-345-9001
Teva Pharmaceutical USA					
1090 Horsham Rd	North Wales	PA	19454	800-545-8800	215-591-3000
NYSE: TEVA					
TruTouch Technologies Inc					
73 Carriage Way	Sudbury	MA	01776	866-721-6221	909-703-5963
UDL Laboratories Inc					
1718 Northrock Ct	Rockford	IL	61103	800-848-0462	
USL Pharma 301 S Cherokee St	Denver	CO	80223	800-654-2299	303-607-4500
X-Gen Pharmaceuticals Inc					
300 Daniels Zenker Dr	Horseheads	NY	14845	866-390-4411	

580 PHARMACEUTICAL & DIAGNOSTIC PRODUCTS - VETERINARY

				Toll-Free	Phone
AbbVie Pharmaceutical Contract Manufacturing					
1401 Sheridan Rd	North Chicago	IL	60064	888-299-7416	847-938-8524
Addison Biological Laboratory Inc					
507 N Cleveland Ave	Fayette	MO	65248	800-331-2530	660-248-2215
Alltech Inc					
3031 Catnip Hill Pk	Nicholasville	KY	40356	800-289-8324	859-885-9613
Bimeda-MTC Animal Health Inc					
420 Beaverdale Rd	Cambridge	ON	N3C2W4	888-524-6332	519-654-8000
Bio-Serv					
3 Foster Ln Ste 201	Flemington	NJ	08822	800-996-9908	908-284-2155
Biomune Co 8906 Rosehill Rd	Lenexa	KS	66215	800-999-0297	913-894-0230
Biovet Inc					
4375 Ave Beaudry	Saint-Hyacinthe	QC	J2S8W2	888-824-6838	450-771-7291
Biovet USA Inc					
1502 E 122nd St	Burnsville	MN	55337	877-824-6838	952-884-3113
Boehringer Ingelheim Vetmedica Inc					
2621 N Belt Hwy	Saint Joseph	MO	64506	800-821-7467	816-233-2571
Delmont Laboratories Inc					
715 Harvard Ave PO Box 269	Swarthmore	PA	19081	800-562-5541	610-543-2747
DMS Laboratories Inc					
2 Darts Mill Rd	Flemington	NJ	08822	800-567-4367	908-782-3353
Dominion Veterinary Laboratories Inc					
1199 Sanford St	Winnipeg	MB	R3E3A1	800-465-7122	204-589-7361
Elanco Animal Health					
2500 Innovation Way	Greenfield	IN	46140	877-352-6261	317-276-2000
IMMVAC Inc 6080 Bass Ln	Columbia	MO	65201	800-944-7563	573-443-5363
King Bio 3 Westside Dr	Asheville	NC	28806	800-237-4100	855-739-7127
Lake Immunogenics Inc					
348 Berg Rd	Ontario	NY	14519	800-648-9990	
Lloyd Inc					
604 W Thomas Ave PO Box 130	Shenandoah	IA	51601	800-831-0004	712-246-4000
Luitpold Pharmaceuticals Inc					
1 Luitpold Dr PO Box 9001	Shirley	NY	11967	800-645-1706	631-924-4000
Merial Ltd					
3239 Satellite Blvd Bldg 500	Duluth	GA	30096	888-637-4251	678-638-3000
MVP Laboratories Inc					
4805 G St	Omaha	NE	68117	800-856-4648	402-331-5106
Nutra-Blend Inc					
3200 Second St	Neosho	MO	64850	800-657-5657	
Pfizer Inc Animal Health Group					
235 E 42nd St	New York	NY	10017	800-879-3477	212-733-2323
Renco Corp					
116 Third Ave N	Minneapolis	MN	55401	800-359-8181	612-338-6124
Texas Vet Lab Inc					
1702 N Bell St	San Angelo	TX	76903	800-284-8403	325-653-4505
Veterinary Pharmacies of America Inc (VPA)					
4802 N Sam Houston Pkwy W Ste 100	Houston	TX	77066	877-838-7979	
Vetoquinol Canada Inc					
2000 Ch Georges	Lavaltrie	QC	J5T3S5	800-363-1700	450-586-2252
XF Enterprises Inc					
500 S Taylor Ste 301 PO Box 229	Amarillo	TX	79101	800-783-5616	806-367-5810

581 PHARMACY ASSOCIATIONS - STATE

SEE ALSO Health & Medical Professionals Associations

				Toll-Free	Phone
Alabama Pharmacy Assn					
1211 Carmichael Way	Montgomery	AL	36106	877-877-3962*	334-271-4222
*General					
California Pharmacists Assn (CPhA)					
4030 Lennane Dr	Sacramento	CA	95834	866-365-7472	916-779-1400
Georgia Pharmacy Assn (GPhA)					
50 Lenox Pointe NE	Atlanta	GA	30324	888-871-5590	404-231-5074
Minnesota Pharmacists Assn (MPhA)					
1000 Westgate Dr Ste 252	St. Paul	MN	55114	800-451-8349	651-697-1771
Missouri Pharmacy Assn					
211 E Capitol Ave	Jefferson City	MO	65101	800-468-4672	573-636-7522
Pharmacists Society of the State of New York					
210 Washington Ave Ext	Albany	NY	12203	800-632-8822	518-869-6595
Texas Pharmacy Assn					
3200 Steck Ave Ste 370	Austin	TX	78757	800-505-5463	512-836-8350

582 PHARMACY BENEFITS MANAGEMENT SERVICES

A pharmacy benefits management service (PBM) is a company that manages various pharmacy-related aspects of a health insurance plan, such as the assignment of pharmacy cards, claims filing and processing, formulary management, etc. For the most part, PBM clients are insurance companies, HMOs, or PPOs rather than individuals or pharmacies.

				Toll-Free	Phone
BioScrip					
1600 Broadway Ste 700	Denver	CO	80202	877-409-2301	720-697-5200
NASDAQ: BIOS					
Caremark Rx Inc					
PO Box 832407	Richardson	TX	75083	877-460-7766	
Health Smart Rx					
1301 E Ninth St	Cleveland	OH	44114	800-681-6912	
Maxor National Pharmacy Services Corp					
320 S Polk St Ste 100	Amarillo	TX	79101	800-658-6146	806-324-5400
Medical Security Card Company LLC					
4911 E Broadway Blvd	Tucson	AZ	85711	800-347-5985	520-888-8070
MedImpact Healthcare Systems Inc					
10680 Treena St Ste 500	San Diego	CA	92131	800-788-2949	858-566-2727
Old Dominion Brush Co					
5118 Glen Alden Dr	Richmond	VA	23231	800-446-9823	
Prescription Solutions					
3515 Harbor Blvd	Costa Mesa	CA	92626	800-788-4863	
Prime Therapeutics Inc					
1305 Corporate Ctr Dr	Eagan	MN	55121	800-858-0723	612-777-4000
Schaefer Brush Manufacturing Company Inc					
1101 S Prairie Ave	Waukesha	WI	53186	800-347-3501	262-547-3500
Script Care Inc					
6380 Folsom Dr	Beaumont	TX	77706	800-880-9988	
Walgreens Health Services					
1411 Lake Cook Rd	Deerfield	IL	60015	800-207-2568	

583 PHARMACY MANAGEMENT SERVICES

Companies that provide long-term care pharmacy services to individuals with special needs (e.g., chronic disease or advanced age); and those that provide pharmacy management services to hospitals or other institutions.

				Toll-Free	Phone
Accredo Health Group Inc					
1640 Century Ctr Pkwy	Memphis	TN	38134	877-222-7336	901-385-3600
McKesson Pharmaceutical					
1 Post St	San Francisco	CA	94104	800-571-2889	415-983-8300
Omnicare Inc					
201 E Fourth St	Cincinnati	OH	45202	800-342-5627	800-990-6664
NYSE: OCR					
Tech Pharmacy Services Inc					
12503 Exchange Dr Ste 536	Stafford	TX	77477	800-378-9020	

584 PHOTO PROCESSING & STORAGE

				Toll-Free	Phone
Advanced Photographic Solutions					
1525 Hardeman Ln	Cleveland	TN	37312	800-241-9234	423-479-5481
Burrell Imaging					
1311 Merrillville Rd	Crown Point	IN	46307	800-348-8732	219-663-3210
Candid Color Systems Inc					
1300 Metropolitan Ave	Oklahoma City	OK	73108	800-336-4550	405-947-8747
Dale Laboratories					
2960 Simms St	Hollywood	FL	33020	800-327-1776	954-925-0103
H & H Color Lab Inc					
8906 E 67th St	Raytown	MO	64133	800-821-1305	816-358-6677
iMemories 9181 E Bell Rd	Scottsdale	AZ	85260	800-845-7986	
McKenna Pro Imaging					
2815 Falls Ave	Waterloo	IA	50701	800-238-3456*	319-235-6265
*General					
Meisel 2019 McKenzie Dr	Carrollton	TX	75006	800-527-5186	214-688-4950

585 PHOTOCOPYING EQUIPMENT & SUPPLIES

SEE ALSO Business Machines - Whol

			Toll-Free	Phone
FlexPrint Inc 2845 N Omaha St	Mesa	AZ 85215	888-353-9774	
Imaging Supplies Company Inc 804 Woodland Ave	Sanford	NC 27330	800-518-1152	919-776-1152
Lasercycle USA Inc 528 S Taylor Ave	Louisville	CO 80027	866-666-7776	303-666-7776
Masterfile Corp 3 Concorde Gate 4th Fl	Toronto	ON M3C3N7	800-387-9010	416-929-3000
Northwest Print Strategies Inc 8175 SW Nimbus Ave	Beaverton	OR 97008	800-648-5156	
Oce-USA Inc 5450 N Cumberland Ave	Chicago	IL 60656	800-877-6232	773-714-8500
R & D Computers Inc 3190 Reps Miller Rd Ste 390	Norcross	GA 30071	800-350-3071	770-416-0103
Sharp Electronics Corp 1 Sharp Plz	Mahwah	NJ 07430	800-237-4277	201-529-8200
Toshiba America Inc 1251 Ave of the Americas 41st Fl	New York	NY 10020	800-457-7777	212-596-0600
Xerox Corp 201 Merritt 7	Norwalk	CT 06856	800-327-9753	888-242-9098
NYSE: XRX				

586 PHOTOGRAPH STUDIOS - PORTRAIT

			Toll-Free	Phone
Cherry Hill Photo Enterprises Inc 4 E Stow Rd	Marlton	NJ 08003	800-969-2440	856-663-1616
Freestyle Photo Biz 5124 Sunset Blvd	Hollywood	CA 90027	800-292-6137	
Gartner Studios 220 Myrtle St E	Stillwater	MN 55082	888-235-0484	
George STREET Photo & Video LLC 230 W Huron St Ste 3W	Chicago	IL 60654	866-831-4103	
Jostens Inc 3601 Minnesota Ave Ste 400	Minneapolis	MN 55435	800-235-4774	952-830-3300
MarathonFoto 3490 Martin Hurst Rd	Tallahassee	FL 32312	800-424-3686	
New England School of Photography 537 Commonwealth Ave	Boston	MA 02215	800-676-3767	617-437-1868
Portrait Express 441 N Water St	Silverton	OR 97381	800-228-3759	503-873-6365
Portraits International 10835 Rockley Rd	Houston	TX 77099	888-838-1495	281-879-8444
Ripcho Studio 7630 Lorain Ave	Cleveland	OH 44102	800-686-7427	216-631-0664

587 PHOTOGRAPHIC EQUIPMENT & SUPPLIES

SEE ALSO Cameras & Related Supplies - Retail

			Toll-Free	Phone
Agfa Corp 611 River Dr	Elmwood Park	NJ 07407	888-274-8626	201-440-2500
Alan Gordon Enterprises Inc 5625 Melrose Ave	Hollywood	CA 90038	800-825-6684	323-466-3561
Anton/Bauer Inc 14 Progress Dr	Shelton	CT 06484	800-422-3473	203-929-1100
Ballantyne Strong Inc 13710 FNB Pkwy	Omaha	NE 68154	800-424-1215*	
*NYSE: BTN ■ *General*				
Beta Screen Corp 707 Commercial Ave	Carlstadt	NJ 07072	800-272-7336	201-939-2400
Carr Corp 1547 11th St	Santa Monica	CA 90401	800-952-2398	310-587-1113
Ceiva Logic Inc 214 E Magnolia Blvd	Burbank	CA 91502	877-693-7263*	818-562-1495
Tech Supp				
Champion Photochemistry 7895 Tranmere Dr	Mississauga	ON L5S1V9	800-387-3430	905-670-7900
Douthitt Corp 245 Adair St	Detroit	MI 48207	800-368-8448	313-259-1565
Draper Shade & Screen Co 411 S Pearl St	Spiceland	IN 47385	800-238-7999	765-987-7999
Identatronics Inc 165 N Lively Blvd	Elk Grove Village	IL 60007	800-323-5403*	847-437-2654
Cust Svc				
InFocus Corp 13190 SW 68th Pkwy Ste 200	Portland	OR 97223	877-388-8385	503-207-4700
Matthews Studio Equipment Group 2405 W Empire Ave	Burbank	CA 91504	800-237-8263	818-843-6715
Navitar Inc 200 Commerce Dr	Rochester	NY 14623	800-828-6778*	585-359-4000
Cust Svc				
Nikon Inc 1300 Walt Whitman Rd	Melville	NY 11747	800-645-6687*	631-547-4200
Cust Svc				
Panavision Inc 6219 DeSoto Ave	Woodland Hills	CA 91367	800-260-1846	818-316-1000
Peter Pepper Products Inc (PPP) 17929 S Susana Rd PO Box 5769	Compton	CA 90224	800-496-0204	
Phase One Inc 200 Broadhollow Rd Ste 312	Melville	NY 11747	888-742-7366	631-757-0400
Research Technology International Inc 4700 W Chase Ave	Lincolnwood	IL 60712	800-323-7520*	847-677-3000
Sales				
Schneider Optics Century Div 7701 Haskell Ave	Van Nuys	CA 91406	800-228-1254	818-766-3715
Sharp Electronics Corp 1 Sharp Plz	Mahwah	NJ 07430	800-237-4277	201-529-8200
Sony Corp of America 550 Madison Ave	New York	NY 10022	800-282-2848	212-833-6800
Stewart Filmscreen Corp 1161 W Sepulveda Blvd	Torrance	CA 90502	800-762-4999	310-784-5300
Tiffen Company LLC 90 Oser Ave	Hauppauge	NY 11788	800-645-2522	631-273-2500

			Toll-Free	Phone
Toshiba America Inc 1251 Ave of the Americas 41st Fl	New York	NY 10020	800-457-7777	212-596-0600
Visual Departures Ltd 48 Sheffield Business Pk	Ashley Falls	MA 01222	800-628-2003	
Vivitar Corp 195 Carter Dr	Edison	NJ 08817	800-592-9541	732-248-1306
Vutec Corp 11711 W Sample Rd	Coral Springs	FL 33065	800-770-4700	

588 PHOTOGRAPHY - COMMERCIAL

			Toll-Free	Phone
Concorde Inc 1835 Market St Ste 1200	Philadelphia	PA 19103	800-662-1676	
Holland Litho Printing Service Inc 10972 Chicago Dr	Zeeland	MI 49464	800-652-6567	616-392-4644
Image Studios Inc 1100 S Lynndale Dr	Appleton	WI 54914	877-738-4080	
Irvin Simon Photographers Inc 146 Meacham Ave	Elmont	NY 11003	800-540-4701	
Telerhythmics LLC 60 Market Center Dr	Collierville	TN 38017	888-333-1003	
Universal Image PO Box 77090	Winter Garden	FL 34787	800-553-5499	407-352-5302

589 PHOTOGRAPHY - STOCK

			Toll-Free	Phone
Alaska Stock Images 2505 Fairbanks St	Anchorage	AK 99503	800-487-4285	907-276-1343
Image Works PO Box 443	Woodstock	NY 12498	800-475-8801	845-679-8500
Photo Researchers Inc 307 Fifth Ave 3rd Fl	New York	NY 10016	800-833-9033	212-758-3420

590 PIECE GOODS & NOTIONS

SEE ALSO Fabric Stores

			Toll-Free	Phone
Advanced Probing Systems Inc 2300 Central Ave	Boulder	CO 80301	800-631-0005	303-939-9345
Associated Fabrics Corp 15-01 Pollitt Dr Unit 7	Fair Lawn	NJ 07410	800-232-4077	
B Berger Co 1380 Highland Rd	Macedonia	OH 44056	800-288-8400*	330-425-3838
Cust Svc				
Baum Textile Mills Inc 812 Jersey Ave	Jersey City	NJ 07310	866-842-7631	201-659-0444
Blank Quilting Corp *Blank Quilting* 49 W 37th St 14th Fl	New York	NY 10018	800-294-9495	
Blumenthal Lansing Co 30 Two Bridges Rd	Fairfield	NJ 07004	800-553-4158	201-935-6220
Bob Barker Company Inc PO Box 429	Fuquay Varina	NC 27526	800-334-9880	
Burch Fabrics Group 4200 Brockton Dr SE	Grand Rapids	MI 49512	800-841-8111	616-698-2800
Criterion Thread Company Inc 21744 98th Ave	Queens Village	NY 11429	800-695-0080*	718-464-4200
General				
Dunlap Industries Inc 297 Industrial Park Rd	Dunlap	TN 37327	800-251-7214	
Duralee Fabrics Ltd Inc 1775 Fifth Ave	Bay Shore	NY 11706	800-275-3872*	631-273-8800
Cust Svc				
EE Schenck Co 6000 N Cutter Cir	Portland	OR 97217	800-433-0722	503-284-4124
Hanes Cos Inc 500 N McLin Creek Rd	Conover	NC 28613	877-252-3052	828-464-4673
Hoffman California Fabrics Inc 25792 Obrero Dr	Mission Viejo	CA 92691	800-547-0100	
Janlynn Corp 2070 Westover Rd	Chicopee	MA 01022	800-445-5565	413-206-0002
Keyston Bros 2801 Academy Way	Sacramento	CA 95815	800-453-1112	916-927-5851
Lew Jan Textile Corp 366 Veterans Memorial Hwy	Commack	NY 11725	800-899-0531	
Marcus Bros Textiles Inc 980 Ave of the Americas	New York	NY 10018	800-548-8295	212-354-8700
McKee Surfaces PO Box 230	Muscatine	IA 52761	800-553-9662*	563-263-2421
Cust Svc				
Miami Corp, The 720 Anderson Ferry Rd	Cincinnati	OH 45238	800-543-0448	513-451-6700
Robert Allen Fabrics Inc 225 Foxboro Blvd	Foxboro	MA 02035	800-333-3777	508-339-9151
Robert Kaufman Company Inc PO Box 59266	Los Angeles	CA 90059	800-877-2066	310-538-3482
Schott Textiles Inc 2850 Gilchrist Rd	Akron	OH 44305	877-661-2121	330-794-2121
Scovill Fasteners Inc 1802 Scovill Dr	Clarkesville	GA 30523	888-726-8455*	706-754-1000
Cust Svc				
Spradling International Inc 200 Cahaba Vly Pkwy PO Box 1668	Pelham	AL 35124	800-333-0955	205-985-4206
Tiger Button Company Inc 307 W 38th St	New York	NY 10018	800-223-2754	212-594-0570
Tingue 535 N Midland Ave	Saddle Brook	NJ 07663	800-829-3864	201-796-4490
United Notions Inc 13800 Hutton St	Dallas	TX 75234	800-527-9447	972-484-8901
US Button Corp 328 Kennedy Dr	Putnam	CT 06260	800-243-1842	860-928-2707
Velcro USA Inc 406 Brown Ave	Manchester	NH 03103	800-225-0180	603-669-4880
Waterbury Button Co 1855 Peck Ln	Cheshire	CT 06410	800-928-1812	

Company / Address	City	State	ZIP	Toll-Free	Phone
World Emblem International Inc 1500 NE 131 St	Miami	FL	33161	**800-766-0448**	
Young Fashions Inc 11111 Coursey Blvd	Baton Rouge	LA	70816	**800-824-4154**	225-766-1010

591 PIPE & PIPE FITTINGS - METAL (FABRICATED)

SEE ALSO Metal Tube & Pipe

Company / Address	City	State	ZIP	Toll-Free	Phone
Alloy Stainless Products Co 611 Union Blvd	Totowa	NJ	07512	**800-631-8372**	973-256-1616
AY McDonald Manufacturing Co 4800 Chavenelle Rd	Dubuque	IA	52002	**800-292-2737***	
*Cust Svc					
BendTec Inc 366 Garfield Ave	Duluth	MN	55802	**800-236-3832**	218-722-0205
Betts Industries Inc 1800 Pennsylvania Ave W	Warren	PA	16365	**800-482-2678**	814-723-1250
Campbell Manufacturing Inc 127 E Spring St	Bechtelsville	PA	19505	**800-523-0224**	610-367-2107
Carpenter Powder Products 600 Mayer St	Bridgeville	PA	15017	**866-790-9092**	412-257-5102
Central Pipe Supply Inc 101 Ware Rd PO Box 5470	Pearl	MS	39288	**800-844-7700**	601-939-3322
Classic Tube 80 Rotech Dr	Lancaster	NY	14086	**800-882-3711**	716-759-1800
Colonial Engineering Inc 6400 Corporate Ave	Portage	MI	49002	**800-374-0234**	269-323-2495
Douglas Bros 423 Riverside Industrial Pkwy	Portland	ME	04103	**800-341-0926**	207-797-6771
Empire Industries Inc 180 Olcott St	Manchester	CT	06040	**800-243-4844**	860-647-1431
Fuller Industrial 65 Nelson Rd	Lively	ON	P3Y1P4	**888-524-3777**	705-682-2777
H-P Products Inc 512 W Gorgas St	Louisville	OH	44641	**800-822-8356**	330-875-5556
Highfield Manufacturing Co 5144 S Intl Dr	Cudahy	WI	53110	**855-443-4353**	414-489-7700
Hydro Tube Enterprises Inc 137 Artino St	Oberlin	OH	44074	**800-226-3553**	440-774-1022
Kelly Pipe Company LLC 11680 Bloomfield Ave	Santa Fe Springs	CA	90670	**800-305-3559**	562-868-0456
McWane Inc 2900 Hwy 280 Ste 300	Birmingham	AL	35223	**800-634-4746**	205-414-3100
MicroGroup Inc 7 Industrial Pk Rd	Medway	MA	02053	**800-255-8823**	508-533-4925
Mills Iron Works Inc 14834 Maple Ave	Gardena	CA	90248	**800-421-2281**	323-321-6520
Milwaukee Valve Company Inc 16550 W Stratton Dr	New Berlin	WI	53151	**800-348-6544**	262-432-2800
Multi Products Company Inc 5301 21st St	Racine	WI	53406	**877-444-1011**	262-554-3700
National Excelsior Co 1999 N Ruby St	Melrose Park	IL	60160	**855-373-9235**	708-343-4225
NIBCO Inc 1516 Middlebury St	Elkhart	IN	46515	**800-234-0227**	574-295-3000
Nor-Cal Products Inc 1967 S Oregon St	Yreka	CA	96097	**800-824-4166**	530-842-4457
Parker Hannifin Corp Brass Products Div 6035 Parkland Blvd	Otsego	MI	49078	**800-272-7537**	269-694-9411
Penn Machine Co 106 Stn St	Johnstown	PA	15905	**800-736-6872**	814-288-1547
Pevco Sys Intl Inc 1401 Tangier Dr	Baltimore	MD	21220	**800-296-7382**	410-931-8800
Piping Technology & Products Inc 3701 Holmes Rd PO Box 34506	Houston	TX	77051	**866-746-9172**	713-731-0030
R & B Wagner Inc PO Box 423	Butler	WI	53007	**888-243-6914**	414-214-0444
Richards Industries Inc 3170 Wasson Rd	Cincinnati	OH	45209	**800-543-7311***	513-533-5600
*Cust Svc					
Romac Industries Inc 21919 20th Ave SE	Bothell	WA	98021	**800-426-9341**	425-951-6200
Star Pipe LLC 4018 Westhollow Pkwy	Houston	TX	77082	**800-999-3009**	281-558-3000
Steico Industries Inc 1814 Ord Way	Oceanside	CA	92056	**800-444-3515**	760-438-8015
Tate Andale Inc 1941 Lansdowne Rd	Baltimore	MD	21227	**800-296-8283**	410-247-8700
Tru-Flex Metal Hose Corp 2391 S St Rd 263 PO Box 247	West Lebanon	IN	47991	**800-255-6291**	765-893-4403
Tubular Fabricators Industry Inc 600 W Wythe St	Petersburg	VA	23803	**800-526-0178**	
Tylok International Inc 1061 E 260th St	Euclid	OH	44132	**800-321-0466**	216-261-7310
US Pipe & Foundry Co 2 Chase Corporate Dr Ste 200	Birmingham	AL	35244	**866-347-7473**	
Vacco Industries Inc 10350 Vacco St	South El Monte	CA	91733	**800-874-7113**	626-443-7121
Victaulic Co 4901 Kesslersville Rd	Easton	PA	18040	**800-742-5842***	610-559-3300
*Sales					
World Wide Fittings Inc 7501 N Natchez Ave	Niles	IL	60714	**800-393-9894**	847-588-2200

592 PIPE & PIPE FITTINGS - PLASTICS

Company / Address	City	State	ZIP	Toll-Free	Phone
Advanced Drainage Systems Inc 4640 Trueman Blvd	Hilliard	OH	43026	**800-821-6710**	
Augusta Fiberglass Coatings Inc 86 Lake Cynthia Rd	Blackville	SC	29817	**800-995-8265**	803-671-4742
Brookdale Plastics 6096 McKee Rd	Madison	WI	53719	**800-541-1535**	608-271-5634
CertainTeed Corp 750 E Swedesford Rd	Valley Forge	PA	19482	**800-782-8777***	610-341-7000
*Prod Info					
Chemtrol Div NIBCO Inc 1516 Middlebury St	Elkhart	IN	46516	**800-234-0227**	574-295-3000
Chevron Phillips Chemical Company Performance Pipe Division 5085 W Pk Blvd Ste 500	Plano	TX	75093	**800-527-0662**	972-599-6600
Cooling Tower Technologies 52410 Clark Rd	White Castle	LA	70788	**800-882-1361**	225-545-3970
Diamond Plastics Corp 1212 Johnstown Rd PO Box 1608	Grand Island	NE	68802	**800-782-7473**	308-384-4400
Endot Industries Inc 60 Green Pond Rd	Rockaway	NJ	07866	**800-443-6368**	973-625-8500
Excalibur Extrusions Inc 110 E Crowther Ave	Placentia	CA	92870	**800-648-6804**	714-528-8834
Extrutech Plastics Inc D/B/A Epi 5902 W Custer St	Manitowoc	WI	54220	**888-818-0118**	
Fernco Inc 300 S Dayton St	Davison	MI	48423	**800-521-1283**	810-653-9626
Genesis Industries Inc 601 Pro Ject Dr	Elmwood	WI	54740	**800-826-3301**	715-639-2435
Hancor Inc PO Box 1047	Findlay	OH	45839	**888-892-2694**	419-422-6521
Hobas Pipe USA LP 1413 E Richey Rd	Houston	TX	77073	**800-856-7473**	281-821-2200
Ideal Window Manufacturing Inc 100 West Seventh St	Bayonne	NJ	07002	**800-631-3400**	
Indepak Inc 2136 NE 194th Ave	Portland	OR	97230	**800-338-1857**	
Intertech Corp 3240 N O'Henry Blvd	Greensboro	NC	27405	**800-364-2255**	336-621-1891
Isco Industries 926 Baxter Ave PO Box 4545	Louisville	KY	40204	**800-345-4726**	502-583-6591
JM Manufacturing Company Inc 5200 W Century Blvd	Los Angeles	CA	90045	**800-621-4404**	
Lasco Fittings Inc 414 Morgan St PO Box 116	Brownsville	TN	38012	**800-776-2756**	731-772-3180
Madan Plastics Inc 108 North Union Ave Ste 3	Cranford	NJ	07016	**888-676-5926**	908-276-8484
Maloney Technical Products 1300 E Berry St	Fort Worth	TX	76119	**800-231-7236**	817-923-3344
Mearthane Products Corp 16 W Industrial Dr	Cranston	RI	02921	**888-883-8391**	401-946-4400
Merrill's Packaging Inc 1529 Rollins Rd	Burlingame	CA	94010	**800-284-5910**	
Mueller Plastics Corp 3070 E Cedar	Ontario	CA	91761	**800-348-8464**	909-930-2060
National Pipe & Plastics Inc 3421 Old Vestal Rd	Vestal	NY	13850	**800-836-4350**	
Nebraska Plastics Inc PO Box 45	Cozad	NE	69130	**800-445-2887**	308-784-2500
North American Pipe Corp 2801 Post Oak Blvd Ste 600	Houston	TX	77056	**855-624-7473**	713-840-7473
Oil Creek Plastics Inc 45619 State Hwy 27 PO Box 385	Titusville	PA	16354	**800-537-3661**	814-827-3661
Pepperell Braiding Company Inc 22 Lowell St	Pepperell	MA	01463	**800-343-8114**	
Plasti Dip International 3920 Pheasant Ridge Dr	Blaine	MN	55449	**800-969-5432**	
Polymer Resources Ltd 656 New Britain Ave	Farmington	CT	06032	**800-243-5176**	
Robert Busse & Company Inc 75 Arkay Dr	Hauppauge	NY	11788	**800-645-6526**	631-435-4711
Santa Fe Extruders & Printing 15315 Marquardt Ave	Santa Fe Springs	CA	90670	**800-645-0626**	
Silvanus Products 40 Merchant St	Sainte Genevieve	MO	63670	**800-822-2788**	
Taylor Made Products *Taylor Made Group* 167 N Main St	Gloversville	NY	12078	**800-628-5188**	
Teraco Inc 2080 Commerce Dr	Midland	TX	79703	**800-687-3999**	
Texas United Pipe Inc 11627 N Houston Rosslyn Rd	Houston	TX	77086	**800-966-8741***	281-448-9463
*Sales					
Tri-Star Plastics Corp 906 Boston Tpke	Shrewsbury	MA	01545	**800-874-7827**	
Trinity Sterile Inc 201 Kiley Dr	Salisbury	MD	21801	**800-829-8384**	
Vinylplex Inc 1800 Atkinson Ave	Pittsburg	KS	66762	**877-779-7473**	620-231-8290
Vinyltech Corp 201 S 61st Ave	Phoenix	AZ	85043	**800-255-3924**	602-233-0071
Viwintech Window & Door Inc 2400 Irvin Cobb Dr	Paducah	KY	42003	**800-788-1050**	

593 PIPELINES (EXCEPT NATURAL GAS)

Company / Address	City	State	ZIP	Toll-Free	Phone
Chevron Pipe Line Co 4800 Fournace Pl	Bellaire	TX	77401	**877-596-2800**	
Colonial Pipeline Co 1185 Sanctuary Pkwy Ste 100	Alpharetta	GA	30009	**800-275-3004**	678-762-2200
Country Mark Co-op 1200 Refinery Rd	Mount Vernon	IN	47620	**800-832-5490**	
Enbridge Energy Partners LP 1100 Louisiana Ste 3300	Houston	TX	77002	**800-481-2804**	713-821-2000
NYSE: EEP					
Genesis Energy LP 919 Milam Ste 2100	Houston	TX	77002	**800-284-3365**	713-860-2500
NYSE: GEL					
Imperial Oil Resources Ltd 237 Fourth Ave SW PO Box 2480 Stn M	Calgary	AB	T2P3M9	**800-567-3776**	
Magellan Midstream Partners LP 1 Williams Ctr	Tulsa	OK	74172	**800-574-6671**	918-574-7000
NYSE: MMP					
MarkWest Energy Partners LP 1515 Arapahoe St Tower 1 Ste 1600	Denver	CO	80202	**800-730-8388**	303-925-9200
NYSE: MWE					
Plains All American Pipeline LP 333 Clay St Ste 1600	Houston	TX	77002	**800-708-5071***	713-646-4100
NYSE: PAA ■ *Mktg					

	City	State	ZIP	Toll-Free	Phone
Sunoco Inc 1735 Market St *NYSE: SUN*	Philadelphia	PA	19103	**800-786-6261**	
Valero LP 1 Valero Way?	San Antonio	TX	78249	**800-333-3377**	210-246-2000

594 PLANETARIUMS

	City	State	ZIP	Toll-Free	Phone
Cernan Earth & Space Ctr 2000 Fifth Ave	River Grove	IL	60171	**800-972-7000**	708-583-3100
Clark Planetarium 110 S 400 W	Salt Lake City	UT	84101	**800-501-2885**	385-468-7827
Dreyfuss Planetarium 49 Washington St	Newark	NJ	07102	**888-370-6765**	973-596-6529
Lick Observatory 7281 Mt Hamilton Rd	Mt Hamilton	CA	95140	**800-866-1131**	408-274-5061

595 PLASTICS - LAMINATED - PLATE, SHEET, PROFILE SHAPES

	City	State	ZIP	Toll-Free	Phone
Chase Plastic Services Inc 6467 Waldon Ctr Dr	Clarkston	MI	48346	**800-232-4273**	248-620-2120
Connecticut Laminating Company Inc 162 James St	New Haven	CT	06513	**800-753-9119**	203-787-2184
Current Inc 30 Tyler St PO Box 120183	East Haven	CT	06512	**877-436-6542**	203-469-1337
DuPont Surfaces 4417 Lancaster Pk CRP 728/3105	Wilmington	DE	19805	**800-448-9835**	302-774-1000
Fiberesin Industries Inc 37031 E Wisconsin Ave PO Box 88	Oconomowoc	WI	53066	**800-450-0051**	262-567-4427
Formica Corp 10155 Reading Rd	Cincinnati	OH	45241	**800-367-6422**	513-786-3400
Franklin Fibre-Lamitex Corp 903 E 13th St	Wilmington	DE	19802	**800-233-9739**	302-652-3621
Hartson-kennedy Cabinet Top Company Inc 522 W 22nd St PO Box 3095	Marion	IN	46953	**800-388-8144**	
Insulfab Plastics Inc 834 Hayne St	Spartanburg	SC	29301	**800-845-7599**	864-582-7506
Insultab Inc 45 Industrial Pkwy *Cust Svc	Woburn	MA	01801	**800-468-4822***	701 035 0800
Iten Industries 4602 Benefit Ave *Orders	Ashtabula	OH	44004	**800-227-4836***	440-997-6134
Lakeland Plastics Inc (LP) 1550 McCormick Blvd	Mundelein	IL	60060	**800-454-4006**	847-680-1550
Madico Inc 64 Industrial Pkwy	Woburn	MA	01801	**800-456-4331**	781-935-7850
Petro Plastics Company Inc 450 S Ave	Garwood	NJ	07027	**800-486-4738**	908-789-1200
Reef Industries Inc 9209 Almeda Genoa Rd	Houston	TX	77075	**800-231-6074**	713-507-4200
Remcon Plastics Inc 208 Chestnut St	Reading	PA	19602	**800-360-3636**	
Rowmark Inc 2040 Industrial Dr	Findlay	OH	45840	**800-243-3339**	419-425-2407
Spaulding Composites Co 55 Nadeau Dr	Rochester	NH	03867	**800-801-0560**	603-332-0555
Techniform Industries Inc 2107 Hayes Ave	Fremont	OH	43420	**800-691-2816**	419-332-8484
V-T Industries Inc 1000 Industrial Pk	Holstein	IA	51025	**800-827-1615**	712-368-4381
Wilmington Fibre Specialty Co 700 Washington St	New Castle	DE	19720	**800-220-5132**	302-328-7525
Wilsonart International Inc 2400 Wilson Pl *Cust Svc	Temple	TX	76504	**800-433-3222***	254-207-7000

596 PLASTICS - UNSUPPORTED - FILM, SHEET, PROFILE SHAPES

SEE ALSO Blister Packaging

	City	State	ZIP	Toll-Free	Phone
Advance Bag & Packaging Technologies 5720 Williams Lake Rd	Waterford	MI	48329	**800-475-2247**	248-674-3126
AEP Industries Inc 125 Phillips Ave *NASDAQ: AEPI*	South Hackensack	NJ	07606	**800-999-2374**	201-641-6600
Anaheim Custom Extruders 4640 E La Palma Ave *Cust Svc	Anaheim	CA	92807	**800-229-2760***	714-693-8508
Arlon Graphics 2811 S Harbor Blvd	Santa Ana	CA	92704	**800-232-7161**	714-540-2811
Atlas Roofing Falcon Foam Div 8240 Byron Ctr Rd SW	Byron Center	MI	49315	**800-917-9138**	
Bemis Company Inc 2301 Industrial Dr *NYSE: BMS*	Neenah	WI	54956	**800-544-4672**	920-527-5000
Catalina Graphic Films Inc 27001 Agoura Rd Ste 100	Calabasas Hills	CA	91301	**800-333-3136**	818-880-8060
Coburn Co, The PO Box 147	Whitewater	WI	53190	**800-776-7042**	262-473-2822
Crown Plastics Co 116 May Dr	Harrison	OH	45030	**800-368-0238**	513-367-0238
CUE Inc 11 Leonberg Rd	Cranberry Township	PA	16066	**800-283-4621**	724-772-5225
Dielectrics Industries Inc 300 Burnett Rd	Chicopee	MA	01020	**800-472-7286**	413-594-8111
Dunmore Corp 145 Wharton Rd	Bristol	PA	19007	**800-444-0242**	215-781-8895
E S Robbins Corp 2802 Avalon Ave	Muscle Shoals	AL	35661	**866-934-6018**	256-248-2400
Enflo Corp 315 Lake Ave	Bristol	CT	06010	**888-887-4093**	860-589-0014
Gary Plastic Packaging Corp 1340 Viele Ave	Bronx	NY	10474	**800-221-8150**	718-893-2200
General Films Inc 645 S High St	Covington	OH	45318	**888-436-3456**	
General Formulations Inc 309 S Union St	Sparta	MI	49345	**800-253-3664**	616-887-7387
GSE Lining Technology Inc 19103 Gundle Rd	Houston	TX	77073	**800-435-2008**	281-443-8564
i2M Inc 755 Oak Hill Rd Crestwood Industrial Pk	Mountain Top	PA	18707	**800-242-3909**	
Kendall Packaging Corp 10335 N Port Washington Rd	Mequon	WI	53092	**800-237-0951**	262-404-1200
Lavanture Products Co 22825 Gallatin Way	Elkhart	IN	46515	**800-348-7625**	574-264-0658
Mitsubishi Polyester Film LLC 2001 Hood Rd	Greer	SC	29650	**800-334-1934**	864-879-5000
MPI Technologies 37 E St	Winchester	MA	01890	**888-674-8088**	781-729-8300
New Hampshire Plastics Inc 1 Bouchard St	Manchester	NH	03103	**800-258-3036**	603-669-8523
Next Generation Films Inc 230 Industrial Dr	Lexington	OH	44904	**800-884-8150**	419-884-8150
Northland Plastics Inc 1420 S 16th St PO Box 290	Sheboygan	WI	53081	**800-776-7163**	
O'Sullivan Films Inc 1944 Valley Ave	Winchester	VA	22601	**800-336-9882**	540-667-6666
Orcon Corp 1570 Atlantic St *General	Union City	CA	94587	**800-227-0505***	510-476-2124
Penn Fibre Plastics 2434 Bristol Rd *Cust Svc	Bensalem	PA	19020	**800-662-7366***	
Plaskolite Inc 1770 Joyce Ave	Columbus	OH	43219	**800-848-9124**	614-294-3281
Polyvinyl Films Inc PO Box 753	Sutton	MA	01590	**800-343-6134**	508-865-3558
Primex Plastics Corp 1235 N 'F' St	Richmond	IN	47374	**800-222-5116**	765-966-7774
Prinsco Inc 1717 16th St NE	Willmar	MN	56201	**800-992-1725**	320-222-6800
Raven Industries Inc 205 E Sixth St *NASDAQ: RAVN*	Sioux Falls	SD	57104	**800-243-5435**	605-336-2750
Shepherd CE Company Inc 2221 Canada Dry St	Houston	TX	77023	**800-324-6733**	713-924-4300
Sinclair & Rush Inc 123 Manufacturers Dr	Arnold	MO	63010	**800-526-6273**	636-282-6800
SLM Manufacturing Corp 215 Davidson Ave	Somerset	NJ	08873	**800-526-3708**	732-469-7500
Soliant LLC 1872 Hwy 9 Bypass	Lancaster	SC	29720	**800-288-9401**	803-285-9401
Southern Film Extruders Inc 2319 English Rd	High Point	NC	27262	**800-334-6101**	336-885-8091
Summit Plastics Inc 107 S Laurel St	Summit	MS	39666	**800-790-7117**	601-276-7500
Thermoplastic Processes Inc 1268 Valley Rd	Stirling	NJ	07980	**888-554-6400**	908-561-3000
VCF Films Inc 1100 Sutton Ave	Howell	MI	48843	**888-905-7680**	517-546-2300
VPI Corp 3123 S Ninth St *Orders	Sheboygan	WI	53081	**800-874-4240***	920-458-4664
Watersaver Company Inc 5870 E 56th Ave	Commerce	CO	80022	**800-525-2424**	303-289-1818
Wilson-Hurd Mfg Co 311 Winton St PO Box 8028	Wausau	WI	54403	**800-950-5013**	
Zippertubing Co 7150 W Erie St	Chandler	AZ	85226	**855-289-1874**	

597 PLASTICS FOAM PRODUCTS

	City	State	ZIP	Toll-Free	Phone
A-Z Sponge & Foam Products Ltd 811 Cundy Ave Annacis Is	Delta	BC	V3M5P6	**800-665-3990**	604-525-1665
ACH Foam Technologies LLC 5250 Sherman St	Denver	CO	80216	**800-525-8697**	303-297-3844
Allied Aerofoam Products LLC 216 Kelsey Ln	Tampa	FL	33619	**800-338-9140**	813-626-0090
Amatech Inc 1460 Grimm Dr	Erie	PA	16501	**800-403-6920**	
American Excelsior Co 850 Ave H E	Arlington	TX	76011	**800-777-7645**	
Balcan Plastics Ltd 9340 Meaux St	Saint Leonard	QC	H1R3H2	**877-422-5226**	514-326-0200
Barger Packaging Inc 2901 Oakland Ave	Elkhart	IN	46517	**888-525-2845**	
Belle-Pak Packaging Inc 7465 Birchmount Rd	Markham	ON	L3R5X9	**800-565-2137**	905-475-5151
Brushfoil LLC 1 Shoreline Dr Unit 6	Guilford	CT	06437	**800-493-2321**	203-453-7403
Bulldog Bag Ltd 13631 Vulcan Way	Richmond	BC	V6V1K4	**800-665-1944**	604-273-8021
Carpenter Co 5016 Monument Ave	Richmond	VA	23230	**800-288-3830**	804-359-0800
CDF Corp 77 Industrial Park Rd	Plymouth	MA	02360	**800-443-1920**	
Cellofoam North America Inc 1917 Rockdale Industrial Blvd	Conyers	GA	30012	**800-241-3634**	770-929-3688
Clark Foam Products Corp 655 Remington Blvd	Bolingbrook	IL	60440	**888-284-2290**	630-226-5900
Clayton Corp 866 Horan Dr *Cust Svc	Fenton	MO	63026	**800-729-8220***	636-349-5333
ClingZ Inc 841 Market St	Nekoosa	WI	54457	**800-826-4886**	
Conglom Inc 2600 Marie-Curie Ave	Saint-Laurent	QC	H4S2C3	**877-333-0098**	514-333-6666
Creative Foam Corp 300 N Alloy Dr	Fenton	MI	48430	**800-529-4149**	810-629-4149
Custom Pack Inc 662 Exton Cmns	Exton	PA	19341	**800-722-7005**	610-363-1900
Dart Container Corp 500 Hogsback Rd	Mason	MI	48854	**800-248-5960**	

Classified Section

Plastics Foam Products (Cont'd)

Company			Toll-Free	Phone
Elliott Company of Indianapolis Inc				
9200 Zionsville Rd	Indianapolis IN	46268	800-545-1213*	317-291-1213
*Orders				
Enduro Composites Inc				
16602 Central Green Blvd	Houston TX	77032	800-231-7271	713-358-4000
Federal Foam Technologies Inc				
600 Wisconsin Dr	New Richmond WI	54017	800-898-9559	715-246-9500
FLEXSTAR Packaging Inc				
13320 River Rd	Richmond BC	V6V1W7	800-663-1177	604-273-9277
Flextron Industries Inc				
720 Mt Rd	Aston PA	19014	800-633-2181	610-459-4600
Foam Fabricators Inc				
950 Progress Blvd	New Albany IN	47150	800-626-1197	812-948-1696
Foam Molders & Specialty Corp				
20004 State Rd	Cerritos CA	90703	800-378-8987	
Free Flow Packaging International Inc				
1090 Mills Way	Redwood City CA	94063	800-866-9946	650-261-5300
Future Foam Inc				
1610 Ave N Council Bluffs	Council Bluffs IA	51501	800-733-8061	712-323-9122
FXI 1400 N Providence Rd	Media PA	19063	800-355-3626	610-744-2300
G & T Industries Inc				
1001 76th St SW	Byron Center MI	49315	800-968-6035	616-452-8611
Gaco Western Inc				
200 W Mercer St Ste 202	Seattle WA	98119	800-456-4226	800-331-0196
General Plastics Mfg Co				
4910 Burlington Way	Tacoma WA	98409	800-806-6051	253-473-5000
Gunther Mele Ltd				
30 Craig St	Brantford ON	N3R7J1	888-486-8437	519-756-4330
Hibco Plastics Inc				
1820 Us 601 Hwy	Yadkinville NC	27055	800-849-8683	336-463-2391
Jif-Pak Manufacturing Inc				
1451 Engineer St	Vista CA	92081	800-777-6613	760-597-2665
Lomont In-Mold Technologies (IMT)				
1516 E Mapleleaf Dr	Mount Pleasant IA	52641	800-776-0380	319-385-1528
Modern Plastics Inc				
88 Long Hill Cross Rd	Shelton CT	06484	800-243-9696	203-333-3128
MonoSol LLC				
707 E 80th Pl Ste 301	Merrillville IN	46410	800-237-9552	
NAP Windows & Doors Ltd				
2150 Enterprise Way	Kelowna BC	V1Y6H7	888-762-5311	250-762-5343
NCFI Polyurethanes				
1515 Carter St	Mount Airy NC	27030	800-346-8229	336-789-9161
Pacific Packaging Products Inc				
24 Industrial Way	Wilmington MA	01887	800-777-0300	978-657-9100
Perfect Turf Inc				
622 Sandpebble Dr	Schaumburg IL	60193	888-796-8873	
Plastipak Industries Inc				
150 Industriel Blvd	Boucherville QC	J4B2X3	800-387-7452	450-650-2200
PMC Biogenix Inc				
1231 Pope St	Memphis TN	38108	800-641-2152	901-325-4930
Poly Molding LLC				
96 Fourth Ave	Haskell NJ	07420	800-229-7161	973-835-7161
Polymer Industries LLC				
10526 Alabama Hwy 40 PO Box 32	Henagar AL	35978	877-489-0039	256-657-5197
Professional Plastics Inc				
1810 E Valencia Dr	Fullerton CA	92831	800-878-0755	714-446-6500
Robbie Manufacturing Inc				
10810 Mid America Ave	Lenexa KS	66219	800-255-6328	913-492-3400
Safas Corp 2 Ackerman Ave	Clifton NJ	07011	800-472-6854	973-772-5252
SBA Materials Inc				
9430-H San Mateo Blvd NE	Albuquerque NM	87113	800-498-9608	
Sekisui Voltek LLC				
100 Shepard St	Lawrence MA	01843	800-225-0668	978-685-2557
Sigma Stretch Film Corp				
Page & Schuyler Aves Bldg 8	Lyndhurst NJ	07071	800-672-9727	201-507-9100
Sonoco 1 N Second St	Hartsville SC	29550	800-377-2692	
NYSE: SON				
Sonoma Graphic Products Inc				
961 Stockton Ave	San Jose CA	95110	800-250-4252	408-294-2072
Storopack Inc				
12007 S Woodruff Ave	Downey CA	90241	800-829-1491	562-803-5582
Syfan USA Corp				
1622 Twin Bridges Rd	Everetts NC	27825	888-597-9326	
ThermoSafe Brands				
3930 N Ventura Dr Ste 450	Arlington Heights IL	60004	800-323-7442	847-398-0110
ThermoServ 3901 Pipestone Rd	Dallas TX	75212	800-635-5559	214-631-0307
TMP Technologies				
1200 Northland Ave	Buffalo NY	14215	866-728-1932	716-895-6100
Topp Industries Inc				
420 N State Rd 25 PO Box 420	Rochester IN	46975	800-354-4534	574-223-3681
UFP Technologies Inc				
172 E Main St	Georgetown MA	01833	800-372-3172	978-352-2200
NASDAQ: UFPT				
Universal Protective Packaging Inc				
61 Texaco Rd	Mechanicsburg PA	17050	800-544-6649	717-766-1578
Western Concord Manufacturing Ltd				
880 Cliveden Ave	Vancouver BC	V3M5R5	800-663-6208	604-525-1061
WinCup 4640 Lewis Rd	Stone Mountain GA	30083	800-292-2877	770-771-5861
Zurn Industries LLC				
511 W Freshwater Way	Milwaukee WI	53204	855-663-9876	

598   PLASTICS MACHINING & FORMING

SEE ALSO Plastics Molding - Custom

Company			Toll-Free	Phone
Bardes Plastics Inc				
5225 W Clinton Ave	Milwaukee WI	53223	800-558-5161*	
*Cust Svc				
Comco Plastics Inc				
98-31 Jamaica Ave	Woodhaven NY	11421	800-221-9555	718-849-9000
East Jordan Plastics Inc				
PO Box 575	East Jordan MI	49727	800-353-1190	
Empire West Inc				
9270 Graton Rd PO Box 511	Graton CA	95444	800-521-4261	707-823-1190
Fabri-Kal Corp				
600 Plastics Pl	Kalamazoo MI	49001	800-888-5054	269-385-5050

Plastics Foam Products (continued — right column)

Company			Toll-Free	Phone
Formall Inc				
3908 Fountain Vly Dr	Knoxville TN	37918	800-643-3676	865-259-6298
Inline Plastics Corp				
42 Canal St	Shelton CT	06484	800-826-5567	203-924-5933
Innovize Inc				
500 Oak Grove Pkwy	Saint Paul MN	55127	877-605-6580	
Kal Plastics				
2050 E 48th St	Los Angeles CA	90058	800-321-3925	323-581-6194
McNeal Enterprises Inc				
2031 Ringwood Ave	San Jose CA	95131	800-562-6325	408-922-7290
Meyer Plastics Inc				
5167 E 65th St	Indianapolis IN	46220	800-968-4131	317-259-4131
Placon Corp 6096 McKee Rd	Madison WI	53719	800-541-1535	608-271-5634
Polygon Co				
103 Industrial Pk Dr PO Box 176	Walkerton IN	46574	800-918-9261	574-586-3145
Quadrant Engineering Plastic Products USA				
2120 Fairmont Ave PO Box 14235	Reading PA	19612	800-366-0300	610-320-6600
Ray Products Company Inc				
1700 Chablis Ave	Ontario CA	91761	800-423-7859	
Thermo-Fab Corp				
76 Walker Rd	Shirley MA	01464	888-494-9777	978-425-2311
Total Plastics Inc				
3316 Pagosa Ct	Indianapolis IN	46226	800-382-4635	317-543-3540

599   PLASTICS MATERIALS - WHOL

Company			Toll-Free	Phone
A Daigger & Company Inc				
620 Lakeview Pkwy	Vernon Hills IL	60061	800-621-7193	847-816-5060
Aetna Plastics Corp				
1702 St Clair Ave	Cleveland OH	44114	800-634-3074	216-781-4421
Aztec Supply				
954 N Batavia St	Orange CA	92867	800-836-3210	714-771-6580
Bamberger Polymers Inc				
2 Jericho Plz	Jericho NY	11753	800-888-8959	516-622-3600
Buckley Industries Inc				
1850 E 53rd St N	Wichita KS	67219	800-835-2779	316-744-7587
Cope Plastics Inc				
4441 Industrial Dr	Godfrey IL	62002	800-851-5510	618-466-0221
Delta Polymers Midwest Inc				
6685 Sterling Dr N	Sterling Heights MI	48312	800-860-6848	586-795-2900
E Hofmann Plastics Inc				
51 Centennial Rd	Orangeville ON	L9W3R1	877-707-7245	519-943-5050
Laird Plastics Inc				
6800 Broken Sound Pkwy Ste 150	Boca Raton FL	33487	800-243-9696	630-451-4688
M Holland				
400 Skokie Blvd Ste 600.	Northbrook IL	60062	800-872-7370	
Maine Plastics Inc				
1817 Kenosha Rd	Zion IL	60099	800-338-7728	847-379-9100
Orange County Industrial Plastics Inc				
4811 E La Palma Ave	Anaheim CA	92807	800-974-6247	
Plastic Film Corporation of America Inc				
1287 Naperville Dr	Romeoville IL	60446	800-654-6589	630-887-0800
Port Plastics Inc				
15325 Fairfield Ranch Rd Ste 150	Chino Hills CA	91709	800-800-0039	480-813-6118
Primepak Co 133 Cedar Ln	Teaneck NJ	07666	800-786-5613	201-836-5060
Regal Plastic Supply Co				
111 E Tenth Ave	North Kansas City MO	64116	800-627-2102	816-421-6290
Ryan Herco Products Corp				
3010 N San Fernando Blvd	Burbank CA	91504	800-848-1141	818-841-1141
San Diego Plastics Inc				
2220 Mckinley Ave	National City CA	91950	800-925-4855	619-477-4855
Seelye Plastics Inc				
9700 Newton Ave S	Bloomington MN	55431	800-328-2728	
Superior Oil Co Inc				
1402 N Capitol Ave Ste 100	Indianapolis IN	46202	800-553-5480	317-781-4400
Tekra Corp				
16700 W Lincoln Ave	New Berlin WI	53151	800-448-3572	

600   PLASTICS MOLDING - CUSTOM

Company			Toll-Free	Phone
Akron Porcelain & Plastics Co				
2739 Cory Ave PO Box 15157	Akron OH	44314	800-737-9664	330-745-2159
Berry Global Inc				
101 Oakley St	Evansville IN	47710	877-662-3779*	413-529-2183
*Sales				
Confer Plastics Inc (CPI)				
97 Witmer Rd	North Tonawanda NY	14120	800-635-3213	716-693-2056
Cuyahoga Molded Plastics Corp				
1265 Babbitt Rd	Cleveland OH	44132	800-805-9549	216-261-2744
D-M-E Co				
29111 Stephenson Hwy	Madison Heights MI	48071	800-626-6653	248-398-6000
Double H Plastics Inc				
50 W St Rd	Warminster PA	18974	800-523-3932	
EFP Corp				
223 Middleton Run Rd	Elkhart IN	46516	800-205-8537	574-295-4690
Elgin Molded Plastics				
909 Grace St	Elgin IL	60120	800-548-5483	847-931-2455
Ensinger Putnam Precision Molding				
11 Danco Rd	Putnam CT	06260	800-752-7865	860-928-7911
Evco Plastics				
100 W N St PO Box 497	DeForest WI	53532	800-507-6000	
Filtertek Inc 11411 Price Rd	Hebron IL	60034	800-248-2461	815-648-1001
Flambeau Inc				
15981 Valplast Rd	Middlefield OH	44062	800-457-5252	440-632-1631
Gruber Systems Inc				
25636 Ave Stanford	Valencia CA	91355	800-257-4070	661-257-4060
Kennerley-Spratling Inc				
2116 Farallon Dr	San Leandro CA	94577	800-523-5474	510-351-8230
Lehigh Valley Plastics Inc				
187 North Commerce Way	Bethlehem PA	18017	800-354-5344	484-893-5500
Midwest Plastic Components				
7309 W 27th St	Minneapolis MN	55426	800-243-3221	952-929-3312

	Toll-Free	Phone
Minnesota Rubber & Plastics		
1100 Xenium Ln N ....Minneapolis MN 55441	800-927-1422	952-927-1400
Molded Fiber Glass Cos		
2925 MFG Pl PO Box 675 ....Ashtabula OH 44005	800-860-0196	440-997-5851
Molding Corp of America		
10349 Norris Ave ....Pacoima CA 91331	800-423-2747	818-890-7877
MXL Industries Inc		
1764 Rohrerstown Rd ....Lancaster PA 17601	800-233-0159	717-569-8711
Plastic Components Inc		
N 116 W 18271 Morse Dr ....Germantown WI 53022	877-253-1496	262-253-0353
PMC Lenco 10240 Deer Pk Rd ....Waverly NE 68462	877-789-5844*	402-786-2000
*Cust Svc		
Royer Corp 805 East St ....Madison IN 47250	800-457-8997	812-265-3133
Seitz LLC		
212 Industrial Ln ....Torrington CT 06790	800-261-2011	860-489-0476
Steere Enterprises Inc		
285 Commerce St ....Tallmadge OH 44278	800-875-4926	330-633-4926
Tuthill Corp Plastics Group		
2050 Sunnydale Blvd ....Clearwater FL 33765	800-634-2695	727-446-8593
Universal Plastic Mold Inc		
13245 Los Angeles St ....Baldwin Park CA 91706	888-893-1587	
Westlake Plastics Co		
PO Box 127 ....Lenni PA 19052	800-999-1700	610-459-1000

601 PLASTICS & OTHER SYNTHETIC MATERIALS

601-1 Synthetic Fibers & Filaments

	Toll-Free	Phone
Consolidated Fibers		
8100 S Blvd ....Charlotte NC 28273	800-243-8621	704-554-8621
DuPont Advanced Fibers Systems		
5401 Jefferson Davis Hwy ....Richmond VA 23234	800-441-7515	804-383-3845
Fairfield Processing Corp		
88 Rose Hill Ave ....Danbury CT 06810	800-980-8000	203-744-2090
Hexcel Corp		
281 Tresser Blvd 16th Fl................Stamford CT 06901	800-444-3923	800-688-7734
NYSE: HXL		
International Fiber Corp		
50 Bridge St ....North Tonawanda NY 14120	888-698-1936	716-693-4040
INVISTA 4123 E 37th St N ....Wichita KS 67220	877-446-0478	316-828-1000
Nylon Corp of America		
333 Sundial Ave ....Manchester NH 03103	800-851-2001	603-627-5150
TenCate Grass America		
1131 Broadway St ....Dayton TN 37321	800-251-1033	423-775-0792
United Plastic Fabricating Inc		
165 Flagship Dr ....North Andover MA 01845	800-638-8265	

601-2 Synthetic Resins & Plastics Materials

	Toll-Free	Phone
Asahi Kasei Plastics North America Inc		
900 E Van Riper Rd ....Fowlerville MI 48836	800-993-5382*	517-223-5100
*Cust Svc		
Bayer Inc 77 Belfield Rd ....Toronto ON M9W1G6	800-622-2937	416-248-0771
Canplas Industries Ltd		
500 Veterans Dr ....Barrie ON L4M4V3	800-461-1771	705-726-3361
Cartec International Inc		
106 Powder Mill Rd ....Canton CT 06019	800-821-4434	860-693-9395
Daikin America Inc		
20 Olympic Dr ....Orangeburg NY 10962	800-365-9570*	792-831-8666
*Cust Svc		
Dow Chemical Co		
2030 Dow Ctr ....Midland MI 48674	800-422-8193*	989-636-1463
NYSE: DWDP ■ *Cust Svc		
DSM Engineering Plastics Inc		
2267 W Mill Rd ....Evansville IN 47720	800-333-4237	812-435-7500
DuPont Engineering Polymers		
Lancaster Pike Rt 141		
Barley Mill Plz Bldg 22 ....Wilmington DE 19805	800-441-7515	302-999-4592
Eastman Chemical Co		
200 S Wilcox Dr ....Kingsport TN 37660	800-327-8626*	423-229-2000
NYSE: EMN ■ *Cust Svc		
Engineered Polymer Solutions Inc		
1400 N State St ....Marengo IL 60152	800-654-4242	
Formosa Plastics Corp USA		
9 Peach Tree Hill Rd ....Livingston NJ 07039	888-664-4040	973-992-2090
Gallagher Corp		
3908 Morrison Dr ....Gurnee IL 60031	800-524-8597	847-249-3440
Goldsmith & Eggleton Inc		
300 First St ....Wadsworth OH 44281	800-321-0954	330-336-6616
Heritage Plastics Inc		
1002 Hunt St ....Picayune MS 39466	800-245-4623	601-798-8663
Huntsman Corp		
500 Huntsman Way ....Salt Lake City UT 84108	888-490-8484	801-584-5700
NYSE: HUN		
Indelco Plastics Corp		
6530 Cambridge St ....Minneapolis MN 55426	800-486-6456	952-925-5075
Interplastic Corp		
1225 Wolters Blvd ....Saint Paul MN 55110	800-736-5497	651-481-6860
Lewcott Corp		
86 Providence Rd ....Millbury MA 01527	800-225-7725*	508-865-1791
*Sales		
Lord Corp 111 Lord Dr ....Cary NC 27511	877-275-5673	919-468-5979
Minova USA Inc		
150 Carley Ct ....Georgetown KY 40324	800-626-2948	502-863-6800
Neville Chemical Co		
2800 Neville Rd ....Pittsburgh PA 15225	877-704-4200*	412-331-4200
*Cust Svc		
NOVA Chemicals Corp		
1000 Seventh Ave SW PO Box 2518..........Calgary AB T2P5C6	800-561-6682	403-750-3600
Perstorp Polyols Inc		
600 Matzinger Rd ....Toledo OH 43612	800-537-0280*	419-729-5448
*Cust Svc		
Plastics Color & Compounding Inc		
14201 Paxton Ave ....Calumet City IL 60409	800-922-9936	

	Toll-Free	Phone
PolyOne Corp		
33587 Walker Rd ....Avon Lake OH 44012	866-765-9663	440-930-1000
NYSE: POL		
Reichhold Inc 2400 Ellis Rd ....Durham NC 27703	800-448-3482	919-990-7500
Resinall Corp PO Box 195 ....Severn NC 27877	800-421-0561	
RheTech Inc		
1500 E N Territorial Rd ....Whitmore Lake MI 48189	800-869-1230	734-769-0585
Rogers Corp 1 Technology Dr ....Rogers CT 06263	800-237-2267	860-774-9605
RTP Co 580 E Front St ....Winona MN 55987	800-433-4787	507-454-6900
Rutland Plastic Technologies		
10021 Rodney St ....Pineville NC 28134	800-438-5134	704-553-0046
Shuman Plastics Inc		
35 Neoga St ....Depew NY 14043	800-803-6242	716-685-2121
Sterling Fibers Inc		
5005 Sterling Way ....Pace FL 32571	800-342-3779*	850-994-5311
*Cust Svc		
Ticona LLC 8040 Dixie Hwy ....Florence KY 41042	800-833-4882	859-372-3244
Vi-Chem Corp		
55 Cottage Grove St SW ....Grand Rapids MI 49507	800-477-8501	616-247-8501
Westlake Chemical Corp		
2801 Post Oak Blvd Ste 600.............Houston TX 77056	888-953-3623	713-960-9111
NYSE: WLK		

601-3 Synthetic Rubber

	Toll-Free	Phone
Akrochem Corp 255 Fountain St ....Akron OH 44304	800-321-2260	330-535-2100
Goodyear Tire & Rubber Co		
200 Innovation Way ....Akron OH 44316	800-321-2136*	330-796-2121
NASDAQ: GT ■ *Cust Svc		
Lanxess Corp		
111 RIDC Pk W Dr ....Pittsburgh PA 15275	800-526-9377	412-809-1000
Midwest Elastomers Inc		
700 Industrial Dr PO Box 412..............Wapakoneta OH 45895	877-786-3539	419-738-8844
Teknor Apex Co		
505 Central Ave ....Pawtucket RI 02861	800-556-3864	401-725-8000
Textile Rubber & Chemical Co Inc		
1300 Tiarco Dr SW ....Dalton GA 30721	800-727-8453	706-277-1300

602 PLASTICS PRODUCTS - FIBERGLASS REINFORCED

	Toll-Free	Phone
Crane Composites Inc		
23525 W Eames St ....Channahon IL 60410	800-435-0080	815-467-8600
Fibergrate Composite Structures Inc		
5151 Beltline Rd Ste 700 ....Dallas TX 75254	800-527-4043	972-250-1633
McClarin Plastics Inc		
15 Industrial Dr ....Hanover PA 17331	800-233-3189	717-637-2241
Red Ewald Inc		
2669 US 181 ....Karnes City TX 78118	800-242-3524	830-780-3304

603 PLASTICS PRODUCTS - HOUSEHOLD

	Toll-Free	Phone
Bow Plastics Ltd		
5700 Cote de Liesse ....Montreal QC H4T1B1	800-852-8527	514-735-5671
GT Water Products Inc		
5239 N Commerce Ave ....Moorpark CA 93021	800-862-5647	
Home Products International Inc		
4501 W 47th St ....Chicago IL 60632	800-457-9881	773-890-8923
Igloo Products Corp		
777 Igloo Rd ....Katy TX 77494	866-509-3503	281-394-6800
Iris USA Inc		
11111 80th Ave ....Pleasant Prairie WI 53158	800-320-4747	262-612-1000
King Plastics Inc		
840 N Elm St ....Orange CA 92867	800-363-9822	714-997-7540
Kraftware Corp 270 Cox St ....Roselle NJ 07203	800-221-1728*	
*Cust Svc		
Maryland Plastics Inc		
251 E Central Ave ....Federalsburg MD 21632	800-544-5582*	410-754-5566
*Cust Svc		
Sterilite Corp PO Box 524 ....Townsend MA 01469	800-225-1046	
TAP Plastics Inc		
6475 Sierra Ln ....Dublin CA 94568	800-894-0827	925-829-4889
Thermos Co		
475 N Martingale Rd Ste 1100 ....Schaumburg IL 60173	800-243-0745	847-439-7821

604 PLASTICS PRODUCTS (MISC)

	Toll-Free	Phone
7-sigma Inc		
2843 26th Ave S ....Minneapolis MN 55406	888-722-8396	612-722-5358
Aco Polymer Products Inc		
9470 Pinecore Dr ....Mentor OH 44060	800-543-4764	440-639-7230
Acrylic Plastic Products Company Inc		
4815 Hwy 80 W ....Jackson MS 39209	800-331-8819	601-922-2651
Aigner Index Inc		
23 Mac Arthur Ave ....New Windsor NY 12553	800-242-3919	845-562-4510
All States Inc		
602 N 12th St ....Saint Charles IL 60174	800-621-5837*	773-728-0525
*Cust Svc		
American Window & Glass Inc		
2715 Lynch Rd ....Evansville IN 47711	877-671-6943	812-464-9400
Amerimade Technology Inc		
449 Mtn Vista Pkwy ....Livermore CA 94551	800-938-3824	925-243-9090
Avery Dennison Fastener Div		
224 Industrial Rd ....Fitchburg MA 01420	800-225-5913	
AXYS Technologies Inc		
2045 Mills Rd ....Sidney BC V8L5X2	877-792-7878	250-655-5850
Bemis Manufacturing Co		
300 Mill St ....Sheboygan Falls WI 53085	800-558-7651	920-467-4621

			Toll-Free	Phone

Blackmore Company Inc
10800 Blackmore Ave .... Belleville MI 48111 **800-874-8660** 734-483-8661

Bowman Mfg Company Inc
17301 51st Ave NE .... Arlington WA 98223 **800-962-4660** 360-435-5005

C L Smith
1311 S 39th St .... Saint Louis MO 63110 **855-551-2625**

CMI Plastics Inc
222 Pepsi Way .... Ayden NC 28513 **877-395-1920** 252-746-2171

Coverbind Corp
3200 Corporate Dr .... Wilmington NC 28405 **800-366-6060** 910-799-4116

Crystal-Like Plastics
21701 Plummer St .... Chatsworth CA 91311 **800-554-6091** 818-846-1818

Den Hartog Industries Inc
4010 Hospers Dr S PO Box 425 .... Hospers IA 51238 **800-342-3408** 712-752-8432

Easyturf 2750 La Mirada Dr .... Vista CA 92081 **866-353-3518** 866-327-9887

Fiberglass Specialties Inc
PO Box 1340 .... Henderson TX 75653 **800-527-1459** 903-657-6522

Garner Industries Inc
7201 N 98th St PO Box 29709 .... Lincoln NE 68507 **800-228-0275** 402-434-9100

Genova Products Inc
7034 E Court St .... Davison MI 48423 **800-521-7488** 888-309-1808

GenPore
1136 Morgantown Rd PO Box 380 .... Reading PA 19607 **800-654-4391** 610-374-5171

Gessner Products Company Inc
241 N Main St PO Box 389 .... Ambler PA 19002 **800-874-7808** 215-646-7667

Glasteel-stabilit America Inc
285 Industrial Dr .... Moscow TN 38057 **800-238-5546** 901-877-3010

GPK Products Inc
1601 43rd St NW .... Fargo ND 58102 **800-437-4670** 701-277-3225

Great Works Internet (GWI)
43 Landry St .... Biddeford ME 04005 **866-494-2020** 207-494-2000

Habasit America
805 Satellite Blvd .... Suwanee GA 30024 **800-458-6431**

Hanscom Inc 331 Market St .... Warren RI 02885 **877-725-6788** 401-247-1999

Harbec Inc 358 Timothy Ln .... Ontario NY 14519 **888-521-4416** 585-265-0010

Hygolet Inc
349 SE Second Ave .... Deerfield Beach FL 33441 **800-494-6538** 954-481-8601

Ideal Pet Products Inc
24735 Ave Rockefeller .... Valencia CA 91355 **800-378-4385** 661-294-2266

Kalwall Corp
1111 Candia Rd PO Box 237 .... Manchester NH 03105 **800-258-9777** 603-627-3861

King Plastic Corp
1100 N Toledo Blade Blvd .... North Port FL 34288 **800-780-5502** 941-493-5502

Lamvin Inc 4675 North Ave .... Oceanside CA 92056 **800-446-6329** 760-806-6400

Landmark Plastic Corp
1331 Kelly Ave .... Akron OH 44306 **800-242-1183** 330-785-2200

Leaktite Corp
40 Francis St .... Leominster MA 01453 **800-392-0039** 978-537-8000

Little Kids Inc
225 Chapman St Ste 202 .... Providence RI 02905 **800-545-5437** 401-454-7600

LSP Products Group Inc
3689 Arrowhead Dr .... Carson City NV 89706 **800-854-3215**

Magic Plastics Inc
25215 Ave Stanford .... Valencia CA 91355 **800-369-0303** 661-257-4485

MedGyn Products Inc
100 W Industrial Rd .... Addison IL 60101 **800-451-9667** 630-627-4105

Micro Plastics Inc
11 Industry Ln Hwy 178 N PO Box 149 .... Flippin AR 72634 **800-466-1467** 870-453-2261

MOCAP Inc 409 Pkwy Dr .... Park Hills MO 63601 **800-633-6775** 314-543-4000

Mold-Rite Plastics LLC
1 Plant St .... Plattsburgh NY 12901 **800-432-5277** 518-561-1812

Neil Enterprises Inc
450 E Bunker Ct .... Vernon Hills IL 60061 **800-621-5584** 847-549-7627

Nordson MEDICAL
3325 S Timberline Rd .... Fort Collins CO 80525 **888-404-5837**

Pac Tec 12365 Haynes St .... Clinton LA 70722 **877-554-2544**

Plastikon Industries Inc
688 Sandoval Way .... Hayward CA 94544 **800-370-0858** 510-400-1010

Plastpro Inc
5200 W Century Blvd 9F .... Los Angeles CA 90045 **800-779-0561** 310-693-8600

Pleiger Plastics Co
PO Box 1271 .... Washington PA 15301 **800-753-4437** 724-228-2244

Plitek LLC 69 Rawls Rd .... Des Plaines IL 60018 **800-966-1250**

Porex Technologies Corp
500 Bohannon Rd .... Fairburn GA 30213 **800-241-0195***
*Cust Svc

Precision Thermoplastic Components Inc
PO Box 1296 .... Lima OH 45802 **800-860-4505** 419-227-4500

Prism Plastics Products Inc
Hwy 65 PO Box 446 .... New Richmond WI 54017 **877-246-7535** 715-246-7535

Randall Mfg LLC
722 Church Rd .... Elmhurst IL 60126 **800-323-7424** 630-782-0001

Rayner Covering Systems Inc
665 Schneider Dr .... South Elgin IL 60177 **800-648-0757** 847-695-2264

Rogan Corp
3455 Woodhead Dr .... Northbrook IL 60062 **800-584-5662** 847-498-2300

Rohrer Corp
717 Seville Rd PO Box 1009 .... Wadsworth OH 44282 **800-243-6640** 330-335-1541

Rubbermaid Commercial Products (RCP)
3124 Valley Ave .... Winchester VA 22601 **800-347-9800** 540-667-8700

Safety Technology International Inc
2306 Airport Rd .... Waterford MI 48327 **800-888-4784** 248-673-9898

Shakespeare Monofilaments & Specialty Polymers
6111 Shakespeare Rd .... Columbia SC 29223 **800-845-2110** 803-754-7011

Simonton Windows Inc
5020 Weston Pkwy Ste 400 .... Cary NC 27513 **800-746-6686**

Smith McDonald Corp
1270 Niagara St .... Buffalo NY 14213 **800-753-8548**

Spears Manufacturing Co
PO Box 9203 .... Sylmar CA 91392 **800-862-1499** 818-364-1611

Spilltech Environmental Inc
1627 Odonoghue St .... Mobile AL 36615 **800-228-3877**

Stant Corp
1620 Columbia Ave .... Connersville IN 47331 **800-822-3121** 765-825-3121

Steinwall Inc
1759 116th Ave NW .... Coon Rapids MN 55448 **800-229-9199** 763-767-7060

Syndicate Sales Inc
PO Box 756 .... Kokomo IN 46903 **800-428-0515** 765-457-7277

			Toll-Free	Phone

Technetics Group
3125 Damon Way .... Burbank CA 91505 **800-618-4701** 818-841-9667

Thombert Inc
316 E Seventh St N .... Newton IA 50208 **800-433-3572**

TMI LLC
5350 Campbells Run Rd .... Pittsburgh PA 15205 **800-888-9750**

Transparent Container Company Inc
625 Thomas Rd .... Bensenville IL 60106 **888-449-8520**

Triad Products Co
1801 W 'B' St .... Hastings NE 68901 **888-253-4227*** 402-462-2181
*General

Trippnt Inc
8830 NE 108th St .... Kansas City MO 64157 **800-874-7768** 816-792-2604

TSE Industries Inc
4370 112th Terr N .... Clearwater FL 33762 **800-237-7634** 727-573-7676

Ultra-Poly Corp
102 Demi Rd PO Box 330 .... Portland PA 18351 **800-932-0619** 570-897-7500

Univenture Inc
16710 Square Dr .... Marysville OH 43040 **800-992-8262** 937-645-4600

World Class Plastics Inc
7695 SR- 708 .... Russells Point OH 43348 **800-954-3140** 937-843-4927

Wren Assoc Ltd
124 Wren Pkwy .... Jefferson City MO 65109 **800-881-2249** 573-893-2249

Zadro Products Inc
5422 Argosy Ave .... Huntington Beach CA 92649 **800-468-4348** 714-892-9200

ZAGG Inc
3855 South 500 West Ste J .... Salt Lake City UT 84115 **800-700-9244** 801-263-0699

605   PLUMBING FIXTURES & FITTINGS - METAL

			Toll-Free	Phone

Accurate Partitions Corp
160 Tower Dr PO Box 287 .... Burr Ridge IL 60527 **800-933-4525** 708-442-6800

Acorn Engineering Co
15125 Proctor Ave
PO Box 3527 .... City of Industry CA 91744 **800-488-8999** 626-336-4561

American Brass Manufacturing Co
5000 Superior Ave .... Cleveland OH 44103 **800-431-6440** 216-431-6565

Anderson Copper & Brass Co
255 Industry Ave .... Frankfort IL 60423 **800-323-5284** 708-535-9030

Barclay Products
4000 Porett Dr .... Gurnee IL 60031 **800-446-9700** 847-244-1234

Bradley Corp
W 142 N 9101 Fountain Blvd .... Menomonee Falls WI 53051 **800-272-3539** 262-251-6000

Champion-Arrowhead LLC
5147 Alhambra Ave .... Los Angeles CA 90032 **800-332-4267** 323-221-9137

Chicago Faucets A Geberit Co
2100 S Clearwater Dr .... Des Plaines IL 60018 **800-323-5060** 847-803-5000

Eljer Inc
1 Centennial Ave .... Piscataway NJ 08855 **800-442-1902**

Elkay Manufacturing Co
2222 Camden Ct .... Oak Brook IL 60523 **800-476-4106** 630-574-8484

Fisher Manufacturing Co
PO Box 60 .... Tulare CA 93275 **800-421-6162**

Fluidmaster Inc
30800 Rancho Viejo Rd .... San Juan Capistrano CA 92675 **800-631-2011** 949-728-2000

Grohe America Inc
241 Covington Dr .... Bloomingdale IL 60108 **800-444-7643** 630-582-7711

Hansgrohe Inc
1490 Bluegrass Lakes Pkwy .... Alpharetta GA 30004 **800-334-0455**

In-Sink-Erator 4700 21st St .... Racine WI 53406 **800-558-5712** 262-554-5432

Josam Co
525 W US Hwy 20 .... Michigan City IN 46360 **800-365-6726**

Keeney Manufacturing Co
1170 Main St .... Newington CT 06111 **800-243-0526*** 860-666-3342
*Cust Svc

LDR Industries Inc
600 N Kilbourn Ave .... Chicago IL 60624 **800-545-5230** 773-265-3000

Microphor Inc 452 E Hill Rd .... Willits CA 95490 **800-358-8280*** 707-459-5563
*Orders

Moen Inc
25300 Al Moen Dr .... North Olmsted OH 44070 **800-289-6636*** 440-962-2000
*Cust Svc

Oatey Co 4700 W 160th St .... Cleveland OH 44135 **800-321-9532*** 216-267-7100
*Cust Svc

Price Pfister Inc
19701 Da Vinci St .... Lake Forest CA 92610 **800-732-8238** 949-672-4000

Sloan Valve Co
10500 Seymour Ave .... Franklin Park IL 60131 **800-982-5839** 847-671-4300

Speakman Co
400 Anchor Mill Rd .... New Castle DE 19720 **800-537-2107**

Sterling Plumbing
444 Highland Dr .... Kohler WI 53044 **888-783-7546*** 920-457-4441
*Cust Svc

Symmons Industries Inc
31 Brooks Dr .... Braintree MA 02184 **800-796-6667**

T & S Brass & Bronze Works Inc
PO Box 1088 .... Travelers Rest SC 29690 **800-476-4103*** 864-834-4102
*Cust Svc

Water Pik Inc
1730 E Prospect Rd .... Fort Collins CO 80553 **800-525-2774**

Waterworks Operating Company LLC
60 Backus Ave .... Danbury CT 06810 **800-899-6757** 203-546-6000

Woodford Manufacturing Co
2121 Waynoka Rd .... Colorado Springs CO 80915 **800-621-6032*** 719-574-0600
*Sales

606   PLUMBING FIXTURES & FITTINGS - PLASTICS

			Toll-Free	Phone

1st Mechanical Services Inc
303 Curie Dr .... Alpharetta GA 30005 **888-346-0792** 770-346-0792

Alpha Mechanical Service Inc
7200 Distribution Dr .... Louisville KY 40258 **888-212-6324**

				Toll-Free	Phone
American Moistening Company Inc					
10402 Rodney St	Pineville	NC	28134	**800-948-5540**	704-889-7281
Apex Piping Systems Inc					
302 Falco Dr	Wilmington	DE	19804	**888-995-2739**	
Aqua Bath Company Inc					
921 Cherokee Ave	Nashville	TN	37207	**800-232-2284**	615-227-0017
Arneg Canada Inc					
18 Rue Richelieu	Lacolle	QC	J0J1J0	**800-363-3439**	450-246-3837
Aurora Contractors Inc					
100 Raynor Ave	Ronkonkoma	NY	11779	**866-423-2197**	631-981-3785
B & B Trade Distribution Centre					
1950 Oxford St E	London	ON	N5V2Z8	**800-265-0382**	519-679-1770
Belding Tank Technologies Inc					
200 N Gooding St PO Box 160	Belding	MI	48809	**800-253-4252**	616-794-1130
Benjamin Manufacturing					
3215 S Sweetwater Rd	Lithia Springs	GA	30122	**800-343-1756**	770-941-1433
Blue Mountain Air Inc					
707 Aldridge Rd	Vacaville	CA	95688	**800-889-2085**	
Blue Sky Energy Inc					
2598 Fortune Way Ste K	Vista	CA	92081	**800-493-7877**	760-597-1642
Boland					
30 W Watkins Mill Rd	Gaithersburg	MD	20878	**800-552-6526**	240-306-3000
Brower Mechanical Inc					
4060 Alvis Ct	Rocklin	CA	95677	**877-816-6649**	916-624-0808
Call-A-Head Corp					
304 Cross Bay Blvd	Broad Channel	NY	11693	**800-634-2085**	
Cambridgeport Air Systems					
8 Fanaras Dr	Salisbury	MA	01952	**877-648-2872**	978-465-8481
Can-am Plumbing Inc					
151 Wyoming St	Pleasanton	CA	94566	**800-786-9797**	925-846-1833
Casto Technical Services Inc					
540 Leon Sullivan Way	Charleston	WV	25301	**800-232-2221**	304-346-0549
Claybar Constracting Inc					
424 Macnab St	Dundas	ON	L9H2L3	**866-801-9305**	905-627-8000
Cole Industrial Inc					
5924 203rd St SW	Lynnwood	WA	98036	**800-627-2653**	425-774-6602
Colite International Ltd					
5 Technology Cir	Columbia	SC	29203	**800-760-7926**	803-926-7926
Continental Fire Sprinkler Co					
4518 S 133rd St	Omaha	NE	68137	**800-543-5170**	402-330-5170
Custom Air					
5338 Pinkney Ave	Sarasota	FL	34233	**888-856-4507**	
D'vontz 7208 E 38th St	Tulsa	OK	74145	**877-322-3600**	918-622-3600
Danamark Watercare Ltd					
2-90 Walker Dr	Brampton	ON	L6T4H6	**888-326-2627**	
Dispensing Dynamics International					
1020 Bixby Dr	City of Industry	CA	91745	**800-888-3698**	626-961-3691
Dornbracht Americas Inc					
1700 Executive Dr S Ste 600	Duluth	GA	30096	**800-774-1181**	770-564-3599
Effective Solar Products LLC					
601 Crescent Ave	Lockport	LA	70374	**888-824-0090**	985-532-0800
Federal Heating & Engineering Company Inc					
611 Main St Ste 202	Winchester	MA	01890	**855-721-2468***	
*Cust Svc					
Ferrandino & Son Inc					
71 Carolyn Blvd	Farmingdale	NY	11735	**866-571-4609**	516-735-0097
Finken Plumbing Heating & Cooling					
628 19th Ave NE	Saint Joseph	MN	56374	**877-346-5367**	320-258-2005
Fitzgerald Electro-mechanical Co					
6 S Linden Ave Ste 4	South San Francisco	CA	94080	**800-448-9832**	650-589-9935
Florestone Products Company Inc					
2851 Falcon Dr	Madera	CA	93637	**800-446-8827**	559-661-4171
Fujitsu General America Inc					
353 Rt 46 W	Fairfield	NJ	07004	**888-888-3424**	973-575-0380
Halvorson Trane					
2220 NW 108th St	Clive	IA	50325	**800-798-0004**	515-270-0004
Heat Transfer Products Group LLC					
201 Thomas French Dr	Scottsboro	AL	35769	**800-288-9488**	256-259-7400
Housh-the Home Energy Experts					
18 S Main St	Monroe	OH	45050	**800-793-6374**	513-793-6374
Hussung Mechanical Contractors					
6913 Enterprise Dr	Louisville	KY	40214	**800-446-2738**	502-375-3500
Imperial Manufacturing Group Inc					
40 Industrial Park St	Richibucto	NB	E4W4A4	**800-561-3100**	506-523-9117
Ingenuity Ieq					
3600 Centennial Dr	Midland	MI	48642	**800-669-9726**	989-496-2233
James Lane Air Conditioning Company Inc					
5024 Old Jacksboro Hwy	Wichita Falls	TX	76302	**800-460-2204**	940-766-0244
Jet Industries Inc					
1935 Silverton Rd NE PO Box 7362	Salem	OR	97303	**800-659-0620**	503-363-2334
Jones Stephens					
3249 Moody Pkwy	Moody	AL	35004	**800-355-6637**	
KITCO Fiber Optics Inc					
5269 Cleveland St	Virginia Beach	VA	23462	**866-643-5220**	757-518-8100
Kohler Canada Company Hytec Plumbing Products Div					
4150 Spallumcheen Dr	Armstrong	BC	V0E1B6	**800-871-8311**	250-546-3067
Kysor Warren Corp					
5201 Transport Blvd	Columbus	GA	31907	**800-866-5596**	706-568-1514
L B Plastics Inc					
482 E Plaza Dr	Mooresville	NC	28115	**800-752-7739**	704-663-1543
Maax Corp					
160 St Joseph Blvd	Lachine	QC	H8S2L3	**888-957-7816**	877-438-6229
Maintenx 2202 N Howard Ave	Tampa	FL	33607	**855-751-0075**	
Mallick Plumbing & Heating					
8010 Cessna Ave	Gaithersburg	MD	20879	**888-805-3354**	
Matco-Norca Inc					
1944 Rt 22 PO Box 27	Brewster	NY	10509	**800-431-2082**	845-278-7570
Meckley Services Inc					
9704 Gunston Cove Rd Ste E	Lorton	VA	22079	**877-632-5539**	703-333-2040
Meier Supply Company Inc					
530 Bloomingburg Rd	Middletown	NY	10940	**800-418-3216**	845-733-5666
Mohr Power Solar Inc					
1452 Pomona Rd	Corona	CA	92882	**800-637-6527**	951-736-2000
National Meter & Automation					
7220 S Fraser St	Centennial	CO	80112	**877-212-8340**	303-339-9100
National Office Systems Inc					
6804 Virginia Manor Rd Ste 400	Beltsville	MD	20705	**800-840-6264**	301-840-6264

				Toll-Free	Phone
North South Supply Inc					
686 Third St	Vero Beach	FL	32962	**800-940-3810**	772-569-3810
Noveo Technologies Inc					
9655 A Ignace St	Brossard	QC	J4Y2P3	**877-314-2044**	450-444-2044
Nupla Corp					
11912 Sheldon St	Sun Valley	CA	91352	**800-872-7661**	818-768-6800
OZZ Electric Inc					
20 Floral Pkwy	Concord	ON	L4K4R1	**844-699-6100**	416-637-7237
Padgett Services					
140 Mountain Brook Dr	Canton	GA	30115	**888-323-0777**	678-880-1600
Pedal Valves Inc					
13625 River Rd	Luling	LA	70070	**800-431-3668**	985-785-9997
PolyJohn Enterprises Corp					
2500 Gaspar Ave	Whiting	IN	46394	**800-292-1305**	
Prier Products Inc					
4515 E 139th St	Grandview	MO	64030	**800-362-1463**	800-362-9055
Pumping Solutions Inc					
1906 S Quaker Ridge Pl	Ontario	CA	91761	**800-603-0399**	
RoboVent					
37900 Mound Rd	Sterling Heights	MI	48310	**888-298-4214**	586-698-1800
Ryan FireProtection Inc					
9740 E 148th St	Noblesville	IN	46060	**800-409-7606**	
Star Services					
4663 Halls Mill Rd	Mobile	AL	36693	**800-661-9050**	251-661-4050
State Supply Co					
597 Seventh St E	Saint Paul	MN	55130	**877-775-7705**	651-774-5985
Therma-Stor LLC					
4201 Lien Rd	Madison	WI	53704	**800-533-7533**	608-237-8400
Thetford Corp					
7101 Jackson Ave PO Box 1285	Ann Arbor	MI	48106	**800-521-3032**	734-769-6000
Thetford Corp Recreational Vehicle Group					
2901 E Bristol St Ste B	Elkhart	IN	46514	**800-831-1076**	574-266-7980
Thompson Industrial Services LLC					
104 N Main	Sumter	SC	29150	**800-849-8040**	803-773-8005
Total Maintenance Solutions					
3540 Rutherford Rd	Taylors	SC	29687	**800-476-2212**	864-268-2891
Tri-state Home Services					
82A Wormans Mill Ct	Frederick	MD	21701	**844-202-2126**	
Verigent LLC					
149 Plantation Ridge Dr Ste 100	Mooresville	NC	28117	**877-637-6422**	704-658-3285
Wisco Supply Inc					
815 S Saint Vrain St	El Paso	TX	79901	**800-947-2689**	915-544-8294
Zehnder America Inc					
6 Merrill Industrial Dr Ste 7	Hampton	NH	03842	**888-778-6701**	603-601-8544

607   PLUMBING FIXTURES & FITTINGS - VITREOUS CHINA & EARTHENWARE

				Toll-Free	Phone
Briggs Plumbing					
597 Old Mt Holly Rd	Goose Creek	SC	29445	**800-888-4458**	
Eljer Inc					
1 Centennial Ave	Piscataway	NJ	08855	**800-442-1902**	
Mansfield Plumbing Products Inc					
150 E First St	Perrysville	OH	44864	**877-850-3060**	419-938-5211
Microphor Inc 452 E Hill Rd	Willits	CA	95490	**800-358-8280***	707-459-5563
*Orders					
Peerless Pottery Inc					
319 S Fifth St	Rockport	IN	47635	**866-457-5785**	812-649-9920
Sterling Plumbing					
444 Highland Dr	Kohler	WI	53044	**888-783-7546***	920-457-4441
*Cust Svc					
Sunrise Specialty Co					
930 98th Ave	Oakland	CA	94603	**800-444-4280**	510-729-7277
Toto USA Inc					
1155 Southern Rd	Morrow	GA	30260	**888-295-8134**	770-282-8686

608   PLUMBING, HEATING, AIR CONDITIONING EQUIPMENT & SUPPLIES - WHOL

SEE ALSO Refrigeration Equipment - Whol

				Toll-Free	Phone
Aaron & Company Inc					
PO Box 8310	Piscataway	NJ	08855	**800-734-4822**	732-752-8200
Agile Sourcing Partners Inc					
2385 Railroad St	Corona	CA	92880	**888-718-1988**	
Air Monitor Corp					
1050 Hopper Ave	Santa Rosa	CA	95403	**800-247-3569**	707-544-2706
American Backflow Specialties					
3940 Home Ave	San Diego	CA	92105	**800-662-5356**	619-527-2525
American Faucet & Coating Corp					
3280 Corporate Vw	Vista	CA	92081	**800-621-8383**	760-598-5895
American Granby Inc					
7652 Morgan Rd	Liverpool	NY	13090	**800-776-2266**	315-451-1100
American Pipe & Supply Company Inc					
4100 Eastlake Blvd	Birmingham	AL	35217	**800-476-9460**	205-252-9460
Anderson Tube Company Inc					
1400 Fairgrounds Rd	Hatfield	PA	19440	**800-523-2258**	215-855-0118
Applied Membranes Inc					
2450 Business Park Dr	Vista	CA	92081	**800-321-9321**	760-727-3711
Applied Thermal Systems					
8401 73rd Ave N Ste 74	Brooklyn Park	MN	55428	**800-479-4783**	763-535-5545
Arizona Partsmaster					
7125 W Sherman St	Phoenix	AZ	85043	**888-924-7278**	602-233-3580
BA Robinson Company Ltd					
619 Berry St	Winnipeg	MB	R3H0S2	**866-903-6275**	204-784-0150
Baker Distributing Co					
14610 Breakers Dr Ste 100	Jacksonville	FL	32258	**844-289-0033**	800-217-4698
Bartle & Gibson Company Ltd					
13475 Ft Rd NW	Edmonton	AB	T5A1C6	**800-661-5615**	780-472-2850
Bascom-Turner Instrument					
111 Downey St	Norwood	MA	02062	**800-225-3298**	781-769-9660
Be-Cool Inc					
903 Woodside Ave	Essexville	MI	48732	**800-691-2667**	989-895-9699

		Toll-Free	Phone
Bender Plumbing Supplies Inc			
580 Grand Ave	New Haven CT 06511	800-573-4288	203-787-4288
Best Plumbing Specialties			
3039 Ventrie Ct	Myersville MD 21773	800-448-6710	
Broedell Plumbing Supply Inc			
1601 Commerce Ln	Jupiter FL 33458	800-683-6363	561-743-6663
Butcher Distributors Inc			
101 Boyce Rd	Broussard LA 70518	800-960-0008	337-837-2088
Caroplast Inc			
PO Box 668405	Charlotte NC 28266	800-327-5797	704-394-4191
City Plumbing & Electric Supply Co			
730 EE Butler Pkwy	Gainesville GA 30501	800-260-2024	770-532-4123
City Supply Corp			
2326 Bell Ave	Des Moines IA 50321	800-400-2377	515-288-3211
Cleveland Plumbing Supply Company Inc			
143 E Washington St	Chagrin Falls OH 44022	800-331-1078	440-247-2555
Coburn Supply Company Inc			
390 Park St Ste 100	Beaumont TX 77701	800-832-8492	409-838-6363
Comfort Products Distributing LLC			
13202 I St	Omaha NE 68137	800-779-8299	402-334-7777
Consolidated Supply Co			
7337 SW Kable Ln	Tigard OR 97224	800-929-5810	503-620-7050
D-S Pipe & Supply Company Inc			
1301 Wicomico St Ste 3	Baltimore MD 21230	800-368-8880	410-539-8000
Dawson Co 1681 W Second St	Pomona CA 91766	800-832-9766	626-797-9710
Delta T Inc			
8323 Loch Lomond Dr	Pico Rivera CA 90660	800-928-5828	310-355-0355
Desco Plumbing & Heating Supply Inc			
65 Worcester Rd	Etobicoke ON M9W5N7	800-564-5146	416-213-1555
Duncan Supply Company Inc			
910 N Illinois St	Indianapolis IN 46204	800-382-5528	317-634-1335
Duravit USA Inc			
2205 Northmont Pkwy Ste 200	Duluth GA 30096	888-387-2848	770-931-3575
East Coast Metal Distributors Inc			
1313 S Briggs Ave	Durham NC 27703	844-227-9531	919-596-2136
Eastern Pennsylvania Supply Co			
700 Scott St	Wilkes-Barre PA 18705	800-432-8075	570-823-1181
Emerson-Swan Inc			
300 Pond St	Randolph MA 02368	800-346-9219	781-986-2000
ETNA Supply			
4901 Clay Ave SW	Grand Rapids MI 49548	855-839-8011	616-245-4373
Everett J Prescott Inc			
32 Prescott St	Gardiner ME 04345	800-357-2447	207-582-1851
Ferguson Enterprises Inc			
12500 Jefferson Ave	Newport News VA 23602	800-721-2590	757-874-7795
Four Seasons Inc			
1801 Waters Ridge Dr	Lewisville TX 75057	888-505-4567	972-316-8100
Fresno Distributing Company Inc			
2055 E McKinley Ave	Fresno CA 93703	800-655-2542	559-442-8800
Gateway Supply Company Inc			
1312 Hamrick St	Columbia SC 29201	800-922-5312	803-771-7160
Gensco Inc 4402 20th St E	Tacoma WA 98424	877-620-8203	253-620-8203
Goodin Co			
2700 N Second St	Minneapolis MN 55411	800-328-8433	612-588-7811
Granite Group Wholesalers LLC			
6 Storrs St	Concord NH 03301	800-258-3690	603-545-3345
Great Western Supply Inc			
2626 Industrial Dr	Ogden UT 84401	866-776-8289	
Greenscape Pump Services Inc			
1425 Whitlock Ln Ste 108	Carrollton TX 75006	877-401-4774	972-446-0037
Habegger Corp, The			
4995 Winton Rd	Cincinnati OH 45232	800-459-4822	513-681-5600
Harry Cooper Supply Company Inc			
605 N Sherman Pkwy	Springfield MO 65802	800-426-6737	417-865-8392
Heat Transfer Sales of the Carolinas Inc			
4101 Beechwood Dr	Greensboro NC 27410	800-842-3328	336-294-3838
Henry Quentzel Plumbing Supply Co			
379 Throop Ave	Brooklyn NY 11221	800-889-2294	718-455-6600
Hercules Industries Inc			
1310 W Evans Ave	Denver CO 80223	800-356-5350	303-937-1000
Hot Water Products			
7500 N 81st St	Milwaukee WI 53223	877-377-0011	414-434-1371
I D Booth Inc			
620 William St PO Box 579	Elmira NY 14902	888-432-6684	607-733-9121
Industrial Pipe & Supply Company Inc			
1779 Martin Luther King Junior Blvd	Gainesville GA 30501	800-426-1458	770-536-0517
J & B Supply Inc			
4915 S Zero PO Box 10450	Fort Smith AR 72917	800-262-2028	479-649-4915
JE Sawyer & Company Inc			
64 Glen St	Glens Falls NY 12801	800-724-3983	
JMF Co 2735 62nd St Ct	Bettendorf IA 52722	800-397-3739	563-332-9200
Johnson Supply Inc			
10151 Stella Link Rd	Houston TX 77025	800-833-5455	713-830-2499
Keeling Co			
PO Box 15310	North Little Rock AR 72231	800-343-9464	501-945-4511
Keller Supply Company Inc			
3209 17th Ave W	Seattle WA 98119	800-285-3302	206-285-3300
Lee Supply Corp			
6610 Guion Rd	Indianapolis IN 46268	800-873-1103	317-290-2500
Mark's Plumbing Parts			
3312 Ramona Dr	Fort Worth TX 76116	800-772-2347	817-731-6211
Martz Supply Co			
5330 Pecos St	Denver CO 80221	800-456-4672	
Masters' Supply Inc			
4505 Bishop Ln	Louisville KY 40218	800-388-6353	
May Supply Company Inc			
1775 Erickson Ave	Harrisonburg VA 22801	800-296-9997	540-433-2611
Mid-Lakes Distributing Inc			
1029 W Adams St	Chicago IL 60607	888-733-2700	312-733-1033
Mid-States Supply Inc			
1716 Guinotte Ave	Kansas City MO 64120	800-825-1410	816-842-4290
Minvalco Inc			
3340 Gorham Ave	Minneapolis MN 55426	800-642-9090	952-920-0131
Morley-Murphy Co			
200 S Washington St Ste 305	Green Bay WI 54301	877-499-3171	920-499-3171
Morrison Supply Company Inc			
311 E Vickery Blvd	Fort Worth TX 76104	877-709-2227	

		Toll-Free	Phone
Morrow Control & Supply Co			
810 Marion Motley Ave NE	Canton OH 44705	800-362-9830	330-452-9791
Mountain States Pipe & Supply Co			
111 W Las Vegas St	Colorado Springs CO 80903	800-777-7173	719-634-5555
Mountain Supply Co			
2101 Mullan Rd	Missoula MT 59808	800-821-1646	406-543-8255
New Wave Enviro Products Inc			
6595 S Dayton St	Greenwood Village CO 80111	800-592-8371	
New York Replacement Parts Corp			
1462 Lexington Ave	Yonkers NY 10128	800-228-4718	
Newton Distributing Company Inc			
245 W Central St	Natick MA 01760	877-837-7745	617-969-4002
Niagara Conservation Corp			
45 Horsehill Rd	Cedar Knolls NJ 07927	800-831-8383	
Northeastern Supply Inc			
8323 Pulaski Hwy	Baltimore MD 21237	877-637-8775	410-574-0010
Northwest Pipe Fittings Inc			
33 S Eigth St W	Billings MT 59102	800-937-4737	406-252-0142
Pasco Specialty & Manufacturing Inc			
11156 Wright Rd	Lynwood CA 90262	800-737-2726	310-537-7782
Pbbs Equipment Corp			
N59W16500 Greenway Cir	Menomonee Falls WI 53051	800-236-9620	262-252-7575
Pepco Sales of Dallas Inc			
11310 Gemini Ln	Dallas TX 75229	877-737-2699	972-823-8700
Plumb Supply Co			
1622 NE 51st Ave	Des Moines IA 50313	800-483-9511	515-262-9511
Plumbers Supply Co			
1000 E Main St	Louisville KY 40206	800-626-5133	502-582-2261
Plumbing Distributors Inc			
1025 Old Norcross Rd	Lawrenceville GA 30046	800-262-9231	770-963-9231
Plymouth Technology Inc			
2925 Waterview Dr	Rochester Hills MI 48309	800-535-5053	248-537-0081
Rampart Supply Inc			
1801 N Union Blvd	Colorado Springs CO 80909	800-748-1837	719-482-7333
Reeves-Wiedeman Co Inc			
14861 W 100th St	Lenexa KS 66215	800-365-0024	913-492-7100
Refrigeration Sales Corp			
9450 Allen Dr	Valley View OH 44125	866-894-8200	216-525-8200
Republic Plumbing Supply Company Inc			
890 Providence Hwy	Norwood MA 02062	800-696-3900	
Robertson Heating Supply Co			
2155 W Main St	Alliance OH 44601	800-433-9532	330-821-9180
Roth 3847 Crum Rd	Youngstown OH 44515	800-872-7684	
Rundle-Spence Mfg Co			
2075 S Moorland Rd	New Berlin WI 53151	800-783-6060	262-782-3000
Schumacher & Seiler Inc			
10 W Aylesbury Rd	Timonium MD 21093	800-992-9356	410-465-7000
Sioux Chief Manufacturing Company Inc			
14940 Thunderbird Rd	Kansas City MO 64147	800-821-3944	
Solco Plumbing Supply Inc			
413 Liberty Ave	Brooklyn NY 11207	800-273-6632	
Standard Air & Lite Corp			
2406 Woodmere Dr	Pittsburgh PA 15205	800-472-2458	412-920-6505
Sunbelt Marketing Investment Corp			
3255 S Sweetwater Rd	Lithia Springs GA 30122	800-257-5566	770-739-3740
Swan 200 Swan Ave	Centralia IL 62801	800-325-7008	
Temperature Systems Inc			
5001 Voges Rd	Madison WI 53718	800-366-0930	608-271-7500
Therm Air Sales Corp			
1413 41st St NW PO Box 9004	Fargo ND 58106	800-726-7520	701-282-9500
Thermal Corp			
1264 Slaughter Rd	Madison AL 35758	800-633-2962	256-837-1122
Trident Technologies Inc			
8885 Rehco Rd	San Diego CA 92121	800-326-4010	619-688-9600
US Airconditioning Distributors			
16900 Chestnut St	City of Industry CA 91748	800-937-7222	
Ward Manufacturing LLC			
117 Gulick St	Blossburg PA 16912	800-248-1027	570-638-2131
Waxman Industries Inc			
24460 Aurora Rd	Bedford Heights OH 44146	800-201-7298	440-439-1830
OTC: WXMN			
Wayne Pipe & Supply Inc			
6040 Innovation Blvd	Fort Wayne IN 46818	800-552-3697	260-423-9577
Webstone Company Inc			
1 Appian Way	Worcester MA 01610	800-225-9529	
Western Nevada Supply Co			
950 S Rock Blvd	Sparks NV 89431	800-648-1230	775-359-5800
Willoughby Industries Inc			
5105 W 78th St	Indianapolis IN 46268	800-428-4065	
Winsupply Inc			
3110 Kettering Blvd	Dayton OH 45439	800-677-4380	937-294-5331
Woodhill Supply Inc			
4665 Beidler Rd	Willoughby OH 44094	800-362-6111	440-269-1100

609 PLYWOOD & VENEERS

SEE ALSO Lumber & Building Supplies ; Home Improvement Centers

		Toll-Free	Phone
Amos-Hill Assoc Inc			
112 Shelby Ave	Edinburgh IN 46124	800-745-1778	812-526-2671
Bacon Veneer Co			
16W273 83rd St Ste A-1	Burr Ridge IL 60527	800-443-7995	630-541-8312
California Panel & Veneer Co			
14055 Artesia Blvd	Cerritos CA 90703	800-451-1745	562-926-5834
Columbia Forest Products Inc Columbia Plywood Div			
7900 McCloud Dr Suit 200	Greensboro NC 27409	800-637-1609	
Constantine's Wood Ctr			
1040 E Oakland Pk Blvd	Fort Lauderdale FL 33334	800-443-9667	954-561-1716
Darlington Veneer Company Inc			
225 Fourth St	Darlington SC 29532	800-845-2388	843-393-3861
Fiber-Tech Industries Inc			
2000 Kenskill Ave	Washington Court House OH 43160	800-879-4377	740-335-9400
Flexible Materials Inc			
1202 Port Rd	Jeffersonville IN 47130	800-244-6492	812-280-7000
G-L Veneer Co Inc			
2224 E Slauson Ave	Huntington Park CA 90255	800-588-5003	323-582-5203

	Toll-Free	Phone

Harbor Sales
1000 Harbor Ct . . . . Sudlersville MD 21668 — **800-345-1712**

Inland Plywood Co
375 N Cass Ave . . . . Pontiac MI 48342 — **800-521-4355** — 248-334-4706

Louisiana-Pacific Corp
414 Union St Ste 2000 . . . . Nashville TN 37219 — **888-820-0325** — 615-986-5600
NYSE: LPX

Murphy Plywood Co
2350 Prairie Rd . . . . Eugene OR 97402 — **888-461-4545** — 541-461-4545

North American Plywood Corp
12343 Hawkins St . . . . Santa Fe Springs CA 90670 — **800-421-1372*** — 562-941-7575
*Sales

Phillips Plywood Company Inc
13599 Desmond St . . . . Pacoima CA 91331 — **800-649-6410*** — 818-897-7736
*Cust Svc

Plywood Supply Inc
7036 NE 175th St . . . . Kenmore WA 98028 — **888-774-9663** — 425-485-8585

Roseburg Forest Products Co
PO Box 1088 . . . . Roseburg OR 97470 — **800-245-1115** — 541-679-3311

States Industries LLC
PO Box 41150 . . . . Eugene OR 97404 — **800-626-1981** — 541-688-7871

Stimson Lumber Co
520 SW Yamhill St Ste 700 . . . . Portland OR 97204 — **800-445-9758** — 503-701-6510
Wurth 1640 Mims Ave SW . . . . Birmingham AL 35211 — **800-272-6486** — 205-925-7601

610 POINT-OF-SALE (POS) & POINT-OF-INFORMATION (POI) SYSTEMS

	Toll-Free	Phone

Checkpoint Systems Inc
101 Wolf Dr . . . . Thorofare NJ 08086 — **800-257-5540** — 856-848-1800
NYSE: CKP

Datalogic Scanning
959 Terry St . . . . Eugene OR 97402 — **800-695-5700** — 541-683-5700

Kiosk Information Systems Inc (KIS)
346 S Arthur Ave . . . . Louisville CO 80027 — **800-509-5471*** — 888-661-1697
*General

Mobile Technologies Inc (MTI)
1050 NW 229th Ave . . . . Hillsboro OR 97124 — **888-684-0040** — 503-648-6500

NextG Networks Inc
890 Tasman Dr . . . . Milpitas CA 95035 — **877-486-9377**

PAR Technology Corp
8383 Seneca Tpke . . . . New Hartford NY 13413 — **800-448-6505** — 315-738-0600
NYSE: PAR

SeePoint Technology LLC
2619 Manhattan Beach Blvd . . . . Redondo Beach CA 90278 — **888-587-1777** — 310-725-9660

TouchSystems Corp
2222 W Rundberg Ln Ste 200 . . . . Austin TX 78758 — **800-320-5944** — 512-846-2424
UTC RETAIL Inc 100 Rawson Rd . . . . Victor NY 14564 — **800-349-0546**

611 POLITICAL ACTION COMMITTEES

SEE ALSO Civic & Political Organizations

	Toll-Free	Phone

AFL-CIO Committee on Political Education
815 16th St NW . . . . Washington DC 20006 — **855-712-8441**

American Assn for Justice PAC
777 Sixth St NW Ste 200 . . . . Washington DC 20001 — **800-622-1791** — 202-965-3500

American Assn of Orthodontists PAC
401 N Lindbergh Blvd . . . . Saint Louis MO 63141 — **800-424-2841** — 314-993-1700

American Association of Nurse Anesthetists PAC (AANAPAC)
222 S Prospect Ave . . . . Park Ridge IL 60068 — **855-526-2262** — 847-692-7050

American Bankers Assn PAC (ABAPAC)
1120 Connecticut Ave NW . . . . Washington DC 20036 — **800-226-5377**

American Bus Association
111 K St NE 9th Fl . . . . Washington DC 20002 — **800-283-2877** — 202-842-1645

American Dental Assn
1111 14th St NW Ste 1100 . . . . Washington DC 20005 — **800-353-2237** — 202-898-2424

American Family Life Assurance Co PAC (AFLAC PAC)
1932 Wynnton Rd . . . . Columbus GA 31999 — **800-992-3522*** — 706-323-3431
*NYSE: AFL ■ *Cust Svc

American Hospital Assn PAC (AHAPAC)
325 Seventh St NW . . . . Washington DC 20004 — **800-424-4301** — 202-638-1100

American Medical Assn PAC
25 Massachusetts Ave NW # 600 . . . . Washington DC 20001 — **800-621-8335** — 312-464-4430

American Nurses Assn PAC (ANA PAC)
8515 Georgia Ave Ste 400 . . . . Silver Spring MD 20910 — **800-274-4262** — 301-628-5000

American Pharmacists Assn PAC
2215 Constitution Ave NW . . . . Washington DC 20037 — **800-237-2742** — 202-628-4410

American Society of Travel Agents PAC
675 N Washington St Ste 490 . . . . Alexandria VA 22314 — **800-275-2782** — 703-739-2782

American Veterinary Medical Assn PAC (AVMA)
1910 Sunderland Pl NW . . . . Washington DC 20036 — **800-321-1473** — 202-789-0007

Associated General Contractors PAC
2300 Wilson Blvd Ste 400 . . . . Arlington VA 22201 — **800-242-1767** — 703-548-3118

Association of Home Appliance Manufacturers PAC (AHAM PAC)
1111 19th St NW Ste 402 . . . . Washington DC 20036 — **800-424-2970** — 202-872-5955

Coca-Cola Nonpartisan Committee for Good Government
PO Box 1734 . . . . Atlanta GA 30301 — **800-438-2653**

College of American Pathologists PAC
1350 I St NW Ste 590 . . . . Washington DC 20005 — **800-392-9994** — 202-354-7100

Credit Union National Association (CUNA)
99 M St SE Ste 300 . . . . Washington DC 20003 — **800-356-9655**

DGA-PAC
7920 W Sunset Blvd . . . . Los Angeles CA 90046 — **800-421-4173** — 310-289-2000

FRAN-PAC
1501 K St Ste 350 . . . . Washington DC 20005 — **800-543-1038** — 202-628-8000

Freedom Alliance
22570 Markey Ct Ste 240 . . . . Sterling VA 20166 — **800-475-6620** — 703-444-7940

Friends Committee on National Legislation (FCNL)
245 Second St NE . . . . Washington DC 20002 — **800-630-1330** — 202-547-6000

IATSE PAC
1430 Broadway 20th Fl . . . . New York NY 10018 — **844-422-9273** — 212-730-1770

Ironworkers
1750 New York Ave NW Ste 400 . . . . Washington DC 20006 — **800-368-0105** — 202-383-4800

	Toll-Free	Phone

Liberal Party of Canada
81 Metcalfe St . . . . Ottawa ON K1P6M8 — **888-542-3725**

NAADAC PAC
44 Canal Center Plz Ste 301 . . . . Alexandria VA 22314 — **800-377-1136** — 703-741-7686

Nareit
1875 'I' St NW Ste 600 . . . . Washington DC 20006 — **800-362-7348** — 202-739-9400

National Active & Retired Federal Employees Assn
606 N Washington St . . . . Alexandria VA 22314 — **800-627-3394** — 703-838-7760

National Association of Home Builders PAC
1201 15th St NW . . . . Washington DC 20005 — **800-368-5242**

National Sunflower Assn PAC
2401 46th Ave SE Ste 206 . . . . Mandan ND 58554 — **888-718-7033** — 701-328-5100

Ontario Pc Party
59 Adelaide St E Ste 400 . . . . Toronto ON M5C1K6 — **800-903-6453** — 416-861-0020

Outdoor Amusement Business Assn Inc (OABA)
1035 S Semoran Blvd Ste 1045A . . . . Winter Park FL 32792 — **800-517-6222** — 407-848-4958

Planned Parenthood Action Fund Inc
1110 Vermont Ave NW . . . . Washington DC 20005 — **800-430-4907** — 202-973-4800

Small Business Investor Alliance (SBIA)
1100 H St NW Ste 1200 . . . . Washington DC 20005 — **800-471-6153** — 202-628-5055

Title Industry PAC (TIPAC)
1800 M St NW Ste 300S . . . . Washington DC 20036 — **800-787-2582** — 202-296-3671

POLITICAL LEADERS

SEE US Senators, Representatives, Delegates ; Governors - State

612 POLITICAL PARTIES (MAJOR)

SEE ALSO Civic & Political Organizations

	Toll-Free	Phone

Libertarian Party
2600 Virginia Ave NW Ste 200 . . . . Washington DC 20037 — **800-735-1776** — 202-333-0008

Republican National Committee (RNC)
310 First St SE . . . . Washington DC 20003 — **800-445-5768** — 202-863-8500

612-1 Democratic State Committees

	Toll-Free	Phone

Delaware Democratic Party
19 E Commons Blvd 2nd Fl . . . . New Castle DE 19720 — **800-685-5544** — 302-328-9036

DEMOCRATIC PARTY OF VIRGINIA
919 E Main St Ste 2050 . . . . Richmond VA 23219 — **800-552-9745** — 804-644-1966

Hawaii Democratic Party
627 S St Ste 105 . . . . Honolulu HI 96813 — **844-596-2980** — 808-596-2980

Idaho Democratic Party
812 W Franklin St . . . . Boise ID 83701 — **800-626-0471** — 208-336-1815

Indiana Democratic Party
115 W Washington St Ste 1165 . . . . Indianapolis IN 46204 — **800-223-3387** — 317-231-7100

Kentucky Democratic Party
190 Democrat Dr . . . . Frankfort KY 40601 — **800-995-3386** — 502-695-4828

Oklahoma Democratic Party
4100 N Lincoln Blvd . . . . Oklahoma City OK 73105 — **800-547-5600** — 405-427-3366

612-2 Republican State Committees

	Toll-Free	Phone

Ohio Republican Party
211 S Fifth St . . . . Columbus OH 43215 — **800-282-0515** — 614-228-2481

Texas Republican Party
1108 Lavaca Ste 500 . . . . Austin TX 78701 — **800-525-5555** — 512-477-9821

613 PORTALS - VOICE

Voice portals permit users to access web-based messaging as well as various types of Internet information (e.g., weather, stock quotes, driving directions, etc.) via the telephone (wired or wireless).

	Toll-Free	Phone

GoSolo Technologies Inc
5410 Mariner St Ste 175 . . . . Tampa FL 33609 — **866-246-7656**

614 PORTS & PORT AUTHORITIES

SEE ALSO Cruise Lines ; Airports

	Toll-Free	Phone

Alabama
Administrative Office of Alabama Courts
300 Dexter Ave . . . . Montgomery AL 36104 — **866-954-9411** — 334-954-5000
Ports Authority 2 Main St . . . . Savannah GA 31402 — **800-342-8012** — 912-964-3811

Hamilton Port Authority
605 James St N 6th Fl . . . . Hamilton ON L8L1K1 — **800-263-2131** — 905-525-4330

Indiana
Agriculture Dept
101 W Washington St . . . . Indianapolis IN 46204 — **800-677-9800**
Port Commission
150 W Market St Ste 100 . . . . Indianapolis IN 46204 — **800-232-7678** — 317-232-9200

Juneau Harbor
155 S Seward St . . . . Juneau AK 99801 — **800-642-0066** — 907-586-5255

Mississippi State Port Authority at Gulfport
2510 14th St Ste 1450 . . . . Gulfport MS 39501 — **877-881-4367** — 228-865-4300

Port Canaveral
445 Challanger Rd . . . . Cape Canaveral FL 32920 — **888-767-8226** — 321-783-7831

Port Everglades
1850 Eller Dr . . . . Fort Lauderdale FL 33316 — **800-421-0188** — 954-523-3404

Port Freeport
1001 N Gulf Blvd . . . . Freeport TX 77541 — **800-362-5743** — 979-233-2667

Port of Anacortes
100 Commercial Ave . . . . Anacortes WA 98221 — **800-874-4434** — 360-293-3134

Port of Anchorage
632 W Sixth Ave . . . . Anchorage AK 99501 — **877-650-8400** — 907-343-6543

				Toll-Free	Phone
Port of Astoria					
10 Pier 1 Bldg Ste 308	Astoria	OR	97103	**800-860-4093**	503-741-3300
Port of Baltimore					
Maryland Port Administration					
401 E Pratt St	Baltimore	MD	21202	**800-638-7519***	
*General					
Port of Brownsville					
1000 Foust Rd	Brownsville	TX	78521	**800-378-5395**	956-831-4592
Port of Corpus Christi					
222 Power St	Corpus Christi	TX	78401	**800-580-7110**	361-882-5633
Port of Duluth					
Duluth Seaway Port Authority					
1200 Port Terminal Dr	Duluth	MN	55802	**800-232-0703**	218-727-8525
Port of Everett					
2911 Bond St Ste 202	Everett	WA	98201	**800-729-7678**	425-259-3164
Port of Jacksonville					
Jacksonville Port Authority					
2831 Talleyrand Ave PO Box 3005	Jacksonville	FL	32206	**800-874-8050**	904-357-3000
Port of New Orleans					
1350 Port of New Orleans Pl	New Orleans	LA	70130	**800-776-6652**	504-522-2551
Port of Pensacola					
700 S Barracks St	Pensacola	FL	32502	**800-711-1712**	850-436-5070
Port of Portland					
7200 NE Airport Way	Portland	OR	97218	**800-547-8411**	503-415-6000
Port of San Diego					
3165 Pacific Hwy	San Diego	CA	92101	**800-854-2757**	619-686-6200
Port of San Francisco					
Pier 1 The Embarcadero	San Francisco	CA	94111	**800-479-5314**	415-274-0400
Port of Seattle					
2711 Alaskan Way	Seattle	WA	98111	**800-426-7817**	206-728-3000
Port of Stockton					
2201 W Washington St	Stockton	CA	95203	**800-344-3213**	209-946-0246
Port of Vancouver					
3103 NW Lower River Rd	Vancouver	WA	98660	**800-475-8012**	360-693-3611
Port of Vancouver					
100 The Pointe 999 Canada Pl	Vancouver	BC	V6C3T4	**888-767-8826**	604-665-9000
Port Panama City					
1 Seaport Dr	Panama City	FL	32401	**855-347-8371**	
Quebec Port Authority					
150 Dalhousie St					
PO Box 80 Stn Haute-Ville	Quebec	QC	G1R4M8	**800-465-1213**	418-648-3640
State Ports Authority					
176 Concord St	Charleston	SC	29401	**800-845-7106**	843-723-8651
Tampa Port Authority					
1101 Channelside Dr	Tampa	FL	33602	**800-741-2297**	813-905-7678
Aging & Rehabilitative Services Dept					
8004 Franklin Farms Dr	Richmond	VA	23229	**800-552-5019**	804-662-7000
Wrangell Harbor PO Box 531	Wrangell	AK	99929	**800-347-4462**	907-874-3736

615   POULTRY PROCESSING

SEE ALSO Meat Packing Plants

				Toll-Free	Phone
American Dehydrated Foods Inc					
3801 E Sunshine	Springfield	MO	65809	**800-456-3447**	417-881-7755
Amick Farms Inc					
2079 Batesburg Hwy	Batesburg	SC	29006	**800-926-4257**	803-532-1400
Brakebush Bros Inc					
N4993 Sixth Dr	Westfield	WI	53964	**800-933-2121**	608-296-2121
Claxton Poultry Farms					
8816 Hwy 301 N	Claxton	GA	30417	**888-739-3181**	912-739-3181
Culver Duck Farms Inc					
12215 CR 10	Middlebury	IN	46540	**800-825-9225**	574-825-9537
Draper Valley Farms					
1500 E College Way PMB449 Ste A	Mount Vernon	WA	98273	**800-682-1468**	
Echo Lake Farm Produce Co					
PO Box 279	Burlington	WI	53105	**800-888-3447**	
Fieldale Farms Corp					
PO Box 558	Baldwin	GA	30511	**800-241-5400**	
Foster Farms Inc					
PO Box 306	Livingston	CA	95334	**800-255-7227**	
Georges Inc					
402 W Robinson Ave	Springdale	AR	72764	**800-800-2449**	479-927-7000
Jennie-O Turkey Store					
2505 Willmar Ave SW PO Box 778	Willmar	MN	56201	**800-621-3505**	320-235-2622
Koch Foods Inc					
1300 Higgins Rd Ste 100	Park Ridge	IL	60068	**800-837-2778**	847-384-5940
Marshall Durbin Co					
2830 Commerce Blvd	Birmingham	AL	35210	**800-245-8204***	205-380-3251
*Sales					
Michael Foods Inc					
301 Carlson Pkwy Ste 400	Minnetonka	MN	55305	**800-328-5474**	952-258-4000
Mountaire Farms					
17269 NC Hwy 71 N	Lumber Bridge	NC	28357	**877-887-1490**	910-843-5942
OK Foods Inc PO Box 1787	Fort Smith	AR	72902	**800-635-9441**	
Olymel LP					
2200 Pratte Ave Pratte	Saint-Hyacinthe	QC	J2S4B6	**800-361-7990**	450-771-0400
Perdue Farms Inc					
31149 Old Ocean City Rd	Salisbury	MD	21804	**800-473-7383**	410-543-3000
Randall Foods Inc					
PO Box 2669	Huntington Park	CA	90255	**800-427-2632**	323-261-6565
Sonstegard Foods Co					
5005 S Bur Oak Pl	Sioux Falls	SD	57108	**800-533-3184**	
Stevens Sausage Company Inc					
3411 Stevens Sausage Rd	Smithfield	NC	27577	**800-338-0561**	919-934-3159
Tip Top Poultry Inc					
327 Wallace Rd	Marietta	GA	30062	**800-241-5230**	770-973-8070
Tyson Foods Inc					
PO Box 219	Kings Mountains	NC	28086	**800-233-6332**	479-290-6397
NYSE: TSN					
West Liberty Foods LLC					
228 W Second St	West Liberty	IA	52776	**888-511-4500**	319-627-6000

616   POWER TRANSMISSION EQUIPMENT - MECHANICAL

SEE ALSO Bearings - Ball & Roller

				Toll-Free	Phone
Allied-Locke Industries					
1088 Corregidor Rd	Dixon	IL	61021	**800-435-7752**	815-288-1471
American Metal Bearing Co					
7191 Acacia Ave	Garden Grove	CA	92841	**800-888-3048**	714-892-5527
Ameridrives					
1802 Pittsburgh Ave	Erie	PA	16502	**800-352-0141**	814-480-5000
Barden Corp 200 Park Ave	Danbury	CT	06810	**800-243-1060**	203-744-2211
Beemer Precision Inc					
230 New York Dr PO Box 3080	Fort Washington	PA	19034	**800-836-2340**	215-646-8440
Bird Precision					
1 Spruce St PO Box 540569	Waltham	MA	02454	**800-454-7369***	
*Cust Svc					
Bishop-Wisecarver Corp					
2104 Martin Way	Pittsburg	CA	94565	**888-580-8272**	925-439-8272
Buckeye Power Sales Company Inc					
6850 Commerce Ct Dr	Blacklick	OH	43004	**800-523-3587**	614-861-6000
Cangro Industries Long Island Transmission Co					
495 Smith St	Farmingdale	NY	11735	**800-422-9210**	631-454-9000
Carlyle Johnson Machine Co (CJM)					
291 Boston Tpke	Bolton	CT	06043	**888-629-4867**	860-643-1531
Certified Power Inc					
970 Campus Dr	Mundelein	IL	60060	**888-905-7411**	847-573-3800
Diamond Chain Co					
402 Kentucky Ave	Indianapolis	IN	46225	**800-872-4246***	317-638-6431
*Cust Svc					
General Bearing Corp					
44 High St	West Nyack	NY	10994	**800-431-1766***	845-358-6000
*Sales					
Hebeler Corp					
2000 Military Rd	Tonawanda	NY	14150	**800-486-4709**	716-873-9300
Helical Products Co Inc					
901 W McCoy Ln	Santa Maria	CA	93455	**877-353-9873**	805-928-3851
Horton Inc					
2565 Walnut St	Saint Paul	MN	55113	**800-621-1320**	651-361-6400
Industrial Clutch					
2800 Fisher Rd	Waukesha	WI	53186	**800-964-3262**	262-547-3357
John Deere Coffeyville Works Inc					
1 John Deere Pl	Moline	IL	61265	**800-844-1337**	309-765-8000
Kingsbury Inc					
10385 Drummond Rd	Philadelphia	PA	19154	**866-581-5464***	215-824-4000
*Sales					
Linn Gear Co					
100 N Eigth St PO Box 397	Lebanon	OR	97355	**800-547-2471**	541-259-1211
Magtrol Inc					
70 Gardenville Pkwy	Buffalo	NY	14224	**800-828-7844**	716-668-5555
Marland Clutch					
23601 Hoover Rd	Warren	MI	48089	**800-216-3515**	
Maurey Manufacturing Corp					
410 Industrial Pk Rd	Holly Springs	MS	38635	**800-284-2161**	
Nook Industries					
4950 E 49th St	Cleveland	OH	44125	**800-321-7800**	216-271-7900
NSK Corp 4200 Goss Rd	Ann Arbor	MI	48105	**800-675-9930**	734-913-7500
NTN Bearing Corp of America					
1600 E Bishop Ct	Mount Prospect	IL	60056	**800-323-2358**	847-298-7500
OPW Engineered Systems					
2726 Henkle Dr	Lebanon	OH	45036	**800-547-9393***	513-932-9114
*Cust Svc					
Peer Bearing Co					
2200 Norman Dr S	Waukegan	IL	60085	**800-433-7337**	847-578-1000
Pic Design Corp					
86 Benson Rd PO Box 1004	Middlebury	CT	06762	**800-243-6125**	203-758-8272
RBC Bearings Inc					
102 Willenbrock Rd	Oxford	CT	06478	**800-390-3300**	
Real Goods Solar					
833 W S Boulder Rd	Louisville	CO	80027	**888-567-6527**	
NASDAQ: RSGE					
Regal-Beloit Corp					
200 State St	Beloit	WI	53511	**800-672-6495**	608-364-8800
NYSE: RBC					
Renold Ajax Inc					
100 Bourne St	Westfield	NY	14787	**800-251-9012**	716-326-3121
Schaeffler Group USA Inc					
308 Springhill Farm Rd	Fort Mill	SC	29715	**800-361-5841**	803-548-8500
Siemens Power Transmission & Distribution Inc					
7000 Siemens Rd	Wendell	NC	27591	**800-347-6659**	919-365-2200
Solomon Corp 103 W Main	Solomon	KS	67480	**800-234-2867**	785-655-2191
Stock Drive Products/Sterling Instrument					
2101 Jericho Tpke	New Hyde Park	NY	11040	**800-737-7436**	800-819-8900
Styberg Engineering					
1600 Gold St PO Box 788	Racine	WI	53401	**800-240-7275**	
TB Wood's Inc					
440 N Fifth Ave	Chambersburg	PA	17201	**888-829-6637**	717-264-7161
Universal Bearings Inc					
431 North Birkey Dr PO Box 38	Bremen	IN	46506	**800-824-7743**	
US Tsubaki Inc					
301 E Marquardt Dr	Wheeling	IL	60090	**800-323-7790**	847-459-9500
Warner Electric					
449 Gardner St	South Beloit	IL	61080	**800-825-6544**	
Whittet-Higgins Co					
33 Higginson Ave PO Box 8	Central Falls	RI	02863	**800-323-7790**	401-728-0700
Zero-Max Inc					
13200 Sixth Ave N	Plymouth	MN	55441	**800-533-1731**	763-546-4300

617   PRECISION MACHINED PRODUCTS

SEE ALSO Machine Shops ; Aircraft Parts & Auxiliary Equipment

				Toll-Free	Phone
Abbott Interfast Corp					
190 Abbott Dr	Wheeling	IL	60090	**800-877-0789**	847-459-6200

				Toll-Free	Phone
Alger Precision Machining LLC 724 S Bon View Ave	Ontario	CA	91761	800-854-9833	
ATEC Inc 12600 Executive Dr	Stafford	TX	77477	800-873-0001	281-276-2700
Biddle Precision Components Inc 701 S Main St	Sheridan	IN	46069	800-428-4387	317-758-4451
Boker's Inc 3104 Snelling Ave	Minneapolis	MN	55406	800-927-4377	612-729-9365
Cox Manufacturing Co 5500 N Loop 1604 E	San Antonio	TX	78247	800-900-7981	210-657-7731
Davies Molding LLC 350 Kehoe Blvd	Carol Stream	IL	60188	800-554-9208	630-510-8188
Delo Screw Products 700 London Rd	Delaware	OH	43015	800-935-9935	740-363-1971
Dirksen Screw Products Co 14490 23 Mile Rd Shelby	Township	MI	48315	800-732-5569	586-247-5400
Elyria Mfg Corp 145 Northrup St PO Box 479	Elyria	OH	44035	866-365-4171	440-365-4171
Enoch Manufacturing Co 14242 SE 82nd Dr	Clackamas	OR	97015	888-659-2660	503-659-2660
Fairchild Auto-mated Parts Inc 10 White St	Winsted	CT	06098	800-927-2545	860-379-2725
Farrar Corp 142 W Burns St	Norwich	KS	67118	800-536-2215	620-478-2212
Greystone of Lincoln Inc 7 Wellington Rd	Lincoln	RI	02865	800-446-1761	401-333-0444
H & H Swiss Screw Machine Products Company Inc 1478 Chestnut Ave	Hillside	NJ	07205	800-826-9985	
Horspool & Romine Manufacturing Inc 5850 Marshall St	Oakland	CA	94608	800-446-2263	
Iseli Co 402 N Main St	Walworth	WI	53184	800-403-8665	262-275-2108
Kenlee Precision Corp 1701 Inverness Ave	Baltimore	MD	21230	800-969-5278	410-525-3800
Kerr Lakeside Inc 26841 Tungsten Rd	Euclid	OH	44132	800-487-5377	216-261-2100
Komet Of America Inc 2050 Mitchell Blvd	Schaumburg	IL	60193	800-865-6638	800-656-6381
Liberty Brass Turning Company Inc 1200 Shames Dr	Westbury	NY	11590	800-345-5939	718-784-2911
Modern Machine & Engineering Corp 9380 Winnetka Ave N	Brooklyn Park	MN	55445	800-443-5117	612-781-3347
MSK Precision Products Inc 10101 NW 67th St	Tamarac	FL	33321	800-992-5010	954-776-0770
Multimatic Products Inc 390 Oser Ave	Hauppauge	NY	11788	800-767-7633	631-231-1515
Nordson XALOY 1399 Countyline Rd	New Castle	PA	16101	800-897-2830	724-656-5600
Omni-Lite Industries Canada Inc 17210 Edwards Rd	Cerritos	CA	90703	800-577-6664	562-404-8510
Pacific Aerospace & Electronics Inc 434 Olds Stn Rd	Wenatchee	WA	98801	855-285-5200	509-667-9600
Precisionform Inc 148 W Airport Rd	Lititz	PA	17543	800-233-3821	717-560-7610
Production Products Co 6176 E Molloy Rd	East Syracuse	NY	13057	800-800-6652	315-431-7200
RB Royal Industries Inc 1350 S Hickory St	Fond du Lac	WI	54937	800-892-1550	920-921-1550
RW Screw Products Inc 999 Oberlin Rd SW	Massillon	OH	44647	866-797-2739	330-837-9211
SFS intec Inc Spring St & Van Reed Rd	Wyomissing	PA	19610	800-234-4533	610-376-5751
Smith & Richardson Manufacturing Co PO Box 589	Geneva	IL	60134	800-426-0876	630-232-2581
Sperry Automatics Company Inc 1372 New Haven Rd PO Box 717	Naugatuck	CT	06770	800-923-3709	203-729-4589
Superior Products Inc 3786 Ridge Rd	Cleveland	OH	44144	800-651-9490	216-651-9400
Talladega Machinery & Supply Co Inc 301 N Johnson Ave PO Box 736 *Cust Svc	Talladega	AL	35161	800-289-8672*	256-362-4124
Trace-A-Matic Inc (T-A-M) 21125 Enterprise Ave	Brookfield	WI	53045	877-375-0217	262-797-7300
Tri Tool Inc 3041 Sunrise Blvd	Rancho Cordova	CA	95742	800-345-5015	916-288-6100
Triumph Group 899 Cassatt Rd Ste 210	Berwyn	PA	19312	800-889-4422	610-251-1000

618 PREPARATORY SCHOOLS - BOARDING

SEE ALSO Preparatory Schools - Non-boarding

Schools listed here are independent, college-preparatory schools that provide housing facilities for students and teachers. All are members of The Association of Boarding Schools (TABS), and many are considered to be among the top prep schools in the United States.

				Toll-Free	Phone
Albert College 160 Dundas St W	Belleville	ON	K8P1A6	800-952-5237	613-968-5726
Army & Navy Academy 2605 Carlsbad Blvd	Carlsbad	CA	92008	888-762-2338	760-729-2385
Avon Old Farms School 500 Old Farms Rd	Avon	CT	06001	800-464-2866	860-404-4100
Bement School 94 Main St PO Box 8	Deerfield	MA	01342	877-405-3949	413-774-7061
Bishop's College School 80 chemin Moulton Hill	Sherbrooke	QC	J1M1Z8	877-570-7542	819-566-0227
Brewster Academy 80 Academy Dr	Wolfeboro	NH	03894	800-842-9961	603-569-7200
Chaminade College Preparatory School 425 S Lindbergh Blvd	Saint Louis	MO	63131	877-378-6847	314-993-4400
Chatham Hall 800 Chatham Hall Cir	Chatham	VA	24531	877-644-2941	434-432-2941
Christ School 500 Christ School Rd	Arden	NC	28704	800-422-3212	828-684-6232
Culver Academies 1300 Academy Rd	Culver	IN	46511	800-528-5837	574-842-7000
Darlington School 1014 Cave Spring Rd	Rome	GA	30161	800-368-4437	706-235-6051
Darrow School 110 Darrow Rd	New Lebanon	NY	12125	877-432-7769	518-794-6000
Dunn School 2555 Hwy 154 PO Box 98	Los Olivos	CA	93441	800-287-9197	805-688-6471
Episcopal High School 1200 N Quaker Ln	Alexandria	VA	22302	877-933-4347	703-933-4062
Gilmour Academy 34001 Cedar Rd	Gates Mills	OH	44040	800-533-5140	440-442-1104
Hargrave Military Academy (HMA) 200 Military Dr	Chatham	VA	24531	800-432-2480	434-432-2481
Hawaii Preparatory Academy 65-1692 Kohala Mountain Rd	Kamuela	HI	96743	800-644-4481	808-885-7321
Hebron Academy 339 Rd PO Box 309	Hebron	ME	04238	888-432-7664	207-966-2100
Hill School 860 Beech St	Pottstown	PA	19464	877-651-2800	610-326-1000
Hillside School 404 Robin Hill Rd	Marlborough	MA	01752	800-344-8328	508-485-2824
Holderness School 33 Chapel Ln	Holderness	NH	03245	877-262-1492	603-536-1257
Howe Military School PO Box 240	Howe	IN	46746	888-462-4693	260-562-2131
Indian Springs School 190 Woodward Dr *General	Pelham	AL	35124	888-843-9477*	205-988-3350
Kent School PO Box 2006	Kent	CT	06757	800-538-5368	860-927-6111
Kiski School 1888 Brett Ln	Saltsburg	PA	15681	877-547-5448	724-639-3586
Landmark School 429 Hale St PO Box 227	Prides Crossing	MA	01965	866-333-0859	978-236-3010
Lawrenceville School 2500 Main St PO Box 6008	Lawrenceville	NJ	08648	800-735-2030	609-896-0400
Linden Hall School for Girls 212 E Main St	Lititz	PA	17543	800-258-5778	717-626-8512
Linsly School 60 Knox Ln	Wheeling	WV	26003	866-648-1893	304-233-3260
Massanutten Military Academy 614 S Main St	Woodstock	VA	22664	877-466-6222	540-459-2167
McCallie School 500 Dodds Ave	Chattanooga	TN	37404	800-234-2163	423-624-8300
Mercersburg Academy 300 E Seminary St	Mercersburg	PA	17236	800-588-2550	717-328-6173
Milton Hershey School PO Box 830	Hershey	PA	17033	800-322-3248	717-520-2100
Northfield Mount Hermon School 1 Lamplighter Way	Gill	MA	01354	866-664-4483	413-498-3227
Perkiomen School 200 Seminary St	Pennsburg	PA	18073	866-966-9998	215-679-9511
Phillips Academy 180 Main St	Andover	MA	01810	877-445-5477	978-749-4000
Phillips Exeter Academy 20 Main St	Exeter	NH	03833	800-245-2525	603-772-4311
Putney School 418 Houghton Brook Rd	Putney	VT	05346	800-999-9080	802-387-5566
Rabun Gap-Nacoochee School 339 Nacoochee Dr	Rabun Gap	GA	30568	800-543-7467	706-746-7467
Randolph-Macon Academy 200 Academy Dr	Front Royal	VA	22630	800-272-1172	540-636-5200
Riverside Military Academy 2001 Riverside Dr	Gainesville	GA	30501	800-462-2338	770-532-6251
Saint Andrew's College 15800 Yonge St	Aurora	ON	L4G3H7	877-378-1899	905-727-3178
Saint John's Northwestern Military Academy 1101 Genesee St	Delafield	WI	53018	800-752-2338	
Saint John's Preparatory School 2280 Watertower Rd PO Box 4000	Collegeville	MN	56321	800-525-7737	320-363-3315
Saint Mary's School 900 Hillsborough St	Raleigh	NC	27603	800-948-2557	919-424-4000
Saint Michael's University School (SMUS) 3400 Richmond Rd	Victoria	BC	V8P4P5	800-661-5199	250-592-2411
San Marcos Academy 2801 Ranch Rd 12 *Admissions	San Marcos	TX	78666	800-428-5120*	512-353-2400
Shattuck-Saint Mary's School 1000 Shumway Ave	Faribault	MN	55021	800-421-2724	507-333-1500
Solebury School 6832 Phillips Mill Rd	New Hope	PA	18938	800-675-6900	215-862-5261
Stuart Hall School 235 W Frederick St PO Box 210	Staunton	VA	24402	888-306-8926	540-885-0356
Valley Forge Military Academy & College 1001 Eagle Rd	Wayne	PA	19087	800-234-8362	610-989-1300
Virginia Episcopal School 400 VES Rd	Lynchburg	VA	24503	800-937-3582	434-385-3607
Wasatch Academy 120 S 100 W	Mount Pleasant	UT	84647	800-634-4690	435-462-1400
Wayland Academy 101 N University Ave *Admissions	Beaver Dam	WI	53916	800-860-7725*	920-356-2120
Webb School PO Box 488	Bell Buckle	TN	37020	888-733-9322	931-389-9322
West Nottingham Academy 1079 Firetower Rd	Colora	MD	21917	866-381-3684	410-658-5556
Wyoming Seminary 201 N Sprague Ave	Kingston	PA	18704	800-325-3252	570-270-2100

619 PREPARATORY SCHOOLS - NON-BOARDING

SEE ALSO Preparatory Schools - Boarding

The schools listed here are among the leading private elementary and secondary schools in the U.S. None of these schools are boarding schools.

				Toll-Free	Phone
Canada School of Public Service 373 Sussex Dr	Ottawa	ON	K1N6Z2	866-703-9598	819-953-5400
Coeur d'Alene Convention & Visitor Bureau Inc 105 N 1st Ste 100	Coeur d'Alene	ID	83814	877-782-9232	
Glen Mills Schools PO Box 5001	Concordville	PA	19331	800-441-2064	610-459-8100
Prairie Valley School Div No 208 3080 Albert St N PO Box 1937	Regina	SK		877-266-1666	306-949-3366

				Toll-Free	Phone
RenWeb School Management Software					
820 SW Wilshire Blvd	Burleson	TX	76028	**866-800-6593**	

620 — PRESS CLIPPING SERVICES

				Toll-Free	Phone
Appian Analytics Inc					
2000 Crow Canyon Pl Ste 300	San Ramon	CA	94583	**877-757-7646**	
Aria Solutions Inc					
110 - 12th Ave SW Ste 600	Calgary	AB	T2R0G7	**866-235-1181**	403-235-0227
Art Resource Inc					
65 Bleecker St 12th Fl	New York	NY	10012	**888-505-8666**	212-505-8700
Attendee Management Inc					
15572 Ranch Rd 12 Ste 1	Wimberley	TX	78676	**877-947-5174**	512-847-5174
BurrellesLuce					
30 B Vreeland Rd PO Box 674	Florham Park	NJ	07932	**800-631-1160**	973-992-6600
Cherry Systems Inc					
2270 Northwest Pkwy Ste 125	Marietta	GA	30067	**800-500-2840**	770-955-2395
Cision US Inc					
130 E Randolph St 7th Fl	Chicago	IL	60601	**800-588-3827**	312-922-2400
CRRG Inc PO Box 170904	Arlington	TX	76003	**800-687-9030**	
Datatech Labs					
8000 E Quincy Ave	Denver	CO	80237	**888-288-3282**	303-770-3282
Florida Newsclips LLC					
PO Box 2190	Palm Harbor	FL	34682	**800-442-0332**	
FlyData Inc					
1043 N Shoreline Blvd Ste 200	Mountain View	CA	94043	**855-427-9787**	
Identifix Inc					
2714 Patton Rd	Saint Paul	MN	55113	**800-745-9649**	651-633-8007
InfySource Ltd					
8345 NW 66th St	Miami	FL	33166	**800-275-7503**	
Kentucky Press Assn					
101 Consumer Ln	Frankfort	KY	40601	**800-264-5721***	502-223-8821
*Cust Svc					
LCS Technologies Inc					
11230 Gold Express Dr Ste 310-140	Gold River	CA	95670	**855-277-5527**	
Michiana Health Information Network Llc					
220 W Colfax Ave Ste 300	South Bend	IN	46601	**800-814-6446**	574-968-1001
Oklahoma Press Service Inc					
3601 N Lincoln Blvd	Oklahoma City	OK	73105	**888-815-2672**	405-499-0020
South Carolina Press Assn					
106 Outlet Pointe Blvd PO Box 11429	Columbia	SC	29210	**888-727-7377**	803-750-9561
South Dakota Newspaper Services					
1125 32nd Ave	Brookings	SD	57006	**800-658-3697**	
Talton Communications Inc					
910 Ravenwood Dr	Selma	AL	36701	**800-685-1840**	334-877-0704
Thrive Networks Inc					
836 North St Bldg 300 Ste 3201	Tewksbury	MA	01876	**866-205-2810**	978-461-3999
United Data Technologies Inc					
8825 NW 21st Terr	Doral	FL	33172	**800-882-9919**	305-882-0435
Virginia Press Services Inc					
11529 Nuckols Rd	Glen Allen	VA	23059	**800-849-8717**	804-521-7570
West Virginia Press Association					
3422 Pennsylvania Ave	Charleston	WV	25302	**800-235-6881**	304-342-1011

621 — PRINTED CIRCUIT BOARDS

SEE ALSO Semiconductors & Related Devices ; Electronic Components & Accessories - Mfr

				Toll-Free	Phone
3Dlabs Inc Ltd					
1901 McCarthy Blvd	Milpitas	CA	95035	**800-464-3348**	408-530-4700
Acromag Inc 30765 S Wixom Rd	Wixom	MI	48393	**877-295-7092**	800-882-2055
Advanced Circuits Inc					
21101 E 32nd Pkwy	Aurora	CO	80011	**800-979-4722**	303-576-6610
All Flex Flexible Circuits & Heaters					
1705 Cannon Ln	Northfield	MN	55057	**800-959-0865**	
Benchmark Electronics Inc					
4141 N Scottsdale Rd	Scottsdale	AZ	85251	**800-322-2885**	623-300-7000
NYSE: BHE					
Bourns Inc					
1200 Columbia Ave	Riverside	CA	92507	**877-426-8767**	951-781-5690
Circuit Express Inc					
229 S Clark Dr	Tempe	AZ	85281	**800-979-4722**	
Crucial Technology					
3475 E Commercial Ct	Meridian	ID	83642	**800-336-8915**	208-363-5790
Dataram Corp					
777 Alexander Rd Ste 100	Princeton	NJ	08540	**800-328-2726**	609-799-0071
NASDAQ: DRAM					
Dynatem Inc					
23263 Madero Ste C	Mission Viejo	CA	92691	**800-543-3830**	949-855-3235
EDGE Tech Corp					
9101 Harlan St Unit 260	Westminster	CO	80031	**800-259-6565**	
El Microcircuits Inc					
1651 Pohl Rd	Mankato	MN	56001	**800-713-4015**	507-345-5786
GE Fanuc Intelligent Platforms Embedded Systems Inc					
7401 Snaproll NE	Albuquerque	NM	87109	**800-433-2682**	505-875-0600
Holaday Circuits Inc					
11126 Bren Rd W	Minnetonka	MN	55343	**800-362-3303**	952-933-3303
Intel Corp					
2200 Mission College Blvd	Santa Clara	CA	95052	**800-628-8686***	408-765-8080
*NASDAQ: INTC ■ *Cust Svc*					
Jabil Circuit Inc					
10560 ML King St N	Saint Petersburg	FL	33716	**877-217-6328**	727-577-9749
NYSE: JBL					
Micron Technology Inc					
8000 S Federal Way	Boise	ID	83707	**888-363-2589**	208-368-4000
NASDAQ: MU					
Natel Engineering Co Inc					
9340 Owensmouth Ave	Chatsworth	CA	91311	**800-590-5774**	818-734-6580
Parallax Inc					
599 Menlo Dr Ste 100	Rocklin	CA	95765	**888-512-1024**	916-624-8333
Plexus Corp					
1 Plexus Way PO Box 156	Neenah	WI	54957	**877-733-7260**	920-722-3451
NASDAQ: PLXS					

				Toll-Free	Phone
Progress Instruments Inc					
807 NW Commerce Dr	Lees Summit	MO	64086	**800-580-9881**	816-524-4442
Promise Technology Inc					
580 Cottonwood Dr	Milpitas	CA	95035	**800-888-0245***	408-228-1400
*Sales					
Quatech Inc					
5675 Hudson Industrial Pkwy	Hudson	OH	44236	**800-553-1170**	330-655-9000
Quest Controls Inc					
208 Ninth St Dr W	Palmetto	FL	34221	**800-373-6331**	
RadiSys Corp					
5445 NE Dawson Creek Dr	Hillsboro	OR	97124	**800-950-0044**	503-615-1100
NASDAQ: RSYS					
SAE Circuits Colorado Inc					
4820 N 63rd St	Boulder	CO	80301	**800-234-9001**	303-530-1900
SigmaTron International Inc					
2201 Landmeier Rd	Elk Grove Village	IL	60007	**800-700-9095**	847-956-8000
NASDAQ: SGMA					
Sopark Corp 3300 S Park Ave	Buffalo	NY	14218	**866-576-7275**	716-822-0434
Spectrum Signal Processing by Vecima					
2700 Production Way Ste 300	Burnaby	BC	V5A4X1	**800-663-8986**	604-676-6700
Unicircuit Inc					
8192 Southpark Ln	Littleton	CO	80120	**800-648-6449**	303-730-0505
Unigen Corp					
45388 Warm Springs Blvd	Fremont	CA	94539	**800-826-0808**	510-668-2088
Westak Inc 1116 Elko Dri	Sunnyvale	CA	94089	**800-893-7825**	408-734-8686
ZTEST Electronics Inc					
523 Mcnicoll Ave	North York	ON	M2H2C9	**866-393-4891**	416-297-5155

622 — PRINTING COMPANIES - BOOK PRINTERS

				Toll-Free	Phone
Adair Printing Technologies					
7850 Second St	Dexter	MI	48130	**800-637-5025**	734-426-2822
Bang Printing Inc					
3323 Oak St	Brainerd	MN	56401	**800-328-0450**	218-829-2877
CJK 3962 Virginia Ave	Cincinnati	OH	45227	**800-598-7808**	513-271-6035
Claitor's Law Books & Publishing Div					
PO Box 261333	Baton Rouge	LA	70826	**800-274-1403**	225-344-0476
Cookbook Publishers					
11633 W 83rd Ter	Lenexa	KS	66214	**800-227-7282**	913-492-5900
Cushing-Malloy Inc					
1350 N Main St	Ann Arbor	MI	48104	**888-295-7244**	734-663-8554
Garlich Printing Co					
525 Rudder Rd	Fenton	MO	63026	**844-449-4752**	
Gospel Publishing House					
1445 N Boonville Ave	Springfield	MO	65802	**800-641-4310***	417-862-2781
*Orders					
Houchen Bindery Ltd					
340 First St	Utica	NE	68456	**800-869-0420**	402-534-2261
John Henry Co					
5800 W Grand River Ave	Lansing	MI	48906	**800-748-0517**	517-323-9000
Jostens Inc					
3601 Minnesota Ave Ste 400	Minneapolis	MN	55435	**800-235-4774**	952-830-3300
Library Reproduction Service					
19146 Van Ness Ave	Torrance	CA	90501	**800-255-5002**	
Moran Printing Inc					
5425 Florida Blvd	Baton Rouge	LA	70806	**800-211-8335**	225-923-2550
Mossberg & Company Inc					
301 E Sample St	South Bend	IN	46601	**800-428-3340**	574-289-9253
Publishers Press Inc					
100 Frank E Simon Ave	Shepherdsville	KY	40165	**800-627-5801**	502-955-6526
Rose Printing Company Inc					
2503 Jackson Bluff Rd	Tallahassee	FL	32304	**800-227-3725**	850-576-4151
RR Donnelley					
111 S Wacker Dr	Chicago	IL	60606	**800-742-4455**	
Sheridan Group					
11311 McCormick Rd Ste 260	Hunt Valley	MD	21031	**800-352-2210**	410-785-7277
Smith-Edwards-Dunlap Co					
2867 E Allegheny Ave	Philadelphia	PA	19134	**800-829-0020**	215-425-8800
Thomson-Shore Inc					
7300 W Joy Rd	Dexter	MI	48130	**800-706-4545**	734-426-3939
United Record Pressing LLC					
453 Allied Dr	Nashville	TN	37211	**866-407-3165**	615-259-9396
Versa Press Inc					
1465 Springbay Rd	East Peoria	IL	61611	**800-447-7829**	
Whitehall Printing Co					
4244 Corporate Sq	Naples	FL	34104	**800-321-9290**	

623 — PRINTING COMPANIES - COMMERCIAL PRINTERS

				Toll-Free	Phone
1-800 Postcards Inc					
121 Varick St	New York	NY	10013	**800-767-8227**	
A&h Lithoprint Inc					
2540 S 27th Ave	Broadview	IL	60155	**855-305-7628**	708-345-1196
ABG Communications					
3810 Wabash Dr	Mira Loma	CA	91752	**888-685-7100**	951-361-7100
Accu-Label Inc					
2021 Research Dr	Fort Wayne	IN	46808	**888-482-5223**	260-482-5223
Acculink					
1055 Greenville Blvd SW	Greenville	NC	27834	**800-948-4110**	252-321-5805
AdMail Express Inc					
31640 Hayman St	Hayward	CA	94544	**800-273-6245**	
Adp Media Group LLC					
7700 Camp Bowie W Blvd Ste B	Fort Worth	TX	76116	**800-925-5700**	817-244-2740
Air Waves Inc					
7750 Green Meadows Dr N	Lewis Center	OH	43035	**844-543-8339**	740-548-1200
AKA Direct Mail Services					
44 Joseph Mills Dr	Fredericksburg	VA	22408	**800-232-1515**	
Aldine 150 Varick St 5th Fl	New York	NY	10013	**800-356-1818**	212-226-2870
All About Packaging Inc					
2200 W Everett St	Appleton	WI	54912	**800-446-1552**	920-830-2700
All-Pro Printing					
11548 Pyramid Dr	Odessa	FL	33556	**866-472-3982**	

Company / Address	City	State	Zip	Toll-Free	Phone
AlphaGraphics Inc 215 S State St Ste 320	Salt Lake City	UT	84111	800-955-6246	801-595-7270
Alpine Packaging Inc 4000 Crooked Run Rd	North Versailles	PA	15137	844-682-2361	412-664-4000
Ambrose Printing Co 210 Cumberland Bend	Nashville	TN	37228	800-334-6524	615-256-1151
Amidon Graphics 1966 Benson Ave	Saint Paul	MN	55116	800-328-6502	651-690-2401
Ampco Manufacturers Inc 9 Burbidge St Ste 101	Coquitlam	BC	V3K7B2	800-663-5482	604-472-3800
Annan & Bird Lithographers Ltd 1060 Tristar Dr	Mississauga	ON	L5T1H9	800-565-5618	905-670-0604
Another Printer Inc 10 Bush River Ct	Columbia	SC	29210	888-689-6399	803-798-1380
ANRO Inc 931 S Matlack St	West Chester	PA	19382	800-355-2676	610-687-1200
Arandell Inc N82 W13118 Leon Rd	Menomonee Falls	WI	53051	800-558-8724	
ArborOakland Group 4303 Normandy Ct	Royal Oak	MI	48073	800-886-5661	248-549-0150
Arkansas Graphics Inc 800 S Gaines St	Little Rock	AR	72201	877-918-4847	501-376-8436
Asap Printing Corp 643 Billinis Rd	Salt Lake City	UT	84119	888-727-2863	
Aus-Tex Printing & Mailing 2431 Forbes Dr	Austin	TX	78754	800-472-7581	512-476-7581
B & D Litho of Arizona 3820 N 38th Ave	Phoenix	AZ	85019	800-735-0375	602-269-2526
B & G House of Printing 1825-A W 169th St	Gardena	CA	90247	800-882-1844	310-532-1533
B H G Inc PO Box 309	Garrison	ND	58540	800-658-3485	701-463-2201
BCW Diversified 514 E 31st St	Anderson	IN	46016	800-433-4229	765-644-2033
Beckmanxmo 376 Morrison Rd	Columbus	OH	43213	800-864-2232	614-864-2232
Berney Office Solutions LLC 10690 John Knight Close	Montgomery	AL	36117	800-239-3025	
Bertek Systems Inc 133 Bryce Blvd	Fairfax	VT	05454	800-367-0210	802-752-3170
Better Label & Products Inc 3333 Empire Blvd SW	Atlanta	GA	30354	800-448-1813	404-763-8440
BFC 1051 N Kirk Rd	Batavia	IL	60510	800-774-6840	630-879-9240
Bibbero Systems Inc 1300 N McDowell Blvd	Petaluma	CA	94954	800-242-2376	
Bolger 3301 Como Ave SE	Minneapolis	MN	55414	866-264-3287	651-645-6311
Bonanza Press Inc 19860 141st Pl NE	Woodinville	WA	98072	800-233-0008	425-486-3399
Bradley Graphic Solutions Inc 941 Mill Rd	Bensalem	PA	19020	800-638-8223	215-638-8771
Brenneman Printing Inc 1909 Olde Homestead Ln	Lancaster	PA	17601	800-222-2423	717-299-2847
Brenner Printing Inc 1234 Triplett St	San Antonio	TX	78216	877-349-4024	210-349-4024
Brimar Industries Inc 64 Outwater Ln	Garfield	NJ	07026	800-274-6271	
Burns Mailing & Printing Inc 6131 Industrial Heights Dr PO Box 52730	Knoxville	TN	37909	866-288-5618	865-584-2265
Burton & Mayer Inc W140 N9000 Lilly Rd	Menomonee Falls	WI	53051	800-236-1770	262-781-0770
Cab Signs 38 Livonia Ave	Brooklyn	NY	11212	800-394-1690	718-385-1600
Canaan Printing 4820 Jefferson Davis Hwy	Richmond	VA	23234	800-332-3580	804-271-4820
Carlson Craft Inc 1750 Tower Blvd	North Mankato	MN	56003	800-774-6848	
Castle Pierce 2247 Ryf Rd	Oshkosh	WI	54904	800-227-8537	
Cathedral Corp 632 Ellsworth Rd Griffis Technology Pk	Rome	NY	13441	800-698-0299	315-338-0021
Century Marketing Solutions LLC 3000 Cameron St	Monroe	LA	71201	800-256-6000	
Challenge Printing Co, The 2 Bridewell Pl	Clifton	NJ	07014	800-654-1234	973-471-4700
Champion Industries Inc PO Box 2968 *OTC: CHMP*	Huntington	WV	25728	800-624-3431	304-528-2791
Circle Graphics LLC 120 Ninth Ave	Longmont	CO	80501	800-367-2472	303-532-2370
Click2mail 3103 Tenth St N Ste 201	Arlington	VA	22201	866-665-2787	703-521-9029
Cober Evolving Solutions 1351 Strasburg Rd	Kitchener	ON	N2R1H2	800-263-7136	519-745-7136
Color Ad Inc 18601 S Santa Fe Ave	Rancho Dominguez	CA	90221	888-264-6991	
Computype Inc 2285 W County Rd C	St. Paul	MN	55113	800-328-0852	
Concord Litho Group 92 Old Tpke Rd	Concord	NH	03301	800-258-3662	603-225-3328
Content Management Corp 4287 Technology Dr	Fremont	CA	94538	877-495-3720	510-505-1100
Control Printing Group Inc 4212 S Hocker Dr Ste 150	Independence	MO	64055	800-333-2820	816-350-8100
Copy Cat Printing 365 N Broadwell Ave	Grand Island	NE	68803	800-400-8520	308-384-8520
Coral Color Process Ltd 50 Mall Dr	Commack	NY	11725	800-564-7303	631-543-5200
Cosmos Communications Inc 11-05 44th Dr	Long Island	NY	11101	800-223-5751	718-482-1800
Courier Graphics Corp 2621 S 37th Ave	Phoenix	AZ	85034	800-454-6381	602-437-9700
Courier Printing 1 Courier Pl	Smyrna	TN	37167	800-467-0444	615-355-4000
Cowan Graphics Inc 4864 - 93 Ave NW	Edmonton	AB	T6B2R9	800-661-6996	780-577-5700
Coyle Reproductions Inc 2850 Orbiter St	Brea	CA	92821	866-269-5373	714-690-8200
CPS Cards 7520 Morris Ct	Allentown	PA	18106	888-817-8121	610-231-1860
Craftsman Printing Inc 120 Citation Ct	Birmingham	AL	35209	800-543-1051	205-942-3939
Creps United Publications 1163 Water St	Indiana	PA	15701	800-752-0555	724-463-8522
Crest Craft Co 3860 Virginia Ave	Cincinnati	OH	45227	800-860-1662	513-271-4858
David A Smith Printing Inc 742 S 22nd St	Harrisburg	PA	17104	800-564-3117	717-564-3719
Davis Direct Inc 1241 Newell Pkwy	Montgomery	AL	36110	877-277-0878	334-277-0878
DESIGNASHIRTCOM 905 N Scottsdale Rd	Tempe	AZ	85281	800-594-1206	480-966-3500
Digital Room Inc 8000 Haskell Ave	Van Nuys	CA	91406	866-266-5047	
Direct Connection Printing & Mailing 1968 Yeager Ave	La Verne	CA	91750	800-420-9937	909-392-2334
Dolphin Shirt Co 757 Buckley Rd	San Luis Obispo	CA	93401	800-377-3256	805-541-2566
Dome Printing 2031 Dome Ln	McClellan Park	CA	95652	800-343-3139	
Downeast Graphics & Printing Inc 477 Washington Jct Rd	Ellsworth	ME	04605	800-427-5582	207-667-5582
Drew & Rogers Inc 30 Plymouth St	Fairfield	NJ	07004	800-610-6210	973-575-6210
Drug Package Inc 901 Drug Package Ln	O'Fallon	MO	63366	800-325-6137	
Dupli Graphics Corp 6761 Thompson Rd N	Syracuse	NY	13211	800-724-2477	
Eagle:XM LLC 5105 E 41st Ave	Denver	CO	80216	800-426-5376	303-320-5411
Eclipse Colour & Imaging Corp 875 Laurentian Dr	Burlington	ON	L7N3W7	800-668-6369	905-634-1900
Edwards Graphic Arts Inc 2700 Bell Ave	Des Moines	IA	50321	800-280-9765	515-280-9765
Electric City Printing Co 730 Hampton Rd	Williamston	SC	29697	800-277-1920	864-224-6331
Embossed Graphics 1175 S Frontenac Rd	Aurora	IL	60504	800-362-6773	
Emerald City Graphics 23328 66th Ave S *General	Kent	WA	98032	877-631-5178*	
Ennis Inc 2441 Presidential Pkwy	Midlothian	TX	76065	800-972-1069	972-775-9801
EPI Marketing Services 5404 Wayne Rd	Battle Creek	MI	49037	800-562-9733	
Expresscopycom 6623 NE 59th Pl	Portland	OR	97218	800-260-5887	
F&M Expressions Inc 211 Island Rd	Mahwah	NJ	07430	888-788-7133	
FCL Graphics Inc 4600 N Olcott Ave	Harwood Heights	IL	60706	800-274-3380	708-867-5500
Fineline Printing Group 8081 Zionsville Rd	Indianapolis	IN	46268	877-334-7687	317-872-4490
Firehouse Image Ctr 2000 N Illinois St	Indianapolis	IN	46202	800-382-9179	317-236-1747
Flagship Press Inc 150 Flagship Dr	North Andover	MA	01845	800-733-1520	978-975-3100
Flexo Impressions 8647 Eagle Creek Pkwy	Savage	MN	55378	800-752-2357	952-884-9442
Fotoprint 975 Pandora Ave	Victoria	BC	V8V3P4	888-382-8211	250-382-8218
Franklin Imaging LLC 500 Schrock Rd	Columbus	OH	43229	877-885-6894	614-885-6894
Fruitridge Printing & Lithograph Inc 3258 Stockton Blvd	Sacramento	CA	95820	800-835-4846	916-452-9213
Fry Communications Inc 800 W Church Rd	Mechanicsburg	PA	17055	800-334-1429	
Garlock Printing & Converting Corp 164 Fredette St	Gardner	MA	01440	800-473-1328	978-630-1028
Garner Printing Co 1697 NE 53rd Ave	Des Moines	IA	50313	800-747-2171	515-266-2171
GE Richards Graphic Supplies Company Inc 928 Links Ave	Landisville	PA	17538	800-233-0410	717-892-4620
General Financial Supply Inc 1235 N Ave	Nevada	IA	50201	800-759-4374	515-382-3549
Genie Repros Inc 2211 Hamilton Ave	Cleveland	OH	44114	877-496-6611	216-696-6677
Georgia Printco 90 S Oak St	Lakeland	GA	31635	866-572-0146	
Goetz Printing Co, The 7939 Angus Ct	Springfield	VA	22153	866-245-0977	703-569-8232
Grandville Printing Company Inc 4719 Ivanrest Ave SW	Grandville	MI	49418	800-748-0248	
Graphics Type & Color Enterprises Inc 2300 NW Seventh Ave	Miami	FL	33127	800-433-9298	305-591-7600
Greenwell Chisholm Printing Co 420 E Parrish Ave	Owensboro	KY	42303	800-844-1876	270-684-3267
Grit Commercial Printing Inc 80 Choate Cir	Montoursville	PA	17754	800-872-0409	570-368-8021
Grove Printing Corp 4225 Howard Ave	Kensington	MD	20895	877-290-5793	301-571-1024
Guide, The 24904 Sussex Hwy PO Box 1210	Seaford	DE	19973	800-984-8433	302-629-5060
Harper Engraving & Printing Co 2626 Fisher Rd	Columbus	OH	43204	800-848-5196	614-276-0700
Hart Industries Inc 11412 Cronridge Dr	Owings Mills	MD	21117	800-638-2700	410-581-1900
Harty Integrated Solutions 25 James St	New Haven	CT	06513	800-654-0562	203-562-5112
HBP Inc 952 Frederick St	Hagerstown	MD	21740	800-638-3508	301-733-2000
Heuss Printing Inc 903 N Second St	Ames	IA	50010	800-232-6710	515-232-6710
Hickory Printing Group Inc 725 Reese Dr SW	Conover	NC	28613	800-442-5679	828-465-3431
HO.T. Printing & Graphics Inc 2595 Tracy Ct	Northwood	OH	43619	800-848-8259	419-242-7000
Hopkins Printing Inc 2246 CityGate Dr	Columbus	OH	43219	800-319-3352	614-509-1080
Ideal Jacobs Corp 515 Valley St	Maplewood	NJ	07040	877-873-4332	973-275-5100
ImageMark Business Services Inc 3145 Northwest Blvd	Gastonia	NC	28098	800-632-9513	

Name / Address	City	State	ZIP	Toll-Free	Phone
Implementix Inc					
4850 Ward Rd	Wheat Ridge	CO	80033	**800-433-2257**	888-831-2536
Indexx Inc					
303 Haywood Rd	Greenville	SC	29607	**800-252-8227**	864-234-1024
Inland Arts & Graphics Inc					
14440 Edison Dr	New Lenox	IL	60451	**800-437-6003**	
Inovar Packaging Group LLC					
10470 Miller Rd	Dallas	TX	75238	**800-285-2235**	
IntegraColor					
3210 Innovative Way	Mesquite	TX	75149	**800-933-9511**	972-289-0705
Intelligencer Printing Co					
330 Eden Rd	Lancaster	PA	17601	**800-233-0107**	
Interprint LLC					
7111 Hayvenhurst Ave	Van Nuys	CA	91406	**800-926-9873**	818-989-3600
J & A Printing Inc					
PO Box 457	Hiawatha	IA	52233	**800-793-1781**	319-393-1781
James Mulligan Printing Corp					
1808 Washington Ave	St. Louis	MO	63103	**800-737-0874**	314-621-0875
John Roberts Co					
9687 E River Rd NW	Minneapolis	MN	55433	**800-551-1534**	763-755-5500
JTS Direct LLC					
1180 Walnut Ridge Dr	Hartland	WI	53029	**877-387-9500**	
Karol Fulfillment					
Hanover Industrial Estates					
375 Stewart Rd	Wilkes-Barre	PA	18706	**800-526-4773**	570-822-8899
Kay Toledo Tag					
6050 Benore Rd PO Box 5038	Toledo	OH	43612	**800-822-8247**	419-729-5479
KDM Signs Inc					
10450 N Medallion Dr	Cincinnati	OH	45241	**855-232-7799**	
Kelly Press Inc					
1701 Cabin Branch Dr	Cheverly	MD	20785	**888-535-5940**	301-386-2800
Kennickell Printing Co					
1700 E President St	Savannah	GA	31404	**800-673-6455**	
Knox Services					
2250 Fourth Ave	San Diego	CA	92101	**800-995-6694**	
Koza Inc 2910 S Main St	Pearland	TX	77581	**800-594-5555**	281-485-1462
l'Usine Tactic Inc					
127th St Ste 2050	Saint George	QC	G5Y2W8	**800-933-5232**	
La Crosse Graphics Inc					
3025 E Ave S	La Crosse	WI	54601	**800-832-2503**	608-788-2500
Label Printers Lp, The					
1710 N Landmark Rd	Aurora	IL	60506	**800-229-9549**	630-897-6970
Label Technology Inc					
2050 Wardrobe Ave	Merced	CA	95341	**800-388-1990**	209-384-1000
Label Works					
2025 Lookout Dr	North Mankato	MN	56003	**800-522-3558**	
Lake Erie Graphics Inc					
5372 W 130th St	Brook Park	OH	44142	**888-293-7397**	216-265-7575
Laminex Inc					
4209 Pleasant Rd	Fort Mill	SC	29708	**800-438-8850**	704-679-4170
Lane Press Inc					
87 Meadowland Dr	Burlington	VT	05403	**877-300-5933**	
Lasting Impressions Inc					
7406 43rd Ave NE	Marysville	WA	98270	**866-859-7625**	360-659-1255
Lawrence Printing Co					
400 Stribling Ave PO Box 886	Greenwood	MS	38935	**800-844-0338**	662-453-6301
Lewisburg Printing Co					
170 Woodside Ave PO Box 2608	Lewisburg	TN	37091	**800-559-1526**	
Litho-Krome Co					
5700 Old Brim Dr	Midland	GA	31820	**800-572-8028**	706-562-7900
Lithotone Inc					
1313 W Hively Ave	Elkhart	IN	46517	**800-654-5671**	
Litigation Solution Inc (LSI)					
5995 Greenwood Plz Blvd					
Ste 160	Greenwood Village	CO	80111	**888-767-7088**	303-820-2000
LogoNation Inc					
PO Box 3847 Ste 102	Mooresville	NC	28117	**800-955-7375**	
Lone Peak Labeling Systems					
1785 South 4490 West	Salt Lake City	UT	84106	**800-658-8599**	801-975-1818
Lowen Corp PO Box 1528	Hutchinson	KS	67504	**800-835-2365**	620-663-2161
Lti Printing Inc					
518 N Centerville Rd	Sturgis	MI	49091	**800-592-6990**	269-651-7574
M Lee Smith Publishers LLC					
PO Box 5094	Brentwood	TN	37024	**800-274-6774**	615-373-7517
M&D Printing					
515 University Ave	Henry	IL	61537	**888-242-7552**	309-364-3957
M&R Companies					
440 Medinah Rd	Roselle	IL	60172	**800-736-6431**	630-858-6101
Magna IV					
2401 Commercial Ln	Little Rock	AR	72206	**800-946-2462**	501-376-2397
Mahaffey's Quality Printing Inc					
355 W Pearl St	Jackson	MS	39203	**800-843-1135**	601-353-9663
Mandel Co					
727 W Glendale Ave Ste 100	Milwaukee	WI	53209	**800-888-6970**	414-271-6970
Marathon Press					
1500 Sq Turn Blvd PO Box 407	Norfolk	NE	68702	**800-228-0629**	
Marina Graphic Ctr					
12901 Cerise Ave	Hawthorne	CA	90250	**800-974-5777**	310-970-1777
Marrakech Express Inc					
720 Wesley Ave Ste 10	Tarpon Springs	FL	34689	**800-940-6566**	727-942-2218
Mercersburg Printing					
9964 Buchanan Trl W	Mercersburg	PA	17236	**800-955-3902**	717-328-3902
Mercury Press Inc					
1910 S Nicklas St	Oklahoma City	OK	73128	**800-423-5984**	405-682-3468
Merrill Corp					
1 Merrill Cir	Saint Paul	MN	55108	**800-688-4400**	651-646-4501
Midland Information Resources Co					
5440 Corporate Pk Dr	Davenport	IA	52807	**800-232-3696**	563-359-3696
Mines Press Inc, The					
231 Croton Ave	Cortlandt Manor	NY	10567	**800-447-6788**	
Minuteman Press International Inc					
61 Executive Blvd	Farmingdale	NY	11735	**800-645-3006**	631-249-1370
Modern Way Printing & Fulfillment					
8817 Production Ln	Ooltewah	TN	37363	**800-603-5135**	423-238-4500
Mr Button Products Inc					
7840 Rockville Rd	Indianapolis	IN	46214	**800-777-0111**	
MWM Dexter Inc					
107 Washington Ave	Aurora	MO	65605	**888-833-1193**	

Name / Address	City	State	ZIP	Toll-Free	Phone
Nameplate & Panel Technology					
387 Gundersen Dr	Carol Stream	IL	60188	**800-833-8397**	630-690-9360
ND Graphic Product Ltd					
55 Interchange Way Unit 1	Concord	ON	L4K5W3	**800-811-0194**	416-663-6416
Northern Ohio Printing Inc					
4721 Hinckley Indus Pkwy	Cleveland	OH	44109	**800-407-7284**	216-398-0000
NPC Inc					
13710 Dunnings Hwy	Claysburg	PA	16625	**800-847-5757**	814-239-8787
Nta Graphics South Inc					
501 Republic Cir	Birmingham	AL	35214	**888-798-2123**	205-798-2123
Nutis Press Inc					
3540 E Fulton St	Columbus	OH	43227	**800-848-6266**	614-237-8626
Original Impressions LLC					
12900 SW 89th Ct	Miami	FL	33176	**888-853-8644**	305-233-1322
OvernightPrints					
7582 S Las Vegas Blvd Ste 487	Las Vegas	NV	89213	**888-677-2000**	
Pacific Color Graphics					
440 Boulder Ct 100d	Pleasanton	CA	94566	**888-551-1482**	925-600-3006
Palmetto Cooperative Services LLC					
7440 Broad River Rd	Irmo	SC	29063	**800-235-4290**	
Paradigm Imaging Group Inc					
3010 Red Hill Ave	Costa Mesa	CA	92626	**888-221-7226**	714-432-7226
Paramount Graphics Inc					
6075 Pkwy North Dr Ste D	Cumming	GA	30040	**800-714-8071**	
Park Printing Inc					
2801 California St NE	Minneapolis	MN	55418	**800-789-3877**	612-789-4333
PBM Graphics Inc					
3700 S Miami Blvd	Durham	NC	27703	**800-849-8100**	919-544-6222
Penmor Lithographers Inc					
8 Lexington St PO Box 2003	Lewiston	ME	04241	**800-339-1341**	
Perkinson Reprographics Inc					
735 E Brill St	Phoenix	AZ	85006	**888-330-8782**	602-393-3131
Plum Grove Inc					
2160 Stoningtone Ave	Hoffman Estates	IL	60169	**866-738-3702**	847-882-4020
Pollock Printing Company Inc					
928 Sixth Ave S	Nashville	TN	37203	**800-349-1205**	615-255-0526
Print Direction Inc					
1600 Indian Brook Way	Norcross	GA	30093	**877-435-1672**	770-446-6446
Print NW 9914 32nd Ave S	Lakewood	WA	98499	**800-826-8260**	253-284-2300
Print Papa					
1920 Lafayette St Ste L	Santa Clara	CA	95050	**800-657-7181**	408-567-9553
Print Works 3850 98 St NW	Edmonton	AB	T6E3L2	**888-452-8921**	780-452-8921
PrintFleet					
1000 Gardiners Rd Ste 202	Kingston	ON	K7K2X5	**866-382-8320**	613-549-3221
Printing Images Inc					
12266 Wilkins Ave A	Rockville	MD	20852	**866-685-4356**	301-984-1140
PrintingForLesscom Inc					
100 PFL Way	Livingston	MT	59047	**800-930-6040**	
PrintPlacecom					
1130 Ave H E	Arlington	TX	76011	**877-405-3949**	817-701-3555
Printswell Inc					
135 Cahaba Valley Pkwy	Pelham	AL	35124	**800-476-4723**	
Prisma Graphic Corp					
2937 E Broadway Rd	Phoenix	AZ	85040	**800-379-5777**	602-243-5777
Production Press Inc					
307 E Morgan St	Jacksonville	IL	62650	**800-231-3880**	217-243-3353
ProForma					
8800 E Pleasant Valley Rd	Independence	OH	44131	**800-825-1525**	216-520-8400
Progress Printing Co					
2677 Waterlick Rd	Lynchburg	VA	24502	**800-572-7804**	
Prosource Fitness Equipment					
6503 Hilburn Dr	Raleigh	NC	27613	**877-781-8077**	919-781-8077
PSPrint LLC					
2861 Mandela Pkwy	Oakland	CA	94608	**800-511-2009**	
Publication Printers Corp					
2001 S Platte River Dr	Denver	CO	80223	**888-824-0303**	303-936-0303
Queen City Printers Inc					
701 Pine St	Burlington	VT	05401	**800-639-8099**	802-864-4566
Quick Color Solutions Inc					
829 Knox Rd	Mc Leansville	NC	27301	**877-698-0951**	336-698-0951
Quick Tab II Inc					
241 Heritage Dr	Tiffin	OH	44883	**800-332-5081**	419-448-6622
Rand Graphics Inc					
500 S Florence St	Wichita	KS	67209	**800-435-7263**	316-942-1218
Regal Press 79 Astor Ave	Norwood	MA	02062	**800-447-3425**	781-769-3900
Reindl Printing Inc					
1300 Johnson St	Merrill	WI	54452	**800-236-9637**	715-536-9537
Reni Publishing Inc					
150 Third St SW	Winter Haven	FL	33880	**800-274-2812**	
RMF Printing Technologies Inc					
50 Pearl St	Lancaster	NY	14086	**800-828-7999**	716-683-7500
RoArk Group Inc, The					
1600 N 35th St	Rogers	AR	72756	**800-569-2616**	479-636-1686
Roberts Company Inc					
180 Franklin St	Framingham	MA	01702	**800-729-1482**	
Robyn Inc					
7717 W Britton Rd	Oklahoma City	OK	73132	**877-211-9711**	
Rogers Printing Inc					
PO Box 215	Ravenna	MI	49451	**800-622-5591**	231-853-2244
Rotary Multiforms Inc					
1340 E 11 Mile Rd	Madison Heights	MI	48071	**800-762-5644**	586-558-7960
Royal Conservatory of Music The					
273 Bloor St W	Toronto	ON	M5S1W2	**800-462-3815**	416-408-2824
Seaway Printing Company Inc					
1609 Western Ave	Green Bay	WI	54303	**800-622-3255**	920-468-1500
Sheridan Group					
11311 McCormick Rd Ste 260	Hunt Valley	MD	21031	**800-352-2210**	410-785-7277
Sigler					
3100 S Riverside Dr PO Box 887	Ames	IA	50010	**800-750-6997**	515-232-6997
Sign-ups & Banners Corp					
2764 W T C Jester Blvd	Houston	TX	77018	**877-682-7979**	713-682-7979
Sir Speedy Inc					
26722 Plaza Dr	Mission Viejo	CA	92691	**800-854-8297**	949-348-5000
Skinner & Kennedy Co					
9451 Natural Bridge Rd	Saint Louis	MO	63134	**800-426-3094**	314-426-2800
SMS Productions Inc					
1340 Charwood Rd Ste g	Hanover	MD	21076	**800-289-7671**	301-953-0011
Solisco Inc 120 10e Rue	Scott	QC	G0S3G0	**800-463-4188**	418-387-8908

		Toll-Free	Phone

Solo Printing Inc
7860 NW 66th St ....Miami FL 33166 — 800-325-0118 — 305-594-8699

Southland Printing Company Inc
213 Airport Dr ....Shreveport LA 71107 — 800-241-8662 — 318-221-8662

Spartan Graphics Inc
200 Applewood Dr ....Sparta MI 49345 — 800-747-4477 — 616-887-8243

Square 1 Art LLC
5470 Oakbrook Pkwy Ste E....................Norcross GA 30093 — 888-332-3294 — 678-906-2291

Stafford Printing Co
2707 Jefferson Davis Hwy ....Stafford VA 22554 — 800-774-6831 — 540-659-4554

Strawbridge Studios Inc
3616 Hillsborough Rd PO Box 3005................Durham NC 27705 — 800-326-9080 — 919-226-3000

Sunset Printing
4522 Rosemead Blvd ....Pico Rivera CA 90660 — 800-427-8980

Super Color Digital LLC
16761 Hale Ave ....Irvine CA 92606 — 800-979-4446

Swift Print Communication
1248 Research Blvd ....Saint Louis MO 63132 — 800-545-1141 — 314-991-4300

Telepress Global
19241 62nd Ave S ....Kent WA 98032 — 800-234-4466

Tenenz Inc
9655 Penn S Ave ....Minneapolis MN 55431 — 800-888-5803

Times Printing Company Inc
100 Industrial Dr ....Random Lake WI 53075 — 800-236-4396 — 920-994-4396

Total Printing Systems
201 S Gregory St ....Newton IL 62448 — 800-465-5200

Transfer Express Inc
7650 Tyler Blvd ....Mentor OH 44060 — 800-622-2280 — 440-918-1900

Travers Printing Inc
32 Mission St ....Gardner MA 01440 — 800-696-0530 — 978-632-0530

Tri-State Financial Press LLC
109 N Fifth St ....Saddle Brook NJ 07663 — 800-866-6375

Tricor Print Communications Inc
7931 NE Halsey St Ste 101....................Portland OR 97213 — 800-635-7778 — 503-255-5595

Tuttle Law Print Inc
414 Quality Ln ....Rutland VT 05701 — 800-776-7682

Valassis Communications Inc
19975 Victor Pkwy ....Livonia MI 48152 — 800-437-0479 — 734-591-3000
NYSE: VCI

Valley Offset Printing Inc
160 S Sheridan Ave ....Valley Center KS 67147 — 888-895-7913 — 316-755-0061

Verified Label & Print Inc
7905 Hopi Pl ....Tampa FL 33634 — 800-764-6110 — 813-290-7721

VictorystoreCom Inc
5200 SW 30th St ....Davenport IA 52802 — 866-241-2295 — 866-241-2294

Vision Envelope Inc
2451 Executive St ....Charlotte NC 28208 — 800-200-9797

Vision Graphics Inc
5610 Boeing Dr ....Loveland CO 80538 — 800-833-4263 — 970-679-9000

Walter Snyder Printer Inc
691 River St ....Troy NY 12180 — 888-272-9774 — 518-272-8881

Warren Printing & Mailing Inc
5000 Eagle Rock Blvd ....Los Angeles CA 90041 — 888-468-6976 — 323-258-2621

Watson Label Products
10616 Trenton Ave ....Saint Louis MO 63132 — 800-678-6715 — 314-493-9300

Watt Printing Co
4544 Hinckley Industrial Pkwy ....Cleveland OH 44109 — 800-273-2170 — 216-398-2000

Waveline Direct Inc
192 Hempt Rd ....Mechanicsburg PA 17050 — 800-257-8830 — 717-795-8830

Weatherall Printing Co
1349 Cliff Gookin Blvd ....Tupelo MS 38801 — 800-273-6043 — 662-842-5284

Weldon Williams & Lick Inc
711 N A St ....Fort Smith AR 72901 — 800-242-4995 — 479-783-4113

Wells & Drew Cos
3414 Galilee Rd ....Jacksonville FL 32207 — 800-342-8636

Wells Printing Company Inc
6030 Perimeter Pkwy ....Montgomery AL 36116 — 800-264-4958 — 334-281-3449

Wentworth Printing Corp
101 N 12th St ....West Columbia SC 29169 — 800-326-0784

West Press Printing & Copying
1663 W Grant Rd ....Tucson AZ 85745 — 888-637-0337 — 520-624-4939

Winston Packaging
8095 N Point Blvd ....Winston-Salem NC 27106 — 800-558-8952 — 336-759-0051

Woolverton Printing Co
6714 Chancellor Dr ....Cedar Falls IA 50613 — 800-670-7713 — 319-277-2616

Xlibris Corp
1663 Liberty Dr Ste 200 ....Bloomington IN 47403 — 888-795-4274

Zebra Print Solutions
9401 Globe Ctr Dr ....Morrisville NC 27560 — 800-545-8835 — 919-314-3700

Zookbinders Inc
151-K S Pfingsten Rd ....Deerfield IL 60015 — 800-810-5745

624 PRINTING & PHOTOCOPYING SUPPLIES

		Toll-Free	Phone

ABCO Printing 512 Trade Rd ....Columbus OH 43204 — 800-821-9435

Buckeye Business Products Inc
3830 Kelley Ave ....Cleveland OH 44114 — 800-837-4323

Chromaline Corp
4832 Grand Ave ....Duluth MN 55807 — 800-328-4261 — 218-628-2217

Color Imaging Inc
4350 Peachtree Industrial Blvd Ste 100 ....Norcross GA 30071 — 800-783-1090 — 770-840-1090

DuraLine Imaging Inc
578 Upward Rd Ste 11 ....Flat Rock NC 28731 — 800-982-3872 — 828-692-1301

Graphic Controls LLC
400 Exchange St ....Buffalo NY 14204 — 800-669-1535

Hurst Chemical Co
2020 Cunningham Rd ....Rockford IL 61102 — 800-723-2004

Image One Corp
13201 Capital St ....Oak Park MI 48237 — 800-799-5377 — 248-414-9955

Ink Technology Corp
18320 Lanken Ave ....Cleveland OH 44119 — 800-633-2826 — 216-486-6720

LexJet Corp
1680 Fruitville Rd 3rd Fl. ....Sarasota FL 34236 — 800-453-9538 — 941-330-1210

Light Impressions
100 Carlson Rd ....Rochester NY 14610 — 800-975-6429

		Toll-Free	Phone

Pad Print Machinery of Vermont Inc
201 Tennis Way ....East Dorset VT 05253 — 800-272-7764 — 802-362-0844

Rayven Inc
431 Griggs St N ....Saint Paul MN 55104 — 800-878-3776* — 651-642-1112
*Cust Svc

WNC Supply LLC
37841 N 16th St ....Phoenix AZ 85086 — 800-538-5108 — 623-594-4602

625 PRINTING & PUBLISHING EQUIPMENT & SYSTEMS

SEE ALSO Printers

		Toll-Free	Phone

Brackett Inc
7115 SE Forbes Ave Bldg 451 J St................Topeka KS 66619 — 800-255-3506 — 785-862-2205

Brandtjen & Kluge Inc
539 Blanding Woods Rd ....Saint Croix Falls WI 54024 — 800-826-7320 — 715-483-3265

Burgess Industries Inc (BII)
7500 Boone Ave N Ste 111....................Brooklyn Park MN 55428 — 800-233-2589 — 763-553-7800

Gravograph-New Hermes Inc
2200 Northmont Pkwy ....Duluth GA 30096 — 800-843-7637 — 770-623-0331

Heidelberg USA Inc
1000 Gutenberg Dr ....Kennesaw GA 30144 — 888-472-9655* — 770-419-6500
*Cust Svc

LasscoWizer Inc
485 Hague St ....Rochester NY 14606 — 800-854-6595 — 585-436-1934

Mark Andy Inc
18081 Chesterfield Airport Rd ....Chesterfield MO 63005 — 800-700-6275 — 636-532-4433

Presstek Inc 55 Executive Dr ....Hudson NH 03051 — 800-422-3616 — 603-595-7000
NASDAQ: PRST

Rosback Co
125 Hawthorne Ave ....Saint Joseph MI 49085 — 800-542-2420 — 269-983-2582

Xerox Corp 201 Merritt 7 ....Norwalk CT 06856 — 800-327-9753 — 888-242-9098
NYSE: XRX

626 PRISON INDUSTRIES

Prison industries are programs established by federal and state governments that provide work for inmates while they are incarcerated as well as on-the-job training to help them become employable on release. At the same time, prison industries provide quality goods and services at competitive prices.

		Toll-Free	Phone

Arizona Correctional Industries
3701 W Cambridge Ave ....Phoenix AZ 85009 — 800-992-1738 — 602-272-7600

Arkansas Correctional Industries (ACI)
6841 W 13th St ....Pine Bluff AR 71602 — 877-635-7213

Badger State Industries (BSI)
3099 E Washington Ave PO Box 8990 ....Madison WI 53708 — 800-862-1086 — 608-240-5200

Cornhusker State Industries
800 Pioneers Blvd ....Lincoln NE 68502 — 800-348-7537 — 402-471-4597

Correctional Enterprises of Connecticut
24 Wolcott Hill Rd ....Wethersfield CT 06109 — 800-842-1146 — 860-263-6839

DEPTCOR 163 N Olden Ave ....Trenton NJ 08625 — 800-321-6524

Federal Prison Industries Inc
320 First St NW ....Washington DC 20534 — 800-827-3168

Georgia Correctional Industries
2984 Clifton Springs Rd ....Decatur GA 30034 — 800-282-7130 — 404-244-5100

Iowa Prison Industries (IPI)
1445 E Grand Ave ....Des Moines IA 50316 — 800-670-4537 — 515-242-5770

Kentucky Correctional Industries
1041 Leestown Rd ....Frankfort KY 40601 — 800-828-9524 — 502-573-1040

Maryland Correctional Enterprises (MCE)
7275 Waterloo Rd ....Jessup MD 20794 — 800-735-2258 — 410-540-5454

Massachusetts Correctional Industries
1 Industries Dr Bldg A PO Box 188................Norfolk MA 02056 — 800-222-2211 — 508-850-1070

New York Correctional Industries
550 Broadway ....Albany NY 12204 — 800-436-6321 — 518-436-6321

Oklahoma Correctional Industries
3402 N Martin Luther King Ave ....Oklahoma City OK 73111 — 800-522-3565 — 405-425-7500

PEN Products
2010 E New York St ....Indianapolis IN 46201 — 800-736-2550 — 317-955-6800

Pennsylvania Correctional Industries
PO Box 47 ....Camp Hill PA 17011 — 877-673-3724* — 717-425-7292
*General

Rough Rider Industries
3303 E Main Ave PO Box 5521................Bismarck ND 58506 — 800-732-0557

Tennessee Rehabilitative Initiative in Correction (TRICOR)
240 Great Cir Rd Ste 310 ....Nashville TN 37228 — 800-958-7426 — 615-741-5705

Washington Correctional Industries
801 88th Ave SE ....Tumwater WA 98501 — 800-628-4738 — 360-725-9100

West Virginia Correctional Industries
617 Leon Sullivan Way ....Charleston WV 25301 — 800-525-5381 — 304-558-6054

627 PROFESSIONAL EMPLOYER ORGANIZATIONS (PEOS)

Companies listed here contractually assume human resources responsibilities for client companies in exchange for a fee, thus allowing the client company to focus on its true company business. The PEO establishes and maintains an employer relationship with the workers assigned to its client companies, with the PEO and the client company each having specific rights and responsibilities toward the employees.

		Toll-Free	Phone

AB Staffing Solutions LLC
3451 Mercy Rd ....Gilbert AZ 85297 — 888-515-3900 — 480-345-6668

Abacus Corp
610 Gusryan St ....Baltimore MD 21224 — 800-230-0043 — 410-633-1900

Adams Keegan Inc
6750 Poplar Ave Ste 400 ....Memphis TN 38138 — 800-621-1308

ADP TotalSource Co
10200 Sunset Dr ....Miami FL 33173 — 800-447-3237 — 800-225-5237

Advice Media LLC
PO Box 982064 ....Park City UT 84098 — 800-260-9497

Agile Frameworks LLC
1826 Buerkle Rd ....Saint Paul MN 55110 — 800-779-1196

				Toll-Free	Phone
Allevity HR & Payroll					
870 Manzanita Ct Ste A	Chico	CA	95926	800-447-8233	530-345-2486
Allied Employer Group					
4400 Buffalo Gap Rd Ste 4500	Abilene	TX	79606	800-495-3836	325-695-5822
AlphaStaff Inc					
800 Corporate Dr Ste 600	Fort Lauderdale	FL	33334	888-335-9545	954-267-1760
Axcet HR Solutions					
Axcet 8325 Lenexa Dr Ste 410	Lenexa	KS	66214	800-801-7557	913-383-2999
Barrett Business Services Inc					
8100 NE Pkwy Dr Ste 200	Vancouver	WA	98662	800-494-5669	360-828-0700
NASDAQ: BBSI					
BlueRange Technology Inc					
9241 Globe Ctr Dr Ste 100	Morrisville	NC	27560	877-928-4800	
Brandmovers Inc					
590 Means St Ste 250	Atlanta	GA	30318	888-463-4933	678-718-1850
Chipton-ross Inc					
343 Main St	El Segundo	CA	90245	800-927-9318	310-414-7800
Co-Advantage Resources					
3350 Buschwood Park Dr Ste 200	Tampa	FL	33618	800-868-1016	855-351-4731
CrowdSource Solutions Inc					
33 Bronze Pointe	Swansea	IL	62226	855-276-9376	877-642-7331
Cubix Labs Inc					
1875 K St NW	Washington	DC	20006	866-978-2220	
Datacore Consulting LLC					
1300 E Granger Rd	Brooklyn Heights	OH	44131	800-244-4241	216-398-8499
Employee & Family Resources (EFR)					
505 Fifth Ave Ste 600	Des Moines	IA	50309	800-327-4692	515-288-9020
Employee Management Services					
435 Elm St	Cincinnati	OH	45202	888-651-1536	513-651-3244
Employer Flexible					
7102 N Sam Houston Pkwy W Ste 200	Houston	TX	77064	866-501-4942	
Extreme Reach Crew Services					
3601 W Olive Ave Ste 500	Burbank	CA	91505	800-301-1992	818-729-0080
FrontPage Local					
1660 Hotel Cir N Ste 600	San Diego	CA	92108	800-219-1755	
GetMeFriends					
7801 Broadway St	San Antonio	TX	78209	888-663-9143	
Human Capital					
2055 Crooks Rd Level B	Rochester Hills	MI	48309	888-736-9071	
Identity Theft Resource Center					
3625 Ruffin Rd Ste 204	San Diego	CA	92123	888-400-5530	
Inspirage Inc					
600 108th Ave NE Ste 540	Bellevue	WA	98004	855-517-4250	
Marvel Consultants Inc					
28601 Chagrin Blvd Ste 210	Cleveland	OH	44122	800-338-1257	216-292-2855
Modern Business Associates Inc					
9455 Koger Blvd Ste 200	St Petersburg	FL	33702	888-622-6460	
Mountain Ltd					
19 Yarmouth Dr Ste 301	New Gloucester	ME	04260	800-322-8627	207-688-6200
Naviant Inc					
201 Prairie Heights Dr	Verona	WI	53593	888-686-4624	
Nexio Group Inc					
2050 de Bleury St Ste 500	Montreal	QC	H3A2J5	888-798-3707	514-798-3707
Oasis Outsourcing Inc					
2054 Vista Pkwy Ste 300	West Palm Beach	FL	33411	888-627-4735*	
*General					
Optimum Logistic Solutions					
3540 Seven Bridges Dr Ste 300	Woodridge	IL	60517	800-356-0595	630-350-0595
OSF Global Services Inc					
6655 Blvd Pierre Bertrand 204-14	Quebec City	QC	G2K1M1	888-548-4344	
Pay Plus Benefits Inc					
1110 N Ctr Pkwy Ste B	Kennewick	WA	99336	888-531-5781	509-735-1143
People Lease Inc					
689 Towne Ctr Blvd	Ridgeland	MS	39157	800-723-3025	601-987-3025
Personnel Management Inc					
PO Box 6657	Shreveport	LA	71136	800-259-4126	318-869-4555
Professional Staff Management Inc					
6801 Lake Plaza Dr Ste D-405	Indianapolis	IN	46220	800-967-5515	317-816-7007
Proficio 1555 Faraday Ave	Carlsbad	CA	92008	800-779-5042	
Progressive Employer Services					
6407 Parkland Dr	Sarasota	FL	34243	888-925-2990	941-925-2990
Recon Management Services Inc					
1907 Ruth St	Sulphur	LA	70663	888-301-4662	337-583-4662
Resource Management Inc					
281 Main St Ste 5	Fitchburg	MA	01420	800-508-0048*	
*Cust Svc					
ScaleMatrix Inc					
5775 Kearny Villa Rd	San Diego	CA	92123	888-349-9994	
Staff One Inc 8111 LBJ Fwy	Dallas	TX	75251	800-771-7823	
Strom Aviation Inc					
109 S Elm St	Waconia	MN	55387	800-356-6440	952-544-3611
Summit Technical Services Inc					
355 Centerville Rd	Warwick	RI	02886	800-643-7372	401-736-8323
T & t Staff Management Inc					
511 Executive Ctr Blvd	El Paso	TX	79902	800-598-1647	915-771-0393
Tilson HR Inc					
1530 American Way Ste 200	Greenwood	IN	46143	800-276-3976	317-885-3838
TriNet Group Inc					
1100 San Leandro Blvd Ste 300	San Leandro	CA	94577	888-874-6388	510-352-5000
VertitechIT Inc					
4 Open Sq Way Ste 310	Holyoke	MA	01040	855-638-9879	
VJV IT 96 Linwood Plz	Fort Lee	NJ	07024	800-614-7561	

628 PUBLIC BROADCASTING ORGANIZATIONS

SEE ALSO Radio Networks ; Television Networks - Broadcast

				Toll-Free	Phone
Alabama Educational Television Commission					
2112 11th Ave S Ste 400	Birmingham	AL	35205	800-239-5233	205-328-8756
Alabama Public Television (APT)					
2112 11th Ave S Ste 400	Birmingham	AL	35205	800-239-5233	205-328-8756
Annenberg Media					
1301 Pennsylvania Ave NW Ste 302	Washington	DC	20004	800-532-7637	
Arkansas Educational Television Network (AETN)					
350 S Donaghey Ave	Conway	AR	72034	800-662-2386	501-682-2386
Blue Ridge Public Television					
1215 McNeil Dr	Roanoke	VA	24015	888-332-7788	540-344-0991

				Toll-Free	Phone
California Public Radio					
4100 Vachell Ln	San Luis Obispo	CA	93401	800-549-8855	805-549-8855
Capitol Steps Productions Inc					
210 N Washington St	Alexandria	VA	22314	800-733-7837	703-683-8330
Commonwealth Club, The					
555 Post St	San Francisco	CA	94102	800-847-7730	415-597-6700
Commonwealth Public Broadcasting					
23 Sesame St	Richmond	VA	23235	800-476-2357	804-320-1301
Connecticut Public Broadcasting Inc (CPBI)					
1049 Asylum Ave	Hartford	CT	06105	877-444-4485	860-278-5310
Corporation for Public Broadcasting (CPB)					
401 Ninth St NW	Washington	DC	20004	800-272-2190	202-879-9600
Georgia Public Broadcasting (GPB)					
260 14th St NW	Atlanta	GA	30318	800-222-6006	
GPB Education					
260 14th St NW	Atlanta	GA	30318	888-501-8960	404-685-2550
Hawaii Public Television					
2350 Dole St	Honolulu	HI	96822	800-238-4847	808-973-1000
Idaho Public Television (IPTV)					
1455 N Orchard St	Boise	ID	83706	800-543-6868	208-373-7220
Independent Television Service (ITVS)					
651 Brannan St Ste 410	San Francisco	CA	94107	888-572-8918	415-356-8383
Louisiana Public Broadcasting					
7733 Perkins Rd	Baton Rouge	LA	70810	800-973-7246	225-767-5660
Maryland Public Television (MPT)					
11767 Owings Mills Blvd	Owings Mills	MD	21117	800-223-3678	410-581-4201
Minnesota Public Radio (MPR)					
480 Cedar St	Saint Paul	MN	55101	800-228-7123	651-290-1212
Montana PBS					
183 Visual Communications Bldg	Bozeman	MT	59717	800-426-8243	866-832-0829
Montana Public Radio					
32 Campus Dr University of Montana	Missoula	MT	59812	800-325-1565	406-243-4931
National Captioning Institute (NCI)					
3725 Concorde Pkwy Ste 100	Chantilly	VA	20151	800-825-6758	703-917-7600
National Public Radio (NPR)					
635 Massachusetts Ave NW	Washington	DC	20001	800-989-8255	202-513-3232
Nebraska Educational Telecommunications (NET)					
1800 N 33rd St	Lincoln	NE	68503	800-868-1868	
New Hampshire Public Television (NHPTV)					
268 Mast Rd	Durham	NH	03824	800-639-8408	603-868-1100
Oregon Public Broadcasting Inc (OPB)					
7140 SW Macadam Ave	Portland	OR	97219	800-241-8123	503-244-9900
Prairie Public Broadcasting Inc					
207 N Fifth St	Fargo	ND	58102	800-359-6900	701-241-6900
Public Broadcasting Council of Central New York					
506 Old Liverpool Rd PO Box 2400	Syracuse	NY	13220	800-451-9269	315-453-2424
Public Broadcasting Northwest Pennsylvania					
8425 Peach St	Erie	PA	16509	800-727-8854	814-864-3001
Public Broadcasting Service (PBS)					
2100 Crystal Dr	Arlington	VA	22202	866-864-0828	703-739-5000
Radio Research Consortium Inc (RRC)					
PO Box 1309	Olney	MD	20830	800-543-7300	301-774-6686
Rocky Mountain Public Broadcasting Network (RMPB)					
1089 Bannock St	Denver	CO	80204	800-274-6666	303-892-6666
Smoky Hills Public Television (SHPTV)					
604 Elm St	Bunker Hill	KS	67626	800-337-4788	785-483-6990
South Carolina Educational Television Commission (ETV)					
1101 George Rogers Blvd	Columbia	SC	29201	800-922-5437	803-737-3200
South Dakota Public Broadcasting (SDPB)					
555 N Dakota St PO Box 5000	Vermillion	SD	57069	800-456-0766	605-677-5861
Texas Public Radio (TPR)					
8401 Datapoint Dr Ste 800	San Antonio	TX	78229	800-622-8977	210-614-8977
ThinkTV 110 S Jefferson St	Dayton	OH	45402	800-247-1614	937-220-1600
TRAC Media Services					
2030 E Speedway Blvd Ste 210	Tucson	AZ	85719	888-299-1866	520-299-1866
Twin Cities Public Television Inc					
172 E Fourth St	Saint Paul	MN	55101	866-229-1300	651-222-1717
University of North Carolina Ctr for Public Television (UNC-TV)					
10 TW Alexander Dr					
PO Box 14900	Research Triangle Park	NC	27709	800-906-5050	919-549-7000
Vermont Public Television (VPT)					
204 Ethan Allen Ave	Colchester	VT	05446	800-639-7811	802-655-4800
WAMC/Northeast Public Radio					
318 Central Ave	Albany	NY	12206	800-323-9262	518-465-5233
West Central Illinois Educational Telecommunications Corp					
PO Box 6248	Springfield	IL	62708	800-232-3605	217-483-7887
Wisconsin Educational Communications Board					
3319 W Beltline Hwy	Madison	WI	53713	800-422-9707	608-264-9600
Wisconsin Public Radio (WPR)					
821 University Ave	Madison	WI	53706	800-747-7444	
Wisconsin Public Television (WPT)					
821 University Ave	Madison	WI	53706	800-422-9707	608-263-2121
Wyoming Public Television					
2660 Peck Ave	Riverton	WY	82501	800-495-9788	307-856-6944

629 PUBLIC INTEREST RESEARCH GROUPS (PIRGS) - STATE

SEE ALSO Consumer Interest Organizations

				Toll-Free	Phone
Florida Public Interest Research Group					
3110 First Ave N Ste 2H	St. Petersburg	FL	33713	800-838-6554	727-431-9686
NYPIRG (NYPIRG) 9 Murray St	New York	NY	10007	800-566-5020	212-349-6460
Rhode Island Public Interest Research Group (RIPIRG)					
11 S Angell St Ste 150	Providence	RI	02906	800-838-6554	401-608-1201

630 PUBLIC POLICY RESEARCH CENTERS

				Toll-Free	Phone
AARP Public Policy Institute					
601 E St NW	Washington	DC	20049	888-687-2277	202-434-2277
Acton Institute					
98 E Fulton St	Grand Rapids	MI	49503	800-345-2286	616-454-3080
American Enterprise Institute for Public Policy Research (AEI)					
1789 Massachusetts Ave NW	Washington	DC	20036	800-862-5801	202-862-5800

	Toll-Free	Phone

Ashbrook Ctr
401 College Ave Ashland University . . . . Ashland OH 44805 **877-289-5411** 419-289-5411

Carter Ctr
1 Copenhill Ave 453 Freedom Pkwy . . . . Atlanta GA 30307 **800-550-3560** 404-420-5100

Center for Law & Social Policy (CLASP)
1015 15th St NW Ste 400 . . . . Washington DC 20005 **800-821-4367** 202-906-8000

Center for Policy Research
Syracuse University 426 Eggers Hall . . . . .Syracuse NY 13244 **800-325-3535** 315-443-3114

Committee for Economic Development (CED)
1530 Wilson Blvd Ste 400 . . . . Arlington VA 22209 **800-676-7353** 202-296-5860

Ethics & Public Policy Ctr
1730 M St NW Ste 910 . . . . Washington DC 20036 **800-935-0699** 202-682-1200

Foundation for Economic Education (FEE)
1819 Peachtree Rd NE Ste 300 . . . . Atlanta GA 30309 **800-960-4333** 404-554-9980

Heritage Foundation
214 Massachusetts Ave NE . . . . Washington DC 20002 **800-546-2843** 202-546-4400

Independent Institute
100 Swan Way . . . . Oakland CA 94621 **800-927-8733** 510-632-1366

Institute for Humane Studies
3434 Washington Blvd MS 1C5 . . . . Arlington VA 22201 **800-697-8799** 703-993-4880

Malcolm Wiener Ctr for Social Policy
John F Kennedy School of Government Harvard Univer
79 John F Kennedy St . . . . .Cambridge MA 02138 **866-845-6596** 617-384-9887

Manpower Demonstration Research Corp
16 E 34th St 19th Fl . . . . New York NY 10016 **800-221-3165** 212-532-3200

Margaret Chase Smith Policy Ctr
5784 York Complex Ste 4 . . . . Orono ME 04469 **877-486-2364** 207-581-1648

RAND Corp 1776 Main St . . . . Santa Monica CA 90401 **877-584-8642** 310-393-0411

Reason Public Policy Institute
3415 S Sepulveda Blvd Ste 400 . . . . Los Angeles CA 90034 **888-732-7668** 310-391-2245

Rockford Institute
928 N Main St . . . . Rockford IL 61103 **800-383-0680** 815-964-5053

Urban Institute
2100 M St NW . . . . Washington DC 20037 **866-518-3874** 202-833-7200

World Policy Institute (WPI)
220 Fifth Ave 9th Fl . . . . New York NY 10001 **800-207-8354** 212-481-5005

Worldwatch Institute
1776 Massachusetts Ave NW . . . . Washington DC 20036 **877-539-9946** 202-452-1999

631   PUBLIC RECORDS SEARCH SERVICES

SEE ALSO Investigative Services

	Toll-Free	Phone

Accufax PO Box 35563 . . . . .Tulsa OK 74153 **800-256-8898**

All-Search & Inspection Inc
1108 E South Union Ave . . . . Midvale UT 84047 **800-227-3152**

AmRent 250 E Broad St . . . . .Columbus OH 43215 **800-324-3681**

Applicant Insight Ltd
5652 Meadowlane St . . . . .New Port Richey FL 34652 **800-771-7703**

Apscreen Inc
PO Box 80639 . . . . .Rancho Santa Margarita CA 92688 **800-277-2733** 949-646-4003

Background Bureau Inc
2019 Alexandria Pk . . . . Highland Heights KY 41076 **800-854-3990** 859-781-3400

Background Information Services Inc
1800 30th St Ste 204 .Boulder CO 80301 **800-433-6010** 303-442-3960

Capitol Lien Records & Research Inc
1010 N Dale St . . . . .Saint Paul MN 55117 **800-845-4077** 651-488-0100

Capitol Services Inc
206 E Ninth St Ste 1300 . . . . Austin TX 78701 **800-345-4647**

CDI Credit Inc
6160 Peachtree Dunwoody Rd NE
Ste B-210 . . . . Atlanta GA 30328 **800-633-3961** 770-350-5070

Charles Jones LLC
PO Box 8488 . . . . .Trenton NJ 08650 **800-792-8888**

Colby Attorneys Service Company Inc
111 Washington Ave Ste 703 . . . . Albany NY 12210 **800-832-1220**

D+H CollateralGuard RC (CSRS)
4126 Norland Ave Ste 200 . . . . Burnaby BC V5G3S8 **866-873-9780** 604-637-4000

Doc-U-Search Inc
63 Pleasant St . . . . .Concord NH 03301 **800-332-3034** 603-224-2871

Driving Records Facilities
PO Box 1086 . . . . Glen Burnie MD 21061 **800-772-5510**

Edge Information Management Inc
1682 W Hibiscus Blvd .Melbourne FL 32901 **800-725-3343**

Employment Screening Services Inc
627 E Sprague St Ste 100 . . . . .Spokane WA 99202 **800-473-7778** 509-624-3851

Explore Information Services LLC
2750 Blue Water Rd Ste 200 . . . . .Eagan MN 55121 **800-531-9125**

Fidelifacts
42 Broadway Ste 1548 . . . . New York NY 10004 **800-678-0007** 212-425-1520

Government Liaison Services Inc (GLS)
200 N Glebe Rd Ste 321 . . . . Arlington VA 22203 **800-642-6564** 703-524-8200

HireRight Inc
5151 California Ave . . . . Irvine CA 92617 **800-400-2761**

IMI Data Search Inc
4333 Park Terrace Dr Ste 220 . . . . .Westlake Village CA 91361 **866-984-1736** 805-920-8617

Information Management Systems Inc
114 W Main St Ste 211 PO Box 2924 . . . . .New Britain CT 06050 **888-403-8347** 860-229-1119

Kress Employment Screening
320 Westcott St Ste 108 . . . . .Houston TX 77007 **888-636-3693** 713-880-3693

Kroll Background America Inc
100 Centerview Dr Ste 300 . . . . Nashville TN 37214 **800-697-7189** 615-320-9800

Laborchex Co, The
2506 Lakeland Dr Ste 200 . . . . Jackson MS 39232 **800-880-0366** 601-664-6760

LegalEase Inc
205 E 42nd St 20th Fl. . . . . New York NY 10017 **800-393-1277** 212-393-9070

MLQ Attorney Services
2000 River Edge Pkwy Ste 885 . . . . Atlanta GA 30328 **800-446-8794** 770-984-7007

OPENonline
1650 Lake Shore Dr Ste 350 . . . . .Columbus OH 43204 **888-381-5656** 614-481-6999

Orange Tree Employment Screening
7275 Ohms Ln . . . . Minneapolis MN 55439 **800-886-4777**

Parasec Inc
2804 Gateway Oaks Dr Ste 200
PO Box 160568 . . . . Sacramento CA 95833 **800-533-7272***
*General

Penncorp Servicegroup Inc
600 N Second St Ste 401 . . . . Harrisburg PA 17101 **800-544-9050** 717-234-2300

Property Owners Exchange Inc
6630 Baltimore National Pk
Ste 208 . . . . .Catonsville MD 21228 **800-869-3200** 410-719-0100

Questel Orbit
1725 Duke St Ste 625 . . . . Alexandria VA 22314 **800-456-7248**

Rental Research Services Inc
7525 Mitchell Rd Ste 301 . . . . Eden Prairie MN 55344 **800-328-0333** 952-935-5700

Search Company International
7700 E Arapahoe Rd Ste 220 . . . . Centennial CO 80112 **800-727-2120** 303-863-1800

Search Network Ltd
1503 42nd St Ste 210 . . . . West Des Moines IA 50266 **800-383-5050** 515-223-1153

Securitech Inc
8230 E Broadway Blvd . . . . .Tucson AZ 85710 **888-792-4473** 520-721-0305

TABB Inc PO Box 10 . . . . .Chester NJ 07930 **800-887-8222**

Unisearch Inc
1780 Barnes Blvd SW . . . . Tumwater WA 98512 **800-722-0708** 360-956-9500

Verified Credentials Inc
20890 Kenbridge Ct . . . . Lakeville MN 55044 **800-473-4934** 952-985-7202

Washington Speakers Bureau
1663 Prince St . . . . Alexandria VA 22314 **833-972-8255**

Westlaw Court Express
1333 H St NW . . . . Washington DC 20005 **877-362-7387** 202-423-2163

632   PUBLIC RELATIONS FIRMS

SEE ALSO Advertising Agencies

	Toll-Free	Phone

Ackermann Public Relations & Marketing
1111 Northshore Dr Ste N-400 . . . . .Knoxville TN 37919 **877-325-9453*** 865-584-0550
*General

Advocal 1000 Q St . . . . .Sacramento CA 95811 **800-446-9121** 916-446-6161

Behan Communications Inc
86 Glen St . . . . New York NY 12801 **877-792-3856**

Charles Ryan Assoc Inc
601 Morris St Ste 301 . . . . .Charleston WV 25301 **877-342-0161**

Connect PR
1 Market St 36th Fl . . . . .San Francisco CA 94105 **800-455-8855** 415-222-9691

Creatine Marketing
2121 Natomas Crossing Ste 200- 105 . . . . Sacramento CA 95834 **800-357-6242** 916-302-4742

E Boineau & Co
128 Beaufain St . . . . Charleston SC 29401 **800-579-2628** 843-723-1462

Epoch 5 Public Relations
755 New York Ave .Huntington NY 11743 **800-628-7070** 631-427-1713

Gard Communications
1140 SW 11th Ave Ste 300 . . . . Portland OR 97205 **800-800-7132** 503-221-0100

Gelia, Wells & Mohr Inc
390 S Youngs Rd .Williamsville NY 14221 **888-711-4884** 716-629-3202

Hanser & Associates
1001 Office Park Rd Ste 210 . . . . .West Des Moines IA 50265 **800-229-4879** 515-224-1086

Jaymie Scotto & Associates
PO Box 20 . . . . .Middlebrook VA 24459 **866-695-3629**

Linden Lab
945 Battery St . . . . .San Francisco CA 94111 **800-294-1067** 415-243-9000

McNeely Pigott & Fox (MP&F)
611 Commerce St Ste 3000 . . . . Nashville TN 37203 **800-818-6953** 615-259-4000

Mercury Public Affairs
200 Varick St Ste 600 . . . . New York NY 10014 **800-325-4151** 212-681-1380

MSR Communications
832 Sansome St 2nd Fl . . . . .San Francisco CA 94111 **866-247-6172** 415-989-9000

Nine Health Services Inc
1139 Delaware St . . . . Denver CO 80204 **800-332-3078** 303-698-4455

Quest Corp of America
17220 Camelot Ct . . . . .Land O' Lakes FL 34638 **866-662-6273**

Sitrick & Co
11999 San Vicente Blvd PH . . . . Los Angeles CA 90049 **800-288-8809** 310-788-2850

SSPR Public Relations Agency
150 N Upper Wacker Dr Ste 2010 . . . . Chicago IL 60606 **800-287-2279**

Sunflower Group
14001 Marshall Dr . . . . Lenexa KS 66215 **800-288-5085**

Thomson Safaris
14 Mt Auburn St . . . . Watertown MA 02472 **800-235-0289** 800-262-6255

PUBLICATIONS

SEE Magazines & Journals ; Newsletters ; Newspapers

633   PUBLISHING COMPANIES

SEE ALSO Book Producers ; Magazines & Journals ; Newsletters ; Newspapers

	Toll-Free	Phone

Idea & Design Works LLC
2765 Truxtun Rd . . . . .San Diego CA 92106 **800-438-7325** 858-270-1315

633-1 Atlas & Map Publishers

	Toll-Free	Phone

MARCOA Publishing Inc
9955 Black Mtn Rd .San Diego CA 92126 **800-854-2935** 858-695-9600

Rand McNally
9855 Woods Dr PO Box 7600 . . . . .Skokie IL 60077 **800-333-0136**

Simon & Schuster Interactive
1230 Ave of the Americas . . . . New York NY 10020 **800-223-2336** 212-698-7000

633-2 Book Publishers

	Toll-Free	Phone

ABC-CLIO Inc 130 Cremona Dr . . . . .Goleta CA 93117 **800-368-6868** 805-968-1911

American Printing House for the Blind
1839 Frankfort Ave PO Box 6085 . . . . Louisville KY 40206 **800-223-1839** 502-895-2405

				Toll-Free	Phone

Antique Collectors Club
116 Pleasant St .... EastHampton MA 01027 800-254-4100 413-529-0861
Applewood Books Inc
1 River Rd .... Carlisle MA 01741 800-277-5312*
*General
Atlantic Publishing Co
315 E Washington St .... Starke FL 32091 800-814-1132
Author House
1663 Liberty Dr .... Bloomington IN 47403 888-519-5121 812-339-6000
Aviation Supplies & Academics Inc
7005 132nd Pl SE .... Newcastle WA 98059 800-272-2359 425-235-1500
Barron's Educational Series Inc
250 Wireless Blvd .... Hauppauge NY 11788 800-645-3476 631-434-3311
Beacon Press Inc
24 Farnsworth St .... Boston MA 02210 800-253-9646 617-742-2110
BRB Publications Inc
PO Box 27869 .... Tempe AZ 85285 800-929-3811 480-829-7475
Brillacademic Publishers Inc
2 liberty Sq 11th Fl .... Boston MA 02109 800-337-9255 617-263-2323
Browntrout Publishers Inc
201 Continental Blvd .... El Segundo CA 90245 800-777-7812 310-607-9010
Catholic News Publishing Co
420 Railroad Way .... Mamaroneck NY 10543 800-433-7771
Cengage Learning
PO Box 6904 .... Florence KY 41022 800-354-9706
Charles C Thomas Publisher
2600 S First St .... Springfield IL 62704 800-258-8980* 217-789-8980
*Sales
Children's Press
557 Broadway .... New York NY 10012 800-724-6527
Chronicle Books
680 Second St .... San Francisco CA 94107 800-722-6657 415-537-4200
Commemorative Brands Inc
7211 Cir S Rd .... Austin TX 78745 800-225-3687
Corwin Press Inc
2455 Teller Rd .... Thousand Oaks CA 91320 800-233-9936*
*Orders
CPP Inc 185 N Wolfe Rd .... Sunnyvale CA 94086 800-624-1765 650-969-8901
CRC Press LLC
6000 Broken Sound Pkwy NW Ste 300 .... Boca Raton FL 33487 800-272-7737* 561-994-0555
*Cust Svc
Creative Communications For The Parish Inc
1564 Fencorp Dr .... Fenton MO 63026 800-325-9414 636-305-9777
Cruising Gide Publications Inc
1130 Pinehurst Rd Ste B .... Dunedin FL 34698 800-330-9542 727-733-5322
Curriculum Assoc Inc
153 Rangeway Rd .... North Billerica MA 01862 800-225-0248
D&B 103 JFK Pkwy .... Short Hills NJ 07078 800-234-3867 973-921-5500
NYSE: DNB
Disney Consumer Products
500 S Buena Vista St .... Burbank CA 91521 855-553-4763* 818-560-1000
*PR
Dorling Kindersley Ltd
375 Hudson St .... New York NY 10014 800-631-8571* 646-674-4047
*Cust Svc
Educators Publishing Service Inc (EPS)
PO Box 9031 .... Cambridge MA 02139 800-225-5750
EMC School
875 Montreal Way .... Saint Paul MN 55102 800-328-1452 651-290-2800
Encyclopaedia Britannica Inc
331 N La Salle St .... Chicago IL 60654 800-323-1229 312-347-7159
FA Davis Co
1915 Arch St .... Philadelphia PA 19103 800-323-3555 215-568-2270
Financial Publishing Co
PO Box 570 .... South Bend IN 46624 800-433-0090* 574-243-6040
*Cust Svc
Forbes Inc 60 Fifth Ave .... New York NY 10011 800-295-0893 212-620-2200
Free Spirit Publishing Inc
217 Fifth Ave N Ste 200 .... Minneapolis MN 55401 800-735-7323 612-338-2068
Gale Cengage Learning
27500 Drake Rd .... Farmington Hills MI 48331 800-877-4253* 248-699-4253
*Cust Svc
Glencoe/McGraw-Hill
8787 Orion Pl .... Columbus OH 43240 800-848-1567
Good Will Publishers Inc
PO Box 269 .... Gastonia NC 28052 800-219-4663 704-865-1256
Goodheart-Willcox Publisher
18604 W Creek Dr .... Tinley Park IL 60477 800-323-0440 708-687-5000
Government Research Service
1516 SW Boswell Ave .... Topeka KS 66604 800-346-6898 785-232-7720
Grey House Publishing
4919 Rt 22 PO Box 56 .... Amenia NY 12501 800-562-2139 518-789-8700
Hachette Book Group
237 Park Ave .... New York NY 10017 800-759-0190
Harlequin
233 Broadway Ste 1001 .... New York NY 10279 800-873-8635 212-553-4200
Health Communications Inc (HCI)
3201 SW 15th St .... Deerfield Beach FL 33442 800-441-5569* 954-360-0909
*Cust Svc
Heinemann 361 Hanover St .... Portsmouth NH 03801 800-541-2086 603-431-7894
Houghton Mifflin Harcourt
222 Berkeley St .... Boston MA 02116 800-225-5425
Human Kinetics
1607 N Market St .... Champaign IL 61820 800-747-4457 217-351-5076
Inner Traditions International
1 Park St .... Rochester VT 05767 800-246-8648 802-767-3174
iUniverse
1663 Liberty Dr .... Bloomington IN 47403 800-288-4677 812-330-2909
Jeppesen Sanderson Inc
55 Inverness Dr E .... Englewood CO 80112 800-353-2107 303-799-9090
John Wiley & Sons Inc
111 River St .... Hoboken NJ 07030 800-225-5945* 201-748-6000
NYSE: JWA ■ *Sales
Judaica Press Inc
123 Ditmas Ave .... Brooklyn NY 11218 800-972-6201 718-972-6200
Kendall/Hunt Publishing Co
4050 Westmark Dr PO Box 1840 .... Dubuque IA 52002 800-228-0810* 563-589-1000
*Cust Svc

Kensington Publishing Corp
119 W 40th St .... New York NY 10018 800-221-2647 212-832-3753
Key Curriculum Press
1150 65th St .... Emeryville CA 94608 800-338-3987 510-595-7000
Lawyers Diary & Manual
890 Mtn Ave Ste 300 .... New Providence NJ 07974 800-444-4041 973-642-1440
Leadership Connect
1407 Broadway Ste 318 .... New York NY 10011 800-627-0311 212-627-4140
Lerner Publishing Group
1251 Washington Ave N .... Minneapolis MN 55401 800-328-4929
LexisNexis Matthew Bender
744 Broad St .... Newark NJ 07102 800-252-9257 973-820-2000
Linden Publishing
2006 S Mary St .... Fresno CA 93721 800-345-4447* 559-233-6633
*Sales
Little Brown & Co
237 Park Ave .... New York NY 10017 800-759-0190* 212-364-1100
*Cust Svc
Llewellyn Worldwide Inc
2143 Wooddale Dr .... Woodbury MN 55125 800-843-6666 651-291-1970
Lonely Planet Publications
50 Linden St .... Oakland CA 94607 800-275-8555 510-893-8555
LRP Publications
360 Hiatt Dr .... Palm Beach Gardens FL 33418 800-621-5463 561-622-6520
Marquis Who's Who
100 Connell Dr Ste 2300 .... Berkeley Heights NJ 07922 800-473-7020 908-673-1000
McFarland & Company Inc
960 NC Hwy 88 W PO Box 611 .... Jefferson NC 28640 800-253-2187 336-246-4460
McGraw-Hill Higher Education Group
1333 Burr Ridge Pkwy .... Burr Ridge IL 60527 800-634-3963 630-789-4000
McGraw-Hill Professional Publishing Group
2 Penn Plz 9th Fl .... New York NY 10121 877-833-5524
Mel Bay Publications Inc
1734 Gilsinn Ln .... Fenton MO 63026 800-863-5229 636-257-3970
Midwest Plan Service
122 Davidson Hall ISU .... Ames IA 50011 800-562-3618 515-294-4337
Mike Murach & Assoc Inc
4340 N Knoll .... Fresno CA 93722 800-221-5528 559-440-9071
National Academy Press
500 Fifth St NW .... Washington DC 20001 800-624-6242 202-334-3313
National Braille Press Inc
88 St Stephen St .... Boston MA 02115 888-965-8965 617-266-6160
National Underwriter Co
4157 Olympic Blvd Ste 225 .... Erlanger KY 41018 800-543-0874
New Generation Research Inc
225 Friend St Ste 801 .... Boston MA 02114 800-468-3810 617-573-9550
New Readers Press
101 Wyoming St .... Syracuse NY 13204 800-448-8878
Nightingale-Conant Corp
6245 W Howard St .... Niles IL 60714 800-557-1660*
*Cust Svc
No Starch Press Inc
38 Ringold St .... San Francisco CA 94103 800-420-7240 415-863-9900
Nolocom 950 Parker St .... Berkeley CA 94710 800-728-3555
Omnigraphics Inc
PO Box 31-1640 .... Detroit MI 48231 800-234-1340
Open Court Publishing Co
70 E Lake St Ste 800 .... Chicago IL 60601 800-815-2280
Pearson Education School Div
1900 E Lake Ave .... Glenview IL 60025 800-348-4474
Penguin Group (USA) Inc
375 Hudson St .... New York NY 10014 800-847-5515* 212-366-2000
*Sales
Penguin Random House
1745 Broadway .... New York NY 10019 800-733-3000 212-782-9000
Peter Lang Publishing Inc
29 Broadway .... New York NY 10006 800-770-5264 212-647-7706
Price Books & Forms Inc
531 E Sierra Madre Ave .... Glendora CA 91741 800-423-8961 909-594-8942
Publications International Ltd
7373 N Cicero Ave .... Lincolnwood IL 60712 800-777-5582* 847-676-3470
*General
Rand McNally
9855 Woods Dr PO Box 7600 .... Skokie IL 60077 800-333-0136
Rosen Publishing Group Inc, The
29 E 21st St .... New York NY 10010 800-237-9932
Rowman & Littlefield Publishers Inc
4501 Forbes Blvd Ste 200 .... Lanham MD 20706 800-462-6420 301-459-3366
RR Bowker LLC
630 Central Ave .... New Providence NJ 07974 888-269-5372 908-795-3500
Sage Publications Inc
2455 Teller Rd .... Thousand Oaks CA 91320 800-818-7243 805-499-9774
Sams Technical Publishing
9850 E 30th St .... Indianapolis IN 46229 800-428-7267*
*Cust Svc
Santillana USA Publishing Co
2023 NW 84th Ave .... Doral FL 33122 800-245-8584 305-591-9522
School Annual Publishing Co
2568 Park Ctr Blvd .... State College PA 16801 800-436-6030
Slack Inc 6900 Grove Rd .... Thorofare NJ 08086 800-257-8290 856-848-1000
Sourcebooks Inc
1935 Brookdale Rd Ste 139 .... Naperville IL 60563 800-432-7444 630-961-3900
Standard & Poor's Corp
55 Water St .... New York NY 10041 877-772-5436 212-438-1000
Sterling Publishing Company Inc
1166 Avenue of the Americas 17th Fl .... New York NY 10036 800-367-9692* 212-532-7160
*Cust Svc
Storey Publishing LLC
210 Mass Moca Way .... North Adams MA 01247 800-827-7444 413-346-2100
Sunset Publishing Corp
80 Willow Rd .... Menlo Park CA 94025 800-777-0117 650-321-3600
Taylor & Francis Group
6000 Broken Sound Pkwy NW Ste 300 .... Boca Raton FL 33487 877-622-5543 207-017-6000
Technology Marketing Corp
1 Technology Plz .... Norwalk CT 06854 800-243-6002* 203-852-6800
Thomas Publishing Co
5 Penn Plz .... New York NY 10001 800-733-1127 212-695-0500

				Toll-Free	Phone

Townsend Press
439 Kelley Dr .... West Berlin NJ 08091 **800-772-6410** 856-753-0554
Triumph Learning
136 Madison Ave .... New York NY 10016 **800-338-6519** 800-586-9940
Tuttle Publishing
364 Innovation Dr .... North Clarendon VT 05759 **800-526-2778*** 802-773-8930
*Sales
University Press of America
4501 Forbes Blvd Ste 200 .... Lanham MD 20706 **800-462-6420** 301-459-3366
Walch Education
40 Walch Dr .... Portland ME 04103 **800-558-2846** 207-772-2846
Walsworth Publishing Co
306 N Kansas Ave .... Marceline MO 64658 **800-972-4968** 660-376-3543
West Group 610 Opperman Dr .... Eagan MN 55123 **800-328-4880*** 651-687-7000
*Cust Svc
Wheatmark Inc
2030 E Speedway Blvd Ste 106 .... Tucson AZ 85719 **888-934-0888** 520-798-0888
Wilderness Press
c/o Keen Communications 2204 First Ave S
Ste 102 .... Birmingham AL 35233 **800-443-7227**
Wiley Publishing Inc
111 River St .... Hoboken NJ 07030 **800-225-5945** 201-748-6000
William H Sadlier Inc
9 Pine St .... New York NY 10005 **800-221-5175**
OTC: SADL
William Morrow & Co
10 E 53rd St .... New York NY 10022 **800-242-7737** 212-207-7000
William S Hein & Company Inc
1285 Main St .... Buffalo NY 14209 **800-828-7571** 716-882-2600
Wimmer Cookbooks
4650 Shelby Air Dr .... Memphis TN 38118 **800-548-2537**
Workman Publishing
225 Varick St .... New York NY 10014 **800-722-7202** 212-254-5900
World Book Inc
180 N LaSalle St Ste 900 .... Chicago IL 60601 **800-967-5325** 312-729-5800
WW Norton & Company Inc
500 Fifth Ave .... New York NY 10110 **800-233-4830** 212-354-5500
Zaner-Bloser Inc
1201 Dublin Rd .... Columbus OH 43215 **800-421-3018** 614-486-0221
Zebra Books
Kensington Publishing Corp
119 West 40th St .... New York NY 10018 **800-221-2647** 212-407-1500

633-3 Book Publishers - Religious & Spiritual Books

				Toll-Free	Phone

Augsburg Fortress
PO Box 1209 .... Minneapolis MN 55440 **800-328-4648** 612-330-3300
Baker Book House Company Inc
6030 E Fulton St .... Ada MI 49301 **800-877-2665*** 616-676-9185
*Orders
Baker Book House Company Inc Revell Div
6030 E Fulton St .... Ada MI 49301 **800-877-2665*** 616-676-9185
*Orders
Bethany House Publishers
11400 Hampshire Ave S .... Bloomington MN 55438 **800-328-6109** 616-676-9185
Brethren Press
1451 Dundee Ave .... Elgin IL 60120 **800-441-3712**
Broadman & Holman Publishers
127 Ninth Ave N MSN 114 .... Nashville TN 37234 **800-448-8032**
Concordia Publishing House Inc
3558 S Jefferson Ave .... Saint Louis MO 63118 **800-325-3040*** 314-268-1000
*Cust Svc
Deseret Book Co
45 W S Temple .... Salt Lake City UT 84101 **800-453-4532** 801-534-1515
Gospel Light Publications
1957 Eastman Ave .... Ventura CA 93003 **800-446-7735** 805-644-9721
Hay House Inc PO Box 5100 .... Carlsbad CA 92018 **800-654-5126** 760-431-7695
Jewish Publication Society
2100 Arch St .... Philadelphia PA 19103 **800-234-3151** 215-832-0600
New Leaf Publishing Group
PO Box 726 .... Green Forest AR 72638 **800-999-3777** 870-438-5288
New World Library
14 Pamaron Way .... Novato CA 94949 **800-972-6657** 415-884-2100
Northwestern Publishing House
1250 N 113th St .... Milwaukee WI 53226 **800-662-6022***
*Orders
Oregon Catholic Press (OCP)
5536 NE Hassalo St .... Portland OR 97213 **877-596-1653** 503-281-1191
Our Sunday Visitor Inc
200 Noll Plz .... Huntington IN 46750 **800-348-2440** 260-356-8400
Pauline Books & Media
50 St Paul's Ave .... Boston MA 02130 **800-876-4463*** 617-522-8911
*Sales
Review & Herald Publishing Assn
55 W Oak Ridge Dr .... Hagerstown MD 21740 **800-456-3991** 301-393-3000
Standard Publishing Co
4050 Lee Vance Dr .... Colorado Springs CO 80918 **800-323-7543**
Standex International Corp Consumer Group
11 Keewaydin Dr .... Salem NH 03079 **800-514-5275** 603-893-9701
NYSE: SXI
Thomas Nelson Inc
501 Nelson Pl PO Box 141000 .... Nashville TN 37214 **800-251-4000**
Tyndale House Publishers Inc
351 Executive Dr .... Carol Stream IL 60188 **800-323-9400**
United Methodist Publishing House
201 Eigth Ave S .... Nashville TN 37203 **800-672-1789** 615-749-6000
Whitaker House/Anchor Distributors
1030 Hunt Vly Cir .... New Kensington PA 15068 **800-444-4484*** 724-334-7000
*General

633-4 Book Publishers - University Presses

				Toll-Free	Phone

Columbia University Press
615 W 131st St .... New York NY 10027 **800-944-8648** 212-459-0600

Cornell University Press
512 E State St .... Ithaca NY 14850 **800-666-2211*** 607-277-2338
*Sales
Duke University Press
905 W Main St Ste 18-B .... Durham NC 27701 **888-651-0122*** 919-687-3600
*Cust Svc
Harvard Business School Publishing
60 Harvard Way .... Boston MA 02163 **800-795-5200**
Harvard University Press
79 Garden St .... Cambridge MA 02138 **800-405-1619** 617-495-2600
Indiana University Press
601 N Morton St .... Bloomington IN 47404 **800-842-6796** 812-855-8817
Johns Hopkins University Press
2715 N Charles St .... Baltimore MD 21218 **800-537-5487*** 410-516-6900
*Orders
MIT Press, The
1 Rogers St .... Cambridge MA 02142 **800-405-1619** 617-253-5646
Naval Institute Press
291 Wood Rd .... Annapolis MD 21402 **800-233-8764** 410-268-6110
Oregon State University Press
1500 Jefferson St .... Corvallis OR 97331 **800-426-3797*** 541-737-3166
Pennsylvania State University Press
820 N University Dr
USB1 Ste C .... University Park PA 16802 **800-326-9180** 814-865-1327
Princeton University Press
41 William St .... Princeton NJ 08540 **800-777-4726** 609-258-4900
Purdue University Press
504 W State St Stewart Ctr 370
.... West Lafayette IN 47907 **800-247-6553*** 765-494-4600
*Orders
Rutgers University Press
106 Somerset St 3rd Fl. .... New Brunswick NJ 08901 **800-848-6224** 848-445-7762
State University of New York Press (SUNY)
22 Corporate Woods 3rd Fl .... Albany NY 12211 **866-430-7869** 518-472-5000
Texas A & M University Press
John H Lindsey Bldg 4354 TAMU
.... College Station TX 77843 **800-826-8911*** 979-845-1436
*Orders
Texas Tech University Press
608 N Knoxville Ave Ste120
Grantham Bldg .... Lubbock TX 79415 **800-832-4042** 806-742-2982
University of Alaska Press
1760 Wwood Wy PO Box 756240 .... Fairbanks AK 99709 **888-252-6657** 907-474-5831
University of California Press
2120 Berkeley Way .... Berkeley CA 94704 **800-343-4499**
University of Chicago Press
1427 E 60th St .... Chicago IL 60637 **800-621-2736*** 773-702-1234
*Sales
University of Hawaii Press
2840 Kolowalu St .... Honolulu HI 96822 **888-847-7377** 808-956-8255
University of Illinois Press
1325 S Oak St .... Champaign IL 61820 **866-244-0626** 217-333-0950
University of Massachusetts Press
671 N Pleasant St .... Amherst MA 01003 **800-562-0112** 413-545-2217
University of Michigan Press
839 Greene St .... Ann Arbor MI 48104 **866-804-0002** 734-764-4388
University of North Carolina Press
116 S Boundary St .... Chapel Hill NC 27514 **800-848-6224** 919-966-3561
University of North Texas Press
1155 Union Cir Ste 311336 .... Denton TX 76203 **800-826-8911** 940-565-2142
University of Pennsylvania Press
3902 Spruce St .... Philadelphia PA 19104 **800-537-5487*** 215-898-6261
*Cust Svc
University of South Carolina Press
1600 Hampton St 5th Fl .... Columbia SC 29208 **800-768-2500*** 803-777-5243
*Orders
University of Texas Press
3001 Lake Austin Blvd 2-200 Stop E4800 .... Austin TX 78703 **800-252-3206*** 512-471-7233
*Sales
University of Virginia Press
210 Sprigg Ln PO Box 400318 .... Charlottesville VA 22904 **800-831-3406*** 434-924-3469
*Orders
University Press of Florida
15 NW 15th St .... Gainesville FL 32603 **800-226-3822*** 352-392-1351
*Sales
University Press of Kentucky
663 S Limestone St .... Lexington KY 40508 **800-537-5487*** 859-257-8400
*Sales
University Press of Mississippi
3825 Ridgewood Rd .... Jackson MS 39211 **800-737-7788** 601-432-6205
University Press of New England (UPNE)
1 Ct St Ste 250 .... Lebanon NH 03766 **800-421-1561*** 603-448-1533
*Orders
Vanderbilt University Press
2014 Broadway .... Nashville TN 37203 **800-627-7377** 615-322-3585
Wesleyan University Press
215 Long Ln .... Middletown CT 06459 **800-421-1561** 860-685-7711

633-5 Comic Book Publishers

				Toll-Free	Phone

Dark Horse Comics Inc
10956 SE Main St .... Milwaukie OR 97222 **800-862-0052** 503-652-8815
Diamond Comic Distributors Inc (DCD)
10150 York Rd Ste 300 .... Hunt Valley MD 21030 **800-452-6642** 443-318-8001
Fantagraphics Books
7563 Lake City Way NE .... Seattle WA 98115 **800-657-1100** 206-524-1967

633-6 Directory Publishers

				Toll-Free	Phone

ASD Data Services LLC
PO Box 1184 .... Manchester TN 37349 **877-742-7297** 931-723-0204
Bresser's Cross Index Directory Co
684 W Baltimore St .... Detroit MI 48202 **800-995-0570** 313-874-0570

Classified Section

Publishing Companies (Cont'd)

Company / Address	City	State	ZIP	Toll-Free	Phone
BurrellesLuce — 30 B Vreeland Rd PO Box 674	Florham Park	NJ	07932	800-631-1160	973-992-6600
Chain Store Guide — 10117 Princess Palm Ave Ste 375	Tampa	FL	33610	800-927-9292	
Cincinnati Bell Directory (CBD) — 312 Plum St Ste 600	Cincinnati	OH	45202	800-877-0475	
Cision US Inc — 130 E Randolph St 7th Fl	Chicago	IL	60601	800-588-3827	312-922-2400
Cole Information Services — 17041 Lakeside Hills Plz Ste 2	Omaha	NE	68130	800-283-2855*	
*Consumer Info					
Contractors Register Inc — 800 E Main St	Jefferson Valley	NY	10535	800-431-2584	914-245-0200
DAG Media Inc — 125-10 Queens Blvd Ste 14	Kew Gardens	NY	11415	800-261-2799	718-263-8454
Haines & Company Inc — 8050 Freedom Ave	North Canton	OH	44720	800-843-8452	
Hoover's Inc — 5800 Airport Blvd	Austin	TX	78752	800-486-8666	512-374-4500
Marc Publishing Co — 600 Germantown Pk	Lafayette Hill	PA	19444	800-432-5478	610-834-8585
Martindale-Hubbell — 121 Chanlon Rd Ste 110	New Providence	NJ	07974	800-526-4902	
Rasansky Law Firm — 2525 McKinnon Ave Ste 550	Dallas	TX	75201	877-405-4313	214-651-6100
OTC: ATTY					
Stewart Directories Inc — 50314 Kings Point Dr PO Box 326	Frisco	NC	27936	800-311-0786	
Valley Yellow Pages — 1850 N Gateway Blvd	Fresno	CA	93727	800-350-8887	559-251-8888
Van Dam Inc — The VanDam Bldg 121 W 27 St	New York	NY	10011	800-863-6537	212-929-0416
World Chamber of Commerce Directory Inc — 446 E 29th St Ste 1029	Loveland	CO	80538	888-883-3231	970-663-3231

633-7 Music Publishers

Company / Address	City	State	ZIP	Toll-Free	Phone
eMedia Music Corp — 664 NE Northlake Way	Seattle	WA	98105	888-363-3424	206-329-5657
Hal Leonard Corp — 960 E Mark St	Winona	MN	55987	800-321-3408	507-454-2920
Lorenz Corp 501 E Third St	Dayton	OH	45402	800-444-1144	
Malaco Music Group Inc — 3023 W Northside Dr	Jackson	MS	39213	800-272-7936*	601-982-4522
*Cust Svc					
Mel Bay Publications Inc — 1734 Gilsinn Ln	Fenton	MO	63026	800-863-5229	636-257-3970
Theodore Presser Co — 588 North Gulph Rd	King of Prussia	PA	19406	800-854-6764	610-592-1222

633-8 Newspaper Publishers

Company / Address	City	State	ZIP	Toll-Free	Phone
Afro-American Newspapers Co — 2519 N Charles St	Baltimore	MD	21218	800-237-6892	410-554-8200
Alameda Times-Star — 7677 Oakport St	Oakland	CA	94621	866-225-5277	510-208-6300
Auburn Publishers Inc — 25 Dill St	Auburn	NY	13021	800-878-5311	315-253-5311
BMH Books — 1104 Kings Hwy PO Box 544	Winona Lake	IN	46590	800-348-2756	
Burlington Hawk Eye Co — 800 S Main St PO Box 10	Burlington	IA	52601	800-397-1708	319-754-8461
Capital City Press Inc — PO Box 588	Baton Rouge	LA	70821	800-960-6397	225-383-1111
Christian Science Publishing Society — 210 Massachusetts Ave P02-15	Boston	MA	02115	800-456-2220	617-450-2300
Daily Globe, The — 118 E McLeod Ave PO Box 548	Ironwood	MI	49938	800-236-2887	906-932-2211
Daily Progress — 685 W Rio Rd	Charlottesville	VA	22901	866-469-4866	434-978-7200
Day Publishing Co — 47 Eugene O'Neill Dr	New London	CT	06320	800-542-3354	860-442-2200
Delphos Herald Inc — 405 N Main St	Delphos	OH	45833	800-589-6950	419-695-0015
Denver Newspaper Agency — 101 W Colfax Ave	Denver	CO	80202	800-336-7678	303-954-1010
Derrick Publishing Co — 1510 W First St	Oil City	PA	16301	800-352-1002	814-676-7444
Detroit Legal News Co — 1409 Allen Rd Ste B	Troy	MI	48083	800-875-5275	248-577-6100
Diocese of Steubenville Catholic Charities — PO Box 969	Steubenville	OH	43952	800-339-7890	740-282-3631
East Hampton Star Inc, The — 153 Main St PO Box 5002	East Hampton	NY	11937	844-324-0777	631-324-0002
Express-News Corp — PO Box 2171	San Antonio	TX	78297	800-555-1551	210-250-3000
Finger Lakes Times — 218 Genesse St	Geneva	NY	14456	800-388-6652	315-789-3333
Fort Wayne Newspapers Inc — 600 W Main St	Fort Wayne	IN	46802	800-444-3303	260-461-8444
Galesburg Printing & Publishing Co — 140 S Prairie St	Galesburg	IL	61401	800-733-2767	309-343-7181
GateHouse Media Inc — 350 Willowbrook Office Pk	Fairport	NY	14450	800-544-9218	585-598-0030
NYSE: GHSE					
Guard Publishing Co — PO Box 10188	Eugene	OR	97440	800-377-7428	541-485-1234
Hastings & Sons Publishing — 38 Exchange St	Lynn	MA	01901	800-243-4636	781-593-7700
Herald Publishing Co — PO Box 153	Houston	TX	77001	888-421-1866	713-630-0391
Herald-Mail Co, The — 100 Summit Ave PO Box 439	Hagerstown	MD	21741	800-626-6397	301-733-5123
Herald-Star — 401 Herald Sq	Steubenville	OH	43952	800-526-7987	740-283-4711
Herald-Times Inc — PO Box 909	Bloomington	IN	47402	800-422-0070	812-332-4401
Hersam Acorn Newspapers — 16 Bailey Ave	Ridgefield	CT	06877	800-372-2790	203-438-6544
High Plains Publishers Inc — 1500 W Wyatt Earp Blvd	Dodge City	KS	67801	800-452-7171	620-227-7171
Home News Enterprises — 333 Second St	Columbus	IN	47201	800-876-7811	
Huse Publishing Co — 525 Norfolk Ave	Norfolk	NE	68701	877-371-1020	402-371-1020
Isanti County News — 234 S Main St	Cambridge	MN	55008	800-927-9233	763-689-1981
Journal & Topics Newspapers — 622 Graceland Ave	Des Plaines	IL	60016	800-719-4881	847-299-5511
Journal Publishing Co — 1242 S Green St	Tupelo	MS	38804	800-264-6397	662-842-2611
Keene Publishing Corp — PO Box 546	Keene	NH	03431	800-765-9994	603-352-1234
Knight Publishing Co — 600 S Tryon St	Charlotte	NC	28202	800-332-0686	704-358-5000
Landmark Community Newspapers Inc — 601 Taylorsville Rd	Shelbyville	KY	40065	800-939-9322	502-633-4334
Lawrence Journal-World — 645 New Hampshire PO Box 888	Lawrence	KS	66044	800-578-8748	785-843-1000
Lee Publications Inc — 6113 State Hwy 5	Palatine Bridge	NY	13428	800-836-2888	518-673-3237
Livingston County Daily Press & Argus — 323 E Grand River Ave	Howell	MI	48843	888-999-1288	517-548-2000
Lowell Sun Publishing Co — 491 Dutton St	Lowell	MA	01854	800-359-1300*	978-458-7100
*Cust Svc					
Madison — 1901 Fish Hatchery Rd PO Box 8056	Madison	WI	53713	800-362-8333*	608-252-6200
*Sales					
Magic Valley Newspapers — 132 Fairfield St W	Twin Falls	ID	83301	800-658-3883	208-733-0931
McClatchy Newspapers — 2100 Q St	Sacramento	CA	95816	866-807-2200	916-321-1000
Meridian Star Inc — 814 22nd Ave	Meridian	MS	39301	800-232-2525*	601-693-1551
*Cust Svc					
MetroActive Publishing Inc — 550 S First St	San Jose	CA	95113	800-831-2345	408-298-8000
Mid-America Publishing Corp — 9 Second St NW	Hampton	IA	50441	800-558-1244	641-456-2585
Missourian Publishing Co — 14 W Main St	Washington	MO	63090	888-239-7701	636-239-7701
Moline Dispatch Publishing Co — 1720 Fifth Ave	Moline	IL	61265	800-660-2472	309-764-4344
Morris Communications Company LLC — 725 Broad St	Augusta	GA	30901	800-622-6358	706-724-0851
News-Herald, The — 1 Heritage Dr Ste 100	Southgate	MI	48195	888-361-6769	734-246-0800
Northwest Herald Inc — PO Box 250	Crystal Lake	IL	60039	800-589-8910	815-459-4040
Oakland Press — 2125 Butterfield Dr Ste 102N	Troy	MI	48084	888-977-3677	248-332-8181
Oshkosh Northwestern Co — 224 State St	Oshkosh	WI	54901	800-924-6168	920-235-7700
Our Sunday Visitor Inc — 200 Noll Plz	Huntington	IN	46750	800-348-2440	260-356-8400
Palm Beach Newspapers Inc — PO Box 24700	West Palm Beach	FL	33416	800-432-7595	561-820-4100
Papers Inc 206 S Main St	Milford	IN	46542	800-733-4111	574-658-4111
PG Publishing Co — 34 Blvd of the Allies	Pittsburgh	PA	15222	800-228-6397*	412-263-1100
*Cust Svc					
Pipestone Publishing Co — PO Box 277	Pipestone	MN	56164	800-325-6440	507-825-3333
Press-Enterprise Inc — 3185 Lackawanna Ave	Bloomsburg	PA	17815	888-484-6345	570-387-1234
Princeton Packet, The — 300 Witherspoon St PO Box 350	Princeton	NJ	08542	888-747-1122	609-924-3244
Progressive Communications Corp — 18 E Vine St	Mount Vernon	OH	43050	800-772-5333	740-397-5333
Quincy Newspapers Inc — 130 S Fifth St	Quincy	IL	62301	800-373-9444	217-223-5100
Republican-American Inc — 389 Meadow St	Waterbury	CT	06702	800-992-3232	203-574-3636
Richmond Times-Dispatch — PO Box 85333	Richmond	VA	23293	800-468-3382	804-649-6000
Rivertown Newspaper Group — 2760 N Service Dr PO Box 15	Red Wing	MN	55066	800-535-1660	651-388-8235
San Angelo Standard Times Inc — 34 W Harris	San Angelo	TX	76901	800-588-1884	325-659-8100
Santa Barbara News-Press Publishing Co — 715 Anacapa St	Santa Barbara	CA	93101	800-654-3292	805-564-5200
Stonebridge Press Inc — 25 Elm St	Southbridge	MA	01550	800-536-5836	508-764-4325
Suburban Life Publications — 1101 W 31st St Ste 100	Downers Grove	IL	60515	800-397-9397	630-368-1100
Telegramcom — 100 Front St 5th Fl	Worcester	MA	01608	800-678-6680	508-793-9100
Tennessee Valley Printing Company Inc — PO Box 2213	Decatur	AL	35609	888-353-4612	256-353-4612
This Week Community Newspapers — 7801 N Central Dr PO Box 608	Lewis Center	OH	43035	888-837-4342	740-888-6000
Times Herald Inc — 639 S Chester Rd PO Box 591	Swarthmore	PA	19081	888-933-4233	610-272-2500
Times-Citizen Communications Inc — 406 Stevens St PO Box 640	Iowa Falls	IA	50126	800-798-2691	641-648-2521
Times-News, The — 707 S Main St	Burlington	NC	27215	800-488-0085	336-227-0131
Tribune Review Publishing Co — 622 Cabin Hill Dr	Greensburg	PA	15601	800-524-5700	724-834-1151

	Toll-Free	Phone
Western Communications Inc 1777 Chandler Ave ....Bend OR 97702	800-503-3933	541-382-1811
Western States Weeklies Inc PO Box 600600 ....San Diego CA 92160	800-628-9466	619-280-2985
World Publishing Co 315 S Boulder Ave ....Tulsa OK 74103	800-444-6552	918-583-2161
Yankton Press & Dakotan 319 Walnut St PO Box 56 ....Yankton SD 57078	800-743-2968	605-665-7811

633-9 Periodicals Publishers

	Toll-Free	Phone
Access Intelligence LLC 4 Choke Cherry Rd 2nd Fl ....Rockville MD 20850	800-777-5006	301-354-2000
Advertising Specialties Institute 4800 St Rd ....Trevose PA 19053	800-546-1350	215-942-8600
American Lawyer Media Inc (ALM) 120 Broadway 5th Fl ....New York NY 10271	877-256-2472	212-457-9400
American Psychiatric Publishing Inc 1000 Wilson Blvd Ste 1825 ....Arlington VA 22209	800-368-5777	703-907-7322
Amos Press Inc 911 S Vandemark Rd ....Sidney OH 45365	866-468-1622	937-498-2111
Annual Reviews 4139 El Camino Way ....Palo Alto CA 94306	800-523-8635	650-493-4400
APN Media LLC PO Box 20113 ....New York NY 10023	800-470-7599	212-581-3380
Atlantic Information Services Inc 1100 17th St NW Ste 300 ....Washington DC 20036	800-521-4323	202-775-9008
Augsburg Fortress PO Box 1209 ....Minneapolis MN 55440	800-328-4648	612-330-3300
BCC Research LLC 49 Walnut Pk Bldg 2 ....Wellesley MA 02481	866-285-7215	781-489-7301
Bottom Line Inc 3 Landmark Sq Ste 201 ....Stamford CT 06901	800-274-5611	203-973-5900
Business & Legal Reports Inc (BLR) 141 Mill Rock Rd E ....Old Saybrook CT 06475	800-727-5257	860-510-0100
Business News Publishing Co 2401 W Big Beaver Rd Ste 700 ....Troy MI 48084	800-837-7370	248-362-3700
Cambridge Whos Who Publishing Inc 498 RXR Plz ....Uniondale NY 11556	866-933-1555	516-535-1515
Challenge Publications Inc 21835 Nordhoff St ....Chatsworth CA 91311	800-562-9182	818-700-6868
Christianity Today International 465 Gundersen Dr ....Carol Stream IL 60188	800-222-1840	630-260-6200
Commodity Information Systems Inc 3030 NW Expy Ste 725 ....Oklahoma City OK 73112	800-231-0477	405-604-8726
Consumers Union of US Inc 101 Truman Ave ....Yonkers NY 10703	800-927-4357	914-378-2000
Crain Communications Inc 1155 Gratiot Ave ....Detroit MI 48207	888-288-6954	313-446-6000
CRC Press LLC 6000 Broken Sound Pkwy NW Ste 300 ....Boca Raton FL 33487 *Cust Svc	800-272-7737*	561-994-0555
Deal, The 14 Wall St 15th Fl ....New York NY 10005 *Cust Svc	888-667-3325*	
Disney Consumer Products 500 S Buena Vista St ....Burbank CA 91521 *PR	855-553-4763*	818-560-1000
Earl G Graves Ltd 130 Fifth Ave 10th Fl ....New York NY 10011 *Cust Svc	800-727-7777*	212-242-8000
Elliott Wave International (EWI) PO Box 1618 ....Gainesville GA 30503 *Cust Svc	800-336-1618*	770-536-0309
Elsevier Science Ltd 360 Park Ave S ....New York NY 10010	888-437-4636	212-989-5800
Entrepreneur Media Inc 18061 Fitch ....Irvine CA 92614	800-779-5295	949-261-2325
Ernst Publishing Co LLC 1 Commerce Plz 99 Washington Ave Ste 309 ....Albany NY 12210	800-345-3822	
Essence Communications Inc 241 37th St 4th Fl ....Brooklyn NY 11232 *Sales	800-274-9398*	
Euromoney Institutional Investor PLC 225 Park Ave S ....New York NY 10003	800-715-9197	212-224-3300
F+W, A Content + eCommerce Co 10151 Carver Rd Ste 300 ....Cincinnati OH 45242 *Sales	800-289-0963*	513-531-2690
Forbes Inc 60 Fifth Ave ....New York NY 10011	800-295-0893	212-620-2200
Forecast International 22 Commerce Rd ....Newtown CT 06470	800-451-4975	203-426-0800
Forum Publishing Co 383 E Main St ....Centerport NY 11721	800-635-7654	631-754-5000
Gardner Publications Inc 6915 Valley Ave ....Cincinnati OH 45244	800-950-8020	513-527-8800
Grand View Media Group Inc (GVMG) 200 Croft St Ste 1 ....Birmingham AL 35242	888-431-2877	205-262-4600
Hanley-Wood LLC 1 Thomas Cir NW Ste 600 ....Washington DC 20005	800-227-8839	202-452-0800
Hart Publications Inc 1616 S Voss Rd Ste 1000 ....Houston TX 77057	800-874-2544	713-260-6400
Hatton Brown Publishers Inc PO Box 2268 ....Montgomery AL 36102	800-669-5613	334-834-1170
Health Forum 155 N Wacker Dr Ste 400 ....Chicago IL 60606	800-821-2039	312-893-6800
Healthy Directions LLC 7811 Montrose Rd ....Potomac MD 20854	866-599-9491	
Highlights for Children Inc 1800 Watermark Dr ....Columbus OH 43216 *Cust Svc	800-255-9517*	614-486-0631
Hli Properties Inc 1003 Central Ave ....Fort Dodge IA 50501	800-247-2000	515-955-1600
Homes & Land Magazine Affiliates LLC 1830 E Park Ave ....Tallahassee FL 32301	800-277-7800	850-701-2300
Honolulu Publishing Co Ltd 707 Richards St Ste PH3 ....Honolulu HI 96813	800-272-5245	808-524-7400
IEEE Computer Society Press 10662 Los Vaqueros Cir PO Box 3014 ....Los Alamitos CA 90720	800-272-6657	714-821-8380
Inside Washington Publishers 1919 S Eads St Ste 201 ....Arlington VA 22202	800-424-9068	703-416-8500
International Data Group Inc (IDG) 492 Old Connecticut Path PO Box 9208 ....Framingham MA 01701 *Orders	800-343-4952*	508-875-5000
JR O'Dwyer Co 271 Madison Ave Ste 600 ....New York NY 10016	866-395-7710	212-683-2750
Lionheart Publishing Inc 506 Roswell St ....Marietta GA 30060	888-303-5639	
Liturgical Publications Inc 2875 S James Dr ....New Berlin WI 53151	800-950-9952	262-785-1188
LRP Publications 360 Hiatt Dr ....Palm Beach Gardens FL 33418	800-621-5463	561-622-6520
Mary Ann Liebert Publishers Inc 140 Huguenot St 3rd Fl ....New Rochelle NY 10801	800-654-3237	914-740-2100
McKnight's Long-Term Care News 900 Skokie Blvd Ste 114 ....Northbrook IL 60062	800-558-1703	847-559-2884
Meister Media Worldwide 37733 Euclid Ave ....Willoughby OH 44094 *Orders	800-572-7740*	440-942-2000
Mergent Inc 477 Madison Ave Ste 410 ....New York NY 10022	800-937-1398	212-413-7700
Merion Publications Inc 2900 Horizon Dr ....King of Prussia PA 19406	800-355-1088	484-804-4888
Miles Media Group LLLP 6751 Professional Pkwy W Ste 200 ....Sarasota FL 34240	800-683-0010	941-342-2300
National Braille Press Inc 88 St Stephen St ....Boston MA 02115	888-965-8965	617-266-6160
National Catholic Reporter Publishing Co 115 E Armour Blvd ....Kansas City MO 64111	800-333-7373	816-531-0538
Nelson Publishing 2500 Tamiami Trl N ....Nokomis FL 34275	800-226-6113	941-966-9521
North American Publishing Co (NAPCO) 1500 Springgarden St 12th Fl ....Philadelphia PA 19130	800-627-2689	215-238-5300
Our Sunday Visitor Inc 200 Noll Plz ....Huntington IN 46750	800-348-2440	260-356-8400
Pacific Press 1350 N Kings Rd ....Nampa ID 83687 *Cust Svc	800-765-6955*	208-465-2500
Paisano Publications LLC 28210 Dorothy Dr ....Agoura Hills CA 91301	800-323-3484	818-889-8740
Platts 2 Penn Plz 25th Fl ....New York NY 10121	800-752-8878	212-904-3070
Pohly Co 867 Boylston St 5th Fl ....Boston MA 02116	800-383-0888	617-451-1700
Progressive Impressions 1 Hardman Dr ....Bloomington IL 61701	800-664-0444	
Publications & Communications Inc 13552 Hwy 183 N Ste A ....Austin TX 78750	800-678-9724	512-250-9023
Publications International Ltd 7373 N Cicero Ave ....Lincolnwood IL 60712 *General	800-777-5582*	847-676-3470
Randall-Reilly Publishing Co 3200 Rice Mine Rd NE ....Tuscaloosa AL 35406 *Cust Svc	800-633-5953*	205-349-2990
Relias 111 Corning Rd Ste 250 ....Atlanta GA 30326 *Cust Svc	800-688-2421*	404-262-5476
RentPath LLC 950 East Paces Ferry Rd NE Ste 2600 ....Atlanta GA 30326	800-216-1423	678-421-3000
Review & Herald Publishing Assn 55 W Oak Ridge Dr ....Hagerstown MD 21740	800-456-3991	301-393-3000
Sage Publications Inc 2455 Teller Rd ....Thousand Oaks CA 91320	800-818-7243	805-499-9774
Saint Croix Press Inc 1185 S Knowles Ave ....New Richmond WI 54017	800-826-6622	715-246-5811
Sandhills Publishing 120 W Harvest Dr ....Lincoln NE 68521	800-331-1978	402-479-2181
Schaeffer's Investment Research Inc 5151 Pfeiffer Rd Ste 250 ....Cincinnati OH 45242	800-448-2080	513-589-3800
Simba Information 11200 Rockville Pk Ste 504 ....Rockville MD 20852	888-297-4622	240-747-3096
Simmons-Boardman Publishing Corp 55 Broad St 26th Fl ....New York NY 10004	800-257-5091	212-620-7200
Sky Publishing Corp 90 Sherman St ....Cambridge MA 02140	800-253-0245	617-864-7360
Slack Inc 6900 Grove Rd ....Thorofare NJ 08086	800-257-8290	856-848-1000
Source Media Inc 1 State St Plz 27th Fl ....New York NY 10004	800-221-1809	212-803-8200
Stamats Communications Inc 615 Fifth St SE ....Cedar Rapids IA 52401	800-553-8878	319-364-6167
Standard Publishing Co 4050 Lee Vance Dr ....Colorado Springs CO 80918	800-323-7543	
Strafford Publications Inc PO Box 13729 ....Atlanta GA 30324	800-926-7926	404-881-1141
Sunset Publishing Corp 80 Willow Rd ....Menlo Park CA 94025	800-777-0117	650-321-3600
Thompson Information Services 4340 E-West Hwy Ste 300 ....Bethesda MD 20814 *Cust Svc	800-677-3789*	202-872-3611
United Methodist Publishing House 201 Eigth Ave S ....Nashville TN 37203	800-672-1789	615-749-6000
University of Chicago Press Journals Div 1427 E 60th St ....Chicago IL 60637	877-705-1878	773-702-1234
Vendome Group LLC 216 E 45th St 6th Fl ....New York NY 10017	800-519-3692	
Warren Communications News Inc 2115 Ward Ct NW ....Washington DC 20037	800-771-9202	202-872-9200
Wright's Media 2407 Timberloch Pl Ste B ....The Woodlands TX 77380	877-652-5295	
Yankee Publishing Inc PO Box 520 ....Dublin NH 03444	800-729-9265	603-563-8111

633-10 Publishers (Misc)

	Toll-Free	Phone
AM Best Co Ambest Rd .... Oldwick NJ 08858	800-424-2378	908-439-2200
American Printing House for the Blind		
1839 Frankfort Ave PO Box 6085 .... Louisville KY 40206	800-223-1839	502-895-2405
Cathedral Press Inc		
600 NE Sixth St .... Long Prairie MN 56347	800-874-8332*	320-732-6143
*Cust Svc		
Chalk & Vermilion Fine Arts Inc		
55 Old Post Rd Ste 2 .... Greenwich CT 06830	800-877-2250	203-869-9500
Channing Bete Co		
1 Community Pl .... South Deerfield MA 01373	800-477-4776	413-665-7611
Clement Communications Inc		
3 Creek Pkwy .... Upper Chichester PA 19061	800-253-6368	610-459-4200
Coastal Training Technologies Corp		
500 Studio Dr .... Virginia Beach VA 23452	866-333-6888	757-498-9014
Drivers License Guide Co		
1492 Oddstad Dr .... Redwood City CA 94063	800-227-8827	650-369-4849
EBSCO Publishing Inc		
10 Estes St .... Ipswich MA 01938	800-633-4604	978-356-6500
FlyerCom 201 Kelsey Ln .... Tampa FL 33619	800-995-4433	
Forecast International		
22 Commerce Rd .... Newtown CT 06470	800-451-4975	203-426-0800
Hadley House Co		
PO Box 245 .... Madison Lake MN 56063	800-423-5390	952-983-8208
Mergent FIS Inc		
580 Kingsley Pk Dr .... Fort Mill SC 29715	800-342-5647	
Microcomputer Applications Inc		
777 S Wadsworth Blvd Bldg 4-220. .... Lakewood CO 80226	800-453-9565	303-801-0338
New York Graphic Society Ltd		
129 Glover Ave .... Norwalk CT 06850	800-221-1032	203-661-2400
OAG Worldwide		
3025 Highland Pkwy Ste 200 .... Downers Grove IL 60515	800-342-5624	
Publicis Touchpoint Solutions Inc		
1000 Floral Vale Blvd Ste 400 .... Yardley PA 19067	800-672-0676	215-525-9800
Somerset Fine Arts		
PO Box 869 .... Fulshear TX 77441	800-444-2540*	
*Sales		
TechTarget 275 Grove St .... Newton MA 02466	888-274-4111	617-431-9200
Thomson CenterWatch Inc		
100 N Washington St Ste 301 .... Boston MA 02114	800-765-9647*	617-948-5100
*Cust Svc		
Wonderlic Inc		
400 Lakeview Pkwy Ste 200 .... Vernon Hills IL 60061	877-605-9496	847-680-4900

633-11 Technical Publishers

	Toll-Free	Phone
Aircraft Technical Publishers		
101 S Hill Dr .... Brisbane CA 94005	800-227-4610	415-330-9500
Faulkner Information Services		
7905 Browning Rd .... Pennsauken NJ 08109	800-843-0460	856-662-2070
Health Forum		
155 N Wacker Dr Ste 400 .... Chicago IL 60606	800-821-2039	312-893-6800
Information Gatekeepers Inc (IGI)		
1340 Soldiers Field Rd Ste 2 .... Brighton MA 02135	800-323-1088	617-782-5033
JJ Keller & Assoc Inc		
3003 Breezewood Ln PO Box 368. .... Neenah WI 54957	800-558-5011	877-564-2333
O'Reilly & Assoc Inc		
1005 Gravenstein Hwy N .... Sebastopol CA 95472	800-998-9938	707-829-0515
Thompson Information Services		
4340 E-West Hwy Ste 300 .... Bethesda MD 20814	800-677-3789*	202-872-3611
*Cust Svc		

634   PULP MILLS

SEE ALSO Paper Mills ; Paperboard Mills

	Toll-Free	Phone
Alberta-Pacific Forest Industries Inc		
PO Box 8000 .... Boyle AB T0A0M0	800-661-5210	780-525-8000
International Paper Co		
6400 Poplar Ave .... Memphis TN 38197	800-223-1268*	901-419-9000
NYSE: IP ■ *Prod Info*		
Kimberly-Clark Corp		
351 Phelps Dr .... Irving TX 75038	888-525-8388	972-281-1200
NYSE: KMB		
Omaha Paper Co 6936 L St .... Omaha NE 68117	800-288-7026	402-331-3243

635   PUMPS - MEASURING & DISPENSING

	Toll-Free	Phone
Bennett Pump Co		
1218 Pontaluna Rd .... Spring Lake MI 49456	800-235-7618	231-798-1310
Brooks Utility Products Group		
23847 Industrial Park Dr .... Farmington Hills MI 48335	888-687-3008	248-477-0250
CID Bio-Science Inc		
4845 NW Camas Meadows Dr .... Camas WA 98607	800-767-0119	360-833-8835
ComSonics Inc		
1350 Port Republic Rd		
PO Box 1106. .... Harrisonburg VA 22801	800-336-9681	540-434-5965
Controlled Access Inc		
1515 W 130th St .... Hinckley OH 44233	800-942-0829	330-273-6185
Electro Static Technology		
31 Winterbrook Rd .... Mechanic Falls ME 04256	866-738-1857	207-998-5140
Gasboy International Inc		
7300 W Friendly Ave .... Greensboro NC 27420	800-444-5579*	336-547-5000
*Sales		
Gerhart Systems & Controls Corp		
754 Roble Rd Ste 140. .... Allentown PA 18109	888-437-4278	610-264-2800
Medicomp Inc		
600 Atlantis Rd .... Melbourne FL 32904	800-234-3278	

	Toll-Free	Phone
O'Day Equipment Inc		
1301 40th St NW .... Fargo ND 58102	800-654-6329	701-282-9260
Rice Lake Weighing Systems Inc		
230 W Coleman St .... Rice Lake WI 54868	800-472-6703	
Standard Imaging Inc		
3120 Deming Way .... Middleton WI 53562	800-261-4446	608-831-0025
Tuthill Transfer Systems		
8500 S Madison .... Burr Ridge IL 60527	800-825-6937	260-747-7529

636   PUMPS & MOTORS - FLUID POWER

	Toll-Free	Phone
Applied Energy Company Inc (AEC)		
1205 Venture Ct Ste 100. .... Carrollton TX 75006	800-580-1171	214-355-4200
Fluid Metering Inc		
5 Aerial Way Ste 500 .... Syosset NY 11791	800-223-3388	516-922-6050
Jetstream of Houston LLP		
4930 Cranswick .... Houston TX 77041	800-231-8192	713-462-7000
Permco Inc		
1500 Frost Rd .... Streetsboro OH 44241	800-626-2801	330-626-2801
TexLoc Ltd		
4700 Lone Star Blvd .... Fort Worth TX 76106	800-423-6551	817-625-5081
TII Network Technologies Inc		
141 Rodeo Dr .... Edgewood NY 11717	888-844-4720	631-789-5000
NASDAQ: TIII		

637   PUMPS & PUMPING EQUIPMENT (GENERAL USE)

SEE ALSO Industrial Machinery, Equipment, & Supplies

	Toll-Free	Phone
Acme Dynamics Inc		
3608 Sydney Rd PO Box 1780 .... Plant City FL 33566	800-622-9355	813-752-3137
Advanced Pressure Systems		
701 S Persimmon St Ste J .... Tomball TX 77375	877-290-4277	281-290-9950
Aermotor Pumps Inc		
293 Wright St .... Delavan WI 53115	800-230-1816	
Air Systems International Inc		
829 Juniper Crescent .... Chesapeake VA 23320	800-866-8100	757-424-3967
Amico Corp		
85 Fulton Way .... Richmond Hill ON L4B2N4	877-462-6426	905-764-0800
AMT Pump Co		
400 Spring St .... Royersford PA 19468	888-268-7867	
Aqua-Dyne Inc		
701 S Persimmon St Ste 85 .... Tomball TX 77375	888-997-1483	
AR Wilfley & Sons Inc		
5870 E 56th Ave .... Commerce CO 80022	800-525-9930	303-779-1777
Armstrong International Inc		
2081 SE Ocean Blvd 4th Fl .... Stuart FL 34996	866-738-5125	772-286-7175
ASM Industries Inc Pacer Pumps Div		
41 Industrial Cir .... Lancaster PA 17601	800-233-3861*	717-656-2161
*Cust Svc		
Barker Air & Hydraulics Inc		
1308 Miller Rd .... Greenville SC 29607	800-922-3324	864-288-3537
Berkeley Pumps		
293 Wright St .... Delavan WI 53115	888-782-7483	262-728-5551
Blackmer		
1809 Century Ave .... Grand Rapids MI 49503	888-363-7886	616-241-1611
Busch Vacuum Technics Inc		
1740 Lionel Bertrand .... Boisbriand QC J7H1N7	800-363-6360	450-435-6899
CDS-John Blue Co		
290 Pinehurst Dr .... Huntsville AL 35806	800-253-2583	256-721-9090
Coffin Turbo Pump Inc		
326 S Dean St .... Englewood NJ 07631	800-568-9798	201-568-4700
Corken Inc		
3805 NW 36th St .... Oklahoma City OK 73112	800-631-4929	405-946-5576
CS & P Technologies LP		
18119 Telge Rd .... Cypress TX 77429	800-262-6103	713-467-0869
Flint & Walling Inc		
95 N Oak St .... Kendallville IN 46755	800-345-9422*	
*Sales		
Flowserve Corp		
5215 N O'Connor Blvd Ste 2300. .... Irving TX 75039	800-543-3927	972-443-6500
NYSE: FLS		
FMG Enterprises Inc		
1125 Memorex Dr .... Santa Clara CA 95050	800-327-6177	408-982-0110
Fristam Pumps USA LP		
2410 Parview Rd .... Middleton WI 53562	800-841-5001	608-831-5001
GIW Industries Inc		
5000 Wrightsboro Rd .... Grovetown GA 30813	888-832-4449	706-863-1011
Graco Inc		
88 11th Ave NE PO Box 1441 .... Minneapolis MN 55413	800-328-0211*	612-623-6000
NYSE: GGG ■ *Cust Svc*		
Graymills Corp		
3705 N Lincoln Ave .... Chicago IL 60613	877-465-7867	773-477-4100
Great Plains Industries Inc		
5252 E 36th St N .... Wichita KS 67220	800-835-0113*	316-686-7361
*Sales		
Hale Products Inc		
700 Spring Mill Ave .... Conshohocken PA 19428	800-220-4253	800-533-3569
Hammelmann Corp		
600 Progress Rd .... Dayton OH 45449	800-783-4935	937-859-8777
Haskel International Inc		
100 E Graham Pl .... Burbank CA 91502	800-743-2720	818-843-4000
Hydromatic Pump Co		
740 E Ninth St .... Ashland OH 44805	888-957-8677	
HydroPressure Cleaning Inc		
413 Dawson Dr .... Camarillo CA 93012	800-934-2399	
Imo Pump 1710 Airport Rd .... Monroe NC 28110	877-853-7867	704-289-6511
Integrated Flow Solutions LLC		
6461 Reynolds Rd .... Tyler TX 75708	800-859-7867	903-595-6511
Kerr Pump & Supply		
12880 Cloverdale .... Oak Park MI 48237	800-482-8259	248-543-3880
Koshin America Corp		
1218 Remington Rd .... Schaumburg IL 60173	800-634-4092	847-884-1570

	City	State	Zip	Toll-Free	Phone
Kraft Fluid Systems Inc 14300 Foltz Pkwy	Strongsville	OH	44149	**800-257-1155**	440-238-5545
Lehigh Fluid Power Inc 1413 Rt 179	Lambertville	NJ	08530	**800-257-9515**	
Liberty Pumps Inc 7000 Apple Tree Ave	Bergen	NY	14416	**800-543-2550**	585-494-1817
Madden Manufacturing Inc PO Box 387	Elkhart	IN	46515	**800-369-6233**	574-295-4292
Magnatex Pumps Inc 3575 W 12th St	Houston	TX	77008	**866-624-7867**	713-972-8666
McNally Industries LLC 340 W Benson Ave	Grantsburg	WI	54840	**800-366-1410**	715-463-8300
Met-Pro Corp Fybroc Div 700 Emlen Way	Telford	PA	18969	**800-392-7621**	215-723-8155
Met-Pro Corp Sethco Div 800 Emlen Way	Telford	PA	18969	**800-645-0500**	215-799-2577
Micropump Inc 1402 NE 136th Ave *Sales	Vancouver	WA	98684	**800-222-9565***	360-253-2008
Moyno Inc 1895 W Jefferson St	Springfield	OH	45506	**877-486-6966**	937-327-3111
MP Pumps Inc 34800 Bennett Dr	Fraser	MI	48026	**800-563-8006**	586-293-8240
MWI Corp 33 NW Second St	Deerfield Beach	FL	33441	**800-296-7004**	954-426-1500
Neptune Chemical Pump Co 22069 Van Buren St	Grand Terrace	CA	92313	**800-255-4017**	215-699-8700
Neptune-Benson Inc 6 Jefferson Dr	Coventry	RI	02816	**800-832-8002**	401-821-2200
NH Yates & Company Inc 117 Church Ln # C	Cockeysville	MD	21030	**800-878-8181**	
PACO Pumps Inc 902 Koomey Rd	Brookshire	TX	77423	**800-955-5847**	281-994-2700
Peerless Pump Co 2005 Dr Martin Luther King Jr St	Indianapolis	IN	46202	**800-879-0182**	317-925-9661
Penn Air & Hydraulics Corp 580 Davies Dr	York	PA	17402	**888-631-7638**	
Pentair 1101 Myers Pkwy	Ashland	OH	44805	**855-274-8948**	
Pentair Water Pool & Spa 1620 Hawkins Ave	Sanford	NC	27330	**800-831-7133**	
Randolph Austin Company Inc 2119 FM 1626 PO Box 988	Manchaca	TX	78652	**800-531-5263**	512-202-1590
RI Deppmann Co 20929 Bridge St	Southfield	MI	48033	**800-589-6120**	248-354-3710
Roper Pump Co 3475 Old Maysville Rd *Sales	Commerce	GA	30529	**800-944-6769***	706-335-5551
Roth Pump Co PO Box 4330	Rock Island	IL	61204	**888-444-7684**	309-787-1791
RS Corcoran Co 500 N Vine St	New Lenox	IL	60451	**800-637-1067**	815-485-2156
Serfilco Ltd 2900 MacArthur Blvd	Northbrook	IL	60062	**800-323-5431**	847-559-1777
SHURflo Pump Mfg Company Inc 5900 Katella Ave	Cypress	CA	90630	**800-854-3218**	562-795-5200
Standard Alloys & Mfg PO Box 969	Port Arthur	TX	77640	**800-231-8240**	409-983-3201
Stansteel Asphalt Plant Products 12700 Shelbyville Rd	Louisville	KY	40243	**800-826-0223**	502-245-1977
Thompson Pump & Mfg Company Inc 4620 City Ctr Dr PO Box 291370	Port Orange	FL	32129	**800-767-7310**	386-767-7310
Townley Engineering & Manufacturing Company Inc 10551 SE 110th St Rd	Candler	FL	32111	**800-342-9920**	352-687-3001
Tuthill Corp 8500 S Madison St	Burr Ridge	IL	60527	**800-634-2695**	630-382-4900
Ultimate Washer Inc 711 Commerce Way Ste 1	Jupiter	FL	33458	**866-858-4982**	561-741-7022
Vaughan Company Inc 364 Monte-Elma Rd	Montesano	WA	98563	**888-249-2467**	360-249-4042
Vogelsang USA 7966 State Rt 44	Ravenna	OH	44266	**800-984-9400**	330-296-3820
Wastecorp Inc PO Box 70	Grand Island	NY	14072	**888-829-2783**	
Waterous Co 125 Hardman Ave	South Saint Paul	MN	55075	**800-488-1228**	651-450-5000
Watson-Marlow Inc 37 Upton Technology Pk	Wilmington	MA	01887	**800-282-8823**	
Zoeller Co 3649 Kane Run Rd *OTC: ZOLR*	Louisville	KY	40211	**800-928-7867**	502-778-2731

638 RACING & RACETRACKS

SEE ALSO Motor Speedways

	City	State	Zip	Toll-Free	Phone
Alameda County Fair Assn (ACFA) 4501 Pleasanton Ave	Pleasanton	CA	94566	**800-874-9253**	925-426-7600
Brainerd International Raceway 5523 Birchdale Rd	Brainerd	MN	56401	**866-444-4455**	218-824-7223
Canterbury Park Holding Corp 1100 Canterbury Rd *NASDAQ: CPHC*	Shakopee	MN	55379	**800-340-6361**	952-445-7223
Charlotte Motor Speedway 5555 Concord Pkwy S	Concord	NC	28027	**800-455-3267**	704-455-3200
Churchill Downs Inc 600 N Hurstbourne Pkwy Ste 400 *NASDAQ: CHDN*	Louisville	KY	40222	**800-283-3729**	502-636-4400
Del Mar Thoroughbred Club 2260 Jimmy Durante Blvd	Del Mar	CA	92014	**800-467-7385**	858-755-1141
Delaware Racing Assn 777 Delaware Park Blvd	Wilmington	DE	19804	**888-850-8888**	
Delta Downs Racetrack 2717 Delta Downs Dr	Vinton	LA	70668	**800-589-7441**	
Dover Downs Hotel & Casino 1131 N DuPont Hwy *NYSE: DDE*	Dover	DE	19901	**800-711-5882**	302-674-4600
Dover International Speedway 1131 N DuPont Hwy PO Box 843	Dover	DE	19901	**800-441-7223**	302-883-6500
Dover Motorsports Inc 1131 N Dupont Hwy PO Box 843 *NYSE: DVD*	Dover	DE	19901	**800-441-7223**	302-883-6500
Fair Grounds Race Course 1751 Gentilly Blvd	New Orleans	LA	70119	**800-262-7983**	504-944-5515
Finger Lakes Gaming & Race Track 5857 Rt 96	Farmington	NY	14425	**877-846-7369**	585-924-3232
Fort Erie Race Track 230 Catherine St PO Box 1130	Fort Erie	ON	L2A5N9	**800-295-3770**	905-871-3200
Grand Prix of Long Beach 3000 Pacific Ave	Long Beach	CA	90806	**888-827-7333**	562-981-2600
Grand River Agricultural Society 7445 Wellington County Rd 21 RR 2	Elora	ON	N0B1S0	**800-898-7792**	519-846-5455
Grays Harbor Raceway 32 Elma McCleary Rd PO Box 911	Elma	WA	98541	**800-667-7711**	360-482-4374
Harrington Raceway 15 W Rider Rd	Harrington	DE	19952	**888-887-5687**	
Hollywood Casino at Charles Town Races 750 Hollywood Dr	Charles Town	WV	25414	**800-795-7001**	304-725-7001
Hoosier Park Racing & Casino 4500 Dan Patch Cir	Anderson	IN	46013	**800-526-7223**	765-642-7223
Illinois State Fairgrounds 801 E Sangamon Ave	Springfield	IL	62702	**866-287-2999**	217-782-4231
Laurel Park Rt 198 & Racetrack Rd PO Box 130	Laurel	MD	20724	**800-638-1859**	301-725-0400
Lone Star Park at Grand Prairie 1000 Lone Star Pkwy	Grand Prairie	TX	75050	**800-795-7223**	972-263-7223
MetraPark 308 Sixth Ave N	Billings	MT	59101	**800-366-8538**	406-256-2400
Northville Downs 301 S Ctr St	Northville	MI	48167	**888-349-7100**	248-349-1000
Oaklawn Park 2705 Central Ave *General	Hot Springs	AR	71901	**800-625-5296***	501-623-4411
Ontario Lottery & Gaming Corp 70 Foster Dr Ste 800	Sault Sainte Marie	ON	P6A6V2	**800-563-5357**	705-946-6464
Pensacola Greyhound Track 951 Dog Track Rd	Pensacola	FL	32506	**800-345-3997**	850-455-8595
Pinnacle Entertainment Inc 3980 Howard Hughes Pkwy *NYSE: PNK*	Las Vegas	NV	89169	**877-764-8750**	702-541-7777
Ravalli County Fair 100 Old Corvallis Rd	Hamilton	MT	59840	**800-225-6779**	406-363-3411
Remington Park Race Track 1 Remington Pl	Oklahoma City	OK	73111	**866-456-9880**	405-424-1000
Saratoga Gaming & Raceway 342 Jefferson St PO Box 356	Saratoga Springs	NY	12866	**800-727-2990**	518-584-2110
Solano County Fair 900 Fairgrounds Dr	Vallejo	CA	94589	**800-700-2482**	707-551-2000
Sunland Park Racetrack & Casino 1200 Futurity Dr	Sunland Park	NM	88063	**800-572-1142**	575-874-5200
Tampa Bay Downs Inc 11225 Racetrack Rd	Tampa	FL	33626	**800-200-4434**	813-855-4401
Texas Motor Speedway 3545 Lone Star Cir	Fort Worth	TX	76177	**800-805-8721**	817-215-8510
TrackMaster 2083 Old Middlefield Way Ste 206	Mountain View	CA	94043	**800-334-3800**	650-316-1020
Turf Paradise Racetrack 1501 W Bell Rd	Phoenix	AZ	85023	**800-639-8783**	602-942-1101
Twin River Casino 100 Twin River Rd	Lincoln	RI	02865	**877-827-4837**	401-475-8505
Woodbine Entertainment Group Inc 555 Rexdale Blvd PO Box 156	Toronto	ON	M9W5L2	**888-675-7223**	416-675-7223
XpressBet LLC 200 Racetrack Rd Bldg 26	Washington	PA	15301	**866-889-7737**	

639 RADIO COMPANIES

	City	State	Zip	Toll-Free	Phone
Bible Broadcasting Network Inc 11530 Carmel Commons Blvd PO Box 7300	Charlotte	NC	28226	**800-888-7077**	704-523-5555
Bott Radio Network 10550 Barkley St Ste 100	Overland Park	KS	66212	**800-875-1903**	913-642-7770
Eagle Communications Inc 2703 Hall St Ste 15	Hays	KS	67601	**877-613-2453**	785-625-5910
Eagle Radio Inc 2703 Hall St Ste 15	Hays	KS	67601	**877-613-2453**	
Educational Media Foundation 5700 W Oaks Blvd *General	Rocklin	CA	95765	**800-525-5683***	800-877-5600
Family Radio 290 Hegenberger Rd	Oakland	CA	94621	**800-543-1495**	
Far East Broadcasting Co Inc 15700 Imperial Hwy PO Box 1	La Mirada	CA	90638	**800-523-3480**	
Shamrock Communications Inc 149 Penn Ave	Scranton	PA	18503	**800-228-4637**	570-348-9100
Telesouth Communications Inc 6311 Ridgewood Rd	Jackson	MS	39211	**888-808-8637**	601-957-1700
Zimmer Radio Group 3215 Lemone Industrial Blvd Ste 200	Columbia	MO	65201	**800-455-1099**	573-875-1099

640 RADIO NETWORKS

	City	State	Zip	Toll-Free	Phone
American Family Association 107 Parkgate Dr	Tupelo	MS	38801	**800-326-4543**	662-844-5036
Black Radio Network 375 Fifth Ave	New York	NY	10016	**866-342-6892**	212-686-6850
Bott Radio Network 10550 Barkley St Ste 100	Overland Park	KS	66212	**800-875-1903**	913-642-7770
Family Life Communications Inc PO Box 35300	Tucson	AZ	85740	**800-776-1070**	

Classified Section

	Toll-Free	Phone
Far East Broadcasting Co Inc		
15700 Imperial Hwy PO Box 1 ....La Mirada CA 90638	800-523-3480	
Radio America		
1100 N Glebe Rd Ste 900 ....Arlington VA 22201	800-807-4703	703-302-1000
Relevant Radio		
1496 Bellevue St Ste 202		
PO Box 10707....................Green Bay WI 54311	877-291-0123	
Tiger Financial News Network		
601 Cleveland St Ste 618 ....Clearwater FL 33755	877-518-9190	727-467-9190
United Stations Radio Network		
1065 Ave of the Americas 3rd Fl..............New York NY 10018	866-989-1975	212-869-1111
Yesterday USA Radio Networks, The		
2001 Plymouth Rock Dr ....Richardson TX 75081	800-624-2272	972-889-9872

641-1 Abilene, TX

	Toll-Free	Phone
KEAN-FM 1051 (Ctry)		
3911 S First St ....Abilene TX 79605	800-588-5326	325-676-5326

641-2 Akron, OH

	Toll-Free	Phone
Summit, The 65 Steiner Ave ....Akron OH 44301	877-411-3662	330-761-3099

641-3 Albany, NY

	Toll-Free	Phone
WAMC-FM 903 (NPR)		
318 Central Ave ....Albany NY 12206	800-323-9262	518-465-5233

641-4 Albuquerque, NM

	Toll-Free	Phone
KNML-AM 610 (Sports)		
500 Fourth St NW 5th Fl...............Albuquerque NM 87102	888-922-0610	505-767-6700
KUNM-FM 899 (NPR)		
1University of New Mexico		
MSC 06 3520........................Albuquerque NM 87131	877-277-4806	505-277-4806

641-5 Amarillo, TX

	Toll-Free	Phone
KACV-FM 90 (Alt)		
PO Box 447 ....Amarillo TX 79178	800-766-0176	
Lonestar 987		
6214 W 34th St ....Amarillo TX 79109	866-930-5225	806-355-9777

641-6 Anchorage, AK

	Toll-Free	Phone
KNBA-FM 903 (NPR)		
3600 San Geronimo Dr Ste 480 ....Anchorage AK 99508	800-996-2848	907-793-3500
KSKA-FM 911		
3877 University Dr ....Anchorage AK 99508	800-478-8255	907-550-8400

641-7 Ann Arbor, MI

	Toll-Free	Phone
WUOM-FM 917 (NPR)		
535 W William St Ste 110......................Ann Arbor MI 48103	888-258-9866	734-764-9210

641-8 Annapolis, MD

	Toll-Free	Phone
WRNR-FM 1031		
179 Admiral Cochrane Dr ....Annapolis MD 21401	877-762-1031	410-626-0103

641-9 Atlanta, GA

	Toll-Free	Phone
Georgia Public Broadcasting		
260 14th St NW ....Atlanta GA 30318	800-222-4788	404-685-2400
WCLK-FM 919		
111 James P Brawley Dr SW ....Atlanta GA 30314	888-448-3925	404-880-8284

641-10 Baltimore, MD

	Toll-Free	Phone
1027Jack FM 711 W 40th St ....Baltimore MD 21211	888-410-1027	410-366-7600
WRBS-FM 951 (Rel)		
3500 Commerce Dr ....Baltimore MD 21227	800-965-9324	410-247-4100

641-11 Bangor, ME

	Toll-Free	Phone
WHCF-FM 885 (Rel)		
PO Box 5000 ....Bangor ME 04402	800-947-2577	207-947-2751
WVOM-FM 1039 (N/T)		
184 Target Industrial Cir ....Bangor ME 04401	800-966-1039	207-947-9100

641-12 Baton Rouge, LA

	Toll-Free	Phone
WRKF-FM 893 (NPR)		
3050 Vly Creek Dr ....Baton Rouge LA 70808	855-893-9753	225-926-3050

641-13 Billings, MT

	Toll-Free	Phone
Yellowstone Public Radio		
1500 University Dr ....Billings MT 59101	800-441-2941	406-657-2941

641-14 Birmingham, AL

	Toll-Free	Phone
1025 The Bull		
600 Beacon Pkwy W Ste 400 ....Birmingham AL 35209	877-811-3369	205-439-9600
WBHM-FM 903 (NPR)		
650 11th St S ....Birmingham AL 35233	800-444-9246	205-934-2606
WZZK-FM 1047 (Ctry)		
2700 Corporate Dr Ste 115................Birmingham AL 35242	866-998-1047	205-916-1100

641-15 Boise, ID

	Toll-Free	Phone
KBXL-FM 941 (Rel)		
1440 S Weideman Ave ....Boise ID 83709	877-207-2276	208-377-3790
KIZN-FM 923 (Ctry)		
1419 West Bannock ....Boise ID 83702	800-529-5264	208-336-3670
KTIK-AM 1350 (Sports)		
1419 W Bannock St ....Boise ID 83702	866-296-1350	208-336-3670

641-16 Boston, MA

	Toll-Free	Phone
WBUR-FM 909 (NPR)		
890 Commonwealth Ave ....Boston MA 02215	800-909-9287	617-353-0909
WGBH-FM 897 (NPR) 1 Guest St ....Boston MA 02135	800-492-1111	617-300-2000
WKLB-FM 1025 (Ctry)		
55 Morrissey Blvd ....Boston MA 02125	888-819-1025	617-822-9600
WUMB-FM 919 (Folk)		
100 Morrissey Blvd ....Boston MA 02125	800-573-2100	617-287-6900

641-17 Branson, MO

	Toll-Free	Phone
KLFC-FM 881		
205 W Atlantic St ....Branson MO 65616	877-410-8592	417-334-5532

641-18 Buffalo, NY

	Toll-Free	Phone
WDCX-FM 995 (Rel)		
625 Delaware Ave Ste 308 ....Buffalo NY 14202	800-684-2848	716-883-3010
WNED		
140 Lower Terr PO Box 1263 ....Buffalo NY 14202	800-678-1873	716-845-7000

641-19 Cedar Rapids, IA

	Toll-Free	Phone
965 FM KISS Country		
600 Old Marion Rd NE ....Cedar Rapids IA 52402	800-258-0096	319-395-0530

641-20 Champaign, IL

	Toll-Free	Phone
WBGL-FM 917 (Rel)		
4101 Fieldstone Rd PO Box 111...............Champaign IL 61822	800-475-9245*	217-359-8232
*Cust Svc		
WDWS-AM 1400 (N/T)		
15 Main St ....Champaign IL 61820	800-223-9397	217-351-5300

641-21 Charleston, WV

	Toll-Free	Phone
WQBE-FM 975 (Ctry)		
817 Suncrest Pl ....Charleston WV 25303	800-222-3697	304-344-9700

641-22 Charlotte, NC

	Toll-Free	Phone
WEND-FM 1065 (Alt)		
801 Wood Ridge Ctr Dr ....Charlotte NC 28217	800-934-1065	704-714-9444
WFAE-FM 907 (NPR)		
8801 JM Keynes Dr Ste 91....................Charlotte NC 28262	800-876-9323*	704-549-9323
*Cust Svc		

641-23 Chicago, IL

	Toll-Free	Phone
WDRV-FM 971 (CR)		
875 N Michigan Ave Ste 1510 ....Chicago IL 60611	800-899-0089	312-274-9710

641-24 Cincinnati, OH

	Toll-Free	Phone
WAKW-FM 933 (Rel)		
6275 Collegevue Pl PO Box 24126 . . . . Cincinnati OH 45224	**888-542-9393**	513-542-9259

641-25 Cleveland, OH

	Toll-Free	Phone
WENZ-FM 1079 (Urban)		
2510 St Clair Ave NE . . . . Cleveland OH 44114	**800-440-1079**	216-579-1111

641-26 Colorado Springs, CO

	Toll-Free	Phone
KILO Radio		
1805 E Cheyenne Rd . . . . Colorado Springs CO 80905	**800-727-5456***	719-633-5456
*General		
KRCC-FM 915 (NPR)		
912 N Weber St . . . . Colorado Springs CO 80903	**800-748-2727**	719-473-4801

641-27 Columbia, SC

	Toll-Free	Phone
FOX Sports Radio 1400		
316 Greystone Blvd . . . . Columbia SC 29210	**844-289-7234**	803-343-1100
WFMV-FM 953		
2440 Milwood Ave . . . . Columbia SC 29205	**888-953-9830**	803-939-9530
WHMC-FM 901 (NPR)		
1041 George Rogers Blvd . . . . Columbia SC 29201	**800-922-5437**	803-737-3200
WLTR-FM 913 (NPR)		
1041 George Rogers Blvd . . . . Columbia SC 29201	**800-922-5437**	803-737-3200

641-28 Columbus, OH

	Toll-Free	Phone
997 Blitz, The		
1458 Dublin Rd . . . . Columbus OH 43215	**800-821-9970**	614-481-7800
WCBE-FM 905 (NPR)		
540 Jack Gibbs Blvd . . . . Columbus OH 43215	**800-241-0421**	614-365-5555
WCOL-FM 923 (Ctry)		
2323 W Fifth Ave Ste 200 . . . . Columbus OH 43204	**800-899-9265**	614-486-6101
WNCI-FM 979 (CHR)		
2323 W Fifth Ave Ste 200 . . . . Columbus OH 43204	**844-289-7234**	
WTVN-AM 610 (N/T)		
2323 W Fifth Ave Ste 200 . . . . Columbus OH 43221	**844-289-7234**	

641-29 Corpus Christi, TX

	Toll-Free	Phone
KEDT 3205 S Staples . . . . Corpus Christi TX 78411	**800-307-5338**	361-855-2213
KSAB-FM		
501 Tupper Ln . . . . Corpus Christi TX 78417	**844-289-7234**	360-289-0111

641-30 Dallas/Fort Worth, TX

	Toll-Free	Phone
Alt 1037		
4131 N Central Expy Ste 1000 . . . . Dallas TX 75204	**877-787-1037**	214-525-7000
KBFB-FM 979 (Urban)		
13760 Noel Rd Ste 1100 . . . . Dallas TX 75240	**844-787-1979**	972-331-5400
KERA-FM 901 (NPR)		
3000 Harry Hines Blvd . . . . Dallas TX 75201	**800-456-5372**	214-871-1390
Kidd Kraddick in The Morning		
220 Las Colinas Blvd E Ste C- 210 . . . . Irving TX 75039	**800-543-3548**	972-432-9094

641-31 Denver, CO

	Toll-Free	Phone
KUVO-FM 893 (Jazz)		
2900 Welton St Ste 200 . . . . Denver CO 80205	**800-574-5886**	303-480-9272

641-32 Des Moines, IA

	Toll-Free	Phone
KIOA-FM 933 (Oldies)		
1416 Locust St . . . . Des Moines IA 50309	**877-984-8786**	515-280-1350

641-33 Duluth, MN

	Toll-Free	Phone
KUMD		
1201 Ordean Ct 130 Humanities . . . . Duluth MN 55812	**800-566-5863**	218-726-7181

641-34 El Paso, TX

	Toll-Free	Phone
KELP Christian Radio		
6900 Commerce Ave . . . . El Paso TX 79915	**800-658-6299**	915-779-0016
KLAQ-FM 955 (Rock)		
4180 N Mesa St . . . . El Paso TX 79902	**844-305-6210**	915-880-4955

641-35 Erie, PA

	Toll-Free	Phone
WQLN-FM 913 (NPR)		
8425 Peach St . . . . Erie PA 16509	**800-727-8854**	814-864-3001

641-36 Eugene, OR

	Toll-Free	Phone
KLCC-FM 897 (NPR)		
136 W Eighth Ave . . . . Eugene OR 97401	**800-922-3682**	541-463-6000

641-37 Evansville, IN

	Toll-Free	Phone
Hot 96 FM		
1162 Mt Auburn Rd . . . . Evansville IN 47720	**888-685-1961**	812-491-9468
WDKS-FM 1061 (CHR)		
117 SE Fifth St . . . . Evansville IN 47708	**888-454-5477**	812-425-4226
WGBF-FM 1031 (Rock)		
20 NW Third St Ste 600 . . . . Evansville IN 47708	**888-900-9423**	812-425-4226
WKDQ 995		
20 NW Third St Ste 600 . . . . Evansville IN 47708	**877-437-5995**	812-425-4226
WNIN-FM 883 (NPR)		
405 Carpenter St . . . . Evansville IN 47708	**855-888-9646**	812-423-2973

641-38 Flagstaff, AZ

	Toll-Free	Phone
KNAU-FM 887 (NPR)		
PO Box 5764 . . . . Flagstaff AZ 86011	**800-523-5628**	928-523-5628

641-39 Fort Wayne, IN

	Toll-Free	Phone
891 WBOI		
3204 Clairmont Ct . . . . Fort Wayne IN 46808	**800-471-9264***	260-452-1189
*General		
WFWI 2915 Maples Rd . . . . Fort Wayne IN 46816	**800-333-1190**	260-447-5511
WLDE FUN 1017		
347 W Berry Ste 600 . . . . Fort Wayne IN 46802	**888-450-1017**	260-423-3676
WOWO-AM 1190 (N/T)		
2915 Maples Rd . . . . Fort Wayne IN 46816	**800-333-1190**	260-447-5511

641-40 Fresno, CA

	Toll-Free	Phone
KMJ-AM 580 (N/T)		
1071 W Shaw Ave . . . . Fresno CA 93711	**800-776-5858**	559-490-5800
KMJ-FM 1059 1071 W Shaw Ave . . . . Fresno CA 93711	**800-491-1899**	559-490-5800
KSKS-FM 937 (Ctry)		
1071 W Shaw Ave . . . . Fresno CA 93711	**800-767-5477**	559-490-5800
Softrock-FM 989 (AC)		
83 E Shaw Ave Ste 150 . . . . Fresno CA 93710	**800-606-7625**	559-230-4300
Y101 FM KWYE-FM		
1071 W Shaw Ave . . . . Fresno CA 93711	**800-345-9101**	559-490-5800

641-41 Grand Rapids, MI

	Toll-Free	Phone
WGRD-FM 979 (Rock)		
50 Monroe Ave NW Ste 500 . . . . Grand Rapids MI 49503	**800-947-3979**	616-451-4800
WGVU-FM 885 (NPR)		
301 W Fulton St . . . . Grand Rapids MI 49504	**800-442-2771**	616-331-6666
Wlav		
60 Monroe Ctr Ste 300 . . . . Grand Rapids MI 49503	**800-882-9528**	616-774-8461

641-42 Green Bay, WI

	Toll-Free	Phone
WDUZ-AM 1400 (Sports)		
810 Victoria St . . . . Green Bay WI 54302	**855-724-1075**	920-468-4100
WOGB-FM 1031 (AC)		
810 Victoria St . . . . Green Bay WI 54302	**800-236-3771**	920-468-4100
WPNE-FM 893 (NPR)		
2420 Nicolet Dr . . . . Green Bay WI 54311	**800-654-6228**	920-465-2444

641-43 Greenville, SC

	Toll-Free	Phone
925 WESC-FM		
101 N Main St Ste 1000 10th Fl . . . . Greenville SC 29601	**800-248-0863**	
His radio 893		
2420 Wade Hampton Blvd . . . . Greenville SC 29615	**800-447-7234**	864-292-6040
WJMZ-FM 1073 (Urban)		
220 N Main St Ste 402 . . . . Greenville SC 29601	**800-767-1073**	864-235-1073
WROQ-FM 1011 (CR)		
25 Garlington Rd . . . . Greenville SC 29615	**888-257-0058**	864-271-9200

641-44 Harrisburg, PA

	Toll-Free	Phone
WITF-FM 895 (NPR)		
4801 Lindle Rd . . . . Harrisburg PA 17111	**800-366-9483**	717-704-3000

Classified Section

641-45 Honolulu, HI

	Toll-Free	Phone
939 The Beat Honolulu		
650 Iwilei Rd Ste 400 .... Honolulu HI 96817	844-289-7234	808-550-9200
KHVH-AM 830 (N/T)		
650 Iwilei Rd Ste 400 .... Honolulu HI 96817	844-289-7234	808-550-9200
KRTR-FM 963 (AC)		
900 Ft St Ste 700 .... Honolulu HI 96813	800-669-1010	808-275-1000

641-46 Houston, TX

	Toll-Free	Phone
1041 KRBE		
9801 Westheimer Rd Ste 700 .... Houston TX 77042	888-955-2993	713-266-1000
KKBQ-FM 929 (Ctry)		
1990 Post Oak Blvd Ste 2300 .... Houston TX 77056	877-745-6591	713-963-1200
KLAT-AM 1010 (Span N/T)		
5100 SW Fwy .... Houston TX 77056	800-646-6779	713-961-1029
KUHF-FM 887 (Clas)		
4343 Elgin St .... Houston TX 77204	877-252-0436	713-748-8888
Rovi Corp		
1990 Post Oak Blvd Ste 2300 .... Houston TX 77056	877-745-6591	713-963-1200

641-47 Hudson, MA

	Toll-Free	Phone
Signalfire Wireless Telemetry Inc		
43 Broad St .... Hudson MA 01749	800-772-0878	978-212-2868
WICN-FM 905 (NPR)		
50 Portland St .... Worcester MA 01608	855-752-0700	508-752-0700

641-48 Huntsville, AL

	Toll-Free	Phone
WLRH Huntsville 893 FM		
UAH Campus John Wright Dr .... Huntsville AL 35899	800-239-9574	256-895-9574

641-49 Indianapolis, IN

	Toll-Free	Phone
WIBC-FM 931 (N/T)		
40 Monument Cir Ste 400 .... Indianapolis IN 46204	800-571-9422	317-266-9422

641-50 Jackson, MS

	Toll-Free	Phone
Mississippi Public Broadcasting		
3825 Ridgewood Rd .... Jackson MS 39211	800-850-4406	601-432-6565

641-51 Jacksonville, FL

	Toll-Free	Phone
WAPE-FM 951 (CHR)		
8000 Belfort Pkwy Ste 100 .... Jacksonville FL 32256	800-475-9595	904-245-8500
X1065		
8000 Belfort Pkwy .... Jacksonville FL 32256	800-460-6394	904-245-8500

641-52 Johnson City, TN

	Toll-Free	Phone
WETS-FM 895 (NPR)		
PO Box 70630 .... Johnson City TN 37614	888-895-9387	423-439-6440

641-53 Kansas City, KS & MO

	Toll-Free	Phone
KCUR-FM 893 (NPR)		
4825 Troost Ave Ste 202 .... Kansas City MO 64110	855-778-5437	816-235-1551
KKFI-FM 901 (Var)		
3901 Main St Ste 203 .... Kansas City MO 64111	888-931-0901	816-931-3122
KLJC-FM 885		
8717 W 110th St Ste 480 .... Overland Park KS 66210	855-474-8850	913-451-8850

641-54 Knoxville, TN

	Toll-Free	Phone
WFIV-FM 1053 517 Watt Rd .... Knoxville TN 37934	800-352-9250	865-675-4105
WUOT-FM 919 (NPR)		
209 Communications Bldg		
University of Tennessee .... Knoxville TN 37996	888-266-9868	865-974-5375

641-55 Las Vegas, NV

	Toll-Free	Phone
KNPR-FM 895 (NPR)		
1289 S Torrey Pines Dr .... Las Vegas NV 89146	888-258-9895	702-258-9895

641-56 Little Rock, AR

	Toll-Free	Phone
KABZ-FM 1037 (N/T)		
2400 Cottondale Ln .... Little Rock AR 72202	800-477-1037	501-661-1037
KKPT-FM 941		
2400 Cottondale Ln .... Little Rock AR 72202	800-844-0094	501-664-9410

641-57 Los Angeles, CA

	Toll-Free	Phone
BAY-FM 945 (AC)		
190 Pk Ctr Plz Ste 200 .... San Jose CA 95113	800-948-5229	408-287-5775
KABC-AM 790 (N/T)		
8965 Lindblade St .... Culver City CA 90232	800-222-5222	310-840-4900
KLOS-FM 955 (CR)		
3321 S La Cienega Blvd .... Los Angeles CA 90016	800-955-5567	310-840-4828
KROQ-FM 1067 (Alt)		
5901 Venice Blvd .... Los Angeles CA 90034	800-520-1067	323-930-1067
KRTH-FM 1011 (Oldies)		
5670 Wilshire Blvd Ste 200 .... Los Angeles CA 90036	800-232-5784	323-936-5784
KUSC		
1149 S Hill St Ste H100		
PO Box 7913 .... Los Angeles CA 90015	800-421-5872	213-225-7400
KXSC-FM 1049 (Alt)		
3607 Trousdale Pkwy .... Los Angeles CA 90089	888-966-5332	415-546-8710

641-58 Louisville, KY

	Toll-Free	Phone
WHAS-AM 840 (N/T)		
4000 One Radio Dr .... Louisville KY 40218	800-444-8484	502-479-2222

641-59 Lubbock, TX

	Toll-Free	Phone
News/Talk 951 & 790 KFYO		
4413 82nd St Ste 300 .... Lubbock TX 79424	800-687-0790	806-798-7078

641-60 Madison, WI

	Toll-Free	Phone
HANK AM 1550 & 977 FM		
730 Ray O Vac Dr .... Madison WI 53711	888-974-4265	608-273-1000
WERN-FM 887 (NPR)		
821 University Ave .... Madison WI 53706	800-747-7444	

641-61 Manchester, NH

	Toll-Free	Phone
News Radio 610		
70 Foundry St Ste 300 .... Manchester NH 03102	866-999-7200	603-625-6915

641-62 Memphis, TN

	Toll-Free	Phone
600 WREC		
2650 Thousand Oaks Blvd Ste 4100 .... Memphis TN 38118	800-474-9732	901-259-1300
957 Hallelujah FM		
2650 Thousand Oaks Blvd Ste 4100 .... Memphis TN 38118	844-885-9425	901-259-1300
WKNO-FM 911 (NPR)		
7151 Cherry Farms Rd .... Cordova TN 38016	800-766-9566	901-325-6544

641-63 Milwaukee, WI

	Toll-Free	Phone
540 ESPN		
310 W Wisconsin Ave Ste 100 .... Milwaukee WI 53203	800-990-3776	414-273-3776
WHAD-FM 907 (NPR)		
310 W Wisconsin Ave Ste 750-E .... Milwaukee WI 53203	800-486-8655	414-227-2040
WJYI-AM 1340 (Rel)		
5407 W McKinley Ave .... Milwaukee WI 53208	800-256-6102	414-978-9000

641-64 Minneapolis/Saint Paul, MN

	Toll-Free	Phone
1500 KSTP-AM LLC		
3415 University Ave .... Minneapolis MN 55414	877-615-1500	651-646-8255

641-65 Miramar, FL

	Toll-Free	Phone
1015 Lite FM		
20450 NW Second Ave .... Miami FL 33169	877-790-1015	
Kiss 999 194 NW 187th St .... Miami FL 33169	866-954-0999	305-654-1700
WINZ-AM 940 (N/T)		
7601 Riviera Blvd .... Miramar FL 33023	844-289-7234	
WIOD-AM 610 (N/T)		
7601 Riviera Blvd .... Miramar FL 33023	866-610-6397	954-862-2000
WMXJ-FM 1027 (Oldies)		
20450 NW Second Ave .... Miami FL 33169	800-924-1027	305-521-5240

641-66 Mishawaka, IN

	Toll-Free	Phone
Federated Media 245 Edison Rd Ste 250 . . . . Mishawaka IN 46545	888-333-6133	
WNDV-FM 929 (CHR) 3371 Cleveland Rd Ste 300 . . . . .South Bend IN 46628	800-242-0100	574-273-9300

641-67 Mobile, AL

	Toll-Free	Phone
WBHY-FM 885 (Rel) PO Box 1328 . . . . Mobile AL 36633	888-473-8488	251-473-8488
WGOK Gospel 900 2800 Dauphin St Ste 104 . . . . Mobile AL 36606	866-992-5660	251-423-9900

641-68 Naples, FL

	Toll-Free	Phone
WAVV-FM 1011 11800 Tamiami Trl E . . . . Naples FL 34113	866-310-9288	239-775-9288

641-69 Nashville, TN

	Toll-Free	Phone
SuperTalk 997 WTN 10 Music Cir E . . . . Nashville TN 37203	800-618-7445	615-321-1067
WPLN-FM 903 (NPR) 630 Mainstream Dr . . . . Nashville TN 37228	877-760-2903	615-760-2903

641-70 New Orleans, LA

	Toll-Free	Phone
WWNO-FM 899 (NPR) University of New Orleans 2000 Lakeshore Dr . . . . .New Orleans LA 70148	800-286-7002	504-280-7000

641-71 New York, NY

	Toll-Free	Phone
NJTV 825 Eighth Ave . . . . New York NY 10019	800-882-6622	609-777-0031
Power 1051 32 Ave of the Americas . . . . New York NY 10013	800-585-1051	212-377-7900
Q 1043 32 Ave of the Americas . . . . New York NY 10013	888-872-1043	212-377-7900
WFAN-AM 66 (Rel) 345 Hudson St 10th Fl . . . . New York NY 10014	866-540-9326	
WQHT-FM 971 (Urban) 395 Hudson St 7th Fl . . . . New York NY 10014	800-223-9797	212-229-9797

641-72 Norfolk/Virginia Beach, VA

	Toll-Free	Phone
WGH 5589 Greenwich Rd Ste 200 . . . . Virginia Beach VA 23462	800-552-9935	757-671-1000

641-73 Oklahoma City, OK

	Toll-Free	Phone
News Radio 1000 KTOK 1900 NW Expy Ste 1000. . . . . .Oklahoma City OK 73118	844-289-7234	405-841-0200

641-74 Omaha, NE

	Toll-Free	Phone
Z92 FM 10714 Mockingbird Dr . . . . .Omaha NE 68127	800-955-9230	

641-75 Orlando, FL

	Toll-Free	Phone
1059 SUNNY FM 1800 Pembrook Dr Ste 400 . . . . Orlando FL 32810	877-919-1059	407-919-1000
WOMX-FM 1051 (AC) 1800 Pembrook Dr Ste 400 . . . . Orlando FL 32810	877-919-1051	407-919-1000
WWKA-FM 923 (Ctry) 4192 N John Young Pkwy . . . . Orlando FL 32804	866-438-0220	407-424-9236

641-76 Ottawa, ON

	Toll-Free	Phone
CBVE-FM 1047 (CBC) PO Box 3220 Sta C . . . . Ottawa ON K1Y1E4	866-306-4636	
Ottawa-AM 1200 (Sports) 87 George St . . . . Ottawa ON K1N9H7	877-670-1200	613-789-2486

641-77 Palm Springs, CA

	Toll-Free	Phone
KCLB-FM 937 (Rock) 1321 N Gene Autry Trl . . . . Palm Springs CA 92262	800-827-2946	760-322-7890

641-78 Pensacola, FL

	Toll-Free	Phone
Rejoice Radio PO Box 18000 . . . . .Pensacola FL 32523	800-726-1191	850-479-6570
WUWF-FM 881 (NPR) 11000 University Pkwy .Pensacola FL 32514	800-239-9893	850-474-2787

641-79 Peoria, IL

	Toll-Free	Phone
WCIC-FM 915 (Rel) 3902 W Baring Trace . . . . Peoria IL 61615	877-692-9242	309-692-9242

641-80 Philadelphia, PA

	Toll-Free	Phone
KYW-NEWSRADIO 1060 (N/T) 1555 Hamilton St . . . . .Philadelphia PA 19130	800-223-8477	215-977-5333
WRTI-FM 901 (NPR) 1509 Cecil B Moore Ave 3rd Fl. . . . . .Philadelphia PA 19121	866-809-9784	215-204-8405

641-81 Phoenix, AZ

	Toll-Free	Phone
1047 Kiss FM 4686 E Van Buren St Ste 300 . . . . Phoenix AZ 85008	844-289-7234	602-374-6000

641-82 Pierre, SD

	Toll-Free	Phone
KMLO-FM 1007 (Ctry) 214 W Pleasant Dr PO Box 1197 . . . . Pierre SD 57501	800-658-5439	605-224-8686
KPLO-FM 945 (Ctry) 214 W Pleasant Dr . . . . Pierre SD 57501 *General	800-658-5439*	605-224-8686

641-83 Pittsburgh, PA

	Toll-Free	Phone
WQED-FM 893 (Clas) 4802 Fifth Ave . . . . .Pittsburgh PA 15213	855-700-9733	412-622-1300

641-84 Providence, RI

	Toll-Free	Phone
94 HJY 75 Oxford St Ste 301 . . . . .Providence RI 02905	844-289-7234	401-224-1994
News Radio 920 AM & 1047 FM 75 Oxford St Ste 301 . . . . .Providence RI 02905	866-920-9455	

641-85 Raleigh/Durham, NC

	Toll-Free	Phone
Foxy 1071 8001-101 Creedmoor Rd . . . . .Raleigh NC 27613	800-467-3699	919-848-9736
Light 1039 FM, The 8001-101 Creedmoor Rd . . . . .Raleigh NC 27613	877-310-9665	919-848-9736
WQOK K975 8001 Creedmoor Rd Ste 101 . . . . .Raleigh NC 27613	800-321-5975	919-848-9736
WSHA-FM 889 (Jazz) 118 E S St . . . . .Raleigh NC 27601	800-241-0421	919-546-8430

641-86 Redlands, CA

	Toll-Free	Phone
KGGI-FM 991 (CHR) 2030 Iowa Ave Ste 100 . . . . Riverside CA 92507	866-991-5444	951-684-1991
KSGN-FM 897 (Rel) 2048 Orange Tree Ln Ste 200 . . . . Redlands CA 92374	888-897-5746	909-583-2150

641-87 Reno/Carson City, NV

	Toll-Free	Phone
KLCA 961 Matley Ln Ste 120 .Reno NV 89502	855-354-9111	775-829-1964
KNIS-FM 913 (Rel) PO Box 21888 . . . . Carson City NV 89721	800-541-5647	775-883-5647
KODS-FM 1037 (Oldies) 961 Matley Ln Ste 120 . . . . .Reno NV 89502	855-354-9111	775-829-1964

641-88 Richmond, KY

	Toll-Free	Phone
WKYL-FM 1021 (NAC) 102 Perkins Bldg 521 Lancaster Ave . . . . .Richmond KY 40475	800-621-8890	

641-89 Richmond, VA

	Toll-Free	Phone
ESPN Richmond 950 2809 Emerywood Pkwy Ste 300 . . . . .Richmond VA 23294	877-994-4950	804-672-9299

641-90 Roanoke, VA

	Toll-Free	Phone
WSLQ-FM 991 (AC)		
3934 Electric Rd SW .... Roanoke VA 24018	800-410-9936	540-387-0234
WVTF-FM 891 (NPR)		
3520 Kingsbury Ln .... Roanoke VA 24014	800-856-8900	540-989-8900

641-91 Sacramento, CA

	Toll-Free	Phone
Capital Public Radio Inc		
7055 Folsom Blvd .... Sacramento CA 95826	877-480-5900	916-278-8900
KHTK-AM 1140 (Sports)		
5244 Madison Ave .... Sacramento CA 95841	800-920-1140	916-338-9200
KTKZ - AM 1380 The Answer		
1425 River Pk Dr Ste 520 .... Sacramento CA 95815	888-923-1380	916-924-9435
KXPR-FM 889 (Clas)		
7055 Folsom Blvd .... Sacramento CA 95826	877-480-5900	916-278-8900

641-92 Saint Louis, MO

	Toll-Free	Phone
KTRS-AM 550 (N/T)		
638 Westport Plz .... Saint Louis MO 63146	888-550-5877	314-453-5500
KWMU-FM 907 (NPR)		
3651 Olive St .... St. Louis MO 63108	866-240-5968	314-516-5968

641-93 Salt Lake City, UT

	Toll-Free	Phone
1430 KLO		
257 East 200 South Ste 400 .... Salt Lake City UT 84111	866-627-1430	801-364-9836
KEGA-FM 1015 (Ctry)		
50 West Broadway Ste 200 .... Salt Lake City UT 84101	866-551-1015	801-524-2600
KZNS-AM 1280 (Sports)		
301 W South Temple .... Salt Lake City UT 84101	855-340-9663	801-325-2043

641-94 San Antonio, TX

	Toll-Free	Phone
930 AM The Answer		
9601 McAllister Fwy Ste 1200 .... San Antonio TX 78216	866-308-8867	210-344-8481
KISS-FM 995 (Rock)		
8122 Datapoint Dr Ste 600 .... San Antonio TX 78229	855-787-2227	210-615-5400
KSTX-FM 891 (NPR)		
8401 Datapoint Dr Ste 800 .... San Antonio TX 78229	800-622-8977	210-614-8977
WOAI-AM 1200 (N/T)		
6222 Interstate 10 .... San Antonio TX 78201	800-383-9624	210-736-9700

641-95 San Diego, CA

	Toll-Free	Phone
1037 KSON		
?9665 Granite Ridge Dr Ste 600 .... San Diego CA 92123	833-287-1037	619-291-9797
KPBS Public Broadcasting		
5200 Campanile Dr .... San Diego CA 92182	888-399-5727	619-265-6438

641-96 San Francisco, CA

	Toll-Free	Phone
985 KFOX		
201 Third St Ste 1200. .... San Francisco CA 94103	877-410-5369	
Autonet Mobile Inc		
3636 N Laughlin Dr Ste 150 .... Santa Rosa CA 95403	800-977-2107	415-223-0316
KQED-FM 885 (NPR)		
2601 Mariposa St .... San Francisco CA 94110	800-723-3566	415-864-2000
KSAN-FM 1077 (Alt)		
750 Battery St Ste300 .... San Francisco CA 94111	888-303-2663	415-995-6800
Wild 949		
340 Townsend St 4th Fl .... San Francisco CA 94107	888-333-9490	415-975-5555

641-97 Savannah, GA

	Toll-Free	Phone
973 Kiss FM 245 Alfred St .... Savannah GA 31408	800-543-3548	912-964-7794
WSVH 911 FM		
13040 Abercorn St Ste 8. .... Savannah GA 31419	877-472-1227	912-344-3565

641-98 Seattle/Tacoma, WA

	Toll-Free	Phone
1061 Kiss Fm Seattle		
645 Elliott Ave W Ste 400 .... Seattle WA 98119	888-343-1061	866-311-9806
965 JACK-FM		
645 Elliott Ave W Ste 400 .... Seattle WA 98119	844-289-7234	
KING-FM 981 (Clas)		
10 Harrison St Ste 100 .... Seattle WA 98109	888-598-9810	206-691-2981
KIRO-FM 973		
1820 Eastlake Ave E .... Seattle WA 98102	800-756-5476	206-726-7000
KJR-AM 950 (Sports)		
645 Elliott Ave W Ste 400 .... Seattle WA 98119	800-829-0950	206-494-2000
KPLZ-FM 1015 (AC)		
140 Fourth Ave N Ste 340 .... Seattle WA 98109	888-821-1015	206-404-4000

	Toll-Free	Phone
KUOW-FM 949 (NPR)		
4518 University Way NE Ste 310 .... Seattle WA 98105	800-289-5869	206-543-2710
KVI-AM 570 (N/T)		
140 Fourth Ave N Ste 340. .... Seattle WA 98109	888-312-5757	206-404-4000

641-99 Shreveport, LA

	Toll-Free	Phone
KDAQ-FM 899 (NPR)		
8675 Youree Dr .... Shreveport LA 71115	800-552-8502	318-798-0102

641-100 Spartanburg, SC

	Toll-Free	Phone
WCQS-FM 881 (NPR)		
73 Broadway .... Asheville NC 28801	866-448-3881	828-210-4800
WSKY 1230 AM		
292 S Pine St PO Box 444 .... Spartanburg SC 29302	888-989-2299	

641-101 Spokane, WA

	Toll-Free	Phone
Spokane Public Radio		
2319 N Monroe St .... Spokane WA 99201	800-328-5729	509-328-5729

641-102 Springfield, IL

	Toll-Free	Phone
NPR Illinois 919 UIS		
University of Illinois at Springfield		
1 University Plz WUIS-130 .... Springfield IL 62703	866-206-9847	217-206-9847

641-103 Springfield, MO

	Toll-Free	Phone
KSMS-FM 905 (NPR)		
Missouri State University		
901 S National .... Springfield MO 65897	800-767-5768	417-836-5878
KSMU-FM 911 (NPR)		
901 S National .... Springfield MO 65897	800-767-5768	417-836-5878
outlaw 1013 KTXR, The		
3000 E Chestnut Expy .... Springfield MO 65802	855-586-8852*	417-862-3751
*General		

641-104 Stamford/Bridgeport, CT

	Toll-Free	Phone
WEBE-FM 108 (AC)		
2 Lafayette Sq .... Bridgeport CT 06604	800-932-3108	203-333-9108

641-105 Stockton, CA

	Toll-Free	Phone
KYCC-FM 901 9019 W Ln .... Stockton CA 95210	800-654-5254	209-477-3690

641-106 Syracuse, NY

	Toll-Free	Phone
WSYR-AM 570 (N/T)		
500 Plum St Ste 400. .... Syracuse NY 13204	844-289-7234	315-472-9797
Y94 iHeartMedia		
500 Plum St Ste 400. .... Syracuse NY 13204	844-289-7234	315-472-9797

641-107 Tallahassee, FL

	Toll-Free	Phone
WFSQ-FM 915 (Clas)		
1600 Red Barber Plz .... Tallahassee FL 32310	855-937-8123	850-645-7200
WFSU-FM 889 (NPR)		
1600 Red Barber Plz .... Tallahassee FL 32310	855-937-8123	850-645-7200

641-108 Tampa/Saint Petersburg, FL

	Toll-Free	Phone
995 QYK		
9721 Executive Ctr Dr N		
Ste 200 .... Saint Petersburg FL 33702	800-992-1099	727-579-1925
Cox Media Group Tampa		
11300 Fourth St N Ste 300 .... Saint Petersburg FL 33716	888-723-9388	727-579-2000
FaithTalk 570 & 910 WTBN		
5211 W Laurel St .... Tampa FL 33607	800-576-3771	813-639-1903
WDAE-AM 620 (Sports)		
4002 W Gandy Blvd .... Tampa FL 33611	888-546-4620	813-832-1000
WHPT-FM 1025 (CR)		
11300 Fourth St N Ste 300 .... Saint Petersburg FL 33716	800-771-1025	727-579-2000
WSUN-FM 971 (Alt)		
11300 Fourth St N Ste 300 .... Saint Petersburg FL 33716	877-327-9797	727-579-2000
WUSF 4202 E Fowler Ave TVB 100 .... Tampa FL 33620	800-741-9090	813-974-8700
WUSF Public Broadcasting		
4202 E Fowler Ave TVB100 .... Tampa FL 33620	800-741-9090	813-974-8700
WXGL-FM 1073 (AC)		
11300 Fourth St N Ste 300 .... Saint Petersburg FL 33716	800-242-1073	727-579-2000

641-109 Tigard, OR

			Toll-Free	Phone
1067 The Eagle 13333 SW 68th Pkwy Ste 310 . . . . .Tigard OR	97223		**844-289-7234**	503-323-6400
923 FM KGON 0700 SW Bancroft St . . . . .Portland OR	97239		**800-222-9236**	503-223-1441
All Classical Portland 211 SE Caruthers St Ste 200 . . . . .Portland OR	97214		**888-306-5277**	503-943-5828
KBNP-AM 1410 (N/T) 278 SW Arthur St . . . . .Portland OR	97201		**888-214-9237**	503-223-6769
KEX-AM 1190 (N/T) 13333 SW 68th Pkwy Ste 310 . . . . .Poland OR	97223		**844-289-7234**	503-323-6400
KNRK-FM 947 (Alt) 0700 SW Bancroft St . . . . .Portland OR	97239		**800-777-0947**	503-733-5470
KPDQ-FM 939 (Rel) 6400 SE Lake Rd Ste 350 . . . . .Portland OR	97222		**800-845-2162**	503-786-0600
KWJJ-FM 995 (Ctry) 0700 SW Bancroft St . . . . .Portland OR	97239		**866-239-9653**	503-733-9653
Rip city radio 620 13333 SW 68th Pkwy Ste 310 . . . . .Tigard OR	97223		**844-289-7234**	503-323-6400

641-110 Toledo, OH

			Toll-Free	Phone
WRQN-FM 935 (Oldies) 3225 Arlington Ave . . . . .Toledo OH	43614		**866-240-1935**	419-725-5700
WXKR-FM 945 (CR) 3225 Arlington Ave . . . . .Toledo OH	43614		**866-240-9945**	419-725-5700

641-111 Topeka, KS

			Toll-Free	Phone
KMAJ-AM 1440 825 S Kansas Ave Ste 100 . . . . .Topeka KS	66612		**877-297-1077**	785-272-2122
KMAJ-FM 1077 (AC) 825 S Kansas Ave Ste 100 . . . . .Topeka KS	66612		**877-297-1077**	785-272-2122
KWIC-FM 993 (Oldies) 825 S Kansas Ave Ste 100 . . . . .Topeka KS	66612		**844-366-8993**	913-795-2665

641-112 Tulsa, OK

			Toll-Free	Phone
KMOD-FM 975 (Rock) 7136 S Yale Ave Ste 500. .Tulsa OK	74136		**844-289-7234**	918-388-5100
KRMG-AM 740 (N/T) 7136 S Yale Ave Ste 500. .Tulsa OK	74136		**855-297-9696**	918-493-7400
Public Radio 895 800 Tucker Dr . . . . .Tulsa OK	74104		**888-594-5947**	918-631-2577

641-113 Tuscaloosa, AL

			Toll-Free	Phone
WHIL-FM 913 (NPR) 920 Paul W Bryant Dr Bryant Denny Stadium Rm N460 . . . . .Tuscaloosa AL	35487		**800-654-4262**	205-348-6644
WUAL-FM 915 (NPR) 920 Paul W Bryant Dr PO Box 870370 . . . . .Tuscaloosa AL	35487		**800-654-4262**	205-348-8620

641-114 Washington, DC

			Toll-Free	Phone
WHUR-FM 963 (Urban AC) 529 Bryant St NW . . . . .Washington DC	20059		**800-221-9487**	202-432-9487

641-115 West Palm Beach, FL

			Toll-Free	Phone
KOOL 1055 3071 Continental Dr . . . . .West Palm Beach FL	33407		**888-415-1055**	561-616-6600
Sunny 1079 Radio *Palm Beach Broadcasting* 701 Northpoint Pkwy Ste 500. . . . . .West Palm Beach FL	33407		**800-919-1079**	561-616-4777
WBZT-AM 1230 (N/T) 3071 Continental Dr . . . . .West Palm Beach FL	33407		**800-889-0267**	561-616-6600
WXEL-FM 907 (NPR) 3401 S Congress Ave . . . . .Boynton Beach FL	33426		**800-915-9935**	561-737-8000

641-116 Wilmington/Dover, DE

			Toll-Free	Phone
WDEL-AM 1150 (N/T) 2727 Shipley Rd .Wilmington DE	19810		**800-544-1150**	302-478-2700
WSTW-FM 937 (CHR) 2727 Shipley Rd .Wilmington DE	19810		**800-544-9370**	302-478-2700

641-117 Winnipeg, MB

			Toll-Free	Phone
CBC Manitoba 541 Portage Ave . . . . .Winnipeg MB	R3C2H1		**877-666-6292**	204-788-3222

641-118 Winooski, VT

			Toll-Free	Phone
WIZN-FM 1067 450 Weaver St . . . . .Winooski VT	05404		**888-873-9496**	802-860-2440

642   RADIO SYNDICATORS

			Toll-Free	Phone
American Urban Radio Networks 938 Penn Ave Ste 701 .Pittsburgh PA	15222		**800-456-4211**	412-456-4099
Car Clinic Productions 5675 N Davis Hwy . . . . .Pensacola FL	32503		**888-227-2546**	850-478-3139
Radio America 1100 N Glebe Rd Ste 900 . . . . .Arlington VA	22201		**800-807-4703**	703-302-1000
Syndication Networks Corp 8700 Waukegan Rd Ste 250 . . . . .Morton Grove IL	60053		**800-743-1988**	847-583-9000
Transmedia 719 Battery St . . . . .San Francisco CA	94111		**800-229-7234**	415-956-3118
TRN (TRN) PO Box 3755 . . . . .Central Point OR	97502		**888-383-3733**	
WCLV 1375 Euclid Ave Idea Ctr . . . . .Cleveland OH	44115		**877-399-3307**	216-916-6100

643   RADIO & TELEVISION BROADCASTING & COMMUNICATIONS EQUIPMENT

SEE ALSO Audio & Video Equipment ; Telecommunications Equipment & Systems

			Toll-Free	Phone
AheadTek Inc 6410 Via Del Oro . . . . .San Jose CA	95119		**800-971-9191**	408-226-9991
Airbiquity Inc 1011 Western Ave Ste 600 . . . . .Seattle WA	98104		**888-334-7741**	206-219-2700
Andersen Manufacturing Inc 3125 N Yellowstone Hwy . . . . .Idaho Falls ID	83401		**800-635-6106**	208-523-6460
AR 160 Schoolhouse Rd . . . . .Souderton PA	18964		**800-933-8181**	215-723-8181
Arris Group Inc 3871 Lakefield Dr .Suwanee GA *NASDAQ: ARRS*	30024		**866-362-7747**	678-473-2000
Artel Video Systems Corp 5B Lyberty Way . . . . .Westford MA	01886		**800-225-0228**	978-263-5775
Ascom North America 300 Perimeter Park Dr . . . . .Morrisville NC	27560		**877-712-7266**	
Atrex Inc 1633 Farm Way Ste 505 . . . . .Middleburg FL	32068		**800-874-4505**	904-264-9600
Avi Systems Inc 9675 W 76th St Ste 200 . . . . .Eden Prairie MN	55344		**800-488-4954**	952-949-3700
Axcera Corp 103 Freedom Dr . . . . .Lawrence PA	15055		**800-215-2614**	724-873-8100
Beacon Wireless 815 Middlefield Rd Unit 1. . . . . .Toronto ON	M1V2P9		**866-867-7770**	416-696-7555
Blonder Tongue Laboratories Inc 1 Jake Brown Rd .Old Bridge NJ *NYSE: BDR*	08857		**877-407-8033**	732-679-4000
Cabot Coach Builders Inc 99 Newark St . . . . .Haverhill MA	01832		**800-544-5587**	978-374-4530
Coaxial Dynamics 6800 Lake Abrams Dr . . . . .Middleburg Heights OH	44130		**800-262-9425**	440-243-1100
Cobalt Digital Inc 2506 Galen Dr . . . . .Champaign IL	61821		**800-669-1691**	217-344-1243
COMARK Communications 104 Feeding Hills Rd . . . . .Southwick MA	01077		**800-288-8364**	413-998-1100
Connecticut Radio Holding Inc 1208 Cromwell Ave PO Box 487. . . . . .Rocky Hill CT	06067		**800-527-8855**	860-563-4867
Conolog Corp 5 Columbia Rd . . . . .Somerville NJ *NASDAQ: CNLG*	08876		**800-526-3984**	908-722-8081
Continental Electronics Corp 4212 S Buckner Blvd .Dallas TX	75227		**800-733-5011**	214-381-7161
Destron Fearing 2805 E 14th St . . . . .Irving TX	75261		**800-328-0118**	
Dielectric Communications Inc 22 Tower Rd . . . . .Raymond ME	04071		**800-341-9678**	
Eagle Comtronics Inc 7665 Henry Clay Blvd . . . . .Liverpool NY	13088		**800-448-7474**	315-622-3402
EFJohnson Technologies 1440 Corporate Dr . . . . .Irving TX	75038		**800-328-3911**	972-819-0700
GAI-Tronics Corp 400 E Wyomissing Ave . . . . .Mohnton PA	19540		**800-492-1212**	610-777-1374
Globecomm Systems Inc 45 Oser Ave . . . . .Hauppauge NY *NASDAQ: GCOM*	11788		**866-499-0223**	631-231-9800
Guardian Mobility Corp 43 Auriga Dr . . . . .Ottawa ON	K2E7Y8		**888-817-8159**	613-225-8885
Harmonic Inc 4300 N First St . . . . .San Jose CA *NASDAQ: HLIT*	95134		**800-322-2885**	408-542-2500
Harris Corp 1025 W NASA Blvd . . . . .Melbourne FL *NYSE: HRS*	32919		**800-442-7747**	321-727-9100
Harris Corp RF Communications Div 1680 University Ave . . . . .Rochester NY	14610		**866-264-8040**	585-244-5830
Hitachi Kokusai Electric America Ltd 150 Crossways Pk Dr . . . . .Woodbury NY	11797		**855-490-5124**	516-921-7200
Honeywell International Inc 101 Columbia Rd PO Box 2245 . . . . .Morristown NJ *NYSE: HON*	07962		**877-841-2840**	480-353-3020
ICOM America Inc 2380 116th Ave NE . . . . .Bellevue WA	98004		**800-872-4266**	425-454-8155
ID Systems Inc 123 Tice Blvd Ste 101. . . . . .Woodcliff Lake NJ *NASDAQ: IDSY*	07677		**866-410-0152**	201-996-9000
Industrial Communications & Electronics Inc 40 Lone St . . . . .Marshfield MA	02050		**800-822-9999**	781-319-1100

			Toll-Free	Phone
Iteris Inc 1700 Carnegie Ave Ste 100 *NASDAQ: ITI*	Santa Ana	CA 92705	**888-254-5487**	949-270-9400
Jampro Antennas Inc 6340 Sky Creek Dr	Sacramento	CA 95828	**800-732-7665**	916-383-1177
Jem Engineering LLC 8683 Cherry Ln	Laurel	MD 20707	**877-317-1070**	301-317-1070
Kenwood USA PO Box 22745	Long Beach	CA 90810	**800-536-9663**	310-639-9000
Klein Electronics Inc 349 N Vinewood St	Escondido	CA 92029	**800-959-2899**	760-781-3220
Kyocera Communications Inc 9520 Towne Centre Dr	San Diego	CA 92121	**800-349-4188**	858-882-1400
L-3 Communications Telemetry East Div 1515 Grundy's Ln	Bristol	PA 19007	**800-351-8483**	267-545-7000
L-3 Communications Telemetry West Div 9020 Balboa Ave	San Diego	CA 92123	**800-351-8483**	858-694-7500
Lightspeed Aviation Inc 6135 Jean Rd	Lake Oswego	OR 97035	**800-332-2421**	503-968-3113
Logitek Electronic Systems Inc 5622 Edgemoor Dr	Houston	TX 77081	**877-231-5870**	713-664-4470
MCL Inc 501 S Woodcreek Rd *Support	Bolingbrook	IL 60440	**800-743-4625***	630-759-9500
MFJ Enterprises Inc 300 Industrial Pk Rd	Starkville	MS 39759	**800-647-1800**	662-323-5869
Midian Electronic Comm Systems 2302 E 22nd St	Tucson	AZ 85713	**800-643-4267**	520-884-7981
Minerva Networks Inc 2150 Gold St	Santa Clara	CA 95002	**800-806-9594**	408-567-9400
Monitor Dynamics Inc 12500 Network Dr Ste 303	San Antonio	TX 78249	**866-435-7634**	210-477-5400
Nautel Ltd 10089 Peggy'S Cove Rd	Hackett'S Cove	NS B3Z3J4	**877-662-8835**	902-823-3900
NSC Communications 6820 Power Line Dr	Florence	KY 41042	**800-543-1584**	859-727-6640
ParkerVision Inc 7915 Baymeadows Way *NASDAQ: PRKR*	Jacksonville	FL 32256	**800-532-8034**	904-732-6100
Pelco 3500 Pelco Way	Clovis	CA 93612	**800-289-9100**	559-292-1981
RA Miller Industries Inc 14500 168th Ave PO Box 858	Grand Haven	MI 49417	**888-845-9450**	616-842-9450
Radio North 2682 Garfield Rd N Ste 22	Traverse City	MI 49686	**800-274-8255**	
RL Drake Co 710 Pleasant Valley Dr	Springboro	OH 45066	**800-276-4523**	937-746-4556
Rockwell Collins Inc 400 Collins Rd NE *NYSE: COL*	Cedar Rapids	IA 52498	**888-721-3094**	319-295-1000
Setcom Corp 3019 Alvin DeVane Blvd Ste 560	Austin	TX 78741	**800-645-1285**	650-965-8020
Shively Labs 188 Harrison Rd PO Box 389	Bridgton	ME 04009	**888-744-8359**	207-647-3327
Sonetics Corp 7340 SW Durham Rd	Portland	OR 97224	**800-833-4558**	
Space Systems/Loral 3825 Fabian Way	Palo Alto	CA 94303	**800-332-6490**	650-852-4000
Tecom Industries Inc 375 Conejo Ridge Ave	Thousand Oaks	CA 91361	**866-840-8550**	805-267-0100
Telepath Systems Inc 49111 Milmont Dr	Fremont	CA 94538	**800-292-1700**	510-656-5600
Thales Communications Inc 22605 Gateway Ctr Dr	Clarksburg	MD 20871	**800-258-4420**	240-864-7000
TPL Communications 3825 Foothill Blvd	La Crescenta	CA 91214	**800-447-6937**	323-256-3000
Ultra Electronics Flightline Systems Inc 7625 Omni Tech Pl	Victor	NY 14564	**888-959-9001**	585-924-4000
Ultra Electronics-DNE Technologies Inc 50 Barnes Industrial Pk N	Wallingford	CT 06492	**800-370-4485**	203-265-7151
Unique Broadband Systems Ltd 400 Spinnaker Way	Vaughan	ON L4K5Y9	**877-669-8533**	905-669-8533
VehSmart Inc 12180 Ridgecrest Rd Ste 412	Victorville	CA 92395	**855-834-7627**	
Vicon Industries Inc 135 Fell Ct *NYSE: VII ■ *Sales*	Hauppauge	NY 11788	**800-645-9116***	631-952-2288
Wilcom Inc 73 Daniel Webster Hwy PO Box 508	Belmont	NH 03220	**800-222-1898**	603-524-2622
Winegard Co 3000 Kirkwood St *Cust Svc	Burlington	IA 52601	**800-288-8094***	319-754-0600
Xcitex Inc 25 First St Ste 105	Cambridge	MA 02141	**800-780-7836**	

644 RAIL TRANSPORT SERVICES

SEE ALSO Logistics Services (Transportation & Warehousing)

			Toll-Free	Phone
Aberdeen & Rockfish Railroad Co 101 E Main St	Aberdeen	NC 28315	**800-849-8985**	910-944-2341
Buffalo & Pittsburgh Railroad Inc (BPRR) 1200-C Scottsville Rd Ste 200	Rochester	NY 14624	**800-603-3385**	585-463-3307
Burlington Northern & Santa Fe Railway (BNSF) 2650 Lou Menk Dr	Fort Worth	TX 76131	**800-795-2673**	
Canadian National Railway Co 935 Rue de la Gauchetiere O *NYSE: CNI*	Montreal	QC H3B2M9	**888-668-4626**	888-888-5909
Canadian Pacific 7550 Ogden Dale Rd SE	Calgary	AB T2C4X9	**888-333-6370**	
CHEP USA 8517 S Pk Cir *Cust Svc	Orlando	FL 32819	**866-855-2437***	407-370-2437
Chicago Southshore & South Bend Railroad 505 N Carroll Ave	Michigan City	IN 46360	**800-356-2079**	219-874-9000
Consolidated Rail Corp 1717 Arch St 13th Fl	Philadelphia	PA 19103	**800-272-0911**	215-209-2000
CSX Transportation Inc 500 Water St	Jacksonville	FL 32202	**800-737-1663**	904-359-3100

			Toll-Free	Phone
Dardanelle & Russellville Railroad Co 4416 S Arkansas Ave	Russellville	AR 72802	**888-877-7267**	479-968-6455
Genesee & Wyoming Inc 66 Field Pt Rd *NYSE: GWR*	Greenwich	CT 06830	**800-230-1059**	203-629-3722
Iowa Interstate Railroad 5900 Sixth St SW	Cedar Rapids	IA 52404	**800-321-3891**	319-298-5400
Kansas City Southern Railway Co 427 W 12th St	Kansas City	MO 64105	**800-468-6527**	816-983-1303
Montana Rail Link Inc 101 International Way	Missoula	MT 59808	**800-338-4750**	406-523-1500
New York Susquehanna & Western Railway Corp (NYSW) 1 Railroad Ave *General	Cooperstown	NY 13326	**800-366-6979***	607-547-2555
Norfolk Southern Railway Co 3 Commercial Pl	Norfolk	VA 23510	**800-635-5768**	800-453-2530
Trans-Continental Systems Inc 10801 Evendale Dr	Cincinnati	OH 45241	**800-525-8726**	513-769-4774
Triple Crown Services 2720 Dupont Commerce Ct	Fort Wayne	IN 46825	**800-325-6510**	260-416-3600
Union Pacific Railroad Co 1400 Douglas St	Omaha	NE 68179	**888-870-8777**	

645 RAIL TRAVEL

SEE ALSO Mass Transportation (Local & Suburban)

			Toll-Free	Phone
Dew Distribution Services Inc 2201 Touhy Ave	Elk Grove Village	IL 60007	**800-837-3391**	
Indiana Rail Road Co, The 101 W Ohio St Ste 1600	Indianapolis	IN 46204	**888-596-2121**	317-262-5140
Iowa Northern Railway Co 305 Second St SE Paramount Theatre Bldg Ste 400	Cedar Rapids	IA 52401	**800-392-3342**	319-297-6000
National Railroad Passenger Corp 60 Massachusetts Ave NE	Washington	DC 20002	**800-872-7245**	202-906-3741
Omega Rail Management 4721 Trousdale Dr Ste 206	Nashville	TN 37220	**800-990-1961**	
Patriot Rail Company LLC 10060 Skinner Lake Dr	Jacksonville	FL 32246	**855-258-4514**	904-423-2540
Twin Cities & Western Railroad 2925 12th St E	Glencoe	MN 55336	**800-290-8297**	320-864-7200
VIA Rail Canada Inc 3 Place Ville Marie Ste 500	Montreal	QC H3B2C9	**888-842-7245**	514-871-6000

646 RAILROAD EQUIPMENT - MFR

SEE ALSO Transportation Equipment & Supplies - Whol

			Toll-Free	Phone
A Stucki Co 2600 Neville Rd	Pittsburgh	PA 15225	**888-266-6630**	412-771-7300
American Railcar Industries Inc 100 Clark St *NASDAQ: ARII*	Saint Charles	MO 63301	**800-489-9888**	636-940-6000
CANAC Inc 6505 Trans-Canada Hwy Ste 405	St Laurent	QC H4T1S3	**800-588-4387**	514-734-4700
Cando Railway Services Ltd 740 Rosser Ave	Brandon	MB R7A0K9	**866-989-5310**	204-725-2627
Cardwell Westinghouse Co 8400 S Stewart Ave	Chicago	IL 60620	**800-821-2376**	773-483-7575
Dayton-Phoenix Group Inc 1619 Kuntz Rd	Dayton	OH 45404	**800-657-0707**	937-496-3900
FreightCar America Inc 17 Johns St *NASDAQ: RAIL*	Johnstown	PA 15901	**800-458-2235**	
Greenbrier Co 1 Centerpointe Dr Ste 200 *NYSE: GBX*	Lake Oswego	OR 97035	**800-343-7188**	503-684-7000
Holland LP 1000 Holland Dr	Crete	IL 60417	**800-895-4389**	708-672-2300
Interstate Transport Inc 324 First Ave N	St Petersburg	FL 33701	**866-281-1281**	727-822-9999
Kasgro Rail Corp 121 Rundle Rd	New Castle	PA 16102	**888-203-5580**	724-658-9061
LB Foster Co 415 Holiday Dr *NASDAQ: FSTR*	Pittsburgh	PA 15220	**800-255-4500**	
Miner Enterprises Inc 1200 E State St	Geneva	IL 60134	**888-822-5334**	630-232-3000
National Railway Equipment Co (NREC) 14400 Robey St	Dixmoor	IL 60426	**800-253-2905**	708-388-6002
New York Air Brake Co 748 Starbuck Ave	Watertown	NY 13601	**888-836-6922**	315-786-5200
Nolan Co 1016 Ninth St SW	Canton	OH 44707	**800-297-1383**	330-453-7922
Pacific Coast Container Inc 432 Estudillo Ave	San Leandro	CA 94577	**800-458-4788**	510-346-6100
Plasser American Corp 2001 Myers Rd PO Box 5464	Chesapeake	VA 23324	**800-388-4825**	757-543-3526
Rail Car Service Co 584 Fairground Rd	Mercer	PA 16137	**800-521-2151**	724-662-3660
Transco Railway Products Inc 200 N LaSalle St Ste 1550	Chicago	IL 60601	**800-472-4592**	312-427-2818
Transportation Research Corp 4305 Business Dr	Cameron Park	CA 95682	**888-676-7770**	530-676-7770
Trinity Mining Service 109 48th St	Pittsburgh	PA 15201	**800-264-2583**	412-682-4700
Trinity Rail Group LLC 2525 N Stemmons Fwy	Dallas	TX 75207	**800-631-4420**	214-631-4420
WABCO Locomotive Products 1001 Air Brake Ave *Cust Svc	Wilmerding	PA 15148	**877-922-2627***	412-825-1000
Wabtec Corp 1001 Air Brake Ave *NYSE: WAB ■ *Cust Svc*	Wilmerding	PA 15148	**877-922-2627***	412-825-1000

647   RAILROAD SWITCHING & TERMINAL SERVICES

					Toll-Free	Phone

Belt Railway Co of Chicago
6900 S Central Ave ....Bedford Park IL 60638 **877-772-5772** 708-496-4000

OmniTRAX Inc
252 Clayton St 4th Fl ....Denver CO 80206 **800-533-9416** 303-398-4500

Public Belt Railroad Commission
4822 Tchoupitulas St ....New Orleans LA 70115 **800-524-3421*** 504-896-7410
*Cust Svc

Railserve Inc
1691 Phoenix Blvd Ste 250 ....Atlanta GA 30349 **800-345-7245** 770-996-6838

Rescar Inc
1101 31st St Ste 250 ....Downers Grove IL 60515 **800-851-5196** 630-963-1114

Roadrunner Transportation Systems Inc
4900 S Pennsylvania Ave ....Cudahy WI 53110 **800-831-4394** 414-615-1500
NYSE: RRTS

Terminal Railroad Assn of Saint Louis
1017 Olive St 5th Fl ....Saint Louis MO 63101 **866-931-0498** 618-451-8400

Vermont Railway Inc
1 Railway Ln ....Burlington VT 05401 **800-639-3088** 802-658-2550

Wheeling & Lake Erie Railway Co
100 E First St ....Brewster OH 44613 **800-837-5622** 330-767-3401

648   REAL ESTATE AGENTS & BROKERS

					Toll-Free	Phone

Assist-2-Sell Inc
1610 Meadow Wood Ln ....Reno NV 89502 **800-528-7816** 775-688-6060

Bailey Properties
106 Aptos Beach Dr ....Aptos CA 95003 **800-347-6830** 831-688-7009

Baird & Warner Inc
120 S LaSalle St 20th Fl ....Chicago IL 60603 **888-661-1176** 312-368-1855

Beach Realty & Construction
4826 N Croatan Hwy ....Kitty Hawk NC 27949 **800-635-1559** 252-261-3815

Bosshardt Realty Services LLC
5542 NW 43rd St ....Gainesville FL 32653 **800-284-6110** 352-371-6100

Bray Real Estate
637 N Ave ....Grand Junction CO 81501 **888-760-4251** 970-242-8450

Brownstone Real Estate Co
1840 Fishburn Rd ....Hershey PA 17033 **877-533-6222** 717-533-6222

Cambria Pines Realty Inc
746-A Main St ....Cambria CA 93428 **800-676-8616** 805-927-8616

Carson Dunlop Home Inspection
120 Carlton St Ste 407 ....Toronto ON M5A4K2 **800-268-7070** 416-964-9415

CENTURY 21 Salvadori Realty
3500 N G St ....Merced CA 95340 **800-557-6033** 209-383-6475

Cityfeetcom Inc
101 California St 43rd Fl ....San Francisco CA 94111 **866-527-0540** 212-924-6450

Coast Property Management
2829 Rucker Ave ....Everett WA 98201 **800-339-3634**

Coldwell Banker Residential Brokerage
600 Grant St Ste 900 ....Denver CO 80203 **833-472-7283*** 303-320-5733
*All

Conterra Ultra Broadband LLC
2101 Rexford Rd Ste 200E ....Charlotte NC 28211 **800-634-1374** 704-365-6701

Corcoran
660 Madison Ave 12th Fl ....New York NY 10065 **800-544-4055** 212-355-3550

Crye-Leike Inc
6525 N Quail Hollow Rd ....Memphis TN 38120 **866-310-3102**

Cutten Realty Inc
2120 Campton Rd Ste C ....Eureka CA 95503 **800-776-4458** 707-445-8811

Dart Appraisalcom
2600 W Big Beaver Rd Ste 540 ....Troy MI 48084 **888-327-8123**

EQUESTRIAN CANADA QUESTRE
2685 Queensview Dr ....Ottawa ON K2B8K2 **866-282-8395** 613-248-3484

ERA Wilder Realty Inc
120A Columbia Ave ....Chapin SC 29036 **866-593-7653** 803-345-6713

Fimc Commercial Realty
1619 Tyler ....Amarillo TX 79102 **800-658-2616** 806-358-7151

H Pearce Real Estate Co
393 State St ....North Haven CT 06405 **800-373-3411** 203-281-3400

Hart Corp 900 Jaymor Rd ....SouthHampton PA 18966 **800-368-4278** 215-322-5100

HomeGaincom Inc
6001 Shellmound St Ste 550 ....Emeryville CA 94608 **888-542-0800** 510-655-0800

HomeServices of America Inc
333 S Seventh St 27th Fl ....Minneapolis MN 55402 **888-485-0018**

Iowa Realty Company Inc
3501 Westown Pkwy ....West Des Moines IA 50266 **800-247-2430** 515-453-6222

Jack Conway
137 Washington St ....Norwell MA 02061 **800-283-1030** 781-871-0080

Janet Mcafee Real Estate
9889 Clayton Rd ....Saint Louis MO 63124 **888-991-4800** 314-997-4800

Jersey Cape Realty Inc
739 Washington St ....Cape May NJ 08204 **800-643-0043** 609-884-5800

John Daugherty Realtors
520 Post Oak Blvd 6th Fl ....Houston TX 77027 **800-231-2821** 713-626-3930

JR Realty
101 E Horizon Dr ....Henderson NV 89015 **800-541-6780** 702-564-5142

Keefe Real Estate
1155 E Geneva St ....Delavan WI 53115 **800-690-2292** 262-728-8757

Keystone Property Group
125 E Elm St Ste 400 ....Conshohocken PA 19004 **866-980-1818** 610-980-7000

Lereta LLC 1123 Parkview Dr ....Covina CA 91724 **800-537-3821**

LG2 Environmental Solutions Inc
10475 Fortune Pkwy Ste 201 ....Jacksonville FL 32256 **800-435-0072** 904-288-8631

Long & Foster Realtors
14501 George Carter Way ....Chantilly VA 20151 **800-237-8800** 703-653-8500

Macdonald Realty
203 5188 Wminster Hwy ....Richmond BC V7C5S7 **877-278-3888** 604-279-9822

MCAP Service Corp
400-200 King St W ....Toronto ON M5H3T4 **800-387-4405** 416-598-2665

National Church Residences Inc
2335 N Bank Dr ....Columbus OH 43220 **800-388-2151**

					Toll-Free	Phone

NP Dodge Real Estate
8701 W Dodge Rd Ste 300 ....Omaha NE 68114 **800-642-5008** 402-255-5099

Ontario Real Estate Assn
99 Duncan Mill Rd ....Don Mills ON M3B1Z2 **866-444-5557** 416-445-9910

Pacific Coast Valuations
740 Corporate Ctr Dr ....Pomona CA 91768 **888-623-4001**

Pacifica Hotels
39 Argonaut ....Aliso Viejo CA 92656 **800-720-0223** 805-957-0095

Patterson-Schwartz & Assoc Inc
7234 Lancaster Pk Ste 100A ....Hockessin DE 19707 **877-456-4663** 302-234-5270

Premier Realty Group
2 N Sewalls Point Rd ....Stuart FL 34996 **800-915-8517** 772-287-1777

Quad Cities Realty
1053 Ripon Ave ....Lewiston ID 83501 **877-798-7798** 208-798-7798

RE/MAX International Inc
5075 S Syracuse St ....Denver CO 80237 **800-525-7452*** 303-770-5531
*Cust Svc

RE/MAX Quebec Inc
1500 rue Cunard ....Laval QC H7S2B7 **800-361-9325** 450-668-7743

Real Estate Express
12977 N 40 Dr Ste 108 ....Saint Louis MO 63141 **866-739-7277**

Real Estate Institute of Bc
1750 - 355 Burrard St ....Vancouver BC V6C2G8 **800-667-2166** 604-685-3702

Real Estate One Inc
25800 NW Hwy ....Southfield MI 48075 **800-521-0508** 248-208-2900

Real Living First Service Realty
13155 SW 42nd St Ste 200 ....Miami FL 33175 **800-899-8477** 305-551-9400

Real Living Real Estate LLC
77 E Nationwide Blvd ....Columbus OH 43215 **800-274-7653** 949-794-7900

RealCapitalMarketscom LLC
5780 Fleet St Ste 130 ....Carlsbad CA 92008 **888-546-5281**

Realty Executives International Inc
645 E Missouri Ave Ste 210 ....Phoenix AZ 85020 **800-252-3366** 480-239-2038

RIS Media Inc 69 E Ave ....Norwalk CT 06851 **800-724-6000** 203-855-1234

Ross Realty Investments Inc
3325 S University Dr Ste 210 ....Davie FL 33328 **800-370-4202** 954-452-5000

Sam Hatfield Realty Inc
4470 Mansford Rd ....Winchester TN 37398 **866-959-7474** 931-968-0500

Select Group Real Estate Inc
409 Century Park Dr ....Yuba City CA 95991 **800-992-3883**

Semonin Realtors
600 N Hurstbourne Pkwy Ste 200 ....Louisville KY 40222 **800-548-1650** 502-425-4760

Shorewest Realtors Inc
17450 W N Ave ....Brookfield WI 53008 **800-434-7350** 262-827-4200

Silicon Valley Assn of Realtors
19400 Stevens Creek Blvd Ste 100 ....Cupertino CA 95014 **877-699-6787** 408 200-0100

Skyline Properties South Inc
50 116th Ave SE Ste 120 ....Bellevue WA 98004 **800-753-6156** 425-455-2065

Sotheby's International Realty
38 E 61st St ....New York NY 10065 **866-899-4747** 212-606-7660

Stan White Realty & Construction
2506 S Croatan Hwy ....Nags Head NC 27959 **800-338-3233** 252-441-1515

Sutton Alliance LLC
515 Rockaway Ave ....Valley Stream NY 11581 **866-435-6600** 516-837-6100

Themlsonline Com Inc
11150 Commerce Dr N ....Champlin MN 55316 **866-657-6654** 763-576-8286

Tri-Land
1 E Oak Hill Dr Ste 302 ....Westmont IL 60559 **800-441-7032** 708-531-8210

United Country Real Estate Inc
2820 NW Barry Rd ....Kansas City MO 64154 **800-999-1020**

Valuation Management Group LLC
1640 Powers Ferry Rd SE Bldg 15
Ste 100 ....Marietta GA 30067 **866-799-7488** 678-483-4420

Virginia Cook Realtors
5950 Sherry Ln Ste 100 ....Dallas TX 75225 **877-975-2665** 214-696-8877

Weichert Realtors
1625 Rt 10 E ....Morris Plains NJ 07950 **800-401-0486** 973-984-1400

Williams & Williams Real Estate Auctions
7120 S Lewis Ave Ste 200 ....Tulsa OK 74136 **800-801-8003** 913-541-8084

ZapLabs LLC
2000 Powell St Ste 700 ....Emeryville CA 94608 **800-225-5947** 510-735-2600
NASDAQ: ZIPR

649   REAL ESTATE DEVELOPERS

SEE ALSO Construction - Building Contractors - Residential ; Construction - Building Contractors - Non-Residential

					Toll-Free	Phone

Al Neyer Inc
302 W Third St Ste 800 ....Cincinnati OH 45202 **877-271-6400** 513-271-6400

AV Homes Inc
8601 N Scottsdale Rd Ste 225 ....Scottsdale AZ 85253 **800-284-6637** 480-214-7400
NASDAQ: AVHI

Cornerstone residential management Llc
2100 Hollywood Blvd ....Hollywood FL 33020 **800-809-4099**

CoStar Group Inc
1331 L St NW ....Washington DC 20005 **888-226-7404** 800-204-5960
NASDAQ: CSGP

CountryTyme Inc
3451 Cincinnati-Zanesville Rd SW ....Lancaster OH 43130 **800-213-8365** 740-475-6001

David Weekley Homes Inc
1111 N Post Oak Rd ....Houston TX 77055 **800-390-6774** 713-963-0500

Double Diamond Co
5495 Belt Line Rd Ste 200 ....Dallas TX 75254 **800-324-7438** 214-706-9801

DR Horton Inc
301 Commerce St Ste 500 ....Fort Worth TX 76102 **800-846-7866** 817-390-8200
NYSE: DHI

Flournoy Development Co
900 Brookstone Ctr Pkwy ....Columbus GA 31904 **888-801-3404** 706-324-4000

Gilbane Inc
7 Jackson Walkway ....Providence RI 02903 **800-445-2263** 401-456-5890

Holiday Builders Inc
2293 W Eau Gallie Blvd ....Melbourne FL 32935 **866-431-2533**

Hunt Midwest Enterprises Inc
8300 NE Underground Dr ....Kansas City MO 64161 **800-551-6877** 816-455-2500

Intervest Construction Inc
2379 Beville Rd ....Daytona Beach FL 32119 **855-215-2974** 844-349-6401

	Toll-Free	Phone

Ivory Homes
970 E Woodoak Ln .... Salt Lake City UT 84117 **888-455-5561**

JA Billipp Co
6925 Portwest Dr Ste 130 .... Houston TX 77024 **800-216-9013** 713-426-5000

John Wieland Homes & Neighborhoods
4125 Atlanta Rd SE .... Smyrna GA 30080 **800-376-4663** 770-996-2400

KB Home
10990 Wilshire Blvd 7th Fl .... Los Angeles CA 90024 **800-304-0657** 310-231-4000
NYSE: KBH

Richmond American Homes Inc
4350 S Monaco St .... Denver CO 80237 **888-402-4663** 303-773-1100

Robson Communities
9532 E Riggs Rd .... Sun Lakes AZ 85248 **800-732-9949**

Schatten Properties Management Company Inc
1514 S St .... Nashville TN 37212 **800-892-1315** 615-329-3011

Sea Pines Resort, The
32 Greenwood Dr .... Hilton Head Island SC 29928 **866-561-8802** 843-785-3333

Sea Trail Corp
75A Clubhouse Rd .... Sunset Beach NC 28468 **888-321-9048** 910-287-1100

Silver Saddle Ranch & Club Inc
20751 Aristotle Dr .... California City CA 93505 **888-430-8728** 760-373-8617

South Shore Harbour Resort & Conference Center
2500 S Shore Blvd .... League City TX 77573 **800-442-5005** 281-334-1000

Stanley Martin Cos
11111 Sunset Hills Rd Ste 200 .... Reston VA 20190 **800-446-4807** 703-964-5000

Stratus Properties Inc
212 Lavaca St Ste 300 .... Austin TX 78701 **800-690-0315** 512-478-5788
NYSE: STRS

Toll Bros Inc
250 Gibraltar Rd .... Horsham PA 19044 **855-897-8655** 215-938-8000
NYSE: TOL

TransCon Builders Inc
25250 Rockside Rd .... Cleveland OH 44146 **800-451-2608** 440-439-2100

Village Green Cos
28411 Northwestern Hwy Ste 400 .... Southfield MI 48034 **866-396-1105**

Villages of Lake Sumter Inc
1000 Lake Sumter Landing .... The Villages FL 32162 **800-245-1081** 352-753-2270

WCI Communities Inc
24301 Walden Ctr Dr .... Bonita Springs FL 34134 **800-924-4005** 239-498-8200

Weyerhaeuser Co
33663 Weyerhaeuser Way S .... Federal Way WA 98003 **800-525-5440** 253-924-2345

650 REAL ESTATE INVESTMENT TRUSTS (REITS)

	Toll-Free	Phone

Apartment Investment & Management Co
4582 S Ulster St Pkwy Ste 1100 .... Denver CO 80237 **888-789-8600*** 303-757-8101
*NYSE: AIV ■ *General*

Arbor Realty Trust Inc
333 Earle Ovington Blvd Ste 900 .... Uniondale NY 11553 **800-272-6710**
NYSE: ABR

Benchmark Group
4053 Maple Rd .... Amherst NY 14226 **800-876-0160** 716-833-4986

BRT Apartments Corp
60 Cutter Mill Rd Ste 303 .... Great Neck NY 11021 **800-450-5816** 516-466-3100
NYSE: BRT

Camden Property Trust
11 Greenway Plz Ste 2400 .... Houston TX 77046 **800-922-6336** 713-354-2500
NYSE: CPT

Capstead Mortgage Corp
8401 N Central Expy Ste 800 .... Dallas TX 75225 **800-358-2323** 214-874-2323
NYSE: CMO

Chesapeake Lodging Trust (CLT)
1997 Annapolis Exchange Pkwy
Ste 410 .... Annapolis MD 21401 **800-698-2820** 571-349-9450
NYSE: CHSP

Commercial Properties Realty Trust
100 North St .... Baton Rouge LA 70802 **800-648-9064** 225-924-7206

Duke Realty Corp
600 E 96th St Ste 100 .... Indianapolis IN 46240 **800-875-3366** 317-808-6000
NYSE: DRE

EastGroup Properties Inc
188 E Capitol St .... Jackson MS 39201 **800-695-1564** 601-354-3555
NYSE: EGP

Federal Realty Investment Trust
1626 E Jefferson St .... Rockville MD 20852 **800-658-8980** 301-998-8100
NYSE: FRT

Franklin Street Properties Corp (FSP)
401 Edgewater Pl .... Wakefield MA 01880 **877-686-9496** 800-950-6288
NYSE: FSP

Highwoods Properties Inc
3100 Smoketree Ct Ste 600 .... Raleigh NC 27604 **866-449-6637** 919-872-4924
NYSE: HIW

Impac Mortgage Holdings Inc
19500 Jamboree Rd .... Irvine CA 92612 **800-597-4101** 949-475-3600
NYSE: IMH

IRET 1400 31st Ave SW Ste 60 .... Minot ND 58702 **888-478-4738** 701-837-4738
NYSE: IRET

Kimco Realty Corp
3333 New Hyde Pk Rd .... New Hyde Park NY 11042 **800-645-6292** 516-869-9000
NYSE: KIM

Kite Realty Group Trust
30 S Meridian St Ste 1100 .... Indianapolis IN 46204 **888-577-5600** 317-577-5600
NYSE: KRG

Lexington Corporate Properties Trust
1 Penn Plz Ste 4015 .... New York NY 10119 **800-850-3948** 212-692-7200

Mack-Cali Realty Corp
343 Thornall St .... Edison NJ 08837 **800-317-4445** 732-590-1000
NYSE: CLI

Parkway Properties Inc
188 E Capitol St Ste 1000 .... Jackson MS 39201 **800-748-1667** 601-948-4091
NYSE: PKY

Pennsylvania Real Estate Investment Trust
200 S Broad St 3rd Fl .... Philadelphia PA 19102 **866-875-0700** 215-875-0700
NYSE: PEI

	Toll-Free	Phone

PMC Commercial Trust
17950 Preston Rd Ste 600 .... Dallas TX 75252 **800-486-3223** 972-349-3200
NASDAQ: CMCT

ProLogis 4545 Airport Way .... Denver CO 80239 **800-566-2706** 400-320-2015
NYSE: PLD

PS Business Parks Inc
701 Western Ave .... Glendale CA 91201 **888-782-6110*** 818-244-8080
*NYSE: PSB ■ *Cust Svc*

Public Storage Inc
701 Western Ave .... Glendale CA 91201 **800-567-0759*** 818-244-8080
*NYSE: PSA ■ *Cust Svc*

Regency Centers
1 Independent Dr Ste 114 .... Jacksonville FL 32202 **800-950-6333** 904-598-7000
NYSE: REG

RioCan Real Estate Investment Trust
2300 Yonge St Ste 500 PO Box 2386 .... Toronto ON M4P1E4 **800-465-2733** 416-866-3033
TSE: REI.UN.CA

Tanger Factory Outlet Centers Inc
3200 Northline Ave Ste 360 .... Greensboro NC 27408 **800-720-6728** 336-292-3010
NYSE: SKT

United Mobile Homes Inc
3499 Rt 9 N Ste 3C .... Freehold NJ 07728 **800-504-0670** 732-577-9997
NYSE: UMH

Ventas Inc
353 N Clark St Ste 3300 .... Chicago IL 60654 **877-483-6827** 312-660-3800
NYSE: VTR

Vornado Realty Trust
888 Seventh Ave .... New York NY 10019 **800-294-1322** 212-894-7000
NYSE: VNO

Washington Real Estate Investment Trust (WRIT)
1775 I St NW .... Washington DC 20006 **800-565-9748** 202-774-3200
NYSE: WRE

Weingarten Realty Investors
2600 Citadel Plaza Dr Ste 125 .... Houston TX 77008 **800-688-8865** 713-866-6000
NYSE: WRI

WP Carey & Company LLC
50 Rockefeller Plz .... New York NY 10020 **800-972-2739** 212-492-1100
NYSE: WPC

651 REAL ESTATE MANAGERS & OPERATORS

SEE ALSO Retirement Communities ; Hotels & Hotel Companies

	Toll-Free	Phone

American Golf Corp
2951 28th St .... Santa Monica CA 90405 **800-238-7267** 310-664-4000

American Motel Management
1872 Montreal Rd Ste A .... Tucker GA 30084 **800-580-8258** 770-939-1801

Apartment Investment & Management Co
4582 S Ulster St Pkwy Ste 1100 .... Denver CO 80237 **888-789-8600*** 303-757-8101
*NYSE: AIV ■ *General*

Brandywine Realty Trust
555 E Lancaster Ave Ste 100 .... Radnor PA 19087 **866-426-5400** 610-325-5600
NYSE: BDN

Brixmor Property Group
450 Lexington Ave 13th Fl .... New York NY 10017 **800-468-7526** 212-869-3000

Calista Corp
301 Calista Ct Ste A .... Anchorage AK 99518 **800-277-5516** 907-279-5516

Camden Property Trust
11 Greenway Plz Ste 2400 .... Houston TX 77046 **800-922-6336** 713-354-2500
NYSE: CPT

ClubCorp Inc
3030 Lyndon B Johnson Fwy Ste 600 .... Dallas TX 75234 **800-433-5079** 972-243-6191

ClubLink Corp
15675 Dufferin St .... King City ON L7B1K5 **800-661-1818**

Developers Diversified Realty Corp
3300 Enterprise Pkwy .... Beachwood OH 44122 **877-225-5337** 216-755-5500
NYSE: DDR

Duke Realty Corp
600 E 96th St Ste 100 .... Indianapolis IN 46240 **800-875-3366** 317-808-6000
NYSE: DRE

EastGroup Properties Inc
188 E Capitol St .... Jackson MS 39201 **800-695-1564** 601-354-3555
NYSE: EGP

Equity Lifestyle Properties Inc
2 N Riverside Plz Ste 800 .... Chicago IL 60606 **800-274-7314** 312-279-1400
NYSE: ELS

Equity Residential
2 N Riverside Plz .... Chicago IL 60606 **800-733-5001** 312-474-1300
NYSE: EQR

Eugene Burger Management Corp
6600 Hunter Dr .... Rohnert Park CA 94928 **800-788-0233** 707-584-5123

Federal Realty Investment Trust
1626 E Jefferson St .... Rockville MD 20852 **800-658-8980** 301-998-8100
NYSE: FRT

Fisher Auction Company Inc
2112 E Atlantic Blvd .... Pompano Beach FL 33062 **800-331-6620** 954-942-0917

General Growth Properties Inc
110 N Wacker Dr .... Chicago IL 60606 **888-395-8037** 312-960-5000
NYSE: GGP

Ghiotto & Associates Inc
2426 Phillips Hwy .... Jacksonville FL 32207 **844-304-7262** 904-886-0071

Goodale & Barbieri Co
818 W Riverside Ave Ste 300 .... Spokane WA 99201 **800-572-9181** 509-459-6109

Gyrodyne Company of America Inc
1 Flowerfield Ste 24 .... Saint James NY 11780 **800-322-2885** 631-584-5400
NASDAQ: GYRO

Highwoods Properties Inc
3100 Smoketree Ct Ste 600 .... Raleigh NC 27604 **866-449-6637** 919-872-4924
NYSE: HIW

Holiday Retirement
480 N Orlando Ave Ste 236 .... Winter Park FL 32789 **800-322-0999**

Hunt Midwest Enterprises Inc
8300 NE Underground Dr .... Kansas City MO 64161 **800-551-6877** 816-455-2500

Irvine Company Apartment Communities
2500 Baypointe Dr .... Newport Beach CA 92660 **844-718-2918**

Kimco Realty Corp
3333 New Hyde Pk Rd .... New Hyde Park NY 11042 **800-645-6292** 516-869-9000
NYSE: KIM

			Toll-Free	Phone
Lexington Corporate Properties Trust				
1 Penn Plz Ste 4015	New York NY	10119	800-850-3948	212-692-7200
Lowe Enterprises				
11777 San Vicente Blvd Ste 900	Los Angeles CA	90049	800-842-2252	310-820-6661
MAA (MAAC) 6584 Poplar Ave	Memphis TN	38138	866-620-1130	
NYSE: MAA				
Mack-Cali Realty Corp				
343 Thornall St	Edison NJ	08837	800-317-4445	732-590-1000
NYSE: CLI				
Mid-Atlantic PenFed Realty Berkshire Hathaway HomeServices (PCR)				
3050 Chain Bridge Rd	Fairfax VA	22030	866-225-5778	703-691-7653
Miller Valentine Group				
137 North Main St Ste 600	Dayton OH	45402	877-684-7687	937-293-0900
Omega Healthcare Investors Inc				
300 International Cir Ste 200	Hunt Valley MD	21030	877-511-2891	410-427-1700
NYSE: OHI				
Parkway Properties Inc				
188 E Capitol St Ste 1000	Jackson MS	39201	800-748-1667	601-948-4091
NYSE: PKY				
Patriot Properties Inc				
123 Pleasant St	Marblehead MA	01945	800-527-9991	781-586-9670
Pennsylvania Real Estate Investment Trust				
200 S Broad St 3rd Fl	Philadelphia PA	19102	866-875-0700	215-875-0700
NYSE: PEI				
ProLogis 4545 Airport Way	Denver CO	80239	800-566-2706	400-320-2015
NYSE: PLD				
PS Business Parks Inc				
701 Western Ave	Glendale CA	91201	888-782-6110*	818-244-8080
NYSE: PSB ■ *Cust Svc				
Realty Income Corp				
11995 El Camino Real	San Diego CA	92130	877-924-6266	858-284-5000
NYSE: O				
Regency Centers				
1 Independent Dr Ste 114	Jacksonville FL	32202	800-950-6333	904-598-7000
NYSE: REG				
Rochdale Village Inc				
169-65 137th Ave	Jamaica NY	11434	800-275-8777	718-276-5700
Schatten Properties Management Company Inc				
1514 S St	Nashville TN	37212	800-892-1315	615-329-3011
Tanger Factory Outlet Centers Inc				
3200 Northline Ave Ste 360	Greensboro NC	27408	800-720-6728	336-292-3010
NYSE: SKT				
Transwestern Commercial Services				
1900 W Loop S Ste 1300	Houston TX	77027	800-531-8182	713-270-7700
United Mobile Homes Inc				
3499 Rt 9 N Ste 3C	Freehold NJ	07728	800-504-0670	732-577-9997
NYSE: UMH				
USAA Real Estate Co				
9830 Colonnade Blvd Ste 600	San Antonio TX	78230	800-531-8182	
Ventas Inc				
353 N Clark St Ste 3300	Chicago IL	60654	877-483-6827	312-660-3800
NYSE: VTR				
Village Green Cos				
28411 Northwestern Hwy Ste 400	Southfield MI	48034	866-396-1105	
Vornado Realty Trust				
888 Seventh Ave	New York NY	10019	800-294-1322	212-894-7000
NYSE: VNO				
Warren Properties Inc				
PO Box 469114	Escondido CA	92046	800-831-0804	
Washington Real Estate Investment Trust (WRIT)				
1775 I St NW	Washington DC	20006	800-565-9748	202-774-3200
NYSE: WRE				
Weingarten Realty Investors				
2600 Citadel Plaza Dr Ste 125	Houston TX	77008	800-688-8865	713-866-6000
NYSE: WRI				
WP Carey & Company LLC				
50 Rockefeller Plz	New York NY	10020	800-972-2739	212-492-1100
NYSE: WPC				

652   REALTOR ASSOCIATIONS - STATE

SEE ALSO Real Estate Professionals Associations
Listed here are the state branches of the National Association of Realtors.

			Toll-Free	Phone
Alabama Assn of Realtors				
522 Washington Ave PO Box 4070	Montgomery AL	36104	800-446-3808	334-262-3808
Alaska Assn of Realtors				
4205 Minnesota Dr	Anchorage AK	99503	800-478-3763	907-563-7133
Arizona Assn of Realtors				
255 E Osborne Rd Ste 200	Phoenix AZ	85012	800-426-7274	602-248-7787
Arkansas Realtors Assn				
11224 Executive Ctr Dr	Little Rock AR	72211	888-333-2206	501-225-2020
Beach Properties of Hilton Head				
64 Arrow Rd	Hilton Head Island SC	29928	800-671-5155	843-671-5155
Buxton Co				
2651 S Polaris Dr	Fort Worth TX	76137	888-228-9866	
Colorado Assn of Realtors				
309 Inverness Way S	Englewood CO	80112	800-944-6550	303-790-7099
Connecticut Assn of Realtors				
111 Founders Plz Ste 1101	East Hartford CT	06108	800-335-4862	860-290-6601
EMG Corp				
10461 Mill Run Cir Ste 1100	Owings Mills MD	21117	800-733-0660	
Flaherty & Collins Properties Inc				
1 Indiana Sq Ste 3000	Indianapolis IN	46240	888-684-0338	317-816-9300
Florida Assn of Realtors				
7025 Augusta National Dr	Orlando FL	32822	800-669-4327	407-438-1400
Georgia Assn of Realtors				
6065 Barfield Rd	Atlanta GA	30328	866-280-0576	770-451-1831
Hawaii Assn of Realtors				
1259 A'ala St Ste 300	Honolulu HI	96817	866-693-6767	808-733-7060
Idaho Assn of Realtors				
10116 W Overland Rd	Boise ID	83709	800-621-7553	208-342-3585
Iowa Assn of Realtors				
1370 NW 114th St Ste 100	Clive IA	50325	800-532-1515	515-453-1064
JEM Strapping Systems				
116 Shaver St	Brantford ON	N3T5M1	877-536-6584	519-754-5432

			Toll-Free	Phone
Kansas Assn of Realtors				
3644 SW Burlingame Rd	Topeka KS	66611	800-366-0069	785-267-3610
Kentucky Assn of Realtors				
2801 Palumbo Dr Ste 202	Lexington KY	40509	800-264-2185	859-263-7377
Maryland Assn of Realtors				
2594 Riva Rd	Annapolis MD	21401	800-638-6425	
Massachusetts Assn of Realtors				
256 Second Ave	Waltham MA	02451	800-725-6272	781-890-3700
Michigan Assn of Realtors				
720 N Washington Ave	Lansing MI	48906	800-454-7842	517-372-8890
Minnesota Assn of Realtors				
5750 Lincoln Dr	Minneapolis MN	55436	800-862-6097	952-935-8313
Mississippi Assn of Realtors				
4274 Lakeland Dr PO Box 321000	Jackson MS	39232	800-747-1103	601-932-9325
Missouri Assn of Realtors				
2601 Bernadette Pl	Columbia MO	65203	800-403-0101	573-445-8400
MLS Property Information Network Inc				
904 Hartford Tpke	Shrewsbury MA	01545	800-695-3000	508-845-1011
Montana Assn of Realtors				
1 S Montana Ave Ste M1	Helena MT	59601	800-477-1864	406-443-4032
Nebraska Realtors Assn				
800 S 13th St Ste 200	Lincoln NE	68508	800-777-5231	402-323-6500
Nevada Assn of Realtors				
760 Margrave Dr Ste 200	Reno NV	89502	800-748-5526	775-829-5911
New York State Assn of Realtors				
130 Washington Ave	Albany NY	12210	800-462-7585	518-463-0300
North Carolina Assn of Realtors Inc				
4511 Weybridge Ln	Greensboro NC	27407	800-443-9956	336-294-1415
North Dakota Assn of Realtors				
318 W Apollo Ave	Bismarck ND	58503	800-279-2361	701-355-1010
O'Keefe Drilling Co				
2000 4 Mile Rd	Butte MT	59701	800-745-5554	406-494-3310
Oklahoma Assn of Realtors				
9807 N Broadway	Oklahoma City OK	73114	800-375-9944	405-848-9944
Oregon Assn of Realtors				
2110 Mission St SE	Salem OR	97308	800-252-9115	503-362-3645
Pennsylvania Assn of Realtors				
500 North 12th St Ste 100	Lemoyne PA	17043	800-555-3390	
Real Estate Institute of Canada				
5407 Eglinton Ave W Unit 208	Toronto ON	M9C5K6	800-542-7342	416-695-9000
Realtors Assn of New Mexico				
2201 Broo Rd	Santa Fe NM	87505	800-224-2282	505-982-2442
RPI Media Inc				
265 Racine Dr Ste 201	Wilmington NC	28403	800-736-0321	910-763-2100
South Carolina Assn of Realtors				
3780 Fernandina Rd	Columbia SC	29210	800-233-6381	803-772-5206
South Dakota Assn of Realtors				
204 N Euclid Ave	Pierre SD	57501	800-227-5877	605-224-0554
Tennessee Assn of Realtors (TAR)				
901 19th Ave S	Nashville TN	37212	877-321-1477	615-321-1477
Texas Assn of Realtors				
1115 San Jacinto Blvd Ste 200	Austin TX	78701	800-873-9155	512-480-8200
Utah Assn of Realtors				
230 W Towne Ridge Pkwy Ste 500	Sandy UT	84070	800-594-8933	801-676-5200
Washington Assn of Realtors				
128 Tenth Ave SW PO Box 719	Olympia WA	98501	800-562-6024*	360-943-3100
*General				
West Virginia Assn of Realtors				
2110 Kanawha Blvd E	Charleston WV	25311	800-445-7600	304-342-7600
Wisconsin Realtors Assn				
4801 Forest Run Rd Ste 201	Madison WI	53704	800-279-1972	608-241-2047
Wyoming Assn of Realtors				
777 Overland Trl Ste 220	Casper WY	82601	800-676-4085	307-237-4085

653   RECORDING COMPANIES

			Toll-Free	Phone
Alligator Records & Artist Management Inc				
PO Box 60234	Chicago IL	60660	800-344-5609	773-973-7736
Integrity Music				
1646 Westgate Cir Ste 106	Brentwood TN	37027	888-888-4726	
Malaco Music Group Inc				
3023 W Northside Dr	Jackson MS	39213	800-272-7936*	601-982-4522
*Cust Svc				
Naxos of America Inc				
1810 Columbia Ave	Franklin TN	37064	877-629-6723	615-771-9393
Nightingale-Conant Corp				
6245 W Howard St	Niles IL	60714	800-557-1660*	
*Cust Svc				
Righteous Babe				
341 Delaware Ave	Buffalo NY	14202	800-664-3769	716-852-8020
Smithsonian Folkways Recordings				
600 Maryland Ave SW Ste 200	Washington DC	20024	800-410-9815	202-633-6450
Soar Corp (SOAR)				
5200 Constitution Ave NE	Albuquerque NM	87110	866-616-4450	505-268-6110
Warner Music Group				
1633 Broadway	New York NY	10019	800-820-1653	212-275-2000
Worldly Voices				
PO Box 218435	Nashville TN	37221	800-286-4237	615-321-8802

654   RECORDING MEDIA - MAGNETIC & OPTICAL

SEE ALSO Photographic Equipment & Supplies

			Toll-Free	Phone
Allied Vaughn				
7600 Parklawn Ste 300	Minneapolis MN	55435	800-323-0281	952-832-3100
Athana International Inc				
602 Faye	Redondo Beach CA	90277	800-421-1591	310-539-7280
Cine Magnetics Inc (CMI)				
9 W Broad St	Stamford CT	06902	800-431-1102	203-989-9955
Conduant Corp				
1501 S Sunset St Ste D	Longmont CO	80501	888-497-7327	303-485-2721
LaserCard Corp				
1875 N Shoreline Blvd	Mountain View CA	94043	800-237-7769	650-969-4428

				Toll-Free	Phone
Maxell Corp of America					
3 Garret Mountain Plz					
3rd Fl Ste 300	Woodland Park	NJ	07424	800-533-2836	973-653-2400
Verbatim Americas LLC					
8210 University Executive Park Dr	Charlotte	NC	28262	800-538-8589	704-547-6500

655 RECREATION FACILITY OPERATORS

SEE ALSO Bowling Centers

				Toll-Free	Phone
Dave & Buster's Inc					
2481 Manana Dr	Dallas	TX	75220	800-842-5369	214-357-9588

656 RECYCLABLE MATERIALS RECOVERY

Included here are companies that recycle post-consumer trash, tires, appliances, batteries, etc. as well as industrial recyclers of plastics, paper, wood, glass, solvents, and so on.

				Toll-Free	Phone
Appliance Recycling Centers of America Inc					
7400 Excelsior Blvd	Minneapolis	MN	55426	800-452-8680	952-930-9000
NASDAQ: ARCI					
Arrow					
9201 E Dry Creek Rd	Centennial	CO	80112	800-393-7627	303-824-4000
Chemtron Corp					
35850 Schneider Ct	Avon	OH	44011	800-676-5091	440-937-6348
Clean Earth of North Jersey Inc					
115 Jacobus Ave	South Kearny	NJ	07032	877-445-3478	973-344-4004
Giordano s Solid Waste Removal					
110 N Mill Rd	Vineland	NJ	08360	800-636-8625	856-696-2068
GreenMan Technologies Inc					
7 Kimball Ln Bldg A	Lynnfield	MA	01940	866-994-7697	781-224-2411
Greentec 95 Struck Ct	Cambridge	ON	N1R8L2	888-858-1515	519-624-3300
Horry County Solid Waste Authority Inc					
1886 Hwy 90	Conway	SC	29526	800-768-7348	843-347-1651
Jupiter Aluminum Corp					
2800 S River Rd	Des Plaines	IL	60018	800-392-7265	219-932-3322
Marborg Industries					
728 E Yanonali St	Santa Barbara	CA	93103	800-798-1852	805-963-1852
Marck Industries Inc					
401 Main St Ste E PO Box 912	Cassville	MO	65625	877-228-2565	
Mason County Garbage & Recycling					
81 E Wilburs Way PO Box 787	Shelton	WA	98584	877-722-0223	360-426-8729
MCF Systems Atlanta Inc					
4319 Tanners Church Rd	Ellenwood	GA	30294	866-315-8116	
Pall Corp					
2200 Northern Blvd	East Hills	NY	11548	800-645-6532	516-484-5400
NYSE: PLL					
Paper Tigers, The					
2201 Waukegan Rd Ste 180	Bannockburn	IL	60015	800-621-1774	847-919-6500
Pioneer Paper Stock					
155 Irving Ave N	Minneapolis	MN	55405	800-821-8512	612-374-2280
Utah Metal Works Inc (UMW)					
805 Everett Ave	Salt Lake City	UT	84116	877-221-0099	

657 RECYCLED PLASTICS PRODUCTS

SEE ALSO Flooring - Resilient

				Toll-Free	Phone
Amazing Recycled Products Inc					
PO Box 312	Denver	CO	80201	800-241-2174	
Bedford Technology LLC					
2424 Armour Rd PO Box 609	Worthington	MN	56187	800-721-9037	507-372-5558
Parkland Plastics Inc					
104 Yoder Dr PO Box 339	Middlebury	IN	46540	800-835-4110	574-825-4336
Plastic Recycling of Iowa Falls Inc					
10252 Hwy 65	Iowa Falls	IA	50126	800-338-1438	641-648-5073
Renew Plastics PO Box 480	Luxemburg	WI	54217	800-666-5207	920-845-2326
Resco Plastics Inc					
93783 Newport Ln	Coos Bay	OR	97420	800-266-5097	541-269-5485
Witt Industries Inc					
4600 Mason-Montgomery Rd	Mason	OH	45040	800-543-7417	

658 REFRACTORIES - CLAY

				Toll-Free	Phone
BNZ Materials Inc					
6901 S Pierce St Ste 260	Littleton	CO	80128	800-999-0890	303-978-1199
RENO Refractories Inc					
601 Reno Dr	Morris	AL	35116	800-741-7366	
RENO Refractories Inc Reftech Div					
601 Reno Dr	Morris	AL	35116	800-741-7366*	
*General					
Resco Products Inc					
2 Penn Ctr W Ste 430	Pittsburgh	PA	15276	888-283-5505	
Shenango Advanced Ceramics LLC					
606 McCleary Ave	New Castle	PA	16101	888-283-5505	
Whitacre Greer Fireproofing Inc					
1400 S Mahoning Ave	Alliance	OH	44601	800-947-2837*	330-823-1610
*Cust Svc					

659 REFRACTORIES - NONCLAY

				Toll-Free	Phone
Fedmet Resources Corp					
PO Box 278	Montreal	QC	H3Z2T2	800-609-5711	514-931-5711
Plibrico Co					
1010 N Hooker St	Chicago	IL	60622	800-255-8793	312-337-9000
Ransom & Randolph Co					
3535 Briarfield Blvd	Maumee	OH	43537	800-800-7496	419-865-9497

				Toll-Free	Phone
RENO Refractories Inc					
601 Reno Dr	Morris	AL	35116	800-741-7366	
RENO Refractories Inc Reftech Div					
601 Reno Dr	Morris	AL	35116	800-741-7366*	
*General					
TYK America Inc					
301 BrickyaRd Rd	Clairton	PA	15025	800-569-9359	412-384-4259

660 REFRIGERATION EQUIPMENT - MFR

SEE ALSO Air Conditioning & Heating Equipment - Commercial/Industrial

				Toll-Free	Phone
Advance Energy Technologies Inc					
1 Solar Dr	Clifton Park	NY	12065	800-724-0198	518-371-2140
American Panel Corp					
5800 SE 78th St	Ocala	FL	34472	800-327-3015	352-245-7055
Applied Process Cooling Corp					
555 Price Ave	Redwood City	CA	94063	877-231-6406	650-595-0665
Arctic Star Refrigeration Mfg Company Inc					
3540 W Pioneer Pkwy	Arlington	TX	76013	800-229-6562	817-274-1396
Beverage-Air Corp					
3779 Champion Blvd	Winston-Salem	NC	27105	800-845-9800	336-245-6400
CIMCO Refrigeration					
65 Villiers St	Toronto	ON	M5A3S1	800-267-1418	416-465-7581
CrownTonka Inc					
15600 37th Ave N Ste 100	Plymouth	MN	55446	800-523-7337	763-541-1410
Delfield Co					
980 S Isabella Rd	Mount Pleasant	MI	48858	800-733-8821	989-773-7981
Dole Refrigerating Co					
1420 Higgs Rd	Lewisburg	TN	37091	800-251-8990	931-359-6211
Eliason Corp 9229 Shaver Rd	Portage	MI	49024	800-828-3655*	269-327-7003
*Cust Svc					
Federal Industries Div Standex Corp					
215 Federal Ave	Belleville	WI	53508	800-356-4206	
Follett 801 Church Ln	Easton	PA	18040	800-523-9361*	610-252-7301
*Cust Svc					
FRL Furniture					
460 Grand Blvd	Westbury	NY	11590	800-529-4375	516-333-4400
Haws Corp 1455 Kleppe Ln	Sparks	NV	89431	888-640-4297	775-359-4712
Heatcraft Refrigeration Products					
2175 W Pk Pl Blvd	Stone Mountain	GA	30087	800-321-1881	770-465-5600
Hill PHOENIX Inc					
1003 Sigman Rd	Conyers	GA	30013	800-518-6630	770-285-3264
Hussmann Corp					
12999 St Charles Rock Rd	Bridgeton	MO	63044	800-592-2060	314-291-2000
Ice-O-Matic 11100 E 45th Ave	Denver	CO	80239	800-423-3367	303-576-2940
IMI Cornelius Inc					
101 Broadway St W	Osseo	MN	55369	800-238-3600	
International Cold Storage Company Inc					
215 E 13th St	Andover	KS	67002	800-835-0001	316-733-1385
KDIndustries 1525 E Lake Rd	Erie	PA	16511	800-840-9577	814-453-6761
Kloppenberg & Co					
2627 W Oxford Ave	Englewood	CO	80110	800-346-3246	303-761-1615
Kolpak 2915 Tennessee Ave N	Parsons	TN	38363	800-826-7036	731-847-5328
Kysor Panel Systems					
4201 N Beach St	Fort Worth	TX	76137	800-633-3426	817-281-5121
Lancer Corp					
6655 Lancer Blvd	San Antonio	TX	78219	800-729-1500	210-310-7000
Leer LP 206 Leer St	New Lisbon	WI	53950	800-766-5337*	608-562-7100
*Cust Svc					
Manitowoc Ice					
2110 S 26th St	Manitowoc	WI	54220	800-545-5720	
Micro Matic USA Inc					
10726 N Second St	Machesney Park	IL	61115	866-291-5756	815-968-7557
MicroMetl Corp					
3035 N Shadeland Ave Ste 300	Indianapolis	IN	46226	800-662-4822	
Nance International Inc					
2915 Milam St	Beaumont	TX	77701	877-626-2322	409-838-6127
Nor-Lake Inc					
727 Second St PO Box 248	Hudson	WI	54016	800-388-5253	715-386-2323
Ontor Ltd 12 Leswyn Rd	Toronto	ON	M6A1K3	800-567-1631	416-781-5286
Perlick Corp					
8300 W Good Hope Rd	Milwaukee	WI	53223	800-558-5592	414-353-7060
Scotsman Ice Systems					
775 Corporate Woods Pkwy	Vernon Hills	IL	60061	800-726-8762*	847-215-4500
*Cust Svc					
Silver King Refrigeration Inc					
1600 Xenium Ln N	Minneapolis	MN	55441	800-328-3329	763-923-2441
True Manufacturing Co					
2001 E Terra Ln	O'Fallon	MO	63366	800-325-6152	636-240-2400
Turbo Refrigerating					
1000 W Ormsby Ave	Louisville	KY	40210	800-853-8648	502-635-3000
Victory Refrigeration Inc					
110 Woodcrest Rd	Cherry Hill	NJ	08003	800-523-5008	856-428-4200
Vintage Air Inc					
18865 Goll St	San Antonio	TX	78266	800-862-6658	210-654-7171
Vogt Ice					
1000 W Ormsby Ave	Louisville	KY	40210	800-853-8648	502-635-3000

661 REFRIGERATION EQUIPMENT - WHOL

SEE ALSO Plumbing, Heating, Air Conditioning Equipment & Supplies - Whol

				Toll-Free	Phone
Allied Supply Company Inc					
1100 E Monument Ave	Dayton	OH	45402	800-589-5690	937-224-9833
Baker Distributing Co					
14610 Breakers Dr Ste 100	Jacksonville	FL	32258	844-289-0033	800-217-4698
Broich Enterprises Inc					
6440 City W Pkwy	Eden Prairie	MN	55344	800-853-3508	952-941-2270
Dennis Supply Co					
PO Box 3376	Sioux City	IA	51102	800-352-4618	712-255-7637
Don Stevens Inc					
980 Discovery Rd	Eagan	MN	55121	800-444-2299	651-452-0872
Ernest F Mariani Company Inc					
573 West 2890 South	Salt Lake City	UT	84115	800-453-2927	

				Toll-Free	Phone
Gustave A Larson Co W233 N2869 Roundy Circle W	Pewaukee	WI	53072	**800-829-9609**	262-542-0200
Hart & Price Corp PO Box 36368	Dallas	TX	75235	**800-777-9129**	214-521-9129
Insco Distributing Inc 12501 Network Blvd	San Antonio	TX	78249	**855-282-4295**	210-690-8400
ISI Commercial Refrigeration LP 640 W Sixth St	Houston	TX	77007	**800-777-5070**	214-631-7980
Luce, Schwab & Kase Inc 9 Gloria Ln	Fairfield	NJ	07007	**800-458-7329**	973-227-4840
Minus Forty Technologies Corp 30 Armstrong Ave	Georgetown	ON	L7G4R9	**800-800-5706**	905-702-1441
Modern Ice Equipment & Supply Co 5709 Harrison Ave	Cincinnati	OH	45248	**800-543-1581**	
Norm's Refrigeration & Ice Equipment Inc 1175 N Knollwood Cir	Anaheim	CA	92801	**800-933-4423**	714-236-3600
RE Lewis Refrigeration Inc 803 S Lincoln St PO Box 92 *Cust Svc	Creston	IA	50801	**800-264-0767***	641-782-8183
Redico Inc 1850 S Lee Ct	Buford	GA	30518	**800-242-3920**	
Rogers Supply Company Inc PO Box 740	Champaign	IL	61824	**800-252-0406**	217-356-0166
Schroeder America 5620 Business Pk	San Antonio	TX	78218	**877-404-2488**	210-662-8200
Southern Refrigeration Corp 3140 Shenandoah Ave	Roanoke	VA	24017	**800-763-4433**	540-342-3493
Stafford-Smith Inc 3414 S Burdick St	Kalamazoo	MI	49001	**800-968-2442**	269-343-1240
Supermarket Systems Inc 6419 Bannington Rd	Charlotte	NC	28226	**800-553-1905**	704-542-6000
SWH Supply Co 242 E Main St	Louisville	KY	40202	**800-321-3598**	502-589-9287
Taylor Freezer Sales Company Inc 2032 Atlantic Ave	Chesapeake	VA	23324	**800-768-6945**	757-545-7900

662 RELOCATION CONSULTING SERVICES

				Toll-Free	Phone
Cartus Corp 40 Apple Ridge Rd	Danbury	CT	06810	**888-767-9357**	203-205-3400
Crye-Leike Inc 6525 N Quail Hollow Rd	Memphis	TN	38120	**866-310-3102**	
RELO Direct Inc 161 N Clark St Ste 1200	Chicago	IL	60601	**800-621-7356**	312-384-5900
Runzheimer International 1 Runzheimer Pk	Waterford	WI	53185	**800-558-1702**	262-971-2200
SIRVA Inc 1 Parkview Plz	Oakbrook Terrace	IL	60181	**800-341-5648**	630-570-3050
Windermere Relocation Inc 5424 Sand Point Way NE	Seattle	WA	98105	**866-740-9589**	206-527-3801

663 REMEDIATION SERVICES

SEE ALSO Waste Management ; Environmental Organizations ; Consulting Services - Environmental

Remediation services include clean-up, restorative, and corrective work to repair or minimize environmental damage caused by lead, asbestos, mining, petroleum, chemicals, and other pollutants.

				Toll-Free	Phone
AAA Environmental Inc 2036 Chesnee Hwy	Spartanburg	SC	29303	**888-296-3803**	864-582-1222
Abmech Inc 976 Forest Ave	West Homestead	PA	15120	**800-686-3626**	412-462-7440
Abscope Environmental Inc 7086 Commercial Dr	Canastota	NY	13032	**800-273-5318**	315-697-8437
Antea Group 5910 Rice Creek Pkwy Ste 100	Saint Paul	MN	55126	**800-477-7411**	651-639-9449
BELFOR (Canada) Inc 3300 Bridgeway St	Vancouver	BC	V5K1H9	**888-432-1123**	604-432-1123
Central Insulation Systems Inc 300 Murray Rd	Cincinnati	OH	45217	**800-544-7502**	513-242-0600
Chemical Waste Management Inc 1001 Fannin St Ste 4000	Houston	TX	77002	**800-633-7871**	713-512-6200
Clean Harbors Inc 42 Longwater Dr PO Box 9149 *NYSE: CLH*	Norwell	MA	02061	**800-282-0058**	781-792-5000
Clean Street Inc 1937 W 169th St	Gardena	CA	90247	**800-225-7316**	
Custom Environmental Services Inc 8041 N I 70 Frontage Rd Unit 11	Arvada	CO	80002	**800-310-7445**	303-423-9949
Cyn Oil Corp 1771 Washington St	Stoughton	MA	02072	**800-242-5818**	781-341-1777
Dec-Tam Corp 50 Concord St	North Reading	MA	01864	**800-332-8261**	978-470-2860
Environmental Enterprises Inc (EEI) 10163 Cincinnati-Dayton Rd	Cincinnati	OH	45241	**800-722-2818**	
Envirovantage 629 Calef Hwy Rt 125	Epping	NH	03042	**800-640-5323**	603-679-9682
H Barber & Sons Inc 15 Raytkwich Rd	Naugatuck	CT	06770	**800-355-8318**	203-729-9000
IEP Technologies LLC 400 Main St	Ashland	MA	01721	**855-793-8407**	
Perma-Fix Environmental Services Inc 8302 Dunwoody Pl Ste 250 *NASDAQ: PESI*	Atlanta	GA	30350	**800-365-6066**	770-587-9898
PW Stephens Inc 15201 Pipeline Ln Unit B	Huntington Beach	CA	92649	**800-750-7733**	714-892-2028
Remediation Services Inc 2735 S Tenth St PO Box 587	Independence	KS	67301	**800-335-1201**	
Safety-Kleen Corp 2600 N Central Expwy Ste 400	Richardson	TX	75080	**800-669-5740**	972-265-2000
SEACOR Holdings Inc 2200 Eller Dr PO Box 13038 *NYSE: CKH*	Fort Lauderdale	FL	33316	**800-516-6203**	954-523-2200

				Toll-Free	Phone
US Ecology 300 E Mallard Dr Ste 300 *NASDAQ: ECOL*	Boise	ID	83706	**800-590-5220**	208-331-8400

664 RESEARCH CENTERS & INSTITUTIONS

SEE ALSO Market Research Firms ; Public Policy Research Centers ; Testing Facilities

				Toll-Free	Phone
Advanced Cell Diagnostics Inc 3960 Point Eden Way	Hayward	CA	94545	**877-576-3636**	510-576-8800
American Institute for Cancer Research 1759 R St NW	Washington	DC	20009	**800-843-8114**	202-328-7744
American Institutes for Research 1000 Thomas Jefferson St NW	Washington	DC	20007	**877-334-3499**	202-403-5000
American Type Culture Collection (ATCC) 10801 University Blvd PO Box 1549 *Cust Svc	Manassas	VA	20108	**800-638-6597***	703-365-2700
Arbor Research & Trading LLC 1000 Hart Rd Ste 260	Barrington	IL	60010	**800-606-1872**	
Argonne National Laboratory (ANL) 9700 S Cass Ave	Argonne	IL	60439	**800-632-8990**	630-252-2000
Autism Research Institute (ARI) 4182 Adams Ave	San Diego	CA	92116	**866-366-3361**	619-281-7165
Barbara Ann Karmanos Cancer Institute 4100 John R St	Detroit	MI	48201	**800-527-6266**	
Battelle Memorial Institute Inc 505 King Ave	Columbus	OH	43201	**800-201-2011**	614-424-6424
BioLegend Inc 11080 Roselle St	San Diego	CA	92121	**877-246-5343**	858-455-9588
bioLytical Laboratories Inc 1108 - 13351 Commerce Pkwy	Richmond	BC	V6V2X7	**866-674-6784**	604-204-6784
California Pacific Medical Ctr Research Institute 475 Brannan St Ste 220	San Francisco	CA	94107	**855-354-2778**	415-600-1600
Center for Grain & Animal Health Research 1515 College Ave	Manhattan	KS	66502	**800-627-0388**	
Center for Space Plasma & Aeronomic Research University of Alabama Huntsville	Huntsville	AL	35899	**800-824-2255**	256-961-7403
Center on Human Development & Disability University of Washington PO Box 357920	Seattle	WA	98195	**800-636-1089**	206-543-7701
National Center for Environmental Health 4770 Buford Hwy NE	Atlanta	GA	30341	**800-232-4636**	
National Institute for Occupational Safety & Health 200 Independence Ave SW	Washington	DC	20201	**800-356-4674**	404-639-3286
Charles River Laboratories Inc 251 Ballardvale St *NYSE: CRL*	Wilmington	MA	01887	**800-772-3271**	781-222-6000
CHI Solutions Inc 5414 Oberlin Dr Ste 202	San Diego	CA	92121	**800-860-5454**	
Children's Research Institute Children's National Medical Ctr 111 Michigan Ave NW	Washington	DC	20010	**888-884-2327**	202-476-5000
Columbia Environmental Research Ctr (CERC) 4200 New Haven Rd	Columbia	MO	65201	**888-283-7626**	703-648-5953
Computer Emergency Response Team (CERT) 4500 Fifth Ave	Pittsburgh	PA	15213	**800-598-6831**	412-268-7090
Coriell Institute for Medical Research 403 Haddon Ave	Camden	NJ	08103	**800-752-3805**	856-966-7377
CRG Global Inc 3 Signal Ave Ste A	Ormond Beach	FL	32174	**800-831-1718**	386-677-5644
CureSearch for Children's Cancer 4600 East-West Hwy Ste 600	Bethesda	MD	20814	**800-458-6223**	301-718-0047
Dana-Farber Cancer Institute 44 Binney St	Boston	MA	02115	**866-408-3324**	617-632-3000
Data Sciences International 119 14th St NW Ste 100	St. Paul	MN	55112	**800-262-9687**	651-481-7400
Data Storage Systems Ctr (DSSC) *Carnegie Mellon University* ECE Department	Pittsburgh	PA	15213	**800-864-8287**	412-268-6600
Diabetes Research Institute 1450 NW Tenth Ave	Miami	FL	33136	**800-321-3437**	954-964-4040
Digital Monitoring Products Inc 2500 N Partnership Blvd	Springfield	MO	65803	**800-641-4282**	417-831-9362
Dycor Technologies Ltd 1851 94 St	Edmonton	AB	T6N1E6	**800-663-9267**	780-486-0091
Edison Biotechnology Institute 1 Ohio University	Athens	OH	45701	**800-444-2420**	740-593-4713
Epitomics Inc 863 Mitten Rd Ste 103	Burlingame	CA	94010	**888-772-2226**	
Evans Data Corp 340 Soquel Ave	Santa Cruz	CA	95062	**800-831-3080**	831-425-8451
Exponent Inc 149 Commonwealth Dr *NASDAQ: EXPO*	Menlo Park	CA	94025	**888-656-3976**	650-326-9400
Federal Aviation Administration (FAA) 800 Independence Ave SW	Washington	DC	20591	**866-835-5322**	
Aviation Research Div 800 Independence Ave SW	Washington	DC	20591	**866-835-5322**	202-267-8442
Fels Institute for Cancer Research & Molecular Biology 3307 N Broad St Pharmacy Allied Health Bldg Rm 154	Philadelphia	PA	19140	**800-331-2839**	215-204-7000
Fox Chase Cancer Ctr 333 Cottman Ave	Philadelphia	PA	19111	**888-369-2427**	215-728-6900
Framingham Heart Study 73 Mt Wayte Ave Ste 2	Framingham	MA	01702	**800-854-7582**	508-935-3418
Friends Research Institute Inc 1040 Park Ave Ste 103	Baltimore	MD	21201	**800-822-3677**	410-823-5116
Social Research Ctr 1040 Park Ave Ste 103	Baltimore	MD	21201	**800-705-7757**	410-837-3977
Gatorade Sports Science Institute 617 W Main St	Barrington	IL	60010	**800-616-4774**	
Genemed Biotechnologies Inc 458 Carlton Ct S San Francisco	San Francisco	CA	94080	**877-436-3633**	650-952-0110
General Atomics 3550 General Atomics Ct PO Box 85608	San Diego	CA	92121	**800-669-6820**	858-455-3000

Classified Section

				Toll-Free	Phone
Glen Research Corp 22825 Davis Dr	Sterling	VA	20164	800-327-4536	703-437-6191
High Performance Computing Collaboratory 2 Research Blvd	Starkville	MS	39762	800-521-4041	662-325-6768
Iconoculture Inc 111 Washington Ave S Ste 600	Minneapolis	MN	55401	866-913-8101	
Idaho National Laboratory (INL) 2525 Fremont Ave	Idaho Falls	ID	83402	866-495-7440	
Institute of Gerontology University of Michigan	Ann Arbor	MI	48109	877-865-2167	734-764-1817
Jackson Laboratory, The 600 Main St	Bar Harbor	ME	04609	800-422-6423	207-288-6000
James, The 460 W Tenth Ave	Columbus	OH	43210	800-293-5066	
Jean Mayer USDA Human Nutrition Research Ctr on Aging 711 Washington St	Boston	MA	02111	800-738-7555	617-556-3000
John F Kennedy Space Ctr	Kennedy Space Center	FL	32899	866-737-5235	321-867-5000
Johns Hopkins University Applied Physics Laboratory 11100 Johns Hopkins Rd	Laurel	MD	20723	800-435-9294	240-228-5000
LIMRA International Inc 300 Day Hill Rd	Windsor	CT	06095	800-235-4672	860-688-3358
Los Alamos National Laboratory (LANL) PO Box 1663	Los Alamos	NM	87545	877-723-4101	505-667-7000
Lovelace Respiratory Research Institute (LRRI) 2425 Ridgecrest Dr SE	Albuquerque	NM	87108	800-700-1016	505-348-9400
Mailman Research Ctr McLean Hospital 115 Mill St	Belmont	MA	02478	800-333-0338	617-855-2000
Martec 105 W Adams St Ste 2900	Chicago	IL	60603	888-811-5755	312-606-9690
Massa Products Corp 280 Lincoln St	Hingham	MA	02043	800-962-7543	781-749-4800
Massey Cancer Ctr Virginia Commonwealth University 401 College St PO Box 980037	Richmond	VA	23298	877-462-7739	804-828-0450
MAX Technologies Inc 2051 Victoria Ave	Saint-Lambert	QC	J4S1H1	800-361-1629	450-443-3332
Memorial Sloan-Kettering Cancer Ctr 1275 York Ave	New York	NY	10065	800-525-2225	212-639-2000
Michigan Mfg Technology Ctr 47911 Halyard Dr	Plymouth	MI	48170	888-414-6682	
Moffitt Cancer Center University of S Florida 12902 Magnolia Dr	Tampa	FL	33612	800-456-3434	888-663-3488
NAHB Research Ctr 400 Prince Georges Blvd	Upper Marlboro	MD	20774	800-638-8556	301-249-4000
National Biodynamics Laboratory (NBDL) University of New Orleans College of Engineering 2000 Lakeshore Dr	New Orleans	LA	70148	888-514-4275	
National Bureau of Economic Research 1050 Massachusetts Ave	Cambridge	MA	02138	800-621-8476	617-868-3900
National Ctr for Genome Resources 2935 Rodeo Pk Dr E	Santa Fe	NM	87505	800-450-4854	505-982-7840
National Ctr for Mfg Sciences (NCMS) 3025 Boardwalk	Ann Arbor	MI	48108	800-222-6267	734-995-3457
National Energy Research Scientific Computing Ctr (NERSC) Lawrence Berkeley National Laboratory	Berkeley	CA	94720	800-666-3772	510-486-5849
National Energy Technology Laboratory (NETL) 3610 Collins Ferry Rd	Morgantown	WV	26505	800-432-8330	304-285-4764
National Hansen's Disease Program (NHDP) 1770 Physicians Pk Dr	Baton Rouge	LA	70816	800-221-9393	
National Institute of Child Health & Human Development (NICHD) 31 Center Dr Bldg 31 Rm 2A32	Bethesda	MD	20892	800-370-2943	
National Institutes of Health (NIH) 9000 Rockville Pk	Bethesda	MD	20892	800-411-1222	301-496-4000
National Cancer Institute 9609 Medical Center Dr BG 9609 MSC 9760	Bethesda	MD	20892	800-422-6237	301-435-3848
National Institute of Arthritis & Musculoskeletal 1 AMS Cir	Bethesda	MD	20892	877-226-4267	301-495-4484
National Institute of Mental Health 6001 Executive Blvd Rm 6200 MSC 9663	Bethesda	MD	20892	866-615-6464	301-443-4513
National Institute of Neurological Disorders PO Box 5801	Bethesda	MD	20824	800-352-9424	301-496-5751
The National Institute on Deafness and Other Communication Disorders 31 Ctr Dr MSC 2320	Bethesda	MD	20892	800-241-1044	301-496-7243
National Optical Astronomy Observatory 950 N Cherry Ave	Tucson	AZ	85719	888-809-4012	520-318-8000
National Research Ctr for Coal & Energy (NRCCE) West Virginia University 385 Evansdale Dr PO Box 6064	Morgantown	WV	26506	800-624-8301	304-293-2867
National Technical Information Service (NTIS) 5285 Port Royal Rd	Springfield	VA	22161	800-553-6847*	703-605-6000
*Orders					
Natural Resources Research Institute (NRRI) University of Minnesota Duluth 5013 Miller Trunk Hwy	Duluth	MN	55811	800-234-0054	218-788-2694
Naval Surface Warfare Ctr Dahlgren Div 6149 Welsh Rd Ste 203	Dahlgren	VA	22448	877-845-5656	
Naval Undersea Warfare Center (NUWC) 1176 Howell St	Newport	RI	02841	800-356-8464	401-832-7742
Neuroscience Curriculum 115 Mason Farm Rd Campus Box 7250	Chapel Hill	NC	27599	800-862-4938	919-843-8536
North American Science Assoc Inc 6750 Wales Rd	Northwood	OH	43619	866-666-9455	419-666-9455
Northern Power Systems Inc 29 Pitman Rd	Barre	VT	05641	877-906-6784	802-461-2955
Oklahoma Medical Research Foundation (OMRF) 825 NE 13th St	Oklahoma City	OK	73104	800-522-0211	405-271-6673
Olon Ricerca Bioscience 7528 Auburn Rd	Concord	OH	44077	888-742-3722	440-357-3300
P&K Research 6323 N Avondale Ave	Chicago	IL	60631	800-747-5522	773-774-3100
Pacific Disaster Ctr 1305 N Holopono St Ste 2	Kihei	HI	96753	888-808-6688	808-891-0525
Pacific Northwest National Laboratory (PNNL) 902 Battelle Blvd PO Box 999	Richland	WA	99352	888-375-7665	509-375-2121
Phantom Laboratory Inc, The 2727 SR-29	Greenwich	NY	12834	800-525-1190	518-692-1190
Pittsburgh Supercomputing Ctr 300 S Craig St	Pittsburgh	PA	15213	800-221-1641	412-268-4960
Pleora Technologies Inc 340 Terry Fox Dr Ste 300	Kanata	ON	K2K3A2	888-687-6877	613-270-0625
Princeton Plasma Physics Laboratory (PPPL) PO Box 451	Princeton	NJ	08543	800-772-2222	609-243-2000
Quantiam Technologies Inc 1651 - 94 St NW	Edmonton	AB	T6N1E6	877-461-0707	780-462-0707
Research Institute on Addictions (RIA) 1021 Main St	Buffalo	NY	14203	800-729-6686	716-887-2566
Research Triangle Institute 3040 Cornwallis Rd PO Box 12194	Research Triangle Park	NC	27709	800-334-8571	919-541-6000
Rodale Institute 611 Siegfriedale Rd	Kutztown	PA	19530	800-432-1565	610-683-1400
Roswell Park Cancer Institute Elm and Carlton St	Buffalo	NY	14263	877-275-7724	716-845-2300
Safety Analysis & Forensic Engineering 5665 Hollister Ave	Goleta	CA	93117	800-426-7866	805-964-0676
San Diego Supercomputer Ctr (SDSC) 9500 Gilman Dr	La Jolla	CA	92093	800-451-4515	858-534-5000
Sandelman & Associates 257 La Paloma Ste 1	San Clemente	CA	92672	888-897-7881	
Sandia National Laboratories - New Mexico (SNL) 1515 Eubank SE	Albuquerque	NM	87123	800-783-5337	505-844-8066
Science Applications International Corp 10260 Campus Pt Dr	San Diego	CA	92121	800-760-4332	866-955-7242
SEDL 4700 Mueller Blvd	Austin	TX	78723	800-476-6861	512-476-6861
SERVE 5900 Summit Ave Ste 201	Browns Summit	NC	27214	800-755-3277	336-315-7400
Siteman Cancer Ctr 4921 Parkview Pl	Saint Louis	MO	63110	800-600-3606	314-362-5196
Social & Economic Sciences Research Ctr (SESRC) Washington State University Wilson Hall Rm 133 PO Box 644014	Pullman	WA	99164	800-932-5393	509-335-1511
Socratic Technologies Inc 2505 Mariposa St	San Francisco	CA	94110	800-576-2728	415-430-2200
Software Engineering Institute (SEI) 4500 Fifth Ave	Pittsburgh	PA	15213	888-201-4479	412-268-5800
Software Engineering Services Corp 1311 Ft Crook Rd S	Bellevue	NE	68005	800-244-1278	402-292-8660
Southern Research 2000 Ninth Ave S	Birmingham	AL	35205	800-967-6774	205-581-2000
Space Science & Engineering Ctr University of Wisconsin-Madison 1225 W Dayton St	Madison	WI	53706	866-391-1753	608-263-6750
Synergy Co of Utah LLC, The 2279 S Resource Blvd	Moab	UT	84532	800-723-0277	
Synexus 11500 Northlake Dr Ste 320	Cincinnati	OH	45249	855-427-8839	513-247-5500
Syracuse Research Corp (SRC) 7502 Round Pond Rd	North Syracuse	NY	13212	800-724-0451	315-452-8000
Technology Service Corp 251 18th St S Ste 705	Arlington	VA	22202	800-324-7700	256-705-2222
Trex Enterprises Corp 10455 Pacific Ctr Ct	San Diego	CA	92121	800-626-5885	858-646-5300
Turner-Fairbank Highway Research Ctr 6300 Georgetown Pk	McLean	VA	22101	800-424-9071	
UAB Comprehensive Cancer Ctr University of Alabama at Birmingham 1824 Sixth Ave S	Birmingham	AL	35294	800-822-0933	205-934-4011
University of Maryland Ctr for Environmental Science (UMCES) 2020 Horn Pt Rd	Cambridge	MD	21613	866-842-2520	410-228-9250
Waisman Ctr University of Wisconsin 1500 Highland Ave	Madison	WI	53705	888-428-8476	608-263-1656
WestEd 730 Harrison St	San Francisco	CA	94107	877-493-7833	415-565-3000
Western Research Institute 365 N Ninth St	Laramie	WY	82072	888-463-6974	307-721-2011
Wistar Institute 3601 Spruce St	Philadelphia	PA	19104	800-724-6633	215-898-3700

665 **RESORTS & RESORT COMPANIES**

SEE ALSO Hotels & Hotel Companies ; Hotels - Conference Center ; Spas - Hotel & Resort ; Casinos ; Dude Ranches

Alabama

				Toll-Free	Phone
Joe Wheeler Resort Lodge & Convention Ctr 4401 McLean Dr	Rogersville	AL	35652	800-544-5639	256-247-5461
Perdido Beach Resort 27200 Perdido Beach Blvd	Orange Beach	AL	36561	800-634-8001	251-981-9811

Alaska

				Toll-Free	Phone
Alyeska Prince Hotel & Resort 1000 Arlberg Ave PO Box 249	Girdwood	AK	99587	800-880-3880	907-754-1111
Pybus Point Lodge PO Box 33497	Juneau	AK	99803	800-947-9287	907-790-4866

Alberta

				Toll-Free	Phone
Fairmont Chateau Lake Louise 111 Lake Louise Dr	Lake Louise	AB	T0L1E0	800-441-1414	403-522-3511
Rimrock Resort Hotel, The 300 Mountain Ave PO Box 1110	Banff	AB	T1L1J2	888-746-7625	403-762-3356
Waterton Lakes Lodge Resort 101 Clematis Ave PO Box 4	Waterton Park	AB	T0K2M0	888-985-6343	403-859-2150

Arizona

				Toll-Free	Phone
Arizona Biltmore Resort & Spa 2400 E Missouri	Phoenix	AZ	85016	**800-950-0086**	602-955-6600
Arizona Golf Resort & Conference Ctr 425 S Power Rd	Mesa	AZ	85206	**800-528-8282**	480-832-3202
Arizona Grand Resort 8000 S Arizona Grand Pkwy	Phoenix	AZ	85044	**866-267-1321**	602-438-9000
Boulders Resort & Golden Door Spa 34631 N Tom Darlington Dr	Scottsdale	AZ	85262	**888-579-2631**	480-488-9009
Camelback Inn JW Marriott Resort Golf Club & Spa 5402 E Lincoln Dr	Scottsdale	AZ	85253	**800-242-2635**	480-948-1700
Canyon Ranch Tucson 8600 E Rockcliff Rd	Tucson	AZ	85750	**800-742-9000**	520-749-9000
CopperWynd Resort & Club 13225 N Eagle Ridge Dr	Scottsdale	AZ	85268	**877-707-7760**	480-333-1900
Enchantment Resort 525 Boynton Canyon Rd	Sedona	AZ	86336	**800-826-4180**	844-244-9489
Fairmont Scottsdale Princess 7575 E Princess Dr	Scottsdale	AZ	85255	**800-257-7544**	480-585-4848
Four Seasons Resort Scottsdale at Troon North 10600 E Crescent Moon Dr	Scottsdale	AZ	85262	**800-332-3442**	480-513-5145
Francisco Grande Hotel & Golf Resort 26000 Gila Bend Hwy *General	Casa Grande	AZ	85222	**800-237-4238***	520-836-6444
Gold Canyon Golf Resort 6100 S Kings Ranch Rd	Gold Canyon	AZ	85118	**800-827-5281**	480-982-9090
Hacienda del Sol Guest Ranch Resort 5501 N Hacienda Del Sol Rd	Tucson	AZ	85718	**800-728-6514**	520-299-1501
Harrah's Ak-Chin Casino Resort 15406 Maricopa Rd *General	Maricopa	AZ	85139	**800-427-7247***	480-802-5000
Lake Powell Resorts & Marinas 100 Lakeshore Dr	Page	AZ	86040	**800-622-6317**	888-896-3829
Legacy Golf Resort 6808 S 32nd St	Phoenix	AZ	85042	**866-729-7182**	602-305-5500
Lodge at Ventana Canyon - A Wyndham Luxury Resort 6200 N Clubhouse Ln	Tucson	AZ	85750	**800-828-5701**	520-577-1400
Loews Ventana Canyon 7000 N Resort Dr	Tucson	AZ	85750	**844-806-9740**	520-299-2020
Los Abrigados Resort 160 Portal Ln	Sedona	AZ	86336	**877-374-2582**	928-282-1777
Millennium Resort Scottsdale McCormick Ranch 7401 N Scottsdale Rd	Scottsdale	AZ	85253	**800-243-1332**	480-948-5050
Phoenician, The 6000 E Camelback Rd	Scottsdale	AZ	85251	**800-888-8234**	480-941-8200
Pointe Hilton at Squaw Peak Resort 7677 N 16th St	Phoenix	AZ	85020	**800-685-0550**	602-997-2626
Pointe Hilton Resort at Tapatio Cliffs 11111 N Seventh St	Phoenix	AZ	85020	**800-947-9784**	602-866-7500
Rancho de los Caballeros 1551 S Vulture Mine Rd	Wickenburg	AZ	85390	**800-684-5030**	928-684-5484
Royal Palms Resort & Spa 5200 E Camelback Rd	Phoenix	AZ	85018	**800-672-6011**	602-840-3610
Saguaro Lake Ranch 13020 Bush Hwy	Mesa	AZ	85215	**800-868-5617**	480-984-2194
Sanctuary on Camelback Mountain 5700 E McDonald Dr	Paradise Valley	AZ	85253	**855-245-2051**	855-421-3522
Scottsdale Camelback Resort 6302 E Camelback Rd	Scottsdale	AZ	85251	**800-891-8585**	480-947-3300
Scottsdale Plaza Resort 7200 N Scottsdale Rd	Scottsdale	AZ	85253	**800-832-2025**	480-948-5000
Sheraton Wild Horse Pass Resort & Spa 5594 W Wild Horse Pass Blvd	Phoenix	AZ	85226	**866-837-4156**	602-225-0100
Westward Look Resort 245 E Ina Rd	Tucson	AZ	85704	**800-722-2500**	520-297-1151

Arkansas

				Toll-Free	Phone
Arlington Resort Hotel & Spa 239 Central Ave	Hot Springs	AR	71901	**800-643-1502**	501-623-7771

British Columbia

				Toll-Free	Phone
Fairmont Chateau Whistler 4599 Chateau Blvd	Whistler	BC	V0N1B4	**800-441-1414**	604-938-8000
Harrison Hot Springs Resort & Spa 100 Esplanade Ave	Harrison Hot Springs	BC	V0M1K0	**800-663-2266**	604-796-2244
Hilton Whistler Resort & Spa 4050 Whistler Way	Whistler	BC	V0N1B4	**800-515-4050**	604-932-1982
Pan Pacific Whistler Mountainside 4320 Sundial Crescent	Whistler	BC	V0N1B4	**888-905-9995**	604-905-2999
River Rock Casino Resort 8811 River Rd	Richmond	BC	V6X3P8	**866-748-3718**	604-247-8900
Tantalus Resort Lodge 4200 Whistler Way	Whistler	BC	V0N1B4	**888-806-2299**	604-932-4146
Whistler Blackcomb Mountain Ski Resort 4545 Blackcomb Way	Whistler	BC	V0N1B4	**800-766-0449**	604-932-3434

California

				Toll-Free	Phone
Alisal Guest Ranch & Resort 1054 Alisal Rd	Solvang	CA	93463	**800-425-4725**	805-693-4208
Bahia Resort Hotel 998 W Mission Bay Dr	San Diego	CA	92109	**800-576-4229**	858-488-0551
Barona Resort & Casino 1932 Wildcat Canyon Rd	Lakeside	CA	92040	**888-722-7662**	619-443-2300
Bear Mountain Golf Course 43101 Gold Mine Dr PO Box 77	Big Bear Lake	CA	92315	**844-462-2327**	
Carmel Valley Ranch Resort 1 Old Ranch Rd	Carmel	CA	93923	**866-405-5037**	855-687-7262
Casa Palmero 1518 Cypress Dr	Pebble Beach	CA	93953	**800-654-9300**	831-622-6650
Chaminade Resort & Spa 1 Chaminade Ln	Santa Cruz	CA	95065	**800-283-6569**	831-475-5600
Claremont Resort & Spa 41 Tunnel Rd	Berkeley	CA	94705	**800-551-7266**	510-843-3000
Costanoa Coastal Lodge & Camp 2001 Rossi Rd	Pescadero	CA	94060	**877-262-7848**	650-879-1100
Desert Springs Marriott Resort & Spa 74855 Country Club Dr	Palm Desert	CA	92260	**888-538-9459**	760-341-2211
Fairmont Sonoma Mission Inn & Spa, The PO Box 1447	Sonoma	CA	95476	**866-540-4499**	707-938-9000
Flamingo Resort Hotel & Conference Ctr 2777 Fourth St	Santa Rosa	CA	95405	**800-848-8300**	707-545-8530
Four Seasons Resort Santa Barbara 1260 Ch Dr	Santa Barbara	CA	93108	**800-819-5053**	805-969-2261
Grand Pacific Palisades Resort & Hotel 5805 Armada Dr	Carlsbad	CA	92008	**800-725-4723**	760-827-3200
Handlery Hotel & Resort 950 Hotel Cir N	San Diego	CA	92108	**800-676-6567**	619-298-0511
Hilton San Diego Resort 1775 E Mission Bay Dr	San Diego	CA	92109	**800-445-8667**	619-276-4010
Hilton Santa Barbara Beachfront Resort 633 E Cabrillo Blvd	Santa Barbara	CA	93103	**800-879-2929**	805-564-4333
Hotel Del Coronado 1500 Orange Ave	Coronado	CA	92118	**800-468-3533**	619-435-6611
Indian Springs Resort & Spa 1712 Lincoln Ave	Calistoga	CA	94515	**800-877-3623**	707-709-8139
Indian Wells Resort Hotel 76-661 Hwy 111	Indian Wells	CA	92210	**800-248-3220**	760-345-6466
Inn at Rancho Santa Fe 5951 Linea Del Cielo PO Box 869	Rancho Santa Fe	CA	92067	**800-843-4661**	858-756-1131
Inn at Spanish Bay, The 2700 17-Mile Dr	Pebble Beach	CA	93953	**800-654-9300**	831-647-7500
Knott's Berry Farm Resort 7675 Crescent Ave	Buena Park	CA	90620	**866-752-2444**	714-995-1111
L'Auberge Del Mar 1540 Camino del Mar PO Box 2889	Del Mar	CA	92014	**800-245-9757**	858-259-1515
La Jolla Beach & Tennis Club 2000 Spindrift Dr	La Jolla	CA	92037	**888-828-0948**	858-454-7126
Lakeland Village Beach & Mountain Resort 3535 Lake Tahoe Blvd	South Lake Tahoe	CA	96150	**888-484-7094**	530-541-7711
Lodge at Pebble Beach 1700 17-Mile Dr	Pebble Beach	CA	93953	**800-654-9300**	831-624-3811
Lodge at Sonoma - A Renaissance Resort & Spa 1325 Broadway	Sonoma	CA	95476	**866-263-0758**	707-935-6600
Mammoth Mountain Resort 10001 Minaret Rd PO Box 24	Mammoth Lakes	CA	93546	**800-626-6684**	760-934-2571
Meadowood Napa Valley 900 Meadowood Ln	Saint Helena	CA	94574	**800-458-8080**	877-963-3646
Miramonte Resort & Spa 45000 Indian Wells Ln	Indian Wells	CA	92210	**800-237-2926**	760-341-2200
Montage Resort & Spa 30801 S Coast Hwy	Laguna Beach	CA	92651	**866-271-6953**	949-715-6000
Morgan Run Resort & Club 5690 Cancha de Golf *Resv	Rancho Santa Fe	CA	92091	**800-378-4653***	800-433-5079
Morongo Casino Resort & Spa 49500 Seminole Dr	Cabazon	CA	92230	**800-252-4499**	951-849-3080
Mount Shasta Resort 1000 Siskiyou Lake Blvd	Mount Shasta	CA	96067	**800-958-3363**	530-926-3030
Northstar-at-Tahoe PO Box 129	Truckee	CA	96160	**800-466-6784**	
Ojai Valley Inn & Spa 905 Country Club Rd	Ojai	CA	93023	**800-422-6524**	805-640-2068
Pacific Palms Conference Resort 1 Industry Hills Pkwy *Cust Svc	City of Industry	CA	91744	**800-524-4557***	626-810-4455
Pala Casino Resort & Spa 11154 Hwy 76	Pala	CA	92059	**877-946-7252**	760-510-5100
Pala Mesa Resort 2001 Old Hwy 395	Fallbrook	CA	92028	**800-722-4700**	760-728-5881
Palm Mountain Resort & Spa 155 S BelaRdo Rd	Palm Springs	CA	92262	**800-622-9451**	760-325-1301
Pechanga Resort & Casino 45000 Pechanga Pkwy	Temecula	CA	92592	**877-711-2946**	951-693-1819
Pismo Coast Village RV Resort 165 S Dolliver St	Pismo Beach	CA	93449	**888-782-3224**	805-755-5406
Quail Lodge Resort & Golf Club 8205 Valley Greens Dr	Carmel	CA	93923	**866-675-1101**	
Rancho Valencia Resort 5921 Valencia Cir PO Box 9126	Rancho Santa Fe	CA	92067	**800-548-3664**	858-756-1123
Renaissance Esmeralda Resort 44-400 Indian Wells Ln	Indian Wells	CA	92210	**888-236-2427**	760-773-4444
Resort at Squaw Creek 400 Squaw Creek Rd PO Box 3333	Olympic Valley	CA	96146	**800-327-3353**	530-583-6300
Ritz-Carlton Half Moon Bay 1 Miramontes Pt Rd *General	Half Moon Bay	CA	94019	**800-241-3333***	650-712-7000
Ritz-Carlton Hotel Company LLC, The 8301 Hollister Ave	Santa Barbara	CA	93117	**800-952-2027**	805-968-0100
Ritz-Carlton Laguna Niguel, The 1 Ritz Carlton Dr	Dana Point	CA	92629	**800-542-8680**	949-240-2000
Shadow Mountain Resort & Club 45-750 San Luis Rey	Palm Desert	CA	92260	**800-472-3713**	760-346-6123
Spa Resort, The 401 E Amado Rd	Palm Springs	CA	92262	**888-999-1995**	760-883-1060
Squaw Valley USA PO Box 2007	Olympic Valley	CA	96146	**800-403-0206**	
Temecula Creek Inn 44501 Rainbow Canyon Rd	Temecula	CA	92592	**888-976-3404**	855-774-8535
Town & Country Resort Hotel 500 Hotel Cir N	San Diego	CA	92108	**800-772-8527**	619-291-7131
Two Bunch Palms Resort & Spa 67425 Two Bunch Palms Trl	Desert Hot Springs	CA	92240	**800-472-4334**	760-329-8791
Ventana Inn 48123 Hwy 1	Big Sur	CA	93920	**800-628-6500**	831-667-2331

				Toll-Free	Phone

Welk Resort Branson
8860 Lawrence Welk Dr .... Escondido CA 92026 · **800-505-9355** · 417-336-3575

Welk Resort San Diego
8860 Lawrence Welk Dr .... Escondido CA 92026 · **800-932-9355*** · 760-749-3000
*Resv

Winner's Cir Resort
550 Via de la Valle .... Solana Beach CA 92075 · **800-874-8770** · 858-755-6666

Colorado

				Toll-Free	Phone

Aspen Meadows Resort
845 Meadows Rd .... Aspen CO 81611 · **800-452-4240** · 970-925-4240

Beaver Run Resort & Conference Ctr
620 Village Rd .... Breckenridge CO 80424 · **800-525-2253** · 970-453-6000

Broadmoor, The
1 Lake Ave .... Colorado Springs CO 80906 · **866-837-9520** · 719-577-5775

C Lazy U Ranch
3640 Colorado Hwy 125 PO Box 379 .... Granby CO 80446 · **800-228-9792** · 970-887-3344

Copper Mountain Resort
209 Ten Mile Cir .... Copper Mountain CO 80443 · **888-219-2441** · 866-841-2481

Crested Butte Mountain Resort (CBMR)
12 Snowmass Rd PO Box 5700 .... Crested Butte CO 81225 · **877-547-5143** · 970-349-2222

Destination Hotels & Resorts Inc
10333 E Dry Creek Rd Ste 450 .... Englewood CO 80112 · **855-893-1011** · 303-799-3830

Grand Lodge Crested Butte
6 Emmons Rd .... Crested Butte CO 81225 · **877-547-5143** · 970-349-8000

Hot Springs Lodge & Pool
415 E Sixth St .... Glenwood Springs CO 81601 · **800-537-7946** · 970-945-6571

Indian Hot Springs
302 Soda Creek Rd PO Box 1990 .... Idaho Springs CO 80452 · **800-884-3201** · 303-989-6666

Keystone Resort
21996 Hwy 6 PO Box 38. .... Keystone CO 80435 · **877-625-1556** · 970-754-0001

Manor Vail Lodge
595 E Vail Vly Dr .... Vail CO 81657 · **800-950-8245** · 970-476-5000

Mountain Lodge at Telluride
457 Mtn Village Blvd .... Telluride CO 81435 · **866-368-6867** · 970-369-5000

Omni Interlocken Resort
500 Interlocken Blvd .... Broomfield CO 80021 · **800-843-6664** · 303-438-6600

Peaks Resort & Golden Door Spa
136 Country Club Dr .... Telluride CO 81435 · **800-789-2220**

Saint Regis Aspen Resort, The
315 E Dean St .... Aspen CO 81611 · **888-627-7198** · 970-920-3300

Sonnenalp Resort of Vail
20 Vail Rd .... Vail CO 81657 · **800-654-8312** · 970-476-5656

Steamboat Grand Resort Hotel & Conference Ctr
2300 Mt Werner Cir .... Steamboat Springs CO 80487 · **877-269-2628** · 970-871-5500

Steamboat Ski & Resort Corp
2305 Mt Werner Cir .... Steamboat Springs CO 80487 · **877-237-2628** · 970-879-6111

Vail Resorts Management Co
390 Interlocken Crescent Ste 1000 .... Broomfield CO 80021 · **800-842-8062** · 303-404-1800
NYSE: MTN

Connecticut

				Toll-Free	Phone

Interlaken Inn
74 Interlaken Rd Rt 12 .... Lakeville CT 06039 · **800-222-2909** · 860-435-9878

Mohegan Sun Resort & Casino
1 Mohegan Sun Blvd .... Uncasville CT 06382 · **888-226-7711** · 860-862-8150

Water's Edge Resort & Spa
1525 Boston Post Rd PO Box 688 .... Westbrook CT 06498 · **800-222-5901** · 860-399-5901

Florida

				Toll-Free	Phone

Amelia Island Plantation
39 Beach Lagoon Rd .... Amelia Island FL 32034 · **800-834-4900** · 904-261-6161

Bahia Mar Beach Resort & Yachting Ctr
801 Seabreeze Blvd .... Fort Lauderdale FL 33316 · **800-755-9558** · 954-627-6309

Banyan Resort
323 Whitehead St .... Key West FL 33040 · **866-371-9222** · 305-296-7786

Bay Hill Golf Club & Lodge
9000 Bay Hill Blvd .... Orlando FL 32819 · **888-422-9445** · 407-876-2429

Biltmore Hotel & Conference Ctr of the Americas
1200 Anastasia Ave ....Coral Gables FL 33134 · **800-727-1926*** · 855-311-6903
*Cust Svc

Boca Raton Resort & Club
501 E Camino Real .... Boca Raton FL 33432 · **888-543-1224** · 561-447-3000

Breakers, The
1 S County Rd .... Palm Beach FL 33480 · **888-273-2537** · 561-655-6611

Casa Marina Resort & Beach Club
1500 Reynolds St .... Key West FL 33040 · **888-303-5719** · 305-296-3535

Casa Ybel Resort
2255 W Gulf Dr ....Sanibel Island FL 33957 · **800-276-4753** · 239-472-3145

Deauville Beach Resort
6701 Collins Ave .... Miami Beach FL 33141 · **800-327-6656** · 305-865-8511

Don CeSar Beach Resort - A Loews Hotel
3400 Gulf Blvd .... Saint Pete Beach FL 33706 · **888-430-4999** · 727-360-1881

Eden Roc - A Renaissance Beach Resort & Spa
4525 Collins Ave .... Miami Beach FL 33140 · **855-433-3676** · 305-531-0000

Fisher Island Club & Resort
1 Fisher Island Dr ....Miami FL 33109 · **800-537-3708*** · 305-535-6000
*Resv

Fontainebleau Miami Beach
4441 Collins Ave .... Miami Beach FL 33140 · **800-548-8886**

Four Seasons Resort Palm Beach
2800 S Ocean Blvd .... Palm Beach FL 33480 · **800-432-2335** · 561-582-2800

Galleon Resort & Marina
617 Front St .... Key West FL 33040 · **800-544-3030** · 305-296-7711

Grand Palms Hotel & Golf Resort
110 Grand Palms Dr .... Pembroke Pines FL 33027 · **800-327-9246** · 954-431-8800

Hammock Beach Resort
200 Ocean Crest Dr .... Palm Coast FL 32137 · **866-841-0287**

Harborside Suites At Little Harbor
536 Bahia Beach Blvd .... Ruskin FL 33570 · **800-327-2773**

Hard Rock Hotel at Universal Orlando Resort
5800 Universal Blvd .... Orlando FL 32819 · **888-430-4999** · 407-503-2000

				Toll-Free	Phone

Hawk's Cay Resort & Marina
61 Hawk's Cay Blvd .... Duck Key FL 33050 · **888-395-5539** · 866-347-2675

Hilton Key Largo Resort
97000 S Overseas Hwy ....Key Largo FL 33037 · **888-871-3437*** · 305-852-5553
*Resv

Hilton Sandestin Beach Golf Resort & Spa
4000 Sandestin Blvd S .... Miramar Beach FL 32550 · **800-559-1805** · 850-267-9500

Holiday Inn Express & Suites Oceanfront
3301 S Atlantic Ave .... Daytona Beach Shores FL 32118 · **800-633-8464** · 386-767-1711

Holiday Isle Beach Resort & Marina
84001 Overseas Hwy .... Islamorada FL 33036 · **855-314-2829** · 305-664-2321

Innisbrook Resort & Golf Club
36750 US Hwy 19 N .... Palm Harbor FL 34684 · **800-492-6899** · 727-942-2000

Jupiter Beach Resort
5 N A1A .... Jupiter FL 33477 · **877-389-0571** · 561-746-2511

JW Marriott Orlando Grande Lakes Resort
4040 Central Florida Pkwy .... Orlando FL 32837 · **800-576-5750** · 407-206-2300

Key Largo Marriott Bay Resort
103800 Overseas Hwy .... Key Largo FL 33037 · **888-731-9056*** · 305-453-0000
*Resv

La Playa Beach & Golf Resort
9891 Gulf Shore Dr .... Naples FL 34108 · **800-237-6883** · 239-597-3123

Lago Mar Resort & Club
1700 S Ocean Ln .... Fort Lauderdale FL 33316 · **855-209-5677** · 954-523-6511

Little Palm Island Resort & Spa
28500 Overseas Hwy .... Little Torch Key FL 33042 · **800-343-8567** · 305-872-2524

Lodge & Club at Ponte Vedra Beach
607 Ponte Vedra Blvd .... Ponte Vedra Beach FL 32082 · **800-243-4304** · 888-839-9145

Longboat Key Club
220 Sands Point Rd .... Longboat Key FL 34228 · **800-237-8821** · 941-383-8821

Marco Beach Ocean Resort
480 S Collier Blvd .... Marco Island FL 34145 · **800-715-8517** · 239-393-1400

Miami Beach Resort & Spa
4833 Collins Ave .... Miami Beach FL 33140 · **866-765-9090** · 305-532-3600

Mission Inn Resort & Club
10400 County Rd 48 .... Howey in the Hills FL 34737 · **800-874-9053** · 352-324-3101

Naples Bay Resort
1500 Fifth Ave S .... Naples FL 34102 · **866-605-1199** · 239-530-1199

Naples Beach Hotel & Golf Club
851 Gulf Shore Blvd N .... Naples FL 34102 · **800-237-7600** · 239-261-2222

Ocean Key Resort & Spa
0 Duval St .... Key West FL 33040 · **800-328-9815** · 305-296-7701

Ocean Manor Resort
4040 Galt Ocean Dr .... Fort Lauderdale FL 33308 · **800-955-0444** · 954-566-7500

Omni Orlando Resort at Championsgate
1500 Masters Blvd ....Champions Gate FL 33896 · **800-843-6664** · 407-390-6664

Palms, The
3025 Collins Ave .... Miami Beach FL 33140 · **800-550-0505** · 305-534-0505

Park Shore Resort
600 Neapolitan Way .... Naples FL 34103 · **855-923-8197**

PGA National Resort & Spa
400 Ave of the Champions .... Palm Beach Gardens FL 33418 · **800-863-2819** · 561-227-2547

Pier House Resort Caribbean Spa
1 Duval St .... Key West FL 33040 · **800-723-2791** · 305-296-4600

Plantation Inn & Golf Resort
9301 W Fort Island Trl ....Crystal River FL 34429 · **800-632-6262** · 352-795-4211

Plaza Resort & Spa
600 N Atlantic Ave .... Daytona Beach FL 32118 · **844-284-2685**

Ponte Vedra Inn & Club
200 Ponte Vedra Blvd .... Ponte Vedra Beach FL 32082 · **800-234-7842** · 866-748-8083

Quality Inn & Suites Naples Golf Resort
4100 Golden Gate Pkwy .... Naples FL 34116 · **800-277-0017** · 239-455-1010

Radisson Resort Parkway
2900 PkwyBlvd .... Kissimmee FL 34747 · **800-333-3333** · 407-396-7000

Reach Resort
1435 Simonton St .... Key West FL 33040 · **888-318-4317** · 305-296-5000

Renaissance Orlando Resort at SeaWorld
6677 Sea Harbor Dr .... Orlando FL 32821 · **800-327-6677** · 407-351-5555

Renaissance Resort at World Golf Village
500 S Legacy Trl .... Saint Augustine FL 32092 · **888-740-7020** · 904-940-8000

Renaissance Vinoy Resort & Golf Club
501 Fifth Ave NE ....Saint Petersburg FL 33701 · **800-468-3571** · 727-894-1000

Ritz-Carlton Naples Golf Resort
2600 Tiburon Dr .... Naples FL 34109 · **877-231-7916*** · 239-593-2000
*Resv

Ritz-Carlton Orlando Grande Lakes
4012 Central Florida Pkwy .... Orlando FL 32837 · **866-922-6882** · 407-206-2400

Rosen Hotels & Resorts Inc
9840 International Dr .... Orlando FL 32819 · **800-204-7234** · 407-996-9840

Royal Pacific Resort at Universal Orlando - A Loews Hotel
6300 Hollywood Way .... Orlando FL 32819 · **800-235-6397** · 407-503-3000

Safety Harbor Resort & Spa
105 North Bayshore Dr .... Safety Harbor FL 34695 · **888-237-8772**

Sandals Resorts International
4950 SW 72nd Ave .... Miami FL 33155 · **888-726-3257** · 305-284-1300

Sandestin Golf & Beach Resort
9300 Emerald Coast Pkwy W ....Sandestin FL 32550 · **800-277-0800** · 850-267-8000

Sanibel Harbour Marriott Resort & Spa
17260 Harbour Pt Dr .... Fort Myers FL 33908 · **800-767-7777** · 239-466-4000

Seminole Hard Rock Hotel & Casino Hollywood
1 Seminole Way .... Hollywood FL 33314 · **866-502-7529**

Sheraton Sand Key Resort
1160 Gulf Blvd .... Clearwater Beach FL 33767 · **800-456-7263** · 727-595-1611

South Seas Island Resort
5400 Plantation Rd .... Captiva FL 33924 · **866-565-5089** · 239-472-5111

Sunset Beach Resort
3287 W Gulf Dr ....Sanibel Island FL 33957 · **866-565-5091** · 239-472-1700

Vanderbilt Beach Resort
9225 Gulf Shore Dr N .... Naples FL 34108 · **800-243-9076** · 239-597-3144

Villas of Grand Cypress Golf Resort
1 N Jacaranda .... Orlando FL 32836 · **877-330-7377** · 407-239-4700

Walt Disney World Dolphin
1500 Epcot Resorts Blvd .... Lake Buena Vista FL 32830 · **888-828-8850** · 407-934-4000

Walt Disney World Swan
1200 Epcot Resorts Blvd .... Lake Buena Vista FL 32830 · **888-828-8850** · 407-934-4000

West Wind Inn
3345 W Gulf Dr .... Sanibel FL 33957 · **800-824-0476** · 239-472-1541

Georgia

	Toll-Free	Phone
Barnsley Resort 597 Barnsley Gardens Rd .... Adairsville GA 30103	877-773-2447	770-773-7480
Brasstown Valley Resort 6321 Hwy 76 .... Young Harris GA 30582	800-201-3205	
Callaway Gardens 17800 Hwy 27 .... Pine Mountain GA 31822	800-225-5292	706-663-2281
Forrest Hills Mountain Resort & Conference Ctr 135 Forrest Hills Rd .... Dahlonega GA 30533	800-654-6313	706-864-6456
Jekyll Island Club Hotel 371 Riverview Dr .... Jekyll Island GA 31527	800-535-9547	912-635-2600
King & Prince Beach & Golf Resort 201 Arnold Rd .... Saint Simons Island GA 31522	800-342-0212	912-638-3631
Reynolds Plantation 100 Linger Longer Rd .... Greensboro GA 30642	800-800-5250	706-467-0600
Ritz-Carlton Lodge Reynolds Plantation 1 Lake Oc1e Trl .... Greensboro GA 30642	877-231-7916	706-467-0600
Sea Palms Golf & Tennis Resort 5445 Frederica Rd .... Saint Simons Island GA 31522	800-841-6268	912-638-3351
St Regis 88 W Paces Ferry Rd .... Atlanta GA 30305	877-787-3447	404-563-7900
Villas by the Sea Resort 1175 N Beachview Dr .... Jekyll Island GA 31527	800-841-6262	912-635-2521

Hawaii

	Toll-Free	Phone
Fairmont Kea Lani 4100 Wailea Alanui Dr .... Maui HI 96753	800-659-4100	808-875-4100
Fairmont Orchid Hawaii 1 N Kaniku Dr .... Kohala Coast HI 96743	800-845-9905	808-885-2000
Four Seasons Resort Hualalai 100 Ka'upulehu Dr .... Kailua-Kona HI 96740	888-340-5662	808-325-8000
Four Seasons Resort Maui at Wailea 3900 Wailea Alanui Dr .... Wailea HI 96753	800-334-6284	808-874-8000
Grand Wailea Resort & Spa 3850 Wailea Alanui Dr .... Wailea HI 96753	800-888-6100	808-875-1234
Hanalei Bay Resort & Suites 5380 Honoiki Rd .... Princeville HI 96722	877-344-0688	808-826-6522
Hapuna Beach Resort 62-100 Kauna'oa Dr .... Kamuela HI 96743	800-882-6060	808-880-1111
Hilton Hawaiian Village 2005 Kalia Rd .... Honolulu HI 96815	800-445-8667	808-949-4321
Hilton Waikoloa Village 425 Waikoloa Beach Dr .... Waikoloa HI 96738	866-931-1679	808-886-1234
Marriott Kaua'i Resort & Beach Club 3610 Rice St Kalapaki Beach .... Lihue HI 96766	800-220-2925	808-245-5050
Mauna Kea Beach Hotel 62-100 Maunakea Beach Dr .... Kohala Coast HI 96743	866-977-4589	808-882-7222
Mauna Lani Bay Hotel & Bungalows 68-1400 Mauna Lani Dr .... Kohala Coast HI 96743	800-367-2323	808-885-6622
Napili Kai Beach Club 5900 Honoapiilani Rd .... Lahaina HI 96761	800-367-5030	808-669-6271
Outrigger Enterprises Group 2375 Kuhio Ave .... Honolulu HI 96815	866-956-4262	
Outrigger Hotels Hawaii *Outrigger Hotels & Resorts* 2375 Kuhio Ave .... Honolulu HI 96815	800-688-7444	866-956-4262
Outrigger Reef on the Beach 2169 Kalia Rd .... Honolulu HI 96815	800-688-7444	808-923-3111
Prince Resorts Hawaii 100 Holomoana St .... Honolulu HI 96815	888-977-4623	808-956-1111
Ritz-Carlton Kapalua 1 Ritz-Carlton Dr Kapalua .... Maui HI 96761 *Resv	800-262-8440*	808-669-6200
Royal Hawaiian 2259 Kalakaua Ave .... Honolulu HI 96815	866-716-8110	808-923-7311
Royal Lahaina Resort 2780 Kekaa Dr .... Lahaina HI 96761	800-222-5642	808-661-3611
Royal Sea Cliff Kona by Outrigger 75-6040 Alii Dr .... Kailua-Kona HI 96740	866-956-4262	808-322-7222
Travaasa Hana 5031 Hana Hwy .... Hana HI 96713	855-868-7282	808-248-8211
Turtle Bay Resort 57-091 Kamehameha Hwy .... Kahuku HI 96731	866-475-2567	808-293-6000

Idaho

	Toll-Free	Phone
Coeur d'Alene Resort 115 S Second St .... Coeur D'Alene ID 83814	800-688-5253	855-703-4648
Red Lion Templin's Hotel on the River 414 E First Ave .... Post Falls ID 83854	800-733-5466	208-773-1611
Sun Valley Resort 1 Sun Valley Rd .... Sun Valley ID 83353	800-786-8259	208-622-4111

Illinois

	Toll-Free	Phone
Eagle Ridge Inn & Resort 444 Eagle Ridge Dr .... Galena IL 61036	800-892-2269	815-777-2444
Eaglewood Resort & Spa 1401 Nordic Rd .... Itasca IL 60143	877-285-6150	630-773-1400

Indiana

	Toll-Free	Phone
Belterra Casino Resort 777 Belterra Dr .... Florence IN 47020	888-235-8377	812-427-7777
French Lick Resort 8670 W State Rd 56 .... French Lick IN 47432	888-936-9360	812-936-9300
Potawatomi Inn Pokagan State Pk 6 Ln 100A Lk James .... Angola IN 46703	877-768-2928	260-833-1077

Iowa

	Toll-Free	Phone
Grand Harbor Resort & Waterpark 350 Bell St .... Dubuque IA 52001	866-690-4006	563-690-4000

Kentucky

	Toll-Free	Phone
General Butler State Resort Park 1608 US Hwy 227 .... Carrollton KY 41008	866-462-8853	502-732-4384
Griffin Gate Marriott Resort 1800 Newtown Pk .... Lexington KY 40511	800-228-9290	859-231-5100

Maine

	Toll-Free	Phone
Atlantic Oceanside Hotel & Event Center 119 Eden St Rte 3 .... Bar Harbor ME 04609	800-336-2463	207-288-5801
Bar Harbor Inn Oceanfront Resort Newport Dr .... Bar Harbor ME 04609	800-248-3351	207-288-3351
Bethel Inn & Country Club 21 Broad St .... Bethel ME 04217	800-654-0125	
Colony Hotel 140 Ocean Ave .... Kennebunkport ME 04046	800-552-2363	207-967-3331
Samoset Resort 220 Warrenton St .... Rockport ME 04856	800-341-1650	207-594-2511
Sebasco Harbor Resort 29 Keynon Rd .... Phippsburg ME 04562	800-225-3819	877-420-1701
Stage Neck Inn 8 Stage Neck Rd Rt 1A PO Box 70 .... York Harbor ME 03911	800-222-3238	207-363-3850
Sugarloaf/USA 5092 Access Rd .... Carrabassett Valley ME 04947	800-843-5623	207-237-2000
Sunday River Ski Resort 15 S Ridge Rd PO Box 4500 .... Newry ME 04261	800-543-2754	207-824-3500

Maryland

	Toll-Free	Phone
Francis Scott Key Family Resort 12806 Ocean Gateway .... Ocean City MD 21842	800-213-0088	410-213-0088
Ritz-Carlton Hotel Co LLC, The 4445 Willard Ave Ste 800 .... Chevy Chase MD 20815	800-241-3333	301-547-4700

Massachusetts

	Toll-Free	Phone
Bayside Resort Hotel 225 Massachusetts 28 .... West Yarmouth MA 02673	800-243-1114	508-775-5669
Blue Water Resort 291 S Shore Dr .... South Yarmouth MA 02664	800-367-9393	
Canyon Ranch 165 Kemble St .... Lenox MA 01240 *Resv	800-742-9000*	413-637-4100
Cape Codder Resort & Spa 1225 Iyanough Rd Rt 132 Bearse's Way .... Hyannis MA 02601	888-297-2200	508-771-3000
Chatham Bars Inn 297 Shore Rd .... Chatham MA 02633	800-527-4884	
Cranwell Resort Spa & Golf Club 55 Lee Rd .... Lenox MA 01240	800-272-6935	413-637-1364
New Seabury Resort 20 Red Brook Rd .... Mashpee MA 02649	877-687-3228	508-539-8200
Ocean Edge Resort & Golf Club 2907 Main St .... Brewster MA 02631	800-343-6074	508-896-9000
Ocean Mist Beach Hotel & Suites 97 S Shore Dr .... South Yarmouth MA 02664	800-655-1972	508-398-2633
Sea Crest Resort & Conference Ctr 350 Quaker Rd .... North Falmouth MA 02556	800-225-3110	508-540-9400

Michigan

	Toll-Free	Phone
Bay Valley Hotel & Resort 2470 Old Bridge Rd .... Bay City MI 48706	888-241-4653	989-686-3500
Boyne Highlands Resort 600 Highlands Dr .... Harbor Springs MI 49740	800-462-6963	844-783-3175
Boyne Mountain Resort 3951 Charlevoix Ave .... Petoskey MI 49770	800-462-6963	231-439-4750
Crystal Mountain Resort 12500 Crystal Mtn Dr .... Thompsonville MI 49683	800-968-7686	231-378-2000
Evergreen Resort 7880 Mackinaw Trl .... Cadillac MI 49601	800-634-7302	
Garland Resort 4700 N Red Oak Rd .... Lewiston MI 49756	877-442-7526	
Grand Traverse Resort & Spa 100 Grand Traverse Blvd PO Box 404 .... Acme MI 49610	800-236-1577	231-534-6000
Inn at Bay Harbor, The 3600 Village Harbor Dr .... Bay Harbor MI 49770	866-585-8123	
Lakewood Shores Resort 7751 Cedar Lake Rd .... Oscoda MI 48750	800-882-2493	
Mission Point Mackinac Island 1 Lakeshore Dr .... Mackinac Island MI 49757	800-833-7711	231-331-3419
Otsego Club 696 M-32 E Main St PO Box 556 .... Gaylord MI 49734	800-752-5510	989-732-5181
Shanty Creek Resort 5780 Shanty Creek Rd .... Bellaire MI 49615	800-678-4111	231-533-8621
Treetops Resort 3962 Wilkinson Rd .... Gaylord MI 49735	866-348-5249	989-732-6711

Minnesota

	Toll-Free	Phone
Arrowwood Resort & Conference Ctr 2100 Arrowwood Ln NW .... Alexandria MN 56308 *Resv	866-386-5263*	320-762-1124
Breezy Point Resort 9252 Breezy Pt Dr .... Breezy Point MN 56472	800-432-3777	
Caribou Highlands Lodge 371 Ski Hill Rd .... Lutsen MN 55612	800-642-6036	218-663-7241
Cascade Lodge 3719 W Hwy 61 .... Lutsen MN 55612	800-322-9543	218-387-1112
Cragun's Conference & Golf Resort 11000 Cragun's Dr .... Brainerd MN 56401	800-272-4867	

	Toll-Free	Phone
Fair Hills Resort		
24270 County Hwy 20 .... Detroit Lakes MN 56501	**800-323-2849***	218-847-7638
*Resv		
Grand Casino Hinckley		
777 Lady Luck Dr .... Hinckley MN 55037	**800-472-6321**	
Grand Casino Mille Lacs		
777 Grand Ave PO Box 343 .... Onamia MN 56359	**800-626-5825**	
Grand Portage Lodge & Casino		
PO Box 233 .... Grand Portage MN 55605	**800-543-1384**	218-475-2401
Grand View Lodge		
23521 Nokomis Ave .... Nisswa MN 56468	**866-801-2951**	218-963-2234
Lake Breeze Motel Resort		
9000 Congdon Blvd .... Duluth MN 55804	**800-738-5884**	218-525-6808
Lutsen Resort		
5700 W Hwy 61 PO Box 9 .... Lutsen MN 55612	**800-258-8736**	218-663-7212
Madden's on Gull Lake		
11266 Pine Beach Peninsula ..... Brainerd MN 56401	**800-642-5363**	800-233-2934
Ruttger's Bay Lake Lodge		
25039 Tame Fish Lake Rd PO Box 400 ..... Deerwood MN 56444	**800-450-4545**	218-678-2885
Superior Shores Resort		
1521 Superior Shores Dr ..... Two Harbors MN 55616	**800-242-1988**	218-834-5671

Mississippi

	Toll-Free	Phone
Beau Rivage Resort & Casino		
875 Beach Blvd .... Biloxi MS 39530	**888-750-7111**	228-386-7111
Gulf Hills Hotel		
13701 Paso Rd .... Ocean Springs MS 39564	**866-875-4211**	228-875-4211
IP Casino Resort & Spa		
850 Bayview Ave .... Biloxi MS 39530	**888-946-2847***	228-436-3000
*Resv		

Missouri

	Toll-Free	Phone
Lilleys' Landing Resort		
367 River Ln .... Branson MO 65616	**866-545-5397**	417-334-6380
Lodge of Four Seasons		
315 Four Seasons Dr .... Lake Ozark MO 65049	**888-265-5500***	573-365-3000
*Resv		
Tan-Tar-A Resort Golf Club & Spa		
494 Tantara Dr PO Box 188TT ..... Osage Beach MO 65065	**800-826-8272***	573-348-3131
*Resv		
Thousand Hills Golf Resort		
245 S Wildwood Dr .... Branson MO 65616	**877-262-0430**	417-336-5873

Montana

	Toll-Free	Phone
Big Sky Resort		
50 Big Sky Resort Rd .... Big Sky MT 59716	**800-548-4486**	406-995-5000
Fairmont Hot Springs Resort		
1500 Fairmont Rd .... Fairmont MT 59711	**800-332-3272**	406-797-3241
Glacier Park Inc		
PO Box 2025 .... Columbia Falls MT 59912	**844-868-7474**	406-892-2525
Meadow Lake Resort		
100 St Andrews Dr .... Columbia Falls MT 59912	**800-321-4653**	406-892-8700
Rock Creek Resort		
6380 US Hwy 212 .... Red Lodge MT 59068	**800-667-1119**	406-446-1111
Triple Creek Ranch		
5551 W Fork Rd .... Darby MT 59829	**800-654-2943**	406-821-4600

Nebraska

	Toll-Free	Phone
Radisson		
11340 Blondo S Ste 100 .... Omaha NE 68164	**888-288-8889**	800-615-7253

Nevada

	Toll-Free	Phone
Alexis Park Resort		
375 E Harmon Ave .... Las Vegas NV 89169	**800-582-2228**	702-796-3300
Aquarius Casino Resort		
1900 S Casino Dr .... Laughlin NV 89029	**888-662-5825**	702-298-5111
Atlantis Casino Resort		
3800 S Virginia St .... Reno NV 89502	**800-723-6500**	775-825-4700
Bellagio Hotel & Casino		
3600 Las Vegas Blvd S .... Las Vegas NV 89109	**888-987-7111**	888-987-6667
Casablanca Resort		
950 W Mesquite Blvd .... Mesquite NV 89027	**800-459-7529**	702-346-7529
Club Cal Neva Hotel Casino, The		
38 E Second St PO Box 2071 .... Reno NV 89501	**877-777-7303**	775-323-1046
Don Laughlin's Riverside Resort & Casino		
1650 Casino Dr .... Laughlin NV 89029	**800-227-3849**	702-298-2535
Golden Nugget Hotel		
129 E Fremont St .... Las Vegas NV 89101	**800-634-3454**	702-385-7111
Golden Nugget Laughlin		
2300 S Casino Dr .... Laughlin NV 89029	**800-950-7700**	702-298-7111
Grand Sierra Resort & Casino		
2500 E Second St .... Reno NV 89595	**800-501-2651**	775-789-2000
Hard Rock Hotel & Casino		
4455 Paradise Rd .... Las Vegas NV 89169	**800-473-7625**	702-693-5000
JW Marriott Resort Las Vegas		
221 N Rampart Blvd .... Las Vegas NV 89145	**877-869-8777**	702-869-7777
Mandalay Bay Resort & Casino		
3950 Las Vegas Blvd S .... Las Vegas NV 89119	**877-632-7800**	702-632-7777
MGM Grand Hotel & Casino		
3799 Las Vegas Blvd S .... Las Vegas NV 89109	**877-880-0880**	702-891-1111
Mirage, The		
3400 Las Vegas Blvd S .... Las Vegas NV 89109	**800-627-6667**	702-791-7111
PARK MGM		
3770 Las Vegas Blvd S .... Las Vegas NV 89109	**800-311-8999**	702-730-7777
Planet Hollywood Resort & Casino		
3667 Las Vegas Blvd S .... Las Vegas NV 89109	**866-919-7472**	

	Toll-Free	Phone
Primm Valley Resort & Casino		
31900 S Las Vegas Blvd .... Primm NV 89019	**800-926-4455**	
Ridge Tahoe		
400 Ridge Club Dr PO Box 5790 ..... Stateline NV 89449	**800-334-1600**	775-588-3553
Treasure Island Hotel & Casino		
3300 Las Vegas Blvd S .... Las Vegas NV 89109	**800-288-7206**	702-894-7111
Tropicana Resort & Casino		
3801 Las Vegas Blvd S .... Las Vegas NV 89109	**800-462-8767***	702-739-2222
*Resv		
Venetian Resort Hotel & Casino		
3355 Las Vegas Blvd S .... Las Vegas NV 89109	**866-659-9643**	702-414-1000

New Hampshire

	Toll-Free	Phone
Mount Washington Hotel & Resort		
310 Mount Washington Hotel Rd ..... Bretton Woods NH 03575	**800-314-1752**	603-278-1000
Waterville Valley Resort		
1 Ski Area Rd PO Box 540 ..... Waterville Valley NH 03215	**800-468-2553**	603-236-8311
White Mountain Hotel & Resort		
87 Fairway Dr PO Box 1828 ..... North Conway NH 03860	**800-533-6301**	603-356-7100

New Jersey

	Toll-Free	Phone
Montreal Beach Resort		
1025 Beach Ave .... Cape May NJ 08204	**800-525-7011**	609-884-7011
Ocean Place Resort & Spa		
1Ocean Blvd .... Long Branch NJ 07740	**800-411-6493**	
Resorts Casino Hotel		
1133 Boardwalk .... Atlantic City NJ 08401	**800-334-6378**	
Tropicana Entertainment		
2831 Boardwalk .... Atlantic City NJ 08401	**800-843-8767**	
OTC: TPCA		
Wyndham Vacation Rentals		
14 Sylvan Way .... Parsippany NJ 07054	**800-467-3529**	

New Mexico

	Toll-Free	Phone
Angel Fire Resort		
PO Box 130 .... Angel Fire NM 87710	**800-633-7463**	575-377-6401
Inn of the Mountain Gods		
287 Carrizo Canyon Rd .... Mescalero NM 88340	**800-545-9011**	
La Posada de Santa Fe Resort & Spa		
330 E Palace Ave .... Santa Fe NM 87501	**866-280-3810**	505-986-0000
Lifts West Condominium Resort Hotel		
PO Box 330 .... Red River NM 87558	**800-221-1859**	505-754-2778

New York

	Toll-Free	Phone
Bonnie Castle Resort		
31 Holland St PO Box 127 ..... Alexandria Bay NY 13607	**800-955-4511**	315-482-4511
Doral Arrowwood Conference Resort		
975 Anderson Hill Rd .... Rye Brook NY 10573	**844-211-0512**	844-214-5500
Gurney's Montauk Resort & Seawater Spa		
290 Old Montauk Hwy .... Montauk NY 11954	**800-848-7639**	631-668-2345
High Peaks Resort		
2384 Saranac Ave .... Lake Placid NY 12946	**800-755-5598**	518-523-4411
Holiday Valley Resort		
6557 Holiday Valley Rd		
PO Box 370 .... Ellicottville NY 14731	**800-323-0020**	716-699-2345
Mohonk Mountain House		
1000 Mtn Rest Rd .... New Paltz NY 12561	**855-883-3798**	845-255-1000
Montauk Yacht Club Resort & Marina		
32 Star Island Rd .... Montauk NY 11954	**888-692-8668**	631-668-3100
Otesaga, The 60 Lake St .... Cooperstown NY 13326	**800-348-6222**	607-547-9931
Peek 'n Peak Resort		
1405 Olde Rd .... Clymer NY 14724	**800-772-6906**	716-355-4141
Point, The PO Box 1327 .... Saranac Lake NY 12983	**800-255-3530**	518-891-5674
Roaring Brook Ranch & Tennis Resort		
Rte 9N S .... Lake George NY 12845	**800-882-7665**	518-668-5767
Rocking Horse Ranch Resort		
600 State Rt 44/55 .... Highland NY 12528	**800-647-2624**	844-402-3214
Sagamore, The		
110 Sagamore Rd .... Bolton Landing NY 12814	**866-384-1944**	518-644-9400
Villa Roma Resort & Conference Ctr		
356 Villa Roma Rd .... Callicoon NY 12723	**800-533-6767**	845-887-4880
Whiteface Club & Resort		
373 Whiteface Inn Ln .... Lake Placid NY 12946	**800-422-6757**	518-523-2551
Woodcliff Hotel & Spa		
199 Woodcliff Dr .... Fairport NY 14450	**800-365-3065**	585-381-4000

North Carolina

	Toll-Free	Phone
Ballantyne Resort Hotel		
10000 Ballantyne Commons Pkwy ..... Charlotte NC 28277	**866-248-4824**	704-248-4000
Eseeola Lodge, The		
175 Linville Ave PO Box 99 .... Linville NC 28646	**800-742-6717**	828-733-4311
Fontana Village Resort		
300 Woods Rd PO Box 68 ..... Fontana Dam NC 28733	**800-849-2258**	828-498-2211
Grove Park Inn Resort & Spa		
290 Macon Ave .... Asheville NC 28804	**800-438-5800**	
High Hampton Inn & Country Club		
1525 Hwy 107 S .... Cashiers NC 28717	**800-334-2551**	
Holiday Inn SunSpree Resort Wrightsville Beach		
1706 N Lumina Ave ..... Wrightsville Beach NC 28480	**888-211-9874**	910-256-2231
Hound Ears Club		
328 Shulls Mill Rd .... Boone NC 28607	**800-243-8652**	828-963-4321
Maggie Valley Resort & Country Club		
1819 Country Club Dr .... Maggie Valley NC 28751	**800-438-3861**	
Mid Pines Inn & Golf Club		
1010 Midland Rd .... Southern Pines NC 28387	**800-747-7272**	910-692-2114
Pine Needles Lodge & Golf Club		
PO Box 88 .... Southern Pines NC 28388	**800-747-7272**	910-692-7111

Classified Section

			Toll-Free	Phone
Pinnacle Inn Resort				
301 Pinnacle Inn Rd	Beech Mountain NC	28604	800-405-7888	828-387-2231
Sanderling Resort & Spa				
1461 Duck Rd	Duck NC	27949	800-701-4111	855-412-7866
Waynesville Inn Golf & Country Club, The				
176 Country Club Dr	Waynesville NC	28786	800-627-6250	828-456-3551
Wolf Ridge Ski Resort				
578 Vly View Cir	Mars Hill NC	28754	800-817-4111	828-689-4111

North Dakota

			Toll-Free	Phone
Prairie Knights Casino & Resort				
7932 Hwy 24	Fort Yates ND	58538	800-425-8277	701-854-7777

Nova Scotia

			Toll-Free	Phone
Atlantica Oak Island Resort & Conference Ctr				
36 Treasure Dr PO Box 6	Western Shore NS	B0J3M0	800-565-5075	902-627-2600
Pines Resort, The				
103 Shore Rd	Digby NS	B0V1A0	800-667-4637	

Ohio

			Toll-Free	Phone
Hueston Woods Lodge & Conference Ctr				
5201 Lodge Rd	College Corner OH	45003	800-282-7275	513-664-3500
Sawmill Creek Resort				
400 Sawmill Creek Dr	Huron OH	44839	800-729-6455	419-433-3800

Oklahoma

			Toll-Free	Phone
Lake Murray Resort Park				
3323 Lodge Rd	Ardmore OK	73401	800-622-6317	580-223-6600
Quartz Mountain Resort & Conference Ctr				
22469 Lodge Rd	Lone Wolf OK	73655	877-999-5567	580-563-2424

Ontario

			Toll-Free	Phone
Deerhurst Resort				
1235 Deerhurst Dr	Huntsville ON	P1H2E8	800-461-6522*	800-461-4393
*Sales				
Pinestone Resort				
4252 County Rd Ste 21	Haliburton ON	K0M1S0	800-461-0357	705-457-1800

Oregon

			Toll-Free	Phone
Black Butte Ranch				
12930 Hawks BeaRd Rd				
PO Box 8000	Black Butte Ranch OR	97759	866-901-2961	541-595-1252
Gearhart By the Sea				
1157 N Marion Ave	Gearhart OR	97138	800-547-0115	503-738-8331
Mount Bachelor Village Resort & Conference Ctr				
19717 Mt Bachelor Dr	Bend OR	97702	800-547-5204	888-691-3069
Salishan Lodge & Golf Resort				
PO Box 118	Gleneden Beach OR	97388	800-452-2300	
Seventh Mountain Resort				
18575 SW Century Dr	Bend OR	97702	877-765-1501	541-382-8711
Sunriver Resort				
17600 Center Dr	Sunriver OR	97707	800-547-3922	855-420-8206
Timberline Lodge				
27500 E Timberline Rd	Government Camp OR	97028	800-547-1406	503-272-3311

Pennsylvania

			Toll-Free	Phone
Carroll Valley Golf Resort				
78 Country Club Trl	Carroll Valley PA	17320	855-784-0330	717-642-8282
Cove Haven Pocono Palace				
5222 Milford Rd	East Stroudsburg PA	18302	800-432-9932	
Fernwood Resort				
5785 Milford Rd	East Stroudsburg PA	18302	888-337-6966	
Hidden Valley Resort & Conference Ctr				
1 Craighead Dr PO Box 4420	Hidden Valley PA	15502	800-452-2223	814-443-8000
Hotel Hershey, The				
100 Hotel Rd	Hershey PA	17033	844-330-1711	717-533-2171
Lancaster Host Resort				
2300 Lincoln Hwy E	Lancaster PA	17602	800-233-0121*	717-299-5500
*Resv				
Mountain Laurel				
81 Treetops Dr	White Haven PA	18661	888-243-9300	570-443-8411
Nemacolin Woodlands Resort & Spa				
1001 Lafayette Dr	Farmington PA	15437	800-422-2736	724-329-7500
Pocono Manor Golf Resort & Spa				
1 Manor Dr Rt 314	Pocono Manor PA	18349	800-233-8150	800-944-8392
Seven Springs Mountain Resort				
777 Waterwheel Dr	Champion PA	15622	800-452-2223	814-352-7777
Skytop Lodge 1 Skytop	Skytop PA	18357	800-345-7759	855-345-7759
Split Rock Resort				
100 Moseywood Rd	Lake Harmony PA	18624	800-255-7625	570-722-9111
Tamiment Resort & Conference Ctr				
Bushkill Falls Rd	Tamiment PA	18371	800-233-8105	570-588-6652
Woodlands Inn, The				
1073 Hwy 315	Wilkes-Barre PA	18702	888-221-6039	

Puerto Rico

			Toll-Free	Phone
El Conquistador Resort & Golden Door Spa				
1000 El Conquistador Ave	Fajardo PR	00738	888-543-1282*	787-863-1000
*Resv				

Quebec

			Toll-Free	Phone
Fairmont Le Chateau Montebello				
392 Notre Dame St	Montebello QC	J0V1L0	800-441-1414	819-423-6341
Hotel Cheribourg				
2603 chemin du Parc	Orford QC	J1X8C8	877-845-5344	819-843-3308
Manoir du Lac Delage				
40 Ave du Lac	Lac Delage QC	G3C5C4	888-202-3242	418-848-2551

Rhode Island

			Toll-Free	Phone
Castle Hill Inn & Resort				
590 Ocean Dr	Newport RI	02840	888-466-1355	401-849-3800

South Carolina

			Toll-Free	Phone
Barefoot Resort & Golf				
4980 Barefoot Resort Bridge Rd	North Myrtle Beach SC	29582	866-638-4818	843-390-3200
Breakers Resort				
3002 N Ocean Blvd	Myrtle Beach SC	29577	800-952-4507	843-448-8082
Caravelle Resort Hotel & Villas				
6900 N Ocean Blvd	Myrtle Beach SC	29572	800-297-3413	843-310-3420
Caribbean Resort & Villas				
3000 N Ocean Blvd	Myrtle Beach SC	29577	800-552-8509	
Charleston Harbor Resort & Marina				
20 Patriots Pt Rd	Mount Pleasant SC	29464	888-856-0028	843-856-0028
Compass Cove Ocean Resort				
2311 S Ocean Blvd	Myrtle Beach SC	29577	800-331-0934	843-448-8373
Coral Beach Resort & Suites				
1105 S Ocean Blvd	Myrtle Beach SC	29577	800-843-2684	800-314-8060
Hilton Head Island Beach & Tennis Resort				
40 Folly Field Rd	Hilton Head Island SC	29928	800-475-2631*	843-842-4402
*Resv				
Hilton Myrtle Beach Resort				
10000 Beach Club Dr	Myrtle Beach SC	29572	800-445-8667	843-449-5000
Kiawah Island Golf Resort				
1 Sanctuary Beach Dr	Kiawah Island SC	29455	800-654-2924*	843-768-2121
*Resv				
Landmark Resort				
1501 S Ocean Blvd	Myrtle Beach SC	29577	800-845-0658	843-448-9441
Litchfield Beach & Golf Resort				
14276 Ocean Hwy	Pawleys Island SC	29585	888-734-8228	843-237-3000
Myrtle Beach Resort Vacations				
5905 S Kings Hwy PO Box 3936	Myrtle Beach SC	29578	888-627-3767	843-238-1559
Mystic Sea Resort				
2105 S Ocean Blvd	Myrtle Beach SC	29577	800-443-7050	843-448-8446
Ocean Reef Resort				
7100 N Ocean Blvd	Myrtle Beach SC	29572	888-322-6411	843-449-4441
Palmetto Dunes Resort				
4 Queens Folly Rd	Hilton Head Island SC	29928	866-380-1778	
Palms Resort				
2500 N Ocean Blvd	Myrtle Beach SC	29577	800-300-1198	843-626-8334
Pawleys Plantation				
70 Tanglewood Dr	Pawleys Island SC	29585	877-283-2122	
Player's Club Resort				
35 Deallyon Ave	Hilton Head Island SC	29928	800-497-7529	843-785-3355
Reef Resort				
2101 S Ocean Blvd	Myrtle Beach SC	29577	800-845-1212*	843-448-1765
*Cust Svc				
Sand Dunes Resort Hotel				
201 74th Ave N	Myrtle Beach SC	29572	800-726-3783	
Sea Mist Resort				
1200 S Ocean Blvd	Myrtle Beach SC	29577	800-793-6507	843-448-1551
Seacrest Oceanfront Resort on the South Beach				
803 S Ocean Blvd	Myrtle Beach SC	29577	888-889-4037	
Wild Dunes Resort				
5757 Palm Blvd	Isle of Palms SC	29451	866-359-5593	
Wyndham Vacation Resorts King Cotton Villas				
1 King Cotton Rd	Edisto Beach SC	29438	800-251-8736	843-869-2561

South Dakota

			Toll-Free	Phone
Spearfish Canyon Resort				
10619 Roughlock Falls Rd	Lead SD	57754	877-975-6343	605-584-3435

Tennessee

			Toll-Free	Phone
Brookside Resort				
463 E Pkwy	Gatlinburg TN	37738	800-251-9597	865-436-5611

Texas

			Toll-Free	Phone
Bahia Mar Resort & Conference Ctr				
3100 Padre Blvd	South Padre Island TX	78597	800-926-6926	
Four Seasons Resort & Club Dallas at Las Colinas				
4150 N MacArthur Blvd	Irving TX	75038	800-332-3442	972-717-0700
Houstonian Hotel Club & Spa				
111 N Post Oak Ln	Houston TX	77024	800-231-2759*	713-680-2626
*Resv				
Inn of the Hills River Resort				
1001 Junction Hwy	Kerrville TX	78028	800-292-5690	830-895-5000
Omni Barton Creek Resort & Spa				
8212 Barton Club Dr	Austin TX	78735	800-336-6158	512-329-4000
Rancho Viejo Resort & Country Club				
1 Rancho Viejo Dr	Rancho Viejo TX	78575	800-531-7400	956-350-4000
Rosewood Hotels & Resorts				
500 Crescent Ct Ste 300	Dallas TX	75201	888-767-3966	214-880-4200

				Toll-Free	Phone
San Luis Resort Spa & Conference Ctr, The					
5222 Seawall Blvd	Galveston Island	TX	77551	800-445-0090*	409-744-1500
*Cust Svc					
Silverleaf Resorts Inc					
1221 Riverbend Dr Ste 120.	Dallas	TX	75247	800-544-8468	214-631-1166
South Shore Harbour Resort & Conference Ctr					
2500 S Shore Blvd	League City	TX	77573	800-442-5005*	281-334-1000
*Resv					
Tapatio Springs Golf Resort & Conference Ctr					
1 Resort Way	Boerne	TX	78006	855-627-2243	

Utah

				Toll-Free	Phone
Alta Lodge PO Box 8040	Alta	UT	84092	800-707-2582*	801-742-3500
*Cust Svc					
Deer Valley Resort Lodging					
PO Box 889	Park City	UT	84060	800-558-3337	435-645-6626
Homestead Resort					
700 N Homestead Dr	Midway	UT	84049	800-327-7220	435-654-1102
Little America Hotels & Resorts					
500 S Main St	Salt Lake City	UT	84101	800-281-7899	801-596-5700
Rustler Lodge					
10380 East Hwy 210 PO Box 8030	Alta	UT	84092	888-532-2582	801-742-2200
Snowbasin Ski Resort					
3925 E Snowbasin Rd	Huntsville	UT	84317	888-437-5488	801-620-1100
Snowbird Ski & Summer Resort					
Hwy 210 PO Box 929000	Snowbird	UT	84092	800-453-3000	801-742-2222
Solitude Mountain					
12000 Big Cottonwood Canyon	Solitude	UT	84121	800-748-4754	801-534-1400
Stein Eriksen Lodge					
7700 Stein Way	Park City	UT	84060	800-453-1302	435-649-3700

Vermont

				Toll-Free	Phone
Basin Harbor Club					
4800 Basin Harbor Rd	Vergennes	VT	05491	800-622-4000	802-475-2311
Equinox, The					
3567 Main St	Manchester Village	VT	05254	800-362-4747	802-362-4700
Hawk Inn & Mountain Resort					
75 Billings Rd	Plymouth	VT	05056	800-685-4295	802-672-3811
Jay Peak Resort 830 Jay Peak Rd	Jay	VT	05859	800-451-4449	802-988-2611
Killington					
4763 Killington Rd	Killington	VT	05751	800-734-9435	802-422-3333
Lake Morey Resort					
1 Clubhouse Rd	Fairlee	VT	05045	800-423-1211	802-333-4311
Smugglers' Notch Resort					
4323 Vermont Rt 108 S	Jeffersonville	VT	05464	800-451-8752	802-644-8851
Stowe Mountain Resort					
5781 Mountain Rd	Stowe	VT	05672	800-253-4754	802-253-3000
Stoweflake Mountain Resort & Spa					
1746 Mountain Rd PO Box 369	Stowe	VT	05672	800-253-2232	802-253-7355
STRATTON MOUNTAIN RESORT					
5 Village Lodge Rd	Stratton Mountain	VT	05155	800-787-2886	802-297-4211
Sugarbush Resort & Inn					
1840 Sugarbush Access Rd	Warren	VT	05674	800-537-8427	802-583-6300
Topnotch at Stowe Resort & Spa					
4000 Mountain Rd	Stowe	VT	05672	800-451-8686	
Trapp Family Lodge					
700 Trapp Hill Rd PO Box 1428	Stowe	VT	05672	800-826-7000	802-253-8511
Woodstock Inn & Resort					
14 The Green	Woodstock	VT	05091	800-448-7900	802-332-6853

Virginia

				Toll-Free	Phone
Alamar Resort Inn					
311 16th St	Virginia Beach	VA	23451	800-346-5681	757-428-7582
Boar's Head Inn					
200 Ednam Dr	Charlottesville	VA	22903	800-476-1988	434-296-2181
Breakers Resort Inn					
16th & Oceanfront	Virginia Beach	VA	23451	800-237-7532	757-428-1821
Great Wolf Lodge Williamsburg					
549 E Rochambeau Dr	Williamsburg	VA	23188	800-551-9653	
Kingsmill Resort & Spa					
1010 Kingsmill Rd	Williamsburg	VA	23185	800-832-5665	757-253-1703
Lansdowne Resort					
44050 Woodridge Pkwy	Leesburg	VA	20176	877-513-8400	703-729-8400
Shenvalee Golf Resort					
9660 Fairway Dr	New Market	VA	22844	888-339-3181	540-740-3181
Turtle Cay Resort					
600 Atlantic Ave	Virginia Beach	VA	23451	888-989-7788	757-437-5565
Virginia Beach Resort Hotel & Conference Ctr					
2800 Shore Dr	Virginia Beach	VA	23451	800-468-2722	

Washington

				Toll-Free	Phone
Alderbrook Resort & Spa					
7101 E SR-106	Union	WA	98592	800-622-9370	360-898-2200
Campbell's Resort					
104 W Woodin Ave PO Box 278	Chelan	WA	98816	800-553-8225	509-682-2561
Desert Canyon Golf Resort					
1030 Desert Canyon Blvd	Orondo	WA	98843	800-258-4173	509-784-1111
Freestone Inn at Wilson Ranch					
31 Early Winters Dr	Mazama	WA	98833	800-639-3809	509-996-3906
Lake Quinault Lodge					
345 S Shore Rd	Quinault	WA	98575	800-562-6672	360-288-2900
Little Creek Casino Resort					
91 W State Rt 108	Shelton	WA	98584	800-667-7711	360-427-7711
Polynesian Resort, The					
615 Ocean Shores Blvd NW	Ocean Shores	WA	98569	800-562-4836	360-289-3361
Resort Semiahmoo					
9565 Semiahmoo Pkwy	Blaine	WA	98230	855-917-3767	360-318-2000
Rosario Resort & Spa					
1400 Rosario Rd	Eastsound	WA	98245	800-562-8820	360-376-2222

				Toll-Free	Phone
Salish Lodge & Spa					
6501 Railroad Ave DE	Snoqualmie	WA	98065	800-272-5474	425-888-2556
Sun Mountain Lodge					
604 Patterson Lake RD	Winthrop	WA	98862	800-572-0493	509-996-2211

West Virginia

				Toll-Free	Phone
Canaan Valley Resort & Conference Ctr					
230 Main Lodge Rd	Davis	WV	26260	800-622-4121	304-866-4121
Glade Springs Resort					
255 Resort Dr	Daniels	WV	25832	866-562-8054	304-763-2000
Greenbrier, The					
300 W Main St	White Sulphur Springs	WV	24986	800-453-4858	304-536-1110
Lakeview Golf Resort & Spa					
1 Lakeview Dr	Morgantown	WV	26508	800-624-8300	304-594-1111
Oglebay Resort & Conference Ctr					
465 Lodge Dr Oglebay Pk.	Wheeling	WV	26003	800-624-6988	304-243-4000
Snowshoe Mountain Resort					
10 Snowshoe Dr	Snowshoe	WV	26209	877-441-4386	
Stonewall Resort					
940 Resort Dr	Roanoke	WV	26447	888-278-8150	304-269-7400
Woods, The					
Mountain Lake Rd PO Box 5.	Hedgesville	WV	25427	800-248-2222	304-754-7977

Wisconsin

				Toll-Free	Phone
Abbey Resort & Fontana Spa					
269 Fontana Blvd	Fontana	WI	53125	800-709-1323	262-275-9000
Alpine Resort					
7715 Alpine Rd PO Box 200	Egg Harbor	WI	54209	888-281-8128	920-868-3000
American Club, The					
419 Highland Dr	Kohler	WI	53044	800-344-2838	920-457-8000
Chanticleer Inn					
1458 E Dollar Lake Rd	Eagle River	WI	54521	800-752-9193	715-479-4486
Chula Vista Resort					
2501 River Rd	Wisconsin Dells	WI	53965	800-388-4782	608-254-8366
Devil's Head Resort & Convention Ctr					
S 6330 Bluff Rd	Merrimac	WI	53561	800-472-6670	608-493-2251
Grand Geneva Resort & Spa					
7036 Grand Geneva Way	Lake Geneva	WI	53147	800-558-3417	262-248-8811
Heidel House Resort					
643 Illinois Ave	Green Lake	WI	54941	800-444-2812	920-294-3344
Holiday Acres Resort					
4060 S Shore Dr PO Box 460	Rhinelander	WI	54501	800-261-1500	715-369-1500
Lake Lawn Resort					
2400 E Geneva St	Delavan	WI	53115	800-338-5253	262-728-7950
Landmark Resort					
7643 Hillside Rd	Egg Harbor	WI	54209	800-273-7877	920-868-3205
Olympia Resort & Spa					
1350 Royale Mile Rd	Oconomowoc	WI	53066	800-558-9573	262-369-4999
Osthoff Resort, The					
101 Osthoff Ave PO Box 151	Elkhart Lake	WI	53020	800-876-3399	855-671-6870
Tundra Lodge Resort & Waterpark					
865 Lombardi Ave	Green Bay	WI	54304	877-886-3725	920-405-8700

Wyoming

				Toll-Free	Phone
Amangani Resort					
1535 NE Butte Rd	Jackson	WY	83001	877-734-7333	307-734-7333
Grand Targhee Resort					
3300 E Ski Hill Rd	Alta	WY	83414	800-827-4433	307-353-2300
Grand Teton Lodge Company & Jackson Lake Lodge					
101 Jackson Lake Lodge Rd	Moran	WY	83013	800-628-9988*	307-543-2811
*Resv					
Jackson Hole Mountain Resort					
3395 Cody Ln PO Box 290	Teton Village	WY	83025	800-450-0477	307-733-2292
Jackson HoleResort Lodging					
3200 W McCollister Dr					
PO Box 510.	Teton Village	WY	83025	800-443-8613	307-733-3990
Jackson Lake Lodge PO Box 250	Moran	WY	83013	800-628-9988	307-543-2811
Rusty Parrot Lodge & Spa					
PO Box 1657	Jackson	WY	83001	800-458-2004	307-733-2000

666   RESTAURANT COMPANIES

SEE ALSO Ice Cream & Dairy Stores ; Bakeries ; Food Service ; Franchises

				Toll-Free	Phone
Al Copeland Investments Inc					
1001 Harimaw Ct S	Metairie	LA	70001	800-401-0401	504-830-1000
BAB Inc					
500 Lake Cook Rd Ste 475	Deerfield	IL	60015	800-251-6101	
OTC: BABB					
Beef O'Bradys Inc					
5660 W Cypress St Ste A	Tampa	FL	33607	800-728-8878	813-226-2333
Bickford's Family Restaurants Inc					
37 Oak St Ext	Brockton	MA	02301	800-969-5653	
Bob Evans Farms Inc					
3776 S High St	Columbus	OH	43207	800-939-2338	
NASDAQ: BOBE					
Bojangles' Restaurants Inc					
9432 Southern Pine Blvd	Charlotte	NC	28273	800-366-9921	704-335-1804
Boston Market Corp					
14103 Denver W Pkwy	Golden	CO	80401	866-977-9090*	303-278-9500
*General					
Boston Pizza Restaurants LP					
14850 Quorum Dr Ste 201	Dallas	TX	75234	866-277-8721	972-484-9022
Brinker International Inc					
6820 LBJ Fwy	Dallas	TX	75240	800-983-4637	972-980-9917
NYSE: EAT					
Brock & Company Inc					
257 Great Vly Pkwy	Malvern	PA	19355	866-468-2783	610-647-5656
Bubba Gump Shrimp Co LLC					
2501 Seawall Blvd	Galveston	TX	77550	800-552-6379	409-766-4952

			Toll-Free	Phone
Buck's Pizza Franchising Corp Inc				
PO Box 405	Du Bois PA	15801	800-310-8848	
Burger King Corp				
5505 Blue Lagoon Dr	Miami FL	33126	866-394-2493	305-378-3000
Burgerville USA				
109 W 17th St	Vancouver WA	98660	888-827-8369	
Captain D's LLC				
624 Grassmere Park Dr Ste 30	Nashville TN	37211	800-314-4819	615-391-5461
Carrols Restaurant Group Inc				
968 James St	Syracuse NY	13203	800-348-1074	315-424-0513
NASDAQ: TAST				
Cask 'n' Cleaver				
8689 Ninth St	Rancho Cucamonga CA	91730	800-995-4452	909-982-7108
CEC Entertainment Inc				
3903 W Airport Frwy	Irving TX	75062	888-778-7193	972-258-8507
NYSE: CEC				
Charleys Philly Steaks				
2500 Farmers Dr Ste 140	Columbus OH	43235	800-437-8325	614-923-4700
Checkers Drive-In Restaurants Inc				
4300 W Cypress St Ste 600	Tampa FL	33607	800-800-8072	813-283-7000
Cousins Submarines Inc				
N83 W13400 Leon Rd	Menomonee Falls WI	53051	800-238-9736	262-253-7700
Cracker Barrel Old Country Store Inc				
PO Box 787	Lebanon TN	37088	800-333-9566	615-235-4054
NASDAQ: CBRL				
D'Angelo Sandwich Shops				
600 Providence Hwy	Dedham MA	02026	800-727-2446	
Denny's Corp				
203 E Main St	Spartanburg SC	29319	800-733-6697*	864-597-8000
*NASDAQ: DENN ■ *Cust Svc*				
Domino's Pizza Inc				
30 Frank Lloyd Wright Dr	Ann Arbor MI	48106	800-253-8182	734-930-3030
NYSE: DPZ				
Donatos Pizza				
935 Taylor Stn Rd	Columbus OH	43230	800-366-2867	
Eat'n Park Hospitality Group				
285 E Waterfront Dr	Homestead PA	15120	800-947-4033	412-461-2000
Edo Japan International Inc				
4838 - 32nd St SE	Calgary AB	T2B2S6	888-336-9888	403-215-8800
El Fenix Corp				
1845 Woodall Rodgers Ste 1100	Dallas TX	75201	877-591-1918	972-241-2171
El Pollo Loco				
3535 Harbor Blvd Ste 100	Costa Mesa CA	92626	877-375-4968	/14-599-5000
Famous Dave's of America Inc				
12701 Whitewater Dr Ste 200	Minnetonka MN	55343	800-929-4040	952-294-1300
NASDAQ: DAVE				
Figaro's Italian Pizza Inc				
1500 Liberty St SE Ste 160	Salem OR	97302	888-344-2767	503-371-9318
Flamer's Grill				
1515 International Pkwy Ste 2013	Heathrow FL	32746	866-749-4889	407-574-8363
Flanigan's				
5059 NE 18th Ave	Fort Lauderdale FL	33334	800-833-5239	954-377-1961
NYSE: BDL				
Friendly Ice Cream Corp				
1855 Boston Rd	Wilbraham MA	01095	800-966-9970	
Frisch's Restaurants Inc				
2800 Gilbert Ave	Cincinnati OH	45206	800-873-3633	513-961-2660
NYSE: FRS				
Frullati Cafe & Bakery				
9311 E Via de Ventura	Scottsdale AZ	85258	866-452-4252	480-362-4800
Gates Bar-Q				
4621 Paseo Blvd	Kansas City MO	64110	800-662-7427	816-923-0900
Gold Star Chili				
650 Lunken Pk Dr	Cincinnati OH	45226	800-643-0465	513-231-4541
Good Eats Inc				
12200 Stemmons Fwy Ste 100	Dallas TX	75234	800-275-1337	972-241-5500
Great Steak & Potato Co				
9311 E Via de Ventura	Scottsdale AZ	85258	866-452-4252	480-362-4800
Great Wraps				
17 Executive Park Dr NE Ste 150	Atlanta GA	30329	888-489-7277	404-248-9900
Hacienda Mexican Restaurants				
1501 N Ironwood Dr	South Bend IN	46635	800-541-3227	
Hard Rock Cafe International Inc				
6100 Old Pk Ln	Orlando FL	32835	888-519-6683	407-445-7625
Hillstone Restaurant Group				
147 S Beverly Dr	Beverly Hills CA	90212	800-230-9787	
Hot Dog on a Stick				
5942 Priestly Dr	Carlsbad CA	92008	877-639-2361	877-922-9215
IHOP Corp 450 N Brand Blvd	Glendale CA	91203	866-444-5144	818-240-6055
Il Fornaio America Corp				
770 Tamalpais Dr Ste 400	Corte Madera CA	94925	888-454-6246	415-945-0500
In-N-Out Burger Inc				
4199 Campus Dr 9th Fl	Irvine CA	92612	800-786-1000*	949-509-6200
*Cust Svc				
International Dairy Queen Corp				
7505 Metro Blvd	Minneapolis MN	55439	866-793-7582	952-830-0200
J Alexander's Corp				
3401 W End Ave Ste 260	Nashville TN	37203	888-528-1991	615-269-1900
NASDAQ: JAX				
Jack in the Box Inc				
9330 Balboa Ave	San Diego CA	92123	800-955-5225	858-571-2121
NASDAQ: JACK				
Jerry's Systems Inc				
702 Russell Ave Ste 306	Gaithersburg MD	20877	800-990-9176	
Jimmy John's Franchise Inc				
2212 Fox Dr	Champaign IL	61820	800-546-6904	217-356-9900
Joey's Seafood Restaurants				
3048 - 9 St SE	Calgary AB	T2G3B9	800-661-2123	403-243-4584
K-Mac Enterprises Inc				
PO Box 6538	Fort Smith AR	72906	800-947-9277	479-646-2053
Kimpton Hotel & Restaurant Group LLC				
222 Kearny St Ste 200	San Francisco CA	94108	800-546-7866	415-397-5572
La Salsa Fresh Mexican Grill				
9311 E Via De Ventura	Scottsdale AZ	85258	866-452-4252	
Landry's Restaurants Inc				
1510 W Loop S	Houston TX	77027	800-552-6379	713-850-1010
Lawry's Restaurants Inc				
225 S Lake Ave Ste 1500	Pasadena CA	91101	888-552-9797	
Little Caesars Inc				
2211 Woodward Ave	Detroit MI	48201	800-722-3727	313-983-6000
LongHorn Steakhouse				
1000 Darden Ctr Dr	Orlando FL	32837	888-221-0642	
Luby's Inc				
13111 NW Fwy Ste 600	Houston TX	77040	800-886-4600	713-329-6800
NYSE: LUB				
Malnati Organization Inc				
3685 Woodhead Dr	Northbrook IL	60062	800-568-8646	847-562-1814
Marie Callender Restaurant & Bakery				
27101 Puerta Real Ste 260	Mission Viejo CA	92691	800-776-7437	
McDonald's Corp				
1 McDonald's Plz	Oak Brook IL	60523	800-244-6227	630-623-3000
NYSE: MCD				
McDonald's Restaurants of Canada Ltd				
PO Box 61023	Winnipeg MB	R3M3X8	888-424-4622	416-443-1000
Melting Pot Restaurants Inc				
8810 Twin Lakes Blvd	Tampa FL	33614	800-783-0867	813-881-0055
Mr Goodcents Franchise Systems Inc				
8997 Commerce Dr	DeSoto KS	66018	800-648-2368	
Mr Hero Restaurants				
7010 Engle Rd Ste 100	Middleburg Heights OH	44130	888-860-5082	440-625-3080
Mr Jim's Pizza Inc				
Franchise Service Ctr				
2521 Pepperwood St	Farmers Branch TX	75234	800-583-5960	972-267-5467
Noble Roman's Pizza Inc				
1 Virginia Ave Ste 300	Indianapolis IN	46204	800-585-0669	
NPC International Inc				
7300 W 129th St	Overland Park KS	66213	866-299-1148	913-327-5555
Orange Julius of America				
7505 Metro Blvd	Minneapolis MN	55439	866-793-7582	952-830-0200
Panda Express				
1717 Walnut Grove Ave	Rosemead CA	91770	800-877-8988	626-312-5401
Papa Gino's Inc				
600 Providence Hwy	Dedham MA	02026	800-727-2446	781-329-1946
Papa John's International Inc				
2002 Papa John's Blvd	Louisville KY	40299	877-547-7272	502-261-7272
NASDAQ: PZZA				
Papa Murphy's International Inc				
8000 NE Pkwy Dr Ste 350	Vancouver WA	98662	877-777-5062	
Pat O'Brien's International Inc				
718 St Peter St	New Orleans LA	70116	800-597-4823	504-525-4823
Patina Restaurant Group				
141 S Grand Ave	Los Angeles CA	90012	866-972-8462	
Penguin Point Franchise Systems Inc				
2691 E US 30	Warsaw IN	46580	800-557-5755	574-267-3107
PF Chang's China Bistro				
7676 E Pinnacle Peak Rd	Scottsdale AZ	85255	866-732-4264	480-888-3000
Piccadilly Circus Pizza				
1007 Okoboji Ave PO Box 188	Milford IA	51351	800-338-4340	
Pizza Boli's				
3 Greenwood Pl Ste 208	Pikesville MD	21208	800-234-2654	
Pizza Factory Inc				
49430 Rd 426	Oakhurst CA	93644	800-654-4840	559-683-3377
Pizza Inn Inc				
3551 Plano Pkwy	The Colony TX	75056	877-574-9924	
NASDAQ: RAVE				
Pizza Pro Inc				
2107 N Second St PO Box 1285	Cabot AR	72023	800-777-7554	501-605-1175
Pizza Ranch Inc				
204 19th St SE	Orange City IA	51041	800-321-3401	
Pretzelmaker				
5555 Glenridge Connector Ste 850	Atlanta GA	30342	877-639-2361	
Quality Dining Inc				
4220 Edison Lakes Pkwy	Mishawaka IN	46545	800-589-3820	574-271-4600
Quiznos Corp				
7595 Technology Way Ste 200	Denver CO	80237	866-486-2783	720-359-3300
Red Hot & Blue Restaurants Inc				
1600 Wilson Blvd	Arlington VA	22209	888-509-7100	703-276-7427
Restaurants Unlimited Inc				
411 First Ave S Ste 200	Seattle WA	98104	877-855-6106	206-634-0550
Rocky Rococo				
105 E Wisconsin Ave	Oconomowoc WI	53066	800-888-7625	262-569-5580
Rubio's Restaurants Inc				
1902 Wright Pl Ste 300	Carlsbad CA	92008	800-354-4199	760-929-8226
Runza National Inc				
PO Box 6042	Lincoln NE	68506	800-929-2394	402-423-2394
Russ' Restaurants Inc				
390 E Eigth St	Holland MI	49423	800-521-1778	616-396-6571
Sagebrush Steakhouse				
129 Fast Ln	Mooresville NC	28117	877-704-5939	704-660-5939
Shari's Restaurant & Pies				
9400 SW Gemini Dr	Beaverton OR	97008	800-433-5334	503-605-4299
Shoney's Restaurants Inc				
1717 Elm Hill Pk Ste B1	Nashville TN	37210	800-708-3558	
Silver Diner Development LLC				
12276 Rockville Pk	Rockville MD	20852	866-561-0518	301-770-0333
Smitty's Canada Inc				
501 18th Ave SW Ste 500	Calgary AB	T2S0C7	800-927-0366	403-229-3838
Sonic Corp				
300 Johnny Bench Dr	Oklahoma City OK	73104	877-828-7868	405-225-5000
NASDAQ: SONC				
Sonic Drive-in Restaurants				
300 Johnny Bench Dr	Oklahoma City OK	73104	877-828-7868	405-225-5000
Stuckey's Corp				
8555 16th St Ste 850	Silver Spring MD	20910	800-423-6171	301-585-8222
Taco Cabana Inc				
8918 Tesoro Dr Ste 200	San Antonio TX	78217	800-580-8668	210-804-0990
Tacoma Inc				
328 E Church St	Martinsville VA	24112	800-352-9417	276-666-9417
Tavistock Restaurants LLC				
4705 S Apopka Vineland Rd Ste 210	Orlando FL	32819	800-424-2753	407-909-7101
Texas Roadhouse Inc				
6040 Dutchmans Ln Ste 400	Louisville KY	40205	800-839-7623	502-426-9984
NASDAQ: TXRH				
Tim Hortons Inc				
874 Sinclair Rd	Oakville ON	L6K2Y1	888-601-1616	905-845-6511
NYSE: QSR				
Tubby's 31920 Groesbeck Hwy	Fraser MI	48026	800-752-0644	

Classified Section

				Toll-Free	Phone
Tumbleweed Inc					
2301 River Rd	Louisville	KY	40206	866-719-3892	502-893-0323
V & J Holding Cos Inc					
6933 W Brown Deer Rd	Milwaukee	WI	53223	800-384-6972	414-365-9003
Village Inn 400 W 48th Ave	Denver	CO	80216	800-800-3644	303-294-0609
Ward's Food Systems Inc					
5133 Lincoln Rd Ext	Hattiesburg	MS	39402	800-748-9273	601-268-9273
Weathervane Seafood Restaurant					
306 US Rt 1	Kittery	ME	03904	800-914-1774	207-439-0330
Wendy's International Inc					
1 Dave Thomas Blvd	Dublin	OH	43017	800-952-5210	614-764-3100
Wingstop Restaurants Inc					
908 Audelia Rd Ste 600	Richardson	TX	75081	877-411-9464	
Yum! Brands Inc					
1441 Gardiner Ln	Louisville	KY	40213	800-225-5532	502-874-1000
NYSE: YUM					

667   RESTAURANTS (INDIVIDUAL)

SEE ALSO Restaurant Companies ; Shopping/Dining/Entertainment Districts
Individual restaurants are organized by city names within state and province groupings.
(Canadian provinces are interfiled among the US states, in alphabetical order.)

Alabama

				Toll-Free	Phone
Dreamland Bar-B-que					
1427 14th Ave S	Birmingham	AL	35205	800-752-0544	205-933-2133

Alaska

				Toll-Free	Phone
Best Western Grandma's Feather Bed					
9300 Glacier Hwy	Juneau	AK	99801	888-781-5005	907-789-5005
Gold Room 127 N Franklin St	Juneau	AK	99801	800-544-0970	907-586-2660

Alberta

				Toll-Free	Phone
Parkallen Restaurant					
7018-109th St NW	Edmonton	AB	T6H3C1	855-822-6854	587-520-6401

Arizona

				Toll-Free	Phone
Sakura Restaurant					
1175 W Rt 66	Flagstaff	AZ	86001	888-288-8889	
On The Border mexican grill & cantina					
1710 S Power Rd	Mesa	AZ	85206	888-682-6882	
T Cook's					
5200 E Camelback Rd	Phoenix	AZ	85018	800-672-6011	602-808-0766
Baja Fresh					
9311 E Via De Ventura	Scottsdale	AZ	85258	866-452-4252	
PF Chang's China Bistro					
7676 E Pinnacle Peak Rd	Scottsdale	AZ	85255	844-737-7333	480-888-3000
PF Chang's China Bistro					
7676 E Pinnacle Peak Rd	Scottsdale	AZ	85255	844-737-7333	480-888-3000
PF Chang's China Bistro					
7676 E Pinnacle Peak Rd	Scottsdale	AZ	85255	844-737-7333	480-888-3000
PF Chang's China Bistro					
7676 E Pinnacle Peak Rd	Scottsdale	AZ	85255	844-737-7333	480-888-3000
PF Chang's China Bistro					
7676 E Pinnacle Peak Rd	Scottsdale	AZ	85255	844-737-7333	480-888-3000
L'Auberge de Sedona					
301 L'Auberge Ln	Sedona	AZ	86336	855-905-5745	800-905-5745
Grill at Hacienda del Sol					
5501 N Hacienda del Sol Rd	Tucson	AZ	85718	800-728-6514	520-529-3500

Arkansas

				Toll-Free	Phone
McClard's Bar-B-Q					
505 Albert Pike Rd	Hot Springs	AR	71901	866-622-5273	501-623-9665
El Chico 8409 I-30	Little Rock	AR	72209	800-242-5353	

British Columbia

				Toll-Free	Phone
Diva at the Met					
645 Howe St	Vancouver	BC	V6C2Y9	800-667-2300	604-602-7788

California

				Toll-Free	Phone
Anaheim Marriott					
700 W Convention Way	Anaheim	CA	92802	800-845-5279	714-750-8000
Catal Restaurant & Uva Bar					
1510 Disneyland Dr	Anaheim	CA	92802	866-972-8462	
Naples Ristorante e Pizzeria					
1510 Disneyland Dr	Anaheim	CA	92802	866-972-8462	
Lawry's the Prime Rib					
100 N La Cienega Blvd	Beverly Hills	CA	90211	877-529-7984	310-652-2827
Hyatt Regency					
Orange County					
11999 Harbor Blvd	Garden Grove	CA	92840	800-233-1234	714-750-1234
Panda Inn 111 E Wilson Ave	Glendale	CA	91206	800-877-8988	
Marine Room, The					
2000 Spindrift Dr	La Jolla	CA	92037	866-644-2351	858-459-7222
Sir Winston's Restaurant & Lounge					
1126 Queens Hwy	Long Beach	CA	90802	877-342-0742	562-499-1739
Cafe Pinot					
700 W Fifth St	Los Angeles	CA	90071	866-972-8462	
Nick & Stef's Steakhouse					
330 S Hope St	Los Angeles	CA	90071	866-972-8462	
Patina 141 S Grand Ave	Los Angeles	CA	90012	866-972-8462	

				Toll-Free	Phone
Cafe Fina					
47 Fisherman's Wharf Ste 1	Monterey	CA	93940	800-843-3462	831-372-5200
Duane's					
3649 Mission Inn Ave	Riverside	CA	92501	800-843-7755	951-784-0300
Panda Inn 506 Horton Plz	San Diego	CA	92101	800-877-8988	
Rancho Bernardo Inn					
17550 Bernardo Oaks Dr	San Diego	CA	92128	877-517-9340	858-675-8500
Westgate Hotel, The					
1055 Second Ave	San Diego	CA	92101	800-522-1564	619-238-1818
La Pastaia					
233 W Santa Clara St	San Jose	CA	95113	800-843-3700	408-286-1000
San Jose Original Joe's					
301 S First St	San Jose	CA	95113	888-841-7030	408-292-7030
50 Forks					
3601 W Sunflower Ave	Santa Ana	CA	92704	855-784-1269	
Tangata 2002 N Main St	Santa Ana	CA	92706	866-972-8462	
Chinois on Main					
2709 Main St	Santa Monica	CA	90405	888-646-3387	310-432-1500

Colorado

				Toll-Free	Phone
Greenbriar Inn, The					
8735 N Foothills Hwy	Boulder	CO	80302	800-253-1474	303-440-7979
Thyme on the Creek					
1345 28th St	Boulder	CO	80302	866-866-8086	303-443-3850
Briarhurst Manor					
404 Manitou Ave	Manitou Springs	CO	80829	877-685-1448	719-685-1864

Delaware

				Toll-Free	Phone
Roma Italian Restaurant					
3 President Dr	Dover	DE	19901	800-711-5882	302-678-1041
Green Room at the Hotel duPont					
42 W 11th St	Wilmington	DE	19801	800-441-9019	302-594-3100
Melting Pot, The					
1601 Concord Pk					
Ste 43-47 Independence Mall	Wilmington	DE	19803	800-783-0867	302-652-6358

District of Columbia

				Toll-Free	Phone
Henley Park Hotel, The					
926 Massachusetts Ave NW	Washington	DC	20001	800-222-8474	202-638-5200

Florida

				Toll-Free	Phone
Hard Rock Cafe International Inc					
5701 Stirling Rd	Davie	FL	33314	888-519-6683	954-585-5703
Angell & Phelps Chocolate Factory					
154 S Beach St	Daytona Beach	FL	32114	800-969-2634	386-252-6531
Dave & Buster's					
3000 Oakwood Blvd	Hollywood	FL	33020	888-300-1515	954-923-5505
IFC Stone Crab					
81532 Overseas Hwy PO Box 283	Islamorada	FL	33036	800-258-2559	
Cafe Marquesa					
600 Fleming St	Key West	FL	33040	800-869-4631	305-292-1244
First Flight Island Restaurant & Brewery					
301 Whitehead St	Key West	FL	33040	800-507-9955	305-293-8484
Hog's Breath Saloon Key West					
400 Front St	Key West	FL	33040	800-826-6969	305-296-4222
Joe's Stone Crab					
11 Washington Ave	Miami Beach	FL	33139	800-780-2722	305-673-0365
Bahama Breeze					
8849 International Dr	Orlando	FL	32819	877-500-9715	407-248-2499
Boheme, The					
325 S Orange Ave	Orlando	FL	32801	866-663-0024	407-313-9000
Palm					
5800 Universal Blvd Hard Rock Hotel	Orlando	FL	32819	866-333-7256	407-503-7256
Shula's Steak House					
4860 W Kennedy Blvd	Tampa	FL	33609	800-888-7012	813-286-4366

Georgia

				Toll-Free	Phone
Country's Barbecue					
2016 12th Ave	Columbus	GA	31901	800-285-4267*	706-327-7702
*General					
Olde Pink House					
29 Abercorn St	Savannah	GA	31401	800-554-1187	

Hawaii

				Toll-Free	Phone
Bali Steak & Seafood					
2005 Kalia Rd	Honolulu	HI	96815	800-445-8667	808-949-4321

Illinois

				Toll-Free	Phone
Giovanni's Restaurant & Convention Ctr					
610 N Bell School Rd	Rockford	IL	61107	877-926-8300	815-398-6411

Indiana

				Toll-Free	Phone
Scholars Inn Gourmet Cafe					
717 N College Ave	Bloomington	IN	47404	800-765-3466	812-332-1892
Circle City Bar & Grille					
350 W Maryland St	Indianapolis	IN	46225	877-640-7666	317-405-6100
Melting Pot of Indianapolis, The					
5650 E 86th St Ste A	Indianapolis	IN	46250	800-783-0867	317-841-3601

Louisiana

	Toll-Free	Phone
Arnaud's 813 Bienville St . . . . New Orleans LA 70112	866-230-8895	504-523-5433
Maison Dupuy Hotel 1001 Rue Toulouse . . . . New Orleans LA 70112	800-535-9177	504-586-8000

Maryland

	Toll-Free	Phone
Famous Dave's Barbeque 181 Jennifer Rd . . . . Annapolis MD 21401	877-833-9335	410-224-2207
Red Hot & Blue Restaurants Inc 200 Old Mill Bottom Rd S . . . . Annapolis MD 21401	888-509-7100	410-626-7427
Marriott International Inc 10400 Fernwood Rd . . . . Bethesda MD 20817 *NASDAQ: MAR*	800-450-4442	301-380-3000
Coral Reef Restaurant 106 N Baltimore Ave . . . . Ocean City MD 21842	866-627-8483	410-289-2612
Fager's Island Restaurant 201 60th St . . . . Ocean City MD 21842	855-432-4377	410-524-5500
Ocean City Maryland Hotels 106 N Baltimore Ave . . . . Ocean City MD 21842	800-837-3588	410-524-5252

Massachusetts

	Toll-Free	Phone
Bristol, The 200 Boylston St . . . . Boston MA 02116	800-819-5053	617-338-4400
Capital Grille 900 Boylston St . . . . Boston MA 02115	866-518-9113	
Kimpton Hotel & Restaurant Group LLC 90 Tremont St . . . . Boston MA 02108	866-906-9090	617-772-5800
Palm restaurant, The 100 Oliver St Lbby Level . . . . Boston MA 02110	866-333-7256	617-867-9292
Water Street 131 N Water St . . . . Edgartown MA 02539	800-225-6005	508-627-7000
Red Inn 15 Commercial St . . . . Provincetown MA 02657	866-473-3466	508-487-7334

Michigan

	Toll-Free	Phone
Chop House Ann Arbor, The 322 S Main St . . . . Ann Arbor MI 48104	888-456-3463	
Hard Rock Cafe 45 Monroe St . . . . Detroit MI 48226	888-519-6683	313-964-7625
English Inn, The 677 S Michigan Rd . . . . Eaton Rapids MI 48827	800-858-0598	517-663-2500

Minnesota

	Toll-Free	Phone
Lindey's Prime Steak House 3600 N Snelling Ave . . . . Arden Hills MN 55112	866-491-0538	651-633-9813
Angie's Cantina 11 E Buchanan St . . . . Duluth MN 55802	800-706-7672	218-727-6117
Grandma's Saloon & Grill 522 Lake Ave S . . . . Duluth MN 55802	800-706-7672	218-727-4192
Kahler Grand Hotel, The 1517 16th St SW . . . . Rochester MN 55902	800-533-1655	

Mississippi

	Toll-Free	Phone
Eat With Us PO Box 1368 . . . . Columbus MS 39703	888-222-9550	662-327-6982

Missouri

	Toll-Free	Phone
Buckingham's Restaurant & Oasis 2820 W Hwy 76 . . . . Branson MO 65616	800-725-2236	417-337-7777
Chateau Grille 415 N State Hwy 265 . . . . Branson MO 65616	888-333-5253	417-334-1161
54th Street Grill 18700 E 38th Terr . . . . Independence MO 64057	866-402-5454	
Capitol Plaza Hotel 415 W McCarty St . . . . Jefferson City MO 65101	800-338-8088	573-635-1234
Jasper's 1201 W 103rd St . . . . Kansas City MO 64114	800-810-3708	816-941-6600
Metropolitan Grill 2931 E Battlefield . . . . Springfield MO 65804	800-225-6343	417-889-4951

Nevada

	Toll-Free	Phone
Bellagio - Las Vegas 3600 Las Vegas Blvd S . . . . Las Vegas NV 89109	866-259-7111	702-693-7111
Caesar's Palace 3570 Las Vegas Blvd S Caesar's Palace . . . . Las Vegas NV 89109	800-634-6001	866-227-5938
Grotto Ristorante 129 E Fremont St . . . . Las Vegas NV 89101	800-634-3454	702-385-7111
Lillie's Asian Cuisine 129 E Fremont St . . . . Las Vegas NV 89101	800-634-3454	702-385-7111
Michael's 9777 Las Vegas Blvd S . . . . Las Vegas NV 89183	866-796-7111	702-796-7111
Second Street Grill 200 E Fremont St . . . . Las Vegas NV 89101	800-634-6460	702-385-3232
SW Steakhouse 3131 Las Vegas Blvd S . . . . Las Vegas NV 89109	888-320-7123	702-770-7000
Atlantis Seafood Steakhouse 3800 S Virginia Ave Atlantis Casino Resort . . . . Reno NV 89502	800-723-6500	
Romanza 2707 S Virginia St Peppermill Hotel Casino . . . . Reno NV 89502	866-821-9996	775-826-2121

New Hampshire

	Toll-Free	Phone
Bedford Village Inn 2 Olde Bedford Way . . . . Bedford NH 03110	800-852-1166	603-472-2001

New York

	Toll-Free	Phone
Kai 20 Jay St Ste 530 . . . . Brooklyn NY 11201	888-832-7832	718-250-4000
Anchor Bar 651 Delaware Ave . . . . Buffalo NY 14202	866-248-9623	716-883-1134
Cafe Centro 200 Park Ave . . . . New York NY 10166	866-972-8462	
Palm Restaurant 250 W 50th St . . . . New York NY 10019	866-333-7256	212-333-7256
Sea Grill Restaurant 19 W 49th St . . . . New York NY 10020	866-972-8462	

North Carolina

	Toll-Free	Phone
Omni Grove Park Inn, The 290 Macon Ave . . . . Asheville NC 28804	800-438-5800	
McCormick & Schmick's 200 S Tryon St . . . . Charlotte NC 28202	800-552-6379	704-377-0201
Melting Pot of Charlotte, The 901 S Kings Dr Ste 140B . . . . Charlotte NC 28204	800-783-0867	704-334-4400
Texas Steakhouse 711 Sutters Creek Blvd . . . . Rocky Mount NC 27804	855-220-7228	

North Dakota

	Toll-Free	Phone
Alumni Center, The 1241 University Dr N . . . . Fargo ND 58102	800-279-8971	701-231-6800

Ohio

	Toll-Free	Phone
Palace, The 601 Vine St . . . . Cincinnati OH 45202	800-942-9000	513-381-6006
Tony Packo's 1902 Front St . . . . Toledo OH 43605	866-472-2567	419-691-1953
Zia's Italian Restaurant 20 Main St . . . . Toledo OH 43605	888-456-3463	

Ontario

	Toll-Free	Phone
Courtyard Cafe 18 St Thomas St . . . . Toronto ON M5S3E7 *Cust Svc	877-999-2767*	416-971-9666

Oregon

	Toll-Free	Phone
Jake's Famous Crawfish 401 SW 12th Ave SW Stark . . . . Portland OR 97205	800-552-6379	503-226-1419
Ringside SteakHouse 2165 W Burnside St . . . . Portland OR 97210	800-688-4142	503-223-1513

Pennsylvania

	Toll-Free	Phone
Cashtown Inn Restaurant 1325 Old Rt 30 PO Box 103 . . . . Cashtown PA 17310	800-367-1797	717-334-9722
Petra 3602 West Lake Rd . . . . Erie PA 16505	866-906-2931	814-838-7197
Gettysburg Hotel 1 Lincoln Sq . . . . Gettysburg PA 17325	866-378-1797	717-337-2000
Herr Tavern & Public House 900 Chambersburg Rd . . . . Gettysburg PA 17325	800-362-9849	717-334-4332
Palm Restaurant 200 S Broad St . . . . Philadelphia PA 19102	866-333-7256	215-546-7256

Quebec

	Toll-Free	Phone
W Montreal Hotel 901 Victoria Sq . . . . Montreal QC H2Z1R1	888-627-7081	514-395-3100
Auberge du Tresor 20 Rue Sainte-Anne . . . . Quebec QC G1R3X2	800-566-1876	418-694-1876
Laurie Raphael 117 Dalhousie St . . . . Quebec QC G1K9C8	877-876-4555	418-692-4555

Rhode Island

	Toll-Free	Phone
Spiced Pear 117 Memorial Blvd . . . . Newport RI 02840	866-793-5664	401-847-2244
Hemenway's Seafood Grille 121 S Main St . . . . Providence RI 02903	888-759-5557	401-351-8570

South Carolina

	Toll-Free	Phone
Grill 225 225 E Bay St . . . . Charleston SC 29401	877-440-2250	843-266-4222
Middleton Place 4300 Ashley River Rd . . . . Charleston SC 29414	800-782-3608	843-556-6020
Trotters Restaurant 2008 Savannah Hwy . . . . Charleston SC 29401	800-334-6660	843-571-1000
Melting Pot of Columbia, The 1410 Colonial Life Blvd . . . . Columbia SC 29210	800-783-0867	803-731-8500
Alexander's Seafood Restaurant & Wine Bar 76 Queens Folly Rd . . . . Hilton Head Island SC 29928	855-706-4319	
Signe's Bakery & Cafe 93 Arrow Rd . . . . Hilton Head Island SC 29928	866-807-4463	843-785-9118

Tennessee

				Toll-Free	Phone
Morton's The Steakhouse					
618 Church St	Nashville TN	37219		800-297-3276	615-259-4558

Texas

				Toll-Free	Phone
Rudy's Texas Bar-B-Q LLC					
2780 N Expressway 77-83a	Brownsville TX	78526		877-609-3337	956-542-2532
Cafe Modern					
3200 Darnell St	Fort Worth TX	76107		866-824-5566	817-738-9215
Goode Co Texas Barbecue					
5109 Kirby Dr	Houston TX	77098		800-627-3502	713-522-2530
Palm Restaurant					
6100 Westheimer Rd	Houston TX	77057		866-333-7256	713-977-2544
Rainbow Lodge					
2011 Ella Blvd	Houston TX	77008		866-861-8666	713-861-8666
Genghis Grill					
8200 Springwood Dr Ste 230	Irving TX	75063		888-436-4447	
Melting Pot of San Antonio, The					
14855 Blanco Rd Ste 110	San Antonio TX	78216		800-783-0867	210-479-6358

Utah

				Toll-Free	Phone
Cafe Rio					
215 N Admiral Byrd Rd Ste 100	Salt Lake City UT	84116		800-223-3746	801-441-5000

Washington

				Toll-Free	Phone
Georgian, The					
411 University St	Seattle WA	98101		888-363-5022	206-621-7889
Sorrento Hotel					
900 Madison St	Seattle WA	98104		800-426-1265	206-622-6400
McMenamins on the Columbia					
1801 S Access Rd	Vancouver WA	98661		800-669-8610	360-699-1521

West Virginia

				Toll-Free	Phone
Tidewater Grill					
1060 Charleston Town Ctr	Charleston WV	25389		888-456-3463	304-345-2620

Wisconsin

				Toll-Free	Phone
Packing House					
900 E Layton Ave	Milwaukee WI	53207		800-727-9477	414-483-5054

668   RETIREMENT COMMUNITIES

SEE ALSO Long-Term Care Facilities

Listed here are senior communities where the majority of residents live independently but where nursing care and/or other personal care is available on-site. The listings in this category are organized alphabetically by state names.

				Toll-Free	Phone
Terraces at Phoenix, The					
7550 N 16th St	Phoenix AZ	85020		800-836-4281	602-906-4024
Bixby Knolls Towers					
3737 Atlantic Ave	Long Beach CA	90807		800-545-1833	562-426-6123
Carmel Valley Manor					
8545 Carmel Valley Rd	Carmel CA	93923		800-544-5546	831-624-1281
Eskaton Inc					
5105 Manzanita Ave	Carmichael CA	95608		800-729-2999	916-334-0810
Eskaton Village					
3939 Walnut Ave	Carmichael CA	95608		800-300-3929	916-974-2000
Freedom Village					
23442 El Toro Rd	Lake Forest CA	92630		800-584-8084	949-472-4700
Grand Lake Gardens					
401 Santa Clara Ave	Oakland CA	94610		800-416-6091	
Lake Park Retirement Residences					
1850 Alice St	Oakland CA	94612		866-384-3130	510-835-5511
Morningside of Fullerton					
800 Morningside Dr	Fullerton CA	92835		800-803-7597	714-256-8000
Mount Miguel Covenant Village					
325 Kempton St	Spring Valley CA	91977		877-321-4895	619-479-4790
O'Connor Woods					
3400 Wagner Heights Rd	Stockton CA	95209		800-957-3308	209-956-3400
Piedmont Gardens					
110 41st St	Oakland CA	94611		800-496-8126	510-596-2600
Plymouth Village					
900 Salem Dr	Redlands CA	92373		800-391-4552	909-793-9195
Regents Point					
19191 Harvard Ave	Irvine CA	92612		800-347-3735*	949-988-0849
*General					
Samarkand, The					
2550 Treasure Dr	Santa Barbara CA	93105		800-510-2020	805-687-0701
Smith Ranch Homes					
400 Deer Valley Rd	San Rafael CA	94903		800-772-6264	415-491-4918
Terraces at Los Altos, The					
373 Pine Ln	Los Altos CA	94022		800-230-2976	650-948-8291
Terraces of Los Gatos					
800 Blossom Hill Rd	Los Gatos CA	95032		800-673-1982	408-356-1006
Valle Verde					
900 Calle de los Amigos	Santa Barbara CA	93105		800-750-5089	805-883-4000
Villa Gardens					
842 E Villa St	Pasadena CA	91101		800-958-4552	626-463-5330
Villa Marin					
100 Thorndale Dr	San Rafael CA	94903		888-926-2030	415-492-2408
Vista del Monte					
3775 Modoc Rd	Santa Barbara CA	93105		800-736-1333	805-687-0793

				Toll-Free	Phone
Parkplace 111 Emerson St	Denver CO	80218		844-431-9875	615-564-8666
Covenant Village of Cromwell & Pilgrim Manor					
52 Missionary Rd	Cromwell CT	06416		800-255-8989	860-635-2690
Elim Park Place					
140 Cook Hill Rd	Cheshire CT	06410		800-994-1776	203-272-3547
Essex Meadows 30 Bokum Rd	Essex CT	06426		866-721-4838	860-767-7201
Evergreen Woods					
88 Notch Hill Rd	North Branford CT	06471		866-413-6378*	203-488-8000
*General					
Cokesbury Village					
726 Loveville Rd	Hockessin DE	19707		800-530-2377	302-235-6000
Country House					
4830 Kennett Pk	Wilmington DE	19807		800-976-7610	302-501-7155
Westminster Village					
1175 Mckee Rd	Dover DE	19904		800-382-1385	302-744-3600
Knollwood					
6200 Oregon Ave NW	Washington DC	20015		800-541-4255	202-541-0400
Abbey Delray					
2000 Lowson Blvd	Delray Beach FL	33445		888-791-9363	561-454-2000
Edgewater Pointe Estates					
23315 Blue Water Cir	Boca Raton FL	33433		888-339-2287*	561-391-6305
*General					
Fleet Landing Retirement Community					
1 Fleet Landing Blvd	Atlantic Beach FL	32233		877-591-6547*	904-246-9900
*General					
Florida Presbyterian Homes					
16 Lake Hunter Dr	Lakeland FL	33803		866-294-3352	863-688-5521
Harbour's Edge					
401 E Linton Blvd	Delray Beach FL	33483		888-417-9281	561-272-7979
Indian River Estates					
2250 Indian Creek Blvd W	Vero Beach FL	32966		800-544-0277*	772-539-4762
*Mktg					
John Knox Village					
651 SW Sixth St	Pompano Beach FL	33060		800-998-5669	
Mayflower Retirement Community					
1620 Mayflower Ct	Winter Park FL	32792		800-228-6518	407-672-1620
Moorings Park					
120 Moorings Pk Dr	Naples FL	34105		866-802-4302	239-643-9111
Saint Mark Village					
2655 Nebraska Ave	Palm Harbor FL	34684		800-706-4513	727-785-2580
Shell Point Village					
15101 Shell Pt Blvd	Fort Myers FL	33908		800-780-1131*	239-466-1131
*Mktg					
Stratford Court					
45 Katherine Blvd	Palm Harbor FL	34684		888-434-4648	727-787-1500
Village on the Green					
500 Village Pl	Longwood FL	32779		888-541-3443*	407-682-0230
*Mktg					
Waterford, The					
601 Universe Blvd	Juno Beach FL	33408		888-335-1678	561-627-3800
Westminster Communities of Florida					
4449 Meandering Way	Tallahassee FL	32308		800-948-1881	850-878-1136
Westminster Manor					
1700 21st Ave W	Bradenton FL	34205		877-382-9036	941-748-4161
Westminster Towers					
70 W Lucerne Cir	Orlando FL	32801		877-382-9036	800-948-1881
Clark-Lindsey Village					
101 W Windsor Rd	Urbana IL	61802		800-998-2581	217-344-2144
Holmstad, The					
700 W Fabyan Pkwy	Batavia IL	60510		877-420-5046	630-879-4000
Providence Life Services					
18601 N Creek Dr	Tinley Park IL	60477		800-509-2800	708-342-8100
Senior Lifestyle					
303 E Upper Wacker Dr Ste 2400	Chicago IL	60601		877-315-0914	
Vi 71 S Wacker Dr	Chicago IL	60606		800-421-1442	312-803-8800
Wesley Towers					
700 Monterey Pl	Hutchinson KS	67502		888-663-9175	620-663-9175
Seniorsplus 8 Falcon Rd	Lewiston ME	04240		800-427-1241	207-795-4010
Asbury Methodist Village					
201 Russell Ave	Gaithersburg MD	20877		800-327-2879	301-216-4001
Carroll Lutheran Village					
300 St Luke Cir	Westminster MD	21158		877-848-0095	410-848-0090
Charlestown Retirement Community (CCI)					
715 Maiden Choice Ln	Catonsville MD	21228		800-917-8649	410-242-2880
Collington Episcopal Community					
10450 Lottsford Rd	Mitchellville MD	20721		888-257-9468	
Ginger Cove					
4000 River Crescent Dr	Annapolis MD	21401		800-299-2683	410-266-7300
Glen Meadows					
11630 Glen Arm Rd	Glen Arm MD	21057		877-246-4744	667-213-1835
Heron Point of Chestertown					
501 E Campus Ave	Chestertown MD	21620		800-327-9138	443-214-3605
Homewood at Williamsport					
16505 Virginia Ave	Williamsport MD	21795		877-849-9244	301-582-1750
Loomis Communities					
246 N Main St	South Hadley MA	01075		800-865-7655	413-532-5325
Willows, The 1 Lyman St	Westborough MA	01581		800-464-8060	508-366-4730
Friendship Village Kalamazoo					
1400 N Drake Rd	Kalamazoo MI	49006		800-613-3984	269-381-0560
Michigan Masonic Home					
1200 Wright Ave	Alma MI	48801		800-321-9357	989-463-3141
Vista Grande Villa					
2251 Springport Rd	Jackson MI	49202		800-889-8499	517-787-0222
Covenant Village of Golden Valley					
5800 St Croix Ave	Minneapolis MN	55422		877-825-9763	763-546-6125
Armed Forces Retirement Home - Gulfport					
1800 Beach Dr	Gulfport MS	39507		800-422-9988	
Havenwood-Heritage Heights Havenwood Campus					
33 Christian Ave	Concord NH	03301		800-457-6833	603-224-5363
RiverMead Retirement Community					
150 RiverMead Rd	Peterborough NH	03458		800-200-5433	603-924-0062
Crestwood Manor 50 Lacey Rd	Whiting NJ	08759		877-467-1652*	732-849-4900
*General					
Evergreens, The					
309 Bridgeboro Rd	Moorestown NJ	08057		877-673-8234	856-242-7435
Medford Leas					
1 Medford Leas Way	Medford NJ	08055		800-331-4302	609-654-3000

				Toll-Free	Phone

Oaks at Denville, The
19 Pocono Rd .... Denville NJ 07834   **877-693-7650**   973-586-6000

La Vida Llena
10501 Lagrima de Oro NE ....Albuquerque NM 87111   **800-922-1344**   505-293-4001

Freedom Village 5275 Rt 14 .... Lakemont NY 14857   **800-842-8679**   607-243-8126

Kendal at Ithaca
2230 N Triphammer Rd .... Ithaca NY 14850   **800-253-6325**   607-266-5300

Arbor Acres
1240 Arbor Rd ....Winston-Salem NC 27104   **866-658-2724**   336-724-7921

Bermuda Village
142 Bermuda Village Dr .... Advance NC 27006   **800-843-5433***
*Mktg

Carol Woods Retirement Community
750 Weaver Dairy Rd ....Chapel Hill NC 27514   **800-518-9333**   919-968-4511

Carolina Meadows
100 Carolina Meadows ....Chapel Hill NC 27517   **800-458-6756**   919-942-4014

Deerfield Episcopal Retirement Community
1617 Hendersonville Rd .... Asheville NC 28803   **800-284-1531**   828-274-1531

Forest at Duke
2701 Pickett Rd .... Durham NC 27705   **800-474-0258**

Pines at Davidson
400 Avinger Ln .... Davidson NC 28036   **877-574-8203**   704-896-1100

First Community Village
1800 Riverside Dr ....Columbus OH 43212   **877-364-2570**   614-324-4455

Kendal at Oberlin
600 Kendal Dr .... Oberlin OH 44074   **800-548-9469***
*Mktg

Laurel Lake Retirement Community
200 Laurel Lake Dr ....Hudson OH 44236   **866-650-2100**

Methodist ElderCare Services
5155 N High St ....Columbus OH 43214   **855-636-2225**   614-396-4990

Otterbein senior lifestyle choices
580 N SR 741 .... Lebanon OH 45036   **888-513-9131**   513-933-5400

Golden Oaks Village
5801 N Oakwood Rd .... Enid OK 73703   **800-259-0914**   580-249-2600

Spanish Cove 11 Palm Ave ....Yukon OK 73099   **800-965-2683**

Friendsview Retirement Community
1301 E Fulton St ....Newberg OR 97132   **866-307-4371**   503-538-3144

Mennonite Village
5353 Columbus St SE .... Albany OR 97322   **800-211-2713**   541-928-7232

Rogue Valley Manor
1200 Mira Mar Ave ....Medford OR 97504   **800-848-7868**   541-857-7214

Willamette View
12705 SE River Rd ....Portland OR 97222   **800-446-0670**   503-654-6581

Brittany Pointe Estates
1001 S Valley Forge Rd ....Lansdale PA 19446   **800-504-2287**   267-656-6008

Cornwall Manor 1 Boyd St ....Cornwall PA 17016   **800-222-2476**   717-273-2647

Cross Keys Village
2990 Carlisle Pk ....New Oxford PA 17350   **888-624-8242***   717-624-2161
*Mktg

Foulkeways at Gwynedd
1120 Meetinghouse Rd .... Gwynedd PA 19436   **800-211-2713**   215-643-2200

Foxdale Village
500 E Marylyn Ave .... State College PA 16801   **800-253-4951**   814-238-3322

Granite Farms Estates
1343 W Baltimore Pk .... Media PA 19063   **888-499-2287**   484-443-0070

Kendal Crosslands Communities
1109 E Baltimore Pk ....Kennett Square PA 19348   **800-216-1920**   610-388-1441

Lima Estates
411 N Middletown Rd .... Media PA 19063   **888-398-2287**   484-443-0090

Lutheran Community at Telford
12 Lutheran Home Dr .... Telford PA 18969   **877-343-7518**   215-723-9819

Passavant Retirement Community
401 S Main St ....Zelienople PA 16063   **888-498-7753**   724-452-5400

Pennswood Village
1382 Newtown-Langhorne Rd ....Newtown PA 18940   **888-454-1122**   215-968-9110

Pine Run Community
777 Ferry Rd ....Doylestown PA 18901   **800-992-8992**   215-345-9000

Sherwood Oaks
100 Norman Dr ....Cranberry Township PA 16066   **800-642-2217**   724-776-8100

Spring House Estates
728 Norristown Rd ....Lower Gwynedd PA 19002   **888-365-2287**   267-460-6116

Willow Valley Lakes Manor
300 Willow Vly Lakes Dr .... Willow Street PA 17584   **800-770-5445**   717-464-0800

Bethea Baptist Retirement Community
157 Home Ave .... Darlington SC 29532   **877-393-2867**   843-393-2867

Westminster Towers
1330 India Hook Rd ....Rock Hill SC 29732   **800-345-6026**   803-328-5000

Army Residence Community
7400 Crestway ....San Antonio TX 78239   **800-725-0083**   210-646-5316

Capital Senior Living Corp
14160 Dallas Pkwy Ste 300 ....Dallas TX 75254   **800-635-1232**   972-770-5600
NYSE: CSU

Manor Park Inc
2208 N Loop 250 W ....Midland TX 79707   **800-523-9898**   432-689-9898

Shenandoah Valley Westminster-Canterbury
300 Westminster-Canterbury Dr ....Winchester VA 22603   **800-492-9463**   540-665-5914

Westminster-Canterbury of Lynchburg
501 VES Rd .... Lynchburg VA 24503   **800-962-3520**   434-386-3500

Westminster-Canterbury on Chesapeake Bay
3100 Shore Dr ....Virginia Beach VA 23451   **800-753-2918**

Westminster-Canterbury Richmond
1600 Westbrook Ave ....Richmond VA 23227   **800-445-9904**   804-264-6000

Williamsburg Landing
5700 Williamsburg Landing Dr ....Williamsburg VA 23185   **800-554-5517**   757-565-6505

Judson Park
23600 Marine View Dr S ....Des Moines WA 98198   **800-401-4113**   206-824-4000

Panorama City 1751 Cir Ln SE ....Lacey WA 98503   **800-999-9807**   360-456-0111

Rockwood Retirement Community
2903 E 25th Ave ....Spokane WA 99223   **800-727-6650**   509-536-6650

Wesley Homes
815 S 216th St ....Des Moines WA 98198   **866-937-5390**   206-824-5000

Fairhaven
435 W Starin Rd ....Whitewater WI 53190   **877-624-2298**   262-473-2140

---

669   RETREATS - SPIRITUAL

The facilities listed here offer basic amenities and services such as bed linens, food preparation, maid service, etc. Although physical activity may play a role in the programs offered, the focus is on the spiritual.

				Toll-Free	Phone

Chopra Ctr at La Costa Resort & Spa
2013 Costa del Mar Rd .... Carlsbad CA 92009   **888-424-6772**   760-494-1600

Expanding Light
14618 Tyler Foote Rd .... Nevada City CA 95959   **800-346-5350**   530-478-7518

Hollyhock
PO Box 127 ....Mansons Landing BC V0P1K0   **800-933-6339**   250-935-6576

ISABELLA FREEDMAN JEWISH RETREAT CENTER
116 Johnson Rd .... Falls Village CT 06031   **800-398-2630**   860-824-5991

Kalani Oceanside Retreat
12-6860 Kapoho Kalapana Rd ....Pahoa HI 96778   **800-800-6886**   808-965-7828

Kirkridge Retreat & Study Ctr
2495 Fox Gap Rd .... Bangor PA 18013   **800-231-2222**   610-588-1793

Kordes Retreat Ctr
802 E Tenth St ....Ferdinand IN 47532   **800-880-2777**   812-367-2777

Louhelen Baha'i School
3208 S State Rd .... Davison MI 48423   **800-894-9716**   810-653-5033

Omega Institute for Holistic Studies
150 Lake Dr ....Rhinebeck NY 12572   **800-944-1001**   845-266-4444

Our Lady of Fatima Retreat House
5353 E 56th St ....Indianapolis IN 46226   **800-382-9836**   317-545-7681

Pendle Hill
338 Plush Mill Rd ....Wallingford PA 19086   **800-742-3150**   610-566-4507

Saint Meinrad Archabbey
200 Hill Dr ....Saint Meinrad IN 47577   **800-682-0988**   812-357-6585

Satchidananda Ashram Yogaville (SAYVA)
108 Yogaville Way ....Buckingham VA 23921   **800-858-9642***   434-969-3121
*Resv

Shambhala Mountain Ctr
151 Shambhala Wy ....Red Feather Lakes CO 80545   **888-788-7221**   970-881-2184

Spiritual Life Ctr
7100 E 45th St N ....Wichita KS 67226   **800-348-2440**   316-744-0167

---

670   ROLLING MILL MACHINERY

SEE ALSO Metalworking Machinery

				Toll-Free	Phone

Bradbury Company Inc
1200 E Cole ....Moundridge KS 67107   **800-397-6394**   620-345-6394

Formtek Metal Forming Inc
4899 Commerce Pkwy ....Cleveland OH 44128   **800-631-0520**   216-292-4460

Magnum Integrated Technologies Inc
200 First Gulf Blvd ....Brampton ON L6W4T5   **800-830-0642**   905-595-1998

---

671   ROYALTY TRUSTS

				Toll-Free	Phone

ARC Resources Ltd
308 Fourth Ave SW Ste 1200 ....Calgary AB T2P0H7   **888-272-4900**   403-503-8600
TSX: ARX

Harvest Operations Corp
700 Second St SW Ste 1500................Calgary AB T2P2W1   **866-666-1178**   403-265-1178

Hugoton Royalty Trust
2911 Turtle Creek Blvd Ste 850
PO Box 962020.........................Dallas TX 75219   **855-588-7839**

Marine Petroleum Trust
2911 Turtle Creek Blvd Ste 850 ....Dallas TX 75219   **800-758-4672**
NASDAQ: MARPS

Obsidian Energy Ltd
Penn W Plz 207 - Ninth Ave SW Ste 200 ....Calgary AB T2P1K3   **866-693-2707**   403-777-2500

Pengrowth Energy Corp
222 Third Ave SW Ste 1600 ....Calgary AB T2P0B4   **800-223-4122**   403-233-0224
TSX: PGF

---

672   RUBBER GOODS

				Toll-Free	Phone

Aero Tec Labs Inc
45 Spear Rd Industrial Pk ....Ramsey NJ 07446   **800-526-5330**   201-825-1400

Alliance Rubber Co
210 Carpenter Dam Rd .... Hot Springs AR 71901   **800-626-5940**   501-262-2700

Biltrite Corp 51 Sawyer Rd ....Waltham MA 02454   **800-877-8775**   781-647-1700

BRP Manufacturing Co
637 N Jackson St .... Lima OH 45801   **800-858-0482**   419-228-4441

Durable Products Inc
PO Box 826 ....Crossville TN 38557   **800-373-3502**   931-484-3502

Flexsys America LP
260 Springside Dr .... Akron OH 44333   **800-455-5622**   330-666-4111

Griswold LLC
1 River St PO Box 638 ....Moosup CT 06354   **800-472-8788**

Hutchinson Aerospace & Industry Inc
82 S St ....Hopkinton MA 01748   **800-227-7962**   508-417-7000

Kent Elastomer Products Inc
1500 St Claire Ave .... Kent OH 44240   **800-331-4762***   330-673-1011
*Cust Svc

Koneta Inc 1400 Lunar Dr .... Wapakoneta OH 45895   **800-331-0775**   419-739-4200

Ludlow Composites Corp
2100 Commerce Dr ....Fremont OH 43420   **800-628-5463**

Mitchell Rubber Products Inc
10220 San Sevaine Way .... Mira Loma CA 91752   **800-453-7526**

MSM Industries Inc
802 Swan Dr ....Smyrna TN 37167   **800-648-6648**   615-355-4355

Musson Rubber Company Inc
1320 E Archwood Ave .... Akron OH 44306   **800-321-2381***   330-773-7651
*Cust Svc

				Toll-Free	Phone
National Rubber Technologies Corp					
35 Cawthra Ave	Toronto	ON	M6N5B3	**800-387-8501**	416-657-1111
Pawling Corp					
32 Nelson Hill Rd PO Box 200	Wassaic	NY	12592	**800-431-3456**	
Proco Products Inc					
PO Box 590	Stockton	CA	95201	**800-344-3246**	209-943-6088
R & K Industrial Products Co					
1945 Seventh St	Richmond	CA	94801	**800-842-7655**	510-234-7212
Regupol America					
11 Ritter Way	Lebanon	PA	17042	**800-537-8737**	
Swarco Industries Inc					
PO Box 89	Columbia	TN	38402	**800-216-8781**	931-388-5900
Teknor Apex Co					
505 Central Ave	Pawtucket	RI	02861	**800-556-3864**	401-725-8000
Vulcan Corp					
30 Garfield Pl Ste 1040.	Cincinnati	OH	45202	**800-447-1146***	513-621-2850
*Sales					

673   RUBBER GOODS - MECHANICAL

Mechanical rubber goods are rubber components used in machinery, such as o-rings, sprockets, sleeves, roller covers, etc.

				Toll-Free	Phone
American National Rubber Co					
Main & High St	Ceredo	WV	25507	**800-624-3410***	304-453-1311
*Cust Svc					
Atlantic India Rubber Co					
1437 Kentucky Rt 1428	Hagerhill	KY	41222	**800-476-6638**	
Colonial Diversified Polymer Products LLC					
2055 Forrest St Ext	Dyersburg	TN	38024	**800-303-3606**	731-287-3636
Fabreeka International Inc					
1023 Tpke St	Stoughton	MA	02072	**800-322-7352***	781-341-3655
*Cust Svc					
Finzer Roller Co					
129 Rawls Rd	Des Plaines	IL	60018	**888-486-1900**	847-390-6200
Griffith Rubber Mills					
2625 NW Industrial St	Portland	OR	97210	**800-321-9677**	503-226-6971
Hiawatha Rubber					
1700 67th Ave N	Minneapolis	MN	55430	**800-782-7776**	763-566-0900
Holz Rubber Company Inc					
1129 S Sacramento St	Lodi	CA	95240	**800-285-1600**	209-368-7171
Jamak Fabrication Inc					
1401 N Bowie Dr	Weatherford	TX	76086	**800-543-4747**	817-594-8771
Jasper Rubber Products Inc					
1010 First Ave	Jasper	IN	47546	**800-457-7457**	812-482-3242
Lauren Mfg					
2228 Reiser Ave SE	New Philadelphia	OH	44663	**800-683-0676**	330-339-3373
Lavelle Industries Inc					
665 McHenry St	Burlington	WI	53105	**800-528-3553**	262-763-2434
Longwood Elastomers Inc					
706 Green Valley Rd Ste 212	Greensboro	NC	27408	**800-829-7231**	336-272-3710
Lord Corp 111 Lord Dr	Cary	NC	27511	**877-275-5673**	919-468-5979
Minor Rubber Company Inc					
49 Ackerman St	Bloomfield	NJ	07003	**800-433-6886**	973-338-6800
MOCAP Inc 409 Pkwy Dr	Park Hills	MO	63601	**800-633-6775**	314-543-4000
OMNI Products Inc					
3911 Dayton St	Mchenry	IL	60050	**800-275-9848**	815-344-3100
Pamarco 171 E Marquardt Dr	Wheeling	IL	60090	**800-323-7735***	847-459-6000
*Sales					
Precision Assoc Inc					
3800 N Washington Ave	Minneapolis	MN	55412	**800-394-6590**	612-333-7464
Precix Inc					
744 Bellville Ave	New Bedford	MA	02745	**800-225-8505**	508-998-4000
RPP Corp 12 Ballard Way	Lawrence	MA	01843	**800-232-2239**	978-689-2800
Sperry & Rice Mfg Company LLC					
9146 US Hwy 52	Brookville	IN	47012	**800-541-9277**	765-647-4141
Thermodyn Corp					
3550 Silica Rd	Sylvania	OH	43560	**800-654-6518**	419-841-7782
West American Rubber Co LLC					
1337 Braden Ct	Orange	CA	92868	**800-245-8748**	714-532-3355

674   SAFETY EQUIPMENT - MFR

SEE ALSO Medical Supplies - Mfr ; Personal Protective Equipment & Clothing

				Toll-Free	Phone
ACR Electronics Inc					
5757 Ravenswood Rd	Fort Lauderdale	FL	33312	**800-432-0227**	954-981-3333
Adams Elevator Equipment Co					
6310 W Howard St	Niles	IL	60714	**800-929-9247**	847-581-2900
Amerex Corp					
7595 Gadsden Hwy	Trussville	AL	35173	**800-654-5980**	205-655-3271
Bradley Corp					
W 142 N 9101 Fountain Blvd	Menomonee Falls	WI	53051	**800-272-3539**	262-251-6000
Carsonite Composites LLC					
19845 US Hwy 76	Newberry	SC	29108	**800-648-7916**	803-321-1185
CSE Corp 1001 Corporate Ln	Export	PA	15632	**800-245-2224**	412-856-9200
Encon Safety Products Co					
6825 W Sam Houston Pkwy N PO Box 3826	Houston	TX	77041	**800-283-6266**	713-466-1449
Gemtor Inc 1 Johnson Ave	Matawan	NJ	07747	**800-405-9048**	732-583-6200
Peerless Chain Co					
1416 E Sanborn St	Winona	MN	55987	**800-533-8056**	507-457-9100
Peerless Industrial Group					
PO Box 949	Clackamas	OR	97015	**800-547-6806**	800 873-1916
Plastic Safety Systems Inc					
2444 Baldwin Rd	Cleveland	OH	44104	**800-662-6338**	
Potter-Roemer					
17451 Hurley St	City of Industry	CA	91744	**800-366-3473**	626-336-4561
Reflexite North America					
315 S St	New Britain	CT	06051	**800-654-7570**	860-223-9247
Rite-Hite Corp					
8900 N Arbon Dr	Milwaukee	WI	53224	**800-456-0600**	414-355-2600
Rostra Precision Controls Inc					
2519 Dana Dr	Laurinburg	NC	28352	**800-782-3379***	910-276-4854
*Cust Svc					

				Toll-Free	Phone
Safety Components International Inc					
40 Emery St	Greenville	SC	29605	**800-896-6926**	864-240-2600

675   SAFETY EQUIPMENT - WHOL

				Toll-Free	Phone
Allstar Fire Equipment Inc					
12328 Lower Azusa Rd	Arcadia	CA	91006	**800-425-5787**	626-652-0900
Arbill PO Box 820542	Philadelphia	PA	19154	**800-523-5367**	
Brooks Equipment Company Inc					
10926 David Taylor Dr Ste 300					
PO Box 481888.	Charlotte	NC	28262	**800-433-9265**	800-826-3473
Broward Fire Equipment & Service Inc					
101 SW Sixth St	Fort Lauderdale	FL	33301	**800-866-3473**	954-467-6625
Calolympic Glove & Safety Company Inc					
1720 Delilah St	Corona	CA	92879	**800-421-6630**	951-340-2229
Continental Safety Equipment					
2935 Waters Rd Ste 140	Eagan	MN	55121	**800-844-7003**	651-454-7233
Empire Safety & Supply Inc					
10624 Industrial Ave	Roseville	CA	95678	**800-995-1341**	
Fire Fighters Equipment Co					
3053 Rt 10 E	Denville	NJ	07834	**800-523-7222**	973-366-4466
LaFrance Equipment Corp					
516 Erie St	Elmira	NY	14904	**800-873-8808**	607-733-5511
LN Curtis & Sons					
1800 Peralta St	Oakland	CA	94607	**800-443-3556**	510-839-5111
Nardini Fire Equipment Company Inc					
405 County Rd E W	Saint Paul	MN	55126	**888-627-3464**	651-483-6631
Orr Safety Corp					
11601 Interchange Dr	Louisville	KY	40229	**800-726-6789**	502-774-5791
PK Safety Supply					
1829 Clement Ave Ste 200	Alameda	CA	94501	**800-829-9580**	510-337-8880
Saf-T-Gard International Inc					
205 Huehl Rd	Northbrook	IL	60062	**800-548-4273**	847-291-1600
Safety Products Inc					
3517 Craftsman Blvd	Lakeland	FL	33803	**800-248-6860**	863-665-3601
Safety Supply South Inc					
100 Centrum Dr	Irmo	SC	29063	**800-522-8344***	
*Cust Svc					
Safeware Inc					
3200 HubbaRd Rd	Landover	MD	20785	**800-331-6707***	301-683-1234
*Cust Svc					
United Fire Equipment Co					
335 N Fourth Ave	Tucson	AZ	85705	**800-362-0150**	520-622-3639

676   SALT

SEE ALSO Spices, Seasonings, Herbs

Companies listed here produce salt that may be used for a variety of purposes, including as a food ingredient or for deicing, water conditioning, or other chemical or industrial applications.

				Toll-Free	Phone
Cargill Salt Inc					
PO Box 5621	Minneapolis	MN	55440	**888-385-7258**	
Compass Minerals International					
9900 W 109th St Ste 100	Overland Park	KS	66210	**866-755-1743***	913-344-9200
NYSE: CMP ■ *Cust Svc					
Morton Salt Inc					
123 N Wacker Dr	Chicago	IL	60606	**800-725-8847**	312-807-2000
United Salt Corp					
4800 San Felipe St	Houston	TX	77056	**800-554-8658**	713-877-2600

677   SATELLITE COMMUNICATIONS SERVICES

SEE ALSO Telecommunications Services ; Cable & Other Pay Television Services ; Internet Service Providers (ISPs)

				Toll-Free	Phone
Bytemobile Inc					
4988 Great America Pkwy	Santa Clara	CA	95054	**800-424-8749**	408-790-8000
Epoch Universal Inc					
9341 Irvine Blvd	Irvine	CA	92618	**877-907-1144**	
Force10 Networks Inc					
1415 N McDowell Blvd	Petaluma	CA	94954	**866-600-5100**	707-665-4400
Globalstar					
300 Holiday Square Blvd	Covington	LA	70433	**877-728-7466**	877-452-5782
Lightriver Technologies					
2150 John Glenn Dre Ste 200.	Concord	CA	94520	**888-544-4825**	925-363-9000
Linkus Enterprises Inc					
5595 W San Madele Ave	Fresno	CA	93722	**888-854-6587**	559-256-6600
ORBCOMM					
22970 Indian Creek Dr Ste 300.	Sterling	VA	20166	**800-672-2666***	703-433-6300
*Cust Svc					
Outerlink Corp					
187 Ballardvale St Ste A260	Wilmington	MA	01887	**877-688-3770**	978-284-6070
Stratos Global Corp					
6550 Rock Spring Dr Ste 650	Bethesda	MD	20817	**800-563-2255**	301-214-8800
ViaSat Inc					
6155 El Camino Real	Carlsbad	CA	92009	**855-463-9333**	760-476-2200
NASDAQ: VSAT					

678   SAW BLADES & HANDSAWS

SEE ALSO Tools - Hand & Edge

				Toll-Free	Phone
California Saw & Knife Works					
721 Brannan St	San Francisco	CA	94103	**888-729-6533**	415-861-0644
Contour Saws Inc					
900 Graceland Ave	Des Plaines	IL	60016	**800-259-6834**	
Diamond Saw Works Inc					
12290 Olean Rd	Chaffee	NY	14030	**800-828-1180**	716-496-7417

	Toll-Free	Phone
Disston Precision Inc		
6795 State Rd ....Philadelphia PA 19135	**800-238-1007***	215-338-1200
*Cust Svc		
Great Neck Saw Manufacturing Inc		
165 E Second St ....Mineola NY 11501	**800-457-0600***	
*Cust Svc		
LS Starrett Co		
121 Crescent St ....Athol MA 01331	**800-482-8710**	978-249-3551
NYSE: SCX		
Marvel Mfg Company Inc		
3501 Marvel Dr ....Oshkosh WI 54902	**800-472-9464**	920-236-7200
MK Diamond Products Inc		
1315 Storm Pkwy ....Torrance CA 90501	**800-421-5830**	310-539-5221
MK Morse Co 1101 11th St SE ....Canton OH 44707	**800-733-3377**	330-453-8187
Simonds International		
135 Intervale Rd ....Fitchburg MA 01420	**800-343-1616**	

679　　SAWMILLS & PLANING MILLS

	Toll-Free	Phone
Anthony Forest Products Co		
309 N Washington Ave ....El Dorado AR 71730	**800-221-2326**	870-862-3414
Buse Timber & Sales Inc		
3812 28th Pl NE ....Everett WA 98201	**800-305-2577**	425-258-2577
Buskirk Lumber Co		
319 Oak St ....Freeport MI 49325	**800-860-9663**	
Ceres Environmental Services Inc		
3825 85th Ave N ....Minneapolis MN 55443	**800-218-4424**	
Collins Cos		
1618 SW First Ave Ste 500......Portland OR 97201	**800-329-1219**	
Cronland Lumber Co		
PO Box 574 ....Lincolnton NC 28093	**800-237-2428**	704-736-2691
Hardwoods of Michigan Inc		
430 Div St ....Clinton MI 49236	**800-327-2812**	517-456-7431
Hunt Forest Products		
401 E Reynolds Dr PO Box 1263 ...Ruston LA 71273	**800-390-8589**	318-255-2245
Impact Guns 2710 S 1900 W ....Ogden UT 84401	**800-917-7137**	
Indiana Dimension Inc		
1621 W Market St ....Logansport IN 46947	**888-875-4434**	
Industrial Timber & Lumber Corp (ITL)		
23925 Commerce Park Rd ....Beachwood OH 44122	**800-829-9663**	216-831-3140
Komo Machine Inc 1 Komo Dr ....Lakewood NJ 08701	**800-255-5670**	732-719-6222
La Crete Sawmills Ltd		
Hwy 697 S PO Box 1090 ....La Crete AB T0H2H0	**888-928-2298**	780-928-2292
Louisiana-Pacific Corp		
414 Union St Ste 2000.............Nashville TN 37219	**888-820-0325**	615-986-5600
NYSE: LPX		
Maibec Inc 202 1984 Fifth St ....Levis QC G6W5M6	**800-363-1930**	418-659-3323
Manke Lumber Company Inc		
1717 Marine View Dr ....Tacoma WA 98422	**800-426-8488**	253-572-6252
Mid South Lumber Inc		
6595 Marshall Blvd PO Box 1185...Lithonia GA 30058	**800-759-3076**	770-482-4800
Parton Lumber Company Inc		
251 Parton Rd ....Rutherfordton NC 28139	**800-624-1501**	828-287-4257
Pike Lumber Company Inc		
PO Box 247 ....Akron IN 46910	**800-356-4554**	574-893-4511
Robbins Inc		
4777 Eastern Ave ....Cincinnati OH 45226	**800-543-1913**	
Roseburg Forest Products Co		
PO Box 1088 ....Roseburg OR 97470	**800-245-1115**	541-679-3311
Rushmore Forest Products		
23848 Hwy 385 PO Box 619.......Hill City SD 57745	**866-466-5254**	605-574-2512
Scott Industries Inc		
1573 Hwy 136 W PO Box 7 ......Henderson KY 42419	**800-951-9276**	270-831-2037
Sierra Forest Products		
13575 Benson Ave ....Chino CA 91710	**800-548-3975**	909-591-9442
Simpson Door Co		
400 Simpson Ave ....Mccleary WA 98557	**800-746-7766**	
Sims Bark Company Inc		
1765 Spring Valley Rd ....Tuscumbia AL 35674	**800-346-3216**	256-381-8323
Stimson Lumber Co		
520 SW Yamhill St Ste 700........Portland OR 97204	**800-445-9758**	503-701-6510
Teal-Jones Group, The		
17897 Triggs Rd ....Surrey BC V4N4M8	**888-995-8325**	604-587-8700
Thompson Mahogany Co		
7400 Edmund St ....Philadelphia PA 19136	**877-589-6637**	
TR Miller Mill Company Inc		
215 Deer St PO Box 708..........Brewton AL 36427	**800-633-6740**	251-867-4331
United Treating & Distribution LLC		
338 E Washington Ave ....Muscle Shoals AL 35661	**877-248-0944**	256-248-0944
Universal Forest Products Inc (UFPI)		
2801 E Beltline Ave NE ....Grand Rapids MI 49525	**800-598-9663**	616-364-6161
NASDAQ: UFPI		
USNR		
1981 Schurman Way PO Box 310......Woodland WA 98674	**800-289-8767**	360-225-8267
Weyerhaeuser Co		
33663 Weyerhaeuser Way S .....Federal Way WA 98003	**800-525-5440**	253-924-2345
NYSE: WY		

680　　SCALES & BALANCES

SEE ALSO Laboratory Apparatus & Furniture

		Toll-Free	Phone
Advance Scale of MD LLC			
2400 Egg Harbor Rd ....Lindenwold NJ	08021	**888-447-2253**	856-627-0700
Avery Weigh-Tronix Inc			
1000 Armstrong Dr ....Fairmont MN	56031	**800-458-7062**	507-238-4461
BRK Brands Inc			
3901 Liberty St Rd ....Aurora IL	60504	**800-323-9005**	630-851-7330
Cardinal Scale Manufacturing Co			
203 E Daugherty St PO Box 151...Webb City MO	64870	**800-441-4237**	417-673-4631
Detecto Scale Co			
203 E Daugherty St PO Box 151...Webb City MO	64870	**800-641-2008**	417-673-4631
Emery Winslow Scale Co			
73 Cogwheel Ln ....Seymour CT	06483	**800-891-3952**	203-881-9333

		Toll-Free	Phone
Fairbanks Scales Inc			
821 Locust St ....Kansas City MO	64106	**800-451-4107**	
Industrial Data Systems Inc			
3822 E La Palma Ave ....Anaheim CA	92807	**800-854-3311**	714-921-9212
Intercomp Co			
3839 County Rd 116 ....Medina MN	55340	**800-328-3336**	763-476-2531
Jarden Consumer Solutions			
2381 Executive Ctr Dr ......Boca Raton FL	33431	**800-777-5452**	561-912-4100
Johnson Scale Company Inc			
36 Stiles Ln ....Pine Brook NJ	07058	**800-572-2531**	973-226-2100
Medela Inc			
1101 Corporate Dr ....Mchenry IL	60050	**800-435-8316**	815-363-1166
Merrick Industries Inc			
10 Arthur Dr ....Lynn Haven FL	32444	**800-345-8440**	850-265-3611
Ohaus Corp			
7 Campus Dr Ste 310..........Parsippany NJ	07054	**800-672-7722**	
Premier Tech Chronos			
1 Premier Ave ....Rivere-du-Loup QC	G5R6C1	**866-571-7354**	418-868-8324
Schenck Trebel Corp			
535 Acorn St ....Deer Park NY	11729	**800-873-2357**	631-242-4010
Scientech Inc			
5649 Arapahoe Ave ....Boulder CO	80303	**800-525-0522**	303-444-1361
Setra Systems Inc			
159 Swanson Rd ....Boxborough MA	01719	**800-257-3872**	978-263-1400
Tanita Corp of America Inc			
2625 S Clearbrook Dr ...Arlington Heights IL	60005	**800-826-4828**	847-640-9241
TCI Scales Inc			
PO Box 1648 ....Snohomish WA	98291	**800-522-2206**	425-353-4384
Thayer Scale			
91 Schoosett St ....Pembroke MA	02359	**855-784-2937**	781-826-8101
Yamato Corp			
1775 S Murray Blvd ......Colorado Springs CO	80916	**800-538-1762**	719-591-1500

681　　SCHOOL BOARDS (PUBLIC)

		Toll-Free	Phone
Albuquerque Public Schools (APS)			
6400 Uptown Blvd NE ....Albuquerque NM	87110	**866-563-9297**	505-880-3700
Anoka-Hennepin School District			
2727 N Ferry St ....Anoka MN	55303	**800-729-6164**	763-506-1000
Arlington School District			
315 N French Ave ....Arlington WA	98223	**877-766-4753**	360-618-6200
Atkinson County School System			
98 Roberts Ave E ....Pearson GA	31642	**800-639-0850**	912-422-7373
Ave Intervision LLC			
1840 W State St ....Alliance OH	44601	**800-448-9126**	
Baltimore City Public Schools			
200 E N Ave ....Baltimore MD	21202	**800-422-0009**	443-984-2000
Barney Trucking Inc			
235 State Rt 24 ....Salina UT	84654	**800-524-7930**	
Battle River Regional Div			
5402 48a Ave ....Camrose AB	T4V0L3	**800-262-4869**	780-672-6131
Beemac Trucking			
2747 Legionville Rd ....Ambridge PA	15003	**800-282-8781**	724-266-8781
Birmingham Board of Education (BCS)			
2015 Park Place North .....Birmingham AL	35203	**800-628-6673**	205-231-4600
Boarder to Boarder Trucking Inc			
PO Box 328 ....Edinburg TX	78541	**800-678-8789**	956-316-4444
Brookline College			
2445 W Dunlap Ave Ste 100....Phoenix AZ	85021	**800-793-2428**	602-242-6265
Brunswick County Board of Education			
35 Referendum Dr ....Bolivia NC	28422	**800-662-7030**	910-253-2900
Campbell Christian Schools			
1075 E Campbell Ave ....Campbell CA	95008	**800-264-7955**	408-370-4900
Cary Academy			
1500 N Harrison Ave ....Cary NC	27513	**800-948-2557**	919-677-3873
Centinela Elementary School			
1123 Marlborough Ave ......Inglewood CA	90302	**800-942-2761**	310-680-5440
Charleston County School District (CCSD)			
75 Calhoun St ....Charleston SC	29401	**800-241-8898**	843-937-6300
Chignecto-central Regional			
60 Lorne St ....Truro NS	B2N3K3	**800-770-0008**	
Circleville City School District			
388 Clark Dr ....Circleville OH	43113	**800-418-6423**	740-474-4340
Clark County School District (CCSD)			
5100 West Sahara Ave ....Las Vegas NV	89146	**866-799-8997**	702-799-5000
Clovis Unified School District			
1450 Herndon Ave ....Clovis CA	93611	**877-544-6664**	559-327-9300
Clyde's Transfer Inc			
8015 Industrial Pk Rd ...Mechanicsville VA	23116	**800-342-8758**	804-746-1135
Collier County School Board			
5775 Osceola Trl ....Naples FL	34109	**800-950-6264**	239-377-0001
Conestoga Valley School District			
2110 Horseshoe Rd ....Lancaster PA	17601	**800-732-0025**	717-397-2421
Crespi Carmelite High School Inc			
5031 Alonzo Ave ....Encino CA	91316	**800-540-4000**	818-345-1672
Cullman City School			
301 First St NE Ste 100 ....Cullman AL	35055	**800-548-2547**	256-734-2233
Culver City Unified School District (CCUSD)			
4034 Irving Pl ....Culver City CA	90232	**855-446-2673**	310-842-4220
Dallas Independent School District			
3700 Ross Ave ....Dallas TX	75204	**866-796-3682**	972-925-3700
Delaware County Intermediate Unit			
200 Yale Ave ....Morton PA	19070	**800-441-3215**	610-938-9000
Des Moines Independent School District			
901 Walnut St ....Des Moines IA	50309	**800-452-1111**	515-242-7911
Duarte Unified School District			
1620 Huntington Dr ....Duarte CA	91010	**888-225-7377**	626-599-5000
Durham Academy Inc			
3130 Pickett Rd ....Durham NC	27705	**888-904-9149**	919-489-9118
Erie 2-Chautauqua Cattaraugus Boces (ECCB)			
8685 Erie Rd ....Angola NY	14006	**800-228-1184**	716-549-4454
Fannin County Board of Education			
2290 E First St ....Blue Ridge GA	30513	**800-308-2145**	706-632-3771
First Bank Of Highland Park			
1835 First St ....Highland Park IL	60035	**877-651-7800**	847-432-7800

Classified Section

Name	Location	ZIP	Toll-Free	Phone
First Farmers & Merchants National Bank 816 S Garden St PO Box 1148 *OTC: FFMH*	Columbia TN	38401	800-882-8378	931-388-3145
Franklin Local School District 4000 Milllers Ln	Duncan Falls OH	43734	800-846-4976	740-674-5203
Fremont Unified School District 4210 Technology Dr	Fremont CA	94538	800-544-5248	510-657-2350
Fulton 58 *Fulton Missouri* 2 Hornet Dr	Fulton MO	65251	800-456-2634	573-590-8000
Gainesville City Schools 508 Oak St	Gainesville GA	30501	800-533-0682	770-536-5275
Garland Independent School District (GISD) 501 S Jupiter PO Box 469026	Garland TX	75042	800-252-5555	972-494-8201
Gray Transportation Inc 2459 GT Dr	Waterloo IA	50703	800-234-3930	319-234-3930
Greenwood School District 50 1855 Calhoun Rd	Greenwood SC	29648	888-260-9430	864-941-5400
Guilford County Schools 712 N Eugene St	Greensboro NC	27401	866-286-7337	336-370-8100
Gulf Coast Bank & Trust Co 200 St Charles Ave	New Orleans LA	70130	800-223-2060	504-561-6100
Guy Shavender Trucking Inc PO Box 206	Pantego NC	27860	800-682-2447	252-943-3379
Harnett County Board of Education 1008 S 11th St	Lillington NC	27546	800-342-9647	910-893-8151
Hawaii Dept of Education Honolulu District Office 4967 Kilauea Ave	Honolulu HI	96816	800-437-8641	808-733-4950
Hillsborough County Public Schools 901 E Kennedy Blvd	Tampa FL	33602	800-962-2873	813-272-4000
Holiday Express Corp 721 S 28th St	Estherville IA	51334	800-831-5078	712-362-5812
Houston Independent School District 228 McCarty St	Houston TX	77029	800-446-2821	713-556-6000
Hueneme Elementary School Dist 205 N Ventura Rd	Port Hueneme CA	93041	866-431-2478	805-488-3588
Huntsville Board of Education 200 White St	Huntsville AL	35801	877-517-0020	256-428-6800
Idaho Falls School District 91 Education Foundation Inc 690 John Adams Pkwy	Idaho Falls ID	83401	888-993-7120	208-525-7500
Ilex Construction & Woodworking 3801 Northampton St NW Ste 3	Washington DC	20015	866-551-4539	410-820-4393
Jackson County School System 1660 Winder Hwy	Jefferson GA	30549	800-760-3727	706-367-5151
Jacksonville Independent School District 800 College Ave	Jacksonville TX	75766	800-583-6908	903-586-6511
JM. Bozeman Enterprises Inc 166 Seltzer Ln *General	Malvern AR	72104	800-472-1836*	
John Cooper School 1 John Cooper Dr	The Woodlands TX	77381	800-295-1162	281-367-0900
Julian Charter School Inc 1704 Cape Horn	Julian CA	92036	866-853-0003	760-765-3847
K12 Inc 2300 Corporate Pk Dr *NYSE: LRN*	Herndon VA	20171	866-512-2273	703-483-7000
Klein Independent School District 7200 Spring Cypress Rd	Klein TX	77379	888-703-0083	832-249-4000
Louis Riel School Div 900 St Mary's Rd	Winnipeg MB	R2M3R3	800-940-3447	204-257-7827
Mardel Inc 7727 SW 44th St	Oklahoma City OK	73179	888-262-7335	
McLeod Express LLC 5002 Cundiff Ct *General	Decatur IL	62526	800-709-3936*	
Merion Mercy Academy 511 Montgomery Ave	Merion Station PA	19066	800-352-7550	610-664-6655
Metropolitan Nashville Public Schools (MNPS) 2601 Bransford Ave	Nashville TN	37204	800-848-0298	615-259-8531
Miami-Dade County Public Schools (M-DCPS) 1450 NE Second Ave	Miami FL	33132	800-955-5504	305-995-1000
Michener Institute for Applied 222 Saint Patrick St	Toronto ON	M5T1V4	800-387-9066	416-596-3101
Midwestern Intermediate Unit Iv 453 Maple St	Grove City PA	16127	800-942-8035	724-458-6700
Minneapolis Public Schools 3345 Chicago Ave	Minneapolis MN	55407	800-543-7709	612-668-0000
Missouri School Boards Assn 2100 I-70 Dr SW	Columbia MO	65203	800-221-6722	573-445-9920
Modesto City Schools 426 Locust St	Modesto CA	95351	800-942-3767	209-574-1500
Murray Co 1215 Fern Ridge Pkwy Ste 213	Saint Louis MO	63141	888-323-5560	314-576-2818
N E Florida Educational Consortium 3841 Reid St	Palatka FL	32177	800-227-6036	386-329-3800
National Outdoor Leadership School (NOLS) 284 Lincoln St	Lander WY	82520	800-710-6657	307-332-5300
Niskayuna Central School District (NCSD) 1239 Van Antwerp Rd	Schenectady NY	12309	866-893-6337	518-377-4666
Norfolk Public Schools 800 E City Hall Ave	Norfolk VA	23510	800-846-4464	757-628-3843
North Ridgeville City School District 5490 Mills Creek Ln	North Ridgeville OH	44039	877-644-6457	440-327-4444
Nye County School District Inc (NCSD) PO Box 113	Tonopah NV	89049	800-796-6273	775-482-6258
Oakland Unified School District 1000 Broadway Ste 680	Oakland CA	94607	888-604-4636	510-879-8200
Orange County Public Schools 445 W Amelia St	Orlando FL	32801	800-378-9264	407-317-3200
Ossining Union Free School District 190 Croton Ave	Ossining NY	10562	877-769-7447	914-941-7700
Palm Beach County School District, The 3300 Forest Hill Blvd	West Palm Beach FL	33406	866-930-8402	561-434-8000
Person County Schools 304 S Morgan St	Roxboro NC	27573	866-724-6650	336-599-2191
Pittsylvania County Schools 39 Bank St SE PO Box 232	Chatham VA	24531	888-440-6520	434-432-2761
Plaquemines Parish School Board 557 F Edward Hebert Blvd	Belle Chasse LA	70037	877-453-2721	504-595-6400
Prairie Lakes Area Education Agency 1235 Fifth Ave S	Fort Dodge IA	50501	800-669-2325	515-574-5500
Princeton Public Schools 25 Valley Rd	Princeton NJ	08540	800-322-8174	609-806-4200
Prior Lake-Savage Area Public School District 719 4540 Tower St SE	Prior Lake MN	55372	855-346-1650	952-226-0000
Proteus Inc 1830 N Dinuba Blvd	Visalia CA	93291	888-776-9998	559-733-5423
Provision Ministry Group 2050 MAIN ST Ste 400	Irvine CA	92614	800-597-9931	
Puget Sound Educational Service District 800 Oakesdale Ave SW	Renton WA	98057	800-664-4549	425-917-7600
Putnam Valley School District Inc 146 Peekskill Hollow Rd	Putnam Valley NY	10579	800-666-5327	845-528-8143
Riverview Intermediate Unit Number 6 Administrative Services 270 Mayfield Rd	Clarion PA	16214	800-672-7123	814-226-7103
Robert e Webber Institute for Worship Studies, The (IWS) 4001 Hendricks Ave	Jacksonville FL	32207	800-282-2977	904-264-2172
Robstown High School 609 W Hwy 44	Robstown TX	78380	800-446-3142	361-387-5999
Romeo Community School District 316 N Main St	Romeo MI	48065	888-427-6818	586-752-0200
Rosetta Stone Ltd 1919 N Lynn St 7th Fl. *NYSE: RST*	Arlington VA	22209	800-788-0822	
Salem-Keizer Public Schools 2450 Lancaster Dr NE	Salem OR	97305	877-293-1090	503-399-3000
Salin Bank 8455 Keystone Xing	Indianapolis IN	46240	800-320-7536	317-452-8000
School District of The Chathams 58 Meyersville Rd	Chatham NJ	07928	800-225-5425	973-457-2500
School Nurse Supply Co 1690 Wright Blvd	Schaumburg IL	60193	800-485-2737	
Seton Home Study School 1350 Progress Dr	Front Royal VA	22630	800-542-1066	540-636-9990
Sidney Transportation Services 777 W Russell Rd PO Box 946	Sidney OH	45365	800-743-6391	937-498-2323
Springfield Public School District #186 1900 West Monroe St	Springfield IL	62704	877-632-7753	217-525-3006
St Clair County Regional Educational Service Agency 499 Range Rd	Marysville MI	48040	800-294-9229	810-364-8990
St Ignatius College Prep 2001 37th Ave	San Francisco CA	94116	888-225-5427	415-731-7500
Stephen Mack Middle School 11810 Old River Rd	Rockton IL	61072	800-252-2873	815-624-2611
Sumner School District 1202 Wood Ave	Sumner WA	98390	866-548-3847	253-891-6000
Thunderbird School of Global Management 1 Global Pl	Glendale AZ	85306	800-848-9084	602-978-7000
Twin Falls School District 411 201 Main Ave W	Twin Falls ID	83301	800-726-0003	208-733-6900
Twin Rivers Unified School District 3222 Winona Way	North Highlands CA	95660	800-260-0659	916-566-1628
US Special Delivery Inc 821 E Blvd	Kingsford MI	49802	800-821-6389	906-774-1931
W N. Morehouse Truck Line Inc 4010 Dahlman Ave	Omaha NE	68107	800-228-9378	402-733-2200
Westfield Board of Education Inc 302 Elm St	Westfield NJ	07090	800-355-2583	908-789-4401
Westminster School District 14121 Cedarwood St	Westminster CA	92683	888-491-6603	714-894-7311
Wharton Independent School District 2100 N Fulton St	Wharton TX	77488	800-818-3453	979-532-3612
William B Meyer Inc 255 Long Beach Blvd	Stratford CT	06615	800-727-5985	203-375-5801
Williamsport Area School District 2780 W Fourth St	Williamsport PA	17701	888-448-4642	570-327-5500
Zanesville City School Board 1701 Blue Ave	Zanesville OH	43701	866-280-7377	740-454-9751

682   SCRAP METAL

SEE ALSO Recyclable Materials Recovery

Name	Location	ZIP	Toll-Free	Phone
Advantage Metals Recycling LLC (AMR) 510 Walnut St Ste 300	Kansas City MO	64106	866-527-4733	816-861-2700
Alter Trading Corp 700 Office Pkwy	Saint Louis MO	63141	888-337-2727	314-872-2400
AMG Resources Corp 2 Robinson Plz # 350	Pittsburgh PA	15205	877-395-8338	412-777-7300
Calbag Metals Co 2495 NW Nicolai St	Portland OR	97210	800-398-3441	503-226-3441
Cleveland Corp 42810 N Green Bay Rd	Zion IL	60099	800-281-3464	847-872-7200
Dimco Steel Inc 3901 S Lamar St	Dallas TX	75215	877-428-8336	214-428-8336
Gachman Metals & Recycling Company Inc 2600 Shamrock Ave	Fort Worth TX	76107	800-749-0423	817-334-0211
Grossman Iron & Steel 5 N Market St	Saint Louis MO	63102	800-969-9423	314-231-9423
Iron & Metals Inc 5555 Franklin St	Denver CO	80216	800-776-7910	303-292-5555
Louis Padnos Iron & Metal Co PO Box 1979	Holland MI	49422	800-442-3509	616-396-6521
Metalico Annaco Inc 943 Hazel St	Akron OH	44305	800-966-1499	330-376-1400
Metro Metals Northwest 5611 NE Columbia Blvd	Portland OR	97218	800-610-5680	503-287-8861
OmniSource Corp 7575 W Jefferson Blvd	Fort Wayne IN	46804	800-666-4789	260-422-5541
Progress Rail Services 1600 Progress Dr PO Box 1037	Albertville AL	35950	800-476-8769	256-505-6600
PSC 5151 San Felipe Ste 1100	Houston TX	77056	800-726-1300	
SA Recycling LLC 2411 N Glassell St	Orange CA	92865	800-468-7272	714-637-4913

	Toll-Free	Phone

Sadoff & Rudoy Industries LLP
240 W Arndt St .... Fond du Lac WI 54936 **877-972-3633*** 920-921-2070
*General

Simon Metals LLC
2202 E River St .... Tacoma WA 98421 **800-562-8464** 253-272-9364

Sims Brothers Recycling
1011 S Prospect St .... Marion OH 43302 **800-536-7465** 740-387-9041

Thermo Fluids Inc
4301 W Jefferson St .... Phoenix AZ 85043 **800-350-7565**

Tube City IMS Corp (TMS)
12 Monongahela Ave .... Glassport PA 15045 **800-860-2442** 412-678-6141
NYSE: TMS

Upstate Shredding LLC
1 Recycle Dr Tioga Industrial Pk. .... Owego NY 13827 **800-245-3133** 607-687-7777

Yaffe Cos Inc, The
1200 S G St .... Muskogee OK 74403 **800-759-2333** 918-687-7543

683   SCREEN PRINTING

	Toll-Free	Phone

Action Screen Print Inc
30w260 Butterfield Rd Unit 203 .... Warrenville IL 60555 **800-661-5892** 630-393-1990

Ares Sportswear Ltd
3704 Lacon Rd .... Hilliard OH 43026 **800-439-8614** 614-767-1950

Art Brands LLC
225 Business Ctr Dr .... Blacklick OH 43004 **877-755-4278** 614-755-4278

Buffalo Specialties Inc
10706 Craighead Dr .... Houston TX 77025 **800-256-0838** 713-271-6107

Designer Decal Inc
1120 E First Ave .... Spokane WA 99202 **800-622-6333** 509-535-0267

Duck Co 5601 Gray St .... Arvada CO 80002 **800-255-3565**

Express Image Inc
2942 Rice St .... Little Canada MN 55113 **866-482-8602**

F&E Sportswear Corp
1230 Newell Pkwy .... Montgomery AL 36110 **800-523-7762** 334-244-6477

Fisher Printing Inc
8640 S Oketo Ave .... Bridgeview IL 60455 **800-366-0006** 708-598-1500

Flow-Eze Co 3209 Auburn St .... Rockford IL 61101 **800-435-4873** 815-965-1062

GFX International Inc
333 Barron Blvd .... Grayslake IL 60030 **800-274-3225** 847-543-4600

Gillespie Graphics
27676 SW Pkwy Ave .... Wilsonville OR 97070 **800-547-6841** 503-682-1122

Hanson Sign Companies
82 Carter St .... Falconer NY 14733 **800-522-2009** 716-484-8564

Image Sport Inc
1115 SE Westbrooke Dr .... Waukee IA 50263 **800-919-0520** 515-987-7699

Kerusso Inc
402 Hwy 62 Spur .... Berryville AR 72616 **800-424-0943** 870-423-6242

Law Elder Law 2275 Church Rd .... Aurora IL 60502 **800-310-3100** 630-585-5200

M & M Designs Inc
1981 Quality Blvd .... Huntsville TX 77320 **800-627-0656**

Motson Graphics Inc
1717 Bethlehem Pk .... Flourtown PA 19031 **800-972-1986** 215-233-0500

New Life Industries Inc
140 Chappells Dairy Rd .... Somerset KY 42503 **800-443-9523** 606-679-3616

Occasions Group, The
1750 Tower Blvd .... North Mankato MN 56003 **800-296-9029**

Petra Manufacturing Co
6600 W Armitage Ave .... Chicago IL 60707 **800-888-7387** 773-622-1475

Primary Color Inc
9239 Premier Row .... Dallas TX 75247 **800-581-9555** 214-630-8800

Print Source Inc, The
404 S Tracy St .... Wichita KS 67209 **800-535-9498** 316-945-7052

Screen Graphics of Florida Inc
1801 N Andrews Ave .... Pompano Beach FL 33069 **800-346-4420**

Serigraph Inc
3801 E Decorah Rd .... West Bend WI 53095 **800-279-6060** 262-335-7200

Service Graphics LLC
8350 Allison Ave .... Indianapolis IN 46268 **800-884-9876** 317-471-8246

Signcraft Screenprint Inc
100 A J Harle Dr .... Galena IL 61036 **800-733-5150** 815-777-3030

Silkworm Inc
102 S Sezmore Dr .... Murphysboro IL 62966 **800-826-0577** 618-687-4077

Technigraph Corp
850 W Third St .... Winona MN 55987 **800-421-4772** 507-454-3830

Top Promotions Inc
8831 S Greenview Dr .... Middleton WI 53562 **800-344-2968** 608-836-9111

Triple Crown Products Inc
814 Ela Ave .... Waterford WI 53185 **800-619-1110** 262-534-7878

Vincent Printing Company Inc
1512 Sholar Ave .... Chattanooga TN 37406 **800-251-7262**

Voss Signs LLC
112 Fairgrounds Dr .... Manlius NY 13104 **800-473-0698** 315-682-6418

684   SCREENING - WOVEN WIRE

	Toll-Free	Phone

ACS Industries Inc
1 New England Way .... Lincoln RI 02865 **866-783-4838** 401-769-4700

Belleville Wire Cloth Inc
18 Rutgers Ave .... Cedar Grove NJ 07009 **800-631-0490** 973-239-0074

Buffalo Wire Works Co
1165 Clinton St .... Buffalo NY 14206 **800-828-7028** 716-826-4666

Cleveland Wire Cloth & Manufacturing Co
3573 E 78th St .... Cleveland OH 44105 **800-321-3234** 216-341-1832

Edward J Darby & Son Inc
2200 N Eigth St PO Box 50049. .... Philadelphia PA 19133 **800-875-6374** 215-236-2203

Gerard Daniel Worldwide
34 Barnhart Dr .... Hanover PA 17331 **800-232-3332** 717-637-5901

IWM International LLC
500 E Middle St .... Hanover PA 17331 **800-323-5585**

Jelliff Corp
354 Pequot Ave .... Southport CT 06890 **800-243-0052** 203-259-1615

King Wire Partitions Inc
6044 N Figueroa St PO Box 42220. .... Los Angeles CA 90042 **800-789-9608** 323-256-4848

	Toll-Free	Phone

TWP Inc 2831 Tenth St .... Berkeley CA 94710 **800-227-1570** 510-548-4434

Universal Wire Cloth Co
16 N Steel Rd .... Morrisville PA 19067 **800-523-0575** 215-736-8981

685   SEATING - VEHICULAR

	Toll-Free	Phone

Custom Aircraft Interiors
3701 Industry Ave .... Lakewood CA 90712 **800-423-2904** 562-426-5098

Freedman Seating Co
4545 W Augusta Blvd .... Chicago IL 60651 **800-443-4540** 773-524-2440

HO Bostrom Company Inc
818 Progress Ave .... Waukesha WI 53186 **800-332-5415** 262-542-0222

Sears Manufacturing Co
PO Box 3667 .... Davenport IA 52808 **800-553-3013*** 563-383-2800
*Cust Svc

Seats Inc
1515 Industrial St .... Reedsburg WI 53959 **800-443-0615** 608-524-8261

686   SECURITIES BROKERS & DEALERS

SEE ALSO Mutual Funds ; Electronic Communications Networks (ECNs) ; Commodity Contracts Brokers & Dealers ; Investment Advice & Management

	Toll-Free	Phone

1&1 Internet Inc
701 Lee Rd Ste 300 .... Chesterbrook PA 19087 **877-461-2631**

1st Discount Brokerage Inc
8927 Hypoluxo Rd Ste A-5. .... Lake Worth FL 33467 **888-642-2811** 561-515-3200

achoo! ALLERGY & AIR Products Inc
3411 Pierce Dr Ste 100. .... Atlanta GA 30341 **800-339-7123**

Ameriprise Brokerage
70040 Ameriprise Financial Ctr .... Minneapolis MN 55474 **800-535-2001**

Andrew Garrett Inc
52 Vanderbilt Ave Ste 510. .... New York NY 10017 **800-899-1883**

Avisen Securities Inc
3620 American River Dr Ste 145. .... Sacramento CA 95864 **800-230-7704** 916-480-2747

Baird Patrick & Company Inc
305 Plz 10 .... Jersey City NJ 07311 **800-221-7747** 201-680-7300

Barclays 745 Seventh Ave . ... New York NY 10019 **888-227-2275** 212-526-7000

BaxterBoo
148 Cypress Ridge Crt .... Ridgeland SC 29936 **888-887-0063**

Bernard L Madoff Investment Securities Co
45 Rockefeller Ctr 11th Fl .... New York NY 10111 **800-334-1343** 212-230-2424

Berthel Fisher Companies
4201 42nd St NE Ste 100. .... Cedar Rapids IA 52402 **800-356-5234** 319-447-5700

BHK Securities LLC
2200 Lakeshore Dr Ste 250 .... Birmingham AL 35209 **888-529-2610** 205-322-2025

Blowfish Direct LLC
6160 Bristol Pkwy Ste 100 .... Culver City CA 90230 **877-725-6934** 310-566-5700

Bourbon & Boots Inc
314 Main St 2th Fl .... North Little Rock AR 72114 **877-435-8977**

Brant Securities Ltd
220 Bay St Ste 300. .... Toronto ON M5J2W4 **888-544-9318** 416-596-4545

Brighton Securities Corp
1703 Monroe Ave .... Rochester NY 14618 **800-388-1703** 585-473-3590

Brill Securities Inc
152 W 57th St 16th Fl. .... New York NY 10019 **800-933-0800** 212-957-5700

Bull Wealth Management Group Inc
4100 Yonge St Ste 612 .... Toronto ON M2P2B5 **866-623-2053** 416-223-2053

Burgundy Asset Management Ltd
Bay Wellington Tower Brookfield Pl 181 Bay St
Ste 4510 .... Toronto ON M5J2T3 **888-480-1790** 416-869-3222

Caldwell Securities Ltd
150 King St W Ste 1710 .... Toronto ON M5H1J9 **800-387-0859** 416-862-7755

Calton & Assoc Inc
2701 N Rocky Point Dr Ste 1000 .... Tampa FL 33607 **800-942-0262** 813-264-0440

Centaurus Financial
2300 E Katella Ave Ste 200. .... Anaheim CA 92806 **800-880-4234**

Ceros Financial Services Inc
1445 Research Blvd Ste 530. .... Rockville MD 20850 **866-842-3356**

Cetera Financial Group Inc
200 N Sepulveda Blvd Ste 1200 .... El Segundo CA 90245 **866-489-3100**

Charles Schwab & Co Inc
211 Main St .... San Francisco CA 94105 **800-648-5300*** 415-667-1009
*Cust Svc

CLS Investments LLC
17605 Wright St .... Omaha NE 68130 **888-455-4244** 402-493-3313

Cobblestone Capital Advisors LLC
140 Allens Creek Rd .... Rochester NY 14618 **800-264-2769** 585-473-3333

Community Banc Investments Inc
26 E Main St .... New Concord OH 43762 **800-224-1013**

Conceptual Financial Planning Inc
2561 E Calumet St .... Appleton WI 54915 **866-809-6411** 920-731-9500

Construction Book Express Inc
990 Park Center Dr Ste E .... Vista CA 92081 **800-253-0541**

Corinthian Partners LLC
850 Third Ave Ste 16C .... New York NY 10022 **800-899-8950** 212-287-1500

CP Capital Securities Inc
3390 Mary St Ste 116. .... Coconut Grove FL 33133 **866-596-5500** 305-702-5500

Crowell Weedon & Co
1 Wilshire Bldg 624 S Grand Ave
26th Fl .... Los Angeles CA 90017 **800-227-0319** 213-620-1850

Davenport & Co LLC
901 E Cary St
1 James Center Ste 1100 .... Richmond VA 23219 **800-846-6666** 804-780-2000

DiscountMugs.com
12610 NW 115th Ave .... Medley FL 33178 **800-569-1980**

Dougherty & Company LLC
90 S Seventh St Ste 4300 .... Minneapolis MN 55402 **800-328-4000** 612-376-4000

E*Trade Financial Corp
1271 Ave of the Americas 14th Fl .... New York NY 10020 **800-387-2331**
NASDAQ: ETFC

eBX LLC
101 Federal St Ste 1010 .... Boston MA 02110 **800-958-4813** 617-350-1600

Company / Address	Location	Toll-Free	Phone
Edward Jones 12555 Manchester Rd	Saint Louis MO 63131	800-441-2357	314-515-2000
EKRiley Investments LLC 1420 Fifth Ave Ste 3300	Seattle WA 98101	800-809-9317	206-832-1520
FIMAC Solutions LLC Denver Technological Ctr 7000 E Belleview Ste 310	Greenwood Village CO 80111	877-789-5905	303-320-1900
Fincantieri Marine Systems North America Inc 800-C Principal Ct	Chesapeake VA 23320	877-436-7643	757-548-6000
Fisc Investment Services Corp 1849 Clairmont Rd	Decatur GA 30033	800-241-3203	404-321-1212
Fisgard Capital Corp 3378 Douglas St	Victoria BC V8Z3L3	866-382-9255	250-382-9255
Franklin Templeton Investments 3344 Quality Dr	Rancho Cordova CA 95670	800-632-2350	650-312-2000
Freedom Investments Inc 375 Raritan Ctr Pkwy	Edison NJ 08837	800-944-4033	
FSC Securities Corp 2300 Windy Ridge Pkwy Ste 1100	Atlanta GA 30339	800-372-5646	800-547-2382
Full Access Brokerage 1240 Charnelton St	Eugene OR 97401	866-890-5743	541-284-5070
Geary Pacific Corp 1908 N Enterprise St	Orange CA 92865	800-444-3279	714-279-2950
Geneos Wealth Management Inc 9055 E Mineral Cir Ste 200	Centennial CO 80112	888-812-5043	303-785-8470
George K Baum & Co 4801 Main St Ste 500	Kansas City MO 64112	800-821-7195	816-474-1100
Georgeson Securities Corp 480 Washington Blvd	Jersey City NJ 07310	800-428-0717	
Global Maxfin Investments Inc 100 Mural St Ste 201	Richmond Hill ON L4B1J3	866-666-5266	416-741-1544
Great Pacific Fixed Income Securities Inc 151 Kalmus Dr Ste H-8	Costa Mesa CA 92626	800-284-4804	714-619-3000
Hampton Securities Ltd 141 Adelaide St W Ste 1800	Toronto ON M5H3L5	877-225-0229	416-862-7800
Harris Financial Services Inc 940 Spokane Ave	Whitefish MT 59937	800-735-7895	406-862-4400
Hogan-Knotts Financial Group, The 298 Broad St	Red Bank NJ 07701	800-801-3190	732-842-7400
Huntleigh Securities Corp 7800 Forsyth Blvd 5th Fl	Saint Louis MO 63105	800-727-5405	314-236-2400
Icor Technology Inc 935 Ages Dr	Ottawa ON K1G6L3	877-483-7978	613-745-3600
IDI Distributors Inc 8303 Audubon Rd	Chanhassen MN 55317	888-843-1318	952-279-6400
Illinois Fair Plan Assn 130 E Randolph PO Box 81469	Chicago IL 60601	800-972-4480	312-861-0385
Index Funds Advisors Inc 19200 Von Karman Ave Ste 150	Irvine CA 92612	888-643-3133	949-502-0050
Interwest Capital Corp 4275 Executive Sq Ste 1020	La Jolla CA 92037	800-792-9639	858-622-4900
Investment Professionals Inc (IPI) 16414 San Pedro Ave Ste 300	San Antonio TX 78232	800-593-8800	210-308-8800
Investrade Discount Securities 950 N Milwaukee Ave Ste 102 *Cust Svc	Glenview IL 60025	800-498-7120*	847-375-6080
ITG Inc 1 Liberty Plz 165 Broadway	New York NY 10006	800-215-4484	212-588-4000
Janney Montgomery Scott LLC 1801 Market St	Philadelphia PA 19103	800-526-6397	215-665-6000
JJB Hilliard WL Lyons Inc 500 W Jefferson St	Louisville KY 40202	800-444-1854	502-588-8400
JonesTrading Institutional Services LLC 32133 Lindero Canyon Rd Ste 208	Westlake Village CA 91361	800-423-5933	818-991-5500
Kingsdale Capital Markets Inc 130 King St W Ste 2950 PO Box 156	Toronto ON M5X1C7	877-373-6007	416-867-4550
Kovack Securities Inc 6451 N Federal Hwy # 1201 Ste 1201	Fort Lauderdale FL 33308	800-711-4078	954-782-4771
L B L Group 3631 S Harbor Blvd Ste 200	Santa Ana CA 92704	800-451-8037	
Lazard 30 Rockefeller Plz *NYSE: LAZ*	New York NY 10112	866-867-4070	212-632-6000
Leaders LLC 14 Maine St Ste 216G PO Box 18	Brunswick ME 04011	888-583-7770	207-318-1893
Legg Mason Inc (LMI) 100 International Dr *NYSE: LM*	Baltimore MD 21202	800-822-5544	800-221-3627
Leigh Baldwin & Company LLC 112 Albany St	Cazenovia NY 13035	800-659-8044	315-734-1410
Lexington Investment Company Inc 2365 Harrodsburg Rd Ste B375	Lexington KY 40504	800-264-7073	859-224-7073
Liberty Group LLC 411 30th St 2nd Fl	Oakland CA 94609	888-588-5818	510-658-1880
Loop Capital Markets LLC 111 W Jackson Blvd Ste 1901	Chicago IL 60604	888-294-8898	312-913-4900
LPL Financial 75 State St 22nd Fl	Boston MA 02109	800-877-7210	
Mailender Inc 9500 Glades Dr	Hamilton OH 45011	800-998-5453	513-942-5453
MB Trading Futures Inc 1926 E Maple Ave	El Segundo CA 90245	866-628-3001	310-647-4281
Mesirow Financial Inc 350 N Clark St	Chicago IL 60654	800-453-0600	312-595-6000
Morgan Stanley 1585 Broadway *NYSE: MS ■ *General*	New York NY 10036	800-223-2440*	212-761-4000
Morgan Stanley Investment Management 1221 Ave of the Americas 5th Fl *General	New York NY 10020	800-223-2440*	212-296-6600
National Securities Corp 410 Park Ave 14th Fl	New York NY 10022	800-742-7730	212-417-8000
Needham & Co Inc 445 Park Ave	New York NY 10022	800-903-3268	212-371-8300
Newbridge Securities Corp 1451 W Cypress Creek Rd	Fort Lauderdale FL 33309	877-447-9625	954-334-3450
NexBank Securities Inc 2515 McKinney Ave Ste 1100	Dallas TX 75201	800-827-4818	972-308-6700
NEXT Financial Holdings Inc 2500 Wilcrest Dr Ste 620	Houston TX 77042	877-876-6398	
Novasel & Schwarte Investments Inc 3170 US Rte 50 Ste 10	South Lake Tahoe CA 96150	800-442-5052	530-577-5050
Nuveen Investments Inc 333 W Wacker Dr	Chicago IL 60606	800-257-8787	312-917-7700
NYLIFE Securities Inc 51 Madison Ave Rm 251	New York NY 10010	800-695-4785	800-695-9873
Oberweis Securities Inc 3333 Warrenville Rd Ste 500	Lisle IL 60532	800-323-6166	630-577-2300
Packaging Material Direct Inc 30405 Solon Rd Ste 9	Solon OH 44139	800-456-2467	
Parnassus Investments 1 Market St Steuart Tower Ste 1600	San Francisco CA 94105	800-999-3505	415-778-0200
Paulson Investment Company Inc 2141 W North Ave 2nd Fl	Chicago IL 60647	855-653-3444	503-243-6000
PDI Financial Group 601 N Lynndale Dr	Appleton WI 54914	800-234-7341	920-739-2303
Pennsylvania Trust Co 5 Radnor Corp Ctr Ste 450	Radnor PA 19087	800-975-4316	610-975-4300
People's Securities Inc 850 Main St	Bridgeport CT 06604	800-894-0300	
Phillips & Company Securities Inc 1300 SW Fifth Ave Ste 2100	Portland OR 97201	800-572-4765	503-224-0858
Piper Jaffray Cos 800 Nicollet Mall Ste 1000 *NYSE: PJC*	Minneapolis MN 55402	800-333-6000	
Precision IBC Inc 8054 Mcgowin Dr	Fairhope AL 36532	800-544-7069	251-990-6789
PRICE Futures Group Inc, The 141 West Jackson Blvd Ste 1340A	Chicago IL 60604	800-769-7021	312-264-4300
Questar Capital Corp 5701 Golden Hills Dr	Minneapolis MN 55416	888-446-5872	
R Seelaus & Company Inc 25 Deforest Ave Ste 304	Summit NJ 07901	800-922-0584	
Raymond James Financial Inc 880 Carillon Pkwy *NYSE: RJF*	Saint Petersburg FL 33716	800-248-8863	727-567-1000
RBC Capital Markets 200 Bay St S Tower 10th Fl	Toronto ON M5J2T6	800-769-2511	
RBC Dain Rauscher Inc 60 S Sixth St	Minneapolis MN 55402	800-933-9946	
Robert W Baird & Company Inc 777 E Wisconsin Ave PO Box 672	Milwaukee WI 53202	800-792-2473	414-765-3500
Roehl & Yi Investment Advisors LLC 450 Country Club Rd Ste 200	Eugene OR 97401	888-683-4343	541-683-2085
Roosevelt & Cross Inc 1 Exchange Plz 55 Broadway 22nd Fl	New York NY 10006	800-348-3426	212-344-2500
Ross Sinclaire & Associates LLC 700 Walnut St Ste 600	Cincinnati OH 45202	800-543-1831	513-381-3939
Royal Alliance Assoc Inc 1 World Financial Ctr 15th Fl	New York NY 10281	800-821-5100	
SagePoint Financial Inc 2800 N Central Ave Ste 2100	Phoenix AZ 85004	800-552-3319	
Samuel A Ramirez & Co Inc 61 Broadway Ste 2924	New York NY 10006	800-888-4086	
Sandler O'Neill + Partners LP 1251 Avenue of the Americas 6th Fl	New York NY 10020	800-635-6851	212-466-7800
Schroder Investment Management North America Inc (SIMNA) 7 Bryant Pk	New York NY 10018	800-730-2932	212-641-3800
Scotiabank 250 Vesey St 23rd & 24th fl	New York NY 10281	877-294-3435	212-225-5000
Securities Center Inc, The 245 E St	Chula Vista CA 91910	800-244-1718	619-426-3550
Securities Service Network Inc 9729 Cogdill Rd Ste 301	Knoxville TN 37932	866-843-4635	
SFE Investment Counsel Inc 801 S Figueroa St Ste 2100	Los Angeles CA 90017	800-445-6320	213-612-0220
Shore Morgan Young 300 W Wilson Bridge Rd	Worthington OH 43085	800-288-2117	614-888-2117
Siebert Cisneros Shank & Co LLC 100 Wall St 18th Fl	New York NY 10005	800-334-6800	646-775-4850
SII Investments Inc 5555 W Grande Market Dr	Appleton WI 54913	800-426-5975	866-275-4422
Silver Legacy Resort Casino 407 N Virginia St	Reno NV 89501	800-687-8733	775-329-4777
Speed Trader 1717 Rte 6	Carmel NY 10512	800-874-3039	845-531-2487
Stephens Inc 111 Ctr St	Little Rock AR 72201	800-643-9691	501-377-2000
Stifel Financial Corp 501 N Broadway *NYSE: SF*	Saint Louis MO 63102	800-679-5446	
Stifel Nicolaus & Co Inc 501 N Broadway	Saint Louis MO 63102	800-679-5446	314-317-6900
StormHarbour Securities LP 140 E 45th St Two Grand Central Tower 33rd Fl	New York NY 10017	800-662-2739	212-905-2500
SunTrust Robinson Humphrey Capital Markets 3333 Peachtree Rd NE	Atlanta GA 30326	800-634-7928	404-926-5000
Tocco Financial Services Inc 1647 N Swan Rd	Tucson AZ 85712	877-881-1149	520-881-1149
Trader's Library LLC 6310 Stevens Forest Rd Ste 200	Columbia MD 21046	800-272-2855	410-964-0026
TradeStation Group Inc 8050 SW Tenth St Ste 2000	Plantation FL 33324	800-871-3577	954-652-7000
Trading Direct 160 Broadway 7th Fl East Bldg	New York NY 10038	800-925-8566	212-766-0230
Tradition Asiel Securities Inc 255 Greenwich St 4th Fl	New York NY 10007	866-220-5771	212-791-4500
Vanguard Brokerage Services PO Box 1110	Valley Forge PA 19482	800-992-8327	610-669-1000
vFinance Inc 1200 N Federal Hwy Ste 400	Boca Raton FL 33432	800-487-0577	
Vining Sparks IBG LP 775 Ridge Lake Blvd	Memphis TN 38120	800-829-0321	901-766-3000
Wayne Hummer Investments LLC 222 S Riverside Pz 28th Fl	Chicago IL 60606	800-621-4477	866-943-4732

				Toll-Free	Phone
Western International Securities Inc					
70 S Lake Ave Ste 700	Pasadena	CA	91101	888-793-7717	
WestPark Capital Inc					
1900 Ave of the Stars Ste 310	Los Angeles	CA	90067	800-811-3487	310-843-9300
William Blair & Company LLC					
222 W Adams St	Chicago	IL	60606	800-621-0687	312-236-1600
Wilson-Davis & Company Inc					
236 S Main	Salt Lake City	UT	84101	800-621-1571	801-532-1313
WR Hambrecht & Co					
909 Montgomery St 3rd Fl	San Francisco	CA	94133	855-753-6484*	415-551-8600
*Cust Svc					
Ziegler Capital Markets Investment Services					
200 S Wacker	Chicago	IL	60606	800-797-4272	414-978-6400

687   SECURITIES & COMMODITIES EXCHANGES

				Toll-Free	Phone
Axial Networks Inc					
443 Park Ave S 8th Fl	New York	NY	10016	800-860-4519	
Border Gold Corp					
15234 N Bluff Rd	White Rock	BC	V4B3E6	888-312-2288	
Chapin Davis Investments					
1411 Clarkview Rd	Baltimore	MD	21209	800-222-3246	410-435-3200
CME Group Inc					
20 S Wacker Dr	Chicago	IL	60606	866-716-7274	312-930-1000
NASDAQ: CME					
Eris Exchange LLC					
311 S Wacker Dr Ste 950	Chicago	IL	60606	888-587-2699	
FIRMA Foreign Exchange Corp					
10205 101 St NW Ste 400	Edmonton	AB	T5J4H5	866-426-2605	780-426-5971
KeyImpact Sales & Systems Inc					
1701 Crossroads Dr	Odenton	MD	21113	800-955-0600	
MAS Capital Inc					
2715 Coney Island Ave	Brooklyn	NY	11235	866-553-7493	
Minneapolis Grain Exchange					
400 S Fourth St					
130 Grain Exchange Bldg	Minneapolis	MN	55415	800-827-4746	612-321-7101
Montreal Exchange					
1800 - 1190 Ave des Canadiens-de-Montr,al					
PO Box 37	Montreal	QC	H3B0G7	800-361-5353	514-871-2424
National Stock Exchange (NSX)					
101 Hudson St Ste 1200	Jersey City	NJ	07302	800-843-3924	201-499-3700
Nations Financial Group Inc					
4000 River Ridge Dr NE					
PO Box 908	Cedar Rapids	IA	52406	800-351-2471	319-393-9541
NMS Capital Advisors LLC					
433 N Camden Dr 4th Fl	Beverly Hills	CA	90210	800-716-2080	
NYSE Arce					
115 Samsone St	San Francisco	CA	94104	877-729-7291	
NYSE Euronext 11 Wall St	New York	NY	10005	866-873-7422	212-656-3000
NYSE: NYX					
Pavilion Financial Corp					
1001 Corydon Ave Ste 300	Winnipeg	MB	R3M0B6	866-954-5101	204-954-5101
RainMaker Securities LLC					
11390 W Olympic Blvd Ste 380	Los Angeles	CA	90064	888-333-1091	
Raymond James (USA) Ltd					
925 West Georgia St Ste 2100	Vancouver	BC	V6C3L2	844-654-7357	
Sprott Global Resource Investments Ltd					
1910 Palomar Point Way Ste 200	Carlsbad	CA	92008	800-477-7853	
Toronto Stock Exchange					
130 King St W The Exchange Tower	Toronto	ON	M5X1J2	888-873-8392	416-947-4670
Wall Street Financial Group Inc					
255 Woodcliff Dr	Fairport	NY	14450	800-303-9255	
Williams Financial Group Inc					
2711 N Haskell Ave Cityplace Tower					
Ste 2900	Dallas	TX	75204	800-225-3650	972-661-8700
World Currency USA Inc					
16 W Main St Ste C	Marlton	NJ	08053	888-593-7927	

688   SECURITY PRODUCTS & SERVICES

SEE ALSO Audio & Video Equipment ; Signals & Sirens - Electric ; Fire Protection Systems

				Toll-Free	Phone
3M 28100 Cabot Dr Ste 200	Novi	MI	48377	877-992-7749	248-374-9600
ADS Security LP					
3001 Armory Dr Ste 100	Nashville	TN	37204	800-448-5852	615-269-4448
ADT Security Services Inc					
14200 E Exposition Ave	Aurora	CO	80012	800-246-9147	800-521-1734
Advantor Systems Corp					
12612 Challenger Pkwy Ste 300	Orlando	FL	32826	800-238-2686	
Akal Global Inc					
7 Infinity Loop	Espanola	NM	87532	888-325-2527	505-692-6600
Alken Inc 40 Hercules Dr	Colchester	VT	05446	800-357-4777	802-655-3159
Allied Fire & Security Inc					
425 W Second Ave	Spokane	WA	99201	888-333-2632*	509-321-8778
*Acctg					
AMAG Technology Inc					
20701 Manhattan Pl	Torrance	CA	90501	800-889-9138	310-518-2380
American Locker Security Systems Inc					
608 Allen St	Jamestown	NY	14701	800-828-9118*	
*Sales					
APi Systems Group Inc					
10575 Vista Park Rd	Dallas	TX	75238	800-566-0845*	214-349-2221
*General					
BI Inc 6400 Lookout Rd	Boulder	CO	80301	800-241-2911	303-218-1000
Black Hat					
1932 First Ave Ste 204	Seattle	WA	98101	866-203-8081	206-443-5489
Bosch Security Systems					
130 Perinton Pkwy	Fairport	NY	14450	800-289-0096	585-223-4060
Brivo Systems LLC					
7700 Old Georgetown Rd Ste 300	Bethesda	MD	20814	866-692-7486*	301-664-5242
*Tech Supp					
BSM Wireless Inc					
75 International Blvd Ste 100	Toronto	ON	M9W6L9	866-768-4771	416-675-1201

				Toll-Free	Phone
Carter Bros LLC					
3015 RN Martin St	East Point	GA	30344	888-818-0152	
Central Signaling					
2033 Hamilton Rd	Columbus	GA	31904	800-554-1101	
Checkpoint Systems Inc					
101 Wolf Dr	Thorofare	NJ	08086	800-257-5540	856-848-1800
NYSE: CKP					
Corby Industries Inc					
1501 E Pennsylvania St	Allentown	PA	18109	800-652-6729*	610-433-1412
*Sales					
DEI Holdings Inc 1 Viper Way	Vista	CA	92081	800-876-0800	760-598-6200
OTC: DEI					
Detex Corp					
302 Detex Dr	New Braunfels	TX	78130	800-729-3839	830-629-2900
deView Electronics USA Inc					
1420 Lakeside Pkwy Ste 110	Lewisville	TX	75057	877-433-8439	214-222-3332
Diebold Nixdorf Inc					
5995 Mayfair Rd	North Canton	OH	44720	800-999-3600	330-490-4000
NYSE: DBD					
Digital Security Controls (DSC)					
3301 Langstaff Rd	Concord	ON	L4K4L2	888-888-7838	905-760-3000
Doyle Security Systems Inc					
792 Calkins Rd	Rochester	NY	14623	866-463-6953	585-244-3400
eDist 97 McKee Dr	Mahwah	NJ	07430	800-800-6624	201-512-1400
ELK Products Inc					
3266 US 70 W	Connelly Springs	NC	28612	800-797-9355	828-397-4200
Fiber SenSys LLC					
2925 NW Aloclek Dr Ste 120	Hillsboro	OR	97124	800-641-8150	503-692-4430
FireKing Security Group					
101 Security Pkwy	New Albany	IN	47150	800-457-2424	812-948-8400
First Action Security Security Team Inc					
525 Northern Ave PO Box 2070	Hagerstown	MD	21742	800-372-7447*	301-797-2124
*Cust Svc					
Fortress Technology Inc					
51 Grand Marshall Dr	Toronto	ON	M1B5N6	888-220-8737	416-754-2898
GE Analytical Instruments Inc					
6060 Spine Rd	Boulder	CO	80301	800-255-6964	303-444-2009
George Risk Industries Inc					
802 S Elm St	Kimball	NE	69145	800-523-1227*	308-235-4645
OTC: RSKIA ■ *Sales					
Guardian Alarm					
20800 Southfield Rd	Southfield	MI	48075	800-782-9688	248-423-1000
HandyTrac Systems LLC					
510 Staghorn Ct	Alpharetta	GA	30004	800-665-9994	678-990-2345
Honeywell Security Group					
2 Corporate Ctr Dr Ste 100	Melville	NY	11747	800-467-5875	516-577-2000
IDenticard Systems Inc					
25 Race Ave 1st Fl	Lancaster	PA	17603	800-233-0298	717-569-5797
Integrated Biometrics Inc					
121 Broadcast Dr	Spartanburg	SC	29303	888-840-8034	864-990-3711
KWJ Engineering Inc					
8430 Central Ave Ste C	Newark	CA	94560	800-472-6626	510-794-4296
Loomis Fargo & Co					
2500 Citywest Blvd Ste 900	Houston	TX	77042	866-383-5069	713-435-6700
Matrix Systems Inc					
1041 Byers Rd	Miamisburg	OH	45342	800-562-8749	937-438-9033
MMF Industries					
1111 S Wheeling Rd	Wheeling	IL	60090	800-323-8181	
Monitor Dynamics Inc					
12500 Network Dr Ste 303	San Antonio	TX	78249	866-435-7634	210-477-5400
NAPCO Security Systems Inc					
333 Bayview Ave	Amityville	NY	11701	800-645-9445	631-842-9400
NASDAQ: NSSC					
National Fingerprint Inc					
6999 Dolan Rd	Glouster	OH	45732	888-823-7873	740-767-3853
Nortek Security & Control LLC					
1950 Camino Vida Roble Ste 150	Carlsbad	CA	92008	800-421-1587*	760-438-7000
*Cust Svc					
Optex Inc					
13661 Benson Ave Bldg C	Chino	CA	91710	800-966-7839	909-993-5770
OSI Systems Inc					
12525 Chadron Ave	Hawthorne	CA	90250	800-579-1639	310-978-0516
NASDAQ: OSIS					
Per Mar Security					
1910 E Kimberly Rd	Davenport	IA	52807	800-473-7627	563-359-3200
PerkinElmer Inc					
940 Winter St	Waltham	MA	02451	800-762-4000	781-663-6050
NYSE: PKI					
protection One Alarm Monitoring					
1035 N Third St Ste 101	Lawrence	KS	66044	800-438-4357	785-371-1884
Revo America Inc					
850 Freeport Pkwy Ste 100	Coppell	TX	75019	866-625-7386	
Seco-Larm USA Inc					
16842 Millikan Ave	Irvine	CA	92606	800-662-0800	949-857-0811
Securitas Security Services USA Inc					
2 Campus Dr	Parsippany	NJ	07054	800-555-0906	973-267-5300
Security Corp 22325 Roethel Dr	Novi	MI	48375	877-374-5700	
Security Defense Systems Corp					
160 Park Ave	Nutley	NJ	07110	800-325-6339	
Security Signal Devices Inc					
1740 N Lemon St	Anaheim	CA	92801	800-888-0444	
Sensormatic Electronics Corp					
6600 Congress Ave	Boca Raton	FL	33487	800-327-1765	561-912-6000
Sentry Group					
900 Linden Ave	Rochester	NY	14625	800-828-1438*	585-381-4900
*Cust Svc					
Sentry Technology Corp					
1881 Lakeland Ave	Ronkonkoma	NY	11779	800-645-4224	
OTC: SKVY					
Sielox LLC					
170 E Ninth Ave	Runnemede	NJ	08078	800-424-2126	856-939-9300
SIRCHIE Finger Print Laboratories Inc					
100 Hunter Pl	Youngsville	NC	27596	800-356-7311	
Sizemore Inc					
2116 Walton Way	Augusta	GA	30904	800-445-1748	706-736-1456
Southern Folger Detention Equipment Co					
4634 S Presa St	San Antonio	TX	78223	888-745-0530	210-533-1231
Tuffy Security Products Inc					
25733 Rd H	Cortez	CO	81321	800-348-8339	

Classified Section

				Toll-Free	Phone

Unisec Inc
2555 Nicholson St . . . . San Leandro CA 94577 **800-982-4587**

Universal Security Instruments Inc
11407 Cronhill Dr . . . . Owings Mills MD 21117 **800-390-4321** 410-363-3000
NYSE: UUU

Vector Security Inc
2000 Ericsson Dr . . . . Warrendale PA 15086 **800-832-8575**

Verint Video Solutions
330 S Service Rd . . . . Melville NY 11747 **800-483-7468**

Winner International LLC
32 W State St . . . . Sharon PA 16146 **800-258-2321** 724-981-1152

---

689   SECURITY & PROTECTIVE SERVICES

SEE ALSO Investigative Services

				Toll-Free	Phone

5 Alarm Fire & Safety Equipment LLC
350 Austin Cir . . . . Delafield WI 53018 **800-615-6789** 262-646-5911

A Bales Security Agency Inc
625 E Twiggs St Ste 101 . . . . Tampa FL 33602 **800-255-7328**

AAA Security
180 Nature Pkwy . . . . Winnipeg MB R3P0X7 **866-949-0078** 204-949-0078

Accsense Inc
8437 Mayfield Rd . . . . Chesterland OH 44026 **800-956-4437** 440-729-2570

Advanced Alarm Systems Inc
101 Lindsey St . . . . Fall River MA 02720 **800-442-5276** 508-675-1937

Am-Gard Security Inc
600 Main St . . . . Pittsburgh PA 15215 **800-554-0412**

Ameriguard Security Services Inc
5470 W Spruce Ave Ste 102 . . . . Fresno CA 93722 **866-836-0117** 559-271-5984

Andy Frain Services Inc
761 Shoreline Dr . . . . Aurora IL 60504 **877-707-4771** 630-820-3820

APL Access & Security Inc
115 S William Dillard Dr . . . . Gilbert AZ 85233 **866-873-2288** 480-497-9471

ASP Inc
460 Brant St Ste 212 . . . . Burlington ON L7R4B6 **877-552-5535** 905-333-4242

Avalon Fortress Security Corp
2407 109th Ave NE Ste 110 . . . . Blaine MN 55449 **844-788-9111** 763-767-9111

AWP Inc 826 Overholt Rd . . . . Kent OH 44240 **800-343-2650**

Brokers International Financial Services LLC
4135 NW Urbandale Dr . . . . Urbandale IA 50322 **877-886-1939**

Business Protection Specialists Inc
1296 E Victor Rd . . . . Victor NY 14564 **800-560-2199**

Cansec Systems Ltd
3105 Unity Dr Unit 9. . . . . Mississauga ON L5L4L2 **877-545-7755** 905-820-2404

Castlegarde Inc
4911 S W Shore Blvd . . . . Tampa FL 33611 **866-751-3203** 813-872-4844

Cook Security Group Inc
5841 SE International Way . . . . Milwaukie OR 97222 **844-305-2665**

Criticom International Corp
715 W State Rd Ste 434 . . . . Longwood FL 32750 **866-705-7705**

Custom Communications Inc
1661 Greenview Dr SW . . . . Rochester MN 55902 **855-288-5522** 507-288-5522

Cypress Security LLC
478 Tehama St . . . . San Francisco CA 94103 **866-345-1277**

DECO Inc
11156 Zealand Ave N . . . . Champlin MN 55316 **800-968-9114**

DIGIOP
9340 Priority Way West Dr . . . . Indianapolis IN 46240 **800-968-3606**

Digistream Investigation
417 Mace Blvd . . . . Davis CA 95618 **800-747-4329**

Digital Watchdog Inc
5436 W Crenshaw St . . . . Tampa FL 33634 **866-446-3595** 813-888-9555

Djg Investigative Services Inc
19501 W Catawba Ave Ste 220 . . . . Cornelius NC 28031 **866-597-7457** 704-536-8025

Dk Security
5160 falcon view ave SE . . . . Grand rapids MI 49512 **800-535-0646** 616-656-0123

DSX Access Systems Inc
10731 Rockwall Rd . . . . Dallas TX 75238 **888-419-8353** 214-553-6140

ECI Systems
68 Stiles Rd Unit C . . . . Salem NH 03079 **800-639-2086** 603-898-6823

Edwards Company Inc
41 Woodford Ave . . . . Plainville CT 06062 **800-336-4206**

eLine Technology
9500 W 49th Ave Ste D106 . . . . Wheat Ridge CO 80033 **800-683-6835**

EMERgency24 Inc
999 E Touhy . . . . Des Plaines IL 60018 **800-800-3624** 773-725-0222

Excelsior Defense Inc
2232 Central Ave . . . . Saint Petersburg FL 33712 **877-955-4636** 727-527-9600

Federal Protection Inc
2500 N Airport Commerce Ave . . . . Springfield MO 65803 **800-299-5400**

Fidelco Guide Dog Foundation Inc
103 Vision Way . . . . Bloomfield CT 06002 **800-225-7566** 860-243-5200

First Alarm Security & Patrol Inc
1111 Estates Dr . . . . Aptos CA 95003 **800-684-1111** 831-476-1111

Fluent 7319 104 St NW . . . . Edmonton AB T6E4B9 **855-238-4826**

Fluke Corp 6920 Seaway Blvd . . . . Everett WA 98203 **800-903-5853** 425-347-6100

GHS Interactive Security Inc
21031 Warner Center Ln Ste D . . . . Woodland Hills CA 91367 **855-447-4961**

Gillmore Security Systems Inc
26165 Broadway Ave . . . . Cleveland OH 44146 **800-899-8995** 440-232-1000

Global Elite Group
825 E Gate Blvd Ste 301 . . . . Garden City NY 11530 **877-425-0999**

Guard Systems Inc
1190 Monterey Pass Rd . . . . Monterey Park CA 91754 **800-606-6711** 323-881-6711

Guardian Alarm
20800 Southfield Rd . . . . Southfield MI 48075 **800-782-9688** 248-423-1000

Guardian Protection Services Inc
174 Thorn Hill Rd . . . . Warrendale PA 15086 **877-314-7092*** 855-779-2001
*Cust Svc

Habitec Security Inc
2926 S Republic Blvd . . . . Toledo OH 43615 **888-422-4832** 419-537-6768

Hepaco Inc
2711 Burch Dr PO Box 26308 . . . . Charlotte NC 28269 **800-888-7689** 704-598-9782

Highcom Security
2451 McMullen Booth Rd Ste 242 . . . . Clearwater FL 33759 **800-987-9098**

Houston Harris Div Patrol Inc
6420 Richmond Ave . . . . Houston TX 77057 **877-975-9922** 713-975-9922

Huffmaster Crisis Management
1055 W Maple Rd . . . . Clawson MI 48017 **800-446-1515**

Information Network Assoc Inc
5235 N Front St . . . . Harrisburg PA 17110 **800-443-0824** 717-599-5505

Innovative Industrial Solutions Inc
2830 Skyline Dr . . . . Russellville AR 72802 **888-684-8249** 479-968-4266

Intec Video Systems Inc
23301 Vista Grande Dr . . . . Laguna Hills CA 92653 **800-468-3254** 949-859-3800

Ipss Inc 150 Isabella St . . . . Ottawa ON K1S1V7 **866-532-2207** 613-232-2228

Itech Digital LLC
4287 W 96th St . . . . Indianapolis IN 46268 **866-733-6673** 317-704-0440

Kent Security Services Inc
14600 Biscayne Blvd . . . . North Miami Beach FL 33181 **800-273-5368** 305-919-9400

Kimmons Investigative Services Inc
5177 Richmond Ave Ste 1190 . . . . Houston TX 77056 **800-681-5046** 713-532-5881

Knight Security Systems LLC
10105 Technology Blvd W Ste 100. . . . . Dallas TX 75220 **800-642-1632** 214-350-1632

Law Enforcement Assoc Corp (LEA-AID)
120 Penmarc Dr Ste 113. . . . . Raleigh NC 27603 **800-354-9669** 919-872-6210
OTC: LAWEQ

Loomis Armored US Inc
2500 Citywest Blvd Ste 900 . . . . Houston TX 77042 **866-383-5069** 713-435-6700

LOREX Corp
3700 Koppers St Ste 504 . . . . Baltimore MD 21227 **888-425-6739**

Mijac Alarm
9339 Charles Smith Ave
Ste 100. . . . . Rancho Cucamonga CA 91730 **800-982-7612** 909-982-7612

Mircom 25 Interchange Way . . . . Vaughan ON L4K5W3 **888-660-4655** 905-660-4655

Monument Security Inc
5 Sierra Gate Plz Ste 305 . . . . Roseville CA 95678 **877-506-1755** 916-564-4234

Murray Guard Inc
58 Murray Guard Dr . . . . Jackson TN 38305 **800-238-3830** 731-668-3400

My Alarm Center LLC
3803 W Chester Pk Ste 100 . . . . Newtown Square PA 19073 **866-484-4800**

National Monitoring Center
26800 Aliso Viejo Pkwy Ste 250. . . . . Aliso Viejo CA 92656 **800-662-1711**

Norred & Associates Inc
1003 Virginia Ave Ste 200 . . . . Atlanta GA 30354 **800-962-6363** 404-761-5058

Nuclear Security Services Corp
701 Willowbrook Centre Pkwy . . . . Willowbrook IL 60527 **800-275-8319** 630-920-1488

Pasek Corp
9 W Third St . . . . South Boston MA 02127 **800-628-2822** 617-269-7110

Pierce County Security Inc
2002 99th St E . . . . Tacoma WA 98445 **800-773-4432** 253-535-4433

Pro Security Group
541 N Valley Mills Dr . . . . Waco TX 76710 **855-753-7766** 254-753-7766

Prodco International Inc
9408 Boul du Golf . . . . Montreal QC H1J3A1 **888-577-6326** 514-324-9796

Rancho Santa Fe Protective Services Inc
1991 Vlg Pk Way Ste 100 . . . . Encinitas CA 92024 **800-303-8877**

Rapid Focus Security LLC
268 Summer St 2nd Fl . . . . Boston MA 02210 **855-793-1337**

Rapid Response Monitoring Services Inc
400 W Division St . . . . Syracuse NY 13204 **800-558-7767**

RECON Dynamics LLC
18323 Bothell Everett Hwy Ste 330. . . . . Bothell WA 98012 **877-480-3551**

RLE Technologies Inc
104 Racquette Dr . . . . Fort Collins CO 80524 **800-518-1519** 970-484-6510

Rodbat Security Services
8125 Somerset Blvd . . . . Paramount CA 90723 **877-676-3228** 562-806-9098

Safe Home Security Inc
1125 Middle St Ste 201 . . . . Middletown CT 06457 **800-833-3211**

Safeguard Security & Communications Inc
8454 N 90th St . . . . Scottsdale AZ 85258 **800-426-6060** 480-609-6200

SDI Presence LLC
33 W Monroe Ste 400. Chicago IL 60603 **888-968-7734** 312-580-7500

Security 101 LLC
2465 Mercer Ave Ste 101 . . . . West Palm Beach FL 33401 **888-909-4101**

Security America Inc
3412 Chesterfield Ave . . . . Charleston WV 25304 **888-832-6732** 304-925-4747

SecurTek Monitoring Solutions Inc
70-1st Ave N . . . . Yorkton SK S3N1J7 **844-321-2712** 877-777-7591

Seico Security Systems
132 Court St . . . . Pekin IL 61554 **800-272-0316** 309-347-3200

Select Engineered Systems
7991 W 26th Ave . . . . Hialeah FL 33016 **800-342-5737** 305-823-5410

Sentry Security LLC
339 Egidi Dr . . . . Wheeling IL 60090 **888-272-7080** 847-353-7200

Sentry Watch Inc
1705 Holbrook St . . . . Greensboro NC 27403 **800-632-4961**

Smith Protective Services Inc
1801 Royal Ln Ste 250 . . . . Dallas TX 75229 **800-631-1384** 214-631-4444

UCIT Online Security
6441 Northam Dr . . . . Mississauga ON L4V1J2 **866-756-7847** 905-405-9898

United Security Inc
4295 Arthur Kill Rd . . . . Staten Island NY 10309 **800-874-6434** 718-967-6820

US Security Assoc Inc
200 Mansell Ct 5th Fl . . . . Roswell GA 30076 **800-730-9599** 770-625-1500

Vanguard Products Group Inc
720 Brooker Creek Blvd Ste 223 . . . . Oldsmar FL 34677 **877-477-4874** 813-855-9639

VeriTainer Corp
1127 Pope St . . . . St. Helena CA 94574 **844-344-8796** 707-967-0944

Vinson Guard Service Inc
955 Howard Ave . . . . New Orleans LA 70113 **800-441-7899** 504-529-2260

Wyvern Consulting Ltd
10 N Main St . . . . Yardley PA 19067 **800-946-4626**

---

690   SEED COMPANIES

SEE ALSO Farm Supplies
Seed production and development companies (horticultural and agricultural).

				Toll-Free	Phone

AgriGold Hybrids
5381 Akin Rd . . . . Saint Francisville IL 62460 **800-262-7333**

				Toll-Free	Phone
Albert Lea Seed House					
1414 W Main St	Albert Lea	MN	56007	**800-352-5247**	507-373-3161
Ampac Seed Co					
32727 Hwy 99 E	Tangent	OR	97389	**800-547-3230**	541-928-1651
Foremostco Inc					
8457 NW 66th St	Miami	FL	33166	**800-421-8986**	305-592-8986
Gries Seed Farms Inc					
2348 N Fifth St	Fremont	OH	43420	**800-472-4797**	419-332-55/1
Johnny's Selected Seeds					
955 Benton Ave	Winslow	ME	04901	**877-564-6697**	
JW Jung Seed Co					
335 S High St	Randolph	WI	53956	**800-297-3123**	920-326-3121
Keithly-Williams Seeds Inc					
420 Palm Ave	Holtville	CA	92250	**800-533-3465**	760-356-5533
Latham Seed Co					
131 180th St	Alexander	IA	50420	**877-465-2842**	641-692-3258
Lebanon Seaboard Corp					
1600 E Cumberland St	Lebanon	PA	17042	**800-233-0628**	717-273-1685
Nunhems USA Inc					
1200 Anderson Corner Rd	Parma	ID	83660	**800-733-9505***	208-674-4000
*Cust Svc					
Park Seed Co					
1 Parkton Ave	Greenwood	SC	29647	**800-845-3369***	
*Orders					
Red River Commodities Inc					
501 42nd St N	Fargo	ND	58102	**800-437-5539**	
Renee's Garden					
6060 Graham Hill Rd	Felton	CA	95018	**888-880-7228**	831-335-7228
Schlessman Seed Co					
11513 US Rt 250	Milan	OH	44846	**888-534-7333**	419-499-2572
Seedway LLC 1734 Railroad Pl	Hall	NY	14463	**800-836-3710**	585-526-6391
Sharp Bros Seed Co					
1005 S Sycamore	Healy	KS	67850	**800-462-8483**	620-398-2231
Stock Seed Farms					
28008 Mill Rd	Murdock	NE	68407	**800-759-1520**	402-867-3771
Stratton Seed Co					
1530 Hwy 79 S	Stuttgart	AR	72160	**800-264-4433**	870-673-4433
W Atlee Burpee Co					
300 Park Ave	Warminster	PA	18974	**800-333-5808***	215-674-4900
*Cust Svc					
Wetsel Inc					
961 N Liberty St	Harrisonburg	VA	22802	**800-572-4018***	540-434-6753
*Cust Svc					

691   SEMICONDUCTOR MANUFACTURING SYSTEMS & EQUIPMENT

				Toll-Free	Phone
Advanced Energy Industries Inc					
1625 Sharp Pt Dr	Fort Collins	CO	80525	**800-446-9167**	
NASDAQ: AEIS					
Brooks Automation Inc					
15 Elizabeth Dr	Chelmsford	MA	01824	**800-698-6149**	978-262-2400
NASDAQ: BRKS					
BTU International Inc					
23 Esquire Rd	North Billerica	MA	01862	**800-998-0666**	978-667-4111
NASDAQ: BTUI					
Data I/O Corp					
6464 185th Ave NE Ste 101	Redmond	WA	98052	**800-426-1045**	425-881-6444
NASDAQ: DAIO					
Ebara Technologies Inc					
51 Main Ave	Sacramento	CA	95838	**800-535-5376**	916-920-5451
EG Systems LLC					
6200 Village Pkwy	Dublin	CA	94568	**800-538-5124**	408-528-3000
Fortrend Engineering					
2220 O'Toole Ave	San Jose	CA	95131	**888-937-3637**	408-734-9311
I.B.I.S. Inc					
420 Technology Pkwy Ste 100	Peachtree Corners	GA	30092	**866-714-8422**	770-368-4000
KLA-Tencor Corp					
1 Technology Dr	Milpitas	CA	95035	**800-600-2829**	408-875-3000
NASDAQ: KLAC					
Kokusai Semiconductor Equipment Corp					
2460 N First St Ste 290	San Jose	CA	95131	**800-800-5321**	408-456-2750
Lam Research Corp					
4650 Cushing Pkwy	Fremont	CA	94538	**800-526-7678**	510-572-0200
NASDAQ: LRCX					
MaxLinear Inc					
2051 Palomar Airport Rd Ste 100	Carlsbad	CA	92011	**888-505-4369**	760-692-0711
NYSE: MXL					
Rudolph Technologies Inc					
16 Jonspin Rd	Wilmington	MA	01887	**877-467-8365**	973-691-1300
NASDAQ: RTEC					
Ultratech Inc					
3050 Zanker Rd	San Jose	CA	95134	**800-222-1213**	408-321-8835
NASDAQ: UTEK					
Universal Instruments Corp (UIC)					
33 Broome Corporate Pk	Conklin	NY	13748	**800-842-9732**	607-779-7522
Veeco Instruments Inc					
1 Terminal Dr	Plainview	NY	11803	**888-724-9511**	516-677-0200
NASDAQ: VECO					

692   SEMICONDUCTORS & RELATED DEVICES

SEE ALSO Printed Circuit Boards ; Electronic Components & Accessories - Mfr

				Toll-Free	Phone
8x8 Inc 810 W Maude Ave	Sunnyvale	CA	94085	**888-898-8733**	408-727-1885
NASDAQ: EGHT					
Actel Corp					
2061 Stierlin Ct	Mountain View	CA	94043	**800-262-1060**	650-318-4200
Advanced Micro Devices Inc (AMD)					
1 AMD Pl PO Box 3453	Sunnyvale	CA	94088	**800-538-8450**	408-749-4000
NYSE: AMD					
Advantage Electronic Product Development					
34 Garden Ctr	Broomfield	CO	80020	**866-841-5581**	303-410-0292

				Toll-Free	Phone
Altera Corp					
101 Innovation Dr	San Jose	CA	95134	**800-767-3753***	408-544-7000
NASDAQ: ALTR ■ *Cust Svc					
Analog Devices Inc					
3 Technology Way	Norwood	MA	02062	**800-262-5643**	781-329-4700
NASDAQ: ADI					
Axsun Technologies Inc					
1 Fortune Dr	Billerica	MA	01821	**866-462-9786**	978-262-0049
B & B Electronics Manufacturing Co					
PO Box 1040	Ottawa	IL	61350	**800-346-3119**	815-433-5100
Cirrus Logic Inc					
2901 Via Fortuna	Austin	TX	78746	**800-888-5016**	512-851-4000
NASDAQ: CRUS					
Clare Inc 78 Cherry Hill Dr	Beverly	MA	01915	**800-272-5273**	978-524-6700
Cree Inc 4600 Silicon Dr	Durham	NC	27703	**800-533-2583**	919-313-5300
NASDAQ: CREE					
Cypress Semiconductor Corp					
198 Champion Ct	San Jose	CA	95134	**800-541-4736**	408-943-2600
NASDAQ: CY					
Enphase Energy Inc					
1420 N Mcdowell Blvd	Petaluma	CA	94954	**877-797-4743**	707-763-4784
Epson Electronics America Inc					
214 Devcon Dr	San Jose	CA	95112	**800-228-3964**	408-474-0500
Exar Corp 48720 Kato Rd	Fremont	CA	94538	**855-755-1330**	510-668-7000
NYSE: EXAR					
Fairchild Imaging Inc					
1801 McCarthy Blvd	Milpitas	CA	95035	**800-325-6975**	408-433-2500
GELPAK 31398 Huntwood Ave	Hayward	CA	94544	**888-621-4147**	510-576-2220
Integrated Device Technology Inc					
6024 Silver Creek Valley Rd	San Jose	CA	95138	**800-345-7015**	408-284-8200
NASDAQ: IDTI					
Intel Corp					
2200 Mission College Blvd	Santa Clara	CA	95052	**800-628-8686***	408-765-8080
NASDAQ: INTC ■ *Cust Svc					
Intermolecular Inc					
3011 N First St	San Jose	CA	95134	**877-251-1860**	408-582-5700
Intersil Corp					
1001 Murphy Ranch Rd	Milpitas	CA	95035	**888-468-3774**	408-432-8888
NASDAQ: ISIL					
Kyocera Solar Inc					
7812 E Acoma Dr	Scottsdale	AZ	85260	**800-544-6466**	480-948-8003
Lattice Semiconductor Corp					
5555 NE Moore Ct	Hillsboro	OR	97124	**800-528-8423**	503-268-8000
NASDAQ: LSCC					
M/A-COM Technology Solutions Inc					
100 Chelmsford St	Lowell	MA	01851	**800-366-2266**	978-656-2500
Maxim Integrated Products Inc					
120 San Gabriel Dr	Sunnyvale	CA	94086	**888-629-4642**	408-737-7600
NASDAQ: MXIM					
Microsemi Corp					
2381 Morse Ave	Irvine	CA	92614	**800-713-4113**	949-221-7100
NASDAQ: MSCC					
Mini-Circuits Laboratories Inc					
13 Neptune Ave	Brooklyn	NY	11235	**800-654-7949**	718-934-4500
NVE Corp					
11409 Vly View Rd	Eden Prairie	MN	55344	**800-467-7141**	952-829-9217
NASDAQ: NVEC					
ON Semiconductor Corp					
5005 E McDowell Rd	Phoenix	AZ	85008	**800-282-9855**	602-244-6600
NASDAQ: ON					
OSI Systems Inc					
12525 Chadron Ave	Hawthorne	CA	90250	**800-579-1639**	310-978-0516
NASDAQ: OSIS					
PerkinElmer Inc					
940 Winter St	Waltham	MA	02451	**800-762-4000**	781-663-6050
NYSE: PKI					
Photronics Inc					
15 Secor Rd	Brookfield	CT	06804	**800-292-9396**	203-775-9000
NASDAQ: PLAB					
Plascore Inc 615 N Fairview	Zeeland	MI	49464	**800-630-9257**	616-772-1220
Powerex Inc					
173 Pavilion Ln	Youngwood	PA	15697	**800-451-1415**	724-925-7272
Powerfilm Inc 2337 230th St	Ames	IA	50014	**888-354-7773**	515-292-7606
Ramtron International Corp					
1850 Ramtron Dr	Colorado Springs	CO	80921	**800-541-4736**	719-481-7000
NASDAQ: RMTR					
Seiko Instruments USA Inc					
21221 S Western Ave Ste 250	Torrance	CA	90501	**800-688-0817***	310-517-7700
*Sales					
Sheldahl Inc					
1150 Sheldahl Rd	Northfield	MN	55057	**800-927-3580**	507-663-8000
Silicon Laboratories Inc					
400 W Cesar Chavez St	Austin	TX	78701	**877-444-3032**	512-416-8500
NASDAQ: SLAB					
Solar Solutions & Distribution LLC					
2500 W Fifth Ave	Denver	CO	80204	**855-765-3478**	303-948-6300
Solatube International Inc					
2210 Oak Ridge Way	Vista	CA	92081	**888-765-2882**	760-477-1120
Spectrolab Inc					
12500 Gladstone Ave	Sylmar	CA	91342	**800-936-4888**	818-365-4611
Tellurex Corp					
1462 International Dr	Traverse City	MI	49686	**877-774-7468**	231-947-0110
Texas Instruments Inc					
12500 TI Blvd	Dallas	TX	75243	**800-336-5236***	972-995-2011
NASDAQ: TXN ■ *Cust Svc					
Tezzaron Semiconductor Corp					
7600 Chevy Chase Dr Bldg 2 Ste 300	Austin	TX	78752	**844-839-7364**	630-505-0404
TT Electronics					
1645 Wallace Dr	Carrollton	TX	75006	**800-341-4747**	972-323-2200
United Microelectronics Corp					
488 De Guigne Dr	Sunnyvale	CA	94085	**800-990-1135**	408-523-7800
NYSE: UMC					
Vishay Intertechnology Inc					
63 Lancaster Ave	Malvern	PA	19355	**800-567-6098**	610-644-1300
NYSE: VSH					
Wallco Inc					
53 E Jackson St # 55	Wilkes-Barre	PA	18701	**800-392-5526**	570-823-6161
Xilinx Inc 2100 Logic Dr	San Jose	CA	95124	**800-594-5469**	408-559-7778
NASDAQ: XLNX					

Classified Section

693 — SHEET METAL WORK

SEE ALSO Plumbing, Heating, Air Conditioning Contractors ; Roofing, Siding, Sheet Metal Contractors

Company	City	State	Zip	Toll-Free	Phone
AC Horn & Co 1269 Majesty Dr	Dallas	TX	75247	800-657-6155	214-630-3311
Air Comfort Corp 2550 Braga Dr	Broadview	IL	60155	800-466-3779	708-345-1900
Air Vent Inc 4117 Pinnacle Pnt Dr Ste 400	Dallas	TX	75211	800-247-8368	
All City Metal inc 54-35 46th St	Maspeth	NY	11378	888-682-5757	718-472-5700
Aluminum Line Products Co 24460 Sperry Cir	Westlake	OH	44145	800-321-3154	440-835-8880
Amuneal Manufacturing Corp 4737 Darrah St	Philadelphia	PA	19124	800-755-9843	215-535-3000
Arizona Precision Sheet Metal 2140 W Pinnacle Peak Rd	Phoenix	AZ	85027	800-443-7039	623-516-3700
ASC Profiles Inc 2110 Enterprise Blvd *Cust Svc	West Sacramento	CA	95691	800-360-2477*	916-372-0933
Associated Materials Inc (AMI) 3773 State Rd	Cuyahoga Falls	OH	44223	800-922-6009	
ATS Systems Inc 30222 Esperanza	Rancho Santa Margarita	CA	92688	800-321-1833	949-888-1744
Automated Quality Technologies Inc 563 Shoreview Park Rd	St Paul	MN	55126	800-250-9297	651-484-6544
Ballew's Aluminum Products Inc 2 Shelter Dr	Greer	SC	29650	800-231-6666	864-272-4453
Berger Bldg Products Inc 805 Pennsylvania Blvd *Cust Svc	Feasterville	PA	19053	800-523-8852*	215-355-1200
Captive-aire Systems Inc 4641 Paragon Pk Rd	Raleigh	NC	27616	800-334-9256	919-882-2410
CID Performance Tooling Inc 6 Willey Rd	Saco	ME	04072	800-964-2331	
Contech Construction Products Inc 9025 Centre Pt Dr Ste 400	West Chester	OH	45069	800-338-1122	513-645-7000
Crown Products Company Inc 6390 Phillips Hwy	Jacksonville	FL	32216	800-683-7144	904-737-7144
Custom Metal Fabricators Inc 7601 Whitepine Rd	Richmond	VA	23237	800-220-4084	
Data-Matique 2110 Sherwin St	Garland	TX	75041	866-706-0981	972-272-3446
Daviess County Metal Sales Inc 9929 E US Hwy 50	Cannelburg	IN	47519	800-279-4299	812-486-4299
Dura-Vent Inc 877 Cotting Ct	Vacaville	CA	95688	800-835-4429	707-446-1786
Eastern Sheet Metal LLC 8959 Blue Ash Rd	Blue Ash	OH	45242	800-348-3440	
Elixir Industries Inc 24800 Chrisanta Dr Ste 210	Mission Viejo	CA	92691	800-421-1942	949-860-5000
Epic Metals Corp 11 Talbot Ave	Rankin	PA	15104	877-696-3742	412-351-3913
Eze Lap Diamond Products 3572 Arrowhead Dr	Carson City	NV	89706	800-843-4815	775-888-9500
Flexbar Machine Corp 250 Gibbs Rd	Islandia	NY	11749	800-879-7575	631-582-8440
FS Tool Corp 71 Hobbs Gate	Markham	ON	L3R9T9	800-387-9723	905-475-1999
Gentek Bldg Products Inc 11 Craigwood Rd	Avenel	NJ	07001	800-489-1144	732-381-0900
Girtz Industries Inc 5262 N E Shafer Dr	Monticello	IN	47960	844-464-4789	
H & H Industrial Corp 7612 Rt 130	Pennsauken	NJ	08110	800-982-0341	856-663-4444
Hagerty Steel & Aluminum Co 601 N Main	East Peoria	IL	61611	800-322-2600	309-699-7251
Hamilton Form Company Ltd 7009 Midway Rd	Fort Worth	TX	76118	800-332-7090	817-590-2111
Hutchinson Manufacturing Inc 720 Hwy 7 W PO Box 487	Hutchinson	MN	55350	800-795-1276	320-587-4653
IMM Inc 758 Isenhauer Rd	Grayling	MI	49738	855-202-6384	989-344-7662
Industrial Louvers Inc 511 Seventh St S	Delano	MN	55328	800-328-3421	763-972-2981
Industrial Revolution Inc 5835 Segale Park Dr C	Tukwila	WA	98188	888-297-6062	
Jensen Bridge & Supply Co 400 Stoney Creek Dr PO Box 151	Sandusky	MI	48471	800-270-2852	810-648-3000
Jones Metal Products Inc 3201 Third Ave	Mankato	MN	56001	800-967-1750	507-625-4436
LB Foster Co 415 Holiday Dr NASDAQ: FSTR	Pittsburgh	PA	15220	800-255-4500	
Link-Burns Mfg Company Inc 253 American Way	Voorhees	NJ	08043	800-457-4358	856-429-6844
Linx Industries Inc 2600 Airline Blvd	Portsmouth	VA	23701	800-797-7476	
Lippincott Marine 3420 Main St	Grasonville	MD	21638	877-437-4193	410-827-9300
M K Specialty Metal Fabricators 725 W Wintergreen Rd	Hutchins	TX	75141	866-814-4617	972-225-6562
Major Industries Inc 7120 Stewart Ave	Wausau	WI	54401	888-759-2678	
Mapes Panels LLC 2929 Cornhusker Hwy PO Box 80069	Lincoln	NE	68504	800-228-2391	
Mayco Industries LLC 18 W Oxmoor Rd	Birmingham	AL	35209	800-749-6061	205-942-4242
McCorvey Sheet Metal Works LP 8610 Wallisville Rd	Houston	TX	77029	800-580-7545	713-672-7545
Metal-Era Inc 1600 Airport Rd	Waukesha	WI	53188	800-558-2162	
Metal-Fab Inc 3025 May St	Wichita	KS	67213	800-835-2830	316-943-2351
Metcam Inc 305 Tidwell Cir	Alpharetta	GA	30004	888-394-9633	770-475-9633
Miller-Leaman 800 Orange Ave	Daytona Beach	FL	32114	800-881-0320	386-248-0500
Mitchell Metal Products Inc 19250 Hwy 12 E PO Box 789	Kosciusko	MS	39090	800-258-6137	662-289-7110
Morse Industries Inc 25811 74th Ave S	Kent	WA	98032	800-325-7513	
Murray Sheet Metal Co Inc 3112 Seventh St	Parkersburg	WV	26104	800-464-8801	304-422-5431
Myrmidon Corp 10555 W Little York Rd	Houston	TX	77041	800-880-0771	713-880-0044
National Metal Fabricators 2395 Greenleaf Ave	Elk Grove Village	IL	60007	800-323-8849	
Newjac Inc 415 S Grant St	Lebanon	IN	46052	800-827-3259	765-483-2190
Nu-Way Industries Inc 555 Howard Ave	Des Plaines	IL	60018	888-488-5631	847-298-7710
OMAX Corp 21409 72nd Ave S	Kent	WA	98032	800-838-0343	253-872-2300
Panavise Products Inc 7540 Colbert Dr	Reno	NV	89511	800-759-7535	775-850-2900
Petersen Aluminum Corp 1005 Tonne Rd	Elk Grove Village	IL	60007	800-323-1960	800-722-2523
Pickwick Co 4200 Thomas Dr SW	Cedar Rapids	IA	52404	800-397-9797	
Platt & Labonia Co 70 Stoddard Ave	North Haven	CT	06473	800-505-9099	203-239-5681
Ply Gem 5020 Weston Pkwy Ste 400	Cary	NC	27513	800-786-2726	888-975-9436
Poly Tech Diamond Co 4 E St PO Box 6	North Attleboro	MA	02761	800-365-7659	508-695-3561
Precision Kidd Steel Company Inc 1 Quality Way	Aliquippa	PA	15001	800-945-5003	724-378-7670
Puritan Manufacturing Inc 1302 Grace St	Omaha	NE	68110	800-331-0487	402-341-3753
Quality Air Heating & Cooling Inc 3395 Kraft Ave SE	Grand Rapids	MI	49512	800-723-8431	713-830-9600
Quality Industries Inc 130 Jones Blvd	La Vergne	TN	37086	800-745-8613	615-793-3000
Quality Metal Products Inc 720 Orange Rd	Dallas	PA	18612	888-251-2805	570-333-4248
Quality Tool Inc 1220 Energy Park Dr	Saint Paul	MN	55108	866-997-4647	651-646-7433
Rollex Corp 800 Chasa Ave *Cust Svc	Elk Grove Village	IL	60007	800-251-3300*	
S & S X-Ray Products Inc 10625 Telge Rd	Houston	TX	77095	800-231-1747	281-815-1300
Saint Regis Culvert Inc 202 Morrell St	Charlotte	MI	48813	800-527-4604	517-543-3430
Skyline Products 2903 Delta Dr	Colorado Springs	CO	80910	800-759-9046	
SMT Inc 7300 ACC Blvd	Raleigh	NC	27617	888-214-4804	919-782-4804
Southwark Metal Mfg Company Inc 2800 Red Lion Rd	Philadelphia	PA	19114	800-523-1052	215-735-3401
Spencer Fabrications Inc 29511 County Rd 561	Tavares	FL	32778	866-277-3623	352-343-0014
Spray Enclosure Technologies 1427 N Linden Ave	Rialto	CA	92376	800-535-8196	
Streimer Sheet Metal Works Inc 740 N Knott St	Portland	OR	97227	888-288-3828	503-288-9393
Structures Unlimited Inc 166 River Rd	Bow	NH	03304	800-225-3895	603-645-6539
T & C Industries Inc Royal Basket Trucks Inc 201 Badger Pkwy	Darien	WI	53114	800-426-6447	262-882-1227
Tenere Inc 700 Kelly Ave	Dresser	WI	54009	866-836-3734	715-294-1577
TF System The Vertical ICF Inc 3030c Holmgren Way	Green Bay	WI	54304	800-360-4634	920-983-9960
Thybar Corp 913 S Kay Ave	Addison	IL	60101	800-666-2872	630-543-5300
Titan Air Inc 13901 16th St	Osseo	WI	54758	800-242-9398	715-597-2050
United Tool & Stamping Co of North Carolina Inc 2817 Enterprise Ave	Fayetteville	NC	28306	800-883-6087	910-323-8588
Unruh Fire 100 Industrial Dr	Sedgwick	KS	67135	800-856-7080	
Vent-A-Hood Ltd PO Box 830426	Richardson	TX	75083	800-331-2492	972-235-5201
Wilson Manufacturing Co 4725 Green Park Rd	Saint Louis	MO	63123	800-634-5248	314-416-8900
Wilson Tool International Inc 12912 Farnham Ave	White Bear Lake	MN	55110	800-328-9646	651-286-6000
Wisco Products Inc 109 Commercial St	Dayton	OH	45402	800-367-6570	937-228-2101
York Metal Fabricators Inc 27 NE 26th St	Oklahoma City	OK	73105	800-255-4703	405-528-7495

694 — SHIP BUILDING & REPAIRING

Company	City	State	Zip	Toll-Free	Phone
Colonna's Shipyard Inc 400 E Indian River Rd	Norfolk	VA	23523	800-265-6627	757-545-2414
Continental Maritime of San Diego Inc 1995 Bay Front St	San Diego	CA	92113	877-631-0020	619-234-8851
Elevating Boats LLC 201 Dean Ct	Houma	LA	70363	800-843-2895	985-868-9655
General Dynamics Electric Boat Corp (GDEB) 75 Eastern Pt Rd	Groton	CT	06340	800-742-9692	860-433-3000
Greenbrier Co 1 Centerpointe Dr Ste 200 NYSE: GBX	Lake Oswego	OR	97035	800-343-7188	503-684-7000
Horizon Shipbuilding Inc 13980 Shell Belt Rd	Bayou La Batre	AL	36509	800-777-2014	251-824-1660
Huntington Ingalls Industries Inc 1000 Access Rd	Pascagoula	MS	39568	877-871-2058	228-935-1122
North River Boats Inc 1750 Green Siding Rd	Roseburg	OR	97471	800-413-6351	541-673-2438
Northrop Grumman Newport News 13560 Jefferson Ave	Newport News	VA	23603	888-493-7386	757-886-7777

		Toll-Free	Phone
Pocock Racing Shells 615 80th St SW .... Everett WA 98203		888-762-6251	425-438-9048
Robishaw Engineering Inc 10106 Mathewson Ln .... Houston TX 77043		800-877-1706	713-468-1706
Tecnico Corp 831 Industrial Ave .... Chesapeake VA 23324 *General		800-786-2207*	757-545-4013
Trinity Marine Products Inc 2525 N Stemmons Fwy .... Dallas TX 75207		877-876-5463	214-631-4420
VT Halter Marine Inc 900 Bayou Casotte Pkwy ...... Pascagoula MS 39581		800-639-2715	228-696-6756

695 SHUTTERS - WINDOW (ALL TYPES)

		Toll-Free	Phone
Atlantic Premium Shutters 29797 Beck Rd .... Wixom MI 48393		866-288-2726	248-668-6408
Champion Window Mfg Inc 12121 Champion Way .... Cincinnati OH 45241		877-424-2674	513-346-4600
Commonwealth Laminating & Coating Inc 345 Beaver Creek Dr ...... Martinsville VA 24112 *General		888-321-5111*	276-632-4991
Perfect Shutters Inc 12213 Rte 173 .... Hebron IL 60034		800-548-3336	815-648-2401
Roll Shutter Systems Inc 21633 N 14th Ave .... Phoenix AZ 85027		800-551-7655	623-869-7057
Roll-A-Way Inc 1661 Glenlake Ave .... Itasca IL 60143		866-749-5424	
Rolling Shield Inc 9875 NW 79th Ave ...... Hialeah Gardens FL 33016		800-474-9404	305-436-6661
Shutter Mill Inc 8517 S Perkins Rd .... Stillwater OK 74074		800-416-6455	405-377-6455
Sunburst Shutters 6480 W Flamingo Rd Ste D ...... Las Vegas NV 89103		877-786-2877	702-367-1600
Tapco Group 29797 Beck Rd .... Wixom MI 48393		800-521-7567	248-668-6400

696 SIGNALS & SIRENS - ELECTRIC

		Toll-Free	Phone
ADDCO LLC 240 Arlington Ave E .... Saint Paul MN 55117		800-616-4408	651-488-8600
ECCO 833 W Diamond St .... Boise ID 83705		800-635-5900	
Econolite Control Products Inc 3360 E La Palma Av .... Anaheim CA 92806		800-225-6480	714-630-3700
Federal Signal Corp Emergency Products Div 2645 Federal Signal Dr .... University Park IL 60466		800-264-3578	708-534-3400

697 SIGNS

SEE ALSO Signals & Sirens - Electric ; Displays - Point-of-Purchase ; Displays - Exhibit & Trade Show

		Toll-Free	Phone
Ace Sign Systems Inc 3621 W Royerton Rd .... Muncie IN 47304		800-607-6010	765-288-1000
Ad Art Co 3260 E 26th St .... Los Angeles CA 90058		800-266-7522	323-981-8941
Advance Corp Braille-Tac Div 8200 97th St S .... Cottage Grove MN 55016		800-328-9451	651-771-9297
Allen Industries Inc 6434 Burnt Poplar Rd .... Greensboro NC 27409		800-967-2553	336-668-2791
APCO Graphics Inc 388 Grant St SE .... Atlanta GA 30312		877-988-2726	404-688-9000
Apex Digital Imaging Inc 16057 Tampa Palms Blvd W ...... Tampa FL 33647		866-973-3034	813-973-3034
ASL Services 3700 Commerce Blvd Ste 216 ...... Kissimmee FL 34741		888-744-6275	407-518-7900
Beyond Digital Imaging 36 Apple Creek Blvd .... Markham ON L3R4Y4		888-689-1888	905-415-1888
Brady Corp 6555 W Good Hope Rd .... Milwaukee WI 53223 NYSE: BRC ■ *Cust Svc		800-541-1686*	414-358-6600
Century Graphics & Metals Inc 550 S N Lake Blvd Ste 1000 .... Altamonte Springs FL 32701		800-373-5330	
Colorado Time Systems 1551 E 11th St .... Loveland CO 80537		800-279-0111	970-667-1000
Couch & Philippi Inc 10680 Fern Ave PO Box A ...... Stanton CA 90680 *Orders		800-854-3360*	714-527-2261
Cummings Signs 15 Century Blvd Ste 200 ...... Nashville TN 37214		800-489-7446	
DiAZiT Company Inc 8105 Diazit Dr .... Wake Forest NC 27587 *Cust Svc		800-334-6641*	919-556-5188
Douglas Corp 9650 Valley View Rd ...... Eden Prairie MN 55344		800-806-6113	
Dualite Sales & Service Inc 1 Dualite Ln .... Williamsburg OH 45176		800-543-7271	513-724-7100
Eastern Metal/USA-SIGN 1430 Sullivan St .... Elmira NY 14901 *Sales		800-872-7446*	607-734-2295
Everbrite Inc 4949 S 110th St PO Box 20020 ...... Greenfield WI 53220		800-558-3888	414-529-3500
FASTSIGNS International Inc 2542 Highlander Way .... Carrollton TX 75006		800-327-8744	214-346-5600
Formetco Inc 2963 Pleasant Hill Rd .... Duluth GA 30096		800-367-6382	770-476-7000
GableSigns Inc 7440 Ft Smallwood Rd ...... Baltimore MD 21226		800-854-0568	410-255-6400
Gemini Inc 103 Mensing Way .... Cannon Falls MN 55009		800-538-8377	507-263-3957
Gopher Sign Co 1310 Randolph Ave .... Saint Paul MN 55105		800-383-3156	651-698-5095

		Toll-Free	Phone
Grandwell Industries Inc 6109 S NC Hwy 55 ...... Fuquay Varina NC 27526 *Cust Svc		800-338-6554*	919-557-1221
Graphic Specialties Inc 3110 Washington Ave N .... Minneapolis MN 55411		800-486-4605	612-522-5287
Hall Signs Inc 4495 W Vernal Pk .... Bloomington IN 47404		800-284-7446	
Hallmark Nameplate Inc 1717 E Lincoln Ave .... Mount Dora FL 32757		800-874-9063	
Hy-Ko Products Co 60 Meadow Ln .... Northfield OH 44067		800-292-0550	330-467-7446
Insignia Systems Inc 8799 Brooklyn Blvd .... Minneapolis MN 55445 NASDAQ: ISIG		800-874-4648	763-392-6200
Kessler Sign Co 5804 Poe Ave .... Dayton OH 45414		800-686-1870	937-898-0633
Lake Shore Industries Inc (LSI) 1817 Poplar St PO Box 3427 .... Erie PA 16508		800-458-0463	
LNI Custom Manufacturing Inc 12536 Chadron Ave .... Hawthorne CA 90250		800-338-3387	310-978-2000
LSI Industries Inc 10000 Alliance Rd .... Cincinnati OH 45242 NASDAQ: LYTS		800-436-7800	513-793-3200
M-R Sign Company Inc 1706 First Ave N .... Fergus Falls MN 56537		800-231-5564	218-736-5681
MC Sign Company Inc 8959 Tyler Blvd .... Mentor OH 44060		800-627-4460	440-209-6200
McLoone 75 Sumner St .... La Crosse WI 54603		800-624-6641	608-784-1260
National Stock Sign Co 1040 El Dorado Ave .... Santa Cruz CA 95062		800-462-7726	
O'Ryan Group Inc 4010 Pilot Ste 108 .... Memphis TN 38118		800-253-0750	901-794-4610
Pannier Graphics 345 Oak Rd .... Gibsonia PA 15044		800-544-8428	724-265-4900
Poblocki Sign Company LLC 922 S 70th St .... Milwaukee WI 53214		800-776-7064	414-453-4010
Quality Manufacturing Inc 969 Labore Industrial Ct .... Saint Paul MN 55110		800-243-5473	651-483-5473
Quiel Bros Sign Co 272 S 'I' St .... San Bernardino CA 92410		800-874-7446	909-885-4476
Safeway Sign Co 9875 Yucca Rd .... Adelanto CA 92301		800-637-7233	
Scioto Sign Company Inc 6047 US Rt 68 N .... Kenton OH 43326		800-572-1686	419-673-1261
Sign Builders Inc 4800 Jefferson Ave PO Box 28380 .... Birmingham AL 35228		800-222-7330	
Sign Designs Inc 204 Campus Way .... Modesto CA 95352		800-421-7446	209-524-4484
Sign Resource Inc 6135 District Blvd .... Maywood CA 90270		800-423-4283	323-771-2098
Signs by Tomorrow USA Inc 8681 Robert Fulton Dr .... Columbia MD 21046		800-765-7446	410-312-3600
Signs Now 5368 Dixie Hwy Ste 1 .... Waterford MI 48329		800-356-3373	248-596-8600
Signtech Electrical Adv Inc 4444 Federal Blvd .... San Diego CA 92102		877-885-1135	619-527-6100
Signtronix 1445 W Sepulveda Blvd .... Torrance CA 90501		800-729-4853	
Tube Art Group (TAG) 11715 SE Fifth St .... Bellevue WA 98005		800-562-2854	206-223-1122
U s Nameplate Co 2100 Hwy 30 W PO Box 10 ...... Mount Vernon IA 52314		800-553-8871	319-895-8804
Vomela Co, The 274 E Fillmore Ave .... Saint Paul MN 55107		800-645-1012	651-228-2200
Walter Haas & Sons Inc 123 W 23rd St .... Hialeah FL 33010		800-552-3845	305-883-2257
World Wide Concessions Inc 1950 Old Cuthbert Rd Ste M .... Cherry Hill NJ 08034		888-377-7666	856-933-9900
Worldwide Sign Systems 446 N Cecil St .... Bonduel WI 54107		800-874-3334	
Young Electric Sign Co 2401 Foothill Dr .... Salt Lake City UT 84109		866-779-8357	801-464-4600
Zumar Industries Inc 9719 Santa Fe Springs Rd .... Santa Fe Springs CA 90670		800-654-7446	562-941-4633

698 SILVERWARE

SEE ALSO Cutlery ; Metal Stampings

		Toll-Free	Phone
Old Newbury Crafters 36 Main St .... Amesbury MA 01913		800-343-1388	978-388-4026
Pfaltzgraff Co PO Box 21769 .... York PA 17402		800-999-2811	
Woodbury Pewterers Inc 860 Main St S .... Woodbury CT 06798		800-648-2014	

699 SIMULATION & TRAINING SYSTEMS

		Toll-Free	Phone
CAE Inc 8585 Cote de Liesse .... Saint Laurent QC H4T1G6 NYSE: CAE		866-999-6223	514-341-6780
Energy Concepts Inc 404 Washington Blvd .... Mundelein IL 60060		800-621-1247	847-837-8191
Evans & Sutherland Computer Corp 770 Komas Dr .... Salt Lake City UT 84108 OTC: ESCC ■ *Sales		800-327-5707*	801-588-1000
Faac Inc 1229 Oak Valley Dr .... Ann Arbor MI 48108		877-322-2387	734-761-5836
Meggitt Training Systems Inc 296 Brogdon Rd .... Suwanee GA 30024		800-813-9046	678-288-1090
Nida Corp 300 S John Rodes Blvd .... Melbourne FL 32904		800-327-6432	321-727-2265

700 — SMART CARDS

			Toll-Free	Phone
CardLogix 16 Hughes Ste 100	Irvine CA	92618	**866-392-8326**	949-380-1312
CCS Plas-Tech 180 Shepard Ave	Wheeling IL	60090	**800-747-1269**	847-459-8320
Clever Devices Ltd 300 Crossways Pk Dr	Woodbury NY	11797	**800-872-6129**	516-433-6100
DataCard Corp 11111 Bren Rd W	Minnetonka MN	55343	**800-328-8623**	952-933-1223
Monitor Dynamics Inc 12500 Network Dr Ste 303	San Antonio TX	78249	**866-435-7634**	210-477-5400

701 — SNOWMOBILES

SEE ALSO Sporting Goods

			Toll-Free	Phone
Yamaha Motor Corp USA 6555 Katella Ave *Cust Svc	Cypress CA	90630	**800-962-7926***	

SOFTWARE

SEE Computer Software

702 — SPAS - HEALTH & FITNESS

SEE ALSO Spas - Hotel & Resort ; Weight Loss Centers & Services ; Health & Fitness Centers

Facilities listed here provide multi-day programs designed to increase health and well-being. Types of programs offered include (but are not limited to) relaxation, smoking cessation, weight loss, and physical fitness.

			Toll-Free	Phone
Amerispa 100 boul From the Navy Ste 2A	Varennes QC	J3X2B1	**866-263-7477**	
Black Hills Health & Education Ctr 13815 Battle Creek Rd PO Box 19 *Cust Svc	Hermosa SD	57744	**866-757-0160***	605-255-4101
Cal-a-Vie Spa 29402 Spa Havens Way	Vista CA	92084	**866-772-4283**	760-945-2055
Calistoga Spa Hot Springs 1006 Washington St	Calistoga CA	94515	**866-822-5772**	707-942-6269
City of Wetaskiwin Recreation 4705-50 Ave	Wetaskiwin AB	T9A2E9	**800-419-2913**	780-361-4446
Cooper Wellness Program 12230 Preston Rd	Dallas TX	75230	**800-444-5192**	972-386-4777
Core Health & Fitness LLC 4400 NE 77th Ave Ste 300	Vancouver WA	98662	**888-678-2476**	360-326-4090
Deerfield Spa 650 Resica Falls Rd	East Stroudsburg PA	18302	**800-852-4494**	570-223-0160
Duke Diet & Fitness Ctr (DFC) 501 Douglas St	Durham NC	27705	**800-235-3853**	
Golden Door 777 Deer Springs Rd	San Marcos CA	92069	**866-420-6414**	760-744-5777
Grand Wailea Resort & Spa 3850 Wailea Alanui Dr	Wailea HI	96753	**800-888-6100**	808-875-1234
Green Mountain at Fox Run 262 Fox Ln	Ludlow VT	05149	**800-448-8106**	802-228-8885
Hilton Head Health Institute 14 Valencia Rd	Hilton Head Island SC	29928	**800-292-2440**	843-785-3919
Himalayan Institute Ctr for Health & Healing 952 Bethany Tpke	Honesdale PA	18431	**800-822-4547**	570-253-5551
Hippocrates Health Institute 1466 Hippocrates Way	West Palm Beach FL	33411	**800-842-2125**	561-471-8876
Kripalu Ctr for Yoga & Health 57 Interlaken Rd	Stockbridge MA	01262	**800-741-7353**	413-448-3400
Miraval AZ Resort & Spa 5000 E Via Estancia Miraval	Tucson AZ	85739	**800-232-3969**	
Nautilus Plus Inc 3550 1e Rue	SiŚge Social QC	J3Y8Y5	**800-363-6763**	514-666-5814
Oaks at Ojai 122 E Ojai Ave	Ojai CA	93023	**800-753-6257**	805-646-5573
Ocean Waters Spa 600 N Atlantic Ave	Daytona Beach FL	32118	**844-284-2685**	386-267-1660
Ojo Caliente Mineral Springs Resort 50 Los Banos Dr PO Box 68	Ojo Caliente NM	87549	**800-222-9162**	505-583-2233
Optimum Health Institute 6970 Central Ave	Lemon Grove CA	91945	**800-993-4325**	619-464-3346
Preventure Inc 2000 Nooseneck Hill Rd	Coventry RI	02816	**888-321-4326**	
Pritikin Longevity Ctr & Spa 8755 NW 36th St	Doral FL	33178	**800-327-4914**	888-988-7168
Raj, The 1734 Jasmine Ave	Fairfield IA	52556	**800-248-9050**	641-472-9580
Sagestone Spa & Salon *Red Mountain Resort* 1275 East Red Mtn Cir	Ivins UT	84738	**877-246-4453**	435-673-4905
Spa at Peninsula Beverly Hills 9882 S Santa Monica Blvd	Beverly Hills CA	90212	**800-462-7899**	310-551-2888
Spa at The Setai 2001 Collins Ave	Miami Beach FL	33139	**888-625-7500**	
Structure House 3017 Pickett Rd	Durham NC	27705	**800-553-0052**	855-736-4009
Tennessee Fitness Spa 299 Natural Bridge Pk Rd	Waynesboro TN	38485	**800-235-8365**	931-722-5589
Tracie Martyn Salon 101 Fifth AVE 11th Fl	New York NY	10003	**866-862-7896**	212-206-9333
Two Bunch Palms Resort & Spa 67425 Two Bunch Palms Trl	Desert Hot Springs CA	92240	**800-472-4334**	760-329-8791
Uchee Pines Lifestyle Center 30 Uchee Pines Rd	Seale AL	36875	**877-824-3374**	334-855-4764
Vail Racquet Club 4695 Vail Racquet Club Dr	Vail CO	81657	**800-428-4840**	970-476-4840

703 — SPAS - HOTEL & RESORT

SEE ALSO Spas - Health & Fitness

			Toll-Free	Phone
100 Fountain Spa at the Pillar & Post Inn 48 John St PO Box 48	Niagara-on-the-Lake ON	L0S1J0	**888-669-5566**	905-468-2123
Abbey Resort & Fontana Spa 269 Fontana Blvd	Fontana WI	53125	**800-709-1323**	262-275-9000
Accent Inns Ltd 3233 Maple St	Victoria BC	V8X4Y9	**800-663-0298**	250-475-7500
AdVantis Hospitality Alliance LLC 615 N Highland Ste 2A	Murfreesboro TN	37130	**866-218-4782**	615-904-6133
Aloft Broomfield Denver 8300 Arista Pl	Broomfield CO	80021	**866-716-8143**	303-635-2000
Aloft Chicago O'hare 9700 Balmoral Ave	Rosemont IL	60018	**866-716-8143**	847-671-4444
Alpine Lodge 434 Indian Creek Cir	Branson MO	65616	**888-563-4388**	417-338-2514
Amoray Dive Resort Inc 104250 Overseas Hwy	Key Largo FL	33037	**800-426-6729**	305-451-3595
Ancient Cedars Spa at the Wickaninnish Inn 500 Osprey Ln PO Box 250	Tofino BC	V0R2Z0	**800-333-4604**	250-725-3100
Aria Athletic Club & Spa 1300 Westhaven Dr	Vail CO	81657	**888-824-5772**	970-479-5942
Arizona Biltmore Resort & Spa 2400 E Missouri	Phoenix AZ	85016	**800-950-0086**	602-955-6600
Au Naturel Wellness & Medical Spa at the Brookstreet Hotel 525 Legget Dr	Ottawa ON	K2K2W2	**888-826-2220**	613-271-1800
Auberge De La Fontaine b & b Inn 1301 Rue Rachel E	Montreal QC	H2J2K1	**800-597-0597**	514-597-0166
Baccarat New York LLC 20 W 53rd St	New York NY	10019	**866-957-5139**	212-765-5300
Bartell Hotels 4875 N Harbor Dr	San Diego CA	92106	**800-345-9995**	619-224-1556
Battery Wharf Hotel, Boston Waterfront 3 Battery Wharf	Boston MA	02109	**866-898-3560**	
Best Western Plus Hood River Inn 1108 E Marina Way	Hood River OR	97031	**800-828-7873**	541-386-2200
Beverly Wilshire, A Four Seasons Hotel 9500 Wilshire Blvd	Beverly Hills CA	90212	**800-545-4000**	310-275-5200
Breakers Palm Beach, The 1 S County Rd	Palm Beach FL	33480	**888-273-2537**	561-655-6611
Cape Codder Resort & Spa 1225 Iyanough Rd Rt 132 Bearse's Way	Hyannis MA	02601	**888-297-2200**	508-771-3000
Carefree Resort & Conference Ctr 37220 Mule Train Rd	Carefree AZ	85377	**888-692-4343**	
Carneros Resort & Spa 4048 Sonoma Hwy	Napa CA	94559	**888-400-9000**	707-299-4900
Centre for Well-Being at the Phoenician 6000 E Camelback Rd	Scottsdale AZ	85251	**800-843-2392**	
Chateau Resort & Conference Center, The 475 Camelback Rd	Tannersville PA	18372	**800-245-5900**	570-629-5900
Chateau Rouge 1505 S Broadway Ave	Red Lodge MT	59068	**800-926-1601**	406-446-1601
Cheeca Lodge & Spa 81801 Overseas Hwy Mile Marker 82	Islamorada FL	33036	**800-327-2888**	305-664-4651
Cliff Spa at Snowbird PO Box 929000	Snowbird UT	84092	**800-453-3000**	801-933-2225
Coral Cay Resort 2300 Caravelle Cir	Kissimmee FL	34746	**866-357-3682**	407-787-0718
Cranwell Resort Spa & Golf Club 55 Lee Rd	Lenox MA	01240	**800-272-6935**	413-637-1364
Cupertino Inn 10889 N De Anza Blvd	Cupertino CA	95014	**800-222-4828**	408-996-7700
El Caribe Resort 2125 S Atlantic Ave	Daytona Beach FL	32118	**800-445-9889**	386-252-1558
Elite Island Resorts Inc 1065 SW 30th Ave	Deerfield Beach FL	33442	**800-771-4711**	954-481-8787
Festival Inn, The 1144 Ontario St	Stratford ON	N5A6Z3	**800-463-3581**	519-273-1150
Ford Hotel Supply Company Inc 2204 N Broadway	Saint Louis MO	63102	**800-472-3673**	314-231-8400
Four Seasons Hotels Ltd 2800 Pennsylvania Ave NW	Washington DC	20007	**800-819-5053**	202-342-0444
Four Seasons Resort Maui *Four Seasons Spa* 3900 Wailea Alanui Dr	Maui HI	96753	**800-334-6284**	808-874-8000
Four Seasons Spa at the Four Seasons Hotel Las Vegas 3960 Las Vegas Blvd S	Las Vegas NV	89119	**800-332-3442**	702-632-5302
Four Seasons Spa at the Four Seasons Hotel Los Angeles at Beverly Hills 300 S Doheny Dr	Los Angeles CA	90048	**800-819-5053**	310-786-2229
Four Seasons Spa at the Four Seasons Resort Jackson Hole 7680 Granite Loop Rd PO Box 544	Teton Village WY	83025	**800-819-5053**	307-732-5120
Four Seasons Spa at the Four Seasons Resort Santa Barbara 1260 Ch Dr *General	Santa Barbara CA	93108	**800-819-5053***	805-565-8250
Fox Harb'r Resort & Spa 1337 Fox Harbour Rd	Wallace NS	B0K1Y0	**866-257-1801**	902-257-1801
Galvestonian Condominium Association 1401 E Beach Dr	Galveston TX	77550	**888-526-6161**	409-765-6161
Garden Spa at MacArthur Place 29 E MacArthur St	Sonoma CA	95476	**800-722-1866**	707-933-3193
Glacial Waters Spa at Grand View Lodge 23521 Nokomis Ave	Nisswa MN	56468	**866-801-2951**	
Grand Hotel Marriott Resort Golf Club & Spa 1 Grand Blvd PO Box 639	Point Clear AL	36564	**800-544-9933**	251-928-9201
Green Valley Ranch Resort Casino & Spa 2300 Paseo Verde Pkwy *Resv	Henderson NV	89052	**866-782-9487***	702-617-7777
Greenbrier, The 300 W Main St	White Sulphur Springs WV	24986	**800-453-4858**	304-536-1110
Grove Park Inn Resort & Spa 290 Macon Ave	Asheville NC	28804	**800-438-5800**	
Hermann Sons Life 515 S Saint Marys St PO Box 1941	San Antonio TX	78205	**800-234-4124**	210-226-9261

	City	State	Zip	Toll-Free	Phone
Hilton Short Hills 41 JFK Pkwy	Short Hills	NJ	07078	**800-445-8667**	973-379-0100
Holly Shores Best Holiday 491 Rt 9	Cape May	NJ	08204	**877-494-6559**	
Homestead Resort 700 N Homestead Dr	Midway	UT	84049	**800-327-7220**	435-654-1102
Hotel Mortagne 1228 Rue Nobel	Boucherville	QC	J4B5H1	**877-655-9966**	450-655-9966
Hotel Valencia Riverwalk 150 E Houston St	San Antonio	TX	78205	**855-596-3387**	210-227-9700
Hotel Villagio 6481 Washington St	Yountville	CA	94599	**800-351-1133**	707-944-8877
Hyatt Regency Waikiki Beach Resort & Spa 2424 Kalakaua Ave	Honolulu	HI	96815	**800-233-1234**	
Indian Springs Resort & Spa 1712 Lincoln Ave	Calistoga	CA	94515	**800-877-3623**	707-709-8139
Jefferson Hotel Washington Dc, The 1200 16th St NW	Washington	DC	20036	**877-313-9749**	202-448-2300
Jiminy Peak Mountain Resort LLC 37 Corey Rd	Hancock	MA	01237	**800-835-2364**	413-738-5500
JW Marriott 221 N Rampart Blvd	Las Vegas	NV	89144	**877-869-8777**	702-869-7807
JW Marriott Desert Springs Resort & Spa 74855 Country Club Dr	Palm Desert	CA	92260	**888-538-9459**	760-341-2211
Kahala Hotel & Resort, The 5000 Kahala Ave	Honolulu	HI	96816	**800-367-2525**	808-739-8938
Kea Lani Spa at the Fairmont Kea Lani Maui 4100 Wailea Alanui Dr	Maui	HI	96753	**800-659-4100**	808-875-2229
Kohler Waters Spa 444 Highland Dr	Kohler	WI	53044	**800-344-2838**	
Lafayette Park Hotel 3287 Mt Diablo Blvd	Lafayette	CA	94549	**855-382-8632**	800-394-3112
Lake Austin Spa Resort 1705 S Quinlan Pk Rd	Austin	TX	78732	**800-847-5637**	512-372-7380
Le Baluchon Eco-resort 3550 chemin des Trembles	Saint-Paulin	QC	J0K3G0	**800-789-5968**	819-268-2555
Lido Beach Resort 700 Ben Franklin Dr	Sarasota	FL	34236	**800-441-2113**	941-388-2161
Living Spa at El Monte Sagrado 317 Kit Carson Rd	Taos	NM	87571	**855-846-8267**	575-758-3502
Loews Hotels 4000 Coronado Bay Rd	Coronado	CA	92118	**800-674-1397**	619-628-8770
Magnuson Hotels 525 E Mission Ave	Spokane	WA	99202	**866-904-1309**	
Mii Amo at Enchantment Resort 525 Boynton Canyon Rd	Sedona	AZ	86336	**888-749-2137**	928-203-8500
Mirbeau Inn & Spa 851 W Genesee St	Skaneateles	NY	13152	**877-647-2328**	315-685-5006
MODERN Honolulu, The 1775 Ala Moana Blvd	Honolulu	HI	96815	**855-599-9604**	808-943-5800
Mokara Hotel & Spa 212 W Crockett St	San Antonio	TX	78205	**866-605-1212**	210-396-5800
Motif Seattle 1415 Fifth Ave	Seattle	WA	98101	**855-515-1144**	206-971-8000
Mountain Laurel Spa at Stonewall Resort 940 Resort Dr	Roanoke	WV	26447	**888-278-8150**	304-269-7400
Music Road Resort Inc 303 Henderson Chapel Rd	Pigeon Forge	TN	37863	**844-993-9644**	
Northern Rockies Lodge Mile 462 Alaska Hwy	Muncho Lake	BC	V0C1Z0	**800-663-5269**	250-776-3481
Ohio House Motel 600 N La Salle Dr	Chicago	IL	60654	**866-601-6446**	312-943-6000
Omni Interlocken Resort 500 Interlocken Blvd	Broomfield	CO	80021	**800-843-6664**	303-438-6600
Osprey Valley Resorts 18821 Main St	Alton	ON	L7K1R1	**800-833-1561**	519-927-9034
Pala Casino Resort & Spa 11154 Hwy 76	Pala	CA	92059	**877-946-7252**	760-510-5100
Peaks Resort & Golden Door Spa 136 Country Club Dr	Telluride	CO	81435	**800-789-2220**	
Pineapple Hospitality Co 155 108th Ave NE	Bellevue	WA	98004	**866-866-7977**	
Portofino Spa at Portofino Island Resort 10 Portofino Dr	Pensacola Beach	FL	32561	**877-523-2016**	
Post Ranch Inn Hwy 1 PO Box 219	Big Sur	CA	93920	**800-527-2200**	831-667-2200
Raindance Spa at the Lodge at Sonoma Renaissance Resort 1325 Broadway	Sonoma	CA	95476	**866-263-0758**	707-935-6600
Resort at Squaw Creek 400 Squaw Creek Rd PO Box 3333	Olympic Valley	CA	96146	**800-327-3353**	530-583-6300
Revere Hotel Boston Common 200 Stuart St	Boston	MA	02116	**855-673-8373**	617-482-1800
Riotel Group 250 Ave du Phare Est	Matane	QC	G4W3N4	**877-566-2651**	418-566-2651
Ritz-Carlton Hotel Co LLC, The 10400 Fernwood Rd	Bethesda	MD	20817	**800-542-8680**	301-380-3000
Safety Harbor Resort & Spa 105 North Bayshore Dr	Safety Harbor	FL	34695	**888-237-8772**	
Sanctuary Beach Resort Monterey Bay 3295 Dunes Rd	Marina	CA	93933	**855-693-6583**	831-883-9478
Scott Resort & Spa, The 4925 N Scottsdale Rd *Resv	Scottsdale	AZ	85251	**800-528-7867***	
Seasons Restaurant at Highland Lake Inn 86 Lilly Pad Ln	Flat Rock	NC	28731	**800-635-5101**	828-696-9094
Secret Garden Spa at the Prince of Wales Hotel 6 Picton St	Niagara-on-the-Lake	ON	L0S1J0	**888-669-5566**	905-468-3246
Senator Inn & Spa of Augusta 284 Western Ave	Augusta	ME	04330	**877-772-2224**	207-622-5804
Shell Island Ocean Front Suites 2700 N Lumina Ave	Wrightsville Beach	NC	28480	**800-689-6765**	910-256-8696
Sheraton Agoura Hills Hotel 30100 Agoura Rd	Agoura Hills	CA	91301	**866-716-8134**	818-707-1220
Sheraton Denver Tech Center Hotel 7007 S Clinton St	Greenwood Village	CO	80112	**800-525-3177**	303-799-6200
Sheraton Fishermans Wharf (San Francisco, CA) 2500 Mason St	San Francisco	CA	94133	**866-716-8134**	415-362-5500
Sheraton Gunter Hotel 205 E Houston St	San Antonio	TX	78205	**866-716-8134**	210-227-3241
Sheraton Lake Buena Vista 12205 S Apopka Vineland Rd	Orlando	FL	32836	**800-325-3535**	407-239-0444
Sheraton Phoenix Downtown Hotel 340 N Third St	Phoenix	AZ	85004	**866-716-8134**	602-262-2500
Sheraton Raleigh Hotel 421 S Salisbury St	Raleigh	NC	27601	**888-627-8319**	919-834-9900
Sheraton Washington North Hotel 4095 Powder Mill Rd	Beltsville	MD	20705	**888-627-8646**	301-937-4422
Shui Spa at Crowne Pointe Historic Inn 82 Bradford St	Provincetown	MA	02657	**877-276-9631**	508-487-6767
Sixty Hotels 206 Spring St 4th Fl	New York	NY	10012	**877-431-0400**	
Solage Calistoga 755 Silverado Trl	Calistoga	CA	94515	**866-942-7442**	
Spa at Big Cedar Lodge 190 Top of the Rock Rd	Ridgedale	MO	65739	**800-225-6343**	417-339-5201
Spa at Kingsmill Resort 1010 Kingsmill Rd	Williamsburg	VA	23185	**800-965-4772**	757-253-8230
Spa at Le Merigot JW Marriott Beach Hotel Santa Monica 1740 Ocean Ave	Santa Monica	CA	90401	**888-236-2427**	310-395-9700
Spa at Pebble Beach 1518 Cypress Dr	Pebble Beach	CA	93953	**800-654-9300**	831-649-7615
Spa at Pinehurst Resort 80 Carolina Vista Dr	Pinehurst	NC	28374	**800-487-4653**	910-235-8320
Spa at the Broadmoor 1 Lake Ave	Colorado Springs	CO	80906	**800-634-7711**	719-634-7711
Spa at the Chattanoogan 1201 Broad St	Chattanooga	TN	37402	**800-619-0018**	423-756-3400
Spa at the Equinox Resort 3567 Main St	Manchester Village	VT	05254	**800-362-4747**	
Spa at the Fairmont Inn Sonoma Mission Inn 100 Boyes Blvd	Sonoma	CA	95476	**866-540-4499**	707-938-9000
Spa at the Hotel Hershey 100 Hotel Rd	Hershey	PA	17033	**877-772-9988**	717-520-5888
Spa at the Norwich Inn 607 W Thames St	Norwich	CT	06360	**800-275-4772**	860-425-3500
Spa at the Saddlebrook Resort 5700 Saddlebrook Way	Wesley Chapel	FL	33543	**800-729-8383**	813-907-4419
Spa at the Sagamore 110 Sagamore Rd	Bolton Landing	NY	12814	**866-384-1944**	518-743-6081
Spa at the Sanderling Resort 1461 Duck Rd	Duck	NC	27949	**855-412-7866**	
Spa at White Oaks Conference Resort 253 Taylor Rd	Niagara-on-the-Lake	ON	L0S1J0	**800-263-5766**	905-641-2599
Spa Terre at LaPlaya Beach & Golf Resort 9891 Gulf Shore Dr	Naples	FL	34108	**800-237-6883**	239-597-3123
Spa Terre at Paradise Point Resort 1404 Vacation Rd	San Diego	CA	92109	**800-344-2626**	858-581-5998
Spa Terre at the Inn & Spa at Loretto 211 Old Santa Fe Trl	Santa Fe	NM	87501	**800-727-5531**	505-984-7997
Spa Toccare at Borgata Hotel Casino 1 Borgata Way	Atlantic City	NJ	08401	**877-448-5833**	609-317-7235
SpaHalekulani at the Halekulani Hotel 2199 Kalia Rd	Honolulu	HI	96815	**800-367-2343**	808-931-5322
Sportsmen's Lodge Hotel 12825 Ventura Blvd	Studio City	CA	91604	**800-821-8511**	818-769-4700
Surf & Sand Resort 1555 S Coast Hwy	Laguna Beach	CA	92651	**877-741-5908**	877-751-5493
Tampa Marriott Waterside Hotel & Marina 700 S Florida Ave	Tampa	FL	33602	**888-268-1616**	813-221-4900
TMI Hospitality 4850 32nd Ave S	Fargo	ND	58104	**800-210-8223**	701-235-1060
Toll House Hotel 140 S Santa Cruz Ave	Los Gatos	CA	95030	**800-238-6111**	408-395-7070
Treasure Island Resort & Casino 5734 Sturgeon Lake Rd	Welch	MN	55089	**800-222-7077**	
Trump Soho New York 725 Fifth Ave	New York	NY	10022	**855-878-6700**	
Tulalip Resort Casino 10200 Quil Ceda Blvd	Tulalip	WA	98271	**888-272-1111**	
U hotel Fifth Avenue 373 Fifth Ave	New York	NY	10016	**800-315-4642**	212-213-3388
Vail Marriott Mountain Resort 715 W Lionshead Cir	Vail	CO	81657	**800-648-0720**	970-476-4444
Vail Mountain Lodge & Spa, The 352 E Meadow Dr	Vail	CO	81657	**888-794-0410**	970-476-0700
Well Spa at Miramonte Resort 45000 Indian Wells Ln	Indian Wells	CA	92210	**800-237-2926**	760-837-1652
Westglow Resort & Spa 224 Westglow Cir	Blowing Rock	NC	28605	**800-562-0807**	828-295-4463
Westin Kierland Resort & Spa 6902 E Greenway Pkwy	Scottsdale	AZ	85254	**800-354-5892**	480-624-1000
Westin Resort & Spa 4090 Whistler Way	Whistler	BC	V0N1B4	**888-627-8979**	604-905-5000
Willow Stream Spa at Fairmont Scottsdale Princess 7575 E Princess Dr	Scottsdale	AZ	85255	**800-908-9540**	480-585-2732
Willow Stream Spa at the Fairmont Banff Springs 405 Spray Ave	Banff	AB	T1L1J4	**800-404-1772**	403-762-1772
Willow Stream Spa at the Fairmont Empress 633 Humboldt St	Victoria	BC	V8W1A6	**866-854-7444**	250-995-4650
Wingate by Wyndham Calgary Hotel 400 Midpark Way SE	Calgary	AB	T2X3S4	**800-228-1000**	403-514-0099

704 SPEAKERS BUREAUS

	City	State	Zip	Toll-Free	Phone
AEI Speakers Bureau 300 Western Ave Ste 2	Allston	MA	02134	**800-447-7325**	617-782-3111
Capitol City Speakers Bureau 1620 S Fifth St	Springfield	IL	62703	**800-397-3183**	217-544-8552
Elk Valley Rancheria 2332 Howland Hill Rd	Crescent City	CA	95531	**866-464-4680**	707-464-4680
Executive Speakers Bureau 3012 Ctr Oak Way Ste 102	Germantown	TN	38138	**800-754-9404**	901-754-9404

	Toll-Free	Phone

Florexpo LLC
1960 Kellogg Ave ....Carlsbad CA 92008 **800-830-3567**

Justifacts Credential Verification Inc
5250 Logan Ferry Rd ....Murrysville PA 15668 **800-356-6885**

Key Speakers Bureau Inc
3500 E Coast Hwy Ste 6 .... Corona del Mar CA 92625 **800-675-1175** 949-675-7856

Leading Authorities Inc
1725 Eye St NW Ste 200............... Washington DC 20006 **855-827-0943**

National Speakers Bureau
1177 W Broadway Ste 300 .... Vancouver BC V6H1G3 **800-661-4110** 604-734-3663

National Speakers Bureau Inc
14047 W Petronalla Dr Ste 102 .... Libertyville IL 60048 **800-323-9442** 847-295-1122

Santa Barbara Speakers Bureau (SBSB)
500 E Montecito St ....Santa Barbara CA 93103 **800-676-1266** 805-966-9222

Speak Inc Speakers Bureau
10680 Treena St Ste 230....................San Diego CA 92131 **800-677-3324** 858-228-3771

Speakers Unlimited
PO Box 27225 ....Columbus OH 43227 **888-333-6676** 614-864-3703

Steven Barclay Agency
12 Western Ave ....Petaluma CA 94952 **888-965-7323** 707-773-0654

705   SPEED CHANGERS, INDUSTRIAL HIGH SPEED DRIVES, GEARS

SEE ALSO Power Transmission Equipment - Mechanical ; Machine Shops ; Motors (Electric) & Generators ; Controls & Relays - Electrical ; Automotive Parts & Supplies - Mfr ; Aircraft Parts & Auxiliary Equipment

	Toll-Free	Phone

Bison Gear & Engineering Corp
3850 Ohio Ave .... Saint Charles IL 60174 **800-282-4766** 630-377-4327

Charles Bond Co
11 Green St PO Box 105.....................Christiana PA 17509 **800-922-0125** 610-596-5171

Cleveland Gear Co
3249 E 80th St .... Cleveland OH 44104 **800-423-3169** 216-641-9000

Columbia Gear Corp
530 County Rd 50 ....Avon MN 56310 **800-323-9838** 320-356-7301

Cone Drive Operations Inc - A Textron Co
240 E 12th St ....Traverse City MI 49684 **888-994-2663*** 231-946-8410
*Sales

Control Techniques Americas
7078 Shady Oak Rd .... Eden Prairie MN 55344 **800-893-2321** 952-995-8000

Curtis Machine Company Inc
2500 E Trl St ....Dodge City KS 67801 **800-835-9166** 620-227-7164

Dalton Gear Co
212 Colfax Ave N .... Minneapolis MN 55405 **800-328-7485** 612-374-2150

Designatronics Inc
2101 Jericho Tpke ....New Hyde Park NY 11040 **800-345-1144*** 800-819-8900
*Orders

Emerson Industrial Automation
8000 W Florissant Ave PO Box 4100 .... St Louis MO 63136 **888-213-0970** 314-553-2000

Fairchild Industrial Products Co
3920 Westpoint Blvd ....Winston-Salem NC 27103 **800-334-8422** 336-659-3400

Hub City Inc
2914 Industrial Ave .... Aberdeen SD 57401 **800-482-2489** 605-225-0360

Kurz Industrial Solutions
1325 McMahon Dr ....Neenah WI 54956 **800-776-3629** 920-886-8200

Lenze 630 Douglas St ....Uxbridge MA 01569 **800-217-9100** 508-278-9100

Nuttall Gear LLC
2221 Niagra Falls Blvd .... Niagara Falls NY 14304 **800-724-6710** 716-298-4100

Piller Inc 45 Turner Rd .... Middletown NY 10941 **800-597-6937**

Regal-Beloit Corp
200 State St ....Beloit WI 53511 **800-672-6495** 608-364-8800
NYSE: RBC

Regal-Beloit Corp Durst Div
PO Box 298 ....Beloit WI 53512 **800-356-0775** 608-365-2563

Richmond Gear PO Box 238 .... Liberty SC 29657 **800-934-2727*** 864-843-9231
*Sales

Rush Gears Inc
550 Virginia Dr ....Fort Washington PA 19034 **800-523-2576**

Sterling Electric Inc
7997 Allison Ave .... Indianapolis IN 46268 **800-654-6220*** 317-872-0471
*Cust Svc

Sumitomo Machinery Corp of America
4200 Holland Blvd .... Chesapeake VA 23323 **800-762-9256** 757-485-3355

Superior Gearbox Co
803 W Hwy 32 .... Stockton MO 65785 **800-346-5745** 417-276-5191

TECO-Westinghouse Motor Co
5100 N IH-35 ....Round Rock TX 78681 **800-451-8798** 512-255-4141

706   SPORTING GOODS

SEE ALSO Cord & Twine ; Tarps, Tents, Covers ; Handbags, Totes, Backpacks ; Firearms & Ammunition (Non-Military) ; Motor Vehicles - Commercial & Special Purpose ; Boats - Recreational ; Bicycles & Bicycle Parts & Accessories ; Personal Protective Equipment & Clothing ; Exercise & Fitness Equipment ; Gym & Playground Equipment ; Swimming Pools ; Snowmobiles ; All-Terrain Vehicles

	Toll-Free	Phone

Acushnet holdings Corp
333 Bridge St ....Fairhaven MA 02719 **800-225-8500** 508-979-2000

AcuSport Corp
1 Hunter Pl ....Bellefontaine OH 43311 **800-543-3150** 937-593-7010

Adams USA Inc
610 S Jefferson Ave ....Cookeville TN 38501 **800-426-9784**

Aldila Inc
14145 Danielson St Ste B.......................Poway CA 92064 **800-854-2786** 858-513-1801
OTC: ALDA

American Sports
74 Albe Dr Ste 1 ....Newark DE 19702 **866-207-3179**

AMF Bowling Worldwide Inc
7313 Bell Creek Rd .... Mechanicsville VA 23111 **800-342-5263**

Aqua-Leisure Industries Inc
PO Box 239 ....Avon MA 02322 **866-807-3998**

	Toll-Free	Phone

Aqualung America Inc
2340 Cousteau Ct ....Vista CA 92083 **800-446-2671** 760-597-5000

Atomic USA 2030 Lincoln Ave ....Ogden UT 84401 **800-258-5020**

Bankshot Sports Organization
330-U N Stonestreet Ave Ste 504 ....Rockville MD 20852 **800-933-0140** 301-309-0260

Bauer Premium Fly Reels
585 Clover Ln Ste 1 ....Ashland OR 97520 **888-484-4165** 541-488-8246

Big Rock Sports LLC
173 Hankison Dr ....Newport NC 28570 **800-334-2661** 252-808-3500

Biscayne Rod Manufacturing Inc
425 E Ninth St ....Hialeah FL 33010 **866-969-0808** 305-884-0808

Bison Inc 603 L St ....Lincoln NE 68508 **800-247-7668** 402-474-3353

Bravo Sports Corp
12801 Carmenita Rd .... Santa Fe Springs CA 90670 **800-234-9737*** 562-484-5100
*Cust Svc

Bridgestone Golf Inc
15320 Industrial Pk Blvd NE ....Covington GA 30014 **800-358-6319** 770-787-7400

Callaway Golf Co
2180 Rutherford Rd ....Carlsbad CA 92008 **800-588-9836** 760-931-1771
NYSE: ELY

Cascade Designs Inc
4000 First Ave S ....Seattle WA 98134 **800-531-9531*** 206-505-9500
*Cust Svc

Century Tool & Mfg
90 McMillen Rd ....Antioch IL 60002 **800-635-3831**

Cleveland Golf Co
5601 Skylab Rd ....Huntington Beach CA 92647 **800-999-6263***
*Cust Svc

Cobra Mfg Co Inc
7909 E 148th St S ....Bixby OK 74008 **800-352-6272**

Coleman Company Inc
3600 North Hydraulic ....Wichita KS 67219 **800-835-3278***
*Cust Svc

Columbia Industries Inc
PO Box 746 ....Hopkinsville KY 42241 **800-531-5920** 270-881-1200

Daisy Outdoor Products
400 W Stribling Dr ....Rogers AR 72756 **800-643-3458** 479-636-1200

Daiwa Corp 11137 Warland Dr .... Cypress CA 90630 **800-736-4653** 562-375-6800

Douglas Industries Co
3441 S 11th Ave ....Eldridge IA 52748 **800-553-8907** 563-285-4162

Dover Saddlery Inc
525 Great Rd ....Littleton MA 01460 **800-406-8204** 978-952-8062
NASDAQ: DOVR

Eagle One Golf Products Inc
1340 N Jefferson St ....Anaheim CA 92807 **800-448-4409** 714-983-0050

Ebonite International Inc
PO Box 746 ....Hopkinsville KY 42241 **800-326-6483** 270-881-1200

Eddyline Kayaks
11977 Westar Ln ....Burlington WA 98233 **800-635-5205** 360-757-2300

Eppinger Manufacturing Co
6340 Schaefer Rd ....Dearborn MI 48126 **888-771-8277** 313-582-3205

Escalade Inc
817 Maxwell Ave ....Evansville IN 47711 **800-426-1421*** 812-467-1200
NASDAQ: ESCA ■ *Cust Svc

Franklin Sports Inc
17 Campanelli Pkwy ....Stoughton MA 02072 **800-225-8649** 781-344-1111

G & H Decoys Inc
PO Box 1208 ....Henryetta OK 74437 **800-443-3269*** 918-652-3314
*Orders

Gamma Sports
200 Waterfront Dr ....Pittsburgh PA 15222 **800-333-0337** 412-323-0335

Gared Sports Inc
707 N Second St Ste 220 ....Saint Louis MO 63102 **800-325-2682** 314-421-0044

Gill Athletics Inc
2808 Gemini Ct ....Champaign IL 61822 **800-637-3090*** 217-367-8438
*Cust Svc

Goal Sporting Goods Inc
37 Industrial Pk Rd PO Box 236 .... Essex CT 06426 **800-334-4625** 860-767-9112

Goals & Poles
7575 Jefferson Hwy ....Baton Rouge LA 70806 **800-275-0317** 225-923-0622

Goalsetter Systems Inc
1041 Cordova Ave ....Lynnville IA 50153 **800-362-4625**

GolfWorks, The
4820 Jacksontown Rd PO Box 3008 ....Newark OH 43058 **800-848-8358** 740-328-4193

HEAD USA Inc
3125 Sterling Cir Ste 101.......................Boulder CO 80301 **800-874-3235**

Hoyt
543 N Neil Armstrong Rd ....Salt Lake City UT 84116 **800-474-8733** 801-363-2990

Hunter Co
3300 W 71st Ave ....Westminster CO 80030 **800-676-4868** 303-427-4626

Intex Recreation Corp
1665 Hughes Way .... Long Beach CA 90810 **800-234-6839***
*Cust Svc

Jayhawk Bowling Supply & Equipment Inc
355 N Iowa St PO Box 685 ....Lawrence KS 66044 **800-255-6436** 785-842-3237

Jerry's Sport Ctr Inc
100 Capital Rd ....Jenkins Township PA 18640 **800-234-2612**

Jugs Sports
11885 SW Herman Rd ....Tualatin OR 97062 **800-547-6843**

K2 Sports 4201 Sixth Ave S ....Seattle WA 98108 **800-426-1617** 206-805-4800

KL Industries Inc
1790 Sun Dolphin Dr ....Muskegon MI 49444 **800-733-2727** 231-733-2725

Kolpin Powersports
9955 59th Ave N ....Plymouth MN 55442 **877-956-5746** 920-928-3118

Kwik Goal Ltd
140 Pacific Dr ....Quakertown PA 18951 **800-531-4252** 215-536-2200

Lamartek Inc
175 NW Washington St ....Lake City FL 32055 **800-495-1046*** 386-752-1087
*Orders

Lifetime Products Inc
Freeport Ctr Bldg D-11
PO Box 160010. ....Clearfield UT 84016 **800-242-3865** 801-776-1532

Lobster Sports Inc
7340 Fulton Ave ....North Hollywood CA 91605 **800-210-5992** 818-764-6000

MacNeill Engineering Company Inc
140 Locke Dr ....Marlborough MA 01752 **800-652-4267** 508-481-8830

Manns Bait Co
1111 State Docks Rd ....Eufaula AL 36027 **800-841-8435** 334-687-5716

			Toll-Free	Phone
Maravia Corp of Idaho				
602 E 45th St	Boise ID	83714	**800-223-7238**	208-322-4949
Mares America Corp				
1 Selleck St	Norwalk CT	06855	**800-874-3236**	203-855-0631
Master Industries Inc				
1001 S Linwood Ave	Santa Ana CA	92705	**800-854-3794**	714-361-9767
Mizuno USA				
4925 Avalon Ridge Pkwy	Norcross GA	30071	**800-966-1211**	770-441-5553
Moultrie Feeders				
150 Industrial Rd	Alabaster AL	35007	**800-653-3334**	205-664-6700
Murrey International Inc				
14150 S Figueroa St	Los Angeles CA	90061	**800-421-1022**	310-532-6091
National Billiard Manufacturing Co				
3315 Eugenia Ave	Covington KY	41015	**800-543-0880**	859-431-4129
North Face, The				
14450 Doolittle Dr	San Leandro CA	94577	**855-500-8639**	877-992-0111
O'Brien International				
14615 NE 91st St	Redmond WA	98052	**800-662-7436**	425-881-5900
O'Neill Wetsuits USA				
1071 41st Ave	Santa Cruz CA	95063	**800-213-6444**	831-475-7500
Ocean Kayak				
125 Gilman Falls Ave Bldg B	Old Town ME	04468	**800-852-9257**	
Ocean Management Systems Inc				
2021 Goshen Tpke	Wallkill NY	12589	**800-325-8439**	619-236-1203
Oceanic USA				
2002 Davis St	San Leandro CA	94577	**800-435-3483**	888-270-8595
Old Town Canoe Co				
125 Gilman Falls Ave Bldg B	Old Town ME	04468	**800-343-1555**	207-827-1530
Orvis International Travel				
178 Conservation Way	Sunderland VT	05250	**800-547-4322**	888-235-9763
Penn Fishing Tackle Manufacturing Co				
7 Science Ct	Columbia SC	29203	**800-892-5444**	
Penn Inc 306 S 45th Ave	Phoenix AZ	85043	**800-289-7366**	
Pentair Ltd				
1351 Rt 55	Lagrangeville NY	12450	**888-711-7487**	845-463-7200
PIC Skate 22 Village Dr	Riverside RI	02915	**800-882-3448**	401-490-9334
Ping Inc				
2201 W Desert Cove Ave PO Box 82000	Phoenix AZ	85071	**800-474-6434**	602-687-5000
Poolmaster Inc				
770 Del Paso Rd	Sacramento CA	95834	**800-854-1492**	916-567-9800
Precision Shooting Equipment Inc				
2727 N Fairview Ave	Tucson AZ	85705	**800-477-7789**	520-884-9065
Resilite Sports Products				
PO Box 764	Sunbury PA	17801	**800-843-6287**	
Riedell Shoes Inc				
122 Cannon River Ave	Red Wing MN	55066	**800-698-6893**	651-388-8251
RL Winston Rod Co				
500 S Main St	Twin Bridges MT	59754	**866-946-7637**	406-684-5674
Rome Specialty Company Inc Rosco Div				
501 W Embargo St	Rome NY	13440	**800-794-8357**	315-337-8200
RSR Group Inc				
4405 Metric Dr	Winter Park FL	32792	**800-541-4867**	407-677-1000
Saunders Archery Co				
1874 14th Ave PO Box 1707	Columbus NE	68601	**800-228-1408***	402-564-7176
*Cust Svc				
Scott Fly Rod Co				
2355 Air Pk Way	Montrose CO	81401	**800-728-7208**	970-249-3180
Scott USA Inc				
PO Box 2030	Sun Valley ID	83353	**800-292-5874**	208-622-1000
Sea Eagle Boats Inc				
19 N Columbia St Ste 1	Port Jefferson NY	11777	**800-748-8066**	631-791-1799
Seeker Rod Co				
700 N Batavia Unit B	Orange CA	92868	**800-373-3537**	714-769-1700
Shakespeare Fishing Tackle Co				
7 Science Ct	Columbia SC	29203	**800-466-5643***	803-754-7000
*Cust Svc				
Simms Fishing Products Corp				
101 Evergreen Dr	Bozeman MT	59715	**800-217-4667**	406-585-3557
Skate One				
30 S La Patera Ln	Santa Barbara CA	93117	**800-288-7528**	805-964-1330
Spalding PO Box 90015	Bowling Green KY	42103	**855-253-4533**	
Storm Products Inc				
165 S 800 W	Brigham City UT	84302	**800-369-4402**	435-723-0403
Toobs Inc 347 Quintana Rd	Morro Bay CA	93442	**800-795-8662**	
True Temper Sports				
8275 Tournament Dr Ste 200	Memphis TN	38125	**800-355-8783**	
Underwater Kinetics (UK)				
13400 Danielson St	Poway CA	92064	**800-852-7483**	858-513-9100
Weed USA Inc				
5780 Harrow Glen Ct	Galena OH	43021	**800-933-3758**	740-548-3881
West Coast Trends				
17811 Jamestown Ln	Huntington Beach CA	92647	**800-736-4568**	714-843-9288
Wiley's Waterski Pro Shop				
1417 S Trenton St	Seattle WA	98108	**800-962-0785**	206-762-1300
Wilson Sporting Goods Co				
8750 W Bryn Mawr Ave	Chicago IL	60631	**800-874-5930**	800-800-9936
Wittek Golf Supply Co Inc				
300 Bond St	Elk Grove Village IL	60007	**800-869-1800**	
Worldwide Golf Shops				
1421 Village Way	Santa Ana CA	92705	**888-216-5252**	714-972-3695
Worth Co, The				
214 Sherman Ave PO Box 88	Stevens Point WI	54481	**800-944-1899**	715-344-6081
Yakima Bait Company Inc				
PO Box 310	Granger WA	98932	**800-527-2711**	509-854-1311
Yamaha Motor Corp USA				
6555 Katella Ave	Cypress CA	90630	**800-962-7926***	
*Cust Svc				
Yonex Corp				
20140 S Western Ave	Torrance CA	90501	**800-449-6639**	424-201-4800

707   SPORTING GOODS STORES

			Toll-Free	Phone
3balls LLC PO Box 90083	Raleigh NC	27675	**888-289-0300**	919-987-3222
5 Star Equine Products Inc				
4589 Hwy 71 S	Hatfield AR	71945	**800-533-3377**	870-389-6328

			Toll-Free	Phone
Academy Sports & Outdoors				
1800 N Mason Rd	Katy TX	77449	**888-922-2336**	281-646-5200
Aero Tech Designs Cycling Apparel				
1132 Fourth Ave	Coraopolis PA	15108	**800-783-8326**	412-262-3255
AFP International LLC				
1730 Berkeley St	Santa Monica CA	90404	**888-895-0547**	310-559-9949
Ambush Boarding Co				
1690 Roberts Blvd NW Ste 105	Kennesaw GA	30144	**800-408-9945**	770-420-9111
American Outfitters Ltd				
3700 Sunset Ave	Waukegan IL	60087	**800-397-6081**	847-623-3959
Apple Saddlery 1875 Innes Rd	Ottawa ON	K1B4C6	**800-867-8225**	613-744-4040
ASLU LLC				
12178 Fourth St Rancho	Cucamonga CA	91730	**800-588-3911**	951-934-4200
Aspen Ski & Board Co				
1170 E Powell Rd	Lewis Center OH	43035	**877-861-0777**	614-848-6600
Athletic Training Equipment Company Inc				
655 Spice Island Dr	Sparks NV	89431	**800-800-9931**	
Austad's Golf				
2801 E Tenth St	Sioux Falls SD	57103	**800-444-1234***	605-331-4653
*Cust Svc				
Backcountry Gear LLC				
1855 W Second Ave	Eugene OR	97402	**800-953-5499**	541-485-4007
Barnes Bullets LLC				
38 N Frontage Rd	Mona UT	84645	**800-574-9200**	435-856-1000
Baseball Express Inc				
5750 NW Pkwy Ste 100	San Antonio TX	78249	**800-937-4824**	210-348-7000
Berg's Ski & Snowboard Shop				
367 W 13th Ave	Eugene OR	97401	**800-800-1953**	541-683-1300
Bicycle Garage of Indy Inc				
4340 E 82nd St	Indianapolis IN	46250	**800-238-7389**	317-842-4140
Big 5 Sporting Goods Corp				
2525 E El Segundo Blvd	El Segundo CA	90245	**800-898-2994**	310-536-0611
NASDAQ: BGFV				
Bike USA Inc				
2811 Brodhead Rd	Bethlehem PA	18020	**800-225-2453**	
Bilenky Cycle Works Inc				
5319 N Second St	Philadelphia PA	19120	**844-889-8823**	215-329-4744
Birdie Golf Balls Golf Equipment				
208 Margate Ct	Margate FL	33063	**800-333-7271**	954-973-2741
Black Bart International LLC				
155 E Blue Heron Blvd Ste R2	Riviera Beach FL	33404	**866-289-7050**	561-842-4550
Blade-Tech Industries Inc				
5530 184th St E	Puyallup WA	98375	**877-331-5793**	253-655-8059
Blue Quill Angler Inc				
1532 Bergen Pkwy	Evergreen CO	80439	**800-435-5353**	303-674-4700
Blue Sky Cycling Inc				
2530 Randolph St	Huntington Park CA	90255	**800-585-4137**	323-585-3934
Bob Ward & Sons Inc				
3015 Paxson St	Missoula MT	59801	**800-800-5083**	406-728-3220
Boyne Country Sports				
1200 Bay View Rd	Petoskey MI	49770	**800-462-6963**	231-439-4906
Burghardt Sporting Goods				
14660 W Capitol Dr	Brookfield WI	53005	**866-790-6606**	262-790-1170
C W I Inc				
650 Three Springs Raod	Bowling Green KY	42104	**888-626-7576**	
Cabela's Inc 1 Cabela Dr	Sidney NE	69160	**800-237-8888**	800-850-8402
NYSE: CAB				
Campmor Inc				
400 Corporate Dr PO Box 680	Mahwah NJ	07430	**800-226-7667**	
Cannon Sports Inc				
12701 Van Nuys Blvd Ste P	Pacoima CA	91331	**800-223-0064**	
Capt Harrys Fishing Supply Company Inc				
8501 NW Seventh Ave	Miami FL	33150	**800-327-4088**	305-374-4661
Carl's Golfland Inc				
1976 S Telegraph Rd	Bloomfield Hills MI	48302	**877-412-2757**	248-335-8095
Century Martial Art Supply Inc				
1000 Century Blvd	Oklahoma City OK	73110	**800-626-2787***	405-732-2226
*Sales				
Coghlan's Ltd 121 Irene St	Winnipeg MB	R3T4C7	**877-264-4526**	204-284-9550
Cole Sport Inc				
1615 Park Ave	Park City UT	84060	**800-345-2938**	435-649-4800
Condor Outdoor Products				
5268 Rivergrade Rd	Irwindale CA	91706	**800-552-2554**	
Coontail				
5466 Park St	Boulder Junction WI	54512	**888-874-0885**	
Cycle-safe Inc				
5211 Cascade Rd SE Ste 210	Grand Rapids MI	49546	**888-950-6531**	616-954-9977
CZ-USA Inc				
PO Box 171073	Kansas City KS	66117	**800-955-4486**	913-321-1811
Dan Bailey Fly Shop				
209 W Park St	Livingston MT	59047	**800-356-4052**	406-222-1673
Dan's Comp				
1 Competition Way	Mount Vernon IN	47620	**888-888-3267**	
Dart World Inc 140 Linwood St	Lynn MA	01905	**800-225-2558**	781-581-6035
Dharma Trading Co				
1604 Fourth St	San Rafael CA	94901	**800-542-5227**	415-456-1211
Diamond Tour				
202 Lucas St Unit A	Sycamore IL	60178	**800-826-5340**	815-787-2649
Dick's Sporting Goods Inc				
345 Court St	Coraopolis PA	15108	**877-846-9997**	
Direct Sports Inc				
1720 Curve Rd	Pearisburg VA	24134	**800-456-0072**	
Dixie Gun Works Inc				
1412 W Reelfoot Ave	Union City TN	38261	**800-238-6785***	731-885-0561
*Orders				
Dolphin Swim School Inc				
1530 El Camino Ave	Sacramento CA	95815	**800-436-5744**	916-929-8188
Doms Outdoor Outfitters				
1870 First St	Livermore CA	94550	**800-447-9629**	925-447-9629
Downtown Athletic Store Inc				
1180 Seminole Trl Ste 210	Charlottesville VA	22901	**800-348-2649**	434-975-3696
Duluth Pack				
365 Canal Park Dr	Duluth MN	55802	**800-777-4439**	
Eagle Grips Inc				
460 Randy Rd	Carol Stream IL	60188	**800-323-6144**	630-260-0400
Eastern Mountain Sports				
1 Vose Farm Rd	Peterborough NH	03458	**888-463-6367**	203-379-2233

		Toll-Free	Phone
Eastern Skateboard Supply Inc			
6612 Amsterdam Way ....Wilmington NC 28405		800-358-7588	910-791-8240
Exerplay Inc			
12001 State Hwy 14 N ....Cedar Crest NM 87008		800-457-5444	505-281-0151
Fanzz			
3775 W California Ave Ste 100............Salt Lake City UT 84104		888-326-9946	
Fibar Group LLC, The			
80 Business Park Dr Suit 300 ....Armonk NY 10504		800-342-2721	914-273-8770
Finlandia Sauna Products Inc			
14010 SW 72nd Ave Ste B ....Portland OR 97224		800-354-3342	503-684-8289
First to The Finish Inc			
1325 N Broad St ....Carlinville IL 62626		800-747-9013	
Fisher Athletic Equipment Inc			
2060 Cauble Rd ....Salisbury NC 28144		800-438-6028	
Fitness Club Warehouse Inc			
2210 S Sepulveda Blvd ....Los Angeles CA 90064		800-348-4537	310-235-2040
Fitness Zone			
3439 Colonnade Pkwy Se 800 ....Birmingham AL 35243		800-875-9145	
Fox Creek Leather Inc			
2029 Elk Creek Pkwy ....Independence VA 24348		800-766-4165	
Gerry Cosby & Company Inc			
11 Pennsylvania Plz ....New York NY 10001		877-563-6464	
Gita Sporting Goods Ltd			
12500 Steele Creek Rd ....Charlotte NC 28273		800-729-4482*	800-366-4482
*Consumer Info			
Gold Tip LLC			
584 E 1100 S Ste 5........................American Fork UT 84003		800-551-0541	
Graf & Sons 4050 S Clark St ....Mexico MO 65265		800-531-2666	573-581-2266
Half Hitch Tackle Company Inc			
2206 Thomas Dr ....Panama City FL 32408		888-668-9810	850-234-2621
Hansen Surfboards			
1105 S Coast Hwy 101 ....Encinitas CA 92024		800-480-4754	
Hoigaards Inc			
5425 Excelsior Blvd ....Minneapolis MN 55416		800-266-8157	952-929-1351
Holabird Sports LLC			
9220 Pulaski Hwy ....Middle River MD 21220		866-860-1416	410-687-6400
Holiday Diver Inc			
180 Gulf Stream Way ....Dania Beach FL 33004		800-348-3872	954-925-7630
Hopkins Sporting Goods Inc			
5485 NW Beaver Dr ....Johnston IA 50131		800-362-2937	515-270-0132
In The Swim Inc			
320 Industrial Dr ....West Chicago IL 60185		800-288-7946	
Island Surf			
1450 Miracle Strip Pkwy SE ....Fort Walton Beach FL 32548		800-272-2065	
Jan's Mountain Outfitters			
1600 Park Ave PO Box 280..................Park City UT 84060		800-745-1020	435-649-4949
Kirkham's Outdoor Products			
3125 S State St ....Salt Lake City UT 84115		800-453-7756	801-486-4161
Kittery Trading Post			
301 US 1 ....Kittery ME 03904		888-587-6246	603-334-1157
Korney Board Aids Sporting			
312 Harrison Ave ....Roxton TX 75477		800-842-7772	903-346-3269
Lacrosse Unlimited Inc			
59 Gilpin Ave ....Hauppauge NY 11788		877-800-5850	
Lancaster Archery Supply Inc			
2195-A Old Philadelphia Pk ....Lancaster PA 17602		800-829-7408	
Leisure Pro 42 W 18th St ....New York NY 10011		800-637-6880	212-645-1234
Mad Dogg Athletics Inc			
2111 Narcissus Ct ....Venice CA 90291		800-847-7746	310-823-7008
Magnum Research Inc			
12602 33rd Ave SW ....Pillager MN 56473		800-772-6168	218-746-4597
Markwort Sporting Goods Co			
1101 Research Blvd ....St. Louis MO 63132		800-280-5555	314-942-1199
McCormick's Group LLC			
216 W Campus Dr ....Arlington Heights IL 60004		800-323-5201	847-398-8680
Midwest Sports Supply Inc			
11613 Reading Rd ....Cincinnati OH 45241		800-334-4580	513-956-4900
Mikasa Sports Usa			
556 Vanguard Way Unit D..................Brea CA 92821		800-854-6927	
Mitchell Golf Equipment Co			
954 Senate Dr ....Dayton OH 45459		800-437-1314	937-436-1314
Modell's Sporting Goods			
498 Seventh Ave 20th Fl ....New York NY 10018		800-275-6633	
Mountain Equipment Co-operative			
149 W Fourth Ave ....Vancouver BC V5Y4A6		800-722-1960	604-707-3300
Mountain Tools			
225 Crossroads Blvd PO Box 222295 ....Carmel CA 93923		800-510-2514	831-620-0911
Mud Hole Custom Tackle Inc			
400 Kane Ct ....Oviedo FL 32765		866-790-7637	407-447-7637
Mueller Recreational Products Inc			
4825 S 16th St ....Lincoln NE 68512		800-925-7665	402-423-8888
Nicros Inc			
845 Phalen Blvd ....Saint Paul MN 55106		800-699-1975	651-778-1975
Nill Bros Sports			
2814 S 44th St ....Kansas City KS 66106		800-748-7221	913-384-4242
NLC Products Inc			
PO Box 8300 ....Little Rock AR 72222		800-648-5483	
No Fault Sports Products			
2101 Briarglen Dr ....Houston TX 77027		800-462-7766	713-683-7101
Norman Shatz Co USA			
3570 St Rd ....Bensalem PA 19020		800-292-0292	
Northwest Outlet			
1814 Belknap St ....Superior WI 54880		800-569-8142	715-392-9838
Nova Fitness Equipment			
4511 S 119th Cir ....Omaha NE 68137		800-949-6682	402-343-0552
NRC Sports Inc			
206 Worcester Rd Ste 36-38..................Princeton MA 01541		800-243-5033	978-464-2433
Olympia Sports			
5 Bradley Dr ....Westbrook ME 04092		844-511-1721	207-854-2794
Palos Sports Inc			
11711 S Austin Ave ....Alsip IL 60803		800-233-5484	708-396-2555
Paragon Sporting Goods Corp			
867 Broadway 18th St ....New York NY 10003		800-961-3030	212-255-8889
Performance Inc			
1 Performance Way ....Chapel Hill NC 27514		800-727-2453*	
*Cust Svc			
Peter Glenn Ski & Sports			
2901 W Oakland Pk Blvd ....Fort Lauderdale FL 33311		800-818-0946	954-484-3606

		Toll-Free	Phone
Planet Bike 2402 Vondron Rd ....Madison WI 53718		866-256-8510	
Playwell Group, The			
4743 Iberia Ave Ste C....................Dallas TX 75207		800-726-1816	
Pro Performance Sports LLC			
2081 Faraday Ave ....Carlsbad CA 92008		877-225-7275	
Proactive Sports Inc			
1200 SE Second Ave ....Canby OR 97013		800-369-8642	503-263-8583
Quarq Technology Inc			
3100 First Ave ....Spearfish SD 57783		800-660-6853	605-642-2226
Recreational Equipment Inc (REI)			
6750 S 228th St ....Kent WA 98032		800-426-4840*	253-395-3780
*Orders			
Reeds Family Outdoor Outfitters			
522 Minnesota Ave NW ....Walker MN 56484		800-346-0019	
Reliable Racing Supply Inc			
643 Glen St ....Queensbury NY 12804		800-223-4448	518-793-5677
Rock Creek Outfitters			
1530 Riverside Dr ....Chattanooga TN 37406		888-707-6708	423-266-8200
Ron Jon Surf Shop			
3850 S Banana River Blvd ....Cocoa Beach FL 32931		888-757-8737	321-799-8888
Runner's Edge Inc, The			
3195 N Federal Hwy ....Boca Raton FL 33431		888-361-1950	561-361-1950
Scuba Com Inc			
1752 Langley Ave ....Irvine CA 92614		800-347-2822	949-221-9300
SeeMore Putter Co, The			
277 Mallory Sta Ste 119....................Franklin TN 37067		800-985-8170	615-435-8015
Sonoma Outfitters			
2412 Magowan Dr ....Santa Rosa CA 95405		800-290-1920	
Sports Imports Inc			
4000 Pkwy Ln ....Hilliard OH 43026		800-556-3198	
Sports Promotion Network			
2895 113th St ....Grand Prairie TX 75050		800-460-9989	866-780-6151
Starline Inc			
1300 W Henry St ....Sedalia MO 65301		800-280-6660	660-827-6640
Stretch Boards			
983 Tower Pl ....Santa Cruz CA 95062		800-480-4754	831-479-7309
Summit Canyon Mountaineering			
205 sixth St ....Glenwood Springs CO 81601		800-360-6994	970-945-6994
Summit Hut			
5045 E Speedway Blvd ....Tucson AZ 85712		800-499-8696	520-325-1554
Sun & Ski Sports			
10560 Bissonnet St Ste 100 ....Houston TX 77099		866-786-3869	281-340-5000
Sundance Beach			
7127 Hollister Ave Ste 25A-323 ....Goleta CA 93117		877-968-0036	
Surf Assoc East Inc			
1701 N Federal Hwy ....Fort Lauderdale FL 33305		800-528-9061	954-564-0202
Tabata US.A. Inc			
2380 Mira Mar Ave ....Long Beach CA 90815		800-482-2282	562-498-3708
Tack Room Too Inc			
201 Lee St SW ....Tumwater WA 98501		800-258-2581	360-357-4268
Tahoe Mountain Sports			
11200 Donner Pass Rd Ste 5e ....Truckee CA 96161		866-891-9177	
Team Connection Inc			
615 Alton Pl ....High Point NC 27263		800-535-3975	
Toledo Physical Education Supply Inc			
5101 Advantage Dr ....Toledo OH 43612		800-225-7749	419-726-8122
Tri-State Pumps Inc			
1162 Chastain Rd ....Liberty SC 29657		800-868-4631	864-843-8100
Triathlete Sports			
186 Exchange St ....Bangor ME 04401		800-635-0528	207-990-2013
Trijicon Inc			
49385 Shafer Ave PO Box 930059 ....Wixom MI 48393		800-338-0563	248-960-7700
Turbo 2 n 1 Grip			
46460 Continental Dr ....Chesterfield MI 48047		800-530-9878	586-598-3948
US. Kids Golf LLC			
3040 Northwoods Pkwy ....Norcross GA 30071		888-387-5437	770-441-3077
Warehouse Skateboards Inc			
1638 Military Cutoff Rd ....Wilmington NC 28403		877-791-9795	
Warrior Custom Golf			
15 Mason Ste A ....Irvine CA 92618		800-600-5113	866-436-6722
Western Power Sports Inc			
601 E Gowen Rd ....Boise ID 83716		800-999-3388	208-376-8400
Wheel & Sprocket Inc			
5722 S 108th St ....Hales Corners WI 53130		866-995-9918	414-529-6600
Xs Sight Systems Inc			
2401 Ludelle St ....Fort Worth TX 76105		888-744-4880	817-536-0136

708   SPORTS COMMISSIONS & REGULATORY AGENCIES - STATE

		Toll-Free	Phone
Judicial Council of California			
455 Golden Gate Ave ....San Francisco CA 94102		800-900-5980	415-865-4200
Delaware			
Aging & Adults with Physical Disabilites Services			
1901 N DuPont Hwy ....New Castle DE 19720		800-223-9074	
Thoroughbred Racing Commission			
2320 S DuPont Hwy ....Dover DE 19901		800-282-8685	302-698-4500
Indiana			
Agriculture Dept			
101 W Washington St ....Indianapolis IN 46204		800-677-9800	
Louisiana			
Agriculture & Forestry Dept			
5825 Florida Blvd ....Baton Rouge LA 70806		866-927-2476	225-922-1234
New York			
Aging Office			
2 Empire State Plz ....Albany NY 12223		800-342-9871	
Athletic Commission			
123 William St 20th Fl ....New York NY 10038		866-269-3769	212-417-5700
North Dakota			
Accountancy Board			
2701 S Columbia Rd Ste D..................Grand Forks ND 58201		800-532-5904	701-775-7100
Pennsylvania State Athletic Commission			
2601 N Third St ....Harrisburg PA 17110		877-868-3772	
Texas			
Aging & Disability Services			
701 W 51st St ....Austin TX 78751		888-388-6332	512-438-3011

SPORTS FACILITIES

SEE Stadiums & Arenas ; Racing & Racetracks ; Motor Speedways

709 SPORTS TEAMS - BASEBALL

SEE ALSO Sports Organizations

				Toll-Free	Phone
3D Lacrosse LLC					
1301 S Jason St Unit K	Denver	CO	80223	800-941-9193	
Cincinnati Reds					
100 Joe Nuxhall Way	Cincinnati	OH	45202	877-647-7337	513-381-7337
Houston Astros					
Minute Maid Pk 501 Crawford St	Houston	TX	77002	800-771-2303	713-259-8000
Kansas City Royals					
Kauffman Stadium 1 Royal Way	Kansas City	MO	64129	800-676-9257*	816-921-8000
*Sales					
Minnesota Twins					
1 Twins Way	Minneapolis	MN	55403	800-338-9467	612-375-1366
Pittsburgh Pirates					
115 Federal St PO Box 7000	Pittsburgh	PA	15212	800-289-2827	412-321-2827
Toledo Mud Hens Baseball Club Inc					
406 Washington St	Toledo	OH	43604	800-736-9520	419-725-4367
Toronto Blue Jays					
1 Blue Jays Way Ste 3200	Toronto	ON	M5V1J1	888-654-6529	416-341-1000

710 SPORTS TEAMS - BASKETBALL

SEE ALSO Sports Organizations

710-1 National Basketball Association (NBA)

				Toll-Free	Phone
Cavaliers Operating Company LLC					
Quicken Loans Arena 1 Ctr Ct	Cleveland	OH	44115	888-894-9424	216-420-2000
Los Angeles Clippers					
1212 S Flower St 5th Fl	Los Angeles	CA	90015	855-895-0872	213-742-7100
Minnesota Timberwolves					
Target Ctr 600 First Ave N	Minneapolis	MN	55403	855-895-0872	612-673-1600
New Jersey Nets					
390 Murray Hill Pkwy	East Rutherford	NJ	07073	800-346-6387	201-935-8888
Sacramento Kings					
1 Sports Pkwy	Sacramento	CA	95834	800-231-8750	916-928-0000
Seattle SuperSonics					
1201 Third Ave Ste 1000	Seattle	WA	98101	800-743-7021	206-281-5800

710-2 Women's National Basketball Association (WNBA)

				Toll-Free	Phone
Chicago Sky					
20 W Kinzie St Ste 1000	Chicago	IL	60610	877-329-9622	312-828-9550
Los Angeles Sparks					
865 S Figueroa St Ste 104	Los Angeles	CA	90017	888-694-3278	213-929-1300

711 SPORTS TEAMS - FOOTBALL

SEE ALSO Sports Organizations

711-1 Canadian Football League (CFL)

				Toll-Free	Phone
Canadian Football League					
50 Wellington St E 3rd Fl	Toronto	ON	M5E1C8	855-264-4242	416-322-9650
Saskatchewan Roughrider Football Club					
1910 Piffles Taylor Way PO Box 1966	Regina	SK	S4P3E1	888-474-3377	306-569-2323

711-2 National Football League (NFL)

				Toll-Free	Phone
Arizona Cardinals					
8701 S Hardy Dr	Tempe	AZ	85284	800-999-1402	602-379-0101
Buffalo Bills					
1 Bills Dr	Orchard Park	NY	14127	877-228-4257	716-648-1800
Carolina Panthers					
Bank of America Stadium					
800 S Mint St	Charlotte	NC	28202	888-297-8673	704-358-7000
Cincinnati Bengals					
1 Paul Brown Stadium	Cincinnati	OH	45202	866-621-8383	513-621-3550
Green Bay Packers					
1265 Lombardi Ave PO Box 10628	Green Bay	WI	54304	800-895-0071	920-569-7500
Indianapolis Colts					
7001 W 56th St	Indianapolis	IN	46254	800-805-2658	317-297-2658
Kansas City Chiefs					
1 Arrowhead Dr	Kansas City	MO	64129	844-323-1227	816-920-9300
Oakland Raiders Inc					
1220 Harbor Bay Pkwy	Alameda	CA	94502	800-724-3377	510-864-5000
San Diego Chargers					
4020 Murphy Canyon Rd	San Diego	CA	92123	877-242-7437	858-874-4500
Seattle Seahawks					
12 Seahawks Way	Renton	WA	98056	888-635-4295	

712 SPORTS TEAMS - HOCKEY

SEE ALSO Sports Organizations

				Toll-Free	Phone
Anaheim Ducks					
2695 E Katella Ave	Anaheim	CA	92806	877-945-3946	

				Toll-Free	Phone
Colorado Avalanche					
Pepsi Ctr 1000 Chopper Cir	Denver	CO	80204	800-559-2333	303-405-1100
Columbus Blue Jackets					
Nationwide Arena 200 W Nationwide Blvd					
Ste Level	Columbus	OH	43215	800-645-2657	
Edmonton Oilers					
10214 104 Ave NW	Edmonton	AB	T5J0H6	800-559-2333	780-414-4625
Los Angeles Kings					
Staples Ctr 1111 S Figueroa St	Los Angeles	CA	90015	888-546-4752	213-742-7100
Montreal Canadiens					
Bell Centre 1275 St-Antoine Ouest	Montreal	QC	H3B5E8	800-363-8162	514-989-2836
New York Islanders					
1535 Old Country Rd	Plainview	NY	11803	800-843-5678	516-501-6700
Ottawa Senators					
1000 Palladium Dr	Ottawa	ON	K2V1A5	800-444-7367	613-599-0250
Penguins 1001 Fifth Ave	Pittsburgh	PA	15219	800-642-7367	412-642-1300

713 SPORTS TEAMS - SOCCER

SEE ALSO Sports Organizations

				Toll-Free	Phone
Chicago Fire					
7000 S Harlem Ave	Bridgeview	IL	60455	888-657-3473	708-594-7200
Colorado Rapids					
6000 Victory Way	Commerce	CO	80022	800-979-3370	303-727-3500
FMC Ice Sports					
100 Schoosett St Bldg 3	Pembroke	MA	02359	888-747-5283	781-826-3085
Los Angeles Galaxy					
18400 Avalon Blvd	Carson	CA	90746	877-342-5299	310-630-2200
New England Revolution					
Gillette Stadium 1 Patriot Pl	Foxboro	MA	02035	877-438-7387	
New York Red Bulls					
600 Cape May St	Harrison	NJ	07029	877-727-6223	

714 SPRINGS - HEAVY-GAUGE

				Toll-Free	Phone
General Wire Spring Co					
1101 Thompson Ave	McKees Rocks	PA	15136	800-245-6200	412-771-6300
Service Spring Corp					
6615 Maumee Western Rd	Maumee	OH	43537	800-752-8522	419-838-6081
Southern Spring & Stamping Inc					
401 Sub Stn Rd	Venice	FL	34285	800-450-5882	941-488-2276

715 SPRINGS - LIGHT-GAUGE

				Toll-Free	Phone
Atlantic Spring					
PO Box 650	Flemington	NJ	08822	877-231-6474	908-788-5800
Century Spring Corp					
222 E 16th St	Los Angeles	CA	90015	800-237-5225	213-749-1466
General Wire Spring Co					
1101 Thompson Ave	McKees Rocks	PA	15136	800-245-6200	412-771-6300
Hickory Springs Mfg Co					
235 Second Ave NW	Hickory	NC	28601	800-438-5341	
Lee Spring Company Inc					
140 58th St Unit 3C	Brooklyn	NY	11220	800-110-2500	718-236-2222
Leggett & Platt Inc					
1 Leggett Rd PO Box 757	Carthage	MO	64836	800-888-4569	417-358-8131
NYSE: LEG					
Mid-West Spring & Stamping Co					
1404 Joliet Rd Unit C	Romeoville	IL	60446	800-619-0909	630-739-3800
Newcomb Spring Corp					
235 Spring St	Southington	CT	06489	888-579-3051	860-621-0111
Southern Spring & Stamping Inc					
401 Sub Stn Rd	Venice	FL	34285	800-450-5882	941-488-2276
Spring Dynamics Inc					
7378 Research Dr	Almont	MI	48003	888-274-8432	810-798-2622
Spring Engineers Inc					
9740 Tanner Rd	Houston	TX	77041	800-899-9488	713-690-9488

716 STADIUMS & ARENAS

SEE ALSO Convention Centers ; Performing Arts Facilities

				Toll-Free	Phone
Air Canada Centre 40 Bay St	Toronto	ON	M5J2X2	800-661-8747	416-815-5500
Alamodome					
100 Montana St	San Antonio	TX	78203	800-884-3663	210-207-3663
Bridgestone Arena					
501 Broadway	Nashville	TN	37203	800-356-4840	615-770-2000
Canal Park Stadium					
300 S Main St	Akron	OH	44308	888-223-6000	330-253-5151
FARGODOME					
1800 N University Dr	Fargo	ND	58102	855-694-6367	701-241-9100
Fenway Park 4 Yawkey Way	Boston	MA	02215	877-733-7699	617-226-6000
Florida Repertory Theatre Inc					
2267 Bay St	Fort Myers	FL	33901	877-787-8053	239-332-4665
Georgia Dome					
1 Georgia Dome Dr NW	Atlanta	GA	30313	888-333-4406	404-223-9200
Greater Austin Performing Arts Center Inc					
701 W Riverside Dr	Austin	TX	78704	800-735-2989	512-457-5100
Independence Bowl Foundation					
PO Box 1723	Shreveport	LA	71166	888-414-2695	318-221-0712
Lambeau Field Atrium					
1265 Lombardi Ave	Green Bay	WI	54304	866-752-1265	920-569-7500
Major League Baseball Ballpark					
333 Camden St	Baltimore	MD	21201	888-848-2473	410-547-6100
Michigan Stadium					
1201 S Main St					
University of Michigan	Ann Arbor	MI	48104	866-296-6849	734-647-2583
Minute Maid Park					
501 Crawford St	Houston	TX	77002	877-927-8767	713-259-8000

Name / Address	City	State	Zip	Toll-Free	Phone
Paul Brown Stadium 1 Paul Brown Stadium	Cincinnati	OH	45202	866-621-8383	513-455-4800
Qualcomm Stadium 9449 Friars Rd	San Diego	CA	92108	800-400-7115	858-694-3900
Quicken Loans Arena 1 Ctr Ct	Cleveland	OH	44115	888-894-9424	216-420-2000
Ralph Wilson Stadium 1 Bills Dr	Orchard Park	NY	14127	877-228-4257	716-648-1800
Scottsdale Stadium 7408 E Osborn Rd	Scottsdale	AZ	85251	877-229-5042	480-312-2586
Seattle Theatre Group 911 Pine St	Seattle	WA	98101	877-784-4849	206-467-5510
Sioux Falls Arena 1201 NW Ave	Sioux Falls	SD	57104	800-338-3177	605-367-7288
Sky Sox Stadium 4385 Tutt Blvd Security Service Field	Colorado Springs	CO	80922	866-698-4253	719-597-1449
State Fair & Exposition 1001 Beulah Ave	Pueblo	CO	81004	800-876-4567	719-404-2018
Times Union Ctr 51 S Pearl St	Albany	NY	12207	866-308-3394	518-487-2000
Toyota Ctr 1510 Polk St	Houston	TX	77002	866-446-8849	713-758-7200
Tropicana Field 1 Tropicana Dr	Saint Petersburg	FL	33705	888-326-7297	727-825-3137
Valley View Casino Ctr 3500 Sports Arena Blvd	San Diego	CA	92110	888-929-7849	619-224-4171
Wake Forest University 2825 University Pkwy	Winston-Salem	NC	27105	888-758-3322	336-758-2410
Will Rogers Memorial Ctr 3401 W Lancaster Ave	Fort Worth	TX	76107	800-433-5747	
Winnipeg Folk Festival 203-211 Bannatyne Ave	Winnipeg	MB	R3B3P2	866-301-3823	204-231-0096

717 STAFFING SERVICES

SEE ALSO Professional Employer Organizations (PEOs) ; Executive Recruiting Firms ; Employment Offices - Government ; Employment Services - Online ; Modeling Agencies

Name / Address	City	State	Zip	Toll-Free	Phone
Allegis Group Inc 7301 Pkwy Dr	Hanover	MD	21076	800-927-8090	
Allied Health Group LLC 6551 Park of Commerce Blvd	Boca Raton	FL	33487	800-873-9182	
Ameri-Force Inc 9485 Regency Sq Blvd Ste 300	Jacksonville	FL	32225	800-522-8998	904-633-9918
AMN Healthcare Services Inc 12400 High Bluff Dr Ste 100 *NYSE: AMN*	San Diego	CA	92130	866-871-8519	
AppleOne 327 West Broadway PO Box 29048	Glendale	CA	91209	800-872-2677	
Aquent LLC 711 Boylston St	Boston	MA	02116	855-767-6333	617-535-5000
ARC Industries Inc 2780 Airport Dr	Columbus	OH	43219	800-734-7007	614-479-2500
BarkerGilmore 1387 Fairport Rd Ste 845	Fairport	NY	14450	877-571-5047	
Bartech Group 17199 N Laurel Park Dr Ste 224	Livonia	MI	48152	800-828-4410	734-953-5050
Brooke Chase Associates Inc 1543 Second St	Sarasota	FL	34236	877-374-0039	
C & A Industries Inc 13609 California St	Omaha	NE	68154	800-574-9829	402-891-0009
Calian Technology Ltd 340 Legget Dr Ste 101 *TSX: CGY*	Ottawa	ON	K2K1Y6	877-225-4264	613-599-8600
CareerStaff Unlimited Inc 6363 N State Hwy 161 Ste 100	Irving	TX	75038	888-993-4599	972-812-3200
Cejka Search Inc 4 Cityplace Dr Ste 300	Saint Louis	MO	63141	800-678-7858	314-726-1603
Command Ctr Inc 3609 S Wadsworth Blvd Ste 250 *NASDAQ: CCNI*	Lakewood	ID	80235	866-464-5844	
Compunnel Software Group Inc 103 Morgan Ln Ste 102	Plainsboro	NJ	08536	800-696-8128	
Cox Elearning Consultants Llc 3848 Macgregor Cmn	Livermore	CA	94551	866-240-3540	925-373-6558
CPC Logistics Inc 14528 S Outer 40 Rd Ste 210	Chesterfield	MO	63017	800-274-3746	314-542-2266
Cross Country Healthcare Inc 6551 Pk of Commerce Blvd *NASDAQ: CCRN*	Boca Raton	FL	33487	800-347-2264	561-998-2232
Davis Cos 325 Donald J Lynch Blvd	Marlborough	MA	01752	800-482-9494	763-231-0700
Eagle Professional Resources Inc 170 Laurier Ave W Ste 902	Ottawa	ON	K1P5V5	800-281-2339	613-234-1810
Ensearch Management Consultants 905 E Cotati Ave	Cotati	CA	94931	888-667-5627	
Entegee Inc 70 BlanchaRd Rd Ste 102	Burlington	MA	01803	800-368-3433	781-221-5800
Express Employment Professionals 9701 Boardwalk Blvd	Oklahoma City	OK	73162	800-222-4057	405-840-5000
Gibson Arnold & Assoc 5433 Westheimer Rd Ste 1016	Houston	TX	77056	800-879-2007	713-572-3000
Hire Image LLC 6 Alcazar Ave	Johnston	RI	02919	888-433-0090	401-490-2202
Interim HealthCare Inc 1601 Sawgrass Corporate Pkwy	Sunrise	FL	33323	800-338-7786	954-858-6000
IPC Technologies Inc 7200 Glen Forest Dr Ste 100	Richmond	VA	23226	877-947-2835	
Joule Inc 1235 Rt 1 S	Edison	NJ	08837	800-341-0341	732-548-5444
Judge Group Inc 300 Conshohocken State Rd Ste 300	West Conshohocken	PA	19428	888-228-7162	610-667-7700
Kforce Inc 1001 E Palm Ave *NASDAQ: KFRC*	Tampa	FL	33605	877-453-6723	813-552-5000
Kimco Staffing Services Inc 17872 Cowan Ave	Irvine	CA	92614	800-649-5627	949-752-6996
Labor Finders 11426 N Jog Rd	Palm Beach Gardens	FL	33418	800-864-7749	561-627-6507
Lucas Assoc Inc 950 E Paces Ferry Rd Ne Ste 2300	Atlanta	GA	30326	800-515-0819	404-239-5620
Lumen Legal 1025 N Campbell Rd	Royal Oak	MI	48067	877-933-1330	248-597-0400
Marketstar Corp 2475 Washington Blvd	Ogden	UT	84401	800-877-8259	
Medical Staffing Associates Inc 6731 Whittier Ave 3rd Fl	McLean	VA	22101	800-235-5105	
Medical Staffing Network 6551 Park of Commerce Blvd	Boca Raton	FL	33487	800-676-8326	
Medvantx Inc 5626 Oberlin Dr Ste 110	San Diego	CA	92121	866-744-0621	866-526-1206
Minute Men Staffing Services 3740 Carnegie Ave	Cleveland	OH	44115	877-873-8856	216-426-9675
NESC Staffing Corp 150 Mirona Rd	Portsmouth	NH	03801	800-562-3463	
Nursefinders Inc 12400 High Bluff Dr	San Diego	CA	92130	800-445-0459	877-214-4105
Oxford Global Resources Inc 100 Cummings Ctr Ste 206L	Beverly	MA	01915	800-536-3562	978-922-7502
Peak Technical Services Inc 583 Epsilon Dr	Pittsburgh	PA	15238	888-888-7325	412-696-1080
Pinnacle Staffing Inc PO Box 17589	Greenville	SC	29606	888-297-4212	
Principal Technical Services Inc 9960 Research Dr Ste 200	Irvine	CA	92618	888-787-3711	
Right at Home Inc 6464 Center St Ste 150	Omaha	NE	68106	877-697-7537	402-697-7537
Robert Half International Inc 2884 Sand Hill Rd Ste 200 *NYSE: RHI*	Menlo Park	CA	94025	855-432-0924	
Robert Half International Inc Accountemps Div 2884 Sand Hill Rd Ste 200	Menlo Park	CA	94025	888-744-9202	650-234-6000
Silicon Valley Staffing 2336 Harrison St	Oakland	CA	94612	877-660-6000	510-923-9898
Southwest Medical Assoc Inc 638 E Market St PO Box 2168	Rockport	TX	78382	800-929-4854	361-729-0646
Special Counsel Inc 10151 Deerwood Park Blvd Bldg 400 3rd Fl	Jacksonville	FL	32256	800-737-3436	904-737-3436
Sterling Computer Corp 600 Stevens Port Dr Ste 200	Dakota Dunes	SD	57049	877-242-4074	605-242-4000
Superior Technical Resources Inc 250 International Dr	Williamsville	NY	14221	800-568-8310	716-929-1400
Surgical Staff Inc 120 St Matthews Ave	San Mateo	CA	94401	800-339-9599	650-558-3999
Sysazzle Inc 15815 S 46th St Ste 116	Phoenix	AZ	85048	800-862-9545	
TAJ Technologies Inc 1168 Northland Dr	Mendota Heights	MN	55120	877-825-2801	651-688-2801
Team Health Inc 265 Brookview Ctr Way Ste 400	Knoxville	TN	37919	800-342-2898	865-693-1000
TEKsystems Inc 7437 Race Rd	Hanover	MD	21076	888-519-0776	410-540-7700
Temporary Solutions Inc 10550 Linden Lake Plz Ste 200	Manassas	VA	20109	888-222-0457	703-361-2220
Thompson Technologies 200 Galleria Pkwy Ste 1100	Atlanta	GA	30339	888-794-7947	770-794-8380
Transforce Inc 5520 Cherokee Ave Ste 200	Alexandria	VA	22312	800-308-6989	
True Blue Inc PO Box 2910 *NYSE: TBI*	Tacoma	WA	98401	800-610-8920	253-383-9101
UltraStaff 1818 Memorial Dr Ste 200	Houston	TX	77007	800-522-7707	713-522-7100
US Legal Support Inc 363 N Sam Houston Pkwy E Ste 1200	Houston	TX	77060	800-567-8757	713-653-7100
White Glove Placement Inc 85 Bartlett St	Brooklyn	NY	11206	866-387-8100	718-387-8181

718 STAGE EQUIPMENT & SERVICES

Name / Address	City	State	Zip	Toll-Free	Phone
Chapman/Leonard Studio Equipment Inc 12950 Raymer St	North Hollywood	CA	91605	888-883-6559	818-764-6726
DreamWorld Backdrops by Dazian 10671 Lorne St	Sun Valley	CA	91352	877-232-9426	
Grosh Scenic Rentals 4114 Sunset Blvd	Los Angeles	CA	90029	877-363-7998	
High End Systems Inc 2105 Gracy Farms Ln	Austin	TX	78758	800-890-8989	512-836-2242
Janson Industries 1200 Garfield Ave SW	Canton	OH	44706	800-548-8982	330-455-7029
Musson Theatrical Inc 890 Walsh Ave	Santa Clara	CA	95050	800-843-2837	408-986-0210
Rosco Laboratories Inc 52 Harbor View Ave	Stamford	CT	06902	800-767-2669	203-708-8900
Screen Works 2201 W Fulton St **Cust Svc*	Chicago	IL	60612	800-294-8111*	312-243-8265
Syracuse Scenery & Stage Lighting Company Inc 101 Monarch Dr	Liverpool	NY	13088	800-453-7775	315-453-8096

719 STEEL - MFR

Name / Address	City	State	Zip	Toll-Free	Phone
AK Steel Corp 9227 Centre Pt Dr *NYSE: AKS*	West Chester	OH	45069	800-331-5050	513-425-5000
Aleris International Inc 25825 Science Pk Dr Ste 400	Beachwood	OH	44122	866-266-2586	216-910-3400
Allegheny Technologies Inc 1000 Six PPG Pl *NYSE: ATI ■ *Sales*	Pittsburgh	PA	15222	800-258-3586*	412-394-2800

Classified Section

				Toll-Free	Phone
American Tank & Fabricating Co (AT&F) 12314 Elmwood Ave	Cleveland	OH	44111	**800-544-5316**	216-252-1500
Bushwick Metals LLC 560 N Washington Ave	Bridgeport	CT	06604	**888-399-4070**	
Canam Group Inc 11535 First Ave Bureau 500 *TSX: CAM*	Saint-Georges	QC	G5Y7H5	**877-499-6049**	418-228-8031
Carpenter Specialty Alloys Operations 101 W Bern St	Reading	PA	19601	**800-654-6543**	610-208-2000
Carpenter Technology Corp PO Box 14662 *NYSE: CRS*	Reading	PA	19612	**800-654-6543**	610-208-2000
Cascade Steel Rolling Mills Inc (CSRM) 3200 N Hwy 99 W PO Box 687	McMinnville	OR	97128	**800-283-2776**	503-472-4181
Charter Mfg Company Inc 1212 W Glen Oaks Ln	Mequon	WI	53092	**800-437-8789**	262-243-4700
Chicago Heights Steel 211 E Main St	Chicago Heights	IL	60411	**800-424-4487**	708-756-5648
Corey Steel Co 2800 S 61st Ct	Cicero	IL	60804	**800-323-2750**	708-735-8000
Creform Corp PO Box 830	Greer	SC	29652	**800-839-8823**	864-989-1700
Crucible Materials Corp 575 State Fair Blvd	Syracuse	NY	13209	**800-365-1180**	315-487-4111
Electralloy Corp 175 Main St	Oil City	PA	16301	**800-458-7273**	814-678-4100
F & D Head Co 3040 E Peden Rd	Fort Worth	TX	76179	**800-451-2684**	817-236-8773
Feroleto Steel Company Inc 300 Scofield Ave	Bridgeport	CT	06605	**800-243-2839**	203-366-3263
Gerdau AmeriSteel Corp 4221 W Boy Scout Blvd Ste 600 *Sales	Tampa	FL	33607	**800-876-7833***	813-286-8383
Gibraltar Industries Inc 3556 Lakeshore Rd *NASDAQ: ROCK*	Buffalo	NY	14219	**800-247-8368**	716-826-6500
GO Carlson Inc 350 Marshallton Thorndale Rd	Downingtown	PA	19335	**800-338-5622**	610-384-2800
Greer Steel Co 624 Blvd *Sales	Dover	OH	44622	**800-388-2868***	
Intsel Steel Distributors LP 11310 W Little York	Houston	TX	77041	**800-762-3316**	713-937-9500
Jersey Shore Steel Co 70 Maryland Ave PO Box 5055	Jersey Shore	PA	17740	**800-833-0277**	570-753-3000
LOKRING Technology LLC 38376 Apollo Pkwy	Willoughby	OH	44094	**800-876-2323**	440-942-0880
Metalex Corp 700 Liberty Dr	Libertyville	IL	60048	**877-667-8634**	847-362-5400
Mill Steel Co 5116 36th St SE	Grand Rapids	MI	49512	**800-247-6455**	
Niagara Corp 667 Madison Ave	New York	NY	10021	**877-289-2277**	212-317-1000
Nucor Corp 1915 Rexford Rd *NYSE: NUE*	Charlotte	NC	28211	**800-294-1322**	704-366-7000
Nucor Corp Cold Finish Div 2800 N Governor Williams Hwy	Darlington	SC	29540	**800-333-0590**	704-366-7000
Nucor-Yamato Steel Co 5929 E State Hwy 18	Blytheville	AR	72315	**800-289-6977**	870-762-5500
Sandmeyer Steel Co 10001 Sandmeyer Ln	Philadelphia	PA	19116	**800-523-3663**	215-464-7100
Scion Steel Inc 21555 Mullin Ave	Warren	MI	48089	**800-288-2127**	586-755-4000
Steel of West Virginia Inc 17th St & Second Ave	Huntington	WV	25703	**800-624-3492**	304-696-8200
Ulbrich Stainless Steels & Special Metals Inc (USSM) 57 Dodge Ave	North Haven	CT	06473	**800-243-1676**	203-239-4481
United Performance Metals 3475 Symmes Rd	Hamilton	OH	45015	**888-282-3292**	513-860-6500
USS-POSCO Industries 900 Loveridge Rd	Pittsburg	CA	94565	**800-877-7672**	
Worthington Steel Co 200 W Old Wilson Bridge Rd	Columbus	OH	43085	**800-944-3733**	614-438-3210

720 STONE (CUT) & STONE PRODUCTS

				Toll-Free	Phone
Akdo Intertrade Inc 1435 State St	Bridgeport	CT	06605	**800-811-2536**	203-336-5199
American Slate Co 1900 Olympic Blvd	Walnut Creek	CA	94596	**888-259-4249**	
AZ Countertops Inc 1445 S Hudson Ave	Ontario	CA	91761	**800-266-3524**	909-983-5386
Bybee Stone Company Inc 6293 N Matthews Dr	Ellettsville	IN	47429	**800-457-4530**	812-876-2215
Coldspring 17482 Granite W Rd	Cold Spring	MN	56320	**800-328-5040**	
Columbus Marble Works Corp 2415 Hwy 45 N *Cust Svc	Columbus	MS	39705	**800-647-1055***	662-328-1477
Continental Cast Stone Manufacturing Inc 22001 W 83rd St	Shawnee	KS	66227	**800-989-7866**	
Dakota Granite Co 48391 150th St PO Box 1351	Milbank	SD	57252	**800-843-3333**	
Dutch Quality Stone 18012 Dover Rd	Mount Eaton	OH	44659	**877-359-7866**	330-359-7866
Glenrock International Inc 985 E Linden Ave	Linden	NJ	07036	**800-453-6762**	
Keystone Retaining Wall Systems Inc 4444 W 78th St	Minneapolis	MN	55435	**800-747-8971**	952-897-1040
Little Falls Granite Works 10802 Hwy 10	Little Falls	MN	56345	**800-862-2417**	
Monumental Sales Inc 537 22nd Ave N PO Box 667	Saint Cloud	MN	56302	**800-442-1660**	320-251-6585
North Carolina Granite Corp 151 Granite Quarry Trl PO Box 151	Mount Airy	NC	27030	**800-227-6242**	336-786-5141
RJ Marshall Co 26776 W 12-Mile Rd *Cust Svc	Southfield	MI	48034	**888-514-8600***	248-353-4100
Rock of Ages Corp 558 Graniteville Rd	Graniteville	VT	05654	**800-421-0166**	802-476-3115
Starrett Tru-Stone Technologies Div 1101 Prosper Dr PO Box 430	Waite Park	MN	56387	**800-959-0517**	320-251-7171
Vermont Structural Slate Company Inc 3 Prospect St PO Box 98	Fair Haven	VT	05743	**800-343-1900**	802-265-4933
Vetter Stone Co (VSC) 23894 Third Ave	Mankato	MN	56001	**800-878-2850**	507-345-4568
WS Hampshire Inc 365 Keyes Ave	Hampshire	IL	60140	**800-541-0251**	847-683-4400

721 STUDENT ASSISTANCE PROGRAMS

				Toll-Free	Phone
Alabama					
Administrative Office of Alabama Courts 300 Dexter Ave	Montgomery	AL	36104	**866-954-9411**	334-954-5000
Prepaid Affordable College Tuition (PACT) 100 N Union St Ste 660	Montgomery	AL	36104	**800-252-7228**	
Alaska					
Arts Council 161 Klevin St Ste 102	Anchorage	AK	99508	**888-278-7424**	907-269-6610
Commission on Postsecondary Education PO Box 110510	Juneau	AK	99811	**800-770-8973**	907-465-6671
Arkansas					
Administrative Office of the Courts 625 Marshall St	Little Rock	AR	72201	**800-950-8221**	501-682-9400
CollegeInvest 1560 Broadway Ste 1700	Denver	CO	80202	**800-448-2424**	303-376-8800
Tuition Assistance Grant Program 810 First St NE	Washington	DC	20001	**877-485-6751**	202-727-2824
Edvest College Savings Plan PO Box 55189	Boston	MA	02205	**888-338-3789**	
FinAid Page LLC PO Box 2056	Cranberry Township	PA	16066	**800-433-3243**	724-538-4500
Prepaid College Board PO Box 6567	Tallahassee	FL	32314	**800-552-4723**	
Student Finance Commission 2082 E Exchange Pl	Tucker	GA	30084	**800-505-4732**	800-436-7442
Student Assistance Commission 1755 Lake Cook Rd	Deerfield	IL	60015	**877-877-3724**	800-899-4722
Indiana					
Agriculture Dept 101 W Washington St	Indianapolis	IN	46204	**800-677-9800**	
Students Assistance Commission 150 W Market St Rm 414	Indianapolis	IN	46204	**888-528-4719**	317-232-2350
Iowa College Student Aid Commission 430 E Grand Ave 3rd Fl	Des Moines	IA	50309	**800-383-4222**	515-725-3400
Higher Education Assistance Authority PO Box 798	Frankfort	KY	40602	**800-928-8926**	
Louisiana					
Agriculture & Forestry Dept 5825 Florida Blvd	Baton Rouge	LA	70806	**866-927-2476**	225-922-1234
Office of Student Financial Assistance 602 N Fifth St	Baton Rouge	LA	70802	**800-259-5626**	225-219-1012
Finance Authority of Maine 5 Community Dr PO Box 949	Augusta	ME	04332	**800-228-3734**	207-623-3263
Education Trust PO Box 30198 *General	Lansing	MI	48909	**800-638-4543***	517-335-4767
Student Financial Services Bureau Austin Bldg 430 W Allegan	Lansing	MI	48922	**888-447-2687**	
Minnesota					
Aging Board 540 Cedar St	Saint Paul	MN	55155	**800-882-6262**	651-431-2500
Office of Higher Education 1450 Energy Pk Dr Ste 350	Saint Paul	MN	55108	**800-657-3866**	651-642-0567
Montana					
Arts Council PO Box 202201	Helena	MT	59620	**800-282-3092**	406-444-6430
Higher Education Board of Regents 2500 Broadway St PO Box 203201	Helena	MT	59620	**877-501-1722**	406-444-6570
Higher Education Student Assistance Authority 4 Quakerbridge Plz PO Box 540	Trenton	NJ	08625	**800-792-8670**	609-584-4480
New York					
Aging Office 2 Empire State Plz	Albany	NY	12223	**800-342-9871**	
Higher Education Services Corp 99 Washington Ave	Albany	NY	12255	**888-697-4372**	518-473-1574
North Carolina State Education Assistance Authority (NCSEAA) PO Box 14103	Research Triangle Park	NC	27709	**800-700-1775**	919-549-8614
North Dakota					
Accountancy Board 2701 S Columbia Rd Ste D	Grand Forks	ND	58201	**800-532-5904**	701-775-7100
Tuition Trust Authority 35 E Chestnut St 8th Fl *Cust Svc	Columbus	OH	43215	**800-233-6734***	614-752-9400
Student Assistance Commission 1500 Valley River Dr Ste 100	Eugene	OR	97401	**800-452-8807**	541-687-7400
Higher Education Assistance Agency 1200 N Seventh St	Harrisburg	PA	17102	**800-213-9827**	
Scholarship America 1 Scholarship Way	Saint Peter	MN	56082	**800-537-4180**	507-931-1682
Tennessee					
Administrative Office of the Cts 511 Union St Ste 600	Nashville	TN	37219	**800-448-7970**	615-741-2687
Student Assistance Corp 404 James Robertson Pkwy Ste 1510	Nashville	TN	37243	**800-342-1663**	615-741-1346
Texas					
Aging & Disability Services 701 W 51st St	Austin	TX	78751	**888-388-6332**	512-438-3011
Higher Education Assistance Authority PO Box 145110	Salt Lake City	UT	84114	**877-336-7378**	801-321-7294
Vermont Student Assistance Corp (VSAC) 10 E Allen St PO Box 2000	Winooski	VT	05404	**800-642-3177**	

	City	State	Zip	Toll-Free	Phone
Aging & Rehabilitative Services Dept					
8004 Franklin Farms Dr	Richmond	VA	23229	**800-552-5019**	804-662-7000
Virginia 529					
9001 Arboretum Pkwy	Richmond	VA	23236	**888-567-0540**	
Higher Education Policy Commission					
1018 Kanawha Blvd E Ste 700	Charleston	WV	25301	**888-825-5707**	304-558-2101
Wyoming					
Aging Div					
2300 Capitol Ave 4th Fl	Cheyenne	WY	82002	**800-442-2766**	307-777-7995

722 SUBSTANCE ABUSE TREATMENT CENTERS

SEE ALSO General Hospitals - US ; General Hospitals - Canada ; Psychiatric Hospitals ; Self-Help Organizations

	City	State	Zip	Toll-Free	Phone
ACI (ACI) 500 W 57th St	New York	NY	10019	**800-724-4444**	212-293-3000
AdCare Hospital of Worcester					
107 Lincoln St	Worcester	MA	01605	**800-252-6465**	508-799-9000
Arms Acres					
75 Seminary Hill Rd	Carmel	NY	10512	**800-989-2676**	845-225-3400
Baltimore Behavioral Health (BBH)					
1101 W Pratt St	Baltimore	MD	21223	**800-789-2647**	410-962-7180
Bradford Health Services					
2101 Magnolia Ave S Ste 518	Birmingham	AL	35205	**800-217-2849**	205-251-7753
Clear Brook Manor					
1100 E Northampton St	Laurel Run	PA	18706	**800-582-6241**	
Coleman Professional Services					
3920 Lovers Ln	Ravenna	OH	44266	**800-673-1347**	330-296-3555
Columbia Community Mental Health					
58646 McNulty Way	Saint Helens	OR	97051	**800-294-5211**	503-397-5211
Conifer Park					
79 Glenridge Rd	Schenectady	NY	12302	**800-989-6446**	518-399-6446
Cornerstone Medical Arts Ctr Hospital					
159-05 Union Tpke	Fresh Meadows	NY	11366	**800-233-9999**	718-906-6700
Daymark Recovery Services Inc Stanly Center					
1000 N First St Ste 1	Albemarle	NC	28001	**866-275-9552**	704-983-2117
Eagleville Hospital					
100 Eagleville Rd	Eagleville	PA	19408	**800-255-2019***	610-539-6000
*General					
Fairbanks Hospital					
8102 Clearvista Pkwy	Indianapolis	IN	46256	**800-225-4673**	317-849-8222
Fellowship Hall Inc					
5140 Dunstan Rd	Greensboro	NC	27405	**800-659-3381**	
Friary of Lakeview Ctr, The					
4400 Hickory Shores Blvd	Gulf Breeze	FL	32563	**800-332-2271**	850-932-9375
Gateway Foundation Inc					
1080 E Park St	Carbondale	IL	62901	**877-505-4673**	618-529-1151
Glenbeigh 2863 SR 45	Rock Creek	OH	44084	**800-234-1001**	440-563-3400
Grand Lake Mental Health Center Inc					
114 W Delaware	Nowata	OK	74048	**800-722-3611**	918-273-1841
Griffin Memorial Hospital					
900 E Main St	Norman	OK	73071	**800-955-3468***	405-321-4880
*General					
Gulf Coast Mental Health Center					
1600 Broad Ave	Gulfport	MS	39501	**800-681-0798**	228-863-1132
Hampton Behavioral Health Center					
650 Rancocas Rd	Westampton	NJ	08060	**800-603-6767**	
Harmony Foundation Inc					
1600 Fish Hatchery Rd	Estes Park	CO	80517	**866-686-7867**	970-586-4491
Hazelden Foundation					
15251 Pleasant Valley Rd	Center City	MN	55012	**800-257-7810**	651-213-4200
Hazelden New York					
322 Eigth Ave 12th Fl	New York	NY	10001	**800-257-7800**	212-420-9520
Hazelden Springbrook					
1901 Esther St	Newberg	OR	97132	**866-866-4662**	503-554-4300
HealthSource Saginaw					
3340 Hospital Rd	Saginaw	MI	48603	**800-662-6848**	989-790-7700
Impact Drug & Alcohol Treatment Ctr					
1680 N Fair Oaks Ave	Pasadena	CA	91103	**866-734-4200**	626-798-0884
Keystone Ctr					
2001 Providence Ave	Chester	PA	19013	**800-558-9600**	610-876-9000
La Hacienda Treatment Ctr					
145 La Hacienda Way	Hunt	TX	78024	**800-749-6160**	830-238-4222
Livengrin Foundation					
4833 Hulmeville Rd	Bensalem	PA	19020	**800-245-4746**	215-638-5200
Mount Regis Center					
125 Knotbreak Rd	Salem	VA	24153	**866-302-6609**	877-217-3447
Oaklawn Psychiatric Center Inc					
330 Lakeview Dr	Goshen	IN	46527	**800-282-0809**	574-533-1234
Ozark Guidance Center Inc					
2400 S 48th St	Springdale	AR	72762	**800-234-7052**	479-750-2020
Phoenix House Foundation Inc (PHF)					
164 W 74th St	New York	NY	10023	**888-671-9392**	646-505-2018
Ridgeview Institute Inc					
3995 S Cobb Dr	Smyrna	GA	30080	**844-350-8800**	
Rimrock Foundation					
1231 N 29th St	Billings	MT	59101	**800-227-3953**	406-248-3175
Rivervalley Behavioral Health Hospital					
1100 Walnut St PO Box 1637	Owensboro	KY	42302	**800-737-0696**	270-689-6800
Schick Shadel Hospital					
12101 Ambaum Blvd SW	Seattle	WA	98146	**800-272-8464**	
Serenity Lane					
1 Serenity Ln PO Box 8549	Coburg	OR	97408	**800-543-9905**	541-687-1110
Sierra Tucson Inc					
39580 S Lago Del Oro Pkwy	Tucson	AZ	85739	**800-842-4487**	520-624-4000
Spencer Recovery Centers Inc					
1316 S Coast Hwy	Laguna Beach	CA	92651	**800-334-0394**	
Talbott Recovery Campus					
5448 Yorktowne Dr	Atlanta	GA	30349	**800-445-4232**	877-345-3301
Turning Point Hospital					
3015 Veterans Pkwy PO Box 1177	Moultrie	GA	31776	**800-342-1075**	229-985-4815
Turning Point of Tampa					
6227 Sheldon Rd	Tampa	FL	33615	**800-397-3006**	813-882-3003
Valley Forge Medical Ctr & Hospital					
1033 W Germantown Pk	Norristown	PA	19403	**888-539-8500**	610-539-8500
Walter B Jones Alcohol & Drug Abuse Treatment Ctr					
2577 W Fifth St	Greenville	NC	27834	**800-422-1884**	252-830-3426
Willingway Hospital					
311 Jones Mill Rd	Statesboro	GA	30458	**800-242-9455**	912-764-6236
Wilmington Treatment Ctr					
2520 Troy Dr	Wilmington	NC	28401	**866-783-6605**	
Youth Home Inc					
20400 Colonel Glenn Rd	Little Rock	AR	72210	**800-728-6452**	501-821-5500

723 SURVEYING, MAPPING, RELATED SERVICES

SEE ALSO Engineering & Design

	City	State	Zip	Toll-Free	Phone
B Jcc Inspections					
1000 Banks Draw	Rexford	MT	59930	**877-248-6006**	406-882-4825
Bock & Clark Corp					
3550 W Market St Ste 200	Akron	OH	44333	**800-787-8397**	330-665-4821
Campbell & Associates Inc					
3485 Fortuna Dr Ste 100	Akron	OH	44312	**800-233-4117**	330-945-4117
Cochrane Technologies Inc					
PO Box 81276	Lafayette	LA	70598	**800-346-3745**	337-837-3334
Cooper Aerial Survey Co					
1692 W Grant Rd	Tucson	AZ	85745	**800-229-2279**	520-884-7580
Day & Zimmermann Group Inc					
1500 Spring Garden St	Philadelphia	PA	19130	**877-319-0270**	215-299-8000
Geophysics GPR International Inc					
100 - 2545 Delorimier St	Longueuil	QC	J4K3P7	**800-672-4774**	450-679-2400
KCI Technologies Inc					
936 Ridgebrook Rd	Sparks	MD	21152	**800-572-7496**	410-316-7800
Landiscor					
3401 E Broadway Rd	Phoenix	AZ	85040	**866-221-8578**	602-248-8989
Landpoint LLC					
5486 Airline Dr	Bossier City	LA	71111	**800-348-5254**	318-226-0100
Print-O-Stat Inc					
1011 W Market St	York	PA	17404	**800-711-8014**	717-854-7821
Sidwell Co Inc					
2570 Foxfield Rd Ste 300	Saint Charles	IL	60174	**877-743-9355**	630-549-1000
Terra Remote Sensing Inc					
1962 Mills Rd	Sidney	BC	V8L5Y3	**800-814-4212**	250-656-0931
Wade-Trim Group Inc					
500 Griswold Ave Ste 2500	Detroit	MI	48226	**800-482-2864**	313-961-3650

724 SWIMMING POOLS

	City	State	Zip	Toll-Free	Phone
Anthony & Sylvan Pools					
3739 Easton Rd Rt 611	Doylestown	PA	18901	**877-729-7946**	215-489-5605
Fox Pool Corp 3490 BoaRd Rd	York	PA	17406	**800-723-1011**	
Hornerxpress Inc					
5755 Powerline Rd	Fort Lauderdale	FL	33309	**800-432-6966**	954-772-6966
Imperial Pools Inc					
33 Wade Rd	Latham	NY	12110	**800-444-9977**	518-786-1200
Radiant Pools Div Trojan Leisure Products LLC					
440 N Pearl St	Albany	NY	12207	**866-697-5870**	518-434-4161
Viking Pools					
121 Crawford Rd PO Box 96	Williams	CA	95987	**800-854-7665**	

725 SWITCHGEAR & SWITCHBOARD APPARATUS

SEE ALSO Transformers - Power, Distribution, Specialty ; Wiring Devices - Current-Carrying

	City	State	Zip	Toll-Free	Phone
Bel Fuse Inc					
206 Van Vorst St	Jersey City	NJ	07302	**800-235-3873**	201-432-0463
NASDAQ: BELFA					
Carlo Gavazzi Inc					
750 Hastings Ln	Buffalo Grove	IL	60089	**800-222-2659**	847-465-6100
Electroswitch Corp					
180 King Ave	Weymouth	MA	02188	**800-572-0479**	781-335-5200
Grayhill Inc					
561 W Hillgrove Ave	La Grange	IL	60525	**800-683-0366**	708-354-1040
Guardian Electric Mfg Company Inc					
1425 Lake Ave	Woodstock	IL	60098	**800-762-0369**	815-334-3600
Inertia Engineering					
6665 Hardaway Rd	Stockton	CA	95215	**800-791-9997**	209-931-1670
ITW Switches					
195 E Algonquin Rd	Des Plaines	IL	60016	**800-544-3354**	847-876-9400
Kasa Industrial Controls Inc					
418 E Ave B	Salina	KS	67401	**800-755-5272**	785-825-7181
Littelfuse Inc					
8755 W Higgins Rd Ste 500	Chicago	IL	60631	**800-227-0029***	773-628-1000
NASDAQ: LFUS ■ *Sales					
Lumitex Inc					
8443 Dow Cir	Strongsville	OH	44136	**800-969-5483**	440-600-3745
Mersen Inc					
374 Merrimac St	Newburyport	MA	01950	**800-388-5428**	978-462-6662
Mitsubishi Electric Power Products Inc					
Thorn Hill Industrial Park 530 Keystone Dr					
	Warrendale	PA	15086	**800-887-7830**	724-772-2555
Otto Engineering Inc					
2 E Main St	Carpentersville	IL	60110	**888-234-6886**	847-428-7171
PDI 4200 Oakleys Ct	Richmond	VA	23223	**800-225-4838**	804-737-9880
Powell Industries Inc					
8550 Mosely Dr	Houston	TX	77075	**800-480-7273**	713-944-6900
NASDAQ: POWL					
Powercon Corp PO Box 477	Severn	MD	21144	**800-638-5055**	410-551-6500
Reliance Controls Corp					
2001 Young Ct	Racine	WI	53404	**800-634-6155**	262-634-6155
Revere Control Systems Inc					
2240 Rocky Ridge Rd	Birmingham	AL	35216	**800-536-2525**	205-824-0004
Romac Supply Company Inc					
7400 Bandini Blvd	Commerce	CA	90040	**800-777-6622**	

				Toll-Free	Phone
Russelectric Inc 99 Industrial Pk Rd	Hingham	MA	02043	**800-225-5250**	781-749-6000
S & C Electric Co 6601 N Ridge Blvd	Chicago	IL	60626	**800-621-5546**	773-338-1000
Tapeswitch Corp 100 Schmitt Blvd	Farmingdale	NY	11735	**800-234-8273**	631-630-0442

726 TABLE & KITCHEN SUPPLIES - CHINA & EARTHENWARE

SEE ALSO

				Toll-Free	Phone
Hall Laughlin China Co 672 Fiesta Dr	Newell	WV	26050	**800-452-4462**	330-385-2900
Heritage Mint Ltd PO Box 13750	Scottsdale	AZ	85267	**888-860-6245**	480-860-1300
Homer Laughlin China Co 672 Fiesta Dr	Newell	WV	26050	**800-452-4462**	304-387-1300
Lenox Corp PO Box 2006	Bristol	PA	19007	**800-223-4311**	
Lipper International Inc 235 Washington St	Wallingford	CT	06492	**800-243-3129**	203-269-8588
Pfaltzgraff Co PO Box 21769	York	PA	17402	**800-999-2811**	
Waterford Wedgwood USA Inc 1330 Campus Pkwy	Wall	NJ	07753	**877-720-3486**	

TAPE - ADHESIVE

SEE Medical Supplies - Mfr

727 TAPE - CELLOPHANE, GUMMED, MASKING, PRESSURE SENSITIVE

SEE ALSO Medical Supplies - Mfr

				Toll-Free	Phone
3M Canada Co 300 Tartan Dr	London	ON	N5V4M9	**888-364-3577**	
American Biltrite Inc Tape Products Div (ABI) 105 Whittendale Dr	Moorestown	NJ	08057	**888-224-6325**	856-778-0700
Avery Dennison Corp 207 Goode Ave *NYSE: AVY* ■ *Cust Svc	Glendale	CA	91203	**888-567-4387***	626-304-2000
Avery Dennison Specialty Tapes 250 Chester St	Painesville	OH	44077	**866-462-8379**	
Bemis Company Inc 2301 Industrial Dr *NYSE: BMS*	Neenah	WI	54956	**800-544-4672**	920-527-5000
Brite-Line LLC 10660 E 51st Ave	Denver	CO	80239	**888-201-6448**	
Decker Tape Products Inc 2 Stewart Pl	Fairfield	NJ	07004	**800-227-5252**	973-227-5350
DeWAL Industries Inc 15 Ray Trainor Dr	Narragansett	RI	02882	**800-366-8356**	401-789-9736
Eternabond 75 E Div St	Mundelein	IL	60060	**888-336-2663**	847-837-9400
Gaska-Tape Inc 1810 W Lusher Ave	Elkhart	IN	46517	**800-423-1571**	574-294-5431
Harris Industries Inc 5181 Argosy Ave	Huntington Beach	CA	92649	**800-222-6866**	714-898-8048
Holland Mfg Co Inc 15 Main St PO Box 404	Succasunna	NJ	07876	**800-345-0492**	973-584-8141
JHL Industries 10012 Nevada Ave	Chatsworth	CA	91311	**800-255-6636**	818-882-2233
Kruse Adhesive Tape Inc 1610 E McFadden Ave	Santa Ana	CA	92705	**800-992-7702**	714-640-2130
M & C Specialties Co 90 James Way *Cust Svc	SouthHampton	PA	18966	**800-441-6996***	215-322-1600
Neptco Inc 30 Hamlet St	Pawtucket	RI	02861	**800-354-5445**	401-722-5500
Plymouth Rubber Company Inc 960 Turnpike St	Canton	MA	02021	**800-458-0336**	
Presto Tape Inc 1626 Bridgewater Rd	Bensalem	PA	19020	**800-331-1373**	215-245-8555
Pro Tapes & Specialties Inc 621 Rte One S	North Brunswick	NJ	08902	**800-345-0234**	732-346-0900
Rudolph Brothers 6550 Oley Speaks Way	Canal Winchester	OH	43110	**800-600-9508**	800-375-0605
Shurtape Technologies LLC 1712 Eigth St Dr SE	Hickory	NC	28602	**888-442-8273**	828-322-2700
Tesa Tape Inc 5825 Carnegie Blvd	Charlotte	NC	28209	**800-426-2181**	704-554-0707
Tommy Tape 378 Four Rod Rd	Berlin	CT	06037	**888-866-8273**	860-378-0111
Vibac SPA 12250 Industrial Blvd	Montreal	QC	H1B5M5	**800-557-0192**	514-640-0250
WTP Inc PO Box 937	Coloma	MI	49038	**800-521-0731**	269-468-3399

728 TARPS, TENTS, COVERS

SEE ALSO Bags - Textile ; Sporting Goods

				Toll-Free	Phone
Aero Industries Inc 4243 W Bradbury Ave *Sales	Indianapolis	IN	46241	**800-535-9545***	317-244-2433
American Pavilion 1706 Warrington Ave	Danville	IL	61832	**800-424-9699**	217-443-0800
Anchor Industries Inc 7701 Hwy 41 N	Evansville	IN	47725	**800-544-4445**	812-867-2421
Canvas Products Co 274 S Waterman St	Detroit	MI	48209	**877-293-1669**	313-496-1000
Clamshell Structures Inc 1101 Maulhardt Ave	Oxnard	CA	93030	**800-360-8853**	805-988-1340
Commonwealth Canvas Inc 5 Perkins Way	Newburyport	MA	01950	**877-922-6827**	978-499-3900
DC Humphrys Inc 5744 Woodland Ave *Sales	Philadelphia	PA	19143	**800-645-2059***	215-724-8181
Eide Industries Inc 16215 Piuma Ave	Cerritos	CA	90703	**800-422-6827**	562-402-8335
Estex Mfg Co Inc 402 E Broad St PO Box 368	Fairburn	GA	30213	**800-749-1224**	
Fisher Canvas Products Inc 415 St Mary St	Burlington	NJ	08016	**800-892-6688**	
John Johnson Co 274 S Waterman St	Detroit	MI	48209	**800-991-1394**	313-496-0600
Loop-Loc Ltd 390 Motor Pkwy	Hauppauge	NY	11788	**800-562-5667**	631-582-2626
Mauritzon Inc 3939 W Belden Ave	Chicago	IL	60647	**800-621-4352**	773-235-6000
Rainier Industries Ltd 18375 Olympic Ave S	Tukwila	WA	98188	**800-869-7162**	425-251-1800
Shur-Co Inc 2309 Shur-Lok St PO Box 713	Yankton	SD	57078	**800-474-8756**	605-665-6000
Steele Canvas Basket Corp 201 William St PO Box 6267 IMCN	Chelsea	MA	02150	**800-541-8929**	617-889-0202
Trimaco LLC 2300 Gateway Centre Blvd Ste 200	Morrisville	NC	27560	**800-325-7356**	919-674-3460
Troy Sunshade Co 607 Riffle Ave	Greenville	OH	45331	**800-833-8769**	937-548-2466
Universal Fabric Structures Inc 2200 Kumry Rd	Telford	PA	18951	**800-634-8368**	215-529-9921

729 TAX PREPARATION SERVICES

				Toll-Free	Phone
AccessPoint LLC 28800 Orchard Lake Rd	Farmington Hills	MI	48334	**866-513-3861**	
Acumen Fiscal Agent 4542 E Inverness Ave Ste 210	Mesa	AZ	85206	**877-211-3738**	
APA Services 4150 International Plaza Tower I Ste 510	Fort Worth	TX	76109	**877-425-5023**	
Arthur Consulting Group Inc 31355 Oak Crest Dr Ste 200	Westlake Village	CA	91361	**800-677-9792**	818-735-4800
Avitus Group 175 N 27th St	Billings	MT	59101	**800-454-2446**	
Bayerkohler & Graff Ltd 11132 Zealand Ave N	Champlin	MN	55316	**866-315-2771**	763-427-2542
Building Block Computer 3209 Terminal Dr Ste 100	Eagan	MN	55121	**800-272-2650**	651-687-9435
Cotlviti Corp 1 Glenlake Pkwy Ste 1400	Atlanta	GA	30328	**800-530-1013**	770-379-2800
Cytak 6001 Shellmound St	Emeryville	CA	94608	**877-759-7464**	
Defense Finance & Acctg Service 8899 E 56th St	Indianapolis	IN	46249	**888-332-7411**	
Eastridge Workforce Solutions 2355 Northside Dr	San Diego	CA	92108	**800-778-0197**	619-260-2100
Eg Tax Service 2475 Niagara Falls Blvd	Amherst	NY	14228	**800-829-9998**	716-632-7886
Exactax Inc 2301 W Lincoln Ave Ste 100	Anaheim	CA	92801	**844-327-6740**	714-284-4802
Exerve Inc 2909 Langford Rd Ste 400B	Norcross	GA	30071	**800-364-0637**	770-447-1566
Farm Business Consultants Inc 150 3015 Fifth Ave NE	Calgary	AB	T2A6T8	**800-265-1002**	403-735-6105
Fiducial 10100 Old Columbia Rd	Columbia	MD	21046	**800-323-9000**	410-290-8296
Global Tax Network US LLC 7950 Main St N Ste 200	Minneapolis	MN	55369	**888-486-2695**	763-746-4556
H & R Block Tax Services Inc 4400 Main St	Kansas City	MO	64111	**800-472-5625**	
Inova Payroll Inc 176 Thompson Ln Ste 204	Nashville	TN	37211	**888-244-6106**	615-921-0600
Jackson Hewitt Inc 3 Sylvan Way Ste 301 *OTC: JHTXQ*	Parsippany	NJ	07054	**800-234-1040**	973-630-1040
JG Tax Group 1430 S Federal Hwy	Deerfield Beach	FL	33441	**866-477-5291**	
Liberty Tax Service Inc 1716 Corporate Landing Pkwy *Cust Svc	Virginia Beach	VA	23454	**800-790-3863***	757-493-8855
Payce Inc 1220B E Joppa Rd Ste 324	Towson	MD	21286	**800-729-5910**	443-279-9000
Paycom 7501 W Memorial Rd	Oklahoma City	OK	73142	**800-580-4505**	
Payworks Inc 1565 Willson Pl	Winnipeg	MB	R3T4H1	**866-788-3500**	
PrO Unlimited Inc 301 Yamato Rd Ste 3199	Boca Raton	FL	33431	**800-291-1099**	
Quantum Management Services Ltd 2000 McGill College Ave Ste 1800	Montreal	QC	H3A3H3	**800-978-2688**	514-842-5555
Questco 100 Commercial Cir	Conroe	TX	77304	**800-256-7823**	936-756-1980
SALT Group, The 1845 Sidney Baker St	Kerrville	TX	78028	**888-257-1266**	830-257-1290
Silver Creek Financial ServicesInc 175 Hwy 82	Lostine	OR	97857	**866-569-0020**	541-569-2272

730 TELECOMMUNICATIONS EQUIPMENT & SYSTEMS

SEE ALSO Modems ; Radio & Television Broadcasting & Communications Equipment

				Toll-Free	Phone
ADTRAN Inc 901 Explorer Blvd *NASDAQ: ADTN*	Huntsville	AL	35806	**800-923-8726**	256-963-8000
AirNet Communications Corp 295 North Dr Ste G	Melbourne	FL	32934	**800-984-1990**	321-984-1990
AltiGen Communications Inc 410 E Plumeria Dr *OTC: ATGN*	San Jose	CA	95134	**888-258-4436**	408-597-9000
Amtelco 4800 Curtin Dr	McFarland	WI	53558	**800-356-9148**	608-838-4194
AT & T Inc 175 E Houston St PO Box 2933 *NYSE: AT&T*	San Antonio	TX	78299	**800-351-7221**	210-821-4105

				Toll-Free	Phone
Atris Inc					
1151 S Trooper Rd Ste E	Norristown	PA	19403	800-724-3384	
Audiovox Corp					
180 Marcus Blvd	Hauppauge	NY	11788	800-645-4994	631-231-7750
NASDAQ: VOXX					
Charles Industries Ltd					
5600 Apollo Dr	Rolling Meadows	IL	60008	800-458-4747	847-806-6300
CiDRA Corp					
50 Barnes Pk N	Wallingford	CT	06492	877-243-7277	203-265-0035
Cisco 3333 Susan St	Costa Mesa	CA	92626	866-398-8749	714-662-5600
ClearOne Communications Inc					
5225 Wiley Post Way	Salt Lake City	UT	84116	800-945-7730	801-975-7200
Communication Technologies Inc					
14151 Newbrook Dr Ste 400	Chantilly	VA	20151	888-266-8358	703-961-9080
Communications Test Design Inc					
1339 Enterprise Dr	West Chester	PA	19380	800-223-3910	610-436-5203
Compunetix Inc					
2420 Mosside Blvd	Monroeville	PA	15146	800-879-4266	
DASAN Zhone Solutions Inc					
7195 Oakport St	Oakland	CA	94621	877-946-6320	510-777-7000
NASDAQ: DZSI					
DynaMetric Inc					
717 S Myrtle Ave	Monrovia	CA	91016	800-525-6925	626-358-2559
Ecessa Corp					
13755 First Ave N Ste 100	Plymouth	MN	55441	800-669-6242	763-694-9949
Electro Standards Laboratories Inc					
36 Western Industrial Dr	Cranston	RI	02921	877-943-1164	401-943-1164
Electronic Tele-Communications Inc					
1915 MacArthur Rd	Waukesha	WI	53188	888-746-4382	262-542-5600
OTC: ETCIA					
FleetBoss Global Positioning Solutions Inc					
241 O'Brien Rd	Fern Park	FL	32730	877-265-9559	407-265-9559
Fujitsu America Inc					
1250 E Arques Ave	Sunnyvale	CA	94085	800-538-8460	408-746-6200
GAI-Tronics Corp					
400 E Wyomissing Ave	Mohnton	PA	19540	800-492-1212	610-777-1374
Genesys Telecommunications Laboratories Inc					
2001 Junipero Serra Blvd	Daly City	CA	94014	888-436-3797	
Harris Corp					
1025 W NASA Blvd	Melbourne	FL	32919	800-442-7747	321-727-9100
NYSE: HRS					
Honeywell International Inc					
101 Columbia Rd PO Box 2245	Morristown	NJ	07962	877-841-2840	480-353-3020
NYSE: HON					
I Wireless					
4135 NW Urbandale Dr	Urbandale	IA	50322	888-550-4497*	
*Cust Svc					
iDirect Technologies Inc					
13865 Sunrise Valley Dr Ste 100	Herndon	VA	20171	888-362-5475	703-648-8118
Infinera Corp					
140 Caspian Ct	Sunnyvale	CA	94089	877-742-3427	408-572-5200
NASDAQ: INFN					
ISCO International LLC					
444 E State Pkwy Ste 123	Schaumburg	IL	60173	888-948-4726	630-283-3100
JTech Communications Inc					
6413 Congress Ave Ste 150	Boca Raton	FL	33487	800-321-6221	
Lantronix Inc					
167 Technology Dr	Irvine	CA	92618	800-526-8766*	949-453-3990
NASDAQ: LTRX ■ *Orders					
Mercury Systems Inc					
50 Minuteman Rd	Andover	MA	01810	866-627-6951	978-256-1300
NASDAQ: MRCY					
Mitel Networks Corp					
350 Legget Dr	Kanata	ON	K2K2W7	800-722-1301	613-592-2122
NEC America Inc					
6555 N State Hwy 161	Irving	TX	75039	866-632-3226*	214-262-2000
*Cust Svc					
Norsat International Inc					
110-4020 Viking Way	Richmond	BC	V6V2L4	800-644-4562	604-821-2800
TSX: NII					
Numerex Corp					
400 Interstate N Pkwy Ste 1350	Atlanta	GA	30339	800-665-5686	770-693-5950
One Inc Systems					
400 Imperial Blvd PO Box 9002	Cape Canaveral	FL	32920	800-749-3160	
Pics Telecom International Corp					
1920 Lyell Ave	Rochester	NY	14606	800-521-7427	585-295-2000
Plantronics Inc					
345 Encinal St	Santa Cruz	CA	95060	800-544-4660	831-426-5858
NYSE: PLT					
Polycom Inc					
4750 Willow Rd	Pleasanton	CA	94588	800-765-9266	
Protel Inc 4150 Kidron Rd	Lakeland	FL	33811	800-925-8882	863-644-5558
Proxim Wireless Corp					
1561 Buckeye Dr	Milpitas	CA	95035	800-229-1630	408-383-7600
OTC: PRXM					
Pulse Communications Inc					
2900 Towerview Rd	Herndon	VA	20171	800-381-1997*	703-471-2900
*Cust Svc					
RAD Data Communications Ltd					
900 Corporate Dr	Mahwah	NJ	07430	800-444-7234	201-529-1100
Samsung Telecommunications America LLP					
1301 E Lookout Dr	Richardson	TX	75082	800-726-7864	972-761-7000
Siemens Canada Ltd					
1550 Appleby Line	Burlington	ON	L7L6X7	800-236-2967	905-319-3600
Superior Essex Communications LP					
6120 Powers Ferry Rd Ste 150	Atlanta	GA	30339	800-551-8948	770-657-6000
Suttle 1001 East Hwy 212	Hector	MN	55342	800-852-8662	320-848-6711
Symmetricom Inc					
2300 Orchard Pkwy	San Jose	CA	95131	888-367-7966	408-433-0910
NASDAQ: MCHP					
System Engineering International Inc (SEI)					
5115 Pegasus Ct Ste Q	Frederick	MD	21704	800-765-4734	301-694-9601
Technical Communications Corp					
100 Domino Dr	Concord	MA	01742	800-952-4082	978-287-5100
NASDAQ: TCCO					
Tekelec					
5200 Paramount Pkwy	Morrisville	NC	27560	800-633-0738	
NASDAQ: TKLC					

				Toll-Free	Phone
Tel Electronics Inc					
313 South 740 East Ste 1	American Fork	UT	84003	800-748-5022	
Telco Systems Inc					
15 Berkshire Rd	Mansfield	MA	02048	800-227-0937	781-255-2120
Telect Inc					
22425 E Appleway Ave Ste 11	Liberty Lake	WA	99019	800-551-4567*	509-926-6000
*Cust Svc					
Teo Technologies Inc					
11609 49th Pl W	Mukilteo	WA	98275	800-524-0024	425-349-1000
Toshiba America Inc					
1251 Ave of the Americas 41st Fl	New York	NY	10020	800-457-7777	212-596-0600
Tricomm Services Corp					
1247 N Church St Ste 12	Moorestown	NJ	08057	800-872-2401	856-914-9001
TSI Global Cos					
700 Fountain Lakes Blvd	Saint Charles	MO	63301	800-875-5605	636-949-8889
Uniden America Corp					
4700 Amon Carter Blvd	Fort Worth	TX	76155	800-297-1023*	817-858-3300
*Cust Svc					
Valcom Inc 5614 Hollins Rd	Roanoke	VA	24019	800-825-2661	540-563-2000
Vbrick Systems Inc					
12 Beaumont Rd	Wallingford	CT	06492	866-827-4251	
VTech Communications Inc					
9590 SW Gemini Dr Ste 120	Beaverton	OR	97008	800-595-9511	503-596-1200
Westell Technologies Inc					
750 N Commons Dr	Aurora	IL	60504	800-323-6883	630-898-2500
NASDAQ: WSTL					

731 TELECOMMUNICATIONS SERVICES

				Toll-Free	Phone
Access America					
673 Emory Valley Rd	Oak Ridge	TN	37830	800-860-2140	865-482-2140
Access Point Inc					
1100 Crescent Green	Cary	NC	27518	877-419-4274	919-851-4838
AirIQ Inc					
1845 Sandstone Manor Unit 10	Pickering	ON	L1W3X9	888-606-6444	905-831-6444
Airvoice Wireless LLC					
2425 Franklin Rd	Bloomfield Hills	MI	48302	888-944-2355	
Alaska Communications Systems Group Inc					
600 Telephone Ave	Anchorage	AK	99503	800-808-8083	855-565-2556
NASDAQ: ALSK					
Allstream Corp					
200 Wellington St W	Toronto	ON	M5V3G2	888-288-2273*	416-345-2000
*Cust Svc					
AmeriCom Inc PO Box 2146	Sandy	UT	84091	800-820-6296	801-571-2446
AT & T Inc					
175 E Houston St PO Box 2933	San Antonio	TX	78299	800-351-7221	210-821-4105
NYSE: AT&T					
Bell Canada					
1050 Beaver Hall Hill	Montreal	QC	H2Z1S4	800-667-0123	
Birch Communications					
2300 Main St Ste 340	Kansas City	MO	64108	866-424-5100	816-300-3000
Bluegrass Cellular Inc					
2902 Ring Rd	Elizabethtown	KY	42701	800-928-2355	270-769-0339
Broadview Networks Holdings Inc					
800 Westchester Ave Ste N-501	Rye Brook	NY	10573	800-260-8766	914-922-7000
Bruce Telecom					
3145 Hwy 21 PO Box 80	Tiverton	ON	N0G2T0	866-517-2000	519-368-2000
Cellhire USA LLC					
3520 W Miller Rd Ste 100	Garland	TX	75041	877-244-7242	
Cesium Telecom Inc					
5798 Ferrier	Montreal	QC	H4P1M7	877-798-8686	514-798-8686
Circa Enterprises Inc					
535 - 10333 Southport Rd SW	Calgary	AB	T2W3X6	877-257-4588	403-258-2011
Citizens Telephone Co-op					
PO Box 137	Floyd	VA	24091	800-941-0426	540-745-2111
Commenco Inc					
4901 Bristol Ave	Kansas City	MO	64129	800-292-9725	816-753-2166
Commonwealth Telephone Co					
1 Newbury St Ste 103	Peabody	MA	01960	800-439-7170	978-536-9500
Comporium Communications					
PO Box 470	Rock Hill	SC	29731	888-403-2667	803-326-6064
Corporate Telephone Services					
184 W Second St	Boston	MA	02127	800-274-1211	617-625-1200
Criticom Inc					
4211 Forbes Blvd	Lanham	MD	20706	800-449-3384	301-306-0600
Dakota Central					
630 Fifth St N	Carrington	ND	58421	800-771-0974	701-652-3184
Deltacom Inc					
7037 Old Madison Pk	Huntsville	AL	35806	800-239-3000	
Eastex Telephone Co-op Inc					
PO Box 150	Henderson	TX	75653	800-232-7839	903-854-1000
EATELCORP Inc					
913 S Burnside Ave	Gonzales	LA	70737	800-621-4211	225-621-4300
Empire Telephone Company					
34 Main St PO Box 349	Prattsburgh	NY	14873	800-338-3300	607-522-3712
Etex Telephone Co-op Inc					
1013 Hwy 155 N	Gilmer	TX	75644	877-482-3839	903-797-4357
Excel Telecommunications					
433 Las Colinas Blvd Ste 400	Irving	TX	75039	877-668-0808	972-910-1900
FairPoint Communications Inc					
521 E Morehead St Ste 250	Charlotte	NC	28202	866-984-2001	704-344-8150
NASDAQ: FRP					
Farmers Telecommunications Co-op (FTC)					
144 McCurdy Ave N PO Box 217	Rainsville	AL	35986	866-638-2144	256-638-2144
Farmers Telephone Co-op Inc					
1101 E Main St	Kingstree	SC	29556	888-218-5050	843-382-2333
Faxaway 417 Second Ave W	Seattle	WA	98119	800-906-4329	206-479-7000
FaxBack Inc					
7007 SW Cardinal Ln Ste 105	Portland	OR	97224	800-329-2225	503-597-5350
Frontier Communications Corp					
3 High Ridge Pk	Stamford	CT	06905	800-877-4390	203-614-5600
NASDAQ: FTR					
Fusion Telecommunications International Inc					
420 Lexington Ave Ste 1718	New York	NY	10170	888-301-1721	212-201-2400
NASDAQ: FSNN					

Listing	Toll-Free	Phone
Golden West Telecommunications 415 Crown St PO Box 411 .... Wall SD 57790	866-279-2161	605-279-2161
Granite Telecommunications LLC 100 Newport Ave Ext .... Quincy MA 02171	866-847-1500	866-847-5500
Guadalupe Valley Telephone Co-op (GVTC) 36101 FM 3159 .... New Braunfels TX 78132	800-367-4882	830-885-4411
Horry Telephone Co-op Inc (HTC) 3480 Hwy 701 N PO Box 1820 .... Conway SC 29528	800-824-6779	843-365-2151
Idc Communications 1385 Niakwa Rd E .... Winnipeg MB R2J3T3	800-474-7771	204-254-8282
Integra Telecom Inc 1201 NE Lloyd Blvd Ste 750 .... Portland OR 97232 *General	866-468-3472*	
Inter-Community Telephone Co (ICTC) PO Box 8 .... Nome ND 58062	800-350-9137	701-924-8815
InterCall 8420 W Bryn Mawr Ste 1100 .... Chicago IL 60631	800-374-2441	773-399-1600
IVCi LLC 601 Old Willets Path .... Hauppauge NY 11788	800-224-7083	631-273-5800
J2 Global Communications Inc 6922 Hollywood Blvd .... Hollywood CA 90028 *Sales	888-718-2000*	323-860-9200
Kaplel (KTC) 220 N Cushing Ave .... Kaplan LA 70548	866-643-7171	337-643-7171
KDDI America Inc 825 Third Ave 3rd Fl .... New York NY 10022	866-348-3370	
Kennebec Telephone Company Inc 220 S Main St PO Box 158 .... Kennebec SD 57544	888-868-3390	605-869-2220
Matanuska Telephone Assn Inc 1740 S Chugach St .... Palmer AK 99645	800-478-3211	907-745-3211
Midcontinent Communications PO Box 5010 .... Sioux Falls SD 57117	800-888-1300	605-274-9810
Molalla Communications Co-op 211 Robbins St PO Box 360 .... Molalla OR 97038	800-332-2344	503-829-1100
Net Access Corp 2300 15th St Ste 300 .... Denver CO 80202	800-638-6336	973-590-5000
Net2Phone Inc 520 Broad St .... Newark NJ 07102	800-386-6438	866-978-8260
Netwolves Corp 4710 Eisenhower Blvd Ste E-8 .... Tampa FL 33634	855-638-9658	
New Ulm Telecom Inc 27 N Minnesota St .... New Ulm MN 56073 OTC: NULM	888-873-6853	507-354-4111
NobelBiz Inc 1545 Faraday Ave .... Carlsbad CA 92008	800-975-2844	760-405-0105
NTT DoCoMo USA Inc 757 Third Ave 16th Fl .... New York NY 10017	888-362-6661	
O1 Communications Inc 4359 Town Ctr Blvd Ste 217 .... El Dorado hills CA 95762	888-444-1111	
Omnitracs 717 North Harwood St Ste 1300 .... Dallas TX 75201	800-348-7227	
OTZ Telephone Co-op Inc PO Box 324 .... Kotzebue AK 99752	800-478-3111	907-442-3114
Panhandle Telecommunication Systems Inc (PTSI) 2222 NW Hwy 64 .... Guymon OK 73942	800-562-2556	580-338-2556
Penasco Valley Telephone Cooperative Inc (PVT) 4011 W Main St .... Artesia NM 88210	800-505-4844	
Pioneer Long Distance Inc PO Box 539 .... Kingfisher OK 73750	888-782-2667	
Pioneer Telephone Assn Inc PO Box 707 .... Ulysses KS 67880	800-308-7536	620-356-3211
Pioneer Telephone Co-op Inc 202 W Broadway Ave PO Box 539 .... Kingfisher OK 73750	888-782-2667	
PWR LLC 6402 Deere Rd .... Syracuse NY 13206	800-342-0878	315-701-0210
Reiko Wireless Inc 55 Mall Dr .... Commack NY 11725	888-797-3456	631-913-6700
Reserve Telephone Company Inc 3750 Nicole St .... Paulina LA 70763	888-611-6111	985-536-1111
Rogers Communications Inc 333 Bloor St E 9th Fl .... Toronto ON M4W1G9 TSX: RCI.B	888-221-1687	877-490-9481
Rural Telephone Service Company Inc PO Box 158 .... Lenora KS 67645	877-625-7872	785-567-4281
Securus Technologies Inc 14651 Dallas Pkwy .... Dallas TX 75254	800-844-6591	972-734-1111
Shawnee Telephone Co PO Box 69 .... Equality IL 62934	800-461-3956	618-276-4211
Shenandoah Telecommunications Co 500 Shentel Way .... Edinburg VA 22824 NASDAQ: SHEN	800-743-6835	540-984-5224
Sirius XM Canada Inc 135 Liberty St 4th Fl .... Toronto ON M6K1A7	888-539-7474	416-408-6000
Skyline Membership Corp 1200 NC Hwy 194 N .... West Jefferson NC 28694	800-759-2226	
SkyTel Corp PO Box 2469 .... Jackson MS 39225 *Cust Svc	800-759-8737*	
Smart City Networks 5795 W Badura Ave Ste 110 .... Las Vegas NV 89118	888-446-6911	702-943-6000
Solarus 440 E Grand Ave .... Wisconsin Rapids WI 54494	800-421-9282	715-421-8111
Southern Communications Services Inc 5555 Glenridge Connector Ste 500 .... Atlanta GA 30342	800-818-5462	
Spok Inc 6850 Versar Ctr Ste 420 .... Springfield VA 22151	888-878-5009	800-611-8488
Spotwave Wireless Inc 500 Van Buren St PO Box 550 .... Kemptville ON K0G1J0	866-704-9750	613-591-1662
Startec Global Communications Corp 11300 Rockville Pk Ste 900 .... Rockville MD 20852	800-827-3374	301-610-4300
TDS Telecommunications Corp 525 Junction Rd .... Madison WI 53717	866-571-6662	608-664-4000
TelAlaska Inc 201 E 56th St .... Anchorage AK 99518	888-570-1792	907-563-2003
Telephone Service Co 2 Willipie St .... Wapakoneta OH 45895	800-743-5707	419-739-2200
Teligent Inc 105 Lincoln Ave .... Buena NJ 08310	800-656-0793	
Thumb Cellular Ltd Partnership PO Box 650 .... Pigeon MI 48755	800-443-5057	
Total Telcom Inc 540 1632 Dickson Ave .... Kelowna BC V1Y7T2	877-860-3762	250-860-3762
Trans National Communications International Inc (TNCI) 2 Charlesgate W .... Boston MA 02215	800-800-8400	617-369-1000
Twin Lakes Telephone Co-op 200 Telephone Ln .... Gainesboro TN 38562 *Cust Svc	800-644-8582*	931-268-2151
United Utilities Inc 5450 A St .... Anchorage AK 99518	800-478-2020	907-561-1674
Unitel Inc PO Box 165 .... Unity ME 04988	888-760-1048	207-948-3900
Universal Service Administrative Co 2000 L St NW Ste 200 .... Washington DC 20036	888-203-8100	
US Cellular Corp (USCC) 8410 W Bryn Mawr Ave Ste 700 .... Chicago IL 60631 NYSE: USM	888-944-9400	773-399-8900
Valley Telephone Co-op Inc 752 E Maley St .... Willcox AZ 85643	800-421-5711	520-384-2231
Verizon Business 1 Verizon Way .... Basking Ridge NJ 07920 *Cust Svc	877-297-7816*	202-789-1432
Verizon Communications Inc 140 W St .... New York NY 10007 NYSE: VZ	800-837-4966	202-789-1432
Verizon Wireless 180 Washington Valley Rd .... Bedminster NJ 07921	800-922-0204	908-306-7000
Virgin Mobile USA Inc 10 Independence Blvd .... Warren NJ 07059	888-322-1122	
Voicecom 5900 Windward Pkwy Ste 500 .... Alpharetta GA 30005	888-468-3554	
Vonage Holdings Corp 23 Main St .... Holmdel NJ 07733 NYSE: VG	877-862-2562	732-528-2600
Vox Mobile 6100 Rockside Woods Blvd Ste 100 .... Independence OH 44131	800-536-9030	
Wabash Telephone Co-op Inc 210 S Church St PO Box 299 .... Louisville IL 62858	877-878-2120	618-665-3311
Warwick Valley Telephone Co 47 Main St PO Box 592 .... Warwick NY 10990 *Cust Svc	800-952-7642*	845-986-8080
Wavedivision Holdings LLC 401 Parkplace Ctr Ste 103 .... Kirkland WA 98033	844-910-8519	425-576-8200
West Central Wireless 3389 Knickerbocker Rd .... San Angelo TX 76904	800-695-9016	
West River Telecommunications Co-op PO Box 467 .... Hazen ND 58545	800-748-7220	701-748-2211
West Texas Rural TelephoneCo-op Inc PO Box 1737 .... Hereford TX 79045	888-440-4331	006 361-3331
XO Communications Inc 13865 Sunrise Vly Dr .... Herndon VA 20171	866-349-0134	703-547-2000
Yak PO Box 71055 Laurier W PO .... Ottawa ON K2P2L9	877-925-4925	

732   TELEMARKETING & OTHER TELE-SERVICES

Both inbound and outbound telephone marketing as well as other tele-services are included here.

Listing	Toll-Free	Phone
AGR GROUP NEVADA LLC 6275 S Pearl St Ste 100-300 .... Las Vegas NV 89120	877-860-5780	
Alta Resources 120 N Commercial St .... Neenah WI 54956	877-464-2582	
America's Call Center Inc 7901 Baymeadows Way Ste 14 .... Jacksonville FL 32256	800-598-2580	904-224-2000
American Home Base Inc PO Box 2430 .... Pensacola FL 32513 *General	800-549-0595*	850-857-0860
Ameridial Inc 4535 Strausser St NW .... North Canton OH 44720	800-445-7128	
Aria Communications 717 W Saint Germain St .... St. Cloud MN 56301	800-955-9924	
Calling Solutions By Phone Power Inc 2200 McCullough Ave .... San Antonio TX 78212 *Cust Svc	800-683-5500*	210-801-9630
Connection, The 11351 Rupp Dr .... Burnsville MN 55337 *Sales	800-883-5777*	952-948-5488
Convergys Corp 201 E Fourth St .... Cincinnati OH 45202 NYSE: CVG	888-284-9900	513-723-7000
Evolve IP LLC 989 Old Eagle School Rd Ste 815 .... Wayne PA 19087	877-459-4347	
Harte-Hanks Response Management 2800 Wells Branch Pkwy .... Austin TX 78728	800-456-9748	512-434-1100
InfoCision Management Corp 325 Springside Dr .... Akron OH 44333	800-210-6269	330-668-1400
Julie Inc 3275 Executive Dr .... Joliet IL 60431	800-892-0123	815-741-5000
Kathy Sisk Enterprises Inc PO Box 1754 .... Clovis CA 93613	800-477-1278	559-323-1472
Lester Inc 19 Business Pk Dr .... Branford CT 06405	800-999-5265	203-488-5265
Mars Stout Inc 4500 Majestic Dr .... Missoula MT 59808	800-451-6277	406-721-6280
Miratel Solutions Inc 2501 Steeles Ave W .... North York ON M3J2P1	866-647-2835	416-650-7850
My Receptionist 800 Wisconsin St Ste 410 .... Eau Claire WI 54703	800-686-0162	
Nordia Inc 3020 Jacques-Bureau 2nd Fl .... Laval QC H7P6G2	866-858-4367	514-415-7088
Telax Voice Solutions 365 Evans Ave Ste 302 .... Toronto ON M8Z1K2	888-808-3529	416-207-0630
Tele Business USA 1945 Techny Rd Ste 3 .... Northbrook IL 60062	877-315-8353	
TeleDevelopment Services Inc 149 Kensington Crt .... Broadview Heights OH 44147	888-788-4441	
TeleTech Holdings Inc 9197 S Peoria St .... Englewood CO 80112 NASDAQ: TTEC ■ *General	800-835-3832*	303-397-8100
Thumbs-Up Telemarketing Inc 11861 Westline Industrial Dr Ste 600 .... Saint Louis MO 63146	800-410-2016	

	Toll-Free	Phone
USA 800 Inc		
9808 E 66th Terr .... Kansas City MO 64133	800-821-7539	816-358-1303
VOX Data		
1155 Metcalfe St 18th Fl. .... Montreal QC H3B2V6	800-861-9599	514-871-1920
West Corp		
11808 Miracle Hills Dr .... Omaha NE 68154	800-232-0900*	
*Sales		
Working Solutions		
1820 Preston Pk Blvd Ste 2000 .... Plano TX 75093	866-857-4800	972-964-4800
Young America Corp		
10 S Fifth St 7th Fl .... Minneapolis MN 55402	800-533-4529	
Your Selling Team		
100 Spectrum Ctr Dr Ste 700 .... Irvine CA 92618	888-387-8002	

TELEVISION - CABLE

SEE Cable & Other Pay Television Services ; Television Networks - Cable

733   TELEVISION COMPANIES

	Toll-Free	Phone
Ask Associates Inc		
1201 Wakarusa Ste C-1 .... Lawrence KS 66049	800-315-4333	785-841-8194
Capitol Broadcasting Co Inc		
2619 Western Blvd .... Raleigh NC 27606	800-234-4857	919-890-6000
Christian Television Network Inc (CTN)		
6922 142nd Ave N .... Largo FL 33771	800-716-7729	727-535-5622
Gannett Company Inc		
7950 Jones Branch Dr .... McLean VA 22107	800-778-3299	703-854-6000
NYSE: GCI		
LeSea Broadcasting Corp		
61300 S Ironwood Rd .... South Bend IN 46614	800-365-3732	574-291-8200
Metrovision Production Group LLC		
508 W 24th St .... New York NY 10011	800-242-2424	212-989-1515
ON Services		
6779 Crescent Dr .... Norcross GA 30071	800-967-2419	770-457-0966
Quincy Newspapers Inc		
130 S Fifth St .... Quincy IL 62301	800-373-9444	217-223-5100

734   TELEVISION NETWORKS - BROADCAST

	Toll-Free	Phone
Public Broadcasting Service (PBS)		
2100 Crystal Dr .... Arlington VA 22202	866-864-0828	703-739-5000

735   TELEVISION NETWORKS - CABLE

	Toll-Free	Phone
Business News Network (BNN)		
299 Queen St W .... Toronto ON M5V2Z5	855-326-6266	416-384-6600
Cable Public Affairs Channel (CPAC)		
PO Box 81099 .... Ottawa ON K1P1B1	877-287-2722	
Christian Broadcasting Network (CBN)		
977 Centerville Tpke .... Virginia Beach VA 23463	800-823-6053	
Daystar Television Network		
3901 Hwy 121 PO Box 610546. .... Bedford TX 76021	800-329-0029	817-571-1229
Discovery Communications Inc		
1 Discovery Pl .... Silver Spring MD 20910	877-324-5850	240-662-2000
NASDAQ: DISCA		
ESPN Deportes		
2 Alhambra Plz .... Coral Gables FL 33134	800-337-6783	305-567-3797
EVINE Live Inc		
6740 Shady Oak Rd .... Eden Prairie MN 55344	800-676-5523	
God's Learning Ch (GLC)		
PO Box 61000 .... Midland TX 79711	800-707-0420	432-563-0420
Hallmark Ch		
12700 Ventura Blvd .... Studio City CA 91604	888-390-7474	818-755-2400
History Ch		
A&E Television Networks LLC		
235 E 45th St .... New York NY 10017	888-371-5848	212-210-1400
Liberty Ch		
1971 University Blvd .... Lynchburg VA 24515	800-332-1883	434-582-2718
Outdoor Ch		
43445 Business Pk Dr Ste 103. .... Temecula CA 92590	800-770-5750	951-699-6991
NASDAQ: OUTD		
QVC Inc 1200 Wilson Dr .... West Chester PA 19380	800-367-9444	484-701-1000
TCT Ministries Inc		
11717 N Rt 37 PO Box 1010. .... Marion IL 62959	800-232-9855	618-997-4700
Telelatino Network Inc (TLN)		
5125 Steeles Ave W .... Toronto ON M9L1R5	800-551-8401	416-744-8200
Trinity Broadcasting Network (TBN)		
PO Box A .... Santa Ana CA 92711	888-731-1000	714-832-2950
Turner Classic Movies Inc (TCM)		
1050 Techwood Dr NW .... Atlanta GA 30318	844-356-7875	
Weather Ch Inc, The		
300 I N Pkwy .... Atlanta GA 30339	866-843-0392	770-226-0000
Worship Network		
PO Box 428 .... Safety Harbor FL 34695	800-728-8723	

736   TELEVISION STATIONS

SEE ALSO Internet Broadcasting

	Toll-Free	Phone
Channel 45 WHFT TV		
3324 Pembroke Rd .... Miami FL 33021	800-447-7235	954-962-1700
CTV 299 Queen St W .... Toronto ON M5V2Z5	866-690-6179	416-384-5000
CW Seattle		
1000 Dexter Ave N Ste 205. .... Seattle WA 98109	866-313-5789	206-441-1111
Detroit WMYD TV20		
20777 W Ten Mile Rd .... Southfield MI 48034	800-825-0770	248-827-7777
Iowa Public Television		
6450 Corporate Dr PO Box 6450 .... Johnston IA 50131	800-532-1290	515-725-9700

	Toll-Free	Phone
KAFT-TV Ch 13 (PBS)		
350 S Donaghey Ave .... Conway AR 72034	800-662-2386	501-682-2386
KBHE-TV Ch 9 (PBS)		
555 N Dakota St PO Box 5000 .... Vermillion SD 57069	800-333-0789	
KCTV-TV Ch 5 (CBS)		
4500 Shawnee Mission Pkwy .... Fairway KS 66205	800-767-7700	913-677-5555
KCWC-TV Ch 4 (PBS)		
2660 Peck Ave .... Riverton WY 82501	800-495-9788	307-856-6944
KELOLAND TV		
501 S Phillips Ave .... Sioux Falls SD 57104	800-888-5356	605-336-1100
Kentucky Educational Television (KET)		
600 Cooper Dr .... Lexington KY 40502	800-432-0951	859-258-7000
KETG 9 Arkadelphia		
350 S Donaghey Ave .... Conway AR 72034	800-662-2386	501-682-2386
KETS-TV Ch 2 (PBS)		
350 S Donaghey Ave .... Conway AR 72034	800-662-2386	501-682-2386
KIMT-TV Ch 3 (CBS)		
112 N Pennsylvania Ave .... Mason City IA 50401	800-323-4883	641-423-2540
KMAX-TV Ch 31 (CBS)		
2713 Kovr Dr .... West Sacramento CA 95605	800-374-8813	916-374-1313
KMIZ-TV Ch 17 (ABC)		
501 Business Loop 70 E .... Columbia MO 65201	800-345-4109	573-449-0917
KMOS-TV Ch 6 (PBS)		
University of Central Missouri .... Warrensburg MO 64093	800-753-3436	
KOMU-TV Ch 8 (NBC)		
5550 Hwy 63 S .... Columbia MO 65201	800-286-3932	573-884-6397
KPDX-TV Ch 49 (MNT)		
14975 NW Greenbrier Pkwy .... Beaverton OR 97006	866-906-1249	503-906-1249
KPTV-TV Ch 12 (Fox)		
14975 NW Greenbrier Pkwy .... Beaverton OR 97006	866-906-1249	503-906-1249
KPXE-TV Ch 50 (I)		
4220 Shawnee Mission Pkwy Ste 110 B. .... Fairway KS 66205	888-467-2988	212-757-3100
KRCG-TV Ch 13 (CBS)		
10188 Old Hwy 54 N .... New Bloomfield MO 65063	800-773-6180	573-896-5144
KSMQ-TV Ch 15 (PBS)		
2000 Eigth Ave NW .... Austin MN 55912	800-658-2539	507-481-2095
KTSD-TV Ch 10 (PBS)		
555 N Dakota St PO Box 5000 .... Vermillion SD 57069	800-333-0789	
KUSD-TV Ch 2 (PBS)		
555 N Dakota St PO Box 5000 .... Vermillion SD 57069	800-333-0789	
KUSM-TV Ch 9 (PBS)		
Visual Communications Bldg Rm 183 .... Bozeman MT 59717	800-426-8243	406-994-3437
KWPX-TV Ch 33 (I)		
8112-C 304th Ave SE PO Box 426 .... Preston WA 98050	888-467-2988	212-757-3100
KWWL-TV Ch 7 (NBC)		
500 E Fourth St .... Waterloo IA 50703	800-947-7746	319-291-1200
UNC-TV Ch 4 (PBS)		
10 TW Alexander Dr		
PO Box 14900. .... Research Triangle Park NC 27709	800-906-5050	919-549-7000
WBNX-TV Ch 55 (CW)		
2690 State Rd .... Cuyahoga Falls OH 44223	800-282-0515	330-922-5500
WBRE-TV Ch 28 (NBC)		
62 S Franklin St .... Wilkes-Barre PA 18701	800-367-9222	570-823-2828
WCAU NBC 10		
10 Monument Rd .... Bala Cynwyd PA 19004	800-847-9228	610-668-5510
WCBB-TV Ch 10 (PBS)		
1450 Lisbon St .... Lewiston ME 04240	800-884-1717	
WCBD-TV Ch 2 (NBC)		
210 W Coleman Blvd .... Mount Pleasant SC 29464	800-861-5255	843-884-2222
WCIA-TV Ch 3 (CBS)		
PO Box 20 .... Champaign IL 61824	800-676-3382	217-356-8333
WDAM-TV Ch 7 (NBC)		
PO Box 16269 .... Hattiesburg MS 39404	800-844-9326	601-544-4730
WEAO-TV Ch 49 (PBS)		
1750 Campus Ctr Dr .... Kent OH 44240	800-554-4549	330-677-4549
WEHT-TV 800 Marywood Dr .... Henderson KY 42420	800-879-8542	800-879-8549
WENH-TV Ch 11 (PBS)		
268 Mast Rd .... Durham NH 03824	800-639-8408	603-868-1100
WETA-TV Ch 26 (PBS)		
3939 Campbell Ave .... Arlington VA 22206	800-662-2386	703-998-2600
WFMY News 2		
1615 Phillips Ave .... Greensboro NC 27405	800-593-3692	212-975-3247
WGBH-TV Ch 2 (PBS)		
1 Guest St .... Brighton MA 02135	800-492-1111	617-300-2000
WGGS-TV Ch 16 (Ind)		
3409 Rutherford Rd Ext .... Taylors SC 29687	800-849-3683*	864-244-1616
*General		
WGHP-TV Ch 8 (Fox)		
2005 Francis St .... High Point NC 27263	800-808-6397	336-841-8888
WHKY-TV Ch 14 (Ind)		
526 Main Ave SE PO Box 1059 .... Hickory NC 28602	800-899-4897	828-322-1290
WHMB-TV Ch 40 (Ind)		
10511 Greenfield Ave .... Noblesville IN 46060	800-535-5542	317-773-5050
WITV-TV Ch 7 (PBS)		
1041 George Rogers Blvd .... Columbia SC 29201	800-277-3245	803-737-3200
WKNO 7151 Cherry Farms Rd .... Cordova TN 38016	877-717-7822	901-729-8765
WMTW-TV Ch 8 (ABC)		
4 Ledgeview Dr .... Westbrook ME 04092	800-248-6397	207-835-3888
WNEM-TV Ch 5 (CBS)		
107 N Franklin St .... Saginaw MI 48607	800-522-9636	989-755-8191
WNEP-TV Ch 16 (ABC)		
16 Montage Mtn Rd .... Moosic PA 18507	800-982-4374	570-346-7474
WNJU-TV Ch 47 (Tele)		
2200 Fletcher Ave 6th Fl. .... Fort Lee NJ 07024	877-478-3536	
WOI-TV Ch 5 (ABC)		
3903 Westown Pkwy .... West Des Moines IA 50266	800-858-5555	515-457-9645
WOUC-TV Ch 44 (PBS)		
35 S College St .... Athens OH 45701	800-456-2044	740-593-1771
WOWK-TV Ch 13 (CBS)		
555 Fifth Ave .... Huntington WV 25701	800-333-7636	304-525-1313
WPXD-TV Ch 31 (I)		
26935 W 11 Mile Rd .... Southfield MI 48033	888-467-2988	212-757-3100
WPXW		
6199 Old Arrington Ln .... Fairfax Station VA 22039	888-467-2988	
WSBT-TV Ch 22 (CBS)		
1301 E Douglas Rd .... Mishawaka IN 46545	877-634-7181	574-232-6397
WSRE-TV Ch 23 (PBS)		
1000 College Blvd .... Pensacola FL 32504	800-239-9773	850-484-1200

	Toll-Free	Phone
WWMT-TV Ch 3 (CBS)		
590 W Maple St .... Kalamazoo MI 49008	800-875-3333	
WXYZ-TV Ch 7 (ABC)		
20777 W 10-Mile Rd .... Southfield MI 48037	800-825-0770	248-827-7777
WYOU-TV Ch 22 (CBS)		
62 S Franklin St .... Wilkes-Barre PA 18701	855-241-5144	570-961-2222

736-1 Albuquerque/Santa Fe, NM

	Toll-Free	Phone
KNME-TV Ch 5 (PBS)		
1130 University Blvd NE		
University of New Mexico .... Albuquerque NM 87102	800-328-5663	505-277-2121
KOAT-TV Ch 7 (ABC)		
3801 Carlisle Blvd NE .... Albuquerque NM 87107	877-871-0165	505-884-7777

736-2 Anchorage, AK

	Toll-Free	Phone
KAKM-TV Ch 7 (PBS)		
3877 University Dr .... Anchorage AK 99508	800-478-8255	907-550-8400
KJUD-TV Ch 8 (ABC)		
2700 E Tudor Rd .... Anchorage AK 99507	877-304-1313	907-561-1313
KTBY-TV Ch 4 (Fox)		
2700 E Tudor Rd .... Anchorage AK 99507	877-304-1313	907-561-1313
KYUR-TV Ch 13 (ABC)		
2700 E Tudor Rd .... Anchorage AK 99507	877-304-1313	907-561-1313

736-3 Asheville, NC/Greenville, SC/Spartanburg, SC

	Toll-Free	Phone
WLOS-TV Ch 13 (ABC)		
110 Technology Dr .... Asheville NC 28803	800-419-6356	828-684-1340
WSPA-TV Ch 7 (CBS)		
250 International Dr .... Spartanburg SC 29303	866-946-6349	864-576-7777
WYFF-TV Ch 4 (NBC)		
505 Rutherford St .... Greenville SC 29609	000 453-9933	864-242-4404

736-4 Atlanta, GA

	Toll-Free	Phone
WGCL-TV Ch 46 (CBS)		
425 14th St NW .... Atlanta GA 30318	800-949-6397	404-327-3194

736-5 Augusta, GA

	Toll-Free	Phone
WFXG-TV Ch 54 (Fox)		
3933 Washington Rd .... Augusta GA 30907	866-974-0487	706-650-5400

736-6 Austin, TX

	Toll-Free	Phone
KLRU-TV Ch 18 (PBS)		
2504-B Whitis Ave PO Box 7158 .... Austin TX 78712	800-239-5233	512-471-4811
KXAN News		
908 W Martin Luther King Jr Bl .... Austin TX 78701	800-843-5678	512-476-3636

736-7 Bangor, ME

	Toll-Free	Phone
WLBZ-TV Ch 2 (NBC)		
329 Mt Hope Ave .... Bangor ME 04401	800-244-6306	207-942-4821

736-8 Baton Rouge, LA

	Toll-Free	Phone
KLPB-TV Ch 24 (PBS)		
7733 Perkins Rd .... Baton Rouge LA 70810	800-272-8161	225-767-5660
WAFB-TV Ch 9 (CBS)		
844 Government St .... Baton Rouge LA 70802	888-677-2900	225-215-4700
WBRZ 2 abc		
1650 Highland Rd .... Baton Rouge LA 70802	800-726-6409	225-383-1111
WLPB-TV Ch 27 (PBS)		
7733 Perkins Rd .... Baton Rouge LA 70810	800-272-8161	225-767-5660

736-9 Billings, MT

	Toll-Free	Phone
KTVQ-TV Ch 2 (CBS)		
3203 Third Ave N .... Billings MT 59101	800-908-4490	406-252-5611

736-10 Birmingham, AL

	Toll-Free	Phone
Abc 33 40		
800 Concourse Pkwy Ste 200 .... Birmingham AL 35244	800-784-8669	205-403-3340
WBIQ-TV Ch 10 (PBS)		
2112 11th Ave S Ste 400 .... Birmingham AL 35205	800-239-5233	205-328-8756
WEIQ-TV Ch 42 (PBS)		
2112 11th Ave S Ste 400 .... Birmingham AL 35205	800-239-5233	205-328-8756
WVTM-TV Ch 13 (NBC)		
1732 Valley View Dr .... Birmingham AL 35209	844-248-7698	205-933-1313

736-11 Boise, ID

	Toll-Free	Phone
KTVB-TV Ch 7 (NBC)		
5407 Fairview .... Boise ID 83706	800-537-8939	208-375-7277

736-12 Boston, MA

	Toll-Free	Phone
WHDH TV 7NEWS 7 Bulfinch Pl .... Boston MA 02114	800-280-8477	855-247-4265

736-13 Buffalo, NY

	Toll-Free	Phone
WIVB-TV Ch 4 (CBS)		
2077 Elmwood Ave .... Buffalo NY 14207	800-794-3687	716-874-4410
WKBW-TV Ch 7 (ABC)		
7 Broadcast Plz .... Buffalo NY 14202	888-373-7888	716-845-6100
WNED-TV Ch 17 (PBS)		
Horizons Plz PO Box 1263 .... Buffalo NY 14240	800-678-1873	716-845-7000

736-14 Cedar Rapids, IA

	Toll-Free	Phone
KCRG-TV Ch 9 (ABC)		
501 Second Ave SE .... Cedar Rapids IA 52401	800-332-5443	319-399-5999
KFXA Fox 28		
600 Old Marion Rd NE .... Cedar Rapids IA 52402	800-222-5426	800-642-6140
KGAN-TV Ch 2 (CBS)		
600 Old Marion Rd NE .... Cedar Rapids IA 52402	800-642-6140	319-395-9060
KPXR-TV Ch 47		
1957 Blairs Ferry Rd NE .... Cedar Rapids IA 52402	888-467-2988	

736-15 Charleston, WV

	Toll-Free	Phone
WCHS-TV Ch 8 (ABC)		
1301 Piedmont Rd .... Charleston WV 25301	888-696-9247	304-346-5358

736-16 Charlotte, NC

	Toll-Free	Phone
WAXN-TV Ch 64		
1901 N Tryon St .... Charlotte NC 28206	855-336-0360	704-335-4786
WSOC-TV Ch 9 (ABC)		
1901 N Tryon St .... Charlotte NC 28206	855-336-0360	704-338-9999

736-17 Chicago, IL

	Toll-Free	Phone
WCPX-TV Ch 38 (I)		
333 S Desplaines St Ste 101 .... Chicago IL 60661	888-467-2988	212-757-3100

736-18 Cincinnati, OH

	Toll-Free	Phone
CET 1223 Central Pkwy .... Cincinnati OH 45214	800-808-0445	513-381-4033
WKRC-TV Ch 12 (CBS)		
1906 Highland Ave .... Cincinnati OH 45219	877-889-5610	513-763-5500

736-19 Cleveland/Akron, OH

	Toll-Free	Phone
WKYC-TV Ch 3 (NBC)		
1333 Lakeside Ave E .... Cleveland OH 44114	877-790-7370	216-344-3333

736-20 Columbia, SC

	Toll-Free	Phone
WHMC-TV Ch 23 (PBS)		
1041 George Rogers Blvd .... Columbia SC 29201	800-277-3245	803-737-3200

736-21 Dallas/Fort Worth, TX

	Toll-Free	Phone
KDFW FOX 4 400 N Griffin St .... Dallas TX 75202	800-677-5339	214-720-4444
KXAS-TV Ch 5 (NBC)		
4805 Amon Carter Blvd .... Fort Worth TX 76155	800-232-5927	214-303-5119
Telemundo 39		
4805 Amon Carter Blvd .... Fort Worth TX 76155	877-266-8365	

736-22 Dayton, OH

	Toll-Free	Phone
WPTD-TV Ch 16 (PBS)		
110 S Jefferson St .... Dayton OH 45402	800-247-1614	937-220-1600

Classified Section

736-23 Denver, CO

	Toll-Free	Phone
Denver7 123 E Speer Blvd .... Denver CO 80203	800-824-3463	303-832-7777
KCEC-TV Ch 50 (Uni) 777 Grant St 5th Fl .... Denver CO 80203	800-420-2757	303-832-0050
KRMA-TV Ch 6 (PBS) 1089 Bannock St .... Denver CO 80204	800-274-6666	303-892-6666

736-24 Des Moines, IA

	Toll-Free	Phone
WHO-TV Ch 13 (NBC) 1801 Grand Ave .... Des Moines IA 50309	800-777-8398	515-242-3500

736-25 Duluth, MN

	Toll-Free	Phone
WDIO-TV Ch 10 (ABC) 10 Observation Rd .... Duluth MN 55811	800-477-1013	218-727-6864
WDSE-TV Ch 8 (PBS) 632 Niagara Ct .... Duluth MN 55811	888-563-9373	218-788-2831

736-26 El Paso, TX

	Toll-Free	Phone
KCOS 13 9050 Viscount Blvd Ste A440 .... El Paso TX 79925	800-683-1899	915-590-1313

736-27 Erie, PA

	Toll-Free	Phone
WICU-TV Ch 12 (NBC) 3514 State St .... Erie PA 16508	800-454-8812	814-454-5201
WQLN-TV Ch 54 (PBS) 8425 Peach St .... Erie PA 16509	800-727-8854	814-864-3001
WSEE-TV Ch 35 (CBS) 3514 State St .... Erie PA 16508	866-571-4553	814-454-5201

736-28 Evansville, IN

	Toll-Free	Phone
WFIE-TV Ch 14 (NBC) 1115 Mt Auburn Rd .... Evansville IN 47720	800-832-0014	812-426-1414
WNIN-TV Ch 9 (PBS) 405 Carpenter St .... Evansville IN 47708	855-888-9646	812-423-2973

736-29 Fargo/Grand Forks, ND

	Toll-Free	Phone
KVLY-TV Ch 11 (NBC) 1350 21st Ave S .... Fargo ND 58103	800-450-5844	701-237-5211
KXJB-TV Ch 4 (CBS) 1350 21st Ave S .... Fargo ND 58103	877-571-0774	701-237-5211
Prairie Public Broadcasting 207 N Fifth St .... Fargo ND 58102	800-359-6900	701-241-6900

736-30 Fresno, CA

	Toll-Free	Phone
KFSN-TV Ch 30 (ABC) 1777 G St .... Fresno CA 93706	800-423-3030	559-442-1170
KFTV-TV Ch 21 (Uni) 601 W Univision Plz .... Fresno CA 93704	866-783-2645	559-222-2121
KMPH-TV Ch 26 (Fox) 5111 E McKinley Ave .... Fresno CA 93727	800-101-2045	559-453-8850

736-31 Grand Rapids, MI

	Toll-Free	Phone
WGVU-TV Ch 35 (PBS) 301 W Fulton St .... Grand Rapids MI 49504	800-442-2771	616-331-6666

736-32 Green Bay, WI

	Toll-Free	Phone
NBC 26 1391 N Rd .... Green Bay WI 54313	800-800-6619	920-494-2626
WBAY-TV Ch 2 (ABC) 115 S Jefferson St .... Green Bay WI 54301	800-261-9229	920-432-3331
WFRV-TV Ch 5 (CBS) 1181 E Mason St .... Green Bay WI 54301	800-236-5550	920-437-5411
WLUK-TV Ch 11 (Fox) 787 Lombardi Ave .... Green Bay WI 54304	800-242-8067	920-494-8711

736-33 Honolulu, HI

	Toll-Free	Phone
ION Media Networks Inc 875 Waimanu St Ste 630 .... Honolulu HI 96813	888-467-2988	808-591-1275
KHON-TV Ch 2 (Fox) 88 Piikoi St .... Honolulu HI 96814	877-926-8300	808-591-4278

	Toll-Free	Phone
KWHE-TV 14 1188 Bishop St Ste 502 .... Honolulu HI 96813	800-218-1414	808-538-1414

736-34 Houston, TX

	Toll-Free	Phone
KXLN-TV Ch 45 (Uni) 5100 SW Fwy .... Houston TX 77056	800-500-4252	713-662-4545

736-35 Huntsville, AL

	Toll-Free	Phone
WHNT-TV Ch 19 (CBS) 200 Holmes Ave .... Huntsville AL 35801	800-533-8819	256-533-1919

736-36 Jackson, MS

	Toll-Free	Phone
WAPT-TV Ch 16 (ABC) 7616 Ch 16 Way .... Jackson MS 39209	800-441-1948	601-922-1607
WLBT-TV Ch 3 (NBC) 715 S Jefferson St .... Jackson MS 39201	800-792-6067	601-948-3333

736-37 Johnson City, TN

	Toll-Free	Phone
WJHL-TV Ch 11 (CBS) 338 E Main St .... Johnson City TN 37601	800-861-5255	423-926-2151

736-38 Kansas City, KS & MO

	Toll-Free	Phone
KCPT-TV Ch 19 (PBS) 125 E 31st St .... Kansas City MO 64108	800-343-4727	816-756-3580

736-39 Las Vegas, NV

	Toll-Free	Phone
Vegas PBS 3050 E Flamingo .... Las Vegas NV 89121	877-727-4483	702-799-1010

736-40 Lexington, KY

	Toll-Free	Phone
WDKY-TV Ch 56 (Fox) 836 Euclid Ave Ste 201 .... Lexington KY 40502	888-404-5656	859-269-5656

736-41 Lincoln, NE

	Toll-Free	Phone
KOLN-TV Ch 10 (CBS) 840 N 40th .... Lincoln NE 68503	800-475-1011	402-467-4321
NET Radio 1800 N 33rd St .... Lincoln NE 68503	800-868-1868	

736-42 Los Angeles, CA

	Toll-Free	Phone
KJLA-TV Ch 57 (Ind) 2323 Corinth Ave .... Los Angeles CA 90064	800-588-5788	310-943-5288

736-43 Louisville, KY

	Toll-Free	Phone
WAVE-TV Ch 3 (NBC) 725 S Floyd St .... Louisville KY 40203	800-223-2579	502-585-2201

736-44 Miami/Fort Lauderdale, FL

	Toll-Free	Phone
WPBT-TV Ch 2 (PBS) 14901 NE 20th Ave .... Miami FL 33181	800-222-9728	305-949-8321

736-45 Milwaukee, WI

	Toll-Free	Phone
WVCY-TV Ch 30 (Ind) 3434 W Kilbourn Ave .... Milwaukee WI 53208	800-729-9829	414-935-3000

736-46 Minneapolis/Saint Paul, MN

	Toll-Free	Phone
KSTP-TV Ch 5 (ABC) 3415 University Ave W .... Saint Paul MN 55114	800-895-1999	651-646-5555

736-47 Mobile, AL

	Toll-Free	Phone
WALA-TV Ch 10 (Fox) 1501 Satchel Paige Dr .... Mobile AL 36606	800-876-8810	251-434-1010

	Toll-Free	Phone
WMPV-TV Ch 21 (TBN)		
1668 W I-65 Service Rd S .... Mobile AL 36693	**855-826-2255**	251-661-2101

736-48 Montgomery, AL

	Toll-Free	Phone
Alabama Newsnet		
3251 Harrison Rd .... Montgomery AL 36109	**800-467-0401**	334-270-9252
WAKA-TV Ch 8 (CBS)		
3020 Eastern Blvd .... Montgomery AL 36116	**800-467-0401**	334-271-8888

736-49 Naples/Fort Myers, FL

	Toll-Free	Phone
WZVN-TV Ch 26 (ABC)		
3719 Central Ave .... Fort Myers FL 33901	**888-232-8635**	239-939-2020

736-50 New Orleans, LA

	Toll-Free	Phone
WDSU-TV Ch 6 (NBC)		
846 Howard Ave .... New Orleans LA 70113	**888-925-4127**	504-679-0600

736-51 New York, NY

	Toll-Free	Phone
WNBC-TV Ch 4 (NBC)		
30 Rockefeller Plz .... New York NY 10112	**866-639-7244**	212-664-4444
WNET-TV Ch 13 (PBS)		
450 W 33rd St .... New York NY 10001	**800-468-9913**	212-560-1313
WPXN-TV Ch 31 (I)		
810 Seventh Ave 30th Fl .... New York NY 10019	**888-467-2988**	212-757-3100
WTBY-TV Ch 54 (TBN)		
111 E 15th St ...., New York NY 10003	**800-201-5200**	714-731-1000

736-52 Oklahoma City, OK

	Toll-Free	Phone
KOCO-TV Ch 5 (ABC)		
1300 E Britton Rd .... Oklahoma City OK 73131	**800-464-7928**	405-478-3000
KWTV-TV Ch 9 (CBS)		
7401 N Kelley Ave .... Oklahoma City OK 73111	**888-550-5988**	212-931-1200

736-53 Omaha, NE

	Toll-Free	Phone
KETV-TV Ch 7 (ABC)		
2665 Douglas St .... Omaha NE 68131	**800-279-5388**	402-345-7777

736-54 Peoria, IL

	Toll-Free	Phone
WTVP-TV Ch 47 (PBS)		
101 State St .... Peoria IL 61602	**800-837-4747**	309-677-4747

736-55 Philadelphia, PA

	Toll-Free	Phone
WPPX-TV Ch 61		
3901 B Main St Ste 301 .... Philadelphia PA 19127	**888-467-2988**	
WTXF-TV Ch 29 (Fox)		
330 Market St .... Philadelphia PA 19106	**800-220-6397**	215-925-2929

736-56 Phoenix, AZ

	Toll-Free	Phone
KPAZ-TV Ch 21 (TBN)		
3551 E McDowell Rd .... Phoenix AZ 85008	**800-447-7235**	602-273-1477
KSAZ-TV Ch 10 (Fox)		
511 W Adams St .... Phoenix AZ 85003	**888-369-4762**	602-257-1234

736-57 Pittsburgh, PA

	Toll-Free	Phone
WQED Multimedia		
4802 Fifth Ave .... Pittsburgh PA 15213	**855-700-9733**	412-622-1300

736-58 Pocatello, ID

	Toll-Free	Phone
KISU-TV Ch 10 (PBS)		
921 S Eighth Ave Stop 8111 .... Pocatello ID 83209	**800-543-6868**	208-282-2857

736-59 Portland, ME

	Toll-Free	Phone
WCSH-TV Ch 6 (NBC)		
1 Congress Sq .... Portland ME 04101	**800-464-1213**	207-828-6666

736-60 Raleigh/Durham, NC

	Toll-Free	Phone
WRAZ FOX 50		
2619 Western Blvd .... Raleigh NC 27606	**877-369-5050**	919-595-5050

736-61 Richmond, VA

	Toll-Free	Phone
WCVE-TV Ch 23 (PBS)		
23 Sesame St .... Richmond VA 23235	**800-476-8440**	804-320-1301

736-62 Rochester, MN

	Toll-Free	Phone
KTTC-TV Ch 10 (NBC)		
6301 Bandel Rd NW .... Rochester MN 55901	**800-288-1656**	507-288-4444

736-63 Rochester, NY

	Toll-Free	Phone
WHAM-TV Ch 13 (ABC)		
4225 W Henrietta Rd .... Rochester NY 14623	**800-322-3632**	585-334-8700

736-64 Sacramento, CA

	Toll-Free	Phone
KVIE-TV Ch 6 (PBS)		
2030 W El Camino Ave .... Sacramento CA 95833	**800-347-5843**	916-929-5843

736-65 Saint Louis, MO

	Toll-Free	Phone
KDNL-TV Ch 30 (ABC)		
1215 Cole St .... St. Louis MO 63106	**800-365-0820**	314-436-3030
KETC-TV Ch 9 (PBS)		
3655 Olive St .... Saint Louis MO 63108	**855-482-5382**	314-512-9000

736-66 Salt Lake City, UT

	Toll-Free	Phone
KUED-TV Ch 7 (PBS)		
101 Wasatch Dr Rm 215 .... Salt Lake City UT 84112	**800-477-5833**	801-581-7777

736-67 San Antonio, TX

	Toll-Free	Phone
KLRN-TV Ch 9 (PBS)		
501 Broadway St .... San Antonio TX 78215	**800-627-8193**	210-270-9000

736-68 San Diego, CA

	Toll-Free	Phone
KGTV-TV Ch 10 (ABC)		
4600 Airway .... San Diego CA 92102	**800-799-8881**	619-237-1010
KPBS-TV Ch 15 (PBS)		
5200 Campanile Dr .... San Diego CA 92182	**888-399-5727**	619-594-1515

736-69 San Francisco, CA

	Toll-Free	Phone
KQED-TV Ch 9 (PBS)		
2601 Mariposa St .... San Francisco CA 94110	**866-573-3123**	415-864-2000

736-70 Seattle/Tacoma, WA

	Toll-Free	Phone
KBTC-TV Ch 28 (PBS)		
2320 S 19th St .... Tacoma WA 98405	**888-596-5282**	253-680-7700

736-71 Shreveport, LA

	Toll-Free	Phone
KSLA-TV Ch 12 (CBS)		
1812 Fairfield Ave .... Shreveport LA 71101	**800-444-5752**	318-222-1212

736-72 Sioux Falls, SD

	Toll-Free	Phone
KDLT-TV Ch 46 (NBC)		
3600 S Westport Ave .... Sioux Falls SD 57106	**800-727-5358**	605-361-5555
KELO-TV Ch 11 (CBS)		
501 S Phillips Ave .... Sioux Falls SD 57104	**800-888-5356**	605-336-1100
KSFY Television		
325 S First Ave Ste 100 .... Sioux Falls SD 57104	**800-955-5739**	605-336-1300

736-73 South Bend, IN

	Toll-Free	Phone
WNIT Public Television 300 W Jefferson Blvd ....South Bend IN 46601	877-411-3662	574-675-9648

736-74 Spokane, WA

	Toll-Free	Phone
KREM-TV 4103 S Regal St ....Spokane WA 99223	888-404-3922	509-448-2000
KREM-TV Ch 2 (CBS) 4103 S Regal St ....Spokane WA 99223	888-404-3922	509-448-2000
KSPS Public TV 3911 S Regal St ....Spokane WA 99223	800-735-2377	509-443-7800

736-75 Springfield, MO

	Toll-Free	Phone
KOZK-TV Ch 21 (PBS) 901 S National Ave ....Springfield MO 65897	866-684-5695	417-836-3500
KY3 999 W Sunshine St ....Springfield MO 65807	888-476-6988	417-268-3000

736-76 Syracuse, NY

	Toll-Free	Phone
WCNY-TV Ch 24 (PBS) 506 Old Liverpool Rd PO Box 2400 ....Syracuse NY 13220	800-638-5163	315-453-2424

736-77 Tampa/Saint Petersburg, FL

	Toll-Free	Phone
WEDU-TV Ch 3 (PBS) 1300 N Blvd ....Tampa FL 33607	800-354-9338	813-254-9338
WFLA-TV Ch 8 (NBC) PO Box 1410 ....Tampa FL 33601	800-338-0808	813-228-8888
WFTS-TV Ch 28 (ABC) 4045 N Himes Ave ....Tampa FL 33607	877-833-2828	813-354-2828
WTVT-TV Ch 13 (Fox) 3213 W Kennedy Blvd ....Tampa FL 33609	800-334-9888	813-876-1313
WUSF-TV Ch 16 (PBS) 4202 E Fowler Ave ....Tampa FL 33620	800-654-3703	813-974-4000

736-78 Toledo, OH

	Toll-Free	Phone
WLMB-TV Ch 40 (Ind) 825 Capital Commons Dr ....Toledo OH 43615	800-218-5740	419-720-9562

736-79 Topeka, KS

	Toll-Free	Phone
KTWU-TV Ch 11 (PBS) 1700 College ....Topeka KS 66621	800-866-5898	785-670-1111

736-80 Toronto, ON

	Toll-Free	Phone
CICA-TV Ch 19 (Ind) 2180 Yonge St Stn Q PO Box 200 ....Toronto ON M4T2T1	800-613-0513	416-484-2600
City 33 Dundas St E ....Toronto ON M5B1B8	888-336-9978	416-764-3003

736-81 Tulsa, OK

	Toll-Free	Phone
KJRH-TV Ch 2 (NBC) 3701 S Peoria Ave ....Tulsa OK 74105	800-727-5574	918-743-2222

736-82 Washington, DC

	Toll-Free	Phone
WHUT-TV Ch 32 (PBS) 2222 Fourth St NW ....Washington DC 20059	800-683-1899	202-806-3200

736-83 West Palm Beach, FL

	Toll-Free	Phone
ION Media Networks Inc 601 Clearwater Pk Rd ....West Palm Beach FL 33401	888-467-2988	561-659-4122
WXEL-TV Ch 42 (PBS) PO Box 6607 ....West Palm Beach FL 33405	800-915-9935	561-737-8000

736-84 Wichita, KS

	Toll-Free	Phone
KPTS-TV Ch 8 (PBS) 320 W 21 St ....Wichita KS 67203	800-794-8498	316-838-3090
KSNW-TV 833 N Main St ....Wichita KS 67203	800-432-3924	316-265-3333

736-85 Winnipeg, MB

	Toll-Free	Phone
CTV-TV Ch 5 (CTV) 345 Graham Ave Ste 400 ....Winnipeg MB R3C5S6	800-461-1542	204-788-3300

736-86 Youngstown, OH

	Toll-Free	Phone
WFMJ-TV Ch 21 (NBC) 101 W Boardman St ....Youngstown OH 44503	800-488-9365	330-744-8611

737   TELEVISION SYNDICATORS

Television syndicators are companies that produce programming in-house and market and distribute the programs to networks on a national or regional basis.

	Toll-Free	Phone
Babe Winkelman Productions PO Box 407 ....Brainerd MN 56401	800-333-0471	
Independent Television Service (ITVS) 651 Brannan St Ste 410 ....San Francisco CA 94107	888-572-8918	415-356-8383
KRCR News Channel 755 Auditorium Dr ....Redding CA 96001	800-222-5727	530-243-7777

738   TESTING FACILITIES

	Toll-Free	Phone
Absolute Standards Inc 44 Rossotto Dr ....Hamden CT 06514	800-368-1131	203-281-2917
Accusource Inc 1240 E Ontario Ave Ste 102-140 ....Corona CA 92881	888-649-6272	951-734-8882
Activation Laboratories Ltd 1336 Sandhill Dr ....Ancaster ON L9G4V5	888-228-5227	905-648-9611
ALine Inc 2206 E Gladwick St ....Rancho Dominguez CA 90220	877-707-8575	
Amplicon Express Inc 2345 NE Hopkins Ct ....Pullman WA 99163	877-332-8080	509-332-8080
Analytics Corp 10329 Stony Run Ln ....Ashland VA 23005	800-888-8061	804-365-3000
Anatom-e Information Systems Ltd 7505 Fannin St Ste 422 ....Houston TX 77054	800-561-0874	
Animal & Plant Health Inspection Service (APHIS) *National Veterinary Services Laboratories* 4700 River Rd ....Riverdale MD 20737	844-820-2234	
Aqua Test Inc 28620 Maple Valley Black Diamond Rd SE ....Maple Valley WA 98038	800-221-3159	
Astro Pak Corp 270 E Baker St Ste 100 ....Costa Mesa CA 92626	888-278-7672	
Bio-Research Products Inc 323 W Cherry St ....North Liberty IA 52317	800-326-3511	319-626-2423
BIOPAC Systems Inc 42 Aero Camino ....Goleta CA 93117	877-524-6722	805-685-0066
Biosan Laboratories Inc 1950 Tobsal Ct ....Warren MI 48091	800-253-6800	586-755-8970
Biothera Pharmaceuticals 3388 Mike Collins Dr Ste A ....Eagan MN 55121	877-699-5100	651-675-0300
bioTheranostics Inc 9640 Towne Centre Dr Ste 200 ....San Diego CA 92121	877-886-6739	
CanWest DHI 660 Speedvale Ave W ....Guelph ON N1K1E5	800-549-4373	519-824-2320
Carrot Medical LLC 22122 20th Ave SE Ste H-166 ....Bothell WA 98021	866-492-3533	425-318-8089
Chardon Laboratories Inc 7300 Tussing Rd ....Reynoldsburg OH 43068	888-660-1724	
Copernicus Group Independent Review Board 5000 CentreGreen Way Ste 200 ....Cary NC 27513	888-303-2224	919-465-4310
CTLGroup 5400 Old OrchaRd Rd ....Skokie IL 60077	800-522-2285	847-965-7500
Cyl-tec Inc 971 W Industrial Dr ....Aurora IL 60506	888-429-5832	630-844-8800
Dairyland Laboratories Inc 217 E Main St ....Arcadia WI 54612	800-658-2481	608-323-2123
DDL Inc 10200 Vly View Rd Ste 101 ....Eden Prairie MN 55344	800-229-4235	952-941-9226
DyAnsys Inc 300 N Bayshore Blvd ....San Mateo CA 94401	888-950-4321	
Dyna Flex Ltd PO Box 99 ....Saint Ann MO 63074	800-489-4020	314-426-4020
Elektro Assemblies 5140 Moundview Dr ....Red Wing MN 55066	800-533-1558	
Embryotech Laboratories Inc 140 Hale St ....Haverhill MA 01830	800-673-7500	978-373-7300
Energy Laboratories Inc 2393 Salt Creek Hwy ....Casper WY 82601	888-235-0515	307-235-0515
EnviroLogix Inc 500 Riverside Industrial Pkwy ....Portland ME 04103	866-408-4597	207-797-0300
Environmental Enterprises Inc (EEI) 10163 Cincinnati-Dayton Rd ....Cincinnati OH 45241	800-722-2818	
EPL Bio Analytical Services 9095 W Harristown Blvd ....Niantic IL 62551	866-963-2143	217-963-2143
Eurofins Spectrum Analytical Inc 830 Silver St ....Agawam MA 01001	800-789-9115	413-789-9018
Everist Genomics Inc 709 W Ellsworth Rd ....Ann Arbor MI 48108	855-383-7478	
Excalibre Engineering 9201 Irvine Blvd ....Irvine CA 92618	877-922-5427	949-454-6603
Fruit Growers Laboratory Inc 853 Corporation St ....Santa Paula CA 93060	800-440-7821	805-392-2000
GE Healthcare Bio-Sciences Corp 800 Centennial Ave ....Piscataway NJ 08855	800-810-9118	732-457-8000

	Toll-Free	Phone

GenePOC Inc
360 Rue Franquet Porte 3 Technology Pk
.....................................Quebec QC G1P4N3 **844-616-1544** 418-650-3535
GenomeDx 1038 Homer St ....Vancouver BC V6B2W9 **888-975-4540**
Glidewell Laboratories Inc
4141 MacArthur Blvd ....Newport Beach CA 92660 **800-854-7256**
H&H X-Ray Services Inc
104 Enterprise St ....West Monroe LA 71292 **800-551-5093**
Huffman Laboratories Inc
4630 Indiana St ....Golden CO 80403 **877-886-6225** 303-278-4455
Hydro-Photon Inc
262 Ellsworth Rd ....Blue Hill ME 04614 **888-783-7473** 207-374-5800
HyGreen Inc
3630 SW 47th Ave Ste 100.............Gainesville FL 32608 **877-574-9473**
iHealth Lab Inc
719 N Shoreline Blvd ....Mountain View CA 94043 **855-816-7705**
Immuno Concepts NA Ltd
9825 Goethe Rd Ste 350..............Sacramento CA 95827 **800-251-5115** 916-363-2649
Inovatia Laboratories LLC
120 E Davis St ....Fayette MO 65248 **800-280-1912** 660-248-1911
Insight Service
20338 Progress Dr ....Strongsville OH 44149 **800-465-4329** 216-251-2510
Integrated BioTherapeutics Inc
4 Research Ct Ste 300 ....Rockville MD 20850 **877-411-2041**
ITEL Laboratories Inc
6676 Corporate Center Pkwy
Ste 107 ....Jacksonville FL 32216 **800-890-4835**
JM Test Systems Inc
7323 Tom Dr ....Baton Rouge LA 70806 **800-353-3411** 225-925-2029
Kanomax Usa Inc
219 US Hwy 206 ....Andover NJ 07821 **800-247-8887** 973-786-6386
Leica Microsystems Inc
1700 Leider Ln ....Buffalo Grove IL 60089 **800-248-0123**
Lumed Science Inc
PO Box 102965 ....Denver CO 80250 **866-526-7120**
Magna Chek Inc
32701 Edward Ave ....Madison Heights MI 48071 **800-582-8947** 248-597-0089
Metcut Research Inc
3980 Rosslyn Dr ....Cincinnati OH 45209 **877-847-1985** 513-271-5100
Micro-Clean Inc
177 N Commerce Way ....Bethlehem PA 18017 **800-523-9852** 610-954-7803
Mira Vista Diagnostics
4705 Decatur Blvd ....Indianapolis IN 46241 **866-647-2847** 317-856-2681
Morgan Schaffer Systems Inc
8300 rue Saint-Patrick Bureau 150 LaSalle
.....................................Montreal QC H8N2H1 **855-861-1967** 514-739-1967
Mountain Research LLC
825 25th St ....Altoona PA 16601 **800-837-4674** 814-949-2034
National Technical Systems Inc (NTS)
2125 E Katella Ave Ste 250............Anaheim CA 92806 **800-879-9225** 818-591-0776
NASDAQ: NTSC
Newport Partners LLC
3760 Tanglewood Ln ....Davidsonville MD 21035 **866-302-0017** 301-889-0017
Nova Biologicals Inc
1775 North Loop 336 E Ste 4 ....Conroe TX 77301 **800-282-5416**
Nsl Analytical
4450 Cranwood Pkwy ....Cleveland OH 44128 **877-560-3943** 877-560-3992
NutriCorp International
4025 Rhodes Dr ....Windsor ON N8W5B5 **888-446-8874** 519-974-8178
NuView Life Sciences Inc
1389 Center Dr Ste 250 ....Park City UT 84098 **888-902-7779**
Ornim Inc
125 Washington St Ste #7 ....Foxboro MA 02035 **866-811-6384**
Phoenix Environmental Laboratories Inc
587 Middle Tpke E ....Manchester CT 06040 **800-827-5426** 860-645-3513
Prezacor Inc
170 Cold Soil Rd ....Princeton NJ 08540 **855-792-3335**
Rothe Development Inc
4614 Sinclair Rd ....San Antonio TX 78222 **800-229-5209** 210-648-3131
Schneider Laboratories Inc
2512 W Cary St ....Richmond VA 23220 **800-785-5227** 804-353-6778
Scion Medical Technologies LLC
90 Oak St ....Newton MA 02464 **888-582-6211**
SHINE Medical Technologies Inc
101 E Milwaukee St Ste 600............Janesville WI 53545 **877-512-6554** 608-210-1060
Simco Electronics
3131 Jay St ....Santa Clara CA 95054 **866-299-6029** 408-734-9750
Southern Petroleum Lab Inc
8850 Interchange Dr ....Houston TX 77054 **877-775-5227** 713-660-0901
Speedie & Assoc Inc
3331 E Wood St ....Phoenix AZ 85040 **800-628-6221** 602-997-6391
Stimwave Technologies Inc
1310 Park Central Blvd S ....Pompano Beach FL 33064 **800-965-5134** 786-565-3342
Test Inc 2323 Fourth St ....Peru IL 61354 **800-659-4659** 815-224-1650
TestAmerica Laboratories Inc
4625 E Cotton Ctr Blvd Ste 189 ....Phoenix AZ 85040 **866-785-5227** 602-437-3340
Testcountry
10123 Carroll Canyon Rd ....San Diego CA 92131 **800-656-0745** 858-784-6904
TGR Industrial Services
8777 Tallyho Rd Bldg 1 ....Houston TX 77061 **800-625-9288** 713-636-2288
Thought Technology Ltd
2180 Belgrave Ave ....Montreal QC H4A2L8 **800-361-3651** 514-489-8251
Toxikon Corp 15 Wiggins Ave ....Bedford MA 01730 **800-458-4141** 781-275-3330
TriLink BioTechnologies Inc
9955 Mesa Rim Rd ....San Diego CA 92121 **800-863-6801** 858-546-0004
Tulsa Welding School Inc
2545 E 11th St ....Tulsa OK 74104 **800-331-2934** 918-856-6416
UL LLC 1559 King St ....Enfield CT 06082 **800-903-5660** 860-749-8371
Verichem Laboratories Inc
90 Narragansett Ave ....Providence RI 02907 **800-552-5859** 401-461-0180
Vibrant Corp
8330A Washington Pl NE ....Albuquerque NM 87113 **800-410-3048** 505-314-1488
VJ Technologies Inc
89 Carlough Rd ....Bohemia NY 11716 **800-858-9729** 631-589-8800
Weecycle Environmental Consulting Inc
1208 Commerce Ct Ste 5B ....Lafayette CO 80026 **800-875-7033** 303-413-0452

739	TEXTILE MACHINERY	

	Toll-Free	Phone

Bowman Hollis Manufacturing Inc
2925 Old Steele Creek Rd ....Charlotte NC 28208 **888-269-2358** 704-374-1500
Eastman Machine Co
779 Washington St ....Buffalo NY 14203 **800-872-5571** 716-856-2200
Gerber Technology Inc
24 Industrial Pk Rd W ....Tolland CT 06084 **800-826-3243** 860-871-8082
HH Arnold Co Inc
529 Liberty St ....Rockland MA 02370 **866-868-9603** 781-878-0346
Hix Corp 1201 E 27th Terr ....Pittsburg KS 66762 **800-835-0606** 620-231-8568
Ioline Corp
14140 NE 200th St ....Woodinville WA 98072 **800-598-0029** 425-398-8282
Lummus Corp
225 Bourne Blvd PO Box 929 ....Savannah GA 31408 **800-458-6687** 912-447-9000
Thermopatch Corp
2204 Erie Blvd E ....Syracuse NY 13224 **800-252-6555** 315-446-8110
TrimMaster
4860 N Fifth St Hwy ....Temple PA 19560 **800-356-4237** 610-921-0203
Tuftco Corp
2318 S Holtzclaw Ave ....Chattanooga TN 37408 **800-288-3826** 423-698-8601

740	TEXTILE MILLS	

740-1 Broadwoven Fabric Mills

	Toll-Free	Phone

American Cotton Growers Textile Div (ACG)
PO Box 2827 ....Lubbock TX 79408 **800-333-8011** 806-763-8011
DeRoyal Textiles
141 E York St ....Camden SC 29020 **800-845-1062** 803-432-2403
Garnet Hill Inc
231 Main St ....Franconia NH 03580 **800-870-3513** 603-823-5545
Hamrick Mills Inc
515 W Buford St PO Box 48 ....Gaffney SC 29341 **800-600-4305** 864-489-4731
Henry Glass & Co
49 W 37th St ....New York NY 10018 **800-294-9495**
JB Martin Co
645 Fifth Ave Ste 400 ....New York NY 10022 **800-223-0525** 212-421-2020
KM Fabrics Inc 2 Waco St ....Greenville SC 29611 **800-845-1896** 864-295-2550
Kuraray America Inc
2625 Bay Area Blvd Ste 600 ....Houston TX 77058 **800-423-9762**
Lantal Textiles Inc
1300 Langenthal Dr PO Box 965 ....Rural Hall NC 27045 **800-334-3309** 336-969-9551
Precision Fabrics Group Inc
301 N Elm St Ste 600 ....Greensboro NC 27401 **800-284-8001**
Scalamandre Silks Inc
350 Wireless Blvd ....Hauppauge NY 11788 **800-932-4361** 631-467-8800
Trelleborg Coated Systems US Inc
1886 Prairie Way ....Louisville CO 80027 **800-344-0714** 303-469-1357
Vectorply Corp
3500 Lakewood Dr ....Phenix City AL 36867 **800-577-4521** 334-291-7704
Warm Co 5529 186th Pl SW ....Lynnwood WA 98037 **800-234-9276** 425-248-2424

740-2 Coated Fabric

	Toll-Free	Phone

Adell Plastics Inc
4530 Annapolis Rd ....Baltimore MD 21227 **800-638-5218** 410-789-7780
Alpha Assoc Inc
145 Lehigh Ave ....Lakewood NJ 08701 **800-631-5399** 732-634-5700
Bondcote Corp PO Box 729 ....Pulaski VA 24301 **800-368-2160** 540-980-2640
Brookwood Laminating
275 Putnam Rd ....Wauregan CT 06387 **800-247-6658** 860-774-5001
Cooley Group 50 Esten Ave ....Pawtucket RI 02860 **800-992-0072*** 401-724-9000
*Cust Svc
Dazian LLC
18 Central Blvd ....South Hackensack NJ 07606 **877-232-9426** 201-549-1000
Deccofelt Corp
555 S Vermont Ave ....Glendora CA 91741 **800-543-3226*** 626-963-8511
*Cust Svc
Der-Tex Corp 1 Lehner Rd ....Saco ME 04072 **800-669-0364**
Duracote Corp
350 N Diamond St ....Ravenna OH 44266 **800-321-2252** 330-296-3487
Emtex Inc
42 Cherry Hill Dr Ste B ....Danvers MA 01923 **800-840-7035** 978-907-4500
Herculite Products Inc
105 E Sinking Springs Ln ....Emigsville PA 17318 **800-772-0036*** 717-764-1192
*Cust Svc
ICG/Holliston
905 Holliston Mills Rd ....Church Hill TN 37642 **800-251-0451** 423-357-6141
Middlesex Research Mfg Company Inc
27 Apsley St ....Hudson MA 01749 **800-424-5188** 978-562-3697
Polyguard Products Inc
PO Box 755 ....Ennis TX 75120 **800-541-4994** 972-875-8421
Reflexite Corp 120 Darling Dr ....Avon CT 06001 **800-654-7570** 860-676-7100
Seaman Corp
1000 Venture Blvd ....Wooster OH 44691 **800-927-8578** 330-262-1111
Taconic
136 Coonbrook Rd PO Box 69 ....Petersburg NY 12138 **800-833-1805** 518-658-3202
Twitchell Corp
4031 Ross Clark Cir ....Dothan AL 36303 **800-633-7550*** 334-792-0002
*General
Uniroyal Engineered Products LLC
501 S Water St ....Stoughton WI 53589 **800-873-8800**
W L Gore & Associates Inc
551 Papermill Rd ....Newark DE 19711 **888-914-4673** 410-506-7787

740-3 Industrial Fabrics

			Toll-Free	Phone
Albany International Corp				
216 Airport Dr	Rochester NH	03867	877-327-5378	518-445-2200
NYSE: AIN				
Amatex Corp				
1032 Stambridge St	Norristown PA	19404	800-441-9680	610-277-6100
AMETEK Inc Chemical Products Div				
455 Corporate Blvd	Newark DE	19702	800-441-7777*	302-456-4431
*Orders				
AstenJohnson				
4399 Corporate Rd	Charleston SC	29405	800-529-7990	843-747-7800
Belton Industries Inc				
1205 Hanby Rd PO Box 127	Belton SC	29627	800-845-8753	864-338-5711
BGF Industries Inc				
3802 Robert Porcher Way	Greensboro NC	27410	800-476-4845	336-545-0011
Carthage Mills				
4243 Hunt Rd	Cincinnati OH	45242	800-543-4430*	
*Sales				
Clear Edge Technical Fabrics				
7160 Northland Cir N	Minneapolis MN	55428	800-328-3036	763-535-3220
FH Bonn Co				
338 W Columbus Rd	South Charleston OH	45368	800-323-0143	937-323-7024
Firestone Fibers & Textiles Co				
100 Firestone Ln PO Box 1369	Kings Mountain NC	28086	800-441-1336	704-734-2132
Mutual Industries Inc				
707 W Grange St	Philadelphia PA	19120	800-523-0888	215-927-6000
Newtex Industries Inc				
8050 Victor Mendon Rd	Victor NY	14564	800-836-1001	585-924-9135
Sefar Printing Solutions Inc				
111 Calumet St	Depew NY	14043	800-995-0531	716-683-4050
Stern & Stern Industries Inc				
188 Thacher St PO Box 556	Hornell NY	14843	800-664-7415	607-324-4485
TenCate Geosynthetics North America				
365 S Holland Dr	Pendergrass GA	30567	888-795-0808	706-693-2226
TenCate Protective Fabrics USA				
6501 Mall Blvd	Union City GA	30291	800-241-8630	
Ultrafabrics LLC				
303 S Broadway	Tarrytown NY	10591	877-309-6648	914-460-1730

740-4 Knitting Mills

			Toll-Free	Phone
Apex Mills Corp				
168 Doughty Blvd	Inwood NY	11096	800-989-2739	516-239-4400
Draper Knitting Co				
28 Draper Ln	Canton MA	02021	800-808-7707	781-828-0029
Lace For Less Inc				
1500 Main Ave	Clifton NJ	07011	800-533-5223	973-478-2955
Monterey Mills Inc				
1725 E Delavan Dr	Janesville WI	53546	800-255-9665	608-754-2866

740-5 Narrow Fabric Mills

			Toll-Free	Phone
Carolina Narrow Fabric Co				
1100 N Patterson Ave	Winston-Salem NC	27101	877-631-3077	336-631-3000
Fulflex Inc				
32 Justin Holden Dr	Brattleboro VT	05301	800-283-2500	802-257-5256
Hickory Brands Inc (HBI)				
429 27th St NW	Hickory NC	28601	800-438-5777	828-322-2600
JRM Industries Inc				
1 Mattimore St	Passaic NJ	07055	800-533-2697	973-779-9340
Julius Koch USA Inc				
387 Church St	New Bedford MA	02745	800-522-3652*	508-995-9565
*Sales				
Name Maker Inc				
4450 Commerce Cir PO Box 43821	Atlanta GA	30336	800-241-2890	404-691-2237
Narrow Fabric Industries Corp				
701 Reading Ave	Reading PA	19611	877-523-6373	610-376-2891
Sequins International Inc				
60-01 31st Ave	Woodside NY	11377	800-221-5801	718-204-0002
South Carolina Elastic Co				
201 S Carolina Elastic Rd	Landrum SC	29356	800-845-6700	864-457-3388
Southern Weaving Co				
1005 W Bramlett Rd	Greenville SC	29611	800-849-8962	864-233-1635
Wayne Mills Co Inc				
130 W Berkley St	Philadelphia PA	19144	800-220-8053	215-842-2134

740-6 Nonwoven Fabrics

			Toll-Free	Phone
Aetna Felt Corp				
2401 W Emaus Ave	Allentown PA	18103	800-526-4451	610-791-0900
Airtex Consumer Products a Div of Federal Foam Technologies				
150 Industrial Pk Blvd	Cokato MN	55321	800-851-8887	
Cerex Advanced Fabrics Inc				
610 Chemstrand Rd	Cantonment FL	32533	800-572-3739	850-937-3365
Fisher Textiles Inc				
139 Business Pk Dr	Indian Trail NC	28079	800-554-8886	704-821-8870
Hobbs Bonded Fibers Inc				
200 Commerce Dr	Waco TX	76710	800-433-3357	254-741-0040
National Nonwovens				
PO Box 150	EastHampton MA	01027	800-333-3469	413-527-3445
Sellars				
6565 North 60th St	Milwaukee WI	53223	800-237-8454	
Tietex International				
3010 N Blackstock Rd	Spartanburg SC	29301	800-843-8390	864-574-0500

740-7 Textile Dyeing & Finishing

			Toll-Free	Phone
Aurora Specialty Textiles Group Inc				
2705 N Bridge St	Yorkville IL	60560	800-864-0303	
Cranston Print Works Co				
1381 Cranston St	Cranston RI	02920	800-876-2756	401-943-4800
Kenyon Industries Inc				
36 Sherman Ave	Kenyon RI	02836	800-247-6658	401-364-3400
Westex Inc 122 W 22nd St	Oak Brook IL	60523	866-493-7839	773-523-7000

740-8 Textile Fiber Processing Mills

			Toll-Free	Phone
Buffalo Industries Inc				
99 S Spokane St	Seattle WA	98134	800-683-0052	206-682-9900
Fabritech Inc				
5740 Salmen St	New Orleans LA	70123	888-733-5009	504-733-5009
JE Herndon Company Inc				
1020 J E Herndon Access Rd	Kings Mountain NC	28086	800-277-0500	704-739-4711

740-9 Yarn & Thread Mills

			Toll-Free	Phone
Coats North America				
3430 Toringdon Way Ste 301	Charlotte NC	28277	800-631-0965	704-329-5800
Eddington Thread Manufacturing Co				
PO Box 446	Bensalem PA	19020	800-220-8901	215-639-8900
Hickory Yarns Inc				
1025 Tenth St NE PO Box 1975	Hickory NC	28601	800-713-1484	828-322-1550
Interstock Premium Cabinets LLC				
6300 Bristol Pk	Levittown PA	19057	800-896-9842	267-442-0026
Kreinik Manufacturing Company Inc				
1708 Gihon Rd	Parkersburg WV	26101	800-537-2166	304-422-8900
Lion Brand Yarn Co				
135 Kero Rd	Carlstadt NJ	07072	800-795-5466	212-243-8995
Parkdale Mills Inc				
531 Cotton Blossom Cir	Gastonia NC	28054	800-331-1843	704-874-5000
Supreme Corp 325 Spence Rd	Conover NC	28613	888-604-6975	828-322-6975
Universal Fibers Inc				
PO Box 8930	Bristol VA	24203	800-457-4759	276-669-1161

741   TEXTILE PRODUCTS - HOUSEHOLD

			Toll-Free	Phone
1888 Mills LLC				
375 Airport Rd	Griffin GA	30224	800-346-3660	
American Textile Co				
10 N Linden St	Duquesne PA	15110	800-289-2826*	412-948-1020
*Cust Svc				
Biddeford Blankets				
300 Terr Dr	Mundelein IL	60060	800-789-6441	
Carole Fabrics Inc				
PO Box 1436	Augusta GA	30903	800-241-0920	706-863-4742
CHF Industries Inc				
1 Park Ave 9th Fl	New York NY	10016	800-243-7090*	212-951-7800
*Cust Svc				
Crown Crafts Inc				
916 S Burnside	Gonzales LA	70737	800-433-9560	225-647-9100
NASDAQ: CRWS				
Custom Drapery Blinds & Shutters				
3402 E T C Jester	Houston TX	77018	800-929-9211	713-225-9211
Echota Fabrics Inc				
1394 US 41 N	Calhoun GA	30701	800-763-9750	706-629-9750
Hollander Home Fashions Corp				
6501 Congress Ave Ste 300	Boca Raton FL	33487	800-233-7666	561-997-6900
Kaslen Textiles				
6099 Triangle Dr	Commerce CA	90040	800-777-5789	323-588-7700
Kay Dee Designs Inc				
177 Skunk Hill Rd	Hope Valley RI	02832	800-537-3433	
Lafayette Venetian Blind Inc				
3000 Klondike Rd PO Box 2838	West Lafayette IN	47996	800-342-5523	
Manual Woodworkers & Weavers Inc				
3737 HowaRd Gap Rd	Hendersonville NC	28792	800-542-3139	828-692-7333
Marietta Drapery & Window Coverings Company Inc				
22 Trammel St PO Box 569	Marietta GA	30064	800-241-7974	
Pacific Coast Feather Co				
1964 Fourth Ave S	Seattle WA	98134	888-297-1778	
Pendleton Woolen Mills Inc				
220 NW Broadway	Portland OR	97209	800-760-4844	503-226-4801
Riegel Consumer Products				
51 Riegel Rd	Johnston SC	29832	800-845-3251	803-275-2541
Surefit Inc				
8000 Quarry Rd Ste C	Alburtis PA	18011	888-796-0500	

742   THEATERS - BROADWAY

SEE ALSO Performing Arts Facilities ; Theater Companies ; Theaters - Resident

			Toll-Free	Phone
Minskoff Theatre				
200 W 45th St	New York NY	10036	800-714-8452	212-869-0550
Richard Rodgers Theatre				
226 W 46th St	New York NY	10036	866-755-3075	212-221-1211

743   THEATERS - MOTION PICTURE

			Toll-Free	Phone
AMC Theatres PO Box 725489	Atlanta GA	31139	888-440-4262	

				Toll-Free	Phone
Brenden Theatres					
531 Davis St	Vacaville	CA	95688	**866-857-5191**	
Cinemark USA Inc					
3900 Dallas Pkwy Ste 500	Plano	TX	75093	**800-246-3627**	972-665-1000
Cineplex Entertainment LP					
1303 Yonge St	Toronto	ON	M4T2Y9	**800-333-0061**	416-323-6600
Landmark Theaters					
2222 S Barrington Ave	Los Angeles	CA	90064	**888-724-6362***	310-473-6701
*Cust Svc					
Marcus Theatres Corp					
100 E Wisconsin Ave Ste 2000	Milwaukee	WI	53202	**800-274-0099***	414-905-1000
*Cust Svc					
Open Air Cinema					
806 North 2800 West	Lindon	UT	84042	**866-319-3280**	801-796-6800
Precision Opinion Inc					
101 Convention Center Dr Plaza 125	Las Vegas	NV	89109	**800-780-2790**	702-483-4000
Regal Entertainment Group					
7132 Regal Ln	Knoxville	TN	37918	**877-835-5734***	865-922-1123
NASDAQ: RGC ■ *Cust Svc					

744   THEATERS - RESIDENT

SEE ALSO Performing Arts Facilities ; Theater Companies ; Theaters - Broadway

All of the theaters listed here are members of the League of Resident Theatres (LORT). In order to become a member of LORT, each theater must be incorporated as a non-profit, IRS-approved organization; must rehearse each self-produced production for a minimum of three weeks; must have a playing season of 12 weeks or more; and must operate under a LORT-Equity contract.

				Toll-Free	Phone
Actors Theatre of Louisville					
316 W Main St	Louisville	KY	40202	**800-428-5849**	502-584-1205
Alabama Shakespeare Festival					
1 Festival Dr	Montgomery	AL	36117	**800-841-4273**	
Arkansas Repertory Theatre					
601 Main St PO Box 110	Little Rock	AR	72203	**866-684-3737**	501-378-0405
Asolo Repertory Theatre					
5555 N Tamiami Tr	Sarasota	FL	34243	**800-361-8388**	941-351-9010
Bb Riverboats Inc					
101 Riverboat Row	Newport	KY	41071	**800-261-8506**	859-261-8500
Guthrie Theater					
818 S Second St	Minneapolis	MN	55415	**877-447-8243***	612-377-2224
*Resv					
Lincoln Ctr Theater					
150 W 65th St	New York	NY	10023	**800-432-7250**	
Maltz Jupiter Theatre					
1001 E Indiantown Rd	Jupiter	FL	33477	**800-445-1666**	561-743-2666
Oregon Shakespeare Festival					
15 S Pioneer St	Ashland	OR	97520	**800-219-8161**	541-482-2111
Seattle Repertory Theatre (SRT)					
155 Mercer St PO Box 900923	Seattle	WA	98109	**877-900-9285**	206-443-2210
Shakespeare Theatre					
516 Eigth St SE	Washington	DC	20003	**877-487-8849**	202-547-3230
Theatre For A New Audience					
154 Christopher St Ste 3D	New York	NY	10014	**866-811-4111**	212-229-2819

745   TICKET BROKERS

				Toll-Free	Phone
All American Ticket Service					
2616 Philadelphia Pk Ste E	Claymont	DE	19703	**800-669-0571**	
Americana Tickets NY					
1535 Broadway	New York	NY	10036	**800-833-3121**	212-581-6660
Broadwaycom					
729 Seventh Ave	New York	NY	10019	**800-276-2392**	212-541-8457
Front Row USA Entertainment					
900 N Federal Hwy	Hallandale beach	FL	33009	**800-277-8499**	
Select-A-Ticket Inc					
25 Rt 23 S	Riverdale	NJ	07457	**800-735-3288**	973-839-6100
Theatre Development Fund					
1501 Broadway 21st Fl	New York	NY	10036	**888-424-4685**	212-221-0885
Ticket Source Inc					
5516 E Mockingbird Ln Ste 100	Dallas	TX	75206	**800-557-6872**	214-821-9011
Ticketscom Inc					
555 Anton Blvd 11th Fl	Costa Mesa	CA	92626	**800-352-0212**	714-327-5400
TicketWeb Inc					
807 S Jackson Rd	Pharr	TX	78577	**866-777-8932***	866-468-3399
*Cust Svc					
Western States Ticket Service					
143 W McDowell Rd	Phoenix	AZ	85003	**800-326-0331**	602-254-3300

746   TILE - CERAMIC (WALL & FLOOR)

				Toll-Free	Phone
Ann Sacks Tile & Stone Inc					
8120 NE 33rd Dr	Portland	OR	97211	**800-278-8453**	
Armstrong World Industries Inc					
2500 Columbia Ave	Lancaster	PA	17603	**800-233-3823***	717-397-0611
NYSE: AWI ■ *Cust Svc					
Crossville Porcelain Stone/USA					
PO Box 1168	Crossville	TN	38557	**800-221-9093**	931-484-2110
Epro Tile Inc					
10890 E CR 6	Bloomville	OH	44818	**866-818-3776**	
Florida Tile Industries Inc					
998 Governors Ln Ste 300	Lexington	KY	40513	**800-352-8453***	859-219-5200
*Cust Svc					
Interstyle Ceramics & Glass Ltd					
3625 Brighton Ave	Burnaby	BC	V5A3H5	**800-667-1566**	604-421-7229
Ironrock Capital Inc					
1201 Millerton St SE	Canton	OH	44707	**800-325-3945**	
ME Tile 447 Atlas Dr	Nashville	TN	37211	**888-348-8453**	
Metropolitan Ceramics					
1201 Millerton St SE	Canton	OH	44707	**800-325-3945**	

				Toll-Free	Phone
Nudo Products Inc					
1500 Taylor Ave	Springfield	IL	62703	**800-826-4132**	217-528-5636
Wood Pro Inc					
421 Washington St PO Box 363	Auburn	MA	01501	**800-786-5577**	508-832-9888

747   TIMBER TRACTS

				Toll-Free	Phone
American Lumber Distributors & Brokers Inc					
2405 Republic Blvd	Birmingham	AL	35201	**800-433-8578**	
Authentic Pine Floors Inc					
4042 Hwy 42	Locust Grove	GA	30248	**800-283-6038**	
Federal Wage & Labor Institute					
7001 W 43rd St	Houston	TX	77092	**800-767-9243**	713-690-5676
Haida Corp PO Box 89	Hydaburg	AK	99922	**800-478-3721**	907-285-3721
Holiday Tree Farms Inc					
800 NW Cornell Ave	Corvallis	OR	97330	**800-289-3684**	541-753-3236
Industrial Timber & Lumber Corp (ITL)					
23925 Commerce Park Rd	Beachwood	OH	44122	**800-829-9663**	216-831-3140
Keim Lumber Company Inc					
4465 State Rt 557 PO Box 40	Charm	OH	44617	**800-362-6682**	330-893-2251
Koopman Lumber Company Inc					
665 Church St	Whitinsville	MA	01588	**800-836-4545**	508-234-4545
McShan Lumber Company Inc					
PO Box 27	McShan	AL	35471	**800-882-3712**	205-375-6277
Moonworks 1137 Park E Dr	Woonsocket	RI	02895	**800-975-6666**	
Olympic Resource Management					
19950 Seventh Ave NE Ste 200	Poulsbo	WA	98370	**800-522-6645**	360-697-6626
NASDAQ: POPE					
Pike Lumber Company Inc					
PO Box 247	Akron	IN	46910	**800-356-4554**	574-893-4511
Roy O Martin					
2189 Memorial Dr PO Box 1110	Alexandria	LA	71301	**800-299-5174**	318-448-0405
Weyerhaeuser Co					
33663 Weyerhaeuser Way S	Federal Way	WA	98003	**800-525-5440**	253-924-2345
NYSE: WY					

748   TIMESHARE COMPANIES

SEE ALSO Hotels & Hotel Companies

				Toll-Free	Phone
Bluegreen Corp					
4960 Conference Way N Ste 100	Boca Raton	FL	33431	**800-456-2582**	561-912-8000
NYSE: BXG					
Disney Vacation Club					
1390 Celebration Blvd	Celebration	FL	34747	**800-500-3990**	407-566-3100
Festiva Resorts					
1 Vance Gap Rd	Asheville	NC	28805	**866-933-7848***	828-254-3378
*Resv					
Four Seasons Hotels & Resorts					
1165 Leslie St	Toronto	ON	M3C2K8	**800-332-3442**	416-449-1750
Hilton Grand Vacations Company LLC					
6355 Metro W Blvd Ste 180	Orlando	FL	32835	**800-230-7068**	407-613-3100
Hyatt Vacation Ownership Inc					
140 Fountain Pkwy N Ste 570	Saint Petersburg	FL	33716	**800-926-4447**	727-803-9400
Interval International Inc					
6262 Sunset Dr	Miami	FL	33143	**800-828-8200**	888-784-3447
Marriott Vacation Club International					
6649 Westwood Blvd Ste 500	Orlando	FL	32821	**800-307-7312**	407-206-6000
Resort Condominiums International (RCI)					
9998 N Michigan Ave	Carmel	IN	46032	**800-338-7777**	317-805-8000
Royal Aloha Vacation Club					
1505 Dillingham Blvd Ste 212	Honolulu	HI	96817	**800-367-5212**	808-847-8050
Silverleaf Resorts Inc					
1221 Riverbend Dr Ste 120	Dallas	TX	75247	**800-544-8468**	214-631-1166
Sunchaser Vacation Villas					
5129 Riverview Gate Rd	Fairmont Hot Springs	BC	V0B1L1	**877-451-1250***	250-345-4545
*Resv					
Vacation Internationale					
1417 116th Ave NE	Bellevue	WA	98004	**800-444-6633**	425-454-8429
WorldMark the Club					
9805 Willows Rd	Redmond	WA	98052	**800-565-0370**	

749   TIRES - MFR

				Toll-Free	Phone
Bridgestone Americas Holding Inc					
535 Marriott Dr	Nashville	TN	37214	**877-201-2373***	615-937-1000
*Cust Svc					
Coker Tire Co					
1317 Chestnut St	Chattanooga	TN	37402	**866-516-3215**	
Cooper Tire & Rubber Co					
701 Lima Ave	Findlay	OH	45840	**800-854-6288**	419-423-1321
NYSE: CTB					
Dunlop Tires					
200 Innovation Way	Akron	OH	44316	**800-522-7458**	
Goodyear Tire & Rubber Co					
200 Innovation Way	Akron	OH	44316	**800-321-2136***	330-796-2121
NASDAQ: GT ■ *Cust Svc					
Hankook Tire America Corp					
1450 Valley Rd	Wayne	NJ	07470	**800-426-5665**	973-633-9000
Hercules Tire & Rubber Co					
16380 E US Rt 224 - 200	Findlay	OH	45840	**800-677-9535**	419-425-6400
K&M Tire Inc					
965 Spencerville Rd PO Box 279	Delphos	OH	45833	**877-879-5407**	419-695-1061
La Cie Canada Tire Inc					
21500 Transcanadienne	Baie-D'Urfe	QC	H9X4B7	**888-267-5097**	514-457-0155
Lyna Manufacturing Inc					
1125 15th St W	North Vancouver	BC	V7P1M7	**800-993-4007**	604-990-0988
Martin Wheel Company Inc, The					
342 W Ave PO Box 157	Tallmadge	OH	44278	**800-462-7846**	330-633-3278
Michelin North America Inc					
1 PkwyS PO Box 19001	Greenville	SC	29615	**866-866-6605***	864-458-5000
*Cust Svc					

	Toll-Free	Phone
Mickey Thompson Tires 4600 Prosper Dr ....Stow OH 44224	800-222-9092	330-928-9092
Millennium Industrial Tires LLC 433 Lane Dr ....Florence AL 35630	800-421-1180	256-764-2900
Mitchell Industrial Tire Co 2915 Eigth Ave ....Chattanooga TN 37407	800-251-7226	423-698-4442
Pete's Road Service Inc 2230 E Orangethorpe Ave ....Fullerton CA 92831	800-352-8349	
Robbins LLC 3415 Thompson St ....Muscle Shoals AL 35661	800-633-3312	256-383-5441
SolidBoss Worldwide Inc 200 Veterans Blvd ....South Haven MI 49090	888-258-7252	269-637-6356
Specialty Tires of America Inc 1600 Washington St ....Indiana PA 15701	800-622-7327	724-349-9010
Superior Tire & Rubber Corp 1818 Pennsylvania Ave W PO Box 308...........Warren PA 16365 *Cust Svc	800-289-1456*	814-723-2370
Tech International 200 E Coshocton St ....Johnstown OH 43031	800-336-8324	740-967-9015
Titan Tire Co 2345 E Market St ....Des Moines IA 50317	800-872-2327	515-265-9200
Toyo Tires 6261 Katella Ave Ste 2B ....Cypress CA 90630	800-678-3250	
Yokohama Tire Corp 601 S Acacia Ave ....Fullerton CA 92831	800-423-4544	714-870-3800

750   TIRES & TUBES - WHOL

	Toll-Free	Phone
4 Wheel Parts 20315 96 Ave ....Langley BC V1M0E4	855-554-2402	778-726-2787
Allied Oil & Supply Inc 2209 S 24th St ....Omaha NE 68108	800-333-3717	402-267-1375
American Tire Depot 14407 Alondra Blvd ....La Mirada CA 90638	855-899-3764	562-677-3950
Ben Tire Distributors Ltd 203 E Madison St PO Box 158 ....Toledo IL 62468	800-252-8961	
BFGoodrich Tires Inc PO Box 19001 ....Greenville SC 29602	877-788-8899	
Big O Tires LLC 4280 Professional Center Dr Ste 400 ....Palm Beach Gardens FL 33410	866-834-2652	
De Ronde Tire Supply Inc 2010 Elmwood Ave ....Buffalo NY 14207	800-227-4647	716-897-6690
Dealer Tire LLC 7012 Euclid Ave ....Cleveland OH 44103	800-933-2537	216-432-0088
East Bay Tire Co 2200 Huntington Dr Unit C.........Fairfield CA 94533	800-831-8473	707-437-4700
Free Service Tire Co Inc PO Box 6187 ....Johnson City TN 37602	855-646-1423	423-979-2250
Friend Tire Co 11 Industrial Dr ....Monett MO 65708	800-950-8473	417-235-7836
Goodyear Canada Inc 450 Kipling ....Toronto ON M8Z5E1	800-387-3288	416-201-4300
K&W Tire Company Inc 735 N Prince St ....Lancaster PA 17603	877-598-4731	800-732-3563
Ken Jones Tire Inc 73 Chandler St ....Worcester MA 01609	800-225-9513	508-755-5255
Kenda USA 7095 Americana Pkwy ....Reynoldsburg OH 43068	866-536-3287	614-866-9803
Kumho Tire USA Inc 10299 Sixth St ....Rancho Cucamonga CA 91730	800-445-8646	909-428-3999
Lakin Tire West Inc 15305 Spring Ave ....Santa Fe Springs CA 90670	800-488-2752	562-802-2752
Michelin Canada Inc 2500 Blvd Daniel-Johnson Ste 500 ....Laval QC H7L23K8	888-871-4444	
Michelin North America Inc 1 PkwyS PO Box 19001 ....Greenville SC 29615 *Cust Svc	866-866-6605*	864-458-5000
Parrish Tire Company Inc 5130 Indiana Ave ....Winston-Salem NC 27106	800-849-8473	336-767-0202
Pete's Tire Barns Inc 114 New Athol Rd ....Orange MA 01364	800-239-1833	978-544-8811
Piedmont Truck Tires Inc PO Box 18228 ....Greensboro NC 27419	800-274-8473	336-668-0091
Pomps Tire Service Inc 1123 Cedar St ....Green Bay WI 54301	800-236-8911	920-435-8301
Reliable Tire Co 805 N Blackhorse Pk ....Blackwood NJ 08012 *All	800-342-3426*	
Royal Tire Inc 3955 Roosevelt Rd ....St. Cloud MN 56301	877-454-7070	320-763-9618
Snyder Tire 401 Cadiz Rd ....Steubenville OH 43953	800-967-8473	740-264-5543
Southeastern Wholesale Tire Co 4721 Trademark Dr ....Raleigh NC 27610 *General	800-849-9215*	
Tire Centers LLC 310 Inglesby Pkwy ....Duncan SC 29334	800-603-2430	864-329-2700
Tire Rack 7101 Vorden Pkwy ....South Bend IN 46628	888-541-1777	574-287-2345
Tire's Warehouse Inc 240 Teller St ....Corona CA 92879	800-655-8851	951-808-0111
Tire-Rama Inc 1429 Grand Ave ....Billings MT 59102	800-828-1642	406-245-3161

751   TOBACCO & TOBACCO PRODUCTS

	Toll-Free	Phone
AMCON Distributing Co 7405 Irvington Rd ....Omaha NE 68122 NYSE: DIT	888-201-5997	402-331-3727
Burklund Distributors Inc 2500 N Main St Ste 3 ....East Peoria IL 61611	800-322-2876	309-694-1900
Cigarcom Inc 1911 Spillman Dr ....Bethlehem PA 18015	800-357-9800	

	Toll-Free	Phone
Eby-Brown Co 1415 W Diehl Rd Ste 300N...........Naperville IL 60563	800-553-8249	630-778-2800
Finck Cigar Co 414 Vera Cruz St ....San Antonio TX 78207 *Orders	800-221-0638*	210-226-4191
Holts Cigar Co 1522 Walnut St ....Philadelphia PA 19102	800-523-1641	215-732-8500
J Polep Distribution Services Inc 705 Meadow St ....Chicopee MA 01013	800-447-6537	413-592-4141
Keilson-Dayton Co 107 Commerce Park Dr ....Dayton OH 45404	800-759-3174	937-236-1070
Klafter's Inc 216 N Beaver St ....New Castle PA 16101	800-922-1233	
Modern Distributors Inc 817 W Columbia St ....Somerset KY 42501	800-880-5543	606-679-1178
National Tobacco Company LP 5201 Interchange Way ....Louisville KY 40229 *Cust Svc	800-579-0975*	502-778-4421

752   TOOL & DIE SHOPS

	Toll-Free	Phone
Aeromet Industries Inc 739 S Arbogast St ....Griffith IN 46319	800-899-7442	219-924-7442
Anchor Manufacturing Group inc 12200 Brookpark Rd ....Cleveland OH 44130	888-341-8910	216-362-1850
Armin Tool & Manufacturing Company Inc 1500 N La Fox St ....South Elgin IL 60177	800-427-3607	847-742-1864
Bowden Manufacturing Corp 4590 Beidler Rd ....Willoughby OH 44094	800-876-8970	440-946-1770
Canadian Tool & Die Ltd 1331 Chevrier Blvd ....Winnipeg MB R3T1Y4	800-204-4150	204-453-6833
Carlson Tool & Manufacturing Corp W57 N14386 Doerr Way ....Cedarburg WI 53012	800-532-2252	262-377-2020
Carr Lane Mfg 4200 Carr Ln Ct ....Saint Louis MO 63119	800-622-4824	314-647-6200
Cbw Automation 3939 Automation Way ....Fort collins CO 80525	800-229-9500	970-229-9500
Claret Canada Inc 1400 Rue Joliot-curie ....Boucherville QC J4B7L9	800-567-7442	450-449-5774
Cleveland Punch & Die Co 666 Pratt St PO Box 769............Ravenna OH 44266	888-451-4342	
Coastal Casting Service Inc 2903 Gano St ....Houston TX 77009	800-433-6223	713-223-4439
Cole Tool & Die Co 241 Ashland Rd ....Mansfield OH 44905	800-837-2653	419-522-1272
Custom Mold Engineering Inc 9780 S Franklin Dr ....Franklin WI 53132	800-448-2005	414-421-5444
D & D Manufacturing Inc 500 Territorial Dr ....Bolingbrook IL 60440	888-300-6869	
D-M-E Co 29111 Stephenson Hwy ....Madison Heights MI 48071	800-626-6653	248-398-6000
Danly IEM 6779 Engle Rd Ste A-F ....Cleveland OH 44130	800-652-6462	
Del-Tech Manufacturing Inc 9703 Penn Rd ....Prince George BC V2N5T6	800-736-7733	250-564-3585
Deluxe Stitcher Company Inc 3747 Acorn Ln ....Franklin Park IL 60131	800-634-0810	847-455-4400
Diamond Tool & Die Inc 508 29th Ave ....Oakland CA 94601	800-227-1084	510-534-7050
Die Services International 45000 Van Born Rd ....Belleville MI 48111	800-555-1212	734-699-3400
EF Precision Design Inc 2301 Computer Rd ....Willow Grove PA 19090	800-536-3900	215-784-0861
Ehrhardt Engineered Solutions 25 Central Industrial Dr ....Granite City IL 62040	877-386-7856	314-436-6900
Excel Machinery Ltd 12100 I-40 E ....Amarillo TX 79120	800-858-4002	806-335-1553
General Carbide Corp 1151 Garden St ....Greensburg PA 15601	800-245-2465	
General Tool Co 101 Landy Ln ....Cincinnati OH 45215	800-314-9817	
GlobalDie 1130 Minot Ave PO Box 1120 ....Auburn ME 04211	800-910-3747	207-514-7252
Hydro Carbide 4439 SR-982 ....Latrobe PA 15650	800-245-2476	724-539-9701
Hygrade Precision Technologies Inc 329 Cooke St ....Plainville CT 06062	800-457-1666	860-747-5773
Indian Creek Fabricators 1350 Commerce Pk Dr ....Tipp City OH 45371	877-769-5880	937-667-5818
Jo-Ad Industries Inc 31465 Stephenson Hwy ....Madison Heights MI 48071	800-331-8923	248-588-4810
Jones Metal Products Co 200 N Ctr St ....West Lafayette OH 43845	888-868-6535	740-545-6381
Kell-Strom Tool Co 214 Church St ....Wethersfield CT 06109	800-851-6851	860-529-6851
Lou-Rich Machine Tool Inc 505 W Front St ....Albert Lea MN 56007	800-893-3235	507-377-8910
Mahuta Tool Corp N118W19137 Bunsen Dr ....Germantown WI 53022	888-686-4940	262-502-4100
Mate Precision Tooling Inc 1295 Lund Blvd ....Anoka MN 55303	800-328-4492	763-421-0230
Moeller Mfg Company Inc Punch & Die Div 43938 Plymouth Oaks Blvd ....Plymouth MI 48170	800-521-7613	734-416-0000
Mold Base Industries Inc 7501 Derry St ....Harrisburg PA 17111	800-241-6656	717-564-7960
Mold-A-Matic Corp 147 River St ....Oneonta NY 13820	866-886-2626	607-433-2121
Motor-Services Hugo Stamp Inc 3190 SW Fourth Ave ....Fort Lauderdale FL 33315	800-622-6747	954-763-3660
Northwestern Tools Inc 3130 Valleywood Dr ....Dayton OH 45429	800-236-3956	937-298-9994
PCS Co 34488 Doreka Dr ....Fraser MI 48026	800-521-0546	586-294-7780
Peddinghaus Corp 300 N Washington Ave ....Bradley IL 60915	800-786-2448	815-937-3800
Penn United Technology Inc 799 N Pike Rd ....Cabot PA 16023	866-572-7537	724-352-1507

Company / Address	City	State	ZIP	Toll-Free	Phone
Pennsylvania Tool & Gages Inc PO Box 534	Meadville	PA	16335	**877-827-8285**	814-336-3136
Porter Precision Products Inc 2734 Banning Rd	Cincinnati	OH	45239	**800-543-7041**	513-923-3777
Precision Metal Works 6901 Preston Hwy	Louisville	KY	40219	**877-511-9695**	
Rome Tool & Die Company Inc 113 Hemlock St	Rome	GA	30161	**800-241-3369**	706-234-6743
RotoMetrics Group 800 Howerton Ln	Eureka	MO	63025	**800-325-3851**	636-587-3600
SB Whistler & Sons Inc PO Box 270	Medina	NY	14103	**800-828-1010**	585-318-4630
Specialty Design & Mfg Co PO Box 4039	Reading	PA	19606	**800-720-0867**	610-779-1357
SPX Corp OTC Div 655 Eisenhower Dr	Owatonna	MN	55060	**800-533-6127**	507-455-7000
Superior Die Set Corp 900 West Drexel Ave	Oak Creek	WI	53154	**800-558-6040**	414-764-4900
Superior Die Tool & Machine Co 2301 Fairwood Ave	Columbus	OH	43207	**800-292-2181**	614-444-2181
Unipunch Products Inc 311 Fifth St NW	Clear Lake	WI	54005	**800-828-7061**	
VRC Inc 696 W Bagley Rd	Berea	OH	44017	**800-872-1012**	440-243-6666
Walker Tool & Die Inc 2411 Walker Ave NW	Grand Rapids	MI	49544	**877-925-5378**	616-735-6660
Weldangrind Ltd 10323 174 St NW	Edmonton	AB	T5S1H1	**866-226-2414**	780-484-3030
Westland Corp 1735 S Maize Rd	Wichita	KS	67209	**800-247-1144**	316-721-1144

753 TOOLS - HAND & EDGE

SEE ALSO Saw Blades & Handsaws ; Lawn & Garden Equipment ; Metalworking Devices & Accessories

Company / Address	City	State	ZIP	Toll-Free	Phone
Allway Tools Inc 1255 Seabury Ave	Bronx	NY	10462	**800-422-5592**	718-792-3636
Ames 1327 Northbrook Pkwy Ste 400	Suwanee	GA	30024	**800-303-1827**	
Ames True Temper Inc 465 Railroad Ave	Camp Hill	PA	17011	**800-393-1846**	
Arrow Fastener Co Inc 271 Mayhill St	Saddle Brook	NJ	07663	**800-776-2228**	201-843-6900
BARCO Industries Inc 1020 MacArthur Rd *Cust Svc	Reading	PA	19605	**800-234-8665***	
Bondhus Corp 1400 E Broadway St PO Box 660 *Cust Svc	Monticello	MN	55362	**800-328-8310***	763-295-2162
Cal-Van Tools 7918 Industrial Village Rd	Greensboro	NC	27409	**800-537-1077**	
Channellock Inc 1306 S Main St *Cust Svc	Meadville	PA	16335	**800-724-3018***	
Charles GG Schmidt & Company Inc 301 W Grand Ave	Montvale	NJ	07645	**800-724-6438**	201-391-5300
Consolidated Devices Inc (CDI) 19220 San Jose Ave	City of Industry	CA	91748	**800-525-6319**	626-965-0668
Cooper Industries 600 Travis St Ste 5400 *NYSE: ETN*	Houston	TX	77002	**866-853-4293**	713-209-8400
Cornwell Quality Tools 667 Seville Rd	Wadsworth	OH	44281	**800-321-8356**	330-336-3506
Dasco Pro Inc 340 Blackhawk Park Ave	Rockford	IL	61104	**800-327-2690**	815-962-3727
Duo-Fast Construction 155 Harlem Ave *Cust Svc	Glenview	IL	60025	**877-489-2726***	
Empire Level Manufacturing Corp 929 Empire Dr PO Box 800	Mukwonago	WI	53149	**800-558-0722**	
Enderes Tool Co 1521 E Hawthorne St	Albert Lea	MN	56007	**800-874-7776**	507-373-2396
Everhard Products Inc 1016 Ninth St SW	Canton	OH	44707	**800-225-0984**	330-453-7786
Fiskars Brands Inc 7800 Discovery Dr	Middleton	WI	53562	**866-348-5661**	
General Machine Products Company Inc 3111 Old Lincoln Hwy *Tech Supp	Trevose	PA	19053	**800-345-6009***	215-357-5500
General Tools Mfg Company LLC 80 White St	New York	NY	10013	**800-697-8665**	212-431-6100
Grobet File Company of America Inc 750 Washington Ave	Carlstadt	NJ	07072	**800-847-4188**	201-939-6700
Hyde Tools Co 54 Eastford Rd	Southbridge	MA	01550	**800-872-4933**	508-764-4344
Ken-Tool Co 768 E N St	Akron	OH	44305	**800-872-4929**	330-535-7177
Klein Tools Inc 450 Bond St *Cust Svc	Lincolnshire	IL	60069	**800-553-4676***	
Leatherman Tool Group Inc 12106 NE Ainsworth Cir	Portland	OR	97220	**800-847-8665**	503-253-7826
LS Starrett Co 121 Crescent St *NYSE: SCX*	Athol	MA	01331	**800-482-8710**	978-249-3551
Mac Tools Inc 505 N Cleveland Ave	Westerville	OH	43082	**800-622-8665**	614-755-7000
Malco Products Inc 14080 State Hwy 55 NW PO Box 400	Annandale	MN	55302	**800-328-3530**	320-274-8246
Marshalltown Co 104 S Eigth Ave	Marshalltown	IA	50158	**800-888-0127**	641-753-5999
Matco Tools 4403 Allen Rd	Stow	OH	44224	**866-289-8665**	330-926-5332
Mayhew Steel Products Inc 199 Industrial Blvd	Turners Falls	MA	01376	**800-872-0037**	413-863-4860
MIBRO Group 111 Sinnott Rd	Toronto	ON	M1L4S6	**866-941-9006**	416-285-9000
Newell Rubbermaid Inc Irwin Tools Div 8935 Northpointe Executive Dr	Huntersville	NC	28078	**800-866-5740**	704-987-4555
QEP Co Inc 1001 Broken Sound Pkwy NW Ste A *OTC: QEPC* ■ *Sales	Boca Raton	FL	33487	**800-777-8665***	561-994-5550
Red Devil Inc 1437 S Boulder	Tulsa	OK	74119	**800-423-3845**	
Reed Manufacturing Co 1425 W Eigth St	Erie	PA	16502	**800-456-1697**	814-452-3691
Relton Corp 317 Rolyn Pl *Cust Svc	Arcadia	CA	91007	**800-423-1505***	323-681-2551
Ripley Co 46 Nooks Hill Rd	Cromwell	CT	06416	**800-528-8665**	860-635-2200
Snap-on Inc 2801 80th St *NYSE: SNA*	Kenosha	WI	53143	**877-762-7664**	262-656-5200
Stabila Inc 332 Industrial Dr PO Box 402	South Elgin	IL	60177	**800-869-7460**	
Stanley Tools Inc 701 E Joppa Rd	Towson	MD	21286	**800-262-2161**	
Stride Tool Inc Imperial Div 30333 Emerald Vly Pkwy	Glenwillow	OH	44139	**888-467-8665**	440-247-4600
Superior Tool Co 100 Hayes Dr Unit C *Cust Svc	Cleveland	OH	44131	**800-533-3244***	216-398-8600
Tamco Inc 1466 Delberts Dr	Monongahela	PA	15063	**800-826-2672**	724-258-6622
Triumph Twist Drill Co Inc 1 SW Seventh St	Chisholm	MN	55719	**800-942-1501**	218-263-3891
Vaughan & Bushnell Manufacturing Co 11414 Maple Ave	Hebron	IL	60034	**800-435-6000**	
Walter Meier Mfg Inc 427 New Sanford Rd	La Vergne	TN	37086	**800-274-6848**	
Warner Manufacturing Co 13435 Industrial Pk Blvd	Plymouth	MN	55441	**800-444-0606**	763-559-4740
Wheeler-Rex Inc 3744 Jefferson Rd PO Box 688	Ashtabula	OH	44005	**800-321-7950**	440-998-2788

TOOLS - MACHINE

SEE Machine Tools - Metal Cutting Types ; Machine Tools - Metal Forming Types

754 TOOLS - POWER

SEE ALSO Lawn & Garden Equipment ; Metalworking Devices & Accessories

Company / Address	City	State	ZIP	Toll-Free	Phone
Alpine Power Systems 24355 Capitol	Redford	MI	48239	**877-993-8855**	
American Pneumatic Tool Inc 1000 S Grand Ave	Santa Ana	CA	92705	**800-532-7402**	562-204-1555
Atlas Copco Tools & Assembly Systems LLC 3301 Cross Creek Pkwy	Auburn Hills	MI	48326	**800-859-3746**	248-373-3000
Blackstone Industries Inc 16 Stoney Hill Rd	Bethel	CT	06801	**800-272-2885**	203-792-8622
Chicago Pneumatic Tool Co 1800 Overview Dr	Rock Hill	SC	29730	**800-624-4735**	803-817-7000
Cooper Industries 600 Travis St Ste 5400 *NYSE: ETN*	Houston	TX	77002	**866-853-4293**	713-209-8400
Dremel Inc 4915 21st St	Racine	WI	53406	**800-437-3635**	262-554-1390
Dynabrade Inc 8989 Sheridan Dr *Cust Svc	Clarence	NY	14031	**800-828-7333***	716-631-0100
Enerpac PO Box 3241 *Cust Svc	Milwaukee	WI	53201	**800-433-2766***	262-293-1600
Florida Pneumatic Manufacturing Corp 851 Jupiter Pk Ln	Jupiter	FL	33458	**800-327-9403**	561-744-9500
Greenlee Textron Inc 4455 Boeing Dr	Rockford	IL	61109	**800-435-0786**	
Hilti Inc 5400 S 122nd E Ave *Cust Svc	Tulsa	OK	74146	**800-879-8000***	
Hougen Manufacturing Inc 3001 Hougen Dr *Orders	Swartz Creek	MI	48473	**800-426-7818***	810-635-7111
Makita USA Inc 14930 Northam St	La Mirada	CA	90638	**800-462-5482**	714-522-8088
Master Appliance Corp 2420 18th St	Racine	WI	53403	**800-558-9413**	262-633-7791
Milwaukee Electric Tool Corp 13135 W Lisbon Rd	Brookfield	WI	53005	**800-729-3878**	262-783-8586
P & F Industries Inc 445 Broadhollow Rd *NASDAQ: PFIN*	Melville	NY	11747	**800-327-9403**	631-694-9800
Pioneer Tool & Forge Inc 101 Sixth St	New Kensington	PA	15068	**800-359-6408**	724-337-4700
Pneutek 17 Friars Dr	Hudson	NH	03051	**800-431-8665**	603-883-1660
Powernail Co 1300 Rose Rd	Lake Zurich	IL	60047	**800-323-1653**	847-847-3000
Robert Bosch Tool Corp 1800 W Central Rd	Mount Prospect	IL	60056	**877-267-2499**	
Ryobi Technologies Inc 1428 Pearman Dairy Rd	Anderson	SC	29625	**800-525-2579**	
SENCO 4270 Ivy Pointe Blvd *Tech Supp	Cincinnati	OH	45245	**800-543-4596***	
Shopsmith Inc 6530 Poe Ave *OTC: SSMH* ■ *Cust Svc	Dayton	OH	45414	**800-543-7586***	937-898-6070
Sioux Tools Inc 250 Snap-on Dr *Orders	Murphy	NC	28906	**800-722-7290***	828-835-9765
Stanley Assembly Technologies Div 5335 Avion Pk Dr	Cleveland	OH	44143	**877-787-7830**	440-461-5500
Stihl Inc 536 Viking Dr *Cust Svc	Virginia Beach	VA	23452	**800-467-8445***	757-486-9100
Thomas C Wilson Inc 21-11 44th Ave	Long Island	NY	11101	**800-230-2636**	718-729-3360

	Toll-Free	Phone

SEE ALSO Bus Services - Charter ; Travel Agencies

		Toll-Free	Phone
Academy Bus LLC			
111 Paterson Ave	Hoboken NJ 07030	800-442-7272	201-420-7000
Adventure Alaska Tours Inc			
PO Box 64	Hope AK 99605	800-365-7057	907-782-3730
Adventure Connection			
PO Box 475	Coloma CA 95613	800-556-6060	530-626-7385
Adventure Life South America			
712 W Spruce St Ste 1	Missoula MT 59802	800-344-6118	406-541-2677
Adventures Out West			
1680 S 21st St	Colorado Springs CO 80904	800-755-0935	
Africa Adventure Co, The			
2601 E Oakland Park Blvd Ste 600	Fort Lauderdale FL 33308	800-882-9453	954-491-8877
African Travel Inc			
330 N Brand Blvd Ste 225	Glendale CA 91203	800-421-8907	818-507-7893
AHI International Corp			
8550 W Bryn Mawr Ave Ste 600	Chicago IL 60631	800-323-7373	
Alaska Collection			
509 W Fourth Ave	Anchorage AK 99501	800-808-8068	907-777-2800
All Aboard USA			
2736 Kanasita Dr	Chattanooga TN 37343	800-499-9877	423-499-9977
Alpine Adventure Trails Tours Inc			
7495 Lower Thomaston Rd	Macon GA 31220	888-478-4004	478-477-4702
AmaWaterways			
26010 Mureau Rd	Calabasas CA 91302	800-626-0126	
American Trails West (ATW)			
92 Middle Neck Rd	Great Neck NY 11021	800-645-6260	516-487-2800
Anderson Coach & Travel			
1 Anderson Plz	Greenville PA 16125	800-345-3435	724-588-8310
ATS Tours			
300 Continental Blvd Ste 350	El Segundo CA 90245	888-410-5770	
Backroads 801 Cedar St	Berkeley CA 94710	800-462-2848	510-527-1555
Badger Coaches Inc			
5501 Femrite Dr	Madison WI 53718	800-442-8259	608-255-1511
Banff Adventures Unlimited			
211 Bear St Bison Courtyard	Banff AB T1L1A8	800-644-8888	403-762-4554
Beamers Hells Canyon Tours			
1451 Bridge St	Clarkston WA 99403	800-522-6966	509-758-4800
Bestway Tours & Safaris			
8678 Greenall Ave	Burnaby BC V5J3M6	800-663-0844	604-264-7378
Big Five Tours & Expeditions			
1551 SE Palm Ct	Stuart FL 34994	800-244-3483	
Bonaventure Tours			
8 Boudreau Ln	Haute-Aboujagane NB E4P5N1	800-561-1213	506-532-3674
Boston Duck Tours Ltd			
4 Copley Pl Ste 4155	Boston MA 02116	800-226-7442	617-267-3825
Breakaway Tours			
337 Queen St W	Toronto ON M5V2A4	800-465-4257	
Brendan Vacations			
801 E Katella Ave	Anaheim CA 92805	800-687-1002	
Brewster Adventures			
PO Box 370	Banff AB T1L1A5	800-691-5085	403-762-5454
Burke International Tours Inc			
PO Box 890	Newton NC 28658	800-476-3900	828-465-3900
California Parlor Car Tours			
500 Sutter St Ste 401	San Francisco CA 94102	800-227-4250	415-474-7500
CEA Study Abroad (CEA)			
2999 N 44th St Ste 200	Phoenix AZ 85018	866-987-8906	800-266-4441
Centennial Travelers			
7697 S Roslyn Ct	Centennial CO 80112	800-223-0675	303-741-6685
Churchill Nature Tours			
PO Box 429	Erickson MB R0J0P0	877-636-2968	204-636-2968
Classic Student Tours			
75 Rhoads Ctr Dr	Dayton OH 45458	800-860-0246	937-439-0032
Club Europa 802 W Oregon St	Urbana IL 61801	800-331-1882	217-344-5863
Coach Tours Ltd			
475 Federal Rd	Brookfield CT 06804	800-822-6224	203-740-1118
Contemporary Tours			
100 Crossways Park Dr W Ste 400	Westbury NY 11797	800-627-8873	516-484-5032
Contiki Holidays			
801 E Katella Ave	Anaheim CA 92805	800-944-5708	866-266-8454
Dash Tours 1024 Winnipeg St	Regina SK S4R8P8	800-265-0000	306-352-2222
Dipert Travel & Transportation Ltd			
PO Box 580	Arlington TX 76004	800-433-5335	
Earthwatch Institute			
114 Western Ave	Boston MA 02134	800-776-0188	978-461-0081
Educational Tours			
1123 Sterling Rd	Inverness FL 34450	800-343-9003	
Educational Travel Consultants (ETC)			
PO Box 1580	Hendersonville NC 28793	800-247-7969	828-693-0412
EF Center 2 Education Cir	Cambridge MA 02141	800-637-8222	800-665-5364
Esplanade Tours			
160 Commonwealth Ave Ste U-1A	Boston MA 02116	800-628-4893	617-266-7465
Explorica Inc 145 Tremont St	Boston MA 02111	888-310-7120	
Fantastic Tours & Travel			
6143 Jericho Tpke	Commack NY 11725	800-552-6262	631-462-6262
Festive Holidays Inc			
5501 New Jersey Ave	Wildwood Crest NJ 08260	800-257-8920	609-522-6316
Friendly Excursions Inc			
PO Box 69	Sunland CA 91041	800-775-5018	818-353-7726
Frontiers International Travel			
600 Warrendale Rd	Gibsonia PA 15044	800-245-1950	724-935-1577
General Tours 53 Summer St	Keene NH 03431	800-221-2216	
Gerber Tours Inc			
100 Crossways Park Dr W Ste 400	Woodbury NY 11797	800-645-9145	516-826-5000
Globus 5301 S Federal Cir	Littleton CO 80123	866-755-8581	
Go Next			
8000 W 78th St Ste 345	Minneapolis MN 55439	800-842-9023	952-918-8950
Go..With Jo! Tours & Travel Inc			
121 W Tyler	Harlingen TX 78550	800-999-1446	956-423-1446

		Toll-Free	Phone
Good Time Tours			
455 Corday St	Pensacola FL 32503	800-446-0886	850-476-0046
Good Times Travel Inc			
17132 Magnolia St	Fountain Valley CA 92708	888-488-2287	714-848-1255
Grand European Tours			
6000 Meadows Rd Ste 520	Lake Oswego OR 97035	877-622-9109	
Gray Line Corporation Inc			
1900 16th St Ste 210	Denver CO 80202	800-472-9546	303-539-8502
Green Tortoise Adventure Travel & Hostels			
494 Broadway	San Francisco CA 94133	800-867-8647	415-834-1000
Gutsy Women Travel LLC			
801 E Katella Ave	Anaheim CA 92806	866-464-8879	
Hagey Coach & Tours Nrt			
210 Schoolhouse Rd	Souderton PA 18964	800-544-2439	215-723-4381
Historic Tours of America Inc			
201 Front St	Key West FL 33040	800-844-7601*	855-629-8777
*Consumer Info			
Hole in One International			
6195 Ridgeview Ct Ste A	Reno NV 89519	800-827-2249	775-828-4653
Holiday River Expeditions			
544 East 3900 South	Salt Lake City UT 84107	800-624-6323	801-266-2087
IWorld of Travel			
25 Broadway 9th Fl	New York NY 10004	800-223-7460	
Jade Travel Group			
1650 Elgin Mills Rd E Unit 403	Richmond Hill ON L4S0B2	800-387-0387	905-787-9288
Julian Tours			
1721 Crestwood Dr	Alexandria VA 22302	800-541-7936	703-379-2300
Ker & Downey Inc 6703 Hwy Blvd	Katy TX 77494	800-423-4236	281-371-2500
Kincaid Coach Lines Inc			
9207 Woodend Rd	Kansas City KS 66111	800-998-1901	913-441-6200
Lakefront Lines Inc			
13315 Brookpark Rd	Brook Park OH 44142	800-543-9912	216-267-8810
Landmark Tours Inc			
4001 Stinson Blvd Ste 430	Minneapolis MN 55421	888-231-8735	651-490-5408
Lindblad Expeditions			
96 Morton St 9th Fl	New York NY 10014	800-397-3348	
Maupintour Inc			
2690 Weston Rd Ste 200	Weston FL 33331	800-255-4266	954-653-3820
Mayflower Tours Inc			
1225 Warren Ave PO Box 490	Downers Grove IL 60515	800-323-7604	630-435-8500
Micato Safaris			
15 W 26th St 11th Fl	New York NY 10010	800-642-2861	212-545-7111
Mid-American Coaches Inc			
4530 Hwy 47	Washington MO 63090	866-944-8687	
Midnight Sun Adventure Travel			
1027 Pandora Ave	Victoria BC V8V3P6	800-255-5057	250-480-9409
MLT Inc 700 S Central Ave	Atlanta GA 30354	800-727-1111	800-800-1504
Moose Travel Network			
192 Spadina Ave Unit 408	Toronto ON M5T2C2	888-244-6673	604-297-0255
Mountain Travel Sobek			
1266 66th St Ste 4	Emeryville CA 94608	888-831-7526	
Natural Habitat Adventures			
PO Box 3065	Boulder CO 80307	800-543-8917	303-449-3711
Networld Inc			
300 Lanidex Plz Ste 1	Parsippany NJ 07054	800-992-3411	973-884-7474
Off the Beaten Path			
7 E Beall St	Bozeman MT 59715	800-445-2995	406-586-1311
Olivia 434 Brannan St	San Francisco CA 94107	800-631-6277	415-962-5700
Onondaga Coach Corp			
PO Box 277	Auburn NY 13021	800-451-1570	315-255-2216
Orange Belt Stages			
PO Box 949	Visalia CA 93279	800-266-7433	559-733-4408
Overseas Adventure Travel			
347 Congress St	Boston MA 02210	800-221-0814	
Panorama Balloon Tours			
2683 Via De La Valle 625G	Del Mar CA 92014	800-455-3592	760-271-3467
Perillo Tours			
577 Chestnut Ridge Rd	Woodcliff Lake NJ 07677	800-431-1515	201-307-1234
Pilgrim Tours & Travel Inc			
3071 Main St PO Box 268	Morgantown PA 19543	800-322-0788	610-286-0788
Pioneer Golf Inc			
609 Castle Ridge Rd Ste 335	Austin TX 78746	800-262-5725	512-327-2680
Pitmar Tours			
7549 140th St Ste 9	Surrey BC V3W5J9	877-596-9670	604-596-9670
Polynesian Adventure Tours Inc			
2880 Kilihau St	Honolulu HI 96819	800-622-3011	808-833-3000
Premier Alaska Tours Inc			
1900 Premier Ct	Anchorage AK 99502	888-486-8725	907-279-0001
Premier Tours Inc			
1120 South St	Philadelphia PA 19147	800-545-1910	
Presley Tours Inc			
16 Presley Pk Dr PO Box 58	Makanda IL 62958	800-621-6100	618-549-0704
Pursuit			
100 Gopher St PO Box 1140	Banff AB T1L1J3	866-606-6700	403-762-6700
REI Adventures PO Box 1938	Sumner WA 98390	800-622-2236	
Rivers Oceans & Mountains Adventures Inc (ROAM)			
24-622 Front St	Nelson BC V1L4B7	888-639-1114	
Roberts Hawaii Inc			
680 Iwilei Rd Ste 700	Honolulu HI 96817	800-831-5541	808-523-7750
RSVP Vacations LLC			
9200 Sunset Blvd Ste 500	West Hollywood CA 90069	800-328-7787	310-432-2300
Scenic Airlines Inc			
1265 Airport Rd	Boulder City NV 89005	800-634-6801	702-638-3300
Short Hills Tours			
46 Chatham Rd	Short Hills NJ 07078	800-348-6871	973-467-2113
Silver Fox Tours & Motorcoaches			
3 Silver Fox Dr	Millbury MA 01527	800-342-5998	508-865-6000
Silverado Stages Inc			
2239 N Black Canyon Hwy	Phoenix AZ 85009	888-383-8109	
Sixthman LTD			
437 Memorial Dr SE Ste A10	Atlanta GA 30312	877-749-8462	404-525-0222
Sports Leisure Vacations			
9812 Old Winery Pl Ste 1	Sacramento CA 95827	800-951-5556	916-361-2051
Sports Travel Inc			
60 Main St PO Box 50	Hatfield MA 01038	800-662-4424	413-247-7678
Straight A Tours & Travel			
6881 Kingspointe Pkwy Ste 18	Orlando FL 32819	800-237-5440	407-896-1242

				Toll-Free	Phone
Student Tours Inc					
60 West Ave	Vineyard Haven	MA	02568	**800-331-7093**	508-693-5078
Student Travel Services Inc					
2431 Solomons Island Rd Ste 302	Annapolis	MD	21061	**800-648-4849**	410-787-9500
Sunny Land Tours Inc					
21 Old Kings Rd N Ste B-212	Palm Coast	FL	32137	**800-783-7839**	386-449-0059
Super Holiday Tours					
116 Gatlin Ave	Orlando	FL	32806	**800-327-2116**	
Tag-A-Long Expeditions					
452 N Main St	Moab	UT	84532	**800-453-3292**	435-259-8946
Tauck World Discovery					
10 Norden Pl	Norwalk	CT	06855	**800-468-2825**	203-899-6500
Timberwolf Tours Ltd					
51404 Range Rd 264 Ste 34	Spruce Grove	AB	T7Y1E4	**888-467-9697**	780-470-4966
Toto Tours					
1326 W Albion Ave	Chicago	IL	60626	**800-565-1241**	773-274-8686
Travcoa					
100 N Sepulveda Blvd Ste 1700	El Segundo	CA	90245	**800-992-2003**	310-649-7104
Tri-State Travel					
4349 Industrial Pk Dr	Galena	IL	61036	**800-779-4869**	815-777-0820
VBT					
426 Industrial Ave Ste 120	Williston	VT	05495	**800-245-3868**	
VentureOut					
575 Pierce St Ste 604	San Francisco	CA	94117	**888-431-6789**	415-626-5678
Wade Tours Inc					
797 Burdeck St	Schenectady	NY	12306	**800-955-9233**	518-355-4500
Walking Adventures International					
14612 NE Fourth Plain Rd Ste A.	Vancouver	WA	98682	**800-779-0353**	
West Coast Connection					
1725 Main St Ste 215.	Weston	FL	33326	**800-767-0227**	954-888-9780
White Mountain Adventures					
131 Eagle Crescent PO Box 4259	Banff	AB	T1L1A6	**800-408-0005**	403-760-4403
White Star Tours					
26 E Lancaster Ave	Reading	PA	19607	**800-437-2323**	610-775-5000
Wilderness Travel					
1102 Ninth St	Berkeley	CA	94710	**800-368-2794**	510-558-2488
Wildland Adventures Inc					
3516 NE 155th St	Lake Forest Park	WA	98155	**800-345-4453**	206-365-0686
Wings Tours Inc					
11350 McCormick Rd Ste 904	Hunt Valley	MD	21031	**800-869-4647**	410-771-0925
WorldStrides					
218 W Water St Ste 400	Charlottesville	VA	22902	**800-999-7676***	
*General					

756 TOY STORES

				Toll-Free	Phone
Alabama Card Systems Inc					
500 Gene Reed Dr Ste 102	Birmingham	AL	35215	**800-985-7507**	205-833-1116
Artists Club, The					
13118 NE Fourth St	Vancouver	WA	98684	**800-574-1323**	
Aruze Gaming America Inc					
955 Grier Dr Ste A	Las Vegas	NV	89119	**877-268-4119**	702-361-3166
Build-A-Bear Workshop Inc					
1954 Innerbelt Business Ctr Dr	Saint Louis	MO	63114	**877-789-2327**	
NYSE: BBW					
Creative Kid Stuff					
3939 E 46th St	Minneapolis	MN	55406	**800-353-0710**	612-929-2431
CRT Custom Products Inc					
7532 Hickory Hills Ct	Whites Creek	TN	37189	**800-453-2533**	615-876-5490
Daron Worldwide Trading Inc					
24 Stewart Pl Unit 4	Fairfield	NJ	07004	**800-776-2324**	973-882-0035
DES Reprographics					
2450 Scott Blvd Ste 300	Santa Clara	CA	95050	**888-788-1898**	408-970-8551
Discount School Supplies					
2 Lower Ragsdale Rd Ste 125	Monterey	CA	93940	**800-919-5238**	
Fat Brain Toys LLC					
20516 Nicholas Cir	Elkhorn	NE	68022	**800-590-5987**	402-779-3181
Fibre Craft Materials Corp					
7603 New Gross Point Rd	Skokie	IL	60077	**800-323-4316**	847-929-5600
Great Lakes Dart Manufacturing Inc					
S84 W19093 Enterprise Dr	Muskego	WI	53150	**800-225-7593**	262-679-8730
Learning Express Inc					
29 Buena Vista St	Devens	MA	01434	**888-725-8697**	978-889-1000
M B Klein Inc					
243-A Cockeysville Rd	Cockeysville	MD	21030	**888-872-4675**	
Mary Maxim Ltd 75 Scott Ave	Paris	ON	N3L3G5	**888-442-2266**	
MGA Entertainment Inc					
16300 Roscoe Blvd Ste 150	Van Nuys	CA	91406	**800-222-4685**	818-894-2525
Thinkfun Inc					
1321 Cameron St	Alexandria	VA	22314	**800-468-1864**	703-549-4999
Thinkway Toys Inc					
8885 Woodbine Ave	Markham	ON	L3R5G1	**800-535-5754**	905-470-8883
Toys 'R' Us (Canada) Ltd					
2777 Langstaff Rd	Concord	ON	L4K4M5	**800-869-7787**	
Trainworld Associates LLC					
751 Mcdonald Ave	Brooklyn	NY	11218	**800-541-7010**	718-436-7072

757 TOYS, GAMES, HOBBIES

SEE ALSO Bicycles & Bicycle Parts & Accessories ; Baby Products ; Games & Entertainment Software

				Toll-Free	Phone
Airmate Co Inc					
16280 County Rd D	Bryan	OH	43506	**800-544-3614**	419-636-3184
American Girl Inc					
8400 Fairway Pl	Middleton	WI	53562	**800-845-0005***	
*Orders					
American Plastic Toys Inc					
799 Ladd Rd	Walled Lake	MI	48390	**800-521-7080**	248-624-4881
Atlas Model Railroad Company Inc					
378 Florence Ave	Hillside	NJ	07205	**800-872-2521***	908-687-0880
*Orders					

				Toll-Free	Phone
Bachmann Industries Inc					
1400 E Erie Ave	Philadelphia	PA	19124	**800-356-3910***	215-533-1600
*Cust Svc					
Ball Bounce & Sport Inc/Hedstrom Plastics					
1 Hedstrom Dr	Ashland	OH	44805	**800-765-9665**	419-289-9310
Bravo Sports Corp					
12801 Carmenita Rd	Santa Fe Springs	CA	90670	**800-234-9737***	562-484-5100
*Cust Svc					
Buffalo Games Inc					
220 James E Casey Dr	Buffalo	NY	14206	**855-895-4290**	
Cardinal Industries Inc					
21-01 51st Ave	Long Island	NY	11101	**800-622-8339**	718-784-3000
Creativity for Kids					
9450 Allen Dr	Cleveland	OH	44125	**800-311-8684**	216-643-4660
Douglas Cuddle Toys Company Inc					
69 Krif Rd PO Box D	Keene	NH	03431	**800-992-9002**	603-352-3414
Estes-Cox Corp 1295 H St	Penrose	CO	81240	**800-525-7561**	719-372-6565
Fisher-Price Inc					
636 Girard Ave	East Aurora	NY	14052	**800-432-5437**	716-687-3000
Five Below Inc					
1818 Market St	Philadelphia	PA	19103	**844-452-3569**	215-546-7909
Gayla Industries Inc					
PO Box 920800	Houston	TX	77292	**800-231-7508**	
Great Planes Model Distributors					
PO Box 9021	Champaign	IL	61826	**800-637-7660**	217-398-3630
Guidecraft USA					
55508 Hwy 19 W	Winthrop	MN	55396	**800-524-3555**	507-647-5030
Gund Inc 1 Runyons Ln	Edison	NJ	08817	**800-448-4863***	732-248-1500
*Cust Svc					
Hasbro Inc					
1027 Newport Ave	Pawtucket	RI	02861	**800-242-7276**	401-431-8697
NASDAQ: HAS					
Imperial Toy LLC					
16641 Roscoe Pl	North Hills	CA	91343	**877-762-8253***	818-536-6500
*Cust Svc					
International Playthings Inc					
75D Lackawanna Ave	Parsippany	NJ	07054	**800-631-1272**	973-316-2500
JAKKS Pacific Inc					
21749 Baker Pkwy	Walnut	CA	91789	**877-875-2557**	909-594-7771
LeapFrog Enterprises Inc					
6401 Hollis St Ste 100	Emeryville	CA	94608	**800-701-5327**	510-420-5000
NYSE: LF					
Learning Resources					
380 N Fairway Dr	Vernon Hills	IL	60061	**800-222-3909**	847-573-8400
LEGO Systems Inc					
555 Taylor Rd	Enfield	CT	06082	**877-518-5346**	860-749-2291
Lionel com LLC					
26750 23 Mile Rd	Chesterfield	MI	48051	**800-454-6635**	586-949-4100
Little Tikes Co, The					
2180 Barlow Rd	Hudson	OH	44236	**800-321-0183***	
*Cust Svc					
Losi 4710 E Guasti Rd	Ontario	CA	91761	**888-899-5674**	909-390-9595
Mag-Nif Inc 8820 E Ave	Mentor	OH	44060	**800-869-5463**	
Maple City Rubber Co					
55 Newton St	Norwalk	OH	44857	**800-841-9434**	419-668-8261
Mattel Inc					
333 Continental Blvd	El Segundo	CA	90245	**800-524-8697**	310-252-2000
NASDAQ: MAT					
Midwest Products Company Inc					
400 S Indiana St	Hobart	IN	46342	**800-348-3497***	219-942-1134
*Orders					
Nintendo of America Inc					
4820 150th Ave NE	Redmond	WA	98052	**800-255-3700***	425-882-2040
*Cust Svc					
Ohio Art Co, The 1 Toy St	Bryan	OH	43506	**800-800-3141**	419-636-3141
OTC: OART					
Pepperball Technologies Inc					
6540 Lusk Blvd Ste C137	San Diego	CA	92121	**877-887-3773**	858-638-0236
Plaid Enterprises Inc					
3225 Westech Dr	Norcross	GA	30092	**800-842-4197**	
Playmobil USA Inc					
26 Commerce Dr	Cranbury	NJ	08512	**800-351-8697**	609-409-1263
Pressman Toy Corp					
3701 W Plano Pkwy Ste 100	Plano	TX	75075	**800-800-0298***	855-258-8214
*Cust Svc					
Radio Flyer Inc					
6515 W Grand Ave	Chicago	IL	60707	**800-621-7613**	773-637-7100
SIG Mfg Company Inc					
401 S Front St	Montezuma	IA	50171	**800-247-5008***	641-623-5154
*Sales					
Spin Master Ltd					
450 Front St W	Toronto	ON	M5V1B6	**800-622-8339**	416-364-6002
Steiff North America					
24 Albion Rd Ste 220	Lincoln	RI	02865	**888-978-3433**	401-312-0080
Swibco Inc 4810 Venture Rd	Lisle	IL	60532	**877-794-2261**	630-968-8900
Testor Corp					
11 Hawthorn Pkwy	Vernon Hills	IL	60061	**800-837-8677**	815-962-6654
TOMY International Inc					
2015 Spring Rd Ste 700	Oak Brook	IL	60523	**800-704-8697**	630-573-7200
Tonner Doll Co PO Box 4410	Kingston	NY	12402	**800-794-2107**	845-339-9537
Uncle Milton Industries Inc					
29209 Canwood St Ste 120	Agoura	CA	91301	**800-869-7555***	818-707-0800
*General					
Universal Mfg Co Inc					
5030 Mackey S	Overland Park	KS	66203	**800-524-5860**	913-815-6230
University Games Corp					
2030 Harrison St	San Francisco	CA	94110	**800-347-4818**	415-503-1600
Upper Deck Co LLC					
5909 Sea Otter Pl	Carlsbad	CA	92010	**800-873-7332***	
*Cust Svc					
Vermont Teddy Bear Company Inc					
6655 Shelburne Rd	Shelburne	VT	05482	**800-988-8277**	802-985-3001
VTech Electronics North America LLC					
1155 W Dundee St Ste 130	Arlington Heights	IL	60004	**800-521-2010**	847-400-3600
William K Walthers Inc					
5601 W Florist Ave	Milwaukee	WI	53218	**800-877-7171**	414-527-0770
Wizards of the Coast Inc					
PO Box 707	Renton	WA	98057	**800-324-6496**	425-226-6500

TRAILERS - TRUCK

SEE Truck Trailers

758 TRAILERS (TOWING) & TRAILER HITCHES

				Toll-Free	Phone
Bright Co-op Inc					
803 W Seale St	Nacogdoches	TX	75964	800-562-0730	936-564-8378
Cequent Towing Products					
47774 Anchor Ct W	Plymouth	MI	48170	800-521-0510	
Cequent Trailer Products					
1050 Indianhead Dr	Mosinee	WI	54455	800-604-9466	715-693-1700
CM Trailers Inc					
200 County Rd	Madill	OK	73446	888-268-7577	
Com-Fab Inc					
4657 Price HilliaRds Rd	Plain City	OH	43064	866-522-1794	740-857-1107
Dethmers Manufacturing Co (DEMCO)					
4010 320th St	Boyden	IA	51234	800-543-3626	712-725-2311
EZ Loader Boat Trailers Inc					
717 N Hamilton St	Spokane	WA	99202	800-398-5623	509-489-0181
Gooseneck Trailer Mfg Co					
4400 E Hwy 21 PO Box 832	Bryan	TX	77808	800-688-5490*	979-778-0034
*Cust Svc					
Midwest Industries Inc					
122 E State Hwy 175	Ida Grove	IA	51445	800-859-3028	712-364-3365
Rigid Hitch Inc					
3301 W Burnsville Pkwy	Burnsville	MN	55337	800-624-7630*	
*Cust Svc					
Sundowner Trailers Inc					
9805 S State Hwy 48	Coleman	OK	73432	800-654-3879	580-937-4255
Take 3 Trailers Inc					
1808 Hwy 105	Brenham	TX	77833	866-428-2533	979-337-9568
Unique Functional Products Corp					
135 Sunshine Ln	San Marcos	CA	92069	800-854-1905	760-744-1610

759 TRAINING & CERTIFICATION PROGRAMS - COMPUTER & INTERNET

				Toll-Free	Phone
Animation Mentor					
1400 65th St Ste 250	Emeryville	CA	94608	877-326-4628	
ASPE Inc					
114 Edinburgh S Dr Ste 200	Cary	NC	27511	877-800-5221	
Career Step LLC					
4692 N 300 W Ste 150	Provo	UT	84604	800-246-7837	801-489-9393
Computer Workshop Inc, The					
5131 Post Rd Ste 102	Dublin	OH	43017	800-639-3535	614-798-9505
Coyne College Inc					
330 N Green St	Chicago	IL	60607	800-707-1922	773-577-8100
ECO Canada					
308 - 11th Ave SE Ste 200	Calgary	AB	T2G0Y2	800-251-7773	403-233-0748
Gainshare Inc					
3110 N Central Ave Ste 160	Phoenix	AZ	85012	800-264-9029	602-266-8500
Global Knowledge Training LLC					
9000 Regency Pkwy Ste 400	Cary	NC	27518	877-200-8866*	919-461-8600
*Cust Svc					
Hands on Technology Transfer Inc					
14 Fletcher St 1 Village Sq Ste 8	Chelmsford	MA	01824	800-413-0939	978-250-4299
Health & Safety Institute Inc					
1450 Westec Dr	Eugene	OR	97402	800-447-3177	
Learning Tree International Inc					
1831 Michael Faraday Dr	Reston	VA	20190	800-843-8733*	703-709-9119
OTC: LTRE ■ *Cust Svc					
Metex Inc					
789 Don Mills Rd Ste 218	North York	ON	M3C1T5	866-817-8137	416-203-8388
My Service Depot					
8774 Cotter St	Lewis Center	OH	43035	888-518-0818	
New Horizons Computer Learning Centers Inc					
1900 S State College Blvd Ste 450	Anaheim	CA	92806	888-236-3625	714-940-8000
New Horizons Worldwide Inc					
1900 S State College Blvd Ste 450	Anaheim	CA	92806	888-236-3625	
Parker University					
2540 Walnut Hill Ln	Dallas	TX	75229	800-637-8337	972-438-6932
PowerScore Inc					
57 Hasell St	Charleston	SC	29401	800-545-1750	
Software Answers Inc					
6770 W Snowville Rd Ste 200	Cleveland	OH	44141	800-638-5212	440-526-0095
Total Seminars LLC					
12550 Fuqua Ste 150	Houston	TX	77034	877-687-2768	281-922-4166

760 TRAINING PROGRAMS - CORPORATE

				Toll-Free	Phone
AchieveGlobal Inc					
8875 Hidden River Pkwy Ste 400	Tampa	FL	33637	800-566-0630	813-631-5517
ActionCOACH					
5781 S Ft Apache Rd	Las Vegas	NV	89148	888-483-2828	702-795-3188
Baker Communications Inc					
10101 SW Fwy #630	Houston	TX	77074	877-253-8506	713-627-7700
ClickSafetycom Inc					
2185 N California Blvd Ste 425	Walnut Creek	CA	94596	800-971-1080	
Creative Training Techniques International Inc					
14530 Martin Dr	Eden Prairie	MN	55344	800-383-9210	952-829-1954
Crestcom International Ltd					
6900 E Belleview Ave	Greenwood Village	CO	80111	800-333-7680	303-267-8200
Dale Carnegie & Assoc Inc					
290 Motor Pkwy	Hauppauge	NY	11788	800-231-5800	
Don Hutson Organization					
516 Tennessee St Ste 219	Memphis	TN	38103	800-647-9166	901-767-0000
Elite PO Box 9630	Rancho Santa Fe	CA	92067	800-204-3548	

				Toll-Free	Phone
Franklin Covey Co					
2200 West PkwyBlvd	Salt Lake City	UT	84119	800-827-1776	801-817-1776
NYSE: FC					
Fred Pryor Seminars					
9757 Metcalf Ave	Overland Park	KS	66212	800-780-8476	
Frontline Group of Texas LLC					
15021 Katy Fwy Ste 575	Houston	TX	77094	800-285-5512	281-453-6000
HealthStream Inc					
209 Tenth Ave S Ste 450	Nashville	TN	37203	800-933-9293	615-301-3100
NASDAQ: HSTM					
Insight Information					
214 King St W Ste 300	Toronto	ON	M5H3S6	888-777-1707	
ITC Learning Corp					
330 Himmarshee St Ste 108	Fort Lauderdale	FL	33312	800-638-3757	703-286-0756
Leadership Management International Inc					
4567 Lake Shore Dr	Waco	TX	76710	800-876-2389	254-776-2060
Levinson Institute Inc					
28 Main St Ste 100	Jaffrey	NH	03452	800-290-5735	603-532-4700
National Businesswomen's Leadership Assn					
PO Box 419107	Kansas City	MO	64141	800-258-7246	
National Seminars Training					
6900 Squibb Rd	Shawnee Mission	KS	66202	800-258-7246	913-432-7755
Pacific Institute					
12101 Tukwila Int'l Blvd Ste 330	Seattle	WA	98168	800-426-3660	206-628-4800
Priority Management Systems Inc					
1595 Cliveden Ave Unit 7	Delta	BC	V3M6M2	800-437-1032	604-214-7772
Productivity Inc					
375 Bridgeport Ave 3rd Fl	Shelton	CT	06484	800-966-5423	203-225-0451
Safety Services Co					
2626 S Roosevelt St	Tempe	AZ	85282	877-894-2566*	877-754-9578
*Cust Svc					
SkillSoft PLC 107 NE Blvd	Nashua	NH	03062	877-545-5763	603-324-3000
Telemedia Inc					
750 West Lake Cook Rd Rd					
Ste 250	Buffalo Grove	IL	60089	800-837-8872	847-808-4000
US Learning Inc					
516 Tennessee St Ste 219	Memphis	TN	38103	800-647-9166	901-767-0000
Voice Pro Inc 2055 Lee Rd	Cleveland	OH	44118	800-261-0104	216-932-8040
Wilson Learning Corp					
8000 W 78th St Ste 200	Edina	MN	55439	800-328-7937	952-944-2880

761 TRAINING PROGRAMS (MISC)

SEE ALSO Training Programs - Corporate ; Training & Certification Programs - Computer & Internet ; Children's Learning Centers

				Toll-Free	Phone
Audio-Digest Foundation					
1577 E Chevy Chase Dr	Glendale	CA	91206	800-423-2308	818-240-7500
Canter & Assoc LLC					
12975 Coral Tree Pl	Los Angeles	CA	90066	800-669-9011*	310-578-4700
*Cust Svc					
Executive Protection Institute					
16 Penn Plz Ste 1570	New York	NY	10001	800-947-5827	212-268-4555
Global University					
1211 S Glenstone Ave	Springfield	MO	65804	800-443-1083	417-862-9533
Mission Essential Personnel LLC					
4343 Easton Commons Ste 100	Columbus	OH	43219	888-542-3447	614-416-2345
Necco 178 Private Dr	South Point	OH	45680	866-996-3226	513-771-9600
Outward Bound					
910 Jackson St Ste 140	Golden	CO	80401	866-467-7651	
Smith & Wesson Academy					
299 Page Blvd	Springfield	MA	01104	800-331-0852	850-850-1250

762 TRANSFORMERS - POWER, DISTRIBUTION, SPECIALTY

				Toll-Free	Phone
AFP Transformers Inc					
206 Talmedge Rd	Edison	NJ	08817	800-843-1215	732-248-0305
Bodine Co PO Box 460	Collierville	TN	38027	800-223-5728	901-853-7211
Controlled Power Co					
1955 Stephenson Hwy	Troy	MI	48083	800-521-4792	248-528-3700
Cooper Power Systems Inc					
2300 Badger Dr	Waukesha	WI	53188	800-223-5227	262-896-2400
DC Group Inc					
1977 W River Rd N	Minneapolis	MN	55411	800-838-7927	
Delta Star Inc					
270 Industrial Rd	San Carlos	CA	94070	800-892-8673	
Dynapower Corp					
85 Meadowland Dr	South Burlington	VT	05403	800-332-1111	802-860-7200
Electric Research & Mfg Co-op Inc					
PO Box 1228	Dyersburg	TN	38025	800-238-5587	731-285-9121
Energy Transformation Systems Inc					
43353 Osgood Rd	Fremont	CA	94539	800-752-8208	510-656-2012
Ensign Corp 201 Ensign Rd	Bellevue	IA	52031	888-797-8658	630-628-9999
Howard Industries Inc					
3225 Pendorff Rd	Laurel	MS	39440	800-663-5598	601-425-3151
Johnson Electric Coil Co					
821 Watson St	Antigo	WI	54409	800-826-9741	715-627-4367
Legend Power Systems Inc					
1480 Frances St	Vancouver	BC	V5L1Y9	866-772-8797	604-420-1500
Mesta Electronics Inc					
11020 Parker Dr	North Huntingdon	PA	15642	800-535-6798	412-754-3000
MGM Transformer Co					
5701 Smithway St	Commerce	CA	90040	800-423-4366	323-726-0888
Micrometals Inc					
5615 E La Palma Ave	Anaheim	CA	92807	800-356-5977	714-970-9400
Mirus International Inc					
31 Sun Pac Blvd	Brampton	ON	L6S5P6	888-866-4787	905-494-1120
MTE Corp					
PO Box 9013	Menomonee Falls	WI	53051	800-455-4683	
Niagara Transformer Corp					
1747 Dale Rd	Buffalo	NY	14225	800-817-5652	716-896-6500
Nova Power Solutions					
23020 Eaglewood Ct Ste 100	Sterling	VA	20166	800-999-6682	

				Toll-Free	Phone

Olsun Electrics Corp
10901 Commercial St . . . . .Richmond IL   60071   **800-336-5786**

Powersmiths International Corp
10 Devon Rd . . . . Brampton ON   L6T5B5   **800-747-9627**   905-791-1493

PWR LLC 6402 Deere Rd . . . . .Syracuse NY   13206   **800-342-0878**   315-701-0210

Shape LLC 2105 Corporate Dr . . . . Addison IL   60101   **800-367-5811**   630-620-8394

SPX Transformer Solutions Inc
400 S Prairie Ave . . . . .Waukesha WI   53186   **800-835-2732**

T & R Electric Supply Company Inc
308 SW Third St . . . . .Colman SD   57017   **800-843-7994**   605-534-3555

T A. Pelsue Co
2500 S Tejon St . . . . .Englewood CO   80110   **800-525-8460**

Unique Lighting Systems Inc
1240 Simpson Way . . . . .Escondido CA   92029   **800-955-4831**

VanTran Industries Inc
7711 Imperial Dr . . . . Waco TX   76712   **800-433-3346**   254-772-9740

Virginia Transformer Corp
220 Glade View Dr . . . . Roanoke VA   24012   **800-882-3944**   540-345-9892

763   TRANSLATION SERVICES

SEE ALSO Language Schools

				Toll-Free	Phone

A William Roberts Jr & Assoc Inc
234 Seven Farms Dr Ste 210 . . . . .Charleston SC   29492   **800-743-3376**   843-722-8414

Argo Translation Inc
1884 Johns Dr . . . . Glenview IL   60025   **888-961-9291**   847-901-4075

Birnbaum Interpreting Services
8730 Georgia Ave Ste 210 . . . . Silver Spring MD   20910   **800-471-6441**   301-587-8885

Boston Language Institute Inc
648 Beacon St . . . . Boston MA   02215   **877-998-3500**   617-262-3500

Bridge-world Language Center Inc, The
110 Second St S Ste 213 . . . . Waite Park MN   56387   **800-835-6870**   320-259-9239

CanTalk (Canada) Inc
250-70 Arthur St . . . . Winnipeg MB   R3B1G7   **800-480-9686**

Certified Languages International LLC
4800 SW Macadam Ave Ste 400. . . . . Portland OR   97239   **800-362-3241**

Deaf-Talk Inc 14 E Main St . . . . Carnegie PA   15106   **877-304-0004**   412-563-3177

Dialog One Llc
2380 Wycliff St Ste 200 . . . . .Saint Paul MN   55114   **877-300-5326**   651-379-8600

Fluent Language Solutions Inc
8801 JM Keynes Dr Ste 400 . . . . .Charlotte NC   28262   **888-225-6056**   704-532-7446

Geo Group Corp, The
6 Odana Ct . . . . Madison WI   53719   **800-993-2262**   608-230-1000

Glyph Language Services Inc
157 S Howard St Ste 603 . . . . Spokane WA   99201   **866-274-3218**

Interpreters Unlimited Inc
10650 Treena St Ste 308. . . . . .San Diego CA   92131   **800-726-9891**

Kane Transport Inc
40925 403rd Ave . . . . Sauk Centre MN   56378   **800-892-8557**   320-352-2762

Language Line Solutions
1 Lower Ragsdale Dr Bldg 2 . . . . Monterey CA   93940   **800-752-6096**

Language Services Associates Inc
455 Business Ctr Dr - Ste 100 . . . . .Horsham PA   19044   **800-305-9673**

Linguistics Systems Inc
201 Broadway . . . . Cambridge MA   02139   **877-654-5006**   617-528-7410

Merritt Interpreting Services
3626 N Hall St Ste 504 . . . . .Dallas TX   75219   **866-761-2585**   214-969-5585

Schreiber Translations Inc
51 Monroe St Ste 101. . . . . .Rockville MD   20850   **800-822-3213**   301-424-7737

Spanish-American Translating
330 Eagle Ave . . . . .West Hempstead NY   11552   **800-870-5790**   516-481-3339

Verbatim Solutions LLC
5200 S Highland Dr Ste 201. . . . . Salt Lake City UT   84117   **800-573-5702**

Versacom
1501 McGill College Ave 6th Fl . . . . Montreal QC   H3A3M8   **866-320-1950**   514-397-1950

Vocalink Global
405 W First St Unit A . . . . Dayton OH   45402   **877-492-7754**

764   TRANSPLANT CENTERS - BLOOD STEM CELL

				Toll-Free	Phone

Arthur G James Cancer Hospital & Richard J Solove Research Institute
Bone Marrow Transplant Program
300 W Tenth Ave . . . . Columbus OH   43210   **800-293-5066**   614-293-5066

Blood Donor Ctr at Presbyterian/St Luke's Medical Ctr
1719 E 19th Ave . . . . Denver CO   80218   **800-231-2222**   303-839-6000

Children's Hospital of Orange County Blood & Donor Services
505 S Main St . . . . Orange CA   92868   **800-228-5234**   714-509-8339

Children's Hospital of Philadelphia Stem Cell Transplant Program
3401 Civic Ctr Blvd . . . . Philadelphia PA   19104   **800-879-2467**

City of Hope National Medical Ctr Hematology & Hematopoietic Cell Transplantation Div
1500 E Duarte Rd . . . . Duarte CA   91010   **800-826-4673**   626-256-4673

Dana-Farber Cancer Institute
450 Brookline Ave . . . . Boston MA   02115   **866-408-3324**   617-632-3591

Froedtert Hospital Bone Marrow Transplant Program
9200 W Wisconsin Ave . . . . Milwaukee WI   53226   **800-272-3666**   414-805-3666

H Lee Moffitt Cancer Ctr & Research Institute Blood & Marrow Transplantation Program
12902 Magnolia Ave . . . . Tampa FL   33612   **888-663-3488**

Helen DeVos Children's Hospital
100 Michigan NE . . . . Grand Rapids MI   49503   **866-989-7999**   616-391-9000

Indiana University Melvin & Bren Simon Cancer Ctr
535 Barnhill Dr . . . . Indianapolis IN   46202   **888-600-4822**   317-278-0070

James Graham Brown Cancer Ctr
529 S Jackson St . . . . Louisville KY   40202   **866-530-5516**   502-562-4369

Karmanos Cancer Institute Bone Marrow/Stem Cell Transplant Program
4100 John R St . . . . Detroit MI   48201   **800-527-6266**

Mount Sinai Hospital Bone Marrow Transplant Program
19 E 98th St . . . . .New York NY   10029   **866-682-9380**   212-241-6021

Nebraska Medicine
987400 Nebraska Medical Ctr . . . . Omaha NE   68198   **800-922-0000**   402-559-2000

Northwell Health
North Shore University Hospital
300 Community Dr
9 Tower Large Conference Rm . . . . .Manhasset NY   11030   **888-321-3627**   888-214-4065

				Toll-Free	Phone

Oregon Health & Science University (OHSU)
Bone Marrow Transplant Clinic
3181 SW Sam Jackson Pk Rd CB569. . . . . .Portland OR   97239   **800-452-1369**   503-494-8500

Penn State Health
500 University Dr . . . . Hershey PA   17033   **800-243-1455**   717-531-6955

Saint Jude Children's Research Hospital
262 Danny Thomas Pl . . . . Memphis TN   38105   **800-822-6344**   901-595-1040

Seattle Cancer Care Alliance
825 Eastlake Ave E PO Box 19023 . . . . Seattle WA   98109   **800-804-8824**   206-606-7222

Strong Memorial Hospital
Stem Cell Transplantation Ctr
601 Elmwood Ave . . . . Rochester NY   14642   **888-661-6162**   585-275-2100

Texas Transplant Institute
7700 Floyd Curl Dr . . . . San Antonio TX   78229   **800-298-7824**   210-575-3817

UMass Memorial Medical Care
Bone Marrow Transplant
55 Lake Ave N . . . . Worcester MA   01655   **855-862-7763**   508-334-1000

University of Maryland Greenebaum Cancer Ctr
22 S Greene St . . . . Baltimore MD   21201   **800-888-8823**   410-328-7904

University of Miami Hospital & Clinics (UMHC)
Sylvester Comprehensive Cancer Ctr
1475 NW 12th Ave . . . . Miami FL   33136   **800-545-2292**   305-243-1000

University of Pittsburgh Medical Ctr (UPMC)
Horizon 110 N Main St . . . . .Greenville PA   16125   **888-447-1122**   724-588-2100

University of Texas Southwestern Medical Ctr Dallas
Hematopoietic Cell Transplant Program
5323 Harry Hines Blvd . . . . Dallas TX   75390   **866-645-6455**   214-648-3111

University of Utah Hospital
Miner's Hospital
50 N Medical Dr Rm 1B295 . . . . Salt Lake City UT   84132   **800-824-2073***   866-864-6377
*General

VA Puget Sound Health Care System - Seattle Div
1660 S Columbian Way . . . . Seattle WA   98108   **800-329-8387**   206-762-1010

Winship Cancer Institute of Emory University
1365 Clifton Rd NE . . . . Atlanta GA   30322   **888-946-7447**   404-778-1900

765   TRANSPORTATION EQUIPMENT & SUPPLIES - WHOL

				Toll-Free	Phone

A & K Railroad Materials Inc
1505 S Redwood Rd . . . . .Salt Lake City UT   84104   **800-453-8812***   801-974-5484
*Sales

AAR Corp
1100 N Wood Dale Rd . . . . .Wood Dale IL   60191   **800-422-2213**   630-227-2000
NYSE: AIR

AAR Defense Systems & Logistics
1100 N Wood Dale Rd . . . . .Wood Dale IL   60191   **877-227-9200**   630-227-2000

Airparts Company Inc
2310 NW 55th Ct . . . . Fort Lauderdale FL   33309   **800-392-4999**   954-739-3575

Argo International Corp
71 Veronica Ave Unit 1 . . . . Somerset NJ   08873   **866-289-2746**   732-979-2996

Atlantic Track & Turnout Co
270 N Broad St . . . . .Bloomfield NJ   07003   **800-631-1274**   973-748-5885

Birmingham Rail & Locomotive Company Inc
PO Box 530157 . . . . Birmingham AL   35253   **800-241-2260**   205-424-7245

Burke Handling Systems
431 Hwy 49 S . . . . Jackson MS   39218   **800-222-5400**   601-939-6600

DAC International Inc
6702 McNiel Dr . . . . Austin TX   78729   **800-527-2531**   512-331-5323

Defender Industries Inc
42 Great Neck Rd . . . . .Waterford CT   06385   **800-628-8225**   860-701-3400

Donovan Marine Inc
6316 Humphreys St . . . . Harahan LA   70123   **800-347-4464**   504-488-5731

Dreyfus-Cortney & Lowery Bros Rigging
4400 N Galvez St .New Orleans LA   70117   **800-228-7660**   504-944-3366

Edmo Distributors Inc
12830 E Mirabeau Pkwy . . . . .Spokane Valley WA   99216   **800-235-3300**   509-535-8280

Fisheries Supply Co
1900 N Northlake Way . . . . Seattle WA   98103   **800-426-6930**   206-632-4462

Formsprag Clutch Inc
23601 Hoover Rd . . . . Warren MI   48089   **800-348-0881**

Freundlich Supply Co Inc
2200 Arthur Kill Rd .Staten Island NY   10309   **800-221-0260**   718-356-1500

Heli-Mart Inc
3184 Airway Ave Unit E . . . . Costa Mesa CA   92626   **800-826-6899**   714-755-2999

Heubel Shaw
6311 NE Equitable Rd . . . . Kansas City MO   64120   **800-283-4177**

Hy-Tek Material Handling Inc
2222 Rickenbacker Pkwy W . . . . .Columbus OH   43217   **800-837-1217**

Industry-Railway Suppliers Inc
577 W Lamont Rd . . . . .Elmhurst IL   60126   **800-728-0029**   630-766-5708

Jerry's Marine Service
100 SW 16th St . . . . Fort Lauderdale FL   33315   **800-432-2231**

JJ MacKay Canada Ltd
1342 Abercrombie Rd PO Box 338 . . . . New Glasgow NS   B2H5C6   **888-462-2529**   902-752-5124

Kellogg Marine Supply Inc
5 Enterprise Dr . . . . Old Lyme CT   06371   **800-243-9303**   860-434-6002

Lagrange Products Inc
607 S Wayne St . . . . Fremont IN   46737   **800-369-6978**   260-495-3025

Marine Depot
14271 Corporate Dr . . . . Garden Grove CA   92843   **800-566-3474**

Markey Machinery Company Inc
7266 Eigth Ave S . . . . Seattle WA   98108   **800-637-3430**   206-622-4697

Muncie Power Products Inc
201 E Jackson St . . . . Muncie IN   47305   **800-367-7867**   765-284-7721

Norlift of Oregon Inc
7373 SE Milwaukie Expy . . . . Portland OR   97222   **800-452-0050**   503-659-5438

O'halloran International Inc
3311 Adventureland Dr . . . . .Altoona IA   50009   **800-800-6503**   515-967-3300

Ottosen Propeller & Accessories Inc
105 S 28th St . . . . Phoenix AZ   85034   **800-528-7551**   602-275-8514

PartsBase Inc
905 Clint Moore Rd . . . . Boca Raton FL   33487   **888-322-6896***   561-953-0700
*Cust Svc

Paxton Co 1111 Ingleside Rd . . . . Norfolk VA   23502   **800-234-7290**   757-853-6781

Railhead Corp
12549 S Laramie Ave . . . . .Alsip IL   60803   **800-235-1782**   708-844-5500

Company	Toll-Free	Phone
Rails Co 101 Newark Way ....Maplewood NJ 07040	800-217-2457	973-763-4320
RS Braswell Company Inc 485 S Cannon Blvd ....Kannapolis NC 28083	888-628-3550	704-933-2269
Shea Concrete Products Inc 87 Haverhill Rd ....Amesbury MA 01913	800-696-7432	978-388-1509
Standard Equipment Company Inc 75 Beauregard St ....Mobile AL 36602	800-239-3442	251-432-1705
Superior Tank Company Inc 9500 Lucas Ranch Rd ....Rancho Cucamonga CA 91730	800-221-8265	
Tanks-A-Lot Ltd 1810 Yellowhead Trail NE ....Edmonton AB T6S1B4	800-661-5667	780-472-8265
Tornado Alley Turbo 300 Airport Rd ....Ada OK 74820	877-359-8284	580-332-3510
Valley Power Systems Inc 425 S Hacienda Blvd ....City of Industry CA 91745	800-924-4265	626-333-1243
Van Bortel Aircraft Inc 4912 S Collins ....Arlington TX 76018	800-759-4295	817-468-7788
Washington Chain & Supply Inc 2901 Utah Ave S PO Box 3645 ....Seattle WA 98124	800-851-3429	206-623-8500
West Marine Inc 500 Westridge Dr ....Watsonville CA 95076 *NASDAQ: WMAR*	800-262-8464	831-728-2700
Wilco Inc 3502 W Harry ....Wichita KS 67213	800-767-7593	
Yingling Aircraft Inc 2010 Airport Rd ....Wichita KS 67209	800-835-0083	316-943-3246

766   TRAVEL AGENCIES

SEE ALSO Travel Agency Networks ; Tour Operators

Company	Toll-Free	Phone
ABC Global Services 6001 Broken Sound Pkwy NW Ste 340 ....Boca Raton FL 33487	800-722-5179	
Adelman Travel Group 6980 N Port Washington Rd ....Milwaukee WI 53217 *Cust Svc	800-248-5562*	414-352-7600
ADTRAV Travel Management 4555 S Lake Pkwy ....Birmingham AL 35244	800-476-2952	205-444-4800
AESU Travel Inc 3922 Hickory Ave ....Baltimore MD 21211	800-638-7640	410-366-5494
Alamo Travel Group 8930 Wurzbach Rd ....San Antonio TX 78240	800-692-5266	210-593-3997
Alaska Tour & Travel 3900 Arctic Blvd Ste 304 PO Box 221011 ....Anchorage AK 99503	800-208-0200	907-245-0200
Alaska Travel Adventures Inc 9085 Glacier Hwy Ste 301 ....Juneau AK 99801	800-323-5757	907-789-0052
All Aboard Cruises Inc 12383 SW 124 Ter ....Miami FL 33186	800-883-8657	305-385-8657
All Cruise Travel 1723 Hamilton Ave ....San Jose CA 95125	800-227-8473	408-295-1200
All-Inclusive Vacations Inc 1595 Iris St ....Denver CO 80215	866-980-6483	303-980-6483
Apple Vacations Inc 101 NW Pt Blvd ....Elk Grove Village IL 60007	800-517-2000	
Avanti Destinations Inc 111 SW Columbia St Ste 1200 ....Portland OR 97201	800-422-5053	503-295-1100
Balboa Travel Management Inc 5414 Oberlin Dr Ste 300 ....San Diego CA 92121	800-359-8773	858-678-3300
Bon Voyage Travel 1640 E River Rd Ste 115 ....Tucson AZ 85718	800-439-7963	520-797-1110
Brownell World Travel 216 Summit Blvd Ste 220 ....Birmingham AL 35243	800-999-3960	205-802-6222
Burkhalter Travel Agency 6501 Mineral Pt Rd ....Madison WI 53705	800-556-9286	608-833-5200
Carefree Vacations Inc 11885 Carmel Mountain Rd Ste 906 ....San Diego CA 92128	800-266-3476	800-795-0720
Casto Travel Inc 2560 N First St Ste 150 ....San Jose CA 95131	800-832-3445	
City Escape Holidays 13470 Washington Blvd Ste 101 ....Marina del Rey CA 90292	800-222-0022	
Classic Custom Vacations 5893 Rue Ferrari ....San Jose CA 95138	800-635-1333	
Clipper Navigation Inc 2701 Alaskan Way Pier 69 ....Seattle WA 98121	800-888-2535	206-443-2560
Conlin Travel Inc 3270 Washtenaw Ave ....Ann Arbor MI 48104	800-426-6546	734-677-0900
Cook Travel 1025 Acuff Rd ....Bloomington IN 47404	800-542-1687	812-336-6811
Covington Travel 4800 Cox Rd Ste 200 ....Glen Allen VA 23060	800-922-9218	804-747-7077
Crown Travel & Cruises 240 Newton Rd Ste 106 ....Raleigh NC 27615	800-869-7447	919-870-1986
Cruise Brokers 2803 W Busch Blvd Ste 100 ....Tampa FL 33618	800-409-1919	813-288-9597
Cruise Concepts 1329 Eniswood Pkwy ....Palm Harbor FL 34683	800-752-7963	727-784-7245
Cruise Connection LLC 7932 N Oak Ste 210 ....Kansas City MO 64118	800-572-0004	816-420-8688
Cruise People Inc 10191 W Sample Rd Ste 215 ....Coral Springs FL 33065	800-642-2469	954-340-2016
Cruise Shop, The 700 Pasquinelli Dr Ste C ....Westmont IL 60559	800-622-6456	858-433-1506
Cruise Specialists Inc 221 First Ave W Ste 210 ....Seattle WA 98119	888-993-1318	
Cruise Vacation Ctr 2042 Central Park Ave ....Yonkers NY 10710	800-803-7245	
Cruise Web Inc 3901 Calverton Blvd Ste 350 ....Calverton MD 20705	800-377-9383	240-487-0155
CruiseOne Inc 1201 W Cypress Creek Rd Ste 100 ....Fort Lauderdale FL 33309	800-278-4731	
Cruises Inc 1201 W Cypress Creek Rd Ste 100 ....Fort Lauderdale FL 33309 *Cust Svc	888-282-1249*	
Direct Travel 95 New Jersey 17 ....Paramus NJ 07652	800-366-2496	201-847-9000
Elegant Voyages 1802 Keesling Ct ....San Jose CA 95125	800-555-3534	408-239-0300
Friendly Cruises 3081 S Sycamore Village Dr ....Superstition Mountain AZ 85118	800-842-1786	480-358-1496
Galapagos Holidays 7800 Red Rd Ste 112 ....South Miami FL 33143	800-327-9854	305-665-0841
Gant Travel Management 400 W Seventh St Ste 233 ....Bloomington IN 47404 *Cust Svc	800-742-4198*	630-227-3800
Gil Tours Travel Inc 1511 Walnut St 2nd Fl ....Philadelphia PA 19102	800-223-3855	215-568-6655
Giselle's Travel Inc 1300 Ethan Way Ste 100 ....Sacramento CA 95825	800-782-5545	916-922-5500
Global Travel 900 W Jefferson St ....Boise ID 83702	800-584-8888	208-387-1000
GOGO WorldWide Vacations 5 Paragon Dr ....Montvale NJ 07645	800-254-3477	
Golden Sports Tours 301 W Parker Rd Ste 206 ....Plano TX 75023	800-966-8258	
Gwin's Travel Planners Inc 212 N Kirkwood Rd ....Saint Louis MO 63122	888-254-7775	314-822-1958
Islands in the Sun Cruises & Tours Inc 348 Thompson Creek Mall Ste 107 ....Stevensville MD 21666	800-278-7786	410-827-3812
Japan Travel Bureau USA Inc (JTB USA Inc) 2 W 45th St Ste 305 ....New York NY 10036	800-223-6104	212-698-4900
Lawyers' Travel Service 71 Fifth Ave ....New York NY 10003 *General	800-431-1112*	
Liberty Travel Inc 69 Spring St ....Ramsey NJ 07446	888-271-1584	
Lorraine Travel Bureau Inc 377 Alhambra Cir ....Coral Gables FL 33134	800-666-8911	305-446-4433
MC & A Inc 615 Piikoi St Ste 1000 ....Honolulu HI 96814 *General	877-589-5589*	808-589-5500
Merit Travel Group Inc 111 Peter St ....Toronto ON M5V2H1	866-341-1777	416-364-3775
Miller Travel Services Inc 4380 W 12th St ....Erie PA 16505	800-989-8747	814-833-8888
Montrose Travel 2349 Honolulu Ave ....Montrose CA 91020	800-666-8767	818-553-3200
More Hawaii for Less 11 Ash Tree Ln ....Irvine CA 92612	800-967-6687	949-724-5050
National Discount Cruise Co 1401 N Cedar Crest Blvd Ste 110 ....Allentown PA 18104	800-788-8108	
Northstar Cruises PO Box 248 ....Essex Fells NJ 07021	800-249-9360	
Omega World Travel Inc 3102 Omega Office Pk Dr ....Fairfax VA 22031	800-756-6342	703-359-0200
Orvis International Travel 178 Conservation Way ....Sunderland VT 05250	800-547-4322	888-235-9763
Paradise Island Vacations 1000 S Pine Island Rd Ste 800 ....Plantation FL 33324 *Resv	888-877-7525*	954-809-2100
Pleasant Holidays LLC 2404 Townsgate Rd ....Westlake Village CA 91361	800-742-9244	818-991-3390
Premier Golf 4355 River Green Pkwy ....Duluth GA 30096	866-260-4409	770-291-4202
Prestige Travel & Cruises Inc 6175 Spring Mountain Rd ....Las Vegas NV 89146	800-758-5693	702-251-5552
Professional Travel Inc 25000 Great Northern Corporate Ctr Ste 170 ....Cleveland OH 44070	800-247-0060	440-734-8800
Protravel International Inc 515 Madison Ave 10th Fl ....New York NY 10022	800-227-1059	212-755-4550
Regal Travel 615 Piikoi St Ste 104 ....Honolulu HI 96814	800-799-0865	808-566-7620
Seaside Golf Vacations 218 Main St ....North Myrtle Beach SC 29582	877-732-6999	
SGH Golf Inc 6805 Mt Vernon Ave ....Cincinnati OH 45227	800-284-8884	513-984-0410
Sita World Travel Inc 16250 Ventura Blvd ....Encino CA 91436	800-421-5643	818-990-9530
Sports Empire PO Box 6169 ....Lakewood CA 90714	800-255-5258	562-920-2350
Sterling Cruises & Travel 8700 W Flagler St ....Miami FL 33174	800-435-7967	305-592-2522
Studentcitycom Inc 8 Essex Ctr Dr ....Peabody MA 01960	888-777-4642	
Tenenbaum's Vacation Stores Inc 300 Market St ....Kingston PA 18704	800-545-7099	570-288-8747
Tower Travel Management 53 Ogden Ave ....Clarendon Hills IL 60514	800-542-9700	
Tramex Travel Inc 4505 Spicewood Springs Rd Ste 200 ....Austin TX 78759	800-527-3039	
Transat AT Inc 300 Leo-Pariseau St Ste 600 ....Montreal QC H2X4C2 *TSE: TRZ*	800-387-0825	514-987-1616
Travel & Transport Inc 2120 S 72nd St ....Omaha NE 68124	800-228-2545	402-399-4500
Travel Destinations Management Group Inc 110 Painters Mill Rd ....Owings Mills MD 21117	800-635-7307	410-363-3111
Travel Impressions Ltd 465 Smith St ....Farmingdale NY 11735	800-284-0044	631-845-8000
Travelennium Inc 556 Colonial Rd ....Memphis TN 38117	800-844-4924	901-767-0761
Traveline Travel Agencies Inc 4074 Erie St ....Willoughby OH 44094	888-700-8747	440-602-8020
TravelStore Inc 11601 Wilshire Blvd ....Los Angeles CA 90025	800-850-3224	310-575-5540
Valerie Wilson Travel Inc 475 Park Ave S ....New York NY 10016	800-776-1116	212-532-3400
Virtuoso 505 Main St Ste 5 ....Fort Worth TX 76102	800-401-4274	817-870-0300
World Travel Holdings (WTH) 100 Fordham Rd Bldg C ....Wilmington MA 01887	877-958-7447	617-424-7990

767 — TRAVEL AGENCY NETWORKS

SEE ALSO Travel Agencies

A travel agency network is a consortium of travel agencies in which a host agency provides technology, marketing, distribution, customer support, and other services to the network member agencies in exchange for a percentage of the member agencies' profits.

				Toll-Free	Phone
Abbey Travel Ltd					
522 N Washington St	Naperville	IL	60563	800-338-0900	630-420-0400
Affordabletourscom					
11150 Cash Rd	Stafford	TX	77477	800-935-2620	
Alice Travel Luxury Cruises & Tour					
277 Fairfield Rd Ste 218	Fairfield	NJ	07004	800-229-2542	973-439-1700
All Direct Travel Services Inc					
19772 MacArthur Blvd Ste 150	Irvine	CA	92612	800-862-1516	949-474-8100
American Express Company Inc					
World Financial Ctr 200 Vesey St	New York	NY	10285	800-528-4800	212-640-2000
NYSE: AXP					
Berkeleys Northside Travel Inc					
1824 Euclid Ave	Berkeley	CA	94709	800-575-3411	510-843-1000
Carlson Wagonlit Travel Inc					
701 Carlson Pkwy	Minnetonka	MN	55305	800-213-7295	
Cascadia Motivation					
4646 Riverside Dr Ste 14	Red Deer	AB	T4N6Y5	800-661-8360	403-340-8687
Chartered Business Valuators					
277 Wellington St W Ste 808	Toronto	ON	M5V3H2	866-770-7315	416-977-1117
Classic Travel Inc					
4767 Okemos Rd	Okemos	MI	48864	800-643-3449	517-349-6200
CP Franchising LLC					
3300 University Dr	Coral Springs	FL	33065	800-683-0206	954-344-8060
Cruise Brothers, The					
100 Boyd Ave	East Providence	RI	02914	800-827-7779	401-941-3999
Cruisecheapcom					
220 Congress Park Dr Ste 330	Delray Beach	FL	33445	800-543-1915	
CruiseOne Inc					
1201 W Cypress Creek Rd					
Ste 100	Fort Lauderdale	FL	33309	800-278-4731	
D&F Travel Inc					
331 Alberta Dr Ste 103	Amherst	NY	14226	800-335-1982	716-835-9227
Ensemble Travel					
256 W 38th St 11th Fl	New York	NY	10018	800-576-2378	212-545-7460
Expedition Tripscom					
5932 California Ave SW	Seattle	WA	98136	877-412-8527	206-547-0700
Forest Travel					
2440 NE Miami Gardens Dr Ste 107	Miami	FL	33180	800-432-2132	305-932-5560
Frosch International Travel Inc					
1 Greenway Plz Ste 800	Houston	TX	77046	800-866-1623	
Gateway Travel Service Inc					
28470 W 13 Mile Rd Ste 200	Farmington Hills	MI	48334	800-423-4898	248-432-8600
Georgia Hardy Tours					
20 Eglinton Ave E	Toronto	ON	M4R1K8	800-813-4509	416-483-7533
Global Travel International					
1060 Maitland Center Commons Ste 305	Maitland	FL	32751	800-715-4440	407-660-7800
Goway Travel Ltd					
3284 Yonge St Ste 300	Toronto	ON	M4N3M7	800-665-4432	416-322-1034
GTI Corporate Travel					
111 Township Line Rd	Jenkintown	PA	19046	800-223-3863	215-379-6800
Happy Time Tours & Travel					
1475 Walsh St W	Thunder Bay	ON	P7E4X6	800-473-5955	807-473-5955
Hume Travel Corp					
1130 W Pender St Ste 510	Vancouver	BC	V6E4A1	800-663-9787	604-682-7581
Jones Travel					
511 S Lincoln St	Elkhorn	WI	53121	800-236-3160	262-723-4309
Kahala Travel					
3838 Camino Del Rio N Ste 300	San Diego	CA	92108	800-852-8338	619-282-8300
Luxe Travel Management Inc					
16450 Bake Pkwy	Irvine	CA	92618	855-665-5900	949-336-1000
Luxury Link LLC					
5200 W Century Blvd Ste 410	Los Angeles	CA	90045	888-297-3299	310-215-8060
Music Celebrations International					
1440 S Priest Dr Ste 102	Tempe	AZ	85281	800-395-2036	
New Wave Travel 1075 Bay St	Toronto	ON	M5S2B1	800-463-1512	416-928-3113
Nexion					
6225 N State Hwy 161 Ste 450	Irving	TX	75038	800-949-6410	408-280-6410
Ohio Travel Association					
1801 Watermark Dr Ste 375	Columbus	OH	43215	800-896-4682	614-572-1931
Pan American Travel Services					
320 East 900 South	Salt Lake City	UT	84111	800-364-4359	801-364-4300
Panda Travel					
1017 Kapahulu Ave	Honolulu	HI	96816	800-303-6702	808-738-3898
Paratransit Services					
4810 Auto Ctr Way	Bremerton	WA	98312	800-933-3468	
Raptim Humanitarian Travel					
6420 Inducon Dr W Ste A	Sanborn	NY	14132	800-272-7846	716-754-9232
Red Label Vacations Inc					
5450 Explorer Dr Ste 100	Mississauga	ON	L4W5N1	866-573-3824	905-283-6020
Signal Travel & Tours Inc					
219 E Main St	Niles	MI	49120	800-811-1522	269-684-2880
Strong Travel Services Inc					
8235 Douglas Ave Ste 1040	Dallas	TX	75225	800-747-5670	214-361-0027
Tangerine Travel Ltd					
16017 Juanita Woodinville Way NE					
Ste 201	Bothell	WA	98011	800-678-8202	425-822-2333
There & Back Again Travel					
35 E Broad St	Savannah	GA	31401	800-782-8222	912-920-8222
Thor Travel Services Inc					
12202 Airport Way Ste 150	Broomfield	CO	80021	800-825-1071	303-439-4100
Tour Edge Golf Manufacturing Inc					
1301 Pierson Dr	Batavia	IL	60510	800-515-3343	630-584-4777
Tourism Richmond Inc					
South Twr 5811 Cooney Rd Ste 205	Richmond	BC	V6X3M1	877-247-0777	604-821-5474
Trading Places International					
25510 Commercentre Dr Ste 100	Lake Forest	CA	92630	800-365-7617	
Travel Berkley Springs					
127 Fairfax St	Berkeley Springs	WV	25411	800-447-8797	304-258-9147

				Toll-Free	Phone
Travel One Inc					
8009 34th Ave S 15th Fl	Minneapolis	MN	55425	800-247-1311	952-854-2551
Travel Society Inc					
650 S Cherry St Ste 200	Denver	CO	80246	800-926-6031	303-321-0900
Travel Turf Inc					
7540 Windsor Dr Ste 202	Allentown	PA	18195	800-222-4432	610-391-9094
Travel-On Ltd					
9000 Virginia Manor Rd Ste 201	Beltsville	MD	20705	800-333-6778	240-387-4000
Travelex International Inc					
2061 N Barrington Rd	Hoffman Estates	IL	60169	800-882-0499	847-882-0400
TRAVELVIDEOSTOREcom Inc					
3420 Boran Dr	Tampa	FL	33610	800-288-5123	813-630-9778
UNIGLOBE Travel USA LLC					
18662 MacArthur Blvd Ste 100	Irvine	CA	92612	877-438-4338	949-623-9000
Vacationcom Inc					
1650 King St Ste 450	Alexandria	VA	22314	800-843-0733	703-740-4100
Vacations To Go Inc					
5851 San Felipe St Ste 500	Houston	TX	77057	800-338-4962	713-974-2121
Virtuoso					
505 Main St Ste 5	Fort Worth	TX	76102	800-401-4274	817-870-0300
Wall Street Inn, The					
9 S William St	New York	NY	10004	877-747-1500	212-747-1500
West University Travel					
3622 University Blvd	Houston	TX	77005	800-256-0640	713-665-4767
Wilcox Travel Sandals					
1550 Hendersonville Rd Ste 214	Asheville	NC	28803	800-294-5269	828-254-0746
World Travel Services LLC					
7645 E 63rd St Ste 101	Tulsa	OK	74133	800-324-4987	918-743-8856
WorldClass Travel Network					
7831 Southtown Ctr Ste A	Bloomington	MN	55431	800-234-3576	952-835-8636
WorldTEK Event & Travel Management					
100 Beard Sawmill Rd Ste 601	Shelton	CT	06484	800-233-5989	203-772-0470
Worldview Travel					
101 W Fourth St Ste 400	Santa Ana	CA	92701	800-627-8726	714-540-7400

TRAVEL INFORMATION - CITY

SEE Convention & Visitors Bureaus

768 — TRAVEL SERVICES - ONLINE

SEE ALSO Hotel Reservations Services

				Toll-Free	Phone
BedandBreakfastcom					
700 Brazos St Ste B-700	Austin	TX	78701	800-462-2632*	512-322-2700
*Sales					
Cruisescom					
100 Fordham Rd Bldg C	Wilmington	MA	01887	800-288-6006	
Hotwire Inc					
PO Box 26285	San Francisco	CA	94126	866-468-9473*	866-381-3981
*Cust Svc					
LastMinuteTravelcom Inc					
220 E Central Pkwy Ste 4000	Altamonte Springs	FL	32701	800-442-0568	407-667-8700
Pricelinecom LLC					
800 Connecticut Ave	Norwalk	CT	06854	800-774-2354	
National Recreation Reservation Service					
PO Box 140	Ballston Spa	NY	12020	877-444-6777	518-885-3639
ReserveAmerica Holdings Inc					
2480 Meadowvale Blvd Ste 120	Mississauga	ON	L5N8M6	877-444-6777	
Vacationcom Inc					
1650 King St Ste 450	Alexandria	VA	22314	800-843-0733	703-740-4100

769 — TRAVEL & TOURISM INFORMATION - CANADIAN

				Toll-Free	Phone
Lion World Travel					
33 Kern Rd	Toronto	ON	M3B1S9	800-387-2706	
Nova Scotia Dept of Tourism & Culture					
8 Water Str PO Box 667	Windsor	NS	B0N2T0	800-565-0000	902-798-6700
NWT Tourism PO Box 610	Yellowknife	NT	X1A2N5	800-661-0788	867-873-7200
Prince Edward Island Tourism					
PO Box 2000	Charlottetown	PE	C1A7N8	800-463-4734	902-368-4000
Tourism New Brunswick					
PO Box 6000	Fredericton	NB	E3B5H1	800-561-0123	
Tourism Saskatchewan					
1621 Albert St	Regina	SK	S4P2S5	877-237-2273	306-787-9600
Tourism Winnipeg					
1 Lombard Pl Ste 810	Winnipeg	MB	R3B0X3	855-734-2489	204-943-1970
Travel Manitoba					
155 Carlton St 7th Fl	Winnipeg	MB	R3C3H8	800-665-0040	204-927-7800
Yukon					
2nd Ave & Lambert St PO Box 2703	Whitehorse	YT	Y1A2C6	800-661-0494	

770 — TRAVEL & TOURISM INFORMATION - FOREIGN TRAVEL

SEE ALSO Embassies & Consulates - Foreign, in the US

				Toll-Free	Phone
A P F Travel Inc					
1721 Garvey Ave 2nd Fl	Alhambra	CA	91803	800-888-9168	
Air Land & Sea Travel Wedding Crdn					
126 N Orlando Ave	Cocoa Beach	FL	32931	800-799-1094	321-783-4900
All World Travel Inc					
314 Gilmer St	Sulphur Springs	TX	75482	866-298-6067	903-885-0896
Anguilla Tourist Marketing Office					
246 Central Ave	White Plains	NY	10606	800-553-4939	914-287-2400
Antigua & Barbuda Dept of Tourism & Trade					
25 SE Second Ave Ste 300	Miami	FL	33131	888-268-4227	305-381-6762
Aruba Tourism Authority					
1750 Powder Springs St Ste 190	Marietta	GA	30064	800-862-7822	404-892-7822
Atlas Travel & Technology Group Inc					
200 Donald Lynch Blvd Ste 323	Milford	MA	01752	800-362-8626	508-478-8626
Bahamas Tourism Office					
1200 S Pine Island Rd Ste 450	Plantation	FL	33324	800-327-7678	954-236-9292

				Toll-Free	Phone
Bermuda Dept of Tourism					
675 Third Ave 20th Fl	New York	NY	10017	**800-223-6106**	212-818-9800
Bike Friday Travel Systems					
3364 W 11th Ave	Eugene	OR	97402	**800-777-0258**	541-687-0487
Blue Ribbon Travel-american					
3601 W 76th St Ste 190	Minneapolis	MN	55435	**800-626-5309**	952-835-2724
Caa Niagara 155 Main St E	Grimsby	ON	L3M1P2	**800-263-7272**	
Canyon Creek Travel Inc					
333 W Campbell Rd Ste 440	Richardson	TX	75080	**800-952-1998**	972-238-1998
Cayman Islands Dept of Tourism					
350 Fifth Ave	New York	NY	10118	**800-235-5888**	212-889-9009
Cayman Islands Dept of Tourism					
8300 NW 53rd St Ste 103	Miami	FL	33166	**800-553-4939**	305-599-9033
China Travel Service Chicago Inc					
2145b S China Pl	Chicago	IL	60616	**800-793-8856**	312-328-0688
Fiji Visitors Bureau					
5777 W Century Blvd Ste 220	Los Angeles	CA	90045	**800-932-3454**	310-568-1616
Go Travel Inc					
2811 W SR 434	Longwood	FL	32779	**800-848-3005**	
Golden Anchor Travel					
1909 Southwood St	Sarasota	FL	34231	**800-299-1125**	941-922-4070
Jamaica Tourist Board					
5201 Blue Lagoon Dr Ste 670	Miami	FL	33126	**800-526-2422**	305-665-0557
Jordan Tourism Board (JTB)					
1307 Dolley Madison Blvd Ste 2A	McLean	VA	22101	**877-733-5673**	703-243-7404
Kenya Tourism Board					
6033 W Century Blvd Ste 900	Los Angeles	CA	90045	**800-223-6486**	310-649-7718
Maritime Travel Inc					
202-2000 Barrington St Cogswell Tower					
	Halifax	NS	B3J3K1	**800-593-3334**	902-420-1554
Mexico Tourism Board (CSTM)					
225 N Michigan Ave Ste 2060	Chicago	IL	60601	**800-446-3942**	
Ministry of Tourism of Dominican Republic					
848 Brickell Ave	Miami	FL	33131	**888-358-9594**	305-358-2899
Monaco Government Tourist Office					
565 Fifth Ave 23rd Fl	New York	NY	10017	**800-753-9696**	212-286-3330
Morley Companies Inc					
1 Morley Plz	Saginaw	MI	48603	**800-336-5554**	989-791-2550
Nova Tours & Travel Inc					
4255 Virgo Course	Liverpool	NY	13090	**800-543-6682**	
Plaza Travel					
16530 Ventura Blvd Ste 106	Encino	CA	91436	**800-347-4447**	818-990-4053
Puerto Rico					
Paseo La Princesa	Old San Juan	PR	00902	**800-866-7827**	787-721-2400
Rail Europe Inc					
44 S Broadway 11th Fl	White Plains	NY	10601	**800-361-7245**	914-682-2999
Russian National Tourist Office					
224 W 30th St Ste 701	New York	NY	10001	**877-221-7120**	646-473-2233
Skyland Travel Inc					
100-445 Sixth Ave W	Vancouver	BC	V5Y1L3	**888-685-6888**	604-685-6885
Switzerland Tourism					
608 Fifth Ave Ste 202	New York	NY	10020	**800-794-7795**	212-757-5944
Tourism Saskatoon					
202 Fourth Ave N	Saskatoon	SK	S7K0K1	**800-567-2444**	306-242-1206
Trois-Rivieres Tourism					
1457 rue Notre-Dame Ctr	Trois-Rivieres	QC	G9A4X4	**800-313-1123**	819-375-1122
Turks & Caicos Islands Tourism Office					
225 W 35th St Ste 1200	New York	NY	10001	**800-241-0824**	646-375-8830
VEGAScom LLC					
2370 Corporate Cir 3rd Fl	Henderson	NV	89074	**866-983-4279**	
Voyages Michel Barrette					
100 Rue Saint-joseph	Alma	QC	G8B7A6	**800-263-3078**	418-668-3078
Williamsburg Travel Management Companies					
570 W Crossville Rd Ste 102	Roswell	GA	30075	**800-952-9922**	770-650-5515

771 TREE SERVICES

SEE ALSO Landscape Design & Related Services

				Toll-Free	Phone
Arborwell Inc					
2337 American Ave	Hayward	CA	94545	**888-969-8733**	
Asplundh Tree Expert Co					
708 Blair Mill Rd	Willow Grove	PA	19090	**800-248-8733**	
Care of Trees Inc					
1500 N Mantua St	Kent	OH	44240	**800-445-8733**	
Davey Tree Expert Co					
1500 N Mantua St	Kent	OH	44240	**800-445-8733**	330-673-9511
FA Bartlett Tree Expert Co					
1290 E Main St	Stamford	CT	06902	**877-227-8538**	203-323-1131
Lewis Tree Service Inc					
300 Lucius Gordon Dr	West Henrietta	NY	14586	**800-333-1593**	585-436-3208
Nature's Trees Inc					
550 Bedford Rd	Bedford Hills	NY	10507	**800-341-8733**	914-241-4999
Nelson Tree Service llc					
3300 Ofc Park Dr	Dayton	OH	45439	**800-522-4311**	937-294-1313

772 TROPHIES, PLAQUES, AWARDS

				Toll-Free	Phone
Architectural Bronze Aluminum Corp					
655 Deerfield Rd Ste 100	Deerfield	IL	60015	**800-339-6581**	
Classic Medallics Inc					
520 S Fulton Ave	Mount Vernon	NY	10550	**800-221-1348**	914-530-6259
F & H Ribbon Co Inc					
3010 S Pipeline Rd	Euless	TX	76040	**800-877-5775**	
Jostens Inc					
3601 Minnesota Ave Ste 400	Minneapolis	MN	55435	**800-235-4774**	952-830-3300
Regalia Manufacturing Co					
2018 Fourth Ave	Rock Island	IL	61201	**800-798-7471**	309-788-7471
RS Owens & Co					
5535 N Lynch Ave	Chicago	IL	60630	**800-282-6200**	773-282-6000
Trophyland USA Inc					
7001 W 20th Ave	Hialeah	FL	33014	**800-327-5820**	305-823-4830
US Bronze Sign Co					
811 Second Ave	New Hyde Park	NY	11040	**800-872-5155**	516-352-5155

				Toll-Free	Phone
Wilson Trophy Co					
1724 Frienza Ave	Sacramento	CA	95815	**800-635-5005**	916-927-9733

TRUCK BODIES

SEE Motor Vehicles - Commercial & Special Purpose

773 TRUCK RENTAL & LEASING

				Toll-Free	Phone
Barco Rent a Truck					
717 South 5600 West	Salt Lake City	UT	84104	**800-453-4761**	801-532-7777
Calmont Leasing Ltd					
14610 Yellowhead Trail NW	Edmonton	AB	T5L3C5	**855-474-2568**	
Carco National Lease Inc					
2905 N 32nd St	Fort Smith	AR	72904	**800-643-2596**	479-441-3200
DeCarolis Truck Rental Inc					
333 Colfax St	Rochester	NY	14606	**800-666-1169**	585-254-1169
Idealease Inc					
430 N Rand Rd	North Barrington	IL	60010	**800-435-3273**	847-304-6000
Lily Transportation Corp					
145 Rosemary St	Needham	MA	02494	**800-248-5459**	
Mendon Truck Leasing & Rental					
8215 Foster Ave	Brooklyn	NY	11236	**877-636-3661**	718-209-9886
MHC Kenworth					
1524 N Corrington Ave	Kansas City	MO	64120	**888-259-4826**	816-483-7035
National Truck Leasing System					
2651 Warrenville Rd Ste 560	Downers Grove	IL	60515	**800-729-6857**	
PACCAR Leasing Corp					
777 106th Ave NE	Bellevue	WA	98004	**800-759-2979**	425-468-7877
Rush Enterprises Inc					
555 IH 35 S Ste 500	New Braunfels	TX	78130	**800-973-7874**	830-626-5200
NASDAQ: RUSHA					
Ryder System Inc					
11690 NW 105th St	Miami	FL	33178	**800-297-9337**	305-500-3726
NYSE: R					
Star Leasing Co					
4080 Business Pk Dr	Columbus	OH	43204	**888-771-1004**	614-278-9999
Star Truck Rentals Inc					
3940 Eastern Ave SE	Grand Rapids	MI	49508	**800-748-0468**	616-243-7033
U-Haul International Inc					
2727 N Central Ave	Phoenix	AZ	85004	**800-528-0361**	

774 TRUCK TRAILERS

SEE ALSO Motor Vehicles - Commercial & Special Purpose

				Toll-Free	Phone
4-Star Trailers Inc					
10 000 NW Tenth St	Oklahoma City	OK	73127	**800-848-3095**	405-324-7827
Beall Corp					
9200 N Ramsey Blvd	Portland	OR	97203	**855-219-5686**	
Brenner Tank LLC					
450 Arlington Ave	Fond du Lac	WI	54935	**800-558-9750**	
Circle J Trailers					
312 W Simplot Blvd	Caldwell	ID	83065	**800-247-2535**	208-459-0842
Clement Industries Inc					
PO Box 914	Minden	LA	71058	**800-562-5948***	318-377-2776
*Cust Svc					
CM Trailers Inc					
200 County Rd	Madill	OK	73446	**888-268-7577**	
Cottrell Inc					
2125 Candler Rd	Gainesville	GA	30507	**800-827-0132***	770-532-7251
*Sales					
Dakota Mfg Company Inc					
1909 S Rowley St	Mitchell	SD	57301	**800-232-5682**	605-996-5571
Doonan Trailer Corp					
36 NE Hwy 156	Great Bend	KS	67530	**800-734-0608**	620-792-6222
East Mfg Corp					
1871 State Rt 44 PO Box 277	Randolph	OH	44265	**888-405-3278**	330-325-9921
Featherlite Trailers					
Hwy 63 & 9 PO Box 320	Cresco	IA	52136	**800-800-1230**	563-547-6000
Floe International Inc					
48473 State Hwy 65	Mcgregor	MN	55760	**800-336-6337**	
Fontaine Trailer Co					
430 Letson Rd PO Box 619	Haleyville	AL	35565	**800-821-6535**	205-486-5251
Hesse Inc					
6700 St John Ave	Kansas City	MO	64123	**800-821-5562**	816-483-7808
Holden Industries Inc					
5624 S State Hwy 43	South West City	MO	64863	**800-488-4487**	417-762-3218
LBT Inc 11502 "I" St	Omaha	NE	68137	**888-528-7278**	402-333-4900
Ledwell & Son Enterprises					
3300 Waco St	Texarkana	TX	75501	**888-533-9355**	903-838-6531
Loadcraft Industries Inc					
3811 N Bridge St	Brady	TX	76825	**800-803-0183**	325-597-2911
Mac Trailer Mfg Inc					
14599 Commerce St NE	Alliance	OH	44601	**800-795-8454**	330-823-9900
MCT Industries Inc					
500 Tierra Montana Loop	Albuquerque	NM	87004	**800-876-8651**	505-345-8651
Merritt Equipment Co					
9339 Brighton Rd	Henderson	CO	80640	**800-634-3036**	303-289-2286
Mickey Truck Bodies Inc					
1305 Trinity Ave	High Point	NC	27261	**800-334-9061**	336-882-6806
Midwest Systems					
5911 Hall St	Saint Louis	MO	63147	**800-383-6281**	314-389-6280
Polar Service Centers					
7600 E Sam Houston Pkwy N	Houston	TX	77049	**800-955-8558**	281-459-6400
Polar Tank Trailer Inc					
12810 County Rd 17	Holdingford	MN	56340	**800-826-6589**	320-746-2255
Redneck Trailer Supplies					
2100 NW By-Pass	Springfield	MO	65803	**877-973-3632**	417-864-5210
Rogers Bros Corp					
100 Orchard St	Albion	PA	16401	**800-441-9880**	814-756-4121
Royal Camp Services Ltd					
7111 - 67 St	Edmonton	AB	T6B3L7	**877-884-2267**	780-463-8000

				Toll-Free	Phone
Schwend Inc					
28945 Johnston Rd	Dade City	FL	33523	**800-243-7757**	352-588-2220
Stoughton Trailers LLC					
416 S Academy St	Stoughton	WI	53589	**800-227-5391**	608-873-2500
Strick Trailers LLC					
301 N Polk St	Monroe	IN	46772	**888-552-3055***	260-692-6121
*Sales					
Summit Trailer Sales Inc					
1 Summit Plz	Summit Station	PA	17979	**800-437-3729**	570-754-3511
Talbert Manufacturing Inc					
1628 W State Rd 114	Rensselaer	IN	47978	**888-489-1731**	
Timpte Inc					
1827 Industrial Dr	David City	NE	68632	**888-256-4884**	402-367-3056
Towmaster Inc					
61381 US Hwy 12	Litchfield	MN	55355	**800-462-4517**	320-693-7900
Trail King Industries Inc					
300 E Norway	Mitchell	SD	57301	**800-843-3324**	
Trailiner Corp					
2169 E Blaine St	Springfield	MO	65803	**800-833-8209**	417-866-7258
Travis Body & Trailer Inc					
13955 FM529	Houston	TX	77041	**800-535-4372**	713-466-5888
Trinity Trailer Manufacturing Inc					
7533 S Federal Way	Boise	ID	83716	**800-235-6577**	208-336-3666
Truck Equipment Service Co					
800 Oak St	Lincoln	NE	68521	**800-869-0363**	402-476-3225
Utility Trailer Mfg Co					
17295 E Railroad St	City of Industry	CA	91748	**800-874-6807**	626-965-1541
Vantage Trailers Inc					
29335 Hwy Blvd	Katy	TX	77494	**800-826-8245**	
Wells Cargo Inc					
1503 W McNaughton St	Elkhart	IN	46514	**800-348-7553**	574-264-9661
Western Trailer Co					
251 W Gowen Rd	Boise	ID	83716	**888-344-2539**	208-344-2539
Wilson Trailer Co					
4400 S Lewis Blvd	Sioux City	IA	51106	**800-798-2002**	712-252-6500

775 TRUCKING COMPANIES

SEE ALSO Logistics Services (Transportation & Warehousing) ; Moving Companies

				Toll-Free	Phone
A & A Express Inc					
PO Box 707	Brandon	SD	57005	**800-658-3549**	605-582-2402
Aaa Moving & Storage Inc					
747 E Ship Creek Ave	Anchorage	AK	99501	**888-995-3331**	888-927-3330
Ace Doran Hauling & Rigging Company Inc					
1601 Blue Rock St	Cincinnati	OH	45223	**800-829-0929**	513-681-7900
Acme Truck Line Inc					
200 Westbank Expy PO Box 183	Gretna	LA	70053	**800-825-6246**	504-368-2510
Alabama Motor Express Inc					
10720 E US Hwy 84 E	Ashford	AL	36312	**800-633-7590**	
Alan Ritchey Inc					
740 S I-35 E Frontage Rd	Valley View	TX	76272	**800-877-0273**	940-726-3276
Allied Automotive Group					
2302 ParkLake Dr Bldg 15 Ste 600	Atlanta	GA	30345	**800-476-2058**	
Ameril-Co Carriers Inc					
1702 E Overland	Scottsbluff	NE	69361	**800-445-5400**	308-635-3157
Amstan Logistics Inc					
101 Knightsbridge Dr	Hamilton	OH	45011	**855-301-7599**	513-817-0937
Anderson Trucking Service Inc					
725 Opportunity St	Saint Cloud	MN	56301	**800-328-2316**	320-255-7400
ArcBest (ABC)					
3801 Old Greenwood Rd	Fort Smith	AR	72903	**800-610-5544**	
NASDAQ: ARCB					
ARG Trucking Corp					
369 Bostwick Rd	Phelps	NY	14532	**800-334-1314**	315-789-8871
Arlo G Lott Trucking Inc					
257 S 100 E	Jerome	ID	83338	**800-443-5688**	208-324-5053
Armellini Express Lines Inc					
3446 SW Armellini Ave	Palm City	FL	34990	**800-327-7887**	772-287-0575
Associated Petroleum Carriers Inc					
PO Box 2808	Spartanburg	SC	29304	**800-573-9301***	864-573-9301
*Cust Svc					
Averitt Express Inc					
1415 Neal St	Cookeville	TN	38501	**800-283-7488**	
B-D-R Transport Inc					
7994 US Rt 5	Westminster	VT	05158	**800-421-0126**	802-463-0606
Barlow Truck Lines inc					
1305 SE Grand Dd Hwy	Faucett	MO	64448	**800-688-1202**	816-396-1430
Bastian Trucking Inc					
440 S Main	Aurora	UT	84620	**800-452-5126**	435-529-7453
Baylor Trucking Inc					
9269 E State Rd 48	Milan	IN	47031	**800-322-9567**	812-623-2020
Bayshore Transportation System Inc					
901 Dawson Dr	Newark	DE	19713	**800-523-3319**	302-366-0220
Beam Mack Sales & Service Inc					
2674 W Henrietta Rd	Rochester	NY	14623	**877-650-8789**	585-424-4860
Beaver Express Service LLC					
4310 Oklahoma Ave PO Box 1147	Woodward	OK	73802	**800-593-2328**	580-256-6460
Beelman Truck Co					
1 Racehorse Dr	East Saint Louis	IL	62205	**800-541-5918***	618-646-5300
*Sales					
Besl Transfer Co					
5700 Este Ave	Cincinnati	OH	45232	**800-456-2375**	513-242-3456
Big G Express Inc					
190 Hawkins Dr	Shelbyville	TN	37160	**800-955-9140**	800-684-9140
Boyd Bros Transportation Inc					
3275 Alabama 30	Clayton	AL	36016	**800-700-2693**	334-775-1400
Bryan Systems					
14020 US 20A Hwy	Montpelier	OH	43543	**800-745-2796**	
Buchanan Hauling & Rigging					
4625 Industrial Rd	Fort Wayne	IN	46825	**888-544-4285**	260-471-1877
Buddy Moore Trucking Inc					
925 34th St N	Birmingham	AL	35222	**877-366-6566**	
Bulk Transit Corp					
7177 Industrial Pkwy	Plain City	OH	43064	**800-345-2855**	614-873-4632

				Toll-Free	Phone
Bulkmatic Transport Co					
2001 N Cline Ave	Griffith	IN	46319	**800-535-8505**	
Burns Motor Freight Inc					
500 Seneca Trl N	Marlinton	WV	24954	**800-598-5674**	304-799-6106
Butler Transport Inc					
347 N James St	Kansas City	KS	66118	**800-345-8158***	
*Cust Svc					
Calex Express Inc					
58 Pittston Ave	Pittston	PA	18640	**800-292-2539**	570-603-0180
California Cartage Company Inc					
2931 Redondo Ave	Long Beach	CA	90806	**888-537-1432**	
Cardinal Transport Inc					
7180 E Reed Rd	Coal City	IL	60416	**800-435-9302**	815-634-4443
Celadon Trucking Services Inc					
9503 E 33rd St	Indianapolis	IN	46235	**800-235-2366**	317-972-7000
Central Freight Lines Inc					
PO Box 2638	Waco	TX	76702	**800-782-5036**	
Central Petroleum Transport Inc (CPT)					
6115 Mitchell St	Sioux City	IA	51111	**800-798-6357**	712-258-6357
Chadderton Trucking Inc					
40 Stewart Way PO Box 687	Sharon	PA	16146	**800-327-6868**	724-981-5050
Coastal Transport Co Inc					
1603 Ackerman Rd	San Antonio	TX	78219	**800-523-8612**	210-661-4287
Coleman Worldwide Moving					
PO Box 960	Midland City	AL	36350	**877-693-7060**	
Colonial Freight Systems Inc					
10924 McBride Ln	Knoxville	TN	37932	**800-826-1402**	865-966-9711
Colonial Truck Co					
1833 Commerce Rd	Richmond	VA	23224	**800-234-8782**	804-232-3492
Combined Transport Inc					
5656 Crater Lake Ave	Central Point	OR	97502	**800-547-2870**	541-734-7418
Comcar Industries Inc					
502 E Bridgers Ave	Auburndale	FL	33823	**800-524-1101***	
*Cust Svc					
Cooke Trucking Co Inc					
1759 S Andy Griffith Pkwy	Mount Airy	NC	27030	**800-888-9502**	336-786-5181
Covenant Transport Inc					
400 Birmingham Hwy	Chattanooga	TN	37419	**800-334-9686**	423-821-1212
NASDAQ: CVTI					
Cox Transportation Services Inc					
10448 Dow Gil Rd	Ashland	VA	23005	**800-288-8118**	804-798-1477
CR England & Sons Inc					
4701 West 2100 South	Salt Lake City	UT	84120	**800-453-8826**	801-972-2712
Craig Transportation Co					
819 Kingsbury St	Maumee	OH	43537	**800-521-9119**	419-872-3333
Cresco Lines Inc					
15220 S Halsted St	Harvey	IL	60426	**800-323-4476**	708-339-1186
Crete Carrier Corp					
400 NW 56th St PO Box 81228	Lincoln	NE	68528	**800-998-4095***	402-475-9521
*Cust Svc					
Crossett Inc 201 S Carver St	Warren	PA	16365	**800-876-2778***	
*General					
Crysteel Truck Equipment Inc					
52248 Ember Rd	Lake Crystal	MN	56055	**800-722-0588***	
*General					
CTI Inc					
11105 Norrth Casa Grande Hwy	Rillito	AZ	85654	**800-362-4952**	520-624-2348
D M Bowman Inc					
10228 Governor Ln Blvd Ste 3006	Williamsport	MD	21795	**800-326-3274**	
D P. Curtis Trucking Inc					
1450 S Hwy 118	Richfield	UT	84701	**800-257-9151**	
D&D Sexton Inc PO Box 156	Carthage	MO	64836	**800-743-0265**	417-358-8727
Daggett Truck Line Inc					
32717 County Rd 10	Frazee	MN	56544	**800-262-9393**	218-334-3711
Dahlsten Truck Line Inc					
101 W Edgar PO Box 95	Clay Center	NE	68933	**800-228-4313**	402-762-3511
Daily Express Inc					
1072 Harrisburg Pk	Carlisle	PA	17013	**800-735-3136**	717-243-5757
Dakota Line Inc					
PO Box 476	Vermillion	SD	57069	**800-532-5682**	605-624-5228
Dana Transport Inc					
210 Essex Ave E	Avenel	NJ	07001	**800-733-3262**	732-750-9100
Davis Express Inc					
PO Box 1276	Starke	FL	32091	**800-874-4270**	
Daylight Transport					
1501 Hughes Way Ste 200	Long Beach	CA	90810	**800-468-9999**	
Decker Truck Line Inc					
4000 Fifth Ave S	Fort Dodge	IA	50501	**800-247-2537**	515-576-4141
Dejana Truck & Utility Equipment Company Inc					
490 Pulaski Rd	Kings Park	NY	11754	**877-335-2621**	631-544-9000
Dick Lavy Trucking Inc					
8848 State Rt 121	Bradford	OH	45308	**800-345-5289**	937-448-2104
Dilmar Oil Company Inc					
1951 W Darlington St PO Box 5629	Florence	SC	29501	**800-922-5823**	
Dino's Trucking Inc					
9615 Continental Indus Dr	Saint Louis	MO	63123	**800-771-7805**	314-631-3001
Dircks Moving Services Inc					
4340 W Mohave St	Phoenix	AZ	85043	**800-523-5038**	602-267-9401
Diversified Transfer & Storage Inc (DTS)					
1640 Monad Rd	Billings	MT	59101	**800-755-5855**	406-245-4695
Duncan & Son Lines Inc					
23860 W US Hwy 85	Buckeye	AZ	85326	**800-528-4283**	623-386-4511
Eagle Transport Corp					
300 S Wesleyan Blvd Ste 202	Rocky Mount	NC	27804	**800-776-9937**	252-937-2464
Earl L Henderson Trucking Inc					
8118 Bunkum Rd	Caseyville	IL	62232	**800-447-8084**	618-623-0057
Epes Carriers Inc					
3400 Edgefield Ct	Greensboro	NC	27409	**800-869-3737**	336-668-3358
EW Wylie Corp					
1520 Second Ave NW	West Fargo	ND	58078	**800-437-4132***	
*Cust Svc					
Falcon Express Inc					
2250 E Church St	Philadelphia	PA	19124	**800-544-6566**	215-992-3140
FFE Transportation Inc					
1145 Empire Central Pl	Dallas	TX	75247	**800-569-9200**	214-630-8090
First Class Services Inc					
9355 US Hwy 60 E	Lewisport	KY	42351	**800-467-8684***	270-295-3746
*General					

Company / Address	City	State	Zip	Toll-Free	Phone
Firstexpress Inc 1137 Freightliner Dr	Nashville	TN	37210	**800-848-9203**	
Five Star Trucking Inc 4380 Glenbrook Rd	Willoughby	OH	44094	**800-321-3658**	440-953-9300
Fort Edward Express Company Inc 1402 Rt 9	Fort Edward	NY	12828	**800-342-1233**	518-792-6571
Forward Air Corp 1915 Snapps Ferry Rd Bldg N *NASDAQ: FWRD*	Greeneville	TN	37745	**800-726-6654**	423-636-3380
Frank C Alegre Trucking Inc PO Box 1508	Lodi	CA	95241	**800-769-2440**	209-334-2112
Fry-Wagner Moving & Storage Co 3700 Rider Trl S	Earth City	MO	63045	**800-899-4035**	314-291-4100
Godfrey Trucking Inc 6173 W 2100 S	West Valley City	UT	84128	**800-444-7669**	801-972-0660
Grammer Industries Inc 6320 E State St	Columbus	IN	47201	**800-333-7410**	812-579-5655
Grask Peterbilt 9201 Sixth St SW	Cedar Rapids	IA	52404	**888-434-2511**	
Groendyke Transport Inc 2510 Rock Island Blvd	Enid	OK	73701	**800-843-2103**	580-234-4663
Guy M Turner Inc 4514 S Holden Rd PO Box 7776	Greensboro	NC	27406	**800-432-4859**	336-294-4660
H & M International Transportation Inc 485B Rt 1 S	Iselin	NJ	08830	**800-446-4685**	732-510-4640
H & W Trucking Company Inc 1772 N Andy Griffith Pkwy PO Box 1545	Mount Airy	NC	27030	**800-334-9181**	336-789-2188
H O Wolding Inc 9642 Western Way	Amherst	WI	54406	**800-950-0054**	715-824-5513
Hazen Transport Inc 27050 Wick Rd	Taylor	MI	48180	**800-251-2120**	313-292-2120
Heartland Express Inc 901 N Kansas Ave *NASDAQ: HTLD*	North Liberty	IA	52317	**800-654-1175**	
Hirschbach Motor Lines Inc 18355 US Hwy 20	East Dubuque	IL	61025	**800-554-2969**	
Holman Transportation Services Inc 1010 Holman Ct	Caldwell	ID	83605	**800-375-2416**	208-454-0779
Hot-Line Freight System Inc PO Box 205	West Salem	WI	54669	**800-468-4686**	608-486-1600
Houff Transfer Inc 46 Houff Rd	Weyers Cave	VA	24486	**800-476-4683**	540-234-9233
Howard F Baer Inc 1301 Foster Ave	Nashville	TN	37210	**800-447-7430**	615-255-7351
Howard Sheppard Inc PO Box 797	Sandersville	GA	31082	**800-846-1726**	478-552-5127
Howell's Motor Freight Inc PO Box 12308	Roanoke	VA	24024	**800-444-0585**	540-966-3200
HVH Transportation Inc 181 E 56th Ave Ste 200	Denver	CO	80216	**866-723-0586**	303-292-3656
Indian River Transport Co 2580 Executive Rd	Winter Haven	FL	33884	**800-877-2430**	863-324-2430
J P Noonan Transportation Inc 415 W St	West Bridgewater	MA	02379	**800-922-8026**	508-583-2880
J-Mar Enterprises Inc PO Box 4143	Bismarck	ND	58502	**800-446-8283**	701-222-4518
Jaro Transportation Services Inc 975 Post Rd	Warren	OH	44483	**800-451-3447**	330-393-5659
Jerry Lipps Inc 3888 Nash Rd	Cape Girardeau	MO	63702	**800-325-3331**	573-335-0196
Jet Star Inc 10825 Andrade Dr	Zionsville	IN	46077	**800-969-4222**	317-873-4222
JH Walker Trucking Company Inc 152 N Hollywood Rd	Houma	LA	70364	**800-581-2600**	985-868-8330
Jim Palmer Trucking 9730 Derby Dr	Missoula	MT	59808	**888-698-3422**	
JNJ Express Inc 3935 Old Getwell Rd	Memphis	TN	38118	**888-383-7157**	901-362-3444
Jones Motor Group 654 Enterprise Dr	Limerick	PA	19468	**800-825-6637**	610-948-7900
KAG West 4076 Seaport Blvd	West Sacramento	CA	95691	**800-547-1587**	800-969-5419
Kaplan Trucking Co 6600 Bessemer Ave	Cleveland	OH	44127	**800-352-2848**	216-341-3322
Keim T S Inc 1249 N Ninth St PO Box 226	Sabetha	KS	66534	**800-255-2450**	
Keith Titus Corp PO Box 920	Weedsport	NY	13166	**800-233-2126**	315-834-6681
Kenan Advantage Group Inc (KAG) 4366 Mt Pleasant St NW	North Canton	OH	44720	**800-969-5419**	
Kenworth Sales Co 2125 Constitution Blvd *General	West Valley City	UT	84119	**800-222-7831***	801-487-4161
KLLM Inc 135 Riverview Dr	Richland	MS	39218	**800-925-5556**	800-925-1000
Knight Transportation Inc 5601 W Buckeye Rd *NYSE: KNX*	Phoenix	AZ	85043	**800-489-2000**	602-269-2000
Kruepke Trucking Inc 2881 Hwy P *Cust Svc	Jackson	WI	53037	**800-798-5000***	262-677-3155
Landair Corp 1110 Myers St	Greeneville	TN	37743	**888-526-3247**	
Landmark International Trucks Inc 4550 Rutledge Pk	Knoxville	TN	37914	**800-968-9999**	865-637-4881
Landstar Express America Inc 13410 Sutton Pk Dr S	Jacksonville	FL	32224	**800-872-9400**	904-398-9400
Landstar Inway Inc 13410 Sutton Pk Dr S	Jacksonville	FL	32224	**800-872-9400**	
Lawrence Companies (LTS) 872 Lee Hwy	Roanoke	VA	24019	**800-336-9626**	
Lightning Transportation Inc 16820 Blake Rd	Hagerstown	MD	21740	**800-233-0624**	301-582-5700
Linden Warehouse & Distribution Co Inc 1300 Lower Rd	Linden	NJ	07036	**800-333-2855**	908-862-1400
Liquid Transport Corp 8470 Allison Pt Blvd Ste 400	Indianapolis	IN	46250	**800-942-3175**	317-841-4200
Lynden Transport Inc 3027 Rampart Dr	Anchorage	AK	99501	**800-327-9390**	
Marten Transport Ltd 129 Marten St *NASDAQ: MRTN*	Mondovi	WI	54755	**800-395-3000**	715-926-4216
Matheson Trucking Inc 9785 Goethe Rd	Sacramento	CA	95827	**800-455-7678**	
Maverick USA Inc 13301 Valentine Rd	North Little Rock	AR	72117	**800-289-6600**	
May Trucking Co 4185 Brooklake Rd	Salem	OR	97303	**800-547-9169**	503-393-7030
Mayfield Transfer Company Inc 3200 West Lake St	Melrose Park	IL	60160	**800-222-2959**	708-681-4440
McKenzie Tank Lines Inc 1966 Commonwealth Ln	Tallahassee	FL	32303	**800-828-6495**	850-576-1221
MCT Transportation LLC 1600 E Benson Rd *Cust Svc	Sioux Falls	SD	57104	**800-843-9904***	605-339-8400
Mercer Transportation Co 1128 W Main St	Louisville	KY	40203	**800-626-5375**	502-584-2301
Mergenthaler Transfer & Storage 1414 N Montana Ave *General	Helena	MT	59601	**800-826-5463***	406-442-9470
Midwest Motor Express Inc 5015 E Main Ave	Bismarck	ND	58502	**800-741-4097**	701-223-1880
Milan Express Company Inc 1091 Kefauver Dr	Milan	TN	38358	**800-231-7303**	
Miller Transporters Inc 5500 Hwy 80 W *Cust Svc	Jackson	MS	39209	**800-645-5378***	601-922-8331
Minuteman Trucks Inc 2181 Providence Hwy	Walpole	MA	02081	**800-231-8458**	508-668-3112
Murrows Transfer Inc PO Box 4095 *Cust Svc	High Point	NC	27263	**800-669-2928***	336-475-6101
National Carriers Inc 1501 E Eigth St	Liberal	KS	67901	**800-835-9180**	
Nationwide Truck Brokers Inc (NTB) 4203 Roger B Chaffee Memorial Blvd SE Ste 2	Grand Rapids	MI	49548	**800-446-0682**	616-878-5554
Navajo Express Inc 1400 W 64 Ave	Denver	CO	80221	**800-525-1969**	303-287-3800
New Penn Motor Express Inc 625 S Fifth Ave *Cust Svc	Lebanon	PA	17042	**800-285-5000***	717-274-2521
Nick Strimbu Inc 3500 PkwyRd	Brookfield	OH	44403	**800-446-8785**	330-448-4046
Northland Trucking Inc 1515 S 22nd Ave	Phoenix	AZ	85009	**800-214-5564**	602-254-0007
Nussbaum Trucking Inc 19336 N 1425 East Rd	Normal	IL	61748	**800-322-7305**	309-452-4426
Old Dominion Freight Line Inc 500 Old Dominion Way *NASDAQ: ODFL*	Thomasville	NC	27360	**800-432-6335**	336-889-5000
Online Transport System Inc 6311 W Stoner Dr	Greenfield	IN	46140	**866-543-1235**	317-894-2159
Ozark Motor Lines Inc 3934 Homewood Rd	Memphis	TN	38118	**800-264-4100**	901-251-9711
Palmetto State Transportation Company Inc 1050 Pk W Blvd	Greenville	SC	29611	**800-269-0175**	864-672-3800
PAM Transportation Services Inc 297 W Henri De Tonti Blvd *NASDAQ: PTSI*	Tontitown	AR	72770	**800-879-7261**	479-361-9111
Paper Transport Inc 1250 Mid Valley Dr	De Pere	WI	54115	**800-317-3650**	
Patriot Transportation Holding Inc 200 West Forsyth St 7th Fl *NASDAQ: PATI*	Jacksonville	FL	32202	**877-704-1776**	
Peet Frate Line Inc 650 S Eastwood Dr PO Box 1129	Woodstock	IL	60098	**800-435-6909**	815-338-5500
Phoenix Transportation Services LLC 335 E Yusen Dr	Georgetown	KY	40324	**800-860-0889**	502-863-0108
Pitt Ohio Express 15 27th St *Cust Svc	Pittsburgh	PA	15222	**800-366-7488***	412-232-3015
Pleasant Trucking 2250 Industrial Dr	Connellsville	PA	15425	**800-245-2402**	
Pozas Bros Trucking Company Inc 8130 Enterprise Dr	Newark	CA	94560	**800-874-8383**	510-742-9939
Predator Trucking Co 3181 Trumbull Ave	McDonald	OH	44437	**800-235-5624**	330-530-0712
Prestera Trucking 19129 US Rt 52	South Point	OH	45680	**855-761-7943**	740-894-4770
Pride Transport Inc 5499 W 2455 S	Salt Lake City	UT	84120	**800-877-1320**	801-972-8890
Prime Inc 2740 N Mayfair PO Box 4208 *Cust Svc	Springfield	MO	65803	**800-321-4552***	417-521-3950
Pritchett Trucking Inc 1050 SE Sixth St PO Box 311	Lake Butler	FL	32054	**800-486-7504**	386-496-2630
Quality Distribution Inc 4041 Pk Oaks Blvd Ste 200 *NASDAQ: QLTY*	Tampa	FL	33610	**800-282-2031**	
Queensborough National Bank & Trust Co 113 E Broad St PO Box 467	Louisville	GA	30434	**800-236-2442**	478-625-2000
R & R Trucking Inc 302 Thunder Rd PO Box 545	Duenweg	MO	64841	**800-625-6885**	417-623-6885
Rbx Inc PO Box 2118	Springfield	MO	65802	**877-450-2200**	800-245-5507
Refrigerated Food Express Inc 57 Littlefield St	Avon	MA	02322	**800-342-8822**	508-587-4600
Relco Systems Inc 7310 Chestnut Ridge Rd	Lockport	NY	14094	**800-262-1020**	716-434-8100
Riechmann Transport Inc 3328 W Chain of Rocks Rd	Granite City	IL	62040	**800-844-4225**	618-797-6700
Roadtex Transportation Corp 13 Jensen Dr	Somerset	NJ	08873	**800-762-3839**	
Robert Bearden Inc 2601 Industrial Pk Dr PO Box 870	Cairo	GA	39828	**888-298-6928**	229-377-6928

			Toll-Free	Phone
Roehl Transport Inc				
1916 E 29th St PO Box 750	Marshfield WI	54449	**800-826-8367**	715-591-3795
Roger Ward Inc				
17275 Green Mtn Rd	San Antonio TX	78247	**888-909-3147***	210-655-8623
*General				
Ross Neely Systems Inc				
1500 Second St	Birmingham AL	35214	**800-561-3357**	205-798-1137
Rountree Transport & Rigging Inc				
2640 N Ln Ave	Jacksonville FL	32254	**800-342-5036**	904-781-1033
Roy Bros Inc				
764 Boston Rd	Billerica MA	01821	**800-225-0830***	978-667-1921
*Cust Svc				
Royal Trucking Co				
1323 Eshman Ave N PO Box 387	West Point MS	39773	**800-321-1293**	
RWH Trucking Inc				
2970 Old Oakwood Rd	Oakwood GA	30566	**800-256-8119**	
S & S Transport Inc				
PO Box 12579	Grand Forks ND	58208	**800-726-8022**	
S-j Transportation Co Inc				
PO Box 169	Woodstown NJ	08098	**800-524-2552**	856-769-2741
Sammons Trucking				
3665 W Broadway	Missoula MT	59808	**800-548-9276**	406-728-2600
Security Van Lines LLC				
100 W Airline Dr	Kenner LA	70062	**800-794-5961**	
Seward Motor Freight				
PO Box 126	Seward NE	68434	**800-786-4469**	402-643-4503
Sherman Bros Trucking				
32921 Diamond Hill Dr PO Box 706	Harrisburg OR	97446	**800-547-8980**	541-995-7751
Shetler Moving & Storage Inc				
1253 E Diamond Ave	Evansville IN	47711	**800-321-5069**	812-421-7750
Shippers Express INC				
1651 Kerr Dr	Jackson MS	39204	**800-647-2480**	601-948-4251
Short Freight Lines Inc				
459 S River Rd PO Box 357	Bay City MI	48707	**800-248-0625**	989-893-3505
Simons Trucking Inc				
920 Simon Dr PO Box 8	Farley IA	52046	**800-373-2580**	563-744-3304
Skinner Transfer Corp				
PO Box 438	Reedsburg WI	53959	**800-356-9350**	608-524-2326
Southeastern Freight Lines Inc				
420 Davega Rd	Lexington SC	29073	**800-637-7335**	803-794-7300
Southwest Freightlines				
11991 Transpark Dr	El Paso TX	79927	**800-776-5799***	915-860-8592
*General				
Star Fleet Inc				
915 S Main St	Middlebury IN	46540	**877-805-9547**	
Star Transportation Inc				
PO Box 100925	Nashville TN	37224	**800-333-3060***	615-256-4336
*Cust Svc				
Steelman Transportation				
2160 N Burton	Springfield MO	65803	**800-488-6287**	417-831-6300
Stevens Transport				
PO Box 279010	Dallas TX	75227	**800-233-9369**	866-551-0337
Styer Transportation Co				
7870 215th St W	Lakeville MN	55044	**800-548-9149**	952-469-4491
Summitt Trucking LLC				
1800 Progress Way	Clarksville IN	47129	**866-999-7799**	812-285-7777
Superior Carriers Inc				
711 Jory Blvd Ste 101-N	Oak Brook IL	60523	**800-654-7707**	630-573-2555
Swift Transportation Company Inc				
2200 S 75th Ave	Phoenix AZ	85043	**800-800-2200**	602-269-9700
NYSE: SWFT				
T & T Trucking Inc				
11396 N Hwy 99	Lodi CA	95240	**800-692-3457***	209-931-6000
*Cust Svc				
T-w Transport Inc				
7405 S Hayford Rd	Cheney WA	99004	**800-356-4070**	
TanTara Transportation Corp				
2420 Stewart Rd	Muscatine IA	52761	**800-650-0292**	563-262-8621
Taylor Truck Line Inc				
31485 Northfield Blvd	Northfield MN	55057	**800-962-5994**	507-645-4531
Teal's Express Inc				
22411 Teal Dr PO Box 6010	Watertown NY	13601	**800-836-0369**	
Tennessee Steel Haulers Inc				
PO Box 78189	Nashville TN	37207	**800-776-4004**	615-271-2400
Tiger Lines LLC Lodi				
927 Black Diamond Way	Lodi CA	95241	**800-967-8443**	
TP Trucking LLC				
5630 Table Rock Rd	Central Point OR	97502	**800-292-4399**	
Trailer Bridge Inc				
10405 New Berlin Rd E	Jacksonville FL	32226	**800-554-1589**	904-751-7100
OTC: TRBRQ				
Trailer Transit Inc				
1130 E US 20	Porter IN	46304	**800-423-3647**	219-926-2111
Trans-Carriers Inc				
5135 US Hwy 78	Memphis TN	38118	**800-999-7383**	901-368-2900
Trans-Phos Inc				
4201 Bonnie Mine Rd	Mulberry FL	33860	**800-940-1575**	
Transport Distribution Co				
PO Box 306	Joplin MO	64802	**800-866-7709**	417-624-3814
Transport Inc				
2225 Main Ave SE	Moorhead MN	56560	**800-598-7267**	218-236-6300
TransWood Carriers Inc				
PO Box 189	Omaha NE	68101	**888-346-8092**	
Tri Star Freight System Inc				
5407 Mesa Dr	Houston TX	77028	**800-229-1095**	713-631-1095
Triple Crown Services				
2720 Dupont Commerce Ct	Fort Wayne IN	46825	**800-325-6510**	260-416-3600
Truline Corp				
9390 Redwood St	Las Vegas NV	89139	**800-634-6489**	702-362-7495
Tryon Trucking Inc				
PO Box 68	Fairless Hills PA	19030	**800-523-5254**	215-295-6622
Underwood Transfer Company LLC				
940 W Troy Ave	Indianapolis IN	46225	**800-428-2372**	317-783-9235
United Road Services Inc				
10701 Middlebelt Rd	Romulus MI	48174	**800-221-5127**	
Universal Logistics Holdings Inc				
12755 E Nine Mile Rd	Warren MI	48089	**800-233-9445**	586-920-0100
NASDAQ: UACL				

			Toll-Free	Phone
US Xpress Enterprises Inc				
4080 Jenkins Rd	Chattanooga TN	37421	**800-251-6291**	423-510-3000
V & S Midwest Carriers Corp				
2001 Hyland Ave	Kaukauna WI	54130	**800-876-4330**	
Vitran Express Inc				
1201 Creditstone Rd	Concord ON	L4K0C2	**800-263-0791**	416-798-4965
Volume Transportation Inc				
2261 Plunkett Rd	Conyers GA	30012	**800-879-5565**	770-482-1400
Waggoners Trucking				
5220 Midland Rd	Billings MT	59101	**800-999-9097**	406-248-1919
Waller Truck Company Inc				
400 S McCleary Rd	Excelsior Springs MO	64024	**800-821-2196**	816-629-3400
Walpole Inc				
269 NW Ninth St	Okeechobee FL	34972	**800-741-6500**	863-763-5593
Warren Transport Inc				
210 Beck Ave	Waterloo IA	50701	**800-526-3053**	
Watsontown Trucking Company Inc				
60 Belford Blvd	Milton PA	17847	**800-344-0313**	570-522-9820
Weaver Bros Inc				
2230 Spar Ave	Anchorage AK	99501	**800-478-4600**	907-278-4526
Wel Companies Inc				
1625 S Broadway PO Box 5610	De Pere WI	54115	**800-333-4415**	
Werner Enterprises Inc				
14507 Frontier Rd	Omaha NE	68138	**800-228-2240**	402-895-6640
NASDAQ: WERN				
West Side Unlimited				
4201 16th Ave SW	Cedar Rapids IA	52404	**800-373-2957**	319-390-4466
Western Express Inc				
7135 Centennial Pl	Nashville TN	37209	**800-316-7160**	877-986-8855
White Bros Trucking Co				
4N793 School Rd	Wasco IL	60183	**800-323-4762**	630-584-3810
Wilson Lines of Minnesota Inc				
2131 Second Ave	Newport MN	55055	**800-525-3333***	651-459-2384
*General				
Wilson Trucking Corp				
137 Wilson Blvd	Fishersville VA	22939	**866-645-7405**	540-949-3200
Wiseway Motor Freight Inc				
PO Box 838	Hudson WI	54016	**800-876-1660**	
Woody Bogler Trucking Co				
PO Box 229	Rosebud MO	63091	**800-899-4120**	573-764-3700
Wragtime Air Freight Inc				
596 W 135th St	Gardena CA	90248	**800-586-9701**	
Wright Transportation Inc				
2333 Dauphin Island Pkwy	Mobile AL	36605	**800-342-4598**	251-432-6390
Wyatt Transfer Inc				
3035 Bells Rd PO Box 24326	Richmond VA	23224	**800-552-5708**	804-743-3800
Wynne Transport Service Inc				
2222 N 11th St PO Box 8700	Omaha NE	68110	**800-383-9330**	402-342-4001
Young's Commercial Transfer				
2075 W Scranton Ave PO Box 871	Porterville CA	93257	**800-289-1639**	559-784-6651
Yourga Trucking Inc				
145 JH Yourga Pl PO Box 607	Wheatland PA	16161	**800-245-1722**	724-981-3600

776 TYPESETTING & RELATED SERVICES

SEE ALSO Printing Companies - Commercial Printers ; Graphic Design

			Toll-Free	Phone
A A Blueprint Company Inc				
2757 Gilchrist Rd	Akron OH	44305	**800-821-3700**	330-794-8803
Allied Bindery LLC				
32501 Dequindre Rd	Madison Heights MI	48071	**800-833-0151**	248-588-5990
Artisan Colour Inc				
8970 E Bahia Dr	Scottsdale AZ	85260	**800-274-2422**	480-948-0009
Auto-Graphics Inc				
430 N Vineyard Ave	Ontario CA	91764	**800-776-6939**	909-595-7004
Bell Litho Inc				
370 Crossen Ave	Elk Grove Village IL	60007	**800-952-3306**	847-952-3300
Carey Digital				
1718 Central Pkwy	Cincinnati OH	45214	**800-767-6071**	513-241-5210
Cohber Press PO Box 93100	Rochester NY	14692	**800-724-3032**	585-475-9100
Color Communication Inc				
4000 W Fillmore St	Chicago IL	60624	**800-458-5743**	
Color House Graphics Inc				
3505 Eastern Ave SE	Grand Rapids MI	49508	**800-454-1916**	616-241-1916
GGS Technical Publications Services				
3265 Farmtrail Rd	York PA	17406	**800-927-4474**	717-764-2222
GotPrint				
7651 N San Fernando Rd	Burbank CA	91505	**877-922-7374**	818-252-3000
Imtech Graphics Inc				
545 Dell Rd	Carlstadt NJ	07072	**800-468-3240**	
Ligature, The				
4909 Alcoa Ave	Los Angeles CA	90058	**800-944-5440**	323-585-6000
Luminite Products Corp				
148 Commerce Dr	Bradford PA	16701	**888-545-2270**	814-817-1420
Presstek 55 Executive Dr	Hudson NH	03051	**800-422-3616**	603-595-7000
NASDAQ: PRST				
Printing Prep Inc				
707 Washington St	Buffalo NY	14203	**877-878-7114**	716-852-5011
Quintessence Publishing Co				
4350 Chandler Dr	Hanover Park IL	60133	**800-621-0387**	630-736-3600
Richards Graphic Communications Inc				
2700 Van Buren St	Bellwood IL	60104	**866-827-3686**	708-547-6000
State & Federal Communications Inc				
80 S Summit St Ste 100	Akron OH	44308	**888-452-9669**	330-761-9960
West Essex Graphics Inc (WEG)				
305 Fairfield Ave	Fairfield NJ	07004	**800-221-5859**	

777 ULTRASONIC CLEANING EQUIPMENT

SEE ALSO Dental Equipment & Supplies - Mfr

			Toll-Free	Phone
Branson 41 Eagle Rd	Danbury CT	06813	**800-732-9262**	
Crest Ultrasonics Corp				
18 Graphics Dr	Ewing Township NJ	08628	**800-992-7378**	609-883-4000
Sonicor Inc 82 Otis St	West Babylon NY	11704	**800-864-5022**	631-920-6555

				Toll-Free	Phone
Sonics & Materials Inc					
53 Church Hill Rd	Newtown	CT	06470	800-745-1105	203-270-4600
OTC: SIMA					
Sterigenics					
2015 Spring Rd Ste 650	Oak Brook	IL	60523	800-472-4508	630-928-1700

778 UNITED NATIONS AGENCIES, ORGANIZATIONS, PROGRAMS

				Toll-Free	Phone
Inter-American Development Bank					
1300 New York Ave NW	Washington	DC	20577	877-782-7432	202-623-1000
International Monetary Fund (IMF)					
700 19th St NW	Washington	DC	20431	800-548-5384	202-623-7000
World Bank Group, The (WBG)					
1818 H St NW	Washington	DC	20433	800-645-7247	202-473-1000

779 UNITED NATIONS MISSIONS

SEE ALSO Embassies & Consulates - Foreign, in the US
All of the missions listed here are permanent missions except the Holy See, which has the status of Permanent Observer Mission to the UN. Two member states, Kiribati and Palau, are not listed because they do not maintain offices in New York. Another member state, Guinea Bissau, has a New York office but is excluded from this list because no telephone number was available for it.

				Toll-Free	Phone
Canada					
885 Second Ave 14th Fl	New York	NY	10017	800-267-8376	212-848-1100
Cuba 315 Lexington Ave	New York	NY	10016	800-553-3210*	212-689-7215
*General					
Libyan Arab Jamahiriya					
309-315 E 48th St	New York	NY	10017	800-253-9646	212-752-5775
Mexico					
2 United Nations Plz Rm DC2-2386	New York	NY	10017	800-553-3210	212-752-0220
Micronesia					
300 E 42nd St Ste 1600	New York	NY	10017	800-469-4828	212-697-8370

780 UNIVERSITIES - CANADIAN

				Toll-Free	Phone
Acadia University 15 University Ave	Wolfville NS	B4P2R6		877-585-1121	902-542-2201
Alberta College of Art & Design 1407 14th Ave NW	Calgary AB	T2N4R3		800-251-8290	403-284-7600
Athabasca University 1 University Dr	Athabasca AB	T9S3A3		800-788-9041	780-675-6111
Bethany Bible College 26 Western St	Sussex NB	E4E1E6		888-432-4444	506-432-4400
Campion College at the University of Regina 3737 Wascana Pkwy	Regina SK	S4S0A2		800-667-7282	306-586-4242
Canadian College of Naturopathic Medicine 1255 Sheppard Ave E	Toronto ON	M2K1E2		866-241-2266	416-498-1255
Canadian Memorial Chiropractic College 6100 Leslie St	Toronto ON	M2H3J1		800-463-2923	416-482-2340
Cape Breton University (CBU) 1250 Grand Lake Rd PO Box 5300	Sydney NS	B1P6L2		888-959-9995	902-539-5300
Carleton University 1125 Colonel By Dr	Ottawa ON	K1S5B6		888-354-4414	613-520-7400
Columbia Bible College 2940 Clearbrook Rd	Abbotsford BC	V2T2Z8		800-283-0881	604-853-3358
Concordia University 1455 de Maisonneuve Blvd W	Montreal QC	H3G1M8		866-333-2271	514-848-2424
Concordia University College of Alberta 7128 Ada Blvd NW	Edmonton AB	T5B4E4		866-479-5200	780-479-9220
Crandall University 333 Gorge Rd	Moncton NB	E1G3H9		888-968-6228	506-858-8970
First Nations University of Canada (FNUniv) *Saskatoon* 229 Fourth Ave S	Saskatoon SK	S7K4K3		800-267-6303	306-931-1800
Heritage College & Seminary 175 Holiday Inn Dr	Cambridge ON	N3C3T2		800-465-1961	519-651-2869
King's University College 9125 50th St	Edmonton AB	T6B2H3		800-661-8582	780-465-3500
Laurentian University 935 Ramsey Lake Rd	Sudbury ON	P3E2C6		800-461-4030	705-675-1151
Laval University 2325 Rue University	Quebec QC	G1V0A6		877-785-2825	418-656-2131
McMaster University 1280 Main St W	Hamilton ON	L8S4L8		800-238-1623	905-525-9140
Mount Saint Vincent University 166 Bedford Hwy	Halifax NS	B3M2J6		877-733-6788	902-457-6117
Nipissing University 100 College Dr PO Box 5002	North Bay ON	P1B8L7		800-655-5154	705-474-3450
Ontario College of Art & Design 100 McCaul St	Toronto ON	M5T1W1		800-382-6516	416-977-6000
Prairie College 350 Fifth Ave NE PO Box 4000	Three Hills AB	T0M2N0		800-661-2425	403-443-5511
Queen's University 99 University Ave	Kingston ON	K7L3N6		800-267-7837	613-533-2000
Redeemer University College 777 Garner Rd E	Ancaster ON	L9K1J4		877-779-0913	905-648-2131
Royal Roads University 2005 Sooke Rd	Victoria BC	V9B5Y2		800-788-8028	250-391-2511
Ryerson University 350 Victoria St	Toronto ON	M5B2K3		866-592-8882	416-979-5000
Saint Francis Xavier University PO Box 5000	Antigonish NS	B2G2W5		877-867-7839*	902-863-3300
*Admissions					
Saint Paul University 223 Main St	Ottawa ON	K1S1C4		800-637-6859	613-236-1393
Taylor University College & Seminary 11525 23rd Ave	Edmonton AB	T6J4T3		800-567-4988	780-431-5200
Thompson Rivers University (TRU) 805 TRU Way	Kamloops BC	V2C0C0		800-663-1663	250-828-5000

				Toll-Free	Phone
Thorneloe University 935 Ramsey Lake Rd	Sudbury ON	P3E2C6		866-846-7635*	705-673-1730
*General					
Trent University 1600 W Bank Dr	Peterborough ON	K9J7B8		888-739-8885	705-748-1011
Trinity Western University 7600 Glover Rd	Langley BC	V2Y1Y1		888-468-6898	604-888-7511
Universite de Moncton *Edmundston* 165 Blvd Hebert	Edmundston NB	E3V2S8		888-736-8623	506-737-5051
Shippagan Campus 218 Blvd JD Gauthier	Shippagan NB	E8S1P6		800-363-8336	506-336-3400
Universite de Sherbrooke 2500 boul de l'Universite	Sherbrooke QC	J1K2R1		800-267-8337	819-821-8000
Universite du Quebec a Trois-Rivieres 3351 Boul des Forges CP 500	Trois-Rivieres QC	G9A5H7		800-365-0922	819-376-5011
Universite Sainte Anne 1695 Rt 1	Pointe-de-l'Eglise NS	B0W1M0		888-338-8337	902-769-2114
University of Alberta *Augustana* 4901-46th Ave	Camrose AB	T4V2R3		800-661-8714	780-679-1100
University of British Columbia 2016-1874 E Mall	Vancouver BC	V6T1Z1		877-272-1422	604-822-9836
University of Guelph 50 Stone Rd E	Guelph ON	N1G2W1		877-674-1610	519-824-4120
University of Manitoba 65 Chancellors Cir 500 University Ctr.	Winnipeg MB	R3T2N2		800-224-7713*	204-474-8880
*Admissions					
University of New Brunswick 100 Tucker Pk Rd PO Box 4400	Fredericton NB	E2L4L5		888-895-3344	506-453-4666
University of Northern British Columbia 3333 University Way	Prince George BC	V2N4Z9		800-627-9931	250-960-5555
University of Ottawa 550 Cumberland St	Ottawa ON	K1N6N5		877-868-8292	613-562-5800
University of Regina 3737 Wascana Pkwy	Regina SK	S4S0A2		800-644-4756	306-585-4111
Saint Thomas More College 1437 College Dr	Saskatoon SK	S7N0W6		800-667-2019	306-966-8900
Western University Canada *King's University College* 266 Epworth Ave	London ON	N6A2M3		800-265-4406	519-433-3491
York University 4700 Keele St	Toronto ON	M3J1P3		800-426-2255	416-736-2100

781 UNIVERSITY SYSTEMS

Listings are organized by state names.

				Toll-Free	Phone
Alabama					
Administrative Office of Alabama Courts 300 Dexter Ave	Montgomery	AL	36104	866-954-9411	334-954-5000
University of Alabama System 401 Queen City Ave	Tuscaloosa	AL	35401	866-362-9476	205-348-5861
Arkansas					
Administrative Office of the Courts 625 Marshall St	Little Rock	AR	72201	800-950-8221	501-682-9400
California State University 401 Golden Shore	Long Beach	CA	90802	800-325-4000	562-951-4000
University of California System 1111 Franklin St 6th Fl	Oakland	CA	94607	800-888-8267	510-987-9074
University of Missouri System 321 University Hall	Columbia	MO	65211	800-225-6075	573-882-2011
University of Nebraska System 3835 Holdrege St Varner Hall	Lincoln	NE	68583	800-542-1602	402-472-2111
Higher Education Dept 2048 Galisteo St	Santa Fe	NM	87505	800-279-9777	505-476-8400
City University of New York (CUNY) 535 E 80th St	New York	NY	10075	800-286-9937	212-997-2869
New York *Aging Office* 2 Empire State Plz	Albany	NY	12223	800-342-9871	
State University of New York, The (SUNY) State University Plz	Albany	NY	12246	800-342-3811	518-320-1888
University of South Dakota Foundation 1110 N Dakota St PO Box 5555	Vermillion	SD	57069	800-521-3575	605-677-6703
Tennessee *Administrative Office of the Cts* 511 Union St Ste 600	Nashville	TN	37219	800-448-7970	615-741-2687
University of Texas System 601 Colorado St	Austin	TX	78701	866-882-2034	512-499-4200
Utah System of Higher Education 60 South 400 West	Salt Lake City	UT	84101	800-418-8757	801-321-7200
Aging & Rehabilitative Services Dept 8004 Franklin Farms Dr	Richmond	VA	23229	800-552-5019	804-662-7000
Community College System 300 Arboretum Pl Ste 200	Richmond	VA	23236	844-897-9096	
Higher Education Policy Commission 1018 Kanawha Blvd E Ste 700	Charleston	WV	25301	888-825-5707	304-558-2101
University of Wisconsin System 1220 Linden Dr 1720 Van Hise Hall	Madison	WI	53706	800-442-6461	608-262-2321
Wyoming *Aging Div* 2300 Capitol Ave 4th Fl	Cheyenne	WY	82002	800-442-2766	307-777-7995

782 UTILITY COMPANIES

SEE ALSO Electric Companies - Cooperatives (Rural) ; Gas Transmission - Natural Gas
Types of utilities included here are electric companies, water supply companies, and natural gas companies.

				Toll-Free	Phone
6D Global Technologies Inc 1500 Broadway Ste 505	New York	NY	10036	800-787-3006	
Acuren Group Inc 7450 - 18th St	Edmonton AB	T6P1N8		800-663-9729	780-440-2131

				Toll-Free	Phone

Alaska Power & Telephone Co
193 Otto St PO Box 3222 ....Port Townsend WA 98368 **800-982-0136*** 360-385-1733
*OTC: APTL ■ *Cust Svc*

Alliant Energy Corp
4902 N Biltmore Ln Ste 1000 ....Madison WI 53718 **800-255-4268**
NYSE: LNT

Alsco Inc
3370 W 1820 S ....Salt Lake City UT 84104 **800-408-0208** 801-973-7771

Ambit Energy LP
1801 N Lamar St Ste 200 ....Dallas TX 75202 **877-282-6248**

Aqua America Inc
762 W Lancaster Ave ....Bryn Mawr PA 19010 **877-987-2782**
NYSE: WTR

Aquarion Co 835 Main St ....Bridgeport CT 06604 **800-732-9678** 203-336-7662

Arizona Public Service Co (APS)
400 N Fifth St PO Box 53999 ....Phoenix AZ 85004 **800-253-9405** 602-371-7171

ATCO Ltd
700 909 11th Ave SW ....Calgary AB T2R1N6 **800-242-3447** 403-292-7500
TSE: ACO/X

Avista Corp
1411 E Mission St ....Spokane WA 99252 **800-227-9187**

Avista Corp
1411 E Mission St ....Spokane WA 99202 **800-936-6629** 509-489-0500
NYSE: AVA

Baltimore Gas & Electric Co
110 W Fayette St ....Baltimore MD 21201 **800-685-0123**

Bangor Hydro Electric Co
PO Box 932 ....Bangor ME 04401 **800-499-6600** 207-945-5621

BPA
Bonneville Power Administration
905 NE 11th Ave ....Portland OR 97232 **800-282-3713** 503-230-3000

Brownstown Electric Supply Company Inc
690 E State Rd 250 ....Brownstown IN 47220 **800-742-8492**

Cabot Oil & Gas Corp
840 Gessner Rd Ste 1400 ....Houston TX 77024 **800-434-3985** 281-848-2799
NYSE: COG

California ISO
151 Blue Ravine Rd PO Box 639014..........Folsom CA 95630 **800-220-4907** 916-351-4400

California Water Service Group
1720 N First St ....San Jose CA 95112 **866-734-0743** 408-367-8200
NYSE: CWI

Cascade Natural Gas Corp (CNGC)
8113 W Grandridge Blvd ....Kennewick WA 99336 **888-522-1130**

Central Maine Power Co
83 Edison Dr ....Augusta ME 04336 **800-565-0121** 207-623-3521

CI Financial Corp
20 Second Queen St E ....Toronto ON M5C3G5 **800-268-9374** 416-585-5420

Citizens Gas & Coke Utility
2020 N Meridian St ....Indianapolis IN 46202 **800-427-4217** 317-924-3311

City Public Service Board
PO Box 1771 ....San Antonio TX 78296 **800-870-1006** 210-353-2222

Cleco Corp
2030 Donahue Ferry Rd PO Box 5000 ....Pineville LA 71361 **800-622-6537***
Cust Svc

Colorado Springs Utilities
111 S Cascade Ave ....Colorado Springs CO 80903 **800-238-5434** 719-448-4800

Columbia Gas of Ohio Inc
200 Civic Ctr Dr ....Columbus OH 43215 **800-807-9781** 800-344-4077

Columbia Gas of Virginia Inc
1809 Coyote Dr ....Chester VA 23836 **800-544-5606*** 800-543-8911
Cust Svc

Consumers Energy Co
1 Energy Plz ....Jackson MI 49201 **800-477-5050*** 517-788-0550
Cust Svc

Coulson Group of Companies
4890 Cherry Creek Rd ....Port Alberni BC V9Y8E9 **800-663-3456** 250-724-7600

Covanta Energy Corp
445 South St ....Morristown NJ 07960 **800-950-8749** 862-345-5000
NYSE: CVA

Dakota Gasification Co
PO Box 5540 ....Bismarck ND 58506 **866-747-3546** 701-221-4400

Dayton Power & Light Co
PO Box 1247 ....Dayton OH 45401 **800-433-8500** 937-331-3900

Delmarva Power
PO Box 231 ....Wilmington DE 19899 **800-898-8042***
Cust Svc

Delta Natural Gas Co Inc
3617 Lexington Rd ....Winchester KY 40391 **800-262-2012** 859-744-6171
NASDAQ: DGAS

Dominion Energy
PO Box 45360 ....Salt Lake City UT 84145 **800-323-5517** 801-324-5111

Dominion Energy
120 Tredegar St ....Richmond VA 23219 **888-216-3718**

Dominion Energy Generation Marketing Inc
701 E Cary St ....Richmond VA 23219 **866-366-4357** 757-857-2112

Dominion Hope
701 E Cary St ....Richmond VA 23219 **866-366-4357** 888-366-8280

Dynasty Gallery
2765 16th St ....San Francisco CA 94103 **800-227-3344** 415-864-5084

Eastern Shore Natural Gas Co
1110 Forest Ave Ste 201........................Dover DE 19904 **877-650-1257** 302-734-6720

El Paso Electric Co
100 N Stanton Stanton Tower ....El Paso TX 79901 **800-351-1621** 915-543-5711
NYSE: EE

Elizabethtown Gas Co
1 Elizabethtown Plz 1085 Morris Ave ....Union NJ 07083 **800-242-5830** 908-289-5000

Empire District Electric Co, The
602 Joplin St PO Box 127 ....Joplin MO 64802 **800-206-2300** 417-625-5100
NYSE: EDE

ENMAX Corp 141 50 Ave SE ....Calgary AB T2G4S7 **877-571-7111** 403-245-7222

ENSTAR Natural Gas Co
401 N International Airport Rd ....Anchorage AK 99518 **800-907-9767** 907-277-5551

Entergy Arkansas Inc
425 W Capitol Ave ....Little Rock AR 72201 **800-368-3749**

Entergy Louisiana Inc
639 Loyola Ave ....New Orleans LA 70113 **800-368-3749*** 504-576-6116
Cust Svc

Entergy Mississippi Inc
PO Box 1640 ....Jackson MS 39215 **800-368-3749**

Entergy New Orleans Inc
639 Loyola Ave ....New Orleans LA 70113 **800-368-3749**

Entergy Texas Inc
350 Pine St ....Beaumont TX 77701 **800-368-3749**

EQT Corp
625 Liberty Ave Ste 1700 ....Pittsburgh PA 15222 **800-242-1776** 412-553-5700
NYSE: EQT

Erie County Water Authority (ECWA)
295 Main St Rm 350........................Buffalo NY 14203 **855-748-1076** 716-849-8484

Eversource 56 Prospect St ....Hartford MA 06103 **800-286-2000** 860-665-3495

Florida City Gas (FCG)
955 E 25th St ....Hialeah FL 33013 **800-993-7546**

Florida Power & Light Co (FPL)
700 Universe Blvd ....Juno Beach FL 33408 **800-226-3545** 561-691-7574

Florida Public Utilities Co (FPUC)
401 S Dixie Hwy ....West Palm Beach FL 33401 **800-427-7712**

Gatco Inc
1550 Factor Ave ....San Leandro CA 94577 **800-227-5640** 510-352-8770

GolfBC Holdings Inc
1800-1030 W Georgia St ....Vancouver BC V6E2Y3 **800-446-5322**

Green Brick Partners Inc
2805 Dallas Pkwy Ste 400 ....Plano TX 75093 **800-374-0137** 469-573-6755

Green Mountain Power Corp
163 Acorn Ln ....Colchester VT 05446 **888-835-4672**

HAWAI'I GAS
515 Kamake'e St ....Honolulu HI 96814 **866-499-3941** 808-535-5933

Hawaiian Electric Industries Inc
1001 Bishop St Ste 2900 ....Honolulu HI 96813 **877-871-8461** 808-543-5662

Hydro One Networks Inc
483 Bay St S Tower 8th Fl Reception ....Toronto ON M5G2P5 **877-955-1155** 888-664-9376

Idaho Power Co
1221 W Idaho St ....Boise ID 83702 **800-488-6151** 208-388-2200

Intermountain Gas Co Inc
555 S Cole Rd ....Boise ID 83709 **800-548-3679*** 208-377-6840
Cust Svc

Jfm Enterprises Inc
1770 Corporate Dr Ste 530....................Norcross GA 30093 **800-462-3449** 770-447-9740

Kansas City Power & Light Co
1200 Main ....Kansas City MO 64141 **888-471-5275** 816-556-2200

Kansas Gas Service
7421 W 129th St ....Overland Park KS 66213 **888-482-4950**

Kimble Companies Inc
3596 State Rt 39 NW ....Dover OH 44622 **800-201-0005**

Kinder Morgan Inc KN Energy Retail Div
370 Van Gordon St ....Lakewood CO 80228 **800-232-1627** 303-989-1740

Kissimmee Utility Authority Inc (KUA)
1701 W Carroll St ....Kissimmee FL 34741 **877-582-7700** 407-933-7777

KP Tissue Inc
1900 Minnesota Ct Ste 200 ....Mississauga ON L5N5R5 **866-600-5869** 905-812-6900

Lineage Power Corp
601 Shiloh Rd ....Plano TX 75074 **877-546-3243** 972-244-9288

Long Island Power Authority
333 Earle Ovington Blvd Ste 403 ....Uniondale NY 11553 **877-275-5472*** 516-222-7700
Cust Svc

Madison Gas & Electric Co
133 S Blair St ....Madison WI 53703 **800-245-1125** 608-252-7000

Marts & Lundy Inc
1200 Wall St W ....Lyndhurst NJ 07071 **800-526-9005** 201-460-1660

Merrithew Corp
2200 Yonge St Ste 500.........................Toronto ON M4S2C6 **800-910-0001** 416-482-4050

Middle Tennessee Natural Gas Utility District (MTNG)
1036 W Broad St PO Box 670.................Smithville TN 37166 **800-880-6373** 615-597-4300

Middlesex Water Co
1500 Ronson Rd PO Box 1500 ....Iselin NJ 08830 **800-549-3802** 732-634-1500
NASDAQ: MSEX

Minnesota Power
30 W Superior St ....Duluth MN 55802 **800-228-4966** 218-722-2625

Missouri Gas Energy
3420 Broadway ....Kansas City MO 64111 **800-582-1234** 816-360-5500

Monroe County Water Authority
475 Norris Dr PO Box 10999 ....Rochester NY 14610 **866-426-6292** 585-442-2000

Montana-Dakota Utilities Co (MDU)
400 N Fourth St ....Bismarck ND 58501 **800-638-3278** 701-222-7900

Morris Products Inc
53 Carey Rd ....Queensbury NY 12804 **888-777-6678** 518-743-0523

MRC Global Inc
2 Houston Ctr ....Houston TX 77010 **877-294-7574**

National Fuel Resources Inc
165 Lawrence Bell Dr Ste 120............Williamsville NY 14221 **800-839-9993** 716-630-6778

Nevada Power Co
6226 W Sahara Ave ....Las Vegas NV 89146 **800-331-3103*** 702-402-5555
*NYSE: NVE ■ *Cust Svc*

New York State Electric & Gas Corp
18 Link Dr PO Box 5240....................Binghamton NY 13904 **800-572-1111**

Nippon Kodo Inc
2771 Plaza Del Amo Ste 805 ....Torrance CA 90503 **888-775-5487** 310-320-8881

North Shore Gas Co
3001 Grand Ave ....Waukegan IL 60085 **866-556-6004**

Northern Electric Inc
12789 Emerson St ....Thornton CO 80241 **877-265-0794** 303-428-6969

Northern Kentucky Water District
2835 Crescent Springs Rd ....Erlanger KY 41018 **800-772-4636** 859-578-9898

Northwest Natural Gas Co
220 NW Second Ave ....Portland OR 97209 **800-422-4012** 503-226-4211
NYSE: NWN

Nova Scotia Power Inc
PO Box 910 ....Halifax NS B3J2W5 **800-428-6230** 902-428-6230

OG & E Electric Services
PO Box 24990 ....Oklahoma City OK 73124 **800-272-9741** 405-553-3000

Ohio Edison Co 76 S Main St ....Akron OH 44308 **800-736-3402** 330-436-4122

Oklahoma Natural Gas Co
401 N Harvey PO Box 401 ....Oklahoma City OK 73101 **800-664-5463**

Olympia Financial Group Inc
125 Ninth Ave SE Ste 2300....................Calgary AB T2G0P6 **888-668-8384** 403-668-8384

Oncor
1616 Woodall Rodgers Fwy 2M-012 ....Dallas TX 75202 **888-313-6862*** 888-313-4747
General

				Toll-Free	Phone

Orange & Rockland Utilities Inc
390 W Rte 59 . . . . Spring Valley NY 10977 **877-434-4100***
*Cust Svc

Otter Tail Power Co
215 S Cascade St . . . . Fergus Falls MN 56537 **800-257-4044** 218-739-8200

Pacific Gas & Electric Co
77 Beale St . . . . San Francisco CA 94105 **800-743-5000*** 415-973-7000
*Cust Svc

Pacific Power & Light
825 NE Multnomah St . . . . Portland OR 97232 **888-221-7070*** 503-813-6666
*Cust Svc

PacifiCorp
825 NE Multnomah St . . . . Portland OR 97232 **888-221-7070** 503-813-5000

Parkway Electric Inc
11952 Jarpes St . . . . Holland MI 49424 **800-574-9553**

Passaic Valley Water Commission
1525 Main Ave . . . . Clifton NJ 07011 **877-772-7077** 973-340-4300

Pennichuck Corp
25 Manchester St . . . . Merrimack NH 03054 **800-553-5191** 603-882-5191
NASDAQ: PNNW

Peoples Gas Light & Coke Co
200 E Randolph St . . . . Chicago IL 60601 **866-556-6001*** 312-744-7000
*Cust Svc

Philadelphia Gas Works (PGW)
800 W Montgomery Ave . . . . Philadelphia PA 19122 **800-242-1776** 215-235-1000

Piedmont Natural Gas
4720 Piedmont Row Dr PO Box 33068 . . . . Charlotte NC 28233 **800-752-7504** 704-364-3120
NYSE: PNY

Portland General Electric
121 SW Salmon St . . . . Portland OR 97204 **800-542-8818** 503-464-8000
NYSE: POR

PPL Electric Utilities Corp
827 Hausman Rd . . . . Allentown PA 18104 **800-342-5775*** 800-358-6623
NYSE: PPL ■ *Cust Svc

PPL Global LLC
2 N Ninth St . . . . Allentown PA 18101 **800-345-3085** 610-774-5151
NYSE: PPL

PS Energy Group Inc
4480 N Shallowford Rd Ste 100 . . . . Dunwoody GA 30338 **800-334-7548** 770-350-3000

Public Service Enterprise Group Inc (PSEG)
80 Park Plz . . . . Newark NJ 07102 **800-436-7734**

Public Works Commission of The City of Fayetteville North Carolina
955 Old Wilmington Rd
PO Box 1089 . . . . Fayetteville NC 28301 **877-687-7921** 910-483-1382

Puget Sound Energy Inc
10885 NE Fourth St . . . . Bellevue WA 98004 **888-225-5773** 425-452-1234

Reliant Energy Retail Services LLC
1201 Fannin St . . . . Houston TX 77002 **866-660-4900** 866-222-7100

Rochester Gas & Electric Corp
89 E Ave . . . . Rochester NY 14649 **800-743-2110**

Roland's Electric Inc
307 Suburban Ave . . . . Deer Park NY 11729 **800-981-8010** 631-242-8080

Salt River Project (SRP)
1521 N Project Dr . . . . Tempe AZ 85281 **800-258-4777** 602-236-5900

San Diego Gas & Electric Co
101 Ash St . . . . San Diego CA 92101 **800-411-7343** 619-696-2000

SETEL UC
720 Cool Springs Blvd Ste 520 . . . . Franklin TN 37067 **800-743-1340** 615-874-6000

Sims Recycling Solutions Holdings Inc
1600 Harvester Rd . . . . West Chicago IL 60185 **800-270-8220** 630-231-6060

Southern California Edison Co
2244 Walnut Grove Ave . . . . Rosemead CA 91770 **800-655-4555** 626-302-1212

Southern California Gas Co
555 W Fifth St . . . . Los Angeles CA 90013 **800-427-2200** 909-305-8261

Southern Co
30 Ivan Allen Jr Blvd NW . . . . Atlanta GA 30308 **800-754-9452*** 404-506-5000
*Cust Svc

Southern Connecticut Gas (SCG)
60 Marsh Hill Rd . . . . Orange CT 06477 **866-268-2887**

Southwest Gas Corp
5241 Spring Mtn Rd PO Box 98510 . . . . Las Vegas NV 89193 **877-860-6020** 702-876-7237
NYSE: SWX

Southwest Gas Corp Northern Nevada Div
400 Eagle Stn Ln . . . . Carson City NV 89701 **877-860-6020**

Southwest Gas Corp Southern Arizona Div
PO Box 98512 . . . . Las Vegas NV 89193 **877-860-6020**

Southwest Gas Corp Southern California Div
13471 Mariposa Rd . . . . Victorville CA 92395 **877-860-6020**

Southwest Gas Corp Southern Nevada Div
5241 Spring Mtn Rd . . . . Las Vegas NV 89150 **877-860-6020** 702-876-7011

Southwestern Energy Co
10000 Energy Dr . . . . Spring TX 77389 **866-322-0801** 832-796-1000
NYSE: SWN

Spire 2828 Dauphin St . . . . Mobile AL 36606 **800-837-3374** 251-476-8052

Stream Gas & Electric Ltd
1950 Stemmons Fwy Ste 3000 . . . . Dallas TX 75207 **866-447-8732**

Summer Infant Inc
1275 Park E Dr . . . . Woonsocket RI 02895 **800-268-6237**

Superior Water Light & Power
2915 Hill Ave PO Box 519 . . . . Superior WI 54880 **800-227-7957** 715-394-2200

System Engineering International Inc (SEI)
5115 Pegasus Ct Ste Q . . . . Frederick MD 21704 **800-765-4734** 301-694-9601

Texas-New Mexico Power Co (TNMP)
577 N Garden Ridge Blvd . . . . Lewisville TX 75067 **888-866-7456** 972-420-4189

Toledo Edison Co PO Box 3687 . . . . Akron OH 44309 **800-447-3333**

Total Insight LLC
310 Main Ave Way SE . . . . Hickory NC 28602 **877-226-9950** 828-485-5000

Trans-Tel Central Inc (TTC)
2805 Broce Dr . . . . Norman OK 73072 **800-729-4636** 405-447-5025

Travel Leaders Group LLC
?119 West 40th? St . . . . New York NY 10018 **800-448-3090** 763-744-3700

Tricomm Services Corp
1247 N Church St Ste 12 . . . . Moorestown NJ 08057 **800-872-2401** 856-914-9001

TXU Electric PO Box 65764 . . . . Dallas TX 75262 **800-242-9113** 972-791-2888

United Electric Supply Inc
10 Bellecor Dr . . . . New Castle DE 19720 **800-322-3374** 302-322-3333

United Illuminating Co
157 Church St . . . . New Haven CT 06510 **800-722-5584*** 203-499-2000
*Cust Svc

				Toll-Free	Phone

United States Information Systems Inc (USIS)
35 W Jefferson Ave . . . . Pearl River NY 10965 **866-222-3778** 845-358-7755

Upland Software Inc
Frost Tower 401 Congress Ave Ste 2950 . . . . Austin TX 78701 **855-944-7526**

Viair Corp 15 Edelman . . . . Irvine CA 92618 **800-618-1994** 949-585-0011

Virginia American Water Co (VAWC)
2223 Duke St . . . . Alexandria VA 22314 **800-452-6863** 703-706-3879

We Energies
231 W Michigan St PO Box 2046 . . . . Milwaukee WI 53203 **800-242-9137** 414-221-2345

Wisconsin Power & Light Co
4902 N Biltmore Ln PO Box 77007 . . . . Madison WI 53718 **800-255-4268**

Wisconsin Public Service Corp
PO Box 19001 . . . . Green Bay WI 54307 **800-450-7260**

Xcel Energy Inc
414 Nicollet Mall . . . . Minneapolis MN 55401 **800-328-8226** 612-330-5500
NYSE: XEL

York Water Co, The
130 E Market St . . . . York PA 17401 **800-750-5561** 717-845-3601
NASDAQ: YORW

Yucaipa Valley Water District
PO Box 730 . . . . Yucaipa CA 92399 **800-304-2226** 909-797-5117

783   VACUUM CLEANERS - HOUSEHOLD

SEE ALSO Appliances - Small - Mfr

				Toll-Free	Phone

Bissell Inc
2345 Walker NW . . . . Grand Rapids MI 49544 **800-237-7691** 616-453-4451

CentralVac International
23455 Hellman Ave PO Box 259 . . . . Dollar Bay MI 49922 **800-666-3133**

Electrolux Home Care Products Inc
PO Box 3900 . . . . Peoria IL 61612 **800-282-2886***
*Cust Svc

Kirby Co 1920 W 114th St . . . . Cleveland OH 44102 **800-437-7170** 216-228-2400

Lindsay Manufacturing Inc
PO Box 1708 . . . . Ponca City OK 74602 **800-546-3729** 580-762-2457

Metropolitan Vacuum Cleaner Co Inc
5 Raritan Rd . . . . Oakland NJ 07436 **800-822-1602** 845-357-1600

Oreck Corp 1400 Salem Rd . . . . Cookeville TN 38506 **800-289-5888**

784   VALVES - INDUSTRIAL

				Toll-Free	Phone

American Cast Iron Pipe Co (ACIPCO)
1501 31st Ave N . . . . Birmingham AL 35207 **800-442-2347** 205-325-7701

Anderson Brass Co
1629 W Bobo Newsome Hwy . . . . Hartsville SC 29550 **800-476-9876** 843-332-4111

Armstrong International Inc
2081 SE Ocean Blvd 4th Fl . . . . Stuart FL 34996 **866-738-5125** 772-286-7175

Barksdale Inc
3211 Fruitland Ave . . . . Los Angeles CA 90058 **800-835-1060** 323-589-6181

C&D Valve Manufacturing Co
201 NW 67th St . . . . Oklahoma City OK 73116 **800-654-9233** 405-843-5621

Cash Acme Inc
2727 Paces Ferry Rd SE Ste 1800 . . . . Atlanta GA 30339 **877-700-4242**

Circle Seal Controls Inc
2301 Wardlow Cir . . . . Corona CA 92880 **800-991-2726** 951-270-6200

Clow Valve Co
902 S Second St . . . . Oskaloosa IA 52577 **800-829-2569** 641-673-8611

Crane Company Stockham Div
2129 Third Ave SE . . . . Cullman AL 35055 **800-786-2542** 203-363-7300

Engineered Controls International Inc (ECII)
100 Rego Dr PO Box 247 . . . . Elon NC 27244 **800-650-0061** 336-449-7707

Fike Corp
704 SW Tenth St . . . . Blue Springs MO 64015 **877-342-3453** 816-229-3405

Flowserve Corp
5215 N O'Connor Blvd Ste 2300 . . . . Irving TX 75039 **800-543-3927** 972-443-6500
NYSE: FLS

Gemini Valve 2 Otter Ct . . . . Raymond NH 03077 **800-370-0936** 603-895-4761

Goulds Pumps Inc Goulds Water Technologies Group
240 Fall St . . . . Seneca Falls NY 13148 **800-327-7700** 315-568-2811

Griswold Industries
1701 Placentia Ave . . . . Costa Mesa CA 92627 **800-942-6326** 949-722-4800

Groth Corp
13650 N Promenade Blvd . . . . Stafford TX 77477 **800-354-7684** 281-295-6800

High Vacuum Apparatus LLC (HVA)
12880 Moya Blvd . . . . Reno NV 89506 **800-551-4422** 775-359-4442

Hudson Valve Company Inc
5301 Office Pk Dr Ste 330 . . . . Bakersfield CA 93309 **800-748-6218** 661-869-1126

Humphrey Products Co
5070 E N Ave PO Box 2008 . . . . Kalamazoo MI 49048 **800-477-8707**

Hunt Valve Company Inc
1913 E State St . . . . Salem OH 44460 **800-321-2757** 330-337-9535

ITT Goulds Pumps Industries/Goulds Industrial Pumps Group
240 Fall St . . . . Seneca Falls NY 13148 **800-327-7700** 315-568-2811

ITT Industries Inc Engineered Valves Div
33 Centerville Rd . . . . Lancaster PA 17603 **800-366-1111** 717-509-2200

Kennedy Valve
1021 E Water St . . . . Elmira NY 14902 **800-782-5831** 607-734-2211

Kraft Fluid Systems Inc
14300 Foltz Pkwy . . . . Strongsville OH 44149 **800-257-1155** 440-238-5545

Lee Co
2 Pellitaug Rd PO Box 424 . . . . Westbrook CT 06498 **800-533-7584** 860-399-6281

Leonard Valve Co
1360 Elmwood Ave . . . . Cranston RI 02910 **800-222-1208** 401-461-1200

Leslie Controls Inc
12501 Telecom Dr . . . . Tampa FL 33637 **800-323-8366** 813-978-1000

Mac Valves Inc 30569 Beck Rd . . . . Wixom MI 48393 **800-622-8587** 248-624-7700

Marotta Controls Inc
78 Boonton Ave PO Box 427 . . . . Montville NJ 07045 **888-627-6882** 973-334-7800

McDantim Inc 750 Shepard Way . . . . Helena MT 59601 **888-735-5607** 406-442-5153

McWane Inc
2900 Hwy 280 Ste 300 . . . . Birmingham AL 35223 **800-634-4746** 205-414-3100

Miller Energy Inc
3200 S Clinton Ave . . . . South Plainfield NJ 07080 **800-631-5454** 908-755-6700

			Toll-Free	Phone
Milwaukee Valve Company Inc				
16550 W Stratton Dr	New Berlin WI	53151	800-348-6544	262-432-2800
Mueller Co				
500 W Eldorado St	Decatur IL	62522	800-423-1323	217-423-4471
NIBCO Inc				
1516 Middlebury St	Elkhart IN	46515	800-234-0227	574-295-3000
Ogontz Corp				
2835 Terwood Rd	Willow Grove PA	19090	800-523-2478	215-657-4770
Parker Hannifin Corp Hydraulic Valve Div				
520 Ternes Ave	Elyria OH	44035	800-272-7537	440-366-5200
Parker Instrumentation Group				
6035 Parkland Blvd	Cleveland OH	44124	800-272-7537	216-896-3000
Peter Paul Electronics Co Inc				
480 John Downey Dr	New Britain CT	06051	800-825-8377	860-229-4884
Plattco Corp 7 White St	Plattsburgh NY	12901	800-352-1731	518-563-4640
Richards Industries Inc				
3170 Wasson Rd	Cincinnati OH	45209	800-543-7311*	513-533-5600
*Cust Svc				
Robert H Wager Co				
570 Montroyal Rd	Rural Hall NC	27045	800-562-7024	336-969-6909
Salina Vortex Corp				
1725 Vortex Ave	Salina KS	67401	888-829-7821	
Sherwood 2200 N Main St	Washington PA	15301	888-508-2583	724-225-8000
Spence Engineering Company Inc				
150 Coldenham Rd	Walden NY	12586	800-398-2493	845-778-5566
Taylor Valve Technology Inc				
8300 SW 8th	Oklahoma City OK	73128	800-805-3401	405-787-0145
United Brass Works Inc				
714 S Main St	Randleman NC	27317	800-334-3035	336-498-2661

785   VALVES & HOSE FITTINGS - FLUID POWER

SEE ALSO Carburetors, Pistons, Piston Rings, Valves

			Toll-Free	Phone
Air-Way Manufacturing Co				
586 N Main St	Olivet MI	49076	800-253-1036*	269-749-2161
*Cust Svc				
Arkwin Industries Inc				
686 Main St	Westbury NY	11590	800-284-2551	516-333-2640
Bosch Rexroth				
14001 S Lakes Dr	Charlotte NC	28273	800-739-7684	330-263-3300
Civacon				
4304 N Mattox Rd	Kansas City MO	64150	888-526-5657*	816-741-6600
*Sales				
Clippard Instrument Lab				
7390 Colerain Ave	Cincinnati OH	45239	877-245-6247	513-521-4261
Control Flow Inc				
9201 Fairbanks N Houston Rd	Houston TX	77064	800-231-9922	281-890-8300
Daman Products Co Inc				
1811 N Home St	Mishawaka IN	46545	800-959-7841	574-259-7841
Deltrol Fluid Products				
3001 Grant Ave	Bellwood IL	60104	800-477-9772	708-547-0500
Dixon Valve & Coupling Company Inc				
800 High St	Chestertown MD	21620	877-963-4966	410-778-2000
Dynaquip Controls				
10 Harris Industrial Pk	Saint Clair MO	63077	800-545-3636	636-629-3700
E H Lynn Industries Inc				
524 Anderson Dr	Romeoville IL	60446	800-633-2948	815-328-8800
Fresno Valves & Castings Inc				
7736 E Springfield Ave PO Box 40	Selma CA	93662	800-333-1658	559-834-2511
Hays Fluid Controls				
114 Eason Rd	Dallas NC	28034	800-354-4297	704-922-9565
Henry Pratt Co				
401 S Highland Ave	Aurora IL	60506	877-436-7977	630-844-4000
Hunt Valve Company Inc				
1913 E State St	Salem OH	44460	800-321-2757	330-337-9535
Hyson Products				
10367 Brecksville Rd	Brecksville OH	44141	800-876-4976	440-526-5900
ITT Industries Inc				
1133 Westchester Ave	White Plains NY	10604	800-254-2823	914-641-2000
NYSE: ITT				
JD Gould Co Inc				
4707 Massachusetts Ave	Indianapolis IN	46218	800-634-6853	
Jetstream of Houston LLP				
4930 Cranswick	Houston TX	77041	800-231-8192	713-462-7000
Mead Fluid Dynamics Inc				
4114 N Knox Ave	Chicago IL	60641	877-632-3872*	773-685-6800
*Cust Svc				
Morrison Bros Co				
570 E Seventh St	Dubuque IA	52001	800-553-4840	563-583-5701
Norgren				
5400 S Delaware St	Littleton CO	80120	800-514-0129	303-794-5000
Omega Flex Inc				
451 Creamery Way	Exton PA	19341	800-355-1039	610-524-7272
NASDAQ: OFLX				
Parker Fluid Connectors Group				
6035 Parkland Blvd	Cleveland OH	44124	800-272-7537*	216-896-3000
*General				
Parker Hannifin Corp Brass Products Div				
6035 Parkland Blvd	Otsego MI	49078	800-272-7537	269-694-9411
Parker Hannifin Corp General Valve Div				
26 Clinton Dr Unit 103	Hollis NH	03049	800-272-7537	
Parker Hannifin Corp Pneumatic Div				
8676 E M 89	Richland MI	49083	877-321-4736	269-629-5000
Parker Hannifin Corp Skinner Valve Div				
95 Edgewood Ave	New Britain CT	06051	800-825-8305	860-827-2300
PBM Inc 1070 Sandy Hill Rd	Irwin PA	15642	800-967-4726	724-863-0550
PerkinElmer Inc				
940 Winter St	Waltham MA	02451	800-762-4000	781-663-6050
NYSE: PKI				
Plattco Corp 7 White St	Plattsburgh NY	12901	800-352-1731	518-563-4640
Rexarc Inc				
35 E Third St	West Alexandria OH	45381	877-739-2721	937-839-4604
Richards Industries Inc				
3170 Wasson Rd	Cincinnati OH	45209	800-543-7311*	513-533-5600
*Cust Svc				

			Toll-Free	Phone
Ross Controls				
1250 Stephenson Hwy	Troy MI	48083	800-438-7677	248-764-1800
Rupe's Hydraulics Sales & Service				
725 N Twin Oaks Valley Rd	San Marcos CA	92069	800-354-7873	760-744-9350
Specialty Manufacturing Co				
5858 Centerville Rd	Saint Paul MN	55127	800-549-4473	651-653-0599
Universal Valve Company Inc				
478 Schiller St	Elizabeth NJ	07206	800-223-0741	908-351-0606

786   VARIETY STORES

			Toll-Free	Phone
1800PetSuppliescom				
395 Oakhill Rd Ste 210	Mountain Top PA	18707	800-738-7877	
99 Cents Only Stores				
4000 Union Pacific Ave	Commerce CA	90023	888-582-5999	323-980-8145
AC Doctor LLC				
2151 W Hillsboro Blvd Ste 400	Deerfield Beach FL	33442	866-264-1479	
All Graphic Supplies				
6691 Edwards Blvd	Mississauga ON	L5T2H8	800-501-4451	
American Muscle 7 Lee Blvd	Malvern PA	19355	888-332-7930	610-251-2397
AutoTruckToyscom				
2814 W Wood St	Paris TN	38242	800-544-6194	731-642-3535
Best Impressions Catalog Co				
345 N Lewis Ave	Oglesby IL	61348	800-635-2378	815-883-3532
Big Lots Inc (BLI)				
300 Phillipi Rd	Columbus OH	43228	877-998-1697	614-278-6800
NYSE: BIG				
Black Forest Decor LLC				
PO Box 297	Jenks OK	74037	800-605-0915	
Blocker & Wallace Service LLC				
1472 Rogers Ave	Memphis TN	38114	800-843-0551	901-274-0708
Camping World RV Sales				
8155 Rivers Ave	Charleston SC	29406	888-586-5446	888-471-3171
Clubfurniturecom				
11535 Carmel Commons Blvd Ste 202	Charlotte NC	28226	888-378-8383	
Coast Guard Exchange System				
510 Independence Pkwy Ste 500	Chesapeake VA	23320	800-572-0230	
DeMesy & Company Ltd				
4514 Cole Ave Ste 808	Dallas TX	75205	800-635-9006	214-855-8777
Diamond Attachments LLC				
2801A S Mississippi	Atoka OK	74525	800-445-1917	580-889-6202
Dollar General Corp				
100 Mission Rdg	Goodlettsville TN	37072	800-678-9258	615-855-4000
NYSE: DG				
Dollar Tree Stores Inc				
500 Volvo Pkwy	Chesapeake VA	23320	877-530-8733	
NASDAQ: DLTR				
Easy Ice LLC				
925 W Washington St Ste 100	Marquette MI	49855	866-327-9423	
Exchange, The				
3911 S Walton Walker Blvd	Dallas TX	75236	800-527-2345	
Family Dollar Stores Inc				
PO Box 1017	Charlotte NC	28201	866-377-6420	844-636-7687
NASDAQ: DLTR				
Howell Tractor & Equipment LLC				
480 Blaine St	Gary IN	46406	800-852-8816	
Hubbard`s Impala Parts Inc				
1676 Anthony Rd	Burlington NC	27215	800-846-7252	336-227-1589
K&D Pratt				
126 Glencoe Dr	Mount Pearl NL	A1N4S9	800-563-9595	709-722-5690
Kerley & Sears Inc				
4331 Cement Valley Rd	Midlothian TX	76065	800-346-4381	972-775-3902
Kryptonite Kollectibles				
1441 Plainfield Ave	Janesville WI	53545	877-646-1728	608-758-2100
Leeco Steel LLC				
1011 Warrenville Rd Ste 500	Lisle IL	60532	800-621-4366	630-427-2100
Lynch Metals Inc				
1075 Lousons Rd	Union NJ	07083	888-272-9464	908-686-8401
McVean Trading & Investments LLC				
850 Ridge Lake Blvd Ste One	Memphis TN	38120	800-374-1937	901-761-8400
Middlesex Gases & Technologies Inc				
292 Second St PO Box 490249	Everett MA	02149	800-649-6704	617-387-5050
Navy Exchange Service Command (NEXCOM)				
3280 Virginia Beach Blvd	Virginia Beach VA	23452	800-628-3924	757-463-6200
New Vitality				
260 Smith St	Farmingdale NY	11735	888-997-2941	888-271-7599
Ollie's Bargain Outlet Inc				
6295 Allentown Blvd Ste 1	Harrisburg PA	17112	800-219-7052	717-657-2300
Overstockcom Inc				
6350 South 3000 East	Salt Lake City UT	84121	800-843-2446*	801-947-3100
*NASDAQ: OSTK ■ *Cust Svc				
PB Hoidale Company Inc				
3801 W Harry	Wichita KS	67213	800-362-0784	316-942-1361
Peach Trader Inc				
6286 Dawson Blvd	Norcross GA	30093	888-949-9613	404-752-6715
Playscripts				
7 Penn Plz Ste 904	New York NY	10001	866-639-7529	
PLH Products Inc				
6655 Knott Ave	Buena Park CA	90620	800-946-6001	714-739-6600
Pride Products Corp				
4333 Veterans Memorial Hwy	Ronkonkoma NY	11779	800-898-5550	631-737-4444
Quadratec Inc				
1028 Saunders Ln	West Chester PA	19380	800-745-6037	
R J Schinner Company Inc				
16950 W Lincoln Ave	New Berlin WI	53151	800-234-1460	262-797-7180
Rakutencom Shopping				
85 Enterprise St	Aliso Viejo CA	92656	800-800-0800	949-389-2000
Rally House & Kansas Sampler				
9750 Quivira Rd	Lenexa KS	66215	800-645-5409	
Rennco LLC 300 Elm St	Homer MI	49245	800-409-5225	
Scout shop PO Box 7143	Charlotte NC	28241	800-323-0736	
SelecTransportation Resources LLC				
9550 N Loop E	Houston TX	77029	800-299-4200	713-672-4115
Shopletcom				
39 Broadway Ste 2030	New York NY	10006	800-757-3015	

Variety Stores (Cont'd)

Name / Address	City	ST	ZIP	Toll-Free	Phone
Southern Company of NLR Inc, The 1201 N Cypress St	North Little Rock	AR	72114	800-482-5493	501-376-6333
Speedway Motors 340 Victory Ln	Lincoln	NE	68528	800-736-3733	800-979-0122
Store Supply Warehouse LLC 9801 Page Ave	St Louis	MO	63132	800-823-0004	314-427-8887
TechStar 802 W 13th St	Deer Park	TX	77536	866-542-0205	
Tiger Supplies Inc 27 Selvage St	Irvington	NJ	07111	888-844-3765	
Trydor Industries (Canada) Ltd 19275 - 25th Ave	Surrey	BC	V3Z3X1	800-567-8558	604-542-4773
Turbo International Inc 2151 Las Palmas Dr Ste E	Carlsbad	CA	92011	800-238-8726	760-476-1444
U-line Corp 8900 N 55th St	Milwaukee	WI	53223	800-779-2547	414-354-0300
Vermeer Mid Atlantic Inc 10900 Carpet St	Charlotte	NC	28273	800-768-3444	704-588-3238
West Springfield Auto Parts 92 Blandin Ave	Framingham	MA	01702	800-615-2392	508-879-6932
Western United Electric Supply Corp 100 Bromley Business Pkwy	Brighton	CO	80603	800-748-3116	303-659-2356

787   VENTURE CAPITAL FIRMS

Companies listed here are investors, not lenders.

Name / Address	City	ST	ZIP	Toll-Free	Phone
Adobe Ventures LP 345 Park Ave	San Jose	CA	95110	877-722-7088	408-536-6000
American Bullion Inc 12301 Wilshire Blvd Ste 650	Los Angeles	CA	90025	800-326-9598	800-465-3472
American Capital Group Inc 23382 Mill Creek Dr Ste 115	Laguna Hills	CA	92653	877-814-6871	949-271-5800
Battery Ventures 1 Marina Pk Dr Ste 1100	Boston	MA	02210	800-449-0645	617-948-3600
BTG International Inc 5 Tower Bridge 300 Barr Harbor Dr Ste 810	West Conshohocken	PA	19428	888-327-1027	610-278-1660
CIBC Wood Gundy Capital 425 Lexington Ave	New York	NY	10017	800-999-6726	212-856-4000
Edison Venture Fund 281 Witherspoon St	Princeton	NJ	08540	800-899-3975	609-896-1900
EQUUS Total Return Inc 700 Louisiana St 48th Fl	Houston	TX	77002	888-323-4533	
Harvest Partners 280 Park Ave 25th Fl	New York	NY	10017	866-771-1000	212-599-6300
InterWest Partners 2710 Sand Hill Rd Ste 200	Menlo Park	CA	94025	866-803-9204	650-854-8585
INVESCO Private Capital Inc 1166 Ave of the Americas 26th Fl	New York	NY	10036	800-959-4246	212-278-9000
LMCG Investments LLC 200 Clarendon St 28th Fl	Boston	MA	02116	877-241-5191	617-380-5600
MDT Advisors Inc 125 High St Oliver St Twr 21st Fl	Boston	MA	02110	800-685-4277	617-235-7100
Mesirow Financial Private Equity 353 N Clark St	Chicago	IL	60654	800-453-0600	312-595-6000
Morgan Stanley Venture Partners 1585 Broadway	New York	NY	10036	866-722-7310	212-761-4000
Northleaf Capital Partners 79 Wellington St W 6th Fl PO Box 120	Toronto	ON	M5K1N9	866-964-4141	
Pomona Capital 780 Third Ave 46th Fl	New York	NY	10017	800-992-0180	
Private Capital Management 8889 Pelican Bay Blvd Ste 500	Naples	FL	34108	800-763-0337	239-254-2500
Technology Funding Inc 460 St Michael's Dr Ste 1000	Santa Fe	NM	87505	800-821-5323	
TEOCO Corp 12150 Monument Dr Ste 400	Fairfax	VA	22033	888-868-3626	703-322-9200
Tortoise Energy Capital Corp 11550 Ash St Ste 300. NYSE: TTP	Leawood	KS	66211	866-362-9331	913-981-1020
UPS Strategic Enterprise Fund 55 Glenlake Pkwy NE Bldg 1 4th Fl	Atlanta	GA	30328	800-742-5877	

788   VETERANS NURSING HOMES - STATE

SEE ALSO Veterans Hospitals

Name / Address	City	ST	ZIP	Toll-Free	Phone
Angels of the Valley Hospice Care 2600 Foothill Blvd Ste 202	La Crescenta	CA	91214	888-344-0880	818-542-3070
Colorado State Veterans Nursing Home-Rifle 851 E Fifth St	Rifle	CO	81650	800-828-4580	970-625-0842
DJ Jacobetti Home for Veterans 425 Fisher St	Marquette	MI	49855	800-433-6760	906-226-3576
Floyd E Tut Fann State Veterans Home 2701 Meridian St	Huntsville	AL	35811	855-212-8028	256-851-2807
Grand Island Veterans' Home 2300 W Capital Ave	Grand Island	NE	68803	800-358-8802	308-385-6252
Idaho State Veterans Home-Pocatello 1957 Alvin Ricken Dr	Pocatello	ID	83201	855-488-8440	208-235-7800
Illinois Veterans Home-Anna 792 N Main St	Anna	IL	62906	800-437-9824	618-833-6302
Indiana Veterans Home 3851 N River Rd	West Lafayette	IN	47906	800-400-4520	765-463-1502
Iowa Veterans Home 7105 NW 70th Ave Camp Dodge Bldg 3465	Johnston	IA	50131	800-838-4692	515-252-4698
Maine Veterans' Homes 310 Cony Rd	Augusta	ME	04330	800-278-9494	207-622-2454
Maine Veterans' Homes 460 Civic Center Dr	Augusta	ME	04330	800-278-9494	
Medicalodges Inc 201 W Eighth St	Coffeyville	KS	67337	800-782-0120	
Mega Care 1883 Whitney Mesa Dr	Henderson	NV	89014	888-883-6342	626-382-9492

Name / Address	City	ST	ZIP	Toll-Free	Phone
Minnesota Veterans Home-Fergus Falls 1821 N Park St	Fergus Falls	MN	56537	877-838-4633	218-736-0400
Minnesota Veterans Home-Minneapolis 5101 Minnehaha Ave S	Minneapolis	MN	55417	877-838-6757	612-548-5700
Minnesota Veterans Home-Silver Bay 56 Outer Dr	Silver Bay	MN	55614	877-729-8387	218-353-8700
Mississippi State Veterans' Home Collins 3261 Hwy 49 S	Collins	MS	39428	877-203-5632	601-765-0403
Missouri Department Of Public Safety Veterans Commission 1600 S Hickory	Mount Vernon	MO	65712	866-838-4636	417-466-7103
Missouri Veterans Home-Cape Girardeau 2400 Veterans Memorial Dr	Cape Girardeau	MO	63701	800-392-0210	573-290-5870
Veterans Home 400 Veterans Dr	Columbia Falls	MT	59912	888-279-7532	406-892-3256
New Mexico State Veterans Ctr 992 S Broadway St	Truth or Consequences	NM	87901	800-964-3976	575-894-4200
Ohio Veterans Home 3416 Columbus Ave *Admissions	Sandusky	OH	44870	800-572-7934*	419-625-2454
Oklahoma Veterans Ctr Ardmore 1015 S Commerce	Ardmore	OK	73401	800-941-2160	580-223-2266
Oklahoma Veterans Ctr Norman 1776 E Robinson St	Norman	OK	73071	800-782-5218	405-360-5600
Oklahoma Veterans Ctr Talihina 10014 SE 1138th Ave PO Box 1168	Talihina	OK	74571	800-941-2160	918-567-2251
Oregon Veterans' Home 700 Veterans Dr	The Dalles	OR	97058	800-846-8460	541-296-7190
Pearl City Nursing Home 919 Lehua Ave	Pearl City	HI	96782	800-596-0026	808-453-1919
Thomson-Hood Veterans Ctr 100 Veterans Dr	Wilmore	KY	40390	800-928-4838	859-858-2814
Veterans Home 1200 E 18th St	Hastings	MN	55033	877-838-3803	651-539-2400
Veterans Home of California-Barstow 100 E Veterans Pkwy	Barstow	CA	92311	800-746-0606	760-252-6200
Veterans Home of California-Chula Vista 700 E Naples Ct	Chula Vista	CA	91911	800-952-5626	
Wisconsin Veterans Home N2665 County Rd QQ	King	WI	54946	877-944-6667	715-258-5586

789   VETERINARY HOSPITALS

Name / Address	City	ST	ZIP	Toll-Free	Phone
Abita Trace Animal Clinic 69142 Hwy 59 Ste E	Mandeville	LA	70471	800-640-3274	985-892-5656
Banfield the Pet Hospital 18101 SE Sixth Way	Vancouver	WA	98683	866-894-7927	
Ieh Laboratories & Consulting Group 15300 Bothell Way NE	Lake Forest Park	WA	98155	800-491-7745	
Imex Veterinary Inc 1001 Mckesson Dr	Longview	TX	75604	800-828-4639	903-295-2196
Millburn Veterinary Hospital 147 Millburn Ave	Millburn	NJ	07041	800-365-8295	973-467-1700
National Veterinary Associates Inc 29229 Canwood St Ste 100	Agoura Hills	CA	91301	888-767-7755	805-777-7722
Oradell Animal Hospital Inc 580 Winters Ave	Paramus	NJ	07652	800-624-1883	201-262-0010
Penn Veterinary Supply Inc 53 Industrial Cir	Lancaster	PA	17601	800-233-0210	717-656-4121
Pipestone Veterinary Clinic LLC 1300 Hwy 75 S PO Box 188	Pipestone	MN	56164	800-658-2523	507-825-4211
PJ Noah PetSalon 27762 Antonio Pkwy Ste L1-622	Ladera Ranch	CA	92694	855-577-7669	
Radiocat 32-A Mellor Ave	Baltimore	MD	21228	800-323-9729	
United Pet Care LLC 6232 N Seventh St Ste 202	Phoenix	AZ	85014	877-872-8800	602-266-5303
VDx Veterinary Diagnostics Inc 2019 Anderson Rd Ste C	Davis	CA	95616	877-753-4285	530-753-4285
Vet-Stem Inc 12860 Danielson Ct Ste B	Poway	CA	92064	888-387-8361	858-748-2004
Western Veterinary Conference 2425 E Oquendo Rd	Las Vegas	NV	89120	866-800-7326	702-739-6698

790   VETERINARY MEDICAL ASSOCIATIONS - STATE

Name / Address	City	ST	ZIP	Toll-Free	Phone
Alaska State Veterinary Medical Assn (AKVMA) 1731 Bragaw St	Anchorage	AK	99508	800-272-1813	907-205-4272
Georgia Veterinary Medical Assn 2200 Century Pkwy Ste 725	Atlanta	GA	30345	800-853-1625	678-309-9800
Indiana Veterinary Medical Assn 1202 E 38th St Discovery Hall Ste 200	Indianapolis	IN	46205	800-270-0747	317-974-0888
Iowa Veterinary Medical Assn 1605 North Ankeny Blvd Ste 110	Ankeny	IA	50023	800-369-9564	515-965-9237
Kentucky Veterinary Medical Assn 108 Consumer Ln	Frankfort	KY	40601	800-552-5862	502-226-5862
Louisiana Veterinary Medical Assn 8550 United Plaza Blvd Ste 1001	Baton Rouge	LA	70809	800-524-2996	225-928-5862
Maine Veterinary Medical Assn (MVMA) 97A Exchange St Ste 305	Portland	ME	04101	800-448-2772	
New York State Veterinary Medical Society 300 Great Oaks Blvd Ste 314	Albany	NY	12203	800-876-9867	518-869-7867
North Carolina Veterinary Medical Assn (NCVMA) 1611 Jones Franklin Rd Ste 108	Raleigh	NC	27606	800-446-2862	919-851-5850
Ohio Veterinary Medical Assn (OVMA) 3168 Riverside Dr	Columbus	OH	43221	800-662-6862	614-486-7253
Oregon Veterinary Medical Assn 1880 Lancaster Dr NE Ste 118	Salem	OR	97305	800-235-3502	503-399-0311
South Carolina Assn of Veterinarians PO Box 11766	Columbia	SC	29211	800-441-7228	803-254-1027
Tennessee Veterinary Medical Assn PO Box 803	Fayetteville	TN	37334	800-697-3587	931-438-0070
Texas Veterinary Medical Assn 8104 Exchange Dr	Austin	TX	78754	800-711-0023	512-452-4224

			Toll-Free	Phone

Virginia Veterinary Medical Assn (VVMA)
3801 Westerre Pkwy Ste D ....Henrico VA 23233 **800-937-8862** 804-346-2611
Washington State Veterinary Medical Assn
8024 Bracken Pl SE ....Snoqualmie WA 98065 **800-399-7862** 425-396-3191
Wisconsin Veterinary Medical Assn (WVMA)
2801 Crossroads Dr Ste 1200 ....Madison WI 53718 **888-254-5202** 608-257-3665
Wyoming Veterinary Medical Assn (WVMA)
2001 Capitol Ave ....Cheyenne WY 82001 **800-272-1813**

791   VIATICAL SETTLEMENT COMPANIES

A viatical settlement is the sale of an existing life insurance policy by a terminally ill person to a third party in return for a percentage of the face value of the policy paid immediately.

			Toll-Free	Phone

Coventry First LLC
7111 Vly Green Rd ....Fort Washington PA 19034 **877-836-8300**
Crystal Wealth Management System Ltd
3385 Harvester Rd Ste 200 ....Burlington ON L7N3N2 **877-299-2854** 905-332-4414
Founders Financial Inc
1020 Cromwell Bridge Rd ....Towson MD 21286 **800-288-3035** 410-308-9988
Francis Investment Counsel LLC
19435 W Capitol Dr ....Brookfield WI 53045 **866-232-6457**
Habersham Funding LLC
3495 Piedmont Rd NE Ste 910 ....Atlanta GA 30305 **888-874-2402** 404-233-8275
Indiana Trust & Investment Management Co
4045 Edison Lakes Pkwy Ste 100 ....Mishawaka IN 46545 **800-362-7905** 574-271-3400
Life Settlement Solutions Inc
9201 Spectrum Ctr Blvd Ste 105 ....San Diego CA 92123 **800-762-3387** 858-576-8067
Page & Assoc Inc
1979 Lakeside Pkwy Ste 200 ....Tucker GA 30084 **800-252-5282**
Pembroke Management Ltd
1002 Sherbrooke St W Ste 1700 ....Montreal QC H3A3S4 **800-667-0716** 514-848-1991
Reilly Financial Advisors
7777 Alvarado Rd Ste 116 ....La Mesa CA 91942 **800-682-3237**
Reinhart Partners Inc
1500 W Market St ....Mequon WI 53092 **800-969-1159** 262-241-2020
Winfield Associatoc Inc
700 W St Clair Ave Ste 404 ....Cleveland OH 44113 **888-322-2575** 216-241-2575

792   VIDEO STORES

SEE ALSO Book, Music, Video Clubs

			Toll-Free	Phone

Amazoncom Inc
1200 12th Ave S Ste 1200 ....Seattle WA 98144 **800-201-7575*** 206-266-1000
NASDAQ: AMZN ■ *Cust Svc
Best Buy Company Inc
7601 Penn Ave S ....Richfield MN 55423 **888-237-8289** 612-291-1000
NYSE: BBY
DVD Empire
2140 Woodland Rd ....Warrendale PA 15086 **888-383-1880**
Facets Multimedia Inc
1517 W Fullerton Ave ....Chicago IL 60614 **800-331-6197*** 773-281-9075
*Cust Svc
Family Video
2500 Lehigh Ave ....Glenview IL 60026 **888-332-6843** 847-904-9000
NetFlix Inc
100 Winchester Cir ....Los Gatos CA 95032 **866-579-7293** 408-540-3700
NASDAQ: NFLX

793   VISION CORRECTION CENTERS

			Toll-Free	Phone

Barnet-Dulaney Eye Ctr
4800 N 22nd St ....Phoenix AZ 85016 **866-742-6581** 602-955-1000
Carolina Eye Assoc PA
2170 Midland Rd ....Southern Pines NC 28387 **800-733-5357** 910-295-2100
Eye Centers of Florida (ECOF)
4101 Evans Ave ....Fort Myers FL 33901 **888-393-2455** 239-939-3456
John-Kenyon Eye Ctr
1305 Wall St ....Jeffersonville IN 47130 **800-342-5393**
Jones Eye Clinic
4405 Hamilton Blvd ....Sioux City IA 51104 **800-334-2015** 712-239-3937
LaserVue Eye Ctr
3540 Mendocino Ave #200 ....Santa Rosa CA 95403 **888-527-3745** 707-522-6200
Minnesota Eye Consultants PA
710 E 24th St Ste 100 ....Minneapolis MN 55404 **800-526-7632** 612-813-3600
Pacific Cataract & Laser Institute
2517 NE Kresky Ave ....Chehalis WA 98532 **800-888-9903** 360-748-8632
TLC Vision Corp
50 Burnhamthorpe Rd W Ste 101 ....Mississauga ON L5B3C2 **877-852-2020**
Will Vision & Laser Centers
8100 NE Pkwy Dr Ste 125 ....Vancouver WA 98662 **877-542-3937**

794   VITAMINS & NUTRITIONAL SUPPLEMENTS

SEE ALSO Diet & Health Foods ; Medicinal Chemicals & Botanical Products ; Pharmaceutical Companies ; Pharmaceutical Companies - Generic Drugs

			Toll-Free	Phone

ADM Natural Health & Nutrition
Archer Daniels Midland Co
4666 Faries Pkwy ....Decatur IL 62526 **800-637-5843** 217-451-7231
AST Sports Science Inc
120 Capitol Dr ....Golden CO 80401 **800-627-2788** 303-278-1420
Atkins Nutritionals Inc
1225 17th St Ste 1000 ....Denver CO 80202 **800-628-5467**
Beehive Botanicals Inc
16297 W Nursery Rd ....Hayward WI 54843 **800-233-4483** 715-634-4274

			Toll-Free	Phone

Cc Pollen Co
3627 E Indian School Rd Ste 209 ....Phoenix AZ 85018 **800-875-0096**
CytoSport
1340 Treat Blvd Ste 350 ....Walnut Creek CA 94597 **888-298-6629**
Douglas Laboratories Inc
600 Boyce Rd ....Pittsburgh PA 15205 **800-245-4440**
Edom Laboratories Inc
100 E Jefryn Blvd Ste M ....Deer Park NY 11729 **800-723-3366** 631-586-2266
Enzymatic Therapy
825 Challenger Dr ....Green Bay WI 54311 **800-783-2286** 920-469-1313
Foodscience Corp
20 New England Dr Ste 10 ....Essex Junction VT 05452 **800-451-5190** 802-878-5508
Fruitful Yield Inc
229 W Roosevelt Rd ....Lombard IL 60148 **800-469-5552**
Garden of Life Inc
4200 NorthCrop Pkwy
Ste 200 ....Palm Beach Gardens FL 33410 **866-465-0051** 561-748-2477
GNC Inc 300 Sixth Ave ....Pittsburgh PA 15222 **877-462-4700** 412-228-4600
NYSE: GNC
Hammer Nutrition Ltd
4952 Whitefish Stage Rd ....Whitefish MT 59937 **800-336-1977***
*Cust Svc
Herbalist, The
2106 NE 65th St ....Seattle WA 98115 **800-694-3727** 206-523-2600
Integrated BioPharma Inc
225 Long Ave ....Hillside NJ 07205 **888-319-6962** 973-926-0816
OTC: INBP
Irwin Naturals
5310 Beethoven St ....Los Angeles CA 90066 **800-297-3273** 310-306-3636
Jarrow Formulas Inc
1824 S Robertson Blvd ....Los Angeles CA 90035 **800-726-0886** 310-204-6936
Labrada Nutrition
403 Century Plaza Dr Ste 440 ....Houston TX 77073 **800-832-9948**
Mega-Pro International Inc
251 W Hilton Dr ....Saint George UT 84770 **800-541-9469** 435-673-1001
Natrol Inc
21411 Prairie St ....Chatsworth CA 91311 **800-262-8765**
Naturade 2030 Main St Ste 630 ....Irvine CA 92614 **800-421-1830**
Natural Alternatives International Inc
1185 Linda Vista Dr ....San Marcos CA 92078 **800-848-2646** 760-744-7340
NASDAQ: NAII
Natural Factors Nutritional Products Ltd
1550 United Blvd ....Coquitlam BC V3K6Y2 **800-663-8900** 604-777-1757
Natural Organics Inc
548 Broadhollow Rd ....Melville NY 11747 **800-645-9500**
Naturally Vitamins
4404 E Elwood St ....Phoenix AZ 85040 **800-899-4499**
Nature's Way Products Inc
825 Challenger Dr Ste 125 ....Green Bay WI 54311 **800-962-8873**
Nickers International Ltd
PO Box 50066 ....Staten Island NY 10305 **800-642-5377** 718-448-6283
Nutraceutical International Corp
1400 Kearns Blvd ....Park City UT 84060 **800-669-8877** 435-655-6000
Pacific Health Laboratories Inc
800 Lanidex Plz Ste 220 ....Parsippany NJ 07054 **877-363-8769*** 732-739-2900
*General
Paragon Laboratories
20433 Earl St ....Torrance CA 90503 **800-231-3670** 310-370-1563
Perrigo Co 515 Eastern Ave ....Allegan MI 49010 **800-719-9260** 269-673-8451
NYSE: PRGO
Phibro Animal Health Corp
300 Frank W Burr Blvd Ste 21 ....Teaneck NJ 07666 **800-223-0434** 201-329-7300
Power Organics
301 S Old Stage Rd PO Box 1626 ....Mount Shasta CA 96067 **877-769-3795** 530-926-6684
SportPharma Inc
3 Terminal Rd ....New Brunswick NJ 08901 **800-872-0101** 732-545-3130
Swanson Health Products Inc
PO Box 2803 ....Fargo ND 58108 **800-824-4491** 701-356-2700
Synutra Ingredients
2275 Research Blvd Ste 500 ....Rockville MD 20850 **866-405-2350** 301-840-3888
Thayers Natural Remedies
65 Adams Rd ....Easton CT 06612 **888-842-9371**
Tishcon Corp
50 Sylvester St ....Westbury NY 11590 **800-848-8442** 516-333-3050
Twinlab Corp
4800 T-Rex Ave ....Boca Raton FL 33431 **800-645-5626**
USANA Health Sciences Inc
3838 West PkwyBlvd ....Salt Lake City UT 84120 **888-950-9595** 801-954-7100
NYSE: USNA
Wachters' Organic Sea Products Corp
550 Sylvan St ....Daly City CA 94014 **800-682-7100** 650-757-9851
Wakunaga of America Company Ltd
23501 Madero ....Mission Viejo CA 92691 **800-421-2998** 949-855-2776
Windmill Health Products
10 Henderson Dr ....West Caldwell NJ 07006 **800-822-4320** 973-575-6591
Young Living Essential Oils
3125 Executive Pkwy ....Lehi UT 84043 **866-203-5666** 801-418-8900

795   VOCATIONAL & TECHNICAL SCHOOLS

SEE ALSO Military Service Academies ; Colleges & Universities - Four-Year ; Universities - Canadian ; Colleges - Community & Junior ; Colleges - Fine Arts ; Colleges - Culinary Arts ; Language Schools ; Children's Learning Centers
Listings in this category are organized alphabetically by states.

			Toll-Free	Phone

Herzing College Birmingham
280 W Valley Ave ....Birmingham AL 35209 **800-425-9432** 205-791-5860
JF Drake State Technical College
3421 Meridian St N ....Huntsville AL 35811 **888-413-7253** 256-539-8161
Lawson State Community College
Bessemer 1100 Ninth Ave SW ....Bessemer AL 35022 **800-373-4879** 205-925-2515
Virginia College
Birmingham
488 Palisades Blvd ....Birmingham AL 35209 **800-584-7290** 205-802-1200

	City	State	ZIP	Toll-Free	Phone
Wallace Community College Selma					
3000 Earl Goodwin Pkwy	Selma	AL	36703	**855-428-8313**	334-876-9227
Phoenix 2149 W Dunlap Ave	Phoenix	AZ	85021	**866-338-7934***	602-749-4500
*Cust Svc					
Southwest Institute of Healing Arts					
1100 E Apache Blvd	Tempe	AZ	85281	**888-504-9106**	480-994-9244
San Bernardino					
201 E Airport Dr	San Bernardino	CA	92408	**800-693-7010**	909-884-8891
San Diego					
4393 Imperial Ave Ste 100	San Diego	CA	92113	**800-693-7010**	619-688-0800
Long Beach					
3880 Kilroy Airport Way	Long Beach	CA	90806	**866-338-7934**	562-427-0861
Sherman Oaks					
15301 Ventura Blvd Bldg D-100	Sherman Oaks	CA	91403	**866-338-7934**	818-713-8111
Everest College Alhambra					
2215 W Mission Rd	Alhambra	CA	91803	**888-223-8556**	626-979-4940
Everest College San Jose					
3095 Yerba Buena Rd	San Jose	CA	95135	**888-223-8556**	408-260-5166
Golden Gate University					
Roseville					
7 Sierra Gate Plz Ste 101	Roseville	CA	95678	**800-448-4968**	415-442-7800
San Francisco					
536 Mission St	San Francisco	CA	94105	**800-448-4968**	415-442-7000
Thornton 9065 Grant St	Thornton	CO	80229	**888-223-8556**	303-457-2757
Bel-Rea Institute of Animal Technology					
1681 S Dayton St	Denver	CO	80247	**800-950-8001**	303-751-8700
Colorado Technical University Denver					
3151 S Vaughn Way	Aurora	CO	80014	**866-813-1836**	303-632-2300
Aurora 111 N Havana St	Aurora	CO	80010	**800-693-7010**	303-861-1151
DeVry University					
Colorado Springs					
1175 Kelly Johnson Blvd	Colorado Springs	CO	80920	**877-784-1997***	719-632-3000
*Help Line					
Denver 1870 W 122nd Ave	Westminster	CO	80234	**866-338-7934**	303-280-7400
Lincoln College of Technology					
11194 E 45th Ave	Denver	CO	80239	**800-254-0547**	303-722-5724
Brandon 3924 Coconut Palm Dr	Tampa	FL	33619	**888-223-8556***	813-621-0041
*Cust Svc					
Orange Park					
805 Wells Rd	Orange Park	FL	32073	**888-223-8556**	904-264-9122
Tampa 3319 W Hillsborough Ave	Tampa	FL	33614	**888-223-8556**	813-879-6000
Miramar 10933 Marks Way	Miramar	FL	33025	**800-693-7010**	954-731-8880
Everest University					
Pompano Beach					
225 N Federal Hwy	Pompano Beach	FL	33062	**800-468-0168**	954-783-7339
Full Sail University					
3300 University Blvd	Winter Park	FL	32792	**800-226-7625**	407-679-6333
Keiser University					
Fort Lauderdale					
1500 W Commercial Blvd	Fort Lauderdale	FL	33309	**800-749-4456**	954-776-4456
Melbourne					
900 S Babcock St	Melbourne	FL	32901	**888-534-7379**	321-409-4800
Sarasota					
6151 Lake Osprey Dr	Sarasota	FL	34240	**866-534-7372**	941-907-3900
Lincoln College of Technology					
2410 Metro Centre Blvd	West Palm Beach	FL	33407	**800-254-0547**	561-842-8324
Brown College of Court Reporting & Medical Transcription (BCCR)					
1900 Emery St NW Ste 200	Atlanta	GA	30318	**800-849-0703**	404-876-1227
Central Georgia Technical College					
3300 Macon Tech Dr	Macon	GA	31206	**866-430-0135**	478-757-3400
Gupton-Jones College of Funeral Service					
5141 Snapfinger Woods Dr	Decatur	GA	30035	**800-848-5352**	770-593-2257
Herzing College					
Atlanta					
3393 Peachtree Rd Ste 1003	Atlanta	GA	30326	**800-573-4533**	404-816-4533
Westwood College Atlanta Northlake					
2309 Parklake Dr NE	Atlanta	GA	30345	**866-552-7536**	
Argosy University Hawaii					
400 ASB Tower 1001 Bishop St	Honolulu	HI	96813	**888-323-2777**	808-536-5555
Remington College Honolulu					
1111 Bishop St Ste 400	Honolulu	HI	96813	**800-208-1950**	808-942-1000
Eastern Idaho Technical College					
1600 S 25th E	Idaho Falls	ID	83404	**800-662-0261**	208-524-3000
MacCormac College					
29 E Madison St	Chicago	IL	60602	**800-621-7740**	312-922-1884
Midstate College					
411 W Northmoor Rd	Peoria	IL	61614	**800-251-4299**	309-692-4092
Northwestern College Chicago Campus					
4829 N Lipps Ave	Chicago	IL	60630	**888-205-2283**	773-777-4220
Brown Mackie College					
Merrillville					
1000 E 80th Pl Ste 205M	Merrillville	IN	46410	**800-258-3321**	219-769-3321
South Bend					
3454 Douglas Rd	South Bend	IN	46635	**800-743-2447**	574-237-0774
College of Court Reporting Inc					
111 W Tenth St Ste 111	Hobart	IN	46342	**866-294-3974**	
International Business College					
5699 Coventry Ln	Fort Wayne	IN	46804	**800-589-6363**	260-459-4500
Ivy Tech Columbus College					
Columbus 4475 Central Ave	Columbus	IN	47203	**800-922-4838**	812-372-9925
Ivy Tech Community College					
Bloomington					
200 Daniels Way	Bloomington	IN	47404	**866-447-0700**	812-330-6137
Central Indiana					
50 W Fall Creek Pkwy N Dr	Indianapolis	IN	46208	**888-489-5463**	317-921-4800
Kokomo 1815 E Morgan St	Kokomo	IN	46901	**800-459-0561**	765-459-0561
Muncie 4301 S Cowan Rd	Muncie	IN	47302	**800-589-8324**	765-289-2291
North Central					
220 Dean Johnson Blvd	South Bend	IN	46601	**888-489-3478**	888-489-5463
Northwest 1440 E 35th Ave	Gary	IN	46409	**888-489-5463**	219-981-1111
Richmond 2357 Chester Blvd	Richmond	IN	47374	**800-659-4562**	765-966-2656
Southeast 590 Ivy Tech Dr	Madison	IN	47250	**800-403-2190**	812-265-2580
Southern Indiana					
8204 old Indiana 311	Sellersburg	IN	47172	**800-321-9021**	812-246-3301
Southwest Indiana					
3501 N First Ave	Evansville	IN	47710	**888-489-5463**	
Wabash Valley					
8000 S Education Dr	Terre Haute	IN	47802	**888-489-5463**	812-298-2293
Lincoln College of Technology					
7225 Winton Dr Bldg 128	Indianapolis	IN	46268	**800-228-6232**	317-632-5553
Western Iowa Tech Community College					
4647 Stone Ave	Sioux City	IA	51102	**800-352-4649**	712-274-6400
Brown Mackie College Lenexa					
9705 Lenexa Dr	Lenexa	KS	66215	**800-635-9101**	913-768-1900
Brown Mackie College Salina					
2106 S Ninth St	Salina	KS	67401	**800-365-0433**	785-825-5422
Concorde Career Colleges Inc					
5800 Foxridge Dr Ste 500	Mission	KS	66202	**800-693-7010**	913-831-9977
Wichita Area Technical College					
301 S Grove St	Wichita	KS	67211	**866-296-4031**	316-677-9400
Brown Mackie College Louisville					
3605 Fern Valley Rd	Louisville	KY	40219	**800-999-7387**	502-968-7191
Brown Mackie College Northern Kentucky					
309 Buttermilk Pk	Fort Mitchell	KY	41017	**800-888-1445**	859-341-5627
Gateway Community & Technical College (GCTC)					
500 Technology Wy	Florence	KY	41042	**855-346-4282**	859-441-4500
Louisville Technical Institute					
Sullivan College of Technology & Design					
3901 Atkinson Sq Dr	Louisville	KY	40218	**800-844-6528**	502-456-6509
National College					
Lexington					
2376 Sir Barton Way	Lexington	KY	40509	**877-540-3494**	859-253-0621
National College of Business & Technology					
8095 Connector Dr	Florence	KY	41042	**888-956-2732**	859-525-6510
Owensboro Community & Technical College					
4800 New Hartford Rd	Owensboro	KY	42303	**866-755-6282**	270-686-4400
Beal College 99 Farm Rd	Bangor	ME	04401	**800-660-7351**	207-947-4591
Central Maine Community College					
1250 Turner St	Auburn	ME	04210	**800-891-2002***	207-755-5100
*Admissions					
Eastern Maine Community College					
354 Hogan Rd	Bangor	ME	04401	**800-286-9357**	207-974-4600
Northern Maine Community College (NMCC)					
33 Edgemont Dr	Presque Isle	ME	04769	**800-535-6682**	207-768-2700
Southern Maine Community College (SMCC)					
2 Ft Rd	South Portland	ME	04106	**877-282-2182**	207-741-5500
National Labor College					
10000 New Hampshire Ave	Silver Spring	MD	20903	**888-427-8100**	301-431-6400
Bay State College					
122 Commonwealth Ave	Boston	MA	02116	**800-815-3276**	617-217-9000
Benjamin Franklin Institute of Technology					
41 Berkeley St	Boston	MA	02116	**877-400-2348**	617-423-4630
Boston Architectural College					
320 Newbury St	Boston	MA	02115	**877-585-0100**	617-585-0100
Cambridge College Inc					
360 Merrimack St 4th fl	Lawrence	MA	01843	**800-829-4723**	617-868-1000
Laboure College 303 Adams St	Milton	MA	02186	**800-877-1600**	617-322-3575
National Aviation Academy					
150 Hanscom Dr	Bedford	MA	01730	**800-659-2080**	727-535-8727
Sanford-Brown College					
Boston 126 Newbury St	Boston	MA	02116	**877-809-2444**	617-578-7100
Cleary University					
2793 Plymouth Rd	Ann Arbor	MI	48105	**800-686-1883**	
Livingston 3750 Cleary Dr	Howell	MI	48843	**800-686-1883**	517-548-3670
Everest Institute					
21107 Lahser Rd	Southfield	MI	48033	**800-611-2101***	248-799-9933
*General					
Anoka Technical College					
1355 W Hwy 10	Anoka	MN	55303	**800-627-3529**	763-433-1100
Dakota County Technical College					
1300 E 145th St	Rosemount	MN	55068	**877-937-3282**	651-423-8301
Duluth Business University (DBU)					
4724 Mike Colalilo Dr	Duluth	MN	55807	**800-777-8406**	218-722-4000
Dunwoody College of Technology					
818 Dunwoody Blvd	Minneapolis	MN	55403	**800-292-4625**	612-374-5800
Hennepin Technical College					
9000 Brooklyn Blvd	Brooklyn Park	MN	55445	**800-345-4655**	952-995-1300
Ridgewater College					
Hutchinson					
2 Century Ave SE	Hutchinson	MN	55350	**800-722-1151**	320-234-8500
Willmar					
2101 15th Ave NW PO Box 1097	Willmar	MN	56201	**800-722-1151**	320-222-5200
Saint Paul College					
235 Marshall Ave	Saint Paul	MN	55102	**800-227-6029**	651-846-1600
Sanford-Brown					
1345 Mendota Heights Rd	Mendota Heights	MN	55120	**888-247-4238**	651-905-3400
Vatterott College Berkeley					
8580 Evans Ave	Berkeley	MO	63134	**888-202-2636**	
Vatterott College Joplin					
809 Illinois Ave	Joplin	MO	64801	**866-200-1898**	888-202-2636
Vatterott College South County					
12900 Maurer Industrial Dr	Saint Louis	MO	63127	**866-312-8276**	888-202-2636
Vatterott College Springfield					
3850 S Campbell	Springfield	MO	65807	**888-202-2636**	
University of Montana					
32 Campus Dr	Missoula	MT	59812	**800-462-8636***	406-243-6266
*Admissions					
Nebraska College of Technical Agriculture					
404 E 7th	Curtis	NE	69025	**800-328-7847**	308-367-4124
Southeast Community College					
Beatrice 4771 W Scott Rd	Beatrice	NE	68310	**800-233-5027**	402-228-3468
Milford 600 State St	Milford	NE	68405	**800-933-7223**	402-761-2131
Berkeley College					
Garrett Mountain					
44 Rifle Camp Rd	Woodland Park	NJ	07424	**800-446-5400**	973-278-5400
Paramus 64 E Midland Ave	Paramus	NJ	07652	**800-446-5400**	201-967-9667
Woodbridge					
430 Rahway Ave	Woodbridge	NJ	07095	**800-446-5400**	732-750-1800
DeVry University North Brunswick					
630 US Hwy 1	North Brunswick	NJ	08902	**866-338-7934**	732-729-3960
Divers Academy International					
1500 Liberty Pl	Erial	NJ	08081	**800-238-3483**	
Central New Mexico Community College					
10549 Universe Blvd NW	Albuquerque	NM	87114	**888-453-1304**	505-224-3000
American Academy McAllister Institute of Funeral Service					
619 W 54th St 2nd Fl	New York	NY	10019	**866-932-2264**	212-757-1190

				Toll-Free	Phone
New York City 3 E 43rd St	New York	NY	10017	**800-446-5400**	212-986-4343
White Plains 99 Church St	White Plains	NY	10601	**800-446-5400**	914-694-1122
Bryant & Stratton College Albany 1259 Central Ave	Albany	NY	12205	**800-836-5627**	518-437-1802
Bryant & Stratton College Syracuse North 8687 Carling Rd	Liverpool	NY	13090	**800-836-5627**	315-652-6500
College of Westchester (CW) 325 Central Ave	White Plains	NY	10606	**800-660-7093**	
Commercial Driver Training 600 Patton Ave	West Babylon	NY	11704	**800-649-7447**	631-249-1330
Long Island City 3020 Thomson Ave	Long Island city	NY	11101	**866-338-7934**	718-361-0004
Helene Fuld College of Nursing 24 E 120th St	New York	NY	10035	**800-262-3257**	212-616-7200
Monroe College 2501 Jerome Ave	Bronx	NY	10468	**800-556-6676**	718-933-6700
Wood Tobe-Coburn School 8 E 40th St	New York	NY	10016	**800-394-9663**	212-686-9040
South College-Asheville 140 Sweeten Creek Rd	Asheville	NC	28803	**800-207-7847**	828-398-2500
Stanly Community College 141 College Dr	Albemarle	NC	28001	**877-275-4219**	704-982-0121
Bradford School 2469 Stelzer Rd	Columbus	OH	43219	**800-678-7981**	614-416-6200
Bryant & Stratton College *Cleveland* 3121 Euclid Ave	Cleveland	OH	44115	**866-948-0571**	216-771-1700
Central Ohio Technical College 1179 University Dr	Newark	OH	43055	**800-963-9275**	740-366-9494
Cincinnati College of Mortuary Science 645 W N Bend Rd	Cincinnati	OH	45224	**888-377-8433**	513-761-2020
Cleveland Institute of Electronics 1776 E 17th St	Cleveland	OH	44114	**800-243-6446**	216-781-9400
Davis College 4747 Monroe St	Toledo	OH	43623	**800-477-7021**	419-473-2700
Eastern Gateway Community College 4000 Sunset Blvd	Steubenville	OH	43952	**800-682-6553**	740-264-5591
Hocking College 3301 Hocking Pkwy	Nelsonville	OH	45764	**877-462-5464**	740-753-3591
North Central State College 2441 Kenwood Cir	Mansfield	OH	44906	**888-755-4899**	419-755-4800
Prentke Romich Co 1022 Heyl Rd	Wooster	OH	44091	**800-262-1984**	330-262-1984
Remington College Cleveland 14445 Broadway Ave	Cleveland	OH	44125	**800-208-1950**	
Stark State College of Technology 6200 Frank Ave NW	North Canton	OH	44720	**800-797-8275**	330-494-6170
Zane State College 1555 Newark Rd	Zanesville	OH	43701	**800-686-8324**	740-454-2501
Indian Capital Technology Ctr 2403 N 41st St E	Muskogee	OK	74403	**800-757-0877**	918-687-6383
Oklahoma State University 219 Student Union Bldg	Stillwater	OK	74078	**800-852-1255**	405-744-5000
Okmulgee 1801 E Fourth St	Okmulgee	OK	74447	**800-722-4471**	918-293-4678
Spartan College of Aeronautics & Technology 8820 E Pine St	Tulsa	OK	74115	**800-331-1204***	918-836-6886
*Admissions					
Altieurs career college 100 Forbes Ave Ste 1200	Pittsburgh	PA	15222	**800-603-2870**	412-261-4520
American College 270 S Bryn Mawr Ave	Bryn Mawr	PA	19010	**888-263-7265**	610-526-1000
Central Pennsylvania College 600 Valley Rd PO Box 309	Summerdale	PA	17093	**800-759-2727**	717-732-0702
Johnson College 3427 N Main Ave	Scranton	PA	18508	**800-293-9675**	570-342-6404
Lansdale School of Business 290 Wissahickon Ave	North Wales	PA	19454	**800-219-0486**	215-699-5700
Penn Commercial Inc 242 Oak Spring Rd	Washington	PA	15301	**888-309-7484**	724-222-5330
Penn Foster Career School 925 Oak St	Scranton	PA	18515	**800-275-4410**	570-342-7701
Pennsylvania College of Technology 1 College Ave	Williamsport	PA	17701	**800-367-9222***	570-326-3761
*Admissions					
Pennsylvania Institute of Technology (PIT) 800 Manchester Ave	Media	PA	19063	**800-422-0025***	610-892-1500
*Admissions					
Philadelphia College of Osteopathic Medicine (PCOM) 4170 City Ave	Philadelphia	PA	19131	**800-999-6998***	215-871-6100
*Admissions					
Pittsburgh Institute of Aeronautics (PIA) 5 Allegheny County Airport	West Mifflin	PA	15122	**800-444-1440**	412-346-2100
Pittsburgh Technical College (PTI) 1111 McKee Rd	Oakdale	PA	15071	**800-784-9675**	412-809-5100
Thaddeus Stevens College of Technology (TSCT) 750 E King St	Lancaster	PA	17602	**800-842-3832**	717-299-7701
Triangle Tech Inc *Du Bois* 225 Tannery Row Rd	Falls Creek	PA	15840	**800-874-8324**	814-371-2090
Erie 2000 Liberty St	Erie	PA	16502	**800-874-8324**	814-453-6016
Greensburg 222 E Pittsburgh St	Greensburg	PA	15601	**800-874-8324**	724-832-1050
Welder Training & Testing Institute 1144 N Graham St	Allentown	PA	18109	**800-923-9884**	610-820-9551
New England Institute of Technology 2500 Post Rd	Warwick	RI	02886	**800-736-7744**	401-467-7744
Central Carolina Technical College 506 N Guignard Dr	Sumter	SC	29150	**800-221-8711**	803-778-1961
Florence-Darlington Technical College 2715 W Lucas St	Florence	SC	29502	**800-228-5745**	843-661-8324
Horry-Georgetown Technical College 2050 E Hwy 501	Conway	SC	29526	**855-544-4482**	843-347-3186
Grand Strand Campus 743 Hemlock Ave	Myrtle Beach	SC	29577	**855-544-4482**	843-477-0808
Piedmont Technical College 620 N Emerald Rd	Greenwood	SC	29646	**800-868-5528**	
Spartanburg Community College 800 Brisack Rd PO Box 4386	Spartanburg	SC	29305	**866-591-3700**	864-592-4800

				Toll-Free	Phone
Tri-County Technical College 7900 Hwy 76	Pendleton	SC	29670	**866-269-5677**	864-646-8361
Trident Technical College (TTC) 7000 Rivers Ave PO Box 118067	North Charleston	SC	29406	**877-349-7184**	843-574-6111
Southeast Technical Institute 2320 N Career Ave	Sioux Falls	SD	57107	**800-247-0789**	605-367-8355
Fountainhead College of Technology 3203 Tazewell Pk	Knoxville	TN	37918	**888-218-7335**	865-688-9422
Nashville State Community College (NSCC) 120 White Bridge Rd	Nashville	TN	37209	**800-272-7363**	615-353-3333
Northeast State Technical Community College PO Box 246	Blountville	TN	37617	**800-836-7822**	423-323-3191
South College 3904 Lonas Dr	Knoxville	TN	37909	**877-557-2575**	865-251-1800
Houston 11125 Equity Dr	Houston	TX	77041	**866-338-7934**	713-973-3026
Wade College 1950 N Stemmons Fwy LB 562 Ste 4080	Dallas	TX	75207	**800-624-4850**	214-637-3530
Latter Day Saints Business College 95 North 300 West	Salt Lake City	UT	84101	**800-999-5767**	801-524-8159
Sterling College PO Box 72	Craftsbury Common	VT	05827	**800-648-3591**	802-586-7711
Vermont Technical College PO Box 500	Randolph Center	VT	05061	**800-442-8821**	802-728-1000
Altierus Career College 14555 Potomac Mills Rd	Woodbridge	VA	22192	**833-692-4264**	571-408-2100
Bryant & Stratton College Richmond 8141 Hull St Rd	Richmond	VA	23235	**866-948-0571**	804-745-2444
Roanoke Valley 1813 E Main St	Salem	VA	24153	**800-664-1886**	540-986-1800
Huntington Junior College 900 Fifth Ave	Huntington	WV	25701	**800-344-4522**	304-697-7550
West Virginia Junior College *Charleston* 1000 Virginia St E	Charleston	WV	25301	**800-924-5208**	304-345-2820
West Virginia Junior College - Bridgeport 176 Thompson Dr	Bridgeport	WV	26330	**800-470-5627**	304-842-4007
Blackhawk Technical College 6004 S County Rd G	Janesville	WI	53546	**800-498-1282**	608-758-6900
Bryant & Stratton College Milwaukee 310 W Wisconsin Ave Ste 500-E	Milwaukee	WI	53203	**866-948-0571**	414-276-5200
Chippewa Valley Technical College 620 W Clairemont Ave	Eau Claire	WI	54701	**800-547-2882**	715-833-6200
Fox Valley Technical College 1825 N Bluemound Dr PO Box 2277	Appleton	WI	54912	**800-735-3882**	920-735-5600
Gateway Technical College 3520 - 30th Ave	Kenosha	WI	53144	**800-247-7122**	262-564-2200
Herzing College Madison 5218 E Terr Dr	Madison	WI	53718	**800-582-1227**	608-249-6611
Lakeshore Technical College 1290 N Ave	Cleveland	WI	53015	**888-468-6582**	920-693-1000
Madison Area Technical College 1701 Wright St	Madison	WI	53704	**800-322-6282**	608-246-6100
Milwaukee Area Technical College 700 W State St	Milwaukee	WI	53233	**866-211-3380**	414-297-6600
Moraine Park Technical College 235 N National Ave	Fond du Lac	WI	54935	**800-472-4554**	920-922-8611
Northcentral Technical College 1000 W Campus Dr	Wausau	WI	54401	**888-682-7144**	715-675-3331
Northeast Wisconsin Technical College PO Box 19042	Green Bay	WI	54307	**800-422-6982**	920-498-5400
Southwest Wisconsin Technical College (SWTC) 1800 Bronson Blvd	Fennimore	WI	53809	**800-362-3322**	608-822-3262
Western Technical College 400 Seventh St N	La Crosse	WI	54601	**800-322-9982**	608-785-9200
Wisconsin Indianhead Technical College *New Richmond Campus* 1019 S Knowles Ave	New Richmond	WI	54017	**800-243-9482**	715-246-6561
Rice Lake Campus 1900 College Dr	Rice Lake	WI	54868	**800-243-9482**	715-234-7082
Superior Campus 600 N 21 St	Superior	WI	54880	**800-243-9482**	715-394-6677

796 VOTING SYSTEMS & SOFTWARE

				Toll-Free	Phone
AI Technology Inc (AIT) 70 Washington Rd	Princeton Junction	NJ	08550	**800-735-5040**	609-799-9388
Diebold Nixdorf Inc 5995 Mayfair Rd	North Canton	OH	44720	**800-999-3600**	330-490-4000
NYSE: DBD					
Dynapar 1675 Delany Rd	Gurnee	IL	60031	**800-873-8731***	
*General					
Election Systems & Software Inc 11208 John Galt Blvd	Omaha	NE	68137	**877-377-8683***	402-593-0101
*General					
Hart InterCivic 15500 Wells Port Dr	Austin	TX	78728	**800-223-4278**	
MicroVote General Corp 6366 Guilford Ave	Indianapolis	IN	46220	**800-257-4901**	317-257-4900

797 WALLCOVERINGS

				Toll-Free	Phone
Fashion Architectural Designs 4005 Carnegie Ave	Cleveland	OH	44103	**800-362-9930***	216-904-1380
*Orders					
Goldcrest Wallcoverings PO Box 245	Slingerlands	NY	12159	**800-535-9513**	518-478-7214
Thibaut Inc 480 Frelinghuysen Ave	Newark	NJ	07114	**800-223-0704**	973-643-1118
York Wallcoverings Inc 750 Linden Ave	York	PA	17404	**800-375-9675**	717-846-4456

Classified Section

798   WAREHOUSING & STORAGE

SEE ALSO Logistics Services (Transportation & Warehousing)

798-1 Commercial Warehousing

				Toll-Free	Phone
Acme Distribution Centers Inc					
18101 E Colfax Ave	Aurora	CO	80011	800-444-3614	303-340-2100
All Source Security Container Mfg Corp					
40 Mills Rd	Barrie	ON	L4N6H4	866-526-4579	705-726-6460
ASW Global LLC					
3375 Gilchrist Rd	Mogadore	OH	44260	888-826-5087	330-798-5172
Dart Entities					
1430 S Eastman Ave	Los Angeles	CA	90023	800-285-0560	323-264-1011
Derby Industries LLC					
4451 Robards Ln	Louisville	KY	40218	800-569-4812	502-451-7373
Gulf Winds International Inc					
411 Brisbane St	Houston	TX	77061	866-238-4909	713-747-4909
Habco 501 Gordon Baker Rd	Toronto	ON	M2H2S6	800-448-0244	416-491-6008
Iron Mountain					
745 Atlantic Ave	Boston	MA	02111	800-899-4766	
NYSE: IRM					
Kenco Group Inc					
2001 Riverside Dr	Chattanooga	TN	37406	800-758-3289	
Longistics Transportation Inc					
10900 World Trade Blvd	Raleigh	NC	27617	800-289-0082	919-872-7626
Offshore International Inc					
8350 E Old Vail Rd	Tucson	AZ	85747	800-897-3158	
Pacific Records					
523 N Hunter St	Stockton	CA	95202	888-823-5467	209-320-6600
Smart Warehousing LLC					
18905 Kill Creek Rd	Edgerton	KS	66021	800-591-2097	
Tejas Logistics System					
PO Box 1339	Waco	TX	76703	800-535-9786	254-753-0301
W O W Logistics Co					
3040 W Wisconsin Ave	Appleton	WI	54914	800-236-3565	920-734-9924

798-2 Refrigerated Storage

				Toll-Free	Phone
Burris Logistics					
501 SE Fifth St	Milford	DE	19963	800-805-8135	302-839-5157
Perley-Halladay Assn Inc					
1037 Andrew Dr	West Chester	PA	19380	800-248-5800	610-296-5800
United Freezer & Storage Co					
650 N Meridian Rd	Youngstown	OH	44509	800-716-1416	330-792-1739

798-3 Self-Storage Facilities

				Toll-Free	Phone
A-American Self Storage Management Co Inc					
11560 Tennessee Ave	Los Angeles	CA	90064	800-499-3524	
Public Storage Inc					
701 Western Ave	Glendale	CA	91201	800-567-0759*	818-244-8080
NYSE: PSA ■ *Cust Svc*					
Shader Bros Corp					
6325 Edgewater Dr	Orlando	FL	32810	866-762-4888	
Stor-All Storage					
1375 W Hillsboro Blvd	Deerfield Beach	FL	33442	877-786-7255	954-421-7888

799   WASTE MANAGEMENT

SEE ALSO Recyclable Materials Recovery ; Remediation Services

				Toll-Free	Phone
Athens Services					
14048 Valley Blvd	La Puente	CA	91746	888-336-6100	626-336-3636
Burrtec Waste Industries Inc					
9890 Cherry Ave	Fontana	CA	92335	888-287-7832	909-429-4200
Casella Waste Systems Inc					
25 Greens Hill Ln	Rutland	VT	05701	800-227-3552	802-775-0325
NASDAQ: CWST					
Consolidated Disposal Services Inc					
12949 Telegraph Rd	Santa Fe Springs	CA	90670	800-299-4898	
Dolphins Plus Inc					
31 Corrine Pl	Key Largo	FL	33037	866-860-7946	305-451-0315
E J Harrison & Sons					
PO Box 4009	Ventura	CA	93007	800-418-7274	805-647-1414
EL Harvey & Sons Inc					
68 Hopkinton Rd	Westborough	MA	01581	800-321-3002	508-836-3000
Kansas Department of Health & Environment					
300 West Douglas Ste 700	Wichita	KS	67202	800-842-0078	316-337-6020
Modern Corp					
4746 Model City Rd	Model City	NY	14107	800-662-0012	716-754-8226
Rumpke 10795 Hughes Rd	Cincinnati	OH	45251	800-582-3107	
Stericycle Inc					
28161 N Keith Dr	Lake Forest	IL	60045	866-783-9816	847-367-5910
NASDAQ: SRCL					
Synagro Technologies Inc					
435 Williams Ct Ste 100	Baltimore	MD	21220	800-370-0035	
Texas Disposal Systems Inc (TDS)					
12200 Carl Rd	Creedmoor	TX	78610	800-375-8375	512-421-1300
Triumvirate Environmental					
61 Innerbelt Rd	Somerville	MA	02143	800-966-9282	617-628-8098
Ute Water Conservancy District					
2190 H 1/4 Rd	Grand Junction	CO	81505	866-768-1732	970-242-7491
Waste Industries USA Inc					
3301 Benson Dr Ste 601	Raleigh	NC	27609	800-647-9946	919-325-3000
Waste Management Inc					
1001 Fannin St Ste 4000	Houston	TX	77002	800-633-7871	713-512-6200
NYSE: WM					

800   WATER - BOTTLED

				Toll-Free	Phone
Absopure Water Co					
8845 General Dr	Plymouth	MI	48170	800-422-7678	
Chester Water Authority					
PO Box 467	Chester	PA	19016	800-793-2323	610-876-8185
Culligan International Co					
9399 W Higgins Rd Ste 1100	Rosemont	IL	60018	800-285-5442	847-430-2800
Distillata Co					
1608 E 24th St	Cleveland	OH	44114	800-999-2906*	216-771-2900
Cust Svc					
DS Services of America Inc					
5660 New Northside Dr Ste 500	Atlanta	GA	30328	800-201-6218*	
Cust Svc					
Frontier Cooperative Herbs					
3021 78th St	Norway	IA	52318	800-669-3275	
Glacier Clear Enterprises Inc					
3291 Thomas St	Innisfil	ON	L9S3W3	800-668-5118*	705-436-6363
Cust Svc					
Le Bleu Corp					
3134 Cornatzer Rd	Advance	NC	27006	800-854-4471	336-998-2894
Lentz Milling Co					
2045 N 11th St	Reading	PA	19604	800-523-8132	
Polar Beverages					
1001 Southbridge St	Worcester	MA	01610	800-734-9800*	
Cust Svc					
Pure-Flo Water Co					
7737 Mission Gorge Rd	Santee	CA	92071	800-787-3356*	619-448-5120
Cust Svc					

801   WATER TREATMENT & FILTRATION PRODUCTS & EQUIPMENT

				Toll-Free	Phone
Aqua-Aerobic Systems Inc					
6306 N Alpine Rd	Loves Park	IL	61111	800-940-5008	815-654-2501
Brita Products Co					
1221 Broadway	Oakland	CA	94612	800-242-7482	510-271-7000
Bucks County Water & Sewer Authority (BCWSA)					
1275 Almshouse Rd	Warrington	PA	18976	800-222-2068	215-343-2538
Carolina Filters Inc					
109 E Newberry Ave	Sumter	SC	29150	800-849-5646	
Court Thomas Wingert					
11800 Monarch St PO Box 6207	Garden Grove	CA	92841	800-359-7337	714-379-5519
Culligan International Co					
9399 W Higgins Rd Ste 1100	Rosemont	IL	60018	800-285-5442	847-430-2800
Deepwater Chemicals Inc					
1210 Airpark Rd	Woodward	OK	73801	800-854-4064	580-256-0500
Dow Liquid Separations					
PO Box 1206	Midland	MI	48642	800-447-4369	989-636-1000
Filterspun					
624 N Fairfield St	Amarillo	TX	79107	800-323-5431	806-383-3840
Graver Technologies LLC					
200 Lake Dr	Newark	DE	19702	800-249-1990	302-731-1700
Kinetico Inc					
10845 Kinsman Rd	Newbury	OH	44065	800-944-9283	440-564-9111
Lancaster Pump Co					
1340 Manheim Pk	Lancaster	PA	17601	800-442-0786	717-397-3521
MSC Filtration Technologies					
198 Freshwater Blvd	Enfield	CT	06082	800-237-7359*	860-745-7475
Cust Svc					
Pall Corp					
2200 Northern Blvd	East Hills	NY	11548	800-645-6532	516-484-5400
NYSE: PLL					
PEP Filters Inc					
322 Rolling Hill Rd	Mooresville	NC	28117	800-243-4583	704-662-3133
Pro Products LLC					
7201 Engle Rd	Fort Wayne	IN	46804	866-357-5063	260-490-5970
Pure & Secure LLC					
4120 NW 44th St	Lincoln	NE	68524	800-875-5915*	402-467-9300
Cust Svc					
Sydnor Hydro Inc					
2111 Magnolia St	Richmond	VA	23223	844-339-6334	804-643-2725
Taylor Technologies Inc					
31 Loveton Cir	Sparks	MD	21152	800-837-8548*	410-472-4340
Cust Svc					
Tomco2 Systems					
3340 Rosebud Rd	Loganville	GA	30052	800-832-4262	770-979-8000
Walker Process Equipment					
840 N Russell Ave	Aurora	IL	60506	800-992-5537	630-892-7921
Waterco USA Inc					
1864 Tobacco Rd	Augusta	GA	30906	800-277-4150*	706-793-7291
General					
Zodiac Pool Systems Inc					
2620 Commerce Way	Vista	CA	92081	800-822-7933	

802   WEAPONS & ORDNANCE (MILITARY)

SEE ALSO Firearms & Ammunition (Non-Military) ; Simulation & Training Systems ; Missiles, Space Vehicles, Parts

				Toll-Free	Phone
Dillon Aero Inc					
8009 E Dillons Way	Scottsdale	AZ	85260	800-881-4231	480-333-5450
Keystone Sporting Arms LLC					
155 Sodom Rd	Milton	PA	17847	800-742-0455	570-742-2777
Mile High Shooting Accessories LLC					
3731 Monarch St	Erie	CO	80516	877-871-9990	303-255-9999
North American Arms Inc					
2150 S 950 E	Provo	UT	84606	800-821-5783	801-374-9990

803 — WEB HOSTING SERVICES

SEE ALSO Internet Service Providers (ISPs)
Companies listed here are engaged primarily in hosting web sites for companies and individuals. Although many Internet Service Providers (ISPs) also provide web hosting services, they are not included among these listings.

			Toll-Free	Phone
Baillio's Inc				
5301 Menaul Blvd NE ....Albuquerque NM	87110		800-540-7511	505-395-5611
Catalogcom Inc				
14000 Quail Springs Pkwy				
Ste 3600 ....Oklahoma City OK	73134		888-932-4376	405-753-9300
Datarealm Internet Services Inc				
PO Box 1616 ....Hudson WI	54016		877-227-3783	
Freeserverscom				
1253 N Research Way Ste Q-2500 ....Orem UT	84097		800-396-1999	
Global Knowledge Group Inc (GKG)				
302 N Bryan Ave ....Bryan TX	77803		866-776-7584	
Homestead Technologies Inc				
180 Jefferson Dr ....Menlo Park CA	94025		800-797-2958	650-944-3100
Host Depot Inc				
4613 N University Dr Ste 227 ....Coral Springs FL	33067		888-340-3527	954-340-3527
Hostcentric Inc				
70 BlanchaRd Rd 3rd Fl ....Burlington MA	01803		866-897-5418*	602-716-5396
*Tech Supp				
Hostedware Corp				
16 Technology Dr Ste 116 ....Irvine CA	92618		800-211-6967	949-585-1500
Hostway Corp				
100 N Riverside Plz 8th Fl ....Chicago IL	60606		866-467-8929	312-238-0125
Media3 Technologies LLC				
33 Riverside Dr N River Commerce Pk ....Pembroke MA	02359		800-903-9327	781-826-1213
NetNation Communications Inc				
550 Burrard St Ste 200 ....Vancouver BC	V6C2B5		888-277-0000	604-688-8946
Radiant Communications Corp				
1600-1050 W Pender St ....Vancouver BC	V6E4T3		888-219-2111	
TSX: RCN				
Superb Internet Corp				
999 Bishop St Ste 1850 ....Honolulu HI	96813		888-354-6128	808-544-0387
Tclus				
630 Ren,-L,vesque Blvd W ....Montreal QC	H3B1S6		877-999-4069	514-665-3050
VPOP Technologies Inc				
1772J Avenida de los Arboles				
Ste 374 ....Thousand Oaks CA	91362		888-811-8767*	805-529-9374
*Sales				

804 — WEB SITE DESIGN SERVICES

SEE ALSO Advertising Agencies ; Advertising Services - Online ; Computer Systems Design Services

			Toll-Free	Phone
Accelian LLC				
1222 Earnestine St ....Mc Lean VA	22101		888-543-0051	703-543-1616
Acro Media Inc				
2303 Leckie Rd Ste 103 ....Kelowna BC	V1X6Y5		877-763-8844	250-763-8884
Applied Logic Inc				
11475 Olde Cabin Rd Ste 100 ....St Louis MO	63141		844-478-7225	314-918-8877
AppNeta Inc				
285 Summer St 4th Fl. ....Boston MA	02210		800-664-4401	800-508-5233
AutoManager Inc				
7301 Topanga Canyon Blvd Ste 200 ....Canoga Park CA	91303		800-300-2808	310-207-2202
Backupify 50 Milk St ....Boston MA	02109		800-571-4984	
Burgess Group LLC, The				
1701 Duke St Ste 300 ....Alexandria VA	22314		800-637-2004	703-894-1800
Champions Way				
4333 Still Creek Dr 2nd Fl ....Burnaby BC	V5C6S6		877-774-5425	
Data Square LLC				
396 Danbury Rd ....Wilton CT	06897		877-328-2738	203-964-9733
eWareness Inc				
1900 S Harbor City Blvd Ste 122 ....Melbourne FL	32901		800-517-4130	321-953-2435
ExpenseVisor				
910 Kenyon Ct Ste 110. ....Charlotte NC	28210		877-219-5448	704-644-0019
Frontline Systems Inc				
PO Box 4288 ....Incline Village NV	89450		888-831-0333	775-831-0300
Function Point Productivity Software Inc				
2034 11th Ave W Ste 140 ....Vancouver BC	V6J2C9		877-731-2522	
Impact Technologies Group Inc				
615 S College St ....Charlotte NC	28202		800-438-6017	704-549-1100
Infopros				
12325 Oracle Blvd Ste 100 ....Colorado Springs CO	80921		888-235-3231	
Langtech Systems Consulting Inc				
733 Frnt St Ste 110. ....San Francisco CA	94111		800-480-8488	415-364-9600
Litehaus Systems Inc				
7445 132nd St Ste 2010. ....Surrey BC	V3W1J8		866-771-0044	
Lux Scientiae Inc				
PO Box 326 ....Westwood MA	02090		800-441-6612	
Msights Inc				
9935 Rea Rd Ste D-301 ....Charlotte NC	28277		877-267-4448	
Nimbix LLC				
800 E Campbell Ste 241 ....Richardson TX	75081		866-307-0819	
Noregon Systems Inc				
7009 Albert Pick Rd ....Greensboro NC	27409		855-889-5776	
ObdEdge LLC				
7117 Florida Blvd ....Baton Rouge LA	70806		888-896-9753	
Orion Systems Integrators LLC				
333 Thornall St 7th Fl. ....Edison NJ	08837		877-456-9922	
OuterBox Corp				
325 S Main St 3rd Fl ....Akron OH	44308		866-647-9218	
Panacore Corp				
2015 E Eighth St Ste 242 ....Odessa TX	79761		877-726-2267	
Partner Software Inc				
PO Box 748 ....Athens GA	30603		844-778-4717	706-612-9494
Pedigree Technologies				
4776 28th Ave S Ste 101 ....Fargo ND	58104		844-407-9307	800-470-6581

			Toll-Free	Phone
Pillar Technology Group LLC				
301 E Liberty St Ste 700 ....Ann Arbor MI	48104		888-374-5527	
Pinestar Technology Inc				
1000 E Jamestown Rd ....Jamestown PA	16134		800-682-2226	724-932-2121
ProCare Rx				
1267 Professional Pkwy ....Gainesville GA	30507		800-377-1037	
QualCorp Inc				
27240 Turnberry Ln Ste 200 ....Valencia CA	91355		888-367-6775	661-799-0033
Quantech Corp				
369 Lexington Ave ....New York NY	10016		833-256-8367	212-323-2660
Radianta Inc				
320 Goddard Ste 100 ....Irvine CA	92618		866-467-9695	
Sapient Corp				
131 Dartmouth St ....Boston MA	02116		866-796-6860	617-621-0200
SECNAP Network Security Corp				
3250 W Commercial Blvd				
Ste 345 ....Fort Lauderdale FL	33309		844-638-7328	561-999-5000
Sentinel Development Solutions Inc				
4015 Beltline Rd Ste 100 ....Addison TX	75001		877-395-8976	515-564-0585
Sharp Innovations Inc				
3113 Main St Bldg B, Main Level ....Conestoga PA	17516		888-575-8977	717-290-6760
ShiftWise Inc				
200 SW Market St Ste 700 ....Portland OR	97201		866-399-2220	
Sierra Creative Systems Inc				
15700 Texaco Ave ....Paramount CA	92723		800-961-4877	562-232-8100
Sigma Business Solutions Inc				
55 York St ....Toronto ON	M5J1R7		855-594-1991	
SoftThinks USA Inc				
11940 Jollyville Rd Ste 225-S ....Austin TX	78759		800-305-1754	
Spindustry Systems Inc				
1370 NW 114th St Ste 300 ....Des Moines IA	50325		877-225-4200	515-225-0920
Team IA Inc				
212 Palmetto Park Blvd ....Lexington SC	29072		888-483-2642	803-356-7676
Techtonic Group Llc				
2000 Central Ave ....Boulder CO	80301		866-382-8280	303-223-3468
Tricycle Inc				
1293 Riverfront Pkwy Ste 1293-B. ....Chattanooga TN	37402		800-808-4809	
Ultryx PO Box 1841 ....Las Vegas NV	89125		866-485-8799	702-940-6900
Velaro Inc				
8174 Lark Brown Rd Ste 201 ....Elkridge MD	21075		800-983-5276	
Verisma Systems Inc				
510 W Third St Ste 200 ....Pueblo CO	81003		866-390-7404	719-546-1849
Viable Solutions Inc				
7802 Kingspointe Pkwy Ste 206. ....Orlando FL	32819		800-679-7626	407-249-9600
VIDA Diagnostics Inc				
2500 Crosspark Rd W150 BioVentures Ctr				
........Coralville IA	52241		855-900-8432	
Vigilistics Inc				
711 Grand Ave Ste 290. ....San Rafael CA	94901		888-235-7540	949-900-8380
W3health Solutions LLC				
115 Franklin TurnPk Ste 352 ....Mahwah NJ	07430		888-934-3258	201-701-0240
Web Presence Architects LLC				
10113 Meadowneck Ct ....Silver Spring MD	20910		888-873-6218	
Webcom				
12808 Grand Bay Pkwy W ....Jacksonville FL	32258		800-338-1771	904-680-6600
XLPrint USA LLC				
213 Rose Ave Ste 1. ....Venice CA	90291		866-275-1290	310-829-7684
Zen Ventures LLC				
3939 S Sixth St Ste 201 ....Klamath Falls OR	97603		888-936-2278	

805 — WEIGHT LOSS CENTERS & SERVICES

SEE ALSO Spas - Health & Fitness ; Health & Fitness Centers

			Toll-Free	Phone
Companions & Homemakers Inc				
613 New Britain Ave ....Farmington CT	06032		800-348-4663	860-677-4948
Jazzercise Inc				
2460 Impala Dr ....Carlsbad CA	92010		800-348-4748*	760-476-1750
*Cust Svc				
NutriSystem Inc				
600 Office Center Dr ....Fort Washington PA	19034		800-585-5483	215-706-5300
NASDAQ: NTRI				
Physicians Weight Loss Centers of America Inc				
395 Springside Dr ....Akron OH	44333		800-205-7887	

806 — WELDING & SOLDERING EQUIPMENT

			Toll-Free	Phone
AGM Industries Inc				
16 Jonathan Dr ....Brockton MA	02301		800-225-9990	508-587-3900
American Torch Tip Co				
6212 29th St E ....Bradenton FL	34203		800-342-8477	
American Ultraviolet Co				
40 Morristown Rd ....Bernardsville NJ	07924		800-288-9288	908-696-1130
Applied Fusion Inc				
1915 Republic Ave ....San Leandro CA	94577		800-704-1078	510-351-4511
Arcos Industries				
1 Arcos Dr ....Mount Carmel PA	17851		800-233-8460	570-339-5200
BUG-O Systems Inc				
161 Hillpointe Dr ....Canonsburg PA	15317		800-245-3186	412-331-1776
CK Worldwide Inc				
3501 C St NE ....Auburn WA	98002		800-426-0877	253-854-5820
Esab Welding & Cutting Products				
256 Midway Dr ....Union SC	29379		800-372-2123	864-466-0921
Eureka Welding Alloys Inc				
2000 E Avis Dr ....Madison Heights MI	48071		800-962-8560	248-588-0001
Eutectic Corp				
N94 W14355 Garwin Mace Dr ....Menomonee Falls WI	53051		800-558-8524	262-532-4677
Gapco Inc				
2151 Centennial Dr ....Gainesville GA	30504		866-534-7928	770-534-7928
Goss Inc				
1511 William Flynn Hwy ....Glenshaw PA	15116		800-367-4677	412-486-6100
Harris Products Group				
4501 Quality Pl ....Mason OH	45040		800-733-4043	513-754-2000
Hobart Bros Co 101 Trade Sq E ....Troy OH	45373		800-424-1543	937-332-4000

Welding & Soldering Equipment (Cont'd)

				Toll-Free	Phone
Lincoln Electric Co					
22801 St Clair Ave	Cleveland	OH	44117	888-935-3878	216-481-8100
M K Products Inc					
16882 Armstrong Ave	Irvine	CA	92606	800-787-9707	949-863-1234
Maine Oxy 22 Albiston Way	Auburn	ME	04210	800-639-1108	207-784-5788
Miller Electric Mfg Co					
1635 W Spencer St	Appleton	WI	54914	888-843-7693	920-734-9821
Smith Equipment Mfg Co					
2601 Lockheed Ave	Watertown	SD	57201	866-931-9730*	605-882-3200
*Cust Svc					
Sonobond Ultrasonics Inc					
1191 McDermott Dr	West Chester	PA	19380	800-323-1269	610-696-4710
Systematics Inc					
1025 Saunders Ln	West Chester	PA	19380	800-222-9353	
Taylor-Winfield Inc					
3200 Innovation Pl	Youngstown	OH	44509	800-523-4899	330-259-8500
Tuffaloy Products Inc					
1400 S Batesville Rd	Greer	SC	29650	800-521-3722	864-879-0763
Uniweld Products Inc					
2850 Ravenswood Rd	Fort Lauderdale	FL	33312	800-323-2111	954-584-2000
Weld Mold Co					
750 Rickett Rd	Brighton	MI	48116	800-521-9755	810-229-9521
Weldaloy Products Co					
24011 Hoover Rd	Warren	MI	48089	888-935-3256	586-758-5550
Western Enterprises Inc					
875 Bassett Rd	Westlake	OH	44145	800-783-7890	

807 — WHOLESALE CLUBS

				Toll-Free	Phone
Costco Wholesale Corp					
999 Lake Dr	Issaquah	WA	98027	800-774-2678*	425-313-8100
NASDAQ: COST ■ *Cust Svc					

808 — WIRE & CABLE

				Toll-Free	Phone
Ace Wire & Cable Co Inc					
7201 51st Ave	Woodside	NY	11377	800-225-2354	718-458-9200
AFC Cable Systems Inc					
960 Flaherty Dr	New Bedford	MA	02745	800-757-6996	508-998-1131
AmerCable Inc					
350 Bailey Rd	El Dorado	AR	71730	800-643-1516	870-862-4919
Astro Industries Inc					
4403 Dayton-Xenia Rd	Dayton	OH	45432	800-543-5810	937-429-5900
Cerro Wire & Cable Company Inc					
1099 Thompson Rd SE	Hartselle	AL	35640	800-523-3869	256-773-2522
Charter Wire					
3700 W Milwaukee Rd	Milwaukee	WI	53208	800-436-9074	414-390-3000
Encore Wire Corp					
1329 Millwood Rd	McKinney	TX	75069	800-962-9473	972-562-9473
NASDAQ: WIRE					
Eubanks Engineering Co					
3022 Inland Empire Blvd	Ontario	CA	91764	800-729-4208	909-483-2456
Fiberwave Inc					
140 58th St Bldg B Unit 6E	Brooklyn	NY	11220	800-280-9011	718-802-9011
Gehr Industries					
7400 E Slauson Ave	Los Angeles	CA	90040	800-688-6606	323-728-5558
Insteel Industries Inc					
1373 Boggs Dr	Mount Airy	NC	27030	800-334-9504	336-786-2141
NASDAQ: IIIN					
Keystone Consolidated Industries Inc					
7000 SW Adams St	Peoria	IL	61641	800-447-6444*	
*Sales					
Major Custom Cable Inc					
281 Lotus Dr	Jackson	MO	63755	800-455-6224	
Mid-South Wire Company Inc					
1070 Visco Dr	Nashville	TN	37210	800-714-7800	615-743-2850
Mount Joy Wire Corp					
1000 E Main St	Mount Joy	PA	17552	800-321-2305	717-653-1461
Owl Wire & Cable Inc					
3127 Seneca Tpke	Canastota	NY	13032	800-765-9473	315-697-2011
Rea Magnet Wire Company Inc					
3400 E Coliseum Blvd Ste 200	Fort Wayne	IN	46805	800-732-9473	
Ribbon Technology Corp					
825 Taylor Stn Rd	Gahanna	OH	43230	800-848-0477	614-864-5444
Sivaco Wire Group					
800 Rue Ouellette	Marieville	QC	J3M1P5	800-876-9473	450-658-8741
Southwestern Wire Inc					
PO Box CC	Norman	OK	73070	800-348-9473	405-447-6900
Southwire Co					
1 Southwire Dr	Carrollton	GA	30119	800-444-1700	770-832-4242
Spotnails					
1100 Hicks Rd	Rolling Meadows	IL	60008	800-873-2239	847-259-1620
Superior Essex Inc					
6120 Powers Ferry Rd	Atlanta	GA	30339	800-551-8948	770-657-6000
Times Fiber Communications Inc					
358 Hall Ave PO Box 384	Wallingford	CT	06492	800-677-2288	434-432-1800
Tree Island Steel					
12459 Arrow Rt	Rancho Cucamonga	CA	91739	800-255-6974	909-594-7511
Wirerope Works Inc					
100 Maynard St	Williamsport	PA	17701	800-541-7673*	570-326-5146
*Cust Svc					
Wrap-On Company LLC					
11756 S Austin Ave	Alsip	IL	60803	800-621-6947	708-496-2150

809 — WIRE & CABLE - ELECTRONIC

				Toll-Free	Phone
Advanced Cable Ties Inc					
245 Suffolk Ln	Gardner	MA	01440	800-861-7228	
Alpha Wire Co					
711 Lidgerwood Ave	Elizabeth	NJ	07207	800-522-5742	908-925-8000
Belden Inc					
2200 US Hwy 27 S	Richmond	IN	47374	800-235-3362	765-983-5200

WIRE & CABLE (cont'd)

				Toll-Free	Phone
Cables to Go Inc					
3599 Dayton Pk Dr	Dayton	OH	45414	800-826-7904	937-224-8646
Champlain Cable Corp					
175 Hercules Dr	Colchester	VT	05446	800-451-5162	
CommScope Inc					
1100 Commscope Pl SE PO Box 339	Hickory	NC	28603	800-982-1708	828-324-2200
Compulink Inc					
1205 Gandy Blvd N	Saint Petersburg	FL	33702	800-231-6685	727-579-1500
Comtran Cable					
330A Turner St	Attleboro	MA	02703	800-842-7809	508-399-7004
Consolidated Electronic Wire & Cable Co					
11044 King St	Franklin Park	IL	60131	800-621-4278	847-455-8830
Corning Cable Systems					
800 17th St NW	Hickory	NC	28603	800-743-2671	607-974-9000
CXtec 5404 S Bay Rd	Syracuse	NY	13221	800-767-3282*	315-476-3000
*Orders					
General Cable Corp					
4 Tessener Dr	Highland Heights	KY	41076	800-572-8000	859-572-8000
NYSE: BGC					
Harbour Industries Inc					
4744 Shelburne Rd PO Box 188	Shelburne	VT	05482	800-659-4733	802-985-3311
Judd Wire Inc					
124 Tpke Rd	Turners Falls	MA	01376	800-545-5833*	413-863-4357
*Cust Svc					
Madison Cable Corp					
125 Goddard Memorial Dr	Worcester	MA	01603	877-623-4766	508-752-2884
Nehring Electric Works Inc					
1005 E Locust St	DeKalb	IL	60115	800-435-4481	815-756-2741
Oleco Inc					
18683 Trimble Ct	Spring Lake	MI	49456	800-575-3282	616-842-6790
Optical Cable Corp (OCC)					
5290 Concourse Dr	Roanoke	VA	24019	800-622-7711	540-265-0690
NASDAQ: OCC					
Prestolite Wire Corp					
200 Galleria Officentre Ste 212	Southfield	MI	48034	800-498-3132	248-355-4422
Rockbestos-Surprenant Cable Corp					
20 Bradley Pk Rd	East Granby	CT	06026	800-327-7625	860-653-8300
Siemon Co					
101 Siemon Co Dr	Watertown	CT	06795	866-548-5814	860-945-4200

810 — WIRING DEVICES - CURRENT-CARRYING

				Toll-Free	Phone
Arlington Industries Inc					
1 Stauffer Industrial Pk	Scranton	PA	18517	800-233-4717	570-562-0270
Bizlink Technology Inc					
3400 Gateway Blvd	Fremont	CA	94538	800-326-4193	510-252-0786
Burndy LLC					
47 E Industrial Park Dr	Manchester	NH	03109	800-346-4175	
Charles E Gillman Co					
907 E Frontage Rd	Rio Rico	AZ	85648	800-783-2589	520-281-1141
Cherry Corp					
11200 88th Ave	Pleasant Prairie	WI	53158	800-510-1689	262-942-6500
Component Enterprises Co Inc					
235 E Penn St PO Box 189	Norristown	PA	19401	877-232-7253	
Cooper Bussmann Inc					
114 Old State Rd	Ellisville	MO	63021	855-287-7626	636-394-2877
Cooper Crouse-Hinds					
1201 Wolf St	Syracuse	NY	13208	866-764-5454	315-477-5531
Cooper Industries					
600 Travis St Ste 5400	Houston	TX	77002	866-853-4293	713-209-8400
NYSE: ETN					
Cooper Wiring Devices Inc					
203 Cooper Cir	Peachtree City	GA	30269	866-853-4293*	770-631-2100
*Cust Svc					
Cord Sets Inc					
1015 Fifth St N	Minneapolis	MN	55411	800-752-0580	612-337-9700
Curtis Industries Inc					
2400 S 43rd St PO Box 343925	Milwaukee	WI	53219	800-657-0853	414-649-4200
Dekko 2505 Dekko Dr	Garrett	IN	46738	800-829-3101	260-357-3621
Edwin Gaynor Corp					
200 Charles St	Stratford	CT	06615	800-342-9667	203-378-5545
EECO Switch					
1240 Pioneer St Ste A	Brea	CA	92821	800-854-3808	
Electroswitch					
2010 Yonkers Rd	Raleigh	NC	27604	888-768-2797	919-833-0707
ERICO Products Inc					
34600 Solon Rd	Solon	OH	44139	800-248-2677	440-248-0100
ETCO Inc 25 Bellows St	Warwick	RI	02888	800-689-3826	401-467-2400
Glenair Inc 1211 Air Way	Glendale	CA	91201	888-465-4094	818-247-6000
Hoffman Products					
9600 Vly View Rd	Macedonia	OH	44056	800-645-2014	216-525-4320
Hubbell Premise Wiring Inc					
23 Clara Dr	Mystic	CT	06355	800-626-0005	
Hubbell Wiring Device-Kellems					
40 Waterview Dr	Shelton	CT	06484	800-288-6000*	203-882-4800
*Cust Svc					
ILSCO 4730 Madison Rd	Cincinnati	OH	45227	800-776-9775*	513-533-6200
*Sales					
Independent Protection Company Inc					
1607 S Main St	Goshen	IN	46526	800-860-8388	574-533-4116
Lumens Light & Living					
2028 K St	Sacramento	CA	95811	877-445-4486	916-444-5585
Marinco					
2655 Napa Valley Corp Dr	Napa	CA	94558	800-307-6702	707-226-9600
Midwest Manufacturing Inc					
5311 Kane Rd	Eau Claire	WI	54703	800-826-7126	715-876-5555
Mill-Max Mfg Corp					
190 Pine Hollow Rd	Oyster Bay	NY	11771	800-333-4237	516-922-6000
Minnesota Wire & Cable Co					
1835 Energy Park Dr	Saint Paul	MN	55108	800-258-6922	651-642-1800
National Standard Parts Assoc Inc					
4400 Mobile Hwy	Pensacola	FL	32506	800-874-6813	850-456-5771
Ohio Associated Enterprises LLC					
97 Corwin Dr	Painesville	OH	44077	888-637-4832	440-354-2100

		Toll-Free	Phone
Omnetics Connector Corp			
7260 Commerce Cir E .... Minneapolis MN 55432		**800-343-0025***	763-572-0656
*Cust Svc			
Panduit Corp			
17301 Ridgeland Ave .... Tinley Park IL 60477		**888-506-5400**	708-532-1800
Phoenix Company of Chicago Inc, The			
22 Great Hill Rd .... Naugatuck CT 06770		**800-323-9562**	203-729-9090
Shape LLC 2105 Corporate Dr .... Addison IL 60101		**800-367-5811**	630-620-8394
Veetronix Inc			
1311 W Pacific Ave .... Lexington NE 68850		**800-445-0007***	308-324-6661
*General			
Weidmuller Inc			
821 Southlake Blvd .... Richmond VA 23236		**800-849-9343***	804-794-2877
*Cust Svc			
Zierick Manufacturing Corp			
131 Radio Cr .... Mount Kisco NY 10549		**800-882-8020**	914-666-2911

811   WIRING DEVICES - NONCURRENT-CARRYING

		Toll-Free	Phone
Allied Moulded Products Inc			
222 N Union St .... Bryan OH 43506		**800-722-2679**	419-636-4217
Bedford Materials Co Inc			
7676 Allegheny Rd .... Manns Choice PA 15550		**800-773-4276**	814-623-9014
Chase & Sons Inc			
295 University Ave .... Westwood MA 02090		**800-323-4182**	781-332-0700
Conduit Pipe Products Co			
1501 W Main St .... West Jefferson OH 43162		**800-848-6125**	614-879-9114
Cooper B-Line Inc			
509 W Monroe St .... Highland IL 62249		**800-851-7415**	
Cottrell Paper Company Inc			
1135 Rock City Rd PO Box 35 .... Rock City Falls NY 12863		**800-948-3559**	518-885-1702
Electri-Flex Co			
222 Central Ave .... Roselle IL 60172		**800-323-6174**	630-529-2920
Flex-Cable Inc			
5822 N Henkel Rd .... Howard City MI 49329		**800-245-3539**	231-937-8000
Gaylord Manufacturing Co			
1088 Montclaire Dr .... Ceres CA 95307		**800-375-0091**	209-538-3313
Hubbell Premise Wiring Inc			
23 Clara Dr .... Mystic CT 06355		**800-626-0005**	
Hughes Bros Inc			
210 N 13th St .... Seward NE 68434		**800-869-0359**	402-643-2991
Ideal Industries Inc			
1375 Park Ave .... Sycamore IL 60178		**800-435-0705**	815-895-5181
LoDan Electronics Inc			
3311 N Kennicott Ave .... Arlington Heights IL 60004		**800-401-4995**	847-398-5311
O-Z/Gedney			
9377 W Higgins Rd .... Rosemont IL 60018		**800-621-1506**	847-268-6000
Opti-Com Mfg Network Co Inc			
259 Plauche St .... New Orleans LA 70123		**800-345-8774**	504-736-0331
RITTAL North America LLC			
Woodfield Corporate Ctr 425 N Martingale Rd			
Ste 400 .... Schaumburg IL 60173		**800-477-4000**	847-240-4600
Saginaw Control & Engineering Inc			
95 Midland Rd .... Saginaw MI 48638		**800-234-6871**	989-799-6871
TJ Cope Inc			
11500 Norcom Rd .... Philadelphia PA 19154		**800-483-3473**	800-882-5543
Varflex Corp 512 West Court St .... Rome NY 13440		**800-648-4014**	315-336-4400
Virginia Plastics Co Inc			
3453 Aerial Way Dr SW .... Roanoke VA 24018		**877-351-1699**	540-981-9700

812   WOOD MEMBERS - STRUCTURAL

		Toll-Free	Phone
Armstrong Lumber Co Inc			
2709 Auburn Way N .... Auburn WA 98002		**800-868-9066**	253-833-6666
Automated Bldg Components Inc			
2359 Grant Rd .... North Baltimore OH 45872		**800-837-2152**	419-257-2152
Enwood Structures Inc			
5724 McCrimmon Pkwy PO Box 2002 .... Morrisville NC 27560		**800-777-8648**	919-518-0464
Fullerton Bldg Systems Inc (FBS)			
34620 250th St PO Box 308 .... Worthington MN 56187		**800-450-9782**	507-376-3128
Giles & Kendall Inc			
3470 Maysville Rd NE PO Box 188 ...... Huntsville AL 35804		**800-225-6738**	256-776-2978
Goodfellow Inc			
225 Goodfellow St .... Delson QC J5B1V5		**800-361-6503**	450-635-6511
HM Stauffer & Sons Inc			
33 Glenola Dr PO Box 567 .... Leola PA 17540		**800-662-2226**	717-656-2811
Laminated Wood Systems Inc (LWS)			
1327 285th Rd PO Box 386 .... Seward NE 68434		**800-949-3526**	
Laminators Inc			
3255 Penn St .... Hatfield PA 19440		**877-663-4277**	215-723-8107
Molpus Co, The			
502 Vly View Rd PO Box 59 .... Philadelphia MS 39350		**800-535-5434**	601-656-3373
Montgomery Truss & Panel Inc			
803 W Main St .... Grove City PA 16127		**800-942-8010**	724-458-7500
RedBuilt LLC 200 E Mallard Dr .... Boise ID 83706		**866-859-6757**	
Robbins Mfg Co			
1003 E 131st Ave .... Tampa FL 33612		**888-558-8199**	813-971-3030
Southern Components Inc			
7360 Julie Frances Dr .... Shreveport LA 71129		**800-256-2144**	318-687-3330
Structural Wood Corp			
4000 Labore Rd .... Saint Paul MN 55110		**800-652-9058**	651-426-8111
Structural Wood Systems			
321 Dohrimier St .... Greenville AL 36037		**800-553-0661**	334-382-6534
Trusco Inc 12527 Porr Rd .... Doylestown OH 44230		**800-847-5841**	330-658-2027
Villaume Industries Inc			
2926 Lone Oak Cir .... Eagan MN 55121		**800-488-3610***	651-454-3610
*Cust Svc			

813   WOOD PRESERVING

		Toll-Free	Phone
Bell Lumber & Pole Co			
778 First St NW PO Box 120786 .... New Brighton MN 55112		**877-633-4334**	651-633-4334

		Toll-Free	Phone
Brown Wood Preserving Company Inc			
6201 Camp Ground Rd .... Louisville KY 40216		**800-537-1765**	502-448-2337
Building Products Plus			
12317 Almeda Rd .... Houston TX 77045		**800-460-8627**	713-434-8008
Conrad Forest Products			
68765 Wildwood Dr .... North Bend OR 97459		**800-356-7146**	
Cox Industries Inc			
860 Cannon Bridge Rd PO Box 1124 ... Orangeburg SC 29116		**800-476-4401**	803-534-7467
Culpeper Wood Preservers Inc			
15487 Braggs Corner Rd PO Box 1148 ... Culpeper VA 22701		**800-817-6215**	
JH Baxter & Co			
PO Box 5902 .... San Mateo CA 94402		**800-556-1098**	650-349-0201
Koppers Inc			
436 Seventh Ave .... Pittsburgh PA 15219		**800-385-4406**	412-227-2001
NYSE: KOP			
Madison Wood Preservers Inc			
216 Oak Park Rd .... Madison VA 22727		**844-623-9663**	
McFarland Cascade			
1640 E Marc St PO Box 1496 .... Tacoma WA 98421		**800-426-8430***	253-572-3033
*Cust Svc			
Osmose Inc			
2475 George Urban Blvd Ste 160 .... Depew NY 14043		**800-877-7653**	770-632-6700
Professional Coaters Inc			
100 Commerce Park Dr .... Cabot AR 72023		**800-962-0344**	
Robbins Mfg Co			
1003 E 131st Ave .... Tampa FL 33612		**888-558-8199**	813-971-3030
Western Wood Preserving Co			
1310 Zehnder St .... Sumner WA 98390		**800-472-7714**	253-863-8191
Wood Preservers Inc			
15939 Historyland Hwy PO Box 158 .... Warsaw VA 22572		**800-368-2536**	804-333-4022

814   WOOD PRODUCTS - RECONSTITUTED

		Toll-Free	Phone
Aya Kitchens & Baths Ltd			
1551 Caterpillar Rd .... Mississauga ON L4X2Z6		**866-292-4968**	905-848-1999
Cabinet Tronix			
280 Trousdale Dr Ste A .... Chula Vista CA 91910		**866-876-6199**	
Homasote Co			
932 Lower Ferry Rd PO Box 7240 ...... West Trenton NJ 08628		**800-257-9491**	609-883-3300
OTC: HMTC			
New England Wood Pellet LLC			
141 Old Sharon Rd .... Jaffrey NH 03452		**877-981-9663**	
Panel Processing Inc			
120 N Industrial Hwy .... Alpena MI 49707		**800-433-7142**	
Rex Lumber Co 840 Main St .... Acton MA 01720		**800-343-0567**	978-263-0055
Tectum Inc 105 S Sixth St .... Newark OH 43055		**888-977-9691**	740-345-9691

815   WOOD PRODUCTS - SHAPED & TURNED

		Toll-Free	Phone
Brown Wood Products Co			
7040 N Lawndale Ave .... Lincolnwood IL 60712		**800-328-5858**	
Frank Edmunds & Co			
6111 S Sayre .... Chicago IL 60638		**800-447-3516**	773-586-2772
Garick Corp			
13600 Broadway Ave .... Cleveland OH 44125		**800-242-7425**	
Humboldt Redwood Co (HRC)			
125 Main St PO Box 565 .... Scotia CA 95565		**888-225-7339**	707-764-4472
Maine Wood Concepts Inc			
1687 New Vineyard Rd .... New Vineyard ME 04956		**800-374-6961**	877-728-4442
TrimJoist Corp			
5146 Hwy 182 E .... Columbus MS 39702		**800-844-8281**	662-327-7950
Western Excelsior Corp			
901 Grand Ave .... Mancos CO 81328		**800-833-8573**	

816   WOODWORKING MACHINERY

		Toll-Free	Phone
Baker Products			
55480 Hwy 21 N PO Box 128 .... Ellington MO 63638		**800-548-6914**	573-663-7711
James L Taylor Manufacturing Co			
108 Parker Ave .... Poughkeepsie NY 12601		**800-952-1320**	845-452-3780
Kimwood Corp			
77684 Oregon 99 .... Cottage Grove OR 97424		**800-942-4401**	541-942-4401
KVAL Inc			
825 Petaluma Blvd So .... Petaluma CA 94952		**800-553-5825**	707-762-4363
Machinery Sales Company Inc			
120 Webster Ave .... Memphis TN 38126		**800-932-8376**	
Mereen-Johnson Machine Co			
4401 Lyndale Ave N .... Minneapolis MN 55412		**888-465-7297**	612-529-7791
Michael Weining Inc			
124 Crosslake Pk Dr PO Box 3158 ...... Mooresville NC 28117		**877-548-0929**	704-799-0100
Oliver Machinery Co			
6902 S 194th St .... Kent WA 98032		**800-559-5065**	253-867-0334
Pendu Manufacturing Inc			
718 N Shirk Rd .... New Holland PA 17557		**800-233-0471**	717-354-4348
Safety Speed Cut Mfg Co Inc			
13943 Lincoln St NE .... Ham Lake MN 55304		**800-772-2327**	763-755-1600
Thermwood Corp			
904 Buffaloville Rd .... Dale IN 47523		**800-533-6901***	812-937-4476
OTC: TOOD ■ *Mktg			
USNR			
1981 Schurman Way PO Box 310 .... Woodland WA 98674		**800-289-8767**	360-225-8267
Viking Engineering & Development Inc			
5750 Main St N .... Fridley MN 55432		**800-545-5112***	763-571-2400
*Sales			
Voorwood Co 2350 Barney St .... Anderson CA 96007		**800-826-0089**	530-365-3311
Yates-American Machine Company Inc			
2880 Kennedy Dr .... Beloit WI 53511		**800-752-6377**	608-364-6333

				Toll-Free	Phone

817 WORLD TRADE CENTERS

Northern California World Trade Ctr
1 Capitol Mall Ste 700 .... Sacramento CA 95814 **855-667-2259** 916-447-9827

Ronald Reagan Bldg & International Trade Ctr
1300 Pennsylvania Ave NW .... Washington DC 20004 **800-984-3775** 202-312-1300

818 ZOOS & WILDLIFE PARKS

SEE ALSO Botanical Gardens & Arboreta ; Aquariums - Public

Abilene Zoological Gardens
2070 Zoo Ln Nelson Pk .... Abilene TX 79602 **800-899-9841** 325-676-6085

African Safari Wildlife Park
267 S Lightner Rd .... Port Clinton OH 43452 **800-521-2660** 419-732-3606

Animal Ark Wildlife Sanctuary & Nature Ctr
1265 Deerlodge Rd .... Reno NV 89508 **866-366-5771** 775-970-3111

Assiniboine Park Zoo
55 Pavilion Crescent .... Winnipeg MB R3P2N6 **877-927-6006** 204-927-8080

Audubon Nature Institute
6500 Magazine St .... New Orleans LA 70118 **800-774-7394** 504-581-4629

Bronx Zoo 2300 Southern Blvd .... Bronx NY 10460 **800-433-4149** 718-220-5100

Calgary Zoo Botanical Garden & Prehistoric Park
1300 Zoo Rd NE .... Calgary AB T2E7V6 **800-588-9993** 403-232-9300

Chahinkapa Zoo Park & Carousel
1004 RJ Hughes Dr .... Wahpeton ND 58075 **800-342-4671** 701-642-8709

Cherry Brook Zoo Inc
901 Foster Thurston Dr .... Saint John NB E2K5H9 **800-321-1433** 506-634-1440

Cincinnati Zoo & Botanical Garden
3400 Vine St .... Cincinnati OH 45220 **800-944-4776** 513-281-4700

Clyde Peeling's Reptiland
18628 US Rt 15 .... Allenwood PA 17810 **800-737-8452** 570-538-1869

Elmwood Park Zoo
1661 Harding Blvd .... Norristown PA 19401 **800-652-4143** 610-277-3825

Felix Neck Wildlife Sanctuary
100 Felix Neck Dr .... Edgartown MA 02539 **866-627-2267** 508-627-4850

Gator Park 24050 SW Eigth St .... Miami FL 33194 **800-559-2205** 305-559-2255

Gatorland
14501 S Orange Blossom Trl .... Orlando FL 32837 **800-393-5297** 407-855-5496

Good Zoo & Benedum Planetarium
465 Lodge Dr .... Wheeling WV 26003 **877-436-1797** 304-243-4030

Grizzly & Wolf Discovery Ctr
201 S Canyon St .... West Yellowstone MT 59758 **800-257-2570** 406-646-7001

Hattiesburg Zoo
107 S 17th Ave .... Hattiesburg MS 39401 **800-733-2767** 601-545-4500

Jacksonville Zoo & Gardens
370 Zoo Pkwy .... Jacksonville FL 32218 **800-241-4113** 904-757-4463

Jungle Adventures
26205 E Colonial Dr .... Christmas FL 32709 **877-424-2867** 407-568-2885

Kentucky Horse Park
4089 Iron Works Pkwy .... Lexington KY 40511 **800-678-8813** 859-233-4303

Minnesota Zoo
13000 Zoo Blvd .... Apple Valley MN 55124 **800-366-7811** 952-431-9200

Nashville Zoo
3777 Nolensville Rd .... Nashville TN 37211 **800-456-6847** 615-833-1534

Rosamond Gifford Zoo at Burnet Park
1 Conservation Pl .... Syracuse NY 13204 **800-724-5006** 315-435-8511

Safari West Wildlife Preserve & Tent Camp
3115 Porter Creek Rd .... Santa Rosa CA 95404 **800-616-2695** 707-579-2551

Saint Louis Zoological Park
1 Government Dr .... Saint Louis MO 63110 **800-966-8877** 314-781-0900

San Diego Zoo Safari Park
15500 San Pasqual Valley Rd ...... Escondido CA 92027 **877-363-6237*** 760-747-8702
*Cust Svc

Sarasota Jungle Gardens
3701 Bay Shore Rd .... Sarasota FL 34234 **877-681-6547** 941-355-5305

Wild Animal Safari
1300 Oak Grove Rd .... Pine Mountain GA 31822 **800-367-2751** 706-663-8744

Wildlife Sanctuary of Northwest Florida
PO Box 1092 .... Pensacola FL 32591 **800-435-7353** 850-433-9453

Wildlife West Nature Park
87 North Frontage Rd .... Edgewood NM 87015 **877-981-9453** 505-281-7655

Wonders of Wildlife
500 W Sunshine St .... Springfield MO 65807 **888-222-6060**

Index to Classified Headings

Citations provided in this index refer to the subject headings under which listings are organized in the Classified Section. The page number given for each citation refers to the page on which a particular subject category begins rather than to a specific company or organization name. "See" and "See also" references are included to help locate appropriate subject categories.

Index

Index

Index

Index

Index

Index

F

Index

Index

Index

Index

Index

Index

Radiological Equipment
See Imaging Equipment & Systems - Medical 706

Radiology Services
See Imaging Services - Diagnostic. 706

Radiopharmaceuticals
See Diagnostic Products 597

Radios - Household & Automotive
See Appliance & Home Electronics Stores 453
    Appliances - Whol. 454
    Audio & Video Equipment 478

Rags - Cleaning, Dusting, Polishing, etc
See Mops, Sponges, Wiping Cloths. 768

Rail Transport Services 836
See also Logistics Services (Transportation & Warehousing) 739

Rail Travel 836
See also Mass Transportation (Local & Suburban) 752

Railings - Metal
See Metal Work - Architectural & Ornamental 763

Railings - Wood
See Millwork 766

Railroad Car Leasing
See Transport Equipment Rental. 619

Railroad Equipment - Mfr 836
See also Transportation Equipment & Supplies - Whol 889

Railroad Equipment - Model
See Toy Stores 887
    Toys, Games, Hobbies 887

Railroad Switching & Terminal Services 837

Railroads
See Logistics Services (Transportation & Warehousing) .. 739
    Rail Transport Services 836

Rain Gear
See Coats (Overcoats, Jackets, Raincoats, etc). 517

Rakes - Agricultural
See Farm Machinery & Equipment - Mfr 621
    Farm Machinery & Equipment - Whol. 622

Ranches
See Agricultural Products. 447
    Dude Ranches 601

Ranges & Ovens
See Appliance & Home Electronics Stores 453
    Appliances - Major - Mfr. 454
    Appliances - Whol. 454

Rapid Transit Cars & Equipment
See Railroad Equipment - Mfr 836

Rapid Transit Services
See Mass Transportation (Local & Suburban) 752

Raspberries
See Berry Growers 643

Rating Organizations - Quality
See Accreditation & Certification Organizations. 457

Ratings Services
See Market Research Firms 751

Rattan Furniture
See Furniture - Mfr. 644

Rayon
See Broadwoven Fabric Mills. 881

Rayon Fibers
See Synthetic Fibers & Filaments. 811

Razor Blades
See Cosmetics, Skin Care, and Other Personal Care Products 590
    Cutlery. 593

Razors - Safety, Straight, Electric
See Appliances - Small - Mfr. 454
    Cosmetics, Skin Care, and Other Personal Care Products 590

Real Estate Agents & Brokers 837

Real Estate Developers 837
See also Construction - Building Contractors - Non-
Residential 565; Construction - Building Contractors -
Residential 566

Real Estate Investment Trusts (REITs) 838

Real Estate Managers & Operators 838
See also Hotels & Hotel Companies 697; Retirement
Communities 852

Real Estate Software
See Professional Software (Industry-Specific) 558

Realtor Associations - State 839
See also Real Estate Professionals Associations 474

Reamers - Machine Tool
See Metalworking Devices & Accessories 765

Reaming Machines
See Machine Tools - Metal Cutting Types 741

Receipt & Transaction Printers
See Printers 548

Receipt Books
See Blankbooks & Binders. 494

Receivables Management Services
See Collection Agencies. 520

Recipes (Cooking) Software
See Personal Software 557

Recognition Products
See Advertising Specialties 447
    Trophies, Plaques, Awards. 892

Record Labels
See Recording Companies. 839

Recording Companies 839

Recording Equipment - Audio or Video
See Audio & Video Equipment 478

Recording Media - Magnetic & Optical 839
See also Photographic Equipment & Supplies 807

Records Storage
See Commercial Warehousing. 904

Recovery Programs
See Self-Help Organizations. 466
    Substance Abuse Treatment Centers 872

Recreation Areas - Outdoor
See Nature Centers, Parks, Other Natural Areas 477

Recreation Associations
See Travel & Recreation Organizations. 467

Recreation Facility Operators 840
See also Bowling Centers 497

Recreational Equipment & Supplies
See Sporting Goods Stores 867
    Toy Stores 887
    Toys, Games, Hobbies. 887

Recreational Equipment & Supplies
See Sporting Goods. 866

Recreational Vehicles
See Campers, Travel Trailers, Motor Homes. 503

Recruiters
See Executive Recruiting Firms 620

Rectifiers
See Electronic Components & Accessories - Mfr. 612
    Semiconductors & Related Devices. 861

Recyclable Materials Recovery 840

Recyclable Metals
See Scrap Metal. 856

Recyclable Textiles
See Textile Fiber Processing Mills 882

Recycled Plastics Products 840
See also Flooring - Resilient 625

Recycling Companies
See Recyclable Materials Recovery 840

Recycling Equipment - Paper
See Paper Industries Machinery 793

Reels - Cable
See Cable Reels 502

Index

Index

Index